EVIDENCE

SANCTIONS

COSTS

JUDGMENTS AND ORDERS

ENFORCEMENT

SPECIALIST COURTS

APPEALS

his edition. This will be available to all Blackstone's Civil Practice subscribers.

BLACKSTONE'S

CIVIL PRACTICE

BLACKSTONE'S

CIVIL PRACTICE

2006

EDITOR-IN-CHIEF

HIS HONOUR JUDGE WILLIAM ROSE

EDITORS

STUART SIME

DEREK FRENCH

CONTRIBUTORS

EVAN ASHFIELD, JULIE BRANNAN
STUART BRIDGE, IAIN COLVILLE, ADRIAN KEANE
CHRIS LETHEM, ANDREW LIDBETTER
ALAN OWENS, CHARLES PLANT
MICHAEL WALKER, MATTHEW WEINIGER,
IVOR WEINTROUB, ANGELA WRIGHT

OXFORD
UNIVERSITY PRESS

OXFORD
UNIVERSITY PRESS

Great Clarendon Street, Oxford OX2 6DP

Oxford University Press is a department of the University of Oxford.
It furthers the University's objective of excellence in research, scholarship,
and education by publishing worldwide in

Oxford New York

Auckland Cape Town Dar es Salaam Hong Kong Karachi
Kuala Lumpur Madrid Melbourne Mexico City Nairobi
New Delhi Shanghai Taipei Toronto

With offices in

Argentina Austria Brazil Chile Czech Republic France Greece
Guatemala Hungary Italy Japan Poland Portugal Singapore
South Korea Switzerland Thailand Turkey Ukraine Vietnam

Oxford is a registered trade mark of Oxford University Press
in the UK and in certain other countries

Published in the United States
by Oxford University Press Inc., New York

First edition published by Blackstone Press, 2000

Seventh edition published 2006

British Library Cataloguing in Publication Data
Data available
Library of Congress Cataloging in Publication Data
Data available

Typeset by RefineCatch Limited, Bungay, Suffolk
Printed in Italy
on acid-free paper by
Legoprint S.p.A.

ISBN 0–19–920721–6 978–0–19–920721–3

1 3 5 7 9 10 8 6 4 2

Preface

NEW TO THE 2006 EDITION

Blackstone's Civil Practice 2006 is up to date to 28 February 2006, and includes rule changes which came into force in the first week of April 2006. The work incorporates all amendments to the Civil Procedure Rules up to those introduced by the Civil Procedure (Amendment No. 4) Rules 2005 (SI 2005/2292) and changes brought in by updates released by the Department for Constitutional Affairs up to Update 41.

The commentary in *Blackstone's Civil Practice 2006* has been fully revised to take into account the wide range of case-law and other developments since the last edition. These include the new provisions on additional claims under Part 20 and Crown proceedings in Part 66, the revised practice on freezing and search orders, the new approach to undertakings in damages, the new practice relating to disclosure of electronic documents, the revised rules dealing with small claims track cases, and the relaxation of the formalities required for conditional fee agreements made by the Conditional Fee Agreements (Revocation) Regulations 2005 (SI 2005/2305). There is extended treatment of the increasingly important area of alternative dispute resolution, and a new chapter dealing with Homelessness and Housing Act 1996 appeals. This edition deals with the reissued Chancery Court Guide, the new Protocol for the Instruction of Experts, the revisions made to all the pre-action protocols (taking effect in April 2006), and the reissued House of Lords Practice Directions and Standing Orders, as well as the Constitutional Reform Act 2005, which will replace the House of Lords with a new Supreme Court.

Among the many case law developments included in the new edition are *Hertsmere Primary Care Trust v Estate of Balasubramanium* on the duty to cooperate; *West Bromwich Building Society v Wilkinson* on the limitation period in mortgage cases; *Collier v Williams* on service and extending the period of validity; *Morgan Est (Scotland) Ltd v Hanson Concrete Products Ltd* on amending after the expiry of limitation; *O'Brien v Chief Constable of South Wales Police* on the use of similar fact evidence in civil claims; and *Trustees of Stokes Pension Fund v Western Power Distribution (South West) plc* on making and withdrawing Part 36 offers.

An online resource centre for *Blackstone's Civil Practice 2006* will also be available with regular updates and useful reading. This can be found at: http://www.oup.com/uk/law/practitioner/cws.

Blackstone's Civil Practice 2006 provides the civil litigation practitioner with a comprehensive and authoritative work covering every topic which the practitioner can reasonably expect to encounter in everyday practice. The objective of the publishers and the editorial team has been to produce a single volume of manageable size and expense. The CD-ROM supplied with the book contains the complete text of the book in easily accessible and searchable form together with 435 court forms and extra statutory material.

Blackstone's Civil Practice occupies a unique place in the civil litigation practitioners library. Commentaries on the Civil Procedure Rules have previously had a limited horizon, in that they address the mechanics of litigation, but fail to study in any depth the substantive law issues with which the practitioner must be fully conversant. Previously the practitioner has had to assemble a series of specialist works on a diverse range of topics, such as evidence, judicial review, and landlord and tenant. *Blackstone's Civil Practice* provides the practitioner with a sufficient study of these and other topics to address the issues which frequently arise in everyday practice. The authors and editors have sought to provide a text which is sufficiently comprehensive, clear and up to date to enable a practitioner easily to assimilate a topic on which he or she may have little knowledge, whilst at the same time providing a depth of analysis and information which will enable those with greater experience of a subject to research in greater detail. We are confident that civil litigation practitioners will find that *Blackstone's Civil Practice* will cover the wide range of issues generally met, and only on rare occasions should it be necessary to consult the highly specialist works.

Our greatest challenge has been to strike the balance between what can be offered in a single volume and the inevitable omission of some specialist academic material on specific topics. We believe that this book has achieved that balance. In addition to a detailed and comprehensive analysis of the Civil Procedure Rules, *Blackstone's Civil Practice 2006* contains authoritative treatment of most of the major subjects of daily civil litigation, including landlord and tenant possession proceedings, company and insolvency law, judicial review, sale of goods and consumer law, as well as chapters on evidence and the influence of human rights law on civil procedure. A team of highly experienced and respected authors has ensured that each subject is given authoritative and specialist attention.

This 2006 edition has built on the achievements of its predecessors in covering the latest changes to the Civil Procedure Rules and practice directions, whilst consolidating and refining previous commentary and anticipating, wherever possible, changes to come. Comprehensive and up-to-date appendices include not only the Civil Procedure Rules, practice directions and pre-action protocols, but also the court guides, court fees orders and many of the statutes most commonly needed in civil litigation. A comprehensive collection of court forms can be found on the accompanying CD-ROM, which provides for on-screen completion of many of the forms. Procedural checklists, which are step-by-step guides to various aspects of civil procedure, can be found in appendix 1. These provide quick and practical guidance on how to comply with the requirements of the rules.

It has been the foresight and enthusiasm of its publishers which has enabled this work to come to fruition. The editors would, in particular, like to thank Alistair MacQueen, Heather Saward and Jeremy Stein of Blackstone Press, because this work would not have seen the light of day without their vision and enthusiasm. We also extend our thanks to Catherine Redmond, Jonathan Kingham, Louise Kavanagh and Andy Redman of Oxford University Press for their guidance, encouragement and total support. We also warmly thank the contributors who have provided authoritative material on their subjects and met a tight schedule notwithstanding their other important commitments.

We thank Mr Benjamin Williams of the Chambers of Mr Richard Davies QC and Mr Richard Wilmot-Smith QC, who made useful comments on chapter 52.

This edition states the law as it was known to the editors and contributors at 28 February 2006 and includes changes to the Civil Procedure Rules and practice directions which took effect on 6 April 2006.

The editors
28 February 2006

Contributors

Evan Ashfield, LLB, Barrister. Evan Ashfield is Head of Chambers, Temple Chambers. He is co-author of *Sale of Goods and Consumer Credit in Practice*, a contributor to Inns of Court School of Law Manuals and former Chairman of the Free Representation Unit.

Julie Brannan, MA (Oxon), Solicitor. Julie Brannan is Director of the Oxford Institute of Legal Practice. She was formerly a litigation partner at Herbert Smith.

Stuart Bridge, MA (Cantab), Barrister. Stuart Bridge is a University Lecturer in Law and a Fellow of Queens' College in the University of Cambridge. He is the author of *Residential Leases* and *Assured Tenancies*, and the editor of *Blackstone's Statutes on Landlord and Tenant.* He is an editor of *Theobald on Wills* and contributed to the sixth edition of Megarry and Wade's *The Law of Real Property*. He is currently a Law Commissioner for England and Wales.

Iain Colville, LLB, Barrister. Iain Colville is a barrister at Arden Chambers. He practises in the fields of housing, landlord and tenant, planning, compulsory purchase, and local government law, and he has extensive experience acting for private individuals, registered social landlords and local authorities. His publications include *A Guide to the Planning Process* (*Arden's Housing Library*); *A Guide to the Greater London Authority Act,* Annotations to the Greater London Authority Act 1999, *Current Law*; and a chapter on 'Planning and Human Rights' in *Human Rights Act 1998 — A Practitioner's Guide.*

Derek French, BSc. Derek French works in legal publishing. He is co-author of *Mayson, French and Ryan on Company Law* and author of *Applications to Wind up Companies* and *How to Cite Legal Authorities.* He is editor of *Blackstone's Statutes on Company Law* and has also written on insolvency law, accountancy and management.

Adrian Keane, LLB, Barrister. Adrian Keane is Professor of Law and Dean of the Inns of Court School of Law, City University, where he teaches evidence and advocacy on the Bar Vocational Course. He is a contributor to *Blackstone's Criminal Practice* and his many publications include *The Modern Law of Evidence.*

District Judge Chris Lethem, BA. Chris Lethem sits at Tunbridge Wells County Court and has written and lectured extensively on costs. He is a member of the Civil Justice Council working party on costs and lectures on costs for the Judicial Studies Board.

Andrew Lidbetter, MA (Oxon), BCL, Solicitor. Andrew Lidbetter is a litigation partner at Herbert Smith specialising in public law including judicial review and human rights. He is the author of *Company Investigations and Public Law,* is on the advisory board of *Judicial Review* and frequently writes and speaks on public law.

Alan Owens, LLB, Solicitor. Alan Owens is a partner in the commercial litigation and arbitration department at Irwin Mitchell, specialising in group claims, particularly in the financial and antitrust sectors. He has lectured widely on civil procedure and is an editor of the *Civil Court Service Newsletter.*

Charles Plant, MA (Cantab), Solicitor. Charles Plant read law at Cambridge University. Throughout his professional life he has been with City firm Herbert Smith, where he became a litigation partner in 1976 and subsequently head of its litigation department. He specialises in the resolution of commercial disputes in the High Court and in arbitration, with particular reference to financial services and the energy and media industries. He is a Governor of the College of Law and an accredited mediator.

His Honour Judge William Rose, Circuit Judge. William Rose was appointed a circuit judge in 1998. He is author of *Pleadings Without Tears* and a contributor to the Inns of Court School of Law Manuals on *Remedies* and *Opinion Writing.* He was a Member of the Board of Examiners of the Inns of Court School of Law between 1990 and 2001. He was Director of Studies at the Judicial Studies Board from 2002 to 2004. He is now resident circuit judge at Wandsworth County Court in south-west London and was appointed a Judicial Member of the Parole Board in 2004.

Stuart Sime, LLB, Barrister. Stuart Sime is the course director of the full-time bar vocational course at the Inns of Court School of Law, where he teaches civil litigation, commercial and company law. He was a practising barrister until 2005. In his early career he spent a number of years in the litigation department of the Treasury Solicitor's Office. He is author of *A Practical Approach to Civil Procedure.*

District Judge Michael Walker. Michael Walker was appointed a district judge in April 1994 and now sits full time at Wandsworth County Court with a mixed workload of civil and family cases. Before that he was a partner in a South London firm of High Street, legal aid, solicitors. Since 1999 he has been active in the affairs of the Association of District Judges.

Matthew Weiniger, MA (Cantab), Solicitor Advocate. Matthew Weiniger is a partner at Herbert Smith practising in the international arbitration group. He specialises in international arbitration and alternative dispute resolution (particularly in banking, investment and joint venture disputes). He also advises on matters relating to public and private international law.

District Judge Ivor Weintroub, LLB. Ivor Weintroub sits in Bournemouth County Court. He is also a Recorder of the Crown and County Courts and is an Honorary Visiting Lecturer to the Business and Law Department of Bournemouth University LPC course. He has lectured and been a tutor judge on civil and family courses for the Judicial Studies Board.

Angela Wright, BA (Hons), solicitor. Angela Wright is a senior lecturer on the corporate legal practice course at the College of Law, London, Moorgate. Previously she was a partner in a Legal 500 London firm of solicitors specialising in family law and was also a consultant in relation to legal aid matters.

Acknowledgments

In addition to the contributors listed above, material used by the editors was supplied by Simon Garner, to whom we are very grateful.

The House of Lords Practice Directions and Standing Orders Applicable to Civil Appeals are reproduced by permission of the Clerk of the Parliaments. The Queen's Bench Guide is reproduced by permission of the Senior Master of the Royal Courts of Justice.

Contents

J EVIDENCE

Appendix 2 Civil Procedure Rules 1998 and Practice Directions

Guide to *Blackstone's Civil Practice*

CHAPTERS AND APPENDICES

Blackstone's Civil Practice has 98 chapters and seven appendices. The chapters are grouped into 20 parts, A to V. For a list of the parts, chapters and appendices see the **Contents** starting on page ix.

Chapters are divided up by numbered headings. The first heading in **chapter 1** is numbered **1.1**, the second is **1.2** and so on. The number of a heading is printed in the margin against the first line of text after the heading. Each chapter begins with a list of its numbered headings. The numbers are used for cross-references throughout the book.

ORGANISATION OF THE SUBJECT MATTER

Subject-focused chapters

The chapters of *Blackstone's Civil Practice* are subject-focused, dealing with all the law on a topic, wherever the source of the law may be in statutes, rules, practice directions or cases. General points are discussed in part A (**chapters 1** to 4), then parts B to P (**chapters 5** to **78**) describe the progress of a civil claim in a county court or the High Court in England and Wales, from consideration of how to fund it (part B) to the methods of enforcing judgment (part P). Part Q (**chapters 79** to **82**) deals with procedure in insolvency proceedings and companies matters in the county courts and High Court. Other special procedures in the county courts and High Court are considered in **chapter 69** (arbitration claims) and **chapter 74** (judicial review, which is conducted in the High Court only) and in the court guides, which are in **appendix** 4. Parts R to T of *Blackstone's Civil Practice* contain compact summaries of the law on topics commonly encountered by practitioners: landlord and tenant and possession proceedings (part R), harassment (part S), sale of goods and consumer credit (part T). Part U deals with human rights and civil procedure.

Blackstone's Civil Practice does not deal with family proceedings.

Procedural checklists

Appendix 1 contains 38 procedural checklists which summarise the steps to be taken in the most commonly encountered stages of a civil claim.

Source-focused appendices

Appendices 2 to 7 of *Blackstone's Civil Practice* are source-focused. **Appendix 2** gives the complete, up-to-date text of the Civil Procedure Rules and supplementing practice directions. Pre-action protocols are in **appendix 3**. Court guides are in **appendix 4**. **Appendix 5** lists the forms which are on the CD-ROM version of *Blackstone's Civil Practice*. **Appendix 6** is court fees orders. **Appendix** 7 gives the up-to-date text of the principal statutes relating to civil procedure. There are further statutes (mostly relating to Parts R to T) on the CD-ROM. Each appendix begins with a list of its contents.

If the title of a legislative provision is set in **bold type** in chapters 1 to 98, the text of the provision will be found in the appropriate appendix to the book.

Contents, index, cross-references and useful references section

Research in *Blackstone's Civil Practice* can be started either from a subject focus or a source focus, because of the comprehensive indexing and cross-referencing of the book.

The index at the end of *Blackstone's Civil Practice* is an in-depth subject index of chapters 1 to 98 and of the Civil Procedure Rules and practice directions. The index is usually the best way of finding where a particular topic is discussed in chapters 1 to 98 of *Blackstone's Civil Practice* and which rules or practice directions are concerned with that topic.

In **appendix 2**, after the heading of each Part of the Civil Procedure Rules, and after the title of each rule, cross-references are given to the headings (by number) in chapters 1 to 98 under which the Part or rule is mentioned. There is a similar system of cross-referencing for the practice directions in **appendix 2. Appendix 2** is usually the best place to start to find commentary on a particular rule or practice direction.

At the beginning of *Blackstone's Civil Practice* there is a **Table of Cases** (page xl), a **Table of Statutes** (page cvii) and a **Table of Rules, Practice Directions and Protocols** (page cxxvii). These tables list all the headings (by number) under which each case, statute etc. is mentioned.

On the inside front cover there is a **Useful References** section. This comprises a list of important and useful paragraphs which often need to be accessed in a hurry.

There is a **Calendar** on the back inside cover.

ADDITIONAL FEATURES OF THE CD-ROM VERSION

The CD-ROM version of *Blackstone's Civil Practice* is provided with links to help navigate the book. All titles of items in contents lists are linked so that clicking on a title will take you to the item. All references in the Table of Cases, Table of Statutes, Table of Rules, Practice Directions and Protocols, and the subject Index, are linked so that clicking on a reference will take you to the paragraph referred to. All cross-references are linked. Almost every reference to the legislation and other materials in the appendices is linked so that clicking on a reference will take you to the material referred to. (Repetitions of nearby references are not linked.)

There are 435 court forms on the CD-ROM, many of which can be filled in on-screen (see **appendix** 5). References in the chapters and appendices to forms are linked.

Because of practical limitations of book production, there are a small number of places where we could not include complete documents in the appendices. For example, we could not include schedule 1 to the Civil Jurisdiction and Judgments Act 1982 in appendix 7. In the printed book, at the point where that schedule should be, you will see a note advising you to go to the same page on the CD-ROM, where you will find a link to the text of that schedule, which is on the CD-ROM only. We have used the same method for guiding you to other items which appear on the CD-ROM only.

Only on the CD-ROM there are some additional pieces of legislation in **appendix** 2 and **appendix** 7 and additional court guides (**appendix** 4). These items are listed in the main contents list in the printed book, and can be accessed from that list on the CD-ROM.

ONLINE RESOURCE CENTRE

This will alert practitioners to key developments taking place during the life cycle of this edition. It will be available to all *Blackstone's Civil Practice 2006* subscribers. Please visit http://www.oup.com/uk/law/practitioner/cws and bookmark the site.

Abbreviations

ADR	alternative dispute resolution
ATE	after-the-event CCA 1974 Consumer Credit Act 1974
CCFA	collective conditional fee agreement
CCFO	County Court Fees Order 1999 (SI 1999/689)
CCR	County Court Rules 1981 (SI 1981/1687) as amended, or as re-enacted in CPR, sch. 2
CDDA 1986	Company Directors Disqualification Act 1986
CFA	conditional fee agreement
CJJA 1982	Civil Jurisdiction and Judgments Act 1982
CLS	Community Legal Service
CPFO	Civil Proceedings Fees Order 2004 (SI 2004/3121)
CPR	Civil Procedure Rules 1998 (SI 1998/3132)
CRU	Compensation Recovery Unit
DCS	debtor-creditor-supplier
ECJ	European Court of Justice
Final Report	Lord Woolf, *Access to Justice. Final Report* (London: HMSO, 1996)
GLO	group litigation order
HL PD	House of Lords Practice Directions and Standing Orders Applicable to Civil Appeals
Interim Report	Lord Woolf, *Access to Justice. Interim Report* (London: Lord Chancellor's Department, 1995)
IR 1986	Insolvency Rules 1986 (SI 1986/1925)
IVA	individual voluntary arrangement
Jurisdiction and Judgments Regulation	Regulation (EC) No. 44/2001
LA 1980	Limitation Act 1980
LSC	Legal Services Commission
MIB	Motor Insurers' Bureau
ord.	order
para.	paragraph
paras	paragraphs
PD	Practice Direction. PD followed by a number is a practice direction supplementing the Part of the CPR with that number and is printed after that Part in **appendix** 2. PD 43–48 is printed after Part 48 in **appendix** 2. PD followed by any other title is one of the general supplementing practice directions which are printed after the CPR in **appendix** 2 (apart from PD Protocols, which is printed in **appendix** 3)
PD Competition Act 1998	Practice Direction — Application for a Warrant under the Competition Act 1998

PD Devolution Issues	Practice Direction — Devolution Issues
PD Directors Disqualification Proceedings	Practice Direction — Directors Disqualification Proceedings
PD Insolvency Proceedings	Practice Direction — Insolvency Proceedings
PD Protocols	Practice Direction — Protocols
PD Welsh Language	Practice Direction Relating to the Use of the Welsh Language in Cases in the Civil Courts in Wales
r.	rule
RCJ	Royal Courts of Justice
RLSC	regional legal services committee
rr.	rules
RSC	Rules of the Supreme Court 1965 (SI 1965/1776) as amended, or as re-enacted in CPR, sch. 1
RTA	road traffic accident
s.	section
SCCO	Supreme Court Costs Office
SCFO	Supreme Court Fees Order 1999 (SI 1999/687)
sch.	schedule
SoGA 1979	Sale of Goods Act 1979
SoG(Am) A 1995	Sale of Goods (Amendment) Act 1995
SoGITA 1973	Supply of Goods (Implied Terms) Act 1973
SoGSA 1982	Supply of Goods and Services Act 1982
ss.	sections
Taking of Evidence Regulation	Regulation (EC) No. 1206/2001
TCC	Technology and Construction Court

Table of Cases

Table of Statutes

European Community treaties

International conventions

Table of Rules, Practice Directions and Protocols

European secondary legislation

Chapter 1 The Overriding Objective and Sources of Procedural Law

INTRODUCTION

This chapter will consider the various sources of the law governing civil proceedings, and will also give general guidance on the interpretation of the main source, the Civil Procedure Rules 1998 ('CPR'). Specific consideration of the detailed provisions of the CPR and related statutory sources and case law can be found in **chapters 2** to **78**. These are supplemented by the procedural checklists in **appendix 1**. The full text of the CPR, and their related practice directions, can be found in **appendix 2**. Pre-action protocols are in **appendix 3**, court guides in **appendix 4**, and forms in **appendix 5**. Court fees orders are in **appendix 6**. Statutes governing civil proceedings are in **appendix 7**. **Chapters 79** to **96** contain text on: 1.1

(a) insolvency proceedings and companies matters (**chapters 79** to **82**);
(b) landlord and tenant law and possession proceedings (**chapters 83** to **90**);
(c) harassment (**chapter 92**);
(d) sale and supply of goods and services (**chapters 92** and **93**);
(e) unfair contract terms (**chapter 95**);
(f) consumer credit (**chapter 96**); and
(g) human rights law (**chapter 97**).

SOURCES OF PROCEDURAL LAW

Statutory sources

1.2 The primary source of law governing procedure in the High Court and Court of Appeal is the **Supreme Court Act 1981**. County courts are governed by the **County Courts Act 1984**. These statutes are the primary source of the jurisdiction exercised by the civil courts in England and Wales. Both statutes are often expressed in very wide terms, leaving the detailed mechanics of many of the procedures used in the courts to be set out in rules of court. The power to make court rules is granted by the **Civil Procedure Act 1997**. The **Access to Justice Act 1999** made provision for funding litigation, and also contains provisions dealing with appeals, courts, judges and civil proceedings. Various other statutes also govern aspects of civil procedure. For example, the **Administration of Justice Act 1969** provides for leapfrog appeals to the House of Lords, certain enforcement procedures are governed by the **Charging Orders Act 1979** and the **Attachment of Earnings Act 1971**, and limitation is governed by the **Limitation Act 1980**. These and other relevant statutes and statutory instruments are set out in **appendix** 7 of this book.

The international dimension is becoming increasingly important in civil procedure. A fundamental change in the approach to many issues, such as the right to a fair trial, has been brought in by the **Human Rights Act 1998**, which incorporates the provisions of the European Convention on Human Rights into English law (see **chapter** 97 and **appendix** 7 of this book). Also important are European Community Regulations dealing with jurisdiction and service of proceedings. These instruments, together with the **Civil Jurisdiction and Judgments Act 1982**, can be found in **appendix** 7 of this book.

Civil Procedure Rules

1.3 By the **Civil Procedure Act 1997, s. 2**, a Civil Procedure Rule Committee was established, with the power to make rules governing the practice and procedure to be followed in:

(a) the civil division of the Court of Appeal;
(b) the High Court; and
(c) the county courts.

The committee is required, by **s. 1(3)**, to exercise its power to make rules 'with a view to securing that the civil justice system is accessible, fair and efficient'. Pursuant to this power, with effect from 26 April 1999, civil proceedings in England and Wales have been governed by a unified set of procedural rules, the Civil Procedure Rules 1998 (CPR, SI 1998/3123). These rules brought into effect the proposals for reform of the civil justice system set out in the *Final Report* compiled by Lord Woolf (*Access to Justice. Final Report* (London: HMSO, 1996)). They embody the most radical reform of civil litigation since the Judicature Acts 1873 to 1875. The full text of the CPR, as amended, can be found in **appendix 2** of this book.

The CPR are divided into Parts, numbered 1 to 76. The rules are numbered within each Part: for example, r. 1.1, r. 1.2, etc. in Part 1; r. 2.1, r. 2.2, etc. in Part 2.

The previous rules governing civil procedure were the Rules of the Supreme Court 1965 (RSC) governing proceedings in the High Court and the Civil Division of the Court of Appeal (these were an extensively revised version of rules set out in sch. 1 to the Supreme Court of Judicature Act 1875, which were themselves in part distilled from pre-existing procedures), and the County Court Rules 1981 (CCR) governing proceedings in the county courts. The fact that the CCR differed in many respects from the RSC added to the complexity of the old civil justice system, and the production of a unified set of rules is one of the main improvements introduced by the CPR.

Practice directions

As permitted by the **Civil Procedure Act 1997, ss. 1** and **5**, and **sch. 1, para. 6**, the CPR are supplemented by practice directions (PDs). The general scheme is that individual areas of civil procedure are governed by Parts of the CPR, with almost every Part being supplemented by one or more PDs. Practice directions set out details of procedure that it is felt do not need to be set out in statutory instruments (as required for amendments to the CPR), which allows for flexible amendment in the light of experience. The full text of the PDs can be found in **appendix** 2 of this book. Each PD is printed after the Part of the CPR which it supplements. **1.4**

Preserved provisions of the old rules

When the CPR were introduced, quite substantial sections of the old RSC and CCR were retained (with minor revisions) in sch. 1 (the preserved provisions of the RSC) and sch. 2 (the preserved provisions of the CCR) to the CPR. These provisions continue in force by virtue of **Part 50 of the CPR**. Since 1998 many provisions of the old rules in the schedules have been replaced by new rules in the main body of the CPR. So the number of Parts of the CPR has increased, with corresponding deletions from the schedules. The rules still in force in sch. 1 and sch. 2 can be found towards the end of **appendix 2** of this book. **1.5**

Tables in **PD 8B** regulate how to commence claims and appeals under the schedules, the appropriate form to use to commence a claim (in particular, when to use a Part 8 claim form), and the procedure to be followed. The rules re-enacted in the schedules are of two general types. First, a number of general procedural rules are retained, such as some of the rules on enforcement of judgments. Secondly, there are various provisions from the old rules dealing with the civil courts' special jurisdiction under a number of statutes. These provisions are mainly in **CCR, ord. 49 in CPR, sch. 2**, and **RSC, ord. 93** to **116 in CPR, sch. 1. Rule 50(2) of the CPR** provides that the CPR apply in relation to the proceedings to which the schedules apply, subject to the provisions in the schedules and the relevant practice directions. This means that the overriding objective (see **1.11**) applies to applications made under these re-enacted provisions from the old rules.

Inherent jurisdiction

Being the successor to the pre-1875 common law courts, the High Court has inherent jurisdiction to control its procedures to ensure its proceedings are not abused to achieve injustice. As Lord Diplock said in *Bremer Vulkan Schiffbau und Maschinenfabrik v South India Shipping Corporation Ltd* [1981] AC 909 at p. 977, the High Court has: **1.6**

> . . . a general power to control its own procedure so as to prevent its being used to achieve injustice. Such a power is inherent in its constitution as a court of justice. . . . it would stultify the constitutional role of the High Court as a court of justice if it were not armed with power to prevent its process being misused in such a way as to diminish its capability of arriving at a just decision of the dispute.

Before the introduction of the CPR, much of the law relating to striking out as a sanction, and the initial development of the jurisdiction to grant freezing injunctions and search orders, was based on the High Court's inherent jurisdiction. In *Re Abermeadow Ltd* [2000] 2 BCLC 824 striking out under the court's inherent jurisdiction was said to survive the introduction of the CPR, but whether this is correct is open to question (see **46.38**). Once an area has been codified, the need for recourse to the inherent jurisdiction recedes or disappears, see *Harrison v Tew* [1990] 2 AC 523, in which it was held that the inherent jurisdiction to order the assessment by the court of a solicitor's bill of costs had been ousted by subsequent statutory codification. In the interests of certainty the High Court extends the ambit of its inherent jurisdiction with some caution.

It is probably the case that the county court, being the creature of statute, has no inherent jurisdiction. There is direct authority to the contrary in *Langley v North West Water Authority* [1991] 1 WLR 697, in which it was held (before the enactment, in the Civil Procedure Act

1997, of the **County Courts Act 1984, s. 74A**) that a county court had inherent jurisdiction to issue a local practice direction. See also the family cases of *D v D (County Court Jurisdiction: Injunctions)* [1993] 2 FLR 802 and *Devon County Council v B* [1997] 1 FLR 591, which probably turn on the effect of the Children Act 1989. The wide scope of the legislation governing county court proceedings, now allows practically no scope or necessity for the exercise of the county court's inherent jurisdiction even if it has one.

Pre-action protocols

1.7 Pre-action protocols have been formulated for clinical negligence, disease and illness, personal injury, construction and engineering, housing disrepair, defamation, professional negligence and judicial review claims. Each protocol contains detailed rules for stating the allegations being made and the reasons for any denial of liability, and for disclosure of documents. **Paragraph 4 of PD Protocols** sets out the similar approach required in cases not covered by specific pre-action protocols. The protocols are intended to enable parties to obtain relevant information at an early stage, and to promote settlement of the dispute (see **chapter 8**). The CPR enable the court to take into account compliance or non-compliance with any relevant protocol when giving directions for the management of proceedings (**CPR, rr. 3.1**(4) and (5) and **3.9**(1)(e)) and when making orders for costs (**r. 44.3(5)(a)**). The text of the relevant protocols can be found in **appendix 3** of this book.

Court guides

1.8 Practical guidance on the conduct of proceedings in the specialist courts and in the main Divisions of the High Court have been published. Court guides were first published before the introduction of the CPR. The first edition of the **Chancery Guide**, for example, was issued in April 1995. The present editions of the guides have been written so as to comply with the provisions of the CPR and relevant PDs. They draw attention to important matters of practice, common errors and failings, give detailed information about forms to use, provide courtroom and telephone numbers for the use of practitioners, and generally supplement the provisions of the CPR and PDs. The various published court guides are included in this book at **appendix 4**.

Forms

1.9 Numerous standard forms have been promulgated to assist practitioners and court users. Many are prescribed forms, made under the authority of statutory instruments, and can be identified by the letter 'N' in their designations (e.g., **form N244** is the standard application notice). Others are 'practice forms', issued under the authority of the masters of the High Court, which can be identified by the letters 'PF' in their designations. All the prescribed and practice forms (many of which can be completed and printed electronically) are in the CD-ROM version of this book: see **appendix 5**. Some PDs contain important precedents, such as the standard-form freezing injunctions and search orders in the annex to **PD 25**. Electronic versions of these precedents can be obtained by cutting and pasting them from the text of the PD using the CD-ROM version of this book.

THE CIVIL PROCEDURE RULES 1998

A new procedural code

1.10 The CPR comprise not merely new rules, but an entirely new procedural code (**CPR, r. 1.1**(1)). As a result authorities under the old rules must be applied with considerable caution when interpreting the new rules (see **1.20**). **Rule 1.1**(1) specifically refers to the CPR as being a 'procedural' code. However, there is a clear distinction between procedure (or how the court system operates) and practice (the principles applied when dealing with procedural problems). **Rule 1.1**(1) does not say, perhaps deliberately, that the CPR are to be regarded as being a new codification of the practice to be adopted by the courts when making procedural decisions. Nor does **r. 1.1** override existing rules of evidence (see *McPhilemy v Times Newspapers Ltd (No. 2)* [2000] 1 WLR 1732).

Overriding objective

The ethos of the CPR is encapsulated in **r. 1.1**, which provides: **1.11**

(1) These Rules are a new procedural code with the overriding objective of enabling the court to deal with cases justly.
(2) Dealing with a case justly includes, so far as is practicable—
  (a) ensuring that the parties are on an equal footing;
  (b) saving expense;
  (c) dealing with the case in ways which are proportionate—
    (i) to the amount of money involved;
    (ii) to the importance of the case;
    (iii) to the complexity of the issues; and
    (iv) to the financial position of each party;
  (d) ensuring that it is dealt with expeditiously and fairly; and
  (e) allotting to it an appropriate share of the court's resources, while taking into account the need to allot resources to other cases.

The court is required to give effect to this overriding objective of dealing with cases justly when exercising any power under the rules, or when interpreting any rule (**r. 1.2**). In control order proceedings under the Prevention of Terrorism Act 2005, this is subject to the provision in **r. 76.2** that the court must ensure that information is not disclosed contrary to the public interest, as defined in **r. 76.1(4)**.

Parties to litigation are required to help the court to further the overriding objective (**r. 1.3**).

Interpretation and the overriding objective

By **CPR, r. 1.2**, the CPR must be interpreted so as to give effect to the overriding objective (in **r. 1.1**, see **1.11**) of enabling the court to deal with cases justly, subject, in control order proceedings under the Prevention of Terrorism Act 2005, to **r. 76.2** (see **1.11**). Where there are no express words in the CPR dealing with a situation, the court is bound to consider which interpretation best reflects the overriding objective when construing the rules (*Totty v Snowden* [2001] EWCA Civ 1415, [2002] 1 WLR 1384 at [34]). As a result, the old 'quasi-statutory' approach to interpretation, based upon a close analysis of the language used in an attempt to find the true intention of the rules, might be thought to be a thing of the past. Lord Woolf commented in the *Final Report*, ch. 14, para. 5, that: **1.12**

> . . . judges exercising appellate functions will have a significant part to play in giving effect to the new system of case management . . . by laying down principles to be followed in exercising the new powers of case management. It should be borne in mind, however, that management decisions are pre-eminently matters of discretion with which an appeal court would seldom interfere.

Purposive interpretation

Lord Woolf himself made clear in the *Final Report* how the overriding objective must be used to interpret the rules. At paras 10–11 of ch. 20 he stated: **1.13**

> Every word in the rules should have a purpose, but every word cannot sensibly be given a minutely exact meaning. Civil procedure involves more judgment and knowledge than the rules can directly express. In this respect, rules of court are not like an instruction manual for operating a piece of machinery. Ultimately their purpose is to guide the court and the litigants towards the just resolution of the case. Although the rules can offer detailed directions for the technical steps to be taken, the effectiveness of those steps depends upon the spirit in which they are carried out. That in turn depends on an understanding of the fundamental purpose of the rules and of the underlying system of procedure.
>
> In order to identify that purpose at the outset, I have placed at the very beginning of the rules a statement of their overriding objective.

In other words, interpretation is to be purposive rather than a matter of close analysis of the meaning of individual words without taking into account their context.

Plain meaning of the rules

1.14 The CPR have been deliberately drafted in a plain English style in order to make them intelligible to lay people using the courts. When construing the rules the courts primarily seek to find the natural meaning of the words used. Although the court must seek to give effect to the overriding objective when interpreting any rule (**CPR, r. 1.2(b)**), this does not enable the court to hold that provisions of the CPR which have a plain meaning should be construed contrary to that meaning, nor that the plain meaning should be ignored (*Vinos v Marks and Spencer plc* [2001] 3 All ER 784 at [20]). The court cannot, therefore, assume a discretion in order to assist a deserving case where there is no jurisdiction to make an order, even by resorting to the overriding objective (*Godwin v Swindon Borough Council* [2001] EWCA Civ 1478, [2002] 1 WLR 997 at [45]).

May, must and should

1.15 There is a clear distinction between a rule that says a court 'may' do something, thereby giving the court a discretion (which ought to be exercised in accordance with the overriding objective), and a rule which says something 'must' be done (which is obligatory). An example is **CPR, Part 13**. Where a default judgment has been entered prematurely or otherwise in circumstances where the claimant is not entitled to judgment, **r. 13.2** provides that the default judgment must be set aside. On the other hand, where there has been compliance with the rules relating to entering a default judgment, setting aside the judgment is a matter of discretion, **r. 13.3** providing that the court 'may' set it aside. Most of the powers given to the courts under the CPR are given in discretionary form.

Most of the steps to be taken by the parties in the course of proceedings are expressed in mandatory terms. This is frequently made clear by use of the word 'must'. For example, **PD 7, para. 3.5A**, which applies where a claim is to be served outside the jurisdiction under **Regulation (EC) No. 44/2001**, that a prescribed endorsement 'must' be included on the claim form. 'Should' is often used interchangeably with the word 'must', for example, in **PD 7, para. 3.5**, which says that a similar endorsement in cases governed by the **Civil Jurisdiction and Judgments Act 1982** 'should' be included. Both paragraphs have almost identical wording, the only significant difference being the use of 'must' in one, and of 'should' in the other.

Problems with mandatory and discretionary language

1.16 The word 'may' is, in certain contexts, used in a mandatory rather than a discretionary sense. An example is **CPR, r. 24.4(1)**, which provides that a claimant 'may' not apply for summary judgment until the defendant has filed an acknowledgment of service or a defence.

Sometimes there are problems in determining who has the power to exercise a discretion created by use of the word 'may'. An example is **r. 32.5(5)**, which provides that if a party who has served a witness statement does not call the witness or use the statement at trial, 'any other party may put the witness statement in as hearsay evidence'. A natural reading of the rule would indicate that the discretion is vested in the other party to the proceedings. Remarkably, in *McPhilemy v Times Newspapers Ltd (No. 2)* [2000] 1 WLR 1732 it was held that the court has a discretion to refuse permission to use such a statement (see **49.22**).

Sometimes the word 'should' is interpreted to mean 'ought, but may do something else'. The prime example of this is *Bloomsbury Publishing Group Ltd v News Group Newspapers Ltd* [2003] EWHC 1205 (Ch), [2003] 1 WLR 1633, in which it was held that it is possible to issue a claim against 'person or persons unknown'. **PD 7, para. 4.1(3)**, provides that the title of a claim form must contain a title which 'should' state the full name of each party. Use of the word 'should' was contrasted by the court with the word 'must', and was held to justify an interpretation allowing proceedings to be issued against persons unknown.

Different meanings given to different expressions

In a number of cases the courts have held that different expressions appearing in a single rule have to be given different meanings. Examples are: 1.17

(a) The difference between 'day' and 'business day' where they appear in **CPR, r. 6.7.** 'Business day' is defined by **r. 6.7(3)** as excluding Saturdays, Sundays and bank holidays (including Christmas Day and Good Friday). In *Anderton v Clwyd County Council (No. 2)* [2002] EWCA Civ 933, [2002] 1 WLR 3174 it was held that 'day' had to bear a different meaning, and was interpreted as meaning any calendar day, including weekends and bank holidays etc.
(b) In *Charles v NTL Group Ltd* [2002] EWCA Civ 2004, LTL 13/12/2002 it was held that different rules apply to giving notice of Part 36 offers as opposed to Part 36 payments. The court relied on the difference in wording between **CPR, r. 36.8(1) and (3)** (on Part 36 offers) and **r. 36.8(2) and (4)** (on Part 36 payments) to justify the distinction drawn. Regarding Part 36 offers, it is provided in r. 36.8(1) and (3) that offers, and improvements on them, are made 'when received by the offeree'. This was interpreted as meaning that the strict rules on service in **Part 6** (see **chapter 15**) do not apply at all to Part 36 offers. On the other hand, in **r. 36.8(2)** and (4) it is provided that Part 36 payments and improvements to them are made 'when written notice of the payment into court is served on the offeree'. This was interpreted as meaning that service in accordance with the rules in **Part 6** is required for Part 36 payments.

The above decisions are based on a literalistic approach to interpretation, and are hard to reconcile with the intended purposive approach advocated by Lord Woolf (see **1.13**).

Interpretation and human rights

The **Human Rights Act 1998, s. 3(1)**, provides that, so far as it is possible to do so, primary legislation and subordinate legislation (which includes the CPR) must be read and given effect in a way which is compatible with the rights set out in the European Convention on Human Rights. In *Goode v Martin* [2001] EWCA Civ 1899, [2002] 1 WLR 1828, s. 3(1) of the Act and **art. 6(1) of the Convention** were used by the court as a basis for reading additional words into **CPR, r. 17.4**, so that it would not prevent the claimant bringing her real claim to trial. The **Human Rights Act 1998, s. 2(1)**, provides that a court determining a question which arises in connection with a Convention right must take into account any judgment, decision, declaration or advisory opinion of the European Court of Human Rights. Although lawyers must take a responsible attitude to raising human rights points (*Daniels v Walker* [2000] 1 WLR 1382), such points do arise on occasion when courts are considering procedural applications, and the CPR and practice directions have been drafted with a view to being compatible with the Convention. 1.18

Reliance on court staff

In *Sayers v Clarke Walker* [2002] EWCA Civ 645, [2002] 1 WLR 3095, the appellant's solicitors said that a breach of the rules had occurred because they had relied on misleading advice given by court staff. It was held to be wrong for solicitors to attempt to rely on conversations with court staff for the purpose of interpreting civil practice, and that being solicitors they should be expected to know such matters themselves. 1.19

Old case law: generally redundant

As a general rule, advocates should not resort to decisions under the old rules for assistance in interpreting the CPR. In *Biguzzi v Rank Leisure plc* [1999] 1 WLR 1926 the Court of Appeal (Lord Woolf MR, Brooke LJ, Robert Walker LJ) held that the pre-CPR cases on abuse of process in the form of wholesale disregard of court rules (such as *Arbuthnot Latham Bank Ltd v* 1.20

Trafalgar Holdings Ltd [1998] 1 WLR 1426) are not binding or persuasive authorities on the exercise of the court's discretion under the CPR. The Court of Appeal said the position under the CPR is fundamentally different from under the old system. It pointed out that under **r. 1.1** the CPR are a 'new procedural code', and now compliance with court orders would be regarded as more serious than under the previous system. Lord Woolf made it clear that, 'Earlier authorities are no longer generally of any relevance once the CPR applies' ([1999] 1 WLR 1926 at p. 1934). Counsel in *Vinos v Marks and Spencer plc* [2001] 3 All ER 784 had made submissions by reference to authorities under the old rules. May LJ said, at [17]:

> . . . these submissions are not in point. The CPR are a new procedural code, and the question for this court in this case concerns the interpretation and application of the relevant provisions of the new procedural code as they stand untrammelled by the weight of authority that accumulated under the former Rules.

In *SSQ Europe SA v Johann & Backes OHG* [2002] 1 Lloyd's Rep 465 the court commented that decisions under similar (but not identical) provisions of the RSC should be treated 'with caution'.

Old cases as a guide to exercise of discretion

1.21 Where the CPR and previous rules have similar or identical wording, and where it can be shown that the operation of old authorities is consistent with the requirement to further the overriding objective as it applies in the particular case, the court may be prepared to take them into account or at least be persuaded by arguments based on principles established in pre-CPR cases. In *Purdy v Cambran* [1999] CPLR 843 May LJ stated:

> Lord Woolf in *Biguzzi v Rank Leisure plc* [1999] 1 WLR 1926 was not saying that the underlying thought processes of previous decisions should be completely thrown overboard. It is clear in my view, that what Lord Woolf was saying was that reference to authorities under the former rules is generally no longer relevant. Rather it is necessary to concentrate on the intrinsic justice of a particular case in the light of the overriding objective.

Previous jurisprudence, for example, on the exercise of the court's discretion to discharge orders for service out of the jurisdiction made without notice, is not binding, although it may still be illuminating (*Bua International Ltd v Hai Hing Shipping Co. Ltd* [2000] 1 Lloyd's Rep 300). Likewise, although prejudice is no longer an essential prerequisite for an order to strike out for delay — as the decision depends on the justice in all the circumstances of the individual case — the courts will consider prejudice as part of the general enquiry into what is just in the circumstances (*Axa Insurance Co. Ltd v Swire Fraser Ltd* [2000] CPLR 142; *Annodeus Entertainment Ltd v Gibson* (2000) *The Times*, 3 March 2000). When dealing with excusing delay in filing a defence, in *Thorn plc v Macdonald* [1999] CPLR 660, Brooke LJ and Robert Walker LJ applied the pre-CPR principles established in *Mortgage Corporation Ltd v Sandoes* [1997] PNLR 263 and *Finnegan v Parkside Health Authority* [1998] 1 WLR 411 (although it ought to be mentioned that these cases were decided with a view to the forthcoming implementation of the Woolf reforms).

Pre-CPR cases were applied as authoritative in relation to applications to reduce Part 36 payments (*Flynn v Scougall* [2004] EWCA Civ 873, [2004] 1 WLR 3069) and on the question whether a judge should withdraw after a premature disclosure of a Part 36 payment (*Garratt v Saxby* [2004] EWCA Civ 341, [2004] 1 WLR 2152). The Court of Appeal in *Nasser v United Bank of Kuwait* [2001] EWCA Civ 556, [2002] 1 WLR 1868, said that the coming into force of the CPR meant that applications for security for costs are now governed by different principles, whereas in *Vedatech Corporation v Seagate Software Information* [2001] EWCA Civ 1924, LTL 29/11/2001, a differently constituted Court of Appeal held that the judge below had been wrong in not applying a principle derived from pre-CPR case law.

Old cases as a guide to principle

Sometimes, it is entirely sensible to have regard to the old authorities. In *Harrison v Bloom Camillin* (1999) *The Independent*, 28 June 1999, Neuberger J said that although the court had to be careful in relying on old cases, in the context of the application he was dealing with (to set aside a witness summons) some regard was to be paid to the authorities under the old rules. Another example is *Hertfordshire Investments Ltd v Bubb* [2000] 1 WLR 2318, in which the Court of Appeal held that the principles set out in *Ladd v Marshall* [1954] 1 WLR 1489, concerning the reception of new evidence on appeal, continue to be relevant as factors which must be considered, rather than as strict rules (the court must also consider the overriding objective, *Gillingham v Gillingham* [2001] EWCA Civ 906, LTL 8/6/2001). **1.22**

Reference to old rules

Generally, because the CPR are a new procedural code, the courts refuse to look at equivalent provisions in the RSC or CCR as an aid to interpretation. *Omega Engineering Inc. v Omega SA* [2003] EWHC 1482 (Ch), *The Times*, 29 September 2003, is an exception. Rule 3.1(2)(a) of the CPR, which provides a general power to extend or abridge time, was construed by reference to the equivalent provision in the RSC, to avoid an unnecessarily restrictive interpretation being placed on the present rule. A more striking example is *Carnegie v Giessen* [2005] EWCA Civ 191, [2005] 1 WLR 2510. In this case the Court of Appeal said that the pre-CPR **Queen's Bench Masters' Practice Direction (11)** (see **61.16**) is to be treated as remaining in effect, because the CPR do not contain express reference to the enforcement of judgments in foreign currency. **1.23**

Rules of practice

As mentioned at **1.10**, there is a distinction between matters of procedure and matters of practice. Quite a few areas of practice have developed in a way that reflects the substantive law (such as the 'cheque rule' and the rules relating to set-offs in summary judgment applications, see **34.35** to **34.40**) or statutory provisions (such as the **Supreme Court Act 1981, s. 37**, on injunctions) which have not been changed by the introduction of the CPR. The practice in such areas has not been changed by the introduction of the CPR. **1.24**

Unreported, unopposed and first-instance decisions

An important point is the extent to which the courts should look at unreported first-instance decisions on the procedure under the CPR and similar decisions reported in the legal periodicals. Often such reports are very short, they are often misleading when compared with the full transcripts, and there is also a worrying tendency for cases which are in fact contrary to the rules to be the subject of such reports. The danger in citing such cases, especially when they are at first instance, is that they can distract the court from applying the overriding objective and the spirit and intention of the CPR in general and the provisions that directly apply to a case. To combat this, Practice Direction (Citation of Authorities) [2001] 1 WLR 1001 prohibits the use of reports of applications attended by one party only, applications for permission to appeal, applications to decide whether the application is arguable, and county court cases (other than to illustrate damages or where no higher authorities are available). Excessive citation of authorities and reliance on summaries of cases which may not have been prepared by professional lawyers will not be tolerated (*Hamblin v Field* (2000) *The Times*, 26 April 2000). **1.25**

APPLICATION OF THE OVERRIDING OBJECTIVE

Dealing with cases justly

The main concept in the overriding objective (**CPR, r. 1.1**) is that the primary concern of the court is to do justice. Shutting a litigant out through a technical breach of the rules will not **1.26** often be consistent with this, because the primary purpose of the civil courts is to decide cases on their merits, not to reject them for procedural default. An example of this is *Jones v Telford and Wrekin Council* (1999) *The Times*, 29 July 1999, where service had been delayed beyond the period of validity because the claimant's solicitors had problems in obtaining psychiatric reports for service with the particulars of claim. The Court of Appeal upheld an extension of time largely because there were no previous authorities dealing with this situation, Lord Woolf MR commenting that the court must not lose sight of the fact that its primary concern is doing justice. The need to deal with cases justly merited a two-day extension of time under **r. 3.1(2)(a)** in *Corus UK Ltd v Erewash Borough Council* [2005] EWHC 2821 (Admin), [2005] NPC 145. For technical reasons this application for extending the validity of a claim form had to be considered under the general power in **r. 3.1(2)(a)** rather than the more restrictive provisions of **r. 7.6**. While firmly discouraging delay, it was held that the court's function is to ensure public bodies act lawfully, and the public are not to be artificially deprived of the opportunity of mounting a challenge to a public act.

In *Adan v Securicor Custodial Services Ltd* [2004] EWHC 394 (QB), [2005] PIQR P79 the claimant asked the court to use **r. 3.1(2)(i)** so that his claim for medical expenses in a personal injuries claim could be dealt with at a later date if and when the claimant was discharged from long-term hospital care. The application was refused as contrary to the overriding objective. It would have exposed the defendant's insurers to an uncertain liability for an indefinite period, which was oppressive and undesirable.

In *Chilton v Surrey County Council* [1999] CPLR 525 the Court of Appeal indicated that dealing with a claim justly involved dealing with the real claim, and allowed the claimant to rely on a revised statement of past and future loss and expense quantifying the claim at about £400,000 rather than the original statement, which indicated a claim value of about £5,000.

In *Cala Homes (South) Ltd v Chichester District Council* (1999) 79 P & CR 430, the principle of dealing with cases justly was invoked in refusing to strike out a claim which was wrongly started in the Central Office of the High Court instead of in the Crown Office. A party who starts a claim using the wrong form, or relying on the wrong statutory provision, is likely to be granted permission to amend in order to deal with the claim justly (particularly if the defendants are not misled by the mistake) (*Thurrock Borough Council v Secretary of State for the Environment, Transport and the Regions* (2000) *The Times*, 20 December 2000). In *Hannigan v Hannigan* [2000] 2 FCR 650, it was held that although proceedings were instituted using the wrong form, and although the form used contained numerous defects, the substance of the claim was fully known to the defendant. The administration of justice would have been better served had the defendants' solicitors pointed out the defects rather than attempted to take a technical point. *Re Osea Road Camp Sites Ltd* [2004] EWHC 2437 (Ch), [2005] 1 WLR 760, where a claim was struck out because the claimant issued a claim form rather than presenting a petition, ignores **r. 2.1** and is probably wrongly decided. When a case is being considered on appeal, dealing with the case justly includes giving weight to the public interest in the finality of the decision at trial, see *Evans v Tiger Investments Ltd* [2002] EWCA Civ 161, [2002] 2 BCLC 185.

Proportionality: the rule

1.27 The overriding objective of dealing with cases justly is defined in terms that include expense and resources, which has caused concern to purists who consider that justice should be done without regard to the cost at which it is achieved. **Rule 1.1(2) of the CPR** provides that dealing with a case justly includes dealing with it in ways which are proportionate to the importance of the case (r. 1.1(2)(c)(ii)) and allotting to it an appropriate share of the court's resources, while taking into account the need to allot resources to other cases (r. 1.1(2)(e)). An assessment of the importance of the case appears to require consideration of factors other than the amount of money involved and the complexity of the case, which are mentioned separately (r. 1.1(2)(c)(i) and (iii)). It is submitted that the importance which is to be considered may be either an exceptional significance to one of the parties or an importance to the public in general or a section of the public (for example, if it is a test case). The court resources to be considered will include not merely available finance but also the availability of judiciary or judicial time to deal with a matter.

Proportionality and costs

There are cases where the cost of achieving justice can exceed or be out of all proportion to the amount in issue between the parties. In these cases costs can assume an importance exceeding that attached to the issues in dispute. An example is *Gould v Armstrong* [2002] EWCA Civ 1159, LTL 23/7/2002, where the claim was worth £4,500 and there was a counterclaim of £3,715, resulting in a net liability of £785. Costs were out of all proportion to this amount. The Court of Appeal commented that the case cried out for a conciliatory approach, and held that the district judge had been right to seek to reduce post-judgment costs by making summary assessments of both sides' costs so as to avoid remitting the case for detailed assessment. **1.28**

Guidance on the practice to be adopted when assessing proportionality in standard-basis assessments was given in *Lownds v Home Office* [2002] EWCA Civ 365, [2002] 1 WLR 2450. In a case where proportionality is an issue, a preliminary judgment as to the proportionality of the costs as a whole should be made at the outset. If the judge concludes that the costs are not disproportionate, the various items of costs are then considered item by item applying the reasonableness tests for standard-basis assessments in **r. 44.4(2)**. If the judge concludes that the costs as a whole may be disproportionate, each item will then be scrutinised applying the tests both for proportionality and reasonableness (see **68.34**).

According to *King v Telegraph Group Ltd* [2004] EWCA Civ 613, [2005] 1 WLR 2282, there are three weapons available to a party who is concerned about the risk of extravagant conduct by the other side:

(a) a prospective cost-capping order (see **66.54**);
(b) a retrospective assessment of costs conducted in accordance with the CPR (see *Lownds v Home Office*); and
(c) a wasted costs order (see **66.70**).

Proportionality: examples

In *Reed v Oury* [2002] EWHC 369 (Ch), LTL 14/3/2002, it was held that having regard to the defendant's conduct in the litigation, the weakness of his counterclaim, and the fact that even if he won on his counterclaim he would still owe a substantial amount to the claimants on the claim (which had already proceeded to judgment), the proportionate way of securing the overriding objective was to stay the counterclaim until he had paid the amount incontestably due to the claimants. In *Mason v First Leisure Corporation plc* [2003] EWHC 1814 (QB), LTL 26/8/2003, it was held that the claimant had been wrongly granted a without-notice order extending the period of validity of the claim form (see **15.7** to **15.10**). Nevertheless, the court refused to set aside service, because the defendant had notice of the claim through the pre-action protocol correspondence, and setting aside would have been unjust and disproportionate. **1.29**

The concept of proportionality will not be applied to prevent a party from instructing lawyers chosen by that party, even if it means one side is represented by far more eminent lawyers than the other (*Maltez v Lewis* (1999) *The Times*, 4 May 1999). Neuberger J said that the right to choose a legal representative, although not absolute, was a fundamental and well-established ingredient in any free society. Proportionality is very important when the court is considering imposing sanctions (see **chapter 46**), with the court being particularly astute to ensure the punishment imposed for procedural default fits the crime. In *Ali v Naseem* (2003) *The Times*, 3 October 2003, it was held that a writ *ne exeat regno* (see **38.42**) would only be granted if proportionate and necessary to secure the ends of justice. The importance of the proportionality principle was underlined by *South Bucks District Council v Porter* [2003] UKHL 26, [2003] 2 AC 558, where the House of Lords used the expression 'just and proportionate' to describe the circumstances in which an interim injunction should be granted rather than the conventional 'just and convenient' formula.

Equal footing

1.30 The case management powers of the court will be exercised so as to ensure, so far as possible, that where the parties have very different financial means the costs thought to be unreasonably incurred by the more affluent party should be paid by that party in any event. In *Maltez v Lewis* (1999) *The Times,* 4 May 1999, it was held that the court had the power to ensure a 'level playing field' by using its case management powers to allow a smaller firm more time, or to require a larger firm to prepare court bundles even though the responsibility would otherwise be that of the smaller firm. Ultimately, the court could ensure compliance with the overriding objective by ensuring that a party was not visited by excessive costs because the other side had instructed unreasonably expensive advisers.

In *McPhilemy v Times Newspapers Ltd* [1999] 3 All ER 775 Lord Woolf MR said that a party which wanted the court to restrain the activities of another party with the object of achieving greater equality, must demonstrate that it is itself conducting the proceedings with a desire to limit expense so far as practical. However, the powers of the court to restrain excess do not extend to preventing a party from putting forward allegations which are central to its case. That said, it is open to the court to attempt to control how those allegations are litigated with a view to limiting costs.

Dealing with cases expeditiously and saving expense

1.31 In *Cadogan Properties Ltd v Mount Eden Land Ltd* (1999) LTL 29/6/99 the court at first instance had made an order for substituted service in circumstances where there were no grounds for doing so. That order was set aside on appeal, with the result that proceedings had not been served and the period of validity had expired. The Court of Appeal relied on **CPR, r. 1.1(2)(d)**, and the need to deal with cases fairly and expeditiously, and also on the need for proportionality (**r. 1.1(2)(c)**), to justify making an order extending the validity of the originating process. The defendant was aware of the proceedings, and suffered no significant prejudice by the course adopted by the court. A court may refuse to hear the merits of an application on the ground of dealing with the case justly, expeditiously and economically where the application will bring no proportionate benefit to the claim as a whole (*Norwich Union Linked Life Assurance Ltd v Mercantile Credit Co. Ltd* (2003) LTL 6/1/2004). Where appropriate and available, parties should use technology, such as videoconferencing, to reduce costs (*Black v Pastouna* [2005] EWCA Civ 1389, The Independent, 2 December 2005). In *Re Hoicrest Ltd* [2000] 1 WLR 414 it was held that, because there was a dispute about crucial facts, the claimant's application under the Companies Act 1985, s. 359, for rectification of a company's register of members, could not proceed under **CPR, Part 8**. The claimant had known all along about the factual dispute and it was his fault for starting the proceedings in the wrong way. The Court of Appeal held that the overriding objective would be furthered by actively managing the case, with appropriate directions, which would be likely to be more cost-effective than striking it out and requiring the claimant to start fresh proceedings. The court may, under its inherent jurisdiction, decline to continue with a trial which has been delayed by the court's own fault (*Re Rocksteady Services Ltd* [2001] BCC 467).

Allotting an appropriate share of the court's resources

1.32 In *S. B. J. Stephenson Ltd v Mandy* [1999] CPLR 500 the defendant appealed against an interim order restraining him from breaching a restrictive covenant in his contract of employment. The appeal against the interim order came before the Court of Appeal on 30 June, but the trial of the main proceedings had been fixed for 20 July. Given the short period before the trial and the fact that the claimant had given the usual undertaking in damages, the court decided that considering the merits of the appeal would not be in accordance with the overriding objective. Expense would not be saved by hearing the appeal, and, given the short time to trial, hearing the appeal would not be a good use of the court's resources.

An appeal was also dismissed (with costs on the indemnity basis) in *Adoko v Jemal* (1999) *The Times*, 8 July 1999, in very different circumstances, on the ground of allotting to it no more than an appropriate share of the court's resources. In this case the appellant had failed to correct the notice of appeal despite a warning from the respondent that it was seriously defective, and had failed to comply with the directions relating to appeal bundles. The Court of Appeal spent over an hour trying to sort out the position, and then decided it was inappropriate that any further share of the court's resources should be allocated to the appeal.

Cooperating

In *Chilton v Surrey County Council* [1999] CPLR 525, referred to above at **1.26**, the Court of Appeal decided against the defendant partly because it seemed to be attempting to take tactical advantage of a mistake by the claimant's solicitors in overlooking to serve the revised statement of past and future loss and expense rather than cooperating with the claimant's solicitors to put matters right. Similar reasoning informed *Hertsmere Primary Care Trust v Administrators of Balasubramanium's Estate* [2005] EWHC 320 (Ch), [2005] 3 All ER 274. The claimant made a Part 36 offer, and was then told by counsel for the defendant that the offer was defective. Despite requests, the defendant declined to explain why. Solicitors for the claimant wrote to ask why, but got no reply. It transpired there was an obvious, but technical, defect. The defendant's conduct was held to be a refusal to cooperate, and the court treated the offer as if it had been in the proper form. **1.33**

In *Hateley v Morris* [2004] EWHC 252 (Ch), [2004] 1 BCLC 582, a striking-out order made by the registrar was overturned on appeal despite an eight-month delay when neither side applied to relist a case management conference. One of the reasons given by the court was that either side could have relisted the matter, and both sides have a duty to cooperate in progressing proceedings.

PRACTICAL IMPACT

Culture

The culture of civil litigation has been changed by the introduction of the CPR. The civil justice system continues to be essentially adversarial in nature, as the ethos of *Access to Justice* is not to undermine the adversarial approach itself, but simply to eliminate its excesses. The effect of the new procedures is that the legal profession will continue to perform its traditional adversarial role, but in a managed environment governed by the courts, and by rules which require the parties to focus their efforts on the key issues. However, it is now less adversarial than before the CPR came into force, and the CPR encourage and require greater cooperation between parties in the preparation of cases for trial. There is an overall emphasis on reducing the role of taking technical points and obstructive tactics, and encouraging the identification and speedy trial of relevant issues only. The parties are required to exhibit openness and cooperation from the outset, to assist the expeditious resolution of their dispute. This requirement is supported by pre-action protocols, the encouragement of ADR, and a system of judicial case management to scrutinise the conduct, cost, and progress of litigation. **1.34**

Case management

Judicial case management effectively removes control of the timescale of litigation from the parties. Procedural judges seek to identify the relevant issues at an early stage, and control the extent to which a party can inflate the costs of the litigation. Particular issues are the curtailment of the rights of parties to adduce expert evidence and to require others to disclose **1.35** documents. The CPR require the parties to do a substantial amount of work investigating and disclosing information and documents early in the litigation process, and this results in the front-loading of costs.

The cost of litigation should be affordable, predictable and proportionate to the value, or to the complexity, of individual cases. Proceedings are therefore allocated by the court to the small claims track, the fast track or the multi-track, depending on the complexity of the matters to be tried, and the amount in issue. These tracks have different timetables and pre-trial procedures. Small claims track cases (see **chapter 43**) are generally given directions requiring minimal pre-trial preparation, and early trial dates. In non-complex proceedings involving between £5,000 and £15,000 (which are allocated to the fast track, **chapter 44**), there are fixed timetables of no more than 30 weeks between track allocation and trial. Strict sanctions are normally applied to parties who do not comply with the procedures or timetables. More complex cases (assigned to the multi-track, **chapter 45**) usually require more judicial attention during the preparation stages, and there are usually a number of case management hearings to ensure they are prepared in an efficient manner. They are usually tried at civil trial centres which have the required resources, including specialist judges.

Active management of the more complex and substantial cases assigned to the multi-track requires practitioners to investigate the facts, research the legal principles and identify the issues at an earlier stage. At case management conferences the judge can ask searching questions about a party's case with the objective of narrowing the issues to be tried, and may eliminate minor issues which are of little or no relevance to the substance of the dispute. In all cases, litigation practitioners must comply with a rigorous timetable, with a regime of real sanctions on default.

Role of the client

1.36 Even if a solicitor is retained, clients have a number of rights and obligations under the CPR. All statements of case must be verified by a statement of truth, declaring the belief of the party that the contents are true and accurate (see **23.11** to **23.16**). A party giving disclosure (**chapter 48**) is required to make a statement setting out the extent of the search which has been made to locate documents which he is required to disclose, and certifying that he understands his duty to disclose and that to the best of his knowledge he has complied with that duty (**CPR, r. 31.10(6)**). The court may order that a judgment or order be served on a party in person as well as any solicitor acting for the party (**r. 40.5**). A solicitor is under a duty to notify a client against whom a costs order is made, if the client was not present when the costs order was made (**r. 44.2**). When deciding what order to make in respect of costs, the court should have regard not only to which party succeeded, but also to the conduct of the parties, including the manner in which a claim was pursued or defended, and whether a claim was exaggerated (**r. 44.3(4)**). Additionally, the conduct of the parties before, as well as during, the proceedings, and efforts made, if any, before or during the proceedings to resolve the dispute, are factors to be taken into account in deciding the amount of costs (**r. 44.3(5)**).

Closer client involvement in civil proceedings is one of the objects of the Solicitors' Costs Information and Client Care Code 1999. This requires solicitors to give clients the best information possible about the overall costs of a case, including giving a realistic estimate or an explanation of why this is not possible. Solicitors should also discuss with the client whether the likely outcome justifies the expense or risk (including the risk of paying the other side's costs). Solicitors must also give their clients a clear explanation of the issues raised, and keep them properly informed about progress in the case.

Role of the solicitor

1.37 Principle 21.01 of the *Guide to the Professional Conduct of Solicitors*, 8th ed. (1999), states that solicitors who act in litigation, whilst under a duty to do their best for their client, must never deceive or mislead the court. If a solicitor is instructed by a client to conduct a case without regard to the overriding objective of the CPR (such as a well-heeled client instructing his solicitor to incur disproportionate expenditure when acting against a client of limited means), the solicitor must warn the client of the potential sanctions in costs that may be incurred as a result. As **CPR, r. 1.3**, requires parties to help the court to further the overriding objective, the question arises whether the solicitor would be in breach of principle 21.01 by carrying out the client's instructions and would thus be forced to withdraw. At present this is unclear and open to interpretation. However, it is likely that the Law Society will review the relevant provision of the Guide in the light of the CPR. The Access to Justice Act 1999, s. 42, has inserted a new provision in the Courts and Legal Services Act 1990, s. 27 (rights of audience), that any person exercising a right of audience before any court has 'a duty to the court to act with independence in the interests of justice' and that the duty 'shall override' any other obligation with which it is inconsistent (other than an obligation under the criminal law).

Role of the barrister

A barrister must 'assist the court in the administration of justice and must not deceive or knowingly or recklessly mislead the court' (Code of Conduct of the Bar of England and Wales, para. 302). The positive manner in which this obligation is expressed may sit more easily beside the overriding objective of the CPR than the obligation of solicitors under principle 21.01 of their code, but may, as a result, make it more likely for a barrister to feel professionally embarrassed when faced with instructions to do some act which may be contrary to the requirement in **CPR, r. 1.3**. **1.38**

Confidentiality and the overriding objective

Conflict may occur between the overriding objective and the duty of a practitioner not to disclose confidential information. For example, **CPR, r. 29.3(2)**, provides for a representative to attend a case management conference 'with sufficient authority to deal with any issues that are likely to arise'. During a case management conference, it is possible that the court may seek information, the disclosure of which would involve a waiver of privilege. The court may well ask about the costs expended to date, the relative financial standing of the parties (one of the issues to be taken into account in meeting the overriding objective), and details of the funding arrangements for the litigation. It is clear the court does not have power to order a representative to disclose privileged information (see **48.40**), but there is an obvious tension between obtaining information for active case management purposes and client confidentiality. If the client is not to attend the case management conference, specific authority will be required to disclose the information which is likely to be sought. **1.39**

Advice to clients

It is important that every client should be advised at an early stage, not only about the general duties to promote the overriding objective, but also other matters, including: **1.40**

(a) the wide-ranging costs and interest sanctions available to the court (see **chapter 46**);
(b) the client's duty in relation to a statement of truth (see **23.13**);
(c) the client's duties of search in relation to disclosure of documents (see **48.14** and **48.8**);
(d) the duties to the court of an expert witness (see **52.4**).

Chapter 2 Court Organisation

INTRODUCTION

2.1 Civil proceedings in England and Wales may be conducted in magistrates' courts, county courts and the High Court. Magistrates' courts have only limited jurisdiction in relation to civil matters, and will not be considered further in *Blackstone's Civil Practice*. Appeals in civil matters are taken to the Court of Appeal, Civil Division, and the House of Lords. Appeals are considered in **chapters** 71 to 73. A wide range of civil disputes are also determined by various tribunals, including employment tribunals and social security tribunals. The composition of and procedure followed by tribunals are regulated by the Tribunals and Inquiries Act 1992 and by rules laid down by statutory instrument for each type of tribunal. They will not be considered further in this book.

This chapter looks at the composition and organisation of the High Court and the county courts and considers the different court personnel and their powers. The rules governing venue, allocation of business and transfer between the High Court and the county courts are dealt with in **chapter 11**.

COUNTY COURTS

2.2 The county courts derive their jurisdiction and powers from statute, principally the **County Courts Act 1984**. There are 219 county courts in England and Wales, each exercising its powers for a limited geographical district (**County Courts Act 1984, s. 1**). On Her Majesty's Courts Service website (www.hmcourts-service.gov.uk) there is a complete list of all county courts with contact details and location maps (click on Court Information and Addresses). For administrative purposes, certain county courts have been designated as civil trial centres at which multi-track cases for their areas will be heard. County courts within the group area which are not civil trial centres are called satellite courts. Each civil trial centre is presided over by a designated civil judge, who is a circuit judge responsible for the effective organisation of each civil trial centre and its satellite courts. Although it was originally envisaged that all multi-track cases would be remitted from satellite courts to the civil trial centre for case management and hearing, some multi-track cases, in particular, possession cases, will remain with the satellite court.

The principal judicial officers of the county courts are circuit judges and district judges. Circuit judges are professional lawyers with a 10-year Crown Court or county court qualification (see Courts Act 1971, s. 16). Most (but not all) circuit judges sit in the Crown Court as well as the county courts, and may be supplemented by recorders, who are part-time judges and who, with limited exceptions, exercise the full powers of a circuit judge (**County Courts Act 1984, s. 5(3)**). Circuit judges conduct most county court trials, sitting alone, and also hear appeals from decisions of district judges. It is preferred for such appeals to be heard by a full-time rather than part-time judge, but this is not always possible.

A circuit judge or recorder may be specifically requested (or 'ticketed'), under the **Supreme Court Act 1981, s. 9**, to sit in the High Court (see **2.7**) or, under **s. 68**, in the Technology and Construction Court (see **2.16**). Where a circuit judge, without being aware she was not duly authorised, heard a High Court case which had not been properly released to her for trial, there was an error of procedure falling within **CPR, r. 3.10** (*Fawdry and Co. v Murfitt* [2002] EWCA Civ 643, [2003] QB 104). This meant the trial judge did have jurisdiction (the de facto doctrine), the error could be remedied, and the result of the trial would stand unless the appeal court so ordered. The result would have been different if the judge had known she was not authorised to hear the case. *Fawdry and Co. v Murfitt* was applied in *Coppard v Commissioners of Customs and Excise* [2003] EWCA Civ 511, [2003] QB 1428, in which it was held that the de facto doctrine does not offend against the **European Convention on Human Rights, art. 6(1)**. *Fawdry and Co. v Murfitt* and *Coppard v Commissioners of Customs and Excise* were both applied in *Baldock v Webster* [2004] EWCA Civ 1869, [2006] 2 WLR 1, in which the de facto doctrine was invoked to uphold the decision of a recorder at the trial of a High Court case which he had not been authorised to hear under the **Supreme Court Act 1981, s. 9**, and which he had dealt with in the mistaken belief that it was proceeding in the county court.

District judges, who must have a seven-year general qualification (**County Courts Act 1984, s. 9**), deal with most interim applications made in the county courts, and normally try all small claims track, and many fast track cases. The allocation of business to different levels of judiciary in the county courts is dealt with in **2.3 to 2.6**.

The correct mode of address for circuit judges and recorders is 'Your Honour'. District judges are addressed as 'Sir' or 'Madam'. Full-time judiciary are addressed as 'Judge', when not formally sitting in court, or in private.

The administrative staff of the county courts are civil servants. They are headed by the court manager and correspondence with the court is usually addressed to that official. The administrative staff draw up and issue court documents, and arrange for them to be served. They also maintain court records.

The county court bailiff is responsible for enforcing judgments by process of execution and serving documents personally. Unlike the High Court enforcement officer, a county court bailiff is a civil servant.

County courts are open to the public from 10.00 a.m. to 4.00 p.m. every day of the year, except weekends, bank holidays and one or two other days specified in **PD 2, para. 3.2**.

Allocation of business to levels of judiciary in the county courts

Trials Circuit judges may exercise the full powers of the county court. By **PD 2B, para. 11.1**, district judges can deal with all small claims and fast track cases, and may also hear cases for the recovery of land, the assessment of damages, and **Part 8** claims allocated to the multi-track (with some exceptions listed in **PD 2B, para. 11.1(a)**). Other claims may be allocated to a district judge only with the permission of the designated civil judge (**PD 2B, para. 11.1(d)**). Cases allocated to the small claims track may only be assigned to a circuit judge with his or her consent (**PD 2B, para. 11.2**). A district judge may not try a case in which an allegation of indirect discrimination is made against a public authority under the Race Relations Act 1976, **2.3**

s. 19B (which makes it unlawful for a public authority to perform a discriminatory act in carrying out its functions) (**PD 2B, para. 15**).

2.4 **Injunctions, anti-social behaviour injunctions and committal** A district judge may grant an injunction:

(a) in any proceedings which he or she has jurisdiction to hear under **PD 2B, para. 11.1** (see 2.3) (**PD 2B, para. 8.1(a)**);
(b) in a money claim which has not yet been allocated to a track, provided the amount claimed is not greater than the fast track limit of £15,000 (**PD 2B, para. 8.1(b); CPR, r. 26.6(4)(b)**);
(c) in terms agreed by the parties (**PD 2B, paras 2.3(a)** and **8.1(c)**);
(d) in connection with or ancillary to a charging order (**PD 2B, paras 2.3(b)** and **8.1(c)**);
(e) in connection with or ancillary to an order appointing a receiver by way of equitable execution (**PD 2B, paras 2.3(c)** and **8.1(c)**);
(f) in proceedings under **RSC, ord. 77, r. 16 in CPR, sch. 1** (an order restraining a person from receiving a sum due from the Crown) (**PD 2B, paras 2.3(c)** and **8.1(c)**);
(g) under the **Housing Act 1996, ss. 153A, 153B** or **153D** (anti-social behaviour injunctions), or the **Protection from Harassment Act 1997, s. 3** (an order restraining a person from conduct which amounts to harassment) (**PD 2B, para. 8.1(d)**).

Otherwise only a circuit judge may grant an injunction in a county court (**PD 2B, para. 8.1**).

A district judge cannot make a committal order to punish breach of an injunction unless authorised by statute (**PD 2B, para. 8.3**, which lists provisions giving such authority). For the circumstances in which a district judge has authority under the Housing Act 1996 to commit see **CPR, r. 65.6(6)**, and **92.11**. It is preferable for committal applications to be heard by a circuit judge rather than a recorder, but this is not always possible.

2.5 **Distribution of business between circuit and district judges** Where both circuit and district judges have jurisdiction, the designated civil judge may make arrangements distributing business between them, including assigning particular cases to individual district judges (**PD 2B, paras 13 and 14**).

2.6 **Case management** By virtue of **PD 29, para. 3.10**, a district judge or a circuit judge may deal with case management issues in respect of cases proceeding in the county courts.

HIGH COURT

2.7 The High Court is one part of the Supreme Court of Judicature of England and Wales. (The other parts are the Crown Court, the Court of Protection, the Supreme Court Costs Office and the Court of Appeal. The Court of Protection will be separated from the Supreme Court of Judicature when the relevant provisions of the Mental Capacity Act 2005 are brought into force.) The High Court's main administrative offices and court facilities are located at the Royal Courts of Justice (RCJ), Strand, London. In addition, there are 132 district registries, which are established by the **Supreme Court Act 1981, ss. 99** to **102**. Each registry serves the districts of the county courts listed in the Civil Courts Order 1983 (SI 1983/713), as amended.

Most trials in the High Court are conducted by High Court judges (puisne judges), who must be practitioners of at least 10 years' standing (**Supreme Court Act 1981, s. 10**). Most interim applications are dealt with in the RCJ by judicial officers known as masters, or by district judges in cases proceeding in the district registries. The allocation of business to different levels of judiciary in the High Court is dealt with in detail in **2.8** to **2.13** below.

Under the **Supreme Court Act 1981, s. 9(1)** and (2), the Lord Chief Justice may request a circuit judge or recorder to act as a High Court judge: when so acting such a judge is informally known as a section 9 judge. A request may be made only after consulting the Lord Chancellor (**s. 9(2B)**) and only with the concurrence of the Judicial Appointments Commission (**s. 9(2D)**). The Lord Chief Justice, after consulting the Lord Chancellor, may appoint as a deputy High Court judge, for a certain period or to sit on certain occasions, any person who is qualified for appointment as a puisne judge (s. 9(4)).

High Court district judges often also hold the office of district judge for the local county court. Masters and district judges must be practitioners of at least seven years' standing (**Supreme Court Act 1981, s. 88** and **sch. 2**).

The correct mode of address for a High Court judge is 'My Lord' or 'My Lady'. Masters are addressed as 'Master'. District judges are addressed as 'Sir' or 'Madam'.

As in the county court, the administrative work of the High Court is performed by civil servants. Enforcement is conducted by enforcement officers who are self-employed practitioners.

The High Court consists of three Divisions, namely the Chancery Division, the Family Division and the Queen's Bench Division. Each High Court judge is attached to a particular Division, by direction of the Lord Chief Justice under the **Supreme Court Act 1981, s. 5(2)**, but may occasionally act as an additional judge of another Division, by direction of the Lord Chief Justice under **s. 5(3)**. Under **s. 5(1)(a)**, the Chancellor of the High Court is president of the Chancery Division. Under **s. 5(1)(b)**, the Lord Chief Justice is a judge of the Queen's Bench Division by virtue of his office and there are also a president and a vice-president of that Division. There is a president of the Family Division (**s. 5(1)(c)**). Each Division has its own judiciary and its own administrative offices for issuing claim forms, arranging interim hearings and trials and for dealing with enforcement. Further, specialist courts exist within the Queen's Bench Division and the Chancery Division to deal with particular classes of cases. These include the Admiralty Court, the Commercial Court, and the Technology and Construction Court in the Queen's Bench Division and the Companies Court and the Patents Court in the Chancery Division (see further **2.15** to **2.21**). Each of these specialist courts also has its own judges and administrative offices. In addition, public law matters, particularly applications for judicial review, are dealt with separately in the Administrative Court (see **2.22**).

The opening times for the various offices of the RCJ are specified in **PD 2, para. 2.1(1) and (2)**. It is usual for a district registry to have the same opening times as the county court offices of which it forms part (**PD 2, para. 2.1(3)**).

Allocation of cases to different levels of the judiciary in the High Court

Paragraphs 2 to 7A of PD 2B state how hearings are allocated between the different levels of the judiciary in the High Court. **PD 2B** does not apply to proceedings in the Family Division, save to the extent that they can also be dealt with in the Chancery Division (**PD 2B, para. 3.2**). **2.8**

Trials Masters and district judges have the power to try **Part 8** claims (subject to **PD 2B, para. 5.1(d)** — see **2.11**), but may not try other cases allocated to the multi-track, or determine a preliminary issue in a multi-track claim, except with the consent of the parties (**PD 2B, para. 4.1**). This does not prevent masters and district judges from hearing applications for summary judgment, or from assessing damages (**PD 2B, paras 4.1 and 4.2**). **2.9**

Deputy High Court judges, masters and district judges cannot try claims under the **Human Rights Act 1998** in respect of judicial acts or for declarations of incompatibility (**PD 2B, para. 7A**).

2.10 **Injunctions and interim remedies** Applications for injunctions, orders for specific performance, freezing injunctions (including orders for disclosure of assets which may become the subject of an application for a freezing injunction), search orders and orders authorising entry on to land to recover, inspect or sample property must be made to a judge. Masters and district judges may grant ordinary injunctions in terms agreed by the parties, or connected to charging orders and receivership by way of equitable execution or in proceedings under **CPR, r. 66.7(3)**, (an order restraining a person from receiving a sum due from the Crown) (**PD 2B, para. 2.3**). Examinations made under freezing orders will usually be dealt with by a master or district judge, or before an examiner they have appointed (**PD 2B, para.** 7). **PD 2B, para. 3.1**, lists a number of orders a master or district judge may not make. These include orders relating to the liberty of a subject, and relating to judicial review claims (except that Queen's Bench Division masters may make orders on interim applications in judicial review claims).

2.11 **Chancery proceedings** **PD 2B, para. 5.1**, contains a list of Chancery applications that must be dealt with by a judge rather than a master or district judge, unless the Chancellor consents. These include approving compromises on behalf of a person under a disability, where the value of the claim exceeds £100,000; hearing **Part 8** claims brought under **PD 8B, para. A. 1(2) or (3)**, to determine a question of law or the construction of a document; and making final orders under the Landlord and Tenant Acts 1927 and 1954, except by consent or for interim rents under **ss. 24A to 24D** of the 1954 Act.

2.12 **Assignment of claims to masters and transfers between masters** **PD 2B, para. 6**, empowers the Senior Master and Chief Master to assign claims in the RCJ to individual masters, or to transfer an assigned case from one master to another. The fact that a case has been assigned to one master does not prevent it being dealt with by another master, where necessary.

2.13 **Case management** By virtue of **PD 29, para. 3.10**, masters will generally deal with case management issues in respect of cases proceeding in the RCJ, and district judges in respect of cases proceeding in the district registries.

High Court Divisions

2.14 Business is allocated between the three High Court Divisions by the **Supreme Court Act 1981, s. 61** and **sch. 1**. However, the jurisdiction of the High Court is exercisable by all three Divisions alike (**Supreme Court Act 1981, s. 5(5)**). Thus, business not specifically allocated to a particular Division may be dealt with by any. In practice, the Divisions have developed their own areas of expertise. The broad position is as follows:

(a) The Queen's Bench Division is usually the most appropriate Division for dealing with claims seeking common law remedies (debt, damages, recovery of land, recovery of goods), including most claims in contract and tort. It will deal, for example, with all personal injury and clinical negligence claims proceeding in the High Court. The Queen's Bench Division has been assigned all cases involving applications for writs of habeas corpus (save those relating to a minor, which would be dealt with by the Family Division), applications for judicial review, control order proceedings, within the meaning of the Prevention of Terrorism Act 2005, and Admiralty claims and claims being dealt with in the Commercial Court (**Supreme Court Act 1981, sch. 1**).

(b) The Chancery Division has been assigned all cases involving the sale, exchange or partition of land; mortgages; execution of trusts; administration of estates; bankruptcy; taking of partnership accounts; rectification etc. of deeds; probate; intellectual property; and applications under the enactments relating to companies. It can also deal with other areas, such as actions in contract and tort not specifically assigned to other divisions (**Supreme Court Act 1981, sch. 1**). Any claim which raises an issue under the EC Treaty, art. 81 (anti-competitive agreements) or art. 82 (abuse of a dominant market position), or the equivalent United Kingdom statutory provisions, chapter 1 or chapter 2 of the Competition Act 1998, which is not proceeding in the Commercial or Admiralty Court must be transferred to the Chancery Division at the RCJ (**CPR, r. 30.8**). For more information on Chancery business see **11.6**.

(c) The Family Division has been assigned all matrimonial matters; matters relating to children, such as adoption, legitimacy and guardianship; non-contentious probate business; and proceedings under the Human Fertilisation and Embryology Act 1990, s. 30 (**Supreme Court Act 1981, sch. 1**). Proceedings which invoke the jurisdiction of the High Court to grant declarations as to the best interests of incapacitated adults (such as permanent vegetative state cases and sterilisation of persons unable to give consent), although they are not allocated to any Division, are more suitable for the Family Division (Practice Direction (Declaratory Proceedings: Incapacitated Adults) [2002] 1 WLR 325). Cases about the best interests of children are also to be litigated in the Family Division (*A v A Health Authority* [2002] EWHC 18 (Fam/Admin), [2002] Fam 213). Cases which only involve issues of public law, even though they are concerned with the welfare of children or incompetent adults, are properly litigated by way of a claim for judicial review (*A v A Health Authority*). Human rights challenges to care plans and placements of children should be heard in the Family Division, preferably by judges with experience of administrative law (*C v Bury Metropolitan Borough Council* [2002] EWHC 1438 (Fam), *The Times*, 25 July 2002). The procedure relating to family matters is not considered in this book.

SPECIALIST COURTS

Within the High Court there are several specialist courts which deal with special types of claim. Some of these courts have issued guides to their own procedure (see **appendix** 4). **2.15**

The jurisdiction of these specialist courts is dealt with at **11.7**. The types of case suitable for the specialist courts, and a brief outline of the procedure to be followed in them is set out below.

Technology and Construction Court

The Technology and Construction Court (TCC) was formerly known as the Official Referees' Department. It consists of judges and other officers nominated under the **Supreme Court Act 1981, s. 68**, to exercise the jurisdiction of the High Court in TCC claims, as defined in **CPR, r. 60.1**. Nomination is by the Lord Chief Justice after consulting the Lord Chancellor. **CPR, Part 60**, and **PD 60** set out the practice relating to TCC claims. They are supplemented by the **Technology and Construction Court Guide** (which is on the CD-ROM version of *Blackstone's Civil Practice*). All TCC cases started in or transferred to London will be classified as suitable for determination either by a High Court judge or a senior circuit judge, and will be allocated accordingly (**Technology and Construction Court Guide, para 3.7**). Parties may make brief representations by letter as to the appropriate classification (**para. 3.7.3**). The TCC deals with technically complex matters, with particular emphasis on construction cases. TCC claims in the High Court outside London may be issued in any district registry, but preferably in one where a TCC judge will usually be available, namely, Birmingham, Bristol, Cardiff, Chester, Exeter, Leeds, Liverpool, Newcastle, Nottingham or Salford (**PD 60, para. 3.3**). The county courts in which a TCC claim may be issued are Birmingham, Bristol, Cardiff, Central London, Chester, Exeter, Leeds, Liverpool, Newcastle, Nottingham and Salford (**PD 60, para. 3.4**). However, a great proportion of TCC claims are conducted in the TCC in Fetter Lane in central London. **2.16**

A claim in the TCC will be assigned to a named TCC judge who will have primary responsibility for the case management of the claim (**PD 60, para. 6.1**). The trial will usually be conducted by the assigned judge (**para. 11.1**).

Commercial Court

2.17 The Commercial Court is part of the Queen's Bench Division. The judges of the Commercial Court are High Court judges who are nominated to be commercial judges (**Supreme Court Act 1981, s. 6**). Nomination is by the Lord Chief Justice after consulting the Lord Chancellor. **CPR, Part 58**, and **PD 58** govern proceedings in the Commercial Court. The Commercial Court hears commercial claims, as defined in **CPR, r. 58.1** (**Supreme Court Act 1981, s. 62(3)**). Claim forms should be marked with the words 'Queen's Bench Division, Commercial Court' (**PD 58, para. 2.3**). All claims in the commercial list are allocated to the multi-track and therefore the rules relating to allocation questionnaires and track allocation do not apply to them (**CPR, r. 58.13(1)**), and generally all pre-trial applications are dealt with by a High Court judge, rather than by a master or district judge (**PD 58, para. 1.3**). The **Admiralty and Commercial Courts Guide** (the text of which is in **appendix** 4) sets out the procedure to be followed in the Commercial Court in matters not covered by the CPR and PDs (Practice Statement (Admiralty and Commercial Courts: Procedure) (2002) *The Times*, 2 April 2002).

Admiralty Court

2.18 The Admiralty Court is the part of the Queen's Bench Division which exercises the High Court's Admiralty jurisdiction, as defined in the **Supreme Court Act 1981, s. 20**, and the High Court's jurisdiction as a prize court (**s. 62(2)**). The judges of the Admiralty Court are High Court judges who are nominated to be Admiralty judges (**s. 6**). Nomination is by the Lord Chief Justice after consulting the Lord Chancellor. All Admiralty proceedings must be commenced in the High Court (Civil Courts (Amendment) (No. 2) Order 1999 (SI 1999/1011)). **CPR, Part 58** (Commercial Court), applies to claims in the Admiralty Court except where **Part 61** provides otherwise (**r. 61.1(3)**). **CPR, Parts 58** and **61**, and **PD 61**, are the principal sources for the practice of the Admiralty Court and are supplemented by the **Admiralty and Commercial Courts Guide**.

Mercantile Courts

2.19 A commercial or business claim, in a broad sense, not specifically required to be brought in the Chancery Division or another specialised court may be brought in one of the Mercantile Courts (**CPR, r. 59.1(2)**), but only if it will benefit from the expertise of one of the judges (known as Mercantile judges: **r. 59.1(3)**) authorised to sit in Mercantile Courts (**PD 59, para. 2.1**). There are Mercantile Courts in the Birmingham, Bristol, Cardiff, Chester, Leeds, Liverpool, Manchester and Newcastle district registries of the High Court, and also at the Central London Civil Justice Centre (where the Mercantile Court is known as the Central London Civil Justice Centre Mercantile List). A claim proceeding in a Mercantile Court is known as a mercantile claim (**CPR, r. 59.1(3)**). Procedure in the Mercantile Courts is governed by **CPR, Part 59**, and **PD 59**. Each Mercantile Court, except Newcastle (which is a very small court), has issued a guide to its own procedures — see the list of contents of **appendix 4**.

Companies Court

2.20 The Companies Court is part of the Chancery Division and exercises the High Court's jurisdiction under the enactments relating to companies, including petitions and applications under the Companies Act 1985 and the Insolvency Act 1986 (see **chapters 79, 81** and **82**).

Patents Court

2.21 The Patents Court hears patents cases within the jurisdiction conferred on it by the Patents Act 1977 (**Supreme Court Act 1981, s. 62(1)**). Patents and other intellectual property claims are governed by **CPR, Part 63**, and **PD 63**, supplemented by the **Patents Court Guide** (the text of which is in **appendix** 4). Patents cases are dealt with either in the Patents Court in the Chancery Division or the Patents County Court. With effect from 1 April 2005, the jurisdiction of patents county courts was extended to include claims under various provisions of the Trade Marks Act 1994. Similar jurisdiction was also conferred on the county courts at Birmingham, Bristol, Cardiff, Leeds, Liverpool, Manchester and Newcastle upon Tyne (**High Court and County Court Jurisdiction Order 1991** (**S.I. 1991/1724**), **art.** 2(7A) and (7B)). The judges of the Patents Court in the Chancery Division are High Court judges who are nominated to be patents judges (**Supreme Court Act 1981, s.** 6). Nomination is by the Lord Chief Justice after consulting the Lord Chancellor.

Administrative Court

The Administrative Court is the part of the Queen's Bench Division which hears judicial review proceedings, which are governed by **CPR, Part** 54, and **PD** 54. There is detailed consideration of judicial review proceedings in **chapter** 74. The Administrative Court also hears habeas corpus applications and some appeals in criminal cases. **2.22**

Chapter 3 Computing Time

APPLICATION OF THE RULES

3.1 **Rules 2.8 to 2.11 of the CPR** deal with calculating time. **Rule 2.8** (see **3.2**, **3.3** and **3.5**) applies to periods of time specified by the CPR, any practice direction or any judgment or order of the court. **Rules 2.9** (see **3.6**) and **2.10** (see **3.4**) apply to any judgment, order, direction or document, but not to the CPR or to practice directions. **Rule 2.11** (see **3.7**) applies to a time specified in the CPR or by the court, but is not relevant to practice directions.

Rules 2.8 and **2.9** apply when calculating the time for 'doing any act' specified in the documents or court orders to which they apply. It was held in *Anderton v Clwyd County Council (No. 2)* [2002] EWCA Civ 933, [2002] 1 WLR 3174, that they do not apply when calculating a time which is not a time by which an act is to be done. **Rules 2.8** and **2.9** therefore apply to calculations of time for doing acts such as filing statements of case, serving application notices, complying with mandatory orders, and most other steps required by the CPR, practice directions and court orders. They do not, however, apply to calculating deemed dates of service, because nothing is to be 'done' by the deemed date.

DAYS

Clear days

3.2 Any period of time expressed as a number of days must be computed as 'clear days' (**CPR, r. 2.8(2)**). This means that if an act must be done a specified number of days before an event occurs, the day on which the act is done and the day on which the event occurs are not counted when calculating whether the required period has elapsed (**r. 2.8(3)**).

For example, if service must be effected at least three days before a hearing on Friday, 20 October, the last date for service is Monday, 16 October.

Five days or less

3.3 If the period of time for doing any act is five days or less, the following days within the period do not count: Saturday, Sunday, a bank holiday, Christmas Day, Good Friday (**CPR, r. 2.8(4)**).

For example, if service must be effected at least three days before a hearing on Monday, 23 October, the last date for service is Tuesday, 17 October.

Rule 2.8(4)(b), which excludes Saturdays, Sundays and bank holidays when calculating periods of five days or less, does not apply when calculating the deemed dates for service under **r. 6.7** relating to service by first-class post (*Anderton v Clwyd County Council (No. 2)* [2002] EWCA Civ 933, [2002] 1 WLR 3174), delivering or leaving the document at a permitted address (*Wilkey v British Broadcasting Corporation* [2002] EWCA Civ 1561, [2003] 1 WLR 1) or (applying the reasoning in *Anderton v Clwyd County Council (No. 2)*) by document exchange or electronic methods (other than fax). This is because the deemed dates of service as set out in **r. 6.7** for these methods of service are calculated by reference to 'days', which is interpreted by these authorities as meaning all calendar days, including weekends and bank holidays. For calculating the deemed date of service by the other prescribed methods of service (fax and personal service) the rules use the term 'business day', which is defined in **r. 6.7(3)** as excluding Saturdays, Sundays and bank holidays (including Christmas Day and Good Friday).

MONTHS

In the CPR, 'month' means calendar month (Interpretation Act 1978, ss. 5 and 22 and sch. 1) and **r. 2.10** of the CPR applies the same definition to any judgment, order, direction or other document. **3.4**

COURT OFFICE CLOSED

Where a period for doing any act at the court offices, such as filing a document, ends on a day when the office is closed, the act will be done in time if done on the next day on which the office is open (**CPR, r. 2.8(5)**). The same rule applies if the court office is closed on the day when a limitation period under the **Limitation Act 1980** expires (*Pritam Kaur v S. Russell and Sons Ltd* [1973] QB 336) or the day when a statutory time limit for bringing an appeal expires (*Aadan v Brent London Borough Council* (1999) *The Times*, 3 December 1999). In *Van Aken v Camden London Borough Council* [2002] EWCA Civ 1724, [2003] 1 WLR 684, a document which was delivered to the court on the last day for filing was held to have been duly filed even though the court office had closed for the day by the time it was delivered. **Paragraphs 2.1** and **3.2 to 3.3 of PD 2** give details of the opening days and times of the RCJ, the district registries of the High Court and of the county courts. **3.5**

TIME LIMITS IN COURT ORDERS

In a court order, judgment or direction which imposes a time limit for doing any act, the last date for compliance must, wherever practicable, be expressed as a calendar date and include a time on that date by which the act must be done (**CPR, r. 2.9(1)**). For example, an order should be drafted to state that an act must be done 'by 4 p.m. on 20 October 2006', rather than 'no later than 14 days after the date of this order'. **3.6**

When the date by which an act must be done is inserted in any document, the date must, wherever practicable, be expressed as a calendar date (**r. 2.9(2)**).

VARIATION BY CONSENT

Rule 2.11 of the CPR makes clear that parties may, by written agreement, vary any deadline specified in the CPR or by the court, unless forbidden to do so by a court order, the CPR or a practice direction. **Rule 3.8(3)** forbids extension of time by agreement of a deadline if the consequence of failure to comply with the deadline is specified in the rule or court order creating it. **Rule 3.8(3)** also applies to deadlines set in practice directions, implying that a practice direction deadline which does not specify the consequence of failure to comply can be varied by agreement. However, authority to vary practice direction deadlines is not given expressly by **r. 2.11**, unless they can be taken to be covered by the phrase 'specified . . . by the court'. **3.7**

An example of the CPR restricting agreement by the parties is **r. 15.5(1)**, which allows an agreement to extend the time for service of a defence by a maximum of 28 days.

The date for filing completed allocation questionnaires cannot be varied by agreement between the parties (**r. 26.3(6A)**). In a fast track claim, the parties are not allowed to vary by consent the date for the return of pre-trial checklists, the trial date or trial window, or any other directions which would impinge on these dates (**r. 28.4**). In a multi-track claim, the parties are not allowed to vary by consent the dates for any case management conference, pre-trial review, the return of pre-trial checklists, the trial date or trial period, or any other directions which would impinge on these dates (**r. 29.5**).

Where parties agree changes to the case management timetable under **r. 2.11**, they need not file the written agreement at court (**PD 28, para. 4.5; PD 29, para. 6.5**).

Chapter 4 Remedies

INTRODUCTION

Many kinds of remedy may be asked for in civil proceedings, with the aim of establishing or changing a legal status, determining legal rights and duties, or rectifying an infringement or denial of legal rights. The remedy which the court decides to grant is embodied in its judgment, which is usually phrased as, and is often called, an 'order'. The remedy sought by a claimant must be specified in the claim form (**CPR, r. 16.2(1)(b)**), though this statement does not limit the remedies which the court may award (**r. 16.2(5)**) (see **23.5**). There is nothing to prevent the court giving a merely declaratory judgment stating what parties' rights are without giving any other remedy (**r. 40.20**) (see **4.18**). **4.1**

Pending a court's decision on what its judgment is to be in a claim, it may make interim orders providing what are usually called 'interim remedies', which are discussed in **chapters 32** and **36** to **41**.

Remedies can be granted only in accordance with established principles of law or under statutory authority: the court does not have an inherent jurisdiction to make any order necessary to ensure that justice is done (*Wicks v Wicks* [1999] Fam 65 at pp. 76–8 and 88–9).

The principal remedies which are available in civil proceedings generally are examined in this chapter, consisting of legal remedies (debt and damages), which are available as of right on proof of infringement of the claimant's legal rights, and equitable remedies (injunction, specific performance, rectification and account), which the court may award, at its discretion, when a legal remedy would be inadequate or unavailable. The discretion to award equitable remedies is exercised in accordance with established principles. In particular, an equitable remedy will not be awarded where it would be inequitable to do so, for example, in the light of the claimant's previous bad behaviour in relation to the subject matter of the claim (the rule that the claimant must come to the court with clean hands), or where the claimant has delayed in claiming the remedy, to the defendant's detriment (the rule against laches, see **10.52**).

Numerous other remedies are available in special types of proceedings, such as the discretionary remedies available in judicial review proceedings (see **chapter 74**), the discretionary remedy of rescission of contract, and many orders created by statute, such as winding-up orders (**chapter 79**), bankruptcy orders (**chapter 80**), orders regulating the affairs of companies (**chapter 82**), director disqualification orders, orders regulating business tenancies (**chapter 91**) and orders declaring that legislative provisions are incompatible with the European Convention on Human Rights (**chapter 97**).

In claims concerning sale of goods to consumers the court now has statutory powers to require the seller to repair or replace the goods (see **chapter 92**).

Methods of enforcing judgments are considered in **chapters 76** to **78**.

EFFECT OF JUDGMENTS

4.2 A judgment or order of a court in civil proceedings takes effect from the day when it is given or made (**CPR, r. 40.7(1)**) and this means from the first moment of that day (*Shelley's Case* (1582) 1 Co Rep 93b). The court may specify a later date on which its judgment or order is to take effect (**r. 40.7(1)**). There are special rules in **r. 40.10** concerning default judgments against foreign States.

It is in the public interest that legal proceedings brought to resolve a dispute should result in a final answer to that dispute. The parties must put their whole case before the court and are not be permitted to relitigate the questions which the court decides.

Judgments are traditionally divided into:

(a) those which are *in personam*, that is, determinative of the rights of the parties to the proceedings, and not challengeable by those parties in other proceedings, but not binding on anyone else, and
(b) those which are *in rem*, that is, determinative of legal status and not challengeable in any proceedings before any tribunal which recognises the jurisdiction of the court which gave the judgment (though it may be possible to question the court's jurisdiction).

The finality of a judgment or order is subject to three qualifications:

(a) A person who was not a party to the proceedings in which the judgment or order was made, but who is directly affected by it, may apply under CPR, **r. 40.9**, for it to be set aside or varied.
(b) Any accidental slip or omission in a judgment or order may be corrected by the court under **r. 40.12**.
(c) It may be possible to appeal against the judgment or order, see **chapters 71** to **73**.

Merger of cause of action into judgment

4.3 When judgment is given, the original cause of action is treated as merged with the judgment, so that no further proceedings can be brought on that cause of action. Where an event gives rise to more than one cause of action, not all of which are litigated, the ones which have not been litigated do not merge in the judgment given on those that were. For example, a claim in contract will not merge with a judgment on a tortious claim which arose from the same event. Merger does not apply to successive causes of action, so that judgment for specific instalments of debt or rent will not bar a claim for further instalments.

Res judicata

4.4 A party who obtains judgment is thereafter estopped from bringing further similar claims. This estoppel takes three distinct forms. First, there is a narrow form of estoppel, known as estoppel by *res judicata* (a thing or matter which has been decided), which is the rule that the issues which were actually adjudicated upon by the court have been finally resolved between the parties to the claim. Secondly, there is a wider form of estoppel, known as cause-of-action estoppel, which is founded on the rule in *Henderson v Henderson* (1843) 3 Hare 100. This rule is based on the public policy of encouraging finality in litigation and (subject to exceptional circumstances) prevents any party to a claim in which judgment has been given from raising in other proceedings any issue which could have been resolved in the adjudicated claim (see **33.14**). The third form of estoppel, known as issue estoppel, is based on the same public policy. The doctrine of issue estoppel is that if, after judgment is delivered in civil proceedings, two of the parties to those proceedings, or their successors in title, are parties to further civil proceedings, then one of those parties cannot repeat, as against the other, in the second proceedings, an assertion which was found to be incorrect by the court in the first proceedings (*Mills v Cooper* [1967] 2 QB 459 per Diplock LJ at pp. 468–9). The doctrine applies only to an assertion — whether of fact, opinion (*Humberclyde Finance Group Ltd v Hicks* (2001) LTL 19/11/2001) or the legal consequences of facts or opinions — which was an essential element of the asserting party's cause of action or defence in the first proceedings. The doctrine affects a party whether the party was an original claimant or defendant in the first proceedings or was joined to those proceedings, but it only affects parties who appear in the same capacity in both sets of proceedings (*Humberclyde Finance Group Ltd v Hicks*). Issue estoppel does not prevent a party repeating an assertion if further material which is relevant to the correctness or incorrectness of the assertion and could not by reasonable diligence have been adduced by that party in the previous proceedings has since become available.

Where a claimant brings proceedings against more than one defendant, entering summary judgment against one defendant may amount to an election to abandon the claim against the other defendants (*Morel Brothers and Co. Ltd v Earl of Westmorland* [1903] 1 KB 64). A default judgment is entered without investigating the merits, unlike summary judgment. Consequently, entering a default judgment against one defendant does not, without more, amount to an election to abandon the claim against the other defendant (*Pendleton v Westwater* (2001) LTL 28/11/2001).

In *Johnson v Gore Wood and Co.* [2002] 2 AC 1 the House of Lords reviewed the circumstances in which public policy permitted a second claim (in this case brought by the majority shareholder of a company after the claim by the company had been compromised) to proceed. The test is whether, taking into account all the public and private interests involved and the facts of the case, a claimant is misusing or abusing the process of the court (see **33.14**).

MONEY JUDGMENTS

The most common judgment given is for payment of a sum of money. The money due will **4.5** usually be a debt (or other liquidated sum) or damages. The distinction between a debt (or other liquidated claim) and damages is no longer as important as it was in the past, but it is still reflected in the CPR by the distinction drawn in several places between claims for specified amounts and claims for unspecified amounts. Interest may be awarded on a money judgment (see **chapter 62**), but this is relief ancillary to the principal remedy of a money judgment, rather than an independent remedy (*Bank voor Handel en Scheepvaart NV v Slatford* [1953] 1 QB 248 at p. 278).

Set-off

If two parties to proceedings make monetary claims against each other (a claim and a cross- **4.6** claim), and both claim and cross-claim are upheld, the court will deduct the smaller of the amounts found due from the larger and give only one judgment for the balance, if the claim and the cross-claim can be set off. There are two sets of rules governing whether a claim and a cross-claim can be set off: one creates a legal set-off, the other an equitable set-off.

In a claim for a liquidated sum the defendant can assert a legal set-off of any liquidated debt or money demand cross-claimed by it from the claimant, provided both the claimant's claim and the defendant's cross-claim can be quantified with certainty at the time of filing a defence (see *Hanak v Green* [1958] 2 QB 9 per Morris LJ at p. 17; *Axel Johnson Petroleum AB v MG Mineral Group AG* [1992] 1 WLR 270; *B. Hargreaves Ltd v Action 2000 Ltd* [1993] BCLC 1111; **CPR, r. 16.6**).

Equitable set-off (also called equitable defence) permits a cross-claim by the defendant to be set off against the claimant's claim if it arises out of the same transaction or is closely connected with that transaction and it goes directly to impeach the claimant's demands — that is, it is so closely connected with those demands that it would be manifestly unjust to allow the claimant to enforce payment without taking the defendant's claim into account (per Lord Denning MR in *Federal Commerce and Navigation Co. Ltd v Molena Alpha Inc.* [1978] QB 927 at pp. 974–5 and Goff LJ at p. 987, point not considered on appeal; *Dole Dried Fruit and Nut Co. v Trustin Kerwood Ltd* [1990] 2 Lloyd's Rep 309). Equitable set-off is not available against a claim for freight (*Aries Tanker Corporation v Total Transport Ltd* [1977] 1 WLR 185) or for payment of a bill of exchange (*Nova (Jersey) Knit Ltd v Kammgarn Spinnerei GmbH* [1977] 1 WLR 713).

A defendant who has an unquantified cross-claim against the claimant which is not connected with the claimant's claim is not entitled to either legal or equitable set-off.

It is possible for the contract governing payment of a debt to prevent the debtor from exercising a right of set-off against the creditor even in legal proceedings brought to enforce payment of the debt (*Coca-Cola Financial Corporation v Finsat International Ltd* [1998] QB 43).

For more on set-off see **34.31 to 34.35**.

DAMAGES

4.7 Damages are a monetary payment as the legal remedy for infringement of legal rights. The amount to be paid primarily reflects the compensation required by the claimant for loss caused by the defendant's wrongdoing (compensatory damages), though the court may increase this compensation because of the additional hurt caused by the objectionable way in which the defendant acted (aggravated damages). In limited circumstances the court, representing the public interest, may mark its disapproval of the defendant's behaviour by adding a penalty element to the damages (exemplary damages). Where there has been a breach of contract, the contract itself may provide how damages for the breach are to be calculated (liquidated damages). An infringement of a legal right which has caused no compensable loss may result in only nominal damages.

Nominal damages

4.8 Nominal damages are awarded where there has been an infringement of a legal right but it has not resulted in any loss for which compensation may be claimed (*The Mediana* [1900] AC 113).

If actual damage to the claimant is an essential element of a cause of action (as it is, for example, for negligence) then failure to prove any damage to the claimant will result in the dismissal of the claim. If actual damage to the claimant is not an essential element of a cause of action (as is the case, for example, with breach of contract or trespass to land), the claimant will be given judgment on proof of the matters that are essential, but cannot be awarded damages beyond a nominal amount.

Aggravated damages

4.9 Aggravated damages are defined in the CPR Glossary as 'Additional damages which the court may award as compensation for the defendant's objectionable behaviour'. A claim for aggravated damages must be made separately in the particulars of claim (**CPR, r. 16.4(1)(c)**). Aggravated damages compensate for injury to feelings caused by the manner in which the wrong was committed, and cannot be awarded to a company, which has no feelings to be injured (*Collins Stewart Ltd v Financial Times Ltd* [2005] EWHC 262 (QB), LTL 25/2/2005). Aggravated damages are quite distinct from exemplary damages and in a suitable case both may be awarded. The most common situation in which both are awarded is unlawful eviction (if statutory damages are not claimed or awarded).

Exemplary damages

Exemplary damages are defined in the CPR Glossary as 'Damages which go beyond compensating for actual loss and are awarded to show the court's disapproval of the defendant's behaviour'. A claim for exemplary damages must be made separately in the particulars of claim (**CPR, r. 16.4(1)(c)**). Exemplary damages can be awarded only in very limited circumstances. The House of Lords in *Rookes v Barnard* [1964] AC 1129 recognised only three categories. They are: **4.10**

(a) oppressive, arbitrary or unconstitutional behaviour by government servants,
(b) cases where the conduct of the defendant is calculated to make a profit which will be in excess of the compensatory damages which are payable, and
(c) where an award of exemplary damages is expressly authorised by statute.

In *Kuddus v Chief Constable of Leicestershire Constabulary* [2002] 2 AC 122 the House of Lords overruled the decision of the Court of Appeal in *AB v South West Water Services Ltd* [1993] QB 507 with the result that the categories of claim which can give rise to an award of exemplary damages are not now limited to those in which awards were made prior to 1964. It now seems that it is the behaviour complained of rather than the precise cause of action which the court must consider. Awards of exemplary damages are certainly available in claims for trespass to the person or property, defamation, false imprisonment and private nuisance. It is now arguable that awards may be made in other categories of case such as misfeasance in public office (the cause of action in *Kuddus*).

Damages may be awarded as exemplary damages even though they have been quantified by reference to specific losses by the claimant (*Borders (UK) Ltd v Commissioner of Police of the Metropolis* [2005] EWCA Civ 197, *The Times*, 15 April 2005).

Liquidated damages

A claim for liquidated damages is a claim for the sum agreed in a contract between the parties as payable in the event of a specified breach of that contract which has in fact occurred. In many cases the amount payable has to be calculated by reference to the circumstances of the breach, such as the number of days' delay in performance. A sum which is a genuine pre-estimate by the parties of the loss occasioned by the breach of contract will be recoverable as liquidated damages, but any other sum will be an irrecoverable penalty (*Dunlop Pneumatic Tyre Co. Ltd v New Garage and Motor Co. Ltd* [1915] AC 79). The circumstances in which a term in a written contract can be challenged so as to avoid this consequence are considered at **93.25**. **4.11**

Compensatory damages

Compensatory damages can be divided into pecuniary and non-pecuniary damages. Pecuniary damages compensate the claimant for measurable financial losses caused by the defendant's wrongdoing. Non-pecuniary damages (often called 'general' damages) are awarded in recognition of suffering which that wrongdoing has caused the claimant. The amount to award as non-pecuniary damages must be assessed according to the court's sense of what would be appropriate in the case before it, in the light of what has been awarded in comparable cases. Information about appropriate awards for pain, suffering and loss of amenity in personal injuries claims is given by the Judicial Studies Board in *Guidelines for the Assessment of General Damages in Personal Injury Cases*, 7th ed. (Oxford University Press, 2004). Conventionally a claimant does not specify the amount sought as non-pecuniary damages, though an estimate of what is likely to be awarded must be made in order to decide which court to start the claim in (see **11.4**). In personal injury claims, pecuniary damages sought must be specified in a schedule of past and future expenses and losses attached to the particulars of claim (**PD 16, para. 4.2**; see **chapter 25**). **4.12**

Traditionally, an award for pecuniary loss is based on the loss which the claimant has sustained and not on what it would be fair or reasonable for the defendant to pay (*General Tire and Rubber Co. v Firestone Tyre and Rubber Co. Ltd* [1975] 1 WLR 819). However, in exceptional cases, where it is just to do so, the court may make orders to ensure that the defendant in a claim for breach of contract retains no benefit from the breach (*Attorney-General v Blake* [2001] 1 AC 268), or, in cases of misuse of property, to award a sum which it would be reasonable for the defendant to pay for that use (*Experience Hendrix llc v PPX Enterprises Inc.* [2003] EWCA Civ 323, [2003] 1 All ER (Comm) 830).

In tortious claims the aim is to award a sum of money which will restore the claimant's position to what it would have been but for the wrong for which the damages are being awarded (*Livingstone v Rawyards Coal Co.* (1880) 5 App Cas 25). Compensatory damages in tort can include heads of loss which have been aggravated by the claimant's impecuniosity (*Lagden v O'Connor* [2003] UKHL 64, [2003] 1 AC 1067, overruling *Liesbosch Dredger (Owners of) v Owners of SS Edison* [1933] AC 449 on this point).

Claims for damages for breach of contract may be made on two different bases:

(a) to restore the claimant's position to what it would have been had the contract been properly performed (loss of bargain); or

(b) to compensate for expenditure rendered futile by the breach (reliance loss).

The claimant can choose the basis on which to claim (*CCC Films (London) Ltd v Impact Quadrant Films Ltd* [1985] QB 16).

DELIVERY UP OF GOODS

4.13 A final judgment ordering delivery up of goods may take one of the three forms permitted by the **Torts (Interference with Goods) Act 1977, s. 3(2)**:

(a) an order for the delivery of the goods and payment of any consequential damages;

(b) an order for delivery of the goods but giving the defendant the alternative of paying the stated value of the goods together, in either case, with the consequential damages; or

(c) judgment for damages.

An order in form (a) is discretionary (**s. 3(3)(b)**), and tends to be made only where the goods are rare or have some special value, or where they are not readily available on the market (*Howard E. Perry and Co. Ltd v British Railways Board* [1980] 1 WLR 1375). If an order in form (a) is obtained but not complied with, the person in whose favour the judgment was given can return to court and the court can revoke the order and make an order for the payment of damages by reference to the value of the goods (**s. 3(4)**). Payment of a judgment for the value of the goods extinguishes the claimant's title to those goods (**s. 5**).

INJUNCTIONS

4.14 An injunction may be either mandatory (requiring some act to be done) or prohibitory (requiring some conduct to stop, or prohibiting threatened conduct). Injunction is an equitable remedy awarded at the court's discretion where a legal remedy would be inadequate (see 4.1).

The general power to grant injunctions has been given statutory form in the **Supreme Court Act 1981, s. 37** (which applies also in the county courts by virtue of the **County Courts Act 1984, s. 38**). This provides that injunctions, whether final or interim, 'may' (emphasising that this is a discretionary power) be granted where it is 'just and convenient'. In cases where rights under the European Convention on Human Rights may be engaged, the test may better be expressed as 'just and proportionate' (see *South Bucks District Council v Porter* [2003] UKHL 26, [2003] 2 AC 558). There are also specific statutory powers to grant injunctions, for example, in the **Housing Act 1996, ss. 153A and 153B** (see **chapter 92**). Power to grant an injunction in judicial review claims is conferred by the **Supreme Court Act 1981, s. 31(2)** (see 74.53).

The discretion to grant an injunction must be exercised judicially, taking into account all the relevant circumstances. Factors include the importance of curbing the defendant's activities, whether breaches of the claimant's rights or the law will continue unless restrained, whether the court would be prepared to impose the sanctions available for breach of the injunction (fining and imprisonment), and, in the case of specific statutory powers to grant injunctions, the purpose for which the power was given (*South Bucks District Council v Porter* at [29] and [32]). The inability to order imprisonment is the reason why injunctions are rarely imposed against children (*G v Harrow London Borough Council* [2004] EWHC 17 (QB), LTL 23/1/2004). When granting an injunction the court does not contemplate that it will be disobeyed (*Castanho v Brown and Root (UK) Ltd* [1981] AC 557 at p. 574). Concern that a defendant might disobey an injunction should not therefore deter a court from granting it. As Lord Bingham of Cornhill said in *South Bucks District Council v Porter* at [32], there is not one law for the law-abiding and another for the lawless and truculent. Consequently, a final injunction was granted in *Mid Bedfordshire District Council v Brown* [2004] EWCA Civ 1709, [2005] NPC 2, where the defendants had moved on to land in breach of an interim order, because the public interest in upholding court orders far outweighed the factors favouring suspension of the injunction.

When a public body applies for an injunction in pursuance of its public functions, one factor which the court may take into account is the lawfulness of the decision to make the application. But this is not the only factor to be taken into account and, in deciding whether to grant the injunction, the court is exercising an original rather than a supervisory jurisdiction (*South Bucks District Council v Porter* at [27]).

The Court may award damages in addition to or in lieu of an injunction (**Supreme Court Act 1981, s. 50; County Courts Act 1984, s. 38**). It is possible to award both an injunction ordering cessation of a breach of the claimant's rights and damages for injury to those rights during the time that the injunction will be in force, for example, where it is clear that the injunction will be evaded (*Brazier v Bramwell Scaffolding (Dunedin) Ltd* [2001] UKPC 59, LTL 20/12/2001). However, if the claimant has established that the claim is one in which the court would usually grant an injunction, the court may not, of its own motion, instead award nominal damages (*Nelson v Nicholson* (2000) LTL 1/12/2000).

When drafting a final injunction it is important that the wording is clear and specific. The order must state what is to be done and when, or what is not to be done from a particular date and time. This is because disobedience of an injunction is contempt of court, for which punishments such as committal and sequestration may be imposed (see **chapter 78**).

SPECIFIC PERFORMANCE

An order for specific performance requires the performance of the obligations of a party to a contract. An order for specific performance is an equitable remedy awarded at the court's discretion where a legal remedy would be inadequate (see **4.1**). In most cases an order for specific performance is asked for as a remedy for a breach of an obligation, but it is also possible to make an order for specific performance in anticipation of a breach. Specific performance is asked for most often in claims for the enforcement of agreements relating to land, but it can also be ordered for the sale of goods, particularly those which are rare or unique such as an original work of art or an heirloom. **4.15**

Certain obligations will not be specifically enforced, including illegal contracts, unenforceable contracts (e.g., sale of land without the necessary written contract), voluntary obligations, contracts for personal skill or work, and obligations which require constant supervision (*Ryan v Mutual Tontine Association* [1983] 1 Ch 116). The claimant must show that he is ready, willing and able to perform his part of the obligation or contract. Specific performance may be refused where there has been a misrepresentation by the claimant, where there has been a serious mistake or misdescription, and in cases of severe hardship.

The Court may award damages in addition to or in lieu of specific performance (**Supreme Court Act 1981, s. 50; County Courts Act 1984, s. 38**).

An order for specific performance must state what is to be done and when. The contract or obligation does not merge completely into the order, but further performance is subject to the control of the court.

RECTIFICATION

4.16 Rectification (alteration of a document to reflect the parties' true intentions) is a discretionary equitable remedy (see 4.1). It is not the bargain which is rectified, but the written record of the transaction. Rectification is not required where the true meaning is revealed by the ordinary rules of construction of written agreements. Where applying those rules of construction to the document shows that it does not reflect the agreement of the parties, the document may be rectified. An order for rectification has retrospective force so that the document is treated as if it was in the rectified form from the date it was signed or created.

ACCOUNTS

4.17 The power of the court to order an account to be taken is considered at **61.28**. Accounts are a common remedy in claims between principal and agent, claims between partners and claims involving jointly owned property. The first stage is to establish that an account should be taken by the court. An account will not be ordered where the parties have already settled the balance between themselves by an account stated or a settled account. If the limitation period for the claim has expired, an account will not be ordered to avoid that limitation period. At the second stage, the court should give directions for the taking of the account, which may involve disclosure and inspection. The party liable to account will usually be ordered to prepare the first account. The receiving party can then raise objections to items in that account. Those disputed items can then be determined by the court.

In cases of jointly owned real property where one party has left the property and the other has remained in occupation until sale, the court may try to avoid taking detailed accounts as the cost of doing so can exceed the sums involved. The party remaining in occupation will have to pay an occupation rent assessed as the fair rental value of the property. If, as is often the case, that person has paid all the outgoings, those will have to be credited. The result in many cases is that the court will refuse to order an account on the ground that the outgoings paid will be broadly the same as the occupation rent (*Bernard v Josephs* [1982] Ch 391; *Dennis v McDonald* [1982] Fam 63).

An account may also be sought (as an alternative to damages) where there has been an infringement of a proprietary right (e.g., misuse of confidential information, or intellectual property rights). A claimant must elect whether to seek damages (based on the loss he can show he has suffered) or an account (based on the net profits made by the defendant). Proving damage is often extremely difficult, so that an account of the profit made by the defendant may be a more attractive remedy.

DECLARATIONS

Final declarations

The power to make binding final declarations can be found in **CPR, r. 40.20**, and the power to make interim declarations is in **r. 25.1(1)(b)**. Power to make a declaration in judicial review claims is conferred by the **Supreme Court Act 1981, s. 31(2)** (see 74.54). When deciding whether to make a declaration the court should take into account justice to the claimant, justice to the defendant, whether the declaration will serve a useful purpose, and any special reasons affecting the decision (*Financial Services Authority v Rourke* (2001) *The Times*, 12 November 2001). A declaration about the lawfulness of future conduct will not be granted unless the circumstances are truly exceptional (*R (Rusbridger) v Attorney-General* [2003] UKHL 38, [2004] 1 AC 357). In deciding whether this test is met, according to *Blackland Park Exploration Ltd v Environment Agency* [2003] EWCA Civ 1795, [2004] Env LR 33, the court will consider the following criteria: **4.18**

(a) the absence of any genuine dispute about the subject matter;
(b) whether the case is fact-sensitive; and
(c) whether there is a cogent public or individual interest that will be advanced by making the declaration.

A declaration may make findings of fact as well as declaring legal rights (*Compagnie Noga d'Importation et d'Exportation SA v Abacha (No. 3)* [2002] EWCA Civ 1142, LTL 31/7/2002).

Interim declarations

The inclusion of the power to grant an interim declaration in **CPR, r. 25.1(1)(b)**, means that such an order is no longer 'a contradiction in terms'. It was recognised in *NHS Trust v T (Adult Patient: Refusal of Medical Treatment)* [2004] EWHC 1279 (Fam), [2005] 1 All ER 387, that there are still difficulties, but: **4.19**

(a) the power to grant interim declarations is not restricted to judicial review claims;
(b) interim declarations can be granted for a one-off medical procedure, for example, a Caesarean section or an amputation (at [44]);
(c) a material change of circumstances can found a reconsideration.

In the case of interim relief in relation to medical treatment of a person said to lack mental capacity, Charles J said the patient should be given an opportunity to make representations. It is for the judge to decide on capacity, then to decide on the best interests of the patient applying the usual civil standard on the best evidence then available.

RESTITUTION

Claims for restitution can be made at law and in equity and are based on the principle of unjust enrichment. The claim is for repayment of the benefit received by the defendant and not the loss suffered by the claimant. The claim will be particularly important where the claimant's damages are less than the benefit received by the defendant, where the claimant may have difficulty proving his damages and where the claimant made a bad bargain. Thus, where a car is purchased without obtaining good title, the purchaser will normally prefer to reclaim the entire purchase price rather than damages based on the lower value of the car when the defect in title is discovered. **4.20**

The most common claims in restitution are for repayment of money had and received which covers both money paid under a mistake and money paid where there has been a total failure of consideration. A claim in restitution may also be made in some tortious actions, particularly those involving interference with proprietary rights. If a defendant takes the claimant's goods and sells them for an advantageous price, it will be more attractive to claim the money received by the defendant rather than the value of the goods. The remedy in tort and the restitutionary remedy are alternatives and the claimant must elect which remedy he seeks. If a claimant seeks restitution he waives the commission of the tort.

Chapter 5 Funding Litigation

INTRODUCTION

There is no doubt that civil litigation is expensive. Potential parties to a claim have to consider their solicitors' fees (which in England are some of the highest in the world), their barristers' fees, court fees (which recently rose very substantially) and, depending on the case, experts' fees. An unsuccessful party can end up paying legal fees twice over or more if he also has to meet a substantial proportion of his opponent's costs. What that means in practice is that every hour spent pursuing a claim can cost one or more of the parties many hundreds, or even thousands, of pounds. 5.1

That cumulative cost means that, aside from the relatively rich, few can afford to bring cases unless they receive some type of financial support from a third party. For those with very low income and limited savings, the State might be prepared to assist through the Community Legal Service, although that has been restricted to only certain types of litigation. Another option for clients is to share the financial risk of litigation with their lawyers or with an insurer.

Conditional fee agreements (CFAs) enable lawyers to share the risk of the litigation with their clients by offering a number of variations on 'no win, no fee' arrangements.

The private insurance market can assist parties by underwriting some or all of the costs of litigation in return for a premium.

CFAs and various insurance products now dominate personal injury litigation. In other civil proceedings the use of CFAs and insurance products has risen steadily, particularly following the **Access to Justice Act 1999**. That Act restricted the scope of public funding but encouraged the use of CFAs, backed by insurance, in a number of ways. In particular, the uplift on the lawyer's fees which becomes payable by the party if the case is won, and which is intended to cover the cost of unsuccessful CFA cases run by the same lawyer, can be recovered from the losing party. Further, any insurance premiums paid to cover the party's risk of paying his opponent's costs can also be recovered from the opponent.

It is perhaps not surprising that when CFAs led to both an increase in the number of claims and the level of costs, a substantial body of satellite litigation relating to the enforceability of CFAs and the recoverability of success fees and insurance premiums followed. While solicitors and clients are becoming more familiar both with the concept and practical requirements of 'risk sharing', the consequent uncertainty has caused considerable disquiet among practitioners, judges, insurance companies and claims management companies. Ongoing reform aimed at ensuring that CFAs in their current form are workable, has led to the introduction of 'predictable costs' in bulk litigation markets, the revocation of the **Conditional Fee Agreements Regulations 2000** and changes to the Solicitors' Practice Rules

1990. The debate continues with the Civil Justice Council's report and recommendations of August 2005, *Improved Access to Justice – Funding Options and Proportionate Costs*, now under consideration.

Of course the question 'Who pays?' is quickly followed by 'How much?' Retrospective assessment of the level of costs is becoming increasingly influenced, and sometimes circumscribed, by prospective, court-approved, budgeting (see **66.54**).

It is no exaggeration to say that the funding of litigation has proved to be one of the most controversial topics in civil practice over recent years and that is set to continue. It remains extremely important for practitioners to keep abreast of the many developments in this field which can have a substantial impact not only on a specific case, but upon the business of running a litigation practice as a whole.

GLOSSARY OF KEY FUNDING TERMS

5.2 **after-the-event (ATE) insurance.** Insurance which is purchased when litigation is contemplated or started and which covers the risk of having to pay the opponent's costs. It can be extended to include cover for the insured's own legal costs and expenses.

before-the-event (BTE) insurance. An insurance product (often linked to other insurance, such as a household or motor policy) which is purchased on a subscription basis prior to any litigation being contemplated or started and which usually pays all of the insured's legal costs and the risk of having to pay the opponent's costs, subject to a financial limit written into the policy. The limit for non-business cases is usually between £15,000 and £50,000.

conditional fee agreement (CFA). A written agreement between a solicitor and his client, or between a barrister and a solicitor, relating to a particular claim, providing that if the case is lost, no fees are payable, but if the case is won, the costs will be calculated by reference to a normal hourly rate plus a percentage uplift (a success fee) which is agreed at the outset. For example, a 100 per cent success fee will double the agreed hourly rate. 100 per cent is the maximum success fee allowed and is the appropriate uplift for a case with a 50–50 chance of success.

contingency fee agreement. An agreement between a solicitor and his client, typically providing that the solicitor's fees for a matter will be calculated by reference to a pre-agreed percentage of the damages recovered. The amount of time the solicitor may spend on the case is irrelevant. This type of agreement is illegal for court proceedings.

detailed assessment. A line-by-line assessment by the court, at the end of a case, of the level of legal costs of a party. This is often undertaken by specialist costs judges.

disbursements. The expenses in a claim, including court fees, travel costs, experts' fees etc.

indemnity principle. The principle that a party who is ordered to pay another party's costs does not have to pay amounts which the receiving party has no enforceable obligation to pay to his own lawyers.

public funding (also known as legal aid). Payment by the State of a person's legal costs, subject to reimbursement from what is recovered in the proceedings. In England and Wales public funding of civil claims is now very restricted. An assisted party has substantial protection against having to pay his opponent's costs even if the case is lost.

statutory charge. A charge on property recovered or preserved in publicly funded legal proceedings, as security for the payment of costs which are not recovered from the losing party.

DUTY TO ADVISE CLIENTS ON FUNDING

Solicitors need to ensure their clients know the funding options available to them, and that they understand the main features of different funding methods. The Solicitors' Costs Information and Client Care Code 1999 provides that solicitors must discuss with their clients how, when and by whom any costs are to be met. This means that a solicitor should consider: **5.3**

(a) whether the client may be eligible and should apply for public funding;
(b) whether the client should be offered the option of funding the claim under a CFA;
(c) the extent to which the client's liability for costs is covered by insurance;
(d) the extent to which an employer, or trade union or other organisation of which the client is a member, may meet the client's liability for costs; and
(e) whether the client's liability for another party's costs may be covered by pre-purchased insurance and, if not, whether it would be advisable for another party's costs to be covered by ATE insurance.

Where a client is represented under a CFA the solicitor should explain:

(a) the circumstances in which the client may be liable for his own costs and for the other party's costs;
(b) the client's right to assessment of costs by the court, wherever the solicitor intends to seek payment of any or all of his costs from the client; and
(c) any interest the solicitor may have in recommending a particular policy or other funding.

A client must be told about the potential liability for the other side's costs if the claim is unsuccessful. The usual rule is that the unsuccessful party in proceedings is ordered to pay the successful party's costs (**CPR, r. 44.3(2)**). The other side's costs generally have to be paid out of the losing party's personal resources. It may be possible for the client to arrange ATE insurance to cover the other side's costs (see **5.9**).

It should be standard practice for a solicitor to consider whether a client's claim could be funded by someone else's legal expenses insurance, for example, that of the householder where the client lives or the driver of a vehicle in which the client was a passenger. A solicitor should always ask a client to bring to the first consultation all relevant insurance policies, if obtaining them is reasonably practicable. The solicitor's duty may extend to making thorough enquiries and reviewing the relevant insurance documentation (*Myatt v National Coal Board* (2005) LTL 4/11/2005). If the client's claim is against the policyholder, and both might be funded by the same insurer, the solicitor must advise whether the degree of control given to the intended defendant's insurer makes it unreasonable to rely on the policy; and this will depend on the size and difficulty of the claim. A failure to follow this practice may mean that the claimant's additional liabilities, such as an ATE insurance premium and/or success fee under a CFA, cannot be recovered. That is on the basis that any additional liability may have been unreasonably incurred and hence not recoverable on an assessment between parties (*Sarwar v Alam* [2001] EWCA Civ 1401, [2002] 1 WLR 125).

Information about funding should be given to the client not only at the outset of litigation but at appropriate stages throughout. The Solicitors' Costs Information and Client Care Code 1999 requires a solicitor to tell his or her client how much the costs are at regular intervals (at least every six months) and in appropriate cases the solicitor should deliver interim bills at agreed intervals. The solicitor should explain to the client and confirm in writing any change in circumstances which will, or which are likely to, affect the amount of the costs, the degree of risk involved or the ratio of cost to benefit to the client of continuing with the matter. The client should be informed in writing as soon as it appears that a cost estimate or agreed upper limit may or will be exceeded. There is an ongoing obligation to consider the client's eligibility for public funding if a material change in the client's means comes to the solicitor's attention.

Forecasting fees can be extremely difficult, but the Code requires the solicitor to give the 'best information possible'. That can include giving a forecast within a possible range of costs or explaining to the client the reasons why it is not possible to fix or give a realistic estimate of the overall costs, and giving instead the best information possible about the costs of the next stage. The client should also be invited to set an upper limit on the firm's costs not to be exceeded without further authority.

A solicitor whose costs exceed what he has estimated may be limited to charging no more than 15 per cent more than the estimate (*Wong v Vizards* (1997) 2 Costs LR 46). A solicitor who gives no estimate at all may be able to recover his fees free of any such restriction (*Garbutt v Edwards* [2005] EWCA Civ 1206, [2006] 1 All ER 553). However, if a complaint of inadequate professional service in not giving an estimate is upheld, the Law Society may vary the fee to what was appropriate and impose a fine of up to £15,000.

Standard information sent out with solicitors' terms of business has an important role to play in ensuring compliance with the requirements of the Code. Assumptions should not be made and solicitor and client should regularly discuss how the litigation is to be funded and whether it deserves funding at all. Not only does that ensure compliance with the Code but it is an essential part of basic client care, and can prevent complaints arising. The unexpectedly high bill at the end of litigation is a fertile source of client dissatisfaction.

PRIVATE FUNDING

Hourly rates and disbursements

5.4 Private funding is the traditional method of paying for litigation. Usually, the client will pay the solicitor's costs of conducting the case at an agreed hourly rate. Charge-out rates are based on the salaries of the staff and fee earners working at the solicitor's office together with an element representing the firm's overheads and profit margins. The modern approach is to fix a single hourly rate for each fee earner (or grade of fee earner) in the firm taking these factors into account. Guideline hourly rates for different grades of fee earners for different parts of the country can be seen in **tables 68.1 to 68.3**. An alternative method, which was used until recently, was to quote a lower hourly rate, but to add a mark-up of a variable percentage (usually 50 per cent for ordinary litigation). Clients tend to find the modern practice of being quoted a simple hourly rate easier to understand.

The client should be informed if the solicitor's charges are likely to be substantially more than a client can expect to recover on an assessment between parties. In *MacDougall v Boote Edgar Esterkin* (2000) SCCO Case Summary No. 15 of 2000 the client agreed to pay the solicitors at the rate of £300 per hour for work done in Manchester from 1992 onwards. Holland J sitting with assessors found that the consent of the client to that rate was not an informed consent. The solicitor had failed to explain the relationship between party and party and solicitor/own client costs and misrepresented what the approach of the costs officer might be. Notwithstanding that the solicitor was held to have given the client 'devoted skilled service on a sustained basis', on a solicitor/own client assessment his hourly rate was substantially reduced.

In addition, the client will be expected to pay for disbursements. These are sums paid by the firm during the course of litigation in respect of experts' and counsel's fees, the cost of making copies of photographs, and similar expenditure. A client care (or 'rule 15') letter, which should include the funding arrangements and, if possible, an estimate of the future costs, should be sent to the client promptly after the firm is retained. It may be appropriate to ask for a sum on account of costs at this stage, and it is sensible to agree to periodical billing of the client (which avoids the client being taken by surprise by a large bill at the end of the case, and also assists with the firm's cash flow).

Fixed fees

Hourly rates are not the only basis for charging. Fixed fees, especially for small claims or fast track litigation, can be agreed. They do, however, require a substantial amount of overall management by the solicitor both in terms of client expectations and the uncertainty of the defendant's conduct. 5.5

In small clinical negligence claims the common interest between the claimants and defendants in agreeing fixed fees has led to a pilot scheme where costs are restricted to £1,500. The scheme remains under review but has, for the most part, been well received by both claimants and defendants.

Following work by the Civil Justice Council, a regime of predictable costs for various classes of personal injury claims has been introduced (**CPR, rr. 45.7** to **45.22**, discussed in **chapter 67**). These rules apply to road accidents from 6 October 2003 and to accidents at work from 1 October 2004. This regime will be reviewed in 2006.

Discounted fees

Practitioners must take particular care with private funding arrangements which offer discounted fees. It is not uncommon, especially when acting for commercial clients, for solicitors to agree, in writing or otherwise, to reduce their normal hourly rate in the event that the litigation is ultimately unsuccessful. Such arrangements are likely to be construed as conditional fee agreements and, if they do not comply with the strict terms of the regulations, may be unenforceable. If the relationship with a particular client deteriorates for one reason or another, the solicitor may find not only that the client refuses to pay any outstanding costs, but may also seek the return of fees paid under a similar arrangement, which may stretch back many years and amount to substantial sums of money. 5.6

PUBLIC FUNDING (LEGAL AID)

The term 'legal aid' was replaced by 'public funding' though the Community Legal Service as from 1 April 2000 (see **chapter 7**). The way in which the system operates has also been altered by the introduction of contracting, which has reduced the number of practitioners who can now undertake publicly funded work. 5.7

Solicitors who are able to offer publicly funded retainers have an additional obligation under the Solicitors' Costs Information and Client Care Code 1999 to explain to a publicly funded client his or her potential liability for his or her own costs and those of any other party, including:

(a) the effect of the statutory charge and its likely amount;
(b) the client's obligation to pay any contribution assessed and the consequences of failing to do so;
(c) the fact that the client may be ordered by the court to contribute to the opponent's costs if the case is lost even though the client's own costs are covered by public funding;
(d) the fact that even if the client wins, the opponent may not be ordered to pay or be capable of paying the full amount of the client's costs.

Publicly funded cases are subject to strict procedural and cost limits which the solicitor must have regard to and advise the client accordingly.

RISK SHARING WITH INSURERS

Before-the-event insurers

5.8 Many clients have the benefit of legal expenses insurance, often as part of their motor or home insurance policies. Legal expenses cover is usually broadly limited to the subject matter of the main policy and to claims of merit, although it is surprising how widely some policies are worded. The level of cover is usually limited to an agreed figure (£25,000 to £50,000 is not unusual) and will cover both the policyholder's liability for their own legal costs, and their liability for an opponent's costs if a case is lost. Legal expenses insurers often require the client's lawyers to provide advice on the merits of the claim from time to time so they can assess whether continuing the litigation can be justified under the terms of the insurance.

Most policies insist that, before the issue of proceedings, the policyholder uses a solicitor selected from a panel appointed by the insurer, which can then retain control over its terms of business with the panel firms. After proceedings have begun the policyholder has a right to instruct a solicitor of his or her choice (Insurance Companies (Legal Expenses Insurance) Regulations 1990, SI 1990/1159). The narrow interpretation of 'proceedings' to exclude pre-issue work, including working through a pre-action protocol, has been endorsed by the Financial Ombudsman Service in a policy statement issued in March 2003 (*Ombudsman News,* issue 26). However, in a different context (when considering costs-only proceedings in *Crosbie v Munroe* [2003] EWCA Civ 350, [2003] 1 WLR 2033) Brooke LJ commented, *obiter*, at [37]:

> . . . lower courts are encountering . . . difficulties over the meaning of the word 'proceedings' as used in **PD Protocols, para. 4A.2.** . . . it appears to me that . . . for instance, the dealings between the parties which lead up to the disposal of a clinical negligence claim are to be treated as 'proceedings' for the purposes of that paragraph even if the dispute is settled without the need to issue a claim form.

More generally the government would like greater use to be made of legal expenses insurance, as it is seen as a cheap and effective way of enabling people to litigate (an aim achieved in part by the continued use of bulk instructions to panel firms). It depends on members of the public and businesses having the foresight to obtain cover before they have disputes; on insurance companies continuing to charge relatively low rates for premiums; and on people with such cover, and their solicitors, being aware that they can make use of it. It is recognised that the people least likely to have such cover are the poorest members of society.

After-the-event insurers

5.9 ATE insurance policies are taken out to help cover the cost of litigation once a dispute has already arisen. If the premium is affordable, it can provide some peace of mind against the possibility of having to pay the total litigation costs if the case is lost. A fixed premium can also provide a certainty of cost exposure which is otherwise missing for a client involved in litigation.

Cover can be obtained to insure both the client's own legal costs, including disbursements, and those of opposing parties. They are commonly, but not exclusively, used in conjunction with conditional fee agreements so that there is risk sharing between both the insurance company and the solicitor. An application for insurance can normally be made at any time in the litigation but many insurance companies encourage applications to be made as early as possible, and preferably before the issue of proceedings.

Whether or not insurance is offered by a particular provider and at what premium will depend primarily on the strength of the case and the level of cover required. As a very rough guide, insurance is generally available for cases with prospects of success greater than 70 per cent. Premiums tend to be about 20 to 30 per cent of the amount of cover required.

The practitioner must exercise caution before assuming any responsibility to give 'best or suitable advice' in relation to the products which may be available. Although it may be incumbent upon the solicitor to suggest to the client a suitable policy, the solicitor should not guarantee that the means of funding adopted will necessarily be the most appropriate to the client's needs. A list of insurance providers is updated quarterly in the Law Society's publication, *Litigation Funding*. Specialist ATE insurance brokers exist, such as TheJudge.co.uk Ltd and Aon Ltd. Brokers may charge a fee for their service but that is often refundable when a policy is taken out. The number of insurers willing to offer ATE insurance cover has begun to contract as the market has matured. However, several different types of policy are available. Some providers offer policies which defer payment of the premium until the conclusion of the case and which rebate the premium if the client is unsuccessful. In *Tilby v Perfect Pizza Ltd* (2002) LTL 28/3/2002 Senior Costs Judge Hirst held that there is no reason why an ATE policy premium must be paid when the policy is taken out. Accordingly an ATE policy can provide for payment of the premium on the conclusion of proceedings without being regarded as providing credit and so subject to the **Consumer Credit Act 1974**. Other policies do specifically offer credit schemes allowing clients to borrow money to pay ongoing disbursements or the insurance premium itself.

A non-party costs order under the **Supreme Court Act 1981, s. 51** (see **66.66**), is unlikely to be made against an ATE insurer provided the agreement with the funder excludes the funder from any control over the conduct of the proceedings (*Arkin v Borchard Lines Ltd* [2003] EWHC 2844 (Comm), LTL 27/11/2003).

Level of ATE insurance premiums

The **Access to Justice Act 1999, s. 29**, allows a successful party to claim the premium paid for ATE cover from the other side as part of the costs of the proceedings. In accordance with the usual rules on the quantification of costs by the court (see **CPR, rr. 44.4** and **44.5**), to be recoverable in full the premium must be reasonably incurred and reasonable and proportionate in amount. There is a considerable body of case law, discussed at **68.51**, on the circumstances in which such a premium can be recovered and what amount is reasonable and proportionate. In considering whether a premium is reasonable, the court must have regard to such evidence as there is, or knowledge that experience has provided, of the relationship between the premium and the risk, and the cost of alternative cover (*Callery v Gray (No. 2)* [2001] EWCA Civ 1246, [2001] 1 WLR 2142, at [69]). **5.10**

In straightforward road traffic claims, only a relative modest premium is likely to be allowed. Thus in *Callery v Gray (No. 2)* the court allowed a premium of £367.50. The courts have to take care when considering premiums charged by claims handling companies, where the payment described as the 'premium' may cover a basket of services only one of which is the ATE insurance cover. See *Sharratt v London Central Bus Co. Ltd (No. 2)* [2004] EWCA Civ 575, [2004] 3 All ER 325, where the Court of Appeal approved the costs judge's approach of investigating how much of the payment in fact related to the cost of the ATE cover. For complex litigation, premiums can be substantial. In *Sarwar v Alam* (2003) LTL 23/3/2003 the claim was an important test case. A premium of £62,500 subject to a 50 per cent no-claims bonus was allowed in full. The costs judge, Master Rogers, commented that although the premium was high, it was unlikely that a lower quotation could have been obtained. In practice, solicitors may have to show they considered more than one insurer if a very large premium is to be recovered in full from the other side.

The fact that a party has taken out an ATE insurance policy must be notified to the court and every other party (**CPR, r. 44.3B(1)(c); PD 43–48, para. 19**). **Form N251** should be used.

PD Protocols, para. 4A.1, requires information about funding arrangements to be given *before* the commencement of proceedings.

The level of the premium does not have to be disclosed (**PD 43–48, para. 19.1(1)**). Non-disclosure can be used to tactical advantage, especially if the party has in fact only taken out a very modest policy to cover only part of the potential liability for costs. That said, in *Henry v British Broadcasting Corporation* [2005] EWHC 2503 (QB), [2006] 1 All ER 154, Gray J held that the defendant's solicitors were entitled to be informed about the extent of the claimant's legal costs insurance cover and were also entitled to be informed if the estimated costs of the claim had risen substantially. If there is difficulty in obtaining that information, the defendant should make an application for the court to exercise its power in **CPR, r. 3.1(2)(II)**, to order the claimant to file and serve an estimate of costs. It may be important that this decision was made in a libel claim and that the use of CFAs in libel proceedings has come under sustained criticism from the media industry and the Court of Appeal (*King v Telegraph Group Ltd* [2004] EWCA Civ 613, [2005] 1 WLR 2282).

Transitional cases

5.11 In *Inline Logistics Ltd v UCI Logistics Ltd* [2002] EWHC 519 (Ch), *The Times*, 2 May 2002, Ferris J was asked to consider whether or not an ATE insurance premium taken out after the Access to Justice Act 1999, s. 29, came into force on 1 April 2000, but before the CPR were amended to reflect the introduction of that section on 3 July 2000, was recoverable from the unsuccessful claimant. The gap between the introduction of s. 29 and the amendment of the Rules was the subject of criticism at the time but to bridge that gap transitional arrangements were put in place. These essentially meant that if a party entered into a funding arrangement prior to 3 July 2000 it had a further 28 days to comply with the new rules, for example, by putting the other party on notice of the arrangement (Civil Procedure (Amendment No. 3) Rules 2000 (SI 2000/1317), r. 39).

However, r. 39 refers to a person who has 'started proceedings'. Ferris J held that this could not apply in the present case as it was the defendant who was seeking recovery of the premium and the defendant could not have been said to have 'started proceedings'. Accordingly it was held that no rules of court applied to defendants who entered into a funding arrangement between 1 April and 2 July 2000. The effect is that r. 39 imposed additional obligations on claimants which, presumably through drafting oversight, it did not impose upon defendants.

RISK SHARING WITH LAWYERS

5.12 Lawyers can share in the risk of litigation with their clients by agreeing to link the recovery of their fees with the outcome of the litigation. These fee agreements are known as 'contingency fees' — the lawyers' fees are contingent on the result obtained.

Contingency fees encompass all types of CFA (where the solicitor charges an uplift on fees if the case is won, and a reduced fee or no fee at all if the case is lost) and agreements to charge fees equivalent to a percentage of the damages awarded (which are common in the USA).

Contingency fees are generally unenforceable in litigation because they are champertous arrangements, contrary to public policy and the common law. There are, however, two important qualifications. First, specific statutory authority has been provided for the use of CFAs in litigation. The whole topic is considered further in **chapter 6**. Secondly, there is no bar to using any type of contingency fee if there is a non-contentious business agreement (**Solicitors Act 1974, s. 57(2)**). This means that they can be used in mediations, arbitrations and employment tribunal cases (save for the Employment Appeal Tribunal). There remains a doubt whether work done during the pre-action protocol period is non-contentious business (see *Crosbie v Munroe* [2003] EWCA Civ 350, [2003] 1 WLR 2033, per Brooke LJ considered at **5.8**). These arrangements are usually considered to be more straightforward for clients to understand than CFAs.

ASSIGNMENT OF CAUSES OF ACTION

Sometimes someone in whom a cause of action is vested will assign it to another person. Doing so, if effective, will allow that other person to bring (or continue) proceedings based on that cause of action. There may be practical reasons for doing this. The cause of action may be vested in a trustee in bankruptcy, who may be unwilling to prosecute the claim. Alternatively, a limited liability company may assign a cause of action to an individual to avoid an order for security for costs. **5.13**

Assignments are sometimes attacked on the ground that they savour of champerty or maintenance (see **14.22** to **14.26**).

Assignments by companies intended to obtain the benefit of public funding and to avoid the risk of having to provide security for costs were upheld by the House of Lords in *Norglen Ltd v Reeds Rains Prudential Ltd* [1999] 2 AC 1. However, 'matters arising out of the carrying on of a business' are now excluded from the scope of public funding by the **Access to Justice Act 1999, sch. 2, para. 1(b)**, and it is difficult to envisage circumstances where public funding will be available following an assignment of this type.

Chapter 6 Conditional Fee Agreements

INTRODUCTION

6.1 A conditional fee agreement (CFA) is defined by the **Courts and Legal Services Act 1990, s. 58(2)(a)**, as an agreement for advocacy or litigation services which provides that the lawyer's fees and expenses, or any part of them, will be payable only in specified circumstances. CFAs are a form of contingency fee arrangement (see **5.12**).

CFAs with success fees are the more familiar arrangements whereby the legal representative charges nothing if the case is lost but the full fee plus an enhancement — calculated as a percentage uplift on the fee — if the case is won. CFAs without success fees effectively replace what were *Thai Trading Co. v Taylor* [1998] QB 781 agreements, i.e., agreements where the client is charged nothing, or a reduced fee, if the case is lost but the full fee where the case is won.

CFAs can be extremely flexible. If the case is lost, the agreement may be that the client will pay nothing at all, or will pay the solicitor's charges at a reduced hourly rate or even a fixed fee depending on the stage reached in the litigation. If the case is won, the agreement can provide for the payment of the solicitor's basic costs without any enhancement, or a percentage uplift on those fees. CFAs can use any combination of these provisions, and, within certain boundaries, set basic hourly rates and the level of discounts and enhancements.

Since 30 July 1998 (Conditional Fee Agreements Order 1998 (SI 1998/1860)) it has been possible to enter into CFAs in all types of civil litigation with the exception of family work. By the **Courts and Legal Services Act 1990, s. 58A(4)**, 'proceedings' for the purposes of CFAs includes any sort of proceedings for resolving disputes and is not limited to proceedings in court. Nor is the term limited to cases where proceedings are commenced as opposed to contemplated. CFAs can be used for many kinds of dispute resolution, including arbitration and tribunal matters.

The concern that it might be possible for the successful defendant to recover costs from a claimant's legal representative on the ground of maintenance or champerty (see **14.23**) was removed by *Hodgson v Imperial Tobacco Ltd* [1998] 1 WLR 1056. An argument that taking a weak case on a CFA is an abuse of process was rejected in *King v Telegraph Group Ltd* [2003] EWHC

1312 (QB), LTL 9/6/2003. The House of Lords has held that the CFA regime (including the recoverability of success fees against defendants) does not breach the **European Convention on Human Rights, art. 10** (right to freedom of expression) (*Campbell v MGN Ltd (No. 2)* [2005] UKHL 61, [2005] 1 WLR 3394). However, concern was expressed about the appropriate balance to be struck between the parties, particularly where a claimant is unable to meet the adverse cost risk if the claim fails. It was suggested that further legislative intervention might be required.

PRACTICAL CONSIDERATIONS

Although most CFAs are entered into by claimants, there is no reason to prevent **6.2** defendants from using them. The definition of 'win' for the purposes of the agreement is a matter for negotiation between the lawyer and the client. When acting for a claimant 'win' will almost always mean an award (but not recovery of) damages. Lawyers who represent a defendant may agree to a definition of 'win' that relates to the amount of damages paid by the defendant at the conclusion of the claim, whether by settlement or trial. The level of those damages could be set at nil, or a figure relating to the claim put in the claimant's statement of case. A successful defendant will be able to benefit from the rules on recovery of a success fee and insurance premium in the same way as a successful claimant, although there is much less of a market for after-the-event insurance for defendants than for claimants.

CFAs are most prevalent in personal injury litigation where they are commonly used in conjunction with ATE insurance (see **5.9**). They are also popular in libel claims. However, the use of CFAs in commercial litigation remains surprisingly underdeveloped. Although many commercial clients do not insist on CFAs now, it is likely that more and more clients will enquire about their use and will increasingly ask their lawyers to give serious consideration to them.

Since the removal of public funding for business-related disputes, CFAs offer a route to funding and progressing meritorious cases when a client may be unable to raise sufficient funds to pay privately. However, disbursements will need funding during the conduct of the claim and there is no statutory protection (unlike in public funding cases) against an adverse order for costs if the claim is unsuccessful. A further disincentive for acting for the impecunious client is that even if the claim is successful, funds may not be available to meet the judgment for damages or costs, for example, because of the insolvency of the unsuccessful party. In that unhappy circumstance, the solicitor may not recover any fees at all, notwithstanding that the client has 'won' for the purposes of the CFA.

CFAs have a potentially important part to play in the effective management of litigation. Entering into a CFA (and paying for insurance against an adverse costs order) can have significant tactical advantages to a client. The client's risk of having to pay legal fees at all will be substantially reduced, or may even be extinguished. However, the opponent's future costs exposure may have more than doubled overnight — something that may be enough to convince the opponent to settle and settle early. CFAs have the effect of raising the stakes in terms of costs while shifting the risk away from the client and sending the message to the opponent that the case is strong enough to attract a CFA.

ENTERING INTO A CFA

Two regimes

From 1 April 2000 to 30 October 2005, a CFA was not effective unless it complied with the **6.3** **Courts and Legal Services Act 1990, ss. 58 and 58A**, and complied with the **Conditional Fee**

Agreements Regulations 2000 (SI 2000/692). The Regulations have been revoked and do not apply to CFAs entered into on or after 1 November 2005. However, they continue to affect agreements entered into before 1 November 2005, under which litigation will be conducted for some time, so the provisions of the Regulations are considered at **6.5** to **6.11**.

Requirements for validity of CFAs entered into on or after 1 November 2005

6.4 A CFA entered into on or after 1 November 2005 must comply with the **Courts and Legal Services Act 1990, ss. 58** and **58A**. This means that a CFA must:

(a) be in writing (**s. 58(3)(a)**);
(b) relate to a type of case that the statute allows to be run on a CFA (**s. 58(3)(b)**); and
(c) specify the success fee, which must not exceed 100 per cent (**s. 58(4); Conditional Fee Agreements Order 2000 (SI 2000/823), art. 4**).

A failure to comply with any of these basic elements is likely to mean that the CFA is unenforceable.

By the **Courts and Legal Services Act 1990, s. 58A(1)**, the only proceedings which cannot be the subject of an enforceable CFA are criminal proceedings and family proceedings, as defined in **s. 58A(2)**, apart from proceedings under the Environmental Protection Act 1990, s. 82 (proceedings in a magistrates' court to abate a statutory nuisance).

The Solicitors' Costs Information and Client Care Code 1999 (the 'Law Society Code') has been amended to include a provision that where a client is represented under a CFA a solicitor should explain:

(a) the circumstances in which the client may be liable for his own costs and for the other party's costs;
(b) the client's right to assessment of costs by the court, wherever the solicitor intends to seek payment of any or all of his costs from the client; and
(c) any interest the solicitor may have in recommending a particular policy or other funding.

Rule 15 of the Solicitors' Practice Rules 1990 requires compliance with the Law Society Code and the Law Society's rules have the force of subordinate legislation (*Swain v Law Society* [1983] 1 AC 598). However, not every breach of the Practice Rules will render a contract unenforceable (*Awwad v Geraghty and Co.* [2001] QB 570). It is also likely that not every breach of the Law Society Code will be a breach of r. 15 of the Practice Rules. For instance, a failure to provide costs estimates (also a potential breach of r. 15 and the Law Society Code) does not render the retainer unenforceable (*Garbutt v Edwards* [2005] EWCA Civ 1206, [2006] 1 All ER 553). In *Garbutt v Edwards* the Court of Appeal said that a breach of the Code by a receiving party's solicitor should affect the paying party's liability only if it had led to a calculable and not immaterial effect on the costs claimed. It is conceivable that a failure to disclose an interest in a policy or funding method may have led to a more expensive policy or funding method being used, although that seems unlikely. Accordingly, although *Garbutt v Edwards* may not prove to be the last word on this subject, it remains a clear statement from the Court of Appeal that the role of the paying party in regulating or challenging the behaviour of the receiving party's solicitors is to be much reduced or even extinguished. If so, it will put an end to the many technical challenges brought by paying parties in recent years and meet one of the express intentions of the revocation of the **Conditional Fee Agreements Regulations 2000 (SI 2000/692)**.

It is clear from *Callery v Gray* [2001] EWCA Civ 1117, [2001] 1 WLR 2112, that the fact that proceedings have not been issued is not a bar to recovery under a CFA and that it is reasonable to enter into a CFA at the outset of the retainer, before the defendant has been approached or has clarified its position.

Requirements for validity of CFAs entered into before 1 November 2005

Before 1 November 2005 a CFA had to comply with the requirements of the **Courts and Legal Services Act 1990, ss. 58 and 58A**, discussed in **6.4** and also the provisions of the **Conditional Fee Agreements Regulations 2000 (SI 2000/692)**. **6.5**

Two types of CFA were permitted by the Regulations. CFAs of the type introduced in 1998 ('normal CFAs', see **6.4**) provide that in the event of success the lawyer's fee and any success fee are payable by the client. Strictly this is so whether or not those fees are ultimately paid by the other side. The second type, introduced in 2003 ('non-indemnity CFAs', see **6.5**), provide that the lawyer's fee and any success fee are payable by the client only to the extent that those fees are paid by the other side.

Normal CFAs

The requirements for normal CFAs entered into before 1 November 2005 were laid down by the **Conditional Fee Agreements Regulations 2000 (SI 2000/692)**. A normal CFA entered into before 1 November 2005 must state: **6.6**

(a) The proceedings to which the agreement relates (reg. 2(1)(a)).
(b) The circumstances in which the legal representative's fees and expenses or part of them are payable (reg. 2(1)(b)).
(c) What happens if those circumstances do not occur (or only partly occur) and the payment due in each scenario (reg. 2(1)(c)(i) and (ii)).
(d) What happens on termination of the agreement (reg. 2(1)(c)(iii)).

The agreement must be in writing and must be signed by both the client and the legal representative (reg. 5).

Agreements that provide for success fees must also contain (by virtue of reg. 3):

(a) Reasons why the success fee has been set at the level that it has. Most agreements include a copy or summary of the risk assessment and success fee calculation carried out by the legal representative.
(b) The extent to which the success fee reflects an allowance for delayed payment, as opposed to the risk of losing.
(c) For agreements covering court proceedings, provision for the legal representative or the client to disclose to the court the reasons behind the success fee (reflecting **CPR, r. 44.15**), and for any shortfall between the success fee stated in the CFA and that allowed by the court or agreed with the paying party to be recoverable from the client only with the court's permission (*Ghannouchi v Houni Ltd* (2004) LTL 19/4/2004).

Certain information had to be given by the legal representative to the client before the CFA was entered into. Those matters are (reg. 4(2)):

(a) The circumstances in which the client may be liable to pay the costs of the legal representative in accordance with the agreement.
(b) The circumstances in which the client may seek assessment of the fees and expenses of the legal representative and the procedure for doing so.
(c) Whether the legal representative considers that the client's risk of incurring liability for costs in respect of the proceedings to which the agreement relates is insured under an existing contract of insurance.
(d) Whether other methods of financing those costs are available, and, if so, how they apply to the client in the proceedings in question.
(e) Whether the legal representative considers that any particular method or methods of financing any or all of those costs is appropriate and, if he considers that a contract of insurance is appropriate or recommends a particular such contract:
    (i) his reasons for doing so; and
    (ii) whether he has an interest in doing so.

The legal representative was also required to explain the general effect of the CFA to the client (reg. 4(3)).

The legal representative must provide such further explanation, advice or information about any of these matters as the client may reasonably require (reg. 4(1)(b)).

Regulation 5 provides that the information set out in reg. 4(2)(a) to (d) must be given orally, but that the matters in reg. 4(2)(e) and the explanation of the effect of the agreement (reg. 4(3)) must be given both orally and in writing.

Non-indemnity CFAs

6.7 **Regulation 3A of the Conditional Fee Agreements Regulations 2000 (SI 2000/692)** came into force on 2 June 2003 and was revoked on 1 November 2005. It enabled a solicitor to enter into an agreement with a client in which it is plainly stated that the solicitor will not seek to recover more than is recovered from others by means of the proceedings, provided the agreement is in the form of a CFA. Before 2 June 2003, such an agreement would have invoked the indemnity principle (see **68.29**) and nothing at all would be recovered under a costs order. However, **r. 43.2(3) of the CPR**, which also came into force on 2 June 2003, provides that costs are recoverable 'notwithstanding that the client is liable to pay his legal representative's fees and expenses only to the extent that sums are recovered in respect of the proceedings by way of costs or otherwise'. This is a direct abrogation of the indemnity principle.

These provisions allow practitioners to offer a simple 'no costs to you' funding product (save for any ATE insurance premium). Whatever the solicitor recovers in costs from other parties is all that the client will be charged. The phrase 'costs or otherwise' has caused some consternation as it permits a solicitor to deduct some or all of his fees from damages. It was included primarily to allow for circumstances where the defendant had the means to pay the damages element of a judgment in whole or in part, but not the entirety of the costs. However, it does raise consumer protection issues, particularly if the defendant offers a global settlement of costs and damages. In those circumstances, it seems that the claimant's solicitor is entitled to deduct the whole of his fee from the amount received as a global settlement.

The simplicity of a non-indemnity CFA is reflected in the less onerous explanations which the solicitor was required to give to the client. **Regulations 2, 3 and 4 of SI 2000/692**, which were the basis of many technical challenges, do not apply to non-indemnity CFAs (**reg. 3A(3)**). Instead, by **reg. 3A(4)(a)**, a non-indemnity CFA need only specify:

(a) the particular proceedings or parts of them to which it relates (including whether it relates to any appeal, counterclaim or proceedings to enforce a judgment or order); and
(b) the circumstances in which the legal representative's fees and expenses, or part of them, are payable.

If a non-indemnity CFA provides for a success fee, it must, by **reg. 3A(4)(b)**, also:

(c) briefly specify the reasons for setting the percentage increase at the level stated in the agreement; and
(d) provide that if, in court proceedings, the percentage increase becomes payable as a result of those proceedings and the legal representative or the client is ordered to disclose to the court or any other person the reasons for setting the percentage increase at the level stated in the agreement, he may do so.

A legal representative was required, before making a non-indemnity CFA, to inform the client of the circumstances in which the client may be liable to pay the legal representative's fees and expenses, and 'provide such further explanation, advice or other information as to those circumstances as the client may reasonably require' (**reg. 3A(6)**).

Regulation **3A(5)** allowed a non-indemnity CFA to contain terms specifying that the client can still be liable to pay the fees under the CFA even if there is no recovery in the proceedings when the client:

(a) fails to cooperate with the legal representative;
(b) fails to attend any medical or expert examination or court hearing which the legal representative reasonably requests him to attend;
(c) fails to give necessary instructions to the legal representative;
(d) withdraws instructions from the legal representative;
(e) (with effect from 2 February 2004, see the Conditional Fee Agreements (Miscellaneous Amendments) (No. 2) Regulations 2003, SI 2003/3344) becomes insolvent; or
(f) (also with effect from 2 February 2004) dies in the course of the proceedings.

Similar provision was made in relation to collective CFAs by **regs 4(1A)** and **5(4), (5) and (6) of the Collective Conditional Fee Agreements Regulations 2000 (SI 2000/2988).**

Failure to comply with the Regulations

The importance of complying with the **Conditional Fee Agreements Regulations 2000** when entering into a CFA before 1 November 2005 cannot be understated. It is only the enabling legislation that prevents CFAs from being unenforceable. If a CFA is unenforceable, the application of the indemnity principle means that all of the successful party's costs will be irrecoverable, giving the paying party a windfall. The argument that the receiving party's fees ought to be reduced, rather than extinguished, in the event of its CFA being found unenforceable was expressly rejected in *Spencer v Wood* [2004] EWCA Civ 352, *The Times*, 30 March 2004. **6.8**

Many applications have been brought by paying parties demanding sight of the receiving party's CFA in assessment proceedings, in the hope of finding breaches of the **Conditional Fee Agreements Regulations 2000** which would relieve them of liability. Appeals from various challenges were consolidated and heard as *Hollins v Russell* [2003] EWCA Civ 718, [2003] 1 WLR 2487. The questions the court had to answer were:

(a) In what circumstances should a CFA be disclosed to the paying party (see **6.9**)?
(b) What is the correct test for compliance with the **Conditional Fee Agreements Regulations 2000** (see **6.10**)?

Disclosure of the CFA In *Hollins v Russell* [2003] EWCA Civ 718, [2003] 1 WLR 2487, the Court of Appeal (distinguishing *Bailey v IBC Vehicles Ltd* [1998] 3 All ER 570) made it clear that when a receiving party relies on a CFA (with or without a success fee) the costs judge should require him to elect whether to disclose the CFA to the paying party or endeavour to prove his entitlement to the costs by other means. The same rule applies to collective CFAs (*Woollam v Cleanaway Ltd* (2004) LTL 4/2/2005). On the other hand he should not ordinarily be required to produce attendance notes. The court expressed the hope that in practice receiving parties will disclose the CFA as part of their normal practice. The Court of Appeal was not impressed by the argument that the CFA was privileged. However, if there are any privileged parts of the agreement, they can be redacted before disclosure. **6.9**

Materially adverse effect In *Hollins v Russell* [2003] EWCA Civ 718, [2003] 1 WLR 2487, the Court of Appeal laid down the following test of whether a CFA complies with the **Conditional Fee Agreements Regulations 2000** (SI 2000/692), namely: **6.10**

> Has the particular departure from a regulation . . . or a requirement in the **Courts and Legal Services Act 1990, s. 58,** either on its own or in conjunction with any other such departure in the case, had a materially adverse effect either upon the protection afforded to the client or upon the proper administration of justice?

If the answer is yes, the conditions have not been satisfied. If the answer is no, the departure is immaterial and the conditions have been satisfied.

If a CFA is unenforceable, any insurance premium and/or disbursements payable by the client are still recoverable from the paying party — it is the client's claim for costs, not the solicitor's — and the right to claim those costs is independent of the CFA, consistent with the **Access to Justice Act 1999, s. 29**.

The test may not prevent defendants from trawling through CFAs in assessment proceedings. However, it does set a further hurdle for defendants to surmount if they seek to show that a particular CFA is unenforceable. Solicitors who use the Law Society's approved model CFA and ensure their staff can adequately explain it to a lay client should be on solid ground. The Court of Appeal in *Hollins v Russell*, when considering a defect in a now superseded version of the Law Society model CFA said, at [128]:

> In the present case we consider that the effect of the CFA read as a whole is sufficiently clear and that the failure to specify the position did not affect the protection given to the client or the administration of justice to any material degree. The result would have been different if the CFA was less clear as to its effect, that is if it would not have been reasonably comprehensible to a lay client.

Much the same approach was taken by Master Seagar Berry in the SCCO in *Ghannouchi v Houni Ltd* (2004) LTL 19/4/2004, again when holding that a defect in a Law Society approved model CFA (in not making clear that the client did not have to pay any shortfall in base costs as well as the success fee) did not amount to a material breach. However, in *Culshaw v Goodliffe* (2003) LTL 23/9/2004, *Adair v Cullen* (Manchester County Court 14 June 2004) and *Samonini v London General Transport Services Ltd* (2005) LTL 2/2/2005, a breach of **SI 2000/692, reg. 4(2)(c)**, was held to be material. The breach concerned the solicitor's failure to advise a client properly about the availability of BTE cover (see also *Sarwar v Alam* [2001] EWCA Civ 1401, [2002] 1 WLR 125). There will also be a materially adverse breach if a solicitor fails to advise a client on the availability of public funding in breach of **reg. 4(2)(d)** (*Bowen v Bridgend County Borough Council* (2004) LTL 4/5/2004).

In *Spencer v Wood* [2004] EWCA Civ 352, *The Times*, 30 March 2004, the Court of Appeal, restating the material breach test set out in *Hollins v Russell*, held the claimant's CFA to be unenforceable for a breach of **reg. 3(1)(b)** (failure to specify how much of the success fee, if any, relates to the cost to the legal representative of postponement of payment of fees and expenses).

The judgment in *Ghannouchi v Houni Ltd* also considered the time at which the issue of materiality should be considered, holding that the court should look at the position at the time the challenge is made, that is, the court should consider with hindsight whether the breach has in fact turned out to be material, rather than whether it was material at the time the CFA was taken out.

However, in *Richard v Davis* (SCCO 25 November 2005) www.hmcourts-service.gov.uk/HMCSJudgments the Senior Costs Judge, Master Hurst, disagreed, holding that the validity of a CFA must instead be judged at the date the CFA was entered into.

6.11 **Delegation of explanations** The Court of Appeal in *Hollins v Russell* [2003] EWCA Civ 718, [2003] 1 WLR 2487, considered whether or not a solicitor could delegate his responsibility to explain the CFA to the client. The point was considered in the context of the procedure adopted by The Accident Group (TAG), where a solicitor sent standard documentation to TAG, which sent one of their employees to see the client and provide the necessary explanations. The Court of Appeal found that, as a matter of agency, the solicitor could delegate his responsibilities, but that the supervision of the representative by the solicitor was all-important. It said, at [217]:

> A national organisation like TAG may be able to achieve economies of scale and standards of client service which are simply not available in an ordinary solicitors' firm. Quality control, however, is all important, and if a solicitor abjures his duty to maintain supervisory responsibility, through an established framework for reporting and accountability, over the TAG representatives when they visit his

clients home on his behalf, it is likely that it would be found that it was not he who gave the information he was required by the **Conditional Fee Agreements Regulations 2000, reg.** 4, to give, and that the regulation has therefore been broken.

It seems likely that if a solicitor delegates responsibility in a situation that he cannot adequately supervise, a material breach of **reg.** 4 will be found, rendering the CFA unenforceable.

In the TAG proceedings the point was dealt with in a mediated agreement, whereby solicitors' costs were recovered in full if explanations in accordance with the regulations were given before, or within 14 days of signing the agreement. Where that had not happened the agreed costs were reduced.

In *Samonini v London General Transport Services Ltd* (2005) LTL 2/2/2005 a CFA was unenforceable because the claims handling company's investigations were inadequate. They had failed to ask the client about any BTE policies other than his motor policy and this breach of the **Conditional Fee Agreements Regulations 2000 (SI 2000/692), reg.** 4(2)(c), was held to have a materially adverse effect.

Setting the success fee

Paragraphs 11.7 to 11.10 of PD 43–48 govern the assessment of what is a 'reasonable' amount for a success fee. The guidance given is as follows: **6.12**

(a) The court will have regard to the facts and circumstances as they reasonably appeared to the solicitor or counsel at the time the funding arrangement was entered into or varied (**para.** 11.7).
(b) The court will assess the level of the success fee by reference to the risk of non-payment of the costs, fees or expenses, the legal representative's liability for any disbursements and what other methods of financing were available (**para. 11.8**).
(c) The court will not reduce the success fee simply because, when added to otherwise reasonable base costs, the total becomes disproportionate (**para. 11.9**). In other words, proportionality for the purposes of costs under the CPR is assessed net of any success fee.

Risk assessment To fix a success fee, the solicitor needs to undertake a risk assessment of the case before him and record that assessment carefully. There are broadly two approaches to assessing risk in litigation claims. Risk can be assessed on case-by-case basis by looking at the particular features of the individual case and assessing those which have a risk of being lost. The alternative approach is to look at generic types of case and consider statistically how many of each type are successful. **6.13**

Generic risk assessment In high-volume, low-value claims a proportionate way of assessing risk is by using the generic model. In *Abrew v Tesco Stores Ltd* (2003) LTL 18/6/2003 the costs judge, when considering the simplistic risk assessment, said, 'I think [the defendant] underestimates the difficulties that would be encountered by a busy solicitor . . . if he had to go into great detail in every single case'. The generic model fits with the concept of staged success fees, which the Court of Appeal was attracted to in *Callery v Gray* [2001] EWCA Civ 1117, [2001] 1 WLR 2112, and which it endorsed later in *Halloran v Delaney* [2002] EWCA Civ 1258, [2003] 1 WLR 28. Lord Woolf in *Callery v Gray* said, '. . . by way of example the uplift might be 100 per cent, subject to a reduction to 5 per cent should the claim settle before the end of the protocol period'. **6.14**

In *Halloran v Delaney* the court applied the reduction to 5 per cent to pre-proceedings settlement, subject to a district judge's discretion to exceed 5 per cent in appropriate cases. Both cases concerned road traffic accident claims. Brooke LJ, who gave the leading judgment in *Halloran v Delaney*, later clarified that the 5 per cent figure only applies to straightforward road traffic accident cases (see *Re Claims Direct Test Cases* [2003] EWCA Civ 136, [2003] 4 All ER 508, at [99]–[101]). He went on to say that it did not require any research evidence or submissions from other parties in the industry to persuade the court that in this type of extremely simple claim a success fee of over 5 per cent was no longer tenable in all the circumstances. He then made it clear that in straightforward road traffic accident cases the prospects of success are virtually 100 per cent and that the 5 per cent is 'to cater for the wholly unexpected risk lurking below the limpid waters of the simplest of claims'.

On 7 October 2003, with the assistance of the Civil Justice Council, an industry agreement in principle was reached to fix recoverable two-stage success fees in road traffic accident cases funded under a CFA. The agreement was the result of a mediation conducted by the Civil Justice Council and involving the Law Society, the Association of British Insurers and main solicitors' organisations such as the Association of Personal Injury Lawyers, the Forum of Insurance Lawyers and the Motor Accident Solicitors' Society. The process was supported by the Department for Constitutional Affairs. The agreement sets out the success fee an insurer will pay the claimant's solicitor in a third-party motor claim. The success fee is 12.5 per cent of base costs recoverable for all successful claims that are settled, whether before or after issue of proceedings. Cases that are tried will attract a 100 per cent success fee.

The agreement, which works in tandem with the predictable costs regime for road traffic cases, is implemented in **CPR, rr. 45.15** to **45.19** (see **67.16** and **67.17**), and applies to accidents occurring on or after 6 October 2003 (**r. 45.15(4)(c)**). Guidance on the assessment of older cases was given in *Atack v Lee* [2004] EWCA Civ 1712, [2005] 1 WLR 2643.

For most road traffic accident claims the success fees are now as follows:

(a) For CFAs signed before 1 August 2001: a band of up to 20 per cent.
(b) For CFAs signed after 1 August 2001: 5 per cent.
(c) For accidents from 6 October 2003: 12.5 per cent, with 100 per cent for trials.
(d) For CFAs on older cases signed after 16 December 2004: 12.5 per cent, with 100 per cent for trials.

Employers' liability accident cases are also now subject to fixed success fees, albeit that (again based on statistical research) the levels are higher than those in road traffic accident cases. **Rules 45.20** to **45.22** (see **67.18** and **67.19**) provide that the CFA success fee in personal injury claims against an employer (save for disease and road traffic accident claims: **r. 45.20(2)(a)(i)** and **(iii)**) will be fixed at 25 per cent for both solicitors and counsel. If a membership organisation is providing ATE cover, the percentage is increased to 27.5 per cent.

Rules 45.20 to **45.22** do not apply to small claims track proceedings (**r. 45.20(2)(b)**), or any injury sustained before 1 October 2004 (**r. 45.20(2)(a)(ii)**).

An application to increase the allowable success fee is discouraged. If the court assesses the success fee in the range of 15–40 per cent, the applicant will still only get 25 per cent (or 27.5 per cent as applicable) and will have to pay the costs of the application (**r. 45.22**).

6.15 **Case-by-case assessment** Notwithstanding *Callery v Gray* [2001] EWCA Civ 1117, [2001] 1 WLR 2112, and *Halloran v Delaney* [2002] EWCA Civ 1258, [2003] 1 WLR 28, the courts' and solicitors' preference for assessing risk on a case-by-case basis remains. For each case common risk areas, such as limitation, evidence, liability, causation, loss and recovery can be identified and assessed. There is necessarily a large element of subjectivity in assessing the risk in any given case, but the more detailed the list of risk factors identified the more likely it is the court will uphold the level of success fee claimed. Complexity does not necessarily increase risk, although it may increase the unknown and therefore unquantifiable factors at the time of assessment. It remains true that even the simplest cases can be lost, often because of evidential difficulties.

Risk factors identified as justifying success fees should be real and not fanciful. For instance, if a simple telephone call will resolve any doubt about the identity of a driver, the call should be made before the success fee is fixed (*Atack v Lee* [2004] EWCA Civ 1712, [2005] 1 WLR 2643).

Probability can be a useful tool in assessing risk. For instance, to succeed at trial a claimant will have to succeed on liability and causation and be able to show a loss. To evaluate the probability of succeeding, the chance of proving all of those elements must be assessed.

If the chance of proving liability in a particular case is 70 per cent and, because of different evidential issues, the chance of proving causation and loss is 80 per cent, the chance of winning the case is 70 per cent multiplied by 80 per cent, that is, 56 per cent.

If there is a further 5 per cent chance of the defendant becoming insolvent, win or lose, the chance of recovering damages is reduced to 53.2 per cent.

What may have appeared at first to be a strong case can, with proper analysis, be shown to have prospects hardly better than predicting the outcome of a tossed coin.

A success fee is ordinarily calculated as: the chances of losing divided by the chances of winning. In a case with 60 per cent prospects, the success fee is 40 per cent divided by 60 per cent, which is 66 per cent. An 80 per cent case will have a success fee of 25 per cent (20/80). The Law Society has published a table for easy reference.

Modest percentages (usually 5 per cent per year) can be added to the success fee to take into account the fact that the solicitor cannot bill the client on an interim basis for costs or disbursements. This additional sum can be claimed against the client, but not between the parties.

There is a limited amount of guidance from the courts on appropriate success fees in particular cases. The following list may be illustrative, but each case should be considered with reference to its particular facts:

Road traffic accident (pre-trial) (mediated industry agreement)	12.5 per cent
Appeal to the Court of Appeal (where it is 'almost certain' that the respondent will successfully resist the appeal) (*Alfa Begum v Supin Klarit* [2005] EWCA Civ 210, *The Times*, 18 March 2005)	15 per cent
Straightforward clinical negligence (*Bensusan v Freedman* (2001) LTL 6/11/2001; *Metcalfe v Clipston* (SCCO 6 April 2004) www.hmcourts-service.gov.uk/HMCSJudgments)	20 per cent
Personal injury claim against an employer (pre-trial) (mediated industry agreement)	25 per cent
Slip and trip (*Abrew v Tesco Stores Ltd* (2003) LTL 18/6/2003)	50 per cent
Personal injury claim where the claimants have sustained serious injuries and liability was uncertain (*Burton v Kingsley* [2005] EWHC1034 (QB), [2006] PIQR P2)	50 per cent
Accident at work (with evidential and causation difficulties) (*Chalk v Hightown Praetorian Housing Association* (Cambridge County Court 1 October 2002))	63 per cent
Asbestosis claims (*Smiths Dock Ltd v Edwards* [2004] EWHC 1116 (QB), LTL 20/5/2004)	87 per cent
Road traffic accident (which is tried) (mediated industry agreement and *Callery v Gray* [2001] EWCA Civ 1117, [2001] 1 WLR 2112)	100 per cent

Fatal accident claim against employer 100 per cent
(*Peto-Williamson v Ivan Housley Poultry Ltd* (Nottingham County Court 10 September 2002))

Intellectual property case lost in the Court of Appeal, successful in the House of Lords 100 per cent
(*Designer Guild Ltd v Russell Williams (Textiles) Ltd (No. 2)* (HL 20 February 2003, SCCO Case Summaries No. 4 of 2003))

Staged success fees

6.16 Staged success fees, starting low and increasing as the case progresses, or starting high and decreasing if admissions of liability are made during the proceedings, are consistent with practical experience of how cases are resolved. Inherently strong claims (generically or by reference to the individual case facts) settle early; the weaker, and therefore riskier, claims often find their way to trial. Such arrangements also give the opponent a clear incentive to make admissions early, and settle cases without reference to the courts at all, consistent with the overriding objective of the CPR.

Staged success fees have been encouraged by the Court of Appeal since *Halloran v Delaney* [2002] EWCA Civ 1258, [2003] 1 WLR 28, and have been adopted in the fixed success fee schemes for road traffic accident and employers' liability claims. The court does not have the power to impose a staged success fee retrospectively (*U v Liverpool City Council* [2005] EWCA Civ 475, [2005] 1 WLR 2657). This is so even after the risks have been substantially reduced, after admissions or on a detailed assessment of costs following the success of the main claim.

A different version of staged success fees was approved in *Benaim (UK) Ltd v Davies Middleton and Davies Ltd* [2004] EWHC 737 (TCC), LTL 29/3/2004, in which the success fee was linked to the amount awarded to the claimant. The definition of the success fee varied the percentage uplift by stages from 40 per cent if the recovery was up to £200,000, to 100 per cent if more than £1 million was recovered.

NOTIFICATION OF FUNDING ARRANGEMENT

6.17 Whether or not the dispute is governed by a pre-action protocol, the parties should inform each other in the pre-action stages whether they are being funded under a conditional fee arrangement (although there is no obligation to give details of the level of 'success fee' that has been agreed — indeed to do so would give valuable and privileged information to the opponent) (see **PD Protocols, paras 4A.1** and **4A.2**). Whether 'should' means 'must' was considered in *Bainbridge v MAF Pipelines Ltd* (2004) LTL 17/5/2004, in which the district judge found that it did, so leading to the disallowance of the success fee, and in *Metcalfe v Clipston* (SCCO 6 April 2004) www.hmcourts-service.gov.uk/HMCSJudgments, in which the master came to the opposite conclusion. *Metcalfe v Clipston* is to be preferred, particularly as the master considered two other conflicting first-instance decisions on the point before reaching his conclusion. That said, good practice still dictates that notice should be given as soon as possible in the pre-action stages.

Once proceedings are started, a party who has retained solicitors under a CFA *must* file and serve notice to that effect in **form N251 (CPR, r. 44.15(1); PD 43–48, para. 19.2)**. Notice must be given at the first opportunity, which means when the claim form is issued (for a claimant) or when filing the acknowledgment of service or defence (for a defendant) in cases where the CFA is already in existence. Where the agreement is entered into at a later stage, notice must be given within seven days of entering into the agreement (**PD 43–48, para. 19.2**(4)). Where funding information becomes inaccurate, notice of the change must be given within seven days (**CPR, r. 44.15(2)**), and this may entail filing a new estimate for costs for the purposes of allocation questionnaires and pre-trial checklists (**r. 44.15(3)**).

In the absence of prejudice, the court may be minded to grant relief to a claimant who has failed to serve the requisite notice but has informed the opponent of the CFA in another way. In *Montlake v Lambert Smith Hampton Group Ltd* [2004] EWHC 1503, LTL 16/7/2004, the claimant failed to serve a form N251 on the defendant or its solicitors. However, the letter of claim stated that 'this claim is now being funded by a conditional fee agreement which provides for a success fee'. In fact the CFA was not finally entered into until a month later and costs were claimed only after that date. The court was informed of the existence of the CFA at the first case management conference. The court found that the defendant had from the outset the information which it was entitled to and the court could not see any conceivable prejudice to the defendant from the breaches of the rule and practice directions. Accordingly the court granted relief (pursuant to **r. 3.9**) from the sanction provided for by **r. 44.3B(1)(c)**, ordering that the claimant was not to be deprived of the opportunity in principle to recover the agreed success fee.

There is no requirement for a party to inform the opponent of a funding arrangement made between the solicitor and counsel or the solicitor and a quasi-expert.

The notification provisions can be used to the tactical advantage of a particular party (see 6.2).

ASSESSMENT OF CFA COSTS

General

Assessment by the court of CFA costs is governed by **CPR, r. 44.3A** and **44.3B**, and **PD 43–48, paras 11.4 to 11.10** (party-and-party assessments), and **CPR, r. 48.8(3)** and **(4)**, and **PD 43–48, paras 54.5** to **54.8** (solicitor-and-client assessments). For the procedure on assessment of costs generally see **68.10** to **68.25**. **6.18**

In a successful conditional fee case the solicitor will calculate his or her fees (referred to in the Law Society's model agreement as 'basic costs') and the barrister's fees at the rates set out in the CFA with the client. The solicitor will seek to recover 100 per cent of the basic costs plus the barrister's fees and disbursements from the unsuccessful paying party. The solicitor may in addition recover from the client:

(a) any part of the solicitor's basic costs, counsel's fees and disbursements not recovered from the paying party;
(b) the agreed success fee (which cannot be more than 100 per cent) calculated as a percentage of the basic costs (and as a separate percentage of the barrister's fees).

When a client receives from the solicitor a bill calculated on the above basis the client is entitled to challenge:

(a) the shortfall in full recovery of the solicitor's basic costs and the barrister's fees,
(b) the solicitor's and barrister's success fees.

The procedure to facilitate such a challenge by the client is set out in **PD 43–48, paras 55.1 to 55.4**.

In order to comply with the Solicitors' Costs Information and Client Care Code 1999, para. 5, a solicitor who intends to seek payment from the client of any or all of his costs should explain to the client, at the outset of the matter and at appropriate stages throughout the matter (para. 3), the client's right to assessment by the court of costs. For a CFA entered into before 1 November 2005 the legal representative, before the agreement was entered into, must have complied with the **Conditional Fee Agreements Regulations 2000, reg.** 4(2)(b), which provided that the client had to be informed about 'the circumstances in which the client may seek assessment of the fees and expenses of the legal representative and the procedure for doing so'.

Assessment of basic costs

6.19 As the basic costs in a CFA are the costs which would have been charged whether or not the solicitor was retained on a conditional fee basis, detailed assessment of them, as between solicitor and client, is governed by the same rules as apply to detailed assessment of any other solicitor's bill, namely, **CPR, r. 48.8(1), (1A) and (2). Rule 48.8(2)** provides that costs are to be assessed on the indemnity basis, in which costs are presumed:

(a) to have been reasonably incurred if they were incurred with the express or implied approval of the client;
(b) to be reasonable in amount if their amount was expressly or impliedly approved by the client;
(c) to have been unreasonably incurred if:
   (i) they are of an unusual nature or amount and
   (ii) the solicitor did not tell the client that as a result he might not recover all of them from the other party.

Assessment of additional liabilities between the parties

6.20 The **Courts and Legal Services Act 1990, s. 58A(6)** , allows the CPR to provide that costs orders may include provision requiring the paying party to pay the success fee as well as the basic costs. The **Access to Justice Act 1999, s. 29**, also enables insurance premiums to be recovered. The insurance premium may be one paid alongside a CFA but the rules are drafted so as to provide for other 'additional liabilities' including stand-alone insurance policies, such as ATE insurance, and even the cost of membership (perhaps to a trade union) as the case may be. The relevant rules are **CPR, r. 44.3A** (costs orders relating to funding arrangements) and **r. 44.3B** (limits on recovery under funding arrangements), as amplified by **PD 43–48, paras 11.4 to 11.10.**

The effect of these rules, taken together, is that an 'additional liability' (whether a success fee or insurance premium or both) may be recovered provided that:

(a) The success fee relates to the risk of losing and not to compensating the legal representative for delayed payment (this, incidentally, is why it is crucial for the conditional fee agreement to split the success fee).
(b) The additional liability does not relate to a period where information about the funding arrangement has not been provided as required by **PD 43–48, para. 19.2.**
(c) The reasons justifying the success fee have been disclosed.
(d) The additional liability is reasonable.

The assessment of the success fee is considered at **6.12** to **6.16**.

Assessment of additional liabilities between solicitor and client

6.21 In a detailed assessment of solicitor-and-client costs under a CFA, when the court is considering the percentage increase, it will have regard to all the relevant factors as they reasonably appeared to the solicitor or counsel when the agreement was entered into or varied (**CPR, r. 48.8**(3) and (4)).

On solicitor-and-client assessments, in addition to the risk of non-payment and the solicitor's liability for disbursements, the court will also take into account the disadvantages relating to the absence of payment on account and whether there is a CFA between solicitor and counsel (**PD 43–48, para. 54.7**). The solicitor cannot seek to recover a greater success fee than that agreed or assessed, unless the court orders otherwise (**Conditional Fee Agreements**

Regulations 2000, reg. 3(2)(b)). The court may adjourn the proceedings to allow the client an opportunity to be separately represented (**CPR, r.** 44.16).

SPECIAL ISSUES RELATING TO CONDITIONAL FEES UNDER THE CPR

Interim costs in conditional fee claims

A special difficulty in a conditional fee case is the summary assessment of costs for interim hearings of less than one day. **6.22**

Paragraphs 14.1 to 14.4 of PD 43–48 provide that the existence of a conditional fee or other funding arrangement is not of itself a reason for declining to assess costs summarily, but that an order for payment of those costs will not be made unless the court has been satisfied that in respect of the costs claimed, the receiving party is at the time liable to pay to his legal representative an amount equal to or greater than the costs claimed. The effect of this is that the order for payment will be postponed until the conclusion of the case unless the client is already liable to his solicitor for the costs, for example, because the client has acted outside the terms of the CFA, perhaps by acting unreasonably. Whether or not the client is liable may be proved by the solicitor filing a statement with the court (**para.** 14.3).

At the end of the case, if the conditional fee client's case is unsuccessful then the costs summarily assessed will form a part of the total costs payable and will generally be paid by the insurer. If the case is won then it will depend on the terms of the policy. However, most insurance policies provide that costs summarily assessed against the client earlier in the case will not be met by the insurer unless those costs exceed the damages recovered. Then, the insurer will pay the difference. Otherwise, the client will have to pay the costs out of the damages.

When summarily assessing costs in conditional fee cases at an interim stage the court should not assess the amount of any additional liability (**CPR, r. 44.3A**) and the statement of costs filed by the receiving party need not say what the amount of that liability is (**PD 43–48, para.** 13.5(5)).

In *Arkin v Borchard Lines Ltd* (2001) LTL 19/6/2001 Colman J permitted the claimant to set off his interim costs liability against costs owed to him by the defendant. The set-off effectively extinguished the claimant's liability and was important to him because without it, under the terms of his conditional fee agreement, he would have been liable to reimburse his solicitors and counsel. Colman J rejected the defendant's argument that no set-off could arise because the costs under the CFA were not immediately payable. On the proper construction of the CFA, he said, 'winning' meant recovering an enforceable payment order — including a pre-trial costs order — not receiving payment.

Colman J then went on to consider what happened when parties sought set-off in cases where there were a number of costs orders going both ways and providing for both summary assessment and detailed assessment. Here, he said, the court should generally preserve the principle of set-off by either delaying the 14-day payment requirement for the costs summarily assessed, otherwise postponing compliance with the summary assessment costs order or having the summarily assessed costs paid into court.

Children, patients and conditional fees

A glaring omission from the statutory and regulatory framework that established conditional fees in 1995 was the lack of attention to the special provisions required for conditional fee cases conducted on behalf of children or patients. **Part 21** of the CPR sets out the basis for court approval of an award of damages to a child or patient. Under the old RSC, ord. 80, at **6.23** the settlement, approval or award of damages to a child or patient the court was also required to approve costs. This caused a problem in conditional fee cases. The solicitor who had entered into a CFA with the litigation friend of a child or patient was vulnerable to the court disapproving the level of the success fee at the approval stage without the protection of the conditional fee taxation procedure under the old RSC, ord. 62, r. 15A (for the new assessment procedure see **6.18**). This anomaly was corrected by **r. 48.9(6)** of the CPR which provided that in a case where the client in a CFA was a child or a patient, the court could not vary the percentage increase except in accordance with r. 48.9(5). Rule 48.9 has been revoked. Although **r. 48.8(3)** makes much the same provision as r. 48.9(5) did, there is now no provision corresponding to r. 48.9(6).

BARRISTERS AND CONDITIONAL FEES

6.24 In a claim where the client has entered into a CFA with the solicitor, it is usual for the solicitor to invite any barrister who may be instructed to enter into a CFA on a similar basis. A high level of mutual understanding is necessary between solicitors and barristers working together as a team on a case where both are acting on a conditional-fee basis. Whilst firms and sets of chambers have developed good working relationships on conditional fee cases, the fact remains that barristers are at a disadvantage because, typically, the greatest financial risk is run in claims that have to be determined at trial and much more work is generally required to be done by counsel in cases as they approach trial than at earlier stages. By the time a case reaches this point the solicitor will still be at risk, but may at the same time have spread that risk by settling large numbers of other cases being run on a conditional-fee basis. Even if the barrister has been involved earlier in the case, he or she will tend to have far fewer cases that succeed through negotiation. Barristers, supported by the Bar Council's CFA working party, are increasingly seeking to have their fees treated as disbursements in the traditional way. Some solicitors prefer counsel not to be on a CFA to avoid any conflict when, for instance, an offer of settlement is made. 'Hybrid' agreements may be an acceptable compromise. In *Designer Guild Ltd v Russell Williams (Textiles) Ltd (No. 2)* (HL 20 February 2003, SCCO Case Summaries No. 4 of 2003) counsel was guaranteed half his fees regardless of the outcome. Accordingly his success fee was approved at 50 per cent, where his solicitors were entitled to a 100 per cent success fee.

To assist with uniformity, a model CFA for barristers in personal injury cases has been produced by collaboration between the Association of Personal Injury Lawyers and the Personal Injury Bar Association. This model agreement has also received the approval of the Bar Council and the Law Society, and is known as APIL/PIBA. In addition the Bar Council has produced a guideline manual about conditional fees and this has been distributed to all sets of chambers. The Bar Council Professional Standards Committee provided further guidance on 1 March 2002. The Chancery Bar Association has produced its own model CFA.

The complex rules in the **Conditional Fee Agreements Regulations 2000** which require certain explanations to be given to the client do not apply to agreements between barristers and their solicitors (see reg. 4(6)).

EXPERTS AND CONDITIONAL FEES

6.25 There is much controversy and some confusion over suggestions that the advent of conditional fees has made it legitimate for solicitors to instruct an expert on a no win no fee basis. Principle 21.11 of the *Guide to the Professional Conduct of Solicitors*, 7th ed., says:

A solicitor must not make or offer to make payments to a witness contingent upon the nature of the evidence given or upon the outcome of a case.

It is permissible to make a deferred fee arrangement by which the expert (particularly one who does a lot of work for a firm of solicitors) agrees not to render a fee note until the end of the case when, if it is lost, the expert may decide to waive the fee. Provided there is no antecedent agreement that the expert will not charge if the case is lost, the deferred arrangement does not breach the professional conduct rules.

In *R (Factortame Ltd) v Secretary of State for Transport, Local Government and the Regions (No. 8)* [2002] EWCA Civ 932, [2003] QB 381, the enforceability of a contingency arrangement made between a quasi-expert and solicitors was considered. At a relatively late stage of the litigation, accountants had been instructed to provide forensic accountancy services to the claimants' fishing industry experts. This support included the assessment of the claimants' financial losses. The accountants had agreed to act in return for 8 per cent of the final settlement achieved (not in fact a conditional fee agreement, but a contingency fee arrangement — the losses being calculated not by an uplift on costs incurred, but by reference to the award of damages). Perhaps surprisingly the court held that the arrangement was enforceable. The Courts and Legal Services Act 1990 was held not to apply as that Act only deals with agreements between clients and 'litigators'. The court was quick to emphasise that this was a 'very rare' case and that the court would not normally consent to an expert being instructed on a contingency fee basis. It noted that experts are frequently in a position to influence litigation in a manner that neither the client nor the lawyer can. To allow an expert to have a financial interest in the outcome of a case carries great dangers for the administration of justice. However, in this case the accountants took care to restrict their role to the provision of support services to the experts who were to be called. Accordingly, their conduct did not offend public policy. The court observed that the accountants' prospect of receiving 8 per cent of the recoveries might have provided a motive for them to inflate the calculation of damages, although not to the extent that a larger percentage might have done. However, there were no grounds for suspecting that the accountants, as reputable members of a respectable profession subject to regulation would do anything other than perform their duties in an honest manner. The court also took some comfort from the fact that, in part at least, the accountants were involved in a joint exercise for the defendant's experts.

In *Papera Traders Co. Ltd v Hyundai Merchant Marine Co. Ltd (No. 2)* [2002] EWHC 2130 (Comm), [2002] 2 Lloyd's Rep 692, the claimant sought to recover as part of its damages fees payable to a firm of marine loss adjusters based on 5 per cent of the recovery made in respect of vehicles which were destroyed in a fire on board the defendant's vessel. The loss adjusters were instructed initially on a fee basis to carry out salvage and general average work and then instructed to carry out recovery services on a percentage basis. The defendant's argument that the agreement was champertous was unsuccessful. The court did agree that the claim was not properly categorised as damages, being too remote, but that the loss adjusters' costs could be assessed on the standard basis, with reference to the amount of time spent on each item.

COLLECTIVE CONDITIONAL FEE AGREEMENTS

Collective conditional fee agreements (collective CFAs) are intended to help bulk users of **6.26** CFAs and their solicitors, by allowing the users to enter into a single agreement with solicitors to allow them to run their members' cases. The agreement need not refer to specific proceedings, but will provide for fees to be payable on a common basis in relation to a class of proceedings. Agreements entered into before 1 November 2005 are subject to the **Collective Conditional Fee Agreements Regulations 2000** (SI 2000/2988).

A collective CFA is an agreement between a solicitor and a bulk provider of work. If the provider is also the claimant (as in debt recovery work) there is no difficulty in establishing the terms of the retainer between the party to the litigation and the solicitor. That is not the case if the work provider is a referrer of work, such as a trade union or insurance company. In this situation there is an implied retainer between the solicitor and the client, alternatively, the client will be regarded as having ratified the appointment of the solicitor by the funder (*Thornley v Lang* [2003] EWCA Civ 1484, *The Times*, 31 October 2003, applying *Adams v London Improved Motor Coach Builders Ltd* [1921] 1 KB 495). This means the client is under a legal obligation to pay the solicitor's bill, even though in practice this may never happen. Consequently, provided there is compliance with the regulations, costs incurred under a collective CFA are recoverable from the opposite party.

Collective CFAs are often commercially sensitive documents and the parties to them are unlikely to consent to their disclosure in costs assessment proceedings. In *Hollins v Russell* [2003] EWCA Civ 718, [2003] 1 WLR 2487, the Court of Appeal considered CFAs to be generally disclosable unless no success fee is claimed (see **6.9**). There is nothing in the judgment which suggests any distinction will be made between CFAs and collective CFAs if the paying party or the court seeks sight of the agreement. However, in practice many collective CFAs do not provide for a success fee, but instead are discounted fee arrangements (see **5.6** and **6.1**).

Collective CFAs are 'funding arrangements' for the purposes of recovery of additional liabilities, such as the cost of membership (**CPR, r. 43.2(1)**).

Chapter 7 Community Legal Service

INTRODUCTION

The Legal Services Commission (LSC) runs two schemes: the Community Legal Service (CLS), which provides advice and legal representation for people involved in civil cases, and the Criminal Defence Service (CDS), which provides advice and legal representation for people facing criminal charges. This chapter covers civil matters only. **7.1**

In the CLS, the LSC has an important role in coordinating and working in partnership with other funders of legal services, such as local authorities. The LSC also directly funds legal services for eligible clients.

Since 2 April 2001 only organisations with a contract with the LSC have been able to provide advice or representation funded by the LSC. For family cases and specialist areas such as immigration and clinical negligence, only specialist firms are funded to do the work. Claims for personal injury, other than clinical negligence, are not usually funded by the LSC because of the availability of conditional fee agreements.

There is a general obligation placed on everyone involved in running the CLS to ensure that it is accessible to those who need it, to ensure that services are provided which are appropriate given the importance and nature of the matter in hand and to seek to achieve the swift and fair resolution of disputes without unnecessary or unduly protracted legal proceedings (**Access to Justice Act 1999, s.** 4). The legal services covered by the scheme are those set out in s. 4(2):

(a) the provision of general information about the law and legal system, and the availability of legal services;
(b) the provision of help by giving advice on how the law applies in particular circumstances;
(c) the provision of help in preventing, or settling or otherwise resolving, disputes about legal rights and duties;
(d) the provision of help in enforcing decisions by which such disputes are resolved; and
(e) the provision of help in relation to legal proceedings not relating to disputes.

The Funding Code prepared by the Commission under s. 8 sets out the general approach to the funding of legal services including levels of service, cost-benefit criteria to be applied in deciding whether or not to fund, and criteria to be applied in particular case categories. The Funding Code is in three parts: criteria, procedures, and decision-making guidance. The procedures have been amended a number of times and the criteria were amended substantially on 25 July 2005. The Code is supplemented by decision-making guidance issued by the Lord Chancellor under s. 23 of the Act and to which all decision-makers must have regard under r. A9 of the Funding Code Procedures.

The Code represents a radical departure from the scheme in place under the Legal Aid Act 1988. Most significantly, rather than the 'demand-led' scheme in place under the 1988 Act, where there was an entitlement to funding provided the relevant merits and means test were satisfied, the Code anticipates a capped scheme where there is a finite fund which is directed according to priorities. A formal cap has not yet been introduced — there is as yet little prospect of an application for funding being refused because the money has run out — but the Code provides the mechanisms for operating within one.

LEVELS OF SERVICE

Introduction

7.2 The LSC will fund only the six levels of legal service described at **7.3** to **7.11**, subject to the provisions of the **Access to Justice Act 1999**, subordinate legislation made under the Act, and the Funding Code made under s. 8. The levels of service are intended to provide a framework through which legal help can be given to individuals at a cost that is appropriate in the circumstances of each case. There is provision for other services to be provided by specific order or direction of the Lord Chancellor.

Legal Help

7.3 Legal Help is the lowest tier of assistance under the Community Legal Service. Legal Help can be provided only as controlled work under contracts, meaning that only a limited number of service providers (whether solicitors or those in the not-for-profit sector) who have satisfied the LSC's quality control criteria can offer Legal Help. These 'contractors' are awarded a budget for a particular kind of work, based on their number of 'case starts' over a given period, but subject to 'tolerances' or margins of error. Contracts are distributed according to regional priorities established by regional legal services committees.

Contracted organisations can provide up to two hours of Legal Help where the client will derive 'sufficient benefit' from it. The old private client test is used for deciding what is and is not sufficient benefit, i.e., would a reasonable private paying client of moderate means pay for this as legal advice? There is also case-specific advice on what can and cannot amount to 'sufficient benefit'. In education, for example, there is guidance on whether the test is satisfied where one child on its own might not gain sufficient benefit from the advice but more than one child is affected. Legal Help may only be provided if it is reasonable for the matter to be funded out of the Community Legal Service Fund having regard to any other potential source of funding.

If the initial two-hour limit is reached and the sufficient-benefit test is still satisfied, contracted organisations can extend Legal Help without reference to the Legal Services Commission, up to a limit of £500. After that, the case must be referred.

Most Legal Help remuneration for matters started from 1 April 2005 is paid as a fixed fee under the Tailored Fixed Fee Scheme for Civil (Non-Immigration) Controlled Work. Firms are paid fixed fees per case based on their average costs.

There are different costs limits for Legal Help in the immigration category which are set out in the Immigration Specification published by the LSC. All individuals performing publicly funded work in the immigration category have to be accredited. From 1 August 2005 the work that immigration advisers can do and the amount they will be paid by the LSC for their work will depend on the level at which they have been accredited.

Legal Help is not available for the issue or conduct of court proceedings, nor for advocacy before any court or tribunal.

Help at Court

Like Legal Help, Help at Court is only available as part of controlled work and so can only be provided by contracted organisations. It is administered using the same form as Legal Help. Help at Court authorises representation for the purposes of a particular hearing, but stops short of full representation, where the representative will be on the court record and for which full Legal Representation (see 7.5) is the appropriate level of service. It is envisaged that the lawyer giving Help at Court will act in a capacity akin to that of a McKenzie friend. It is intended to be a quick and informal way of helping clients who need someone to speak for them in court. **7.4**

General Family Help

General Family Help is licensed work. This means that an application for a certificate must be made to the LSC and the service can only be provided by firms with a Specialist Quality Mark (SQM) for family work. General Family Help can be used to assist in resolving a family dispute through negotiation or otherwise, or to obtain a necessary consent order following settlement of part or all of the dispute and related conveyancing work. It can be used for issuing proceedings, but it does not include representation at a contested final hearing. **7.5**

Legal Representation

Funding for Legal Representation authorises the provision of legal services for a party to legal proceedings, or for an individual who is contemplating bringing proceedings. It includes: **7.6**

(a) litigation services;
(b) advocacy services;
(c) all the legal assistance that is usually given by a person providing representation in civil proceedings, including steps preliminary or incidental to such proceedings; and
(d) all the legal assistance that is usually given by a legal representative in achieving or giving effect to a compromise to avoid or bring an end to civil proceedings.

Funding for Legal Representation does not include the provision of mediation or arbitration, but this does not prevent help being given in relation to mediation or arbitration, or the payment of a mediator's or arbitrator's fees as a disbursement.

Controlled Legal Representation Legal Representation is generally licensed work and is provided under certificates of public funding issued by the LSC. Some Legal Representation before a mental health review tribunal or the Asylum and Immigration Tribunal is, however, controlled work for which the application for funding is made to the supplier, not to the LSC. Many firms no longer have devolved powers for immigration work and will need to apply for authority from the LSC, but the funding of the work remains within the Controlled Work Budget. **7.7**

A first appeal to the Asylum and Immigration Tribunal will be funded under Controlled Legal Representation. The costs of an application to review a decision of the tribunal and, if successful, any subsequent reconsideration hearing can be claimed as Controlled Legal Representation only if a costs order is successfully obtained under the Nationality, Immigration and Asylum Act 2002, s. 103D (see Community Legal Service (Asylum and Immigration Appeals) Regulations 2005 (SI 2005/966)).

There are two levels of funding within the Legal Representation service: Investigative Help and Full Representation.

7.8 **Investigative Help** This is a form of funding for Legal Representation which is limited to investigation of the strength of a proposed claim. Investigative Help can include the issue and the conduct of proceedings, but only in so far as may be necessary to obtain disclosure of relevant information or to protect the client's position in relation to any urgent hearing or time limit for the issue of proceedings.

Investigative Help is intended for cases that need a substantial amount of investigative work before the prospects of success can be assessed. Funding for this purpose is somewhat speculative. It may be refused if there is the potential for a conditional fee agreement, and if the damages are likely to be less than £5,000 and there is no significant wider public interest at stake.

The criteria for Investigative Help vary depending on the type of legal matter. Investigative Help is likely to be refused if it is more appropriate for the client to pursue a complaints procedure.

7.9 **Full Representation** This is the second form of Legal Representation and covers any grant of Legal Representation other than Investigative Help. It is therefore the equivalent of full civil legal aid, and covers the conduct of litigation beyond the initial investigative stages. Full Representation will be considered once it is possible to make a reasonable assessment of the prospects of success. It is intended for strong cases, and exacting criteria have been laid down for determining whether the claim is strong enough to justify this form of funding (see 7.20).

Help with Mediation

7.10 Help with Mediation is licensed work. The certificate is normally granted by the firm under its devolved powers and the service can only be provided by firms with an SQM for family work. Help with Mediation authorises help and advice to a client in support of Family Mediation (see 7.11), help in drawing up any agreement reached in mediation and, where appropriate, help in confirming such an agreement in a court order and related conveyancing work.

Family Mediation

7.11 Family Mediation is the sixth level of service under the Funding Code. It authorises mediation of a family dispute and an assessment of whether mediation appears suitable to the parties and all the circumstances of the dispute. Family Mediation is always funded as Other Contracted Work through the Commission's family mediation contracts with mediators.

EXCLUDED CATEGORIES

7.12 Under the **Access to Justice Act 1999, sch. 2**, the following categories of claims and matters may not be funded as part of the Community Legal Service:

(a) allegations of personal injury or death, other than allegations relating to clinical negligence;
(aa) allegations of negligently caused damage to property;
(b) conveyancing;
(c) boundary disputes;
(d) making of wills;
(e) matters of trust law;
(f) defamation and malicious falsehood;

(g) matters of company or partnership law;
(h) other matters arising out of the carrying on of a business; and
(i) attending an interview conducted on behalf of the Secretary of State with a view to his reaching a decision on a claim for asylum (as defined by the Immigration and Asylum Act 1999, s. 167(1)).

The denial of public funding in the libel case of *Steel v United Kingdom* (application 68416/01) (2005) 41 EHRR 22, was found to be a breach of the **European Convention on Human Rights, art. 6(1).** The question of whether public funding is necessary for a fair hearing depends on the particular facts of the case. Factors to be considered include the importance of what is at stake, the complexity of the relevant law and procedure, and the party's ability to represent himself effectively.

Schedule 2 also prohibits public funding of advocacy in tribunal proceedings, except before a mental health review tribunal, the Asylum and Immigration Appeal Tribunal, the Special Immigration Appeals Commission or the Proscribed Organisations Appeal Commission. Some other tribunal proceedings have been brought into the scope of public funding by the Lord Chancellor's direction discussed next.

There is provision in the **Access to Justice Act 1999, s. 6(8)**, to bring back into the scheme cases that would otherwise be excluded. The section is not very happily drafted but it appears there are three routes. First, s. 6(8)(a) permits the Lord Chancellor, by direction, to *require* the Commission to fund cases in specific circumstances. Secondly, under s. 6(8)(b), the Lord Chancellor can *authorise* the Commission to fund cases in specified circumstances. Both the requirement and the authorisation are achieved by direction.

One such direction was issued on 2 April 2001. Paragraph 7(f) of the Funding Code Decision-making Guidance brings back in professional negligence actions 'save where the alleged negligence relates to services provided to the client's business'. Other matters brought back in include:

(a) Any judicial review claim arising out of the conduct of a business which concerns serious wrongdoing, abuse of position or power or significant breach of human rights.
(b) Any case concerning a business tenancy where the client's home is in issue.
(c) All cases, other than business cases, which have a significant wider public interest.
(d) Any case where the liberty of the client is in issue.
(e) Proceedings arising out of allegations of the abuse of a child or vulnerable adult.
(f) Proceedings arising out of allegations of sexual assault.
(g) Proceedings under the Proceeds of Crime Act 2002 (if not already specified under the **Access to Justice Act 1999, sch. 2**).

More tribunals have been brought into the scope of public funding, such as death-in-custody inquests, proceedings before the Care Standards Tribunal (previously the Protection of Children Act Tribunal) and proceedings before the General and Special Commissioners of Income Tax, and proceedings before the VAT and Duties Tribunal where public funding is in the interests of justice and the proceedings are criminal in nature for the purposes of the **European Convention on Human Rights, art. 6** (see *Han v Commissioners of Customs and Excise* [2001] EWCA Civ 1040, [2001] 1 WLR 2253, and **97.20**).

Under the Lord Chancellor's guidelines the Commission is authorised to provide funding where a public authority has allegedly committed a serious wrongdoing, breach of duty or power. In *R (G) v Legal Services Commission* [2004] EWHC 276 (Admin), LTL 11/2/2004, it was held the Commission had erred in concluding the guidance required deliberate, malicious or dishonest conduct by the public authority. Rather, the guidance addresses the quality of the duty and the circumstances in which it was breached.

The third route is also under s. 6(8)(b), which provides for applications for 'exceptional funding'. The Lord Chancellor's revised guidance on applications for exceptional funding came into force on 1 November 2001 (partially in response to *R (Jarrett) v Legal Services Commission* [2001] EWHC 389 (Admin), [2002] ACD 160).

Exceptional funding may be granted for representation at inquests. If the LSC finds that the client is financially eligible for Legal Representation and that no other source of funding is available, the Lord Chancellor will consider funding if:

(a) there is a significant wider public interest in the client being represented at the inquest; or
(b) funded representation for the family of the deceased is likely to be necessary to enable the coroner to carry out an effective investigation into the death, as required by the **European Convention on Human Rights, art. 2.** In considering whether funded representation may be necessary to comply with this obligation, all the circumstances of the case must be taken into account, including:
    (i) the nature and seriousness of any allegations which are likely to be raised at the inquest, including in particular any allegations against public authorities or other agencies of the State;
    (ii) whether other forms of investigation have taken place, or are likely to take place, and whether the family have or will be involved in such investigations;
    (iii) whether the family may be able to participate effectively in the inquest without funded legal representation.

Exceptional funding may also be granted for other proceedings, provided that the LSC is satisfied that the client is financially eligible, relevant criteria in the Funding Code are satisfied (such as the ratio of costs to benefit) and the client has produced evidence to demonstrate that no alternative means of funding is available, whether through conditional fees or otherwise. Provided the LSC is satisfied, the Lord Chancellor is prepared to consider funding where:

(a) there is a significant wider public interest in the resolution of the case and funded representation will contribute to it; or
(b) the case is of overwhelming importance to the client; or
(c) there is convincing evidence that there are other exceptional circumstances such that, without public funding for representation, it will be practically impossible for the client to bring or defend proceedings, or the lack of public funding would lead to obvious unfairness in the proceedings.

The case of *Jarrett* concerned director disqualification proceedings. However, any complex litigation which has merit but for which the applicant cannot reasonably obtain alternative sources of funding may fall to be considered. Exceptional funding could even be granted to those whose financial means disqualify them from public funding but who could not fund the entirety of a trial or final hearing. The Lord Chancellor will use as a benchmark those exceptional cases where the European Court of Human Rights has indicated that the right of access to courts has effectively been denied because of the lack of public funding (see *X v United Kingdom* (1984) 6 EHRR 136).

All applications for exceptional funding must be made to the LSC in the first instance and can be made directly to the LSC's Special Cases Unit, 29–37 Red Lion Street, London WC1R 4PP. All applications should be accompanied by the normal merit and means forms as if applying for a certificate for Legal Representation. It is important that applications are made as early as possible to allow time for the LSC to decide whether or not to request funding from the Lord Chancellor, and subsequently for the Lord Chancellor to make that decision.

FINANCIAL ELIGIBILITY

7.13 Public funding under the CLS is only available to those who are financially eligible in accordance with the Community Legal Service (Financial) Regulations 2000 (SI 2000/516).

Table 7.1 Financial eligibility for public funding from 10 April 2006

Level of service	Disposable income limit	Disposable capital limit
Legal representation before the Asylum and Immigration Tribunal or High Court under the Nationality, Immigration and Asylum Act 2002 (SI 2000/516, reg. 5(2))	£649 per month	£3,000 (immigration matters) £8,000 (asylum matters)
Legal Help, Help at Court, Family Mediation, Help with Mediation (reg. 5(3), (4))	£649 per month	£8,000
Legal Representation (not covered in the above), General Family Help and Support Funding (reg. 5(6))	£649 per month	£8,000

For some categories of cases there are no financial eligibility requirements (see regs 3 and 5B to 5E, dealing with cases, for example, under the Children Act 1989, and injunctions seeking protection from harm to the person). For other cases, there is a general rule that no one with a gross monthly income of more than £2,350 may receive any funding (reg. 5A(4)) and there are further complex financial eligibility tests set out in the Regulations. To assist practitioners the LSC has piloted a financial eligibility calculator which is available at www.legalservices.gov.uk/calculator.

By reg. 4(2), clients who are directly or indirectly in receipt of the following benefits are eligible for all the levels of LSC service set out in reg. 2(3) (which is fairly comprehensive) without making any contributions:

(a) income support;
(b) income-based jobseeker's allowance;
(c) guarantee state pension credit;
(d) payments from the National Asylum Support Service (NASS) under the Immigration and Asylum Act 1999, s. 95.

Other clients must meet criteria based on disposable income and disposable capital. Regulations 6 to 37 set out the rules on calculating the client's income and capital, including matters such as disregarding certain State benefits (reg. 19), the effect of paying maintenance (reg. 20), and assets to be taken into account in assessing capital. Where eligibility is being assessed for Legal Representation (other than Controlled Legal Representation for immigration work), only the first £100,000 of capital assets that are the subject matter of the dispute are disregarded (reg. 32A). The first £100,000 of the client's interest in his principal dwelling are disregarded (reg. 32B). There are additional capital disregards for persons over 60 years of age and with a monthly disposable income of less than £279.

With effect from 10 April 2006, by reg. 5, the main eligibility limits are as set out in **table** 7.1. The LSC may disregard the disposable income limit for the funding of Legal Representation in proceedings where the client seeks an injunction to protect against harm to the person or committal for breach of such an order (reg. 5E). For cases coming within reg. 5(6) (see **table** 7.1), the client can be required to pay contributions under reg. 38 out of income and/or capital if monthly disposable income exceeds £279 or disposable capital exceeds £3,000.

CRITERIA FOR PUBLIC FUNDING

Introduction

Different criteria will be applied to the different levels of service available when deciding **7.14**
whether individuals who are financially eligible ought to obtain the benefit of funding by the Community Legal Service. The aim of the criteria is that public funding will be provided only

where there is no other alternative funding method available, and where the prospects of success and benefit expected from the legal services provided meet the required thresholds. Although the Funding Code describes them as criteria, they are often conditions that must be satisfied if funding is to be given.

The standard criteria (Funding Code, part 1, section 4) apply to all cases (see **7.16**). There are criteria for different levels of service (section 5) which are discussed in **7.17** to **7.25**.

Further criteria, which will not be discussed in this book, are applied in very expensive claims (section 6), judicial review cases (section 7), claims against public authorities (section 8), clinical negligence claims (section 9), housing cases (section 10), family matters (section 11), mental health matters (section 12), immigration cases (section 13) and quasi-criminal proceedings (section 14).

Prospects of Success

7.15 The Funding Code divides cases into six categories regarding the prospects of success on the substantive dispute (although the prospects of success are not relevant to every level of funding):

(a) 'Very good' meaning prospects of 80 per cent or more.
(b) 'Good' meaning 60–80 per cent.
(c) 'Moderate' meaning 50–60 per cent.
(d) 'Borderline' meaning that because of difficult disputes of fact, law or expert evidence, it is not possible to say that the prospects of success are better than 50 per cent, but not being so weak as to fall into the 'poor' category.
(e) 'Poor' meaning clearly less than 50 per cent, so the claim is likely to fail.
(f) 'Unclear' meaning that the case does not fall into any of the other categories because further investigation is needed.

Standard criteria

7.16 In setting the criteria for public funding the Legal Services Commission has divided and subdivided by levels of service and case type. The criteria applying to all cases and all levels of service are the standard criteria in the Funding Code, part 1, section 4. They are:

(a) It must be a matter of English law.
(b) It must not be a service excluded under the **Access to Justice Act 1999, sch. 2**, and not brought back into scope by direction or order.
(c) The applicant must be an individual, not a company or partnership.
(d) Public funding must be provided via a recognised supplier.
(e) If the work is to be carried out under the terms of a contract, it must comply with those contract terms.
(f) Funding Code procedures must be followed.
(g) The financial eligibility criteria must be satisfied.
(h) Public funding may be refused if it appears reasonable to do so having regard to the conduct of the applicant.

Legal Help and Help at Court

7.17 The two main criteria for Legal Help are:

(a) Is there sufficient benefit to the client, having regard to the circumstances of the matter, including the personal circumstances of the client, to justify work or further work being carried out?
(b) Is it reasonable for the matter to be funded out of the Community Legal Service Fund, having regard to any other potential sources of funding?

The main criteria for Help at Court are:

(a) Sufficient benefit, which is the same as criterion (a) for Legal Help.

(b) Reasonableness, which is the same as criterion (b) for Legal Help.
(c) Are the nature of the proceedings and the circumstances of the hearing and the client such that representation is appropriate and will be of real benefit to the client?
(d) Help at Court will not be given if the contested nature of the hearing is such that, if any help is to be provided, it is more appropriate that it should be given through legal representation (in which event, obviously, funding should be provided through legal representation rather than Help at Court).

In addition, there is case-specific guidance for all the categories of controlled work (family, employment, debt, consumer/general contract, housing, immigration, welfare benefits, mental health, clinical negligence and education).

Legal Representation

There are six general criteria that apply to all levels of assistance by way of Legal Representation, all of which should be satisfied. In addition, there are further criteria for the different forms of assistance within these categories, which must also be satisfied. The six general criteria are: **7.18**

(a) An application may be refused if there is alternative funding available to the client through insurance or otherwise, or if there are other persons or bodies, particularly those who might benefit from the proceedings, who can reasonably be expected to bring or fund the case.
(b) An application may be refused if there are complaint systems, ombudsman schemes or forms of alternative dispute resolution which should be tried before litigation is pursued.
(c) An application may be refused if it appears premature.
(d) An application may be refused if it appears more appropriate for the client to be assisted by some other level of service (Legal Help or Help at Court).
(e) An application may be refused if it appears unreasonable to fund the case, for example, in light of the nature and complexity of the issues, the existence of other proceedings, or the interests of other parties in the proceedings.
(f) An application will be refused if the claim has been or is likely to be allocated to the small claims track.

Legal Representation may be granted as a matter of urgency only where it appears to be in the interests of justice to do so.

Criteria for Investigative Help

In addition to the general criteria set out at 7.18, when considering funding for Investigative Help the following criteria should be applied: **7.19**

(a) Investigative Help may be refused if the nature of the case and the circumstances of the client are such that investigative work should be carried out privately with a view to entering into a conditional fee agreement.
(b) Investigative Help may only be granted where the prospects of success are uncertain and substantial investigative work is required before the prospects can be assessed.
(c) Investigative Help will be refused if the damages (if it is a money claim) are unlikely to exceed £5,000, unless there is a significant wider public interest.
(d) Investigative Help may be granted only if there are reasonable grounds for believing that when the investigative work has been done the prospects of success and of benefits compared with costs will satisfy the criteria for Full Representation (for which see 7.20).

Criteria for Full Representation

In addition to the general criteria set out at 7.18, when considering funding for Full Representation the following criteria should be applied: **7.20**

(a) Full Representation will be refused in claims suitable for funding under conditional fee agreements, provided the client is likely to be able to enter into such an agreement.

(b) Full Representation will be refused if:
  (i) the prospects of success are unclear (in this situation it may be appropriate to grant funding for Investigative Help); or
  (ii) the prospects are borderline, and the case does not appear to have a significant wider public interest or to be of overwhelming importance to the client; or
  (iii) the prospects of success are poor.

(c) Full Representation will or may be refused on cost-benefit grounds (see 7.21).

Comparison of benefits and costs

7.21 As a general proposition, Full Representation will be refused if the benefit expected to be obtained from the proceedings does not justify the level of costs likely to be incurred. For this purpose an estimate must be made of the likely total gross costs (excluding VAT) to be incurred on behalf of the client through to the disposal of the proceedings. This includes counsel's fees, disbursements, and the solicitor's costs, including any enhancement or uplift. Where appropriate, the likely costs should be calculated using standard or prescribed remuneration rates set by the Lord Chancellor or the Commission. In money claims an estimate must also be made of the amount likely to be recovered from the other side. This involves making a realistic estimate of the size of the money claim if the client is successful, taking into account any deduction through contributory negligence or otherwise. There should also be a realistic discount for any risk that the defendant may not pay.

Counsel (or solicitors with higher rights qualifications) may be instructed to advise on the merits of cases for the purposes of obtaining continued public funding. Guidelines for this purpose have been drafted by the LSC and appear as Annex E to the Bar Code of Conduct. Counsel instructed for this purpose should consider whether it is necessary to have a conference in order to assess the reliability of the evidence where it is likely to be contested. In making this decision counsel should take into account whether such a conference is likely to be cost-effective. The written opinion produced should state the level of service for which it is being written, and the category of case involved. Any relevant excluded work should be identified. It should then address the issues so as to provide the information and counsel's opinion on the law that the LSC will require in making its decision whether to grant public funding. It should be written in sufficient detail to enable the LSC to assess the relative strength of opposing cases, and to form a view on the likely outcome of legal points, without having to go outside the opinion. It should also draw attention to any lack of material which might have a bearing on the outcome. It should address the relevant criteria for the funding decision (although that does not mean that every criterion needs to be mentioned), and also any relevant wider public interest.

An important issue is counsel's view on the merits for the purposes of the cost-benefit assessment and the solicitor should be ready to assist counsel in estimating the likely level of costs.

In money claims having no wider public interest, Full Representation will be refused in the following circumstances:

(a) if the prospects of success are very good (80 per cent or more), but the likely damages do not exceed the likely costs;
(b) if the prospects of success are good (60–80 per cent), but the likely damages do not exceed the likely costs by a ratio of 2 : 1; or
(c) if the prospects of success are moderate (50–60 per cent), but the likely damages do not exceed the likely costs by a ratio of 4 : 1.

In *Oakes v Legal Services Commission* [2003] EWHC 1948 Admin, LTL 27/8/2003, a judicial review challenge to the refusal of public funding of a claim against the LSC was refused, because the prospects of success in the claim were poor, so there was no unfairness in refusing public funding on cost-benefit grounds. On the other hand, in *Alliss v Legal Services Commission* [2002]

EWHC 2079 Admin it was held that it was irrational and in breach of the **European Convention on Human Rights, art.** 6(1), to withdraw public funding at a late stage of a complex claim where the litigant could not realistically be expected to conduct the trial in person (even with the assistance of a McKenzie friend, see **59.32**). This was so despite the prospects of success being less than 50 per cent and the combined costs of both parties being about four times the likely damages.

In non-money claims having no wider public interest, full representation will be refused unless the likely benefits from the proceedings justify the likely costs, such that a reasonable private paying client would be prepared to litigate, having regard to the prospects of success and all other circumstances. This test is also applied to cases where the applicant for funding is the defendant, and in money claims where the proceedings have an overwhelming importance to the claimant.

In claims having a wider public interest, Full Representation may be refused where the likely benefits to the applicant and the public do not justify the likely costs, having regard to the prospects of success and all other circumstances.

As from 3 October 2005, Legal Representation for family proceedings may be refused if it appears reasonable in all the circumstances for the proceedings to be funded privately, having regard to the financial circumstances (including ability to borrow) of the client and the value of the assets in dispute.

Criteria for emergency representation

Funding for representation may be granted on an emergency basis in urgent cases. Even in emergency cases the normal criteria should be applied, but if the urgency results in limited information being available, emergency funding should be granted only if it appears likely on the information available that the ordinary criteria will be satisfied. The solicitor should be satisfied that the client will satisfy not only the merits test, but also the funding eligibility requirements. A full application has to be made as soon as is reasonably practicable after the emergency application has been made. If the client is found not to be financially eligible for funding, the certificate will be revoked (see 7.27). **7.22**

Criteria for Help with Mediation

Funding for Help with Mediation is only available if the client is involved in family mediation or has been involved and has reached agreement. Help with Mediation may be refused if it is more appropriate for the client to be assisted by way of Legal Help. Funding may only be provided where there is sufficient benefit to the client, having regard to the circumstances of the matter, including the personal circumstances of the client, to justify work or further work being carried out. **7.23**

Criteria for General Family Help

A family dispute must first be referred to a mediator to determine whether it is suitable for mediation. If mediation is appropriate General Family Help may be refused. If the application is premature, it may be refused. **7.24**

General Family Help will be refused unless the benefits to be gained from representation for the client justify the likely costs, such that a reasonable private paying client would be prepared to proceed in all the circumstances.

Criteria for Family Mediation

On initial assessment of a dispute for which Family Mediation is sought, the standard criteria (see 7.16) need to be satisfied. Beyond that, mediation may be provided only where the mediator is satisfied that mediation is appropriate for the dispute and the parties and all the circumstances. **7.25**

Right to a fair trial

7.26 Funding in civil proceedings is a matter for the LSC, and the courts have no power to order a party to be provided with State-funded legal representation (*Perotti v Collyer-Bristow* [2003] EWCA Civ 1521, [2004] 2 All ER 189). If a court decides that legal representation is desirable in order to comply with the European Convention on Human Rights, art. 6(1) for example, if legal representation is necessary in order for the court to grasp the facts and principles governing the case, it can give an indication to that effect. In such cases funding is likely to be made available by the LSC (*Perotti v Collyer-Bristow* and para. 6.5 of the Funding Code).

WITHDRAWAL OF FUNDING

7.27 The three most important general grounds for withdrawing funding under a certificate are:

(a) where the criteria under which the funding was originally granted are no longer satisfied (including a change in merits and/or ratio of costs to benefits or an increase in the client's financial means);

(b) where it is unreasonable for funding to continue in all the circumstances of the case (which includes the death or bankruptcy of the client, or the client's unreasonable conduct);

(c) where funding is no longer needed because all the work has been completed.

A certificate can be brought to an end by being either revoked or discharged. If the certificate is revoked, it is treated as never having existed. Accordingly revocation can have very serious consequences for the client, who must repay to the Legal Services Commission all the costs paid or payable under the certificate. The client also loses (retrospectively) any cost protection against adverse costs orders made in favour of the opponent in the litigation. Revocation takes place primarily where the client has been dishonest or has failed to comply with obligations under the Funding Code. It can also take place where a client in receipt of emergency representation is shown to be financially ineligible or fails to accept an offer of funding subject to a contribution.

Discharge of a certificate is much more common, and simply means that funding ceases from the date of the discharge.

After discharge or revocation the client can make further representations for a review by the Regional Director of the LSC who may restore the certificate if appropriate. The client can apply to the Funding Review Committee of the LSC if still not satisfied.

'Show cause' procedure: embargo on a certificate

7.28 Unless the reason for the discharge of a certificate is on financial grounds, the death or bankruptcy of the client, completion of the work or if the client agrees to the discharge, no non-emergency certificate will be discharged or revoked without reference to the 'show cause' procedure. This gives the client time in which to make further representations to the LSC as to why the certificate should stay in force. Since 8 April 2002, the LSC has had the power to embargo further work under a certificate pending completion of the 'show cause' procedure (in response to *R (Machi) v Legal Services Commission* [2001] EWCA Civ 2010, [2002] 1 WLR 983). When an embargo is imposed the LSC retains a discretion to authorise work under the embargoed certificate. If a certificate is embargoed, the solicitor can apply to come off the court record as acting (see **chapter 22**). If the certificate is later discharged, the client will lose protection against an adverse costs order (under the Legal Aid Act 1988, s. 17, or the **Access to Justice Act 1999, s. 11(1)**) from the date of beginning to act in person, not from the later date of discharge (*Burridge v Stafford* [2000] 1 WLR 927; **Community Legal Service (Cost Protection) Regulations 2000 (SI 2000/824), reg. 3**). It is unclear whether the client loses cost protection for the period of acting in person if the certificate is not in fact discharged at the end of the 'show cause' procedure. It is submitted that he should not, because by successfully showing cause why the certificate should not be discharged, the client has shown that he is entitled to be publicly funded throughout the period. The contrary view would encourage opposing parties to seek to trigger the 'show cause' procedure and thereby prejudice the assisted party's interests (since he will become exposed to a liability for the costs incurred while the embargo is in place). Further, if a litigant were to lose the statutory protection against an adverse costs order during the embargo, this will have an unfairly one-sided effect, as the statutory charge will remain to protect the LSC, and all damages and costs awarded to the litigant after the embargo takes effect will be available to meet the statutory charge — including any extra sums entirely attributable to the litigant's unaided efforts.

STATUTORY CHARGE

By virtue of the **Access to Justice Act 1999, s. 10**(7), the sums paid by the LSC in funding a claim and any other sums which the funded client is required to pay by regulations (such as interest on late payments of contributions) constitute a first charge on any property recovered or preserved in the proceedings or by any settlement or compromise to the dispute. The underlying principle is to place the publicly funded party in a similar position to a party privately funding litigation whose primary responsibility at the end of the proceedings is to pay the costs incurred by his or her own solicitors in bringing or defending the claim. In this way public funding is often described as a 'loan' to pay legal costs which is repayable if a client gains or keeps money or property with the help of public funding. **7.29**

The charge only applies if there is a net liability to the LSC. This usually arises because of the gap between the solicitor/own client costs and the costs recovered on a party/party assessment. Solicitors often waive their claim for costs not recovered from the opponent, but there is no obligation on them to do so.

Property covered by the charge

The charge attaches to any property recovered or preserved in the claim. This includes any property or money which was the subject matter of the proceedings or any property or money received under a settlement (even if it was not claimed in the proceedings) (*Van Hoorn v Law Society* [1985] QB 106). Property is 'recovered' if the publicly funded client gains ownership or possession of it through the proceedings or settlement. It is 'preserved' if another party's claims to ownership or possession are defeated. **7.30**

In *Curling v Law Society* [1985] 1 WLR 470 it was held that property was recovered, and was subject to the statutory charge, even if title to the property was not in issue, if proceedings were necessary to obtain possession of the property. This was distinguished in *Patel v Legal Services Commission* [2004] EWHC 743 (Ch), LTL 13/4/2004, a case involving a boundary dispute over a strip of land not more than 7 inches wide which was part of the claimant's back garden. A declaration was granted that the claimant's property was not subject to the statutory charge because the strip was of only nominal value, and only the strip was in issue in the claim, not the whole of the claimant's property.

The statutory charge does not apply in every case (Community Legal Service (Financial) Regulations 2000 (SI 2000/516), reg. 44). In particular, it does not apply:

(a) To maintenance payments.
(b) To advice in relation to a family mediation.
(c) Where advice only is given under the Legal Help Scheme in any matter other than family or personal injury after 1 April 2000.

The £3,000 exemption in family law cases was revoked with effect from 1 April 2005 (Community Legal Service (Financial) (Amendment) Regulations 2005 (SI 2005/589), reg.

14). A solicitor also has limited powers to waive the statutory charge in family or personal injury cases where advice has been given only under the Legal Help Scheme.

Giving effect to the charge

7.31 Whenever property is recovered or preserved for a publicly funded person, the solicitor has a duty to inform the LSC immediately so that the charge can be registered and enforced. Because costs and damages are subject to the charge, under no circumstances should damages or costs be paid to the publicly funded party directly. If the money is paid to the solicitor, it must be paid straightaway to the LSC (**Community Legal Service (Costs) Regulations 2000 SI 2000/441), reg. 20**).

This can mean a delay in publicly funded clients actually receiving the balance of costs and damages from a successful claim pending the assessment of costs. In practice, it is sometimes possible, with the agreement of the LSC, to give interim payments provided sufficient funds are retained to satisfy the statutory charge.

Enforcement of the charge can be postponed if the property is a home for the client or his or her dependants or if property or money recovered or preserved is to be used to pay for a home. In that case, the charge will be registered as a mortgage for the full amount of the outstanding costs. Interest will be added. The rate of interest is set in the Community Legal Service (Financial) Regulations 2000, reg. 53(3), as:

Until 31 March 2002	8 per cent per annum
1 April 2002 to 30 September 2005	5 per cent per annum
From 1 October 2005	8 per cent per annum

The LSC may postpone the enforcement of a statutory charge only if it would be unreasonable for the client to repay the amount of the charge (reg. 52A). Any decision to postpone a charge may be reviewed at any time resulting in the charge being either enforced or continuing to be postponed on terms that the client pays interim capital payments and/or interest (reg. 52B).

The LSC has no power to reduce the statutory charge and where it applies it must be paid. The client has a direct interest in ensuring that costs do not rise unnecessarily, especially if the other side has public funding or for any reason is unlikely to pay all or some of the costs. On assessment of the publicly funded costs, the client can raise objections to the level of solicitor's charges, which can have the overall effect of reducing the amount of the charge. Credit will be given for any contribution paid during the time the certificate is in force.

Practitioners have a professional duty to advise clients who apply for public funding of the effects of the statutory charge. This should be done orally and in writing. The LSC has produced a leaflet called *Paying Back the Legal Services Commission*, which should ordinarily be provided to the client in every case.

COST PROTECTION

7.32 The **Access to Justice Act 1999, s. 11**, provides what is known as 'cost protection' for an individual whose legal proceedings have been publicly funded but unsuccessful. By **s. 11(1)**, any costs ordered against such an individual must not exceed what is a reasonable sum for the individual to pay, having regard to all the circumstances, including:

(a) the financial resources of all the parties to the proceedings, and
(b) their conduct in connection with the dispute to which the proceedings relate.

Cost protection does not apply in prescribed circumstances (**s. 11(1)**), that is, the circumstances prescribed in the **Community Legal Service (Cost Protection) Regulations 2000 (SI 2000/824), reg. 3**. See **66.57** to **66.65**.

DUTIES TO THE LSC

Both publicly funded clients and their legal representatives are under a continuing duty to comply with the provisions of the Access to Justice Act 1999 and associated Regulations and the Funding Code. **7.33**

Legal representatives (including counsel) owe a duty to bring to the attention of the LSC any matter which might affect the client's entitlement to funding or the terms of the certificate. This includes the client's financial eligibility as well as the other criteria. The client also has an ongoing duty to the LSC to advise it of any changes in his or her financial circumstances. Solicitors must never succumb to any pressure from a client to keep matters from the LSC. Not only is this a breach of the duties owed by the solicitor to the LSC, but it may lead to the revocation of the certificate, which can have substantial financial implications for the client.

CONTRACTING

Under the **Access to Justice Act 1999, s. 6(3)**, the Legal Services Commission acquired the power to procure services for civil work by way of contract. It is generally only firms who hold an SQM who are entitled to bid for a contract. **7.34**

Firms must now be contracted to undertake any new civil publicly funded work. Legal Help, Help at Court and Legal Representation before a mental health review tribunal or the Asylum and Immigration Tribunal is limited by a centrally controlled budget, and is called Controlled Work. Legal Representation in any other civil matter is known as Licensed Work. Certain work, including personal injury and clinical negligence, will only be authorised if the firm has an SQM in that specific area. Otherwise an SQM in any category will usually be sufficient to allow a firm to undertake work in any civil matter.

Several ideas underlie the concept of contracting. First, contracted organisations have passed the quality threshold in the same way as franchised organisations. Secondly, contracting enables the LSC, through its regional legal services committees (RLSCs), to set geographical priorities rather than respond to demand under the old scheme. One criticism of the old scheme was that it led to supplier-induced demand. For example, it might be said that legal aid spent in one area was particularly high not because that had been prioritised as a deprived area but because the local legal culture meant that suppliers were particularly adept at selling their services there. By contrast, under the new scheme, the Commission and its RLSCs are expected to develop and acquire quite sophisticated information about local need for particular legal services and award contracts accordingly.

Thirdly, contracting introduces the means for capping the Community Legal Service budget. The government sets the budget and the LSC decides where the priority areas are and sets its contracts accordingly. Both the number of cases covered by a contract and the remuneration rates payable under it can be varied.

Finally, contracting with approved suppliers enables the LSC to build in various mechanisms for providing information about the way suppliers (solicitors and volunteers) spend public funds. It is expected that the LSC will monitor this information carefully and use it as the basis for future reforms in this area, particularly the proposals relating to preferred suppliers.

The Legal Services Commission General Civil Contract for Solicitors operates like other commercial contracts. Clause 23 is an arbitration clause. Litigation based on a dispute amenable to arbitration under the clause is liable to be stayed on the application of the other side in accordance with usual contract law principles (*Asghar v Legal Services Commission* [2004] EWHC 1803 (Ch), LTL 26/8/2004).

Many changes to public funding took place in 2005 (known as 'New Focus' from the 2004 consultation document, *A New Focus for Civil Legal Aid*) and more changes are proposed as a Fundamental Legal Aid Review (FLAR) is taking place. A number of pilot schemes are in place such as a Preferred Supplier pilot and a pilot scheme testing a proposed new devolved level of Family Help to replace Legal Help and General Family Help.

LEGAL SERVICES COMMISSION MANUAL

7.35 All the material governing the public funding of civil cases, including the legislation, regulations, guidance and the standard civil contract terms between the Commission and suppliers is set out in the four-volume loose-leaf *Legal Services Commission Manual*. The latest version of the Manual (release 03) was published in December 2005 to take into account the 2005 changes to the Funding Code. It is supplemented by the very useful Legal Services Commission journal, *Focus*, which is usually published four times a year. The LSC's website at www.legalservices.gov.uk is a useful resource for practitioners. For contract holders the LSC is piloting a specialist support helpline. The intention is to provide legal advice and support from some of the leading legal aid practitioners in the country together with a system of referrals for more complex cases.

Chapter 8 Pre-action Protocols

The following procedural checklists, which are in **appendix 1**, are relevant to this chapter:

Procedural checklist 1 Pre-action Protocol for Personal Injuries
Procedural checklist 2 Pre-action procedure where no protocol applies

PURPOSE OF PRE-ACTION PROTOCOLS

The *Final Report* recommended the development of pre-action protocols: 'to build on and increase the benefits of early but well-informed settlements which genuinely satisfy both parties to a dispute' (ch. 10, para. 1). **8.1**

The protocols provide a simple system which sets out guidelines of best practice by providing timetables for the exchange of information before litigation commences as well as pro forma letters before action, to assist each party in knowing the case that may have to be met.

If court proceedings do become necessary, following the relevant protocol should ensure that the litigation proceeds quickly and efficiently from the moment of issue of the claim, as a result of the parties' previous compliance with what will come to be regarded as 'normal pre-action behaviour'. This will be supported by greater control by the courts in ensuring compliance with the protocols.

The **Pre-action Protocol for Personal Injury Claims** summarises the objectives of the protocols as follows (at **para. 1.2**):

(a) more pre-action contact between the parties;
(b) better and earlier exchange of information;
(c) better pre-action investigation by both sides;
(d) to put the parties in a position where they may be able to settle cases fairly and early without litigation;
(e) to enable proceedings to run to the court's timetable and efficiently, if litigation does become necessary.

Thus, the aim of the protocols, in keeping with the general ethos of the Woolf reforms, is to avoid litigation if at all possible, through greater contact between the parties and exchange of information at a very early stage, in the hope that settlements can be achieved without resort to court proceedings.

CURRENT PROTOCOLS

8.2 The pre-action protocols currently in force cover claims for personal injury, clinical negligence, disease and illness, housing disrepair, construction and engineering disputes, defamation, professional negligence and judicial review.

Before proceedings are started in cases falling outside these categories, the parties must follow the general guidance laid down by **PD Protocols, para.** 4, which is discussed at 8.52 to 8.54.

CONSEQUENCES OF FAILURE TO COMPLY WITH PROTOCOLS

Substantial compliance

8.3 The court will expect all parties to have complied, in substance, with the terms of an approved protocol (**PD Protocols, para. 2.2**).

The use of the word 'substance' in para. 2.2 is reinforced by para. 3.4, which states that the court will not be concerned with minor infringements, for example, failure by a short period to provide information, and indeed a minor infringement by one party will not excuse other parties from continuing to follow the protocol.

Paragraphs 3.1 and 3.2 of PD Protocols provide examples of non-compliance, such as:

(a) a claimant not providing sufficient information to the defendant, or not following the procedure required to be followed by the relevant protocol,
(b) a defendant failing to make a preliminary response to the letter of claim within the time limits fixed by the relevant protocol, not making a full response within the time specified in the relevant protocol or not disclosing documents to the claimant, as required by the relevant protocol.

Sanctions for non-compliance

8.4 The CPR enable the court to take into account compliance or non-compliance with an applicable protocol when giving directions for the management of proceedings (**rr. 3.1(4) and** (5) and **3.9(1)(e)**) and when making orders for costs (**r. 44.3(5)(a)**). **PD Protocols, para. 2.3,**

sets out orders which the court may make if, in its opinion, non-compliance with a protocol:

(a) has led to the commencement of any proceedings which might not otherwise have needed to be commenced, or
(b) has led to costs being incurred in proceedings that might otherwise not have been incurred.

The court has power to make a variety of orders, which include:

(a) an order that the party at fault pay the costs of the proceedings, or part of those costs, of the other party or parties;
(b) an order that the party at fault pay those costs on an indemnity basis;
(c) if the party at fault is the claimant in whose favour an order for the payment of damages or some specified sum is subsequently made, an order depriving that party of interest on such sum and in respect of such period as may be specified, and/or awarding interest at a lower rate than that at which interest would otherwise have been awarded;
(d) if the party at fault is a defendant and an order for the payment of damages or some specified sum is subsequently made in favour of the claimant, an order awarding interest on such sum and in respect of such period as may be specified at a higher rate, not exceeding 10 per cent above base rate, than the rate at which interest would otherwise have been awarded.

The court will exercise its powers to sanction the defaulting party with the object of placing the innocent party in no worse a position than he would have been in if the protocol had been followed (**PD Protocols, para. 2.4**). For example, in *Paul Thomas Construction Ltd v Hyland* [2001] CILL 1748 the court ordered the claimant to pay the defendant's costs on the indemnity basis after finding that the claimant had ignored repeated requests for further information and proposals for resolution of the matter by some form of ADR and had commenced wholly unnecessary proceedings.

The court has a general power to impose sanctions under **CPR, r. 3.8**, where a party has failed to comply with a rule, practice direction or court order, which sanctions remain effective unless the party in default applies for and obtains relief from them. **Rule 3.9** provides that the court, when considering whether to grant relief, will take into account factors set out in **r. 3.9(1)**, which include (**r. 3.9(1)(e)**) the extent to which the party in default has complied with other rules, practice directions, court orders and any relevant pre-action protocol.

Failure to comply with a protocol can, therefore, lead to an immediate sanction or to sanctions later during the course of proceedings, or to sanctions, by way of costs, at the conclusion of the proceedings.

The list of sanctions for non-compliance with the pre-action protocols set out in **PD Protocols, para. 2.3**, is not exhaustive. General sanctions which the court may impose include:

(a) if the claimant is in default, a stay of proceedings to allow the defendant to gather its information and, so to speak, catch up;
(b) costs, which may be ordered to be paid forthwith;
(c) an order refusing permission to call evidence from an expert who has been instructed by one or other party without compliance with the relevant protocol;
(d) under **CPR, r. 3.1(5)**, the court may order any party to pay a sum of money into court if that party has without good reason failed to comply with a rule, practice direction or relevant pre-action protocol. If applied to a claimant, this sanction could amount to giving security for costs, and in the case of a defendant, a payment into court in respect of the whole or part of the claim. The court is reluctant to use this sanction unless breaches have been repeated or there has been lack of good faith (*Mealey Horgan plc v Horgan* (1999) *The Times*, 6 July 1999).

Costs

8.5 Rule 44.3(4)of the CPR lists factors to be taken into account by the court when deciding to make an order for costs. One of them is the conduct of the parties, which is defined in **r. 44.3(5)** to include: 'conduct, before, as well as during the proceedings and in particular the extent to which the parties followed any relevant pre-action protocol'.

In *King v Telegraph Group Ltd* [2004] EWCA Civ 613, [2005] 1 WLR 2282, one of the factors which inclined the court towards making a prospective cost-capping order (see **66.54**) was that the letter of claim was written in a vituperative tone calculated to raise the temperature and inflate the parties' costs.

COSTS OF MATTERS DROPPED AT THE PRE-ACTION STAGE

8.6 It has always been clear that costs incurred in complying with pre-action protocols (and general pre-action work) are recoverable as 'incidental to' proceedings if a claim is subsequently issued (**Supreme Court Act 1981, s. 51**; *Callery v Gray* [2001] EWCA Civ 1117, [2001] 1 WLR 2112). The costs of such work are therefore recoverable as part of the general costs of the proceedings. In the absence of agreement between the parties, it has always been the case that costs are not recoverable between parties in dispute if proceedings are not issued.

In *McGlinn v Waltham Contractors Ltd* [2005] EWHC 1419 (TCC), [2005] 3 All ER 1126 it was argued that a successful claimant who raised a number of issues in pre-action correspondence, but abandoned some of them before issuing proceedings, was to be treated as only partially successful. A partially successful party is usually awarded just a percentage of the costs of the claim (see **66.10**). It was held that save in exceptional circumstances (such as where there is unreasonable conduct) the costs of the abandoned issues will not be 'incidental to' the subsequent proceedings. It would be contrary to the whole purpose of the pre-action protocols if claimants were routinely penalised if they dropped matters included in their letters of claim. The protocols are designed to narrow the issues, and allow a defendant to persuade a claimant that claims would not succeed.

ALTERNATIVE DISPUTE RESOLUTION

8.7 **Practice Direction Protocols, para.** 4.7, was expanded with effect from 1 October 2005. It reminds parties that the courts increasingly take the view that litigation should be the last resort, and draws attention to a Legal Services Commission booklet on *Alternatives to Court.* It says that parties may be required to provide evidence that alternative means of dispute resolution were considered. ADR is considered in detail in **chapter 70**.

NOTIFICATION OF FUNDING ARRANGEMENT

8.8 Whether or not the dispute is governed by a pre-action protocol, the parties should inform each other in the pre-action stages whether they have the benefit of public funding under legal aid or the Community Legal Service. Likewise, a party who is being funded under a conditional fee arrangement should notify the other potential parties of this fact, although there is no obligation to give details of the level of 'success fee' that has been agreed (see **PD Protocols, paras 4A.** 1 and **4A.2,** and **6.15**).

PERSONAL INJURY CLAIMS PROTOCOL

The **Pre-action Protocol for Personal Injury Claims** is primarily drafted for road traffic, slipping and tripping and accident at work claims which include an element of personal injury with a value of less than £15,000 and which are likely to be allocated to the fast track (**para. 2.3**). The protocol is intended to assist in the preparation of a claim, which, on the fast track, must be ready to be tried within 30 weeks of allocation. **8.9**

The protocol applies to the whole of a claim, not just the personal injury element.

The protocol lays down a timetable for the pre-action period but **para. 2.3** envisages that there may be claims where some flexibility in the timetable will be necessary. Arrangements for disclosure and expert evidence may need to be varied to suit the particular circumstances of individual cases. There may be difficulties, for example, in a claim with a modest personal injury element, which is easily resolved, but a substantial claim for vehicle repairs, where the claimant may wish to move expeditiously to have the vehicle examined and repaired or scrapped and replaced. It may well be considered reasonable for the claimant to give the defendant's insurers much less notice of his or her intention in relation to the vehicle, and to insist on an inspection far more quickly than the timescale indicated by the protocol. It is undesirable for a claimant to be put in the position of wondering whether a defendant's dilatory insurer will or will not accept the claimant's figures for repairs particularly when an alternative vehicle may have to be hired. It is submitted that common sense must prevail in allowing for variations of the timetable set by the protocol.

If it is considered, by either or both parties to a claim, that the detail of the protocol is not appropriate to it, and proceedings are subsequently issued, the court will expect an explanation of why the protocol has not been followed or has been varied (**para. 2.5**). A space is provided in the allocation questionnaire for giving such an explanation.

The steps required by the protocol are summarised in **procedural checklist 1**, which is in **appendix 1**, and are discussed in detail in **8.10** to **8.41**.

Early notification

The **Pre-action Protocol for Personal Injury Claims** promotes early notification of the possibility of a claim to the person against whom it may be made. **Paragraph 2.6** recognises that it may not be possible to provide all the relevant details immediately but that it may be best to put the potential defendant on notice by writing an initial letter as soon as it is apparent that a claim is likely to be made. An early notification of this kind will not start the timetable for responding. **8.10**

Letter of claim

The timetable set by the **Pre-action Protocol for Personal Injury Claims** is initiated by the letter of claim. This should be as detailed as possible and a specimen letter appears at annex A to the protocol. The letter should concentrate on providing sufficient information for the defendant to assess liability. It should also provide sufficient information to enable the defendant to estimate the likely size of the claim (**para. 2.9**). In a road traffic claim the letter should provide the name and address of the hospital where the claimant was treated, and, if available, the claimant's hospital reference number (**para. 2.8**). Normally two copies of a letter of claim are sent to the defendant, who is asked to pass one copy to the insurers responsible (**paras 3.1** and **3.4**). If the insurers are already known, the second copy should be sent direct to them (**para. 3.4**). After sending a letter of claim the claimant should do no more work on investigating liability until the defendant responds indicating whether liability is accepted or denied (**para. 2.10**). **8.11**

Defendant's acknowledgment

8.12 The defendant is required to acknowledge receipt of the letter of claim within 21 days of posting, identifying the insurers, if any (**Pre-action Protocol for Personal Injury Claims, para. 3.6**). If the defendant or the insurers fail to respond within 21 days, the claimant is entitled to issue proceedings (**para. 3.6**). Bearing in mind the spirit of reasonable pre-action behaviour, if the defendant delays passing the letter of claim on to the insurers, it would be reasonable to allow the insurers additional time for responding to it (**para. 2.7**).

Investigation and response

8.13 Having acknowledged the letter of claim, the defendant (or insurers) then has three months to investigate and to reply stating whether liability is denied and, if it is, giving reasons for denial and any alternative version of the events relied upon (**Pre-action Protocol for Personal Injury Claims, para. 3.7**). Proceedings should not be issued in this period. For some claims this may not be possible. For example, if the claimant consults a solicitor towards the end of a relevant limitation period, a protective claim form will have to be issued, so as not to deprive the claimant of a remedy. In these circumstances, the protocol recommends, at **para. 2.11**, that the claimant's solicitor should give as much notice as is practicable and the parties should consider whether the court might be invited to extend the time for service of the claimant's supporting documents and the service of any defence, or alternatively to stay the proceedings while the recommended steps in the protocol are followed. This may only be done where there is an expectation that there is a valid claim to be pursued. In *West Bromwich Building Society v Mander Hadley and Co.* [1998] CLC 814 the Court of Appeal held that the issue of protective proceedings, when a claimant had no intention of prosecuting the claim and was unaware of any valid basis for it, was an abuse of process.

Status of letters of claim and response

8.14 Although a letter of claim and its response should be as full as possible, in order to meet the 'cards on the table approach', it is not intended that they should bear the same status as formal statements of case (**Pre-action Protocol for Personal Injury Claims, para. 2.12**). It is recognised that various matters may well come to light as a result of investigations after the letter of claim has been sent or after the defendant has responded, especially in a situation where the disclosure of documents takes place outside the recommended three-month period. Circumstances such as these could mean that particulars of claim and/or the defence may present a party's case in a slightly different way than in the letter of claim and/or response, and it would be inconsistent with the spirit of the protocol for a party to take a point on this in the proceedings, provided there was no deliberate intention to mislead (**para. 2.12**). Indeed it is clear from the comments of Lord Woolf MR in *McPhilemy v Times Newspapers Ltd* [1999] 3 All ER 775 that contests over the terms of statements of case are to be avoided.

Disclosure of documents and schedule of special damages

8.15 The **Pre-action Protocol for Personal Injury Claims, para. 3.10**, provides for pre-action disclosure of documents where the defendant denies liability. The defendant should enclose documents material to the issues with the letter of reply. Annex B to the protocol lists documents likely to be material in different types of claim. No charge is to be made for supplying documents under the protocol (**para. 3.13**). The claimant is required to send the defendant a schedule of special damages with supporting documents as soon as practicable (**para. 3.14**). This is particularly important where the defendant has admitted liability, where the schedule should be sent to the defendant at least 21 days before proceedings are issued to give the defendant a chance to make a Part 36 offer (**para. 5.3**).

The aim of early disclosure of documents is not to encourage 'fishing expeditions' by the claimant but to promote an early exchange of relevant information to assist in clarifying or resolving the issues in dispute (**para. 2.13**). The claimant's solicitors can assist by identifying in the letter of claim or in a subsequent letter the particular categories of documents which they consider are relevant (**para. 2.13**).

Experts

The **Pre-action Protocol for Personal Injury Claims** encourages the joint selection of, and access to, experts (**para. 2.14**). In most claims this will apply to medical experts, but there may be occasions when it will also apply to others, such as engineers. The protocol also promotes the practice of the claimant obtaining a medical report, disclosing it to the defendant, who then has the opportunity to ask questions on the report and/or agree it without the need to obtain a second report (**para. 2.14**). At **para. 3.15**, the protocol suggests that before instructing any expert a party should provide the other party with a list of names of experts in the relevant area who are considered suitable to instruct. **8.16**

It is often the case that the claimant will wish the medical practitioner who provided the medical treatment to be retained as the expert in the claim. In most cases this is best avoided, as the court may well reach the conclusion that the medical expert is no longer sufficiently objective, because, first, he or she will have developed a relationship with the patient/claimant and secondly, may regard his or her views on prognosis as unchallengeable. It is suggested that the procedure for the joint selection of experts set out in **paras 3.15** to **3.19** of the protocol is preferable in order that a mutually acceptable expert can be instructed.

Claimants who choose to instruct their own expert unilaterally, may well discover that the court will later refuse permission to call that expert and insist that an expert be jointly instructed (**CPR, r. 35.7**). The consequence of this is that the costs of the first expert will not be recoverable, regardless of the outcome of the case. The question relating to experts in the allocation questionnaire asks whether reports have been disclosed and if it is not proposed to use a joint expert, reasons must be given. This allows arguments to be put for a separate defence expert and for the court to enquire whether the defendant's position cannot be protected by simply delivering written questions to the claimant's expert.

Furthermore, the protocol does maintain the flexibility for either party to obtain their own expert's report, if necessary, once proceedings have been commenced, but with the permission of the court. It is also for the court to decide whether the costs of more than one expert report should be recoverable (see **CPR, r. 35.4(4)**).

It is clear from the foregoing that the provisions of the CPR and those of the protocol do not lie easily with each other. However, with cooperation between practitioners together with appropriate judicial intervention, common sense should prevail. In applying the overriding objective, the court will decide whether it is more efficient to order a report from a second expert for the opposing side and will probably determine the question of costs at a later stage. Whether the costs of the additional expert will be recoverable will depend upon the degree and extent to which the protocol was complied with, or whether it would have been more advantageous to instruct a new joint expert.

Joint selection **Paragraphs 3.15 to 3.21 of the Pre-action Protocol for Personal Injury Claims** lay down the procedure for the joint selection of experts. Joint selection of an expert means that one party's choice of expert to be instructed is agreed by the other party, but it does not mean that the expert is jointly instructed by both parties. Only the party who instructed the jointly selected expert is entitled to see the expert's report, which is protected by legal professional privilege unless the instructing party chooses to disclose it (*Carlson v Townsend* [2001] EWCA Civ 511, [2001] 1 WLR 2415). In contrast, if an expert is jointly instructed, both parties are entitled to see his or her report. The party who instructed a jointly selected expert is solely liable to pay the expert's fee, but both parties are liable to pay a jointly instructed expert. **8.17**

Medical agencies Some solicitors have adopted the practice of obtaining medical reports via **8.18**

medical agencies rather than directly from a specific doctor or hospital (**Pre-action Protocol for Personal Injury Claims, para. 2.15**). The protocol does not discourage this but emphasises that in such a case, the defendant's prior consent should be sought and, if the defendant so requests, the agency should be asked to provide in advance the names of the doctors whom they are considering instructing (**para. 2.15**).

Negotiation, rehabilitation and settlement

8.19 **Paragraph 2.16** of the **Pre-action Protocol for Personal Injury Claims**, which in its present form came into effect on 6 April 2006, requires the parties to consider whether some form of ADR would be more suitable than litigation. Both sides may be required to provide the court with evidence that ADR was considered. Litigation is regarded as a last resort, and proceedings should not be issued while settlement is being actively explored. It is expressly recognised that the parties cannot be forced to mediate or enter into any form of ADR (**para. 2.19**), but a failure to comply with the aim of **para. 2.16** may be taken into account on costs.

As early as possible both sides should consider whether the claimant has reasonable needs that could be met by rehabilitation treatment or other measures (**para. 4.1**). Annex D to the protocol is a Rehabilitation Code which gives guidance on how to identify the claimant's needs. This may involve obtaining a report assessing the claimant's rehabilitation needs. An assessment report should be produced using the seven headings set out in **para. 5.2 of the Rehabilitation Code**. It will not deal with diagnostic criteria, causation or long-term care requirements (**Code, para. 5.3**). Instead it must deal with short- and medium-term rehabilitation treatment, its likely benefits, and cost (**Code, para. 5.2**). The defendant's insurer will pay for the report within 28 days of receipt (**Code, para. 6.5**). It is for the parties to agree that any particular regime of rehabilitation or treatment shall be put in place (**Code, para. 6.4**). Any funds laid out by the insurer for treatment are treated as voluntary interim payments (**Code, para. 7.2**). Provided the claimant uses such funds for the recommended purpose, the insurer warrants it will not dispute the reasonableness or the agreed cost of the treatment in subsequent proceedings (**Code, para. 7.2**). Any assessment report must not be used in the litigation except by consent (**Pre-action Protocol for Personal Injury Claims, para. 4.4**). Any notes and reports created in connection with the assessment process shall not be disclosed in any litigation, and any person involved in the preparation of the assessment report shall not be a compellable witness (**Code, para. 6.3**).

Preparation for proceedings

8.20 Where a claim is not resolved, even though the parties have followed the protocol, they might wish to carry out a 'stocktake' of the issues in dispute and the evidence that the court is likely to require to resolve those issues, prior to the commencement of proceedings (**Pre-action Protocol for Personal Injury Claims, para. 2.17**).

If the pre-action steps on the defendant's side have been taken by insurers, the protocol recommends that, seven to 14 days before the intended issue date, the claimant's solicitor should invite the insurers to nominate solicitors to act in the proceedings.

Application to the small claims track

8.21 Strictly, **PD Protocols, para. 4** (see 8.52 to 8.54), applies to small-value personal injuries claims rather than the **Pre-action Protocol for Personal Injury Claims**. Acting reasonably may involve adopting some features from the **Pre-action Protocol for Personal Injury Claims**, but much will depend on the circumstances of the case. In particular, it may be appropriate to rely on a short report from a general practitioner rather than obtaining a jointly selected consultant's report. **PD Protocols, para. 4.3**, suggests that a month will usually be sufficient time for the defendant to investigate and respond. Further, it is submitted that, given the restricted costs regime on the small claims track, solicitors representing claimants in small-value claims should not be criticised for issuing proceedings soon after receiving a response, save where there has been the most flagrant disregard of the need for cooperation provided for in the protocols.

Personal injury claims worth more than £15,000

The strict requirements, and timetables, laid down in the **Pre-action Protocol for Personal Injury Claims** apply to personal injury claims up to £15,000 (**para. 2.3**). In claims worth more than £15,000 the courts will expect to see reasonable pre-action behaviour (**para. 2.14**). This is likely to mean that the parties must comply with the protocol as far as possible, particularly in respect of letters of claim, exchanging information and agreeing experts (**para. 2.14**). Where a claim is initially believed to have a value under £15,000, but on investigation appears to have a value exceeding that figure, the claimant should notify the defendant as soon as possible (**para. 3.9**). **8.22**

CLINICAL NEGLIGENCE PROTOCOL

The **Pre-action Protocol for the Resolution of Clinical Disputes** came about following detailed investigation by the Clinical Disputes Forum, a body formed in 1997 following Lord Woolf's Access to Justice Inquiry. One of the aims of the Forum is to establish less adversarial and more cost-effective ways of resolving disputes relating to healthcare and medical treatment. According to the **Executive Summary, para. 3, the Clinical Negligence Protocol**: **8.23**

(a) encourages a climate of openness when something has 'gone wrong' with a patient's treatment or the patient is dissatisfied with that treatment and/or the outcome;
(b) provides general guidance on how this more open culture might be achieved when disputes arise;
(c) recommends a timed sequence of steps for patients and healthcare providers, and their advisers, to follow when a dispute arises. This should facilitate and speed up exchanging relevant information and increase the prospects that disputes can be resolved without resort to legal action.

It is recognised in **paras 1.3** and **1.4** of the protocol that, in the past, there has been mistrust on both sides, patient and healthcare provider, meaning that patients fail to raise their concerns regarding treatment as early as possible and that healthcare providers are reluctant to be honest with patients, fail to provide prompt and clear explanations and tend to 'close ranks' once a claim has been made. Despite having complaints about treatment, patients often wish to maintain their relationships with medical practitioners. Thus the general aims of the protocol are (**para. 2.1**):

(a) to maintain or restore the patient-healthcare provider relationship;
(b) to resolve as many disputes as possible without litigation.

The specific objectives are (**para. 2.2**):

(a) to encourage early communication of perceived problems between patients and their healthcare providers;
(b) to encourage patients to voice their concerns regarding treatment;
(c) to encourage healthcare providers to develop systems of early reporting and investigation for serious adverse treatment outcomes and to provide full and prompt explanations to dissatisfied patients;
(d) to ensure that sufficient information is disclosed by both parties to enable each to understand the other's perspective and case, and to encourage early resolution.

The protocol encourages a timely approach to investigation by recommending that any investigations are carried out promptly and that all relevant medical records are provided to patients or their advisers on request, to a realistic timetable, by healthcare providers (**para. 2.2**).

The protocol does not attempt to usurp the function of the NHS Executive or the National Health Service Litigation Authority by providing any detailed guidance to healthcare providers on clinical risk management, or adverse outcome reporting (**para. 2.3**). Nor does the protocol recommend changes to the codes of conduct of healthcare professionals, although it is understood that the General Medical Council is currently preparing guidance to doctors regarding their duty to report adverse incidents and to cooperate with inquiries.

Code of good practice

8.24 The protocol does not set out to be a comprehensive code governing all the steps which need to be taken in a clinical dispute but attempts to set out a code of good practice which parties should follow where litigation is contemplated (**para. 3.1**). There is a 'commitments' section (**para. 3.4**) which sets out some guiding principles both to healthcare providers and patients and their advisers, which each side is invited to endorse when dealing with potential complaints and claims.

Steps required by the Clinical Negligence Protocol

8.25 **Paragraphs 3.6 to 3.27 of the Pre-action Protocol for the Resolution of Clinical Disputes** set out the sequence of actions to be followed if litigation is a prospect.

The first step is the request by the patient or his or her legal advisers for records. That request should be made in standard form as provided at **annex B** to the protocol. Records should be provided within 40 days of the request. If there is a failure by the healthcare provider to make records available and no explanation has been given, the potential claimant can apply to the court for an order for pre-action disclosure. Sanctions are also likely to be imposed where there is an unreasonable delay in providing records.

The letter of claim will follow and it should be as detailed as possible. A template for the recommended contents is provided at **annex C1** to the protocol.

A template for the letter of response appears at **annex C2**. The letter of claim should be acknowledged by the healthcare provider within 14 days of receipt. The healthcare provider should identify who will be dealing with the matter. The healthcare provider then has three months in which to provide a 'reasoned answer'. Thus proceedings should not be issued until after three months from the letter of claim, unless there is a limitation problem or the patient's position needs to be protected by early issue.

The parties are encouraged to resolve their dispute without recourse to litigation and **para. 5.2** (inserted with effect from 6 April 2006) of the protocol provides details of a number of forms of alternative dispute resolution.

DISEASE AND ILLNESS PROTOCOL

8.26 The **Pre-action Protocol for Disease and Illness Claims**, which came into force on 8 December 2003, applies to all personal injuries claims where the injury takes the form of an illness or disease rather than a physical injury (**para. 2.1**). It applies to any illness, whether physical or psychological, any disorder, ailment, affliction, complaint, malady or derangement, other than a physical or psychological injury caused solely by an accident or other similar single event (**para. 2.2**). It covers diseases and illnesses occurring in the workplace, and also those caused by, for example, the occupation of premises (where there may be an overlap with the **Pre-action Protocol for Housing Disrepair Cases**) or the use of products (including medications). The Disease and Illness Protocol is not intended to cover cases dealt with as group or class claims (**para. 2.3**).

Disclosure of occupational and health records, and product data

8.27 Before sending a letter of claim, under the **Pre-action Protocol for Disease and Illness**

Claims, the potential claimant is permitted to request copies of any relevant occupational or health records, and also to request copies of product data which may be relevant to a causation issue. The potential defendant should provide copies of the claimant's records within 40 days (**para.** 4.3), and the protocol says it is good practice to provide product data. If a defendant is in difficulties in providing the documents in time, this should be explained, with a reasonable time estimate for compliance (**para.** 4.4). Failure to comply may provide grounds for an application for pre-action disclosure (**para.** 4.5, and see **chapter** 48).

Records with third parties

Employment records with previous employers, and general practitioner records, should, if relevant, be sought by the claimant (**Pre-action Protocol for Disease and Illness Claims, para.** 5.1). If, on considering the records, the claimant decides not to pursue the claim, this decision should be communicated to any defendants previously notified of the claim (**para.** 5.3). **8.28**

Letter of claim, chronology and schedule of damages

Two copies of a letter of claim, primarily addressing liability issues, should be sent to the defendant (one copy is for any insurer) (**Pre-action Protocol for Disease and Illness Claims, paras 6.1 to 6.3**). The standard format for the letter is laid down in **annex B of the protocol.** It should identify relevant documents (**para. 6.5**) and identify any other potential defendants (**para. 6.6**). A chronology, including dates of exposure to the substance alleged to be the cause of the complaint, should be sent with the letter of claim (**para. 6.4**). A schedule of special damages, with copies of supporting documents, should be sent to the defendant as soon as practicable, particularly where the defendant admits liability (**para. 8.1**). **8.29**

Response

The defendant should send an acknowledgment identifying any liability insurer within 21 calendar days of posting of the letter of claim (**Pre-action Protocol for Disease and Illness Claims, para.** 7.1). The defendant will need to investigate the claim, and must provide a reasoned answer to the letter of claim, stating the extent to which the claim is admitted or denied, within three months of the date of the acknowledgment letter (**para.** 7.3). Copies of documents material to the issues should be sent with the reply. If three months is insufficient time, the defendant may seek an agreed extension if there is a reasonable justification (**para.** 7.5). **8.30**

Experts in disease and illness claims

Expert evidence may be required dealing with: **8.31**

(a) knowledge, fault and causation;
(b) the claimant's condition and prognosis; and
(c) valuing aspects of the claim.

The **Pre-action Protocol for Disease and Illness Claims** recognises that it is important to adopt a flexible approach to the decisions that have to be made about obtaining expert evidence in these claims (**paras 9.2 and 9.3**). Joint selection, joint instruction, separate experts, and claimants disclosing medical evidence before defendants take a view on causation are all canvassed in the protocol. Different approaches may be appropriate for different issues within a claim. Care must be taken before the parties decide on instructing their own experts, because the court may subsequently rule that doing so was unreasonable (**para.** 9.7).

Commencing proceedings and negotiations

Proceedings should not be commenced within the three month investigation period unless there is a limitation problem or some other reason for needing to protect the claimant's position (**Pre-action Protocol for Disease and Illness Claims, paras 6.10 and 6.11**). Further, **8.32** the defendant should be given 21 days from disclosure of reports to allow for attempts to settle the claim without the need for proceedings (**paras 10.1 and 10.3**). With effect from 6 April 2006, **para. 2A.1** requires the parties to consider whether some form of ADR would be more suitable than litigation. Both sides may be required to provide the court with evidence that ADR was considered. Litigation is regarded as a last resort, and proceedings should not be issued while settlement is being actively explored. It is expressly recognised that the parties cannot be forced to mediate or enter into any form of ADR (**para. 2A.4**), but a failure to comply with the aim of **para. 2A.1** may be taken into account on costs.

Before proceedings are commenced the parties should carry out a 'stocktake' of the issues in dispute and the evidence required (**para. 10.2**). If an insurer is acting for the defendant, it is good practice to give the insurer seven to 14 days' notice to nominate solicitors to act in the proposed proceedings (**para. 10.5**).

HOUSING DISREPAIR PROTOCOL

8.33 The **Pre-action Protocol for Housing Disrepair Cases** came into force on 8 December 2003. It applies to all civil claims arising from the condition of residential premises (**para. 3.1**), except when raised as a counterclaim or set-off (because, by definition, a claim has already commenced, see **para. 4.2**). Where housing disrepair is raised by a counterclaim or set-off, the landlord and tenant will still be expected to act reasonably in exchanging information and trying to settle the claim at an early stage (**para. 4.2(a)**).

The protocol is aimed primarily at claims with a value between £1,000 and £15,000 (**para. 4.2(b)**), but applies also to claims which are likely to be allocated to the small claims track and multi-track. It applies to disrepair claims brought by tenants, members of the tenant's family (**para. 3.1(c)**), and to 'lessees', which is presumably a typographical error for licensees. The Housing Disrepair Protocol applies where the claim includes a personal injury element, and in these claims the **Pre-action Protocol for Personal Injury Claims** should be followed as well, unless the personal injury is relatively minor and suitable for being dealt with by reliance on a general practitioner's letter (**Pre-action Protocol for Housing Disrepair Cases, para. 4.4(d)**).

Early notification

8.34 As a matter of substantive law (see *O'Brien v Robinson* [1973] AC 912), the tenant must show that the landlord has received sufficient information about the alleged defects to put a reasonable person on inquiry as to whether repairs are necessary. Nothing in the **Pre-action Protocol for Housing Disrepair Cases** avoids this requirement, the protocol being aimed at seeking to resolve cases where the problem persists despite notice (**para. 4.3(a)**).

Under the protocol, where the landlord fails to remedy the situation despite knowing of the defects, the claimant should send an early notification letter to the landlord as soon as possible (**para. 3.2(a)**). Detailed requirements for this letter, which should include all the alleged defects, are set out in **para. 3.2(a)**, with a template letter at **annex A** and a template schedule of defects at **annex G**. It should request a copy of the tenancy agreement and copies of the landlord's documents dealing with notice of the defects and work done (**para. 3.2(b)**). **Paragraph 3.2** says that an early notification letter is not required in every case, but is a helpful tool.

Letter of Claim

8.35 A letter of claim should be sent at the earliest reasonable opportunity (**Pre-action Protocol for Housing Disrepair Cases, para. 3.3(a)**). Detailed requirements for the information to be included in this letter, in so far as it has not been given in an early notification letter, are set out in **para. 3.3(a)**, with template letters at **annex B**, a template schedule of special damages at

annex E, and a template schedule of defects at **annex G**. A letter of claim should identify the proposed expert, and enclose a proposed letter of instruction (in the form of the template at **annex C**). Copies of documents the tenant relies upon should also be enclosed, together with a list of the documents the tenant wishes the landlord to disclose.

Landlord's response

The landlord should provide a written response within 20 working days of receipt of the first letter from the tenant (**Pre-action Protocol for Housing Disrepair Cases, para. 3.5.1**). The letter should include copies of the landlord's disclosure documents and a response on appointing an expert (**para. 3.5.1**). This letter may state whether liability is admitted, take any point about lack of notice or difficulty in gaining access, include a full schedule of intended works, and any offer of compensation or costs, although a response on these points may be delayed until up to 20 working days from receipt of the report of a single joint expert (**para. 3.5.2**). **8.36**

Evidence

The **Pre-action Protocol for Housing Disrepair Cases** reminds tenants that photographic and video evidence may be useful in disrepair claims (**para. 3.6(a)**). **8.37**

Experts

There will be some cases where no expert evidence is required (**Pre-action Protocol for Housing Disrepair Cases, para. 3.6(a)**), but generally it is expected that the parties will agree on a single joint expert (**para. 3.6(d)**). The expert should be asked to report on all the defects the landlord ought reasonably to have known, or which the expert should reasonably report on, and should be asked to prepare a schedule of works and an estimate of the costs of repair, and to list any urgent works (**para. 3.6(b)**). If the parties cannot agree on a jointly instructed expert, the landlord should send the tenant a copy of its letter of instruction (the tenant having already done so, see **8.35**), and the parties should attempt to agree to a joint inspection of the premises (**para. 3.6(d), (e)**). The tenant should give reasonable access for inspection (and repairs) (**para. 3.6(k)**). **8.38**

Costs, negotiations and proceedings

If the tenant's claim is settled without proceedings on terms that justify raising the claim, the landlord 'will' pay the tenant's reasonable costs or out-of-pocket expenses (**Pre-action Protocol for Housing Disrepair Cases, para. 3.7(a)**). **Annex F to the protocol** is a standard statement of costs for this purpose. **8.39**

The purpose of the protocol is to prevent unnecessary proceedings, so the parties are required to consider whether some form of ADR would be more suitable than litigation (**para. 4.1(a)**, substituted with effect from 6 April 2006). Both sides may be required to provide the court with evidence that ADR was considered. A number of different ADR procedures that might be appropriate are set out in **para. 4.1(b)**. It is expressly recognised that the parties cannot be forced to mediate or enter into any form of ADR (**para. 4.1(d)**), but a failure to comply with the aim of **para. 4.1(a)** may be taken into account on costs. The parties will be expected to have attempted to agree a schedule of works, a timetable for implementation, and any claim for compensation before a claim is issued. If limitation is an issue, the tenant should ask for an extension of the limitation period in the first letter to the landlord. If this is refused, the court will decide whether this was reasonable (**para. 4.8**).

CONSTRUCTION AND ENGINEERING DISPUTES PROTOCOL

The **Pre-action Protocol for Construction and Engineering Disputes** applies to all construction and engineering disputes, including professional negligence claims against **8.40** architects, engineers and quantity surveyors. However, a claimant is not expected to follow the protocol where the proposed proceedings:

(a) are for the purpose of enforcing an adjudicator's decision under the Housing Grants, Construction and Regeneration Act 1996, s. 108;
(b) include a claim for an interim injunction;
(c) are expected to proceed to an application for summary judgment; or
(d) relate to the same or substantially the same issues as have been the subject of a recent adjudication under the 1996 Act or some other formal ADR procedure.

Requirements of the Construction and Engineering Protocol

8.41 The protocol timetable starts with a letter of claim being sent by the claimant to the proposed defendants (**Pre-action Protocol for Construction and Engineering Disputes, para. 3**). This should include details of all the proposed defendants, a clear summary of the facts on which the claim or claims are based, and the allegations forming the basis of each claim. This will include reference to the contractual terms and statutory provisions relied upon, the nature of the relief claimed, and a breakdown of how any damages are quantified or liquidated claim is calculated. If a claim has previously been made and rejected, the claimant must explain the reasons for disagreeing with the rejection of the claim. If any experts on whom the claimant wishes to rely have already been instructed, the letter of claim must include their names and state the issues to which the experts' evidence is directed.

The defendants should acknowledge receipt of the letter of claim within 14 days (**para. 4.1**). If there is no response, the claimant becomes entitled to issue proceedings. It may also be necessary for a claimant to issue proceedings at an early stage if the expiry of the limitation period is approaching (**para. 6**).

If a defendant intends to dispute the court's jurisdiction, or allege that the claim should be referred to arbitration, or allege that the wrong defendant has been identified, this should be made clear by a letter of objection which should be sent within 28 days after the letter of claim (**para. 4.2.1**). If a letter of objection is sent, there is no need to make a substantive response to the letter of claim (**para. 4.2. 2**). If there is no letter of objection, the defendants have to send a letter of response (**para. 4.3.1**). This should normally be sent within 28 days after the letter of claim, although the parties may agree to a longer period of up to four months. A letter of response will set out in detail which parts of the claim are agreed, which parts are rejected and why. If a defendant raises an allegation of contributory negligence, a summary of the facts relied on should be included in the letter of response and the claimant should reply with detailed responses within 28 days (**para. 4.4**).

After this correspondence has been completed, the parties should normally arrange a 'without prejudice' meeting to seek to agree what are the main issues, identify the root problem and consider how to resolve matters without recourse to litigation (**para. 5.2**). If litigation cannot be avoided, at the meeting the parties should seek to agree the steps they should take in accordance with the overriding objective, including how best to obtain any expert evidence that might be necessary, the extent of the disclosure of documents required, and how best to minimise costs and prevent delay (**para. 5.5**). Although the meeting is 'without prejudice', this does not prevent any of the parties disclosing that it did or did not take place, any refusal to attend and the result of any agreements made (**para. 5.6**).

DEFAMATION PROTOCOL

8.42 Since the primary limitation period for defamation claims is only one year, it is recognised that time is of the essence regarding pre-action skirmishing in this area. The claimant is, under the protocol, required to notify the defendant in writing of the claim at the earliest reasonable opportunity (**Pre-action Protocol for Defamation, para. 3.1**). The letter of claim should include as much detail as possible, including an identification of the publication or broadcast containing the words complained of, factual inaccuracies, where relevant, any facts tying the claimant to the alleged defamatory statement and any special facts relevant to interpretation, and the nature of the remedies sought (**para. 3.2**). The defendant is required to respond as soon as reasonably possible, and normally within 14 days (**para. 3.4**). The letter of response should say whether or the extent to which the claim is accepted. If the claim is rejected, the defendant should explain why, indicating any facts relied upon in support of any substantive defence. If more information is sought, this should be stated in the response (**para. 3.5**). Both parties are expected to act reasonably so as to keep costs proportionate, and should consider whether the matter could be referred to ADR (**paras 3.6** to **3.9**).

PROFESSIONAL NEGLIGENCE PRE-ACTION PROTOCOL

Introduction

The **Professional Negligence Pre-action Protocol** applies to any claim against a professional, other than a construction professional or healthcare provider, as a result of that professional's alleged negligence or breach of fiduciary duty, although there may be other types of claim for which the protocol is appropriate (**para. A1**). This protocol is not intended to replace existing alternative forms of dispute resolution, such as the Surveyors and Valuers Arbitration Scheme (**para. A3**). Indeed, parties are encouraged to use these procedures where available but to use the protocol where alternative procedures fail and prior to litigation (**para. A3**). The standards set in this protocol will be treated by the courts as the normal, reasonable approach in professional negligence cases (**para. A4**). The protocol contains no definition of 'professional'. Should it become an issue whether a defendant is or is not a professional, the parties are reminded of the overriding need to act reasonably and rather than argue about the definition of 'professional', it is recommended that they use the protocol, adapting it where appropriate (**para. C2.3**). **8.43**

Preliminary notice

Immediately there is a reasonable chance that a claim will be brought against a professional, the potential claimant is encouraged to notify the professional by letter, referred to as a preliminary notice (**Professional Negligence Pre-action Protocol, para. B1.1**) informing the recipient of the claimant's identity, a brief outline of the complaint against the professional and, if possible, an indication of the financial value of the claim (**para. B1.2**). The letter should also request the professional to notify his or her professional indemnity insurers, if any (**para. B1.3**). Receipt of the letter is required to be acknowledged by the professional within 21 days (**para. B1.4**). At this stage there is no obligation on the professional to take any further action (**para. B1.4**). **8.44**

Letter of claim

As soon as the claimant considers that there are grounds for a claim against the professional a detailed letter of claim should be sent (**Professional Negligence Pre-action Protocol, para. B2.1**). Normally a letter of claim should not be expressed to be without prejudice and it should include (**para. B2.2**): **8.45**

(a) the identity of any other parties to the dispute;
(b) a chronological summary of the facts on which the claim is based identifying and enclosing copies of key documents;
(c) acts and omissions alleged against the professional;
(d) explanation of how the error has caused the loss claimed;
(e) estimate and calculation of the loss together with documentary evidence in support or an explanation of why details of the loss cannot be supplied, if this is the case;
(f) whether the claimant seeks any form of non-financial redress;

(g) confirmation of whether or not an expert has been appointed and if so, the identity of the expert, his or her discipline and the date of appointment;
(h) request that the letter of claim is immediately forwarded to the professional's insurers.

Although the letter of claim is not intended to have the same status as a statement of case, if it differs materially from a statement of case in subsequent proceedings, the court may decide to impose sanctions (**para. B2.3**). Where the claimant has sent other letters of claim to other parties in relation to this or a related dispute, those letters should also be copied to the professional (**para. B2.4**). The letter of claim should be acknowledged by the professional in a letter of acknowledgment within 21 days of receipt (**para. B3.1**). If the claimant is claiming against a person to whom the protocol does not apply, there are a number of potential problems recognised in **para. C4.2**. It is possible that different protocols will apply to different defendants, that defendants will claim against each other, and that other parties will be drawn into the dispute. It is possible that the protocol timetable against one party will not be synchronised with the protocol timetable against a different party. Parties are expected to act reasonably, which will depend on the individual facts of each case (**para. C4.3**). The protocol does not provide solutions to specific problems but encourages parties to cooperate and to discuss how problems might be resolved.

Investigations

8.46 The professional will have three months from the date of the letter of acknowledgment to investigate the claim (**Professional Negligence Pre-action Protocol, para. B4.1**). Any difficulty in complying with that period should be notified to the claimant as soon as possible, together with an explanation of what is being done to resolve the problem and when the professional expects to complete the investigations. The claimant should agree to any reasonable request for an extension of the three-month period (**para. B4.2**). During this stage and throughout, the parties should provide each other with whatever relevant information or documentation is reasonably requested (**para. B4.3**). As with the other protocols, the early exchange of information is considered conducive to early settlement.

Letter of response and letter of settlement

8.47 As soon as the professional has completed his investigations, the claimant should be sent:

(a) a letter of response, or
(b) a letter of settlement, or
(c) both.

These may be contained within a single letter (**Professional Negligence Pre-action Protocol, para. B5.1**).

The letter of response will normally not be expressed to be without prejudice (**para. B5.2**). It should be a reasoned answer to the claimant's allegations. If the claim is admitted, the letter of response should say so.

If only part of the claim is admitted, the letter of response should make clear which parts of the claim are admitted and which are denied.

If the claim is denied in whole or in part, the letter of response should include specific comments on the allegations against the professional and, if the claimant's version of events is disputed, the professional should provide his or her version of events.

If the professional is unable to admit or deny the claim, any further information which is required should be identified.

If the professional disputes the estimate of the claimant's financial loss, the letter of response should set out the professional's estimate. If an estimate cannot be provided, the professional should explain why and should state when it will be possible to provide an estimate. This information should be sent to the claimant as soon as reasonably possible.

Where additional documents are relied upon in the letter of response, copies should be provided.

The letter of response is not intended to have the same formal status as a defence. However, if it differs materially from the defence in subsequent proceedings, the court may decide to impose sanctions (**para. B5.3**).

A letter of settlement will normally be a without-prejudice letter and should be sent if the professional intends to make proposals for settlement (**para. B5.4**). It should contain the professional's views on the claim identifying those issues which the professional believes are likely to remain in dispute and those which are not. This information is not required if the professional has sent a letter of response. The letter of settlement should contain a settlement proposal or identify any further information which is required before the professional can formulate proposals. Copies of additional documents should be provided where these are relied upon.

Effect of letter of response and/or letter of settlement

Where the letter of response denies the claim in its entirety and there is no letter of settlement, **8.48** it is open to the claimant to commence proceedings (**Professional Negligence Pre-action Protocol, para. B5.5**). Otherwise, the professional and the claimant should begin negotiations with the aim of reaching a conclusion within six months of the date of the letter of acknowledgment (*not* from the date of the letter of response) (**para. B5.6**). If the claim cannot be resolved within this period, the parties should agree within 14 days of the end of the period whether the period should be extended and, if so, by how long (**para. B5.7**). They should also identify the issues which remain in dispute and those which are agreed. If an extension of time for settlement negotiations cannot be agreed, the claimant may commence proceedings.

Alternative dispute resolution

With effect from 6 April 2006, the **Professional Negligence Pre-action Protocol, para. B6.1** **8.49** (replacing earlier provisions also dealing with ADR), requires the parties to consider whether some form of ADR would be more suitable than litigation. Both sides may be required to provide the court with evidence that ADR was considered. Litigation is regarded as a last resort, and proceedings should not be issued while settlement is being actively explored. It is expressly recognised that the parties cannot be forced to mediate or enter into any form of ADR (**para. B6.4**), but a failure to comply with the aim of **para. B6.1** may be taken into account on costs.

Experts

If the claimant has obtained expert evidence prior to sending the letter of claim, the **8.50** professional will have an equal right to obtain expert evidence prior to sending the letter of response and/or letter of settlement (**Professional Negligence Pre-action Protocol, para. B7.1**). If the claimant has not previously obtained expert evidence, the parties are encouraged to appoint a joint expert (**para. B7.2**). If they do so, they should seek to agree the identity of the expert and the terms of the expert's appointment (**para. B7.2**). In the event that such agreement cannot be reached, all parties are free to appoint their own experts (**para. B7.3**). The protocol recognises the range of complexity and amounts of financial loss that may be involved in professional negligence cases and is thus very flexible on the issue of experts, leaving it to the parties to reach agreement on the instruction of experts, their payment and how and to whom the expert should report.

Proceedings

Unless it is necessary, for example, to obtain protection against the expiry of a relevant **8.51** limitation period, court proceedings should not be commenced until the letter of response denies the claim in its entirety and there is no letter of settlement, or the period for negotiation has come to an end (**Professional Negligence Pre-action Protocol, para. B8.1**). If the claimant does intend to institute proceedings, where possible 14 days' written notice should be given to the professional, indicating the court within which the claimant is intending to commence litigation (**para. B8.2**). Proceedings should be served on the professional, unless the professional's solicitor has notified the claimant in writing that he or she is authorised to accept service on the professional's behalf (**para. B8.3**). If proceedings are commenced prior to the parties following the procedures in the protocol, they are encouraged to agree to apply to the court for a stay of proceedings while the protocol procedures are followed (**para. C7.2**).

CASES NOT SUBJECT TO SPECIFIC PRE-ACTION PROTOCOLS

8.52 The pre-action protocols are drafted to apply to specific types of claim, but the approach which they embody should be applied generally. For example, although the **Pre-action Protocol for Personal Injury Claims** is designed to facilitate either negotiation or more expeditious and efficiently managed litigation in the fast track, 'The spirit, if not the letter of the protocol' should be followed in higher-value claims (**para. 2.4**). 'In accordance with the sense of the civil justice reforms, the court will expect to see the spirit of reasonable pre-action behaviour applied in all cases, regardless of the existence of a specific protocol' (**para. 2.4**).

PD Protocols, para. 4.1, provides:

> In cases not covered by any approved protocol, the court will expect the parties, in accordance with the overriding objective and the matters referred to in **CPR, r. 1.1(2)(a), (b) and (c)**, to act reasonably in exchanging information and documents relevant to the claim and generally in trying to avoid the necessity for the start of proceedings.

The parties should follow a reasonable procedure, suitable to the particular circumstances of the case (**PD Protocols, para. 4.2**). For a summary of the steps required when there is no specific pre-action protocol see **procedural checklist 2**, which is in **appendix 1**. For more detail see 8.53 and 8.54

Letter of claim

8.53 The claimant should send a detailed letter of claim enclosing copies of the essential documents and asking for an acknowledgment within 21 days and a full response within a stated period (**PD Protocols, paras 4.2 and 4.3**). It is generally inappropriate to commence proceedings without at the very least a letter before action, unless the matter is one of extreme urgency. A claimant who brings and loses a claim without having sent a letter before action may be ordered to pay costs on the indemnity basis, even if the claim is not covered by a specific protocol (*Phoenix Finance Ltd v Fédération Internationale de l'Automobile* [2002] EWHC 1028 (Ch), *The Times*, 27 June 2002). In *Reid v Capita Group plc* [2005] EWHC 2448 (Ch), LTL 17/10/2005, the claimant brought proceedings to obtain documents relating to a commercial transaction without having sent a letter of claim, and without having identified the documents sought. It was held the proceedings were premature, and the claimant was ordered to pay the defendant's costs of the proceedings.

It is suggested that in all cases a letter of claim be sent to the potential defendant which sets out a clear and concise summary of the facts on which a claim may be based, together with details of the remedy sought. In *King v Telegraph Group Ltd* [2004] EWCA Civ 613, [2005] 1 WLR 2282, solicitors who sent a 10-page letter of claim, settled by junior counsel (at [60]), failed to comply with the spirit of cooperation required by the protocols. Among other things it accused the newspaper of cant, reckless falsehood, and a malicious agenda of incriminating misrepresentation. Its effect was to remove the prospect of conciliation between the parties, making litigation almost inevitable.The proposed defendant may not be represented at this stage and therefore the letter should state that independent legal advice should be sought. The letter should indicate what, if any, information is required from the potential defendant.

The letter should also state the date by which a reply is sought, and provide ample time for the potential defendant to supply any information sought by the proposed claimant. It should be made clear in the letter that if the proposed defendant fails to respond or fails to respond within the period given, the potential claimant may issue proceedings without further notification. The length of time which should be allowed by the potential claimant for the potential defendant to investigate the claim and for the early exchange of information will depend on the complexity of the issues raised by the claim. Normally this will be one month (**para. 4.3**) but for many claims a three-month investigation period would not be unreasonable. In a simple debt case it may be reasonable to stipulate seven or 14 days for the response.

Subsequent steps

The defendant's full response should say whether liability is accepted in full or in part or denied (**PD Protocols, para. 4.5**). If liability is denied, the response must give detailed reasons and enclose the essential documents relied upon (**para. 4.6**). In defended cases, both sides: **8.54**

(a) are entitled to ask for copies of documents in the possession of the other side, which must not be used by the recipient for purposes other than resolving the dispute (**para. 4.8**);
(b) should state whether they are prepared to enter into mediation or some other method of dispute resolution (**paras 4.3(f) and 4.6(e)**);
(c) should consider appointing an agreed expert if expert evidence is required (**para. 4.9**).

With effect from 6 April 2006, a new **para. 4.7** imposes a duty on both sides to consider whether some form of ADR would be more suitable than litigation. Both sides may be required to provide evidence that ADR was considered. While it is recognised that no party can be forced to mediate or enter into any form of ADR, there is a warning in the new **para. 4.7** that a failure to comply with the protocol will be taken into account on the question of costs.

Chapter 9 Notices before Action

LETTER OF CLAIM

9.1 Whether a claim is governed by a pre-action protocol or not, and unless urgent or secret relief is being sought, a letter of claim should be sent before proceedings are issued. This is necessary either to comply with an applicable protocol, or to comply with the general ethos of the protocols (see **chapter 8**). The court has a discretion to order a claimant who issues proceedings without giving warning to the other side to pay indemnity-basis costs (*Phoenix Finance Ltd v Fédération Internationale de l'Automobile* [2002] EWHC 1028 (Ch), *The Times*, 27 June 2002; and see **8.53**).

ROAD TRAFFIC CASES

Introduction

9.2 A person who sustains injury in a road traffic accident has a cause of action against a negligent driver but not against his or her insurers. Damages may be recovered direct from the insurers provided the claimant gives the insurers notice of the proceedings against the defendant driver either before or within seven days after the commencement of the proceedings (Road Traffic Act 1988, s. 152). The phrase 'commencement of proceedings' has its ordinary meaning (*Silver v Goodall* [1997] PIQR P451). The **Pre-action Protocol for Personal Injury Claims, para. 3.4**, states that a letter of claim should ask a potential defendant for insurance details.

Notice must be something more formal than a casual mention of proceedings in conversation (*Herbert v Railway Passengers Assurance Co.* [1938] 1 All ER 650). However, notice given in a telephone conversation, dealing mainly with obtaining details of the insured driver, with a secretary employed by the insurer was held to be sufficient in *Nawaz v Crowe Insurance Group* [2003] EWCA Civ 316, *The Times*, 11 March 2003. A loosely written letter may not be sufficient notice (*Weldrick v Essex and Suffolk Equitable Insurance Society Ltd* (1949) 83 Ll L Rep 91, in which the letter which purported to give notice was found to be no more than an intimation that proceedings might be brought).

A pre-action protocol letter of claim is insufficient notification of the proceedings for the purposes of the Road Traffic Act 1988, s. 152(1)(a) (*Wylie v Wake* [2000] RTR 291). Lack of notice may be raised as a defence at any stage of the proceedings and the fact that a claim has been defended on its merits does not constitute a waiver of lack of notice (*Wylie v Wake*).

Motor Insurers' Bureau

9.3 It sometimes happens that a claimant sustains injury in a road traffic accident arising out of the negligence of a driver who is uninsured or untraceable. In return for the business generated by compulsory motor insurance, the insurance industry has set up the Motor Insurers' Bureau (MIB) to enable claimants to obtain compensation in circumstances in which they would be unable to bring effective proceedings. There are two agreements between the MIB and the Minister for Transport, one dealing with uninsured drivers and the other with untraced drivers. For more details see Donald B. Williams, *Guide to Motor Insurers' Bureau Claims*, 8th ed. (London: Blackstone Press, 2000).

Uninsured drivers

Under the Motor Insurers' Bureau (Compensation of Victims of Uninsured Drivers) Agreement 1999, the claimant must satisfy a number of conditions in order for the MIB to pay an award of damages in respect of an uninsured driver. Provided the claim is one that the MIB is obliged to satisfy and the claimant fulfils the requisite conditions, the MIB will pay any award of damages if the judgment is not satisfied within seven days. Two conditions of the agreement are particularly relevant to pre-action conduct. First, under cl. 13(a) of the agreement, the claimant must have demanded the information, and where appropriate, the particulars, specified in the Road Traffic Act 1988, s. 154, in accordance with that section or, if so required by MIB, have authorised MIB to do so on the claimant's behalf. Section 154 requires the person against whom a claim is made to provide the claimant with details of the name and address of his insurers, details of his insurance and the policy number. This can be dealt with very simply in the letter of claim. The MIB does not have to wait for a judgment to be obtained before intervening in a case. Claimants may wish to apply to the MIB before the commencement of proceedings, but any claim must comply with cl. 7 of the agreement. This means that the claim must be in the form required by the MIB and must give such information about the proceedings and other relevant matters and be accompanied by such documents as the MIB may require. Wherever possible, claims should be made on the MIB application form, accompanied by supporting documents. Using the correct forms is likely to avoid delays occurring in the claim being processed. **9.4**

A further condition is that the claimant must give written notice of proceedings to the MIB or identified insurer not later than 14 days after commencement of proceedings and that such notice should be accompanied by a copy of the sealed claim form, particulars of claim, schedule of past and future loss and expense, medical report and and any other relevant documents, for example, correspondence with the defendant. A pre-action protocol letter of claim is insufficient notification of the proceedings for these purposes (*Wylie v Wake* [2000] RTR 291, a case under the Road Traffic Act 1988, s. 152(1)(a)). The particulars of claim, schedule and medical report may, alternatively, be served within seven days after service on the defendant (cl. 9(3)). Furthermore, notice of service of the claim form must be given to the MIB or identified insurer within seven days of notification by the court (or 14 days of deemed service) (see cl. 10). It is recommended that the claimant's notice, if sent by post, be sent by recorded delivery, which will provide confirmation to the claimant that the notice has in fact been received by the MIB. The MIB does, however, prefer service by fax because it is speedy and can be confirmed equally quickly. Service of documents by DX is not permitted.

Under cl. 6(1)(e)(ii) of the uninsured drivers' agreement, the MIB is absolved from liability where the injured passenger 'knew or ought to have known' that the vehicle was uninsured. Article 1(4) of the Second Council Directive (84/5/EEC) (to which the uninsured drivers' agreement is intended to give effect) entitles member States to exclude liability only if the injured person 'knew' the vehicle was uninsured. This was held by the House of Lords in *White v White* [2001] 1 WLR 481 to include actual knowledge and cases where the injured party deliberately refrained from asking questions about the insured status of the vehicle. It does not cover cases where the passenger was careless or negligent about whether the vehicle was insured. This exception of the MIB from liability does not apply unless the passenger's presence in the vehicle was voluntary. A passenger who knows the driver is uninsured on entering a vehicle will continue being voluntarily in the vehicle until he or she either gets out or unequivocally requests the driver to stop (*Pickett v Roberts* [2004] EWCA Civ 6, [2004] 1 WLR 2450).

Untraced drivers

9.5 The MIB's other agreement with the Minister of Transport seeks to provide compensation for any victim of any untraced driver. The current agreement relating to untraced drivers, was concluded in 2003 and applies to accidents on or after 14 February 2003. The European Court of Justice has decided that the untraced drivers' agreement broadly complies with Council Directive 84/5/EEC (*Evans v Secretary of State for the Environment, Transport and the Regions* (case C-63/01) [2005] All ER (EC) 763). The Court pointed out, however, that art. 1(4) of the Directive has to be interpreted to mean that compensation awarded under the agreement must take account of the passage of time between the accident and payment. This is now provided for by cl. 9 of the 2003 agreement. Costs need not be included in the scheme, unless reimbursement of costs is necessary to safeguard the rights derived from the Directive (see cl. 10 of the 2003 agreement).

An application arising out of an accident alleged to have been caused by an untraced driver must be made within three years of the accident where the application includes a claim for compensation for personal injuries or death, or within nine months of the accident where the claim is limited to compensation for damage to property (cl. 4(3)(a)). The applicant must, unless this was not reasonably possible, have reported the accident to the police within 14 days of the accident (within five days if limited to damage to property (cl. 4(3)(c)). When it receives the application, the MIB makes a preliminary investigation (cl. 7(1)(a)) to decide whether the case is one to which the agreement applies and whether there is, in addition to the untraced driver, a second person partly liable for the accident (for which see cl. 13). If the preliminary investigation indicates that the agreement applies and that cl. 13 does not apply, the MIB may notify the applicant that it is using the accelerated procedure in cl. 26 and make an offer to settle the claim. The offer will include reasons for the assessment of the award. The applicant then has six weeks to notify the MIB whether the offer is accepted or rejected. If the offer is accepted, the MIB has to pay the compensation within the next 14 days, and is discharged from all liability under the agreement (cl. 27).

If the accelerated procedure is not adopted by the MIB, or if the applicant rejects an offer made under that procedure, the MIB arranges for a full investigation to be made of the accident by a delegated member of the Bureau. The subsequent report enables the MIB to decide whether an award will be made and if so, the amount of that award. Decisions are based on ordinary principles of negligence and quantification of damage, but with some minor adjustments regarding quantum, as they would apply to the accident (cl. 8).

Under the normal procedure, the MIB's decision is sent, together with reasons, to the claimant (cl. 16). If the claimant does not disagree with the decision or the amount of any award within the period of six weeks from the notice of the decision, the MIB will pay the award to the claimant. An applicant who is unwilling to accept the MIB's decision or determination has six weeks from being notified by the MIB of its decision to send a written notice of appeal to the MIB (cl. 19(1)). The matter will then be referred to arbitration in accordance with cll. 19 to 25 of the agreement.

Procedure on Motor Insurers' Bureau claims

9.6 The agreements are between the MIB and the Minister of Transport. Claimants are not parties to the agreements, though the agreements were clearly made for their benefit and the MIB has never tried to rely on the lack of privity of a claimant as a defence to a claim, because doing so would make the agreements pointless. In *Albert v Motor Insurers' Bureau* [1972] AC 301 Lord Donovan said:

> The question immediately suggests itself as to how the appellant as a third party can claim the benefit of this agreement. The point was looked at in *Hardy v Motor Insurers' Bureau* [1964] 2 QB 745 where, at p. 757,

Lord Denning MR remarks that the agreement is on the face of it a contract between two parties for the benefit of a third, and that no point was taken by the Bureau that the agreement was not enforceable by the third person.

Diplock LJ also considered the matter in *Gurtner v Circuit* [1968] 2 QB 587, saying that on a number of occasions the court had turned a blind eye to the position and that unless the point were specifically raised the court was 'entitled to proceed upon the assumption that the Bureau has, before action is brought, contracted for good consideration with the [claimant] to perform the obligations specified in its contract with the Minister or has by its conduct raised an estoppel which would bar it from relying on absence of privity of contract'.

As the uninsured drivers agreement was made before the Contracts (Rights of Third Parties) Act 1999 was passed it is not covered by the Act, but it is clear that when it is renewed it will be.

The effective paying party in uninsured drivers cases is the MIB, but the named defendant will be the driver, who will often play no active role in the litigation. It is therefore common practice for the court to grant permission for the MIB to be added as a defendant under what is now **CPR, r. 19.2(2)(a)** (see *Gurtner v Circuit* [1968] 2 QB 587). The same does not apply to untraced drivers (see *White v London Transport Executive* [1971] 2 QB 721).

There is no formal procedure for making claims to the MIB under either of the agreements. The notification of the claim may usually be made in a letter to the MIB from the claimant or the claimant's legal representatives, after which the MIB sends out a claim form which should be completed and returned. The rest is up to the MIB, either in the case of untraced drivers to appoint a member to investigate or in the case of uninsured drivers to make enquiries of anyone such as witnesses and experts who may be able to piece together the accident. In cases where the driver is untraced, there is little a victim can do but apply to the MIB for assistance. In the case of the uninsured driver, however, claimants and those representing them would do well to make their own enquiries to ensure that there was no insurance cover at the time of the accident. The MIB should not be notified unless and until the claimant is aware of the true position, in order to avoid time being wasted and unnecessary expense.

LANDLORD AND TENANT NOTICES

Various pre-action notices must be given in landlord and tenant disputes. These include: **9.7**

(a) *Notice to quit.* This is a means of terminating a periodic tenancy. At common law, notice to quit could be given orally, but had to be of the correct length (generally that corresponding to a period of the tenancy, although for tenancies from year to year, only six months' notice was required). Difficulties of proof have resulted in notices to quit invariably being given in writing. In relation to residential premises, the notice must set out certain prescribed information (see **chapter 90**).
(b) *Statutory notices in claims for possession of residential property.* There are different statutory codes dealing with security of tenure for residential tenants (see **chapters 85** to **88**). Before possession proceedings can be brought, various forms of notice must be served on the tenant, which are described more fully in the relevant chapters.
(c) *Business tenancies.* There is a regime of serving pre-action notices and counter-notices in relation to the termination of business tenancies and seeking new business leases under the **Landlord and Tenant Act 1954, part II** (see **chapter 91**).
(d) *Law of Property Act 1925, s. 146.* This section provides that where the landlord seeks to enforce a right of re-entry or forfeiture for breach of covenant or condition (other than non-payment of rent), the landlord must first serve a notice specifying the breach; requiring it to be remedied (if capable of remedy) within a reasonable, specified, time; and

requiring the payment of any compensation. For further details, see works on landlord and tenant law.

(e) *Notice of disrepair.* In a claim for housing disrepair, whether brought for breach of the tenancy agreement or in tort, the tenant must show that the landlord has received sufficient information about the alleged defects to put a reasonable person on inquiry as to whether repairs are necessary (*O'Brien v Robinson* [1973] AC 912). A landlord will be assumed to have notice of defects in the common parts of a building as these areas are under the landlord's care and control (*British Telecommunications plc v Sun Life Assurance plc* [1996] Ch 69).

BILLS OF EXCHANGE

Notice of dishonour

9.8 A claim against a person for liability on a bill of exchange which has been dishonoured by non-acceptance or non-payment cannot be made unless notice of dishonour has been given (Bills of Exchange Act 1882, s. 48). Notice must be sent off on the day after dishonour, or, if there is no convenient post on that day, by the next post, unless the person giving, and the person to be given, the notice reside in the same place, in which case notice must be sent off in time to reach the latter on the day after dishonour (s. 49(12)).

Section 50(2) provides several exceptions from the requirement to give notice of dishonour. In particular, it dispenses with the need to give notice of dishonour in practically all instances where a cheque (which is a bill of exchange drawn on a banker payable on demand: s. 73) is dishonoured by non-payment. (There is no need to present a cheque for acceptance: s. 39.) Normally the only person liable on a dishonoured cheque is the drawer and usually it is not necessary to give notice of dishonour to the drawer of a cheque because s. 50(2)(c)(4) provides that notice is dispensed with if the drawee (the bank) is under no obligation (as between drawee and drawer) to pay the cheque, and normally this is the only reason why a cheque is dishonoured. A bank has no obligation to pay its customer's cheque if, for example, there are insufficient funds in the account on which the cheque is drawn, or the customer has countermanded (stopped) payment (ss. 50(2)(c)(5) and 75) or the bank has notice that the customer has died (s. 75). The answer given on the cheque when it is returned by the paying bank will indicate whether any of these apply.

If notice of dishonour of a bill of exchange is not dispensed with by s. 50(2), the notice, in order to be valid and effectual, must be given in accordance with the rules in s. 49.

Notice can be given only by or on behalf of the holder of the bill, or by or on behalf of an endorser who is at the time liable on the bill (s. 49(1)), but written notice need not be signed (s. 49(7)). Notice may be given to a duly authorised agent of the party sought to be made liable (s. 49(8)).

There is no prescribed form of notice, which need not even be written, but it must sufficiently identify the bill and state whether the dishonour was by non-acceptance or non-payment (s. 49(5)). If notice is given of non-acceptance, it is unnecessary to give a further notice of non-payment, unless the bill has been accepted in the meantime (s. 48, proviso (2)). In fact there is no need to present a non-accepted bill for payment (s. 43(2)). Misdescription of the bill does not vitiate the notice unless the recipient of the notice has in fact been misled by it (s. 49(7)). Simply returning the bill to the drawer or an endorser is sufficient notice (s. 49(6)), but in practice it is usual to retain possession of the bill for the purposes of taking proceedings on it.

Notice of dishonour must be given within a reasonable time after the dishonour (s. 49(12)). In the absence of special circumstances, notice is not deemed to have been given within a reasonable time, unless (s. 49(12)):

(a) where the person giving, and the person to receive, notice reside in the same place, the notice is given or sent off in time to reach the latter on the day after the dishonour;
(b) otherwise, the notice is sent off on the day after the dishonour, unless there is no post at a convenient time on that day, in which case it must be sent by the next post.

Whether persons are in the same place for the purposes of s. 49(12)(a) seems to be determined by facilities for travel rather than administrative boundaries (*Hamilton Finance Co. Ltd v Coverley Westry Walbaum and Tosetti Ltd* [1969] 1 Lloyd's Rep 53, in which Upper Brook Street, London W1 and Seething Lane EC3 were held to be in the same place as they are 'a modest bus or tube journey apart, both in the central area').

Where a notice of dishonour is duly addressed and posted, the sender is deemed to have given due notice of dishonour, 'notwithstanding any miscarriage by the post office' (s. 49(15)).

Where a bill which has been dishonoured is in the hands of an agent, for example, a bank collecting payment for its customer, notice of dishonour may be given by the agent either direct to the person liable on the bill or to the agent's principal, who then has a reasonable time (as specified in s. 49(12), see above) to give notice to the person liable (s. 49(13)).

Delay in giving notice of dishonour is excused where the delay is caused by circumstances beyond the control of the party giving notice (s. 50(1)).

Section 50(2) lists circumstances in which notice of dishonour is not required. They are:

(a) when, after the exercise of reasonable diligence, notice as required by the Act cannot be given or does not reach the drawer or endorser sought to be made liable;
(b) where it has been waived (waiver may be express or implied and may be after notice should have been given).

Notice to the drawer is not required where (s. 50(2)(c)):

(a) drawer and drawee are the same person (as with a bank draft);
(b) the drawee is fictitious or has no capacity to contract;
(c) presentation was to the drawer;
(d) as between drawee/acceptor and drawer, the drawee/acceptor is under no obligation to pay/accept the bill (see above, in relation to cheques);
(e) the drawer has countermanded payment.

Notice to an endorser is not required where (s. 50(2)(d)):

(a) at the time of endorsing the bill the endorser was aware that the drawee was fictitious or had no capacity to contract;
(b) presentation was to the endorser;
(c) the bill was drawn or accepted for the accommodation of the endorser.

Notice given by or on behalf of the holder of a bill enures for the benefit of all prior endorsers who have a right of recourse against the person notified, and also for the benefit of any subsequent holder (s. 49(3)). Notice given by or on behalf of an endorser enures for the benefit of the holder and all subsequent endorsers (s. 49(4)).

Protesting foreign bills

A foreign bill which has been dishonoured by non-acceptance must be protested for non-acceptance, and a foreign bill which is dishonoured by non-payment must be protested for non-payment, unless it has been previously dishonoured by non-acceptance (Bills of Exchange Act 1882, s. 51(2)). A foreign bill is a bill of exchange which is not an inland bill (s. 4) and an inland bill is one which is either (a) both drawn and payable within the British Islands or (b) drawn within the British Islands upon some person resident in the British Islands. The British Islands are the United Kingdom, the Isle of Man and the Channel Islands **9.9**

(s. 4(1)). Failure to protest a foreign bill discharges the liability of the drawer and endorsers. A protest is made by a notary public in the form prescribed in s. 51(7). It is usual to ask a notary to note a dishonoured bill, which must be done on the day of dishonour or the next business day (s. 51(4)), so that a later protest will take effect, under s. 51(4), as from the date of noting. Protest is required in addition to notice of dishonour and is dispensed with in the same circumstances (s. 51(9)).

Letter before claim on a bill of exchange

9.10 Even if a statutory notice of dishonour of a bill of exchange is not required, in a letter of claim sent before proceedings are started, the dishonoured bill should be identified and a photocopy provided, the nature of the dishonour should be stated and the amount claimed should be set out in detail.

DEMANDS IN MONEY CLAIMS

9.11 In the case of a bank owing money to a customer (perhaps being money held to the customer's credit on a current or deposit account), subject to contrary agreement, a demand from the customer is a condition precedent to repayment (*N. Joachimson v Swiss Bank Corporation* [1921] 3 KB 110) and the demand must be made at the branch where the account is kept (*Clare and Co. v Dresdner Bank* [1915] 2 KB 576). In all other situations where money has been borrowed with no time specified for repayment, including lending repayable on demand (such as bank overdrafts, which, subject to contrary agreement, are repayable on demand: *Paget's Law of Banking*, 11th ed. (1996), p. 167, citing *Titford Property Co. Ltd v Cannon Street Acceptances Ltd* (22 May 1975, ChD, unreported)), at common law the demand was not regarded as a condition precedent to repayment (*Re Brown's Estate* [1893] 2 Ch 300; *Bradford Old Bank v Sutcliffe* [1918] 2 KB 833). This meant that the limitation period ran from the time of making the loan. However, the effect of the **Limitation Act 1980, s. 6**, is that in relation to loans which are not for a fixed term, time only starts running for limitation purposes from the making of a demand. Demands have a further importance in lending cases, because under the terms of any security agreements (such as guarantees and mortgages), resort to the security or the right to appoint a receiver is usually only possible after a demand has been made.

To be effective, a demand must be a clear intimation that payment is required. It must be peremptory in character and unconditional, but the language used is immaterial, and the word 'demand' need not be used (*Re Colonial Finance, Mortgage, Investment and Guarantee Corporation Ltd* (1905) 6 SR (NSW) 6, followed in *Re a Company* [1985] BCLC 37). However, it need not state the amount to be repaid (*Bank of Baroda v Panessar* [1987] Ch 335).

In England and Wales the rule is that a borrower of money repayable on demand must have the money ready to repay at all times, so that the only time that need be allowed between making a demand and regarding the borrower as being in default is the time necessary to effect the mechanics of payment, and if it is known that the borrower has not got the money then no time at all need be allowed (*Sheppard and Cooper Ltd v TSB Bank plc* [1996] 2 All ER 654). The commercially unrealistic mechanics-of-payment test has been rejected in Canada in favour of a reasonable-time test, and may be due for re-examination at appellate level in England (see *Lloyds Bank plc v Lampert* [1999] BCC 507).

A claim for restitution after rescission of a contract cannot be made until notice of rescission has been given, but no demand is necessary before claiming restitution in a case of unjust enrichment (*Fuller v Happy Shopper Markets Ltd* [2001] 1 WLR 1681).

NOTICE OF ASSIGNMENT

Where there has been a legal assignment of a debt or other thing in action, express written notice must be given to the debtor or other person against whom the right can be enforced. See the Law of Property Act 1925, s. 136, and **14.26**. **9.12**

DIRECTOR DISQUALIFICATION

A person intending to apply to a county court or the High Court for a disqualification order (generally the Secretary of State for Trade and Industry) is required to give 10 days' notice of this intention to the former director against whom the order is to be sought (Company Directors Disqualification Act 1986, s. 16(1)). An application made without giving the correct period of notice is not a nullity (*Secretary of State for Trade and Industry v Langridge* [1991] Ch 402), but may be an abuse of process, for which one possible sanction would be to strike out the claim (*Secretary of State for Trade and Industry v Swan* [2003] EWHC 1780 (Ch), [2004] BCC 877, at [93]). **9.13**

Chapter 10 Limitation

INTRODUCTION

10.1 Expiry of a limitation period provides a defendant with a complete defence to an action. Lord Griffiths in *Donovan v Gwentoys Ltd* [1990] 1 WLR 472 said, 'The primary purpose of the limitation period is to protect a defendant from the injustice of having to face a stale claim, that is a claim with which he never expected to have to deal'. If a claim is brought a long time after the events in question, the likelihood is that evidence which may have been available earlier may have been lost, and the memories of witnesses who may still be available will inevitably have faded or become confused. Further, it is contrary to general policy to keep people perpetually at risk.

Limitation is a procedural defence. It will not be taken by the court of its own motion, but must be specifically set out in the defence (**PD 16, para. 13.1**). Time-barred cases rarely go to trial. If the claimant is unwilling to discontinue the claim (see **chapter 53**), it is usually possible for the defendant to apply successfully for the claim to be struck out (see **chapter 33**) as an abuse of the court's process.

Normally, the only consequence of the expiry of a limitation period is that the defendant acquires a technical defence to the claim. The claimant still has a cause of action, but one that cannot be enforced. In cases of adverse possession of land and conversion, expiry of the limitation period has the additional consequence of extinguishing the party's title to the land or goods.

LIMITATION PERIODS

Most limitation periods are laid down in the **Limitation Act 1980** (LA1980) as amended. **10.2**
Several other statutes lay down limitation periods, and some procedural rules impose time limits which act rather like limitation periods. There has been a move in recent legislation towards flexible limitation periods for some types of cases, which will be considered at **10.42** to **10.50**. However, the usual rule is that no objection can be taken to a claim started on the last day of the limitation period, but there is a complete defence if proceedings are issued one day late. Time runs until the issue of the claim form in the present proceedings. An earlier claim form based on the same alleged cause of action which is not proceeded with does not affect the question whether the claim form in the present claim was issued before limitation expired (*Markfield Investments Ltd v Evans* [2001] 1 WLR 1321). **Table 10.1** sets out the limitation periods for the most important classes of cases.

Cases outside the Limitation Act 1980

A claim which is outside the provisions of the **Limitation Act 1980** is not subject to a strict **10.3**
period of limitation (*Nelson v Rye* [1996] 1 WLR 1378). It may, however, be subject to a time limit by analogy to the **LA 1980** (see **LA 1980, s. 36**, and *Coulthard v Disco Mix Club Ltd* [1999] 2 All ER 457), or it may be subject to the defences of laches and acquiescence (as in *Nelson v Rye* [1996] 1 WLR 1378, but see the discussion at **10.4**). For example, a claim against a mortgagee for failing to obtain a proper price on the sale of mortgaged property was held to be governed by a six-year limitation period by analogy with **LA 1980, s. 2**, in *Raja v Lloyds TSB Bank plc* (2000) *The Times*, 16 May 2000. In *Companhia de Seguros Imperio v Heath (REBX) Ltd* [2001] 1 WLR 112 a six-year limitation period was imposed on a claim for breach of fiduciary duty, by analogy with **LA 1980, ss. 2** and **5**. A six-year time limit applies to a claim for specific performance of a contract by analogy with **LA 1980, s. 5** (*P and O Nedlloyd BV v Arab Metals Co.* [2005] EWHC 1276 (Comm), [2005] 1 WLR 3733). Undue influence claims fall outside the LA 1980 (*Clarke v Marlborough Fine Art (London) Ltd* (2001) *The Times*, 5 July 2001, but see **10.52** below). Further, if there is no limitation period, the court may still strike out the proceedings as an abuse of process. In *Taylor v Ribby Hall Leisure Ltd* [1998] 1 WLR 400 an application to commit was delayed by about five years. It was struck out, the court taking into account factors such as the prospects of the court exercising its supervisory powers at the hearing, and the public interest in the efficient administration of justice and the compliance with court orders and undertakings.

Breach of trust

The main limitation periods are six years in claims for breach of trust and to recover trust **10.4**
property (**LA 1980, s. 21(3)**), and the unlimited period for bringing claims in respect of any fraud or fraudulent breach of trust to which the trustee was party or privy (**s. 21(1)(a)**) and for claims to recover from a trustee trust property in the possession of the trustee or which was previously received by the trustee and converted to the trustee's use (**s. 21(1)(b)**). A claim for an account of profits against a director following a deliberate non-disclosure of an interest was held in *Gwembe Valley Development Co. Ltd v Koshy (No. 3)* [2003] EWCA Civ 1478, [2004] 1 BCLC 131, to be a fraudulent breach of trust within **s. 21(1)(a)**, with the result, there was no period of limitation. It was held that a breach of trust was fraudulent if it was dishonest. *J. J. Harrison (Properties) Ltd v Harrison* [2001] EWCA Civ 1467, [2002] 1 BCLC 162, in which it was held

Table 10.1 Limitation periods

Class of claim		Limitation period
1	Fraudulent breach of trust	None (LA 1980, s. 21(1))
2	Recovery of land	12 years (LA 1980, s. 15(1))
3	Recovery of money secured by mortgage	12 years (LA 1980, s. 20(1))
4	Specialty	12 years (LA 1980, s. 8(1))
5	Recovery of a sum due under statute	6 years (LA 1980, s. 9(1))
6	Enforcement of a judgment	6 years (LA 1980, s. 24(1))
7	Contract	6 years (LA 1980, s. 5)
8	Recovery of trust property and breach of trust	6 years (LA 1980, s. 21(3))
9	Recovery of arrears of rent	6 years (LA 1980, s. 19)
10	Tort (except those listed below)	6 years (LA 1980, s. 2)
11	Defective Premises Act 1972 claims	6 years (Defective Premises Act 1972, s. 1(5))
12	Personal injuries claims	3 years (LA 1980, s. 11(4))
13	**Fatal Accidents Act 1976** claims	3 years (LA 1980, s. 12(2))
14	Personal injuries or damage to property claims under the Consumer Protection Act 1987	3 years (LA 1980, s.11A)
15	Carriage by Air Act 1961 claims	2 years (Carriage by Air Act 1961, sch. 1)
16	Claims for personal injuries or damage to vessel, cargo or property or personal injuries to passengers at sea	2 years (Merchant Shipping Act 1995, s. 190(3) and sch. 6, part I, art. 16)
17	Disqualification of company directors under the Company Directors Disqualification Act 1986, s. 6	2 years (Company Directors Disqualification Act 1986, s. 7(2))
18	Contribution under the **Civil Liability (Contribution) Act 1978**	2 years (LA 1980, s. 10(1))
19	Contribution under the Maritime Conventions Act 1911	1 year (Merchant Shipping Act 1995, s. 190(4))
20	Carriage of Goods by Road Act 1965 claims	1 year (Carriage of Goods by Road Act 1965, sch., art. 32)
21	Defamation and malicious falsehood	1 year (**LA 1980, s. 4A**)
22	Applications for judicial review	3 months (**CPR, r. 54.5**)
23	Unfair dismissal under the Employment Rights Act 1996	3 months (Employment Rights Act 1996, s. 111(2))
24	Applications for new business tenancies under the **Landlord and Tenant Act 1954, Part II**	If made by the tenant, not before 2 months after the tenant's request for a new tenancy under s. 26 (s. 29A(3)), and whether by the tenant or landlord, not after the date specified in any s. 25 notice or the day before the date specified in any s. 26 request (s. 29A(2))
25	Claims for an account	Period applicable to claim on which account is based (LA 1980, s. 23)

that a claim to recover property conveyed to a director who was in breach of fiduciary duty came within **s. 21(1)(b)** (also resulting in there being no limitation period), was distinguished in *Gwembe Valley Development Co. Ltd v Koshy (No. 3)*. In *Re Pantone 485 Ltd, Miller v Bain* [2002] 1 BCLC 266 it was held that use of a beneficiary's money for the benefit of the fiduciary amounts to a conversion for the use of the fiduciary, and thereby brings the claim within **s. 21(1)(b)** (so there is no limitation period). A trustee who had negligently left trust money with a solicitor, who then embezzled it, but who was not a party to or privy to the solicitor's fraud, was held in *Thorne v Heard* [1894] 1 Ch 599 to be entitled to rely on a limitation defence after six years (class 8 in **table 10.1**).

Breach of fiduciary duty

10.5 In *Nelson v Rye* [1996] 1 WLR 1378 it was held that a claim for breach of fiduciary duty *simpliciter* is outside the provisions of the **LA 1980**, and so is not subject to any limitation period. This case has been called into question by subsequent decisions, particularly *Paragon Finance plc v D. B. Thakerer and Co.* [1999] 1 All ER 400. In *Nelson v Rye* the claimant was a musician and sought accounts from his former manager stretching back 11 years before proceedings were issued. Millett LJ in *Paragon Finance plc v D. B. Thakerer and Co.* pointed out that every agent owes fiduciary duties to his principal, and without something more the claim would have been subject to the usual six-year limitation period. The defendant in *Nelson v Rye* was no more than an accounting party who had failed to account. To have been entitled to a longer limitation period, the claimant would have had to show, among other things, that the defendant owed fiduciary duties in relation to the money.

Constructive trusts

Millett LJ in *Paragon Finance plc v D. B. Thakerer and Co.* [1999] 1 All ER 400 (and followed in **10.6**
Coulthard v Disco Mix Club Ltd [1999] 2 All ER 457) pointed out that there is a distinction between two categories of constructive trust claim:

(a) Where the constructive trustee, although not expressly appointed as a trustee, has assumed the duties of a trustee before the events which are alleged to constitute the breach of trust. In this category the defendant is a real trustee, and the provisions of the **LA 1980, s. 21(1)**, may apply if the other conditions of the subsection are satisfied, with the result that there may be an unlimited period for bringing proceedings. An example is *James v Williams* [2000] Ch 1.

(b) Where the constructive trust is merely the creation of the court as a remedy to meet the alleged wrongdoing. In this category there is no real trust, and usually no prospect of a proprietary remedy. The defendant is merely said to be liable to account as a constructive trustee. In this category the other provisions of the **LA 1980** apply, with the result that the period will usually be six years from accrual.

When considering the boundary between cases where the defendant is a true trustee under an express or constructive trust, and those where he is not, the key factor is whether there is trust property (*Clarke v Marlborough Fine Art (London) Ltd* (2001) *The Times*, 5 July 2001).

Personal injuries claims

Claims for personal injuries (class 12 in **table 10.1**) comprise all claims in negligence, **10.7**
nuisance and breach of duty (including contractual and statutory duties) where the claim to relief consists of or includes damages in respect of personal injuries to the claimant or any other person (**LA 1980, s. 11(1)**). Under **LA 1980, s. 11(4)**, the basic limitation period for such claims is three years. An attempt was made to avoid this limitation period in *Letang v Cooper* [1965] 1 QB 232. The claimant was injured when the defendant drove his car over her legs while she was sunbathing on the grass in the car park of a hotel. Proceedings were issued four years afterwards, but the cause of action was pleaded both in negligence and in trespass to the person. The Court of Appeal overruled the trial judge and held the claim was time-barred. Two reasons were advanced. One was that where an injury is inflicted negligently rather than intentionally, the only cause of action is in negligence, so the claimant is unable to rely on the six-year limitation period in trespass (class 10 in **table 10.1**). The second reason was that the phrase 'breach of duty' in what is now **LA 1980, s. 11(1)**, covered a breach of any duty under the law of tort.

A claim by an employee against an employer for failing to advise on the benefits available after suffering a personal injury is a claim for negligent advice (class 10), see *Gand v Leeds Health Authority* (1999) *The Times*, 14 May 1999. On the other hand, a claim in professional negligence against a solicitor arising out of the firm's handling of a divorce ancillary relief claim, which included a claim for anxiety and stress arising out of the firm's alleged mishandling of her claim, became, for that reason, a claim in respect of personal injuries and subject to a three-year limitation period (class 12) rather than the usual six-year period in claims in tort and breach of contract (*Oates v Harte Reade and Co.* [1999] PIQR P120). A negligent failure by an education authority to improve the consequences of the claimant's dyslexia by appropriate teaching, or a negligent failure to treat a physical injury, are both claims for personal injuries (*Adams v Bracknell Forest Borough Council* [2004] UKHL 29, [2005] 1 AC 76).

In *Ackbar v C. F. Green and Co. Ltd* [1975] QB 582 a claim against an insurance broker for damages for breach of contract for failing to effect cover for a passenger who later suffered personal injuries in a road accident was held to be a claim in contract (class 7). A claim for breach of statutory duty to insure a motor vehicle on the road was, in contrast, held to be a claim for personal injuries in *Norman v Ali* [2000] RTR 107.

Deliberate trespass to the person

10.8 Although the decision in *Letang v Cooper* [1965] 1 QB 232 (see **10.7**) was approved by the later House of Lords decision of *Stubbings v Webb* [1993] AC 498, the second of the reasons for the decision was rejected. The claimant in *Stubbings v Webb* alleged she had suffered mental illness as a result of being sexually abused and raped by each of the defendants respectively over a period between 16 and 28 years before the proceedings were issued. It was held that the phrase 'breach of duty' in the **LA 1980, s. 11(1)**, had to be construed as a duty not to cause personal injury rather than an obligation not to infringe any legal right of another person. Cases of deliberate assault therefore do not fall within s. 11, with the result that they are governed by the six-year limitation period in s. 2, and cannot take the benefit of the date-of-knowledge provisions in s. 14 (discussed at **10.23** to **10.27**) nor the discretionary power to disapply the primary limitation period contained in s. 33 (discussed at **10.44** to **10.50**). As the claim was time-barred it was struck out. *Stubbings v Webb* was confirmed by the European Court of Human Rights in *Stubbings v United Kingdom* (applications 22083/93 and 22095/93) (1996) 23 EHRR 213, and applied in *A v Hoare* [2005] EWHC 2161 (QB), *The Times*, 27 October 2005.

In *Seymour v Williams* [1995] PIQR P470 a 29-year-old woman brought a claim against her parents in respect of sexual abuse she alleged she had suffered during her childhood. Her claim against her father, the alleged perpetrator, was struck out following *Stubbings v Webb*. However, her claim against her mother for alleged breach of parental duty to protect her against the foreseeable risk of injury from sexual abuse by her father was allowed to continue, because it was a claim for 'breach of duty' within s. 11, and it was possible that the court might exercise its discretion under s. 33 in her favour. It is debatable whether the *Stubbings v Webb* rule applies in cases of unauthorised or excessive medical treatment, as these cases are in essence claims in trespass in which the patient may have given consent by signing the usual consent forms used by hospitals. Some support for the view that these cases are also governed by the six-year limitation period can be found in the Master of the Rolls's judgment in *Dobbie v Medway Health Authority* [1994] 1 WLR 1234. However, a claim based on a failed sterilisation, as happened in *Walkin v South Manchester Health Authority* [1995] 1 WLR 1543, is a claim for personal injuries, and is governed by the usual three-year limitation period.

Statutes and specialties

10.9 A claim for damages for infringement of a right conferred by Community law amounts to a breach of statutory duty. It is therefore a claim founded on tort, and subject to a six-year limitation period under the **LA 1980, s. 2** (*R v Secretary of State for Transport, ex parte Factortame Ltd (No. 7)* [2001] 1 WLR 942). A claim to recover rent due under a lease under seal is governed by the six-year limitation period in class 9, not the 12 years in class 4 (*Romain v Scuba TV Ltd* [1997] QB 887). Although statutes are specialties, money claims pursuant to statute are governed by the six-year period in s. 9 (class 5) (see *Central Electricity Board v Halifax Corporation* [1963] AC 785 and *Re Farmizer (Products) Ltd* [1997] 1 BCLC 589), whereas claims for other remedies pursuant to statute will be governed by the 12-year period in s. 8 (class 4). Consequently, a claim to reopen an extortionate credit bargain under the **Consumer Credit Act 1974, s. 139**, has a 12-year limitation period running from the date of the agreement (*Rahman v Sterling Credit Ltd* [2001] 1 WLR 496). Direct claims against insurers under the **Third**

Parties (Rights against Insurers) Act 1930, s. 1, are governed by the same limitation period, accruing on the same date, as is applicable against the original tortfeasor (*Matadeen v Caribbean Insurance Co. Ltd* [2002] UKPC 69, [2003] 1 WLR 670).

Mortgages and deeds

A claim for the recovery of the principal due under a mortgage, even after the property has been repossessed and sold, is governed by the 12-year period in the **LA 1980, s. 20** (class 3 in **table 10.1**), but claims for interest are subject to a six-year limitation period as set out in s. 20(5) (*Bristol and West plc v Bartlett* [2002] EWCA Civ 1181, [2003] 1 WLR 284). A claim to enforce a charge by deed securing moneys guaranteed by the defendant is a claim on a specialty and governed by the 12-year limitation period (*Securum Finance Ltd v Ashton* [2001] Ch 291). It seems from *Global Financial Recoveries Ltd v Jones* (1999) *The Times*, 23 February 2000, that whether a claim for any shortfall after the realisation of mortgaged property (the mortgage being by deed) is one based on simple contract or specialty depends on whether the terms of the mortgage include the consequences of any shortfall. A claim to enforce a charge made under the Insolvency Act 1986, s. 313 (charge on a bankrupt's home imposed by court order), is subject to the 12-year time limit in **LA 1980, s. 20**, and time runs from the date of the charge (*Doodes v Gotham* [2005] EWHC 2576 (Ch), [2005] NPC 134). **10.10**

In *West Bromwich Building Society v Wilkinson* [2005] UKHL 44, [2005] 1 WLR 2303, the defendants bought a property with a loan secured by a legal charge. The charge contained a proviso for redemption in conventional form. It also provided for a power of sale which was exercisable on demand of the money advanced or on five other events of default, including non-payment. Only two of the monthly instalments were paid. Default on the monthly payments, and obtaining and execution of an order for possession, occurred more than 12 years before the present proceedings, which sought judgment on the shortfall after sale of the property. Sale of the property was less than 12 years before the claim was issued. The building society argued that under the charge it had no right to recover the mortgage advance until the shortfall was quantified, which was when the property was sold. The House of Lords held that on the true construction of the charge, the principal money outstanding became payable when the power of sale became exercisable. Although the relevant clause did not in terms say this, the natural meaning of the clause was that the money became payable on making the demand or on the occurrence of any of the other events of default (at [19]). This was more than 12 years before the date of issue, so the claim was time-barred under **LA 1980, s. 8**.

Foreign limitation periods

Where, in accordance with the rules of private international law, the law of any other country is to be taken into account in any claim in England and Wales, the law of that other country relating to limitation must be applied (Foreign Limitation Periods Act 1984). **10.11**

ACCRUAL OF CAUSE OF ACTION

The rules on accrual fix the date from which time begins to run for limitation purposes. Lindley LJ in *Reeves v Butcher* [1891] 2 QB 509 said: '. . . it has always been held that the statute runs from the earliest time at which an action could be brought'. In *Read v Brown* (1888) 22 QBD 128 Lord Esher MR defined 'cause of action' as encompassing 'every fact which it would be necessary for the [claimant] to prove, if traversed, in order to support his right to the judgment of the court'. In other words, time runs from the point when facts exist establishing all the essential elements of the cause of action. A distinction is drawn between the substantive elements and mere procedural requirements. Thus, a solicitor can commence a claim to recover costs from a client only if at least a month has elapsed since a bill for those costs has been delivered to the client (**Solicitors Act 1974, s. 69(1)**). In *Coburn v Colledge* [1897] 1 QB 702 it was held that the requirement to furnish a bill was only a procedural matter, and time **10.12** ran from completion of the work as opposed to delivery of the bill. Sometimes this can be a difficult distinction to draw. *Sevcon Ltd v Lucas CAV Ltd* [1986] 1 WLR 462 concerned the Patents Act 1949, s. 13(4), which contained a proviso: 'Provided that an applicant shall not be entitled to institute any proceedings for infringement until the patent has been sealed'. It was held that the cause of action accrued on the date of the infringement, but could not be enforced until the procedural requirement of sealing was met.

In addition to the elements of the cause of action being present, there must be a party capable of suing and a party liable to be sued. So, if goods are converted after the owner has died intestate, time would only run from the date letters of administration were taken out (*Thomson v Lord Clanmorris* [1900] 1 Ch 718 per Vaughan Williams LJ). However, if it is necessary to restore to the register of companies a company against which a claim is to be made, the date of accrual remains based on the date of the breach (or other element of the cause of action), not on the date of restoration (*Smith v White Knight Laundry Ltd* [2001] EWCA Civ 660, [2002] 1 WLR 616). Although the court has power under the Companies Act 1985, s. 651(6), to direct that the period between dissolution and restoration shall not count for the purposes of limitation, a direction under this provision should not normally be made unless notice of the application had been served on all parties who could be expected to oppose it. Also, time continues running during a period in which the defendant is an undischarged bankrupt (*Anglo Manx Group Ltd v Aitken* [2002] BPIR 215).

Accrual in claims for the recovery of land

10.13 For recovery of land cases not governed by the Land Registration Act 2002 (see **10.14** below), there are detailed rules dealing with accrual in **LA 1980, sch. 1**. For adverse possession against Crown land, and the 30-year period in **LA 1980, sch. 1, para. 10**, see *Hill v Transport for London* [2005] EWHC 856 (Ch), [2005] Ch 379. Broadly, time runs from the taking of adverse possession where the person bringing the claim has a present interest in the land but will be delayed until the determination of the preceding interest in the case of future interests. Use of the phrase 'adverse possession' is well established, but was regretted by the House of Lords in *J. A. Pye (Oxford) Ltd v Graham* [2002] UKHL 30, [2003] 1 AC 419, because it may be misleading. The question is whether the squatter dispossessed the paper owner by going into ordinary possession of the land for the requisite 12 years without the consent of the owner. There are two elements:

(a) Factual possession. This requires an appropriate degree of physical control, which depends on the circumstances, such as the nature of the land and the manner in which such land is commonly used. It has to be shown that the squatter has dealt with the land as an occupying owner might be expected to do, and that no one else has done so. Parking vehicles and delivering goods on the disputed land amounted to no more than use of the land in *Tennant v Adamczyk* [2005] EWCA Civ 1239, (2005) 41 EG 205 (CS).

(b) Intention to possess. What must be proved is an intention to possess, not a more extensive intention to own, or to acquire ownership, or to exclude the true owner. Lord Browne-Wilkinson described as heretical and wrong the concept, stemming from *Leigh v Jack* (1879) 5 ExD 264, that it must be shown that acts have been done which were inconsistent with the true owner's enjoyment of the land for the purposes for which he intended to use it. What is required is proof of an intention, in the squatter's own name and on his own behalf, to exclude the world at large, including the paper owner so far as was reasonably practicable and so far as the processes of the law would allow. Consequently, evidence that the squatter was willing to pay for his occupation if asked by the paper owner does not prevent time running against the paper owner.

10.14 **Registered land** The provisions of the LA 1980 as regards registered land were replaced as from 13 October 2003 by the Land Registration Act 2002, sch. 6 and sch. 12. These support the principle under the 2002 Act that the register is to be a complete and accurate record of the state of the title to registered land at any given time, so that it will be possible to investigate title to land online and with the absolute minimum of additional enquiries and inspections. A person claiming adverse possession of registered land for at least 10 years is allowed to apply for registration. The usual evidence of adverse possession is required. The registered owner and any chargees and other interested persons is then served with notice of the application, and they may serve counter-notice. If they fail to do so, the applicant will be registered as the registered proprietor in place of the former proprietor, and free from former charges. If counter-notice is served, the application is dismissed unless one of three grounds is established. These are that it would be unfair to dispossess the applicant because of an equity by estoppel; that the applicant has an independent right which suggests he ought to be registered as the owner; or that there has been a reasonable mistake over boundaries. If an exception applies, the applicant is registered in place of the registered proprietor, and this happens notwithstanding objections from registered chargees. However, charges will continue to apply unless as a matter of general law the applicant's rights have priority over the charge. Where prior charges continue to apply the applicant can apply for an apportionment of the charges between the land acquired by adverse possession and the remainder of the original title.

If an application under the 2002 Act is dismissed the registered owner then has two years to take action to evict the person claiming adverse possession or otherwise regularise the position. If this is not done, once the two years has elapsed the person claiming adverse possession may reapply for registration, and, if still in possession, will be automatically registered in place of the existing registered owner. If this happens, the applicant is registered with a new, separate title, and takes free of any former registered charges.

Extinction of title and the European Convention on Human Rights

The European Court of Human Rights in *J. A. Pye (Oxford) Ltd v United Kingdom* (application 44302/02) (2005) *The Times*, 23 November 2005, laid down the following propositions: **10.15**

(a) The extinction of the owner's title under the Land Registration Act 1925 and the **LA 1980** after 12 years' adverse possession is an interference with the owner's rights under art. 1 of the First Protocol to the European Convention on Human Rights in the **Human Rights Act 1998, sch. 1** (no one shall be deprived of his possessions except in the public interest).
(b) Although extinction of title might serve a legitimate aim, it is more difficult to justify this result in the case of registered land than it is in a jurisdiction not having a system of land registration.
(c) The pre-Land Registration Act 2002 system of extinction of title without adequate procedural safeguards and with no compensation imposed an excessive burden on the landowner, did not create a fair balance, and violated art. 1 of the First Protocol.

A similar conclusion was reached in *Beaulane Properties Ltd v Palmer* [2005] EWHC 817 (Ch), [2006] Ch 79. It was declared that the defendant had not acquired title to land occupied for grazing his horses for more than 12 years despite the Land Registration Act 1925, s. 75. The judge held that art. 1 of the First Protocol applied. Extinction of title was an expropriation of registered land without compensation, and the circumstances did not advance any legitimate aims of the statutory provisions, and was disproportionate. (The legitimate statutory aim of the Land Registration Act was regarded as covering things like inaccurately placed boundary fences.)

J. A. Pye (Oxford) Ltd v United Kingdom did not specifically decide whether the additional safeguards implemented by the Land Registration Act 2002 (formal notice to the owner, and the need to show special reasons where the owner opposes the application) redress the balance. However, the implication of the decision is that the 2002 Act system is Convention compliant.

Beneficiaries

10.16 Different types of claims by beneficiaries have no time limits, 12-year and six-year time limits, see **LA 1980, ss. 21 and 22.** A right of action for non-fraudulent breach of trust does not accrue until a future interest falls into possession (**LA 1980, s. 21(3)**). Claims to the personal estate of a deceased person accrue on 'the date on which the right to receive the share or interest accrued'. Time was held to run from the end of the executor's year (one year from death) in *Re Loftus* [2005] EWHC 406 (Ch), [2005] 1 WLR 1890.

Money due under statute

10.17 In *Swansea City Council v Glass* [1992] QB 844 the council brought a claim to recover the cost of repairing a house owned by the defendant and let to a tenant where the defendant had failed to effect necessary repairs. The claim was brought under the Housing Act 1957, s. 10(3), and was commenced over six years after the work was done, but less than six years after a demand for payment. It was held that time ran from completion of the work, so the claim was statute-barred.

Contract

10.18 Time runs from the breach of contract. When this is depends on the nature of the obligation sued on and the terms of the contract, and also on whether a repudiatory breach is accepted by the claimant. Applying the general rule, causes of action in breach of contract will accrue as follows:

(a) In claims for breach of the implied terms as to satisfactory quality etc. in the **Sale of Goods Act 1979** (SoGA 1979), time normally starts running on delivery of the goods (*Battley v Faulkner* (1820) 3 B & Ald 288).

(b) In claims for late delivery of goods, time runs from the contractual date for delivery.

(c) In claims based on the implied term as to title to goods sold, time runs from the date of the contract, or, in the case of an agreement to sell, from the date title was to pass (see **SoGA 1979, s. 12(1)**).

(d) Claims for the price of goods sold accrue on the contractual date for payment (**SoGA 1979, s. 49(2)**), failing which on the date property in the goods passes to the buyer (s. 49(1)) or the date the buyer is informed that the seller is ready and willing to deliver (s. 28).

(e) In a construction contract where the price is payable by stated instalments at the end of each month, time runs in respect of each instalment from the end of the relevant month (*Henry Boot Construction Ltd v Alstom Combined Cycles Ltd* [2005] EWCA Civ 814, [2005] 1 WLR 3850, at [60]).

(f) In a construction contract where stage and final payments are payable after certification by an architect or engineer, the certificate is a condition precedent to payment, so time runs from the date the certificate is issued or ought to be issued (*Henry Boot Construction Ltd v Alstom Combined Cycles Ltd* [2005] EWCA Civ 814, [2005] 1 WLR 3850, at [23] to [28] and [50]). This case also pointed out that there are separate causes of action based on interim and final certificates, even if the amounts certified are the same (at [56]).

(g) In claims based on defective building work, time usually starts running on practical or substantial completion (*Tameside Metropolitan Borough Council v Barlow Securities Group Services Ltd* [2001] BLR 113).

(h) Claims for the price of entire contracts for work and services accrue on completion of the work (*Emery v Day* (1834) 1 Cr M & R 245). In many building contracts the parties agree to stage payments, and time starts running in relation to these at the contractual date for payment.

(i) Claims by banks to recover overdrafts from customers normally accrue on service of a demand in writing (**LA 1980, s. 6**). There is an exception in s. 6 relating to loans where the debtor also enters into a collateral obligation to pay, such as by delivering a promissory note, but most bank overdrafts fall into the main category.

(j) Claims against sureties and guarantors usually accrue on default by the principal debtor (*Parr's Banking Co. v Yates* [1898] 2 QB 460).

(k) Accrual in the case of negotiable instruments is somewhat complicated. Claims against acceptors and makers based on non-payment accrue on the maturity of the instrument, unless it is a bill of exchange which is accepted after maturity, in which case time runs from the date of acceptance (Bills of Exchange Act 1882, s. 10(2)). Bills of exchange often mature on fixed dates, but if they mature (say) a fixed period of time after sight, time starts running that fixed period after acceptance (or after noting or protesting if it is not accepted) (s. 14(3)). A claim against a drawer or endorser after dishonour by non-payment accrues when the bill is duly presented for payment and payment is refused or cannot be obtained, or, if presentment is excused, when the bill is overdue and unpaid (s. 47(2)).

(l) Accrual in claims against insurers depends on the terms of the policy. The general rule is that time starts running at the date of the loss. For example, claims for constructive total loss accrue on the date of the casualty (*Bank of America National Trust v Chrismas* [1994] 1 All ER 401). However, it is open to the parties to displace the general rule by creating conditions precedent to the insured's right to payment. For example, in *Virk v Gan Life Holdings plc* [2000] Lloyd's Rep IR 159 critical illness benefit became payable under a policy if the insured survived 30 days after suffering a stroke. It was held that time started running 30 days after the stroke.

In cases where the claimant has accepted an anticipatory breach as a repudiation, time starts running from the date of acceptance rather than the contractual date for performance of the obligation in question (*Reeves v Butcher* [1891] 2 QB 509). Claims for consequential losses, such as salvage charges arising out of a claim based on the loss of a ship against an insurer, are not separate causes of action, so accrual turns on the date of the underlying cause of action (the casualty) not on the date the consequential loss was incurred (*Bank of America National Trust v Chrismas* [1994] 1 All ER 401). There are several types of contractual obligation that give rise to continuing or repeated breaches. An example of a continuing breach is a failure to comply with a covenant to keep in repair (*Spoor v Green* (1874) LR 9 Ex 99 at p. 111), and an example of a repeated breach is a failure to pay rent (*Archbold v Scully* (1861) 9 HL Cas 360). In these cases the claimant will be able to succeed in respect of the consequences of breach over the six-year period (12 years for claims on a specialty) before the claim form is issued.

General claims in tort

The general rule is that in addition to proving the defendant is guilty of some wrongful conduct, liability in tort can only be established on proof of damage. Usually, damage is the final matter to come into existence, so the usual rule is that time runs in tort from the date when damage is sustained. It was held in *Law Society v Sephton and Co.* [2004] EWCA Civ 1627, [2005] QB 1013, that there is a distinction between a measurable relevant loss (which starts time running) and a mere risk of loss (which does not). The claim was against a firm of accountants and rested on an allegation that they had negligently prepared accounts for a firm of solicitors which failed to find misappropriations of clients' money which might have been prevented if the accounts had been prepared properly. On the facts the claim against the accountants accrued when the claimant resolved to make a payment to a client of the solicitors arising out of the misappropriations. 10.19

The important date is the date damage was sustained, not the date on which the claimant discovered the damage (*Cartledge v E. Jopling and Sons Ltd* [1963] AC 758). There are, of course, many cases where measurable damage and its discovery coincide (*Abbott v Will Gannon and Smith Ltd* [2005] EWCA Civ 198, [2005] BLR 195). In *Pirelli General Cable Works Ltd v Oscar Faber and*

Partners [1983] 2 AC 1 it was held that a cause of action for negligent design of a chimney arose when cracking in the structure first developed, and not when the damage could have been or was in fact discovered. Likewise, where additional damage is suffered after the tortious act complained of, time continues to run from the original tortious act (*Iqbal v Legal Services Commission* [2005] EWCA Civ 623, LTL 10/5/2005).

The decision in *Darley Main Colliery v Mitchell* (1886) 11 App Cas 127 on continuing torts is probably confined to subsidence claims (*Iqbal v Legal Services Commission*). Conversely, it was held in *Phonographic Performance Ltd v Department of Trade and Industry* [2004] EWHC 1795 (Ch), [2004] 1 WLR 2893, that where the tort is one which is not actionable per se, there is a continuing breach of duty and a fresh cause of action every time the claimant suffers loss. Where work done by a developer is defective, and the developer does further work intended to rectify defects but which is also defective, the further work is a fresh cause of action and time starts running again (*Alderson v Beetham Organization Ltd* [2003] EWCA Civ 408, [2003] 1 WLR 1686).

Professional negligence

10.20 In a claim against a solicitor for negligent advice, actual damage is suffered when the advice is acted upon, such as by executing a document (*Forster v Outred and Co.* [1982] 1 WLR 86) or entering into an agreement (*McCarroll v Statham Gill Davis* [2003] EWCA Civ 425, [2003] PNLR 509). A claim against a solicitor based on alleged negligent advice on inheritance tax accrues when the client relies on the advice (*Daniels v Thompson* [2004] EWCA Civ 307, [2004] PNLR 33). Where a claimant seeks to sue a solicitor for negligently allowing a claim to be struck out as a sanction for breach of directions or the requirements of the CPR, time runs from the date when the claimant had no arguable basis for avoiding the claim being struck out, not from the date on which it was actually struck out (*Khan v R. M. Falvey and Co.* [2002] EWCA Civ 400, [2002] PNLR 28; *Hatton v Chafes* [2003] EWCA Civ 341, LTL 13/3/2003, disapproving *Hopkins v MacKenzie* (1994) 6 Med LR 26). A related, but different point, was considered in *Cohen v Kingsley Napley* [2006] EWCA Civ 66, LTL 10/2/2006. Pill LJ at [19] said that even if the original claim would have been struck out if an application had been made by the original opponent at the point six years before the present claim was issued against the solicitors, the claim against the solicitors will not be time-barred if:

(a) on the evidence the original opponent would not have applied to strike out at that time;
(b) with the result that the original claim still had some value at the point six years before the current proceedings.

There are not many cases where the first point will be satisfied. *Cohen v Kingsley Napley* was a strike-out application, and the Court of Appeal said it was a matter that could be argued at trial. The court was swayed by the fact the original claim was a counterclaim, so the original opponent was a claimant, and so may have been reluctant to strike out the counterclaim for delay given the claim would also be in danger of being struck out.

Applying the rule that a claim accrues when actual damage is sustained, a professional negligence claim against solicitors based on failing to serve a claim form in time, or based on wrongly relying on an order (later set aside) extending time for service, accrues when the original period of validity of the claim form expires (*Polley v Warner Goodman and Street Solicitors* [2003] EWCA Civ 1013, [2003] PNLR 784). A continuing duty on a solicitor to advise will continually renew the accrual of limitation until the duty to advise ends, usually on termination of the retainer (*Workman v Pannone and Partners* [2002] EWHC 2366 (QB), LTL 18/11/2002).

Where the claim is in respect of a transaction entered into through a breach of duty owed by the defendant to the claimant (such as a loan agreement entered into in reliance on a negligent property valuation), time will run from the date the transaction was entered into if the claimant suffered a loss there and then. If there was no immediate loss, such as where the security for a loan was worth more than the loan when it was first advanced (albeit not as much as the defendant's valuation), time will start running only when the value of the security falls below the amount of the loan (see the discussion in *First National Commercial Bank plc v Humberts* [1995] 2 All ER 673).

Trespass and libel

These are actionable per se, so time runs from the wrongful act since there is no requirement to prove damage. **10.21**

Conversion

Time runs from the date the goods were converted. A number of special rules apply: **10.22**

(a) where goods are converted more than once, the original six-year period continues to run and is not renewed (**LA 1980, s. 3(1)**);
(b) at the end of the original six-year period the true owner's title is extinguished (**LA 1980, s. 3(2)**);
(c) subject to (d) below, there is no time limit where goods are stolen (**LA 1980, s. 4**);
(d) where goods are converted (but not stolen) and are then stolen at a later date, proceedings in respect of the theft are barred once the true owner's title is extinguished under **s. 3(2)** by virtue of the original conversion (**LA 1980, s. 4(1)**).

Personal injuries claims: date of knowledge

Time runs in personal injuries claims from the date the cause of action accrued, or, if later, the date of the claimant's date of knowledge (**LA 1980, s. 11(4)**). Date of knowledge is defined by **s. 14(1)** as: **10.23**

> . . . the date on which [the claimant] first had knowledge of the following facts—
> (a) that the injury in question was significant; and
> (b) that the injury was attributable in whole or in part to the act or omission which is alleged to constitute negligence, nuisance or breach of duty; and
> (c) the identity of the defendant; and
> (d) if it is alleged that the act or omission was that of a person other than the defendant, the identity of that person and the additional facts supporting the bringing of an action against the defendant.

The subsection concludes by providing that knowledge that any acts or omissions did or did not, as a matter of law, involve negligence, nuisance or breach of duty is irrelevant.

The provision for time to run from date of knowledge was first introduced in July 1963 by the Limitation Act 1963 and has no application to any claim already time-barred before it was introduced (*McDonnell v Congregation of Christian Brothers Trustees* [2003] UKHL 63, [2003] 1 AC 1101, applying *Arnold v Central Electricity Generating Board* [1988] AC 228).

Personal injuries claims: constructive knowledge

A claimant seeking to rely on **LA 1980, s. 14**, is taken to know facts observable or ascertainable by him or her, and also facts ascertainable with the help of expert advice which it would have been reasonable to obtain (**LA 1980, s. 14(3)**). This is a mixed test, and is said to require the court to decide what would reasonably have been known by someone with the claimant's age, background, intelligence and disabilities (*Davis v City and Hackney Health Authority* (1989) 2 Med LR 366). In *Forbes v Wandsworth Health Authority* [1997] QB 402, however, the Court of Appeal doubted the relevance of the claimant's individual characteristics in what is expressed to be an objective test. This means that personal characteristics of the claimant, such as a lack of confidence or a need to avoid contention, are irrelevant under **s. 14**. Rather, the court has to consider how a reasonable person in the claimant's situation, suffering from the claimant's medical condition, would have acted. It is to be expected that claimants who have suffered significant injuries will seek professional advice on the cause of their problems, even if they have serious difficulties with reading and writing (*Adams v Bracknell Forest Borough Council* [2004] UKHL 29, [2005] 1 AC 76). **10.24**

The *Forbes* approach was applied in *Parry v Clwyd Health Authority* [1997] PIQR P1, where in context the knowledge of the 'reasonable man' was regarded as being that of a person who knew no more of the subject than what might have been learnt at school, from parents or friends or the media. A claimant who is clear in her own mind that there was a connection between the defendant's conduct and her injury has sufficient knowledge even if other people would want to get expert advice before making up their minds (*Spargo v North Essex District Health Authority* [1997] PIQR P235). A claimant who eventually makes a claim against a drug company in respect of the effects of an allegedly defective drug may well have consulted a doctor at an early stage when possibly drug-related symptoms first became apparent. A doctor is likely to concentrate on a solution to the patient's problems rather than give advice on attributing blame. Therefore, whether the doctor's knowledge about the cause of the claimant's symptoms should be attributed to the claimant depends on whether in the circumstances it would have been reasonable to expect the claimant to have asked the doctor about cause as well as cure (*Nash v Eli Lilly and Co.* [1993] 1 WLR 782).

In *Ali v Courtaulds Textiles Ltd* [1999] Lloyd's Rep Med 301 the Court of Appeal held that the claimant in an industrial deafness case could not be said to know his deafness was attributable to his working conditions, as opposed to being age-induced, until after he had been advised by his doctors. In *Henderson v Temple Pier Co. Ltd* [1998] 1 WLR 1540 the claimant was injured as she boarded a moored ship. She did not know the identity of the owners. She instructed solicitors about a month after the accident. If they had acted competently, they could have discovered the identity of the defendant from the General Register of Shipping and Seamen fairly soon after they were retained, but in the event they only discovered the defendant's identity about 18 months after the accident. Proceedings were issued 4 years and 3 months after the accident. It was held that the proviso to s. 14(3) was not intended to give an extended period to a person whose solicitor acted in a dilatory manner in obtaining information which is obtainable without particular expertise, and the claimant was fixed with constructive knowledge which her solicitors ought to have acquired. The same reasoning applies where a solicitor fails to identify a defendant through failing to request a copy of a police road accident report (*Copeland v Smith* [2000] 1 WLR 1371).

Date of knowledge: significant injury

10.25 The 'injury in question' for the purposes of **LA 1980, s. 14(1)(a)**, is the injury for which the claim is brought (*McManus v Mannings Marine Ltd* [2001] EWCA Civ 1668, LTL 29/10/2001). Therefore, where a claimant sues for the exacerbation of a previous injury following further exposure to hazardous working conditions, time runs from the date the claimant knew the exacerbated injury was significant. It is legitimate for a claimant to restrict a claim to post-traumatic stress disorder which arose in a delayed form, and not to include a claim for the alleged underlying (and earlier) physical abuse. In such a case the 'injury in question' for the purposes of **s. 14** is the post-traumatic stress disorder, for which the claimant's date of knowledge may be later than for the underlying abuse (*H v Northampton County Council* [2004] EWCA Civ 526, [2005] PIQR P87, per Pill LJ at [18], relying on *KR v Bryn Alyn Community (Holdings) Ltd* [2003] EWCA Civ 85, [2003] EWCA Civ 783, [2003] QB 1441 at [39] and *Stubbings v Webb* [1992] QB 197 at p. 208). The limitation issue was remitted back to be dealt with at trial.

An injury is 'significant' for the purposes of **s. 14(1)(a)** if it is sufficiently serious to justify proceedings against a defendant who does not dispute liability and is able to satisfy any judgment. It could be objected that *any* injury will satisfy this test. However, it was held in *Stephen v Riverside Health Authority* (1989) *The Times*, 29 November 1989, that the early symptoms of cancer arising from excessive radiation received from a medical X-ray did not amount to a significant injury. Reasons for not bringing proceedings outside the merits of the claim, such as reluctance to sue an employer, have been held to be irrelevant under s. 14, although they can be relevant under s. 33 (see **10.44**) (*McCafferty v Metropolitan Police District Receiver* [1977] 1 WLR 1073). In claims alleging childhood abuse, it might be that the claimant will only realise there is a link between the abuse and later psychiatric problems after receiving advice from a psychiatrist (*KR v Bryn Alyn Community (Holdings) Ltd* [2003] EWCA Civ 85, [2003] EWCA Civ 783, [2003] QB 1441). *James v East Dorset Health Authority* (1999) *The Times*, 7 December 1999, is a relatively rare case where a patient who underwent an unsuccessful operation did not realise he might have suffered an injury until he was put on notice that this was a possibility by an independent consultant five years later. Time did not start running against the claimant over the subsequent 17 months either, because it was not unreasonable for him to have taken at least that time to obtain confirmation that the original operation had caused him injury.

Date of knowledge: attributable to defendant's conduct

The knowledge mentioned in **LA 1980, s. 14(1)(b)**, is not knowledge detailed enough to enable the claimant's advisers to draft particulars of claim, and there is no requirement that the claimant must be aware that the defendant's conduct is actionable. To hold that this is the case would be contrary to the final words of s. 14(1) that knowledge that any acts or omissions do or do not constitute negligence as a matter of law is irrelevant. In *Spargo v North Essex District Health Authority* [1997] PIQR P235, Brooke LJ laid down the following four principles: **10.26**

(a) The knowledge required to satisfy s. 14(1)(b) is a broad knowledge of the essence of the causally relevant act or omission to which the injury is attributable.
(b) 'Attributable' in this context means 'capable of being attributed to' in the sense of being a real possibility.
(c) An injured person has the requisite knowledge when he or she knows enough to make it reasonable to begin to investigate whether or not there is a case against the person responsible. This will be the case if the injured person so firmly believes that his condition is capable of being attributed to an act or omission which he can identify (in broad terms) that he goes to a solicitor to seek advice about making a claim for compensation.
(d) An injured person will not have the requisite knowledge if he thinks he knows of acts or omissions which he should investigate, but in fact is barking up the wrong tree; or if his knowledge is so vague or general that he cannot fairly be expected to know what he should investigate; or if his state of mind is such that he thinks his condition could be attributable to the act or omission alleged to constitute negligence, but he is not sure about this, and would need to check with an expert before he could properly be said to know that it was.

In *Broadley v Guy Clapham and Co.* [1994] 4 All ER 439 the claimant had gone into hospital for a knee operation, and left suffering from a condition known as foot drop. It was held that time started to run when the claimant had both a 'broad knowledge' that the operation had caused an injury to her foot, and specific knowledge that the operation had been carried out in such a way as to damage a nerve in her leg (the cause of her foot drop condition). She had the requisite broad knowledge shortly after the operation, and should have had the specific knowledge within a few months after the operation if she had taken the appropriate expert advice. In *Dobbie v Medway Health Authority* [1994] 1 WLR 1234 it was alleged that a hospital carried out a mastectomy without conducting the usual tests, and that the operation was entirely unnecessary. The surgeon was alleged to have told the claimant afterwards that at least she was fortunate that there was no malignancy. It was held that within days of the operation the claimant had the requisite broad knowledge that she had suffered a significant injury, and time started running from that point, even though it was not until several years later that she realised she could make a claim. Whether the relevant facts could only be known after obtaining an expert's report depends on the complexity of the case (*Hendy v Milton Keynes Health Authority* (1991) 3 Med LR 114). Thus, in *Forbes v Wandsworth Health Authority* [1997] QB 402 the claimant was admitted to hospital for an operation to cure circulation problems in his leg. The operation was not a success, and a fortnight later his leg was amputated. He did not obtain actual knowledge of the default of the hospital that he later relied on in proceedings for medical negligence until he received advice from a consultant 10 years later. It was held that, where an operation was expected to be successful, but ended up with disappointing results, the patient had to be allowed a reasonable time in which to get over the shock and to take stock of the situation before being expected to seek advice for the purpose of bringing a claim. Where the results were serious, as in this case, the taking-stock period would be in the region of 12 to 18 months. From that point the patient would be fixed with constructive knowledge, and time would start running for limitation purposes.

Date of knowledge: defendant's identity

10.27 Typical cases where time is postponed under **LA 1980, s. 14(1)(c)**, are hit-and-run accidents and cases where claimants are rendered unconscious and have no recollection of the accident. Claimants injured at work almost always have immediate knowledge of the identity of their employer. However, there are cases where the exact identity of the claimant's employer does not become clear until some time after an accident. In *Simpson v Norwest Holst Southern Ltd* [1980] 1 WLR 968 time was postponed where the claimant's employer 'hid' (to use the word used by Lawton LJ at p. 974) its identity by calling itself 'Norwest Holst Group'. Time was also postponed in *Cressey v E. Timm and Son Ltd* [2005] EWCA Civ 763, [2005] 1 WLR 3926, where the actual employer was one company in the group (Holdings), but the claimant's pay slips were issued by another company (Limited). Rix LJ made the point (at [29]) that application of **s. 14(1)(c)** does not depend on deliberate 'hiding' of the defendant's identity. At [35] Rix LJ said that knowing the defendant's 'identity' in **s. 14(1)(c)** requires something specific enough to enable a person to be identified for the purposes of a claim form. This in turn means that time will run against a claimant who knows who the defendant is, but does not have the defendant's correct name (at [33]).

Fatal accidents and death: date of knowledge

10.28 Time runs in claims brought by dependants under the **Fatal Accidents Act 1976** from the date of death or the 'date of knowledge' (as set out in **10.23**) of the person for whose benefit the proceedings are brought (**LA 1980, s. 12**). In proceedings brought for the benefit of the deceased's estate under the **Law Reform (Miscellaneous Provisions) Act 1934** time runs from the date of death or the personal representative's 'date of knowledge' (**LA 1980, s. 11(5)**).

Defective products

10.29 Claims under the Consumer Protection Act 1987 in respect of personal injuries or damage to property accrue on the date of damage or the 'date of knowledge' (**LA 1980, s. 11A(4)**).

Indemnity and contribution claims

10.30 At common law, an indemnity accrued on actual payment to the third party rather than on the event giving rise to the liability to the third party (*Huntley v Sanderson* (1833) 1 Cr & M 467). Equity, on the other hand, allowed a party to preserve its position by claiming an indemnity as soon as the liability was incurred, and to recover once the liability was established or quantified (*British Union and National Insurance Co. v Rawson* [1916] 2 Ch 476). The leading modern case is *Telfair Shipping Corporation v Inersea Carriers SA* [1985] 1 WLR 553. Accrual depends on the construction of the indemnity clause. The key question is usually whether the clause gives rise to the indemnity once primary liability to the third party has been ascertained or established, or whether the indemnity arises only after payment to the third party (*Socony Mobil Oil Co. Inc. v West of England Ship Owners Mutual Insurance Association (London) Ltd (No. 2)* [1989] 1 Lloyd's Rep 239).

A contribution claim accrues on the date the amount of the underlying liability is fixed, disregarding any possible appeal. If the amount of underlying liability is determined by the court, time runs from judgment (**LA 1980, s. 10(3)**), which means judgment on quantum, not merely liability (see *Aer Lingus v Gildacroft Ltd* [2006] EWCA Civ 4, [2006] NPC 4). If the amount of the underlying liability is fixed by agreement, time runs from the date of settlement (s. 10(4)). Where a firm agreement to settle the primary claim is made, time starts running immediately under **s. 10(4)**, and does not start again if the agreement is subsequently recorded in a consent order (*Knight v Rochdale Healthcare NHS Trust* [2003] EWHC 1831 (QB), [2004] 1 WLR 371). However, if the agreement requires the making of a consent order before it takes effect, time starts running from the consent order (ibid.).

Compulsory purchase compensation claims

In *Hillingdon London Borough Council v ARC Ltd* [1998] 1 WLR 174 it was held that a cause of action in respect of a claim for compensation under the Compulsory Purchase Act 1965, s. 9, accrues on the date of the acquiring authority's entry on the land. In *Halstead v Manchester City Council* [1998] 1 All ER 33 it was held that the statutory right to recover interest on compensation under the 1965 Act did not accrue until the amount on which interest became due was awarded or agreed. **10.31**

CALCULATING THE LIMITATION PERIOD

Limitation and the date of issue

Time runs from the day following the day on which the cause of action arose, as parts of a day are ignored (*Marren v Dawson Bentley and Co. Ltd* [1961] 2 QB 135). A claim is brought for limitation purposes 'when the [claim form] or other originating process is issued by the central office of the High Court and not when it is brought to the knowledge of the defendant by service upon him' (per Lord Diplock in *Thompson v Brown* [1981] 1 WLR 744). **Part 20** proceedings are commenced for limitation purposes on the date the **Part 20** claim form is issued (**LA 1980, s. 35(1)(a)**). If the court office is closed on the final day of the limitation period, proceedings are deemed to be in time if they are issued on the next day the court office is open (*Pritam Kaur v S. Russell and Sons Ltd* [1973] QB 336). A claimant may send a claim form to the court office for issue. Letters requesting the issue of claim forms will be date-stamped on receipt, and the date of receipt will stop time running for limitation purposes if the court does not issue the claim form on the same day (**PD 7, paras 5.1 and 5.2**). An enquiry as to the date on which a claim form was received by the court should be directed to a court officer (**para. 5.3**). **Paragraph 5.4** goes on to say that parties should recognise the importance of establishing the date of receipt if a limitation period is approaching, and should take steps to record the date of receipt. To avoid difficulties in cases where limitation might be a problem, it is usually best to make a personal attendance at court to issue the proceedings. **10.32**

Disability

There are two categories of persons under disability: children and persons of unsound mind. By virtue of **LA 1980, s. 28**, time does not run against a child until that person's 18th birthday. Also by virtue of **s. 28**, time does not run against a person of unsound mind if that person was under disability at the date the cause of action accrued. Thus, an adult who is immediately rendered of unsound mind by an accident is not subject to limitation until he or she recovers. The same applies to a child who has a cause of action while of sound mind, but who becomes of unsound mind before reaching the age of majority. However, time will continue to run during a period of mental disorder where a cause of action accrues to an adult who was of sound mind at the date of accrual. **10.33**

Fraud

In claims based on fraud, the limitation period does not begin to run until the claimant discovers the fraud or could with reasonable diligence have discovered it (**LA 1980, s. 32(1)(a)**). This provision applies only where fraud is the essence of the claim. An action in **10.34** conversion where the defendant has incidentally been guilty of fraud or dishonesty does not bring the provision into effect (*Beaman v ARTS Ltd* [1949] 1 KB 550).

Concealment

10.35 Time does not run where any fact relevant to the claim has been deliberately concealed by the defendant until the concealment is discovered or with reasonable diligence could have been discovered (**LA 1980, s. 32(1)(b)**). For the purposes of s. 32(1)(b), deliberate commission of a breach of duty in circumstances in which it is unlikely to be discovered for some time amounts to deliberate concealment of the facts involved in that breach of duty (s. 32(2)). This was interpreted by a number of authorities as meaning that time did not run where a professional person deliberately provided a service, even if the professional did not realise that the service was being provided in a negligent way (*Brocklesby v Armitage and Guest* [2002] 1 WLR 598 and *Liverpool Roman Catholic Archdiocese Trustees Inc. v Goldberg* [2001] 1 All ER 182). This line of authorities was overruled by *Cave v Robinson Jarvis and Rolf* [2002] UKHL 18, [2003] 1 AC 384, in which it was held that s. 32(1)(b) deprives a defendant of a limitation defence:

(a) where the defendant has taken active steps to conceal his breach of duty after he has become aware of it; and
(b) where the defendant is guilty of deliberate wrongdoing and conceals or fails to disclose it in circumstances where the wrongdoing is unlikely to be discovered for some time.

However, the mere fact that the defendant intended to do the act complained of does not mean that s. 32(1)(b) applies to prevent time running. If the defendant is unaware of his alleged error or that he may have failed to take proper care, there is nothing for the defendant to disclose, and time is not prevented from running by s. 32(1)(b). Consequently, to use examples referred to in *Cave v Robinson Jarvis and Rolf*, time will run where a surgeon negligently leaves a swab inside a patient; and where an anaesthetist negligently administers the wrong drug; and where a solicitor gives a client negligent advice. Time will not run if the surgeon deliberately left the swab inside the patient, or if the lawyer after giving negligent advice fails to disclose other facts which he is under a duty to disclose to the client which would have alerted the client to the negligent nature of the advice. Thus, there was concealment by a solicitor sued for the negligent conduct of litigation who failed to inform the client that that claim had been compromised and failed to tell the client he had agreed to a consent order (*Williams v Fanshaw Porter and Hazelhurst* [2004] EWCA Civ 157, [2004] 1 WLR 3185). In *Sheldon v R. H. M. Outhwaite (Underwriting Agencies) Ltd* [1996] AC 102 the claim was governed by a six-year limitation period and was allowed to continue although it was commenced 10 years after accrual. The defendants were alleged to have deliberately concealed material facts two years after accrual, and it was held that s. 32(1)(b) applies both where the concealment of the relevant facts was contemporaneous with the accrual of the cause of action and where it occurred subsequently. Concealment, for the purposes of **s. 32(1)(b)**, will almost inevitably occur after the cause of action has arisen. In *Skerratt v Linfax Ltd* [2003] EWCA Civ 695, LTL 6/5/2003, it was held that there had not been concealment for the purposes of **s. 32(1)(b)** when, before allowing the claimant to take part in the activity which injured him, the defendant required him to sign a document which misled him to believe that he could not make a claim, and more than three years elapsed before a solicitor advised him that this was not so.

Mistake

10.36 Where the claim is for relief from the consequences of a mistake, time does not run until the mistake is, or could with reasonable diligence have been, discovered (**LA 1980, s. 32(1)(c)**). In *Kleinwort Benson Ltd v Lincoln City Council* [1999] 2 AC 349 the House of Lords held that **LA 1980, s. 32(1)(c)**, applies to all mistakes, whether of fact or of law, so that it could apply where the claimant had paid money to the defendant under a mistake of law. Conversely, a restitutionary claim made by a person who makes a payment to the HM Revenue and Customs pursuant to an unlawful demand (see *Woolwich Equitable Building Society v*

Commissioners of Inland Revenue [1993] AC 70) accrues when the payment is made. These cases where analysed in *Deutsche Morgan Grenfell Group plc v Commissioners of Inland Revenue* [2005] EWCA Civ 78, [2006] 2 WLR 103. It was held at [208] that a claimant who makes a payment to the Revenue under a mistake of law is not entitled to a restitutionary remedy otherwise than under the *Woolwich* principle (where the demand is unlawful) or under the relevant statutory regime (where the demand is lawful). For unlawful demands, therefore, **LA 1980, s. 32(1)(c)**, does not arise (at [228]).

What amounts to 'reasonable diligence' is a question of fact. In *Peco Arts Inc. v Hazlitt Gallery Ltd* [1983] 1 WLR 1315, a case involving an alleged mistake over whether a 19th-century drawing was an original signed by the artist, it was held that the term meant doing what an ordinary prudent buyer of a valuable work of art would do. Depending on the facts, this might include taking suitable expert advice. See also *West Sussex Properties Ltd v Chichester District Council* (2000) LTL 28/6/2000. By way of exception, none of the provisions in **s. 32** applies to the time bar on interest on judgment debts in **s. 24(2)** (see **10.41**), because execution on a judgment is not an 'action' within the meaning of **s. 32** (*Lowsley v Forbes* [1999] 1 AC 329).

Acknowledgments and part payments

Under the **LA 1980, s. 29**, acknowledging title to land, acknowledging a debt and making part payments have the effect of renewing the limitation period from the date of acknowledgment or payment. A letter in which the defendant said he was 'happy to confirm that you suggest the following amounts are owed by me to you' was held to be a sufficient acknowledgment in *Ross v McGrath* [2004] EWCA Civ 1054, LTL 14/7/2004. *Bradford and Bingley plc v Rashid* [2005] EWCA Civ 1080, LTL 22/7/2005, was essentially the same as *West Bromwich Building Society v Wilkinson* [2005] UKHL 44, [2005] 1 WLR 2303 (discussed at **10.10**). To avoid the claim being time-barred the lender sought to rely on letters from the defendant saying he was unable to pay the shortfall, but offering to pay £500 towards the outstanding amount. It was held that the letters were to be regarded as without prejudice, and were inadmissible for the purpose of establishing an acknowledgement under **LA 1980, ss. 29** and **30**. Under **s. 30** any acknowledgment must be in writing and signed by the person liable or by that person's agent. A typed signature on a telex is a sufficient signature for this purpose (*Good Challenger Navegante SA v Metalexportimport SA* [2003] EWCA Civ 1668, [2004] 1 Lloyd's Rep 67). However, the part payment of rent or interest due at any time does not extend the time for claiming the balance (**s. 29(6)**). A payment made outside a repayment schedule therefore has the effect of renewing the limitation period (*International Finance Corporation v Utexafrica sprl* [2001] CLC 1361). **10.37**

Latent damage

It follows from the decision in *Pirelli General Cable Works Ltd v Oscar Faber and Partners* [1983] 2 AC 1 noted at **10.19** that it is possible for a claim in tort to be statute barred before the claimant knows that damage has been sustained, because time runs from the date of damage rather than discovery. To mitigate this position the Latent Damage Act 1986 inserted **ss. 14A** and **14B** into the **LA 1980**. These provisions apply to claims for negligence other than for personal injuries (**s. 14A(1)**). They are restricted to claims in tort, and do not extend to claims for 'contractual negligence' (*Société Commerciale de Réassurance v ERAS (International) Ltd* [1992] 2 All ER 82). It was thought that the most frequent use of the provisions would be in claims in respect of defective buildings, but the practical scope of the provisions was significantly reduced when the House of Lords in *Murphy v Brentwood District Council* [1991] 1 AC 398 overruled *Anns v Merton London Borough Council* [1978] AC 728 and so restricted the duty of care of local authorities when supervising compliance with building regulations. **10.38**

Latent damage: starting date Two alternative periods of limitation are provided by **LA 1980, s. 14A(4)**, namely, six years from accrual and three years from the 'starting date'. The first of these periods is simply the usual period for claims in tort. The 'starting date' is the earliest date the claimant knew: **10.39**

(a) that the relevant damage was sufficiently serious to justify proceedings; and
(b) that the damage was attributable to the alleged negligence; and
(c) the defendant's identity.

These concepts are very similar to those in s. 14 (see **10.23 to 10.27**) and it was accepted in *Hallam-Eames v Merrett* (1995) *The Times*, 25 January 1995, that the authorities on s. 14 apply to applications under s. 14A. 'Knowledge' in **s. 14A** means knowing with sufficient confidence to justify embarking on the preliminaries to issuing proceedings (*Haward v Fawcetts* [2006] UKHL 9, [2006] 1 WLR 682). Regarding condition (b), it is clear the claimant does not need to know he has a cause of action, or that the defendant's acts would be characterised by the law as negligence. It is enough if the claimant has broad knowledge of the facts on which the complaint is based, and knows there is a real possibility that the defendent's acts or omissions caused the damage under condition (a) (*Haward v Fawcetts*). In *Gravgaard v Aldridge and Brownlee* [2004] EWCA Civ 1529, [2005] PNLR 19, the defendant solicitors negligently failed to advise the claimant that it was not necessary for her to transfer the matrimonial home into joint names with her husband before charging it as security to pay her husband's debts. It was held that the claimant did not have actual knowledge for the purposes of condition (b) until she knew that the exposure of her husband's share of the home to her husband's creditors was caused by the solicitors' wrongful advice.

The knowledge of a loss adjuster appointed by the claimant's insurer in a subrogated claim can be attributed to the claimant for the purposes of **s. 14A(5)** (*Graham v Entec Europe Ltd* [2003] EWCA Civ 1177, [2003] 4 All ER 1345).

Section 14A(9) provides that knowledge that any acts or omissions did or did not, as a matter of law, involve negligence is irrelevant for the purposes of the provisions on date of knowledge in s. 14A. In *Bowie v Southorns* [2002] EWHC 1389 (QB), 152 NLJ 1240, it was held that this covers both knowledge of breach and knowledge that the defendant owed a duty of care, both of which are irrelevant for the purposes of date of knowledge under s. 14A(5).

10.40 **Latent damage: longstop** In order to give some protection to defendants who might otherwise be perpetually at risk, LA 1980, s. 14B, provides a longstop or overriding time-limit for bringing proceedings of 15 years from the act or omission alleged to constitute the negligence causing the claimant's damage.

Judgments

10.41 By **LA 1980, s. 24(1)**, an action may not be brought upon any judgment after the expiration of six years from the date on which the judgment became enforceable. A judgment for costs to be assessed is not enforceable for the purposes of **s. 24(1)** until the costs have been assessed (*Chohan v Times Newspapers Ltd* [2001] 1 WLR 1859). Insolvency proceedings, whether personal or corporate, are not 'actions' within the meaning of s. 24(1). Accordingly, a winding-up petition based on a judgment for costs obtained more than six years before the winding-up petition was held not to be time-barred in *Ridgeway Motors (Isleworth) Ltd v ALTS Ltd* [2005] EWCA Civ 92, [2005] 1 WLR 2871. Similarly, bringing an 'action' on a judgment does not include proceedings by way of execution (*Lowsley v Forbes* [1999] 1 AC 329). If enforcement proceedings are brought more than six years after judgment, the **LA 1980, s. 24(2)**, will limit the interest that can be claimed on the judgment debt to that accrued over six years.

Judicial review: discretionary extension

10.42 The three-month time-limit for bringing a claim for judicial review can be extended if good reasons are shown, see **74.33**.

Defamation: discretionary extension

10.43 Where defamation or malicious falsehood proceedings are not commenced within the one-year time limit, the court may direct that the limitation period shall not apply if it appears equitable to allow the claim to proceed, having regard to the balance of prejudice between the claimant and the defendant (**LA 1980, s. 32A**, as substituted by the Defamation Act 1996, s. 5). This section is modelled on s. 33, which provides a similar discretion in personal injuries cases, and which is considered in some detail at **10.44** to **10.50**. Permission was granted in *Wood v Chief Constable of West Midlands Police* [2004] EWCA Civ 1638, *The Times*, 13 December 2004, to add an alternative claim for slander four years after the event by way of an amendment at the close of evidence in a libel trial. The discretion was exercised against the claimant in *Hinks v Channel 4 Television Corporation* (2000) LTL 3/3/2000, principally because the claimant's solicitor had missed the one-year limitation period by relying, in April 1999, on a textbook written in 1994, which was before the limitation period was reduced from three years to one year in 1996. Another case where solicitors overlooked the one-year limitation period is *Steedman v British Broadcasting Corporation* (2001) *The Times*, 13 December 2001, in which it was held that an absence of prejudice to the ability to defend by reason of the delay is simply a factor, and in this case it was outweighed by the strong claim against the solicitors.

Personal injuries claims: discretionary extension

A wide discretion is given to override the usual three-year limitation period in personal injuries claims by **LA 1980, s. 33**, which in part provides: **10.44**

(1) If it appears to the court that it would be equitable to allow an action to proceed having regard to the degree to which—
   (a) the provisions of section 11 or 11A or 12 of this Act prejudice the plaintiff or any person whom he represents; and
   (b) any decision of the court under this subsection would prejudice the defendant or any person whom he represents;

   the court may direct that those provisions shall not apply to the action, or shall not apply to any specified cause of action to which the action relates. . . .

(3) In acting under this section the court shall have regard to all the circumstances of the case and in particular to—
   (a) the length of, and the reasons for, the delay on the part of the plaintiff;
   (b) the extent to which, having regard to the delay, the evidence adduced or likely to be adduced by the plaintiff or the defendant is or is likely to be less cogent than if the action had been brought within the time allowed by section 11, by section 11A or (as the case may be) by section 12;
   (c) the conduct of the defendant after the cause of action arose, including the extent (if any) to which he responded to requests reasonably made by the plaintiff for information or inspection for the purpose of ascertaining facts which were or might be relevant to the plaintiff's cause of action against the defendant;
   (d) the duration of any disability of the plaintiff arising after the date of the accrual of the cause of action;
   (e) the extent to which the plaintiff acted promptly and reasonably once he knew whether or not the act or omission of the defendant, to which the injury was attributable, might be capable at that time of giving rise to an action for damages;
   (f) the steps, if any, taken by the plaintiff to obtain medical, legal or other expert advice and the nature of any such advice he may have received.

Interpretation of s. 33 The factors set out in LA 1980, s. 33(3), are those which experience had indicated were of real importance in considering where the balance of prejudice was likely to lie. The delay referred to in para. (a) is the same as that referred to in para. (b), namely, the delay after the expiry of the primary limitation period as extended, if appropriate, by the claimant's date of knowledge under s. 14 (*Long v Tolchard and Sons Ltd* (1999) *The Times*, 5 January 2000). The reasons for the delay to be considered are those of the claimant: it is a subjective test (*Coad v Cornwall and Isles of Scilly Health Authority* [1997] 1 WLR 189). Having found what the reason is for the delay, the court must then decide whether the reason is good or bad. The general rule is that the longer the delay, the more likely it is that the balance of prejudice will move away from granting relief to the claimant. Under para. (a) it is wrong to concentrate mainly on the claimant's reasons for the delay, without sufficient emphasis on the length of the delay (*Buckler v Sheffield City Council* [2004] EWCA Civ 920, [2005] PIQR P36). Only limited **10.45**

weight will be given to reasons for delay after the date of knowledge in cases where **s. 14** (see **10.23** to **10.27**) extends the normal limitation period (*KR v Bryn Alyn Community (Holdings) Ltd* [2003] EWCA Civ 85, [2003] EWCA Civ 783, [2003] QB 1441).

The question of cogency in para. (b) is only concerned with the loss or adverse effect on evidence through the passage of time. A court is not entitled in an application under s. 33 to find prejudice to the defendant by assuming that omissions or contradictions in the claimant's evidence may be excused by the trial judge (*Nash v Eli Lilly and Co.* [1993] 1 WLR 782). Any prejudice to contribution proceedings, such as tracing witnesses, has to be taken into account under **s. 33(3)(b)** (*Buckler v Sheffield City Council* [2004] EWCA Civ 920, [2005] PIQR P36). The period of disability referred to in para. (d) is one of mental disability arising after the accrual of the cause of action, and hence one which does not prevent time running (see **10.33**).

The leading authority on s. 33 is *Thompson v Brown* [1981] 1 WLR 744, in which the House of Lords held that the court has a discretion unfettered by any rules of practice, that the court must consider all the circumstances of the case, and is not restricted to the matters specifically set out in s. 33(3). Lord Diplock said in that case that a direction under s. 33 is always prejudicial to the defendant, but the extent of the prejudice is related to the strength or otherwise of the claim or defence.

10.46 **Cross-claims against solicitor** One factor not mentioned in LA 1980, s. 33(3), but of considerable importance, is whether the claimant has an alternative claim in negligence against his or her solicitor for failing to issue proceedings in time (*Thompson v Brown* [1981] 1 WLR 744). This factor can be discounted if there is real doubt about the strength of the claim against the solicitor, and in any event the claimant will suffer some prejudice through further delay, instructing unknown solicitors to pursue the new claim, the old solicitors knowing the weaknesses of the original claim, and possible restrictions in obtaining disclosure against the original defendants (see disclosure against non-parties in **chapter 48**). In *Steeds v Peverel Management Services Ltd* (2001) *The Times*, 16 May 2001, the claimant's solicitors had, through oversight, issued proceedings 49 days after the expiry of limitation. The Court of Appeal held that the judge at first instance had erred in law in assuming that the solicitors' failings were those of the claimant, and in criticising a period of delay after the solicitors were instructed. Despite the strong claim in negligence against the solicitors, if the claim were defeated by the expiry of the limitation period, greater prejudice would be suffered by the claimant than the defendant, and the claim was allowed to proceed.

10.47 **Date of notification** A second factor not mentioned in LA 1980, s. 33(3), which is always regarded as being of considerable importance is the delay between the accident and the defendant being informed of the claim. The reason is that a defendant who is informed of the potential claim at an early stage has the opportunity to investigate the facts while the events are still fresh in witnesses' memories, even if proceedings are issued rather late, and hence cannot complain of significant prejudice under s. 33(3)(b). This seems to have been a significant factor in *Thompson v Brown* [1981] 1 WLR 744 and also in *Hartley v Birmingham City District Council* [1992] 1 WLR 968. Conversely, in *Donovan v Gwentoys Ltd* [1990] 1 WLR 472 there was a delay in excess of six years before the defendants were given full details of the claim. In fact proceedings were issued only six months late, as the claimant was a child at the date of the accident. She instructed solicitors 19 days before her 18th birthday, so she had an alternative claim against her solicitors. It was held that the delay in notifying the defendants was an extremely important consideration, that it would be inequitable to require the defendants to meet such a stale claim, and the claimant would suffer only the slightest prejudice in being required to sue her solicitors. Permission was refused.

10.48 **Merits of substantive claim** Parker LJ in *Hartley v Birmingham City District Council* [1992] 1 WLR 968 expressed the view that the merits of the claimant's case are of little importance, on the ground that the stronger the merits the greater the prejudice to both the claimant and the defendant of the decision under LA 1980, s. 33, going against them. This is inconsistent with Lord Diplock's speech in Thompson v Brown, and contrary to subsequent cases. These include *Nash v Eli Lilly and Co.* [1993] 1 WLR 782, where a finding that the claims were weak was regarded as an important factor in refusing to make orders under s. 33, and *Long v Tolchard and Sons Ltd* (1999) *The Times*, 5 January 2000, where it was said that if the claimant has a strong, or even a cast-iron, case against the original tortfeasor, that is an important factor to place into the balance that has to be struck. Of course, like all the other factors, the strength of the case is not determinative of the application. Where the question of the merits arises at an interim hearing, all the court should do is to determine the overall prospects (*Dale v British Coal Corporation (No. 2)* (1992) *The Times*, 2 July 1992), although a determination to the usual civil standard may be appropriate where the matter is raised as a preliminary issue.

Other factors In *Das v Ganju* [1999] PIQR P260 the Court of Appeal held that delays caused by incorrect advice given by the claimant's lawyers should not be laid at the claimant's door, and allowed a claim to continue despite a delay of many years. **10.49**

As mentioned at **10.25**, many reasons for not bringing a claim, such as a reluctance to sue one's present employer, are irrelevant under LA 1980, s. 14. However, they can be important factors under s. 33. So, in *McCafferty v Metropolitan Police District Receiver* [1977] 1 WLR 1073 Lawton LJ said, in relation to an application under s. 33, '... the court should be understanding of men who, after taking an overall view of their situation, come to the conclusion that they would prefer to go on working rather than become involved in litigation'.

Discretionary extension of the limitation period under s. 33 has no application in cases governed by the two-year limitation period under the Convention relating to the Carriage of Passengers and their Luggage by Sea (as enacted by the Merchant Shipping Act 1995; class 16 in **table 10.1**), see *Higham v Stena Sealink Ltd* [1996] 1 WLR 1107.

Procedure Applications under LA 1980, s. 33, should generally be made to a judge, although in the county courts they can be made to a district judge if the value of the claim does not exceed £15,000 (the trial jurisdiction for district judges) (*Hughes v Jones* [1996] PIQR P380). It is incumbent on the claimant to disclose all relevant circumstances at the hearing of the application, and if this is breached, the decision may be set aside (*Long v Tolchard and Sons Ltd* (1999) *The Times*, 5 January 2000). **10.50**

Issuing a second claim

Where proceedings are issued and come to naught through inactivity on the part of the claimant, they can be abandoned or discontinued, and, provided the limitation period has not expired, fresh proceedings can be commenced in respect of the same cause of action. There are exceptions where the original proceedings are dismissed for contumelious conduct or are struck out as an abuse of process. Given that the court has a discretion to allow personal injuries cases to continue despite being commenced after the expiry of the limitation period under **LA 1980, s. 33**, the question arose whether a second claim could be issued in a personal injuries case after the expiry of limitation where a first claim commenced within the limitation period was flawed in some way (such as the proceedings not being served in circumstances where they would not be renewed — see **15.7** — or where the first claim had been dismissed or struck out). The answer, according to *Walkley v Precision Forgings Ltd* [1979] 1 WLR 606, is no. As Lord Wilberforce said, s. 33 contemplates: **10.51**

> a case in which, because the three years have expired without an action being brought, [s. 11] applies to the prejudice of the [claimant]. But if the [claimant] has brought his action within the three years, how has he been prejudiced by [s. 11]? ... He brought his first action within the normal limitation period, and if he has suffered any prejudice, it is by his own inaction and not by the operation of the Act.

Claims were struck out in *Piggott v Aulton* [2003] EWCA Civ 24, [2003] RTR 540, where a claimant issued the first claim against the estate of a deceased person before personal representatives were appointed, and the second claim was issued against the personal representative, and in *Young v Western Power Distribution (South West) plc* (2003) *The Times*, 19 August 2003, where a widow started a second claim after the first claim had failed before her husband died.

The principle only applies where the same defendant is sued on the same cause of action in both sets of proceedings. Where the first claim is against a driver's employer alleging vicarious liability, a direction under s. 33 may be made in a second claim arising out of the same accident brought against the driver personally (*Shapland v Palmer* [1999] 1 WLR 2068).

In *Deerness v John R. Keeble and Son (Brantham) Ltd* [1983] 2 Lloyd's Rep 260, a second claim was struck out as an abuse of process despite an interim payment having been made in the original claim, Lord Diplock saying that s. 33 cannot be used to heal such self-inflicted wounds.

Surprisingly, *Walkley v Precision Forgings Ltd* was distinguished in *White v Glass* (1989) *The Times*, 18 February 1989, where the first claim was irregular in that it named the defendant as 'Corby Hazeltree Football Club', an unincorporated association. The claim was not a nullity, so it is difficult to see any real distinction from *Walkley v Precision Forgings Ltd*. *Forward v Hendricks* [1997] 2 All ER 395, however, is in line with the House of Lords authorities in holding there is no jurisdiction to make an order under s. 33 where the first claim fails due to defective service of the proceedings.

Agreement extending Landlord and Tenant Act 1954, part II, time limits

10.52 The statutory period for commencing applications by landlords or tenants for new business tenancies under the **Landlord and Tenant Act 1954, s. 24**, and by landlords for orders terminating part II tenancies under **s. 29(2)** is set out in **s. 29A(2)**. Where the landlord gave a notice under **s. 25**, the statutory period ends on the date specified in that notice, and where the tenant made a request for a new tenancy under **s. 26**, it ends immediately before the date specified in the request.

In the period between the landlord's notice under **s. 25** or the tenant's request under **s. 26** and the expiry of the statutory period, the parties may agree to extend the time for bringing an application under the Act for a specified period (**s. 29B(1)**). The parties may from time to time agree further, specified, extensions, but such agreements must be made before time has expired under the current agreement (**s. 29B(2)**).

EQUITABLE REMEDIES, LACHES AND ACQUIESCENCE

10.53 By **LA 1980 s. 36(1)**, the usual time limits in the Act do 'not apply to any claim for specific performance of a contract or for an injunction or for other equitable relief, except in so far as any such time limit may be applied by the court by analogy'. Claims for equitable damages or equitable compensation are claims to which **s. 36** applies the six-year limitation periods in **ss. 2** and **chapter 5** by analogy (*Companhia de Seguros Imperio v Heath (REBX) Ltd* [2001] 1 WLR 112). In such cases the question is whether prior to 1 July 1940 a court facing such a case would have applied a limitation period by analogy. However, trawling through ancient authorities to find actual instances where this had been done in the past is deprecated.

In *Clarke v Marlborough Fine Art (London) Ltd* (2001) *The Times*, 5 July 2001, it was said that it is probable that in undue influence claims the only time-related defences available are laches and acquiescence (and presumably, affirmation). The defences of laches and acquiescence are preserved by s. 36(2). The essence of the defence of acquiescence is that there has been an encouragement or allowance of a party to believe something to his detriment. Principles dealing with this defence were laid down in *Jones v Stones* [1999] 1 WLR 1739, which considered the older cases of *Willmott v Barber* (1880) 15 ChD 96 and *Habib Bank Ltd v Habib Bank AG Zurich*

[1981] 1 WLR 1265. The first question is whether one party, by its action or inaction, has encouraged the other party to believe a certain state of affairs. The second question is whether there was reliance on that encouragement. Thirdly, whether in all the circumstances of the case it would be unconscionable for the first party to then insist on its legal rightIt is incorrect to concentrate on the period of delay as being enough of itself.

The period of delay likely to give rise to these equitable defences depends on the nature of the relief claimed and the facts of the case. Delay in the context of interim injunctions is considered in **37.51**. In the case of actions to redeem mortgages, a period of 20 years was said to be a convenient guide in *Weld v Petre* [1929] 1 Ch 33. Laches was held to be a defence in *Lynch v James Lynch and Sons (Transport) Ltd* (2000) LTL 8/3/2000 where a shareholder failed to assert his rights for 24 years.

Chapter 11 Where to Start Proceedings

JURISDICTION OF THE HIGH COURT AND THE COUNTY COURTS

Concurrent jurisdiction

11.1 The High Court and the county courts have concurrent jurisdiction over most claims. These include claims:

(a) in contract and tort (**County Courts Act 1984, s. 15**);
(b) for the recovery of land (s. 21);
(c) under the Inheritance (Provision for Family and Dependants) Act 1975 (**County Courts Act 1984, s. 25**);
(d) for relief from forfeiture (s. 139); and
(e) under the **Landlord and Tenant Act 1954, part II**, in relation to the security of tenure of business tenants (Landlord and Tenant Act 1954, s. 63).

Cases where the jurisdiction of the county courts is limited

11.2 The jurisdiction of the county courts is limited in certain cases to claims which fall below particular financial limits. For example, county courts have jurisdiction over claims in equity where the estate, fund or value of property does not exceed £30,000 (**County Courts Act 1984, s. 23**) (parties can in certain cases agree to vary this limit: s. 24). Other limits to the jurisdiction of county courts are set out in the **High Court and County Courts Jurisdiction Order 1991, art. 2.**

Further, the following claims may not be conducted in a county court, whatever their financial value, unless (in the case of paragraphs (c) and (d)) the parties agree in writing:

(a) a claim for judicial review, as a county court does not have the power to make any of the orders asked for in judicial review claims (**County Courts Act 1984, s. 38(3)(a)**): judicial review is assigned to the Queen's Bench Division by the **Supreme Court Act 1981, sch. 1, para. 2(b)** (referred to in **PD 7, para. 2.6**), and claims are dealt with in the Administrative Court (**PD 54, para. 2.1**);
(b) an application for a writ of habeas corpus, which must be made in the Queen's Bench Division (**Supreme Court Act 1981, sch. 1, para. 2(a); PD 7, para. 2.6**), unless it is an application by a parent or guardian of a child in relation to the custody, care or control of the child, in which case it must be made in the Family Division (**RSC, ord. 54, r. 11 in CPR, sch. 1**);
(c) a claim for libel or slander (**County Courts Act 1984, s. 15(2)(c); PD 7, para. 2.9**);
(d) a claim in which the title to any toll, fair, market or franchise is in question (**County Courts Act 1984, s. 15(2)(b); PD 7, para. 2.9**);
(e) applications concerning the decisions of local authority auditors (**High Court and County Courts Jurisdiction Order 1991, art. 6**).

A claim under the **Human Rights Act 1998, s.** 7(1)(a), in respect of a judicial act may only be brought in the High Court. Any other claims under that section may be brought in any court (**CPR, r.** 7.11).

County courts no longer have Admiralty jurisdiction as defined in the **County Courts Act 1984, s.** 27 (Civil Courts (Amendment) (No. 2) Order 1999 (SI 1999/1011)). Most Admiralty claims must be started in the Admiralty Court in the Queen's Bench Division (**CPR, r.** 61.2).

Cases which must be brought in a county court

Certain claims must be brought in a county court: **11.3**

(a) Claims under the **Consumer Credit Act 1974** may only be brought in a county court, normally the county court where the debtor resides or carries on business (**PD 7B, para.** 4).
(b) A mortgage possession claim must be brought in the county court for the district in which the land is situated unless circumstances such as complex factual disputes or points of law of general importance justify starting a claim in the High Court (**CPR, r.** 55.3; **PD** 55, **para.** 1)
(c) Applications under the Access to Neighbouring Land Act 1992, s. 1, must be started in a county court (**High Court and County Courts Jurisdiction Order 1991, art. 6A**).
(d) Proceedings to enforce claims of sex discrimination made unlawful under the Sex Discrimination Act 1975, part III, may be brought only in a county court (Sex Discrimination Act 1975, s. 66). A High Court judge dealing with a judicial review claim arising out of facts including an allegation of unlawful sex discrimination must refuse to decide the discrimination issue, and related legal points, as these are matters for the county court (*R v South Bank University, ex parte Coggeran* (2000) *The Times*, 19 September 2000).

ALLOCATION OF BUSINESS BETWEEN THE HIGH COURT AND COUNTY COURTS

Where the High Court and the county courts have concurrent jurisdiction, business is allocated according to the following rules: **11.4**

(a) A claim for damages or for a specified sum may be issued in the High Court only where the value of the claim is more than £15,000 (**PD 7, para. 2.1**).
(b) **PD 29, para. 2.2**, restricts a claimant's right to continue proceedings issued in the Central Office or Chancery Chambers of the Royal Courts of Justice (RCJ). Although any money claim worth over £15,000 may be issued in the RCJ, claims with an estimated value less than £50,000 will generally be transferred to a county court, unless one of the following exceptions applies:
    (i) The claim is required by statute to be tried in the High Court.
    (ii) The claim falls within a specialist list as defined in **CPR, r. 2.3(2)**. The specialist lists are the lists of proceedings in the Commercial Court (**r. 58.2(1)**), Mercantile Courts (**r. 59.1(3)(a)**), the Patents Court and the Patents County Court (**r. 63.4**), and the Technology and Construction Court (**r. 60.2(1)**).
    (iii) The claim falls into one of the following categories: professional negligence, fraud or undue influence, defamation, malicious prosecution or false imprisonment, claims against the police, claims under the **Fatal Accidents Act 1976**, or contentious probate claims (**PD 29, para. 2.6**).
    (iv) The claim is otherwise 'within the criteria of art. 7(5) of the **High Court and County Courts Jurisdiction Order 1991**' (SI 1991/724). This article has in fact now been repealed by the High Court and County Courts Jurisdiction (Amendment) Order 1999 (SI 1999/1014). It stated the following criteria: the financial substance of the

action; its importance, and in particular whether it raises questions of importance to non-parties or the general public; its complexity; and whether transfer is likely to result in a more speedy trial of the action (although transfer may not be ordered on this ground alone).

(c) A claim for personal injuries must not be started in the High Court unless the value of the claim is £50,000 or more (**PD 7, para. 2.2**).

(d) A claim must be issued in the High Court or in a county court, as appropriate, where an enactment requires it (**PD 7, para. 2.3**).

(e) Subject to paragraphs (a) and (c) above, a claim should be started in the High Court if the claimant believes it should be tried by a High Court judge because of the financial value of the claim and the amount in dispute, its complexity or its importance to the general public (**PD 7, para. 2.4**). In other words, the £15,000 and £50,000 limits are the lowest thresholds for issuing a claim in the High Court. But, even where a case is worth more than these amounts, the claimant should not issue automatically in the High Court but should go on to consider the factors listed in para. 2.4 in deciding whether trial by a High Court judge is really necessary.

By **PD 7, para. 2.2**, the value of a claim is determined in accordance with the High Court and County Courts Jurisdiction Order 1991, art. 9. This simply cross-refers to **CPR, r. 16.3(6)**. Thus, the following must all be disregarded:

(a) interest;
(b) costs;
(c) any reduction for contributory negligence against the claimant;
(d) the value of any counterclaim or set-off; and
(e) the recoupment of benefits under the Social Security (Recovery of Benefits) Act 1997.

Table 11.1 Summary of the rules on allocation of business where both the High Court and the county courts have jurisdiction

Nature of claim	Venue
Money claim (i.e., claim for debt or liquidated demand or damages)	May be commenced in the High Court only if the claimant expects to recover more than £15,000.
Money claim issued in the RCJ	May be commenced in the RCJ, but will generally be transferred to a county court, if worth less than £50,000, unless one of the exceptions stated in **PD 29, para. 2.2**, applies.
Claim for personal injuries	May be commenced in the High Court only if the value of the claim is £50,000 or more.

ALLOCATION OF BUSINESS TO THE QUEEN'S BENCH DIVISION OF THE HIGH COURT

11.5 The following claims must be issued in the Queen's Bench Division of the High Court:

(a) applications for a writ of habeas corpus (**Supreme Court Act 1981, sch. 1, para. 2(a); PD 7, para. 2.6**) except applications by a parent or guardian in relation to a child (see 11.2);

(b) applications for judicial review (**Supreme Court Act 1981, sch. 1, para. 2(b); PD 7, para. 2.6**);

(c) all control order proceedings within the meaning of the Prevention of Terrorism Act 2005 (**Supreme Court Act 1981, sch. 1, para. 2(ba)**);

(d) matters involving the exercise of the High Court's jurisdiction as a prize court (**Supreme Court Act 1981, sch. 1, para. 2(c)**);

(e) Commercial Court claims (**Supreme Court Act 1981, sch. 1, para. 2(d)**; see further **11.7(d)**).

A claim in the High Court ordered to be tried by jury will be transferred to the Queen's Bench Division, if not already being conducted there (**PD 7, para. 2.8**).

CHANCERY BUSINESS

Claims involving Chancery business may be dealt with either in the High Court or in a county court (**PD 7, para. 2.5**). The claim form must be marked 'Chancery Division' in the top right corner, if issued in the High Court, and 'Chancery Business' if issued in the county court (**PD 7, para. 2.5**). The county court's jurisdiction over equity claims is limited to £30,000 (**County Courts Act 1984, s. 23**), though parties may agree to vary this in certain types of proceedings (s. 24). **11.6**

PD 7, para. 2.5, defines 'Chancery business' as including any of the matters specified in the **Supreme Court Act 1981, sch. 1, para. 1**. Those matters are:

(a) the sale, exchange or partition of land, or the raising of charges on land;
(b) the redemption or foreclosure of mortgages;
(c) the execution of trusts;
(d) the administration of the estates of deceased persons;
(e) bankruptcy;
(f) the dissolution of partnerships or the taking of partnership or other accounts;
(g) the rectification, setting aside or cancellation of deeds or other instruments in writing;
(h) probate business, other than non-contentious or common form business;
(i) patents, trade marks, registered designs, copyright or design right;
(j) the appointment of a guardian of a minor's estate,
(k) all causes and matters involving the exercise of the High Court's jurisdiction under the enactments relating to companies.

Within the £30,000 limit in the **County Courts Act 1984, s. 23**, any county court can deal with any Chancery business claim except:

(a) county court probate claims must be brought in a court where there is a Chancery district registry (**CPR, r. 57.2(3)**); and
(b) county court intellectual property claims must be brought in a court where there is a Chancery district registry or in the Patents County Court(**r. 63.13, PD 63, para. 18**).

This means that there will be claims designated as Chancery business which are commenced in county courts with no Chancery expertise. Detailed guidance on transferring these cases, and also claims from the Chancery Division to an appropriate county court (and in particular to the Central London County Court, Chancery List), is given in the **Chancery Guide, paras 13.4** to **13.15**.

Any claim which raises an issue under the EC Treaty, art. 81 (anti-competitive agreements) or art. 82 (abuse of a dominant market position), or the equivalent United Kingdom statutory provisions, chapter 1 or chapter 2 of the Competition Act 1998, must be transferred to the Chancery Division at the RCJ if commenced in any court other than the Commercial and Admiralty Court (**CPR, r. 30.8**). If a commercial claim, as defined in **r. 58.1(2)**, which raises a competition issue is commenced in the Queen's Bench Division or a Mercantile Court, any party may apply for the claim to be transferred to the Commercial Court instead of the Chancery Division. If the application to transfer to the Commercial Court is refused, the claim must be transferred to the Chancery Division at the RCJ in the usual way (**r. 30.8(4)**).

SPECIALIST CLAIMS

11.7 Various rules and practice directions regulate the place where the specialist proceedings to which they relate should be started. In brief, the position is as follows:

(a) Probate claims: **CPR, Part** 57, and **PD** 57. A probate claim to be conducted in the High Court must be issued in the Chancery Division, that is, either Chancery Chambers of the Royal Courts of Justice, or a Chancery district registry. (Chancery district registries are to be found at Birmingham, Bristol, Cardiff, Leeds, Liverpool, Manchester, Newcastle upon Tyne and Preston.) A probate claim may be issued in a county court, but only where the value of the estate does not exceed £30,000 (**County Courts Act 1984, s. 32**). A probate claim in the county court can only be brought in a county court where there is also a Chancery district registry or in the Central London County Court (**CPR, r. 57.2(3)**).

(b) Companies Act applications: **PD 49B**. Applications under the Companies Act 1985, and related legislation (see **82.4**), to be conducted in the High Court must be issued in the Companies Court of the Chancery Division, in the Royal Courts of Justice, or in a Chancery district registry. Applications under the Companies Act 1985 may be made in the county court only in respect of companies whose paid-up capital is no more than £120,000 (Insolvency Act 1986, s. 117(2)). (See further 79.7.)

(c) Technology and Construction Court (TCC): **CPR, Part 60**, and **PD 60**. Claims that involve issues or questions which are technically complex, or for which a trial by a judge of the TCC is desirable, may be issued in the TCC. TCC claims may be brought either in the High Court or certain county courts. In the High Court outside London, they may be issued in any district registry, but preferably in a district registry where a TCC judge will usually be available. These are: Birmingham, Bristol, Cardiff, Chester, Exeter, Leeds, Liverpool, Newcastle, Nottingham and Salford (**PD 60, para. 3.3**). TCC claims may be issued only in the following county courts: Birmingham, Bristol, Cardiff, Central London, Chester, Exeter, Leeds, Liverpool, Newcastle, Nottingham and Salford (**PD 60, para. 3.4**). However, a great proportion of TCC claims are conducted in the TCC in Fetter Lane in London.

(d) Commercial Court: **CPR, Part 58**, and **PD 58**. Commercial claims as defined by **CPR, r. 58.1(2)**, may be conducted in the commercial list in the Royal Courts of Justice and, if they are, they should be issued out of the Admiralty and Commercial Registry (**PD 58, para. 2.1**). By **CPR, r. 58.1(2)**, any case arising out of trade and commerce in general may be commenced in the Commercial Court, including any case relating to:
   (i) a business document or contract;
   (ii) the export or import of goods;
   (iii) the carriage of goods by land, sea, air or pipeline;
   (iv) the exploitation of oil and gas reserves or other natural resources;
   (v) insurance and reinsurance;
   (vi) banking and financial services;
   (vii) the operation of markets and exchanges;
   (viii) the purchase and sale of commodities;
   (ix) the construction of ships;
   (x) business agency; and
   (xi) arbitration.

(e) Mercantile Courts: **CPR, Part 59**, and **PD 59**. Claims which are broadly commercial in nature, and which are not required to proceed in the Chancery Division or in any other specialist list may be issued in a Mercantile Court (**CPR, r. 59.1(2)**). There are Mercantile Courts at the Central London Civil Justice Centre and at the following district registries: Birmingham, Bristol, Cardiff, Chester, Leeds, Liverpool, Manchester and Newcastle. By **PD 59, para. 2.3**, claims worth less than £15,000 may not be issued in the mercantile list at the Central London Civil Justice Centre without the court's permission.

(f) Patents etc.: **CPR, Part 63**, and **PD 63**. The jurisdiction of the Patents Court and the Patents County Court is conferred by the statutes concerning intellectual property rights.

(g) Admiralty proceedings: **CPR, Part 61**, and **PD 61**. An Admiralty claim listed in **CPR, r. 61.2(1)**, must be commenced in the Admiralty Court. County courts no longer have Admiralty jurisdiction (Civil Courts (Amendment) (No. 2) Order 1999 (SI 1999/1011)).

(h) The business assigned to the Family Division is listed in **2.14**.

APPLICATIONS BEFORE ISSUE

Applications made before a claim has started should be made to the court where it is likely that the claim to which the application relates will be issued, unless there is good reason to make the application to a different court (**CPR, r. 23.2(4)**). There is no explanation in the rules of what is meant by 'good reason' but one circumstance in which it would be appropriate to make an application in a different court is where a freezing injunction or search order (which may be made only by the High Court or a duly authorised judge, see **37.2**) is sought in relation to a claim to be issued in a county court. **11.8**

COMMENCING IN THE WRONG COURT

Generally, when proceedings are commenced in the wrong court they will be transferred to the correct court using the procedure in **CPR, Part 30**, and the claimant will usually be penalised by being ordered to pay the costs involved in the transfer. In addition, where proceedings which, in the court's opinion, should have been commenced in a county court have been commenced in the High Court, the court may reduce any award of costs by up to 25 per cent (**Supreme Court Act 1981, s. 51(8)** and **(9)**). However, if a claimant brings a claim in the High Court in breach of a requirement that it should be in a county court (or vice versa), the court may either transfer the claim, or, if it is satisfied that the person bringing the claim knew of the requirement, strike out the proceedings (**County Courts Act 1984, ss. 40(1)(b)** and **42(1)(b)**; see *Adshead v Royal Bank of Scotland plc* [2002] EWHC 192 (Ch), LTL 25/2/2002). According to *Restick v Crickmore* [1994] 1 WLR 420, striking out is inappropriate for bona fide mistakes, but would be a proper response to instances where starting in the wrong court was a deliberate attempt to harass a defendant, or a deliberate attempt to run up unnecessary costs, or was done despite the claimant being told by the defendant where the claim should be commenced. **11.9**

Where a claimant seeks to issue proceedings, and the court manager believes they are being issued in the wrong court, the court should nevertheless accept the papers. Court officials have no power to make judicial determinations as to whether they should accept a claim (*Gwynedd County Council v Grunshaw* [2000] 1 WLR 494). Once the claim is issued, it may be transferred or struck out by judicial determination, as above.

Chapter 12 Issuing Proceedings

The following procedural checklists, which are in **appendix 1**, are relevant to this chapter and **chapter 15**:

Procedural checklist 9 Issue and service where service of the claim form is to be effected by the court

Procedural checklist 10 Issue and service where service of the claim form is to be effected by the claimant

METHODS OF COMMENCING CIVIL PROCEEDINGS

12.1 Lord Woolf's *Final Report* commented that 'A prime example of [the complexity of the old rules] is the fact that there are four different ways of starting proceedings in the High Court, and another four in the county courts' (ch. 12, para. 1). In order to further the aim of achieving simplicity in civil proceedings, Lord Woolf recommended that there should be a single claim form which could be used for every case (ch. 2, para. 3).

This radical simplification has not worked out in practice. First, during the drafting of the CPR it was realised that it is possible to use a simplified procedure (now in **CPR, Part 8**; see **chapter 13**) for certain classes of proceedings in which it is normal for there to be no disputes over facts. Secondly it was decided to create a special form of process for third-party and other subsidiary claims (**CPR, Part 20**; see **chapters 28** and **29**). Thirdly it was not possible, in time for the introduction of the CPR in April 1999, to assimilate the numerous varieties of specialist proceedings for which special forms of originating process existed under the old rules, and at present they remain exceptions under the CPR. Some of these exceptional procedures are prescribed by statute and some were excluded from the terms of reference of Lord Woolf's inquiry.

The result is that there are still at least 13 different ways of commencing claims in civil courts. These are by:

(a) Claim form (**form N1**; see **chapter 23**), which is the standard method under the CPR. (Three special claim forms are prescribed for use in Admiralty claims (**ADM 1, ADM 1A** and **ADM 15**); there is a special version of **form N1** for use in the Commercial Court (**form N1(CC)**); and a special claim form (**N461**) is prescribed for judicial review proceedings.)

(b) **Part 8** claim form (**form N208**), for use in proceedings in which there are no substantial factual disputes and where required by a practice direction (see **chapter 13**). A special **Part 8** claim form (**N500**) has been prescribed for director disqualification proceedings.

(c) **Part 20** claim form (**form N211**), for additional claims (see **chapters 28** and **29**).

(d) Arbitration claim form (**form N8**), which is used in arbitration applications (see **69.2** and **69.3**).

(e) Special claim forms for starting a claim for possession of land (**N5** and **N5B**), for relief against forfeiture of a lease (**N5A**) and for demotion of tenancy (**N6**).
(f) Special claim form (N2) for use in probate claims.
(g) Petition, which is required by statute or statutory instrument for various proceedings, such as divorce and judicial separation (which are not considered in this work), winding up of companies (see **chapter** 79) and bankruptcy (see **chapter 80**), and has been adopted by practice direction for some companies matters (see **chapter** 82).
(h) Administration application, to obtain an order appointing an administrator of a company (see **79.101** to **79.115**).
(i) Originating application, which is required for an application under the Insolvency Act 1986 or the Insolvency Rules 1986 (SI 1986/1925) if it is not in pending proceedings (see **chapter 81**).
(j) Interpleader notice, which is used in certain circumstances in county court interpleader proceedings (**CCR, ord. 33** in CPR, sch. 2), but is not used in the High Court.
(k) Summons in respect of alleged offences contrary to the **County Courts Act 1984, ss. 14**, **92**, and **124** (**CCR, ord. 34** in CPR, sch. 2), which is a procedure more of a criminal nature than civil.
(l) Request, such as under the rules for enforcing parking penalties under the Road Traffic Act 1991 (**CPR, r. 75.3**).
(m) Some cases can be brought very informally simply by making an application by witness statement or affidavit, an example being an application under the Deeds of Arrangement Act 1914, s. 7 (**RSC, ord. 94, r.** 4(1) in CPR, sch. 1).

The point is made in **PD Protocols, para** 4.7, and in most of the pre-action protocols themselves, that litigation is a last resort (see **chapter 8**). Complaints procedures and other forms of alternative dispute resolution should at least be considered before most forms of litigation are started: even if the whole dispute cannot be resolved by these means, the parties and their legal advisers should resolve the dispute as far as possible without litigation (*R (Cowl) v Plymouth City Council* [2001] EWCA Civ 1935, [2002] 1 WLR 803).

Use of incorrect form

If a claimant has used the wrong form to start proceedings, the court should not strike out the claim, but should permit the claimant to rectify it, provided all the information the defendant needed to understand the case to be met has been given (*Hannigan v Hannigan* [2000] 2 FCR 650). If use of a particular procedure is prescribed by statute, the court does not have any power under the CPR to waive that requirement (*Re Osea Road Camp Sites Ltd* [2004] EWHC 2437 (Ch), [2005] 1 WLR 760, which is criticised at **1.26**). **12.2**

ISSUING A CLAIM FORM

Under the CPR, unless another method of commencing proceedings is required or permitted (see **12.1**), proceedings are started when the court issues, at the request of the claimant, a claim form (**form** N1) prepared by or on behalf of the claimant (**r.** 7.2(1)). Issue, rather than service, is the relevant date for the purposes of limitation (see *Thompson v Brown* [1981] 1 WLR 744) and for the supply of court records of proceedings under **r.** 5.4(1) (*Advance Specialist Treatment Engineering Ltd v Cleveland Structural Engineering (Hong Kong) Ltd* [2000] 1 WLR 558). On the other hand, service is the relevant date for proceedings being definitively pending under **Regulation** (EC) **No. 44/2001** (the Jurisdiction and Judgments Regulation) (see **16.38**). An issue fee is payable in accordance with the **CPFO** (see **appendix** 6). The court will issue the claim form by affixing the court seal (**CPR, r.** 2.6(1)), which it may do by hand or by printing a facsimile of the seal on the document, electronically or otherwise (**r.** 2.6(2)). If the claimant has entered into a funding arrangement (as defined in **r.** 43.2(1)(k)), a notice of funding of claim (**form N251**) must be filed at court with the claim form (**PD 43–48, para.** 19.2(2)(a)). **12.3**

Likewise, in LSC-funded claims a copy of the certificate must be lodged when the claim is issued (**PD 43–48, para. 21.6**). There is nothing to prevent a claim being issued with a stated value well below the full value of the damage done, even though the effect may be that a lower issue fee will be payable (*Khiaban v Beard* [2003] EWCA Civ 358, [2003] 1 WLR 1626). The procedure for issuing and serving a claim is summarised in **procedural checklist 9** and **procedural checklist 10**, in **appendix 1**. Those procedural checklists should be read in conjunction with **chapter 15**.

Number of copies required

12.4 In order to have a claim form issued, the claimant must take or send to court one copy of the completed claim form for the court and one for each defendant. The rules do not mention a copy for the claimant's own use. However, a claimant who wants a file copy of the claim form as issued may provide a further copy of the claim form which the court will seal and return to the claimant marked 'claimant's copy' (**Queen's Bench Guide, para. 4.1.5**).

Time of issue

12.5 For the purposes of the CPR, proceedings are started when the claim form is issued by the court (**CPR, r. 7.2(1)**). The date of issue is entered on the form by the court (**r. 7.2(2)**). For the purposes of the **Limitation Act 1980** and other statutes a claim is 'brought' when received by the court office, if this date is earlier than the date on which the court office issued the claim form (**PD 7, para. 5.1**; and see **10.32**). Court officials will record the date of receipt of the claim form either on the claim form itself, or on its covering letter (**PD 7, para. 5.2**). However **PD 7, para. 5.4**, enjoins claimants for whom the date of receipt is crucial to make their own arrangements for recording it.

Notice of issue

12.6 Once the court has issued a claim form, it will assign the claim a number, create a case management file and send a notice of issue to the claimant, using form N205A, N205B or N205C, depending on whether the claim is for a specified or unspecified amount of money or whether it is a non-money claim.

Issue by fax in the Admiralty and Commercial Registry

12.7 Appendix A to **PD 58** provides a procedure for claimants to make a request by fax for the issue of a claim form in the Admiralty and Commercial Registry in the RCJ when that registry is closed. Provided the procedure is followed, the claim form is treated as issued at the time when the fax is received.

CLAIM PRODUCTION CENTRE

12.8 Claim forms may be issued in bulk in debt recovery claims brought by, for example, credit card companies and public utilities, from the Production Centre in Northampton, in accordance with **PD 7C**. A code of practice provides for the forms of magnetic media that may be used when delivering data to the Centre. Claims that may be issued at the Production Centre are restricted to county court claims for specified sums, in pounds sterling, up to £100,000 brought against no more than two defendants, none of whom is to be served out of the jurisdiction, where the claimant is not publicly funded, and where none of the parties is a child or patient. The Centre will not deal with claims against the Crown. The Centre can deal with cases through service, entry of default judgment and judgment on admissions, and to the registration of judgment and issuing warrants of execution. It can also handle defences, but when a defence is filed it will send a notice to the claimant requiring a reply within 28 days stating whether the claimant wishes the claim to proceed. If no such notification is given the claim will be stayed. If, however, notification is received that the claim is to continue, the proceedings will be transferred to the defendant's home court (if the defendant is an individual), or (if the defendant is not an individual) to the claimant's home court (or that of the claimant's solicitors) (**PD 7C, paras 1.3(2)(e)** and **5.2**). A claim will also be transferred to the defendant's home court where an order for oral examination or enforcement (other than by warrant of execution, charging order or third party debt order) is made (**PD 7C, para. 1.3(2)(f)**).

CLAIMS UNDER THE CONSUMER CREDIT ACT 1974: FIXED-DATE CLAIMS

The court may in certain cases fix a date for a hearing upon issue of a claim form (**CPR, r. 7.9**). The claims for which the court will adopt this procedure are listed in **PD 7B, para. 3**. They are all claims under specified sections of the **Consumer Credit Act 1974**. A modified procedure applies to these claims, as set out in **PD 7B, para. 5**. It is as follows: **12.9**

(a) The court will fix a hearing date on the issue of the claim form. Each party must be given at least 28 days' notice of the hearing date. Notice of the hearing date must be served at the same time as the claim form, unless the hearing date is specified in the claim form.
(b) The claimant must serve particulars of the claim with the claim form.
(c) The defendant should not file an acknowledgment of service. A defendant who wishes to defend the claim should file a defence, within 14 days after service of the claim form.
(d) Where the defendant fails to file a defence within 14 days, the claimant may not apply for judgment in default: **CPR, part 12**, does not apply where the claimant is using the **PD 7B** procedure. The defendant may file a defence after the expiry of the 14-day time limit, but the court may take account of the delay in the costs order it makes.
(e) The court will usually dispose of the claim at the hearing, provided the defendant has not served a defence. If a defence has been served, the court may allocate the claim to a track and give directions.

MONEY CLAIM ONLINE

A claimant may start a claim electronically at the Money Claim Online website, www.moneyclaim.gov.uk, where a request can be made for the issue of a claim form by Northampton County Court (**CPR, r. 7.12; PD 7E, para. 1.2(1) and 1.4**). Once a claim has been started in this way, the claimant can also file electronically a request for judgment in default, or judgment on acceptance of an admission of the whole of the amount claimed or the issue of a warrant of execution (paras **1.2(2)** and **13**). The claimant can also view an electronic record of the progress of the claim. The record of each claim will be reviewed and, where necessary, updated every day until the claim is either transferred from the Northampton County Court or a party files a defence, or a part admission or an application notice requiring a hearing (**para. 15.2**). **12.10**

By **para. 4**, Money Claim Online may only be used for money claims in sterling which are for less than £100,000. It may not be used where the claimant is a child or patient, or is funded by the Legal Services Commission. Nor may it be used against more than one defendant (or more than two, where the claim is for a single amount against each of them) or where the defendant is the Crown or a child or patient. The defendant's address for service must be within England and Wales.

The claimant requests the issue of a claim form by completing and sending an online claim form (including the particulars of claim) and electronically paying the appropriate issue fee at www.moneyclaim.gov.uk (**para. 5.1**). The claim is brought for the purposes of the **Limitation Act 1980** on the date on which the online claim form is received by the court's computer system (**PD 7E, para.** 5.5). The court will serve a hard copy of the claim form on the defendant, and will also send the claimant notice of issue by post (**para.** 5.6). The claim form is deemed to be served on the fifth day after issue, whether that day is a business day or not (**para.** 5.7).

The defendant may then acknowledge service or file a defence and/or counterclaim in the conventional way or alternatively by sending either document by email to the email addresses specified in **para 6.1**.

By **para.** 14, where the Northampton County Court is not the defendant's home court, the court will transfer the claim to the defendant's home court (or, where the defendant is not an individual, the court for the district in which the claimant's address for service is situated) if:

(a) the defendant applies to set aside or vary judgment under **CPR, r. 13.4**;
(b) there is to be a hearing for a judge to determine the time and rate of payment under **r. 14.2**;
(c) a defence is filed to all or part of the claim under **r. 26.2**; or
(d) either party makes an application which cannot be dealt with without a hearing.

Chapter 13 Part 8 Claims

The following procedural checklists, which are in **appendix 1**, are relevant to this chapter:

Procedural checklist 3 Claim under standard Part 8 procedure
Procedural checklist 4 Modified Part 8 procedure for claims listed in PD 8B, Section B, Table 2

TYPES OF CLAIM TO WHICH PART 8 APPLIES

Introduction

The **Part 8** procedure is intended for cases where the nature of the relief or remedy sought, or the lack of factual dispute, would make the standard procedure unnecessarily cumbersome. It provides a speedy mechanism for disposing of claims without the need for particulars of claim (**CPR, rr. 8.9(a)(i)** and **16.1**), a defence (**rr. 8.9(a)(ii)** and **15.1**), or an allocation questionnaire (because all Part 8 claims are allocated to the multi-track: **r. 8.9(c)**). Judgment in default is not available (**r. 12.2(b)**). By **r. 8.1(2)** and **(6)**, and **PD 8, paras 1.1** and **1.2**, a claimant may use the **Part 8** procedure to seek the court's decision on a question which is unlikely to involve a substantial dispute of fact (see **13.2**), or where a rule or practice direction requires or permits use of the procedure (see **13.3** and **13.4**). **13.1**

General claims unlikely to involve a substantial dispute of fact

Claims for which the **Part 8** procedure may be used on the ground that they are unlikely to involve a substantial dispute of fact would include claims which turn on a question of law, claims relating to the construction of a document and applications for a declaration. In some cases, the claimant will have the choice between (a) invoking the **Part 8** procedure, and (b) issuing a **Part** 7 claim form and applying for summary judgment. However, as the **Part 8** procedure does not permit the exchange of particulars of claim or defences, it will not be suitable for claims where the parties need to set out their respective cases in complicated or lengthy statements of case. Nor will **Part 8** be suitable for a claim where the claimant does not know until the defence is available whether the defendant admits the factual basis of the claim. But where a claim is suitable for determination under **Part 8**, the claimant may well find it a speedier mechanism for disposing of the claim than issuing proceedings under **Part 7**, even where these are dealt with by way of summary judgment. **13.2**

PD 8, para. 1.4, gives the following examples where the **Part 8** procedure may be used:

(a) Where a claim by or against a child or patient has been settled before the commencement of proceedings and the sole purpose of issuing the claim form is to obtain the approval of the court to the settlement.

(b) Where a claim for provisional damages has been settled before the commencement of proceedings and the sole purpose of the claim is to obtain a consent judgment.
(c) Where a summary claim for possession is made against named or unnamed defendants occupying land or premises without the licence or consent of the person claiming possession, and the claim is unlikely to involve a substantial dispute of fact.

It is the claimant, or the claimant's legal advisers, who must choose whether to use the Part 8 procedure, but the rules enable the court to weed out claims for which the chosen procedure appears to be inappropriate. Where the court receives a **Part 8** claim form, a court officer who believes it may not be appropriate for the claim may refer it to a judge for consideration (**PD 8, para. 1.5**). The court may at any stage order a **Part 8** claim to continue using the standard procedure, and give appropriate directions (**CPR, r. 8.1(3)**).

Claims under re-enacted provisions of the old rules

13.3 **PD 8B** explains whether the **Part 8** procedure should be used for the many provisions for the commencement of proceedings contained in the old RSC and CCR, re-enacted in sch. 1 and 2 to the CPR.

PD 8B is divided into two sections. For each section, there is a table listing the rules in CPR, sch. 1 and 2, to which that section applies.

Claims to which Section A applies must be brought using the standard **Part 8** procedure (subject to any contrary provision in a statute, practice direction or rule contained in CPR, sch. 1 or 2). By **PD 8B, para. A.1**, Section A applies where:

(a) the claim is listed in Table 1 of **PD 8B**;
(b) the claim or application is brought in the High Court, and an Act specifies that the application must be brought by originating summons; or
(c) before 26 April 1999, the claim or application would have been brought by originating summons,

and no other method of bringing the claim or application on or after 26 April 1999 is specified in an Act, rule or practice direction.

Claims to which Section A applies include interpleader proceedings.

Cases that fall within **Section B of PD 8B** must be brought using a modified form of the **Part 8** procedure. This is set out at **PD 8B, paras B.2 to B.15** (see **procedural checklist 4**). By **PD 8B, para. B.1**, Section B applies where:

(a) the claim is listed in Table 2 of **PD 8B**; or
(b) before 26 April 1999, the claim would have been brought in the High Court by originating motion or in a county court by originating application or petition,

and no other procedure is prescribed in an Act, rule or practice direction for the claim.

Claims which fall within Section B include applications and appeals to the High Court under a number of statutory provisions such as the Coroners Act 1988, s. 13, the Town and Country Planning Act 1990, s. 289(6), and the Drug Trafficking Act 1994.

PD 8B, para. B.1(3), by no means abolishes county court petitions, because **PD 8B** only supplements the CPR and the CPR do not apply to the most common forms of proceedings brought by petition, such as insolvency and family proceedings (**CPR, r. 2.1(2)**).

Other rules and practice directions

13.4 **PD 49B, para. 2(1)**, requires applications under most provisions of the Companies Act 1985 and other legislation relating to companies to be brought under **CPR, Part 8** (see **chapter 82**). PD Directors Disqualification Proceedings requires disqualification proceedings to use the **Part 8** procedure but prescribes a special claim form. A Part 8 claim form must be used for a claim under the Inheritance (Provision for Family and Dependants) Act 1975, s. 1 (**CPR,**

r. 57.16(1)), and for an application for a stop order which is not made in existing proceedings (CPR, r. 73.12(2)). **CPR, r. 19.7B**, requires applications under the Postal Services Act 2000, s. 92, for permission to bring proceedings in the name of the sender or addressee of a postal packet or his personal representative to be made in accordance with **CPR Part 8**. An arbitration claim must be brought under the Part 8 procedure (**rr. 62.3(1)** and **62.13(1)**).

PART 8 PROCEDURE

The **Part 8** procedure is straightforward (see **procedural checklist 3**). The claim is begun by the issue of a **Part 8** claim form. Evidence in support must be filed and served at the same time as the claim form is issued and served. Save in cases where **PD 8B, section B**, applies, the defendant responds by filing and serving an acknowledgment of service and evidence in opposition, but not a defence. The claimant may then serve evidence in reply. The court will automatically allocate the case to the multi-track, and will give directions for the disposal of the case. In most cases there will be a hearing, usually on written evidence only. **13.5**

Issue and service of Part 8 claim

The claim is issued on claim **form N208** (or such other form as is specified in **PD 8B, section B, Table 2**). The rules on issue and service contained in **CPR, Part 6** and 7 (see **chapters** 12 and 15), apply to **Part 8** claims, save that the only forms which should be served with the claim form when it is served on the defendant are the form for acknowledging service (**form N210**) and, if the claimant has entered into a funding arrangement (as defined in **r. 43.2(1)(k)**), a notice of funding of claim (**form N251**) (**PD 43–48, para. 19.2(2)(b)**). Forms for defending or admitting the claim are not required (**rr. 7.8(2)** and **8.9(a)(iv)** and **(b)(ii)**). **13.6**

Forms N208(CC) and **N210(CC)** are special versions of the Part 8 claim and acknowledgment forms for use in the Commercial Court (**PD 58, paras 2.4** and **5.2**).

In the case of claims to which **PD 8B, Section B**, applies, forms of acknowledgment are not needed either, as the defendant is not required to file an acknowledgment (**PD 8B, para. B.12**). In such cases the court will fix a hearing date upon issuing the claim form (**PD 8B, para. B.9**), and notice of the hearing date should be served on the defendant with the claim form (**PD 8B, para. B.11**).

Contents of Part 8 claim form

The following requirements for **Part 8** claim forms are made by **r. 8.2**: **13.7**

(a) The form must state that **Part 8** applies to the claim.
(b) The form must set out the question which the claimant wants the court to decide or the remedy the claimant is seeking, and the legal basis for the remedy claimed.
(c) If the claim is being made under an enactment, the claimant must identify the enactment.
(d) If the claimant is claiming, or the defendant is being sued, in a representative capacity, the claim form must state that fact and state what the capacity is.

In *Szekeres v Alan Smeath and Co.* [2005] EWHC 1733 (Ch), LTL 2/8/2005, a **Part 8** claim form which was intended to seek an order for detailed assessment of a solicitor's bills failed to state the question to be decided, did not state the remedy sought, did not refer to the **Solicitors Act 1974**, did not state that **CPR, Part 8**, applied and did not contain a statement of truth. Despite these defects, it was held that the claim form contained enough information to convey the nature of the claim. That being so, the claim form was sufficient to commence the proceedings and there was no basis on which the court could decline putting the document into formal order.

As with any other claim form, a **Part 8** claim form must be served within four months after issue, or six months where it is served out of the jurisdiction (r. 7.5). The provisions of **r. 7.6** permitting a claimant to apply for an extension of time for service of the claim form apply also to Part 8 claims (*Barker v Casserly* (2000) LTL 24/10/2000).

Where **PD 8B, section B**, applies to the claim, the claim form must be served no less than 21 days before the hearing date (**PD 8B, para. B.10**).

Because of the nature of the procedure, it is not necessary in a claim started by a **Part 8** claim form to serve particulars of claim, and **Part 16** does not apply to **Part 8** claims (**r. 8.9(a)(i)**). Instead, any written evidence on which a **Part 8** claimant intends to rely must be filed and served with the **Part 8** claim form (**r. 8.5(1) and (2)**). Written evidence will usually be in the form of a witness statement or affidavit, but the matters included in the claim form may stand as the claimant's evidence, where the claim form is verified by a statement of truth (which it must be by virtue of **Part 22**) (**PD 8, para. 5.2**).

Under **CPR, r. 8.2A**, a Part 8 claim form may be issued without naming a defendant, provided the court's permission is obtained first. This enables proceedings to be issued under Part 8 where there is no defendant to a claim, or where the defendant is unascertained.

Acknowledgment of service

13.8 The defendant responds to service of a **Part 8** claim form by filing an acknowledgment of service, and serving a copy on the claimant and any other parties (**CPR, r. 8.3(1)**). Acknowledgment may be made either in the appropriate form (**N210**) or in an informal document such as a letter (**PD 8, para. 3.2**).

An acknowledgment of service in a Part 8 claim must be verified by a statement of truth (**CPR, r. 22.1(1)(d)**).

The acknowledgment must be filed no more than 14 days after service of the claim form (**CPR, r. 8.3**) (unless **r. 10.3(2)** applies: see 18.2). It is in the nature of the sort of claims which are suitable for determination by the **Part 8** procedure, that a pleaded defence is inappropriate. Accordingly, the rules state that the defendant should not file a defence. Rather, any points which the defendant wishes to rely on in reply to the claim should be set out in a witness statement or affidavit. The provisions of **Part 15** in relation to defences do not apply to **Part 8** claims (**r. 8.9(a)(ii)**) nor do **rr. 14.4 to 14.7** in relation to judgments on an admission (**r. 8.9(b)(i)**).

In the acknowledgment of service the defendant must:

(a) indicate whether he contests the claim (**r. 8.3(2)(a)**);
(b) if he seeks a different remedy from that set out in the claim form, state what remedy he seeks (**r. 8.3(2)(b)**);
(c) include his address for service (**r. 10.5**).

The acknowledgment must be signed by the defendant or his legal representative (**r. 10.5**). **Paragraphs 4.2 to 4.4 of PD 10** specify who should sign the acknowledgment where the defendant is a company, corporation or partnership.

If the defendant has entered into a funding arrangement (as defined in **r. 43.2(1)(k)**), a notice of funding of case (**form N251**) must be filed at court with the acknowledgment of service and a copy served on every other party (**PD 43–48, para. 19.2(3)**).

Where **PD 8B, section B**, applies to the claim, the defendant is not required to file or serve an acknowledgment (**PD 8B, para. B.12**).

Consequences of failure to file an acknowledgment

13.9 Due to the nature of the proceedings, in a **Part 8** claim the claimant may not obtain default judgment under **CPR, Part 12**, if the defendant fails to acknowledge service in time, or at all (**r. 8.1(5)**). However, a defendant who has not acknowledged service may not take part in the hearing of the claim unless the court gives permission, although he may attend the hearing (**r. 8.4**). Clearly the likelihood of permission being granted will depend on the reasons for the failure, the circumstances of the claim, the nature of the defendant's interest and the speed with which the claimant and the court were notified of the wish to be heard.

Defendant's evidence

A defendant to a **Part 8** claim who wishes to rely on written evidence (which by **PD 8, para. 5.2**, may be in the form either of a witness statement or affidavit) should file and serve it when filing and serving the acknowledgment of service (**CPR, r. 8.5(3) and (4)**). **13.10**

In practice, 14 days may not be long enough to prepare evidence in opposition to the claim. After filing the acknowledgment, a party may apply to the court for an extension of time for filing and service of evidence, or for permission to serve additional evidence (**r. 8.6(1)(b)**; **PD 8, para. 5.5**). Alternatively, parties can agree an extension of up to 14 days for service of the defendant's evidence. The agreement must be in writing, and a copy of the agreement must be filed at court at the same time as the acknowledgment (**PD 8, para. 5.6**).

Contesting jurisdiction

A defendant to a **Part 8** claim may contest the jurisdiction of the English courts in the usual way provided for in **CPR, Part 11** (see **chapter 19**), by filing an acknowledgment of service, completing section C, and proceeding to make an application for an order that the court does not have jurisdiction. Any such application must be made within 14 days after filing the acknowledgment of service (**r. 11(4)(a)**). **13.11**

Objecting to use of the Part 8 procedure

A defendant to a **Part 8** claim who believes that the **Part 8** procedure should not be used, should file an acknowledgment of service, completing section D, but at the same time should file and serve a statement of reasons for opposing the procedure (**CPR, r. 8.8(1)**; **PD 8, para. 3.6**). Where this contains matters of evidence, it should be verified by a statement of truth. **13.12**

The court has power to order the claim to continue as if it were an ordinary claim not governed by **Part 8**, and give appropriate directions (**CPR, r. 8.1(3)**). Upon receipt of the defendant's acknowledgment and evidence opposing the procedure, the court will consider how the claim should continue, and will give directions as to its future management (**r. 8.8(2)**).

Claimant's evidence in reply

If the defendant to a **Part 8** claim files evidence, the claimant may file and serve evidence in reply within 14 days (**CPR, r. 8.5(5) and (6)**). Evidence may be served after this deadline with the permission of the court (**CPR, r. 8.6(1)(b)**; **PD 8, para. 5.5**). Alternatively, parties can agree an extension of up to 14 days for service of the claimant's evidence in reply. Any such agreement must be in writing (**PD 8, para. 5.6**). **13.13**

Parties may also apply to the court for permission to serve and file additional evidence (**CPR, r. 8.6(1)**; **PD 8, para. 5.5**).

Case management of a Part 8 claim

All **Part 8** claims (save those to which **PD 8B, section B**, applies) are automatically allocated to the multi-track (**CPR, r. 8.9(c)**) and there is no need to complete allocation questionnaires. **Part 26** does not apply. In the case of claims under **PD 8B, section B**, however, the presumption is that the claim will be disposed of at its first hearing, without the need for it to be allocated to a track. Where that does not happen, the court may give directions, including **13.14** directions for the allocation of the claim to a particular track (**PD 8B, paras B.13** and **B.14**), and **CPR, rr. 26.5(3)** to **(5)** and **26.6** to **26.10** apply (**PD 8B, para. B.15**).

The court may give directions immediately a **Part 8** claim form is issued, either upon application of a party or on its own initiative (**PD 8, para. 4.1**). The directions can include fixing a hearing date either where there is no dispute (for example, in child and patient settlements) or where there is a dispute but it is convenient to give a hearing date (for example, in mortgage possession claims or applications for the appointment of trustees). If it has not fixed a hearing date earlier, the court will give directions for the disposal of the claim as soon as practicable after the defendant has acknowledged service and filed any written evidence or after the time has expired for this to be done (**para. 4.2**).

CPR, Part 29, applies to **Part 8** claims automatically allocated to the multi-track, and, as in all multi-track claims, the parties should try to agree appropriate directions for the management of the claim. Parties should submit these to the court either at the same time as filing the acknowledgment or at the latest by the time any case management conference is fixed.

Hearing of a Part 8 claim

13.15 Most claims will be disposed of with a hearing. However, the court has a discretion to deal with claims without a hearing (**PD 8, para. 4.3**) or without the parties needing to attend court (**CPR, r. 1.4(2)(j)**).

Evidence at the hearing of a **Part 8** claim will normally be adduced in written form. A party may only rely on evidence served after the time limits specified in **CPR, r. 8.5** (i.e., at the time of service of the claim form or acknowledgment of service, or in reply 14 days thereafter) with the court's permission (**r. 8.6(1)(b)**).

However, the court has power to require or permit oral evidence or to require a witness who has given written evidence to attend for cross-examination (**r. 8.6(2) and (3)**). Such cases will be rare. Oral evidence is unlikely to be necessary in cases where there is no factual dispute between the parties.

Additional claims and the Part 8 procedure

13.16 Counterclaims and other additional claims do not sit easily with **Part 8** claims. A defendant to a **Part 8** claim who wishes to bring any other claim may do so only with the permission of the court (**CPR, r. 8.7**). (See **chapters 28** and **29 on additional claims.**)

Chapter 14 Joinder and Parties

The following procedural checklists, which are in **appendix 1**, are relevant to this chapter:

Procedural checklist 5 Application for joinder
Procedural checklist 6 Interpleader proceedings: High Court
Procedural checklist 7 Interpleader proceedings: county court
Procedural checklist 8 Approval of settlement or compromise to which a child or patient is party, where sole purpose of claim is to obtain court approval

DESCRIPTION OF PARTIES

14.1 Under the CPR the party who makes a claim is known as 'the claimant' (**r. 2.3(1)**). The party against whom proceedings are brought is 'the defendant' (**r. 2.3(1)**). Parties to applications are referred to as 'applicant' and 'respondent' (**r. 23.1**). Parties to petitions are known as the 'petitioner' and the 'respondent'. Before 6 April 2006, parties to additional claims under **Part 20** were known as the 'Part 20 claimant' and 'Part 20 defendant'. From 6 April 2006, parties to additional claims are known by their titles as they appeared in the original claim (if they were claimants or defendants: **PD 20, para. 7.3**), but if they have been brought in under **CPR, Part 20**, they are known as the 'third party', 'fourth party' etc. (**PD 20, para. 7.4**).

The heading of a claim form must include the full name of each party (**PD 16, para. 2.6**). The name of a party who is an individual must include the title by which he or she is known (**para. 2.6(a)**).

The form of words to be used in describing different types of parties in the headings of statements of case and other court documents is set out in **PD16, para. 2.6**, and in **table 14.1**.

JOINDER OF CAUSES OF ACTION AND PARTIES

14.2 The **Supreme Court Act 1981, s. 49(2)**, requires the court to exercise its discretion to ensure that:

> as far as possible, all matters in dispute between the parties are completely and finally determined, and all multiplicity of legal proceedings with respect to any of those matters is avoided.

This is reflected in **r. 7.3** of the CPR, which states that a single claim form may be used to start all claims which can be conveniently disposed of in the same proceedings. This does not require a claimant to include in his pleaded case all the heads of damage he could possibly argue against a defendant (*Khiaban v Beard* [2003] EWCA Civ 358, [2003] 1 WLR 1626). **Rule 19.1** states that any number of claimants or defendants may be joined as parties to one claim. There must, however, be a cause of action against all those joined (*Douihech v Findlay* [1990] 1 WLR 269, but see *Individual Homes Ltd v Macbream Investments Ltd* (2002) *The Times*, 14 November 2002, where a bank was joined as a party to enable it to recover the costs of complying with a witness summons). Joint claimants must have the same interest in the claim and must be represented by the same solicitors and counsel.

Rule 19.3 (which does not apply to probate claims: **r. 19.3(3)**) deals with claims in respect of rights held by two or more persons jointly (as opposed to severally held rights, alternative claims and related claims). All persons jointly entitled to a remedy must be parties to the claim, either as joint claimants, if they are willing, or as defendants, if they are not (**r. 19.3(1)**

Table 14.1 Names of parties

Class of party	Form of words
An individual	His or her full unabbreviated name and the title by which he or she is known, e.g., Mr Richard John Brown
A child under 18	Miss Jane Mary Brown (a child by Joe Bloggs her litigation friend)
A child under 18 who is conducting proceedings on his or her own behalf	Miss Jane Mary Brown (a child)
A child reaching full age	Ms Jane Mary Brown (formerly a child but now of full age)
An individual who is a patient within the meaning of the Mental Health Act 1983	Mrs Jane Mary Brown (by Joe Bloggs, her litigation friend)
An individual who is trading under another name	John Smith, trading as (or T/as) 'Smith's Groceries'
An individual who is suing or being sued in a representative capacity	Miss Jane Mary Brown, as the representative of Hilda Marion Brown (deceased)
An individual who is suing or being sued in the name of a club or other unincorporated organisation	Miss Jane Mary Brown, suing/sued on behalf of the Northtown Under 16 Football Club
A firm	Brown & Co. (A Firm)
A corporation (other than a company)	The full name of the corporation, including indication of legal form ('Corporation', 'Incorporated', etc.), where appropriate
A company, whether registered in England and Wales, or an overseas company, or a limited liability partnership	The full registered name, including indication of legal form (plc, Ltd, llp, etc.)

and (2)). When claiming to recover land it is good practice, though not a legal requirement, to name as co-claimants, all the persons in whom title to possession is vested (*Dearman v Simpletest Ltd* (1999) *The Times*, 14 February 2000).

The court may consider the constitution of proceedings, and make appropriate orders of its own initiative, as part of its duty to manage a case. The case management powers given to the court expressly include power to direct that part of a claim (such as a counterclaim) be dealt with separately, power to consolidate (i.e., to order two separate claims to continue and be tried as if they were a single claim), and power to try two or more claims on the same occasion (r. 3.1(2)).

No guidance is provided about which claims it might be considered convenient to dispose of in the same proceedings. However, the court will take into account the overriding objective in coming to its decision, in particular the objectives of saving expense and of ensuring that cases are dealt with expeditiously and fairly. Thus claims involving common questions of law or fact between different parties, or different causes of action involving the same parties, should be dealt with in the same proceedings.

ADDITION AND SUBSTITUTION OF PARTIES

Principles

The court is given a wide discretion under the CPR to order that a person be added, removed or substituted as a party to a claim, provided that (in the case of adding a party) the limitation 14.3

period has not yet expired. The court's attitude is permissive, provided the other party can be appropriately protected in costs. The court's power may be exercised upon application by a party, or by a person who wishes to intervene in proceedings to become a party, or by the court acting on its own initiative (**CPR, r. 19.4(2); PD 19, para. 1.1**). Addition of a party after the expiry of a limitation period is considered at **14.8**.

The court is empowered by **CPR, r. 19.2(2)**, to add a party where it is desirable:

(a) to enable it to resolve all the matters in dispute in the proceedings; or
(b) to resolve an issue between an existing party and a proposed new party, which is connected to the matters in dispute in the claim.

In *United Film Distribution Ltd v Chhabria* [2001] EWCA Civ 416, [2001] 2 All ER (Comm) 865, the Court of Appeal stated that the discretion to add a party under **CPR, r. 19.2(2)**, is as wide as under the predecessors to that paragraph, namely, RSC, ord. 15, rr. 4 and 2(b). However, claims that are quite separate will not be joined (*Turner v Haworth Associates* [2001] EWCA Civ 370, LTL 23/2/2001).

Where an application is made to re-join a defendant against whom a claim in the same action has previously been struck out, the court should exercise its discretion under **CPR, r. 19.2**, in accordance with the test for bringing a second claim on the same facts as a claim struck out, established in *Securum Finance Ltd v Ashton* [2001] Ch 291 (see **33.25**) (*Kent v M and L Management and Legal Ltd* [2005] EWHC 2546 (Ch), LTL 28/11/2005). In *Kent v M and L Management and Legal Ltd* the court refused permission to re-join the defendant because it was no longer possible for him to have a fair trial. He had become mentally ill and could not give live evidence. Further, part of the evidence against him was contained in written statements from his mother who had since died.

In *C Inc. plc v L* [2001] 2 Lloyd's Rep 459, the court considered the meaning of the words 'all matters in dispute in the proceedings' in **CPR, r. 19.2(2)(a)**. It held that the phrase embraced all stages of a claim from the time it is started until it is finally complete. Thus, in this case, where judgment had already been entered against the only existing party, there remained issues in dispute relating to enforcement for which it was desirable to add a new party. In *The Selby Paradigm* [2004] EWHC 1804 (Admlty), [2004] 2 Lloyd's Rep 714, the court allowed an underwriter to be added as a defendant to a claim even though judgment in default had already been entered against the existing defendant (the assured), on the grounds that there was a defence with a reasonable prospect of success which had not been run by the assured, and the underwriter now wished to apply to set aside the default judgment. The court rejected the argument that there can be no 'matters in dispute' once judgment has been entered. The test is whether, taking into account the overriding objective, it is desirable in all the circumstances to join the intended defendant. This decision may be contrasted with *Kooltrade Ltd v XTS Ltd* (2001) IPD 25018, where the court refused to allow new defendants to be added to a claim after judgment had been entered. However, here the application was brought by the claimant, the judgment was not capable of being reopened, and joining new defendants at this stage therefore deprived them of potential defences.

Under **r. 19.2(2)** the court will add a person who is bound to satisfy any judgment given in the claim (such as the Motor Insurers' Bureau: see *Gurtner v Circuit* [1968] 2 QB 587) but not a person who runs the risk of being ordered to pay costs (such as a person funding one of the parties: see *Hamilton v Al Fayed* (2000) *The Times*, 13 October 2000).

The court may, by **r. 19.2(3)**, remove a party if it is not desirable for that person to be a party to the proceedings.

The court may, by **r. 19.2(4)**, substitute a new party for an existing one if:

(a) the existing party's interest or liability has passed to the new party; and

(b) it is desirable to substitute the new party so that the court can resolve the matters in dispute in the proceedings.

Adding a person as a claimant may not be done without the person's written consent, which must be filed at court (**r. 19.4(4)**). Any order made by the court joining a new claimant will not take effect unless and until the signed, written consent of the person joined has been filed (**PD 19, para. 2.2**). The Commissioners for HM Revenue and Customs may be added as a party only if they consent (**CPR, r. 19.4(4A)**).

Procedure

A party may only be added, removed or substituted with the permission of the court, unless the claim form has not been served. Thus where an existing party, or the proposed new party, wishes to change the parties to a claim, an application for permission to do so must be made under **CPR, Part 23** (**r. 19.4(1); PD 19, para. 1.4**). The procedure is summarised in **procedural checklist** 5, in **appendix** 1, and there is detailed commentary at **14.5** to **14.7**. **14.4**

Application Application is made by filing an application notice in accordance with **CPR, r. 23.3** (**PD 19, para. 1.4**). The application must be made on notice (save in the case of the substitution of a party following a transfer of interest or liability) and, where it is on notice, a copy of the application notice must be filed and served in accordance with **CPR, rr. 23.3** and **23.4** (**PD 19, para. 1.4**). An application to add or substitute a party must be supported by evidence setting out the proposed new party's interest in or connection with the claim (**PD 19, para. 1.3**). Where the application is to substitute a party following the transfer of an interest or liability, the evidence in support must show the stage reached by the proceedings and set out the change which has occurred to cause the transfer of interest or liability (**PD 19, para. 5.2**). The rules contain no requirement for evidence to be submitted in support of an application to remove a party. The party applying for the amendment will usually be ordered to pay the costs of the application and any additional costs arising from the amendment. **14.5**

Where the party to be added or substituted is a claimant, a copy of the proposed amended claim form and particulars of claim and the signed written consent of the new party must be filed with the application notice (**PD 19, para. 2.1**).

Hearing Where all parties (and the proposed new party) agree the change, the application may be dealt with without a hearing (**PD 19, para. 1.2**). The application must still be approved by a judicial officer, and the procedural judge has a discretion to refuse or allow an agreed order. **14.6**

Order and consequential directions Where the court makes an order adding a party it will normally also make consequential directions (**CPR, r. 19.4(6)**). In addition to directions about the management of the proceedings, these will normally include orders that: **14.7**

(a) the claimant or the party who made the application file the amended claim form and particulars of claim within 14 days (**PD 19, paras 2.3(3)** and **3.2(1)**);
(b) the new party be served with a copy of the existing statements of case (and documents referred to in them) (**paras 2.3(2)** and **3.2(3)**);
(c) any new defendant (and, unless the court orders to the contrary, any other defendants) be served with the amended claim form and particulars of claim and the usual response pack (forms for admitting, defending and acknowledging the claim) (**para. 3.2(3)**); and
(d) a copy of the order be served on the parties, and any other person affected by it (**CPR, r. 19.4(5); PD 19, paras 2.3(1)** and **3.2(2)**).

A new defendant does not become a party to the proceedings until served with the amended claim form (**PD 19, para. 3.3**). Thus it is this step (not the making of the application) which will interrupt the running of the limitation period against that person (*Ketteman v Hansel Properties Ltd* [1987] AC 189).

When a party is removed, the claimant must file in court an amended claim form and particulars of claim, and a copy of the order must be served on every party and on any other person affected (**CPR, r. 19.4(5); PD 19, para. 4**). The court may give consequential directions about the management of the proceedings (**CPR, r. 19.4(6)**).

The procedure for amending a statement of case is dealt with in **PD 17, para.** 2 (see **chapter** 31).

An order giving permission to amend should normally be drawn up. The court will serve it, unless the parties wish, or the court orders them, to do so (**PD 19, para. 1.5**).

Addition or substitution of a party after the expiry of the limitation period

14.8 The addition or substitution of parties after the expiry of a limitation period is considered at **14.8** to **14.13**. For the related topic of adding new causes of action after a limitation period has expired see **31.16** to **31.20**.

In accordance with the **Limitation Act 1980, s. 35, r. 19.5** of the CPR restricts the power of the court to add a new party after the expiry of a statutory limitation period. The provisions to which **r. 19.5** applies include **s. 11A** of the 1980 Act (claims in respect of defective products) (*Horne-Roberts v SmithKline Beecham plc* [2001] EWCA Civ 2006, [2002] 1 WLR 1662). In claims other than for personal injury, the court may grant permission only where the limitation period had not expired when the claim was issued, and the addition or substitution is necessary. It will be 'necessary' only if one of the circumstances discussed in **14.9** to **14.13** exists. In *Martin v Kaisary* (2005) EWCA Civ 594, LTL 16/3/2005, the court held that whether it is 'necessary' to add a defendant depends on whether the claim against the existing defendant can be determined without the addition of the new defendant. Adding an alternative claim against a new defendant is not 'necessary' within the meaning of the rule.

14.9 **Correcting a mistake** Under **CPR, r. 19.5(3)(a)**, which implements the **Limitation Act 1980, s. 35**, the court may substitute a new party for an existing party, after the expiry of a relevant limitation period, where the existing party was named in mistake for the new party. **Rule 19.5(3)(a)** allows the substitution of a new party for an existing party named in error, but not the addition of a new party, and so contemplates only a change in the persons named as parties, not an increase in their number. However, if there are two or more distinct claims against a party, substitution is possible under **r. 19.5(3)(a)** in respect of only some of the claims, leaving the others to continue against the original party (*Procter and Gamble (Health and Beauty Care) Ltd v Carrier Holdings Ltd* [2003] EWHC 83 (TCC), [2003] BLR 255; *Ultra Furniture Ltd v KPMG Audit plc* [2003] All ER (D) 302).

In *Morgan Est (Scotland) Ltd v Hanson Concrete Products Ltd* [2005] EWCA Civ 134, [2005] 1 WLR 2557, Jacob LJ considered the test to be applied to applications under **r. 19.5(3)(a)** and criticised the endorsement by three post-CPR authorities (*Horne-Roberts v SmithKline Beecham plc* [2001] EWCA Civ 2006, [2002] 1 WLR 1662; *Parsons v George* [2004] EWCA Civ 912, [2004] 1 WLR 3264; and *Kesslar v Moore and Tibbits* [2004] EWCA Civ 1551, [2005] PNLR 17) of the pre-CPR test set out in *The Sardinia Sulcis* [1991] 1 Lloyd's Rep 201.

In *The Sardinia Sulcis* Lloyd LJ had sought to clarify the types of mistake which were covered by the predecessor to **r. 19.5(3)(a)**, which was RSC, ord. 20, r. 5. He held that it would be too broad to permit joinder in any case where the applicant named a person other than the person who was liable for the wrong, as permission to substitute would always be granted. Instead, to come within the rule, a claimant had to be able to identify a defendant by a description specific to the particular case. If the claimant got the right description but used the wrong name, there was likely to be little doubt about the identity of the intended defendant. If the claimant got the wrong description and used the wrong name, the position would be otherwise.

In *Morgan Est (Scotland) Ltd v Hanson Concrete Products Ltd* Jacob LJ took the view that this approach was too narrow. There was no reason to construe 'mistake' restrictively. The purpose of the **Limitation Act 1980, s. 35**, was to liberalise the previous position. In any event, *The Sardinia Sulcis* was not actually a decision on the **Limitation Act, s. 35** at all, and therefore could not be an authority on **CPR, r. 19.5**. Further, the interpretation of **r. 19.5** should not turn on authorities under the old RSC. The correct approach is to construe **r. 19.5** without regard to *The Sardinia Sulcis*, but with regard to the overriding objective.

The facts in *Morgan Est (Scotland) Ltd v Hanson Concrete Products Ltd* were that company A contracted to buy concrete pipes from the defendant, which were alleged to be defective. Company A assigned its cause of action to company B, which later assigned the cause of action to company C. Shortly before the limitation period expired, solicitors for company B, unaware of the second assignment, issued a claim in the name of company B against the defendant. They discovered their mistake after the limitation period had expired and then made an application to substitute company A and company C as the claimants.

Whether **r. 19.5** applied was held to depend on three questions:

(a) Has the limitation period expired (**r. 19.1**)?
(b) Is the substitution necessary (**r. 19.5(2)(a)**)? This depended on whether the new party was to be substituted for a party who was named in the claim form in mistake for the new party.
(c) Is the original party named 'in mistake' for the new party?

Applying this test, the court allowed the substitution of company A for company B under **r. 19.5(3)(a)** and the addition of company C under **r. 19.5(3)(c)** (see **14.11**). There was no prejudice to the defendants in being deprived of an unmeritorious defence arising solely from a blunder by the other side.

The new approach has the benefit of being far simpler than the *Sardinia Sulcis* test. However, there are a number of criticisms which can be made of the decision. The overriding objective cannot be used to interpret substantive law, namely, the meaning of 'in mistake' in the **Limitation Act 1980, s. 35**. Further, the phrase used in **s. 35(6)(a)** is 'whose name was given in any claim made in the original action in mistake for the new party's name'. The new test fails to give effect to the need for the mistake to be related to the party name. Finally, although rules of court made under the **Limitation Act 1980** can be the same as or more restrictive than **s. 35(6)**, **s. 35(4)** prohibits them from relaxing the provisions of **s. 35(6)**.

Nevertheless, *Morgan Est (Scotland) Ltd v Hanson Concrete Products Ltd* has since been followed in *AMB Generali Holding AG v SEB Trygg Liv Holding AB* [2005] EWCA Civ 1237, [2006] 1 All ER 437.

CPR, r. 19.5(3)(a), should be read in conjunction with **r. 17.4(3)**, which provides that the court may make an amendment to correct a mistake as to the name of a party, but only where the mistake was genuine and not one which would cause reasonable doubt as to the identity of the party in question. In *Gregson v Channel Four Television Corporation* (2000) *The Times*, 11 August 2000 (approved in *Morgan Est (Scotland) Ltd v Hanson Concrete Products Ltd*), the Court of Appeal considered the relationship between **r. 17.4(3)** and **r. 19.5(2)** and **(3)**. It held that **r. 19.5** deals with cases where the claimant mistakenly names the wrong person as defendant, whereas **r. 17.4** deals with cases where the claimant misnames the defendant. The court made clear that there is no significant conflict between the two rules, thus confirming the decision in *International Distillers and Vintners Ltd v J. F. Hillebrand (UK) Ltd* (1999) *The Times*, 25 January 2000.

Claim cannot properly be continued The court may add or substitute a new party as **14.10**
claimant or defendant after the expiry of a relevant limitation period if the claim cannot properly be continued without the addition or substitution of the new party (**CPR, r. 19.5(3)(b)**). The operation of the equivalent provision in the old rules (RSC, ord. 15, r. 6(6)) was limited to five categories of case in which, for technical reasons, claims were liable to be defeated for want of the correct parties. These were where: the claim concerned property

vested in the new party at law or in equity and the claimant had an equitable interest in the property; the claim was vested in the claimant and the new party jointly but not severally; the new party was the Attorney-General and the proceedings should have been brought as relator proceedings in his name; the new party was a company in which the claimant was a shareholder whose claim was liable to be defeated by the rule in *Foss v Harbottle* (1843) 2 Hare 461 (see **14.41**); and the claim should have been brought against new party and the existing defendant jointly. It remains to be seen whether **CPR, r. 19.5(3)(b)**, will be interpreted in a similar, restrictive way, but it is submitted that it should be, so as to accord with the policy of the **Limitation Act 1980, s. 35**. This view is supported by *Merrett v Babb* [2001] EWCA Civ 214, [2001] QB 1174, where permission to add the claimant's mother as second claimant was granted after the expiry of the limitation period on the ground that the cause of action was vested in them jointly, so the claim could not be maintained by the original claimant without joining her mother. In *Martin v Kaisary* [2005] EWCA Civ 594, (2005) LTL 16/3/2005, joinder of a new defendant was not permitted as it was not necessary to establish the liability of the original defendant.

14.11 **Death and bankruptcy** If a party to a claim dies or is adjudicated bankrupt, the court may, even if a relevant limitation period has expired, add or substitute as a party the person to whom the deceased or bankrupt party's interest or liability has passed (**CPR, r. 19.5(3)(c)**). In *Morgan Est (Scotland) Ltd v Hanson Concrete Products Ltd* [2005] EWCA Civ 134, [2005] 1 WLR 2557, the court used **r. 19(5)(3)(c)** to permit the addition of a claimant to whom the claim had been assigned, despite the fact that the rule does not refer to transmission by assignment.

14.12 **Alteration of capacity** The court may, after a relevant limitation period has expired, allow an amendment to alter the capacity in which a party claims, if the new capacity is one which that party had when the proceedings started or has since acquired (**CPR, r. 17.4(4)**). In *Haq v Singh* [2001] 1 WLR 1594 the court held that 'capacity' in r. 17.4(4) has the same meaning as it has in the **Limitation Act 1980, s. 35**. Thus the alteration in capacity referred to is an alteration from a representative capacity or personal capacity to another representative capacity, or (in the case of a representative claim) from a representative capacity to a personal capacity. The claimant could not take advantage of **r. 17.4(4)** to cure her lack of standing by taking an assignment of the cause of action which had previously been vested in her trustee in bankruptcy. The reality was that the claim was being brought by her in her personal capacity both before and after the assignment.

14.13 **Personal injury claims** **Rule 19.5(4) of the CPR** gives the court an additional power in a personal injuries case to add a new party after the expiry of the limitation period:

(a) where it has exercised its discretion under the **Limitation Act 1980, s. 33**, to override the usual three-year limitation period for a personal injuries claim (**Limitation Act 1980, s. 11**) or a claim under the fatal accidents legislation (**Limitation Act 1980, s. 12**); or
(b) where it directs that this issue should be decided at trial.

Claims for wrongful interference with goods

14.14 A claimant bringing a claim for wrongful interference with goods must state in the particulars of claim the name and address of every person who, to the claimant's knowledge, has or claims an interest in the goods, but who is not a party to the claim (**CPR, r. 19.5A**). The defendant may then apply to the court for any person named to be made a party to the claim. If the defendant makes such an application, but the person sought to be joined fails to attend the hearing of the application or to comply with any directions made, the court may order that person to be deprived of any claim against the defendant in respect of the goods.

This rule gives effect to the provisions of the **Torts (Interference with Goods) Act 1977, ss. 7** and **8**. These sections deal with the potential wrong of a defendant being doubly liable in damages to competing owners of goods. They deal with this wrong in two ways:

(a) **Section** 7 of the Act requires any order for relief in proceedings for wrongful interference to which two or more persons interested in goods are parties to be such as to avoid the double liability of the wrongdoer as between those persons. Where only one of two or more persons interested in goods is a party, and receives more from the wrongdoer than is properly due, the overpayment must be passed on to other persons interested or repaid to the defendant.

(b) **Section 8** of the Act entitles the defendant to show that a third party has a better right to the goods which are the subject matter of the claim, and to rely on this as a defence to the claim or in reduction of the damages claimed.

INTERPLEADER PROCEEDINGS

Introduction

Interpleader proceedings are used to determine ownership of disputed property in two circumstances: **14.15**

(a) where a person ('the stakeholder') owes a debt, or has possession of goods or money, and does not claim the property personally, but is being, or expects to be, sued by competing claimants to the property;

(b) where a High Court enforcement officer (a term which will be used in **14.16** to **14.18** to mean sheriff or enforcement officer) or county court bailiff has seized goods in execution which a person other than the judgment debtor claims to own.

The stakeholder, enforcement officer or bailiff in effect calls on the competing claimants to claim against each other (to 'interplead') so that title to the property can be decided by the court. The stakeholder, enforcement officer or bailiff may then dispose of the property in accordance with the court's order, safe from being sued by the competing claimants.

The rules governing interpleader proceedings are to be found in **RSC, ord.** 17 in CPR, sch. 1, and **CCR, ord.** 33 in CPR, sch. 2. The two sets of rules are similar, but not identical. Regrettably, the opportunity to unify the procedure has not yet been taken. The procedure is summarised in **procedural checklist** 6 (High Court) and **procedural checklist** 7 (county court), in **appendix 1**, and there is detailed commentary in **14.16** to **14.21**.

In a county court, the district judge is technically responsible for bailiffs. So the rules refer to the district judge being in possession of the goods seized, when in practice it will be the bailiff who has custody of them.

Procedure in the High Court

Goods seized in execution A person who claims to own goods seized in execution by a High Court enforcement officer should notify the enforcement officer of the claim, and provide details of an address for service (**RSC, ord.** 17, **r.** 2(1) in CPR, sch. 1). The enforcement officer must notify the judgment creditor immediately of the claim. The judgment creditor then has seven days to inform the enforcement officer whether the claim is admitted or disputed. If the claim is admitted, the judgment creditor will not be liable for any fees or expenses incurred by the enforcement officer after receipt of the notice of admission (**RSC, ord.** 17, **r.** 2(2) in CPR, sch. 1) and the enforcement officer may apply to the court for an order restraining the bringing of a claim against the enforcement officer for having taken possession of the goods (**RSC, ord.** 17, **r.** 2(3) and (4) in CPR, sch. 1). Where the judgment creditor disputes the claim, or fails to respond within the seven days, and the third party does not withdraw the claim, the enforcement officer may issue interpleader proceedings in order to have the court resolve the question of ownership. The interpleader application may be **14.16**

made either in the court where the underlying claim was proceeding, or in the court where the judgment is being executed, if different (**RSC, ord.** 17, **r.** 4 in CPR, sch. 1).

14.17 **Application for interpleader relief** Application for interpleader relief other than in existing proceedings is made by **Part 8** claim form (**PD 8B, table 1**). An application in existing proceedings should be made by issuing an application notice under **CPR, Part 23** (**RSC, ord.** 17, **r.** 3(1) in CPR, sch. 1).

It is required by **RSC, ord.** 17, **r.** 3(4) in CPR, sch. 1 that, save where the application is brought by an enforcement officer, the claim form or application notice must be supported by evidence (in the form permitted under **CPR, rr.** 32.6 and 32.15) that the applicant:

(a) claims no interest in the subject matter in dispute, other than for charges or costs;
(b) does not collude with any of the claimants to the subject matter; and
(c) is willing to pay or transfer that subject matter into court or to dispose of it as the court may direct.

Under the old version of this rule, the affidavit was required to be made by the applicant personally, rather than by a solicitor, save where there were practical difficulties, such as the applicant being abroad (*Wood v Lynne* (1850) 4 De G & Sm 16). Under the CPR, if the evidence is adduced in the form of a witness statement, it should still be that of the applicant rather than the applicant's solicitor, as the applicant will have the first-hand knowledge of the matters about which evidence is being given.

Once issued, the claim form or notice must be served on all claimants to the property (*Lambert v Townsend* (1832) 1 LJ Ex 113; **RSC, ord.** 17, **r.** 3(2) in CPR, sch. 1).

Where the claim relates to goods seized in execution, the claimant then has 14 days in which to serve a witness statement or affidavit on the enforcement officer and the judgment creditor. This must identify the property claimed and the grounds for asserting rights in the property (**RSC, ord.** 17, **r.** 3(6) in CPR, sch. 1).

14.18 **Powers of the court hearing the claim** In interpleader proceedings the court has a wide discretion to make any order, including any order as to costs, which it thinks just (**RSC, ord.** 17, **r.** 8 in CPR, sch. 1). Where there are several different existing claims, even in different divisions of the High Court, the court may make an order which binds the parties to all of them (**RSC, ord.** 17, **r.** 9 in CPR, sch. 1).

Trial of the interpleader issue. The court may order the trial of an interpleader issue. In this case, at the first return date, it will give directions dealing with the constitution of the action, for example, directing which of the competing claimants is to be claimant and which is to be defendant. In relation to an existing claim concerning the disputed property, in which the applicant is the defendant:

(a) the court may order a person claiming the property to become the defendant, in substitution for or in addition to the applicant (**RSC, ord.** 17, **r.** 5(1)(a) in CPR, sch. 1);
(b) the court may stay all further proceedings in the claim (**RSC, ord.** 17, **r.** 7 in CPR, sch. 1).

Where appropriate, the court may also order disclosure under **CPR, Part 31**, or the provision of further information under **CPR, Part 18**. The trial itself will take place in the usual way and **CPR, Part 39**, will apply (**RSC, ord.** 17, **rr.** 10 and 11(1) in CPR, sch. 1).

Orders in relation to the property. The court may also give directions as to the safe custody of the property in dispute, pending trial. If the property is money, the court will usually order it to be paid into court. If it is goods, the court may make orders for its safe custody or sale. Where the applicant is an enforcement officer and the claimant alleges that the property is security for a debt, the court may order the sale of the property and the application of the proceeds of sale as it thinks just (**RSC, ord.** 17, **r.** 6 in CPR, sch. 1).

Summary judgment. Where the applicant is an enforcement officer, or with the consent of all claimants, or at the request of any of them, or if the case turns on a question of law, the court may order the summary determination of the claim (**RSC, ord. 17, r. 5(2)** in CPR, sch. 1).

Barring a claimant. Where a claimant to the property does not appear at the hearing, or fails to comply with an order in the proceedings, the court may make an order barring that claimant from making any future claim against the applicant. This order does not affect any rights the interpleader claimants have as between themselves (**RSC, ord. 17, r. 5(3)** in CPR, sch. 1).

County court procedure

Goods seized in execution A person who claims to own goods seized by a county court bailiff must give notice to the bailiff of the claim. The notice must include the claimant's name and address, the grounds of the interpleader claim, and, where the claim is for rent, particulars of the amount of rent in arrears and the period in respect of which it is due, as required by the **County Courts Act 1984, s. 102(2)** (**CCR, ord. 33, r. 1(1)** in CPR, sch. 2). Save where the claim is for the proceeds or value of goods, the court will require the claimant to make a deposit or provide security for the claim, in accordance with the **County Courts Act 1984, s. 100** (**CCR, ord. 33, r. 1(2)(b)** in CPR, sch. 2). The court will also notify the judgment creditor of the claim (**CCR, ord. 33, r. 1(2)(a)** in CPR, sch. 2). **14.19**

The judgment creditor must notify the court, within four days of receipt of the notice of claim, whether the claim is disputed or admitted or whether the district judge (i.e., the bailiff, see **14.15**) is requested to withdraw from possession of the disputed property. If the claim is admitted or the district judge is requested to withdraw from possession, the judgment creditor will not be liable for any fees or expenses incurred by the district judge after receipt of the notice (**CCR, ord. 33, r. 2** in CPR, sch. 2). In addition, the district judge can apply to the circuit judge for an order restraining the bringing of a claim against the district judge for having taken possession of the goods (**CCR, ord. 33, r. 3** in CPR, sch. 2).

Where the judgment creditor gives notice disputing a claim, the court will issue an interpleader notice in form N88 or N88(1). A hearing date will be fixed, and the court will serve the notice on the judgment creditor and the interpleader claimant at least 14 days before the return date.

Claims by stakeholders A stakeholder who is defending a claim should apply for interpleader relief to the court in which the claim is proceeding, and one threatened with a claim should apply to the court where the claim might be brought (**CCR, ord. 33, r. 6(2)** in CPR, sch. 2). **14.20**

Whether in a pending action or not, by **CCR, ord. 33, r. 6(3)** in CPR, sch. 2, the stakeholder makes an application for interpleader relief by filing a witness statement or affidavit showing that the applicant:

(a) claims no interest in the subject matter in dispute other than for charges or costs;
(b) does not collude with any of the interpleader claimants; and
(c) is willing to pay or transfer the subject matter into court or to dispose of it as the court may direct.

One copy of the witness statement or affidavit should be filed for the court, together with an additional copy for each competing interpleader claimant (**CCR, ord. 33, r. 6(3)** in CPR, sch. 2).

The witness statement or affidavit of a stakeholder who is a defendant in a pending claim must be filed within 14 days after service of the claim form on the stakeholder. On receipt of this evidence, the court will fix a date for a pre-trial review and will send notice of the application to all parties to the pending claim. These notices will be served at least 21 days before the return date. Each must be accompanied by a copy of the affidavit or witness statement together with the claim form and particulars of claim in the underlying action (**CCR, ord. 33, r.** 7 in CPR, sch. 2).

Where the stakeholder is not a defendant in a pending claim, the court will fix a date for a pre-trial review, will issue an interpleader notice in form N89 and will serve a copy of the notice together with the witness statement or affidavit on each of the competing claimants at least 21 days before the return date (**CCR, ord. 33, r. 8** in CPR, sch. 2).

In either case, each interpleader claimant must, within 14 days after service of the notice under r. 7 or r. 8, either file a notice that no interpleader claim is to be made, or file particulars of the grounds for a claim. The claimant should file copies for service on all other parties. The court will forward these documents (**CCR, ord. 33, r. 10** in CPR, sch. 2).

14.21 **Powers of the court** At the final hearing, the court will give judgment determining the rights and claims of the competing parties (**CCR, ord. 33, r. 11(3)** in CPR, sch. 2). The court also has the power to make an order barring and striking out the claim of an interpleader claimant who does not appear at a pre-trial review or at the final hearing (**CCR, ord. 33, r. 11(1)** and (2) in CPR, sch. 2). The court may also bar the claim of an interpleader claimant who fails or refuses to comply with an order made in the proceedings (**CCR, ord. 33, r. 11(1)** in CPR, sch. 2).

ASSIGNMENT OF CAUSES OF ACTION: MAINTENANCE AND CHAMPERTY

Introduction

14.22 It sometimes happens that a litigant's rights and liabilities in a claim are voluntarily transferred to a non-party before judgment has been obtained. Whether such a transfer can be validly made depends on whether the transaction is tainted by maintenance or champerty. For a case on a defective assignment, see *Smith v Henniker-Major and Co.* [2002] EWCA Civ 762, [2003] Ch 182.

Maintenance and champerty

14.23 Maintenance is the support of litigation by a stranger without just cause. Champerty is an aggravated form of maintenance. The distinguishing feature of champerty is the support of litigation by a stranger in return for a share of the proceeds (*Giles v Thompson* [1994] 1 AC 142). Until 1967 champerty and maintenance gave rise to both criminal and tortious liability. The Criminal Law Act 1967 abolished champerty and maintenance as crimes and torts. But s. 14(2) of the Act expressly preserved the common law rule that contracts which are tainted by champerty or maintenance are 'to be treated as contrary to public policy or otherwise illegal'.

There are two circumstances in which the rule against champerty and maintenance continues to be of relevance:

(a) The rule may invalidate agreements whereby a stranger to litigation provides funding to enable a party to bring or continue a claim. Historically, this has precluded solicitors from entering into contingency fee arrangements with their clients. The decision of the Court of Appeal in *Thai Trading Co. v Taylor* [1998] QB 781 appeared to remove the prohibition against the type of contingency fee arrangement in which the solicitor agrees with the client not to charge if the claim fails, but to seek costs from the other side if the claim succeeds. Subsequent decisions (*Hughes v Kingston upon Hull City Council* [1999] QB 1193; *Awwad v Geraghty and Co.* [2001] QB 570) preserved the original rule. **CPR, r. 43.2(3),** permits recovery of costs under a CFA (see **chapter 6**) which provides that the legal representative's fees are payable only to the extent that sums are recovered in respect of the proceedings, whether by way of costs or otherwise (see further **6.5** and **68.29**). However, in *Ahmed v Powell* [2003] PNLR 22 it was held that the basis on which costs negotiators charged fees was champertous. In an arrangement with the defendant's insurers, the costs negotiators were to receive a percentage of the reduction in the amount of costs which they achieved. On the other hand, in *Benaim (UK) Ltd v Davies Middleton and Davies Ltd* [2004] EWHC 737 (TCC), LTL 29/3/2004, the court upheld a CFA which provided for an uplift of up to 100 per cent depending upon the amount of damages recovered. A CFA which complies with the provisions of the **Courts and Legal Services Act 1990, s. 58**, and, if entered into before 1 November 2005 the **Conditional Fee Agreements Regulations 2000**, is enforceable, even though the success fee is calculated by reference to the amount of damages recovered (see further **6.14**).

(b) The rule may invalidate assignments of causes of action.

Scope of maintenance and champerty The scope of the rule against champerty and maintenance, in so far as it affects both funding of litigation and assignments of causes of action, has been progressively narrowed. The current position can be summarised as follows: **14.24**

(a) Liquidated claims in contract, such as the right to sue for the price of goods sold and delivered for which the defendant had failed to pay, can be assigned (*County Hotel and Wine Co. Ltd v London and North Western Railway Co.* [1918] 2 KB 251).

(b) An administrator, administrative receiver or liquidator of a company has a statutory power under the Insolvency Act 1986, sch. 1, para. 2, and sch. 4, para. 6, to sell the company's property, which includes assigning a cause of action on terms that the assignees, by way of consideration, will pay over a share of the recoveries. Property which could be acquired for the company's estate by the exercise of a statutory power to bring proceedings given to a liquidator or administrator by the Insolvency Act 1986, ss. 127, 213, 214, 238, 239, 244 or 245, is not the company's property and cannot be assigned in return for funding the proceedings (*Re Oasis Merchandising Services Ltd* [1998] Ch 170). A trustee in bankruptcy has a similar power under the Insolvency Act 1986, sch. 5, para. 9 (*Grovewood Holdings plc v James Capel and Co. Ltd* [1995] Ch 80). These powers must be exercised in the best interests of the creditors. So, for example, in *Faryab v Smith* [2001] BPIR 246 a trustee in bankruptcy was ordered not to assign a right of action of the bankrupt to the potential defendant without evaluating the claim.

(c) The status of the assignment of a damages claim in contract or tort is more complex. The current approach of the courts is set out in *Giles v Thompson* [1994] 1 AC 142. The first question the court will ask is whether the contract of assignment has the characteristics of champerty or maintenance and is therefore prima facie unlawful. In other words, has a stranger to the dispute agreed to involve itself in litigation (maintenance) in a way which yields it a financial benefit from a successful outcome (champerty)? If it does, the court will then inquire whether the transaction is validated by the legitimate interest of the person supporting the action in its outcome. A proprietary interest in the subject matter of the litigation has been held to be a sufficient interest (*Alabaster v Harness* [1894] 2 QB 897), as has a genuine commercial interest in the outcome of the litigation (*Trendtex Trading Corporation v Credit Suisse* [1982] AC 679). A member of a family has been held justified in maintaining a claim by another member of the family (*Bradlaugh v Newdegate* (1883) 11 QBD 1).

The court will also look at public policy considerations. It will examine the question of maintenance and champerty in the light of their 'origins as a principle of public policy designed to protect the purity of justice and the interests of vulnerable litigants' (*Giles v Thompson*, per Lord Mustill).

Examples *Giles v Thompson* [1994] 1 AC 142 involved car insurance arrangements, whereby **14.25**

the insurance company loaned its insured a replacement vehicle at no charge in return for the assignment of the insured's right to claim hire charges against the defendant. The House of Lords considered whether such arrangements would harm the administration of justice or the interests of the motorist. It concluded that they did not, and therefore, that even though the insurance companies had no interest in the outcome of the litigation, the arrangements were not champertous.

This approach was upheld by the Court of Appeal in *R (Factortame Ltd) v Secretary of State for Transport, Local Government and the Regions (No. 8)* [2002] EWCA Civ 932, [2003] QB 381. The question in that case was whether the provision of expert accounting services to the claimants in return for an assignment of 8 per cent of the damages to be received by the claimants was champertous. Lord Phillips of Worth Matravers MR said that:

> It is necessary to look at the agreement under attack in order to see whether it tends to conflict with existing public policy that is directed to protecting the due administration of justice with particular regard to the interests of the defendant.

The court held first that the agreement was not in breach of the **Courts and Legal Services Act 1990, s. 58** (which invalidates any conditional fee agreements outside its ambit), as the section applies only to the provision of litigation services by a legal representative, not by an expert. Secondly, the court held that giving evidence on a contingency fee basis gives an expert a significant financial interest in the outcome of the case, which is undesirable. The court would only rarely permit an expert to operate under a contingency fee agreement. However, the court concluded that in this case the agreement was not champertous and did not put justice in jeopardy. The accountants did not perform the role of expert witnesses. Their involvement was limited to assisting the quantification of damages. They had no involvement in the court's decision on the merits of the claim.

In *Stocznia Gdanska SA v Latreefers Inc.* [2001] 2 BCLC 116 the Court of Appeal considered the status of an agreement to fund litigation where the funder had a clear commercial interest in the litigation, but the funding agreement gave it a substantial profit in the form of a division of the damages which was in excess of its preceding loss. Morritt LJ considered the circumstances in which the court would stay a claim on the grounds of champerty or maintenance. He stated that the court was concerned with abuses of the court's process, but that not every abuse will result in a stay. The court was concerned to prevent 'trafficking in litigation'. He declined to define 'trafficking', but continued:

> . . . it seems to us to connote unjustified buying and selling of rights to litigation where the purchaser has no proper reason to be concerned with the litigation. . . . A large mathematical disproportion between any pre-existing financial interest and the potential profit of funders may in particular cases contribute to a finding of abuse, but is not bound to do so.

In this case, the funding agreement did not constitute trafficking in litigation, and there was no abuse of process.

In *Papera Traders Co. Ltd v Hyundai Merchant Marine Co. Ltd (No. 2)* [2002] EWHC 2130 (Comm), [2002] 2 Lloyd's Rep 692, the court considered whether an agreement to pay 5 per cent of the amount recovered in litigation against insurers to a firm of marine loss adjusters was champertous. Again, the question for the court was whether the agreement impugned the integrity of the English legal system and in coming to a decision the court had to consider the precise nature of the loss adjusters' interest in the outcome of the litigation. In this case, the agreement was not champertous as their activities were subject to the control of solicitors and counsel, the agreement was not exclusively concerned with litigation and there was a good commercial reason to retain them.

Procedure for substitution following assignment

14.26 Rule 19.2(4) of the CPR provides that:

> The court may order a new party to be substituted for an existing one if—

(a) the existing party's interest or liability has passed to the new party; and
(b) it is desirable to substitute the new party so that the court can resolve the matters in dispute in the proceedings.

An application for such an order may be made without notice but must be supported by evidence (**r. 19.4(3)**) showing the stage the claim has reached and setting out details of the transfer of interest or liability (**PD 19, para. 5.2**).

A new claimant must consent in writing to being added as a claimant, and the consent must be filed at court (**r. 19.4(4)**). The order substituting the new party must then be served on all parties and any other person affected by it (**r. 19.4(5)**). The court will order service of the existing statements of case on the new party. See further **14.3** to **14.13**.

PERSONS UNKNOWN

PD 7, para. 4.1, provides that a claim form must be headed with the title of the proceedings and that the title should include the full name of each party. All known forenames and the surname should be used. But a claimant who does not know the identity or name of a defendant may use a description rather than a name, or sue 'Persons Unknown', provided the description is sufficiently clear to identify who is included within it and who is not (*Bloomsbury Publishing Group Ltd v News Group Newspapers Ltd* [2003] EWHC 1205 (Ch), [2003] 1 WLR 1633; approved by the Court of Appeal in *South Cambridgeshire District Council v Persons Unknown* [2004] EWCA Civ 1280, *The Times*, 11 November 2004). This is of particular application in intellectual property claims where there is a clear case for an injunction against a defendant whose identity is not known to the claimant. **14.27**

DECEASED PARTIES

Survival of causes of action

Under the **Law Reform (Miscellaneous Provisions) Act 1934, s. 1(1)**, most causes of action subsisting against or vested in an individual survive his or her death, against or for the benefit of his or her estate. Even a claim for unlawful racial discrimination survives the claimant's death (*Lewisham and Guys Mental Health NHS Trust v Andrews* [2000] 3 All ER 769). The principal exception to this is that a defamation claim comes to an end upon the claimant's death. **14.28**

Death of party before claim issued

If an individual who has, or against whom there is, a claim, dies before the claim is started, it must be brought by or against the personal representatives of the deceased if they have been granted probate or letters of administration (**CPR, r. 19.8(2)**). The capacity of the executor or administrator must be made clear in their description in the claim form, for example, 'Joe Bloggs as the personal representative of Sharon Bloggs (deceased)' (**PD 7, para. 5.5; CPR, r. 19.8(3)(a)**). A claim brought against a person who was in fact dead at its commencement will be treated as if it had been commenced against his or her estate (**r. 19.8(3)(b)**). However, the irregularity must be corrected by the making of an application for a person to represent the deceased for the purposes of the claim. Until that happens there is no defendant with legal personality (*Piggott v Aulton* [2003] EWCA Civ 24, [2003] RTR 540). **14.29**

A claimant who wishes to start proceedings against the estate of a deceased defendant before there has been a grant of probate or letters of administration should bring a claim against 'the estate' of the deceased (**r. 19.8(2)(b)(i)**). However, the claim form may not be served in this form, because it does not identify the defendants upon whom it should be served. So the next step in the claim is for the claimant to apply, within the time limited for service of the claim form (which is four months within the jurisdiction, six months outside), for an order appointing a person to represent the deceased person for the purpose of the claim and for the action to continue against the representative (**PD 7, para. 5.5; CPR, r. 19.8(2)(b)(ii)**).

Death of party after claim issued

14.30 Where a claimant or defendant dies after the claim has been issued, an order may be obtained under **CPR, r. 19.2(4)**, for the claim to be carried on by or against his or her personal representatives. Application should be made by application notice, with evidence in support, in accordance with the procedure set out **CPR, Part 19**, and **PD 19** (see **14.3** to **14.13**).

Where a party to a claim has died but has no personal representatives, the court may order the claim to proceed in the absence of a person representing the estate, or may order the appointment of a person to represent the estate for the purpose of the proceedings (**CPR, r. 19.8(1)**). This enables the court to dispense with the need for a formal grant of probate or letters of administration. In *Re Berti* [2001] EWCA Civ 2079, LTL 16/11/2001 the Court of Appeal emphasised that a person who wishes to represent a deceased's estate may obtain a representation order under **r. 19.8(1)(b)** as an alternative to being granted probate or letters of administration, and the court should not insist on such a person going to the expense of obtaining probate or administration, especially where the estate is small. The court may require notice of the application to be given to anyone who may have an interest in the estate (**r. 19.8(4)**). Any judgment or order made in the claim will then bind the estate of the deceased person (**r. 19.8(5)**).

Notice of claim to non-parties

14.31 In a claim relating to the estate of a deceased person, the court has power under **CPR, r. 19.8A**, to require notice of the claim or a judgment or order in it to be given to any person who is not a party but who may be affected by any judgment. An application for an order under this rule may be made without notice but must be supported by written evidence which includes the reasons why the person to be served should not be bound by the judgment in the claim. Notice must be given in form 52, accompanied by a copy of the claim form, a form for acknowledging service and any affidavits, witness statements or statements of case ordered by the court to be served. Once the person served acknowledges service, that person becomes a party to the claim. Even if there is no acknowledgment of service, the person will be bound by any judgment or order made in the claim. Provision is made for him to apply to vary or set aside the order (**CPR, r. 19.8A(8)(b)**).

CHILDREN AND PATIENTS

Introduction

14.32 The CPR contain special provisions governing proceedings involving children and patients.

A child is a person under 18 (**r. 21.1(2)(a)**). A patient is an individual who is incapable of managing and administering his or her own property and affairs by reason of mental disorder within the meaning of the Mental Health Act 1983 (**CPR, r. 21.1(2)(b)**). Section 1(2) of the Mental Health Act 1983 defines 'mental disorder' as 'mental illness, arrested or incomplete development of mind, psychopathic disorder and any other disorder or disability of mind'. In order for a litigant to be declared a patient, however, mental disorder of itself is not sufficient: the mental disorder must result in the litigant being incapable of managing or administering his or her own affairs. Mental capacity is a matter of fact. See *Assessment of Mental Capacity: Guidance for Doctors and Lawyers* (2004) published jointly by the Law Society and the British Medical Association. The burden of proving a person is a patient rests on the party asserting incapacity (*Masterman-Lister v Brutton and Co. (Nos. 1 and 2)* [2002] EWCA Civ 1889, [2003] EWCA Civ 70, [2003] 1 WLR 1511; see also *Phillips v Symes* [2004] EWHC 1887 (Ch), LTL 18/8/2004). The question is whether the litigant is capable of understanding, with assistance from his legal representatives and other experts, the issues on which his consent or decision is likely to be necessary in the course of the proceedings. Similar issues arise when considering whether a party has the mental capacity to approve a settlement of liability or quantum, where the enquiry has to be directed to the transaction which is to be approved, and the question is whether the party is able to understand the proceedings and make an informed decision, with the help of any explanation from his or her advisers (*Bailey v Warren* [2006] EWCA Civ 51, *The Times*, 20 February 2006).

The court will almost certainly require a medical report before being able to find a party to be under a mental incapacity. In cases where no one recognises the fact that one of the parties is under a mental incapacity, the court can regularise the position retrospectively, provided everyone is acting in good faith. The rules on capacity are not designed to allow a party to reopen litigation which has apparently been conducted properly (*Phillips v Symes*).

Litigation friends

Both patients and children (subject, in the latter case to any order by the court to the contrary, see **14.36**) must have a litigation friend to conduct proceedings on their behalf (**CPR, r. 21.2**). The title to an action to which a patient is a party should read 'AB (by CD his litigation friend)'. In the case of a child, it should read 'AB (a child, by CD her litigation friend)' (**PD 21, paras 1.3** and **1.5**). **14.33**

A claimant who sues a child or patient who has no litigation friend may take no step in a claim other than issuing and serving the claim form, or making an application for the appointment of a litigation friend (**CPR, r. 21.3(2)**). If a party to proceedings becomes a patient, no further step in the claim may be taken without the court's permission until he or she has a litigation friend (**r. 21.3(3)**). Any step taken before the appointment of the litigation friend has no effect, subject to any order by the court to the contrary (**r. 21.3(4)**).

Judgment on an admission may not be entered against a child or patient (**r. 14.1(4)(a)**). Default judgment may be entered against a child or patient only with the court's permission (**r. 12.10(a)(i)**) and only after a litigation friend has been appointed by the court (**PD 12, para. 4.2(1)**). It would seem that a litigation friend appointed out of court under **CPR, r. 21.5** (see **14.35**), is not acceptable.

By **r. 14.1(4)(b)**, where a child or patient makes a claim, judgment on an admission by the defendant may be entered only if the admission is under **r. 14.5** (admission of part of a claim for a specified amount of money) or **r. 14.7** (admission of liability to pay claim for unspecified amount of money where defendant offers a sum in satisfaction of the claim).

Who may be a litigation friend?

By **CPR, rr. 21.4(1)** and **(2)** and **21.6**, a litigation friend may be: **14.34**

(a) a person appointed by the court (see **14.35**);
(b) a person authorised under part VII of the Mental Health Act 1983 to conduct legal proceedings in the name of a patient; or
(c) a person who can fairly and competently conduct proceedings on behalf of the child or patient and who has no adverse interest in the claim.

A litigation friend who acts for a claimant (but not a defendant) must also undertake to pay any costs which the claimant may be ordered to pay (subject to any right that the friend may have to be repaid from the assets of the child or patient) (**CPR, r. 21.4(3)**). A litigation friend who incurs expenses on behalf of a child or patient in the course of proceedings is entitled to recoup them out of any money recovered from the opposing party or from a payment into court, provided the expenses are of a reasonable amount and were reasonably incurred (r. 21.11A). Any such application must be supported by a witness statement setting out the nature and amount of the expense being claimed and the reason it was incurred (**PD 21, para. 8A.2**).

PD 21, para. 2.1, places a litigation friend under a duty to conduct the proceedings fairly and competently, and to take all decisions and steps in the claim for the benefit of the child or patient.

In practice, a child's litigation friend will normally be a parent, guardian or other relative who can comply with these requirements. A patient's litigation friend may be a receiver appointed under the Mental Health Act 1983 or, where no such person has been appointed, the person with whom the patient lives or who is caring for the patient. Alternatively, in either case the litigation friend can be the Official Solicitor, although he will normally consent to act only where there is no one else suitable who is willing to act.

How is a litigation friend appointed?

14.35 There are two methods in the CPR whereby a litigation friend may be appointed.

First, a person may become a litigation friend without a court order, under **r. 21.5**, by filing either:

(a) in the case of a patient, his or her authorisation to act under part VII of the Mental Health Act 1983; or

(b) in the case of a child or a patient without such authorisation, a certificate of suitability in **form N235**. The details of what the certificate must state are set out at **PD 21, para. 2.3(2)**.

These documents must be filed when proceedings are first issued (where the litigation friend acts on behalf of the claimant) or when the litigation friend first takes a step in the proceedings (where acting on behalf of the defendant). A copy of the certificate of suitability must, by **CPR, r. 21.5(6)**, be served on every person on whom the claim form must be served under **r. 6.6** (see **15.29**) and a certificate of service must be filed with the certificate of suitability.

Alternatively, a litigation friend may be appointed by court order under **r. 21.6**. An application for an order under this rule may be made by any person who wishes to be appointed as litigation friend or by any party to the action (**r. 21.6(2)**). The application should be made under the **Part 23** procedure. It must, by **PD 21, para. 3.4**, be supported by evidence that the person proposed for appointment:

(a) consents to act;
(b) can conduct proceedings fairly and competently;
(c) has no adverse interest to the child or patient; and
(d) in the case of a claimant, undertakes to pay any costs order (subject to any right to be repaid from the assets of the child or patient).

The last three of these conditions are also specified in **CPR, r. 21.4(3)**.

By **r. 21.8(1)**, an application to appoint a litigation friend must be served on every person on whom the claim form should be served under **r. 6.6** (see **15.29**). An application to appoint a litigation friend for a patient must also be served on the patient, unless the court orders otherwise (**r. 21.8(2)**).

On an application under **r. 21.6** the court may, under **r. 21.8(4)** appoint the person proposed in the application or any other person who complies with the conditions in **r. 21.4(3)**.

When may a child conduct proceedings without a litigation friend?

In the case of a child (but not a patient) the court has a discretion to make an order permitting the child to conduct proceedings without a litigation friend (**CPR, r. 21.2(3)**). The order may be made on application by the child, on notice to the litigation friend if the child already has one. The court has power to rescind any such order (**CPR, r. 21.2(3) to (5)**). **14.36**

The court will only authorise a child to conduct proceedings without a litigation friend where it is satisfied that the child is of sufficient maturity and understanding (*Gillick v West Norfolk and Wisbech Area Health Authority* [1986] AC 112).

Where a child is conducting proceedings on his or her own behalf, the action should be headed 'A. B. (a child)' (**PD 21, para. 1.5(2)**).

Terminating the appointment of a litigation friend

The court may direct that a person may not act as a litigation friend, or may substitute or remove a litigation friend (**CPR, r. 21.7**). Application for such an order should be made under the **Part 23** procedure, and should be supported by evidence (**PD 21, para. 4**). **14.37**

By **CPR, r. 21.8(1)** and **(3)**, an application to substitute or remove a litigation friend must be served on every person on whom the claim form should be served (see **15.29**) and on the person acting, or purporting to act, as litigation friend. A person proposed for substitution as a litigation friend must comply with the conditions specified in **r. 21.4(3)** (see **14.35**) (**r. 21.7(3)**) and must be served with the application, unless he or she is the applicant (**r. 21.8(3)**).

By **r. 21.8(4)**, on an application for substitution the court may appoint the person proposed in the application or any other person who complies with the conditions in **r. 21.4(3)**.

When a child (who is not a patient) reaches 18, the appointment of his or her litigation friend ceases (**CPR, r. 21.9(1)**). No application to the court to terminate the appointment is necessary. Either the friend or the individual for whom he or she has been acting may serve a notice under **PD 21, para. 5.2**, stating that the individual has reached full age and that the litigation friend's appointment has ceased, giving an address for service and stating whether the individual intends to continue the proceedings. The heading in the action then becomes: 'A. B. (formerly a child but now of full age') (**PD 21, para. 5.3**).

When a patient recovers, an application to court must be made in order to terminate the appointment of the litigation friend (**CPR, r. 21.9(3)**). The application must be supported by medical evidence that the patient is capable of managing and administering his or her own affairs (**PD 21, para. 5.7**). The former patient must file in court a notice that the litigation friend's appointment has ceased, giving an address for service and stating whether he or she intends to continue to pursue or defend the proceedings (**para. 5.8**). Any order made must be served on other parties to the proceedings.

Court approval of settlement of a claim to which a child or patient is party

In a claim by, or on behalf of, or against a child or patient, no settlement, compromise or payment, and no acceptance of money paid into court, is valid without the court's approval (**CPR, rr. 21.10(1)** and **36.18(1)**). Whether proceedings have been started or not, until a proposed settlement is approved by the court there is no binding contract, and either party may renege on it (*Dietz v Lennig Chemicals Ltd* [1969] 1 AC 170; *Drinkall v Whitwood* [2003] EWCA Civ 1547, [2004] 1 WLR 462). **Rule 21.10(1)** is intended to enable a defendant to obtain a valid discharge from a claim, and to ensure that any settlement etc. is fair on the child or patient. The court will weigh the claimant's prospects of success against the likely level of damages, assuming full liability, and decide whether the proposed settlement etc. is in the interests of the child or patient. **Paragraphs 6.4, 6.4A** and **6.4B of PD 21** set out the procedure to be used where the parties have agreed that damages are to be paid in instalments. **14.38**

An application for approval of a settlement etc. in proceedings is made using the **Part 23** procedure (see **chapter 32**). In the Chancery Division the application will be heard by a judge, not a master, where the claim exceeds £100,000 or is in respect of absent, unborn or unascertained persons (**PD 2B, para. 5.1(a)**).

It is possible to bring proceedings solely for the purpose of obtaining the court's approval for a settlement of a claim before it has been issued. Court approval of a settlement reached in these circumstances is necessary to prevent a defendant repudiating the settlement at a later stage (*Drinkall v Whitwood* [2003] EWCA Civ 1547, [2004] 1 WLR 462). Such proceedings should be brought using the **Part 8** procedure (see **chapter 13**). For a summary of the approval procedure see **procedural checklist 8** in **appendix 1**. The **Part 8** claim form should set out the details of the claim and request the court's approval of the settlement. The proposed terms may be set out either in the body of the claim form or in a draft consent order in **form N292** (**CPR, r. 21.10(2)** and **PD 21, para. 6.1**). The court must satisfy itself that the parties have considered whether payment in instalments is appropriate (**PD 21, para. 6.4A**). Where periodic payments are included in the settlement, **para. 6.4B** sets out further information which the parties should provide.

PD 21, para. 6.2, sets out details of the information the court will need in order to approve the settlement. This includes whether and to what extent the defendant admits liability, the age and occupation (if any) of the child or patient, the litigation friend's approval of the proposed settlement and, in a personal injury case arising from an accident, the circumstances of the accident, any medical reports, schedules of damages, and details of any relevant criminal proceedings.

For limitations on default judgments and judgments on admissions see **14.33**.

Investment of money recovered for a child or patient

14.39 Any money recovered on behalf of a patient or child may be dealt with only as directed by the court (**CPR, r. 21.11**). The court has power to appoint a guardian of a child's estate (**r. 21.12**). **Paragraphs** 7 to 12 of **PD 21** set out details concerning how money recovered for a child or patient should be applied.

BANKRUPTCY

14.40 A bankrupt's estate becomes vested in the trustee in bankruptcy immediately on the trustee's appointment taking effect (Insolvency Act 1986, s. 306(1)). Property vests in the trustee without the need for any conveyance, assignment or transfer (s. 306(2)). By s. 283, a bankrupt's estate comprises all property belonging to or vested in the bankrupt at the commencement of the bankruptcy, and property which by virtue of the Insolvency Act 1986 is treated as belonging to the bankrupt. There are certain exceptions, such as tools and basic domestic belongings. By s. 436, 'property' includes money, goods, things in action, land and every description of property, and every description of interest in property. Consequently, most causes of action vested in an individual become vested in the trustee in bankruptcy once the trustee is appointed. However, personal claims, and in particular claims for defamation and personal injuries, remain vested in the bankrupt notwithstanding the appointment of a trustee in bankruptcy (*Heath v Tang* [1993] 1 WLR 1421), provided the claim is solely of a personal nature (*Ord v Upton* [2000] Ch 352). Where a claim in negligence gives rise to heads of damage personal to the bankrupt (such as for pain, suffering and loss of amenity) and others which have vested in the trustee (such as for loss of earnings up to the date of discharge from bankruptcy or for loss of reputation), the whole cause of action vests in the trustee, who is therefore the proper claimant. The trustee does not hold such a mixed cause of action on a bare trust for the bankrupt alone, but for the benefit of both the bankrupt and the creditors

(*Mulkerrins v PricewaterhouseCoopers* [2001] BPIR 106, point not considered on appeal). However, in such a case the trustee will hold the damages recovered in respect of the personal heads on a constructive trust for the bankrupt (*Ord v Upton* [2000] Ch 352).

Where the trustee refuses to bring proceedings on a cause of action in which part of the damages will be held on trust for the bankrupt, one solution is for the bankrupt (after discharge) to negotiate an assignment of the cause of action from the trustee. It appears there may be jurisdiction for the court to give directions for such an assignment (*Smith and Williamson v Sims Pipes* (2000) LTL 17/3/2000).

For control of litigation against individuals subject to insolvency procedures, see **81.15** to **81.36**.

COMPANIES

A company registered under the Companies Act 1985 or an earlier Companies Act must sue and be sued using the full, registered company name. Where the company is in liquidation, the words '(in liquidation)' should be included in the heading. A company which is not required to end its name with 'Ltd' or 'plc' (or their Welsh equivalents) should be referred to by its name followed by an appropriate description, such as '(a company limited by guarantee)'. The full name of a foreign company should be followed, if helpful, by '(a company incorporated under the law of . . .)'. **14.41**

The articles of association of a registered company usually confer on its directors a general power to manage the business of the company (see, for example, Table A, art. 70, in the Companies (Tables A to F) Regulations 1985 (SI 1985/805)). The power to litigate in the name of a company is part of this general power of management and so may be exercised by the directors, not the members (shareholders) (*John Shaw and Sons (Salford) Ltd v Shaw* [1935] 2 KB 113; *Breckland Group Holdings Ltd v London and Suffolk Properties Ltd* [1989] BCLC 100; *Mitchell and Hobbs (UK) Ltd v Mill* [1996] 2 BCLC 102). The members may take a decision to litigate in the company's name only if there is no board of directors capable of acting (*Alexander Ward and Co. Ltd v Samyang Navigation Co. Ltd* [1975] 1 WLR 673).

If a company is in administration, or an administrative receiver has been appointed, the administrator or receiver has a power to bring or defend any claim in the name and on behalf of the company (Insolvency Act 1986, s. 42, sch. B1, para. 60, and sch. 1, para. 5). During administration, any power of the company or its officers, including the power to litigate, that could be exercised in such a way as to interfere with the administrator's exercise of his or her powers is not exercisable except with the consent of the administrator (sch. B1, para. 64).

In *Newhart Developments Ltd v Cooperative Commercial Bank Ltd* [1978] QB 814 it was held that the appointment of a receiver does not divest the directors of their power to institute proceedings in the company's name, provided they do not interfere with the receiver's work of realising the charged assets (cf. *Shanks v Central Regional Council* 1987 SLT 410, affirmed 1988 SLT 212). In *Tudor Grange Holdings Ltd v Citibank NA* [1992] Ch 53 Browne-Wilkinson V-C said that he had substantial doubts that *Newhart Developments Ltd v Cooperative Commercial Bank Ltd* was correctly decided, and thought that, at present, it should only be followed in cases where, as in the *Newhart Developments* case, the directors proposing litigation undertook to meet any award of costs against the company if the litigation should fail. The Vice-Chancellor had two specific criticisms of the *Newhart Developments* decision. First, he pointed out that any cause of action of a company in administrative receivership would be covered by the charge under which the receiver was appointed and should therefore be under the control of the receiver. Secondly, allowing directors to start proceedings of their own but leaving the receiver to defend any counterclaim would be chaotic.

If a company is in liquidation, its liquidator has a power to bring or defend any claim in the name and on behalf of the company (Insolvency Act 1986, ss. 165(3) and 167(1)(a) and sch. 4, para. 4), but in a compulsory liquidation (a winding up by the court) the liquidator must obtain the permission of the court or of the liquidation committee.

For control of litigation against companies subject to insolvency proceedings see **81.15** to **81.36**.

Foss v Harbottle and derivative claims

14.42 It is not possible for a company's rights to be enforced in proceedings brought in the name of a member of the company (*Foss v Harbottle* (1843) 2 Hare 461), because the company is the proper claimant to enforce its own rights. There is an exception to this proper claimant principle where the directors have improperly decided not to bring a claim. The impropriety required is usually described as a fraud on the minority (that is, a minority of the members, who, because they lack the necessary votes in general meetings, are incapable of dismissing the directors) and typically involves personal benefit to the directors. Where this exception occurs, a member of the company may bring what is known as a derivative claim to vindicate the company's rights. The company must be made a co-defendant to a derivative claim so that it can enforce any judgment (**CPR, r. 19.9(2)**). After issuing a claim form making a derivative claim, the claimant must apply to the court (under **Part 23**) for permission to continue the claim (**r. 19.9(3)**). This application must be supported by written evidence (**r. 19.9(4)**). It is submitted that, as suggested by the Court of Appeal in *Prudential Assurance Co. Ltd v Newman Industries Ltd (No. 2)* [1982] Ch 204 before the rule was introduced, a claimant must establish a prima facie case (a) that the company is entitled to the relief claimed, and (b) that the claim falls within the proper boundaries of the exception to the proper claimant principle. The court should consider whether the company is disabled from pursuing the claim and whether pursuing it is in the company's interests (*Fraser v Oystertec plc* [2004] EWHC 2225 (Ch), LTL 8/10/2004, at [29]).

The onus is on the claimant to establish a positive case for being allowed to sue on behalf of the company (*Portfolios of Distinction Ltd v Laird* [2004] EWHC 2071 (Ch), [2004] 2 BCLC 741). The court will usually not allow a derivative claim to proceed if, rather than being pursued bona fide for the benefit of the company, the claim has been brought for an ulterior purpose (*Barrett v Duckett* [1995] 1 BCLC 243; *Portfolios of Distinction Ltd v Laird*), or if there is another adequate remedy (*Barrett v Duckett*; *Cooke v Cooke* [1997] 2 BCLC 28; *Portfolios of Distinction Ltd v Laird*; *Mumbray v Lapper* [2005] EWHC 1152 (Ch), *The Times*, 31 May 2005). The court will not allow a derivative claim to be brought by a person who participated in the wrongful act complained of (*Whitwam v Watkin* (1898) 78 LT 188; *Towers v African Tug Co.* [1904] 1 Ch 558; *Nurcombe v Nurcombe* [1985] 1 WLR 370).

Until permission to continue a derivative claim is given, the claimant may not take any other steps in the claim (unless the court gives specific permission) apart from serving the claim form, the application notice (for the application to proceed) and written evidence in support of the application (**r. 19.9(3)** and **(5)**). These documents must be served within the period available for service of the claim form (**r. 19.9(5)**).

If permission to proceed is given, a defence to the claim must be filed within 14 days after the date on which it is given, unless the court specifies a different time (**r. 19.9(6)**).

Continuing supervision by the court of a derivative claim is required. Permission is often given to continue only to a certain point, which is usually service of defence and completion of disclosure. There should be a review of permission to proceed if there is a material change of circumstances or if the derivative claimant decides to add a new cause of action (*Fraser v*

Oystertec plc [2004] EWHC 2225 (Ch), LTL 8/10/2004). The supervising judge should not be the trial judge (ibid.).

If a claim vested in a company arises out of facts which also disclose unfairly prejudicial conduct of the company's affairs, a petition by a member under the Companies Act 1985, s. 459 (see **82.9** to **82.18**), may be used as an alternative to a derivative claim (*Re a Company (No. 005287 of 1985)* [1986] 1 WLR 281; *Lowe v Fahey* [1996] 1 BCLC 262; *Clark v Cutland* [2003] EWCA Civ 810, [2004] 1 WLR 783).

A derivative claim may be brought in relation to a foreign company as well as a company incorporated in England and Wales. However, the appropriate forum for such a claim is likely to be the country of incorporation, unless it is an offshore haven with no connection to the dispute other than being the place of incorporation (*Konamaneni v Rolls-Royce Industrial Power (India) Ltd* [2002] 1 WLR 1269).

Reflective loss

It follows from the proper claimant principle (**14.42**) that a member holding shares in a company cannot claim any compensation for the diminution in value of those shares which merely reflects a loss which the company could recover (the 'no reflective loss principle'). The diminution in value of the shares due to the company's loss will be reversed when the company recovers compensation for that loss (*Prudential Assurance Co. Ltd v Newman Industries Ltd (No. 2)* [1982] Ch 204 at pp. 222–3; *Johnson v Gore Wood and Co.* [2002] 2 AC 1). A member of the company also cannot sue for any other losses which merely reflect losses which the company could recover, such as lost dividends and any other payments which the shareholder might have obtained from the company if it had not been deprived of its funds, including payments which might have been made in the shareholder's capacity as an officer or employee of the company. **14.43**

If a company has been injured by a breach of the European Convention on Human Rights, a member of the company is not a victim of that breach and so has no standing to apply to the European Court of Human Rights or to bring proceedings under the **Human Rights Act 1998, s. 7** (*Agrotexim v Greece* (application 14807/89) (1995) 21 EHRR 250; *Weir v Secretary of State for Transport* [2005] EWHC 2192 (Ch), LTL 14/10/2005, at [294]–[298]). The European Court of Human Rights has, however, allowed a form of derivative claim, in which a member of a company presents an application in the company's name, where it is clear that it is not possible for those responsible for the company's litigation to make the application (*Credit and Industrial Bank v Czech Republic* (application 29010/95) ECHR 2003-XI at paras 46–52).

If a company with a right to sue a person, D, to recover a loss fails to recover all or part of that loss, for example, because it settles the claim before trial, or refuses to take any action at all, then all or part of members' reflective losses will not be recovered. This does not give the members a right to sue D for the unrecovered amount of the reflective losses, because the shortfall in recovery is caused by the company, not D (*Johnson v Gore Wood and Co.*). There is an exception if it is D's wrongdoing which has caused the company to be unable to sue, for example, because that wrongdoing has left it without enough money to fund litigation (*Giles v Rhind* [2002] EWCA Civ 1428, [2003] Ch 618).

The no reflective loss principle ensures that D can only be sued once for the same loss. It prevents a person other than the company suing even if that person has a cause of action against D and even if that cause of action differs from the company's (*Day v Cook* [2001] EWCA Civ 592, [2002] 1 BCLC 1, at [79]). It applies whether the cause of action lies in common law or equity, and whether the remedy is damages or restitution (*Gardner v Parker* [2004] EWCA Civ 781, [2004] 2 BCLC 554). It applies to prevent a member suing whether the member has a controlling or a minority interest (*Gardner v Parker*, rejecting doubts expressed in *Humberclyde Finance Group Ltd v Hicks* (2001) LTL 19/11/2001 and in *Floyd v John Fairhurst and Co.* [2004] EWCA Civ 604, [2004] PNLR 41, at [77]).

The no reflective loss principle is not an infringement of the European Convention on Human Rights, protocol 1, art. 1 (protection of property), in the **Human Rights Act 1998, sch. 1** (*Humberclyde Finance Group Ltd v Hicks* (2001) LTL 19/11/2001).

The mere fact that D has caused a company to suffer loss does not give a holder of shares in that company a right of action to sue for the diminution in share value resulting from that loss. However, it is possible for a company to suffer loss because of something done by D but have no right of action against D while a shareholder does have a right of action against D. In such a case, the shareholder is permitted to claim for loss in value of the shareholding due to a loss which the company itself has no cause of action to recover (*George Fischer (Great Britain) Ltd v Multi Construction Ltd* [1995] 1 BCLC 260; *Gerber Garment Technology Inc. v Lectra Systems Ltd* [1997] RPC 443).

It is possible, when both company and shareholder have causes of action against the same defendant, that some of the shareholder's claims are not for reflective losses and can be pursued by the shareholder personally (see, for example, *R. P. Howard Ltd v Woodman Matthews and Co.* [1983] BCLC 117; *Giles v Rhind*).

It has been suggested that a defendant applying to strike out a claim, on the ground that it reflects a loss which a company could have sued for, but did not, must show that the supposed claim by the company would have been likely to succeed (*Perry v Day* [2004] EWHC 1398 (Ch), LTL 18/6/2004, per Rimer J at [65]).

By analogy with the no reflective loss principle, if a defendant's wrongful act is found to have caused both a loss to a claimant and a gain to a company in which the claimant is a shareholder, the claimant's loss and the company's gain must be set off, at least where the claimant effectively owns all the shares in the company (*Floyd v John Fairhurst and Co.* [2004] EWCA Civ 604, [2004] PNLR 41).

PARTNERSHIPS

Name

14.44 The liability of partners is generally joint and several (Partnership Act 1890, ss. 9 and 12). Partners may sue or be sued in their individual names. Alternatively, partners carrying on business within the jurisdiction may sue or be sued in the name of their firm (**RSC, ord. 81, r. 1** in CPR, sch. 1; **CCR, ord. 5, r. 9(1)** in CPR, sch. 2). In this case, the words '(a firm)' must be added to the name of the firm in the title of the action. Partners in a firm which is not carrying on business in England or Wales may only sue and be sued individually in their own names.

Disclosure of partners' names

14.45 **RSC, ord. 81, r. 2** in CPR, sch. 1, and **CCR, ord. 5, r. 9(2)** in CPR, sch. 2, permit a party suing or being sued by partners in the name of their firm to serve a notice requiring the partners to disclose the names and addresses of all the firm's partners at the time when the cause of action accrued. In the High Court, if the notice is not complied with, an order can be obtained compelling disclosure or, if the firm is the claimant, staying the claim. In the county court, if a disclosure demand is not complied with, the court may order disclosure and direct that, in default, if the firm is the claimant, the claim will be stayed, or if the claim is against the firm, the partners will be debarred from defending it (**CCR, ord. 5, r. 9(3)** in CPR, sch. 2).

SOLE TRADERS

A sole trader may be sued, but may not sue, in his or her trading name, and the provisions of **RSC, ord. 81, r. 2** in CPR, sch. 1, and **CCR, ord. 5, r. 9** in CPR, sch. 2, will apply (**RSC, ord. 81, r. 9** in CPR, sch. 1; **CCR, ord. 5, r. 10** in CPR, sch. 2). Thus, for example, a claimant may apply for disclosure of a defendant sole trader's real name and private address (see **14.45**). **14.46**

A claimant sole trader should sue in his or her own name, adding the words 'trading as' and the trading name. A defendant sole trader whose real name is not known may be sued in the business name, followed by the words 'a trading name' (**RSC, ord. 81, r. 9** in CPR, sch. 1; **CCR, ord. 5, r. 10** in CPR, sch. 2).

OTHER INCORPORATED AND UNINCORPORATED ASSOCIATIONS

Trade unions and employers' associations

A trade union which is not a special register body under the Trade Union and Labour Relations (Consolidation) Act 1992, s. 117, is not a body corporate. However, even if unincorporated, a trade union is capable of suing or being sued in its own name (Trade Union and Labour Relations (Consolidation) Act 1992, s. 10(1)(b)). It may not, however, unless it is a special register body and therefore a body corporate, sue in its own name for damages for defamation. This is because a libel is a wrong to the person and therefore no action may be brought unless the trade union has a legal personality (*Electrical, Electronic, Telecommunication and Plumbing Union v Times Newspapers Ltd* [1980] QB 585). **14.47**

An employers' association may be either a body corporate or an unincorporated association. However, even where unincorporated, it may sue or be sued in its own name (Trade Union and Labour Relations (Consolidation) Act 1992, s. 127(2)(b)).

Building societies

A building society must be incorporated under the Building Societies Act 1986 and can sue or be sued in its corporate name. **14.48**

Charities

A charitable corporation, which may sue or be sued in its own name, may be created in a number of ways: by royal charter, or by the Charity Commissioners under the Charities Act 1993, or as a charitable company incorporated under the Companies Act 1985. **14.49**

Where a charitable institution is unincorporated, proceedings may be brought against it by suing an officer of the charity 'on behalf of the charity [naming it]'. Alternatively, the charity's trustees may be named as parties (*Muman v Nagasena* [2000] 1 WLR 299).

Proceedings under the court's jurisdiction with respect to charities, or with respect to trusts in relation to the administration of a trust for charitable purposes, cannot be brought without the permission of the Charity Commissioners for England and Wales (Charities Act 1993, s. 33). The Commissioners will not give permission if, in their opinion, they can deal with the matter themselves under the 1993 Act (s. 33(3)). If the Commissioners refuse to give permission, it may be given instead by a judge of the Chancery Division (s. 33(5)). These rules do not apply to proceedings brought by the Commissioners themselves or by the Attorney-General (s. 33(6)) and do not apply to the exempt charities listed in sch. 2 to the 1993 Act (s. 33(2)).

Local government bodies

14.50 London boroughs (London Government Act 1963, s. 1), metropolitan districts and non-metropolitan counties and districts (Local Government Act 1972, s. 2) are bodies corporate, and may sue or be sued by name.

A local authority (which includes a county council, a district council, a London borough council and a parish council: Local Government Act 1972, s. 270) may institute civil proceedings where it considers it expedient for the promotion or protection of the interests of the inhabitants of its area (Local Government Act 1972, s. 222).

Central government departments

14.51 Most central government departments may sue or be sued in their own name: see **14.76**.

Quasi-governmental public bodies

14.52 There are numerous quasi-governmental public bodies which are not formal departments of State. These bodies will usually have an implicit power to bring proceedings to protect their special interests in the performance of their functions (*Broadmoor Special Health Authority v Robinson* [2000] QB 775).

Clubs

14.53 An unincorporated members' social or sporting club is not a separate legal entity and may not sue or be sued in the name of the club. Nor can the secretary or any other officer of such a club sue or be sued on behalf of the club. Where proceedings are necessary, there are two main options:

(a) Bring proceedings against individual members of the club. However, members who are not made parties will have no direct interest in the action, and any judgment obtained may not be enforced against them.

(b) Bring representative proceedings (see **14.55**) (*Campbell v Thompson* [1953] 1 QB 445). A judgment in a representative action binds the members represented, but may not be enforced against any member who is not a party to the proceedings, without the court's permission.

A proprietary club is one where the property and funds of the club belong to the proprietor, who usually conducts it with a view to profit. Where such a club is unincorporated, the proprietor may sue or be sued, either in his or her own name or in the name of the club (*Firmin and Sons Ltd v International Club* (1889) 5 TLR 694). Where it is incorporated, it should sue and be sued in its corporate name.

TRUSTS AND TRUSTEES

14.54 A claim by or against a trust is brought by joining its trustees. Trustees should act jointly and all should be named in any proceedings (as defendants, if they will not consent to act as claimants).

It is provided in **CPR, r. 19.7A** that beneficiaries need not be joined as parties to a claim brought by or against a trust. Any judgment or order made in the claim will bind the beneficiaries unless the court orders otherwise. The predecessor to this rule (RSC, ord. 15, r. 14(1)) empowered the court to order otherwise only because the trustees could not or did not represent the beneficiaries' interests. In practice this is likely to remain the principal reason for ordering that a judgment is not binding on beneficiaries.

In a High Court claim relating to trust property, the court has power under **CPR, r. 19.8A**, to order notice of the claim to be given to anyone who is not a party but who may be affected by any judgment. An application for an order under this rule may be made without notice but must be supported by written evidence which includes the reasons why the person to be served should not be bound by the judgment in the claim. Notice must be given in form 52, accompanied by a copy of the claim form, all other statements of case, and a form for acknowledging service. The person served becomes a party to the claim on acknowledging service. Even if there is no acknowledgment of service, the person will be bound by any judgment or order made in the claim.

REPRESENTATIVE PARTIES

Principles

Where it is difficult or impossible for all persons affected by a claim to be parties to the proceedings, the court may, under **CPR, rr. 19.6** and **19.7**, order one or more persons to be made party to the claim as representative of persons who are not parties and direct that orders made in the claim are to bind represented persons. **Rule 19.6** also permits a claim to be commenced by or against a representative party without a court order. **Rule 19.6** applies to any kind of claim. **Rule 19.7** (see **14.57**) is available only in the kinds of claims listed in **r. 19.7(1)**. The rules provide for two different sorts of 'representative proceedings': **14.55**

(a) representation under **r. 19.6** of one person by another with the same interest in the claim (see below); and
(b) representation under **r. 19.7** of one person by another, where the person represented cannot be identified (see **14.57**).

An alternative method of dealing with the interests of several persons is by a group litigation order, or 'GLO' (see **14.60**).

It is provided in **CPR, r. 19.6(1)**, that:

> Where more than one person has the same interest in a claim—
> (a) the claim may be begun; or
> (b) the court may order that the claim be continued,
> by or against one or more of the persons who have the same interest as representatives of any other persons who have that interest.

In *Duke of Bedford v Ellis* [1901] AC 1 (followed in *Independiente Ltd v Music Trading On-Line (HK) Ltd* [2003] EWHC 470 (Ch), LTL 25/3/2003) it was held that there are three elements to be satisfied in deciding whether the representative party and the persons represented have the same interest:

(a) a common interest;
(b) a common grievance; and
(c) a remedy beneficial to all.

A representation order in respect of a defendant may be made only where everyone within the class has a common interest in the claim. Where different defendants have different defences there is no common interest within **r. 19.6(1)**.

The court must also take account of the overriding objective. In *National Bank of Greece SA v R. M. Outhwaite 317 Syndicate at Lloyd's* [2001] Lloyd's Rep IR 652 it was held in the Commercial Court that it was proper to begin proceedings against one individual as representative of all members of 39 Lloyd's syndicates which had subscribed an insurance policy, even though the chosen individual was a member of only one of the syndicates and there was no leading underwriter clause in the policy. Andrew Smith J said that the phrase 'the same interest in a claim' in r. 19.6 is to be interpreted with a view to giving effect to the overriding objective in the CPR. Specifically, it should be interpreted in a way that makes representative proceedings available in cases where they would save expense and enable a matter to be dealt with expeditiously.

Procedure

14.56 The representative capacity of the claimant or defendant, and the class of persons represented, must be made clear in the description of the parties in the claim form. For example, 'AB, as representing himself and all other members of the British Phonographic Industry Ltd'.

It is not necessary for a representative claimant to obtain the authority of the represented persons to bring the claim. The authority to bring the proceedings is provided by **CPR, r. 19.6**, itself, *Independiente Ltd v Music Trading On-Line (HK) Ltd* [2003] EWHC 470 (QB), LTL 25/3/2003; *Howells v Dominion Insurance Co. Ltd* [2005] EWHC 552 (QB), LTL 8/4/2005. Nor is it necessary for a claimant to obtain the court's permission to issue a claim form either as a representative of other claimants, or against a representative defendant. But the court is expressly empowered by **CPR, r. 19.6(2)**, to order that a person may not act as a representative. Any party may make an application for such an order.

The representative claimant is fully empowered to choose how to run the litigation on behalf of the class. However, those represented are not parties to the litigation, so, for example, disclosure may be ordered against them only as non-parties (*Ventouris v Mountain* [1990] 1 WLR 1370, QBD). Nor are the persons represented individually liable for costs (*Howells v Dominion Insurance Co. Ltd*).

By virtue of **r. 19.6**, unless the court orders otherwise, any judgment or order is binding on the persons represented. It may be enforced by or against any represented person. However, it may not be enforced by or against a person who is not a named party without the court's permission (*Howells v Dominion Insurance Co. Ltd*).

Representation of unascertained persons

14.57 In claims involving:

(a) the estate of a deceased person,
(b) trust property, or
(c) the meaning of a document (including a statute),

the court has power to appoint a representative for another person or class, for the purposes of the claim (**CPR, r. 19.7**). The court may exercise the power where:

(a) the person or persons to be represented are unborn, or cannot be found or easily ascertained; or
(b) in the case of a class, the members of the class have the same interest in the claim and:
 (i) one or more members are unborn, or cannot be found or easily ascertained; or
 (ii) appointing a representative would further the overriding objective.

If the court does appoint such a representative, any judgments or orders made in the action are binding on the person(s) represented, but may only be enforced by or against a person who is not a party with the permission of the court (**r. 19.7(7)**).

CONSOLIDATION

14.58 The court may order closely connected claims to be consolidated (**CPR, r. 3.1(2)(g)**). After consolidation the claims continue as if they were a single claim. Consolidation is only likely to be ordered where there is a strong overlap, or where there is a risk of irreconcilable judgments. Where there is minimal overlap, consolidation is inappropriate (*Law Debenture Trust Corporation (Channel Islands) Ltd v Lexington Insurance Co.* (2001) LTL 12/11/2001).

A consolidation order can only be made if all the claims are before the court on the same occasion. Therefore applications will have to be made in each of the claims returnable in the same court (perhaps after some of the claims are transferred) at the same time. Alternatively, a single application can be issued (again after ensuring all claims are proceeding in the same court and Division) stating the titles of all the claims proposed to be consolidated. If the order is made, one of the claims is nominated as the lead claim.

INTERVENTION

In cases where there is no effective respondent and which raise issues likely to be of wider importance than the immediate interests of the parties, the court may adjourn so that a suitable person, or advocate to the court (*amicus curiae*), be appointed to ensure arguments are raised in the public interest. The Pensions Ombudsman was invited to appear on this basis in *Legal and General Assurance Society Ltd v CCA Stationery Ltd* [2003] EWHC 1491 (Ch), LTL 11/6/2003. 14.59

GROUP LITIGATION

Group litigation orders

Until May 2000, no special provision was made in rules of court for multi-party group litigation, or class actions. Representative proceedings under **CPR, r. 19.7** (see **14.55** to **14.57**) are one way of dealing with multi-party actions, but are not designed for group litigation. In particular, they do not provide an effective mechanism for managing group litigation, for identifying generic issues applicable to the entire group or for resolving cases at a cost which is proportionate to the value of an individual claim. By the early 1990s there was wide agreement that a new approach was needed (see *Nash v Eli Lilly and Co.* [1993] 1 WLR 782). Recommendations by Lord Woolf in ch. 17 of his *Final Report* for a new framework for multi-party actions led (albeit with some differences) to the introduction of **CPR, r. 19.11**, and **PD 19B**. The court may, under **CPR, r. 19.11**, make a 'group litigation order' or 'GLO', where a number of claims give rise to common or related, issues of fact or law. The order may be made upon the application of any party, or by the court acting of its own initiative (**PD 19B, paras 3.1** and **4**). The types of cases suitable for a GLO include mass product liability claims, claims arising out of a public transport disaster, and housing claims involving similar claims by numerous tenants. 14.60

The key features of the rules on GLOs are:

(a) Either before or after the commencement of litigation, a party may apply for a GLO.
(b) The GLO will identify the issues to be managed as part of the group litigation (the 'GLO issues'). Any individual claim (a 'GLO claim') must raise these issues to fall under the terms of the order.
(c) A register will be established for the GLO claims, and a specified court will be given responsibility for managing them.
(d) The managing court is given wide powers to give case management directions to ensure the effective coordination and resolution of the GLO claims (see **14.65**).
(e) Any judgment made on a GLO issue will bind all the GLO claims (see **14.66**). The rules do not, however, provide any guidance on how a settlement, or proposed settlement, should be managed.

Preliminary steps

Solicitors acting for potential applicants for a GLO should contact the Law Society's Multi-Party Actions Information Service (telephone 0870 606 2522) to identify other potential claims giving rise to the same issues (**PD 19B, para. 2.1**). (Members of the public should ring 0870 606 6575.) Consideration should also be given to forming a solicitors' group and to identifying a solicitor to lead the application for a GLO and the litigation of the GLO issues. 14.61

PD 19B, para. 2.2, advises that the lead solicitor's role and relationship with other members of the solicitors' group should be defined in writing. In any event, the lead solicitor will be subject to any directions given by the court.

PD 19B, para. 2.3, advises that the applicant should consider whether it would be more appropriate to seek any other order, in particular, an order for claims to be consolidated or for a representative to be appointed under **CPR, rr. 19.6** to **19.9**.

The Law Society publishes practice guidelines for those conducting or wishing to conduct disaster litigation under a GLO. A copy is available on the Law Society website (www.lawsociety.org).

Applying for a GLO

14.62 Application for a GLO, whether before or after issue of the claim, is made by the **Part 23** procedure (see **chapter 32**), and can be made by any party to the claim (**PD 19B, para. 3.1**). Alternatively the court may make an order of its own motion. The application should be made to the Senior Master in the Queen's Bench Division of the High Court, or the Chief Chancery Master in the Chancery Division. For claims likely to proceed in a specialist list (see **11.4**), the application should be made to a senior judge of that list. For claims likely to proceed in a district registry, application should be made to the presiding judge, or to the supervising Chancery judge. County court applications should be made to the designated civil judge for the area in which the court is situated (**PD 19B, paras 3.5 to 3.7**).

By **PD 19B, para. 3.2**, either the application notice itself, or the written evidence in support should include the following information:

(a) a summary of the nature of the litigation;
(b) the number and nature of claims already issued;
(c) the number of parties likely to be involved;
(d) the common issues of fact or law; and
(e) whether there are any matters that distinguish smaller groups of claims within the wider group.

A GLO may not be made without the consent of the Lord Chief Justice, in the case of claims proceeding in the Queen's Bench Division, or the Chancellor, in the case of claims proceeding in the Chancery Division, or the Head of Civil Justice in the case of claims proceeding in a county court (**PD 19B, para. 3.3**). It is for the court, not the parties, to seek such consent, by sending to the Lord Chief Justice, or the Chancellor, or the Head of Civil Justice, as appropriate, a copy of the application notice, any relevant written evidence in support and a written statement of the reasons a GLO is thought to be desirable. This step may be taken before or after hearing the application. Indeed, in the county court, the applicant should request the court to refer the application notice to the designated civil judge as soon as possible to enable him or her to consider seeking the consent of the Head of Civil Justice prior to the hearing of the application (**PD 19B, para. 3.8**).

Nature of the order

14.63 A GLO must, by **CPR, r. 19.11(2)**:

(a) identify the issues which a claim must raise if it is to be managed under the order (the 'GLO issues');
(b) set up a register for such claims; and
(c) specify the court that will manage the claims (the 'management court').

The management court is the court to which any application to vary the GLO should be made (**PD 19B, para. 12.2**).

Once a GLO has been made, a copy should be supplied to the Law Society and to the Senior Master of the Queen's Bench Division (**PD 19B, para. 11**). There is a list of GLOs on Her

Majesty's Courts Service website: www.hmcourts-service.gov.uk. The list includes details of the lead solicitors and defined issues.

Group register

The group register of claims managed under a GLO is normally maintained by the management court, but that court may direct it to be kept by a solicitor for one of the parties to a case entered on it (normally the lead solicitor) (**PD 19B, para. 6.5**). In this case, the solicitor must permit the register to be inspected by the public during business hours, upon reasonable notice and upon paying an appropriate fee (**PD 19B, para. 6.6(2)**). **14.64**

Any party to a case may apply to be entered on or removed from a group register (**PD 19B, para. 6.2; CPR, r. 19.14**). An order for a case to be entered may be made where the case raises at least one of the GLO issues (**PD 19B, para. 6.3**). However, even where a case does raise a GLO issue, the court has a discretion to refuse registration (or to order the removal of a case from the register) on the grounds that it cannot conveniently be managed with the other cases on the register, or that its inclusion would adversely affect the management of the other cases (**PD 19B, para. 6.4**).

The management court may specify a cut-off date after which no claim may be added to the register without the court's permission (**CPR, r. 19.13; PD 19B, para. 13**). In *Taylor v Nugent Care Society* [2004] EWCA Civ 51, [2004] 1 WLR 1129, the claimant issued separate proceedings arising out of alleged abuse in a childrens' home, an issue which was the subject of a GLO. He applied unsuccessfully to join the group litigation, some two and a half years after the cut-off date set by the court. The defendant made an application to strike out the claim. The Court of Appeal refused the application on the grounds that it was a disproportionate reaction to the claimant's delay and there were other steps, such as staying the claimant's action pending case management directions, which adequately protected the defendant's interests. The Court of Appeal also considered the relationship between a GLO and a claim on the same issue not included in the group. The court stated that although there is no requirement in **CPR, Part 19**, for a claimant to join a GLO, if he chooses not to do so he is still subject to the management powers of the court. If he brings proceedings in parallel to a GLO, the court is entitled to manage those separate proceedings in a way which takes account of the position of those who have joined the GLO. Those who have joined the GLO are entitled to have their interests given a higher priority than those of a defendant who has not joined. This is partly because of their number but also because by joining the GLO they are cooperating with the proper management of the claim.

Managing the GLO claims

After a GLO is made, all existing claims which raise any of the GLO issues will, where necessary, be transferred to the management court, be listed on the group register and, where appropriate (for example, where one claim is proceeding as a test claim or to await group case management directions), be stayed pending further order (**CPR, r. 19.11(3)**). Every claim entered on the group register will automatically be allocated to the multi-track. Any case management directions already given will be set aside and any hearing date already fixed other than for the purpose of the group litigation will be vacated (**PD 19B, para. 7**). **14.65**

The management court will normally require all new claims to be commenced in it. Failure to comply with any such order will not invalidate a claim, but the claim should be transferred to the management court and entered on the group register as soon as possible after issue (**PD 19B, para. 9**).

A GLO claim will be managed by a single assigned judge, assisted by a district judge or master and a costs judge (**PD 19B, para. 8**). Case management directions may be given when the GLO is made, or subsequently. Such directions may include orders for one claim to proceed as a test claim, appointing a lead solicitor and specifying a cut-off date for joining the group, and provision for allocation of costs (**CPR, r. 19.13; PD 19B, paras 12** and **13**).

Directions will normally also address the form that the particulars of claim should take. In particular, **PD 19B, para. 14**, makes provision for the service of 'group particulars of claim' — i.e., one statement of case which sets out details of all the claims on the group register at the time it is filed. **PD 19B** suggests that the particulars should contain details of the general allegations common to all claims and a schedule (or a series of questionnaires, in a form approved by the court) setting out specific facts relating to particular claimants on the group register (**paras 14.1** and **14.3**).

The management court may also give directions for the trial of the action, addressing how the issues common to the group claims and those raised by particular claims should be dealt with (**PD 19B, para. 15.1**). While common issues will normally be tried in the management court, the separate issues raised by individual claims may be tried at a court which suits the convenience of the parties to that particular claim (**PD 19B, para. 15.2**).

Judgment

14.66 Subject to any court order to the contrary, any judgment or order made by the court in relation to a GLO issue is binding on the parties to all the other claims which are by then already on the GLO register (**CPR, r. 19.12(1)(a)**). An appeal against the judgment or order may only be made with the permission of the court (**CPR, r. 19.12(2)**).

The court may also direct to what extent any order or judgment should bind parties to claims entered subsequently on the GLO register (**CPR, r. 19.12(1)(b)**). However, in this case, an affected party may apply to the court for an order that the judgment or order is not binding on him (**CPR, r. 19.12(3)**).

Any document disclosed by a party to any claim on the GLO register is disclosed to all parties to claims on the GLO register at the time disclosure is made and to those subsequently entered (**CPR, r. 19.12(4)**).

Costs

14.67 In assessing costs, the court will need to apportion costs between those relating to common issues and those which relate to issues in particular cases. The question of costs in group actions is governed by **CPR, r. 48.6A**, and is considered more fully at **66.52**.

VEXATIOUS LITIGANTS

Means of restraining vexatious litigants

14.68 A small minority of litigants misuse the freedom of access to the courts by launching large numbers of unmeritorious claims or numerous interim applications, wasting court resources and causing a great deal of anxiety, trouble and expense to the persons they litigate against. Following amendments to the CPR made as a consequence of the decision in *Bhamjee v Forsdick* [2003] EWCA Civ 1113, [2004] 1 WLR 88, there are now two mechanisms for restraining the activities of a vexatious litigant. They are:

(a) Civil proceedings and all proceedings orders under the **Supreme Court Act 1981, s. 42**, made by the Divisional Court on the application of the Attorney-General, preventing a vexatious litigant issuing proceedings without permission of the court for an indefinite period (see 14.69).

(b) One of three kinds of civil restraint orders, as defined in **CPR, r. 2.3(1)**. The procedure for making these is simpler than for orders under the **Supreme Court Act 1981, s. 42**, and does not require the involvement of the Attorney-General. Civil restraint orders can be made by the court acting on its own initiative (**CPR, r. 3.3(7)**). See **14.70** to **14.73**.

Civil proceedings orders and all proceedings orders

Where it is proved that a litigant has 'habitually and persistently and without any reasonable ground' instituted vexatious proceedings or applications, the High Court is given power under the **Supreme Court Act 1981, s. 42**, to make: **14.69**

(a) a civil proceedings order; or
(b) an all proceedings order applying both to all civil proceedings and applications and specified criminal proceedings.

A person subject to either order is prevented from continuing or commencing a civil claim, or making applications in a civil claim, without the permission of the High Court. Permission will not be granted unless the High Court is satisfied that the claim or application is not an abuse of process and that there are reasonable grounds for bringing it. The order will remain in force indefinitely, unless it is expressed to be for a specific period.

Application for an order under s. 42 must be made by the Attorney-General and is heard by a Divisional Court. Application is by **Part 8** claim form (**PD 8B, table 2**) and the special procedure set out in **PD 8B, Section B**, must be followed. The application must be made by claim form, which, with a witness statement or affidavit in support, must be filed in the Administrative Court Office and served on the person against whom the order is sought (**RSC, ord. 94, r. 15** in CPR, sch. 1).

The procedure whereby a litigant against whom an order has been made under s. 42 makes an application for permission to commence or continue a claim is set out in **para. 7 of PD 3**. An application notice should be issued in the High Court and signed by the litigant who is subject to the order. The application notice must state:

(a) the title and reference number of the proceedings in which the order was made;
(b) the full name and address of the litigant;
(c) the order the litigant is seeking; and
(d) briefly, why the order is sought.

Written evidence may be filed in support of the application. Either in the application notice, or the supporting evidence, the litigant must list the previous occasions on which he or she has made an application for permission.

The application will then be placed before a High Court judge, who may:

(a) make an order granting or dismissing the application without the attendance of the applicant;
(b) ask for further written evidence from the litigant; or
(c) give directions for there to be a hearing of the application. Such directions may include an order that the application notice be served on the Attorney-General and on anyone against whom the litigant wishes to bring the new claim.

No appeal is possible against a decision refusing permission (**Supreme Court Act 1981, s. 42(41)**).

If permission is given for a vexatious litigant to commence a new claim, at a hearing of which the proposed defendant was not given notice, the defendant to the new claim may apply to set it aside (**PD 3, para. 7.9**).

In *Ewing v Office of the Deputy Prime Minister* [2005] EWCA Civ 1583, *The Independent*, 20 January 2006, the court considered concurrent applications by a vexatious litigant under the **Supreme Court Act 1981, s. 42,** for permission to bring proceedings and for permission to seek judicial review. The court stated that a vexatious litigant should not allow his name to be included in a claim form (even as a 'proposed' claimant) unless and until he has obtained the necessary permission, and went on to give guidance on dealing with an application for permission under s. 42 in the context of a proposed judicial review claim. It also held that the procedure under s. 42 is designed to provide a mechanism to ensure that a vexatious litigant has access to the court to pursue his own genuine legal grievances, not to set himself up as a public champion. Where the court considers that the vexatious litigant does not have sufficient standing in the substantive action, it should refuse permission under s. 42 to bring the claim.

An order under the **Supreme Court Act 1981, s. 42**, does not violate **art. 6(1) of the European Convention on Human Rights** (*Attorney-General v Covey* [2001] EWCA Civ 254, *The Times*, 2 March 2001). The Convention requires a fair and reasonable opportunity to address the court, not an unlimited and uncontrolled opportunity.

Civil restraint orders

14.70 By virtue of **CPR, r. 3.11**, and **PD 3C**, the court has power to make civil restraint orders. These provisions give effect to the recommendations in *Bhamjee v Forsdick* [2003] EWCA Civ 1113, [2004] 1 WLR 88, extending the old '*Grepe v Loam*' orders which restrained a party from making further applications in current proceedings (*Grepe v Loam* (1887) 37 ChD 168). **CPR, r. 2.3(1)**, defines three kinds of civil restraint orders:

(a) a limited civil restraint order, restraining a party from making any further applications in current proceedings (see **14.71**);
(b) an extended civil restraint order, restraining a party from issuing particular claims or making particular applications in specified courts (see **14.72**); and
(c) a general restraint order, restraining a party from issuing any claim or making any application in specified courts (see **14.73**).

Court orders must record whether any application (including an application for permission to appeal or for permission to apply for judicial review), statement of case or appeal has been struck out or dismissed as being totally without merit. Whenever it makes any such order, the court must go on to consider whether to make a civil restraint order (**rr. 3.3(7), 3.4(6), 23.12** and **52.10(6)**). **Rule 3.3(7)** gives the court power to make a civil restraint order on its own initiative.

Sometimes the court must go further and protect its staff from a litigant who persists in wasting their time and disturbing the orderly conduct of court business. The appropriate way of doing this is by an injunction prohibiting the litigant from entering the court building unless summoned by the court (*Attorney-General v Ebert* [2001] EWHC Admin 695, [2002] 2 All ER 789). See also *Mahajan v Department for Constitutional Affairs* [2004] EWCA Civ 946, *The Times*, 13 July 2004, in which an order was made restraining the claimant from addressing or corresponding with court staff in a rude or abusive manner.

In *Ebert v Venvil* [2000] Ch 484 the Court of Appeal made an extended civil restraint order restraining a party from taking any steps, including the issuing of new proceedings, in any Division of the High Court or any county court, arising out of the same matter. It rejected an argument that this would be contrary to the **European Convention on Human Rights, art. 6**, or the common law approach indicated in *R v Lord Chancellor, ex parte Witham* [1998] QB 575. The same view was taken in *Mahajan v Department for Constitutional Affairs* [2004] EWCA Civ 946, *The Times* 13 July 2004, in which the Court of Appeal confirmed that, so long as the right of access to the court is not being extinguished, the court is entitled to regulate its affairs so as to protect its process and the interests of other parties against whom vexatious litigation is persistently brought.

Limited civil restraint orders

14.71 A limited civil restraint order restrains a party from making any further applications in current proceedings without obtaining the permission of a particular judge specified in the order (**PD 3C, para. 2.2(1)**). An order may be made by a judge of any court, where a party has made two or more applications which are totally without merit (**para. 2.1**). The order will remain in force for the duration of the proceedings (**para. 2.9**). This is the only form of civil restraint order which may be made by a master, circuit judge or district judge under **PD 3C**. For the position before **PD 3C** came into force see *Wickramaratna v Cambridge University Chemistry Department* [2004] EWCA Civ 1532, LTL 2/11/2004.

A party subject to a limited civil restraint order may apply to vary or discharge the order only with the permission of the judge specified in the order (**para. 2.2(2)**). The restrained party may also appeal against the order, but again only with permission (**para. 2.2(3)**). Making an application without permission will result in automatic dismissal (**para. 2.3(1)**). Where a person who is subject to a civil restraint order makes repeated applications for permission which are totally devoid of merit, by **para. 2.7**, a Court of Appeal judge, a High Court judge or master, or a designated civil judge or his deputy may make a further order refusing any further right of appeal unless the judge who refused permission to appeal now grants it (**para. 2.3(2)**).

Notice of an application, by a party who is subject to a limited civil restraint order, for permission under **para. 2.2(1)** or (2) must be served by that party on any other parties to the proceedings, setting out the nature and grounds of the application and giving the other parties at least seven days in which to respond. The application must be in writing, must include the other parties' written responses and will be determined without a hearing (**para. 2.6**). Any appeal against the refusal of permission under **para. 2.2(1) or (2)** must also be in writing and will also be determined without a hearing (**para. 2.8**).

Extended civil restraint orders

An extended civil restraint order restrains a party from issuing claims or applications in specified courts which involve, relate to, touch upon or lead to the proceedings in which the order is made (**PD 3C, para. 3.2(1)**). By **para. 3.1** a Court of Appeal judge, a High Court judge or a designated civil judge or his deputy may make such an order where a party has persistently issued claims or applications which are totally without merit. The fact that the party has also made some successful, or partially successful, applications is relevant to the exercise of the discretion to grant an extended civil restraint order, but is not a bar (*Thakerar v Lynch Hall and Hornby* (2005) *The Times*, 30 November 2005). Masters, circuit judges and district judges have no power to make such an order. If they consider that an order should be made in a case before them, they must transfer it to a High Court or designated civil judge (**para. 3.11**). **14.72**

An extended civil restraint order will apply to claims or applications in:

(a) any court, where the order is made by a Court of Appeal judge;
(b) the High Court or the county court, where the order is made by a High Court judge; or
(c) any county court where the order is made by a designated civil judge or his deputy.

An extended civil restraint order will remain in force for a specified period not exceeding two years, although it may be extended for periods of up to two years at a time (**paras 3.9** and **3.10**).

A person subject to an extended civil restraint order may apply to vary or discharge the order only with the permission of the judge specified in the order (**para. 3.2(2)**). The restrained person may also appeal against the order, but again only with permission (**para. 3.2(3)**). Issuing a claim or making an application without permission will result in automatic striking out or dismissal (**para. 3.3(1)**). Where a person who is subject to an extended civil restraint order makes repeated applications for permission which are totally devoid of merit, by **para. 3.7**, a Court of Appeal judge, a High Court judge or a designated civil judge or his deputy may make a further order refusing any further right of appeal unless the judge who refused permission to appeal now grants it (**para. 3.3(2)**).

Notice of an application, by a party who is subject to an extended civil restraint order, for permission under **para.** 3.2(1) **or** (2), must be served by that party on any other parties to the proceedings, setting out the nature and grounds of the application and giving the other parties at least seven days in which to respond. The application for permission must be in writing, must include the other parties' written responses and will be determined without a hearing (**para.** 3.6). Any appeal against the refusal of permission under **para.** 3.2(1) **or** (2) must also be in writing and will be determined without a hearing (**para.** 3.8).

As an alternative to making any form of civil restraint order, the court may accept an appropriate assurance from the litigant. In *Wilkes v Ballam Delaney Hunt* [2005] EWCA Civ 1104, the court declined to order an extended civil restraint order against a litigant who had given an assurance to the court not to commence fresh proceedings against specified individuals and had kept to his assurance.

General civil restraint orders

14.73 A general civil restraint order restrains a person from issuing any claim or making any application in specified courts without obtaining the permission of a particular judge specified in the order (**PD 3C, para.** 4.2(1)). By **paras** 4.2(1) and 4.1 a Court of Appeal judge, a High Court judge, or a designated civil judge or his deputy may make an order where, despite being subject to an extended civil restraint order, a person has persistently issued claims or applications which are totally without merit. Masters, circuit judges and district judges have no power to make general civil restraint orders. If they consider that an order should be made in a case before them, they must transfer it to a High Court or designated civil judge (**para.** 4.11).

Where a litigant had repeatedly breached an extended civil proceedings order and there was no indication that the extended order had effectively limited his activities, it was appropriate to make a general civil proceedings order against him. This was particularly so, given that he had made applications in relation to third parties to the main litigation (*Carroll v Kynaston* [2005] EWHC 927, LTL 2/6/2005).

A general civil restraint order will apply to claims or applications in:

(a) any court, where the order is made by a Court of Appeal judge;
(b) the High Court or the county court, where the order is made by a High Court judge; or
(c) any county court where the order is made by a designated civil judge or his deputy (**para.** 4.2(1)).

A general civil restraint order will remain in force for a specified period not exceeding two years, although it may be extended for periods of up to two years at a time (**paras** 4.9 and 4.10).

A person subject to a general civil restraint order may apply to vary or discharge the order only with the permission of the judge specified in the order (**para.** 4.2(2)). The restrained person may also appeal against the order, but again only with permission (**para.** 4.2(3)). Issuing a claim or making an application without permission will result in automatic striking out or dismissal (**para.** 4.3(1)). Where a person who is subject to a general civil restraint order makes repeated applications for permission which are totally devoid of merit, by **para.** 4.7, a Court of Appeal judge, a High Court judge or a designated civil judge or his deputy may make a further order refusing any further right of appeal unless the judge who refused permission to appeal now grants it (**para.** 4.3(2)).

Notice of an application, by a party who is subject to a general civil restraint order, for permission under **para.** 4.2(1) or (2), must be served by that party on any other parties to the proceedings, setting out the nature and grounds of the application and giving the other parties at least seven days in which to respond. The application for permission must be in writing, must include the other parties' written responses and will be determined without a hearing (**para. 4.6**). Any appeal against the refusal of permission under **para. 4.2(1)** or **(2)** must also be in writing and will also be determined without a hearing (**para. 4.8**).

CROWN PROCEEDINGS

Introduction

Proceedings by and against the Crown are governed by the **Crown Proceedings Act 1947** and **CPR, Part 66**, which, with effect from 1 October 2005, replaced RSC, ord. 77, and CCR, ord. 42. The intention behind the **Crown Proceedings Act 1947** is that proceedings involving the Crown should be governed by broadly the same procedure as between private litigants. The new **CPR, Part 66**, has removed some of the procedural advantages which the Crown had under the old rules. There are still special rules for Crown proceedings concerning the content of a claim form (see **23.17**), service (**14.76** and **15.34**), venue (**14.75**), forms of relief (**14.77**), default judgment (**20.7**), counterclaims (**28.2**) and enforcement (**76.38**). Crown proceedings cannot be undertaken through the Claim Production Centre (**12.8**) or Money Claim Online (**12.10**). **14.74**

Venue

The new rules remove the Crown's power to determine venue and to transfer proceedings from a county court to the High Court. Instead, it is now for the court to determine the appropriate venue case by case. The **Crown Proceedings Act, s. 20(2)**, provides that the usual rules on transfer from a county court to the High Court, or the transfer of proceedings from the High Court to a county court, apply in relation to proceedings against the Crown. However, a new **CPR, r. 30.3(2)(h)**, adds to the factors to which the court must have regard in considering whether or not to transfer the claim 'the location of the relevant government department or officers of the Crown and, where appropriate, any relevant public interest that the matter should be tried in London'. A note by the Attorney-General to assist judges and practitioners with matters relevant to the venue of Crown proceedings is annexed to **PD 66**. **14.75**

Parties to the proceedings

Only authorised government departments may sue or be sued in their own name (**Crown Proceedings Act 1947, s. 17(2)** and **(3)**). Where a department is not authorised under the Act, proceedings by or against it may be instituted in the name of the Attorney-General. A new **CPR, r. 19.4(4A)**, provides that the Commissioners for HM Revenue and Customs may be added as a party to proceedings only if they consent in writing. The Cabinet Office publishes a list of government departments authorised for the purposes of the Act. The list appears in this book after the text of the Act in **appendix** 7. See also **15.34**. **14.76**

Forms of relief available against the Crown

Apart from the cases set out below, the court has power to grant the same relief against the Crown as it has in proceedings between private litigants. By the **Crown Proceedings Act 1947, s. 21**, the court may not, however, make an order for any of the following against the Crown: **14.77**

(a) an injunction (although the court may require the Crown to provide a cross-undertaking in damages in support of an application for an interim injunction: *F. Hoffmann-La Roche & Co. AG v Secretary of State for Trade and Industry* [1975] AC 295);
(b) specific performance; or
(c) an order for the recovery of land or other property.

In these cases, the court will instead make a declaration against the Crown.

Human rights: joining minister

14.78 The court cannot make a declaration of incompatibility under the **Human Rights Act 1998, s. 4**, unless 21 days' notice has been given to the Crown (**CPR, r. 19.4A(1)**). The minister, or other person permitted by the Act, is entitled to be joined on giving notice to the court. Where a claim is made for damages in respect of a judicial act under the **Human Rights Act 1998, s. 9**, notice must be given to the Crown (**CPR, r. 19.4A(3)**), but in this situation, if the appropriate person does not apply to be joined within 21 days or such other time as may be allowed by the court, the court may join that person as a party (**r. 19.4A(4)**). A notice to the Crown under **r. 19.4A** must be served on the person named in the list published under the **Crown Proceedings Act 1947, s. 17** (**PD 19, para. 6.4(1)**; the list is printed after the 1947 Act in **appendix** 7; for more on service on the Crown see **15.34**). In *Poplar Housing and Regeneration Community Association Ltd v Donoghue* [2001] EWCA Civ 595, [2002] QB 48 the Court of Appeal said that, in addition to the formal notice required under **r. 19.4A**, the party intending to raise the issue of incompatibility should also give informal notice of its intention to do so, both to the court and to the Crown, at the earliest possible opportunity. Directions under these provisions will usually be made at the case management conference (**PD 19, paras 6.2 and 6.6**).

RIGHTS AGAINST INSURERS IN ROAD TRAFFIC CASES

14.79 Under the **European Communities (Rights against Insurers) Regulations 2002** (SI 2002/3061), a claimant who is resident in an EEA county (the EU plus Iceland, Liechtenstein, Norway and Switzerland) bringing proceedings in tort arising out of a road accident may issue proceedings against the insurer of the vehicle alleged to be responsible for the accident (reg. 3). An 'accident' for the purposes of the Regulations means an accident on a road or other public place in the United Kingdom caused by, or arising out of, the use of any insured vehicle (reg. 2(1)). A 'vehicle' is any vehicle normally based in the United Kingdom intended for travel on land which is propelled by mechanical power, but not running on rails, and includes any trailer whether or not it is coupled (reg. 2(1)). A vehicle is 'insured' if there is a policy of insurance in force fulfilling the requirements of the Road Traffic Act 1988, s. 145 (SI 2002/3061, reg. 2(3)). If the Regulations apply, the insurer is directly liable to the claimant (reg. 3(2)), and the right to sue the insurer is in addition to the existing right of action against the driver (reg. 3(2)). The full text of the Regulations can be found in **appendix** 7.

FOREIGN STATES AND DIPLOMATS

Foreign States

14.80 The State Immunity Act 1978 gives foreign States immunity from the jurisdiction of the United Kingdom courts for acts of a governmental nature. The Act applies to any foreign or Commonwealth State, and to its government, head of State and governmental departments (s. 14(1)). Entities which are distinct from the executive organs of State are also immune if the proceedings relate to something done by the separate entity in the exercise of sovereign authority and the circumstances are such that a State would have been immune under the Act (s. 14(2)). A certificate issued by the Secretary of State of the Foreign and Commonwealth Office is conclusive evidence as to whether a territory is a State, and as to the person or persons to be regarded as the head of the government or State (s. 21(a)).

The 1978 Act sets out the categories of claims for which a foreign State is not immune. Acts which could be performed by a company or a private individual will not enjoy immunity.

These include where the proceedings relate to a commercial transaction (s. 3), to a contract of employment made or to be performed within the United Kingdom (s. 4), to death or personal injury caused by an act in the UK (s. 5) (so an allegation of torture against the Saudi Arabian Ministry of the Interior alleged to have occurred in Saudi Arabia did not fall within s. 5 and was covered by State immunity, but the State officials alleged to be responsible for the acts of torture were not entitled to immunity (*Jones v Ministry of the Interior of Saudi Arabia* [2004] EWCA Civ 1394, [2005] UKHRR 57)), to immovable property within the United Kingdom (s. 6), or to intellectual property rights (s. 7).

In *Grovit v De Nederlandsche Bank* [2005] EWHC 2944 (QB), [2006] 1 All ER (Comm) 397, a claim was brought before the English courts under **Regulation 44/2001** ('the **Jurisdiction and Judgments Regulation**'), **art.** 5(3), alleging libel against the defendant Dutch bank. The court held that the **Jurisdiction and Judgments Regulation** had to be read subject to the international law of State immunity, as expressed in the State Immunity Act 1978. It also held, approving *Jones v Ministry of the Interior of Saudi Arabia* [2004] EWCA Civ 1394, [2005] UKHRR 57, that some acts, such as torture, were outside the scope of any proper exercise of sovereign authority and so could not be protected by State immunity. However, the allegations of malicious libel in this case fell well below the seriousness required for the claim of State immunity not to be upheld. The court also considered the relationship between the State Immunity Act 1978 and the **European Convention on Human Rights, art. 6**. The European Court of Human Rights has accepted that a plea of State immunity does in principle interfere with art. 6 rights (e.g., *McElhinney v Ireland* (2002) 34 EHRR 13, para. 26; *Fogarty v United Kingdom* (2002) 34 EHRR 12, para. 28; and *Al-Adsani v United Kingdom* (2002) 34 EHRR 273, para. 52). The courts also recognise, however, the importance of complying with international law to promote comity and good relations between States through respect of another State's sovereignty. The courts' approach should therefore be to consider whether, on the facts of the individual case, the claim to State immunity is proportionate to the denial of a hearing. In this case, comity and respect for the dignity of other States made it wholly proportionate that the claimants should be precluded from pursuing their claim in an English court.

A claim may be brought against a State where it has submitted voluntarily to the jurisdiction. It may do this by filing an acknowledgment of service and not taking any step to contest jurisdiction, or by prior written agreement, or by instituting, or intervening in, proceedings (s. 2).

Foreign diplomats

Both at common law, and under the provisions of the Diplomatic Privileges Act 1964, foreign diplomats, their families and their servants are immune from civil or criminal proceedings. A certificate of immunity issued by the Secretary of State will be conclusive (s. 4). Accordingly, service of a claim form on a person with diplomatic immunity is null and void, unless immunity is waived by the defendant filing an acknowledgment of service, and not following it up by an application under **CPR, Part 11**. **14.81**

Chapter 15 Filing and Service

The following procedural checklists, which are in **appendix 1**, are relevant to this chapter and **chapter 12**:

Procedural checklist 9 Issue and service where service of the claim form is to be effected by the court

Procedural checklist 10 Issue and service where service of the claim form is to be effected by the claimant

The following procedural checklist is relevant to this chapter:

Procedural checklist 11 Application to extend time for service of claim form

INTRODUCTION

15.1 The rules on service in the CPR have probably been among the least successful of the Woolf reforms. They are complicated and have generated a large volume of new case law. In *Collier v Williams* [2006] EWCA Civ 20, *The Times*, 3 February 2006, Dyson LJ noted that the rules were proving difficult to understand and apply. He commented with dismay that the intention of reducing cost, complexity and delays in litigation by the introduction of rules which were simple, straightforward and not susceptible to satellite litigation had not been achieved in this area.

With this in mind, the rules on service are to be reviewed by the Civil Procedure Rule Committee.

TIME FOR SERVING A CLAIM FORM

Period of validity

Proceedings are started when the court issues a claim form (see **chapter 12**) at the request of the claimant, on the date entered on the form by the court (**CPR, r.** 7.2). Once issued, a claim form must be served within four months after issue, or six months where it is to be served out of the jurisdiction (**r.** 7.5). A concurrent claim form will initially be valid for four months (*Pirelli Cables Ltd v United Thai Shipping Corporation Ltd* [2000] 1 Lloyd's Rep 663). By **r. 6.5(1)**, service must be within the jurisdiction unless service out of the jurisdiction is permitted under **rr. 6.17** to **6.31** (see **16.42** to **16.63**). Service of a claim form within the jurisdiction may be performed on any day, including Saturdays, Sundays and bank holidays, but will only be effective on the deemed date of service, which depends on the method of service (see **15.36** and **15.37**). **15.2**

Calculating the period of validity

In the CPR 'month' means calendar month (Interpretation Act 1978, ss. 5 and 22 and sch. 1). **Rule** 7.5 defines periods for service of claim forms as within a number of months after issue, so the period begins the day after issue and service must occur before the end of the last day of the period. The last day of the period is found by applying the 'corresponding date rule' (*Dodds v Walker* [1981] 1 WLR 1027). So a claim form issued on 21 July 2006 must be served within the jurisdiction on or before 21 November 2006. When there is no corresponding date in the month in which the period ends, it will end on the last day of the month. For example, a claim form issued on 29 October 2006 must be served within the jurisdiction on or before 28 February 2007. The validity period of a claim form under the CPR is one day longer than the period for a writ under the RSC, because that period began on the day of issue of the writ (RSC, ord. 6, r. 8(1)(c); *Smith v Probyn* (2000) *The Times*, 29 March 2000). **15.3**

The day on which a claim form is deemed to be served is determined by **r. 6.7** and depends on the method of service (see **15.36** and **15.37**). For example, service by first-class post is deemed to occur on the second day after posting. So to achieve service by first-class post within the period of validity of a claim form issued on 21 July 2006, it must be posted no later than 19 November 2006.

Effect on period of validity of applying to serve outside the jurisdiction

In *National Bank of Greece SA v R. M. Outhwaite 317 Syndicate at Lloyd's* [2001] Lloyd's Rep IR 652 the court considered the effect of an application to serve a claim form out of the jurisdiction on the period for service. It held that a claim form which specifies an address within the jurisdiction can still become a claim form 'to be served out of the jurisdiction' within the meaning of **CPR, r.** 7.5(3), if permission to serve out of the jurisdiction is subsequently granted. This is so, even where the application for permission is made after the expiry of the four-month period for service within the jurisdiction. However, if the effect of permission for service out of the jurisdiction is to breathe new life into a claim form after the four-month period has expired, this will be an important factor in deciding whether or not to grant permission. Although **r. 7.6(3)** does not apply directly to an application for permission to serve out of the jurisdiction, the court will not ignore the strict approach stipulated there to extending service periods that have expired (see **15.10**). Doubt is shed on this case by *Anderton v Clwyd County Council (No. 2)* [2002] EWCA Civ 933, [2002] 1 WLR 3174, in which the court confirmed that the criteria of **r. 7.6(3)** do not apply directly or indirectly to applications for permission to serve a claim form out of the jurisdiction, whether before or after the period of **15.4** four months from the date of issue. Such applications are governed by the criteria set out in **r. 6.20**. The court did not agree that the discretionary criteria which apply to an application made more than four months after the issue of the claim form differ from those that apply to an application made within that period.

Failure to serve claim form in time

15.5 The consequences of failure to serve a claim form within these time limits, particularly when the limitation period for the claim has by then expired, are extremely dangerous for the claimant and for the claimant's legal advisers. There is a serious risk of a successful application being made to strike out the claim on the ground of non-compliance with the rules and of the cause of action then being statute-barred. The court's attitude to applications of this nature has been illustrated in *Godwin v Swindon Borough Council* [2001] EWCA Civ 1478, [2002] 1 WLR 997, and *Anderton v Clwyd County Council (No. 2)* [2002] EWCA Civ 933, [2002] 1 WLR 3174. In *Anderton v Clwyd County Council (No. 2)* the Court of Appeal (per Mummery LJ) said, at [2]:

> Now that the disputed interpretations of the CPR have been resolved by *Godwin v Swindon Borough Council* and by this judgment, there will be very few (if any) acceptable excuses for future failures to observe the rules for service of a claim form. The courts will be entitled to adopt a strict approach, even though the consequences may sometimes appear to be harsh in individual cases.

Godwin v Swindon Borough Council and *Anderton v Clwyd County Council (No. 2)* are discussed in more detail at various points in this chapter, in particular at **15.10**.

Documents to be served with the claim form

15.6 The documents which must be served on the defendant are:

(a) Claim form.

(b) Particulars of claim (unless the claim form states that they are to follow).

(c) Response pack, which consists of forms for acknowledging service, and for admission, defence and counterclaim (CPR, r. 7.8(1)). Where the claim is for a specified sum, **forms N9A** and **N9B** should be used. Where the claim is for an unspecified sum, or is a non-money claim, **forms N9C** and **N9D** should be used. Where the **Part 8** procedure is being used **r.** 7.8(1) does not apply, but the claim form must be accompanied by a form for acknowledging service (**r. 7.8(2)**). Any written evidence on which a claimant using the **Part 8** procedure intends to rely must be filed and served with the claim form (**r. 8.5(1)** and (2)).

(d) Where the claimant has entered into a funding agreement, **form N251** must be served with the claim form (**PD 43–48, para. 19.2(2)**).

(e) In personal injury claims, the particulars of claim (not the claim form, if served alone) should be accompanied by a medical report and schedule of expenses and losses (**PD 16, paras** 4.2 and 4.3).

(f) In a claim based upon a written contract, a copy of the contract or documents constituting the agreement, or any relevant general conditions of sale should accompany the particulars of claim (not the claim form, if served alone) (**PD 16, para. 7.3**).

EXTENDING TIME FOR SERVING A CLAIM FORM

Procedure

15.7 If it is not possible to serve a claim form within the time limit set out at **15.1**, the claimant can apply under CPR, r. 7.6, for an extension. Applications to extend **Part 8** claim forms are governed by the same rules (*Barker v Casserly* (2000) LTL 24/10/2000). The procedure is summarised in **procedural checklist 11**, in **appendix 1**, and there is detailed commentary from here to 15.12.

An application for extending time for serving a claim form should be made using the **Part 23** procedure (see **chapter 32**). It may be made without serving a copy of the application notice on the defendant (or any other respondent) (**r. 7.6(4)(b)**). A defendant who is served with an order made without notice, extending time for service of a claim form, has seven days in which to apply for it to be set aside (**r. 23.10**).

The application must be supported by evidence (**r. 7.6(4)(a)**). The evidence will either be set out in the application notice (which must then be verified by a statement of truth) or be in the form of a witness statement (which must also be verified by a statement of truth) (**r. 32.6**). Alternatively, evidence may be in affidavit form, although any additional cost of producing the evidence in this form may not be recovered from any other party without a court order (**r. 32.15(2)**).

PD 7, para. 8.2, requires the evidence to include the following details:

(a) all the circumstances relied on;
(b) the date of issue of the claim;
(c) the expiry date of any extension already granted under **r. 7.6**; and
(d) a full explanation of why the claim form has not been served.

In stating the circumstances relied on the evidence should cover both those relating to the cause of action and the reasons for seeking an extension. The former will include the dates of accrual and expiry of the limitation period. As an application for extending time for service is made without notice, the applicant has a duty of full and frank disclosure, which includes an obligation to make reasonable inquiries into the matters relevant to the application.

An applicant who wishes to have the application dealt with without a hearing should request this in the application notice (**PD 23, para. 2.1(5)**). The court has the power to dispense with a hearing where it does not consider a hearing appropriate (**CPR, r. 23.8(c)**). In practice, it is very common for these applications to be considered without a hearing and without notice to the defendant. However, in *Collier v Williams* [2006] EWCA Civ 20, *The Times*, 3 February 2006, the Court of Appeal stated that courts should consider whether that is an appropriate way of proceeding. Where the application is made shortly before expiry of the period for service of the claim form and where the cause of action has become time-barred since the date on which the claim form was issued, the application is potentially crucial. It is highly desirable that applications of this type, where time is running out, should normally be dealt with by an urgent hearing. Where pressure of business means it is not possible to deal with the application other than on paper, consideration should be given to dealing with it by telephone. It is likely that the court will dispense with a hearing in cases where there are clear grounds for granting an extension.

Order extending time for serving

There is no limit on the length of any extension, or on the number of extensions which a court may grant. It will be for the applicant to justify the length of extension sought. Bearing in mind the court's duty as part of the overriding objective to ensure that cases are dealt with expeditiously it is unlikely that the court will be prepared to grant long or multiple extensions in the absence of good reason (see **15.9**). Under the old rules the maximum period of any extension was 12 months at a time (this was renewable), but the courts insisted on a justification for the period of any extension sought. **15.8**

Where an order is made (whether granting or dismissing the application) without notice to the defendant, a copy of the order, the application notice and any evidence in support must be served on the defendant, unless the court orders to the contrary (**CPR, r. 23.9**). The order must contain a statement of the defendant's right to apply to have the order set aside or varied (**r. 23.9(3)**). The defendant has seven days from the date of service to apply to the court for the order to be varied or set aside (**r. 23.10**).

Grounds on which the court will grant an extension

15.9 The general rule is that an application to extend the time for service of a claim form should be made within the usual period of service (or that period as already extended by the court) (CPR, r. 7.6(2)). The application is 'made' when the notice is issued, not when it is heard (r. 23.5; *Collier v Williams* [2006] EWCA Civ 20, *The Times*, 3 February 2006). The CPR are silent on the test to be applied in deciding whether to allow an extension under r. 7.6(2), but guidance was given in *Hashtroodi v Hancock* [2004] EWCA Civ 652, [2004] 1 WLR 3206, in which the Court of Appeal made clear that the authorities on extending the period of validity of a writ under RSC, ord. 6, r. 8, no longer apply. *Hashtroodi v Hancock* was clarified by *Collier v Williams*. As now clarified, the approach of the court to applications under r. 7.6(2) should be as follows:

The critical enquiry the court must undertake is to evaluate why the claimant did not serve the claim form within the specified period. Whereas under the old law a plaintiff who was unable to show a good reason for not serving in time failed to satisfy the former threshold condition (*Kleinwort Benson Ltd v Barbrak Ltd* [1987] AC 597), under the CPR a more calibrated approach is adopted. If there is a good reason for the failure to serve the claim form within the specified period, an extension of time will usually be granted. The weaker the reason, the readier the court will be to refuse the application and where there is no reason or only a very weak reason the court is most unlikely to grant an extension of time. In *Collier v Williams*, the reason for the failure to serve in time was the claimant's erroneous belief as to the whereabouts of the defendant's usual or last known residence. So the court needed to consider the reasonableness of that belief. If the claimant had been misled by the defendant as to his residence, the court would be likely to hold that the claimant had reasonable grounds for his belief, that there was a very good reason for the claimant's failure to serve in time and would grant an extension of time under r. 7.6(2). But it is always incumbent on the claimant to take reasonable steps to ascertain the defendant's last known residence. What is reasonable must depend on the circumstances of the case. The claimant in this case had made an assumption about the defendant's address based on little evidence and so there was no good reason to extend the period for service of the claim form.

The discretion must be exercised in accordance with the overriding objective. However, the exercise of going through the checklist of factors set out in r. 1.1(2) will often not be necessary. Where there is no good reason justifying the failure to serve the claim form in time, there should normally be no need to go further.

On the facts of the case, the court refused to grant an extension because the reason for failing to serve within the period of validity was the incompetence of the claimant's advisers.

Hashtroodi v Hancock was applied in *Mersey Docks Property Holdings v Kilgour* [2004] EWHC 1638 (TCC), [2004] BLR 412, in which the court held that the focus of an application to extend time is whether the claimant has taken reasonable steps to serve the claim form in time. The question of prejudice to the defendant is irrelevant. The court refused to grant the extension which was needed only because the claimant's solicitors had made insufficient efforts to investigate the defendant's last known place of business and had waited to the last moment before attempting to serve the claim form.

The Court of Appeal has made clear in *Collier v Williams* that while the r. 7.6(3) requirements (see 15.9) are relevant to the exercise of the discretion given by r. 7.6(2), there is a clear difference between the two paragraphs and the fact that the preconditions stated in r. 7.6(3) are not satisfied is not necessarily determinative of the outcome of an application under r. 7.6(2). In particular, in deciding whether to grant an extension under r. 7.6(2), the court is required to make a judgment about how good a reason there is for the failure to serve in time (assuming that the application is being dealt with after the expiry of the four-month period for service). Under r. 7.6(3) the position is that unless all reasonable steps have been taken, the court cannot extend time.

In *NV Procter and Gamble International v Gartner KG* [2005] EWHC 960 (Comm), [2006] 1 Lloyd's Rep 82, the court upheld orders made without notice to the defendant extending the time for service of a claim form, even though a full explanation of why the claim form had not been served had not been provided, as required by **PD 7, para. 8.2** (see **15.6**). It was not clear that the delay in serving the proceedings had prejudiced the defendant, which was aware that the claim was being pursued and had given no indication it wished to have the dispute settled speedily. In these circumstances it would not be proportionate to deprive the claimant of its claim by setting aside the extensions of time which had already been granted.

In *Steele v Mooney* [2005] EWCA Civ 96, [2005] 1 WLR 2819, the Court of Appeal considered the relationship between **CPR, r. 3.10** (the power to cure an irregularity), and **r. 7.6(2)**. In this case, an application to extend time for service of the particulars of claim had by mistake failed to refer to the claim form, so an application to extend time for service of the claim form had not been made within the four-month period for service. The court held that the error was procedural in nature and did fall within the ambit of **r. 3.10**, which should not be given an artificially restrictive meaning. However, **r. 3.10** should not be used to circumvent something that is prohibited under another rule (an application of the decision in *Vinos v Marks and Spencer plc* [2001] 3 All ER 784 — see **15.11**). The application now fell to be considered under the provisions of **r. 7.6(2)** (not **r. 7.6(3)**, see **15.11**) as the original application for an extension had been made within the usual time limit for service. The application would have succeeded under **r. 7.6(2)** if it had been made correctly, so **r. 3.10** could be used to correct the error now and extend time for service of the claim form.

Applications made after the usual period of service has expired

The rules permit the making of an application after the expiry of time for service of the claim form. But in this case, the court may only grant an extension where (**r. 7.6(3)**): **15.10**

(a) the court has been unable to serve the claim form, or
(b) the claimant has taken all reasonable steps to serve the claim form but has been unable to do so, and
(c) in either case the claimant has acted promptly in making the application.

The application may be made without notice, but must be supported by evidence (**r. 7.6(4)**). For the distinction between this test and the test under **r. 7.6(2)**, see **15.8**.

The meaning of **r. 7.6(3)** was considered in *Latreefers Inc. v Hobson* [2002] EWHC 1586 (Ch), LTL 31/7/2002, in which it was held that the regime of the CPR required parties to use the whole of a period allowed for a specific purpose. If they do nothing until the last moment, and what they then do is ineffective, they cannot expect a second chance. In this case, the claimants' solicitors had instructed foreign lawyers to effect service abroad, and those lawyers had not effected valid service under local law. However, the solicitors had taken no step to serve the claim form out of the jurisdiction for five out of the six months allowed. Such conduct did not satisfy the requirement of **r. 7.6(3)(b)**. 'Promptly' is to be construed in accordance with the ordinary meaning of the word, 'readily, quickly, at once' (*Chare v Fairclough* [2003] EWHC 180 (QB), LTL 20/1/2003).

The phrase 'the court has been unable to serve the claim form' in **r. 7.6(3)** includes a case where the court overlooks the claim form and makes no attempt to serve it (*Cranfield v Bridgegrove Ltd* [2003] EWCA Civ 656, [2003] 1 WLR 2441). In most cases of court neglect it will be appropriate to grant an extension of time provided the claimant has acted promptly. However, if failures on the part of the claimant or his solicitors are the real reason why the claim form is not served within the period of validity, it will often be inappropriate to grant an extension. In *Smith v Probyn* (2000) *The Times*, 29 March 2000, the court refused to extend the time for service of a claim form where the claimant had sought to serve solicitors who had no authority to accept service on the defendants' behalf, on the grounds that the claimant had failed to take all reasonable steps to serve the claim form.

In *Kaur v CTP Coil Ltd* (2000) LTL 10/7/2000, the Court of Appeal held that the word 'serve' in **r. 7.6(3)(b)** means the actual process of service, and therefore does not extend to difficulties in the preparation of schedules of special damage in a personal injury claim.

Attempts to evade rule 7.6(3)

15.11 In *Vinos v Marks and Spencer plc* [2001] 3 All ER 784 the Court of Appeal construed **CPR, r. 7.6(3)**, in effect as a self-contained code and held that the court has power to extend time for serving the claim form after the period for its service has run out 'only if' the stipulated conditions are fulfilled. This means that, once the period of validity of a claim form has expired, the court cannot, under the general power to extend time in **r. 3.1(2)(a)** or the power in **r. 3.10** to cure an irregularity, grant an extension. This approach was upheld in *National Bank of Greece SA v R. M. Outhwaite 317 Syndicate at Lloyd's* [2001] Lloyd's Rep IR 652 and in *Nanglegan v Royal Free Hampstead NHS Trust* [2001] EWCA Civ 127, [2002] 1 WLR 1043. Nor, by parity of reasoning, can an extension in effect be granted by resorting to the power in **r. 3.9** to give relief from sanctions (*Kaur v CTP Coil Ltd* (2000) LTL 10/7/2000). (See also *Amerada Hess v C. W. Rome* (2000) *The Times*, 15 March 2000.) In *Elmes v Hygrade Food Products plc* [2001] EWCA Civ 121, LTL 27/2/2001, it was held that if the conditions in **r. 7.6(3)** cannot be satisfied, it is not possible to make an order for service by an alternative method under **r. 6.8**, because **r. 6.8** orders only operate prospectively. In *Infantino v Maclean* [2001] 3 All ER 802 the court considered itself to be bound by the decisions in *Vinos v Marks and Spencer plc* and *Kaur v CTP Coil Ltd* and therefore unable to rely on **rr. 3.9** or **3.10** to cure a defect in service.

In summary, attempts to use **rr. 3.1** (extending time), **3.9** (relief from sanctions), **3.10** (correcting errors of procedure), **6.8** (alternative service) and **6.9** (dispensing with service) have all been rejected. There remain three exceptions:

(a) An order under **r. 3.10** can be made to remedy an error in an application notice, issued while the claim form was current, which sought permission to extend time for service of the particulars of claim but which had forgotten to ask for permission to extend the claim form as well (*Steele v Mooney* [2005] EWCA Civ 96, [2005] 1 WLR 2819). This is to be distinguished from *Kaur v CTP Coil Ltd* (2000) LTL 10/7/2000, where **r. 3.10** could not be used to correct service after the claim form had expired.

(b) If the court grants permission to serve outside the jurisdiction, the validity of the claim form will be extended by two months (see **15.4**).

(c) An order can be made dispensing with service under **r. 6.9** if there are exceptional circumstances (see **15.12**).

Dispensing with service because of problems with serving

15.12 The court in *Infantino v Maclean* [2001] 3 All ER 802 granted an order dispensing with service of the claim form under **CPR, r. 6.9(1)** (see **15.41**), on the grounds that to do so was necessary to give effect to the overriding objective of dealing with a case justly. The claimant's solicitors had behaved impeccably, apart from using the wrong DX address for the defendant, which resulted in the claim form being served a day late. *Infantino v Maclean* was disapproved in *Godwin v Swindon Borough Council* [2001] EWCA Civ 1478, [2002] 1 WLR 997, in which the court held that the discretionary power to dispense with service under **r. 6.9** should not be used as a means of circumventing and rendering nugatory the clear provisions of **r. 7.6(3)**. However, in *Anderton v Clwyd County Council (No. 2)* [2002] EWCA Civ 933, [2002] 1 WLR 3174, the Court of Appeal distinguished two categories.

Category 1 is where no attempt to serve a claim form has been made. In this circumstance, as stated in *Godwin v Swindon Borough Council*, **r. 6.9** cannot be relied on retrospectively to circumvent the consequences of late service. The court can only dispense with service where there has been an attempt to effect service during the period of validity.

Category 2 is where, as in *Infantino v Maclean*, an ineffective attempt to serve within four months has been made, and the defendant does not dispute that he or his legal adviser has in fact received and had his attention drawn to the claim form within the four months. Here, the claimant is in effect seeking to be excused the need to prove service in accordance with the rules. In such cases, the court in *Godwin* concluded that **r. 6.9** is sufficiently widely worded to entitle the court to dispense retrospectively with service of the claim form in an appropriate case. It was decided in *Wilkey v British Broadcasting Corporation* [2002] EWCA Civ 1561, [2003] 1 WLR 1, that the discretion to make an order under **r. 6.9** should ordinarily be exercised in category 2 cases provided the attempt to serve was made before the decision in *Anderton v Clwyd County Council (No. 2)*, which was 3 July 2002 (the decision was reported in the *All England Law Reports* on 14 August 2002). In category 2 cases since 3 July 2002 the discretion under **r. 6.9** will only be exercised in exceptional cases, with the court applying a strict approach and considering matters such as the claimant's explanation for the late attempt to serve and any other criticisms that may be appropriate about the claimant's conduct of the proceedings. It may also be appropriate to make an order dispensing with service where there has been some minor departure from the permitted methods of service (*Cranfield v Bridgegrove Ltd* [2003] EWCA Civ 656, [2003] 1 WLR 2441). Where a draft, unsealed, claim form was sent to the defendant's insurers during the period of validity, but service was not duly effected on the defendant, it could not be said that the circumstances were exceptional so as to justify dispensing with service (*Cranfield v Bridgegrove Ltd*). In *Cranfield v Bridgegrove Ltd* the Court of Appeal, at [32], stated emphatically that:

> The *Godwin* principle is important and must not be subverted. It will be subverted unless the power to dispense with service retrospectively is confined to truly exceptional cases.

The Court of Appeal again reviewed the authorities on **r. 6.9** in *Kuenyehia v International Hospitals Group Ltd* [2006] EWCA Civ 21, *The Times*, 17 February 2006. Neuberger LJ confirmed the approach in *Godwin v Swindon Borough Council*, as refined in *Anderton v Clwyd County Council (No. 2)*, *Wilkey v British Broadcasting Corporation* and *Cranfield v Bridgegrove Ltd*. He summarised the reasoning required by a court in exercising its discretion under **r. 6.9** as follows.

First it requires an exceptional case before the court will exercise its power to dispense with service under **r. 6.9** where the time limit for service of a claim form in **r. 7.5(2)** has expired before service was effected in accordance with **Part 6**.
Secondly and separately, the power is unlikely to be exercised save where the claimant has either made an ineffective attempt in time to serve by one of the methods permitted by **r. 6.2** or has served in time in a manner which involved a minor departure from one of those permitted methods of service.
Thirdly, however, it is not possible to give an exhaustive guide to the circumstances in which it would be right to dispense with service of a claim form.
In this case, the claimants, on the last day for service of the claim form, couriered a copy of the claim form to the defendant's solicitors who did not have instructions to accept service and faxed a copy of the claim form to the defendants' head office, even though the defendants had not stated in writing that they were willing to receive service by fax. Neither of these steps was good service under the rules. The court held there were no exceptional circumstances, and that service by fax without the defendant's consent was more than a minor departure from the permitted methods. Accordingly, it set aside the order made at first instance dispensing with service of the claim form.

Thus errors in effecting service have been held not to amount to exceptional circumstances: see *Nathoo v Ashford and St Peter's Hospital Trust* [2004] EWHC 1571 (QB), LTL 24/11/2003 (service by fax when the defendants had not consented to it, the same error as in *Kuenyehia v International Hospitals Group Ltd*); *Horn v Dorset Healthcare NHS Trust (No. 2)* (2004) LTL 17/9/2004 (holding back from serving the defendant's solicitors when they did in fact have authority to accept service); *Kitt v South West Peninsula Health Authority* (2004) LTL 10/1/2005 (serving the defendant's solicitors who were not authorised to accept service). In each of these cases, the defendant or its legal advisers had in fact received the claim form in time. This is not an exceptional circumstance as it occurs in all category 2 cases.

Factors considered in *Lakah Group v Al Jazeera Satellite Channel* [2003] EWHC 1297 (QB), LTL 11/6/2003, [2003] EWCA Civ 1781, LTL 9/12/2003, a 'category 2' case for dispensing with service, were (a) the defendant's knowledge of the details of the claim; (b) the defendant's non-residential status; (c) the claimant's attempt to effect service; (d) the claimant's conduct in the claim; (e) prejudice to the defendant; and (f) prejudice to the claimant.

SERVICE OF PARTICULARS OF CLAIM

15.13 Where particulars of claim (see **chapter 24**) are not contained in or served with the claim form, the claim form must contain a statement that particulars will follow (**PD 7, para. 6.2**). The particulars must be served within 14 days after serving the claim form (**CPR, r. 7.4(1)**) and no later than the latest time for serving the claim form (**r. 7.4(2)**). Where a claimant is late in serving the particulars of claim, the court has a general discretion under **r. 3.1(2)(a)** to extend time. This is so even where the delay extends beyond the period of validity of the claim form, and such applications are not bound by the requirements in **r. 7.6(3)** (see **15.10**) (*Totty v Snowden* [2001] EWCA Civ 1415, [2002] 1 WLR 1384).

In a case of any complexity, when a court is considering an application for an extension of time made after the time prescribed for the taking of a step in proceedings has expired, the court should follow the checklist given in **r. 3.9** (*Sayers v Clarke Walker* [2002] EWCA Civ 645, [2002] 1 WLR 3095). It is not necessary for the court to apply the **r. 3.9** checklist in an application for an extension of time made before the deadline for service has expired: the court's discretion should be exercised simply by having regard to the overriding objective and the factors listed in **r.1.1(2)** (*Robert v Momentum Services Ltd* [2003] EWCA Civ 299, [2003] 1 WLR 1577).

Totty v Snowden and *Sayers v Clarke Walker* were applied in *Price v Price* [2003] EWCA Civ 888, [2003] 3 All ER 911, in which the Court of Appeal signalled that the courts should take care not to relax the disciplinary framework created by the CPR. In this case an extension of time for service of particulars of claim was granted, but subject to a condition restricting the value of the claim, using the case management powers under **r. 3.1(2)(a) and (3)(a)**.

An intentional delay in serving particulars of claim would, if made out, be highly significant if not determinative of whether to grant relief (*Bournemouth and Boscombe Athletic Football Club Ltd v Lloyds TSB Bank plc* [2003] EWCA Civ 1755, LTL 10/12/2003).

If particulars of claim are served separately from the claim form, a copy of the particulars must be filed, with a certificate of service, within seven days of service on the defendant (**r. 7.4(3)**). If practicable, the particulars of claim should be set out in the claim form (**PD 16, para. 3.1**).

FILING DOCUMENTS

15.14 The CPR distinguish between serving a document, which is the procedure whereby a document is brought to the attention of another party and filing a document, which is the procedure whereby the court receives a copy of a document. 'Filing' is defined in **r. 2.3(1)** as: 'delivering [a document], by post or otherwise, to the court office'. Filing takes effect immediately documents are posted through the court's letter box, even if the court is then closed to the public and there are no officials to take delivery of the document (*Van Aken v Camden London Borough Council* [2002] EWCA Civ 1724, [2003] 1 WLR 684). The problem with this approach is that it will be impossible for court officials to establish the time (and therefore the date) of filing without making further enquiry of the person who delivered the document. Under **r. 5.5** practice directions may provide for filing by fax or other electronic means. Filing by fax is covered by **PD 5, para. 5.3**, which provides that a fax received after 4 p.m. is treated as filed on the next day that the court office is open. Over 50 courts now accept filing by email, including the Chancery Division and the Commercial Court at the RCJ: see **PD 5B** and **A Guide to Emailing the Civil and Family Courts**, which is in appendix 4. Electronic filing is used in Money Claim Online (**PD 7E**; see **12.10**). A pilot scheme extending the ambit of electronic filing is being conducted in the Preston County Court.

A document sent by post is filed when it is delivered, not when it is posted (*Morshead Mansions Ltd v Langford* [2003] EWHC 2023 (QB), LTL 29/8/2003). The deeming rules discussed at **15.36** only apply to service, so for filing it is the actual delivery date that counts. The Interpretation Act 1978, s. 7, applies (by s. 23(1) and (2)), so a document filed by post is deemed to be filed at the time at which the letter containing it would be delivered in the ordinary course of post, unless the contrary is proved.

The CPR make clear which documents must be filed, and when. The detailed requirements are addressed at relevant points in this work. The general rule is that a copy of most formal documents generated in the course of a claim must be filed at court. Thus, all statements of case must be filed, and witness statements and experts' reports may be ordered to be filed. The purpose of the requirement is clear: it is only by having access to information about the case as it progresses that the court is able to exercise its case management powers.

Officials will record the date and time when a document was received at court for filing in court records (**PD 5, para. 5.2**). The actual date of filing will be stamped on the document itself (**PD 5, para. 5.1**).

Inspecting the court file

Public right of access to court register and to court documents Under **CPR, r. 5.4(1)**, the Queen's Bench and Chancery Divisions and the Admiralty and Commercial Court registry in the RCJ keep a register of the claims which they have issued (**PD 5, para. 4.1**). The register is open to members of the public to search upon payment of the prescribed fee (**CPR, r. 5.4(2)**). There are no registers of claims in any district registries or other offices of the High Court or any county courts (**PD 5, para. 4.2**). **15.15**

Subject to any court order to the contrary, members of the public may obtain a copy of a claim form (but not documents filed with, or attached to, or intended to be served with, the claim form) and any judgment or order once the defendant has filed an acknowledgment of service or defence (or, where there is more than one defendant, all have done so or at least one has and the court gives permission), or the claim has been listed for hearing or judgment has been entered (**r. 5.4(5)(a)**). The entitlement under **r. 5.4(5)(a)** applies only to judgments or orders made in public. A witness statement which stands as the evidence-in-chief of a witness is open for inspection during the trial unless the court directs otherwise (**r. 32.13**). Members of the public may obtain a copy of any other document filed by a party or any communication between the court and a party or other person, but here the court's permission is always required (**r. 5.4(5)(b)**).

In *Dian AO v David Frankel and Mead* [2004] EWHC 2662 (Comm), LTL 13/10/2004, the court held that an application under **r. 5.4(5)**, must identify with reasonable precision the documents or class of documents the applicant wishes to search for and explain why it wants them. The principle of open justice which lies behind the rules must be borne in mind in any application for access to the court file. Thus, the court will more readily grant permission for documents which have been read by the court or otherwise used as part of the judicial process. In this case the court held, in granting permission for copies of specified documents to be provided, that the relevance of those documents on the court file to proceedings in which the applicant was involved abroad constituted a legitimate reason for seeking access to the court file.

This decision was followed in *Chan U Seek v Alvis Vehicles Ltd* [2004] EWHC 3092 (Ch), [2005] 1 WLR 2965, in which Park J made clear that the court is generally in favour of disclosure of materials which have entered the public domain in proceedings in open court. These include statements of case and witness statements that have been confirmed in general terms by their makers and have stood as evidence-in-chief. The purpose of **rr. 5.4** and **32.13** is to give the public access to documents which will provide a proper understanding of the case. If the documents sought by a member of the public fall within the categories stated in these rules, the burden of showing that the public should not be allowed to inspect documents is on the person objecting to disclosure. No distinction can be drawn between documents used at trial and those used at the interim stages of a case (*Cleveland Bridge UK Ltd v Multiplex Constructions (UK) Ltd* [2005] EWHC 2101 (TCC), LTL 31/8/2005). In balancing the competing interests of open justice and the protection of the legitimate interests of parties and persons named in documents, it may be appropriate to order the replacement of names with initials in the inspection copies (*Cox v Jones* [2004] EWHC 1006 (Ch), LTL 18/5/2004). It is not necessary for the application to be made to the court seised of the underlying case: the court referred to in **r. 5.4(5)** is the High Court.

In *Glidepath BV v Thompson* [2005] EWHC 818 (Comm), [2005] 2 Lloyd's Rep 549, the court refused to order disclosure of documents filed in court proceedings which had subsequently been stayed pursuant to the Arbitration Act 1996, s. 9. The private and confidential character of proceedings ancillary to the arbitral process ought to be protected. Disclosure should be granted only if all parties consented or if there were an overriding reason in the interests of justice.

15.16 **Parties' right of access to court documents** Subject to an order to the contrary, **CPR, r. 5.4(3)**, and **PD 5, para. 4.2A**, give parties to proceedings the right to obtain copies of the following documents from the court file:

(a) a certificate of suitability of a litigation friend;
(b) a notice of funding;
(c) a claim form or other statement of case, together with any documents filed with, or attached to, or intended by the claimant to be served with, it;
(d) an acknowledgment of service, together with any documents filed with, or attached to, or intended by the party acknowledging service to be served with, it;
(e) a certificate of service, other than a certificate of service of an application notice or order in relation to a type of application mentioned in sub-paragraph (h)(i) or (ii) below;
(f) a notice of non-service;
(g) an allocation questionnaire;
(h) an application notice, other than in relation to:
  (i) an application by a solicitor for an order declaring that he has ceased to be the solicitor acting for a party; or
  (ii) an application for an order that the identity of a party or witness should not be disclosed;
(i) any written evidence filed in relation to an application, other than a type of application mentioned in sub-paragraph (h)(i) or (ii);
(j) a judgment or order given or made in public (whether made at a hearing or without a hearing);
(k) a statement of costs;
(l) a list of documents;
(m) a notice of payment into court;
(n) a notice of discontinuance;

(o) a notice of change; or
(p) an appellant's or respondent's notice of appeal.

A party to proceedings or any person identified in the claim form may apply to the court for an order restricting the right to obtain copies to particular individuals or categories (**r. 5.4(7)(a)**). Alternatively the court may order that particular individuals or categories of people can only obtain an edited copy of the claim form (**r. 5.4(7)(b)**), or it may make other orders restricting the right of access, as it considers appropriate (**r. 5.4(7)(c)**).

Procedure An application under **CPR, r. 5.4(4), (5)(b)** or **(6)(b)(ii)**, to obtain a copy of a document from the court records must be made in accordance with **Part 23** (**r. 5.4(8)(a)**) and must identify the document or class of documents sought and the grounds relied on (**PD 5, para. 4.3**). An application under **CPR, r. 5.4(7)**, for restrictions on inspection must be made in accordance with **Part 23** and must be made to a master or district judge, unless the court orders otherwise (**PD 5, para. 4.4**). An application for permission to inspect or for restrictions on inspection may be made without notice, but the court may direct notice to be given to any person who would be affected by its decision (**CPR, r. 5.4(9)**). Inspecting a document without the court's permission is an interference with the administration of justice, and is a criminal contempt of court if done in the knowledge that the court's permission is required (*Dobson v Hastings* [1992] Ch 394). **15.17**

The provisions of **r. 5.4** are subject to any contrary provision in a rule or practice direction (**r. 5.4(10)**). Provisions disapplying **r. 5.4** include:

(a) **r. 57.5(5)**, which provides that, unless the court gives permission, a party to a probate claim may not inspect testamentary documents or written evidence filed by any other party until he has filed his own testamentary documents and evidence;
(b) **PD 62, para. 5.1**, which states that an arbitration claim form may only be inspected with the permission of the court (reflecting the privacy of arbitration proceedings);
(c) **PD Application for a Warrant under the Competition Act 1998, paras. 3.3** and **3.4**, under which no Part 8 claim form issued on an application by the Office of Fair Trading for a warrant under the Competition Act 1989 may be inspected by a member of the public unless a High Court judge grants permission.

WHO MAY SERVE DOCUMENTS?

Regardless of whether a claim is proceeding in the High Court or a county court, service of any document which the court has issued or prepared may be effected either by the court or the party on whose behalf the document is to be served, at the option of the party concerned, unless otherwise required by a rule, court order or practice direction (**CPR, r. 6.3(1)**). **15.18**

This option of court service extends to more than just the claim form: the court may also serve application notices and court orders. But the court will not serve particulars of claim unless they are to be served with the claim form.

For several specialist proceedings the option of court service is not available. The Commercial Court will not serve any statement of case (which includes a claim form) (**PD 58, para. 9**). The High Court will not serve documents in companies matters (**PD 49B, para. 11**) or in insolvency proceedings (**PD Insolvency Proceedings, para. 1.3**). Neither the High Court nor county courts will serve claim forms in directors disqualification proceedings (**PD Directors Disqualification Proceedings, para. 7.1**).

SERVICE BY THE COURT

15.19 Where a party prepares any document (including the claim form) which it wishes to be served by the court, a copy of the document, together with a copy for each party to be served must be filed at court (**CPR, r. 6.3(3)**).

The court will then decide which method of service to use (**r. 6.3(2)**). The method will normally be first-class post (**PD 6, para. 8.1**).

Where the court serves a claim form (but not other documents), it will notify the claimant that the claim form has been served in the notice of issue, which will also indicate the deemed date of service (**CPR, r. 6.14**). If a document, which the court has attempted to serve by post, is returned to the court, it must inform the party who requested service that this has happened (**r. 6.11**). Similarly, it must notify the party who requested service of a document by the bailiff if the bailiff is unable to serve it (**r. 6.11A**). Provided the address used was a legitimate address for service (see **15.23**), there is no need to take further steps, because the rules on deemed service will apply (see **15.36** and **15.37**).

Where the court file contains no record that service has taken place there can be no presumption that service has indeed been effected by the court (*Patel v Smeaton* [2000] WL 1675263). Where a court fails to effect service and the period for service of the claim form therefore expires, the claimant may apply for an extension under **r. 7.6(3)(a)** (*Cranfield v Bridgegrove Ltd* [2003] EWCA Civ 656, [2003] 1 WLR 2441; see **15.10**).

The CPR do not require the court to give notice of service in the case of documents other than the claim form, but when other documents are returned to the court undelivered, the court will notify the party who requested court service (**r. 6.11**). Despite being returned, the documents will usually be deemed to have been delivered, under **r. 6.7**.

The procedure is summarised in **procedural checklist 9**, in **appendix 1**.

SERVICE BY A PARTY

15.20 Although the option of asking the court to serve a document is available in many cases, it is always open to a party required to serve a document to make other arrangements to achieve service. As explained in **15.16**, for some documents the option of service by the court is not available. Many practitioners may prefer to serve documents themselves, either to retain control over the process (for example, because they do not wish the claim form to be served immediately upon issue, or because a contractual limitation period requires issue and service by a specific date) or to take advantage of the wider methods of service available when a party serves (see **15.21** to **15.28**).

A party intending to effect service itself must notify the court of that intention when the document concerned is filed at court (**CPR, r. 6.3(1)(b)**). The rules do not specify the form that notification should take. In practice a party may notify the court informally by letter that it wishes to effect service. In the RCJ, solicitors are invited to indicate at the commencement of proceedings whether they wish to effect service themselves, and if this is done, the file will be marked accordingly and no further application will be necessary.

A claimant who effects service of the claim form himself must file a certificate of service (**form N215**) within seven days of service giving the details set out in the table at **r. 6.10** (which is reproduced in **table 15.1**). As from 30 June 2004, a certificate of service is no longer required to state that the document served has not been returned undelivered. This change makes the CPR consistent with the policy that there is an irrebuttable presumption of service on proof of one of the methods of service under **rr. 6.2** and **6.7** (see **15.35** and *Anderton v Clywd County*

Table 15.1 Contents of certificate of service

Method of service	Details to be certified
Post	Date of posting
Personal	Date of personal service
Document exchange	Date of delivery to the document exchange
Delivery of document to or leaving it at a permitted place	Date when the document was delivered or left at the permitted place
Fax	Date and time of transmission
Other electronic means	Date of transmission and the means used
Alternative method permitted by the court	As required by the court

Council (No. 2) [2002] EWCA Civ 933, [2002] I WLR 3174). A certificate of service must be verified by a statement of truth (**r. 22.1(1)(f)**). It is not possible to obtain judgment in default under **Part 12** until the certificate of service has been filed (**r. 6.14(2)(b)**).

If the particulars of claim are served by the claimant separately from the claim form, a certificate of that service must be filed with the particulars (**r. 7.4(3)**). The procedure is summarised in **procedural checklist 10**, in **appendix 1**.

METHODS OF SERVICE

Prescribed methods of service

The methods of service permitted under **CPR, Part 6**, are listed in **r. 6.2(1)**. They are: **15.21**

(a) personal service in accordance with **r. 6.4** (see **15.19**);
(b) first-class post or, from 6 April 2006, another delivery service that provides for delivery on the next working day;
(c) leaving the document at a place specified in **r. 6.5** (see **15.20**);
(d) through a document exchange in accordance with **PD 6, para. 2**;
(e) by fax or other electronic means in accordance with **PD 6, para. 3**.

Rule 6.2(1) provides an exhaustive list of the methods of service, and no other method may be used unless the court permits an alternative under **r. 6.8** (see **15.35**) or the person being served agrees to accept service by another method (see **15.28** and **15.40**) (*Anderton v Clwyd County Council (No. 2)* [2002] EWCA Civ 933, [2002] 1 WLR 3174). Any of the methods listed in **r. 6.2(1)** can be used to serve claim forms as well as any other document generated in the course of the proceedings. However, the rules on service in **Part 6** do not apply to Part 36 offers (*Charles v NTL Group Ltd* [2002] EWCA Civ 2004, LTL 13/12/2002; see **15.27**).

There are special rules for service on the Crown (see **15.34**) and service in proceedings for the recovery of land and mortgage possession claims (**CPR, Part 55**). There are also special guidelines for service on members of the US Air Force and members of HM Forces contained in **PD 6**.

General provisions about service of documents are considered in **15.22** to **15.29**.

The CPR do not define what is meant by service other than prescribing how it may be done. In *Asia Pacific (HK) Ltd v Hanjin Shipping Co. Ltd* [2005] EWHC 2443 (Comm), [2005] 2 CLC 747, the question arose whether a claim form which had been transmitted to a defendant by fax, and therefore in a manner provided for under **CPR, r. 6.2**, was intended to be served or was for information only. The court held that when a claim form was delivered to the recipient in a manner provided for by the rules it was served unless it was made clear by the person who delivered it that whilst he was delivering the form by such a method he was not in fact serving it. The facts that no response pack was served, that the claim form was marked 'Claimant's Copy' and that the fax did not state that the claim form was faxed 'by way of service' did not demonstrate that no service was intended at all.

Personal service

15.22 A document may be served personally on the person to be served, unless a solicitor has been authorised to accept service on that person's behalf and has given written notice to the party serving the document that he is so authorised (**CPR, r. 6.4**). For service on a party's solicitor, see **15.24**.

A document is served personally on an individual by leaving it with that individual (**r. 6.4(3)**). Provision for service by leaving a document with a person was made under the old rules and it is likely that, as under those rules, where the individual to be served under **r. 6.4(3)** is uncooperative, service will be effective if the individual to be served is informed of what the document is and it is left as nearly as possible in his or her possession or control (*Thomson v Pheney* (1832) 1 Dowl Pr Cas 441). Once a document which is to be served on an individual has been handed to that individual and the individual knows what it is, the document is served and it makes no difference that the individual gives it back to the process server (*Nottingham Building Society v Peter Bennett and Co.* (1997) *The Times*, 26 February 1997).

Address for service

15.23 A party must give an address for service within the jurisdiction, including (unless the court orders otherwise) a full postcode, where all documents to be served by any method other than personal service must be served (**CPR, r. 6.5(2) and (4)**). A party who resides, or carries on business, within the jurisdiction, and who does not give the business address of his solicitor as his address for service, must give his residence or place of business as his address for service (**r. 6.5(3)**).

Where no solicitor is acting for the party to be served (see **15.24** where a solicitor is acting), and no address for service has been given, a table in **r. 6.5(6)** shows the place where documents must be served. This is reproduced in **table 15.2**. The phrase 'no solicitor acting'

Table 15.2 Service when there is no address for service

Nature of party to be served	Place of service
Individual	• Usual or last known residence.
Proprietor of a business	• Usual or last known residence; or • Place of business or last known place of business.
Individual who is suing or being sued in the name of a firm	• Usual or last known residence; or • Principal or last known place of business of the firm.
Corporation incorporated in England and Wales other than a company	• Principal office of the corporation; or • Any place within the jurisdiction where the corporation carries on its activities and which has a real connection with the claim.
Company registered in England and Wales	• Principal office of the company; or • Any place of business of the company within the jurisdiction which has a real connection with the claim.
Any other company or corporation	• Any place within the jurisdiction where the corporation carries on its activities; or • Any place of business of the company within the jurisdiction.

means 'no solicitor acting so that he can be served'. Where a defendant has a solicitor acting for him in some capacity but without instructions to accept service, service should be effected in accordance with **table 15.2** (*Collier v Williams* [2006] EWCA Civ 20, *The Times*, 3 February 2006). Service at an individual's last known residence, in accordance with the table, is valid even if it is known by the serving party that the individual no longer resides there (*Cranfield v Bridgegrove Ltd* [2003] EWCA Civ 656, [2003] 1 WLR 2441). The description 'last known' means the address last known to the claimant, having taken reasonable steps to ascertain it (*Mersey Docks Property Holdings v Kilgour* [2004] EWHC 1638 (TCC), [2004] BLR 412).

This interpretation was supported in *Collier v Williams* [2006] EWCA Civ 20, *The Times*, 3 February 2006, when Dyson LJ suggested that the knowledge referred to in 'last known' was either the serving party's actual knowledge or his constructive knowledge, i.e., knowledge which he could have acquired exercising reasonable diligence. The Court of Appeal also held that 'usual or last known address' could not include an address where the defendant had never resided, regardless of the reasonableness of the belief of the serving party that the defendant did reside there.

The address of a person who is the tenant of a room in a house is the address of the house, not the room (*Akram v Adam* [2004] EWCA Civ 1601, [2005] 1 WLR 2762).

Premises rented by the defendant to tenants could not be classified as the defendant's place of business for the purposes of **table 15.2** (*O'Hara v McDougal* [2005] EWCA Civ 1623, LTL 22/11/2005).

Service on any other person, for example, the defendant's insurer, is ineffective unless the claimant first obtains an order under **r. 6.8** for service by an alternative method (*Elmes v Hygrade Food Products plc* [2001] EWCA Civ 121, LTL 27/2/2001).

An address owned by someone else, but used occasionally by the defendant and other members of his family when they visited England was not the defendant's residence for the purpose of **r. 6.5** (*Chellaram v Chellaram (No. 2)* [2002] EWHC 632 (Ch), [2002] 3 All ER 17). Provided the address used was at one time the defendant's residence, and provided it is the last address known to the claimant as such, it would follow from *Godwin v Swindon Borough Council* [2001] EWCA Civ 1478, [2002] 1 WLR 997, that once it is proved that documents were sent or left there in accordance with one of the permitted methods of service (see **15.21**), they will be deemed to have been served, and evidence will not be admissible to prove they were not received by the defendant (see **15.36**). In *Cranfield v Bridgegrove Ltd*, it was held that service at the defendant's last known address was valid even though the claimant knew the defendant had not been resident there for over 19 months. For the purpose of service of a claim form (as opposed to service of other types of documents, which are also governed by **r. 6.5**), service at the defendant's last known address will only be effective if, in addition, the defendant was present in the jurisdiction when service was effected (*Chellaram v Chellaram (No. 2)*) (at least where the defendant is domiciled outside the jurisdiction, although the passage dealing with this at [47] of the judgment is stated in untrammelled terms, as is the similar case of *Fairmays v Palmer* [2006] EWHC 96 (Ch), LTL 7/2/2006). See also the discussion in **20.14** of setting aside a default judgment where the defendant had no actual knowledge of a claim form which is deemed to have been served.

Service on a party represented by a solicitor

Where a defendant is represented by a solicitor, service may be effected on the solicitor instead of the defendant himself under the provisions of **CPR, rr. 6.4** and **6.6**. In *Collier v Williams* [2006] EWCA Civ 20, *The Times*, 3 February 2006, Dyson LJ drew a distinction between personal service under **r. 6.2(1)(a)** and service by the other methods specified in **r. 6.2(1)(b)** to **(e)**. **15.24**

(a) *Personal service.* A claimant who wishes to serve a document on a defendant personally must serve the defendant, unless the defendant's solicitor is authorised to accept service and the solicitor has notified the claimant in writing that he is so authorised (**r. 6.4(2)**).

Thus, where a solicitor's address has been given as a defendant's address for service, it is still open to the claimant to serve the defendant personally, unless the claimant has been notified by the solicitor in accordance with **r. 6.4(2)**.

(b) *Service by another method.* If a claimant wishes to serve a document by one of the other methods of service specified in **r. 6.2(1)**, such as service by first class post, and he has been provided with a solicitor's address as the address for service, no confirmation is required from the solicitor. In these circumstances the claimant must post the document to the solicitor and he will be unable to post the document to the defendant himself. However, if the document to be served is a claim form, the solicitor must be authorised to accept service on the defendant's behalf. Authority for this is to be found in the words in parentheses at the end of **r. 6.5(5)**, directing attention to **r. 6.13**. In the case of documents other than the claim form, a party's address for service under **r. 6.5** is the business address of the solicitor acting for him (**r. 6.5(5)**) and no explicit authority to accept service is required.

The reference in **r. 6.5(6)** to 'no solicitor is acting' means 'no solicitor acting so that he can be served'. Thus where a claimant is told that a solicitor is acting for a defendant but that the solicitor does not have instructions to accept service, service on the defendant in accordance with **r. 6.5(6)** will be good service.

A solicitor cannot be authorised to accept service on behalf of a party to a claim unless authorised in relation to the claim itself: acting in relation to the events which are the subject of the claim is not sufficient (*Nagusina Naviera v Allied Maritime Inc.* [2002] EWCA Civ 1147, LTL 10/7/2002, in which service of a claim form, in an appeal from an arbitration award, on the solicitor who had acted for the defendant in the arbitration was held to be ineffective). Similarly, an indication by solicitors that they were authorised to accept service of proceedings brought by a claimant to recover a debt, did not mean that they were also authorised to accept service in relation to a separate claim for the same debt brought by the assignee of the debt. A solicitor's authority to accept service of a claim form must be defined not only by reference to the subject matter of the claim, but also by reference to the identity and capacity of the claimant (*Firstdale Ltd v Quinton* [2004] EWHC 1926 (Comm), [2005] 1 All ER 639). On the other hand, a letter agreeing that all further correspondence in relation to a notice to concur in arbitration proceedings should be sent to a firm of solicitors did constitute a representation that the solicitors should be served with court proceedings in relation to the same underlying claim (*Peacocks Ltd v Chapman Taylor* [2004] EWHC 2898 (TCC), LTL 18/4/2005).

Service by DX

15.25 Service by document exchange (DX) is permitted where the party's address for service, or the headed notepaper of the party or of the party's legal representative, includes a DX address, provided there has been no specific indication by the party or the party's legal representative that service by DX will not be acceptable (**PD 6, para. 2**).

Service by fax, email or other electronic means

15.26 Before service is permitted by fax, email or other electronic means, the party who is to be served, or his legal representative, must have expressly indicated in writing that he is willing to accept service by electronic means, and must provide his fax number, email address or other electronic identification (**PD 6, para. 3.1(1)**).

The following are regarded by **PD 6, para. 3.1(2)**, as a sufficient express indication of willingness to accept service electronically:

(a) including a fax number on the legal representative's writing paper;

(b) including a fax number, email address or electronic identification on a statement of case or a response to a claim filed with the court.

The following are not, by themselves, regarded by **PD 6** as sufficient express indication of willingness to accept service electronically:

(a) a fax number on the writing paper of a party (*Molins plc v GD SpA* [2000] 1 WLR 1741);
(b) an email address or electronic identification on a legal representative's writing paper.

Solicitors may be tempted to make the position clear beyond doubt on their letterhead by including a statement that they do not accept service by email. However, relying on this to refuse service by email in an emergency, and then opposing an application under **CPR, r. 3.9**, by the opponents for relief from sanctions, is unlikely to attract the court's sympathy (*RC Residuals Ltd v Linton Fuel Oils Ltd* [2002] EWCA Civ 911, [2002] 1 WLR 2782).

A party who seeks to serve electronically should first enquire whether the recipient has any limitations on matters such as on the format of transmitted documents or the size of attachments (**PD 6, para. 3.2**). This allows conditions to be imposed, but should not be read as allowing the intended recipient to decline such service. In order to comply with the requirement in CPR, r. 6.5(2), that addresses for service must be within the jurisdiction, any fax number given for the purpose of service must be at the address for service, and email and other electronic identifications are deemed to be at the address for service (**PD 6, para. 3.3**). There is no need to serve a hard copy after using fax or electronic methods of service (**para. 3.4**). Until 2 June 2003, there used to be a provision in PD 6 that not serving a hard copy after disputed service by fax or email could be taken into account. This has been deleted, because **CPR, r. 6.7**, gives rise to an irrebuttable presumption of due service after service by one of the prescribed means (*Anderton v Clwyd County Council (No. 2)* [2002] EWCA Civ 933, [2002] 1 WLR 3174), so service of a hard copy adds nothing to the presumption (and would be inadmissible as evidence).

It remains to be seen whether litigants or their legal representatives will use electronic methods of service often. One of the problems with these methods of service is that the recipient receives only a representation of a document, not an officially sealed copy. All these methods require the cooperation of the party being served, and email can be used only where legal representatives have been appointed. Service by email on a defendant whose physical address is unknown would be possible only if authorised by the court under **r. 6.8** (see **15.38**).

Service of Part 36 offers and notices of Part 36 payments

In a decision based on a legalistic interpretation of the rules, the Court of Appeal in *Charles v NTL Group Ltd* [2002] EWCA Civ 2004, LTL 13/12/2002, has held that different rules apply to giving notice of Part 36 offers as opposed to Part 36 payments (see **chapter 64**). The court relied on the difference in wording between **CPR, r. 36.8(1)** and (3) (on Part 36 offers) and **r. 36.8(2) and** (4) (on Part 36 payments) to justify the distinction drawn. Regarding Part 36 offers, **r. 36.8(1)** and (3) provide that Part 36 offers, and improvements on Part 36 offers, are made 'when received by the offeree'. This was interpreted as meaning that the strict rules on service in **Part 6** do not apply at all to Part 36 offers. On the other hand, **r. 36.8(2)** and (4) provide that Part 36 payments and improvements to Part 36 payments are made 'when written notice of the payment into court is served on the offeree'. This was interpreted as meaning that service in accordance with the rules in **Part 6** is required for Part 36 payments. It is difficult to see any justification for this distinction. It means that if the intended recipient has not indicated willingness to accept service by fax, that will not prevent the other side making a Part 36 offer by fax if the claim seeks non-monetary remedies, but will be effective to prevent service of a notice of a Part 36 payment by fax if the claim seeks a monetary remedy. It also means that a party making a Part 36 offer has to prove receipt, whereas a party serving a notice of a Part 36 payment can rely on the irrebuttable presumption of due service in **r. 6.7**, discussed at **15.36**. **15.27**

Service pursuant to contract

Where a contract contains a provision for service, a claim form containing a claim only in respect of that contract may be served by the method specified in it (**CPR, r. 6.15(1)**). **15.28**

However, by **r. 6.15(2)**, where the claim form is served out of the jurisdiction, service in accordance with the contractually agreed method will not be valid unless either:

(a) the claimant has obtained an order for service out of the jurisdiction under **r. 6.20**; or
(b) service out of the jurisdiction can be effected without permission under **r. 6.19**.

Only parties to the contract, their transferees and assignees can take advantage of a contractual method of service (*Argo Capital Investors Fund SPC v Essar Steel Ltd* [2005] EWHC 2587, LTL 28/11/2005).

PARTICULAR TYPES OF PARTY

Children and patients

15.29 Where proceedings are begun against a child, the claim form must be served on one of his or her parents or guardians, or, if there is no such person, on the person with whom the child resides or who has care of the child (**CPR, r. 6.6(1)**). In the case of a patient, the claim form must be served on the person authorised under the Mental Health Act 1983 to conduct proceedings on the patient's behalf, or, where there is no person so authorised, on the person with whom the patient resides or who has care of the patient (**r. 6.6(1)**). There is no requirement for the child or the patient to be served, or given any other form of notification of the existence of the proceedings, although the court has a discretion to make an order to that effect (**r. 6.6(2)**). Where the court has made an order allowing a child to conduct proceedings without a litigation friend, the usual rules for service on an individual apply (**r. 6.6(5)**).

Once proceedings have been commenced with a litigation friend acting on behalf of the child or patient, any document which would otherwise be served on the child or patient should be served on his or her litigation friend (**r. 6.6(1)**).

These rules are subject to any order to the contrary made by the court (**r. 6.6(2)**). Where a document has been served on some other person, the court may make an order that service should stand (**r. 6.6(4)**).

Companies

15.30 By **CPR, r. 6.2(2)**, a company registered, or treated as if registered, under the Companies Act 1985 may be served by any of the methods permitted under **Part 6** (see 15.21).

Personal service on a company is effected by leaving a document with a person holding a senior position within the company (**r. 6.4(4)**). The following hold a senior position for the purpose of the CPR: a director, secretary, treasurer, chief executive, manager or other officer of the company (**PD 6, para. 6.2(1)**). Whether a person falls within the ambit of **CPR, r. 6.4(4)**, and **PD 6, para. 6.2(1)**, is a matter of fact (*Lakah Group v Al Jazeera Satellite Channel* [2003] EWHC 1231 (QB), *The Times*, 18 April 2003, [2003] EWCA Civ 1781, LTL 9/12/2003).

Service by any other method under the CPR, on a company which has neither provided an address for service under **r. 6.5(2)**, nor authorised a solicitor to accept service under **r. 6.13**, may be effected at its principal office or any place of business of the company within the jurisdiction which has a real connection with the claim (**r. 6.5(6)**).

As an alternative to service under the CPR, a company may be served at its registered office under the Companies Act 1985, s. 725 (**CPR, r. 6.2(2)**). Section 725(1) provides that: 'A document may be served on a company by leaving it at, or sending it by post to, the company's registered office'. Where the document is sent by post, it may be sent either by first or second-class post. Unless the contrary is proved, service is deemed to be effected at the time when the letter would be delivered in the ordinary course of post (**Interpretation Act 1978, s. 7**). Service on a registered company at its registered office takes effect under the Companies

Act 1985, s. 725, and not under the CPR. Service under the Companies Act 1985 and under the CPR are true alternatives. There are the following differences between the two methods. If service of a document is effected by post under the Companies Act 1985, the document will be deemed to have been served, unless the contrary is proved, when the letter would have been delivered in the ordinary course of post (**Interpretation Act 1978, s.** 7; *Cranfield v Bridgegrove Ltd* [2003] EWCA Civ 656, [2003] 1 WLR 2441). Service by second-class post is allowed by the Companies Act 1985, but not by the CPR. Under the Companies Act 1985 the deemed date of delivery depends on which day the letter is posted and whether first or second class is used, and the deemed date can be displaced by evidence to the contrary.

The Companies Act 1985, s. 725, also applies to limited liability partnerships (Limited Liability Partnerships Regulations 2001 (SI 2001/1090), reg. 4(1) and sch. 2, part I).

Service on a company registered in Scotland at its registered office in Scotland will be service outside the jurisdiction (see **chapter 16**).

Oversea companies

By **CPR**, **r.** **6.2(2)**, a company incorporated outside Great Britain which has established a place of business in Great Britain (known as an 'oversea company': see the Companies Act 1985, s. 744) can be served either: **15.31**

(a) by any of the methods permitted under **CPR, Part 6** (see **15.21**), at any place of business of the company in the jurisdiction or any place in the jurisdiction where the company carries on its activities (**r. 6.5(6)**; *Sea Assets Ltd v PT Garuda Indonesia* [2000] 4 All ER 371); or
(b) under the provisions of the Companies Act 1985, s. 694A (which provides for service on an oversea company which has established a branch in Great Britain and is required to register the branch under s. 690A) or s. 695 (which provides for service on an oversea company which has established a place of business in Great Britain but is required to register under s. 691 rather than s. 690A).

Service will not be valid under **r. 6.5(6)** at an address with which the company has no more than a transient or irregular connection (*Lakah Group v Al Jazeera Satellite Channel* [2003] EWHC 1231, *The Times*, 18 April 2003, [2003] EWCA Civ 1781, LTL 9/12/2003).

In *Harrods Ltd v Dow Jones and Co. Inc.* [2003] EWHC 1162 (QB), LTL 29/5/2003, at [32] and [33], Eady J held that a company incorporated outside Great Britain which had not established a place of business in Great Britain and so could not be served under the Companies Act 1985, s. 695, also cannot be served by any of the methods permitted by **CPR, Part 6**. In particular, it cannot be served, under **r. 6.5(6)**, at a place in the jurisdiction where its activities are carried on. In *Reuben v Time Inc.* [2003] EWHC 1430 (QB), LTL 3/7/2003, Morland J said, at [31], that he agreed with this statement of the law. In *Lakah Group v Al Jazeera Satellite Channel* Gray J, at first instance, thought that **Part 6** allows for service on a wider range of foreign companies than those which can be served under the Companies Act 1985. However, when refusing permission to appeal against Gray J's decision, the Court of Appeal found it unnecessary to discuss the point.

Whether a company has an established place of business in Great Britain, and where that place of business is, are questions of fact (*Rakusens Ltd v Baser Ambalaj Plastik Sanayi Ticaret AS* [2001] EWCA Civ 1820, [2002] 1 BCLC 104, at [8]; *Matchnet plc v William Blair and Co. llc* [2002] EWHC 2128 (Ch), [2003] 2 BCLC 195). A place may be a company's place of business even if only an ancillary part of the company's business is carried on there (*South India Shipping Corporation Ltd v Export-Import Bank of Korea* [1985] 1 WLR 585). A place where a person takes orders for a company incorporated outside Great Britain, without authority to decide whether to accept or reject them, is not a place of business established by the company in Great Britain (*Rakusens Ltd v Baser Ambalaj Plastik Sanayi Ticaret AS*; *Harrods Ltd v Dow Jones and Co. Inc.* [2003] EWHC 1162 (QB), LTL 29/5/2003). In *Harrods Ltd v Dow Jones and Co. Inc.* the criteria used to determine whether the place of business of an agent of a foreign company was that company's place of business were the criteria suggested by the Court of Appeal in *Adams v Cape Industries plc* [1990] Ch 433 at pp. 530–1 for determining whether the activities of an agent here of a foreign company make the company subject to the jurisdiction of the courts here. The same approach was taken in *Reuben v Time Inc.*

A company incorporated outside Great Britain which has established a place of business in Great Britain must register with the registrar of companies under either:

(a) the Companies Act 1985, s. 690A and sch. 21A, if the British place of business is a branch; or

(b) the Companies Act 1985, s. 691, otherwise.

A company incorporated in Gibraltar or Northern Ireland cannot register under s. 690A.

Registration of a company's branch under s. 690A and sch. 21A involves informing the registrar of the address of the branch and the business carried on at it, and giving a list of the names and addresses of all persons resident in Great Britain authorised to accept on the company's behalf service of process in respect of the business of the branch (sch. 21A, para. 3(a), (c) and (e)). Any process required to be served on the company in respect of the carrying on of the business of the branch is sufficiently served if addressed to any such person and left at or sent by post to the address given (s. 694A). Process is in respect of the carrying on of the business of a branch for the purposes of s. 694A even if it is only partly in respect of that business and partly in respect of the company's business elsewhere (*Saab v Saudi American Bank* [1999] 1 WLR 1861). Process which is not in respect of the business of the branch at all must be served under **CPR, Part 6**, rather than the Companies Act 1985, s. 694A.

Registration of a company's place of business under s. 691 involves providing the registrar with a list of the names and addresses of some one or more persons resident in Great Britain authorised to accept on the company's behalf service of process (s. 691(1)(b)(ii)). Any process required to be served on the company is sufficiently served if addressed to any such person and left at or sent by post to the address given (s. 695(1)).

Where the document is sent by post, it may be sent either by first or second-class post. Unless the contrary is proved, service is deemed to be effected at the time when the letter would be delivered in the ordinary course of post (**Interpretation Act 1978, s. 7**).

If the only address given by an oversea company of a British resident authorised to accept service is in Scotland, service under s. 694A or s. 695 will be service outside the jurisdiction (see **chapter 16**).

To be served in accordance with s. 694A or s. 695(1), a document must be addressed to the person resident in Great Britain who is authorised to accept service — addressing it to the company and leaving it at the authorised person's address is not sufficient (*Boocock v Hilton International Co.* [1993] 1 WLR 1065).

If a company has complied with s. 691, a document can be served under s. 695(1) even after the company has ceased to have a place of business in Great Britain (*Sabatier v Trading Co.* [1927] 1 Ch 495) and even though the registrar has been notified of the cessation of business and the person whose name has been delivered to the registrar has left Great Britain (*Rome v Punjab National Bank (No. 2)* [1989] 1 WLR 1211).

Where an oversea company fails to provide the necessary information to the registrar of companies, or if service cannot be effected on the authorised person(s), because they have died or have moved, or for any other reason, service may be effected at any place of business established by the company in Great Britain (Companies Act 1985, ss. 694A(3) and 695(2)) and used as its place of business at the time of service (*Deverall v Grant Advertising Inc.* [1955] Ch 111).

Other corporations

A corporation, incorporated in England and Wales, which cannot be served under the Companies Act 1985, s. 725 (registered company or limited liability partnership, see **15.30**), must be served by one of the methods listed in **CPR, r. 6.2(1)** (see **15.21**). This applies to entities such as building societies and incorporated friendly societies. 15.32

Personal service on a corporation is effected by leaving the document to be served with a person holding a senior position within the corporation (**r. 6.4(4)**). The following hold a senior position for this purpose: a director, the treasurer, secretary, chief executive, manager or other officer of the corporation, the mayor, chairman, president, town clerk or similar officer (**PD 6, paras 6.1** and **6.2**).

Service by any other method under the CPR on a corporation incorporated in England and Wales, which has neither provided an address for service under **r. 6.5(2)** nor authorised a solicitor to accept service under **r. 6.13**, may be effected at either the principal office of the corporation or any place within the jurisdiction where the corporation carries on business and which has a real connection with the claim (**r. 6.5(6)**).

Rule 6.5(6) names the place of service (other than personal service) for a company not registered in England and Wales and a corporation (other than a company) not incorporated in England and Wales where no solicitor is acting and no address for service in the jurisdiction has been given. This is 'any place within the jurisdiction where the *corporation* carries on its activities; or any place of business of the *company* within the jurisdiction'. However, it seems that a company incorporated outside Great Britain cannot be served in this way unless it is liable to service under the Companies Act 1985, s. 649A or s. 695 (see **15.31**).

Partnerships

Service on a partnership may be effected by any of the methods permitted by **CPR, r. 6.2(1)** (see **15.21**). 15.33

Where partners are sued in the firm name, personal service is effected by leaving the document to be served with a partner, or, alternatively, at the firm's principal place of business, with a person having, at the time of service, control or management of the partnership business (**CPR, r. 6.4(5)**). In the latter case, if the claim form or particulars of claim are being served, the person served must also be served with a notice stating whether he or she is being served as a partner, as a person having control or management of the partnership business, or both (**PD 6, para. 4.2**).

Where a firm has neither provided an address for service under **CPR, r. 6.5(2)**, nor authorised a solicitor to accept service under **r. 6.13**, service on a partnership by any method other than personal service should be effected by sending the document to be served either to the usual or last known residential address of a partner, or to the principal or last known place of business of the firm (**r. 6.5(6)**).

Partners sued in their individual names must be served as individual defendants.

By **PD 10, para. 4.4**, an acknowledgment served on a firm may be signed by any partner or by a person with control or management of the partnership business.

If partners are sued as partners in the name of their firm, they may acknowledge service only in their own names (**RSC, ord. 81, r. 4(1)** in CPR, sch. 1).

Where a person served as a partner denies being a partner in the defendant firm, or denies being a partner at the time the cause of action accrued, an acknowledgment should be filed under protest stating the denial (**RSC, ord. 81, r. 4(2)** in CPR, sch. 1). The claimant may then apply to have the acknowledgment set aside on the ground that the person was a partner, or may leave the question to be decided later in the proceedings. Likewise, the person served may apply to set aside service of the claim form immediately, on the ground of not being a partner, or may take the point in defence.

Under the old version of **RSC, ord. 81**, only certain forms of wording were permitted in an acknowledgment of service filed by a partnership. No such express provision is made in the CPR. Indeed, **form N9** makes no provision at all for completing an acknowledgment under protest in accordance with **RSC, ord. 81, r.** 4(2) in CPR, sch. 1. Litigants in this position will have to amend the printed form in order to comply with the rule.

Schedule 2 to the CPR naturally contains no provision for acknowledging service, as this was not a step which existed under the old CCR. However, it is now open to a defendant to county court proceedings to acknowledge service under **CPR, r. 10**.

Where a defendant partnership wishes to acknowledge service of county court proceedings, it would be prudent to follow the procedure set out in **RSC, ord. 81** in CPR, sch. 1, even though technically this applies only to proceedings issued in the High Court (**CPR, r.** 50(3)(c)), taking care to acknowledge under protest only, if appropriate. For the effect of acknowledging service on enforcement against the assets of individual partners see **76.37**.

Crown proceedings

15.34 By **CPR, r.** 6.4(2A) documents required to be served on the Crown may not be served personally. Further, **r.** 6.5(8) stipulates that service on the Attorney-General must be effected on the Treasury Solicitor and service on a government department must be effected on the solicitor acting for that department as required by the **Crown Proceedings Act 1947, s. 18**. The list published under the **Crown Proceedings Act, s. 17**, of the solicitors acting for the different government departments on whom service is to be effected, and of their addresses follows the text of the **Crown Proceedings Act, 1947** in **appendix** 7.

Agent of a principal who is overseas

15.35 By **CPR, r.** 6.16(1) and (2), a claimant may, with the court's permission, serve a claim form on the agent of a principal who is overseas, where:

(a) the claim relates to a contract entered into within the jurisdiction, with or through the agent; and
(b) at the time of the application for permission, the agent's authority has not been terminated or the agent is still in business relations with the principal.

Application for permission should be made in accordance with the **Part 23** procedure. No notice need be given, but the application must, by **r. 6.16(3)**, be supported by evidence setting out details of the contract, confirming that it was entered into in the jurisdiction through an agent residing or carrying on business in the jurisdiction and providing the other information specified in **PD 6, para. 9.2.** Any order made under the rule must give a time limit within which the defendant must respond to the particulars of claim (not the claim form) (**r. 6.16(4)**). A copy of the order and of the claim form must be served on the defendant (**r. 6.16(6)**).

A Practice Direction (1920)150 LT Jo 388 was issued in relation to an earlier version of this rule. It contains the following guidance for practitioners, which the courts may still take into account:

(a) The court's power to make an order under the rule is discretionary, and to be exercised with caution. It should not be used where there is no difficulty in getting an order and serving out of the jurisdiction in the usual way.
(b) The court will look at the nature of the agency relationship. If it is 'casual', the court will be less ready to make an order.

DEEMED DATES OF SERVICE

Rule 6.7(1) of the CPR sets out a table showing deemed dates of service for service by first-class post, by delivering a document to or leaving it at the place of service, through a document exchange, by fax or by other electronic method. This is reproduced in **table 15.3**. The Court of Appeal has held that **r. 6.7(1)** creates an irrebuttable presumption that service occurred on the deemed day of service: the presumption cannot be displaced by proving the actual day of receipt (*Godwin v Swindon Borough Council* [2001] EWCA Civ 1478, [2002] 1 WLR 997; *Anderton v Clwyd County Council (No. 2)* [2002] EWCA Civ 933, [2002] 1 WLR 3174). **15.36**

Calculating deemed dates of service

The deemed dates for service by post, document exchange, delivery to or leaving at a permitted address, and by electronic methods other than fax, take effect on the calendar dates set out in **table 15.3**, ignoring weekends and bank holidays. For example, a document put into the first-class post on a Friday is deemed to be served on the following Sunday. This is so even though there is no postal delivery on Sundays, and even if, on the deemed date of service, there is no one at the address (such as a place of work that is not occupied at weekends). See *Anderton v Clwyd County Council (No. 2)* [2002] EWCA Civ 933, [2002] 1 WLR 3174. The reason is that **r. 6.7 of the CPR** uses the term 'day' rather than 'business day' for these methods of service, and **r. 2.8(4)** (which disregards weekends and bank holidays) does not apply because it is restricted to calculating periods 'for the doing of an act' (**r. 2.8(1)**), whereas **r. 6.7** does not relate to the doing of any act at all, but is simply a deeming provision (see *Anderton v Clwyd County Council (No. 2)* at [39]). Thus a document posted on a Friday is deemed to be served (on the following Sunday) before a document which is faxed on a Friday, but after 4 p.m., because, by r. 6.7(1), the fax is deemed to be served on the next business day, which would be the following Monday (see below). **15.37**

Personal service takes effect immediately, unless it is performed after 5 p.m. on a business day, or at any time on Saturday, Sunday or bank holiday, in which case it is deemed to be service on the next business day (**CPR, r. 6.7(2)**). 'Business day' here means any day except Saturday, Sunday or a bank holiday, and Christmas Day and Good Friday are counted as bank holidays (r. 6.7(3)).

The deemed dates for service for faxes sent after 4 p.m., and for personal service after 5 p.m. or on a Saturday, Sunday or bank holiday, are calculated applying **r. 6.7(3)**, and therefore ignoring Saturdays, Sundays and bank holidays. This is because **r. 6.7** provides in these cases for deemed dates of service calculated as business days (see *Anderton v Clwyd County Council*

Table 15.3 Deemed days of service

Method of service	Deemed day of service
First-class post or, from 6 April 2006, another delivery service that provides for delivery on the next working day	The second day after it was posted.
Document exchange	The second day after it was left at the document exchange.
Delivering the document to or leaving it at a permitted address	The day after it was delivered to or left at the permitted address.
Fax	• If it is transmitted on a business day before 4 p.m., on that day; or • in any other case, on the business day after the day on which it is transmitted.
Other electronic method	The second day after the day on which it is transmitted.

(No. 2)). Consequently, a fax sent at 6 p.m. on Friday will be deemed to have been served on the following Monday. In *Home Office v Dorgan* [2002] EWCA Civ 933, [2002] 1 WLR 3174, however, the Court of Appeal upheld an order dispensing with service where a claim form was received by fax at 4.03 p.m., and the defendant had contacted the claimant on receipt.

Rule 2.8(2), which requires a period, expressed as a number of days, for 'doing any act' (**r. 2.8(1)**) to be calculated as clear days, does not apply to the calculation of a deemed date of service, because a deemed date is not a date by which any act is to be done (*Anderton v Clwyd County Council (No. 2)* at [39]).

SERVICE BY AN ALTERNATIVE METHOD

15.38 The court may authorise service by an alternative method where 'there is a good reason' to do so (**CPR, r. 6.8(1)**). This is equivalent to the old rules in the RSC and CCR on substituted service. There is no guidance in the CPR about what constitutes a 'good reason'. The desirability of serving a defendant in the jurisdiction in order to ensure that England is the jurisdiction first seised of proceedings for the purposes of art. 21 of the Brussels Convention does not constitute a good reason under **r. 6.8** (*Knauf UK GmbH v British Gypsum Ltd* [2001] EWCA Civ 1570, [2002] 1 WLR 907).

Under the old rules, an order could be made where there was evidence that the defendant was evading service or could not easily be found. The applicant normally also had to show that service in the manner sought would be effective to bring the existence of proceedings to the defendant's attention. Substituted service would not be ordered where one of the prescribed methods of service would be effective, nor simply because it had been impractical to serve proceedings in time (*Paragon Group Ltd v Burnell* [1991] Ch 498).

These principles were applied in *National Justice Compania Naviera SA v Prudential Assurance Co. Ltd (No. 3)* 2001 WL 753347, where an order was made under **r. 6.8(1)** for service on the defendant's solicitors, who did not have instructions to accept service, on the grounds that the defendant was refusing to cooperate over service and his solicitors were clearly in contact with him.

Under the old RSC, orders were regularly made for substituted service on the insurers of drivers of motor vehicles who had disappeared but were not 'untraced drivers' for the purposes of the Motor Insurers' Bureau agreements (see *Gurtner v Circuit* [1968] 2 QB 587). Similarly, in a claim for professional negligence by a solicitor who had disappeared, substituted service was allowed at the address of the Solicitors' Indemnity Fund in *Abbey National plc v Frost* [1999] 1 WLR 1080.

Also under the old rules, where the defendant was abroad on the date of issue, an order for substituted service would not normally be made unless either the plaintiff had obtained an order for service out of the jurisdiction or the case was one where service out of the jurisdiction could be effected without permission under the Brussels or Lugano Conventions (*Myerson v Martin* [1979] 1 WLR 1390; *Cadogan Properties Ltd v Mount Eden Land Ltd* (1999) LTL 29/6/99). The position under the CPR is the same: **CPR, r. 6.5(1)**, provides that a document must be served within the jurisdiction 'except as provided by Section III of this Part (service out of the jurisdiction)'. **Rule 6.8** may not be used to avoid the provisions of the relevant conventions on effecting service abroad (*Knauf UK GmbH v British Gypsum Ltd* [2001] EWCA Civ 1570, [2002] 1 WLR 907). In *Marconi Communications International Ltd v PT Pan Indonesia Bank Ltd TBK* [2004] EWHC 129 (Comm), [2004] 1 Lloyd's Rep 594, permission to serve out of the jurisdiction on an Indonesian defendant was granted together with an order under **r. 6.8** for service on its English solicitors. Steel J, commenting that the court's discretion under **r. 6.8** is broader than under the RSC, upheld the order for service by an alternative method. Even though it could not be said that service in Indonesia was impractical, evidence that it would take at least one year in a case where delay was the sole aim of the defendant, constituted 'good reason'.

It would seem that there is no power to make an order under **r. 6.8** retrospectively to cure an error already made in effecting service (*Elmes v Hygrade Food Products plc* [2001] EWCA Civ 121, LTL 27/2/2001).

Procedure

An application for an order permitting service by an alternative method should be made using the **Part 23** procedure. The application may be made without notice to other parties (**CPR, r. 6.8(2)(b)**). It must be supported by evidence showing why the order is sought and what steps have been taken to serve by permitted means (**r. 6.8(2)(a); PD 6, para. 9.1**). 15.39

Where the court makes an order permitting such service, it will specify the method of service and the date of deemed service (**CPR, r. 6.8(3)**). Commonly ordered alternative methods of service include newspaper advertisement, service at an address which the defendant is known to frequent, and service on a person who is likely to draw the attention of the defendant to the proceedings, such as a relative or a solicitor who has been acting for the defendant, but who has no instructions to accept service.

SERVICE BY MEANS OUTSIDE THE CPR

Under the RSC it was possible to effect service by a method outside the rules, provided the defendant had agreed to accept service by the method chosen. In *Kenneth Allison Ltd v A. E. Limehouse and Co.* [1992] 2 AC 105 a process server effected service on the defendant partnership by leaving the writ with the receptionist, who took it only after she had consulted one of the partners and he had authorised her to accept it. The House of Lords held that although service by this method was outside the rules, it was nevertheless valid as it had been effected pursuant to an ad hoc agreement. The decision was followed in *Finn v Girobank plc* (2000) LTL 19/1/2000, which was a case on the old RSC, ord. 10. 15.40

The Court of Appeal in *Anderton v Clwyd County Council (No. 2)* [2002] EWCA Civ 933, [2002] 1 WLR 3174, appears to have held that the list of methods for service in **CPR, r. 6.2**, is exhaustive and that provision of the claim form to the defendant by any other method, even where it is effective to bring the existence of the claim to the defendant's attention, does not constitute service under the rules. In that case, the Court of Appeal did not consider the effect of an agreement by the defendant to the use of an alternative method of service. In *Cranfield v Bridgegrove Ltd* [2003] EWCA Civ 656, [2003] 1 WLR 2441, though, it approved, *obiter*, *Kenneth Allison Ltd v A. E. Limehouse and Co.* as authority for the proposition that an ad hoc agreement for service in a manner outside the CPR is legally effective.

DISPENSING WITH SERVICE

The court may dispense with service of a document (**CPR, r. 6.9(1)**). An application for an order to dispense with service may be made without notice (**r. 6.9(2)**). An application for an order dispensing with service can be made after the event (*Godwin v Swindon Borough Council* [2001] EWCA Civ 1478, [2002] 1 WLR 997; *Anderton v Clwyd County Council (No. 2)* [2002] EWCA Civ 933, [2002] 1 WLR 3174). However, an order dispensing with service will only be made in exceptional cases if it has the effect of avoiding the strict requirements of **r. 7.6(3)** where a claim form has not been served within its period of validity (*Wilkey v British Broadcasting Corporation* [2002] EWCA Civ 1561, [2003] 1 WLR 1). (For a more detailed discussion see **15.12**.) 15.41

In *Collier v Williams* [2006] EWCA Civ 20, *The Times*, 3 February 2006, Dyson LJ held that an order dispensing with service of the claim form under r. 6.9 can be made in conjunction with an order extending time for service under r. 7.6. If the defendant has already received the claim form, the court may well dispense with service on the ground that once a decision has been made to extend the time for service there is no point in requiring the claimant to re-serve the document.

DEFENDANT REQUIRING SERVICE

15.42 Where the claimant has issued but not yet served the claim form, the defendant can serve a notice under CPR, r. 7.7, requiring the claimant either to do so, or to discontinue the claim by a date which is at least 14 days after the date of service of the notice. If the claimant fails to comply, the defendant may apply to the court for an order dismissing the claim. This rule enables the defendant to require the claimant to proceed with the claim, rather than wait for the four or six months during which the claim form may be served. In practice, the provision is rarely used.

Chapter 16 Service outside the Jurisdiction

The following procedural checklist, which is in **appendix 1**, is relevant to this chapter:

Procedural checklist 12 Application for permission to serve claim form out of the jurisdiction

INTRODUCTION

16.1 Inevitably, there are a number of complexities where the intended defendant to proceedings lives outside the jurisdiction. At common law, an action *in personam* (i.e., an action against a legal person as opposed to an action *in rem* against a ship or other property) could only be brought against a defendant served with process while in England or Wales. This, at least superficially, had the merit of ensuring the courts of this country did not purport to exert an exorbitant jurisdiction over defendants who were not amenable to the coercive powers of the courts. The superficiality stemmed from the fact that jurisdiction could be established by service on a defendant while on a temporary visit to this country (**16.2**) or by a foreign defendant submitting to the jurisdiction (**16.3**). In any event, the restrictive common law rule has been subject to a discretionary power to allow English proceedings against defendants outside the jurisdiction since the enactment of the Common Law Procedure Act 1852. This discretionary power is governed by **CPR, r. 6.20**, and is discussed at **16.43** to **16.53**. These rules will be referred to in this chapter as the common law rules.

If a defendant is domiciled in another EU country, other than Denmark, the common law rules are replaced by **Council Regulation** (EC) **No. 44/2001** on jurisdiction and the recognition and enforcement of judgments in civil and commercial matters (the 'Jurisdiction and Judgments Regulation', referred to in **CPR, Part 6**, as the 'Judgments Regulation'). This lays down a general rule that a defendant domiciled in an EU State (apart from Denmark) must be sued in the courts of that State (**16.17**). (The same rule applies to Denmark under the earlier Brussels Convention, see below.) This is subject to a number of wide-ranging exceptions, which are discussed in **16.18** to **16.37**.

The text of the Jurisdiction and Judgments Regulation is based on, and is substantially the same as, an earlier treaty which all member States of the EU (including Denmark) agreed to. This was the Brussels Convention on Jurisdiction and the Enforcement of Judgments in Civil and Commercial Matters (the 'Brussels Convention'). Unlike a Council Regulation, which has direct effect, the Brussels Convention had to be incorporated into United Kingdom law by an Act of Parliament: the **Civil Jurisdiction and Judgments Act 1982** ('CJJA 1982'). The Brussels Convention is set out in **sch. 1 to the CJJA 1982**. Denmark has opted out of the Jurisdiction and Judgments Regulation, so questions of jurisdiction between Denmark and the United Kingdom must still be decided by the Brussels Convention. The EU States in which the Jurisdiction and Judgments Regulation takes effect are listed in **table 16.1**.

Until 31 April 2004 questions of jurisdiction and judgment, as between the United Kingdom (and all other EU States) and Iceland, Norway, Poland and Switzerland, were governed by the Lugano Convention, which is in practically the same terms as the Brussels Convention. As from 1 May 2004, between Poland and the United Kingdom and all EU States other than Denmark the regime for determining these questions is the **Jurisdiction and Judgments Regulation.**

Denmark has agreed to apply the **Jurisdiction and Judgments Regulation** (OJ L299, 16/11/2005, pp. 62–7), but the date when the agreement is to enter into force was not known when this edition went to press.

In this chapter, where appropriate, we refer to the provisions of both the Jurisdiction and Judgments Regulation and the Brussels Convention. Unless the contrary is stated, references

Table 16.1 EU States in which the Jurisdiction and Judgments Regulation takes effect

Until 30 April 2004	As from 1 May 2004
Austria	Austria
Belgium	Belgium
	Cyprus
	Czech Republic
	Estonia
Finland	Finland
France	France
Germany	Germany
Greece	Greece
	Hungary
Republic of Ireland	Republic of Ireland
Italy	Italy
	Latvia
	Lithuania
Luxembourg	Luxembourg
	Malta
Netherlands	Netherlands
	Poland
Portugal	Portugal
	Slovakia
	Slovenia
Spain	Spain
Sweden	Sweden
United Kingdom	United Kingdom

to articles are to articles of the Jurisdiction and Judgments Regulation, with the equivalent article of the Brussels Convention given in parentheses afterwards. As it is so similar to the Brussels Convention, we will not consider the Lugano Convention separately in this chapter.

Within the United Kingdom, separate jurisdiction is exercised by the courts of England and Wales, Scotland and Northern Ireland. Under the **CJJA 1982** these three areas are known as 'parts' of the United Kingdom. Allocation of jurisdiction between the courts of the various parts of the United Kingdom is regulated by a modified form of the Jurisdiction and Judgments Regulation, which can be found in the CJJA 1982, sch. 4. The substantive provisions of the Brussels Convention are applied as between Gibraltar and the United Kingdom by the Civil Jurisdiction and Judgments Act 1982 (Gibraltar) Order 1997 (SI 1997/2602).

Where a claim can be brought in the courts of more than one country, there is a general concern that it should be brought in the courts of the most appropriate country. The courts are also concerned that the same dispute should not be litigated in several countries at the same time, with the risk of irreconcilable judgments and difficulties regarding the recognition of judgments for enforcement purposes. These problems are addressed under the common law rules by the courts' powers to stay English proceedings on the ground of *forum non conveniens* (**16.65** to **16.70**) and to grant injunctions to restrain foreign proceedings (**16.71**). Similar problems in Jurisdiction and Judgments Regulation and Brussels Convention cases are dealt with by requirements that courts other than the one first seised of the matter must either decline jurisdiction or stay their proceedings (see **16.38** and **16.40**). Determining the system of law to be applied to resolve an action where one or more of the parties is foreign is a matter of private international law. As such it is outside the scope of this book, and specialist works should be consulted.

SERVICE ON A FOREIGN DEFENDANT WITHIN THE JURISDICTION

16.2 Under the common law rules, a foreign defendant is amenable to the jurisdiction of the courts in this country if process is served upon the defendant within the jurisdiction. Applying this rule, jurisdiction was established in *Maharanee Seethaderi Gaekwar of Baroda v Wildenstein* [1972] 2 QB 283, where the proceedings were served on the defendant while on a temporary visit to this country to attend the Ascot Races. This rule has been abolished for cases governed by the **Jurisdiction and Judgments Regulation**, which by **art. 3** (Brussels Convention, art. 3) provides that jurisdiction against EU defendants can no longer be founded by service during the defendant's temporary presence in this country. It is possible to issue a claim form against a foreign defendant marked 'Not to be served out of the jurisdiction' (**PD 6B, para. 1.4**). The intention when this is done is usually either to effect service on the defendant during a temporary visit to this country (unless the defendant lives in the EU) or to secure the defendant's agreement to service within the jurisdiction (often on English solicitors). The period of validity of an originating process intended to be served within the jurisdiction is four months, not six (**CPR, r. 7.5(2) and (3)**).

If a domestic claim form has been issued, and it is later discovered that the defendant is outside the jurisdiction, or if a claim form marked 'Not to be served out of the jurisdiction' cannot be served within the jurisdiction for any reason, the proper procedure is to apply for permission to issue a concurrent claim form for service outside the jurisdiction. Although the CPR contain no provision for issuing concurrent claim forms, this practice has continued and express reference is made to it in the **Admiralty and Commercial Courts Guide, app. 15, para. 4**.

It is not possible to serve a defendant with originating process within the jurisdiction unless the defendant is present in the jurisdiction at the time of actual or deemed service (*Chellaram v Chellaram (No. 2)* [2002] EWHC 632 (Ch), [2002] 3 All ER 17, applying *Barclays Bank of Swaziland Ltd v Hahn* [1989] 1 WLR 506). Whether this is consistent with *Anderton v Clwyd County Council (No. 2)* [2002] EWCA Civ 933, [2002] 1 WLR 3174, is open to question: see **15.36**. However, *Chellaram v Chellaram (No. 2)* has been followed in *Fairmays v Palmer* [2006] EWHC 96 (CH), LTL 7/2/2006.

SUBMISSION TO THE JURISDICTION

16.3 Regardless of whether the court would otherwise have jurisdiction, a defendant may submit to the jurisdiction of the courts of this country. It may be, for example, to save the costs of disputing jurisdiction, that a defendant will agree to English proceedings being served at the offices of a solicitor in England. Alternatively, a domestic claim form may be sent to a defendant outside the jurisdiction in breach of the rules requiring permission to serve (**16.43** to **16.52**) and the defendant may proceed to contest the action on its merits without objecting to the defect in service. In the absence of any express agreement to submit to the jurisdiction, it is a question of whether the defendant's conduct, when viewed objectively in the context of all the circumstances of the case, is inconsistent with maintaining an objection to the jurisdiction of the court. It is always dangerous to do anything more than to acknowledge service and to make an application under **CPR, Part 11**, to contest the jurisdiction (see **chapter 19**). It is easy to submit to the jurisdiction inadvertently by, for example:

(a) instructing a solicitor to accept service in the jurisdiction (*Manta Line Inc. v Sofianites* [1984] 1 Lloyd's Rep 14); or

(b) appearing to contest the merits. An example is *Marc Rich & Co. AG v Società Italiana Impianti PA (No. 2)* [1992] 1 Lloyd's Rep 624, where the defendant was held to have submitted to the jurisdiction of the courts in Italy by delivering a statement of case disputing the merits of the claim. See, however, *SSQ Europe SA v Johann & Backes OHG* [2002] 1 Lloyd's Rep 465, which is discussed in **19.3** and **19.4**.

A claimant who has commenced proceedings gives the court jurisdiction to hear a counterclaim.

A similar principle applies in Jurisdiction and Judgments Regulation cases, where **art. 24** (Brussels Convention, art. 18) provides that the courts of a member State have jurisdiction where the defendant 'enters an appearance' unless the appearance is entered solely to contest jurisdiction. The reference to entering an appearance is to acknowledging service or filing a defence. From *Elefanten Schuh GmbH v Jacqmain (case 150/80)* [1981] ECR 1671, a decision of the European Court of Justice ('ECJ'), it appears that a defence contesting jurisdiction and the merits in the alternative does not constitute a submission to the jurisdiction (there is no equivalent to the word 'solely' in the French text of the Convention). However, it is not possible to submit to the jurisdiction of a court where the courts of another country have exclusive jurisdiction under **art. 22** of the Regulation (Brussels Convention, art. 16).

CASES OUTSIDE THE GENERAL RULES

Certain types of proceedings affect rights *in rem*. Both under the common law rules and under the Jurisdiction and Judgments Regulation special rules govern where many of these types of proceedings must be litigated. The main policy consideration justifying these special rules is that rights *in rem* are often protected by detailed national laws, and the courts of the country in question are in the best position to apply them. These special rules are considered at **16.5** to **16.14**. **16.4**

Under the common law rules

Land disputes Claims founded on a dispute as to the title to, or possession of, land must be brought in the courts of the country where the land is situated. The authority for this is *British South Africa Co. v Companhia de Mocambique* [1893] AC 602 as interpreted by later decisions. Where a question as to the title of foreign land is no more than a collateral issue in a claim, the rule does not prevent the courts in this country exercising jurisdiction (see *St Pierre v South American Stores (Gath and Chaves) Ltd* [1936] 1 KB 382 and, in relation to claims for trespass, CJJA 1982, s. 30). It was established by *Penn v Lord Baltimore* (1750) 1 Ves Sen 444 that the rule can be circumvented if the defendant is subject to the general jurisdiction of the courts in this country, such as through presence here, and if the claim can be framed so as to impose a personal obligation on the defendant. An example is a claim for rent due under a lease of foreign land (*St Pierre v South American Stores (Gath and Chaves) Ltd* [1936] 1 KB 382). **16.5**

Intellectual property Claims founded on the validity or infringement of foreign copyrights, trade marks and patents have to be brought in the country where they are registered (*Tyburn Productions Ltd v Conan Doyle* [1991] Ch 75). This is a recent extension of the preceding rule, and it is possible that it is restricted to cases where an English judgment would not be recognised in the country of registration. **16.6**

Divorce, nullity and judicial separation Under the Domicile and Matrimonial Proceedings Act 1973, s. 5(2), the courts in England have jurisdiction over proceedings for divorce, nullity and judicial separation if either of the parties to the marriage, at the time the proceedings are commenced, either: **16.7**

(a) is domiciled in England; or
(b) has been habitually resident in England for the previous year.

No permission is required for service abroad of family proceedings. A translation must be provided if the respondent does not understand English, and an enhanced period must be allowed for giving notice of intention to defend (Family Proceedings Rules 1991 (SI 1991/1247), r. 10.6).

16.8 **Insolvency proceedings** Service outside the jurisdiction of any document in proceedings under the In solvency Act 1986 or the Insolvency Rules 1986 is governed by the Insolvency Rules 1986 (SI 1986/1925), r. 12.12 (see **81.5**).

Proceedings under the 1986 Act or Rules, apart from petitions to wind up solvent companies, are outside the scope of the Regulation (by **art. 1** of the Regulation; Brussels Convention, art. 1). Instead jurisdiction in insolvency proceedings in EU States other than Denmark is governed by Council Regulation (EC) No. 1346/2000 (see **79.9** to **79.12** and **80.3**).

Under the Jurisdiction and Judgments Regulation

16.9 **Exclusive jurisdiction** **Article 22** of the Jurisdiction and Judgments Regulation (art. 16 of the Brussels Convention) allocates exclusive jurisdiction, regardless of the domicile of the parties, over five categories of cases. The courts of the member States are required, of their own motion, to declare they have no jurisdiction in these cases (Regulation, **art. 25**; Brussels Convention, art. 19).

16.10 **Land** **Article 22(1)** of the Jurisdiction and Judgments Regulation (Brussels Convention, art. 16(1)) provides that proceedings which have as their object rights *in rem* in immovable property or tenancies of immovable property are subject to the exclusive jurisdiction of the courts of the Regulation State or Convention territory in which the property is situated. This is subject to an exception in respect of actions concerning tenancies between natural persons domiciled in the same country for temporary private use for periods of up to six months, which may be brought in the country where the defendant is domiciled.

Regarding rights *in rem*, the article has been interpreted by the ECJ in *Reichert v Dresdner Bank* (case C-115/88) [1990] ECR 27 as being restricted to actions to determine the extent, content, ownership or possession of immovable property, or the existence of other rights *in rem* therein. In *Webb v Webb* (case C-294/92) [1994] QB 696 an apartment in France had been bought in the defendant's name with money provided by the claimant. An action was brought in England claiming a declaration that the property was held on an express or resulting trust for the claimant. It was held, by reasoning analogous to that in *Penn v Lord Baltimore* (1750) 1 Ves Sen 444 (see **16.5**), that the claim affected the defendant's obligations *in personam* and did not have as its object rights *in rem*, and so was outside the scope of **art. 22** (Brussels Convention, art. 16).

Conversely, the provision regarding tenancies has been construed widely. It covers cases where the existence of a lease is disputed (*Sanders v Van der Putte* (case 73/77) [1977] ECR 2383) and to any dispute concerning the respective obligations of the parties under a lease (*Rösler v Rottwinkel* (case 241/83) [1986] QB 33). It therefore applies to claims in respect of unpaid rent and other breaches of covenant under a lease. There are limits, however. In *Jarrett v Barclays Bank plc* [1999] QB 1, claims by consumers against the bank under the **Consumer Credit Act 1974** arising out of loans to purchase timeshares in properties in Portugal did not have as their object tenancies in immovable property. The foundation of the claims was the loan agreement, and so the claims were not prevented by **art. 22** (Brussels Convention, art. 16) from being commenced in England.

16.11 **Companies and associations** **Article 22(2)** of the Jurisdiction and Judgments Regulation (Brussels Convention, art. 16(2)) provides that proceedings having as their object the validity of the constitution, nullity or dissolution of companies or associations of legal or natural persons, or of their organs, must be brought in the country where the relevant body has its 'seat'. Under the Regulation a court in a member State determines where a company has its seat by applying its rules of private international law. For the purposes of the operation of the

Brussels Convention in the United Kingdom the place where a company, legal person or association has its seat is determined by the **CJJA 1982**, and is the country where the company or association was incorporated or formed, or where its central management and control is exercised (CJJA 1982, s. 43(2)). In *Newtherapeutics Ltd v Katz* [1991] Ch 226 the claimant company, which was registered in England, brought an action in England against a French director claiming:

(a) that certain transactions were signed by the defendant without the approval of a meeting of the board of directors; and
(b) that the transactions were such that no reasonable directors could properly have entered into.

The first of these was held to be within the exclusive jurisdiction of the courts in England as it concerned the validity of a decision of one of the company's organs, whereas the second claim fell outside art. 16(2) of the Brussels Convention. The question then was whether the action had as its 'object' the validity of the decision of one of its organs. This depended on which of the two claims was the principal claim. In the circumstances of the case this was held to be the first claim, so the action was properly brought in England.

Public registers **Article 22(3)** of the Jurisdiction and Judgments Regulation (Brussels Convention, art. 16(3)) gives exclusive jurisdiction over proceedings concerning the validity of entries in a public register to the courts of the State where the register is kept. **16.12**

Intellectual property **Article 22(4)** of the Jurisdiction and Judgments Regulation (Brussels Convention, art. 16(4)) gives exclusive jurisdiction over proceedings concerning the registration or validity of patents, trade marks, designs and similar rights to the courts of the State where the property in question has been registered or where registration has been applied for. This does not extend to claims for infringement of patents, which are claims in tort and may be brought in accordance with art. 5(3) (see **16.29**). **Article 22(4)** (Brussels Convention, art. 16(4)) does not apply to proceedings in respect of copyright in which no question of registration arises (*Pearce v Ove Arup Partnership Ltd* [2000] Ch 403). **Article 22(4)** includes a paragraph, which is not in the Brussels Convention, providing that the courts of a member State have exclusive jurisdiction in proceedings concerned with the registration or validity of a European patent granted for that State. **16.13**

Enforcement of judgments **Article 22(5)** of the Jurisdiction and Judgments Regulation (Brussels Convention, art. 16(5)) gives exclusive jurisdiction in enforcement proceedings to the courts of the State in which the judgment is to be enforced. **16.14**

JURISDICTION UNDER THE JURISDICTION AND JUDGMENTS REGULATION

The Jurisdiction and Judgments Regulation gives effect to art. 293 of the Treaty establishing the European Community. It is designed to determine the international jurisdiction of the courts of the member States, to facilitate recognition, and to introduce a simple procedure for securing the international enforcement of judgments. Enforcement under the Regulation is considered in **chapter** 77. **16.15**

The main rule (**16.17**) is that a claim must be brought in the courts of the country where the defendant is domiciled. However, there are many types of claim that can be brought in other countries (**16.18 to 16.37**). Where the other country is England, English proceedings may be issued and served without permission. As there is a possibility that the courts of more than one country may have jurisdiction over a case, provision has been made for jurisdiction being declined or subsequent claims being stayed (**16.38** and **16.40**).

Under the 1971 Protocol on the interpretation of the Brussels Convention by the European

Court, questions of interpretation of the Brussels Convention may be referred to the European Court of Justice.

It is important that the Convention is interpreted in the same way in all the contracting States. Obviously, there are many differences in the domestic laws applied in the various contracting States, particularly between the civil and common law systems. The ECJ has therefore regularly decided that legal concepts used in the Convention must be given a 'Community meaning'. This involves attempting to discover shared principles, a far from simple task.

As the Jurisdiction and Judgments Regulation is an act of the institutions of the Community, the European Court of Justice may give preliminary rulings on its interpretation under art. 234 of the EC Treaty (see **chapter** 75) and it may be assumed that the ECJ will interpret the Regulation in the same way as it interpreted the Brussels Convention.

Scope of the Jurisdiction and Judgments Regulation

16.16 The Jurisdiction and Judgments Regulation applies to civil and commercial proceedings whatever the nature of the court or tribunal (**art.** 1, Brussels Convention, art. 1). It does not apply to revenue, customs, social security, insolvency, arbitration or administrative matters, nor to proceedings relating to the status or legal capacity of natural persons, rights in property arising out of a matrimonial relationship, wills and succession. As the ECJ explained in *Marc Rich & Co. AG v Società Italiana Impianti PA* (case C-190/89) [1991] ECR I-3855, arbitration matters were excluded from the scope of the Brussels Convention because they were already covered by international conventions, particularly the New York Convention, 1958. The ECJ held that in order to determine whether a dispute falls within the scope of the Brussels Convention, the court is only entitled to consider the subject matter of the dispute. If the subject matter, such as the appointment of an arbitrator, falls into one of the excluded categories, the existence of a preliminary issue (such as whether the arbitration agreement exists or is valid) could not justify the application of the Brussels Convention. A claim for a declaration that a valid arbitration agreement exists and a claim for an anti-suit injunction restraining proceedings in another member State in breach of an arbitration agreement are both claims to which the Regulation does not apply (*Navigation Maritime Bulgare v Rustal Trading Ltd* [2002] 1 Lloyd's Rep 106).

Domicile: the general rule

16.17 The general rule laid down by the Jurisdiction and Judgments Regulation is that proceedings must be brought in the courts of the country where the defendant is domiciled. **Article** 2 (Brussels Convention, art. 2) provides:

> Subject to this Regulation, persons domiciled in a member State shall, whatever their nationality, be sued in the courts of that member State.

Domicile is defined for the purposes of the Regulation by the Civil Jurisdiction and Judgments Order 2001 (SI 2001/3929), sch. 2, paras 9 to 12. Similar provisions are made for the purposes of the Conventions by the **CJJA 1982, ss. 41 to 46**. The domicile of individuals is governed by SI 2001/3929, sch. 2, para. 9, which provides in sub-para. (2):

> An individual is domiciled in the United Kingdom if and only if—
> (a) he is resident in the United Kingdom; and
> (b) the nature and circumstances of his residence indicate that he has a substantial connection with the United Kingdom.

By sub-para. (6) an individual is presumed to have a substantial connection with the United Kingdom after being resident in the United Kingdom for three months.

For the purposes of CJJA 1982, a corporation's 'seat' is treated as its domicile (s. 42(1)). By s. 42(3):

A corporation or association has its seat in the United Kingdom if and only if—
(a) it was incorporated or formed under the law of a part of the United Kingdom and has its registered office or some other official address in the United Kingdom; or
(b) its central management and control is exercised in the United Kingdom.

Article 60 of the Jurisdiction and Judgments Regulation provides that a corporation is domiciled where it has its 'seat', central administration or principal place of business. A company's seat is its registered office or, if it does not have one, the place where it was incorporated. The 'principal place of business' of a company within art. 60 is the place at the heart of its operations (*King v Crown Energy Trading AG* [2003] EWHC 163 (Comm), *The Times*, 14 March 2003). This can often be determined by listing the important individuals running and working for the company, and identifying where they are based.

The time for judging whether there is a defendant domiciled within the jurisdiction for the purposes of art. 60 is the date of issue, not the date of service (*Canada Trust Co. v Stolzenberg (No. 2)* [2002] 1 AC 1).

Exceptions to the rule that jurisdiction is based on domicile

16.18 Although **art. 2** of the Jurisdiction and Judgments Regulation (Brussels Convention, art. 2) lays down the general rule, a claimant often has a choice of forum under the Regulation. This is because, in a wide variety of cases, the claimant is given the option of suing in another country. **Article 3** of the Regulation (Brussels Convention, art. 3) provides that 'Persons domiciled in a member State may be sued in the courts of another member State only by virtue of the rules set out in sections 2 to 7 of this Chapter'. These sections encompass **arts 5** to **24** of the Regulation. **Article 22** was considered at **16.9** to **16.14**. **Articles 5, 6, 8** to **21** and **23** (Brussels Convention, arts 5 to 15 and 17 and 18) will be considered at **16.19** to **16.37**.

The basic scheme, as confirmed by **CPR, r. 6.19(1A)**, is that the courts of England and Wales will have jurisdiction to hear and determine a claim under the Regulation if:
(a) the case falls within one of the provisions set out in **arts 5** to **24**;
(b) there are no proceedings pending involving the same claim in another part of the United Kingdom or another member State (other than Denmark); and
(c) the defendant is domiciled in a member State (other than Denmark).

Similar provision is made in relation to Denmark, Iceland, Norway, Poland and Switzerland by **CPR, r. 6.19(1)**. The requirement of having a defendant domiciled in a Regulation or Convention State is dispensed with in cases falling within **art. 22** of the Regulation (Brussels Convention, art. 16) (exclusive jurisdiction, see **16.9** to **16.14**) and is modified in cases within **art. 23** (Brussels Convention, art. 17) (jurisdiction clauses, see **16.25**), where the requirement is that *any* one of the parties must be domiciled in a member State.

Contract

16.19 **Main provision** Article 5(1) of the Jurisdiction and Judgments Regulation (Brussels Convention, art. 5(1)) provides in part that a person domiciled in one member State may alternatively 'be sued in matters relating to a contract, in the courts for the place of performance of the obligation in question'.

The Regulation goes on to provide that the place of performance of the obligation in question shall be, in the case of the sale of goods, the place in a member State where, under the contract, the goods were delivered or should have been delivered, and in the case of the provision of services, the place in a member State where, under the contract, the services were provided or should have been provided (**art. 5(1)(b)**). There is no equivalent provision in the Brussels Convention. The revision was introduced by the Regulation to counter criticism that the operation of art. 5(1) of the Brussels Convention tended to give jurisdiction to the courts of the claimant's domicile not the courts of the country with the closest connection to the dispute.

16.20 **Scope of article 5(1)** In *Arcado SPRL v Haviland SA* (case 9/87) [1988] ECR 1539 the ECJ confirmed that, in the **Jurisdiction and Judgments Regulation, art. 5(1)** (Brussels Convention, art. 5(1)), the phrase 'matters relating to a contract':

> . . . is to be regarded as an independent concept which, for the purpose of the application of the Convention, must be interpreted by reference principally to the system and objectives of the Convention in order to ensure that it is fully effective.

In another case in the same year, *Kalfelis v Bankhaus Schröder, Münchmeyer, Hengst & Co.* (case 189/87) [1988] ECR 5565 the ECJ laid down the general principle that the special jurisdiction given by **art. 5** must be interpreted restrictively as it derogates from the principle that jurisdiction is vested in the courts of the country where the defendant is domiciled. An earlier decision of the ECJ, *Martin Peters Bauunternehmung GmbH v Zuid Nederlandse Aannemers Vereniging* (case 34/82) [1983] ECR 987, decided that as membership of an association creates close links between members of the same kind as those between the parties to a contract, jurisdiction over a dispute between an association and one of its members could be given by **art. 5(1)**. The effect is that **art. 5(1)** can be invoked where either there is a contractual relationship giving rise to an actual contract, or there is a consensual obligation similar to a contract giving rise to a comparable obligation.

In *Kleinwort Benson Ltd v Glasgow City Council* [1999] 1 AC 153, the House of Lords held that restitutionary claims based on void contracts did not fall within **art. 5(1)**. Where the only connection with this country is an alleged non-disclosure or misrepresentation in relation to the making of a contract, jurisdiction may be given by **art. 5(1)**. This is because the word 'obligation' in **art. 5(1)** is not limited to contractual obligation, and in suitable cases the objects of the Convention can be achieved by bringing proceedings where the negotiations in a matter related to a contract were conducted (*Agnew v Länsförsäkringsbolagens AB* [2001] 1 AC 223).

In *Effer SpA v Kantner* (case 38/81) [1982] ECR 825 the ECJ held that **art. 5(1)** applies even where the existence of the contract on which the claim is based is disputed by the defendant. Otherwise, a defendant could oust the jurisdiction granted by **art. 5(1)** merely by saying there is a dispute. This decision was interpreted by the Court of Appeal in *Tesam Distribution Ltd v Schuh Mode Team GmbH* [1990] ILPr 149 as meaning that a court cannot accept jurisdiction under **art. 5(1)** on the mere assertion or pleading of the claimant. There must be evidence from which it would be proper to conclude that a contract existed and that the place of performance was the country in which the action was brought. This concept was also applied by the Court of Appeal in *Boss Group Ltd v Boss France SA* [1997] 1 WLR 351 where Saville LJ's judgment is to the effect that a claimant relying on **art. 5(1)** does not have to establish finally and conclusively that the place of performance of the obligation was in England, but does have to establish a 'good arguable case that that was so'.

16.21 **Place of performance of obligation** If the **Jurisdiction and Judgments Regulation, art. 5(1)** (Brussels Convention, art. 5(1)), applies, proceedings may be brought in the courts of 'the place of performance of the obligation in question'. In *Etablissements A. de Bloos SPRL v SCA Bouyer* (case 14/76) [1976] ECR 1497 the ECJ held that the 'obligation' in **art. 5(1)** refers to the contractual obligation forming the basis of the legal proceedings. Regard must be had to the contractual obligation under consideration, and not to the contract as a whole. In *Medway Packaging Ltd v Meurer Maschinen GmbH & Co. KG* [1990] 2 Lloyd's Rep 112 an English claimant brought an action in England against a German defendant alleging the defendant had repudiated an exclusive distribution agreement without giving reasonable notice. It was held, first, that the defendant's alleged obligation to give due notice terminating the contract had to be performed at the claimant's place of business in England. Secondly, the agreement granting the claimant exclusive rights to distribute the defendant's machines was essentially negative in character, and could be broken in either England or Germany. That was held to be sufficient to give the courts in England jurisdiction under **art. 5(1)**. In *MBM Fabri-Clad Ltd v Eisen und Hüttenwerke Thale AG* (1999) LTL 3/11/99, the Court of Appeal held that in a claim for damages for breach of a contract to design, manufacture and supply goods, the obligation in question was the obligation to supply goods which met the contractual specification, rather than the defendant's acts and omissions in Germany which led to the goods failing to meet the specification. Since the goods were to be supplied to the claimant in England, the English courts had jurisdiction under **art. 5(1)**.

Where a claimant brings a claim concerning a number of obligations under a single contract, it is the principal obligation that determines jurisdiction under **art. 5(1)** (*Shenavai v Kreischer* (case 266/85) [1987] ECR 239). This was applied in *Union Transport plc v Continental Lines SA* [1992] 1 WLR 15, where the claimant had claims under a voyage charter for failing to nominate a vessel (which was to be performed in England) and for failure to provide a vessel (which was to be performed in the USA). It was held that nominating a vessel was the principal obligation as it triggered the other contractual obligations, and therefore proceedings had validly been brought in England.

Contracts of employment Articles 18 to 21 of the Jurisdiction and Judgments Regulation deal with jurisdiction over individual contracts of employment and have no equivalent in the Brussels Convention. The Regulation provides that the employee may be sued only in the courts of the member State in which the employee is domiciled (save that a counterclaim may be brought against an employee in the courts where the original claim is pending) (**art. 20**). The employer, on the other hand, under **art. 19**, may be sued either in: **16.22**

(a) the courts where the employer is domiciled; or
(b) in the courts for the place where the employee habitually carries out his or her work, or last did so; or
(c) if the employee does not or did not habitually carry out his or her work in any one country, in the courts for the place where the business which engaged the employee is or was situated.

In any disputes with its employees, an employer who is not domiciled in a member State is deemed to be domiciled in the member State where it operates any branch or agency (**art. 18**, overriding the provisions of **arts 4** and **5(5)**).

The provisions of the Brussels Convention relating to contracts of employment are set out in art. 5(1), which states that:

> . . . in matters relating to individual contracts of employment, [the place of performance of the obligation in question] is that where the employee habitually carries out his work, or if the employee does not habitually carry out his work in any one country, the employer may also be sued in the courts for the place where the business which engaged the employee was or is now situated.

The rights given to employees in the Brussels Convention, and now enhanced in the Regulation, are in accordance with one of the policies of the Convention, carried forward in the Regulation, namely, the protection of the weaker party in contractual relationships. This was emphasised by *Mercury Publicity Ltd v Wolfgang Loerke GmbH* (1991) *The Times*, 21 October 1991, where the Court of Appeal said the rule was restricted to relationships of master and servant of a personal nature, and refused to extend the rule to a contract of commercial agency.

Consumer contracts Articles 15 to 17 of the Jurisdiction and Judgments Regulation (Brussels Convention, arts 13 to 15) apply to consumer contracts, ousting the special jurisdiction granted by **art. 5(1)**. Again, these provisions are designed to protect the weaker **16.23**

party to certain contracts. A restrictive meaning has been given by **art. 15** of the Regulation to the term 'consumer contract'. To qualify as a consumer a party must not have entered the contract in the course of a trade or profession. The contract must then be either:

(a) for the sale of goods on instalment credit terms; or
(b) for a loan repayable by instalments, or for any other form of credit, made to finance the sale of goods; or
(c) concluded with a person who pursues commercial or professional activities in the member State of the consumer's domicile or, by any means, directs such activities to that member State or to several States including that member State, and the contract falls within the scope of such activities.

Article 13 of the Brussels Convention is narrower in that the third alternative is limited to contracts for the supply of goods or services (not transport) entered into in response to advertising or a specific invitation addressed to the consumer.

By **art. 16** of the Regulation (Brussels Convention, art. 14), a consumer acting as a claimant may bring proceedings in the courts where either party is domiciled, but a consumer may only be sued in the courts of the country in which he or she is domiciled.

16.24 **Insurance contracts** Jurisdiction in insurance matters is governed by **arts 8** to **14** of the Jurisdiction and Judgments Regulation (Brussels Convention, arts 7 to 12A), and **art. 5(1)** is ousted. These provisions are designed to protect the insured, who is regarded as being the weaker party in insurance matters. It is not always the case that an insured will be in a weaker negotiating position than the insurer, especially where the insured is a large commercial corporation. Nevertheless, the Court of Appeal held in *New Hampshire Insurance Co. v Strabag Bau AG* [1992] 1 Lloyd's Rep 361 that the concept of 'matters relating to insurance' in these provisions has to be given a literal interpretation, and is not restricted to insurance for domestic or private purposes. However, reinsurance contracts are outside the scope of the provisions (*Universal General Insurance Co. v Group Josi Reinsurance Co. SA* (case C-412/98) [2001] QB 68).

By **arts 9** and **10** (Brussels Convention, arts 8 and 9) an insurer domiciled (or having a branch, agency or establishment) in a member State may be sued:

(a) in the courts of the State where it is domiciled; or
(b) in the courts of the State where the policyholder, insured or beneficiary (in the Brussels Convention only the insured) is domiciled, provided that State is a member State; or
(c) if there are co-insurers, in the courts of a member State where proceedings have been brought against the leading insurer; or
(d) if the case involves liability insurance or insurance over immovable property, in the courts for the place where the harmful event occurred.

The insured is protected by **art. 12** (Brussels Convention, art. 11), which provides that an insurer may bring proceedings only in the courts of the country where the insured is domiciled.

16.25 **Jurisdiction agreements** **Article 23(1)** of the Jurisdiction and Judgments Regulation provides:

> If the parties, one or more of whom is domiciled in a member State, have agreed that a court or the courts of a member State are to have jurisdiction to settle any disputes which have arisen or which may arise in connection with a particular legal relationship, that court or those courts shall have jurisdiction. Such jurisdiction shall be exclusive unless the parties have agreed otherwise. Such an agreement conferring jurisdiction shall be either—
> (a) in writing or evidenced in writing; or
> (b) in a form which accords with practices which the parties have established between themselves; or

(c) in international trade or commerce, in a form which accords with a usage of which the parties are or ought to have been aware and which in such trade or commerce is widely known to, and regularly observed by, parties to contracts of the type involved in the particular trade or commerce concerned.

Article 23(2) goes on to provide that any communication by electronic means which provides a durable record of the agreement shall be equivalent to 'writing'.

Article 17 of the Brussels Convention is in similar terms, save that there is no equivalent to **art.** 23(2) of the Regulation, and, more importantly, a jurisdiction agreement is always deemed to give the court(s) on which it confers jurisdiction exclusive jurisdiction.

In the form of the Regulation which determines jurisdiction within the United Kingdom (Civil Jurisdiction and Judgments Act 1982, sch. 4, para. 12), the sentence 'Such jurisdiction shall be exclusive unless the parties have agreed otherwise' is omitted. Nevertheless, according to the Inner House of the Scottish Court of Session in *McGowan v Summit at Lloyds* (2002) *The Times*, 15 July 2002, construing the modified form of the Brussels Convention which previously determined jurisdiction within the United Kingdom, the parties are still free to agree whether or not their jurisdiction agreement is to confer exclusive jurisdiction, and whether the agreement does so or not is to be determined by the ordinary rules of construction of contracts.

Application of article 23(1) General words of incorporation might be effective to incorporate a jurisdiction clause for the purposes of the Jurisdiction and Judgments Regulation, art. 23(1)(a) (Brussels Convention, art. 17(a)), but will only do so if they clearly and precisely demonstrate the existence of a consensus to that effect (*AIG Europe SA v QBE International Insurance Ltd* [2001] 2 All ER (Comm) 622; *Tradigrain SA v Siat SpA* [2002] CLC 574). **16.26**

In order for **art. 23** (Brussels Convention, art. 17) to apply the parties must have 'agreed' to give jurisdiction to the courts of a member State. *Dresser UK Ltd v Falcongate Freight Management Ltd* [1992] QB 502 concerned a jurisdiction clause in a bill of lading relied on by a bailor of goods against a sub-bailee. Bingham LJ said that the article demands a contract between the parties. Consequently, the clause would operate between the immediate parties to the bill, and between an agent and an immediate party. It would also operate between an immediate party and a party to whom all the rights and obligations under the contract of carriage have been assigned (*Partenreederei ms Tilly Russ v Haven & Vervoebedriff Nova NV* (case 71/83) [1985] QB 931). However, the relationship between a bailor and a sub-bailee does not depend on agreement, so the clause did not satisfy the requirements of **art. 23** (Brussels Convention, art. 17). In *Powell Duffryn plc v Petereit* (case C-214/89) [1992] ECR I-1745 the ECJ held that a jurisdiction clause in the articles of association of a company was to be regarded as being part of a contract for the purposes of **art. 23** (Brussels Convention, art. 17) as between the company and the shareholders and also between the shareholders *inter se*.

The rule in the Brussels Convention that a jurisdiction agreement is always deemed to confer exclusive jurisdiction has caused some problems and has been dropped from the Jurisdiction and Judgments Regulation. It was decided by the ECJ in *Meeth v Glacetal Sarl* (case 23/78) [1978] ECR 2133 that a clause providing that the parties could only be sued in the courts of their respective countries was within art. 17 of the Brussels Convention, despite the risk that two countries could have 'exclusive' jurisdiction if both parties decided to sue. This decision was applied in *Kurz v Stella Musical Veranstaltungs GmbH* [1992] Ch 196, where it was held that a clause giving both parties a choice of suing in either England or Germany was effective under art. 17 of the Brussels Convention. This may be contrasted with *Dresser UK Ltd v Falcongate Freight Management Ltd* [1992] QB 502, where the Court of Appeal applied the *contra proferentem* rule of construction so as to restrict the scope of an ambiguous jurisdiction clause. A contract which provided that the courts of Poland had non-exclusive jurisdiction was held in *Insured Financial Structures Ltd v Elektrocieplownia Tychy SA* [2003] EWCA Civ 110, [2003] QB 1260, to mean that Poland was an alternative jurisdiction to England, which was otherwise granted jurisdiction by the Lugano Convention, so proceedings were validly brought in England.

Article 23(1) of the Regulation (Brussels Convention, art. 17) also lays down certain requirements as to the form of jurisdiction clauses. A distinction is drawn between international trading and commercial contracts and, on the other hand, more general contracts. A jurisdiction clause in a general contract must be in writing or evidenced in writing, or else accord with the practices of the parties. The ECJ held in *Colzani v Rüwa* (case 24/76) [1976] ECR 1831 that if the jurisdiction clause is contained in written standard terms, the contract must contain an express reference to those standard terms. In international trade or commerce, a jurisdiction clause may alternatively be in a form which accords with a widely known usage in that trade or commerce of which the parties are or ought to have been aware.

Article 23(3) of the Regulation (Brussels Convention, art. 17) provides:

> Where such an agreement is concluded by parties, none of whom is domiciled in a member State, the courts of other member States shall have no jurisdiction over their disputes unless the court or courts chosen have declined jurisdiction.

Jurisdiction given by **art.** 23 (Brussels Convention, art. 17) does not take precedence over the rules on *lis pendens* and related actions in **arts** 27 and 28 (Brussels Convention, arts 21 and 22) (see **16.38** and **16.40**), even where there is excessive delay in the first court (*Erich Gasser GmbH v MISAT Srl* (case C-116/02) [2005] QB 1). **Article** 23 (Brussels Convention, art. 17) does take precedence over the provisions of art. 6(2) (see **16.37**) (*Hough v P and O Containers Ltd* [1999] QB 834).

16.27 **Restrictions on jurisdiction clauses** Parties are not completely free to confer jurisdiction by means of jurisdiction clauses. The following restrictions should be noted:

(a) a jurisdiction clause cannot override exclusive jurisdiction conferred by **art.** 22 of the Jurisdiction and Judgments Regulation (Brussels Convention, art. 16) (for which, see **16.9** to **16.14**);
(b) a jurisdiction clause inserted for the benefit of one party may be waived by that party;
(c) in actions relating to individual contracts of employment, consumer contracts and insurance contracts, jurisdiction agreements are only effective (in broad terms) if entered into after the dispute has arisen or if invoked by the employee, consumer or insured (see **arts** 13, 14, 17 and 21 (Brussels Convention, arts 12,12A, 15 and 17));
(d) submission to the jurisdiction (**16.3**) overrides a jurisdiction clause (*Elefanten Schuh GmbH v Jacqmain* (case 150/80) [1981] ECR 1671).

Maintenance

16.28 Article 5(2) of the Jurisdiction and Judgments Regulation (Brussels Convention, art. 5(2)) provides that in matters relating to maintenance, as an alternative to bringing proceedings in the debtor's country of domicile, proceedings may be brought in the courts where the creditor is domiciled or habitually resident or, if the matter is ancillary to proceedings concerning the status of a person, in the court which has jurisdiction to entertain those proceedings (unless that jurisdiction is based solely on nationality). This provision, like several already considered, is designed to protect the financially dependent and hence weaker party.

Tort

16.29 A claim in tort may be brought in the country where the defendant is domiciled, or where the harmful event occurred or, under the Regulation only, where the harmful event may occur (Jurisdiction and Judgments Regulation, **art.** 5(3); Brussels Convention, art. 5(3)).

On the same lines as jurisdiction in contract under **art.** 5(1), the Court of Appeal in *Mölnlycke AB v Procter and Gamble Ltd* [1992] 1 WLR 1112 held that the court has power to filter off frivolous or vexatious use of the jurisdiction given by art. 5(3) by insisting that the claimant must establish a good arguable case on the merits. This test was applied in *Bank of Tokyo-Mitsubishi Ltd v Baskan Gida Sanayi ve Pazarlama AS* [2004] EWHC 945 (Ch), [2004] 2 Lloyd's Rep 395.

Meaning of 'tort' Like matters relating to contract (**16.19**), it is important that the **Jurisdiction and Judgments Regulation, art.** 5(3) (Brussels Convention, art. 5(3)), should be construed consistently in all the contracting States despite differences in the types of conduct regarded as tortious in the various countries. Accordingly, the ECJ in *Kalfelis v Bankhaus Schröder, Münchmeyer, Hengst & Co.* (case 189/87) [1988] ECR 5565 decided that 'tort' must be regarded as an autonomous concept which is to be interpreted by reference to the scheme and objectives of the Brussels Convention. **16.30**

As to what is meant by the independent concept of tort, the ECJ in the *Kalfelis* case said:

> . . . the term 'matters relating to tort, delict or quasi-delict' within the meaning of article 5(3) of the Convention must be regarded as an independent concept covering all actions which seek to establish the liability of a defendant and which are not related to a 'contract' within the meaning of article 5(1).
>
> . . . it must be observed . . . that the 'special jurisdictions' enumerated in articles 5 and 6 of the Convention constitute derogations from the principle that jurisdiction is vested in the courts of the State where the defendant is domiciled and as such must be interpreted restrictively. It must therefore be recognised that a court which has jurisdiction under article 5(3) over an action in so far as it is based on tort or delict does not have jurisdiction over that action in so far as it is not so based.

The first half of this passage has been frequently misunderstood as meaning that **art.** 5(3) is a catch-all provision. Such an interpretation is inconsistent with the second half of the quotation. In fact, the word 'liability' in the first passage must be understood as connoting liability within the scope of **art.** 5(3). 'Mainstream' torts, such as negligence, nuisance, defamation and patent infringement, all come within the definition. A claim that the defendant was constructive trustee of money which, with the dishonest assistance of the defendant, had been taken from the claimant by a senior employee in breach of duty was held to be a matter 'relating to tort, delict or quasi-delict' within **art.** 5(3) in *Casio Computer Co. Ltd v Kaiser* [2001] EWCA Civ 661, LTL 11/4/2001.

Harmful event It was held by the ECJ in *Handelskwekerij G. J. Bier BV v Mines de Potasse d'Alsace SA* (case 21/76) [1978] QB 708 that art. 5(3) of the Brussels Convention gives the claimant the option of commencing proceedings either in the country where the wrongful act or omission took place, or in the country where the damage occurred. The place where the damage occurred is not the place where the damage was quantified or where steps were taken to mitigate the effects of the wrongful conduct of the defendant (*Netherlands v Rüffer* (case 814/79) [1980] ECR 3807). In the Jurisdiction and Judgments Regulation there is the further alternative of commencing proceedings in the country where the harmful event may occur. This alternative is not available in the Brussels Convention and it has been held that in the Convention the 'place where damage occurred' cannot be construed as encompassing any place where adverse consequences of an event which have already caused actual damage elsewhere could be felt (*Marinari v Lloyds Bank plc* (case C-364/93) [1996] QB 217). It therefore does not include a place where a claimant claimed to have suffered loss consequential on initial damage suffered in another contracting State. These principles were applied in *Mazur Media Ltd v Mazur Media GmbH* [2004] EWHC 1566 (Ch), [2004] 1 WLR 2966. **16.31**

In *Shevill v Presse Alliance SA* (case C-68/93) [1995] 2 AC 18 (ECJ); [1996] AC 959 (HL), the claimants commenced proceedings in England against a French defendant complaining that they had been libelled in one of the defendant's newspapers. The newspaper had a daily circulation of 200,000 copies in France, and about 250 copies in England. Their particulars of claim relied only on publication in England. It was held that as the 'harmful event' in art. 5(3) included the place where the damage was suffered, the action had been validly brought in

England, although the English courts had jurisdiction solely in respect of the harm caused in England.

In *Henderson v Jaouen* [2002] EWCA Civ 75, [2002] 1 WLR 2971, the claimant was injured in a road accident in France, and obtained a final award of damages from the civil courts in France. Under French law he was entitled to bring a fresh action, which was regarded in French law as a fresh cause of action, if his injuries subsequently deteriorated. His injuries did deteriorate, and by this time the claimant was living in England. He brought English proceedings based on this deterioration, alleging that the deterioration was a 'harmful event' engaging art. 5(3). The Court of Appeal held that this second claim had to be brought in France, because the 'harmful event' was the original 'tort, delict or quasi-delict', which was the original road traffic accident in France. That was a single event, which had no extraterritorial effect.

The court should adopt a restrictive approach to the application of art. 5 (*Kleinwort Benson Ltd v Glasgow City Council* [1999] 1 AC 153). Applying this principle, it is the place where the tortious event takes place that matters for art. 5(3), not the place where the decision is made to commit the tort (*Anton Durbeck GmbH v Den Norske Bank ASA* (2002) LTL 17/6/2002). Although the decision (in this case, to arrest a ship in Panama, which was alleged to be wrongful interference with goods), which was made in England, was a connecting factor with England, it was not a 'particularly close connecting factor'.

Criminal compensation

16.32 Where a civil claim is made based on an act giving rise to criminal proceedings, jurisdiction is given by **art.** 5(4) of the Jurisdiction and Judgments Regulation (Brussels Convention, art. 5(4)) to the courts of the country dealing with criminal proceedings.

Branches, agencies and establishments

16.33 Article 5(5) of the Jurisdiction and Judgments Regulation (Brussels Convention, art. 5(5)) provides that alternative jurisdiction is given as regards disputes arising out of the operations of a branch, agency or other establishment to the courts for the place in which the branch, agency or other establishment is situated. This provision has been restrictively interpreted. From the Jenard Report and the opinion of the advocate general in *Etablissements A. de Bloos SPRL v SCA Bouyer* (case 14/76) [1976] ECR 1497 it is accepted that the branch, agency or other establishment referred to must be that of the proposed defendant, and the claimant's arrangements in this respect are irrelevant. Further, the mere fact that some person in the country where the claimant wishes to commence proceedings acted as the proposed defendant's agent for the purposes of the law of agency is not enough, on its own, to satisfy **art.** 5(5). 'Agency' must be interpreted *eiusdem generis* with 'branch' and 'establishment'. The effect is that **art.** 5(5) is dealing with emanations of the defendant's business which are subject to the defendant's control and which give the defendant a corporate presence within the relevant jurisdiction. Even if the defendant does have a branch, agency or establishment within the meaning of **art.** 5(5), it is further necessary that the dispute must arise out of the activities of that branch, agency or establishment. This will comprehend, according to *Somafer SA v Saar-Ferngas AG* (case 33/78) [1978] ECR 2183, the following types of activities by the branch, agency or establishment:

(a) management matters, such as the local engagement of staff;
(b) contractual undertakings given in the name of the parent;
(c) tortious and other non-contractual liability.

If a dispute arises out of the operations of a branch, there is no further requirement that the obligation in question must be performed in the State where the branch is situated. So, in *Lloyd's Register of Shipping v Société Campenon Bernard* (case C-439/93) [1995] ECR I-961 the claimant entered into a contract with the French branch of the defendant under which the defendant agreed to do certain work in Spain. The work was carried out by the defendant's Spanish branch. A dispute arose, and proceedings were commenced in France, the claimant relying on **art.** 5(5). The ECJ held the proceedings had been validly commenced in France, and there was no requirement in **art.** 5(5) for performance to be in the State where proceedings were commenced.

It was held in *Anton Durbeck GmbH v Den Norske Bank ASA* [2003] EWCA Civ 147, [2003] QB 1160, applying *Lloyd's Register of Shipping v Société Campenon Bernard* (case C-439/93) [1995] ECR I-961, that there has to be a nexus between the operations of the branch and the dispute to render it natural to describe the dispute as arising out of the operations of the branch. It is, however, unnecessary for the activities of the branch to bring about the harmful event giving rise to the dispute. In contract claims the nexus required could be derived from the negotiations giving rise to the contract. Tort claims vary widely, so whether the necessary nexus exists depends on the facts of the particular case.

Trusts

A settlor, trustee or beneficiary of a trust created by the operation of a statute, or by a written instrument, or created orally and evidenced in writing, may be joined as a party to proceedings brought in the courts of the country where the trust is domiciled (Jurisdiction and Judgments Regulation, **art.** 5(6); Brussels Convention, art. 5(6)). This form of wording excludes implied and constructive trusts. For the purposes of the Brussels Convention, a trust is domiciled in England if English law is the system of law with which the trust has its closest and most real connection (CJJA 1982, s. 45(3)). **16.34**

Salvage and freight

Under **art.** 5(7) of the Jurisdiction and Judgments Regulation (Brussels Convention, art. 5(7)) claims for freight or salvage of cargo may be brought where the freight or cargo has been or could be arrested. **16.35**

Co-defendants

It is provided by **art.** 6(1) of the Jurisdiction and Judgments Regulation (Brussels Convention, art. 6(1)) that a person domiciled in a member State may also be sued, 'where he is one of a number of defendants, in the courts for the place where any one of them is domiciled'. In the Regulation only this is followed by a proviso that the claims must be so closely connected that it is expedient to hear and determine them together to avoid the risk of irreconcilable judgments resulting from separate proceedings. In order to use this provision to join persons domiciled outside England and Wales to a claim against a person domiciled in England and Wales there must, first of all, be a valid claim against the defendant domiciled within the jurisdiction (*The Rewia* [1991] 2 Lloyd's Rep 325). That defendant must have been domiciled here at the time the claim was issued (*Canada Trust Co. v Stolzenberg (No. 2)* [2002] 1 AC 1). It is then necessary to consider whether the joinder is valid. The nature of the connection justifying joinder of a defendant not domiciled in England is given an independent Community meaning, and it is not necessarily enough that the joinder satisfies **CPR, r. 7.3** (for which see **14.2**) (*Kalfelis v Bankhaus Schröder, Münchmeyer, Hengst & Co.* (case 189/87) [1988] ECR 5565). According to the ECJ, the proper use of art. 6(1) of the Brussels Convention is to avoid the risk of irreconcilable judgments and to prevent related actions proceeding in different contracting States. The provisio added to the Regulation makes this principle explicit. *Aiglon Ltd v Gau Shan Co. Ltd* [1993] 1 Lloyd's Rep 164, in so far as it holds that art. 6(1) of the Brussels Convention gives a claimant an unfettered right of choice of forum when one co-defendant is domiciled in England, is inconsistent with *Kalfelis* and must be wrong. **16.36**

In *Société Commerciale de Réassurance v ERAS (International) Ltd (No. 2)* [1995] 2 All ER 278 the applicant issued proceedings seeking injunctions restraining the claimants in four actions pending in the High Court from bringing claims against the applicant in the USA. Two of the claimants were not domiciled in England, and sought declarations that the High

Court had no jurisdiction to grant the proposed injunctions against them. The applicant relied on art. 6(1) as the other claimants were domiciled in England. Potter J held there was no requirement in art. 6(1) for the 'defendants' (in this case the claimants in the four actions) to be jointly liable, or even that the defendants be sued in the same action. The applicant was seeking identical relief against each of the claimants based upon similar acts on the part of each of them, and his lordship held he was permitted to take a broad view of what was meant in *Kalfelis* as to the risk of irreconcilable judgments. On this basis the declarations sought by the foreign claimants were refused, and it was held that the High Court had jurisdiction over all the claimants. This is inconsistent with the decision at first instance of Hirst J in *Barclays Bank plc v Glasgow City Council* [1993] QB 429, where it was held that a number of closely connected, but technically separate, actions did not come within art. 6(1). Whichever decision is correct, it is arguable that consolidated actions satisfy the requirements of art. 6(1).

In *Gascoine v Pyrah* (1991) *The Times*, 26 November 1991, the second defendant, a German veterinary surgeon, was struck out of an English action against an English defendant over the sale of a horse. The reasons for doing so were that the place of performance of the principal obligation was Germany, the event causing the damage occurred in Germany, and there was no real risk of irreconcilable judgments if the first defendant was sued in England and the second defendant was sued in Germany.

Counterclaims and Part 20 proceedings

16.37 By **art. 6(2) and** (3) of the Jurisdiction and Judgments Regulation (Brussels Convention, art. 6(2) and (3)), counterclaims arising from the same contract or facts as those founding the claim, and **Part 20** proceedings, may be brought in the court in which the claimant's claim is pending. In *Kinnear v Falconfilms NV* [1996] 1 WLR 920 a claim was commenced in England by the administrators of an actor's estate against a film company claiming damages arising out of a riding accident during the shooting of a film in Spain. The film company issued an additional claim seeking an indemnity or a contribution against the Spanish hospital that treated the actor, claiming that the actor's death was caused by the negligence of the hospital. It was held that the hospital could be brought in as a third party defendant in the English proceedings, because the nexus required for bringing claims against third parties under what is now **CPR, Part 20** (see **chapter 29**), was in practical terms sufficient to satisfy the requirements of the special jurisdiction conferred by **art. 6(2)**. A cross-claim made by a party who was not an original defendant to the claim is not within the definition of art. 6(3) (*Dollfus Mieg et Cie v CDW International Ltd* (2003) *The Times*, 19 April 2003).

At first instance, it has been held that a contribution notice under **CPR, r. 20.6**, is not a claim form and cannot be served outside the jurisdiction (*Knauf UK GmbH v British Gypsum Ltd* [2002] EWHC 739 (Comm), [2002] 2 Lloyd's Rep 416). Further, a contribution notice will be set aside if the defendant served with the notice ceases to be a defendant by an order setting aside service on that defendant (ibid.).

Lis pendens

16.38 **Article** 27 of the Jurisdiction and Judgments Regulation (Brussels Convention, art. 21) provides:

> (1) Where proceedings involving the same cause of action and between the same parties are brought in the courts of different member States, any court other than the court first seised shall of its own motion stay its proceedings until such time as the jurisdiction of the court first seised is established.
> (2) Where the jurisdiction of the court first seised is established, any court other than the court first seised shall decline jurisdiction in favour of that court.

This article is designed to prevent parallel proceedings before the courts of different contracting States, and to avoid the conflicts that might otherwise result. It is to be interpreted broadly, and covers all situations of *lis pendens*, irrespective of the parties' domicile (*Overseas Union Insurance Ltd v New Hampshire Insurance Co.* (case C-351/89) [1992] QB 434). The phrase 'proceedings involving the same cause of action' must be given an independent Community meaning (*Gubisch Maschinenfabrik KG v Palumbo* (case 144/86) [1987] ECR 4861). The article obviously covers the situation where a claimant brings identical proceedings in two countries. It also covers the situation where a claimant brings proceedings in one country for a declaration that there has been no breach of a contract and the defendant to that action brings proceedings in another country claiming damages for breach of that contract (see *The Maciej Rataj* (case C-406/92) [1994] ECR I-5439). It even covers a case where one party to a contract brings an action for rescission of a contract and the other party to the contract brings proceedings in another country to enforce the same contract. However, **art.** 27 (Brussels Convention, art. 21) only operates to the extent that the parties to the second claim are the same as those in the first.

Court first seised Priority under the **Jurisdiction and Judgments Regulation, art.** 27 (Brussels Convention, art. 21), is given to the court 'first seised'. Under the Brussels Convention, this means, according to the ECJ in *Zelger v Salinitri* (case 129/83) [1984] ECR 2397, the court before which the requirements for proceedings to become definitively pending are first fulfilled. Such requirements are to be determined in accordance with the national law of each of the courts concerned. English actions with no international aspect become pending when proceedings are issued. However, they only become 'definitively' pending when the defendant becomes subject to the court's jurisdiction by service of the originating process (*Dresser UK Ltd v Falcongate Freight Management Ltd* [1992] QB 502). In *Neste Chemicals SA v DK Line SA* [1994] 3 All ER 180 the Court of Appeal held there were no exceptions to this simple rule. Under the **Jurisdiction and Judgments Regulation**, an English court becomes seised when a claim form (or other originating process) is lodged at court for issue, provided the claimant does not subsequently fail to effect service (**art. 30**(1)). Slightly different rules apply in some other Regulation States (**art. 30**(2)) where domestic law requires the originating process to be served before being lodged in court. In such cases the court becomes seised when the document is received by the authority responsible for service, provided the claimant has not subsequently failed to take any required steps to lodge the document with the court. **16.39**

The court should not seek to advance the date on which an English court is seised of the claim for the purposes of the Regulation or the Brussels Convention to prevent the courts in another EU or Convention State from having jurisdiction (*Knauf UK GmbH v British Gypsum Ltd* [2001] EWCA Civ 1570, [2002] 1 WLR 907).

Where an action is brought in one country, and the defendant to that action brings a second action in another country and alleges that the courts of the country first seised have no jurisdiction under the Brussels Convention, the second court may either decline jurisdiction or stay its proceedings to await the outcome of any challenge made to the jurisdiction of the first court. What the second court is not allowed to do is to investigate the jurisdiction of the first court (*Overseas Union Insurance Ltd v New Hampshire Insurance Co.* (case C-351/89) [1992] QB 434). This is so even where there is a choice-of-forum clause conferring jurisdiction on the second court, and even where there are excessive delays in the first court (*Erich Gasser GmbH v MISAT Srl* (case C-116/02) [2005] QB 1).

Related actions

Article 28 of the Jurisdiction and Judgments Regulation (Brussels Convention, art. 22) provides: **16.40**

(1) Where related actions are pending in the courts of different member States, any court other than the court first seised may stay its proceedings. . . .

(3) For the purposes of this article, actions are deemed to be related where they are so closely connected that it is expedient to hear and determine them together to avoid the risk of irreconcilable judgments resulting from separate proceedings.

The Brussels Convention article is expressed to apply only while the actions are pending at first instance.

Article 28 (Brussels Convention, art. 22) is dealing with the area between situations where two claims are the same (where the second claim must be stayed under **art. 27** (Brussels Convention, art. 21)) and situations where it is right for two claims to proceed at the same time. In considering whether to grant a stay, the court must apply the simple test set out in the article, which is designed to cover a range of circumstances. The purpose of art. 28 is to harmonise courts' jurisdiction and avoid irreconcilable judgments (*Sarrio SA v Kuwait Investment Authority* [1999] 1 AC 32). A stay was granted in *Sarrio SA v Kuwait Investment Authority*, where there was an overlap between the issues raised in insolvency proceedings in Spain and later proceedings in England claiming damages for negligent misrepresentation. It would cover a claim *in rem* and a claim *in personam* in respect of the same loss, where technically the parties are not the same (*The Sylt* [1991] 1 Lloyd's Rep 240). It was conceded in *Dresser UK Ltd v Falcongate Freight Management Ltd* [1992] QB 502 that it would cover proceedings for limitation of liability for loss of cargo at sea and a claim for damages for the loss of the same cargo. Once it is held that proceedings are related, the court has a discretion whether to grant a stay, but it will be unusual for the stay to be refused (*The Linda* [1988] 1 Lloyd's Rep 175). In a case where there were two English claims (both of which raised similar questions of English law) and a distantly related action in France, it was held to be a wrong exercise of discretion to stay one of the English claims (so it could be litigated with the French claim), as doing so raised a risk of conflicting decisions (*Abkco Music and Records Inc. v Jodorowsky* [2003] ECDR 3). In *Bank of Tokyo-Mitsubishi Ltd v Baskan Gida Sanayi ve Pazarlama AS* [2004] EWHC 945 (Ch), [2004] 2 Lloyd's Rep 395, the courts in Italy were first seised of proceedings brought by the second defendant against the claimant and the first defendant, claiming that the first defendant was liable in fraud and that the claimant was liable for making unlawful demands for payment. The claimant then issued proceedings in England claiming damages in contract against the first and second claimants and also claims for conspiracy and knowing receipt of trust property and a tracing claim. The court stayed the claims in contract on the grounds of **art. 27**, because the facts and law relied on as the basis of the English claim were substantially the same as in the Italian proceedings, despite differences in formulation and detail. However, it held that neither **art. 27** nor **art. 28** applied to the claimant's tortious claims, as no such claims had been asserted when the Italian proceedings were commenced, and the contractual and tortious claims did not raise any common issues. Nor, for the purposes of **art. 28**, were there any grounds for suggesting that they were so closely connected that it was expedient to hear and determine them together to avoid the risk of irreconcilable judgments.

Interim relief

16.41 The **CJJA 1982, s. 25(1)**, and the Civil Jurisdiction and Judgments Act 1982 (Interim Relief) Order 1997 (SI 1997/302) confer on the High Court in England power to grant interim relief in the absence of substantive proceedings, provided proceedings have been or will be commenced in another jurisdiction (see **38.6**).

Section 25 is not confined to freezing injunctions, subsection (7) defining 'interim relief' as relief of any kind which the court has power to grant in proceedings within its jurisdiction other than warrants for arrest and orders for obtaining evidence. It is perhaps doubtful whether the definition includes security for costs (*Bank Mellat v Helliniki Techniki SA* [1984] QB 291).

PROCEDURE ON COMMENCING PROCEEDINGS PURSUANT TO THE REGULATION OR CONVENTIONS

A claim form may be served on a defendant out of the jurisdiction, without the court's permission, if each claim being made against that defendant can be determined by the court under **CJJA 1982 (CPR, r. 6.19(1))**, or the **Jurisdiction and Judgments Regulation (CPR, r. 6.19(1A))** or any other enactment (**r. 6.19(2)**). The only formality is that the claim form must contain a statement of the grounds on which the claimant is entitled to serve it out of the jurisdiction (**r. 16.19(3)**). **Paragraphs 1.1** to 1.3D of **PD 6B** provide standard wordings for the required statement in various situations. A claim form which is issued against a defendant who appears to be out of the jurisdiction, but which does not contain a statement of the grounds for entitlement to serve outside, will be marked 'not for service out of the jurisdiction' (**PD 6B, para. 1.4**). A failure to comply with **CPR, r. 6.19**, can be cured under **r. 3.10** where there is no prejudice to the defendant (*Bank of Tokyo-Mitsubishi Ltd v Baskan Gida Sanayi ve Pazarlama AS* [2004] EWHC 945 (Ch), [2004] 2 Lloyd's Rep 395). **16.42**

ASSUMED JURISDICTION

The rules discussed at **16.44** to **16.53** deal with the situation where it is desired to serve English proceedings on a defendant outside the jurisdiction in proceedings outside the scope of the **Jurisdiction and Judgments Regulation** or the Brussels and Lugano Conventions. Under the old RSC, leave was needed both to issue and to serve proceedings out of the jurisdiction. Under the CPR, permission is no longer needed to issue a claim form intended for service out of the jurisdiction (although until permission to serve is granted it will be stamped 'not for service out of the jurisdiction': **PD 6B, para. 1.4**). Nevertheless, the former practice continues, and the Queen's Bench Guide makes clear that a claimant may either issue his claim form for service abroad first and then apply for permission to serve (in which case the court will stamp the claim form 'not for service out of the jurisdiction') or may apply for permission to issue a claim form for service out of the jurisdiction in the old way (**Queen's Bench Guide, paras 4.2.11** and **4.2.14**). However, permission is still required to serve a claim form out of the jurisdiction if an English court does not have jurisdiction under the **Jurisdiction and Judgments Regulation** or the Conventions. **16.43**

Basic principles governing applications for permission

The requirements that need to be satisfied if the English courts are to grant permission to serve proceedings outside the jurisdiction under the court's assumed jurisdiction were laid down by the House of Lords in *Seaconsar Far East Ltd v Bank Markazi Jomhouri Islami Iran* [1994] 1 AC 438 and modified by **CPR, r. 6.21(1)(b)**. The intending claimant must establish that: **16.44**

(a) There is a good arguable case that the court has jurisdiction within one of the 18 grounds set out in **CPR, r. 6.20**. These are discussed at **16.46** to **16.52**. The need to show a good arguable case is not as strict a requirement as satisfying the court to the civil standard of proof (*Agrafax Public Relations Ltd v United Scottish Society Inc.* (1995) *The Times*, 22 May 1995).

(b) There is a reasonable prospect of success on the merits (**r. 6.21(1)(b)**, modifying the *Seaconsar* test that there should be a serious issue to be tried). Before *Seaconsar* it was generally thought that the intending claimant had the rather more onerous task of showing a 'good arguable case' on the merits. Judges have tended to be rather lax in their use of expressions such as 'good arguable case', 'dispute which can properly be heard' and 'reasonable prospect of success' (see the almost interchangeable use of these expressions in *MRG (Japan) Ltd v Englehard Metals Japan Ltd* [2003] EWHC 3418 (Comm), LTL 2/1/2004). In *Ophthalmic Innovations International (UK) Ltd v Ophthalmic Innovations International Inc.* [2004] EWHC 2948 (Ch), LTL 4/1/2005, Lawrence Collins J commented that the test under

r. 6.21(1)(b) of a 'reasonable prospect of success' is unlikely to be any different to the requirement under RSC, ord. 11, of a serious question to be tried or a substantial question of fact or law or both.

(c) The case is a proper one for service outside the jurisdiction. This is considered further at **16.53**.

Obviously, putting a foreigner to the inconvenience of defending an action in this country is a serious matter, so the courts have always exercised the power to allow service abroad with caution.

Procedure on seeking permission

16.45 As there is no defendant on the record, an application for permission to serve a claim form out of the jurisdiction, or to issue a claim form for service out of the jurisdiction, should be made without notice. There will be no hearing. In the RCJ, a copy of the application notice and evidence in support should be left in the Master's Secretary's Department, room E16.

The evidence must state, according to **CPR, r. 6.21**:

(a) the grounds on which the application is made and the paragraph or paragraphs of **r. 6.20** relied on;

(b) that the claimant believes that the claim has a reasonable prospect of success;

(c) the defendant's address, or, if that is not known, in what place or country the defendant is or is likely to be found;

(d) where the application is made under **r. 6.20(3)** (that the defendant is a necessary and proper party), the grounds for believing that there is a real issue between the claimant and the existing defendant which it is reasonable for the court to try.

The procedure is summarised in **procedural checklist 12 in appendix 1**.

Because service out of the jurisdiction is an assertion of extra-territorial jurisdiction which could have international repercussions, it was the rule under RSC, ord. 11, that irregularities should be cured only in exceptional cases (*Camera Care Ltd v Victor Hasselblad AB* [1986] 1 FTLR 348). In *Ophthalmic Innovations International (UK) Ltd v Ophthalmic Innovations International Inc.* [2004] EWHC 2948 (Ch), LTL 4/1/2005, Lawrence Collins J stated that the same principle applies under the CPR.

As the application is made initially without notice, the claimant is under an obligation to make full and frank disclosure of all material facts. In deciding whether that duty has been complied with, the primary question is whether in all the circumstances the effect of the evidence in support of the application is such as to mislead the court in any material respect concerning its jurisdiction and the discretion under the rules (*BP Exploration Co. (Libya) Ltd v Hunt* [1976] 1 WLR 788). The existence of overlapping proceedings in a foreign jurisdiction between the same or related parties (whether pending or prospective) is likely to be a particularly relevant matter which in normal circumstances must be disclosed, and the non-disclosure of which may well lead to the order for permission being set aside (*Konamaneni v Rolls-Royce Industrial Power (India) Ltd* [2002] 1 WLR 1269. The failure fully to disclose concurrent proceedings in the United States in the witness statement in support of the claimant's application to serve out of the jurisdiction was one reason why service was ordered to be set aside in *Ophthalmic Innovations International (UK) Ltd v Ophthalmic Innovations International Inc.* [2004] EWHC 2948 (Ch), LTL 4/1/2005.

Grounds for granting permission

16.46 **General interpretation** The grounds in **CPR, r. 6.20**, were formerly in RSC, ord. 11, r. 1(1), and have been amended several times over the years. The grounds were reformulated in 1983 and again in 2000, so some caution is necessary with earlier case law. However, it is likely that case law on the basic principles governing applications for permission to serve a claim form out of the jurisdiction remains valid.

As **r. 6.20** allows the court to exercise an exorbitant jurisdiction, its provisions are to be strictly construed in favour of the foreigner (*The Hagen* [1908] P 189). Furthermore, the case must fall within the overall purposes of the rule, not merely its strict letter (*Johnson v Taylor Bros and Co.* [1920] AC 144). Service out is not allowed unless the claim falls into one or other of the grounds set out in the rule (*Holland v Leslie* [1894] 2 QB 346), and there must be a good arguable case that this is so. Although the claimant can choose which ground or grounds to rely on (*Matthews v Kuwait Bechtel Corporation* [1959] 2 QB 57), the claimant must specifically state those grounds in the evidence in support of the application, and will not be permitted to raise alternative grounds on a defendant's application to discharge the order granting permission (*Metall und Rohstoff AG v Donaldson Lufkin and Jenrette Inc.* [1990] 1 QB 391). The principle was followed in *United Film Distribution Ltd v Chhabria* [2001] EWCA Civ 416, [2001] 2 All ER (Comm) 865. An attempt by charterers to bring interpleader proceedings against a non-resident party for the purpose of compelling that party not just to pursue a claim against the interpleading party in this jurisdiction but also to pursue a dispute with the others who had competing claims against the interpleading party failed in *Cool Carriers AB v HSBC Bank USA* [2001] 2 Lloyd's Rep 22, because **r. 6.20** is concerned with claims asserted by, not against, the claimant.

An application, made before the end of the six months allowed for service of a claim form, for permission to serve it out of the jurisdiction is governed by **rr. 6.20** and **6.21**, not by **r. 7.6(3)** (*Anderton v Clwyd County Council (No. 2)* [2002] EWCA Civ 933, [2002] 1 WLR 3174).

Domicile A claim form may be served out of the jurisdiction if the claim is for a remedy against a person domiciled within the jurisdiction (**CPR, r. 6.20(1)**). **Article 2 of the Jurisdiction and Judgments Regulation** (Brussels Convention, art. 2) permits a person to be sued where domiciled, and, by CPR, **r. 6.18(g)**, domicile for the purposes of **r. 6.20** is to be determined: **16.47**

(a) in relation to EU States other than Denmark, in accordance with the **Jurisdiction and Judgments Regulation** and the Civil Jurisdiction and Judgments Order 2001 (SI 2001/3929), sch. 2, paras 9 to 12, and
(b) in relation to Denmark, Iceland, Norway, Poland (until 30 April 2004) and Switzerland, by the rules in the CJJA 1982, ss. 41 to 46.

Injunctions and interim relief The injunction referred to in **CPR, r. 6.20(2)**, has to be final as opposed to interim (*The Siskina* [1979] AC 210). The injunction must be the real form of relief sought, and must not simply be tacked on in order to found jurisdiction (*Rosler v Hilbery* [1925] Ch 250). **16.48**

However, the **CJJA 1982, s. 25(1)** (see **16.41**), enables the court to grant interim relief in the absence of substantive proceedings, regardless of whether the defendant is domiciled in a country which is a party to the Brussels or Lugano Conventions. Since **r. 6.20(2)** of the CPR applies only to final injunctions, **r. 6.20(4)** enables the court to permit service out of the jurisdiction in such cases where the defendant is not resident in a Convention country.

Necessary or proper party Rule 6.20(3) of the CPR may be compared with **art. 6(1) of the Jurisdiction and Judgments Regulation** (Brussels Convention, art. 6(1)) (**16.36**). It is no longer a requirement, as it was under RSC, ord. 11, that the claim form be served before making the application to join a defendant as a necessary or proper party. The ground in **CPR, r. 6.20(3)**, applies where 'a claim is made against someone on whom the claim form has been or will be served (otherwise than in reliance on this paragraph)'. The words in parentheses were added with effect from 1 October 2004. They make clear that **r. 6.20(3)** only permits the claimant to join a defendant to proceedings brought against another defendant against whom jurisdiction can be established in reliance on some other provision. The claimant's evidence must depose to the grounds for believing that there is a real issue which it is reasonable for the court to try between the claimant and the defendant (see **16.45**). Once this has been established, the claimant must further show that the second defendant is a **16.49**

necessary and proper party to the action. There is particular reluctance to allow service under this paragraph given its anomaly (in relation to the other grounds) in not being founded upon any territorial connection between the claim and the jurisdiction of the English courts (*Multinational Gas and Petrochemical Co. v Multinational Gas and Petrochemical Services Ltd* [1983] Ch 258). However, a claim against a foreign defendant could be brought under the old RSC, ord. 11, provided it was bona fide and constituted a good cause of action, even if the predominant reason for including the English defendant was to found an application against a foreign defendant (*Multinational Gas and Petrochemical Co. v Multinational Gas and Petrochemical Services Ltd* [1983] Ch 258). This approach was followed in relation to **CPR, r. 6.20(3)**, by *Credit Agricole Indosuez v Unicof Ltd* [2003] EWHC 2676 (Comm), [2004] 1 Lloyd's Rep 196. An example of where **r. 6. 20(3)** might be used is where a partnership has been served in England, and it is sought to serve a foreign partner (*West of England Steamship Owners' Protection and Indemnity Association Ltd v John Holman and Sons* [1957] 1 WLR 1164).

In *Petróleo Brasileiro SA v Mellitus Shipping Inc.* [2001] 2 Lloyd's Rep 203, the Court of Appeal held that in deciding whether or not to permit service outside the jurisdiction on a defendant on the ground that it was a necessary and proper party, the court could have regard to the fact that the competing foreign jurisdiction did not recognise a right to contribution. In *United Film Distribution Ltd v Chhabria* [2001] EWCA Civ 416, [2001] 2 All ER (Comm) 865, the Court of Appeal held that the ground for serving a defendant out of the jurisdiction, that it is a necessary and proper party, is the same as would justify adding a party to existing proceedings under **r. 19.2**. The court's power to add a party under **r. 19.2** is no narrower than it was under its predecessors, RSC, ord. 15, rr. 4.4(1) and 6(2)(b). Where, as in this case, the claims give rise to common questions of fact and arise out of the same series of transactions, permission would be granted. The decision in *United Film Distribution Ltd v Chhabria* has been followed in *Trumann Investment Group Ltd v Societe Generale SA* [2004] EWHC 1769 (Ch), LTL 3/9/2004, and in *Philips Domestic Appliances and Personal Care BV v Salton Europe Ltd* [2004] EWHC 2092 (Ch), (2004) LTL 30/7/2004. In *C Inc. plc v L* [2001] 2 Lloyd's Rep 459, the Commercial Court gave permission for a husband, who was liable under the terms of an indemnity to his wife, to be served out of the jurisdiction on the ground that he was a necessary and proper party to the claim against his wife.

By **r. 6.20(3A)**, permission may be given to serve a claim form for an additional claim on persons who are necessary and proper parties to that claim.

16.50 **Contract** Claims under **CPR, r. 6.20(5)**, presuppose the existence of a contract between the claimant and the defendant. Claims seeking a declaration that such a contract never existed fall instead under **r. 6.20(7)**.

Rule 6.20(5)(a) has no equivalent in the Jurisdiction and Judgments Regulation or the Brussels Convention. Whether a contract was made within the jurisdiction depends on general contractual principles (see *Brinkibon Ltd v Stahag Stahl und Stahlwarenhandelsgesellschaft mbH* [1983] 2 AC 34). This case involved an exchange of telexes between parties in different countries. It was held that the contract was made in the country where the telex accepting the offer was received. A contract made within the jurisdiction which is subsequently amended outside the jurisdiction still comes within **r. 6.20(5)(a)** unless the amendment substitutes a new contract (*BP Exploration Co. (Libya) Ltd v Hunt* [1976] 1 WLR 788). Unlike **art. 5(5)** of the Regulation (Brussels Convention, art. 5(5)) (**16.33**), **r. 6.20(5)(b)** is given a wide interpretation, and even includes a case where the defendant's London agent merely sent the claimant the defendant's price list and forwarded the claimant's order to the defendant (*National Mortgage and Agency Co. of New Zealand Ltd v Gosselin* (1922) 38 TLR 832). The 'agent', however, must be that of the defendant, not the claimant (*Union International Insurance Co. Ltd v Jubilee Insurance Co. Ltd* [1991] 1 WLR 415). There is no equivalent to **r. 6.20(5)(c)**, that the contract is governed by English law, in the Regulation or the Brussels Convention. An express term to this effect should not cause difficulties. An implication that a contract is governed by

English law may arise by course of dealings where earlier transactions between the parties were governed by English law (*Banque Paribas v Cargill International SA* [1992] 1 Lloyd's Rep 96). An express jurisdiction clause (**r. 6.20(5)(d)**) will almost always be given effect by the courts (compare **16.25**), but there are sometimes questions as to whether the claimant is a party entitled to rely on the clause in cases where there are interlocking contracts (see, for example, *The Mahkutai* [1996] AC 650).

Rule 6.20(6), breach within the jurisdiction, should be compared with **art. 5(1)** of the Regulation (Brussels Convention, art. 5(1)) (see **16.19**). Where the breach consists of a failure to perform a contractual obligation, it is necessary to find the place where performance should have taken place (*Brinkibon Ltd v Stahag Stahl und Stahlwarenhandelsgesellschaft mbH* [1983] 2 AC 34).

Tort Jurisdiction in tort under **CPR, r. 6.20(8)**, has been modelled on the Brussels Convention, art. 5(3) (see **16.29**). Jurisdiction may be founded either on the basis of damage being suffered in England or through the tortious act being committed in England. In a case on the meaning of RSC, ord. 11, r. 1(1)(f), the predecessor to **CPR, r. 6.20(8)**, the Court of Appeal held that it was sufficient if the cause of action in substance arose in England. If separate acts constituting a single tort were committed here and abroad, the question was whether the tort was in substance committed within the jurisdiction (*Metall und Rohstoff AG v Donaldson Lufkin and Jenrette Inc.* [1990] 1 QB 391). In *Booth v Phillips* [2004] EWHC 1437 (Comm), [2004] 1 WLR 3292, the court considered the meaning of the word 'damage' in **r. 6.20(8)**, and stated that it should be given its natural and ordinary meaning. It referred to harm which had been sustained by the claimant, whether physical or economic, and it was sufficient if some damage (not necessarily all of the damage) was sustained within the jurisdiction. There was no requirement that the damage sustained within the jurisdiction should be that which completed the cause of action. **16.51**

Trusts The equivalent to **CPR, r. 6.20(11)**, in the Jurisdiction and Judgments Regulation is **art. 5(6)** (Brussels Convention, art. 5(6)) (see **16.34**). **Rule 6.20(11)** may be used against an absconding trustee even after trust assets have been removed from the jurisdiction. Like **art. 5(6)**, **r. 6.20(11)** is restricted to trusts under written instruments. The provision now in **r. 6.20(14)** was added in 1990 to allow claims arising from acts committed within the jurisdiction to be brought in England against constructive trustees who cannot be served within the jurisdiction. There has to be evidence that substantial and efficacious acts had been committed within the jurisdiction (*Nycol (UK) Ltd v Lacey* [1994] CLC 11). **16.52**

The proper place to bring the claim (*forum conveniens*)

It is provided in **CPR, r. 6.21(2A)**, that the court will not give permission for service out of the jurisdiction 'unless satisfied that England and Wales is the proper place in which to bring the claim', i.e., is the *forum conveniens*. The leading case is *Spiliada Maritime Corporation v Cansulex Ltd* [1987] AC 460. The claimant shipowner sought permission to serve English proceedings on Canadian sulphur exporters, claiming damages in respect of severe corrosion to the hold of the claimant's ship, the *Spiliada*, allegedly caused by a cargo of wet sulphur. An almost identical claim, *The Cambridgeshire*, had just reached trial in England. The defendants in both claims were the same, and the claimants in both claims had the same insurer (through subrogation, the insurer rather than the nominal claimants had the real interest in bringing the actions). *The Cambridgeshire* was in the nature of a test case. The scientific investigations made approached the limits of scientific knowledge. The claimant's experts came from England, whereas the defendant had instructed two English and four foreign experts. A total of 15 counsel were instructed, each being armed with 75 files of evidence and documents, and the trial was estimated for six months. Many of the potential witnesses of fact would be Canadian, but many witnesses would come from other places (the *Spiliada* was registered in Liberia). **16.53**

Lord Goff of Chieveley laid down the general principle that the court has to identify the forum in which the case can be most suitably tried in the interests of all the parties and for the ends of justice. The burden of proof rests on the claimant to show that England is clearly the most appropriate place for the trial of the action. Factors to be considered by the court when deciding whether to exercise its discretion to grant permission include the residence or place of business of the defendant and the ground invoked by the claimant. The availability of legal aid (or its equivalent) is, however, irrelevant, see *Connelly v RTZ Corporation plc* [1996] QB 361. The weight to be attached to the relevant factors depends on all the circumstances of the case. As Lord Goff said:

> . . . the defendant's place of residence may be no more than a tax haven to which no great importance should be attached. It is also significant to observe that the circumstances specified in ord. 11, r. 1(1), as those in which the court may exercise its discretion to grant leave to serve proceedings on the defendant outside the jurisdiction, are of great variety, ranging from cases where, one would have thought, the discretion would normally be exercised in favour of granting leave (e.g., where the relief sought is an injunction ordering the defendant to do or refrain from doing something within the jurisdiction) to cases where the grant of leave is far more problematical. In addition, the importance to be attached to any particular ground invoked by the plaintiff may vary from case to case. For example, the fact that English law is the putative law of the contract may be of very great importance (as in *BP Exploration Co. (Libya) Ltd v Hunt* [1976] 1 WLR 788, where, in my opinion, Kerr J rightly granted leave to serve proceedings on the defendant out of the jurisdiction); or it may be of little importance as seen in the context of the whole case.

On the facts, the extent and depth of preparation undertaken in *The Cambridgeshire* proceedings, and the fact that English law was the proper law of the contract, meant that England was the appropriate forum, and permission to serve outside the jurisdiction was granted. The doctrine of *forum non conveniens* will be considered further at **16.65** to **16.70**.

An English court may have jurisdiction to hear a derivative claim concerning a foreign company in an appropriate case, and if so, it will give permission for the claim form to be served on the company out of the jurisdiction, because the company is a necessary party to the claim (**CPR, r. 6.20(3)(b)**; *Konamaneni v Rolls-Royce Industrial Power (India) Ltd* [2002] 1 WLR 1269). However, the courts of the place of incorporation of a company will almost invariably be the most appropriate forum for determining whether a shareholder may sue on behalf of the company (*Konamaneni v Rolls-Royce Industrial Power (India) Ltd*). In *SMAY Investments Ltd v Sachdev* [2003] EWHC 474 (Ch), [2003] 1 WLR 1973, the court held, following *Konamaneni*, that the appropriate forum for the resolution of a dispute about the ownership of, and investment in, an Indian company was India, despite the existence of an agreement made in England to provide financial assistance to the company.

In *King v Lewis* [2004] EWCA Civ 1329, [2005] EMLR 4, the court considered the appropriate forum to hear a claim in relation to a libel published on the Internet. For a tort claim, the starting point for ascertaining the most appropriate forum is to identify the place where the tort was committed. The alleged defamation had occurred in England when the libel had been viewed on a computer here, and permission to serve out had been obtained on the basis of publication here. But the more tenuous the claimant's connection with this jurisdiction (and the more substantial the publication abroad) the weaker this consideration would become. Whilst every case would depend on its own circumstances, the court's discretion would have to be more open-textured in order to give effect to the publisher's choice of a global medium.

SERVICE ABROAD

Effecting service abroad

It is provided in **CPR, r. 6.24**, that service abroad must be effected either: **16.54**

(a) by a method permitted by the law of the country in which it is to be served (**r. 6.24(1)(a)**); or

(b) through diplomatic channels, judicial authorities or British consular authorities under the provisions of the Hague Convention or of a bilateral convention or of the EU Service Regulation (**Council Regulation (EU) No. 1348/2000**) (see **16.57** and **16.58**) (**CPR, r. 6.24(1)(b)** and (c)); or

(c) in the case of a State, under the rules set out in **r. 6.27** (see **16.56**).

In practice, this means that as an alternative to service through diplomatic channels, service may be effected informally by the claimant, provided this is permitted under local law. **Rule 6.24(1)(a)**, permitting such service, should be applied with a reasonable degree of flexibility when applied to foreign systems of law. The burden of proof lies on the claimant to show, by expert evidence, what the requirements of local law are and that the method of service adopted complied with them (*Arros Invest Ltd v Nishanov* [2004] EWHC 576 (Ch), LTL 24/3/2004). A default judgment entered following service which was not effected in accordance with local law will be set aside as of right under **r. 13.2** (*Credit Agricole Indosuez v Unicof Ltd* [2003] EWHC 77 (Comm), LTL 4/2/2003). In *Shiblaq v Sadikoglu (No. 2)* [2004] EWHC 1890 (Comm), LTL 16/8/2004 it was held that none of **rr. 3.10**, **6.8** or **6.9** should normally be used if their deployment is for the purpose of substituting a form of service or avoiding a defect in service which is inconsistent with a service convention binding as between England and Wales and the country of service. Likewise, in *Knauf UK GmbH v British Gypsum Ltd* [2001] EWCA Civ 1570, [2002] 1 WLR 907, the court declined to make an order for service by an alternative method under **r. 6.8** where it would have the effect of advancing the date on which the English court was seised of the claim which would prevent the courts of another EU or Convention State from having jurisdiction. However, in *Phillips v Symes* [2005] EWHC 1880 (Ch), LTL 26/8/2005, the court held that it retained a discretion under **r. 6.9** to dispense with service in international cases. The discretion should be exercised only in exceptional cases, and what these were would depend on the facts of the particular case. Here, errors in service in Switzerland by the court office in removing the claim form from the package to be served on one defendant and by the Swiss post office in failing to serve the claim form at the right address in the case of another defendant justified the making of orders dispensing with service and holding that the English court was definitively seised of proceedings on the date when the package from which the claim form had been removed was served.

Scotland Service in Scotland can be undertaken only by a messenger-at-arms (appropriate for High Court claims) or a sheriff officer (appropriate for county court claims). Further information is available on the website of the Society of Messengers-at-Arms and Sheriff Officers at: www.ednet.co.uk/psmaso/. **16.55**

Service on a foreign State Service of a claim form or any other document on a foreign State must be effected in the manner set out in **r. 6.27**. A request for service, a copy of the claim form and a certified translation of it, must be filed in the Foreign Process Department, RCJ (room E10). The Senior Master will send the documents filed to the Foreign and Commonwealth Office to be transmitted to the Ministry of Foreign Affairs of the State which is to be served. Service is deemed to have been effected when the claim form or other document is received at the Ministry (State Immunity Act 1978, s. 12(1)). **16.56**

A foreign State may agree to an alternative method of service. Where it does, service may be effected either under the provisions of **CPR, r. 6.27**, or by the agreed method (**r. 6.27(6)**).

Service through diplomatic channels under the Hague Convention

16.57 The United Kingdom is one of the 52 contracting States to the Hague Convention on the Service Abroad of Judicial and Extra-judicial Documents in Civil or Commercial Matters (1965) ('the Hague Convention'). Each contracting State has designated a central authority to receive and transmit requests for service from other contracting States. A claim form may be served in another contracting State either through the central authority in the State in question, or, if permitted by the law of that country, through the judicial authorities of that country or the British consular authority in that country (**CPR, r. 6.25(1)**). The member States of the EU (apart from Austria and Malta) are also parties to the Hague Convention, but as between all of the EU States except Denmark the provisions of the EU Service Regulation (**Council Regulation** (EU) **No. 1348/2000**, see **16.59**) prevail over the provisions of the Hague Convention (Service Regulation, art. 20). The Service Regulation also applies to the French overseas departments of French Guiana, Guadeloupe, Martinique and Réunion, which are part of the EU territory. The Netherlands and the United Kingdom have extended the operation of the Hague Convention to some of the overseas countries and territories for which they are responsible and which are not part of the EU territory, so that the Service Regulation does not apply to them. The countries in which English process may be served under the Hague Convention are listed in **table 16.2**. The text of the Convention and the declarations of the contracting States on the details of how it applies in their territories can be seen on the website of the Hague Conference on Private International Law: www.hcch.net.

Table 16.2 Countries in which English process may be served under the Hague Convention. In case of doubt contact the Foreign Process Department, RCJ, room E10 (telephone (020) 7947 6691; fax (020) 7947 6237), or consult the Hague Conference website, www.hcch.net

Anguilla, Antigua and Barbuda, Argentina, Aruba, Bahamas, Barbados, Belarus, Bermuda, Botswana, British Virgin Islands, Bulgaria, Canada, Cayman Islands, China, Denmark, Egypt, Falkland Islands and dependencies, Gibraltar, Guernsey, Hong Kong SAR, Israel, Isle of Man, Japan, Jersey, Republic of Korea, Kuwait, Macau SAR, Malawi, Mexico, Montserrat, Norway, Pakistan, Pitcairn, Romania, Russian Federation, San Marino, Seychelles, Sri Lanka, St Helena and dependencies, St Vincent and the Grenadines, Switzerland, Turkey, Turks and Caicos Islands, Ukraine, United States of America, Venezuela

By **CPR, rr. 6.26(2)**, **6.28** and **6.29**, and **PD 6B, paras 1.5**, **2** and **4**, the following documents should be filed at the Foreign Process Department, RCJ, room E10 for onward transmission to the central authority in the receiving country:

(a) request for service;
(b) the claim form, plus a duplicate for every defendant to be served;
(c) particulars of claim, and any documents accompanying them, where these are to be served with the claim form;
(d) the response pack (**form N9**), or **form N1C** (notes for defendants) where the claim form is served without particulars of claim — both **form N9** and **N1C** must be amended to show the relevant deadline for filing the acknowledgment and/or the defence;
(e) unless the claim form is to be served in a country where English is an official language or on a British subject, a certified translation into the language of the jurisdiction where service is to be effected of the claim form, particulars of claim and **form N9** or **N1C**; and
(f) an undertaking to be responsible for the expenses incurred by the Foreign and Commonwealth Office.

Service under a bilateral civil procedure convention

16.58 The United Kingdom has entered into bilateral conventions for service of proceedings with the countries listed in **table 16.3** where the Service Regulation (see **16.59**) does not apply.

A claim form may be served in a country in **table 16.3** either through the judicial authorities of that country or through a British consul, subject to any provisions of the applicable convention governing the nationality of a person who may be served by a British consul (**CPR, r. 6.25(2)**).

As in Hague Convention cases (see **16.57**), the documents to be served should be filed in the Foreign Process Section for onward transmission. The documents are the same as in Hague Convention cases.

Table 16.3 Countries party to bilateral civil procedure conventions with the UK. In case of doubt contact the Foreign Process Department, RCJ, room E10 (telephone (020) 7947 6691; fax (020) 7947 6237), or consult the Foreign and Commonwealth website, www.fco.gov.uk

Denmark, Iraq, Israel, Lebanon, Norway, Romania, Switzerland, Turkey, (Yugoslavia — convention continues to apply to Bosnia-Herzegovena, Croatia and Yugoslavia FR)

Service under the EU Service Regulation

The Service Regulation (**Council Regulation (EU) No. 1348/2000**) came into force on 31 May 2001, and binds all EU member States with the exception of Denmark, to which it does not apply. The Service Regulation applies to service between member States of documents in civil and commercial matters. The full text of the Regulation is on the CD-ROM version of *Blackstone's Civil Practice*. As between EU States other than Denmark, the Service Regulation supersedes all earlier treaties including any earlier bilateral conventions and the Hague Convention (Service Regulation, art. 20). **16.59**

The Service Regulation requires member States to establish transmitting and receiving agencies to effect service of judicial documents (art. 2(1) and (2)). Under the Service Regulation, documents are transmitted directly between courts, without going through a central authority as under the Hague Convention. For England and Wales the transmitting and receiving agency is the Foreign Process Department, room E10, in the RCJ (telephone (020) 7947 6691; fax (020) 7947 6237). To achieve service under the Service Regulation the claimant must file with the claim form any translations and other documents required by the Service Regulation (**CPR, r. 6.26A(2)**). The court officer will then seal the copy of the claim form and forward the documents to the Senior Master (**r. 6.26A(3)**). The documents will then be transmitted to the receiving agency in the State where they are to be served and that agency will serve them.

The Service Regulation attempts to deal with the delays which are often inherent in other methods of service through formal channels by providing that the receiving agency must send a receipt for any document it receives to the transmitting agency as soon as possible, and in any event within seven days of receipt (art. 6(1)). All steps necessary to effect service must be taken as soon as possible, and the receiving agency must notify the transmitting agency if it has not proved possible to effect service within one month of receipt (art. 7(2)).

Article 9 establishes a mechanism for calculating the date of service of a document served under the Service Regulation. Where the document has to be served within a particular time under the law of the sending State, the rules of the sending State will determine the date of service. Otherwise, the date of service will be determined by the law of the receiving State.

Article 19 sets out the conditions which must be satisfied before judgment in default of acknowledgment can be entered against a defendant served under the provisions of the Service Regulation. See **16.64**.

The European Union publishes a manual (OJ L298, 15.11.2001) containing details of the receiving agencies established by the member States under the terms of the Service Regulation, the geographical areas in which they have jurisdiction, the means of receipt of documents available and the languages that may be used for the completion of the standard form for service. It also publishes a glossary of the documents which may be served under the Service Regulation (OJ L125, 13.5.2002). An updated version of this manual is maintained online at the website of the European Judicial Atlas in Civil Matters, europa.eu.int/comm/justice_home/judicialatlascivil/html/index_en.htm. The necessary forms are available at that website for completion on-screen.

Service through diplomatic channels where there is no civil procedure convention

16.60 It is possible for service to be effected through diplomatic channels even where there is no civil procedure convention between the United Kingdom and the country where it is sought to effect service. By **CPR, r. 6.25(3)**, in such cases, provided the law of the relevant jurisdiction permits it, the claim form may be served either:

(a) through the government of that country, where that government is willing to effect service; or

(b) through a British consular authority in that country.

However, given that the receiving country has not bound itself by international treaty to permit service through these channels, there is no guarantee that service will be effective under local law. In practice, the advice of a local lawyer must be sought.

The same documents as in Hague Convention cases must be filed at the Foreign Process Section (see **16.57**).

Service cannot be effected under **r. 6.25(3)** in other parts of the United Kingdom, the Isle of Man, the Channel Islands, any Commonwealth State or any United Kingdom Overseas Territory (**r. 6.25(4)**). Service in any of these places can be effected either under the Hague Convention, where it applies (see **16.57**), or (except in Malta or Singapore) by the claimant or his agent (**PD 6B, para. 3.1**). Since 1 May 2004 service in Cyprus and Malta is governed by the EU Service Regulation (see **16.59**). The United Kingdom Overseas Territories are listed in **PD 6B, para. 3.2**: the Hague Convention has been extended to most of them (see **table 16.2**).

Service by informal methods

16.61 In practice, service through diplomatic channels is often a slow and laborious process. It is often quicker, where permitted under local law, for the claimant to effect service by an informal method, for example, by instructing a local process server to effect service personally on the defendant.

Service by such informal methods may be permitted even where a civil procedure convention exists with the country where it is sought to serve the claim form, but the relevant bilateral convention would need to be checked. The Hague Convention expressly preserves the possibility of using the traditional modes of service such as service by post, through a 'competent person', or through judicial officers, provided that the State of destination does not object (art. 10). The right of a claimant to effect service by informal means is also preserved by the EU Service Regulation (**Council Regulation (EU) No. 1348/2000, art. 15**).

Personal service by the claimant's agent is permitted in most common law countries. The position in civil law countries, where service is seen as a judicial act, is more problematic. However, even here, it is possible in some countries to use a local agent to transmit documents direct to the local *huissier* or other court official responsible for effecting service of court documents. For service in Scotland see **16.55**.

Where it is sought to effect service by an informal method, the documents listed in **16.57** (with the exception of the request for service and the expenses undertaking) must be served on the defendant.

Under the old RSC, service of English process abroad was restricted to the method specified in RSC, ord. 10, r. 1(1) (personal service) (RSC, ord. 11, r. 5(1)). Service abroad by post was therefore not permitted, save under an order for substituted service. On the other hand, in *Noirhomme v Walklate* (1991) *The Times*, 2 August 1991, service by post of foreign process on a defendant in England and Wales was held to be valid on the grounds that art. 10 of the Hague Convention did not exclude service by post, and this was a method permitted under English law.

The old restriction does not appear in **CPR, r. 6.24**. It may well be, therefore, that the English courts would uphold postal service of English process abroad, provided it is valid under local law. A further question is whether service abroad by the electronic methods now permitted under **CPR, Part 6**, would be good service. In theory, provided that electronic methods of service are not contrary to local law, and in particular to the provisions of any relevant convention, the answer should be yes. In *Molins plc v GD SpA* [2000] 1 WLR 1741 it was held that service by fax effected by an Italian litigant on a defendant in England could have been good service under art. 15 of the Hague Convention if the requirements of **PD 6, para. 3.1**, had been met.

Some light is shed on this by *Burns-Anderson Independent Network plc v Wheeler* [2005] EWHC 575 (QB), [2005] 1 Lloyd's Rep 580. Here, service on a defendant in France by registered post was held not to be good service, even though service by registered post was valid under French law, because in fact no service took place and the package containing the claim form was returned unopened. The claimant could not rely on the deeming provisions of **CPR, r. 6.7(1)**, because registered post fell outside the methods of service permitted under that rule. This leaves unanswered the question whether service by registered post out of the jurisdiction would have been good under the CPR if it had been effective to draw the existence of the proceedings to the defendant's attention. Certainly, in *Knauf UK GmbH v British Gypsum Ltd* [2001] EWCA Civ 1570, [2002] 1 WLR 907, the Court of Appeal commented, *obiter*, that it disagreed with the parties' contention that, as a matter of English law, service by post out of the jurisdiction is not permitted. It did not, however, consider the contention that the only method of postal service then permitted under **r. 6.2** (first-class post) is available only in the UK. As from 6 April 2006 it has been possible to use any other service which provides for delivery on the next working day. So far as service abroad by other methods permitted under **r. 6.2** is concerned, it is implicit in *Burns-Anderson Independent Network plc v Wheeler* that service by fax or other electronic method which complies with the relevant rules would be good service on a defendant abroad, provided it is good service under local law.

For service on a defendant who is abroad under **CPR, r. 6.8** (service by an alternative method) see **15.36**.

Responding to service

Where a court in England and Wales has jurisdiction under **Council Regulation (EC) No. 44/2001** (the Jurisdiction and Judgments Regulation) or the Brussels or Lugano Convention, or the modified Regulation which applies within the United Kingdom, over a claim against a defendant out of the jurisdiction and the claim form is served on the defendant in a European territory of a contracting State or a Regulation State (or in Scotland or Northern Ireland), the defendant must acknowledge service or file a defence within 21 days after service of the claim form, or, where the claim form states that particulars of claim are to follow, of the particulars (**CPR, r. 6.22(2)**). The defendant is not obliged to acknowledge service at all, but where an acknowledgment is filed, the period for filing a defence is extended by 14 days (**PD 6B, para. 7.4(2)**). **Rule 6.22(3)** prescribes a response period of 31 days where a claim form is **16.62** served in 'any other territory of a Contracting State' (i.e., other than European territory, which is covered in r. 6.22(2)). This rule was not amended when the Jurisdiction and Judgments Regulation came into force. It seems that it can only ever have referred to the French overseas departments (French Guiana, Guadeloupe, Martinique and Réunion) and the African territories of Portugal (Madeira) and Spain (Canary Islands, Ceuta and Melilla), so that r. 6.22(3) should have been amended to refer to Regulation States rather than Contracting States.

Where proceedings are served on a defendant outside the jurisdiction who resides outside the territories of contracting States (either where permission to serve has been obtained, or where arts 16 or 17 of the Conventions apply and the defendant is not in the territory of a contracting State), the period for acknowledging service is set out in the table at the end of **PD 6B**. The periods for acknowledging service or filing an admission in the response pack included with a claim form served outside the jurisdiction have to be amended accordingly. After service of the claim form the defence must be served within the number of days set out in the table. But a defendant who has acknowledged service is given an extra 14 days to file the defence (**PD 6B, para. 7.4(2)**).

Where application notices or orders have to be served out of the jurisdiction, the period for responding to service is seven days less than the periods set out in the table (**para. 8.1**). Apart from pre-action applications and orders made in undefended cases, this latter provision should have a limited application, as it is provided in **CPR, r. 6.5(2)**, that all parties must give an address for service within the jurisdiction.

Proof of service

16.63 Where service is effected through diplomatic channels, the claimant will be provided with an official certificate of service (which is evidence that service has been effected) and with a note of the expenses incurred.

Where service is effected through informal methods, service should be evidenced by a certificate of service (or affidavit or witness statement of service) from the person who effected service.

JUDGMENT IN DEFAULT

16.64 No special rule applies in cases of assumed jurisdiction regarding entering judgment in default other than the need for waiting the enhanced period laid down by **PD 6B**.

Where service outside the jurisdiction has been effected without permission under **CPR, r. 6.19**, judgment in default can only be entered by application under **CPR, Part 12** (**CPR, r. 12.10(b)(i)**). These provisions give effect to **art. 26 of the Jurisdiction and Judgments Regulation** (Brussels Convention, art. 20), which requires the courts of contracting States to declare of their own motion that they have no jurisdiction where proceedings involving the same cause of action have already been commenced in another contracting State and the defendant fails to 'enter an appearance' (i.e., acknowledge service). A default judgment entered following service which was not effected in accordance with local law will be set aside as of right under **CPR, r. 13.2** (*Credit Agricole Indosuez v Unicof Ltd* [2003] EWHC 77 (Comm), LTL 4/2/2003).

Where a hearing date is fixed when a claim is issued, and a defendant who is served with the claim form outside the jurisdiction does not appear at the hearing, the claimant may not take any further step without filing written evidence of service of the claim form (**CPR, r. 6.31**). **Rule 6.31** does not apply where service has been effected under the EU Service Regulation (see **16.58**) (**r. 6.26A(4)**).

Where service is effected under the Service Regulation, judgment in default cannot be given until it is established that service was effected by a method prescribed by the internal law of the receiving State or that the documents were actually delivered to the defendant or to the defendant's residence by another method provided by the Regulation and that, in either case, the defendant had sufficient time to defend the claim (art. 19).

Council Regulation (EC) No. 805/2004, which applies from 21 October 2005, provides that a court which has given judgment in an uncontested money claim may, on the application of the claimant, certify it as a European enforcement order, which is enforceable in any EU State (other than Denmark) without any further formality. A judgment can only be certified if given in proceedings which meet minimum procedural standards laid down in the Regulation.

STAYS ON THE GROUND OF *FORUM NON CONVENIENS*

General

English proceedings can be served as of right on a defendant within the jurisdiction irrespective of the degree of connection with this country of the defendant or the cause of action (see **16.2**). A claim form for an Admiralty claim *in rem* may be served within the jurisdiction on a ship or sister ship while at port in the country, even if there is absolutely no other connection with this country. **16.65**

To prevent completely unsuitable actions proceeding, the courts have a discretion to stay English proceedings on the principle of *forum non conveniens*. The leading case is *Spiliada Maritime Corporation v Cansulex Ltd* [1987] AC 460 (see **16.53**). The principles applied are the same as on applications for permission under **CPR, r. 6.20** (see **16.43** to **16.53**), but the burden of proof is reversed to take into account the fact that here the claimant has commenced proceedings as of right, whereas under **r. 6.20** the claimant requires permission to serve outside the jurisdiction.

The court will not grant a stay on the ground of *forum non conveniens* on the application of the claimant, where there has been no challenge to the court's jurisdiction by the defendant, unless there are exceptional circumstances (*Ledra Fisheries Ltd v Turner* [2003] EWHC 1049 (Ch), LTL 15/4/2003). In *Ledra Fisheries Ltd v Turner* the court also refused the claimant's application for stay of a counterclaim by the defendant.

Appropriate forum

In *Spiliada Maritime Corporation v Cansulex Ltd* [1987] AC 460 Lord Goff of Chieveley said: **16.66**

> The basic principle is that a stay will only be granted on the ground of *forum non conveniens* where the court is satisfied that there is some other available forum, having competent jurisdiction, which is the appropriate forum for the trial of the action, i.e. in which the case may be tried more suitably for the interests of all the parties and the ends of justice.

The burden of proof rests on the defendant to show there is some other clearly more appropriate forum. If there is no other more suitable forum, the stay should usually be refused. So, for example, in *The Vishva Abha* [1990] 2 Lloyd's Rep 312 the owners of cargo on board a ship named the *Dias* made a claim *in rem* against the owners of a ship named the *Vishva Apurva*. The collision happened on the high seas. The only connection with England other than the fact that the defendant's ship was arrested here was that the defendant's ships regularly docked in this country. The suggested alternative forum was South Africa, on the ground that the *Dias* had been arrested there in litigation between the owners of the two ships. The only connection with South Africa was that proceedings had been served there while the *Dias* was in port. It was pure chance that litigation was pending in South Africa over the same collision as opposed to any other country, so there was no other distinctly more appropriate forum.

Real and substantial connection

16.67 In considering whether there is an alternative forum, the court will look for the country 'with which the action has the most real and substantial connection' (*The Abidin Daver* [1984] AC 398 per Lord Keith of Kinkel). Sometimes, the natural forum of the action will be obvious. In *MacShannon v Rockware Glass Ltd* [1978] AC 795, a Scots employee sued his employer, which was registered in England, in respect of an accident in Scotland. All the witnesses lived in Scotland. Clearly, Scotland was the natural forum. *Gulf Oil Belgian SA v Finland Steamship Co. Ltd* [1980] 2 Lloyd's Rep 229 arose from a collision between two ships in Swedish waters caused by a misunderstanding between two Swedish pilots speaking in Swedish by VHF radio. It was patently obvious that the case should be tried in Sweden. The places of residence or business of the parties must be considered. A stay will be more readily granted if service was effected during a temporary visit to England and Wales. On the other hand, where the defendant has an established place of business within the jurisdiction, very clear and weighty grounds must be shown for refusing to exercise jurisdiction (*Banco Atlantico SA v British Bank of the Middle East* [1990] 2 Lloyd's Rep 504). The court will also consider the availability of factual and expert witnesses, the law governing the dispute and whether the parties have conferred jurisdiction on any particular court. Usually, it is best for proceedings to be continued in the country whose law governs the dispute (*Standard Steamship Owners' Protection and Indemnity Association (Bermuda) Ltd v Gann* [1992] 2 Lloyd's Rep 528). An alternative forum which simply applies its own laws irrespective of the generally accepted rules on the conflict of laws is unlikely to be regarded as a suitable alternative (*Banco Atlantico SA v British Bank of the Middle East* [1990] 2 Lloyd's Rep 504). Convincing reasons must usually be shown before the court will go behind an express agreement between the parties as to jurisdiction (*Kuwait Oil Co. (KSC) v Idemitsu Tankers KK* [1981] 2 Lloyd's Rep 510).

Reasons of justice

16.68 If there is some more appropriate forum, the court may refuse a stay if, in all the circumstances of the case, justice requires that a stay should not be granted (*Spiliada Maritime Corporation v Cansulex Ltd* [1987] AC 460). The burden of proof regarding showing some reason for not granting a stay despite there being some more suitable forum is on the claimant. A stay may be refused, for example, where the claimant has cogent evidence that justice will not be done in the foreign jurisdiction (*The Abidin Daver* [1984] AC 398). However, a fear that justice will not be done in the claimant's own country, if that is the appropriate forum, is irrelevant (*Jeyaretnam v Mahmood* (1992) *The Times*, 21 May 1992). In a group action, the lack of established procedures for handling such claims together with the strong likelihood that funding will be unavailable in the foreign jurisdiction to investigate complex factual and legal issues may mean that substantial justice would not be done there (*Lubbe v Cape plc* [2000] 1 WLR 1545).

Legitimate personal or juridical advantage

16.69 There are many cases where a claimant can secure some advantage by commencing proceedings in one jurisdiction rather than another. Examples include the measure of damages, the vigour of the procedures on disclosure, the power to award interest, and the length of the limitation period. Generally, an advantage to the claimant will give rise to an equal disadvantage to the defendant. Stays have been granted in cases where doing so deprives the claimant of some advantage, as in *Trendtex Trading Corporation v Credit Suisse* [1982] AC 679. Generally, the court seeks to do 'practical justice' between the parties (see *Lord Goff of Chieveley* in *Spiliada Maritime Corporation v Cansulex Ltd* [1987] AC 460), being less worried about depriving a claimant of a benefit secured by 'forum shopping'. Any injustice that may be caused by granting a stay may be avoided by making the order subject to conditions. For example, a stay may be granted in favour of a jurisdiction with a shorter limitation period on condition that the defendant shall waive any limitation defence. Indeed, the parties may try to pre-empt arguments along these lines by voluntarily undertaking not to take advantage of procedural differences in advance of the hearing for the stay.

Brussels Convention cases

The CJJA 1982, s. 49, provides that nothing in the Act shall prevent the court from staying proceedings 'on the ground of *forum non conveniens* or otherwise, where to do so is not inconsistent with the 1968 Convention'. This means that there is no power to stay where that is inconsistent with the Brussels Convention. Generally, the Brussels Convention provides a complete code, so a stay would be inconsistent with the Convention. The English courts have taken the approach that where the defendant is domiciled in England, but the dispute as to jurisdiction is between the courts of this country and the courts of a non-contracting State, English proceedings may be stayed on the ground of *forum non conveniens* (*Re Harrods (Buenos Aires) Ltd* [1992] Ch 72). However, doubt is shed on this approach by the recent decision of the European Court of Justice in *Universal General Insurance Co. v Group Josi Reinsurance Co. SA* (case C-412/980) [2001] QB 68 that (apart from the exceptional cases where the Convention expressly provides that jurisdiction is dependent on the claimant's domicile being in a contracting State) the Brussels Convention is applicable where the defendant's domicile or seat is in a contracting State, even if the claimant is domiciled in a non-member country. This would therefore exclude the possibility of a stay on the grounds of *forum non conveniens* where the defendant is domiciled in England — or any Convention territory. It seems that this ECJ case was not cited to Longmore J, who, in *ACE Insurance SA-NV v Zurich Insurance Co.* [2000] 2 Lloyd's Rep 423, stayed proceedings in England against a defendant domiciled in Switzerland on the ground that Texas was the more appropriate forum. Longmore J's decision was upheld by the Court of Appeal [2001] 1 Lloyd's Rep 618. 16.70

In *Owusu v Jackson* [2002] EWCA Civ 877, LTL 19/6/2002, the Court of Appeal referred to the Court of Justice of the European Communities the following question:

(a) whether it is inconsistent with the Brussels Convention, where a claimant contends that jurisdiction is founded on art. 2, for a court of a contracting State to exercise a discretionary power, available under its national law, to decline to hear proceedings brought against a person domiciled in that State in favour of the courts of a non-contracting State if: (i) the jurisdiction of no other contracting State under the Convention is in issue; and (ii) the proceedings have no connecting factors with any other contracting State; and
(b) if the answer to (a)(i) or (a)(ii) is yes, whether it is inconsistent in all circumstances or only in some, and if so, which.

In *Owusu v Jackson* (case C-281/02) [2005] QB 801 the European Court of Justice held that art. 2 is mandatory and can be derogated from only by express provision in the Convention.

INJUNCTIONS TO RESTRAIN FOREIGN PROCEEDINGS

In rare circumstances, an English court may grant an injunction restraining the institution or continuance of foreign proceedings. Such an injunction is only granted when it is required for the ends of justice (*Castanho v Brown and Root (UK) Ltd* [1981] AC 557). The injunction is directed to a party, not to the foreign court, so is only available against a party who is amenable to the jurisdiction of the English courts. It is a jurisdiction which must be exercised with a great deal of caution. There are two main categories of case in which an anti-suit injunction will be awarded. First, where the pursuit of the foreign proceedings is vexatious and oppressive (see further below) and second, in order to restrain proceedings brought in a foreign country in breach of either a jurisdiction or an arbitration agreement between the 16.71

parties (see *Continental Bank NA v Aeakos Compania Naviera SA* [1994] 1 WLR 588 and *Aggeliki Charis Compania Maritima SA v Pagnan SpA* [1995] 1 Lloyd's Rep 87).

The leading case concerning the first of these categories is now *Société Nationale Industrielle Aérospatiale v Lee Kui Jak* [1987] AC 871. The principle laid down was that where a remedy for a particular wrong is available both in England and in a foreign country, an injunction will only be granted to restrain the foreign proceedings if pursuit of those proceedings would be vexatious and oppressive. This presupposes that England is the natural forum for the trial. Account must be taken of the balance of injustice to the parties depending on whether the injunction is either granted or refused, bearing in mind the possibility of removing any injustice by the imposition of suitable terms or the giving of undertakings.

The facts were that the deceased, who had lived in Brunei, was killed in a helicopter crash in Brunei. A government report on the accident concluded that the accident was caused by metal debris in the rotating assembly. The administrators of the deceased's estate started proceedings, *inter alia*, against the manufacturer of the helicopter and the maintenance company in both Brunei and Texas. The maintenance company had been served with a contribution notice in Brunei where they did not object to the jurisdiction of the court, but were vigorously resisting the jurisdiction of the court in Texas. Brunei was obviously the natural forum for the action, but an injunction could only be granted if the proceedings in Texas were vexatious or oppressive. Vexation on the ground that under Texan law there was strict liability and punitive damages was neutralised by undertakings by the claimants that neither of these would be pursued. However, there was a distinct possibility that the defendants would be unable to claim contribution from the maintenance company in Texas, whereas they could in Brunei, with the result that the proceedings in Texas could be described as oppressive. An injunction was granted.

The existence of two concurrent proceedings in different jurisdictions is not of itself 'vexatious and oppressive' and will not alone justify the granting of an anti-suit injunction (*Dornoch Ltd v Mauritius Union Assurance Co. Ltd* [2005] EWHC 1887 (Comm), LTL 30/8/2005).

The European Court of Justice held, in *Turner v Grovit* (case C-159/02) [2005] AC 101, that a court in a country which is a party to the Brussels Convention may not issue an injunction prohibiting another party from commencing or continuing proceedings in another Convention State on the ground that the proceedings are vexatious and oppressive. The reasoning was that an anti-suit injunction constitutes an interference with the jurisdiction of the foreign court and is therefore inconsistent with the system of the Convention. There is no reason to suppose that the position will be different in relation to the Jurisdiction and Judgments Regulation. Further, the Court of Appeal has recently commented on the European Court's decision in *Erich Gasser GmbH v MISAT Srl* (case C-116/02) [2005] QB 1 that, because the court first seised must decide issues of jurisdiction including the jurisdiction of the court second seised, where the English court is the court second seised, it is therefore unable to grant an anti-suit injunction on the grounds that the foreign court did not have jurisdiction (*Through Transport Mutual Insurance Association (Eurasia) Ltd v New India Assurance Co. Ltd* [2004] EWCA Civ 1598, [2005] 1 Lloyd's Rep 67). In the same case, however, the court drew a distinction between anti-suit injunctions in support of a jurisdiction clause and those in support of an arbitration clause. In the latter case, it held that there was nothing in the Jurisdiction and Judgments Regulation to prevent the courts of a contracting State from granting an injunction, because arbitration is outside the scope of the Regulation. Nor does such an injunction offend comity. The decision has been followed in *West Tankers Inc. v Ras Riuione Adriatica di Sicurtà SpA* [2005] EWHC 454, [2005] 2 Lloyd's Rep 257.

An application for an anti-suit injunction does not have to be made by a formal claim or counterclaim (*Glencore International AG v Exter Shipping Ltd* [2002] EWCA Civ 528, [2002] 2 All ER (Comm) 1). In this case it was held there was territorial, *in personam* jurisdiction to grant the injunction against a party who had submitted to the jurisdiction, and on the facts there was a clear need to protect the English proceedings.

An application for an anti-suit injunction should be made promptly. It is unlikely to be granted once judgment has been obtained in the foreign claim, or where it has been allowed to continue almost to the point of judgment (*Toepfer International GmbH v Molino Boschi Srl* [1996] 1 Lloyd's Rep 510). On the other hand, the foreign action must be more than merely anticipated (*Pan American World Airways v Andrews* 1992 SLT 268).

If a company is in compulsory liquidation in England and Wales, the winding-up court may restrain any person subject to its jurisdiction from taking proceedings outside the jurisdiction which would distort the distribution of the company's assets in accordance with English law (*Re Oriental Inland Steam Co., ex parte Scinde Railway Co.* (1874) LR 9 Ch App 557; *Re Vocalion (Foreign) Ltd* [1932] 2 Ch 196). This will be applied to a voluntary winding up on an application under the Insolvency Act 1986, s. 112 (*Re Jenkins and Co. Ltd* (1907) 51 SJ 715).

In *OT Africa Line Ltd v Hijazy* [2001] 1 Lloyd's Rep 76 the court considered whether an anti-suit injunction restraining proceedings before a foreign court was a breach of **art. 6 of the European Convention on Human Rights** in that it would prevent a party's case being considered by an independent and impartial tribunal established by law. The court held that **art. 6** does not give a person an unfettered choice of tribunal in which to pursue or defend civil rights. **Article 6** does not deal with the place where the right to a fair trial is to be exercised by a litigant: it simply requires a fair trial to be available somewhere. Accordingly **art. 6** does not prevent an anti-suit injunction being granted.

Chapter 17 Admitting the Claim and Requesting Time to Pay

The following procedural checklist, which is in **appendix 1**, is relevant to this chapter:
Procedural checklist 13 Admitting a claim and requesting time to pay

DEFENDANT'S OPTIONS ON RECEIVING PARTICULARS OF CLAIM

17.1 A defendant to a claim is not required by the CPR to do anything until particulars of claim are served. On receipt of particulars of claim, **Part 9** provides for three alternative responses:

(a) A defendant who wishes to admit the claim should file a form of admission (see **17.2** to 17.7).

(b) A defendant who wishes to contest the claim should file a defence within 14 days of service of the particulars of claim (see **18.4** to **18.6**).

(c) A defendant who wishes to contest the claim but needs more than 14 days to prepare the defence, or who wishes to contest the jurisdiction of the court, should file an acknowledgment of service (see **18.1** to **18.3**).

ADMISSION BY NOTICE IN WRITING

17.2 Any party may admit the truth of the whole or any part of another party's case at any stage of the proceedings (**CPR, r. 14.1(1)**), by giving notice in writing either in a statement of case or by letter (**r. 14.1(2)**). Where a defendant makes an admission by notice under **r. 14.1**, the claimant is then entitled to apply for judgment (**r. 14.3(1)**). The court will enter such judgment as it appears to the court that the applicant is entitled to on the admission (**r. 14.3(2)**).

The provisions of **Part 14** do not apply to an admission of liability made before proceedings commenced (*Sowerby v Charlton* [2005] EWCA Civ 1610, [2006] 1 WLR 568).

WITHDRAWAL OF AN ADMISSION

17.3 CPR, r. 14.1(5), makes provision for a party to withdraw an admission with the court's permission. The court may make its consent subject to conditions, which are most likely to be that the party making the application bear its own and the other side's costs of the application.

In *Braybrook v Basildon and Thurrock University NHS Trust* [2004] EWHC 3352 (QB), LTL 7/1/2005, it was held that in exercising its discretion the court should consider all the circumstances of the case and seek to give effect to the overriding objective. Amongst the matters to be considered would be:

(a) the reasons and justifications for the application which had to be made in good faith;
(b) the balance of prejudice to the parties;
(c) whether any party had been the author of any prejudice it might suffer;
(d) the prospects of success of any issue arising from the withdrawal of an admission; and
(e) the public interest in avoiding where possible satellite litigation, disproportionate use of court resources and the impact of any strategic manoeuvring.

The nearer the application is to a final hearing the less chance of success it will have, even if the party making the application can establish clear prejudice.

The test set out in *Braybrook* has received *obiter* support from the Court of Appeal in *Sowerby v Charlton* [2005] EWCA Civ 1610, [2006] 1 WLR 568. The Court of Appeal commented that the old approach under the leading pre-CPR authority of *Gale v Superdrug Stores Plc* [1996] 1 WLR 1089, in which the court looked only at the balance of prejudice to the parties, should now be approached with caution.

ADMISSION OF A MONEY CLAIM WITHIN 14 DAYS OF SERVICE OF THE PARTICULARS OF CLAIM

In money claims (whether for a specified sum or not), the CPR contain a procedure for the admission of the claim at an early stage. This procedure (which is in addition to the procedure described in 17.2) is aimed primarily at individual defendants in debt claims. It provides a mechanism whereby the rate and time by which the admitted claim is to be paid can be agreed between the parties or fixed by the court. **17.4**

There are separate rules for four different categories of admission:

(a) admission of the whole of a claim for a specified sum (r. 14.4; see 17.5);
(b) admission of part of a claim for a specified sum (r. 14.5; see 17.6);
(c) admission of liability to pay the whole of a claim for an unspecified amount of money (r. 14.6; see 17.6); and
(d) admission of liability to pay the whole of a claim for an unspecified amount of money, where the defendant offers a sum in satisfaction of the claim (r. 14.7; see 17.8).

The claimant may not enter judgment in default under these rules against a child or a patient, nor may a claimant who is a child or patient enter judgment where the admission has been made under r. 14.5 or r. 14.7 (r. 14.1(4)).

Any admission by the defendant under rr. 14.4 to 14.7 must be made within 14 days after service of the claim form, or, where the claim form states that particulars of claim will follow, within 14 days after service of the particulars of claim (r. 14.2). Rule 14.2(2) extends this deadline in two cases:

(a) Where the claim form has been served out of the jurisdiction in circumstances where the court's permission is not required, in which case the time limits set out in r. 6.22 apply. (Where the court's permission is required for service out of the jurisdiction the court's order will specify the time for filing or serving an admission (r. 6.21(4)) calculated by reference to the table at the end of **PD 6B** (**PD 6B, para. 7.2**).)
(b) Where the court makes an order for service on an agent of an overseas principal under CPR, r. 6.16, in which case the deadline for filing the acknowledgment will be that specified in the order.

In any event, the defendant may return an admission under **rr. 14.4** to **14.7** after the deadline specified in **r. 14.2**, provided judgment in default has not already been entered (**r. 14.2(3)**).

When particulars of claim are served on a defendant, the response pack will include a series of forms for responding to the claim. These will include forms for making an admission (**r. 7.8(1)**; **PD 14, para. 2.1**). The defendant will need to choose the correct form from the pack for making his admission.

Admission of the whole of a claim for a specified sum

17.5 Under **CPR, r. 14.4**, a defendant who admits the whole of a claim for a specified sum has three options:

(a) If he is able, he may simply pay the sum claimed in full (together with interest, and the amount of fixed costs (see **chapter 67**) and issue fee endorsed on the claim form) direct to the claimant in full within 14 days after service.

(b) Alternatively, the defendant may ask for time to pay, or ask to pay by instalments (**r. 14.9**), by returning **form N9A** to the claimant having completed the details sought about his means (**r. 14.4(2)**). Where the claimant accepts the defendant's proposals, he may obtain judgment by filing request **form N225** (**r. 14.9(4)**). The court will then enter judgment for payment at the time and rate specified in the defendant's request (**r. 14.9(5)**). If the claimant does not accept the defendant's proposals, he should still file request **form N225**, but give notice that he does not accept the proposals (**r. 14.10(2)**). The court will then decide the time and rate at which payment should be made (**r. 14.10(4)**).

(c) The defendant may simply admit the claim without seeking time to pay, by returning **form N9A** to the claimant. In this case, the claimant may obtain judgment by filing a request for judgment in **form N225** (**r. 14.4(3)**). The claimant may specify the date by which the judgment should be paid or the times and rates at which it is to be paid by instalments (**r. 14.4(4)**). Judgment will then be entered by the court in the terms specified by the claimant (**r. 14.4(5) and (6)**).

Admission of only part of a claim for a specified sum

17.6 A defendant who, under **CPR, r. 14.5**, admits part of a claim for a specified sum should complete **forms N9A** and **N9B** and return them to the court within 14 days after service. The claimant then has the choice of accepting the partial admission and entering judgment, or refusing the admission altogether, in which case the claim will continue as a defended claim.

On receipt of the defendant's admission, the court will serve notice on the claimant requiring notification to the court within 14 days of whether the claimant wishes to accept the defendant's offer, reject it or accept the amount of the offer but reject the proposals for payment (**r. 14.5(3)**). If the claimant does not reply within 14 days, the claim will be stayed until the reply is filed (**r. 14.5(4)** and **(5)**).

The defendant may or may not have asked for time to pay. Where the claimant has accepted the partial admission in principle, the procedure in 17.5 (b) and (c) then applies in relation to proposals for payment (except that **form N225A** is used instead of **N225**).

Admission of liability on a claim for an unspecified sum

17.7 A defendant who, under **CPR, r. 14.6**, admits liability for the whole of a claim for an unspecified sum should complete **form N9C** and return it to the court within 14 days after service. This form is then sent by the court to the claimant, who may request the court to enter judgment on liability, with damages to be assessed. The court will then enter judgment and give directions for the assessment of damages. If appropriate, the case may be allocated to a track (**r. 14.8**). The procedure for assessing damages is considered at **42.26** to **42.31**.

If the claimant does not file a request for judgment within 14 days after service of the admission on him, the claim is stayed until the request is filed (**r. 14.6(5)**).

Admission of liability for a claim for an unspecified sum and offer of an amount to satisfy the claim

A defendant who, under **CPR, r. 14.7**, admits liability for a claim for an unspecified sum and offers an amount of money to satisfy the claim should complete **form N9C** and send it to the court within 14 days after service. The court will forward it to the claimant. The claimant may then either accept the amount offered and request judgment to be entered in that amount, or reject the amount offered and request judgment to be entered for an amount to be decided by the court and costs. The claimant's choice must be notified to the court within 14 days of being served with a notice of request. If the claimant does not reply within 14 days, the claim will be stayed until the reply is filed. **17.8**

The defendant may or may not ask for time to pay. Where the claimant accepts the admission in principle, the procedure in **17.5** (b) and (c) then applies in relation to proposals for payment (except that **form N266** is used instead of N225).

Chapter 18 Acknowledging Service and Filing a Defence

The following procedural checklist, which is in **appendix 1**, is relevant to this chapter:

Procedural checklist 14 Time limits for responding to claim by acknowledging service and/or filing a defence

ACKNOWLEDGING SERVICE

18.1 When particulars of claim are served on the defendant, the response pack will include a form (**form N9**) for acknowledging service of the claim (**CPR, r. 7.8(1)**). Except in the case of **Part 8** claims (see **chapter 13**), contentious probate claims and claims issued in the Commercial and Mercantile Courts (see below), a defendant is under no obligation to file an acknowledgment, even if there is an intention to defend the claim. Instead of filing an acknowledgment, a defendant may proceed immediately to file and serve a defence.

By **r. 10.1(3)**, an acknowledgment may be filed in any case where:

(a) the defendant is not able to file a defence within 14 days after service of the particulars of claim; or
(b) the defendant wishes to dispute the court's jurisdiction.

In the latter case, filing an acknowledgment indicating an intention to contest the jurisdiction will not constitute a submission to the jurisdiction (**r. 11(3)**) (see further **chapter 19** on disputing the court's jurisdiction).

If the claim has been brought under the **Part 8** procedure (in which case the claim form must state that **Part 8** applies), the claim form is accompanied only by a form of acknowledgment of service (**r. 7.8(2)(b)**). The defendant must then file and serve an acknowledgment within 14 days after service of the claim form (**r. 8.3**). See further **chapter 13**.

The general provisions for acknowledging service are modified for claims issued in the Commercial and Mercantile Courts. In those courts the defendant must always file an acknowledgment of service (**rr. 58.6(1)** and **59.5(1)**) within 14 days after service of the claim form (whether or not it is accompanied by particulars of claim) (**rr. 58.6(2)** and **59.5(2)**). An adapted version of N9(CC) has been approved for use in the Commercial Court (**form N9(CC)**). The period for acknowledging service is extended in the situations listed in **rr. 58.6(3)** and **59.5(3)**. There are special rules for Admiralty claims in **rr. 61.3** and **61.4**.

TIME FOR FILING THE ACKNOWLEDGMENT

18.2 An acknowledgment of service must, by **CPR, r. 10.3(1)**, be filed:

(a) within 14 days after service of the particulars of claim, where the particulars of claim are served after the claim form; or

(b) within 14 days after service of the claim form, where the particulars of claim are included in or served with the claim form.

In contentious probate proceedings, the time limits are 28 days after service of the claim form or particulars of claim, where the particulars are served after the claim form (**r. 57.4**).

In *Coll v Tattum* (2001) *The Times*, 3 December 2001, Neuberger J held that, although the CPR are silent on the point, a defendant who wishes to acknowledge service or file a defence after these time limits have expired but before judgment in default is entered needs either the other side's consent or the court's permission. Granting permission is a matter for the court's discretion, which will normally be exercised in favour of extending time where there is a defence with a realistic prospect of success (see **20.9**). *Coll v Tattum* has been followed in *Boeing Capital Corporation v Wells Fargo Bank Northwest* [2003] EWHC 1364 (Comm), LTL 17/7/2003.

These deadlines are extended where the claim form has been served out of the jurisdiction (**r. 10.3(2)(a)**). Where service out of the jurisdiction has been effected without the court's permission, under **r. 6.19**, the time limits set out in **r. 6.22** apply. Where an order for service out of the jurisdiction has been obtained, it will include the date by which acknowledgment should be filed (**r. 6.21(4)**) calculated by reference to **PD 6B, para. 7.3**, and the table at the end of **PD 6B** (**PD 6B, para. 7.2**). In contentious probate proceedings, these time limits are extended by a further 14 days (**CPR, r. 57.4(3)**).

Where the court makes an order under **r. 6.16**, for service on an agent of an overseas principal, any acknowledgment of service must be filed within the period specified by the court under **r. 6.16(4)** for responding to particulars of claim (**r. 10.3(2)(b)**).

In judicial review cases, acknowledgment of service must be filed within 21 days after service of the claim form, and must be served on the claimant and any other person named in the claim form (**r. 54.8(2)**).

The court must notify the claimant in writing that an acknowledgment has been filed (**r. 10.4**).

CONTENTS OF THE FORM OF ACKNOWLEDGMENT

The form of acknowledgment of service (**form N9**) requires the defendant: **18.3**

(a) to indicate the intention to defend all or part of the claim; and
(b) to state whether it is intended to contest the jurisdiction.

The acknowledgment must give the defendant's full name, if it is different from the name given on the claim form. It must give an address for service in the jurisdiction (**CPR, r. 10.5(b)**). If the defendant's legal representative has signed the acknowledgment, the representative's business address will be the defendant's address for service (**PD 10, para. 3.2**).

The acknowledgment must be signed either by the defendant or by the defendant's legal representative (**CPR, r. 10.5(a)**). In the case of a company or other corporation, the acknowledgment must be signed by a person in a senior position. Persons who fall into this category are set out at **PD 10, para. 4.3**. Where the defendant is a partnership, the acknowledgment may be signed by any partner or a person having control or management of the partnership business (**PD 10, para. 4.4**) (see further **15.33**, and **76.36** for the effect of acknowledgment on enforcement against the personal assets of a partner). A child or patient may sign an acknowledgment only through his or her litigation friend or solicitor, unless the court orders to the contrary (**PD 10, para. 4.5**).

An acknowledgment of service in a claim begun using the **CPR, Part 8**, procedure (but not other types of claim) must be verified by a statement of truth (**r. 22.1(1)(d)**).

The same form may be used for two or more defendants, if they are represented by the same solicitor (**PD 10, para. 5.3**).

If the defendant has entered into a funding arrangement (as defined in **r. 43.2(1)(k)**), a notice of funding of case (**form N251**) must be filed at court with the acknowledgment of service and a copy served on every other party (**PD 43–48, para. 19.2(3)**).

An acknowledgment of service may be amended or withdrawn only with permission of the court (**PD 10, para. 5.4**).

FILING A DEFENCE

18.4 Save in the case of **Part 8** claims (**CPR, r. 15.1**), a defendant who wishes to defend all or part of a claim must file a defence (**r. 15.2**). A defendant's privilege against self-incrimination does not give rise to a right not to plead a defence in civil proceedings (*Versailles Trade Finance Ltd v Clough* [2001] EWCA Civ 1509, [2002] CP Rep 8). If a defence is not filed within the specified period, default judgment (see **chapter 20**) may be entered (**r. 15.3**). A copy of the defence must be served on every other party (**r. 15.6**).

If the defendant has entered into a funding arrangement (as defined in **r. 43.2(1)(k)**) and the defence is the first document to be filed by the defendant, a notice of funding of case (**form N251**) must be filed at court with the defence and a copy served on every other party (**PD 43–48, para. 19.2(3)**).

None of the rules relating to the filing of defences applies to **Part 8** claims (**r. 15.1**). They do, however, apply to cases where a defence is filed to a counterclaim (**r. 20.3**).

Period for filing a defence

18.5 The general rule is that a defence must be filed within 14 days after service of the particulars of claim (**CPR, r. 15.4(1)(a)**). Where a claim form is served which does not include, and is not accompanied by, particulars of claim, the defendant should wait for the particulars, which should be served by the claimant within 14 days after service of the claim form (**r. 7.4**).

If more time is needed in which to file and serve a defence, the defendant may file an acknowledgment of service under **Part 10**. The time for filing a defence is then extended until 28 days after service of the particulars of claim (**r. 15.4(1)(b)**).

There are different time limits for filing a defence where the claim form is served out of the jurisdiction without the court's permission, under **r. 6.19** (see **r. 6.23**). Where an order for service out of the jurisdiction has been obtained, it will include the date by which a defence should be filed (**r. 6.21(4)**) calculated by reference to **PD 6B, paras 7.3 and 7.4**, and the table at the end of **PD 6B** (**PD 6B, para. 7.2**). Where a claim form is served on the agent of a principal who is overseas the court will, under **CPR, r. 6.16(4)**, specify the period for responding.

There are two further exceptions to the general rule:

(a) A defendant who makes an application disputing the jurisdiction of the court (see **chapter 19**) need not file a defence before the hearing of the application (**r. 11(9)**).

(b) Where the claimant makes an application for summary judgment under **Part 24** (see **chapter 34**) before the defendant has filed a defence, the defendant need not then do so before the hearing of the application (**r. 24.4(2)**).

If either application is unsuccessful, and the claim continues, the court will make a direction for filing and service of the defence within a stated period. **Rules 11(9)** and **24.4(2)** do not prevent a defendant filing a defence in the period before the hearing of the application.

Late filing of the defence

Under **CPR, r. 15.4**, the general rule is that the period for filing a defence is 14 days after service of the particulars of claim. This period can be extended by filing an acknowledgment of service, obtaining the claimant's consent, or obtaining an order for an extension. Once this period has elapsed, the claimant is usually entitled to enter a default judgment under **Part 12**, and the only consequence stated in the CPR as flowing from not filing a defence within the stated time is the danger that the claimant might enter judgment in default (**r. 15.3**). A default judgment may only be entered where the defendant has failed to file an acknowledgment of service or a defence (**r. 12.1**). This means that if the claimant delays in entering judgment in default, the question is which side then acts first. If the claimant enters judgment first, all the defendant can do is to apply to set the judgment aside under **Part 13**. If the defendant files a defence first, it is no longer open for the claimant to enter judgment in default because of **r. 12.1**. In this situation, the claim proceeds as normal, but the delay by the defendant may be taken into account on costs or in general case management. **18.6**

In a number of situations, judgment in default can only be entered after the claimant issues an application for permission to enter judgment (see **20.8** and **20.9**). Typically, these are claims where the relief sought includes equitable remedies. What is the position if the defendant purports to acknowledge service or file a defence in the period between the claimant issuing an application for the entry of default judgment and the hearing of the application? In *Coll v Tattum* (2001) *The Times*, 3 December 2001, Neuberger J said that as the defendant was seeking to file the defence outside the time limit, he needed either the consent of the claimant or the permission of the court. Permission would normally be granted where there was a genuine defence. A similar result was achieved in *Boeing Capital Corporation v Wells Fargo Bank Northwest* [2003] EWHC 1364 (Comm), LTL 17/7/2003, a case like *Coll v Tattum* where the claimant needed permission because the claim was for equitable relief. Neither of these cases considered the test for what amounts to a genuine defence, but it is suggested that the appropriate standard is that the defence must have a real prospect of success within the meaning of *Swain v Hillman* [2001] 1 All ER 91 and *E. D. and F. Man Liquid Products Ltd v Patel* [2003] EWCA Civ 472, [2003] CPLR 384 (see **34.10**).

Extending the time for service of a defence

Under **CPR, r. 15.5**, the defendant and the claimant may agree an extension of the time for filing a defence of up to 28 days only. Where they do so, they must notify the court in writing (**r. 15.5(2)**). **18.7**

A defendant who requires additional time must make an application, using the **Part 23** procedure, under **r. 3.1(2)(a)**. Guidance on the exercise of the court's discretion when making orders under **r. 3.1(2)(a)** is to be found in *Sayers v Clarke Walker* [2002] EWCA Civ 645, [2002] 1 WLR 3095, and *Robert v Momentum Services Ltd* [2003] EWCA Civ 299, [2003] 1 WLR 1577 (see **15.13**).

Filing and serving a defence in the Commercial Court

The Commercial Court no longer has special rules on filing and serving defences. **18.8**

Chapter 19 Disputing the Court's Jurisdiction

The following procedural checklist, which is in **appendix 1**, is relevant to this chapter:

Procedural checklist 15 Procedure for disputing the court's jurisdiction

INTRODUCTION

19.1 **Part 11** of the CPR makes provision for the defendant to challenge the jurisdiction of the English court, or to argue that the court should not exercise any jurisdiction which it may have. The procedure is available whenever a party wishes to challenge the jurisdiction of the court in which a claim has been issued. It is of particular relevance when the defendant has been served out of the jurisdiction, or if he wishes to argue that the claim is subject to an arbitration agreement. The rules on jurisdiction are considered in **chapter 16**. The procedure for disputing the court's jurisdiction is considered below.

ACKNOWLEDGMENT OF SERVICE

19.2 The defendant must first file an acknowledgment of service within the usual time limit (i.e., within 14 days after service of the claim form, or of the particulars of claim, if served later, or, where served out of the jurisdiction, the time limits given under **CPR, r. 6.22**, and **PD 6B, para.** 7.3) stating an intention to contest the jurisdiction (**CPR, r. 11(2)**). To avoid any ambiguity about submitting to the jurisdiction, the defendant should tick only the 'intention to contest the jurisdiction' box and not also tick the 'intention to defend' box (see **19.4**).

APPLICATION DISPUTING JURISDICTION

19.3 Within 14 days after filing an acknowledgment of service, the defendant should make an application for the order sought, using the **Part 23** procedure (**CPR, r. 11(4)(a)**). In the Commercial and Mercantile Courts the time limit is 28 days after filing an acknowledgment (**rr. 58.7** and **59.6**). Failure to make the application within this time limit will be taken as a submission to the jurisdiction (**r. 11(5)(b)**). The application must be supported by evidence (**r. 11(4)(b)**). No defence need be served before the hearing of the application (**r. 11(9)**). Serving a defence may constitute a voluntary submission to the jurisdiction (see **19.4**).

As originally drafted, **r. 11(4)** expressed the time limit for making an application as 'the period for filing a defence'. It became clear in *Monrose Investments Ltd v Orion Nominees Ltd* [2001] CP Rep 109 that it was confusing to express the time limit in this way as the reference was to the time limit in **r. 15.4**, not the time as it might have been extended by the court. The current wording of **r. 11(4)** deals with this problem. It was also held in *Monrose Investments v Orion Nominees* that if a party needs additional time to make an application to contest the jurisdiction, it should make an application for an extension of the time limit laid down in **r. 11(4)** and the court has a discretion under **r. 3.1(2)(a)** to extend it. The decision on this point was followed in *SSQ Europe SA v Johann & Backes OHG* [2002] 1 Lloyd's Rep 465, in which the court confirmed that an extension of time for service of a defence does not carry with it an extension of time for an application to challenge the court's jurisdiction.

In *Sawyer v Atari Interactive Inc.* [2005] EWHC 2351 (Ch), LTL 9/11/2005, Lawrence Collins J held that he had discretion under **r. 3.1(2)(a)** retrospectively to extend the period for making an application to dispute the jurisdiction. It was appropriate to exercise the discretion where the application was made promptly, there was no prejudice to the claimant and the solicitor's error in not making the application in time was understandable, if not excusable in that he erroneously believed the relevant time limit to be the period for filing the defence.

SUBMISSION TO JURISDICTION

Acknowledging service does not affect any right the defendant might have to contest the jurisdiction of the court (**CPR, r. 11(3)**). Although the CPR do not address the point explicitly, taking any step in the claim other than acknowledging service and applying under **Part 11** to contest the court's jurisdiction is extremely dangerous. Any such action may constitute a voluntary submission to the jurisdiction of the English courts. It was held in *Monrose Investments Ltd v Orion Nominees Ltd* [2001] CP Rep 109 (applying *Sage v Double A Hydraulics Ltd* (1992) *The Times*, 2 April 1992) that applying for an extension of time for service of a defence, without any reference to an intention to contest the jurisdiction, constituted a submission to the jurisdiction. In *SSQ Europe SA v Johann & Backes OHG* [2002] 1 Lloyd's Rep 465 it was held that service of a defence and counterclaim accompanied by an express challenge to the jurisdiction did not constitute a submission. It did not amount to the unconditional entry of an appearance or unequivocal conduct required by art. 18 of the Brussels Convention (now **Council Regulation (EC) No. 44/2001, art. 24**) (*Elefanten Schuh GmbH v Jacqmain* (case 150/80) [1981] ECR 1671). In *SMAY Investments Ltd v Sachdev* [2003] EWHC 474 (Ch), [2003] 1 WLR 1973, it was held that neither (a) ticking both the 'intention to defend' and the 'intention to contest the jurisdiction' boxes on the acknowledgment of service nor (b) obtaining an extension of time for service of the defence and offering undertakings to the court accompanied by an intention to contest the jurisdiction constituted an unequivocal intention to submit to the jurisdiction. Attending before a judge to challenge a freezing injunction obtained without notice does not amount to submitting to the jurisdiction, unless the party agrees to an order regulating his position pending trial (*SMAY Investments Ltd v Sachdev*). **19.4**

SUSPENSION OF TIME IN MAIN CLAIM

Making an application to contest the jurisdiction suspends time in the main claim. Thus, a defendant need not file a defence (**CPR, r. 11(9)(a)**); a defendant to a Part 8 claim need not file evidence in opposition (**r. 11(9)(b)**) and in claims in the Commercial or Mercantile Courts where the application has been made before service of the particulars of claim, the claimant need not file particulars of claim (**rr. 58.7** and **59.6**). **19.5**

ORDERS

The court may make a declaration that it has no jurisdiction over the claim, or that it will not exercise its jurisdiction. Under **CPR, r. 11(6)**, the order may also: **19.6**

(a) set aside the claim form;
(b) set aside service of the claim form;

(c) discharge any order made before the claim was commenced or the claim form served;
(d) stay the proceedings.

SECOND ACKNOWLEDGMENT

19.7 Where the court does not make any declaration that it does not have, or should not exercise, jurisdiction, the acknowledgment of service already filed by the defendant will cease to have effect and the defendant should complete and file another form within 14 days or such period as the court may order (**CPR, r. 11(7)**). This acknowledgment will be treated as a submission to the jurisdiction (**r. 11(8)**). The court will give directions for the filing and service of the defence, in a Part 7 claim, or for the filing of evidence in a Part 8 claim (**r.11(7)(c)**).

Chapter 20 Default Judgment

The following procedural checklists, which are in **appendix 1**, are relevant to this chapter:

Procedural checklist 16 Request for entry of judgment in default
Procedural checklist 17 Application for entry of judgment in default

INTRODUCTION

Failure to file an acknowledgment or a defence within the time limits laid down in the CPR may result under **Part 12** in the claimant entering judgment in default, that is, judgment without a trial of the claim. In most cases the entry of judgment in default is a purely administrative act, not involving any judicial determination of the merits of the claim. **20.1**

There are two mechanisms under the rules for entering default judgment:

(a) A simple request-for-judgment procedure under **Part 12** is available in money claims (**r. 12.4(1)**), which include claims for specified sums, claims for unquantified damages and some other types of claim. Under this procedure, judgment is entered over the counter on filing a request for default judgment, without any consideration of the merits of the claim. (See **20.3** to **20.6**.) This will apply in the overwhelming majority of cases.

(b) In a claim for a remedy other than a money claim, in a claim only for costs (other than fixed costs) and in certain other cases set out in **r. 12.10**, an application for judgment must be made using the **Part 23** procedure (see **chapter 32**). On an application for the entry of a default judgment there will be a hearing and the court will give 'such judgment as it appears to the court that the claimant is entitled to on his statement of case' (**r. 12.11(1)**). In this case, then, the court will, in a limited way, consider the merits of the claim. (See **20.8** to **20.9**.)

A default judgment obtained using the request procedure in error instead of the application-for-judgment procedure was irregular and capable of being set aside as of right under **r. 13.2** (*Intense Investments Ltd v Development Ventures Ltd* [2005] EWHC 1726 (TCC), [2005] BLR 478 (see further **20.12**).

CASES WHERE DEFAULT JUDGMENT MAY NOT BE ENTERED

20.2 CPR, r. 12.2, and PD 12, para. 1.2, provide that judgment in default may not be entered:

(a) on a claim where the **Part 8** procedure has been used (see further **13.9**);
(b) on a claim for 'delivery of goods' (i.e., delivery up of goods) subject to an agreement regulated by the **Consumer Credit Act 1974**; and
(c) in any case where a practice direction provides that a claimant may not obtain a default judgment.

Default judgment cannot be obtained in a possession claim to which **CPR, Part 55**, applies (**r. 55.7(4)**) or in a probate claim (**r. 57.10(1)**). In the Admiralty Court the procedure is modified by **r. 61.9** and **PD 61, para. 8.1**. Default judgment cannot be obtained in arbitration claims under **CPR, Part 62**, because they are brought under the Part 8 procedure (**rr. 62.3(1)** and **62.13(1)**). Nor can default judgment be entered in a case involving a claim for provisional damages, unless the claimant abandons the claim for provisional damages. If the defendant does not file his acknowledgment or defence in time, and the claimant does not wish to abandon the claim for provisional damages, he should apply to the court for directions under **Part 23** (**PD 41, para. 5.1**).

Where a defendant has made an admission, the correct response is for the claimant to proceed under **CPR, Part 14** (see **chapter 17**), rather than by way of entry of judgment in default.

CONDITIONS FOR ENTERING JUDGMENT IN DEFAULT

20.3 In order to enter judgment in default, the court is required by **CPR, r. 12.3**, and **PD 12, para. 4.1**, to be satisfied:

(a) that the particulars of claim have been served (a certificate of service on the court file will be sufficient evidence where service was effected by the claimant);
(b) that either the defendant has not filed an acknowledgment of service or has not filed a defence, and, in either case, time for doing so has expired;
(c) that the defendant has not satisfied the claim;
(d) that the defendant has not filed or served an admission together with a request for time to pay;
(e) that the defendant has not made an application to strike out the claim or for summary judgment which has not been disposed of; and
(f) where it is sought to enter judgment in default against a child or patient, that a litigation friend has been appointed.

Point (a) does not have to be satisfied in the Commercial and Mercantile Courts, where default judgment may be entered before the claimant has served particulars of claim (**CPR, rr. 58.8** and **59.7**).

For the purpose of (b) above, the filing of any document purporting to be a defence will prevent the claimant obtaining judgment in default (**PD 12, para. 1.1**). If a purported defence discloses no substantial grounds of defence, the claimant may consider applying to strike it out (see **chapter 33**) or may seek summary judgment (see **chapter 34**).

REQUEST FOR DEFAULT JUDGMENT

20.4 The procedure for requesting entry of judgment in default is summarised in **procedural checklist 16**, which is in **appendix 1**.

By **CPR, r. 12.4**, a claimant may obtain judgment in default by filing a form requesting judgment to be entered where the claim is for:

(a) a specified sum of money (save where the claim is only for costs other than fixed costs);
(b) an amount of money to be decided by the court;
(c) delivery of goods where the claim form gives the defendant the alternative of paying their value; or
(d) any combination of these remedies.

If the claimant (rather than the court) served the claim form, judgment in default cannot be obtained unless a certificate of service of the claim form has been filed (**r. 6.14(2)**).

Judgment in default can be obtained under **r. 12.4** for a claim which includes a claim or claims for a remedy other than money provided the non-money claims are abandoned in the request form (**r. 12.4(3)**). However, where this is done and default judgment is entered only to be later set aside, the abandoned claim will be restored when judgment is set aside (**r. 13.6**).

Claim for specified sum

To obtain judgment in default on a claim for a specified sum, the claimant files a request for judgment in form N205A or N225. **20.5**

Judgment will be entered for the amount sought in the claim form, plus fixed costs (set out in the table at **CPR, r. 45.4**, and see **chapter 67**). Alternatively, the claimant may give the defendant time to pay or permit the defendant to pay in instalments. This is done by setting out the rate and times of payment acceptable in the request for judgment form. Judgment will then be entered on this basis (**r. 12.5**).

By **r. 12.6**, the default judgment will include interest on claims for specified sums which has accrued due up to the date on which the default judgment was entered, provided that:

(a) full particulars of interest were set out in the particulars of claim;
(b) on a claim for statutory interest, the rate sought is no higher than that payable on judgment debts; and
(c) the request for judgment sets out a calculation of the interest claimed between the date to which interest has been calculated in the claim form, and the date of the request for judgment.

Otherwise, judgment will be entered for interest to be decided by the court (**r. 12.6(2)**).

Claim for unspecified sum

To obtain judgment in default on a claim for an unspecified sum, the claimant files form N205B or N227 and judgment will be for an amount to be decided by the court, plus costs (**CPR, r. 12.5(3)**). A default judgment on liability for an amount to be decided by the court is conclusive on liability in respect of all matters pleaded. But all questions going to quantification of the damage remain open. Any point may be raised by the defendant at the assessment of damages, provided it is consistent with the judgment on liability. Thus it is not open to the defendant to say that its acts or omissions had not caused any damage, but it could say that its acts or omissions had not caused certain individual items of damage (*Lunnun v Singh* (1999) *The Times*, 19 July 1999, followed in *Pugh v Cantor Fitzgerald International* [2001] EWCA Civ 307, *The Times*, 19 March 2001). **20.6**

In any case where the court enters judgment for:

(a) an amount to be decided by the court,
(b) the value of goods to be decided by the court, or
(c) interest to be decided by the court,

it will also give any directions it considers appropriate and may allocate the case to a track (**r. 12.7**). However, it will normally only allocate the case (other than in small claims track cases) where there is a substantial dispute between the parties as to the amount payable (**PD 26, para. 12.3**).

The detailed procedure governing the assessment of damages is set out in **PD 26, para. 12.** On the entry of the default judgment, the court will fix an appointment for a disposal hearing, at which it may either give case management directions, or, where it has sufficient information, quantify the claim immediately. Where the value of the claim is below the limit for the small claims track, the court will allocate the case to that track and may treat the disposal hearing as the final hearing of the case (**PD 26, para. 12.3(2)**). The types of order the court may make are set out in **PD 26, para. 12.2**, and include the filing of allocation questionnaires and stays for the purpose of ADR. The court may also fix further hearings, and, to enable it to come to a decision on quantum, it might order disclosure, the filing of expert evidence and the exchange of witness statements on the issues which remain live between the parties.

Claims against the Crown

20.7 Default judgment in claims against the Crown may now be entered upon filing a request for judgment. An application is no longer necessary. However, a request for a default judgment against the Crown must be considered by a master or district judge, who must be satisfied that the claim form and particulars of claim have been properly served on the Crown in accordance with the **Crown Proceedings Act 1947, s. 18,** and **CPR, r. 6.5(8)**.

APPLICATION FOR DEFAULT JUDGMENT

20.8 The procedure for applying for entry of judgment in default is summarised in **procedural checklist 17**, which is in **appendix 1**.

CPR, rr. 12.9(1)(b) and **12.10**, and **PD 12, para. 2.3**, specify certain types of claim on which default judgment may only be obtained by making an application under **CPR, Part 23**. Cases where the claimant must make an application are where:

(a) The claim is:
   (i) not a money claim;
   (ii) a claim against a child or patient;
   (iii) a claim in tort by one spouse or civil partner against the other;
   (iv) a claim for costs other than fixed costs;
   (v) for delivery up of goods where the defendant will not be allowed the alternative of paying their value; or
(b) The defendant is:
   (i) a person who has been served with the claim out of the jurisdiction without the court's permission under **r. 6.19(1)** or **(1A)**;
   (ii) a State;
   (iii) a diplomatic agent who enjoys diplomatic immunity by virtue of the Diplomatic Privileges Act 1964;
   (v) a person or organisation which enjoys immunity from civil claims under the International Organisations Acts 1968 and 1981.

A claimant who has served a claim form and particulars of claim on a child or patient cannot apply immediately for default judgment, because no step may be taken in the proceedings (other than issuing and serving a claim form) until a litigation friend has been appointed for the defendant (**CPR, r. 21.3(2)**). Therefore, the correct procedure is to apply for the appointment of a litigation friend under **r. 21.6** before applying for default judgment (**PD 12, para. 4.2(1)**).

Where service is effected under **Council Regulation (EU) No. 1348/2000** (the Service Regulation), judgment in default cannot be given until it is established that service was effected by a method prescribed by the internal law of the receiving State or that the documents were actually delivered to the defendant or to the defendant's residence by another method provided by the Regulation and that, in either case, the defendant had sufficient time to defend the claim (**art. 19**).

Application procedure

A notice of application for default judgment must be filed in accordance with the procedure in **CPR, Part 23**. Where the defendant is an individual, the claimant must provide the defendant's date of birth (if known) in part C of the application notice, for use in the registration of judgments (**r. 12.4(2)**). Notice of the application must then be given to the defendant in all cases except claims served under **r. 6.19** and claims against a State where the defendant has not acknowledged service (**r. 12.11(4); PD 12, para. 5.1**). **20.9**

A defendant who seeks to prevent judgment being entered in default by filing an acknowledgment of service or a defence on or just before the hearing must apply for an extension of time. Whether permission will be granted is a matter for the court's discretion, but normally it will be exercised in favour of extending time where, in the case of late acknowledgement, it is a genuine preliminary to a defence to the claim (*Coll v Tattum* (2001) *The Times*, 3 December 2001, followed in *Boeing Capital Corporation v Wells Fargo Bank Northwest* [2003] EWHC 1364 (Comm), LTL 17/7/2003). Neither of these cases considers the test to be applied in evaluating the genuineness of the defence. However, logically, the defence must have a real prospect of success within the meaning of *Swain v Hillman* [2001] 1 All ER 91 and *E. D. and F. Man Liquid Products Ltd v Patel* [2003] EWCA Civ 472, [2003] CPLR 384.

There will be a hearing, and judgment will be entered for what it appears to the court that the claimant is entitled to on the statement of case (**CPR, r. 12.11(1)**). In other words, the court will consider the merits of the claim, albeit only as they appear in the particulars of claim.

On an application for default judgment against a child or a patient or a claim in tort between spouses or civil partners, evidence must be produced to satisfy the court that the claimant is entitled to the judgment claimed (**r. 12.11; PD 12, para. 4.2**).

On an application for default judgment in a claim where service was effected under the **Civil Jurisdiction and Judgments Act 1982** or a claim against a foreign State, evidence must establish the points listed in **PD 12, paras 4.3 or 4.4**, respectively, and must be given by affidavit (**para. 4.5**).

TWO OR MORE DEFENDANTS

If there are two or more defendants, the claimant may obtain a judgment on request against one defendant and proceed with the claim against any other defendants (**CPR, r. 12.8(1)**). However, where a claimant applies for default judgment against some defendants and not others, the court will only enter default judgment where the claim can be dealt with separately from the claim against other defendants (**r. 12.8(2)**). **20.10**

Having obtained the default judgment, a claimant may enforce it against only some defendants, save where it is for the possession of land or delivery of goods. Here, the defendant may enforce only after obtaining judgment against all defendants, or where the court gives its permission (**r. 12.8(3)**).

SETTING ASIDE A DEFAULT JUDGMENT

Principles upon which a default judgment will be set aside

20.11 A defendant against whom judgment in default has been entered may apply for it to be varied or set aside under **CPR, Part 13**.

A judgment which has been entered wrongly (as defined in the CPR) must be set aside by the court. In other cases, the court has a discretion to set the judgment aside and it will normally require the defendant to show a real prospect of successfully defending the claim before it will do so.

In any case where the court sets aside a default judgment, it may attach conditions, such as the payment of money into court (**r. 3.1(3)**).

Where the default judgment was entered wrongly

20.12 The court must set aside any judgment entered wrongly (**CPR, r. 13.2**). The phrase 'entered wrongly' is defined precisely under the rules. By **r. 13.2(a) to (c)**, it is limited to the following cases:

(a) time for acknowledging service, or for serving a defence (as the case may be) had not expired by the time the default judgment was entered;
(b) a summary judgment application or an application to strike out the claim made by the defendant was pending when the default judgment was entered; or
(c) the defendant had satisfied the whole claim or, on a money claim, filed an admission and a request for time to pay at the time the default judgment was entered.

Judgment was set aside as of right under **r. 13.2(a)** in *Credit Agricole Indosuez v Unicof Ltd* [2003] EWHC 77 (Comm), LTL 4/2/2003. The claimant purported to serve the claim form by leaving it with the defendant's company secretary in Kenya, whereas service in Kenya had to be by leaving the claim form at the company's registered office. As the claim form had not been served, the defendant was entitled to have the judgment set aside. In *Shiblaq v Sadikoglu* [2004] EWHC 1890 (Comm), [2004] 2 All ER (Comm) 596, the court took the same approach.

Where service in a foreign jurisdiction has not complied with local law, neither **r. 6.8** (by which the court may grant an order for service by an alternative method) nor **r. 6.9** (by which the court may dispense with service) can normally be used either retrospectively to cure the defect in service or prospectively to authorise a different form of service to that permitted in the country of service. Nor can **r. 3.10** be used to cure an error in service. (See further **16.54**.)

A default judgment obtained using the request procedure in error instead of the application for judgment procedure was irregular and capable of being set aside as of right under **r. 13.2** (*Intense Investments Ltd v Development Ventures Ltd* [2005] EWHC 1762 (TCC), [2005] BLR 478). It is submitted that this decision ignores the constraints of **r. 13.2** which specifies precisely the circumstances in which the court must set aside a default judgment. These do not include using the wrong procedure to enter the default judgment.

WHERE THE DEFAULT JUDGMENT WAS NOT ENTERED WRONGLY

20.13 The court has a discretion to set aside a default judgment which was not entered wrongly. It may exercise its discretion if (**CPR, r. 13.3(1)**):

(a) the defendant has a real prospect of successfully defending the claim; or
(b) it appears to the court that there is some other good reason why:
 (i) the judgment should be set aside or varied; or
 (ii) the defendant should be allowed to defend the claim.

In considering whether to set aside or vary a judgment entered under **Part 12**, the matters to which the court must have regard include whether the person seeking to set aside the judgment made an application to do so promptly (**r. 13.3(2)**).

The wording of **r. 13.3(1)(a)** mirrors the test established in *Alpine Bulk Transport Co. Inc. v Saudi Eagle Shipping Co. Inc.* [1986] 2 Lloyd's Rep 221, that the defendant must have a case with a reasonable prospect of success, and it is not enough to show a merely arguable defence. In *E. D. and F. Man Liquid Products Ltd v Patel* [2003] EWCA Civ 472, [2003] CPLR 384, the Court of Appeal confirmed that the test is the same as the test for summary judgment. The only significant difference is that in a summary judgment application the burden of proof rests on the claimant to show that the defendant has no real prospect of success whereas in an application to set aside a default judgment it is for the defendant to show that his defence has a real prospect of success. For this reason it might be harder for a defendant to succeed in an application to set aside than to resist an application for summary judgment. The test was considered in detail in *Swain v Hillman* [2001] 1 All ER 91 (see **34.10**).

There may be a good reason for setting aside a default judgment under **r. 13.3(1)(b)** where a claimant has an unanswerable claim which would effectively be lost if the judgment were not set aside (*Messer Griesheim GmbH v Goyal MG Gases Pvt Ltd* [2006] EWHC 79 (Comm), *The Times*, 14 February 2006).

Defendant unaware that service has been deemed to have occurred

Once it is proved (such as by a certificate of service) that proceedings have been served by **20.14** one of the methods prescribed by the CPR, service is deemed to take effect on the date laid down by **r. 6.7**, and evidence to prove the contrary is not admissible (see *Anderton v Clwyd County Council (No. 2)* [2002] EWCA Civ 933, [2002] 1 WLR 3174). Where a default judgment has been entered after the expiry of 14 days from the deemed date of service in a case where the defendant did not in fact receive the proceedings, setting aside is subject to the court's discretion rather than as of right (*Godwin v Swindon Borough Council* [2001] EWCA Civ 1478, [2002] 1 WLR 997). The decisions in *Anderton v Clwyd County Council (No. 2)* and *Godwin v Swindon Borough Council* concerned the effect of the deeming provisions on a claimant who delays serving a claim form until the end of the period for service. However, in *Akram v Adam* [2004] EWCA Civ 1601, [2005] 1 WLR 2762, the Court of Appeal looked at the position of a defendant who says that he had no notice of the proceedings at all until after he heard of the default judgment. The court dismissed the contention that a defendant in this situation should be entitled to have the judgment set aside as of right on the grounds that he had received no notification of the proceedings and was therefore a stranger to them. It also held that the deeming provisions on service in the CPR did not contravene the European Convention on Human Rights, art. 6 in the **Human Rights Act 1998, sch. 1**. It confirmed that a judgment entered on a claim served in accordance with the rules, but of which the defendant had no notice, has not been entered wrongly and the defendant can have it set aside only on the grounds specified in **CPR, r. 13.3(1)** (see **20.13**). Such a defendant will therefore either have to show a defence with a real prospect of success, or rely on non-service as 'some other good reason' for setting aside the judgment. According to May LJ in *Godwin v Swindon Borough Council* at [49] this may arise where a defendant would have paid instead of having an embarrassing judgment entered, and it may give grounds for departing from the usual rule of the defendant being ordered to pay the costs thrown away (see **66.26**). In *Manx Electricity Authority v JP Morgan Chase Bank* [2002] EWHC 867 (Comm), LTL 16/5/2002, the court agreed that a judgment entered in this situation should be set aside under **r. 13.3(1)(b)**; alternatively that the claimant should have taken steps under **r. 13.5** to set aside the judgment (see **20.20**). Doubts about the effectiveness of alternative service in the circumstances of the case appear to have been treated as a factor in setting aside a default judgment in *Black Arrow Finance Ltd v Orderdaily Co. Ltd* [2002] EWCA Civ 289, LTL 31/1/2002.

Real prospect of success

20.15 In *International Finance Corporation v Utexafrica sprl* [2001] CLC 1361 it was stated that the test in CPR, r. 13.3(1)(a), of having a real prospect of success means that the prospects must be better than merely arguable. In *E. D. and F. Man Liquid Products Ltd v Patel* [2003] EWCA Civ 472, [2003] CPLR 384, the Court of Appeal confirmed this proposition and that the test is higher than it was under RSC, ord. 14.

Discretion to set aside

20.16 In *Rahman v Rahman* (1999) LTL 26/11/99 the court considered the nature of the discretion to set aside a default judgment under **CPR, r. 13.3**. It concluded that the elements the judge had to consider were the nature of the defence, the period of delay (i.e., why the application to set aside had not been made before), any prejudice the claimant was likely to suffer if the default judgment was set aside, and the overriding objective.

In *Thorn plc v Macdonald* [1999] CPLR 660 the Court of Appeal approved the following principles:

(a) while the length of any delay by the defendant must be taken into account, any pre-action delay is irrelevant;
(b) any failure by the defendant to provide a good explanation for the delay is a factor to be taken into account, but is not always a reason to refuse to set aside;
(c) the primary considerations are whether there is a defence with a real prospect of success, and that justice should be done; and
(d) prejudice (or the absence of it) to the claimant also has to be taken into account.

In *Law v St Margarets Insurance Ltd* [2001] EWCA Civ 30, LTL 18/1/2001, the Court of Appeal allowed judgment in default to be set aside despite the defendant's solicitors' procedural errors in failing to file an acknowledgment of service and in failing to ensure that the statement of truth in relation to the evidence in support of the application was signed by the right person. The overriding objective required that the default judgment be set aside in order to enable the merits of the defence to be determined.

In *Lloyds Investment (Scandinavia) Ltd v Ager-Hansen* (2001) LTL 7/11/2001 a default judgment was set aside on the ground that the defendant had a real prospect of success. Although the claimant had raised serious questions about the defendant's credibility, no finding could be made without oral evidence and cross-examination.

Where summary judgment had been refused against defendants who appeared on the application but default judgment had been entered against a defendant who did not appear, the court subsequently set aside the default judgment, because there had been no examination of the evidence against that defendant. Given that the question of a real prospect of successfully defending the claim had been determined in favour of the defendants who had filed defences, it would have been wrong to come to a different conclusion in relation to the defendant who had not participated (*Huntingdon Life Sciences Ltd v Stop Huntingdon Animal Cruelty* [2004] EWHC 3145 (QB), LTL 11/11/2004).

The privilege against self-incrimination does not afford an excuse for failing to serve a defence with a realistic prospect of success, and will not provide grounds for setting aside a judgment in default (*Versailles Trade Finance Ltd v Clough* [2001] EWCA Civ 1509, [2002] CP Rep 8).

The provisions governing default judgments in Admiralty claims are in **r. 61.9**. Although **r. 61.9(5)** gives the court power to set aside a default judgment, it does not prescribe the criteria. It was held in *The Selby Paradigm* [2004] EWHC 1804 (Admlty), [2004] 2 Lloyd's Rep 714, that the burden on the defendant is to show that it has a real prospect of success in defending the claim, and is not akin to that imposed on an appellant.

Setting aside under the Service Regulation

Where service was effected under **Council Regulation (EU) No. 1348/2000** (the Service Regulation), the court has power under art. 19(4) to relieve the defendant from the effect of any judgment entered in default if: **20.17**

(a) the defendant, without any fault on his part, did not have knowledge of the documents served in sufficient time to defend; and
(b) the defendant discloses a prima facie defence to the claim on its merits.

Procedure

A defendant must apply for judgment in default to be varied or set aside under the **Part 23** procedure (see **chapter 32**). An application to set aside a default judgment which has not been entered wrongly must be supported by evidence (**CPR, r. 13.4(3)**). Commonly, a draft defence is attached to a witness statement in support of the application. **20.18**

Where the claim is for a specified sum of money, has not been started in a specialist list and the judgment is entered against an individual in a court which is not the defendant's home court (defined in **r. 2.3(1)**), the court will automatically transfer the application there (**r. 13.4(1)**).

If the defendant has entered into a funding arrangement (as defined in **r. 43.2(1)(k)**) and the application to set aside default judgment is the first document to be filed by the defendant, a notice of funding of case (**form N251**) must be filed at court with the application and a copy served on every other party (**PD 43–48, para. 19.2(3)**).

Setting aside on conditions

If the court sets aside a default judgment, it may do so on terms (**CPR, r. 3.1(3)**). In most cases the defaulting defendant will be ordered to pay the claimant's costs thrown away. In addition, the court may consider imposing a condition that the defendant must pay a specified sum of money into court to await the final disposal of the claim. This is effectively a sanction requiring the defendant to pay the money immediately (albeit into court), rather than being able to wait until judgment. The sum paid into court also assists the claimant, who obtains a secure fund from which the amount found due can be paid, which also operates as a secured fund if the defendant becomes insolvent (*Re Ford* [1900] 2 QB 211). **20.19**

In deciding whether to impose such a condition, the court will consider factors such as whether there was any delay in applying to set aside, doubts about the strength of the defence on the merits, and conduct of the defendant indicating a risk of dissipation of assets (see *Creasey v Breachwood Motors Ltd* [1993] BCLC 480). As to the amount, this is in the court's discretion, which should be exercised applying the overriding objective. However, a condition requiring payment into court of a sum that the defendant will find impossible to pay ought not to be ordered (*M. V. Yorke Motors v Edwards* [1982] 1 WLR 444; *Training in Compliance Ltd v Dewse* (2000) LTL 2/10/2000), as that would be tantamount to refusing to set aside.

The court may also find it appropriate to exercise other of its case management powers under **r. 3.1(2)**. For example, it may order trial of a preliminary issue raised in any draft defence or allow judgment to be set aside on the issues raised in the draft defence which have a real prospect of success and not on those which do not.

FORMER DUTY OF CLAIMANT TO SET ASIDE A WRONGLY ENTERED DEFAULT JUDGMENT

The provision formerly in **CPR, r. 13.5**, which placed a duty on a claimant who had entered default judgment, but subsequently became aware that the particulars of claim had not **20.20** reached the defendant before judgment was entered, to request that the default judgment be set aside or apply for directions, has been revoked. It was inconsistent with the policy that there is an irrevocable presumption of service on the date set out in **r. 6.7** on proof of one of the permitted methods of service under **r. 6.2.** See **15.35** and *Anderton v Clwyd County Council (No. 2)* [2002] EWCA Civ 933, [2002] 1 WLR 3174.

DEFAULT JUDGMENT ON AN ADDITIONAL CLAIM

20.21 There are special rules which apply in relation to entering judgment in default on an additional claim. These are dealt with in **29.10**.

Chapter 21 Acting by a Solicitor

INTRODUCTION

This chapter deals with a number of issues that arise when litigation is conducted, as it often is, by solicitors. A solicitor is an officer of the court, and is therefore under certain duties to the court and subject to the disciplinary jurisdiction of the High Court. Once proceedings are issued by a solicitor on behalf of a client, or acknowledged by a solicitor on behalf of a client, the solicitor will be regarded as being on the record. All further steps taken on behalf of that client should be taken by that solicitor, and all further documents served on that client should be served on that solicitor, until formal notice of change has been served. While on the record the solicitor will have apparent authority (and often actual authority) to take all steps on behalf of the client, who will be bound by the action taken. A number of other topics are also considered. **21.1**

OFFICER OF THE COURT

The **Solicitors Act 1974, s. 50**, provides as follows: **21.2**

(1) Any person duly admitted as a solicitor shall be an officer of the Supreme Court.
(2) Subject to the provisions of this Act, the High Court, the Crown Court and the Court of Appeal respectively, or any division or judge of those courts, may exercise the same jurisdiction in respect of solicitors as any one of the superior courts of law or equity from which the Supreme Court was constituted might have exercised immediately before the passing of the Supreme Court of Judicature Act 1873 in respect of any solicitor, attorney or proctor admitted to practise there.
(3) An appeal shall lie to the Court of Appeal from any order made against a solicitor by the High Court or the Crown Court in the exercise of its jurisdiction in respect of solicitors under subsection (2).

As officers of the court, solicitors are under duties not to mislead the court, to bring to the court's attention authorities relevant to the case which may go against their clients, and various other duties conveniently summarised in *Cordery on Solicitors*, 9th ed. (London: Butterworths, 1995) and the Law Society's *Guide to the Professional Conduct of Solicitors*, 8th ed. (1999). Counsel owe similar duties under the Code of Conduct of the Bar of England and Wales. Solicitors and counsel must, moreover, be regarded as owing a duty to assist the court in achieving the overriding objective by reason of **CPR, r. 1.3** (which in fact places the duty on the legal representatives' clients), and the fact that solicitors are officers of the court.

The High Court has a summary disciplinary jurisdiction over solicitors. In *Myers v Elman* [1940] AC 282 Lord Wright said that the underlying principle of the summary jurisdiction is that the High Court has a right and a duty to supervise the conduct of solicitors, and to impose penalties where the conduct of a solicitor is of such a nature as to tend to defeat justice. The jurisdiction is compensatory rather than punitive, but does have a disciplinary slant. There was formerly a body of case law dealing with applications for costs orders against solicitors pursuant to the court's inherent jurisdiction over them. This particular area is now covered by the detailed rules on wasted costs applications, which is considered further in **chapter 66**.

Disciplinary proceedings against solicitors are nowadays mainly investigated by the Office for Supervision of Solicitors and, where appropriate, brought before the Solicitors' Disciplinary Tribunal. Powers still exist, however, to apply to the High Court to strike the name of a solicitor off the roll of solicitors, or to answer certain allegations, under the Solicitors Act 1974, ss. 51 to 55.

SOLICITOR ON THE RECORD

21.3 Every party to litigation must provide an address for service within the jurisdiction (**CPR, r. 6.5(2)**), which, where a solicitor is acting for a party, will be the business address of the party's solicitor (**r. 6.5(5)**). The claim form will identify whether the claimant is acting by a solicitor, and the acknowledgment of service form, defence, or defence and counterclaim, will similarly identify whether the defendant is acting by a solicitor.

Once a solicitor is on the court record as acting for a party, by **rr. 42.1** and **42.2(5)**, that solicitor will be considered to be continuing to act for that party until due notice is given or an order is made in accordance with **Part 42**. The rules on giving notice of change are considered further in **chapter 22**.

ACTING FOR JOINT CLAIMANTS

21.4 Before the introduction of the CPR, the usual rule where there were joint claimants was that they were not allowed to take inconsistent steps (such as by just one of them making an interim application within the proceedings), they had to act by a common firm of solicitors, and be represented at trial and other hearings by the same counsel (*Re Wright* [1895] 2 Ch 747; *Re Mathews* [1905] 2 Ch 460; *Lewis v Daily Telegraph Ltd (No. 2)* [1964] 2 QB 601). Pearson LJ in *Lewis v Daily Telegraph Ltd (No. 2)* said that there may be scope for making a special order for separate representation of joint claimants, but indicated a distinct reluctance to do this. The disinclination against separate representation of joint claimants must be stronger under the CPR, given the elements of the overriding objective relating to saving expense and ensuring that cases are dealt with expeditiously. A defendant faced with separately represented claimants should consider applying for a stay (**chapter 54**).

CONFLICTS BETWEEN CLIENTS

No-conflict rule

21.5 A solicitor will be unable to act for two or more clients in the same matter (whether as claimants or defendants) where there is a conflict of interest between the clients. If the clients whose interests are in conflict are intending claimants, the best course is for them all to go to new solicitors and, if proceedings are necessary, to bring separate proceedings so that they can be separately represented. The original solicitor will have to consider carefully whether he or she is able to act for one of the parties in view of the initial contact with another party, bearing in mind the advice in the Law Society's *Guide to the Professional Conduct of Solicitors.* A solicitor who discovers a conflict of interest in representing a client must inform the client of his or her inability to act, and that the client should seek legal advice from other solicitors, starting afresh and not relying on any advice already given by the solicitor (*Hilton v Barker Booth and Eastwood* [2005] UKHL 8, [2005] 1 WLR 567).

Nor can a solicitor generally act for a client where that client's interests conflict with those of a former client. For example, in *Saminadhen v Khan* [1992] 1 All ER 963 Lord Donaldson of Lymington MR said he could conceive of no circumstances in which it would be proper for a solicitor who had acted for one defendant in criminal proceedings, in which a cut-throat defence had been advanced between two defendants, to act subsequently for the other defendant after the first retainer had terminated. However, the full position is more complicated than this, because the courts dealing with this problem are in fact seeking to balance two conflicting public interests:

(a) The public interest in enabling the client to repose the fullest confidence in the solicitor he retains, and ensuring there is no risk or perception of a risk that confidential information relating to a client will be conveyed to anyone else. The information that the court will seek to protect will have the following characteristics:
   (i) It was originally communicated to the solicitor in confidence.
   (ii) It is still confidential, and reasonably capable of being considered capable of being recalled. It might lose this characteristic by becoming common knowledge, or (in certain circumstances) if it has been communicated to an opponent during the course of litigation. Alternatively, it might be so eminently forgettable that it should not be protected. A client complaining that confidential information might be at risk must identify it with some particularity, but the degree of particularity required depends on the facts of the case (*Re a Firm of Solicitors* [1997] Ch 1).
   (iii) It is relevant to the subject matter of the subsequent retainer.
(b) The public interest in the freedom of the solicitor to obtain instructions from any member of the public, and for all members of the public to instruct the solicitor of their choice.

A solicitor who continues to act without disclosing a conflict between duty of loyalty to the first client and duty of confidentiality to a second client, is liable for any loss suffered by the first client. The duty of loyalty to the first client is not modified by the fact that complying with it will involve breaching the duty of confidentiality to the second client: the predicament is the solicitor's own fault in allowing the conflict to arise (*Hilton v Barker Booth and Eastwood* [2005] UKHL 8, [2005] 1 WLR 567).

Further, a solicitor cannot simultaneously act for two clients in separate matters if the clients have potentially conflicting interests and there is a reasonable relationship between the two transactions (*Marks and Spencer plc v Freshfields Bruckhaus Deringer* [2004] EWHC 1337 (Ch), [2004] 1 WLR 2331).

As a matter of practice, it is wise for solicitors to run computer conflict checks when instructed and when parties are added to existing proceedings.

Restraining a solicitor from acting

A solicitor who is possessed of relevant confidential information will be restrained from acting against the former client (*Re a Firm of Solicitors* [1992] QB 959). In the case of a firm previously retained by a client, the partners and employees who are in possession of confidential information may be restrained from acting against the former client, and this extends to them if they change firms. Members and employees of the firm who never had possession of relevant confidential information are in a rather more complex position. While they remain 21.6

with the firm they will, generally, be precluded from acting against the former client of the firm, but it is possible they may be allowed to act if there is no real (as opposed to fanciful) risk that relevant confidential information may have been communicated to them (*Re a Firm of Solicitors* [1992] QB 959).

Real risk of disclosure

21.7 In *Bolkiah v KPMG* [1999] 2 AC 222 the claimant had retained the defendant firm of accountants in his private capacity to provide extensive litigation support services of a kind commonly provided by solicitors in relation to proceedings he was involved in. In the course of this retainer the defendants became privy to detailed information relating to the claimant's financial affairs, and no less than 168 of the defendants' employees were involved. Some months after the conclusion of the claimant's action, the defendants were retained by the claimant' s former employer (the Brunei Investment Agency, BIA) to investigate the location of substantial funds that had been transferred during his period of employment. Aware of a possible conflict of interest, the defendants erected an information barrier (also known as a 'Chinese wall') around the department conducting the BIA investigation. The defendants did not, however, ask for the claimant's consent to them acting for the BIA. It was held that the claimant was entitled to an injunction restraining the defendants from continuing to act in the BIA investigation. Such injunctions will be granted unless the firm produces clear and convincing evidence that effective measures have been taken to ensure that no disclosure of the former client's affairs will be made to the department acting for the new client, and that there is no risk of the former client's information reaching the department acting for the new client. Although, in some cases, Chinese walls may be sufficient protection, there is a very heavy burden on the firm to prove this, and it will be very difficult for the firm to do so unless those measures were an established part of the firm's organisational structure. See also the first-instance decision in *Re a Firm of Solicitors* [2000] 1 Lloyd's Rep 31.

Following *Bolkiah v KPMG* the question is whether there is a real, as opposed to a fanciful, risk of disclosure. Whether there is such a risk is a question of fact. Where a solicitor acted for a party many years before, but neither the solicitor nor the client have any material recollection of the previous matter, there is no material conflict (*Re T and A (Children) (Risk of Disclosure)* [2000] 1 FLR 859). Each case turns on its own facts. In *Koch Shipping Inc. v Richards Butler* [2002] EWCA Civ 1280, [2003] PNLR 11, it was held that fears of inadvertent disclosure of confidential information by the solicitor formerly with day-to-day conduct of a case for one side who then joined the firm representing the other side (where she had no dealings with the case) were fanciful.

In *Bodle v Coutts and Co.* [2003] EWHC 1865 (Ch), LTL 17/7/2003, Farrer and Co. ('the solicitors') had acted for the claimant some years previously in matrimonial proceedings. Subsequently, the claimant sued the defendant bank, who were now represented by the solicitors. The claimant had not paid the solicitors, who exerted a lien over her matrimonial papers. An application was made to restrain the solicitors from acting for the bank. The court directed the solicitors to produce the papers (which were not shown to the claimant), and the judge concluded they contained nothing relevant to the present proceedings. This procedure was held not to infringe the European Convention on Human Rights, art. 6(1), as production had been directed by the court, rather than the papers being voluntarily deployed by the solicitors. On the solicitors giving undertakings restricting access to the papers and discussion of their contents, the claimant's application was refused.

Staff moving to new firms

21.8 Once members or employees, who never had possession of confidential information about a former client of a firm, move to new firms, they will be free from constraint. To come into this more favoured class, the burden is on the solicitor to prove not only that he or she did not have possession of relevant confidential information, but that there is no real risk that he or she has such information (*Re a Firm of Solicitors* [1997] Ch 1).

Other examples

A different problem was considered in *Re Schuppan* [1996] 2 All ER 664. A well-known firm of solicitors had acted for the judgment creditor in hard-fought High Court proceedings involving allegations of fraud and a detailed investigation of the assets of the judgment debtor. The judgment was not satisfied, and the debtor was declared bankrupt. The trustee in bankruptcy retained the solicitors who had been acting for the judgment creditor to act in the bankruptcy. It was held that having a blanket rule that it is never allowable for a creditor's solicitors to act for the trustee in bankruptcy was a counsel of perfection, and this could be allowed if no difficulty was expected in quantifying the provable debts (which generally is the most obvious area of possible conflict of interest), provided there were good reasons for retaining the creditor's solicitors. In this case there were good reasons, as they already had a good grasp of the bankrupt's finances, and it would have been very expensive for any new firm to read into the case. In addition, there were further unresolved issues arising from the original litigation, including a wasted costs application against the creditor's solicitors and an inquiry based on the creditor's undertaking in damages in respect of a discharged freezing order. These issues did give rise to a possible conflict of interest, but it was held that the risk could be averted by a division of responsibility (with another firm being retained to deal with these issues), and then a balancing exercise would be undertaken (which on the facts favoured allowing the creditor's solicitor to act). 21.9

In *Re L (Minors) (Care Proceedings: Solicitors)* [2001] 1 WLR 100 Wilson J in the Family Division made a declaration that the solicitor acting for the local authority in care proceedings was not so acting, thus removing her from the record, because the fact of her cohabiting with the solicitor for two of the seven respondents to the proceedings could give rise to an apprehension of bias by lay persons.

There may be a conflict of interest where a solicitor has a financial interest in a transaction which may conflict with the interests of a client (*Hilton v Barker Booth and Eastwood* [2005] UKHL 8, [2005] 1 WLR 567).

Orders available

Where a party establishes a conflict of interest, the most the court can do is to grant an injunction forbidding the solicitor from continuing to act for the other party and, if necessary, a stay unless and until new solicitors are instructed. There is no power to order a party to instruct new solicitors (*SMC Engineering (Bristol) Ltd v Fraser* (2000) *The Times*, 26 January 2001). 21.10

AUTHORITY OF SOLICITORS

A solicitor retained by a client is, of course, the client's agent, and has actual or apparent authority to do all things that may reasonably be expected to arise in litigation being conducted for the client (*Prestwich v Poley* (1865) 18 CB NS 806). As against an opposing litigant, the only limitation on the apparent authority of a solicitor to compromise litigation is that it cannot be taken to include the compromise of matters collateral to the proceedings. A matter will only be regarded as collateral where it really is extraneous to the proceedings (*Waugh v H. B. Clifford and Sons Ltd* [1982] Ch 374). However, as between solicitor and client, there will be a breach of authority by the solicitor unless any action taken (particularly compromising the claim) is within his or her express or implied authority. It may well be that a proposed compromise of a claim will be within the apparent authority of the solicitor as against the other side (because it does not include anything collateral to the claim), but will be outside 21.11

the actual authority of the solicitor as between himself and his client. The solicitor will generally only be safe in concluding the proposed compromise if the client gives express instructions. See *Waugh v H. B. Clifford and Sons Ltd*. In general, death of a client will terminate a solicitor's authority. However, where the client is a company, death of its sole shareholder and director will not have this effect, as the company will continue to exist (*Donsland Ltd v Van Hoogstraten* [2002] EWCA Civ 253, [2002] PNLR 26). A solicitor with a 'general retainer' in litigation is required to act for the client to the end and to take all necessary steps to bring the claim to a conclusion. Difficulties in obtaining instructions does not affect the authority of solicitors acting under a general retainer (*Euroafrica Shipping Lines Co. Ltd v Zegluga Polska SA* [2004] EWHC 385 (Comm), [2004] 2 BCLC 97).

AUTHORITY OF COUNSEL

21.12 In *Swinfen v Lord Chelmsford* (1860) 5 Hurl & N 890 Pollock CB said that a barrister has complete authority over the conduct of litigation and all that is incidental to it, but not over matters which are collateral to the case. In *Matthews v Munster* (1887) 20 QBD 141 Lord Esher MR said, at p. 143:

> . . . when the client has requested counsel to act as his advocate . . . he thereby represents to the other side that counsel is to act for him in the usual course, and he must be bound by that representation so long as it continues. . . . The request does not mean that counsel is to act in any other character than that of advocate or to do any other act than such as an advocate usually does. The duty of counsel is to advise his client out of court and to act for him in court, and until his authority is withdrawn he has, with regard to all matters that properly relate to the conduct of the case, unlimited power to do that which is best for his client.

In *Worldwide Corporation Ltd v Marconi Communications Ltd* (1999) *The Times*, 7 July 1999, an application for permission to amend to set up a different cause of action, leading counsel for the claimant had abandoned the cause of action originally pleaded, in a strategy to try to obtain permission to amend. Permission was refused, with the result that, as the original claim had been abandoned, the claim was dismissed. An attempt was then made on behalf of the claimant to resuscitate the original claim, and new leading counsel was briefed. Although it left open the possibility that there may be exceptional cases, the Court of Appeal held that the court had to be able to rely on counsel, and the client was not able to retreat from the abandonment of the original claim.

WARRANTY OF AUTHORITY

Breach of warranty of authority

21.13 By issuing proceedings a firm of solicitors warrant that they have authority from the claimant to do so. Similarly, by filing a defence or taking any other step in the proceedings a firm purporting to act for a defendant warrant that they have authority to act for the defendant. According to Buxton LJ in *AMB Generali Holding AG v SEB Trygg Liv Holding AB* [2005] EWCA Civ 1237, [2006] 1 All ER 437, the solicitor warrants:

(a) that he has a client; and
(b) that the client has instructed him to assert or deny the claims made in the proceedings.

There is no warranty that the solicitor's client has the same name as that used in the proceedings. Otherwise the solicitor would be liable for every misnomer, including typographical errors and changes in company names (*AMB Generali Holding AG v SEB Trygg Liv Holding AB*).

If solicitors do not have authority to issue proceedings, they will be in breach of warranty of authority and liable to the other parties. This rarely occurs through the deliberate action of the solicitors. However, the cases show that it is no defence that the solicitors acted perfectly innocently and without knowledge of the defect in their authority. Solicitors have been held to be in breach of warranty of authority in the following circumstances:

(a) Where the claimant is a child or under a mental disability (*Geilinger v Gibbs* [1897] 1 Ch 479; *Yonge v Toynbee* [1910] 1 KB 215).
(b) Where the claimant does not exist (*Simmons v Liberal Opinion Ltd* [1911] 1 KB 966).
(c) Where the claimant is a limited company which has no directors or officers with authority to give instructions to the solicitors (*West End Hotels Syndicate Ltd v Bayer* (1912) 29 TLR 92).
(d) Where the claimant has died before proceedings were commenced (*Tetlow v Orela Ltd* [1920] 2 Ch 24).
(e) Where the claimant is a company that has been dissolved (*Babury Ltd v London Industrial plc* (1989) 139 NLJ 1596).

Being without instructions

There is a difference between a solicitor being without instructions and being without authority. It is only in the latter case that damages may be awarded against the solicitor for breach of warranty of authority (*Donsland Ltd v Van Hoogstraten* [2002] EWCA Civ 253, [2002] PNLR 26). Where a sole director and shareholder of a company died during the course of proceedings, the company's solicitors, acting under a general retainer, continued to have authority to make applications in those proceedings even though they did not have anyone to give them specific instructions (*Donsland Ltd v Van Hoogstraten*). **21.14**

Practice after a breach of warranty of authority

Where a breach of warranty of authority occurs, the court has jurisdiction to make a summary order against the solicitor where the issues are reasonably clear, but where there are real issues of fact or law the injured party should be left to bring the claim by issuing separate proceedings (*Skylight Maritime SA v Ascot Underwriting* [2005] EWHC 15 (Comm), [2005] PNLR 25). In both cases the jurisdiction is compensatory rather than punitive, so proof of loss is essential (*Skylight Maritime SA v Ascot Underwriting*). Where the summary procedure is used, the innocent party should make an application using **form N244** seeking an order striking out the claim (or the defence) and that the solicitor should be ordered to pay the costs on the indemnity basis. (The principles established in the old cases are unlikely to have been altered in this respect by the introduction of the CPR. The earlier cases indicate that the solicitor in breach should be ordered to pay its client's costs on the indemnity basis.) The application should be served on the solicitors and on the party (if it exists) for whom the solicitor has purported to act. **21.15**

There are some breaches that can be cured, such as by the appointment of a litigation friend (*Cooper v Dumnett* [1930] WN 248) or the passing of necessary company resolutions and ratification of the actions of the solicitors (*East Pant Du United Lead Mining Co. Ltd v Merryweather* (1864) 2 Hem & M 254), and in these cases the court may be prepared to grant a stay for these steps to be taken. In some cases there may be a dispute of fact as to whether there was a want of authority. For example, it may be disputed whether the claimant is of unsound mind. In these cases the court may dismiss or adjourn the application, and leave the applicant to bring separate proceedings for damages for breach of warranty of authority (*Yonge v Toynbee* [1910] 1 KB 215). Otherwise, an order dismissing the claim (or defence) and for indemnity basis costs follows almost as a matter of course.

SOLICITORS' AGENTS

21.16 It is common practice for solicitors to appoint local agents to deal with court hearings, particularly simple interim applications and short trials. There is also a common practice for provincial firms to appoint London agents for trials and important hearings at the Royal Courts of Justice. In these situations the London or local agent's principal is the firm of solicitors originally retained by the lay client, subject to contrary express agreement. The local or London agents must therefore look to their principals for payment of their costs, rather than the client (*Collins v Griffin* (1734) Barnes 37; *Scrace v Whittington* (1823) 2 B & C 11). If the agent is negligent, the client is able to sue the principal, who will be liable for the acts and omissions of the agent (*Re Ward* (1862) 31 Beav 1). In most such cases the principal could seek a contribution or indemnity from the agent using the **Part 20** procedure. As regards the other side, the solicitor agent has apparent authority within the scope of the application under consideration. If that is the trial, the agent has apparent authority to compromise the claim (*Re Newen* [1903] 1 Ch 812), and if an application, to agree terms relevant to the application.

ENFORCING SOLICITORS' UNDERTAKINGS

Binding nature of undertakings

21.17 Undertakings are regularly given by solicitors in a variety of circumstances, and include undertakings that payments will be made, or that things will or will not be done. An undertaking will bind not only the individual solicitor giving it, but also his or her firm, if it is made by a partner in the usual way of business of the kind carried on by the firm (see Partnership Act 1890, and *United Bank of Kuwait Ltd v Hammoud* [1988] 1 WLR 1051). Where the underlying transaction is unusual, the other partners will be bound only if they expressly consent (*see Hirst v Etherington* (1999) 149 NLJ 1110).

Failing to implement a solicitor's undertaking is regarded by the courts and the Solicitors' Disciplinary Tribunal as professional misconduct, even if the solicitor has not been guilty of dishonourable conduct. As solicitors are officers of the court, the High Court has a general jurisdiction to enforce undertakings given by solicitors in their capacities as solicitors (*United Mining and Finance Corporation Ltd v Becher* [1910] 2 KB 296). This jurisdiction is not limited to undertakings given in the course of litigation. The court also has the power to grant a solicitor relief from an undertaking on sufficient cause being shown (*John Fox v Bannister, King and Rigbeys* [1988] QB 925). It may do so, for example, to give relief from a mistake or where there has been impropriety by the other side.

Practice on enforcing solicitors' undertakings

21.18 In *Udall v Capri Lighting Ltd* [1988] QB 907 Balcombe LJ said there are three ways in which a party seeking to enforce a solicitor's undertaking can proceed:

(a) by an action at law;
(b) by an application to the High Court to exercise its inherent supervisory jurisdiction over solicitors; and
(c) by an application to the Law Society. The only remedy available to the Law Society is to take disciplinary action against the solicitor. It cannot order specific performance or grant compensation.

In *Rooks Rider v Steel* [1994] 1 WLR 818 the claimant solicitors acted for a company based in Louisiana in a complex transaction under which the Louisiana company agreed to lend money to a hotel company. The hotel company's solicitors undertook in writing to pay the claimant's fees in connection with the transaction 'whether the matter proceeds to completion or not'. The transaction was never completed, and it transpired the Louisiana company did not have the funds to make the loan, and used the proposed transaction for fraudulent purposes. The defendant solicitors refused to honour their undertaking, relying on the fraud as absolving them from liability. It was found that the claimant solicitors were not involved in their client's fraud. It was accordingly held there was no lawful justification for not complying with the undertaking, and an order was made requiring the defendants to comply. In *Bentley v Gaisford* [1997] QB 627 it was held to be a breach of an undertaking given by the defendant firm to hold documents, which were the subject of a lien against unpaid fees, to the order of the claimant firm, when a partner in the defendant firm, acting in good faith and in what he regarded as his duty to his client, copied all the documents to the client. Doing so rendered the lien worthless.

Where on an application under the supervisory jurisdiction over solicitors it is shown that there has been a breach of an undertaking by a solicitor, the court will usually make an order requiring the solicitor to comply with the undertaking (*Re a Solicitor* [1966] 1 WLR 1604). If compliance with the undertaking will be impossible (perhaps because it involves actions which are not within the control of the solicitor), the court may order the solicitor to pay compensation to any person who suffers loss as a result of the breach of undertaking (*Udall v Capri Lighting Ltd* [1988] QB 907). In *Bentley v Gaisford* [1997] QB 627 the court refused to order the defendant solicitors to pay compensation despite their breach of undertaking because the partner who had copied the documents to the client was not guilty of inexcusable conduct meriting reproof.

Chapter 22 Change of Solicitor

TERMINATION OF RETAINER

22.1 A retainer to conduct litigation is generally regarded as an entire contract, with the effect that a solicitor once retained must see the litigation through to its conclusion. However, the retainer is subject to an implied term that the solicitor may withdraw if there is good cause and provided reasonable notice is given to the client. The client may terminate the retainer without cause at any time. When a party changes solicitors, or retains a solicitor having previously been acting in person, or starts acting in person having previously retained a solicitor, the other parties and the court need to be informed so that future correspondence and court applications, orders and other documents can be sent to the correct address.

SOLICITOR ON THE RECORD

22.2 **Part 6** of the CPR contains general rules on service of documents. Although there are several refinements, some of the basic rules on where litigation documents should be served are:

(a) Under **r. 6.5(2)**, each party to litigation must provide an address for service within the jurisdiction.

(b) **Rule 6.5(5)** provides that where a solicitor is acting for a party, that party's address for service for all purposes other than service of the claim form is the business address of the solicitor.

(c) The address for service of a party who is acting in person is usually the party's residential address or place of business (**r. 6.5(3)**).

(d) Any change of address of a party or of a party's solicitor (without changing the identity of the person acting for that party) must be notified in writing to the court and to other parties as soon as the change takes place (**PD 6, para.** 7).

(e) In recent times the practice has been that if one solicitor acts for a number of parties in a claim, it is sufficient to serve on that solicitor a single copy of any documents that need to be served (see, for example, **PD 10, para.** 5.3).

The claim form will identify whether the claimant is acting by a solicitor or in person, and the defence or defence and counterclaim will similarly identify whether the defendant is acting in person or by a solicitor. **Part** 42 of the CPR contains rules dealing with giving notice of changes relating to representation by solicitors.

PRESUMED CONTINUANCE

22.3 Once a solicitor is on the court record as acting for a party, by **CPR, rr.** 42.1 and 42.2(5), that solicitor will be considered to be continuing to act for that party until due notice is given or an order is made in accordance with **Part** 42. However, a solicitor appointed solely for the purpose of acting as an advocate at a hearing is not considered to be acting for the client for the purposes of **Part 42** (**PD 42, para. 1.3**).

NOTICE OF CHANGE

By **CPR, r. 42.2**, notice of change stating the change and the new address for service (which must be within the jurisdiction, see **r. 6.5(3)**) must be filed at court and served on all other parties whenever: **22.4**

(a) a party who has been acting by a solicitor changes solicitor;
(b) a party who has been acting in person appoints a solicitor; or
(c) a party who has been acting by a solicitor intends to act in future as a litigant in person.

In the circumstances set out in (a) and (c) above the notice of change must also be served on the former solicitor. The form of notice of change of solicitor is **form N434**. It should not be filed until every other party has been served (**PD 42, para. 1.2**), and should be filed in the court office in which the claim is proceeding (**para. 2.5**). Where the claim is the subject of an appeal to the Court of Appeal, the notice should also be filed in the Civil Appeals Office (**para. 2.7**). The copy of the notice filed at court must state that it has also been served on the other parties, and, if appropriate, the former solicitor.

REVOCATION OR DISCHARGE OF PUBLIC FUNDING

The retainer of any solicitor acting on behalf of a publicly funded client determines forthwith upon receipt of a notice of revocation or discharge (Civil Legal Aid (General) Regulations 1989 (SI 1989/339), reg. 83; **Community Legal Service (Costs) Regulations 2000** (SI 2000/441), reg. 4). As soon as the retainer of a solicitor is ended under either of these regulations, the solicitor is required by **CPR, r. 42.2(6)(a)**, to cease acting for the formerly funded or assisted litigant. If the litigant wishes to continue the litigation despite the cessation of public funding, a notice of change (see **22.4**) must be given (**r. 42.2(6)(b)**; **PD 42, para. 2.2**), even if the same solicitor is retained (because the previous solicitor is deemed by **CPR, r. 42.2(6)(a)**, to have ceased to act and **r. 42.2(6)(b)(i)** treats the litigant as previously having acted in person). Where a solicitor is appointed the notice of change does not have to be served on the former solicitor (again because **r. 42.2(6)(b)(i)** treats the litigant as previously having acted in person). The notice must give the last known address of the formerly funded or assisted person (**PD 42, para. 2.2**). **22.5**

COMING OFF THE RECORD

Once retained, a solicitor may withdraw only for good cause and upon giving reasonable notice to the client. There may be good cause to withdraw (see *Underwood, Son and Piper v Lewis* [1894] 2 QB 306) where the client fails to give instructions, acts unreasonably, or fails or refuses to pay a reasonable sum on account of the past and future costs of the litigation within a reasonable time of a request for payment (**Solicitors Act 1974, s. 65(2)**). A solicitor who withdraws in the absence of good cause is in breach of the contract of retainer, and, as it is an entire contract, will be unable to recover any fees from the client (and may be required to refund fees previously paid). **22.6**

When a solicitor ceases to act for a client, whether or not there is a breach of contract as between the solicitor and client, the change ought to be entered in the court records by one means or another. In most cases this will be done by the client or any new solicitor retained by the client giving notice of change as discussed in 22.4. If this does not happen, the former solicitor will in practical terms be obliged to take steps to come off the record. To do this it is necessary to apply for an order under **CPR, r. 42.3**. It is reasonably clear from *Plenty v Gladwin* (1986) 67 ALR 26 (High Court of Australia) that such an application has nothing to do with whether or not the solicitor was right to withdraw, but is simply a matter of ensuring the court's record accords with the reality of whether the solicitor is continuing to act for the client. Unless there are special circumstances to the contrary, orders that a solicitor has ceased to act are generally made as a matter of course when it is shown that the solicitor is no longer acting for the party, and that no notice of change has been given.

An application under **r. 42.3** is made by application notice, which must be served on the client unless the court directs otherwise, and must be supported by evidence, usually by witness statement (see **r. 42.3(2)** and **Part 23**). The application and evidence must not be served on the other parties as it will often contain information which is confidential between the solicitor and client (*Re Creehouse Ltd* [1983] 1 WLR 77).

If an order is made under **r. 42.3** that a solicitor has ceased to act, the order must be served on all the parties to the proceedings, and if the order is not served by the court, the serving party or solicitor must also file a certificate of service in **form N215** (**r. 42.3(3)**).

REMOVAL OF SOLICITOR ON APPLICATION OF ANOTHER PARTY

22.7 Where a solicitor has died, become bankrupt, ceased to practise or gone missing, the court and other parties should be informed and the client's address for service duly altered. Although this is not expressly provided by the CPR, ceasing to practise covers a multitude of circumstances, including retirement, changing professions, and also being struck off the roll of solicitors, failing to take out a practising certificate and being suspended from practising. In the circumstances mentioned in this paragraph there is a strong likelihood of the Law Society intervening in the solicitor's practice, under the Solicitors Act 1974, s. 35 and sch. 1.

Normally the client will appoint a new solicitor who will serve and file the appropriate notice of change. However, if no notice of change is served, the position can be regularised on the application of any other party under **CPR, r. 42.4**, for an order declaring the solicitor has ceased acting for the relevant party. Under the RSC the phrase 'any other party', which appeared in a number of contexts in the old rules and also appears in **CPR, r. 42.4(1)**, was until recently interpreted restrictively by cases such as *Shaw v Smith* (1886) 18 QBD 193 as limited to opposite parties, with the result that a co-defendant was not included. More recently, in *Manatee Towing Co. v Oceanbulk Maritime SA* [1999] 1 Lloyd's Rep 876, a decision under the old rules, it was held that this restrictive interpretation of the phrase no longer applied to the latest version of the old rules. There is no prospect of the old restrictive interpretation being carried forward into the CPR. The result is that an application under **r. 42.4** may be made by any party other than the party whose solicitor is no longer available.

An application notice seeking a declaration under **r. 42.4** must be supported by evidence (**PD 42, para. 4.2**) and, unless the court otherwise directs, must be served on the client whose solicitor is unavailable. If the declaration is made, a copy of the order must be served on all the other parties, and if the order is not served by the court, the serving party must also file a certificate of service in **form N215** (**CPR, r. 42.4(3)**).

Chapter 23 Claim Form

INTRODUCTION

The standard method of starting a claim under the CPR is by the court issuing a claim form (**form N1**), prepared for or by the claimant (the other methods and the circumstances in which they are used are summarised in 12.1). A claim form is required by the CPR to set out essential details of the claim, including a concise statement of the nature of the cause of action and a statement of the remedy sought. The CPR also require the claimant to provide rather fuller particulars of claim (see **chapter** 24), which must include, among other prescribed matters, a concise statement of the facts on which the claimant relies. If practicable the particulars of claim should be set out in the claim form, though they may be in a separate document either accompanying the claim form or served and filed separately (see 15.1). 23.1

Claim forms and separate particulars of claim are examples of what the CPR calls 'statements of case', a term which applies to all documents in which a party's case is set out for the other parties and for the court. The former term for statements of case, 'pleadings', is still commonly used. **Rule** 2.3(1) includes the following definition:

'statement of case'—

(a) means a claim form, particulars of claim where these are not included in a claim form, defence, **Part** 20 claim, or reply to defence; and

(b) includes any further information given in relation to them voluntarily or by court order under **rule** 18.1.

Every statement of case, including a claim form and particulars of claim, must be verified by a statement of truth (see 23.11). A person who makes a false statement in a document verified by a statement of truth, without an honest belief in its truth, is guilty of a contempt of court (CPR, r. 32.14(1)). Thus there is now a degree of consanguinity between statements of case, witness statements and affidavits, and it would not perhaps be surprising were there to be further blurring between such documentation in the fullness of time.

CONTENTS OF A CLAIM FORM

Form N1 is the form used to start most proceedings under the CPR. Other forms and the circumstances in which they are used are described in 12.1. There is a special version of form N1 for use in the Commercial Court (**form N1 (CC)**). It is not appropriate to strike out a claim merely because the wrong form has been used to bring it, even if important elements such as the royal arms have been omitted, provided it is clear to the defendant (or, at least, the 23.2

defendant's lawyers) what case has to be met and what type of proceedings are being brought (*Hannigan v Hannigan* [2000] 2 FCR 650). In *Hannigan v Hannigan* the mistake was made by the claimant's professional advisers and the Court of Appeal indicated that its judgment was not to be taken as giving general permission to practitioners not to bother about using correct forms. However, a claimant using the wrong form of originating process may well be granted permission to correct the position in the interests of dealing with the case justly (see *Thurrock Borough Council v Secretary of State for the Environment, Transport and the Regions* (2000) *The Times*, 20 December 2000). The court does not have any power under the CPR to waive a failure to use a form (such as a petition) prescribed by Act of Parliament (*Re Osea Road Camp Sites Ltd* [2004] EWHC 2437 (Ch), [2005] 1 WLR 760, which is criticised at **1.26**).

Heading

23.3 On page 1 of **form N1** there must be stated:

(a) The court in which the claimant wishes to issue the claim. If the claim is to be issued in the High Court, the form must specify (a) the Division and (b) whether the claim is to be issued in the Royal Courts of Justice or a named district registry. The name of the court must be stated on the claim form for a claim in the Commercial Court (**PD 58, para. 2.3**), a Mercantile Court (**PD 59, para. 2.2**), the Patents Court (**PD 63, para. 3.1**) or the Technology and Construction Court (**PD 60, para. 3.2**).

(b) The parties, who should be described as in **table 14.1**. From 6 April 2006 a number of changes came into effect, including a requirement to include the full unabbreviated names and titles of parties who are individuals (see **PD 16, para. 2.6**). If the claimant is claiming in a representative capacity, the claim form must state what that capacity is (**CPR, r. 16.2(3)**). If the defendant is sued in a representative capacity, the claim form must likewise state what that capacity is (**r. 16.2(4)**).

(c) The addresses of all parties, as specified in **table 15.2** in **15.20**. From 6 April 2006, an address for service must include a full postcode unless the court orders otherwise (**r. 6.5**). Postcode information can be obtained from www.royalmail.com or the Royal Mail Address Management Guide. The claimant's address goes under the heading 'Claimant' on page 1. This address must be that at which the claimant resides or carries on business, even if the business address of the claimant's solicitor is the claimant's address for service (**PD 16, para. 2.2**). If the claimant's address for service is different from the address on page 1, it should be entered on page 2 in the box headed 'Claimant's or claimant's solicitor's address'. The defendant's name and address go in the space provided at the foot of page 1. Where the defendant is an individual, the claimant should (if the information is available) include the address at which the defendant resides or carries on business, even though solicitors may have agreed to accept service on the defendant's behalf (**para. 2.3**). A separate claim form must be prepared for each defendant, giving that defendant's name and address in this box.

If a claim form does not include full addresses for either the claimants or defendants, it will still be issued, but will be retained by the court and will not be served (**para. 2.5**). The court will notify the claimant, and will retain the claim form until the claimant provides full addresses including postcodes, or until the court dispenses with the requirement to provide full addresses (**para. 2.5**).

In clinical negligence claims the words 'clinical negligence' must be inserted at the top of every statement of case (**PD 16, para. 9.3**).

Brief details of claim

23.4 Every claim form must contain a concise statement of the nature of the claim (**CPR, r. 16.2(1)(a)**). This should be inserted in page 1 of **form N1** under the heading 'Brief details of claim'. It is suggested that, save in the most straightforward cases where the particulars of claim will be included in the claim form, this will be a simple statement such as:

The claimant's claim is for damages for personal injuries and interest arising out of a collision caused by the defendant's negligence when driving a motor car along Oxford Street, London W1 on 1 July 2005.

More precise details of the allegations and issues will be contained in the particulars of claim, and from a drafting standpoint, it would perhaps not be amiss to state that in the brief details.

By **PD 16, para. 1.4**, if exceptionally a statement of case exceeds 25 pages (excluding schedules) an appropriate short summary must also be filed and served.

Remedy sought

Every claim form must specify the remedy which the claimant seeks (**CPR, r. 16.2(1)(b)**). There is no separate heading for this statement in **form N1** and so the remedies sought should be included in the section of the claim form dealing with the brief details of claim. **23.5**

An important departure from previous practice is that a failure to specify a particular remedy will not limit any power of the court to grant such a remedy if the claimant is entitled to it (**r. 16.2(5)**). Likewise, in *Slater v Buckinghamshire County Council* [2004] EWCA Civ 1478, LTL 10/11/2004, it was held that the trial judge was entitled to make a finding of fact on an issue which had not been specifically pleaded, but which the parties clearly regarded as live and crucial to the case, and which they adequately dealt with at trial. Thus it should not be possible for a defendant to rely on a technical but unmeritorious defence that a particular remedy has not been set out, in order to escape the full scope of the court's powers (but see the cases discussed at **31.11**). It is suggested that the best practice is to set out all the remedies that are being claimed against the defendant, and there may be costs penalties if this is not done.

STATEMENT OF VALUE

Where the claimant is making a claim for money, the claim form must contain a statement of value (**CPR, r. 16.2(1)(c)**). The term 'claim for money' includes both a claim for a debt or liquidated demand and a claim for damages. **23.6**

The clear objective of this rule is not merely to ensure precision and avoid ambiguity, but also to enable the court to allocate the case to the appropriate court and track. A statement of value on a claim form does not, however, limit the power of the court to give judgment for the amount to which it considers the claimant to be entitled (**r. 16.3(7)**).

By **r. 16.2(1)(c)**, a statement of value must be in accordance with **r. 16.3**, and additional requirements are set out in **PD 7, para. 3**. On page 1 of **form N1** there is a space headed 'Value'. By **r. 16.3(2)** a statement of value must specify:

(a) the amount of money being claimed;
(b) that the claimant expects to recover:
  (i) not more than £5,000, or
  (ii) more than £5,000 but not more than £15,000, or
  (iii) more than £15,000
  (these are the basic delineations between cases on the small claims track, the fast track, and the multi-track); or
(c) that the amount which the claimant expects to recover cannot be stated.

If the claim is one for personal injuries, the claimant must state whether the amount that he or she expects to recover as general damages for pain, suffering and loss of amenity is not more than £1,000 or more than £1,000 (**r. 16.3(3); PD 7, para. 3.8**). This declaration is in addition to the statement of the overall expected value of the claim required by **CPR, r. 16.3(2)**, as it relates solely to the general damages aspect of the claim value. This may be important if the overall value of the claim is less than £5,000 (in which event it would normally fall to be tried on the small claims track) but where the general damages aspect of the case is expected to be over £1,000, the claim will normally be dealt with on the fast track, by virtue of **r. 26.6(1)(a)**. Curiously, the 'notes for claimant' (**form N1A**), which are served with the claim form, only require the statement of value for the personal injury claim to be inserted in a case where the overall value does not exceed £5,000, but this guidance does not accord with the requirements of **r. 16.3(3)**.

If the claim includes a claim by a tenant of residential premises against his or her landlord seeking an order requiring the landlord to carry out repairs or other work to the premises, the claimant must state whether the estimated cost of those repairs or other work is not more than £1,000 or more than £1,000; and whether or not the claimant expects to recover more than £1,000 in respect of any other claim for damages (**r. 16.3(4); PD 7 para. 3.9**). This will determine whether the claim can be allocated to the small claims track (see **CPR, r. 26.6(1)(b)**).

For other matters concerning claim forms in specialist jurisdictions, or using special procedures, see 23.17.

Reason for starting claim in High Court

23.7 If the claim form is to be issued in the High Court, it must include an explanation of why it is being filed there, by stating (**r. 16.3(5)**):

(a) that the claimant expects to recover more than £15,000; or
(b) that some other enactment provides that the claim may be commenced only in the High Court (stating the relevant enactment); or
(c) if the claim is one for personal injuries, that the claimant expects to recover £50,000 or more; or
(d) that the claim needs to be in one of the specialist High Court lists, stating which list.

The way in which the financial details are to be entered in the claim form is set out in the notes for claimant on **form N1**.

Computation of values

23.8 In calculating how much it is expected to recover, the following matters should be disregarded (**CPR, r. 16.3(6)**):

(a) interest;
(b) costs;
(c) any potential finding of contributory negligence;
(d) any potential counterclaim or defence of set-off;
(e) any potential payments that the defendant may have to make, out of any award to the claimant, to the Secretary of State for Social Security under the Social Security (Recovery of Benefits) Act 1997, s. 6.

Foreign currency claim

23.9 Where a claim is for a sum of money expressed in a foreign currency, the claim form should expressly state (**PD 16, para. 9.1**):

(a) that the claim is for payment in a specified foreign currency;
(b) why it is for payment in that currency;
(c) the sterling equivalent of the sum at the date of the claim; and
(d) the source of the exchange rate used in calculating the sterling equivalent.

STATEMENT OF TRUTH

Requirements

By **CPR, r. 2.3(1)**, a claim form and, if separate, the particulars of claim are classified as statements of case. **Rule 22.1(1)(a)** requires every statement of case to be verified by a statement of truth, that is, a statement that the party putting forward the document believes the facts stated in the document are true (**r. 22.1(4)**). The basic format of a statement of truth is (**PD 22, para. 2.1**): 23.10

I believe that the facts stated in this [name of document being verified] are true.

It is possible for the legal representative of a party to make a statement of truth verifying a document put forward by that party (**CPR, r. 22.1(6)**), in which event the basic format of the statement is:

The [claimant/defendant] believes that the facts stated in this [name of document being verified] are true.

There is a pro forma statement of truth on **form N1** for use when the particulars of claim are included in the statement of claim.

A statement of truth may be contained in the document it verifies, or it may be in a separate document served subsequently (**PD 22, para. 1.5**). If it is in a separate document, the formalities set out in **PD 22, para. 2.3**, must be observed.

Who may sign a statement of truth

A statement of truth verifying a document put forward by a party must be signed by the party or his or her litigation friend (**CPR, r. 22.1(6)(a)(i)**). Alternatively it can be signed by the party's legal representative (**r. 22.1(6)(a)(ii)**), provided the capacity in which the representative signs and the name of his or her firm are stated (**PD 22, para. 3.7**). The term 'legal representative' is defined by **CPR, r. 2.3**, as a barrister or a solicitor, solicitor's employee or other authorised litigator (as defined in the **Courts and Legal Services Act 1990**) who has been instructed to act for a party in relation to a claim. A statement of truth signed by a legal representative will refer to the client's belief and not the representative's but must be signed in the representative's own name and not that of his or her firm or employer (**PD 22, para. 3.10**). The individual who signs a statement of truth must print his or her full name clearly beneath the signature (**PD 22, para. 3.9**). 23.11

In the case of a company or other corporation, the statement of truth must be signed by one of the persons 'holding a senior position' listed in **PD 22, para. 3.5**, giving his or her position in the organisation (**PD 22, para. 3.4**). The list in **para. 3.5** includes 'manager or other officer of the company or corporation'. A footnote in **para. 3.4** refers to **CPR, r. 6.4(4)**, which in turn refers to **PD 6** for the definition of 'senior position'. **PD 6, para. 6.2**, however, defines persons holding a senior position in a company or corporation in precisely the same terms as **PD 22, para. 3.5**. A manager signing a statement of truth must be someone who has personal knowledge of the contents of the document being verified or is responsible for managing those who have that knowledge. In a large company this may be the manager of a claims, insurance or legal department. In a small company it may be that the only persons who hold senior positions are the directors. An employee of a company who works in a legal department managed by an employed solicitor is employed by the company, not by the solicitor, and so cannot qualify as the company's legal representative, though, depending on his or her responsibilities, such an employee might be regarded as holding a senior position.

If an insurer or the Motor Insurers' Bureau has a financial interest in the result of the proceedings for which the document is created, the insurer or Bureau may sign the statement of truth verifying the document (**PD 22, para. 3.6A**). A claims manager may be a person holding a senior position who can sign for the insurer (**para. 3.11**). Signature of a statement of truth when insurers are conducting proceedings on behalf of several claimants or defendants, is dealt with in **para. 3.6B**.

When the claimant is a partnership, the statement of truth may be signed by any of the partners or a person having the control or management of the partnership business (**para. 3.6**). It is not thought that there is any significance in the difference between the word 'must' used in **para. 3.4** and 'may' used in **para. 3.6**.

An agent who manages property or investments for a party cannot sign a statement of truth to verify that party's documents (**para. 3.11**).

It is stated in **para. 3.11** that 'Where some or all of the trustees [of a trust] comprise a single party one, some or all of the trustees comprising the party may sign a statement of truth. The legal representative of the trustees may sign it.' It seems that this permits one trustee to sign on behalf of all.

Mechanically reproduced signatures

23.12 It is submitted that it is not good practice for a statement of truth to be signed otherwise than by the hand of the person making the statement. If a mechanically reproduced signature is added by the person making the statement and is an assertion that the signatory's mind has been applied to the contents of the verified document, it is highly arguable that **CPR, r. 22.1(6)**, has been complied with, but it is difficult to see why the signature could not have been written. If a mechanically reproduced signature is applied by someone other than the purported signatory, **r. 22.1(6)** has not been complied with (*Birmingham City Council v Hosey* 2002 Legal Action 20). Although the defect is an irregularity which could be cured by order of the court under **r. 3.10**, until that is done, the statement of case cannot be relied on as evidence of any of the matters set out in it (**r. 22.2(1)**; see **23.16**).

In *Goodman v J. Eban Ltd* [1954] 1 QB 550 it was held that a solicitor's bill of costs accompanied by a letter, on which the solicitor's signature had been rubber-stamped, was 'signed by' the solicitor, as required by what is now the **Solicitors Act 1974, s. 69(2)**, the rubber stamp having been applied by the solicitor himself, but the practice was disapproved by the court. In *Birmingham City Council v Hosey* a statement of truth was rubber-stamped with the name of an employee in the council's legal services department who had never seen the papers, checked the facts or read any of the source documents. He had merely authorised more junior employees to apply the rubber stamp. Judge MacDuff QC held that the statement had not been properly signed, saying that the requirement in r. 22.1(6) was not a mere technicality or a matter of form only. **Rule 5.3**, which allows a document to be signed by 'computer or other mechanical means' did not apply, because a statement of truth is not a document but a statement in a document.

Liability for a statement of truth

23.13 A person who makes a false statement in a document verified by a statement of truth, or who causes such a statement to be made, without an honest belief in its truth, is guilty of contempt of court (**CPR, r. 32.14(1)**). It must be shown that the person knew (a) that the statement was false, (b) that it was likely to interfere with the course of justice (*Malgar Ltd v R.E. Leach (Engineering) Ltd* [2000] FSR 393; *KK Sony Computer Entertainment v Ball* [2004] EWHC 1984 (Ch), LTL 11/8/2004). Proceedings for such contempt can only be brought by the Attorney-General or with the permission of the court (**r. 32.14(2)**; **PD 32, paras 28.1 to 28.4**). This is to ensure that proceedings are brought only when required in the public interest (*Malgar Ltd v R.E. Leach (Engineering) Ltd*, in which the court refused permission because the alleged contempt was not sufficiently serious; *KK Sony Computer Entertainment v Ball*, in which the court granted permission and imposed a fine of £2,000).

The belief stated in a statement of truth (and the consequent responsibility for making a false statement) is that of the party putting forward the document, save in the case where a party is conducting proceedings with the aid of a litigation friend, in which event the statement of belief is that of the litigation friend (**r. 22.1(5)**). Although it could possibly be argued that both a litigation friend and the party on whose behalf such friend is acting, could be jointly or independently responsible for the accuracy of the statement of truth in the (possibly rare) circumstances where it could be shown that the party was aware that the statement was false, this seems to be precluded by the terms of **r. 22.1(5)**.

When a statement of truth verifying a document is signed by a legal adviser of the party putting forward the document, its contents and the consequences of signing it are deemed, by virtue of the signature, to have been explained to the claimant, and the signature will be taken by the court as meaning that the client has authorised the representative to sign (**PD 22, para. 3.8**).

For the position of an insurer or the Motor Insurers' Bureau signing a statement of truth see **PD 22, paras 3.6A** and **3.6B**.

The effect of this rule is to rest the responsibility for the contents of the document squarely on the shoulders of the person putting forward the facts. It is not sufficient for a legal representative to put forward matters in the belief (however genuine) that what his client has told him is the truth — it is incumbent on him to ensure that he has received direct instructions to that effect. This is particularly important in view of the explanation deemed to have been made to the client by **PD 22, para. 3.8**, which, if not actually given, could well lead to an allegation of professional misconduct. Provided that such instructions have been given, the legal representative signing a statement should not incur personal liability in respect of any default, unless he is aware that the contents are false, notwithstanding his instructions to the contrary.

Use of a verified statement of case as evidence

The principal reason for the requirement for a statement of case to be verified by a statement of truth is to ensure that litigants do not lightly put forward false cases. A secondary purpose is to enable a statement of case to be used as evidence in interim proceedings. By **r. 32.6(2)**, at hearings other than the trial, matters set out in a party's statement of case or application notice may be relied on in support of that party's application, provided that the statement or notice is verified by a statement of truth. **23.14**

Effect of verification requirement

In many ways the requirement for verification of statements of case equates them with affidavits and witness statements. All effectively contain declarations which render a party liable to proceedings for contempt of court should statements be proved to have been made without honest belief in their truth, although the precise means by which a party becomes so liable varies according to the nature of the document. It is perhaps difficult to see how the requirement to verify the contents of a statement of case is much of a disincentive to a groundless (or even dishonest) claim or defence. It seems unlikely that a client will inform his legal adviser that the substance of his statement of case is false, and in such an event it will presumably not be signed by the adviser in any event. It is also difficult to envisage a situation serious enough to warrant proceedings for contempt where the court's powers to punish contemnors will have to be predicated solely upon the fact that the claimant or defendant is proved not to have had an honest belief in the truth of his statement of case. We no longer live in an age in which the threat of one's soul being consigned to perdition provides a compelling sanction against making false declarations, and the court's willingness or desire to investigate the honesty of a belief in order to impose penal sanctions once it has resolved a civil dispute must surely be open to doubt. Although permission is required under **CPR, r. 32.14(2)(b)**, for proceedings for contempt, the procedure could be open to tactical abuse and/or a desire to inflict additional retribution on the losing side. Granting permission will rarely be consistent **23.15** with the overriding objectives of saving expense, ensuring expedition and fairness, and appropriate allocation of resources (**r. 1.1**).

Consequence of failure to verify a statement of case

23.16 If a statement of case is not verified by a statement of truth, it will remain effective unless struck out, but the party putting it forward may not rely on it as evidence of any of the matters set out in it (**CPR, r. 22.2(1)**). The omission simply means that the statement of case cannot be used for the purpose of supporting an application under **r. 32.6(2)**.

Where a statement of case remains unverified, any party may apply either:

(a) under **r. 22.4** for an order that the statement be verified within such period as the court may specify, or be struck out in default (**PD 22, para. 4.2**); or

(b) under **r. 22.2(2)** for an order that the statement be struck out.

The costs of such an application will normally be ordered to be paid by the defaulting party in any event, and forthwith (**PD 22, para. 4.3**). It is probable that the majority of such applications will be as a result of oversight on the part of the party putting forward the document, rather than as a result of any deliberate intention to avoid the rule.

OTHER MATTERS TO BE SET OUT IN THE CLAIM FORM

23.17 Special rules concerning claims against the Crown are set out in **CPR, r. 16.2(1A)**.

A claim form must contain such other matters as may be set out in a practice direction (**CPR, r. 16.2(1)(d)**).

For entering fixed costs on a claim form see **67.6**. Where fixed costs do not apply, the words 'to be assessed' should be entered in the box for Solicitor's costs (**PD 43–48, para. 24A**).

Paragraphs 14 and 15 **of PD 16** specify matters which must be included in a claimant's statement of case and so could either be in the claim form or in the particulars of claim. **Paragraph 14** is concerned with certain proceedings under the Competition Act 1998 and specifies information which must be presented by a claimant intending to rely on a determination of the Director General of Fair Trading. **Paragraph 15** specifies what must be set out in a statement of case by a claimant who seeks to rely on any provision of, or right arising under, the **Human Rights Act 1998**, or seeks a remedy under that Act.

If a claim form is to be served outside the jurisdiction under the **Civil Jurisdiction and Judgments Act 1982** it must be endorsed in accordance with **PD 7, para. 3.5A**. A claim form which is to be served out under **Regulation (EC) No. 44/2001** must be endorsed in accordance with **PD 7, para. 3.5B**.

Particulars of claim (see **chapter 24**) must be set out in the claim form in claims issued through the Claims Production Centre (**PD 7C, para. 2.3(3)**) or through Money Claim Online (**PD 7E, para. 5.2(1)**).

The other practice directions supplementing Part 7 (**PD 7B** and **PD 7D**) do not make any provisions concerning claim forms.

If the claimant has entered into a funding arrangement (as defined in **r. 43.2(1)(k)**), a notice of funding of claim (**form N251**) must be filed at court with the claim form and served on every other party (**PD 43–48, para. 19.2(2)**).

Chapter 24 Particulars of Claim

REQUIREMENT

Particulars of claim are required by **CPR, r. 7.4(1)**. They must include the matters specified in **r. 16.4**, the first of which is a concise statement of the facts on which the claimant relies (see **24.3**). Particulars of claim should, if practicable, be set out in the claim form (**PD 16, para. 3.1**). Page 2 of **form N1** has a space headed 'Particulars of Claim'. If it is not practicable to state the particulars of claim on the claim form, they may be in a separate document accompanying the claim form, or they may be served and filed separately within the time limits stated in **15.1**. In the **PD 7B** procedure, which applies to most claims under the **Consumer Credit Act 1974**, particulars of claim must be served with the claim form (**PD 7B, para. 5.2**). Particulars of claim must be set out in the claim form in claims issued through the Claims Production Centre (**PD 7C, para. 2.3(3)**) or through Money Claim Online (**PD 7E, para. 5.2(1)**). **24.1**

Particulars of claim are not required in the **Part 8** procedure, to which **Part 16** does not apply (**r. 8.9(a)(i)**).

POWER TO DISPENSE WITH STATEMENTS OF CASE

If a claim form has been properly issued and served on a defendant, the court has the power under **r. 16.8** to order that the claim will then continue without any statements of case having to be filed. This will presumably be reserved for cases of considerable urgency where the matter can be dealt with expeditiously without formal disclosure of the respective parties' cases, or matters where the issue is extremely simple, and where the service of statements of case would only add to the delay and expense of the proceedings. **24.2**

CONTENT

Where the particulars of claim are served separately from the claim form, they must state (**PD 16, para. 3.8**): **24.3**

(a) the name of the court in which the claim is proceeding;

(b) the claim number;
(c) the title of the proceedings (parties should be described as in **table 14.1**); and
(d) the claimant's address for service.

The body of the particulars of claim must include:

(a) A concise statement of the facts on which the claimant relies (**CPR, r. 16.4(1)(a)**). Particulars of claim extending to 109 pages with 162 numbered paragraphs could not be regarded as concise (*Diamantides v J. P. Morgan Chase Bank* [2005] EWHC 263 (Comm), LTL 5/3/2005, at [10]). The word 'facts', it is submitted, equates to the concept of 'material particulars' in previous pleading practice, and the rules should not be read or interpreted as suggesting that the particulars of claim should contain evidence. This distinction between material facts (relevant), and the evidence by which those facts are to be proved (irrelevant), was contained in the old RSC, ord. 18, r. 7(1), and still remains good practice. For a discussion of the degree and extent to which it may be argued that the CPR require the inclusion of matters of evidence in statements of case generally, see **24.7** and **24.18**.
(b) Details of any interest claimed (**CPR, r. 16.4(1)(b)** and **(2)**). A claimant who is seeking interest must state whether it is being claimed under the terms of a contract, or under a specified enactment, or for some other (defined) reason (**r. 16.4(2)(a)**). If the claim is for a specified sum of money, the particulars of claim should state the percentage rate claimed, the date from which interest is claimed, the date to which it is calculated (being not later than the date of issue of the claim form), the amount claimed up until that date, and the daily rate of interest accruing after that date (**r. 16.4(2)(b)**). Thus, on a specified sum, a claim for interest 'pursuant to statute' or 'at such rate and for such period as the court shall deem fit' will not comply with the rule.
(c) Where appropriate, a statement to the effect that aggravated or exemplary damages (or both) are being claimed; together with the grounds on which they are claimed (**r. 16.4(1)(c)**). This rule requires the claimant to give details of the grounds on which such additional damages are claimed, and not merely the fact that they are claimed. It may well be necessary under the CPR to give more details of such grounds than would have been the case under the previous rules.
(d) Where appropriate, a statement to the effect that provisional damages are being claimed, together with the grounds on which they are claimed (**r. 16.4(1)(d)**).
(e) Where a claim is brought to enforce a right to recover possession of goods, a statement showing the value of the goods (**PD 16, para. 7.2**).
(f) Where a claim is based upon a written agreement, a copy of the contract or contractual documents should be attached to or served with the particulars of claim; together with relevant parts of the contract or documents incorporating any general conditions of sale (**PD 16, para. 7.3**). (This does not apply to claims issued through the Claims Production Centre (**PD 7C, para. 1.4(4)**) or Money Claim Online (**PD 7E, para. 5.3**).) The original documents should be available at the hearing.
(g) Where a claim is based upon an oral agreement, the contractual words relied upon, including by whom, to whom, when and where they were spoken (**PD 16, para. 7.4**).
(h) Where a claim is based upon an agreement by conduct, particulars of the conduct relied on, stating by whom, when and where the acts constituting the conduct were done (**PD 16, para. 7.5**).
(i) In a claim issued in the High Court relating to a **Consumer Credit Act 1974** agreement, a statement that the action is not one to which s. 141 of the Act applies (**PD 16, para. 7.6**).
(j) Any other matters required by practice directions to be included in respect of certain types of claim (**CPR, r. 16.4(1)(e); PD 16, para. 3.6(2)**).
(k) Where a party seeks to raise a human rights point, the particulars of claim (and any other type of statement of claim or appeal notice filed on behalf of that party) must set out

precise details of the Convention right relied upon. It must also give details of the alleged infringement and it must state the relief sought (**PD 16, para. 15.1**).

(l) In a claim for wrongful interference with goods the particulars of claim must state the name and address of every person (who is not a party) who the claimant knows claims an interest in the goods (**CPR, r. 19.5A(1)**).

Additionally, the following specific matters are required by **PD 16, para. 8.2**, to be set out in particulars of claim, if the claimant wishes to rely on them:

(a) any allegation of fraud (see *Rigby v Decorating Den Systems Ltd* (1999) LTL 15/3/99; **Chancery Guide, paras. 2.6** and **2.7**);
(b) the fact of any illegality;
(c) details of any misrepresentation;
(d) details of all breaches of trust;
(e) notice or knowledge of a fact;
(f) details of unsoundness of mind or undue influence;
(g) details of wilful default;
(h) any facts relating to mitigation of loss or damage.

It has always been good drafting practice to deal with these matters so as to ensure that the relevant issues are exposed at the earliest possible moment.

Signature when drafted by legal representative

Statements of case and other documents drafted by a legal representative must be signed. Documents drafted by counsel must bear counsel's signature, and those drafted by a solicitor must be signed in the name of the firm (**PD 5, para. 2.1**). In practice, counsel's handwritten signature appears only on the draft as settled by counsel. The version of the document used for service and filing simply has the barrister's name typed in capitals. For the use of mechanically reproduced signatures see **23.12**. **24.4**

Statement of truth

The particulars of claim, being a statement of case, must be verified by a statement of truth (**CPR, r. 22.1(1)(a)**; see **23.10** to **23.16**). The purpose of requiring a statement of truth is to eliminate claims in which a party has no honest belief and to discourage the pleading of claims unsupported by evidence and which are put forward in the hope that something may turn up on disclosure or at trial (*Clarke v Marlborough Fine Art (London) Ltd* [2002] 1 WLR 1731). **24.5**

Special rules for certain types of claim

For special requirements in: **24.6**

(a) personal injury claims, see **PD 16, para. 4**;
(b) fatal accident claims, see **PD 16, para. 5**;
(c) possession claims, see **PD 55, paras 2.1 to 2.6**;
(d) hire-purchase claims, see **PD 16, para. 6**;
(e) claims under the **Consumer Credit Act 1974** to which **PD 7B** applies, see **PD 7B, para. 7**;
(f) defamation claims, see **PD 53, para. 2**;
(g) claims made for an injunction or declaration in respect of land or its possession, see **PD 16, para. 7.1**;
(h) claims for recovery of goods, see **PD 16, para. 7.2**;
(i) cases where a claimant wishes to rely on the provisions of the Civil Evidence Act 1968, s. 11 or s. 12, concerning evidence of conviction of an offence, or a finding of adultery or paternity, see **PD 16, para. 8.1**.

Paragraphs 14 and 15 of **PD 16** specify matters which must be included in a claimant's statement of case and so could either be in the claim form or in the particulars of claim. **Paragraph** 14 is concerned with certain proceedings under the Competition Act 1998 and specifies information which must be presented by a claimant intending to rely on a determination of the Director General of Fair Trading. **Paragraph** 15 specifies what must be set out in a statement of case by a claimant who seeks to rely on any provision of, or right arising under, the **Human Rights Act 1998**, or seeks a remedy under that Act.

If a claim form is to be served outside the jurisdiction under the **Civil Jurisdiction and Judgments Act 1982** or **Regulation** (EC) **No. 44/2001**, the particulars of claim (unless they are set out in the claim form) must be endorsed in accordance with **PD 7, para. 3.5** (1982 Act) or **para. 3.5A** (Regulation).

Points of law, witnesses and documents

24.7 PD 16, para. 13.3, states that a statement of case may include:

(a) a reference to any point of law on which the party's claim or defence is based;
(b) the name of any witness whom the party proposes to call; and
(c) (by way of service or attachment) a copy of any document which the party considers is necessary to the claim or defence (including any expert's report to be filed in accordance with **Part 35**).

It is interesting that there is no reference to this option in the guidance notes on drafting particulars of claim which are given to claimants on **form N1A**.

PD 16, para. 13.3, represents a fundamental and radical departure from previous pleading practice, where a strict distinction has always been maintained between material particulars on the one hand, and evidence on the other (see **24.18**). There is a potential scope for tactical manoeuvring as a result of this practice direction, whereby one party may attempt to take the point that its case is to be preferred as a result of having been more expeditious in the declaration of its evidence than the other. It is suggested that such attempts will be actively discouraged and disapproved by the courts, in line with the general emphasis on resolving a case on its merits, rather than as a result of tactics — in line with the overriding objective.

STRUCTURE OF PARTICULARS OF CLAIM

24.8 It is not intended to provide precedents of statements of case in this work, as some of the worst excesses of the previous system came about as a result of over-reliance on formulaic pleading, to the detriment of clear and objective thought. It is suggested that the basic objective of particulars of claim should be to inform the court and the other side what the case is all about, including (in the vast majority of cases) the duty that was allegedly owed, the fact that it was broken, how it was broken, and the remedies sought as a result. It is hoped that the following advice on structure will be of assistance.

Identification of the parties

24.9 It is, of course, essential to ensure that the correct parties appear as claimant(s) and defendant(s). Although in most cases these may be self-evident, there are instances in which the correct parties may only be ascertained by reference to the cause of action (for example, where there are special rules as to the parties entitled to claim relief, or against whom relief can be claimed). It may be necessary to sue 'persons unknown', who are identified by description rather than name (see **14.27**).

The manner in which a claim form, and every other statement of case should be headed, is now set out specifically in **PD 7, paras** 4.1 and 4.2, and **PD 16, para. 2.6**. The title should state:

(a) the number of proceedings (i.e., the case number);
(b) the court or Division in which they are proceeding;
(c) each party's full unabbreviated name and title by which he is known;

(d) each party's status in the proceedings (i.e., claimant or defendant).

Where there is more than one claimant and/or defendant, the parties should be described in the title as:

(1) Mr AB	
(2) Miss CD	
(3) Mrs EF	Claimants
— and —	
(1) Mr GH	
(2) Ms IJ	
(3) Master KL	Defendants

It is perhaps unfortunate that **PD 7** takes no account of the useful distinction that used normally to be made between parties suing (or more commonly being sued) jointly and parties whose interests are separate. In the past, it was usual to identify parties whose interests were, or may have been, separate as, for example:

GH	1st Defendant
— and —	
IJ	2nd Defendant

Parties suing or being sued jointly were described as, for example:

GH	
IJ	Defendants

or

(a) GH	
(b) IJ	Defendants

This also made the drafting of the claim far more straightforward, as a clear distinction could be drawn between the 'First Defendant' and the 'Second Defendant' in the particulars of a claim where the defendants were not sued jointly. In the rather less common event that it was necessary to refer to an individual defendant in a case where liability was joint and several, the term 'the first-named Defendant' etc., could be employed. If **PD 7** is followed rigidly, this may now be more difficult to set out clearly, and the resulting draft will be less concise, and indeed more clumsy than hitherto. It therefore seems unlikely that in appropriate circumstances, the retention of the previous format will attract much criticism!

Although it may be helpful for some description of the parties to be given in the first paragraph of the particulars of claim, it is not necessary to do this when their business, profession or relationship to the other parties is not relevant to the claim. If, however, it is necessary to assert the identity and status of the claimant or defendant in order to set out the legal basis on which the claim is being brought, this should be done. Thus, it may be necessary to state the nature of a company's business where a claim is being brought by or against a company arising out of matters concerning its business. Similarly it may be important to set out the fact that a party is a landlord or tenant of premises, or the owner of a particular chattel, or an employer or employee.

Background

Before turning to the precise nature of the duty owed, it will often (but not invariably) be necessary to 'set the scene', by giving a short description of the circumstances in which the duty came about. This should be done with sufficient precision to enable the defendant precisely to identify what will subsequently be alleged, and to put it into context. This may vary from a short description of the circumstances in which an accident occurred, to the **24.10** events which ultimately gave rise to a concluded agreement between the parties. In many cases, the CPR or PDs will require the insertion of material here, such as supporting documentation, or particulars of words spoken.

Duty alleged

24.11 The vast majority of claims involve allegations of breaches of duty. It is thus essential first to state what the duty is (and if necessary how it is alleged to have arisen) before alleging the breach or breaches relied on. Often this will be no more than stating the fact that a contract has come into being with various terms. Sometimes the relationship between the parties has given rise to a duty. In road traffic cases, it is conventional not to allege the fact that the presence of a motor vehicle on a road gave rise to a duty of care towards other road users, because that is taken for granted.

Breach of duty

24.12 Once the existence and nature of the duty have been alleged, it is necessary to set out precisely the manner in which it is alleged that the duty has been breached. It is in this regard that particulars of claim are prone to criticism. In the past, the habit grew up, particularly in road traffic cases, of inserting 'stock' particulars, which told little or nothing about the real nature of the claim. A specimen of such unsatisfactory particulars appears in example 24.3 in **24.19**. Such particulars will almost inevitably be struck out today.

It must be remembered that the objectives of particulars of breach are twofold — first to describe the nature of the breach, and secondly to do so in such a way that it is clear to the defendant and the court how the breach actually took place. In particulars of negligence, for example, it is essential that each particular should not only describe a breach of the duty, but set out the manner and circumstances (singly or collectively) in which that breach occurred. See example 24.1 for an annotated description of properly drafted particulars.

The above example not merely describes the alleged breaches of duty, but puts them in a context which enables the claimant's case to be understood, so that an appropriate response can be made. This does not, of course mean that the case is unassailable — the defence in the above example may well be to the effect that the claimant was emerging from a minor road and that the defendant had the right of way. He would not, however, be in a position to assert this had the context of the claim not been fully particularised.

In *Uren v First National Home Finance Ltd* [2005] EWHC 2529 (Ch), *The Times*, 17 November 2005, the claim simply pleaded a sequence of events and stated that as a result of those events the defendant had been unjustly enriched. This was struck out. It failed to set out facts which were capable of bringing the claim within one of the established restitutionary categories, or some justifiable extension of them.

A party is obliged to plead its positive case on an issue, even if the burden of proof rests with the other side (*Baxter Healthcare Corporation v Abbott Laboratories* [2005] EWHC 2878 (Pat), LTL 6/12/2005).

Loss suffered

24.13 Although the claim **form N1** contains a section into which the value of the claim has to be inserted (the 'statement of value', see **23.6**), it will normally be necessary to set out what loss has been suffered in consequence of the breaches alleged in the previous paragraph(s). Without this, logically, there will be no sustainable claim, as there is no formal averment that the relief being sought is as a result of the breach previously alleged. Such particulars may well include, for example, brief details of any injury suffered (attaching or serving any evidence from a medical practitioner on which reliance is made: **PD 16, para. 4.3**) as well as details of the effect of the breaches on the claimant, in support of the relief sought at the end of the particulars of claim. Where there is a money claim, it will be necessary to make clear whether

Example 24.1 Properly drafted particulars

PARTICULARS OF NEGLIGENCE

The defendant was negligent in that he:

1. Drove his car along Litigation Avenue towards the junction with Blackstone Road, at a speed that was excessive in the circumstances.

(The conventional phrase 'drove too fast', says very little if anything about the breach, and often appears to be inserted as a matter of form. It is often incorrectly thought that this allegation means that the defendant was exceeding the speed limit. The duty is to drive at a safe speed in the circumstances. The manner in which the particulars are set out makes this clear, and also starts to build up the picture which, when all the particulars are complete, will properly identify the claimant's case, so that it can be answered by the defendant.)

2. Failed to keep a proper lookout.

(This is a straightforward example of an allegation of breach of a generic duty. It should later be qualified by particulars of how precisely it is alleged that the breach took place.)

3. Failed to see or heed the presence of the claimant's vehicle, which was in the process of entering into Litigation Avenue from Blackstone Road into the path of the defendant's car.

(This paragraph comprises specific particulars of the generic allegation made in paragraph 2, and adds further details which, in conjunction with paragraph 1, clarifies the circumstances in which the accident took place. Essentially, this paragraph could be silently prefaced by the words, 'because he failed to keep a proper lookout, he . . .'.

4. Failed to brake, steer or otherwise manoeuvre his car in order to avoid colliding with the claimant.

(Again, this paragraph runs logically on from the last one: 'Because he failed to see the claimant, he failed to brake etc.'. Once again, specific breaches of duty are alleged here in the context of the events that are being described.)

5. Caused his car to collide with that of the claimant.

(Often, and wrongly, omitted in many particulars, this is the actual breach of duty which gives rise to the claim.)

it is a claim for general and/or special damages. In many cases it will be necessary to deal with the amount of special damages by means of a schedule attached to the particulars of claim. This must be done when the claim is for personal injury, where the claimant is claiming past and future expenses and losses (**PD 16, para. 4.2**), and in all cases where the damages claimed are anything other than short and straightforward.

Other relevant matters

Many types of claim require certain information to be inserted in the particulars of claim, and care should be taken to ensure that these requirements are complied with. For example, claims for aggravated or exemplary damages must be specifically set out together with the grounds for claiming them (**CPR, r. 16.4(1)(c)**). Claims for interest must comply with **r. 16.4(2)**. **24.14**

In many cases some of this information will have to be given in previous paragraphs or particulars. In others, it will be sufficient to set them out formally in separate paragraphs. Often it will be a combination of the two (see, for example, the required matters in claims for the recovery of land in **PD 55, para. 2**, where it is clear that the special requirements will have to be inserted at various places in the particulars of claim). Further special rules are set out in 24.6.

Although there is no express requirement for a statement of value to be included in the particulars of claim (**CPR, r. 16.3**, referring specifically to it being set out in the claim form), it may nevertheless be good practice to repeat it in the particulars of claim, particularly when that document is likely to be the principal one referred to in the course of the trial.

Alternative and contradictory claims

24.15 The purpose of requiring statements of truth is to deter parties from advancing cases which are inherently untrue or wholly speculative. Nevertheless, if it would further the overriding objective, a party should be allowed to rely on more than one version of the facts (*Binks v Securicor Omega Express Ltd* [2003] EWCA Civ 993, [2003] 1 WLR 2557). There is, therefore, no objection to a claimant advancing alternative claims, provided the alternative sets of facts are clearly set out. Examples are where:

(a) The claimant advances one set of facts, and the defence advances a different set of facts. The claimant seeks to amend, saying that even on the defendant's version of the facts liability is established.
(b) The claimant, perhaps because of injuries suffered in the accident, has no personal recollection of the material events, and has to rely on independent witnesses, who give different versions of those events, each of which is consistent with liability being established.
(c) The claimant, perhaps through having honestly convinced himself of the truth of his version of events as set out in the particulars of claim, gives evidence, but a different version of events emerges from the body of evidence at the trial. Permission may be sought to amend at trial to adopt the version that has emerged at trial.

Subject to the court's discretion based on the overriding objective, a claimant in each of these situations may be given permission to rely on the alternative or new versions of events (*Binks v Securicor Omega Express Ltd*). The claimant's statement of truth has the effect of stating the claimant's honest belief that on either one set of facts or the other the claim is made out (*Clarke v Marlborough Fine Art (London) Ltd* [2002] 1 WLR 1731). It may be necessary to seek the court's permission in cases like the examples set out above to amend without verifying the amended statements of case with a new statement of truth, or to use an amended statement of truth making clear that the primary case is not an assertion of the truth (say) of the defendant's alternative version, but that the defendant's version is relied on as an alternative basis for liability if the court finds the facts to be as pleaded by the defendant (*Binks v Securicor Omega Express Ltd*).

A claimant cannot make a unified claim relying on contradictory allegations of fact, because in such a case the claimant cannot honestly sign a statement of truth (*Clarke v Marlborough Fine Art (London) Ltd*).

Relief claimed

24.16 In pre-CPR pleadings, the particulars of claim would invariably end with a 'prayer', in which the plaintiff set out a summary of the relief claimed, in tabulated form, so that the extent of the action could clearly be seen. The CPR contain no requirement for there to be a 'prayer' (and it would certainly not, in any event, be referred to as such in present terminology). The claim form contains a box for 'brief details of the claim' and another for the value, but it is suggested that it is best practice for a summary (whatever it may be called) to be included at the conclusion of the particulars of claim as a useful means by which the extent of the claim can be seen at a glance. A claim for costs has always conventionally been omitted from the summary, and such an omission does certainly not preclude the court awarding costs to the claimant at the conclusion of the case.

EFFECT OF THE CPR ON DRAFTING STYLE

Criticism of former drafting style

Pleadings under the old rules had been much criticised for being over-stylised and complex, with much use of anachronistic language and obscure terminology. The growth and availability of precedents of pleading often led to formalistic drafting in which the objectives of the pleading process were at best obscured, and at worst often ignored altogether. Additionally, pleadings were increasingly drafted with tactical considerations in mind, which are inconsistent with the overriding objective. The *Final Report* took pains to criticise the system by which time and expense have in the past been taken up in interim proceedings concerning the pleadings process, and the avowed aim of the CPR is to ensure that matters progress on their merits, and not on technicalities. **24.17**

Is evidence required in a claim form or particulars of claim?

The requirement set out in **CPR, r. 16.2(1)(a)**, that the claim form must contain a concise statement of the nature of the claim, has led some to take the view that some evidence must be set out in the claim form, and if such evidence is omitted, it would be possible to have the claim struck out for containing insufficient particulars. Support for this argument is gained by the fact that the claim form is required to be verified by a statement of truth (see **23.10**), which, by its very nature, implies that the claim form is to contain matters of evidence. **24.18**

Nevertheless, it is submitted that the CPR do not impose any additional *requirement* to include evidence in a statement of case, but in making it clear that the claim form must contain a concise statement of the nature of the claim (**r. 16.2(1)(a)**) and that particulars of claim must include a concise statement of the facts on which the claimant relies (**r. 16.4(1)(a)**), the original (and often forgotten) principles of pleading are reaffirmed in mandatory form. In practice, there appear to be few instances of statements of case containing much evidential matter.

The fact that there is no direct rule to the effect that evidence should *not* be contained in a statement of case does not mean that a statement of case is automatically defective if evidence is not included. If that was the intention of the rules, **r. 16.2(1)** would surely say so. Furthermore, although statements of case are required to be verified by a statement of truth, and when so verified can stand as the evidence on interim applications, the notice of application (**form N244**) provides space for evidence to be inserted separately or attached as witness statements or affidavits, which would be unnecessary if the evidence was required already to have been fully incorporated into the statement of case. It may of course be that in some instances a verified statement of case will contain all the particulars and evidence necessary to entitle an applicant to the remedy sought, but there will be many instances in which it will not.

There has always been a grey area between what used to be called 'material particulars' and 'evidence', and even a pleading properly drafted under the old rules contained matters which were essentially matters of fact. A situation in which particulars would be sufficient to support an interim application, without necessarily involving the inclusion of evidence, is set out in example 24.2.

If the statement of case in example 24.2 was verified by a statement of truth, there seems little doubt that it would be sufficient, on its own, to support an application made in the case (e.g., for an interim injunction under **CPR, Part 25**), yet it would be hard to argue that the statement of case actually contains any evidence. Put another way, the example sets out the relevant material such that the defendants are made aware of the nature and extent of the claimant's case, but not the means by which he intends to prove it. Verification of the particulars by a statement of truth will suffice for the purposes of an interim application, but for a final hearing, the claimant's case must be proved in the conventional manner.

Example 24.2

1. The claimant is and was at all relevant times the owner of residential premises known as 1 Acacia Gardens, Boggle, Kent. The premises comprise a house together with a 100 foot back garden.

2. On at least 3 occasions per week since 1 March 2006, the defendants have unlawfully entered into the claimant's garden and remained there for periods of up to 2 hours, using the same for football practice. The last 3 occasions on which the defendants have trespassed into the garden were [a], [b] and [c].

3. Despite being orally requested to leave the garden by the claimant on several occasions, the defendants have refused to do so, and the claimant fears that unless an injunction is granted restraining such acts of trespass, they will be frequently repeated.

4. Further, by reason of the acts of trespass described in paragraph 2, the claimant has suffered damage to his garden plants and furniture . . . [particulars etc.].

True purpose of statements of case

24.19 A good claim or defence should enable the parties and the court to narrow down and identify the central issues in dispute. This has always been the case. For example, a defendant is entitled to know not merely the cause of action against him, but also the manner in which it is alleged that he was in breach of his duty, thereby causing the claimant to seek redress against him. To achieve that objective requires no more than a properly detailed set of particulars (as opposed to evidence), thereby allowing him to set out his case in response.

Thus, as in the past, a claim or defence which discloses little or nothing about the party's case is liable to be (and today almost certainly will be) struck out. The following is an example of a common type of defective claim, which will almost certainly be struck out under the new rules (relevant parts of the claim only are illustrated):

Example 24.3 Unsatisfactory drafting

IN THE BLACKSTONE COUNTY COURT Claim No. BD 003456

BETWEEN:

Mr ADAM BROWN Claimant

— and —

Mr CHARLES DAVIS Defendant

Brief details of claim: The Claimant claims damages for loss and personal injuries caused in a road traffic accident on 21 May 2005.

Value: more than £5,000 but not more than £15,000. The claim includes a claim for personal injuries and the amount expected to be recovered exceeds £1,000.

Particulars of claim: On 21 May 2005 an accident occurred at the junction of Fairfax Road and Grove Hill, London SW99 between the Claimant's Renoir Nicole R 123 ABC and a Bergman P 456 JKL driven by the Defendant.

The accident was caused by the Defendant's negligence, in that he:

(a) drove too fast;
(b) failed to keep a proper lookout;
(c) failed to brake in time or at all to avoid the accident.

As a result, the Claimant suffered injuries and loss.

(Particulars etc.)

(Statement of truth etc.)

Similarly a 'block and parry' defence, confining itself merely to admitting, requiring proof of or denying the allegations in the claim, but not containing any particulars of the defendant's case, will also be liable to be struck out.

A proposed amendment to include a defence of justification in a libel claim was refused in *Al Rajhi Banking and Investment Corporation v Wall Street Journal Europe Sprl* [2003] EWHC 1358 (QB), LTL 24/6/2003, because the draft amended statement of case lacked clarity and precision.

Good drafting involves the concise and clear identification of the subject matter of the claim, the issues in the case, and the parties' respective positions in respect of those issues.

Drafting language

There is little doubt that the aims and objectives of the CPR militate against much of the previously conventional and archaic language of pleadings. Not only is the use of Latin terms now obsolete, but many of the more 'old-fashioned' English words such as 'hereinbefore' and 'thereafter' may be thought to be inconsistent with the new objectives. Such changes are perhaps not wholly to be welcomed — the price of drafting in modern language is frequently a lack of elegance and an increase rather than saving in verbiage. The very term 'statement of case' rather than 'pleading' is an example in point. **24.20**

The use of a standard claim form means that the drafting of statements of case is less of a specialised art than before, as the procedure is designed for use by laypersons as well as lawyers. However, the CPR are not intended to encourage sloppy drafting, and although it is clear that the overriding objective does not permit cases to be won or lost on purely technical points of pleading, the need for precision in the drafting of statements of case (particularly in more complex matters) is still paramount.

A short list of some of the conventional Latin and English phrases previously used, and possible modern counterparts, appears in **table 24.1**.

Table 24.1 Suggested replacements for traditional legal language

Old term	Suggested equivalent
Aforesaid	Above
Aver	Contend
By reason of the matters aforesaid	Due to the above matters, or As a result of the above
Due to (meaning 'because of')	Because of
Hereinafter set out	Set out below
Hereinbefore set out	Set out above
In the premises	In the circumstances
In so far (or insofar)	To the extent that
Inter alia	Among other things
Material	Relevant
Mutatis mutandis	With all necessary changes
Notwithstanding	Despite (the fact that)
Pursuant to	In consequence of, or as a result of, or in the course of, or under
Seriatim	Individually
Without prejudice to the generality of the foregoing	Without prejudice to the matters set out above

MEANINGS OF COMMON DRAFTING TERMS

At all material times

24.21 'At all material times' is perhaps the most commonly used stock phrase in drafting statements of case. When used in relation to breach by the defendant, it means 'material to the period of the breach' as detailed in the particulars of claim (*Convergence Group plc v Chantrey Vellacott* [2005] EWCA Civ 290, *The Times*, 25 April 2005).

Include, but not limited to

24.22 Where a statement of case is drafted when inquiries are incomplete, it is common to plead such particulars as are known, but prefaced by a phrase such as 'include but are not limited to' the particulars that immediately follow or which are set out in a schedule. This device is used at various times when giving particulars of breach and particulars of loss. Its use prevents the statement of case being treated as deliberately excluding details not specifically set out (*Deutsche Morgan Grenfell Group plc v Commissioners of Inland Revenue* [2005] EWCA Civ 78, [2006] 2 WLR 103, at [257]). If used, the statement of case should be amended to include the full particulars when these become known. Until amended, such a statement of case remains vulnerable to being struck out as embarrassing, as the other side are entitled to know the full case being asserted against them (*Deutsche Morgan Grenfell Group plc v Commissioners of Inland Revenue* at [247]).

FAILURE TO INCLUDE PARTICULARS

24.23 A judge should not normally make a finding of fact on an issue which depends on evidence and which has not been raised in statements of case, so that all parties did not have a proper opportunity to address it, even if it was raised in correspondence after statements of case have been served (*Sivanandan v Executive Committee of Hackney Action for Racial Equality* [2002] EWCA Civ 111, LTL 25/1/2002). However, if a factual issue has been adequately dealt with at trial and is clearly regarded by all parties as a live issue which is crucial to the case, the judge is entitled to make a finding of fact, even if the issue was not raised in the statements of case, which could have been amended during the trial (*Slater v Buckinghamshire County Council* [2004] EWCA Civ 1478, LTL 10/11/2004). In *Strover v Strover* [2005] EWHC 860 (Ch), [2005] NPC 64, it was held that where the essential allegations to establish proprietary estoppel had not been pleaded, but had formed the central planks in the evidence of the claimant in support of his original plea, the court could grant the relief flowing from the estoppel. An allegation which is not included in the particulars of claim cannot provide a sustainable ground for an appeal (*Dunnett v Railtrack plc* [2002] EWCA Civ 303, [2002] 1 WLR 2434).

Chapter 25 Schedule of Loss and Damage

INTRODUCTION

The purpose of a schedule of loss and damage is to display, in concise and digestible form, the extent of the special damage that the claimant wishes to obtain from the defendant. This is not merely to enable the value of the claim to be appreciated, but also to allow the defendant to agree with or dispute the contents (independently of whether or not liability is admitted), and to draft a counter-schedule indicating any areas of contention. As a result, the parties and court will know the degree and extent to which damages are disputed, and the areas of dispute should clearly be defined. This is, of course, precisely what the system of statements of case is intended to achieve. **25.1**

CONTENTS OF THE SCHEDULE

No format for a schedule of loss and damage is prescribed by the CPR or any practice direction. Logic dictates that different heads of damage should be separately calculated in the body of the schedule, and that subtotals should be calculated wherever possible. This will normally cause no problems where specific amounts have already been expended or loss of earnings incurred, but items of alleged future loss may be more difficult to set out. The appropriate manner in which to do this is by reference to the multiplier that it is alleged is appropriate in the particular case, thus making the basis of the calculation quite clear, and enabling the preparation of a counter-schedule in similar format on the defendant's side. **25.2**

A schedule or counter-schedule must be verified by a statement of truth (**PD 22, para. 1.4(3)**).

EXAMPLES

Two examples of a schedule of loss and damage are given below, showing how different heads of loss should be set out. **25.3**

Example 25.1

IN THE BLACKSTONE COUNTY COURT — Claim No. BL01234

BETWEEN:

Ms ANNA BRIGHT — Claimant

— and —

(1) Mr CHARLES DAVIS

(2) Mrs ELEANOR FOWKES — Defendants

SCHEDULE OF PAST AND FUTURE LOSS AND EXPENSE

The calculations in this Schedule are made to 10 February 2006.

Loss of Earnings

1. Prior to the accident, which occurred on 6 June 2003, the Claimant, who is a State Enrolled Nurse, worked for the Loganberry Nursing Home, Beresford Road, Blackstone BL5 1AB. At the

time of the accident the Claimant's average net weekly earnings were £130.61. Since the accident the Claimant has been unable to return to work, and has received no pay from her previous (or any other) employer. The Claimant claims the loss of income as follows:

6.6.2003 to 31.12.2003, being 30 weeks at £130.61 per week	£3,918.30
1.1.2004 to 31.12.2004, being 52 weeks at £135.83 per week	£7,063.16
1.1.2005 to 31.12.2005, being 52 weeks at £141.26 per week	£7,345.52
1.1.2006 to 10.2.2006, being 6 weeks at £146.91 per week	£881.46
Total claim under this part	£19,208.44

2. The Claimant's loss of earnings will continue until the date she would have retired had she not been injured in the accident. The Claimant contends that but for the accident she would have retired on 28 May 2006. From 11 February 2006 her net loss of earnings will be £146.91 per week. The Claimant claims:

11.2.2006 to 28.5.2006, being 15 weeks at £146.91 per week	£2,203.65

3. The Claimant would have worked part-time from 29 May 2006 for a period of 5 years earning approximately half her pre-retirement income, being £73.45 net per week. Her annual loss of income during this period is therefore £3,819.66. The appropriate multiplier is 4.

The Claimant therefore claims future loss of earnings in the sum of	£15,278.64

Medication

4. Prescriptions, 2 at £6.40 each	£12.80

5. Paracetamol.

(i) The Claimant takes four paracetamol tablets a day, and has done since the accident. Estimated cost	£100.00
(ii) This loss will continue at the approximate rate of £1.50 per week, equivalent to £78.00 per annum. The appropriate multiplier is 13.	
The Claimant therefore claims the sum of	£1,014.00
Total claim under this paragraph	£1,114.00

Taxi Fares

6. As a result of her injuries the Claimant has not been as mobile as she was before the accident, and has had to travel by taxi or minicab, whereas before being injured she would have walked or travelled by public transport. The Claimant claims the costs of the said taxi and minicab fares and/or the difference in costs between the said fares and the costs of travel by public transport. The Claimant walks to the supermarket once a week, but has to have a minicab back home with her shopping. This minicab fare is paid out once a week and has been since April 2004.

(i) 1.4.2004 to 10.2.2006, being 97 weeks at £3.00 per week	£291.00
(ii) This loss continues at the rate of £3.00 per week, and will continue for the rest of her life. The annual loss is £156.00, and the appropriate multiplier is 13.	
The Claimant therefore claims the sum of	£2,028.00
Total loss under this head	£2,319.00

Care and Assistance

7. Since the accident the Claimant has received considerable care and assistance from her husband. The Claimant's husband does all the vacuum cleaning in the house. He assists with the washing. The Claimant puts washing in the washing machine a piece at a time but her husband has to empty the machine and hang out the washing. The Claimant is unable to do gardening and her husband now spends about one hour per week keeping weeds under control. He also strips the beds. He does his own cooking and a little shopping for the Claimant.

(i) For the period from 6.6.2003 to 10.2.2006, being 139 weeks, comprising 8 hours per week at £4.04 per hour £4,492.48

(ii) Continuing at the annual rate of £1,680.64 (8 hours per week, at an hourly rate of £4.04). The appropriate multiplier is 13.

The Claimant therefore claims the sum of £21,848.32

Total loss under this head £26,340.80

Knitting

8. Before the accident the Claimant used to knit as a hobby, and she would produce approximately four jumpers per year worth in addition to materials approximately £50 each. She would produce one set of baby clothes a year worth approximately £50. The annual value of the Claimant's knitting was therefore £250.

Since the accident the Claimant has been unable to continue with her knitting, and therefore claims:

(i) £250 per annum between 6.6.2003 and 10.2.2006	£625.00
(ii) Continuing loss at £250 per annum with a multiplier of 13	£3,250.00
Total loss under this head	£3,875.00

Summary

Para. 1	£19,208.44
Para. 2	£2,203.65
Para. 3	£15,278.64
Para. 4	£12.80
Para. 5	£1,114.00
Para. 6	£2,319.00
Para. 7	£26,340.80
Para. 8	£3,875.00
TOTAL CLAIM UNDER THIS SCHEDULE	£70,352.33

STATEMENT OF TRUTH

I believe that the facts stated in this schedule of past and future loss and expense are true.

Signed:

DATED 10 February 2006.

Messrs O'Reilly & Mackman, Bank Chambers, Edinburgh Road, Blackstone BL3 8GC, Solicitors for the Claimant.

Example 25.2

In this example, various heads of damage are claimed which cannot presently be quantified.

IN THE BLACKSTONE COUNTY COURT Claim No. BL934753

BETWEEN:

Mr GARTH HOPKINS Claimant

— and —

Mr IAN JACKS Defendant

SCHEDULE OF PAST AND FUTURE LOSS AND EXPENSE

Loss of Earnings

1. At the time of the accident the Claimant was employed by Closestaff Limited as a trainee manager. He was paid at his standard salary rates despite a protracted period off work as a result of

his injuries. On 31 January 2004 he was made redundant. His gross average monthly earnings at the time he was made redundant were £650, with deductions of £62.40 for tax and £43.48 for National Insurance (net £544.12 per month). Thereafter he was unemployed for 6 months 16 days until he commenced work on 17 August 2004 with Opendoors Limited. He was offered another job with the Finalposition Limited on 26 August 2004, which he accepted and commenced work on 14 September 2004. His current annual salary is £8,500, so there is no continuing loss of earnings while he remains in this employment.

2. By reason of his injuries the Claimant was unable to apply for jobs in the period between his redundancy and August 2004 which involved an element of manual work and had to restrict himself to office-based jobs. He also would have been able to put more energy into his job search but for the accident. If he had not been injured he would have commenced work about 3 months earlier than he did.

Total claim for loss of earnings:

3 months at £544.12 net per month	£1,632.36

Disadvantage on the Labour Market

3. The Claimant has a 12-month contract in his current employment ending on 10 September 2006.

4. By reason of his elbow injury the Claimant has been left with residual pain and restricted movements which compromise the overall function of his dominant right arm. This substantially limits the amount of physical work he can do with his arms, and also interferes with his driving in that he finds it difficult to steer. He is therefore effectively restricted to purely clerical work, whereas before the accident he could take jobs which included physical work. He is also going to be unable to take jobs involving any substantial amount of driving. He is consequently disadvantaged if he needs to look for work in the future, and he claims:

Damages to be assessed

Care and Assistance

5. Before the accident the Claimant lived in his own house. On being discharged from hospital on 24 June 2003 he moved in with his parents because he was totally reliant on them. In particular he needed assistance with washing, shaving and personal hygiene, with dressing and drinking and eating. In the period until 5 November 2003 he was unable to wash or iron his clothes, do his shopping or cooking, and was reliant entirely on his parents. 5 November 2003 was the first occasion on which he was able to assist his mother with preparing meals and some washing up. The Claimant was unable to drive until 11 December 2003. Until then he was dependent on his parents for lifts to hospital and physiotherapy sessions and for all other purposes. From the beginning of November 2003 until the end of January 2004 the Claimant was given reducing levels of assistance, until he was able to cope with most domestic tasks by himself by the beginning of February 2004. The Claimant required additional assistance in late October and November 2004 when he returned to hospital for removal of the plate and screws in his elbow. The Claimant claims for the care and assistance he has been given

Damages to be assessed

Gardening, DIY etc.

6. As a result of his injuries the Claimant has been unable to carry out gardening or domestic jobs requiring heavy lifting, and has had to obtain assistance from members of his family. He has also been unable to do any decorating, and will have to seek assistance from his family for decorating and DIY work at his own property and will be restricted in assistance he can give to his parents. He has also been unable to continue doing maintenance work on his car, and has had to seek the help of his brother-in-law. All these are continuing. The annual values for these are:

(a) Gardening	£100.00
(b) Heavy domestic work	£50.00
(c) Decorating	£250.00
(d) DIY	£100.00
(e) Assistance to parents	£50.00
(f) Car maintenance	£100.00
Total	£650.00

7. The Claimant therefore claims under this head:

(a) Value to date of gardening, heavy domestic work, decorating, DIY, assistance to parents and car maintenance from 13 June 2003 to 13 January 2006 (2 years 7 months) at £650.00 per annum	£1,679.16
(b) Future value of gardening, heavy domestic work, decorating, DIY, assistance to parents and car maintenance from 14 January 2005 with a multiplier of 20	£13,000.00
Total claim under this head	£14,679.16

Power Steering

8. By reason of his elbow injury the Claimant needs to buy cars with power steering. His car at the time of the accident was a Kurosawa Benidorm 1.1, which was replaced by another Benidorm 1.1 registration number LG53 DAB. These cars do not come with power-assisted steering, and there is no practical method of converting them to power steering. In order to buy cars with power steering the Claimant will have to buy cars which are more expensive than if he did not have this restriction. The Claimant estimates the price difference to be about £1,000, and that he will replace his vehicles approximately every 3 years. His annual loss is therefore about £330.

Additional annual cost of buying cars with power steering, with a multiplier of 20	£6,600.00

Future Surgery

9. There is an approximately 30% chance that the Claimant will require either elbow replacement surgery or an arthrodesis of his elbow within the next 30 years. Such an operation is likely to cost about £5,000 to £6,000. The Claimant will give credit for advanced receipt as appropriate.

To be assessed

10. There is an approximately 30% chance that the Claimant will require an arthrodesis of his great toe within the next 30 years. Such an operation is likely to cost about £2,000 to £2,500. The Claimant will give credit for advanced receipt as appropriate.

To be assessed

Accidental Damage

11. Excess	£50.00
12. Loss of use of car and inconvenience from 13 June 2003 to 14 August 2003	£450.00
13. Damage to clothing	£57.00
Total claim under this head	£557.00

Other Out-of-pocket Expenses

14. Loss of deposit for holiday	£20.00
15. Loss of deposit for railway ticket	£23.00
16. Miscellaneous expenses for telephone, letters and photographs and the like	£70.00
Total claim under this head	£113.00

Travel Costs

17. Taxis

(a) Before 19 November 2003	£39.00	
(b) 19 November 2003	£10.00	
(c) 11 December 2003	£10.00	
(d) 12 November 2004	£5.00	
Subtotal		£64.00

18. Driving to hospital, physiotherapy etc. at £0.35 per mile

(a) To Blackstone General Hospital up to 20 November 2003 (13 visits)	£50.00	
(b) 8 January 2004 (6 miles)	£2.10	

(c) 10 January 2004 (6 miles)	£2.10
(d) 5 February 2004 (6 miles)	£2.10
(e) 30 April 2004 (6 miles)	£2.10
(f) 18 June 2004 (6 miles)	£2.10
(g) 8 July 2004 (6 miles)	£2.10
(h) Parking on 8 July 2004	£1.40
(i) 11 July 2004 (6 miles)	£2.10
(j) 16 July 2004 (6 miles)	£2.10
(k) 10 September 2004 (6 miles)	£2.10
(l) 27 October 2004 (20 miles)	£7.00
(m) 1 December 2004 (10 miles)	£3.50
(n) 7 January 2005 (6 miles)	£2.10
(o) 8 June 2005 (20 miles)	£7.00
(p) 5 visits for physiotherapy (the Claimant walked for the other 26 sessions) at 3 miles each round trip	£5.25
(q) Additional trips to physiotherapy (78 miles)	£27.30
(r) 9 August 2005 (24 miles)	£8.40
Subtotal	£130.85

Total claim under this head £194.85

Medication

19. To November 2003 £21.60

20. From November 2003 to January 2006 at £12.00 a year £24.00

21. Continuing need for medications at £12.00 a year, with a multiplier of 20 £240.00

Total claim under this head £285.60

STATEMENT OF TRUTH

I believe that the facts stated in this schedule of past and future loss and expense are true.

Signed:

DATED this day of 2006.

Messrs O'Reilly & Mackman, Bank Chambers, Edinburgh Road,
Blackstone BL3 8GC,
Solicitors for the Claimant.

Chapter 26 Defending a Claim

INTRODUCTION

The principal rules concerning the drafting of the defence can be found in **CPR, Parts 15** and **16**, and their associated practice directions. **26.1**

The matters discussed below do not apply where the claimant uses the **Part 8** procedure, and apply with limited effect to specialist claims. They do, however, apply to cases where a defence is drafted to a counterclaim.

Although it is not mandatory, **form N9B** (specified amount) or **N9D** (unspecified amount or non-money claims) may be used for the purpose of setting out a defence (**PD 15, para. 1.3**). Copies of the forms are included in the response pack served on the defendant with the particulars of claim.

WHEN A DEFENCE IS REQUIRED

A defendant who wishes to defend all or part of a claim must file a defence (**CPR, r. 15.2**). If a defence is not filed, default judgment (see **chapter 20**) may be entered if allowed by **Part 12** (**r. 15.3**). A copy of the defence must be served on every other party (**r. 15.6**). **26.2**

PERIOD FOR FILING A DEFENCE

The general rule is that a defence must be filed within 14 days after service of the particulars of claim (**CPR, r. 15.4(1)(a)**). Therefore, no defence need be filed where a claim form is served which does not include, and is not accompanied by, particulars of claim (which can be served within 14 days thereafter: see **15.1**). As the particulars of claim can be contained within the body of the claim form (as opposed to served with it, or at a later date) care should therefore be taken to ensure whether the claim form contains the full particulars of claim, or merely the basic information required. **26.3**

The defendant is allowed to gain an additional 14 days for filing the defence simply by filing the acknowledgment of service form included in the response pack (see **chapter 18**). If this is done, the time for filing a defence is extended to 28 days after service of the particulars of the claim (**r. 15.4(1)(b)**).

There are different periods for filing a defence where the claim form is served out of the jurisdiction (see **r. 15.4(2)(a)**). If the court grants permission for a claim form to be served on the agent of a principal who is overseas, the court will, at the same time, under **r. 6.16(4)**, specify the period for responding.

There are three further exceptions to the above rules:

(a) Where the defendant makes an application disputing the jurisdiction of the court under **Part 11** (see **chapter 19**), the defence need not be filed before the hearing of the application (**r. 11(9)**).
(b) Where the claimant applies for summary judgment under **Part 24** (see **chapter 34**) before the defendant has filed a defence, the defendant need not file a defence before the summary judgment hearing (**r. 24.4(2)**).
(c) Where the defendant has applied for summary judgment under **Part 24**, or for the claimant's statement of case to be struck out under **r. 3.4**, default judgment may not be entered for the claimant until that application has been disposed of (**r. 12.3(3)(a)**).

The words of **r. 15.4** do not appear to prohibit the filing of a defence in the exceptional circumstances should the defendant wish. Where an application for summary judgment has been made by the claimant under **Part 24**, the defendant would appear to have a choice:

(a) His response may be supported by evidence, usually by witness statement, which may exhibit a draft defence. In practice this is usually the simplest and best approach.
(b) Alternatively, under **r. 32.6(2)**, a party may rely on his statement of case in hearings other than the trial, provided that it is verified by a statement of truth. Thus it appears, should the defendant wish to file his defence, he may do so, and then rely on it in addition to any witness statement he may wish to file.

EXTENDING THE TIME FOR SERVICE OF A DEFENCE

26.4 The defendant and the claimant may, under **CPR, r. 15.5**, agree that the period for filing a defence shall be extended by up to 28 days. Where this is done, the defendant must notify the court in writing (**r. 15.5(2)**). Thus there is a strict limit to the degree of 'slippage' which the parties may, by consent, allow. This is consistent with the principles of *Access to Justice* in that whereas there is an acknowledgment that the time limits set out in the rules may have to be extended, the principle of judicially led case management precludes the parties from agreeing further (or even open-ended) extensions of time. Any party wishing a further extension of time (whether by consent or otherwise) will have to make an application to the court under **r. 3.1(2)(a)**.

STAY OF CLAIM WHERE NO ACTION TAKEN

26.5 Where at least six months have expired since the end of the period for filing a defence, and no defendant has served or filed any admission, defence or counterclaim, and the claimant has not entered or applied for default judgment under **CPR, Part 12**, or summary judgment under **Part 24**, the claim shall be stayed, although any party can apply for such stay to be lifted (**r. 15.11**). The evidence in support of an application to lift the stay must give the reason for the delay in proceeding with or responding to the claim (**PD 15, para. 3.4**).

CONTENTS OF A DEFENCE — GENERAL MATTERS

26.6 The defence of a defendant who is an individual must include the defendant's residential or business address, unless it has been correctly given on the claim form (**PD 16, para. 10.4**).

The address must include the postcode unless the court orders otherwise (**para. 10.6**). Postcode information can be obtained from www.royalmail.com or the Royal Mail Address Management Guide. This address determines which court is the defendant's home court and must be established even if it is not the defendant's address for service (**para. 10.5**).

A defendant who is an individual must provide his or her date of birth (if known) in the defence (or acknowledgment of service, admission, defence and counterclaim, or reply or other response) (**para. 10.7**). This is primarily to identify the defendant if a judgment is to be registered (see **61.41**).

Admit, require to prove, deny

A defence to a claim must say which of the allegations in the particulars of claim are admitted, which are denied and which allegations the defendant is unable to admit or deny, but requires the claimant to prove (**CPR, r. 16.5(1)**). Every allegation made in a claim should be dealt with in the defence (**PD 16, para. 10.2**). **26.7**

It may be useful to restate the established principles behind the three possible responses to an allegation in particulars of claim, and their consequences so far as the claimant is concerned. If an allegation is *admitted*, the claimant is absolved from any obligation to bring any further evidence in support of that allegation. This is apart from any other consequences that may flow from the admission made. Allegations should be admitted if they are accepted by the defendant or if they make no material difference. A defendant who wishes to admit the truth of all or part of the other party's case may adopt the admissions procedure set out in **Part 14** (see **17.2**). The principles governing applications for permission to withdraw admissions are considered at **34.25**.

A defendant may *require the claimant to prove* an allegation which the defendant is unable to admit or deny (**CPR, r. 16.5(1)(b)**), usually because the defendant does not have sufficient information on the point. Often this will be because the evidence relevant to the allegation is in the possession of another party or person, or has been lost. Allegations which the claimant is required to prove are still in issue, but the defendant will not be making a positive alternative case on the point.

Where an allegation is *denied*, this normally implies that the defendant intends to put up a positive case to the contrary. Indeed, **r. 16.5(2)** specifically provides that where the defendant denies an allegation, he must state his reasons for doing so; and if he intends to put forward a different version of events from that given by the claimant, he must state his own version. This essentially restates what always was required under the old rules of pleading, even though often omitted.

A defendant who fails to answer a specific allegation will nevertheless be taken to require that allegation to be proved, provided that in his defence, he has set out the nature of his case in relation to the issue to which that allegation is relevant (**r. 16.5(3)**). In such an event, it will presumably be open to the claimant to apply to the court that the defendant give further information under **Part 18**, or for the court to order it of its own volition. However if the defendant totally fails to deal with an allegation, he shall be taken to have admitted it (**r. 16.5(5)**), unless it is an allegation relating to the value of a money claim, in which case he shall be taken to require that any allegation relating to the amount of money claimed by proved, unless he expressly admits the allegation (**r. 16.5(4)**).

Stand-alone defences and positive case

In addition to responding to the particulars of claim by admitting, requiring proof and denying the allegations made by the claimant, the defendant is obliged to set out his own case in sufficient detail to ensure the claimant can prepare for trial and understand the case which has to be met. This is the effect of **PD 18, para. 1.2**. The obligation extends beyond stating **26.8** reasons and any alternative version where the defence uses denials (see 26.7). It means the defence must give full details of:

(a) Any stand-alone defence relied upon. Examples are reliance on limitation periods, exemption and limitation of liability clauses in contracts, and equitable and legal defences, such as laches, delay, consent, illegality, lack of writing etc. The obligation is to set out sufficient facts to establish the elements of the defence based on the circumstances of the case.
(b) Any positive case relied upon by the defendant on an issue, even if the burden of proof rests with the claimant (*Baxter Healthcare Corporation v Abbott Laboratories* [2005] EWHC 2878 (Pat), LTL 6/12/2005).

CONTENTS OF A DEFENCE — SPECIFIC MATTERS

Dispute about statement of value

26.9 A claim form is required by **CPR, r. 16.3**, to contain a statement of value (see 23.6). If this statement is disputed, the defendant must state why he disputes it, and if he can, give his own statement of the value of the claim (**r. 16.5(6)**).

Claims already paid

26.10 Where (apart from costs and interest) the only claim against a defendant is for a specified sum of money, and a defence is filed stating that the sum has been paid to the claimant, the special procedure in **CPR, r. 15.10** applies.

Defendant in representative capacity

26.11 A defendant who is defending in a representative capacity must state that fact in the defence, and also say what that capacity is (**CPR, r. 16.5(7)**).

Address for service

26.12 Rule 16.5(8) of the CPR requires a defence to contain an address for service, within the jurisdiction (r. 6.5(2)), to which documents can be sent to the defendant, if no acknowledgment of service has been filed.

Personal injury claim

26.13 Where a defended claim is one in respect of personal injury, and the claimant has attached a medical report in respect of his or her alleged injuries, **PD 16, para. 12.1**, provides that the defence should state whether the defendant:

(a) agrees with the medical report; or
(b) disputes it (in which event the reasons for doing so should be stated (**para. 12.1(2)**); or
(c) neither agrees nor disputes it, but has no knowledge of the matters contained in the medical report.

If a medical report has been obtained by the defendant, on which the defendant intends to rely, it should be attached to the defence (**para. 12.1(3)**). It is submitted that 'should' in **PD 16, para. 12.1**, has the same mandatory force as 'must' in **CPR, r. 16.5**, and that no technical distinction should be drawn between the two.

Thus, there is an obligation on a defendant who disputes medical evidence served with the particulars of claim to attach his own medical report to his defence, when it has been obtained by the time the defence is drafted. There is, interestingly, no mandatory requirement to attach a medical report to a defence *whenever* the claimant's report is in dispute, but only where the defendant has already obtained his own medical report at the time of drafting the defence. However, it may well be difficult to dispute the claimant's report (particularly when reasons have to be given) save on grounds obtained as a result of a defence medical report, which is frequently not predicated upon a defence medical examination of the claimant, but upon an examination of medical records. If a defence medical report is not attached to a defence when detailed reasons for dispute are given, it would almost certainly prompt the claimant to question the basis for the response and apply for disclosure of the report. If the defendant has not had the opportunity to obtain his own expert evidence by the time the defence is drafted, it is likely that he would then have to state that he had 'no knowledge of the matters contained in the [claimant's] medical report', under **PD 16, para. 12.1(1)(c)**. Such a situation should be rare. In the vast majority of personal injury claims, and particularly when the amount of damages claimed is less than £15,000 and consequently allocated to the fast track, the parties will have been expected to have complied with the **Pre-action Protocol for Personal Injury Claims** (paras **2.2** and **2.3** of the Protocol). By **para. 2.14** of the Protocol, the joint selection of experts is encouraged, and is an almost invariable requirement in fast track cases. Thus it is likely that if the Protocol has been complied with, and proceedings are then issued, the medical report will have been agreed or obtained on a joint basis, and it is unlikely that the defendant will have obtained one of his own. If separate experts are instructed, it will be for the court ultimately to decide whether either party had acted unreasonably (**para. 3.18** of the Protocol). For detailed discussion of the pre-action protocols, see **chapter 8**.

Where, in a personal injuries case, the claimant has included a schedule of past and future expenses and losses, the defendant must include in or attach to his defence a counter-schedule stating which items are agreed, in dispute, or neither agreed nor disputed, because of lack of knowledge (**PD 16, para. 12.2(1)**). Where items are disputed, alternative figures, where appropriate, should be supplied (**para. 12.2(2)**). The counter-schedule must be verified by a statement of truth (**PD 22, para. 1.4(3)**).

Whole claim alleged to be fraudulent

There are occasions where the defendant alleges the whole claim is fraudulent or fabricated. A typical example is a low velocity impact road traffic accident. The argument is that the two vehicles collided at such a low speed that it is impossible for the injuries alleged by the claimant to have been caused by the collision. In such a case there is no burden on the defendant to prove fraud, and no obligation on the defendant to plead fraud or fabrication in the defence (*Kearsley v Klarfeld* [2005] EWCA Civ 1510, *The Independent*, 16 December 2005). It is sufficient simply to set out in the defence the facts from which the defendant will invite the judge to infer that the claimant had not suffered the injuries being claimed (*Cooper v P and O Stena Line Ltd* [1999] 1 Lloyd's Rep 734). In these cases the court will expect the parties to be particularly open and cooperative on matters such as access to the vehicles for expert examination and access to medical notes, and these claims are likely to be suitable for the multi-track even if below the usual threshold (*Kearsley v Klarfeld*). **26.14**

Limitation defence

A defendant who relies on the expiry of any limitation period, must give in his defence details of the date on which it is alleged the relevant limitation period expired (**PD 16, para. 13.1**). **26.15**

Human Rights Act 1998

A defendant who seeks to rely on any provision of, or right arising under, the **Human Rights Act 1998**, or seeks a remedy under that Act, must state in the defence the matters set out in **PD 16, para. 15.1**. **26.16**

Defamation

For particular rules in cases of defamation etc., see **PD 53, para. 2**. **26.17**

Tender

26.18 For particular rules where the defence is one of tender before action see **PD 16, para. 13.2**, CPR, r. 37.3, and PD 37, para. 2.

Competition Act 1998

26.19 In certain proceedings under the Competition Act 1998, a defendant who intends to rely on a determination of the Director General of Fair Trading must comply with **PD 16, para. 14**.

SET-OFFS

26.20 A defendant who wishes to rely wholly or in part on a defence of set-off may, by **CPR, r. 16.6**, include this in the defence, whether or not it will also form the subject of a counterclaim under **Part 20**. Interestingly, the rule does not *require* this to be done, but as set-off was almost invariably pleaded in the defence under the old rules, there seems no reason why that practice should not continue.

STATEMENT OF TRUTH

26.21 A defence must be verified by a statement of truth (see 23.11 to 23.16). The form of statement is (**PD 16, para. 11.2**):

[I believe] [the defendant believes] that the facts stated in the defence are true.

DRAFTING STYLE

26.22 With certain exceptions, there is no radical departure from the principles of pleading that applied under the old RSC and CCR. However, the matters which led to the criticism of the pleadings process, and need for reform (discussed in 24.17) applied as much to the defence as to the claim. In particular it appeared often to be forgotten that it was (and is) as incumbent upon a defendant to state full particulars of his case, as it was and is for the plaintiff/claimant. In addition to stating his position with regard to the allegations made against him, the defendant, when denying an allegation, must state his reasons for doing so, and if he intends to put forward a different version of events from that given by the claimant, he must state his own version (**CPR, r. 16.5(2)**). Too often in the past, defences concentrated point by point on the allegations set out in the claim, stating whether they were admitted, denied or not admitted, but then wholly neglected to set out the defendant's own case on the issues. To do this today will render the defence in grave danger of being struck out. The incorrect and correct approaches are illustrated in example 26.1.

Example 26.1

Insufficiently set out

It is denied that the defendant was negligent as alleged or at all.

Insufficiently set out

It is denied that the defendant drove along Litigation Avenue at an excessive speed, and/or failed to keep a proper lookout, and/or failed to brake or steer his car so as to avoid colliding with the claimant, as alleged or at all.

Correctly set out

It is denied that the defendant was negligent in any of the ways set out in the particulars of negligence, or at all. The defendant was driving at a safe speed down Litigation Avenue, which is a major road. The accident was caused when the claimant drove his car out of Blackstone Road, which was a minor road, into the path of the defendant's car, giving the defendant no opportunity to avoid the collision. In the circumstances, the collision was wholly caused by the negligence of the claimant, as set out below:

PARTICULARS OF NEGLIGENCE

etc.

Chapter 27 Reply and Subsequent Statements of Case

GENERAL AND PROCEDURAL REQUIREMENTS

27.1 Although a claimant may file a reply to a defence, he does not have to do so, and failure to file a reply must not be taken as an admission of any of the matters raised in the defence (**CPR, r. 16.7(1)**). If a reply is filed, but fails to deal with a matter raised in the defence, the claimant shall nevertheless be taken to require that matter to be proved. Thus, strictly speaking, it is unnecessary for the reply to commence with a statement joining issue with the defendant upon all matters not specifically admitted in the defence (the old 'general traverse'), as there is an implied joinder of issue. Where, however, the defence includes a counterclaim to which it is intended to file a defence, it is suggested that a formal reply should also be filed in the conventional manner, joining issue with the defendant on his defence and counterclaim, although the rules do not specifically provide for, or require, this to be done.

When a claimant intends to file a reply, this must be done when he files his allocation questionnaire under **r. 26.3(6)**, and the reply must be served on the other parties at the same time as it is filed (**r. 15.8**).

CONTENTS OF A REPLY

27.2 Conventionally, a reply may respond to any matters raised in the defence which were not, and which should not have been, dealt with in the particulars of claim, and exists solely for the purpose of dealing disjunctively with matters which could not properly have been dealt with in the particulars of claim, but which require a response once they have been raised in the defence. It has always been a cardinal principle of pleading (which has certainly not been altered by the CPR) that a claim should not anticipate a potential defence (popularly known as 'jumping the stile'). Once, however, a defence has been raised which requires a response so that the issues between the parties can be defined, a reply becomes necessary for the purpose of setting out the claimant's case on that point. The reply is, however, neither an opportunity to restate the claim, nor is it, nor should it be drafted as, a 'defence to the defence'.

Where the defence takes issue with a fact set out in the particulars of claim, and the claimant accepts that the fact is incorrect, the proper course should be for the claimant to seek to amend his statement of case accordingly (see **chapter 31**), and not to deal with the matter in a reply (**PD 16, para. 9.2**). Thus where, for example, the particulars of claim contain an error as to the quantity of goods ordered, and the correct quantity is set out in the defence, the error should be corrected by way of amendment, rather than reply.

A reply must be verified by a statement of truth (see **23.11** to **23.16**; **CPR, r. 22.1(1)(a)**).

SUBSEQUENT STATEMENTS OF CASE

27.3 A party may not file or serve any statement of case beyond a reply, without the permission of the court (**CPR, r. 15.9**). Such permission should rarely be required, and presumably will rarely be granted. Under the previous rules, leave had to be granted to file a rejoinder, surrejoinder, rebutter or surrebutter, and such instances were so rare as to have almost fallen into disuse. Save in the most exceptional cases the supposed need for additional pleadings normally evidenced a failure to plead the case properly in the first place. Problems of this kind can be resolved either by amendment or by requests for further information.

Chapter 28 Counterclaims

The following procedural checklist, which is in **appendix 1**, is relevant to this chapter:

Procedural checklist 18 Counterclaim (Part 20)

INTRODUCTION

28.1 The rules governing counterclaims are contained in **CPR, Part 20**, and **PD 20**. For claims against co-defendants and other parties (which are also covered by **Part 20**) see **chapter 29**.

Any claim other than a claim by a claimant against a defendant, is classed as an 'additional claim', an expression which includes a counterclaim by a defendant (whether against the claimant or against the claimant and some other person) (**r. 20.2(2)**). Until changes made by the Civil Procedure (Amendment No. 4) Rules 2005 (SI 2005/3515) came into effect on 6 April 2006, counterclaims (together with the types of proceedings described in **chapter 29**) were known as 'Part 20' claims.

The ability to bring a counterclaim within existing proceedings allows a defendant to wrest some of the initiative away from the claimant. Its main purpose, however, is to promote the general policy of ensuring that, so far as convenient, all issues between the parties are resolved together, with a view to saving costs, avoiding a multiplicity of claims, and avoiding the risk of irreconcilable judgments. Under **CPR, r. 3.1(2)(e)** and **(j)**, the court has general case management powers to order part of proceedings to be dealt with as separate proceedings, and to decide the order in which issues are tried. Specific factors that the court should take into account in making such decisions in the context of additional claims like counterclaims are set out in **r. 20.9**.

PERMISSION TO MAKE A COUNTERCLAIM

28.2 Provided it is filed with the defence, the court's permission is not required to make a counterclaim (**CPR, r. 20.4(2)(a)**). However, permission is required for filing a counterclaim after service of the defence (**r. 20.4(2)(b)**), and the procedure and conditions laid down in **Part 20** and **PD 20** will have to be followed. A copy of the proposed counterclaim must be filed together with the application notice seeking permission (**PD 20, para. 1.2**). The evidence in support must state the stage reached in the main proceedings, the nature of the additional claim, a summary of the facts on which the additional claim is based, and the name and address of any proposed additional party (**para. 2.1**). Where possible the applicant should provide a timetable of the proceedings to date (**para. 2.3**).The permission of the court is required for a counterclaim against the Crown if:

(a) the proceedings were brought in the name of a government department and the counterclaim does not relate to that department (**CPR, r. 66.4(4)**); or
(b) the proceedings were brought in the name of the Attorney-General (**r. 66.4(3)**).

A defendant who wishes to counterclaim against a person other than the claimant must apply to the court for an order adding that person as a defendant to the counterclaim (**r. 20.5(1)**). An application for such an order may be made without notice, unless the court directs otherwise (**r. 20.5(2)**), and if the order is made, the court will at the same time give directions for the management of the case (**r. 20.5(3)**).

PROCEDURE

A defendant may make a counterclaim against a claimant by filing particulars of the counterclaim (**CPR, r. 20.4(1)**). The counterclaim will attract an additional fee, equal to that of starting fresh proceedings (**CPFO, fee 1.6**). A fee of £35 in a county court, £50 in the High Court, is payable if a party is added to the claim (**CPFO, fee 1.5**). If the issue fee is not paid after due warning by the court, the counterclaim will be struck out automatically (**CPR, r. 3.7A**). **28.3**

The defence and counterclaim should normally form one document with the counterclaim following on from the defence (**PD 15, para. 3.1; PD 20, para. 6.1**).

The usual rule once judgment has been obtained and fully satisfied is that it is not possible to bring a counterclaim, because there is no subsisting claim against which the counterclaim can be brought. This rule has been held to be subject to an exception where the claim is for possession of land, see *Laib v Aravindan* [2003] EWHC 2521 (QB), *The Times*, 13 November 2003.

In a claim by the Crown for taxes, duties or penalties, the defendant cannot bring a counterclaim or raise a set-off (**CPR, r. 66.4(1)**). Similarly, in a claim by the Crown, the defendant cannot bring a counterclaim or raise a set-off based on a claim for repayment of taxes, duties or penalties (**r. 66.4(2)**).

Where the permission of the court to make a counterclaim is not required, the counterclaim should also be served on every other party when a copy of the defence is served (**r. 20.8(1)(a)**), or within 14 days after the date on which the counterclaim was issued by the court, if it is to be served on a person who is not an existing party (**r. 20.8(1)(b)**). **Rule 20.8(1)(a)** refers to a counterclaim against an 'additional' party only. This is an obvious drafting error (a counterclaim against an additional party only is not a counterclaim at all, but a third party claim), and should refer to a counterclaim against an 'existing' party only. Where the permission of the court is required, the court will give directions as to service (**r. 20.8(3)**). If a counterclaim is made against an additional party, the copy served on that additional party must be accompanied by forms for admitting and defending the counterclaim, and for acknowledging service. Also, that additional party must be served with copies of all statements of case which have been served in the proceedings, together with any other documents which the court may direct (**r. 20.12(1)**). A copy of the additional claim form must be served on every existing party (**r. 20.12(2)**).

HEADING A COUNTERCLAIM

Before 6 April 2006

The manner in which a counterclaim against both the claimant and another party was headed in counterclaims filed before 6 April 2006 was set out in the former version of **PD 20, para. 7.2**. Where there was more than one Part 20 claim, the heading had to be as set out in **PD 20, para. 7.3**. Suggestions for simplifying more complex headings were given in **PD 20, paras 7.4** and **7.5**. It is perhaps unfortunate that the practice direction did not differentiate between the situation where the counterclaim was against the existing claimant and where it was against a new party, when setting out the Part 20 heading. Thus, even when the counterclaim was against the claimant only, it appears that the heading had to read as in example 28.1, **28.4**

Example 28.1

IN THE BLACKSTONE COUNTY COURT Claim No. BP 12345

BETWEEN

AB Claimant/Part 20 Defendant

— and —

CD Defendant/Part 20 Claimant

which could potentially make drafting the counterclaim a little cumbersome. From the point of pure drafting technique, there was no reason why such a counterclaim could not refer to the parties as 'claimant' and 'defendant' respectively, rather than adopt the Part 20 nomenclature. The two contrasting styles are set out in examples 28.2(a) and 28.2(b) respectively, and it is suggested that the former is to be preferred.

Example 28.2(a)

COUNTERCLAIM

8. The Defendant repeats the matters set out paragraphs 3 to 7 of the Defence above.

9. By an oral agreement made in the course of a telephone conversation on 29 June 2005 between the Defendant and the Claimant, it was agreed that the Defendant would supply the Claimant with 15 boxes of widgets at a price of £277 per box inclusive of VAT.

Example 28.2(b)

COUNTERCLAIM

8. The Part 20 Claimant repeats the matters set out paragraphs 3 to 7 of the Defence above.

9. By an oral agreement made in the course of a telephone conversation on 29 June 2005 between the Part 20 Claimant and the Part 20 Defendant, it was agreed that the Part 20 Claimant would supply the Part 20 Defendant with 15 boxes of widgets at a price of £277 per box inclusive of VAT.

From 6 April 2006

28.5 The draft PD 20, which is expected to come into effect on 6 April 2006, broadly adopts the practice set out in example 28.2(a) above. This provides that claimants and defendants in the original claim should always be referred to as such in the title to the proceedings, even if they subsequently acquire an additional procedural status (**para.** 7.3). In a simple counterclaim there is no change in the parties, with the counterclaim being brought by the defendant against the claimant. Where the defendant brings a counterclaim against the claimant and an additional party, the additional party is called the 'third party' (**para.** 7.4(c)), unless there has been an earlier additional claim within the proceedings. In that event there will already be a third party, so the additional party on the counterclaim will be the 'fourth party' (or whatever in accordance with the order in which this person is added to the proceedings, see **para.** 7.4).

A counterclaim brought against the original claimant is simply described as the counterclaim. A counterclaim brought against the claimant and an additional party has to be described in the title as such. For example, 'defendant's counterclaim against claimant and third party' (see **para.** 7.10).

STATUS OF A COUNTERCLAIM

Save where **CPR, Part 20**, states to the contrary, the provisions of the CPR apply to counterclaims as if they were claims (**r. 20.3(1)**). In particular, as **PD 20, para. 3**, points out, the provisions relating to any failure to respond will apply as much to a counterclaim as they do to a claim. **Part 15** of the CPR applies to a defence to a counterclaim. Thus it is, for example, open to a defendant to obtain judgment in default of a defence to a counterclaim, subject to the conditions and procedure laid down in **Part 12**. However, a claimant wishing to defend a counterclaim is not permitted to file an acknowledgment of service (**r. 20.4(3)**), and various consequential rules pertaining to time limits, statements of value for the purposes of issue in the High Court, and preliminary case management under **Part 26** also do not apply (see **r. 20.3(2)** for details). **28.6**

CONTENTS OF A COUNTERCLAIM

As a counterclaim is treated as if it was a claim for the purposes of the CPR, it should be set out in the same format, and with the same particularity as particulars of claim. **28.7**

The contents of a counterclaim must be verified by a statement of truth (see **23.11** to **23.16**; **CPR, r. 22.1(1)(a)**; **PD 20, para. 4.1**). The form of statement is (**PD 20, para. 4.2**; **PD 22**):

[I believe] [the defendant believes] that the facts stated in this counterclaim are true.

DEFENCE TO COUNTERCLAIM

General and procedural requirements

A claimant who files a reply and a defence to a counterclaim should normally put them in one document, with the reply followed by the defence to counterclaim (**CPR, r. 15.4(2)**; **PD 20, para. 6.2**). **28.8**

Where a defence is filed to a counterclaim or other Part 20 claim, the court must consider the future conduct of the proceedings and give appropriate directions, in the course of which it must ensure that both the main claim and the Part 20 claim are managed together, so far as is practicable (**CPR, r. 20.13**). For this purpose the court will arrange a case management conference. Normally this will be fixed for the same time as a case management hearing for the original claim and any other additional claims (**PD 20, para. 5.1**).

Contents of defence to counterclaim

A defence to a counterclaim is governed by the same rules as a defence to a claim (see **chapter 26**) and must be verified by a statement of truth (see **23.11** to **23.16**). **28.9**

Chapter 29 Additional Claims under Part 20

The following procedural checklist, which is in **appendix 1**, is relevant to this chapter:

Procedural checklist 19 Additional claim (against third party)

INTRODUCTION

29.1 Part 20 of the CPR concerns both counterclaims, and what formerly were known as third party proceedings. Counterclaims have already been discussed in **chapter 28**. This chapter considers claims made by a defendant, either against a co-defendant, seeking a contribution or indemnity, or against a third party. Together with counterclaims, these are now generically known as 'additional claims'. Until 6 April 2006 they were known as 'Part 20 claims'.

An indemnity is an obligation to reimburse someone, i.e., it is a claim for the fulfilment of an obligation, not for damages for breach of one. A contribution is essentially a partial indemnity.

CONTRIBUTION

29.2 A right to a contribution can arise as between joint tortfeasors, debtors or contractors, or by statute, for example, under the **Civil Liability (Contribution) Act 1978, s. 1(1)**, which provides that where two or more persons are liable to the same claimant for the same damage, each may claim contribution towards that liability from the others. The 'damage' referred to in s. 1(1) is the wrong causing the injury: it is not the injury itself (*Jameson v Central Electricity Generating Board* [1998] QB 323). Note also that the word used is 'damage' rather than 'damages' (see *Birse Construction Ltd v Haiste Ltd* [1996] 1 WLR 675). There is no limit or restriction on this concept. For example, a building contractor who remedies defective building work at no cost to the employer can claim a contribution from a consulting engineer based on the value of the remedial work (*Baker and Davies plc v Leslie Wilks Associates* [2005] EWHC 1179 (TCC), [2005] 3 All ER 603). The 1978 Act extends the reach of the contribution principle to cover cases whatever the legal basis of the liability, whether in tort, breach of contract, breach of trust or otherwise (see s. 6(1)).

In deciding whether the defendant and the third party are 'liable for the same damage', the words from s. 1(1) must be given their natural and ordinary meaning, without any restrictive or expansive gloss (*Royal Brompton Hospital NHS Trust v Hammond* [2002] UKHL 14, [2002] 1 WLR 1397). The words do not cover damage which is merely substantially or materially similar (per

Lord Steyn). The defendants in *Royal Brompton Hospital NHS Trust v Hammond* were architects who were sued by the hospital for negligently issuing certificates to building contractors, the effect of which was to give the contractors a defence to a claim the hospital had against the contractors for breach of contract for delays in completing building work. It was held that the hospital's claims against the contractors and against the architects were different, so the architects could not claim a contribution against the contractors. If the third party has no liability to the claimant, such as through a term in a contract absolving the third party from liability, the defendant cannot claim contribution from the third party (*Cooperative Retail Services Ltd v Taylor Young Partnership Ltd* [2002] UKHL 17, [2002] 1 WLR 1419).

A relevant liability under the Civil Liability (Contribution) Act 1978, s. 1, includes a liability under a court order, even if the amount of that liability has not been determined (*Abbey National plc v Matthews and Son* [2003] EWHC 925 (Ch), [2003] 1 WLR 2042, applying *R. A. Lister and Co. Ltd v E. G. Thomson (Shipping) Ltd (No. 2)* [1987] 1 WLR 1614).

An additional claim under Part 20 was struck out in *Abbey National plc v Matthews and Son* on the ground of circularity. The building society sued solicitors for failing to disclose material relevant to a loan agreement, and the solicitors issued an additional claim against surveyors seeking a contribution on the ground of an alleged negligent valuation. The solicitors settled with the building society, and assigned their additional claim to the building society. By virtue of the settlement arrangements, the building society, using the assigned additional claim, could only claim a contribution from the surveyors if the solicitors were liable to the building society, but the solicitors were only liable to the building society if and to the extent that the building society obtained a contribution order from the surveyors.

The personal innocence of a person vicariously liable for the acts of an employee or partner is not relevant for the purpose of contribution proceedings between that person and another wrongdoer (*Dubai Aluminium Co. Ltd v Salaam* [2002] UKHL 48, [2003] 2 AC 366).

INDEMNITY

Entitlement to an indemnity can arise by contract, under statute, or by virtue of the relationship between the parties. It is reasonably common for commercial and standard-form contracts to include provisions requiring one party to indemnify the other in specified circumstances, such as where one party incurs a liability to another person through the fault or breach of the other contracting party. General principles of contract law apply to such terms. **29.3**

The principal purpose of a contract of insurance is to provide an indemnity to the assured. It has long been the practice not to allow a defendant to join its insurer as a third party in claims where the defendant is insured against the potential liability. Traditionally this has been because jurors were thought to be unduly influenced by the presence of insurance (*Harman v Crilly* [1943] KB 168), but even today joining an insurer can only be justified in accordance with the overriding objective if the insurer is denying liability under the insurance contract.

Indemnities arising by statute (such as the Law of Property Act 1925, s. 76(1)(D) and sch. 2, part IV, and the Companies Act 1985, s. 322(3)(b)) are mostly of a specialised nature.

Indemnities arising out of the relationship between the parties depend on the substantive law. For example, a principal is required to indemnify an agent in respect of liabilities incurred by the agent when acting within the agent's authority (*Adamson v Jarvis* (1827) 4 Bing 66; *Frixione v Tagliaferro and Sons* (1856) 10 Moo PC 175). Similarly, a surety who is sued may claim an indemnity against the principal debtor (*Ascherson v Tredegar Dry Dock and Wharf Co. Ltd* [1909] 2 Ch 401; *Thomas v Nottingham Incorporated Football Club Ltd* [1972] Ch 596).

A contractual clause giving an indemnity for all actions, claims, costs, proceedings and demands was considered in *Lomax Leisure Ltd v Fabric London Ltd* [2003] EWHC 307 (Ch), LTL 19/3/2003.

REQUIREMENT FOR PERMISSION

29.4 The permission of the court is not required in order to bring an additional claim, save in the following circumstances:

(a) where a defendant wishes to counterclaim against a claimant after having already filed his defence (**CPR, r. 20.4(2)(b)**; see **chapter 28**);
(b) where a defendant wishes to counterclaim against a person other than the claimant (**r. 20.5(1)**; see **chapter 28**);
(c) where a defendant wishes to make a claim for contribution or indemnity against a co-defendant, but does not file the notice of claim with his defence (**r. 20.6**);
(d) where a defendant who has already filed a defence wishes to make a claim for contribution or indemnity against a co-defendant added to the proceedings after the defence was filed, but does not file the notice of claim within 28 days of the filing of the new defendant's defence (**r. 20.6**); and
(e) where a defendant wishes to make a claim (whether for a contribution or indemnity or otherwise) against a person who is not a co-defendant, and where the claim is not a counterclaim, and where such claim is not issued before or at the same time as he files his defence (**r. 20.7(1)** and **(3)**).

It follows that the permission of the court to make an additional claim is not required:

(a) where a defendant wishes to counterclaim against the claimant at the same time that he files his defence (see **chapter 28**);
(b) where a defendant wishes to make a claim against a co-defendant for a contribution or an indemnity at the same time as filing his own defence (**r. 20.6**);
(c) where a defendant who has filed a defence wishes to make a claim for a contribution or an indemnity against a new co-defendant added after the defence was filed and does so within 28 days of the filing of the new co-defendant's defence (**r. 20.6**);
(d) where a defendant wishes to make any claim against a third party before or at the same time as he files his defence (**r. 20.7(3)(a)**). The expression 'defendant' in **r. 20.7(3)** is presumably intended to apply to a third (or fourth) party wishing to make a further claim against a person not already a party. This was perfectly clear on the pre-6 April 2006 wording of **r. 20.7(3)**, because at that time a third party brought in by the original defendant was known as the 'Part 20 defendant'. It is not so clear under the present version of **r. 20.7(3)**, because it is worded on the basis that the 'defendant' means the defendant to the original claim (see **PD 20, paras** 7.3 and 7.4), and the person brought in by the defendant is known as the 'third party'. However, this should not prevent a third party who acts quickly being allowed to issue a fourth party claim without permission. This is because **CPR, r. 20.3(1)**, provides that an additional claim is to be treated as if it were a claim for the purposes of the CPR, and there is no reason to read **r. 20.7(3)** as derogating from that for this purpose.

PROCEDURE FOR COMMENCING AN ADDITIONAL CLAIM WHEN PERMISSION IS NOT REQUIRED

29.5 The claim and particulars must be served on the person against whom it is made within 14 days after the date on which the additional claim is issued by the court (**CPR, r. 20.8(1)(b)**). There is no express provision that copies must also be served on every other party, which apparently only has to be done, under **r. 20.12(2)**, when an additional claim is served on a person who is not already a party (**r. 20.12(2)** refers to 'the additional claim form', referring to the form which is the subject of **r. 20.12(1)**). However, it is suggested that it would be good practice to do so. **Rule 20.8(1)** does not apply to a defendant's claim against a co-defendant for contribution or indemnity, for which see **29.11** (**r. 20.8(2)**).

PROCEDURE FOR FILING AN ADDITIONAL CLAIM WHEN PERMISSION IS REQUIRED

A party requiring permission to make an additional claim may apply without notice unless the court directs otherwise (**CPR, r. 20.7(5)**). The application notice should be filed together with a copy of the proposed additional claim (**PD 20, para. 1.2**), and the evidence in support should set out (**PD 20, para. 2.1**): **29.6**

(a) the stage which the proceedings have reached;
(b) the nature of the additional claim, or details of the question or issue which needs to be decided;
(c) a summary of the facts on which the additional claim is based; and
(d) the name and address of any proposed additional party.

Where there has been delay which has caused or contributed to the need to apply for permission an explanation of the delay should be given in the evidence in support (**PD 20, para. 2.2**).

Additionally, where possible, the evidence should include a timetable of the proceedings to date (**PD 20, para. 2.3**).

Relevant considerations in applications for permission to file an additional claim

When considering whether or not to give permission for the filing of an additional claim, the court clearly has the power either to grant the application, dismiss it, or, under **CPR, r. 3.1(2)(e)**, require the additional claim to be dealt with separately from the claim by the claimant against the defendant. Apart from the question of whether or not it would be proper to allow the claim to be filed on its merits, or when there has been any delay, the court may also, by **r. 20.9(2)**, have regard to: **29.7**

(a) the connection between the additional claim and the claim made by the claimant against the defendant;
(b) whether the party making the additional claim is seeking substantially the same remedy which some other party is claiming from him;
(c) whether the party making the additional claim wants the court to decide any question connected with the subject matter of the proceedings not only between existing parties, but between existing parties and a third party; or against an existing party in some different capacity in which he may stand, as well as in the capacity in which he is already a party.

There is no reason to believe that the approach of the courts in deciding whether or not to grant permission to bring an additional claim will differ substantially from the manner in which discretion was exercised under the old rules. In *Chatsworth Investments Ltd v Amoco (UK) Ltd* [1968] Ch 665 Russell LJ held that the court had to take a wide approach in exercising its discretion, and had to ask whether the third-party claim accorded with the general functions of third-party proceedings. In *Barclays Bank Ltd v Tom* [1923] 1 KB 221 Scrutton LJ identified these functions as safeguarding against differing results, ensuring the third party is bound by the decision between the claimant and the defendant, ensuring the additional claim is decided close in time to the proceedings commenced by the claimant, and to save the expense of having two trials.

Essentially, therefore, the establishment of some factual, legal or personal connection between the additional claim and the original claim will be helpful in ensuring the success of the application.

Permission to issue an additional claim may be refused if the application is made after an unjustified delay. In *Borealis AB v Stargas Ltd* [2002] EWCA Civ 757, LTL 9/5/2002, there was a counterclaim against the claimant, and the claimant had sought to bring an additional claim against a non-party, SA, to contribute towards any liability on the counterclaim. The claimant's additional claim was set aside by the House of Lords in March 2001. In September 2001 there was a case management conference and a trial was fixed for July 2002. In March 2002 the defendant, for the first time, sought to bring its own additional claim against SA to contribute towards any liability the defendant might have. Although it was held that the defendant had a good arguable case on its additional claim, permission was refused because there was an inexcusable delay of a year after the House of Lords decision, and granting permission would have resulted in the trial being vacated.

CONTENTS OF AN ADDITIONAL CLAIM

29.8 An additional claim under **CPR, Part 20**, must contain particulars, or particulars must be served with the claim (**r. 20.7(4)**). **Rule 20.7** does not apply to a defendant's claim against a co-defendant for contribution or indemnity, for which see **29.11** (**r. 20.7(1)**). The title of an additional claim should, where there are additional parties, comprise a list of all the parties, describing them by giving each party a separate identification (**PD 20, para 7.2**). This identification should be used throughout. Claimants and defendants in the original claim should be described as such, a position that does not change even if they acquire an additional procedural status (**para. 7.3**). The first party added under **Part 20** is called the 'third party'. Subsequently added parties are the 'fourth party', 'fifth party' etc., in the order in which they are joined to the proceedings (**para. 7.4**). If an additional claim is brought against more than one party jointly, they are known as the 'first named third party' and 'second named third party' (etc.) (**para. 7.5**). If an additional party ceases to be a party, all the remaining parties retain their existing nominal status (**para. 7.9**).

The description of an additional claim (traditionally set out in tramlines beneath the names of the parties in the title) must reflect the nature of the document and its relation to the parties. Thus:

(a) A 'defendant's additional claim against third party' is an additional claim brought by the defendant against a single additional party, the third party.

(b) A 'third party's defence to defendant's additional claim' would be the defence filed by the third party in the previous example.

It is established drafting practice to set out in the opening paragraphs of the particulars of an additional claim summaries of the original and any existing additional claims, to state that copies of the previous statements of case are being served with the present statement of case (in compliance with **CPR, r. 20.12**), and a denial of the claim made against the drafting party. This provides a context for the rest of the draft against the new additional party, and also allows certain terms to be defined for use in the rest of the draft. See example 29.1.

In proceedings where there are fourth or subsequent parties, they should be referred to in the text of statements of case, witness statements etc. by name, suitably abbreviated if appropriate (**PD 20, para. 7.11**). If parties have similar names, suitable distinguishing abbreviations should be used.

Example 29.1

IN THE HIGH COURT OF JUSTICE Claim No. ....

QUEEN'S BENCH DIVISION

BETWEEN:

Mr ALAN BEST Claimant

— and—

Miss CATHERINE DAY Defendant

— and —

Ms ELAINE FRASER Third Party

— and —

Ms GAIL HARVEY Fourth Party

THIRD PARTY'S ADDITIONAL CLAIM AGAINST FOURTH PARTY

1. In his claim against the Defendant the Claimant claims damages and interest for alleged breach of a contract in writing dated 13 June 2005 ('the third contract') for the sale of a Bergman car registration number ML02 TYS ('the car'). Copies of the third contract, Claim Form and Particulars of Claim are served with these particulars of additional claim.
2. The Defendant denies she is liable to the Claimant on the grounds set out in the Defence, a copy of which is served with these particulars of additional claim.

3. In her additional claim against the Third Party, the Defendant claims damages and interest for alleged breach of a contract in writing dated 5 June 2005 ('the second contract') for the car. Copies of the second contract, Additional Claim Form and Defendant's Additional Claim against Third Party are served with these particulars of additional claim.

4. The Third Party denies she is liable to the Defendant on the grounds set out in the Third Party's Defence to Defendant's Additional Claim, a copy of which is served with these particulars of additional claim. If, contrary to the Third Party's Defence to Defendant's Additional Claim, the Third Party is held liable in whole or in part to the Defendant, the Third Party claims against the Fourth Party ('Ms Harvey') [to be indemnified against] [, alternatively, a contribution towards] [her liability, if any, to the Defendant] [damages and interest for alleged breach of a contract in writing dated 25 May 2005 ('the first contract') for the car] for the reasons set out below.

5. [*Continue with details of the claim against the Fourth Party as in normal particulars of claim.*]

An additional claim should be verified by a statement of truth (see **23.11** to **23.16**; **CPR, r. 22.1(1)(a)**; **PD 20, para. 4.1**). The form of statement is (**PD 20, para. 4.2; PD 22**):

[I believe] [the [defendant] believes] that the facts stated in this additional claim are true.

PROCEDURE AND CASE MANAGEMENT AFTER FILING

Although **CPR, Part 12** (obtaining judgment in default of a defence), applies to counterclaims (see **28.3**), it does not apply to other additional claims (**r. 20.3(3)**). Instead, the procedure where no acknowledgment of service or defence is filed to an additional claim is set out in **r. 20.11** (which does not apply to a defendant's claim against a co-defendant for contribution or indemnity: **r. 20.11(1)(a)**). **29.9**

Part 14 (admissions) also does not apply (**r. 20.3(4)**), save for the provisions relating to the ability to admit in writing the truth of another party's case (under **r. 14.1(1)** and **(2)**), so that the other party can obtain judgment under **r. 14.3**.

Where the court gives permission to make an additional claim it will at the same time give directions as to its service (**r. 20.8(3)**).

Once an additional claim is served on a person, he either becomes a party if he is not one already, or if he is already a party but the additional claim is served on him for the purpose of requiring the court to decide a question against him in a further capacity, he also becomes a party in such further capacity (**r. 20.10**).

If an additional claim form is served on a person who is not already a party, **r. 20.12(1)** requires it to be accompanied by:

(a) a form for defending the claim;
(b) a form for admitting the claim;
(c) a form for acknowledging service;
(d) a copy of every statement of case which has already been served in the proceedings; and
(e) such other documents as the court may direct.

A copy of the additional claim form must also be served on every existing party (**r. 20.12(2)**).

Where a defence is filed to an additional claim, the court must consider the future conduct of the proceedings and give appropriate directions (**r. 20.13(1)**). In order to do so, the court will arrange a hearing to consider case management of the additional claim, and will give notice of the hearing to each party likely to be affected by any order made at the hearing (**PD 20, paras 5.1** and **5.2**). When giving directions, the court must ensure that, so far as practicable, the additional and the main claims are managed together (**CPR, r. 20.13(2)**). An additional claim which is unsuitable for hearing with the main claim may be filtered out at an earlier stage if it requires the court's permission before it can be made (see **29.7**). However, if the permission of the court was not required, the question of the best means by which the two matters should be heard will be decided at this stage.

At the hearing, the court may (**PD 20, para. 5.3**):

(a) treat the matter as a summary judgment hearing (whether on the application of the defendant, third party, or of its own volition);
(b) order that the additional claim be dismissed (presumably as an outcome of (a) above);
(c) give directions as to the manner in which any matter set out in or arising from the additional claim should be dealt with, and as to the part, if any, that the third party will take at the trial of the claim, and the extent to which he is to be bound by any judgment or decision to be made in the claim.

Any of the above orders can be made either before or after any judgment in the claim has been entered by the claimant against the defendant (**PD 20, para. 5.4**).

Where an additional claim had proceeded to trial without an order expressly stating that permission had been granted, contrary to **r. 20.7(3)**, it was held in *Lloyds Bank plc v Ellicott* [2003] BPIR 632 to have been wrong to have struck out the additional claim. Rather, the judge should have exercised his case management powers under **r. 3.10** to cure the irregularity and proceeded on the basis that permission had been granted.

Where third parties were added at a late stage in a case where there were good reasons for not granting an adjournment of the trial of the main claim, the judge was held to have been entitled to order that the third parties would not be added to the trial between the claimant and the defendant (*Powell v Pallisers of Hereford Ltd* [2002] EWCA Civ 959, LTL 1/7/2002). The Court of Appeal in this case also advised the parties to reach a consensual agreement whereby the third parties were given an opportunity (such as by being allowed to ask questions at trial) to test the defendant's witnesses, with a view to reducing the costs caused by duplication at the later trial of the additional claim.

DEFAULT JUDGMENT IN ADDITIONAL CLAIMS

Where no acknowledgment of service or defence is filed in respect of an additional claim, the procedure is governed by **CPR, r. 20.11**. The provisions for judgment in default under **Part 12** are not applicable, because a default judgment in an additional claim may depend on the success or otherwise of the principal claim against the defendant. **29.10**

A failure to file acknowledgment of service or defence will be deemed to be an admission of the additional claim, and, to the extent that it is relevant, the third party will be bound by any judgment or decision in the main proceedings (**r. 20.11(2)(a)**). The consequences of default are set out in the notes for the third party which are sent with the additional claim.

If a default judgment under **Part 12** is given against a defendant who has made an additional claim, then, if no acknowledgment of service or defence has been filed by the third party, the defendant may, in turn, obtain judgment in respect of the additional claim, by filing a request in the relevant practice form (**r. 20.11(2)(b)**). Until Her Majesty's Courts Service issues a form it is suggested that **form N227** may be adapted for this purpose. This may be done without the court's permission, provided that the defendant has satisfied the default judgment against himself, and does not wish to obtain judgment against the third party for any other remedy than a contribution or indemnity (**r. 20.11(3)**). However, if he has not satisfied the judgment against himself, or if he wishes to obtain judgment for some remedy other than a contribution or indemnity, the permission of the court has to be obtained, on an application which can be made without notice, unless the court otherwise directs (**r. 20.11(4)**). Such a judgment can be set aside or varied by the court at any time (**r. 20.11(5)**). The rule requiring prior payment (unless the court's permission is obtained) is presumably to ensure that a defendant does not profit by a default judgment against him, by keeping the proceeds of a default judgment against the third party, and failing to pass it on to the claimant. **Rule 20.11(3)(b)** does not appear to preclude the obtaining of a default judgment against a third party where a claim has been made against him for a remedy in addition to that of a contribution or indemnity, provided that it is not intended to pursue that part of the claim — the rule uses the words 'he wishes to obtain judgment for any remedy' rather than 'the claim is for any remedy'.

DEFENDANT'S CLAIM AGAINST A CO-DEFENDANT FOR CONTRIBUTION OR INDEMNITY

Under **CPR, r. 20.6**, a defendant may make an additional claim against a co-defendant for contribution or indemnity by: **29.11**

(a) filing a notice containing a statement of the nature and grounds of the claim; and
(b) serving that notice on the co-defendant against whom the claim is to be made.

Unless this notice is filed with the defendant's defence, the court's permission is required. If the only reason for not filing the notice with the defence is that the co-defendant was not added to the claim until after the defence was filed, the court's permission is not required if the notice is filed and served within 28 days after the new co-defendant's defence is filed.

Rules 20.7 to **20.12** are either irrelevant to or are expressed not to apply to a defendant's claim against a co-defendant for contribution or indemnity. There is apparently no provision for any form of judgment in default of defence. The co-defendant against whom the claim is made will presumably remain a party to the main action (unless he fails to file a defence to that action, in which event judgment in default will presumably be obtained in the main action), and thus all issues will be heard together.

At first instance, it has been held that a contribution notice under **r. 20.6** is not a claim form and cannot be served outside the jurisdiction (*Knauf UK GmbH v British Gypsum Ltd* [2002] EWHC 739 (Comm), [2002] 2 Lloyd's Rep 416). Defendants who are outside the jurisdiction, once they come on the record by acknowledging service or filing a defence, are obliged to provide an address for service within the jurisdiction (**r. 6.5(2)**), which is the address to be used for serving contribution notices.

RESOLVING CLAIMS BETWEEN A DEFENDANT AND A THIRD PARTY

29.12 There will be occasions when a claim by a claimant against a defendant is intimately connected with a dispute between the defendant and a third party which involves the same facts or a common point of law, but does not affect the defendant's liability to the claimant. In such an event, the defendant has a choice of either commencing separate proceedings against the third party, or applying that the third party be joined to the existing claim under **CPR, r. 19.2(2)(b)**, on the ground that there is an issue between the defendant and the new party which is connected to the matters in dispute, and that it is desirable to add the new party to resolve that issue.

The advantage of the latter procedure is that bringing the claim within existing proceedings will normally provide a speedier and more cost-effective means of resolving the dispute, and will also avoid the potentially difficult situation of different tribunals arriving at different conclusions on what are essentially the same facts and issues. See also **chapter 14**.

Chapter 30 Further Information

PRINCIPLES

30.1 CPR, Part 18, and PD 18 provide procedures by which, subject to any rule of law or procedure to the contrary, one party to proceedings can obtain from any other party:

(a) clarification of any matter which is in dispute in the proceedings; and/or
(b) additional information in relation to any such matter.

Initially this is to be done by making a request directly to the other party, under **PD 18**, without the court's involvement. If the other party does not respond to the request, or the response is considered inadequate, an application may be made to the court for an order under **r. 18.1** to give further information.

The distinction between the old 'request for further and better particulars' and 'interrogatories' has been abolished. Formerly the distinction between the two was that the request for further and better particulars was part of the pleadings process, and was (at least technically) limited to matters which should have been disclosed in the first place, so that a proper response to the pleading could be made. Although the process had no application to the discovery of evidence, being limited merely to material particulars, the tactical potential of the medium to cause embarrassment to the other side and reveal weaknesses in their case was such that the line was frequently overstepped. Interrogatories, on the other hand, were technically part of the discovery process and were answered on affidavit. Occasionally a creature of fashion, and, when well drafted, a devastating means of exposing shortcomings in the other side's argument, they nevertheless were not used in the vast majority of cases.

The doctrine of proportionality and the more 'utilitarian' approach to statements of case generally, should mean that requests for further information should be used with some caution. Although they can be used to advantage in some claims, considerable care must be taken in selecting the areas to be investigated by a request, and in formulating the questions to be put. Experience has shown that the CPR have been effective in severely curtailing, if not extinguishing altogether, the use of the request for further information for tactical purposes, and requests for further information appear to be employed much more rarely than the old request for further and better particulars.

REQUEST FOR FURTHER INFORMATION

30.2 A party should not make an application to the court for an order under **CPR, r. 18.1**, without having first served a written request on the party from whom the information or clarification is sought. The request must give a reasonable time to respond, and set a date by which the response should be served (**PD 18, para. 1.1**). Such request should be made, as far as possible, in a single comprehensive document, and not piecemeal (**para. 1.3**). It should be concise, and strictly confined to matters which are reasonably necessary and proportionate to enable the party requesting the information to prepare his own case or to understand the case he has to meet (**para. 1.2**). The requirement of proportionality is, of course, to ensure compliance with the overriding objective in **Part 1**, and provides the recipient with a new ground for refusing to give further information (although, it is suggested, not clarification) even though the request might otherwise be legitimate.

Form and content of request

30.3 There is no requirement that a request for further information should be in a particular form, save that a party who has indicated willingness to be served by email (see **15.24**) should be served with a request by email (**PD 18, para.** 1.7). If the text is brief, and the reply likely to be so as well, it may be made by letter (**PD 18, para. 1.4**). Such a letter should expressly state that it contains a request made under **CPR, Part 18**, and should deal with no matters other than the request (**PD 18, para. 1.5**). It is required to contain the same formalities as a request made in a separate document (**para. 1.6**). These requirements tend to blur the distinction between the two formats to the extent that there seems little advantage in making the request other than by way of a formal separate document.

Whether made by letter or in a separate document, the request must (**PD 18, para. 1.6(1)**):

(a) be headed with the name of the court and the title and number of the claim;
(b) state in its heading that it is a request made under **Part 18**;
(c) identify the party making the request and the party to whom the request is made (referred to in **PD 18** as the 'first party' and the 'second party');
(d) set out in a separate numbered paragraph, each request for information or clarification;
(e) identify any document referred to in the request, and (if relevant) the paragraph or words to which the request relates;
(f) state the date by which the response is expected.

A further advantage of making the request by way of a separate document rather than by letter is that, if convenient, it may be prepared with the numbered paragraphs set out on the left-hand half of each sheet, leaving room for the response to appear on the same document on the right. Thus the entire request and response would appear on the same document. If the request is prepared in this manner, an extra copy should be served for the use of the recipient (**PD 18, para. 1.6(2)**). It may well be, however, that, save in straightforward cases, limitations of space, and word-processing difficulties may make it easier for the 'second party' to adopt the alternative response procedure, where the text of the request is repeated, followed by the response (**PD 18, para. 2.3(1)(c)**) (as was formerly the case when responding to a request for further and better particulars).

Until experience has been gained of using the new rules there may be difficulty in adapting the different techniques formerly used for interrogatories and for requests for further and better particulars, now that there is no distinction between them. This may particularly be so when there is some intermixing of the different types of request. Example 30.1 provides some suggestions as to the manner in which a request could be approached.

Example 30.1

IN THE BLACKSTONE COUNTY COURT — Claim No. 0000

BETWEEN

AB — Claimant

— and —

CD — Defendant

REQUEST FOR FURTHER INFORMATION ABOUT THE CLAIMANT'S CASE UNDER PART 18

Sought on behalf of the Claimant (the first party) from the Defendant (the second party), and made on 20 January 2006.

[*Example of a straightforward request for clarification of the claim*]

Under Paragraph 2 of the Particulars of Claim

Of: 'It was a term of the agreement between the parties that the propellers would be delivered to the Claimant within 7 working days of receipt of the order by the Defendant'.

Request

1. Please state whether the alleged term was made orally or in writing. If the request was made orally, please give full information as to the parties agreeing the same, the date, time and place that it was allegedly agreed, and the gist of all words spoken. If it is alleged that the term was made in writing, please give the above information with all necessary changes, identifying any document or documents relied on, and attaching a copy of the same to the response.

[*Example of a request not directly referable to the particulars of claim*]

2. Is it not the case:

(a) that on 23 May 2005 the Claimant was handed a cheque for £2,350 by the Defendant, in the course of a meeting at the Defendant's premises, being a refund in respect of propellers that the Defendant was unable to supply?
(b) that the Claimant, or some other person on his behalf, subsequently presented the cheque and that it was duly met and cleared through the Defendant's bank account on 2 June 2005?
(c) that such sum falls therefore to be deducted from the Claimant's claim against the Defendant?

[*Example of a request referable to a document attached to the particulars of claim*]

Please look at the letter dated 28 May 2005 from the Claimant to the Defendant, attached to the Particulars of Claim.

Request

3. Please state whether it is the Claimant's case:

(a) that the propellers referred to in the final paragraph on page 1 are of model PDG 234, or PDG 236, or some other, and if so, which model?
(b) that the signature on the letter is that of the Claimant, or some other person (and if so, please identify the alleged signatory)?

Take notice that these requests must be answered no later than 4.00 p.m. on 10 February 2006.

Dated 20 January 2006

The request need not be verified by a statement of truth, although the response must be (see **23.10 to 23.16; CPR, r. 22.1(1)(a); PD 18, para. 3**).

FORM AND CONTENT OF RESPONSE

The response to a request for further information must be in writing and must be dated and signed by the second party or his legal representative (**PD 18, para. 2.1**). It must be verified by a statement of truth (see **23.10 to 23.16; CPR, r. 22.1(1)(a); PD 18, para. 3**). Where the request is made by letter, the response may be in like form, or in a formal reply (**para. 2.2(1)**), but if the response is made in a letter it should identify itself as a response, and deal with no matters other than the response (**para. 2.2(2)**). To this extent the format of the letter will be similar to that containing the original request. By analogy, it is submitted, a response to an email request should be sent by email. **30.4**

If the original request was prepared in the form set out in **para. 1.6(2)** (so that the response could be made on the same form as the request), the second party may choose whether to use it, or to reply in a separate document. If he uses the original form, no additional formalities are required (save for the date, signature and statement of truth). However, if the response is made in a formal document, it must (**para. 2.3(1)**):

(a) be headed with the name of the court and the title and number of the claim;

(b) in its heading, identify itself as a response to the request;
(c) repeat the text of each separate paragraph of the request and set out under each paragraph the response to it;
(d) refer to and have attached to it, a copy of any document not already in the possession of the first party, which forms part of the response.

A second or supplementary response must identify itself as such in its heading (**para.** 2.3(2)). It seems clear from the practice direction, that where the original request is made in a formal document, the response should not be by way of letter.

The response must be served on all parties (in addition to the first party), and a copy should be filed with the court together with a copy of the request (**para.** 2.4).

OBJECTIONS TO RESPONDING

30.5 The second party appears to be allowed four principal grounds on which to object to part or all of a request:

(a) that it is a request for information or clarification that is unnecessary, irrelevant or improper;
(b) that he is unable to provide the information or clarification requested;
(c) that insufficient time has been given to him to formulate a reply;
(d) that the request can only be complied with at an expense which is disproportionate to the claim, or is otherwise contrary to the overriding objective;
(e) that he is protected from answering by privilege.

In the event of an objection being taken on the basis of one or more of (a) to (c) above, the second party must inform the first party promptly, and in any event within the time stipulated in the request (**PD 18, para.** 4.1(1)). Such information may be by letter, or by way of a formal response in a separate document, but in either event must be accompanied by reasons for the objection, and, where relevant, a date by which he expects to be able to comply with the request (**para.** 4.1(2)). Presumably, there is no reason why such objection(s) could not be taken in the course of a response that does answer other requests, although this is not specifically dealt with in **PD 18**.

Where the objection is one of disproportionate expense, it seems that it will not be sufficient for the second party to adopt the above course. Instead, he must serve a reply, and explain in it briefly why he has taken the view (**para.** 4.2(2)). Where the objection is founded on privilege, a reply should be served setting out the nature of the privilege relied upon.

Once the second party has indicated his objection(s) in the appropriate format, there is no need for him to make any application to the court (**para.** 4.2(1)). Upon receipt of the response or objection, it will be for the first party to decide whether or not to make an application to the court for an order that the information be provided.

A 'fishing' request will be improper. A request is fishing where the party making the request does not have evidence supporting the cause of action or defence being put forward, but is hoping that something may turn up in response to the request (*Best v Charter Medical of England Ltd* [2001] EWCA Civ 1588, *The Times*, 19 November 2001).

COURT ORDER TO PROVIDE FURTHER INFORMATION

30.6 Under **CPR, r.** 18. 1, a party to proceedings may ask the court to order another party:

(a) to clarify any matter which is in dispute in the proceedings; or
(b) to give additional information in relation to any such matter.

This may be done whether or not the matter is contained in or referred to in a statement of case. The court may exercise the power to make an order under **r. 18.1** at any time, but the power is expressed by **r. 18.2** to be subject to any rule of law to the contrary.

If a party makes no response to a request (in whole or in part) or it is considered that such response as is made is inadequate, an application can be made to the court in the manner laid down in **CPR, Part 23** (see **chapter 32**) for an order under **r. 18.1**. The application notice should set out, or have attached to it, the text of the order sought, and in particular should specify the matter or matters in respect of which the clarification or information is sought (**PD 18, para.** 5.2). In practice, it would presumably be helpful to set out or attach the request (or that part of it that is said still to be unanswered) in the format in which it was originally sent to the 'second party'. If no request had originally been sent to the 'second party', an explanation for this should be set out in the application notice (**PD 18, para.** 5.3(1)), as should any response made by the 'second party' to any request that had been made (**PD 18, para.** 5.3).

If a request has been served, and no response received, the party making the application need not serve the application notice on the second party, and the court may deal with the application without a hearing, provided that at least 14 days have passed since the request was served, and the time stated in it for a response has expired (**PD 18, para.** 5.5). In all other cases, the application notice must be served on the second party and on all other parties to the claim (**PD 18, para.** 5.6).

Both parties to the application (or just the first party if an application notice is not served) should consider whether evidence in support of or in opposition to the application is required (**PD 18, para.** 5.4).

Where an order is made, the party required to provide the clarification or information must file his response and serve it on the other parties within the time specified (**r. 18.1(3)**). The order itself must be served on all parties to the claim (**PD 18, para.** 5.7), regardless of whether or not notice of the application was originally given. The order may also make a summary assessment of costs (**PD 18, para.** 5.8). If the order makes no reference to costs, no party is entitled to claim them (**PD 18, para.** 5.8(2)).

RESTRICTIONS ON THE USE OF FURTHER INFORMATION

Whether or not further information is given voluntarily or following an order of the court, **30.7**
the court may direct that such information must not be used for any purpose except for that of the proceedings in which it is given (**CPR, r. 18.2**).

Chapter 31 Amendments to Statements of Case

INTRODUCTION

31.1 The CPR provide a system under which a party can amend a statement of case, although the degree and extent to which this can be done are somewhat more restricted than under the old rules.

WHEN PERMISSION IS NOT REQUIRED FOR AMENDMENT

31.2 A party may amend a statement of case at any time before it has been served on any other party (**CPR, r. 17.1(1)**), and in such an event, the permission of the court is not required. However, such an amendment can subsequently be disallowed by the court (**r. 17.2(1)**) on the application, within 14 days of service of the amended statement of case, by the party on whom it is served (**r. 17.2(2)**). The rules do not presently state any specific matters that the court will take into consideration when deciding whether or not to grant such an application, but it is almost certain that the overriding objective and general principles of case management will be applied.

If a statement of case has been served, an amendment can be made without permission of the court, provided the written consent of all the other parties has been obtained (**r. 17.1(2)(a)**). It will not be sufficient under this rule simply to obtain the consent of the party to whom the statement of case has been directed.

If, however, the application is to amend by removing, adding or substituting a party, the application must be made in accordance with **r. 19.4** (which deals more specifically with the addition and substitution of parties; see **14.3 to 14.8**).

Where an amended statement of case is filed without the need for the permission of the court, it should be endorsed in the following manner (**PD 17, para. 2.1(2)**):

Amended [particulars of claim/defence (or as may be)] under CPR, [rule 17.1(1) or 17.1(2)(a)], dated . . .

For the format of an amended statement of case, see **31.10**.

WHEN PERMISSION IS REQUIRED FOR AMENDMENT

Where a statement of case has been served, and the written consent of all the other parties has not been obtained, or is not forthcoming, a party may apply to the court for permission to make an amendment (**CPR, r. 17.1(2)(b)**). The applicant should file the application notice with the court, together with a copy of the statement of case with the proposed amendments (**PD 17, para. 1.2**). By **PD 17, para. 2.2**, the statement of case in its amended form need not show the original text (see **31.10**), but it is difficult to see how the court will be assisted in making a decision on an application to amend, if the original text is not shown in the copy to be filed with the application. **31.3**

The application may be dealt with at a hearing, or, where all parties consent, without a hearing (i.e., on written submissions) (**PD 17, para. 1.1**). If permission to amend is given, the court may (not must) give directions as to amendments to be made to any other statement of case, and service of any amendments (**CPR, r. 17.3(1)**). Thus provision can (and it is suggested normally will) be made by the court for the service of any amendments that will have to be made by other parties consequent upon the service of the amended statement of case on them. In any event, the amended statement of case should be filed by the applicant within 14 days of the date of the order, unless the court directs otherwise (**PD 17, para. 1.3**). A copy of the amended statement of case and the order should be served on every party to the proceedings unless the court directs otherwise (**PD 17, para. 1.5**). The court's power to give permission is subject to the rules on change of parties, both before and after the end of a relevant limitation period, set out in **CPR, rr. 19.2** and **19.5**, and to **r. 17.4** dealing with amendments after the expiry of a relevant limitation period (**r. 17.3(2)**).

Where an amended statement of case is filed with the permission of the court, it should be endorsed in the following manner (**PD 17, para. 2.1(1)**):

Amended [particulars of claim/defence (or as may be)] by order of [Master . . . /District Judge . . . or as may be] dated . . .

PRINCIPLES ON WHICH PERMISSION IS GRANTED

The court has a general discretion to permit amendments where this is just and proportionate. If no arguable claim is raised by a proposed amendment, permission will be refused (*Collier v Blount Petre Kramer* [2004] EWCA Civ 467, LTL 1/4/2004). This general discretion is not overridden by the common law concept of 'abandonment' (*Kuwait Airways Corporation v Iraqi Airways Co.* [2002] EWCA Civ 515, LTL 27/3/2002). It was held in *Charlesworth v Relay Roads Ltd* [2000] 1 WLR 230 that the court will still apply the principle from *Clarapede and Co. v Commercial Union Association* (1883) 32 WR 262 that: **31.4**

However negligent or careless may have been the first omission, and however late the proposed amendment, the amendment should be allowed if it can be made without injustice to the other side. There is no injustice if the other side can be compensated in costs.

See also *HIH Casualty and General Insurance Ltd v JLT Risk Solutions Ltd* [2004] EWHC 1687 (Comm), LTL 26/7/2004. Even if costs will not adequately compensate the other party, amendments will be allowed if they are required in the interests of justice (*Gabriel v Hayward* [2004] EWHC 2363 (TCC), LTL 29/10/2004).

Amendments which introduce a new cause of action after a relevant limitation period has expired raise special problems which are considered at **31.13** to **31.20**. For addition and substitution of parties see **chapter 14**.

Late amendments

31.5 Although amendments can be made during the course of the trial, and even during closing speeches (see **31.11**), lateness is one factor to be considered on an application for permission to amend. Lateness is often combined with related factors, such as impact on the trial date, and whether the party seeking to amend can be criticised for failing to apply earlier because they have known for some time of the material forming the basis of the amended case. Lateness, combined with a weak case, albeit one with some prospect of success (see **31.6**), resulted in permission being denied in *Savings and Investment Bank Ltd v Fincken* [2003] EWCA Civ 1630, [2004] 1 WLR 667. Permission to make an apparently small amendment, which in fact amounted to a complete volte-face by the defendant, sought two weeks before trial in a substantial claim, was refused in *Calenti v North Middlesex NHS Trust* (2001) LTL 10/4/2001.

An amendment sought at a late stage in an attempt to save a claim that would otherwise have been struck out as disclosing no reasonable claim was refused in accordance with the overriding objective in *Christofi v Barclays Bank plc* [2000] 1 WLR 937. It is not clear how late the application was made, but it may have been during the appeal hearing itself. On the other hand, amendments were allowed in accordance with the overriding objective in *Finley v Connell Associates* (1999) *The Times*, 23 June 1999. In *Mark v Associated Newspapers Ltd* (2002) LTL 6/2/2002 permission to make amendments was granted even though the amendments represented a complete change of tack and involved allegations which were always open and obvious to the claimant, because permission was sought at an early stage in the proceedings (even though there had been delay before issue) and the amendments would not prejudice the defendant. A careless error resulting in the wrong defendant being named was allowed to be corrected by amendment under what is now **CPR, r. 19.5**, in *Virk v Gan Life Holdings plc* [2000] Lloyd's Rep IR 159 as there was no suggestion of prejudice to the defendant being brought in by the amendment.

Where a claimant had failed to file an amended schedule of special damages and this had clearly been an obvious mistake and had been foreshadowed, the overriding objective meant that the parties should have cooperated with each other to allow a late amendment at a time where the mistake could have obviated satellite litigation (*Chilton v Surrey County Council* [1999] CPLR 525). Refusal of permission to amend was held to have been wrong in *Kelly v Chief Constable of South Yorkshire Police* [2001] EWCA Civ 1632, LTL 25/10/2001, even though it was sought at the end of the trial and changed the basis of the case against the defendant. Where proposed amendments had been raised in earlier statements of case and affidavits, delay in applying to amend should not, of itself, preclude permission being granted (*Stansburys v Pashley* (2000) LTL 6/4/2000). See also **31.11**.

Amendments with no real prospect of success

31.6 A proposed amendment will be refused where the amended case has no real prospect of success (*Oil and Mineral Development Corporation Ltd v Sajjad* (2001) LTL 6/12/2001; *Savings and Investment Bank Ltd v Fincken* (2001) *The Times*, 15 November 2001; *Clarke v Slay* [2002] EWCA Civ 113, LTL 25/1/2002). In *Hussain v Cuddy Woods and Cochrane* (1999) LTL 19/10/99 an application to amend particulars of claim was refused where the claimant had no prospect of success against the solicitor and barrister defendants in his claim that a settlement reached was inadequate. Similarly, permission will be refused to make an amendment adding a claim which cannot succeed (*Laws v Society of Lloyd's* [2003] EWCA Civ 1887, *The Times*, 23 January 2004; *Collier v Blount Petre Kramer* [2004] EWCA Civ 467, LTL 1/4/2004).

Substantial amendments

31.7 In *Cook v News Group Newspapers Ltd* [2002] EWHC 1070 (QB), LTL 21/6/2002, permission to make substantial amendments to the defences in a libel claim was sought five months before trial. The amendments would have entailed substantial amendments to the replies, together with extensive further disclosure and additions to the witness statements. In such cases the court needed to have regard to the public interest in enabling the defendant to deploy the defences it wished to use, while fulfilling the overriding objective. Such applications are therefore considered with great care, being astute to avoid granting permission to allegations which failed to address (in the context of a libel claim) the real sting of the publication. The court would be more accommodating where the proposed amendments related to matters which had only emerged at a late stage with the discovery of evidence which previously had been genuinely unavailable. On the facts, permission was granted restricted to allegations genuinely supporting the central allegations. A similar case, *Morris v Bank of America National Trust and Savings Association* (2001) LTL 11/1/2002, resulted in all the substantial proposed amendments being disallowed, with permission being granted only for one amendment, which narrowed the issues. Late permission to add a single, but important, paragraph to a defence was allowed in *Electronic Data Systems Ltd v National Air Traffic Services Ltd* [2002] EWCA Civ 13, LTL 15/1/2002.

It is incumbent on a party, particularly in complex litigation, to state clearly the nature of his case (*Law Debenture Trust Corporation (Channel Islands) Ltd v Lexington Insurance Co.* [2002] EWCA Civ 1824, LTL 13/12/2002). It is preferable as a matter of case management to allow amendments which set out details of a party's allegations, rather than simply let matters take their natural course at trial based on general allegations (*Three Rivers District Council v Bank of England* [2003] EWHC 1269 (Comm), LTL 9/6/2003).

An amendment order should not require a party to plead its case in accordance with the judge's view of the law where the party has a different view which is at least arguably correct (*Coflexip SA v Stolt Offshore MS Ltd* [2003] EWCA Civ 296, [2003] FSR 728).

Cause of action accruing after issue

The modern approach is flexible, with amendments being granted in accordance with the justice of the case. There is no longer any absolute rule of law or practice which precludes an amendment to rely on a cause of action which has arisen after the commencement of the proceedings where otherwise the claim would fail (*Maridive and Oil Services (SAE) v CNA Insurance Co. (Europe) Ltd* [2002] EWCA Civ 369, [2002] 2 Lloyd's Rep 9). Likewise, amendments may be allowed adding heads of claim which have arisen after the proceedings were commenced (*British Credit Trust Holdings v UK Insurance Ltd* [2003] EWHC 2404 (Comm), LTL 28/10/2003). **31.8**

Abandonment

In *British Credit Trust Holdings v UK Insurance Ltd* [2003] EWHC 2404 (Comm), LTL 28/10/2003, the claim form sought damages and declaratory relief. The original particulars of claim only sought damages. It was held that the particulars of claim could be amended to include the declaratory relief, which had not been abandoned. There was no intention to abandon and no detriment. **31.9**

FORMAT OF AN AMENDED STATEMENT OF CASE

The amended form of the statement of case need not show the original text, unless the court thinks that it is desirable for it to do so, in which event it may direct that the amendments should be shown either by coloured amendments (either manuscript or computer-generated) or by use of a numerical code in a monochrome computer-generated document (**PD 17, para. 2.2**). (Many word processing packages include the facility to print an amended text automatically showing corrections and deletions.) Where colour is used, the deleted text should be struck through in colour, and any replacement text should be inserted or underlined in the same colour (**PD 17, para. 2.3**). The order for successive amendments is, as has always been the case: red for the first amendment, green for the second, violet for the third, and yellow for the fourth (**PD 17, para. 2.4**). **31.10**

The court will normally direct whether the original text should be shown together with the amendment at the time that it gives the permission for the amendment to be made. However, if no such permission is required, such a direction would have to be given after service. The principal purpose of displaying the original text has always been to enable the parties and the court to see the degree and extent to which a party has departed from its original stated case. Obviously, if the amendment is comparatively minor, and has been undertaken under **CPR, r. 17.1(1)**, the case for showing the original text is far less persuasive. In cases where it is wished to amend a statement of case after it has been served, there seems no reason why, as a precondition of giving written consent, the other party should not require the amendment to display the original text as well, failing which the 'amending party' will have to apply to the court, which may well be persuaded by the opposing party to order that the original text be shown.

If the substance of the statement of case is changed by reason of the amendment, the statement of case should be re-verified by a statement of truth (**PD 17, para. 1.4**). When a statement of case is amended, the court has a power in **r. 22.1(2)** to dispense with the need to re-verify with another statement of truth. This power may be exercised, or a suitably drafted statement of truth may be used making it clear that there is a primary and a secondary case, where a party relies on the facts asserted by the other side (which are inconsistent with the primary case) as an alternative basis for a finding in his favour (*Binks v Securicor Omega Express Ltd* [2003] EWCA Civ 993, [2003] 1 WLR 2557, and see **24.15**).

CHANGING BASIS OF CASE AT TRIAL

31.11 A not infrequent occurrence is that a party will seek to rely on a secondary case at trial that is not fully reflected in the way that party's case was previously put in its statement of case. Where this is done to reflect a version of the facts that only emerges with the evidence at the trial, an amendment is generally permitted as this accords with the overriding objective (*Binks v Securicor Omega Express Ltd* [2003] EWCA Civ 993, [2003] 1 WLR 2557). Where the party seeking to amend is aware of the alternative version in advance of the trial, an application to amend should be made a reasonable time before the trial. Likewise, seeking permission to argue a point which is raised for the first time at or shortly before the hearing will generally be granted, as refusing may be an unduly harsh penalty and represent a windfall to the other side (*E. I. Du Pont de Nemours and Co. v S. T. Dupont (No. 2)* [2002] EWHC 2455 (Ch), *The Times*, 28 November 2002). Neuberger J in this case said that permission may be refused if there are special factors, such as the point being raised at a late stage combined with:

(a) the other side needing a significant adjournment to adduce evidence in response; or
(b) the point being new and difficult, again requiring a long adjournment.

An example of a party seeking to amend to rely on a secondary case is *Sturton v Sutherland Holdings plc* (2000) LTL 27/10/2000, in which the counterclaim set out a claim for damages for breach of warranty, relying on one set of accounts. At trial, the defendant sought to rely on a fall-back case based on amended accounts, which had not been mentioned in the counterclaim (although they had been referred to in the defence). It was held that the defendant had been under a duty to make clear it was relying on the fall-back case well in advance of trial, so that the claimant could answer that case and call appropriate evidence.

In *Bowerbank v Amos* [2003] EWCA Civ 1161, LTL 31/7/2003, a re-re-re-re-re-amendment was allowed during the course of the trial changing the case from one pleaded in breach of trust to one pleaded in breach of contract. It was held that this was permissible, especially as otherwise a meritorious claim would have been defeated on a pleading point. Once such an amendment was allowed, the judge had to be scrupulous to minimise any prejudice to the other party. The judge had refused permission to recall the claimant for further cross-examination after the amendment was made, so the case was remitted back to the judge to hear the further cross-examination and to reconsider his findings.

In *Hall v Motor Sport Vision Ltd* (2002) LTL 1/5/2002 an appeal was dismissed against a refusal of permission sought at trial to allow amendments and additional evidence. These had the effect of raising certain allegations as separate breaches of the defendant's obligations, whereas in the original particulars of claim they were pleaded only as particulars of breach.

A judge is not permitted to give judgment on the basis of a claim that is not included in the statements of case. If this is done, there may be no option but to order a retrial (*Rosengrenstann Ltd v Ayres* (2001) LTL 22/6/2001).

CHANGING TRACK AT TRIAL

There are no additional problems if an amendment at trial involves changing between the small claims and fast tracks, or from the multi-track to the fast track. However, an amendment involving changing from the fast track to the multi-track may involve having to change judges, because multi-track claims cannot be tried by district judges without the consent of the designated civil judge (**PD 2B, para. 11.1**(a) and (d)). Having to adjourn (for example, where the new value of the claim is substantially above the normal fast track limit of £15,000) may be a sufficient reason for refusing permission to amend (*Maguire v Molin* [2002] EWCA Civ 1083, [2002] 4 All ER 325). Another option is for the district judge to allow the amendment without changing tracks (*Maguire v Molin*), but this may lead to an inappropriate fast track costs limitation (see **44.22**). **31.12**

AMENDMENT AFTER A RELEVANT LIMITATION PERIOD HAS EXPIRED

Effect of expiry of limitation

For the purposes of the **Limitation Act 1980** (LA 1980), an amendment to add or substitute a new party (a situation discussed at **14.3** to **14.8**) or a new cause of action is deemed to be a separate claim and to have been commenced on the same date as the original claim (**LA 1980, s. 35(1)** and **(2)**). Consequently, if the original claim was commenced within the relevant limitation period, and an amendment is allowed adding a party or cause of action after the expiry of the limitation period, the defendant will be deprived of the limitation defence, and will usually suffer injustice not compensable by an order for costs. The usual rule, therefore, is that such amendments are not permitted (**LA 1980, s. 35(3)**). There are, however, a number of exceptions which are considered below. It seems that if there is a dispute about whether a limitation period has expired, the test is whether the claim is unarguably time-barred (*Leicester Wholesale Fruit Market Ltd v Grundy* [1990] 1 WLR 107). **31.13**

The statutory relation back in the **LA 1980, s. 35(1)**, only applies to the procedural time bars in the LA 1980. It does not apply to contractual or substantive time limits, like that in the Hague-Visby Rules, art. III, para. 6 (Carriage of Goods by Sea Act 1971, sch.), which have the effect that on expiry of the period laid down the claimant's cause of action ceases to exist (*Payabi v Armstel Shipping Corporation* [1992] QB 907).

Permission to amend after expiry of limitation

Provision is made in **CPR, r. 17.4**, for the problem which can arise when a party wishes to amend a statement of case after a period of limitation has expired. The rule is expressed to apply where a party applies to amend a statement of case under **Part 17**, and a period of limitation has expired under the **Limitation Act 1980**, the Foreign Limitation Periods Act **31.14**

1984 or other statutory provision (**CPR, r. 17.4(1)**). No provision is made in **r. 17.4** for a situation in which no application is made because a party is entitled to amend without permission. Clearly, if the statement of case has been served, it is unlikely that the other party will give written permission under **r. 17.1(2)(a)**, and an application would have to be made to the court. However, if proceedings are filed immediately before the expiry of the limitation period, but have not been served, and the claimant wishes to amend them before service, no application would ordinarily be made to the court. Of course, the court may disallow the amendment on an application under **r. 17.2**, but it is suggested that **r. 17.4** implies that such an amendment should only be made upon application to the court.

Rule 17.4(1) was amended with effect from 26 March 2001 to make it clear that **r. 17.4** applies only to cases governed by enactments (including the **Limitation Act 1980** and the Foreign Limitation Periods Act 1984) providing for limitation periods but which allow amendments to add or substitute new claims.

If the effect of a proposed amendment will be to add or substitute a new claim after a limitation period has expired, the court may allow it, but only in the circumstances discussed in **31.16**.

An amendment may be allowed after the expiry of a relevant limitation period to alter the capacity in which a party claims, if that capacity was one which that party had when the proceedings started, or has since acquired (**r. 17.4(4)**).

New cause of action

31.15 In assessing whether proposed amendments in fact amount to a new cause of action (rather than a clarification of the existing cause of action), it is necessary to consider the statement of case as a whole (*Leeds and Holbeck Building Society v Ellis* (2000) LTL 5/10/2000). To determine whether a proposal amendment introduces a new cause of action for the purposes of LA 1980, s. 35(5)(a), it is necessary to examine the duty alleged, the nature and extent of the breach alleged and the nature and extent of the damage claimed. If the new plea introduces an essentially distinct allegation, it will be a new cause of action. 'The policy of the section is that, if factual issues are in any event going to be litigated between the parties, the parties should be able to rely upon any cause of action which substantially arises from those facts' (per Hobhouse LJ in *Lloyds Bank plc v Rogers* (1996) *The Times*, 24 March 1997).

Where the only difference between the original case and the case set out in the proposed amendments is a further instance of breach, or the addition of a new remedy, there is no addition of a new cause of action (*Savings and Investment Bank Ltd v Fincken* [2001] EWCA Civ 1639, *The Times*, 15 November 2001). Amendments changing page references from the American edition of a magazine to the European page references were held not to involve making a new claim in *Reuben v Time Inc.* [2003] EWCA Civ 6, LTL 22/1/2003. An amendment adding a new duty or obligation usually raises a new cause of action, whereas pleading additional facts, or better particulars, allegedly constituting a breach of the duty already pleaded usually will not (*Darlington Building Society v O'Rourke James Scourfield* [1999] PNLR 365). It is necessary to examine the duty alleged, the nature and extent of the breach alleged, and the nature and extent of the damage claimed. If the new plea introduces an essentially distinct allegation, it will be a new cause of action. An amendment to plead a claim under the law of a different State raises a new claim within s. 35 (*Latreefers Inc. v Hobson* [2002] EWHC 1586 (Ch), LTL 31/ 7/2002). In *Abbey National plc v John Perry and Co.* [2001] EWCA Civ 1630, LTL 24/10/2001, it was held that deleting the word 'constructive' from a claim, thereby altering the basis of the claim from one in constructive trust to one in implied trust, was a matter of semantics and did not involve the substitution of a new cause of action.

Where a claimant has brought proceedings as an assignee of a claim, a valid assignment is an essential element of the cause of action (*Smith v Henniker-Major and Co.* [2002] EWCA Civ 762, [2003] Ch 182 at [99]). An amendment after limitation to plead an assignment can therefore only be allowed if it comes within s. 35(5)(a). In *Smith v Henniker-Major and Co.* the claim as originally formulated relied on an invalid assignment from a company purportedly signed at an inquorate board meeting. After limitation expired, the claimant procured a resolution from the company purporting to ratify parts of the invalid assignment. Although the amendment to plead the ratification arose out of substantially the same facts as the original claim, permission was refused, because a party seeking to ratify a transaction had to adopt it in its entirety, and because of prejudice to the defendant caused by the delays.

AMENDMENT OF CAUSES OF ACTION AFTER EXPIRY OF LIMITATION

A new cause of action (as opposed to a new party) may be added to an existing claim after the relevant period of limitation has expired in three situations: **31.16**

(a) Where the action is in respect of personal injuries and the court makes a direction under the **LA 1980, s. 33** (see **10.43**), that the usual limitation period shall not apply (**LA 1980, s. 35(3)**).
(b) Where the new cause of action is an original set-off or counterclaim (**LA 1980, s. 35(3)**). An original set-off or counterclaim is one made by an original defendant who has not previously raised any counterclaim under **CPR, Part 20**, in the claim, and the counterclaim must be made against the original claimant (see *Kennett v Brown* [1988] 1 WLR 582, which is still good law on this point). If bringing a counterclaim in effect evades an accrued limitation period, the claimant should consider making an application to strike out the counterclaim under **CPR, r. 3.4**. The principles on which such an application will be decided were considered in *Ernst and Young v Butte Mining plc (No. 2)* [1997] 1 WLR 1485.
(c) Where the new cause of action arises out of the same facts or substantially the same facts as are already in issue in the original claim (**LA 1980, s. 35(5)(a)**; see **31.17**).

Same or substantially the same facts

Raised by either party The **LA 1980, s. 35(5)(a)**, permits rules of court to allow a claimant to add, after a limitation period has ended, a new claim which arises out of the same facts as are already in issue on any claim previously made in the original claim. This includes facts which are put in issue in the defence to the original claim (*Goode v Martin* [2001] EWCA Civ 1899, [2002] 1 WLR 1828). **Rule 17.4(2)** of the CPR is expressed to allow a new claim to be added only if it arises out of the same facts as the original claim, but it must be read as also allowing a new claim which arises out of the same facts as are already in issue on the original claim, because otherwise the rule would impede a claimant's access to a court for determination of civil rights, contrary to the **European Convention on Human Rights, art. 6**. In *Goode v Martin* the claimant had originally alleged that the defendant had negligently caused personal injuries to the claimant in the factual circumstances set out in the claim. The defendant served a defence asserting that the personal injuries happened in different circumstances. After the limitation period had expired the claimant was allowed to add a claim that, even if the defendant's version of events was true, the injuries were caused by the defendant's negligence. **31.17**

The test Whether amendments involve the same or substantially the same facts as those already in issue is largely a matter of impression (*Darlington Building Society v O'Rourke James Scourfield* [1999] PNLR 365). Facts are substantially the same if there are no more than minor differences likely to be the subject of inquiry but not involving any major investigation and/or differences merely collateral to the main substance of the new claim, proof of which would not necessarily be essential to its success (*P and O Nedlloyd BV v Arab Metals Co.* [2005] EWHC 1276 (Comm), [2005] 1 WLR 3733, Colman J at [42]). In *Hoechst UK Ltd v Commissioners of Inland* **31.18**

Revenue [2003] EWHC 1002 (Ch), LTL 11/4/2003, it was held that it is not enough that the background facts of the two claims are the same: the central facts of both causes of action must be the same or based on substantially the same facts. In making this assessment the judge must not confine himself to the original statements of case, but must consider the facts that would have had to be litigated on the original statements of case (*Hemmingway v Roddam* [2003] EWCA Civ 1342, LTL 18/9/2003).

31.19 **Examples** Spanish fishermen were refused permission to amend their claim to add further claims for compensation for breach of Community law (in being prevented from fishing by unlawful UK legislation) in respect of additional vessels. This was because the facts they needed to prove were largely specific to each boat, and so the additional claims did not arise out of substantially the same facts as were already in issue (*R v Secretary of State for Transport, ex parte Factortame Ltd (No. 7)* [2001] 1 WLR 942). A claim in negligent misrepresentation, which focused on what the defendant should have done, was held in *Law v Society of Lloyd's* [2003] EWCA Civ 1887, *The Times*, 23 January 2004, not to arise out of substantially the same facts as the original case pleaded in fraud (which was based on an allegation that the defendant knew the representations were false). In *Senior v Pearsons and Ward* (2001) LTL 26/1/2001 the claim originally alleged that the defendant solicitors had acted contrary to their instructions. The claimant was permitted to amend the particulars of claim after the expiry of limitation to add allegations of failing to advise fully, as the additional allegations arose out of the same facts, or substantially the same facts, as those originally pleaded.

In *Brickfield Properties Ltd v Newton* [1971] 1 WLR 862 the general endorsement on the writ (the equivalent of a claim form giving just a concise statement of the nature of the claim under **CPR, r. 16.2(1)(a)**) claimed damages against an architect for negligent supervision of certain building works. The particulars of claim were served after the expiry of the limitation period, and contained claims both for negligent supervision and negligent design. It was held that the negligent design claim arose substantially out of the same facts as the negligent supervision claim and in its discretion the court allowed the amendment. In *Hancock Shipping Co. Ltd v Kawasaki Heavy Industries Ltd* [1992] 1 WLR 1025, permission to amend the particulars of claim was sought three years after service of the original statement of case and after the limitation period had expired. In considering whether it is just to allow an amendment in such circumstances, the court held that it had to take into account that granting permission will deprive the defendant of an accrued limitation defence, but could exercise its discretion to allow the amendment in the light of all the relevant factors. An important factor is the degree to which the defendant is prejudiced in being unable to investigate the facts of the new claim through the disappearance of evidence. The Court of Appeal in *Hancock Shipping Co. Ltd v Kawasaki Heavy Industries Ltd* disallowed certain of the proposed amendments on the ground that the defendant would be prejudiced through the loss of evidence, but allowed certain other amendments which were closely related to the claim already made as there was likely to be little prejudice through the loss of evidence.

Amendments after the limitation period affecting accrued rights

31.20 A defendant will not be given permission to amend where the effect of the proposed amendment is to transfer responsibility for the claim on to a non-party who cannot be sued by the claimant as a result of the expiry of the relevant limitation period. An example is *Steward v North Metropolitan Tramways Co.* (1886) 16 QBD 556, where the claimant sued the tramway for personal injuries. After the expiry of the limitation period, the defendant sought to amend its defence. The effect of the proposed amendment was to transfer the defendant's liability for the claimant's injuries to the local road authority. Permission to amend was refused, because even an order for costs could not put the claimant into the same position as if the proposed defence had been pleaded at the proper time. This approach was confirmed by *Cluley v R. L. Dix Heating* [2003] EWCA Civ 1595, LTL 31/10/2003, where the court dismissed an argument that the prejudice was caused by the claimant having failed to identify the proper person to bring proceedings against rather than by the defendant seeking, after the expiry of limitation, to withdraw an admission of having entered into a contract with the claimant.

Much depends on whether the defendant has been at fault in not pleading the proposed defence at the proper time. In *Weait v Jayanbee Joinery Ltd* [1963] 1 QB 239, through no fault of their own, the defendants discovered after the expiry of the limitation period that the claimant's injuries were probably worse than they should have been through the intervening negligence of the doctor who treated the claimant. An amendment to the defence to plead the doctor's negligence was allowed despite the fact that the claimant could not make a claim against the doctor as that claim was time-barred. Further, an amendment blaming a non-party may be allowed if it alleges facts within the knowledge of the claimant, since in such a case the prejudice to the claimant arises from the claimant's own failure to sue the non-party in time, rather than by some line of defence being made known at a late stage. An example is *Turner v Ford Motor Co. Ltd* [1965] 1 WLR 948. The claimant sued the occupier and a building contractor (but not his own employer) for injuries suffered when he was struck by a falling brick. After disclosure of documents by the first defendant, and after the expiry of the limitation period, the second defendant discovered that the claimant had not been wearing a safety helmet at the relevant time, and sought to amend its defence to allege contributory negligence on the part of the claimant. The claimant opposed the amendment on the ground that he was now out of time in suing his employer for failing to provide him with a helmet. The amendment was allowed, because the claimant must have known whether he was wearing a safety helmet at the time of the accident, so the amendment told him nothing he did not know in order to commence his claim. If the first defendant, who had knowledge of the claimant not wearing a helmet, had sought an amendment to plead contributory negligence after the expiry of the limitation period, permission would have been refused.

Chapter 32 Applications and Interim Orders

The following procedural checklists, which are in **appendix 1**, are relevant to this chapter:

Procedural checklist 20 Interim application without notice
Procedural checklist 21 Interim application with notice

INTRODUCTION

32.1 Interim applications are made when a party to proceedings seeks an order or directions from the court prior to the substantive hearing of the claim. Parties seeking interim orders or directions in general have to issue an application notice in **form N244**, pay a court fee, and often have to provide written evidence in support. The application notice and evidence must in general be served at least three clear days before the return date. Generally, service will be effected by the court, although an applicant may notify the court that he wishes to serve himself (**CPR, r. 6.3(1)**).

Chapters 33 to **41** deal with various types of interim application, such as for summary judgment, interim injunctions, freezing injunctions and search orders. Applications for disclosure orders, such as specific disclosure and pre-action disclosure, are dealt with in **chapter 48**. Various other types of application are considered elsewhere, such as applications for alternative service in **15.38**, setting aside default judgments in **20.11** to **20.18**, for further information in **30.6** and for amendment in **chapter 31**. There is a separate code of procedure for applications in insolvency proceedings, which is considered in **chapter 81**.

In most cases there should be a limited need for making interim applications because of the level of involvement of the judiciary in case management. Part of the obligation placed on the courts in furthering the overriding objective is to consider whether the likely benefits of taking a particular step will justify the cost of taking it (**r. 1.4(2)(h)**). The court is also required to deal with as many aspects of the case as is practicable on the same occasion (**r. 1.4(2)(i)**).

In fast track and multi-track cases the procedural judge will scrutinise defended claims shortly after defences are filed, and there will be further judicial consideration of the case at the listing for trial stage (see **chapters 42, 44** and **45**). A party contemplating a particular order may ask the court to consider it during the scrutiny process.

Whenever the parties are notified that an interim hearing, such as a case management conference or listing hearing, has been fixed, they must consider and make any application which may be appropriate for the court to deal with at the hearing (**PD 23, para. 2.8; PD 28, para. 2.5** (fast track cases); **PD 29, para. 3.5** (multi-track cases)).

Consequently, most interim orders are made as part of the regular case management system. Further, there is a general obligation to make all interim applications as soon as it becomes apparent they are necessary or desirable (**PD 23, para. 2.7**).

The CPR permit the court to make interim orders on its own initiative, and to hold hearings by telephone or other direct means of communication. Solicitors should keep correspondence with masters and district judges to a minimum, and must ensure that opposing parties receive copies (**Chancery Guide, para. 5.41**). The ordinary rule is that interim hearings are in public, although there are significant exceptions.

A distinction needs to be drawn between applications for directions and applications for interim remedies. A somewhat more formal approach is taken with applications for interim remedies, which should in almost all cases be supported by written evidence (see **CPR, r. 25.3(2)**). The distinction is between:

(a) case management matters, such as standard disclosure of documents, exchange of factual and expert evidence, and trial directions, and
(b) applications for specific remedies, such as specific disclosure, interim injunctions, interim payments and striking out.

There is a further important distinction between interim applications made without giving notice to any other parties, and those made on notice. This distinction will be considered further at **32.7** and **32.10**.

TO WHICH COURT SHOULD AN APPLICATION BE MADE?

In general an application must be made to the court where the claim is presently being dealt with. This will be the court where the proceedings were commenced (**CPR, r. 23.2(1)**), unless: **32.2**

(a) the claim has been transferred (**r. 23.2(2)**);
(b) the claim has been listed for trial at another court, in which event the application should be made to the trial court (**r. 23.2(3)**); or
(c) the application is made after judgment, in which event the application may need to be made to the court dealing with enforcement (**r. 23.2(5)**).

An application for pre-action remedies (such as some injunction, freezing injunction and search order applications) should be made to the court where the substantive proceedings are likely to be brought, unless there is a good reason for applying to another court (**r. 23.2(4)**).

Rule 2.7 gives the court a general power to deal with a case at any place that it considers appropriate. This power may be used in courts with shared listing arrangements, and where a court with congested lists arranges to release some cases to another court to reduce listing delays.

WHICH JUDGE SHOULD DEAL WITH AN APPLICATION?

32.3 Unless otherwise provided for by an Act, rule or practice direction, interim applications can be dealt with by judges, masters and district judges (**CPR, r. 2.4**). The most significant exceptions are freezing injunctions and search orders, which are dealt with by High Court judges, and ordinary interim injunctions, which are generally dealt with by a judge who would have jurisdiction to try the claim (see **PD 25, para. 1.3; PD 2B, para. 2**). In the county courts this means that circuit judges will deal with interim injunction applications in most multi-track claims, but district judges may hear such applications in small claims and fast track cases (see 2.4), and also in a number of other types of claim (**PD 2B, para. 11.1**). High Court masters and district judges may grant interim injunctions by consent, in connection with charging orders and receivers and in aid of execution (see 2.10). Apart from injunctions, most applications are dealt with by masters and district judges, but they may refer particular applications to be dealt with by a judge (**PD 23, para. 1**).

Applications to a High Court judge in the Chancery Division are made to the interim applications judge (**Chancery Guide, paras. 5.8** and **5.9**). An application notice must be used, which should usually state that it is to be heard by 'the interim applications judge'.

In the Chancery and Queen's Bench Divisions there are arrangements for assigning claims to individual masters. Once assigned a claim may be transferred to another master, and the fact that a claim has been assigned does not prevent it being dealt with by another master (**PD 2B, para. 6.2**). However, the usual rule is that once a claim is assigned all applications in that claim will be dealt with by the assigned master.

STAGE WHEN INTERIM REMEDIES SHOULD BE SOUGHT OR CONSIDERED

32.4 The basic rules are that interim applications should be made as early as possible (**PD 23, para.** 2.7), but after the party making the application has come on to the court record. For a claimant this is after proceedings are issued, and for a defendant it is after service is acknowledged or a defence is filed (**CPR, r. 25.2(2)**).

PRE-ACTION INTERIM REMEDIES

32.5 A claimant may exceptionally make an application for an interim order before the commencement of proceedings (see **CPR, r. 25.2(2)(b)**) if either:

(a) the matter is urgent; or

(b) it is otherwise desirable to grant the interim remedy before the claim is brought in the interests of justice.

The courts may thus entertain pre-commencement applications for urgent interim injunctions (such as some libel cases where publication is threatened within hours of the applicant finding out about the matter) and some applications for freezing injunctions and search orders.

If a pre-action interim remedy is granted, the court should give directions requiring a claim to be commenced (**r. 25.2(3)**). **Rule** 25.2(4) points out that such directions need not be given where an order is made for pre-action disclosure or inspection under the **Supreme Court Act**

1981, s. 33, or the **County Courts Act 1984, s. 52** (see **48.70**). This is because such an order may result in the applicant deciding not to bring substantive proceedings at all, as recognised in *Dunning v United Liverpool Hospitals' Board of Governors* [1973] 1 WLR 586. The same can be said for *Norwich Pharmacal* orders (see **48.83**), which may not result in the true wrongdoer being identified. Normally directions for bringing substantive proceedings are made in other types of pre-action order.

Superficially similar to pre-action applications are applications for permission to bring certain proceedings under the Mental Health Act 1983, s. 139. The Mental Health Act 1983, s. 139, provides that no civil proceedings shall be brought against any person in any court in respect of any act purporting to have been done under the Act without the leave of the High Court. Although this type of application is similar to other types of pre-action order, it has the significant difference that the court's jurisdiction is invoked by issuing a self-contained Part 8 claim limited to preparing for later separate, substantive proceedings.

OBLIGATION TO APPLY EARLY

The obligation to apply early for an interim remedy stems from the overriding objective, which includes ensuring that cases are dealt with expeditiously (**CPR, r. 1.1(2)(d)**). **32.6**

Parties should normally notify the court of any intention to apply for interim remedies when they file their allocation questionnaires (**PD 26, para. 2.2**).

In multi-track cases the appropriate time to consider most forms of interim relief, if possible, is the first case management conference. A party that wishes to invite the court to make directions or orders of types not usually dealt with on case management conferences, and which are likely to be opposed, is required by **PD 29, para. 5.8**, to issue and serve an application returnable at the same time as that set for the case management conference (with a time estimate if it is clear that the time originally allowed for the case management conference will be insufficient, so a fresh date can be fixed). **Paragraph 3.8** expressly says that applications in multi-track cases must be made as early as possible so as to minimise the need to change the directions timetable, and an application to vary a directions timetable laid down by the court (perhaps on its own initiative) must ordinarily be made within 14 days of service of the directions (**para. 6.2**).

There are some express restrictions in the CPR about when some types of application can be made. Examples include summary judgment, which can be applied for only after the defendant has acknowledged service or entered a defence (**r. 24.4(1)**), and interim payments, where a similar restriction applies (**r. 25.6(1)**). Nevertheless, summary judgment (and striking-out) applications should normally be made on or before filing of allocation questionnaires (**PD 26, para. 5.3(1)**).

Of course the need for an interim remedy may not become apparent until some later stage. **Rule 25.2(1)(b)** of the CPR provides that applications can be made even after final judgment has been given. Where it becomes necessary to make an application shortly before trial, it should be dealt with on the pre-trial review if there will be one (there is a pre-trial review about eight to 10 weeks before the trial in some multi-track cases, see **45.21**). If this is not possible, another option is to make the application at the start of the trial itself.

APPLICATIONS WITHOUT NOTICE

The general rule is that all applications must be made on notice to the other parties (**CPR, r. 23.4(1)**). Exceptions to this rule are only allowed where permitted by a provision in the CPR, a practice direction, or a court order (**r. 23.4(2)**). For example, applications to extend **32.7** the time for serving a claim form (renewal of process) are permitted without notice (**r. 7.6(4)**), as are applications for permission to issue additional claims after filing of the defence (**r. 20.7(5)**). These are both examples of applications where the opposite party will not be on the court record when the application is made. Other situations where applications may be made without giving notice to the other parties are:

(a) Where the application arises in urgent circumstances, so there is no practical possibility of giving the required minimum of three clear days' notice to the other side. In cases of this sort informal notification should be given to the other parties unless the circumstances require secrecy (**PD 23, para. 4.2**).
(b) Where a party decides to make an application at a hearing that has already been fixed, but there is insufficient time to serve an application notice. In cases of this sort the applicant should inform the other parties and the court (preferably in writing) as soon as possible of the nature of the application, the reason for it, and then make the application orally at the hearing (**PD 23, para. 2.10**).
(c) Where the application depends on secrecy for its efficacy, such as most applications for freezing injunctions and search orders.

Procedure on applications without notice

32.8 The procedure for an interim application without notice is summarised in **procedural checklist 20**, which is in **appendix 1**.

Like applications on notice, applications without notice should normally be made by filing an application notice (**CPR, r. 23.3(1)**) in **form N244**, which must state the order being sought and the reasons for seeking the order (**r. 23.6**). Letters must not be used in place of formal application notices (**Chancery Guide, para. 5.41**). The prescribed fee is £35 in the county court, £50 in the High Court (**CPFO, fee 2.6**). The application notice must also be signed, and include the title of the claim, its reference number and the full name of the applicant. If the applicant is not already a party it should also give the applicant's address for service. If the applicant wants a hearing, that too must be stated (**PD 23, para. 2.1**). The application should normally be supported by evidence, which should, in addition to setting out the evidence in support of the relief sought, state the reasons why notice was not given (**CPR, r. 25.3(3)**).

By virtue of **r. 39.2**, which applies to all types of hearings, including interim hearings and trials, applications made without notice will in general be held in public. However, sometimes one of the exceptions may apply, such as publicity defeating the object of the application (as in applications for freezing injunctions and search orders) or the application being made without notice and it being unjust to the respondent for there to be a public hearing (**r. 39.2(3)(a)** and **(e)**). In any event, most applications will be heard in chambers even if technically they are being dealt with in public.

Where an application is made for an order to be made against a person without notice to that person, **r. 23.9(2)** provides that the order made on the application must be served on the person together (unless the court orders otherwise) with the application notice and any evidence in support. The order must, by virtue of **r. 23.9(3)**, contain a statement to the effect that the person against whom it is made has a right to apply to set aside or vary the order within seven clear days of service of the order. In *Dadourian Group International Inc. v Simms* [2005] EWHC 268 (Ch), [2005] 2 All ER 651, a without-notice order was not served in accordance with **r. 23.9(2)** and did not contain the notice required by **r. 23.9(3)**. The defendant was a solicitor. It was held at [24] that while the parties must not flout the CPR, the court had to retain a sense of balance in deciding the consequences of any breach, and refused to discharge the order on this ground. Legal representatives acting for the applicant are under a duty to provide full notes of the hearing to all parties affected by the order (*Interoute Telecommunications (UK) Ltd v Fashion Gossip Ltd* (1999) *The Times*, 10 November 1999, freezing injunctions and search orders; *Cinpres Gas Injection Ltd v Melea Ltd* [2005] EWHC 3180 (Pat), *The*

Times, 21 December 2005, interim injunctions). This is to ensure other parties know exactly what happened, the basis and material on which the order was made, and so they can make an informed decision whether to apply to discharge the order. Applications to set aside or vary are normally made back to the judge who made the original order.

Duty of full and frank disclosure

Any application made without notice is subject to a duty of full and frank disclosure of matters adverse to the application. These include matters which are known to the applicant and matters which the applicant should have known on making reasonable inquiries. The duty is a continuing one, continuing until the application is renewed on notice or until the without notice order is acted upon (*Network Telecom (Europe) Ltd v Telephone Systems International Inc* [2003] EWHC 2890 (QB), LTL 21/10/2003). This duty, and the question of discharging for material non-disclosure, has frequently been an issue in applications for freezing injunctions (see **38.35** for a full discussion), but the principles apply to all applications made without notice. **32.9**

APPLICATIONS WITH NOTICE

The general rule is that all other parties should be given three clear days' notice of any interim application that may be made (**CPR, rr. 23.4(1)** and **23.7(1)**). Advance notice should be given of the grounds on which an interim order is sought. A particular example is an application to discharge a freezing injunction on the ground of material non-disclosure, where specific notice of the grounds of the application must be given (*Bracken Partners Ltd v Guttridge* (2001) LTL 16/1/2002). The procedure for an interim application with notice is summarised in **procedural checklist 21**, which is in **appendix 1**, and there is a detailed discussion in **32.11** to **32.28**. Even if an application is misconceived or hopeless, the respondent should not cross-apply to strike out the first application, but should simply oppose it, as issuing such a cross-application wastes costs (*Arkin v Borchard Lines Ltd (No. 2)* (2001) LTL 21/6/2001). **32.10**

Documentation

An interim application should normally be made by filing an application notice stating the order being sought and the reasons for seeking the order (**CPR, rr. 23.3(1)** and **23.6**). The application notice must be signed, and should include the title of the claim, its reference number and the full name of the applicant. If the applicant is not already a party it should also give the applicant's address for service. If the applicant seeks a hearing, that must be stated (**PD 23, para. 2.1**). If the applicant wants the application dealt with by a telephone hearing, that must also be stated (**para. 6.1A**). The application should normally be supported by written evidence setting out the facts justifying the relief sought (**CPR, r. 25.3(2)**). The notice must be filed at court together with the prescribed fee (£100 in the High Court, £65 in the county court, **CPFO, fee 2.5**), and served as soon as possible thereafter (**r. 23.7(1)**). The standard form of application notice is **form N244**. **32.11**

On receipt of the application notice the court may either notify the parties of the time and date of the hearing, or notify them that it proposes to consider the application without a hearing (**PD 23, para. 2.3; CPR, r. 23.8(c)**).

Applications by persons who are not parties

Persons who are not parties may make applications in existing proceedings in a number of circumstances. These include applications to intervene in the proceedings (see **14.59**) and applications by third parties to vary the terms of injunctions (see **38.31**). In urgent cases an intending claimant may apply for injunctive relief before a claim form is issued (see **37.4** and **37.5**). **32.12**

With effect from 6 April 2006, a person who is not already a party who issues an application notice must include a postcode in his address for service on the application notice (**PD 23, para. 2.1(4)**).

Evidence in support

32.13 The general rule is that applications for interim remedies must be supported by evidence (**CPR, r. 25.3(2)**), but evidence in support is not required when applying for case management directions. Some judgment is required from lawyers when deciding whether they need evidence for their applications. **PD 23, para. 9.1**, specifically mentions that, as a practical matter, the court will often need to be satisfied by evidence of the facts that are relied on in support of, or for opposing, an application. Sometimes the matter will be put beyond doubt if the court gives directions for filing evidence when it fixes a hearing.

The evidence in support must be filed at court, although the exhibits should not be filed unless the court otherwise directs (**PD 23, para. 9.6**). The evidence (including exhibits) in support must be served with the application (**CPR, r. 23.7(3)**). Any evidence which a respondent wishes to rely upon must be served as soon as possible, and in any event in accordance with any directions the court may have given (**PD 23, para. 9.4**). The court will not take kindly to respondents who serve evidence in response at the last minute, particularly if this results in a wasted hearing and a need to adjourn.

Four options are available to the applicant regarding the format of the evidence to be used in support of an interim application. They are:

(a) To provide sufficiently full factual information in support of the application in the body of the application notice itself (**CPR, rr. 22.1(3)** and **32.6(2)(b)**), and include a statement of truth in the notice. This is a signed statement that the applicant believes that any facts stated in the application are true (**r. 22.1(4)** and **(6)**; **PD 22, para. 2.1**).

(b) To rely on the facts stated in a statement of case filed in the proceedings, provided it contains a statement of truth (**CPR, r. 32.6(2)(a)**). This will usually have been previously served and filed, and if so there is no need to reserve or refile (**r. 23.7(5)**).

(c) To rely on witness statements each with statements of truth signed by the witnesses (**rr. 22.1(4)** and **32.6(1)**). The witness statements used may be ones drafted specifically for the interim application, or it may be possible to rely on the main witness statements that have been disclosed on the substantive issues in the case. The general rule is that any fact that needs to be proved at any hearing other than the trial should be proved by the evidence of witnesses in writing (**r. 32.2(1)**), and it is further provided by **r. 32.6(1)** that at hearings other than the trial evidence is to be by witness statement unless the court, a practice direction or any other enactment requires otherwise. Consequently, evidence by witness statement is the primary means of adducing evidence at interim hearings.

(d) To rely on affidavit evidence. **Rule 32.15(2)** allows a witness to give evidence by affidavit at any hearing other than a trial if he or she chooses to do so. This also allows the use of affirmations (**PD 32, para. 1.7**). However, using affidavits may result in the loss of the additional costs over and above the cost of using an ordinary witness statement. There are situations where affidavit evidence is required either by specific court order, or by virtue of a practice direction or other enactment. Affidavits are required, for example, in applications under the **Protection from Harassment Act 1997, s. 3(5)(a)** (see **91.4**); for certain applications relating to confiscation and forfeiture in connection with criminal proceedings; under the environmental control legislation; and in director disqualification proceedings. **PD 32** and **PD 25** require affidavit evidence in support of applications for:
   (i) search orders,
   (ii) freezing injunctions,
   (iii) orders to require an occupier to permit another to enter land, and
   (iv) orders for contempt of court.

Affidavits are not used in applications for other types of interim injunction unless specifically ordered by the court.

Unless the form which the evidence in support has to take is prescribed, a party to an interim application may choose the method of adducing evidence in support from the above options. This allows flexibility, and should assist in ensuring applications are prepared in a cost-efficient manner. **Form N244** requires the applicant to indicate which type of evidence will be relied upon by ticking an appropriate box. It may on occasion be appropriate to use a combination of these methods. It may also be important to place the background facts of the case before the court (which could be done by use of the statement of case), as well as facts relevant solely to the application in hand (which could be adduced by a specifically drawn-up witness statement or affidavit). **Form N244** militates against this by allowing only one of the boxes to be ticked.

Weight attached to written evidence

The courts will give the same weight to all forms of written evidence whether they have statements of truth or are sworn. It has always been the case that, unless deponents are called for cross-examination, written evidence adduced on an interim application will usually be accepted as correct for the purposes of the application. The reluctance of accepting a challenge to witness statement evidence in an interim application in the absence of cross-examination was emphasised in *Wallis v Valentine* [2002] EWCA Civ 1034, [2003] EMLR 8. Cases such as *National Westminster Bank plc v Daniel* [1993] 1 WLR 1453 established that the court would only go behind written evidence if its contents are incredible. In *Shyam Jewellers Ltd v Cheeseman* (2001) LTL 29/11/2001 it was stated that choosing between witnesses is the function of the trial judge, and it is only permissible for a judge to go behind a witness statement in an interim application if there is some inherent improbability being asserted or there is extraneous evidence contradicting it. **32.14**

Facts may be inferred on an interim application from a failure to deal adequately with an issue in response to correspondence or the written evidence in an interim application. In *Pattihis v Jackson* [2002] EWHC 2480 (QB), LTL 22/11/2002, an assistant solicitor left his employment with the claimant to work for the second defendant, taking with him a large number of the claimant's client files. The fact of the removal of the files, and the second defendant's failure to demonstrate a right to the files in the two days following demands for the return of the files, enabled the court to find the files were unlawfully in the second defendant's possession. In *Zappia Middle East Construction Co. Ltd v Clifford Chance* [2001] EWCA Civ 946, in an application for security for costs, there was a conflict of evidence on the claimant's place of residence. The court refused to accept unparticularised second-hand evidence from the claimant's solicitor, the claimant obviously being able to give first-hand and detailed evidence on the matter, and decided the point in a summary way in favour of the applicant.

Facts can also be inferred from the nature of the situation. In *Aims Asset Management Sdn Bhd v Kazakhstan Investment Fund Ltd* [2002] EWHC 3225 (Ch), LTL 23/5/2002 the court found, based on the respondent's location in Kazakhstan but no further evidence, that there was a very substantial, but unquantifiable, risk that enforcement in that country of an English judgment would be extremely difficult and expensive, if not impossible. This comes close to taking judicial knowledge (see **47.26** to **47.33**) of such facts.

Bundles of documents

Sometimes it is appropriate to prepare bundles of documents for interim applications. Often it is sufficient to rely on the application notice, written evidence and exhibits without the need to go to the expense of compiling formal bundles. It is stated in the **Chancery Guide, para.** 7.9, and the **Queen's Bench Guide, para.** 7.11.7, that bundles should be prepared for applications heard by judges whenever more than 25 pages are involved, although it must be **32.15** said that even in straightforward applications it is easy to exceed this. In the Chancery Division, bundles are also required for case management conferences and any interim hearing likely to last at least an hour (**Chancery Guide, para. 7.40**). The whole point of compiling bundles is to save time and expense (as recognised in the paragraphs of the court guides just cited). If they are used, the general guidance discussed in **chapter 57** should be followed, but bearing in mind that for an interim application it ought to be possible to restrict the number of documents that need to be included. There are plenty of interim applications that do not need all the statements of case, witness statements etc.

All parties should cooperate in agreeing bundles (see, for example, **Chancery Guide, para. 7.12**), and should make clear whether they are simply agreeing which documents should be included in the bundles, or whether they are also agreeing that the included documents are to be treated as evidence of the facts stated in them and/or that the documents to be included are agreed to be authentic (**Chancery Guide, para. 7.13, CPR, r. 32.19**).

For applications, the applicant should ensure that one copy of the bundle is lodged at court at least two clear days before the hearing (though for a Queen's Bench master's appointment, the bundle should be brought to the hearing, unless the master otherwise directs: **Queen's Bench Guide, para. 7.11.8**), and that all parties and the court have identical bundles.

Skeleton arguments

32.16 Skeleton arguments are not often used on interim applications before district judges, masters and bankruptcy and Companies Court registrars, but are usually required for hearings before High Court judges and are often used for interim hearings before county court judges. Even before High Court judges they are not insisted on if the application is likely to be short or if it is so urgent that preparation of a skeleton argument is impracticable. For applications estimated at one hour or more (**Chancery Guide, para. 7.47**) skeletons should be delivered to the court two clear days before the hearing. For shorter applications, or urgent applications, they may be delivered the day before the hearing or at the hearing.

According to the **Chancery Guide, app. 7**, a skeleton argument should provide a concise summary of the party's submissions on the issues raised by the application, and should be as brief as the nature of the case allows. There is a general ceiling of 20 pages of double-spaced A4 paper. It should cite the main authorities relied upon, be divided into numbered paragraphs, be paginated, make use of abbreviations (such as 'C' for claimant, 'A/345' for page 345 of bundle A) and give dates in the form '26.4.2006'. It should not go so far as to argue the case on paper. In more substantial applications it should have a reading list for the judge of the core documents.

Authorities in skeleton arguments

32.17 Practice Direction (Citation of Authorities) [2001] 1 WLR 1001 provides that the following types of authorities should not be cited unless they establish a new principle or extend the law:

(a) law reports of applications attended by one party only;
(b) applications for permission to appeal;
(c) applications that only decide the application is arguable; and
(d) county court cases (other than to illustrate damages in personal injuries claims or to illustrate current authority where no higher authorities are available).

Lawyers were criticised in *Bank of Scotland v Henry Butcher and Co.* [2003] EWCA Civ 67, [2003] 2 All ER (Comm) 557, for using the *All England Law Reports* and *All England Law Reports Reprint* rather than the *Weekly Law Reports* and *English Reports.*

Practice Direction (Citation of Authorities [2001] 1 WLR 1001 says that skeleton arguments will have to justify reliance on decisions that merely apply decided law to the facts, and also decisions from other jurisdictions. Decisions of the ECJ and organs of the European

Convention on Human Rights are treated as domestic authorities for this purpose. For each authority cited, the skeleton must state the proposition of law the case demonstrates, and refer to the passages in support. Any bundle or list of authorities must contain a certificate by the advocate that these requirements have been complied with.

Practice Direction (Judgments: Form and Citation) [2001] 1 WLR 194 and Practice Direction (Judgments: Neutral Citations) [2002] 1 WLR 346 introduced a method of neutral citation in the format *Smith v Jones* [2001] EWCA Civ 10 at [30], [2001] QB 124. 'EWCA' stands for England and Wales, Court of Appeal. 'Civ 10' stands for Civil Division, 10th case of 2001. 'At [30] ' stands for paragraph 30 of the judgments (with the paragraph numbering continuing into the second and subsequent judgments). This innovation is designed to assist publication of judgments on the Internet. Reports cited in court should be taken from the official *Law Reports*, and only from other series if unavailable from the *Law Reports*. Practice Direction (Judgments: Form and Citation) [2001] 1 WLR 194 also provides that it is permissible to cite judgments by means of copies reproduced from electronic sources. Such copies should preferably be in 12-point fonts (although 10 or 11-point fonts are acceptable), and the advocate presenting the report must be satisfied that it has not been reproduced in a garbled form. More detailed guidance on the use of authorities in appeals, including the use of *Hansard*, which should also be followed in first-instance skeleton arguments, can be found at **71.48** to **71.49**.

Chronologies

Skeleton arguments are often accompanied by chronologies. Good chronologies have short **32.18** entries for the material events, phrased in a non-contentious way to promote agreement with the other parties.

Draft orders

Paragraph 12.1 of PD 23 says that except in the most simple applications the applicant **32.19** should bring to the hearing a draft of the order sought. The standard **form N244** contains words, which may be deleted, saying that a draft of the order sought is attached. If the order is unusually long or complex, the draft should be supplied on disk as well as on hard copy (**PD 23, para. 12.1**). Preparing draft orders is particularly important in all types of interim injunction applications, and (although strictly this is turning **PD 23** on its head) whenever the order is at all complicated or unusual. Draft orders are also useful if a detailed directions timetable needs to be laid down. For almost all other types of application the short particulars of the orders sought normally inserted in the N244 will be sufficient.

Service

Unless the applicant notifies the court to the contrary, the normal rule is that the court will **32.20** serve the application notice and documents in support by first-class post (**CPR, rr. 6.3** and **23.7(3)**, and **PD 6, para. 8.1**). Alternatively, the applicant may notify the court that he wishes to effect service himself. When the court is to effect service, the applicant must file with the court copies of the evidence in support for service on the respondents and a copy of any draft order prepared on behalf of the applicant. There is, however, no requirement to refile or re-serve documents which have already been filed or served at an earlier stage (**CPR, r. 23.7(5)**).

Service must be effected as soon as possible after the application is issued, and in any event not less than three clear days before it is to be heard (**r. 23.7(1)**). In accordance with the general rules on computing time in **r. 2.8**, this means clear days (excluding the date of effective service and the date of the hearing), and, because the period is less than five days, also excluding weekends, bank holidays, Christmas and Good Friday. Take, for example, a hearing which is listed for Wednesday 8 November 2006. Assume the solicitor for the applicant decides to serve the application and evidence in support by document exchange. The three clear days before the hearing are Friday 3, Monday 6 and Tuesday 7 November 2006. The documents must therefore arrive on Thursday 2 November, and given the provision in **r. 6.7** that documents transmitted by DX are deemed to be served on the second day after being left at the document exchange, the latest the documents could be left at the document exchange would be Tuesday 31 October 2006.

Disposal without a hearing

32.21 Rule 23. 8 of the CPR provides that the court may deal with an interim application without a hearing if:

(a) the parties agree the terms of the order; or
(b) the parties agree that the court should dispose of the application without a hearing (the applicant's view on whether there should be a hearing should be stated in the application notice); or
(c) the court does not consider that a hearing would be appropriate.

A party dissatisfied with any order or direction made without a hearing is able to apply to have it set aside, varied or stayed (**r. 3.3(5)(a)**). Such an application must be made within seven days after service of the order, and the right to make such an application must be stated in the order (**r. 3.3(5)(b) and (6)**).

In *Irwin Mitchell Solicitors v Patel* (2003) LTL 15/4/2003 an application for disclosure of documents, which resulted in an 'unless order', was marked to be dealt with without a hearing. Although the respondent should have been served with the application, this was not done. Ultimately, all the orders flowing from the application notice were set aside because of the procedural irregularity.

Hearings by telephone

32.22 Active case management in accordance with the overriding objective includes dealing with cases without the parties needing to attend court, and by making use of technology (**CPR, r. 1.4(2)(j) and (k)**). Both may be achieved by dealing with some applications by telephone conference calls, which is specifically provided for by **r. 3.1(2)(d)**. The rule enables the court to hold a hearing by telephone or any other method of direct oral communication, so other means of electronic communication may be used as technology develops.

Normally a telephone hearing will not be permitted unless every party entitled to notice of, and to attend, the hearing has consented (**PD 23, para. 6.2**).

Any party who is acting in person must be accompanied by a responsible person who knows the litigant and can confirm that person's identity to the court (**PD 23, para. 6.3(1)**). A 'responsible person' may be a barrister, solicitor, legal executive, doctor, clergyman, police officer, prison officer or someone of similar status (**para. 6.3(2)**).

If the court decides to hold a telephone hearing, it will allocate a time and give suitable directions. The applicant will be responsible for ensuring all the legal representatives (or litigants) are put on line in order (applicant followed by respondents, then the judge) and also for ensuring that the conference is tape-recorded by the telephone service provider. **PD 23, para. 6**, contains detailed provisions for setting up and paying for telephone hearings.

Telephone hearings pilot scheme

32.23 Between 1 September 2003 and 1 October 2006 there is a pilot scheme for telephone hearings at Newcastle Combined Court Centre and Bedford and Luton County Courts. During this period all allocation hearings, listing hearings, all case management conferences and interim applications with time estimates up to one hour, and any other hearing with the parties' consent and court agreement will be conducted by telephone unless the court otherwise orders. Further details are contained in **PD 23B**.

Orders made on the court's own initiative

As part of the ethos of active case management, the courts are encouraged to exercise their powers on their own initiative where this is appropriate, and to this end **r. 3.3(1)** of the CPR gives the court the power to make orders of its own initiative. This power is intended to be exercised for the purpose of managing the case and furthering the overriding objective (see **r. 3.1(2)(m)**). Orders made in this way must, by virtue of **r. 3.3(5)(b)** and **(6)**, include a statement that parties who are affected may apply within seven days (or such other period as the court may specify) after service for the order to be set aside, varied or stayed. Failing to make an application to vary or set aside is likely to result in the court assuming the orders or directions made were correct in the circumstances then existing (**PD 28, para. 4.2(2)**, for fast track cases; **PD 29, para. 6.2(2)**, for multi-track cases). **32.24**

There is a related power enabling the court to make orders on its own initiative after giving the parties an opportunity of making representations on the matter. Where the court proposes to make such an order it will specify a time within which the representations must be made (**CPR, r. 3.3(2)**). If the court on its own initiative strikes out a statement of case or application, and it considers the claim or application was totally without merit, that fact must be recorded in the court's order, and the court must consider whether to make a civil restraint order (see **r. 3.3(7)** and **14.70**).

Hearings convened on the court's own initiative

In addition, the court has power to fix a hearing for the purpose of deciding whether to make any order it might propose to make of its own initiative. For example, in order to reduce the issues in a case it might convene a summary judgment hearing. Unless some other period is specified in the rules regarding notice, any application convened by the court must be notified to parties likely to be affected by the proposed order at least three clear days in advance (**CPR, r. 3.3(3)**). **32.25**

Court hearing

The general rule is that interim hearings will be in public (**CPR, r. 39.2**). In practice the public do not attend most hearings before masters and district judges, even if notionally they are heard in public, because most interim applications are conducted in chambers, with limited facilities for accommodating the public. It is sufficient if the door is open, or if there is no sign on the door indicating that the hearing is in private (**PD 39, para. 1.10**). There is no obligation to provide space for the public, although the judge may, if he or she thinks it appropriate, adjourn to a larger room or court (**para. 1.10**). **32.26**

In addition to dealing with the specific application that has been made, the court may wish to review the conduct of the case as a whole and give any necessary case management directions. The parties will therefore have to be prepared for this and be able to answer any questions the court may ask (**PD 23, para. 2.9**). The procedural judge will keep, either by way of a note or a tape recording, brief details of all proceedings, including a short statement of the decision taken at each hearing (**PD 23, para. 8**).

In most courts applications are given specific hearing times, and are called in one at a time. The main exception are judge's applications in the Chancery Division (see **Chancery Guide, para. 5.10**). For these the judge sitting has a discretion as to the order in which applications are heard. However, urgent applications and applications affecting the liberty of the subject are given priority, followed by ineffective applications (those which are to be adjourned or have settled), then effective applications usually in order of their time estimates, with the shortest applications being heard earliest. Applications estimated for more than two hours are usually made applications by order. In these cases the applications judge may make a temporary order to preserve the position pending a full hearing of the application. Solicitors or counsel's clerks must then apply to the Chancery Listing Office for a date for the hearing of the application. There is also a procedure for interim applications by order by consent. See **Chancery Guide, paras. 5.11 and 5.14.**

Summary determination of interim costs

32.27 Where an interim application is disposed of in less than a day (which will cover the vast majority of such applications), the court will normally make a summary assessment of the costs of the application immediately after making its order (**PD 43–48, para. 13.2**). In the absence of a specific order to the contrary, costs assessed summarily are payable within 14 days of the order (**CPR, r. 44.8**). To assist the judge in assessing costs the parties are required by **PD 43–48, para.** 13.5, to file and serve not less than 24 hours before the interim hearing signed statements of their costs for the interim hearing in **form N260** setting out:

(a) the number of hours claimed;
(b) the hourly rate claimed;
(c) the grade of the earner;
(d) the amount and nature of disbursements;
(e) the solicitor's costs for attending or appearing at the hearing; (f)counsel's fees; and
(g) VAT on the above.

Any failure to file or serve a statement of costs, without reasonable excuse, will be taken into account in deciding the costs order to be made on the application (**PD 43–48, para. 13.6**). In the absence of any aggravating factors, mere failure to serve a statement of costs in compliance with **para.** 13.5 should not result in the successful party being deprived of its costs. Instead, the court should consider whether the failure has resulted in any prejudice to the paying party and decide on a proportionate response which will deal with any prejudice found (*MacDonald v Taree Holdings Ltd* [2001] CPLR 439). Options are:

(a) giving the paying party a brief adjournment to consider the statement of costs, then proceeding with the summary assessment, with the judge erring towards a lighter figure;
(b) standing the matter over for a detailed assessment;
(c) standing the matter over for a summary assessment at a later date; and
(d) provided all the parties agree, standing the matter over for the summary assessment to be dealt with in writing.

Immediate summary assessment of costs will be appropriate only where the court decides to order costs in any event. Where the interim costs are to be in the case, assessment will almost certainly be left to the conclusion of the case. In cases where costs are awarded in any event, the court should make a summary assessment there and then, but may decide to give directions for a further hearing to deal with the costs (**PD 43–48, para. 13.8**). Summary assessment will be unnecessary in cases where the parties have agreed the amount of costs (**para.** 13.4). The court must not make a summary assessment of the costs of a publicly funded party (**para.** 13.9). Nor may it make a summary assessment of the costs of a party under a disability, unless that party's solicitor has waived the right to further costs (**para.** 13.11(1)). These last two sentences do not prevent the court making a summary assessment of any interim costs which it decides are payable by an assisted party or a party under a disability (**paras** 13.10 and 13.11(2)), although the court should not make such costs payable immediately (in the case of an assisted paying party) unless it also makes a determination under the Legal Aid Act 1988, s. 17, or the **Access to Justice Act 1999, s. 11**(1) (for which, see **66.57**).

Non-attendance

32.28 The court may proceed in the absence of any party to an application (**CPR, r. 23.11(1)**). When this happens the court has a general discretion to relist the application (see **60.1**).

GENERAL POWERS REGARDING INTERIM RELIEF AND ORDERS

Rule 3.1(2) of the CPR sets out a non-exhaustive list of orders that may be made for the purpose of managing cases, and **r. 25.1(1)** sets out a non-exhaustive list of interim remedies that may be granted by the court. The **r. 3.1(2)** list includes orders: **32.29**

(a) extending or shortening time for compliance with rules, orders and practice directions (see **46.21**;
(b) adjourning or bringing forward hearing dates (see **59.7** and **59.9**);
(c) requiring a party or a legal representative to attend court;
(d) directing part of proceedings, such as a counterclaim, to be dealt with as separate proceedings;
(e) dealing with part of a case as a preliminary issue (see **59.41**);
(f) staying all or part of the proceedings generally or to a specified date or event (see **chapter** 54);
(g) consolidating two or more claims, or trying two or more claims on the same occasion (see **14.58**);
(h) deciding the order in which issues are to be tried;
(i) excluding an issue from consideration (see **42.25**); and
(j) (with effect from 1 October 2005), a power to order any party to file and serve a statement of costs (see **63.19**).

The **r. 25.1(1)** list of interim remedies includes:

(a) Interim injunctions (see **chapter** 37).
(b) Interim declarations (see **4.18**).
(c) Freezing injunctions, which may also include ancillary disclosure orders (see **chapter** 38).
(d) Search orders (see **chapter** 39).
(e) Orders for the detention, custody, preservation, inspection or sale of, taking samples from or carrying out of experiments on relevant property, or for the payment of income from relevant property (see **chapter** 41). The order may include authority to enter land in the possession of a party to the proceedings for one of these purposes. 'Relevant property' means property which is the subject of a claim, or as to which any question may arise in a claim.
(f) Orders for interim delivery up of goods pursuant to the **Torts (Interference with Goods) Act 1977, s. 4** (see **chapter** 40).
(g) Orders for pre-action disclosure and inspection pursuant to the **Supreme Court Act 1981, s. 33**, or the **County Courts Act 1984, s. 52**. For the application of these provisions to disclosure of documents, see **chapter** 48. For their application to inspection of property, see **chapter** 41.
(h) Disclosure or inspection orders against non-parties pursuant to the **Supreme Court Act 1981, s. 34**, or the **County Courts Act 1984, s. 53**. For the application of these provisions relate to disclosure of documents, see **chapter** 48. For their application to inspection of property, see **chapter** 41.
(i) Interim payments orders (see **chapter** 36).
(j) An order that a specified fund be paid into court or otherwise secured. (**CPR, r. 25.1(1)(l)**). This power is limited to money which forms all or part of a 'specified fund'. This phrase is not a term of art, and is capable of a number of meanings depending on the context. It can include the proceeds from the sale of property, but an order may only be appropriate if the claimant has a proprietary interest in those proceeds. The power cannot be used to order the payment into court of a sum merely representing a debt owed to the claimant (*Myers v Design Inc. (International) Ltd* [2003] EWHC 103 (Ch), [2003] 1 WLR 1642).
(k) An order permitting a party seeking to recover personal property to pay money into court pending the outcome of the case, and directing that if this is done, the property shall be

given to the party (see **r. 25.1(1)(m)**). This type of order provides a useful means of recovering disputed property while protecting the defendant by means of the security provided by the payment into court. This also provides the court with jurisdiction to order a solicitor to deliver up documents by overriding a disputed solicitor's lien (*Paragon Finance plc v Rosling King* (2000) LTL 26/5/2000).

(l) An order directing a party to prepare and file accounts relating to the dispute or directing an account to be taken or inquiry to be made by the court (see **r. 25.1(1)(n)** and **(o)** and **chapter 61**).

(m) An order in intellectual property proceedings under Directive (EC) 2004/48, art. 9, making the continuation of an alleged infringement subject to the lodging of guarantees (see **r. 25.1(1)(p)**).

Where an order imposes a time limit for doing any act, the date for compliance must be expressed as a calendar date, and must include the time of day by which the act must be done (**CPR, r. 2.9(1)**). Orders may be made subject to conditions, and may, at the court's discretion, specify the consequences of failing to comply (**r. 3.1(3)**).

If the court dismisses an application, and it considers the application was totally without merit, that fact must be recorded in the court's order, and the court must consider whether to make a civil restraint order (see **r. 23.12** and **14.70**).

CONSENT ORDERS

32.30 Consent orders are divided into those which can be entered on a purely administrative basis, without seeking the approval of a judicial officer, and those that need approval. The court may deal with an application without a hearing if the parties agree on the terms of the order sought (**CPR, r. 23.8(a)**).

Administrative consent orders

32.31 Administrative entry of consent orders is only permitted where none of the parties is a litigant in person (**CPR, r. 40.6(2)(b)**). By **r. 40.6(3)** only the following types of orders may be entered by this process:

(a) judgments and orders for the payment of money;
(b) judgments and orders for the delivery up of goods with or without the option of paying the value of the goods or an agreed value;
(c) orders for the dismissal of the whole or part of proceedings;
(d) Tomlin orders (for the stay of proceedings on agreed terms, which are usually set out in a schedule to the order) and other stays on agreed terms disposing of the proceedings;
(e) orders for the stay of enforcement of a judgment, either unconditionally or on condition that the money due under the judgment be paid by specified instalments;
(f) orders setting aside unsatisfied default judgments;
(g) orders for the payment out of money paid into court;
(h) orders for the discharge from liability of any party; and
(i) orders for the payment, assessment or waiver of costs.

Approved consent orders

32.32 Proposed orders or directions which are agreed between the parties must be submitted to the court for scrutiny if either (a) one or more of them is a litigant in person, or (b) any of the orders or directions fall outside the list set out at **32.31**. The procedural judge has a discretion to allow or refuse agreed orders and directions. The court will be particularly concerned to ensure that orders and directions that may have been agreed between the parties are consistent with the overriding objective and with the case management structure for the case. The parties may agree the terms for interim orders at or shortly before a hearing, and to submit them to the court for approval. As at present the court will usually expect the agreed terms to be reduced into writing before being submitted to the court, which is often done in a fairly informal manner. If there is time, it may be possible to draw up a formal Tomlin order or other suitable order for approval by the court.

Costs in consent orders

Where the parties agree to an order by consent in an interim application, they should also agree a figure for costs to be inserted in the consent order, or agree that there should be no order for costs (**PD 43–48, para. 13.4**). If they cannot agree on a figure for costs, they will need to attend on the appointment. If this happens, no costs will be allowed for the attendance unless good reason can be shown for the failure to agree the figure for the costs (para. 13.4). **32.33**

DRAWING UP INTERIM ORDERS

Drawing up consent orders

A consent order must be drawn up in the terms that have been agreed, must be expressed to be 'by consent', and must be signed by the legal representatives of all parties (or, if approved by the court, any litigant in person) affected by the order (**CPR, r. 40.6(7)**). Letters sent to the court by the respective parties signifying their consent to a draft order are sufficient (**PD 23, para. 10.2**). The order is then filed with the court, which will arrange for it to be sealed, entered in the court records, and sent out to the parties. **32.34**

Drawing up non-consent interim orders

Rules 40.2(2) and **40.3(1)(c)** of the CPR provide that all interim orders have to be drawn up and sealed by the court, unless the court dispenses with the need to do so. Normally the court will take responsibility for drawing up, but: **32.35**

(a) unless otherwise ordered, every judgment or order in the Queen's Bench Division (including the Admiralty, Commercial, and Technology and Construction Courts, but excluding the Administrative Court) must be drawn up by the parties (**rr. 40.3** and **60.7**);
(b) in any court, the court may order a party to draw up an order; or
(c) a party may, with the permission of the court, agree to draw up an order; or
(d) the court may direct a party to draw up the order subject to checking by the court before it is sealed; or
(e) the court may direct the parties to file an agreed statement of the terms of the order before the court itself draws up the order; or
(f) the order may be entered administratively by consent, in which event the parties will submit a drawn-up version of their agreement for entry.

A party who is required to draw up a judgment is allowed seven days to file it, together with sufficient copies for all relevant parties, failing which any other party may draw it up and file it for sealing (**rr. 40.3(3)** and **40.4(1)**).

Every judgment (apart from judgments on admissions, default judgments and consent judgments) must state the name and judicial title of the judge who made it (**r. 40.2(1)**).

Once an order has been drawn up the court will serve sealed copies on the applicant and respondent, and also on any other person the court may order to be served (**r. 40.4(2)**). (Service will not be by the court if one of the exceptions set out in **r. 6.3** applies.) The court is given a specific power by **r. 40.5** to order service on a litigant as well as the litigant's solicitor.

Judgments and orders normally take effect from the day they are given or made, not from the time they are drawn up, sealed or served (**r. 40.7**). However, the court is given the power to specify some later date from which the order shall take effect.

REVIEW OF INTERIM DECISIONS

Reconsideration

32.36 The court has a power to reconsider its decision in an interim application at any point up to the time the order is drawn up (*Pittalis v Sherefettin* [1986] QB 868; *Charlesworth v Relay Roads Ltd* [2000] 1 WLR 230). This jurisdiction will only be exercised in exceptional cases where it is in the interests of justice to do so (*Re Blenheim Leisure (Restaurants) Ltd (No. 3)* (1999) *The Times*, 9 November 1999). Circumstances where it may be appropriate to ask the court to reconsider the matter include cases where there has been a plain mistake on the part of the court; a failure to draw to the court's attention facts or points of law that are plainly relevant; the discovery of new facts; and being taken by surprise in circumstances where a party did not have a fair opportunity to present its arguments.

Varying and revoking orders

32.37 The court has the power to vary or revoke a previous order made under a power conferred by the CPR (**CPR, r. 3.1(7)**). It is suggested that this power should only be used in relation to an interim order where:

(a) there has been a material change of circumstances (see **45.30**);
(b) the original order was made on a without notice application (see **37.60**); or
(c) where a third party is adversely affected by an order made in his absence (see **37.60** and **38.31**).

It is probable that the specific power to revoke given by **r. 3.1(7)** only applies to orders made since the CPR came into force (*DEG-Deutsche Investitions- und Entwicklungsgesellschaft mbH v Koshy (No. 2)* [2004] EWHC 2896 (Ch), [2005] 1 WLR 2434).

Renewing interim applications

32.38 The general principle is that it is incumbent on the parties to bring their whole case to the court at the relevant hearing. If they choose to hold back some of their evidence or arguments, they are not, generally, permitted to have a second attempt, deploying further arguments. There are limits to this general principle:

(a) Most decisions can be reviewed on appeal (see **chapter 71**). There are restricted grounds on which an appeal can be brought (see **72.6**), and generally permission must be sought if an appeal is to be brought (see **71.11**). Although sometimes fresh evidence can be adduced on an appeal, there are severe restrictions on when this will be permitted (see **72.13**).
(b) Interim orders can be varied or revoked by a court at the same level as the court that made the original order where there has been a change of circumstances (see **32.37**).
(c) Where the court makes an order of its own initiative, without hearing the parties or giving them an opportunity to make representations, a party affected by the order may apply, within seven days of being served with it, for it to be set aside, varied or stayed (**CPR, r. 3.3(4) and (5)**). This applies also where the court does not consider that a hearing would be appropriate under **r. 23.8(c)**. In *Collier v Williams* [2006] EWCA Civ 20, *The Times*, 3 February 2006, it was decided that this power to review also applies where an applicant asks the court to consider an application without notice on the papers, and then asks the court to set aside or vary the order made on the paper application at a renewed application involving a hearing.
(d) The court has power to adjourn a hearing under **CPR, r. 3.1(2)(b)**, which it can use while

a hearing is part-heard to allow a party to return on a future date with additional evidence.

Beyond this, it is submitted, the court should not go. A first-instance decision, *Laemthong International Lines Co Ltd v ARTIS* [2004] EWHC 2226 (Comm), [2004] 2 All ER (Comm) 797, appears to have taken an additional, forbidden step. Colman J held that a judge has jurisdiction to hear a without notice application for a freezing injunction despite the same application having been heard and dismissed on two previous occasions by two different judges. Plainly, the applicant will have to inform the court on the subsequent hearings of the earlier applications in compliance of its duty of full and frank disclosure (see **32.9**). While Colman J said that another judge will normally dismiss a renewed application, this is not strong enough, and the correct position is that the renewed application must be dismissed unless there has been a material change of circumstances.

Chapter 33 Striking Out

The following procedural checklist, which is in **appendix 1**, is relevant to this chapter:

Procedural checklist 22 Application for striking out

INTRODUCTION

33.1 By **CPR, r. 3.4**, the court has the power to order the whole or any part of a statement of case to be struck out. This power may be resorted to on an application by a party seeking to attack the statement of case drafted by the other side. It may also be used by the court of its own initiative. This may be because of failure to comply with the requirement to give a concise statement of the facts on which the claimant relies (**r. 16.4(1)(a)**) or the requirement to give the reasons for any denial in a defence (**r. 16.5(2)(a)**). A related use of the power is where it is alleged that a statement of case, even if its contents are assumed to be true, does not amount to a sustainable claim or defence as a matter of law. Striking out is also used to prevent the misuse of the right to issue proceedings, on the ground that proceedings are an abuse of process. These facets of the jurisdiction to strike out will be considered in this chapter.

Striking out is also used as a means of enforcing compliance with the general provisions of the CPR, practice directions and court orders and directions as part of the court's case management functions. This aspect of striking out will be considered in **chapter 46**.

It is recognised in several places in the CPR that striking out under **r. 3.4** is closely related to the jurisdiction to enter summary judgment under **Part 24**, discussed in **chapter 34** (see, for example, **PD 3, paras 1.2,1.7** and **6.1**; the note to **CPR, r. 24.2**; and **PD 26, para. 5.2**). Both powers are used to achieve the active case management aim of summarily disposing of issues that do not need full investigation at trial (**CPR, r. 1.4(2)(c)**). As they are closely related, it is very common for parties to make applications in suitable cases for striking out and summary judgment in the alternative, although in *Clarke v Davey* [2002] EWHC 2342 (QB), LTL 11/11/2002, it was said that the right course is to apply only for summary judgment. In *Three Rivers District Council v Bank of England (No. 3)* [2001] UKHL 16, [2003] 2 AC 1 Lord Hope of Craighead said, that under **r. 3.4** the court generally is only concerned with the statement of case which it is alleged discloses no reasonable grounds for bringing or defending the claim.

In *Monsanto plc v Tilly* [2000] Env LR 313 Stuart-Smith LJ said that **r. 24.2** gives a wider scope for dismissing a claim or defence. The court should look to see what will happen at the trial and, if the case is so weak that it has no reasonable prospects of success, summary judgment should be entered. There is an inevitable overlap between the two concepts. Some allegations will be factually weak and aptly described as disclosing no reasonable grounds within the meaning of r. 3.4. Procedural judges are under a duty to narrow the issues as part of their case management functions under **Part 1** and have the power to treat an application to strike out as one for summary judgment in order to dispose of issues or claims that do not deserve full investigation at trial (*Three Rivers District Council v Bank of England (No. 3)* at [88]).

THE MAIN RULE

Rule 3.4(2) **of the CPR** provides: **33.2**

> The court may strike out a statement of case if it appears to the court—
> (a) that the statement of case discloses no reasonable grounds for bringing or defending the claim;
> (b) that the statement of case is an abuse of the court's process or is otherwise likely to obstruct the just disposal of the proceedings; or
> (c) that there has been a failure to comply with a rule, practice direction or court order.

By **r. 3.4(1)** references in **r. 3.4(2)** to a statement of case include references to part of a statement of case. A claim may fall within **r. 3.4(2)(b)** where it is vexatious, scurrilous or obviously ill-founded (**PD 3, para. 1.5**).

In addition, the High Court retains its power to strike out under its inherent jurisdiction, as **CPR, r. 3.4(5)**, provides that **r. 3.4(2)** does not limit any other power of the court to strike out a statement of case (*Re Abermeadow Ltd* [2000] 2 BCLC 824).

PROCEDURE ON APPLICATIONS MADE BY PARTIES

An application to strike out made by a party should be brought by issuing an application notice in accordance with the procedure in **CPR, Part 23** (see **chapter 32**). **PD 3, para. 5.2**, says that while many applications to strike out can be made without evidence in support (the poor drafting of the statement of case may be self-evident, or the point may be one of law on which no evidence would be required), the applicant should always consider whether facts need to be proved. If so, evidence in support should usually be filed and served, unless the facts relied upon have already been adequately evidenced in, say, a statement of case which included a statement of truth. However, careful consideration should be given before relying on a statement of case in this way. **33.3**

In accordance with **PD 23, para.** 2.7, any application to strike out should be made as soon as it becomes apparent that it is desirable to make it. Applications to strike out should normally be made in the period between acknowledgment of service and filing of allocation questionnaires (**PD 26, para. 5.3(1)**, and see also **PD 3, para. 5.1**).

There will be cases where it may be appropriate to seek striking out or summary judgment in the alternative (**PD 3, para. 1.7**; see **33.1**).

Effect on default and summary judgment and allocation

If a striking-out application is issued before the defence is filed, default judgment cannot be entered until the striking out application has been disposed of (**CPR, r. 12.3(3)**). If a striking-out application is dealt with before allocation and the claim survives, the court may be in a position to dispense with the need to file allocation questionnaires, and may allocate the case and make case management directions at the end of the striking-out hearing (**PD 26**, **33.4**

para. 2.4). If a striking-out application is contemplated, but has not been dealt with by the time allocation questionnaires have to be returned, the intention to make the application should be included as extra information provided when the questionnaire is returned (**PD 26, para. 2.2(3)(a)**).

PD 26, para. 5.3(2), provides that where a party makes an application to strike out before the claim has been allocated to a track the court will not allocate the claim before hearing the application. By **PD 26, para. 5.3(3)** and (4), where a party files an allocation questionnaire and states an intention to strike out but has not yet done so, the judge will usually direct that an allocation hearing is listed. The striking-out application may be heard at the allocation hearing if the application notice has been issued and served in sufficient time.

REFERENCES BY COURT OFFICERS

33.5 A claim form that has been lodged for issuing may be referred by a court official to the judge (**CPR, r. 3.2**), and this power may be exercised where it is felt that the claim form (which in context means the particulars of claim) is amenable to being struck out under **r. 3.4** (see **PD 3, para. 2.1**). The judge may then make an order designed to ensure that the claim is disposed of, or proceeds, in a way that accords with the rules. The judge has a discretion whether to hear the claimant before making such order as may be appropriate (**para. 2.3**). If an order is made without giving notice to the claimant, **rr. 23.9** and **23.10** of the CPR apply, so that the order has to include a statement that the claimant has the right within seven days after service of the order to apply to vary or set it aside.

One option available to the judge is to order a stay to allow the claimant an opportunity of putting the claim on a proper footing. This may take the form of a simple stay until further order, or an order that the claim form shall not be served until the stay is lifted, or an order that no application to lift the stay shall be made until the claimant files specified further documents, such as amended particulars of claim or a witness statement (**PD 3, para. 2.4**). If the claimant does what the judge requires, and the stay is lifted, the judge may give directions regarding service of the order and any other documents on the court file (**para. 2.5**). The fact that the judge allows the claim to proceed does not preclude the defendant from making an application to strike out or for summary judgment once proceedings are served (**para. 2.6**).

Similar powers are available where a court official believes a document purporting to be a defence is amenable to being struck out (**para. 3**). A stay would be inappropriate in this situation, but the judge may strike out the defence on his or her own initiative, or allow the defendant an opportunity to file an amended defence, or may require the defendant to provide further information to clarify the defence within a stated time, failing which the judge may order the defence to be struck out. The fact that a judge does not strike out a defence under this power does not prejudice the claimant's right to apply for such an order or any other order.

GENERAL TEST

33.6 Under the old rules it was well settled that the jurisdiction to strike out was to be used sparingly. The reason was, and this has not changed, that the exercise of the jurisdiction deprives a party of its right to a trial, and of its ability to strengthen its case through the process of disclosure and other court procedures such as requests for further information. Further, it has always been true that the examination and cross-examination of witnesses often changes the complexion of a case. It was accordingly the accepted rule that striking out was limited to plain and obvious cases where there was no point in having a trial.

Under the CPR it is part of the court's active case management role to identify the issues at an early stage and to decide which issues need full investigation at trial, and to dispose summarily of the others (**CPR, r. 1.4(2)(b)** and (c)). In *Swain v Hillman* [2001] 1 All ER 91 (a summary judgment case), Lord Woolf MR said that **Part 24** applications had to be kept within their proper limits, and were not meant to be used to dispense with the need for a trial where there were issues which should be considered at trial. The same could be said in relation to striking out under **r. 3.4**. In the same vein, before using **r. 3.4** to dispose of 'side issues', care should be taken to ensure that a party is not deprived of the right to trial on issues essential to its case. In *McPhilemy v Times Newspapers Ltd* [1999] 3 All ER 775, one of the first cases decided under the CPR, the Master of the Rolls said that the powers of the court to restrain excess do not extend to preventing a party from putting forward allegations which are central to its case. That said, it is open to the court to attempt to control how those allegations are litigated with a view to limiting costs.

The leading case under the old rules was *Williams and Humbert Ltd v W and H Trade Marks (Jersey) Ltd* [1986] AC 368. The claimant's application to strike out the defence took seven days to argue before the judge, six days in the Court of Appeal, and four days in the House of Lords. The case reiterated the point that striking out was only appropriate in plain and obvious cases. Sometimes, a case would only become clear after protracted argument. Lord Templeman said that:

> . . . if an application to strike out involves a prolonged and serious argument the judge should, as a general rule, decline to proceed with the argument unless he not only harbours doubts about the soundness of the pleading but, in addition, is satisfied that striking out will obviate the necessity for a trial or will substantially reduce the burden of preparing for trial or the burden of the trial itself.

A judge may therefore refuse to hear a striking-out application if: (a) the application is unlikely to succeed; or (b) the application will not be decisive or appreciably simplify the eventual trial (see *Morris v Bank of America National Trust* [2000] 1 All ER 954). It is generally improper to conduct what is in effect a mini-trial involving protracted examination of the documents and facts as disclosed in the written evidence on a striking-out application (*Wenlock v Moloney* [1965] 1 WLR 1238), although such a detailed analysis is sometimes appropriate in striking-out applications in relation to unfair prejudice petitions under the Companies Act 1985, s. 459 (*Morris v Bank of America National Trust*).

The principles from *Williams and Humbert Ltd v W and H Trade Marks (Jersey) Ltd*, *Wenlock v Moloney* and *Morris v Bank of America National Trust* were approved in *Three Rivers District Council v Bank of England (No. 3)* [2001] UKHL 16, [2003] 2 AC 1 at [96, 97].

If an application to strike out is unsuccessful, the claim will proceed towards trial. In such cases it may be considered undesirable for the judge or master to express any reasons as to why that decision has been made (*Re Baltic Real Estate Ltd (No. 1)* [1993] BCLC 498).

NO REASONABLE GROUNDS FOR BRINGING OR DEFENDING THE CLAIM

Applications under **CPR, r. 3.4(2)(a)**, may be made on the basis that the statement of case under attack fails on its face to disclose a claim or defence which is sustainable as a matter of law. On hearing such an application it will be assumed that the facts alleged are true (see *Morgan Crucible Co. plc v Hill Samuel and Co. Ltd* [1991] Ch 295 per Slade LJ). **33.7**

For purists it ought to be unnecessary to seek to undermine the claim or defence with evidence in support. The rules do not, however, contain any express ban on adducing evidence in support: **r. 25.3(2)** provides that applications must be supported by evidence unless the court otherwise orders, and **PD 3, para. 5.2**, leaves open the option of adducing evidence in support.

In deciding whether to strike out, the judge should consider the effect of the order. In *Watson v Ian Snipe and Co.* [2002] EWCA Civ 293, LTL 21/2/2002, there were parallel proceedings against two firms of solicitors, which had successively been retained by the claimants in an unsuccessful claim. It was held to have been inconsistent with sound case management principles to have struck out the claim against one of the firms, because this added to the overall complexity of the proceedings.

A number of examples of statements of case open to attack under **CPR, r. 3.4(2)(a)**, are given by **PD 3**. A claim may be struck out if it sets out no facts indicating what the claim is about (such as a claim simply saying it is for 'Money owed £5,000'), or if it is incoherent and makes no sense, or if the facts it states, even if true, do not disclose a legally recognisable claim against the defendant. A defence may be struck out if it consists of a bare denial or otherwise fails to set out a coherent statement of facts, or if the facts it sets out, even if true, do not amount in law to a defence to the claim. Many institutional defendants have been in the habit of filing short defences making blanket denials without stating any positive case. These defences ought to be a thing of the past. See **chapters 24** and **26**.

Some prospects of success

33.8 Under the old rules, a cause of action with some prospects of success would not be struck out. Provided the statement of case raised some question fit to be tried, it did not matter that the case was weak or unlikely to succeed (*Wenlock v Moloney* [1965] 1 WLR 1238), one of the leading cases under the old rules, and *Chan U Seek v Alvis Vehicles Ltd* [2003] EWHC 1238 (Ch), *The Times*, 16 May 2003, which adopted the same test under the CPR). The apparent implausibility of a case on paper is not in itself enough to justify striking it out (*Merelie v Newcastle Primary Care Trust* [2004] EWHC 2554 (QB), *The Times*, 1 December 2004). Nor is it appropriate to strike out a claim where the central issues are in dispute (*King v Telegraph Group Ltd* [2003] EWHC 1312 (QB), LTL 9/6/2003). Cases where striking out under **CPR, r. 3.4(2)(a)**, is appropriate according to Potter LJ in *Partco Group Ltd v Wragg* [2002] EWCA Civ 594, [2002] 2 Lloyd's Rep 343, at [46], include:

(a) where the statement of case raises an unwinnable case where continuing the proceedings is without any possible benefit to the respondent and would waste resources on both sides (*Harris v Bolt Burdon* [2000] CPLR 9); and
(b) where the statement of case does not raise a valid claim or defence as a matter of law (*Price Meats Ltd v Barclays Bank plc* [2000] 2 All ER (Comm) 346).

A cause of action that is unknown to the law will be struck out; as will, subject to the court giving permission to amend, a statement of case that omits some material element of the claim or defence. A statement of case ought also to be struck out if the facts set out do not constitute the cause of action or defence alleged, or if the relief sought would not be ordered by the court. A defence may be struck out if it does not answer the claim being made. However, purely technical objections to the form of statements of case will not be entertained, provided the statement of case is sufficient to allow the other side to have a fair trial (*Morris v Bank of America National Trust* [2000] 1 All ER 954).

In *Taylor v Inntrepreneur Estates (CPC) Ltd* (2001) LTL 7/2/2001 the claimant brought a claim seeking a declaration that a lease agreement had come into force, damages for breach of the lease, and damages for misrepresentation resulting from having entered into the alleged lease. On the documents it was clear that throughout the parties had negotiated on a 'subject to contract' basis. It was held that as no written agreement had been signed, no lease had been entered into. It followed that there was no reasonable cause of action, and the claim was struck out. Conversely, in *Cornelius v Hackney London Borough Council* [2002] EWCA Civ 1073, [2003] LGR 178, an application to strike out a misfeasance claim was dismissed because liability turned on whether an official had abused his public office, which was a question of fact. In *Kirk v London Borough of Brent* [2005] EWCA Civ 1701, LTL 8/12/2005, the Court of Appeal said it had been wrong to strike out a nuisance claim which alleged the claimant's property had been damaged by tree roots. While the defendant had been notified of the claim very late, a letter about a similar problem involving a neighbouring property written a year after the damage to the claimant's property had been discovered raised implications about the defendant's state of knowledge which meant the claim was not suitable for striking out.

Points of law

Where the argument involves a substantial point of law which does not admit of a plain and obvious answer, it may be best not to have it determined on a striking-out application. One thing the courts are anxious to avoid is expensive satellite litigation. Instead, sensible case management may indicate that it would be better dealt with as a preliminary issue, although dealing with issues in this way sometimes increases costs and delay — see **59.55**. **33.9**

Where the law is in a state of development, it will usually be inappropriate to decide questions, such as whether a duty of care exists in a novel situation, on hypothetical facts. Such questions are usually best dealt with at trial (*D v East Berkshire Community Health NHS Trust* [2005] UKHL 23, [2005] 2 AC 373, per Lord Bingham of Cornhill at [4]; *Brooks v Commissioner of Police of the Metropolis* [2005] UKHL 24, [2005] 1 WLR 1495, per Lord Bingham of Cornhill at [3]; *Hughes v Richards* [2004] EWCA Civ 266, [2004] PNLR 35).

Claim meriting further investigation

A similar approach is taken in striking-out applications to that adopted in summary judgment applications (see **34.19**) where the strength of a case may not be clear because it has not been fully investigated. Where there is a real possibility that, on a full investigation of the factual background, any uncertainty on the merits might be remedied, striking out should be refused (*Kyrris v Oldham* [2003] EWCA Civ 1506, [2004] 1 BCLC 305). **33.10**

Amendment and disclosure

The court may allow a party to amend rather than striking out. There have been cases where amendments have been allowed at a very late stage (see, under the old rules, *CBS Songs Ltd v Amstrad Consumer Electronics plc* [1987] RPC 417), but the power to amend will be exercised in accordance with the overriding objective, and this may militate against giving permission depending on the circumstances of the case (see *Finley v Connell Associates* (1999) *The Times*, 23 June 1999, where permission to amend was granted, and *Christofi v Barclays Bank plc* [2000] 1 WLR 937, where permission was refused). An amendment should only be permitted as an alternative to striking out if there is a real prospect of establishing the amended case (*Charles Church Developments plc v Cronin* [1990] FSR 1; *Savings and Investment Bank Ltd v Fincken* (2001) *The Times*, 15 November 2001). **33.11**

Where a claim is arguably so speculative that it discloses no reasonable cause of action or amounts to an abuse of process, instead of striking out the court may be prepared to allow the claim to proceed to enable the claimant to obtain disclosure from the defendant to see whether there is evidence substantiating the claim. If it does not, the defendant would be allowed to reapply for striking out (*Arsenal Football Club plc v Elite Sports Distribution Ltd* [2002] EWHC 3057 (Ch), [2003] FSR 26, where the circumstances pointed towards the defendant having committed some tort, but it was unclear which one).

ABUSE OF PROCESS

The first half of CPR, r. 3.4(2)(b), gives the court power to strike out a statement of case **33.12** which is an abuse of the court's process. This is a power '. . . which any court of justice must possess to prevent misuse of its procedure in a way which, although not inconsistent with the literal application of its procedural rules, would nevertheless be manifestly unfair to a party to litigation before it, or would otherwise bring the administration of justice into disrepute among right-thinking people' (per Lord Diplock in *Hunter v Chief Constable of the West Midlands Police* [1982] AC 529 at p. 536). Applications to strike out for abuse of process should be made shortly after service. Once the defendant has filed a defence and defended on the merits he is taken to have acquiesced, and it is too late to take the point (*Johnson v Gore Wood and Co.* [2002] 2 AC 1; *Coca-Cola Co. v Ketteridge* [2003] EWHC 2488 (Ch); LTL 4/11/2003).

The court has the power to strike out even a valid claim where there has been an abuse of process, but it is not always correct to do so. Striking out should be the last option. If the abuse can be addressed in some less draconian way, it should be (*Reckitt Benckiser (UK) Ltd v Home Pairfum Ltd* [2004] EWHC 302 (Pat), [2004] FSR 37).

Some striking-out applications are brought on the basis that it is an abuse of process to litigate a very weak claim. It is submitted that this is a misuse of the term 'abuse of process', and that weak claims should be dealt with either as disclosing no reasonable grounds for bringing or defending the claim (see **33.7** to **33.10**) or on an application for summary judgment (**chapter 34**). In so far as there is any validity in striking out on this basis, it was held in *Barrett v Universal-Island Records Ltd* [2003] EWHC 625 (Ch), *The Times*, 24 April 2003, that the court needed to have a high degree of confidence that the claim or defence would not succeed before striking it out as an abuse of process.

General examples of abuse of process

33.13 A claim that is issued after the expiry of limitation may be struck out as an abuse of process (alternatively, the limitation point may be determined as a preliminary issue, or at trial, or by way of an application for a direction under the **LA 1980, s. 33**), but cannot be struck out on the ground of there being no reasonable cause of action. The reason is that limitation is a procedural defence, so does not prevent there being a cause of action. See *Ronex Properties Ltd v John Laing Construction Ltd* [1983] QB 398.

Generally, it is an abuse of process for a claimant complaining about a public authority's infringement of the claimant's public law rights to seek redress by way of an ordinary claim rather than by way of judicial review (see *O'Reilly v Mackman* [1983] 2 AC 237). In considering whether to strike out on this ground, the court will take into account whether the claimant has used the ordinary procedure to obtain some advantage not available in judicial review proceedings, and generally whether striking out accords with the overriding objective (*Clark v University of Lincolnshire and Humberside* [2000] 1 WLR 1988). The prohibition is limited to bringing claims, so there is no restriction on raising public law issues in a defence (*Rhondda Cynon Taff County Borough Council v Watkins* [2003] EWCA Civ 129, [2003] 1 WLR 1864).

In *Barton Henderson Rasen v Merrett* [1993] 1 Lloyd's Rep 540 Saville J said that it is an abuse of the court's process to issue proceedings with no intention of taking the case any further. In contentious matters the courts exist for the purpose of determining claims. Therefore, starting a claim with no intention of pursuing it is not using the court's processes for the purposes for which they were designed. 'Parking' proceedings in an attempt to achieve a settlement with other defendants justified striking out with indemnity costs in *Sodeca SA v NE Investments Inc.* [2002] EWHC 1700 (QB), LTL 27/8/2002. Litigating for the purpose of causing expense, harassment or commercial prejudice beyond that normally encountered in the course of properly conducted litigation justifies striking out as an abuse of process (*Wallis v Valentine* [2002] EWCA Civ 1034, [2003] EMLR 8). A claim based on comments made in without-prejudice communications is an abuse of process (*Unilever plc v Procter and Gamble Co.* [2000] 1 WLR 2436).

According to *McDonald's Corporation v Steel* [1995] 3 All ER 615, it is an abuse of process where the statement of case is incurably incapable of proof. The fact that a party's case may be incapable of proof may become apparent after disclosure of documents or after exchange of witness statements. However, in *McDonald's Corporation v Steel* it was said that striking out on this basis will be fairly unusual, as there are few cases which are sufficiently clearly and obviously hopeless that they deserve the draconian step of being struck out. A clinical negligence claim commenced five years after the event and which was not supported by the medical experts instructed for the claimant was regarded as unwinnable in *Harris v Bolt Burdon* [2000] CPLR 9.

Framing a claim in malicious falsehood rather than the more natural cause of action in libel, in order to gain the benefit of public funding for the claim, was not regarded as an abuse of process in *Joyce v Sengupta* [1993] 1 WLR 337. In *R v Richmond upon Thames London Borough Council, ex parte C* [2001] LGR 146, bringing judicial review proceedings relating to obtaining a place for a child in a preferred school in the name of the child rather than his parent in order to obtain public funding was regarded by Kennedy LJ as an abuse of process. A claim by a police informer for contractual payments for information provided was struck out in *Carnduff v Rock* [2001] 1 WLR 1786, because trying the allegations in the claim would have required evidence of specialist police operations which were protected by public interest immunity. In those circumstances the claim could not be tried justly.

Relitigation amounting to an abuse of process

There have been several cases dealing with whether a claim which is inconsistent with an earlier claim or evidence given by the claimant in earlier proceedings (such as an affidavit used in an application to discharge a freezing injunction) should be struck out as an abuse of process. Further, a party to litigation is required to bring forward his whole case, and is generally not permitted to bring later proceedings raising matters that could have been resolved in the earlier proceedings (the rule in *Henderson v Henderson* (1843) 3 Hare 100). It is clear from cases such as *Bradford and Bingley Building Society v Seddon* [1999] 1 WLR 1482 that there are two main elements: **33.14**

(a) that the second claim is one that could have been brought in the first claim, or is in conflict with an earlier claim or evidence; and
(b) an additional element, such as a collateral attack on the earlier decision, or dishonesty, election, or unjust harassment.

Thus, in *Hunter v Chief Constable of the West Midlands Police* [1982] AC 529 a claim against the police was struck out as it was held to be no more than a collateral attack upon the decision of another court of competent jurisdiction.

Issue estoppel Where the issues raised in an earlier claim are identical to the issues raised in a later claim, there is an absolute bar on the later proceedings unless fraud or collusion is alleged (*Arnold v National Westminster Bank plc* [1991] 2 AC 93). Where an issue decided in a previous claim between the parties is central to a second claim between the same parties, the whole second claim will be struck out (*Kennecott Utah Copper Corporation v Minet Ltd* [2002] EWHC 1622 (Comm), [2003] PNLR 18). Issue estoppel applies where an order is made, and it does not matter whether the order was made by consent or after argument (*Lennon v Birmingham City Council* [2001] EWCA Civ 435, LTL 27/3/2001). Issue estoppel also arises to prevent a party reopening a liability issue after a judgment for damages to be decided by the court on the assessment of damages (*Item Software (UK) Ltd v Fassihi* (2003) LTL 28/1/2003). There is no issue estoppel if there is no definitive decision on the issue in the first claim (*Tannu v Moosajee* [2003] EWCA Civ 815, LTL 20/6/2003). **33.15**

Where the parties in the two claims are not the same, issue estoppel does not apply (*Sweetman v Nathan* [2003] EWCA Civ 1115, *The Times*, 1 September 2003), and further, the factual findings in the first claim are not admissible evidence in the second claim (*Hollington v F. Hewthorn and Co.*

Ltd [1943] KB 587). A person claiming title to goods or land is treated as being privy to the interests of those through whom title is claimed, and so will be bound by the decision in proceedings in which any predecessor in title was a party, but only if judgment in those proceedings was given before the presently claimed title was acquired. A person who purchased title before judgment is not regarded as a privy (*Powell v Wiltshire* [2004] EWCA Civ 534, [2005] QB 117).

33.16 **Issue which should have been raised in earlier proceedings** It is an abuse of process to raise in a second claim an issue which should have been raised against someone who was a party to earlier proceedings (*Henderson v Henderson* (1843) 3 Hare 100; *Talbot v Berkshire County Council* [1994] QB 290). Where it is alleged that an issue was or should have been raised in earlier proceedings, it is first necessary to consider whether issue estoppel applies, which can only be negatived by fraud or collusion (see **33.15**). It is only if there is no such estoppel that it is appropriate to consider whether raising the issue now would be an abuse of process under the principle in *Henderson v Henderson* (see *Coflexip SA v Stolt Offshore MS Ltd* [2004] EWCA Civ 213, [2004] FSR 34; *Kennecott Utah Copper Corporation v Minet Ltd* [2003] EWCA Civ 905, [2004] 1 All ER (Comm) 60; *Bim Kemi AB v Blackburn Chemicals Ltd* [2004] EWCA Civ 1490, *The Times*, 22 November 2004). In *Johnson v Gore Wood and Co.* [2002] 2 AC 1 the House of Lords held that when considering whether a second claim is an abuse of process a broad, merits-based judgment has to be made, taking into account all the public and private interests involved, and all the facts. A second claim should be struck out only if, in all the circumstances, it should, rather than merely could, have been brought in the first claim. Mr Johnson was a shareholder in a company which had sued the defendant solicitors. That first claim was settled, with the compromise agreement containing a clause seeking to limit the defendants' liability to Mr Johnson personally. Mr Johnson then sued the solicitors in his personal capacity, and the defendants applied to strike out his personal claim as an abuse. Certain heads of claim were struck out, as they merely reflected losses suffered by the company in which Mr Johnson held shares, but others were arguably recoverable by Mr Johnson in his own right, and it was held that even though his personal claim could have been joined with the first claim by the company, it was not on the facts an abuse to have brought the personal claim by separate proceedings. Contrast *Giles v Rhind* [2002] EWCA Civ 1428, [2003] Ch 18, where a shareholder's claim was allowed to proceed because it was not reflective of the company's loss. The question of reflected losses is discussed further at **14.41**.

In *Dexter Ltd v Vlieland-Boddy* [2003] EWCA Civ 14, LTL 24/1/2003, the defendant in the second claim was the brother of the defendant in an earlier claim based on the same facts. It was held that the burden was on the defendant to show that the second claim was abusive. Applying a broad merits-based approach, taking into account the fact the defendants were different and that the first claim resulted in an unsatisfied judgment, the second claim was allowed to proceed. In *De Crittenden v Bayliss* [2005] EWCA Civ 1425, LTL 13/10/2005, the claimant became aware of an alternative cause of action after issuing the first claim, and issued a second claim form. It was held that the second claim should have been brought by amending the first claim, so issuing separate proceedings was an abuse of process.

It will only be an abuse of process to challenge the findings in the earlier claim if it would be manifestly unfair to a party in the later claim for the issues to be relitigated, or if relitigating will bring the administration of justice into disrepute (*Secretary of State for Trade and Industry v Bairstow* [2003] EWCA Civ 321, [2004] Ch 1). Where an issue, which is raised on taking accounts following judgment, was before the trial judge, but was not decided definitively, the question is whether a party is misusing or abusing the process of the court in raising the issue again (*Tannu v Moosajee* [2003] EWCA Civ 815, LTL 20/6/2003). A judge's evaluation of the facts on an application to strike out was treated as an exercise of discretion in *De Crittenden v Bayliss*, with the result that the decision will be difficult to reverse on appeal (see **72.9**).

Where the first and second claims are of a different nature, compelling reasons are required before the later claim will be struck out (*Specialist Group International Ltd v Deakin* [2001] EWCA Civ 77, LTL 23/5/2001). In *Heffernan v Grangewood Securities Ltd* [2001] EWCA Civ 1082, LTL 19/6/2001, proceedings were commenced by a mortgagee which were compromised in 1995 on terms that the mortgagors would pay the arrears over the remaining term of the mortgage. In 1997 the mortgagors commenced their own claim seeking a declaration that the original mortgage was not binding. This second claim was struck out because the mortgagors should have raised this issue in the first claim.

Estoppel preventing application to strike out In *Johnson v Gore Wood and Co.* [2002] 2 AC 1 **33.17**
the House of Lords considered whether a court should refuse to strike out a second claim, which is alleged to be an abusive relitigation of an earlier claim, because of the defendant's previous conduct, in particular where the second claim was taken into consideration when reaching a settlement of the first claim. This is best considered as an estoppel by representation, with the key question being whether it would be unconscionable for the defendant to apply for striking out.

Fresh evidence Claims have been allowed even though they involve questioning the **33.18**
decision of a court of competent jurisdiction if fresh evidence has come to light since the earlier decision, or where the second claim is a professional negligence claim against the solicitors acting for the claimant in the first claim, see *Walpole v Partridge and Wilson* [1994] QB 106. A damages claim was permitted to proceed, subject to stringent conditions, in *Sweetman v Shepherd* (2000) *The Times*, 29 March 2000, despite the fact that it could have been brought by contribution proceedings in an earlier claim.

Reviving earlier claim In *Buckland v Palmer* [1984] 1 WLR 1109 it was held to be an abuse of **33.19**
process to commence a second claim in respect of the same cause of action as was raised in an earlier claim. The claimant's car had been damaged in a motor accident. Repairs cost £1,142. She claimed on her insurance, and brought proceedings against the defendant claiming the £50 excess not paid by her insurer. This claim was stayed when she accepted a payment into court. The insurer then commenced a second claim in the name of the claimant claiming £1,092, and this claim was struck out as an abuse of process. However, it was possible for the insurer to apply for the first claim to be revived (as it had not proceeded to judgment) and for the original claim to be amended to include the full costs of repairs. A comment was made in *Bradford and Bingley Building Society v Seddon* [1999] 1 WLR 1482 that abuse of process cases of this nature will perhaps be less frequent under the CPR, because of the requirement that the claimant must sign a statement of truth in relation to the second claim, which might be difficult given an earlier, inconsistent, claim.

Settlement acting as a bar to later proceedings

Settling a claim can act as a bar to later proceedings. In *Jameson v Central Electricity Generating* **33.20**
Board [2000] 1 AC 455, the deceased accepted £80,000 from his former employer in 'full and final settlement and satisfaction of all the causes of action' set out in his statement of claim against his employer in respect of asbestos-related disease. After his death his widow brought a claim against the Board as the owner of premises where the deceased had been exposed to asbestos. It was held, on the assumption that the employer and the Board were concurrent and not joint tortfeasors, and as the settlement could not be construed as only a partial settlement, that the compromise with the employer operated to extinguish the claims against all the tortfeasors. The claim against the Board was therefore struck out. *Jameson v Central Electricity Generating Board* was interpreted by the House of Lords in *Heaton v AXA Equity and Law Life Assurance Society plc* [2002] UKHL 15, [2002] 2 AC 329, as laying down the following principles:

(a) A claim for unliquidated damages, whether in contract or tort, is capable of being fixed in a specific sum of money either on judgment or by agreement.

(b) Although a judgment invariably fixes the full measure of the claimant's loss, whether a compromise fixes the full measure depends on the proper construction of the compromise agreement. Lord Bingham of Cornhill said that in construing a compromise agreement for this purpose one significant factor is whether the claimant has expressly reserved the right to sue other persons, although the absence of such a reservation is by no means conclusive in favour of an argument that other claims are extinguished.

(c) If a compromise, on its proper construction, fixes the full measure of the claimant's loss, the compromise extinguishes the claim so that other claims for the same damage cannot be pursued against other persons, whether in contract or tort.

Following *Heaton v AXA Equity and Law Life Assurance Society plc*, in *Cape and Dalgleish v Fitzgerald* [2002] UKHL 16, LTL 25/4/2002, it was held that a settlement between the original claimant and the defendant was not intended or understood to represent full compensation, so the original claimant had been able to commence a second claim against another party (Cape). The consequence was that Cape was then entitled, in a third claim, to seek a contribution against the defendant in respect of the damages Cape was ordered to pay the claimant in the second claim.

Although a party can agree to release claims or rights of which he is unaware if appropriate language is used in the agreement, the court will be very slow to accept that this is the effect of a release (*Capital Trust Investments Ltd v Radio Design TJ AB* [2002] EWCA Civ 135, [2002] 2 All ER 159).

In *Minton v Kenburgh Investments (Northern) Ltd* [2000] CPLR 551 liquidators brought misfeasance proceedings under the Insolvency Act 1986, s. 212, against former directors alleging breach of fiduciary duty, which were compromised with sums payable in full and final settlement of the proceedings. The liquidators then brought proceedings against the company's former solicitors arising out of the same transaction as had formed the basis of the first claim for breach of their duties to the company. It was held that as the causes of action were different in the two claims the *Jameson* principle did not apply.

Destruction of evidence

33.21 Destruction of evidence before proceedings are commenced in an attempt to pervert the course of justice may result in a claim or defence being struck out. Destruction of evidence after proceedings are issued may be visited by striking out if a fair trial is no longer achievable (*Douglas v Hello! Ltd (No. 2)* [2003] EWHC 55 (Ch), [2003] 1 All ER 1087).

OBSTRUCTING THE JUST DISPOSAL OF THE PROCEEDINGS

33.22 The second half of **CPR, r. 3.4(2)(b)**, allows the court to strike out a statement of case which obstructs the just disposal of the proceedings. This is expanded upon by **PD 3, para. 1.5**, which provides that a claim may come within **r. 3.4(2)(b)** if it is vexatious, scurrilous or obviously ill-founded. Generally, the court will know a claim of this kind when it sees it.

Whether a statement of case is vexatious depends 'on all the circumstances of the case: the categories are not closed and the considerations of public policy and the interests of justice may be very material' (per Stuart-Smith LJ in *Ashmore v British Coal Corporation* [1990] 2 QB 338). The applicant in *Ashmore v British Coal Corporation* was one of 1,500 women claiming they were employed on less favourable terms than certain male comparators. Fourteen cases were selected for determination, and the eventual finding was in favour of the employer. The applicant then sought to proceed with her claim. Although the previous determination was not strictly binding, the applicant's claim was struck out as being frivolous and vexatious. Pleadings under the old system have also been struck out on this ground where a party has been joined merely to obtain disclosure of documents or costs (*Burstall v Beyfus* (1884) 26 ChD

35) or where a claim is a disguised action for gaming debts (*Day v William Hill (Park Lane) Ltd* [1949] 1 KB 632).

Poor drafting

A party confronted with a poorly drafted statement of case cannot insist on it being amended, but can take the initiative by applying to have the whole or offending parts of the statement of case struck out. If the statement of case fails to comply with the principles discussed in **chapter 24**, it is likely to obstruct the just disposal of the claim. Statements of case which fail to inform the other side of the case it will have to meet tend to be described as 'embarrassing' (a term that does not appear in the CPR). **33.23**

Rassam v Budge [1893] 1 QB 571 concerned a claim for damages for slander. Instead of pleading to the words alleged by the claimant, the defence set out the defendant's rather different version of what he had said, and alleged the words he alleged he had spoken were true. These allegations were struck out as tending to prejudice the fair trial of the action, because they left it unclear whether the issue was whether the words complained of by the claimant were spoken and published, or whether those words were true.

In *Philipps v Philipps* (1878) 4 QBD 127 Cotton LJ said, at p. 139:

> . . . in my opinion it is absolutely essential that the pleading, not to be embarrassing to the defendants, should state those facts which will put the defendants on their guard and tell them what they have to meet when the case comes on for trial.

Deutsche Morgan Grenfell Group plc v Commissioners of Inland Revenue [2005] EWCA Civ 78, [2006] 2 WLR 103, was a claim for restitution of money paid to the Inland Revenue. The particulars of claim sought repayment of sums which 'include but are not limited to' certain payments set out in a schedule. As this only stated part of the sum actually sought, Jonathan Parker LJ said it was embarrassing (at [247]).

A defence will be struck out if it does not make clear how much of the claim is admitted and how much is denied (*British and Colonial Land Association Ltd v Foster* (1887) 4 TLR 574). Mere prolixity or setting out of inconsistent claims or defences would be unlikely to result in striking out (see, for example, *Re Morgan* (1887) 35 ChD 492), although costs sanctions may be imposed if the case is protracted as a result.

POWERS AFTER A STRIKING-OUT APPLICATION

When a court strikes out a statement of case it may enter such judgment as the successful party appears entitled to (**PD 3, para. 4.2**) and make any consequential order it considers appropriate (**CPR, r. 3.4(3)**). If the court strikes out a claimant's statement of case, and it considers the claim was totally without merit, that fact must be recorded in the court's order, and the court must consider whether to make a civil restraint order (see **r. 3.4(6)** and **14.70**). If a claim survives a striking-out application, the court may dispense with the need to file allocation questionnaires, may allocate the claim to a track, and make case management directions (**PD 26, para. 2.4**). **33.24**

COMMENCING A SECOND CLAIM

Endorsing the rule laid down in *Gardner v Southwark London Borough Council (No. 2)* [1996] 1 WLR 561, **CPR, r. 3.4(4)**, provides that where a claim is struck out and the claimant is ordered to pay the defendant's costs, if the claimant commences a second action (within the limitation period) arising out of substantially the same facts as those forming the basis of the struck-out **33.25** claim, the defendant may apply for a stay of the second action until the costs of the first action have been paid.

A second claim based on the same facts as those forming the basis of a claim that has been struck out is itself at risk of being struck out as an abuse of process. In *Securum Finance Ltd v Ashton* [2001] Ch 291 it was said that a claimant's wish to have a 'second bite of the cherry' had to be weighed against the overriding objective, and in particular to the need to allot the court's limited resources to other cases. On the facts of the case, however, the first claim had been based on payment due under a guarantee, whereas the second claim was to enforce a charge (albeit both claims were based on enforcing security over the same borrowing). In these circumstances it was held that there was no basis for striking out the second claim.

Chapter 34 Summary Judgment

The following procedural checklists, which are in **appendix 1**, are relevant to this chapter:

Procedural checklist 23 Application by a party for summary judgment
Procedural checklist 24 Proposal by court for order for summary judgment

INTRODUCTION

34.1 In cases where the defendant fails to defend it is usually possible to enter a default judgment (see **chapter 20**). Where there is no real defence, a defendant may go through the motions of defending in order to delay the time when judgment may be entered. It is possible for defendants to put up the pretence of having a real defence to such an extent that some cases run all the way through to trial before judgment can be entered. The CPR provide several ways of preventing this happening. The court can use its power to strike out (see **chapter 33**) to knock out hopeless defences, such as those that simply do not amount to a legal defence to a claim. Entering summary judgment is a related procedure, and is used where a purported defence can be shown to have no real prospect of success and there is no other compelling reason why the case should be disposed of at trial. Indeed, **PD 3, para. 1.7**, recognises that there will be cases where applications for summary judgment and striking out may be sought in the alternative (but see *Clarke v Davey* [2002] EWHC 2342 (QB), LTL 11/11/2002, in which it was said that the application should be restricted to summary judgment).

The procedure for entering summary judgment is not limited to use by claimants against defendants. Defendants may apply for summary judgment to attack weak claims brought by claimants. Further, summary judgment can be used by the court of its own initiative to perform the important function of stopping weak cases from proceeding. The procedure can also be used for the purpose of obtaining a summary determination of some of the issues in a case, thereby reducing the complexity of the trial.

TIME AT WHICH THE APPLICATION MAY BE MADE

34.2 Summary judgment can be applied for by a claimant or a defendant (see **procedural checklist 23** in **appendix 1**) or can be proposed by the court of its own initiative (see **34.5** and **procedural checklist 24**).

A claimant may apply for summary judgment only after the defendant has filed either an acknowledgment of service or a defence (**CPR, r. 24.4(1)**). If the defendant fails to do either of these within the time limited by the CPR, the claimant may enter a default judgment, which, depending on the nature of the claim, may require the court's permission (see **chapter 20**). By analogy with **r. 25.2(2)(c)**, a defendant likewise can only apply for summary judgment after either filing an acknowledgment of service or a defence.

With effect from 1 October 2005, where the claimant has failed to comply with any relevant pre-action protocol, an application for summary judgment will not normally be entertained before the defence has been filed, or the time for doing so has expired (**PD 24, para. 2(6)**).

Applications for summary judgment should normally be made in the period between acknowledgment of service and filing of the applicant's allocation questionnaire (**PD 26, para. 5.3(1)**). This is normally the appropriate time, because, if the other side have no realistic prospects of success, entering summary judgment early prevents unnecessary costs being incurred. Question D in the allocation questionnaire (**form N150**) specifically asks whether there is any intention of making an application for summary judgment. If for any reason the application is not made before allocation, there is still a general obligation to apply as soon as it becomes apparent that it is desirable to do so (**PD 23, para. 2.7**).

Under the old rules there was nothing to prevent a late application for summary judgment (see, for example, *Brinks Ltd v Abu-Saleh (No. 1)* [1995] 1 WLR 1478), but as a practical matter the judge dealing with a late application might well have felt there was a lack of conviction on the part of the applicant if the application was significantly delayed. For summary judgment at trial, see **59.35**.

Summary judgment applications made before filing the defence

34.3 If the application is made after filing an acknowledgment of service, but before filing of the defence, there is no need to file a defence before the hearing (**CPR, r. 24.4(2)**). At that stage the court will give directions, which will include providing a date for filing the defence. The permissive wording of the rule confirms *Natural Resources Inc. v Origin Clothing Ltd* [1995] FSR 280, in which it was held that there is nothing to prevent a defendant from serving a defence in the period before the hearing if the defendant chooses to do so.

Summary judgment applications made before allocation to a track

34.4 PD 26, para. 5.3(2), provides that where a party makes an application for summary judgment before the claim has been allocated to a track the court will not allocate the claim before hearing the application. If a party files an allocation questionnaire stating an intention to apply for summary judgment but has not yet made an application, the judge will usually direct the listing of an allocation hearing (**para. 5.3(3)** and **(4)**). The summary judgment application may be heard at the allocation hearing if the application notice has been issued and served in sufficient time.

Hearings fixed by the court of its own initiative

The rules specifically mention that the court may fix a summary judgment hearing of its own initiative (**CPR, r. 24.4(3)**), and doing so may further the overriding objective, which includes deciding promptly which issues need full investigation and trial, and accordingly disposing summarily of the others (**r. 1.4(2)(c)**). If the court is minded to make use of this power, it is most likely to do so on the initial scrutiny at the track allocation stage shortly after filing of the defence. If the court uses the power, it will not allocate the case to a track, but instead it will fix a hearing, giving the parties 14 days' notice and informing them of the issues it proposes to decide (**PD 26, para. 5.4**). 34.5

DEFENDANT'S APPLICATION FOR SUMMARY JUDGMENT: NO DEFAULT JUDGMENT

Where a defendant has applied for summary judgment against a claimant, the claimant cannot obtain a default judgment until the summary judgment application has been disposed of (**CPR, r. 12.3(3)(a)**). 34.6

EXCLUDED PROCEEDINGS

Under **CPR, r. 24.3(2)**, an application for summary judgment cannot be brought against the defendant in: 34.7

(a) residential possession proceedings against a mortgagor or a tenant or person holding over whose occupancy is protected by the **Rent Act 1977** or the **Housing Act 1988**; or
(b) Admiralty claims *in rem*.

Until 30 September 2005 the Crown was exempt from summary judgment applications (**Crown Proceedings Act 1947, s. 35**; RSC, ord. 77; CCR, ord. 42). These provisions were repealed with effect from 1 October 2005 (Civil Procedure (Modification of Crown Proceedings Act 1947) Order 2005, SI 2005/2712, art. 8), so the Crown is now treated in the same way as other parties.

Summary judgment will not be granted in a libel claim where there is a material issue of fact between the parties, because such issues must be decided by the jury (**Supreme Court Act 1981, s. 69**; and *Safeway Stores plc v Tate* [2001] QB 1120). However, where the evidence, taken at its highest, is such that no properly directed jury could reach a verdict contended for by one of the parties, summary judgment is available (*Alexander v Arts Council of Wales* [2001] 1 WLR 1840).

In applications against claimants there are no excluded types of proceedings (**CPR, r. 24.3(1)**).

PROCEDURE

The general rules on making interim applications (see **chapter 32**) apply on making an application for summary judgment, with certain refinements. The application is made by application notice, which must be supported by evidence (**CPR, r. 25.3(2)**). The evidence in support is most likely to be contained either in part C of the application notice, or in a separate witness statement. The facts supporting the claim will have been verified by a statement of truth included in the particulars of claim. The evidence in support of an 34.8

application by a claimant will have to state a belief that there is no defence with a reasonable prospect of success. It may be prudent to go further and to give details of the background facts and to exhibit relevant documentation to show there is no reasonable defence. On an application by the defendant there may or may not be a filed defence. If not, clearly the evidence will have to explain why the claim is unlikely to succeed, and will probably have to go into the background in some detail.

Instead of the usual notice period of three clear days which applies to most types of interim application, the notice period in applications for summary judgment is 14 clear days (r. 24.4(3)). The 14-day period of notice may be varied by practice directions (**r. 24.4(4)**), and has been shortened for specific performance claims (see **34.43**).

The respondent must file and serve any evidence in reply at least seven clear days before the hearing (**r. 24.5(1)**). The application notice must inform the respondent of this time limit (**PD 24, para. 2(5)**). If the applicant wishes to respond to the respondent's evidence, the further evidence must be served and filed at least three clear days before the hearing of the application (**r. 24.5(2)**).

In cases where the hearing is fixed by the court on its own initiative, all parties must file and serve their evidence at least seven clear days before the return day, and if they want to respond to their opponents' evidence, that must be done at least three clear days before the return day (**r. 24.5(3)**).

ORDERS AVAILABLE

34.9 **Paragraph 5.1 of PD 24** says that the range of orders available on a summary judgment application include:

(a) giving judgment on the claim;
(b) striking out or dismissal of the claim;
(c) dismissal of the application; and
(d) making a conditional order.

Where the defendant has a defence to only part of the claim the most natural order would be to grant judgment for the part of the claim against which there is no defence, and to dismiss the application as to the balance. Although **CPR, r 24.2**, expressly says that the court can give summary judgment on particular issues, this is most appropriate where resolving the issue or issues will resolve or help to resolve the litigation (*Kent v Griffiths (No. 3)* [2001] QB 36 at p. 51). The court must apply the overriding objective, and may consider that where there are connected issues, some of which should go to trial, summary judgment should be refused on the others as well (*Redevco Properties v Mount Cook Land Ltd* [2002] EWHC 1647 (Ch), LTL 30/7/2002). The court should be slow to entertain an application for summary judgment on certain issues where there is going to be a full trial in any event, particularly where dealing with such an application may delay (because of possible appeals) the final disposal of the claim (*Partco Group Ltd v Wragg* [2002] EWCA Civ 594, [2002] 2 Lloyd's Rep 343, at [27]).

This is not a comprehensive list (note the use of the word 'include' in **PD 24, para. 5.1**), and the court can make other orders, such as allowing the claim to continue to trial on condition that a party pay money into court as security for costs (*Olatawura v Abiloye* [2002] EWCA Civ 998, [2003] 1 WLR 275).

TEST FOR ENTERING SUMMARY JUDGMENT

Rule 24.2 of the CPR provides: **34.10**

> The court may give summary judgment against a claimant or defendant on the whole of a claim or on a particular issue if—
> (a) it considers that—
> (i) that claimant has no real prospect of succeeding on the claim or issue; or
> (ii) that defendant has no real prospect of successfully defending the claim or issue; and
> (b) there is no other compelling reason why the case or issue should be disposed of at a trial.

An application for summary judgment is decided applying the test of whether the respondent has a case with a real prospect of success, which is considered having regard to the overriding objective of dealing with the case justly. This has been said to be consistent with the need for a fair trial under art. 6(1) of the European Convention on Human Rights (*Three Rivers District Council v Bank of England (No. 3)* [2001] UKHL 16, [2003] 2 AC 1). Whether there is a real prospect of success is the same test as that applied in applications to set aside default judgments (see **20.13** and *E. D. and F. Man Liquid Products Ltd v Patel* [2003] EWCA Civ 472, [2003] CPLR 384).

In *Swain v Hillman* [2001] 1 All ER 91 Lord Woolf MR said that the words 'no real prospect of succeeding' did not need any amplification as they spoke for themselves. The word 'real' directed the court to the need to see whether there was a realistic, as opposed to a fanciful, prospect of success. The phrase does not mean 'real and substantial' prospect of success. Nor does it mean that summary judgment will only be granted if the claim or defence is 'bound to be dismissed at trial'.

A claim may be fanciful where it is entirely without substance, or where it is clear beyond question that the statement of case is contradicted by all the documents or other material on which it is based (*Three Rivers District Council v Bank of England (No. 3)*). The judge should have regard to the witness statements and also to the question of whether the case is capable of being supplemented by evidence at trial (*Royal Brompton Hospital NHS Trust v Hammond* [2001] BLR 297). The question of whether there is a real prospect of success is not approached by applying the usual balance of probabilities standard of proof (*Royal Brompton Hospital NHS Trust v Hammond*). Applying a test of whether the claim is arguable will give grounds for appeal (*Sinclair v Chief Constable of West Yorkshire* (2000) LTL 12/12/2000).

In *E. D. and F. Man Liquid Products Ltd v Patel* Potter LJ at [6] regarded the terms 'real prospect' and 'realistic prospect' as interchangeable. Lord Woolf MR in *Swain v Hillman* said that summary judgment applications have to be kept within their proper role. They are not meant to dispense with the need for a trial where there are issues which should be considered at trial. Further, summary judgment hearings should not be mini-trials. They are simply summary hearings to dispose of cases where there is no real prospect of success. Without allowing the application to become a mini-trial, there are occasions when the court has to consider fairly voluminous evidence in order to understand the facts that are in issue (*Miles v ITV Networks Ltd* [2003] EWHC 3134 (Ch), LTL 9/12/2003).

Burden of proof

An important issue on many applications for summary judgment is whether the burden of proof is on the applicant to show the respondent's case has no real prospect of success, or whether the burden of proof rests with the respondent to establish a case with a real prospect of success. In *E. D. and F. Man Liquid Products Ltd v Patel* [2003] EWCA Civ 472, [2003] CPLR 384, Potter LJ said at [9] that the burden of proof is on the applicant to show the respondent's case has no real prospect of success. Strictly this is no more than an *obiter dictum*, because the learned judge was dealing with an application to set aside a default judgment, and was contrasting his view of the burden of proof on the two types of application. Whether Potter LJ's view is correct is open to question. **34.11**

Under the old rules the incidence of the burden of proof was perfectly clear, because RSC, ord. 14, r. 3(1), said in terms: 'Unless . . . the defendant satisfies the court with respect to the claim, or part of the claim, to which the application relates that there is an issue or question in dispute which ought to be tried . . . the court may give such judgment for the plaintiff'.

The present rule, **CPR, r. 24.2**, is not explicit on the burden of proof, saying: 'The court may give summary judgment against a [defendant] . . . if (a) it considers that (ii) that defendant has no real prospect of successfully defending the claim or issue' (and similarly if the application is against the claimant). Lord Woolf 's *Final Report* says, at p. 123, regarding applications for summary judgment:

> The test for making an order would be that the court considered that a party had no realistic prospect of succeeding at trial on the whole case or on a particular issue. A party seeking to resist such an order would have to show more than a merely arguable case; it would have to be one which he had a real prospect of winning.

The wording of PD 24, paras 4.1 and 4.2, when first issued, made it clear that the burden of proof was on the respondent, providing:

> 4.1 Where a claimant applies for judgment on his claim, the court will give that judgment if:
> (1) the claimant has shown a case which, if unanswered, would entitled him to that judgment, and
> (2) the defendant has not shown any reason why the claim should be dealt with at trial.
> 4.2 Where a defendant applies for judgment in his favour on the claimant's claim, the court will give that judgment if either:
> (1) the claimant has failed to show a case which, if unanswered, would entitle him to judgment, or
> (2) the defendant has shown that the claim would be bound to be dismissed at trial.

Thus, under the old para. 4.1(1), a claimant applying for summary judgment had to adduce evidence establishing his claim (but not disproving any purported defence), as is clear from the phrase 'which, if unanswered'.

In *Swain v Hillman* [2001] 1 All ER 91 Lord Woolf MR commented on the revocation of the original paras 4.1 and 4.2 of PD 24 as follows:

> The reason for that deletion is obvious. It was perceived that there was a conflict between paras 4.1 and 4.2 and the provisions of Part 24. The PD was laying down a different standard which indicated that the approach required was one of certainty. The judge could only exercise his power under Part 24 if he was certain or, to read the actual language of the PD, he thought that a claim 'would be bound to be dismissed at trial'. If that was thought to be the effect of the PD, that would be putting the matter incorrectly because that did not give effect to the word 'real' to which I have already referred.

Paragraphs 4.1 and 4.2 were deleted because they imposed, or were perceived to impose, too high a standard of proof on an application for summary judgment. It was not because they imposed the wrong burden of proof. The true burden of proof, it is suggested, is still on the respondent to show a case with a real prospect of success.

Complex claims

34.12 Complex claims, cases relying on complex inferences of fact, and cases with issues involving mixed questions of law and fact where the law is complex are likely to be inappropriate for summary judgment (*Three Rivers District Council v Bank of England (No. 3)* [2001] UKHL 16, [2003] 2 AC 1; *Arkin v Borchard Lines Ltd (No. 2)* (2001) LTL 21/6/2001). The high standard of proof required at trial in fraud claims means that it will be difficult to succeed on a summary judgment application in such a case (*Allied Dunbar Assurance plc v Ireland* [2001] EWCA Civ 1129, LTL 12/6/2001).

If an application for summary judgment involves prolonged serious argument, the court should, as a rule, dismiss it without hearing the argument, unless it harbours doubt about the soundness of the statement of case and is satisfied that granting summary judgment would avoid the need for a trial or would substantially reduce the burden of the trial (*Three Rivers*

District Council v Bank of England (No. 3); *Partco Group Ltd v Wragg* [2002] EWCA Civ 594, [2002] 2 Lloyd's Rep 343, at [28]; *Equitable Life Assurance Society v Ernst and Young* [2003] EWCA Civ 1114, [2003] 2 BCLC 603). Summary judgment is also inappropriate in cases in areas of developing jurisprudence, which should only be decided on the basis of actual findings of fact (*Farah v British Airways plc* (1999) *The Times*, 26 January 2000; *Barrett v Enfield London Borough Council* [2001] 2 AC 550).

Defence on the merits

On an application for summary judgment by a claimant, the defendant may seek to show a defence with a real prospect of success by setting up one or more of the following: **34.13**

(a) a substantive defence, e.g., *volenti non fit injuria*, frustration or illegality;
(b) a point of law destroying the claimant's cause of action;
(c) a denial of the facts supporting the claimant's cause of action;
(d) further facts answering the claimant's cause of action, e.g., an exclusion clause, or that the defendant was an agent rather than a principal.

An example under the old rules was *Mercer v Craven Grain Storage Ltd* [1994] CLC 328. The claimant was a farmer who deposited a quantity of grain with the defendant storage company. Later, the claimant requested redelivery, but the defendant was only able to deliver a small fraction of the grain. The defendant alleged that the claimant had entered into an agreement with a marketing company, and that the missing grain had been withdrawn from the store with the authority of the marketing company. By a bare majority it was held that this defence raised triable legal and factual issues, and leave to defend was given. With the change in the test, this case would now perhaps result in a conditional order being made.

Points of law and construction

Although summary judgment applications should not be allowed to turn into mini-trials, where the case turns on an issue of construction of a term in a contract the court will usually determine the point and give judgment accordingly (*Wootton v Telecommunications UK Ltd* (2000) LTL 4/5/2000). **34.14**

Where a clear-cut issue of law is raised by way of defence in an application for summary judgment, the court should decide it immediately. This is so even if the question is, at first blush, of some complexity and therefore will take some time to argue fully (see Lord Greene MR in *Cow v Casey* [1949] 1 KB 474). Not deciding a case once full argument has been addressed to the court on the issue will result in the case going to trial, where the argument will be rehearsed again, with consequent delay and unnecessary expense. Likewise, where the point at issue is one of the construction of contractual documents, the court will decide the point on the summary judgment application, provided it is relatively straightforward (*Coastal (Bermuda) Ltd v Esso Petroleum Co. Ltd* [1984] 1 Lloyd's Rep 11). In *GMAC Commercial Credit Ltd v Dearden* (2002) LTL 31/5/2002 summary judgment was given to the claimant against four of the defendants, with a conditional order against the fifth defendant. The claim was to enforce personal guarantees given by directors to secure borrowing by their company. It was held that defences of economic duress had no real prospect of success, the claimant having acted in good faith and its conduct not going beyond what was normal and legitimate in commercial arrangements.

However, it is quite a different matter, per Lord Donaldson of Lymington MR in *R. G. Carter Ltd v Clarke* [1990] 1 WLR 578:

> if the issue of law is not decisive of all the issues between the parties or, if decisive of part of the [claimant's] claim or of some of those issues, is of such a character as would not justify its being determined as a preliminary point, because little or no savings in costs would ensue. It is an a fortiori case if the answer to the question of law is any way dependent upon undecided issues of fact.

Summary judgment should also be refused where the point requires protracted argument (*Home and Overseas Insurance Co. Ltd v Mentor Insurance Co. (UK) Ltd* [1990] 1 WLR 153). Summary judgment was refused in *System Control plc v Munro Corporate plc* [1990] BCLC 659, in which it was held that whether the claimants had irrevocably elected to treat a contract as discharged, or whether they could enforce it, was an issue which should be decided at trial. In *I-Way Ltd v World Online Telecom Ltd* [2002] EWCA Civ 413, LTL 8/3/2002, the claimant sued to recover the benefits it alleged were due to it under an oral variation of a written contract. The defendant resisted the claim relying on a clause of the written contract that there was to be no addition or amendment to the contract unless it was in writing and signed by both parties. An application by the defendant for summary judgment against the claimant was dismissed, because there was no direct authority on the issue whether the parties could prevent oral variations of a contract by use of such a clause, and an important point of principle such as the one in issue needed to be tried rather than determined by summary judgment.

Disputes of fact

34.15 Where there are issues of fact, which, if decided in the respondent's favour, would result in judgment for the respondent, it is inappropriate to enter summary judgment, even if there is substantial evidence in support of the applicant's case (*Munn v North West Water Ltd* (2000) LTL 18/7/2000). Primarily the court will consider the written evidence adduced by the parties, and if it discloses a dispute with a real prospect of success, the summary judgment application will be dismissed. However, the court is not always obliged to accept written evidence at face value, and may disregard evidence which is incredible (see **32.14**).

In *Public Trustee v Williams* (2000) LTL 10/2/2000 the claimant sought to recover for a deceased's estate the sum of £74,000 which was received by one of the defendants and used by her to buy a house. The evidence of the recipient filed in response to an application for summary judgment was at its best unclear and at its worst confusing as to where she thought the money had come from. However, there was no clear evidence that the money had come from the estate, and it was held it was not a suitable case for summary judgment. In *Bates v Microstar Ltd* (2000) LTL 4/7/2000 summary judgment had been granted based on a purported contract written on hotel notepaper. There were two other documents purporting to be the contract between the parties, and a number of the terms in the hotel notepaper document were arguably too vague. The judgment was set aside on appeal. In *Mehdi v Bates* (2001) LTL 3/12/2001 the contractual documentation was unclear on the issue of whether the contract had been entered into by the defendant personally or by the defendant's company. It was held that the judge had not been justified in entering summary judgment against the claimant on the basis that it was unlikely that a businessman would have entered into this contract personally.

Claims involving allegations of fraudulent or deceitful misconduct which are not admitted and which are not capable of being substantiated by inference from the documentary or written evidence are inappropriate for summary judgment (*Esprit Telecoms UK Ltd v Fashion Gossip Ltd* (2000) LTL 27/7/2000). Conversely, where a challenge to a fraud claim has no real prospects of success, summary judgment may be appropriate (*Sinclair Investment Holdings SA v Cushnie* (2006) LTL 6/2/2006).

Cases involving disputes over whether employers are vicariously liable for the tortious acts of employees who might not be acting in the course of their employment are fact-sensitive and inappropriate for summary judgment (*Cercato-Gouveia v Kiprianou* [2001] EWCA Civ 1887, LTL 30/11/2001).

Where the applicant has the burden of proving a disputed issue, such as the reasonableness of an exclusion clause under the **Unfair Contract Terms Act 1977**, it will be difficult for the applicant to establish that the respondent has no real prospect of success (see, for example, *Lalji v Post Office Ltd* [2003] EWCA Civ 1873, LTL19/12/2003).

In a proprietary estoppel claim, where the context and meaning of the words used needs to be investigated, summary judgment is inappropriate (*Century (UK) Ltd SA v Clibbery* [2003] EWCA Civ 1374, LTL 17/7/2003). Where there is no arguable evidence on an essential element of the claim (or defence), or where a claimant will be unable to establish any loss flowing from a breach not actionable per se, summary judgment should be entered (*Morshead Mansions Ltd v Langford* [2003] EWHC 2023 (QB), LTL 29/8/2003). In *Shamil Bank of Bahrain EC v Beximco Pharmaceuticals Ltd* [2003] EWHC 2118 (Comm), [2003] 2 All ER (Comm) 849, a defence to a claim by the bank for repayment of moneys lent was that there was an oral agreement suspending payment until a further agreement had been reached. This was dismissed as fanciful, as it made no commercial sense for a bank to enter such an arrangement, because if the parties failed to reach a further agreement the defendants would be released from liability (different issues were raised on the appeal, [2004] EWCA Civ 19, [2004] 1 WLR 1784).

Negligence claims and previous convictions

Although there is nothing in principle preventing a claimant from applying for summary judgment in claims seeking damages for negligence, such cases invariably involve disputed factual issues, so it is rare for a court to find there is no real defence once liability is denied. An exception was *Dummer v Brown* [1953] 1 QB 710, where summary judgment was given against the defendant, a coach driver, who had previously pleaded guilty of dangerous driving in respect of the accident giving rise to the claim. Even if there is a conviction, summary judgment may be refused if there are good reasons for believing the conviction was erroneous (*McCauley v Vine* [1999] 1 WLR 1977). **34.16**

Previous disciplinary proceedings

Adverse findings in disciplinary proceedings against a solicitor may mean the solicitor has no real prospect of success in related proceedings (*Simms v Law Society* [2005] EWCA Civ 849, [2005] ACD 98). **34.17**

Housing Grants, Construction and Regeneration Act 1996 claims

The Housing Grants, Construction and Regeneration Act 1996, part II, provides for the speedy resolution of construction industry disputes. It requires that every written construction contract must contain a right to refer disputes to adjudication under a procedure that complies with s. 108. To the extent that a construction contract does not do this, the adjudication provisions contained in the Scheme for Construction Contracts (England and Wales) Regulations, SI 1998/649, apply (see s. 108(5)). By s. 108(2) an adjudicator is required to reach a decision within 28 days after a referral, or such longer term as may be agreed by the parties. By s. 108(3) the construction contract must provide that the adjudicator's decision is binding until the dispute is finally determined by legal proceedings, by arbitration or agreement. The parties may agree to accept the decision of the adjudicator as finally determining the dispute. **34.18**

Adjudications are intended to be provisional, but binding, decisions (*Macob Civil Engineering Ltd v Morrison Construction Ltd* [1999] BLR 93 at [14]). The policy is 'pay now, argue later' (*RJT Consulting Engineers Ltd v DM Engineering (Northern Ireland) Ltd* [2002] EWCA Civ 270, [2002] 1 WLR 2344). A party with the benefit of an adjudicator's decision may bring enforcement proceedings by issuing a **Part 8** claim form, and then applying for summary judgment. In most cases it is to be expected that summary judgment will be entered in accordance with the policy of the Act.

Summary judgment will be refused, however, if the defendant advances a properly arguable jurisdictional objection, such as a dispute about whether there was a written construction contract between the parties (*Pegram Shopfitters Ltd v Tally Weijl (UK) Ltd* [2003] EWCA Civ 1750, [2004] 1 WLR 2082). A list of nine questions which are relevant where there is a dispute over an adjudicator's jurisdiction was suggested in *McAlpine PPS Pipeline Systems Ltd v Transco plc* [2004]

EWHC 2030 (TCC), [2004] BLR 352. If the defendant has agreed that the adjudicator can rule on the issue of jurisdiction and that he will be bound by the adjudicator's decision, summary judgment will be entered even if the adjudicator is wrong (*Thomas-Fredric's (Construction) Ltd v Wilson* [2003] EWCA Civ 1494, [2004] BLR 23, at [20]). Summary judgment may also be entered if the defendant has not submitted to the adjudicator's jurisdiction, provided the adjudicator's decision is plainly right (*Thomas-Fredric's (Construction) Ltd v Wilson*).

Summary judgment will also be entered where the defendant has not paid the amount due under an architect's certificate, unless the defendant has given an effective notice of intention to withhold payment under s. 111. This is so even if the certificate might be wrong (*Rupert Morgan Building Services (LLC) Ltd v Jervis* [2003] EWCA Civ 1563, [2004] 1 WLR 1867).

Evidence not yet investigated

34.19 Summary judgment was regarded as inappropriate in *Derksen v Pillar* (2002) LTL 17/12/2002 because evidence was still being acquired or investigated and the claim raised complex issues. In *Creative Resins International Ltd v Glasslam Europe Ltd* [2005] EWHC 777 (QB), LTL 11/5/2005, the claimant sued the second defendant (the solicitors acting for the first defendant) in libel based on a letter sent by the solicitors to one of the claimant's customers. The second defendant applied for summary judgment, arguing that the letter was protected by qualified privilege. The first defendant had not at this point waived legal professional privilege in respect of solicitor and client communications leading up to the allegedly libellous letter. The possibility that legal professional privilege might be waived before trial, combined with the complexity surrounding cases raising qualified privilege, meant this was not a suitable case for summary judgment.

Where an issue requires the court to consider conduct over a period of time, it is unlikely that the issue can be disposed of on an application for summary judgment (*Celador Productions Ltd v Melville* [2004] EWHC 2362 (Ch), 28(1) IPD 10). On the other hand, in *Mancini v Telecommunications UK Ltd* [2003] EWHC 211 (Ch), LTL 16/1/2003, the lack of evidence produced by the claimant resulted in the claim being struck out. It was reasonable to expect the claimant to have numerous documents, and to be able to produce witnesses, to explain what had happened in relation to the key issue. The court was not impressed by the explanation, first raised on appeal, that the documents had been destroyed in a flood, and there was no explanation for not adducing witness statements dealing with the facts.

Conduct

34.20 In *Penningtons v Abedi* (1999) LTL 13/8/99 there had been ongoing litigation in which the defendant had advanced a series of defences which had each been shown to be false. An application was made for summary judgment, and it was held that the defendant's conduct of the litigation was such that there was no realistic prospect of her successfully defending the claim.

Contemporaneous documentation

34.21 There are cases where the contemporaneous documentation shows that the respondent will never be able to establish its case at trial, and in those cases, such as *Collins v Union Bank of Switzerland* (2000) LTL 25/5/2000, summary judgment will be entered. In *Abelene Ltd v Cranbrook Finance Inc.* (2000) LTL 25/8/2000 it was held that although it was open to a court to accept documents produced at the last moment by a respondent to an application for summary judgment, if there was no explanation as to the circumstances in which the documents were executed or why they were not produced at the proper time, it would also be open to the court to be sufficiently suspicious of their genuineness to disregard them. Summary judgment was entered in *Musical Fidelity Ltd v Vickers* [2002] EWCA Civ 1989, LTL 2/12/2002, where the contents of the defendant's website established a clear case of infringement of the claimant's trade mark. Likewise, in *National Westminster plc v Szirtes* (2003) LTL 27/6/2003, the cumulative effect of all the evidence, and in particular the correspondence between the parties, strained the credibility of the defendants' evidence that they were unaware of the guarantees relied upon by the bank to such an extent that they had no real prospect of success. A slightly different formulation was applied in *Hussain v Cuddy Woods and Cochrane* [2001] Lloyd's Rep PN 134, where it was said in a professional negligence claim against a barrister that, from a consideration of the voluminous documentation available, it was 'difficult to see how the claimant could establish' his claim, and summary judgment was entered in favour of the defendant.

Amendment

There are many cases where the defective nature of one side's statement of case becomes clear at the hearing of an application for summary judgment. If the defect is one of how the case is put rather than of substance, the court has a wide power to allow an amendment to correct the problem, which can be exercised at the hearing (*Stewart v Engel* [2000] 1 WLR 2268). **34.22**

ADMISSIONS

In *E. D. and F. Man Liquid Products Ltd v Patel* [2003] EWCA Civ 472, [2003] CPLR 384, a defence which might have had a real prospect of success was destroyed by clear, written admissions made by the defendant. Likewise, in *Soir Contracting and General Trading Co. v Desai* (2006) LTL 14/2/2006, despite a lack of documentary evidence substantiating the claim, and an allegation that the defendant was the victim of a dishonest fabrication, clear, signed acknowledgments of the debt by the defendant meant the defence had no real prospect of success. In *Equant SAS v Ives* [2002] EWHC 1992 (Ch), LTL 4/10/2002, the defendant was permitted to resile from an admission in the defence, and on the amended case there were disputes of fact which resulted in summary judgment being refused. A defendant seeking to avoid summary judgment being entered on an admission has to issue an application for permission to amend, otherwise the court is entitled to enter judgment on the unamended statement of case (*Loveridge v Healey* [2004] EWCA Civ 173, *The Times*, 27 February 2004). **34.23**

Whether an apparent admission is binding on a party and such as to justify the entry of summary judgment is considered further at **34.25** to **34.29**.

Whether the admission binds the other party

In the case of parties which are artificial bodies, such as registered companies, an issue arises as to whether the individual said to have made the admission was authorised in fact or in law to bind the party in question in this way. Much depends on the seniority of the individual within the body in question, and on the nature of the relationship between the individual and that body. So, a limited company's directors or solicitor would have authority to bind it when making an admission, whereas an ordinary employee would not in the absence of express authority from the directors. Questions of actual, apparent or ostensible and usual authority of agents may arise, for which see the general works on agency. **34.24**

Under the general law of evidence, binding admissions can sometimes be made by persons connected with a party. Typical examples are admissions made by partners (see the Partnership Act 1890, s. 15), predecessors in title and referees.

Formal and informal admissions

Admissions may be formal or informal. As discussed in **chapters** 17, 26 and 27, the statements of case, and in particular the defence and any reply, may well contain admissions. These reduce the area of dispute, and can be very helpful in summary judgment applications. Admissions in statements of case are one example of formal admissions, which have the effect of establishing the facts admitted without the need to call evidence, and which can only **34.25** be withdrawn with the permission of the court. Other examples of formal admissions are admissions made and recorded at a case management conference or pre-trial review, admissions made in reply to a notice to admit facts (see **47.8**) and admissions made by counsel at trial (for which see *Worldwide Corporation Ltd v Marconi Communications Ltd* (1999) *The Times*, 7 July 1999).

Informal admissions, on the other hand, are merely items of evidence and may be disproved or explained away by other evidence at trial. Informal admissions may be oral statements made by a party or person connected to a party which are at least partially adverse to that party's case, or may be made in correspondence. Admissions made in statements of case in other proceedings, or by witnesses called by a party in other proceedings, are not binding as informal admissions in the present proceedings (*British Thomson-Houston Co. Ltd v British Insulated and Helsby Cables Ltd* [1924] 2 Ch 160). Rather inconsistently, it was held in the old case of *Brickell v Hulse* (1837) 7 Ad & El 454 that reliance on written evidence in earlier proceedings can amount to an informal admission of anything contained in that evidence. Possibly this can be explained on the basis that by relying on written evidence the party is to be taken as adopting it, whereas the details of oral testimony are uncertain until the evidence has been called, and that statements of case are delivered for the purposes of the present litigation only. Admissions made in answers to requests for further information in the present action are probably formal admissions because of the need to include a statement of truth.

Permission to withdraw admissions

34.26 It is provided by **CPR, r. 14.1(5)**, that the court may allow a party to amend or withdraw an admission. It was held in *Sowerby v Charlton* [2005] EWCA Civ 1610, [2006] 1 WLR 568, that **r. 14.1(5)** does not apply to admissions made before proceedings. This means that court permission is not required if a party wishes to withdraw such an admission. It remains to be seen whether this undermines the **Pre-action Protocol for Personal Injury Claims, para. 3.9**, which provides that where liability is admitted, the presumption is that the defendant is bound by the admission for all claims with a total value of up to £15,000. *Sowerby v Charlton* concerned a serious injury worth considerably more than that figure.

The result is that permission under **CPR, r. 14.1(5)**, is required only where the defendant seeks to withdraw an admission made after proceedings were issued. The Court of Appeal in *Sowerby v Charlton* said that the pre-CPR authorities on withdrawing such admissions, and in particular *Gale v Superdrug Stores plc* [1996] 1 WLR 1089, are to be approached with caution. Brooke LJ endorsed the following guidance given by Sumner J in *Basildon and Thurrock University NHS Trust v Braybrook* (2004) LTL 7/1/2005 on exercising the discretion under **r. 14.1(5)**:

(a) in exercising its discretion, the court must consider all the circumstances of the case and seek to give effect to the overriding objective;
(b) among the factors to be considered are:
  (i) the reasons and justification for the application, which must be made in good faith;
  (ii) the balance of prejudice to the parties;
  (iii) whether any party had been the author of any prejudice he might suffer;
  (iv) the prospects of success of any issue arising from the withdrawal of the admission;
  (v) the public interest in avoiding, where possible, satellite litigation, disproportionate use of court resources, and the impact of any strategic manoeuvring;
(c) the nearer any application is to a final hearing the less chance of success it will have, even if the party making the application can establish clear prejudice. This factor might be decisive if the application is made shortly before the hearing.

As Brooke LJ said in *Sowerby v Charlton*, the exercise of any discretion depends on the facts of the individual case. Permission may be granted, for example, where an admission was made by mistake (*Hamilton v Hertfordshire County Council* [2003] EWHC 3018 (QB), LTL 19/12/2003).

Admissions made without knowledge and as to law

An 'admission' made without knowledge of the facts said to have been admitted has little if any evidential value (see *Comptroller of Customs v Western Lectric Co. Ltd* [1966] AC 367). Also, the 'admission' must be one of fact, not law. In *Ashmore v Corporation of Lloyd's* [1992] 1 WLR 446 the House of Lords held that statements made by members of the Committee of Lloyd's said to be admissions that the defendants owed a duty of care to 'names' (members of underwriting syndicates) concerned a question of law and so the statements were neither relevant nor admissible. 34.27

Obtaining judgment on admissions

There is rarely any doubt about formal admissions, although occasionally points of construction are taken in respect of admissions said to have been made in statements of case. Informal admissions, on the other hand, need to be proved. In *Re Beeny* [1894] 1 Ch 499 judgment was entered on the basis of informal oral admissions made by the defendant to the claimant's solicitor. The admissions were proved by an affidavit sworn by the solicitor, the court having to decide whether the admissions were sufficiently proved and sufficiently clear. As North J said in this case: 34.28

> No doubt, if the alleged admission is only verbal, there is more difficulty in treating it as sufficient, if there be any dispute as to the fact of its having been made.

CONDITIONAL ORDERS

PD 24, para. 4, provides that where it appears to the court possible that a claim or defence may succeed but improbable that it will do so, the court may make a conditional order. **Paragraph 5.2** provides that a conditional order is an order which requires a party: 34.29

(a) to pay a sum of money into court, or
(b) to take a specified step in relation to his claim or defence, as the case may be,

and which provides that that party's claim will be dismissed or his statement of case will be struck out if he does not comply.

Conditional orders are appropriate for cases in the grey area between granting judgment and dismissing the application. In *Homebase Ltd v LSS Services Ltd* (2004) LTL 28/6/2004, the claimant made a claim against the defendant seeking five months' licence fees for occupying a site. The defendant filed a witness statement to the effect that the claimant had orally agreed that the defendant need pay nothing until the claimant had obtained consent from its landlord to assign the land to the defendant. The claimant denied there was any such agreement. Despite the absence of contemporaneous documents, it could not be said that the defendant's version of events was incredible. Entering summary judgment was therefore inappropriate, but because of the justifiable doubts about the defendant's version, a conditional order was made requiring the whole sum claimed to be paid into court.

Amount to be paid in

If the court decides to make the respondent to the application pay money into court under a conditional order, it must decide how much should be paid in. The starting point has traditionally been the full amount of the claim. However, the court has a discretion, which it will exercise in accordance with the overriding objective. Obviously, the more uncertain the defence, the more likely it is that the court will order the full amount to be paid in. Another factor is the defendant's ability to pay. Under the old rules (and similar principles are applied under the CPR, see *Sweetman v Shepherd* (2000) *The Times*, 29 March 2000), Lord Diplock in *M. V. Yorke Motors v Edwards* [1982] 1 WLR 444 endorsed the following principles: 34.30

(a) Defendants seeking to limit a financial condition must make full and frank disclosure of their finances. This is done on affidavit or witness statement. It is common for defendants who realise that a conditional order may be made to produce such written evidence in advance of the summary judgment hearing, and to disclose it to the claimant on the claimant undertaking not to refer to it unless a conditional order is made.

(b) Reliance on a legal aid certificate as evidence of impecuniosity is not enough.

(c) The test is whether it will be impossible for the defendant to comply with the financial condition, as opposed to merely finding it difficult. An impossible condition is tantamount to entering judgment.

M. V. Yorke Motors were suing Mr Edwards for breach of warranty of title in relation to a contract for the sale of a car for £23,520. Conditional leave to defend was given, because the court was sceptical about his defence that he was only acting as the agent for a foreign buyer. By the time of the hearing Mr Edwards was unemployed, living with his father, and in receipt of legal aid with a nil contribution. The House of Lords substituted a condition of bringing £3,000 into court.

A claimant who intends to invite the court to make a conditional order if summary judgment is not granted should give the defendant notice of that intention in advance of the hearing. If this is not done, the judge should not make such an order without giving the defendant an opportunity to be heard (and adduce evidence) on questions such as whether the defendant has the means to pay the amount contemplated (*Anglo-Eastern Trust Ltd v Kermanshahchi* [2002] EWCA Civ 198, LTL 22/2/2002).

Where money is paid into court in compliance with a conditional order, the claimant is a secured creditor for that amount in the event of the defendant's bankruptcy (*Re Ford* [1900] 2 QB 211).

CROSS-CLAIMS

34.31 Cross-claims fall into three categories. Where the only answer to the claim is a cross-claim, the nature and effect of the three types are as follows:

(a) Cross-claims unconnected with the claim. Here, summary judgment should be entered. An example is *Rotheram v Priest* (1879) 41 LT 558, where the claimant claimed arrears of rent, and the defendant counterclaimed in libel. It was held that the counterclaim was totally foreign to the claim, so summary judgment was given to the claimant. The result would be the same under the CPR.

(b) Counterclaims linked to the claim. The appropriate order used to be for judgment subject to a stay of execution pending trial of the counterclaim. In *Drake and Fletcher Ltd v Batchelor* (1986) 130 SJ 285 Sir Neil Lawson said that in considering whether to grant a stay of execution, 'The question is whether the two contracts are so closely linked that it would be fair and equitable to deprive the [claimant] of the fruits of its judgment until resolution of the counterclaim'. The judge said there were three matters which needed to be considered:

   (i) The degree of connection between the claim and the counterclaim.

   (ii) The strength of the counterclaim. The weaker it was, the weaker the case for granting a stay.

   (iii) The claimant's ability to satisfy any judgment on the counterclaim. Any doubt on this matter strengthened the case for granting a stay.

   There is some doubt about how cases where the only matter raised by the defendant is a connected counterclaim should be dealt with under the CPR. There is no longer any equivalent to the former RSC, ord. 14, r. 3(2), which provided for a stay of execution in summary judgment applications where there was a connected counterclaim. Early drafts of the CPR had a directly equivalent provision, and the probable consequence of removing it from the final version of the rules is that the court should simply enter judgment for the claimant. If this is correct, there is no longer any practical difference between this type of counterclaim and totally unconnected cross-claims.

(c) Set-offs. Where a counterclaim amounts to a set-off it is a defence to the claim and any summary judgment application should be dismissed, provided the value of the set-off is at least equal to the value of the claim. Where a set-off is not worth as much as the claim, the appropriate order is for summary judgment for the undisputed balance. The nature of set-offs is considered in **34.31**.

Set-offs

The following are established set-off situations: **34.32**

(a) Mutual debts. By virtue of the 18th-century Statutes of Set-off, mutual debts owed between the claimant and the defendant can be set off against each other. There is no need for the transactions giving rise to the debts to be connected other than through the parties. They need not be debts, strictly so-called, but may sound in damages provided they are capable of being ascertained with precision at the time of the application (*Morley v Inglis* (1837) 4 Bing NC 58, applied in *Axel Johnson Petroleum AB v MG Mineral Group AG* [1992] 1 WLR 270). A former partner was held in *Hurst v Bennett* [2001] 2 BCLC 290 to be unable to set off claims for money allegedly owed to him on the taking of partnership accounts against the claim of certain of the former partners to be indemnified against expenses they had incurred on the ground of lack of mutuality.

(b) Sale of goods. By virtue of the **Sale of Goods Act 1979, s. 53(1)**, a buyer may set off counterclaims for breach of the statutory implied conditions about satisfactory quality, fitness for purpose and correspondence to description against a claim by the seller for the price.

(c) On a claim for the price of services, for example, where a builder is suing for the price of building work done, the defendant can set off a counterclaim for damages for poor workmanship in respect of the contract the claimant is suing on (*Basten v Butler* (1806) 7 East 479).

(d) Arrears of rent. Where a landlord brings a claim for arrears of rent, the tenant is allowed to set off a counterclaim for damages against the landlord for breach of a covenant in the lease in respect of which the landlord is claiming (*British Anzani (Felixstowe) Ltd v International Marine Management (UK) Ltd* [1980] QB 137, not following *Hart v Rogers* [1916] 1 KB 646, confirmed by *Agyeman v Boadi* (1996) 28 HLR 558). A tenant does not have a similar right of set-off in respect of a counterclaim for breach of repairing obligations against a claim for service charges as against a manager appointed by the court under the Landlord and Tenant Act 1987, s. 24(1) (*Taylor v Blaquiere* [2002] EWCA Civ 1633, *The Times*, 21 November 2002), nor where the tenant's failure to pay has the intended consequence that the landlord will be unable to meet the repairing covenant (*Bluestorm Ltd v Portvale Holdings Ltd* [2004] EWCA Civ 289, (2004) 22 EG 142).

(e) Equitable set-off. Although it is clear that an equitable set-off is a defence, and hence is a defence to a claim, it is difficult to be precise about the ambit of the doctrine. Nevertheless, 'One thing is clear — there must be some equity, some ground for equitable intervention, beyond the mere existence of a cross-claim' (per Lord Wilberforce in *Aries Tanker Corporation v Total Transport Ltd* [1977] 1 WLR 185). It is not necessary that the claim and cross-claim arise out of the same transaction, but there must be an 'inseparable connection' between them (*Bim Kemi AB v Blackburn Chemicals Ltd* [2001] EWCA Civ 457, [2001] 2 Lloyd's Rep 93). Perhaps the leading case is *Hanak v Green* [1958] 2 QB 9, where the claimant sued her builder for breach of contract for failing to complete certain building works at her home. The defendant sought to set off counterclaims for a *quantum meruit* for extra work done outside the original contract, for damages for loss sustained through the claimant's refusal to admit his workmen, and for damages for trespass to his tools. It was held that all three cross-claims were equitable set-offs, because the courts of equity before the Judicature Acts would have required the claimant to take the cross-claims into account before insisting on her own claim. Broadly, what is required is a sufficient degree of connection between the two transactions such that the one should not be enforced without taking the other into account (*Dole Dried Fruit and Nut Co. v Trustin Kerwood Ltd* [1990] 2 Lloyd's Rep 309). It does not matter whether or not either or both claims are unliquidated (*Axel Johnson Petroleum AB v MG Mineral Group AG* [1992] 1 WLR 270). Overpayments of rent can be set off against claims for rent as an equitable set-off (*Fuller v Happy Shopper Markets Ltd* [2001] 1 WLR 1681).

Mutual debts amount to set-offs whether or not the relevant transactions are connected, but they must be liquidated. Set-offs in categories (b) to (d) above involve liquidated claims and unliquidated cross-claims arising from the same transaction. Equitable set-offs can arise where both the claim and the cross-claim are unliquidated, but there must be a sufficient connection between the two.

34.33 **Parties to set-off** Although set-offs usually arise between the immediate parties to a transaction, this is not always the case. A defendant who has guaranteed payment of a debt owed to the claimant by a principal debtor can rely on set-offs and cross-claims available to the debtor. This principle extends to certain types of bonds entered into in building contracts (whereby the party giving the bond promises to pay a specified sum to the claimant if one of the contractors fails to perform) provided the bond is construed as a guarantee, see *Trafalgar House Construction (Regions) Ltd v General Surety and Guarantee Co. Ltd* [1996] AC 199.

Unliquidated damages claims which can be set off as between the original parties can also be set off against an assignee (*Hanak v Green* [1958] 2 QB 9), because an assignee of a chose in action takes subject to all rights of set-off available against the assignor (*Roxburghe v Cox* (1881) 17 ChD 520). A tenant is therefore entitled to set off any damages for disrepair due from the original landlord against a claim for arrears of rent brought by the landlord's assignee (*Smith v Muscat* [2003] EWCA Civ 962, *The Times*, 12 August 2003).

34.34 **Excluding rights of set-off** It is open to the parties to a contract to exclude any right to set-off by an express term to that effect (*Hong Kong and Shanghai Banking Corporation v Kloeckner & Co. AG* [1990] 2 QB 514), but it is possible that such a term may be unreasonable and rendered ineffective by virtue of the **Unfair Contract Terms Act 1977**, as happened in *Stewart Gill Ltd v Horatio Myer and Co. Ltd* [1992] QB 600.

The cheque rule

34.35 Cheques are one form of bill of exchange. Where goods or services are paid for by cheque, two contracts are entered into by the parties. The first contract is the underlying contract for the sale of goods or for the provision of services. The second contract is contained in the cheque, whereby the drawer of the cheque undertakes to pay the payee the sum stated. If a cheque is dishonoured, the seller has the option of suing on the underlying contract or on the cheque. If the seller sues on the underlying contract, the buyer is entitled to rely on any set-off that may be available in respect of that contract by way of defence to an application for summary judgment. However, if the seller sues on the cheque, the buyer is only permitted to raise defences relating to the cheque itself. The reason probably stems from the unconditional nature of a bill of exchange, as provided by the Bills of Exchange Act 1882, s. 3(1). As Lord Wilberforce said in *Nova (Jersey) Knit Ltd v Kammgarn Spinnerei GmbH* [1977] 1 WLR 713, bills of exchange 'are taken as equivalent to deferred instalments of cash. Therefore English law does not allow cross-claims or defences to be made.' The rule is regarded as being of considerable importance to the business community, and the courts will not 'whittle away [the] rule of practice by introducing unnecessary exceptions to it under influence of sympathy-evoking stories' (per Sachs LJ in *Cebora SNC v SIP (Industrial Products) Ltd* [1976] 1 Lloyd's Rep 271). It is only in exceptional circumstances that the court will allow a stay of execution when entering summary judgment for non-payment of a cheque. The fact the claimant is a company in administration is not an exceptional circumstance (*Isovel Contracts Ltd v ABB Building Technologies Ltd* [2002] 1 BCLC 390).

The cheque rule applies to:

(a) cheques and bills of exchange;
(b) direct debits (*Esso Petroleum Co. Ltd v Milton* [1997] 1 WLR 938);
(c) letters of credit (*SAFA Ltd v Banque du Caire* [2000] 2 All ER (Comm) 567); and
(d) performance bonds (*Solo Industries UK Ltd v Canara Bank* [2001] 1 WLR 1800).

The cheque rule does not apply in the context of statutory demands (*Hofer v Strawson* [1999] 2 BCLC 336, a case which turns on the wording of the Insolvency Rules 1986 (SI 1986/1925), r. 6.5(4)).

There are some exceptional cases where summary judgment will not be given in a claim on a bill of exchange (see **34.38** to **34.40**). Before looking at these it is necessary to consider the nature of the claimant's title to the bill of exchange.

Types of holder of a bill of exchange Under the Bills of Exchange Act 1882 there are four types of holder of a bill of exchange. A mere holder is a person in possession of the bill. Although a mere holder can sue on the bill and give a valid discharge (s. 38), any claim is prone to be defeated for want of consideration. A holder for value is a person in possession of a bill who has given consideration sufficient to support a simple contract, or who derives title directly or indirectly from a previous holder who gave value for the bill (s. 27). A holder for value cannot be defeated on the ground of want of consideration. A holder in due course is broadly a holder of a complete and regular bill who gave value for it in good faith without notice of any defect in the title of the person who negotiated it (s. 29). A holder in due course obtains title to the bill free from equities and defects in the title of the transferor. The fourth type of holder is one who derives title through a holder in due course, and who broadly has all the rights of a holder in due course (s. 29(3)). **34.36**

An application for summary judgment by a mere holder will always be defeated by a plea of want of consideration, whereas an application by a holder in due course should always succeed as such a holder takes free of equities. If the claimant's title as a holder in due course is challenged by the defendant, judgment will only be given for the claimant if the claim to be a bona fide holder for value is supported by unchallenged or unchallengeable contemporary documents (*Bank für Gemeinwirtschaft AG v City of London Garages Ltd* [1971] 1 WLR 149). Holders for value are the most problematic category. They are also the most numerous, given that an immediate party to a bill cannot be a holder in due course (*R. E. Jones Ltd v Waring and Gillow Ltd* [1926] AC 670).

Fraud, duress and illegality To amount to a defence against a holder for value, an allegation of fraud, duress or illegality must be supported by evidence. A mere allegation in the defendant's written evidence is insufficient (*Bank für Gemeinwirtschaft AG v City of London Garages Ltd* [1971] 1 WLR 149). Such a defence will not, however, avail against a holder in due course (see the Bills of Exchange Act 1882, s. 30(2)). **34.37**

No consideration As explained in **34.35**, there will be a defence where the claimant is a mere holder who has given no consideration for the bill sued on. A total failure of consideration arises where a buyer lawfully rejects goods sold, the buyer being entitled to recover the price from the seller. Again summary judgment should be refused. Likewise, a liquidated partial failure of consideration is a defence *pro tanto* (*Thoni GmbH & Co. KG v RTP Equipment Ltd* [1979] 2 Lloyd's Rep 282). In *Isovel Contracts Ltd v ABB Building Technologies Ltd* [2002] 1 BCLC 390 the defendant countermanded a cheque given to a subcontractor in payment of the sum due under an interim certificate in a building project. The certificate had been issued by the main contractor, and, before payment of the cheque, had been shown to be wrong, because later certificates showed no money at all was due at the time the cheque **34.38**

was given. The subcontract provided that in this event any overpayment would be deducted from the amounts payable under subsequent interim certificates. It was held that in these circumstances the defendant could not rely on failure of consideration as a defence to an application for summary judgment.

34.39 **Misrepresentation** In *Clovertogs Ltd v Jean Scenes Ltd* [1982] Com LR 88 the Court of Appeal held that an allegation that the claimant had procured two cheques by misrepresentation amounted to a defence in an application for summary judgment. This decision was described as surprising in *Famous Ltd v Ge Im Ex Italia SRL* (1987) *The Times*, 3 August 1987, and should be regarded as wrongly decided as it is inconsistent with other cases on bills of exchange. Following *SAFA Ltd v Banque du Caire* [2000] 2 All ER (Comm) 567 and *Solo Industries UK Ltd v Canara Bank* [2001] 1 WLR 1800, a distinction needs to be drawn between:

(a) Cases where there is a misrepresentation by a beneficiary which was made directly to induce the execution of the bill of exchange (or other payment obligation covered by the cheque rule). In such cases, provided there is a real prospect of establishing the misrepresentation, summary judgment on the cheque (or other payment obligation) should be refused.

(b) Cases where an allegation of misrepresentation is in reality an allegation relating to the underlying contract of services or sale on which the payment obligation is based. In these cases summary judgment should be entered on the cheque (or other payment obligation), with no stay of execution. The courts need to be particularly astute in ensuring the cheque rule is not diluted by treating cases in this category as ones affecting the cheque or other payment obligation.

International trade

34.40 Irrevocable letters of credit are treated as cash and must be honoured. If the bank refuses to honour such a transaction, the court will grant summary judgment to the claimant (*Power Curber International Ltd v National Bank of Kuwait SAK* [1981] 1 WLR 1233). Summary judgment will also be given on a claim for freight even if there is a cross-claim relating to the cargo (*Aries Tanker Corporation v Total Transport Ltd* [1977] 1 WLR 185).

SOME OTHER REASON FOR A TRIAL

34.41 Summary judgment will be refused if there is some other compelling reason why the case should be disposed of at a trial (**CPR, r. 24.2(b)**). An assertion that pleading a defence would infringe the defendant's privilege against self-incrimination does not amount to a compelling reason for a trial, nor for staying or adjourning a summary judgment application (*Versailles Trade Finance Ltd v Clough* [2001] EWCA Civ 1509, [2002] CP Rep 8). The privilege does not amount to a defence in civil proceedings, nor does it provide a right not to plead a defence. It does not, therefore, provide any basis for resisting an application for summary judgment (although the defendant in *Versailles Trade Finance Ltd v Clough* was allowed 14 days to file a full defence). Seeking an adjournment to negotiate with the claimant was not regarded as a compelling reason in *Phonographic Performance Ltd v Planet Ice (Peterborough) Ltd* [2004] EWHC 486 (Ch), LTL 2/2/2004. Reasons for going to trial include:

(a) The respondent is unable to contact a material witness who may provide material for a defence.

(b) The case is highly complicated such that judgment should only be given after mature consideration at trial.

(c) The facts are wholly within the applicant's hands. In such a case it may be unjust to enter judgment without giving the respondent an opportunity of establishing a defence in the light of disclosure or after serving a request for further information (*Harrison v Bottenheim* (1878) 26 WR 362). However, summary judgment will not necessarily be refused in cases where the evidence for any possible defence could only lie with the applicant if there is nothing devious or artificial in the claim *State Trading Corporation of India v Doyle Carriers Inc.* [1991] 2 Lloyd's Rep 55).

(d) The applicant has acted harshly or unconscionably, or the facts disclose a suspicion of dishonesty or deviousness on the part of the applicant such that judgment should only be obtained in the light of publicity at trial. An example is *Miles v Bull* [1969] 1 QB 258, where possession proceedings had the appearance of a device to evict the defendant.

DIRECTIONS ON SUMMARY JUDGMENT HEARING

If a summary judgment application is dismissed or otherwise fails finally to dispose of the claim, the court will give case management directions for the future conduct of the case (**PD 24, para. 10**), which may include directions for filing and service of a defence (**CPR, r. 24.6**), and may dispense with allocation questionnaires and allocate the case to a case management track. **34.42**

SPECIFIC PERFORMANCE, RESCISSION AND FORFEITURE IN PROPERTY CASES

An even speedier process for obtaining summary judgment is available by virtue of **PD 24, para.** 7, in claims for specific performance and similar claims arising out of the sale, purchase, exchange, mortgage or charge of any property, or for the grant or assignment of a lease or tenancy of any property. Specific performance as a remedy requires an exceptional case (*Cooperative Insurance Society Ltd v Argyll Stores (Holdings) Ltd* [1998] AC 1), and the same applies on an application for summary judgment. The judge is not entitled to enter into a mini-trial on an application for summary judgment, and it is wrong to attempt to resolve disputes of fact on such an application on the balance of probabilities (*North East Lincolnshire Borough Council v Millenium Park (Grimsby) Ltd* [2002] EWCA Civ 1719, *The Times*, 31 October 2002). Summary judgment was not appropriate in *Greenacre Properties Ltd v Tower Hamlets London Borough Council* (2002) LTL 24/7/2002 where it was arguable that the sale of land was beyond the council's power as it had not obtained ministerial consent. **34.43**

Where there is no defence, summary judgment can be sought at any time after the claim is served, rather than having to wait until after acknowledgment or defence, and the application can be made even in the absence of particulars of claim. The application notice, evidence in support and a draft order must be served no less than four clear days before the hearing.

SUMMARY ORDERS FOR ACCOUNTS AND INQUIRIES

By **CPR, r. 25.1(1)(o)**, the court may make an interim order directing accounts to be taken or inquiries to be made. The application notice seeking such an order should ask: **34.44**

(a) for specified accounts to be taken or specified inquiries to be made;
(b) for directions for the taking of the account or for making the inquiries; and
(c) for payment of the amount found to be due on taking the accounts.

Written evidence is not always required in support, but if the matter is at all contentious such evidence should be filed and served with the application. The court may refuse to make the order if there is a preliminary question that ought to be tried, such as whether the defendant is under a duty to account.

The practice on taking accounts and conducting inquiries is dealt with by **PD 40**. When making an order for accounts and inquiries the court may also at the same time or later give directions as to how the account is to be taken or the inquiry conducted (**PD 40, para.** 1.1). Among the directions that may be made are the following:

(a) that the relevant books of account shall be evidence of their contents, subject to the parties having the right to make objections (**para.** 1.2);
(b) that an accounting party must make out his account and verify it by exhibiting it to an affidavit or witness statement (**para.** 2(1)); and
(c) that, if appropriate, and at any stage in the proceedings, the parties must serve points of claim and points of defence (**para.** 5).

A party alleging that an account drawn by an accounting party is inaccurate (or making similar allegations) must give written notice of the objections to the accounting party (**para.** 3.1). These objections must give full particulars, specify the grounds on which it is alleged the account is inaccurate, and be verified by a statement of truth (or exhibited to an affidavit or witness statement).

Unless the court orders otherwise, accounts and inquiries are conducted by a master or district judge (para. 9). Detailed provisions dealing with inquiries into estates, trusts and for beneficiaries and next of kin can be found in paras 10 to 15.

SUMMARY DETERMINATION OF CONSTRUCTION OF WILLS

34.45 The High Court may make an order authorising trustees or personal representatives to act in reliance on an opinion of counsel of 10 years' call on the construction of a will or trust (Administration of Justice Act 1985, s. 48). Applications under s. 48 are made in the Chancery Division without notice supported by written evidence stating the names of all persons who may be affected by the order sought; all admissible surrounding circumstances; counsel's call and experience; the value of the fund; and details of any known dispute. Instructions to counsel, counsel's opinion, and draft minutes of the order sought must be exhibited to the evidence in support. The papers are considered by a judge without hearing argument, who will make the order sought if that order is appropriate and if there appears to be no tenable argument contrary to counsel's opinion.

Chapter 35 Possession Claims against Trespassers

INTRODUCTION

Machinery for obtaining possession orders without undue delay against trespassers and similar categories of unauthorised occupiers is provided by **CPR, Part 55**. Landowners seeking possession against squatters frequently do not know the identity of those on their land. One of the main objects of the rules governing claims against trespassers is to avoid the need for the claimant to investigate the identities of the people in unauthorised occupation, and to allow possession orders to be made even against 'persons unknown'. Where the summary procedure against trespassers is not available, ordinary possession proceedings (see **35.14**) should be used. **35.1**

POLICE

There are occasions when trespassers enter on to land and refuse to leave. A person entitled to possession who attempts to turn trespassers off the land without the sanction of a court order risks a breach of the peace and may incur civil or criminal liability for doing so. A court order is not needed, however, if the person entitled to the land can make use of the Criminal Law Act 1977, s. 7, as substituted by the Criminal Justice and Public Order Act 1994, s. 73. This makes it an offence for any person who is on premises as a trespasser to fail to leave on being required to do so by the residential occupier or a protected occupier. A constable in uniform may arrest such a trespasser without a warrant. The section only applies to residential property, and not to commercial property or open land. **35.2**

PROCEDURE ON POSSESSION CLAIMS AGAINST TRESPASSERS

Definition

Possession claims against trespassers are claims for the recovery of land which is alleged to be occupied by persons who entered or remained on the land without the consent of a person entitled to possession of the land (**CPR, r. 55.1(b)**). They do not include claims against tenants or sub-tenants, whether the defendant's tenancy has terminated or not. These claims can include claims against licensees who remain in occupation after the termination of their licences. **35.3**

In addition to the obvious situation of the owner in fee simple in possession claiming against a squatter, the summary procedure against trespassers may be used:

(a) By the owner of the premises against a person who had gone into possession as a licensee, but whose licence has expired (*Greater London Council v Jenkins* [1975] 1 WLR 155). This also applies where the occupant is a former employee whose right to remain was terminated on dismissal, even where the employee has applied to an employment tribunal for reinstatement if the employer has expressed an intention not to reinstate in any event (*Whitbread West Pennines Ltd v Reedy* [1988] ICR 807).

(b) By a tenant of premises against a person who, while the tenant was absent, was let into occupation with the consent of the landlord (*Borg v Rogers* (1981) 132 NLJ 134).

(c) By a licensee who was not in occupation of the land against a trespasser where possession was necessary to give effect to the licensee's contractual rights of occupation (*Manchester Airport plc v Dutton* [2000] QB 133). The land in this case was owned by the National Trust, and the airport was given a licence in order to fell some trees for purposes connected with the construction of a second runway. The trespassers were protesters. It was held that an order for possession would not interfere with the prior rights of the National Trust.

Situations not amounting to claims against trespassers

35.4 The summary procedure in claims against trespassers cannot be used against a tenant or sub-tenant or a former tenant or sub-tenant holding over at the end of the tenancy (see **CPR, r. 55.1(b)**). In addition, the following situations have been considered by the courts:

(a) Where the defendant was allowed into the premises by a tenant, the landlord was held not to be entitled to use the summary procedure unless the tenancy had been determined or surrendered (*Auto Finance Ltd v Pugh* (unreported, 10 June 1985)).

(b) A number of cases have considered claims brought by councils which may be in breach of statutory duty to provide accommodation for the defendants. It has been held that the fact that the council is in breach of its statutory duty, and that the breach has caused the presence of the defendants on the council's land, does not by itself provide the defendants with any defence (*Southwark London Borough Council v Williams* [1971] Ch 734). However, if the decision to use the summary procedure against trespassers is void on the ground of unreasonableness in the *Wednesbury* sense (see *Associated Provincial Picture Houses Ltd v Wednesbury Corporation* [1948] 1 KB 223), then the defendants can seek to have the possession proceedings struck out (*Bristol District Council v Clark* [1975] 1 WLR 1443). In *Cannock Chase District Council v Kelly* [1978] 1 WLR 1 Megaw J said that overwhelming proof of the unreasonableness would be required. A case in which possession was refused on this basis is *West Glamorgan County Council v Rafferty* [1987] 1 WLR 457.

(c) Where a complicated issue arises as to title (*Cudworth v Masefield* (1984) *The Times*, 16 May 1984) or as to whether there has been a surrender of a tenancy by operation of law (*Cooper v Vardari* (1986) 18 HLR 299), the summary procedure against trespassers may be inappropriate.

(d) A doubtful situation is where a head landlord seeks possession against unlawful sub-tenants. This was held to be a situation where summary possession could be ordered under the old rules (*Moore Properties (Ilford) Ltd v McKeon* [1976] 1 WLR 1278), but the words 'or sub-tenant' in r. 55.1(b) may be regarded as extending even to an unlawful sub-tenant, with the effect that the summary procedure will not be available in such a claim.

County court or High Court

35.5 Possession claims must normally be started in the county court for the district in which the land is situated (**CPR, r. 55.3(1)**). The High Court may be appropriate where there are complicated issues of fact, points of law of general importance, or the claim is against trespassers and there is a substantial risk of public disturbance or of serious harm to persons or property which require immediate determination (**PD 55, para. 1.3**). If the claim is started in the High Court when it should have been started in a county court, the claim will either be struck out or transferred (**PD 55, para. 1.2**).

Claim form, particulars of claim and evidence in support

A special claim form (**form** N5) must be used in claims against trespassers. The claim form should name as defendants all the persons in occupation whose identities are known to the claimant. Where the claimant does not know the names of all the occupiers, the claim is brought against 'persons unknown' in addition to any named defendants. There is nothing to be gained, therefore, by making inquiries as to who might be in occupation, but there will be extra people to serve if some of those in occupation become known to the claimant. Where the claimant is a large organisation, it is important for the solicitor conducting the case to find out what may be known by any of the employees of the claimant, as there have been cases where delays have occurred through the need to amend by adding extra defendants when it later becomes clear that some of the occupiers were known to local employees of the claimant. **35.6**

The particulars of claim must be in **form N121**, which is specifically for claims against trespassers. This must identify the land, state whether it is residential property, state the claimant's interest in the property or the basis for claiming possession, the circumstances in which it has been occupied without the claimant's licence or consent, and give details of every person who, to the best of the claimant's knowledge, is in possession of the property (**PD 55, paras 2.1** and **2.6**). Particulars of claim and witness statements in support must be filed when the claim is issued (**CPR, rr. 55.4** and **55.8(5)**). When the claim is issued the court will fix a date for the hearing, which will usually be just a few days after issue.

Service

No acknowledgment of service form is required (**CPR, r. 55.7(1)**), so the only documents that need to be served are the claim form, particulars of claim, any additional evidence in support, and any notice of the return day. Service copies of the claim form must be sealed (see **12.3**). **35.7**

Individually named defendants must be served in accordance with the normal rules on service (see **chapter 15**). Service by the means described below for 'persons unknown' will not suffice for individually named defendants (*Greater London Council v Tully* (1976) 120 SJ 555).

Where the claim is against, or includes, persons unknown, in addition to serving the named defendants in the normal way, the documents must, by **r. 55.6**, be served by:

(a) attaching copies to the main door or some other part of the land so they are clearly visible, and, if practicable, by inserting another set of the documents through the letter box in a sealed transparent envelope addressed to 'the occupiers'; or

(b) attaching copies, contained in sealed transparent envelopes addressed to 'the occupiers', to stakes placed in the land in places where they are clearly visible. This method is used where the trespassers are on open land. Where service is to be effected by the court, the claimant must provide sufficient transparent envelopes and stakes (**PD 55, para. 4.1**).

In *Westminster City Council v Chapman* [1975] 1 WLR 1112, the county court bailiff served the proceedings, but did not affix a copy to the main door or other conspicuous part of the premises. The defendants learnt of the matter by reading the copy inserted through the letter box. It was held that service was irregular (rather than a nullity), and as there was no prejudice to the defendants, the irregularity was cured under what is now **CPR, r. 3.10**.

Service must be effected not less than five days before the hearing in the case of residential property, and not less than two days before the hearing in respect of commercial property and open land (**r. 55.5(2)**). Time is calculated from service on each of the various defendants. Time may be shortened under **r. 3.1(2)(a) and (b)** where the occupiers have threatened to assault the claimant or to cause serious damage to the property or other property in the locality (**PD 55, para. 3.2**).

Defence

35.8 The form for a defence in a possession claim against trespassers (**form N11**) simply provides a space for giving the reasons for disputing the claim and a statement of truth. However, in possession claims against trespassers **r. 15.2** of the CPR does not apply, and there is no need for a defendant to file a defence (**r. 55.7(2)**). The provisions on default judgment do not apply (**r. 55.7(4)**).

Application by occupier to be made a party

35.9 By **CPR, r. 19.4**, an occupier who is not named as a defendant and who wishes to be heard on the return day may apply at any stage to be joined as a defendant. An application notice should be filed and served in accordance with **Part 23** (**PD 19, para. 1.4**). Such applications are often heard on the day of the hearing. All that need be shown is that the occupier wishes to be heard on whether an order for possession should be made, so permission to join is usually granted quite readily.

Hearing in claims against trespassers

35.10 Summary possession hearings are generally heard by masters in the Royal Courts of Justice and by district judges in the county courts. Unless the court orders otherwise, the facts are placed before the court at the hearing by relying on the evidence in the witness statements served with the claim form (**CPR, r. 55.8(3)**). The fact of service is proved by producing a certificate of service (**r. 55.8(6)** and **form N215**).

If the defendants need an opportunity to file evidence in reply, the first hearing may be used for giving directions (particularly where there is not much time between service and the return date). If the necessary five or two clear days have not elapsed since service, the court should ordinarily adjourn the hearing to enable the proper time to elapse (*Westminster City Council v Monahan* [1981] 1 WLR 698). If the maker of a witness statement does not attend the hearing, and another party disputes material evidence contained in the statement, the court will normally adjourn the hearing so that oral evidence can be given (**PD 55, para. 5.4**). Adjournments are usually very short, as the whole point of the procedure is to provide an expeditious means of obtaining possession orders where there is no defence.

The summary procedure against trespassers is only appropriate where the defendants have no real defence. If the court takes the view that the case is not suitable for summary possession, it may dismiss the claim (particularly where it does not come within the scope of the procedure). If the defendants attend and adduce evidence showing a substantial defence, the claim is usually converted into an ordinary possession claim.

Possession orders against trespassers

35.11 Normally, if the court is satisfied that there are grounds for granting possession of the land, the order will be for possession forthwith. Where the defendants' original entry on to the land was unlawful, the court has no discretion to make a suspended order in the absence of consent from the landowner (*Swordheath Properties Ltd v Floydd* [1978] 1 WLR 550). However, if the original occupation was lawful, such as under a service agreement, the court may exercise any power which it could have exercised if possession had been sought in an ordinary possession claim.

Usually the order will grant possession of the land actually occupied by the defendants. This may not provide sufficient protection for the claimant, and the court can make an 'area' possession order, covering the land actually occupied by the defendants and also other land owned by the claimant. Such an order can only be made if there is convincing evidence of a real danger that the defendants or people associated with them will occupy other land owned by the claimant when they are removed from the land they presently occupy (*Secretary of State for the Environment, Food and Rural Affairs v Drury* [2004] EWCA Civ 200, [2004] 1 WLR 1906). In such cases it is sensible to mark the various parcels of land intended to be covered on a map attached to the order, rather than simply describing the land covered as 'all land owned by the claimant', so as to be clear about what is covered and to assist with enforcement.

Warrant of possession

A warrant of possession to enforce a possession order against a trespasser may be issued immediately after the order is made. However, permission to issue a warrant of possession is required if the warrant is not issued within the next three months (**CCR, ord. 24, r. 6**, in CPR, sch. 2). Orders for permission to enforce out of time are made on application to the master or district judge without notice (unless the court otherwise directs). If permission is granted, the defendants may apply to vary or set it aside by making an application within seven days of service of the order granting permission (**CPR, r. 23.10**). **35.12**

Interim possession orders

An interim order for possession can be sought in a claim for possession against trespassers by following the procedure in **CPR, rr. 55.20** to **55.28**. Such an order is available if the following conditions are satisfied: **35.13**

(a) the only claim in the proceedings is for possession so there can be no money claim;
(b) the claim is in respect of premises (and not open land); and
(c) the claim is made within 28 days of the claimant knowing (or reasonably being able to know) of the wrongful occupation.

The claim must be brought by issuing an application for possession in **form N130**, supported by written evidence in the prescribed form, and a notice of application for an interim possession order must also be issued (in **form N131**). Once the proceedings have been issued the court will fix a date for consideration of the application, which must be not less than three days after the proceedings were issued. Service must be effected by the applicant within 24 hours after issue. Service is effected by fixing one set of copies to the main door or other conspicuous part of the premises, and inserting a second set through the letter box in a transparent envelope addressed to 'the occupiers'.

The defendant is permitted to file written evidence in reply, and a standard form for this must be used (**form N133**). If the court decides to make an interim possession order, the claimant is required to give a number of undertakings set out in **CPR, r. 55.25(1)** including a promise to reinstate the defendant if the court later holds that the interim possession order should not have been made. An interim possession order requires the defendant to vacate within 24 hours of service (r. 55.25(3)). A defendant who does not comply commits an offence contrary to the Criminal Justice and Public Order Act 1994, s. 76, punishable by imprisonment for up to six months and/or a fine not exceeding level 5 on the standard scale. The only means of enforcement is under the 1994 Act, which requires the involvement of the police.

After an interim possession order is made there is a second return date when the court will consider whether to make a final order for possession, or to dismiss the claim for possession.

OTHER POSSESSION PROCEEDINGS

Ordinary possession claims

Ordinary possession claims, like possession claims against trespassers, are governed by **CPR, Part 55**, and **PD 55** (and see **chapters 83** to **89**). The court has a power to allocate these claims to the fast track or multi-track (r. 55.8(2)), may give case management directions, and may require the facts to be proved by calling witnesses at the trial. **35.14**

The claim form to be used in possession claims is **form N5**; the claim form for relief against forfeiture is **form N5A**; the form for particulars of claim in claims in respect of rented residential premises is **form N119**; the form for particulars of claim in claims for possession of mortgaged residential premises is **form N120**; the form for a defence in mortgage possession claims is **form N11M**; and the form for a defence in claims in respect of rented residential premises is **form N11R**.

ACCELERATED PROCEDURE FOR ASSURED SHORTHOLD TENANCIES

35.15 **Rules 55.11 to 55.19** of the CPR provide an accelerated procedure for obtaining possession orders to recover possession of residential properties let under assured shorthold tenancies. There are prescribed claim forms and defence forms, and the papers are referred to a district judge or judge, who may strike out the claim if it discloses no reasonable grounds (**r. 55.16(1)(c)**), or may make an order for possession without requiring the attendance of the parties (**r. 55.17**). Although an application can be made to set aside such an order (**r. 55.19**), the procedure is intended to provide a speedy and inexpensive means of obtaining possession orders in cases where there is unlikely to be any defence.

There is a special claim form (**form N5B**) for use in accelerated procedure claims in respect of assured shorthold property and it includes the particulars of claim. The form for a defence to such a claim is **form N11B**.

Chapter 36 Interim Payments

The following procedural checklist, which is in **appendix** 1, is relevant to this chapter:

Procedural checklist 25 Application for an order for interim payment

ORDERS FOR INTERIM PAYMENT

An order for interim payment is defined in **CPR, r. 25.1(1)(k)**, as an order for payment of a sum of money by a defendant on account of any damages, debt or other sum (except costs) which the court may hold the defendant liable to pay. Such orders are likely to be made in claims where it appears the claimant will achieve at least some success, and where it would be unjust to delay, until after the trial, payment of the money to which the claimant appears to be entitled. The purpose behind this procedure is to alleviate the hardship that may otherwise be suffered by claimants who may have to wait substantial periods of time before they recover any damages in respect of wrongs they may have suffered. In addition to providing resources to the claimant, sometimes making an interim payment will enable the claimant to pay for treatment, or to save assets which would otherwise be lost, or to have an asset repaired earlier than might otherwise be the case, and may thereby reduce the amount of the claim. Further, making an early interim payment will reduce the defendant's liability to pay interest. **36.1**

Cases on the small claims track are unlikely to be large enough to justify the expense of applications for interim payments, and small claims and fast track cases, unless delayed, are likely to proceed to final hearing with such speed that there will be little point in making an application, unless the hearing results in a judgment for damages to be assessed. Most applications for interim payments are therefore likely to be made in multi-track cases (or cases likely to be allocated to the multi-track when track allocation is considered).

Voluntary interim payments and rehabilitation

There is nothing to prevent the parties agreeing to voluntary interim payments, and these are quite common in cases where liability is not in dispute but where quantum is still being investigated. Payments made by insurers for intervention or treatment pursuant to the Rehabilitation Code (**Annex D to the Pre-action Protocol for Personal Injury Claims**) are treated as interim payments on account of damages (**Code, para. 7.2**). The permission of the court must be obtained if a voluntary interim payment is being considered where the claimant is a person under disability (**PD 25B, para. 1.2**). **36.2**

EC law and informal interim payments under CPR, r. 25.1

36.3 In *R (Teleos plc) v Commissioners of Customs and Excise* [2005] EWCA Civ 200, [2005] 1 WLR 3007, the company brought judicial review proceedings to challenge a VAT assessment which the Commissioners had levied through a set-off. The Commissioners refused to make an interim payment to the company under the Value Added Tax Act 1994, and it was clear there were no grounds for granting an interim payment under **CPR, r. 25.7**. The company applied for interim relief under **r. 25.1** and/or the court's inherent jurisdiction for an interim payment of 50 per cent of the assessed VAT. Dyson LJ said at [23] that if there were no mechanism for a taxpayer in these circumstances to obtain an interim payment of VAT withheld by the Commissioners, there would be an infringement of the principle of proportionality (see *Garage Molenheide BVBA v Belgium* (cases C-286/94, C-340/95, C-401/95 and C-47/96) [1997] ECR I-7281). This did not apply to the present case, given the Commissioners' power to make interim payments and the right to challenge their decisions through judicial review. Accordingly, it was unnecessary to give a strained interpretation of **CPR, r. 25.1**, to provide such a power, nor did the court need such a power as a consequence of EC law (at [33]).

PROCEDURE

Who may apply

36.4 The rules (**CPR, rr. 25.1(1)(k)** and **25.6(1)**) refer to interim payments being applied for by claimants against defendants. This should be interpreted as meaning that interim payments may also be applied for by claimants in additional claims, so that defendants may bring interim payment applications against the defendants to their counterclaims, and defendants may seek interim payments against additional parties.

Time for applying

36.5 An application for an order for an interim payment cannot be made until the period for filing an acknowledgment of service has expired (**CPR, r. 25.6(1)**). However, voluntary interim payments may be made at any time, including the period before proceedings are issued. It is possible to make several applications for interim payments during the life of a claim (**r. 25.6(2)**).

Application and evidence

36.6 The procedure for applying for an interim payment is summarised in **procedural checklist** 25, which is in **appendix** 1. Applications for interim payments are made on notice, and must be served at least 14 clear days before the hearing of the application. Rather unnecessarily, it is specifically stated as a requirement by **CPR, r. 25.6(3)**, that applications for interim payments must be supported by evidence which must be served with the application. **PD 25B, para. 2.1**, provides that the evidence in support should set out all relevant matters including:

(a) the amount sought by way of interim payment;
(b) what the money will be used for (see **36.15**);
(c) the likely amount of money that will be awarded;
(d) the reasons for believing the relevant ground (see **36.7**) is satisfied;
(e) in a personal injuries claim, details of special damages and past and future loss; and
(f) in a claim under the **Fatal Accidents Act 1976**, details of the persons on whose behalf the claim is made and the nature of the claim.

All relevant documents in support should be exhibited. In personal injuries claims these will include the medical reports.

Respondents who wish to rely on written evidence in reply must file and serve their evidence at least seven clear days before the hearing. In personal injuries claims the respondent will need to obtain a certificate of recoverable benefits from the Secretary of State under the Social Security (Recovery of Benefits) Act 1997, which is needed for the purposes of framing the order. If the applicant wants to respond to the respondent's evidence, any further evidence must be filed and served at least three clear days before the return day (**CPR, r.** 25.6(4) and (5)).

GROUNDS

The conditions which must be satisfied before an interim payment order can be made are set out in **CPR, r.** 25.7. Under **CPR, r.** 25.7(1), an interim payment may be ordered against a specific defendant only if: **36.7**

(a) the defendant has admitted liability to pay damages or some other sum of money to the claimant (**r.** 25.7(1)(a)); or
(b) the claimant has obtained judgment against the defendant for damages or some other sum (other than costs) to be assessed (**r.** 25.7(1)(b)); or
(c) the court is satisfied that, if the claim went to trial, the claimant would obtain judgment against the defendant from whom the interim payment is sought for a substantial sum of money (other than costs) (**r.** 25.7(1)(c)); or
(d) the claimant is seeking possession of land, and the court is satisfied that if the case went to trial the defendant would be held liable to pay the claimant a sum of money for use and occupation of the land while the claim is pending (**r.** 25.7(1)(d)).

Where there are two or more defendants and the court, though satisfied that the claimant will obtain judgment, cannot determine which of the defendants will be found liable, **r.** 25.7(1)(e), which is discussed in **36.11**, provides an alternative ground for granting an interim payment.

Former additional condition in personal injuries cases

Rule 25.7 of the CPR was amended with effect from 1 April 2005 by revoking the additional conditions that applied in personal injuries claims which were set out in **r.** 25.7(2). Before 1 April 2005 interim payments could only be made in personal injuries claims where the defendant was insured or a public body, or where the defendant's liability would be met by an insurer under the **Road Traffic Act 1998, s. 151**, or an insurer acting under the Motor Insurers' Bureau Agreement or by the Motor Insurers' Bureau itself. Until 1 April 2005, these conditions applied in all personal injuries claims regardless of how many defendants were named in the claim. For the present position see **36.10** and **36.11**. **36.8**

STANDARD OF PROOF

On an application under **CPR, r.** 25.7(1)(c), **(d)** or **(e)**, the court has to be satisfied on the balance of probabilities that the claimant 'would' obtain judgment. This wording is identical to that used in the old rules (RSC, ord. 29, rr. 11(1)(c) and 12(1)(c)), and it ought to be the case, despite the new approach to interpretation, that the same principles will apply regarding the standard of proof on these two grounds. If so, it has to be shown that the claimant will win on the balance of probabilities, but at the upper end of the scale, the burden being a high one. Being likely to succeed at trial is not enough. The leading authorities under the old rules establishing these principles were *Shearson Lehman Brothers Inc. v Maclaine Watson and Co. Ltd* [1987] 1 WLR 480 and *British and Commonwealth Holdings plc v Quadrex Holdings Inc.* [1989] QB 842. **36.9**

MULTIPLE DEFENDANTS

Where the court is satisfied a specific defendant is liable

36.10 The conditions set out in **CPR, r. 25.7(1)(a)** to **(d)** (see **36.7**) confirm the effect of *Ricci Burns Ltd v Toole* [1989] 1 WLR 993 in applications for interim payments in claims where there is more than one defendant. As from 1 April 2005, an interim payment order can be made against a specific defendant if the claimant establishes one of the conditions in **r. 25.7(1)(a)** to **(d)** to the required standard against that specific defendant. Where this can be done there is no need to satisfy the additional requirements of **r. 25.7(1)(e)** described at **36.11**.

Where the court cannot determine which defendant is liable

36.11 By **CPR, 25.7(1)(e)**, an interim payment may be ordered where all the following conditions are satisfied:

(a) there are two or more defendants;
(b) the court is satisfied that if the claim went to trial the claimant would obtain judgment for a substantial sum of money (other than costs) against at least one of the defendants;
(c) the court cannot determine under **r. 25.7(1)(c)** which of the defendants will lose; and
(d) all the defendants are either insured, public bodies, or are defendants whose liability will be met by an insurer under the **Road Traffic Act 1988, s. 151**, or an insurer acting under the Motor Insurers' Bureau Agreement or by the Motor Insurers' Bureau itself.

The provision in **r. 25.7(1)(e)(ii)(b)** (see (d) above) should be construed as including cases where liability will be met by an insurance company under the Domestic Regulations Agreement between the Motor Insurers' Bureau and its members pursuant to the Uninsured Drivers' Agreement (*Sharp v Pereira* [1991] 1 WLR 195, considering a provision in the same form introduced in 1996).

If it transpires that the wrong defendant was required to make the interim payment, the requirement that all the defendants must be insured etc. means it should be possible to make effective adjustments (see **36.16**) after the final determination of the case.

EFFECT OF COUNTERCLAIMS AND DEFENCES

36.12 When deciding on an order for interim payment the court 'must take into account' any relevant set-off or counterclaim and any contributory negligence (**CPR, r. 25.7(5)**). From the context of this provision it clearly applies at the second stage of an interim payment application when the court is considering the amount to be ordered by way of an interim payment. Counterclaims and allegations of contributory negligence with reasonable prospects of success obviously affect the likely amount of the final judgment. **Rule 25.7(5)**, however, has no express restriction to quantum. Unlike unconnected cross-claims, set-offs are also defences. Consequently, the existence of a set-off with a reasonable prospect of success should also be taken into account at the first stage when the court is considering the grounds for granting an interim payment, and may prevent the court being satisfied that the claimant will obtain judgment for the purposes of **r. 25.7(1)(c)**. This was the position under the previous rules (see *Shanning International Ltd v George Wimpey International Ltd* [1989] 1 WLR 981).

RELATIONSHIP WITH SUMMARY JUDGMENT

36.13 It is quite common to combine applications for summary judgment with applications for interim payments. Summary judgment is available where the defence has no real prospect of success, and interim payments are available where the claimant can show that liability will be established. Obviously these are similar concepts. Further, on the summary judgment application the court may make a 'relevant order' (**PD 26, para. 12.1**) entering judgment for damages to be assessed, which would itself provide grounds for making an order for an interim payment. Another possibility is that the court may make a conditional order on the summary judgment application, with the condition being compliance with an interim payment order.

Under the old rules before the CPR there were several reported cases that considered the question of whether it was possible to make an interim payment order if a summary judgment application was unsuccessful (see, for example, *Schott Kem Ltd v Bentley* [1991] 1 QB 61 and *Andrews v Schooling* [1991] 1 WLR 783). The better view under the old rules was that an interim payment order would not be made in such cases, although it was possible to make an interim payment order if conditional leave to defend (the old equivalent to a conditional order) was granted. With the increased availability of summary judgment under the CPR, there can be no doubt that if summary judgment is refused it would be inconsistent for the court then to decide that the claimant 'would' succeed so as to give grounds for an interim payment. There may even be a little doubt about whether making an interim payment order can be consistent with making a conditional order, again because of the change in the test for summary judgment. If the defence is on the border of having a real prospect of success (the situation where conditional orders are appropriate), it is difficult to see how the court can simultaneously find that the claimant will win for the purposes of making an interim payment order.

DISCRETION

Even if the claimant establishes a ground for making an interim payment, the court retains a discretion whether to make an order. In one of the old cases (*British and Commonwealth Holdings plc v Quadrex Holdings Inc.* [1989] QB 842) it was said that the court may take into account the respondent's lack of means in either refusing to make an order or in fixing its amount. **36.14**

AMOUNT TO BE ORDERED

The court is not permitted to order an interim payment of more than a reasonable proportion of the likely amount of any final judgment, taking into account any contributory negligence and any relevant set-off or counterclaim (**CPR, r. 25.7(4) and(5)**). This is the same test as before the CPR, when different judges took very different views of what a 'reasonable proportion' of the final award might be. Generally, most judges err on the side of caution. In personal injuries cases many judges are very reluctant to look further than the statement of past and future loss and damage, and then take a view on which heads are likely to survive at the hearing, and disregard general damages for pain, suffering and loss of amenity. Very cautious judges limit themselves to past financial losses. Other judges are prepared to look at the likely level of damages in the round, and include all heads of damage. In the non-personal injuries field, the pre-CPR case of *Andrews v Schooling* [1991] 1 WLR 783 is helpful. This was a claim for damages against builders under the Defective Premises Act 1972. The court ignored the claimant's quantification of the claim at £12,000, but made an order for an interim payment of £7,500 given an estimate of £10,000 for necessary remedial works. **36.15**

The small claims limit may be a reasonable guide for what is meant by 'a substantial amount of money' in **r. 25.7(1)(c)**. This may lead to a threshold of £1,000 in personal injuries claims, and of £5,000 for most other claims.

Paragraph 2.1(2) of PD 25B states that the evidence in support of the application must deal with the items or matters in respect of which the interim payment is sought. In general, the claimant's intended use of the money if an interim payment is awarded is irrelevant to the court's decision. As stated in *Schott Kem Ltd v Bentley* [1991] 1 QB 61, commercial people always have a need for money for the purposes of their business interests. Once an interim payment is made they will invest it somewhere. It is generally the same in personal injuries claims (*Stringman v McArdle* [1994] 1 WLR 1653). The court is not concerned with how a claimant of full capacity spends a final award in damages, and should not try to prescribe what an interim payment is spent on either. Despite the general principle, the rule in *Stringman v McArdle* must not be applied in a mechanistic way, and there are cases where the proposed use of the interim payment has a significant bearing on the decision of the court (*Tinsley v Sarker* [2004] EWCA Civ 1098, LTL 23/7/2004). The intended use of the money may be relevant where the payment may prejudice the trial or the position of the defendant in the proceedings or prejudge an issue to be determined at the trial (Thorpe LJ at [48]). Of course, if the applicant can point to specific purchases which are related to dealing with the consequences of the applicant's cause of action, it will be easier to persuade the court when it comes to the exercise of the court's discretion.

In personal injuries claims the defendant will need to obtain a certificate of recoverable benefits from the Secretary of State under the Social Security (Recovery of Benefits) Act 1997. A copy of the certificate should be filed at the hearing, and any order made must set out the amount by which the payment to be made to the claimant has been reduced in accordance with the Act and the Social Security (Recovery of Benefits) Regulations 1997 (SI 1997/2205) (**PD 25B, paras 4.1 to 4.4**).

Rule 25.6(7) of the CPR allows an interim payment order to require payment by instalments. Where this happens, the order should set out the total amount of the interim payment, the amount of each instalment, the number of instalments and the date they are to be paid, and to whom the payments should be made (**PD 25B, para. 3**).

Undertaking for repayment

36.16 In *Ultraframe (UK) Ltd v Eurocell Building Plastics Ltd* [2005] EWHC 2111 (Ch), LTL 30/8/2005, as a condition for granting an interim payment, the claimant and its holding company were required to give a cross-undertaking to repay the interim payment, and to provide a guarantee. Such undertakings are comparatively rare.

FURTHER APPLICATIONS

36.17 The claimant is permitted to make more than a single application for an interim payment (**CPR, r. 25.6(2)**). In practice, a second or subsequent application will have to be justified by a change in circumstances or other cause being shown, such as an increase in the special damages claim through additional loss of income or expenses being incurred, or through unforeseen delays in determining the claim.

NON-DISCLOSURE

36.18 The fact that a defendant has made an interim payment must not be disclosed to the trial judge until all questions of liability and quantum have been determined (**CPR, r. 25.9**), unless the defendant agrees. This is important, as the trial judge may (unwittingly) be influenced by knowing that the court has previously decided that the claimant will win, and that the claim is worth more than the amount of the interim payment. Where a claimant (usually through ignorance) does disclose this information prematurely, the judge will usually abort the trial and consider making a wasted costs order against the lawyer responsible.

ADJUSTMENT

The court has powers to order all or part of an interim payment to be repaid, to vary or discharge an interim payment order, and to order a co-defendant to reimburse a defendant who has made an interim payment (provided the defendant who made the interim payment has claimed a contribution, indemnity or other remedy against the co-defendant being ordered to reimburse) (**CPR, r. 25.8**). Interest may be ordered in favour of the defendant on any overpaid interim payment. These powers are usually exercised, if at all, at trial. **PD 25B, para. 5**, and **PD 40B, para. 6**, contain detailed rules on recording the effect of interim payments and any order for adjustment on the final award for damages. **36.19**

Chapter 37 Interim Injunctions

INTRODUCTION

37.1 Interim injunctions are temporary orders made with the purpose of regulating the position between the parties to an action pending trial. Imposing an interim injunction is a serious matter, and should be restricted to appropriate cases. Such an order is particularly useful where there is evidence that the respondent's alleged wrongdoing will cause irreparable damage to the applicant's interests in the period between issue of process and trial.

Interim injunctions should be distinguished from perpetual injunctions, which are final orders, usually made at trial (but see 37.46) and which continue with no limitation of time. Further distinctions are:

(a) Injunctions made without notice. These are a form of interim injunction, usually made in circumstances of urgency, which are expressed to continue in force for a limited period, usually a few days, sufficient for the application to be renewed on a hearing with notice being given to the respondent.

(b) Mandatory injunctions require the other side to do specified acts (such as to deliver up documents or to demolish a wall), whereas prohibitory injunctions require the other side to refrain from doing specified acts (such as publishing a libel or breaching a confidence). It is the substance of the order (rather than its wording) which makes it mandatory or prohibitory. Both types of injunction can be granted on an interim basis, but the courts are more wary of granting mandatory orders (see **37.50**).

(c) Where the other side have not yet committed a civil wrong, but have threatened to do so in the future, it is possible to obtain an interim injunction on a *quia timet* basis.

Interim injunctions can be applied for even in claims allocated to the small claims track (**CPR, r. 27.2(1)**).

Any party to proceedings can apply for an interim injunction, and can do so whether or not a claim for the injunction was included in that party's originating process or statement of case (**CPR, r. 25.1(4)**).

JUDGES ABLE TO GRANT INJUNCTIONS

Given the serious nature of injunctions and the consequences of breach, subject to the following exceptions, all applications for interim injunctions must be made to a judge rather than a master or district judge. **37.2**

There are several exceptions and restrictions. The detailed rules are to be found in **PD 25, paras 1.1 to 1.4**, which have to be read together with **PD 2B**. The effect of the various rules is set out in **table 37.1**.

Table 37.1 Power to grant interim injunctions

Type of order	Judges with power to grant
Search order	High Court judge and any other 'duly authorised' judge.
Freezing injunction	High Court judge and any other 'duly authorised' judge.
Other High Court interim injunction	Generally, only High Court judges. However, masters and district judges have power to grant injunctions: (a) in terms agreed by the parties; (b) in connection with charging orders and appointment of receivers; and (c) restraining a person receiving a sum due from the Crown.
County court interim injunctions	Judge with trial jurisdiction. Generally this will be the circuit judge, but may be the district judge in claims on the small claims and fast tracks, where the terms have been agreed by the parties, in relation to charging orders and the appointment of receivers, and certain Housing Act 1996 and harassment claims.
Variation of interim injunctions	Generally by a judge of the same level as the judge who granted the original injunction. Masters and district judges have jurisdiction as well if all parties consent to the variation or discharge.

PRE-ACTION APPLICATIONS FOR INTERIM INJUNCTIONS

37.3 Rule 25.2(1) of the CPR empowers the court to grant an interim injunction before a claim form has been issued. An application for an interim injunction at that stage must be made under **Part 23 (PD 23, para. 5)**. By **CPR, r. 25.2(2)**, an interim injunction can be obtained prior to issue of proceedings provided:

(a) no rule or practice direction prohibits the granting of the order;
(b) the matter is urgent or it is otherwise desirable to make the order in the interests of justice;
(c) in the less common circumstance in which the applicant is an intended defendant, the defendant has obtained the court's permission to make the application. The defendant cannot without this permission apply for an interim remedy prior to the filing of an acknowledgment of service or defence (which can only happen after issue). It seems that the defendant could apply for permission and for the injunction in the same application and at the same hearing.

Urgent cases

37.4 A case is 'urgent' where there is a true impossibility in giving the requisite three clear days' notice or in arranging for the issue of process. There has to be an element of threatened damage, requiring the immediate intervention of the court, which may occur between the without notice hearing and the hearing of an effective application (*Mayne Pharma (USA) Inc. v Teva UK Ltd* [2004] EWHC 3248 (Ch), LTL 3/12/2004). An 'impossibility' resulting from delay on the part of the claimant will not suffice (*Bates v Lord Hailsham of St Marylebone* [1972] 1 WLR 1373).

Reasons for applying without notice have to be given to the judge. It is especially important to give notice where grave allegations are to be made on the application. Thus, in *Cinpres Gas Injection Ltd v Melea Ltd* [2005] EWHC 3180 (Pat), *The Times*, 21 December 2005, a without-notice interim injunction to restrain the defendant from threatening, intimidating or harassing any witnesses was set aside because it should have been made on notice. Although the court will not usually consider an application made without notice where there is no true impossibility in notifying the defendant, there is a suggestion in *Bates v Lord Hailsham of St Marylebone* that the court may do so if the case is overwhelming on the merits. The relief sought on a without-notice application must be necessary and proportionate to the reasons for applying without notice (*Moat Housing Group-South Ltd v Harris* [2005] EWCA Civ 287, [2005] 3 WLR 691).

Where a case is urgent, the usual procedural requirements are relaxed in so far as is necessary to do justice between the parties. For example:

(a) The application may be made before issue of process.
(b) The application may be made without notice. However, it is still incumbent on the applicant to give the other side such notice as is possible, such as by telephone or by fax unless secrecy is essential (such as on applications for search orders and freezing injunctions). A defendant who is notified in this way may decide to attend the hearing, a situation which is known as an 'opposed hearing without notice'.
(c) Informal evidence may be relied on. This may be in the form of an unsworn draft affidavit, or a witness statement, correspondence or even simply facts related to the court by counsel on instructions.
(d) Although very much a last resort, the court may make an order without a draft having been prepared by counsel on behalf of the applicant. It is very rare for there to be no time for anything to be drafted in advance of appearing before the judge.
(e) In particularly urgent cases it is possible to interrupt the judge's list, or even to see the judge out of normal hours or to apply to the judge over the telephone.

Procedure on pre-action applications

For a summary of the procedure, see **procedural checklist 20** in **appendix 1.** **37.5**

The application itself will normally be in a written application notice (**CPR, r. 23.3(1)**), the general requirement for which is that it should set out the order sought and why the order is being sought (**r. 23.6**). In the High Court **form N244** should usually be used for the application notice, but in the county court there is a special form for applying for injunctions (**form N16A**) which must be used. It must include the title of the proposed claim, the full name of the applicant, and, as the applicant is not yet a party, the applicant's address for service. It should contain a request for a hearing or ask that the application be dealt with without a hearing (**PD 23, para. 2.1**). It will be very rare for injunctions to be sought without hearings. Dispensing with a hearing is only permissible if the parties agree to the terms of the order sought, or agree that the court should dispose of the application without a hearing, or if the court does not consider a hearing would be appropriate (**CPR, r. 23.8**). None of these is very likely in the case of pre-action injunctions. **PD 25, para. 2.1**, provides that an application notice for an interim injunction should:

(a) state the order sought, and
(b) give the date, time and place of the hearing.

It is good practice to annex a draft order to the application notice where time allows. **Form PF 39 CH** must be used for pre-action applications.

Many pre-action applications for injunctions are made in cases of real urgency. Drafting and issuing an application notice may delay matters to the detriment of the applicant, and the court may in such cases exercise its power in **CPR, r. 23.3(2)(b)**, to dispense with the requirement for an application notice. If the court dispenses with the application notice, it will usually only do so for the purposes of the initial hearing. **PD 25, para. 5.1(4)**, provides that in these circumstances the court will, unless it orders otherwise, require an undertaking from the applicant to file an application notice and pay the appropriate fee on the same or the next working day.

An application for an interim remedy must be supported by evidence, unless the court orders otherwise (**CPR, r. 25.3(2)**). The evidence required is discussed further in **37.13**.

The application should be made in the court in which the substantive proceedings are likely to be be issued unless 'there is good reason to make the application to a different court' (**CPR, r. 23.2(4)**).

Especially where the terms of the injunction sought are complex, it is good practice to attach a draft of the order to the application notice and to provide it on computer disk (**PD 25, para. 2.4**).

If the court is to serve the application on the respondent, a suitable number of copies of the application notice and evidence in support must be filed with the court. Unless the court orders otherwise, or an application without service of an application notice can be justified, the application notice should be served as soon as practicable and in any event at least three clear days before the hearing (**CPR, r. 23.7**). Obviously, if three days' notice can be given of an application for an interim injunction, there will be time to issue proceedings. Pre-action applications will therefore always be made without full notice to the respondent. This can only be justified if there are 'good reasons for not giving notice' (**r. 25.3(1)**). Urgency and/or the need for secrecy will be accepted as good reasons.

Arrangements for pre-action injunction hearings

Pre-action interim injunction applications will almost always be considered at a hearing but **37.6**
without full (or any) notice to the respondent. Such applications will almost certainly be of an urgent nature. If they arise during or shortly before the ordinary times when the court is

sitting, the hearing will take place in court as soon as the circumstances permit. This means that generally such applications are heard before other matters that are listed, either as soon as the court sits in the morning or immediately after lunch. The necessary arrangements must be made with the court staff, who will invariably do all they can to ensure urgent applications are dealt with at the first available opportunity. Solicitors should therefore contact the court by telephone as soon as they know they will need to make an urgent application, so as to allow the court time to make the necessary arrangements. Sometimes urgent applications arise during the course of the morning or afternoon in circumstances where it is not possible to wait to the beginning of the next session. If the case is sufficiently urgent the court will invariably interrupt whatever it is doing at a convenient moment so that it can hear the urgent application.

On other occasions the need for a pre-action interim injunction may arise at a time when it is not possible to wait until the next occasion when the court will be sitting. If the application is of extreme urgency it may be dealt with by telephone (**PD 25, para. 4.2**). If the problem has arisen during business hours, but in circumstances where it will not be possible to go before a judge before the close of business, initially it is necessary to telephone the court (either the High Court on (020) 7947 6000 or the appropriate county court) asking to be put in touch with a High Court judge of the appropriate division or county court judge available to deal with an emergency application (**PD 25, para. 4.5(1)**).

If the problem has arisen outside office hours, the applicant should telephone either the High Court (on the same number as above) asking to be put in touch with the clerk to the appropriate duty judge (or the appropriate area circuit judge where known), or should telephone the urgent court business officer of the appropriate circuit, who will contact the local duty judge.

If the facilities are available, a draft of the order sought will usually be required to be sent by fax to the duty judge who will be dealing with the application.

Telephone hearings are only available if the applicant is acting by solicitors or counsel (**PD 25, para. 4.5(5)**).

The pre-action order and related matters

37.7 The order should be in **form PF 39 CH**. If the order is granted, the court may give directions requiring a claim to be commenced (**CPR, r. 25.2(3)**). **PD 25, para. 5.1(5)**, gives effect to this by providing that an order made before issue of the claim form will, unless the court orders otherwise, include 'an undertaking to issue and pay the appropriate fee on the same or next working day' or contain directions for the commencement of the claim. In other respects the order will follow the same form as other interim injunctions, see **37.52**.

As the application will invariably have been made without notice to the respondent, the order must, by **PD 25, para. 5.1(2)** and (3), include, unless the court orders otherwise:

(a) an undertaking by the applicant to the court to serve the respondent with the application notice, evidence in support and any order made, as soon as practicable; and
(b) a return date for a further hearing at which the other party can be present.

Counsel and solicitors have a responsibility to take a full note of what is said on a hearing where the respondent is not present, so the respondent can know the case that was made against him. There are too many technical problems in the recording system at the Royal Courts of Justice for lawyers to rely on official transcripts for this purpose (*Cinpres Gas Injection Ltd v Melea Ltd* [2005] EWHC 3180 (Pat), *The Times*, 21 December 2005).

Service of pre-action interim injunctions

37.8 Generally, pre-action applications for interim injunctions are made without notice to the respondent. Therefore, **r. 23.9** of the CPR applies. This requires a copy of the application notice and any evidence in support to be served with the injunction order on all parties and persons against whom the order was sought or made. The order must contain a statement of the right to apply under r. 23.10 to set aside or vary the order within seven days after it is served.

Where possible the claim form should be served with the injunction order (**PD 25, para. 4.4(2)**).

APPLICATIONS FOR INTERIM INJUNCTIONS DURING THE COURSE OF PROCEEDINGS

Time for applying for general interim injunctions

An application for an interim injunction in proceedings must be made after the claim form commencing the proceedings is issued if applying before issue is prevented by the conditions laid down in CPR, r. 25.2(2) (see 37.3). This will be the case where a pre-action application is prohibited by a rule or practice direction, or the matter is not urgent and it is not desirable to grant an injunction before issue in the interests of justice, or the applicant is an intended defendant and the court refuses permission. **Paragraphs** 2.7 and 2.8 of **PD 23** say that any application during proceedings should be made as soon as it becomes apparent that it is necessary or desirable, but should preferably be made at a hearing for which a date has already been, or is about to be, fixed. In many cases this means that the right time to apply for an interim injunction will be at the allocation stage, but an earlier, separate hearing would be justified if delay would make it more difficult to preserve the status quo. **37.9**

If the applicant is a defendant who has yet to file either an acknowledgment or a defence, the applicant must obtain the court's permission to make the application (CPR, r. 25.2(2)(c)).

Procedure on applications during proceedings

The procedure will be as described in 37.5 for pre-action applications except that: **37.10**

(a) The application notice need not give the applicant's address for service.
(b) The application will be made:
   (i) to the court in which the substantive proceedings were started (**CPR, r. 23.2(1)**), or
   (ii) to the court in which the proceedings were subsequently transferred (**r. 23.2(2)**), or
   (iii) if a date has been fixed for trial, to the court where the trial is to take place (**r. 23.2(3)**), or
   (iv) if after enforcement proceedings have been started, to the court dealing with enforcement 'unless any rule or practice direction provides otherwise' (**r. 23.2(5)**).
(c) It is good practice to annex a draft order to the application notice where time allows. **Form PF 40 CH** must be used for applications made after a claim has been issued.

For a summary of the procedure, see **procedural checklist 20** and **procedural checklist 21** in **appendix 1**.

Where the court is to serve, sufficient copies of the application notice and evidence in support should be provided for the court and each respondent (**PD 25, para.** 2.3). Service should be effected as soon as possible, and in any event not less than three clear days before the hearing.

Although **PD 23, para.** 2.8, provides that 'Applications should wherever possible be made so that they can be considered at any other hearing for which a date has already been fixed or for which a date is about to be fixed', clearly an application for an injunction, even where both parties are to appear at the hearing, will very often be of sufficient urgency to make it inappropriate to wait to make it until, say, the case management conference. Given the requirement to save expense (**CPR, r. 1.1(2)(b)**) and to allot to the case an appropriate share of the court's resources, while taking into account the need to allot resources to other cases (**r. 1.1(2)(e)**), an applicant should expect to be called on to justify the need for a separate hearing.

Respondents to applications made on notice are not under any specific duty under the rules to disclose their evidence in reply in advance of the hearings. However, deliberately holding back evidence in reply to the last minute will be a clear breach of the overriding objective. If the minimum of three clear days' notice was given by the applicant, it might be difficult or impossible for a respondent to compile and serve evidence in reply, which is why the CPR require the applicant to serve the application notice and evidence in support as soon as practicable after issue. The greater the notice given to the respondent, the greater is the effective obligation on the respondent to serve evidence in advance of the hearing. The rules seek to avoid multiple hearings (**CPR, r. 1.4(2)(i)**), and although the court may be prepared to give directions as to the service of evidence on the first hearing, it may well impose sanctions if it considers the need to give directions was caused by the default of either party.

Hearing of interim injunction applications in pending proceedings

37.11 Normally the hearing of an application for an interim injunction will be listed in the usual way for disposal in public (see **CPR, r. 39.2**). There are exceptional circumstances in which the hearing will be in private, such as where the hearing involves confidential information, the interests of children or patients, or where it would be unjust to proceed in public because the respondent has not been given due notice.

If the application is of an urgent nature justifying giving less than the usual three clear days' notice (see 37.4), unless secrecy is essential, the applicant should give the respondents informal notice (**PD 25, para. 4.3(3)**), which should be explained in the evidence in support. If the urgency justifies making the application without first issuing an application notice, a draft order (at least) should be provided at the hearing. Normally the court will direct that an application notice and evidence in support must be filed with the court on the same or the next working day (**PD 25, para. 4.3(2)**). If possible, even in the case of urgent applications, the application notice, evidence in support and draft order should be filed with the court at least two hours before it is intended to go before the judge (**PD 25, para. 4.3(1)**).

In cases of extreme urgency, the court may interrupt its list, or conduct the hearing by telephone with the duty judge, in the same way as extremely urgent pre-action applications (see 37.6).

Where there is to be a hearing, then with consent of all parties (and provided no party is acting in person), the court can order the hearing to be dealt with by telephone (**PD 23, para. 6.1**) or by video conference (**PD 23, para. 7**).

Both parties should be prepared to deal with the future case management of the action. **PD 23, para. 2.9**, warns them that: '. . . at any hearing the court may wish to review the conduct of the case as a whole and give any necessary case management directions. They should be ready to assist the court in doing so and to answer questions the court may ask for this purpose.' Indeed if the application takes place before allocation, the court may deal with allocation at the hearing (**PD 26, para. 2.4**).

Order obtained without notice

37.12 When an interim injunction is obtained in the course of proceedings without notice to the respondent, **rr. 23.9** and **23.10** of the CPR apply as they do to pre-action injunctions (see 37.8). Lawyers acting for the applicant have to make and serve on the respondent a note of what was said at the without notice hearing (*Cinpres Gas Injection Ltd v Melea Ltd* [2005] EWHC 3180 (Pat), *The Times*, 21 December 2005).

EVIDENCE IN SUPPORT OF AN APPLICATION FOR AN INTERIM INJUNCTION

An application for an interim injunction must be supported by evidence unless the court orders otherwise (**CPR, r. 25.3(2)**). The evidence must cover the substantive issues and also, if the application is without notice, explain why notice has not been given (**r. 25.3(3); PD 25, para. 3.4**). If the application is made before the issue of a claim form, the evidence should also address the urgency of the application or why it is 'desirable . . . in the interests of justice' to make the order (**CPR, r. 25.2(2)(b)**). The evidence should also address the relevant principles for granting injunctive relief (see below). **37.13**

PD 25, para. 3.2, states that unless the court or an Act requires evidence by affidavit, evidence is to be:

(a) by witness statement;
(b) set out in the application, provided it is verified by a statement of truth; or
(c) set out in a statement of case, provided it is verified by a statement of truth.

The provision whereby a statement of case can be relied on as evidence is more likely to be of use where an application for an interim injunction is made during the course of proceedings.

PD 25, para. 3.3, provides that 'The evidence must set out the facts on which the applicant relies for the claim being made against the respondent, including all material facts of which the court should be made aware'. This provision is not restricted to applications without notice. It appears to import at least some of the concepts of the previous duty of full and frank disclosure in relation to *ex parte* applications. The extent to which there is any duty, in any applications on full notice, to make reasonable inquiries remains obscure. Further, the 'material facts of which the court should be made aware' are likely to be more wide-ranging in an application made without notice than one made with the required three clear days' notice. Nevertheless, this paragraph of the practice direction is clearly intended to make parties address adverse facts in their evidence, even where the application is on notice and the respondent has a clear ability to file evidence and make representations at the hearing.

Where the application is on notice the respondent may, of course, file evidence in opposition (**PD 23, para. 9.4**).

STATUTORY AUTHORITY

Like all forms of equitable relief, the granting of interim injunctions is a matter within the discretion of the court. The fundamental principle is contained in the **Supreme Court Act 1981, s. 37(1)**, which (using pre-CPR terminology) provides: **37.14**

> The High Court may by order (whether interlocutory or final) grant an injunction or appoint a receiver in all cases in which it appears to the court to be just and convenient to do so.

The same principle applies in the county courts, where the **County Courts Act 1984, s. 38**, provides in part:

> (1) Subject to what follows, in any proceedings in a county court the court may make any order which could be made by the High Court if the proceedings were in the High Court.
> (2) Any order made by a county court may be—
> (a) absolute or conditional;
> (b) final or interlocutory.

With the introduction of the **Human Rights Act 1998**, the test to be applied may be whether granting relief is just and proportionate rather than just and convenient (*South Bucks District Council v Porter* [2003] UKHL 26, [2003] 2 AC 558).

SUBSTANTIVE CAUSE OF ACTION

37.15 Injunctions are only remedies, so can usually only be granted if the applicant has a substantive cause of action. As stated by Lord Diplock in *The Siskina* [1979] AC 210:

> A right to obtain an [interim] injunction is not a cause of action. It cannot stand on its own. It is dependent upon there being a pre-existing cause of action against the defendant arising out of an invasion, actual or threatened by him, of a legal or equitable right of the [claimant] for the enforcement of which the defendant is amenable to the jurisdiction of the court. The right to obtain an [interim] injunction is merely ancillary and incidental to the pre-existing cause of action.

In *The Siskina* the claimant had a cause of action against the defendant, but it was only actionable in a foreign country. It was therefore held that the English courts had no jurisdiction to grant an interim injunction to protect the applicant's position. This principle was restated by Lord Brandon of Oakbrook in *South Carolina Insurance Co. v Assurantie Maatschappij 'De Zeven Provincien' NV* [1987] AC 24, where he said that, apart from freezing injunctions and injunctions to restrain foreign proceedings, the court has discretion to grant injunctions in only two situations:

(a) where a party has invaded or threatened to invade a legal or equitable right of another party which is amenable to the jurisdiction of the court;
(b) where a party has behaved or threatened to behave in an unconscionable manner.

Lord Brandon's reference to freezing injunctions should not be taken as referring to all freezing injunction applications, as that would be contrary to *The Siskina*, where the injunction sought was in fact a freezing injunction. Rather, it must be a reference to the **CJJA 1982, s. 25** (discussed at **16.41**), which provides that the High Court in England and Wales has power to grant interim relief in relation to proceedings which have been or could be commenced in another Regulation State or contracting State to the Brussels and Lugano Conventions (i.e., EU and EFTA countries other than Liechtenstein). The **CJJA 1982, s. 25**, is not restricted to freezing injunctions, but is most commonly invoked in those cases.

Examples

37.16 Lord Browne-Wilkinson in *Channel Tunnel Group Ltd v Balfour Beatty Construction Ltd* [1993] AC 334 in the House of Lords expressed doubt on whether the law as stated in *The Siskina* [1979] AC 210 was correct in restricting the power to grant injunctions to certain exclusive categories. The question was, however, reserved for consideration when it arises. A rather marginal case was *Newport Association Football Club Ltd v Football Association of Wales Ltd* [1995] 2 All ER 87, where it was held that an interim injunction could be granted in a case where the only final relief sought was a declaration. This was somewhat surprising as there was, until 26 April 1999, no jurisdiction to grant an interim declaration.

The *South Carolina Insurance Co.* principles were applied in *Ali v Westminster City Council* [1999] 1 WLR 314, in which it was held that the county court had no jurisdiction to grant an injunction in favour of applicants seeking interim mandatory injunctions to require their local housing authorities to provide them with accommodation pending the resolution of their appeals against decisions that they were not homeless persons within the meaning of the Housing Act 1996.

A company law claim for relief under the Companies Act 1985, s. 459, based on unfairly prejudicial mismanagement is not in itself a substantive cause of action, and it is only if there is a claim that the directors are in breach of fiduciary duty or some other established cause of action that an injunction can be granted in such proceedings (*Re Premier Electronics (GB) Ltd* [2002] 2 BCLC 634).

Person unknown as defendant

Under the pre-CPR rules it was an almost invariable rule that proceedings and orders could only be granted against named parties (*Friern Barnet Urban District Council v Adams* [1927] 2 Ch 25). The only exception related to claims for summary possession of land. 37.17

In a radical decision, *Bloomsbury Publishing Group Ltd v News Group Newspapers Ltd* [2003] EWHC 1087 Ch, [2003] 1 WLR 1633, the claimant was allowed to join 'person or persons unknown' as second defendants to a claim where an interim injunction was granted restraining disclosure of the contents of, or information from, a book prior to its publication date. Laddie J said that if somebody could be identified clearly enough, a court should do what it could to allow injunctive relief to be ordered against him even if it was not possible to identify him by name. Under the CPR, the rules merely say that the defendant 'should' be named (**PD 7, para. 4.1**), and if proceedings are started against an unnamed person, they can be remedied under **CPR, r. 3.10**, unless the court thinks otherwise. On the facts, the injunction would be effective once it was brought to the attention of other people who, knowing of the order, assisted in its breach or nullified the purpose of a trial. The significance attached in this decision to the use of the word 'should' instead of 'must' in **PD 7, para. 4.1**, is hard to justify. These words are often used interchangeably in the CPR: see, for example, the phrases 'should be endorsed' and 'must be endorsed' in **paras 3.5** and **3.5A** of **PD 7**. Nevertheless, *Bloomsbury Publishing Group Ltd v News Group Newspapers Ltd* has been approved by the Court of Appeal in *South Cambridgeshire District Council v Persons Unknown* [2004] EWCA Civ 1280, *The Times*, 11 November 2004.

INJUNCTIONS IN SUPPORT OF THE CRIMINAL LAW

The High Court has jurisdiction to grant injunctions in support of the criminal law. In *Attorney-General v Chaudry* [1971] 1 WLR 1614 Lord Denning MR said: 37.18

> There are many statutes which provide penalties for breach of them — penalties which are enforceable by means of a fine — or even imprisonment — but this has never stood in the way of the High Court granting an injunction. Many a time people have found it profitable to pay a fine and go on breaking the law. In all such cases the High Court has been ready to grant an injunction. . . .
>
> Whenever Parliament has enacted a law and given a particular remedy for the breach of it, such remedy being in an inferior court, nevertheless the High Court always has reserve power to enforce the law so enacted by way of an injunction or declaration or other suitable remedy. The High Court has jurisdiction to ensure obedience to the law whenever it is just and convenient so to do.

These injunctions are exceptional. The main questions are whether criminal proceedings are likely to be effective to achieve the public-interest purposes of the legislation and whether there are good grounds for believing that compliance would not be secured by prosecution (*Guildford Borough Council v Hein* [2005] EWCA Civ 979, *The Times*, 21 September 2005).

In the 1980s there were cases (*Chief Constable of Kent v V* [1983] QB 34; *West Mercia Constabulary v Wagener* [1982] 1 WLR 127; *Chief Constable of Hampshire v A Ltd* [1985] QB 132; *Chief Constable of Leicestershire v M* [1989] 1 WLR 20) dealing with applications for injunctions brought by chief constables to freeze suspected proceeds of crime in advance of any conviction for the crime in question. In *Chief Constable of Leicestershire v M* it was said that the detailed interventions by Parliament in part VI of the Criminal Justice Act 1988 (now in the Proceeds of Crime Act 2002) suggested that the civil courts should not indulge in parallel creativity by extension of the common law principles. In *Attorney-General v Blake* [2001] 1 AC 268 the claimant sought an injunction restraining the defendant from receiving any payment from a publisher resulting from the defendant's criminal conduct as a spy. The defendant had escaped to Moscow in 1966 and there was no realistic prospect of him returning to the United Kingdom. It was held that there was no common law power to confiscate property (the royalties) without compensation and no statutory confiscatory powers applied, so the court had no jurisdiction to grant the injunction.

THE *AMERICAN CYANAMID* GUIDELINES

37.19 In *American Cyanamid Co. v Ethicon Ltd* [1975] AC 396 Lord Diplock laid down guidelines on how the court's discretion to grant interim injunctions should be exercised in the usual types of cases. Although these guidelines are of great authority, they must not be read as if they were statutory provisions, and in practice they are applied with some degree of flexibility. However, it is not unknown for judges to give reasoned judgments in interim injunction cases following the sequence of steps set out by Lord Diplock (for example, *Rottenberg v Monjack* [1993] BCLC 374). The court must also be careful to apply the overriding objective, and to grant an injunction only if it is 'just and convenient'.

The underlying purpose of the guidelines is to enable the court to make an order that will do justice between the parties, whichever way the decision goes at trial, while interfering with the parties' freedom of action to the minimum extent necessary (see *Polaroid Corporation v Eastman Kodak Co.* [1977] RPC 379 per Buckley LJ at p. 395). The guidelines are described in 37.20 to 37.32, but there are exceptions, which are discussed in 37.33 to 37.49.

Serious question to be tried

37.20 Before *American Cyanamid Co. v Ethicon Ltd* [1975] AC 396, the courts would only grant an interim injunction if the applicant could establish a prima facie case on the merits. Consequently, the courts needed to consider the respective merits of the parties' cases in some detail. This encouraged the filing of detailed written evidence supported by voluminous exhibits, and resulted in lengthy interim hearings. As Lord Diplock said at p. 407:

> It is no part of the court's function at this stage of the litigation to try to resolve conflicts of evidence on affidavits as to facts on which the claims of either party may ultimately depend nor to decide difficult questions of law which call for detailed argument and mature consideration.

Therefore, the court only needs to be satisfied that there is a serious question to be tried on the merits. The result is that the court is required to investigate the merits to a limited extent only. All that needs to be shown is that the claimant's cause of action has substance and reality. Beyond that, it does not matter if the claimant's chance of winning is 90 per cent or 20 per cent (*Mothercare Ltd v Robson Books Ltd* [1979] FSR 466 per Megarry V-C at p. 474; *Alfred Dunhill Ltd v Sunoptic SA* [1979] FSR 337 per Megaw LJ at p. 373).

37.21 **Examples** Convincing the court that the claim brought by an applicant for an interim injunction raises a serious question to be tried is not a difficult hurdle to surmount. In *Porter v National Union of Journalists* [1980] IRLR 404, the issue was whether a strike instruction by the union affected a majority of its members. If it did, the union's rule book required a ballot. Neither party adduced accurate figures of the total numbers in the union, nor of the numbers affected by the strike instruction. It was held there was a serious question to be tried.

On the other hand, if there is no serious question to be tried on the substantive claim, the injunction must be refused. *Morning Star Co-operative Society Ltd v Express Newspapers Ltd* [1979] FSR 113 should be regarded as not having passed this hurdle. At the time of the case, the *Daily Star* newspaper was about to be launched. The claimant alleged that it was going to be passed off as the established *Morning Star* newspaper. Apart from the fact that they were both newspapers and had the word 'Star' in their names, they were different in about every other respect. As Foster J commented, 'Only a moron in a hurry would be misled' into thinking that the *Daily Star* was the *Morning Star*, so the claimant had failed to show a serious issue to be tried on the alleged cause of action. A weak claim on the merits combined with relatively little financial harm to the claimant through the defendant's alleged infringement of intellectual property rights resulted in a refusal of relief in *GMG Radio Holdings Ltd v Tokyo Project Ltd* [2005] EWHC 2188 (Ch), LTL 21/10/2005.

In *Boobyer v David Holman and Co. Ltd* [1993] 1 Lloyd's Rep 96 the claimant, a name at Lloyd's, applied for an interim injunction to restrain the defendant underwriting agent from paying cash calls on the claimant for being a member of a number of syndicates. Saville J refused the injunction without considering the balance of convenience as the claimant had failed to show even a serious issue to be tried. In *News Datacom Ltd v Satellite Decoding Systems* [1995] FSR 201 the claimant alleged that the defendant was selling a computerised 'smart card' for decoding satellite television programmes by copying the computer program supplied by the claimant to its customers. It was accepted that the defendant's card enabled its customers to decode the claimant's satellite broadcasts. In its application for an interim injunction the claimant exhibited an expert's report in which the expert stated an opinion that the defendant's product must have been copied from the claimant's program. This opinion was based on the complexity of the program and the implausibility of the defendant's product not being a copy, and not on a comparison of the two products. The High Court of Ireland held that as the claimant had failed to adduce evidence comparing the two products it had failed to show a serious question to be tried.

Sometimes there are arguments about whether the claimant's allegations amount to a cause of action known to the law. An example was *Khorasandjian v Bush* [1993] QB 727. In this case the claimant sought an injunction to restrain the defendant from making harassing and pestering telephone calls. The parties were not married and had never cohabited. There was therefore no jurisdiction to grant an injunction against 'molestation' under the Domestic Violence and Matrimonial Proceedings Act 1976, s. 1. The claimant lived with her mother and had no proprietary interest in the parental home, so had no cause of action in nuisance. The Court of Appeal held by a majority that the tort of harassment exists, and on the facts the judge had been entitled to grant an interim injunction restraining the defendant from 'harassing, pestering or communicating' with the claimant. In a related case, it was held in *Burris v Azadani* [1995] 1 WLR 1372 that, when granting an interim injunction to restrain future assaults or harassment, the court has power to impose an exclusion zone at the same time.

Adequacy of damages to the applicant

If there is a serious question to be tried on the merits of the substantive claim, the court should then consider whether the applicant will be adequately compensated by an award of damages at trial. The test was stated in the following way by Lord Diplock in *American Cyanamid Co. v Ethicon Ltd* [1975] AC 396 at p. 408: 37.22

> If damages in the measure recoverable at common law would be an adequate remedy and the defendant would be in a financial position to pay them, no [interim] injunction should normally be granted.

Damages will often be an adequate remedy for the claimant in claims for breach of contract, including contracts of employment (see *Ali v Southwark London Borough Council* [1988] ICR 567, but the position regarding claims in respect of contracts of employment is not completely free from doubt, see *Powell v Brent London Borough Council* [1988] ICR 176). A term providing for liquidated damages may be inadequate for the applicant where these will be lower than the probable loss caused by a breach of the contract (*Bath and North East Somerset District Council v Mowlem plc* [2004] EWCA Civ 115, [2004] BLR 153). A claimant bringing an action for breach of copyright or confidence may also (depending on the facts) be refused injunctive relief on the ground that damages would be an adequate remedy (*Hubbard v Vosper* [1972] 2 QB 84). However, damages will be inadequate if:

(a) The defendant is unlikely to be able to pay the sum likely to be awarded at trial.
(b) The wrong is irreparable, e.g., loss of the right to vote.
(c) The damage is non-pecuniary, e.g., libel, nuisance, trade secrets.

(d) There is no available market. In *Howard E. Perry and Co. Ltd v British Railways Board* [1980] 1 WLR 1375 the defendant refused to allow the claimant to remove a consignment of steel during a steelworkers' dispute. The claimant sought an order that the defendant permit the claimant to remove it. As steel was otherwise unobtainable at the time, damages were not an adequate remedy.

(e) Damages would be difficult to assess. Examples are loss of goodwill (*Foseco International Ltd v Fordath Ltd* [1975] FSR 507), disruption of business (*Evans Marshall and Co. Ltd v Bertola SA* [1973] 1 WLR 349) and where the defendant's conduct has the effect of killing off a business before it is established (*Mitchelstown Co-operative Society Ltd v Société des Produits Nestlé SA* [1989] FSR 345).

As where the claimant fails to show a serious question to be tried, if damages would be an adequate remedy, that is the end of the matter and the injunction must be refused.

Undertakings in damages

37.23 Subject to some limited exceptions, an undertaking in damages is always required when an interim injunction is granted. The court has a discretion to order an interim injunction subject to a limited undertaking in damages (*RBG Resources plc v Rastogi* (2002) LTL 31/5/2002). By the undertaking the claimant is required to compensate the defendant for any loss incurred by the defendant during the currency of the injunction if it later appears that the injunction was wrongly granted. Its purpose is to provide a safeguard for the defendant who may be unjustifiably prevented from doing something it was entitled to do. As stated in *Wakefield v Duke of Buccleugh* (1865) 12 LT 628, this assists the court '. . . in doing that which was its great object, viz. abstaining from expressing any opinion on the merits of the case until the hearing'.

Undertakings in damages are not required where the Crown or a local authority is seeking an interim injunction to enforce the law (*Kirklees Metropolitan Borough Council v Wickes Building Supplies Ltd* [1993] AC 227), nor from the Financial Services Authority (formerly the Securities and Investments Board) when enforcing provisions of the Financial Services Act 1986 (now replaced by the Financial Services and Markets Act 2000, see *Securities and Investments Board v Lloyd-Wright* [1993] 4 All ER 210), unless the defendant shows a strong prima facie case that its conduct is lawful (*F. Hoffmann-La Roche & Co. AG v Secretary of State for Trade and Industry* [1975] AC 295). In *Customs and Excise Commissioners v Anchor Foods Ltd* [1999] 1 WLR 1139 the Commissioners applied to restrain the disposal of certain assets by the defendant. The purpose of the application was to protect funds which the Commissioners contended should be paid to them. Neuberger J said that in these circumstances the presence or absence of an undertaking in damages was a factor to be weighed when considering the balance of convenience, and was only prepared to grant an injunction if the Commissioners gave an undertaking in damages.

An undertaking is also dispensed with where the injunction is in the nature of final relief (*Fenner v Wilson* [1893] 2 Ch 656), and where an injunction is granted in aid of execution after judgment (*Gwembe Valley Development Co. Ltd v Koshy (No. 4)* (2001) *The Times*, 28 February 2002).

37.24 **Fortifying the undertaking in damages** Where there is doubt about the claimant's solvency and hence the value of the usual undertaking in damages, the claimant may be required to 'fortify the undertaking' by bringing money into court or by providing security. A defendant seeking an order that the claimant must fortify an undertaking needs to satisfy the court that the injunction is likely to cause the defendant significant loss and there must be satisfactory evidence that the claimant may be unable to pay (*Bhimji v Chatwani (No. 2)* [1992] BCLC 387). See also 38.16.

37.25 **Whether the undertaking in damages is an adequate protection for the defendant** In *American Cyanamid Co. v Ethicon Ltd* [1975] AC 396 Lord Diplock said at p. 408:

> If . . . damages would not provide an adequate remedy for the [claimant] in the event of his succeeding at the trial, the court should then consider whether, on the contrary hypothesis that the defendant were to succeed at the trial in establishing his right to do that which was sought to be enjoined, he would be adequately compensated under the [claimant's] undertaking as to damages for the loss he would have sustained by being prevented from doing so between the time of the application and the time of the trial. If damages in the measure recoverable under such an undertaking would be an adequate remedy and the [claimant] would be in a financial position to pay them, there would be no reason upon this ground to refuse an [interim] injunction.
>
> It is where there is doubt as to the adequacy of the respective remedies in damages available to either party or to both, that the question of balance of convenience arises.

It is clear from this that, unlike the question whether the claimant would be adequately compensated in damages, the adequacy of the undertaking will rarely be determinative of the application. If it is an adequate protection, that is 'no reason' for refusing the injunction. The court will then consider the balance of convenience, but the fact that the defendant is adequately protected will be a substantial factor in favour of granting the injunction (see *Bunn v British Broadcasting Corporation* [1998] 3 All ER 552). If the undertaking does not adequately protect the defendant, although that is a reason for refusing the injunction, normally the court will go on to consider the balance of convenience. Even a freezing injunction has been granted in favour of a legally aided claimant (who obviously could not give a valuable undertaking in damages) where otherwise it was a proper case for granting the injunction (*Allen v Jambo Holdings Ltd* [1980] 1 WLR 1252). If the claimant is unable to give an undertaking in damages, care must be exercised before granting an injunction. It was said in *Belize Alliance of Conservation Non-Governmental Organisations v Department of the Environment* [2003] UKPC 63, *The Times*, 25 September 2003, that it is particularly important to form a view on the merits of the claim in such cases, and to grant an injunction only if the claimant has a strong case. Where defendants in an application for a freezing injunction had failed to put in any evidence of the sort of loss they might suffer as a result of the order, it was held in *Bracken Partners Ltd v Guttridge* (2001) LTL 16/1/2002 that there was no present basis for regarding the claimant's undertaking in damages as being insufficient.

Refusal of injunction in extreme cases In extreme cases where the claimant cannot give an adequate undertaking in damages, the court will refuse the injunction without considering the balance of convenience. *Morning Star Co-operative Society Ltd v Express Newspapers Ltd* [1979] FSR 113 was such a case, referred to at **37.21**. In addition to the weak cause of action, the claimant had assets of £170,000 and liabilities of £260,000, so there was no realistic chance of it being able to honour the undertaking, especially as the defendants were likely to suffer appreciable, unquantifiable, damages. In *Merrell Dow Pharmaceuticals Inc. v N. H. Norton and Co. Ltd* [1994] RPC 1 a patentee would probably have had to make a permanent reduction in its prices as a result of an alleged infringement, which was an ascertainable loss, whereas the defendant had an unascertainable loss represented by the possible market share it would not achieve if the injunction was granted. On this basis the injunction was refused. **37.26**

Balance of convenience

Most injunction cases are determined on the balance of convenience. In *American Cyanamid Co. v Ethicon Ltd* [1975] AC 396 Lord Diplock said, at p. 408: **37.27**

> . . . it would be unwise to attempt even to list all the various matters which may need to be taken into consideration in deciding where the balance lies, let alone to suggest the relative weight to be attached to them. These will vary from case to case.

In other cases, such as *Cayne v Global Natural Resources plc* [1984] 1 All ER 225, the courts have insisted that it is not mere convenience that needs to be weighed, but the risk of doing an injustice to one side or the other.

Lord Diplock in *American Cyanamid Co. v Ethicon Ltd* said the extent to which the disadvantages to each party would be incapable of being compensated in damages is always a significant factor in assessing where the balance of convenience lies. In *Dyrlund Smith A/S v Turberville Smith Ltd* [1998] FSR 774 the apparent inability of the defendants to meet an award of damages was regarded as the decisive factor in favour of granting an interim injunction.

A claimant can reduce the potential injustice to the defendant by drafting the terms of the injunction as narrowly as is consistent with preserving the claimant's interests, or by offering undertakings to provide extra safeguards for the defendant.

37.28 **Examples** The claimants in *American Cyanamid Co. v Ethicon Ltd* [1975] AC 396 sought an interim injunction to prevent the defendants marketing a surgical suture alleged to be in breach of patent. The claimants' patented suture had recently been introduced, and the claimants were expanding their market. The defendants' product had not at that time been introduced. They asserted that their product did not infringe the claimants' patent, alternatively, that the patent was invalid. If the injunction had been granted no factories would have closed, but if refused the claimants might have failed to increase their market and would effectively have lost the benefit of their patent. Therefore, the balance favoured the claimants. In *Douglas v Hello! Ltd* [2001] QB 967 an interim injunction to restrain a magazine from publishing wedding photographs alleged to infringe the first two claimants' rights of privacy was refused. If the event had been more intimate and private, the court would have been more willing to assist, but the first two claimants had already sold the rights to their wedding photographs to the third claimant, and the third claimant was adequately protected by an award of damages. On the other side, an injunction would have prevented publication of an issue of the defendant's magazine.

Each case turns on its own facts, but matters found to be important include:

(a) being deprived of employment (*Fellowes and Son v Fisher* [1976] QB 122);
(b) damage to business through picketing (*Hubbard v Pitt* [1976] QB 142);
(c) damage to the goodwill of a business (*Associated Newspapers plc v Insert Media Ltd* [1991] 1 WLR 571);
(d) closing down a factory, which was described as being catastrophic in *Potters-Ballotini Ltd v Weston-Baker* [1977] RPC 202;
(e) although the fact that an injunction may result in a company being wound-up is a weighty matter, in *Astor Chemicals Ltd v Synthetic Technology Ltd* [1990] BCLC 1 this was outweighed by other considerations, particularly the fact that the company wanted to continue trading on a very speculative venture while hopelessly insolvent;
(f) preserving confidential information (*X AG v A Bank* [1983] 2 All ER 464);
(g) the public interest in keeping a drug with life-saving qualities on the market (*Roussel-Uclaf v G. D. Searle and Co. Ltd* [1977] FSR 125);
(h) preserving a substantial financial investment (*Catnic Components Ltd v Stressline Ltd* [1976] FSR 157);
(i) a failure by the claimant to respond to a letter from the defendant frankly stating its plans and enclosing sample containers, use of which is alleged by the claimant to amount to passing off (*Dalgety Spillers Foods Ltd v Food Brokers Ltd* [1994] FSR 504).

Status quo

37.29 In *American Cyanamid Co. v Ethicon Ltd* [1975] AC 396 Lord Diplock said at p. 408 that, in considering the balance of convenience: 'Where other factors appear to be evenly balanced it is a counsel of prudence to take such measures as are calculated to preserve the status quo'. From *Garden Cottage Foods Ltd v Milk Marketing Board* [1984] AC 130, it appears that the status quo ante is the state of affairs before the defendant started the conduct complained of, unless there has been unreasonable delay, when it is the state of affairs immediately before the application. Therefore, it behoves the claimant to act quickly. An apparently unreasonable delay may be excused if sufficiently explained by the claimant.

Special factors

As Lord Diplock said in *American Cyanamid Co. v Ethicon Ltd* [1975] AC 396 at p. 409, '... there may be many special factors to be taken into consideration [in the balance of convenience] in the particular circumstances of individual cases'. If American Cyanamid Co. had been refused interim relief, but had established its claim at trial, it was probable that it would have been commercially impracticable for it to have insisted on Ethicon's sutures then being withdrawn, as doctors would have by then become used to using Ethicon's new sutures. **37.30**

Merits of the claim

In *American Cyanamid Co. v Ethicon Ltd* [1975] AC 396 Lord Diplock said at p. 409 that, as a last resort: **37.31**

> ... it may not be improper to take into account in tipping the balance the relative strength of each party's case as revealed by the affidavit evidence adduced on the hearing of the application. This, however, should be done only where it is apparent upon the facts disclosed by evidence as to which there is no credible dispute that the strength of one party's case is disproportionate to that of the other party. The court is not justified in embarking upon anything resembling a trial of the action upon conflicting affidavits in order to evaluate the strength of either party's case.

An example of a case where the merits were considered under this principle is *Cambridge Nutrition Ltd v British Broadcasting Corporation* [1990] 3 All ER 523. The merits were considered, because the incompensable damage to each party did not differ widely.

Less formal approaches

Although the *American Cyanamid* principles are well established, there are occasions where judges adopt slightly different approaches when deciding whether it is just and convenient (the **Supreme Court Act 1981, s. 37**, test, see 37.14) to grant an injunction. There are some judges who, despite the principles set out above, habitually weigh the respective merits of the parties' cases as disclosed in the written evidence and exhibits in deciding whether or not to grant interim injunctive relief. This approach finds expression in the judgment of Laddie J in *Series 5 Software Ltd v Clarke* [1996] 1 All ER 853. In his judgment Laddie J said the following were the guidelines to be adopted on a proper analysis of the *American Cyanamid* decision: **37.32**

(a) that interim injunctions are discretionary and all the facts of the case must be considered;
(b) there are no fixed rules, and the relief must be kept flexible;
(c) the court should rarely attempt to resolve complex issues of disputed fact or law;
(d) important factors in exercising the jurisdiction to grant interim injunctions are:
  (i) the extent to which damages are likely to be an adequate remedy to either side, and the ability of the other party to pay;
  (ii) the balance of convenience;
  (iii) maintaining the status quo; and
  (iv) any clear view the court may reach about the relative strength of the parties' cases.

In *Carlisle Cumbria United Independent Supporters Society Ltd v Courtnay* (2005) LTL 25/11/2005 the questions asked by Sir Donald Rattee in considering whether to continue an injunction restraining the defendant from acting contrary to an agreement between the parties (a case close to the negative covenant exception discussed at 37.41) were:

(a) whether the claimant had shown a good arguable case on the merits; and
(b) whether the continuation of the injunction would better preserve the court's ability to do justice between the parties at trial than a refusal to continue the injunction.

EXCEPTIONAL CASES

There are some well-settled categories of cases where the *American Cyanamid* guidelines (see 37.19 to 37.32) are not applied. The usual difference is that in these cases the courts will **37.33** investigate the merits of the cause of action. How these various cases can be reconciled with *American Cyanamid Co. v Ethicon Ltd* [1975] AC 396 is a question of some theoretical controversy. Suggestions are that they are examples of the 'special factors' mentioned by Lord Diplock; that the *American Cyanamid* guidelines only apply where the facts are in dispute; that *American Cyanamid* only applies where a trial is likely; and that the existence of some or all of the categories were not directly considered by Lord Diplock.

Final disposal of the claim

37.34 In *NWL Ltd v Woods* [1979] 1 WLR 1294 Lord Diplock said at p. 1306:

> *American Cyanamid Co. v Ethicon Ltd* [1975] AC 396 . . . was not dealing with a case in which the grant or refusal of an injunction at that stage would, in effect, dispose of the action finally in favour of whichever party was successful in the application, because there would be nothing left on which it was in the unsuccessful party's interest to proceed to trial.

Two questions arise (see *Cayne v Global Natural Resources plc* [1984] 1 All ER 225; *Channel Tunnel Group Ltd v Balfour Beatty Construction Ltd* [1993] AC 334). First, on the assumption that the injunction is refused, and taking into account the likely length of time it will take to get to trial and the probable factual situation at that time, is there any realistic possibility that the claimant will wish to proceed to trial? Assertions by claimants that they will in any event proceed to trial to recover damages may be disregarded if in reality a trial would be a meaningless gesture (*Lansing Linde Ltd v Kerr* [1991] 1 WLR 251). Secondly, on the assumption that the injunction is granted, is there any realistic prospect of the defendant insisting on going to trial to vindicate its defence and having the injunction discharged? Where neither party has a real interest in going to trial, the interim application will finally determine the action. In such a case, Lord Diplock in *NWL Ltd v Woods* [1979] 1 WLR 1294, said at p. 1307:

> . . . the degree of likelihood that the [claimant] would have succeeded in establishing his right to an injunction if the action had gone to trial, is a factor to be brought into the balance by the judge in weighing the risks that injustice may result from his deciding the application one way rather than the other.

The degree to which the claimant must establish the merits of the case vary with the circumstances. Thus, in *Cayne v Global Natural Resources plc* [1984] 1 All ER 225, the claimants, who were shareholders in the defendant company, sought injunctions, *inter alia*, to restrain the company from implementing a merger transaction without first obtaining the approval of the company in general meeting. There was no realistic prospect of a trial, because by the time the claim could be tried either the deal would have been implemented or the general meeting would have taken place. The claimants alleged the purpose of the transaction was to maintain the directors in office. The defendants served evidence which, if true, completely destroyed the claimants' case. Instead of applying the *American Cyanamid* guidelines the court had to apply the broad principle of doing its best to avoid injustice. Eveleigh LJ said, at p. 233:

> . . . it would be wrong to run the risk of causing an injustice to a defendant who is being denied the right to trial where the defence put forward has been substantiated by affidavits and a number of exhibits.

Accordingly, an injunction would only have been granted if the claimants' case was overwhelming on its merits. It was not, so the injunction was refused. Conversely, the case of *Lansing Linde Ltd v Kerr* [1991] 1 WLR 251, concerned an application for an injunction to enforce a covenant in restraint of trade. It was not possible for the claim to be tried before the expiry of the period of the restraint; the claimants were not realistically interested in pursuing their claim for damages; so there was no prospect of a trial. Staughton LJ said that in the circumstances justice simply required 'some assessment of the merits . . . more than merely a serious issue to be tried'. A case just on the other side of the line regarding final disposal was *Astor Chemicals Ltd v Synthetic Technology Ltd* [1990] BCLC 1. The main issue on this aspect of the case was whether the defendant had any real interest in taking the case to trial if the injunction was granted, given that the effect of the injunction was almost certainly to force it into liquidation.

It was held that there was some prospect of the liquidator taking the claim to trial for the defendant, so *American Cyanamid Co. v Ethicon Ltd* had to be applied.

Right to freedom of expression

Article 10(1) of the European Convention on Human Rights provides that everyone has the right to freedom of expression. This right is subject to safeguards in **art. 10(2)**, which include restrictions for the protection of the reputation or rights of others. The **Human Rights Act 1998, s. 12(3)**, provides that no relief to restrain publication before trial which might affect the **art. 10(1)** right is to be allowed 'unless the court is satisfied that the applicant is likely to establish that the publication should not be allowed'. In *Cream Holdings Ltd v Banerjee* [2004] UKHL 44, [2005] 1 AC 253, the House of Lords rejected an argument that s. 12(3) simply required the applicant to show a 'real prospect of success', even one convincingly established. Instead, a flexible approach has to be taken. To satisfy the test in s. 12(3) the applicant must in most cases advance a case which will probably ('more likely than not') succeed at trial (Lord Nicholls of Birkenhead at [22]). The court will then exercise its discretion, taking into account the jurisprudence on art. 10 and any other relevant matters. Where this approach does not achieve the legislative intention behind s. 12(3), or fails to give effect to countervailing Convention rights, a lesser degree of likelihood will suffice to satisfy the test. Exceptional cases suggested by Lord Nicholls were where the potential adverse consequences of disclosure are particularly grave, and where a short-term injunction is needed to enable the court to give proper consideration to an application for an interim injunction. A duty of confidentiality expressly assumed under a contract should be given greater weight than an implied duty arising from the general principles of equity (*London Regional Transport v Mayor of London* [2001] EWCA Civ 1491, [2003] EMLR 4; *Attorney-General v MGN Ltd* [2003] EWHC 3201 (Ch), LTL 24/11/2003). 37.35

Defamation claims at common law

Since *Bonnard v Perryman* [1891] 2 Ch 269, it has been held that interim injunctions will not generally be granted in defamation cases if the defendant intends to plead justification. In *Bestobell Paints Ltd v Bigg* [1975] FSR 421 it was held that this principle is unaltered by *American Cyanamid Co. v Ethicon Ltd* [1975] AC 396, because of the overriding public interest in protecting the right to free speech. In *Greene v Associated Newspapers Ltd* [2004] EWCA Civ 1462, [2005] QB 972, it was held that the rule in *Bonnard v Perryman* is also unaltered by the **Human Rights Act 1998, s. 12(3)** (see **37.35**) or by the **Human Rights Act 1998, s. 6** (which requires public authorities to act in ways compatible with the Convention, see **97.6**). There are two conditions: 37.36

(a) The defendant must state in the evidence in reply that it is intended to set up the defence of justification.
(b) The alleged libel must not be obviously untruthful. The claimant may accordingly adduce evidence to prove the falsity of the words published. However, the burden on the claimant is a heavy one (*Holley v Smyth* [1998] QB 726).

In *Holley v Smyth* the claimants could not discharge the burden of proving that the alleged libel was obviously untruthful, but argued that an injunction should nevertheless be granted on account of the defendant's motive. The defendant alleged that the first two claimants were guilty of fraud and that the third and fourth claimants were guilty of negligence in relation to the fraud. He wrote to the claimants enclosing copies of press releases he proposed publishing if the sums he alleged had been lost were not repaid. It was accepted in the Court of Appeal that his motive was not so much to publish the truth, but the less high-minded one of obtaining the sum he considered he was owed by the claimants. It was held that this was insufficient to allow the court to go behind the principle in *Bonnard v Perryman*. However, if the defendant's conduct had gone further and amounted to the crime of blackmail, an injunction would have been granted.

Similar principles apply where the defendant intends to plead fair comment on a matter of public interest (*Fraser v Evans* [1969] 1 QB 349) and where the publication is privileged, unless, in the case of qualified privilege, there is overwhelming evidence of malice (*Harakas v Baltic Mercantile and Shipping Exchange Ltd* [1982] 1 WLR 958). There is even greater reluctance to restrain publication of an expression of opinion. The rule in *Bonnard v Perryman* cannot be evaded by pleading the claim in both libel and breach of confidence, where it is clear that the main claim is in libel (*Woodward v Hutchins* [1977] 1 WLR 760). However, the rule in *Bonnard v Perryman* is ousted where the publication amounts to a contempt of court as well as a libel (*Attorney-General v News Group Newspapers Ltd* [1987] QB 1).

Copyright, privacy and confidentiality claims

37.37 In *Hubbard v Vosper* [1972] 2 QB 84 Lord Denning MR said that in copyright claims defendants with reasonable defences of fair dealing under what is now the Copyright, Designs and Patents Act 1988, s. 30, should not be restrained by injunctions. The reason is that a defendant with such a defence 'is entitled to publish it: and the law will not intervene to suppress freedom of speech except when it is abused'.

Interim injunctions in proceedings to restrain newspapers from publishing articles that invade the claimant's privacy should normally be governed by the *American Cyanamid* guidelines (see **37.19** to **37.32**), as adapted by the Human Rights Act 1998, s. 12(3) (see **37.35**). *Douglas v Hello! Ltd* [2001] QB 967, which is discussed at **37.28** was widely interpreted as opening the door to a new cause of action to protect individual privacy based on the European Convention on Human Rights, art 8. The House of Lords has made clear there is no common law tort of invasion of privacy, with or without the Human Rights Act 1998 (*Wainwright v Home Office* [2003] UKHL 53, [2004] 2 AC 406). Following *Wainwright v Home Office* it will be necessary to frame any claim using the established principles relating to breach of confidence. Information will be private for the purposes of a claim in confidentiality where a reasonable person in the position of the subject of the disclosure would find the publication offensive (*Campbell v MGN Ltd* [2004] UKHL 22, [2004] 2 AC 457). In this case details of the claimant's drug addiction therapy published by the newspaper went beyond the level of detail required to give credibility to the story. Taking account of all the circumstances, the claimant's right to respect for her private life under the European Convention on Human Rights, art. 8, outweighed the newspaper's right to freedom of expression under art. 10. Detailed guidance was given in *A v B plc* [2002] EWCA Civ 337, [2003] QB 195, on how the courts should balance the competing interests in protecting private and family life under art. 8(1), freedom of expression under art. 10(1), and the protection of the reputation and rights of others under art. 10(2). In *Re A Local Authority (Inquiry: Restraint on Publication)* [2003] EWHC 2746 (Fam), [2004] Fam 96, the balance came down in favour of granting an injunction to restrain publication of a report on fostering children as the art. 8 rights of the children and vulnerable adults identified in the report outweighed the local authority's right to publish under art. 10. A confidentiality injunction will be refused where the information is already in the public domain (*D v L* [2003] EWCA Civ 1169, LTL 31/7/2003).

Industrial disputes

37.38 After *American Cyanamid Co. v Ethicon Ltd* [1975] AC 396, whenever an interim injunction was sought against a trade union that claimed it was acting in contemplation or furtherance of a trade dispute, the courts refused to investigate the respective merits of the case on each side, and tended to concentrate on the balance of convenience. Unions could rarely point to significant inconvenience if they were restrained from striking, whereas employers could readily identify their continuing financial losses. The result was that injunctions were invariably granted against unions involved in trade disputes despite the statutory defences.

Legislation was accordingly passed to ensure the merits of the statutory defences are considered before injunctions are granted against trade unions. This legislation is now contained in the Trade Union and Labour Relations (Consolidation) Act 1992, s. 221(2), which provides:

Where—
(a) an application for an interlocutory injunction is made to a court pending the trial of an action, and
(b) the party against whom it is sought claims that he acted in contemplation or furtherance of a trade dispute,

the court shall, in exercising its discretion whether or not to grant the injunction, have regard to the likelihood of that party's succeeding at the trial of the action in establishing any matter which would afford a defence to the action under section 219 (protection from certain tort liabilities) or section 220 (peaceful picketing).

Differing views have been expressed on the interpretation of this section. The approach favoured by Lord Scarman in *NWL Ltd v Woods* [1979] 1 WLR 1294 was that the court must consider:

(a) whether the cause of action against the union discloses a serious action to be tried;
(b) the balance of convenience; and
(c) the likelihood of the union establishing the statutory defence.

Lord Fraser of Tullybelton in the same case pointed out that the word 'likelihood' is a word of degree, and the weight to be given to establishing the trade dispute defence varies according to the degree of the likelihood.

Claims against public authorities

Smith v Inner London Education Authority [1978] 1 All ER 411 is authority for the proposition that public authorities should not be restrained from exercising their statutory powers and duties unless the claimant has an extremely strong case on the merits. If the evidence indicates that the authority is exceeding the law, often upholding the rule of law will prevail over administrative inconvenience (*Bradbury v Enfield London Borough Council* [1967] 1 WLR 1311). Most cases of this nature should now be brought by proceedings for judicial review (**chapter 74**). Where interim injunctions are sought in judicial review proceedings, the *American Cyanamid* principles (see **37.19** to **37.32**) will be applied (see *R v Ministry of Agriculture, Fisheries and Food, ex parte Monsanto plc* [1999] QB 1161). The *Monsanto plc* case also considered how those principles ought to be applied in a public law case. An interim injunction may be granted to restrain the enforcement of a UK statute where there are strong grounds for finding that the statute contravenes EC law (*R v Secretary of State for Transport, ex parte Factortame Ltd (No. 2)* (case C-213/89) [1991] 1 AC 603). **37.39**

In considering an application to disapply national legislation by injunction pending a reference to the ECJ, the Court of Appeal in *R v Her Majesty's Treasury, ex parte British Telecommunications plc* [1994] 1 CMLR 621 said the following factors must be taken into account:

(a) The apparent strength of the Community right asserted. This is not to be considered in depth, as this is a matter for the ECJ. However, if the English court is almost persuaded that the applicant will succeed before the ECJ, albeit having enough doubt to refer the point to the ECJ, an injunction is far more likely to be granted than where the Community right is more speculative.
(b) The importance, in political terms, of the impugned legislation. An injunction is more likely to be granted where the legislation is obscure than where it is a major piece of legislation on which an election was fought.
(c) Other factors include whether the economic survival of the applicant depends on injunctive relief being granted, and the degree to which the applicant can be compensated in damages.

Town and Country Planning Act 1990 injunctions

37.40 For the factors to be taken into account in applications for injunctions under the Town and Country Planning Act 1990, s. 187B, including the personal circumstances of the persons in occupation, see *South Bucks District Council v Porter (No. 2)* [2004] UKHL 33, [2004] 1 WLR 1953, and *South Cambridgeshire District Council v Gammell* [2005] EWCA Civ 1429, [2006] 1 WLR 658.

Negative covenants and covenants in restraint of trade

37.41 A perpetual injunction has been held to issue 'as of course' where it is established that the defendant is in breach of a valid express negative covenant (*Doherty v Allman* (1878) 3 App Cas 709). The same principle applies to applications for interim injunctions (*Attorney-General v Barker* [1990] 3 All ER 257).

As a matter of competition law, a negative covenant which is in restraint of trade will not be enforced unless it is in a contract of employment or a contract for the sale of a business and its terms relating to activities restrained, duration and geographical limits are reasonably required to protect the covenantee's legitimate interests. In *Office Overload Ltd v Gunn* [1977] FSR 39, the defendant was the branch manager of the claimant's employment agency in Croydon. In his contract of employment he covenanted not to work for or set up a competing business in the Croydon area for one year after ceasing to work for the claimant. After giving notice the defendant immediately started competing. The claimant applied for an interim injunction. Given that to be valid a covenant has to be for a limited period of time, refusal of interim relief will usually deprive a claimant of the benefit of the covenant. Lord Denning MR accordingly said:

> Covenants in restraint of trade are in a special category . . . if they are prima facie valid and there is an infringement the courts will grant an injunction.

A covenant will be prima facie valid if:

(a) all the facts are before the court; and

(b) the covenant is reasonable in ambit, area and duration.

37.42 **Restraint of trade cases to which the *American Cyanamid* guidelines apply** The rule that an interim injunction will be issued to prevent breach of a valid covenant in restraint of trade (*Office Overload Ltd v Gunn* [1977] FSR 39) applies only where there is no sustainable dispute concerning the claimant's cause of action. If there is real doubt about the claimant's case, the *American Cyanamid* guidelines apply. Thus, in *Lawrence David Ltd v Ashton* [1991] 1 All ER 385, the claimant had dismissed the defendant from his employment, and there was a real issue as to whether that amounted to a repudiatory breach of the employment contract (and if so, it could not insist on the covenant being observed). Further, the terms of the covenant were perhaps too wide. Given those two matters, the case was not an open-and-shut one in favour of the claimant, and the *American Cyanamid* guidelines were applied.

As the foundation of this exception is the effective deprivation of the employer of the benefit of the covenant due to the effluxion of time before trial, the exception does not apply if a trial can be arranged before the period of the covenant expires (for example, through ordering a speedy trial) (*Dairy Crest Ltd v Pigott* [1989] ICR 92). An example of what can be done with cooperation from all sides is *Symphony Group plc v Hodgson* [1994] QB 179, where the action was tried six weeks after the employee gave his notice.

Injunctions to restrain breaches of covenants in employment contracts are often combined with injunctions to restrain the misuse of confidential information obtained during the defendant's employment. Injunctions to restrain breach of confidence are decided in accordance with *American Cyanamid* guidelines, see *Lock International plc v Beswick* [1989] 1 WLR 1268, or the guidelines in *A v B plc* [2002] EWCA Civ 337, [2003] QB 195, and 37.37.

Enforced inactivity ('garden leave') If a covenant in a contract of employment against working for competitors is too wide and therefore void, the employer may still be able to obtain some injunctive relief if the employee resigns and starts working for a competitor under the principle in *Evening Standard Co. Ltd v Henderson* [1987] ICR 588. In this case the Court of Appeal found that a newspaper production manager, whose contract provided that he had to give a year's notice, was in clear breach of his contract of employment when he purported to give two months' notice after which he intended to work for a competitor. The claimant refused to accept the defendant's repudiation of his contract, and undertook to pay the defendant his full normal salary during his period of notice. Applying the *American Cyanamid* guidelines, an injunction was granted restraining the defendant from working for any competitor for his contractual period of notice, thereby giving the defendant a period of 'garden leave'. It is not always possible to obtain a 'garden leave' injunction even if the employee fails to give the contractual period of notice. The cases fall into two categories (see *Langston v Amalgamated Union of Engineering Workers (No. 2)* [1974] ICR 510). In the first, the employment contract extends to an obligation to permit the employee to do the contractual work. Theatrical engagements usually fall into this category. In these cases the employer needs a provision in the employment contract entitling the employer to send the employee home on garden leave. There will be little scope for implying such a term into the contract. Without such a term, no injunction will be granted. In the second category the employment contract is confined to the employer agreeing to pay wages for the work done. In this category the employer is entitled to send the employee home on garden leave even in the absence of an express or implied term, because there is no contractual obligation to prevent this. Garden leave injunctions are therefore far more likely to be granted in this category. See *William Hill Organisation Ltd v Tucker* [1999] ICR 291. Other decisions have shown that enforcing a period of idleness on the defendant is a factor to be taken into account in the balance of convenience against granting such an injunction (*Euro Brokers Ltd v Rabey* [1995] IRLR 206), and it may be appropriate to impose the injunction for a period shorter than the contractual period of notice where other 'defectors' are on shorter periods of notice than the defendant (*GFI Group Inc. v Eaglestone* [1994] IRLR 119). 37.43

Injunction equivalent to specific performance

The House of Lords in *Scandinavian Trading Tanker Co. AB v Flota Petrolera Ecuatoriana* [1983] 2 AC 694 held that specific performance will not be ordered of a non-demise time charter. Under this type of charterparty the owner provides the ship and the crew, and the charterer provides the cargo. It is therefore a contract for services, which the law never enforces by specific performance. In *Lauritzencool AB v Lady Navigation Inc.* [2005] EWCA Civ 579, [2005] 1 WLR 3686, it was held that nevertheless the court could grant an interim injunction prohibiting a shipowner from employing the vessel in a manner inconsistent with a charterparty. Such an order does not juristically amount to an order for specific performance, even if in practical reality it compels the owner to perform the charterparty. 37.44

Arbitration Act 1996 injunctions

The Arbitration Act 1996, s. 44, provides: 37.45

(1) Unless otherwise agreed by the parties, the court has for the purposes of and in relation to arbitral proceedings the same power of making orders about the matters listed below as it has for the purposes of and in relation to legal proceedings.
(2) Those matters are—
 (a) the taking of the evidence of witnesses;
 (b) the preservation of evidence;
 (c) making orders relating to property which is the subject of the proceedings or as to which any question arises in the proceedings . . .;
 (d) the sale of any goods the subject of the proceedings;
 (e) the granting of an interim injunction or the appointment of a receiver.

(3) If the case is one of urgency, the court may, on the application of a party or proposed party to the arbitral proceedings, make such orders as it thinks necessary for the purpose of preserving evidence or assets.

In *Cetelem SA v Roust Holdings Ltd* [2005] EWCA Civ 618, [2005] 1 WLR 3555, a dispute arose between parties to a share sale contract containing a London arbitration clause. A condition precedent under the contract was that approval had to be given by the Russian Central Bank. Five weeks before the expiry of the time for obtaining approval, no action had been taken by the defendant, so the claimant applied for an urgent mandatory interim injunction requiring the defendant to lodge the necessary papers in Russia. It was held that such an order could only be made if it was necessary for the preservation of evidence or assets, and there was no jurisdiction to make the order on any wider basis. Nevertheless the injunction satisfied the test. 'Assets' to be preserved under s. 44(3) could include choses in action. In this case the injunction was necessary to preserve the claimant's contractual right to purchase the shares, because the right to purchase them would be lost if no application was made for Russian Central Bank approval.

Apart from the Arbitration Act 1996, s. 44, the High Court also has an inherent jurisdiction to grant interim injunctions. This jurisdiction can be invoked even if there is an arbitration clause in the contract underlying the dispute which might be invoked at a later stage and lead to a stay of the court proceedings (*Glidepath Holding BV v Thompson* [2004] EWHC 2234 (Comm), [2005] 1 All ER (Comm) 434).

No defence

37.46 In *Official Custodian for Charities v Mackey* [1985] Ch 168 Scott J said that the *American Cyanamid* principles: 'are not, in my view, applicable to a case where there is no arguable defence to the [claimant's] claim'. The court will not consider the balance of convenience, but will grant the relief claimed subject to the usual equitable considerations. Injunctions have been granted on this basis in cases of clear trespass (*Patel v W. H. Smith (Eziot) Ltd* [1987] 1 WLR 853) and of clear breach of contract (*Sheppard and Cooper Ltd v TSB Bank plc* [1996] 2 All ER 654). Similarly, if all that is at issue on the merits is a simple point of construction, the court will resolve it and dismiss or grant the application accordingly (*Associated British Ports v Transport and General Workers Union* [1989] 1 WLR 939 at p. 979).

Alternatively, where there is no defence with real prospects of success the claimant may apply for summary judgment including a final order for an injunction, instead of applying for an interim order (*Viscount Chelsea v Muscatt* [1990] 2 EGLR 48). Summary judgment was entered and an injunction granted in *WWF-World Wide Fund for Nature v World Wrestling Federation Entertainment Inc.* [2002] EWCA Civ 196, [2002] FSR 504, in a claim to enforce a settlement of an earlier trade-mark dispute. A settlement is presumed to represent a reasonable division of the parties' trading interests for the purposes of the restraint-of-trade doctrine, and it is for the party seeking to go behind the settlement to show grounds for doing so, such as the settlement being contrived, or there being no reasonable basis for the rights claimed, or the settlement being otherwise contrary to the public interest.

Restraint of legal proceedings

37.47 *American Cyanamid* principles do not govern the exceptional jurisdiction of the courts to restrain the commencement of legal proceedings. Most commonly this arises in relation to preventing the presentation of petitions to wind up companies (see **79.28** to **79.32**). An injunction may also be sought to restrain foreign proceedings to prevent 'forum shopping', if it can be established that the foreign proceedings would be vexatious or oppressive (*Société Nationale Industrielle Aérospatiale v Lee Kui Jak* [1987] AC 871, see **16.71**).

Worldwide injunctions

In exceptional cases the courts may make injunctive orders having a worldwide effect. Such orders have been made in a small number of freezing injunction cases (see **38.9**), and also in an application to enforce a covenant of confidentiality against a former employee of the Royal household (*Attorney-General v Barker* [1990] 3 All ER 257). **37.48**

Medical treatment

In *Re J (A Minor) (Child in Care: Medical Treatment)* [1993] Fam 15 an application was made for an interim injunction to compel doctors to give a child in an intensive care unit a specific form of medical treatment. It was held that there was absolutely no room in such a case for the application of the *American Cyanamid* principles. The proper approach was to consider the options available to the court, and in the proper exercise of its inherent powers to make such orders as would best serve the interests of the child pending a final decision. There was no question of considering whether damages were an adequate remedy, of finding the balance of convenience or of preserving the status quo. In the event, no order was made, with the result that there was no fetter on the clinical judgment of the doctors treating the child. **37.49**

INTERIM MANDATORY INJUNCTIONS

In *Shepherd Homes Ltd v Sandham* [1971] Ch 340 Megarry J said that an interim mandatory injunction would only be granted if the court felt a 'high degree of assurance' about the merits of the claimant's cause of action. This formulation was approved in *Locabail International Finance Ltd v Agroexport* [1986] 1 WLR 657, where the Court of Appeal refused a mandatory injunction for the payment of money. Nevertheless, there are exceptions (see *Zockoll Group Ltd v Mercury Communications Ltd* [1998] FSR 354). In *Leisure Data v Bell* [1988] FSR 367, a dispute arose about the copyright in a computer program developed by the defendant for the claimant. The claimant was granted a mandatory injunction despite the merits being equally arguable either way. Partly this was because the claimant was prepared to give wide-ranging undertakings to protect the defendant's position, and partly because the practical reality of the situation was that of the two parties only the claimant was in a position to make commercial use of the program. **37.50**

The importance of taking the course carrying the least risk of injustice was emphasised in *Nikitenko v Leboeuf Lamb Greene and Macrae* (1999) *The Times*, 26 January 1999. Rather surprisingly, Pumfrey J in *Incasep Ltd v Jones* (2001) LTL 26/10/2001 said that an application for an interim mandatory injunction requiring a company to reinstate the claimant as an executive director pending the outcome of his unfair prejudice petition under the Companies Act 1985, s. 459, was governed by the *American Cyanamid* guidelines, albeit having regard to particular factors concerning the potential injustice that such injunctions could cause. On the facts the injunction was refused.

DEFENCES

Any of the following equitable defences and bars to relief may be raised on an application for an interim injunction: **37.51**

(a) Acquiescence. This arises where the claimant's conduct (usually inactivity) induces the defendant to believe something to his detriment (*Davies v Marshall* (1861) 10 CB NS 697; *Jones v Stones* [1999] 1 WLR 1739; see **10.52**).
(b) Delay or laches. Simply allowing time to elapse may persuade a court to refuse injunctive relief even if the conduct does not amount to acquiescence. Delay is a more significant factor in interim applications than at trial (*Johnson v Wyatt* (1863) De G J & S 18). The

length of delay meriting refusal of relief depends on the nature of the case and whether the defendant has been prejudiced, but usually will need to be measured in months. See, for example, *Century Electronics Ltd v CVS Enterprises Ltd* [1983] FSR 1 and *Newport Association Football Club Ltd v Football Association of Wales Ltd* [1995] 2 All ER 87, where the facts were sufficiently exceptional to excuse a two-year delay. Furthermore, what may appear to be an unreasonable delay may be justified by the claimant (*Carroll v Tomado Ltd* [1971] FSR 218). On the other hand, a delay of 20 days was held to bar relief in *Bunn v British Broadcasting Corporation* [1998] 3 All ER 552, where an application to restrain the broadcast of confidential information was made just two working days before the intended date of the broadcast. Delay interrelates with the status quo (for which, see **37.29**).

(c) Hardship. This is taken into account in the balance of convenience.

(d) Clean hands. Inequitable conduct by the claimant may be a bar to equitable relief (*Hubbard v Vosper* [1972] 2 QB 84).

(e) Equity does not act in vain. In *Attorney-General v Guardian Newspapers Ltd (No. 2)* [1990] 1 AC 109 an injunction to restrain breach of confidence was refused where there had already been widespread publication.

(f) 'The court will not and ought not to make an order performance or obedience to which it cannot enforce' (per Astbury J in *Amber Size and Chemical Co. Ltd v Menzel* [1913] 2 Ch 239). Injunctions are therefore rarely granted against children, because they cannot be committed to prison and can rarely pay a fine (*G v Harrow London Borough Council* [2004] EWHC 17 (QB), LTL 23/1/2004).

(g) An injunction will be refused if its effect is to enforce an agreement for personal services (e.g., *Warren v Mendy* [1989] 1 WLR 853).

(h) Difficulty in compliance. An injunction was refused in *Unique Pub Properties Ltd v Licensed Wholesale Co. Ltd* (2003) LTL 13/10/2003 as it would have imposed on the defendant a serious obligation to check information given to it by its tenants, any error constituting a breach.

THE ORDER

37.52 There are currently four standard forms for interim injunction orders:

(a) **PF 39 CH**, order for an injunction (intended action) (introduced in March 2005);

(b) **PF 40 CH**, order for interim injunction (for use where substantive proceedings have been issued) (introduced in March 2005);

(c) Freezing injunction order (**PD 25, Annex**, revised 1 October 2005);

(d) Search order (**PD 25, Annex**, revised 1 October 2005).

All these forms are for use in the county courts and High Court, and both the Queen's Bench Division and the Chancery Division.

A penal notice must be inserted on the front page of the order warning the defendant that breach may result in imprisonment or other penalties. By **PD 40B, para. 9.1**, the standard form of penal notice is in the following form:

> If you the within-named [ ] do not comply with this order you may be held to be in contempt of court and imprisoned or fined, or [in the case of a company or corporation] your assets may be seized.

Undertakings

37.53 Undertakings given by the claimant, such as undertakings given in applications without notice (37.7), and the undertaking in damages (**PD 25, para. 5.1(1)**), are incorporated into an order for an interim injunction. An impecunious claimant may be required to fortify the undertaking in damages by providing security or paying money into court (37.24). The general principle is that the amount of security should be based on the highest arguable figure for the likely damage to the defendant that is supported by the evidence (*Business Online Group plc v MCI Worldcom Ltd* [2001] EWCA Civ 1399, LTL 9/8/2001).

Until the standard form injunctions were changed in March 2005, there was no need in most interim injunctions, other than freezing injunctions, to include an undertaking to pay the reasonable costs of any third party incurred as a result of the order (*Miller Brewing Co. v Ruhi Enterprises Ltd* (2003) *The Times*, 6 June 2003). In *Smithkline Beecham plc v Apotex Europe Ltd* [2005] EWHC 1655 (Ch), [2006] 1 WLR 872, the claimant obtained an interim injunction in the pre-2005 form against alleged infringement of patented pharmaceuticals by the original defendants. These defendants were supplied by related companies based in Canada (the additional defendants). The additional defendants were made parties two days before the injunction was discharged, and then sought to recover on the claimant's undertaking in damages. As this was a pre-2005 injunction there was no express undertaking to compensate third parties. It was held that the additional defendants only took the benefit of the undertaking from the day they were joined, not retrospectively, which was regarded as *de minimis*. It was also held that the injunction could not be corrected under the slip rule (**CPR, r. 40.12**) to include an undertaking to compensate third parties. The slip rule can only be used to correct mistakes on matters which the court or party had in mind. Here no one had thought of including an undertaking to compensate third parties until after the new standard forms were introduced. **Forms PF 39 CH** and **PF 40 CH** contain undertakings to compensate both parties and third parties who suffer loss caused by the order. Unless there is a convincing reason for amending the undertaking (ultimately the judge has a discretion on the wording of the order), this should be included in all interim injunction orders.

Operative provisions

The operative part of the order for an interim injunction should not be in terms wider than is necessary to do justice between the parties. In *Moat Housing Group-South Ltd v Harris* [2005] EWCA Civ 287, [2005] 3 WLR 691, Brooke LJ said that the relief granted must be limited to that which is necessary and proportionate as a means of avoiding the apprehended harm. *Hall v Save Newchurch Guinea Pigs (Campaign)* [2005] EWHC 372 (QB), *The Times*, 7 April 2005, was an application under the **Protection from Harassment Act 1997, s. 3**, for an injunction and an exclusion zone of seven parishes, covering 200 square kilometres. Although there had been extreme conduct in the past, only a prohibitory injunction was granted. The judge said that an exclusion zone might be added later if the initial injunction was not effective. 37.54

The injunction should be worded so that the defendant can know with certainty what is and what is not permitted (**PD 25, para. 5.3**). Thus, an order which restrained, among other things, the defendant 'from otherwise infringing' a patent lacked sufficient specificity (*Hepworth Plastics Ltd v Naylor Bros (Clayware) Ltd* [1979] FSR 521). It is usually best to avoid using legal terms of art, especially the names of torts, which often include matters of degree with the result that the defendant will often not know whether specific conduct will breach the order. A proposed order restraining disclosure of 'confidential information' is oppressive, excessively general and wide. Instead, it needs to be limited to defined confidential information (*Raks Holdings AS v TTPCom Ltd* [2004] EWHC 2137 (Ch), LTL 29/7/2004). The judge will have regard to the draft prepared by the claimant, and may initial the draft without amendment. Ultimately, however, the choice of wording is a matter within the discretion of the judge (*Khorasandjian v Bush* [1993] QB 727). It will not usually be appropriate to qualify the terms of an injunction to protect the defendant from the consequences of any misbehaviour by its employees (*British Telecommunications plc v Nextcall Telecom plc* [2000] FSR 679). Where the order is made in the presence of all relevant parties (or at least at a hearing of which they had notice even if they did not attend), it may be expressed to last 'until trial or further order' (**PD 25, para. 5.2**).

Injunctions affecting third parties

37.55 The standard-form injunction orders **PF 39 CH** and **PF 40 CH** include undertakings to compensate third parties served with or notified of the order who suffer loss as a result of the order (see 37.58). With effect from 1 October 2005, where an injunction will affect a third party who was not present at the hearing, that person may request copies of any materials read by the judge, any documents prepared after the hearing in compliance with directions of the judge, and the note of the hearing (**PD 25, para. 9.2**). The applicant is required to comply with such a request promptly, unless the court orders otherwise.

Suspending the operation of an injunction

37.56 The court has the power to suspend the operation of an injunction. This is generally exercised where it is necessary to ensure injunctions operate in a just and convenient (or just and proportionate, see 37.14) manner. See *Waverley Borough Council v Lee* [2003] EWHC 29 (Ch), LTL 14/1/2003.

INQUIRY AS TO DAMAGES

37.57 Where it transpires that an interim injunction should not have been granted (for example, if the claimant loses at trial) the defendant may seek to enforce the undertaking in damages by applying for an order for an inquiry as to damages. If a claimant discontinues (for which, see **chapter 53**), the court should consider the circumstances and the reasons why this has been done before ordering an inquiry as to damages (*Goldman Sachs International Ltd v Lyons* (1995) *The Times*, 28 February 1995).

Excessive, inexcusable delay may result in an application for an inquiry as to damages being dismissed (*Barratt Manchester Ltd v Bolton Metropolitan Borough Council* [1998] 1 WLR 1003). An order for an inquiry is not penal and does not depend on fault on the part of the claimant.

Where an interim injunction is discharged before trial, the court has a number of options on an application for an inquiry as to damages. These were identified in *Cheltenham and Gloucester Building Society v Ricketts* [1993] 1 WLR 1545, as being:

(a) To accede to the application and immediately proceed to determine the question of damages. This should be done only in the most straightforward cases.
(b) To allow the application, and to order the inquiry by a master or district judge. The judge making the order will give directions for the inquiry.
(c) To stand the application over (that is, adjourn it) to a specified time. This is perhaps the usual order where an injunction is discharged during the interim stages of a claim. It is the most appropriate option where matters material to the question whether it is just to order an inquiry are still in issue and will only be determined at trial. The application is most frequently stood over to trial, when all the facts should be known.
(d) To order an inquiry and to direct that the question of liability on the undertaking be determined at the inquiry. This is unusual.
(e) To refuse the application. This is only done in straightforward cases where, for example, it is clear the defendant has suffered no loss as a result of the injunction.
(f) To make an order setting off the sum found on making an inquiry against an earlier judgment. Such an order was made in *Keller v Cowen* [2001] EWCA Civ 1704, LTL 6/11/2001, where the earlier judgment was obtained in a foreign court, and despite there being no mutuality of debts.

Example 37.1 High Court interim injunction (form PF 40 CH)

IN THE HIGH COURT OF JUSTICE Claim No. 73635
QUEEN'S BENCH DIVISION

BEFORE the Honourable Mr Justice Collier (judge in private)
Monday the 16th day of January 2006

BETWEEN

CASPKEELER PRODUCTS LIMITED Claimants

— and —

LOAMER TECHTRONICS LIMITED Defendants

ORDER FOR AN INJUNCTION

Important

NOTICE TO THE DEFENDANTS

(1) This Order prohibits you from doing the acts set out in this Order. You should read it carefully. You are advised to consult a Solicitor as soon as possible. You have a right to ask the Court to vary or discharge this Order.
(2) If you disobey this Order you may be guilty of Contempt of Court [and any of your directors may be sent to prison or fined] and you may be fined or your assets may be seized.

Include the words in square brackets in the case of a corporate defendant. This notice is not a substitute for the endorsement of a penal notice

An Application was made on 16 January 2006 by Counsel for the Claimants to the Judge and was attended by Counsel for the Defendants. The Judge heard the Application and read the witness statements listed in Schedule 1 and accepted the undertakings in Schedule 2 of this Order.

IT IS ORDERED that

THE INJUNCTION

(1) Until after final judgment in this claim the Defendants must not:
   (a) license the right to distribute the Loamer Techtron Capacitor anywhere in the world in the term of six years from 16 September 2002 granted to the Claimants Caspkeeler Products Limited under an agreement between the Claimants and the Defendants dated 16 September 2002;
   (b) sell Loamer Techtron Capacitors otherwise than through the Claimants Caspkeeler Products Limited;
   (c) assert or represent to customers that the Claimants Caspkeeler Products Limited are not the sole distributors of the Loamer Techtron Capacitor.

Costs of the Application

(2) [The Defendant shall pay the Claimant's costs of this Application.] [The costs of this Application are reserved to be dealt with by the Judge who tries this Claim.] [The costs of this Application are to be costs in the case.] [The costs of this Application are to be the Claimant's costs in the case.]

Variation or Discharge of This Order

The Defendants may apply to the Court at any time to vary or discharge this Order, but if they wish to do so they must first inform the Claimants' Solicitors in writing at least 48 hours beforehand.

Name and Address of Claimants' Solicitors

The Claimant's Solicitors are:
Collins, Brown and Heath, of 7 Ingrave Road, Birmingham B5 8EP
Ref: JGB/4663, Telephone: 01212158349.

Interpretation of This Order

(1) In this Order the words 'he' 'him' or 'his' include 'she' 'her' or 'hers' and 'it' or 'its'.
(2) Where there are two or more Defendants then (unless the contrary appears):
  (a) references to 'the Defendant' mean both or all of them;
  (b) an Order requiring 'the Defendant' to do or not to do anything requires each Defendant to do or not to do it.

The Effect of This Order

(1) A Defendant who is an individual who is ordered not to do something must not do it himself or in any other way. He must not do it through others acting on his behalf or on his instructions or with his encouragement.
(2) A Defendant which is a corporation and which is ordered not to do something must not do it itself or by its directors, officers, employees or agents or in any other way.

Service of This Order

This Order shall be served by the Claimants on the Defendants.

SCHEDULE 1

Witness Statements

The Judge read the following witness statements before making this Order:
(1) Rachel Helen Radcliffe, made on 11 January 2006,
(2) Daniel Jordan Loamer, made on 12 January 2006.

SCHEDULE 2

Undertaking given to the Court by the Claimants

If the Court later finds that this Order has caused loss to the Defendants or any other Party served with or notified of this Order and decides that the Defendant or other Party should be compensated for that loss, the Claimants will comply with any Order the Court may make.

All communications to the Court about this Order should be sent to Room 307, Royal Courts of Justice, Strand, London WC2A 2LL quoting the case number. The office is open between 10 a.m. and 4.30 p.m. Monday to Friday. The telephone number is (020) 7936 6148.

Quantification of damages

37.58 An application for an inquiry as to damages made by a successful defendant at the end of the trial will normally only be refused if it is unlikely that the defendant has suffered any provable loss (*McDonald's Hamburgers Ltd v Burgerking (UK) Ltd* [1987] FSR 112). Ordinary contractual principles are applied on causation and quantum, though it is possible for aggravated or exemplary damages to be awarded in cases where the claimant has acted oppressively. Where defendants had sought enormous damages and failed, the court was justified in refusing any order rather than seeking out a smaller loss (*Tyco European Metal Framing Ltd v New Systems Ltd* (2001) LTL 7/12/2001). As a term for granting permission to discontinue, the court in *FSL Services Ltd v MacDonald* [2001] EWCA Civ 1008, LTL 21/6/2001, had made a direction that there be an inquiry as to damages in respect of a freezing injunction that had previously been granted. The losses claimed by the defendant were the costs incurred by the defendant and ordered to be paid to the claimant by the defendant in contesting the injunction at the earlier stage. The claimant applied for an order striking out the inquiry. It was held that although there is jurisdiction to strike out an inquiry, on the facts it was inappropriate to do so, as the objections to the recovery of the costs were matters that could best be raised on the inquiry itself. Inquiries are normally conducted by masters and district judges.

UNDERTAKINGS GIVEN BY THE DEFENDANT

Instead of contesting an application for an interim injunction, a defendant may give undertakings in similar terms to the injunction sought by the claimant. Such undertakings have the same force as an injunction ordered by the court, with the result that the defendant will be in contempt of court if the undertakings are broken. In return, the claimant will be required to give a cross-undertaking in damages to safeguard the defendant. **37.59**

A defendant can be released from an undertaking only in special circumstances and where this will not occasion an injustice. (*Eronat v Tabbah* [2002] EWCA Civ 950, LTL 10/7/2002). In the absence of special circumstances, a claim commenced in breach of an undertaking will be struck out as an abuse of process, unless striking out would not further the overriding objective (*Di Placito v Slater* [2003] EWCA Civ 1863, [2004] 1 WLR 1605).

DISCHARGE

Applications to vary or discharge injunctions are made by application notice to a judge, often the same judge who granted the initial injunction. The normal practice where there are cross-applications to continue an interim injunction and to discharge the original interim injunction is for both applications to be heard at the same time. However, the court could hear the applications separately (*Network Multimedia Television Ltd v Jobserve Ltd* (2000) *The Times*, 25 January 2001) applying the following factors: the likely delay if they are heard together; prejudice to the defendant if the injunction were to be discharged after being renewed; prejudice to the claimant if the injunction is discharged and later reimposed; the grounds relied upon for discharging the injunction; the interrelationship of the two applications; the circumstances in which the injunction was obtained; and any special facts. Grounds for varying or discharging injunctions include: **37.60**

(a) Material non-disclosure if the injunction was granted without notice. In *Network Multimedia Television Ltd v Jobserve Ltd (No. 2)* (2001) LTL 9/4/2001 it was found there were non-deliberate material non-disclosures. The injunction obtained without notice was therefore discharged. On a full consideration of the *American Cyanamid* factors (see 37.19 to 37.32) the judge decided that it was an appropriate case for reimposing an injunction, albeit recognising that this discretion should be used sparingly after a previous injunction had been discharged.
(b) The particulars of claim being inconsistent with the written evidence on an application without notice.
(c) The facts not justifying relief without giving notice.
(d) The claimant's failure to comply with the undertakings incorporated into the order.
(e) The order having an oppressive effect.
(f) Unreasonable interference with the rights of innocent third parties. Affected third parties are entitled to apply for a variation of the order. All the circumstances have to be considered, and it is sometimes within the court's powers to grant an injunction to restrain a defendant from fulfilling a contract already entered into with an innocent third party. An example is where this is necessary in order to protect the claimant's trade secrets (*PSM International plc v Whitehouse* [1992] IRLR 279).
(g) Material change in the circumstances.
(h) A failure to prosecute the substantive claim with due speed.
(i) If the claim is stayed other than by agreement between the parties, any interim injunction, other than a freezing injunction, will be set aside unless the court orders that it should continue in force (CPR, r. 25.10).
(j) If the claim is struck out for non-payment of the fees payable at allocation or listing, the interim injunction will lapse 14 days after the claim is struck out. However, if within

that 14-day period the claimant applies to reinstate the claim, the injunction will remain in force until the hearing of that application (unless the court otherwise orders) (**r. 25.11**).

Non-disclosure at on-notice hearing

37.61 Traditionally, material non-disclosure has only been a ground for discharging an injunction granted without notice (see **37.60**). In *DEG-Deutsche Investitions- und Entwicklungsgesellschaft mbH v Koshy (No. 2)* [2005] EWHC 2896 (Ch), [2005] 1 WLR 2434, a freezing injunction (granted before the introduction of the CPR) was continued after an on-notice hearing. The defendant argued that the facts found by the trial judge showed there had been material non-disclosure by the claimant. It was held that, apart from provision made by rules of court, there is no jurisdiction to discharge a freezing injunction based on alleged non-disclosure at an on-notice hearing. **Rule 3.1**(7) provides, 'A power of the court under these Rules to make an order includes a power to vary or revoke the order.' As the case was decided under the old rules, Hart J did not express an opinion on whether the wording of **r. 3.1**(7) has changed the position. It is doubtful whether it has. The rule is expressed as conferring a jurisdiction to vary or revoke, but does not deal in terms with the grounds for doing so. A provision more likely to assist the argument is **PD 25, para. 3.3**, which says that the evidence in support of applications for interim injunctions must include 'all material facts of which the court should be made aware'. The counter-argument is that what the court should be made aware of depends on the nature of the application.

BREACH

37.62 Breach of an injunction is a contempt of court punishable by imprisonment or sequestration. Contempt must be proved beyond reasonable doubt. Punishment for contempt of court is considered in more detail in **chapter 78**.

Clearly, the person against whom the order was made will be in contempt if he or she acts in breach of an injunction after having notice of it (*Z Ltd v A-Z and AA-LL* [1982] QB 558 per Eveleigh LJ). A non-party who aids and abets the defendant in breaching the terms of an injunction, or who acts with the intention of impeding the administration of justice, will also be in contempt of court (*Attorney-General v Times Newspapers Ltd* [1992] 1 AC 191). The Attorney-General had obtained interim injunctions against a number of national newspapers restraining them from publishing materials from a book (*Spycatcher*) pending trial. The substantive action was based on alleged breach of confidence. The present defendants were not named in the injunction. They obtained serialisation rights in the book, and published their first instalment. The purpose of the injunctions was to prevent publication pending trial. Publication nullified the purpose of the trial by putting into the public domain what was alleged to be confidential material, and thereby impeded or interfered with the administration of justice. As the defendants had acted knowingly, they were in contempt of court. To establish a contempt by a non-party it must be demonstrated both that the non-party's acts defeated, in whole or in part, the court's purpose in granting the injunction, and that the non-party appreciated that what he was doing was what the injunction was intended to prevent. There is no need to prove an intention to thwart the court's purpose (*Attorney-General v Punch Ltd* [2002] UKHL 50, [2003] 1 AC 1046).

Attorney-General v Times Newspapers Ltd and the Court of Appeal's decision in *Attorney-General v Punch Ltd* [2001] QB 1028 were interpreted in *Jockey Club v Buffham* [2002] EWHC 1866 (QB), [2003] QB 462, as only protecting from interference with pending proceedings. On that basis it was held that the *Spycatcher* principle does not extend to final injunctions. *Jockey Club v Buffham* might have been decided differently if the committal had been brought on the basis that the third party had aided and abetted a breach of the injunction rather than on the basis of interfering with the administration of justice (see *Attorney-General v Punch Ltd* [2002] UKHL 50, [2003] 1 AC 1046).

EFFECT OF NOT APPLYING FOR INTERIM RELIEF

Failing to apply for interim relief is a factor in considering at trial whether the claimant is guilty of acquiescence (*Shaw v Appelgate* [1977] 1 WLR 970). It may also provide grounds for awarding damages in lieu of an injunction (*Jaggard v Sawyer* [1995] 1 WLR 269). Delay in issuing proceedings after the claimant is aware of the defendant's breach, and deciding not to apply for an interim injunction to avoid giving an undertaking in damages, were considered by the Court of Appeal in *Mortimer v Bailey* [2004] EWCA Civ 1514, LTL 29/10/2004. These are both matters to be taken into account in considering whether to grant a final injunction, but do not bar granting such an injunction where the claimant has made clear his objection to the defendant's conduct. *Blue Town Investments Ltd v Higgs and Hill plc* [1990] 1 WLR 696, which said that continuing proceedings was an abuse of process after failing to apply for an interim injunction to avoid having to give an undertaking in damages, should be regarded as wrongly decided. (Another first-instance decision, *Oxy-Electric Ltd v Zainuddin* [1991] 1 WLR 115, reached the opposite conclusion.) **37.63**

Chapter 38 Freezing Injunctions

NATURE OF A FREEZING INJUNCTION

38.1 A freezing injunction is an interim order restraining a party from removing assets located within the jurisdiction out of the country, or from dealing with assets whether they are located within the jurisdiction or not (**CPR, r. 25.1(1)(f)**). Usually the order will be restricted to assets not exceeding the value of the claim. Until the CPR came into force on 26 April 1999 this form of order was known as a *Mareva* injunction, taking its name from *Mareva Compania Naviera SA v International Bulkcarriers SA* [1980] 1 All ER 213.

The purpose of a freezing injunction is to prevent the injustice of a defendant's assets being salted away so as to deprive the claimant of the fruits of any judgment that may be obtained. However, as Ackner LJ said in *A. J. Bekhor and Co. Ltd v Bilton* [1981] QB 923, the jurisdiction to grant freezing injunctions has not rewritten the law of insolvency, and the imposition of such an order does not give the claimant any priority or security if the defendant becomes insolvent. It is a relief *in personam* which simply prohibits certain acts in relation to the assets frozen.

In *Mareva Compania Naviera SA v International Bulkcarriers SA* [1980] 1 All ER 213 the Court of Appeal refused to consider itself bound by *Lister v Stubbs* (1890) 45 ChD 1, which had held that a defendant could not be compelled to give security before judgment, and decided that what is now the **Supreme Court Act 1981, s. 37(1)**, is wide enough to permit the court to grant an interim injunction restraining the dissipation of assets. Parliament has subsequently acknowledged the jurisdiction in the **Supreme Court Act 1981**, s. 37(3), the **County Court Remedies Regulations 1991** (SI 1991/1222) and the **CPR, r. 25.1(1)(f)**.

It has always been recognised that freezing orders are draconian measures, and they will be granted only if a number of onerous conditions are fulfilled. The most significant of these conditions is that there must be a real risk that the defendant will dissipate assets to frustrate any judgment the claimant may obtain.

Although freezing injunctions are most commonly sought by claimants, they may be sought by any party, such as a counterclaiming defendant or a defendant against a **Part 20** defendant.

PROCEDURE

For a summary of the procedure, see **procedural checklist 20**. **38.2**

County courts do not generally have jurisdiction to grant freezing injunctions, so applications must usually be made in the High Court (**County Court Remedies Regulations 1991, regs 2** and **3**). Freezing injunctions may be granted by a county court where a High Court or Court of Appeal judge sits, in Business List and Patents County Court cases, certain family proceedings, and in aid of execution (reg. 3(2) and (3)(a), (c) and (d)). Another exception where a freezing injunction can be ordered by a county court is where the proposed order seeks to preserve or detain property which is or may form the subject-matter of the proceedings or proposed proceedings (reg. 3(3)(b)). Where a freezing injunction is sought in a county court claim (and none of the exceptions in the **County Court Remedies Regulations 1991** applies), the application for the freezing injunction must be made in the High Court (**High Court and County Courts Jurisdiction Order 1991 (SI 1991/724), art. 3**). The application must be made returnable to a judge, and the application notice must (see *Schmidt v Wong* [2005] EWCA Civ 1506, [2006] 1 WLR 561) carry the following endorsement:

> This application is being made in the course of [in anticipation of] proceedings in the [ ] county court pursuant to article 3 of the High Court and County Courts Jurisdiction Order 1991. The county court has no jurisdiction to grant the relief sought by reason of regulation 3(1) of the County Court Remedies Regulations 1991.

Given that a freezing injunction can only be ordered against an unscrupulous defendant who is prepared to dissipate assets to prevent the claimant recovering on any judgment obtained, the application is, in practice, made without informing the defendant to ensure the injunction is effective. They are often sought on an urgent basis (see **37.4**) before proceedings are issued, in which event the applicant will be required to give an undertaking to issue proceedings as soon as practicable (*Fourie v Le Roux* [2005] EWCA Civ 204, *The Times*, 25 April 2005). Where the claimant had been pursuing the defendant for some time, and there had been other applications for relief in other jurisdictions, it was not wrong to refuse to deal with an application for a freezing order without notice (*Kensington International Ltd v Republic of Congo* [2003] EWCA Civ 709, LTL 13/5/2003). The application is made to a judge sitting in private and is made before service of the claim form so as not to alert the defendant.

Papers in support

An application for a freezing injunction must be supported by an affidavit making full and frank disclosure of all material facts, including those going against the grant of the order. This type of application is one of the exceptions where affidavits must be used (**PD 25, para. 3.1**). The affidavit must be clear and fair, and claimants should avoid the temptation to flood the court with voluminous exhibits, particularly where this will tend to obscure the real issues. Counsel must produce a draft minute of the order sought. The form of the order is considered in **38.31**. In urgent cases the application can be made before issue of the proceedings, and may be supported by evidence in draft or referred to orally on instructions, but in such cases **38.3** the applicant will be required to confirm on affidavit all the evidence presented at the hearing (*Flightwise Travel Services Ltd v Gill* [2003] EWHC 3082 (Ch), *The Times*, 5 December 2003).

The papers must, wherever possible, be delivered to the court at least two hours before the hearing to allow the judge to read them in advance (**PD 25, para. 4.3(1)**). Further, even on applications without notice and especially where 'worldwide' freezing injunctions (see **38.9**) are sought, counsel should consider drafting a skeleton argument indicating how the requirements for granting the order are made out (see *ALG Inc. v Uganda Airlines Corporation* (1992) *The Times*, 31 July 1992). Judges dealing with freezing injunctions applications made without notice to the respondents must be astute to ensure the provisions of **PD 25** are complied with, and must be sure that the evidence adduced by the applicant justifies the order in the terms sought (*Thane Investments Ltd v Tomlinson* [2003] EWCA Civ 1272, LTL 29/7/2003).

Paragraph 3 of the standard-form freezing injunction order in the **annex to PD 25** provides for a return day for a further hearing on notice, which is normally a few days after the without-notice hearing. The respondent must be fully informed of the case against him well in advance of the hearing on notice, including being provided with the evidence and being told of the arguments used (and, if appropriate, any observations made by the judge) at the without-notice hearing (*Flightwise Travel Services Ltd v Gill* [2003] EWHC 3082 (Ch), The Times, 5 December 2003). Consequently, a full note of the hearing must be provided to all parties affected by the order to ensure they know exactly what happened, the basis and material on which the order had been made (*Interoute Telecommunications (UK) Ltd v Fashion Gossip Ltd* (1999) *The Times*, 10 November 1999). Full notes must be provided without respondents needing to ask for them (*Thane Investments Ltd v Tomlinson* [2002] EWHC 2972 (Ch), *The Times*, 10 December 2002).

A third party who did not attend the hearing at which a freezing injunction was made, but who is served with the order, may request copies of the materials read by the judge, material prepared at the direction of the judge, and the note of the hearing (**PD 25, para. 9.2**). Unless the court otherwise orders, the applicant must comply promptly with the request.

CONDITIONS FOR GRANTING FREEZING INJUNCTIONS

38.4 The jurisdiction to grant freezing injunctions derives from the **Supreme Court Act 1981, s. 37(1)**. This section enables the court to grant interim injunctions on such terms and conditions as the court thinks just where it appears 'just and convenient' to do so. The requirements laid down by the courts for granting freezing injunctions are:

(a) a cause of action justiciable in England and Wales;
(b) a good arguable case;
(c) the defendant having assets within the jurisdiction;
(d) a real risk that the defendant may dissipate those assets before judgment can be enforced;
(e) that the defendant will be adequately protected by the claimant's undertaking in damages (the discussion at **37.25** applies equally to freezing injunctions).

The above principles cover the general run of cases. Because injunctions are granted where it is just and convenient, the court retains a discretion to refuse relief, and, in rare, exceptional cases, has power to stretch the usual rules if that is in the interests of justice. This power is used only in truly exceptional cases. Otherwise, the above requirements must be established, and it is not sufficient to say that a freezing injunction should be granted because there is no immediate and obvious prejudice to the respondent (*Flightwise Travel Services Ltd v Gill* [2003] EWHC 3082 (Ch), *The Times*, 5 December 2003).

Claim justiciable in England and Wales

38.5 The claimant must have a substantive cause of action which can be brought in England and Wales. The leading case is *The Siskina* [1979] AC 210. The claimant, a Saudi Arabian cargo owner, claimed damages against Panamanian shipowners over the discharge of the cargo in Cyprus. The bills of lading were issued in Italy and conferred exclusive jurisdiction on the courts of Genoa. An English freezing injunction was sought, because insurance money had become payable to the defendants in London. The order was refused, because a freezing injunction is a remedy, not a cause of action, and the claimant did not have a substantive claim which could be brought in England.

In *Al-Abbas v Al-Dabbagh* (2002) LTL 21/11/2002 the solicitors acting for one of the parties in a matrimonial case intervened for the purpose of obtaining an order that the respondent should pay their former client's costs pursuant to a compromise between the parties. The solicitors also obtained a freezing injunction against the respondent, which was set aside on appeal on the ground that in the circumstances the court did not have jurisdiction to grant the injunction without an order for costs.

A defendant who is abroad can be sued in England and Wales if:

(a) permission to serve proceedings out of the jurisdiction has been granted under **CPR, r. 6.20**; or
(b) the defendant submits to the jurisdiction; or
(c) the claim form can be served in another EU or EFTA State under **r. 6.19**.

Injunctions in support of foreign proceedings

If proceedings have been, or are to be, commenced in another jurisdiction, the High Court is empowered by the **Civil Jurisdiction and Judgments Act 1982, s. 25**, and the Civil Jurisdiction and Judgments Act 1982 (Interim Relief) Order 1997 (SI 1997/302) to grant interim relief, including freezing injunctions, in support of those foreign proceedings (see **16.41**). (*The Siskina* [1979] AC 210 was decided before the **CJJA 1982**, so could be decided differently today if its facts were to reoccur, given the exclusive jurisdiction clause in favour of the courts of Italy.) There is no requirement that the foreign proceedings have to correspond precisely with the equivalent English claim, but there must be a pre-existing foreign cause of action that would be enforceable in England and Wales (*Fourie v Le Roux* [2005] EWCA Civ 204, *The Times*, 25 April 2005). Particular caution is shown before granting freezing injunctions under s. 25 (*Crédit Suisse Fides Trust SA v Cuoghi* [1998] QB 818), because this can result in the English freezing order overlapping with similar orders made in other countries, which can lead to double jeopardy for the defendants and the opportunity for forum shopping by the claimants (*Ryan v Friction Dynamics Ltd* (2000) *The Times*, 14 June 2000). **38.6**

A court in England and Wales can grant interim relief in aid of foreign courts unless the fact the court has no jurisdiction over the case apart from s. 25 'makes it inexpedient' (s. 25(2)) for the court to grant relief. According to *Motorola Credit Corporation v Uzan (No. 2)* [2003] EWCA Civ 752, [2004] 1 WLR 113, the following factors are relevant in deciding expediency:

(a) whether making the order would interfere with the management of the case in the primary court;
(b) whether it is the policy in the primary jurisdiction to refuse to make worldwide freezing or disclosure orders;
(c) whether there is a danger that the order would give rise to disharmony or confusion and/or the risk of conflicting, inconsistent or overlapping orders in other jurisdictions;
(d) whether at the time the order is sought there is likely to be potential conflict as to jurisdiction; and
(e) whether the worldwide order could be enforced. In such cases each defendant falls to be considered separately.

Of course the other basic requirements must also be satisfied (*Refco Inc. v Eastern Trading Co.* [1999] 1 Lloyd's Rep 159). Where it is appropriate to grant a freezing order that overlaps with an order from a foreign court, it is sensible to state in the order which court is to have the primary role in enforcing the overlapping orders, and for the English order, if it is a secondary order, to be in substantially the same terms as the primary foreign order (*Ryan v Friction Dynamics Ltd*).

Lawyers in England and Wales have to exercise extreme caution when instructed to apply for freezing injunctions in aid of foreign proceedings under the **Civil Jurisdiction and Judgments Act 1982, s. 25**. These applications often involve copious and complex financial or commercial information which is difficult to digest, and because the lawyers in this jurisdiction will not be as familiar with the case as the foreign lawyers, it can mean that important features of the case are not covered in the evidence or otherwise not disclosed to the judge (see *Lewis v Eliades* (2002) *The Times*, 28 February 2002).

Good arguable case

38.7 Regarding the merits of the substantive claim, the minimum threshold for the exercise of the discretion is the establishment of a 'good arguable case' (*Ninemia Corporation v Trave Schiffahrtsgesellschaft mbH & Co.* [1983] 1 WLR 1412). According to Mustill J in *Ninemia Corporation v Trave Schiffahrtsgesellschaft mbH & Co.* at first instance [1983] 2 Lloyd's Rep 600, at p. 605, the expression means 'a case which is more than barely capable of serious argument, and yet not necessarily one which the judge believes to have a better than 50 per cent chance of success'. In *Attock Cement Co. Ltd v Romanian Bank for Foreign Trade* [1989] 1 All ER 1189 (a case on service outside the jurisdiction), it was said that a judge considering whether there is a good arguable case had to reach a provisional or tentative conclusion on all the admissible material that the claimant is probably right on the disputed question of fact. This test will not be satisfied if the claimant does not have the evidence to substantiate the case relied upon, or if the case is likely to be struck out, and may not be satisfied if there is an arguable defence. Freezing injunctions against directors were refused in an unfair prejudice case under the Companies Act 1985, s. 459, where there was no personal cause of action against the directors (*Re Premier Electronics (GB) Ltd* [2002] 2 BCLC 634). The courts have on occasion been reluctant to find there is a good arguable case where fraud is alleged, as in *Cheltenham and Gloucester Building Society v Ricketts* [1993] 1 WLR 1545, given the difficulty of proving this particular allegation. An arguable set-off may be taken as reducing or extinguishing the value of the claim. Anticipation that the defendant will be in breach of contract in the future has been held to be insufficient to satisfy this part of the test (*Veracruz Transportation Inc. v VC Shipping Co. Inc.* [1992] 1 Lloyd's Rep 353, overruling *A v B* [1989] 2 Lloyd's Rep 423).

In *Softwarecore Ltd v Pathan* [2005] EWHC 1845 (Ch), LTL 1/8/2005, Pumfrey J used a 'triable issue' test for the merits of the claim, rather than the traditional 'good arguable case' test. This was satisfied on the facts, where the issue was whether the defendant was knowingly involved in certain alleged frauds. The judge took into account the pattern of trading, the lack of any formal written terms of agreement, the lack of investigations into the other parties' creditworthiness, and suspicious figures for profits in various transactions.

Assets

38.8 The requirement of proving that the defendant has assets within the jurisdiction stems from the principle that equity will not act in vain so that if an injunction will not be effective it will not be granted. The claimant must show 'some grounds for believing' that the defendant has assets within the jurisdiction. 'Assets' includes money, shares, securities, insurance money, bills of exchange, motor vehicles, ships, aircraft, trade goods, office equipment, jewellery and paintings. Ownership may be legal or beneficial, but must be in the same capacity as the defendant is or will be a party to the claim.

The existence of an overdrawn bank account was held in one case, *Third Chandris Shipping Corporation v Unimarine SA* [1979] QB 645, to be some evidence of assets within the jurisdiction.

This is so particularly where the court can infer that the account is likely to be secured in some way. Assets in the name of a third party will not usually be included in a freezing injunction unless the claimant establishes a good arguable case that the assets are beneficially owned by the defendant (*TSB Private Bank International SA v Chabra* [1992] 1 WLR 231; approved by the Court of Appeal in *Yukong Line Ltd v Rendsburg Investments Corporation* [2001] 2 Lloyd's Rep 113). In *TSB Private Bank International SA v Chabra* it was clear that the claimant had a good cause of action against the first defendant, and equally clear there was no independent cause of action against the second defendant, a company owned by the first defendant and/or his wife. As there was credible evidence that the assets apparently owned by the second defendant in fact belonged to the first defendant, Mummery J granted a freezing injunction against the second defendant on the ground that it was ancillary and incidental to the claim against the first defendant.

Worldwide freezing injunctions

Generally, freezing injunctions do not extend to assets outside the jurisdiction. A freezing injunction having extraterritorial effect can be granted only in an exceptional case. Typically, exceptional cases are those having the three following characteristics: **38.9**

(a) the defendant has acted dishonestly or fraudulently on a large scale;
(b) the defendant has the ability to transfer large sums of money around the world quickly; and
(c) the defendant is able to hide assets behind companies or in countries where they are unlikely to be found.

Examples are *Derby and Co. Ltd v Weldon (No. 1)* [1990] Ch 48, and *Republic of Haiti v Duvalier* [1990] 1 QB 202. An extraterritorial freezing injunction should not be made where the defendant has sufficient assets within the jurisdiction to satisfy the claim. It has been held that the court can make a worldwide order in cases where the defendant has no assets in England (*Derby and Co. Ltd v Weldon (Nos. 3 and 4)* [1990] Ch 65).

If the case is otherwise a suitable one for a worldwide freezing injunction, such an order may be made even if the court is dealing with the application under the **CJJA 1982, s. 25**, in support of proceedings in another EU or EFTA State (*Crédit Suisse Fides Trust SA v Cuoghi* [1998] QB 818, not following *S & T Bautrading v Nordling* [1997] 3 All ER 718).

Undertakings Worldwide freezing orders must include a *Babanaft* proviso that the order will not affect third parties outside the jurisdiction until, and to the extent that, it has been recognised, registered or enforced by a foreign court. See *Babanaft International Co. SA v Bassatne* [1990] Ch 13 and clause 19 of the standard-form freezing injunction in **PD 25**. They must also include a 'Baltic' proviso to the effect that third parties served with the order may comply with what they reasonably believe to be their civil and criminal obligations in the country where the assets are located (*Bank of China v NBM LLC* [2001] EWCA Civ 1933, [2002] 1 WLR 844, and clause 20 of the standard-form freezing injunction). The claimant is further required to undertake not to enforce the order in a foreign court without first obtaining permission from the English court (*Derby and Co. Ltd v Weldon (No. 1)* [1990] Ch 48 and sch. B, para. 10, of the standard-form freezing injunction). **38.10**

In *Re Bank of Credit and Commerce International SA* [1994] 1 WLR 708 the English liquidators of foreign companies had obtained worldwide freezing injunctions in proceedings brought against two individuals alleging fraud in connection with the companies' affairs. The defendants sought an undertaking that the liquidators would not commence criminal proceedings against them outside the jurisdiction without the court's permission, but the court refused to impose such an undertaking, because it would impede investigation of the companies' affairs by regulatory and prosecuting authorities which the liquidators had a duty to assist.

Schedule B, para. 10, of the standard-form freezing injunction is an undertaking by the applicant not to seek to enforce the order outside the jurisdiction without the permission of the court. This undertaking takes effect as if it were an injunction, and can be replaced by an express injunction to the same effect (*Grupo Torras SA v Al Sabah* [2005] EWCA Civ 1370, LTL 24/8/2005).

38.11 **Seeking permission to enforce outside the jurisdiction** Guidance on the procedure to be followed on an application for permission to enforce a worldwide freezing order outside the jurisdiction was given in *Dadourian Group International Inc. v Simms* [2005] EWHC 268 (Ch), [2005] 2 All ER 651:

(a) Applications should normally be made on notice.
(b) The evidence in support should include information on the local law and practice, because the court must be satisfied that any satellite proceedings will go no further than equivalent proceedings in England and Wales.

On an application for permission to enforce outside the jurisdiction, the claimant needs to demonstrate only a real prospect that there are assets in the country where enforcement is sought. When exercising its discretion, the court must take into account the possible oppression caused by a proliferation of foreign proceedings (*Dadourian Group International Inc. v Simms*). The court will also consider whether granting permission is appropriate in the interests of justice, and whether information obtained under the injunction is intended to be used for a purpose which is not a purpose of the worldwide injunction (*Bates v Microstar Ltd* [2003] EWHC 661 (Ch), *The Times*, 15 April 2003).

Risk of disposal

38.12 The claimant must establish that there is a real risk that the defendant will dissipate assets if unrestrained (*Ninemia Maritime Corporation v Trave Schiffahrtsgesellschaft mbH & Co. KG* [1983] 1 WLR 1412). In *Customs and Excise Commissioners v Anchor Foods Ltd* [1999] 1 WLR 1139 Neuberger J said that what is required is a good and arguable case for a risk of dissipation. This was found to be so where the defendant proposed to dispose of its entire business at a price which had been independently verified by a partner in a leading accountancy firm, because the purchaser was a company controlled by the same people who controlled the defendant and there was contrary valuation evidence (also from very eminent experts) indicating that the price was too low. A real risk of disposal of assets may be established by reference either to previous conduct which tends to show a want of probity or to a course of dealing suggesting the defendant will deal with his assets to make himself judgment-proof, or by raising an inference that such is the case by other evidence (*Re Industrial Services Group Ltd (No. 1)* [2003] BPIR 392). However, being short of money is not to be equated with an intention to dissipate assets (*Midas Merchant Bank plc v Bello* (2002) LTL 14/10/2002). It may be difficult to establish a real risk of dissipation if the respondent is a well-established business (*Vinprom Rousse v Bulgarian Vintners Co. Ltd* (2000) LTL 8/5/2001).

In *Oaktree Financial Services Ltd v Higham* [2004] EWHC 2098 (Ch), LTL 11/5/2004, one of the solicitors involved in the case wrote to the defendant unwittingly but in effect warning him of the possibility of an application being made for a freezing injunction. Laddie J was almost minded to refuse the injunction on this ground alone, as there was a strong prospect that any funds would have been dissipated once the defendant was put on notice.

At one time it was thought that freezing injunctions could only be granted against foreign defendants. The **Supreme Court Act 1981, s. 37(3)**, now provides that the jurisdiction to grant these orders 'shall be exercisable in cases where [the defendant] is, as well as in cases where he is not, domiciled, resident or present within [the] jurisdiction'. Lord Denning MR in *Third Chandris Shipping Corporation v Unimarine SA* [1979] QB 645 said, at p. 669:

> The mere fact that the defendant is abroad is not by itself sufficient. . . . But there are some foreign companies whose structure invites comment. We often see in this court a corporation which is

> registered in a country where the company law is so loose that nothing is known about it — where it does no work and has no officers and no assets. . . . Judgment cannot be enforced against it. There is no reciprocal enforcement of judgments. . . . In such cases the very fact of incorporation there gives some ground for believing there is a risk that, if judgment or an award is obtained, it may go unsatisfied.

Reciprocal enforcement of judgments is considered in **chapter** 77.

Assessing risk In *Barclay-Johnson v Yuill* [1980] 1 WLR 1259 Megarry V-C said: 38.13

> A reputable foreign company, accustomed to paying its debts, ought not to be prevented from removing its assets from the jurisdiction, especially if it has substantial assets in countries in which English judgments can be enforced.

Factors relevant to the question of risk of dissipation include:

(a) whether the defendant is domiciled or incorporated in a tax haven or country with lax company law;
(b) whether English judgments are enforceable in the country where the defendant's assets are situated (*Montecchi v Shimco (UK) Ltd* [1979] 1 WLR 1180). This is a particularly important factor where the assets are in an EU country, due to the ease of enforcement under the **Jurisdiction and Judgments Regulation**;
(c) whether the evidence supporting the substantive cause of action discloses dishonesty or a suspicion of dishonesty on the part of the defendant. This is a weighty factor when it is present, and this is so whether or not it is pleaded as fraud (*Guinness plc v Saunders* (1987) *The Independent*, 15 April 1987);
(d) whether there is evidence that the defendant has been dishonest, outside the actual cause of action. This includes matters such as contrivances designed to generate an appearance of wealth;
(e) past incidents of debt default by the defendant, although it is not essential for the claimant to have such evidence (*Third Chandris Shipping Corporation v Unimarine SA* [1979] QB 645);
(f) evidence that the defendant has already taken steps to remove or dissipate its assets (*Aiglon Ltd v Gau Shan Co. Ltd* [1993] 1 Lloyd's Rep 164);
(g) any history of non-compliance with court orders and other action by the defendant taken in total disregard of court orders (*Great Future International Ltd v Sealand Housing Corporation* (2002) LTL 16/5/2002).

Discretion

In its discretion, the court can refuse a freezing injunction even if the usual requirements are made out. In *Rasu Maritima SA v Perusahaan Pertambangan Minyak Dan Gas Bumi Negara* [1978] QB 644 the Court of Appeal refused to grant an order partly because the 'cleanliness' of the claimant's hands was open to question, and partly in the exercise of its discretion. The assets frozen were parts for a fertiliser plant, and were valued at $12 million in the hands of the defendants, but were only worth $0.35 million as scrap. This was regarded as only a 'drop in the ocean' in comparison with the size of the claim. 38.14

A freezing order against a defendant bank was discharged in the exercise of the court's discretion in *Polly Peck International plc v Nadir (No. 2)* [1992] 4 All ER 769. The claimants claimed the bank, the fourth defendant, was liable as a constructive trustee in respect of money allegedly misapplied by the first defendant. The freezing injunction covered 60 per cent of the bank's assets, and would almost certainly have severely damaged its day-to-day banking business, and also was likely to result in a loss of confidence among investors with the possibility of a run on its deposits. In those circumstances, the granting of the order was inimical to the purpose for which the freezing injunction jurisdiction existed. Lord Donaldson of Lymington MR said that the judgments in this case should not be taken as meaning that it will never be possible to obtain a freezing injunction against a bank, but the circumstances would have to be unusual. At the other end of the scale, freezing injunctions will not be granted where the assets in question are relatively modest. The defendant in *Indosuez International Finance BV v National Reserve Bank* [2002] EWHC 774 (Comm), LTL 26/4/2002, applied to discharge a freezing injunction in support of a foreign judgment on the ground that sufficient funds had been frozen under a Belgian order also in support of that judgment. The application was refused, partly because the defendant was strenuously resisting enforcement in Belgium, and partly because the value of the Belgian assets (bonds) was highly volatile, so the Belgian assets were not adequate protection. In *Sions v Price* (1988) *The Independent*, 19 December 1988, an order was refused where the claim was £2,000. The current small claims limit of £5,000 may be a good guide to where the line should be drawn.

CONTENTS OF A FREEZING INJUNCTION

Undertakings

38.15 The following undertakings by the claimant must be given to the court and incorporated into the order:

(a) as with other interim injunctions, to pay damages to the defendant if it transpires that the order should not have been granted. The court has a discretion to order a freezing injunction subject to a limited undertaking in damages (*RBG Resources plc v Rastogi* (2002) LTL 31/5/2002);
(b) to notify the defendant forthwith of the terms of the order, often by telex or fax, and to serve the defendant with the affidavit and exhibits in support. This is a consequence of applying without notice;
(c) to pay the reasonable costs and expenses incurred by third parties in complying with the order;
(d) to indemnify third parties in respect of any liability incurred in complying with the order.

In urgent cases, the following further undertakings may be required:

(e) to issue a claim form in the terms of the draft used on the application;
(f) to swear and file affidavits deposing to the facts relied on before the judge.

Under the **Supreme Court Act 1981, s. 37(2)**, interim injunctions can be granted on such terms and conditions as the court thinks fit. A little latitude is permissible. So, in *Allen v Jambo Holdings Ltd* [1980] 1 WLR 1252 the Court of Appeal continued a freezing injunction in favour of a legally aided claimant who could not give a valuable undertaking in damages. The case was unusual in that the defendants had sworn an affidavit blatantly exaggerating the effects of the order and had been less than forthcoming on a number of points. Also, in any event, the defendants could have obtained the release of their frozen aeroplane by providing security.

38.16 **Fortifying the undertaking in damages** In appropriate cases the court can order the applicant to fortify the undertaking in damages by paying money into court or providing other security. The usual undertaking is intended to provide a means of compensating for potential loss, and the court should consider whether it is an adequate protection. A respondent may apply for the order to be varied to include a requirement to fortify the undertaking, and in such a case it is for the respondent to establish a sufficient risk of loss (*Sinclair Investment Holdings SA v Cushnie* [2004] EWHC 218 (Ch), LTL 23/3/2004). Factors that the court should consider are similar to those on applications for security for costs (see **65.16** to **65.24**). Therefore, the court should not usually take into account the merits of the claim, but should consider whether requiring the applicant to fortify the undertaking may stifle a genuine claim (*Sinclair Investment Holdings SA v Cushnie*).

Assets covered by the order

Considered in relation to the assets they cover, freezing injunctions can be divided into three types: 38.17

(a) General orders, which cover all the defendant's assets.
(b) Maximum-sum orders, which cover the defendant's assets up to the amount of the claim together with interest and costs. An appropriate sum should be included for the applicant's estimated costs (*Fourie v Le Roux* [2005] EWCA Civ 204, *The Times*, 25 April 2005). If the claim is unliquidated, the maximum sum is calculated by reference to the sum the claimant is likely to recover. Where there is a dispute about the value of the claim, the order should freeze assets in the largest sum for which there is a good arguable case (*Great Future International Ltd v Sealand Housing Corporation* (2002) LTL 16/5/2002).
(c) Orders attaching to specific assets, such as a ship, a cargo or an aeroplane.

Often, orders attaching to specific assets are combined with either general or maximum-sum orders. The choice between general and maximum-sum orders was considered in *Z Ltd v A-Z and AA-LL* [1982] QB 558. Maximum-sum orders are the norm. A general order is likely to provoke an application for a variation down to a maximum-sum order. One drawback with maximum-sum orders is that banks will not necessarily know if they can honour transactions on the defendant's accounts as they will not know the total value of the defendant's assets covered by the order at any particular time. Where such practical difficulties result in a larger sum being 'frozen' than the sum stated in the order, the claimant may be held liable on its undertakings in damages. General orders may accordingly be used where the defendant's assets are not fully known by the claimant, and are also appropriate in fraud cases where the amount of the claim may be unknown.

Where the claimant asks for a freezing injunction to cover assets which the defendant or some third party alleges belong to someone other than the defendant, the court has a wide power to do whatever is just and convenient, including ordering the question of ownership to be tried as an issue between the claimant and the third party (*SCF Finance Co. Ltd v Masri* [1985] 1 WLR 876). Unless specifically excluded, the defendant's assets subject to a freezing order will include assets over which the defendant claims to have only legal title (for example, as executor or bare trustee) as well as assets in respect of which the defendant is beneficial owner (*Federal Bank of the Middle East Ltd v Hadkinson* [2000] 1 WLR 1695). Any dispute about whether the defendant is only a legal owner can be dealt with by trying an issue, as suggested in *SCF Finance Co. Ltd v Masri*. In *C Inc. plc v L* [2001] 2 Lloyd's Rep 459, the claimant obtained judgment against the defendant, and sought a freezing injunction in aid of execution against both the defendant and her husband. On the facts the defendant had an arguable right to an indemnity from her husband in respect of the judgment, and it was held that in those circumstances it was right to add the husband as a party and to extend the freezing injunction to cover his assets.

Bank accounts

Bank accounts are one of the most common assets covered by freezing injunctions. The following points should be noted: 38.18

(a) A joint account will not be affected by a freezing injunction unless it is specifically covered by the wording of the order (*SCF Finance Co. Ltd v Masri* [1985] 1 WLR 876).
(b) If the defendant has an account containing money over which the claimant asserts a proprietary interest, mixed with the defendant's own money and/or money held by the defendant on behalf of a third party, the court has jurisdiction to freeze the entire account (*Chief Constable of Kent v V* [1983] QB 34).
(c) The claimant must give the fullest possible details (bank, branch, account name and number) in the affidavit in support. If it is necessary to ask the bank to search for an account, the number of branches involved should be as limited as possible. The claimant

will be required to pay the costs of such searches immediately, which may or may not be recoverable from the defendant as costs of the action.

(d) The bank should honour transactions entered into before the order is made. The bank must also honour cheques backed by guarantee cards and irrevocable letters of credit, see, for example, *Cretanor Maritime Co. Ltd v Irish Marine Management Ltd* [1978] 1 WLR 966, and *Lewis and Peat (Produce) Ltd v Almatu Properties Ltd* (1992) *The Times*, 14 May 1992. Cheque cards should be recalled once the order has been served on the bank.

(e) A freezing injunction can apply to the *proceeds* of a letter of credit when received (*Z Ltd v A-Z and AA-LL* [1982] QB 558).

(f) A provision must be incorporated into the order to allow any bank served with the order to exercise any right of set-off it may have in respect of facilities given to the defendant before the order (*Oceanica Castelana Armadora SA v Mineralimportexport* [1983] 1 WLR 1294).

38.19 **Duty owed by banks to the claimant** The negligence liability of banks after being notified of freezing orders was considered by the Court of Appeal in *Commissioners of Customs and Excise v Barclays Bank plc* [2004] EWCA Civ 1555, [2005] 1 WLR 2082. Under its usual practice, the bank would have frozen the defendant's accounts on being notified of a freezing injunction. Due to human error it allowed the defendant to withdraw £2 million two hours after notification. Shortly afterwards the bank wrote to the claimant confirming it would comply with the order. At first instance it was held that the bank only came under a duty of care in negligence when it assumed responsibility, which was when it wrote to the claimant saying it was willing to abide by the terms of the order. This was overturned on appeal. Longmore LJ pointed out that the various so-called tests for duty of care (threefold test of foreseeability, proximity and fairness; assumption of responsibility; and incremental approach) are really just labels which are conclusionary (at [40]). Here the threefold test pointed to the imposition of a duty of care, which was supported by the incremental approach (at [48]) and was not displaced by the apparent lack of any assumption of responsibility.

Port authorities

38.20 Where a freezing injunction affects a ship in harbour, the claimant will be required to undertake to reimburse the port authority for lost income, and a proviso will be incorporated into the order giving the port authority a discretion to move the ship for operational reasons (*Clipper Maritime Co. Ltd v Mineralimportexport* [1981] 1 WLR 1262).

Land

38.21 Freezing injunctions can be granted over land, although it may be difficult to prove there is a 'risk of disposal'. An order, if granted, would not be made for the purpose of enforcing a judgment, so would not be registrable as a land charge (*Stockler v Fourways Estates Ltd* [1984] 1 WLR 25).

Living expenses

38.22 A freezing injunction must allow an individual defendant to use a reasonable sum each week or month to pay his or her ordinary living expenses. As decided in *PCW (Underwriting Agencies) Ltd v Dixon* [1983] 2 All ER 158, a defendant is not dissipating his assets by living as he has always lived. It is a misuse of the jurisdiction to grant freezing injunctions to seek to apply pressure on the defendant (perhaps with a view to obtaining a favourable settlement) by unreasonably limiting the money available for ordinary living expenses. Living expenses money must not, however, be spent on extraordinary items, such as expensive motor cars (see *TDK Tape Distributor (UK) Ltd v Videochoice Ltd* [1986] 1 WLR 141). More caution must be shown before allowing a defendant to use frozen assets where the claim is a proprietary one, because the allegation is that the frozen assets belong to the claimant (*Halifax plc v Chandler* [2001] EWCA Civ 1750, [2002] CPLR 41). Spending in excess of the living expenses clause is not a breach of the injunction if it is funded by borrowing from another source (*Cantor Index Ltd v Lister* (2001) LTL

23/11/2001). Retrospective variation to allow frozen assets to be used to pay for substantial living expenses is unlikely to be allowed (*Cantor Index Ltd v Lister*).

Trade debts

A freezing injunction must allow a defendant who is engaged in trade to pay any legitimate trade debts as they would be paid in the ordinary course of the defendant's business. The philosophy behind this is that a freezing injunction is not intended to confer priority over other trade creditors. A defendant should be allowed to pay a trade debt, if the defendant is acting in good faith and in the ordinary course of business, even if the debt is not strictly enforceable (*Iraqi Ministry of Defence v Arcepey Shipping Co. SA* [1981] QB 65). Ordinary business expenses may usually be paid from frozen funds, and, in the event of a dispute, the court does not usually consider whether the business venture is reasonable nor whether the business expenses are reasonable. Further, it does not balance the strength of the defendant's case against that of the claimant, nor does it take into consideration that money will not be available to the claimant if it gets judgment (*Halifax plc v Chandler* [2001] EWCA Civ 1750, [2002] CPLR 41). Whether the defendant should use assets not covered by the order where such are available depends ultimately on the defendant's motive (*Campbell Mussels v Thompson* (1984) 81 LS Gaz 2140, interpreting *A v C (No. 2)* [1981] QB 961). A payment by a defendant as an agent to its principal was accepted as amounting to an abuse of a freezing injunction in *Atlas Maritime Co. SA v Avalon Maritime Ltd (No. 1)* [1991] 4 All ER 769, where the relationship of principal and agent was held not to exist on the facts. The defendants were being sued on an alleged contract for the sale of a ship. The claimants obtained a freezing injunction over the defendants' assets. The defendants' shares were wholly owned by its parent company. The defendants sought a variation of the order to allow it to pay all its funds to its parent company, it being alleged that all the defendants' assets had been advanced to the defendants by way of loan. It was held that in the circumstances it was appropriate to look behind the corporate veil, with the result that the proposed repayment to the parent company was not a repayment in the 'ordinary course of business', but was an attempt to avoid the defendants' responsibilities to the claimants if they were ultimately successful in obtaining judgment against the defendants. **38.23**

Costs of litigation

A freezing injunction should normally also allow the defendant to pay the ordinary costs of the present proceedings if no other funds are available. Even substantial expenditure, and expenditure on VAT advice which is necessary for the defendant's solicitor to formulate the defence, may be allowed under this proviso (*Furylong Ltd v Masterpiece Technology Ltd* (2004) LTL 13/7/2004). A case where the Court of Appeal held there were other funds available to pay the defendant's costs was *Atlas Maritime Co. SA v Avalon Maritime Ltd (No. 3)* [1991] 1 WLR 917. In this case it was found that the defendants' parent company operated the defendants in such a way that all funds received by the defendants were immediately paid to the parent company, and any sums payable by the defendants were paid by the parent company. **38.24**

The permission to use money to pay reasonable legal costs (or living expenses or trade debts) does no more than to permit the expenditure without the defendant being in contempt of court. Thus, where the underlying cause of action asserts a proprietary claim against the defendant, the permission to use money to pay reasonable legal expenses is no guarantee that the recipients of that money will escape a later claim in constructive trust for knowing receipt should the claim be established (*United Mizrahi Bank Ltd v Doherty* [1998] 1 WLR 435).

A freezing injunction should not prevent, and may be varied if it does, bona fide expenditure on the legal costs of litigation other than the case in hand, where the other case has a reasonable prospect of success and was on foot when the freezing injunction was granted (*Halifax plc v Chandler* [2001] EWCA Civ 1750, [2002] CPLR 41).

Ancillary orders

38.25 The court has power under **CPR, r. 25.1(1)(g)**, to make ancillary orders for disclosure and answers to requests for further information to ensure the effectiveness of the main freezing injunction. Clause 9 of the standard freezing injunction order in **PD 25** requires the defendant to provide information confirmed on affidavit giving details of all his assets. Clause 18 of the standard search order requires the defendant to provide information confirmed on affidavit of the whereabouts of all listed items, the names and addresses of the persons who supplied them or to whom they have been supplied, and dates and quantities of each transaction. Orders may be made requiring disclosure of the nature and whereabouts of all the defendant's assets within the jurisdiction. Defendants should be given a realistic time for compliance (*Oystertec plc v Davidson* [2004] EWHC 627 (Ch), LTL 7/4/2004, where four working days was regarded as extremely short). In addition, the defendant's bank may be ordered, even if not a party, to give disclosure of documents relating to the defendant's bank account (*A v C* [1981] QB 956).

Orders requiring disclosure of the nature and whereabouts of all the defendant's assets within the jurisdiction are a standard requirement in freezing injunctions, and are generally required if freezing injunctions are to be effective (*Motorola Credit Corporation v Uzan* [2002] EWCA Civ 989, *The Times*, 10 July 2002, in which the defendant was required to disclose the whereabouts of his assets notwithstanding a pending application to set aside the freezing order). There are three major limits on the jurisdiction to make ancillary disclosure orders. First, as with other forms of disclosure, such orders will not be granted if they are merely 'fishing' (see *Faith Panton Property Plan Ltd v Hodgetts* [1981] 1 WLR 927). Essentially, an application for disclosure will be 'fishing' if it is based on no more than suspicion as opposed to some evidence.

Secondly, similar problems arise in relation to the privilege against self-incrimination as can arise in relation to search orders (see **chapter 39**).

Thirdly, there is no free-standing power under **r. 25.1(1)(g)** to order the disclosure of information which might be of assistance in seeking a freezing injunction if the applicant has no material at present justifying an application for a freezing injunction (*Parker v CS Structured Credit Fund Ltd* [2003] EWHC 391 (Ch), [2003] 1 WLR 1680).

Freezing injunction against third party

38.26 There is an undoubted jurisdiction to make a freezing injunction against a third party where there is good reason to believe that assets in the name of the third party are really those of the principal defendant (*SCF Finance Co. Ltd v Masri* [1985] 1 WLR 876). This power is ancillary to para. 6 of the standard-form freezing injunction order, which states the order covers assets over which the respondent has a direct or indirect power to dispose of or deal with as if they were his own. Assets held on a bare trust can be frozen up to the amount of the principal defendant's assets (*TSB Private Bank International SA v Chabra* [1992] 1 WLR 231). Likewise, ancillary freezing orders can be made where there is a good arguable case that the principal defendant has hidden assets in offshore trusts and companies in tax havens (*International Credit and Investment Co. (Overseas) Ltd v Adham* [1998] BCC 134). Even where the principal defendant has no strict legal or equitable right to the assets, such as where assets are held under a discretionary trust, an ancillary freezing injunction can be made if the principal defendant has some right in respect of the assets, or has control over them, or other rights of access to them (*Dadourian Group International Inc. v Azuri Ltd* (2005) LTL 26/7/2005).

Cross-examination as to assets

38.27 It is only in exceptional circumstances that cross-examination will be ordered on an affidavit of assets sworn pursuant to a freezing order. However, where the claimant has justifiable concerns as to whether the defendant has made a full disclosure as required by the order, the court may order the defendant to be cross-examined (*Den Norske Bank ASA v Antonatos* [1999] QB 271). Following *Den Norske Bank ASA v Antonatos*, while it is legitimate for claimants to have information in order to enable them to trace their money, ancillary orders cannot require the defendant to reveal whether he has obtained bribes other than those identified by the claimant. The purpose of the cross-examination is solely to discover what assets the defendant has, with a view to freezing them, and so will be unnecessary if sufficient assets are known to meet the value of the claim (*Great Future International Ltd v Sealand Housing Corporation* [2001] CPLR 293). The examination will be conducted by a master or district judge unless the judge making the order otherwise directs (**PD 2B, para. 7**).

Duration

38.28 A freezing injunction made without notice will remain in force for a limited period until the 'return date', which will be fixed by the judge when the order is granted. So far as practicable, any application to discharge or vary the injunction should be dealt with on the return date. The standard forms of freezing injunction in **PD 25** contain a clause enabling the defendant or any third party notified of the order to apply to the court at any time (i.e., less than the usual three clear days' notice), but must first notify the claimant's legal representatives. The standard-form freezing injunctions in the annex to **PD 25** say the orders are to continue 'until further order'. This is a reference to an order which expressly or impliedly discharges the freezing injunction. A freezing injunction does not therefore lapse when final judgment is entered against the defendant (*Cantor Index Ltd v Lister* (2001) LTL 23/11/2001).

Standard-form orders

38.29 A combined standard-form freezing injunction order for domestic freezing injunctions and worldwide freezing injunctions can be found in the annex to **PD 25**. The current form was revised with effect from 1 October 2005. This form should always be used, with only such modifications as are essential to fit the circumstances of the case. Any substantial variation from the form should be brought to the attention of the judge at the hearing. Wherever possible, a draft of the order sought should be filed with the application notice, with a copy on disk (**PD 25, para. 2.4**).

EFFECT OF THE ORDER

38.30 A defendant or anyone else with notice of a freezing injunction will be in contempt of court if they dispose or assist in the disposal or dissipation of enjoined assets (*Z Ltd v A-Z and AA-LL* [1982] QB 558 at p. 572 per Lord Denning MR). A non-party who hands an asset covered by a freezing injunction back to the defendant does not thereby dissipate or dispose of it (*Law Society v Shanks* [1988] 1 FLR 504), unless the non-party knows of a probability that after receiving it the defendant will dispose of it in breach of the order (*Bank Mellat v Kazmi* [1989] 1 QB 541).

A freezing injunction covering unspecified assets has an ambulatory effect (*see Cretanor Maritime Co. Ltd v Irish Marine Management Ltd* [1978] 1 WLR 966 per Buckley LJ). Assets acquired by the defendant after the order is granted will be covered by it, up to the maximum sum (if any) stated in the order (*TDK Tape Distributor (UK) Ltd v Videochoice Ltd* [1986] 1 WLR 141).

VARIATION OR DISCHARGE OF A FREEZING INJUNCTION

Procedure on application to vary or discharge

38.31 Applications to vary or discharge freezing injunctions are made to a judge, either pursuant to the liberty to apply provision in the order itself, or on the claimant's application to renew the order on the return date. The application will be made in accordance with **CPR, Part 23** (see **chapter 32**). It is inappropriate to entertain an application to discharge a freezing injunction where a defendant has given no warning of an intention to argue that it should be discharged on the ground of material non-disclosure (*Bracken Partners Ltd v Guttridge* (2001) LTL 16/1/2002).

A non-party who is affected by the terms of a freezing injunction can apply to intervene in the proceedings under **CPR, r. 19.2(2)**, and for the terms of the order to be varied. However, formal intervention may be unnecessary, as Buckley LJ in *Cretanor Maritime Co. Ltd v Irish Marine Management Ltd* [1978] 1 WLR 966 said that a non-party may apply for a variation of a freezing injunction order without intervening provided the non-party had a clear interest. Provided the intervention (whether formal or on the lines indicated by Buckley LJ) is justified, the non-party should be entitled to its costs on the indemnity basis (see *Project Development Co. Ltd SA v KMK Securities Ltd* [1982] 1 WLR 1470).

Where it is clear that the order should be varied or discharged, the parties may agree to this in the form of a consent order.

Grounds for variation

38.32 Variations of freezing injunctions may be allowed where the original order is more onerous to the defendant than is necessary, or if it imposes unnecessary obligations on a non-party. Examples are failures to include necessary provisos, such as for ordinary living expenses, paying trade debts, allowing banks the usual set-off, or making a general order when a maximum-sum order is appropriate. Hardship to third parties may also give grounds for a variation. In *Camdex International Ltd v Bank of Zambia (No. 2)* [1997] 1 WLR 632 a freezing injunction had caught a large quantity of banknotes for issue in Zambia. It was varied to allow the release of the banknotes, to prevent serious damage being inflicted on the general population of the country.

Discharge where the claim is not one in which a freezing injunction order may be made

38.33 A freezing injunction may be discharged on the ground that one of the usual requirements has not been made out. This may be on the basis, for example, that the claimant does not have a good arguable case, as in *Cheltenham and Gloucester Building Society v Ricketts* [1993] 1 WLR 1545. Alternatively, what may have appeared to be a good arguable case on the application without notice may be wiped out by an arguable defence or set-off. It may be that evidence concerning the defendant's financial status, business history or links with this country (or other countries where an English judgment would be enforceable) will persuade the court that there is no real risk of the defendant dissipating the enjoined assets in order to frustrate any judgment the claimant may obtain. Further, a change in the management of a company defendant may remove the risk of dissipation and merit a freezing injunction being discharged (*Capital Cameras Ltd v Harold Lines Ltd* [1991] 1 WLR 54).

Discharge on provision of security

38.34 A freezing injunction will cease to have effect where the defendant provides sufficient security for the claim (clause 11(4) of the standard freezing injunction order). Security can be provided by bond or guarantee, paying money into an account in the joint names of the parties' solicitors or by paying money into court. The standard security provision in a freezing injunction in cl. 11(4) only gives 'security' against the risk of dissipation of assets. It does not confer priority over the defendant's other creditors (*Technocrats International Inc. v Fredic Ltd* [2004] EWHC 2674 (QB), [2005] 1 BCLC 467). Likewise, a payment into a bank account in the joint names of the parties' solicitors was held not to confer any security rights in *Flightline Ltd v Edwards* [2003] EWCA Civ 63, [2003] 1 WLR 1200. For an equitable charge to be created it is necessary for the terms on which the 'security' is given to include an obligation on the debtor to pay the debt out of the fund (*Palmer v Carey* [1926] AC 703). This can be done by including a clause that the respondent has to satisfy any judgment obtained by the applicant out of the moneys in the joint account. Giving security can be to the advantage of the defendant, since it may be that the order 'freezes' an asset worth more to the defendant than the cost of the security being offered, and in any event it is often important for defendants for freezing injunctions to be discharged as such orders carry a significant financial stigma, and usually result in banking facilities being withdrawn.

Discharge on the basis of material non-disclosure

A consequence of freezing injunction applications being made without notice is that a claimant applying for a freezing injunction is under a duty to give full and frank disclosure of any defence or other facts going against the grant of the relief sought. This duty extends both to facts within the actual knowledge of the claimant, and to facts which would have been known on the making of reasonable inquiries. It also extends to breaches of an advocate's duty to the court (*Memory Corporation plc v Sidhu (No. 2)* [2000] 1 WLR 1443). **38.35**

To determine whether there has been a material non-disclosure, it is first necessary to consider the affidavit in support to see whether any adverse facts which the applicant either knew or could have discovered have been omitted. All material facts must appear in the affidavit itself, not in documents exhibited to it (see *National Bank of Sharjah v Dellborg* (1992) *The Times*, 24 December 1992). Secondly, it is necessary to consider whether anything omitted was 'material' in the sense that it would have affected the judgment of a reasonable tribunal when deciding whether to grant the freezing injunction in question (*Lloyds Bowmaker Ltd v Brittania Arrow Holdings plc* [1988] 1 WLR 1337). Facts are material if they are necessary to enable the court to exercise its discretion on a proper basis, bearing in mind the need to act fairly between the parties, the fact that the defendant has not been heard, and the inherent hardship and inconvenience caused by a freezing injunction. There is obviously a distinction between what are material facts and documents for the purposes of the application for the injunction and those which will be relevant at the trial of the action, and a claimant should not feel it is necessary to exhibit more than a few key documents to the affidavit in support of the application without notice (*National Bank of Sharjah v Dellborg* (1992) *The Times*, 24 December 1992). Instances where omitted facts have been held to be material include:

(a) mistakes in framing the cause of action (*Bank Mellat v Nikpour* [1985] FSR 87);
(b) failing to disclose the existence of proceedings in another country (*Behbehani v Salem* [1989] 1 WLR 723) or this country (*Elvee Ltd v Taylor* [2001] EWCA Civ 1943, [2002] FSR 48);
(c) misstating the source of information (*St Merryn Meat Ltd v Hawkins* (2001) LTL 2/7/2001, where the affidavit said that information about the defendants' activities was obtained using a bugged telephone in the claimants' offices, whereas in fact it was obtained using an interception device at one of the defendant's homes);
(d) failing to correct an assertion that the defendant was outside the jurisdiction once the claimant knew that was wrong (*Lombard North Central plc v Bradley* (2002) LTL 3/2/2002, but this was an innocent non-disclosure and did not justify discharging a worldwide freezing injunction);
(e) failing to disclose weaknesses in the claimant's financial position, which are relevant to the value of the claimant's undertaking in damages and to the undertaking to indemnify third parties.

Continuing duty of disclosure

The duty to make full and frank disclosure is a continuing one until the first hearing on notice, so the applicant has a duty to bring to the attention of the court any material changes in the circumstances after a freezing injunction has been granted (*Commercial Bank of the Near East plc v A* [1989] 2 Lloyd's Rep 319). There is a continuing duty on the claimant to draw the defendant's attention to any material change in the claimant's financial position (*Staines v Walsh* [2003] EWHC 1486 (Ch), *The Times*, 1 August 2003). **38.36**

Discretion to forgive a non-disclosure

38.37 Finding a material non-disclosure is not necessarily the end of the matter. As Lord Denning said in *Bank Mellat v Nikpour* [1985] FSR 87, at p. 90, 'It is not for every omission that the injunction will be automatically discharged. A *locus poenitentiae* may sometimes be afforded.' The court has a discretion to continue the order, or to make a new order on terms (such as on costs or payment of damages) 'if the original non-disclosure was innocent and if an injunction could properly be granted even had the facts been disclosed' (per Glidewell LJ in *Lloyds Bowmaker Ltd v Brittania Arrow Holdings plc* [1988] 1 WLR 1337). 'Innocence' in this connection depends on whether the omission was made intentionally, but, of course, there are degrees of culpability. Much depends on the quality of the facts that have not been disclosed. Some facts are so important that the court will readily infer that the non-disclosure was deliberate. For example, in *St Merryn Meat Ltd v Hawkins* (2001) LTL 2/7/2001 the claimants stated in the affidavits in support of the without notice application that certain information was obtained using a bugged telephone in the claimants' offices. It later transpired that the conversations were taped using an interception device at one of the defendant's homes. The order was discharged and not re-granted to mark the gravity of the claimants' conduct. Others, being material but not central to the application, will be more readily forgiven. See the judgment of Woolf LJ in *Behbehani v Salem* [1989] 1 WLR 723.

In deciding what sanctions, if any, to impose for any breach of duty, it is necessary to take into account all the relevant circumstances, including the gravity of the breach, the excuse or explanation offered, the severity and duration of any prejudice occasioned, and whether the consequences of the breach were remediable and had been remedied. The court must also apply the overriding objective and the need for proportionality (*Memory Corporation plc v Sidhu (No. 2)* [2000] 1 WLR 1443). It is important that the rule against material non-disclosure does not itself become an instrument of injustice (*Brink's Mat Ltd v Elcombe* [1988] 1 WLR 1350).

Discharge on the basis of unfair conduct

38.38 In *Negocios Del Mar SA v Doric Shipping Corporation SA* [1979] 1 Lloyd's Rep 331 the claimants had agreed to buy a ship from the defendants. Before paying the agreed price, they discovered it was damaged. So they obtained a freezing injunction, which they served immediately on the exchange of the ship for the price. The effect was that the proceeds of the sale were immediately frozen in the hands of the sellers. On appeal, this was regarded as being unfair conduct on the part of the claimants, and the injunction was discharged.

Discharge on the basis of delay

38.39 It was stated by Glidewell LJ in *Lloyds Bowmaker Ltd v Brittania Arrow Holdings plc* [1988] 1 WLR 1337 that:

> . . . a plaintiff who succeeds in obtaining a Mareva injunction is in my view under an obligation to press on with his action as rapidly as he can so that if he should fail to establish liability in the defendant the disadvantage which the injunction imposes upon the defendant will be lessened so far as possible.

A failure to press on with the substantive action will therefore provide grounds for discharging a freezing injunction. A fully and sufficiently explained delay will not result in the injunction being discharged (*Walsh v Deloitte and Touche Inc.* [2001] UKPC 58, LTL 18/12/2001).

FREEZING INJUNCTIONS AFTER JUDGMENT

38.40 There is nothing in the decision in *Lister v Stubbs* (1890) 45 ChD 1 to prevent an injunction being granted *after* judgment to restrain a judgment debtor from disposing of assets in order to prevent the judgment creditor enforcing the judgment that has been obtained. Indeed, it was expressly held in *Orwell Steel (Erection and Fabrication) Ltd v Asphalt and Tarmac (UK) Ltd* [1984] 1 WLR 1097 that a freezing injunction may be granted in aid of the execution of a judgment debt, and in *Faith Panton Property Plan Ltd v Hodgetts* [1981] 1 WLR 927, that a freezing injunction may be granted to restrain the disposal of assets to frustrate the enforcement of an order for costs. In the latter case, the proceedings for the assessment of costs were likely to take about four or five months to complete, but the Court of Appeal held that it was appropriate to grant the injunction under principles established before *Mareva Compania Naviera SA v International Bulkcarriers SA* [1980] 1 All ER 213.

Regarding the principles to be applied on a post-judgment application, provided the judgment is enforceable in England and Wales, the requirements that the claimant must have a cause of action justiciable in England and Wales and a good arguable case are satisfied by the judgment itself. Consequently, the only requirements are that the defendant has assets within the jurisdiction and there is a real risk of those assets being dissipated before judgment can be enforced. A freezing injunction in aid of execution should operate in the same way as a freezing injunction granted in the course of proceedings. So, for example, a bank served with an order freezing a customer's account should still honour routine banking transactions such as bills of exchange or letters of credit (see *Lewis and Peat (Produce) Ltd v Almatu Properties Ltd* (1992) *The Times*, 14 May 1992).

The usual practice in applications for freezing injunctions after judgment is to grant them without requiring an undertaking in damages. The reason is that no protection is required because there is no question of the injunction being reversed at a later date (*Gwembe Valley Development Co. Ltd v Koshy (No. 4)* (2001) *The Times*, 28 February 2002). Likewise, a claimant who obtained a pre-trial freezing injunction is usually entitled to be discharged from his undertakings in costs and damages once judgment is obtained (*Oystertec plc v Davidson* [2004] EWHC 2004 (Ch), LTL 6/8/2004). An undertaking may be required, however, where the trial judge has granted permission to appeal (*Gwembe Valley Development Co. Ltd v Koshy (No. 4)*).

TRACING CLAIMS

Unlike a claim for damages, an equitable tracing claim is a claim of a proprietary character. **38.41**
The only interim protection that can be sought in a damages claim is a freezing injunction. On the other hand, the sum subject to a tracing claim may be protected by an ordinary interim injunction, which will be granted on the usual *American Cyanamid Co. v Ethicon Ltd* [1975] AC 396 principles (for which, see **chapter 37**) (*Polly Peck International plc v Nadir (No. 2)* [1992] 4 All ER 769).

WRIT *NE EXEAT REGNO*

The writ *ne exeat regno* prevents a person from leaving the jurisdiction. It originated in the **38.42**
thirteenth century as a prerogative writ, but was subsequently adapted by equity as a means of coercing a defendant to give bail on pain of arrest in cases where the defendant owed a debt that was equitable (so that the defendant was not liable under the old procedure of arrest on mesne process). It may be granted where the defendant may leave the jurisdiction to the damage of a claimant to whom the defendant is indebted until he or she gives security for the debt. A good deal of caution is applied before the writ will be issued (*Allied Arab Bank Ltd v Hajjar* [1988] QB 787), and the court must be satisfied that issuing the writ is proportionate and necessary to secure the ends of justice (*Ali v Naseem* (2003) *The Times*, 3 October 2003). The requirements for such a writ were stated by Megarry J in *Felton v Callis* [1969] 1 QB 200 as being:

(a) The claim must be one in which the defendant would formerly have been liable to arrest at law.
(b) A good cause of action for at least £50 must be established.

(c) There must be good probable cause for believing the defendant is about to leave the jurisdiction unless he or she is arrested.
(d) It must be shown that the absence of the defendant from the jurisdiction will materially prejudice the claimant in the prosecution of the claim.
(e) The claim must be an equitable one.

In *Allied Arab Bank Ltd v Hajjar* [1988] QB 787 a writ *ne exeat regno* was discharged on a number of grounds, one of them being that it had been obtained for the primary purpose of requiring the defendant to identify his assets for the purposes of a freezing injunction, rather than prejudicing the prosecution of the claim (condition (d)). Freezing injunctions are remedies in aid of execution, and are therefore distinct from prosecuting the substantive claim. It also follows from this condition that the writ is only available before trial, and not in aid of execution (*Hume v Druyff* (1873) LR 8 Ex 214).

However, in *Bayer AG v Winter* [1986] 1 WLR 497 the Court of Appeal allowed an appeal to add terms to a freezing injunction (combined with a search order) requiring the defendant to deliver up his passports and restraining him from leaving the jurisdiction until execution of the freezing and search orders. The jurisdiction relied upon derived from the **Supreme Court Act 1981, s. 37(1)**, rather than the restrictive rules governing writs *ne exeat regno*. In *B v B (Injunction: Jurisdiction)* [1997] 1 WLR 329 Wilson J held the power to restrain a party from leaving the jurisdiction and to surrender his passport exists where the applicant has established a right to interim relief (such as a freezing order) which would otherwise be rendered nugatory and where a hearing is shortly to take place. His lordship also said the process was available in aid of all the court's procedures leading to a disposal of the proceedings, and after judgment. However, the power to make such an order would be exercised with considerable caution, and only for a short period. It certainly would not be granted in order to pressurise a defendant into paying a claim. After judgment was obtained against the claimant in *Robinson v Robinson* (2003) LTL 15/10/2003 an order for the surrender of his passport was made for the purpose of ensuring that he complied with an order to swear an affidavit of assets in support of a freezing injunction. It was feared that he would leave for his home in the USA.

Chapter 39 Search Orders

NATURE OF A SEARCH ORDER

A search order is a bundle of interim orders which require the respondent to admit another party to premises for the purpose of preserving evidence which might otherwise be destroyed or concealed by the respondent (see **CPR, r. 25.1(1)(h)**). Statutory authority for the jurisdiction is given by the **Civil Procedure Act 1997, s. 7**. Prior to the introduction of the CPR this form of order was commonly known as an *Anton Piller* order, taking its name from *Anton Piller KG v Manufacturing Processes Ltd* [1976] Ch 55. **39.1**

A search order is both injunctive and mandatory in nature. It requires the intended defendant to allow a named supervising solicitor from an independent firm, a partner from the claimant's own solicitors, and a limited number of additional people to enter on to the defendant's premises, and any vehicles in the defendant's control in the vicinity of those premises, so that they can search for, inspect, take photocopies and remove specified items and documents. The specified items and documents are those likely to be probative in the proceedings. The order will also often require the intended defendant to deliver up relevant documents not located at the premises searched, and to verify information on affidavit. The potential oppression inherent in such an order is recognised by the courts, and a search order is regarded as at the extremity of the court's powers. Although the jurisdiction to make search orders may be invoked in any type of claim, it is most frequently encountered in claims for infringement of intellectual property rights in the entertainment industry.

PROCEDURE ON APPLICATIONS FOR SEARCH ORDERS

Court

Search orders are, by virtue of the **County Court Remedies Regulations 1991** (SI 1991/1222 as amended by SI 1995/206), available: **39.2**

(a) In the High Court, which is the usual venue. Intellectual property claims, which form the bulk of the cases where this type of application is likely to be made, are assigned to the Chancery Division (**Supreme Court Act 1981, sch, 1, para. 1(i)**). If an application for a search order in an intellectual property case is not made in the Chancery Division, the applicant should tell the court that applications should normally be made in the Chancery Division and explain why the present application is not being made there (*Elvee Ltd v Taylor* [2001] EWCA Civ 1943, [2002] FSR 48).

(b) In the patents county court.

(c) In any county court, provided the judge dealing with the application is a High Court or Court of Appeal judge.

Where a search order is sought in a county court claim (and none of the exceptions in the **County Court Remedies Regulations 1991** applies), the application for the search order must be made in the High Court (**High Court and County Courts Jurisdiction Order 1991 (SI 1991/724), art. 3**). Such an application is deemed to include an application for the transfer of the proceedings to the High Court (**County Court Remedies Regulations 1991, reg. 4**). The application must be made returnable to a judge, and the application notice must (see *Schmidt v Wong* [2005] EWCA Civ 1506, [2006] 1 WLR 561) carry the following endorsement:

This application is being made in the course of [in anticipation of] proceedings in the [ ] county court pursuant to article 3 of the High Court and County Courts Jurisdiction Order 1991. The county court has no jurisdiction to grant the relief sought by reason of regulation 3(1) of the County Court Remedies Regulations 1991.

Procedure

39.3 Search orders are only obtainable against defendants who are likely to destroy relevant evidence if an application on notice were to be made (see **39.9**). Consequently, secrecy is essential, so the application will be made without notice and the court will sit in private. Many applications are also urgent, and many are made before proceedings are issued. The general procedure for applications for interim injunctions applies, for which see **37.5** to **37.13** and **procedural checklist 20** in **appendix 1**. Essentially, the claimant must:

(a) have issued a claim form in respect of the substantive cause of action, unless the application is too urgent to wait for this to be done;
(b) issue an application notice in **form N244**;
(c) provide affidavit evidence in support (witness statements are not acceptable: **PD 25, para. 3.1**);
(d) provide a draft order, together with a copy on disk;
(e) provide a skeleton argument in support; and
(f) after the hearing, provide all affected parties with a full note, for which they do not have to ask, of what happened at the hearing, including the basis and materials on which the order was made (*Interoute Telecommunications (UK) Ltd v Fashion Gossip Ltd* (1999) *The Times*, 10 November 1999).

It is very common to combine applications for search orders with other forms of urgent interim relief. It is not unknown, to use the old terminology, to 'pile *Piller* upon *Mareva*' in fraud and pirating claims.

Full and frank disclosure

39.4 As the application is made without notice, the claimant has the usual duty of full and frank disclosure. The courts have insisted that this is especially important in applications for search orders, and the claimant should err on the side of excessive disclosure. The supporting affidavit must disclose in very full terms the reason for seeking the order, including the probability that relevant material will disappear if the order is not made (**PD 25, para. 7.3**).

Supervising solicitor

39.5 The affidavit supporting an application for a search order must state the name and experience of the proposed supervising solicitor, and give the name and address of his or her firm. The proposed supervising solicitor must be someone experienced in the operation of search orders (**PD 25, para. 7.2**) and must not be a member or employee of the claimant's solicitors (**para.** 7.6). Names of suitable supervising solicitors can be obtained through the Law Society and (for the London area) the London Solicitors Litigation Association. If the court orders that a search order need not be served by the supervising solicitor, the reason for so ordering must be set out in the order (**para.** 7.7). Various undertakings given by the supervising solicitor appear in the standard-form search order in sch. E. These include an undertaking by the supervising solicitor to keep the existence of the removed items confidential.

Documents to third parties

A third party who did not attend the hearing at which a search order was made, but who is served with the order, may request copies of the materials read by the judge, materials prepared at the direction of the judge, and the note of the hearing (**PD 25, para.** 9.2). Unless the court otherwise orders, the applicant must comply promptly with the request. **39.6**

PRINCIPLES

Ormrod LJ in *Anton Piller KG v Manufacturing Processes Ltd* [1976] Ch 55 laid down the following preconditions for granting search orders: **39.7**

(a) There must be an extremely strong prima facie case on the merits. It is worth contrasting this with the requirement of merely showing a good arguable case in applications for freezing orders.
(b) The defendant's activities must be proved to result in very serious potential or actual harm to the claimant's interests.
(c) There must be clear evidence that incriminating documents or materials are in the defendant's possession.
(d) There must be a real possibility that such items may be destroyed before any applications on notice can be made. This is considered at 39.9.
(e) The defendant will be adequately protected by the claimant's undertaking in damages (the discussion at 37.25 applies equally to search orders).

Insistence on strict compliance

In the early 1980s it was thought that the conditions set out in 39.5 had been relaxed by *Yousif v Salama* [1980] 1 WLR 1540 and *Dunlop Holdings Ltd v Staravia Ltd* [1982] Com LR 3. In the former it was inferred that there was a real risk of the defendant disobeying any orders made on applications on notice from evidence that he had forged a signature on a cheque. In the latter, Oliver LJ said: **39.8**

> . . . it has certainly become customary to infer the probability of disappearance or destruction of evidence where it is clearly established on the evidence before the court that the defendant is engaged in a nefarious activity which renders it likely that he is an untrustworthy person. It is seldom that one can get cogent or actual evidence of a threat to destroy material or documents.

The claimant's solicitors in *Columbia Picture Industries Inc. v Robinson* [1987] Ch 38 had applied for some 300 search orders between 1974 and 1985, and none of their applications had been refused.

Since *Booker McConnell plc v Plascow* [1985] RPC 425 there has been a marked change in judicial attitude, and nowadays the courts insist on strict compliance with the principles enunciated by Ormrod LJ in *Anton Piller KG v Manufacturing Processes Ltd* [1976] Ch 55. The order is regarded as a serious stigma on the defendant's commercial reputation, and will often result in banks refusing further credit or even calling in loans. The order itself often allows the claimant's representatives to remove the defendant's stock-in-trade, and the net result is often to drive the defendant out of business. Accordingly, the order is regarded as a remedy of last resort, and should be made only 'when there is no alternative' (per Ormrod LJ in *Anton Piller KG v Manufacturing Processes Ltd*). As Dillon LJ explained in *Booker McConnell plc v Plascow*:

. . . the courts have always proceeded, justifiably, on the basis that the overwhelming majority of people in this country will comply with the court's order, and that defendants will therefore comply with orders to, for example, produce and deliver up documents without it being necessary to empower the [claimants'] solicitors to search the defendant's premises.

Putting the matter slightly differently, Hoffmann J in *Lock International plc v Beswick* [1989] 1 WLR 1268 said at p. 1281: ' . . . there must be *proportionality* between the perceived threat to the [claimant's] rights and the remedy granted'. Before embarking on an application for a search order, it is therefore necessary to consider whether some less draconian measure, such as applying on notice for negative injunctions or for an order that the documents be delivered up to the defendant's solicitor, or even awaiting disclosure in the usual way, would adequately protect the claimant.

REAL RISK OF DESTRUCTION

39.9 In *Anton Piller KG v Manufacturing Processes Ltd* [1976] Ch 55 it was said that a search order would not be made unless there is 'real possibility' that material evidence will be destroyed if an application for disclosure were to be made on notice to the defendant. This formula has been adopted in numerous cases since then. It is possible that the CPR have made a slight alteration in this requirement. **PD 25, para.** 7.3(2), referring to the evidence needed in support of an application for a search order, says it must cover 'the probability' that relevant material would disappear if the order were not made. There is a slight difference between a 'real possibility' and a 'probability', in that the latter expression means that the risk of destruction has to be proved on the balance of probabilities, whereas the earlier expression can be satisfied by evidence coming a little distance short of establishing the risk on the balance of probabilities. However, it is doubtful that **para.** 7.3(2), which is a provision dealing with the evidence required in support of an application, can have been intended to alter the established conditions for the remedy.

The requirement of showing there is a real risk that the defendant will destroy vital evidence lies at the heart of the jurisdiction to grant search orders. Sometimes it is possible to infer this risk from the nature of the defendant's alleged conduct, for instance, in video pirating claims and commercial fraud actions. Even in these cases, however, the claimant is still obliged to give full and frank disclosure of anything known about the defendant, including past responsible conduct or other matters which tend to show the defendant would obey the court's orders.

Outside the area of actions based directly on dishonesty, it will be rare for the claimant to have evidence of a real risk of destruction. An example is *Lock International plc v Beswick* [1989] 1 WLR 1268, where the claimant alleged the defendants, who were former employees now competing with the claimant, were making use of its trade secrets and confidential information. A search order was executed, and the defendants successfully applied to discharge the order. Hoffmann J said the claimant's evidence:

> . . . came nowhere near [establishing] . . . a 'grave danger' or 'real possibility' that the defendants might destroy evidence. . . . these defendants were no fly-by-night video pirates. They were former long-service employees with families and mortgages, who had openly said that they were entering into competition and whom the plaintiff knew to be financed by highly respectable institutions.

FORM OF THE ORDER

39.10 A standard form of search order is provided in the annex to **PD 25** (as refined from time to time). This form is described in **PD 25, para.** 7.11, as an 'example', and should be used with such modifications as are necessary to fit the circumstances of the case. Any substantial variation from the form should be brought to the attention of the judge at the hearing. A number of significant amendments were made to the standard search order with effect from 1 October 2005. Before these amendments came into force, the practice was (pre-1 October 2005 version of PD 25, para. 8.4) to delete provisions in the standard order relating to documents protected by the privilege against self-incrimination in cases where the privilege has been removed by statute (see **39.16**). The present practice is to retain all the standard wording in the order even where the privilege has been removed by statute (present version of **PD 25, para.** 7.9).

The main provision is clause 6, which provides that the defendant 'must permit [certain named people, referred to as "the search party"] to enter' the defendant's premises. Other clauses in the order are designed to give effect to the basic purpose of the order, which is to allow the search party to enter the defendant's premises and to take documents which might be disclosable in the proceedings or otherwise be relevant, while providing suitable safeguards for the defendant. These include the appointment of an independent supervising solicitor to ensure the order is not misused by the claimant. Clause 22 may be used to set out prohibitory injunctions ancillary to the main part of the order. Schedule B sets out the items that may be seized, and must extend no further than the minimum necessary to preserve the evidence which might otherwise be concealed or destroyed (*Columbia Picture Industries Inc. v Robinson* [1987] Ch 38).

Service of the order

Since *Universal Thermosensors Ltd v Hibben* [1992] 1 WLR 840 execution of search orders has been subject to oversight by supervising solicitors who are independent of the claimant's usual solicitors. Before this case there was mounting concern about the execution of search orders by enthusiastic but inexperienced persons. Execution by a solicitor related to the claimant or by one of the claimant's directors was deprecated in *Manor Electronics Ltd v Dickson* [1988] RPC 618. **39.11**

The order must be served personally by the supervising solicitor, unless the court otherwise orders. Together with the order there must be served an application notice for a hearing on notice in respect of the search order (see **39.21**). The affidavits in support and any exhibits capable of being copied must be served at the same time as the order (**PD 25, para. 7.4(1)**). Confidential exhibits need not be served, but they must be made available for inspection by the defendant in the presence of the claimant's solicitors while the order is being executed. Copies of confidential exhibits may be retained by the defendant's solicitors on their undertaking not to permit the defendant to see them except in their presence, nor to allow the defendant to make or take away any note or record of them (**para.** 7.4(2)). Unless the court otherwise orders, service may only be effected between 9.30 a.m. and 5.30 p.m. Monday to Friday (**para.** 7.4(6)). The reason for this is that the defendant is entitled to seek legal advice, and this will only be effective if the order is executed during office hours. It is recognised that mistakes (on both sides) are less likely to occur if these orders are executed during office hours (for an example, see *Adam Phones Ltd v Goldschmidt* [1999] 4 All ER 486).

Planning is essential for effective execution. If several addresses are included in the order, it is important that execution is simultaneous. To reduce its oppressive effect the order will limit the number of persons who can assist with its execution at each address specified. Further, if the defendant is a woman living alone, a woman must accompany those executing the order (**para.** 7.4(5)). The police will be informed beforehand if there is any prospect of a breach of the peace.

Gaining access and explaining the order

A search order is not a search warrant, and does not authorise the use of force to gain access. In cases where the defendant has committed both a civil wrong against the claimant and a criminal offence, a search order must not be executed at the same time as a police search **39.12** warrant (**PD 25, para.** 7.8; clause 8 of the standard form of search order). Clause 6 is a mandatory order that the defendant 'must permit' access to the supervising solicitor. But before entering, the supervising solicitor must explain the terms and effect of the order in everyday language and must inform the defendant that legal advice may be sought before entry is permitted and of the defendant's right to apply to vary or discharge the order.

With effect from 1 October 2005, by **PD 25, para.** 7.4(4), the supervising solicitor must also advise the respondent that he may avail himself of:

(a) legal professional privilege; and
(b) the privilege against self-incrimination. Situations where the privilege against self-incrimination do not apply are listed in **para.** 7.9 (see **39.16** and **39.17**).

A solicitor who negligently failed to explain the effect of the order to the defendant in a fair and accurate manner was held to be in contempt of court in *VDU Installations Ltd v Integrated Computer Systems and Cybernetics Ltd* [1989] FSR 378. The right to seek legal advice means that the obligation to give permission for entry only arises after a reasonable period of time has elapsed for legal advice to be obtained (*Bhimji v Chatwani* [1991] 1 WLR 989). Thereafter, the defendant must give permission, or else will be in contempt of court. Even if there are grounds for seeking an order for the immediate discharge of the search order, while it subsists it is an order of the court and must be obeyed (*Wardle Fabrics Ltd v G. Myristis Ltd* [1984] FSR 263). However, if entry is refused and the order is successfully discharged shortly thereafter, that will give the court grounds for imposing no penalty on an application to commit for contempt of court. Matters to be taken into account include whether an application to discharge is merely a device to delay the search, and whether the defendant has interfered with the evidence during the delay (*Bhimji v Chatwani*).

Executing the order

39.13 There is a heavy duty on the supervising solicitor to comply strictly with the terms of the order as to the premises which can be searched and the items which can be removed.

The defendant's premises must not be searched, and no items may be removed, except in the presence of the defendant or a person who appears to be a responsible employee of the defendant (**PD 25, para.** 7.5(2)). If any of the items covered by the order exist only in computer-readable form, the defendant must immediately give the claimant's solicitors effective access, including any necessary passwords, and arrange for the material to be printed out. The claimant must take all reasonable steps to ensure that no damage is done to the defendant's computer system, and must ensure that the person searching the defendant's system has sufficient expertise to avoid causing damage (**para.** 7.5(8) to (10)). Items seized must be recorded by the supervising solicitor in a list, and must be retained by the claimant's solicitors for the minimum time necessary to take copies and in any case for no more than two days, after which they must be returned to their owner (**para.** 7.5(3) and (6)). Nothing should be removed until the defendant has had a reasonable opportunity to check it against the list (**para.** 7.5(7)). Where ownership of the material seized is in dispute, the claimant's solicitors should place it in the custody of the defendant's solicitors pending trial on the defendant's solicitors undertaking to retain it in safekeeping and to produce it to the court when required (**para.** 7.5(4)). It may be appropriate for the order to require the claimant to insure the materials seized (**para.** 7.5(5)).

Execution of a search order in an excessive or oppressive manner will render the claimant liable under the undertaking in damages. Seizing documents not specified in the order may be penalised by an award of aggravated damages. An award of £10,000 against the claimant was made on this ground in *Columbia Picture Industries Inc. v Robinson* [1987] Ch 38.

It is important that neither the claimant nor the claimant's employees are allowed to conduct searches for documents belonging to a trade competitor. Safeguards must be built into the order to protect the confidentiality of the defendant's trade secrets.

Additional powers and duties of the supervising solicitor

It may become apparent that it is impracticable to comply fully with the requirement that the defendant be allowed to check the claimant's list of materials before anything is removed from the premises, or the conditions for accessing material stored on computer. If the supervising solicitor is satisfied that compliance is impracticable, he or she may permit the search to proceed and for items to be removed without full compliance (**PD 25, para. 7.5(13)**). **39.14**

Once the search has been completed, the supervising solicitor must provide the claimant's solicitors with a report on the carrying out of the order. The claimant's solicitors must then serve a copy on the defendant and file a copy with the court (**PD 25, para. 7.5(11)** and **(12)**).

Contempt by the defendant

In *Alliance and Leicester Building Society v Ghahremani* (1992) 142 NLJ 313 a search order was executed at the premises of a firm of solicitors. The order required the defendant solicitor to disclose 'documents' of various categories. There was evidence that the defendant erased information stored on computer while the order was being executed. Hoffmann J held that the word 'document' in the order was, in the light of the earlier decision of *Derby and Co. Ltd v Weldon (No. 9)* [1991] 1 WLR 652, wide enough to include information stored on computer, and that the defendant was guilty of contempt of court. It is probable that if the defendant had not been a lawyer the court would have held that the wording was insufficiently clear to found an application for committal. It is for this reason that the standard search order contains specific provision in clause 17 for copying information stored on computer. In addition to being a contempt of court, 'the refusal to comply may be the most damning evidence against the defendant at the subsequent trial' (per Ormrod LJ in *Anton Piller KG v Manufacturing Processes Ltd* [1976] Ch 55). **39.15**

On the other hand, a petty breach of a search order in circumstances where the defendant had honestly tried to obey it should be ignored by the parties. Under the CPR, given the emphasis on proportionality, an application to commit for no more than a technicality is likely to be dismissed with costs (*Adam Phones Ltd v Goldschmidt* [1999] 4 All ER 486).

PRIVILEGE AGAINST SELF-INCRIMINATION

The House of Lords in *Rank Film Distributors Ltd v Video Information Centre* [1982] AC 380 held that where a criminal charge was more than a contrived, fanciful or remote possibility, the defendant could refuse to provide information by relying on the privilege against self-incrimination. In many cases where the evidence is strong enough for a search order, it will also amount to a breach of the criminal law. The privilege applies in relation to any piece of information or evidence on which the prosecution might wish to rely in establishing guilt or in deciding whether to prosecute or not (*Den Norske Bank ASA v Antonatos* [1999] QB 271). The scope of the privilege is discussed at **48.38**. **39.16**

The *Rank* decision threatened to destroy the utility of many search orders, and was swiftly reversed by the **Supreme Court Act 1981, s. 72**. This is not the only provision making inroads into the privilege against self-incrimination (see **PD 25, para. 7.9**), the relevant provisions being:

(a) the **Supreme Court Act 1981, s. 72**, which focuses on the civil cause of action, applying to intellectual property and passing-off civil claims, and removes the privilege in respect of 'related offences' and the recovery of 'related penalties';

(b) the Theft Act 1968, s. 31(1), which removes the privilege in civil proceedings for the recovery or administration of any property, for the execution of any trust, or for an account, notwithstanding that compliance may expose the witness or his spouse to a charge under the Theft Act 1968;

(c) the Children Act 1989, s. 98, which removes the privilege in applications relating to the care, supervision or protection of a child;
(d) various statutes and statutory instruments where the privilege has been impliedly removed (see *Bank of England v Riley* [1992] Ch 475).

The above statutory provisions do not completely remove the privilege against self-incrimination, which still applies, for example, in civil fraud proceedings. In such cases, it was held in *Tate Access Floors Inc. v Boswell* [1991] Ch 512 that the privilege entitles a defendant served with a search order to refuse:

(a) permission to enter;
(b) to deliver up documents covered by the order; and
(c) to verify information about suppliers and customers.

However, as was also held in *Tate Access Floors Inc. v Boswell*, it is a privilege against *self*-incrimination. The privilege may be relied on by persons ordered to give information whether they are natural persons or artificial persons such as limited companies (for which see *Triplex Safety Glass Co. Ltd v Lancegaye Safety (1934) Glass Ltd* [1939] 2 KB 395) provided they do so on their own behalf. However, one person cannot refuse to give information which might incriminate another, except where the other is the person's spouse. In *Tate Access Floors Inc. v Boswell* the court left open the question whether the connection between the controller of a company and the company might be so strong that they should be allowed to refuse to incriminate each other. In *Sociedade Nacional de Combustiveis de Angola UEE v Lundqvist* [1991] 2 QB 310 the court said that a company officer nominated to transmit the company's information (which in that case was information about assets subject to a freezing injunction) could refuse to transmit evidence which might incriminate him or her, but that the court would immediately nominate another person to transmit the information.

The above problems can be avoided if the risk of the information supplied being used in criminal proceedings can be removed. This can be achieved if the Crown Prosecution Service indicate in writing that they will not make use of the information for the purposes of any criminal prosecution against the defendant or the defendant's spouse, and if a clause stating that no disclosure made in compliance with the order will be used in evidence in the prosecution or any offence committed by the defendant of the defendant's spouse is included in the order (*AT and T Istel Ltd v Tully* [1993] AC 45).

Privilege and terms of the search order

39.17 Until *Den Norske Bank ASA v Antonatos* [1999] QB 271 an attempt was sometimes made to add a clause to a search order to the effect that a defendant who claimed to be entitled to the benefit of the privilege against self-incrimination still had to provide the allegedly privileged information to the supervising solicitor, who would hold the information to the order of the court. It was held in *Den Norske Bank ASA v Antonatos* that such a clause is inconsistent with the privilege if it applies, and should no longer be used.

A respondent who wishes to claim that listed documents are protected by privilege may gather them together and hand them over to the supervising solicitor to assess whether they are privileged as claimed (standard search order, cl. 11(1)). On assessing the materials, the supervising solicitor may:

(a) Decide they are privileged (standard search order, cl. 11(2)). In such a case the materials will be excluded from the search. The supervising solicitor will list them for inclusion in his report, and return them to the respondent.
(b) Decide they may be privileged (standard search order, cl. 11(3)). In such a case the supervising solicitor will exclude the material from the search, but will retain it in his possession pending further order of the court.

Clause 11(3) of the standard search order states the same procedure as in (b) above applies 'if the respondent claims to be entitled to withhold production on [the grounds that the documents may be privileged or incriminating]'. It is probable, but not clear from cls. 11(1) and (3), that this applies only where the respondent does not hand the documents over to the supervising solicitor to assess whether they are privileged (under cl. 11(1)). It is possible to read cl. 11(3) as applying also where cl. 11(1) has been invoked and the supervising solicitor has decided the documents are clearly not privileged, but the respondent then claims to be entitled to withhold them.

DISCHARGE AND VARIATION OF SEARCH ORDERS

Discharge of search orders

Applications to discharge or vary search orders are largely governed by the principles already discussed in relation to freezing injunctions at **38.32** to **38.39**. However, if a search order has been executed, there is a strong argument that it is an unjustified waste of costs and of the court's time to seek its discharge before trial. Doing so was said by Browne-Wilkinson V-C in *Dormeuil Frères SA v Nicolian International (Textiles) Ltd* [1988] 1 WLR 1362 to be little more than an empty gesture, and that the right course was normally to adjourn an application to set aside the order to be dealt with at trial. Unless there is not even a prima facie case of abuse, where a search order has been executed at the defendant's home, the court should allow the defendant a hearing on an application to discharge the search order (*Indicil Salus Ltd v Chandrasekaran* (2006) LTL 16/2/2006). Where the order had not been complied with at the time of the application to set aside, as in *Arab Monetary Fund v Hashim* [1989] 1 WLR 565, it was necessary to consider whether the order would be made in the light of the full facts. In *Tate Access Floors Inc. v Boswell* [1991] Ch 512 the Vice-Chancellor reconsidered his decision in *Dormeuil Frères SA* in the light of the freezing injunction case of *Behbehani v Salem* [1989] 1 WLR 723. There is a conflict between the public interest in ensuring that applications made without notice are made in good faith, and the public interest in ensuring the courts are not clogged up with long interim hearings. The Vice-Chancellor suggested the solution may be that the circumstances in which an order without notice was obtained should only be investigated at the pre-trial stage if it is clear there has been a material non-disclosure or where the nature of the alleged non-disclosure is so serious as to demand immediate investigation. If the ground for seeking to have the order discharged is that the claimant is guilty of material non-disclosure over a matter relevant to the granting of relief without notice, being a matter which has no relevance to the merits of the substantive action (such as the value of the claimant's undertaking in damages), it may be more appropriate to determine the matter immediately rather than waiting until trial. **39.18**

Further, it is sometimes argued that even if the original order was granted on insufficient grounds, the fruits of the search may indicate that justice was done in the event. Such an argument was rejected in *Manor Electronics Ltd v Dickson* [1988] RPC 618 in the face of a clear material non-disclosure.

A search order was discharged in *Gadget Shop Ltd v Bug.Com Ltd* [2001] FSR 26, for multiple breaches of procedure. Small variations in the standard form of order had not been drawn to the attention of the judge on the initial application; the lack of experience of the supervising solicitor had not been adequately explained in the evidence in support; and the evidence in support did not give adequate full and frank disclosure, for example, that some of the allegedly confidential material said to have been taken by the defendants had been published on the applicant's own web site.

Exclusion of evidence obtained under a discharged search order

The question of whether any documents seized under a search order which is subsequently **39.19** discharged should be held to be inadmissible at trial was left open by the Vice-Chancellor in *Tate Access Floors Inc. v Boswell* [1991] Ch 512. The general rule has been that there is no exclusionary discretion in civil cases, and if the documents are otherwise relevant and admissible it should not matter how they were obtained. This has been changed by **CPR, r. 32.1**, as decisively held in *Grobbelaar v Sun Newspapers Ltd* (1999) *The Times*, 12 August 1999. The defendant also has a remedy under the claimant's undertaking in damages.

Variation on grounds of intimidation

39.20 One of the defendants in *Coca-Cola Co. v Gilbey* [1995] 4 All ER 711 argued that he should not be required to disclose the identities of other persons involved with him in a highly organised passing-off operation, and other information, as required by a search order, on the ground that doing so might expose himself and his family to physical violence from those other persons. It was held that, although violence or threats of violence would be legitimate grounds if put forward by innocent parties, when put forward by actual participants, public policy and the interests of the victim carried more weight, and disclosure was ordered forthwith.

AFTER EXECUTION

39.21 After executing the order, the supervising solicitor is required to compile a report of what happened (see **39.14**). The report is served on the defendant. Clause 3 of the model form of search order specifies a return date when there will be a second hearing, this time on notice to the defendant. The applicant's solicitors are required to provide the supervising solicitor with an application for hearing on the return date (sch. D, para. 1(iii)), which will be served on the defendant when the main order is executed by the supervising solicitor.

On the hearing the court will consider the supervising solicitor's report and the defendant may apply to discharge the order. Once a search order has been executed, there is an enhanced duty on the claimant to prosecute the main action without delay. In *Hytrac Conveyors Ltd v Conveyors International Ltd* [1983] 1 WLR 44, the claimant delayed for 10 weeks after obtaining a search order without serving a statement of claim. The claim was dismissed, Lawton LJ saying that claimants 'must not use [search] orders as a means of finding out what sort of charges they could make'.

If the claim was transferred to, or commenced in, the High Court for the purposes of applying for a search order, but is otherwise more suitable for the county court, after the application for the search order has been disposed of the claim will be transferred down to the county court (**County Court Remedies Regulations 1991** (SI 1991/1222), **reg. 5**). The application is not treated as disposed of until any application to set the order aside has been heard, or until the expiry of 28 days during which no such application is made.

USE FOR COLLATERAL PURPOSES OF MATERIAL OBTAINED USING A SEARCH ORDER

39.22 As with other forms of disclosure (see **chapter 48**), the claimant gives an implied undertaking not to use items seized under a search order for any collateral purposes. The court may sanction a relaxation of this undertaking in a proper case. The leading case is *Crest Homes plc v Marks* [1987] AC 829. In 1984 the claimant brought a claim against the defendant seeking injunctions to restrain breach of copyright in certain house designs. In the course of that claim a search order was obtained and executed. In 1985 the claimant commenced a second copyright claim against the defendant in relation to another house design, and obtained and executed a second search order. Some of the documents seized under the second search order were alleged by the claimant to show the defendant had not given full disclosure under the first search order. The claimant therefore sought to use those documents in contempt proceedings in relation to the first search order. The House of Lords held that although there were technically two separate actions, in substance they were a single set of proceedings. As the defendant would suffer no injustice by lifting the implied undertaking, permission was given to allow the claimant to use the documents in the contempt proceedings.

Chapter 40 Interim Delivery Up of Goods

INTRODUCTION

40.1 An order for the interim delivery up of goods operates in a similar way to freezing injunctions, but instead of merely restraining the defendant from disposing of or otherwise dealing with the goods covered by the order, actually requires the defendant to deliver up the goods to the claimant or someone else specified in the order. These orders are only available in proceedings for wrongful interference with goods.

JURISDICTION

40.2 The jurisdiction to make orders for interim delivery up is conferred by the **Torts (Interference with Goods) Act 1977, s. 4**, which provides:

(1) In this section 'proceedings' means proceedings for wrongful interference.
(2) On the application of any person in accordance with rules of court, the High Court shall, in such circumstances as may be specified in the rules, have power to make an order providing for the delivery up of any goods which are or may become the subject matter of subsequent proceedings in the court, or as to which any question may arise in proceedings.
(3) Delivery shall be, as the order may provide, to the claimant or to a person appointed by the court for the purpose, and shall be on such terms and conditions as may be specified in the order.

By the **Torts (Interference with Goods) Act 1977, s. 4**(5), orders under **s. 4** can be made in county court claims on the same basis as equivalent orders in the High Court. The power to make **s. 4** orders is listed among the interim remedies available to the court under **CPR, r. 25.1(1)(e)**.

'Wrongful interference', for the purpose of the **Torts (Interference with Goods) Act 1977, s. 4**(1), is defined by **s. 1** to mean:

(a) conversion of goods (a claim in conversion is expanded by s. 2(2) to cover the loss or destruction of goods which a bailee has allowed to happen in breach of his duty to his bailor, to balance the abolition of detinue, see (d) below);
(b) trespass to goods;
(c) negligence so far as it results in damage to goods or to an interest in goods; and
(d) any other tort so far as it results in damage to goods or to an interest in goods (but the tort of detinue was abolished by s. 2(1)).

By the Torts (Interference with Goods) Act 1977, s. 14, for the purposes of the Act the term 'goods' includes all chattels personal other than things in action and money.

PROCEDURE

40.3 The procedure in **CPR, Part 23**, should be followed on making an application under the **Torts (Interference with Goods) Act 1977, s. 4** (see **chapter 32** and **procedural checklist 21** in **appendix 1**). An application notice in **form N244** should be issued seeking delivery up of the goods, which must be specified, usually in a schedule to the application notice. It is not uncommon to combine the application with requests for orders for the detention, custody or preservation of the goods under **CPR, r. 25.1(1)(c)**, in the alternative. The application will need to be supported by written evidence (**r. 25.3(2)**).

Usually, applications for the interim delivery up of goods will be made on notice in the course of pending proceedings. However, if the case is of an urgent nature, the application may be made before the claim form is issued (as recognised in the **Torts (Interference with Goods) Act 1977, s. 4(2)** itself). If there is reason to believe the defendant may destroy or otherwise dispose of the goods if notice is given, the application may be made without giving notice, but the need for this will have to be justified in the evidence in support, and the usual duty of full and frank disclosure will apply to any application without notice.

Hearings for orders for interim delivery up of goods are usually dealt with by masters and district judges (see **CPR, r. 2.4**, and **PD 2B**). However, if the order will require permission to enter land, it is submitted that the hearing should be dealt with by a judge, as is required by **PD 2B, para. 2.1**, in the case of other types of interim orders involving entry on to land.

PRINCIPLES

A court considering an application for interim delivery up must first decide whether the goods are or may become the subject matter of proceedings for wrongful interference with goods (see **40.2**), and then consider whether to exercise its discretion to make the order. All that is required at the first stage is an arguable case. In *Pattihis v Jackson* [2002] EWHC 2480 (QB), LTL 22/11/2002, an assistant solicitor left his employment with the claimant to work for the second defendant, taking with him a large number of the claimant's client files. It was held that the second defendant had converted the files when it failed to return them by the third day after receiving a request for their return. **40.4**

Once it is established that there is an arguable case for one of the forms of wrongful interference with goods, the court has a discretion whether to make an interim delivery-up order. There is no need to show that there is an urgent need for the order, or that there might be a danger or risk that the goods might be lost or destroyed if the order is not made (*Howard E. Perry and Co. Ltd v British Railways Board* [1980] 1 WLR 1375). However, the order may be refused in the court's discretion where there would be no grounds for making an order for specific delivery (for which, see the **Torts (Interference with Goods) Act 1977, s. 3**, and **4.13**), because the order in effect gives an advance order for specific delivery (*Howard E. Perry and Co. Ltd v British Railways Board*).

The court will not usually order the delivery up of documents over which an accountant or solicitor is asserting a lien for unpaid fees, but it has a discretion to do so, particularly where there is a lack of evidence in support of the work alleged to have been done and which is said to give rise to the lien (*Thaper v Singh* 1987 FLR 369). Otherwise, the discretion is exercised by the balancing of considerations from each side (*Howard E. Perry and Co. Ltd v British Railways Board*).

If the order is refused, the court may make an order for the detention or preservation of the goods, falling short of delivery up, if the application includes this in the alternative. Normally, orders in this form are very readily made, as there are usually few reasons why the subject matter of the claim should not be preserved so it can be available at the trial. Countervailing considerations may be that the defendant has some legitimate reason for selling the goods for business reasons or because the goods are of a perishing nature.

THE ORDER

40.5 The order may provide for delivery up to the claimant or to anyone else appointed by the court for the purpose (**Torts (Interference with Goods) Act 1977, s. 4(3)**). The order may have to make provision for how delivery up is to be effected, and whether the claimant is to be allowed to collect the goods himself. The court must consider whether to include in the order similar provisions to those specified in **PD 25, paras** 5.1 to 5.3 (ordinary injunctions) and **paras** 7.1 to 7.11 (search orders) for the benefit or protection of the parties (**PD 25, para.** 8.2). Suitable provisions may well include undertakings in damages, and provisions dealing with the listing, insurance and custody of the goods to be delivered up.

HYBRID DELIVERY-UP ORDERS

40.6 According to the Court of Appeal in *CBS United Kingdom Ltd v Lambert* [1983] Ch 37, the court has a power deriving from either its inherent jurisdiction or from the **Supreme Court Act 1981, s. 37(1)**, to order the interim delivery up of assets as an adjunct to a freezing order. The defendant had admitted his involvement in the large-scale counterfeiting of musical recordings, and the evidence pointed to the defendant having deliberately put the proceeds of his activities into easily disposable chattels such as expensive motor cars. It was held to be a clear case for ordering delivery up of his assets. A number of guidelines were laid down for this type of order:

(a) There should be clear evidence that the defendant is likely, unless restrained by order, to dispose of or otherwise deal with the goods in order to deprive the claimant of the fruits of any judgment which may be obtained. The court will be slow to order the delivery up of property belonging to the defendant unless there is some evidence or inference that the property has been acquired as a result of the defendant's alleged wrongdoing.

(b) No order should be made for the delivery up of a defendant's clothes, bedding, furnishings, tools of his trade, farm implements, livestock or machinery (including motor vehicles) or stock-in-trade which it is likely that the defendant uses for the purposes of a lawful business. However, furnishings consisting of *objets d'art* of substantial value which the evidence indicates were bought with the fruits of the wrongdoing may be included in the order.

(c) The order should specify as clearly as possible the goods or classes of goods to be delivered up. If the claimant is unable to identify the goods in question, that points towards refusing an order.

(d) The order must not authorise the claimant to enter the defendant's premises or to seize the defendant's property save with the defendant's permission.

(e) The order should not require delivery up to anyone other than the claimant's solicitor or a receiver appointed by the court. The court will need to be satisfied that the claimant's solicitor, if to be the person taking possession of the goods, has facilities for suitable safe custody.

(f) Suitable safeguards should be built into the order for the protection of the defendant along the lines of freezing injunctions. These will include an undertaking in damages, and provision for the defendant's living expenses.

(g) The order should give the defendant liberty to apply to stay, vary or discharge the order.

Chapter 41 Inspection of Property

INTRODUCTION

By **CPR, r. 25.1(1)(c)**, the High Court and county courts have powers to make orders, on the application of one party to proceedings, for the inspection and preservation of property in the possession of another party. There are ancillary powers to authorise the taking of samples, and conducting experiments on and with property in the possession of the other party. There is a further power to authorise entry on to any land or building in the possession of the other party where the property that needs to be inspected is located (**r. 25.1(1)(d)**). These powers are useful for ensuring that the subject matter of the claim is still in existence when the proceedings reach trial. They are also used to give all sides a fair and proper opportunity to obtain informed expert evidence relevant to the issues in the claim. For example, in a claim arising out of an accident at work it may be necessary for the claimant's engineering expert to be able to inspect and test the machinery involved in the accident, which is likely to be located in the defendant's premises. In a claim arising out of the sale of goods it may be necessary for the seller's expert to take a sample of the goods in question and to test them or comment on their quality, and the goods may well be in the possession of the buyer. In a claim for negligence against a valuer the defendant's expert will almost inevitably have to inspect the claimant's property for the purposes of considering both liability and quantum. **41.1**

The most usual situation arises where the property that needs to be inspected is in the possession of an opposite party, and the request for inspection arises during the course of proceedings. However, the rules also make provision for inspection (and related orders) before the claim is issued, and for orders for inspection against persons who are not parties to the proceedings.

When making an order for the preservation of property the court must consider whether to include in the order similar provisions to those specified in **PD 25, paras 5.1 to 5.3** (ordinary injunctions) and **paras** 7.1 to 7.11 (search orders) for the benefit or protection of the parties (**PD 25, para. 8.2**). Suitable provisions are likely to include undertakings in damages, and provisions dealing with the listing, insurance and custody of the property to be preserved.

INSPECTION DURING THE COURSE OF PROCEEDINGS AGAINST A PARTY

Rule 25.1(1)(c) of the CPR provides that the courts have power to make orders for: **41.2**

(a) the detention, custody or preservation of relevant property (for the purpose of ensuring that the property is still available at trial); and
(b) the inspection of, taking samples of, carrying out of experiments on or with relevant

property (for the purpose of ensuring that experts can provide informed evidence at the trial, and to ensure fairness to both sides).

The order may include authority to enter land in the possession of a party to the proceedings for any of these purposes (**r. 25.1(1)(d)**). 'Relevant property' means property which is the subject of a claim, or as to which any question may arise in a claim (**r. 25.1(2)**).

Detention and preservation orders are usually sought where there is some risk that the other side may deliberately or accidentally get rid of the property before trial. If there is some risk, the order should be made quite readily as, unless there is some legitimate reason for the party with possession of the property wishing to sell it or use it up, justice points strongly towards it being preserved for the purposes of the proceedings.

Regarding orders for inspection etc., it is usually unarguably in the interests of justice and in accordance with the overriding objective for such orders to be made. It is usual, given the requirement of cooperation (**r. 1.3**), for the parties to seek consent to any necessary inspections before resorting to the assistance of the court. An order should only be sought if the other side do not respond in a reasonable time, or refuse their consent, or insist on unreasonable conditions.

Meaning of 'property'

41.3 Before the introduction of the CPR it was held that the rules allowing inspection of 'property' did not extend to inspecting the defendant's manufacturing process (*Tudor Accumulator Co. Ltd v China Mutual Steam Navigation Co. Ltd* [1930] WN 200). Nevertheless, under the old system it was held that there was inherent jurisdiction to make such an order (*Ash v Buxted Poultry Ltd* (1989) *The Times*, 29 November 1989). Technical limitations like those identified in *Tudor Accumulator Co. Ltd v China Mutual Co.* are precisely the sorts of restrictions the CPR were intended to sweep away, and inspection of a manufacturing process is almost certainly included within the meaning of 'relevant property' as set out in **r. 25.1(2)**. In *Huddleston v Control Risks Information Services Ltd* [1987] 1 WLR 701 (a case on the related pre-action procedure in the **Supreme Court Act 1981, s. 33(1)**, discussed at **41.5**) it was held that a document could be an item of 'property' for these purposes, but whether it was depended on whether the application sought inspection or detention of the physical document. If the application in substance sought the disclosure of the information recorded on the document, it was a disclosure application (for which, see **chapter 48**) rather than an application relating to 'property'.

Procedure on applications for inspection etc. during proceedings

41.4 Where an order for the preservation, detention or inspection of relevant property is required, the proper time for seeking it is at the track allocation stage, if the need for the order can be identified at that time. If so, the terms of the order sought should be provided to the court in the form of a draft order and sent to the court with the allocation questionnaire (see **PD 26, para. 2.2(3)(d); PD 28, paras 3.4** and **3.5; PD 29, para. 4.7**). The parties should seek to agree suitable directions, but failing that, the minimum is that the party seeking inspection etc. should send details of the proposed orders to the other side no later than the time the questionnaire is sent to the court.

There are cases where the need for preservation, detention or inspection orders only becomes apparent at a later stage. If so, the application should be made at a case management conference or pre-trial review or other hearing, and having a hearing just for this purpose is a last resort. In the latter situation an application notice in **form N244** will need to be issued. If a hearing is necessary because of the default of a party, sanctions may be imposed (**PD 28, para. 2.3; PD 29, para. 3.6**).

Written evidence in support is required unless the court otherwise orders (**CPR, r. 25.3(2)**). There will be some cases where the need for the order is so self-evident that no evidence is required.

Generally, these orders may be granted by a master or district judge. However, where the order seeks authorisation of entry on to land to recover, inspect or sample property, it must be made to a judge (**PD 2B, para. 2.3**).

INSPECTION BEFORE COMMENCEMENT OF PROCEEDINGS

There is jurisdiction to make orders for the inspection, detention and preservation of relevant property even before proceedings are issued, under the **Supreme Court Act 1981, s. 33(1)**, and the **County Courts Act 1984, s. 52(1)**. The **Supreme Court Act 1981, s. 33(1)**, provides: **41.5**

On the application of any person in accordance with rules of court, the High Court shall, in such circumstances as may be specified in the rules, have power to make an order providing for any one or more of the following matters, that is to say—

(a) the inspection, photocopying, preservation, custody and detention of property which appears to the court to be property which may become the subject matter of subsequent proceedings in the High Court, or as to which any question may arise in such proceedings; and
(b) the taking of samples of any such property as is mentioned in paragraph (a), and the carrying out of any experiment on or with any such property.

The **County Courts Act 1984, s. 52(1)**, is in essentially the same terms, but refers to the power being vested in the county court.

The only condition laid down by the statutory provisions is that an order for inspection etc. must be in respect of 'property which may become the subject matter of subsequent proceedings'. The discussion of what constitutes 'property' in **41.3** also applies for the purposes of these sections. However, the importance of *Huddleston v Control Risks Information Services Ltd* [1987] 1 WLR 701 has all but disappeared since the jurisdiction to make pre-commencement orders for disclosure of documents (see **chapter 48**) was widened by the Civil Procedure (Modification of Enactments) Order 1998 (SI 1998/2940) to extend these orders to all types of proceedings (and not just personal injuries claims).

There are no other restrictions, apart from the application of the overriding objective. An order may be refused on the grounds of proportionality and saving expense if it is not necessary to obtain the order until after proceedings are issued, or if no attempt has been made to obtain the inspection by consent. Also, it is less likely that the court will be prepared to make an order against someone who is not likely to be a party to the substantive proceedings than a respondent who is the likely opposite party.

Procedure on pre-commencement application for inspection

The general rules governing applications made before the commencement of proceedings are considered in **chapter 32**, particularly at **32.2** and **32.5**. Pre-commencement inspection orders are applied for by issuing an ordinary application notice in **form N244** in the anticipated proceedings, supported by written evidence. **Rule 25.5(2)** of the CPR requires the evidence in support of the application to show, if practicable by reference to any statement of case prepared in relation to the anticipated proceedings, that the property: **41.6**

(a) is or may become the subject matter of such proceedings; or
(b) is relevant to the issues that will arise in relation to such proceedings.

A copy of the application and a copy of the evidence in support must be served on the person against whom the order is sought (**r. 25.5(3)**). If the order is made, the court will probably decide against giving directions requiring a claim to be commenced, as the decision to commence will usually turn on the nature of the evidence gathered from the inspection (see **r. 25.2(3)** and **(4)**).

INSPECTION AGAINST NON-PARTIES

41.7 There is jurisdiction to make orders in pending proceedings for the inspection, detention and preservation of relevant property against persons who are not parties to the substantive claim, under the **Supreme Court Act 1981, s. 34(3)**, and the **County Courts Act 1984, s. 53(3)**. The **Supreme Court Act 1981, s. 34(3)**, provides:

> On the application, in accordance with rules of court, of a party to any proceedings, the High Court shall, in such circumstances as may be specified in the rules, have power to make an order providing for any one or more of the following matters, that is to say—
> (a) the inspection, photographing, preservation, custody and detention of property which is not the property of, or in the possession of, any party to the proceedings but which is the subject matter of the proceedings or as to which any question arises in the proceedings;
> (b) the taking of samples of any such property as is mentioned in paragraph (a) and the carrying out of any experiment on or with any such property.

The **County Courts Act 1984, s. 53(3)**, is in essentially the same terms, but refers to the power being vested in the county court. Before amendment by the Civil Procedure (Modification of Enactments) Order 1998 (SI 1998/2940), the provisions applied only to personal injuries claims, but now they cover all types of proceedings.

There are two conditions:

(a) substantive proceedings must have been issued before the application is made; and
(b) the property must be the subject matter of the proceedings, or a question relating to the property must arise in the proceedings. The discussion of what constitutes 'property' in **41.3** also applies for the purposes of these sections.

If the conditions are satisfied, the court has a discretion whether to make the order, which will be exercised in accordance with the overriding objective.

Procedure on application for inspection against a non-party

41.8 An order for inspection of property against a non-party is sought by issuing an application notice in **form N244** supported by evidence during the course of the proceedings. The fact that such an application is contemplated should be mentioned in further information filed with the allocation questionnaire. If possible the application should be made returnable at any case management hearing that may already have been listed. The evidence in support of an application for inspection against a non-party must, by **CPR, r. 25.5(2)**, show, if practicable by reference to any statement of case prepared in relation to the proceedings, that the property in question is the subject matter of the proceedings, or is relevant to the issues that will arise in relation to the proceedings.

A copy of the application notice and a copy of the evidence in support must be served on the person against whom the order is sought and every party to the proceedings other than the applicant (**r. 25.5(3)**).

ORDERS FOR SALE AND IN RELATION TO INCOME

41.9 Power is conferred on the civil courts by **CPR, r. 25.1(1)(c)(v) and (vi)**, to make orders:

(a) for the sale of relevant property which is of a perishable nature, or which for any other good reason should be sold quickly; and
(b) for the payment of income from relevant property until the claim is decided.

'Relevant property' means property which is the subject of a claim, or as to which any question may arise in a claim (**r. 25.1(2)**). In *On Demand Information plc v Michael Gerson (Finance) plc* [2002] UKHL 13, [2003] 1 AC 368, an interim order for sale of the subject matter of the proceedings was made under the equivalent provisions of the old rules (RSC, ord. 29,

r. 4). The claimants had leased video and editing equipment from the defendants on three-year lease agreements which provided that after expiry of the three-year term the claimants could sell the equipment and retain 95 per cent of the price. The claimants went into receivership, which under the terms of the leases allowed the defendants to terminate the leases. The receiver wished to sell the claimants' business as a going concern, together with the leased equipment, and brought a claim seeking relief from forfeiture (so as to preserve the claimants' right to retain 95 per cent of the proceeds of sale). An interim order was made under what would now be **CPR, r. 25.1(1)(c)(v)**, allowing the equipment to be sold on the ground that there was good reason for it to be sold quickly. At trial it was held that because the equipment had been sold under the interim order, the court no longer had jurisdiction to grant relief from forfeiture, such relief only being available if the relevant asset remained unsold. In the House of Lords it was said that the whole purpose of this type of interim order is to preserve the value of the parties' rights. Once the equipment was sold the proceeds of sale stood in the place of the equipment for the purposes of the litigation, and although relief from forfeiture was no longer possible (because of the sale), the court could still give effect to the respective rights of the parties by formulating an order deciding the proportions in which the parties were entitled to the proceeds of sale.

A party seeking an order under **r. 25.1(1)(c)(v)** or **(vi)** should issue an application notice in form **N244** supported by written evidence. The application should, if possible, be listed with any subsisting pending case management hearing.

Chapter 42 Case Management

INTRODUCTION

42.1 Judicial case management of civil litigation is one of the central planks of the CPR. The *Final Report* stressed the idea that ultimate responsibility for the control of litigation should move from the litigants and their advisers to the court. Under the CPR, the legal profession is intended to perform its traditional adversarial role in a managed environment governed by the courts. One of the purposes behind the CPR is to require the parties to focus their efforts on the key issues rather than allowing every issue to be pursued regardless of expense and time. Case management is seen as the principal means by which the judiciary will ensure this happens.

In exercising their powers to manage cases, the courts seek to secure the overriding objective of ensuring that cases are dealt with justly. **Rule 1.1(2)** provides that dealing with cases justly includes ensuring they are dealt with expeditiously and fairly, allotting to them an appropriate share of the court's resources, and ensuring they are dealt with proportionately bearing in mind factors such as the importance and complexities of the issues and the monetary value of the claim.

Rule 1.3, which is discussed at **1.37** and **1.38**, requires the parties to assist the court in furthering the overriding objective. This means that the parties must ensure the court has the information required if effective directions are to be made, and must inform the court of events which may affect directions previously made which cannot be dealt with by the consent of the parties. Examples are case management hearings, permission to call experts, pre-trial checklist dates and the trial date or window. Failure to do so may result in sanctions being imposed, including costs sanctions for any resulting applications and even striking out under r. 3.4(2)(c).

The *Final Report*, ch. 1, para. 4, envisaged there would be active case management by the courts, with procedural judges identifying the issues in the case, summarily disposing of some issues and deciding the order in which other issues are to be resolved, fixing timetables for the procedural steps in preparing cases for trial, and limiting evidence, particularly documentary and expert evidence. These ideas are put into effect by **r. 1.4(1)**, which provides that the court must further the overriding objective by actively managing cases. The rule goes on to list 12 methods that may be adopted to achieve this, a number of which adopt the ideas listed at the beginning of this paragraph. It is accordingly intended that procedural judges should be willing to intervene during the early stages of proceedings to ensure that the issues are narrowed, that cases are prepared economically and speedily, and disposed of fairly and without undue delay or expense.

To ensure that case management is proportionate the *Final Report* envisaged there would be active judicial intervention only in cases which would require and repay it. Basic management, with a fixed timetable and standard procedure, is used wherever possible, on the multi-track as well as on the fast track. Standard directions are laid down for the small claims track (**PD 27, app.** A), fast track (**PD 28, app.**) and multi-track (PF 52, see **appendix** 5). Keeping case management proportionate can, however, prove quite difficult, particularly on the multi-track, or where the parties fail to identify the issues or fail to consider properly the expert evidence required to prove the case. Directions may be given without hearings and by consent (see **32.21** and **32.30**). The CPR give the courts powers to hold four types of procedural hearing (allocation hearings, case management conferences, pre-trial reviews and hearings under **rr. 28.5(4)** and **29.6(4)**), which, unless kept under control, could result in substantial increases in the use of court resources and expense to the parties. The overall result is that the majority of defended cases proceed between the filing of a defence and trial with directions in a more or less standard form, but tailored to the needs of the particular case.

PROCEDURAL JUDGES

Case management decisions are generally dealt with by masters for cases proceeding in the Royal Courts of Justice, and by district judges in High Court district registry and county court cases. The governing rule (**CPR, r. 2.4**) in fact gives the courts a great deal of flexibility, allowing performance by any judicial officer, whether a district judge, master or judge, subject to any specific contrary provision in any enactment, rule or practice direction. However, **PD 29, para. 3.10**, says (in relation to multi-track cases) that masters will in general perform case management functions in the Royal Courts of Justice, district judges in district registry matters, and either district judges or circuit judges in county court cases. Much the same is said, in effect, by **PD 2B, para. 1.1. PD 2B** enables masters and district judges to deal with all types of application, but with express exceptions set out in the practice direction. Exceptions include most interim injunction applications, and applications affecting the liberty of the subject, which must be dealt with by a High Court or circuit judge. Detailed lists of exceptions can be seen in **para. 3.1** (Queen's Bench Division), **para. 5.1** (Chancery Division) and **paras 8** and **9** (county courts). A county court district judge can deal with interim injunctions (see **para. 8.1**) before allocation where the claim has a monetary limit not exceeding the fast track limit, also in cases where district judges have trial jurisdiction as listed in **para. 11.1**, and under the legislation on protection from harassment and anti-social behaviour (see **chapter 92**). **42.2**

Cases in the Chancery and Queen's Bench Divisions are assigned to individual masters (**PD 2B, para. 6.1**), although from time to time hearings may be dealt with by other masters or deputies as the circumstances may require, and cases may be transferred from one master to another.

References to circuit judges include recorders and references to masters and district judges include deputies (**PD 2B, para. 1.1**).

TRANSFER TO APPROPRIATE COURT

42.3 Subject to the rules relating to commencing proceedings in the High Court, a claimant has a free choice of which court to use when commencing proceedings (see **11.4**). The first case management intervention may be to transfer the case to the most appropriate court. General powers to order transfers can be found in the **County Courts Act 1984, ss. 40** to **42**. One restriction is that transfers to and from specialist lists can only be made by judges dealing with claims in the specialist list (**CPR, r. 30.5(2)** as substituted on 6 April 2006). Allocation of cases to Divisions and specialist courts is discussed in **chapter 11**.

Defended claims for specified sums of money against individuals are automatically transferred to the defendant's home court on receipt by the court of a defence (**CPR, r. 26.2**). In county court claims the defendant's home court is the county court for the district in which the defendant resides or carries on business. For High Court claims, the home court is the district registry for the district where the defendant resides or carries on business or, where there is no such registry (such as where the defendant is outside the jurisdiction), the Royal Courts of Justice (**r. 2.3(1)**).

Transfers in other cases are governed by **Part 30**, with criteria for deciding whether to transfer being set out in the **High Court and County Courts Jurisdiction Order 1991** (SI 1991/724). These criteria include the financial value of the claim, and whether it would be more convenient to try the case in another court. The convenience of the defendant is always a strong factor, because the defendant has not chosen to be sued (*Pepin v Taylor* [2002] EWCA Civ 1522, LTL 10/10/2002). Simply inserting a high value on the claim form does not ensure the claim will not be transferred to a county court (*Kohanzad v Derbyshire Police Authority* [2004] EWCA Civ 1387, LTL 8/10/2004, where the amount was £5 million). For transfers to the Royal Courts of Justice where the Crown is a party, see the Attorney-General's note annexed to **PD 66**.

Transfer to civil trial centre

42.4 Cases commenced in courts that are not civil trial centres (such courts are described as 'feeder courts') are considered by a procedural judge when defences are filed. If it appears that the case is suitable for allocation to the multi-track, the district judge will normally make an order allocating the case to the multi-track, will give case management directions, and transfer the claim to a civil trial centre (**PD 26, para. 10.2(5)**). A case may be allocated to the multi-track and be retained in a feeder court, if it is envisaged that there may need to be more than one case management conference and the parties or their legal advisers are located inconveniently far from the designated civil trial centre (**PD 26, para. 10.2(10)**) or where pressure of work in the trial centre has led to the designated civil judge approving retention of the case by the feeder court. If it is not possible to decide whether a case should be allocated to the fast or multi-track, the procedural judge will either hold an allocation hearing at the feeder court, or transfer the case to a civil trial centre for the allocation decision to be made there (**paras 10.2(6) and (8)**). Once a case is transferred, a judge will consider the file when it is received at the civil trial centre and give any further directions that appear necessary or desirable (**para. 10.2(9)**).

ALLOCATION

42.5 Every defended claim must be allocated to one of the three tracks (small claims track, fast track, multi-track) by a procedural judge's order. To assist the court the parties are usually required to file allocation questionnaires in **form N149** or **N150** shortly after defences are filed (see 42.7), to provide the court with additional information about the progress that has been made to date in seeking a resolution with the other parties and in preparing the evidence for trial, and with information relevant to the likely length of the trial and about costs.

PD 26 contains a note reminding practitioners that **PD 43–48, para.** 6.4(1) requires parties in claims outside the financial scope of the small claims track to file and serve estimates of their base costs, following **precedent** H in the schedule to **PD 43–48**, at the same time as they file their allocation questionnaires. See **63.19**.

TIME WHEN TRACK ALLOCATION IS DECIDED

The usual position is that the procedural judge will decide which track to allocate a case to when every defendant has filed an allocation questionnaire, or when the period for filing allocation questionnaires has expired, whichever is the sooner (**CPR, r. 26.5(1)**). Although the rule only mentions questionnaires filed by defendants, it is to be expected that the court will wait for the claimant's questionnaire if the specified period has not expired. There are some additional provisions dealing with track allocation in special cases, as follows: **42.6**

(a) In cases where there is a stay for settlement (see **42.24**), allocation is dealt with at the end of the period of the stay (**r. 26.5(2)**).
(b) In cases which are automatically transferred, allocation decisions are taken after the transfer takes place and are made by a procedural judge of the destination court.
(c) In cases which could be allocated either to the fast track or to the multi-track, allocation decisions are usually taken in the court where the proceedings are commenced, but occasionally they will be transferred to the appropriate civil trial centre for allocation and directions.
(d) Where a claimant enters a default judgment for an amount of money to be decided by the court or for the value of goods or the amount of interest to be decided by the court, the case will not be 'defended' in that a defence will not have been filed. These cases therefore are not governed by the standard track allocation provisions. Instead, when judgment is entered the court will give any necessary directions and will, if appropriate, allocate the case to one of the three tracks (**r. 12.7(2)(b)**). These cases are considered further at **42.26**.
(e) When judgment is entered for damages to be decided on an admission by the defendant in a claim for money that has not been specified, then, as in (d), the court will give any necessary directions and, if appropriate, allocate the case to one of the three tracks (**r. 14.8**). These cases are also considered at **42.26**.
(f) **Part 8** claims are treated as allocated to the multi-track (**r. 8.9(c)**). Nevertheless, the court can allocate a Part 8 claim to a different track when giving directions (see **rr. 8.1(3)** and **8.8(2)** and **PD 8B, para. B.14**).
(g) Most types of specialist proceedings are treated as allocated to the multi-track. This includes claims in the Commercial Court (**r. 58.13(1)**), mercantile claims (**r. 59.11(1)**), claims allocated to the Technology and Construction Court (**r. 60.6(1)**), Admiralty Court claims (**r. 61.1(3)**, applying **Part 58**), arbitration claims (r. 62.7(2)), claims retained at the Royal Courts of Justice in the Queen's Bench Division (**Queen's Bench Guide, para. 6.5.8**), claims retained in the Chancery Division (**Chancery Guide, para. 2.5**), claims in the Patents Court (**r. 63.7**), applications under the Companies Act 1985 (**PD 49B, para. 10**), directors disqualification proceedings (**PD Directors Disqualification Proceedings, para. 2.1**) and insolvency proceedings (Insolvency Rules 1986 (SI 1986/1925), r. 7.51(2)).

ALLOCATION QUESTIONNAIRES

When a defendant files a defence (or, in the case of multiple defendants, when they have all filed defences or the time limited for doing so has expired), the court will serve allocation questionnaires in **form N149** or N150 on each party (for fees payable, see **42.12**), or will make a direction dispensing with the need for questionnaires (**CPR, r. 26.3(1) and (2)**). **42.7**

Questionnaires may be dispensed with if there has already been an application, such as for summary judgment, which has been treated as an allocation hearing (**PD 26, para. 2.4**). The obligation of serving allocation questionnaires rests with the court where proceedings were commenced, even in claims that are automatically transferred to the defendant's home court. The allocation questionnaire form will state the date by which it must be filed, which should be at least 14 days after the date it is deemed to have been served on the party in question. The parties cannot, by agreement among themselves, vary the date for filing the allocation questionnaire (**CPR, r. 26.3(6A)**).

The questionnaire asks for details of whether the relevant pre-action protocol procedure was complied with. Unjustified failure to follow the protocol may result in sanctions being imposed (see **8.4**). It also asks whether a stay is sought for settlement (see **42.24**), about possible transfer to another court, for the party's view on the appropriate track for the case, for details about expert and factual witnesses, and for details of any contemplated application for summary judgment. It should provide information to enable the judge to gauge the value of the claim, to see how many expert witnesses are required, and how long the trial is likely to take. The form also requires costs estimates for the work done to date, and for the overall conduct of the claim. The questionnaire is obviously an important document, and care in completing it will assist the court in deciding whether to transfer the case to a more appropriate venue, on the appropriate track for the case, on the nature of any directions that may be appropriate, and whether a case management conference will be required if the case is allocated to the multi-track. If the estimated costs are felt to be disproportionate, the judge may consider making a costs capping order (see **66.50**), and inaccurate estimates may result in costs being disallowed (see **63.19**).

The parties are encouraged to consult one another and cooperate in completing their allocation questionnaires, and also in deciding on any additional information, which may include suggested directions (see **42.9**), they may send to the court with their questionnaires (**PD 26, para. 2.3**). They should not allow consultation to delay filing of questionnaires.

Cases where allocation questionnaires are not used

42.8 Allocation questionnaires are not, in general, used in specialist cases automatically allocated to the multi-track (the types of cases automatically allocated to the multi-track were mentioned at 42.6(g), and see, for example, **PD 49B, para. 10**, for applications under the Companies Act 1985, and **CPR, r. 60.6**, for claims in the Technology and Construction Court). Each specialist court has its own procedure dealing with case management at the allocation stage. In the Technology and Construction Court, for example, the court will send the parties a case management information sheet and a case management directions form (see **PD 60, para. 8.2** and app. A and B). In the Commercial Court, within 14 days after service of the defence, the claimant must apply for a case management conference (**PD 58, para. 10.2**). The legal representatives for each party must liaise for the purpose of preparing a short case memorandum and an agreed list of important issues (with a separate section dealing with matters which are common ground between all or some of the parties), and the claimant's solicitors must prepare a case management bundle (**PD 58, para. 10.8**). Seven days before the case management conference each party must file a completed case management information sheet, in the form set out in the **Admiralty and Commercial Courts Guide, app. 6**, and it is this form that takes the place of the allocation questionnaire (**PD 58, para. 10.7**). On the other hand, allocation questionnaires are used in Chancery Division cases despite the fact they are automatically allocated to the multi-track.

Voluntary extra information

42.9 Parties may file additional information with their allocation questionnaires if this will assist the court in making its decisions regarding track allocation and case management. However, such additional information should only be filed if all the parties have agreed the information is correct and that it should be put before the court, or if the party intending to file the information confirms that copies have been delivered to all the other parties (**PD 26, para. 2.2(2)**). Information and matters that might assist the court include:

(a) whether any of the parties intends to apply for summary judgment or to strike out or some other order that might dispose of the case or reduce the amount in dispute or the issues to be decided;
(b) whether any of the parties intends to make an additional claim or to apply to add another party;
(c) information about the steps taken and intended to be taken regarding preparing the evidence for trial; and
(d) suggested case management directions for the case.

Order for further information

The documents filed by the parties may not be sufficiently informative for the court to decide on the appropriate track for the case. In such cases, **r. 26.5(3)** of the CPR provides that the court may order a party to provide further information about its case. Usually any such order will stipulate a time and date expiring after 14 days for compliance (**PD 26, para. 4.2(2)**). Before allocating a claim to the small claims track and giving directions, the court may require a party to give further information about his case (**PD 27, para. 2.3**). The standard notice of allocation or listing hearing form (**N153**) incorporates a section for the court to set out the further information it requires from the parties. How the court may deal with cases where inadequate information is given is considered further at **45.5**. **42.10**

Failure to file an allocation questionnaire

If a party fails to file an allocation questionnaire, the court may give any direction it considers appropriate (**CPR, r. 26.5(5)**). The court's response may well depend on whether the other parties have filed their questionnaires, and the court may simply act on the information given by the other parties. If the court decides it does not have enough information, it will list the matter for an allocation hearing (**PD 26, para. 2.5(2)(b)**), although it may accede to a request for a telephone hearing (see **42.13**). The Court will almost certainly order the costs of the hearing to be paid by the party in default on the indemnity basis, usually with a summary assessment of those costs and an order for them to be paid forthwith or within a stated period (**PD 26, para. 6.6(2)**). If all the parties are in default, the court will make an unless order striking out the claim or defence unless the questionnaire is returned within the next seven days (**PD 26, para. 2.5(1)**). **42.11**

Allocation fees and non-payment

On filing an allocation questionnaire the claimant is required to pay a fee, which is £100 in the county courts and £200 in the High Court (**CPFO, sch 1, fee 2.1**). If the court dispenses with the need to file allocation questionnaires, the fee is payable within 14 days of the dispatch of the notice of allocation to a track. In cases which are automatically allocated to a track, the fee is payable within 28 days of the filing of the last defence. In claims proceeding only on a counterclaim the fee is payable by the defendant. No fee is payable in a **Part 8** claim, or a claim managed under a GLO or in proceedings in the county court in which the only claim is to recover a sum of money which does not exceed £1,500. Rules on exemptions and reductions of court fees can be found in **CPFO, art. 4**. **42.12**

Rule 3.7 of the CPR provides that claims will be struck out automatically if allocation or listing fees are not paid after due warning, which the court gives by sending the claimant a **form N173**. Automatic striking out after due warning also covers non-payment of the issue fee on filing a counterclaim, and dishonouring cheques used to pay fees (**rr. 3.7A** and **3.7B**). **PD 3B** says that if a claim is struck out, the court will send the defendant a notice which will explain the effect of **r. 25.11**, which provides that any interim injunction will cease having any effect after 14 days unless the claimant applies to reinstate the claim. This notice will prompt most defendants to apply for their costs against the defaulting claimant. Once the claim has been struck out the court retains a power to reinstate it (**r. 3.7**(7)), and on such an application the court will apply the criteria set out in **r. 3.9** relating to applications for relief from sanctions (see **chapter 46**). However, any order for reinstatement will be made conditional on either paying the fee or filing evidence of exemption from payment, or remission, of the fee (r. 3.7(7)). The time limit for payment or filing such evidence is two days from the date of the order if the claimant is present or represented, otherwise seven days from the date of service of the order (r. 3.7(8)).

ALLOCATION HEARING

42.13 The court may hold an allocation hearing if it thinks it is necessary (**CPR, r. 26.5(4)**). If the solicitors are not local, this is often organised as a telephone hearing. Alternatively, the court may treat any other interim hearing as an allocation hearing, the most likely candidates being applications for summary judgment and interim injunctions. At such a hearing the procedural judge will consider which track will be most suitable for the case, bearing in mind its financial value and the other factors set out at **42.19**, and give suitable case management directions. Consequently, the person attending for the parties should, if possible, be the person responsible for the case. In any event, the representative must be familiar with the case, be able to provide the court with the information it is likely to require, and have sufficient authority to deal with any issues that are likely to arise (**PD 26, para. 6.5**).

If an allocation hearing was listed because one of the parties was in default of the requirement to file an allocation questionnaire, and that party fails to attend the hearing, the court will usually make an order specifying the steps which that party is required to take, and providing that unless those steps are taken within stated periods of time that party's statement of case will be struck out (**PD 26, para. 6.6(3)**).

ALLOCATION RULES

42.14 The primary rules for track allocation are based on the financial value of the claim. This is the monetary value of the claim disregarding any amount not in dispute, any claim for interest or costs, and also disregarding any allegation of contributory negligence (**CPR, r. 26.8(2)**). It is for the court to assess the financial value of the claim, though it will take into account the way in which the claim is formulated in the particulars of claim and any information given in the allocation questionnaire. Any sum for which the defendant does not admit liability is in dispute, but the court will not regard the following as in dispute (**PD 26, para. 7.4**):

(a) sums for which summary judgment on a part of a claim has been entered;
(b) any distinct items in the claim for which the defendant has admitted liability; and
(c) any distinct items in the claim which have been agreed between the parties.

Generally claims are allocated in accordance with their financial value, but a claim may be allocated to a track which is not the one normally appropriate to its value if the procedural judge decides that it can be dealt with more justly on that other track, taking into account a number of factors set out in **CPR, r. 26.8** (see **42.19**). However, because of the costs consequences (see, for example, **r. 27.14(5)**), a claim will not be allocated to a lower track than its financial value indicates is appropriate, unless all the parties consent to the lower track allocation (**r. 26.7(3)**).

Small claims track

The small claims track is intended to provide a proportionate procedure for the most straightforward types of cases, such as consumer disputes, small accident claims, disputes about the ownership of goods, and landlord and tenant cases other than opposed claims under **Part 56**, disputed claims for possession under **Part 55**, and demotion claims (**PD26, para. 8.1(1)(c)**). This is the normal track for defended claims with a value not exceeding £5,000 (**CPR, r. 26.6(3)**). **42.15**

Although most claims under £5,000 will end up in the small claims track, the following types of claim will not normally be allocated there even if they have a value under £5,000:

(a) personal injuries cases where the value of the claim for pain, suffering and loss of amenity exceeds £1,000 (**r. 26.6(1)(a) and (2)**);
(b) claims by tenants of residential premises seeking orders that their landlords should carry out repairs or other works to the premises where the value of the claim exceeds £1,000 (**r. 26.6(1)(b)**);
(c) claims by residential tenants seeking damages against their landlords for harassment or unlawful eviction (**r. 26.7(4)**); and
(d) claims involving a disputed allegation of dishonesty (**PD 26, para. 8.1(1)(d)**).

Even if the claim is worth less than £5,000 there may be other reasons why it should not be allocated to the small claims track. One relates to expert evidence, which is not allowed in small claims track cases, either by calling an expert at the hearing or simply relying on an expert's report, unless the court gives permission (**CPR, r. 27.5**). Although permission may be granted, there are also severe restrictions on the costs recoverable for expert evidence in small claims track cases, including a limit of £200 for each expert's fees (**PD 27, para. 7.3(2)** and see also **CPR, r. 35.4(4)**), which may make it unjust for a small case which requires expert evidence to be allocated to the small claims track.

An explanatory note following **PD 26, para. 7.4**, is to the effect that if, in relation to a claim with a value above the small claims limit of £5,000, the defendant makes an admission before allocation reducing the amount in dispute below £5,000, the normal track for the claim will be the small claims track. Where such an admission is made, it may be in the interests of the claimant to apply for judgment on the admission under **CPR, Part 14**, in order to recover costs, although even in such an application recovery of costs will be discretionary (see **r. 44.5(3)**).

If the claim is worth more than £5,000, the parties may consent to it being allocated to the small claims track (**r. 26.7(3)**). However, the court retains control, and may refuse to allocate the case in accordance with the parties' wishes if it feels the case is not suitable for the small claims track (**PD 26, para. 8.1(2)(b)**). For example, it is unlikely to agree to a case being allocated to the small claims track if the hearing is likely to take more than a day (**PD 26, para. 8.1(2)(c)**). If the court agrees with the parties and allocates the case to the small claims track, the case is treated for the purposes of costs as a fast track case, except that trial costs are in the discretion of the court (except they cannot exceed the amount that would be allowed by **CPR, r. 46.2**, see **r. 27.14(5)**).

Fast track

The fast track is the normal track for cases broadly falling into the £5,000 to £15,000 bracket, and which can be disposed of by a trial which will not exceed a day. There are therefore two factors for deciding whether the fast track is the normal track for defended cases that are not allocated to the small claims track. The first factor, financial value (**CPR, r. 26.6(1) to (4)**), is to the effect that the following cases will normally be allocated to the fast track: **42.16**

(a) personal injuries cases with a financial value between £5,000 and £15,000;
(b) personal injuries cases with an overall value under £5,000, but where the damages for pain, suffering and loss of amenity are likely to exceed £1,000;
(c) claims by residential tenants for orders requiring their landlords to carry out repairs or

other work to the premises where the financial value of the claim is between £1,000 and £15,000;

(d) claims by residential tenants for damages against their landlords for harassment or unlawful eviction where the financial value of the claim does not exceed £15,000; and

(e) other categories of cases where the financial value of the claim is between £5,000 and £15,000.

The second factor, disposal at trial (**r. 26.6(5)**), is to the effect that cases falling within the normal limits for allocation to the fast track must also be likely to be disposed of by a trial lasting no more than a day, and with oral expert evidence limited to experts in no more than two expert fields and to one expert per party per field of expertise. The possibility that the trial might last longer than a day (which in this context means five hours) is not necessarily a conclusive reason for allocating a case to the multi-track (**PD 26, para. 9.1(3)(c)**), though in practice such cases are almost always so allocated, because on the fast track there will be no costs allowed beyond the first day. The assessment of likely trial length and the nature of the expert evidence necessary usually has to be made in the early stages of the proceedings, although it can arise again on a subsequent application to reallocate the case.

Multi-track

42.17 The multi-track is the normal track for claims not falling within the rules in **42.15** and **42.16** for allocation to either the small claims or fast tracks (**CPR, r. 26.6(6)**). Typically these will be cases involving claims exceeding £15,000, and cases worth less than that sum where the trial is likely to exceed a day.

Claims with no monetary value

42.18 Claims with no financial value will be allocated to the track which the procedural judge considers to be most suitable to enable it to be dealt with justly, taking into account the factors discussed at **42.19** (**CPR, r. 26.7(2)**). In these cases the importance of careful completion of the allocation questionnaire cannot be overemphasised.

Discretionary factors

42.19 In addition to the financial value of the claim (if it has one), when deciding which track to allocate it to the court is required to have regard to the following factors (**CPR, r. 26.8**):

(a) the nature of the remedy sought;

(b) the likely complexity of the facts, law or evidence;

(c) the number of parties or likely parties;

(d) the value of any counterclaim or other additional claim and the complexity of any matters relating to those claims (the court will not aggregate the sums claimed in the claim, counterclaim and so on, but will generally simply look at the value of the largest of the cross-claims: **PD 26, para. 7.7**);

(e) the amount of oral evidence which may be required;

(f) the importance of the claim to persons who are not parties to the proceedings;

(g) the views expressed by the parties, which will be regarded as important, though not binding on the court (**PD 26, para. 7.5**); and

(h) the circumstances of the parties.

These factors are not exclusive, and the court exercises its discretion taking into account all the circumstances including the nature of the case as disclosed by the statements of case and other relevant information provided by the parties. Complex claims are usually allocated to the multi-track, partly for case management reasons, and partly to ensure they are tried by a sufficiently senior judge. In practice, the following types of cases are allocated to the multi-track even if the amount at stake was within the normal financial value for allocation to the fast track:

(a) cases involving issues of public importance;

(b) test cases;
(c) medical negligence cases; and
(d) cases where there is a right to trial by jury, including deceit cases.

Other professional negligence cases and building cases that fall within the financial parameters of the fast track vary considerably in complexity, and should be allocated to the most suitable track depending on the complexity of each case.

TRIAL IN THE ROYAL COURTS OF JUSTICE

In principle only the most important cases should be managed and tried in the Royal Courts of Justice as opposed to another civil trial centre, because only the most important cases justify use of the resources of the Royal Courts of Justice. Thus, in general cases with an estimated value of less than £50,000 will be transferred out of the Royal Courts of Justice to a county court (**PD 29, para. 2.2**). Exceptions are listed in **11.4**. **42.20**

NOTICE OF ALLOCATION

After the court has decided on the track to which a case is allocated, it will send a notice of allocation to the parties, together with copies of all relevant allocation questionnaires and further information provided by the other parties (**CPR, r. 26.9**). Several forms of notice of allocation have been devised for different circumstances. There are four different forms for cases allocated to the small claims track (N157 to N160), one for the fast track (N154) and one for the multi-track (N155). Each has a space for allocation directions and for the judge's reasons for the allocation decision. **42.21**

ALLOCATION DIRECTIONS

The type of directions the court will make at the allocation stage depends on which track the case is allocated to, and the circumstances of the case. Typically the court will make standard directions in small claims track cases (see **chapter 43**). In fast track and multi-track cases it will consider making directions covering disclosure of documents, exchange of witness statements, disclosure of experts' reports and narrowing the expert evidence issues, and listing the claim for trial. There are standard directions for fast track claims in the appendix to **PD 28**. In multi-track cases the court will also consider whether to convene a case management conference or a pre-trial review. These matters are considered in more detail in **chapters 44** and **45**. **42.22**

When making directions the court will be astute to apply the overriding objective in all its aspects. It will seek to ensure that the case is prepared properly so that the claim can be determined justly, but it will also seek to avoid unnecessary expense. Where appropriate it will impose timetables, seek to narrow the issues, or use its power under **CPR, r. 32.1**, to control the evidence that is prepared. A trial date or window is often set as part of allocation directions. It gives the parties a target date for the trial, enables witnesses (especially expert witnesses) to be warned at an early stage, and emphasises the fact that the court has control over the timetable. Any party unable to keep to the timetable has to explain to the court why the case may not be ready for the set trial date or window, and should understand that the court may refuse to vacate the date set for the trial unless there are exceptional circumstances (**PD 28, para. 5.4(1); PD 29, para. 7.4(1)**). **Rule 32.1** of the CPR gives the court a wide-ranging power to give directions about the issues on which it requires evidence, the nature of the evidence which it requires to decide those issues, and the way in which the evidence is to be placed before the court. The power under the rule may be used to exclude evidence that would otherwise be admissible (**r. 32.1(2)**; *Grobbelaar v Sun Newspapers Ltd* (1999) *The Times*, 12 August 1999). However, it is primarily a case management power designed to enable the court to stop cases getting out of hand (*Post Office Counters Ltd v Mahida* [2003] EWCA Civ 1583, *The Times*, 31 October 2003). See also the more detailed discussion at **47.7**, and compare the power to extend time, discussed at **46.21** to **46.25**.

CHANGING TRACKS

42.23 After a claim has been allocated to a track the court may make a subsequent order reallocating it to a different track (**CPR, r. 26.10**). Where a claim was initially allocated to the small claims track, and is later reallocated to another track, the small claims costs restrictions cease to apply from the date of reallocation (**r. 27.15**).

A party who is dissatisfied with an allocation decision may challenge the decision either by appealing up to the next higher court or by making an application back to the judge who made the initial decision (**PD 26, para. 11.1(1)**). Applications should be used where the decision was made without any hearing of which the party was given due notice or if there has been a material change of circumstances. If the party was present, represented or given due notice of the hearing where the decision was made, the only appropriate route is by way of appeal (**PD 26, paras 11.1 and 11.2**).

If an additional claim is issued, it may be necessary to redetermine the most suitable track for the proceedings. Mere issue of an additional claim will not have this effect, but where a defence to an additional claim has been filed the proceedings will be reconsidered by the procedural judge to determine whether the claim should remain on its existing track (particularly in cases on the small claims and fast tracks) and whether there needs to be any adjustment to the timetable. At the same time the procedural judge will consider whether the additional claim should be dealt with separately from the main claim.

When an amendment increases or reduces the amount of a claim, the court may consider reallocating the case to a different case management track. It will only do so if there is a good reason (*Maguire v Molin* [2002] EWCA Civ 1083, [2002] 4 All ER 325). In addition to the factors in **CPR, r. 26.8** (see **42.19**), the amount by which the claim now exceeds the normal limit for the allocated track is a highly relevant consideration. If the new value is substantially above the normal limit, the case will normally need to be reallocated. Another important factor is whether the trial date will be lost as a result of reallocating the claim (perhaps because of the limited trial jurisdiction of district judges, see **PD 2B, para. 11.1**), particularly if the amendment is sought after the trial has started (*Maguire v Molin*, where permission to amend was refused).

STAY TO ALLOW FOR SETTLEMENT

42.24 One of the court's case management functions is to help the parties to settle the whole or part of the case (**CPR, r. 1.4(2)(f)**), and another is to encourage the parties to use alternative dispute resolution procedures if appropriate, and to facilitate the use of such procedures (**r. 1.4(2)(e)**). Although the court cannot force the parties to use mediation or any other form of ADR, it is part of its function to consider whether the parties should be encouraged to use ADR in an attempt to resolve the dispute. Particularly at case management hearings the judge may steer the parties towards using such a process. The strength of the encouragement, if any, given by the judge may affect the decision on costs when the claim is finally determined (see *Halsey v Milton Keynes General NHS Trust* [2004] EWCA Civ 576, [2004] 1 WLR 3002). ADR is discussed in **chapter 70**. It is with these objectives in mind that the CPR provide for the court to order a stay of proceedings to allow for settlement of the case.

The allocation questionnaire allows a party to include a request for the proceedings to be stayed while the parties try to settle the case. If all the parties make such a request, or if the court on its own initiative considers that such a stay would be appropriate, a direction will be made staying all or part of the proceedings for one month or for such specified period as it considers appropriate (**r. 26.4(2)**). Until it was amended with effect from 1 October 2005, **r. 26.4(2)** provided that stays for negotiation were (unless extended) always for a period of one month. The court has power to extend the stay for such specified period as it thinks appropriate (**r. 26.4(3)**), which it will generally exercise on receipt of a letter from either party confirming that the extension is sought with the agreement of all the parties and giving a reasonable explanation of the steps being taken and the identity of the mediator or expert assisting with the process (**PD 26, para. 3.1(1)**). Extensions will not usually exceed four weeks at a time unless there are clear reasons to justify a longer time. During the period of such a stay the claimant is under a duty to inform the court if a settlement is reached (**CPR, r. 26.4(4)**). If, by the end of the defined period of the stay, the claimant has not told the court that the case has been settled, the court will often seek a report on progress, and will give such directions for the management of the case as it considers appropriate, including allocating it to an appropriate track (**rr. 26.4(5)** and **26.5(2)**). The periods of stays under these rules are carefully restricted so as to prevent the procedure being used to secure protracted 'authorised' delays after proceedings are commenced, under the guise of attempting to settle.

A complex commercial dispute which could be solved by means going outside the remedies available in a court or in commercial arbitration was particularly suitable for being stayed for the purpose of mediation (*C v RHL* [2005] EWHC 873 (Comm), LTL 12/5/2005).

LIMITING THE ISSUES TO BE TRIED

The court has power under **CPR, r. 32.1**, to give directions limiting the issues on which it wishes to be addressed, and on the evidence that may be adduced at trial on those issues, despite the fact that doing so may result in the exclusion of material that would otherwise be admissible under the law of evidence, and may take this into account when allocating (**PD 26, para. 9.1(3)(b)**). This power should only be exercised in accordance with the overriding objective. This requires that cases must be dealt with justly and fairly, so limiting evidence should not be so intrusive that it prevents either or both parties from proving their cases at trial. Some guidance was given in *McPhilemy v Times Newspapers Ltd* [1999] 3 All ER 775, where Lord Woolf MR said that the courts' case management powers to restrain excess do not extend to preventing a party from putting forward allegations which are central to its case. That said, it is open to the court to attempt to control how those allegations are litigated with a view to limiting costs. This means that the procedural judge may cut out peripheral matters. In a libel claim this may mean that the judge can decide that a plea even of justification is either central or peripheral: it is essentially a matter within the discretion of the procedural judge (*Tancic v Times Newspapers Ltd* (1999) *The Times*, 12 January 2000). An alternative approach is to separate certain issues for determination as preliminary issues (*GKR Karate UK Ltd v Yorkshire Post Newspapers Ltd* (2000) *The Times*, 9 February 2000). **42.25**

CLINICAL CASE MANAGER

Clinical case managers are in some cases appointed to assist a severely injured person to deal with a dispute, typically involving litigation. The cost involved in having a clinical case manager is habitually included in any relevant damages claim. A clinical case manager must act in the best interests of his or her client, the injured person, and owes duties to that person, not to the court (*Wright v Sullivan* [2005] EWCA Civ 656, [2006] 1 WLR 172). This case held that **42.26** where a clinical case manager attends a conference with legal advisers at which advice is being sought, the client can assert legal professional privilege, which can only be waived by the client. Conversely, where a clinical case manager enters into communications with an expert where obtaining legal advice is not the dominant purpose (see =*Waugh v British Railways Board* [1980] AC 521), the occasion is not privileged, and the communications must be disclosed on standard disclosure.

TIME APPLICATIONS, IRREGULARITY, THE SLIP RULE ETC.

42.27 The courts possess a range of powers to assist with the just disposal of civil claims, and to deal with cases of procedural default. These powers are:

(a) Time applications for extending time for complying with provisions in orders, directions, rules and practice directions under **CPR, r. 3.1(2)(a)**, see **15.13**, **46.21** to **46.26**.
(b) Time applications to abridge time for taking steps in litigation under **r. 3.1(2)(a)**, see **46.21**.
(c) Applications to extend the period of validity of a claim form under **r. 7.6**, see **15.7** to **15.12**.
(d) Miscellaneous case management powers are set out in **rr. 3.1(2)** and **25.1(1)**, see **32.29**.
(e) Applications to cure procedural irregularities under **r. 3.10**, see **15.11**; **46.27**.
(f) The slip rule enabling the correction of slips and errors in orders and judgments under **r. 40.12(1)**, see **37.53**, **61.35**.
(g) Relief from sanctions under **r. 3.9**, see **46.31** to **46.35**.
(h) The form of orders and judgments, see **61.7** to **61.14**.
(i) The requirement that orders and directions imposing time limits must include the time and date by which the step must be taken (**r. 2.9(1)**), see **61.8**.

ASSESSMENT OF DAMAGES CASES

42.28 Cases where judgment is entered for damages to be decided by the court do not fall into the usual pattern of 'defended' cases. In such a case the court will make what is called a 'relevant order', which is defined by **PD 26, para. 12.1(1)**, as meaning any order or judgment which requires the amount of money that has to be paid to be decided by the court. This includes orders that require:

(a) the assessment of damages;
(b) the assessment of interest;
(c) the taking of an account;
(d) the making of an inquiry as to any sum due, but does not include an order for the assessment of costs.

According to **PD 26, para. 12.1(2)**, relevant orders may be made on entry of judgment in default, on entry of judgment on an admission, on the striking out of a statement of case, on a summary judgment application, on the determination of a preliminary issue or on a split trial as to liability, or even by consent or at trial.

When making a relevant order, the court will give directions, which may (**PD 26, para. 12.2(1)**):

(a) list the claim for a disposal hearing (see **42.27**);
(b) allocate or reallocate the claim to a track;
(c) direct the parties to file allocation questionnaires by a specified date;
(d) stay the claim while the parties try to settle by ADR or other means.

Stays for settlement are dealt with as described at **42.24**

The directions given when making a relevant order in a claim which is not stayed for ADR depend, principally, on whether the financial value of the claim is such that the claim would, if defended, be allocated to the small claims track (**PD 26, para. 12.3**). Normally, if a relevant order is made in a claim which would otherwise be a small claim but has not previously been allocated to a track, the court will allocate it to the small claims track and list it for a disposal hearing at which the amount payable will be decided. If the claim is not a small claim and the amount payable appears to be genuinely disputed on substantial grounds, or if the dispute is not suitable to be dealt with at a disposal hearing, the court will allocate the claim to an appropriate track for further hearing (see **42.30**). As a result, most personal injuries claims above the fast-track threshold, where there are arguments about causation or quantum, are allocated to a track rather than being dealt with at a disposal hearing.

Disposal hearings

A disposal hearing of a relevant order is a hearing which will not normally last longer than 30 minutes, but at which the court will decide and give judgment for the amount payable under the relevant order, or will give directions for the future conduct of the proceedings (**PD 26, para. 12.4**(1) and (2)). If a claim in which a relevant order has been made is a small claim, the amount payable under the order will normally be decided at a disposal hearing and the court may treat the disposal hearing as a final hearing for the purposes of **CPR, Part** 27 (**PD 26, para. 12.4**(3)). **42.29**

The court will not normally hear oral evidence at a disposal hearing (**PD 26, para. 12.4**(1)(b)). Evidence may, unless the court otherwise directs, be adduced under **CPR, r. 32.6** (see **PD 26, para. 12.4**(4)). This means that reliance may be placed on the matters set out in the particulars of claim (provided it is verified by a statement of truth) or by witness statement. The evidence relied upon must be served on the defendant at least three clear days before the disposal hearing.

Where the hearing is likely to exceed 30 minutes, or where the evidence is disputed, the court may allocate the case to a track and give assessment directions.

Assessment directions

If a relevant order is made by consent, the parties should file agreed directions with the draft consent order which they should invite the court to give (**PD 26, para. 12.2**(3)). For other relevant orders, other than those dealt with by stays for settlement or by way of a disposal hearing, the court will give directions, which may include allocating or reallocating the case to a case management track, directing that pre-trial checklists be filed within a stated period of time, and directing that the case be listed for a hearing or a further hearing (**para. 12.2**(1)). Allocating a case to the fast track or multi-track on making a relevant order should only happen if the amount payable is genuinely disputed on grounds that appear to be substantial, or if the dispute is not suitable to be dealt with at a disposal hearing (**para. 12.3**). If a claim has not been allocated to a track, and at the disposal hearing it becomes clear that its value is less than £5,000, in the ordinary case the small claims track costs regime should apply (*Voice and Script International v Alghafar* [2003] EWCA Civ 736, LTL 8/5/2003). **42.30**

Hearing to assess damages

A master or district judge may decide the amount payable under a relevant order, irrespective of the financial value of the claim and of the track to which it has been allocated (**PD 26, para. 12.6**). But, when making a relevant order, the court may give directions specifying the level or type of judge who is to deal with the case (**para. 12.2**(2)). The designated circuit judge will from time to time set local guidelines for this purpose based on the value of the claim and the nature of any equitable relief sought. Hearings involving substantial damages or complex issues should usually be directed before a circuit judge or judge (*Sandry v Jones* (2000) *The Times*, 3 August 2000). **42.31**

On an assessment of damages the defendant can raise any point which goes to quantification of the damage, provided that it is not inconsistent with any issue settled by the judgment (*Lunnun v Singh* [1999] CPLR 587). Where judgment for damages to be assessed was entered after the court rejected a defence that the claimant was guilty of gross misconduct disentitling him to any damages, it was still open for the defence to raise mitigation of damages on the assessment (*Pugh v Cantor Fitzgerald International* [2001] CPLR 271).

SUBSEQUENT CASE MANAGEMENT

42.32 The following three chapters deal in more detail with the further progress of cases on each of the three case management tracks following allocation. **Figure 42.1** shows the routes which cases may take from either a defence being filed or a 'relevant order' being made, up to the decision to allocate the case to a case management track. **Figure 42.2** shows in broad terms what happens to cases on the three case management tracks from the time they are allocated to a track until trial.

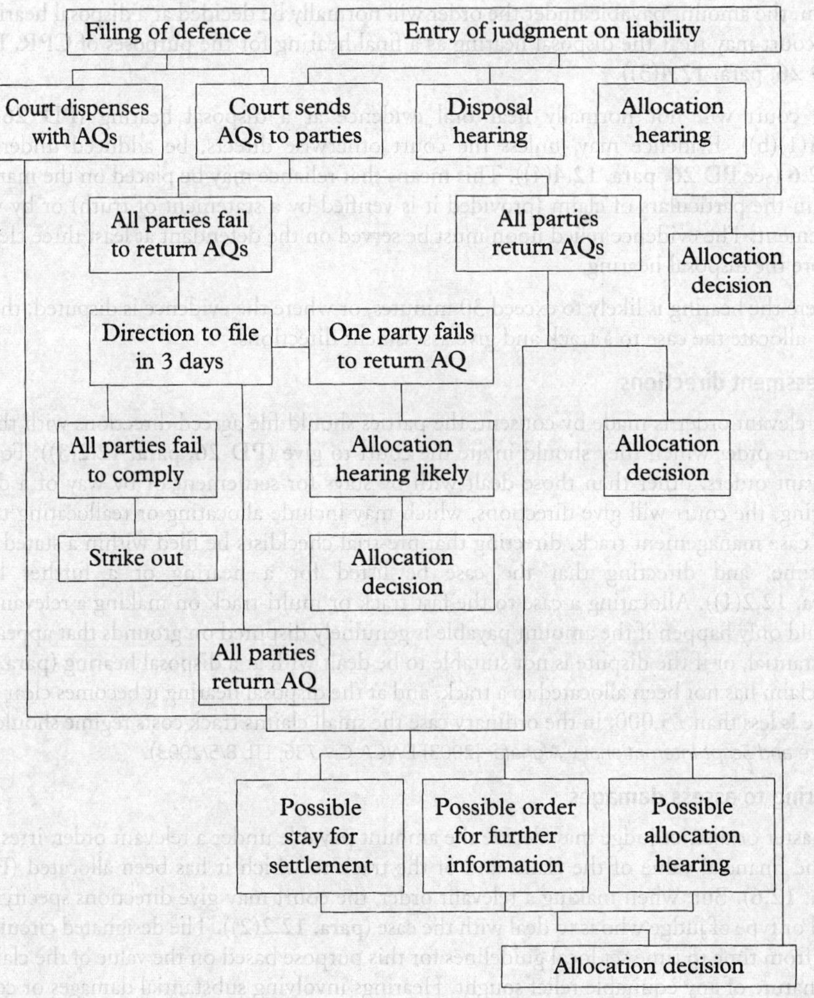

Figure 42.1 Routes to making track allocation decision
AQ = Allocation questionnaire

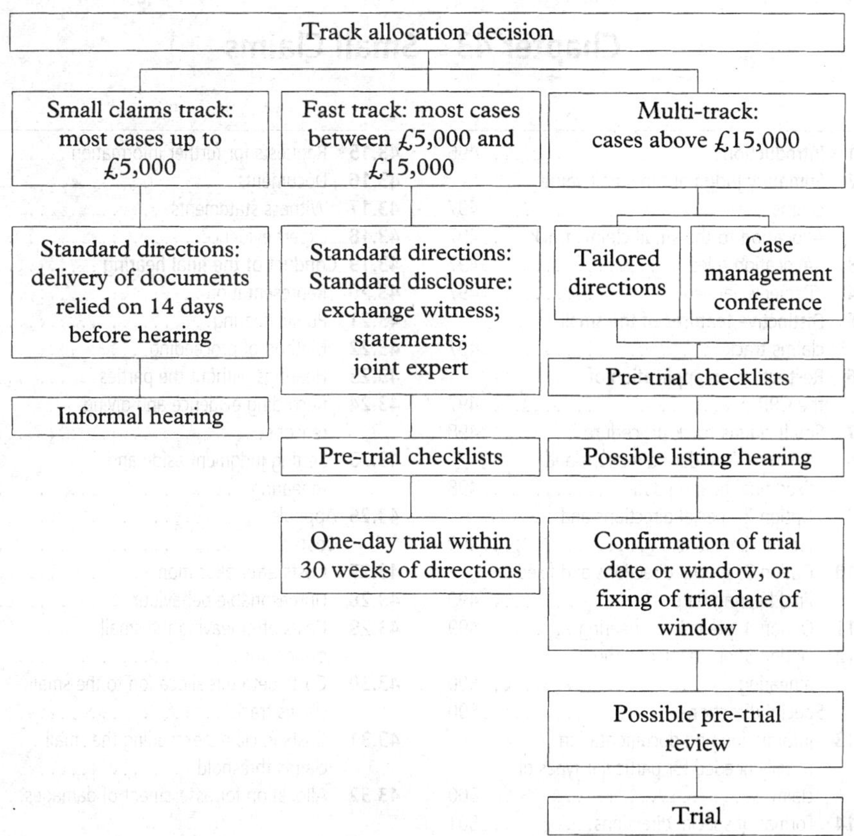

Figure 42.2 The case management tracks

Chapter 43 Small Claims

INTRODUCTION

43.1 The small claims track is the normal track for claims up to £5,000 in value (see 42.15). Despite the adjective 'small', the track is of immense significance to the civil justice system. Every year over 55,000 judicial determinations are made of cases in the small claims track representing over 75 per cent of all cases disposed of by way of final hearing.

The term 'small claim' is unfortunate given that the upper limit of the financial jurisdiction represents a sum which many would consider a large claim. Cases within the small claims track can range from very modest consumer disputes or arguments over dry-cleaning through to technically complex disputes over credit hire and factually complicated disagreements over building extensions. Many small claims relate to road traffic accidents.

The small claims track provides an entirely different type of dispute determination from that offered by the other two tracks. The basic 'no costs' rule positively encourages parties to represent themselves. Pre-hearing preparation is less formal than on the other case management tracks. Standard disclosure does not apply. Witness statements are exchanged on the small claims track only where the nature of the case makes this desirable. There are severe restrictions on the use of expert evidence. At the hearing the district judge may well adopt an interventionist approach designed to elicit the relevant information as quickly and as informally as possible.

For professional legal advisers the challenges are considerable. It is necessary to form a view of the merits of a case very quickly and often on the basis of a paucity of evidence. The client may not wish to incur the cost of legal representation at the hearing; in that case the role of the professional adviser is to advise on the merits of the case, to ensure that the client discloses copies of all the documents on which he intends to rely and to ensure that, if appropriate, the client's case is adequately set out in a witness statement. If necessary, the legal adviser may also assist in the preparation of an expert's report.

SUMMARY JUDGMENT IN SMALL VALUE CLAIMS

It is open to a claimant or defendant to apply for summary judgment (see **chapter** 34). This should normally be done before track allocation (**PD 26, para.** 5.3(1)). If summary judgment is given before allocation in a claim which is otherwise suitable for the small claims track, the successful party can apply for costs in the ordinary way and is not subject to the rule providing for only modest fixed costs on the small claims track (see 43.27). **43.2**

ALLOCATION TO THE SMALL CLAIMS TRACK

Allocation rules

The rules governing allocation to the small claims track are considered in **chapter** 42, especially at 42.14 and 42.15. **43.3**

Remedy claimed

There is no restriction on the nature of remedies which can be granted on the small claims track (**CPR, r.** 27.3). Thus injunctions, possession, restitution, specific performance and the like are available to the same extent as on the other tracks, though jurisdiction to grant freezing injunctions and search orders is restricted to the High Court (County Court Remedies Regulations 1991 (SI 1991/1222), regs 2 and 3). **43.4**

DISTINCTIVE FEATURES OF THE SMALL CLAIMS TRACK

The important differences between small claims and the other tracks are: **43.5**

(a) Some rules and procedures have no application on the small claims track (see 43.6).
(b) The procedures after allocation are different (see 43.7 to 43.12).
(c) Pre-trial checklists are not used on the small claims track.
(d) The procedure at the hearing is different (see 43.13 to 43.25).
(e) The procedure on appeals (see 43.26).
(f) Costs provisions are different (see 43.27 to 43.31).

RESTRICTION ON APPLICATION OF THE CPR

Rule 27.2 of the CPR provides that on the small claims track the following parts of the CPR do not apply: **43.6**

(a) **Part** 25 (interim remedies) except as it relates to interim injunctions;
(b) **Part** 31 (disclosure and inspection);
(c) **Part** 32 (evidence) except **r.** 32.1, which gives the court a general power to control evidence;
(d) **Part** 33 (miscellaneous rules about evidence);
(e) **Part** 35 (experts and assessors) except **r.** 35.1, which restricts the use of expert evidence, **r.** 35.3, which sets out the expert's overriding duty to the court and **rr.** 35.7 and 35.8 (use of a single joint expert);
(f) **Part** 18 (further information), but see 43.15;

(g) **Part 36** (offers to settle and payments into court), but see **43.28**; and
(h) **Part 39** (hearings) except **r. 39.2**, which is the general rule that hearings are to be in public.

In principle the other parts of the CPR apply to small claims except to the extent that any rule limits such application.

SMALL CLAIMS TRACK PROCEDURE

43.7 Figure 43.1 is a flowchart of the small claims track procedure.

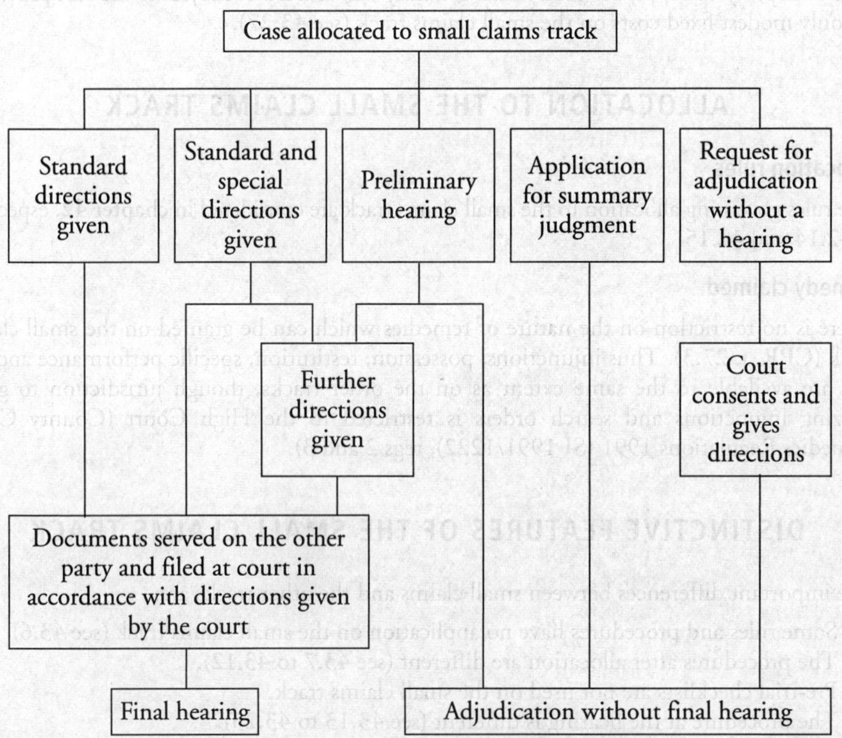

Figure 43.1 Small claims track procedure

Under **CPR, r. 27.4** once a case has been allocated to the small claims track the court has five options (described below) on how the case will be dealt with through to final disposal. Most small claims are given standard directions and a fixed hearing date (option 1). A party may ask the court to give particular directions (**PD 27, para. 2.4**), and should normally do so when returning the allocation questionnaire. The court is given a general power under **CPR, r. 27.7**, to add to, vary or revoke directions.

Option 1: standard directions and fixed final hearing date

43.8 The court may give standard directions and fix a date for the final hearing (**CPR, r. 27.4(1)(a)**).

By **r. 27.4(3)(a)**, read together with **PD 27, para. 2.2**, and **app. B**, 'standard directions' means directions:

(a) that each party shall, at least 14 days before the date fixed for the final hearing, file and serve on every other party copies of all documents (including the letter of claim, any reply, and any expert's report) on which he intends to rely at the hearing;

(b) that the original documents must be brought to the hearing;

(c) fixing the hearing date and time allowed;

(d) encouraging the parties to contact each other with a view to trying to settle the claim or narrow the issues, and requiring the parties to notify the court immediately if the claim is settled; and

(e) informing the parties that they cannot rely on expert evidence at the hearing without a direction giving express permission to do so.

The relevant set of standard directions will be sent out by the court in the form of an order along with notification of the hearing date.

District judges' experience will usually enable them to give a reasonable estimate of the length of hearing for routine cases. Most courts adopt a 'back-to-back' system for listing small claims cases so that, for example, two or more district judges are jointly listed to hear many hours' worth of cases whose litigants are all instructed to attend court at 10.00 a.m. or 2.00 p.m. Experience shows that it is usually safe for the court to list twice or even three times the number of cases that could in fact be properly dealt with if all parties attended. Most small claim hearings take less than an hour; very few take more than one day.

Option 2: special directions and further directions

Instead of using the standard directions in **PD 27, appendix B**, the court can give 'special directions' and consider what further directions are to be given no later than 28 days after giving special directions (**CPR, r. 27.4(1)(c)**). The power is seldom used. More usually a district judge will either vary the standard directions, give special directions and fix a final hearing or alternatively fix a preliminary hearing. **43.9**

Option 3: special directions and fixed final hearing date

The court may give special directions and fix a date for the final hearing (**CPR, r. 27.4(1)(b)**). **43.10** This will be appropriate where the district judge can formulate special directions for the case without needing to hold a preliminary hearing. 'Special directions' are often based on the standard directions, although they can be completely tailor-made (**r. 27.4(3)(b)**). In formulating special directions, district judges use their experience, the information and requests for directions in the allocation questionnaires, and the guidance in **PD 27, app. A** (see **43.13**) on the information and documentation usually required for certain types of claim.

Option 4: preliminary hearing

The court may fix a date for a preliminary hearing (**CPR, r. 27.4(1)(d)**). **43.11**

Consistent with the policy that the parties should attend court only when it is essential for them to do so, **r. 27.6** provides that the court may hold a preliminary hearing for the consideration of a small claim only in one of three situations:

(a) Where the court considers that special directions under **r. 27.4** are needed to ensure a fair hearing, and it appears necessary for a party to attend court to ensure that the party understands what must be done to comply with the special directions. This will be where the court considers (possibly from the content of the documents received) that it may be necessary to have the parties before the court to ensure that they understand what they must do in order that the case may be properly and efficiently progressed. Alternatively, it may be that special directions need to be considered, and that it would be inappropriate for the district judge to make them without hearing the parties.

(b) To enable the court to dispose of the claim on the basis that one of the parties has no real prospect of success. This may be obvious from the documents, for example, where the claim is based on a cause of action not known to English law. In less clear-cut cases, particularly where the only witnesses are the parties themselves, the better course would often be to have the case listed for a short final hearing. That would permit the party with no apparent prospect of success an opportunity to present his evidence before the judicial decision is reached.

(c) To enable the court to strike out the whole or part of a statement of case where it discloses no reasonable grounds for bringing or defending the claim. This provision follows on from the one before. Alternatively, if the failure to disclose a cause of action or defence is due to sloppy drafting, an opportunity should be given to amend.

By **r. 27.6(4)**, the court may treat a preliminary hearing as the final hearing of the claim if all parties agree. It is unlikely that this will commonly apply unless the point is a very short one, as it would otherwise mean that the preliminary appointment could take the same time as the substantive hearing.

After the preliminary hearing, the court will fix the date of the final hearing and inform the parties of the amount of time allowed, together with any other appropriate directions (**r. 27.6(5)**).

Option 5: proceeding without a hearing

43.12 The court may, if all parties agree, deal with a small claim without a hearing (**CPR, r. 27.10**). **Rule 27.10** is infrequently used. It appears to give the court a discretion to refuse to deal with a claim on paper even if that is what the parties want. Dealing with a small claim without a hearing might be appropriate where, for example, one party is living outside the jurisdiction and is either unable or unwilling to return for an oral hearing. In such a case the district judge would direct that copies of the relevant documents and witness statements be lodged; he would then give a written judgment.

SPECIAL DIRECTIONS

Information and documentation usually needed for particular types of claim

43.13 Appendix A of PD 27 sets out the type of information and documentation normally required for four types of claim frequently met on the small claims track. In the following lists, entries in square brackets have been added by the editors of this work.

(a) Road traffic accident claims:
- witness statements, including from the parties themselves;
- invoices and estimates for repairs;
- agreements and invoices for any car hire costs;
- the police accident report;
- sketch plan, which should be agreed if possible;
- photographs of the scene of the accident and the damage.

(b) Building disputes, repairs, sale of goods, and similar contract claims:
- any written contract [or correspondence evidencing the contract, including any specification for the contract works];
- photographs;
- any plans;
- a list of the works complained of;
- [written complaints by the customer and any responses];
- a list of any outstanding works;
- any relevant estimate, invoice or receipt including any relating to repairs to each of the defects;
- invoices for work done or goods supplied;
- estimates for work to be completed;
- a valuation of work done to date.

(c) Landlord and tenant claims:
- a calculation of the amount of rent alleged to be owing, showing amounts received;
- details of breaches of an agreement which are said to justify withholding any deposit itemised showing how the total is made up and with invoices and estimates to support them;
- [the tenancy agreement, or correspondence evidencing the agreement];
- [contemporaneous documentation proving rent received];
- [documents showing complaints by the tenant];
- [documents showing work done on behalf of the landlord].

(d) Breach of duty cases (negligence, deficient professional services etc). Details of the following:
- what it is said by the claimant was done negligently by the defendant;
- why it is said that the negligence is the fault of the defendant;
- what damage is said to have been caused;
- what injury or losses have been suffered and how any (and each) sum claimed has been calculated;
- the response of the defendant to each of the above.

Format of special directions

To assist court users, **PD 27, app.** C, sets out model special directions dealing with: **43.14**

(a) further information to clarify a party's case;
(b) inspection of property;
(c) final hearing to take place at a location other than the court;
(d) requiring items to be brought to court;
(e) exchange of witness statements;
(f) warning that evidence will not be allowed if directions are not complied with;
(g) the form of an unless order;
(h) expert evidence;
(i) video evidence.

Requests for further information

The parties to a small claim are not permitted to make requests for further information under **CPR, Part 18**, see **r. 27.2(1)(f)**. With effect from 1 October 2005 this is subject to **r. 27.2(3)**, which says the court of its own initiative may order a party to provide further information if it considers it appropriate to do so. This is useful where the particulars of claim or defence are unclear and the court needs further information to clarify the case that the litigant intends to advance. **43.15**

Documents

Parties to cases on the small claims track are not subject to the standard disclosure obligations of disclosing documents which adversely affect their case or support another party's case (**CPR, rr. 27.2(1)(b)** and **31.6**). Standard small claims directions do, however, require parties to file and serve, at least 14 days before the hearing, copies of the documents on which they intend to rely at the hearing (**r. 27.4(3)(a)**). When this is read together with the lists of documentation usually required in the types of cases considered in **PD 27, app. A**, it is clear that there is a fairly extensive obligation on the parties in small claims cases to provide documentation in support of their side of the dispute. **43.16**

Witness statements

In deciding whether to make an order for the exchange of witness statements in a small claim, **PD 27, para. 2.5** (introduced on 1 October 2005), provides that the court must have regard to: **43.17**

(a) whether either or both parties are represented;
(b) the amount in dispute;
(c) the nature of the matters in dispute. **PD 27, app. A**, says that witness statements will usually be required in road traffic accident claims. They may also be needed in more complex small claims, such as building disputes and holiday claims;
(d) whether the need for any party to clarify his case could better be dealt with by ordering him to provide further information under **PD 27, para. 2.3**;
(e) the need for the parties to have access to justice without undue formality, cost or delay.

By **CPR, r. 27.2(1)(c)**, the provisions of **rr. 32.2** to **32.19** (which include the provisions concerning the form and use of witness statements) do not apply to cases on the small claims track. Subject to the precise terms of the relevant direction, it is therefore permissible to use informal witness statements when these are ordered in small claims track cases.

Expert evidence

43.18 Most small claims can be resolved without expert evidence. The court is obliged to restrict expert evidence to that which is reasonably required to resolve the proceedings (**CPR, r. 35.1**). Where experts are required, permission must be expressly granted (**r. 27.5**). Usually the court will direct the evidence to be given through a written report of a jointly instructed expert (**PD 27, app. C; PD 35, annex (Protocol for the Instruction of Experts), para. 17.2; CPR, rr. 35.7** and **35.8**, on the power to direct evidence to be given by a single joint expert, and on instructions to a single joint expert, apply to cases on the small claims track, see **r. 27.2(1)(e)**). The court will normally also give directions allowing the parties to put written questions to the expert. If the court allows each side to instruct an expert, any discussions between the experts should be by telephone or letter (**PD 35, annex (Protocol for the Instruction of Experts), para. 18.4**). The costs which may be recovered by a successful party are limited to £200 for each expert (**PD 27, para. 7.3(2)**). While an expert on this track still owes an overriding duty to the court (**CPR, r. 35.3**), his or her report need not comply with all the requirements of **Part 35** (most of which is disapplied by **r. 27.2(1)(e)**). An informal letter from the expert will often suffice.

CONDUCT OF THE FINAL HEARING

43.19 The final hearing of a small claim will normally be before a district judge. The hearing may be assigned to a circuit judge (**PD 27, para. 1**), with that judge's consent (**PD 2B, para. 11.2**), but this rarely happens, not least because any appeal would have to be taken to the High Court.

Hearings are informal, the strict rules of evidence do not apply, and expert evidence (whether written or oral) may be given only with the court's permission (**CPR, rr. 27.5** and **27.8**). The district judge may well adopt an interventionist approach. In a small claim hearing the court will not always insist on the production of expert evidence, whereas it might be required for a similar case on one of the other tracks (*Bandegani v Norwich Union Fire Insurance Society Ltd* (1999) LTL 20/5/99, in which the claimant did not produce expert evidence for the value of a car which had been damaged in an accident).

Representation

43.20 By **PD 27, para. 3.2(1)**, at a hearing on the small claims track, a party's case may be presented:

(a) by the party personally;
(b) by a lawyer; or
(c) by a lay representative.

A 'lawyer' means a barrister, a solicitor or legal executive employed by a solicitor (**para. 3.1(1)**). A 'lay representative' means any other person (**para. 3.1(2)**).

By **para. 3.2(2) and (3)**, the court's permission must be obtained for representation by a lay representative in the following circumstances:

(a) if the party being represented by the lay person is not present;
(b) if judgment has been given in the claim; or
(c) if the hearing is of an appeal against any decision made by the district judge in the proceedings.

The court may refuse to hear a lay representative in any proceedings if it is of the opinion that he or she is acting in an unruly manner in those proceedings (Courts and Legal Services Act 1990, s. 11(4)). The court must specify the conduct which warranted its refusal (s. 11(5)).

An individual may be prohibited by an order of a county court judge under s. 11(6) from acting as a lay representative. An order under s. 11(6) may be made where the judge has reason to believe that, in the present proceedings or any other proceedings, the individual has intentionally misled the court, or otherwise demonstrated unsuitability to exercise a right of audience. In *Paragon Finance plc v Noueiri* [2001] EWCA Civ 1402, [2001] 1 WLR 2357 (where a prohibition order was made by the Court of Appeal under its inherent jurisdiction), the representative's unsuitability was demonstrated by:

(a) his failure, or refusal, to understand crucial procedural rules;
(b) his bankruptcy, which meant that it would be futile to order him to pay wasted costs.

A corporate party is physically incapable of presenting its own case, but may be represented by a lawyer or a lay representative (*Avinue Ltd v Sunrule Ltd* [2003] EWCA Civ 1942, [2004] 1 WLR 634) or by any officer or employee (**PD 27, para. 3.2(4)**).

Public hearing

According to **PD 27, para. 4.1**, the hearing of a small claim will usually be in public, but the judge may decide to hold it in private if: **43.21**

(a) the parties agree, or
(b) a ground mentioned in **CPR, r. 39.2(3)**, applies.

PD 27 goes on to say at **para. 4.2** that a hearing that takes place at the court will generally be in the judge's room, but it may take place in a courtroom. It may involve a site visit if the time involved is proportionate, though judgment will be given in the judge's room rather than on site.

Method of proceeding

Rule 27.8 of the CPR allows the court to adopt any method of proceeding at a small claims hearing that it considers to be fair. The hearings are informal, evidence need not be taken on oath (and in practice rarely is) and the court may limit cross-examination. **PD 27, para. 4.3**, provides that the judge may in particular: **43.22**

(a) ask questions of any witness before allowing any other person to do so,
(b) ask questions of all or any of the witnesses before allowing any other person to ask questions of any witnesses,
(c) refuse to allow cross-examination of any witness until all the witnesses have given evidence-in-chief,
(d) limit cross-examination of a witness to a fixed time or to a particular subject or issue or both.

All the above is consistent with the interventionist approach. The district judge will have pre-read all the papers and is thus able to focus on areas of evidence materially in dispute. Such an approach is favoured by most unrepresented parties although it remains important to ensure that every party has a reasonable opportunity to say or ask all they want to.

If both parties are legally represented, matters may proceed more efficiently if the usual sequence of a court trial is observed, with short opening speeches if of assistance, formal evidence given in chief (although a direction for witness statements to stand as evidence-in-chief may be useful), cross-examination, re-examination and closing speeches. With unrepresented litigants, the district judge will assess the situation and the parties and decide what he or she needs to hear in order both to do justice and to ensure that the parties feel that within reason they have had their say. Although a district judge may control cross-examination by the parties, it would not be appropriate to forbid cross-examination entirely (*Chilton v Saga Holidays plc* [1986] 1 All ER 841).

Hearings without the parties

43.23 Under **CPR, r. 27.9(1)**, a party to a small claim may request the court, by written notice given at least seven days before the hearing, to decide the claim without that party being present. A party who wishes to make use of this facility must serve every other party with copies of the documents filed at court at least seven days before the hearing (**r. 27.9(1)(b)**). If these steps are taken (and the party, as indicated, does not attend the hearing), the court will take into account the statement of case and any other documents filed by that party when deciding the claim (**r. 27.9(1)**).

If a *claimant* has not given notice under **r. 27.9(1)** but then does not attend the hearing, the court may, and usually will, strike out the claim (**r. 27.9(2)**).

The word 'may' in **r. 27.9(2)** gives the court a discretion and thus a party who has misunderstood the requirement to give seven days' notice and perhaps sends in a fax on the morning of the hearing, requesting the court to deal with the case on the basis of his written statements, will no doubt be given some indulgence. If the opposing party can demonstrate any prejudice caused by the lack of notice of the other party's non-appearance, an adjournment may be permitted. This may be, for example, because the party who is present needed to cross-examine the absent party about some feature of his case which would have demonstrated, e.g., the falseness of a particular piece of evidence, or that a certain document was not authentic. There may well also be a class of case where one party needs the other to attend in order to establish quantum, e.g., claims by former employees to commission payments based on sales. Generally speaking, a party who attends is likely to fare better than a party who does not attend.

If a *defendant* does not attend a hearing or give notice under **r. 27.9(1)**, and the claimant either does attend or has given the notice referred to, the court may, and usually will, decide the claim on the basis of the evidence of the claimant alone (**r. 27.9(3)**).

If *neither party* attends or gives notice, the court may strike out the claim and any defence and counterclaim (**r. 27.9(4)**).

Nothing in these provisions affects the general power of the court to adjourn a hearing for good reason, e.g., where a party who wishes to attend cannot do so because of illness.

Recording evidence and giving reasons

43.24 A court hearing of a small claim is tape-recorded by the court (**PD 27, para. 5.1**) and a party may thereafter obtain a transcript on payment of the proper charges. The fact that a party is exempt from paying court fees does not mean that he or she can obtain a transcript without charge, since such charges are not made by Her Majesty's Courts Service directly.

The court must give reasons for its decision (**CPR, r. 27.8(6)**) and will do so 'as briefly and simply as the nature of the case allows' (**PD 27, para. 5.3(1)**). Reasons are normally given orally at the hearing although they may be given later, either in writing or at a hearing fixed for that purpose (para. 5.3(2)).

Where the judge decides the case without a hearing under **CPR, r. 27.10**, or a party who has given notice under **r. 27.9(1)** does not attend the hearing, the judge will prepare a note of his or her reasons and the court will send a copy to each party (**PD 27, para. 5.4**).

One practical difficulty is that of an impecunious and unrepresented party who is unable to afford the cost of a transcript. In such circumstances a circuit judge, before hearing an appeal or when deciding whether to give permission to appeal, may be of the opinion that a note from the district judge setting out the main reasons for his decision would be of assistance; such a note from the district judge to the circuit judge should be made available to all the parties.

Setting judgment aside and rehearing

A party to a small claim who was neither present nor represented at the hearing of the claim, and who did not give written notice to the court under **CPR, r. 27.9(1)**, may apply for an order that judgment shall be set aside and the claim reheard (**r. 27.11(1)**). **43.25**

To do this, application must be made not more than 14 days after the day on which notice of the judgment was served on that party (**r. 27.11(2)**). The court may then, by **r. 27.11(3)**, grant an application *only* if the applicant:

(a) had a good reason for not attending or being represented at the hearing or giving written notice to the court under **r. 27.9(1)**; and
(b) has a reasonable prospect of success at the hearing.

Compare **r. 39.3(5)**, discussed in **60.2**, which applies to setting aside a judgment given in the absence of a party on the fast track or multi-track, but does not (by **r. 27.2(1)(h)**) apply to the small claims track.

A party may not apply to set judgment aside under **r. 27.11** if the court dealt with the claim without a hearing under **r. 27.10** (i.e., by an order of the court with the consent of the parties dispensing with the hearing (**r. 27.11(5)**)).

A party who was deliberately absent from court without a proper reason has no right to have a rehearing, however strong that party's case may be. If the court concludes that there is good reason for the absence, there is still an obligation on the party applying to show a reasonable prospect of success. This may go beyond consideration of whatever documents have been previously filed and may lead to the court asking for written evidence or further documentary evidence.

If judgment is set aside, the court must fix a new hearing (**r. 27.11(4)(a)**). The new hearing may take place immediately after the hearing of the application to set aside the judgment and may be dealt with by the judge who set aside the judgment (**r. 27.11(4)(b)**).

APPEALS

The procedure for appeals is considered in **chapters** 71 and 72. An appeal against a court's order may be made only with the permission of that court or of the appeal court (**CPR, r. 52.3**). An appellant's notice in a small claim appeal must be in form **N164** (**PD 27, para. 8A; PD 52, para. 5.8(1A)**). A party to a case on the small claims track who wishes to appeal against an order made under **r. 27.10**, without a hearing, or in that party's absence in accordance with a request under **r. 27.9**, must apply to the appeal court for permission (**PD 27, para. 8.2**). When a decision has been made by a district judge (as is usual on the small claims track), the 'appeal court' for these purposes is the circuit judge at the same county court (**PD 52, para. 2A.1**). If permission to appeal has not been given by the district judge, it must be requested in the appellant's notice (**CPR, r. 52.4(1)**). **43.26**

There are simplified rules in **PD 52, para. 5.8**, setting out the documents to be filed. These require only the filing of an appellant's notice, a sealed copy of the order under appeal, and any order granting or refusing permission to appeal. An appellant may file additional documents, and may be ordered to file a suitable record of the reasons for the judgment of the lower court (**para. 5.8(4)**) and (5), which may be an agreed note prepared by the parties or a note from the district judge (see **43.18**).

If an appeal against an order made on the small claims track is allowed, the appeal court will, if possible, dispose of the case at the same time, rather than referring it back to the lower court or ordering a new hearing (**PD 27, para. 8.3**). The appeal court may dispose of the case without hearing further evidence (**para. 8.3**).

COSTS

Costs after allocation

43.27 After a claim has been allocated to the small claims track there are considerable restrictions on the costs that the successful party may recover. In principle (**CPR, r. 27.14(2)**) the court may not order a party to pay a sum to another party in respect of that other party's costs except:

(a) the fixed costs payable under **Part 45** (or which would be payable if **Part 45** applied) attributable to issuing the claim;
(b) in proceedings which include a claim for an injunction or specific performance, an amount not exceeding £260 for legal advice and assistance relating to that claim (**PD 27, para. 7.2**);
(c) costs assessed by the summary procedure in relation to an appeal; and
(d) such further costs as the court may assess by the summary procedure and order to be paid by a party who has behaved unreasonably (see **43.28**).

Under **r. 27.14(3)** the court may also order a party to pay all or part of:

(a) any court fees paid by the other party (r. 27.14(3)(a));
(b) travelling and subsistence expenses of a party or witness reasonably incurred for the purpose of attending a hearing (r. 27.14(3)(b));
(c) loss of earnings or loss of leave caused by a party or witness attending a hearing, limited to £50 per person per day (r. 27.14(3)(c); **PD 27, para. 7.3(1)**);
(d) experts' fees, limited to £200 per expert (r. 27.14(3)(d); PD 27, para. 7.3(2)).

Unreasonable behaviour

43.28 Instead of the limited costs normally recoverable on the small claims track (see 43.27), a successful party may seek to recover all of his costs from a party who has behaved unreasonably (**CPR, r. 27.14(2)(d)**). This inevitably involves the court exercising a wide discretion. The following may, it is suggested, be considered to be unreasonable:

(a) making a claim which the court has found to be wholly false;
(b) failure to inform the court of the non-attendance of a witness;
(c) deliberate delay in dealing with an undeniable claim so as to force a party to issue proceedings;
(d) filing a spurious defence and then not attending the final hearing;
(e) paying the claim in full just before the final hearing;
(f) making unnecessary procedural applications;
(g) possibly, rejecting a Part 36 offer (see below).

A material factor may be that the rules in **Part 36** on payments into court and offers to settle have no application in small claims proceedings (**r. 27.2(1)(g)**). With effect from 1 October 2005, **r. 27.14(2A)** provides that a party's rejection of an offer in settlement will not of itself constitute unreasonable behaviour under **r. 27.14(2)(d)**, but the court may take it into consideration when it is applying the unreasonableness test. A note to **r. 27.14** refers to **r. 36.2(5)**, and says this latter rule allows the court to order Part 36 costs consequences in a small claim. **Rule 36.2(5)** is in fact worded the other way round, saying that Part 36 offers will not have the consequences provided by Part 36 unless the court orders otherwise.

Accordingly, a strong case should be required before the court holds that rejection of an offer is unreasonable behaviour.

When the court concludes that a party has behaved unreasonably, the court must conduct an immediate and summary assessment of the costs to be paid (r. 27.14(2)(d)). It will thus be important for a party who expects to be able successfully to press a claim for costs to have information available on the status of the fee earner, time claimed for attendances, correspondence, documents and so on, or even to have completed a formal statement of costs.

Costs after leaving the small claims track

If a case is reallocated from the small claims track to another track, the small claims costs provisions cease to apply after the claim has been reallocated and the fast track or multi-track rules will thereafter apply (CPR, r. 27.15). **43.29**

Costs before reallocation to the small claims track

If a claim has been on some other track before being reallocated to the small claims track, the rules applicable to the first track will apply up to the date of reallocation and the small claims track rules will apply after that date, unless the court orders otherwise (CPR, r. 44.11(2)). **43.30**

Costs in claims exceeding the small claims threshold

If the parties have consented to a claim being allocated to the small claims track, even though the financial value of the claim exceeds the limit for the small claims track, until 30 September 2005 for costs purposes the claim was treated as if it were proceeding on the fast track. With effect from 1 October 2005 such a case is treated for costs purposes as on the small claims track unless the parties agree to it being treated for costs as if it is on the fast track (r. 27.14(5) and (6)). **43.31**

Allocation for assessment of damages

Claims may be allocated to the small claims track for determination of quantum after judgment has been entered for damages to be assessed. When this happens the limitation on costs in respect of the small claims hearing will apply, although costs of earlier stages will be based on the sums available on the track concerned. It is likely that if proceedings are to be transferred to the small claims track for the assessment of damages, the court will undertake a summary assessment of the costs incurred before the allocation to the small claims track. **43.32**

Chapter 44 Fast Track

INTRODUCTION

44.1 The fast track is intended to cover the majority of defended claims within the £5,000 to £15,000 monetary band. It will also deal with non-monetary claims such as injunctions, declarations and claims for specific performance which are unsuitable for the small claims track and do not require the more complex treatment of the multi-track. The fast track provides a 'no-frills' procedure for medium-sized cases that do not justify the detailed and meticulous preparation appropriate for complex and important cases. Instead, a case allocated to this track will be progressed to trial within a short timescale after the filing of a defence. **Rule 1.1(2)(c)** of the CPR provides that part of the overriding objective is that cases should be dealt with proportionately, and it is this idea that underlies the whole concept of having a fast track with limited costs. The intention is to increase access to justice by removing the uncertainty faced by many litigants over the cost of litigating, and to provide a means of obtaining justice speedily.

When claims are allocated to the fast track, directions will be given setting out the timetable to be followed, with a fixed trial date or trial period no more than 30 weeks later. Such a timetable will be long enough for the parties to undertake the work necessary for preparing the case for trial, but sufficiently tight to discourage elaboration. The court will use its case management powers (see **chapter 42**) and its power to impose sanctions (**chapter 46**) to provide protection against oppressive or unreasonable behaviour, and in particular against a powerful opponent driving up the costs so as to overwhelm a weaker litigant.

Under the CPR the court is expected to enforce the timetable it sets so as to ensure that it is not simply ignored by those conducting litigation, and that fast track cases really do proceed to a speedy resolution by trial if they are not settled beforehand. It is for this reason that, as will be seen in this chapter, although some scope is given for the parties to alter some of the dates in the timetable set by the court, changing the date of the trial is only a matter of last resort. To ensure the timetable is not invalidated by listing difficulties, the *Final Report* also envisaged that any applications that might be needed in the period between allocation to the fast track and trial would be dealt with speedily, in a matter of days rather than weeks, and with applications wherever possible being dealt with on paper rather than requiring hearings (*Final Report*, ch. 2, para. 33 and 34).

The full range of interim applications is available in fast track cases. It has always been notorious that intended short cuts, such as applications for summary judgment and trials of preliminary issues, have a habit of turning out to be time-consuming and expensive detours.

Trenchant comments to this effect were made by Lord Donaldson of Lymington MR in *R.G. Carter Ltd v Clarke* [1990] 1 WLR 578, a summary judgment case, and by Lord Roskill in *Allen v Gulf Oil Refining Ltd* [1981] AC 1001, a preliminary issue case.

ADVANCE PREPARATION

Once a case is allocated to the fast track and directions are given, there will be a limited period of no more than seven months in which to prepare the case for trial. Such is the importance of ensuring fast track claims are dealt with expeditiously that **PD 28, para. 3.12**, lays down a typical directions timetable providing for a trial 30 weeks after the notice of allocation. **Paragraph 3.13** envisages shortening this period in cases where some of the typical steps in the timetable are thought unnecessary. Claimants will therefore be well advised to ensure that their cases are in an advanced state of preparation before they issue proceedings, to make sure they do not fall behind schedule once the timetable starts running. They should ensure they have available for disclosure all disclosable documents, both on liability and the amount of damages. They should also have identified and if necessary traced all material witnesses, and preferably have reduced into writing at least draft statements for each witness. They should also have made some progress regarding obtaining any expert evidence that might be necessary. It is to be expected that in most fast track cases the court will direct that there should be joint instruction of experts. Prospective claimants will therefore be well advised to have identified possible experts to be instructed, and sought agreement with their prospective defendants for the joint instruction of agreed experts. Anything less than this will be storing up trouble for later on. **44.2**

Defendants are in a similar, and sometimes more precarious, position. They too will easily find themselves in time difficulties later on unless they have completed at least some of the necessary preparation before the claim is issued. Full compliance with any relevant pre-action protocol will at least put them in a reasonably advanced state of preparedness. They should, at the very least, have available for disclosure their documentation on liability, and have draft statements from material witnesses. They should also be in the process of seeking agreement on the joint instruction of experts. Like claimants, failing to have these matters in hand will mean there will be little time to get the case ready before the trial arrives.

DIRECTIONS

When it allocates a case to the fast track, the court will at the same time give case management directions and set a timetable for the steps to be taken from that point through to trial (**CPR, r. 28.2(1)**). The directions given will be designed to ensure the issues are identified and the necessary evidence is prepared and disclosed (**PD 28, para. 3.3**). Usually the court will give directions of its own initiative without a hearing, and will take into account the respective statements of case, the allocation questionnaires, and any further information provided by the parties. Occasionally it may hold a directions hearing, such as when it is proposing to make an unusual order, for example, to appoint an assessor (see **PD 28, para. 3.11**). It is the duty of the parties to ask for all directions that might be needed on any hearing that may be fixed (**para. 2.5**). If any direction or order is required that has not been provided for, it is the duty of the parties to make an application as soon as possible so as to avoid undue interference with the overall timetable (**para. 2.8**). If a directions hearing becomes necessary because of the default of any of the parties, the court will usually impose a sanction (**para. 2.3**). **44.3**

Typically, by **CPR, rr. 28.2(2)** and **28.3**, the matters to be dealt with in directions given on allocation to the fast track will include:

(a) disclosure of documents;
(b) service of witness statements;
(c) expert evidence; and
(d) fixing a date for the trial, or a period (not exceeding three weeks) in which the trial is to take place.

Standard directions to be used in fast track cases are set out in the Appendix to **PD 28**. They include matters, such as orders for the provision of further information, which are not included in the basic list. This is because the directions given will be tailored by the procedural judge to the circumstances of each individual case. The time periods for taking the various steps will also be tailored to the requirements of each individual case, but a few indications of the probable times allowed for different steps will be given in the following paragraphs. Further directions may be given after consideration of pre-trial checklists (**CPR, r. 28.6(1)**, see **44.16** to **44.20**) or after failure to file or complete them (**r. 28.5(3)** and **(4)**, see **44.11**). The date for filing pre-trial checklists will be not more than eight weeks before the trial date or the beginning of the trial period (**r. 28.5(2)**). Further directions are usually given about four to six weeks before trial.

Disclosure

44.4 Disclosure is discussed fully in **chapter 48**. Disclosure in some form should have taken place before proceedings were issued in compliance with the pre-action protocols. Information about this should have been given with the allocation questionnaire. Based on the respective statements of case and these questionnaires, the procedural judge may direct the parties to give standard disclosure as one of the directions made at this stage, or may direct that no disclosure need take place (where the parties confirm that disclosure has taken place and no further disclosure is required), or may specify the documents or classes of documents which the parties must disclose (**CPR, r. 28.3(2); PD 28, para. 3**). The standard directions will provide for disclosure to be given by service of lists of documents, which must be delivered by a specified calendar date. It is also possible for disclosure to be given more informally without a list and with or without a disclosure statement. Disclosure is likely to be ordered for 28 days after service of the notice of allocation (**PD 28, para. 3.12**).

Witness statements

44.5 The exchange of witness statements is considered further in **chapter 49**. Standard directions will usually provide for simultaneous exchange by a specified calendar date of statements from all the factual witnesses on whose evidence each party intends to rely. Exchange is likely to be required about 10 weeks from the order for directions (**PD 28, para. 3.12**). By **CPR, r. 32.9(1)**, witness summaries may be used in circumstances where witness statements cannot be obtained for practical reasons, but such instances should be exceptional. **Rule 32.5(4)** points firmly in the direction of full witness statements, as witnesses will only be allowed to amplify their statements if there is 'good reason' not to confine them to their disclosed witness statements. Trial judges usually take a strict view against allowing additional questions in-chief seeking to introduce new matters or to insulate a witness against cross-examination under the guise of 'amplifying' an exchanged statement.

Expert evidence

44.6 For detailed consideration of directions about experts see **52.6** to **52.15**. Under the CPR cases will not normally be on the fast track unless oral expert evidence at trial is limited to one expert per party in each expert field, and to two fields of expertise (**CPR, r. 26.6(5)**). It is difficult to see how any more experts could give evidence within the time limit for a fast track hearing. One of the powers available to the court is that of directing that the evidence on particular issues may be given by a single expert jointly instructed by the opposing parties (**r. 35.7**). In order to keep down costs and to reduce the length of fast track trials, it will be usual for the court to make directions for the joint instruction of a single expert unless there is good reason for doing something else (**PD 28, para.** 3.9(4)). In addition, in fast track cases the court will not direct an expert to attend at trial unless it is necessary to do so in the interests of justice (**CPR, r.** 35.5(2)). It is expected that such directions will be rare.

If the parties are given permission to instruct their own experts, the court has a power under **r. 35.12** to direct a discussion between the experts with a view to producing an agreed statement of the issues on which they agree and the areas on which they are in disagreement. If the experts cannot reach agreement, the interests of justice are likely to be served only by allowing both parties to call their experts at the trial so the areas of disagreement can be adjudicated upon by the judge. In such cases it may not be possible to deal with the case in a single day, and the court may need to consider reallocating the case to the multi-track. This will be considered by the procedural judge on filing of pre-trial checklists by the parties.

Normally expert evidence should be prepared and/or exchanged about 14 weeks after the order giving directions (**PD 28, para. 3.12**). The standard fast track directions have several different options regarding expert evidence, as alternatives to the joint instruction of experts. Options provided within the standard directions are:

(a) Sequential service of experts' reports. Normally it will be the claimant who will serve first.
(b) Simultaneous exchange of reports on some issues, with sequential service on the others.
(c) Holding of a discussion between experts in cases where the other side's reports cannot be agreed within a short time (usually 14 days) after service. This form of direction provides for a specified calendar date by which the discussion must take place, and the filing of a joint statement of the agreed issues and those in dispute (with reasons for the lack of agreement) by another specified date (which will often be close to the date for filing listing questionnaires).
(d) That expert evidence is not necessary and no party has permission to call or rely on expert evidence at the trial without permission expressly given by the court following an application.
(e) That the parties may rely on experts' reports at trial, but cannot call oral expert evidence.
(f) That the parties may rely on experts' reports, and the court will reconsider whether there is any need for experts to be called on consideration of the filed pre-trial checklists.

Questions to experts

The standard directions also make provision pursuant to the power given by **CPR, r. 35.6**, for written questions to be put to the experts for the purpose of clarifying their reports. Questions should be sent, if at all, usually within 14 days of receiving the relevant report, but **PD 35, para. 5.1**, provides this should be done no later than 28 days after receiving the report. Questions can be sent direct to the expert, but copies should be sent to the other side's solicitors. No time is laid down for the answers (although this may be done by a specific court order), but 28 days would seem to be reasonable. Sensible questions can only be asked if the party (or more commonly its solicitor) is guided by its own expert. If its own expert knows the answers, there will be little point in asking the questions in the first place, so it must be sensible to clear the written questions with the party's own experts first. It will take a little time for a party to receive the other side's expert reports, consider them, decide if it is a case where written questions should be put, contact its own expert and take its expert's advice about the written questions to be put, formulate the questions, and then serve them. Experts are often busy consultants and professionals with many calls on their time, so a period of 28 days for questions and answers may seem rather tight, but is necessary if a fast track timetable is to be met. Solicitors must send copies of directions orders to experts so they are aware of the court's timetable (**PD 35, para. 6A**). Solicitors should also ensure that experts are aware of their rights and duties under **CPR, Part 35**, particularly **r. 35.14**, which allows an expert to apply to the court for directions. **44.7**

Further statements of case

44.8 When giving directions the procedural judge may also direct that a party must file a further statement of case, such as a reply or defence to counterclaim. The direction will specify a calendar date and time for doing so.

Requests for further information

44.9 Requests for further information are considered in more detail in **chapter 30**. Standard directions provide for two possible times for service of such requests (with either, both or neither being directed in any particular case):

(a) Within a short, specified, time after directions are given, where the request is based on the other side's statement of case. The direction will also specify the date by which the request must be dealt with. A response is usually required within 14 days.
(b) After disclosure or exchange of witness statements. The direction will lay down a limited time after disclosure or service of the statement within which the request must be served, and a limited time within which it must be dealt with.

LISTING QUESTIONNAIRES: PRE-TRIAL CHECKLISTS

44.10 Standard fast track directions provide for all parties to file completed pre-trial checklists, previously known as listing questionnaires, no later than specific dates set out in the directions, unless the court considers the claim can be listed for trial without them. They are used to ensure the case is on course for being ready for trial, and to enable the procedural judge to set a trial timetable. If a party wants additional directions, the form has to be accompanied by an application notice and draft directions. Explanations must be given for witness dates to avoid. Information about experts includes whether opposing experts have signed a joint statement. If the time estimate has changed, the parties must say whether they have agreed a new estimate. When they are used, pre-trial checklists must be returned within the time specified by the court, which will be no later than eight weeks before the trial date or the beginning of the trial period (**CPR, r. 28.5(2)**). At the same time each party must file an estimate of costs (costs precedent H). The estimate of costs must be divided into parts showing the costs already incurred and an estimate of the future costs to trial (**PD 43–48, para. 6.2**). A fee is payable whether or not pre-trial checklists are used. The fee, of £275, is payable by the claimant (**CPFO, fee 2.2**). If the fee is not paid, the court will send a notice to pay in **form N173**, and failing payment within the time stated in the notice, the claim will be struck out (**r. 3.7**). As an incentive to settle, this fee is refundable if the court is notified at least 14 days before trial that the case has settled or has been discontinued.

Failure to file or complete pre-trial checklists

44.11 If a party fails to file a completed pre-trial checklist by the time specified or fails to give the information required, the court may give such directions as it considers appropriate (**CPR, r. 28.5(4)**). The court may require the parties to attend a hearing for this purpose, and if so will give at least three days' notice (unless abridged under **r. 3.1(2)(b)**) of the directions hearing using form N153 (**PD 28, para. 6.3**). Particularly where any of the parties are in default, the court may consider imposing sanctions and making 'unless' orders.

If none of the pre-trial checklists is returned within the stated time, the court will order that unless a completed pre-trial checklist is filed within seven days from service of that order, the claim, defence and any counterclaim will be struck out without further order (**r. 28.5(3)**). If only some of the parties are in default, the court will give directions based on the checklists that are returned (**PD 28, para. 6.5**). Notice of a pre-trial directions hearing will be in **form N153**.

FIXING THE DATE FOR TRIAL

When giving directions the court will fix the trial date or a period, not exceeding three weeks, in which the trial is to take place, and which will be specified in the notice of allocation (**CPR, r. 28.2(2) to (4)**). A trial window will usually be given at the allocation stage and the trial directions will be given on consideration of pre-trial checklists. A trial date or window may be altered, but only as a last resort or where it is necessary to avoid injustice (see **44.15**). Whichever course is taken, the court must give the parties at least three weeks' notice of the date of the trial unless, in exceptional circumstances, the court directs that shorter notice will be given (**r. 28.6(2)**). **44.12**

Rule 28.2(4) provides that the 'standard' period between the giving of directions and the trial will be not more than 30 weeks. It is therefore open for procedural judges to lay down even tighter timetables, which depends on the complexity of the case and whether any of the usual steps have already been taken (**PD 28, para. 3.13**). There is also scope, if the procedural judge can be persuaded that it is necessary, for the timetable to be longer than the standard period. Factors such as those mentioned at **44.15** may influence the court when considering a longer timetable in an individual case.

STANDARD FAST TRACK TIMETABLE

Table 44.1 charts the progress of a fast track case from issue, through allocation to the fast track, up to trial. The case illustrated takes 39 weeks, or about nine months, from issue to trial. The various stages will vary from case to case (such as where there is a stay for negotiation or if the claimant effects service rather than the court) and, as mentioned in **44.12**, even the 30-week period between directions and trial may be considerably reduced in some cases. It will be obvious that the parties will have to be in a high state of preparedness before proceedings are issued in all but the very simplest of cases if they are to have any real prospect of adhering to such tight timetables without being forced on the mercy of the courts. **44.13**

Table 44.1 Progress of fast track case to trial

Week after allocation	Step in the proceedings	Time limit
	Issue of proceedings Service by court (takes effect on second day after posting)	Usual limitation period 4 months from issue (6 months if outside the jurisdiction)
	Acknowledgment ofserviceor filing of defence	14 days after deemed service of the particulars of claim
	Service of allocation questionnaires (may be dispensed with)	Not before all defendants have filed defences, or expiry of time for filing defences
	Possible transfer to defendant's home court	On filing defence
	Return of allocation questionnaires and service and filing of statements of costs	Not less than 14 days after service of the questionnaire
0	Allocation decision and directions given by the procedural judge	After return of questionnaires
4	Disclosure of documents	Usually 4 weeks after allocation
10	Exchange of witness statements	Usually 10 weeks after allocation
10	Service of hearsay notices	With exchanged witness statements
14	Experts' reports	Usually 14 weeks after allocation

Week after allocation	Step in the proceedings	Time limit
(Say) 17	Written questions to experts	Between reports and pre-trial checklists
(Say) 19	Answers from experts	Usually 2 weeks from written questions
20	Service of pre-trial checklists (may be dispensed with)	Usually 20 weeks after
22	Return of pre-trial checklists with statements of costs	Usually 22 weeks after allocation
(Say) 24	Any directions arising out of the pre-trial checklists	Optional
(24)	Hearing if pre-trial checklists not returned	Only if parties in default
27	Confirmation of trial date	3 weeks before trial
27	Service of notice to admit	3 weeks before trial
28/29	Lodge trial bundle	3 to 7 days before trial
29	Service and filing of statements of costs	Not less than 24 hours before the hearing
30	Trial	30 weeks after allocation

AGREED DIRECTIONS

44.14 The parties are encouraged to seek to agree suitable directions to be submitted to the court with their allocation questionnaires. If this is done, the court will at least take them into account when giving directions, and if they are suitable, will simply approve them. To be approved the directions should essentially follow the above rules (see **PD 28, para. 3**), which means they must deal with disclosure, witness statements and expert evidence, lay down a timetable by calendar dates, and provide for a trial or trial period no more than 30 weeks after the start of the timetable.

VARYING THE DIRECTIONS TIMETABLE

44.15 A party that wishes to vary the date fixed by the court's directions for returning allocation questionnaires, pre-trial checklists or for the trial must apply to the court (**CPR, rr. 26.3(6A)** and **28.4(1)**). Any other date set by the court also cannot be varied by the parties if the variation would make it necessary to vary the dates for either filing pre-trial checklists or trial (**r. 28.4(2)**). The effect of these rules is that it is quite permissible for the parties to agree to the variation of the other directions for service of lists of documents, witness statements and experts' reports without troubling the court, provided the two key dates (filing pre-trial checklists and trial) are not affected by slippage elsewhere. If the parties agree to a variation which does not impinge on any of the key dates, they can act on their agreement without having to file anything at court (**PD 28, para. 4.5(1)**).

Under the CPR the parties are required to help the court to further the overriding objective (**r. 1.3**), and the court must encourage the parties to cooperate with each other in the conduct of proceedings (**r. 1.4(2)(a)**). If a party falls a little behind on the timetable, one would expect the other side to assist by agreeing to a slight revision to the timetable, rather than insisting on strict compliance. The court has a general power to extend and abridge the time for compliance with any rule, practice direction or court order, even if the application is made after the time for compliance has elapsed (**r. 3.1(2)(a)**).

A party who disagrees with the directions timetable laid down should either appeal or apply to the court for it to reconsider its directions (**PD 28, para.** 4.3(1)). Orders and directions made at hearings attended by a party or his representative or regarding which the party was given due notice, should be appealed (**para.** 4.3(2)), whereas an application is necessary in relation to directions made of the court's own initiative (**para.** 4.3(3)). Any appeal or application must be made as soon as possible (**PD 28, para.** 4.2(1)). The court will assume for the purposes of any later application that a party who did not appeal, and who made no application to vary any directions given within 14 days, was content that they were correct in the circumstances then existing (**PD 28, para.** 4.2(2)). Some courts expressly abridge this period to seven days after service, to be consistent with **CPR, r.** 3.3(5). Obviously, parties should not feel forced into making speculative applications in relation to directions that are based on future events (such as requests for further information and questions to experts), and applications to extend these (and some of the other) time limits are dealt with realistically when the need arises.

It is made very clear by **PD 28, para.** 5.4(6), that variations involving loss of the trial date will be considered matters of last resort. Examples include cases where there are significant problems with the evidence, where medical evidence requires re-tracking or further investigation, where there is a change of solicitor, where proceedings are issued at the very end of the limitation period, and in personal injuries cases where the prognosis is uncertain (*Final Report*, ch. 3, para. 19). If there is no option but to postpone the trial, the postponement will be for the shortest possible time, and the court will give directions for taking the necessary steps outstanding as rapidly as possible. In some of these cases the best course may be to have split trials of liability and quantum, or to proceed only on those issues that are ready (**PD 28, para.** 5.4(4)). Where this happens the court may disallow the costs of the remaining issues, or order them to be paid by the party in default in any event. If necessary the judge can decide issues while the case is allocated to the fast track, then re-allocate the claim, if re-allocating the claim immediately would cause substantial disruption to the litigation or unreasonable delay (*Maguire v Molin* [2002] EWCA Civ 1083, [2002] 4 All ER 325).

PRE-TRIAL DIRECTIONS

On receipt of the pre-trial checklists, under **CPR, r.** 28.6(1), the court will: **44.16**

(a) Fix the date for the trial (or, if it has already done so, confirm the date).
(b) Give any further directions for the trial as may seem necessary, including setting a trial timetable. Standard directions for this stage are set out in the Appendix to **PD 28**.
(c) Specify any further steps that need to be taken before trial.

The parties should seek to agree directions, and they may submit a proposed order (**PD 28, para.** 7.2(1)). They should give reasons for any unusual directions. Usually directions will be made by the court without a hearing, but it may decide to hold a pre-trial directions hearing, giving the parties three clear days' notice (**PD 28, para.** 6.3).

Confirmation of expert directions

Pre-trial directions will confirm or make provision for the permission granted to the parties regarding reliance on written experts' reports and calling expert witnesses at trial. The direction will specify the experts by name, and say whether they can be called or whether it is only the expert's report that can be relied upon. Oral evidence from experts will only be allowed if the court believes it is necessary in the interests of justice (**PD 28, para.** 7.2(4)). **44.17**

Trial timetable

The court may, if it considers that it is appropriate to do so, set a timetable for the trial. Setting a timetable is discretionary (**CPR, r.** 28.6(1)(b)), and is easier if the managing judge **44.18** will be the trial judge. If it decides to set a timetable, the court must consult with the parties (**r. 39.4**). A trial timetable defines how much time the court will allow at trial for the various stages of the trial itself. A simple direction may limit the time to be spent by each party in calling its evidence and in addressing the court in closing submissions. More sophisticated timetables will define how much time will be allowed for each witness, or even for cross-examination and re-examination. If a timetable is set, it will usually provide for a five-hour trial, to include all stages including judgment and the summary assessment of costs.

Trial bundles

44.19 Standard pre-trial directions will provide that an indexed, paginated, bundle of documents contained in a ring binder must be lodged with the court not more than seven days or less than three days before the trial. Slightly inconsistently, the standard direction in the Appendix to **PD 28** provides that trial bundles must be lodged at least seven days before trial. The parties must seek to agree the contents of the trial bundle a reasonable time in advance, which in practical terms means no later than 14 days before the trial. For further details on the contents of the trial bundles, see **chapter 57**. The claimant is responsible for lodging the bundle. Lodgment at court is required so that the trial judge can read the case papers in advance of the trial. Judges are likely to take a very dim view if the bundle is not lodged in time. Identical bundles will be needed for each of the parties, with an additional bundle for the witness box.

Case summary

44.20 Standard pre-trial directions give the procedural judge the option of directing that a case summary should be included in the trial bundle. This document is intended to be non-partisan, and to be agreed if possible. It should usually be no more than 250 words, and should outline the matters in issue, referring where appropriate to the relevant documents in the trial bundle. Again, responsibility for this rests with the claimant.

FAST TRACK TRIALS

44.21 The trial of a fast track claim will usually take place in the county court where it is proceeding, but may take place in a civil trial centre or any other court if it is appropriate because of listing difficulties, the needs of the parties or for other reasons. The judge may be a district judge or a circuit judge. The trial judge will generally have read the trial bundle and will usually dispense with opening speeches. Unless the trial judge otherwise directs, the trial will be conducted in accordance with any order previously made (see **44.18**), although the judge is free to set a fresh trial timetable (**PD 28, para. 8.3**). Given the time constraints and the need for proportionality, the trial judge will almost invariably order witness statements to stand as the evidence-in-chief and otherwise control the evidence to be presented. If a trial is not concluded on the day it is listed, the judge will normally sit on the following day to complete it (**PD 28, para. 8.6**; though in many county courts this does not reflect reality). In such an event no further costs will be allowed to the parties.

COSTS IN FAST TRACK CASES

44.22 **Rule 28.2(5)** of the CPR provides that the court's power to award trial costs is limited in accordance with **Part 46**, which sets fixed amounts for the costs of trial depending on the amount recovered, with a small uplift if counsel is attended by a solicitor, see **68.6**).

The general rule is that at the end of a fast track trial the court will make a summary assessment of the costs of the whole claim immediately after giving judgment (**PD 43–48, para. 13.2**). To assist the judge in assessing costs, the parties are required to file and serve, not less than 24 hours before the trial, signed statements of their costs for the interim hearing in **form N260**. A statement of costs must, by **PD 43–48, para. 13.5(2)**, set out:

(a) the number of hours claimed;
(b) the hourly rate claimed;
(c) the grade of the earner;
(d) the amount and nature of disbursements;
(e) the solicitor's costs for attending or appearing at the hearing;
(f) counsel's fees; and
(g) VAT on the above.

Any failure to file or serve a statement of costs, without reasonable excuse, will be taken into account in deciding the costs order to be made regarding the claim, the trial, and/or any detailed assessment hearing that might become necessary as a result of that failure (**PD 43–48, para. 13.6**; see **32.26**). Summary assessment (see **68.3**) is not permitted of an assisted party's costs, nor of the costs of a person under disability, unless the solicitor representing the person under disability waives the right to further costs (**PD 43–48, paras 13.9 and 13.11**).

Parties should try to ensure that their costs statements are realistic. The fact that a party's costs statement is inflated may well be used against that party by the court and the other side if costs are awarded to the other side. Underpricing a party's costs may assist in attacking its opponent's costs if it loses, but will be counterproductive if it is awarded costs.

The judge retains responsibility for ensuring that the costs claimed are not disproportionate or unreasonable, even if they are not disputed by the paying party (**PD 43–48, para. 13.13**). The fact that the paying party does not dispute the amount claimed can be taken as some indication that the amount is proportionate and reasonable.

Chapter 45 Multi-track

INTRODUCTION

45.1 A vast range of cases are allocated to the multi-track from simple contractual disputes involving little more than £15,000, to complex commercial cases involving difficult issues of fact and law with values of several million pounds, to cases where perhaps no money is at stake but which raise points of real public importance. Case management on the multi-track is intended to reflect this. Simpler cases are given standard directions without the need for hearings, and the parties are expected to comply with those directions without complicating or delaying matters. At the other end of the scale, the courts adopt a far more active approach, possibly with several directions hearings in the form of case management conferences and pre-trial reviews. The first case management conference is often an allocation and directions hearing. The courts adopt a flexible approach to ensure each case receives the right amount of case management input from the court (**PD 29, para. 3.2(2)**). Straightforward multi-track cases may be given tight timetables from defence to trial that are similar to those on the fast track. In such cases, the comments made in **44.1** apply with equal force about the need to be well prepared before commencing proceedings, the main difference being on costs. Even in complex multi-track cases it will be important for case preparation to be reasonably advanced before issue, because under the CPR there is a great deal 'front loading', and the procedural judge will want to be assisted by the parties in identifying the issues and the evidence required at the first case management conference.

Cases on the multi-track will generally be dealt with either in the Royal Courts of Justice or other civil trial centre (see **PD 29, paras 2** and **3.1**). The procedural judge may need to order a transfer on first consideration or at an allocation hearing, see **42.3**. Case management will generally be dealt with by masters and district judges (see **PD 2B**). It is the duty of the parties at all hearings to consider whether any directions should be made, as this can avoid the need for additional case management hearings later on (**PD 29, para. 3.5**).

CASE MANAGEMENT STAGES IN MULTI-TRACK CASES

Track allocation is decided after filing of the defence and return of allocation questionnaires (see **42.6**). Once a case is allocated to the multi-track the court will give directions and hold such procedural hearings as may be appropriate in order to progress the case to trial or resolution by other means. **Figure 45.1** illustrates the main stages in the progress of a multi-track case to trial. **45.2**

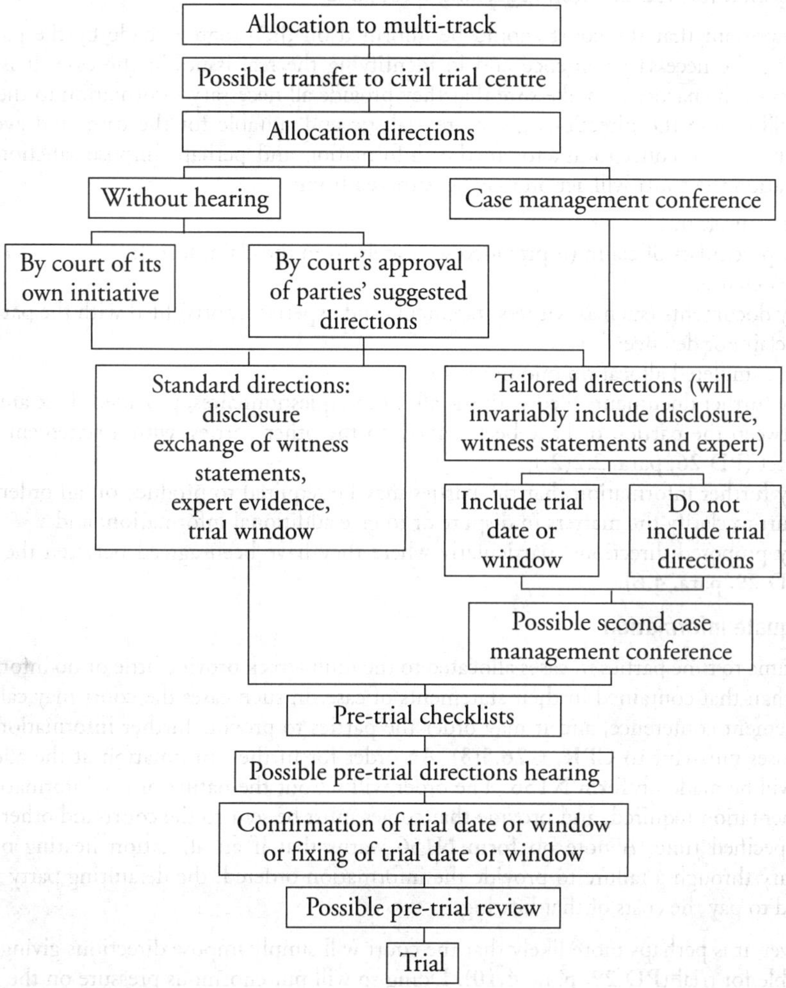

Allocation to multi-track

Possible transfer to civil trial centre

Allocation directions

Without hearing

Case management conference

By court of its own initiative

By court's approval of parties' suggested directions

Standard directions: disclosure exchange of witness statements, expert evidence, trial window

Tailored directions (will invariably include disclosure, witness statements and expert)

Include trial date or window

Do not include trial directions

Possible second case management conference

Pre-trial checklists

Possible pre-trial directions hearing

Confirmation of trial date or window or fixing of trial date or window

Possible pre-trial review

Trial

Figure 45.1 The multi-track

Directions on allocation

At the same time as a case is allocated to the multi-track the procedural judge will decide whether to give directions or to fix a case management conference or pre-trial review (or both a case management conference and a pre-trial review) and such other directions as are thought fit (CPR, r. 29.2(1)). The procedural judge will therefore take a view as to the complexity of the case, and the amount of work required to get it ready for trial, and decide whether or not it is necessary to call the parties in before the court for a procedural hearing. The judge **45.3** will also consider whether the case should be stayed while ADR procedures are attempted, see 42.24.

The court will seek to tailor its directions to the needs of the case, and the steps the parties have already taken to prepare it for trial. It will also take into account the extent to which the parties have complied with any pre-action protocol (see **chapter 8**). The court's concern will be to ensure the issues between the parties are identified, and that the evidence required for the trial is prepared and disclosed (**PD 29, para. 4.3**).

Making an informed decision regarding directions

45.4 It is important that the court should be informed on the progress made by the parties in gathering the necessary evidence and in identifying the real issues in the case. It is in the interests of the parties to make sure that they provide all necessary information to the court. This will ensure the directions given are realistic and suitable for the case, and avoid the necessity for the court to ask for further information and perhaps impose sanctions. The information the court will act on may be gathered from:

(a) the claim form;
(b) the particulars of claim (if provided separately from the claim form);
(c) the defence;
(d) any documents (such as witness statements and experts' reports) filed with the particulars of claim or defence;
(e) the completed allocation questionnaires;
(f) any further documents filed with the allocation questionnaires, provided these are agreed between the parties, or have been served on the other parties, with a statement to that effect (**PD 26, para. 2.2(2)**);
(g) any further information that the parties may be required to produce on an order by the court to clarify the matters in dispute or to give additional information; and
(h) any proposed directions, particularly where they have been agreed between the parties (**PD 29, para. 4.6**).

Inadequate information

45.5 From time to time parties in cases allocated to the multi-track provide little or no information other than that contained in their statements of case. In such cases the court may call a case management conference, and it may order the parties to provide further information about their cases pursuant to **CPR, r. 26.5(3)**. An order for further information at the allocation stage will be made on **form N156**. The order will set out the nature of the information and documentation required, and provide that copies must be sent to the court and other parties by a specified time. A note on **form N156** warns that if an allocation hearing becomes necessary through a failure to provide the information ordered, the defaulting party may be ordered to pay the costs of that hearing.

However, it is perhaps more likely that the court will simply impose directions giving a tight timetable for trial (**PD 29, para. 4.10**). Doing so will put enormous pressure on the parties. They will either have to comply, or will find themselves in considerable difficulty unless they apply promptly for tailored directions. This is because the court will assume for the purposes of any later application (in the absence of any appeal or application within 14 days to vary) that the parties were content that the directions were correct in the circumstances then existing (**PD 29, para. 6.2(2)**).

The general approach in these cases where there is inadequate information is for directions along the following lines to be made by the court of its own initiative:

(a) filing and service of any further information required to clarify either party's case;
(b) standard disclosure (for further details on which, see **chapter 48**) between the parties;

(c) simultaneous exchange of witness statements;
(d) for the appointment of a single expert unless there is good reason for not doing so;
(e) simultaneous exchange of experts' reports in cases or on issues where single expert directions have not been given (unless expert evidence is required on both liability and quantum, in which event the direction may be for simultaneous exchange on the liability issues, but sequential exchange on quantum issues);
(f) if experts' reports are not agreed, that there be a discussion between the experts for the purpose of identifying the expert evidence issues, and, if possible, reaching agreement between the experts, and the preparation of a statement setting out the issues on which they are agreed and a summary of their reasons on the issues where they disagree;
(g) listing a case management conference after the final date in the above directions;
(h) specifying a trial period; and
(i) if appropriate, directions for the parties to consider ADR.

An ADR direction may include provisions requiring the parties to file witness statements if they consider the case to be unsuitable for ADR giving their reasons for saying that the case is unsuitable (**PD 29, para. 4.10(9)**). This approach to ADR directions applies where the court does not hold a case management conference and where the court does not know what steps have been taken by the parties other than the exchange of statements of case, so is relatively unusual.

Avoiding the need for a directions hearing

If the parties in a multi-track case agree proposals for the management of the case and the court considers that the proposals are suitable, the court may simply approve them without the need for a directions hearing (**CPR, r. 29.4; PD 29, para. 4.6** and **4.7**). This is encouraged, as it obviously saves costs and court time. In order to obtain the court's approval the agreed directions must: **45.6**

(a) if appropriate, include a direction regarding the filing of a reply;
(b) if appropriate, provide for amending any statement of case;
(c) include provision about the disclosure of documents;
(d) include provision about both factual and expert evidence (the provision about expert evidence may be to the effect that no expert evidence is required);
(e) if appropriate, include dates for service of requests for further information and/or questions to experts, and when they should be answered;
(f) include a date or a period when it is proposed the trial will take place; and
(g) if appropriate, a date for a case management conference.

It will be seen that only items (c), (d) and (f)are obligatory in all cases, although the others will frequently arise in practice. Proposed agreed directions must lay down a timetable by reference to calendar dates. The court will scrutinise the timetable carefully, with particular attention to the proposals for the trial and case management conference, and will be astute to ensure these are no later than is reasonably necessary (**PD 29, para. 4.7(2)**).

The provision in any agreed directions relating to disclosure may:

(a) limit disclosure to standard disclosure, or less than that; and/or
(b) direct that disclosure will take place by the supply of copy documents without a list of documents, but if so, it must say either that the parties must serve a disclosure statement with the copies, or that they have agreed to disclose in this way without a disclosure statement.

The provision regarding factual and expert evidence should, if appropriate, deal with:

(a) whether the evidence should be disclosed simultaneously or sequentially;
(b) the use of a single expert; and
(c) without prejudice discussions between the experts if a single expert is not going to be instructed.

The court is free to reject directions that have been agreed between the parties, but will take them into account when making its own directions (either without a hearing or on a case management conference). The ultimate responsibility for case management remains at all times with the court, and parties will be unwise to assume that agreed directions will be automatically approved.

Once directions have been made by consent, the court retains control, and can override them in the future if this is justified in the circumstances (*Re Debtors (Nos. 13-MISC-2000 and 14-MISC-2000)* (2000) *The Times*, 10 April 2000).

CASE MANAGEMENT CONFERENCES

45.7 Case management conferences are an integral part of the new system of active case management by the courts. They are not simply directions hearings, but are intended to ensure that the real issues between the parties are identified. Side issues will be dispensed with either by agreement between the parties with due encouragement from the judge, or by means of summary judgment or striking-out determinations at an early stage. Case management conferences may be held immediately after a case is allocated to the multi-track or at any time thereafter through to the listing stage. They can be used as the vehicle for laying down directions at the allocation stage, or may be used later in order to assess how the case is progressing when the initial directions on allocation should have been completed. Normally the court has a discretion whether to call a case management conference. However, where it is contemplated that an order may be made either for the evidence on a particular issue to be given by a single expert, or that an assessor should be appointed, **PD 29, para. 4.13**, provides that a case management conference must be held unless the parties have consented to the order in writing. Some procedural judges use some case management conferences as mediation-style hearings to promote settlement. Judges adopting this practice will have extensive knowledge of the case, and will attempt to assist settlement so as to restrict and identify the issues to be tried. Whether this is a legitimate use of the judicial office, with the inherent pressure exerted by the presence of a judge and the lack of clear rules governing the roles of those present and how the hearing should be conducted, has yet to be decided.

Where a case management conference is or may be dealt with by the trial judge, no reference should be made to any Part 36 offers or payments whether in the case management bundle or at the hearing (see **64.5**). **CPR, r. 36.19**, does not prevent disclosure to procedural judges who will not be conducting the trial.

Case management conferences will also be called in cases where the court feels it cannot properly give directions on its own initiative, and where no agreed directions have been filed which it feels can be approved (**PD 29, para. 4.12**).

By encouraging the parties to settle their dispute or resolve it outside the court system, and by forcing the parties into identifying the real issues at an early stage, case management conferences are a means of using court time to save more time.

Listing of case management conferences

45.8 There is a commitment towards having case management conferences listed as promptly as possible (**PD 29, para. 4.12(2)**). The minimum period of notice the court will give to the parties of the date for the case management conference is three clear days (**CPR, r. 3.3(3); PD 29, para. 3.7**).

Attendance at case management conferences

45.9 If a case management conference is to be attended by a legal representative on behalf of a party, the representative must be someone familiar with the case (**CPR, r. 29.3(2)**). It is unacceptable to send a trainee with a two-page briefing note on such a hearing. Instead it will have to be the fee-earner concerned, or someone (possibly counsel) who is fully familiar with the file, the issues and the proposed evidence, who must attend. They must be able to field the questions that are likely to be covered at the hearing, and have the authority to agree and/or make representations on the matters reasonably to be expected to arise. Where the inadequacy of the person attending or his or her instructions leads to the adjournment of the hearing, it will be normal for a wasted costs order to be made (**PD 29, para. 5.2(3)**), or even an order for indemnity-basis costs and interest on damages at a higher rate than usual (see *Baron v Lovell* [1999] CPLR 630). Where a direction is made for the attendance of the parties and one of the parties is a company, the order should be that individuals with knowledge of the history of the case should attend (*Tarajan Overseas Ltd v Kaye* [2001] EWCA Civ 1859, *The Times*, 22 January 2002).

In the Chancery Division, whenever possible, the advocates instructed or expected to appear at trial should attend case management conferences and other case management hearings (**Chancery Guide, para. 3.7**). In the Admiralty and Commercial Courts, case management conferences should be attended on behalf of each party both by the fee earner with conduct of the case and by at least one of the advocates retained (**Admiralty and Commercial Courts Guide, para. D8.2**). Case management conferences in complex cases in the Admiralty and Commercial Courts are regarded as particularly significant stages in the litigation, and are conducted by a judge who will usually form part of the two-judge team that will manage the case, one of whom will usually subsequently be the trial judge (**paras D4.1, D4.2** and **D8.3**).

Business at case management conferences

At a case management conference the court will, as stated by **PD 29, para. 5.1**: **45.10**

(a) make a thorough review of the steps the parties have taken to date in preparing the case for trial;
(b) consider the extent to which they have complied with any previous orders and directions;
(c) decide on the directions needed to progress the action in accordance with the overriding objective;
(d) ensure that reasonable agreements are made between the parties about the matters in issue and the future conduct of the action; and
(e) record all such agreements.

To assist the court the legal representatives for all parties should ensure that all documents (and in particular witness statements and expert reports) the court is likely to ask to see are brought to court. The court may give directions for preparing a case management bundle. Legal representatives should consider whether the parties themselves should attend, and consider in advance what orders and directions may be appropriate (**PD 29, para. 5.6**). If the witness statements and experts' reports have not been exchanged at the time of the case management conference, it should follow from *General Mediterranean Holdings SA v Patel* [2000] 1 WLR 272 that the only reports and statements that can legitimately be called for are those that have been disclosed or that may be voluntarily disclosed at the hearing.

Case summary

An additional matter the parties are required by **PD 29, para. 5.6**, to consider is whether the court may be assisted by a written case summary. This should be a short document not exceeding 500 words which is designed to assist the court in understanding and dealing with the issues raised in the case (**PD 29, para. 5.7**). It should give a brief chronology of the claim, and state the factual issues that are agreed and those in dispute, and the nature of the evidence needed to decide them. Responsibility for preparing the document rests with the claimant, and if possible it should be agreed by the other parties. **45.11**

In the Admiralty and Commercial Courts, the legal representatives for each party must liaise for the purpose of preparing a short case memorandum, which will be included in the case management bundle. They must also prepare an agreed list of important issues (with a separate section dealing with matters which are common ground between all or some of the parties), and the claimant's solicitors must prepare the case management bundle (**Admiralty and Commercial Courts Guide, paras D5.1, D6.1** and **D7.1**). The case management bundle must contain these documents, together with the claim form and statements of case (or case summaries under **para. C1.4** if any of the statements of case exceed 25 pages), and any orders etc. made so far (see **para. D7.2**), being careful to avoid any reference to interim payments and **Part 36** offers and payments (as the case management judge could well be the trial judge, see **para. D5.4**). The case management bundle must be lodged with the Listing Office at least seven days before the first case management conference (**para. D7.4**).

In the Technology and Construction Court, the court will fix a case management conference within 14 days of filing of the acknowledgment of service or defence or any order transferring the claim to the TCC (**PD 60, para. 8.1**). The court will then notify the parties of the date for the case management conference, and send them a case management information sheet and a case management directions form (see **PD 60, para. 8.2**, app. A and app. B). These should be completed and exchanged, and then filed by 4 p.m. two days before the case management conference (**para. 8.3**). The parties are encouraged to agree directions.

Usual directions

45.12 In all cases the court will set a timetable at the case management conference for the steps it decides are necessary for preparing the case for trial (**PD 29, para. 5.3 and 5.4**). Typically the court will consider giving directions on the following matters:

(a) Whether the claimant has made clear the claim that is being made and the amount being claimed, and whether the defence is no more than a bare denial or is otherwise unclear. Orders for amendment and/or for further information may be appropriate if the statements of case are insufficiently clear for the other side to understand the case that has to be met.
(b) The scope of disclosure of documents required.
(c) The nature of the expert evidence required, and how and when it should be obtained. The court will not give permission for the use of expert evidence unless it can identify each expert by name or field of expertise, and say whether each expert's evidence should be given orally or by use of a report. Further matters that may be considered are whether the evidence on a particular issue should be given by a single expert, or that an assessor should be appointed, and whether there should be discussions between the experts.
(d) Disclosure of witness statements and summaries.
(e) Whether further information should be provided on matters other than statements of case, such as witness statements.
(f) Arrangements for questions that may be put to experts.
(g) Whether it would be just and save costs to have split trials on liability and quantum, or whether there should be the trial of one or more preliminary issues.
(h) Whether there should be another case management conference or a pre-trial review.
(i) Whether it is possible to fix a date for the trial, or to give a trial 'window'. The court will be anxious to comply with the rule that the trial should be fixed as soon as practicable (**CPR, r. 29.2(2)**).
(j) Whether the trial should be dealt with by a High Court judge, or by a specialist judge. If so, the court will also consider transferring the case to the appropriate court (**PD 29, para. 5.9**).

At case management conferences in Admiralty or Commercial Court cases the judge will, if practicable, fix the entire pre-trial timetable, or as much of it as practicable (see **Admiralty and Commercial Courts Guide, para. D8.7**). A standard set of directions is set out in the **Admiralty and Commercial Courts Guide, app. 8**. The same practice is followed where possible in county courts, provided trial windows and the availability of judges are known. In a High Court district registry, trial dates are fixed by liaising with the presiding judge through the diary manager. On each circuit the district judges, designated civil judges and the presiding judge cooperate closely on timetabling issues.

Unusual directions

45.13 It is the duty of the parties to ensure that all interim matters are dealt with at the case management conference. If they want an order dealing with a matter that is not normally dealt with at a case management conference, such as an order for an interim payment or for specific disclosure, and they know the application is likely to be opposed, they should issue and serve an application notice (**form N244**) in time for it to be heard at the conference. If the time allowed for the conference is insufficient to deal also with the contested application, they must inform the court at once so that a fresh date can be fixed. Failure to take these steps may result in a costs sanction (**PD 29, para. 5.8**). **PD 23, para. 2.10**, provides that where a party decides to make an application at a hearing that has already been fixed, but there is insufficient time to serve an application notice, it may be sufficient simply to give such written notice as is possible, and to make the application orally at the original hearing.

Other directions from those provided for by **CPR, r. 3.1(2)**, that may be considered in appropriate cases include:

(a) directing that part of the proceedings, such as a counterclaim, be dealt with as separate proceedings;
(b) staying the whole or part of the proceedings either generally or until a specified date or event;
(c) consolidating proceedings;
(d) trying two or more actions at the same time;
(e) deciding the order in which issues are to be tried; and
(f) excluding an issue from consideration.

Plans, photographs, models and video evidence

45.14 Generally a party intending to use photographs, plans, models and similar items as evidence at trial must give notice to the other parties by the date for disclosing witness statements (**CPR, r. 33.6(4)**). Video recordings fall into the wide definition of 'documents' for the purposes of **Part 31**, so the usual rules on disclosure and inspection apply (see **chapter 48**). Furthermore, there is an obligation to inform the court at the first opportunity that such evidence will be relied upon, as arrangements need to be made to ensure video equipment is available at trial, and extra time will be required for the trial for showing the evidence (*Rall v Hume* [2001] EWCA Civ 146, [2001] 3 All ER 248).

FIXING THE DATE FOR TRIAL

45.15 The court will fix the trial date or the period in which the trial is to take place as soon as practicable (**CPR, r. 29.2(2)**). This may be possible when it gives allocation directions, but in complex cases (and also, perhaps, badly prepared cases and cases where the facts are developing, such as many personal injuries claims) this may have to be delayed, perhaps for a considerable period of time. Where fixing the trial date is postponed, it may be revisited either at a later case management conference, or on the application of the parties, or after further scrutiny by the court.

When the court fixes the date for trial (or lays down a trial period or 'window'), it will give written notice to the parties, and will also specify a date by which the parties must file pre-trial checklists (**r. 29.2(3)**). The court may alternatively make an order for an early trial on a fixed date and dispense with pre-trial checklists (**PD 29, para. 8.1(2)**), or may simply list the case for trial when it reconsiders the case at the time when pre-trial checklists would be sent out, dispensing with the need for checklists at that stage (**CPR, r. 29.6(1)**).

In Queen's Bench Division cases proceeding in the Royal Courts of Justice in London, other than cases in the Admiralty and Commercial Courts and the Technology and Construction Court, a direction will be given as early as possible (often the first case management conference) with a view to fixing the trial or trial window (see **Queen's Bench Guide, para. 8.4.4**). The court will often direct that the trial is not to begin before a specified date, or that it will be held within a specified period (**para. 8.4.5**). The claimant must then, within the next seven days, take out an appointment with the Listing Officer and give notice of the appointment to the other parties (**para. 8.4.7**). At the listing hearing the claimant must bring any case summary, the particulars of claim and any orders relevant to listing, and all parties must have details of the dates of availability of their witnesses, experts and counsel. The Listing Officer will try to provide the earliest firm trial date or trial window consistent with the case management directions (**para. 8.4.8**).

In most cases in the Admiralty and Commercial Courts, a fixed trial date will be given immediately after the pre-trial timetable has been set at the case management conference (**Admiralty and Commercial Courts Guide, para. D16.1**).

Fixed dates are given on the basis that if previous fixtures have been substantially underestimated, or urgent matters arise, the trial may be delayed for a few days. Where such a delay might cause particular inconvenience, the Clerk to the Commercial Court should be informed well in advance (**para. D16.2**).

In the Technology and Construction Court, the trial date is usually fixed at the first case management conference (**PD 60, para. 8.6**).

The power to adjourn the trial is considered at **59.9** to **59.14**, and listing and adjourning problems caused by the restricted availability of experts are discussed at **59.8**.

LISTING QUESTIONNAIRES: PRE-TRIAL CHECKLISTS

45.16 Pre-trial checklists, which used to be known as listing questionnaires, in **form N170** will (unless dispensed with) be sent out to the parties by the court. These must be completed and returned by the date specified in the directions given when the court fixed the date or period for trial (**CPR, r. 29.6**). In multi-track claims directions for listing for trial are usually given on a case management conference at some stage after allocation. On this track, like the fast track (see **44.10**), the title 'listing questionnaire' was regarded as misleading, because the forms are used as checklists for ensuring cases are being properly prepared for trial. The forms should be served by the court at least 14 days before they must be returned. **PD 43–48, para. 6.4(2)**, states that costs estimates must be filed and served at the same time as pre-trial checklists are filed. Each party is under an obligation to return a completed checklist before the specified date, and the claimant is required to pay a fee of £600 in the High Court, £500 in a county court (**CPFO, fee 2.2**). If pre-trial checklists are dispensed with, the fee is payable within 14 days of dispatch of the notice of the trial date or period. In cases which are proceeding on a counterclaim alone the fee is payable by the defendant. The fee is refundable if the party who paid it gives written notice to the court at least seven days before the trial (or before the trial date has been fixed) that the claim has been settled or discontinued. There is a possible sanction of automatic striking out for non-payment after a reminder from the court (**CPR, r. 3.7**).

Purpose of checklists

45.17 Pre-trial checklists are used to check that earlier orders and directions have been complied with, and to provide up-to-date information to assist the court with deciding when to hold the trial and how long it will take, and in making trial timetable directions. Once all the checklists have been received, or the time limit has expired, the file will be placed before the procedural judge, who will make directions for trial along the same lines as those set out in 45.24, or direct that there should be a pre-trial directions hearing or pre-trial review. A case management conference may be convened specifically to consider and limit issues.

Exchange of checklists

The CPR do not require the parties to exchange copies of their pre-trial checklists, but doing so may avoid the parties giving conflicting or incomplete information to the court (**PD 29, para. 8.1(5)**). Getting this right may avoid the need for a pre-trial directions hearing or pre-trial review. **45.18**

Failure to file checklists

If no one returns a pre-trial checklist by the specified date, the court will order that unless a completed pre-trial checklist is filed within seven days from service of that order, the claim, defence and any counterclaim will be struck out without further order (**CPR, r. 29.6(3)**). Where only some of the parties file pre-trial checklists the court will fix a pre-trial directions hearing, under **r. 29.6(4)** (see **PD 29, para. 8.5**). It will also fix a directions hearing if any of the questionnaires do not provide the necessary information, or if the court considers that such a hearing is necessary to decide what further directions should be given to complete the preparations for trial (**CPR, r. 29.6(4)**). **45.19**

PRE-TRIAL DIRECTIONS HEARINGS

Pre-trial directions hearings serve a similar purpose to pre-trial reviews, but concentrate on making the decisions relevant to fixing the date of the trial. They are fixed for dates as early as possible, and the parties are given at least three clear days' notice of the date. Even if a pre-trial directions hearing is fixed because some of the parties did not file their pre-trial checklists, the court will normally fix or confirm the trial date and make orders about the steps to prepare the case for trial (**PD 29, para. 8.3(2)**). The court is likely to make further directions similar to those set out in 45.24. **45.20**

PRE-TRIAL REVIEW

If a pre-trial review (rather than a pre-trial directions hearing, see 45.20) is listed, it is likely to take place about eight to 10 weeks before trial. The pre-trial review gives the court a further opportunity to check that the parties have complied with earlier orders and directions, and may help in promoting settlement. Pre-trial reviews are not held in all cases, but only in those that merit the additional hearing. The intention is that they should be conducted by the eventual trial judge. **45.21**

Before the pre-trial review

In some cases a pre-trial review may be required by directions made by the court at an earlier stage, such as on allocation or at a case management conference. In other cases the court may decide to hold a pre-trial review of its own initiative, such as when it considers the pre-trial checklists. In this event it will give the parties at least seven clear days' notice of the hearing of a pre-trial review (**CPR, r. 29.7**). **45.22**

In the Chancery Division the claimant should, seven days before the pre-trial review, circulate a list of matters to be considered at the pre-trial review, including suggestions for how the case should be tried. Other parties must respond at least two days before the hearing (**Chancery Guide, para. 3.20**). The claimant should deliver to the Chancery Judges' Listing Office, by

10 a.m. on the day before the hearing of the pre-trial review, a bundle containing the lists of matters to be considered and proposals served by the parties on each other and the trial timetable, together with the results of the discussions between the parties on those matters, and any other useful documents (**para. 3.21**).

In the Commercial Court the parties should have completed Commercial Court pre-trial checklists (in the form set out in the **Admiralty and Commercial Courts Guide, app. 13**) in accordance with the pre-trial timetable directions. Before the pre-trial review, the parties must discuss and, if possible, agree a draft written timetable for the trial (**PD 58, para. 11.3**). The claimant's solicitor must ensure that the case management bundle is up to date (**PD 58, para. 10.9**).

Attendance

45.23 The same rules about a fully informed representative being present apply to pre-trial reviews as apply to case management conferences (see 45.9) and in the specialist courts in particular they should be attended by the trial advocates.

Pre-trial review directions

45.24 At a pre-trial review the court will not readily change earlier directions, and will apply the same principles as are applied generally when the parties fail to apply within 14 days for variation of case management directions (**PD 29, paras 6** and **9.3**; see 45.5).

Perhaps the most important task on a pre-trial review is to determine the timetable for the trial itself. This can lay down time limits for examination and cross-examination of witnesses, and for speeches. Doing this is intended to force advocates to focus their preparation, and to produce well managed trials. Other matters to be dealt with are:

(a) Evidence, particularly expert evidence. At this stage there should have been full disclosure and perhaps also discussions between the experts. It may be possible to make more rigorous directions about which experts really do need to be called at the trial, and which experts (or which parts of the expert evidence) can be taken from the experts' reports.
(b) A time estimate for the trial.
(c) Preparation and organisation of trial bundles.
(d) Fixing a trial date or week.
(e) Fixing the place of trial. This will normally be at a civil trial centre but may be at another court depending on the convenience of the parties and the availability of court resources (**PD 29, para. 10.1**).

Agreed pre-trial review directions

45.25 The parties are required to seek to agree the directions to be made on the pre-trial review, and may file an agreed order (**PD 29, para. 9.2**). The court may then make an order in the terms agreed, or make some other order, or reject the proposals and continue with the pre-trial review.

DIRECTIONS GIVEN AT OTHER HEARINGS

45.26 The court is not restricted to making case management directions on the occasions described above, but can do so on any occasion the case comes before the court (**PD 29, para. 3.4**). In fact, whenever there is a hearing it is the duty of the parties to consider whether any directions should be made, and to make any appropriate application on that occasion (**PD 29, para. 3.5**). Further, the court may hold a directions hearing on its own initiative on three clear days' notice whenever it appears necessary to do so. This can include situations where progress is delayed because one or other of the parties is in default of directions previously made (**PD 29, para. 3.6**). It can also occur because a party needs a direction not already in place, perhaps because a need to amend, or to ask for further information, has arisen since the last case management hearing. In such cases the application must be made as soon as possible so as to minimise the disruption to the original timetable (**PD 29, para. 3.8**).

VARIATION OF CASE MANAGEMENT TIMETABLE

As mentioned in 45.5, the court will assume for the purposes of any later application that the parties were content that any case management directions given were correct in the circumstances existing when they were given, unless an appeal or application to vary is made within 14 days. It is also regarded as essential that any party wanting to vary the timetable should take steps to do so as soon as possible (**PD 29, para. 6.2**). A delay in making an essential application to vary the timetable may well have the effect of losing all the time used before the application is eventually heard, which is not going to be looked upon favourably given the objective of dealing with cases expeditiously (**CPR, r. 1.1(2)(d)**). **45.27**

Variation by agreement

Case management directions fall into two categories: **45.28**

(a) Those that can be varied only by an order made by the court on an application by a party seeking a variation (**CPR, r. 29.5(1)**). These 'key dates' are:
   (i) dates fixed for holding a case management conference;
   (ii) dates fixed for holding a pre-trial review;
   (iii) dates specified for the return of pre-trial checklists; and
   (iv) dates fixed for trial (including a trial 'window').
(b) All other types of case management direction. These may be varied by the parties by consent, provided the variation does not affect any of the 'key dates' in category (a) above. There is no need to file anything with the court when a variation is agreed that does not affect any of the 'key dates' (**PD 29, para. 6.5(1)**).

Consensual variation of 'key dates'

If the parties agree to a variation of any of the key dates in the case management timetable as laid down by the court, they must apply for an order by consent, file a draft of the order sought, and also file an agreed statement of the reasons why the variation is sought (**PD 29, para. 6.5(2)**). If the procedural judge is satisfied with the stated reasons, an order will be made without a hearing, either in the terms agreed or as thought fit by the procedural judge. Otherwise, the application will be listed for hearing, at which the parties will need to justify their position. **45.29**

Variation by court

The court has power to vary directions at any hearing of its own initiative (**PD 29, para. 3.4**). A court may vary previous directions without the need for an appeal where there has been a change of circumstances (**para. 6.4**). Courts act with considerable caution before making substantial variations in previous directions (such as cancelling previous directions for the trial of a preliminary issue), because doing so comes close to overruling the decision-making process of the earlier directions hearing. Whether a substantial variation should be allowed depends on the circumstances of the case, and an application of the overriding objective (*Umm Qarn Management Co. Ltd v Bunting* [2001] CPLR 21). If there has been a real change in circumstances there is usually no objection to the court reviewing previous directions. Where there are no changed circumstances, any review of directions made on notice has to be made by way of appeal (*Jameson v Lovis* [2001] EWCA Civ 1264, LTL 24/7/2001). **45.30**

Objecting to directions made without prior notice

This paragraph deals with directions made in two circumstances: **45.31**

(a) by the court of its own initiative; and
(b) where a party can establish it did not receive notice of the hearing where the directions were made.

A party who is dissatisfied with the directions given in such circumstances must apply for the court to reconsider its decision, and the application will normally be heard by the same judge as gave the original directions (**PD 29, para. 6.3**). The court will give the parties at least three clear days' notice of the hearing to reconsider the directions. At the hearing the court may confirm the original directions, or may make such different order as it thinks just.

Objecting to directions made after due notice

45.32 Directions made after due notice, where there has been no change of circumstances, can be varied only by mounting an appeal (**PD 29, para. 6.3(2)**). The procedure for appealing is considered in **chapter 71**.

Chapter 46 Non-compliance, Sanctions and Relief

INTRODUCTION

46.1 So that the court can ensure that its case management directions and orders are complied with, and to retain control over the conduct of litigation, it needs to be armed with suitable coercive powers. These are provided in the CPR in the form of sanctions. The most draconian sanction that may be imposed is striking out. **Rule 3.4(2)(c)** provides that the court may strike out the whole or part of a statement of case if it appears that there has been a failure to comply with a rule, practice direction or court order. Striking out the whole of a party's statement of case ought to be reserved for the most serious, or repeated, breaches or defaults (see *UCB Corporate Services Ltd v Halifax (SW) Ltd* [1999] CPLR 691). In less serious cases of default or breach the court may be prepared to impose a sanction which, to use a phrase used in some of the cases under the old rules, 'fits the crime'.

It is to be expected that from time to time one or other of the parties to proceedings will be unable to keep to the directions timetable that will have been imposed by the court. This will not generally be a problem provided the parties cooperate and can still keep to the directions relating to the 'key dates' for filing allocation questionnaires, case management conferences, pre-trial reviews, filing pre-trial checklists and trial (**rr. 26.3(6A), 28.4 and 29.5**). If the non-compliance is through events outside the control of the defaulting party or is otherwise not deliberate, normally it would be expected that the parties would cooperate in compliance with **r. 1.4(2)(a)** and resolve the difficulty by agreeing a new timetable that preserves the key dates. The time specified by any provision of the CPR or by the court for doing any act may be varied by the written agreement of the parties, unless there is an express prohibition on variation in the rules (**r. 2.11**). If non-compliance cannot be resolved without, say, impinging on one of the key dates, or if the other side insist on compliance, the matter is likely to come before the court.

In addition to situations where an innocent party applies for an order imposing a sanction for default, similar problems arise where a defaulting party seeks an extension of time for complying with directions, in that a failure to secure an extension may result in evidence being inadmissible. Where a sanction is applied, it is possible for the defaulting party to apply for relief from the sanction (**r. 3.9**). These topics will also be considered in this chapter.

NON-COMPLIANCE WITH DIRECTIONS

46.2 **PD 28, para.** 4.2(2), and **PD 29, para.** 6.2(2), are relevant to whether a sanction should be imposed for non-compliance with directions. They provide that the court will assume for the purposes of any later application that a party who did not appeal, and who made no application to vary within 14 days of service of any order containing directions, was content that the directions were correct in the circumstances then existing.

Where a party has failed to comply with the court's directions, the court may make an order against the defaulting party providing that a sanction will be imposed if the order is not complied with (an 'unless order', see **46.28**). Compliance with time limits is now regarded as being more important than under the old rules (*Biguzzi v Rank Leisure plc* [1999] 1 WLR 1926). It was an accepted principle under the old system that unless orders were not made on the first default of a party, but were a last resort to ensure compliance (see *Hytec Information Systems Ltd v Coventry City Council* [1997] 1 WLR 1666). Such an approach is often unworkable under the CPR, particularly in cases on the fast track, where there is a very limited time between any breach and the date or window fixed for the trial. There simply will not be time for orders without sanctions to be made after non-compliance with directions if trial dates are not to be lost. Consequently, courts are prepared to make orders with sanctions where a defaulting party is still in breach at the time the application is heard, even on a first breach by a defaulting party.

RESPONDING TO THE OTHER SIDE'S DEFAULT

46.3 A party not in default faced with an opponent who has not complied with the court's directions is not entitled to try to make matters worse for the defaulting party by sitting back and waiting for the other side's default to get worse by the additional passage of time. Nor is the innocent party entitled to jump the gun by making an immediate application for an order with sanctions. In *Chilton v Surrey County Council* [1999] CPLR 525, which is discussed further at **46.6**, the Court of Appeal took against the defendant partly because it seemed the defendant was attempting to take tactical advantage of a mistake by the claimant's solicitors in overlooking to serve the revised statement of past and future loss and expense rather than cooperating with the claimant's solicitors to put matters right.

Instead, the correct procedure is that laid down in **PD 28, paras. 5.1 to 5.3** (for fast track cases) and **PD 29, paras 7.1 to 7.3** (which are in identical terms and apply in multi-track cases). The innocent party should first write to the defaulting party referring to the default, asking for it to be rectified within a short reasonable period (usually seven or 14 days), and giving warning of an intention to apply for an order if the default is not remedied. If there is continued default, the innocent party may apply for an order to enforce compliance or for a sanction to be imposed or both. Any application for such an order must be made without delay. If the innocent party does delay in making the application, the court may take the delay into account when it decides whether to make an order imposing a sanction or whether to grant relief from a sanction imposed by the rules or any practice direction.

Last-minute applications to strike out for breach of orders, particularly applications made without notice for hearing on the day of trial, were discouraged by the Court of Appeal in *Whittaker v Soper* [2001] EWCA Civ 1462, LTL 28/9/2001.

PRINCIPLES

Flexible approach

The Court of Appeal in *Biguzzi v Rank Leisure plc* [1999] 1 WLR 1926, in affirming a decision to strike out for wholesale disregard of the court's rules, commented that striking out would not always be the correct approach. Under the CPR the court has much wider powers than under the earlier rules for imposing proportionate sanctions. It is therefore possible to formulate suitable sanctions for breach of directions without resorting to draconian responses such as striking out. The CPR powers include making orders for indemnity costs, for paying money into court, and awarding interest at higher or lower rates. By a proper exercise of case management powers it should be possible for the courts to ensure that parties do not disregard timetables, whilst producing a just result. **46.4**

However, *Biguzzi v Rank Leisure plc* must not be understood as promoting an unduly lenient approach to the imposition of sanctions. Each case has to be considered on its own facts, with the court seeking to do justice between the parties in the light of the overriding objective. There will, accordingly, be a number of cases where there has been serious default where immediate striking out is appropriate (*UCB Corporate Services Ltd v Halifax (SW) Ltd* [1999] CPLR 691; *Purdy v Cambran* [1999] CPLR 843).

When considering cases of delay, the court should be astute to apply the overriding objective to the facts of the case in hand, and should not be flooded with excessive citation of authorities, particularly short case summaries (*Hamblin v Field* (2000) *The Times*, 26 April 2000).

Preservation of trial date

The general approach that will be adopted where there has been a breach of case management directions that may impinge on the date or window fixed for the trial of a claim is set out in **PD 28, para.** 5.4 (fast track), and **PD 29, para.** 7.4 (multi-track). It is to be expected that a similar approach will be taken where the breach is of a practice direction or provision in the CPR. According to the relevant paragraphs of PD 28 and PD 29: **46.5**

(a) The court will not allow a failure to comply with directions to lead to the postponement of the trial unless the circumstances of the case are exceptional (see *AC Electrical Wholesale plc v IGW Services Ltd* (2000) LTL 10/10/2000).
(b) If practicable to do so, the court will exercise its powers in a manner that enables the case to come on for trial on the date or within the period previously set.
(c) In particular, the court will assess what steps each party should take to prepare the case for trial, direct that those steps are taken in the shortest possible time and impose a sanction for non-compliance. Such a sanction may, for example, deprive a party of the right to raise or contest an issue or to rely on evidence to which the direction relates.
(d) Where it appears that one or more issues are or can be made ready for trial at the time fixed while others cannot, the court may direct that the trial will proceed on the issues that are or will then be ready, and order that no costs will be allowed for any later trial of the remaining issues or that those costs will be paid by the party in default.
(e) Where the court has no option but to postpone the trial, it will do so for the shortest possible time and will give directions for the taking of the necessary steps in the meantime as rapidly as possible.

(f) Litigants and lawyers must be in no doubt that the court will regard the postponement of a trial as an order of last resort. The court may exercise its power to require a party, as well as the party's legal representative, to attend court at a hearing where such an order is to be sought.

In *Holmes v SGB Services plc* (2001) LTL 19/2/2001 a jointly instructed expert reported shortly before the trial date. The report did not support the claimant's pleaded case, but suggested an alternative explanation consistent with the claimant succeeding. The claimant therefore applied to amend, but this meant having to adjourn the trial. This created a tension between doing justice (**CPR, r. 1.1**) and preserving the trial date (**PD 29, para.** 7), which was essentially a matter for the judge's discretion. On the facts permission to amend and an adjournment were granted.

Dealing with cases justly

46.6 The main concept in the overriding objective in **CPR, r. 1.1**, is that the primary concern of the court is doing justice. Shutting a litigant out through a technical breach of the rules will not often be consistent with this, because the civil courts are established primarily for deciding cases on their merits, not in rejecting them through procedural default. An example is *Jones v Telford and Wrekin Council* (1999) *The Times*, 29 July 1999, where service had been delayed beyond the period of validity because the claimant's solicitors had problems in obtaining psychiatric reports for service with the particulars of claim. The Court of Appeal upheld an extension of time largely because there were no previous authorities dealing with this situation, Lord Woolf MR commenting that the court must not lose sight of the fact that its primary concern was doing justice. Another example is *Chilton v Surrey County Council* [1999] CPLR 525, where the Court of Appeal indicated that dealing with a claim justly involves dealing with the real claim, and allowed the claimant to rely on a revised statement of past and future loss and expense served 12 days before trial quantifying the claim at about £400,000 rather than the original statement, which indicated a claim value of about £5,000. The fact that the real value of the claim was substantially greater than the figures stated in the original statement of past and future loss and expense was revealed many months previously when an employment expert's report was disclosed. The revised statement had not been served through a mistake by the claimant's solicitors, who believed it had already been served. The Court of Appeal disapproved of the defendant's tactics, but also commented that if the revised statement was to be excluded it was for the defendant to point to details of any prejudice it might suffer because of late service.

See also the discussion on non-compliance with expert and witness statement directions at 46.24 and 46.26, and seeking to rectify defective performance (46.25).

Allotting an appropriate share of the court's resources

46.7 An appeal was dismissed (with costs on the indemnity basis) in *Adoko v Jemal* (1999) *The Times*, 8 July 1999, on the ground that hearing it would be a waste of the court's resources. The appellant had failed to correct the notice of appeal despite a warning from the respondent that it was seriously defective, and had failed to comply with the directions relating to appeal bundles. The Court of Appeal spent over an hour trying to sort out the problem, and then decided it was inappropriate that any further court resources should be allocated to the appeal.

Client or solicitor at fault

46.8 Where protracted delay is the fault of the client rather than its solicitor, striking out may be justified (*Habib Bank Ltd v Jaffer* (2000) *The Times*, 5 April 2000), whereas if the fault is that of the solicitor combined with other circumstances, the claim may be allowed to continue (*Western Trust and Savings Ltd v Acland and Lensam* (2000) LTL 19/6/2000). Reduced weight was given to defects in complying with a court order in *Whittaker v Soper* [2001] EWCA Civ 1462,

LTL 28/9/2001, because the defects were the fault of the solicitor rather than the party. An inconsistent decision is *Daryanani v Kumar and Co.* (2000) LTL 12/12/2000, where it was held that it is inappropriate to draw a distinction or to apportion responsibility between the litigant himself and his advisers on the issue of delay. This should be contrasted with applications for relief from sanctions, where it is provided by **CPR, r. 3.9(1)(f)**, that one of the factors to be considered is whether the failure to comply was caused by the party or his representative. Where a party failed to comply with a time limit because his solicitors in error amended the wrong document, it was held that striking out was too great a penalty (*Austin v Newcastle Chronicle and Journal Ltd* [2001] EWCA Civ 834, LTL 18/5/2001).

Both parties in default

Both parties have obligations regarding compliance with court directions and the provisions of the CPR, and are required to cooperate with each other (see **r. 1.4(2)(a)**). Where both sides are in breach of directions, it is difficult to justify imposing a sanction purely on the claimant, provided it is reasonably possible to have a fair trial notwithstanding the breach (*Western Trust and Savings Ltd v Acland and Lensam* (2000) LTL 19/6/2000). Some cases go further, pointing out that both sides have a duty to help the court to further the overriding objective (**r. 1.3**). Consequently it is inappropriate for defendants to sit back and let a claim go to sleep, and then complain about delay when the claimant resumes the claim (*Khalili v Bennett* [2000] EMLR 996; *Dainty v Reynolds* (2000) LTL 28/11/2000). **46.9**

In *Hateley v Morris* [2004] EWHC 252 (Ch), [2004] 1 BCLC 582, there was an eight-month delay when neither side applied to relist a case management conference in an unfair prejudice petition. A striking-out order made by the registrar was overturned on appeal because:

(a) striking out was not fair or proportionate, given the delay was not that great;
(b) either side could have relisted the matter, and both sides have a duty to cooperate in progressing proceedings; and
(c) it was unlikely the quality of the evidence had been damaged due to the delay.

Unless orders

Applying the above principles, the court may take the view that the best way to ensure its directions are complied with by a defaulting party and that the trial date will be met, is to make an unless order. This gives the defaulting party a final opportunity to comply, and imposes a sanction in default. Often a costs sanction will be imposed at the same time. The form of unless orders is considered at **46.28**. **46.10**

In *Forrester Ketley and Co. v Brent* [2005] EWCA Civ 270, LTL 2/3/2005 it was held that the court below had been fully entitled to make unless orders, with striking out in default, on both the following grounds, where the defendant:

(a) had failed to provide a single document which clearly stated his case; and
(b) had failed to pay earlier interim costs orders.

SANCTIONS

Sanctions available

The following is a non-exhaustive list of possible sanctions that may be imposed: **46.11**

(a) striking out the entire claim or defence (see **46.13**);
(b) striking out part of the defaulting party's statement of case (see **46.16**);
(c) debarring a party from amending or updating part of its statement of case or a schedule of future loss and expense (see **46.20**);
(d) debarring a party from calling one or more witnesses, including expert witnesses (see **46.24, 46.26**);

(e) depriving a claimant who is in default of all or some of the interest that would otherwise have been awarded (see **62.14**);
(f) increasing the rate of interest otherwise payable (if the default comprises non-compliance with a pre-action protocol) (see **8.3**);
(g) requiring a defaulting party to pay all or some of the other party's costs of the proceedings (see **46.17**);
(h) requiring the defaulting party to pay the costs of and occasioned by the application in which the default is considered;
(i) ordering adverse costs orders to be paid on the indemnity basis (see **46.17**);
(j) requiring adverse costs orders to be paid forthwith;
(k) requiring the defaulting party to provide security as a condition for being allowed to continue with the proceedings;
(l) ordering security for costs (see **46.19**).

There are various provisions in the CPR and practice directions that impose various sanctions in default of due compliance. For example, **r. 35.13** provides that a party failing to disclose an expert's report may not use the report at the trial or call the expert to give evidence orally unless the court gives permission. A more severe sanction is imposed by **r. 3.7**, which provides for the striking out of claims for non-payment of allocation and listing fees after the time set by a notice of non-payment. An example from the practice directions is **PD 32, para. 25**, which provides that if an affidavit, witness statement or exhibit does not comply with the requirements of **CPR, Part 32**, or **PD 32**, the court may refuse to admit it as evidence and may refuse to allow the costs arising from its preparation. This last example differs from the previous two in that it provides for a sanction which the court may choose to impose, whereas the other two provide for sanctions which apply unless the court grants relief. The court will usually impose a sanction if it holds a hearing to give directions because of the default of a party or its legal representatives (**PD 29, para. 3.6**).

Non-compliance with applicable pre-action protocols

46.12 If, in the opinion of the court, non-compliance with a pre-action protocol leads to the commencement of proceedings which might otherwise not have been necessary, or leads to costs being incurred in the proceedings that might otherwise not have been incurred, **PD Protocols, para. 2.3**, provides that the orders the court may make include:

(a) an order that the party at fault pay the costs of the proceedings, or part of those costs, of the other party or parties;
(b) an order that the party at fault pay those costs on an indemnity basis;
(c) if the party at fault is a claimant in whose favour an order for the payment of damages or some specified sum is subsequently made, an order depriving that party of interest on such sum and in respect of such period as may be specified, and/or awarding interest at a lower rate than that at which interest would otherwise have been awarded;
(d) if the party at fault is a defendant and an order for the payment of damages or some specified sum is subsequently made in favour of the claimant, an order awarding interest on such sum and in respect of such period as may be specified at a higher rate, not exceeding 10 per cent above base rate, than the rate at which interest would otherwise have been awarded.

PD Protocols, para. 2.4, provides that the court will exercise its powers under **para. 2.3** with the object of placing the innocent party in no worse a position than he would have been in if the protocol had been complied with.

The **Pre-action Protocol for Personal Injury Claims, para. 1.5**, says that if the court has to consider the question of compliance, it will not be concerned with minor infringements, such as the failure by a short period to provide relevant information. A single minor breach will not exempt the 'innocent' party from complying with the protocol.

STRIKING OUT

Situations where striking out is appropriate

An applicant seeking a straight striking-out order has the burden of proof, whereas on an application for relief from sanctions (under **CPR, r. 3.9**, see **46.30**) after non-compliance with an unless order (see **46.28, 46.29**) the onus is on the defaulting party (*Malekout v Medical Sickness Annuity and Life Assurance Society Ltd* (2003) LTL 30/10/2003). **46.13**

In *UCB Corporate Services Ltd v Halifax (SW) Ltd* [1999] CPLR 691 the claimant had repeatedly failed to comply with court directions and provisions in the rules, and there was an unexplained delay of two years, at which point the defendant made an application to strike out. The claimant was regarded as being guilty of a total disregard of court orders, amounting to an abuse of process. Accordingly, the judge was held to have been entitled to strike out the claim rather than imposing a lesser penalty. Where there has been a history of delay, and several different orders have been breached, there will come a point when the court will say it is right to apply the ultimate sanction of striking out (*Necati v Metropolitan Police Commissioner* (2000) LTL 19/1/2001), or that 'enough is enough' (*Duggan v Wood* [2001] EWCA Civ 1942, LTL 22/11/2001). *Tulsiani v Albin, Hunt and Stein Solicitors* [2001] EWCA Civ 2066, LTL 21/12/2001, was a professional negligence claim against solicitors. The solicitors had been retained in 1983 to defend a claim, with judgment being entered in 1989. The present claim was issued in 1993, and no steps were taken for six years after service of the defence in January 1994. There was further, albeit shorter, delay after the CPR were directed to apply to the claim in April 2000. It was held that the claimant's difficulty in obtaining legal aid did not excuse the delay. Delay of this magnitude of itself indicated an abuse of process; the fair determination of the claim required oral evidence of events leading up to the trial in 1989; and it was held to be plain that the claim should be struck out.

Protracted delay combined with a weak case on the merits may lead the court to conclude it is in accordance with the overriding objective to strike out the claim (*O'Donnell v Charly Holdings Inc.* (2000) LTL 14/3/2000). The court can take into account apparent weakness in the underlying claim even in a case which has survived an application to strike out on the merits or for summary judgment (*Cohort Construction Co. UK Ltd v Melchior* (2000) LTL 20/10/2000).

In *Annodeus Entertainment Ltd v Gibson* (2000) *The Times*, 3 March 2000, Neuberger J stressed the windfall effect of striking out for delay. In *Arrow Nominees Inc. v Blackledge* [2000] 2 BCLC 167 one of the parties admitted falsifying or tampering with a number of material documents. It was held that where a litigant was guilty of conduct that put the fairness of any trial in jeopardy, or which was such as to render further proceedings unsatisfactory and to prevent the court from doing justice, the court was bound to refuse him taking any further part in the proceedings, and, if appropriate, to determine the proceedings against him.

In *Circuit Systems Ltd v Zuken-Redac (UK) Ltd* [2001] BLR 253 a claim issued 11 years previously was struck out. An unless order had been made giving the claimant a final opportunity to plead the case in a form fit to be carried through to trial, after which a reamended statement of case had been served, which was still deficient. Although the claim was assumed to be meritorious, the claimant had failed without adequate explanation to put matters right after having been given a final chance to do so, and the failure meant that a six-week trial had to be adjourned. On the other hand, striking out for failure to give disclosure pursuant to an order not framed as an unless order would be inappropriate (*Johnson v Valks* (2000) LTL 15/3/2000).

Prejudice

In *Axa Insurance Co. Ltd v Swire Fraser Ltd* [2000] CPLR 142, a case where the Court of Appeal held the judge had been wrong to strike out the claim despite a protracted failure to provide further information, it was said that proof of prejudice is not a requirement for an order for **46.14** striking out under **CPR, r. 3.4(2)(c)**. That said, prejudice to the innocent party is clearly an important factor, and where it is present, such as in *Purdy v Cambran* [1999] CPLR 843, where the defendant's expert died in the period of delay, it may offset an argument that striking out would be a disproportionate sanction.

In *Arogundade v Brent London Borough Council* (2000) LTL 16/10/2000 the judge was regarded as acting proportionately in striking out the claim where the claimant was in default of a number of orders to provide a properly pleaded reply and defence to counterclaim, and where the defendant was prejudiced by the default (because of mounting rent arrears). Where there is no prejudice it is correspondingly difficult to justify striking out (*Gaddafi v Telegraph Group Ltd* (2000) LTL 22/8/2000), and accordingly some lesser sanction will usually be imposed.

Fair trial

46.15 It has often been the approach of the courts under the CPR to say that it is unlikely to be consistent with the overriding objective or with the **European Convention on Human Rights, art. 6**, to strike out for delay where it is still possible to have a fair trial. In deciding whether it is still possible to have a fair trial the court should consider the effect of the delay on both the claim and any counterclaim which might extinguish the claim (*Habib Bank Ltd v Abbeypearl Ltd* (2001) LTL 26/1/2001). The right to a fair trial in art. 6 is a right to have a fair hearing within a reasonable time. In this context it is therefore important to note that the defendant, as well as the claimant, has rights under the article (*Circuit Systems Ltd v Zuken-Redac (UK) Ltd* [2001] BLR 253). In *Powell v Boladz* [2003] EWHC 2160 (QB), LTL 22/9/2003, a libel claim was issued in 1995, and was still about a year from trial in 2003. Although it was held that such a trial would not take place within a reasonable time as required by art. 6(1), the delays were not the claimants' fault, and a fair trial was still possible. Balancing the claimants' right to a fair trial with the defendant's right to a trial within a reasonable period, it was held that it would be disproportionate to strike out the claim.

Where striking out is based on delay, what is required is not considerable doubt, but a considerable risk or impossibility of a fair trial taking place (*Taylor v Anderson* [2002] EWCA Civ 1680, [2003] RTR 305). This test was approved by *Fay v Chief Constable of Bedfordshire Police* [2003] EWHC 673 (QB), *The Times*, 13 February 2003. However, Davies J said that the *Taylor v Anderson* test, although highly relevant, is not the only consideration. The *Taylor v Anderson* test does not apply in application for relief from sanctions (see **46.31**; *Hansom v E. Rex Makin* [2003] EWCA Civ 1801, LTL 18/12/2003). An order striking out a claim was overturned on appeal in *Asiansky Television plc v Bayer-Rosin* [2001] EWCA Civ 1792, [2002] CPLR 111. Breach of an order to set down for trial was not, in the context of the claim, so serious as to justify striking out, and the case could still be fairly tried. Where a claim has gone stale, with no sufficient explanation for the delay and a real risk that any trial will not be truly fair, it is appropriate to strike it out (*Rio Guadalete SA v Hopwood* [2001] EWCA Civ 445, LTL 27/3/2001).

In *Beegum v Yousaf* [2002] EWCA Civ 60, LTL 23/1/2002, a claim for the rescission of a transfer of property, the outcome turned on the recollection of witnesses. This, combined with delays and the rejection of the claimant's explanation, meant that striking out the claim was not disproportionate. In *Al Chalabi v Kentucky Fried Chicken (Great Britain) Ltd* (2001) LTL 14/12/2001 Keith J said that it is possible to take the argument of the unreliability of witnesses too far. The passage of time always affects a person's memory. This was a claim alleging misstatement and/or breach of warranty concerning the profitability of a business, so most the evidence was documented. Consequently the claim was not dismissed despite delays. The death of the claimant during a period of delay was regarded as not affecting the fair trial of the claim so far as the defendant was concerned in *Anyiam-Osigwe v Gillam* (2001) LTL 13/7/2001. Any prejudice affected the claimant.

LESSER SANCTIONS

Striking out part of a statement of case

For example, a party may be in default of an order to provide further information on a single issue in a case where several issues are raised. A suitable sanction in such circumstances may be striking out the part of the statement of case dealing with that issue (see *QPS Consultants Ltd v Kruge Tissue (Manufacturing) Ltd* [1999] BLR 366). 46.16

Payment of costs

The normal costs order on a successful application to set aside a judgment entered in default of an unless order (see **46.26**) is that the claimant pay the defendant's costs, including the costs of and occasioned by the application to set aside. Orders requiring a defaulting party to pay the costs of the proceedings to date as a sanction involve a substantial risk of impairing that party's right of access to the courts. A reasonably lenient approach to this type of order should be adopted, at least in cases which have not reached the appeal stage (*Ford v Labrador* [2003] UKPC 41, [2003] 1 WLR 2082). Nevertheless, an order depriving the claimant of all her costs to date, and providing that the claimant would pay certain defence costs in any event, was made as an alternative to striking out in *Parnall v Hurst* [2003] EWHC 2164 (Ch), *The Times*, 10 July 2003. A mere failure to comply with an unless order is not enough to justify an order requiring the defaulting party to pay all the other side's costs (*Gore v Jones* (2000) *The Times*, 21 February 2001). Adverse costs orders covering all or part of the costs of the claim to date are not uncommon orders where the court allows a late amendment of a statement of case if the amendment makes a fundamental change to the nature of the case being advanced (*Beoco Ltd v Alfa Laval Co. Ltd* [1995] QB 137). However, the court will almost certainly impose a costs sanction, covering the costs of the application, on the defaulting party, even if it successfully opposes a striking-out application, because default is seen as bringing such applications on the defaulting party's own head (*Axa Insurance Co. Ltd v Swire Fraser Ltd* [2000] CPLR 142). 46.17

A sanction limited to indemnity costs was imposed despite protracted delay in *Royal Bank Invoice Finance Ltd v Bird* (2001) LTL 19/2/2001, because striking out or discharging a freezing injunction (the other options) were regarded as too draconian and unjust.

Paying security

In *Mealey Horgan plc v Horgan* (1999) *The Times*, 6 July 1999, the defendant served his witness statements two weeks late. The claimants sought an order requiring the defendant to pay a sum into court as a sanction for late service. Buckley J refused the order and said a sanction of that nature would be appropriate only in cases of repeated breach of timetables, or where the defaulting party's conduct gave rise to suspicion that it was not acting in good faith. 46.18

A striking-out order was set aside in *Grundy v Naqvi* (2001) LTL 1/2/2001 on the ground that this was a disproportionate response to a failure to comply with an order to disclose witness statements. The defaulting party had some reason for not having complied (in that she wanted to amend her statement of case, which would have impacted the content of the witness statements), albeit she was also guilty of delay in seeking permission to amend. An order was made requiring the defaulting party to pay £50,000 into court.

Ordering security for costs

In *Olatawura v Abiloye* [2002] EWCA Civ 998, [2003] 1 WLR 275, factors to be taken into account when making an order tantamount to security for costs as a sanction were said to include: 46.19

(a) the ability of the respondent to pay;
(b) the respondent's conduct, including compliance with orders and pre-action protocols; and
(c) the apparent strength of the claim or defence (this is only to be taken into account where

the defaulting party's case has no real prospect of success: *Ali v Hudson* [2003] EWCA Civ 1793, LTL 11/12/2003).

The court must be sensitive to the risk that it might be denying the respondent access to the court when making such an order (*Olatawura v Abiloye*). An order should not ordinarily be made unless the defaulting party can be shown to have regularly flouted court procedures or otherwise demonstrated a lack of good faith (*Ali v Hudson*). An order for security for costs was imposed as a sanction for defective performance of an unless order for disclosure of documents in *Carlco Ltd v Chief Constable of Dyfed-Powys Police* [2002] EWCA Civ 1754, LTL 18/11/2002. A distinction was drawn in *CIBC Mellon Trust Co. v Mora Hotel Corporation NV* [2002] EWCA Civ 1688, [2003] 1 All ER 564, between ordering security for costs incurred before the relevant default (which may be hard to justify if there is evidence that the defaulting party cannot afford to pay) and ordering security for the costs of the application, which may well be justifiable. In *Dardana Ltd v Yukos Oil Co.* [2002] EWCA Civ 543, [2002] 1 All ER (Comm) 819, it was held that an order for security for costs was wholly inappropriate when imposed on granting an adjournment at the request of the party obtaining the benefit of the security.

Depriving of interest and related sanctions

46.20 In *Walsh v Misseldine* [2000] CPLR 201 the claimant was guilty of inadequately justified delay of over four years. Liability was not in issue. If the claim had progressed normally it would have been tried in Spring 1995. During the period of delay a revised schedule of special damages was prepared, substantially increasing the special damages claim. The Court of Appeal was able to substitute its own discretion for that of the judge below. It found that it was still possible, in 1999, to have a fair trial of the issues as they stood in 1995, but that it would not be fair to have a trial of the additional issues raised by the increased special damages claim. The Court of Appeal allowed the claim to proceed, but restricted to the issues as they stood in 1995. Stuart-Smith LJ made it clear that there is a real distinction between cases where liability is and is not in dispute. Where liability is admitted, depriving the claimant of interest or requiring the claimant to pay costs which can be set off against the damages award are effective sanctions for delay. They are not necessarily so if the claim turns out to be unsuccessful. A similar decision was reached in *Price v Price* [2003] EWCA Civ 888, [2003] 3 All ER 911, where the court allowed the claim to continue on condition that damages were restricted to the amount that might be substantiated by any medical report written before a stated date.

EXTENSIONS OF TIME

Applying to extend time

46.21 The court has a general power to extend and abridge time (**CPR, r. 3.1(2)(a)**). It also has a general power to impose conditions (**r. 3.1(3)**. A party who will be unable to comply with an order or direction in time (or who is already in breach), and who has not been able to agree an extension with the other side, may make an application asking the court to extend time for compliance. The discretion given to the court under **r. 3.1** is unfettered other than by the general requirement to further the overriding objective. A party who is late in taking a particular step and who has not yet taken it may be treated differently from a party who has been late in taking a step but has rectified the position. The power to extend time may be exercised even where a rule says a step 'must' be taken within a stated period (*USF Ltd v Aqua Technology Hanson NV/SA* (2001) LTL 31/1/2001). The power to extend time in **r. 3.1(2)(a)** is wide enough to enable the court to extend the time for compliance with the provisions of an order previously made by the same court (*Omega Engineering Inc. v Omega SA* [2003] EWHC 1482 (Ch), *The Times*, 29 September 2003).

A two-day extension of time for serving a claim form issued under the Town and Country

Planning Act, 1990, s. 287, and **RSC, ord. 94 in CPR, sch. 1**, was granted under **r. 3.1(2)(a)** in *Corus UK Ltd v Erewash Borough Council* [2005] EWHC 2821 (Admin), [2005] NPC 145. While delay was firmly discouraged, the court's function is to ensure public bodies acted lawfully, and the public were not to be artificially deprived of the opportunity of mounting a challenge to a public act. It is wrong to use the **r. 3.1(2)(a)** power to extend time for the purpose of nullifying the effect of a mandatory provision in the CPR (*Walker Residential Ltd v Davis* (2005) LTL 9/12/2005, where the Court of Appeal overturned an extension of time for paying into court under **r. 36.10(3)(a)**, the effect of which had been to deprive the claimant of the mandatory costs order provided by **r. 36.13(1)**).

Applying to extend time before time expires

There is a fundamental difference between applying for an extension of time before a time limit has expired, and seeking relief from a sanction after the event (*Robert v Momentum Services Ltd* [2003] EWCA Civ 299, [2003] 1 WLR 1577). In simple time applications under **CPR, r. 3.1**, the court applies the overriding objective, with the principal consideration being whether there is any prejudice caused to the other side through the delay in taking the step in question. The court is not required to consider the checklist of factors set out in **r. 3.9**. **46.22**

An application made very close to the trial may be refused where its effect would be unfair on the other party (*Calenti v North Middlesex NHS Trust* (2001) LTL 10/4/2001).

An extension of time was allowed in *Glauser International SA v Khan* [2002] EWCA Civ 368, [2002] BLR 224, as there was no prejudice, and striking out was wholly disproportionate given the extension was very short and there had been no unless order. In *Becker v Baileys Shaw and Gillett* (1999) LTL 4/11/1999 a decision to refuse to extend time for complying with an unless order to supply particulars of loss was described as 'plainly wrong'. Part of the reasoning was that the particulars were complex and required the evidence of a forensic accountant experienced in Lloyd's claims.

Extending time for compliance with an unless order

Where a party seeks an extension of time for complying with an unless order before the time for complying has elapsed, the list of factors laid down by **CPR, r. 3.9**, for relief from sanctions (see **46.31**) is a convenient list of the factors that should be considered in deciding whether to grant an extension (*Keith v CPM Field Marketing Ltd* (2000) *The Times*, 29 August 2000; *Circuit Systems Ltd v Zuken-Redac (UK) Ltd* [2001] BLR 253 at [42]; *Price v Price* [2003] EWCA Civ 888, [2003] 3 All ER 911). **46.23**

Where the parties have agreed an unless order by consent, with a sanction to take effect in default, the court retains a power to extend the time for compliance (*Ropac Ltd v Inntrepreneur Pub Co.* (2000) *The Times*, 21 June 2000). However, where there is a clear agreement between the parties, the court will give great weight to the agreement, and would be slow, in the absence of special circumstances, to depart from the parties' agreement.

Non-compliance with expert directions

In *Newton v Dorset Travel Service Ltd* (1999) LTL 5/5/99 the defendants had sought additional time for serving their psychiatric evidence in a personal injuries claim, and an unless order had been made to the effect that unless they served their report by Friday, 29 January 1999, they would be debarred from calling psychiatric evidence. There were delays in obtaining their report. The report, once it had been obtained, disclosed a marked disagreement with the claimant's expert evidence. It was sent by fax to the claimant's solicitors first thing on Monday, 1 February. The judge refused the defendants a one-day extension, saying the rules had to be obeyed. The Court of Appeal said that although the defendants' solicitors should have pushed their expert for the report, they had not deliberately flouted the order, the extension sought was minimal, and the need to enforce orders with vigour had to be tempered by proportionality. It was held that an extension should have been granted. *O'Hara v Rye* (1999) **46.24**

LTL 12/2/1999 was a case under the old system, but the judgment of the Court of Appeal makes express reference to the impact of the CPR. The Court of Appeal stressed that when it becomes impossible to adhere to a directions timetable, it is important to disclose all material difficulties to the court so that the court can give directions that are realistic. The Court of Appeal also said that where an unless order gives a bias to a case which is inappropriate, the court is entitled to exercise its discretion by refusing to strike out. In *Great Future International Ltd v Sealand Housing Corporation* (2002) LTL 24/5/2002 the defendants failed to comply with the original timetable for disclosure of expert reports, which was made on 5 March 2002. On 10 May Lightman J ordered that unless the defendants disclosed their reports by 4.00 p.m. on 27 May they would be debarred from defending the hearing, which was listed for the beginning of July 2002. On appeal the defendants explained they were unable to obtain their reports by 27 May, and the Court of Appeal substituted orders that reports be served by dates between 31 May and 6 June, with orders refusing permission to rely on the experts in default.

On the other hand, if a party holds on to a report for some time, and then serves it at the last minute, permission to adduce the report may well be refused. In *Baron v Lovell* [1999] CPLR 630 the defendant obtained a medical report (which did not differ very greatly from that produced for the claimant) in February 1999 which was disclosed in June 1999, on the day of a pre-listing hearing when the trial was fixed for hearing in August 1999. The defendant was in substantial breach of the direction on disclosure of medical evidence. The Court of Appeal held that in the circumstances, particularly the narrow difference between the two sides' medical evidence, the defendant had been correctly refused permission to rely on any medical evidence. Permission to call an additional expert two weeks before trial where the need to call that expert had been identified several months beforehand, and where there was no sufficient explanation for the delay, was refused in *Calenti v North Middlesex NHS Trust* (2001) LTL 10/4/2001. In *Hanley v Stage and Catwalk Ltd* [2001] EWCA Civ 1739, LTL 7/11/2001, it was held that the judge had been justified in granting the defendant permission two weeks before trial to call an expert in a new area of expertise. This was largely because at the same time the claimant was seeking permission to adduce evidence from an expert who had previously reported in the claim, but which was a substantial departure from the earlier report.

It will generally be just to allow a party in a personal injuries claim permission to adduce additional medical evidence to cover further evidence coming to light at a later stage, even after a notional trial date, but before the actual trial, as in *Snowdon v Thurstan Hoskins and Partners* (2002) LTL 19/11/2002.

Expert failing to answer written questions

46.25 Where an expert fails to answer written questions by the time stated in directions (see 52.23), the court may impose sanctions against the party instructing the expert. If there is continued non-compliance, the court may debar a party from relying on the report (**PD 35, annex (Protocol for the Instruction of Experts) para. 16.1**).

Non-compliance with directions on witness statements

46.26 On an application for permission to use a witness statement served out of time, the court will exercise its discretion in accordance with the following principles:

(a) The court's discretion must be exercised in accordance with the overriding objective.

(b) Any sanction imposed, or order made, must be proportionate to the default.

(c) Generally it is contrary to the overriding objective and contrary to the principle of ensuring a fair trial to make an order effectively depriving a party from being able to call any factual witness evidence. In most cases this is tantamount to deciding the case against the defaulting party. This principle is not absolute. There are cases of repeated or deliberate default where an order equivalent to striking out is appropriate (*UCB Corporate*

Services Ltd v Halifax (SW) Ltd [1999] CPLR 691; *Mealey Horgan plc v Horgan* (1999) *The Times*, 6 July 1999).

(d) The period of delay, and the period between disclosure and the start of the trial, are important. Short delays are generally forgiven, as are protracted delays where there is still sufficient time before the start of the trial to ensure the innocent party is not prejudiced by the delay. The court should be very slow before refusing permission to rely on a witness statement served several weeks before trial (*Roberts v Williams* [2005] EWCA Civ 1086, LTL 18/5/2005, where the statements were served six weeks before trial).

(e) The more important the evidence is, the more likely permission will be granted. Permission was refused in *Coore v Chief Constable of Leicestershire* (1999) LTL 10/5/99 where the evidence did not address the essential issue in the case.

(f) Prejudice to the innocent party is an important factor if present. In most cases of delay the innocent party will not have served its witness statements, as most directions require the mutual exchange of statements. Consequently, usually there should be no danger of the defaulting party taking advantage of its own default and 'trimming' the statements of its witnesses.

(g) If the additional evidence will significantly change the basis of the defaulting party's case, permission might be refused, particularly if permission is sought shortly before trial (*British Sugar plc v Cegelec Ltd* [2004] EWCA Civ 1450, LTL 7/10/2004).

(h) Whether the additional evidence comes from a witness who was available to both parties is a factor to be taken into consideration. There is no property in a witness (*Cowland v District Judges of the West London County Court* (1999) LTL 20/7/99), although there are practical and professional conduct problems in obtaining witness statements from employees of, and persons connected with, the other side.

In *Mealey Horgan plc v Horgan* witness statements were served two weeks late and six weeks before the trial. Buckley LJ said that making an order depriving the defaulting party of its evidence was out of proportion to the default. In *I. N. Newman Ltd v Adlem* [2004] EWCA Civ 1492, LTL 16/11/2004, permission was granted to serve witness statements five weeks before the trial, and the innocent party was ordered to pay the costs of the application for permission because it should have consented to the late service. In *Cowland v District Judges of the West London County Court* permission was granted for the use of a witness statement served on the morning of the trial where the witness was available to both sides and where the evidence plainly went to the heart of the issue between the parties. In *Hayes v Transco plc* [2003] EWCA Civ 1261, LTL 17/9/2003, an appeal was allowed partly on the ground that permission to adduce two supplementary witness statements had been wrongfully refused. The judge had refused permission to use the statements, but had granted the other side permission to use documents disclosed late, which was a failure to hold a fair balance between the parties.

Rectifying defective performance

On some occasions a default may arise through the defective performance of the requirements of a rule, practice direction or court order. For example, it may be that the wrong form was used, or that it was sent to the wrong address (but still came to the attention of the other side), or that the document used was not completed correctly. These are errors of procedure. By **CPR, r. 3.10**, such errors do not invalidate the step purportedly taken, unless the court so orders. The court may make an order invalidating a step if it was so badly defective that the other side were misled, or where the defects are so great that it would not be right to regard the purported performance as performance at all. Further, by **r. 3.10(b)** the court may make an order to remedy any error of procedure. A defaulting party should consider seeking such an order where there is an objection made regarding defective performance. An obvious and technical defect in a Part 36 offer was ignored in *Hertsmere Primary Care Trust v Administrators of Balasubramanium's Estate* [2005] EWHC 320 (Ch), [2005] 3 All ER 274 (and it is submitted would have been cured under **r. 3.10**). **46.27**

Where a party purports to serve a claim form within its period of validity, but by an incorrect method, or at an incorrect address, the court has a discretion whether to grant relief under **r. 3.10**, which is exercised in accordance with the overriding objective. On an application for an order remedying such an error in procedure, the court will consider whether the claimant has taken all reasonable steps to put the matter right once the problem was discovered (*Nanglegan v Royal Free Hampstead NHS Trust* [2001] EWCA Civ 127, [2002] 1 WLR 1043, where relief was refused).

An order rectifying an error in procedure was made in *Fawdry and Co. v Murfitt* [2002] EWCA Civ 643, [2003] QB 104, where a judge, without being aware she was not duly authorised, heard a case which had not been properly released to her for trial.

FORM OF ORDER WITH SANCTIONS

46.28 Like all other orders, orders with sanctions must specify the time within which the step under consideration must be taken by reference to a calendar date and a specific time (**CPR, r. 2.9**). The sanction part of the order may take the form of an unless provision. This is to the effect that if the terms of the order are breached, the other party may file a request for judgment to be entered and costs (**r. 3.5**). **PD 40B, para. 8.2**, lays down formulae for drafting unless orders. These are in the following forms (to be adapted as necessary):

(a) 'Unless the claimant serves his list of documents by 4.00 p.m. on Friday, 27 October 2006 his claim will be struck out and judgment entered for the defendant.' This is the preferred form.

(b) 'Unless the claimant serves his list of documents within 14 days of service of this order . . . .' This should be used where the defaulting party did not attend the hearing where the order was made.

NON-COMPLIANCE WITH ORDER IMPOSING A SANCTION

46.29 If a party fails to comply with a rule, practice direction or court order imposing any sanction, the sanction will take effect unless the defaulting party applies for and obtains relief from the sanction (**CPR, r. 3.8**). **Rule 3.8(3)** provides that extensions cannot be agreed between the parties. Where a rule, practice direction or order uses the terms:

- 'shall be struck out or dismissed'; or
- 'will be struck out or dismissed',

the meaning is that the striking out or dismissal takes place automatically, and no further order from the court is necessary (**PD 3, para. 1.9**, inserted with effect from 1 October 2005).

The reasoning in *Langtree Group plc v Richardson* [2004] EWCA Civ 1447, LTL 14/10/2004, fails to give effect to **r. 3.8(1)**, and must be regarded as unsound. An unless order provided that the claim would be struck out if not complied with by a date six weeks before trial. The claimant defaulted. By **r. 3.8(1)** the unless order took effect, there being no application for relief from sanctions, so the defendant was entitled to request the entry of judgment under **r. 3.5** (see **46.28, para. (a)**). Instead, the defendant, who was a litigant in person, tried to get the claimant to comply with the unless order, and rather inconsistently, at trial made an application for the claim to be struck out for breach of the unless order. The Court of Appeal felt that these events, combined with a lack of prejudice to the defendant, justified a refusal to enter judgment. The court also seems to have considered that it was necessary for the innocent defendant to have made an application for the entry of judgment, which is a different concept from making a request, as required by **r. 3.5(2)** on the facts.

Procedure for entering judgment in default of an unless order

Where the court has made an order providing that a statement of case shall be struck out if a party does not comply with the order, **r. 3.5** sets out the procedure for obtaining judgment on non-compliance with the order. A number of different situations are dealt with: **46.30**

(a) Where the party in default is the claimant and the order provides for the striking out of the whole of the particulars of claim, the defendant may enter judgment with costs by filing a request (there is no prescribed form) stating that the right to enter judgment has arisen because the court's order has not been complied with (**r. 3.5(2)(a)** and **(3)**).
(b) Where the party in default is the defendant and the order provides for the striking out of the whole of the defence, and the claim is limited to one of the following forms of relief, namely, a specified sum of money, damages, and/or delivery of goods with the alternative of paying their value, the claimant may enter judgment with costs by filing a request (again there is no prescribed form) stating that the right to enter judgment has arisen because the court's order has not been complied with (**r. 3.5(2)(b) and (3)**).
(c) Where neither (a) nor (b) applies, such as where the order provided for striking out of only part of a statement of case, or where the defendant is in default and the claimant has claimed equitable relief, the party seeking to enter judgment for non-compliance with the order must make an application in accordance with **Part 23** (**r. 3.5(4)**). This means that an application notice must be issued for a hearing on notice. As entering judgment for non-compliance with an order is not strictly an 'interim remedy', **r. 25.3(2)** does not apply and there is no specific requirement for evidence in support. However, particularly where equitable relief is sought, it will often be sensible to provide written evidence in support.

RELIEF FROM SANCTIONS

Principles governing applications for relief

A party in breach of a rule, practice direction or order imposing a sanction for non-compliance may apply for relief from the sanction (**CPR, r. 3.8(1)**). This is done by issuing an application notice, which must be supported by evidence. On such an application, **r. 3.9(1)** provides that the court will consider all the circumstances, and then sets out nine factors which will be considered: **46.31**

(a) the interests of the administration of justice;
(b) whether the application for relief has been made promptly;
(c) whether the failure to comply was intentional;
(d) whether there is a good explanation for the failure;
(e) the extent to which the party in default has complied with other rules, practice directions, court orders and any relevant pre-action protocol;
(f) whether the failure to comply was caused by the party or his legal representative;
(g) whether the trial date or the likely trial date can still be met if relief is granted;
(h) the effect which any failure to comply had on each party; and
(i) the effect which the granting of relief would have on each party.

Full consideration of an application for relief from a sanction involves considering each of the factors listed in **r. 3.9(1)** systematically and then weighing the various factors to decide whether granting relief would accord with the overriding objective. This is particularly necessary in complex cases, see *Bansal v Cheema* (2000) LTL 13/9/2000 (where a failure to do so was held to render the decision open to appeal), *Woodhouse v Consignia plc* [2002] EWCA Civ 275, [2002] 1 WLR 2558, and *RC Residuals Ltd v Linton Fuel Oils Ltd* [2002] EWCA Civ 911, [2002] 1 WLR 2782. On the other hand, in *Jones v Williams* [2002] EWCA Civ 897, LTL 27/5/2002, the Court of Appeal thought that it was sufficient that the judge considered the relevant factors from the list and applied them to the case.

Woodhouse v Consignia plc is authority for saying that it has to be kept in mind that refusing relief deprives the defaulting party of access to the court, which has particular importance given **art. 6(1) of the European Convention on Human Rights**. Similarly, depriving the defaulting party of the ability to call any oral evidence because of late service of witness statements by about two days was regarded as devastating and therefore wrong in *Jones v Williams*. The possibility of having a fair trial is highly important in applications for relief from sanctions, but not to the almost determinative extent in applications for the imposition of sanctions (for which see **46.15**; *Hansom v E. Rex Makin* [2003] EWCA Civ 1801, LTL 18/12/2003).

The factors listed in **r. 3.9(1)** are used generally when the court is exercising a discretion to relieve against provisions having an adverse effect, such as on applications to lift stays imposed for not taking steps (see **54.3**, para (h)) and on applications for extending the time for appealing (see **71.21**). **Rule 3.9(1)** does not apply on an application to be released from, or an extension of time to comply with, an undertaking arrived at by bargaining between the parties (*Di Placito v Slater* [2003] EWCA Civ 1863, [2004] 1 WLR 1605). In such cases 'special circumstances' must be established, such as unintended or unforeseen matters arising (*Eronat v Tabbah* [2002] EWCA Civ 950, LTL 10/7/2002; *Di Placito v Slater*).

Relief and deliberate default

46.32 Relief from an order resulting in judgment being entered for breach of 'unless orders' was refused in *CIBC Mellon Trust Co. v Stolzenberg* [2004] EWCA Civ 827, *The Independent*, 2 July 2004. The court took into account the factors set out in **CPR, r. 3.9**, but was particularly influenced by a finding that there had been deliberate non-compliance with the unless orders. The fact that a fair trial was still possible did not mean that relief had to be granted. Deliberate breach of the time period for serving particulars of claim was the most important factor in refusing relief under r. 3.9 in *Bournemouth and Boscombe Athletic Football Club v Lloyds TSB Bank plc* [2003] EWHC 834 (Ch), LTL 24/4/2003.

In *RC Residuals Ltd v Linton Fuel Oils Ltd* [2002] EWCA Civ 911, [2002] 1 WLR 2782, there had been previous defaults before breach of an 'unless' order relating to expert evidence. It was held that the previous defaults, and an earlier adjournment of the trial date, were weighty factors. Nevertheless relief was given as these factors were offset by the facts that the present default was not intentional and did not affect the parties, the new trial date could still be met, and a full explanation had been given.

No serious prejudice

46.33 Relief was granted in *IBS Technologies (Pvt) Ltd v APM Technologies SA (No. 2)* (2003) LTL 17/4/2003, where the fault in not complying with the full terms of an unless order was that of the solicitors rather than the party, and the default was capable of remedy without serious prejudice to the other party.

In *Woodward v Finch* [1999] CPLR 699 the claimant applied for relief from the consequences of failing to comply with an unless order for service of his witness statements. Proceedings had been issued in April 1994 and there was a history of delay, including a default in serving a schedule of special damages, which was only remedied when the defendant issued an application to strike out. When the claimant failed to serve his witness statements in accordance with directions, the court made an unless order expiring on 29 July 1999. On 2 August 1999 the claimant issued an application for relief from sanction. He explained his delay by pointing to a change in solicitors, and problems in transferring his legal aid certificate. He purported to serve his witness statements the day before his application was heard. The Court of Appeal refused to interfere with the judge's decision to grant relief, despite the history of non-compliance and the fact that the excuse put forward was not a good one. The main reasons were that relief had been applied for promptly; the default was more muddle-headedness than anything else; the trial date could still be met; there was not much effect on either party through the default; and refusing relief would have a devastating effect on the claimant.

No explanation for the delay

46.34 It is common in applications for relief from sanctions for the defaulting party to be unable to point to any adequate reason for the delay. This is sometimes because no reasons are advanced, and sometimes because the 'reasons' suggested on behalf of the defaulting party are regarded as unconvincing or inadequate by the court. At one time, under the old rules, it was held that once it was established that there was no adequate explanation for the delay, there was no material on which the court could be asked to exercise its discretion to allow more time (or relief from sanctions), with the result that the sanction took effect. This rather harsh approach was rejected decisively by the Court of Appeal in *Finnegan v Parkside Health Authority* [1998] 1 WLR 411. In that case it was held that the court considering an application for more time in the absence of any good reason for the delay still had to consider all the circumstances of the case, recognising the overriding principle that justice had to be done, and the absence of a reason was just one of the factors that had to be weighed. The reference to the overriding objective obviously shows the court had the principles of the CPR in mind.

It appears from *Thorn plc v Macdonald* [1999] CPLR 660 that the *Finnegan v Parkside Health Authority* approach continues to be good law even though a stricter attitude is being taken under the CPR (see, for example, *Shikari v Malik* (1999) *The Times*, 20 May 1999). The court should consider all the circumstances in accordance with the overriding objective even if there is no explanation for the delay, but the fact that the delay is unexplained should be a very weighty factor in the exercise of the discretion to grant relief from a sanction (or to extend time).

Improperly obtained unless order

46.35 Where an unless order (see **46.28**) is obtained to enforce an order which was improperly obtained without giving notice to the respondent, the original order and the unless order should be set aside without needing to consider the **CPR, r. 3.9**, factors (*Irwin Mitchell Solicitors v Patel* (2003) LTL 15/4/2003).

PROHIBITION FROM MAKING FURTHER APPLICATIONS

46.36 Where a litigant makes repeated applications of a similar nature, it is sometimes appropriate to make a civil restraint order to the effect that no further applications of a specified type can be made by the named litigant without the permission of a judge (see **14.68** to **14.73**).

SECOND CLAIMS

46.37 Where a claim is struck out for delay, the claimant is entitled to issue fresh proceedings based on the same cause of action, which will not have been determined on its merits. Such a second claim may be met by an application to strike out if the limitation period has expired. Even if the limitation period has not expired, the court has the power to strike out the second claim as an abuse of process if doing so accords with the overriding objective, particularly on the ground that it constitutes a misuse of the court's resources. See *Securum Finance Ltd v Ashton* [2001] Ch 291, where the second claim raised a different cause of action, and was allowed to continue. In *Collins v CPS Fuels Ltd* [2001] EWCA Civ 1597, LTL 9/10/2001, the first claim was struck out for repeated breaches of orders for disclosure of documents, and because the claimant's solicitors failed to attend two case management conferences. A second claim was then issued, making the same allegations. There were no limitation difficulties because the claimant was a child. The judge balanced the prejudice to the claimant in having to sue her solicitors and the possibility of the original allegations being fairly dealt with, against the conduct giving rise to the first claim being struck out and the effect of the delays, and concluded that the second claim should be struck out. This decision was approved on appeal, where it was held that the decision to strike out has to be made by balancing all the competing arguments and reasons. Putting a gloss on this exercise, by saying (as previous authorities have said) that the claimant has to establish 'special reasons', grounds that are 'good enough' or 'sufficient reasons', was regarded as unhelpful.

INORDINATE DELAY

46.38 Under the pre-CPR law, there were three bases on which claims could be struck out for delay:

(a) On the ground of inordinate and inexcusable delay (also known as dismissal for want of prosecution, see *Birkett v James* [1978] AC 297). This was only available against a party in the position of a plaintiff; where there was inordinate and inexcusable delay; which had either given rise to a substantial risk that it would not be possible to have a fair trial, or which was likely to cause, or had caused, serious prejudice to the defendant; and, generally, the limitation period had to have expired.

(b) On the ground of non-compliance with a peremptory order. Guidelines for this type of case were laid down in *Hytec Information Systems Ltd v Coventry City Council* [1997] 1 WLR 1666 and other cases. These included the principle that unless orders were made as a last resort (which is no longer the case under the CPR) and a failure to comply would therefore usually result in the sanction being imposed; that late compliance would only be excused if there were compelling reasons, usually beyond the control of the defaulting party; that a party who deliberately flouted an order would not generally be absolved; that each case was considered on its own merits, with the key consideration being the interests of justice.

(c) On the ground that the delay amounted to an abuse of process (*Grovit v Doctor* [1997] 1 WLR 640; *Arbuthnot Latham Bank Ltd v Trafalgar Holdings Ltd* [1998] 1 WLR 1426). Where the defaulting party's conduct, which could be prolonged inactivity, amounted to an abuse of the court's process the court would be justified in striking out the claim even where the limitation period had not expired and even where the defendant could not point to any prejudice arising from the delay.

The problems under the old law with dealing justly with cases where there had been delay was one of the main motivating factors in introducing the CPR, and it has been hoped that the old principles, and the considerable case law that developed around them, could be consigned to history. These concepts, however, may still have some life on the basis that even in CPR cases they survive as part of the court's inherent jurisdiction (see *Re Abermeadow Ltd* [2000] 2 BCLC 824 at pp. 829 and 830 and **CPR, rr. 3.3(1)** and **3.4(5)**), though whether this is a sound approach is open to question. In *Re Abermeadow Ltd* the court refused on the facts to dismiss a director disqualification claim after eight years' delay, and also refused an argument based on the **European Convention on Human Rights, art. 6(1)**, of not having a hearing within a reasonable time. On the latter point, in *GJ v Luxembourg* [2000] BPIR 1021 it was held that the length of time taken for the purposes of **art. 6(1)** had to be assessed in the light of the particular circumstances of the case, having regard to the complexity of the case and any special features. On the facts, six years for a liquidation breached **art. 6(1)**.

Chapter 47 General Law of Evidence

FACTS OPEN TO PROOF

47.1 The only facts which are open to proof, or disproof, are facts in issue, relevant facts and collateral facts.

Facts in issue

47.2 In a civil trial, the facts in issue are those which the claimant must prove in order to succeed in his claim together with those which the defendant must prove in order to succeed in his defence. The facts in issue in a case are therefore determined partly by reference to the substantive law and partly by reference to what the parties allege, admit, do not admit and deny. They should be identifiable by reference to the statements of case, which should set out the issues on which the parties agree and disagree so that it is known in advance what facts have to be proved or disproved at trial. Under **CPR, r. 16.4(1)**, particulars of claim must include a concise statement of the facts on which the claimant relies, and under **r. 16.5(1)** a defence must state which of the allegations in the particulars of claim are denied or not admitted, and which are admitted, by the defendant. See further, as to the circumstances in which a party shall be taken to require that an allegation be proved or shall be taken to admit an allegation, **r. 16.5(3) to (5)**. However, the CPR make it clear that the court also has a role to play in determining what the facts in issue are in any given case. **Rule 32.1** provides that 'the court may control the evidence by giving directions as to—

(a) the issues on which it requires evidence;
(b) the nature of the evidence which it requires to decide those issues; and
(c) the way in which the evidence is to be placed before the court'.

This provision invests the court with an extraordinarily wide power whereby it can override the views of the parties not only as to the nature of the evidence appropriate to decide the issues in the case, and as to the way in which the evidence should be given, for example, in documentary form rather than orally, but also as to the very issues that do or do not call for evidence. Thus if the court is of the opinion, for example, that the parties have misunderstood the substantive law in such a way as to lead them to believe, erroneously, that a certain matter does or does not have to be proved, then it may give appropriate corrective directions.

Relevant facts

47.3 Relevant facts are facts from which the existence or non-existence of a fact in issue may be inferred, and evidence of relevant facts is properly described as 'circumstantial evidence'. Some types of circumstantial evidence arise so often that they are referred to as presumptions of fact (see further, **47.21 to 47.23**). Typical examples of circumstantial evidence include evidence of motive to do a particular act, evidence of plans or other preparations for the performance of a particular act, evidence of opportunity, or lack of it, evidence of identity and evidence of lies. Two final examples relate to the failure to give evidence or call witnesses, and standards of comparison. Where one party fails to give evidence or call witnesses, the court may be justified in drawing all reasonable inferences from the evidence given by an opponent of the facts which the first party chose to withhold (per Lord Diplock in *British Railways Board v Herrington* [1972] AC 877 at p. 930). Where it is necessary to decide whether a person's conduct meets some objective standard, evidence of what others would do in the same circumstances is admissible to show what that standard is. See, for example, *Chapman v Walton* (1833) 10 Bing 57, where for the purpose of deciding whether a broker had exercised a reasonable degree of care, skill and judgment in the performance of his duties, evidence was received from other brokers as to what they would have done in the same circumstances. See also *Noble v Kennoway* (1780) 2 Doug KB 510, which concerned the practice of delaying the discharge of a ship's cargo, and *Fleet v Murton* (1871) LR 7 QB 126.

Collateral facts

Collateral facts are of three kinds. The first kind affects the credibility of witnesses, for example, the fact that a witness is biased towards one of the parties or has made a previous inconsistent statement. The second type of collateral fact, often referred to as a preliminary fact, is a fact which must be proved as a condition precedent to the admissibility of an item of evidence. For example, under the Bankers' Books Evidence Act 1879, s. 4, a copy of an entry in a banker's book is only admissible under s. 3 of the Act if it is proved, *inter alia*, that the book was at the time of the making of the entry one of the ordinary books of the bank. See further at 47.77. The third kind of collateral fact affects the competence of witnesses, for example, the fact that a potential expert witness is properly qualified in the subject calling for expertise. 47.4

RELEVANCE, ADMISSIBILITY AND THE DISCRETION TO EXCLUDE

The two governing principles underlying the English law of evidence are that: 47.5

(a) evidence must be sufficiently relevant in order to be admissible, but
(b) such evidence will only be admissible in so far as it is not excluded by the court either by virtue of a rule of law or in the exercise of its discretion.

However, there is no principle of law or practice which dictates that a judge cannot read or hear material that is actually or potentially inadmissible, especially if he or she is a judge of both law and fact (*Barings plc v Coopers and Lybrand* [2001] EWCA Civ 1163, [2001] CPLR 451). In that case, in which the judge, before the trial, was proposing to read background documentation by way of preparation for what was bound to be a long and complex case, it was held that there was no danger of his being so influenced by what he read that he would not decide the case only on the basis of the admissible evidence.

In general, disputes about the admissibility of evidence in civil proceedings are best resolved by the judge at the substantive hearing of an application or at the trial of a claim, rather than at a separate preliminary hearing, because the judge at a preliminary hearing will usually be less well informed about the case and preliminary hearings can cause unnecessary costs and delays (*Stroude v Beazer Homes Ltd* [2005] EWCA Civ 265, [2005] NPC 45).

The exclusionary rules of evidence, for example, the rules relating to opinion evidence and legal professional privilege, are covered elsewhere in this work. The following paragraphs consider relevance and discretionary exclusion.

Relevance

47.6 The word 'relevance' means that 'any two facts to which it is applied are so related to each other that according to the common course of events one either taken by itself or in connection with other facts proves or renders probable the past, present or future existence or non-existence of the other' (Stephen, *Digest of the Law of Evidence*, 12th ed., art. 1). Whether evidence is relevant is often a question of degree and determined not by strict logic but by common sense and experience.

Sometimes, evidence is plainly irrelevant. *Holcombe v Hewson* (1810) 2 Camp 391 concerned an alleged breach of covenant by the defendant, a publican, to buy his beer from the claimant, a brewer. The defence was that the claimant had previously supplied bad beer. Evidence purporting to rebut this, that the claimant had supplied other publicans with good beer, was held to be inadmissible because irrelevant: the issue was the quality of the beer supplied to the defendant, not the quality of different beer supplied to others. Similarly, in *Hollingham v Head* (1858) 27 LJ CP 241, where the defendant sought to establish that a contract was made on certain special terms, evidence that the claimant had entered into contracts with other customers on similar terms was held to be inadmissible because irrelevant: it afforded no reasonable inference as to the terms of the contract in question.

In other cases, relevance will be a question of degree. For example, evidence that after an accident the working practices of a defendant to a negligence action were altered and improved will not necessarily be relevant to the issue whether the accident was caused by negligence (see *Hart v Lancashire and Yorkshire Railway Co.* (1869) 21 LT 261). Conversely, in *Great Future International Ltd v Sealand Housing Corporation* (2002) LTL 25/7/2002 evidence of an attempt by an employee (who was not called as a witness) of one of the claimants to persuade an expert retained for one of the defendants not to testify was held to be relevant to the question of mitigation of damage. In some cases evidence will be excluded because although it is undoubtedly of *some* relevance to the issues, it will give rise to a number of subsidiary issues which might well distract the court from the main issue. This may involve the court in a protracted investigation (see *Attorney-General v Hitchcock* (1847) 1 Ex 91 at p. 105) or a difficult controversy of the same kind as that which it has to decide (see *Metropolitan Asylum District Managers v Hill* (1882) 47 LT 29). A good illustration is *Agassiz v London Tramway Co.* (1872) 21 WR 199, in which a passenger in an omnibus claimed damages for personal injuries suffered as a result of a collision alleged to have been caused by the negligence of the driver. After the accident another passenger had suggested to the conductor that the driver's conduct should be reported, to which the conductor had replied that the driver had been reported because he had been off the points five or six times that day. This evidence was held to have been properly excluded on the basis that it did not relate to the conduct of the driver at the relevant time and did not explain the cause of the collision, but gave rise to a multiplicity of side issues.

Discretion to exclude

47.7 Prior to the introduction of the CPR, a judge in a civil case had no discretion to exclude evidence admissible as a matter of law, and that principle applied even if the evidence in question had been obtained improperly or unlawfully (see per Lord Denning MR in *Helliwell v Piggott-Sims* [1980] FSR 582). On one view, there was an exception to this general rule whereby a judge could permit a witness, whether a party to the proceedings or not, to refuse to disclose information, typically information given and received under the seal of confidence, where disclosure would be a breach of some ethical or social value and non-disclosure would be unlikely to result in serious injustice in the case in which it was being claimed: see 16th Report of the Law Reform Committee, *Privilege in Civil Proceedings* (1967) Cmnd 3472, para. 1, and per Lords Hailsham of St Marylebone and Kilbrandon in *D v National Society for the Prevention of Cruelty to Children* [1978] AC 171. In that case, however, both Lord Simon of Glaisdale and Lord Edmund-Davies doubted the existence of such a wide discretionary power. Lord Simon was of the view that the judge can exercise a considerable moral authority on the course of a trial, and is therefore entitled to say to counsel, for example: 'You see that the witness feels that he ought not in conscience to answer that question. Do you really press it in the circumstances? ' However, Lord Simon was also of the view that this was far from the exercise of a formal discretion, and said that, 'if it comes to the forensic crunch . . . it must be law not discretion which is in command'.

Rule 32.1(2) of the CPR has introduced an exclusionary discretion of general application in civil cases, including claims allocated to the small claims track (see **CPR, r. 27.2(1)**). Under **r. 32.1(1)** the court may control the evidence by giving directions as to the issues on which it requires evidence, the nature of the evidence which it requires to decide those issues, and the way in which the evidence is to be placed before the court. **Rule 32.1(2)** provides that 'the court may use its power under this rule to exclude evidence that would otherwise be admissible' and **r. 32.1(3)** states that 'the court may limit cross-examination'. In exercising its powers under either **r. 32.1(2) or r. 32.1(3)**, the court must seek to give effect to the 'overriding objective' of the rules, to enable the court 'to deal with cases justly' (**r. 1.1**). The power conferred by **r. 32.1(2)** is extremely wide. Subject to **r. 1.1**, there are no express limitations as to the manner and extent of the exercise of the power (*Grobbelaar v Sun Newspapers Ltd* (1999) *The Times*, 12 August 1999). The court has always had the power to rule evidence inadmissible if it is of no more than marginal relevance (see **47.6**). **Rule 32.1(2)**, however, goes further: the court may exclude any type of otherwise admissible evidence, even if plainly relevant, although obviously the more relevant it is, the more reluctant the courtest is likely to be to exercise its power to exclude it. This was emphasised in *Great Future International Ltd v Sealand Housing Corporation* (2002) LTL 25/7/2002, where it was said that the power under **r. 32.1(2)** has to be exercised with great circumspection. In *Post Office Counters Ltd v Mahida* [2003] EWCA Civ 1583, *The Times*, 31 October 2003, Hale LJ said, at [24], that the power to exclude admissible evidence under **r. 32.1(2)** is principally a case management power designed to allow the court to stop cases getting out of hand. This means the rule may be used by the court when managing cases with the aim of minimising the burden on litigants of slender means by excluding all peripheral material which is not essential to the just determination of the real issues between the parties and whose examination would be disproportionate to its importance to those issues (*McPhilemy v Times Newspapers Ltd* [1999] 3 All ER 775 per May LJ at p. 791). As to the exclusion of expert evidence by reason of non-compliance with **PD 35**, see *Stevens v Gullis* [2000] 1 All ER 527.

The court may also use **r. 32.1(2)** to restrict the number of witnesses to be called, and to exclude any evidence thought to be superfluous.

In appropriate circumstances, the court may properly take the view that in order to give effect to the 'overriding objective' it should also exercise the discretion in **r. 32.1(2)** to exclude evidence that has been obtained illegally (for example, by a crime, tort or breach of contract or statute), improperly (for example, by trickery, deception, bribes, threats or inducements) or in breach of the right to respect for private and family life in the **European Convention on Human Rights, art. 8** (for example, by covertly video-recording employees or claimants in personal injuries litigation). In *Jones v University of Warwick* [2003] EWCA Civ 151, [2003] 1 WLR 954, the defendant was allowed to use as evidence a video of the claimant obtained in breach of art. 8 and by trespass, inquiry agents acting for the defendant's insurers having filmed the claimant without her knowledge after having gained access to her home by deception. Lord Woolf CJ held that the court had to consider two competing public interests: that in litigation the truth should be revealed and that the courts should not acquiesce in or encourage a party to use unlawful means to obtain evidence. Thus the judge's responsibility requires him, when exercising his discretion in accordance with the overriding objective, to consider not only the litigation before the court but also the effect of his decision on litigation generally. The weight to be attached to the two competing interests will vary according to the circumstances. The significance of the evidence will differ as will the gravity of the breach of art. 8. On the facts, it was held that it was not a case where the conduct of the insurers was so outrageous that the defence should be struck out and that it would be artificial and undesirable for the evidence to be excluded, which would have required the instruction of fresh medical experts. However, it was also stressed that the conduct of the insurers was improper and unjustified and that the trial judge should take it into account when deciding the appropriate order for costs. See also *Niemietz v Germany* (1992) 16 EHRR 97 and *Halford v United Kingdom* (1997) 24 EHRR 523.

Rule 32.1(3) may be used by the court to impose limits on the time permitted for cross-examination of witnesses at trial (see, for example, *Rall v Hume* [2001] 3 All ER 248). This supplements the pre-existing discretionary powers of the judge to prevent questions in cross-examination which, in his or her opinion, are unnecessary, improper or oppressive. At common law, cross-examination should be conducted with restraint and with a measure of courtesy and consideration to the witness (see per Sankey LC in *Mechanical and General Inventions Co. Ltd v Austin* [1935] AC 346 at p. 360; and the Code of Conduct of the Bar of England and Wales (2000), sect. 1, para. 708 and sect. 3, paras 5.10 and 5.11). Counsel should be restrained from embarking on lengthy cross-examination on matters that are not really in issue (*Mechanical and General Inventions Co. Ltd v Austin* at p. 359) or from framing questions in such a way as to invite argument rather than elicit evidence on the facts in issue (per Lord Hewart CJ in *R v Baldwin* (1925) 18 Cr App R 175).

In order to call into question a witness's credibility, the witness may be asked about his or her conviction for any offence, even if it is not one of dishonesty (see **47.65**), but the court may exercise its discretion under **CPR, r. 32.1(3)**, to limit such cross-examination to convictions for offences involving dishonesty. However, a judge sitting without a jury should be more hesitant to exclude otherwise relevant evidence and cross-examination, because a judge does not need to be protected from giving undue weight to evidence relating to a witness's credibility (*Watson v Chief Constable of Cleveland Police* [2001] EWCA Civ 1547, LTL 12/10/2001).

Circumstances vary infinitely, and for this reason it is submitted that it will normally be unnecessary and undesirable for the courts to provide general guidance, additional to that to be found in the inclusionary definition of 'dealing with a case justly' in **r. 1.1(2)**, on the way in which the discretionary powers under **r. 32.1(2) and (3)** should be exercised. For the same reason the exercise of these discretionary powers should only be open to appeal on the limited grounds discussed in **72.9**).

FORMAL ADMISSIONS

47.8 A fact which is formally admitted ceases to be in issue. Evidence of such a fact, being unnecessary, is inadmissible. Legal advisers owe a duty to their clients to consider whether any formal admissions can properly be made. Formal admissions should be made by a party in the case of facts as to which there is no serious dispute, thereby saving the other party to the case the unnecessary trouble and expense of proving them. A party may admit the truth of the whole or any part of another party's case (**CPR, r. 14.1(1)**), although once an admission has been made, the court may allow a party to amend or withdraw it (**r. 14.1(5)**). A fact may be formally admitted in a variety of ways: by a defendant, in his or her defence, expressly (**r. 16.5(1)(c)**) or by default, i.e., by failing to deal with an allegation (**r. 16.5(5)**), and by either party in response to a notice to admit facts (**r. 32.18**) or in response to a written request, or court order, to give additional information (see **rr. 18.1** and **26.5(3)** and **PD 18**). Prior to the trial, a formal admission may also be made by a letter written by a legal adviser acting on behalf of a party (*Ellis v Allen* [1914] 1 Ch 904). According to **CPR, r. 14.1(2)**, a party may make an admission 'by giving notice in writing (such as in a statement of case or by letter)'.

However, it would seem that it remains possible for a formal admission to be made by a party or a party's legal adviser orally, either at the trial itself (see *Urquhart v Butterfield* (1887) 37 ChD 357) or in interim proceedings, in which case the admission may subsequently be withdrawn, provided that the other party has not acted on it so as to give rise to an estoppel (*H. Clark (Doncaster) Ltd v Wilkinson* [1965] Ch 694).

PRESUMPTIONS

Introduction

There are numerous common law, equitable and statutory presumptions. The following paragraphs deal with some of the most important of them. The presumption of legal origin and the equitable presumptions of undue influence and advancement are not considered. **47.9**

Rebuttable presumptions of law

Where a rebuttable presumption of law operates, on the proof or admission of basic or primary facts, and in the absence of further evidence, another fact must be presumed. The party relying on the presumption bears the burden of establishing the basic facts, and his adversary bears either an evidential burden to adduce some evidence in rebuttal of the presumed fact or, as the case may be, a legal burden to disprove the presumed fact. A rebuttable presumption which operates to put an evidential burden on the party against whom it operates is referred to as an evidential presumption. If the party relying on an evidential presumption proves the basic facts, the presumed fact will be treated as having been established unless his opponent adduces some evidence in rebuttal, but where the opponent discharges the evidential burden in the usual way (see 47.35) the effect will be as if the presumption had never come into play at all: the party relying on the presumption bears the legal burden to prove on a balance of probabilities the fact that otherwise could have been presumed. It follows from this, of course, that if at the end of the day, on all the evidence before the court, the probability of the existence of the presumed fact is equal to the probability of its non-existence, the opponent will succeed. A rebuttable presumption which operates to put a legal burden on the party against whom it operates is referred to as a 'persuasive' or 'compelling' presumption. If a party relying on a persuasive presumption proves the basic facts, a legal burden is placed on the opponent to disprove the presumed fact. The opponent will therefore lose on the issue not only by adducing no evidence to disprove the presumed fact, but also where on all the evidence before the court the probability of the existence of the presumed fact is equal to the probability of its non-existence. **47.10**

Some rebuttable presumptions, such as the presumption of mental capacity, operate without the proof or admission of basic facts, and in truth, therefore, are nothing more than rules relating to the incidence of the burden of proof that have been cast in the language pertaining to presumptions.

Presumption of marriage There appear to be three types of presumption of marriage, a presumption of formal validity, a presumption of essential validity, and a presumption of marriage arising from cohabitation. They are considered here in outline only. (For a fuller treatment, see Keane, *The Modern Law of Evidence*, 5th ed. (2000) at pp. 639ff.) **47.11**

The formal validity of a marriage depends upon the *lex loci celebrationis*. Under English law, for example, there are formal requirements, in the case of a Church of England marriage, to publish banns and to obtain a common licence, and in the case of other marriages to give due notice to the superintendent registrar. Under the presumption of the formal validity of a marriage, on the proof or admission of the basic facts that a marriage was celebrated between persons who intended to marry, the formal validity of the marriage will be presumed in the absence of sufficient evidence to the contrary. The presumption is a persuasive presumption.

The leading authority relating to an English marriage is *Piers v Piers* (1849) 2 HL Cas 331, where a marriage performed in a private house was held to be formally valid despite the absence of evidence that the bishop of the diocese had granted the necessary special licence. For an example of the application of the presumption to a foreign marriage, see *Mahadervan v Mahadervan* [1964] P 233. It has been said that the standard of proof to be met by the party with the legal burden of disproving formal validity is high (see *Piers v Piers*), but it is submitted that under the modern law there is little likelihood of the courts applying the decision in *Mahadervan v Mahadervan*, where Sir Jocelyn Simon P held that the presumption can only be rebutted by evidence which satisfies beyond reasonable doubt that there was no valid marriage (see further at **47.40** to **47.43**).

Under the presumption of the essential validity of a marriage, on proof or admission of the basic facts that a formally valid marriage was celebrated, in the absence of sufficient evidence to the contrary, the essential validity of the marriage will be presumed, i.e., it will be presumed that the parties had the capacity to marry, and therefore, under English law, for example, were not related within the prohibited degrees, were aged 16 or over and were not already married (see *Tweney v Tweney* [1946] P 180). The presumption is probably a persuasive presumption. Evidence of a valid prior marriage will suffice to rebut the presumption (*Gatty v Attorney-General* [1951] P 444; *Re Peete* [1952] 2 All ER 599), but not where the prior marriage is itself of doubtful validity (*Taylor v Taylor* [1967] P 25).

Under the persuasive presumption of marriage arising from cohabitation, on proof or admission of the basic fact that a man and woman have cohabited as if man and wife, it is presumed, in the absence of sufficient evidence to the contrary, that they were living together in consequence of a valid marriage (see *Sastry Velaider Aronegary v Sembecutty Vaigalie* (1881) 6 App Cas 364). The presumption applies even in the absence of evidence that a marriage ceremony has taken place (see *Re Taplin* [1937] 3 All ER 105 and *Re Taylor* [1961] 1 WLR 9). Evidence in rebuttal is required to meet a high standard (see *Re Taplin* and *Re Taylor*).

47.12 **Presumption of legitimacy** Under the persuasive presumption of legitimacy, on proof or admission of the basic fact that a child was born or conceived during lawful wedlock, it is presumed, in the absence of sufficient evidence to the contrary, that the child is legitimate. The presumption applies where there is a maintenance order in force against the husband, unless it contains a non-cohabitation clause (*Bowen v Norman* [1938] 1 KB 689), where proceedings for divorce or nullity have commenced (*Knowles v Knowles* [1962] P 161) and where the parties are living apart, whether or not under a separation agreement (*Ettenfield v Ettenfield* [1940] P 96). The presumption does not apply where a decree of judicial separation or a magistrate's separation order is in force (see *Hetherington v Hetherington* (1887) 12 PD 112).

The presumption applies both where a child is born so soon after a marriage ceremony that premarital conception is indicated (*Poulett Peerage Case* [1903] AC 395) and where a child is born so soon after the mother's termination of her marriage that conception during the marriage is indicated (*Maturin v Attorney-General* [1938] 2 All ER 214; *Re Heath* [1945] Ch 417). In *Re Overbury* [1955] Ch 122, six months after her first husband's death, a woman remarried, and two months later gave birth to a girl. It was held that the child was the legitimate daughter of the first husband, there being insufficient evidence to rebut the presumption.

The standard of proof to be met by the party seeking to rebut the presumption is governed by the Family Law Reform Act 1969, s. 26. It provides as follows:

> Any presumption of law as to the legitimacy or illegitimacy of any person may in any civil proceedings be rebutted by evidence which shows that it is more probable than not that the person is illegitimate or legitimate as the case may be and it shall not be necessary to prove that fact beyond reasonable doubt in order to rebut the presumption.

Thus even weak evidence against legitimacy must prevail if there is no other evidence to counterbalance it, but where the evidence is such that legitimacy is as probable as illegitimacy, the party seeking to rebut the presumption will fail (see *S v S* [1972] AC 24 at p. 41, applied in *T (HH) v T (E)* [1971] 1 WLR 429).

The presumption of legitimacy may be rebutted by evidence that the husband and wife did not have sexual intercourse as a result of which the child was conceived (*Banbury Peerage Case* (1811) 1 Sim & St 153), evidence of the husband's impotence (*Legge v Edmonds* (1855) 25 LJ Ch 125), an admission of paternity by another man (*R v King's Lynn Justices, ex parte M* [1988] 2 FLR 79), evidence of the wife's cohabitation with another man for an appropriate period of time before the birth of the child (*Re Jenion* [1952] Ch 454), evidence of a DNA test excluding the husband as the father, coupled with evidence of the putative father's refusal to comply with an order for a blood test (*F v Child Support Agency* [1999] 2 FLR 244) or evidence of the conduct of the wife and illicit partner towards the child (*Kanapathipillai v Parpathy* [1956] AC 580). The inference of paternity to be drawn from a refusal to undergo DNA testing outweighs the presumption of legitimacy (*Secretary of State for Work and Pensions v Jones* (2003) *The Times*, 13 August 2003). Evidence in rebuttal may also take the form of evidence of non-access or the use of reliable contraceptives. Evidence of adultery on the part of the mother will not rebut the presumption unless accompanied by evidence that at the time of conception sexual intercourse between the husband and wife did not take place (*Gordon v Gordon* [1903] P 141).

Presumption of death Under the presumption of death, if there is no acceptable affirmative evidence that a person was alive at some time during a continuous period of seven years or more, on the proof or admission of the basic facts that: **47.13**

(a) there are persons who would be likely to have heard of him or her over that period,
(b) those persons have not heard of him or her, and
(c) all due enquiries have been made appropriate to the circumstances,

that person will be presumed to have died at some time within that period (per Sachs J in *Chard v Chard* [1956] P 259 at p. 272). The decision of the House of Lords in *Prudential Assurance Co. v Edmonds* (1877) 2 App Cas 487 suggests that this is an evidential presumption rebuttable by adducing sufficient evidence to raise the possibility of the existence of the absent person. As to the first of the basic facts, friends and relatives will not be treated as persons likely to have heard of the absent person where there are reasons which might have led the latter not to wish to be heard of by the former (see *Chard v Chard*) or where it is shown that the latter did not intend the former to hear of him or her (see *Watson v England* (1844) 14 Sim 28 and *Re Lidderdale* (1912) 57 SJ 3).

The authorities conflict on whether (c) above is among the basic facts to be proved or admitted before the presumption can arise (see *Willyams v Scottish Widows' Fund Life Assurance Society* (1888) 4 TLR 489; *Chipchase v Chipchase* [1939] P 391; and *Bradshaw v Bradshaw* [1956] P 274), the explanation for which is probably that in some cases the circumstances are such that it would not be appropriate to make any enquiries at all (see *Bullock v Bullock* [1960] 1 WLR 975).

Under the presumption of death, the court presumes only the fact of a person's death. Thus if it is sought to establish that the deceased died unmarried, childless or without next-of-kin, these additional facts require additional evidence (*Re Jackson* [1907] 2 Ch 354), although less evidence seems to be required than if the presumption had not applied (see *Dunn v Snowden* (1862) 32 LJ Ch 104; *Rawlinson v Miller* (1875) 1 ChD 52; *Greaves v Greenwood* (1877) 2 ExD 289). Additional evidence is also required to prove that the death took place at a particular period (per Giffard LJ in *Re Phené's Trusts* (1870) LR 5 Ch App 139 at p. 144). As to the date on which one may presume the fact of death, the authorities are in conflict. *Re Phené's Trusts* was taken by the Privy Council in *Lal Chand Marwari v Mahant Ramrup Gir* (1925) 42 TLR 159 at p. 160 to be an authority for the proposition that the fact of death is presumed at the date of the proceedings. However, the decisions in *Re Westbrook's Trusts* [1873] WN 167 (criticised in *Re Rhodes* (1887) 36 ChD 586) and *Chipchase v Chipchase* [1939] P 391 are only consistent with the conflicting view that the fact of death may be presumed at the end of the continuous period of absence for seven years.

47.14 **Presumption of regularity** Under this evidential presumption, often expressed in the maxim *omnia praesumuntur rite esse acta* (all acts are presumed to have been duly done), on the proof or admission of the basic fact that a person has acted in a public or official capacity, it is presumed, in the absence of sufficient evidence to the contrary, that the person was regularly and properly appointed and that the act was regularly and properly performed. Those presumed to have been duly appointed have included a police officer (*R v Gordon* (1789) 1 Leach 515), an officer of the Post Office (*R v Borrett* (1833) 6 Car & P 124), a judge (*R v Roberts* (1878) 38 LT 690) and an inspector of the Health and Safety Executive (*Campbell v Wallsend Slipway and Engineering Co. Ltd* [1978] ICR 1015). In *R v Langton* (1876) 2 QBD 296 the presumption was used to establish the due incorporation of a company which had acted as such. In *R v Inland Revenue Commissioners, ex parte T. C. Coombs and Co.* [1991] 2 AC 283 a tax inspector, with the consent of a General Commissioner, had served notice under the Taxes Management Act 1970, s. 20, requiring stockbrokers to deliver documentary information relevant to the tax liability of one of their former employees. It was presumed, in the absence of evidence to the contrary, that both the inspector and the Commissioner had acted within the limits of their authority, with honesty and discretion.

47.15 **Presumption of mental capacity** A party or witness is presumed to have mental capacity until the contrary is proved, the burden of proving the contrary resting on the party asserting incapacity (*Masterman-Lister v Brutton and Co. (Nos. 1 and 2)* [2002] EWCA Civ 1889, [2003] EWCA Civ 70, [2003] 1 WLR 1511). The court as a matter of practice should investigate the question of capacity whenever there is reason to suspect its absence, even if the matter is not in contention. The test is issue specific and depends on the nature and complexity of the transactions involved. The test is whether the person was capable of understanding the issues on which his or her consent or decision was necessary. However, although the decisions made are likely to be important indicators of the existence or lack of understanding, a person is not to be regarded as unable to make any rational decision merely because the decision made would not have been made by a person of ordinary prudence and, conversely, is not to be regarded as having mental capacity merely because his or her decision appears rational. The court must be astute not to accept a plea of incompetence when the evidence does not suggest a lack of competence (*Phillips v Symes* [2004] EWHC 1887 (Ch), LTL 18/8/2004).

47.16 **Presumptions in testamentary cases** Under this evidential presumption, on the proof or admission of the basic fact that a rational will has been duly executed, it is presumed, in the absence of sufficient evidence to the contrary, that the testator was sane. Thus, in *Sutton v Sadler* (1857) 3 CB NS 87, in which the heir-at-law brought an action against the devisee alleging the insanity of the testator, it was held that the devisee bore the legal burden of proving that he was the devisee under a duly executed will; that proof of the due execution of a rational will gave rise to the presumption, placing an evidential burden on the heir-at-law; and that if the heir-at-law had raised sufficient evidence for the issue of sanity to go before the tribunal of fact, that tribunal should find against the devisee unless satisfied that he had discharged the legal burden of proving on a balance of probabilities that the testator was sane.

There is a presumption of due execution on proof that a will contains the signatures of the deceased, two witnesses and an attestation clause. Although this is an evidential presumption, it can only be rebutted by the strongest evidence that the witness did not intend to attest the deceased's signature (*Sherrington v Sherrington* [2005] EWCA Civ 326, *The Times*, 24 March 2005). It is not rebutted merely because the attesting witnesses have no recollection of having signed (*Channon v Perkins* [2005] EWCA Civ 1808, LTL 1/12/2005).

47.17 **Principle of *res ipsa loquitur*** Under the principle of *res ipsa loquitur*, on proof or admission of the basic facts that some thing was under the management of the defendant or his or her employees and an accident occurred, being an accident which in the ordinary course of things does not occur if those who have the management of the thing use proper care, it may or must be presumed, in the absence of sufficient evidence to the contrary, that the accident was caused by the negligence of the defendant (see generally per Sir William Erle CJ in *Scott v London and St Katherine Docks Co.* (1865) 3 Hurl & C 596 at p. 601). This definition reflects the fact that in different cases the principle has been treated in different ways, as a persuasive presumption, as an evidential presumption (see **47.10**), and as a presumption of fact or provisional presumption (see 47.21). In both *Woods v Duncan* [1946] AC 401 at pp. 419, 425 and 439 and *Barkway v South Wales Transport Co. Ltd* [1948] 2 All ER 460 at p. 471, it was treated as a persuasive presumption, shifting the onus of proof onto the defendant to show on the balance of probabilities that he was not negligent. See also per Lords Reid and Donovan in *Henderson v Henry E. Jenkins and Sons* [1970] AC 282. In *The Kite* [1933] P 154, however, it was treated as an evidential presumption, so that if the defendant gives a reasonable explanation for the accident, which is equally consistent with the accident happening without his or her negligence as with it, then the burden of proof is on the claimant to show, as the claimant has to show from the beginning, that it was the negligence of the defendant that caused the accident. See also per Lord Pearson in *Henderson v Henry E. Jenkins and Sons*, per Lawton LJ in *Ward v Tesco Stores Ltd* [1976] 1 WLR 810 and *Ng Chun Pui v Lee Chuen Tat* [1988] RTR 298. Finally, there is authority that the principle of *res ipsa loquitur* is no more than a presumption of fact, so that proof of the basic facts gives rise to an inference of negligence which, in the absence of evidence to the contrary, may but need not be drawn (see per Greer LJ in *Langham v Wellingborough School Governors and Fryer* (1932) 101 LJ KB 513 at p. 518 and per Goddard LJ in *Easson v London and North Eastern Railway Co.* [1944] KB 421). There may be no anomaly in this diversity of approach. As it has been put elsewhere:

> Given that the facts calling for the application of the principle vary enormously from case to case so that in some the inference of negligence is slight, in others all but irresistible, efforts aimed at confining the principle to a single category seem ill-founded. At the risk of uncertainty, classification according to the facts of the case in question seems preferable. If the thing speaks for itself, it may do so with degrees of conviction. The hardship caused to the claimant may be remedied by placing the tactical, evidential or legal burden on the defendant depending on the strength of the basic facts in question. (Keane, *The Modern Law of Evidence*, 5th ed. (2000), at p. 654.)

Presumption that a time clause is not of the essence of a contract The Law of Property Act 1925, s. 41, contains a provision, first enacted in 1873, which fuses the common law and equitable rules on time in contracts. The effect is that, subject to three exceptions, a stipulation as to time in a contract (a time clause) is not deemed to be of the essence of the contract, and consequently it cannot be asserted that breach of such a stipulation repudiates the contract. The exceptions are: **47.18**

(a) where the contract expressly states that time of performance is of the essence of the contract or must be strictly complied with;
(b) where the circumstances of the contract or its subject matter indicate that stipulations as to time must be strictly complied with; and
(c) where one party is guilty of undue delay and the innocent party gives notice that performance is required within a reasonable time.

There is a rebuttable presumption that stipulations as to time in rent review clauses are not of the essence of the contract (*United Scientific Holdings Ltd v Burnley Borough Council* [1978] AC 904). This presumption was rebutted in *Starmark Enterprises Ltd v CPL Distribution Ltd* [2001] EWCA Civ 1252, [2002] Ch 306, by a clause which stated that the tenant 'shall be deemed' to have agreed to an increased rent on failing to serve a counter-notice within one month of receipt of the rent notice. For a general discussion of when time is of the essence see *Re Gray* [2004] EWHC 1538 (Ch), [2005] 1 WLR 815.

Presumption that a fraudulent representation induced a contract On proof of a fraudulent representation of such a nature that it would be likely to have affected a reasonable person, it will be presumed that the representation induced the claimant to enter into the contract, unless the representor satisfies the court to the contrary. In *County NatWest Ltd v Barton* [2002] **47.19**

4 All ER 494 it was held that the presumption alters the burden of proof, that the alteration remains unless and until the presumption is rebutted, and that the presumption continues to apply even if the representee gives evidence at the trial.

Irrebuttable presumptions of law

47.20 On the operation of an irrebuttable or conclusive presumption of law, on the proof or admission of basic or primary facts, another fact must be presumed and the party against whom the presumption operates is barred from adducing any evidence in rebuttal. For an example, see the Civil Evidence Act 1968, s. 13(1) (considered at **47.94**)

Presumptions of fact

47.21 On the operation of a presumption of fact, sometimes referred to as a provisional presumption, on the proof or admission of basic or primary facts, another fact may be presumed in the absence of sufficient evidence to the contrary, so that the party against whom the presumption operates bears a provisional or tactical burden in relation to the fact which may be presumed, not an evidential or legal burden. Presumptions of fact, therefore, are simply examples of circumstantial evidence, i.e., relevant facts, facts from which the existence or non-existence of a fact in issue may be inferred. In civil proceedings the only important examples of circumstantial evidence which have recurred so frequently as to be referred to as presumptions of fact are the presumption of continuance of life and the presumption of seaworthiness.

47.22 **Presumption of continuance of life** On the operation of this presumption of fact, on the proof or admission of the basic or primary fact that a person was alive on a certain date, it may be presumed, in the absence of sufficient evidence to the contrary, that he or she was alive on a subsequent date (*McDarmaid v Attorney-General* [1950] P 218; *Re Peete* [1952] 2 All ER 599; *Chard v Chard* [1956] P 259). The strength of the presumption depends on the strength of the basic facts. If, for example, it were to be proved that a person was young and in good health on a certain date then, without more, the inference would be very strong that he or she was alive on the following day. If, on the other hand, it were to be proved that at a certain date a person was suffering from a terminal illness, then without more this would be unlikely to afford a reasonable inference that he or she was alive a year later (see *R v Lumley* (1869) LR 1 CCR 196 at p. 198).

47.23 **Presumption of seaworthiness** On the operation of this presumption of fact, on the proof or admission of the basic fact that a ship sank or became unable to continue her voyage shortly after putting out to sea, it may be presumed, in the absence of sufficient evidence to the contrary, that she was unseaworthy on leaving port. It has been held that if, in the absence of evidence in rebuttal, the tribunal of fact were not to presume unseaworthiness, but were to find the contrary, then it would be such a finding against the reasonable inference to be drawn that it would amount to a verdict against the evidence (per Brett LJ in *Pickup v Thames and Mersey Marine Insurance Co. Ltd* (1873) 3 QBD 594 at p. 600; and see also *Ajum Goolam Hossen and Co. v Union Marine Insurance Co.* [1901] AC 362).

47.24 **Presumption of proper working order** There is a presumption, which comes into operation without the need for proof or admission of any basic or primary facts, that in the absence of sufficient evidence to the contrary, mechanical or other instruments of a kind that are usually in proper working order, were in proper working order at the time of their use. The party against whom the presumption operates bears an evidential burden to adduce some evidence to the contrary. The presumption has been applied, e.g., in the case of speedometers (*Nicholas v Penny* [1950] 2 KB 466) and traffic lights (*Tingle Jacobs and Co. v Kennedy* [1964] 1 WLR 638).

Conflicting presumptions

47.25 Where two evidential or two persuasive presumptions are relied upon in the same case, and as a result the court finds itself obliged to draw two conclusions, the one in conflict with the other, then the two presumptions can be treated as having cancelled each other out, with the effect that the case can be decided on the basis of the ordinary rules pertaining to the burden of proof. This solution was adopted in *Monckton v Tarr* (1930) 2 BWCC 504, where the presumption of essential validity of marriage applied to two different ceremonies, but when a similar conflict arose in *Taylor v Taylor* [1967] P 25, the court preferred to preserve the existing marriage, rather than avoid it by virtue of an earlier effectively moribund one, an approach which suggests that the court may reach its decision not only on the basis of the comparative likelihood of the two presumed facts, but also having regard to policy considerations.

It is submitted that where two conflicting presumptions are relied upon in the same case, but they are of unequal strength, as when a rebuttable presumption of law conflicts with a presumption of fact, the conflict is more apparent than real, because the determinative factor will be the incidence of the legal burden of proof: the party bearing the legal burden will lose on the issue in question if he fails to discharge it to the requisite standard of proof. The outcome in *R v Willshire* (1881)6 QBD 366 is consistent with this view. See also *Re Peatling* [1969] VR 214 (Supreme Court of Victoria).

JUDICIAL NOTICE

The doctrine of judicial notice takes two distinct forms, which were defined and distinguished by Lord Sumner in *Commonwealth Shipping Representative v Peninsular and Oriental Branch Service* [1923] AC 191 at p. 212: 'Judicial notice refers to facts, which a judge can be called upon to receive and to act upon, either from his general knowledge of them, or from enquiries to be made by himself for his own information from sources to which it is proper for him to refer'. These two forms of judicial notice require separate consideration. Consideration is also given to the extent to which, if at all, a judge may make use of his or her personal knowledge of facts in issue or of facts relevant to the facts in issue. 47.26

Judicial notice without inquiry at common law

If a fact is so notorious or of such common knowledge that it requires no proof, the judge, without recourse to any extraneous sources of information, may take judicial notice of it and thereby treat it as proved, notwithstanding that it has not been established by evidence. The doctrine may be illustrated by the following examples: the duration of the normal period of human gestation is about nine months (*Preston-Jones v Preston-Jones* [1951] AC 391); cats are ordinarily kept for domestic purposes (*Nye v Niblett* [1918] 1 KB 23); the streets of London are full of traffic (*Dennis v A. J. White and Co.* [1916] 2 KB 1); and a postcard is the sort of document which might be read by anyone (*Huth v Huth* [1915] 3 KB 32). In all of these examples, the doctrine was expressly applied, but in the case of facts beyond all serious dispute, for example, that Tuesday follows Monday, or that there are seven days in the week, it is common for judicial notice to be taken tacitly. 47.27

At common law, judicial notice is also taken of public Acts passed before 1851, but in the absence of express provision to the contrary, a private Act passed before 1851 must be proved by evidence, for which purpose production of a Queen's Printer's copy or an HMSO copy suffices (Evidence Act 1845, s. 3, and Documentary Evidence Act 1882, s. 2). Statutory instruments also call for proof, for which purpose Queen's Printer's or Stationery Office copies also suffice (*see R v Ashley* (1967) 52 Cr App R 42 and Documentary Evidence Act 1868, s. 2), but some have acquired such notoriety that judicial notice may be taken of them (*see R v Jones* (1968) 54 Cr App R 63).

As a general rule, foreign law, being a question of fact normally calling for expert evidence, cannot be the subject of judicial notice (*Brenan and Galen's Case* (1847) 10 QB 492 at p. 498). The exceptions to this general rule include:

(a) the common law of Northern Ireland (*Re Nesbitt* (1844) 14 LJ MC 30 at p. 33);
(b) Scots law in civil cases, of which judicial notice may be taken by the House of Lords; and
(c) in civil cases only, notorious points of foreign law, e.g., that in Monte Carlo roulette is legal (see *Saxby v Fulton* [1909] 2 KB 208 and *R v Ofori (No. 2)* (1993) 99 Cr App R 223).

Judicial notice without inquiry pursuant to statute

47.28 Judicial notice of a fact, without inquiry, may be required by statute. Most of the statutory provisions require judicial notice to be taken of the fact that a judicial or other official document has been signed by the person by whom it purports to have been signed or has been sealed by the court by which it purports to have been sealed. This applies in the case of:

(a) a judicial or official document purporting to have been signed by a judge of the Supreme Court (Evidence Act 1845, s. 2);
(b) summonses and other documents issuing out of a county court and purporting to be sealed or stamped with the seal of the court (County Courts Act 1984, s. 134(2)).

At common law, judicial notice is taken of public Acts passed before 1851 (see 47.27). In the case of a UK statute (whether general, local and personal, or private) passed after 1850, the Interpretation Act 1978, s. 3, as supplemented by s. 22(1) and sch. 2, para. 2, requires judicial notice to be taken of it, unless the contrary is expressly provided by the Act. Evidence is therefore not required to prove either the contents of such an Act or that it has been duly passed by both Houses of Parliament. Judicial notice must also be taken of the European Community Treaties, the Official Journal of the Communities, and decisions of, or opinions by, the European Court of Justice (European Communities Act 1972, s. 3(2)).

Judicial notice after inquiry

47.29 If a fact is not sufficiently notorious to be the subject of judicial notice without inquiry, the judge may take judicial notice of it and thereby treat it as proved, notwithstanding that it has not been established by evidence, after referring to reliable extraneous sources of information, such as certificates from ministers, learned treatises, works of reference and expert witnesses. The inquiry is distinct from proof by evidence because the rules of evidence do not apply, the results of the inquiry are not open to evidence in rebuttal, and the result constitutes a precedent, except in the case of facts lacking constancy, such as the status of a foreign government. There is obvious scope for abuse of the doctrine, but this has to be balanced against the reality that some facts are readily demonstrable by reference to sources of virtually indisputable authority and are likely to be in issue again, in other cases, so that proof in the normal way is undesirable, having regard to considerations of cost and the need for uniformity of decision. This may go some way towards explaining *McQuaker v Goddard* [1940] 1 KB 687, where it was held that judicial notice after inquiry could be taken of the fact that a camel is a domestic animal.

Judicial notice after inquiry has usually been taken of three kinds of fact:

(a) facts which are readily demonstrable after reference to appropriate authoritative works of reference or learned treatises;
(b) customs and professional practices; and
(c) facts of a political nature.

47.30 **Readily demonstrable facts** Examples include the day of the week on which a certain date fell, after reference to a diary or almanac; the longitude and latitude of a place, after reference to an atlas; and the date and place of a well-known historical event, after reference to an authoritative historical work.

47.31 **Customs and professional practices** After consultation with suitably qualified expert witnesses, judicial notice may be taken of general customs and professional practices, such as the custom of the general lien of bankers on the securities of their customers (*Brandao v Barnett*

(1846) 12 Cl & F 787; *George v Davies* [1911] 2 KB 445 at p. 448) and the practices of conveyancers (*Re Rosher* (1884) 26 ChD 801), ordnance surveyors (*Davey v Harrow Corporation* [1958] 1 QB 60) and accountants (*Heather v P-E Consulting Group Ltd* [1973] Ch 189).

Political facts Judicial notice after inquiry has been taken of facts of a political nature such as the status of foreign governments, the membership of diplomatic suites and the extent of territorial sovereignty. The inquiry will usually be made of a minister, whose certificate will be treated as accurate because as a matter of public policy it is desirable to avoid a conflict between the courts and the executive on such issues. Examples include the fact that a country exists as an independent sovereign state (*Duff Development Co. v Government of Kelantan* [1924] AC 797, and see also *Mighell v Sultan of Johore* [1894] 1 QB 149 and *Carl Zeiss Stiftung v Rayner and Keeler Ltd (No. 2)* [1967] 1 AC 853); the fact that this country is in a state of war with another (*R v Bottrill, ex parte Kuechenmeister* [1947] KB 41); the membership of the staff of an ambassador (*Engelke v Mussmann* [1928] AC 433); and the classification 'secret' appearing on a document originating in a government office, meaning that the document contains information and material the unauthorised disclosure of which would cause serious injury to the interests of the nation (*Secretary of State for Defence v Guardian Newspapers Ltd* [1985] AC 339 per Lord Diplock at p. 354). **47.32**

Personal knowledge

When a judge takes judicial notice of a notorious fact, he or she makes use of his or her general knowledge. The extent to which, if at all, a judge may make use of his or her personal and particular knowledge of facts in issue or relevant to the facts in issue, is unclear. There is certainly authority that a judge may use personal knowledge of matters within the common knowledge of people in the locality, but that is a principle which derives from cases decided under the Workmen's Compensation Acts, under which county court judges sat as arbitrators and took into account, in assessing compensation, personal knowledge of the labour market (see *Keane v Mount Vernon Colliery Co. Ltd* [1933] AC 309 and *Reynolds v Llanelly Associated Tinplate Co. Ltd* [1948] 1 All ER 140). In *Mullen v Hackney London Borough Council* [1997] 1 WLR 1103 the Court of Appeal held that a county court judge, in deciding which penalty to impose on the council for its failure to carry out an undertaking to the court, was entitled to take judicial notice of his own knowledge of the council's conduct in relation to previous undertakings. As to judicial notice, the facts in this case were clearly not notorious or of the kind of which judicial notice has been held to have been properly taken after enquiry. The Court of Appeal appears to have treated the principle deriving from cases such as *Keane v Mount Vernon Colliery Co. Ltd* as one of general application in any county court case (see Allen, *International Journal of Evidence and Proof* (1998) vol. 2, No. 1, 37). **47.33**

THE BURDEN AND STANDARD OF PROOF

Legal burden

In this chapter, the phrase 'the legal burden' will be used to denote what has been variously described as 'the burden of proof', the 'probative burden', 'the ultimate burden', 'the burden of proof on the pleadings', 'the risk of non-persuasion' and 'the persuasive burden'. The legal burden is the obligation imposed on a party by a rule of law to prove (in some cases to negative or disprove) a fact in issue: a party which fails to discharge the burden will lose on the issue in question. In civil proceedings the standard of proof required to discharge the burden is proof on the balance of probabilities (see 47.40). Whether a party has discharged the burden is decided by the tribunal of fact, whether judge or jury, once only, after the parties to the litigation have called all of their evidence. **47.34**

In exceptional cases, a judge may find it impossible to make a finding, one way or the other, on a disputed issue of fact, and therefore may decide the issue by resort to the legal burden.

The principles to be derived from the authorities, in this respect, were summarised in *Stephens v Cannon* [2005] EWCA Civ 222, *The Times*, 2 May 2005, at [46] as follows:

(a) The situation in which the court finds itself before it can dispatch a disputed issue by resort to the burden of proof has to be exceptional.
(b) Nevertheless the issue does not have to be of any particular type. . . . It may be more likely to arise following an enquiry into, for example, the identity of the aggressor in an unwitnessed fight; but it can arise even after an enquiry, aided by good experts, into, for example, the cause of the sinking of a ship.
(c) The exceptional situation which entitles the court to resort to the burden of proof is that, notwithstanding that it has striven to do so, it cannot reasonably make a finding in relation to a disputed issue.
(d) A court which resorts to the burden of proof must ensure that others can discern that it has striven to make a finding in relation to a disputed issue and can understand the reasons why it has concluded that it cannot do so. The parties must be able to discern the court's endeavour and to understand its reasons in order to be able to perceive why they have won and lost. An appellate court must also be able to do so because otherwise it will not be able to accept that the court below was in the exceptional situation of being entitled to resort to the burden of proof.
(e) In a few cases the fact of the endeavour and the reasons for the conclusion will readily be inferred from the circumstances and so there will be no need for the court to demonstrate the endeavour and to explain the reasons in any detail in its judgment. In most cases, however, a more detailed demonstration and explanation in [the] judgment will be necessary.

Judges sometimes refer to the 'shifting' of a burden from a party to that party's opponent. In the case of the legal burden, this can only happen at common law on the operation of a rebuttable presumption of law of the persuasive variety: once the party relying on the presumption has proved the primary or basic facts giving rise to the presumption, the legal burden can be said to have shifted, in that the opponent will then bear the legal burden to disprove the fact that will otherwise be presumed (see 47.10). When reference is made to the shifting of the burden in other circumstances, it is merely to signify that at a given moment in the course of the trial the burden appears to have been satisfied by the party on whom it lies, but in so far as this places a burden on the opponent, it is a tactical burden, not a legal or evidential burden (see per Mustill LJ in *Brady v Group Lotus Car Companies plc* [1987] 3 All ER 1050 at p. 1059): as already noted, whether a legal burden has been discharged is determined only once, at the end of the trial.

Evidential burden and right to begin

47.35 The evidential burden, sometimes referred to as 'the burden of adducing evidence' and 'the duty of passing the judge', is the obligation to adduce sufficient evidence of a fact to allow the issue in question to go before the tribunal of fact. The burden is discharged when there is sufficient evidence to justify, as a possibility, a favourable finding by the tribunal of fact. Whether a party has discharged the burden is decided only once in the course of the trial, and is decided by the judge, as opposed to the tribunal of fact. Thus a claimant who bears the evidential and legal burden on a particular issue, and fails to discharge the evidential burden, necessarily fails on the issue, since the judge will refuse to let the issue go before the tribunal of fact. However, discharge of the evidential burden will not necessarily result in discharge of the legal burden: the issue goes to the tribunal of fact, which may or may not find in favour of the claimant, although a defendant who adduces no evidence in rebuttal clearly runs the risk of losing on the issue.

As with the legal burden, judges sometimes refer to the 'shifting' of the evidential burden. However, this can only happen at common law on the operation of a rebuttable presumption of law of the evidential variety: where the party relying on such a presumption adduces sufficient evidence of the primary or basic facts, the adversary will bear an evidential burden to adduce some evidence in rebuttal of the presumed fact (see 47.10). When reference is made to the shifting of the evidential burden in other circumstances, it is to signify that at a given moment during the course of the trial, the burden appears to have been discharged by the party on whom it lies, but this is to place no more than a provisional or tactical burden, as opposed to an evidential burden, on his opponent, because as has been said, an opponent who adduces no evidence in rebuttal clearly runs the risk of losing on the issue in question (see *Sutton v Sadler* (1857) 3 CB NS 87).

The right to be the first party to adduce evidence is determined by the incidence of the evidential burden. Usually the claimant will adduce his evidence first, but where the evidential burden on all the issues in the action lies on the defendant, or one of the defendants, the defendant or that defendant is entitled to begin (see *Pontifex v Jolly* (1839) 9 Car & P 202 and *Re Parry* [1977] 1 WLR 93). In *Mercer v Whall* (1845) 14 LJ QB 267 a clerk brought an action for unliquidated damages for wrongful dismissal. The defendant admitted the dismissal but claimed justification on the grounds of the clerk's misconduct. Although the defendant would have had the right to begin if the claim had been for a liquidated sum, because then the only issue would have been the issue of misconduct, on which the defendant bore the evidential burden, it was held that the clerk had the right to begin because he bore the evidential burden in relation to damages.

Incidence of the legal and evidential burden

Subject to cases in which reliance is placed upon evidential presumptions (see 47.10 to 47.25), the evidential burden in relation to any given fact in issue will lie on the party bearing the legal burden on that fact in issue. As to the incidence of the legal burden, this may be fixed by agreement of the parties, but otherwise falls to be determined by rules of law to be found in statutes and at common law, where the general guiding principle to be derived from the precedents is that 'he who asserts must prove'. **47.36**

By agreement The parties themselves may expressly agree upon the incidence of the legal burden (see, e.g., *Levy v Assicurazioni Generali* [1940] AC 791 and *Fred Chappell Ltd v National Car Parks Ltd* (1987) *The Times*, 22 May 1987), but where a written agreement such as an insurance policy contains no such express provision, the court may nonetheless have regard to the terms of the agreement and may treat the issue as a matter of construction. In *Munro, Brice and Co. v War Risks Association* [1918] 2 KB 78, a ship had disappeared for reasons unknown and a claim was made under a policy of insurance which covered the ship subject to an exemption in respect of loss by capture or in consequence of hostilities. The issue was whether the claimant had to prove that the ship was not lost by reason of enemy action. The court found for the claimant on the basis that it was for the defendant to prove that the facts fell within the exception, which they had failed to do. (Contrast, but question, *Hurst v Evans* [1917] 1 KB 352; and see also *Gorman v Hand-in-Hand Insurance Co.* (1877) IR 11 CL 224.) However, where a claimant in such a case relies upon a proviso to an exemption clause, the court may conclude that the claimant must prove that the facts fall within the proviso. This was the outcome in *The Glendarroch* [1894] P 226. In that case, an action in negligence for non-delivery of goods, the goods having been lost when the boat carrying them sank, the bill of lading contained a clause exempting the defendants in respect loss or damage caused by perils of the sea, provided that they were not negligent. It was held that it was for the claimants to prove the contract and non-delivery; for the defendants, if they relied upon the exemption clause (loss caused by perils of the sea), to prove that the facts fell within it; and for the claimants, if they relied upon the proviso to the exemption clause (negligence on the part of the defendants), to prove that the facts fell within that proviso. **47.37**

By statute The incidence of the legal burden may be determined by statute. For example, under the Consumer Credit Act 1974, s. 171(7), if a debtor alleges that a credit bargain is extortionate within the meaning of ss. 137 and 138 of that Act, it is for the creditor to prove the contrary. A further example is to be found in the Employment Rights Act 1996, s. 98: in a claim of unfair dismissal, it is for the former employee to prove that he or she was dismissed, but it is for the employer to show the reason for the dismissal and that it amounts to one of the five grounds set out and for which a dismissal is capable of being fair, failing which the **47.38**

dismissal is treated as automatically unfair. See also the Sex Discrimination Act 1975, s. 63A, the Race Relations Act 1976, s. 54A, and the Disability Discrimination Act 1995, s. 17A(1C) (and, as to their construction, *Igen Ltd v Wong* [2005] EWCA Civ 142, [2005] ICR 931).

47.39 **At common law** As to the incidence of the legal burden at common law, the general guiding principle to be derived from the precedents is that 'he who asserts must prove, not he who denies' (*Joseph Constantine Steamship Line Ltd v Imperial Smelting Corporation Ltd* [1942] AC 154, per Lord Maugham at p. 174). For example, in *Wakelin v London and South Western Railway Co.* (1886) 12 App Cas 41, an action in negligence, brought by a widow under the Fatal Accidents Act 1846, in which the only evidence was that the husband had been found dead near a level crossing at the side of a railway line, it was held that the claim must fail: the widow bore the burden of proving that the death had been caused by the defendants' negligence, but the evidence adduced was as capable of indicating negligence on the part of the husband as on the part of the defendants (cf. *Jones v Great Western Railway Co.* (1930) 144 LT 194). The principle is most useful, as in *Wakelin v London and South Western Railway*, when the issues are straightforward. Thus in an action for negligence, the claimant bears the legal burden of proving duty of care, breach of the duty and consequential loss, and the defendant bears the burden of proving contributory negligence, *volenti non fit injuria*, or any other defence which goes beyond a bare denial of the claimant's allegations. Similarly, in an action for breach of contract, the claimant bears the legal burden of proving the contract, its breach and consequential loss, and the defendant bears the burden of proving any defence which goes beyond a bare denial of the claimant's allegations, e.g., discharge by agreement or frustration.

The burden of proving a failure to mitigate rests on the defendant (*Geest plc v Lansiquot* [2002] UKPC 48, [2002] 1 WLR 3111, in which the Privy Council reviewed the authorities and agreed with both parties that the decision in *Selvanayagam v University of the West Indies* [1983] 1 WLR 585, that the burden lay on the claimant, cannot be relied upon).

In *BHP Billiton Petroleum Ltd v Dalmine SpA* [2003] EWCA Civ 170, [2003] BLR 271, it was held that in most cases the statements of case are likely to be a good guide to the incidence of the legal burden. The defendant manufactured and provided steel pipes used in the construction of a pipeline serving oil and gas fields in the Irish Sea. The pipeline failed after cracks developed in the welds which joined the pipes together. The defendant had fraudulently misrepresented that the pipes complied with the contractual specification, and the claimants, in reliance on this misrepresentation, had accepted and used the pipes which otherwise they would have rejected. On the question of causation, it was accepted by the claimants that they bore the burden of proving that the incorporation of non-compliant pipe caused the pipeline to fail and they succeeded in discharging this burden. However, the defendant in its defence averred that a pipeline made only of compliant pipe would have failed in any event. It was held that the defendant bore the burden of proving what it had averred.

It was accepted in *BHP Billiton Petroleum Ltd v Dalmine SpA* that although the statements of case are likely to be a good guide to the incidence of the legal burden, they cannot be definitive, because a party cannot, by poor pleading, take upon himself a burden which the law does not impose on him or free himself from a burden which the law does impose on him. Equally, a party cannot avoid a legal burden by an assertion cast in the form of a negative allegation, seeming to oblige his or her opponent to allege a positive. For example, in *Soward v Leggatt* (1836) 7 Car & P 613, the claimant landlord alleged that his tenant 'did not repair' a certain house, to which the defendant replied that he 'did well and sufficiently repair the house'. It was held that it was not the form of the issue which required consideration, but its substance and effect: the claimant, who might have pleaded instead that the defendant 'let the house become dilapidated', was alleging breach of covenant and therefore he had to prove it.

The limitations of the maxim 'he who asserts must prove' are highlighted by *Abrath v North*

Eastern Railway (1883) 11 QBD 440 (affirmed on appeal, (1886) 11 App Cas 247, and applied in *Reynolds v Metropolitan Police Commissioner* (1984) 80 Cr App R 125). In that case, an action for malicious prosecution, the Court of Appeal held that the burden was on the claimant to prove not only that the defendant had instituted proceedings against him, but also that he had done so without reasonable and probable cause. Rejecting the submission that the burden of showing reasonable and probable cause fell on the defendant, Bowen LJ held that the assertion of a negative being an essential part of the claimant's case, the burden rested on him. The case illustrates the point that, in the absence of a precedent, if it is unclear whether an assertion is an essential part of the claim of the claimant or the defence of the defendant, the court must decide the matter. The authorities show that in these circumstances, the courts decide the matter having regard to matters of policy, such as the ease or otherwise that the respective parties would encounter in seeking to discharge the legal burden, and whether the objective of the rule of substantive law in question, whether a common law or statutory rule, would be likely to be achieved better by placing the burden on the one party or the other (see generally Stone (1944) 60 LQR 262).

An example, in the case of a statutory tort, is *Nimmo v Alexander Cowan and Sons Ltd* [1968] AC 107, a Scottish case brought by an injured workman under the Factories Act 1961, s. 29(1), which provided that 'every place at which any person has at any time to work . . . shall, so far as is reasonably practicable, be made and kept safe for any person working therein'. The workman alleged that his place of work was not kept safe, but did not aver that it was reasonably practicable to make it safe. By a majority, the House of Lords held that there was no burden on the workman to prove that it was reasonably practicable to keep the premises safe: it was for the defendant employers to prove that it was not reasonably practicable to keep the premises safe. The majority, in reaching this decision, were of the view that where, on the face of a statute, it is unclear on whom the burden should lie, a court, in order to determine Parliament's intention, may go beyond the mere form of the enactment and look to policy considerations such as the mischief at which the Act was aimed, and the ease or difficulty that the respective parties would encounter in discharging the burden. The defendant was clearly in a better position to discharge the burden. Furthermore the decision of the House, it is submitted, was the best way of achieving the object of the enactment, the provision of safe places of work.

A common law example is *Joseph Constantine Steamship Line Ltd v Imperial Smelting Corporation Ltd* [1942] AC 154. A ship on charter was destroyed by an explosion, the cause of which was unclear. The charterers claimed damages from the owners for failure to load. The defence was frustration. The charterers argued that the owners could not rely upon frustration unless they proved that the explosion was not caused by their fault. The House of Lords held that in order to defeat the defence, the burden was upon the charterers to prove fault on the part of the owners. The cause of the explosion being unclear, the appeal of the owners was allowed. The outcome may be justified on the basis that it is generally easier to prove fault than its absence, but there is no inflexible rule to that effect. Thus in bailment cases, the bailor having proved bailment, it is for the bailee to prove that the goods were lost or damaged without fault on his part (see *Coldman v Hill* [1919] 1 KB 443 and cf. *Levison v Patent Steam Carpet Cleaning Ltd* [1978] QB 69). Similarly, in cases of conversion, the burden of proof is on the bailee to show that he dealt with the goods in good faith and without notice (*Marcq v Christie Manson and Woods Ltd* [2002] EWHC 2148 (QB), [2002] 4 All ER 1005, affirmed [2003] EWCA Civ 731, [2004] QB 286).

Standard of proof

In civil proceedings, the standard of proof generally required to be met by either party seeking to discharge a legal burden is proof on a balance of probabilities. This standard of proof is normally used at the end of the trial, after all the evidence has been called, but should also be used in reaching a decision on a submission of no case to answer when the defendant has elected not to adduce any evidence (*Miller v Cawley* [2002] EWCA Civ 1100, *The Times*, 6 September **47.40**

2002). There are exceptions to this general rule. The standard in committal proceedings for civil contempt of court is proof beyond reasonable doubt (*Re Bramblevale Ltd* [1970] Ch 128; *Dean v Dean* [1987] 1 FLR 517). The standard of beyond reasonable doubt may also be required pursuant to statute (see *Judd v Minister of Pensions and National Insurance* [1966] 2 QB 580). An exacting civil standard of proof, which for all practical purposes is indistinguishable from the criminal standard, applies to applications for sex offender orders under the Crime and Disorder Act 1998, s. 2 (*B v Chief Constable of Avon and Somerset Constabulary* [2001] 1 WLR 340 at p. 354) and for football banning orders under the Football Spectators Act 1989, s. 14B (*Gough v Chief Constable of the Derbyshire Constabulary* [2002] EWCA Civ 351, [2002] QB 1213). The position is the same for anti-social behaviour orders, in relation to the Crime and Disorder Act 1998, s. 1(1), but pragmatism dictates that magistrates must in all such cases apply the *criminal* standard, which makes their task more straightforward (*R (McCann) v Crown Court at Manchester* [2002] UKHL 39, [2003] 1 AC 787, at [37], [83] and [114]–[117]).

In *Miller v Minister of Pensions* [1947] 2 All ER 372 at p. 374, Denning J referred to the degree of cogency required to discharge the legal burden in a civil case in the following way: 'It must carry a reasonable degree of probability, but not so high as is required in a criminal case. If the evidence is such that the tribunal can say: "we think it more probable than not", the burden is discharged, but if the probabilities are equal it is not'. However, the degree of cogency required can vary from case to case according to the seriousness of the allegations made and the potential consequences of the decision for the parties. In *Re Dellow's Will Trusts* [1964] 1 WLR 451, Ungoed-Thomas J put the matter thus: 'The more serious the allegation the more cogent is the evidence required to overcome the unlikelihood of what is alleged and thus to prove it'. To similar effect, it has been said that 'the very elements of gravity become a part of the whole range of circumstances which have to be weighed in the scale when deciding as to the balance of probabilities' (per Morris LJ in *Hornal v Neuberger Products Ltd* [1957] 1 QB 247 at p. 266, a dictum approved and adopted by the House of Lords in *Khera v Secretary of State for the Home Department* [1984] AC 74 at pp. 113–14). The same point has been conveyed by referring to degrees of probability within the one standard of the preponderance of probability (per Denning LJ in *Bater v Bater* [1951] P 35 at p. 36). In relation to a number of issues, therefore, it has been held that the standard is higher than the ordinary civil standard or that what is alleged is so serious or improbable as to call for stronger or more cogent evidence than would otherwise be required. Such issues defy comprehensive classification, but the following important examples may be given.

47.41 **Allegations of crime or fraud** In *Hornal v Neuberger Products Ltd* [1957] 1 QB 247 the claimant claimed damages for breach of warranty or alternatively for fraud. The company had sold a lathe to the claimant. The issue was whether, as the claimant alleged, one of the directors of the defendant company had represented that the lathe had been reconditioned. If such a representation was made, there had been a fraudulent misrepresentation, because the director knew that the lathe had not been reconditioned. The trial judge was satisfied on a balance of probabilities, but not beyond reasonable doubt, that the representation was made and awarded damages for fraud, but dismissed the claim for damages for breach of warranty on the basis that the parties did not intend the representation to have contractual effect. On appeal, the Court of Appeal held that on an allegation of crime in civil proceedings, the standard was not, as a number of previous authorities had indicated, the criminal standard of proof, beyond reasonable doubt, but the ordinary, and flexible, civil standard of proof, on a balance of probabilities. Denning LJ said (at p. 37):

> The degree [of probability] depends on the subject matter. A civil court, when considering a charge of fraud, will naturally require for itself a higher degree of probability than that which it would require when asking if negligence is established. It does not adopt so high a degree as a criminal court, even when it is considering a charge of a criminal nature; but still it does require a degree of probability which is commensurate with the occasion.

Hornal v Neuberger Products Ltd was applied in *Re Dellow's Will Trusts* [1964] 1 WLR 451, where the issue was whether a woman had feloniously killed her husband, and also in *Post Office v Estuary Radio Ltd* [1967] 1 WLR 1396, which involved an allegation of a criminal offence under the Wireless Telegraphy Act 1949. See also *Piermay Shipping Co. SA v Chester* [1979] 1 Lloyd's Rep 55 (an allegation of deliberately scuttling a ship), *Brazier v Bramwell Scaffolding (Dunedin) Ltd* [2001] UKPC 59, LTL 20/12/2001 (an allegation of conduct akin to fraud) and *Parks v Clout* [2003] EWCA Civ 1030, LTL 10/6/2003 (an allegation of obtaining letters of administration by fraud).

Grounds of divorce Prior to the Divorce Reform Act 1969, the old grounds for divorce were largely based on the concept of the matrimonial offence. For reasons of this kind, and because of the importance of divorce proceedings to both the parties and the state, the earlier authorities required the application of the criminal standard: see, in the case of allegations of cruelty, *Bater v Bater* [1951] P 35; in the case of al legations of adultery, *Ginesi v Ginesi* [1948] P 179, and also *Preston-Jones v Preston-Jones* [1951] AC 391 and *F v F* [1968] P 506, in both of which the finding of adultery would have rendered a child illegitimate; and see generally *Blyth v Blyth* [1966] AC 643. However, in *Bastable v Bastable* [1968] 1 WLR 1684, where adultery was in issue, Wilmer LJ and Winn LJ adopted as appropriate the dicta of Denning LJ in *Bater v Bater*, approved by the Court of Appeal in *Hornal v Neuberger Products Ltd* [1957] 1 QB 247, to the effect that the civil standard applies, but the court requires a degree of probability proportionate to the subject matter. Bearing in mind the present philosophy of divorce law, it is submitted that the approach taken in *Bastable v Bastable* should now be followed in all matrimonial causes. **47.42**

Other cases Other facts and matters, in relation to which it has been held that the appropriate standard is higher than the ordinary civil standard, are set out below. In so far as some of the cases, on some of these issues, require, or seem to require, a standard at least as high as the criminal standard, it is submitted that they are unlikely to be followed, especially now that it is clear that the civil standard of proof is appropriate to allegations of crime in civil cases (see 47.41). **47.43**

(a) *Change of domicile.* A party seeking to prove an intention to change domicile must do so 'clearly and unequivocally' (*Moorhouse v Lord* (1863) 10 HL Cas 272 at p. 236; see also *Re Fuld (No. 3)* [1968] P 675 at p. 685).
(b) *Rebutting the presumption of the formal validity of a marriage.* The evidence in rebuttal of this strong common law presumption is required to be 'strong, distinct and satisfactory' (*Piers v Piers* (1849) 2 HL Cas 331 at p. 389) or 'evidence which satisfied beyond reasonable doubt that there was no valid marriage' (*Mahadervan v Mahadervan* [1964] P 233 at p. 246).
(c) *Rectification.* A party claiming rectification must prove his case by 'strong irrefragable evidence' (*Countess of Shelburne v Earl of Inchiquin* (1784) 1 Bro CC 338 at p. 341; and see also *Earl v Hector Whaling Ltd* [1961] 1 Lloyd's Rep 459).
(d) *Child abuse.* In cases involving the care of children, the more serious or improbable an allegation of abuse or harm, the stronger the evidence required to prove it and the identity of the perpetrator (see *Re H (Minors) (Sexual Abuse: Standard of Proof)* [1996] AC 563 and *Re G (A Child) (Non-accidental Injury: Standard of Proof)* [2001] 1 FCR 97). It is incorrect, in such cases, to apply the criminal standard of proof or to treat the distinction between criminal and civil standards of proof as largely illusory (*Re U (A Child)* [2004] EWCA Civ 567, [2005] Fam 134).
(e) *Paternity.* The standard of proof required to make a finding of paternity is a heavy one, commensurate with the gravity of the issue, and although not the criminal standard, is more than the ordinary civil standard (*W v K* [1988] 1 FLR 86; and see also *Serio v Serio* (1983) 4 FLR 756).
(f) *Medical treatment for the mentally ill.* In order for a court to approve proposed medical treatment for an incompetent mentally ill patient without infringing the **European Convention on Human Rights, art. 3**, it must be 'convincingly shown' that the treatment is medically necessary. This standard of proof may be met notwithstanding the

existence of a responsible body of opinion against the proposed treatment (*R (N) v Dr M* [2002] EWCA Civ 1789, [2003] 1 WLR 562).

WITNESSES: COMPETENCE, COMPELLABILITY, OATHS AND PROCEDURE

Competence and compellability — the general rule

47.44 The general rule may be put in the form of two propositions:

(a) any person is competent in any proceedings; and
(b) all competent witnesses are compellable.

The only remaining exceptions to these two propositions relate to children, persons of unsound mind, the Sovereign, heads of other sovereign states, diplomats and, in prescribed circumstances, bankers. At common law there were many exceptions to the first proposition, but these have been swept away, over the centuries, by judicial and statutory reform: see *Omychund v Barker* (1745) 1 Atk 21 and the Evidence Further Amendment Act 1869 (non-Christians and atheists); the Civil Rights of Convicts Act 1828 and the Evidence Act 1843 (convicts and those with a personal pecuniary or proprietary interest in the outcome of the proceedings); the Evidence Act 1851 and the Evidence Further Amendment Act 1869 (the parties to proceedings); and the Evidence Amendment Act 1853 and the Evidence Further Amendment Act 1869 (the spouses of the parties to proceedings). Concerning the parties to the proceedings, the consequence is that any party to civil proceedings may give evidence and may compel any other party to those proceedings to give evidence. As to the spouses of the parties to proceedings, in *Monroe v Twistleton* (1802) Peake Add Cas 219 (followed in *O'Connor v Marjoribanks* (1842) 4 Man & G 435) it was held that a former spouse is incompetent following the termination of his or her marriage in so far as his or her evidence relates to events which occurred during the marriage. Reversal of this decision is plainly long overdue, although it is arguable that it can be ignored on the basis that the words 'husbands' and 'wives' in the Evidence Amendment Act 1853, by which the spouses of parties were rendered competent and compellable, can be taken to cover former husbands and wives (but cf. *Shenton v Tyler* [1939] Ch 620).

Children

47.45 The Children Act 1989, s. 96, which resembles the Children and Young Persons Act 1933, s. 38(1), upon which it appears to have been modelled, provides as follows:

(1) Subsection (2) applies where a child who is called as a witness in any civil proceedings does not, in the opinion of the court, understand the nature of an oath.
(2) The child's evidence may be heard by the court if, in its opinion—
 (a) he understands that it is his duty to speak the truth; and
 (b) he has sufficient understanding to justify his evidence being heard.

A child, for the purposes of s. 96, is a person under the age of 18 (Children Act 1989, s. 105). In deciding whether a child 'understands the nature of an oath', it is submitted that the courts are likely to be guided by the authorities which governed in both civil and criminal cases before the law was changed, in criminal cases, by the Criminal Justice Act 1991, s. 52. Thus, in order to form an opinion on the issue, the judge will put preliminary questions to the child (*see R v Surgenor* (1940) 27 Cr App R 175), although whether the child warrants such an examination is a matter of judicial discretion. There is no fixed age at which a child should be treated as competent and below which he or she should be examined, but as a general working rule inquiry should be made of a child under the age of 14, although much depends on the type of child in question (*R v Khan* (1981) 73 Cr App R 190; and cf. *Bains v Director of Public Prosecutions* [1992] Crim LR 795). The watershed dividing children who are normally considered old enough to take the oath and those normally considered too young to do so probably falls between the ages of eight and 10 (*see R v Hayes* [1977] 1 WLR 234). The former practice was for judges to ask questions designed to discover whether the child was aware of the divine sanction of the oath, but in *R v Hayes* this practice was abandoned in favour of a secular approach. In that case, the Court of Appeal held that the important consideration is, 'whether the child has a sufficient appreciation of the solemnity of the occasion and the added responsibility to tell the truth, which is involved in taking an oath, over and above the duty to tell the truth which is an ordinary duty of social conduct'. If the child fails this secular test, then his or her evidence may be given unsworn if, in the opinion of the court, the conditions set out in s. 96(2)(a) and (b) are met. It is submitted that 'the duty to speak the truth' to which s. 96(2)(a) refers, means the duty to tell the truth which is an ordinary duty of normal social conduct.

Persons of unsound mind

In *R v Hill* (1851) 2 Den 254 it was established that if, in the opinion of the judge, a proposed witness, by reason of unsound mind, does not understand the nature and sanction of an oath, he or she is incompetent to testify; and that a person of unsound mind who does understand the oath may testify, in which case it will be for the tribunal of fact to attach such weight to his or her testimony as it sees fit, disregarding it altogether if it is so tainted with insanity as to be unworthy of credit. These propositions remain the law, except in one respect. The test to be applied should be the secular one adopted in *R v Hayes* [1977] 1 WLR 234 (see 47.45): whether the proposed witness has a sufficient appreciation of the seriousness of the occasion and a realisation that taking the oath involves something more than the duty to tell the truth in ordinary day-to-day life (see *R v Bellamy* (1985) 82 Cr App R 222). **47.46**

The Sovereign, heads of State and diplomats

The Sovereign and heads of foreign sovereign States are competent but not compellable. Diplomats, consular officials, and various officers of prescribed international organisations also enjoy varying degrees of immunity from compellability (see the Diplomatic Privileges Act 1964, the Consular Relations Act 1968, the International Organisations Act 1968, the Diplomatic and other Privileges Act 1971, and the State Immunity Act 1978). **47.47**

Bankers

The Bankers' Books Evidence Act 1879 provides for the admissibility of copies of entries in bankers' books as evidence of their contents (see 47.77). Section 6 of the Act provides as follows: **47.48**

> A banker or official of a bank shall not, in any legal proceedings to which the bank is not a party, be compellable to produce any banker's book the contents of which can be proved under this Act, or to appear as a witness to prove the matters, transactions, and accounts therein recorded, unless by order of a judge made for special cause.

Oaths and affirmations

The general rule is that all witnesses must give sworn evidence, i.e. after having taken an oath or having made an affirmation. A judgment founded on unsworn evidence may be set aside as a nullity (*R v Marsham, ex parte Pethick Lawrence* [1912] 2 KB 362). In civil proceedings there are the following four exceptions to the general rule. **47.49**

(a) In claims which have been allocated to the small claims track, the court need not take evidence on oath (CPR, r. 27.8(4)).

(b) Children under the age of 18 may be permitted to give their evidence unsworn (see 47.45).

(c) A witness called only to produce a document may give unsworn evidence if the identity of the document is either not in dispute or is to be established by another witness (*Perry v Gibson* (1834) 1 Ad & E1 48).

(d) Counsel may give unsworn evidence of the terms of a compromise reached by the parties (*Hickman v Berens* [1895] 2 Ch 638).

The form and manner of the administration of the oath in the case of Christians and Jews is governed by the **Oaths Act 1978, s. 1(1)**. The officer administering the oath shall administer it in this form and manner without question unless the witness objects thereto, or is physically incapable of so taking the oath (s. 1(2)). For those of other religious belief, the oath shall be administered 'in any lawful manner' (s. 1(3)), upon such holy book as is appropriate. Whether an oath is administered in a lawful manner for these purposes depends on whether the oath appears to the court to be binding on the conscience of the witness and is one which the witness considers to be binding on his or her conscience, rather than on the intricacies of the witness's particular religion. Thus in *R v Kemble* [1990] 1 WLR 1111, an oath taken by a Muslim on the New Testament was held to have been administered in a lawful manner notwithstanding that under the strict tenets of Islam, an oath taken by a Muslim is only valid if taken on a copy of the Koran in Arabic. If the ground is properly laid for an expectation that a witness will take the oath on a particular holy book, but the witness affirms, the judge has a discretion to allow the reason why the witness did not take the oath on the holy book to be explored sensitively (*R v Mehrban* [2002] 1 Cr App R 561). Section 3 of the 1978 Act permits a person to be sworn with uplifted hand, in the form and manner in which an oath is usually administered in Scotland. Where an oath has been duly administered and taken, the fact that the person to whom it was administered had, at the time of taking it, no religious belief, shall not for any purpose affect its validity (s. 4(2)).

Any person who objects to being sworn shall be permitted to make his or her solemn affirmation instead (s. 5(1)), which shall be of the same force and effect as an oath (s. 5(4)). Where it is not reasonably practicable without inconvenience or delay to administer an oath in the manner appropriate to a person's religious belief, then he or she may be permitted, or required, to make his or her solemn affirmation instead (s. 5(2) and (3)).

Oral evidence and evidence by video link or other means

47.50 Under **CPR, r. 32.2**, the general rule is that any fact which needs to be proved by the evidence of witnesses is to be proved:

(a) at trial, by their oral evidence given in public; and
(b) at any other hearing, by their evidence in writing.

Under **r. 32.2(2)**, however, the general rule is subject:

(a) to any provision to the contrary contained in the CPR or elsewhere; or
(b) to any order of the court.

An example of the former is to be found in **r. 32.3**, which provides that the court may allow a witness to give evidence through a video link 'or by other means', e.g., by means of a telephone. No defined limit or set of circumstances should be placed upon this discretionary power, which is not restricted to cases in which the witness is seriously ill or cases of pressing need (*Rowland v Bock* [2002] 4 All ER 370). Lord Nicholls of Birkenhead in *Polanski v Condé Nast Publications Ltd* [2005] UKHL 10, [2005] 1 WLR 637, said that videoconferencing orders are readily available to all litigants in civil proceedings. This decision is discussed further at **56.11**. As to the use at trial of witness statements, see **chapter 49**. As to the power to direct that certain facts may not be proved by the oral evidence of proposed witnesses, see further at **47.51**, and generally at 47.7.

Directions in relation to witnesses

47.51 Before the CPR came into effect, the choice of witnesses to support a party's case, and the order in which they were to be called, were matters entirely for that party (*Briscoe v Briscoe* [1966] P 501). The judge had no right to call witnesses against the will of the parties (*Re Enoch and Zaretzky, Bock and Co.'s Arbitration* [1910] 1 KB 327), except in cases of civil contempt (*Yianni* *v Yianni* [1966] 1 WLR 120). Under **CPR, r. 32.1(1)**, the court may now control the evidence by giving directions as to not only the issues on which it requires evidence, but also as to the nature of the evidence which it requires to decide those issues and the way in which the evidence is to be placed before the court. Furthermore, under **r. 32.1(2)**, the court may use its power under the rule to exclude evidence that would otherwise be admissible. In exercising these powers, the judge must seek to give effect to the 'overriding objective'. **Rule 32.1(1)** does not empower the court to order a party to call a witness (*Society of Lloyd's v Jaffray* (2000) *The Times*, 3 August 2000). However, it is submitted that in appropriate circumstances a judge may take the view that in furtherance of the 'overriding objective' directions should be given under **r. 32.1(1)** as to the order in which witnesses should give their evidence, and as to which potential witnesses should not be called, on the basis either that the issue to which their evidence relates only requires evidence in written form or that their evidence, although admissible in law, should be excluded in the exercise of the judge's discretion. The judge also has the power to recall a witness called by a party (*Fallon v Calvert* [1960] 2 QB 201).

Time at which evidence should be adduced

As a general rule of practice, rather than law, a party should adduce all the evidence on which he intends to rely before the close of his case. The authorities in this regard, which are almost all criminal cases, indicate that there are two common law exceptions to the general rule and a 'wider discretion' to be exercised outside the two exceptions only very rarely. Under the first exception, evidence is allowed in rebuttal of matters arising *ex improviso*, which no ingenuity could have foreseen (*R v Frost* (1839) 4 St Tr NS 85). Under this exception, it is for the judge, in the exercise of his or her discretion, to decide whether the relevance of the evidence could reasonably have been anticipated (*R v Scott* (1984) 79 Cr App R 49; *R v Day* (1940) 27 Cr App R 168). A party may rely on the exception where the evidence in question was not at the outset clearly relevant, but only marginally, minimally or doubtfully relevant (*R v Levy* (1966) 50 Cr App R 198), or constituted fanciful and unreal statements, e.g., allegations which were obviously ridiculous and untrue (*R v Hutchinson* (1985) 82 Cr App R 51). Under the second exception, the judge has a discretion to admit evidence which has not been adduced by reason of inadvertence or oversight. The evidence is usually of a formal or uncontentious nature (see *R v Waller* [1910] 1 KB 364; *Price v Humphries* [1958] 2 QB 353; and *Palastanga v Solman* [1962] Crim LR 334), but sometimes relates to a matter of substance (see *Piggott v Sims* [1973] RTR 15 and *Middleton v Rowlett* [1954] 1 WLR 831). It has been held that the judge's discretion to admit evidence after the close of a party's case is not confined to the two well-established exceptions, but the wider discretion should be exercised only on the rarest of occasions (*R v Francis* [1991] 1 WLR 1264), as when an important witness arrives late for reasons beyond his or her control (see, e.g., *James v South Glamorgan County Council* (1994) 99 Cr App R 321). **47.52**

Although the exceptions to the general rule of practice are well-established, more recent authorities permit the court to take a generalised discretionary approach to admissibility, having regard to whether the defendant will be unfairly prejudiced (as when the defence would have been conducted differently had the evidence in question been adduced at an earlier stage). In *Jolly v Director of Public Prosecutions* [2000] Crim LR 471, applied in *Cook v Director of Public Prosecutions* [2001] Crim LR 321, it was said to be 'beyond argument' that there is a general discretion to permit the prosecution to call evidence after closing its case. Before exercising the discretion, the court would look carefully at the interests of justice overall and, in particular, the risk of any prejudice whatsoever to the defence. The result is that the discretion would be sparingly exercised, but it is doubtful whether it assists a court to speak in terms of 'exceptional circumstances'. Each case must be considered on its own facts. In civil cases, where obviously regard must be had to the overriding objective, a broadly similar approach has been adopted. In *Stocznia Gdanska SA v Latvian Shipping Co.* (2000) LTL 12/2/2001 the claimants, after the close of the trial but before judgment had been handed down, sought to adduce further relevant evidence, namely, a document which ought to have been disclosed by one of the defendants and which the claimants could not have obtained by other means. It was held that the claimants could rely on the document and that, in accordance with the overriding objective, it would not be just to ignore it.

REFRESHING THE MEMORY

Refreshing memory in court

47.53 A witness who, in examination-in-chief, experiences difficulty in recollecting the events to which his or her evidence relates, may refer to a document such as a diary, log or other written statement, or, it seems, to a tape recording (see *R v Bailey* (2001) LTL 19/3/2001), in order to refresh his or her memory, provided that:

(a) it was made or verified by the witness at the time of the events to which it relates, or so shortly afterwards that the facts were still fresh in the witness's memory;
(b) it is produced for inspection by the court and opposite party; and
(c) it is, in prescribed cases, the original.

The principle operates not only where the witness does in fact refresh his or her memory, but also where the witness has no recollection of the events in question, but simply gives evidence as to the accuracy of the contents of the document. In both cases, however, it is the testimony of the witness, and not the document, which constitutes the evidence in the case. In *Maugham v Hubbard* (1828) 8 B & C 14 a witness called to prove that he had received a sum of money, looked at an unstamped acknowledgment that he had signed, and then gave evidence that he had no doubt that he had received the money, but had no recollection of having done so. It was held that his oral evidence sufficed to establish receipt of the money, the acknowledgment being incapable of being received in evidence because it was unstamped. In these circumstances, it is submitted that rather than preserve a fiction, it would be better to concede that the court is, in effect, admitting the written statement for the truth of its contents by way of exception to the hearsay rule. In fact the statement itself is admissible, with the permission of the court, as evidence of the truth of its contents, under the Civil Evidence Act 1995, s. 6(2)(a) (see **51.7**). Indeed, under the modern law, the scope for refreshing memory in court has been much reduced by reason of the existence of s. 6(2)(a) and the fact that in most cases it will be a witness's witness statement that stands as his or her evidence-in-chief (see **chapter 49**).

47.54 **Conditions** The document 'must have been written either at the time of the transaction or so shortly afterwards that the facts were fresh in [the witness's] memory' (*Phipson on Evidence*, 11th ed., 1970, at p. 634, para. 1528), a definition which provides a measure of elasticity and should not be taken to confine witnesses to an over-short period (*R v Richardson* [1971] 2 QB 484). The question is obviously one of fact and degree, and for this reason the precedents are of limited, if any, value. The entry in the document may have been made or verified by the witness. As to the former, the document may be used even if based on earlier notes or jottings, provided that when written up, the facts were still fresh in the memory (*Attorney-General's Reference (No. 3 of 1979)* (1979) 69 Cr App R 411). The witness may also refresh his or her memory from a copy of the original document, where the original has been destroyed, provided that the court is satisfied that the copy is accurate or substantially reproduces the original (*Topham v McGregor* (1844) 1 Car & K 320). See also *R v Mills* [1962] 1 WLR 1152 (notes written up by a witness with the assistance of a tape recording made by him but which was not itself admitted in evidence). The document may have been prepared by another, provided that the witness has verified it while the events were still fresh in his or her memory (*Burroughs v Martin* (1809) 2 Camp 112). Thus in *Anderson v Whalley* (1852) 3 Car & K 54, entries in a ship's log made by the mate and verified by the captain about a week later could be used by the latter to refresh his memory. A witness may also make use of a note dictated to another and then verified, whether by reading it personally or listening to it being read out, provided, in the latter case, that the other is called to prove that the note used in court is the note that was dictated and read back (*R v Kelsey* (1981) 74 Cr App R 213). In all cases, the document must be produced for inspection by the opposite party, who may wish to cross-examine the witness on its contents (*Beech v Jones* (1848) 5 CB 696). In cases, like *Maugham v Hubbard* (1828) 8 B & C 14, in which the witness has no recollection of the events in question but gives evidence as to the accuracy of what is recorded in the document, the original document must be produced (*Doe d Church and Phillips v Perkins* (1790) 3 TR 749), but where the original has been lost or destroyed, a verified or accurate copy will suffice (*Topham v McGregor* (1844) 1 Car & K 320).

Cross-examination on the document Cross-examining counsel may inspect the document without thereby making it evidence in the case. Counsel may also cross-examine on it without thereby making it evidence, but only if the cross-examination does not go beyond the parts used by the witness to refresh his or her memory. Cross-examination on other parts of the document entitles the party calling the witness to put the document in evidence and to let the tribunal of fact see the document on which the cross-examination has been based (*Gregory v Tavernor* (1833) 6 Car & P 280; *Senat v Senat* [1965] P 172 at p. 177). The document will then be admissible as evidence of the truth of its contents. The Civil Evidence Act 1995, s. 6 provides as follows: **47.55**

(4) Nothing in this Act affects any of the rules of law as to the circumstances in which, where a person called as a witness in civil proceedings is cross-examined on a document used by him to refresh his memory, that document may be made evidence in the proceedings.
(5) Nothing in this section shall be construed as preventing a statement of any description referred to above from being admissible by virtue of section 1 as evidence of the matters stated.

It seems reasonably clear that the intention underlying these two subsections, when taken together, was to perpetuate the rule formerly stated with clarity in the Civil Evidence Act 1968, s. 3(2), that where a memory-refreshing document is made evidence in the proceedings, any statement made in the document will be admissible as evidence of the matters stated. It is submitted that the subsections should be construed in this way notwithstanding that whereas subsection (5) refers to 'a statement of any description referred to above', subsection (4) refers not to 'a statement', but to 'a document'.

Refreshing memory out of court

It is a common practice for a witness, before giving testimony, to refresh his or her memory from statements or notes made by him or her at a time closer to the events in question, whether a private note or record, a proof of evidence, or a witness statement as such. Any rule to the contrary would be unenforceable, would make testimony more a test of memory than truthfulness, and would tend to create difficulties for honest witnesses, but be likely to do little to hamper dishonest witnesses (*R v Richardson* [1971] 2 QB 484). The conditions which apply in the case of a witness refreshing his memory while giving evidence do not apply to the witness who refreshes his or her memory outside the witness box (*R v Richardson*). However, as in t he case of refreshing memory while giving evidence, cross-examining counsel is entitled to call for, inspect and cross-examine on a document which a witness has used to refresh his or her memory outside court but has not used while giving evidence, and if counsel cross-examines on material which has not been referred to by the witness, the party calling the witness may put the document in evidence, rendering it admissible as evidence of the matters it states (see *Owen v Edwards* (1983) 77 Cr App R 191 at p. 195, and the Civil Evidence Act 1995, s. 6(4) and (5), considered at 47.55). **47.56**

It is open to the judge, in the exercise of his or her discretion and in the interests of justice, to permit a witness who has begun to give his or her evidence, to withdraw and refresh his or her memory from a statement made by him or her closer to the time of the events in question, even if not made at the time of the events or so soon thereafter that the facts were fresh in the memory, if the following conditions are met:

(a) the witness says that he or she cannot now recall the details of the events because of the lapse of time;
(b) the witness made a statement much nearer the time of the event, the contents of which represented his or her recollection at that time;
(c) the witness did not read the statement before giving evidence; and
(d) the witness wishes to read the statement before continuing to give evidence.

The witness may withdraw from the witness box to read the statement, in which case there must be no communication with the witness, or the statement may be read by the witness in the witness box, but either way, the statement must be removed from the witness when he or she continues to give evidence, and the witness should not be permitted to refer to it again (see *R v Da Silva* [1990] 1 WLR 31). An alternative solution to the problem, in appropriate circumstances, would be for the party calling the witness to seek leave to admit the previous statement for the truth of its contents under the Civil Evidence Act 1995, s. 6(2)(a) (see further at 51.7).

R v Da Silva has not created a rule of law that a witness, once in the witness box, can refer to a statement only if all four of the conditions specified in that case are met, because the court has a discretion whether to allow a witness to refresh his or her memory from a non-contemporaneous statement: see *R v South Ribble Magistrates, ex parte Cochrane* [1996] 2 Cr App R 544, where a witness who had read his statement before giving evidence, but had not taken it in properly, was allowed to refresh his memory. See also *R v Gordon* [2002] EWCA Crim 1, LTL 7/2/2002, where a witness, who was unable, because of dyslexia, to read his statement, adopted it after it was read out by counsel. It was held that there are no fixed and immutable rules to be followed before a witness can refresh memory by a document prepared when his or her memory was clearer, but there is a broad fact-sensitive judicial discretion to be exercised in the interests of fairness and justice.

PREVIOUS CONSISTENT STATEMENTS

The rule

47.57 At common law, as a general rule a previous consistent or self-serving statement of a witness is excluded as evidence of his or her consistency. Thus, a witness may not be asked in examination-in-chief about former oral or written statements made by him or her and consistent with the testimony which he or she is giving, and evidence about those statements should not be elicited from any other witness. The rule is usually justified on the basis that without it, a witness could manufacture evidence with ease (see, e.g., *R v Roberts* [1942] 1 All ER 187 at p. 191). In *Corke v Corke* [1958] P 93 a husband petitioned for divorce on the ground of adultery. One night he had accused his wife of having recently committed adultery with a lodger. The Court of Appeal held that the wife, who denied adultery, had been improperly permitted to give evidence that shortly after the husband's accusation, she had telephoned her doctor and asked him to examine herself and the lodger with a view to showing that there had been no recent sexual intercourse.

Exceptions

47.58 In civil proceedings, there are only three exceptions to the rule, under each of which the previous statement is admitted not only as evidence of consistency, but also as evidence of the facts it contains. They are:

(a) previous statements admissible, with the permission of the court, under the Civil Evidence Act 1995, s. 6(2);

(b) statements in documents used by a witness to refresh his or her memory, in cases in which cross-examination on the document has gone beyond the parts of it relied on by the witness, so that the document has become evidence in the case; and
(c) statements in rebuttal of allegations of recent fabrication.

The first two of these exceptions are considered at 51.7 and 47.55 respectively.

There is no general further exception to the effect that a witness who has been cross-examined to show inconsistencies, can be re-examined to show consistency by reference to a previous statement (*R v Beattie* (1989) 89 Cr App R 302 at p. 307). However, the court does have a residual discretion to permit such re-examination to ensure that the tribunal of fact is not positively misled by the cross-examination as to the existence of some fact or the terms of an earlier statement (*R v Ali* [2003] EWCA Crim 3214, [2004] 1 Cr App R 501).

Statements admissible to rebut allegations of recent fabrication

A previous consistent statement will not be admissible to bolster the credibility of a witness simply because his or her evidence was impeached in cross-examination, even if the impeachment took the form of showing a contradiction or inconsistency between his or her evidence and something he or she said on a previous occasion (see *R v Coll* (1889) 25 LR Ir 522 at p. 541 and *R v Beattie* (1989) 89 Cr App R 302 at pp. 306–7, and contrast, but question, *Ahmed v Brumfitt* (1967) 112 SJ 32). However, if in cross-examination it is suggested that his or her version of events is a recent fabrication, evidence of his or her previous statements to the same effect will become admissible, and will normally be elicited in re-examination (*R v Oyesiku* (1971) 56 Cr App R 240; and see also *Flanagan v Fahy* [1918] 2 IR 361 and *Fox v General Medical Council* [1960] 1 WLR 1017). In *R v Oyesiku* the Court of Appeal adopted as a correct statement of the law the judgment of Dixon CJ in *Nominal Defendant v Clement* (1961) 104 CLR 476 (High Court of Australia), from which the following propositions derive: **47.59**

(a) The exception requires a suggestion in cross-examination that the witness's account has been recently invented or reconstructed, even though not with conscious dishonesty.
(b) The previous statement is admissible if it was made contemporaneously with the event or at a time sufficiently early to be inconsistent with the suggestion of recent fabrication.
(c) The judge should exercise care to assure himself or herself that:
   (i) the account given is attacked on the ground of recent invention or reconstruction or a foundation for such an attack has been laid;
   (ii) the contents of the previous statement are to like effect as the account given in evidence; and
   (iii) the previous statement, having regard to the time and circumstances in which it was made, rationally tends to answer the attack.

In civil proceedings, a previous statement admissible under the exception is admissible not merely to confirm the witness's credit, but also as evidence of the facts contained in it. The Civil Evidence Act 1995, s. 6, provides as follows:

> (2) A party who has called or intends to call a person as a witness in civil proceedings may not in those proceedings adduce evidence of a previous statement made by that person, except—
> . . .
> (b) for the purpose of rebutting a suggestion that his evidence has been fabricated.
> . . .
> (5) Nothing in this section shall be construed as preventing a statement of any description referred to above from being admissible by virtue of section 1 as evidence of the matters stated.

UNFAVOURABLE AND HOSTILE WITNESSES

Rule against attacking the credit of one's own witnesses

47.60 At common law, if a witness fails to come up to proof, or gives adverse evidence, such as evidence in support of the other party's version of the facts in issue, the party calling the witness is not thereby entitled to turn around and seek to impeach his or her credit or otherwise cross-examine the witness as if he or she were a witness for the opposite party: the party calling the witness will not be allowed, therefore, to question the witness about, or adduce evidence of, such matters as his or her bias or bad character, any previous convictions, or any previous inconsistent statements. The rule has now been put on a statutory basis (see Criminal Procedure Act 1865, s. 3, at **47.62**). There are limited exceptions to this general rule in the case of hostile witnesses, but not in the case of witnesses who are merely unfavourable.

Unfavourable witnesses

47.61 An unfavourable witness is one who, displaying no hostility to the party calling him or her, fails to come up to proof or gives evidence unfavourable to that party. At common law, the party calling the witness is not permitted to impeach his or her credit, but may call other witnesses to give evidence of those matters as to which it was expected that the unfavourable witness would testify. In *Ewer v Ambrose* (1825) 3 B & C 746 a witness called by the defendant to prove a certain partnership, gave evidence to the contrary. It was held that the defendant, although not entitled to adduce general evidence to show that the witness was not to be believed on his oath, could contradict him by calling other witnesses. As Littledale J observed, were the rule otherwise, it would attach undue importance to the order in which witnesses are called: if a party with four witnesses to prove his case were to call first the one who happened to disprove it, he would be deprived of the evidence of the other three.

Hostile witnesses

47.62 A hostile witness is one who, in the opinion of the judge, shows no desire to tell the truth at the instance of the party calling him or her, to whom he or she displays a hostile animus (Stephen, *Digest of the Law of Evidence*, 12th ed., art. 147). In criminal cases, the prosecution may call a person as a witness even if that person has shown signs that he or she is likely to be a hostile witness, e.g., by retracting a statement or by making a second statement (*see R v Mann* (1972) 56 Cr App R 750 and *R v Dat* [1998] Crim LR 488). Similarly, in civil proceedings it seems that a party may call a witness who has indicated that he or she may be hostile, e.g., by refusing to make a statement or by refusing to testify having agreed to do so. (**CPR, r. 32.9**, under which a party unable to obtain a witness statement may seek permission to serve a witness summary instead, is discussed at **49.18**.)

At common law the judge has a discretion whether to treat a witness as hostile and allow the witness to be cross-examined by the party calling him or her, and the judge's decision will seldom be challenged successfully on appeal (*Rice v Howard* (1886) 16 QBD 681; *Price v Manning* (1889) 42 ChD 372). If a witness fails to give the evidence expected, or gives evidence contrary to an earlier statement, the judge should first consider inviting the witness to refresh his or her memory from material which can properly be used for that purpose, rather than simply proceeding to treat the witness as hostile, unless he or she displays such an excessive degree of hostility that that is the only appropriate course (*R v Maw* [1994] Crim LR 841). The judge will have regard to the attitude and demeanour of the witness, his or her willingness to cooperate, and any previous contradictory or inconsistent statements.

Under the Criminal Procedure Act 1865, s. 3, if a witness is treated as hostile, the party calling the witness may prove prior statements made by the witness and inconsistent with his or her evidence. Section 3 provides as follows:

> A party producing a witness shall not be allowed to impeach his credit by general evidence of bad

character, but he may, in case the witness shall, in the opinion of the judge, prove adverse, contradict him by other evidence, or, by leave of the judge, prove that he has made at other times a statement inconsistent with his present testimony; but before such last mentioned proof can be given the circumstances of the supposed statement, sufficient to designate the particular occasion, must be mentioned to the witness, and he must be asked whether or not he made such statement.

The word 'adverse', in s. 3, means hostile (*Greenough v Eccles* (1859) 5 CB NS 786, a decision under the Common Law Procedure (Amendment) Act 1856, s. 22, which was repealed but re-enacted by s. 3 of the 1865 Act). The first part of s. 3 applies to both unfavourable and hostile witnesses and is nothing more than a statutory re-statement of the common law rule against attacking the credit of one's own witnesses (see **47.60**). The next part of the section, which allows the party calling the witness to contradict him or her by other evidence, applies only to hostile witnesses, but has not affected the rule at common law that a party may contradict an *unfavourable* witness by calling other witnesses (*Greenough v Eccles*). The final part of the section, which permits proof of previous inconsistent statements, applies only in the case of hostile witnesses.

If a witness is treated as hostile, at common law the party calling the witness may ask him or her leading questions. Section 3 of the 1865 Act has not removed this right. Thus, where a witness has made a statement in favour of a party, but when called to testify, stands mute of malice and is treated as hostile, then although the case may not be governed by s. 3, because the witness has given no 'testimony', at common law he or she may be asked leading questions and the witness's previous statement may be put to him or her (*R v Thompson* (1976) 64 Cr App R 96, relying upon *Clarke v Saffery* (1824) Ry & M 126 and *Bastin v Carew* (1824) Ry & M 127). However, it is submitted that if, in these circumstances, the witness were to deny making the previous statement, it could not be proved at common law.

A hostile witness who is cross-examined on a previous inconsistent statement under s. 3 of the 1865 Act may or may not accept the truth of the contents of the statement. If its truth is accepted, the previous statement in effect becomes part of the witness's evidence and, subject to the assessment of his or her credibility, is capable of being accepted (*R v Maw* [1994] Crim LR 841). If its truth is not admitted by the witness, the previous statement is admissible as evidence of the matters stated by virtue of the Civil Evidence Act 1995, s. 6, which provides as follows:

(3) Where in the case of civil proceedings section 3 . . . of the Criminal Procedure Act 1865 applies, which [makes] provision as to—
 (a) how far a witness may be discredited by the party producing him, . . .
 this Act does not authorise the adducing of evidence of a previous inconsistent or contradictory statement otherwise than in accordance with those sections.

. . .

(5) Nothing in this section shall be construed as preventing a statement of any description referred to above from being admissible by virtue of section 1 as evidence of the matters stated.

It follows that if the witness does not admit the truth of the previous statement, the tribunal must decide whether to accept as true the contents of the previous statement or the evidence of the witness. The more recent criminal authorities suggest that there is no inflexible rule to the effect that a hostile witness's evidence should be regarded as unreliable where he or she is shown to have made previous inconsistent statements (see, e.g., *R v Pestano* [1981] Crim LR 397; *R v Governor of Pentonville Prison, ex parte Alves* [1993] AC 284 and *R v Goodway* [1993] 4 All ER 894 at p. 899; and contrast *R v Golder* [1960] 1 WLR 1169 at pp. 1172–3, approved in *R v Oliva* [1965] 1 WLR 1028). This more recent approach, it is submitted, has much to commend it, not least because in some cases the witness will be able to give a convincing explanation for the inconsistency: whether the judge can give any credence to the witness, and if so, which parts of his or her evidence, if any, the judge should accept, are questions which fall to be resolved in the light of the particular circumstances of each case.

FINALITY ON COLLATERAL ISSUES

The rule

47.63 The general rule at common law is that the answers given by a witness under cross-examination to questions on collateral issues, i.e. issues which are not directly relevant to the facts in issues in the case, must be treated as final, not in the sense that the tribunal of fact must accept the truth of the answers, but in the sense that the cross-examining party should not be allowed to call further evidence with a view to contradicting the witness. The rationale of the rule is to prevent the proliferation of issues of minimal or marginal relevance to the facts in issue, which would prolong the trial unnecessarily. Thus, it has been held that where a witness gives evidence through an interpreter and under cross-examination about his knowledge of English, denies that he is able to speak the language, the matter will normally be quite irrelevant to any matter directly in issue in the proceedings, and therefore evidence in rebuttal will normally be inadmissible (see *R v Burke* (1858) 8 Cox CC 44). In *Attorney-General v Hitchcock* (1847) 1 Ex 91, in which a prosecution witness, under cross-examination, denied that he had made an out-of-court statement to a certain Cook to the effect that Excise officers had offered to give him £20 to give false evidence, it was held that the defence were not allowed to call Cook to give evidence in rebuttal, on the basis that it was irrelevant to the matters in issue that someone had thought fit to offer a bribe, which was not accepted, to give an untrue account of a transaction. The decision is not easily reconciled with *R v M* [2004] EWCA Crim 2085, LTL 6/7/2004. In that case, the sexual offences which formed the basis of the charge came to light when a private investigator and enquiry agents, being used by a man, S, whose wife had been having an affair with the accused, interviewed the victims. The accused said that S had induced the victims to give evidence against him by offers of financial reward, but all the victims denied any such financial inducement. It was held that the accused should have been allowed to call a witness to give evidence that she had been approached by the private investigator, and that when she had refused to give adverse information, had been told that S had unlimited funds for the right information. The court was of the view that although the witness's evidence, viewed in isolation, was collateral and 'borderline', it was relevant as showing that the victims might have been offered money or been influenced by the offer of money.

According to Pollock CB in *Attorney-General v Hitchcock*, if the witness's answer is a matter on which the cross-examining party would be allowed to introduce evidence-in-chief, because of its connection with the issues in the case, then the matter is not collateral and may be rebutted. This test seems to be circular, and the cases show that it is not always easy to tell whether an issue is collateral. The explanation probably lies in the fact that relevance is a question of degree on which views may differ and the answer to which may turn on whether the matter which the cross-examining party seeks to prove is a single fact which is easy of proof or a broad issue involving a difficult and complex fact-finding task (see *R v S* [1992] Crim LR 307). Questions which go *merely* to the credit of the witness are clearly collateral, but it does not follow that questions on all other matters are not collateral. This is because in some cases the difference between questions going to credit and questions going to the issue will be barely discernible, if it can be said to exist at all. *R v Busby* (1981) 75 Cr App R 79 illustrates the point well. In that case, police officers under cross-examination denied two matters, that they had made up statements attributed to the accused and indicative of his guilt and that they had threatened W, a potential defence witness, to stop him from testifying. The Court of Appeal held that W should have been allowed to give evidence that he had been threatened by the officers, because it was evidence relevant to an issue in the case in that, if true, it showed that the police were prepared to go to improper lengths to secure a conviction, which would have supported the defence case that the statements attributed to him had been fabricated. Of this case, it has since been said that it has created a new exception to the general rule (see *R v Funderburk* [1990] 2 All ER 482 at p. 486), but it has also been said that the facts came within the exception of bias (see 47.66) and that if the case cannot be explained on that basis, it is inconsistent with the general rule itself (*R v Edwards* [1991] 1 WLR 207 at p. 215).

To the general rule there are exceptions in the case of the previous convictions of a witness, his or her bias, a physical or mental disability affecting his or her reliability, and his or her reputation for untruthfulness. It is also convenient and usual to treat as an exception to the general rule proof of a witness's previous inconsistent statement, although strictly speaking such proof is not covered by the general rule, because permitted only where the statement is 'relative to the subject matter of the . . . proceeding' (Criminal Procedure Act 1865, ss. 4 and 5, considered at 47.64).

Previous inconsistent statements

The proof of previous oral or written statements in civil proceedings is governed by the Criminal Procedure Act 1865, ss. 4 and 5. Section 4 applies to both oral and written statements; s. 5 applies to written statements only (per Lord Taylor of Gosforth CJ in *R v Derby Magistrates' Court, ex parte B* [1996] AC 487 at pp. 498–9). They provide as follows: **47.64**

4. If a witness, upon cross-examination as to a former statement made by him relative to the subject matter of the indictment or proceeding, and inconsistent with his present testimony, does not distinctly admit that he has made such a statement, proof may be given that he did in fact make it; but before such proof can be given, the circumstances of the supposed statement, sufficient to designate the particular occasion, must be mentioned to the witness, and he must be asked whether or not he made such statement.
5. A witness may be cross-examined as to previous statements made by him in writing or reduced into writing relative to the subject matter of the indictment or proceeding, without such writing being shown to him; but if it is intended to contradict such witness by the writing, his attention must, before such contradictory proof can be given, be called to those parts of the writing which are to be used for the purpose of so contradicting him; provided always, that it shall be competent for the judge, at any time during the trial, to require the production of the writing for his inspection, and he may thereupon make such use of it for the purposes of the trial as he may think fit.

Both sections assume, correctly, the common law right to cross-examine a witness about previous inconsistent statements, and although they are not confined to previous statements made on oath (*R v Hart* (1957) 42 Cr App R 47; *R v O'Neill* [1969] Crim LR 260), they are confined to statements 'relative to the subject matter of the . . . proceeding'. Under s. 4, proof may be given that the witness made a previous inconsistent statement if 'he does not distinctly admit that he has made such a statement', wording which covers not only the witness who denies that he or she made the statement, but also the witness who, when asked whether he or she made the statement, gives an equivocal answer, or states that he or she has no recollection of having done so, or declines to answer at all.

Under s. 5, a witness may be cross-examined about a previous inconsistent statement contained in a document, without the document being shown to the witness, but the cross-examining party must have the document with him or her, even if that party does not intend to contradict the witness with it, because under the section the judge may require production of the document for inspection and may make such use of it as he or she may think fit (*R v Anderson* (1929) 21 Cr App R 178). In the first instance, counsel may have the document handed to the witness, mentioning the circumstances 'sufficient to designate the particular occasion', draw the witness's attention to the relevant passage, ask the witness to read it to himself or herself, and then ask whether the witness adheres to the evidence already given. If the witness accepts the truth of the previous statement, it becomes part of his or her evidence which, to that extent, will have changed. If the witness adheres to the evidence he or she has already given, there is no obligation to prove the document, a course which counsel may wish to avoid if the discrepancy is minor or the statement taken as a whole tends to confirm rather than contradict the witness. This is because in civil proceedings, where a previous inconsistent statement is put in evidence, whether under s. 4 or s. 5 of the 1865 Act, it is admissible not only to impugn the credibility of the witness, but as evidence of the truth of its contents. The Civil Evidence Act 1995, s. 6 provides as follows:

> (3) Where in the case of civil proceedings section . . . 4 or 5 of the Criminal Procedure Act 1865 applies, which make provision as to—
>
> . . .
>
> (b) the proof of contradictory statements made by a witness, and
>
> (c) cross-examination as to previous statements made in writing,
>
> this Act does not authorise the adducing of evidence of a previous or contradictory statement otherwise than in accordance with those sections.
>
> . . .
>
> (5) Nothing in this section shall be construed as preventing a statement of any description referred to above from being admissible by virtue of section 1 as evidence of the matters stated.

Previous convictions

47.65 The Criminal Procedure Act 1865, s. 6, provides as follows:

> If, upon a witness being lawfully questioned as to whether he has been convicted of any felony or misdemeanour, he either denies or does not admit the fact, or refuses to answer, it shall be lawful for the cross-examining party to prove such conviction.

Although s. 6 appears to cover cross-examination and proof of any conviction of any witness, irrespective of relevance to either credibility or the issues in the case (see per Cairns J in *Clifford v Clifford* [1961] 1 WLR 1274 at p. 1276), it is submitted that the section operates subject to the general common law power of the judge to restrain unnecessary, irrelevant or unduly oppressive questions in cross-examination (see, e.g., per Lawton J in *R v Sweet-Escott* (1971) 55 Cr App R 316). *R v Sweet-Escott* applies equally to civil claims (*Watson v Chief Constable of Cleveland Police* [2001] EWCA Civ 1547, LTL 12/10/2001), so that convictions that are not relevant should not be put to witnesses. It is not only convictions for offences of dishonesty that reflect on the credibility of witnesses (*Clifford v Clifford*) and a number of offences can affect credibility. The operation of the section is also restricted by the Rehabilitation of Offenders Act 1974, whereby cross-examination of any witness about 'spent' convictions is prohibited (s. 4(1)), unless the judge is satisfied that it is not possible for justice to be done except by admitting the convictions (s. 7(3)). Evidence of the conviction may be admitted under s. 7(3) not only if relevant to an issue in the case, but also if relevant merely to credit, but the judge should weigh its relevance against its prejudicial effect and admit it only if satisfied that otherwise the parties would not have a fair trial or the witness's credit could not be fairly assessed (*Thomas v Commissioner of Police of the Metropolis* [1997] QB 813).

Bias

47.66 Evidence is admissible to rebut a witness's denial of bias or partiality towards one of the parties and to show that he or she is prejudiced in relation to the case in which he or she appears (see per Geoffrey Lane LJ in *R v Mendy* (1976) 64 Cr App R 4 at p. 6). Thus where a female employee of a party is called as his witness and under cross-examination denies that she is his kept mistress, the other party may call evidence to contradict her (*Thomas v David* (1836) 7 Car & P 350). Likewise evidence will be admissible to rebut the evidence of a witness who, under cross-examination, denies having threatened to be revenged on the cross-examining party following a quarrel with him or her (*R v Shaw* (1888) 16 Cox CC 503), or denies acceptance of a bribe to testify against the cross-examining party (*Attorney-General v Hitchcock* (1847) 1 Ex 91).

Evidence of disability affecting reliability

47.67 Expert medical evidence is admissible to show that a witness is suffering from some physical or mental disability that affects the reliability of his or her evidence. Such evidence is not confined to a general opinion of the unreliability of the witness, but may cover all the matters necessary to show not only the foundation of and reasons for the diagnosis, but also the extent to which the credibility of the witness is affected. Thus, if a witness says that he or she saw something from a distance of 50 yards, it is possible to adduce the evidence of an oculist to show that the witness cannot see beyond 20 yards, or the evidence of a surgeon who had removed a cataract from which the witness was suffering at the material time. Equally, it is permissible to call medical evidence of mental illness which makes a witness incapable of giving reliable evidence, whether through the existence of delusions or otherwise.

The principle only operates if the disability from which the witness suffers is a proper subject of expert evidence: partiality, prejudice, self-interest, imagination and inaccuracy are matters which, generally speaking, the tribunal of fact, helped by cross-examination and common sense, must assess without expert assistance (see per Lord Pearce in *Toohey v Metropolitan Police Commissioner* [1965] AC 595 at pp. 608–9. In *R v MacKenney* [2003] EWCA Crim 3643, [2004] 2 Cr App R 32, the accused were convicted of murder. At their trial, they alleged that the chief prosecution witness had fabricated his evidence and sought to call a psychologist by whom the witness had refused to be assessed. The psychologist watched the witness testify and formed the opinion that he was a psychopath who was likely to be lying and whose mental state meant that his demeanour and behaviour in giving evidence would not betray the usual indications to the jury that he was lying. The psychologist's evidence was ruled inadmissible and the convictions were upheld on appeal. On a subsequent referral to the Court of Appeal by the Criminal Cases Review Commission, there was fresh evidence from a psychiatrist, who also had not assessed the witness, whose opinion was very similar to that of the psychologist who had observed the witness at the trial. It was held that the evidence of the psychologist would today be admissible, and on that basis the conviction was quashed. It was held that the absence of a pre-trial assessment by the expert went to the weight to be attached to the opinion, not to its admissibility.

A party, A, cannot call a witness of fact, W, and then call a psychologist or psychiatrist to give reasons why the tribunal of fact should regard W as reliable. But if the other party, B, proposes to call an expert to say that W should be regarded as unreliable because of some mental abnormality calling for expert evidence, then A may call an expert in rebuttal or, anticipating B's evidence, as part of his own case. Where B does not call an expert, but puts a case in cross-examination that W is unreliable by reason of mental abnormality, this may also be open to rebuttal by expert evidence, although much may depend on the nature of the abnormality and of the cross-examination. If such expert evidence is admitted, it must be restricted to the specific challenge, and should not extend to 'oath-helping' (*R v Robinson* [1994] 3 All ER 346).

Evidence of reputation for untruthfulness

There is a long-established rule at common law that a party may call a witness to give evidence that in his or her opinion a witness called by the opposite party is not to be believed on his or her oath. The details of the rule, in its present form, are to be found in *R v Richardson* (1968) 52 Cr App R 317 at p. 323 and are not rehearsed here. The rule is rarely used, even in criminal proceedings, and it is submitted that in civil cases it would be better forgotten, because it encourages exactly that which the rule of finality was designed to prevent, namely the undue prolongation of trials from too close an examination of the credit of witnesses (see also per Lord Pearce in *Toohey v Metropolitan Police Commissioner* [1965] AC 595 at p. 606). **47.68**

EVIDENCE OF CHARACTER AND DISPOSITION

Character as a fact in issue or relevant to a fact in issue

47.69 Evidence of the character of a party or non-party is clearly admissible if it is in issue or of direct relevance to the facts in issue in a case. The law of defamation provides a number of examples. Thus on the question of liability, in an action in which justification is pleaded, the claimant's character will clearly be in issue; the claimant, in order to rebut a defence of fair comment, may adduce evidence of his or her good reputation at the time of publication of the allegedly defamatory material; and the character of the claimant, if he or she succeeds, is of direct relevance to the quantum of recoverable damages (see *Cornwell v Myskow* [1987] 1 WLR 630).

Character relevant to credit

47.70 Anyone who testifies, whether or not a party to the proceedings, is open to cross-examination on his or her character in so far as it is relevant to his or her credibility as a witness, subject to the general discretion of the judge to prevent any questions in cross-examination which, in the judge's opinion, are unnecessary, improper or oppressive, and subject also to CPR, r. 32.1(3), which baldly provides that, 'The court may limit cross-examination'. In *Hobbs v Tinling* [1929] 2 KB 1 at p. 51, Sankey LJ held that the court, in the exercise of its discretion to disallow questions as to credit in cross-examination, should have regard to the following principles, which derive from the Indian Evidence Act (I of 1872), s. 148:

(1) Such questions are proper if they are of such a nature that the truth of the imputation conveyed by them would seriously affect the opinion of the court as to the credibility of the witness on the matter to which he testifies.
(2) Such questions are improper if the imputation which they convey relates to matters so remote in time, or of such a character, that the truth of the imputation would not affect, or would affect in a slight degree, the opinion of the court as to the credibility of the witness on the matter to which he testifies.
(3) Such questions are improper if there is a great disproportion between the importance of the imputation made against the witness's character and the importance of his evidence.

There are similar, but more detailed, provisions dealing with the character of witnesses in criminal cases in the Criminal Justice Act 2004, ss. 100 to 106 (see *Blackstone's Criminal Practice 2006*, F12–14). In *O'Brien v Chief Constable of South Wales Police* [2005] UKHL 26, [2005] 2 AC 534, the House of Lords said that while the Criminal Justice Act 2004 does not apply as such to civil claims, ss. 100 to 106 contain policy considerations which a civil judge will wish to keep in mind when exercising the discretion to exclude under CPR, r 32.1.

In *R v Sweet-Escott* (1971) 55 Cr App R 316 at p. 320 Lawton J, in answer to the question, 'How far back is it permissible for advocates when cross-examining as to credit to delve into a man's past and to drag up such dirt as they can find there?', said, 'Since the purpose of cross-examination as to credit is to show that the witness ought not to be believed on his oath, the matters about which he is questioned must relate to his likely standing after cross-examination with the tribunal which is trying him or listening to his evidence'.

As a general rule, the cross-examining party is not allowed to adduce evidence to contradict a witness's answer to a question going to his or her credit, but there are exceptions in the case of such matters as previous convictions and prejudice or bias on the part of the witness (see 47.63 to 47.68).

Evidence of disposition

47.71 There is a dearth of modern authority on the question whether evidence of disposition towards good conduct on the part of the parties to civil litigation is admissible. It is submitted that such evidence should be admissible provided that it meets the ordinary requirement of relevance (but see *Attorney-General v Bowman* (1791) 2 Bos & P 532n). In *Hatton v Cooper* [2001] RTR 544, a case arising out of a collision between two cars in which there was an unusual dearth of relevant evidence, it was held that, on the question of liability, the trial judge had improperly relied on evidence from the claimant's employer that the claimant was an excellent driver, calm and assured, who never took risks. Jonathan Parker LJ said: 'In the context of a collision such as that which occurred in the instant case, the opinion of a third party as to the driving ability of either party is, in my judgment, completely worthless'.

As to so-called 'similar fact evidence', i.e., evidence of the disposition of the defendant towards wrongdoing, or the commission of a particular kind of civil wrong, whereas in criminal cases the test for admissibility has properly reflected a concern to safeguard the accused from the admission of unduly prejudicial evidence, in civil cases tried by a judge alone, the test approximates to the ordinary test of relevance, the question being whether the evidence in question is of sufficient probative force in relation to the facts in issue. For example, in *Hales v Kerr* [1908] 2 KB 601, an action in negligence in which the claimant alleged that he had contracted ringworm from a dirty razor used by the defendant, a hairdresser, evidence was admitted that two other customers shaved by the defendant had contracted ringworm. In *Joy v Phillips, Mills and Co. Ltd* [1916] 1 KB 849, a claim for workmen's compensation by the father of a deceased stable boy who had been kicked by a horse and had been found nearby holding a halter, evidence that the boy had previously teased horses with a halter was admitted in rebuttal of the allegation that the accident had occurred in the course of the boy's employment. In *Jones v Greater Manchester Police Authority* [2001] EWHC Admin 189, [2002] ACD 4, in proceedings for a sex offender order under the Crime and Disorder Act 1998, s. 2, it was held that evidence of propensity to commit sexual offences is relevant and admissible, because the court seeks to predict the extent to which past events give rise to reasonable cause for believing that an order is necessary to protect the public from serious harm, and that the admission of such evidence breaches neither **art. 6** nor **art. 8** of the **European Convention on Human Rights**. See also *Barrett v Long* (1851) 3 HL Cas 395, *Osborne v Chocqueel* [1896] 2 QB 109 and *Sattin v National Union Bank* (1978) 122 SJ 367.

In *Mood Music Publishing Co. Ltd v De Wolfe Publishing Ltd* [1976] Ch 119, an action for infringement of copyright in which the defendants admitted the similarity between the musical work in which the claimants owned the copyright and the work which they had produced, but alleged that the similarity was coincidental, evidence was admitted to show that on other occasions the defendants had produced musical works bearing a close resemblance to works which were the subject of copyright. It was held that the evidence had been properly admitted to rebut the allegation of coincidence. Lord Denning MR added a gloss to the ordinary test of relevance, although in so far as it relates to giving the other party fair notice of the intention to adduce the evidence, under the current cards-on-the-table approach to civil litigation it is of little significance. He said (at p. 127): 'In civil cases, the courts will admit evidence of similar facts if it is logically probative, that is, if it is logically relevant in determining the matter which is in issue: provided that it is not oppressive or unfair to the other side: and also that the other side has fair notice of it and is able to deal with it' (cf. *EG Music v SF (Film) Distributors Ltd* [1978] FSR 121 and *Berger v Raymond and Son Ltd* [1984] 1 WLR 625). This dictum, however, only applies to civil cases tried by a judge alone, who is trained to distinguish between what is probative and what is not: where there is a jury, the court must be more careful about admitting the evidence (per Dillon LJ in *Thorpe v Chief Constable of Greater Manchester Police* [1989] 1 WLR 665 at p. 670).

The leading authority is *O'Brien v Chief Constable of South Wales* [2005] UKHL 26, [2005] 2 AC 534. The claimant was convicted of murder. After serving 11 years in prison, his case was referred to the Criminal Cases Review Commission and his appeal was allowed. He then brought proceedings against the Chief Constable for misfeasance in public office and malicious prosecution, alleging that he had been 'framed' by a Detective Inspector L and a Detective

Chief Superintendent C, who was alleged to have approved some aspects of the misconduct alleged against L. The House of Lords held that evidence had properly been admitted to show that L had behaved with similar impropriety on two other occasions and that C had done so on one other occasion. The House of Lords held that the test of admissibility in civil cases is different from that which applies in criminal cases. There is no warrant for the automatic application of the criminal test in a civil suit. To do so would be to introduce an inflexibility which is inappropriate and undesirable. Lord Phillips of Worth Matravers said (at [53] to [56]):

> [53] I would simply apply the test of relevance as the test of admissibility of similar fact evidence in a civil suit. Such evidence is admissible if it is potentially probative of an issue in the action.
>
> [54] That is not to say that the policy considerations that have given rise to the complex rules . . . in the Criminal Justice Act 2003, ss. 100 to 106 [see generally *Blackstone's Criminal Practice 2006*, F12] have no part to play in the conduct of civil litigation. They are policy considerations which the judge who has the management of the civil litigation will wish to keep well in mind. **CPR, r. 1.2**, requires the court to give effect to the overriding objective of dealing with cases justly. This includes dealing with the case in a way which is proportionate to what is involved in the case, and in a manner which is expeditious and fair. **Rule 1.4** requires the court actively to manage the case in order to further the overriding objective. **Rule 32.1** gives the court the power to control the evidence. This power expressly enables the court to exclude evidence that would otherwise be admissible and to limit cross-examination.
>
> [55] Similar fact evidence will not necessarily risk causing any unfair prejudice to the party against whom it is directed . . . It may, however, carry such a risk. Evidence of impropriety which reflects adversely on the character of a party may risk causing prejudice that is disproportionate to its relevance, particularly where the trial is taking place before a jury. In such a case the judge will be astute to see that the probative cogency of the evidence justifies this risk of prejudice in the interests of a fair trial.
>
> [56] Equally, when considering whether to admit evidence, or permit cross-examination, on matters that are collateral to the central issues, the judge will have regard to the need for proportionality and expedition. He will consider whether the evidence in question is likely to be relatively uncontroversial, or whether its admission is likely to create side issues which will unbalance the trial and make it harder to see the wood from the trees.

DOCUMENTARY EVIDENCE

Proof of contents

47.72 Proof of the contents of a document on which a party seeks to rely is now largely, but not exclusively, governed by the Civil Evidence Act 1995, ss. 8 and 9, which are considered in detail at **51.15** to **51.17**. Under s. 8, where a statement contained in a document is admissible in evidence in civil proceedings, it may be proved by the production of that document, or, whether or not that document is still in existence, by the production of a copy of that document or the material part of it, authenticated in such manner as the court may approve (s. 8(1)); and it is immaterial for this purpose how many removes there are between a copy and the original (s. 8(2)). Under s. 9, a document which is certified as forming part of the records of a business or public authority may be received in evidence without further proof (s. 9(1) and (2)); and the absence of an entry in the records of a business or public authority may be proved by the affidavit of an officer of the business or authority. A document, for the purposes of both sections, means 'anything in which information of any description is recorded' (s. 13), a definition wide enough to cover maps, plans, graphs, drawings, discs, audiotapes, soundtracks, photographs, negatives, videotapes and films; and for the purposes of s. 8, a copy, in relation to a document, means, 'anything onto which information recorded in the document has been copied, by whatever means and whether directly or indirectly' (s. 13).

Section 8 of the 1995 Act appears to be of general application, i.e., to apply to any statement contained in a document, and not merely statements admissible for the truth of their contents by virtue of the 1995 Act; and likewise s. 9 seems to apply to any document forming part of the records of a business or public authority. On this construction, these provisions have reversed the general common law rule (see 47.73) that a party seeking to rely on the contents of a document must adduce primary evidence of those contents, i.e., usually the original. In any event, ss. 8 and 9 are permissive as to the means of proof. Section 14(2) of the Act provides that, 'Nothing in this Act affects the proof of documents by means other than those specified in section 8 or 9'. Sections 8 and 9, therefore, do not affect the operation of:

(a) the common law rule that where secondary evidence of the contents of a private document is admissible, it may take the form of oral evidence, which is not permitted under the 1995 Act;
(b) various statutory provisions, mostly relating to public and judicial documents, which provide for proof of their contents by copies which are required to take a particular form, such as an examined or certified copy (see 47.76); or
(c) the Bankers' Books Evidence Act 1879, whereby copies of entries in bankers' books are admissible if certain conditions are met (see 47.77).

Section 14(3) of the 1995 Act provides that nothing in the Act affects the operation of the following enactments:

(a) Documentary Evidence Act 1868, s. 2, which relates to the proof of certain official documents (see 47.76);
(b) Documentary Evidence Act 1882, s. 2, which relates to documents printed under the superintendence of the Stationery Office (see 47.76);
(c) Evidence (Colonial Statutes) Act 1907, which relates to proof of statutes of certain legislatures (see 47.98);
(d) Evidence (Foreign, Dominion and Colonial Documents) Act 1933 (proof and effect of registers and official certificates of certain countries); and
(e) Oaths and Evidence (Overseas Authorities and Countries) Act 1963 (provision in respect of public registers of other countries).

Given the general saving in s. 14(2) of the 1995 Act, it is unclear why s. 14(3) refers to only some of the many pre-existing statutory provisions governing the proof of various specific types of document.

General rule at common law

The general rule at common law is that a party seeking to rely on the contents of a document **47.73**
must adduce primary evidence of the contents, that is:

(a) the original;
(b) an official copy, in the case of an enrolled document; or
(c) an informal admission.

As to originals, duplicates of a deed which have been executed by all parties are all originals (*Forbes v Samuel* [1913] 3 KB 706); a copy of a document which is signed or otherwise duly executed is an original; and a counterpart lease executed by the lessee alone is the original if tendered against him or her, and the other part is the original if tendered against the lessor (*Doe* d *West v Davis* (1806) 7 East 363). If a private document is required to be enrolled, i.e., officially filed in a court or other public office, the copy issued by the court or office is treated as the original. For example, where a grant of probate has been obtained, the probate copy of the will is treated as primary evidence of the contents of the will. Where a party to litigation makes an informal admission as to the contents of a document, it constitutes primary evidence of the contents and is admissible against him or her (*Slatterie v Pooley* (1840) 6 M & W 664; but see now the Civil Evidence Act 1995, s. 7(1), considered at 51.20 to 51.22).

The general rule only applies where a party relies on the contents of the document. Thus whereas proof of the length of a tenancy or of the amount of rent due requires production of the lease, proof of the existence or fact of the tenancy, albeit created by a lease which defines its terms, may be proved by other means, such as parol evidence as to the payment of rent (see *Augustien v Challis* (1847) 1 Ex 279 (the amount of rent due) and *Twyman v Knowles* (1853) 13 CB 222 (the length of the tenancy); and cf. *R v Holy Trinity, Hull (Inhabitants)* (1827) 7 B & C 611 (the fact of a tenancy) and *Alderson v Clay* (1816) 1 Stark 405 (the fact of a partnership). Equally the rule does not apply where reference is made to a document merely for the purpose of establishing the bare fact of its existence (see *R v Elworthy* (1867) LR 1 CCR 103) or identifying it (see *Boyle v Wiseman* (1855) 11 Ex 360 at p. 367).

The general rule is well-established, as are the common law exceptions to it, which are considered at 47.76 and 47.78 to 47.81. However, the Court of Appeal in *Springsteen v Flute International Ltd* [2001] EMLR 654 appeared to reject the notion that, at common law, there is a general rule accompanied by a number of exceptions, in favour of a more generalised approach whereby the admissibility of secondary evidence of the contents of a document depends upon the weight to be attached to the secondary evidence. Observing 'with confidence' that the best evidence rule had finally expired, the court held that:

(a) Where the party seeking to adduce the secondary evidence could readily produce the document, it might be expected that, absent some special circumstances, the court would decline to admit the secondary evidence on the ground that it was worthless.
(b) At the other extreme, where that party genuinely could not produce the document, it might be expected that, absent some special circumstances, the court would admit the secondary evidence and attach such weight to it as it considered appropriate in the circumstances.
(c) In cases falling between these two extremes, it was for the court to make a judgment as to whether in all the circumstances any weight should be attached to the secondary evidence.
(d) Thus the admissibility of secondary evidence of the contents of documents is entirely dependent on whether or not any weight is to be attached to the evidence, which is a matter for the court to decide.

A similar approach was adopted in *Post Office Counters Ltd v Mahida* [2003] EWCA Civ 1583, *The Times*, 31 October 2003. The claimant had destroyed the primary documentary evidence proving the sums owed by the defendant, and relied on secondary evidence in the form of schedules drawn up by the claimant of the claims for payments and receipts submitted to it by the defendant. It was held to have been permissible to adduce this secondary evidence, but the judge had given it too much weight. The judge should have taken into account the claimant's delay in responding to the defendant's requests for the primary documents, and the claimant's failure to take proper care of that evidence.

Exceptions

47.74 Under the exceptions to the general rule, in the case of private documents, secondary evidence of the contents of a document may take the form of a copy, a copy of a copy (*Lafone v Griffin* (1909) 25 TLR 308), or oral evidence. Where a copy is produced, proof is required that it is a true copy of the original (see *R v Collins* (1960) 44 Cr App R 170).

It has been said that 'there are no degrees of secondary evidence' (per Lord Abinger CB in *Doe d Gilbert v Ross* (1840)7 M & W 102), which means that although less weight may attach to inferior forms of secondary evidence, there is no obligation to tender the best type of secondary evidence available. For example, oral evidence of the contents of a document is admissible even if a copy of the document is available. To this principle, however, there are numerous exceptions: many public documents may be proved by oral evidence only if examined, certified or other types of copy are unavailable (see 47.76); bankers' books are generally proved by examined copies (see 47.77); and the contents of a will admitted to probate may not be proved by oral evidence if the original or probate copy exists.

Hearsay statements Where the contents of a document, including a computer-produced document, are admissible by virtue of Civil Evidence Act 1995, they may be proved in accordance with ss. 8 and 9 of that Act (see 47.72 and generally at **51.15** to **51.17**). **47.75**

Public and judicial documents At common law, secondary evidence of the contents of public documents is admissible on the grounds that production of the originals would cause a high degree of inconvenience: see, e.g., *Mortimer v M'Callan* (1840)6 M & W 58 (books of the Bank of England). A number of statutes also provide for the proof of different types of public and judicial document by secondary evidence, which is usually required to take the form of: **47.76**

(a) an examined copy, i.e., a copy proved by oral evidence to correspond with the original;
(b) a certified copy, i.e., a copy signed and certified to be accurate by an official who has custody of the original;
(c) an office copy, i.e., a copy prepared by a court officer who has custody of an original judicial document and the power to provide copies authenticated with the seal of the court; or
(d) a Queen's Printer's or Stationery Office copy.

There are two statutory provisions of general importance, the Evidence Act 1845, s. 1, and the Evidence Act 1851, s. 14. Under the former, where a statute provides for proof of a document by a certified, sealed, or stamped copy, the copy, provided that it purports to be signed, sealed or stamped, is admissible without any proof of the signature, seal or stamp, as the case may be. Under the Evidence Act 1851, s. 14, certified or examined copies may be used to prove the contents of any document provided that it is of such a public nature that it is admissible in evidence on production from proper custody and no other statute provides for proof of its contents by means of a copy.

Specific statutory provision is made for the proof by secondary evidence of the contents of the following types of public and judicial documents:

(a) Acts of Parliament and journals of either House of Parliament. Private Acts of Parliament and journals of either House may be proved by Queen's Printer's or Stationery Office copies (Evidence Act 1845, s. 3 and Documentary Evidence Act 1882, s. 2). As to public Acts, every Act passed after 1850 is a public Act to be judicially noticed as such unless the contrary is expressly provided by the Act (Interpretation Act 1978, s. 3). At common law, judicial notice is taken of earlier public Acts (see 47.27).
(b) Royal proclamations and orders or regulations issued by the government. These documents may be proved by Queen's Printer's or Stationery Office copies, by a copy of the *Gazette* purporting to contain them, or by copies certified to be true by the appropriate official (Documentary Evidence Act 1868, ss. 2,3, 5 and 6, and Documentary Evidence Act 1882, s. 2).
(c) By-laws. By-laws may be proved by certified printed copies (Local Government Act 1972, s. 238).
(d) Court proceedings. Every document purporting to be sealed or stamped with the seal or stamp of the Supreme Court shall be received in evidence without further proof (Supreme Court Act 1981, s. 125). Likewise, under **CPR, r. 2.6(3)**, a document purporting to bear the court's seal is to be admissible in evidence without further proof. Records of proceedings in the county courts and magistrates' courts may be proved by certified copies (**County Courts Act 1984, s. 12** and Magistrates' Courts Rules 1981, r. 68).
(e) Proclamations, treaties and other acts of state of foreign states or British colonies and judgments, decrees, orders, and other judicial proceedings of any court of justice in any foreign state or in any British colony, and affidavits, pleadings and other legal documents filed or deposited in any such court. These documents may be proved by examined copies or by copies authenticated with the seal of the foreign state, colony or court, as the case may be (Evidence Act 1851, s. 7).

(f) Foreign and colonial laws. Colonial statutes may be proved by certified copies (Colonial Laws Validity Act 1865, s. 6) or copies purporting to be printed by the Government printer of the possession in question (Evidence (Colonial Statutes) Act 1907, s. 1). Subject to these provisions, and excepting law ascertained by the British Law Ascertainment Act 1859, foreign and colonial law, including Scots law, cannot be proved merely by the production of documentary evidence, but generally requires proof by a suitably qualified expert (see *Sussex Peerage Case* (1844) 11 Cl & F 85 and generally at **47.98**).

(g) Public records. Public records kept in the Public Record Office may be proved by examined, certified copies which have been sealed or stamped (Public Records Act 1958, s. 9).

(h) Births, deaths and marriages. An entry in the register of births or deaths may be proved by a certified copy purporting to be sealed or stamped with the seal of the General Register Office and is admissible evidence of the birth or death to which it relates (Births and Deaths Registration Act 1953, s. 34; and see also the Adoption Act 1976, s. 50(2)). Proof of the celebration of a marriage may be effected by the production of a certified copy of an entry kept at the General Register Office (Marriage Act 1949, s. 65(3)). Births, deaths and marriages out of England may be proved by entries properly and regularly recorded in foreign registers kept under the sanction of public authority (*Lyell v Kennedy* (1889) 14 App Cas 437 at pp. 448–9). See also the Foreign Marriages Act 1892, s. 16 (ambassadors' or consular registers of marriages under British law by British subjects); the Registration of Births, Deaths and Marriages (Scotland) Act 1854 and the Registration of Births, Deaths and Marriages (Scotland) Amendment Act 1860; the Registration of Births, Deaths and Marriages (Army) Act 1879, s. 3; the Merchant Shipping Act 1995, s. 108 and the Merchant Shipping (Returns of Births and Deaths) Regulations 1979 (SI 1979/1577); and the Registration of Births, Deaths and Marriages (Special Provisions) Act 1957, s. 2 (births, deaths and marriages on Her Majesty's ships at sea and service aircraft).

(i) Minute-books of local authorities. The signed minutes of the proceedings of local authorities shall be received in evidence without further proof (Local Government Act 1972, sch. 12, para. 41); and a certified copy of the minutes shall be evidence of their terms (Local Government (Miscellaneous Provisions) Act 1976, s. 41(1)).

(j) Documents relating to insolvency. In this regard, any document purporting to be or to contain any order, direction or certificate issued by the Secretary of State shall be received in evidence and be deemed to be (or contain) that order or certificate or those directions without further proof, unless the contrary is shown (Insolvency Rules 1986 (SI 1986/1925), r. 12.6). As to use of copies of the *Gazette*, see also SI 1986/1925, r. 12.20.

47.77 **Bankers' books** The Bankers' Books Evidence Act 1879 provides for the admissibility of entries in bankers' books as evidence of the matters they record by way of exception to the common law rule against hearsay; and in order to avoid the inconvenience involved in the production of the originals of such books, permits the admission of copies. The Act provides as follows:

> **3. Mode of proof of entries in bankers' books**
> Subject to the provisions of this Act, a copy of an entry in a banker's book shall in all legal proceedings be received as prima facie evidence of such entry, and of the matters, transactions, and accounts therein recorded.
>
> **4. Proof that book is a bankers' book**
> A copy of an entry in a banker's book shall not be received in evidence under this Act unless it be first proved that the book was at the time of the making of the entry one of the ordinary books of the bank, and that the entry was made in the usual and ordinary course of business, and that the book is in the custody or control of the bank.
>
> Such proof may be given by a partner or officer of the bank, and may be given orally or by an affidavit sworn before any commissioner or person authorised to take affidavits.

5. **Verification of copy**
A copy of an entry in a banker's book shall not be received in evidence under this Act unless it be further proved that the copy has been examined with the original entry and is correct.
Such proof shall be given by some person who has examined the copy with the original entry, and may be given either orally or by an affidavit sworn before any commissioner or person authorised to take affidavits.
6. **Case in which banker, etc., not compellable to produce book, etc.**
A banker or officer of a bank shall not, in any legal proceedings to which the bank is not a party, be compellable to produce any banker's book the contents of which can be proved under this Act . . . or to appear as a witness to prove the matters, transactions, and accounts therein recorded, unless by order of a judge made for special cause.
7. **Court or judge may order inspection, etc.**
On the application of any party to a legal proceeding a court or judge may order that such party be at liberty to inspect and take copies of any entries in a banker's book for any of the purposes of such proceedings. An order under this section may be made either with or without summoning the bank or any other party, and shall be served on the bank three clear days before the same is to be obeyed, unless the court or judge otherwise directs.
8. **Costs**
The costs of any application to a court or judge under or for the purposes of this Act, and the costs of anything done or to be done under an order of a court or judge made under or for the purposes of this Act shall be in the discretion of the court or judge, who may order the same or any part thereof to be paid to any party by the bank, where the same have been occasioned by any default or delay on the part of the bank. Any such order against a bank may be enforced as if the bank was a party to the proceeding.
9. **Interpretation of 'bank', 'banker', and 'bankers' books'**
(1) In this Act the expression 'bank' and 'banker' mean—
(a) a deposit-taker;
(c) the National Savings Bank.
(1A) 'Deposit taker' means—
(a) a person who has permission under Part 4 of the Financial Services and Markets Act 2000 to accept deposits; or
(b) an EEA firm of the kind mentioned in paragraph 5(b) of Schedule 3 to that Act which has permission under paragraph 15 of that Schedule (as a result of qualifying for authorisation under paragraph 12(1) of that Schedule) to accept deposits or other repayable funds from the public.
(1B) But a person is not a deposit-taker if he has permission to accept deposits only for the purpose of carrying on another regulated activity in accordance with that permission.
(1C) Subsections (1A) and (1B) must be read with—
(a) section 22 of the Financial Services and Markets Act 2000;
(b) any relevant order under that section; and
(c) Schedule 2 to that Act.
(2) Expressions in this Act relating to 'bankers' books' include ledgers, day books, cash books, account books and other records used in the ordinary business of the bank, whether those records are in written form or are kept on microfilm, magnetic tape or any other form of mechanical or electronic data retrieval mechanism.
10. **Interpretation of 'legal proceeding', 'court', 'judge'**
In this Act—
The expression 'legal proceeding' means any civil or criminal proceeding or inquiry in which evidence is or may be given, and includes an arbitration and an application to, or an inquiry or other proceedings before, the Solicitors Disciplinary Tribunal . . .
The expression 'the court' means the court, judge, arbitrator, persons or person before whom a legal proceeding is held or taken;
The expression 'a judge' means with respect to England a judge of the High Court . . .
The judge of a county court may with respect to any action in such court exercise the powers of a judge under this Act.

In s. 9(2), the words 'other records used in the ordinary business of the bank' mean other records of the same type as ledgers, day books, cash books and account books, which are the means by which a bank records day-to-day financial transactions, and therefore records kept by the bank of conversations between its employees and customers or others or internal memoranda are not bankers' books (*Re Howglen Ltd* [2001] 1 All ER 376).

Paid cheques and paying-in slips retained by a bank after the conclusion of a banking transaction to which they relate are not bankers' books under the Act, because even if bundles of such documents can be treated as 'records used in the ordinary business of the bank', the addition of an individual cheque or paying-in slip cannot be regarded as making an 'entry' in those records (*Williams v Williams* [1987] 3 All ER 257). If such documents relate to the bank account of the other party to the action, an order for disclosure may be made and the bank, as agent holding the documents on that party's behalf, may then be required to disclose them. In other cases, the party seeking inspection may obtain a witness summons addressed to the appropriate officer of the bank and requiring him or her to attend at the hearing with all the relevant documents in the possession of the bank relating to the account in question.

Although s. 7 of the Act allows an application to be made without summoning the bank or any other party, there is much to be said for notice being given (per Widgery LJ in *R v Marlborough Street Magistrates' Court, ex parte Simpson* (1980) 70 Cr App R 291 at p. 294). An order may be made under s. 7 to inspect the account of a person who is not a party to the proceedings, even if that person is not compellable as a witness (*R v Andover Justices, ex parte Rhodes* [1980] Crim LR 644). However, an application under s. 7 in respect of the bank account of a third party will only be granted if:

(a) the court is satisfied that the account is in fact the account of the other party to the action or an account with which the other party is so much concerned that items in it would be admissible against him; and
(b) the applicant shows very strong grounds for suspicion, almost amounting to certainty, that there are items in the account which would be material evidence against the other party

(*South Staffordshire Tramways Co. v Ebbsmith* [1895] 2 QB 669 (a pre-trial application) and *D. B. Deniz Nakliyati TAS v Yugopetrol* [1992] 1 WLR 437 (an application against a judgment debtor)).

Save in exceptional circumstances, a foreign bank which is not a party to the proceedings should not be ordered to produce documents which are outside the jurisdiction and concern business transacted outside the jurisdiction, even if it carries on business within the jurisdiction, because an order under the 1879 Act is an exercise of sovereign authority to assist in the administration of justice and foreign banks owe their customers a duty of confidence regulated by their own laws (*MacKinnon v Donaldson Lufkin and Jenrette Securities Corporation* [1986] Ch 482). A party seeking to obtain documents from a foreign bank may apply to a master under **CPR, r. 34.13**, for the issue of letters of request to the courts of the country in question, or may apply directly to such a court under the relevant local law, having first obtained the permission of the English court on a hearing with notice.

The 1879 Act may not be used to compel disclosure of incriminating material (see *Waterhouse v Barker* [1924] 2 KB 759 and *R v Bono* (1913) 29 TLR 635).

47.78 **Failure to produce after notice** A party may produce the contents of a document by secondary evidence where the original is in the possession or control of another party to the proceedings who, having been served with a notice to produce it, has failed to do so (see *Dwyer v Collins* (1852)21 LJ Ex 225). It is submitted that this rule subsists notwithstanding that the CPR make no provision for service of a formal notice to produce (see, formerly, RSC, ord. 24, r. 10). A notice to produce does not compel production of a document: a party who wishes to rely at the trial on the original of a document should serve a summons requiring a witness to produce the original to the court (see **CPR, r. 34.2**).

47.79 **Non-party's lawful refusal to produce** Secondary evidence of the contents of a document will be admissible where the original is in the possession of a stranger to the litigation who, having been served with a witness summons requiring production of the document to the court (see **CPR, r. 34.2**), lawfully refuses to do so, e.g., by reason of a valid claim to privilege (*Mills v Oddy* (1834) 6 Car & P 728), diplomatic immunity (*R v Nowaz* [1976] 3 All ER 5) or because he cannot be compelled to produce it, being outside the jurisdiction (*Kilgour v Owen* (1889)88 LT Jo 7). If the stranger unlawfully refuses to produce the original, secondary evidence is inadmissible (see, but doubt, *R v Llanfaethly (Inhabitants)* (1853) 2 El & Bl 940).

Lost documents Secondary evidence of the contents of a document is admissible on proof that the original has been destroyed or cannot be found after due search, the quality of the proof required depending on the nature and value of the document in question (*Brewster v Sewell* (1820) 3 B & Ald 296). **47.80**

Production of original impossible Secondary evidence is obviously admissible where production of the original is impossible, either physically, e.g., because it is an inscription on a tombstone (per Alderson B in *Mortimer v M'Callan* (1840) 6 M & W 58), or legally, e.g., because a notice required by statute to be constantly affixed at a factory (*Owner v Bee Hive Spinning Co. Ltd* [1914] 1 KB 105) or a document in the custody of a foreign court (*Alivon v Furnival* (1834) 1 Cr M & R 277). **47.81**

Proof of due execution

The general rule at common law is that a document will only be admitted in evidence on proof of due execution. A major exception exists in the case of public and judicial documents, proof of the contents of which are governed by statute: most of the relevant statutory provisions also exempt from proof of due execution (see 47.76). As to private documents, proof of due execution is frequently formally admitted, and in certain circumstances may be presumed, but otherwise usually involves proving handwriting, a signature, or attestation. Some documents are also required to be stamped for the purposes of stamp duty. **47.82**

Presumptions It is provided in **CPR, r. 32.19(1)**, that a party to whom a document is disclosed under **Part 31** shall be deemed to admit its authenticity, unless he serves notice that he wishes the document to be proved at trial. Without such a notice, therefore, a party will be taken to admit that a document was printed, written, signed or executed as it purports to have been. Proof of due execution is also unnecessary where the document in question is in the possession of an opponent who has refused to comply with a notice to produce it (*Cooke v Tanswell* (1818) 8 Taunt 450). A document which is more than 20 years old and comes from proper custody is presumed to have been duly executed (see Evidence Act 1938, s. 4, whereby the period of 20 years was substituted for the 30-year period required at common law). Proper custody, for these purposes, does not require that the document comes from 'the best and most proper place of deposit', but if it is found elsewhere, the court must be satisfied that the other place was 'reasonable and natural' in the circumstances (*Meath (Bishop) v Marquis of Winchester* (1836) 3 Bing NC 183; cf. *Doe d Lord Arundel v Fowler* (1850) 14 QB 700). **47.83**

There are three other common law presumptions relating to documents:

(a) that a document was made on the date which it bears (*Anderson v Weston* (1840) 6 Bing NC 296);
(b) that a deed was duly sealed (but see *Re Sandilands* (1871) LR 6 CP 411); and
(c) that an alteration or erasure in a deed was made before execution, but in a will was made after execution (per Lord Campbell CJ in *Doe d Tatum v Catomore* (1851) 16 QB 745).

Handwriting and signatures Proof that a document was written or signed by the person by whom it purports to have been written or signed may be effected by the following means: **47.84**

(a) by the direct oral evidence of the author or signatory or by any witness to the execution of the document, or by admissible hearsay assertions to the same effect;
(b) by the opinion evidence of someone acquainted with the handwriting or signature (*Doe d Mudd v Suckermore* (1837) 5 Ad & El 703), although the weight to be attached to such evidence will obviously vary according to the circumstances; or

(c) by comparison of the disputed handwriting or signature with another document which is proved or admitted to have been written by the person in question, under Criminal Procedure Act 1865, s. 8, which provides as follows:

Comparison of a disputed writing with any writing proved to the satisfaction of the judge to be genuine shall be permitted to be made by witnesses; and such writings, and the evidence of witnesses respecting the same, may be submitted to the court and jury as evidence of the genuineness or otherwise of the writing in dispute.

The court need only be satisfied as to the genuineness of the specimen handwriting on a balance of probabilities. The judge, in comparing the disputed and specimen writing, may be assisted by an expert in handwriting or by someone who, although not an expert, is familiar with the handwriting in question (*Fitzwalter Peerage Claim* (1844) 10 Cl & F 193). A witness who has not seen the original of the 'disputed writing', e.g., because it is lost, is entitled to use a photocopy of it to make the comparison (*Lockheed-Arabia Corporation v Owen* [1993] QB 806).

Any of the above-mentioned means of proving handwriting may be used in the case of documents which, although not required by law to be attested, were in fact attested: the Criminal Procedure Act 1865, s. 7 provides that such a document may be proved as if there had been no attesting witness thereto.

47.85 **Attestation** Except where probate is sought in common form, to prove the due execution of a will (or other testamentary document), one of the attesting witnesses, if available, must be called. Such witnesses are treated as the court's witnesses and may be cross-examined by the party seeking to prove due execution (*Oakes v Uzzell* [1932] P 19). Other evidence becomes admissible if the witness denies the execution (*Bowman v Hodgson* (1867) LR 1 P & D 362) or refuses to give evidence (*Re Ovens Goods* (1892) 29 LR Ir 451). If all the attesting witnesses are dead, insane, outside the jurisdiction or untraceable, proof is required of the handwriting of one of the attesting witnesses; and if, despite every effort to do so, it is impossible to prove such handwriting, other evidence of due execution becomes admissible, such as the evidence of a non-attesting witness to the execution (*Clarke v Clarke* (1879) 5 LR Ir 451).

Under the Evidence Act 1938, s. 3, except in the case of a will or other testamentary document, any document required by law to be attested may, instead of being proved by an attesting witness, be proved in the manner in which it might be proved if no attesting witness were alive (e.g., by evidence of the handwriting of an attesting witness or by the evidence of a non-attesting witness to the execution).

47.86 **Stamped documents** A document requiring a stamp for the purposes of stamp duty shall not be given in evidence unless it is duly stamped in accordance with the law in force at the time when it was first executed or, the court having objected to the omission or insufficiency of the stamp, and the document being one which may be legally stamped after its execution, payment is made of the amount of unpaid duty, together with any penalty payable on stamping, and a further sum of one pound (Stamp Act 1891, s. 14). The parties cannot waive these rules (*Bowker v Williamson* (1889) 5 TLR 382). If a document requiring a stamp cannot be found or is in the possession of a party who refuses to comply with a notice to produce it, it is presumed to have been duly stamped; but if there is evidence to show that it was not duly stamped, then it is presumed, in the absence of sufficient evidence to the contrary, that this remained the case (*Closmadeuc v Carrel* (1856) 18 CB 36).

REAL EVIDENCE

Material objects and documents

47.87 Real evidence usually takes the form of a material object examined by the tribunal of fact as a means of proving its existence, condition or value; but subject to a formal admission by the party against whom it is tendered, and subject also to **CPR, r. 33.6** (which is considered at 47.91), it needs to be accompanied by testimony to at least identify it or explain its provenance. A document may constitute real evidence, as when it is introduced not for the statements that it contains but as a material object, to show that it exists or the condition that it is in. There is no rule to the effect that oral evidence regarding a material object is inadmissible unless the object itself is produced, or its non-production excused (*Hocking v Ahlquist Brothers Ltd* [1944] 1 KB 120), but non-production of the object may affect the weight to be attached to the oral evidence and give rise to an inference adverse to the party failing to produce (see, e.g., *Armory v Delamirie* (1722) 1 Str 505).

Demeanour and appearance

47.88 The demeanour and attitude of a witness in the course of giving his or her evidence may be regarded as a form of real evidence which is relevant to the witness's credit and the weight to be attached to his or her evidence. Real evidence may also take the form of a person's physical appearance, as when injuries or scars are examined on a question of causation or quantum. The facial resemblance of a child to its alleged father and mother may be relevant on the question of legitimacy, although in many cases little weight should be attached to it (*C v C (Legitimacy: Photographic Evidence)* [1972] 1 WLR 1335; cf. *Slingsby v Attorney-General* (1916) 33 TLR 120 at pp. 122–3). The appearance of an animal may also constitute real evidence, as in *Line v Taylor* (1862) 3 F & F 731, where a dog alleged to be of a vicious disposition was examined in court.

Printouts, photographs, videotapes and films

47.89 A computer printout (or photograph, videotape or film) is a document for the purposes of the Civil Evidence Act 1995 (see **51.15**) and under that Act may be used to prove the matters stated therein. They are also documents for the purposes of disclosure and inspection (see **chapter 48**). At common law, where a computer or other device is used as a calculator, (i.e., as a tool which does not contribute its own knowledge, but merely performs a calculation, albeit sophisticated, which could have been performed manually), the resulting printout is not hearsay, but is treated as an item of real evidence. The actual proof and relevance of the printout depend on the evidence of the person using the computer, the computer programmer or other experts involved, who can testify as to such matters as the function and operation of the computer (see per Lord Lane CJ in *R v Wood* (1982) 76 Cr App R 23 at p. 26, in which a laborious mathematical process had been undertaken by a computer operated by chemists investigating the chemical composition of metal; and see also, in the case of a printout from a breathalyser, *Castle v Cross* [1984] 1 WLR 1372). The principle applies not only where the device in question processes information supplied to it, but also where it gathers information itself (*R v Spiby* (1990) 91 Cr App R 186, in which the printout came from a computerised machine used to monitor telephone calls and automatically record such information as the numbers to and from which calls were made, and the duration of the calls). In *R (O'Shea) v Coventry Magistrates' Court* [2004] EWHC 905 (Admin), [2004] Crim LR 948, automatically generated computer records of access and attempted access to web pages, including details matching O's credit card, email and home address, were admitted to show what had been recorded and not as evidence of the truth of what had been recorded. It was, therefore, real evidence and not hearsay. See also *R v Governor of Brixton Prison, ex parte Levin* [1997] AC 741.

In appropriate circumstances, the same principle applies in the case of photographs, videotapes and films: see *R v Dodson* (1984) 79 Cr App R 220 (photographs taken by security cameras) and *Khan v Armaguard Ltd* [1994] 1 WLR 1204 (a videotape inconsistent with the claimant's claims about the nature of his injuries). It has been said that the photograph, together with the sketch and the photofit, are in a class of evidence of their own to which neither the rule against hearsay nor the rule against previous consistent statements applies (per Watkins LJ in *R v Cook* [1987] QB 417 at p. 425). In *The Statue of Liberty* [1968] 1 WLR 739, an action concerning a collision between two ships, a cinematograph film of radar echoes recorded by a shore radar station and produced mechanically and without human intervention was held to be admissible in evidence. Sir Jocelyn Simon P said (at p. 740):

> If tape recordings are admissible, it seems that a photograph of radar reception is equally admissible — or indeed, any other type of photograph. It would be an absurd distinction that a photograph should be admissible if the camera were operated manually by a photographer, but not if it were operated by a trip or clock mechanism. Similarly, if evidence of weather conditions were relevant, the law would affront common sense if it were to say that those could be proved by a person who looked at a barometer from time to time, but not by producing a barograph record. So, too, with other types of dial recordings.

Regarding video recordings, there is an obligation to inform the court at the first opportunity that such evidence will be relied upon, as arrangements need to be made to ensure video equipment is available at trial, and extra time will be required for the trial for showing the evidence (*Rall v Hume* [2001] 3 All ER 248). Use of videos at trial takes two forms. They can be used as part of a party's affirmative case. In this event the videotapes may need to be played in their entirety. Alternatively, a party may wish to use a videotape in cross-examination of the opposing party by playing certain parts of the video for comment by the witness being cross-examined in order to undermine the witness. Use of a tape in this way will usually be legitimate, even if an application for such use is made quite close to the trial date. However, a direction is likely to be made limiting the footage to be shown (in *Rall v Hume* the limit was 20 minutes). Some inquiry agents are not very discriminating when shooting covert videos, and the court will be astute to ensure that the footage used does not infringe the **European Convention on Human Rights, art. 8(1)** (the right to private life).

Views

47.90 A view is an inspection of a site or of an object that it is impossible or inconvenient to bring to court, e.g., an omnibus (see *London General Omnibus Co. Ltd v Lavell* [1901] 1 Ch 135). In some circumstances it will also be appropriate to conduct out-of-court demonstrations or reenactments, before which, it is submitted, the demonstrator should take the oath and thereby offer himself or herself for cross-examination (see *Buckingham v Daily News Ltd* [1956] 2 QB 534; and cf. *Goold v Evans and Co.* [1951] 2 TLR 1189 at pp. 1191–2). Each of the parties must be given the opportunity of being present at a view, and a failure to do so may result in a re-trial (*Goold v Evans and Co.*). However, it has been said that the judge may visit the *locus in quo* in order to see that which has previously been represented to him or her in court by plan and photograph on his or her own and without reference to the parties at all (per Widgery LJ in *Salsbury v Woodland* [1970] 1 QB 324 at pp. 343–4).

Notice and inspection of plans, photographs, models etc.

47.91 Rule 33.6 of the CPR governs the admissibility of 'evidence (such as a plan, photograph or model) which is not—

(a) contained in a witness statement, affidavit or expert's report;
(b) to be given orally at trial; or
(c) evidence of which prior notice must be given under rule 33.2' (hearsay evidence; see 51.9).

Unless the court orders otherwise, the evidence shall not be receivable at a trial unless the party intending to put it in evidence has given notice to the other parties of his intention and given each of them an opportunity to inspect it and to agree to its admission without further proof. In *Orford v Rasmi Electronics Ltd* [2002] EWCA Civ 1672, [2003] CPLR 213, one of the reasons for ordering a retrial was that a plan was not shown to the claimant until the morning of the trial, though it had been in existence for over five months. The rule is wide enough to cover not only the illustrations given, i.e., plans, photographs and models, but also films and video films and other varieties of real evidence. The rule also covers documents which may be received in evidence without further proof under the Civil Evidence Act 1995, s. 9 (see **51.16**). Where the evidence forms part of expert evidence, the notice must be given when the expert's report is served on the other party (**r. 33.6(6)**). Subject to this, where the intention is to use the evidence as evidence of any fact, then notice must be given not later than the latest date for serving witness statements. If there are not to be witness statements, or the intention is to put the evidence in solely in order to disprove an allegation made in a witness statement, notice must be given at least 21 days before the hearing (**r. 33.6(5)**). Where the evidence is being produced to the court for any reason other than as part of factual or expert evidence, notice must also be given at least 21 days before the hearing (**r. 33.6(7)**).

JUDGMENTS AS EVIDENCE

The decision of the Court of Appeal in *Hollington v F. Hewthorn and Co. Ltd* [1943] KB 587 tipped the balance in favour of the view supported by the bulk of authority by which it was preceded, that verdicts in criminal proceedings (or judgments in civil proceedings) are not admissible in subsequent proceedings as evidence of the facts on which they were based. Thus, in that case, an action in negligence against the driver of a car who had been convicted of careless driving at the time and place of the accident in question, it was held that the conviction was inadmissible as evidence of negligence, being inadmissible as evidence of the fact that the driver had committed the offence. The court was of the view that the civil court would know nothing of the evidence before the criminal court, and the arguments that were addressed to it, and that the opinion of the criminal court was irrelevant. The rule in *Hollington v F. Hewthorn and Co. Ltd* understandably attracted much criticism and, in so far as it applies not only to previous convictions, but also to findings of adultery and paternity in previous civil proceedings, it has been reversed by the Civil Evidence Act 1968, ss. 11 to 13. **47.92**

Previous convictions

Civil Evidence Act 1968, s. 11 Section 11 of the Civil Evidence Act 1968 reverses the decision in *Hollington v F. Hewthorn and Co. Ltd* [1943] KB 587, and creates a persuasive presumption that the person convicted shall be taken to have committed the offence in question unless the contrary is proved. A claimant who wishes to rely on evidence of a conviction under s. 11 must include in his or her particulars of claim a statement to that effect and give details of the type of conviction and its date, the court or court-martial which made it, and the issue in the claim to which it relates (**PD 16, para. 8.1**). Section 11 provides as follows: **47.93**

(1) In any civil proceedings the fact that a person has been convicted of an offence by or before any court in the United Kingdom or by a court-martial there or elsewhere shall (subject to subsection (3) below) be admissible in evidence for the purpose of proving, where to do so is relevant to any issue in those proceedings, that he committed that offence, whether he was so convicted upon a plea of guilty or otherwise and whether or not he is a party to the civil proceedings; but no conviction other than a subsisting one shall be admissible in evidence by virtue of this section.

(2) In any civil proceedings in which by virtue of this section a person is proved to have been convicted of an offence by or before any court in the United Kingdom or by a court-martial there or elsewhere—
   (a) he shall be taken to have committed that offence unless the contrary is proved; and
   (b) without prejudice to the reception of any other admissible evidence for the purpose of identifying the facts on which the conviction was based, the contents of any document which is admissible as evidence of the conviction, and the contents of the information, complaint,

indictment or charge-sheet on which the person in question was convicted, shall be admissible in evidence for that purpose.

(3) Nothing in this section shall prejudice the operation of section 13 of this Act or any other enactment whereby a conviction or a finding of fact in any criminal proceedings is for the purposes of any other proceedings made conclusive evidence of any fact.

(4) Where in any civil proceedings the contents of any document are admissible in evidence by virtue of subsection (2) above, a copy of that document, or of the material part thereof, purporting to be certified or otherwise authenticated by or on behalf of the court or authority having custody of that document shall be admissible in evidence and shall be taken to be a true copy of that document or part unless the contrary is shown.

(5) Nothing in . . .

(a) section 14 of the Powers of Criminal Courts (Sentencing) Act 2000 (under which a conviction leading to discharge is to be disregarded except as therein mentioned) . . . shall affect the operation of this section. . . .

(6) In this section 'court-martial' means a court-martial constituted under the Army Act 1955, the Air Force Act 1955 or the Naval Discipline Act 1957 or a disciplinary court constituted under section 52G of the said Act of 1957, and in relation to a court-martial 'conviction' means a finding of guilty which is, or falls to be treated as, the finding of the court, and 'convicted' shall be construed accordingly.

Section 18 provides that, for the purposes of s. 11, 'civil proceedings':

includes, in addition to civil proceedings in any of the ordinary courts of law—

(a) civil proceedings before any other tribunal, being proceedings in relation to which the strict rules of evidence apply; and

(b) an arbitration or reference, whether under an enactment or not,

but does not include civil proceedings in relation to which the strict rules of evidence do not apply.

A 'subsisting' conviction includes a conviction against which an appeal is pending, but not one which has been quashed on appeal; and therefore rather than finally dispose of civil proceedings in reliance on a conviction subsequently liable to be quashed, it is better to adjourn the civil proceedings pending the outcome of the appeal (see *Re Raphael* [1973] 1 WLR 998). Section 11 does not apply to foreign convictions (see *Union Carbide Corporation v Naturin Ltd* [1987] FSR 538). However, although *Hollington v F. Hewthorn and Co. Ltd* therefore continues to apply to foreign convictions, they may be referred to in an affidavit in support of a freezing injunction where they are part of the narrative explanation of the case against the defendant and enable the claimant to comply with his or her duty to make full and frank disclosure to the court (*Arab Monetary Fund v Hashim (No. 2)* [1990] 1 All ER 673).

Section 11(2)(b) is 'without prejudice to the reception of any other admissible evidence for the purpose of identifying the facts on which the conviction was based'. Such other evidence could include a copy of the summing up, which would be admissible under the Civil Evidence Act 1995 (see *Brinks Ltd v Abu-Saleh (No. 2)* [1995] 1 WLR 1487, a decision under the Civil Evidence Act 1968), as would a transcript of the evidence given in the criminal case.

Section 11(2)(a) imposes on a party who wishes to 'go behind' a conviction the burden of proving, on the balance of probabilities, that the person convicted did not commit the offence, and therefore it is not sufficient to establish that the conviction is unsafe, that the judge in the criminal trial (or the Court of Appeal) made an error or that the prosecution was an abuse of process (*Raja v Van Hoogstraten* [2005] EWHC 1642 (Ch), LTL 22/8/2005).

There is a divergence of judicial opinion as to what weight should be attached to the conviction, in deciding whether a party has discharged the burden of proving 'the contrary' under s. 11(2)(a). In *Taylor v Taylor* [1970] 1 WLR 1148, in which the petitioner wife, in support of her allegation that her husband had committed adultery, relied upon his conviction of incest, Davies LJ was of the view that the standard to be met in order to upset the conviction was the balance of probabilities but that the verdict of the jury was entitled to very great weight (at p. 1152). Similar views were expressed by Lord Denning MR in *Stupple v Royal Insurance Co. Ltd* [1971] 1 QB 50. Stupple, who had been convicted of robbery from a bank which had been indemnified by the defendant company, brought a claim for the recovery of money which had been found by the police in his possession and which had been paid over to the defendant company under the Police (Property) Act 1897. Judgment was given for the company and Stupple's appeal was dismissed. Lord Denning MR was of the opinion that the conviction does not merely shift the burden of proof, but is a weighty piece of evidence of itself (at p. 72). Buckley LJ, however, was of the view that the statutory presumption would give way to evidence establishing the contrary on the balance of probability without itself affording any evidential weight when deciding whether that onus had been discharged (at p. 76). In *McIlkenny v Chief Constable of the West Midlands* [1980] QB 283 at p. 320 Lord Denning MR suggested, *obiter*, that a convicted man could only prove 'the contrary' under s. 11(2)(a) by proving that the conviction was obtained by fraud or collusion or by adducing fresh evidence which must be 'decisive' and 'conclusive'. On appeal, however, Lord Diplock disapproved the dictum, being of the opinion that the standard to be met, in proving 'the contrary' was proof on a balance of probabilities, but added that 'in the face of a conviction after a full hearing this is likely to be an uphill task' (*Hunter v Chief Constable of the West Midlands Police* [1982] AC 529 at p. 544).

Civil Evidence Act 1968, s. 13 Section 13 of the Civil Evidence Act 1968, which applies to defamation proceedings, reverses the decision in *Hollington v F. Hewthorn and Co. Ltd* [1943] KB 587 (47.92) and creates a conclusive presumption, that the person convicted shall be conclusively taken to have committed the offence in question. Thus a defamation claim based on the defendant's statement that the claimant committed an offence in respect of which he has been convicted, will be struck out as an abuse of the process of the court, unless the statement also contains some other legally defamatory matter (*Levene v Roxhan* [1970] 1 WLR 1322). Section 13 provides as follows: **47.94**

(1) In an action for libel or slander in which the question whether the plaintiff did or did not commit a criminal offence is relevant to an issue arising in the action, proof that at the time when that issue falls to be determined, he stands convicted of that offence shall be conclusive evidence that he committed that offence; and his conviction thereof shall be admissible in evidence accordingly.

(2) In any such action as aforesaid in which by virtue of this section the plaintiff is proved to have been convicted of an offence, the contents of any document which is admissible as evidence of the conviction, and the contents of the information, complaint, indictment or charge-sheet on which he was convicted, shall, without prejudice to the reception of any other admissible evidence for the purpose of identifying the facts on which the conviction was based, be admissible in evidence for the purpose of identifying those facts.

(2A) In the case of an action for libel or slander in which there is more than one plaintiff—
 (a) the references in subsections (1) and (2) above to the plaintiff shall be construed as references to any of the plaintiffs, and
 (b) proof that any of the plaintiffs stands convicted of an offence shall be conclusive evidence that he committed that offence so far as that fact is relevant to any issue arising in relation to his cause of action or that of any other plaintiff.

(3) For the purposes of this section a person shall be taken to stand convicted of an offence if but only if there subsists against him a conviction of that offence by or before a court in the United Kingdom or by a court-martial there or elsewhere.

(4) Subsections (4) to (6) of section 11 of this Act shall apply for the purposes of this section as they apply for the purposes of that section, but as if in the said subsection (4) the reference to subsection (2) were a reference to subsection (2) of this section.

Previous findings of adultery and paternity

The Civil Evidence Act 1968, s. 12, reverses the rule in *Hollington v F. Hewthorn and Co. Ltd* [1943] KB 587 (47.92), in so far as it applied to previous findings of adultery and paternity, and creates two persuasive presumptions, that the person found guilty of adultery shall be taken to have committed the adultery, and that the person found to be the father of a child shall be taken to be, or have been, the father of the child. A claimant who wishes to rely on evidence **47.95** under s. 12 of a finding or adjudication of adultery or paternity must include in his or her particulars of claim a statement to that effect and give details of the finding or adjudication and its date, the court which made it, and the issue in the claim to which it relates (**PD 16, para. 8.1**). Section 12 provides as follows:

(1) In any civil proceedings—
  (a) the fact that a person has been found guilty of adultery in any matrimonial proceedings; and
  (b) the fact that a person has been found to be the father of a child in relevant proceedings before any court in England and Wales or Northern Ireland or has been adjudged to be the father of a child in affiliation proceedings before any court in the United Kingdom;

shall (subject to subsection (3) below) be admissible in evidence for the purpose of proving, where to do so is relevant to any issue in those civil proceedings, that he committed the adultery to which the finding relates or, as the case may be, is (or was) the father of that child, whether or not he offered any defence to the allegation of adultery or paternity and whether or not he is a party to the civil proceedings; but no finding or adjudication other than a subsisting one shall be admissible in evidence by virtue of this section.

(2) In any civil proceedings in which by virtue of this section a person is proved to have been found guilty of adultery as mentioned in subsection (1)(a) above or to have been found or adjudged to be the father of a child as mentioned in subsection (1)(b) above—
  (a) he shall be taken to have committed the adultery to which the finding relates or, as the case may be, to be (or have been) the father of that child, unless the contrary is proved; and
  (b) without prejudice to the reception of any other admissible evidence for the purpose of identifying the facts on which the finding or adjudication was based, the contents of any document which was before the court, or which contains any pronouncement of the court, in the other proceedings in question shall be admissible in evidence for that purpose.

(3) Nothing in this section shall prejudice the operation of any enactment whereby a finding of fact in any matrimonial or affiliation proceedings is for the purposes of any other proceedings made conclusive evidence of any fact.

(4) Subsection (4) of section 11 of this Act shall apply for the purposes of this section as if the reference to subsection (2) were a reference to subsection (2) of this section.

(5) In this section—

'matrimonial proceedings' means any matrimonial cause in the High Court or a county court in England and Wales or in the High Court in Northern Ireland, any consistorial action in Scotland, or any appeal arising out of any such cause or action; 'relevant proceedings' means—
  (a) proceedings on a complaint under section 42 of the National Assistance Act 1948 or section 26 of the Social Security Act 1986;
  (b) proceedings under the Children Act 1989;
  (c) proceedings which would have been relevant proceedings for the purposes of this section in the form in which it was in force before the passing of the Children Act 1989;
  (e) proceedings which are relevant proceedings as defined in section 8(5) of the Civil Evidence Act (Northern Ireland) 1971;

'affiliation proceedings' means, in relation to Scotland, any action of affiliation and aliment; and in this subsection 'consistorial action' does not include an action of aliment only between husband and wife raised in the Court of Session or an action of interim aliment raised in the sheriff court.

As to the meaning of 'civil proceedings', see s. 18(1), which is considered at **47.93**. Under s. 12(2) the party seeking to disprove the adultery or paternity bears the legal burden of doing so, and the standard of proof required to discharge the burden is the ordinary civil standard of proof on a balance of probabilities (*Sutton v Sutton* [1970] 1 WLR 183).

Previous acquittals

47.96 Parliament rejected the Law Reform Committee's recommendation that in defamation proceedings evidence of an acquittal should be conclusive evidence of innocence (see 15th Report (1967) Cmnd 3391, para. 26 et seq.) The question still remains, however, whether the principle of *Hollington v F. Hewthorn and Co. Ltd* [1943] KB 587 (**47.92**) should apply to previous acquittals so as to render them inadmissible as evidence of innocence in subsequent civil proceedings. It is submitted that, on balance, the question should be answered in the affirmative because although it is desirable that a person acquitted of an offence should be granted some measure of immunity from assertions to the contrary, an allegation which was not proved beyond reasonable doubt may still be susceptible to proof on a balance of probabilities, as it was in *Loughans v Odhams Press* [1963] 1 QB 299, a libel suit arising out of the publication of a statement suggesting that the claimant had committed a murder in respect of which he had been acquitted. However, in *Packer v Clayton* (1932) 97 JP 14, a decision pre-dating *Hollington v F. Hewthorn and Co. Ltd*, Avory J expressed the opinion that in affiliation proceedings, the respondent's acquittal of a sexual offence against the applicant would be admissible to show that the jury were not convinced by her evidence.

Other previous findings

The principle of *Hollington v F. Hewthorn and Co. Ltd* [1943] KB 587 would appear to apply, in civil proceedings, to all judicial findings in previous civil proceedings, except findings of adultery and paternity (see Civil Evidence Act 1968, s. 12, at **47.95**). In *Secretary of State for Trade and Industry v Bairstow* [2003] EWCA Civ 321, [2004] Ch 1, the Secretary of State began proceedings under the Company Directors Disqualification Act 1986, s. 8, seeking a disqualification order against B, the managing director of a company. By the time of the proceedings, B had been dismissed and his claim for damages for wrongful dismissal had been unsuccessful, both at first instance and on appeal. In the proceedings under the 1986 Act, the Court of Appeal held that the factual findings and conclusions of the judge at first instance in the wrongful dismissal proceedings were not admissible as evidence of the facts found in those proceedings. The principle of *Hollington v F. Hewthorn and Co. Ltd* has also been held to apply to previous findings of inspectors appointed under what is now the Companies Act 1985, part XIV (*Savings and Investment Bank Ltd v Gasco Investments (Netherlands) BV* [1984] 1 WLR 271), an arbitration award, in later proceedings for the determination of a fair market rent (*Land Securities plc v Westminster City Council* [1993] 1 WLR 286) and the findings of Lord Bingham in his extra-statutory report into the collapse of BCCI (*Three Rivers District Council v Bank of England (No. 3)* [2001] UKHL 16, [2003] 2 AC 1). However, in *Hill v Clifford* [1907] 2 Ch 236 the Court of Appeal held that a finding by the General Medical Council that a dentist had been guilty of professional misconduct was admissible as prima facie evidence of the misconduct in subsequent civil proceedings concerning the dissolution of his partnership. A report of inspectors appointed under the Companies Act 1985, part XIV, is material on which, unless it is substantially challenged, a court may proceed to make a winding-up order on a petition by the Secretary of State (*Re Travel and Holiday Clubs Ltd* [1967] 1 WLR 711; *Re SBA Properties Ltd* [1967] 1 WLR 799 at p. 804; *Re Allied Produce Co. Ltd* [1967] 1 WLR 1469). See also *Faulder v Silk* (1811) 3 Camp 126 (inquisitions in lunacy as prima facie evidence of a person's unsoundness of mind). As to statements contained in public documents, which at common law are admissible for the truth of their contents, see **51.24** to **51.26**. Although a person who was not a party to the earlier proceedings cannot be bound by the result, they can be affected by it. **47.97**

FINDINGS ON QUESTIONS OF FOREIGN LAW

Points of foreign law are questions of fact, and therefore fall to be decided on the evidence adduced, normally expert evidence, except in the case of: **47.98**

(a) points of foreign law which are formally admitted (see 47.8) or of which judicial notice may be taken (see 47.27) and
(b) the construction of provisions of foreign legislation admitted under the Evidence (Colonial Statutes) Act 1907, whereby copies of Acts, ordinances and statutes passed by the legislature of any part of Her Majesty's dominions exclusive of the United Kingdom and of orders, regulations and other instruments issued or made under the authority of any such Act, ordinance or statute, if purporting to be printed by the Government printer of the possession, shall be received in evidence by all courts in the United Kingdom

without proof that the copies were so printed (see the authorities cited in *Jasiewicz v Jasiewicz* [1962] 1 WLR 1426).

Under the British Law Ascertainment Act 1859, English courts may state a case on a point of foreign law for the opinion of a superior court in another part of Her Majesty's dominions, and the opinion pronounced is admissible in evidence on the point. See also the Foreign Law Ascertainment Act 1861.

Points of foreign law must always be decided by the judge. Under the Supreme Court Act, 1981, s. 69, where, for the purposes of disposing of any action or other matter which is being tried by a judge with a jury, it is necessary to ascertain the law of any other country which is applicable to the facts of the case, any question as to the effect of the evidence given with respect to that law shall, instead of being submitted to the jury, be decided by the judge alone. To like effect, see also the **County Courts Act 1984, s. 68.**

Foreign law will usually be established by the opinion evidence of an expert, who may refer to foreign statutes, decisions and texts. If the evidence of the experts conflicts, the judge is bound to look at the sources of knowledge upon which they have relied in order to reach a decision (see per Lord Langdale MR in *Earl Nelson v Lord Bridport* (1845) 8 Beav 527 at p. 537; and per Scarman J in *Re Fuld (No. 3)* [1968] P 675 at pp. 700–3), but should not conduct his or her own research into those sources and rely on material not adduced in evidence in order to reject the expert testimony (per Lord Chelmsford in *Duchess di Sora v Phillipps* (1863) 10 HL Cas 624 at p. 640; and per Purchas LJ in *Bumper Development Corporation Ltd v Metropolitan Police Commissioner* [1991] 1 WLR 1362 at pp. 1368–71).

Although points of foreign law are questions of fact, if a point has been decided, and the same point arises again in a subsequent case, it does not necessarily need to be decided afresh on new expert evidence. The Civil Evidence Act 1972, s. 4, provides as follows:

(2) Where any question as to the law of any country or territory outside the United Kingdom, or of any part of the United Kingdom other than England and Wales, with respect to any matter has been determined (whether before or after the passing of this Act) in any such proceedings as are mentioned in subsection (4) below, then in any civil proceedings (not being proceedings before a court which can take judicial notice of the law of that country, territory or part with respect to that matter)—
- (a) any finding made or decision given on that question in the first-mentioned proceedings shall, if reported or recorded in citable form, be admissible in evidence for the purpose of proving the law of that country, territory or part with respect to that matter; and
- (b) if that finding or decision, as so reported or recorded, is adduced for that purpose, the law of that country, territory or part with respect to that matter shall be taken to be in accordance with that finding or decision unless the contrary is proved:

Provided that paragraph (b) above shall not apply in the case of a finding or decision which conflicts with another finding or decision on the same question adduced by virtue of this subsection in the same proceedings.

(3) Except with the leave of the court, a party to any civil proceedings shall not be permitted to adduce any such finding or decision as is mentioned in subsection (2) above by virtue of that subsection unless he has in accordance with rules of court given to every other party to the proceedings notice that he intends to do so.

(4) The proceedings referred to in subsection (2) above are the following, whether civil or criminal, namely—
- (a) proceedings at first instance in any of the following courts, namely the High Court, the Crown Court, a court of quarter sessions, the Court of Chancery of the county palatine of Lancaster and the Court of Chancery of the county palatine of Durham;
- (b) appeals arising out of any such proceedings as are mentioned in paragraph (a) above;
- (c) proceedings before the Judicial Committee of the Privy Council on appeal (whether to Her Majesty in Council or to the Judicial Committee as such) from any decision of any court outside the United Kingdom.

(5) For the purposes of this section a finding or decision on any such question as is mentioned in subsection (2) above shall be taken to be reported or recorded in citable form if, but only if, it is

> reported or recorded in writing in a report, transcript or other document which, if that question had been a question as to the law of England and Wales, could be cited as an authority in legal proceedings in England and Wales.

'Civil proceedings', for the purposes of s. 4(2) and (3), means civil proceedings before any tribunal, in relation to which the strict rules of evidence apply, whether as a matter of law or by agreement of the parties (s. 5). **Rule 33.7** of the CPR sets out the procedure which must be followed by a party who intends to put in evidence a finding under s. 4(2). He or she must give notice of his or her intention:

(a) if there are to be witness statements, not later than the latest date for serving them, or
(b) otherwise, not less than 21 days before the hearing;

and the notice must specify the question on which the finding was made and enclose a copy of a document where it is reported or recorded.

Section 4(2)(b) effectively raises a presumption that the earlier decision is correct. The weight to be attached to the earlier decision, however, is a matter for the trial judge, and although it is obviously desirable to reach consistent conclusions, the section is not to be construed as if it laid down a general rule that the presumption can only be displaced by particularly cogent evidence (*Phoenix Marine Inc. v China Ocean Shipping Co.* [1999] 1 Lloyd's Rep 682).

EVIDENCE OF CONSENT OF TRUSTEE TO ACT

A document purporting to contain the written consent of a person to act as trustee and to bear his or her signature, verified by some other person, is evidence of such consent (CPR, r. 33.8). **47.99**

Chapter 48 Disclosure

The following procedural checklists, which are in **appendix 1**, are relevant to this chapter:

Procedural checklist 26 Standard disclosure
Procedural checklist 27 Specific disclosure
Procedural checklist 28 Non-party disclosure

INTRODUCTION

Disclosure is the formal process by which parties to claims give each other copies of the documents in their control which are material to the issues in the claim. Formal disclosure under **CPR, Part 31**, applies to claims on the fast track and multi-track, but not to claims on the small claims track (see **43.16**). Disclosure should take place in accordance with directions made by the court. In most fast track and multi-track claims directions for disclosure are made when the claim is allocated to a track (**rr. 28.2(1), 28.3, 29.2(1)(a); PD 29, para. 4**). Otherwise, directions are given at a case management conference (**CPR, r. 29.2(1)(b)**). The usual direction is for standard disclosure (see **48.4**), which covers documents in the control of the party making disclosure which that party intends to rely on at the trial, and also documents which adversely affect that party or which support the other side. Disclosure takes place in two stages. First, the parties exchange lists of documents using **form N265**. This form identifies all the documents which support or adversely affect any of the parties to the claim, and also asserts any privilege claimed against disclosure in respect of identified documents or categories of documents (see **48.37** to **48.69**). Secondly, the parties allow their opponents to inspect the non-privileged disclosed documents. Usually this happens by providing photocopies, but there is provision for physical inspection of the originals. The court has a discretion to limit the issues on which disclosure is to be provided, and to order disclosure in stages (see **48.25**, **48.26**). **48.1**

'Documents' for the purposes of disclosure include anything on which information is recorded (**CPR, r. 31.4**), including paper documents, pictures, photographs, computer files and disks, emails, audio recordings and videos. Documents within a party's 'control' include those which are or have been in that party's possession, or of which that party has or has had a right to possession or to inspect or to take copies (**r. 31.8**). The scope of disclosure is therefore very wide, but it does not include what are traditionally called 'train of inquiry' documents (which are considered at **48.17**).

Features of the disclosure system include:

(a) application of the principle of proportionality to limit the extent of the searches required for find disclosable documents;
(b) a requirement to include a 'disclosure statement' in the list of documents to the effect that the party giving disclosure has complied with its duties under **CPR, Part 31**;
(c) a requirement that litigants, rather than their lawyers, must sign the disclosure statement. This obligation is intended to bring home to litigants that it is their personal responsibility to give full disclosure (*Arrow Trading and Investments Est 1920 v Edwardian Group Ltd* [2004] EWHC 1319 (Ch), [2005] 1 BCLC 696).

Where an opponent fails to give disclosure in accordance with directions, the innocent party should still usually comply with its own disclosure obligations, but may apply for a sanction (usually an 'unless' order, see **chapter 46**) or for specific disclosure (see **48.29**).

Documents disclosed under **Part 31** are deemed to be authentic (see **48.31**), and if this is disputed, the party receiving the copies should serve a notice to prove. Disclosed documents are provided for the purposes of the present litigation and must not be used for any collateral purpose (**48.33**), although this protection is usually lost once the documents are referred to in open court.

DOCUMENTATION ON THE SMALL CLAIMS TRACK

48.2 The rules on disclosure in **CPR, Part 31**, do not apply at all to the small claims track (**r.** 27.2(1)(b)). On the small claims track, parties are required to disclose only the documents on which they intend to rely at trial (see **r.** 27.4(3)(a) and **43.16**).

DISCLOSURE ORDERS IN AID OF ARBITRATION

48.3 Where a dispute is referred to arbitration, the Arbitration Act 1996, s. 43, provides that court procedures to procure documents or other material evidence may be used only with the permission of the arbitral tribunal or the agreement of the other parties. This provision does not prevent a court making a *Norwich Pharmacal* order (see **48.83**) in the period before a dispute has been referred to arbitration, where the power is used for preserving assets or remedies (*Glidepath Holding BV v Thompson* [2004] EWHC 2234 (Comm), [2005] 1 All ER (Comm) 434). Unless otherwise agreed by the parties, the court has under s. 44 five specified powers relating to the taking of evidence from witnesses, the preservation of evidence and making orders in relation to property. These specified powers do not include orders for non-party disclosure under **CPR, r. 31.17** (see **48.76**). Where there is a risk that documents may cease to exist or become unavailable, it may be possible to obtain an order for their preservation, such as by copying, under s. 44(2)(b), see *Assimina Maritime Ltd v Pakistan National Shipping Corporation* [2004] EWHC 3005 (Comm), [2005] 1 All ER (Comm) 460).

STANDARD DISCLOSURE

48.4 By **CPR, r. 31.5(1)**, a court order requiring a party to give disclosure is an order to give standard disclosure, unless the court directs otherwise. However, in the exercise of its case management powers in furtherance of the overriding objective, the court may decide to make orders limiting disclosure, and it should not be assumed that an order for standard disclosure will simply be rubber-stamped by the court (see **48.25**).

By **r. 31.6**, standard disclosure requires a party to disclose only:

(a) the documents on which he relies; and
(b) the documents which—
  (i) adversely affect his own case;
  (ii) adversely affect another party's case; or
  (iii) support another party's case; and
(c) the documents which he is required to disclose by a relevant practice direction.

Although these categories do not include 'train of inquiry' documents (see **48.17**), they are nevertheless wide ranging, and many clients are surprised at the breadth of documentation that they are required to disclose. To ensure the system works fairly between the opposing parties, lawyers are under professional duties to advise their clients on their disclosure obligations (**48.15**), and clients must take personal responsibility by signing a disclosure statement (48.18). Whether a document falls into any of these categories is to be judged against the statements of case, and not by reference to matters raised elsewhere, even in exchanged witness statements (*Paddick v Associated Newspapers Ltd* [2003] EWHC 2991 (QB), LTL 12/12/2003).

Rule 31.7 requires a party ordered to give standard disclosure to 'make a reasonable search for documents falling within **r. 31.6(b)** and (c)' (adverse material and documents specifically required by a practice direction). The effect of this, reinforced by **PD 31, para.** 2, is to apply the principle of proportionality to searching for the purposes of standard disclosure. The searcher must search for the documents required by **CPR, r. 31.6(b)** and (c), but may make a policy decision not to search in places where the cost of searching could not be justified by the small chance of finding anything disclosable. The factors relevant in deciding what kind of search would be reasonable are discussed in **48.8**.

List of documents

48.5 The procedure for standard disclosure is summarised in **procedural checklist** 26, which is in **appendix** 1. When standard disclosure has been ordered, each party should make a list of the documents in its control which come within the categories set out in **CPR, r.** 31(6) (see 48.4). Lists of documents should be on **form N265**, and have to be served by the date stated in the court's directions on every other party (**r. 31.10(2); PD 31, para.** 3.1). Although a party will usually give disclosure in a list of documents, the requirement in **CPR, r. 31.2**, to disclose a document 'by stating that the document exists or has existed' can be satisfied by referring to a document's existence in a witness statement or expert's report (*SmithKline Beecham plc v Generics (UK) Ltd* [2003] EWCA Civ 1109, [2004] 1 WLR 1479, at [29]). On **form N265**, as required by **rr. 31.10(4)** and **31.19(4)**, the list is in three parts:

(a) Documents presently in the disclosing party's control which the controlling party does not object to being inspected.
(b) Documents presently in the disclosing party's control which the controlling party objects to be inspected, giving the reason for the objection. According to **PD 31, para.** 4.5, a right or duty to withhold a document, or part of a document, from inspection must be claimed in writing with a statement of the grounds on which it is claimed, and, according to **para.** 4.6, should normally be included in the disclosure statement (see 48.20), although **form N265** is not laid out in that way.
(c) Documents that have been, but are no longer, in the disclosing party's control. The list must state when each document was last in the party's control and where each is now.

Rule 31.10(8) provides that the parties may agree in writing to disclose documents without making a list, and to disclose documents without the disclosing party making a disclosure statement, but such agreement must be put into writing and lodged with the court (**PD 31, para.** 1.4). Such agreements are comparatively uncommon and **form N265** is normally used.

PD 31, para. 3.2, provides that compliance with **CPR, r. 31.10(3)**, will be achieved by listing documents in chronological order, numbering them consecutively, and giving each of them a concise description, for example, 'letter, claimant to defendant, 17 Jan 2005'. Where there is a large number of documents which all fall into a particular category, the disclosing party is permitted to list those documents as a category, rather than individually, thus, for example: '50 bank statements relating to account number 1234546 at Anywhere Bank, January 2000–November 2005'.

Standard disclosure in personal injury claims

48.6 Annex B to the **Pre-Action Protocol for Personal Injury Claims** contains detailed lists of categories of documents that should be disclosed in various types of personal injury claims. For example, in tripping cases the highway authority should disclose its records for the 12 months prior to the accident dealing with inspections of the relevant stretch of highway;

maintenance including records of independent contractors working in the relevant area; minutes of highway authority meetings where maintenance or repair policy was discussed or decided; complaints about the state of highways; and other accidents on the relevant stretch of highway. Annex B has even more detailed lists for accidents at work. Standard disclosure imposes similar obligations, but will include claims-handling documents and party-and-party correspondence, and (although, because privileged, inspection will not be required) documents relating to legal advice on the claim.

The combined effect of **CPR, rr. 31.3, 31.6, 31.8** and **31.12(3)**, is to oblige a claimant in a personal injuries claim to disclose and give inspection of the claimant's GP and hospital records (*Bennett v Compass Group UK and Ireland Ltd* [2002] EWCA Civ 642, [2002] ICR 1177). Where the claimant fails to cooperate in providing these records (which are under the claimant's control as defined by **r. 31.8(2)**), the court has the power to make an order that the claimant must provide the defendant with a signed authority for the release of the records, but such an order has to be carefully worded to ensure the claimant's rights are not infringed (*Bennett v Compass Group UK and Ireland Ltd*). This means that care should be taken to ensure the records to be disclosed are not wider (in terms of dates or nature of the document to be disclosed) than the nature of the case merits.

Standard disclosure in commercial and contract claims

48.7 Contractual and commercial claims often generate considerable disclosable documentation. This will include the contractual documents, including the contract, tenders, offers, orders, shipping documents, delivery notes, invoices, documents recording or effecting payment, statements of account, and receipts; correspondence relating to forming the contract, its performance, and alleged breach; documents dealing with the effects of breach and any steps taken to mitigate damage; and often financial documentation, such as business accounts, tax records and financial records dealing with loss of profits or other heads of loss and damage.

In *Marlton v Tektronix UK Holdings Ltd* [2003] EWHC 383 (Ch), LTL 10/2/2003) there was a dispute about whether a contractual document was sent by email, so disclosure was ordered of the relevant hard disks, back-ups and server. Diaries containing business and personal details, which were relevant to establishing how much time a director had spent in managing a business, were ordered to be disclosed in *Re Cawgate Ltd* [2004] EWHC 1773 (Ch), LTL 30/6/2004. In an unfair prejudice case under the Companies Act 1985, s. 459, where it was alleged the directors were receiving excessive remuneration, standard disclosure included financial documents such as accounts and budgets (*Arrow Trading and Investments Est 1920 v Edwardian Group Ltd* [2004] EWHC 1319 (Ch), [2005] 1 BCLC 696).

Standard disclosure in libel claims

48.8 Standard disclosure of various categories of documents was considered in the libel case of *Beckham v News Group Newspapers Ltd* [2005] EWHC 2252 (QB), LTL 25/10/2005:

(a) Disclosure of documents relating to the claimants' public relations strategies was refused, because there was no sufficient foundation to the defendant's case that the claimants had presented a false image to the public.

(b) Disclosure was also refused of documents relating to the claimants' move to Madrid, their commercial arrangements with a particular photographer, and the termination of an agency agreement with a public relations company.

(c) Disclosure of tapes of a television documentary about the claimants, including all unedited versions, was dealt with by an order that the claimants must use their best endeavours to find out from those involved in making the documentary about incidents relied on by the defendant and to communicate such information to the defendant.

(d) Disclosure of notes and tapes made by journalists when interviewing the claimants' former nanny was ordered. This was because the court needed to have regard to the totality of what the nanny said to the journalists, and because the items might be relevant to whether the nanny had appeared to be a credible source of information to the defendant's journalists.

MATERIALS TO BE DISCLOSED

Documents

The regime for disclosure and inspection in **CPR, Part 31**, is concerned only with documents, and not any other type of evidence. A 'document' is defined in **r. 31.4** as 'anything in which information of any description is recorded' and 'copy' in relation to a document, means anything onto which information recorded in the document has been copied, by whatever means and whether directly or indirectly'. Thus a 'document' is not confined to paper, but includes electronic documents, audio and video cassettes, and other similar material. **48.9**

Electronic documents

The definition of 'documents' in **CPR, r. 31.4**, extends to electronic documents, including emails, messages on mobile telephones, word-processed documents and databases. In addition, the definition covers documents that are stored on servers and back-up systems and electronic documents that have been 'deleted'. It also extends to additional information stored and associated with electronic documents known as metadata (**PD 31, para. 2A.1**, inserted on 1 October 2005). Where disclosure of electronic documents is likely to go beyond readily accessible documents, the parties should discuss the issues that arise, and provide technical information to each other, before the first case management conference. If the matter proves difficult or if there is disagreement, directions should be sought at an early stage, preferably the first case management conference (**PD 31, para. 2A.2**). **48.10**

Control of documents

By **CPR, r. 31.8(1)**, a party's duty to disclose documents is limited to documents which are now or have been previously within the party's control. **Rule 31.8(3)** provides that a document is or was in a party's control if: **48.11**

(a) it is or was in the party's physical possession;
(b) the party has or has had a right to possession of it; or
(c) the party has or has had a right to inspect or take copies of it.

This does not seem any different from the 'possession, custody or power' criterion for giving discovery under the old rules. Therefore, it may be possible to require the controller of a company to disclose the company's documents in a claim to which the controller, but not the company, is a party (*B v B (Matrimonial Proceedings: Discovery)* [1978] Fam 181; *Lonrho Ltd v Shell Petroleum Co. Ltd* [1980] 1 WLR 627; *Re Tecnion Investments Ltd* [1985] BCLC 434).

Disclosure of copies

By **CPR, r. 31.9**, a copy of a document must be treated as a separate document, and therefore separately disclosed, if it contains a modification, obliteration or other marking or feature: **48.12**

(a) on which 'a party' (which clearly means the disclosing party) intends to rely; or
(b) which adversely affects the disclosing party's own case or supports another party's case.

So if, for example, several copies of a memorandum have been produced and some have been returned to the originator with other people's comments on them, and those comments are within (a) or (b) above, the copies must be disclosed. Otherwise it is not necessary to disclose the existence of copies of disclosed documents (**r. 31.9(1)**).

Extent of the search

48.13 The duty to disclose under an order for standard disclosure is qualified by reasonableness. **Rule 31.7(2)** of the CPR provides that the factors relevant in deciding the reasonableness of a search include the following:

(a) the number of documents involved;
(b) the nature and complexity of the proceedings;
(c) the ease and expense of retrieval of any particular document; and
(d) the significance of any document which is likely to be located during the search.

This list of factors is not intended to be exhaustive, and there may well be others which affect the reasonableness of disclosing documents.

Electronic documents present particular difficulties. Given the wealth of electronic documents that might fall within a party's standard disclosure obligations under **r. 31.6** (see **PD 31, para. 2A.1** and **48.10**), there may be time and expense reasons for limiting the search for electronic documents under **CPR, r. 31.7**. Factors relevant in deciding the reasonableness of a search for electronic documents are set out in **PD 31, para. 2A.4** (inserted on 1 October 2005). They include the number of documents, the nature and complexity of the proceedings, the significance of the documents, and the ease and expense of retrieval of the relevant documents. It may be reasonable to search for electronic documents using defined keywords (**para. 2A.5**). Sub-paragraph (4) of the disclosure statement on **form N265** is a declaration of the extent of the search carried out for electronic documents.

A party who has not searched for a category or class of document on the grounds that to do so would be unreasonable, must state this in the disclosure statement (see **48.18**) and identify the category or class of document (**r. 31.7(3)**).

The extent of the search should be discussed by legal representative and client at all stages of litigation planning. Clients must provide their legal advisers with realistic information about the quantity of documents and the time and expense that may be involved in carrying out the search. It is the task of the lawyer to assess the legal significance and relevance of what might be disclosed if the search was extended, and all these factors must be taken into account and balanced against the value of the claim itself when deciding what kind of search would be reasonable.

DUTIES ON PARTIES AND LAWYERS

Client's duty

48.14 The person responsible for making standard disclosure must certify, amongst other matters, that the duty to disclose is understood, and that to the best of his or her knowledge and belief, the duty has been discharged (**r. 31.10(6)(b) and (c)**). The certification is included in the disclosure statement required by **r. 31.10(5)** (see **48.18**) and has profound implications for the way in which a party should approach the whole disclosure process.

Standard disclosure requires disclosure of *only* the documents listed in **r. 31.6**, and so it is not sufficient to conduct an indiscriminate trawl through all documentation in the control of the party, extracting every single item which may have some relevance to the litigation. Whilst this may attract criticism as being expensive, or for 'front-loading' the costs of the case, it is submitted that the resultant saving in time and expense amply redresses the balance.

Under **r. 31.10(6)** and **PD 31, para. 4.4**, it is clear that the person signing the disclosure statement must have an understanding of the duty to search and all that it entails, and also knowledge of the documents and issues in the case. The responsible person should normally be present at case management conferences and any other hearings where the issue of disclosure is likely to arise. For large corporate parties, or organisations such as local authorities, that person will normally be an in-house lawyer with responsibility for the case, but this situation can occasionally present problems. It may well be that the person with first-hand knowledge of the dispute is a departmental head who does not occupy a senior position in the organisation and who may, therefore, not be the appropriate person to sign the disclosure statement. Administrative problems may arise when documents that have to be disclosed emanate from different departments within the organisation. Organisations need to have sound and efficient document management systems. It may well be that 'documents officers' will have to be appointed within organisations for this purpose, as it is clear from the format of the disclosure statement that it cannot be signed by a legal representative. Parties may be well advised to seek legal advice on compliance with the duty.

Legal representative's duties to advise

At an early stage in a claim, a solicitor should advise his or her client of the obligations of standard disclosure (*Rockwell Machine Tool Co. Ltd v E. P. Barrus (Concessionaires) Ltd* [1968] 1 WLR 693). Solicitors owe a duty to the court to ensure their clients make full disclosure. As Salmon J said in *Woods v Martins Bank Ltd* [1959] 1 QB 55 at p. 60: **48.15**

> It cannot be too clearly understood that solicitors owe a duty to the court, as officers of the court, carefully to go through the documents disclosed by their client to make sure, as far as possible, that no relevant documents have been omitted from their clients' affidavit [or list of documents].

It will often be sensible to give advice about keeping receipts and other documents commonly thrown away, and stopping routine destruction of documents. There may also be an obligation to advise a client to make an early and thorough search for documents which may need to be disclosed. It will often be sensible to explain the breadth of meaning of the word 'document' for this purpose (see **48.9** and **48.10**), emphasising that it includes emails and computer records. Solicitors (Law Society's Code for Advocacy, para. 5.1) and counsel (Code of Conduct of the Bar of England and Wales, para. 608(d)) must withdraw from a case if the client refuses to authorise the disclosure of documents which should be disclosed to the other side.

ILLEGALLY OBTAINED DOCUMENTS

The Data Protection Act 1998, s. 55(1), provides that a person must not (and by s. 55(3) it is an offence to) knowingly or recklessly, without the consent of the data controller: **48.16**

(a) obtain or disclose personal data of the information contained in personal data; or
(b) procure the disclosure to another person of the information contained in personal data.

Section 55(2)(a) provides that s. 55(1) does not apply to a person who shows that the obtaining, disclosing or procuring of the personal data or information:

(a) was necessary for the purpose of preventing or detecting crime; or
(b) was required or authorised by or under any enactment, by any rule of law or by order of a court.

In *Guidance Note (Illegally Obtained Evidence in Civil and Family Proceedings)* issued by the General Council of the Bar (September 2003), the following principles were set out for the guidance of the profession (which it is submitted are of equal relevance for solicitors):

(a) Legal representatives must never advise that evidence be obtained illegally, including by methods infringing the Data Protection Act 1998. Updating or clarifying such evidence is just as illegal as obtaining it in the first place.
(b) There is an important distinction between obtaining such data in the first place, which is illegal, and disclosure of such material in civil proceedings. If disclosure is compulsory, it is likely to be lawful. Standard disclosure under **CPR, r. 31.6**, is a rule of law within

the meaning of the Data Protection Act 1998, s. 55(2)(a)(ii), and so will be regarded as compulsory for the purposes of s. 55.

(c) A party who has obtained relevant documents illegally is not entitled to claim legal professional privilege over them (see **48.40** and *Dubai Aluminium Co. Ltd v Al Alawi* [1999] 1 WLR 1964). In addition to the illegally obtained evidence, the source of the evidence and the letters of instruction to the person who obtained it must also be disclosed.

(d) If a client refuses to comply with these disclosure obligations, the legal representatives will be obliged to withdraw.

(e) If disclosure is made, the data can be used in evidence in the claim in the usual way.

(f) If there is doubt about the use of data, or the need to disclose it, the Guidance Note suggests a without notice application should be made to the court. The need for tactical secrecy may justify the application being made without notice. Any order made by the court for disclosure or use will provide the necessary compulsion within the last five words of s. 55(2)(a)(ii).

'TRAIN OF INQUIRY' DOCUMENTS

48.17 One of the principal problems that beset the old system of discovery flowed from the decision of the Court of Appeal in *Compagnie Financiere et Commerciale du Pacifique v Peruvian Guano Co.* (1882) 11 QBD 55, where Brett LJ said, at p. 63:

> . . . every document relates to the matters in question in the action, which not only would be evidence upon any issue, but also which, it is reasonable to suppose, contains information which *may* — not which *must* — either directly or indirectly enable the party [seeking discovery] either to advance his own case or to damage the case of his adversary. . . . a document can properly be said to contain information which may enable the party [seeking discovery] either to advance his own case or to damage the case of his adversary, if it is a document which may fairly lead him to a train of inquiry, which may have either of these two consequences.

This concept of the 'train of inquiry' made discovery of documents an extensive and costly process and was a principal cause of complaint by practitioners and litigants alike. In *O Co. v M Co.* [1996] 2 Lloyd's Rep 347 Colman J, perhaps in anticipation of the new approach, and certainly out of frustration with the old, stated, at pp. 350–1:

> The principle was never intended to justify demands for disclosure of documents at the far end of the spectrum of materiality which on the face of it were unrelated to the pleaded case of the plaintiff or defendant and which were required for purely speculative investigation. . . . That formulation [Brett LJ's 'train of inquiry'] must not, in my judgment, be understood as justifying discovery demands which would involve parties to civil litigation being required to turn out the contents of their filing systems as if under criminal investigation merely on the off-chance that something might show up from which some relatively weak inference prejudicial to the case of the disclosing party might be drawn.

Train of inquiry documents are not covered by the definition of standard disclosure (see **48.2**), and are rarely required to be disclosed in fast track claims. It is also comparatively rare for them to be required in multi-track claims, and a specific order to this effect must be obtained if disclosure is to reach this far. Before making such an order the court will take into account all the circumstances of the case with particular regard to the overriding objective (**PD 31, para. 5.4**). An order was made in *Commissioners of Inland Revenue v Exeter City AFC Ltd* (2004) [2004] BCC 519 for the disclosure of communications between the Inland Revenue and 20 to 30 football clubs connected to proposed and actual entry into insolvency of those football clubs. These were train of inquiry documents which could have advanced the defendant football club's case that the Inland Revenue had not been unfairly treated by the club's voluntary arrangement.

DISCLOSURE STATEMENT

Who must make a disclosure statement

The disclosing party's list of documents (**form N265**) must include a disclosure statement (**CPR, r. 31.10(5)**) and the form of statement, which is set out in the annex to **PD 31**, is included in **form N265** with a signature box. A disclosure statement is the statement of the disclosing party, or that party's insurer or the Motor Insurers' Bureau, rather than a legal representative (**CPR, r. 31.10(6)**). A disclosure statement is not a mere technicality. Its purpose is to impose a positive duty on each party to give full standard disclosure. If there are several defendants in a case, each should sign a disclosure statement. Providing a single composite list of documents does not satisfy **r. 31.10** (*Arrow Trading and Investments Est 1920 v Edwardian Group Ltd* [2004] EWHC 1319 (Ch), [2005] 1 BCLC 696). **48.18**

Where an insurer, or the Motor Insurers' Bureau, has a financial interest in the outcome of the proceedings, it may sign a disclosure statement on behalf of a party (**r. 31.10(9); PD 31, para.** 4.7).

If the disclosing party is an individual, the disclosure statement is either the party's own statement, signed by the party or the party's litigation friend, or is the statement of the party's insurer or the Motor Insurers' Bureau.

If the disclosing party is not an individual, the disclosure statement must identify the person who is making and signing it and explain why he or she is considered an appropriate person to make it (**CPR, r. 31.10(7)**). It must state t hat person's name and address and the office or position he or she holds in the disclosing party (**PD 31, para.** 4.3). The same rules apply when a disclosure statement is signed by an insurer or the Motor Insurers' Bureau (**PD 31, para.** 4.7).

If a disclosure order requires a particular person to make disclosure on behalf of a party, that person cannot delegate the duty (*Carlco Ltd v Chief Constable of Dyfed-Powys Police* [2002] EWCA Civ 1754, LTL 18/11/2002). At present, company law permits a company to have officers who are not individuals (it is proposed to change this in the next revision of the law). In *Carlco Ltd v Chief Constable of Dyfed-Powys Police* a disclosure order required disclosure to be made by the claimant company's 'officer' and as its only officers were themselves companies, which could not delegate to individuals, no disclosure could be made.

Contents of disclosure statement

By **CPR, r. 31.10(6)**, a disclosure statement must: **48.19**

(a) set out the extent of the search that has been made to locate documents which are required to be disclosed;
(b) certify that the signatory understands the duty to disclose documents; and
(c) certify that to the best of his or her knowledge he or she has carried out that duty.

The disclosure statement certifies that a reasonable and proportionate search has been carried out to disclose all the documents required by the court's order.

PD 31, para. 4.2, requires a disclosure statement expressly to state that the disclosing party believes the extent of the search to have been reasonable in all the circumstances; and **r.** 31.7(3) of the CPR requires a party who has not searched for a category or class of document on the grounds that to do so would be unreasonable, to state this in the disclosure statement, and identify the category or class of document not searched for. In the prescribed form of disclosure statement in **PD 31, annex**, and **form N265** the statement required by **r.** 31.7(3) is turned into a description of the boundaries of a search:

I did not search for documents—
pre-dating——

located elsewhere than——
in categories other than——
for electronic documents (if electronic documents were searched for, further details must be given of the limits of the search)

In the disclosure statement the disclosing party should draw attention to any particular limitations which were adopted for proportionality reasons and give the reasons why the limitations were adopted (**PD 31, para.** 4.2(2)).

The searcher must search for the documents required by **CPR, r. 31.6(b) and** (c), but may make a policy decision not to search in places where the cost of searching could not be justified by the small chance of finding anything disclosable.

Rule 31.3(2) requires a party who considers that it would be disproportionate to the issues in the case (see 48.24) to permit inspection of a category or class of documents to state that fact in the disclosure statement.

PD 31, para. 4.4, requires the legal representative of a disclosing party to endeavour to ensure that the individual making the disclosure statement understands the duty of disclosure under **CPR, Part 31**. It is submitted that the requirement in **r. 31.6(b)** to disclose adverse documents is a concise restatement of the previous requirement to give honest discovery.

Conclusive nature of statements on the status of documents

48.20 There is a general rule that statements by a party about the status of documents in his control are conclusive at all stages up to the trial. In *Paddick v Associated Newspapers Ltd* [2003] EWHC 2991 (QB), LTL 12/12/2003, the claimant gave standard disclosure of extracts from two witness statements, and stated that the undisclosed parts were irrelevant. Disclosure of these parts was refused, the claimant's assertion as to relevance being conclusive. See also *Loutchansky v Times Newspapers* [2001] EWCA Civ 536, [2002] QB 321; *GE Capital Corporate Finance Group Ltd v Bankers Trust Co.* [1995] 1 WLR 172. Where a party credibly asserts that a category of documents is privileged, that assertion is also ordinarily a complete answer to an application for disclosure (*Beckham v News Group Newspapers Ltd* [2005] EWHC 2252 (QB), LTL 25/10/2005).

INSPECTION AND COPYING OF DOCUMENTS

48.21 The right of inspection of a disclosed document is contained in **CPR, r. 31.3**, which provides that a party to whom a document has been disclosed has a right to inspect it, except where:

(a) the document is no longer in the control of the party who disclosed it;
(b) the party disclosing the document has a right or duty to withhold inspection of it (see 48.37 to 48.68); or
(c) the disclosing party considers that it would be disproportionate to the issues in the case to permit inspection of documents within a category or class of document disclosed under **r. 31.6(b)** (adverse documents) (see 48.24).

Written notice of a wish to inspect a document must be given to the party who disclosed it (**r. 31.15(a)**) and inspection must be permitted not more than seven days after the date of receipt of that notice (**r. 31.15(b)**). A party may, instead of physical inspection, request a copy of the document, and, provided there is also an undertaking to pay reasonable copying costs, the party who disclosed the document must supply a copy not later than seven days after the date of receipt of the request (**r. 31.15(c)**). This rule is unclear, but it is submitted that the seven-day period in respect of supplying copies should begin when the undertaking to pay for the copies is given.

The parties should cooperate at an early stage in an endeavour to agree the format in which electronic documents should be inspected (**PD 31, para. 2A.3**, introduced on 1 October

2005). In case of difficulty or disagreement, the matter should be resolved by directions, preferably at the first case management conference.

Under **r. 31.12** the court may make an order for specific inspection, which is an order that a party permit inspection of a document, named in the order, which the party sought to exclude from inspection under **r. 31.2(2)** (permission to inspect would be disproportionate to the issues in the case, see **48.24**). An application for an order under **r. 31.12** must be made by application notice (see **48.29**).

Inspection of documents referred to in statements of case, etc.

Apart from the general right to inspect documents disclosed either by standard or specific disclosure (see **48.21**), a party has, under **CPR, r. 31.14(1)**, the right to inspect a document referred to in: **48.22**

(a) a statement of case;
(b) a witness statement;
(c) a witness summary; or
(d) an affidavit.

This particular right arises as soon as the document concerned is mentioned, even prior to it being referred to in **form N265**. It is submitted that the limitations on inspection listed in **r. 31.3** (see **48.21**), apply here too. It further seems that the words 'referred to' indicate that the right to inspect arises only once a specific reference to a document has been made. Where there is no more than an inference (as opposed to a specific reference) to the existence of a document, it seems to be more appropriate to make an application for specific disclosure under **r. 31.12** or to wait for standard disclosure. If a party makes reference to a document which is not in its control, the appropriate course will be to seek to obtain the document by means of an order under **r. 31.17** (orders for disclosure against a person not a party), **r. 34.2(4) and (5)** (witness summons), or **r. 34.8** (evidence by deposition).

In *Bennett v Compass Group UK and Ireland Ltd* [2002] EWCA Civ 642, [2002] ICR 1177, it was held that the defendants were entitled to inspect the claimant's GP and hospital notes under **CPR, r. 31.14**, because they had been referred to in the medical report attached to the particulars of claim. This case was decided under the rule before it was amended on 25 March 2002. The current version of **r. 31.14**, by sub-para. (2), requires a court order for inspection of documents referred to in experts' reports. An expert's report must state the substance of all material instructions on which the report is based (**r. 35.10(3)**). However, in relation to those instructions, the court will not order disclosure of any specific document or permit any questioning in court other than by the party who instructed the expert, unless it is satisfied that there are reasonable grounds to consider that the statement of material instructions is inaccurate or incomplete (**r. 35.10(4)**).

REFUSAL TO DISCLOSE OR PERMIT INSPECTION

A person holding a document may dispute aspects of disclosure or inspection on a number of bases, namely: **48.23**

(a) there may be factual disputes about the disclosability or existence of the document;
(b) there may be factual disputes about whether the document is or has ever been under the party's control;
(c) there may be a claim by a person under **CPR, r. 31.3(2)**, that it would be 'disproportionate' to the issues in the case to permit inspection of documents (see **48.24**);
(d) there may be a claim to withhold inspection on the basis of private privilege, i.e.,

professional legal privilege, litigation privilege, or the privilege against self-incrimination (see **48.37** to **48.65**);

(e) there may be a claim to withhold disclosure on the basis of public interest immunity (see **48.66** to **48.68**).

Under **CPR, r. 31.19(3)**, a person who claims to have a right or a duty to withhold inspection of a document or part of a document must assert the right or duty in writing and state the grounds on which it is claimed. That assertion must be in the list in which the document is disclosed, or, if there has been no list, in a notice to the person wishing to inspect the document (**r. 31.19(4)**). Any party may then apply to the court under **r. 31.19(5)** to decide whether a claim made under **r. 31.19(3)** should be upheld. Thus an application for the court's decision on whether a claim to withhold inspection is justified may be made either by the party seeking inspection or the party resisting it. It is suggested in **PD 31, para. 6.1**, that a claim to withhold inspection of a document does not require an application to the court, so that, generally speaking, it is the party who wishes to challenge that claim who must apply to the court. Although this is applicable in the case of disputes about private privilege, in the case of public interest immunity **r. 31.19(1)** provides that a person may apply to the court, without notice to other parties, for an order permitting disclosure of a document to be withheld on the ground that disclosure would damage the public interest. To decide an application under **r. 31.19(1)** or **(3)**, the court may require the person seeking to withhold inspection of a document to produce it to the court, and it may invite any person, whether or not a party, to make representations (**r. 31.19(6)**).

Inspection disproportionate to the case

48.24 Under **CPR, r. 31.3(2)**, a party who considers that it would be disproportionate to the issues in the case to permit inspection of documents within a category or class of document, is not required to permit inspection of those documents, but must state in the disclosure statement that inspection of those documents will not be permitted on the ground that to do so would be disproportionate.

This basis for withholding inspection of a document, whose existence and disclosability appear to be admitted, did not exist before the CPR came into effect. The concept of proportionality is an important one in considering the CPR purposively. It imports considerations not merely of technical relevance to the litigation, but of how expensive or time-consuming the carrying out of inspection is likely to be. Given that by this time the party having the documents will have presumably found them and identified them so that any search is likely to have been successful, this would seem to focus the court's attention on the cost of carrying out inspection and therefore presumably on the fact that inspection would need, perhaps, to be in some distant place, or that the time to be taken in view of the number of documents would be excessive, or the like.

It is difficult to see how **r. 31.3(2)** will operate in practice. If the disclosing party has concluded that the documents fall within the proper bounds of standard disclosure, on what basis is the court to determine that the costs of the opposite party inspecting them will be disproportionate? If the disclosing party's search has been carried out properly under the rules, and documents have been examined to determine disclosability, the cost of physical inspection of the documents would seem likely to be only a small proportion of the cost of finding and identifying them in the first place. If the documents were not sufficiently relevant, they need not have been disclosed at all. Disputes will presumably focus on how peripheral to the litigation the documents are, and the cost of inspecting them, although on the face of it, one might think that whether or not to incur the cost should initially be a matter for the inspecting party, no further costs to the disclosing party being involved, save those of permitting the inspecting party access to the documents. Guidance from the higher courts on the concept of 'proportionality' in this context would be welcome.

ORDERS OR AGREEMENTS LIMITING OR AFFECTING DISCLOSURE

Standard disclosure may be dispensed with or limited by the court under **CPR, r. 31.5(2)**, or, under **r. 31.5(3)**, by written agreement between the parties, which should be lodged with the court (**PD 31, para. 1.4**). On the fast track the court may decide not to direct standard disclosure, but may direct that no disclosure takes place, or specify the documents or classes of documents which the parties must disclose (**CPR, r. 28.3(2)**). This is likely to occur if, for example, whether in pursuance of a pre-action protocol or otherwise, there has already been substantial or total disclosure at some early stage. **48.25**

The fact that the ultimate responsibility for case management rests with the court precludes the parties from agreeing a form of disclosure without approval. It may well be that the court will not be prepared to accept an agreement between the parties, in which event it will supplant the agreement with its own orders under **r. 28.3** in fast track cases or **r. 29.2** in cases on the multi track (**r. 31.5**). Often this may be because the court, having scrutinised the documents before it, decides that it would be appropriate to limit standard disclosure to what it perceives to be the relevant issues. For example, where the respective statements of case make it clear that the whole litigation turns on whether a written contract was or was not subsequently varied by agreement between the parties, the court might limit disclosure to 'documents relevant to the issue as to whether or not the contract dated 25 February 2004 was varied in the course of correspondence between the parties, between 15 April and 8 May 2004'.

Staged disclosure

Under **CPR, r. 31.13**, the court may direct, or the parties may agree in writing, that disclosure or inspection, or both, shall take place in stages. This may be appropriate, for example, in personal injuries claims if the court has ordered split trials of liability and quantum. It may also be appropriate in complex litigation, where to ensure the claim is managed efficiently the court may order the parties to disclose documents limited to selected issues, with a view to the case being reappraised at a later case management hearing. Although the rules are silent on the point, it is submitted that an agreement for staged disclosure should also be lodged with the court, in the same manner as an agreement for disclosure has to be lodged under **PD 31, para. 1.4**. **48.26**

Clarification of material

The court has the ability to order a party, under **CPR, Part 18**, to clarify any matter which is in dispute in the proceedings, or to give additional information in relation to any such matter, whether or not the matter is contained or referred to in a statement of case (see **chapter 30**). **48.27**

FAILURE TO DISCLOSE DOCUMENTS

Under **CPR, r. 31.21**, a party who has not disclosed, or not permitted inspection of, a document may not rely on it, unless the court gives permission. In deciding whether or not to grant such permission, the court will doubtless consider the principles of proportionality, as well as the reasons why the document was not disclosed in the first place. In the absence of an inadvertent mistake it is perhaps difficult to see why a court should grant any latitude to a party who, having failed to disclose and allow inspection of a document as required by the court's order, then seeks to use the document at trial. The key issue will, of course, be prejudice to the other party, although given the obvious default of the party seeking to introduce the document, the court may not be inclined to enquire too nicely into the matter. **Rule 31.21** will permit the court some residual discretion, which may perhaps be more liberally exercised in the case of accidental non-disclosure, especially by unrepresented parties. **48.28**

Solicitors will need to protect themselves by writing comprehensively to clients about the nature of the duty of disclosure in order to protect themselves from potential wasted costs orders.

SPECIFIC DISCLOSURE

Jurisdiction and procedure

48.29 A party who wishes to obtain copies of particular documents which are believed to be in the custody of another party may make an application for specific disclosure under **CPR, r. 31.12**, and **PD 31, para. 5.1**. Applications for specific disclosure are most frequently made after standard disclosure has been given, and the disclosed documents have been inspected. There is no restriction in this respect, and the court also has jurisdiction to order specific disclosure before standard disclosure has taken place (*Dayman v Canyon Holdings Ltd* (2006) LTL 11/1/2006). An early application may not accord with the overriding objective, particularly if its effect is to increase costs. The procedure is summarised in **procedural checklist** 27, which is in **appendix 1**.

If the application is made and granted, the court may make an order under **CPR, r. 31.12**, ordering a party to do one or more of the following:

(a) disclose documents or classes of documents specified in the order;
(b) carry out a search to the extent stated in the order;
(c) disclose any documents located as a result of that search.

Any application for an order under **r. 31.12** must be made by application notice, specifying the order that the applicant intends to ask the court to make, and must be supported by evidence (**PD 31, para. 5.2**). The rules do not provide what this evidence should contain, but it is suggested that it should briefly explain the nature of the dispute, the stage reached in the proceedings, and the facts which lead the applicant to conclude that the documents sought exist, are disclosable and are within the control of the opposing party. The documents sought from the other side are commonly described in a schedule to the draft order. They must be described with reasonable precision. An application for disclosure of 'all documents relating to [the other side's] financial and tax affairs which are necessary to prove the quantum of his counterclaim' was held to be too imprecise in *Morgans v Needham* (1999) *The Times*, 5 November 1999.

PD 31, para. 5.3, provides that 'the grounds on which the order is sought' may be set out in the application notice itself or in the evidence filed in support. **Rule 31.12** of the CPR does not specify the form in which compliance with an order for specific disclosure should be undertaken. **Form N265** (which is expressed to be for standard rather than specific disclosure) could be adapted, but it is likely that the court will want more formality and would require the party against whom the order is made to file evidence, or certify in some form whether the documents exist, and the extent of any search made.

The court may make an order for costs on such an application, or, where appropriate, may reserve the costs to abide the determination of the issue as to whether or not the documents disclosed are relevant.

Discretion to order specific disclosure

48.30 **Paragraph 5.4 of PD 31** provides that in deciding whether or not to make an order for specific disclosure, the court will take into account all the circumstances of the case, and in particular, the overriding objective. The overriding objective requires the parties, so far as possible and so far as economically reasonable, to have access to documents which might help their case (*Commissioners of Inland Revenue v Exeter City AFC Ltd* [2004] BCC 519). In this case extensive disclosure was ordered of Inland Revenue documents relating to voluntary arrangement cases involving about 20 to 30 other football clubs. The issue raised had national importance, and the costs of the exercise were not disproportionate. In *Chantrey Vellacott v Convergence Group plc* (2006) LTL 6/2/2006 specific disclosure, in the form of an order to conduct a proper search for emails and draft documents, was ordered primarily because the claim was likely to turn on the documents. *Simba-Tola v Elizabeth Fry Hostel* [2001] EWCA Civ 1371, LTL 30/7/2001, concerned an allegation of racial discrimination against the claimant by other residents at the hostel. The hostel had disclosed its file on the claimant and its log book. None of the alleged incidents were recorded in these documents. The claimant sought disclosure of the hostel's files on other residents to see whether the incidents were recorded on those files. The Court of Appeal held it would not be proportionate to make an order for disclosure that would result in duplication. Further, as the court had seen the disclosed file and log book, it was possible to conclude that the further files would not have any relevant information. Further disclosure was therefore refused.

Paragraph 5.4 continues by warning that:

> . . . if the court concludes that the party from whom specific disclosure is sought has failed adequately to comply with the obligations imposed by an order for disclosure (whether by failing to make a sufficient search for documents or otherwise) the court will usually make such order as is necessary to ensure that those obligations are properly complied with.

AUTHENTICITY OF DOCUMENTS DISCLOSED

The authenticity of documents disclosed to a party under **CPR, Part 31**, is deemed to be admitted, unless the party serves notice requiring the document to be proved at trial (**r. 32.19**). A notice to prove a document must be served by the latest date for serving witness statements, or within seven days of disclosure of the document, whichever is later (**r. 32.19(2)**). **48.31**

CONTINUING DUTY TO DISCLOSE

The duty imposed by an order to give disclosure continues until the conclusion of the proceedings, that is, until the court gives its final judgment or order in the proceedings (which take effect when made: **CPR, r. 40.7**). If documents, to which a duty of disclosure extends, come to a party's notice at any time during the proceedings, every other party must be notified immediately (**r. 31.11(2)**). **PD 31, para. 3.3**, provides that this should be done by a 'supplemental list', presumably in **form N265**. This further reinforces the suggestion made above that the duty of honest disclosure is precisely parallel to that under the previous rule. **48.32**

COLLATERAL USE OF DISCLOSED DOCUMENTS

Following previous law and practice, it is provided in **CPR, r. 31.22**, that a party to whom a document has been disclosed may use such document only for the purposes of the proceedings in which it is disclosed. There are exceptions to this rule where: **48.33**

(a) the document has been read to or by the court, or referred to, at a hearing that has been held in public; or
(b) the court gives permission; or
(c) the party who disclosed the document and the person to whom the document belongs, agree.

The court may, however, make an order restricting or prohibiting the use of a document which has been disclosed, even though that document has been read to or by the court, or referred to at a public hearing (**r. 31.22(2)**). An application for such an order may be made by a party or by any person to whom the document belongs (**r. 31.22(3)**).

This preserves the principle that, as one is required to complete disclosure with absolute honesty and thus confidential documents may be disclosed, it is right that a party should have the protection of knowing that the documents are to be used only for the current litigation. The rule, which evolved from *Riddick v Thames Board Mills Ltd* [1977] QB 881, is that a document disclosed in proceedings may not be used, for example, for unrelated commercial purposes, or as the basis on which to found another claim. Indeed, misuse of such documents will constitute a serious contempt of court. The prohibition against using material for collateral purposes does not apply to documents referred to in affidavits and witness statements, as these are regarded as having been voluntarily disclosed (*Cassidy v Hawcroft* [2000] CPLR 624).

After use in a public hearing

48.34 The prohibition against collateral use of disclosed documents disappears once the documents have been used in a public hearing (**CPR, r. 31.22(1)**, although the words 'or referred to' in **r. 31.22(1)(a)** may cause some difficulty). In *SmithKline Beecham Biologicals SA v Connaught Laboratories Inc.* [1999] 4 All ER 498, documents pre-read by the judge and 'economically' referred to in court were held to be in the public domain. The phrase 'read to or by the court' has been interpreted as including documents made available to the judge with the reading list before the trial starts (*Derby v Weldon (No. 2)* (1988) *The Times*, 20 October 1988).

Once documents have been used in open court, an order restricting or prohibiting subsequent use will only be made if there are very good reasons for departing from the usual rule of publicity (*Lilly Icos Ltd v Pfizer Ltd* [2002] EWCA Civ 2, [2002] 1 WLR 2253). Merely asserting a document is confidential is insufficient. Specific reasons why a party would be damaged by subsequent use are required. Permission to use disclosed material will be refused where there is a very strong risk of dishonest or malicious use of the material (*Eronat v Tabbah* [2002] EWCA Civ 950, LTL 10/7/2002).

Permission for collateral use

48.35 An order may, in any event, be made by the court permitting a party to use a document for other purposes, in its general discretion (**CPR, r. 31.22(1)(b)**). One example is *Apple Corps Ltd v Apple Computer Inc.* [1992] 1 CMLR 969, where documents, which had been disclosed in English proceedings, were required for the purposes of parallel proceedings before the European Commission, which constituted a cogent reason why the documents were permitted to be used outside the English proceedings. A material consideration in deciding whether to lift an order under **r. 31.22** is whether an order for non-party disclosure under **r. 3.17** (see **48.76**) could have been obtained (*SmithKline Beecham plc v Generics (UK) Ltd* [2003] EWCA Civ 1109, [2004] 1 WLR 1479, at [37]). There are cases where the discretion has to be exercised by balancing competing public interests (see *Marlwood Commercial Inc. v Kozeny* [2004] EWCA Civ 798, [2005] 1 WLR 104, where the competing interests were the due administration of justice of the civil claim and the investigation of an alleged serious fraud).

Family proceedings documents

48.36 Information about children cases is covered by privacy and secrecy, and no information may be disclosed after the end of the case without the permission of the court (Family Proceedings Rules 1991 (SI 1991/1247), r. 10.20A). Information disclosed under compulsion in ancillary relief proceedings, together with voluntary disclosure, information in affidavits, statements of case and witness statements, is protected from collateral use. Other family proceedings are not automatically covered by secrecy even if heard in private. See *Clibbery v Allan* [2002] EWCA Civ 45, [2002] Fam 261, in which publication was allowed.

PRIVILEGE

Introduction

A disclosed document may be withheld from inspection if the disclosing party has a right or duty to withhold it (**CPR, r. 31.3(1)(b)**). Such a right or duty is called a 'privilege'. A party asserting a privilege must do so in writing and state the grounds on which it is claimed (**r. 31.19(3)**). This must be done in the list in which the document is disclosed, if a list is given (r. **31.19(4)**). Space is provided in the middle of the second page of **form N265** for this purpose. **48.37**

There are three heads of privilege: the privilege against self-incrimination (**48.38** and **48.39**); legal professional privilege (**48.40** to **48.50**); and 'without prejudice' communications (**48.54**). The three heads of privilege confer a right to withhold disclosure. Public interest immunity (**48.66** to **48.68**) arises from a duty to withhold disclosure. When considering these different heads of privilege, it is worth bearing in mind the comment made by Lord Edmund-Davies in *Waugh v British Railways Board* [1980] AC 521, at p. 543:

> . . . we should start from the basis that the public interest is, on balance, best served by rigidly confining within narrow limits the cases where material relevant to litigation may be lawfully withheld. Justice is better served by candour than by suppression.

The court will not order disclosure and/or inspection where disclosing and/or allowing inspection would be an offence under English criminal law, but the court has a discretion whether to order disclosure and/or inspection which would be an offence under a foreign law to which the disclosing party is subject (*Morris v Banque Arabe et Internationale d'Investissement SA* (1999) *The Times*, 23 December 1999).

PRIVILEGE AGAINST SELF-INCRIMINATION

Common law rule

In *Blunt v Park Lane Hotel Ltd* [1942] 2 KB 253, Goddard LJ said, at p. 257: **48.38**

> . . . the rule is that no one is bound to answer any question [or to produce any document] if the answer thereto would, in the opinion of the judge, have a tendency to expose [him] to any criminal charge, penalty, or forfeiture which the judge regards as reasonably likely to be preferred or sued for.

The claimant had objected to answering questions in a slander claim on the ground that her answers would tend to expose her to the risk of ecclesiastical penalties. It was held that it was purely fantastic to suppose that in 1942 she would be subject to any ecclesiastical penalty if she admitted adultery, and permission was granted to ask the questions. In civil proceedings the right applies only as regards criminal offences under the law of any part of the United Kingdom and penalties provided for by such law (Civil Evidence Act 1968, s. 14(1)). Exposure to the risk of a penalty under EU legislation forming part of the law of the UK by virtue of the European Communities Act 1972 is a penalty for these purposes (see *Rio Tinto Zinc Corporation v Westinghouse Electric Corporation* [1978] AC 547).

In *Rank Film Distributors Ltd v Video Information Centre* [1982] AC 380 it was held that where a criminal charge was more than a contrived, fanciful or remote possibility, the defendant could refuse to provide information by relying on the privilege. The privilege may arise, not only when answering might increase the risk of being prosecuted, but also where the prosecution may make use of the answer in deciding whether to prosecute, and where the prosecution may seek to rely on the answer in establishing guilt (*Den Norske Bank ASA v Antonatos* [1999] QB 271). Merely asserting there is a risk is not enough: the risk must be real and appreciable (*Rank Film Distributors Ltd v Video Information Centre*), and it is a matter for the court to determine the likelihood of a prosecution (*Rio Tinto Zinc Corporation v Westinghouse Electric Corporation* [1978] AC 547).

It has been held that subsequent committal proceedings for contempt of court are penal for this purpose (*Cobra Golf Inc. v Rata* [1998] Ch 109; *Memory Corporation plc v Sidhu* [2000] Ch 645), but disqualification proceedings under the Company Directors Disqualification Act 1986 are regulatory rather than penal (*Official Receiver v Stern* [2000] 1 WLR 2230). *Memory Corporation plc v Sidhu* discusses a possible exception to the privilege against incrimination where the risk of prosecution is for perjury arising out of the witness's conduct in the instant case. The cases on this exception are old and unsatisfactory, but the exception is probably good law. *Memory Corporation plc v Sidhu*, however, holds that even if the exception is good law relating to perjury, it does not extend to the risk of proceedings for contempt of court if the answers of a witness to an order requiring disclosure of assets are defective and hence a breach of the order.

The privilege extends to providing documents or answers that tend to expose the wife or husband of the person asserting the privilege to criminal proceedings or proceedings for the recovery of a penalty (Civil Evidence Act 1968, s. 14(1)). As a corporation has legal personality it can claim the privilege (*Triplex Safety Glass Co. Ltd v Lancegaye Safety (1934) Glass Ltd* [1939] 2 KB 395). It may be necessary to distinguish between the corporation and its officers and employees, and to consider whether all or only some of them may be at risk of criminal proceedings (*Sociedade Nacional de Combustiveis de Angola UEE v Lundqvist* [1991] 2 QB 310).

The privilege against self-incrimination may be lost by the turn of events. Obviously, once the party has been tried, whether resulting in a conviction or an acquittal, there is no possibility under the present law of a further trial in the criminal courts. The party may be given a pardon, which again eliminates the risk of prosecution (*R v Boyes* (1861) 1 B & S 311). If the Crown Prosecution Service indicate in writing that they will not make use of the information sought for the purposes of any criminal proceedings against the party or the party's spouse, and if a clause stating that no disclosure made in compliance with the order will be used in evidence in the prosecution of any offence committed by the party or spouse is included in the order, the court may conclude there is no realistic risk of use by the prosecution, and hold that the privilege does not apply (*AT and T Istel Ltd v Tully* [1993] AC 45).

Statutory limitations on the rule

48.39 One of the consequences of the privilege against self-incrimination is that the risk of documents being used against the party for the purposes of criminal proceedings is obviously greater in cases where the defendant is alleged to have been particularly dishonest, and the worse the conduct alleged the greater the prospect of a successful claim to the privilege. After *Rank Film Distributors Ltd v Video Information Centre* [1982] AC 380 there were fears that the privilege would operate to frustrate the use of search orders in intellectual property piracy claims, and Parliament intervened by enacting the **Supreme Court Act 1981, s. 72**, which has the effect of removing the privilege against self-incrimination in relation to claims involving the infringement of intellectual property rights and passing off, but also provides that the answers given shall not be used in any related criminal prosecution.

Similarly, where the information sought for the purposes of civil proceedings may lead to a prosecution under the Theft Act 1968, the privilege against self-incrimination has been removed by the Theft Act 1968, s. 31(1). These various provisions do not, of course, completely remove the privilege from civil proceedings. It still has an effect, for example, in civil fraud cases, and in motoring claims.

LEGAL PROFESSIONAL PRIVILEGE

There are two classes of legal professional privilege: one arises out of the relationship of legal adviser and client, even where no litigation is contemplated (legal advice privilege, see **48.42**); and the other relates to communications connected with contemplated or pending litigation (see **48.47**). The privilege belongs to the client, not to the solicitor, though the solicitor is under a duty to the client to assert it unless it is waived by the client. A clinical case manager appointed to assist a severely disabled person who attends a conference or other occasion normally attracting legal professional privilege, is obliged to respect the claimant's privilege (*Wright v Sullivan* [2005] EWCA Civ 656, [2006] 1 WLR 172). **48.40**

Legal professional privilege is a fundamental human right long established in the common law (*R v Derby Magistrates' Court, ex parte B* [1996] AC 487). As Lord Taylor of Gosforth CJ said in this case, unless the privilege is waived by the client or abrogated it is absolute, so that:

> legal professional privilege is thus much more than an ordinary rule of evidence, limited to the facts of a particular case. It is a fundamental condition on which the administration of justice as a whole rests.

The policy behind litigation privilege was described by Sir George Jessel MR in *Anderson v Bank of British Columbia* (1876) 2 ChD 644 as follows, at p. 649:

> as, by reason of the complexity and difficulty of our law, litigation can only be properly conducted by professional men, it is absolutely necessary that a man, in order to prosecute his rights or to defend himself from an improper claim, should have recourse to the assistance of professional lawyers, and it being so absolutely necessary, it is equally necessary, to use a vulgar phrase, that he should be able to make a clean breast of it to the gentleman whom he consults with a view to the prosecution of his claim, or the substantiating his defence against the claim of others; that he should be able to place unrestricted and unbounded confidence in the professional agent, and that the communications he so makes to him should be kept secret, unless with his consent (for it is his privilege, and not the privilege of the confidential agent), that he should be enabled properly to conduct his litigation.

There is a slightly different policy justification for legal advice privilege, which is based on the sanctity of the rule of law. As Lord Scott of Foscote said in *Three Rivers District Council v Bank of England (No. 6)* [2004] UKHL 48, [2005] 1 AC 610, at [34]:

> it is necessary in our society, a society in which the restraining and controlling framework is built upon a belief in the rule of law, that communications between clients and lawyers, whereby the clients are hoping for the assistance of the lawyers' legal skills in the management of their (the clients') affairs, should be secure against the possibility of any scrutiny from others, whether the police, the executive, business competitors, inquisitive busybodies or anyone else.

In recent times legal professional privilege has been regarded as part of the right of privacy guaranteed by the **European Convention on Human Rights, art. 8** (*Campbell v United Kingdom* (1992) 15 EHRR 137) and part of European Community law (*AM and S Europe Ltd v Commission of the European Communities* (case 155/79) [1983] QB 878). This is subject to **art. 8(2)**, which means the privilege can be overridden for example where this is necessary in the interests of the welfare or protection of children (*Essex County Council v R* [1994] Fam 167).

Statutory exclusion of legal professional privilege

A statute will not exclude legal professional privilege unless it does so expressly or by necessary implication (*R (Morgan Grenfell and Co. Ltd) v Special Commissioner of Income Tax* [2002] UKHL 21, [2003] 1 AC 563). Following *R (Morgan Grenfell and Co. Ltd) v Special Commissioner of Income Tax*, it was held in *B v Auckland District Law Society* [2003] UKPC 38, [2003] 2 AC 736, that the statute in question did not override legal professional privilege either expressly or by necessary implication. Unlike questions relating to confidential documents, protection of legally privileged documents does not depend on balancing competing private and public interests, nor will the privilege be excluded by any common law right to compel production. Circumstances in which a statute **48.41** will be held to have excluded legal professional privilege by necessary implication will be rare. The presumption against the removal of legal professional privilege is even stronger where general words in a statute merely delegate a power to legislate (*General Mediterranean Holdings SA v Patel* [2000] 1 WLR 272).

Legal advice privilege

48.42 Confidential communications between a legal representative and client made for the giving or receiving of legal advice are protected by legal professional privilege. This is so whether or not litigation is contemplated. The privilege applies to communications between a client and his legal advisers, to documents evidencing such communications, and to documents intended to be such communications even if they are not in fact communicated. However, these are the limits of the privilege, and it is not open to the court to extend them (*Three Rivers District Council v Bank of England (No. 5)* [2003] EWCA Civ 474, [2003] QB 1556).

The principle is that a client should be able to get legal advice in confidence. This raises issues as to who is the client (see **48.43**), and what is legal advice (see **48.44**), for this purpose. Another issue is whether obtaining legal advice must be the dominant purpose of the communication (see **48.45**). Examples are given at **48.46**.

48.43 **Client.** Where an individual seeks legal advice, it will usually be obvious that that individual is the client. The answer may not be so obvious where a litigation friend, trustee in bankruptcy, person acting under a power of attorney, or a personal representative is acting for someone else or an estate. In these cases the solicitor's retainer letter will or should make this clear. Where a solicitor is retained by a company or other corporation, it follows from *Three Rivers District Council v Bank of England (No. 5)* [2003] EWCA Civ 474, [2003] QB 1556, that the 'client' will be restricted to those personnel who have been authorised by the company or corporation to retain the services of the solicitor. On the facts the Bank had appointed three officials to deal with the Bank's communications with a private inquiry conducted by Lord Bingham of Cornhill as its 'Bingham Inquiry Unit', or 'BIU'. The BIU had sought legal assistance from a firm of solicitors. It was held that the BIU was the client for the purposes of legal advice privilege, so that communications between the solicitors and any other Bank official, even the Governor of the Bank, would not be protected. This decision may be too restrictive. There are hints in *Three Rivers District Council v Bank of England (No. 6)* [2004] UKHL 48, [2005] 1 AC 610, for example, at [118], that *Three Rivers District Council v Bank of England (No. 5)* might not survive if the matter were to be considered afresh by the House of Lords, but none of their lordships expressed a clear opinion on the issue.

As a practical consequence, corporate clients would be well advised to nominate a defined group of suitable employees or officers who will be the client when retaining a solicitor. To ensure that all sensitive communications are covered by the privilege, solicitors should ensure the legal context of the retainer is set out in clear terms in the retainer letter, and should advise the client that only employees and officers in the defined 'client' group prepare documents for use in seeking advice under the retainer.

48.44 **Legal advice.** 'Legal advice' covers telling a client the law, and also includes advice as to what should prudently and sensibly be done in the relevant legal context (Taylor LJ in *Balabel v Air India* [1988] Ch 317 at p. 330). To be protected the advice must be sought or given in a relevant legal context. So, if a solicitor becomes a client's 'man of business' with responsibility for advising the client on all matters of business, such as investment policy and financial matters, the privilege does not apply because without more there is no legal context (*Three Rivers District Council v Bank of England (No. 6)* [2004] UKHL 48, [2005] 1 AC 610, at [38]). In doubtful cases, according to Lord Scott of Foscote, there are two questions. First, did the advice sought relate to the rights, liabilities, obligations or remedies of the client under private law or under public law? Secondly, if so, did the occasion on which the communication took place and its purpose make it reasonable to expect that the privilege would apply? Putting it a different way, according to Lord Rodger of Earlsferry, the important question is whether the lawyer is being asked in his capacity as a lawyer to provide legal advice (at 58]).

In *Balabel v Air India*, approved in *Three Rivers District Council v Bank of England (No. 6)* at [111], Taylor LJ said the privilege is not restricted to specific requests for advice from clients and documents containing legal advice from solicitors. Where information is passed by the solicitor or the client to the other as part of a continuum aimed at keeping both informed, so that advice may later be given, privilege will attach. Further, legal advice is not confined to telling the client the law. It includes advice on what should prudently be done in the relevant legal context.

Legal advice privilege and dominant purpose. In *Three Rivers District Council v Bank of England (No. 5)* [2003] EWCA Civ 474, [2003] QB 1556, and *Three Rivers District Council v Bank of England (No. 6)* [2004] EWCA Civ 218, [2004] QB 916, the Court of Appeal were of the view that seeking or giving legal advice must be the dominant purpose of the communication if the occasion was to be protected by legal advice privilege. One result was that each communication between the client and solicitor had to be looked at before deciding whether the privilege applied on each occasion (see *United States of America v Philip Morris Inc.* [2004] EWCA Civ 330, *The Times*, 16 April 2004). These Court of Appeal authorities must be considered as wrongly decided on this point given the decision of the House of Lords in *Three Rivers District Council v Bank of England (No. 6)* [2004] UKHL 48, [2005] 1 AC 610, and the approval of the continuum of advice approach in *Balabel v Air India* [1988] Ch 317. Establishing a dominant purpose of obtaining legal advice is, however, a requirement for litigation privilege, see **48.48**. **48.45**

Examples of legal advice privilege. Applying the above principles, legal advice privilege applies, for example, to the following: **48.46**

(a) communications for the primary object of actual or contemplated civil or criminal proceedings (*Three Rivers District Council v Bank of England (No. 6)* [2004] UKHL 48, [2005] 1 AC 610, at [56]);
(b) conclusions reached by a solicitor from such communications (*Marsh v Sofaer* [2003] EWHC 3334, [2004] PNLR 24);
(c) advice from the solicitor on matters such as the conveyance of property or drawing up of a will (*Three Rivers District Council v Bank of England (No. 6)* [2004] EWCA Civ 218, [2004] QB 916, at [39]; [2004] UKHL 48, [2005] 1 AC 610, at [55]);
(d) confidential information given to a solicitor in the course of giving instructions relating to the drawing up of a will about matrimonial or financial difficulties, or about an anticipated inheritance (*Three Rivers District Council v Bank of England (No. 6)* [2004] UKHL 48, [2005] 1 AC 610, at [106]);
(e) confidential information given to a solicitor retained to give tax advice about family finances and family businesses (*Three Rivers District Council v Bank of England (No. 6)* [2004] UKHL 48, [2005] 1 AC 610, at [106]);
(f) advice or assistance from a lawyer to the promoter or opponent of a private Bill in Parliament (*Three Rivers District Council v Bank of England (No. 6)* [2004] UKHL 48, [2005] 1 AC 610, at [40]);
(g) advice from a solicitor on the best way to present evidence to a private, non-statutory inquiry, a coroner's inquest, a statutory inquiry or an ad hoc inquiry (*Three Rivers District Council v Bank of England (No. 6)* [2004] UKHL 48, [2005] 1 AC 610, at [44]);
(h) advice to a client about public law ramifications of a public inquiry (*Three Rivers District Council v Bank of England (No. 6)* [2004] UKHL 48, [2005] 1 AC 610);
(i) advice from in-house lawyers in the same circumstances as outside lawyers, provided the advice relates to legal as opposed to administrative matters (*Alfred Crompton Amusement Machines Ltd v Commissioners of Customs and Excise (No. 2)* [1974] AC 405); and

(j) instructions and briefs to counsel, and counsel's opinions, drafts and notes.

Legal advice privilege will not apply to the following:

(a) investment advice, or advice given by a solicitor as a patent or estate agent, because the advice is not given by the solicitor in his capacity as a solicitor;
(b) the actual conveyancing documents prepared by the solicitor (*R v Inner London Crown Court, ex parte Baines and Baines* [1988] QB 579, because they are not communications);
(c) a solicitor's client ledger accounts (*Nationwide Building Society v Various Solicitors* [1999] PNLR 53, because they are internal records, not communications dealing with advice);
(d) counsel's endorsement on a brief of the result of a hearing, because it is regarded as *publici juris* (*Nicholl v Jones* (1865) 2 Hem & M 588);
(e) documents prepared by the client's employees with the intention of sending them to the solicitors and in fact sent to the solicitors (*Three Rivers District Council v Bank of England (No. 5)* [2003] EWCA Civ 474, [2003] QB 1556);
(f) documents prepared by the client's employees with the dominant purpose of obtaining legal advice, but which are not sent to the solicitor (*Three Rivers District Council v Bank of England (No. 5)*); or
(g) communications with third parties, including documents obtained from third parties for the purpose of showing them to a solicitor for advice (*Wheeler v Le Marchant* (1881) 17 ChD 675).

Communications connected to litigation

48.47 Confidential communications between a solicitor or a client and a third party where the dominant purpose in creating the document is to use it or its contents in order to obtain legal advice or to help in the conduct of litigation which is at that time reasonably in prospect are privileged. This includes:

(a) obtaining and collecting evidence to be used in litigation; and
(b) obtaining information which may lead to the obtaining of evidence to be used in litigation (*Anderson v Bank of British Columbia* (1876) 2 ChD 644; *Wheeler v Le Marchant* (1881) 17 ChD 675; *Southwark and Vauxhall Water Co. v Quick* (1878) 3 QBD 315).

This head of privilege is sometimes called litigation privilege. The rule is relatively straightforward in relation to solicitors' communications, and covers letters to and statements from witnesses, and letters to and reports from experts. In *Southwark and Vauxhall Water Co. v Quick* (1878) 3 QBD 315 the Court of Appeal held that, if litigation is reasonably in prospect, privilege attaches to documents brought into existence for the purpose of enabling lawyers to advise whether a claim should be made or resisted, whether or not a decision to instruct lawyers had been made at the time they were brought into being, as long as such purpose was the dominant purpose behind creating the documents.

Documents which came into existence otherwise than for the purposes of the present litigation, but which have been obtained for a party's solicitor for the purpose of use in the present litigation, are not privileged and must be produced to the other for inspection (*Ventouris v Mountain* [1991] 1 WLR 607, CA).

There is a general rule that 'once privileged, always privileged' (*Calcraft v Guest* [1898] 1 QB 759). Thus, the privilege applies in the existing or contemplated proceedings, and also in any other proceedings. However, the privilege can only be claimed by the person originally entitled to it, or by that person's successor in title to the document. There is no requirement that the person asserting the privilege should be a party to the subsequent proceedings, or that the subsequent claim should have any connection with the original claim (*The Aegis Blaze* [1986] 1 Lloyd's Rep 203).

This head of legal professional privilege does not, according to *Re L (A Minor) (Police Investigation: Privilege)* [1997] AC 16, apply to documents commissioned for the purposes of proceedings under part IV of the Children Act 1989. This is because proceedings under part IV are investigative and non-controversial, and are conducted with the welfare of the child as the primary consideration.

Litigation privilege: dominant purpose

48.48 In relation to clients' communications with persons other than their lawyers litigation privilege has a narrower scope than in relation to communications through their lawyers. In *Waugh v British Railways Board* [1980] AC 521 the claimant sought disclosure of an internal enquiry report prepared by two of the defendant's officers two days after the accident which was the subject of the claim. The report was headed 'For the information of the Board's solicitor', but the written evidence on the application for disclosure made it clear that there were in fact two purposes in preparing the report. One was to establish the cause of the accident so that safety measures could be introduced, and the second was to obtain legal advice in the event of any claim. The Board regarded both purposes as of equal importance. It was held that the report had to be disclosed. It would only have been protected by legal professional privilege if the legal advice aspect had been the dominant purpose. According to Lord Edmund-Davies, a dominant purpose is one with a 'clear paramountcy'. A solicitor's assertion that the dominant purpose of a particular communication was the obtaining of legal advice is not conclusive. This has to be determined by the court on the whole of the evidence (*United States of America v Philip Morris Inc.* [2003] EWHC 3028 (Comm), LTL 10/12/2003). In *Lask v Gloucester Health Authority* (1991) 2 Med LR 379 it was held that an accident report which was required by National Health circulars was not privileged, because the dominant purpose was the prevention of similar accidents, rather than seeking legal advice.

Just because a report is compiled shortly after the relevant event does not mean that it cannot be privileged. In *Re Highgrade Traders Ltd* [1984] BCLC 151 the Court of Appeal held that an insurer who instructed experts in fire investigation in a suspected insurance arson case was primarily interested in the question of liability, not the prevention of recurrence, so the report was privileged. This case is also authority for the proposition that the dominant purpose must be that of the person commissioning the report, not necessarily that of the author. The time at which the dominant purpose is to be judged is the time at which the document was created. The privileged status of the document will not be affected by any subsequent use to which it is put, or the subsequent intentions of the author or the person commissioning it. Thus, documents which were procured for the purpose of valuing goods for the purpose of purchase tax could not become privileged through some subsequent intention to use them for the purposes of litigation (*Alfred Crompton Amusement Machines Ltd v Commissioners of Customs and Excise (No. 2)* [1974] AC 405).

Copies of documents

48.49 Where a document is not privileged when a party receives it, a copy of that document made by the party and forwarded to its solicitor for the purpose of contemplated or pending proceedings does not become privileged (*Dubai Bank Ltd v Galadari* [1990] Ch 98; *Ventouris v Mountain* [1991] 1 WLR 607, CA). On the other hand, a selection of documents assembled or copied by a party's solicitor which would betray the trend of advice given to the party will be privileged (*Lyell v Kennedy* (1884) 27 ChD 1), provided the documents assembled were originally third-party, non-disclosable, documents. In principle, an assembly of translations of third-party documents will also be privileged if it will betray the trend of legal advice given. However, own-party documents (unprivileged documents disclosable by the party claiming privilege) are not protected by the *Lyell v Kennedy* principle (*Sumitomo Corporation v Credit Lyonnais Rouse Ltd* [2001] EWCA Civ 1152, [2002] 1 WLR 479).

Iniquity

48.50 Legal professional privilege does not apply where the purpose behind seeking legal advice is 'iniquitous', such as to devise a structure for a transaction to prejudice the interests of the client's creditors (see *Barclays Bank plc v Eustice* [1995] 1 WLR 1238). According to *Kuwait Airways Corporation v Iraqi Airways Co. (No. 6)* [2005] EWCA Civ 286, [2005] 1 WLR 2734:

(a) the fraud exception can apply both to litigation privilege and legal advice privilege;
(b) where the issue of fraud is one of the issues in the claim, there must be a very strong prima facie case of fraud;
(c) where fraud is not one of the issues in the claim, a prima facie case of fraud may be enough.

The privilege was lost on this ground in a case where a search order was obtained using information which had been gathered in breach of the Data Protection Act 1984 (*Dubai Aluminium Co. Ltd v Al Alawi* [1999] 1 WLR 1964). Communications in furtherance of a fraud or crime are not protected by privilege (*Finers v Miro* [1991] 1 WLR 35). It does not matter whether or not the solicitor was aware of the client's intent (*Gamlen Chemical Co. (UK) Ltd v Rochem Ltd* [1979] CA Transcript 777). The principle applies whether or not the claim is founded on the particular fraud in question (*Dubai Bank Ltd v Galadari (No. 6)* (1991) *The Times*, 22 April 1991). Communications which are criminal in themselves, or intended to further a criminal purpose, are not covered by legal professional privilege. An affidavit setting out the details of an abusive telephone call (which was an offence contrary to the Telecommunications Act 1984, s. 43(1)(a)) and a threat to rip someone's throat out (which was a threat to kill contrary to the Offences against the Person Act 1861, s. 16) was held not to be privileged in *C v C (Privilege: Criminal Communications)* [2001] EWCA Civ 469, [2002] Fam 42.

Common interest privilege

48.51 Common interest privilege is a form of legal professional privilege, see *Buttes Gas and Oil Co. v Hammer (No. 3)* [1981] QB 223. It is a privilege in aid of anticipated litigation in which several persons have a common interest, and applies to cases where some only of the persons who have sought legal advice are eventually made parties to the litigation. For example, owners of adjoining houses complain of a nuisance which affects them both. Both take legal advice, and both exchange relevant documents. However, only one becomes a claimant (for whatever reasons). The various documents shared between the persons who took the legal advice will be privileged provided they had a common interest in advancing or defending the anticipated proceedings (*R v Trutch* [2001] EWCA Crim 1750, LTL 27/7/2001).

Other confidential relationships

48.52 In *Alfred Crompton Amusement Machines Ltd v Commissioners of Customs and Excise (No. 2)* [1974] AC 405 the House of Lords held that legal professional privilege extends to in-house lawyers. The privilege also extends to communications with barristers and to other persons authorised to provide advocacy, litigation, conveyancing and probate services (**Courts and Legal Services Act 1990, s. 63**). Communications with patent agents in pending or contemplated proceedings are also privileged by virtue of the Civil Evidence Act 1968, s. 15. Privilege does not extend to doctors, priests or others entrusted with confidences (see *Wheeler v Le Marchant* (1881) 17 ChD 675), because confidentiality is only an element of the privilege, not its foundation. However, a third party, whether official or unofficial, who receives information in confidence with a view to conciliation between the parties will not be compelled by the courts to disclose what was said without the parties' agreement (*McTaggart v McTaggart* [1949] P 94; *D v National Society for the Prevention of Cruelty to Children* [1978] AC 171). This privilege, which is based on the sanctity of marriage, also extends to proceedings under the Children Act 1989 (*Re D (Minors) (Conciliation: Disclosure of Information)* [1993] Fam 231).

Danger and confidentiality

48.53 A dilemma from time to time faced by professional people is whether they should alert the authorities to some danger when knowledge of the danger has come to them through a confidential relationship. In *Re B (Children: Patient Confidentiality)* [2003] EWCA Civ 786, [2003] 2 FLR 813, it was held to be proper for a psychiatrist to report to the local authority child protection services information giving rise to a concern of child abuse. The Court of Appeal stated that the psychiatrist should have limited herself to making a report, and should not have gone further and provided a witness statement on the matter.

WITHOUT-PREJUDICE COMMUNICATIONS

Without-prejudice communications, whether oral or in writing, which are made with the intention of seeking a settlement of litigation, are privileged from disclosure. The policy is to encourage litigants to settle their differences rather than litigate them to the finish (see Lord Griffiths in *Rush and Tompkins Ltd v Greater London Council* [1989] AC 1280). Privilege does this by removing the potential embarrassment of concessions made in the course of negotiations being used at trial against the party who made them. So, on an application for costs, it is not permissible to adduce without-prejudice communications, without the joint consent of the parties, to establish whether a party unreasonably refused a proposal for ADR. Further, it is impermissible to draw adverse inferences from a party's reluctance to waive the joint privilege (*Reed Executive plc v Reed Business Information Ltd* [2004] EWCA Civ 887, [2004] 1 WLR 3026). **48.54**

The privilege applies even if the words 'without prejudice' are not used, provided the purpose was to seek a settlement (*Chocoladefabriken Lindt & Sprungli AG v Nestlé Co. Ltd* [1978] RPC 287). It applies, for example, to joint settlement meetings, unless they are stated to be 'without prejudice save as to costs' (*Jackson v Ministry of Defence* [2006] EWCA Civ 46, LTL 12/1/2006). The question is whether the communication was genuinely intended to be a negotiating document (*Schering Corporation v Cipla Ltd* [2004] EWHC 2587 (Ch), *The Times*, 2 December 2004). In making this assessment the court must determine the author's intention, and must put itself in the position of a reasonable recipient to determine the message the communication conveyed (*South Shropshire District Council v Amos* [1986] 1 WLR 1271). Use of the words 'without prejudice' will not attach privilege to communications intended to prejudice the recipient or which are no more than an assertion of one party's rights (*Buckinghamshire County Council v Moran* [1990] Ch 623). A failure to use the words, coupled with a finding that the purpose of the communications was more administrative than with a view to settling a claim, meant that documents were not protected in *Prudential Assurance Co. Ltd v Prudential Insurance Co. of America* [2002] EWCA Civ 1154, LTL 31/7/2003. A letter marked 'without prejudice' proposing terms of a lease was not privileged, and the possibility of a dispute arising in the event the negotiations broke down was not sufficient to attract privilege (*Bath and North East Somerset District Council v Nicholson* (2002) LTL 22/2/2002).

Where the parties enter into 'without-prejudice' negotiations, continuing negotiations will be privileged until one party brings it home to the other party that the 'without-prejudice' basis of the negotiations is at an end. Thus, in *Cheddar Valley Engineering Ltd v Chaddlewood Homes Ltd* [1992] 1 WLR 820 it was held that prefacing one telephone offer with the word 'open' was insufficient to bring home the change in basis when further telephone negotiations and a letter did not repeat the word 'open'.

The public policy rationale of the privilege is, according to *Murrell v Healy* [2001] EWCA Civ 486, [2001] 4 All ER 345, directed solely to protecting admissions, and if documents are to be used for a different purpose, such as to show the amount of compensation paid for an earlier injury, they are admissible. This is not entirely consistent with *Unilever plc v Procter and Gamble Co.* [2000] 1 WLR 2436, in which it was held that, while admissions are the most important class of statements protected by the without-prejudice rule, it would create huge practical difficulties to dissect out identifiable admissions and withhold protection of the rest of without-prejudice communications. In *Re New Gadget Shop Ltd* [2005] EWHC 1606 (Ch), LTL 5/8/2005, the petitioner sought to dissect identifiable admissions out of without-prejudice communications, crafting its witness statements so as to include the alleged admissions but avoiding reference to any of the without-prejudice negotiations.

It was held that this approach was prohibited by *Unilever plc v Procter and Gamble Co.* [2000] 1 WLR 2436. The paragraphs seeking to achieve this were struck out.

A draft expert's report sent by the claimant 'without prejudice' in the early stages is inadmissible at trial on the question of deciding the amount of interest, even where the defendant is arguing that the award of interest should be reduced because of delays in formulating the value of the claim, and where the report dealt with quantifying the claim (*UYB Ltd v British Railways Board* (2000) *The Times*, 15 November 2000). This was not a legal professional privilege matter (in which event the claimant could have waived privilege), because the issue was when the defendant was first notified of the value of the claim.

Proof of settlement

48.55 Without-prejudice negotiations which result in a settlement are admissible to prove the terms of the settlement (*Walker v Wilsher* (1889) 23 QBD 335). Where the terms of settlement reached in without-prejudice communications are relevant in determining the extent of the liability of another person who is then sued by one of the parties to the settlement for a contribution towards the original liability, the privilege will not prevent inspection of the without-prejudice communications (*Gnitrow Ltd v Cape plc* [2000] 1 WLR 2327).

Abuse of without-prejudice rule

48.56 *Unilever plc v Procter and Gamble Co.* [2000] 1 WLR 2436 reiterated in a modern context the old rule that the without-prejudice rule will not protect statements made in circumstances where the rule is being unequivocally abused. Threats or other conduct which could be described as oppressive, dishonest or dishonourable could fall into this category. Thus, marking a letter 'without prejudice' will not protect the evidence of a threat of what will happen if an offer is not accepted (*Kitcat v Sharp* (1882) 48 LT 64).

A mere inconsistency between an admission made on a without-prejudice occasion and the pleaded case or the facts stated in a witness statement of the party making the admission will not result in the privilege being lost (*Savings and Investment Bank Ltd v Fincken* [2003] EWCA Civ 1630, [2004] 1 WLR 667). This is so even if persistence in the inconsistent position might lead to perjury. The strength of the public policy protecting without-prejudice communications is such that it should be lost only in truly exceptional circumstances (*Savings and Investment Bank Ltd v Fincken*) or where there is a very clear case of abuse of a privileged occasion (*Berry Trade Ltd v Moussavi* [2003] EWCA Civ 715, *The Times*, 3 June 2003). In *Berry Trade Ltd v Moussavi* the privilege was not lost where the alleged admissions were made orally in a lengthy without-prejudice meeting which was not tape-recorded or made the subject of a detailed note, and where the alleged admissions were small, selected parts of the discussion.

Use in interim applications

48.57 Without-prejudice correspondence is often used in interim applications, particularly applications seeking sanctions for default, or relief from sanctions (*Family Housing Association (Manchester) Ltd v Michael Hyde and Partners* [1993] 1 WLR 354). Before using without-prejudice material the other side should be informed and given an opportunity to object, and before placing the material before the judge the court should be informed so it can react and rule on its use before the judge's knowledge is affected (*Berg v IML London Ltd* [2002] 1 WLR 3271). Use of without-prejudice material on an interim application by one party entitles the other party to use that material at trial, at least where the issues on the interim application included consideration of the underlying merits of the claim (*Somatra Ltd v Sinclair Roche and Temperley* [2000] 1 WLR 2453).

Use of without-prejudice material in subsequent proceedings

Once a document is protected by without-prejudice privilege, it will always (subject to the principles discussed in 48.55 to 48.57) be privileged. Thus, an admission made in without-prejudice communications by one party will not be admissible in other proceedings against that party (*Rush and Tompkins Ltd v Greater London Council* [1989] AC 1280). If without-prejudice documents are used to found subsequent proceedings, those proceedings will be struck out as an abuse of process, unless the claimant in the subsequent proceedings can show that the statements relied upon were made improperly, or that there is some public interest favouring their subsequent use (*Unilever plc v Procter and Gamble Co.* [2000] 1 WLR 2436). **48.58**

WAIVER OF PRIVILEGE

Legal professional privilege belongs to, and can be waived by, the client. The privilege against self-incrimination belongs to the witness, and can only be waived by him. The privilege in without-prejudice communications belongs to both sides jointly, and can only be waived if both sides consent (*Rush and Tompkins Ltd v Greater London Council* [1989] AC 1280). Adverse inferences will not be drawn from a refusal to waive privilege (*Sayers v Clarke Walker* [2002] EWCA Civ 910, LTL 26/6/2002; *Reed Executive plc v Reed Business Information Ltd* [2004] EWCA Civ 887, [2004] 1 WLR 3026). **48.59**

Waiver of privilege may be given expressly, or implicitly by disclosing a privileged document to the other side. Examples include disclosure by service of a hearsay notice; by inclusion as an exhibit to a witness statement; by using the document to refresh the memory of a witness while giving evidence; and use of documents in re-examination to rebut an allegation of recent fabrication. Use by both parties of incidents (or the denial of incidents) which are alleged to have occurred during mediation amounts to mutual waiver of privilege as both parties have chosen to plead privileged matter in public documents (*Hall v Pertemps Group Ltd* (2005), *The Times*, 23 December 2005). A consent order in proceedings in Minnesota was held, on the wording of the order, not to be an implied waiver of privilege in *British American Tobacco (Investments) Ltd v United States of America* [2004] EWCA Civ 1064, LTL 30/7/2004. A party waives privilege for trial purposes by using materials in an interim application (*Derby and Co. Ltd v Weldon (No. 10)* [1991] 1 WLR 660).

In *Great Atlantic Insurance Co. v Home Insurance Co.* [1981] 1 WLR 529 the Court of Appeal held that where part of a document is used in counsel's opening, privilege in the whole of the document is waived unless it is a clearly separable document with different parts dealing with completely different subjects. A single letter can be a severable document if different parts of the letter are so distinct that they amount to different documents (*Pozzi v Eli Lilley and Co.* (1986) *The Times*, 3 December 1986). Where a document is severed, with privilege being asserted as to a part, the other parties must be informed that this has been done (*Nea Karteria Maritime Co. Ltd v Atlantic and Great Lakes Steamship Corporation (No. 2)* [1981] Com LR 138). If a document deals with a single subject matter, a party cannot waive privilege on a part, and assert privilege on the rest (*Great Atlantic Insurance Co. v Home Insurance Co.*). As Denning LJ said in *Burnell v British Transport Commission* [1956] 1 QB 187:

> It would be most unfair that cross-examining counsel should use part of the document which was to his advantage and not allow anyone else, not even the judge or the opposing counsel, a sight of the rest of the document, much of which might have been against him.

Once privilege on a subject has been waived, the waiver will be taken to extend to any associated material (*Derby and Co. Ltd v Weldon (No. 10)*), but the court will seek to define the subject matter of the waiver quite restrictively (*General Accident Fire and Life Assurance Corporation Ltd v Tanter* [1984] 1 WLR 100). In *United Building and Plumbing Contractors v Kajla*

[2002] EWCA Civ 628, LTL 26/4/2002, a party who put in evidence of meetings between the parties for settlement negotiations was held to have waived the privilege in the without-prejudice negotiations at those meetings.

Where a party allows documents which were protected by legal professional privilege to be used by a third party for a limited purpose, there is a limited waiver restricted to that purpose. A limited waiver does not destroy the privilege for all purposes (*B v Auckland District Law Society* [2003] UKPC 38, [2003] 2 AC 736).

Implied waiver

48.60 In a claim against the claimant's former solicitor the claimant's privilege over all documents concerned with the claim is impliedly waived to the extent necessary to enable the court to adjudicate the dispute fully and fairly. In *Lillicrap v Nalder and Son* [1993] 1 WLR 94 property developers sued their solicitors for negligently failing to advise them about a right of way over some land they purchased. The claimants had retained the solicitors to advise on a number of other transactions, and the solicitors said their files on those other transactions showed the claimants habitually ignored their warnings, so would have bought the land even if they had been properly advised. The Court of Appeal held that the previous transactions were relevant to an issue in the present proceedings, so the implied waiver extended to them as well as to the transaction in question. However, there are limits on the implied waiver of privilege in solicitors' negligence claims. In *Paragon Finance plc v Freshfields* [1999] 1 WLR 1183 the first firm of solicitors had acted for the finance company in relation to a number of mortgage transactions. The finance company made a number of claims against insurance policies entered into in relation to the mortgages, which the insurer disputed. The finance company then retained a second firm of solicitors to pursue outstanding insurance claims, and later sued the first firm of solicitors for professional negligence. A question arose as to whether the finance company had, by suing the first firm of solicitors, impliedly waived its privilege in respect of the work done by the second firm in pursuing the insurance claims. It was held that by suing the first firm of solicitors the finance company had only put its relationship with that firm into the public domain, and had not done so in respect of the work done by the second firm, and so had not waived its privilege in respect of the work done by the second firm.

Secondary evidence

48.61 It was held in *Calcraft v Guest* [1898] 1 QB 759 that secondary evidence, such as a copy, of otherwise privileged material is admissible at trial. In *Goddard v Nationwide Building Society* [1987] QB 670 Nourse LJ said that it makes no difference how the privileged material was obtained. Even if confidential documents have been obtained by theft, it is said that they will be admissible. However, the party who would otherwise be able to claim privilege may apply for an injunction to restrain use of such material if it has not yet been used in the litigation (*Goddard v Nationwide Building Society*). This was before the introduction of **CPR, r. 32.1(2)**, under which it is possible for the court to exercise its discretion to exclude stolen documents (see 47.7). Alternatively, the court has always had a jurisdiction to grant an injunction to restrain use of privileged material which has fallen into the hands of another party, as long as the application is made before the material has been used in the litigation (*Goddard v Nationwide Building Society*).

Injunctions to restrain use of privileged material

48.62 In *ISTIL Group Inc. v Zahoor* [2003] EWHC 165 (Ch), [2003] 2 All ER 252, the claimant sought an injunction to restrain the defendant from using documents which the claimant had sent to a person who then gave them to the defendant. The claimant alleged that the documents were protected by legal professional privilege. The defendant said that he should be allowed to use the documents because they came into existence as part of a scheme by the claimant to present a false case to the court. Unlike the situation considered at **48.41** (where disclosure is sought from the party asserting legal professional privilege), in the present situation the allegedly privileged documents are already in the hands of the other side. Here the court will balance the public interest in supporting legal professional privilege against the public interest in the administration of justice. On the facts there had been forgery and an attempt to place a misleading case before the court, so the injunction was refused.

The manner in which otherwise privileged materials came into the possession of the other party is important. If this happened illegally, the principles discussed at **48.10** apply. Alternatively, the circumstances may be taken as indicating that the party seeking to assert privilege has waived its privilege.

Waiver may arise inadvertently (*Great Atlantic Insurance Co. v Home Insurance Co.* [1981] 1 WLR 529). In *Guinness Peat Properties Ltd v Fitzroy Robinson Partnership* [1987] 1 WLR 1027 a privileged letter was inadvertently disclosed. The defendant allowed the claimant to inspect certain files before serving a list of documents. By accident, the letter was left in one of the files, and the claimant took a copy of it. The document later appeared in the defendant's list of documents, without a claim for privilege, and the claimant was again allowed to inspect it at the defendant's solicitors' office, but was not given a copy. Slade LJ said, at p. 1044:

> Care must be taken by parties to litigation in the preparation of their lists of documents and no less great care must be taken in offering inspection of the documents disclosed. Ordinarily, in my judgment, a party to litigation who sees a particular document referred to in the other side's list, without privilege being claimed, and is subsequently permitted inspection of that document, is fully entitled to assume that any privilege which might otherwise have been claimed for it has been waived.

As Slade LJ said, this is ordinarily the position. It is subject to two exceptions:

(a) where a party or its solicitor procures inspection of the relevant document by fraud; and
(b) where a party or its solicitor realises on inspection that the document has been disclosed as a result of an obvious mistake.

Where either of these exceptions applies, Slade LJ in *Guinness Peat Properties Ltd v Fitzroy Robinson Partnership* said the court should ordinarily intervene, unless there is some equitable reason for not doing so, such as delay.

Guinness Peat Properties Ltd v Fitzroy Robinson Partnership was an example of an obvious mistake, as, being a trained lawyer, the claimant's solicitor must have realised the privileged nature of the letter as soon as he read it. Another, more obvious, example is *English and American Insurance Co. Ltd v Herbert Smith* [1988] FSR 232, where counsel's clerk allowed counsel's instructions and papers (including witness statements and counsel's written opinion) to be sent to the other side's solicitors. An injunction was granted restraining use being made of any of the information in the papers.

Principles governing applications for injunctions In *Al Fayed v Commissioner of Police for the* **48.63**
Metropolis [2002] EWCA Civ 780, *The Times*, 17 June 2002, an injunction was refused because the recipient solicitors genuinely thought the other side's counsel's opinions had been disclosed on purpose. This case has a useful statement of the principles governing applications for injunctions to prevent use of privileged documents:

(a) A party giving inspection of documents has to decide what privileged documents to disclose before doing so.
(b) Although the privilege belongs to the client, the solicitor has ostensible authority to waive the privilege.
(c) A solicitor inspecting another party's documents owes no duty of care to the other party, and is generally entitled to assume that any privilege has been intentionally waived.
(d) Where privileged documents are given to the other side by mistake, it is generally too late thereafter to claim privilege by seeking an injunction to restrain use of those documents.

(e) Nevertheless, the court does have jurisdiction to grant such injunctions where justice requires.
(f) An injunction would be granted where documents were made available for inspection through an obvious mistake.
(g) A mistake was likely to be obvious where the receiving solicitor appreciated that a mistake had been made before making use of the documents or if it would have been obvious to a reasonable solicitor in the position of the receiving solicitor that a mistake had been made.
(h) In considering whether a mistake was obvious, it is relevant but not conclusive that a solicitor had considered the question and honestly concluded that the documents had not been made available by mistake.
(i) Even if there has been an obvious mistake, an injunction may be refused if it would be unjust or inequitable to grant an injunction.
(j) There are no rigid rules, because the court is exercising an equitable discretion.
(k) The same principles apply to the exercise of the discretion under **CPR, r. 31.20**.

The provisions of the CPR appear to reverse the common law position described above, with **r. 31.20** providing that where a party inadvertently allows a privileged document to be inspected, the party who has inspected the document may use it or its contents only with the permission of the court. Procedurally this means that there is no longer any need for the party making the inadvertent disclosure to apply for an injunction, and the onus must now be on the other party to seek an order giving permission to rely on the documents. However, in *Breeze v John Stacey and Sons Ltd* (1999) *The Times*, 8 July 1999, it was held that **r. 31.20** does no more than confirm the long-established principles set out above, and does not alter the law in any way.

Documents *publici juris*

48.64 Notes of proceedings in open court and counsel's endorsement on the brief of the order of the court are *publici juris* (in the public domain) and are not privileged (*Nicholl v Jones* (1865) 2 Hem & M 588). Likewise, public records and documents are also *publici juris.* However, a collection of extracts or copies from public documents may be protected from production by legal professional privilege where the collection is a product of the professional knowledge, research and skill of a party's legal advisers (*Lyell v Kennedy* (1884) 27 ChD 1).

Beneficiaries and shareholders

48.65 There is a general rule that a cestui que trust (for which see *Tugwell v Hooper* (1847) 10 Beav 348) and a shareholder (for which see *W. Dennis and Sons Ltd v West Norfolk Farmers' Manure and Chemical Co-operative Co. Ltd* [1943] Ch 220) are entitled to see opinions from counsel and advice from solicitors paid for out of the fund or the assets of the company (respectively) for the purpose of administering the fund or the company. The rule is subject to an exception where the legal advice is sought by the trustees or company in hostile litigation against the beneficiary or shareholder in question. It applies to a company whether it is public or private and however many shareholders it has (*CAS Nominees Ltd v Nottingham Forest plc* [2001] 1 All ER 954). But where a company is merely a necessary but nominal defendant in proceedings between its shareholders and directors there is no 'hostile' litigation for this purpose, and the general rule applies (*Re Hydrosan Ltd* [1991] BCLC 418).

PUBLIC INTEREST IMMUNITY

General principles

48.66 Certain documents must be withheld from disclosure and/or inspection on the ground that revealing the existence and/or contents of the documents would be injurious to the public interest. Claims to public interest immunity are of two types: (a) claims that all documents of certain classes must be protected; (b) claims that individual documents need to be protected because of their particular 'contents'. Contents immunity attaches, for example, to diplomatic dispatches and documents relating to national security. There is a wide variation in the 'classes' of documents protected, from Cabinet minutes to more routine documents such as local authority social work records (*Re M (A Minor)* (1989) 88 LGR 841).

Ministerial certificates

The usual practice is that the responsible minister provides a certificate stating the grounds of the objection to disclosure and/or inspection, identifying the document in question. Such a certificate is not conclusive (*Conway v Rimmer* [1968] AC 910) and the court may require the document to be produced to it (**CPR, r. 31.19(6)**). It is, though, for the party seeking inspection to show that the claim to immunity should be rejected (*Air Canada v Secretary of State for Trade* [1983] 2 AC 394). If the party seeking disclosure establishes a counteracting interest to the claim for immunity, the court must balance the public interest in concealment against the public interest in the due administration of justice in favour of disclosure (see Lord Fraser of Tullybelton in the *Air Canada* case). **48.67**

Procedure

Under **CPR, r. 31.19(1)**, a person (who need not be a party) may apply, without notice, for an order permitting him to withhold disclosure of a document on the ground that disclosure would damage the public interest. Usually the applicant for such an order is the Secretary of State for the government department asserting public interest immunity in the document. By **r. 31.19(2)**, unless the court otherwise orders, any order made under this rule must not be served on any other person, and must not be open to inspection by any other person. Claims for protection may alternatively be made in the list of documents served by a party (**r. 31.19(4)**), or may be insisted upon by the court of its own initiative. **48.68**

It is questionable whether these procedures, particularly the procedure under **r. 31.19(1)**, comply with the European Convention on Human Rights, art. 6(1). In *Rowe v United Kingdom* (2000) 30 EHRR 1, the European Court of Human Rights considered the procedural aspects of withholding evidence in *criminal* trials on the grounds of public interest. It was held that to comply with art. 6(1) the accused had to be given information about the withheld information appropriate to the category of the evidence involved, and that it was for the trial judge (rather than a court on appeal) to decide whether the evidence should be withheld. **Rule 31.19** allows orders to be made without giving any information to the parties (or to just one side if one of the parties is the government department seeking to withhold disclosure), and for decisions to be made by judges other than the trial judge, which would seem to fall short of the safeguards contemplated by the European Court. In criminal trials there are the additional minimum rights given by art. 6(3), which do not apply to civil cases, but this difference is unlikely to have a substantial effect on the implications of the decision in civil cases.

Confidential documents

Confidentiality is not of itself a ground of privilege or public interest immunity, although it is an element in these concepts. Although there is a reluctance to order disclosure of confidential documents, if disclosure is necessary in the interests of the litigation, those interests override mere confidentiality (*Science Research Council v Nassé* [1980] AC 1028; *Three Rivers District Council v Bank of England (No. 5)* [2002] EWHC 2309 (Comm), LTL 8/11/2002, a point not dealt with on the appeal [2003] EWCA Civ 474, [2003] QB 1556). In such cases the court may consider whether confidentiality may be preserved while satisfying the needs of the litigation by ordering redactions, disclosure from other sources, and other appropriate means (*Science Research Council v Nassé*; *Wallace Smith Trust Co. Ltd v Deloitte Haskins and Sells* [1997] 1 WLR 257; *Three Rivers District Council v Bank of England*). **48.69**

PRE-ACTION DISCLOSURE

48.70 The procedure for applying for disclosure of documents before proceedings have started is governed by **CPR, r. 31.16. Rule 31.17** deals with applications, after proceedings have started, for disclosure by a person who is not a party to the proceedings. These applications are made under the **Supreme Court Act 1981, ss. 33(2)** and **34**, or the **County Courts Act 1984, ss. 52(2)** and **53**. Until these sections were amended by the Civil Procedure (Modification of Enactments) Order 1998 (SI 1998/2940) such orders were available only in proceedings in respect of personal injury and wrongful death. Now they may be made in any type of case. The court may not make an order under these provisions if it considers that complying with the order would be injurious to the public interest (**Supreme Court Act 1981, s. 35(1); County Courts Act 1984, s. 54(1)**).

Requirements for pre-action disclosure

48.71 The court has power to make an order for pre-action disclosure where the following conditions are satisfied:

(a) The respondent must be likely to be a party to subsequent proceedings (**CPR, r. 31.16(3)(a)**). 'Likely' means 'may well' as opposed to 'more probable than not' (*Black v Sumitomo Corporation* [2001] EWCA Civ 1819, [2002] 1 WLR 1569). The proceedings may be an additional claim as much as a Part 7 or 8 claim (*Moresfield Ltd v Banners* [2003] EWHC 1602 (Ch), LTL 3/7/2003).

(b) The applicant must be likely to be a party to subsequent proceedings (**r. 31.16(3)(b)**).

(c) Although the **Supreme Court Act 1981, s. 35(1)**, and the **County Courts Act 1984, s. 54(1)**, refer to the applicant and the respondent being likely to be parties to 'subsequent proceedings', there is no requirement that such proceedings are likely to be brought (*Black v Sumitomo Corporation*). Instead, the applicant must usually establish a worthwhile claim, or a reasonable basis for the intended claim (*Burns v Shuttlehurst Ltd* [1999] 1 WLR 1449), or a claim which is properly arguable or which has a real prospect of success (*Rose v Lynx Express Ltd* [2004] EWCA Civ 447, [2004] 1 BCLC 455), although in *Snowstar Shipping Co. Ltd v Graig Shipping plc* [2003] EWHC 1367 (Comm), LTL 17/6/2003, an order was made even though the substantive claim was described as speculative (see **48.72**).

(d) An order can be made only if, had proceedings been started, the respondent's duty by way of standard disclosure set out in **r. 31.6** would extend to the documents or classes of documents of which the applicant seeks disclosure (**r. 31.16(3)(c)**). Thus, pre-action disclosure cannot be granted in respect of documents which would not be disclosable had proceedings actually been commenced.

(e) By **r. 31.16(3)(d)**, the court may only make an order if disclosure before the proceedings have started is desirable in order:
   (i) to dispose fairly of the anticipated proceedings;
   (ii) to assist the dispute to be resolved without proceedings; or
   (iii) to save costs.

It follows from requirements (c) and (d) that the court has to be clear what the issues are likely to be in the anticipated proceedings, and must make sure that the documents being asked for are likely to adversely affect the case of one side or the other. Where there is no clear issue between the parties, the application should be refused (*Medisys plc v Arthur Andersen* [2002] PNLR 22; *Laurence v Commissioner of Police of the Metropolis* (2006) LTL 13/2/2006).

When considering requirement (e), the court has to undertake a balancing exercise to determine whether pre-action disclosure is 'desirable' in one of the three ways set out in **r. 31.16(3)(d)** (*Bermuda International Securities Ltd v KPMG* [2001] CPLR 252). Where the applicant has enough material to plead a claim, albeit not as perfectly as might be possible with further documentation from the respondent, it is unlikely to be 'desirable' to order pre-action disclosure (*First Gulf Bank v Wachovia Bank National Association* [2005] EWHC 2827 (Comm), LTL 15/12/2005).

The test for granting an order for pre-action disclosure is strict, in that it requires not only that the document sought is disclosable, but that disclosing it at that stage will further one of the purposes set out in r. **31.16(3)(d)**, for example, that its disclosure will indicate whether or not the claimant has a case (*Burrells Wharf Freeholds Ltd v Galliard Homes Ltd* [1999] 33 EG 82). Where a pre-action protocol applies, there should be little need for an application of this nature, as the protocols normally provide for the early exchange of documents and information before a claim is issued.

Discretion to order pre-action disclosure

48.72 All applications will obviously turn on their own facts, and the Court of Appeal has said that it is inappropriate to lay down guidelines (*Bermuda International Securities Ltd v KPMG* [2001] CPLR 252). Orders for pre-action disclosure are not exceptional, but they are unusual. The discretion is likely to be exercised against an applicant who has enough material to plead a claim against the respondent, but is applying for pre-action disclosure to improve its case (*First Gulf Bank v Wachovia Bank National Association* [2005] EWHC 2827 (Comm), LTL 15/12/2005). Where the likely defendant had supplied a substantial proportion of the documents requested, an order for pre-action disclosure of the rest was refused, as the likely claimant had enough material to decide whether to bring proceedings (*Meretz Investments NV v First Penthouse Ltd* [2003] EWHC 2324 (Ch), LTL 16/10/2003). The court will not make an order for pre-action disclosure which would be oppressive, for example, where the proposed claim is speculative and there is real doubt that the documents sought would actually produce evidence to support the claim, rather than merely suggesting a possible line of inquiry (*Black v Sumitomo Corporation* [2001] EWCA Civ 1819, [2002] 1 WLR 1569). It may be appropriate to make an order even if the substantive claim appears speculative, for example, where the likely defendant has refused to provide a clear answer to the alleged claim (*Jay v Wilder Coe* [2003] EWHC 1786 (QB) 1786, LTL 28/8/2003). Any weakness in the substantive claim is relevant to the court's discretion, and will make the court less inclined to make an order for pre-action disclosure (*Snowstar Shipping Co. Ltd v Graig Shipping plc* [2003] EWHC 1367 (Comm), LTL 17/6/2003).

Pre-action provision of information

48.73 The court does not have the power under **CPR, r. 31.16**, to make an order to confirm or give information, as opposed to disclosure of documents (*Snowstar Shipping Co. Ltd v Graig Shipping plc* [2003] EWHC 1367 (Comm), LTL 17/6/2003). This might be possible under the *Norwich Pharmacal* jurisdiction, see **48.84**.

Procedure on applying for pre-action disclosure

48.74 An application for pre-action disclosure is brought by issuing an application notice in **form N244**, and must be supported by written evidence (**CPR, r. 31.16(2)**). The evidence must explain, for each document or class of documents sought from the likely defendant, how the requirements discussed in **48.71** are satisfied.

An order (and any draft order) for pre-action disclosure must specify the documents or classes of documents to be disclosed (**r. 31.16(4)(a)**). It is suggested, therefore, that a general application for 'standard disclosure' will fail. The order will further require the respondent to list any of the specified documents which are no longer in the respondent's control, or in respect of which the respondent claims a right or duty to withhold inspection (**r. 31.16(4)(b)**). It may require the respondent to indicate what has happened to any documents no longer in his control, and may specify the time and place for disclosure and inspection (**r. 31.16(5)**).

Costs of pre-action disclosure applications

48.75 Most applications for pre-action disclosure will be made on behalf of the potential claimant, although there may be exceptional cases where a potential defendant, having been notified of a possible claim, will seek to take the initiative in obtaining documents which are believed go to the heart of the action and which have not been voluntarily provided in advance by the claimant.

The rules on costs relating to special cases (**CPR, Part 48**) apply to pre-action disclosure, and applications for disclosure against non-parties. The general rule is that the person against whom an order for pre-action disclosure is sought will be awarded the costs of the application and of complying with any order made (**r. 48.1(2)**). Such costs will almost invariably be determined by summary assessment, although it may not be possible for the assessment to take place immediately after the application, simply because the respondent may not know what the cost of complying with the order will be.

The court may, however, by **r. 48.1(3)**, make a different costs order, having regard to all the circumstances, which include the extent to which it was reasonable for the person against whom the order was sought to oppose the application, and whether the parties to the application have complied with any relevant pre-action protocol. It may be unreasonable where the respondent had an obligation to provide the documents in compliance with a pre-action protocol. Even where the respondent is regarded as acting unreasonably, costs against the respondent should be limited to the costs of the application, with the applicant still paying the costs of the exercise of disclosing the documents (*Bermuda International Securities Ltd v KPMG* [2001] CPLR 252).

Thus, as with all costs orders, the court will have regard to the general duty of cooperation between the parties and reasonableness of their conduct. In personal injury and clinical negligence cases, the protocols provide guidance as to reasonable pre-action behaviour, including the early exchange of information and documents. Any successful application for pre-action disclosure in such cases is almost certainly an indication that the pre-action protocols have not been complied with, and will therefore strongly suggest unreasonable behaviour on the part of the respondent, who should expect to be ordered to pay the applicant's costs.

DISCLOSURE BY NON-PARTIES

48.76 The procedure for applying for a non-party disclosure order is summarised in **procedural checklist 28**, which is in **appendix** 1. Once proceedings have started, an application for an order for disclosure by a person who is not a party to the proceedings must be made in accordance with **CPR, Part 23** (see **chapter 32**), and must be supported by evidence (**r. 31.17(2)**). Notice of the application must be served on the respondent (**r. 23.4(1)**). The procedure enables the court to order a witness to produce relevant documents well before the trial, rather than having to wait until the trial and obtaining the documents from the witness under a witness summons. This can be extremely useful, as early disclosure can prevent the need to adjourn the trial.

The ability of the court to make an order for non-party disclosure in all types of cases will diminish, but not totally extinguish, the need for practices of the kind used in *Khanna v Lovell White Durrant* [1995] 1 WLR 121, in which the court invented the concept of the 'production appointment' for witnesses to attend under subpoena to bring documents to a hearing before the trial, in order that they could be photocopied for use in the proceedings (see **48.81**).

Requirements for non-party disclosure orders

48.77 An order for the disclosure of documents may be made against a non-party if:

(a) the documents sought are likely to support the case of the applicant or adversely affect the case of another party (**CPR, r. 31.17(3)**);
(b) the documents sought actually exist; and
(c) disclosure is necessary for the purpose of disposing of the claim fairly or saving costs (r. 31.17(3)).

'Likely' in this context means 'may well' support the applicant's case or adversely affect the case of another party (*Three Rivers District Council v Her Majesty's Treasury* [2002] EWCA Civ 1182, [2003] 1 WLR 210).

Disclosure against non-parties will only be granted where the documents sought are relevant (as opposed to disclosable under standard disclosure) (see *American Home Products Corporation v Novartis Pharmaceuticals UK Ltd* (2001) LTL 13/2/2001). The court should primarily consider relevance in the context of the statements of case, and should not embark on determining disputes of substance as to whether the documents are relevant (*Clark v Ardington Electrical Services* (2001) LTL 4/4/2001). There must be some evidential basis for the allegations in respect of which the documents are said to be relevant (*Re Skyward Builders plc* [2002] EWHC 1788 (Ch), [2002] 2 BCLC 750). The court is required to apply the test to each document sought, although the court is permitted to consider the documents on a sub-class by sub-class basis (*Three Rivers District Council v Her Majesty's Treasury* [2002] EWCA Civ 1182, [2003] 1 WLR 210).

Discretion to order non-party disclosure

Where the documents are relevant, it is then necessary to consider whether the court should refuse the order in its discretion, or impose some limit on disclosure, such as by ordering disclosure of documents only between stated dates. It will require a very exceptional case to justify ordering the disclosure of a non-party's confidential medical documents (*A v X* [2004] EWHC 447 (QB), LTL 6/4/2004). Further, the court will not make an order if it is not satisfied that the documents sought in fact exist. In *Re Howglen Ltd* [2001] 1 All ER 376 an application was made in general terms for documents against a non-party bank for bank records and interview notes. An order was made limited to the notes of three interviews identified in the evidence in support. **48.78**

It will sometimes be possible to make an application under the Access to Health Records Act 1990, or the Bankers' Books Evidence Act 1879, as an alternative to making an application for non-party disclosure under the Supreme Court Act 1981, s. 34 or the County Courts Act 1984, s. 53.

An applicant for an order under **CPR, r. 31.17**, should consider carefully all alternative ways of obtaining the required documents. For example, it may be argued, in a particular case, that it is not necessary to see the document in advance of the trial, and that a witness summons or deposition will suffice. However, there will not be many cases in which the many documents sought will be sufficiently straightforward that they can be digested and properly dealt with by both parties on the morning of the trial, and without appearing in the trial bundle for pre-reading, and general principles of case management militate against last-minute surprises.

Form of order for non-party disclosure

An order for non-party disclosure must specify the documents or the classes of documents which the respondent must disclose, and require the respondent, when making disclosure, to specify any of these documents which are no longer in the respondent's control, or in respect of which the respondent claims a right or duty to withhold inspection (**CPR, r. 31.17(4)**). In addition, the court may order that the respondent be required to indicate what has happened to any documents now outside the respondent's control, and specify the time and place for disclosure and inspection (**r. 31.17(5)**). **48.79**

The order may restrict access to the disclosed documents to the applicant's legal advisers and/or experts (**Supreme Court Act 1981, s. 34(2); County Courts Act 1984, s. 52(2)**). This may be appropriate where the documents include trade secrets (*Premier Profiles Ltd v Tioxide Europe Ltd* (2002) LTL 25/9/2002).

The court may order the applicant to provide a sum of money to the respondent as a condition of compliance in advance of inspection (*Re Skyward Builders plc* [2002] EWHC 1788 (Ch), [2002] 2 BCLC 750, where the sum of £1,000 was ordered to be paid).

Costs of application for non-party disclosure

48.80 The rules on costs in **CPR, r. 48.1** (see **48.75**), apply equally to the costs of non-party disclosure as they do to the costs of pre-action disclosure. The presumption is that the court will award the non-party the costs of the application and of complying with the terms of any order made (**r. 48.1(2)**). However, the court has the power to make a different order to reflect what it may consider to be the reasonableness of the non-party's opposition to the application (**r. 48.1(3)**).

Additional powers to order pre-action and non-party disclosure

48.81 **Rule 31.18** of the CPR provides that **rr. 31.16** and **31.17** do not limit any other power which the court may have to order disclosure before proceedings have started, or to order disclosure against a person who is not a party to the proceedings. This allows continuation of the practice in *Khanna v Lovell White Durrant* [1995] 1 WLR 121 of production appointments (see **48.76**) if considered preferable to an order for non-party disclosure. **Rule 31.18** also preserves the jurisdiction to make a *Norwich Pharmacal* order (see **48.83**). Additionally, orders may be made under the Data Protection Act 1998 (see **48.82**) and pursuant to the decision in *Bankers Trust Co. v Shapira* [1980] 1 WLR 1274 (see **48.88**).

Data protection

48.82 The **Data Protection Act 1998, s. 7**, applies where personal data about an individual are held by a data controller. On making a request in writing and paying a fee (if applicable), the individual is entitled to have communicated to him in an intelligible form any personal data relating to him and any information about the source of that data. For this purpose 'data' means information which is processed automatically (generally by computer), and also information recorded as part of a filing system, or which forms part of an accessible record (which, by s. 68, means health, education and accessible public records). A manual filing system will only be regarded as 'data' within the meaning of the **Data Protection Act 1998** if it is of sufficient sophistication to provide the same or similar ready accessibility as a computerised filing system. This means the files must be referenced or indexed in a way that makes it possible to identify with reasonable certainty and speed whether they contain personal data without having to leaf through the files themselves (*Durant v Financial Services Authority* [2003] EWCA Civ 1746, [2004] FSR 28). 'Personal data' is defined as meaning data relating to a living individual who can be identified from that data (or other information in the possession of the data controller), and includes expressions of opinion about the individual (**s. 1(1)**). According to *Durant v Financial Services Authority* information will come within this definition if:

(a) the information is biographical in a significant sense, going beyond mere involvement in the events described in the file; and
(b) the data subject (the applicant) is the focus of the information.

Thus, a file dealing with a complaint made to the Financial Services Authority by the applicant about a bank was not personal data because its focus was the complaint, not biographical information about the applicant.

There are various exemptions and further detailed provisions, such as a restriction on revealing information that would identify other individuals without their consent (**s. 7(4)**). When complying with a request for personal data which will also reveal details about other individuals, the data controller is required to balance the interests of the other individuals with the interests of the data subject. It may be permissible to redact the names of the other individuals if it is reasonable to do so.

The data controller is required to comply with a request promptly, and can be ordered to comply by the High Court or a county court (ss. 7(9) and 15(1)). For the purpose of determining whether the applicant is entitled to the information under s. 7, the court may require the information to be made available for inspection by the court (but not the applicant, who will not be allowed to inspect the information until after a determination in his favour (s. 15(2)). On an application for an order under ss. 7(9) and 15(1), the court has an untrammelled discretion whether to grant an order, but the main factor is that access under the Act is mainly for the purpose of correcting inaccuracy (*Durant v Financial Services Authority*). An individual who is refused an order under s. 7 on the ground that the information held is not personal data may subsequently be allowed access to the same information under any of the powers under **CPR, Part 31**, such as an application for specific disclosure (*Johnson v Medical Defence Union* [2004] EWHC 2509 (Ch), [2005] 1 WLR 750).

NORWICH PHARMACAL ORDERS

In *Norwich Pharmacal Co. v Commissioners of Customs and Excise* [1974] AC 133 it was held that a person who, albeit innocently, became 'mixed up in the tortious acts of others so as to facilitate their wrongdoing' was under a duty to assist the person who had been wronged by giving that person full information and disclosing the identity of the wrongdoers. **48.83**

The jurisdiction is based on the ancient Chancery bill of discovery, and is useful where a party has a cause of action but does not have the names and addresses of persons who should be named as the defendants. Using Lord Reid's terminology from *Norwich Pharmacal Co. v Commissioners of Customs and Excise*, the court may make an order compelling a person to provide information identifying wrongdoers if:

(a) The respondent has become mixed up in the wrongdoing. The respondent may be perfectly innocent, and may not even realise that there has been any wrongdoing (as in *Norwich Pharmacal Co. v Commissioners of Customs and Excise* itself). Where the respondent is a party to the wrongdoing it is usually named as defendant in the substantive claim, and is also under a duty to identify other wrongdoers (*British Steel Corporation v Granada Television Ltd* [1981] AC 1096). In cases of wilful evasion of court orders, it may be enough that the respondent has got mixed up in the affairs of the wrongdoer (*Mercantile Group (Europe) AG v Aiyela* [1994] QB 366).

(b) The respondent has facilitated the wrongdoing. Unwitting facilitation of the infringement of the claimants' patent by allowing infringing products into the country was sufficient in *Norwich Pharmacal Co. v Commissioners of Customs and Excise*. However, a person who has done nothing to facilitate the wrongdoing, and is a mere witness, is under no obligation to disclose the identity of the wrongdoers (*Ricci v Chow* [1987] 1 WLR 1658). In *Harrington v Polytechnic of North London* [1984] 1 WLR 1293 the claimant was a student who claimed he was prevented from attending the polytechnic by student pickets. Photographs were taken of the pickets, and the claimant sought an order compelling the lecturers to identify the pickets. It was held that the lecturers were mere witnesses when acting in their private capacities, but the polytechnic was ordered to provide the information as it had become mixed up in and facilitated the wrongdoing.

(c) The applicant has a sufficient interest. Generally this is satisfied by showing a genuine intention to bring legal proceedings against the wrongdoers. The condition will also be satisfied if the applicant has no intention to sue, but does intend to discipline employee wrongdoers (*Ashworth Hospital Authority v MGN Ltd* [2002] UKHL 29, [2002] 1 WLR 2033). Disclosure of the names of customers of someone alleged to be infringing the claimant's patent will not usually be ordered unless there is some real grievance or some significant purpose in doing so (*Smith Kline and French Laboratories Ltd v Doncaster Pharmaceuticals Ltd* [1989] FSR 407).

(d) The court exercises its discretion to make the order (the relief being equitable). It was held by *Mitsui and Co. Ltd v Nexen Petroleum UK Ltd* [2005] EWHC 625 (Ch), [2005] 3 All ER 511, that *Norwich Pharmacal* orders against third parties will only be granted if there is no other practicable way of obtaining the information. The remedy is one of last resort, so will not be granted if the information could be obtained on an application for pre-action disclosure.

Scope of *Norwich Pharmacal* jurisdiction

48.84 The *Norwich Pharmacal* jurisdiction is not restricted to claims in tort, but is of general application, and applies to claims in breach of confidence and breach of contract (*British Steel Corporation v Granada Television Ltd* [1981] AC 1096; *Ashworth Hospital Authority v MGN Ltd* [2001] 1 WLR 515 (CA); [2002] UKHL 29, [2002] 1 WLR 2033). In most cases where *Norwich Pharmacal* orders have been made it has been clear, or nearly so, that some tort or other civil wrong has been committed. Provided the conditions laid down by Lord Reid (see **48.83**) are satisfied, an order can be made even if the underlying cause of action has not been clearly made out (*P v T Ltd* [1997] 1 WLR 1309). *Re an Intended Claim, Carlton Film Distributors Ltd v VDC Ltd* [2003] EWHC 616 (Ch), LTL 21/3/2003, concerned an application for disclosure of information against an identified proposed defendant. Extending the jurisidiction further than *P v T Ltd*, the application was allowed, even though its purpose was to secure documents which the proposed claimant needed in order to formulate a claim against the proposed defendant. The principle was further extended in *Murphy v Murphy* [1999] 1 WLR 282, where an order was made against a settlor to disclose to a potential beneficiary the names and addresses of the trustees under a settlement, to enable the potential beneficiary to communicate with the trustees with a view to being considered for the distribution of trust property held on discretionary trusts. The trustees were obviously not wrongdoers for the purpose of the *Norwich Pharmacal* principle.

Journalists' sources

48.85 The Contempt of Court Act 1981, s. 10 (which was enacted in response to *British Steel Corporation v Granada Television Ltd* [1981] AC 1096), provides:

> No court may require a person, nor is any person guilty of contempt of court for refusing to disclose, the source of information contained in a publication for which he is responsible, unless it be established to the satisfaction of the court that disclosure is necessary in the interests of justice or national security or for the prevention of disorder or crime.

The section provides a general protection to journalists' sources. It applies despite any proprietary claim for the delivery up of stolen documents if the documents could lead to the identification of the source (*Secretary of State for Defence v Guardian Newspapers Ltd* [1985] AC 339). It also applies even if there has been no publication of the information, provided the information was supplied with a view to publication (*X Ltd v Morgan-Grampian (Publishers) Ltd* [1991] 1 AC 1). In *Totalise plc v Motley Fool Ltd* [2001] EMLR 750 a website operator was ordered to disclose the identity of a person who, it was alleged, had posted defamatory comments on the website. It was held that the Contempt of Court Act 1981, s. 10, had no application to the facts because the defendant took no responsibility for items posted on its website, since the section applied to information 'contained in a publication for which he is responsible'.

Disclosure of a journalist's source under one of the exceptions to s. 10 will only be ordered if 'necessary' for one of the exceptional reasons. The phrase 'interests of justice' is interpreted so 'that persons should be enabled to exercise important legal rights and to protect themselves from serious legal wrongs whether or not resort to legal proceedings in a court of law will be necessary to attain these objectives' (see Lord Bridge of Harwich in *X Ltd v Morgan-Grampian (Publishers) Ltd*). 'Prevention of crime' includes the detection and prosecution of crimes which are shown to have been committed and where detection and prosecution can sensibly be said to act as a practical deterrent to future criminal conduct of a similar type (see Lord Oliver of Aylmerton in *Re an Inquiry under the Company Securities (Insider Dealing) Act 1985* [1988] AC 660).

If one of the exceptions applies and is necessary, the court must then weigh the importance of disclosure for the exceptional reason against the importance of protecting the source of the information. Factors to be taken into account include the degree of confidentiality attaching to the information, the manner in which the information was obtained, the public interest in concealing journalists' sources, and whether the information brings to light iniquity on the part of the claimant. According to Lord Bridge in *X Ltd v Morgan-Grampian (Publishers) Ltd* disclosure should only be ordered if the balance is clearly on the side of disclosure, since otherwise the courts would be undermining the policy stated in the section. The interrelation between the Contempt of Court Act 1981, s. 10, the **European Convention on Human Rights, art. 10** (freedom of expression), and *Norwich Pharmacal* orders was further considered in *Ashworth Hospital Authority v MGN Ltd* [2002] UKHL 29, [2002] 1 WLR 2033, and its first-instance sequel, *Mersey Care NHS Trust v Ackroyd* [2006] EWHC 107 (QB), *The Times*, 9 February 2006, and in *Interbrew SA v Financial Times Ltd* [2002] EWCA Civ 274, [2002] 2 Lloyd's Rep 229.

Procedure for seeking *Norwich Pharmacal* orders

Norwich Pharmacal orders are usually sought by issuing a claim form against the facilitator, **48.86** and then by issuing an application notice within that claim seeking the disclosure order. Applications have to be supported by witness statement evidence. It is possible in an urgent case to seek the order without giving notice (*Loose v Williamson* [1978] 1 WLR 639).

The order

Normally a successful applicant for a *Norwich Pharmacal* order should pay the costs of the **48.87** party ordered to make disclosure, including the costs of making the disclosure (*Totalise plc v Motley Fool Ltd (No. 2)* [2001] EWCA Civ 1897, [2002] 1 WLR 1233). These costs may be recovered against the wrongdoer in the same or a subsequent claim (*Smith Kline and French Laboratories Ltd v R. D. Harbottle (Mercantile) Ltd* [1980] RPC 363). The person from whom disclosure is sought may contact the person whose identity is sought and invite that person to submit reasons why disclosure should not be ordered: the court may require such contact to be made and may hear the person whose identity is sought (*Totalise plc v Motley Fool Ltd (No. 2)*). Where disclosure is sought of information which is controlled by the Data Protection Act 1998 no order is to be made for disclosure of the data subject's identity unless the court has first considered whether the disclosure is warranted having regard to the rights and freedoms and the legitimate interests of the data subject (*Totalise plc v Motley Fool Ltd (No. 2)*). The court must be careful not to make an order which unjustifiably invades the right of an individual to respect for his or her private life, contrary to the **European Convention on Human Rights, art. 8** (*Totalise plc v Motley Fool Ltd (No. 2)*). The interrelation between the Contempt of Court Act 1981, s. 10, and the **European Convention on Human Rights, art. 10** (freedom of expression) was considered by the Court of Appeal in *Ashworth Hospital Authority v MGN Ltd* [2001] 1 WLR 515 and it was concluded that the section's aims coincided with those of art. 10.

BANKERS TRUST ORDERS

In *Bankers Trust Co. v Shapira* [1980] 1 WLR 1274 a bank, which was a defendant in proceedings, **48.88** was ordered to disclose to the claimant certain confidential information, such as copies of correspondence, cheques, debit vouchers, transfer applications and internal memoranda, relating to two co-defendants, notwithstanding that those co-defendants had not yet been served with proceedings. The purpose of the order was to enable the applicant to trace the existence of and protect the assets claimed in the proceedings, in which, it was found, there was very strong evidence that the co-defendants had been guilty of fraud. Given the confidential nature of the documents to be disclosed, a party claiming an order of this kind must give an undertaking not to use the information obtained other than in the course of the proceedings. See also *Arab Monetary Fund v Hashim (No. 5)* [1992] 2 All ER 911 and *Omar v Omar* [1995] 1 WLR 1428.

Chapter 49 Witness Statements

INTRODUCTION

A witness statement is a written statement signed by a person which contains the evidence which that person would be allowed to give orally (**CPR, r. 32.4(1)**). The text of the statement must, if practicable, be in the witness's own words, and should be expressed in the first person (**PD 32, para. 18.1**). They are used for two main purposes: **49.1**

(a) for setting out the evidence in support of interim applications; and
(b) for setting out the evidence witnesses are expected to give at trial.

Witness statements take much the same form as traditional affidavits and affirmations (see **chapter 50**), except that they are not sworn or affirmed, and instead contain a simple statement of truth. Consequently most of the formalities required for affidavits, such as corner markings, and the rules on paragraphing, exhibits etc., have to be complied with. However, a witness statement will not have a commencement, and it will not have a jurat. Also, because it is not sworn there will be a saving of the fees payable for swearing an affidavit (£5 for the affidavit plus £2 per exhibit).

An example of a witness statement for use in an interim application is shown in **figure 49.1**.

PRINTING AND BINDING

Witness statements must be typed on one side only of durable A4 paper with a 35 mm margin (**PD 32, para. 19.1(1)** and **(2)**). The pages should be numbered consecutively (**para. 19.1(4)**. Wherever possible they should be securely bound in a manner that will not hamper filing (**para. 19.1(3)**). If they are not securely bound each page should bear the claim number and initials of the witness (**para. 19.1(3)**). **49.2**

CORNER MARKINGS

At the top right-hand corner of the first page of the witness statement and of the backsheet there must appear the following details (**PD 32, para. 17.2**): **49.3**

(a) the party on whose behalf it is filed;
(b) the initials and surname of the maker of the statement;

(c) the number of the witness statement in relation to that deponent;
(d) the identifying initials and numbers of the exhibits referred to in the witness statement (if the statement is not the first one by this witness, the numbering of the exhibits must run consecutively from one statement to the next, and not start again with each statement: **para. 18.6**);
(e) the date it is signed.

HEADING

49.4 A witness statement should contain a formal heading with the title of the proceedings (**PD 32, para. 17.1**). It should be headed with the number of the claim, the court (and Division) where it is proceeding, the full names of the parties and their capacities (such as whether they are claimants or defendants). It is sufficient to identify the parties as being 'Between AB (and others) Claimants/Applicants and CD (and others) Defendants/Respondents' (**PD 32, para. 17.1; PD 7, para. 4**).

BODY OF WITNESS STATEMENT

49.5 A witness statement must, if practicable, be in the deponent's own words and should be expressed in the first person (**PD 32, para. 18.1**). A witness statement is not to be used as a vehicle for conveying legal argument (*Alex Lawrie Factors Ltd v Morgan* (1999) *The Times*, 18 August 1999). Nor should it contain lengthy quotations from documents (**Admiralty and Commercial Courts Guide, para. H1.1(iii)**).

The opening paragraph should give details of the witness's occupation or description and his or her place of residence (**PD 32, para. 18.1**). If the statement is made in the witness's professional, business or other occupational capacity, the address given may be the address where the witness works, and the name of his or her firm or employer, and the position he or she holds, should be given. The statement should also state if the witness is a party in the proceedings, or employed by a party.

It is usually convenient to follow the chronological sequence of events. Each paragraph should be numbered, and, so far as possible, be confined to a distinct portion of the subject (**paras 19.1(5) and 19.2**). All numbers, including dates, should be expressed in figures (**para. 19.1(6)**). Documents referred to in the statement should be formally exhibited.

Allegations of serious misconduct (whether or not they amount to fraud) must be set out clearly and with adequate particularity. Matters on which the witness can give direct evidence must be clearly distinguished in the witness statement from anything which is stated as a matter of inference (*Secretary of State for Trade and Industry v Swan* [2003] EWHC 1780 (Ch), [2004] BCC 877).

Since the Civil Evidence Act 1995 has been in force it has been no objection that some of the evidence in a witness statement might be hearsay, but where it is, the witness should identify it as a matter based on information or belief, and give the source of that information or belief (**PD 32, para. 18.2**). This requirement is merely a procedural provision requiring the witness to identify, for the information of the other parties, the source of hearsay in the statement. There is no requirement that the source be identified using only admissible evidence, and the witness may use either recollection or opinion (*Clarke v Marlborough Fine Art (London) Ltd* [2002] 1 WLR 1731). Service of a witness statement containing hearsay evidence is sufficient notice of proposal to adduce hearsay evidence for the purposes of the Civil Evidence Act 1995, s. 2 (**CPR, r. 33.2(1)**). If it is not proposed to call the witness to give oral evidence at trial, the party intending to rely on the hearsay evidence must, when serving the witness statement, inform the other parties that the witness is not being called to give oral evidence and give the reason for not calling the witness (r. 33.2(2)). There is no duty to give notice under the Civil Evidence Act 1995, s. 2, of an intention to adduce hearsay evidence at hearings other than trials (CPR, r. 33.3(a)).

EXHIBITS

The requirements for exhibits to affidavits, which are set out in **PD 32, paras** 11.3 to 15.5, apply to exhibits to witness statements (**para.** 18.5). Numbering of exhibits has already been referred to (see **49.3**). In the body of the witness statement exhibits must be introduced with the words: **49.6**

I refer to the [description of exhibit] marked '[witness's initials and exhibit number]'

followed by a description of the exhibit. Exhibits must be kept separate from the witness statement. They should have a frontsheet having the same markings in the top right corner and heading as the witness statement. Where an exhibit contains several documents the frontsheet should list them with their dates, and/or state the nature of the documents exhibited (such as so many original letters and so many copy letters). The frontsheet needs to bear the correct exhibit mark, and needs to be signed by the maker of the statement. Documents of a similar nature, such as correspondence, should be gathered together into a single exhibit, and arranged chronologically with the earliest document on top, and with each page numbered consecutively at the bottom centre. It is permissible to use copy documents in exhibits, provided the originals are available at the hearing should they be needed (**para.** 13.1). Illegible pages should be followed with a typed version with an 'a' number.

Exhibits other than documents should be clearly marked with the appropriate exhibit number in such a manner that the mark cannot become detached from the exhibit. Small items may be placed in a container, with the container being appropriately marked (**para.** 14).

A common mistake is to exhibit court documents. This is unnecessary as sealed copies of these documents prove themselves (**CPR, r.** 2.6(3), a point specifically made by **PD 32, para.** 13.2).

Exhibits must not be stapled, but should be securely fastened in a way that does not hinder the reading of the documents they contain (**para.** 15.1(1)).

Bulky exhibits

Where, on account of their bulk, the service of exhibits on other parties would be difficult or impracticable, directions should be sought dealing with arrangements for bringing the exhibits to the attention of the other parties and their custody pending trial (PD 32, para. 15.4). **49.7**

Marginal references

A witness statement must 'give the reference to any document or documents mentioned either in the margin or in bold text in the body of the statement' (**PD 32, para.** 19.1(7)). It appears that this refers to the page references in the application or trial bundle, which will be added after the witness statement is signed. There is no objection to these references being added in manuscript (**Admiralty and Commercial Courts Guide, app.** 10, **para.** 3(i)). Time should be allowed for adding marginal references when preparing bundles. **49.8**

STATEMENT OF TRUTH

A witness statement must include a signed statement that the witness believes the facts it contains are true. False statements may be punished as contempt of court (CPR, r. 32.14; PD 32, para. 28). The form of statement of truth (see **PD 32, para.** 20.2) is: **49.9**

I believe that the facts stated in this witness statement are true.

In *Aquarius Financial Enterprises Inc. v Certain Underwriters at Lloyd's Subscribing to Contract KD 970212* (2001) LTL 20/5/2001 there was evidence that one of the witness statements had been obtained by bullying, threats and inducements. Toulson J said that where a witness statement is prepared by someone other than the witness, there should be a written declaration by the person who prepared the statement giving information about its preparation, and certifying compliance with any appropriate code of practice. Whether this will become the practice remains to be seen. It is improper to put pressure on a witness to give anything other than his own account of the matters in question, and it is also improper to serve a witness statement which is known to be false or which it is known the maker does not in all respects believe to be true (**Admiralty and Commercial Courts Guide, para. H1.2**).

Witness unable to read or sign

49.10 Where a witness statement is made by a person who is unable to read or sign the statement, it must contain a certificate made by an 'authorised person' (**PD 22, para. 3A.1**). An authorised person is someone able to administer oaths and take affidavits, but need not be independent of the parties or their representatives. The certificate must be in the form set out in annex 1 to **PD 22**. It says that the witness statement has been read to the witness, who appeared to understand it and approved its contents, that the statement of truth has been read to the witness, that the witness appeared to understand it and the consequences of making a false statement, and that the witness signed or made his or her mark in the presence of the authorised person.

ALTERATIONS

49.11 Alterations to a witness statement must be initialled by the person taking the statement or, if the witness is unable to read or sign, by the 'authorised person' (see **49.10**) (**PD 32, para. 22.1**). A witness statement which contains an alteration that has not been initialled may be used in evidence only with the permission of the court (**para. 22.2**).

FAILURE TO COMPLY WITH PD 32

49.12 If a witness statement or exhibit fails to comply with **PD 32**, the court may refuse to admit it as evidence and may refuse to allow the costs arising out of its preparation (**PD 32, para. 25.1**). Permission to use a defective witness statement may be obtained from a judge (meaning judge, master or district judge: **CPR, r. 2.3(1)**) of the court.

Striking out witness statements

49.13 There is no specific power in the CPR equivalent to the old RSC, ord. 41, r. 6, providing for the striking out of written evidence which is scandalous, irrelevant or oppressive. The general exclusionary discretion in **CPR, r. 32.1**, is probably the source for the continuing power to control evidence which it would be embarrassing for the court to have to keep on file, although **r. 32.2(2)(b)** seems to have been relied upon in *Stroude v Beazer Homes Ltd* [2004] EWHC 676 (Ch), LTL 15/3/2004. That there is such a power under the CPR was regarded as beyond doubt in *Sandhurst Holdings Ltd v Grosvenor Assets Ltd* (2001) LTL 25/10/2001. The court said that the jurisdiction would be exercised sparingly, and made it clear that the court's business would be seriously impeded if parties made striking-out applications as a matter of course whenever they perceived scandalous or irrelevant material was included in their opponents' evidence. A witness statement was ordered to be redacted to exclude inadmissible evidence of negotiations in *Stroude v Beazer Homes Ltd*. Likewise, in *Re New Gadget Shop Ltd* [2005] EWHC 1606 (Ch), LTL 5/8/2005, paragraphs in witness statements which used privileged material were struck out (see **48.54**).

FILING

If the court directs that a witness statement is to be filed, filing should be at the court (or Division of the court) where the case is or will be proceeding (**PD 32, para. 23.1**). **49.14**

FOREIGN LANGUAGE

Where the court directs that a witness statement in a foreign language is to be filed, the party relying on it must have the statement translated, and the translator must make an affidavit verifying the translation, exhibiting both the translation and a copy of the foreign language witness statement. Both the original statement and the translator's affidavit must be filed (**PD 32, para. 23.2**). The importance of the witness first making and signing a statement in his own language, followed by a translation into English, rather than a statement being made in English, and then translated into the witness's language prior to signing, was reiterated in *Re Phoneer Ltd* [2002] 2 BCLC 241. **49.15**

VOLUMINOUS WITNESS STATEMENTS AND EXHIBITS

The courts have for some time generally deprecated the use of voluminous written evidence. However, there are cases where it is inevitable, and then the witness statements and exhibits to be used should be put into separate bundles, with the pages numbered consecutively throughout (**PD 32, paras 15.3 and 18.5**). **49.16**

Figure 49.1 Witness statement seeking to set aside a judgment in default and transfer of action

Made on behalf of the Defendant
Witness: B. Parkes
1st statement of witness
Exhibits: BP 1 to BP 3
Made: 15.9.2006

IN THE HIGH COURT OF JUSTICE HC06Q 98744

QUEEN'S BENCH DIVISION

BETWEEN

SHILTON MACHINE TOOLS LIMITED Claimant

— and —

BANKS PLASTIC MOULDINGS LIMITED Defendant

WITNESS STATEMENT OF BRIAN PARKES

1. I am Brian Parkes, of Unit 6, Elland Trading Estate, Leeds LS8 3AN. I am a director of the Defendant company. I have full knowledge of the facts of this case and I am duly authorised to make this statement on behalf of the Defendant in support of its application to set aside a default judgment entered on 8 August 2006. In so far as the contents of this statement are within my personal knowledge they are true, otherwise they are true to the best of my knowledge, information and belief.
2. The Defendant has a trading account with the Claimant, and it is true that it ordered 4 moulding machines from the Claimant on 14 April 2005 at a price of

£60,000 plus VAT. Although the machines were delivered, they have been the subject of repeated breakdowns and have suffered a number of faults. The main problem with 2 of the machines is that despite a number of site attendances by the claimant's engineers they have proved incapable of producing mouldings to industry standards. I have been advised by Mr Edward Knight, a consulting engineer of 36 Harrogate Road, Leeds LS3 8DQ, that these two machines are so badly designed that it will be impossible to put them right.

3. As a result of the problems with all 4 machines the Defendant has suffered a substantial loss of business. In particular, it has lost a contract with United Plastic Containers plc, under which the Defendant was producing goods valued at between £10,000 and £20,000 per month. I refer to the bundle containing true
pp. 41–65 copies of the Defendant's contractual documentation with United Plastic Containers plc, monthly invoices, and recent correspondence marked 'BP 1' in which the termination of the contract is explained. I have been advised by the
pp. 66–94 Defendant's solicitors and believe that it has a substantial counterclaim with a value significantly above the value of the claim.

4. As soon as I received the court papers in this action I raised the matter with Mrs Elaine Stepney, the finance director of the Claimant. I refer to the bundle of
p. 95 correspondence marked 'BP 2', at page 1 of which is a true copy of my letter to
p. 96 her dated 19 July 2006. Her reply, at page 2, says she will look into the matter. Nevertheless, judgment was entered on 8 August 2006.

p. 98–102 5. For the reasons set out above, I ask that this judgment be set aside on the merits. I refer to the draft Defence and Counterclaim marked 'BP 3' which the Defendant intends to file if judgment is set aside, and I confirm the truth of the contents of the draft Defence and Counterclaim.

6. If judgment is set aside and the case allowed to continue, I respectfully ask that the action be transferred to the Leeds County Court, the local court of the Defendant.

STATEMENT OF TRUTH

I believe the facts stated in this witness statement are true.

Signed:

Position: Director

Dated: 15 September 2006.

DIRECTIONS FOR THE EXCHANGE OF WITNESS STATEMENTS

49.17 Witness statements are sometimes required in cases allocated to the small claims track (see 43.17). Directions dealing with witness statements tend to be made only in the slightly more complex small claims. The technical rules on witness statements (in **CPR, Part 32**) do not apply to claims on the small claims track (**r. 27.2(1)(c)**), so the following discussion is largely limited to claims on the fast and multi-tracks. For these cases, directions for the exchange of witness statements are mandatory.

The court will order a party to serve on the other parties any witness statement of the oral evidence which the party serving the statement intends to rely on in relation to any issues of fact to be decided at the trial (**CPR, r. 32.4(2)**). The court may give directions as to the order in which witness statements are to be served, and whether or not they should be filed (**r. 32.4(3)**).

When directions are made on allocating a case to the fast track or multi-track, or at a case management conference, the court will make provision for the date by when witness statements must be exchanged. Normally mutual exchange is required, and it usually takes place a few weeks after disclosure and inspection of documents. Part of the reason why witness statements are exchanged after disclosure of documents is that the witnesses may need to comment on some of the documentation in their statements. If a witness statement is not served within the time specified in the directions, the witness may only be called with permission.

WITNESS SUMMARIES

A party who is unable to obtain signed witness statements before the time prescribed for exchange may apply, without notice, for permission to serve witness summaries instead of witness statements (**CPR, r. 32.9**). A witness summary is simply a summary of the evidence that would have been included in a witness statement. A witness summary could be an unsigned draft statement or even just an indication of the issues it is hoped the witness could deal with. Permission to serve a witness summary can only be granted if the party is unable to obtain the relevant witness statement. Unless the court orders otherwise, a witness summary must be served within the period in which a witness statement would have had to be served. **49.18**

LATE SERVICE OF WITNESS STATEMENTS

If a witness statement or witness summary for use at trial is not served in respect of an intended witness within the time specified by the court, the witness may not be called to give oral evidence unless the court gives permission (**CPR, r. 32.10**). The case law dealing with non-compliance with directions for the exchange of witness statements is discussed at **46.24**. **49.19**

USE OF WITNESS STATEMENTS AT TRIAL

A party who has served a witness statement, and wishes to rely at trial on the evidence of the witness who made the statement, must call the witness to give oral evidence, unless the court orders otherwise or the statement is put in as hearsay evidence (**CPR, r. 32.5(1)**). A party who has disclosed witness statements pursuant to directions cannot be ordered to call those witnesses at trial (*Society of Lloyd's v Jaffray* (2000) *The Times*, 3 August 2000), but should give prompt notice to the other parties that the witnesses will not be called. Despite the provisions of the Civil Evidence Act 1995, there are several reasons why judges tend to attach limited weight to statements relied upon as hearsay without calling the maker at trial. The fact that the witness is not present, in the absence of some good reason, tends to indicate that the witness does not have confidence in the statement. It will not have been tested by cross-examination. It may not have been possible to show weaknesses or limitations in the evidence, such as the distance from the scene of the witness, whether there were any obstructions, whether the witness saw what is dealt with in the statement rather than constructing it after the event, etc. Live witnesses are also thought to have great impact with the court (for better or for worse, depending on how they perform in the witness box). The result is that, wherever possible, witnesses are called to give evidence at trials. **49.20**

Exchanged witness statements stand as the witnesses' evidence-in-chief unless the court otherwise orders (**CPR, r. 32.5(2)**). A witness may, however, and provided the court considers there is good reason not to confine the witness to the contents of the disclosed statement, amplify his or her witness statement and give evidence in relation to new matters that have arisen since the statement was served (**r. 32.5(3) and (4)**). These conditions are very restrictive, and the result is that generally witnesses should not be allowed to go outside their witness statements when they give evidence-in-chief. This also means that a witness statement should contain the whole of the evidence-in-chief that it is anticipated the witness will be able to give, as the judge may refuse permission to ask any supplementary questions. Consideration should be given to serving a supplementary statement if a witness needs to correct or materially add to an exchanged statement (see **Admiralty and Commercial Courts Guide, para. H1.6**).

Cross-examination

49.21 A witness who is called to give evidence at trial may be cross-examined on his or her witness statement, whether or not the statement or any part of it was referred to during the witness's evidence-in-chief (**CPR, r. 32.11**).

Use by other parties

49.22 **Rule 32.5(5)** of the CPR provides that where a witness statement is served, but the party on whose behalf it is served decides not to call the maker to give evidence at trial or to rely on the statement as hearsay evidence, any other party may introduce the witness statement as hearsay evidence. This rule effectively resolves the dispute under the old rules as to whether or not any vestiges of legal professional privilege continued to attach to a witness statement after it was exchanged, and it is now clear that service of witness statements waives the privilege (see *Society of Lloyd's v Jaffray* (2000) *The Times*, 3 August 2000).

Once it becomes clear that a party who has served a witness statement is not going to use it, and it is indicated that another party wishes to use the disclosed statement, the judge has a discretion whether to permit use of the statement (*McPhilemy v Times Newspapers Ltd (No. 2)* [2000] 1 WLR 1732). Generally the discretion will be exercised in accordance with the overriding objective. However, **r. 32.5(5)** cannot be used to override established rules of evidence. This means that permission will not be given for a witness statement to be put in evidence by a party if it substantially conflicts with the party's own case and the party will say that a substantial part of the statement must be disbelieved as untrue (*McPhilemy v Times Newspapers Ltd (No. 2)* [2000] 1 WLR 1732). This is because, with the exception of hostile witnesses, a party is not allowed under the rules of evidence to impeach his own witnesses (see *Ewer v Ambrose* (1825) 3 B & C 746 and **47.61**).

Availability of witness statements for inspection

49.23 Witness statements that stand as evidence-in-chief are open to inspection by the public during the course of the trial, unless the judge otherwise directs (**CPR, r. 32.13**). Normally witness statements used in this way have to be open to inspection, because proceedings are conducted in public and the public are entitled to know what evidence has been presented by a witness. The burden is accordingly on any person opposing an application for inspection. It is permissible for the court to allow inspection of a statement subject to editing out of details relating to issues which have been withdrawn before the witness testifies (*Cox v Jones* [2004] EWHC 1006 (Ch), LTL 18/5/2004). The right to inspect does not extend to documents referred to in the statements used at trial (*GIO Personal Investment Services Ltd v Liverpool and London Steamship Protection and Indemnity Association Ltd* [1999] 1 WLR 984). Anyone may ask the judge to make a direction that a witness statement should not be open to inspection, but such a direction will only be made in limited circumstances, such as where it is in the interests of justice or the public interest that it should not be made available to the public. The court also has a power to blank out certain passages from witness statements open to inspection by the public (**r. 32.13(4)**).

COLLATERAL USE

49.24 Once served, witness statements may be used only for the purposes of the proceedings in which they were served (**CPR, r. 32.12(1)**). This restriction does not apply if and to the extent either:

(a) the witness gives consent in writing to some other use of the statement;
(b) the court gives permission for some other use; or
(c) the witness statement has been put in evidence at a hearing held in public.

The prohibition against using material for collateral purposes does not apply to documents referred to in affidavits and witness statements, as these are regarded as having been voluntarily disclosed (*Cassidy v Hawcroft* [2000] CPLR 624).

ABSOLUTE PRIVILEGE

A statement made by a witness or prospective witness to a legal representative for the purposes of preparing a witness statement, proof of evidence or affidavit for use in court proceedings, or in contemplation of doing so, attracts absolute privilege for the purposes of possible defamation proceedings, unless it has no reference at all to the subject matter of the proceedings (*Smeaton v Butcher* (2000) *The Times*, 17 May 2000). The statement will also attract absolute privilege if used in other proceedings to which it relates (*Smeaton v Butcher*). **49.25**

Chapter 50 Affidavits

INTRODUCTION

50.1 Affidavits are sworn written statements. They take much the same form as modern witness statements (see **chapter** 49), but they have a few formal differences (principally the commencement and jurat). They were formerly the main means by which evidence was placed before the court on interim applications. That role has now largely been taken over by the use of witness statements, although there are a small number of situations where affidavits must still be used in interim applications. Their remaining main use is for putting evidence before the court at the final hearings of certain types of proceedings, particularly matrimonial and family proceedings, insolvency proceedings, director disqualification proceedings and proceedings brought using **Part 8** of the CPR.

FORM OF AFFIDAVITS

50.2 **Rule** 32.16 of the CPR provides that affidavits must be in the form set out in the appropriate PD, which is **PD 32, paras 2 to 16**. The form of an affidavit is broadly similar to that of a witness statement, described in **chapter 49**:

(a) An affidavit must be typed on one side only of consecutively numbered sheets of durable A4 paper with a 35 mm margin (**PD 32, para. 6.1(1), (2) and (4)**).
(b) It must have the same corner markings as witness statements (**PD 32, para. 3.2**; see **49.3**).
(c) It must be headed in the same way as witness statements (see **49.4**).
(d) After the heading and before the body of the affidavit there should appear a commencement (**PD 32, para. 4.1**). This should read:

> I [full name] of [address, which can be a business address if sworn in the deponent's professional, business or occupational capacity] state on oath:

(e) The comments about the body of the text in witness statements at **49.5** apply equally to affidavits (**PD 32, paras 4.1 and 4.2**).
(f) The same provisions apply to exhibits to affidavits as apply to exhibits to witness statements (see **49.6** and **49.7**).
(g) The comments about marginal references in witness statements at **49.8** apply equally to affidavits (**PD 32, para. 6.1(7)**).
(h) Alterations need to be initialled by both the deponent and the person taking the affidavit (**PD 32, para. 8.1**).
(i) Instead of a statement of truth (see **49.9**), an affidavit ends with a jurat. The jurat must follow on from the body of the affidavit, and must not appear on a separate page. After giving the oath the affidavit has to be signed by all deponents (exceptionally an affidavit may be sworn by more than one person) and be completed by the person taking the affidavit. The person taking the affidavit must insert his or her full address, sign the jurat, and print his or her name and qualification under the signature (**PD 32, para. 5**).

QUALIFICATION OF PERSON TAKING AN AFFIDAVIT

A person who takes an affidavit must be duly qualified (solicitors, commissioners for oaths, magistrates, certain court officials and judges, British consuls and others authorised by statute, such as barristers), and independent of the parties and their representatives (**PD 32, para. 9**). **50.3**

AFFIRMATIONS

Affirmations are similar to affidavits, but the deponent will affirm rather than swear when executing the document. They can be used whenever an affidavit may or must be used. All the provisions in **PD 32** relating to affidavits apply also to affirmations (**PD 32, para. 16**). For affirmations the commencement should read: **50.4**

I [full name] of [address] do solemnly and sincerely affirm:

In an affirmation, the word 'sworn' in the jurat is replaced by the word 'affirmed'.

INABILITY OF DEPONENT TO READ OR SIGN AN AFFIDAVIT

Where an affidavit is sworn by a person who is unable to read or sign it, the person before whom it is sworn must certify in the jurat that he or she has read the affidavit to the deponent and that the deponent appeared to understand it (**PD 32, para. 7.1(1) and (2)**). The person who took the affidavit must also certify that, in his or her presence, the deponent signed it or made his or her mark (**para. 7.1(3)**). Two versions of the form of the certificate appear in annex 1 to **PD 32**. If such a certificate is not included in the jurat, the affidavit may not be used unless the court is satisfied that it was read to the deponent and he or she appeared to understand it (**para. 7.2**). **50.5**

FILING AND MISCELLANEOUS TOPICS

Identical provisions apply to filing of affidavits and affirmations, in relation to foreign language affidavits, and the use of voluminous affidavits and exhibits, as apply to witness statements (see **49.13** to **49.16**, and **PD 32, paras 10** and **15.3**). Likewise as regards failing to comply with **PD 32** (see **49.13** and **49.15**, and **PD 32, para. 25**). **50.6**

SITUATIONS WHERE AFFIDAVITS MUST BE USED

Affidavits must be used whenever sworn evidence is required by an enactment, rule, order or practice directions (**PD 32, para. 1.4**). Examples include applications under the **Protection from Harassment Act 1997, s. 3(5)(a)**, certain applications relating to confiscation and forfeiture in connection with criminal proceedings, and under the environmental control legislation. **PD 32** and **PD 25** require affidavit evidence in support of applications for freezing injunctions and search orders, orders to require an occupier to permit another to enter land, and applications for contempt of court. Verification of a translation of a witness statement or affidavit must be on affidavit (**PD 32, paras 10.2** and **23.2**). Evidence in support of applications for judgment in default after service outside the jurisdiction without permission or against a State must be given on affidavit (**PD 12, para. 4.5**). **50.7**

Chapter 51 Hearsay Evidence

INTRODUCTION

51.1 The Civil Evidence Act 1995 gives effect to the main recommendations of the Law Commission in its report, *The Hearsay Rule in Civil Proceedings* (Law Com. No. 216, Cm 2321, 1993). These were as follows:

(a) The hearsay rule should be abolished.
(b) A party calling a person as a witness should not adduce evidence of a previous statement made by that person without the permission of the court.
(c) A party intending to rely on hearsay evidence should be required to give notice of that fact, if it is reasonable and appropriate to do so, but failure to do so should not render the evidence inadmissible, although it may detract from its weight and result in the imposition of a costs sanction.
(d) A party should have the power to call a witness for cross-examination on his or her hearsay evidence.
(e) There should be guidelines to assist the court in assessing the weight of hearsay evidence.
(f) There should be no special conditions of admissibility or safeguards for business and other records, and the means of proving such records should be simplified.
(g) There should be no special conditions of admissibility or safeguards for statements contained in computer-produced documents: the potential for misuse of computers should be taken into account in considering the weight to be attached to such evidence.

The overall effect of the Civil Evidence Act 1995 has been to simplify the law and procedure relating to hearsay in civil cases and to render admissible much that would have been inadmissible under the regime of the Civil Evidence Act 1968 and its accompanying and unduly complex notice provisions.

ADMISSIBILITY OF HEARSAY UNDER THE 1995 ACT

The Civil Evidence Act 1995, s. 1, provides as follows: **51.2**

(1) In civil proceedings evidence shall not be excluded on the ground that it is hearsay.
(2) In this Act—
  (a) 'hearsay' means a statement made otherwise than by a person while giving oral evidence in the proceedings which is tendered as evidence of the matters stated; and
  (b) references to hearsay include hearsay of whatever degree.

'Civil proceedings' means civil proceedings before any tribunal in relation to which the strict rules of evidence apply, whether as a matter of law or by agreement of the parties (s. 11). Thus the Act does apply in tribunals and arbitrations in which the strict rules of evidence are applied, but does not apply to the wardship jurisdiction of the High Court (see *Official Solicitor to the Supreme Court v K* [1965] AC 201) or to magistrates when considering, under the Local Government (Miscellaneous Provisions) Act 1976, whether there is reasonable cause to suspend a private hire vehicle licence (*Westminster City Council v Zestfair Ltd* (1989) 88 LGR 288; *Leeds City Council v Hussain* [2002] EWHC 1145 (Admin), *The Times*, 8 July 2002). Applications to commit for contempt, founded on breaches of orders made in civil proceedings, are themselves civil proceedings, despite the criminal standard of proof appropriate to such applications and their possible penal consequences (see *Savings and Investment Bank Ltd v Gasco Investments (Netherlands) BV (No. 2)* [1988] Ch 422, a decision under the equivalent provision of the Civil Evidence Act 1968).

Under s. 1(1), 'evidence shall not be excluded on the ground that it is hearsay', wording which makes it clear that hearsay evidence will only be admissible if not open to exclusion on some other basis. The point is reinforced by s. 14(1) of the Act:

Nothing in this Act affects the exclusion of evidence on grounds other than that it is hearsay.

This applies whether the evidence falls to be excluded in pursuance of any enactment or rule of law, for failure to comply with rules of court or an order of the court, or otherwise.

The only 'hearsay' to which the safeguards and supplementary provisions of the Act apply is that defined in s. 1(2). The definition corresponds to the definition of hearsay at common law, and the Law Commission was of the view that there is likely to continue to be reference to the existing case law in cases in which the boundary of the definition is unclear (Law Com. No. 216, para. 4.6). 'Statement' means 'any representation of fact or opinion, however made' (s. 13). As to representations of opinion, these will only be admissible if admissible under the Civil Evidence Act 1972. The phrase 'however made' ensures that the Act covers statements made orally, in writing, whether manually or by any other means, and by conduct. A written statement in an affidavit, however, may perhaps not be covered (see per Harman J in *Rover International Ltd v Cannon Film Sales Ltd* [1987] 1 WLR 1597, at pp. 1603–4, doubting whether affidavits were documents under the Civil Evidence Act 1968). It is also unclear whether a 'representation' covers implied assertions, such as protests (e.g., 'Don't, Bill!'), greetings (e.g., 'Hello, Harriet') or other verbal utterances (e.g., 'Jack, please supply six tons of wheat'). It is debatable whether assertions of this kind should be treated as stating the facts which they imply (in the examples given, that Bill was doing something unwelcome to the person who protested, that Harriet was present at the place where she was greeted, and that Jack can supply wheat). It is equally unclear whether a 'representation' covers assertions which can be implied from conduct, as when customers who have ordered beer, taste it, do not finish it and then either leave it or throw it away (see per Farwell J in *Manchester Brewery Co. Ltd v Coombs* (1901) 82 LT 347 at p. 349, who was of the opinion, *obiter*, that such evidence would be admissible at common law). The Law Commission was content to duck the issue, being of the view that the question whether assertive or non-assertive conduct should come within the definition of hearsay was 'a matter for judicial consideration and development' (Law Com. No. 216, para. 4.35).

To come within the definition of hearsay in s. 1(2), the statement must have been made otherwise than by a person while giving 'oral evidence'. 'Oral evidence', for these purposes, includes evidence which, by reason of a defect of speech or hearing, a person called as a witness gives in writing or by signs (s. 13).

Hearsay and human rights

51.3 It is unnecessary and unwarranted to imply words into the Civil Evidence Act 1995 to give the court the power to exclude hearsay evidence. The admission of hearsay evidence under the 1995 Act is not incompatible with the **Human Rights Act 1998** and will not necessarily or automatically infringe a defendant's right to a fair trial under the **European Convention on Human Rights, art. 6(1)** (*R (McCann) v Crown Court at Manchester* [2002] UKHL 39, [2003] 1 AC 787 at [35]). *McCann's* case concerned applications for anti-social behaviour orders. It was held (at [113], [116] and [117]) that, having regard to s. 4 of the 1995 Act, which lays down guidelines for assessing the weight of hearsay evidence (see **51.13**), a fair balance between the general interests of the community (represented by the weak and vulnerable who are the potential victims of anti-social behaviour) and protection of defendants' rights, requires the scales to come down in favour of the community and of the admission of hearsay evidence.

Defamation claims

51.4 The admissibility of hearsay evidence under the Civil Evidence Act 1995 has altered the common law rule in defamation claims that in establishing a defence of justification it was not permissible to rely upon hearsay (see *Shah v Standard Chartered Bank* [1999] QB 241 at p. 270C, which overlooked the 1995 Act). The present position is that hearsay evidence of whatever degree is admissible to prove the truth of the particulars of justification (*Chase v News Group Newspapers Ltd* [2002] EWCA Civ 1772, [2003] EMLR 11).

ADMISSIBILITY OF HEARSAY UNDER OTHER STATUTORY PROVISIONS

51.5 Apart from the Civil Evidence Act 1995, various statutory provisions and statutory instruments provide for the admissibility of particular types of hearsay evidence. These include, for example, the Bankers' Books Evidence Act 1879 (considered at 47.77), the Marriage Act 1949, s. 65(3), the Births and Deaths Registration Act 1953, s. 34, the Solicitors Act 1974, s. 18, and the Children (Admissibility of Hearsay Evidence) Order 1993 (SI 1993/621). The purpose of s. 1(3) and (4) of the 1995 Act is to preserve the effect of all such provisions and to make it clear that evidence admissible under other statutory provisions is not subject to the requirements of competence and permission and the other safeguards set out in the 1995 Act. The subsections provide as follows.

> (3) Nothing in this Act affects the admissibility of evidence admissible apart from this section.
> (4) The provisions of sections 2 to 6 (safeguards and supplementary provisions relating to hearsay evidence) do not apply in relation to hearsay evidence admissible apart from this section, notwithstanding that it may also be admissible by virtue of this section.

COMPETENCE

51.6 Hearsay evidence may only be admitted under the Civil Evidence Act 1995 if the maker of the out-of-court statement would have been competent to give evidence at the time when he or she made the statement and, in cases in which the hearsay statement is to be proved by the statement of another (as when A's out-of-court oral statement is to be proved by B's written record of what was said), if that other person would have been competent to give evidence at the time when he or she made the statement. Section 5(1) provides as follows:

Hearsay evidence shall not be admitted in civil proceedings if or to the extent that it is shown to consist of, or to be proved by means of, a statement made by a person who at the time he made the statement was not competent as a witness.

For this purpose 'not competent as a witness' means suffering from such mental or physical infirmity, or lack of understanding, as would render a person incompetent as a witness in civil proceedings; but a child shall be treated as competent as a witness if he satisfies the requirements of section 96(2)(a) and (b) of the Children Act 1989 (conditions for reception of unsworn evidence of child).

The provisions of the Children Act 1989, s. 96(2)(a) and (b), are considered at **47.45**.

The burden of proof, under the Civil Evidence Act 1995, s. 5(1), is on the party seeking to exclude the hearsay evidence (*JC v CC* [2001] EWCA Civ 1625, LTL 25/10/2001).

PREVIOUS STATEMENTS

At common law, there is a general rule that a witness cannot be asked in examination-in-chief **51.7** about former oral or written statements made by that witness and consistent with his or her evidence in the proceedings. In civil cases, the rule was subject to only two common law exceptions: statements admissible to rebut allegations of recent fabrication and memory-refreshing documents rendered admissible as a result of cross-examination. The general effect of s. 6 of the Civil Evidence Act 1995 has been to relax the rule, by providing that previous statements may be admissible with permission, and to preserve the two exceptions to the rule. As to the rule, s. 6 reflects the view that a requirement for permission is necessary in the case of the previous consistent statements of a person called as a witness in order to prevent the pointless proliferation of superfluous evidence, which would needlessly prolong trials and increase costs (Law Com. No. 216, para. 4.30). In fact, s. 6 goes further and imposes a requirement of permission in the case of *any* previous statement, i.e. whether consistent or merely relating to matters other than those as to which the witness will give evidence. However, the concluding words of the section make it clear that it cannot be used to prevent a witness statement from standing as the witness's evidence-in-chief under **CPR, r. 32.5(2)** (see **49.20**). As to the common law exceptions to the rule against previous consistent statements, they have been preserved by s. 6(2)(b) (statements in rebuttal of allegations of recent fabrication, considered at **47.59**) and s. 6(4) (memory-refreshing documents, considered at **47.55**).

Section 6 of the Act provides as follows:

(1) Subject as follows, the provisions of this Act as to hearsay evidence in civil proceedings apply equally (but with any necessary modifications) in relation to a previous statement made by a person called as a witness in the proceedings.

(2) A party who has called or intends to call a person as a witness in civil proceedings may not in those proceedings adduce evidence of a previous statement made by that person, except—
(a) with the leave of the court, or
(b) for the purpose of rebutting a suggestion that his evidence has been fabricated.

This shall not be construed as preventing a witness statement (that is, a written statement of oral evidence which a party to the proceedings intends to lead) from being adopted by a witness in giving evidence or treated as his evidence.

The question naturally arises as to when permission should be granted. It is submitted that where the witness is incapable of giving direct evidence on the matter in question, then provided that his or her statement is sufficiently relevant to the facts in issue and its admission would not be unjust to the other parties to the proceedings, permission should normally be granted. Typically, the witness will be incapable of giving direct evidence where he or she has no recollection of the matter at all or where, although the witness is not incapable of giving direct evidence on the matter, his or her evidence is of questionable reliability, inconsistent or not wholly intelligible by reason of partial loss of memory, lapse of time, age or physical or mental infirmity. Such an approach would be in line with that taken in *Morris v Stratford-on-Avon Rural District Council* [1973] 1 WLR 1059, a decision under the equivalent leave requirement of the Civil Evidence Act 1968 (s. 2(2)). In that case, a claim for damages against the Council for the alleged negligence of one its employees, the trial only began some five years after the cause of action had arisen. The employee gave confused and inconsistent evidence. At the conclusion of his examination-in-chief, counsel for the defendant was granted leave to admit in chief a written statement made by the employee and given to the defendant's insurers about nine months after the events in question. The Court of Appeal held that the trial judge had not erred in allowing the evidence to be admitted.

Where permission is given to admit a previous statement under s. 6, there are no restrictions as to when it may be introduced in evidence. In some cases, therefore, it may be appropriate to give evidence of the statement before or during the examination-in-chief of the witness, as when this might render more intelligible the direct evidence to be given.

ADVANCE NOTICE

51.8 The principal objectives of the notice provisions under the Civil Evidence Act 1995 are the same as they were in the case of the notice provisions under the Civil Evidence Act 1968: to deal with all issues arising out of the adduction of hearsay evidence pre-trial and therefore to avoid surprise at trial. The current provisions, however, are simpler and more flexible. They are based on the following principles (see generally Law Com. No. 216, paras 4.9 and 4.10):

(a) The notice provision should require a party to give notice of the fact that he or she proposes to adduce hearsay, but should put the onus on the receiving party to demand such particulars as he or she requires in order to be able to make a proper assessment of the weight and cogency of the hearsay and to be in a position to respond to it adequately.
(b) Circumstances can arise in litigation rendering compliance with a notice requirement impracticable. For example, some hearings need to be arranged urgently. In other cases, albeit rarely, advance notification may carry a real risk of danger to the witness or someone else. For reasons of this kind, the new provisions make allowance for the possibility that in some circumstances it would be unreasonable and impracticable to give any notice at all.
(c) The notice provisions should be subject to rules of court to allow them to be disapplied in certain classes of proceedings if, as experience is gained, this is felt to be appropriate.
(d) The parties should be free to agree to exclude the notice provisions.

Section 2 of the 1995 Act provides as follows:

(1) A party proposing to adduce hearsay evidence in civil proceedings shall, subject to the following provisions of this section, give to the other party or parties to the proceedings—
 (a) such notice (if any) of that fact, and
 (b) on request, such particulars of or relating to the evidence, as is reasonable and practicable in the circumstances for the purpose of enabling him or them to deal with any matters arising from its being hearsay.
(2) Provision may be made by rules of court—
 (a) specifying classes of proceedings or evidence in relation to which subsection (1) does not apply, and
 (b) as to the manner in which (including the time within which) the duties imposed by that subsection are to be complied with in the cases where it does apply.
(3) Subsection (1) may also be excluded by the agreement of the parties; and compliance with the duty to give notice may in any case be waived by the person to whom notice is required to be given.

Notice of intention to rely on hearsay evidence

51.9 The relevant rules on notice of intention to rely on hearsay evidence are to be found in CPR, Part 33, which does not apply to claims which have been allocated to the small claims track.

Under **CPR, r. 33.2(1)**, where a party intends to rely on hearsay evidence at trial and either that evidence is to be given by a witness giving oral evidence or is contained in a witness statement of a person who is not being called to give oral evidence, that party complies with s. 2(1)(a) of the Act by serving a witness statement on the other parties in accordance with the court's order. A party who intends to rely on a witness statement containing hearsay evidence without calling the maker of the statement, must, when serving the witness statement, inform the other parties that the witness is not being called to give oral evidence and give the reason why the witness will not be called (**r. 33.2(2)**). In all other cases where a party intends to rely on hearsay evidence at trial, for example where a party intends to rely on the contents of a letter or diary written by a person since deceased, or the contents of a computer printout, that party complies with s. 2(1)(a) of the Act by serving a notice on the other parties which:

(a) identifies the hearsay evidence;
(b) states that the party serving the notice proposes to rely on the evidence at trial; and
(c) gives the reason why the witness will not be called (**r. 33.2(3)**).

This notice must be served no later than the date for serving witness statements and, if the hearsay evidence is to be in a document, supply a copy to any party who requests him or her to do so (**r. 33.2(4)**). See further, in the case of documents which are shown to form part of the records of a business or public authority, **51.16**.

Consequences of failure to comply with the notice procedure

Section 2(4) of the 1995 Act provides as follows: **51.10**

(4) A failure to comply with subsection (1), or with rules under subsection (2)(b), does not affect the admissibility of the evidence but may be taken into account by the court—
  (a) in considering the exercise of its powers with respect to the course of proceedings and costs, and
  (b) as a matter adversely affecting the weight to be given to the evidence in accordance with section 4.

Thus where a party does not give notice, when in all the circumstances of the case it would have been reasonable and practicable for him or her to have done so, or fails to give proper notice, or gives late notice, although the court may not refuse to admit the evidence, there are a number of other potential consequences:

(a) under s. 2(4)(a), the court, in the exercise of its powers with respect to the course of proceedings, may grant an adjournment in order to compel a party to give notice, to perfect an inadequate notice, or to allow the other party time to deal with the effect of late notification;
(b) under s. 2(4)(a), the court may also impose a costs sanction; and
(c) under s. 2(4)(b), the court may reduce the weight to be given to the evidence.

Circumstances in which notice of intention is not required

It is provided in **CPR, r. 33.3** that the duty to give notice of intention to rely on hearsay evidence does not apply: **51.11**

(a) to evidence at hearings other than trials [i.e., on interim applications];
(aa) to an affidavit or witness statement which is to be used at trial but which does not contain hearsay evidence;
(b) to a statement which a party to a probate claim wishes to put in evidence and which is alleged to have been made by the person whose estate is the subject of the proceedings; or
(c) where the requirement is excluded by a practice direction.

POWER TO CALL WITNESSES FOR CROSS-EXAMINATION

Section 3 of the Civil Evidence Act 1995 provides as follows: **51.12**

3. Rules of court may provide that where a party to civil proceedings adduces hearsay evidence of a statement made by a person and does not call that person as a witness, any other party to the proceedings may, with the leave of the court, call that person as a witness and cross-examine him on the statement as if he had been called by the first-mentioned party and as if the hearsay statement were his evidence-in-chief.

The relevant rule of court is **CPR, r. 33.4**, which provides that where a party proposes to rely on hearsay evidence and does not propose to call the person who made the original statement to give oral evidence, the court may, on the application of any other party, permit that party to call the maker of the statement to be cross-examined on the contents of the statement. An application for permission to cross-examine under this rule must be made not more than 14 days after the day on which a notice of intention to rely on the hearsay evidence was served on the applicant (r. 33.4(2)).

In the normal case, r. 33.4 applies where a party has served a witness statement but does not propose to call its maker as a witness. It also applies where a party neither calls the maker of one of its witness statements nor puts the statement in as hearsay, and another party, under r. 32.5(5) (see 49.22), puts the witness statement in as hearsay, so that the first party may then, with the permission of the court, call the witness and cross-examine him on the statement (*Douglas v Hello! Ltd* [2003] EWCA Civ 332, [2003] EMLR 633).

WEIGHT TO BE GIVEN TO HEARSAY EVIDENCE

51.13 Section 4 of the Civil Evidence Act 1995 sets out the various matters to which the court shall or may have regard in estimating the weight, if any, to be given to hearsay evidence. The provision was introduced for two reasons. First, since the 1995 Act all but abolishes the hearsay rule, the courts need to be particularly vigilant in testing the reliability of such evidence. Secondly, such a provision can operate to deter parties from abusing abolition of the rule, for example, by deliberately failing to give notice, by giving late or inadequate notice, by relying on hearsay rather than calling a dubious witness who can give direct evidence, or by amassing hearsay statements on a point in an attempt to conceal an essential witness (see Law Com. No. 216, para. 4.19). Section 4 provides as follows:

(1) In estimating the weight (if any) to be given to hearsay evidence in civil proceedings the court shall have regard to any circumstances from which any inference can reasonably be drawn as to the reliability or otherwise of the evidence.
(2) Regard may be had, in particular, to the following—
   (a) whether it would have been reasonable and practicable for the party by whom the evidence was adduced to have produced the maker of the original statement as a witness;
   (b) whether the original statement was made contemporaneously with the occurrence or existence of the matters stated;
   (c) whether the evidence involves multiple hearsay;
   (d) whether any person involved had any motive to conceal or misrepresent matters;
   (e) whether the original statement was an edited account, or was made in collaboration with another or for a particular purpose;
   (f) whether the circumstances in which the evidence is adduced as hearsay are such as to suggest an attempt to prevent proper evaluation of its weight.

Section 13 provides that, in relation to hearsay evidence, 'the original statement':

means the underlying statement (if any) by:
(a) in the case of evidence of fact, a person having personal knowledge of that fact, or
(b) in the case of evidence of opinion, the person whose opinion it is.

As to s. 4(2)(a), it is submitted that an inference as to unreliability may be drawn even if, had the maker of the original statement been called as a witness, the court would have granted leave under s. 6(2) to adduce evidence of the statement (see further at 51.7). However, it is also submitted that such an inference is unlikely to be drawn under s. 4(2)(a) where the other party or parties have not applied for permission to call the maker of the original statement for cross-examination under s. 3 (see further at 51.12).

Concerning s. 4(2)(d), the phrase 'any person involved' will cover not only the maker (or, in cases of collaboration, makers) of 'the original statement', but also, in all cases in which the statement is proved at trial other than by the maker of the original statement, the person who claims to have heard the statement or to have recorded it in a document, and, in all cases of multiple hearsay, the intermediaries through whom the information contained in 'the original statement' was supplied.

In estimating the weight to be attached to hearsay evidence contained in computer-generated documents, the courts are likely to use s. 4 to have regard to a variety of circumstances, in addition to those set out in s. 4(2), from which inferences can be drawn as to the reliability or otherwise of the evidence, including in particular the following circumstances:

(a) the reliability or otherwise of the hardware and software;
(b) the accuracy or otherwise with which data was input; and
(c) the potential for misuse of the computer through the capacity to hack, corrupt and alter information.

IMPEACHING THE CREDIBILITY OF ABSENT WITNESSES

The general purpose of s. 5(2) of the Civil Evidence Act 1995 is to ensure that where the maker of 'the original statement' (see further at 51.13), or the maker of any statement relied upon to prove 'the original statement', is not called as a witness, evidence relating to his or her credibility is as admissible as it would have been if he or she had been called as a witness. Section 5(2) provides as follows: **51.14**

> (2) Where in civil proceedings hearsay evidence is adduced and the maker of the original statement, or of any statement relied upon to prove another statement, is not called as a witness—
> (a) evidence which if he had been so called would be admissible for the purpose of attacking his credibility as a witness is admissible for that purpose in the proceedings; and
> (b) evidence tending to prove that, whether before or after he made the statement, he made any other statement inconsistent with it is admissible for the purpose of showing that he had contradicted himself.
>
> Provided that evidence may not be given of any matter of which, if he had been called as a witness and had denied that matter in cross-examination, evidence could not have been adduced by the cross-examining party.

The meaning of the phrase 'the maker . . . of any statement relied upon to prove another statement' is unclear. It is submitted that the words 'another statement' should not be taken to mean a statement other than the original statement, but should be given a purposive construction so as to cover the statement of someone who has heard the original statement or recorded it in a document and, in the case of multiple hearsay, the statements of any intermediaries through whom the information contained in 'the original statement' was supplied. For example, if A makes an oral statement to B ('the original statement'), B tells C what A said, and C makes a written record of her conversation with B (by which means A's statement is to be proved), and if A, B and C are all unavailable to give evidence, it is submitted that for the purposes of s. 5(2), evidence relating to the credibility of A, B or C should be admissible.

The purpose of the proviso to s. 5(2) is to ensure that the rule on finality of answers to questions on collateral issues (see 47.63) operates to restrict the evidence admissible under the subsection against the maker of the statement who is not called as a witness in the same way as it applies in relation to a person who is called as a witness. Evidence admissible for the purpose of attacking credibility under s. 5(2)(a) therefore includes the types of evidence admissible under exceptions to the rule on finality, namely evidence of bias, evidence of previous convictions, and evidence of mental or physical disability affecting reliability (see 47.65 to 47.67). As to s. 5(2)(b), it seems that whereas a previous inconsistent statement of a person called as a witness is admissible not only to impugn his or her credibility but also as evidence of any matter stated (see s. 6(3) and (5) at 47.64), a previous inconsistent statement of a maker of a statement not called as a witness and admissible under s. 5(2)(b) is admissible 'for the purpose of showing that he had contradicted himself', i.e., only for the purpose of impugning credibility.

By **CPR, r. 33.5**, a party who, in reliance on s. 5(2), wishes to call evidence to attack the credibility of 'the maker of the original statement', must give notice of intention to do so, to the party who proposes to give the hearsay statement in evidence, not more than 14 days after being served with the notice of intention to rely on the hearsay evidence. Somewhat curiously, there is no equivalent notice requirement where a party intends to attack the credibility of 'the maker . . . of any statement relied upon to prove another statement'.

PROOF OF STATEMENTS CONTAINED IN DOCUMENTS

51.15 Documents certified as forming part of the records of a business or public authority are capable of being received in evidence without further proof (see **51.16**). Notarial acts and instruments may also be received in evidence without further proof (see **51.18**).The proof of statements contained in other documents is governed by s. 8 of the Civil Evidence Act 1995, which provides as follows:

(1) Where a statement contained in a document is admissible as evidence in civil proceedings, it may be proved—
  (a) by the production of that document, or
  (b) whether or not that document is still in existence, by the production of a copy of that document or of the material part of it,

authenticated in such manner as the court may approve.

(2) It is immaterial for this purpose how many removes there are between a copy and the original.

A 'document', for the purposes of s. 8, means 'anything in which information of any description is recorded' (s. 13), a definition wide enough to embrace maps, plans, graphs, drawings, discs, CD-ROMs, computer-generated printouts, audiotapes, videotapes, negatives, photographs, films and microfilms. A 'copy', in relation to a document, means 'anything onto which information recorded in the document has been copied, by whatever means and whether directly or indirectly' (s. 13), a definition sufficiently wide to include transcripts of audiotapes. It is submitted that the requirement of 'authentication' at the end of s. 8(1) relates not to proof of the original of a document, but calls for authentication that a copy of a document is a true copy of the original (see *Ventouris v Mountain (No. 2)* [1992] 1 WLR 887, a decision under the Civil Evidence Act 1968). It is further submitted that, as under s. 6(1) of the 1968 Act, 'production' for the purposes of s. 8 of the 1995 Act refers not to counsel handing the document to the court, but to a witness who is qualified to do so in accordance with the rules producing the document and saying what it is (see per Staughton LJ in *Ventouris v Mountain (No. 2)* at p. 901). However, it seems that a statement contained in a document may also be proved by another hearsay statement. Thus, where it is sought to admit a statement which has been deliberately tape-recorded, but whose maker is unavailable to produce the tape and give direct evidence that it is the tape that he or she made, the tape may be proved by his or her out-of-court statements to the same effect (*Ventouris v Mountain (No. 2)*).

DOCUMENTS FORMING PART OF THE RECORDS OF A BUSINESS OR PUBLIC AUTHORITY

Entries in the records of a business or public authority

Record keeping within many organisations has largely been taken over by technology and there is often no one witness who can give direct evidence of all aspects of the way in which the records were compiled. For reasons of this kind, provision has been made for documents certified as forming parts of the records of a business or public authority to be received in evidence without further proof (see Law Com. No. 216, paras 3.12 and 4.39). Section 9 of the Civil Evidence Act 1995 provides as follows: **51.16**

(1) A document which is shown to form part of the records of a business or public authority may be received in evidence in civil proceedings without further proof.

(2) A document shall be taken to form part of the records of a business or public authority if there is produced to the court a certificate to that effect signed by an officer of the business or authority to which the records belong.
For this purpose—
(a) a document purporting to be a certificate signed by an officer of a business or public authority shall be deemed to have been duly given by such an officer and signed by him; and
(b) a certificate shall be treated as signed by a person if it purports to bear a facsimile of his signature.

'Records' means 'records in whatever form' (s. 9(4)), a definition which gives the courts scope to abandon the narrow definition of the word under the Civil Evidence Act 1968, for the purposes of which it was taken to mean 'records which a historian would regard as original or primary sources, that is documents which either give effect to a transaction itself or which contain a contemporaneous register of information supplied by those with direct knowledge of the facts' (see *H v Schering Chemicals Ltd* [1983] 1 WLR 143). Section 9(4) provides that '"business" includes any activity regularly carried on over a period of time, whether for profit or not, by any body (whether corporate or not) or by an individual', and '"public authority" includes any public or statutory undertaking, any government department and any person holding office under Her Majesty'. Not all businesses, as defined, will have 'officers' in the strict sense of that word, and so in s. 9(4) 'officer' is defined to include 'any person occupying a responsible position in relation to the relevant activities of the business or public authority or in relation to its records'.

Although business and other records can often be regarded as likely to be reliable, there are bound to be exceptions, and for this reason the court has been given the discretionary power to disapply the certification provisions in s. 9. Section 9(5) provides that:

(5) The court may, having regard to the circumstances of the case, direct that all or any of the above provisions of this section do not apply in relation to a particular document or record, or description of documents or records.

Unless the court orders otherwise, a document which may be received in evidence under s. 9 shall not be receivable at trial unless the party intending to put it in evidence has given notice to the other parties (**CPR, r. 33.6(2)** and **(3)**). A party intending to use a s. 9 document as evidence of any fact must give notice not later than the latest date for serving witness statements (**r. 33.6(4)**), unless the evidence forms part of expert evidence, in which case notice must be given when the expert's report is served on the other party (**r. 33.6(6)**). A party who has given notice of intention to put in evidence under s. 9 must give every other party an opportunity to inspect it and to agree to its admission without further proof (**r. 33.6(8)**).

Absence of an entry in the records of a business or public authority

At common law it seems that the non-existence of a fact can be inferred, without offending the hearsay rule, by evidence of the absence of a recording of that fact in a record which, **51.17** having regard to its compilation and custody, one would have expected that fact, had it existed, to have been recorded. Thus, it has been said that in order to prove that A is an illegal immigrant, an officer responsible for the compilation and custody of Home Office records of persons entitled to a certificate of registration in the UK, in which A's name does not appear, may give evidence that the method of compilation and custody of the records is such that if A's name is not there, he or she must be an illegal immigrant (per Bristow J in *R v Patel* [1981] 3 All ER 94 at p. 96, applied in *R v Shone* (1983) 76 Cr App R 72). Section 9(3) of the Civil Evidence Act 1995 facilitates the proof of the absence of an entry in the records of a business or public authority. It provides as follows:

> (3) The absence of an entry in the records of a business or public authority may be proved in civil proceedings by affidavit of an officer of the business or authority to which the records belong.

In cases in which the court has any reason to suspect that the records are unlikely to be reliable, then it may direct that s. 9(3) does not apply by exercising its discretionary power under s. 9(5) (see **51.16**), in which case the absence of the entry will need to be proved either by calling the officer of the business or authority to give direct evidence or, if he or she cannot be called, by relying on a hearsay statement to the same effect.

NOTARIAL ACTS AND INSTRUMENTS

51.18 Notarial acts and instruments are bills of exchange which a notary has 'noted' or protested and documents which a notary has authenticated in private or public form (see *Halsbury's Laws of England*, 4th edn, reissue, vol. 33, paras 728 and 732). At common law, it was necessary to call the notary or his clerk to prove authentication etc. (*Sutton v Gregory* (1797) Peake Add Cas 150). However, **CPR, r. 32.20**, provides as follows:

> A notarial act or instrument may be received in evidence without further proof as duly authenticated in accordance with the requirements of law unless the contrary is proved.

HEARSAY FORMERLY ADMISSIBLE AT COMMON LAW

General

51.19 Section 9 of the Civil Evidence Act 1968 preserved and gave statutory force to a number of common law exceptions to the rule against hearsay, without purporting to amend the law relating to those exceptions. The exceptions included informal admissions, works of reference, and public documents and records. The Civil Evidence Act 1995 perpetuates this state of affairs, except in the case of informal admissions, which are therefore now subject to the general provisions of the 1995 Act, including those relating to notice and weight. The other common law exceptions have been preserved for three reasons:

(a) statutory provisions such as the Evidence (Foreign, Dominion and Colonial Documents) Act 1933, s. 1, and the Oaths and Evidence (Overseas Authorities and Countries) Act 1963, s. 5, which are unaffected by the 1995 Act, presuppose the existence of the common law exceptions relating to public records;
(b) the procedural burden of the notice procedure should not be introduced where it has not been borne before; and
(c) the weight to be given to evidence admissible under the exceptions is rarely a matter for debate (see Law Com. No. 216, para. 4.33).

Informal admissions

51.20 Section 7(1) of the Civil Evidence Act 1995 provides that 'the common law rule effectively preserved by section 9(1) and (2)(a) of the Civil Evidence Act 1968 (admissibility of admissions adverse to a party) is superseded by the provisions of this Act'. 'Admissions adverse to a party' means informal admissions, i.e., statements by a party to the proceedings, or someone in privity with him or her, made other than while testifying in those proceedings, and adverse to his or her case. By virtue of s. 7(1), therefore, an informal admission shall not be excluded on the ground that it is hearsay (see s. 1(1) at **51.2**), but will be subject to the general provisions of the Act, including those relating to notice (s. 2) and weight (s. 4). The weight to be attached to an informal admission depends upon a variety of special considerations additional to those set out in s. 4 itself (see **51.13**). For example, regard should always be had to the whole statement, including any passages favourable to its maker which qualify, explain or even nullify those parts of the statement relied upon as an admission, because the favourable parts of the statement are as much evidence of the facts they state as the parts relied upon as constituting an admission. Equally, regard should be had to any contradictory evidence adduced by the maker of the statement at the trial. Regard should also be had to the circumstances in which the admission was made, including, for example, whether it was made as a result of some inducement or threat. There are two other important considerations: whether the admission contains facts of which its maker had personal knowledge, and whether the admission was vicarious, i.e., made by someone in privity with the party to the legal proceedings.

Personal knowledge There is no requirement under the 1995 Act that the hearsay statement tendered, in order to be admissible, must have been made by someone with personal knowledge of the matters stated. However, the weight to be attached to a statement containing facts of which its maker has no personal knowledge will vary according to the circumstances. For example, an admission made by a party as to his or her age is obviously not based on personal knowledge, but it concerns a matter as to which it is reasonable to suppose that he or she has been accurately informed (see *R v Turner* [1910] KB 346 and *Lustre Hosiery Ltd v York* (1936) 54 CLR 134 (High Court of Australia)). However, an admission made as to the countries of origin of certain imported goods made solely in reliance on the fact that the goods bear marks and labels indicating that they came from those countries, is likely to be evidentially worthless (see per Lord Hodson in *Comptroller of Customs v Western Lectric Co. Ltd* [1966] AC 367 at p. 371). **51.21**

Vicarious admissions Prior to the 1995 Act, an informal admission could only be received in evidence if it had been made by a party to the proceedings personally, or vicariously, i.e., by someone in privity with him. Under the 1995 Act, an out-of-court statement adverse to the case of a party may be admitted whether made by that party or by any other person. However, the weight to be attached to an admission made by someone who, at common law, would have been in privity with a party, is likely to be greater than an adverse statement made by someone else. Those in privity included the following: **51.22**

(a) a predecessor in title of a party to proceedings, provided that the admission concerned title to the property and was made at a time when he or she had an interest in it (*Woolway v Rowe* (1834) 1 Ad & El 114);
(b) a partner, provided that the admission concerned the partnership affairs and was made in the ordinary course of its business (see the Partnership Act 1890, s. 15);
(c) a referee (*Williams v Innes* (1808) 1 Camp 364); and
(d) agents, provided that:
    (i) the admission was made at a time when the agency existed (*Edwards v Brookes (Milk) Ltd [1963] 1 WLR 795*);
    (ii) the communication in which it was made was authorised, expressly or by implication, by the principal (*Wagstaff v Wilson* (1832) 4 B & Ad 339; *G (A) v G (T)* [1970] 2 QB 643); and
    (iii) the admission was made in the course of a communication with some third party, as opposed to the principal (*Re Devala Provident Gold Mining Co.* (1883) 22 ChD 593).

At common law there was no privity between:

(a) spouses, merely by virtue of the marital relationship;
(b) parent and child, merely by virtue of that relationship (*G(A) v G(T)*);
(c) co-claimants or co-defendants; or
(d) a witness and the party calling him or her (*British Thomson-Houston Co. Ltd v British Insulated and Helsby Cables Ltd* [1924] 2 Ch 160).

Works of reference

51.23 It is provided in the Civil Evidence Act 1995, s. 7(2)(a), that:

> (2) The common law rules effectively preserved by section 9(1) and (2)(b) to (d) of the Civil Evidence Act 1968, that is, any rule of law whereby in civil proceedings—
> (a) published works dealing with matters of a public nature (for example, histories, scientific works, dictionaries and maps) are admissible as evidence of facts of a public nature stated in them . . .
>
> shall continue to have effect.

The effect of s. 7(2)(a) is to preserve the common law rule that authoritative published works of reference dealing with matters of a public nature are admissible to prove, or to assist the court in deciding whether to take judicial notice of, facts of a public nature stated therein. Examples include:

(a) historical works concerning public facts (*Read v Bishop of Lincoln* [1892] AC 644);
(b) standard medical texts concerning the nature of a disease (*McCarthy v The Melita (Owners)* (1923) 16 BWCC 222);
(c) engineers' reports, within the common knowledge of engineers, on the nature of soil (*East London Railway Co. v Thames Conservators* (1904) 90 LT 347);
(d) Carlisle Tables, on average life expectancy (*Rowley v London and North Western Railway Co.* (1873) LR 8 Ex 221);
(e) dictionaries, on the meaning of English words (*Marchioness of Blandford v Dowager Duchess of Marlborough* (1743) 2 Atk 542; *R v Agricultural Land Tribunal, ex parte Benney* [1955] 2 QB 140); and
(f) published maps and plans concerning facts of geographical notoriety (*R v Orton* (1873) and *R v Jameson (1896), Stephen's Digest of the Law of Evidence, 10th ed. at p. 48*).

Public documents and records

51.24 It is provided in the Civil Evidence Act 1995, s. 7(2)(b) and (c), that:

> (2) The common law rules effectively preserved by section 9(1) and (2)(b) to (d) of the Civil Evidence Act 1968, that is, any rule of law whereby in civil proceedings—
> . . .
> (b) public documents (for example, public registers, and returns made under public authority with respect to matters of public interest) are admissible as evidence of the facts stated in them, or
> (c) records (for example, the records of certain courts, treaties, Crown grants, pardons and commissions) are admissible as evidence of facts stated in them,
>
> shall continue to have effect.

51.25 Examples This common law exception to the hearsay rule applies to a wide variety of documents made under public authority in relation to matters of public concern, and may be justified on the grounds of reliability and convenience. Examples include:

(a) recitals in public Acts of Parliament (*R v Sutton* (1816) 4 M & S 532);
(b) entries relating to acts of State and public matters in parliamentary journals and governmental gazettes (*Attorney-General v Theakston* (1820) 8 Price 89);
(c) entries in parish registers (and foreign registers) of baptisms, marriages and burials (see per Lord Selborne in *Lyell v Kennedy* (1889) 14 App Cas 437 at pp. 448–9);
(d) entries in the public books of a corporation relating to matters of public interest (*Shrewsbury v Hart* (1823) 1 Car & P 113);

(e) the contents of a file from the Companies Register containing the statutory returns made by a company (*R v Halpin* [1975] QB 907);
(f) entries in university records relating to degrees conferred (*Collins v Carnegie* (1834) 1 Ad & El 695);
(g) records of assessment by commissioners of land tax (*Doe d Strode v Seaton* (1834) 2 Ad & El 171); and
(h) findings of professional misconduct by the General Medical Council (*Hill v Clifford* [1907] 2 Ch 236).

Conditions of admissibility The conditions of admissibility for statements in public documents vary to some extent according to the particular type of document in question. In general terms, however, a public document will only be admissible as evidence of the facts it contains if: 51.26

(a) it concerns a public matter;
(b) it was made by a public officer acting under a duty to inquire and record the results of his or her inquiry; and
(c) it was intended to be retained for public reference or inspection (see per Lord Blackburn in *Sturla v Freccia* (1880) 5 App Cas 623 at pp. 643–4).

As to the first of these conditions, 'public' must not be taken to mean the whole world: the matter in question may concern either the public at large or a section of the public (*Sturla v Freccia*; *Heath v Deane* [1905] 2 Ch 86). Under the second condition, the statement must have been made by a public officer, as opposed to a private individual, acting in discharge of a strict duty to inquire into, and satisfy himself or herself as to the truth of, the facts recorded (*Doe d France v Andrews* (1850) 15 QB 756; *White v Taylor* [1969] 1 Ch 150; *Wilton and Co. v Phillips* (1903) 19 TLR 390; *Brierly v Brierly* [1918] P 257; and cf. *Bird v Keep* [1918] 2 KB 692 at pp. 697–8 and 701 and *Re Stollery* [1926] Ch 284 at p. 322). In more recent times, however, it seems that strict compliance with the requirement of personal knowledge of the facts recorded is no longer required. Thus, where a duty is cast upon a company by statute to make accurate returns of company matters to the Registrar of Companies so that those returns can be filed and inspected by members of the public, all statements on the return are prima facie proof of the truth of their contents, notwithstanding that the relevant official at the Companies Register has no duty to inquire and satisfy himself or herself as to the truth of the recorded facts (*R v Halpin* [1975] QB 907).

The fact that the public official fails to record the matter in question promptly may affect the weight to be attached to the evidence, but does not affect its admissibility (*R v Halpin*, at p. 916). The position is the same where the record in question was made by an interested party (*Irish Society v Bishop of Derry* (1846) 12 Cl & F 641, in which the Bishop's statements relating to advowsons in his diocese were admitted notwithstanding that some of them belonged to him).

Declarations as to pedigree or the existence of a marriage

At common law a declaration as to pedigree was admissible, after its maker's death, as evidence of the truth of its contents (see, e.g., *Johnson v Lawson* (1824) 2 Bing 86 and the *Berkeley Peerage Case* (1811) 4 Camp 401). Matters of pedigree concern the relationship by blood or marriage between persons, including the fact and date of births, marriages and deaths, legitimacy, celibacy, failure of issue and intestacy. This exception to the hearsay rule would cover, for example, oral declarations by deceased parents that one of their children, whose legitimacy was in issue, was born before their marriage, and written declarations such as entries in family Bibles or pedigrees hung up in the family home. There was no requirement, on the part of the declarant, of personal knowledge of the facts stated, which might amount to nothing more than reputation or family tradition handed down from one generation to another. Declarations as to pedigree are now admissible pursuant to the Civil Evidence Act 1995, and s. 7(3) of that Act provides as follows: 51.27

(3) The common law rules effectively preserved by section 9(3) and (4) of the Civil Evidence Act 1968, that is, any rule whereby in civil proceedings—

...

(b) evidence of reputation or family tradition is admissible—

(i) for the purpose of proving or disproving pedigree or the existence of a marriage . . .

shall continue to have effect in so far as they authorise the court to treat such evidence as proving or disproving that matter.

Where any such rule applies, reputation or family tradition shall be treated for the purposes of this Act as a fact and not as a statement or multiplicity of statements about the matter in question.

Evidence of reputation or family tradition is usually made up of a multiplicity of hearsay statements, but if it were to be treated as such, strict application of the provisions of the 1995 Act relating to notice and weight would be impossible (see Law Com. No. 216, para. 4.34). For this reason, s. 7(3) requires such evidence to be treated as evidence of fact. The effect is that the party proposing to adduce such evidence, in complying with the notice requirement under s. 2 of the Act (see **51.8** and **51.9**), will not be expected to give to the other parties particulars of the person who had personal knowledge of the matters in question and of the intermediaries through whom the information was conveyed to him or her. A further effect is that the court, in assessing the weight of the evidence under s. 4 of the Act (see **51.13**), will not be expected to have regard to such matters as whether the person with personal knowledge of the matters stated made the 'original statement' contemporaneously with the occurrence or existence of the matters stated.

Declarations as to public and general rights

51.28 At common law, a declaration as to the reputed existence of a public or general right was admissible, after its maker's death, as evidence of the existence of the right in question. Public rights are those common to the public at large, such as rights to use paths (see *Radcliffe v Marsden Urban District Council* (1908) 72 JP 475) or landing places on the banks of a river (*Drinkwater v Porter* (1835) 7 Car & P 181). General rights are those common to a section of the public or a considerable class of persons, such as the inhabitants of a parish or the tenants of a manor (*Nicholas v Parker* (1805) 14 East 331n). Any person was competent to make a declaration as to the reputed existence of a public right, and the fact that the declarant had no knowledge of the subject went only to weight, not admissibility. A declaration as to general rights, however, was only admissible if it was made by a person with some connection with or knowledge of the matters in question (see *Rogers v Wood* (1931) 2 B & Ad 245 and *Crease v Barrett* (1835) 1 Cr M & R 919). Declarations as to public and general rights are now admissible pursuant to the Civil Evidence Act 1995, and s. 7(3) of that Act provides as follows:

(3) The common law rules effectively preserved by section 9(3) and (4) of the Civil Evidence Act 1968, that is, any rule whereby in civil proceedings—

...

(b) evidence of reputation or family tradition is admissible—

...

(ii) for the purpose of proving or disproving the existence of any public or general right or of identifying any person or thing,

shall continue to have effect in so far as they authorise the court to treat such evidence as proving or disproving that matter.

Where any such rule applies, reputation or family tradition shall be treated for the purposes of this Act as a fact and not as a statement or multiplicity of statements about the matter in question.

As to the rationale of the concluding part of s. 7(3), see **51.27**.

Chapter 52 Experts and Assessors

INTRODUCTION

Expert evidence was one of the factors attracting the greatest criticism under the old rules before the CPR. Notwithstanding that experts were not supposed to be partisan witnesses, it was perfectly clear that there was a perhaps not unnatural desire to please the party that was instructing (and paying the bill), and all too often cases became polarised into a battle between two experts — a battle in which the interests of the parties frequently took second place. **52.1**

The effect of the CPR has been to restrict what was formerly the parties' almost unhindered right to call their own experts to give evidence in court. **Rule 35.4(1)** provides that no party may call an expert, or put in evidence an expert's report, without the court's permission.

The duty of the expert, by **r. 35.3(1)**, is no longer to the instructing party, but to the court. This is an overriding duty, which, it is hoped, liberates an expert from what may previously have been perceived as a pressure to win the case for the instructing party. The fact that experts are frequently jointly instructed on behalf of both parties means it is comparatively rare to find an expert in civil litigation who is overtly biased towards one of the parties.

Sanctions for failing to serve an expert's report in time, and where an expert fails to answer written questions, are considered at **46.24** and **46.25**.

ADMISSIBILITY OF OPINION EVIDENCE

It is a general rule that opinion evidence is inadmissible. A witness may only attest to facts which are within his or her personal knowledge and is not permitted to draw inferences from those facts. By way of exception a witness may express an opinion on matters which can only realistically be conveyed in that way, such as when describing a person's age, or the speed of a **52.2** vehicle, or the state of the weather. An ancient exception to the general rule is that a properly qualified expert may state his or her opinion on matters calling for his or her particular area of expertise, if it is an expertise that the court does not possess (*Buckley v Thomas* (1554) Plowd 118 per Saunders J at p. 124; *Folkes v Chadd* (1782) 3 Doug KB 157).

In most cases it will be obvious whether or not expert evidence is admissible, but in disputed cases the inquiry has two stages (*Barings plc v Coopers and Lybrand* [2001] PNLR 22).

The first stage requires an examination of whether the evidence qualifies as admissible expert evidence within the Civil Evidence Act 1972, s. 3. At this stage the court must be satisfied by the party seeking to call the evidence that there is a body of expertise governed by recognised standards or rules of conduct capable of influencing the court's decision on any of the issues which it has to decide, and that the witness has sufficient familiarity with and knowledge of the area of expertise to be of value to the court (see also *Liverpool Roman Catholic Archdiocesan Trustees Inc. v Goldberg (No. 3)* [2001] 1 WLR 2337).

There is no requirement that the expertise must have been acquired in a professional capacity or in the course of the expert's business. An expert is a competent expert witness if the court considers that he or she has the necessary expertise, however it was obtained (*R v Silverlock* [1894] 2 QB 766). A person suitably qualified by his or her knowledge or experience is competent to give expert evidence on the law of a foreign jurisdiction, whether or not he or she has practised law in that jurisdiction (Civil Evidence Act 1972, s. 4(1)).

At the second stage the court must inquire whether the evidence should actually be admitted. This turns on the nature of the evidence sought to be given (*Liverpool Roman Catholic Archdiocesan Trustees Inc. v Goldberg (No. 3)*). Experts may not be called on matters which reasonably fall within the knowledge and experience of the tribunal of fact. Expert evidence is not usually admitted on questions of credibility of a witness, even where the witness under consideration is a child (*Re N (A Minor) (Sexual Abuse: Video Evidence)* [1997] 1 WLR 153, but contrast *Re M and R (Minors) (Sexual Abuse: Expert Evidence)* [1996] 4 All ER 239). Although an employment consultant may give expert evidence on the employment opportunities in an area, and the claimant's prospects of finding work, expert evidence is not admissible on a claimant's motivation for finding work (*Larby v Thurgood* [1993] ICR 66). An accident reconstruction expert is permitted to give scientific evidence based on physical evidence of the road layout, vehicle positions, skid marks and the positions of debris, gouge and paint marks, and from that evidence to deduce minimum speeds and movements of the vehicles. However, such an expert is not permitted to analyse the witness statements and to draw conclusions as to what the drivers did, whether they should have seen each other, or taken avoiding action, as these are matters on which the trial judge does not need expert assistance (*Liddell v Middleton* [1996] PIQR P36). Permission to adduce a report from a lawyer specialising in art law was refused in *Clarke v Marlborough Fine Art (London) Ltd* [2002] EWHC 11 (Ch), LTL 21/1/2002, because the report was unlikely to provide the court with material assistance on the issues (whether transactions were to the deceased's manifest disadvantage and whether the deceased had received independent legal advice). Experts may not be called on questions of English law, as this is within the expertise of the court (*Midland Bank Trust Co. Ltd v Hett, Stubbs and Kemp* [1979] Ch 384).

Independence

52.3 It is important that expert evidence should be, and should be seen to be, the independent product of the expert uninfluenced by the exigencies of the litigation (*Whitehouse v Jordan* [1981] 1 WLR 246 per Lord Wilberforce). A useful test for 'independence' is whether the expert would express the same opinion if given the same instructions by the opposite party (**PD 35, annex, para. 4.3**). In *Liverpool Roman Catholic Archdiocesan Trustees Inc. v Goldberg (No. 3)* [2001] 1 WLR 2337 it was said that a professional relationship between a litigant and an expert prevented the expert from having the necessary independence to be called as an expert witness. This case was doubted, as being inconsistent with *Field v Leeds City Council* [2000] 1 EGLR 54 (where an employee was allowed to give expert evidence on behalf of the Council, see **52.10**), in *Admiral Management Services Ltd v Para-Protect Europe Ltd* [2002] EWHC 233 (Ch), [2002] 1 WLR 2722 at [33], and is probably wrong. It was also disapproved in *R (Factortame Ltd) v Secretary of State for Transport, Local Government and the Regions (No. 8)* [2002] EWCA Civ 932, [2003] QB 381, where Lord Phillips of Worth Matravers MR said at [70] the *Liverpool Roman Catholic Archdiocesan Trustees Inc.* case applied the wrong test (the test for apparent bias in a tribunal). In *DN v Greenwich London Borough Council* [2004] EWCA Civ 1659, [2005] LGR 597, an educational psychologist was held to be entitled to give expert evidence on his own behalf on why in his opinion his conduct did not fall below the relevant standard of care.

Where an expert has an interest in the proceedings, this should be disclosed to the court as soon as possible. Whether the expert's evidence should be allowed should be determined during the course of case management. In considering that question the judge will have to weigh the alternative choices available if the expert's evidence is excluded, having regard to the overriding objective (*R (Factortame Ltd) v Secretary of State for Transport, Local Government and the Regions (No 8)#* at [70]).

DUTIES OF EXPERTS AND THE COURT'S POWER TO RESTRICT EXPERT EVIDENCE

Rule 35.1 of the CPR provides that expert evidence shall be restricted to that which is reasonably required to resolve the proceedings. In order to achieve impartiality of experts, **r. 35.3** provides that: **52.4**

(a) it is the duty of an expert to help the court on the matters within his or her expertise; and
(b) this duty overrides any obligation to the person from whom the expert has received instructions or by whom the expert is paid.

Practitioners should advise their clients of the expert's overriding duty to the court, so that the client understands that the expert will consider the matter objectively and not with a view to advancing the interests of the client.

Whether or not expert evidence is necessary to resolve the issues in a case is a decision for the court as set out in **r. 35.4(1)**, which provides that 'No party may call an expert or put in evidence an expert's report without the court's permission'. Practitioners should apply in good time for permission to call an expert or such permission will not be granted. In *Calenti v North Middlesex NHS Trust* (2001) LTL 10/4/2001, the defendant was refused permission to call a medical expert two weeks prior to trial because to do so would work a significant injustice on the claimant. A party applying for permission either to call an expert or to put in evidence an expert's report must identify (**r. 35.4(2)**):

(a) the field in which it is sought to rely on expert evidence; and
(b) where practicable, the expert in that field whose evidence the party wishes to call.

If permission is granted under **r. 35.4**, it will be in relation only to the expert named or the field identified (**r. 35.4(3)**).

The court has power to limit the amount of an expert's fees and expenses that the party who wishes to rely on the expert may recover from any other party (**r. 35.4(4)**). The court may also exercise its discretion to terminate the expert's appointment in appropriate circumstances (*Kranidiotes v Paschali* (2001) EWCA 357, LTL 8/5/2001). This power is in addition to the court's general powers to restrict experts' fees on a subsequent detailed assessment of costs under **Part 44**. An expert who has caused significant expense to be incurred through flagrant, reckless disregard of his duties to the court may be ordered to pay those costs (*Phillips v Symes (No. 2)* [2004] EWHC 2330 (Ch), [2005] 1 WLR 2043). Where an expert adopts a biased or irrational approach, it may be appropriate for the judge to refer the witness's conduct to the relevant professional body, after giving the witness a suitable period of time to make representations (*Pearce v Ove Arup Partnership Ltd* (2001) LTL 8/11/2001).

In the absence of a duty of confidence, it is contrary to public policy for an expert to agree not to act for another party (*Lilly Icos LLC v Pfizer Ltd* (2000) LTL 26/1/2001).

DIRECTIONS ABOUT EXPERTS

52.5 The court may give directions about expert evidence under **CPR, Part 35** (expert evidence), or under **PD 28** (fast track) or **PD 29** (multi-track). Experts are comparatively rare on the small claims track, see **43.18**. No expert may give evidence, whether written or oral, at a hearing without the permission of the court (**CPR, r. 35.4(1)**). Where directions require an act to be done by an expert, or otherwise affect an expert, the party instructing the expert must serve a copy of the order on the expert (**PD 35, para. 6A**).

The first stage at which the court may give directions in relation to experts is at the allocation stage. By this time the parties to proceedings will have completed their allocation questionnaires in **form N149** or **N150**. Question D asks whether the party completing the form wishes to use expert evidence at the hearing and whether any expert reports have yet been copied to the other parties. The party completing the form is required to list the experts whose evidence it may wish to use and their fields of expertise. A party must also indicate whether it will use the same expert as the other parties: reasons must be given if the answer is no. Reasons must also be given for wanting one's expert to give evidence orally at the hearing or trial. These answers will assist the court in deciding on track allocation as well as the form of directions to be made on allocation.

Although the court has power to limit the expert evidence the parties may call at trial, it does not have power to limit the experts a party can instruct. The court cannot impose a condition that a party must obtain the court's permission before instructing an expert (*Vasiliou v Hajigeorgiou* [2005] EWCA Civ 236, [2005] 1 WLR 2195).

Directions on the fast track

52.6 Where a case has been allocated to the fast track, **PD 28, para. 3.2**, provides:

> The court will seek to tailor its directions to the needs of the case and the steps of which it is aware that the parties have already taken to prepare the case. In particular it will have regard to the extent to which any pre-action protocol has or (as the case may be) has not been complied with.

It is also possible for the parties to agree the directions sought and if this is the case, the proposed directions should where necessary contain a provision regarding the use of a single joint expert, or in cases where the use of a single expert has not been agreed, the exchange and agreement of expert reports (including whether exchange is to be simultaneous or sequential) and without-prejudice discussions of the experts (**PD 28, para. 3.7**). It is possible that the court will not approve the directions submitted by the parties and will instead substitute its own directions, having regard to the parties' suggested directions (**PD 28, para. 3.8**). Alternatively, the court may hold an allocation hearing at which directions will be given.

Where the court gives directions of its own initiative, and is not aware of any steps taken by the parties other than the service of statements of case, its general approach in relation to experts will be to give directions for a single joint expert unless there is good reason not to do so (**PD 28, para. 3.9(4)**). Indeed in *Baron v Lovell* [1999] CPLR 630, it was held that a judge was entitled at a pre-trial review to direct that the medical evidence needed to determine the issues relating to the claimant's personal injury action could be provided by the claimant's medical expert only.

According to **PD 28, para. 3.9(5)**, where a direction for a single joint expert is not given, the court's general approach will be:

(a) to direct disclosure of experts' reports by way of simultaneous exchange; and
(b) if experts' reports are not agreed, to direct a discussion between the experts for the purpose set out in **CPR, r. 35.12(1)** (identification of and agreement of the issues in the case) and the preparation of a report under **r. 35.12(3)** (see **52.22**).

Where expert reports are to be exchanged, generally this should be done within 14 weeks of the directions order (**PD 28, para. 3.12**).

The court will not direct an expert to attend a hearing of a fast track claim, unless it is necessary to do so in the interests of justice (**CPR, r. 35.5(2)**).

Directions on the multi-track

Paragraphs 4.2, 4.6, 4.7, 4.9 and 4.10 of PD 29 make virtually the same provisions about directions on the multi-track concerning experts as the paragraphs of **PD 28** considered in 52.7 do for the fast track. There is a greater willingness to allow the parties to instruct their own experts (*S (A Minor) v Birmingham Health Authority* (1999) LTL 23/11/99) and, as these claims are usually more complex than fast track claims, the time for exchanging experts' reports is likely to be longer than for fast track claims. There is also a greater willingness to allow experts to give oral evidence at trial in multi-track cases. The spirit and effect of the rules mean that even in multi-track claims great care will be taken before making expert directions. For example, in claims relating to the alleged infringement of registered designs, expert evidence may not be useful (see *Oren v Red Box Toy Factory Ltd* [1999] FSR 785) and may well not be allowed (see *Thermos Ltd v Aladdin Sales and Marketing Ltd* (1999) *The Independent*, 13 December 1999). In *Mann v Chetty and Patel* (2000) LTL 26/10/2000 the Court of Appeal agreed that the judge had been right in a multi-track claim to refuse permission to call various experts, because the evidence would have been of minimal value, would not have been conclusive on the issues, and would have been disproportionate. In *Rawlinson v Cooper* [2002] EWCA Civ 392, LTL 11/3/2002, it was held that both an original report from a medical expert and a second report from the same witness, which included references to published papers on life expectancy and their application to the claimant's case, should be admitted in evidence. **52.7**

Directions for the exchange of scholarly information

In *Wardlaw v Farrar* [2003] EWCA Civ 1719, [2003] 4 All ER 1358, it was pointed out that there is a standard direction dealing with disclosure of scholarly information used by medical experts for use in clinical disputes, based on the direction used by Masters Ungley and Yoxall, which should be followed in all courts dealing with medical negligence claims. The direction, which is set out below, can also be used in other categories of claim. **52.8**

> Any unpublished literature upon which any expert witness proposes to rely shall be served at the same time as service of his [report] together with a list of published literature and copies of any unpublished material. Any supplementary literature upon which any expert witness proposes to rely shall be notified to all other parties at least one month before trial. No expert witness shall rely upon any publications that have not been disclosed in accordance with this direction without [permission] of the trial judge on such terms as to costs as he deems fit.

Reports and privilege

Until an expert's report is disclosed to the other side, instructions to the expert and the expert's report will be protected by legal professional privilege (see **48.47**). While privilege applies, the court will not make an order compelling disclosure, as that would run counter to the privilege (*Worrall v Reich* [1955] 1 QB 296). By disclosing a report, whether voluntarily or pursuant to directions, a party waives privilege (**48.59**). Disclosing the final version of an expert's report does not waive privilege in earlier drafts of the report (*Jackson v Marley Davenport* **52.9**

Ltd [2004] EWCA Civ 1225, [2004] 1 WLR 2926). For privilege in respect of jointly instructed and jointly selected experts, see **52.11**.

The status of instructions to experts once a report is disclosed is considered at **52.21**.

JOINT AND SEPARATE EXPERTS

Single joint expert

52.10 Under **CPR, r. 35. 7**, where two or more parties wish to submit expert evidence on a particular issue, the court has power to direct that evidence is to be given by a single joint expert only. The parties for whom that person is a joint expert are called the 'instructing parties'. It may be that the instructing parties cannot agree on who that expert should be, in which case the court may:

(a) select the expert from a list prepared or identified by the instructing parties, or
(b) direct that the expert be selected in such other manner as the court may direct.

The court may give directions about the payment of a single joint expert's fees and expenses and about any inspection, examination or experiments which the expert may wish to carry out (**r. 35.8(3)**). Before a single joint expert is instructed the court may limit the amount that can be paid by way of fees and expenses to the expert and direct that the instructing parties pay that amount into court (**r. 35.8(4)**). In any event, where a single joint expert is instructed, the instructing parties are jointly and severally liable for the payment of the expert's fees and expenses, unless the court directs otherwise (**r. 35.8(5); PD 35, annex, para. 17.8**). In this way, the parties will know in advance what their financial commitment is in the way of experts' fees.

The reasons for directing that a report be obtained from a single joint expert are that it saves time and costs and is usually proportionate to the issues in the case. It may be the case that in order to fulfil these objectives, it is simpler to use an employee of one of the parties, who is expert in the relevant discipline. Given that **r. 35.3** provides that the expert has an overriding duty to the court rather than to the parties, an employee of a party involved in litigation can be an independent expert (*Field v Leeds City Council* [2000] 1 EGLR 54). A party proposing to use its employee's expert evidence should be given an opportunity to demonstrate that the employee has relevant experience and is aware of the primary duty to the court when giving expert evidence. It may help to demonstrate objectivity if training has been given to the employee on the special position of expert witnesses (*Field v Leeds City Council*).

A number of disciplines may be relevant to an issue in a claim. If this is so, an expert in the dominant discipline should be identified as the single joint expert who will prepare the general part of the report and be responsible for annexing or incorporating the contents of any reports from experts in other disciplines (**PD 35, para. 6**). This is more likely to happen in a multi-track case and should be dealt with at a case management conference, where the judge would be informed that several expert disciplines are relevant to a particular issue.

Joint selection of expert

52.11 Joint selection is to be contrasted with joint instruction of experts. A jointly instructed expert receives instructions from both sides, who both contribute to the expert's fees, and both are entitled to the expert's report. A jointly selected expert is one who is chosen (usually by one side providing a list of proposed experts, and the other side deciding whether to object to any of those named) by both sides, but who is instructed by one side only. That party is entirely responsible for the expert's fees, and is entitled to assert legal professional privilege over the report (*Carlson v Townsend* [2001] EWCA Civ 511, [2001] 1 WLR 2415). Pre-action protocols often recommend joint selection of experts. Court directions tend to provide for joint instruction.

Joint expert or own experts

Whether a direction should be given for the instruction of a single joint expert depends on the nature of the issue being considered. In substantial claims where the central issues can only be resolved by expert evidence it is likely to be wrong for the court to insist on a single joint expert. This is particularly so if there is more than one school of thought on the central issues (*Oxley v Penwarden* [2001] CPLR 1). In clinical disputes, it was suggested in *Peet v Mid-Kent Healthcare Trust* [2001] EWCA Civ 1703, [2002] 1 WLR 210, that the balance between proportionality and expense could be achieved by allowing the parties to call their own experts on the medical issues, but to direct the instruction of a joint expert on the non-medical issues. This is so even where the sums at stake are substantial. **52.12**

Challenging joint report

Where a single joint expert has been agreed by the parties and the court has directed that expert to report, a party who is unhappy with that expert's conclusions will not be permitted to call further expert evidence by way of their own expert unless it would be unjust pursuant to the overriding objective not to allow that evidence (*Daniels v Walker* [2000] 1 WLR 1382). A preliminary requirement if further expert evidence is to be allowed is whether there is any rational criticism of the joint expert's report. A significant discrepancy between the valuation evidence of a single joint expert and a second expert instructed by one of the parties may be a sufficient basis for allowing the second expert's evidence (*Marston v Lewis* [2004] EWHC 2833 (Ch), LTL 4/11/2004). There are cases where a pivotal issue depends on expert evidence and the jointly instructed expert's view is not easily capable of challenge in the absence of other expert opinion. If so, justice may require permission to be granted to seek a second opinion (*W v Oldham Metropolitan Borough Council* [2005] EWCA Civ 1247, *The Times*, 7 November 2005, a family law case). **52.13**

Factors bearing on the exercise of the discretion to allow additional expert evidence after a jointly instructed expert has reported include the reasons for seeking another report, the nature of the case and the amount at stake, the effect of allowing another expert to report and its impact on delay and the trial (*Cosgrove v Pattison* [2001] CPLR 177). See also **52.29** for cross-examination of a joint expert.

If there is no basis for rational criticism of a joint expert's report, and if the joint report totally undermines one side's case, the court may enter summary judgment. Thus, in *Smith v Peter North and Partners* [2001] EWCA Civ 1553, [2002] PNLR 12, a joint expert reported in a claim for damages against a surveyor that the value of the property was the same with and without the defects. Summary judgment was entered for the defendant because there was no prospect of the claimant persuading the court that the cost of repairs was the correct measure of damages. Contrast *Layland v Fairview New Homes plc* [2002] EWHC 1350 (Ch), LTL 10/7/2002, in which, after considering various criticisms of a single jointly instructed valuation expert's report (which concluded the claimants had suffered no loss), Neuberger J allowed the claim to go to trial as there was material which could fruitfully be exploited in cross-examination.

Experts instructed only to advise

Parties on occasion instruct an expert with no present intention of using the expert's opinions in court proceedings. This may arise: **52.14**

(a) in complex claims where a party to a dispute needs expert assistance as part of the investigative process; and
(b) where a litigant wants another expert to comment on a single joint expert's report.

In these circumstances, and while the report in question is not intended for use in the proceedings, neither **CPR, Part 35**, nor the Experts Protocol in **PD 35, annex** applies (**PD 35, annex, paras 5.1** and **5.2**). The expert's fees are unlikely to be recoverable as costs in the proceedings (**para. 17.5**). An expert who has advised in this way should only be proposed as a single joint expert if the other parties are given all relevant information about the previous involvement (**para. 17.4**).

Retaining an expert before directions are given

52.15 Retaining an expert without trying to agree a single joint expert with one's opponent carries the risk that the costs of the expert will not be allowed. Where it is necessary to instruct an expert before commencement of proceedings, the pre-action protocols encourage the joint selection of, and access to, experts (**Pre-action Protocol for Personal Injury Claims, para. 2.14**). If no specific protocol applies, the parties should, if possible, engage an agreed expert (**PD Protocols, para. 4.9**).

Retaining one's own expert may lead to the following consequences:

(a) The court may not grant permission for the expert's report to be used, so that the party who wishes to rely on the report may not recover the costs of instructing the expert.
(b) The court may order that a different, jointly instructed expert be used, so that the costs of the first expert are wasted.
(c) The court may allow the report to be used, but disallow the costs, and allow the opponent to instruct and call its own expert.
(d) An attempt to persuade one's opponent to use one's expert's report as the only report in the case may involve disclosing it earlier than might have been ordered by the court and the opponent may still not agree to its use.

There are, however, circumstances in which it is important to obtain an expert's report for the claimant, for example:

(a) In many cases, it may not be until an expert's report has been obtained that a claimant can be sure of having a case at all.
(b) There may be such lengthy waiting lists to get a report from the chosen expert that the claimant needs to initiate these procedures as soon as solicitors are instructed.
(c) In straightforward cases and given that the letter of instructions will be disclosed, if the expert who is instructed is well-known and accepted as reputable by the opponent, time may be saved and the report may be accepted, perhaps subject to further questions being put by the opponent under **CPR, r. 35.6**.

It is nonetheless clear that the preferred approach is to communicate with one's opponent in an effort to agree on a mutually acceptable expert (*Carlson v Townsend* [2001] EWCA Civ 511, [2001] 1 WLR 2415).

INSTRUCTING EXPERTS

Appointment of experts

52.16 Before an expert is formally instructed, or the court's permission is sought, solicitors should establish (see **PD 35, annex, para. 7.1**):

(a) that the expert is suitably qualified;
(b) that the expert is familiar with his or her duties as an expert in court proceedings;
(c) that the expert can provide a report and answer written questions within a suitable time frame;
(d) whether the expert will be available for the trial;
(e) that there is no potential conflict of interest.

Terms of appointment should be agreed at the outset (**para. 7.2**). These should include the services required from the expert, time for delivery of the report, the basis of the expert's charges including cancellation fees and fees for attending court, and arrangements for answering written questions. Agreement to delay payment of fees until the end of the case is permissible, but fees contingent on the nature of the expert's advice, or dependent on the outcome of the case, are not (**paras** 7.6 and 7.7).

Instructions

Solicitors must give clear instructions to retained experts (**PD 35, annex, para.** 8.1). These should include: **52.17**

(a) basic information, such as names, addresses, dates of birth, telephone numbers and dates of incidents;
(b) the nature and extent of the expertise called for;
(c) the purpose of the report, a description of what needs to be investigated and of the issues in the case;
(d) copies of the statements of case, witness statements and disclosed documents relevant to the report;
(e) where proceedings have not been commenced, whether that is the intention, and whether the expert is asked only for advice;
(f) an outline programme for all stages of the expert's work, consistent with good case management;
(g) where proceedings have started, the dates of any hearings and details of matters such as the case management track for the case, together with copies of relevant court directions and orders.

The expert should confirm, without delay, whether he or she accepts the instructions, and should inform the instructing party without delay of any problems or insufficiency in the instructions (**para.** 9.1). Once instructions are accepted, the expert must not withdraw without first discussing the reasons with those who gave the instructions (**para.** 10.1), and should consider whether it might be more appropriate to seek directions under **CPR, r.** 35.14.

Instructions to a single joint expert

Where a direction has been given by the court, in accordance with **CPR, r.** 35.7, for a single joint expert to be used, the parties should try to agree joint instructions, and should try to agree what documents should be included with the instructions (**PD 35, annex, para.** 17.6). In the event of disagreement, they should try to agree where the areas of disagreement lie and their instructions should make this clear (**para.** 17.7). Where they cannot agree, each instructing party may give instructions to the expert (**CPR, r.** 35.8(1)), but must send a copy, at the same time, to the other instructing parties (**r.** 35.8(2)). There is no rule, and in fact it is contrary to the express terms of **r.** 35.8(1), that a party should be bound to the instructions to a single joint expert proposed by the other side. The court should not order one side to sign instructions they object to (*Yorke v Katra* [2003] EWCA Civ 867, LTL 9/6/2003). **52.18**

It may be the case that one or other of the parties has access to information which is not reasonably available to another party and which may assist the expert in preparing his or her report. In these circumstances, the court may direct the party who has such access to prepare and file a document recording the information and to serve a copy of that document on the other party (**r.** 35.9). The document must include sufficient details of all the facts, tests, experiments and assumptions which underlie any part of the information to enable the party on whom it is served to make, or to obtain, a proper interpretation of the information and an assessment of its significance (**PD 35, para.** 3).

Single joint experts owe an equal duty to all parties, and must maintain independence, impartiality and transparency at all times (**PD 35, annex, para.** 17.11). They should keep all instructing parties informed of material steps they may take by copying correspondence to all parties (**para.** 17.10). A party will not be permitted to invite a jointly instructed expert to a conference without the written consent of the other parties or where the court has directed the meeting should take place (*Peet v Mid-Kent Healthcare Trust* [2001] EWCA Civ 1703, [2002] 1 WLR 210).

WRITTEN REPORTS

Oral or written evidence at trial

52.19 Expert evidence is to be given in a written report, unless the court directs otherwise (**CPR, r. 35.5(1)**). If a claim is on the fast track, the court will not direct an expert to attend a hearing, unless it is necessary to do so in the interests of justice (**r. 35.5(2)**).

However, in the Commercial and Admiralty Courts a sole expert should be available to give oral evidence, unless his or her report is on discrete and substantially non-controversial matters collateral to the main issues (*Voaden v Champion* (2000) LTL 2/6/2000).

If oral expert evidence is to be given it has been made clear that it is up to the party calling the witness to make sure that he or she will be available at the hearing and this is best achieved by planning well ahead and cooperating with the other side (*Matthews v Tarmac Bricks and Tiles Ltd* [1999] CPLR 463; *Rollinson v Kimberly Clark Ltd* [1999] CPLR 581).

An expert's report must be disclosed, otherwise it cannot be used at trial without the court's permission (**r. 35.13**). If an expert's report has not been disclosed, the expert cannot be called to give oral evidence without the court's permission (**r. 35.13**). Once an expert's report has been disclosed by the party which commissioned it, any other party may use it as evidence at the trial (**r. 35.11**). By parity of reasoning with *McPhilemy v Times Newspapers Ltd (No. 2)* [2000] 1 WLR 1732, the court has a discretion to refuse permission where another party seeks to use such a report.

If an expert who has been commissioned to prepare a report refuses to do so because of a reasonable fear that it will not be paid for, the court will not allow a witness summons to be issued requiring the expert to give evidence (*Brown v Bennett* (2000) *The Times*, 2 November 2000).

Contents of expert's report

52.20 PD 35, para. 2, deals with the form and content of experts' reports. An expert's report should be addressed to the court and not to the party from whom instructions were received (para. 2.1). It must (**para. 2.2**):

(a) give details of the expert's qualifications;
(b) give details of any literature or other material which the expert has relied on in making the report;
(c) contain a statement setting out the substance of all facts and instructions given to the expert which are material to the opinions expressed in the report or upon which those opinions are based;
(d) make clear which of the facts stated in the report are within the expert's own knowledge;
(e) say who carried out any examination, measurement, test or experiment which the expert has used for the report, give the qualifications of that person, and say whether or not the test or experiment has been carried out under the reporting expert's supervision;
(f) where there is a range of opinion on the matters dealt with in the report:
 (i) summarise the range of opinion, and
 (ii) give reasons for the reporting expert's own opinion;
(g) contain a summary of the conclusions reached;
(h) if the expert is not able to give his or her opinion without qualification, state the qualification; and

(i) contain a statement that the expert understands his or her duty to the court and has complied with that duty (this statement is required by **CPR, r. 35.10(2)**).

Extra detail is given in **PD 35, annex, paras 13.1** to **13.15**. An expert's report must be verified by a statement of truth (**PD 35, para. 2.3**; see **23.11**to **23.16**). The form of the statement of truth is (**para. 2.4**):

I confirm that in so far as the facts stated in my report are within my own knowledge I have made clear which they are and I believe them to be true, and that the opinions I have expressed represent my true and complete professional opinion.

Experts must not be asked to amend, expand or alter their reports in a manner which distorts their true opinion, and must refuse to do so if asked (**PD 35, annex, para. 15.2**). This prohibition does not prevent an expert being invited to amend or expand a report to ensure its accuracy, internal consistency, completeness, relevance to the issues and clarity (**para. 15.2**).

Where an expert's report fails to comply with the provisions of **PD 35, para. 2.2**, concerning contents it is a proper use of judicial discretion not to excuse that failure, and to debar the expert from giving evidence. It would not then be open to the parties to invite the court to make a consent order granting an extension of time for compliance (*Stevens v Gullis* [2000] 1 All ER 527).

Providing details of instructions

An expert's report must contain a statement setting out the substance of all material instructions (whether written or oral) on the basis of which the report was written (**CPR, r. 35.10(3)**). It should summarise the facts and instructions given to the expert which are material to the opinions expressed in the report or upon which those opinions are based. This can cause particular problems when expert's reports are disclosed before the disclosure of factual witness statements. If the expert was instructed with the provision of draft witness statements, those witness statements lose their privileged status because they form part of the expert's instructions (**r. 35.10(4)**). **Rule 35.10(4)** goes on to say that the court will not order disclosure of the expert's instructions or disclosure of any specific document unless it is satisfied that there are reasonable grounds for believing the statement of instructions in the report is inaccurate or incomplete. The aim of these rules is to ensure that the factual basis on which an expert prepares a report is transparent. An expert's 'instructions' are not limited to any letters of instruction, but include materials, earlier experts' reports and witness statements supplied to the expert as part of the instructions (*Morris v Bank of India* (Hart J, 15 January 2001); *Lucas v Barking, Havering and Redbridge Hospitals NHS Trust* [2003] EWCA Civ 1102, [2004] 1 WLR 220). A party who is served with an expert's report is not allowed, as a matter of course, to call for all the documents referred to in the report. Before being entitled to do so, there has to be some concrete fact giving rise to reasonable grounds for questioning the expert's statement of instructions (*Lucas v Barking, Havering and Redbridge Hospitals NHS Trust*). If the expert was asked to provide a report based on hypothetical facts posed by the solicitor providing the instructions, that should be made clear in the expert's report (*Morris v Bank of India* (2001) LTL 16/11/2001). 52.21

DISCUSSION BETWEEN EXPERTS

Rule 35.12 of the CPR provides that the court may, at any stage, direct a discussion between experts for the purpose of requiring them: 52.22

(a) to identify and discuss the expert issues in the proceedings; and
(b) where possible, to reach an agreed opinion on those issues.

Arrangements for such a discussion should be proportionate to the value of the case, and may take place by telephone or through correspondence as an alternative to a face-to-face meeting (**PD 35, annex, para. 18.4**). Primary responsibility for producing an agenda for the meeting rests with the parties' solicitors (**para. 18.5**). The agenda should indicate the matters agreed between the parties and contain a concise summary of the matters still in issue. It is often helpful to include a list of the questions to be answered by the experts (**para. 18.6**). The court may specify the issues which the experts must discuss (**r. 35.12(2)**) and may also direct that following a discussion between them, the experts must prepare a statement for the court showing (**r. 35.12(3)**):

(a) the issues on which they agree; and
(b) issues on which they disagree and a summary of their reasons for disagreeing.

The parties' lawyers may only be present at discussions between experts if all the parties agree or the court so orders. If lawyers do attend, they should not normally intervene except to answer questions put to them by the experts or to advise about the law (*Hubbard v Lambeth, Southwark and Lewisham Health Authority* [2001] EWCA Civ 1455, [2002] Lloyd's Rep Med 8). A joint statement is produced for the court to assist in case management and is not a document for which a party can claim privilege (*Robin Ellis Ltd v Malwright Ltd* [1999] BLR 81). However, the content of the experts' discussion is not to be referred to at the trial unless the parties agree (**r. 35.12(4)**). Where experts reach agreement on an issue during their discussions, that agreement will not bind the parties unless they expressly agree to be bound by it (**r. 35.12(5)**).

Thus whether or not the parties request it, the court has power to direct that the experts have without prejudice discussions in an attempt to narrow the issues in the case upon which their expertise has been sought. Such discussions will normally be ordered in multi-track cases only where there are opposing experts. It is helpful that where the experts reach agreement on an issue in their without prejudice discussions, the parties are not bound by it (**r. 35.12(5)**). First, this permits the experts more freedom in their discussions, without fear of binding their respective instructing parties and secondly, if the parties were bound by the agreement then effectively there would be compulsory arbitration by a panel of experts.

WRITTEN QUESTIONS TO EXPERTS

52.23 **Rule 35.6** of the CPR provides that a party may put written questions to an expert instructed by another party or to a single joint expert.

Written questions may only be put once and must be put within 28 days of service of the expert's report (**r. 35.6(2)(a) and (b)**). They must be for the purpose only of clarification of the report, unless the court gives permission or the other party consents (**r. 35.6(2)(c)**). Questions must be purely for clarification if they are put to the expert without permission, but it is possible to ask about matters not in the expert's report (as long as they are within the expert's expertise) with the consent of the other side or the court's permission (*Mutch v Allen* [2001] CPLR 200). Where a party sends a written question direct to an expert, a copy of the question should, at the same time, be sent to the other party or parties (**PD 35, para. 5.2**). The party or parties who instructed the expert must pay his or her fees for answering questions put under **CPR, r. 35.6**, but this does not affect any decision by the court about who is ultimately to bear the expert's costs (**PD 35, para. 5.3**). The expert's answers to the questions put under **r. 35.6** are treated as forming part of his or her report (**CPR, r. 35.6(3)**). Where a party has put a written question to an expert instructed by another party in accordance with **r. 35.6** and the expert does not answer that question, the court may make an order that the party who instructed the expert may not rely on the evidence of that expert and/or that the party may not recover the fees and expenses of that expert from any other party (**r. 35.6(4)**). No sanction is specifically provided for failure by a jointly instructed expert to reply, but the failure may reduce the evidential value of the report.

The 28-day time limit in which questions are to be put to an expert requires that practitioners act speedily once an expert's report is served on them. It may be, in very complex cases, that a party would wish to instruct its own expert for the purpose of raising appropriate questions of the reporting expert and there may be some cases in which it will be necessary to have the questions themselves expertly drafted by counsel. It will be important to be able to justify increasing the costs of expert evidence in this way, or suffer disallowance of the extra costs on assessment.

If questioning reveals a fundamental disagreement with a single joint expert, it will be necessary to apply to the court for further directions.

Where there is an application that the court should, under **r. 35.6(4)**, disallow an expert's evidence on the ground of non-response to questions, the appropriateness of the questions may be examined and those which are clearly unreasonable or beyond the expert's area of expertise may themselves be disallowed and the application dismissed, which may result in costs sanctions.

EXPERT'S RIGHT TO ASK COURT FOR DIRECTIONS

It is clear from **CPR, r. 35.3**, that it is an expert's duty to assist the court rather than the **52.24**
parties from whom he or she has received instructions. Further, the court has control over an expert in respect of the issues on which he or she should report and has a power to give directions regarding any examination, inspection or experiment that an expert is to carry out. The court also has power to restrict the amount of fees and expenses to be paid to an expert. It would be wholly inappropriate, therefore, if an expert were to be unable to communicate with the court to clarify these matters from time to time. For example, an expert may find that it is necessary to carry out tests which had not been authorised by the court. Lines of communication between expert and court are opened by **r. 35.14**, under which an expert may file a written request for directions from the court, to assist the expert in carrying out his or her function as an expert. An expert who proposes to request directions must, unless the court orders otherwise, provide a copy of the proposed request to his or her instructing party at least seven days before filing it, and to all other parties at least four days before filing it (**r. 35.14(2)**). When the court gives directions to the expert, it may also order that a party be served with a copy of the directions (**r. 35.14(3)**). The wording of **r. 35.14(3)** is rather odd, stating that the court can order 'a party' to be served with a copy of the directions, but as the singular includes the plural, is to be interpreted as enabling the court to direct service on all the parties or such of the parties as may be specified in the directions.

INSPECTION, EXAMINATION AND TESTING OF PROPERTY

Invariably experts need to inspect, measure, examine and/or test the subject matter on which **52.25**
they are asked to report. The expert may delegate these tasks, but where this is done the report must identify and state the qualifications of the person who did the delegated tasks, and say whether they were done under the supervision of the retained expert (**PD 35, para. 2.2(5)**). The subject matter could be goods, land, buildings or machinery relevant to the issues in the claim. Where the subject matter is under the control of the party instructing the expert there should be no problem. Where it is under the control of the other side or a non-party, it will be necessary to secure their consent to the expert having access for the purpose of conducting

any necessary inspection, examination etc. If consent is not given, it is usually possible to obtain an order (usually on a case management conference) giving access, a subject dealt with in detail in **chapter 41**.

In *SKB plc v Apotex* (2003) LTL 4/2/2003, a patent claim, the court held that a confidentiality agreement between the parties had the effect that **CPR, r. 31.22** (undertaking not to use information disclosed for collateral purposes, see **48.33**), applied to the test results on samples of the defendant's products. It is possible that an implied undertaking in similar terms would be imposed even without a confidentiality agreement, although it is better for collateral use to be expressly dealt with when permission to inspect property is sought.

MEDICAL EXAMINATION

52.26 In personal injuries claims the defendant is entitled to test the severity of the claimant's injuries by obtaining expert medical evidence on the claimant's history, present condition and prognosis. This is often done on a joint basis, particularly in claims suitable for the fast track, either in compliance with the Pre-action Protocol for Personal Injury Claims (see **8.16**) or as part of case management directions after proceedings are issued (see **44.6** and **52.6**). In these cases consent to the necessary medical examination is not usually an issue.

Where the parties intend to instruct competing experts, the defendant needs to request the claimant's consent to the medical examination by the defendant's experts. In practice, the defendant will usually provide a written consent form to be signed by the claimant for the release of the claimant's medical records at the same time. If the claimant fails to consent to the proposed medical examination, the court will not make a direct order requiring the claimant to comply. This is because any medical examination involves at least a technical assault on the patient, which is an infringement of the fundamental human right to liberty and security of person, and it is seen to be wrong to order a person to consent to an assault with the sanction of committal to prison in default. Instead, where a claimant refuses a reasonable request for a medical examination the court will make an order imposing a stay on the claim until the claimant submits to the examination (*Edmeades v Thames Board Mills Ltd* [1969] 2 QB 67). Where the medical examination relates to only part of a claim, it is likely that a limited stay will be imposed on the relevant issues only (*James v Baily Gibson and Co.* [2002] EWCA Civ 1690, LTL 30/10/2002).

In *Edmeades v Thames Board Mills Ltd* it was held that a stay will be imposed if it is just and reasonable in the circumstances. In *Starr v National Coal Board* [1977] 1 WLR 63 Scarman LJ said this has two elements:

(a) the defendant's request for the medical examination must be reasonable; and
(b) the claimant's refusal to consent to the examination, or consent subject to conditions, must be such as to prevent the just determination of the claim.

In complex claims it may be reasonable for the defendant to request the claimant to consent to examinations by experts in a number of different fields of medical science, and to consent to examinations for initial and updating reports.

A claimant is not allowed to consent to an examination by anyone other than certain experts (or even anyone other than a single named expert). The reason is that the claimant can go to anyone in the medical profession for a report, and the same freedom has to be allowed to the defendant (*Starr v National Coal Board* [1977] 1 WLR 63). Sometimes the claimant will refuse to consent because the proposed examination is particularly invasive, or even carries a risk of further injury. In these cases the court has to balance the need for the examination and proposed tests, for the proper preparation of the defendant's case, against the reasonableness of the claimant's objections based on the degree of pain, risk to health and inconvenience

(*Prescott v Bulldog Tools Ltd* [1981] 3 All ER 869; see also *Aspinall v Sterling Mansell Ltd* [1981] 3 All ER 866).

Stays may also be imposed against defendants (*Cosgrove v Baker* (14 December 1979 unreported); *Lacey v Harrison* (1992) *The Times*, 22 April 1992) and in non-personal injuries claims (*Jackson v Mirror Group Newspapers Ltd* (1994) *The Times*, 29 March 1994, a libel claim) if the relevant party's medical condition is relevant to an issue in the case.

Conditions imposed by claimants

Claimants are entitled to require reasonable conditions to be met before consenting to a medical examination. Conditions usually regarded as reasonable include: **52.27**

(a) that the defendant pays any loss of earnings incurred by the claimant in attending;
(b) that the defendant pays any out-of-pocket expenses incurred in attending;
(c) that the expert will not discuss or question the claimant about the accident except so far as is necessary for the purpose of compiling the medical report;
(d) that a friend, relative or legal representative attends with the claimant for moral support, unless that person will interfere with the examination (such as may happen in psychiatric consultations: *Whitehead v Avon County Council* (1995) 29 BMLR 152).

Disclosure of defendant's report

It has been held that it is never reasonable to insist that the defendant must disclose the report compiled after the examination as a condition of consenting to an examination (*Megarity v D. J. Ryan and Sons Ltd* [1980] 1 WLR 1237). This is because the report is protected by legal professional privilege, and would give the claimant an advantage not enjoyed by the defendant. An exception was recognised in *Hookham v Wiggins Teape Fine Papers Ltd* [1995] PIQR P392 where past delay in the claim or the proximity of the trial may justify such a condition in the particular circumstances. In *Beck v Ministry of Defence* [2003] EWCA Civ 1043, [2005] 1 WLR 2206, the defendant was required to disclose a copy of the first report it had commissioned on the claimant's injuries as a condition for being given permission to instruct a second expert. **52.28**

CROSS-EXAMINATION

The substance of the instructions sent to an expert must be stated in his or her report (**CPR, r. 35.10(3)**; see 52.20) and are not privileged against disclosure, but the court will not either order disclosure of any specific document or permit any questioning in court, other than by the party who instructed the expert, unless it is satisfied that there are reasonable grounds to consider the statement of instructions to be inaccurate or incomplete (**r. 35.10(4)**). If the court is so satisfied, it will permit cross-examination of the expert on the contents of his or her instructions where it appears to the court that it is in the interests of justice to do so (**PD 35, para. 4**). **52.29**

In the normal course of things, a jointly instructed expert's report should be the evidence in the case on the issues covered by that report. Normally there should be no need for such a report to be amplified or tested by cross-examination (*Peet v Mid-Kent Healthcare Trust* [2001] EWCA Civ 1703, [2002] 1 WLR 210). It might be appropriate to order attendance for cross-examination where a single joint expert delivers his report shortly before the trial, or where the expert has not considered all the written questions put to him (*Coopers Payen Ltd v Southampton Container Terminal Ltd* [2003] EWCA Civ 1223, [2004] 1 Lloyd's Rep 331, at [41]). If, exceptionally, the expert is called at trial, any cross-examination should be restricted as far as possible (*Peet v Mid-Kent Healthcare Trust*).

ASSESSORS

52.30 **Rule 35.15** of the CPR applies where the court appoints one or more persons as assessors under the **Supreme Court Act 1981, s. 70**, or the **County Courts Act 1984, s. 63**. An assessor is someone who assists the court in dealing with a matter within his or her skill and expertise and who generally sits with the judge. Factors to be considered when considering whether to appoint an assessor include the complexity of the arguments and the amount in issue (*Agrimex Ltd v Tradigrain SA* [2003] EWHC 1656 (Comm), [2003] 2 Lloyd's Rep 537). Under **CPR, r. 35.15(3)**, an assessor shall take such part in the proceedings as the court may direct and, in particular, the court may direct the assessor to prepare a report for the court on any matter at issue in the proceedings and direct the assessor to attend the whole or any part of the trial to advise the court on any such matter. Where the assessor prepares the report for the court before the commencement of the trial, the court will send a copy to each of the parties enabling the parties to use the report at trial, although they are not permitted to question or cross-examine the assessor (**PD 35, para. 7.4**). To comply with the European Convention on Human Rights, art. 6(1), in the **Human Rights Act 1998, sch. 1**, it is permissible for the judge to put questions to an assessor after discussion with counsel. The answers should then be disclosed to counsel, either orally or in writing, who are then permitted to make submissions to the judge on whether the advice of the assessor should be followed (*Bow Spring (Owners) v Manzanillo II (Owners)* [2004] EWCA Civ 1007, [2005] 1 WLR 144; *The Global Mariner* [2005] EWHC 380 (Admlty), [2005] 2 All ER (Comm) 389 at [14]).

Where it is intended to appoint an assessor to assist the court, at least 21 days before the appointment, the court will notify each party in writing of the name of the proposed assessor, of the matter in respect of which his or her assistance is sought and the qualifications of the assessor to give that assistance (**PD 35, para. 7.1**). An objection by a party to the appointment of an assessor, either on personal grounds or in relation to his or her qualifications, must be made in writing and filed with the court within seven days of receipt of the notification (**paras 7.2 and 7.3**). The court will consider any objections when deciding whether or not to make the appointment (**para. 7.3**).

Any consultation between assessors and the court must take place openly as part of the assembling of the evidence, and the parties are entitled to an opportunity to address the court on the assessor's advice (*Bow Spring (Owners) v Manzanillo II (Owners)*). The judge is not bound to accept the advice received from assessors (*Admiralty Commissioners v SS Ausonia (Owners)* (1920) Ll L Rep 123 at p. 124).

The remuneration to be paid to the assessor for his or her services will be determined by the court and forms part of the costs of the proceedings (**CPR, r. 35.15(5)**). The court may order any party to deposit in the court office a specified sum in respect of the assessor's fees and, where it does so, the assessor will not be asked to act until the sum has been deposited (**r. 35.15(6)**), except in cases where the remuneration of the assessor is to be paid out of money provided by Parliament (**r. 35.15(7)**).

Chapter 53 Discontinuance

INTRODUCTION

From time to time a claimant may think better of having commenced proceedings, and will want to discontinue without incurring all the costs of litigating to trial. It may be, for example, that after seeing the evidence available to the defendant it will be clear that the claim has limited prospects of success. A claimant in this situation may be able to negotiate a compromise with the defendant, who may agree terms which are not too onerous on the claimant. Before the CPR, a claimant could simply allow the case to go to sleep. Under the new system it is very much more difficult to allow a case simply to go to sleep, given the active case management regime now in place. In most situations, a claimant who decides not to proceed should therefore now either seek to come to an accommodation with the defendant, or should discontinue. Any other course will almost certainly result in increased costs liabilities, particularly if there is a contested hearing. **53.1**

A claimant who wishes to discontinue proceedings must file a notice of discontinuance. The general rule is that once a claim is discontinued, the claimant has to pay the defendant's costs of the claim.

DISTINCTION BETWEEN DISCONTINUING AND ABANDONING

Discontinuance as a concept is restricted to causes of action. If a single cause of action gives rise to more than one remedy (or more than one head of damages), some of the remedies or heads of damage may be abandoned without producing a formal discontinuance (**CPR, r. 38.1(2)**). A claimant abandoning some of the relief claimed simply has to comply with the rules on amendment (see **chapter 31**). The result is that if some of the relief claimed is abandoned, the claimant will almost certainly have to pay the costs of and arising from the amendments to the statements of case, but will incur no wider liability in relation to the costs of the claim. **53.2**

WHAT MAY BE DISCONTINUED

A claimant may discontinue: **53.3**

(a) the whole claim (**CPR, r. 38.1(1)**); or
(b) part of the claim (i.e., some of the causes of action pleaded: **r. 38.1(1)**); and
(c) against all of the defendants (**r. 38.2(3)**); or
(d) against some of the defendants (**r. 38.2(3)**).

PERMISSION TO DISCONTINUE

53.4 Generally, a claimant has the right to discontinue without seeking permission first (**CPR, r. 38.2(1)**). However, in some circumstances permission is required. These are:

(a) If an interim injunction has been granted in relation to the claim being discontinued, permission has to be sought from the court (**r. 38.2(2)(a)**).

(b) If any party has given an undertaking to the court in relation to the claim being discontinued, permission has to be sought from the court (**r. 38.2(2)(a)**).

(c) If the claimant has received an interim payment (whether by agreement or pursuant to a court order) in relation to the claim being discontinued, permission must be sought from the court or consent must be given in writing by the defendant (**r. 38.2(2)(b)**).

(d) Where there is more than one claimant, the claimant wishing to discontinue must either obtain permission to discontinue from the court, or must obtain consent in writing from all the other claimants (**r. 38.2(2)(c)**). In group litigation, permission to discontinue is not required where the claim form of the claimant who is seeking to discontinue only has a single named claimant (*Sayers v Smithkline Beecham plc* [2004] EWHC 1899 (QB), [2005] PIQR P8).

(e) Where a claim is brought by a person under a disability, and the discontinuance of the claim amounts to a settlement or a compromise, approval of the court is required under **r. 21.10** (see **14.38** and *Sayers v Smithkline Beecham plc*).

If consent is required, the signed consent(s) must be obtained before the claimant files the notice of discontinuance. If the court's permission has to be sought, a separate application for permission must be issued, and the claimant is only allowed to file the notice of discontinuance after the order granting permission is made. There may be greater reluctance to give permission to discontinue in probate claims (*Green v Briscoe* (2005) LTL 9/5/2005).

PROCEDURE FOR DISCONTINUING

53.5 A claimant discontinues all or part of the claim by filing a notice of discontinuance (**form N279**) with the court, and serving a copy on all other parties. Regarding contents:

(a) The notice of discontinuance that is filed at court must state that copies have been served on all other parties (**CPR, r. 38.3(2)**).

(b) In cases where the consent of another party is required, all copies of the notice of discontinuance must have copies of the consent annexed (**r. 38.3(3)**).

(c) In cases where there is more than one defendant, the notice of discontinuance must identify the defendants against whom the claim is being discontinued (**r. 38.3(4)**).

SETTING ASIDE NOTICE OF DISCONTINUANCE

53.6 A defendant may apply for an order setting aside a notice of discontinuance served without consent or permission, provided the application is made within 28 days of the notice (**CPR, r. 38.4**). A notice of discontinuance was set aside in *Fakih Brothers v A. P. Moller (Copenhagen) Ltd* [1994] 1 Lloyd's Rep 103, where it was served to avoid the imposition of an onerous term in a consent order, and in *Ernst and Young v Butte Mining plc* [1996] 1 WLR 1605, where it was served in order to pre-empt the effective service of a counterclaim.

EFFECT OF DISCONTINUANCE

Notice of discontinuance takes effect, and brings the proceedings to an end as against each defendant, on the date it is served upon that defendant. This of course is subject to any right to apply to set aside the notice, and does not affect the court's power to deal with costs (**CPR, r. 38.5**). **53.7**

Unless the court orders otherwise, the claimant is liable for the defendant's costs up to the date of service of the notice of discontinuance (**r. 38.6(1)**). A costs liability taking effect by virtue of **r. 38.6(1)** is for costs on the standard basis. Alternatively, it is open to a defendant to seek an order for costs to be payable on the indemnity basis (*Jarvis plc v PricewaterhouseCoopers* (2000) *The Times*, 10 October 2000). The power to make some other order is exercised applying the factors set out in **r. 44.3** (see **66.5**) (*Longstaff International Ltd v Evans* [2005] EWHC 4 (Ch), LTL 26/1/2005). Unreasonably continuing a claim after it has become clear it is doomed to failure may justify an order for indemnity-basis costs from that date (*Wates Construction Ltd v HGP Greentree Allchurch Evans Ltd* [2005] EWHC 2174 (TCC), LTL 4/11/2005; and see **66.21**).

It may be appropriate to depart from the usual rule where there has been a change of circumstances since proceedings were issued making it uneconomic to continue (*Walker v Walker* (2005) LTL 27/1/2005). The court can reverse the usual costs rule on a discontinuance where the claimant has in effect obtained all the relief sought in the proceedings (*Amoco (UK) Exploration Co. v British American Offshore Ltd* (2000) LTL 13/12/2000). On the facts of *Dooley v Parker* [2002] EWCA Civ 1188, it was ordered, following a discontinuance by the claimant, that the justice of the matter was best served by making no order as to costs up to service of the notice of discontinuance, and to award the claimant costs thereafter. The fall-back order where an appeal from an Immigration Appeal Tribunal is discontinued before the hearing with the Secretary of State consenting to a rehearing of the decision being appealed is to make no order as to costs (*Sengoz v Secretary of State for the Home Department* [2001] EWCA Civ 1135, *The Times*, 13 August 2001). There are no costs consequences regarding discontinued small claims track cases (**r. 38.6(3)**).

If only part of the claim is discontinued, the claimant's liability is limited to the costs of the part of the claim that has been discontinued. Usually the claimant does not have to pay the defendant's costs following a partial discontinuance until the conclusion of the action. However, the court may in its discretion order these costs to be paid immediately, either after they have been agreed between the parties or after they have been assessed by the court (**r. 38.6(2)**). Where the claimant is required to pay the costs of the discontinued part of the claim straight away, the liability to do so arises 14 days after the relevant costs are agreed or assessed by the court. Failure to pay gives grounds for the court imposing a stay on the remainder of the proceedings until the costs are paid (**r. 38.8**).

SUBSEQUENT PROCEEDINGS

A claimant who discontinues after a defence has been filed is not allowed to commence new proceedings against the same defendant arising out of the same or substantially the same facts as the original claim, unless the court first gives permission for the second claim to be issued (**CPR, r. 38.7**). If permission is granted, the court will normally give directions regarding issuing the substantive second claim (**r. 25.2(3)**). **53.8**

Chapter 54 Stays

INTRODUCTION

54.1 By **CPR, r. 3.1(2)(f)**, the court has a general case management power to stay the whole or any part of any proceedings or judgment either generally or until a specified date or event. This rule derives from the **Supreme Court Act 1981, s. 49(3)**, which provides that nothing in the Act affects the power of the High Court and Court of Appeal to stay proceedings where the court thinks fit to do so, either of its own motion or on the application of any person, whether or not a party to the proceedings. A stay may apply to only part of the proceedings, and where this applies obviously the remaining parts of the proceedings will continue. A stay may be lifted on proper grounds being shown (*Cooper v Williams* [1963] 2 QB 567).

The glossary to the CPR says a 'stay' imposes a halt on proceedings, apart from taking any steps allowed by the CPR or the terms of the stay. Proceedings can be continued if the stay is lifted. This is quite important, because in times past (particularly in the late nineteenth century) the courts were in the habit of ordering stays when nowadays they would strike out or dismiss the proceedings. Old cases used to speak of absolute stays (meaning orders dismissing proceedings) and conditional stays (having the modern meaning of stays). This old misuse of the word 'stay' should be a thing of the past.

Stays may be imposed in a great variety of different circumstances, and for widely varying reasons.

STAY ON SETTLEMENT

54.2 For the stay of a claim when a **Part 36** offer or **Part 36** payment is accepted see **64.48**. Ordinary consent orders following a compromise of a claim frequently provide for the stay of the proceedings (see *Rofa Sport Management AG v DHL International (UK) Ltd* [1989] 1 WLR 902). Similarly, a Tomlin order (see **61.14**) provides for the stay of the proceedings on the terms set out in a schedule to the order, with liberty to apply.

STAYS FOR LITIGATION REASONS

54.3 There may be reasons relating to the efficient progress of the proceedings which make granting a stay desirable. Examples are:

(a) Where there is no issue on liability in a personal injury case, but a clear prognosis will not be possible for some time. This possibility is referred to in **PD 51, para. 19(3)(b)**, where the machinery referred to is an adjournment to determine prognosis.

(b) Where a personal injuries claim is issued without complying with the pre-action protocol because the solicitor acting for the claimant is instructed shortly before the expiry of the limitation period. A stay may be granted in the early stages of the proceedings to enable the steps of the protocol to be completed (**Pre-action Protocol for Personal Injury Claims, para. 2.11**).

(c) Where a personal injuries claim is issued close to the expiry of limitation without sufficient medical evidence substantiating the claimant's injuries because of difficulties in obtaining the necessary evidence. This arose in *Knight v Sage Group plc* (1999) LTL 28/4/99, where the court gave the claimant three months to obtain and disclose the necessary evidence.
(d) Where a claim is commenced, and subsequent events show that there is a possibility that the proceedings will not serve a useful purpose. For example, a claim may be brought in professional negligence seeking an indemnity in respect of the claimant's potential liability to a stranger to the proceedings. If it transpires there is a possibility that the stranger to the litigation may never make a claim against the claimant, it may be appropriate to order a stay until the stranger's claim becomes time-barred. Similarly, a stay may be ordered under the court's inherent jurisdiction where the issues have been compromised between all but one of the parties, and the court may also make an order for costs involving the non-consenting party (although it is unlikely to be appropriate to make an order for costs against that party, see *Clark v Rice* (2000) LTL 29/6/2000). If costs are still in issue, usually the only way a determination can be made is if the issues are tried (*Markos v Goodfellow* (2000) LTL 7/6/2000).
(e) The court may order a stay at the allocation stage to allow for the possibility of settlement under **CPR, r. 26.4** (see **42.24**).
(f) The usual stay ordered as part of an order making a reference to the European Court of Justice (see **chapter 75**).
(g) Stays imposed pending the resolution of a test case (*Woods v Duncan* [1946] AC 401).

STAYS TO ENFORCE COMPLIANCE WITH ORDERS

Sometimes the court imposes stays as a means of enforcing compliance with its orders. This is only going to be effective against a claimant or a party in the position of a claimant, such as a defendant making a counterclaim. Examples are: **54.4**

(a) Stays which are normally imposed pending the provision of security for costs (see **chapter 65**).
(b) A stay imposed where the claimant in a personal injuries claim refuses a reasonable request for a medical examination (see *Edmeades v Thames Board Mills Ltd* [1969] 2 QB 67; see **52.26**).
(c) A stay pending a satisfactory undertaking as to costs or otherwise connected with the way in which a claim is funded (*Grovewood Holdings plc v James Capel and Co. Ltd* [1995] Ch 80; *Abraham v Thompson* (1997) *The Times*, 15 May 1997).
(d) A second claim may be stayed pending payment of the costs of an earlier discontinued claim (see **53.8**) or the costs of an earlier claim that was struck out (**CPR, r. 3.4(4)**, confirming *Gardner v Southwark London Borough Council (No. 2)* [1996] 1 WLR 561). A stay pending payment of the costs of an earlier claim does not conflict with the **European Convention on Human Rights, art. 6(1)**. Such a stay can be imposed even where the parties were not entirely the same, provided the second claim arose out of substantially the same facts as the previous claim (*Stevens v School of Oriental and African Studies* (2000) *The Times*, 2 February 2001). A stay can also be imposed where the claimant is the successor in title to the claimant in the previous claim (*Sinclair v British Telecommunications plc* [2001] 1 WLR 38).
(e) Where partners fail to comply with a demand for their names and addresses under **RSC, ord. 81, r. 2** in CPR, sch. 1.

STAYS TO PROTECT CONCURRENT CLAIMS

There is a general public interest in avoiding a multiplicity of claims. Sometimes it is simply an abuse of process to bring duplicate sets of proceedings, with the result that the later **54.5** proceedings will be struck out (see *Buckland v Palmer* [1984] 1 WLR 1109). The following examples stop a little way short of being suitable for striking out, but stays may be imposed instead:

(a) Where the dispute should be dealt with by arbitration rather than by litigation (see **chapter 69**).
(b) Where the dispute should be dealt with in the administration of an insolvent person's estate (see **chapter 81**).
(c) Stays on the ground of *forum non conveniens* (see **chapter 16**).
(d) Stays under various provisions of **Council Regulation** (EC) **No. 44/2001** (see **arts 27** to **28** and **chapter 16**).
(e) Stays pending the resolution of connected criminal proceedings. There must be a pending criminal case, not merely the possibility of one (*Caledonian Contracting Partnership Ltd v Rodger* (2004) LTL 7/4/2004). Applications for such stays may be made by any party to the civil claim, or the prosecutor or any defendant to the criminal proceedings (**PD 23, para. 11A. 1**). The evidence in support of the application must contain an estimate of the expected duration of the stay, and must identify the respects in which continuing the civil claim may prejudice the criminal trial (**para. 11A. 3**).
(f) Stays of civil proceedings raising the same main issue as proceedings in the Competition Commission Appeal Tribunal (see *Synstar Computer Services (UK) Ltd v ICL (Sorbus) Ltd* (2001) *The Times*, 1 May 2001).

EFFECT OF A STAY

54.6 While a stay is in place the proceedings remain alive, but no further steps may be taken to progress the claim other than applying to lift the stay. For some purposes time will continue to run during a stay, such as the limited period of validity for service of an originating process (*Aldridge v Edwards* [2000] CPLR 349). There is no need to apply to lift the stay imposed by a Tomlin order before making an application for a wasted costs order (*Wagstaff v Colls* [2003] EWCA Civ 469, [2003] PNLR 561). A stay on a judgment prevents any steps being taken to enforce it, until the stay is lifted.

AUTOMATIC STAY OF PRE-CPR PROCEEDINGS

54.7 Unless proceedings which were commenced before 26 April 1999 came before a judge (including a master or district judge), whether on paper or at a hearing, by 25 April 2000, they were stayed as from 26 April 2000 by virtue of **PD 51, para. 19(1)**. The stay would have been avoided if the court made an order of its own initiative under **CPR, r. 3.3**, or if a party made an application under **Part 23**. However, merely writing a letter to the court, even if it came to a judge's attention before 26 April 2000, did not prevent the stay taking effect (*Reliance National Insurance Co. (Europe) Ltd v Ropner Insurance Services Ltd* [2001] 1 Lloyd's Rep 477). For this purpose a claim and an additional claim are separate proceedings, and it is possible for one of them to be stayed under **PD 51, para. 19**, despite activity on the other (*National Westminster Bank plc v Feeney* [2003] EWCA Civ 950, LTL 12/6/2003). A stay imposed under **para. 19(1)** may be lifted on the application of any party (**para. 19(2)**). A court considering an application to lift the stay will apply the principles laid down for granting relief from sanctions (see **CPR, r. 3.9(1)**, discussed at **46.31**; see *Audergon v La Baguette Ltd* [2002] EWCA Civ 10, [2002] CPLR 192; *Woodhouse v Consignia plc* [2002] EWCA Civ 275, [2002] 1 WLR 2558). A refusal to lift the stay was held to be wrong in that it was disproportionate and contrary to the overriding objective in *Overseas and Commercial Developments Ltd v Cox* [2002] EWCA Civ 635, LTL 25/4/2002.

Chapter 55 Witness Summonses

NATURE OF WITNESS SUMMONSES

A witness summons is a document issued by the court requiring a witness to attend court to give evidence or produce documents to the court (CPR, **r. 34.2(1)**). A witness summons must be in **form N20** (**r. 34.2(2)**) and there must be a separate witness summons for each witness required to attend court (**r. 34.2(3)**). Two copies of the witness summons should be filed with the court for sealing, one of which will be retained on the court file (**PD 34, para. 1.2**). A witness summons may, by **r. 34.2(4)**, require a witness to produce documents to the court either: 55.1

(a) on the date fixed for a hearing; or
(b) on such date as the court may direct.

The only documents that a summons under **Part 34** can require a person to produce before a hearing are documents which that person could be required to produce at the hearing (**r. 34.2(5)**). This means that they must be relevant to the issues and otherwise admissible in evidence at trial, and so is narrower than the scope of standard disclosure. **Rule 34.2(4)** may be considered as an alternative to non-party disclosure. It also incorporates the device used by the court in *Khanna v Lovell White Durrant* [1995] 1 WLR 121, in which the court invented the concept of the 'production appointment' for witnesses to attend under summons to bring documents to a hearing earlier than the trial, where, for example, the documents were required by one or other party to prepare the case properly for trial and production on the morning of the trial would have been insufficient.

ISSUE OF A WITNESS SUMMONS

A witness summons is issued on the date entered on the summons by the court (CPR, **r. 34.3(1)**). It must be issued by (**r. 34.3(3)**): 55.2

(a) the court where the case is proceeding; or
(b) the court where the hearing in question will be held.

The procedure is a simple one in which the party wishing to obtain a witness summons attends at court with the completed summons in **form N20**, which the court then seals for service. Where the witness summons is for the witness to attend at a trial, there is no requirement to obtain the court's permission, but permission must be obtained from the court under **r. 34.3(2)** where a party wishes:

(a) to have a summons issued less than seven days before the date of the trial;
(b) to have a summons issued for a witness to attend court to give evidence or to produce documents on any date except the date fixed for trial; or
(c) to have a summons issued for a witness to attend court to give evidence or to produce documents at any hearing except the trial.

Thus the permission of the court is necessary where the witness summons is to be issued very close to the date of the trial, where a witness summons is required for attendance at an interim hearing or where a witness is required to attend to give oral evidence or produce documents at such a hearing. Applications for permission are made without notice to a district judge or master. There is no provision in **Part 34** for evidence in support of such applications and therefore it would seem sufficient to indicate orally, at the hearing of the application, the purpose for which the witness summons is sought.

Witness summons in aid of inferior court or tribunal

55.3 The High Court and the county courts have a discretion to issue a witness summons in aid of any court or tribunal that does not have power to issue a witness summons in relation to proceedings before it (**CPR, r. 34.4(1)**). The court which issued a witness summons under this rule may set it aside (**r. 34.4(2)**). Such an application will be heard (**PD 34, para. 2.3**):

(a) in the High Court by a master at the Royal Courts of Justice or by a district judge in a district registry, and
(b) in a county court by a district judge.

Unless the court directs otherwise, the applicant on the application to set aside must give no less than two days' notice of the application to the party that issued the witness summons. The application to set aside will normally be dealt with at a hearing (**PD 34, para. 2.4**).

SERVICE OF WITNESS SUMMONS

Time for serving a witness summons

55.4 The general rule, as set out in **CPR, r. 34.5(1)**, is that a witness summons is binding if it is served at least seven days before the date on which the witness is required to attend before the court or tribunal. However, the court has a discretion to direct that the witness summons is binding even though it will be served less than 7 days before that date (**r. 34.5(2)**). **Rule 34.5(3)** provides that a witness summons which is served in accordance with **r. 34.5**, and requires the witness to attend court to give evidence, is binding until the conclusion of the hearing at which the attendance of the witness is required.

Service by the court or the party

55.5 A witness summons is served by the court unless it is indicated in writing, at the time of asking the court to issue the summons, that the party on whose behalf it is issued will serve it.

The usual practice is for the court to serve a witness summons either by post or by county court bailiff. Practitioners who wish to ensure certainty and expeditious service are likely to prefer to undertake service themselves.

Witness expenses

55.6 At the time of service of a witness summons the witness must be offered or paid a sum reasonably sufficient to cover his or her expenses in travelling to and from the court and compensation for loss of time (**CPR, r. 34.7**). The amount to be paid as compensation for loss of time is to be based on the sums payable to witnesses in the Crown Court (**PD 34, paras 3.1 to 3.3**). These are determined by the Lord Chancellor under the Costs in Criminal Cases (General) Regulations 1986 (SI 1986/1335), reg. 17.

A witness required to produce documents under a witness summons will only be paid conduct money, so will not be compensated for the expense of producing the documents, unlike the position on an application for non-party disclosure under **CPR, rr. 31.17** and **48.1(2)** (see *Re Howglen Ltd* [2001] 1 All ER 376 at p. 384 and **48.80**). However, in *Individual Homes Ltd v Macbream Investments Ltd* (2002) *The Times*, 14 November 2002, an order was made joining the witness as a party for the purpose of making a costs order in its favour for complying with a witness summons to produce documents.

If the witness summons is to be served by the court, the sum for expenses must be deposited in the court office (**CPR, r. 34.6(2)**). If the witness summons is to be served by the party issuing it, the sum must be offered to the witness when the summons is served (**PD 34, para. 3.4**).

FAILURE TO OBEY A WITNESS SUMMONS

County courts

A person who refuses or neglects, without sufficient cause, to appear, or produce documents, **55.7**
as required by a witness summons issued by a county court may be fined up to £1,000 (**County Courts Act 1984, s. 55(1) and (2)**). A fine may also be imposed if a summoned witness attends court but refuses to be sworn or give evidence (**s. 55(1)**). A fine cannot be imposed unless witness expenses (see **55.6**) were paid or tendered at the time of serving the summons (**s. 55(3)**). A judge imposing a fine may, at his or her discretion, direct that all or part of it (after deducting costs) is to be applied to indemnifying the party injured by the refusal or neglect (**s. 55(4)**). These are statutory versions of the inherent powers of the High Court (see **55.8**), but a county court has no power to issue a bench warrant for the arrest of a witness.

The power to impose a fine under **s. 55** may be exercised by a circuit judge, district judge, assistant district judge or deputy district judge (**s. 55(1) and (4A)**).

A judge who has fined, or is contemplating fining, a person under **s. 55** may invite the person to show cause why the fine should not have been, or should not be, imposed (**CCR, ord. 34, r. 2** in CPR, sch. 2). Although the rule is expressed to confer a discretion on the judge, it is clear that, in the light of the **European Convention on Human Rights, art. 6**, a fine should not be imposed without giving the offender an opportunity of submitting a defence. A witness who attends the trial but refuses to give evidence may give an explanation there and then. Otherwise the judge should direct the court officer to issue a notice naming a day on which cause is to be shown by witness statement, affidavit or otherwise. Repayment may be ordered of part or all of any fine already paid if, on considering the cause shown, the judge decides that the fine should have been of a lesser amount, not imposed at all or not enforced (**CCR, ord. 34, r. 4** in CPR, sch. 2).

If a fine imposed for failure to obey a witness summons is not paid, the court must report the matter to the circuit judge (**CCR, ord. 34, r. 3(1)** in CPR, sch. 2), who may, under the **County Courts Act 1984, s. 129**, order the fine to be enforced by any method available for the enforcement of a county court judgment debt or a magistrates' court fine.

High Court

In the High Court failure to obey a witness summons is contempt of court (*Wyat v Wingford* (1729) 2 Ld Raym 1528), as is appearing in response to a summons but refusing to be sworn or **55.8**
to answer questions or to produce documents (*R v Daye* [1908] 2 KB 333). No penalty may be imposed unless witness expenses (see **55.6**) were paid or tendered with the summons (*Fuller v Prentice* (1788) 1 H Bl 49; *Re Working Men's Mutual Society* (1882) 21 ChD 831). If disobedience was not wilful, no penalty will be imposed (*Horne v Smith* (1815) 6 Taunt 10; *Scholes v Hilton* (1842) 10 M & W 15) or enforcement of a penalty will be stayed (*R v Daye*). A person who has disobeyed a witness summons may be sued for damages by the party who obtained the summons, provided actual loss is proved (*Crewe v Field* (1896) 12 TLR 405; *Roberts v J. and F. Stone Lighting and Radio Ltd* (1945) 172 LT 240).

The High Court has an inherent power to issue a bench warrant for the arrest of a person required as a witness so as to secure his or her attendance in court (*Astrovlanis Compania Naviera SA v Linard (No. 2)* [1972] 2 Lloyd's Rep 187; *Zakharov v White* [2003] EWHC 2463 (Ch), *The Times*, 13 November 2003).

SETTING ASIDE OR VARYING A WITNESS SUMMONS

55.9 Under CPR, r. 34.3(4), the court may set aside or vary a witness summons. This may be on the application of any party or by the witness. The presumption is that the interests of justice are best served by the grant of a witness summons (*Tilbury Consulting Ltd v Gittins* [2004] STC (SCD) 1). A witness summons may be set aside if the witness has no connection with the claim, or where the witness summons is used for tactical purposes, as was the case in *Harrison v Bloom Camillin* (1999) *The Independent*, 28 June 1999, in which it was found that the defendants were attempting to conduct a fishing expedition. A witness summons to produce documents was set aside in *Tajik Aluminium Plant v Hydro Aluminium AS* [2005] EWCA Civ 1218, [2006] 1 WLR 767, on the ground that it did not identify the documents required with sufficient certainty. The documents must be sufficiently described so as to leave no doubt in the mind of the witness what he is required to produce. It is not necessary to describe documents individually. A compendious description will suffice provided it enables the witness to know specifically what is covered.

Chapter 56 Giving Evidence without Attending Court

INTRODUCTION

At both the allocation and pre-trial checklist stages, the court will timetable certain events in order to progress a case to trial, and at the pre-trial checklist stage in particular, the trial will be fixed for a date or period of time when it is thought that all the witnesses will be able to attend to give evidence. Prudent practitioners will have asked clients and witnesses to identify dates to avoid but it sometimes happens that, despite planning in advance, a witness is unable, physically, to attend court. On both the fast track and multi-track, the postponement of a trial is considered as an order of last resort (**PD 28, para. 5.4(6); PD 29, para. 7.4(6)**). Therefore, where a witness does have difficulties in attending court to give evidence in person, alternative means of giving evidence should be considered, in order that the trial is not postponed. 56.1

It may also be the case that in the period leading up to the trial, a hearing is necessary in respect of an interim remedy, for which a crucial witness is unable or refuses to provide a witness statement, without which the party wishing to make the application is unable to proceed.

One way of overcoming these difficulties is to take the witness's evidence by deposition.

DEPOSITIONS

Rule 34.8 of the CPR provides that a party to a claim may apply for an order for a person to be examined before the trial of the claim or an interim hearing takes place. The person from whom evidence is to be obtained is referred to as a deponent and the evidence itself is referred to as a deposition. 56.2

An order under **r. 34.8** is for the deponent to be examined on oath before either a judge, an examiner of the court or such other person as the court appoints (**r. 34.8(3)**). The order may also require the production of any document which the court considers is necessary for the purposes of the examination (**r. 34.8(4)**). Persons appointed by the Lord Chancellor as examiners of the court must be barristers or solicitor-advocates who have been practising for a period of at least three years (**r. 34.15**).

Witness expenses must be offered or paid when an order for examination is served (**r. 34.8(6)**) just as when a witness summons is served (see 55.6).

An order for a deposition to be taken may also order the party who obtained the order to serve a witness statement or witness summary in relation to the evidence to be given by the person to be examined (**r. 34.8(7)**).

The party who obtains an order for the examination of a deponent before an examiner of the court must (**PD 34, para. 4.2**):

(a) apply to the Foreign Process Section of the Masters' Secretary's Department at the Royal Courts of Justice for the allocation of an examiner; and
(b) provide the allocated examiner with copies of all documents in the proceedings necessary to inform the examiner of the issues.

Conduct of examination

56.3 Rule 34.9 of the CPR provides details of the procedure to be adopted in conducting the examination of a deponent. Subject to any directions contained in the order for examination, the examination must be conducted in the same way as if the witness were giving evidence at a trial (**r. 34.9(1)**). If all the parties are present, the examiner may conduct the examination of a person not named in the order for examination if the parties and the person to be examined consent (**r. 34.9(2)**). Therefore, as all parties are present, they effectively have the right to ask questions under the usual rules of evidence, albeit via the examiner. If the examiner considers it appropriate, he or she may conduct the examination in private (**r. 34.9(3)**).

In ensuring that the deponent's evidence is recorded in full, as required by **r. 34.9(4)**, the court or the examiner may permit it to be recorded on audiotape or videotape, but the deposition must always be recorded in writing by the examiner or by a competent shorthand writer or stenographer (**PD 34, para. 4.3**). If the deposition is not recorded verbatim, it must contain, as nearly as may be, the statement of the deponent; the examiner may record word for word any particular questions and answers, which appear to him or her to have special importance (**PD 34, para. 4.4**).

PD 34, para. 4.12, provides that once an examination is completed the examiner must sign the deposition, both the examiner and the deponent must initial any amendments to it, and it must be endorsed by the examiner with:

(a) a statement of the time occupied by the examination, and
(b) a record of any refusal by the deponent to sign the deposition and of his or her reasons for not doing so.

The examiner must send a copy of the deposition to the person who obtained the order for the examination of the witness, and to the court where the case is proceeding, for filing on the court file (**CPR, r. 34.9(5)**; **PD 34, para. 4.12(4)**). The party who obtained the order must then send each of the other parties a copy of the deposition received from the examiner (**CPR, r. 34.9(6)**).

Enforcing attendance for examination

56.4 If a person served with an order to attend before an examiner fails to attend or refuses to be sworn for the purpose of the examination or to answer any lawful question or produce any document at the examination, a certificate of that failure or refusal, signed by the examiner, must be filed by the party requiring the deposition (**CPR, r. 34.10(1)**).

If a deponent objects to answering any question or where any objection is taken to any question, the examiner must (**PD 34, para. 4.5**):

(a) record in the deposition or a document attached to it:
   (i) the question,
   (ii) the nature of and grounds of the objection, and
   (iii) any answer given; and
(b) give his or her opinion on the validity of the objection and any question of costs arising from it.

By **CPR, r. 34.10(2)**, on the certificate of failure or refusal being filed, the party requiring the deposition may apply, without notice, to the court for an order requiring the deponent to attend or to be sworn or to answer any question or produce any document, as the case may be. The court may order the person against whom an order is made under this rule to pay any costs resulting from the failure or refusal.

Fees and expenses of examiner

An examiner of the court may charge a fee for an examination (**CPR, r. 34.14(1)**) and is not required to send the deposition to the court unless the fee is paid (**r. 34.14(2)**). The examiner's fees and expenses must be paid by the party who obtained the order for examination (**r. 34.14(3)**) and if not paid within a reasonable time, the examiner may report that fact to the court (**r. 34.14(4)**). **56.5**

The court may order the party who obtained on order for examination to deposit in the court office a specified sum in respect of the examiner's fees, and the examiner will not be asked to act until that sum has been deposited (**r. 34.14(5)**).

Use of deposition at a hearing

A deposition ordered under **CPR, r. 34.8**, may be given in evidence at a hearing unless the court orders otherwise. A party intending to put a deposition in evidence at a hearing must serve notice of that intention on every other party at least 21 days before the day fixed for the hearing (**r. 34.11(1), (2) and (3)**). Under **r. 34.11(4)** the court may require a deponent to attend the hearing and give evidence orally. Where a deposition is given in evidence at trial, it shall be treated as if it were a witness statement for the purposes of **r. 32.13** (availability of witness statement for inspection) (see **49.23**). **56.6**

Restrictions on subsequent use of deposition taken for the purpose of any hearing except the trial

Rule 34.12 of the CPR provides that where the court orders a party to be examined about assets (whether the party's or any other person's) for the purpose of any hearing except the trial, the deposition may be used only for the purpose of the proceedings in which the order was made. It may, however, be used for some other purpose: **56.7**

(a) by the party who was examined;
(b) if the party who was examined agrees; or
(c) if the court gives permission.

Rule 34.12 is expressed to apply only to depositions relating to assets and will therefore be relevant to procedures concerning the enforcement of judgment, freezing orders, search orders and the like.

EXAMINATION OUT OF THE JURISDICTION

Requests to EU Regulation States

Council Regulation (EC) No. 1206/2001 on cooperation between the courts of Member States in the taking of evidence in civil and commercial matters (the 'Taking of Evidence Regulation') provides for taking evidence in one EU State for use in civil proceedings in another EU State. It does not apply to Denmark (art. 1). Each Regulation State has designated courts where evidence can be taken (in England and Wales these are the Royal Courts of Justice and the court centres at Birmingham, Bristol, Cardiff, Manchester and Leeds, see **PD 34, annex C**). Each Regulation State also has a central body (in England and Wales this is the Senior Master of the Queen's Bench Division, see **PD 34, para. 9.2**) who is responsible for supplying information, seeking solutions to any difficulties that may arise, and, in exceptional cases, forwarding requests to the competent court. **56.8**

A party to English civil proceedings seeking to obtain a deposition from a witness in a Regulation State must apply for an order for the issue of a request to a designated court in the

Regulation State (**CPR, r. 34.23(2)**). The party seeking the order must undertake to be responsible for the costs sought by the requested court for fees for experts, interpreters and for the court's expenses (**r. 34.23(3)**). Requests for the taking of evidence under the Taking of Evidence Regulation need to be made in the official language of the requested court (art. 5), and must be in form A in the annex to the Taking of Evidence Regulation (art. 4). The request must include the questions to be put to the witness or a statement of the facts about which he is to be examined, and also include any request for the examination to be under oath or affirmation, and any special form to be used (such as recording the evidence in a deposition).

Within seven days of receipt of the request the requested court must send an acknowledgment to the requesting court (art. 7(1)). Where necessary, coercive measures (the local equivalent of a witness summons) may be applied by the requested court to secure the attendance of the witness (art. 13). A request should be executed within 90 days, failing which the requested court should inform the requesting court, stating the reasons for the delay (arts 10 and 15). Representatives of the requesting court should be able to be present when the evidence is taken if this is compatible with the law of the requesting court (art. 12), and representatives of the parties have the right to participate on such conditions as may be laid down by the requested court in accordance with local law (art. 11).

The requesting court can ask for use of communications technology, including video-conferencing and teleconferencing, for the purpose of taking the evidence (art. 10(4)). The party seeking the order must undertake to be responsible for the costs sought by the requested court for any communications technology used (**CPR, r. 34.23(3)**).

Direct taking of evidence in Regulation States

56.9 A party can seek an order pursuant to **CPR, r. 34.23(5)**, for the submission of a request under art. 17 of the **Taking of Evidence Regulation** for the direct taking of evidence from a witness by the requested court. The party seeking the request must undertake to pay the court's expenses (**CPR, r. 34.23(6)(c)**). Direct taking of evidence is only permitted if it can be performed on a voluntary basis without the need for coercive measures (**Taking of Evidence Regulation, art. 17(2)**). The request must be in form I of the Taking of Evidence Regulation, and must be accompanied by a translation (**CPR, r. 34.23(6)(b)**). The central body of the requested court may only refuse the direct taking of evidence if the request does not fall within the scope of art. 1, or does not contain all the information required by art. 4, or if the direct taking of evidence is contrary to the fundamental principles of law of the requested State (art. 17(5)).

Non-EU countries: letters of request

56.10 Rule 34. 13 of the CPR provides for a deposition to be taken from a witness in Denmark or a non-EU State for use in English proceedings. The High Court, not a county court, may order the issue of a letter of request to the judicial authorities of the country in which the proposed deponent is. All applications are dealt with at the RCJ. A letter of request is a request to a judicial authority to take the evidence of that person, or arrange for it to be taken (**r. 34.13(2)**). The High Court may make an order under this rule in relation to county court proceedings (**r. 34.13(3)**).

An application for an order to issue a letter of request should be made by application notice in accordance with **Part 23** (**PD 34, para. 5.2**). The documents listed in **CPR, r. 34.13(6)**, should be filed with the application notice, together with a draft order (**PD 34, para. 5.3**). A draft letter of request should be in the form set out in Annex A to **PD 34**. The application will be dealt with by the Senior Master of the Queen's Bench Division of the High Court who will, if appropriate, sign the letter of request.

In exercising the discretion whether to order the issue of a letter of request the most important factor is the need to achieve justice. Thus, in *Banerji v Devi* (2005) LTL 29/6/2005 it was held to be wrong to refuse an order to take the evidence of a lawyer in India who had witnessed a signature which was alleged to have been forged, as the evidence was crucial on the forgery issue.

If the government of a country allows a person appointed by the High Court to examine a person in that country, the High Court may make an order appointing a special examiner (**r. 34.13(4)**), who may be the British consul or the consul-general or his or her deputy in the country where the evidence is to be taken (**PD 34, para. 5.8**). If the country in question is not a party to a civil procedure convention providing for evidence to be taken, it will be necessary to obtain the Secretary of State's consent to the appointment of a consul.

Examination in a foreign country may be on oath or affirmation or in accordance with any procedure permitted in that country (**CPR, r. 34.13(5)**).

The procedural requirements set out in **PD 34, paras 4.1 to 4.12**, relating to depositions taken in England and Wales for proceedings before courts in England and Wales apply to depositions to be taken abroad (**para. 5.9**).

The Criminal Justice (International Cooperation) Act 1990 empowers a judge in criminal proceedings to issue a letter of request to obtain evidence outside the United Kingdom. Section 3(7) provides that the evidence obtained shall not, without the consent of the appropriate authority, be used for any purpose other than that specified in the request. It was held in *BOC Ltd v Barlow* (2001) *The Times*, 10 July 2001, that, notwithstanding the apparently wide terms of s. 3(7), the provision is implicitly concerned only with the use of the evidence by the prosecuting authority or defendant in the criminal proceedings, and does not restrict use in civil proceedings.

Video links

A further means of presenting oral testimony from a witness who has difficulty in attending a hearing or trial is to have the witness's evidence given by video link, or other means which the court may allow under **CPR, r. 32.3**. If a party wishes to use this method, it is advisable to ascertain from the court whether the necessary technical facilities are available. **56.11**

Where the witness is in an EU State (other than Denmark), taking evidence by video link has to comply with the requirements of Council **Regulation (EC) No. 1206/2001**, which is discussed at **56.8**.

In *Polanski v Condé Nast Publications Ltd* [2005] UKHL 10, [2005] 1 WLR 637, the claimant brought libel proceedings in England, and sought permission to give evidence at the trial through a video link. In 1977 he had pleaded guilty in criminal proceedings in California, but had fled from the United States before sentence, and was living in France where he was safe from extradition. If he came to England to give evidence at his libel trial, there was a risk that he would be extradited to face the consequences of his United States conviction. Lord Nicholls of Birkenhead described videoconferencing facilities as being readily available to all litigants, and should not be denied to a party solely on the ground that he was a fugitive from justice. Indeed, the fact that he was a fugitive could be, and on the facts was, a sufficient reason for making a videoconferencing order. Videoconferencing directions were given in *Bank of Credit and Commerce International SA v Rahim* (2005) LTL 30/11/2005, where a witness in Pakistan was said to be in poor health (despite there being no medical evidence to this effect) and feared he might be arrested if he entered the UK. Other factors were the expense and inconvenience of bringing him from Pakistan, and the fact that as he was simply a witness, being outside the jurisdiction meant he could not be compelled to attend. Consideration should be given to allowing an expert to give evidence by video link where this is appropriate (**PD 35, annex, para. 19.2(c)**).

Detailed guidance on arranging and conducting videoconferencing is contained in **annex 3 to PD 32**. A list of the sites which are available for videoconferencing can be found on HM Courts Service website at www.hmcourts-service.gov.uk (**PD 32, para. 29.1**).

LETTERS OF REQUEST FROM FOREIGN COURTS

56.12 The statutory provisions on obtaining evidence for foreign courts are in the Evidence (Proceedings in Other Jurisdictions) Act 1975. The rules of court are in **CPR, rr. 34.16** to **34.21**, which should be read in conjunction with **PD 34, paras 6.1 to 6.8**.

Some letters of request from foreign courts are dealt with by officials and do not require action by legal representatives in England and Wales. Where a foreign court's letter of request cannot be dealt with in this way an application by an agent in England or Wales of a party to the foreign proceedings to give effect to the request should be made to the High Court by **Part 8** claim form and should be supported by a witness statement or affidavit exhibiting the documents listed in **PD 34, para.** 6.3. It may be made without notice being served on any other party (**CPR, r. 34.17(b)**).

A letter of request should be for the purpose of taking evidence on behalf of a foreign court. The High Court will not make an order for the examination of a witness where the letter of request is mainly of an investigatory nature. This is so even if the court is satisfied the witness can give some relevant and admissible evidence, unless it is possible to exclude the impermissible areas of the request without undue difficulty (*Re State of Norway's Application* [1987] QB 433; *United States of America v Philip Morris Inc.* [2003] EWHC 3028 (Comm), LTL 10/12/2003).

The order for the deponent to attend and be examined together with the evidence upon which the order was made must be served on the deponent (**PD 34, para. 6.5**). Arrangements for the examination to take place at a specified time and place before an examiner of the court or such other person as the court may appoint shall be made by the applicant for the order and approved by the Senior Master (**CPR, r. 34.18**).

CPR, rr. 34.9 and **34.10**, and **PD 34, paras 4.2 to 4.12**, apply to examinations requested by foreign courts, except that the examiner must send the deposition to the Senior Master (**PD 34, para. 6.6**).

Requests from Regulation States

56.13 Requests for the taking of evidence in England and Wales from other Regulation States under the **Taking of Evidence Regulation** must be made to a designated court (the Royal Courts of Justice and the court centres at Birmingham, Bristol, Cardiff, Manchester and Leeds, see **CPR, r. 34.24(2)** and **PD 34, Annex C**). The courts in England and Wales will act on requests in either English or French (**PD 34, para** 11.4), but otherwise translations are required. Once a request is received it is sent to the Treasury Solicitor (PD 34, para 11.2) who may apply on form N244 for an order for the evidence to be taken. The application is usually considered without notice (**CPR, r. 34.24(2)(c)**). The order and evidence in support must be served on the witness (**PD 34, para.** 11.5). Arrangements for the taking of the evidence will be made by the Treasury Solicitor and approved by the court (**para. 11.6**), and the court will provide these details to the parties and the representatives of the foreign court (if they have indicated they wish to be present when the evidence is taken (**para. 11.7**). The evidence will be taken in accordance with **CPR, rr. 34.9, 34.10** and **34.18**, for which see **56.3** and **56.12** (**r. 34.24(3)**).

The examiner will send the deposition to the requested court for transmission to the requesting court, and a copy of the deposition to the Treasury Solicitor (**r. 34.24(4)**).

Collateral use of depositions

A deposition obtained under **CPR, Part 34**, is obtained subject to an undertaking, implied at common law, not to use it for a collateral purpose without the consent of the witness or the permission of the requesting court. This includes depositions obtained under the **Taking of Evidence Regulation**. In exercising its discretion whether to grant permission for the collateral use of depositions, the court applies similar principles as apply in relation to the collateral use of disclosed documents (see **48.35**). The court also takes into account the purpose of the relevant power to take evidence on deposition. Thus, in *Dendron GmbH v Regents of the University of California* [2004] EWHC 589 (Pat), [2005] 1 WLR 200, permission was granted for the use of depositions obtained under the **Taking of Evidence Regulation** in related proceedings in other Regulation States, but not for use in the United States. **56.14**

Chapter 57 Trial Bundles

TIME FOR PREPARING TRIAL BUNDLES

57.1 All the documents likely to be referred to at trial should be placed into paginated trial bundles for use by the judge, witnesses and parties. Directions regarding the preparation and lodging of trial bundles will commonly be included with the directions made at the listing stage, but the rules in any event require the claimant to lodge the bundle not more than seven and not less than three days before the trial (**CPR, r. 39.5(2)**). If there is a trial 'window', presumably these periods are to be calculated from the start of the window. Although there is no duty to do so in the rules, defendants should, as a matter of practicality, notify the solicitor for the claimant about 14 days before the start of the trial of the documents the defendants want to be included in the trial bundles.

CONTENTS OF TRIAL BUNDLES

57.2 Detailed rules governing the format of trial bundles in non-specialist proceedings are to be found in **PD 39, para. 3**. These are that:

(a) The bundles should contain copies of:
   (i) the claim form and all statements of case;
   (ii) a case summary and/or a chronology where appropriate;
   (iii) all requests for further information and responses to the requests;
   (iv) all witness statements and witness summaries to be relied upon;
   (v) any hearsay notices;
   (vi) any notices of intention to rely on plans, photographs, etc. under **CPR, r. 33.6**;
   (vii) all experts reports and responses to questions to those experts;
   (viii) any order giving trial directions; and
   (ix) any other necessary documents. This last category will include all the relevant contemporaneous documentation and documentary evidence, as well as relevant correspondence.

(b) The bundles should be continuously paginated throughout, and indexed with a description of each document with its page number.

(c) If any of the documents is illegible they should be followed by a typed transcript given an 'A' number and with a suitable cross-reference.

(d) Where the bundle exceeds 100 pages numbered dividers should be used between groups of documents.

(e) If the documentation is particularly voluminous, a separate core bundle should be compiled containing the most important documents with cross-references to where the documents it contains can be found in the main bundles.

(f) The bundles should normally be contained in ring or lever-arch files. If more than one file is needed they should be in different colours or should be clearly marked by distinguishing letters, and obviously the same coding should be used for each set of the bundles. It is sometimes convenient to have a separate file containing the expert evidence.

The contents of the bundles should be agreed where possible (**PD 39, para. 3.9**). The parties should also, if possible, agree which of the documents in the bundles are authentic, and which of the documents are to be treated as evidence of the facts they state even if hearsay notices have not been served. The last point seems to contain a misunderstanding of the Civil Evidence Act 1995, which provides in s. 1(1) that in civil proceedings evidence will not be excluded on the ground that it is hearsay, and by s. 2(4) any failure to serve a hearsay notice (even if required) does not affect admissibility, but only goes to the questions of costs and weight.

Where it is not possible to agree the contents of the bundles, a summary of the points on which the parties are unable to agree should be included.

PREPARING BUNDLES

The claimant will need to compile identical bundles for the court, for each of the parties, and one for use by the witnesses at the trial (**PD 39, para. 3.10**). Under no circumstances should rival bundles be presented to the court (**Chancery Guide, app. 6, para. 5**). The originals of the documents in the bundle should be available for production at the hearing (**PD 39, para. 3.3**). **57.3**

The CPR provide that it is for the claimant to file the trial bundles (**r. 39.5(1)**) unless the court orders otherwise. It was said in *Maltez v Lewis* (1999) *The Times*, 4 May 1999, by Neuberger J that where the defendant is in a better financial position than the claimant the court might order the bundles to be prepared by the defendant's solicitors in order to ensure a level playing field for the purposes of **CPR, r. 1.1**.

There is no provision in the rules relating to the preparation of trial bundles (unlike **CPR, r. 31.15(c)**, in relation to disclosure of documents) for payment for the copy sent to the defendant. The cost of preparing the bundles is therefore simply part of the general costs of the claimant.

OTHER PROVISIONS DEALING WITH BUNDLES

Different requirements apply to bundles used in the following situations: **57.4**

(a) interim applications in non-specialist proceedings (**32.15**);
(b) Chancery Division hearings (see **Chancery Guide, paras 7.9** to **7.19** and **app. 6**);
(c) Admiralty and Commercial Court applications (see **Admiralty and Commercial Courts Guide, paras F6.4** to **F6.8** and **F11** to **F13** and **app. 10**);
(d) Admiralty and Commercial Court case management bundles (see **PD 58, para. 10.8; Admiralty and Commercial Courts Guide, para. D7** and **app. 10**);
(e) Admiralty and Commercial Court trials (see **Admiralty and Commercial Courts Guide, para. J3** and **app. 10**);
(f) Patents Court (see **Patents Court Guide, para. 9** and standard direction 15);
(g) appeals (see **PD 52, paras 5.6, 5.6A, 15.2** to **15.4** and **15.11**); and
(h) judicial review (see **74.36, PD 52, para. 15.4** and **PD 54, paras 5.6** to **5.9**).

USE OF BUNDLES AT THE HEARING

All the documents in an agreed bundle (see **57.2**) are admissible at the hearing unless the court orders otherwise or if a party gives a written notice objecting to the admissibility of particular documents (**PD 32, para. 27.2**). **57.5**

In *Gough v Mummery* [2002] EWCA Civ 1573, LTL 4/10/2002, the trial bundle contained one version of a letter from an expert, but a different (and more favourable) version (with the same date) was in the papers of counsel for the side relying on the letter. It was held that the trial judge's decisions to refuse an adjournment to investigate the differences between the two versions of the letter, and to refuse permission to rely on the version in counsel's papers, were discretionary matters and were not plainly wrong.

READING LISTS AND TIME ESTIMATES

57.6 In all Queen's Bench Division and Chancery Division claims where bundles must be lodged, the claimant or applicant must at the same time lodge:

(a) a reading list for the judge who will conduct the hearing;
(b) an estimated length of reading time; and
(c) an estimated length for the hearing.

This must be signed by all the advocates who will appear at the hearing. Each advocate's name, business address and telephone number must appear below his or her signature. In the event of disagreement about any of these matters, separate reading lists and estimates must be signed by the appropriate advocates. See Practice Direction (Royal Courts of Justice: Reading Lists and Time Estimates) [2000] 1 WLR 208.

Chapter 58 Trial by Jury

INTRODUCTION

Almost all civil trials nowadays are tried before a judge sitting alone. The last vestiges of the former practice of conducting civil trials before juries are statutory rights in the **County Courts Act 1984, s. 66**, and the **Supreme Court Act 1981, s. 69**, for trial by jury in actions in deceit, libel, slander, malicious prosecution and false imprisonment. There are exceptions relating to cases involving prolonged examination of documents or accounts, or scientific or local investigations which cannot conveniently be made by a jury. Juries are not looked on favourably for a number of reasons. These include the fact they do not give reasons for their decisions, the experience that jury trials tend to take considerably longer than trials before a judge sitting alone, and the risk that a jury will fail to reach even a majority verdict. **58.1**

STATUTORY RIGHTS TO TRIAL BY JURY

The **Supreme Court Act 1981, s. 69(1)**, provides: **58.2**

> Where, on the application of any party to an action to be tried in the Queen's Bench Division, the court is satisfied that there is in issue—
> (a) a charge of fraud against that party; or
> (b) a claim in respect of libel, slander, malicious prosecution or false imprisonment; or
> (c) any question or issue of a kind prescribed for the purposes of this paragraph,
> the action shall be tried with a jury, unless the court is of opinion that the trial requires any prolonged examination of documents or accounts or any scientific or local investigation which cannot conveniently be made with a jury.

The **County Courts Act 1984, s. 66(3)**, is in essentially the same terms for county court proceedings. The result is that the right to a jury only arises to claims proceeding in the Queen's Bench Division of the High Court and the county courts, and not while a claim is in the Chancery Division. Claims may be transferred to the Queen's Bench Division for the purpose of securing trial by jury, if appropriate. Note also that the right to trial by jury in fraud cases is only available to the defendant, but that either party has the right to a jury in claims for libel, slander, malicious prosecution and false imprisonment. 'Fraud' for this purpose is limited to claims in deceit (*Stafford Winfield Cook and Partners Ltd v Winfield* [1981] 1 WLR 458).

In considering whether the proviso to the **Supreme Court Act 1981, s. 69(1)**, applies, according to *Phillips v Commissioner of Police of the Metropolis* [2003] EWCA Civ 382, *The Times*, 2 April 2003, three questions must be asked:

(a) Would there be a prolonged examination of documents or any scientific investigation?
(b) If so, could the examination be conveniently made with a jury?
(c) If not, should the court nevertheless exercise its discretion to order trial with a jury?

In *Oliver v Calderdale Metropolitan Borough Council* (1999) *The Times*, 7 July 1999, it was said as a secondary ground for refusing a jury that a substantial dispute between the experts dealing with the psychological effects of an alleged malicious prosecution rendered the case unsuitable for trial by a jury. 'Documents' for the purpose of the proviso to s. 69 includes video footage. Whether the examination of that material could be made conveniently with a jury depends on factors such as the quality of the recordings and the quantity of material (*MacIntyre v Chief Constable of Kent* (2002) LTL 6/2/2002). In *Beta Construction Ltd v Channel Four Television Co. Ltd* [1990] 1 WLR 1042 Stuart Smith LJ made the point that some cases are inconvenient for juries because of the physical problems of jurors trying to follow documentation being taken from several files simultaneously, or trying to grapple with large plans within the confined space of most jury boxes. Where a case involves prolonged examination of documents which cannot conveniently be made with a jury, it is within the judge's case management discretion to order trial by judge of those issues, with jury trial for the rest (*Phillips v Commissioner of Police of the Metropolis*). Being a matter of discretion, it is unlikely that a successful appeal could be mounted against such a decision (*Gregson v Channel Four Television Corporation* [2002] EWCA Civ 941, LTL 4/7/2002).

TIME TO APPLY FOR TRIAL BY JURY

58.3 The **Supreme Court Act 1981, s. 69(2)**, provides that an application for trial by jury must be made not later than such time before trial as may be prescribed, which is within 28 days after service of the defence (**CPR, r. 26.11**).

DISCRETION TO ORDER TRIAL BY JURY

58.4 In cases outside the categories where there is a right to a jury the court retains, in most cases, a discretion to make an order for jury trial. There is no power to grant a jury even on a discretionary basis in county court admiralty proceedings, and certain proceedings under the Rent (Agriculture) Act 1976, the **Rent Act 1977**, the Protection from Eviction Act 1977 and the **Housing Act 1988** (see the **County Courts Act 1984, s. 66(1)**).

In other categories of case the court has a discretion, which must be exercised judicially and in accordance with the overriding objective, whether to make an order for trial by jury. However, the requirements of the **CPR, Part 1**, point strongly against the discretion being exercised, particularly the need for expedition and saving costs. Under the old rules it was in any event almost impossible to obtain a discretionary order for a jury, see *Ward v James* [1966] 1 QB 273, and *Williams v Beesley* [1973] 1 WLR 1295, and it was said in *Goldsmith v Pressdram Ltd* [1988] 1 WLR 64 that 'the emphasis now is against trial with juries, and the court should take this emphasis into account when exercising its discretion', per Lawton LJ.

JURY SELECTION

58.5 Juries must be selected randomly in accordance with the **Juries Act 1974, ss. 2, 5 and 6** (see *R v Tarrant* (1997) *The Times*, 29 December 1997). The former practice of allowing peremptory challenges to prospective jurors has been abolished (Criminal Justice Act 1988, s. 118), but it is still possible to challenge for cause (**Juries Act 1974, s. 12**).

RELEASING JURORS

58.6 Releasing jurors part way through a trial is inconvenient, and can lead to the need to discharge the entire jury and for the trial to start again. In an effort to avoid this happening, particularly in lengthy trials, the trial judge should inquire of prospective jurors whether they will suffer inconvenience or hardship through having to serve for the estimated length of the trial, and excuse those who will be so affected (see Practice Direction (Juries: Length of Trial) [1981] 1 WLR 1129, which should be applied even under CPR).

During the course of the trial the judge may discharge a juror on the ground of evident necessity. An example from criminal proceedings is *R v Richardson* [1979] 1 WLR 1316, where the judge discharged by telephone a juror whose husband had died during the night. It was held there was no material irregularity in the trial despite the fact the decision to discharge the juror had not been made in open court.

COMMUNICATIONS WITH THE JURY

All communications between the judge and jury should be conducted in open court and with the whole jury present (*R v Woods* (1987) 87 Cr App R 60). **58.7**

SUMMING UP

It is not the function of the judge to embark on a fact-finding exercise when sitting with a jury. The judge must sum up the case, with an agreed list of issues where there is a conflict (*Balchin v Chief Constable of Hampshire Constabulary* (2001) *The Times*, 4 May 2001). Where an expert in an assault claim against the police gave evidence which contradicted the account given by the claimant, the judge had to give adequate assistance to the jury on how to approach the conflicting evidence (*Masters v Chief Constable of Sussex* [2002] EWCA Civ 1482, LTL 3/10/2002). **58.8**

JURY VERDICTS

The jury should be told by the judge that they should deliberate on their verdict only when they are all together in the jury room (*R v Hastings* [2003] EWCA Crim 3730, *The Times*, 12 December 2003). A party who expressly asks for a question to be left to the jury cannot appeal against the jury's decision on the grounds that it is perverse (*McPhilemy v Times Newspapers Ltd (No. 3)* [2001] EMLR 832). **58.9**

If, after being discharged, the jury indicate that they have given the wrong verdict, the judge may invite them to retire again to reconsider their verdict and may accept a changed verdict if it is in the interests of justice to do so (*Igwemma v Chief Constable of Greater Manchester Police* [2001] EWCA Civ 953, [2002] QB 1012). In considering whether it is in the interests of justice, the judge should take into account: the time that has elapsed since the original verdict was returned; the reasons for seeking further assistance from the jury; and whether the jury may have been persuaded to change their view by anything said or done since they gave their original verdict.

Majority verdicts

High Court civil juries have 12 members. County court juries are eight strong. The jury must seek to reach a unanimous verdict, and the trial judge may only give a majority verdict direction where it appears that the jury has had such sufficient time for deliberation as the judge considers reasonable given the nature and complexity of the case (**Juries Act 1974, s. 17(4)**). **58.10**

Permissible majority verdicts where there are not less than 11 jurors are 11 : 1,10 : 2 and 10 : 1. Where there are only 10 jurors a 9 : 1 majority is permitted. In the county courts a majority of 7 : 1 is permissible. In addition, the court may accept a majority verdict with the consent of the parties (such as a simple majority verdict), and the parties may further agree to proceed with an incomplete jury (s. 17(5)).

Hung jury

58.11 Where the jury cannot reach a verdict, even a majority verdict, they should be discharged and the trial discontinued. The normal rule is that the costs of the inconclusive trial should be made to be in the case, so that whoever wins the subsequent trial recovers the costs of the first trial (*Camiller v Commissioner of Police of the Metropolis* (1999) *The Times*, 8 June 1999).

Chapter 59 Trial

The following procedural checklist, which is in **appendix 1**, is relevant to this chapter:

Procedural checklist 29 Trial preparation

INTRODUCTION

A key feature of the CPR is that the court must retain control of the progress of claims, and one of the ways in which this is achieved is by giving the parties trial dates or windows at an early stage. Trial directions are often given when a claim is allocated to a track, particularly in small claims and fast track claims. Small claims track cases are determined by district judges at informal hearings where the strict rules of evidence do not apply. They are usually conducted in the district judge's chambers. Hearings in small claims cases are discussed further in **chapter 43**. This chapter is principally concerned with trials in fast track and multi-track **59.1** claims. The standard period between directions and the trial date or window in fast track claims is 30 weeks (**CPR, r. 28.2(4)**). Even in multi-track claims the court will fix a trial date or window as soon as practicable (**r. 29.2(2)**). Further ways in which the court maintains control, particularly over the trial process, include:

(a) holding pre-trial reviews in selected multi-track cases a few weeks before trial — these will usually be heard by the trial judge, and one of their main purposes is to decide how to conduct the trial in the most efficient manner;
(b) setting of trial timetables in advance, limiting the amount of time allowed for speeches and questioning of witnesses;
(c) an emphasis on written preparation;
(d) the use of Fridays as preparation days in long trials (although this is not set out anywhere in the CPR or practice directions, and is a matter for individual courts and judges).

PRE-TRIAL CHECKLISTS AND FIXING THE DATE OF TRIAL

59.2 These topics have already been considered in the context of the discussion of fast track cases (see **44.12** and **44.16**) and multi-track cases (see **45.15** and **45.16**). Essentially, directions made either on track allocation or at a case management conference or other directions hearing will fix a date for pre-trial checklists, and trial dates will be fixed as soon as possible. In fast track cases this means at the allocation stage. In multi-track cases, fixing the trial date as soon as possible may mean doing this at the allocation stage, but may mean doing so considerably later. If a trial date is given at an early stage it may be altered later, perhaps after the court considers the pre-trial checklists. Trial dates may either be fixtures, which obviously means that the trial will commence on a specific date, or may be given by means of a trial 'window' of up to three weeks.

Fast track listing

59.3 A trial date or a period in which the trial is to take place will usually be given in fast track cases as part of the standard directions at the track allocation stage. If a trial period is given, it should not exceed three weeks. The trial date or period should not be more than 30 weeks from the date of the directions. The trial date or period will be confirmed or altered at the listing stage, which is fixed as one of the standard fast track directions, and is usually about eight weeks before trial.

In his *Final Report*, ch. 3, para. 28, Lord Woolf said in relation to fast track listing, 'I attach great importance to trial dates being honoured and I know that the Court Service is already working towards developing an effective listing system to meet the needs of the fast track'. The report went on to explain the difficulties and delays that are likely if all cases are given fixed dates, which stem largely from the fact that most cases settle, and the probability that when this happens the courts will not be in use for a substantial part of the working week. It also identified a number of well-known problems in the present listing system. These include Her Majesty's Courts Service being unable to find a judge or court for some trials when they are listed; urgent applications being listed immediately before trials, resulting in trials being delayed or adjourned; the practice of the courts deliberately 'overbooking' in the hope that most of the cases booked for one particular day will settle; and 'block listing' a number of cases for the same time in circumstances where it is almost inevitable that the parties and witnesses in some of the cases blocked together will have to wait in court for a substantial time before their cases are reached. All these problems, if they persist, will have a substantial impact on fast track cases. These cases are intended to be tried within a single day, and have restrictions on the costs recoverable, both of which may be rendered meaningless if listing shortcomings result in adjournments and part-heard trials.

As recognised by the *Final Report*, ch. 3, para. 31, ensuring fast track cases are tried as intended will involve the cooperation of everyone involved. Practitioners are under an obligation to provide accurate information in their pre-trial checklists to enable hearing times to be calculated on a realistic basis. District judges need to make realistic assessments of hearing times based on the information on the court files. Listing officers need to make provision for hearing urgent matters in ways that do not interfere with fast track trials, and must provide specific staggered times for hearings rather than block lists.

Multi-track listing

The key obligation in the CPR regarding fixing multi-track cases for trial is in **r. 29.2(2)**, which provides that the court must fix the trial date or period in which the trial will take place as soon as practicable. Given the wide variety of cases on the multi-track this will vary considerably from case to case. For some cases the trial date or period may be given in the directions made at the track allocation stage. In other cases it may not be possible until a considerable time later, perhaps in a case management conference or pre-trial review. Like fast track cases, there is a pre-trial checklist procedure in multi-track cases (see 45.16). Directions for filing these checklists will be made at some stage in the directions process, normally with a view to the checklists being filed about 10 weeks before the intended trial. The trial date will be confirmed or altered at that stage. **59.4**

As multi-track trials may sometimes stretch over several days or weeks, minor delays due to urgent applications being listed first are not so likely to have such an impact as in fast track cases, so the concerns noted in 59.3, although still important, are not so fundamental.

It is interesting to note that if the court gives a trial window in a multi-track case instead of a fixture, the period should be just one week (**r. 29.8(ii)**), rather than the possible three-week period for fast track cases.

Fixing trial dates and windows in claims proceeding in the Royal Courts of Justice

In Admiralty, Commercial and Technology and Construction Court claims, trials are usually fixed at, or in consequence of, the first case management conference. In other Queen's Bench Division claims in the Royal Courts of Justice (see **Queen's Bench Guide, para. 8.4.5**), the court may: **59.5**

(a) direct that the trial is not to begin earlier than a specified date; and/or
(b) direct that the trial date be within a specified period; and/or
(c) specify the trial date or window.

If either option (a) or (b) is used, the court will also direct the parties to attend upon the listing officer to fix the trial date or window. The claimant (unless another party agrees to do it) must within the next seven days of a date directed by the court for the purpose take out an appointment with the listing officer and give notice of the appointment to the other parties. At the listing hearing the trial will be fixed in accordance with the main direction.

Chancery Division listing

There are three main Chancery Division lists called the trial list (for trials to be heard with witnesses), the interim hearings list (for interim applications and appeals from masters), and the general list (for all other matters) (**Chancery Guide, paras 6.3** to **6.6**). There is a warned list which is published on Fridays showing the cases liable to be heard in the following week. **Chapter 6 of the Chancery Guide** also deals with time estimates, appeals from masters, and listing of bankruptcy applications and appeals, companies applications and petitions, short applications and summary judgment, as well as revenue appeals and hearings in claims for the variation of trusts. **59.6**

Expedited hearing

In cases of real urgency the court may order an expedited hearing, exercising its power under **CPR, r. 3.1(2)(b)**. Granting such an order has an impact on all other cases listed for hearing, **59.7** so can rarely be justified. An argument that effective enforcement cannot be started until a final judgment has been obtained is not a convincing reason for expediting a trial, and generally any such application should be made in the early stages of the litigation (*Daltel Europe Ltd v Makki* [2004] EWHC 1631 (Ch), LTL 17/6/2004). An example where an order was granted is *Wembley National Stadium Ltd v Wembley (London) Ltd* (2000) LTL 16/11/2000, where funding for a project which was dependent on the success of the proceedings was likely to be withdrawn within a limited time. In addition to ordering an expedited hearing, the court will lay down a timetable with strict deadlines.

Availability of experts and listing

59.8 Two important concepts are that trials should be listed as soon as practicable, and once fixed should not be adjourned unless absolutely necessary. If a party wants to change experts in the run-up to trial, or to instruct an expert for the first time shortly before trial, they are obliged to instruct experts who will report in sufficient time and be available for the trial. In *Rollinson v Kimberly Clark Ltd* [1999] CPLR 581 an expert instructed about six months before trial was unable to attend trial. On an application made about three months before trial the judge refused to break the fixture, and her decision was upheld by the Court of Appeal. A decision of great practical importance is *Matthews v Tarmac Bricks and Tiles Ltd* [1999] CPLR 463. There had been some difficulty in fixing the trial, and the court convened a listing hearing which was attended by a young member of the Bar on behalf of the defendant. Counsel had been provided with a list of unavailable dates, which included 15 July. The judge asked why the defendant's two experts were unavailable on 15 July, to which counsel replied she had no instructions. The judge then said, 'I can do two things. I can fix July 15 or I can adjourn this matter so that you can make phone calls and then I'll fix July 15. Which would you prefer?' Given the judge was going to fix the trial for 15 July anyway, counsel replied, 'You might as well fix July 15'. On being informed of the result the defendant's solicitors then wrote to the court saying they would like permission to appeal, but did not tell the court why their experts were unavailable. The judge refused permission, and did not list the matter for a hearing. In fact one was booked to be on holiday, and the other was due to appear as a witness in another trial. The Master of the Rolls said it was not enough simply to tell the court which dates experts could not attend, but that reasons had to be given as well. Even if the actual reasons had been given, it did not follow that the court would not have still listed the case for 15 July. The two courts could have consulted together to produce trial timetables to allow the expert to attend both trials. An effort should have been made with the other doctor to change his holiday plans: doctors holding themselves out as practising in the medico-legal field have to be prepared to arrange their affairs to meet the commitments of the courts where that is practical. The case clearly underlines the importance of having someone familiar with the case and fully briefed attend at case management hearings (see **CPR, r. 29.3(2)**). However, it may be that the decision in this case turned on the history of difficulties in fixing the trial, and should not be seen as always applicable in other cases.

ADJOURNMENT

Power to adjourn

59.9 **Rule 3.1(2)(b)** of the CPR gives the court a general power to adjourn. Adjournments may be necessary due to shortages of court resources. They may be sought by a party on the ground of some event outside their control which prevents them from presenting their full case at the hearing. They are also, regrettably, sometimes sought because a party or their lawyers have failed to prepare the case in time, and adjournments in these circumstances are often attended by breaches of case management directions previously made by the court.

The power to grant an adjournment is discretionary, and should be exercised in accordance with the overriding objective. Where an adjournment is sought for reasons outside the control of the party, it should usually be granted. Examples are where vital witnesses are unavoidably out of the country, or too ill to attend court. Adjournments are unlikely to be granted where a party is not ready for trial through their own fault, or where they have been given a previous adjournment and are still not ready, unless the circumstances are exceptional.

An adjournment was refused in *Powell v Pallisers of Hereford Ltd* [2002] EWCA Civ 959, LTL 1/7/2002, where the defendant wanted more time to enable a third-party to take part in the trial, but where an early trial date, which would ensure that the claim was tried by the time of the 2002 harvest, had been set because the claimant was a farmer in financial difficulties. A judge has a wide discretion whether to adjourn, and it is not easy for an appeal court to interfere with that discretion (*Roshdi v Thames Trains Ltd* [2002] EWCA Civ 284, LTL 20/2/2002).

Problems obtaining representation

In *Bates v Croydon London Borough Council* (2001) LTL 23/1/2001 an adjournment should have **59.10** been given as the appellant was awaiting a determination of an application for legal aid, and she had been served with the respondents' witness statements and other documents very shortly before the hearing. The court should respect the right of a party to seek public funding by granting adjournments where appropriate (*Berry Trade Ltd v Moussavi* [2002] EWCA Civ 477, [2002] 1 WLR 1910). An adjournment should have been granted in *Henry Butcher International Ltd v KG Engineering* [2004] EWCA Civ 1597, LTL 22/10/2004, to enable a party to obtain legal representation where the case had a complex history and raised complex legal issues. Similarly, in *Ghadami v Harlow District Council* [2004] EWCA Civ 891, LTL 21/6/2004, an adjournment should have been given where the date listed conflicted with an earlier direction and would have deprived a party of his counsel of choice. In *Joyce v King* (1987) *The Times*, 13 July 1987, the claimant was unable to obtain expert evidence without legal aid, and there were problems in obtaining legal aid. It was held that the trial should have been adjourned because it was not possible for the claimant to obtain justice without being given further time. An adjournment was granted in *Islam v Meah* [2005] EWCA Civ 1485, LTL 11/11/2005, where the defendant had limited understanding of English, and the adjournment was needed so he could obtain legal funding and legal representation.

Breach of case management directions

The general approach that will be adopted where an adjournment is sought after there has **59.11** been a breach of case management directions is set out in **PD 28, para. 5.4** (fast track) and **PD 29, para. 7.4** (multi-track). These provide that the court will not allow a failure to comply with directions to lead to the postponement of the trial unless the circumstances of the case are exceptional. Litigants and lawyers must be in no doubt that the court will regard the postponement of a trial as an order of last resort. If practicable to do so, the court will exercise its powers in a manner that enables the case to come on for trial on the date or within the period previously set, and it may set a new, but tight, timetable, with sanctions for non-compliance. Where it appears that one or more issues are or can be made ready for trial at the time fixed while others cannot, the court may direct that the trial will proceed on the issues that are or will then be ready, and order that no costs will be allowed for any later trial of the remaining issues or that those costs will be paid by the party in default. Where the court has no option but to postpone the trial it will do so for the shortest possible time and will give directions for the taking of the necessary steps in the meantime as rapidly as possible.

An adjournment of a fast track claim based on an argument that the claimant had suffered psychiatric injuries (which were not mentioned in the disclosed medical evidence) and that the claim should be reallocated to the multi-track was refused in *Taylor v Graham* (2000) LTL 25/5/2000, largely because evidence was not adduced substantiating the more complex nature of the claim justifying reallocation. Failing to prepare for trial because there were ongoing negotiations for a settlement is unlikely to be regarded as a sufficient reason for an adjournment (*Assiouti v Hosseini* (1999) LTL 26/11/99). An application to adjourn in *AC Electrical Wholesale plc v IGW Services Ltd* (2000) LTL 10/10/2000 based on a need to include a claim for loss of profits in a counterclaim was refused as there were no exceptional circumstances to explain why this had not been pleaded earlier.

Late applications to adjourn

59.12 The fact that a party has not applied to adjourn until the day of the trial, despite knowing for many weeks that it is in difficulties, may be a sufficient reason to refuse an adjournment (*National Westminster Bank plc v Aaronson* [2004] EWHC 618 (QB), LTL 9/3/2004). Where both parties are to blame for the failure to instruct an expert and in not informing the court of the need to adjourn until the last minute, it is wrong to refuse to adjourn if only one party will suffer detriment from the lack of adjournment (*Thomson v O'Connor* [2005] EWCA Civ 1533, LTL 7/11/2005). In *Alderson v Stillorgan Sales Ltd* [2001] EWCA Civ 1060, LTL 13/6/2001, the claimants were refused permission to call their own expert, and the court directed that the parties jointly instruct an expert, who was to report just over two weeks before the trial. The expert was late, and delivered his report, which was favourable to the defendants, five days before trial. The day before trial the claimants sought an adjournment, which was refused, and a renewed application on the day of the trial was also refused. On appeal it was held that waiting to the day before trial was inappropriate. The appeal was dismissed partly because the claimants should have appealed the original order, or applied to adjourn when the expert missed the date for delivering his report, and partly because their case was weak in any event.

Witness availability and medical reasons

59.13 In *Green v Northern General Transport* (1970) 115 SJ 59 a new trial was ordered after the judge refused to adjourn despite a material witness being unavailable. In *Re A (A Child)* [2005] EWCA Civ 862, LTL 14/7/2005, the judge was held entitled to conclude that the medical evidence about the father's post-operative condition did not justify an adjournment of more than about a week. Justice is a two-way street, and the other parties are as entitled to a fair and expeditious hearing as the party seeking the adjournment. An adjournment was refused in *Ahmed v Butt* [2005] EWCA Civ 1448, LTL 1/11/2005, where a litigant in person complained of having a sore throat. The judge said he would reassess the matter as the hearing progressed, but allowed the hearing to continue even though the litigant in person became inaudible. It was held that the judge was entitled to refuse the initial application on this provisional basis, but erred in not adjourning when it became apparent the party was not capable of making himself heard.

Cold feet and tactical reasons

59.14 In *Skipsey v O'Rourke* [2005] EWCA Civ 912, LTL 30/6/2005, medical evidence that the claimant was 'not in a fit frame of mind' to attend was rightly held to be insufficient to justify an adjournment. (It later transpired that the doctor had understated the claimant's condition, and an adjournment was allowed on that basis.) The court felt in *Law Debenture Trust Corporation plc v Elektrim Finance BV* [2005] EWCA Civ 1354, LTL 8/11/2005, that an adjournment was sought in order to leave the present proceedings unresolved, so as to secure a forensic advantage in related proceedings in Poland. On that basis the adjournment was refused.

SETTLEMENT BEFORE TRIAL

59.15 If a claim is settled, whether by agreement or acceptance of a **Part 36** offer, or is discontinued, in the period between the giving of a trial date or 'window' and the commencement of the trial, it is the duty of the parties to notify the listing officer for the trial court immediately (**PD 39, para. 4.1**). Giving written notice to the court at least 14 days before the trial date will result in the listing fee being refunded (**CPFO, note following fee 2.2**). If an order is drawn up giving effect to a settlement or discontinuance, a copy of the order should be lodged with the listing officer.

PRE-TRIAL ARRANGEMENTS

Trial timetables

59.16 The court must, in consultation with the parties, set a timetable for the trial, unless it considers that it would be inappropriate to do so (**CPR, rr. 28.6 and 29.8**). In multi-track cases, if there is a pre-trial review, that is the occasion when the court should set the trial timetable. In other cases on the fast or multi-tracks, the court sets the timetable either at a listing hearing (which should rarely be required) or when (or shortly after) it lists the case for trial (**rr. 28.6(1)** and **29.8(i)**). When the court sets a trial timetable it will do so in consultation with the parties (**r. 39.4**). If no trial timetable is laid down before trial, the trial judge may lay down a timetable at the start of the trial (**PD 28, para. 8.3**, for fast track cases; **PD 29, para. 10.3**, for cases on the multi-track).

Parties will need to make sure that any views they might have regarding the trial timetable are notified to the court at the same time as they file their listing questionnaires. Among the matters to be considered are:

(a) whether an opening speech is required on behalf of the claimant, and if so, how long will be required for this;
(b) how much time will be required in chief to elucidate or expand upon the witness statements relied upon on behalf of the client;
(c) which of the other side's witnesses it will be necessary to cross-examine, and which of their witnesses' evidence can be agreed, whether in whole or in part (and if the latter, which parts);
(d) how much of the expert evidence can be agreed, and how many of the experts need to be called to give oral evidence at the trial;
(e) how long each of the closing speeches will require.

Other factors will include whether the trial should be limited to certain specified issues; the order in which witnesses should be called; and the length of time required for delivery of judgment and arguments about costs and any other outstanding matters. It is important that the trial timetable laid down is realistic because, unless the trial judge makes an order to the contrary, the trial will follow the pattern laid down in the timetable (**rr. 28.7** and **29.9**).

One of the objects in setting trial timetables is to limit the length of trials. The time given will therefore usually be restrictive. Advocates will consequently be forced to give even more careful consideration to the questions they want to put to the various witnesses, as time in court will be at a premium. The *Final Report* recognised that more time will be required for preparation, which is why recommendation 50 was that there would be no sittings on Fridays.

Statement of issues

59.17 One of the matters to be considered on a pre-trial review (if one is held) is the preparation of a statement of the issues to be tried. In complex cases this document will assist in focusing on the matters that need to be dealt with. In Admiralty and Commercial Court cases a list of issues must be compiled in accordance with the **Admiralty and Commercial Courts Guide, para. D6**, after the defence has been served. The court may decide to use some of its more far-reaching case management powers to ensure the trial is focused on what the court regards as the real issues in the case, rather than what the parties may want to keep in issue if they can. The court, for example, has power to:

(a) decide which issues need full investigation at trial, and to dispose of the others summarily (such as by fixing a summary judgment hearing of its own initiative: **CPR, r. 1.4(2)(c)**);

(b) direct that part of the proceedings be dealt with separately (**r. 3.1(2)(e)**);

(c) order the trial of preliminary issues, or the split trial of liability and quantum or other issues (**r. 3.1(2)(i), (l)**, and see **59.41 to 59.56**);

(d) decide the order in which issues are to be resolved or tried (**rr. 1.4(2)(d)** and **3.1(2)(j)**);

(e) give directions on the issues on which it requires evidence (**r. 32.1(1)(a)**);

(f) give directions on the nature of the evidence it requires to decide the issues it identifies (**r. 32.1(1)(b)**); and

(g) direct how the evidence is to be placed before the court (**r. 32.1(1)(c)**).

In multi-track cases, **PD 29, paras 5.6** and **5.7**, provide that the parties are required to consider, before the court holds a case management conference, whether a case summary will be helpful. This is not quite the same thing as a statement of issues, but is a document designed to assist the court in understanding the issues and questions in the case. The document should be no more than 500 words, should set out a brief chronology, must state the issues of fact which are agreed and in dispute, and should set out the evidence required to decide the disputed issues.

Reading guides and skeletons

59.18 Skeleton arguments are required for almost all High Court trials, and are often desirable for county court trials. Directions for the exchange of skeletons are often incorporated in ordinary case management directions. Normally skeletons are exchanged simultaneously. In complex claims sequential disclosure may be ordered, but the time between disclosure of the claimant's skeleton and that of the defendant should be short, giving the defendant time simply to refashion a draft rather than to formulate the entire argument (*Brown v Bennett* (2000) *The Times*, 13 June 2000). The discussion on skeleton arguments at **32.16** applies equally to trial skeletons. For the practice in the Admiralty and Commercial Courts see the **Admiralty and Commercial Courts Guide, paras J5** and **J6** and **app. 9**. In the High Court, advocates must also provide reading lists for the trial judge, see **57.6**.

In addition to the trial bundles the trial judge has a discretion about what other material to read by way of pre-trial preparation, and may read material containing inadmissible evidence (*Barings plc v Coopers and Lybrand* [2001] EWCA Civ 1163, [2001] CPLR 451).

Disposal without an oral hearing

59.19 The *Final Report*, recommendation 49, was that suitable cases be determined on the statements of case without the need for an oral hearing, where this would save time and costs. **Rule** 1.4(2)(j) of the CPR implements this by providing that active case management includes a power to deal with cases without the parties needing to attend at court. This power is used most often in cases raising straightforward points of construction or law, where the facts are agreed or not in dispute. However, the power cannot be exercised without the consent of the parties given the provisions of the **European Convention on Human Rights, art. 6(1)**.

Hearings in public and in private

59.20 The general rule in **CPR, r. 39.2(1)**, is that trials will be conducted in public. The general rule does not, however, impose an obligation to make special arrangements for accommodating members of the public. By way of exception to the general rule, **r. 39.2(3)** provides that hearings may be conducted in private if:

(a) publicity would defeat the object of the hearing;

(b) it involves matters relating to national security;

(c) it involves confidential information (including information relating to personal financial matters) and publicity would damage that confidentiality;

(d) a private hearing is necessary to protect the interests of any child or patient;

(e) it is a hearing of an application made without notice and it would be unjust to any respondent for there to be a public hearing;
(f) it involves uncontentious matters arising in the administration of trusts or in the administration of a deceased's estate; or
(g) the court considers this to be necessary, in the interests of justice.

Further, the court may order that the identity of any party or witness must not be disclosed if it considers non-disclosure necessary in order to protect the interests of that party or witness (**CPR, r. 39.2(4)**).

This accords with the **European Convention on Human Rights, art. 6(1)**, which provides that everyone is entitled to a fair and public hearing, and goes on to say that:

> Judgment shall be pronounced publicly but the press and public may be excluded from all or part of the trial in the interests of morals, public order or national security in a democtratic society, where the interests of juveniles or the protection of the private life of the parties so require, or to the extent strictly necessary in the opinion of the court in special curcumstances where publicity would prejudice the interests of justice.

PD 39, para. 1.4A, provides that in deciding whether to hold a hearing in public or private the judge must have regard to the **European Convention on Human Rights, art. 6(1)**.

A newspaper making an unsuccessful application for a hearing to be held in public may be ordered to pay costs if the application causes unnecessary disruption to the hearing (*A v Times Newspapers Ltd* [2002] EWHC 2444 (Fam), [2003] 1 All ER 587).

Hearings in private

The general principle (see **European Convention on Human Rights, art. 6(1)**) is that trials are conducted in public. Hearing all or part of a trial in private is exceptional, and should be ordered only where it is necessary, in the interests of justice, to do so (*Three Rivers District Council v Bank of England* [2005] EWCA Civ 933, LTL 18/8/2005). A number of specific types of proceedings which will be conducted in private are set out in **PD 39, para. 1.5**, broadly as follows: **59.21**

(a) mortgage possession claims against individuals;
(b) repossession claims for non-payment of rent in respect of dwelling houses;
(c) most hearings relating to the enforcement and execution of judgments, including applications to suspend warrants, applications to vary or suspend payment of judgment debts by instalments, applications for charging orders, third party debt orders, attachment of earnings, administration orders, the appointment of receivers, and obtaining information from judgment debtors;
(d) the determination of an assisted person's liability for costs under the **Community Legal Service (Costs) Regulations 2000 (SI 2000/441), regs 9** and **10**, and the Civil Legal Aid (General) Regulations 1989, reg. 127;
(e) applications for security for costs under the Companies Act 1985, s. 726(1) (nothing is said about applications under **CPR, r. 25.13**);
(f) proceedings under the **Consumer Credit Act 1974**;
(g) proceedings under the Inheritance (Provision for Family and Dependants) Act 1975;
(h) proceedings under the **Protection from Harassment Act 1997**;
(i) hearings which involve the interests of a child or patient **CPR, r. 39.2(3)(d)**; **PD 39, para. 1.6**); and
(j) application by a trustee or personal representative for directions as to bringing or defending legal proceedings. It has been held in *Re Trusts of X Charity* [2003] EWHC 1462 (Ch), [2003] 1 WLR 2751, that applications by trustees for directions are essentially administrative, designed to provide guidance to the fiduciary, and therefore do not engage the **European Convention on Human Rights, art. 6(1)**, at all, and so may be conducted entirely in private.

All arbitration claims (see **chapter 69**) other than hearings determining points of law under the Arbitration Act 1996, s. 45, and appeals under s. 69, are, subject to any order of the court, heard in private (**CPR, r. 62.10**). The presumption is that most arbitration claims will be heard in private (*Moscow City Council v Bankers Trust Co.* (2003) *The Times*, 1 September 2003).

Under **r. 39.8** the court may exclude the claimant and his or her representatives from proceedings under the Race Relations Act 1976, s. 57(1), on the ground that doing so is in the interests of national security. Where this power is exercised the court may allow the excluded party to make a statement, and the Attorney-General may appoint a special advocate to represent the interests of the claimant under s. 67A(2). The court may order the special advocate not to communicate with any person (including the excluded claimant) on any matter discussed or referred to or with regard to any material disclosed (**PD 39C**).

Where a hearing is to proceed in private a sign will be place on the door to the court or room where a hearing is taking place to that effect. After a hearing in private the order drawn up will be clearly marked in the title 'Before [name of judge] sitting in private'. Anyone other than a party will not be allowed to obtain a copy of the judgment or the order except with the permission of the judge who decided the matter (**PD 39, para. 1.12**). On the other hand, if the hearing was in public anyone can obtain copies of the judgment and order after paying the appropriate fee.

Privacy of family cases

59.22 No confidentiality attaches to witness statements, affidavits and the events in proceedings in the Family Division relating to money or property where no children are involved, even if the proceedings are heard in chambers (*Clibbery v Allan* [2002] EWCA Civ 45, [2002] Fam 261). Restricting publication of such material would be a restriction on the freedom of expression guaranteed by the **European Convention on Human Rights, art. 10**, and such a restriction could not be justified by reference to **arts 8** (right to respect for private and family life) and **6** (right to a fair trial). The denial of a hearing and pronouncement of judgment in public in child custody proceedings under the Family Proceedings Rules 1991 (SI 1991/1247), r. 4.16(7), is justifiable under **art. 6(1) of the Convention** (*B v United Kingdom* (2001) 34 EHRR 19).

Mortgage possession claims

59.23 Regarding claims by mortgagees against individuals for possession of land, where the hearing is listed to be held in private (as will be normal), **PD 39, para. 1.15**, provides that any fact which needs to be proved by the evidence of witnesses may be proved by evidence in writing.

Sittings

59.24 Sittings of the High Court and Court of Appeal, and the vacation arrangements for the High Court, are dealt with in **PD 39B**. The four sittings are:

Michaelmas: from 1 October to 21 December;

Hilary: from 11 January to the Wednesday before Easter Sunday;

Easter: from the second Tuesday after Easter Sunday to the Friday before the spring holiday at the end of May; and Trinity: from the second Tuesday after the spring holiday to 31 July.

Where a claim proceeding in London needs to be heard immediately or promptly during a vacation, an application should be made for the claim to be heard in vacation (**PD 39B, para. 2.1**(2)). For proceedings in the Queen's Bench Division, **para. 2.5** lists 10 types of application which may be listed for hearing before a master during August without first seeking permission. They include applications such as for extensions of time, setting aside judgment and approval of settlements. Likewise, Queen's Bench Division appeals to the judge during August will generally be limited to the 10 listed types of hearing. Applications to the judge in the Queen's Bench Division during August should be restricted to matters of real urgency (**para. 2.3(2)**). During September all types of applications and appeals may be made in the Queen's Bench Division, but a September hearing date may not be obtainable. Where it is important to have a Queen's Bench Division application or appeal heard in August or September it is wise to include a request with the papers to have the application marked 'fit for August' or 'fit for vacation' (see **para. 2.3(3)**).

In the Chancery Division masters deal with all types of application throughout the summer, with deputies dealing with much of the work during this period (**para. 2.4**). For High Court district registry cases circuit arrangements may be made for sittings in vacation (**para. 2.2**).

Trial location

Normally trials will take place at the court where the case has been proceeding, but it may be transferred to another court for trial if this is appropriate having regard to the convenience of the parties and the availability of court resources (**PD 28, para. 8.1**, for the fast track; **PD 29, para. 10.1**, for cases on the multi-track). Multi-track cases will generally have been transferred to Civil Trial Centres when allocated to the multi-track (if commenced in a feeder court), but they may be allowed to proceed elsewhere if that is appropriate given the needs of the parties and the availability of court resources. **59.25**

Allocation to judiciary

District judges have jurisdiction to try all small claims and fast track cases (**PD 2B, para. 11.1**). District judges may also hear cases seeking the recovery of land, for the assessment of damages, with the consent of the parties, and **Part 8** claims allocated to the multi-track. Injunction and committal applications may only be heard by a district judge if the claim has been allocated to the fast or small claims tracks; or if the financial value is below £15,000 (in cases that have not been allocated at the time of the application); or if the terms have been agreed by the parties, or if the injunction is connected to a charging order or receivership order by way of equitable execution. **59.26**

Most multi-track cases will be tried by High Court judges and, in the county courts, by circuit judges and recorders. There is no restriction on masters and district judges trying **Part 8** claims, but other cases on the multi-track may be tried by a master or district judge only with the consent of the parties (**PD 2B, para. 4.1**). Hearings to assess damages may be dealt with by masters and district judges without limit (**para. 4.2**).

Impartiality of judge

It has long been established that a judge must not sit in his or her own cause. The rule laid down in *Dimes v Proprietors of Grand Junction Canal* (1852) 3 HL Cas 759 by Lord Campbell is now interpreted as not being confined to a claim in which the judge is a party, but applies also to a claim in which the outcome could, realistically, affect an interest of the judge. In *R v Bow Street Metropolitan Stipendiary Magistrate, ex parte Pinochet Ugarte (No. 2)* [2000] 1 AC 119 the House of Lords held that the principle that a judge is automatically disqualified from hearing a matter in his or her own cause is not limited to cases where the judge has a pecuniary interest in the outcome, but applies also to cases where the judge's decision would lead to the promotion of a cause in which the judge was involved together with one of the parties. The automatic disqualification rule is subject to the *de minimis* principle, in that some supposed financial interests are so small they can be ignored (*Locabail (UK) Ltd v Bayfield Properties Ltd* [2000] QB 451). The same principles apply to arbitrators (*AT and T Corporation v Saudi Cable Co.* [2000] 2 Lloyd's Rep 127). **59.27**

Under the **European Convention on Human Rights, art. 6(1)**, litigants are entitled to a fair hearing before an impartial tribunal. ECHR jurisprudence has established that there will be a breach where the existence of a legitimate reason or fear of a lack of impartiality is objectively justified. Before the implementation of the Convention, the House of Lords had held that a judge should not sit if there is a real danger of bias (*R v Gough* [1993] AC 646). A synthesis of the two tests was accomplished by the Court of Appeal in *Re Medicaments and Related Classes of Goods (No. 2)* [2001] 1 WLR 700, where the court laid down a two-stage test. In *Porter v Magill* [2001] UKHL 67, [2002] 2 AC 357, Lord Bingham of Cornhill approved this two-stage test, but said that the reference to 'a real danger' of bias in the test should be deleted. The words no longer serve any useful purpose and have not been used in the jurisprudence of the European Court of Human Rights. Following *Porter v Magill*, the test for bias can, according to *Taylor v Lawrence* [2002] EWCA Civ 90, [2003] QB 528, and *Lawal v Northern Spirit Ltd* [2003] UKHL 35, [2003] ICR 856, be formulated as follows:

> The court must first ascertain all the circumstances which have a bearing on the suggestion that the judge was biased. It must then ask whether those circumstances would lead a fair-minded and informed observer to conclude that there was a real possibility that the tribunal was biased.

It was also said in *Taylor v Lawrence* that a judge should be circumspect about declaring the existence of a relationship where there is no real possibility of a fair-minded and informed observer regarding it as raising a possibility of bias. If it is clear that there is no possibility of bias being perceived, no purpose is served by mentioning the relationship. If it is clear that bias might be perceived, it is important that disclosure should be made. If the position is borderline, disclosure should be made so that the judge can consider, having heard the parties' submissions, whether to withdraw.

59.28 **Application of the informed observer test** An informed observer will be aware of the legal traditions and culture of this jurisdiction. In England and Wales judges are members of the legal profession and have regular contract with other members of the profession. The fact that a judge receives free legal services from the solicitors representing a party to a claim being heard by the judge would not, according to a five-judge Court of Appeal in *Taylor v Lawrence* [2002] EWCA Civ 90, [2003] QB 528, lead a fair-minded and informed observer to conclude that there was a real possibility that the judge was biased. Nor is there any apparent bias where the judge calls counsel into the judges' corridor to inform them that he thinks the case is weak and that the parties should consider a settlement (*Hart v Relentless Records Ltd* [2002] EWHC 1984 (Ch), *The Times*, 8 October 2002). There was no apparent bias in *Taylor v Williamsons* [2002] EWCA Civ 1380, *The Times*, 9 August 2002, where the judge forgot he had not heard final submissions, and had to withdraw his judgment when this was pointed out, and so could give judgment after considering final submissions.

Observing at the start of a trial that a party has no case gives the appearance of an inability to try the claim objectively (*Co-operative Group Ltd v International Computers Ltd* [2003] EWCA Civ 1955, *The Times*, 19 January 2004). A judge should have recused himself in *Ealing London Borough Council v Jan* [2002] EWCA Civ 329, LTL 7/2/2002, having on a previous occasion twice stated in strong terms that he did not trust the defendant, even though the comments related to a different issue from the one to be determined in the subsequent hearing.

In *Re Medicaments and Related Classes of Goods (No. 2)* [2001] 1 WLR 700 one of the three members of the Restrictive Practices Court was an economist who had applied for a job during the course of the proceedings with a firm, one of whose members was providing expert evidence for one of the parties. When the member of the court realised the problem she immediately cancelled her job application and informed the parties, and the firm wrote stating that it had no jobs available in any event. It was held that a fair-minded observer would apprehend there was a real danger that the member of the court could not make an objective and impartial appraisal of the expert evidence. Before the start of a tribunal hearing in *Turner v Harada Ltd* [2001] EWCA Civ 599, LTL 6/4/2001, the chairman said: 'This is the seventh time that [Harada] have appeared here in the last six months. . . . [They] turn up with excuses and arguments to avoid matters going to trial . . . it is not as though [they] come here with a slate which is exactly clean. ' It was held that a fair-minded observer would have concluded there was a real danger of bias. In *Lawal v Northern Spirit Ltd* [2003] UKHL 35, [2003] ICR 856, it was held that the practice of leading counsel who have appeared as advocates before the Employment Appeal Tribunal being appointed to sit as part-time judges in the same tribunal did not infringe the bias rule. However, it tended to undermine public confidence in the system and should be discontinued.

There will be an injustice if the judge was predisposed or prejudiced against one party's case for reasons unconnected with the merits of the case (see *R v Inner West London Coroner, ex parte Dallaglio* [1994] 4 All ER 139). Guidance on situations where there may be a real danger of bias was given by the Court of Appeal in *Locabail (UK) Ltd v Bayfield Properties Ltd* [2000] QB 451, which is of particular relevance to cases dealt with by solicitor and barrister deputy judges. The Court of Appeal could not conceive of circumstances in which an objection could be soundly based on the religion (see also *Seer Technologies Inc. v Abbas* (2000) *The Times*, 16 March 2000), ethnic or national origin, gender, age, class, means or sexual orientation of the judge. Nor, at least ordinarily, could there be a valid objection based on the judge's social, educational, service or employment background, nor that of any member of his or her family. Nor could an objection be based on previous political associations, membership of social, sporting or charitable bodies, or Masonic associations; previous judicial decisions; extra-curial utterances, whether in textbooks, lectures, speeches, articles (but see *Hoekstra v HM Advocate (No. 2)* 2000 JC 391 discussed in **97.48**), interviews, reports or responses to consultation papers; previous receipt of instructions to act for or against any party, solicitor or advocate engaged in the current case; or membership of the same Inn, circuit, local Law Society or chambers. By contrast, there might be a real danger of bias if there was personal friendship or animosity between the judge and anyone other than the lawyers involved in the present case; or if the judge was closely acquainted with a witness whose credibility was in issue; or if the judge had ruled against the credibility of a witness in a previous case in outspoken terms such as to cast doubt on whether the judge could deal with the witness in the current case with an open mind (but not if the judge had commented adversely on a party or witness in a previous case in temperate terms); or if the judge had expressed views on a matter also in issue in the present case in such extreme terms as to throw into doubt his or her ability to try the case objectively. If there is any doubt, it should be exercised in favour of refusing to sit.

Impartiality may be thrown into doubt where a judge has had a direct involvement in the passage of legislation or of executive rules relevant to the case (*McGonnell v United Kingdom* (2000) 30 EHRR 289, in which the European Court of Human Rights held there was an infringement of art. 6(1) of the European Convention on Human Rights in Guernsey). An appearance of bias where a witness is well known to the judge cannot be removed, even by the party intending to call the witness deciding not to call him, and substituting alternative witnesses (*Morrison v AWG Group Ltd* [2006] EWCA Civ 6, *The Independent*, 25 January 2006). In such a case the safe course is to remove all possibility of apparent bias by recusal of the judge.

Disclosing conflicting interests: procedure Judges are obliged to mention any possible conflict when they become aware of its existence. Wherever possible this is done in advance of the commencement of the trial, so as to avoid the expense of an adjournment. If the matter becomes apparent at the commencement of a hearing (or during its course), the judge should mention it and the parties must consider whether they will waive the difficulty or ask the judge to decline to act or withdraw. The judge will give great weight to the parties' wishes, particularly if the hearing has already commenced (or if there is no other available judge). A judge who doubts his or her ability to be impartial will withdraw, even if the parties do not require it. If the parties waive their right to object, they cannot later raise the matter by way of appeal. See *Locabail (UK) Ltd v Bayfield Properties Ltd* [2000] QB 451. **59.29**

Where proceedings are abandoned because of the appearance of bias on the part of a member of the court, the Lord Chancellor is not liable for any of the costs incurred at the wasted hearing (*Re Medicaments and Related Classes of Goods (No. 4)* [2001] EWCA Civ 1217, [2002] 1 WLR 269).

Rights of audience

59.30 Under the Courts and Legal Services Act 1990, s. 27, the following persons have rights of audience at trial:

(a) litigants in person;
(b) counsel;
(c) solicitors;
(d) members of the Institute of Legal Executives;
(e) persons given express permission by the court; and
(f) persons given an express right of audience by statute (an example being the right given to local authority officers to present rent and possession claims on behalf of their employers under the **County Courts Act 1984, s. 60**).

Counsel, solicitors and legal executives have rights of audience subject to the terms of the **Courts and Legal Services Act 1990** and the regulations of their professional body. At present counsel have unrestricted rights of audience, but it is expected that practising certificates will be introduced at some stage (see the Access to Justice Act 1999, s. 46). Solicitors must comply with the Law Society advocacy qualifications before they can conduct High Court trials. The rights of audience of employed advocates have been increased by ss. 31A and 31B of the Courts and Legal Services Act 1990 (this particularly affects lawyers employed by the Crown Prosecution Service and the Legal Services Commission).

Costs negotiators are not properly instructed as agents of solicitors and therefore do not have rights of audience under the Courts and Legal Services Act 1990, s. 27 (*Ahmed v Powell* [2003] PNLR 22). A person with an enduring power of attorney does not have, in that capacity, a right of audience under the Courts and Legal Services Act 1990, s. 28(2) (*Gregory v Turner* [2003] EWCA Civ 183, [2003] 1 WLR 1149).

59.31 **Legal representative prejudicing administration of justice** The court has a power to grant an injunction to restrain a legal representative from appearing at a hearing if continued participation would lead to any order made being set aside on appeal (*Geveran Trading Co. Ltd v Skjevesland* [2002] EWCA Civ 1567, [2003] 1 WLR 912). Such applications are not governed by the same principles as apply regarding the impartiality of judges (see **59.27 to 59.28**), and the court must not be too ready to remove an advocate from a case. Advocates have no obligation not to be partisan. An advocate who is aware of a personal factor making his or her continued participation likely to prejudice the administration of justice or cause a procedural irregularity should withdraw, and must disclose to the other side any personal factor which might reasonably be regarded as open to objection.

59.32 **McKenzie friends** The position of 'McKenzie friends' has been controversial for some time. The name is derived from *McKenzie v McKenzie* [1971] P 33 and refers to a person who attends court with a litigant in person to render assistance in presenting the case, but is not qualified to address the court. In *R v Bow County Court, ex parte Pelling* [1999] 1 WLR 1807, the Court of Appeal considered the effect of the **CPR, Part 1**, and how it related to the assistance given by McKenzie friends, and laid down the following principles:

(a) In relation to proceedings in public a litigant in person should be allowed to have the assistance of a McKenzie friend unless the judge is satisfied that fairness and the interests of justice do not require a litigant in person to have this assistance.
(b) The position is the same if an application is dealt with in chambers (i.e., the judge's room) provided the hearing is still in public.
(c) If the hearing is in private (whether in the judge's room or an ordinary courtroom) that might make it undesirable in the interests of justice for a McKenzie friend to assist.

A McKenzie friend is not entitled to address the court. Addressing the court on behalf of a litigant is advocacy, which requires the discretionary grant of a right of audience (*Noueiri v Paragon Finance plc* (2001) *The Times*, 4 October 2001). Allowing a McKenzie friend to address the court is an indulgence which the court will not lightly accord, particularly where the friend is a bankrupt, or the subject of a civil restraint or vexatious litigant order (*Izzo v Philip Ross and Co.* (2001) *The Times*, 9 August 2001, and see **14.68 to 14.72**).

There is greater reluctance in allowing unconnected, but unqualified, persons to act as advocates for litigants in person (see *D v S (Rights of Audience)* [1997] 1 FLR 724, where it was said that exceptional circumstances must be shown) than in cases where the representation is to be given by a member of the litigant's family (*Clarkson v Gilbert* (2000) *The Times*, 4 July 2000). Generally, the litigant in person should apply for permission at the first hearing on notice, and it is the litigant, rather than the proposed advocate, who should explain why permission should be granted. If representation is allowed, the litigant should normally be present in court during hearings.

There are different rules for small claims track hearings, see **43.14**.

Representation of companies at hearings **Paragraphs 5.2** to **5.6** of **PD 39** deal with the representation of companies and corporations at hearings by employees (which is of some importance following the abolition of the rule that companies have to act by solicitors in the High Court). **Rule 39.6 of the CPR** provides that a company or corporation may appear at a hearing through a duly authorised employee provided the court gives permission. **PD 39, para. 5.3**, says that permission should usually be given unless there is some particular and sufficient reason why it should be withheld. Additional factors, according to *Tracto Teknik GmbH v LKL International Pty Ltd* [2003] EWHC 1563 (Ch), [2003] 2 BCLC 519, are: whether the company is able to afford legal representation, the ability of the proposed representative to do the work required in the litigation, and whether the representative is able to understand and discharge the obligations (such as disclosure of documents) involved in the litigation. **59.33**

Permission should generally be sought on an occasion prior to the hearing, but may be granted at the hearing itself. Permission may be sought informally. Like all representatives, the employee's status has to be included in the written statement of representatives pursuant to **PD 39, para. 5.1**. In this case the statement must include the full name and registered number of the company or corporation, the employee's position within the company, and details of the board or other authorisation for the employee to act for the company.

In considering whether to grant permission for a company or other corporation to be represented by an employee, the matters to be taken into account include the complexity of the issues and the experience and position in the company or corporation of the proposed representative (**para. 5.3**). The trial judge in *Watson v Bluemoor Properties Ltd* [2002] EWCA Civ 1875, [2003] BCC 382, refused to permit a company to be represented by a former director who had been disqualified. The Court of Appeal said that the better course in such circumstances is to adjourn to give the company an opportunity to consider whether it wishes to continue, rather than entering judgment on the basis of non-attendance. Permission should not normally be granted in jury trials or contempt proceedings (**para. 5.6**). The **Admiralty and Commercial Courts Guide, para. M3**, says that, because of their complexity, in most Commercial Court cases it is not appropriate for a company litigant to be represented by an employee. See **43.14** for representation of companies in small claims track hearings.

CONDUCT OF THE TRIAL

Specific guidance for Chancery Division trials is given in the **Chancery Guide, ch. 8**, and for Admiralty and Commercial Court trials by the **Admiralty and Commercial Courts Guide,** **59.34** section J. The normal sequence of events in non-specialist cases is discussed in the following paragraphs and in **59.39** to **59.47**.

Before the hearing the court should be provided with a written statement of the name and professional address of each advocate, his or her qualification as an advocate, and the party he or she acts for (**PD 39, para. 5.1**). This is usually done by advocates completing a slip provided by the court on the day of the hearing.

The rules give the courts a great deal of flexibility regarding how they will deal with trials. As previously discussed, the court can lay down trial timetables prescribing how the time available for the trial will be used, and allocating specified, limited times, for examination-in-chief, cross-examination and so on. The trial will then follow the timetable previously laid down, or laid down by the trial judge at the start, or will follow the traditional sequence of events.

Generally it will be the claimant who begins. However, it will be the defendant if the defendant has admitted all the issues on which the burden of proof rests on the claimant, so that the only live issues have to be proved by the defendant.

Summary disposal of issues at the start of a trial

59.35 Under **CPR, r. 1.4(2)(c)**, a trial judge has a power to make an order excluding certain issues from the trial. This power is additional to those for striking out (**chapter 33**) and summary judgment (**chapter 34**), but should be used sparingly and by applying the test of whether the issues in question have a real prospect of success. In most cases weak issues should be disposed of well before trial, and generally use of the procedure at trial is deprecated as potentially time wasting and expensive (see *Royal Brompton Hospital NHS Trust v Hammond* [2001] BLR 297). **Rules 3.3** and **24.4(3)**, which require notice to be given to the parties of striking-out and summary judgment hearings listed by the court on its own initiative, only cover cases where the hearing is specifically set up for that purpose, and do not cover summary disposal at trial (*James v Evans* [2003] CPLR 163). However, a failure by the trial judge to give the claimant sufficient notice of an intention to give summary judgment against the claimant at trial justified setting aside the judgment in *Orford v Rasmi Electronics Ltd* [2002] EWCA Civ 1672, [2003] CPLR 213.

Concessions by advocates and abandonment of issues

59.36 In order to simplify the issues, or for tactical reasons, trial advocates may concede specified facts, issues, or legal arguments. In the absence of exceptional circumstances, failing to argue a point at a hearing which is raised in a party's statement of case or witness statements will result in the point being taken as abandoned (*Adams v Mason Bullock* [2004] EWHC 2910 (Ch), *The Times*, 6 January 2005). The court has a discretion to allow a concession to be withdrawn. Where a party to an appeal seeks to withdraw a concession made in the court below, the appeal court has a discretion to permit this, but will be very cautious before granting permission (*Grobbelaar v News Group Newspapers Ltd* [2002] UKHL 40, [2002] 1 WLR 3024).

Permission to withdraw a concession was granted in *New Zealand Meat Board v Paramount Export Ltd* [2004] UKPC 45, LTL 27/7/2004, where there was no possibility that the outcome would have been affected had the point been taken earlier.

Rulings by the judge

59.37 Trial judges frequently hear and determine all manner of procedural and evidential applications during the course of a trial. After ruling on such matters the judge is *functus officio*. Subject to the rules discussed at **71.51**, advocates are not permitted to ask for such rulings to be reopened: if they wish to take the matter further they should seek permission to appeal (*R v Lashley* [2005] EWCA Crim 2016, *The Times*, 28 September 2005).

Daily trial transcripts

Her Majesty's Courts Service does not provide daily transcripts of the evidence and submissions made at hearings. Instead, hearings are recorded, and may be transcribed after the event. Requests for transcripts should be made to the court transcribing service. They are quite expensive, and tend to be used for appeal purposes (see **71.25**). **59.38**

Sometimes one of the parties, particularly in important cases, will arrange for daily transcripts to be produced. Often these are purely for the use of the lawyers acting for the party who has arranged for the transcripts. Where copies are provided to the judge, they must also be provided to the other parties (*Lloyds Bank plc v Cassidy* [2004] EWCA Civ 1767, *The Times*, 11 January 2005).

Opening speech

The trial judge will generally have read the papers in the trial bundle before the trial. It will often be the case that in those circumstances there is no need for an opening speech, which may be dispensed with (**PD 28, para. 8.2**, for the fast track; **PD 29, para. 10.2**, for cases on the multi-track). If an opening speech is allowed, counsel for the claimant will usually describe the nature of the claim, and will identify the issues to be tried by reference to the statements of case and/or the statement of issues. Some of the documentary evidence may be referred to. It sometimes happens that the judge will rise during the course of the opening to read some of the documents. **59.39**

Claimant's case

After the claimant's opening speech evidence will be called on behalf of the claimant. Broadly, evidence adduced at trial will be real evidence (i.e., physical items), contemporaneous documentary evidence, views of the site, and the evidence of witnesses (see **chapter 47**). **59.40**

Real evidence and documents admitted into evidence are made exhibits and are labelled with individual exhibits numbers. The judge has a discretion to inspect the *locus in quo* if there are compelling reasons to do so, outweighing the time and expense of a view. Inspections should generally be conducted in the presence of the parties.

There are occasions when evidence is adduced in a deposition, by affidavit or in the form of hearsay statements.

It is rather more usual for evidence from witnesses to be produced by calling the witnesses to give evidence from the witness box. Witnesses are sometimes asked to leave the court until they are called so they are not influenced by the evidence given by other witnesses, but they remain in court in the large majority of cases. Subject to any trial directions they may be called in any order. When called they are sworn or affirm in a manner they consider binding (**Oaths Act 1978**). A witness will be afforded anonymity, for example, by being allowed to give evidence behind a screen and without stating his or her name and address aloud, only in highly exceptional cases (*Re W (Children) (Care Proceedings: Witness Anonymity)* [2002] EWCA Civ 1626, *The Times*, 1 November 2002).

Exhibits which are handed in and proved during the course of the trial will be recorded in an exhibit list and kept in the custody of the court until the conclusion of the trial, unless the judge directs otherwise (**PD 39, para. 7**). At the conclusion of the trial the parties have the responsibility for taking away and preserving the exhibits pending any possible appeal.

Examination-in-chief

Traditionally witnesses would give their evidence in answer to non-leading questions put to them by counsel for the party calling them. However, under the CPR witness statements of witnesses called at trial will stand as the evidence-in-chief unless the court otherwise orders (**r. 32.5(2)**). Technically, it is only possible to augment the evidence contained in the **59.41** exchanged statements if, by virtue of **r. 32.5(3)** and (4), the court considers there is good reason not to confine the witness to the contents of his or her witness statement, and for the purpose of either:

(a) amplifying the witness statement; or
(b) giving evidence in relation to new matters which have arisen since the witness statement was served on the other parties.

What will be regarded as a sufficiently 'good reason' to allow supplementary questions remains to be seen. There is a fear that different judges will take different views. Witness statements drafted in a deliberately concise way in accordance with the ethos of the *Final Report* as contemplated at ch. 12, paras 54 to 59, of avoiding elaborate over-drafting therefore may fall into the trap (which was also mentioned in the *Final Report* at chapter 12, para. 55) of encountering a trial judge who refuses to allow the witness to depart from or amplify his or her witness statement.

Cross-examination

59.42 After being examined in chief, each witness may be cross-examined by counsel for the defendant. Where there is more than one defendant, they cross-examine in the order they appear on the court record. Cross-examination may be conducted using leading questions (i.e. questions which suggest the required answer). Cross-examination is permitted on the witness's statement, whether or not the statements are referred to in chief (**CPR, r. 32.11**). Cross-examination provides the other side the opportunity to test and seek to undermine the evidence given in chief. One of the main obligations on an advocate cross-examining a witness is to put his or her client's case. This means that the witness must be challenged and given an opportunity to comment on the points of conflict between the evidence he or she has given and the case being advanced by the cross-examining party. If this is not done, the court may decide that the witness's account is accepted. Peter Smith J gave a reminder of the importance of putting one's case positively to the other side's witnesses in *EPI Environmental Technologies Inc. v Symphony Plastic Technologies plc* [2004] EWHC 2945 (Ch), [2005] 1 WLR 3456. A failure to do so usually means the point cannot be taken against the witness in the closing speech. This has become even more important with witness statements usually standing as the examination-in-chief, as it allows the judge to assess the witness's response by reference to his or her demeanour and the overall context of the case. It was held in *Re Share* [2002] BPIR 194 that the judge was wrong to reject the evidence of two witnesses which had not been tested in cross-examination (the petitioner having elected not to cross-examine in order to save costs), even though there was documentary evidence which was flatly inconsistent with the oral testimony of those witnesses. For further discussion see **chapter** 47, particularly 47.7.

A witness who has been cross-examined may be re-examined by counsel for the claimant on matters covered in cross-examination. Leading questions are not allowed.

Witness called by the judge

59.43 A witness who is not relied upon by either side may be called by the judge, who may conduct the examination. As the witness is not called by another party, neither has a right to cross-examine, although the judge has a discretion to (and will usually) allow either or both parties to do so (*Fallon v Calvert* [1960] 2 QB 201).

Submissions of no case to answer

59.44 At the conclusion of the case for the claimant, the defendant may make a submission of no case to answer. This is made on the basis that on the evidence adduced by the claimant the claim cannot succeed. In *Benham Ltd v Kythira Investments Ltd* [2003] EWCA Civ 1794, LTL 15/12/2003, it was said that a submission of no case to answer should rarely, if ever, be entertained in a civil case tried without a jury. As the judge is the trier both of law and fact, it is embarrassing for the judge to be asked to rule on the merits of the claim while the evidence is still incomplete.

Further, if the judge's ruling were to be reversed on appeal, there would be the added cost of having a retrial. It has therefore been the practice that a defendant seeking to make a submission of no case to answer had to elect to call no evidence before making the submission (*Alexander v Rayson* [1936] 1 KB 169; *Young v Rank* [1950] 2 KB 510).

Under the CPR it remains the case that, in general, the judge may require a defendant to elect to call no evidence before making a submission of no case to answer (*Blinkhorn v Hall* (2000) LTL 13/4/2000; *Miller v Cawley* [2002] EWCA Civ 1100, *The Times*, 6 September 2002). However, there may be circumstances where a submission may be entertained without putting the defendant to an election, as in *Mullan v Birmingham City Council* (1999) *The Times*, 29 July 1999. The power to dismiss on a submission of no case to answer without putting the defendants to their election whether to call evidence should be exercised with considerable caution (*Boyce v Wyatt Engineering* [2001] EWCA Civ 692, *The Times*, 14 June 2001).

Where the court allows a defendant to make a submission of no case to answer without being required to elect whether to call no evidence, the test by which the submission is determined is whether the claim has no real prospect of success (*Benham Ltd v Kythira Investments Ltd*). On the other hand, if the defendant is required to call no evidence, the submission of no case to answer is decided on the basis of whether the claimant has established the case on the balance of probabilities (*Miller v Cawley* [2002] EWCA Civ 1100, *The Times*, 6 September 2002). It is the judge's duty to survey the expert evidence together with that of the defendant before deciding to accede to a submission of no case to answer (*Youssif v Jordan* [2003] EWCA Civ 1852, *The Times*, 22 January 2004).

Defence case

Where the defence decide to call evidence, they may be allowed to make an opening speech (though this is now rather unusual). They then call their evidence in the same way as the claimant. Where there is more than one defendant, they present their evidence in the order they appear on the record. **59.45**

Closing speeches

Where the defence has called evidence, the defence closing speech is made before that of the claimant. Speeches usually deal with how the evidence that has been adduced and the inferences that can be drawn from that evidence support the case for the party in question on the factual issues involved. Counsel also argue any legal points that arise, sometimes making use of skeleton arguments. Where a case has overrun, the judge may adjourn, or may take other measures, such as ordering closing submissions to be made in writing, to be followed by a written judgment (*Sleeman v High Care Ltd* (1999) *The Times*, 3 November 1999). **59.46**

A judge who, after the close of evidence, realises he may decide the case on a new footing not addressed earlier in the trial, should give the parties a specific warning that this course may be taken, and invite them to make submissions on the matter (*Maersk Co. Ltd v Wilson* [2004] EWCA Civ 313, LTL 25/3/2004).

Role of the judge

During the course of the trial the judge may put questions to the witnesses, particularly if matters remain obscure after counsel's questions. Depending on the circumstances, it may be the judge's duty to ask questions, including leading questions, to ensure an accurate picture of the events is adduced (*Currey v Currey* [2004] EWCA Civ 1799, *The Times*, 26 November 2004). Judges should be careful to avoid interrupting the flow of counsel's questions, particularly during cross-examination (*Jones v National Coal Board* [1957] 2 QB 55). Frequent or intemperate interventions may give grounds for an appeal (*Re R (Children)* [2001] EWCA Civ 1880, LTL 7/12/2001, where there were interventions on average every 50 seconds, but compare *Priestley v Harrogate Healthcare NHS Trust* [2002] EWCA Civ 183, LTL 7/2/2002 and *Cairnstores Ltd v AB Hässle* (2002) LTL 22/10/2002, where appeals based on excessive intervention by the judge were **59.47** dismissed). The judge will have to rule on any applications and any objections to the admissibility of evidence or questions during the course of the trial.

After hearing the evidence the judge must decide where the truth lies, decide any points of law, and give judgment. The claimant has the burden of proof on a balance of probabilities. It is for the claimant to prove the case, and the judge should beware of too much speculative reconstruction (*Lynch v James Lynch and Sons (Transport) Ltd* (2000) LTL 8/3/2000). Some allegations are inherently unlikely, so the standard of proof in civil cases is of necessity a flexible one (*Hornal v Neuberger Products Ltd* [1957] 1 QB 247). In the absence of cross-examination (for example, where a witness statement is simply read to the court) the court cannot make findings against a party who denies what is alleged against him, unless the denial is self-evidently wrong, for example, because of other facts which are admitted or because the denial is plainly contradicted by reliable documents (*Re Hopes (Heathrow) Ltd* [2001] 1 BCLC 575).

Deciding between witnesses

59.48 In evaluating evidence given at trial, Peter Smith J in *EPI Environmental Technologies Inc. v Symphony Plastic Technologies plc* [2004] EWHC 2945 (Ch), [2005] 1 WLR 3456 at [74] gave the following guidance:

(a) It is essential to evaluate a witness's performance in the light of the entirety of his or her evidence. Witnesses can make mistakes, but those mistakes do not necessarily affect other parts of their evidence.
(b) Witnesses can regularly lie. However, lies themselves do not mean necessarily that the entirety of that witness's evidence is rejected. A witness may lie in a stupid attempt to bolster a case, but the actual case nevertheless remains good irrespective of the lie. Alternatively, a witness may lie because the case is a lie.
(c) It is essential that a witness is challenged with the other side's case. This involves putting the case positively. It is for the judge then to assess the witness's oral response and demeanour, and the likely veracity of the response in the overall context of the litigation.

In *Powell v Streatham Manor Nursing Home* [1935] AC 243, Lord Macmillan, referring to fraud cases, said, at p. 256, he found it essential to test the credibility of witnesses against objective facts proved independently, particularly the documents in the case. He also took into account their motives, and the overall probabilities of the case. Adopting a two-stage approach of making preliminary findings on the evidence of lay witnesses, and then testing those findings against the expert evidence, is likely to be wrong. In *Hall v Jakto Transport Ltd* [2005] EWCA Civ 1327, *The Times*, 28 November 2005, an engineering expert's evidence was relevant to how an accident might have happened. It was held that the judge should have considered the expert's evidence when reaching his conclusions on the credibility of the other witnesses, rather than making preliminary findings based only on the lay witnesses, then reassessing those findings in the light of the expert's evidence.

When faced with competing property valuations, the judge does not necessarily have to decide that one rather than the other is correct. An alternative approach is to seek to find the probable value of the property in the light of the evidence of both valuers (*Stephens v Cannon* [2005] EWCA Civ 222, *The Times*, 2 May 2005).

Adjudicating on expert evidence

59.49 It is common for judges to have to decide between conflicting expert evidence. When this happens the duty of the judge is to make findings of fact and resolve the conflict (*Sewell v Electrolux Ltd* (1997), *The Times*, 7 November 1997). In *Roadrunner Properties Ltd v Dean* [2003] EWCA Civ 1816, LTL 21/11/2003, the claimant's expert gave evidence that cracks in a party wall were caused by the defendants' use of a jackhammer. The Court of Appeal held the judge had been wrong to prefer the evidence of the defendants' expert, who advanced a hypothesis that the damage was due to climate change, a theory otherwise unsupported by evidence. The court commented that the trial judge had given too much credence to a comment by the defendants' expert that coincidence (that the claimant's damage occurred after use of the jackhammer) was not a forensic tool.

Where there is a conflict between an expert and lay witnesses, generally the judge should refuse to accept the lay evidence in preference to uncontradicted expert evidence (*Re B (A Minor) (Split Hearings: Jurisdiction)* [2000] 1 WLR 790). However, the judge is not obliged to accept expert evidence if there are sufficient grounds for rejecting it, such as where it does not speak to a relevant issue (see *R v Lanfear* [1968] 2 QB 77), or where the judge does not believe the expert or is otherwise unconvinced by the expert's evidence (*Dover District Council v Sherred* (1997) *The Times*, 11 February 1997). In *Coopers Payen Ltd v Southampton Container Terminal Ltd* [2003] EWCA Civ 1223, [2004] 1 Lloyd's Rep 331, Lightman J said at [67] that if there is no other direct evidence, the evidence given by a single joint expert is likely to be compelling. A judge may depart from it only in exceptional circumstances and after fully explaining the reasons. It is different if an expert, including a single joint expert, gives evidence on an issue of fact on which there is lay evidence. Where both the expert and the lay witness are credible, there is no rule of law or practice requiring the judge to prefer the evidence of the expert. The judge must consider whether the expert and lay evidence can be reconciled. If not, the judge must consider whether there is any explanation for the conflict or a possible error by a witness, and in the light of the circumstances, make a considered choice on which evidence to accept. The court in *Armstrong v First York Ltd* [2005] EWCA Civ 277, [2005] 1 WLR 2751, rejected the evidence of a jointly instructed expert who was called at the trial to give evidence in an emerging area of expertise (bio-mechanical accident reconstruction). Ultimately, litigation is conducted by trial by judge, not by experts (see Brooke LJ in *Armstrong v First York Ltd*).

The judge should not develop his own theory on a matter requiring expertise without recalling the experts for their guidance on the theory (*Deveron Joinery Co. Ltd v Perkins* [2003] EWCA Civ 1241, LTL 30/7/2003). In *Breeze v Ahmad* [2005] EWCA Civ 223, LTL 8/3/2005, the judge preferred the defendant's expert, who the judge said was 'compellingly supported' by the expert literature. None of the literature was introduced at the trial or shown to the claimant's expert. In fact it provided no support for the defendant's expert at all. The failure to adduce the literature was held to be a serious procedural irregularity, and a retrial was ordered. In *Re M (Child: Residence)* [2002] EWCA Civ 1052, [2002] 2 FLR 1059, it was held that it was not open to the judge to reject the uncontested evidence of three expert witnesses that the core personality of a father had been so damaged by childhood experiences as to make him unsuitable to be a child's primary carer simply on the basis of impressions while in the witness box. However, on issues such as future placement and parent-child attachment, a judge could depart from unanimous expert opinion. Also, there are cases where lay evidence may be preferred to expert evidence, such as where attesting witnesses are preferred to a handwriting expert over a contested will (*Fuller v Strum* (2000) *The Times*, 14 February 2001, reversed on other grounds [2001] EWCA Civ 1879, [2002] 1 WLR 1097).

Resorting to the burden of proof

An appeal was allowed in *Cooper v Floor Cleaning Machines Ltd* [2003] EWCA Civ 1649, [2004] RTR 59.50
254, where the judge found that both drivers in a road traffic accident were not to be believed, and dismissed both the claim and counterclaim on the basis that neither side had proved its case on the balance of probabilities. Scott-Baker LJ said, at [3]:

> It is, on any view, a wholly exceptional situation for a judge to conclude, particularly in a case concerning a road traffic accident, that a claim and counterclaim both fail on the basis of failure to discharge the burden of proof.

In *Stephens v Cannon* [2005] EWCA Civ 222, *The Times*, 2 May 2005, Wilson J laid down the following principles:

(a) There have to be exceptional circumstances before the court can be justified in deciding a disputed issue by resorting to the burden of proof.
(b) The circumstances will be exceptional where, despite striving to make a finding on the evidence, the court finds it is not reasonable to do so.
(c) A judge resorting to the burden of proof must analyse the evidence and set out in the judgment the steps taken to make a finding on the evidence, and the reasons why the judge has concluded this is not possible, unless these can readily be inferred from the circumstances of the case.

There have been exceptional cases which have been validly decided on the burden of proof. *Ashaf v Akram* (22 January 1999), for example, was a case where there were conflicting stories producing 'an intractable evidential tangle' such that resort to the burden of proof was permissible. In other cases, like *Baker v Market Harborough Industrial Co-operative Society Ltd* [1953] 1 WLR 1472, where two vehicles collided head-on in the middle of the road leaving no survivors, the proper inference may be that both drivers were equally to blame.

Judgment

59.51 Judgment is often given immediately, but in complicated cases may be reserved. Particularly in the High Court, there are cases where the judge will reserve judgment and provide the legal representatives with a written draft judgment usually about one day before the date fixed for pronouncing judgment (see **Admiralty and Commercial Court Guide, para. J12; Chancery Guide paras 9.1** to **9.3; Queen's Bench Guide, paras 9.3.5** to **9.3.7**). Such a judgment is not delivered until it is formally pronounced in court. Retaining the word 'draft' after a judgment is pronounced does not render the judgment invalid (*Birmingham City Council v Yardley* [2004] EWCA Civ 1756, *The Times*, 13 December 2004). The draft usually contains a confidentiality notice to the effect that it must not be communicated to clients until an hour before the hearing. Advocates should familiarise themselves with the draft and be ready to deal with any points that arise when judgment is delivered, and should refer any typographical errors to the judge's clerk not later than 12 noon on the day before pronouncement.

If judgment is reserved, the court retains the power to entertain further evidence, but will consider factors similar to those laid down in *Ladd v Marshall* [1954] 1 WLR 1489 (see **72.13**) in deciding whether allowing further evidence will accord with the overriding objective (*Townsend v Achilleas* (2000) LTL 6/7/2000; see **61.37** to **61.40**). The whole of any hearing, whether in the High Court or a county court, will be recorded, unless the judge directs otherwise (**PD 39, para. 6.1**). Unofficial tape-recording without permission (which will rarely be given) is a contempt of court. **Paragraphs 6.3** to **6.5** of **PD 39** deal with obtaining transcripts of proceedings on payment of authorised charges.

After judgment is given the court will deal with the question of costs, the form of the judgment, and any application for permission to appeal.

Further evidence after judgment and before order

59.52 The trial judge has a discretion to permit a party to adduce additional evidence after judgment has been handed down and before the final order has been made (*Navitaire Inc. v Easyjet Airline Co. Ltd* [2005] EWHC 282, LTL 18/3/2005). Applications are considered applying the *Ladd v Marshall* [1954] 1 WLR 1489 principles, discussed at **72.13** and **72.14**, but with more flexibility than in appeals to the Court of Appeal (see *Navitaire Inc. v Easyjet Airline Co. Ltd* at [37]–[39]). Nevertheless, the jurisdiction is exercised sparingly and only in exceptional cases. Particular emphasis is placed on the first of the *Ladd v Marshall* principles, and an application was refused in *Fisher v Cadman* [2005] EWHC 2424 (Ch), *The Times*, 23 June 2005, principally because the evidence could have been made available at the right time if the applicant had exercised reasonable diligence.

PRELIMINARY ISSUES

As a general rule, it is in the interests of the parties and the administration of justice that all issues arising in a dispute are tried at the same time. However, particularly in complex actions, costs and time can sometimes be saved if decisive, or potentially decisive, issues can be identified and ordered to be tried before or separately from the main trial. **59.53**

There are three types of order that can be made:
(a) for the trial of a preliminary issue on a point of law;
(b) for the separate trial of preliminary issues or questions of fact;
(c) for separate trials of liability and quantum.

The jurisdiction to make these orders derives from **CPR, r. 3.1(2)**.

Factors to be taken into account when deciding whether to order the determination of a preliminary issue were laid down by Neuberger J in *Steele v Steele* (2001) *The Times*, 5 June 2001, as follows:

(a) Whether the determination of the preliminary issue will dispose of the whole case or at least one aspect of the case.
(b) Whether the determination of the preliminary issue will significantly cut down the cost and the time involved in pre-trial preparation and in connection with the trial itself.
(c) If the preliminary issue is an issue of law, the amount of effort involved in identifying the relevant facts for the purposes of the preliminary issue.
(d) If the preliminary issue is an issue of law, whether it can be determined on agreed facts. If there are substantial disputes of fact it is unlikely to be safe to determine the legal issue until the facts are found.
(e) Whether the determination of the preliminary issue will unreasonably fetter either of the parties or the court in achieving a just result.
(f) The risk that an order will increase the costs or delay the trial, and the prospects that such an order may assist in settling the dispute.
(g) The more likely it is that the issue will have to be determined by the court the more appropriate it is to have it determined as a preliminary issue.
(h) The risk that the determination may lose its effect by subsequent amendment of the statements of case.
(i) Whether it is just and right to order the determination of the preliminary issue.

Procedure for trial of preliminary issues

Orders for the trial of preliminary issues are made either on the application of a party or by the court of its own initiative. It is rare for the court to make such an order without the concurrence of at least one of the parties. It is not possible to make such an order by consent. Normally the application is made at the allocation or listing stage, or on a case management hearing, although it is not unknown for an application to be made to the trial judge at the beginning of a trial. **59.54**

Where an order for the preliminary trial of an issue of law or fact is made, the court must formulate the issue to be tried. It is important that the issue is defined with precision so as to avoid future difficulties of interpretation. If it is impossible to define the issue, no order should be made (*Allen v Gulf Oil Refining Ltd* [1981] AC 1001). If the issue is one of law, the court must further order the issue to be tried either:

(a) on the statements of case;
(b) on a case stated; or
(c) on an agreed statement of facts.

In *Keays v Murdoch Magazines (UK) Ltd* [1991] 1 WLR 1184, an issue as to whether words were capable of a defamatory meaning was ordered to be tried on the pleadings in conjunction with the copy of the magazine in which the offending article appeared.

Preliminary issues of law or fact

59.55 In *Allen v Gulf Oil Refining Ltd* [1981] AC 1001, Lord Roskill said:

> The preliminary point procedure can in certain classes of case be invoked to achieve the desirable aim of economy and simplicity. But cases in which invocation is desirable are few.

Situations identified by Lord Roskill as being suitable for trial as preliminary issues include:

(a) where a single issue of law can be isolated from the other issues in a case, and its decision may be finally determinative of the case as a whole;
(b) where the facts are agreed and the sole issue is one of law.

Neuberger J in *Re Bank of Credit and Commerce International SA, Banque Arabe Internationale d'Investissement SA v Morris* [2001] 1 BCLC 263 said that preliminary issues of law would not be ordered unless:

(a) they are so formulated that they can be answered without making artificial findings of fact (i.e., findings of fact which are not agreed and are disputed);
(b) they would, if determined one way, enable the court to dismiss at least one of the claims made in the proceedings; and
(c) the point can be formulated into a reasonably arguable issue.

In *Ashmore v Corporation of Lloyd's* [1992] 1 WLR 446, preliminary points of law were ordered to decide:

(a) whether Lloyd's owed a duty of care to the claimants who were 'names' (underwriting members of Lloyd's organised in syndicates); and
(b) whether Lloyd's had immunity from suit under the Lloyd's Act 1982, s. 14.

Issues raised in personal injuries cases as to the claimant's 'date of knowledge' under the **Limitation Act 1980, s. 14**, may be suitable for trial as preliminary issues. In *Keays v Murdoch Magazines (UK) Ltd* [1991] 1 WLR 1184, the issue whether the words published were capable of bearing a defamatory meaning was determined as a preliminary issue. One of the key factors is whether the procedure is likely to achieve a saving in costs, or whether it is likely to increase expense and delay.

The House of Lords has on several occasions disapproved the practice of making orders to determine points of law on assumed facts. As Lord Scarman said in *Tilling v Whiteman* [1980] AC 1, they are 'too often treacherous short cuts. Their price can be delay, anxiety and expense.' If the court finds against the point of law, the case will be no further advanced than when the order was made. If the facts are found or agreed first, the hearing on the preliminary issue should finally determine the proceedings.

There appears to be a slightly increased willingness to order the trial of preliminary issues under the CPR. The way it is put in the **Chancery Guide**, for example, at **para. 3.11**, is that costs can sometimes be saved by identifying decisive issues, or potentially decisive issues, and ordering that they be tried first. The decision of one issue, which in itself may not be decisive, may still be appropriate, because it may enable the parties to settle the remainder of their dispute.

Separate trials of liability and damages

59.56 Such orders are regarded as exceptional, and are only made where a clear demarcation line between the issues of liability and quantum can be drawn (*Marks v Chief Constable of Greater Manchester Police* (1992) *The Times*, 28 January 1992). Where certain items of evidence would need to be called at both trials, an order should not be made. In personal injuries cases where the long-term prognosis will only become clear some years after the event, unless quantum can be dealt with by provisional damages, it may be best for liability to be tried early while events are still relatively fresh, leaving quantum to be determined when the prognosis becomes clear (*Hawkins v New Mendip Engineering Ltd* [1966] 1 WLR 1341). If judgment is entered for damages to be assessed, it would be possible for the claimant to apply for an interim payment under **CPR, rr. 25.6 to 25.9** (see **chapter 36**). In these cases disclosure is normally initially limited to the issue of liability (*Baldock v Addison* [1995] 1 WLR 158).

Chapter 60 Non-attendance

NON-ATTENDANCE AT INTERIM HEARINGS

60.1 The court may proceed in the absence of any party to an application (**CPR, r. 23.11(1)**). When this happens the court has a general discretion to relist the application, which it may exercise of its own initiative or on application by the absent party (**r. 23.11(2)**). This gives the court power to rehear the application in full and make such order as may be appropriate (*Riverpath Properties Ltd v Brammall* (2000) *The Times*, 16 February 2000). Matters to be taken into account when exercising the discretion include the reasons for the absence, the interests of justice, any undue delay since the missed hearing, whether either party has acted on the order, and whether there is a real prospect of the court changing the original order (see *Shocked v Goldschmidt* [1998] 1 All ER 372, which is discussed in **60.2**, and *Riverpath Properties Ltd v Brammall*).

NON-ATTENDANCE AT TRIAL

60.2 A trial may proceed despite the non-attendance of any of the parties, and the court may simply strike out the claim or defence, and any counterclaim or defence to counterclaim (**CPR, r. 39.3(1)**). If a party is not present but its legal representative is, the court should not exercise its power to strike out (*Rouse v Freeman* (2001) *The Times*, 8 January 2002). The court has a power to restore the proceedings (or any part of the proceedings) that may have been struck out due to non-attendance (**r. 39.3(2)**), and may set aside any judgment entered in such circumstances (**r. 39.3(3)**). Applications to set aside or restore must be supported by evidence (**r. 39.3(4)**). **Rule 39.3(5)** provides that orders to restore or set aside may only be granted if the applicant:

(a) acted promptly on finding out about the order;
(b) had a good reason for not attending; and
(c) has a reasonable prospect of success at a reconvened trial.

These conditions are similar to those enunciated in *Shocked v Goldschmidt* [1998] 1 All ER 372, but under the CPR they are cumulative. If any of the conditions is not satisfied, there is no residual discretion to set aside (*Barclays Bank plc v Ellis* (2000) *The Times*, 24 October 2000).

In this context, acting 'promptly' means acting with alacrity (*Regency Rolls Ltd v Carnall* (2000) LTL 16/10/2000). An application issued six weeks after trial in a complex claim was regarded as 'prompt' in *Watson v Bluemoor Properties Ltd* [2002] EWCA Civ 1875, [2003] BCC 382. The phrase 'good reason' in r. 39.3(5)(b) is sufficiently clear and does not need further definition (*Brazil v Brazil* [2002] EWCA Civ 1135, *The Times*, 18 October 2002, where judgment was set aside because the applicant, who was illiterate, did not receive notice of the trial date). An application to set aside in *Neufville v Papamichael* (1999) LTL 23/11/99) was refused, primarily because there was no adequate explanation for the claimant, who failed to attend trial, not having kept in contact with his solicitors. *Barclays Bank plc v Ellis* shows that the court will take a rigorous approach to the question of whether the party who failed to attend has a reasonable prospect of success at a reconvened trial. See also *Stock v Stock* (2000) LTL 17/10/2000. The requirements of r. 39.3 were held to be satisfied in *Thakerar v Northwich Park and St Mark's NHS Trust* [2002] EWCA Civ 617, LTL 24/4/2002, where the claimant had been admitted to hospital with a heart condition and was discharged during the course of the first day of the trial. Once the conditions are satisfied, the discretion under r. 39.3 should be exercised in favour of restoring the claim unless there is material justifying a refusal of the order.

Hackney London Borough Council v Driscoll [2003] EWCA Civ 1037, [2003] 1 WLR 2602, is a difficult case. On its facts the Court of Appeal applied **r. 39.3(5)** and refused to set aside a judgment entered against the defendant who was not notified of the new trial date after an adjournment of a hearing which he had attended. The difficulty rests in the fact that the case reached the Court of Appeal in order to settle, once and for all, the question whether the principle in *White v Weston* [1968] 2 QB 647 (in which the Court of Appeal held that a default judgment entered without notice to the defendant would be set aside as of right, and with the claimant paying the costs) applies not only where a defendant has no notice of the proceedings, but also where the defendant knew about the proceedings but was not notified of the trial date. Although the Court of Appeal was plainly right to refuse the argued extension of the principle, the entire decision in *White v Weston* has no place under the scheme of the CPR. **Rule 39.3** provides a complete code for applications to set aside judgments after hearings. Setting aside a default judgment after the defendant fails to respond to the particulars of claim is governed by **Part 13**. If service is not effected in accordance with **Part 6**, any default judgment will be set aside as of right under **r. 13.2**. If service is effected in accordance with Part 6, that creates an irrebuttable presumption of due service (see *Godwin v Swindon Borough Council* [2001] EWCA Civ 1478, [2002] 1 WLR 997; *Anderton v Clwyd County Council (No. 2)* [2002] EWCA Civ 933, [2002] 1 WLR 3174 and **15.36**), and default judgment can only be set aside applying the criteria in **r. 13.3**.

A counterclaim was reinstated in *Watson v Bluemoor Properties Ltd* on terms that the party applying to reinstate made an interim payment and provided security for future costs.

Chapter 61 Judgments and Orders

INTRODUCTION

61.1 Although there is likely to be a delay between judgment being pronounced and the judgment being sealed and served, **r. 40.7(1)** of the CPR provides that judgment in fact takes effect from the day it was given. Where a written judgment is sent in draft to the legal representatives of the parties under Practice Statement (Supreme Court: Judgments) [1998] 1 WLR 825, it is not given or made for the purposes of **r. 40.7(1)** until it is pronounced in court (*Prudential Assurance Co. Ltd v McBains Cooper* [2000] 1 WLR 2000). After a judgment or order has been pronounced by the court, the next step is to have it drawn up. In *Holtby v Hodgson* (1889) 24 QBD 103 Lord Esher MR said, at p. 107, 'Pronouncing judgment is not entering judgment; something has to be done which will be a record'. The distinction between judgments and orders is that a judgment is the final decision which disposes of a claim (subject to appeal), whereas an order is an interim decision. However, there is no practical difference between the two, and both are enforceable in the same way.

A party seeking to dispute an order or judgment is usually limited to applying for permission to appeal (see **chapters** 71 and 72). There are exceptions where an application to review an order can be made back to the same judge as made the original order (or to a judge at the same or equivalent level) without appealing. Orders made wi thout noti ce can be reviewed by applying to set aside or vary within seven days of service of the order (**r. 23.10**). Default judgments can be set aside using the procedure in **Part 13**. If there is a change of circumstances it may be possible to vary case management directions (see **45.30**). If there is an accidental slip or error in an order, it may be corrected under the slip rule (see **61.34**). Orders and judgments can be reviewed by the judge in the period between pronouncement and drawing up (see **61.35**). It may be right to refuse an application to set aside or vary an order where an appeal from that order is pending (*Barrie v J. Barrie (Plant Hire) Ltd* (2001) LTL 14/2/2001).

SETTLEMENTS

Where the parties have agreed terms for settling the substantive issues in the claim, or on an interim application, they must also decide how those terms should be recorded. An important consideration in this regard is how the agreement can be enforced in the event of either party failing to abide by its terms. The simplest form of judgment provides for immediate payment of the sum agreed together with costs (often on the standard basis, to be the subject of a detailed assessment if not agreed). Enforcement proceedings can be taken on such a judgment on the same day as it is entered. Agreements are not always this simple. Five further ways of recording agreed terms were discussed by Slade J in *Green v Rozen* [1955] 1 WLR 741 (in the context of an agreement reached at the door of the court): **61.2**

(a) Where a claim is settled on terms as to the payment of money, judgment may be entered for the agreed sum, subject to a stay of execution pending payment of stated instalments. If the instalments fall into arrears, the stay will be lifted, and the judgment creditor can immediately take enforcement proceedings.
(b) A consent order may be drawn up embodying the undertakings of both parties in a series of numbered paragraphs. If any of the terms are not complied with, enforcement may be possible immediately or on application to the court depending on the nature of the term in question.
(c) The agreement may be recorded in a Tomlin order. A Tomlin order has the effect of staying the proceedings save for the purpose of carrying the terms set out in a schedule to the order into effect. See **61.14**.
(d) A consent order may be drawn up staying all further proceedings upon the agreed terms. If the agreement is reached immediately before the hearing its terms will usually be endorsed on counsel's briefs and the court will be asked to make a consent order in those terms. Unlike Tomlin orders, the courts are very unwilling to remove the stay imposed by such orders, so enforcement can usually only be effected by bringing fresh proceedings for breach of the contract embodied in the compromise (see *Rofa Sport Management AG v DHL International (UK) Ltd* [1989] 1 WLR 902).
(e) The court may be informed merely that the case has been settled upon terms endorsed on counsel's briefs. This is the most informal way of compromising a claim. Its effect is to supersede the existing claim with the compromise. Any breach can only be enforced by issuing fresh proceedings.

A sixth method was the subject of *Atkinson v Castan* (1991) *The Times*, 17 April 1991, where a consent order made 'no order' save as to costs, but set out the agreed terms in recitals. It was held that the claimants were entitled to enforce the terms stated in the recitals without the need to bring a fresh action.

Notifying court and effect of settling claim

Where terms are agreed in advance of a hearing, each party has a responsibility to inform the court so that the time set aside for the hearing can be reallocated to other litigants. The court should be notified even if the settlement is reached at a late hour on the day before the hearing, and this certainly should be done where the case is being heard in the High Court. The High Court switchboard is open all night, and even a late notification may prevent a judge wasting time on pre-reading a case that has settled (see *Tasyurdu v Immigration Appeal* **61.3**

Tribunal [2003] EWCA Civ 447, [2003] CPLR 343, where the hearing was in the Court of Appeal). If an order giving effect to the settlement is drawn up, a copy should be filed with the listing officer (**PD 39, para. 4.2**). Whether the hearing can be completely vacated depends on whether the terms agreed are suitable for a judgment or order by consent. If they are not, the court should still be informed because the time estimate will almost certainly be considerably reduced. Settlements of the substantive dispute reached in advance of trial are usually made between the parties' solicitors in correspondence (by letter or fax) or over the telephone. The agreed settlement is itself a contract, so is binding even if it is not made into a formal order of the court (*Thakrar v Ciro Citterio Menswear plc* [2002] EWHC 1975 (Ch), LTL 1/10/2002, where the court had refused to approve a draft Tomlin order). However, as discussed above, it is usually desirable to incorporate the agreed terms in a judgment or order to facilitate enforcement in the event of breach. The options are largely as described above, except that entering the agreement on counsels' papers does not arise.

If the court is notified in writing at least 14 days before the hearing that the case has been settled or discontinued, the listing fee will be refunded (**CPFO, note following fee 2.2**).

Costs and terms of settlement

61.4 Settlements agreed after proceedings have been issued should deal with the costs of the parties and with the future status of the claim. Options on the latter include entering final judgment, dismissing the claim, granting a stay or discontinuing or withdrawing it. Care should be taken to ensure the wording used reflects the parties' intentions, especially as regards any previous interim costs orders. It should be kept in mind that if a claim is discontinued, the claimant is required to pay the defendant's costs unless specific provision is made to the contrary, and that the claimant is not necessarily barred from commencing fresh proceedings in respect of the same claim (see **chapter 53**). Care is also needed when drafting a consent order to ensure it reflects the parties' intentions on enforcement in the event of breach. For example, in landlord and tenant claims, a compromise may give the landlord a suspended possession order, which allows the landlord to proceed to enforcement by eviction if the tenant fails to comply. Alternatively, a compromise may reinstate the defendant as the lawful tenant, which merely allows the landlord to apply to the court to enforce compliance with any additional terms in the event of breach (*Gibb v Pubmaster Ltd* (2002) LTL 9/10/2002).

ORDERS MADE AT HEARINGS

61.5 Counsel are under a duty to take notes of the court's judgment, and must endorse a note of the court's decision on the backsheet of their briefs. Instructing solicitors may use this as the basis for drawing up the court's order, so accuracy in noting is of great importance. If the orders are at all complex, counsel for both sides will often consult each other immediately after the hearing to ensure that both sides are clear on what the court has ordered. Counsel's endorsement of the order is not protected by legal professional privilege.

In addition, in interim applications the master, district judge or judge will either:

(a) initial the relevant paragraphs of the application notice or draft minutes of the order; or
(b) initial together with making amendments; or
(c) endorse the order on the affidavit, witness statement or application notice in abbreviated form or longhand.

Judgments in Queen's Bench Division trials are certified by the court associate.

The associate's function in this regard is to record what the judge said, and an order recording what the associate believed to be the judge's unexpressed intention was rectified in *Memminger-IRO GmbH v TripLite Ltd (No. 2)* (1992) *The Times*, 9 July 1992.

Remedies and findings beyond the statements of case

Remedies asked for by the claimant must be set out in the claim form (**CPR, r. 16.2(1)(b)**). **61.6**
Only exceptionally will relief be granted, without an amendment, where the relief claimed is based on implied allegations (*Kirin Amgen Inc. v Hoechst Marion Roussel Ltd* (2001) LTL 8/8/2001). Where the particulars of claim include a claim for 'further or other relief', unless the claimant obtains permission to amend, relief, according to *Kirin Amgen Inc. v Hoechst Marion Roussel Ltd*, will not normally be granted in respect of a claim which:

(a) is not pleaded; or
(b) is inconsistent with the relief specifically pleaded; or
(c) is not supported by the allegations in the pleaded case; or
(d) takes the defendant by surprise, unless there are exceptional circumstances.

The danger of a judge making findings of bad faith and giving false evidence when no bad faith had been pleaded is highlighted by *Co-operative Group Ltd v International Computers Ltd* [2003] EWCA Civ 1955, *The Times*, 19 January 2004, where an appeal was allowed partially on this ground.

FORM OF JUDGMENTS AND ORDERS

The heading of a judgment or order is the same as that for the claim, except that the name of **61.7**
the judge, master or district judge, if any, is included above the names of the parties (**CPR, r. 40.2(1)**). Certain consent orders do not need to be approved by a judicial officer. There then follow any recitals. These are followed by the body of the order, which may be short or may be complex, and should include the court's pronouncement on costs. Undertakings tend to be set out in schedules to orders. The terms of the orders must accurately reflect the pronouncement made by the court. Often it is necessary to amplify the court's words, or to put them in imperative form. To simplify this task and to ensure consistency, in both the High Court and the county courts there are many prescribed forms for judgments and orders. There are also model form orders contained in some of the practice directions, such as those for freezing injunctions and search orders in **PD 25**. These must be used where applicable, with such variations as the circumstances of the case may require.

Every judgment and order must bear the date on which it was given or made, and be sealed by the court (**r. 40.2(2)**).

Where an application or appeal is dismissed, and the judge considers that it was totally without merit, this fact must be recorded in the order (and the judge must consider whether to make a civil restraint order). See **rr. 3.3(7)**, **3.4(6)**, **23.12** and **52.10(6)**, and the discussion on civil restraint orders at **14.70** to **14.73**.

Appeals against almost all interim orders can only be made with permission (**r. 52.3**). Usually permission must initially be sought from the lower court, with a right to renew the application for permission to the appeal court. Where a party has sought permission to appeal from the lower court, that court's order must by **r. 40.2(4)** state:

(a) whether or not the judgment or order is final (for which, see **71.5**);
(b) whether an appeal lies from the judgment or order, and if so, to which appeal court (for which, see **71.3**);
(c) whether the lower court has given permission to appeal; and
(d) if not, the appeal court to which any further application for permission to appeal may be made (this requirement is to assist litigants in person who are often confused about which court deals with appeals).

Time limits

61.8 Where an order imposes a time limit for doing any act, the date for compliance must be expressed as a calendar date, and must include the time of day by which the act must be done (**CPR, r. 2.9(1)**). Orders may be made subject to conditions, and may, at the court's discretion, specify the consequences of failing to comply (**r. 3.1(3)**).

Orders requiring an act to be done ('unless orders')

61.9 Orders requiring an act to be done, other than the payment of money, must specify the time within which the act must be done. The consequences of failing to comply with the order must also be set out (**PD 40B, paras 8.1** and **8.2**). There are two suitable forms of wording, and the first form should be used wherever possible. The second form should be used where the defaulting party does not attend:

Unless the claimant serves his list of documents by 4.00 p.m. on Friday, 22 September 2006, his claim will be struck out and judgment entered for the defendant.

Unless the defendant serves his list of documents within 14 days of service of this order . . .

Injunction orders and penal notice

61.10 Injunction orders, whether prohibitory or mandatory, are intended to have penal consequences and can be punished as a contempt of court. These orders need to be endorsed with a penal notice in the following form (**PD 40B, para. 9.1**):

If you the within-named [ ] do not comply with this order you may be held to be in contempt of court and imprisoned or fined, or [in the case of a company or corporation] your assets may be seized.

Undertakings given in lieu of injunctions are treated in the same way. A person giving an undertaking may also be required to sign a statement, which is endorsed on the court's copy of the order, to the effect that he or she understands the terms of the undertaking and the consequences of failure to comply with it (**PD 40B, para. 9.3**).

Consent orders

61.11 Many orders are made 'by consent'. A true consent order is based on a contract between the parties. As such, the contract is arrived at by bargaining between the parties, perhaps in correspondence, and the consent order is simply evidence of that contract (*Wentworth v Bullen* (1840) 9 B & C 840). To be a true consent order there must be consideration passing from each side. If this is the case, then, unlike other orders, it will only be set aside on grounds, such as fraud or mistake, which would justify the setting aside of a contract (*Purcell v F. C. Trigell Ltd* [1971] 1 QB 358; *Centrehigh Ltd v Amen* (2001) LTL 18/7/2001). A common mistake of law can vitiate a consent order (applying the principles from *Kleinwort Benson Ltd v Lincoln City Council* [1999] 2 AC 349), but consent orders should not be set aside lightly. In *Brennan v Bolt Burdon* [2004] EWCA Civ 1017, [2005] QB 303, the claimant sought to set aside an agreement to discontinue a claim entered into on a mistaken view of the law before the law was clarified by *Anderton v Clwyd County Council (No. 2)* [2002] EWCA Civ 933, [2002] 1 WLR 3174. At the time of the agreement the law was in doubt, but the claimant entered into the agreement anyway, so there was no operative mistake. A consent order may be set aside on the ground that neither party intended to be bound by it (*Goodway v Zurich Insurance Co.* [2004] EWHC 137 (TCC), 96 Con LR 49). In theory a consent order may be void for uncertainty, but this applies only where it is legally or practically impossible to give the agreement any sensible content. This is likely to be extremely rare, because the court will lend its assistance in the working out of its orders or in their clarification (*Scammell v Dicker* [2005] EWCA Civ 405, [2005] 3 All ER 838). A consent order may have contractual effect, but leave the mechanics to be worked out by directions of the court, which may include giving one of the parties additional time to perform (*Chaggar v Chaggar* [2002] EWCA Civ 1637, LTL 30/10/2002). The court has jurisdiction to vary a consent order by discharging a term which is an unlawful restraint of trade while leaving the rest of the order in place (*Gerrard Ltd v Read* (2002) 152 NLJ 22).

In *Green v Vickers Defence Systems* [2002] EWCA Civ 904, *The Times*, 1 July 2002, the deceased and the defendants entered into a consent order, settling a personal injuries claim arising out of the deceased having developed pleural plaques, under which the defendants paid a sum of money on a full-liability basis and on the assumption the deceased would not develop mesothelioma. It was held that the agreement meant that a subsequent claim based on the deceased developing mesothelioma would be paid on a full-liability basis. There is a common misapprehension that where a party fails to honour a term of a compromise agreement settling litigation the original claim is reopened. Although this can be the position where there are grounds for avoiding the contract, in most cases an agreement to compromise a claim brings proceedings on the claim to an end and replaces them with the contractual arrangements in the compromise. Breach of the compromise agreement gives rise to a new claim for breach of contract (*Lewis v Barnett* [2004] EWCA Civ 807, LTL 29/7/2004).

Tomlin orders made in commercial disputes are interpreted in the same way as other commercial agreements (*Sirius International Insurance Co. (Publ) v FAI General Insurance Ltd* [2004] UKHL 54, [2004] 1 WLR 3251). This means the court will seek to ascertain the contextual meaning of the language used. An objective approach is taken, with the court asking what a reasonable person would have understood the parties to have meant by the language used in the order.

However, there is a distinction between a real contract and a simple submission to an order (*Ropac Ltd v Inntrepreneur Pub Co.* (2000) *The Times*, 21 June 2000). In *Siebe Gorman and Co. Ltd v Pneupac Ltd* [1982] 1 WLR 185, Lord Denning MR said at p. 189:

> It should be clearly understood by the profession that, when an order is expressed to be made 'by consent', it is ambiguous . . . One meaning is this: the words 'by consent' may evidence a real contract between the parties. In such a case the court will only interfere with such an order on the same grounds as it would with any other contract. The other meaning is this: the words 'by consent' may mean 'the parties hereto not objecting'. In such a case there is no real contract between the parties. The order can be altered or varied by the court in the same circumstances as any other order that is made by the court without the consent of the parties.

Consent judgments and orders must be expressed as being 'by consent' (**CPR, r. 40.6(7)(b)**) and must be signed by the legal representatives for each party (or by the litigants in person where this is allowed, see **61.31**). **Paragraph 3.4 of PD 40B** provides that the signatures of the legal representatives may be those of the solicitors or counsel acting for the parties.

Consent orders in family proceedings A further distinction relates to family proceedings. In these the legal effect of a consent order derives from the order, not the agreement of the parties. Consequently, there is no jurisdiction to vary a matrimonial consent order (*Thwaite v Thwaite* [1982] Fam 1). Where such an order was obtained by fraud, misrepresentation or mistake, the remedy is to appeal or bring fresh proceedings (*De Lasala v De Lasala* [1980] AC 546 per Lord Diplock). **61.12**

Consent orders as estoppels A consent order can act as an estoppel which can be raised if fresh proceedings are brought alleging matters encompassed by the compromise (*Keith v Walcott* [1929] AC 482). However, whether this is the effect depends on what was agreed in the consent order, and it may be that one party has reserved the right to bring proceedings on certain allegations although they were raised in the compromised action (*Rice v Reed* [1900] 1 QB 54 and contrast *Jameson v Central Electricity Generating Board* [2000] 1 AC 455, where the terms of the settlement extinguished a claim against a concurrent tortfeasor). Particular care must be taken when entering into a consent order to compromise a claim for specific performance. Such a consent order may be construed as replacing the agreement on which the proceedings were based, or it may be construed as simply replacing the terms of the original **61.13**

contract expressly dealt with in the consent order, with the rest of the original contract still subsisting (as in *Paige v Webb* [2001] EWCA Civ 1220, LTL 26/7/2001).

Tomlin orders

61.14 Tomlin orders are so named after Tomlin J who, in a Practice Note [1927] WN 290, said that where terms of compromise are agreed and it is intended to stay the claim with the terms scheduled to the order, the order should be worded:

> And, the [claimant] and the defendant having agreed to the terms set forth in the schedule hereto, it is ordered that all further proceedings in this claim be stayed, except for the purpose of carrying such terms into effect. Liberty to apply as to carrying such terms into effect.

Tomlin orders are used where complex terms are agreed, or where the terms of a compromise go beyond the boundaries of the claim (for example, *E. F. Phillips and Sons Ltd v Clarke* [1970] Ch 322), or where it is sought to avoid publicity of the agreement. In the event of the scheduled terms being breached, enforcement is a two-stage process. First, the claim must be restored under the 'liberty to apply' clause, and an order obtained to compel compliance with the term breached. Secondly, if that order is itself breached, enforcement can follow in the usual way.

By **PD 40B, para. 3.5**, where a consent order is in the form of a stay of proceedings on agreed terms recorded in a schedule (a Tomlin order), any direction for the payment of money out of court or for the payment and assessment of costs must be contained in the body of the order and not the schedule. The reason is that these two forms of direction require action on the part of the court, and must therefore be included in the public part of the order and not concealed in the schedule. If the amount of costs has been agreed this can be included in the schedule.

Money judgments and payment by instalments

61.15 A judgment for the payment of money (including costs) must be complied with within 14 days of the judgment, unless the court specifies some other date for compliance (**CPR, r. 40.11**). It may, for example, instead of requiring immediate payment, impose an order for payment by instalments. A judgment for payment by instalments must state the total amount of the judgment, the amount of each instalment, the number of instalments and the date on which each is to be paid, and to whom the instalments should be paid (**PD 40B, para. 12**).

Judgments in foreign currency

61.16 Since *Miliangos v George Frank (Textiles) Ltd* [1976] AC 443, the general rule has been that in cases with a foreign element it has been possible to enter judgment in a foreign currency, and the date of conversion into sterling for enforcement purposes is the date of payment. As Lord Fraser said at p. 502,

> Any conversion date earlier than the date of payment would, in my opinion, be open to the same objection as the breach date, *viz.* that it would necessarily leave a considerable interval of time between the conversion date and the date of payment. During that interval currency fluctuations might cause the sterling award to vary appreciably from the sum in foreign currency to which the creditor was entitled. . . . [Hence the date of conversion is] the date when the court authorises enforcement of the judgment.

For further discussion of the law on this subject, see *McGregor on Damages*.

Where a claimant intends to seek judgment in a foreign currency, the particulars of claim must specify the foreign currency, and must state why the claim is for payment in that currency, the sterling equivalent, and the source of the exchange rate relied upon (**PD 16, para. 9.1**). If the court orders a judgment to be entered in a foreign currency, by **PD 40B, para. 10**, the order must be in the following form:

> It is ordered that the defendant pay the claimant [*state the sum in the foreign currency*] or the sterling equivalent at the time of payment.

The CPR contain no express provisions on the *enforcement* of judgments in foreign currency. In *Carnegie v Giessen* [2005] EWCA Civ 191, [2005] 1 WLR 2510, the Court of Appeal held that the relevant pre-CPR practice direction, Queen's Bench Masters' Practice Direction (11), is to be treated as remaining in force. The text of this practice direction, updated to comply with CPR terminology, appears in **appendix 2.**

Counterclaims

The court has power to give separate judgments when dealing with cases where there are claims and counterclaims. It also has power, as at present, to order a set-off between the two claims, and simply enter judgment for the balance (**CPR, r. 40.13(2)**). Where it does so, it retains power to make separate costs orders in respect of the claims and counterclaims (**r. 40.13(3)**). **61.17**

State benefits recoupment

In personal injuries cases where some or all of the damages are subject to recovery under the Social Security (Recovery of Benefits) Act 1997, the judgment should include a preamble setting out the amounts awarded under each head of damage, and the amount by which it has been reduced in accordance with the Act (**PD 40B, para. 5.1**). The judgment should then provide for entry of judgment and payment of the balance. **61.18**

Interim payments

Detailed rules for the form of judgments given in cases where there have been interim payments are laid down in **PD 25B**. In a preamble to the judgment in such a case there should be set out the total amount awarded and the amounts and dates of all interim payments. The total amount awarded should then be reduced by the total amount of the interim payments, with judgment being given for the balance. If the interim payments exceed the amount awarded at trial, by virtue of **CPR, r. 25.8(2)**, the judgment should set out any orders made for repayment, reimbursement, variation or discharge, and any award of interest on the overpaid interim payments. **61.19**

Provisional damages

At common law an award of damages had to be by way of a single lump sum. This did not always produce a just result in personal injuries cases involving a risk of the claimant suffering some future deterioration related to the original injury. Although the court would increase the damages awarded to take into account the risk of the future deterioration, the uplift would only be a fraction of the true loss if it occurred, and the claimant would be overcompensated if it did not occur. To remedy this shortcoming, the courts have been given power to award provisional damages by the **Supreme Court Act 1981, s. 32A**, and the **County Courts Act 1984, s. 51.** **61.20**

These sections provide that an award of provisional damages may be made in an:

> ... action for damages for personal injuries in which there is proved or admitted to be a chance that at some definite or indefinite time in the future the injured person will, as a result of the act or omission which gave rise to the cause of action, develop some serious disease or suffer some serious deterioration in his physical or mental condition.

A provisional damages award has two elements:

(a) immediate damages in respect of the existing injuries, calculated on the assumption that the claimant will not develop the future disease or that the future deterioration will not be suffered; and
(b) an entitlement to return to court to apply for further damages if the disease develops or the deterioration is suffered.

Conditions for awarding provisional damages There are four conditions: **61.21**

(a) The particulars of claim must include a claim for provisional damages (**CPR, r. 41.2(1)(a)**).

(b) The future disease or deterioration must be to the claimant's physical or mental condition. A risk that the claimant may be discharged from long-term state-paid hospital care, with the result that he would then need a great deal of private medical care, is not a 'disease or deterioration' (*Adan v Securicor Custodial Services Ltd* [2004] EWHC 394 (QB), [2005] PIQR P79). An injury suffered in a second accident resulting from the injury suffered in the accident for which the defendant is responsible may be a 'deterioration' for these purposes (see *Hughes v Cheshire County Council* (2 March 1989 unreported), mentioned in and doubted by *Willson v Ministry of Defence* [1991] 1 All ER 638).

(c) The future disease or deterioration must be 'serious'. According to Scott Baker J in *Willson v Ministry of Defence*, this connotes something beyond the ordinary or commonly experienced consequences of the injury in question. It is relevant to consider the effect on the particular claimant, for example, a hand injury will be more serious to a concert pianist than to most other claimants. One matter particularly considered in *Willson v Ministry of Defence* was whether possible future osteoarthritis could be the subject of a provisional damages award. An increased risk of the onset of osteoarthritis is a common factor where an accident victim has suffered fractured bones. As such, it is not beyond the ordinary, and Scott Baker J took the view that even if the future risk of osteoarthritis involved a possible need for surgery or a change in employment it would not be 'serious'.

(d) There must be a 'chance' that the future deterioration 'will' be suffered. If this is not admitted by the defendant, it must be proved on the balance of probabilities. The 'chance' that must be proved is one that is measurable as opposed to being fanciful. In *Patterson v Ministry of Defence* [1987] CLY 1194, Simon Brown J found that the claimant had about a 5 per cent risk of developing further pleural thickening, and decided there was a 'plain' chance of that happening for the purposes of making a provisional damages award.

61.22 **Discretion to award provisional damages** Once the above conditions have been established, the court has a discretion whether to make a provisional damages award as opposed to a conventional lump-sum award. The most important factor in the exercise of this discretion would appear to be one of balancing the desirability of putting an end to litigation against the possibility of doing better justice by reserving the claimant's right to return to court for further damages. Provisional damages are more appropriate where the risk of the future deterioration is high and the nature of the possible future deterioration is very serious (for example, a future risk of severe epilepsy). Provisional damages are also more likely to be awarded if the claimant can point to some clear-cut future event that will trigger the entitlement to return to court for further damages.

61.23 **Provisional damages orders** A provisional damages order:

(a) must specify the disease or type of deterioration in respect of which an application may be made for further damages as a future date;

(b) must specify the period within which that application may be made. The period for applying for further damages may be extended; and

(c) may be made in respect of more than one disease or type of deterioration, and may, in respect of each disease or type of deterioration, specify a different period for applying for further damages.

A model form of provisional damages judgment is set out in **PD 41**. This includes the filing of a case file of documents to be preserved until the expiry of the period (or any extension) during which the claimant is entitled to apply for further damages if the specified disease develops or the specified deterioration is suffered. The documents that will usually be included in the case file are the judgment, the statements of case, a transcript of the judge's oral judgment, all medical reports relied upon, and a transcript of the claimant's own evidence in so far as the judge regards it as necessary (**PD 41, para. 3.2**). The fact there may be a few 'loose ends' where the parties cannot agree does not prevent the court making a provisional damages award (*Hurditch v Sheffield Health Authority* [1989] QB 562).

Other matters dealt with in **PD 41** are the entering of consent orders for provisional damages (**para.** 4) and default judgments (which can only be entered with the court's permission, with the master or district judge having to decide whether the case is an appropriate one for a provisional damages award, **para.** 5).

Applying for further damages If the deterioration occurs, an application for further damages should be made within the period specified in the order (as extended from time to time). Only one application for further damages can be made in respect of each disease or deterioration specified in the order. The claimant must give 28 days' notice of the intention to ask for further damages. Within 21 days of the expiry of the 28 days' notice the claimant has to apply to the court for directions. **61.24**

Structured settlements and awards of periodical payments

By virtue of an agreement between the Inland Revenue and the Association of British Insurers in 1987, periodic payments made under certain settlements are deemed to be instalments of antecedent debts. The result is that the payments are capital and not income and therefore are not taxable. This tax advantage is obtained by using the whole or a part of the lump sum which would otherwise be available on settling a personal injury claim to purchase an annuity. There are four types of annuity which qualify under the scheme: **61.25**

(a) a basic term annuity, which runs for a fixed number of years;
(b) an index-linked (i.e., one which rises with inflation) fixed-term annuity;
(c) an annuity for life or for a minimum number of years (which survives for the claimant's beneficiaries);
(d) an index-linked life or minimum-term annuity.

Annuities are bought from life offices. A life office will quote a price of an annuity if given certain details about the claimant (age, sex, medical reports, level of income required, etc.). A quotation will normally only remain open for a limited time. The basic idea is that the tax advantage should be shared between the parties, so that the claimant obtains a more favourable settlement which will provide more income than that obtainable under a lump-sum award, and the defendant will pay less for the annuity than the conventional award. Both parties need to agree on a settlement being structured, and it is generally thought that structuring is only viable where damages run into six figures.

In addition to the established structured settlements, the court can make an award in the form of periodical payments (Damages Act 1996, s. 2, as substituted by the Courts Act 2003, s. 100, from 1 April 2005). An award in the form of periodical payments can be made where both parties agree, or may be ordered by the court where it awards damages for future pecuniary loss in respect of personal injuries. Such an award can only be made if the court is satisfied the continuity of payments under the order is reasonably secure (Damages Act 1996, s. 2(3)). Rules on continuity of payments are in s. 2(4), **CPR, r. 41.9**, and **PD 41B, para. 3**.

In a personal injuries claim, either side may state in its statement of case whether it considers periodical payments or a lump sum is the more appropriate form for all or part of any award of damages (**CPR, r. 41.5**). The court is under a duty to consider and indicate to the parties its view on the matter as soon as practicable (**r. 41.6**). In considering whether periodical payments might be appropriate, and whether to make a periodical payments award, the court must have regard to all the circumstances of the case, and which form of award will best meet the claimant's needs (**r. 41.7**). Factors to take into account include, by **PD 41B, para.** 1:

(a) the scale of the annual payments taking into account any contributory negligence;

(b) the claimant's preference, including his reasons for that preference and the nature of any financial advice received; and
(c) the defendant's preference, and his reasons for that preference.

A periodical payments award must specify the annual amount of the award, how each payment is to be made and at what intervals, and the amounts of the main heads of loss (**CPR, r. 41.8(1)**). There are further requirements where the court orders the award to continue after death for the benefit of the claimant's dependents, where the award is to increase or decrease, and where there is an award for substantial capital purchases (**r. 41.8(2)** to (4), supplemented by **PD 41B, para.** 2). Variations may be permitted pursuant to the Damages (Variation of Periodical Payments) Order 2005 (SI 2005/841). Where the court is satisfied under the Damages Act 1996, s. 2(6)(a), that special circumstances make an assignment or charge of periodical payments necessary, it must also take into account whether the capitalised value of the assignment or charge represents value for money, whether the assignment or charge is in the claimant's best interests, and how the claimant will be financially supported thereafter (**CPR, r. 41.10, and PD 41B, para. 4**).

As a result of the Damages Act 1996, s. 2, there are special rules on making Part 36 offers and payments where a personal injuries claim includes damages for future pecuniary loss (**CPR, r. 36.2A, see 64.12**).

Where a claim which includes damages for future pecuniary loss is settled on behalf of a claimant under a disability, the usual rules in **Part 21** have to be complied with (see **14.38**), and also the rules in **PD 21, paras 6.3** to **6.9**. Where court approval is sought for a compromise, the court must be satisfied that the parties have considered whether there should be periodical payments (**paras 6.4A** and **6.7**). Where the settlement includes periodical payments, the draft consent order must comply with **CPR, rr. 41.8** and **41.9** (see above). The court must be supplied with an opinion on the merits of the settlement or compromise given by counsel or the solicitor acting for the child or patient (except in very clear cases), and a copy or record of any financial advice (**PD 21, paras 6.3** and **6.9**).

Part-owners in relation to claims for the detention of goods

61.26 In a claim by a person who is one of several people with interests in goods which are the subject of proceedings for wrongful interference and which is not based on a right to possession, any judgment can only be for damages unless every other part-owner gives written authority to the claimant to bring the claim on the part-owner's behalf as well as on the claimant's (**CPR, r. 40.14**).

Miscellaneous technical requirements in orders

61.27 A number of technical provisions for different types of judgment are contained in **PD 40B. Paragraph 14** gives examples of forms that can be used for judgments, and lays down certain matters to be included in the preamble of a judgment, such as the questions put to a jury and their findings, any orders made during the trial regarding the use of evidence, and the findings of the judge in respect of each head of damage in a personal injury case.

EMBARGOED JUDGMENTS

61.28 PD 40E, which was introduced on 1 October 2005, applies to all judgments in the Court of Appeal (Civil Division), the Queen's Bench Division and Chancery Division, including judgments given by masters, registrars and costs judges (**para. 1.1**). Where judgment is reserved, a copy will normally be provided to the parties' legal representatives by 4 p.m. on the second working day before the day listed for handing down the judgment (**para. 2.3**). Any proposed corrections should be sent to the clerk of the judge, with a copy to the other parties (**para. 5**).

The draft judgment must be kept confidential until the judgment is formally handed down. During the two-day period between circulation and handing down, the draft judgment can be shown, in confidence, to the parties (**para. 2.4**). If this is done, neither the judgment nor its substance may be disclosed to any other person, and no action may be taken on it other than internally (**para. 2.4**).

The parties should consider whether they can agree a draft order based on the circulated draft judgment. If they can, they should fax or email a copy to the clerk to the judge or presiding judge, and file four copies in the relevant court office by 12 noon on the working day before handing down (**para. 4.1**). If consequential orders are agreed, there is no need for advocates to attend when judgment is handed down, and costs may be disallowed if they do (**paras 3.1** and **3.2**).

ACCOUNTS AND INQUIRIES

At any stage of proceedings, on application by a party or of its own initiative, the court may make an order directing accounts to be taken or inquiries to be made (**CPR, r. 25.1(1)(o)**). The practice on taking such accounts and conducting such inquiries is dealt with in **PD 40**. When making such an order the court may also at the same time or later give directions as to how the account is to be taken or the inquiry conducted (**PD 40, para. 1.1**). Among the directions that may be made are the following: **61.29**

(a) that the relevant books of account shall be evidence of their contents, subject to the parties having the right to make objections (**para. 1.2**);
(b) that an account must be made out and verified by an accounting party by exhibiting it to an affidavit or witness statement (**para. 2(1)**);
(c) that, if appropriate, and at any stage in the proceedings, the parties must serve points of claim and points of defence (**para. 5**);
(d) that the matter should be advertised (**para. 10**);
(e) (in an account of debts or other liabilities) that a party examine the claims of those alleging they are owed money, and to file written evidence on his findings and reasons (**para. 11.1(1)**); and
(f) (in an inquiry for next of kin or unascertained beneficiaries) that a party examine the claims made and file written evidence with his findings and reasons (**para. 11.1(3)**).

Unless the court orders otherwise, accounts and inquiries are conducted by masters or district judges (**para. 9**). The court may direct the inquiry to be investigated in any manner, and direct the person making the claim to give further details, file written evidence and attend court (**para. 12**).

A party alleging that an account drawn by an accounting party is inaccurate (or making similar allegations) must give written notice of the objections to the accounting party (**para. 3.1**). These objections must give full particulars, specify the grounds on which it is alleged the account is inaccurate, and be verified by a statement of truth (or exhibited to an affidavit or witness statement).

GENERAL RULES RELATING TO DRAWING UP ORDERS AND JUDGMENTS

Rules 40.2(2), 40.3(1) and 60.7 of the CPR provide that all judgments and orders have to be drawn up and sealed by the court, unless it dispenses with the need to do so. Normally the court will take responsibility for drawing up, but: **61.30**

(a) unless otherwise ordered, every judgment or order in the Queen's Bench Division,

including the Admiralty and Commercial Courts, and the Technology and Construction Court (but not the Administrative Court) must be drawn up by the parties;
(b) the court may order a party to draw up an order; or
(c) a party may, with the permission of the court, agree to draw up an order; or
(d) the court may direct a party to draw up the order subject to checking by the court before it is sealed; or
(e) the court may direct the parties to file an agreed statement of the terms of the order before the court itself draws up the order; or
(f) the order may be entered administratively by consent, in which event the parties will submit a drawn up version of their agreement for entry.

A party who is required to draw up a judgment is allowed seven days to file the relevant document, together with sufficient copies for all relevant parties, failing which any other party may draw it up and file it for sealing (**CPR, rr. 40.3(3)** and **40.4(1)**).

Every judgment or order (apart from judgments on admissions, default judgments, consent judgments and orders made by court officers under **rr. 70.5** and **71.2**) must state the name and judicial title of the judge who made it (**r. 40.2(1)**).

Once an order has been drawn up the court will serve sealed copies on the applicant and respondent, and also on any other person the court may order to be served (**r. 40.4(2)**). It will be the court that effects service unless one of the exceptions set out in **r. 6.3** applies. The court is given a specific power by **r. 40.5** to order service on a litigant as well as the litigant's solicitor.

Entering administrative consent orders

61.31 In order to save time and costs, **r. 40.6** of the CPR allows certain types of consent orders to be entered by a purely administrative process without the need for obtaining the approval of a judge. However, this process may not be used if any of the parties is a litigant in person (**r. 40.6(2)(b)**). The types of orders covered are:

(a) judgments or orders for the payment of money;
(b) judgments or orders for the delivery up of goods (other than specific delivery);
(c) orders to dismiss the whole or part of the proceedings;
(d) orders for stays on agreed terms which dispose of the proceedings, including Tomlin orders;
(e) orders setting aside default judgments;
(f) orders for the payment out of money in court;
(g) orders for the discharge from liability of any party; and
(h) orders for the payment, waiver or assessment of costs.

The consent order has to be drawn up in the agreed terms, has to bear the words 'By Consent', and be signed by the solicitors or counsel acting for each of the parties. In cases where terms are annexed in a schedule, provisions dealing with the payment of money out of court and for the payment and assessment of costs should be contained in the body of the order rather than in the schedule (**PD 40B, para. 3.5**).

Consent orders approved by the court

61.32 If an order is agreed between the parties, but includes a provision going beyond the types of orders referred to in **61.31**, or if one of the parties is a litigant in person, it will have to be approved by a judge (often a district judge or master). It will be drawn up as above. The name of the judge will not be known, so the draft will have to include a space for the judge's details to be inserted (**PD 23, para. 10.3**). If all the parties write to the court expressing their consent, the court will treat that as sufficient signing of the consent order (**PD 23, para. 10.2**). The court will not necessarily make the order in accordance with the agreement between the parties, as the court retains ultimate control, particularly over case management matters. However, it will always take the terms agreed between the parties into account in whatever order it decides to make (see, for example, **PD 28, para. 3.8**).

In cases where the court's approval must be sought, either party may make the application for approval, and the application may be dealt with without a hearing (**CPR, r. 40.6(5)** and **(6)**).

Chancery Division orders

Most Chancery Division orders are drawn up by the court (**Chancery Guide, para. 9.8**). This can usually be done more quickly if a draft order is handed in by the party for whom it is being made (**para. 9.4**). In all but the simplest cases a draft order should be prepared and brought to the hearing (**para. 9.4**) and it is helpful if the draft is provided by email or on disk (see **para. 9.6** for details). **61.33**

REVIEW OF JUDGMENT

Appealing (see **chapters** 71 and 72) is the main way of impugning a decision. In limited circumstances a judgment or order may be corrected under the slip rule (**61.35**), or may be reconsidered (**61.36**) or recalled (**61.38**) before it is drawn up. There is also an exceptional power to reopen the whole proceedings where no appeal is possible (**61.39**). **61.34**

Slip rule

The court has power to correct any accidental slip or omission in any judgment (**CPR, r. 40.12(1)**). The slip rule can be used to amend an order to give effect to the intention of the court, but cannot be used to enable the court to have second or additional thoughts (*Bristol-Myers Squibb Co. v Baker Norton Pharmaceuticals Inc. (No. 2)* [2001] RPC 913) or to correct a substantive issue (*Markos v Goodfellow* (2002) LTL 11/10/2002). An order in *Gesek v Nazdrowicz-Woodley* (1998) LTL 13/11/98 appointing a representative for a deceased claimant referred to 'proceedings to be instituted'. In fact the relevant proceedings had already been issued. It was held that the order should be corrected under the slip rule, even though the correction was sought at trial. **Paragraphs** 4.1 to 4.5 of **PD 40B** deal with applications to correct errors in judgments and orders. If the error is obvious the court may deal with the application without notice. Opposed applications will normally be listed before the judge who gave the judgment or made the order. **61.35**

Reconsideration before judgment is drawn up

The court may reconsider a judgment after it has been pronounced provided this is done before it is drawn up. During this period factual errors can be corrected (*Spice Girls Ltd v Aprilia World Service BV (No. 3)* (2000) *The Times*, 12 September 2000). The Court of Appeal may reconsider a judgment in the period between draft judgments being sent to the parties and formal delivery in court (*Royal Brompton Hospital NHS Trust v Hammond* [2001] BLR 317; see also the power to reopen an appeal under **CPR, r. 52.17**, discussed at **71.51**). The power to reconsider a judgment is not affected by **r. 40.7**, which provides that a judgment takes effect from the time of pronouncement (*Stewart v Engel* [2000] 1 WLR 2268), or by **r. 52.4(2)**, which provides that the time limit for filing an appellant's notice is normally calculated from the time of pronouncement (*Kirin Amgen Inc. v Transkaryotic Therapies Inc.* (2001) *The Times*, 1 June 2001). Reconsideration should be sought only in exceptional circumstances (*Stewart v Engel*). The examples of exceptional circumstances justifying reconsideration of interim decisions, given by Neuberger J in *Re Blenheim Leisure (Restaurants) Ltd (No. 3)* (1999) *The Times*, 9 November 1999 (see **32.36**), would also justify reconsideration of a final judgment (*Stewart v Engel*). The fact that the party against whom judgment has been pronounced has a change of mind about not pursuing a particular cause of action is not an exceptional circumstance justifying reconsideration (*Stewart v Engel*). It would be a misuse of the jurisdiction to argue that a judge should reconsider an issue which was in dispute and already argued: that would **61.36** be to subvert the appeal process (*Compagnie Noga d'Importation et d'Exportation SA v Abacha* [2001] 3 All ER 513).

Reconsideration of case management decisions

61.37 It may sometimes be appropriate for one judge to reconsider case management directions made on a previous occasion by another judge. Each case turns on its own facts, with the court seeking to give effect to the overriding objective, but if there has been a change of circumstances it may well be appropriate to interfere with the procedural regime previously laid down (*Umm Qarn Management Co. Ltd v Bunting* [2001] CPLR 21). It is only if there is a significant change in circumstances that a case management decision can be revisited on a later occasion (*Jameson v Personal Representatives of Smith* [2001] EWCA Civ 1264, [2001] CPLR 489). It is incumbent on a party to claim interim relief based on the same facts once and once only (*Halifax plc v Chandler* [2001] EWCA Civ 1750, [2002] CPLR 41, where there were two applications to vary a freezing injunction). In *Leadmill Ltd v Omare* [2002] EWHC 1226 (Ch), LTL 23/4/2002, an interim injunction was granted restraining the defendant from calling his tapas bar 'The Treadmill', being sited close to the claimant's nightclub, 'The Leadmill'. The defendant applied to discharge the order on the basis he intended to change the colour and font of his signs. It was held that the defendant could have raised this at the initial hearing. As afterthoughts are not permitted, the application was refused. On the other hand, the production of extra evidence was regarded as a change of circumstances in *Bass Taverns Ltd v Carford Catering Equipment Ltd* (2002) LTL 23/4/2002.

Recalling judgment

61.38 A judge is under a positive obligation to recall a draft judgment sent to the legal representatives of the parties in advance of formal pronouncement (see **59.47**) if it becomes clear that the draft is wrong (*Robinson v Bird* [2003] EWCA Civ 1820, *The Times*, 20 January 2004). In *Taylor v Williamsons* [2002] EWCA Civ 1380, *The Times*, 9 August 2002, after hearing evidence on a preliminary issue, the case was adjourned with directions for the exchange and filing of written submissions. Before the deadline, and before receiving the claimant's submissions, the judge issued a written judgment dismissing the claim. When the mistake was discovered, the judge recalled his judgment, refused to recuse himself, and again gave judgment for the defendant. An appeal by the claimant was dismissed. It was held that a judge has a wide discretion to amend a judgment before it is perfected and to recall such a judgment, and there was no reason to think the judge in this case had not reconsidered the case fairly in the light of the further submissions.

Reopening proceedings

61.39 Like the Court of Appeal (*Taylor v Lawrence* [2002] EWCA Civ 90, [2003] QB 528, see **71.51**), the High Court has jurisdiction to reopen proceedings after they have been concluded to hear more evidence or further argument (*Seray-Wurie v Hackney London Borough Council* [2002] EWCA Civ 909, [2003] 1 WLR 257). The power should only be exercised where there has been a significant injustice and where there is no alternative remedy. There may be no alternative remedy where an appeal court has refused permission to appeal (see **71.16** and the **Access to Justice Act 1999, s. 54(4)**, which is a point made at **CPR, r. 52.17(7)**). Applications for permission to reopen should be made on paper (*Taylor v Lawrence*).

The decisions referred to in the previous paragraph were both based on the court's inherent jurisdiction. This means they have no direct relevance to the question of whether there is jurisdiction for a county court circuit judge to reopen a decision (*Seray-Wurie v Hackney London Borough Council*, a point which appears to be confirmed by **r. 52.17(3)**).

PRESERVED PROVISIONS OF THE CCR RELATING TO JUDGMENTS AND ORDERS

The following provisions of the CCR have been preserved in the CPR, sch. 2: **61.40**

(a) **CCR, ord. 22, r. 8**, on obtaining a certificate of judgment;
(b) **CCR, ord. 22, r. 10**, on applying to vary the date or rate of payment;
(c) **CCR, ord. 22, r. 11**, on setting off cross-judgments; and
(d) **CCR, ord. 22, r. 13**, on filing in the county court orders of the High Court and Court of Appeal after appeals have been determined.

REGISTER OF JUDGMENTS

With effect from 6 April 2006 (see Courts Act 2003 (Commencement No. 12 and Transitional Provision) Order 2005, SI 2005/3518): **61.41**

(a) The former provisions in the County Courts Act 1984, ss. 73 and 73A, were repealed. These sections set up machinery for the operation of the register of county court money judgments, which was operated by Registry Trust Ltd.
(b) The provisions of the Courts Act 2003, s. 98(1) and (3) were brought into effect. This section provides for the registration of money judgments from the High Court and the county courts, and also criminal fines.

Under the Courts Act 2003, the register may be kept either by a body corporate in accordance with terms agreed with the Lord Chancellor, or it may be kept by the Lord Chancellor (Register of Judgments, Orders and Fines Regulations 2005, SI 2005/3595, regs 6 and 7). Appropriate officers in the High Court and county courts are required to provide the registrar with periodic returns of judgments and orders for the payment of money (reg. 8(1) and the definition of 'judgment' in reg. 3). The following are, by reg. 9, exempt from registration:

(a) judgments in family proceedings;
(b) judgments in the Administrative Court;
(c) judgments in the Technology and Construction Court;
(d) judgments under appeal, until the appeal has been determined;
(e) broadly, judgments in contested proceedings, until an order or application is made for payment by instalments, or the judgment creditor takes any step to enforce the judgment; and
(f) broadly, orders for the payment of money in claims for the recovery of land, until the judgment creditor takes any step to enforce the order.

Details given by the appropriate officer to the registrar include the debtor's full name, date of birth (which explains why this information is required in acknowledgments of service and defences), and the amount of the judgment debt (reg. 10). The amount may be increased, for example, after the assessment of costs (reg. 20). Registrations are removed after six years in any event (reg. 26). Registration may be cancelled if the judgment is satisfied within one month from the date of the judgment, or if it is set aside or reversed (reg. 11(2)). If the judgment is satisfied more than a month after judgment, the appropriate officer should notify the registrar who will endorse the entry with the fact the judgment has been satisfied (reg. 11(3)).

Chapter 62 Interest

INTRODUCTION

62.1 At common law interest was payable only when provided for by contract (*London, Chatham and Dover Railway Co. v South Eastern Railway Co.* [1893] AC 429). However, equity, the law merchant and statute have made such widespread inroads into the common law rule that today if money is recovered in legal proceedings then interest on the money is recoverable in almost all cases up to the date of judgment, and in most cases in the period between judgment and payment. Where interest is recoverable it is usually awarded at the **Judgments Act 1838** rate, which is currently 8 per cent a year. Interest awarded by the court will generally be simple interest, although there are exceptions where compound interest is awarded.

GENERAL POWER TO INCLUDE INTEREST IN JUDGMENTS

Damages claims

62.2 Statutory authority for adding interest to any sum recovered by way of damages is provided by the **Supreme Court Act 1981, s. 35A(1)**, and by the **County Courts Act 1984, s. 69(1)**, both of which are in identical terms (except for referring to the High Court and county courts respectively). The **County Courts Act 1984, s. 69(1)**, provides:

> Subject to rules of court, in proceedings (whenever instituted) before a county court for the recovery of a debt or damages there may be included in any sum for which judgment is given simple interest, at such rate as the court thinks fit or as may be prescribed, on all or any part of the debt or damages in respect of which judgment is given, or payment is made before judgment, for all or any part of the period between the date when the cause of action arose and—
> (a) in the case of any sum paid before judgment, the date of the payment; and
> (b) in the case of the sum for which judgment is given, the date of the judgment.

Interest on damages is therefore discretionary, and may be awarded on all or part of the amount recovered, and for such period and at such rates as the court may think fit. However, it is a discretion which is usually exercised in favour of the party obtaining judgment. The principle on which the courts act is that interest should be paid to compensate the claimant for being kept out of the money which the judgment shows should have been paid at an earlier time (*Wentworth v Wiltshire County Council* [1993] QB 654). Since the time at which the money should have been paid, the claimant will have been forced either to borrow money, or to use funds which could have been employed profitably for other purposes, or have been deprived of the use of the money awarded by the judgment. An award of interest compensates for this loss.

The statutory provisions only allow the court to award simple interest. It is therefore wrong in principle to award damages for things such as bank interest if an award of statutory interest on the other heads of damage is made, as that would amount to double recovery (*Wentworth v Wiltshire County Council* [1993] QB 654).

In personal injuries claims it is even clearer that interest should ordinarily be awarded in addition to damages. The **Supreme Court Act 1981, s. 35A(2)**, and the **County Courts Act 1984, s. 69(2)**, both provide:

In relation to a judgment given for damages for personal injuries or death which exceed £200 subsection (1) shall have effect—

(a) with the substitution of 'shall be included' for 'may be included'; and
(b) with the addition of 'unless the court is satisfied that there are special reasons to the contrary' after 'given', where first occurring.

The **Supreme Court Act 1981, s. 35A(7)** and the **County Courts Act 1984, s. 69(6)**, state that the term 'personal injuries' includes any disease or impairment of a person's physical or mental condition.

Debt claims

The main provisions in the **Supreme Court Act 1981, s. 35A(1)**, and the **County Courts Act 1984, s. 69(1)** (see **62.2**), by their terms apply to debt claims as well as claims for damages. Accordingly, the court is given a general discretion to award simple interest on judgments for debts at such rates and for such periods as the court thinks fit. In addition, s. 35A(3) of the 1981 Act and s. 69(3) of the 1984 Act (both of which are in the same terms apart from references to the High Court and county courts respectively) provide for the recovery of simple interest on debt claims which are paid after the commencement of proceedings even in the absence of a judgment. The **County Courts Act 1984, s. 69(3)**, provides: **62.3**

Subject to rules of court, where—

(a) there are proceedings (whenever instituted) before a county court for the recovery of a debt; and
(b) the defendant pays the whole debt to the [claimant] (otherwise than in pursuance of a judgment in the proceedings),

the defendant shall be liable to pay the [claimant] simple interest, at such rate as the court thinks fit or as may be prescribed, on all or any part of the debt for all or any part of the period between the date the cause of action arose and the date of payment.

These provisions do not apply if interest is payable on the debt for some other reason (see **62.5**), because s. 35A(4) of the 1981 Act and s. 69(4) of the 1984 Act provide:

Interest in respect of a debt shall not be awarded under this section for a period during which, for whatever reason, interest on the debt already runs.

Payment before judgment

The reason why subsection (3) is in the **Supreme Court Act 1981, s. 35A** and the **County Courts Act 1984, s. 69**, is that payment in full of a debt extinguishes the debt, and so subsection (3) is required to preserve a right to interest despite payment of the principal before judgment (see *Edmunds v Lloyds Italico & l'Ancora Compagnia di Assicurazione e Riassicurazione SpA* [1986] 1 WLR 492). On the other hand, payment of the sum claimed in a damages case does not extinguish the cause of action, and the court may still enter judgment for damages (even though full credit will be given so that no further damages will be paid) and interest. Consequently, there is no need for an equivalent provision to subsection (3) in relation to damages claims (*Edmunds v Lloyds Italico & l'Ancora Compagnia di Assicurazione e Riassicurazione SpA* [1986] 1 WLR 492). **62.4**

Interest is not payable by virtue of s. 35A of the 1981 Act or s. 69 of the 1984 Act unless proceedings have been commenced (*President of India v La Pintada Navigacion SA* [1985] AC 104), though interest may be payable under other provisions (see **62.5** and **62.6**). In a damages claim there is nothing to stop the claimant insisting on an element representing interest to be included in any agreed settlement before proceedings are issued. In a debt claim where there is no defence, the debtor is well advised to pay the whole sum due before proceedings are commenced so as to avoid an order to pay interest as well. Once proceedings are commenced, interest may be claimed for the periods both before and after issue.

INTEREST PURSUANT TO OTHER STATUTES

62.5 In addition to the general provisions in the **Supreme Court Act 1981, s. 35A**, and the **County Courts Act 1984, s. 69**, there are other statutes giving rights to interest. Examples are:

(a) The Bills of Exchange Act 1882, s. 57, which provides:

Where a bill is dishonoured, the measure of damages, which shall be deemed to be liquidated damages, shall be as follows:

(1) The holder may recover from any party liable on the bill and the drawer who has been compelled to pay the bill may recover from the acceptor, and an indorser who has been compelled to pay the bill may recover from the acceptor or from the drawer, or from a prior indorser:

(a) The amount of the bill:

(b) Interest thereon from the time of presentment for payment if the bill is payable on demand, and from the maturity of the bill in any other case:

(c) The expenses of noting, or, when protest is necessary, and the protest has been extended, the expenses of protest.

[(2) Repealed]

(3) Where by this Act interest may be recovered as damages, such interest may, if justice require it, be withheld wholly or in part, and where a bill is expressed to be payable with interest at a given rate, interest as damages may or may not be given at the same rate as interest proper.

(b) In a claim against a carrier under the Convention on the Contract for the International Carriage of Goods by Road, the claimant is entitled to claim interest at 5 per cent per annum (Carriage of Goods by Road Act 1965, sch., art. 27).

(c) Under the Partnership Act 1890, s. 24(3), a partner who contributes more capital than the partnership agreement calls for is entitled to interest at 5 per cent per annum on the additional contribution from the date of payment, unless otherwise agreed.

(d) Under the Solicitors' (Non-contentious Business) Remuneration Order 1994 (SI 1994/2616), art. 14, a solicitor may charge interest at a rate not exceeding that payable on judgments on the amount of his or her unpaid costs in respect of non-contentious business or common form probate business, plus disbursements and VAT, subject to various conditions set out in the Order.

(e) Various revenue statutes provide for the payment of interest, such as the Taxes Management Act 1970, ss. 86 to 92.

INTEREST PURSUANT TO CONTRACT

62.6 Interest may be payable under the express terms of a contract between the parties. Where this is the case, the interest is payable as of right, and is not a matter for the court's discretion. The only exception is where the rate of interest is extortionate within the meaning of the **Consumer Credit Act 1974**. Mortgage agreements and many other forms of credit agreement purport to give the lender an unfettered discretion to vary the rate of interest charged. Dyson LJ in *Paragon Finance plc v Nash* [2001] EWCA Civ 1466, [2002] 1 WLR 685, said that such a discretion is subject to an implied term that it is not to be exercised dishonestly, capriciously, arbitrarily or for an improper purpose. Express terms for the payment of interest often also provide that interest at the agreed rate shall be payable before and after proceedings, and even before and after judgment, until actual payment. The latter type of clause presents some difficulty over the form any judgment should take. One school of thought is to the effect that the judgment should only include contractual interest to the date of the judgment, leaving the creditor to bring a second action (if thought fit) to recover the post-judgment interest. The other school of thought would allow the court to make a judgment to include the interest to the date of judgment together with continuing interest at the contractual daily rate to payment.

Interest has also been awarded in cases where money has been lent on terms that it should be repaid on a set date with interest being payable until then. Where the loan is not repaid on the due date, the courts have awarded interest from the due date for repayment as damages (*see Cook v Fowler* (1874) LR 7 HL 27). As the award has been for damages, the courts have not always used the original interest rate as the measure of the damages for late payment.

LATE PAYMENT OF COMMERCIAL DEBTS

The Late Payment of Commercial Debts (Interest) Act 1998 was passed in compliance with Directive 2000/35/EC on combating late payment. Section 1(1) makes it an implied term in a contract to which the Act applies that any qualifying debt created by the contract carries simple interest subject to the terms of ss. 1 to 6 of the Act. The Act applies to contracts for the sale of goods and for the supply of services and related matters (s. 2), and a 'qualifying debt' is an obligation to pay the price under such a contract (s. 3(1)). With the exception of advance payments, interest runs from 30 days after the supplier performs its obligations under the contract, or 30 days after invoice or other notification of the price (s. 4(2), (4) and (5)). The rate of interest will be as prescribed by statutory instrument (s. 6); see The Late Payment of Commercial Debts (Rate of Interest) (No. 2) Order 1998 (SI 1998/2765), which sets the rate at 8 per cent over the Bank of England's official dealing rate. The rate of interest may be reduced in the interests of justice on account of any misconduct by the supplier (s. 5). **62.7**

The 1998 Act has been brought into effect as follows:

Phase	Applies to contracts from	Scope
1	1 November 1998	Small businesses can claim statutory interest for late payment from large businesses and most public-sector bodies.
2	1 November 2000	Small businesses can claim statutory interest from small businesses, large businesses and most public-sector bodies.
3	7 August 2002	All businesses and public-sector bodies can claim statutory interest.

Under phase 3, a payment is deemed to be late when an agreed credit period has expired, or, if there is none, 30 days after the later of:

(a) delivery of the goods or performance of the services under the contract; and
(b) the date the purchaser was notified of the amount of the debt.

There are special rules for advance payments. Where the parties have a system of payment by the end of the month following the month in which the invoice is received, payment will be late for the purposes of the legislation at the end of the month following the month in which the invoice was received.

A seller making use of the legislation must notify the purchaser. Notification may be oral, but written notice is preferable in the event of a dispute. The notice should state the amount owed, what it is owed for, how the statutory interest is calculated, should quote the original invoice number, and state to whom and where payment should be made, by what date and by what method.

The Bank of England base rate on 31 December will be the 'reference rate' for the following 1 January to 30 June. Base rate on 30 June will be the reference rate for the period 1 July to 31 December. Statutory interest under the late payment legislation is 8 per cent above the appropriate reference rate. So, if the reference rate is 4 per cent p.a., the rate payable under the late payment legislation would be simple interest at 12 per cent p.a. (but fluctuating every six months with any variations in Bank of England base rate).

In addition, a seller is entitled to charge statutory compensation on late payments. The amount of compensation varies with the amount of the debt, as follows:

Size of unpaid debt	Amount of compensation
Up to £999.99	£40.00
£1,000 to £9,999.99	£70.00
Over £9,999.99	£100.00

Parties to a contract can contract out of the late-payment legislation, provided they make their own arrangements for contractual interest. To prevent abuse, contractual interest must be 'substantial', otherwise it will be void and the late-payment legislation will apply. In considering whether a contractual remedy is substantial, the court must consider all the circumstances, including the rate of interest applicable to late payments and the length of credit periods. If the credit period is considered excessive, the court can strike it down and replace it with a 30-day default period. 'Representative bodies' are given standing to challenge contractual terms which are grossly unfair on behalf of small and medium-sized enterprises (SMEs). SMEs are independent enterprises which have fewer than 250 employees and either a turnover of less than 40 million euro or an annual balance sheet total not exceeding 27 million euro.

ADMIRALTY CASES

62.8 There is a long-established practice of awarding damages in the Admiralty Court on damages arising out of collisions at sea and salvage awards (*The Aldora* [1975] QB 748; *The Rilland* [1979] 1 Lloyd's Rep 455).

EQUITY CASES

62.9 There is a long-established practice of awarding interest in the Chancery Division ancillary to equitable remedies such as the taking of an account or specific performance. Awarding interest has been used as a remedy in claims where defendants owing fiduciary duties have been found to have misapplied or withheld money, or been guilty of fraud (*Johnson v R* [1904] AC 817).

EXCEPTIONAL CASES WHERE INTEREST IS NOT AWARDED

62.10 Interest is not normally awarded on awards in libel cases, nor in claims for wrongful arrest or false imprisonment (*Holtham v Commissioner of Police for the Metropolis* (1987) *The Independent*, 26 November 1987). In *Saunders v Edwards* [1987] 1 WLR 1116 it was held that interest should not have been awarded on a sum for inconvenience and disappointment made in a misrepresentation claim.

RULES OF COURT

The main statutory provisions giving a discretion to award interest (see 62.2 and 62.3) are subject to rules of court. The main rule of court to be considered is **CPR, r. 16.4(2)**. This provides that if the claimant is seeking interest, the particulars of claim must: **62.11**

(a) state whether the claim is:
  (i) under the terms of a contract; or
  (ii) under an enactment, and if so which; or
  (iii) on some other basis, and if so which basis;
(b) if the principal claim is for a specified sum of money, the particulars of claim must:
  (i) state the percentage rate claimed for the interest and the date from which it is claimed;
  (ii) contain an interest calculation, giving a date (which should be no later than the date of issue of the claim form) to which past interest is calculated; and
  (iii) the daily rate at which future interest accrues.

If the claim is for an unspecified amount of money (as most damages claims are), it is sufficient, in addition to stating the basis on which interest is claimed, to say in the particulars of claim that interest is sought at such rates and for such periods on the sums found due to the claimant as the court may think fit, to be decided by the court.

RATE OF INTEREST

Interest pursuant to contract should be at the contract rate. Some statutes (such as the Partnership Act 1890) lay down specific rates for interest recoverable. Otherwise, the rate of interest is in the discretion of the court. Where this is so, in practical terms the starting point in most classes of case is the **Judgments Act 1838** rate, which has been 8 per cent a year since 1 April 1993. **62.12**

In commercial cases and actions on bills of exchange, traditionally interest has been awarded at 1 per cent above base rate. However, this is no more than a practice, and may be displaced by evidence showing that the rate is unfair to either party (*Shearson Lehman Hutton Inc. v Maclaine Watson and Co. Ltd (No. 2)* [1990] 3 All ER 723). In *Jaura v Ahmed* [2002] EWCA Civ 210, *The Times*, 18 March 2002, the court recognised that borrowing costs for small businesses are higher than those available to first-class borrowers, and awarded interest at 3 per cent above base rate.

In personal injuries claims, interest on damages for pain, suffering and loss of amenity has in recent years been awarded at 2 per cent a year from the date proceedings are issued (*Wright v British Railways Board* [1983] 1 AC 352). Despite the decision in *Wells v Wells* [1999] 1 AC 345, the rate applied remains at 2 per cent (see *Lawrence v Chief Constable of Staffordshire* (2000) *The Times*, 25 July 2000). Past special damages (such as loss of earnings and out-of-pocket expenses) usually attract interest at half the appropriate rate of interest (to reflect the fact that the losses will usually be ongoing between the date of the accident and the trial, the court adopting a broad-brush approach to the precise dates when individual losses were incurred). The 'appropriate rate' for this purpose is the average rate allowed for money in the Special Account (formerly the short-term investment account). Where the bulk of the losses were incurred a long time before trial, it may be appropriate to award interest on special damages at a higher (and perhaps the full) rate (see *Dexter v Courtaulds Ltd* [1984] 1 WLR 372; *Prokop v Department of Health and Social Security* [1985] CLY 1037). Interest is recoverable in full on past loss of earnings despite the recoupment of State benefits under the Social Security (Recovery of Benefits) Act 1997 (see *Wisely v John Fulton (Plumbers) Ltd* [2000] 1 WLR 820). Obviously, no interest is allowed on future loss and expense or loss of earning capacity. An action in professional negligence against a solicitor based on mishandling of a personal injuries claim will usually attract ordinary interest at the **Judgments Act 1838** rate rather than under the rules discussed in this paragraph (*Pinnock v Wilkins and Sons* (1990) *The Times*, 29 January 1990).

There are other methods of determining the rate of interest to be paid. The court may assess interest by reference to the rates provided by index-linked government stock, or by reference to the base rate of the Bank of England, or one of the clearing banks (usually at a stated percentage above that rate).

Interest, including ordinary statutory interest under the **Supreme Court Act 1981, s. 35A**, or **County Courts Act 1984, s. 69**, at a rate up to 10 per cent above base rate may be awarded where the claimant has made a successful claimant's **Part 36** offer (see **CPR, r. 36.21(2)**), or where the defendant has failed to comply with a pre-action protocol leading to proceedings being commenced which might not have needed to be commenced (**PD Protocols, para. 2.3(4)**). In deciding whether to award interest as high as 10 per cent above base rate under **r. 36.21**, the court should evaluate whether doing so would itself work an injustice or result in a disproportionate advantage to the claimant, or a disproportionate disadvantage to the defendant (*Little v George Little Sebire and Co.* (1999) *The Times*, 17 November 1999).

Table 62.1 Judgments Act 1838 and Special Account rates of interest

Date (from)	Judgments Act 1838 rate	Special Account rate
1.4.1984	12% (from 10.11.1982)	12%
16.4.1985	15%	12%
1.8.1986	15%	11.5%
1.1.1987	15%	12.25%
1.4.1987	15%	11.75%
1.11.1987	15%	11.25%
1.12.1987	15%	11%
1.5.1988	15%	9.5%
1.8.1988	15%	11%
1.11.1988	15%	12.25%
1.1.1989	15%	13%
1.11.1989	15%	14.25%
1.4.1991	15%	12%
1.10.1991	15%	10.25%
1.2.1993	15%	8%
1.4.1993	8%	8%
1.8.1999	8%	7%
1.2.2002	8%	6%

COMPOUND INTEREST

62.13 The general rule is that awards of interest are for simple interest. However, to mark the court's disapproval in cases of breach of fiduciary duty the courts of equity would (and the Chancery Division will continue to) award compound interest with yearly (or such other as may seem appropriate) rests (*Wallersteiner v Moir (No. 2)* [1975] QB 373). Further it is the common practice of banks to charge their customers compound interest, and they are entitled to judgment at their usual compounded rates up to judgment or earlier payment (*National Bank of Greece SA v Pinios Shipping Co. (No. 1)* [1990] 1 AC 637). A deed of priority between two mortgagees giving priority to one mortgagee in the sum of £160,000 'together with interest thereon' was construed as meaning compound interest in *Whitbread plc v UCB Corporate Services Ltd* (2000) *The Times*, 22 June 2000. Giving full compensation under Community law was held by *Sempra Metals Ltd v Commissioners of Inland Revenue* [2005] EWCA Civ 389, [2006] QB 37, to require compound interest. The domestic measure, with simple interest, failed to provide full compensation.

PERIOD OF INTEREST

Interest normally runs from the date the cause of action accrued until judgment or earlier payment. In the case of a claim on an unpaid invoice, the terms of the contract will determine when the invoice matured. In the absence of other evidence the practice is to take the date of maturity as being 30 days after the date of the invoice. In a contract for the sale of land, interest runs from the contractual date for completion notwithstanding the transfer has not been stamped or that the vendor was unable to comply with a request from the purchaser to register the transfer (*P and O Overseas Holdings Ltd v Rhys Braintree Ltd* [2002] EWCA Civ 296, *The Times*, 5 April 2002). Interest on property damaged by negligence is payable from the date of the repairs (or when a decision was made to write off the property damaged). See also *BP Exploration Co. (Libya) Ltd v Hunt (No. 2)* [1979] 1 WLR 783. **62.14**

Where either party is guilty of unjustifiable delay, the court may increase or reduce the rate of interest, or alter the period over which interest is payable, to reflect this fact (*Birkett v Hayes* [1982] 1 WLR 816; *Spittle v Bunney* [1988] 1 WLR 847). In *Beahan v Stoneham* (2001) LTL 16/5/2001 it was held that the judge had been wrong not to reduce the interest awarded on the claim for damages as the claimant had been guilty of delay. It is unnecessary for the defendant to establish prejudice. The starting point is to decide when the case could reasonably have been brought to trial. Interest for two years was disallowed. Reducing interest, even in the event of gross delay, may be unjust and give the defendant an unwarranted windfall if the defendant has been holding on to money that should have been paid to the claimant (*Adcock v Co-operative Insurance Society Ltd* (2000) *The Times*, 26 April 2000). In a case where there was unreasonable delay for two years, during which time there were high interest rates, the claimants were awarded interest at half the usual rate during the period of the delay (*Quorum AS v Schramm* [2002] CLC 77). Ultimately the decision is one within the discretion of the trial judge. The **Supreme Court Act 1981, s. 35A(5)**, and the **County Courts Act 1984, s. 69(5)**, provide that interest under the respective Acts may be calculated at different rates in respect of different periods.

INTEREST ON JUDGMENTS IN FOREIGN CURRENCY

Where judgment is given in a foreign currency, the rate of interest will be that appropriate for the relevant country (usually the rate at which money could be borrowed in that country). Evidence of the rate contended for should be adduced. See *Miliangos v George Frank (Textiles) Ltd (No. 2)* [1977] QB 489. **62.15**

INTEREST ON JUDGMENT DEBTS

The **Judgments Act 1838, s. 17**, and the **County Courts Act 1984, s. 74**, are general provisions which allow simple interest, currently at 8 per cent a year, on all High Court money judgments and on relevant county court money judgments (see below). The **Judgments Act 1838, s. 17**, provides: **62.16**

(1) Every judgment debt shall carry interest at the rate of 8 per cent per annum from such time as shall be prescribed by rules of court, until the same shall be satisfied, and such interest may be levied under a writ of execution on such judgment.
(2) Rules of court may provide for the court to disallow all or part of any interest otherwise payable under subsection (1).

Interest on a judgment runs from the date it is pronounced, not the date it might be drawn up (*Erven Warnink BV v J. Townend and Son (Hull) Ltd (No. 2)* [1982] 3 All ER 312). In the case of a judgment for damages to be decided by the court, **Judgments Act 1838** interest runs on the damages from the date the damages are finally decided. Until then, the claimant can only claim interest on damages under the ordinary principles (which, in a personal injuries case, will be at considerably lower rates). See *Hunt v R. M. Douglas (Roofing) Ltd* [1990] 1 AC 398.

The **County Courts Act 1984, s. 74,** on the other hand, is an enabling provision allowing the Lord Chancellor to make orders that county court judgments shall carry interest at such rates and for such periods as the rules may prescribe. The relevant rules are the County Courts (Interest on Judgment Debts) Order 1991 (SI 1991/1184), which provide that 'relevant judgments' are those for not less than £5,000 and those which are qualifying debts for the purposes of the Late Payment of Commercial Debts (Interest) Act 1998 (see **62.7**), and that interest at the **Judgments Act 1838** rate (art. 5) shall be payable from the date the judgment was given (art. 2(1)). However, there are exceptions. Interest is not payable:

(a) on claims based on regulated agreements under the **Consumer Credit Act 1974** (SI 1991/1184, art. 2(3)(a));
(b) on judgments granting suspended orders for possession of dwelling houses, where the order is in favour of a landlord or mortgagee (art. 2(3)(b));
(c) in the case of a judgment deferring payment, until the date specified for payment (art. 3(a)); and
(d) in the case of a judgment payable by instalments, until instalments are in arrears, and then only on the arrears (art. 3(b)) (the same applies to High Court judgments, see *Caudery v Finnerty* (1892) 66 LT 684 and *Morse v Muir* [1939] 2 KB 106).

Where a judgment creditor takes enforcement proceedings on a relevant county court judgment, accrual of interest ceases from that point unless the enforcement proceedings fail (art. 4). For these purposes applying for a charging order is not regarded as proceeding for enforcement.

INTEREST ON COSTS

62.17 Under the **CPR, r. 40.8**, interest on costs runs from the date the judgment is given, unless a rule or practice direction provides otherwise, or the court orders otherwise. Interest on costs where judgment has been entered for damages to be assessed therefore generally runs from the date of the liability judgment, but the court has a discretion to award interest on costs from some other date. This discretion may be exercised to reflect the periods over which the costs in assessing damages were in fact incurred (**r. 44.3(6)(g)**; *Powell v Herefordshire Health Authority* [2002] EWCA Civ 1786, [2003] 3 All ER 253). As regards interest on costs after a claim is automatically struck out for non-payment of the fees payable at the allocation or listing stages, or after acceptance of a payment in or an offer to settle, or after a claim is discontinued, by virtue of **r. 44.12** interest runs from the date of the event giving rise to the entitlement to costs (i.e., the date of striking out, acceptance, or the date of service of the notice of discontinuance).

Conducting litigation for commercial reasons regardless of the rights and wrongs of the claim, with much of that party's evidence being rejected followed by a resounding defeat, was said in *Amoco (UK) Exploration Co. v British American Offshore Ltd* [2002] BLR 135 to give grounds for awarding interest on costs for the period before judgment from the time those costs were paid.

Chapter 63 Solicitor and Own Client Costs

INTRODUCTION

The purpose of this chapter is to deal with some of the core issues which arise in relation to solicitor and own client billing. It is somewhat remarkable in this market-driven age that the legal profession is still regulated in how it charges for its services. The primary regulatory scheme governing the solicitor and client relationship is in the **Solicitors Act 1974**, which is supported by the Solicitors (Non-contentious Business) Remuneration Order 1994 (SI 1994/2616), the Non-contentious Probate Rules 1987 (SI 1987/2024) and **CPR, Parts 43 to 48**, in relation to contentious business. This chapter will concentrate on contentious business. **63.1**

By tradition the profession, in observing the statutory framework, had generally grown used to basing charges for services upon an expense rate for the particular grade of fee-earner plus a mark-up for care and conduct, the latter being determined by reference to RSC, ord. 62, app. 1, part 1, generally known as the 'seven pillars of wisdom'. There was a growing resistance in the marketplace to the application of the variable percentage uplift on expense rates, particularly from those who were volume buyers of legal services. They preferred to agree that solicitors' charges would be based on a composite hourly rate or rates per grade of fee-earners. This also reflected the more general public mood that there should be more transparency and certainty in solicitors' charges. Solicitors are required to give detailed costs information to their clients (see **63.3** to **63.6**) to ensure a client is fully aware of how the solicitor will charge for the work done.

One of the aims of the CPR was to bring into focus the costs of achieving justice as it was recognised that in some cases the costs could exceed or be out of all proportion to the amount at issue between the parties.

With the advent of summary assessment of costs and the consultation paper on benchmark costs, it is felt that the next phase of change will be a move away from the somewhat rigid approach of basing charges on the number of hours at specified hourly rates and towards a fee for a particular piece of work or for an entire case.

AGREEING SOLICITORS' CHARGES

It is of the utmost importance that the client responsible for giving instructions and incurring the liability for costs is clearly identified as being responsible for payment of those costs. This **63.2** is of particular concern, for example, where acting for companies or a group of clients. A solicitor instructed to act for a company must make certain that the person giving instructions has proper authority to incur the costs which ultimately the company will be liable to pay. When acting for a group of clients it is necessary to determine how the costs are to be discharged and by whom.

Where solicitors are retained by executors to deal with non-contentious business, it is best practice for the solicitor to obtain prior agreement for the proposed charges not only from the executors, but also from any residuary beneficiary who is a statutory entitled party under the Solicitors' (Non-Contentious Business) Remuneration Order 1994 (SI 1994/2616) (*Jemma Trust Co. Ltd v Liptrott* [2003] EWCA Civ 1476, [2004] 1 WLR 646).

A written retainer from the client is always advisable and nearly always required by r. 15 of the Solicitors' Practice Rules 1990. Having a clear written agreement on charges should reduce the risk to the solicitor at a later stage when a bill of costs is rendered for the services provided. Indeed, with regard to contentious business, it is the duty of the solicitor to obtain a written authority from the client before a claim is commenced. Such authority must be signed by the party responsible for the solicitor's bill of costs and it must clearly identify the work to be carried out and extent of the retainer. This has long been the recognised position, see *Allen v Bone* (1841) 4 Beav 493.

CLIENT CARE

63.3 Rule 15 of the Solicitors' Practice Rules 1990 provides that solicitors shall:

(a) give information about costs and other matters; and
(b) operate a complaints handling procedure.

The main object of the Solicitors' Costs, Information and Client Care Code 1999 is to make sure that the fullest information is given to a client on the progress of the client's case and, in particular, with regard to the costs of legal services at the outset and as the matter progresses. In addition, the code requires firms to offer a complaints handling procedure. The code also states that it is good practice to record in writing all information required to be given by the code, including decisions relating to costs and any arrangements for making changes. If information required by the code has not been given in a particular matter, the reasons for not giving it should be recorded. The code recognises that it may not be appropriate to give the full information specified in every case, for example, for a regular client for whom repetitive work is done or if compliance with the code may be insensitive or impractical, but that such information should be given as soon as reasonably practical.

Compliance with the code is required even where a client is publicly funded, because the client may have a financial interest in terms of contributions or the statutory charge. The code also applies to contingency fee and conditional fee arrangements.

The code provides that the costs information must not be inaccurate or misleading and that any costs information required to be given must be given clearly, in a way and at a level that is appropriate to the particular client. Information on the overall costs, the basis of the firm's charges, ancillary further information and costs-benefit risk should be given to the client at the outset and at appropriate stages throughout the matter and confirmed in writing.

Explaining costs liabilities

63.4 Where the client is publicly funded, the solicitor should explain the client's potential liability, including:

(a) the costs of any other party;
(b) the effect of the statutory charge and its likely amount;

(c) the liability to contribute to the opponent's costs if the case is lost, even though the client's own costs are covered by public funding; and
(d) the fact that, even if the client wins, the opponent may not be ordered to pay or be capable of paying the full amount of the client's costs.

For privately paying clients, the solicitor should explain the potential liability for the client's own costs and those of any other party and:
(a) the fact that the client will be responsible for paying the firm's bill in full, regardless of any order for costs made against an opponent;
(b) the probability that the client will have to pay the opponent's costs as well as the client's own costs if the case is lost;
(c) the fact that even if the client wins, the opponent may not be ordered to pay or be capable of paying the full amount of the client's costs; and
(d) if the opponent is publicly funded, that the client may not recover costs even if successful.

Keeping the client informed

A solicitor should keep his or her client properly informed about costs as the matter progresses and should tell the client, unless otherwise agreed, how much the costs are at regular intervals, and at least every six months. In appropriate cases interim bills may be rendered at agreed intervals. It is important to explain to the client, and confirm in writing, any changed circumstances which will, or which are likely to, affect the amount of costs, the degree of risk involved, or the ratio of costs to the benefits likely to be achieved by continuing the matter. The client should be informed in writing as soon as it appears that a costs estimate or agreed upper limit may or will be exceeded. If a material change in the client's means comes to the solicitor's attention, consideration should be given to the client's eligibility for or help under the Community Legal Service. **63.5**

Client care letter

The document generally referred to as a 'client care letter' has achieved a greater status in more recent times. In *Bailey v IBC Vehicles Ltd* [1998] 3 All ER 570 Judge LJ stated that 'in the ordinary case in which a "client care letter" has been provided (and certainly if and when the client care letter becomes obligatory) the hourly rate claimed in the bill of costs should coincide with the terms of that letter' and further that 'in future, copies of the relevant documents (where they exist) or a short written explanation of the kind eventually provided in this case in September 1997, should normally be attached to the bill of costs'. This has been given effect by **PD 43–48, para. 40.2(i)**, which stipulates that where there is a dispute as to the receiving party's liability to pay costs to the solicitors who are acting for the receiving party, any letter or other written information provided by the solicitor to his or her client, explaining how the solicitor's charges are to be calculated, is to be lodged at the Supreme Court Costs Office together with the request for a detailed assessment hearing. The relevance of client care letters was further reinforced by *General of Berne Insurance Co. v Jardine Reinsurance Management Ltd* [1998] 1 WLR 1231 in the context of contentious business agreements. **63.6**

A breach of the Solicitors' Practice Rules 1990, r. 15, is a breach of subordinate legislation (*Swain v Law Society* [1983] 1 AC 598) which might have an effect on the solicitor's right to remuneration. In *Garbutt v Edwards* [2005] EWCA Civ 1206, [2006] 1 All ER 553, the solicitors representing the successful party failed to provide their client with any costs estimate in breach of the Solicitors' Costs, Information and Client Care Code. The Court of Appeal held this did not render the retainer unlawful or unenforceable, so was not a knock-out blow to the assessment of the successful party's costs. Although this did not arise on the facts, the court said the paying party may be able to obtain a reduction in the amount payable if the costs incurred would have been lower if the solicitor had complied with the Code. Compare the approach to estimates between the parties, see **63.19**.

A requirement for greater transparency is shown in *Ralph Hume Garry v Gwillim* [2002] EWCA Civ 1500, [2003] 1 WLR 510, in which the court considered what constituted a bill for assessment under the Solicitors Act 1974. A bill may be for a gross sum (see **63.13**), but it must contain sufficient narrative to identify what the client is being charged for and to enable the client to decide whether to ask for detailed assessment (*Haigh v Ousey* (1857) 7 El & Bl 578). Nowadays it is common for solicitors to record all work done in a computerised time costing system. Where this happens, the least that a client is entitled to is a printout of that record suitably redacted (*Ralph Hume Garry v Gwillim*). A bill can only charge for the services which the client contracted to pay for. Thus, where a client asked for a solicitor but was represented by a legal executive, the solicitors were not entitled to any fee as the client had not received the representation he contracted for (*Pilbrow v Peerless De Rougemont and Co.* [1999] 3 All ER 355; *Adrian Alan Ltd v Fuglers* [2002] EWCA Civ 1655, [2003] PNLR 305).

SOLICITORS ACT 1974

63.7 Sections 59 to 71 of the Solicitors Act 1974 regulate contentious business.

Section 59 permits solicitors to enter into written agreements, called 'contentious business agreements', concerning remuneration for contentious business (see **63.11**).

Sections 67 to 70 deal with the situation where there is no contentious business agreement with the client and the requirements for delivery of a bill of costs, proceedings to recover costs by the solicitor and applications by the client or the solicitor for the detailed assessment of the bill of costs.

Section 69 provides that no action shall be brought to recover any costs due before the expiration of one month from the date on which a bill of costs was delivered, subject to two exceptions. If the client is about to quit the jurisdiction, become bankrupt or compound with creditors, or is about to do any other act which would prevent or delay the solicitor obtaining payment, the High Court may, upon application, permit the solicitor to commence an action to recover his or her costs and may also order that those costs be referred to detailed assessment. A signed bill must have been delivered to the party to be charged.

Application for detailed assessment

63.8 Section 70 of the Solicitors Act 1974 provides for detailed assessment upon application of the party chargeable or the solicitor. If before the expiration of one month from delivery of a bill of costs, an application is made by the party chargeable, the court shall, without requiring any sum to be paid into court, order detailed assessment of the bill and that no claim be commenced until the assessment is completed. If no such application is made before expiration of the one-month period, the court may order detailed assessment on such terms, if any, as it thinks fit, but not terms as to costs of the assessment. Where an application is made by the party chargeable with the bill more than 12 months from its delivery, or after judgment has been obtained for recovery of the costs, or after the bill has been paid, no order for detailed assessment may be made except in special circumstances and, if an order is made, it may contain such terms as regards the costs of the detailed assessment as the court may think fit. The party chargeable with a bill is unable to obtain a detailed assessment under the Solicitors Act 1974 after 12 months from payment of the bill (s. 70(4)).

In *Connollys v Harrington* (2002) LTL 27/8/2002 it was held that the High Court has an inherent jurisdiction to order detailed assessment, even where the provisions of the Solicitors Act 1974 have not been complied with, and that the specific provisions in the Act do not oust that jurisdiction. Whether any such inherent jurisdiction exists in parallel with the Act is dubious and is inconsistent with *Harrison v Tew* [1990] 2 AC 523.

Two cases heard by the Court of Appeal have permitted detailed assessment more than 12 months after delivery of the bill (*Thomas Watts and Co. v Smith* (1998) 2 Costs LR 59 and *Turner and Co. v O. Palomo SA* [2000] 1 WLR 37). In each case the clients were entitled to challenge the solicitor's claim on the grounds that the fees claimed were unreasonably high even though the time for detailed assessment had expired. The statutory right to seek an order for detailed assessment was held not to exclude any other common law right to challenge the bills.

Section 71 provides that where a person other than the party chargeable with the bill has paid, or is or was liable to pay, a solicitor's bill, that person may apply for a detailed assessment of the bill as if that person were the party chargeable with it, and the court may make the same order as it might have made had the application been made by the party chargeable with the bill. However, where the court has no power to make an order, except in special circumstances, it may in considering whether there are special circumstances sufficient to justify the making of an order, take into account circumstances which affect the applicant but do not affect the party chargeable with the bill. The prohibition against a party chargeable with a bill seeking a detailed assessment more than 12 months after paying the bill in s. 70(4) does not apply in applications under s. 71, where the passing of time after payment is simply a factor to be taken into account in exercising the discretion in s. 71(3) whether to order the assessment of the bill (*McIlwraith v McIlwraith* (2002) LTL 1/8/2002).

Conduct of detailed assessment

The procedure for seeking orders under the **Solicitors Act 1974, part III**, leading up to the possible detailed assessment of the solicitor's charges, is laid down by **CPR, r. 48.10** and **Part 67**, and **PD 43–48, paras 56.1** to **56.19**; see **68.19**. The detailed assessment may deal with the profit costs or disbursements or both and the court may allow a claim to be commenced or to be continued for any costs not being challenged (s. 70(6)). The CPR apply in determining the amounts recoverable, see **63.18**. **63.9**

CONTENTIOUS AND NON-CONTENTIOUS BUSINESS

It is important to remember that contentious and non-contentious costs must not be intermingled and put in one bill (see *Re a Solicitor* [1955] 2 QB 252). Essentially, contentious and non-contentious business are each governed by different sections of the **Solicitors Act 1974** and in the case of non-contentious business additionally by the Solicitors (Non-contentious Business) Remuneration Order 1994 (SI 1994/2616). A solicitor conducting non-contentious business is entitled to charge both for the time spent on an hourly basis and a separate fee based on the value of the transaction or estate (*Jemma Trust Co. Ltd v Liptrott* [2003] EWCA Civ 1476, [2004] 1 WLR 646). **63.10**

Contentious business is defined in the **Solicitors Act 1974, s. 87(1)**, as involving proceedings actually begun before a court or arbitrator. Any other business is non-contentious. Any work done preparatory to the issue of proceedings, for example, the instruction of counsel to settle a statement of case and writing letters pursuant to a pre-action protocol, is deemed to be non-contentious business, unless and until the proceedings are formally issued.

CONTENTIOUS BUSINESS AGREEMENTS

A contentious business agreement made under the **Solicitors Act 1974, s. 59**, is not subject to a detailed assessment unless the agreement provides for the solicitor's remuneration to be by reference to an hourly rate (**s. 60(1)**). A contentious business agreement may provide that the solicitor be remunerated by a gross sum, an hourly rate or rates, salary or otherwise and at a higher or lower rate than the solicitor would ordinarily be entitled to (s. 59(1)). **Sections 59** to **63** do not enable a solicitor to purchase an interest in the whole or part of the proceedings. **63.11**

Any agreement pursuant to s. 59 must be in writing. The existence of a contentious business agreement does not affect the amount of, or any rights or remedies for recovery of, any costs payable by the client to, or to the client by, any person other than the solicitor, and that person may, unless bound by an agreement to the contrary, require the costs to be referred to detailed assessment (s. 60(2)). The client is not entitled to recover from any other person under an order for payment of any costs to which the contentious business agreement relates more than the amount payable by the client to the solicitor (s. 60(3); this is the indemnity principle — see **68.29**).

Since 2 June 2003 it has been possible for a solicitor to enter into a non-indemnity CFA under which the solicitor's costs are limited to those recoverable from the losing party (see 6.5). The paying party will no longer be able to use the indemnity principle to defeat such an agreement. This and the more formal CFAs (see **chapter 6**) are the only exceptions to the general rule against conditional fees.

Enforcement of contentious business agreements

63.12 The Solicitors Act 1974, s. 61, provides that no action shall be brought to enforce a contentious business agreement, but on application a party to the agreement, or representative of a party, or a person who is liable to pay, or to be paid, the costs due, may apply to the court to enforce or set aside the agreement and determine its validity and effect. On any application, the court may enforce the agreement if it considers the same to be fair and reasonable or, if the contrary view is taken, may refer the agreement to detailed assessment.

If on a detailed assessment of any costs, a contentious business agreement is relied upon by the solicitor and the client objects, but does not allege that the agreement is unfair or unreasonable, the costs officer may review and consider the number of hours claimed by the solicitor and whether the number of hours claimed are excessive (s. 61(4B)).

Contentious business agreements have become more attractive in recent years particularly because they bring some certainty to the solicitor on the question of hourly rates and remove the entitlement to a detailed assessment, unless the court considers that the agreement is not fair and reasonable. The client also benefits from certainty on the question of hourly rates.

ASSESSMENT WHERE THERE IS NO CONTENTIOUS BUSINESS AGREEMENT

63.13 Section 64 of the Solicitors Act 1974 stipulates that a solicitor's bill of costs may, at the option of the solicitor, be either a bill containing detailed items or a gross sum bill. A client who receives a gross sum bill may, at any time before being served with proceedings for recovery of the costs included in the bill and before the expiration of three months from the date on which the bill was delivered, require the solicitor to replace it with a bill containing detailed items and upon making such request the gross sum bill will be of no effect (s. 64(2)). Where proceedings are commenced on a gross sum bill, the court will, if requested by the party chargeable with the bill before the expiration of one month from service, order that the bill be referred to detailed assessment and that the solicitor shall provide the court with such further details of the costs as the costs officer may require (s. 64(3) and (4)).

PERIODIC BILLING

63.14 The modern trend is to bill clients on a more regular periodic basis. At the very least this helps the cash flow of the solicitor and keeps the client informed about the costs of the matter.

However, there are pitfalls for the unwary. There must be an agreement with the client at the outset that interim or periodic bills will be delivered and become payable, otherwise there is no right to render an interim bill, unless it coincides with a natural break in the litigation. It is important also to distinguish between two classes of bills which can be rendered during the course of litigation:

(a) an interim bill which is final for the period of work covered by it; and
(b) an interim bill which is on account of a final bill which is yet to be delivered.

A bill of type (a) is covered by the **Solicitors Act 1974** and can be referred to detailed assessment and sued upon by the solicitor for non-payment. A bill of type (b) cannot be referred to detailed assessment nor can the solicitor issue proceedings for recovery. This interpretation of the two classes of bill was dealt with in *Davidsons v Jones-Fenleigh* (1980) 124 SJ 204.

BILL OF COSTS

It has long been established that any bill to a client must be a complete bill containing sufficient information to enable the client to obtain advice about its detailed assessment (see *Haigh v Ousey* (1857) 7 El & Bl 578). The purpose of the **Solicitors Act 1974, ss. 64** and **69**, is to protect the innocent or ignorant client by providing adequate information to justify the amount charged. It is not to provide an unscrupulous client with an unmeritorious defence. The detail required in the narrative of a bill therefore varies from case to case, and deficiencies in the detail provided in a bill can be made good from the client's own knowledge and documents sent with the bill and other information already in the possession of the client (*Ralph Hume Garry v Gwillim* [2002] EWCA Civ 1500, [2003] 1 WLR 510). To prevent disputes it may be sensible to provide clients with printouts of accounts department records see **63.6**. **63.15**

A bill of costs must include an adequate description of the work carried out coupled with the dates within which the services were rendered. Disbursements must relate to the period in question otherwise upon any detailed assessment there is a risk that any disbursements outside the scope of the period in question will be struck out and become irrecoverable.

There is a tendency not to pay much attention to the subject of billing and there is sometimes a remarkable lack of care and attention to detail, which is not lost on an astute client. Very often, the solicitor's bill of costs is the final professional service that the client receives on a particular matter and it represents the last opportunity that a firm has to promote itself positively. A sloppily composed bill of costs containing errors or incorrect information will leave the wrong impression with the client. There is also the temptation to add unnecessary narrative or explanation to the bill, in order, it would seem, to justify the fee. The majority of clients, and particularly commercial clients, can see through this. If there is an agreement to render interim bills, they should be delivered on the due dates.

DISBURSEMENTS

Only expenses which a solicitor incurs in order to provide his or her professional service are disbursements which can be so described in a bill of costs to the client (see **68.45**). Any other amounts paid on the client's behalf, such as payments into court, payments of damages and payment of other side's costs, should form part of the cash account which should accompany a bill of costs. **63.16**

It is also important to ensure that any disbursements which are not paid as at the date of rendering the bill of costs, are described as 'not yet paid'. Otherwise, there is a real risk that these disbursements will not be recoverable.

INTEREST

63.17 Interest is recoverable for costs for non-contentious business, provided sufficient notice is given as required by the Solicitors (Non-contentious Business) Remuneration Order 1994 (SI 1994/2616). For contentious business, the opposite is the case. Ordinarily, a solicitor is not entitled to interest unless it is specified and agreed with the client at the inception of the retainer. Upon detailed assessment under the **Solicitors Act 1974**, if application is made to the costs officer, interest will be granted only upon disbursements already paid out by the solicitor.

As well as allowing interest to be charged on outstanding bills, the initial retainer may provide for the solicitor to receive a share of any interest to which the client may become entitled under the **Judgments Act 1838, s. 17** (*Hunt v R. M. Douglas (Roofing) Ltd* [1990] 1 AC 398).

DETAILED ASSESSMENT

63.18 **Rule 48.8** of the CPR sets out the basis of detailed assessment of solicitor and own client costs and applies to every assessment of a solicitor's bill to his or her client except a bill which is to be paid out of the Community Legal Service Fund or where the solicitor and the client have entered into a conditional fee agreement as defined by the **Courts and Legal Services Act 1990, s. 58**. The **Solicitors Act 1974, s. 74(3)**, applies unless the solicitor and client have entered into a written agreement which expressly permits payment of an amount of costs greater than that which could be recovered from another party to proceedings in the county court. **Section** 74(3) does not limit the costs between solicitor and client to the amount assessed between the parties (*Lynch v Paul Davidson Taylor* [2004] EWHC 89 (QB), [2004] 1 WLR 1753).

Pursuant to **CPR, r. 48.8(2)**, costs payable to a solicitor by his or her client are to be assessed on the indemnity basis. They are presumed to have been reasonably incurred if they were incurred with the expressed or implied approval of the client, to be reasonable in amount if the amount is expressly or impliedly approved by the client and to have been unreasonably incurred if they are of an unusual nature or amount and the solicitor did not tell the client that it might not be possible to recover all of them from the other parties. Questions of proportionality do not arise.

The assessment procedure is prescribed in **CPR, r. 48.10** (see **68.19**).

ESTIMATES

63.19 From time to time the court will require estimates of costs in order to keep the parties informed about their potential liability in respect of costs and to assist the court with decisions about costs and case management (see **CPR, r. 3.1(2)(ll)**).

An estimate of costs, which means an estimate of base costs, including disbursements, incurred and to be incurred (**PD 43–48, para. 6.2**), is required in the following circumstances:

(a) On filing an allocation questionnaire for a claim which is outside the financial scope of the small claims track (see **42.15** and **43.3**), a party's solicitor must file in court, and serve on his client and every other party, a costs estimate (**PD 43–48, para. 6.4(1)**).

(b) On filing a pre-trial checklist in a Part 8 claim or any claim on the fast track or multi-track, a party's solicitor must file in court, and serve on his client and every other party, an updated costs estimate (**PD 43–48, para. 6.4(2)**).

(c) When the court orders an estimate to be filed, which it may do at any stage in a case, particularly to show the cost of making a particular case management direction (**PD 43–48, para. 6.3**).

(d) Where the funding arrangement has changed, the party must file and serve notice of the change (**CPR, r. 44.15(2)**), and must at the same time file and serve an estimate of costs (**PD 43–48, para. 6.4(2)** (inserted on 1 October 2005)).

A costs estimate should be in the form of **precedent H (PD 43–48, para. 6.5)**.

A court assessing costs can have regard to any estimate previously provided by any of the parties to the proceedings and an estimate may be taken into account in deciding the reasonableness of the costs (**PD 43–48, para. 6.6**). A poor or unreliable costs estimate is potentially misleading to the court, the client (see **63.20**) and the paying party.

As discussed at **63.6**, on an assessment of costs between solicitor and client the solicitor's recoverable charges may be disallowed to the extent that they significantly exceed an estimate given to the client. In assessments between party and party, the question is whether **PD 43–48, para. 6.6** provides scope for reducing the amount allowed on assessment where there is a significant discrepancy between an estimate served with an allocation questionnaire or pre-trial checklist and the final bill. In *Leigh v Michelin Tyre plc* [2003] EWCA Civ 1766, [2004] 1 WLR 846, a remarkably tolerant approach was adopted in a claim that settled before trial. The estimate in the allocation questionnaire put overall costs at £6,000 plus VAT, whereas the final bill was for £21,891.28. It was held that as the paying party had not relied on the estimate, and as the court would not have made different case management directions if it had known the true cost of the claim, there was no scope for reducing the assessed costs under **para. 6.6**. In other words, **para. 6.6** cannot be used simply to punish a party who provides an inadequate costs estimate. The Court of Appeal did say that where there is a substantial difference between an estimate and the final bill, that difference calls for an explanation. In the absence of a satisfactory explanation a court is entitled to conclude that the costs claimed are unreasonable.

As a result of *Leigh v Michelin Tyre plc*, with effect from 1 October 2005, **para. 6.6** has been revised and a new **para. 6.5A** has been inserted. If there is a 20 per cent difference between an estimate of costs and the amount claimed in a bill of costs, the receiving party must provide a statement of the reasons for the difference in his bill of costs. If the paying party claims to have reasonably relied on the estimate, he must serve a statement setting out his case (**para. 6.5A(2)**). Where, on the assessment, there is a 20 per cent or more difference between the base costs claimed and a previous estimate, the court may regard the difference as evidence (as one factor among others) that the costs claimed are unreasonable or disproportionate (**para. 6.6(2)**) if either:

(a) the receiving party has not provided a satisfactory explanation; or
(b) the paying party reasonably relied on the estimate.

Experience suggests that many allocation questionnaires and pre-trial checklists are being filed without a costs estimate. When this is done, it is open to a party to apply for an order requiring the defaulting party to comply with the rules by filing and serving the costs estimate.

It is suggested that it is good practice to provide revised costs estimates to the opposing party on a voluntary basis periodically.

Client estimates

In compliance with r. 15 of the Solicitors' Practice Rules 1990, in providing costs information for clients particular regard needs to be given to any estimates given. This is of vital importance, for example, where hourly rates are agreed with the client at the outset. Where the litigation is likely to span a number of years the solicitor should make provision for annual revision of those hourly rates. However, the client must be informed of any increase made on an annual review. **63.20**

In *Wong v Vizards* (1997) 2 Costs LR 46 the solicitors had informed the client that they would charge him an hourly rate of £125 for partners' time and £110 for an assistant solicitor, both rates to be subject to review. That agreement was recorded in an attendance note on the solicitors' file. Subsequently in November 1993 the client was provided with a letter making a fee proposal in response to the client's request to know how much it might cost to take the particular matter to trial which was fixed for July 1994. The fee proposal reflected an hourly rate for an assistant solicitor of £110 per hour and no reference was made to partners' time or indeed any increase in hourly rates. The fee proposal of November 1993 allowed for profit costs of £9,955 plus disbursements. After the trial, a bill of costs was rendered to the client for work carried out from 20 October 1993 in the sum of £32,015.93 including disbursements and VAT, which contrasted starkly with the total sum estimated in the November 1993 letter of £21,805 plus VAT of £3,815.87, which the writer had said, 'hopefully sets out the fullest extent of your liability to this firm for costs likely to be incurred in the future'.

No indication was ever given to the client that the costs being incurred were outrunning the fee proposal. Toulson J ordered that the solicitors' profit costs for the period November 1993 to conclusion of the trial in July 1994 should be limited to £9,955 plus VAT, being the maximum shown in the fee proposal (excluding counsel's and expert's fees). It was argued that this figure should have been reduced even further, because the proposal was based on the trial lasting two days longer than it actually did. However, the judge held that the fee proposal was a projection or an estimate rather than a warranty. In not reducing the figure of £9,955, the judge effectively allowed the solicitors a margin of approximately 15 per cent over the worst-case estimate given. The judge said, 'I consider that a greater divergence would be substantial and unreasonable'.

It naturally follows from what has been explained above that one has to be cautious in formulating costs estimates for the client's benefit and use. It has long been recognised that in formulating an estimate required by the client a number of imponderables could crop up during the course of the litigation that were unexpected and not budgeted for. Suffice it to say that where an estimate has been given it must be regularly reviewed and updated with the client in order to protect the solicitor's position.

Care must be given in expressing a costs estimate that it does not change in character and become a costs quotation. An estimate may vary, but not substantially, whereas a quotation is a fixed price for the piece of work to be carried out. The latter is particularly unattractive where the course of the litigation may take an unplanned (and therefore unbudgeted) course or certain steps envisaged prove to be more time consuming than originally envisaged. It must be made abundantly clear to the client at the inception of the retainer that any estimate given is purely an estimate and does not represent a fixed price for the work.

Chapter 64 Part 36 Offers and Payments

The following procedural checklists, which are in **appendix 1**, are relevant to this chapter:

Procedural checklist 30 Defendant's Part 36 offer
Procedural checklist 31 Part 36 payment

INTRODUCTION

64.1 **Part 36** of the CPR sets out procedures for making formal offers to settle and payments into court which have costs and other consequences if not accepted. There is an important public interest in assisting parties to settle without the need to issue proceedings, or to avoid the need to go to trial, which the availability of Part 36 offers and payments promotes. Among the things the court must take into account in deciding what order to make on costs is whether there has been any payment into court or admissible offer to settle, whether or not made in accordance with **Part 36 (r. 44.3(4)(c))**. Although costs are always discretionary (**r. 44.3(1)**), in practice this means:

(a) if the claim fails, the defendant is usually awarded costs in accordance with the principle that costs usually follow the event (**r. 44.3(2)(a)**);

(b) if the claim is successful and exceeds any Part 36 offer or payment, the offer or payment is ignored when making an order on costs, and usually the claimant will be awarded costs under **r. 44.3(2)(a)**;

(c) if the claim is successful, but the remedy awarded is less favourable to the claimant than the terms of a Part 36 offer or payment, usually this will be reflected in the costs order, the theory being that the claimant should have accepted the offer within the period it was open. Under **Part 36** this period is 21 days from making the offer. Consequently, the usual costs order in these circumstances is that the claimant will recover costs (because the claim succeeded) until the 21st day after the offer or payment was made, but the defendant recovers its costs thereafter. Usually these competing costs orders are stated to be set off against each other.

Nothing in **Part 36** prevents a party from making an offer to settle in any other manner (**r. 36.1(2)**). However, if an offer is not made in accordance with **Part 36**, it will have the consequences specified in **Part 36** only if the court so orders (**r. 36.1(2)**; see **64.47** to **64.49**). The courts have shown a remarkably tolerant approach where offers do not comply with the requirements of **Part 36**, see *Trustees of Stokes Pension Fund v Western Power Distribution (South West) plc* [2005] EWCA Civ 854, [2005] 1 WLR 3595, discussed at **64.48**. A common situation is where a party uses a Part 36 offer when it should have made a Part 36 payment (see **64.6** and **64.8**). There have been several cases where such offers have been taken into account on costs (see **64.47** to **64.49**).

Part 36 applies to counterclaims and any additional claim under **Part 20** by virtue of **r. 20.3**.

Part 36 does not apply to the small claims track (**r. 27.2**), but this does not prevent a party making an offer to settle a small claims case, though the costs and other financial consequences set out in **Part 36** will not apply unless the court orders otherwise (**r. 36.2(5)**). A party's rejection of a Part 36 offer does not of itself amount to unreasonable behaviour under **r. 27.14(2)(d)** so as to justify an award of costs despite the no-costs rule on the small claims track, but may be taken into consideration when the court is asked to apply the unreasonableness test (**r. 27.14(2A)**).

TERMINOLOGY

64.2 • *Part 36 payment.* Also known as a 'payment into court'. This is a formal offer to settle, made on **form N242A**, by which the defendant offers to pay a sum of money in settlement of all or a specified part of the claim. The defendant must lodge the sum offered in court. The claimant has 21 days from service of the notice of the Part 36 payment to decide whether to accept. If a Part 36 payment is accepted (on **form N243A**), the claim is stayed, the money in court will be paid to the claimant's solicitors, and the defendant becomes liable to pay the claimant's standard basis costs (**r. 36.13(2)**). If a Part 36 payment is not accepted, the money remains in court to await the final outcome of the claim. Part 36 payments may only be made in respect of money claims (**r. 36.3(1)**) and only after proceedings are issued (**r. 36.3(2)**). An offer to settle a threatened money claim may be made under **r. 36.10**, followed by a Part 36 payment of the amount offered if proceedings are actually issued.

- *Part 36 offer*. Occasionally known as '*Calderbank*' offers and as offers 'without prejudice save as to costs' (the former from *Calderbank v Calderbank* [1976] Fam 93, where the practice was first approved, and the latter from the words used in the heading of the letter containing a Part 36 offer). A Part 36 offer is made in a letter to the other side expressed to be without prejudice save as to costs, which means that if it is not accepted, the letter cannot be referred to at trial until all issues as to liability and quantum have been dealt with (except with the joint consent of both parties), but that it can be disclosed to the judge on the question of costs. A Part 36 offer must be expressed to be open for acceptance for 21 days from receipt (**rr. 36.5(6) and (7)**, and **36.8(1)**). If accepted, the proceedings (or such part as is covered by the offer) will be settled, and the claimant will be entitled to standard basis costs from the defendant (**r. 36.13(2)**). Part 36 offers can be used in any type of dispute before proceedings are issued (**r. 36.10**), but once a claim is issued they can only be used in respect of non-monetary relief (subject to an exception for recoupment of State benefits, see **r. 36.23(2)**).
- *Claimant's Part 36 offer*. This is a Part 36 offer made by a claimant, rather than the usual case of a Part 36 offer being made by a defendant. Like a defendant's Part 36 offer, this is a formal written offer made without prejudice save as to costs, which is stated to remain open for 21 days from receipt. If accepted, the proceedings or such part as is covered by the offer will be settled, and the claimant will in addition be entitled to standard basis costs from the defendant (**r. 36.14**). A claimant's Part 36 offer can be made in any type of dispute, and before or after proceedings are issued. The real difference from defendants' Part 36 offers rests in the consequences of non-acceptance, discussed at **64.50**.
- *Offeror*. The person making a Part 36 payment or Part 36 offer (**r. 36.2(2)**).
- *Offeree*. The person receiving a notice of a Part 36 payment or Part 36 offer (**r. 36.2(3)**).

SCOPE AND PARTIES

A Part 36 offer or payment may relate to the whole or part of a claim or to any issue arising in a claim (**CPR, rr. 36.5(2)** and **36.6(1)**). **64.3**

A Part 36 offer or payment may be made at any time after proceedings have started and may also be made in appeal proceedings (**r. 36.2**). Part 36 offers can also be made before proceedings are issued (**r. 36.10**), but Part 36 payments can only be made after proceedings are started (**r. 36.3(2)**). The provisions in relation to Part 36 payments make no reference to claimants and provide no means by which a claimant could make a Part 36 payment, save as a defendant to a counterclaim or other additional claim. It is difficult to imagine any other circumstances in which a claimant would make such a payment.

ADVISING ON PART 36 OFFERS AND PAYMENTS

Advising on the amount to pay in, or the terms to offer, under **CPR, Part 36**, requires a great deal of professional judgment. Likewise, advising on whether an offer or payment should be accepted requires a balancing of a number of factors, including risks on liability (including any contributory negligence and counterclaim or set-off) and risks on the amount of damages, as well as considering the likely level of interest that might be awarded. In claims where the prospects turn on whether evidence might be allowed in or disallowed, either in a future application or at trial, assessing the risks is even more difficult. A legal adviser will be **64.4** expected to give reasons for advice on whether offers should be accepted, and should concentrate on giving clear advice that can be readily understood by the client. Legal advisers are not required, particularly if advice is being given on the day of a trial, to engage in defensive advocacy by giving their clients a catalogue of every factor that might have a bearing on whether an offer should be accepted (*Moy v Pettman Smith* [2005] UKHL 7, [2005] 1 WLR 581).

DISCLOSURE OF PART 36 OFFERS AND PAYMENTS

64.5 There are restrictions on disclosure of Part 36 offers or payments. **Rule 36.19(1)** of the CPR provides that a Part 36 offer will be treated as 'without prejudice except as to costs'. The fact that a Part 36 payment has been made is not to be communicated to the trial judge until all questions of liability and quantum have been decided (**r. 36.19(2)**). Similar restrictions apply to appeals (see **r. 52.12(1)**). However, **r. 36.19(2)** will not apply where (**r. 36.19(3)**):

(a) the defence of tender before claim has been raised;
(b) the proceedings have been stayed under **r. 36.15** following acceptance of a **Part 36** offer or payment; or
(c) the issue of liability has been determined before any assessment of the money claimed and the fact that there has or has not been a **Part 36** payment may be relevant to the question of the costs of the issue of liability.

The embargo in **r. 36.19** on disclosing the existence of Part 36 offers and payments to the judge until all questions of liability and damages have been decided means that they are only relevant in deciding orders as to costs. They cannot be used on questions relating to the date for assessing damages or on the amount of interest to allow (*Johnson v Gore Wood and Co. (No. 2)* [2004] EWCA Civ 14, *The Times*, 17 February 2004).

If there is an inadvertent disclosure of a Part 36 offer or payment, the judge has a discretion whether to order a new trial, but may continue if satisfied that no injustice will be done (*Millensted v Grosvenor House (Park Lane) Ltd* [1937] 1 KB 717). *Millensted v Grosvenor House (Park Lane) Ltd* was approved by *Garratt v Saxby* [2004] EWCA Civ 341, [2004] 1 WLR 2152. If, after inappropriate disclosure of a Part 36 offer or payment, the judge thinks it proper or necessary for the due administration of justice, he may refuse to hear the trial any further and direct that it be tried by another judge. However, the judge should not be too ready to adopt this course, and if satisfied that no injustice will be done, may continue with the trial. Matters to consider include the overriding objective, saving expense and dealing with claims justly and proportionately. If a new trial is ordered, the court will almost certainly consider making a wasted costs order against the legal representative at fault.

Disclosure of a Part 36 offer or payment outside the proceedings in a way which will not come to the judge's attention does not harm or infringe the integrity of the court's process and requires no action by the court (*Re a Company (No. 007466 of 2003)* [2004] EWHC 35 (Ch), [2004] 1 WLR 1357).

SPLIT TRIALS AND PART 36 OFFERS

64.6 *HSS Hire Services Group plc v BMB Builders Merchants Ltd* [2005] EWCA Civ 626, [2005] 1 WLR 3158, deals with cases where a claimant wins on liability at a split trial after the defendant has made a Part 36 offer or payment. Other than in the most exceptional case, the question of costs should be reserved until determination of quantum. After the trial on liability the conditions for disclosing the amount of the offer in **CPR, r. 36.19(2)**, have not been met, and it will be only after the determination of quantum that the court can decide whether the Part 36 offer was effective for costs purposes.

OFFERS MADE BEFORE COMMENCEMENT OF PROCEEDINGS

It is open to any party to make an offer to settle, in accordance with the provisions of **CPR, r. 36.10**, before proceedings are started. This is eminently sensible given the existence of pre-action protocols, and the general expectation that parties to all claims will try to avoid starting proceedings (**PD Protocols, para. 4.1**). **64.7**

To comply with **CPR, r. 36.10**, an offer must be expressed to be open for at least 21 days after the date it was made and, if it is made by a person who would be a defendant if proceedings were commenced, must include an offer to pay the costs of the offeree incurred up to the date 21 days after the date it was made (**r. 36.10(2)**). The offer must also otherwise comply with **Part 36** (**r. 36.10(2)(c)**). An offer under **r. 36.10** is 'made' when it is received by the offeree (**r. 36.10(5)**).

If proceedings are started after a pre-commencement offer complying with **r. 36.10** has been made, the offer cannot be accepted without the court's permission (**r. 36.10(4)**) and, whether or not the offer is accepted, the court will take it into account when making any order as to costs (**r. 36.10(1)**). If, however, proceedings are not started, the court has no jurisdiction to make any orders.

If a defendant to a money claim makes a pre-commencement offer, and proceedings are then commenced, the defendant must, in order to obtain the costs advantages provided by **Part 36**, make a Part 36 payment within 14 days of service of the claim form and the amount of the payment must not be less than the sum offered before proceedings began (**r. 36.10(3)**). This payment cannot be accepted by the offeree without the court's permission (**r. 36.10(4)**). A defendant who needs more time than the 14 days allowed by **r. 36.10(3)** can apply for permission to extend time under **r. 3.1(2)(a)**, see *Walker Residential Ltd v Davis* [2005] LTL 9/12/2005. The power to extend time under **r. 3.1(2)(a)** cannot be used once money in court has been accepted without permission, because such an extension will overreach the mandatory costs order in favour of the claimant provided by **r. 36.13(1)** (for which see **64.40**).

PART 36 OFFERS AND PAYMENTS

Part 36 payments in money claims

An offer to settle a claim by means of a Part 36 payment can be made only after proceedings have been commenced (**CPR, rr. 36.2(4)** and **36.3(2)**) and is only available in money claims (**r. 36.3(1)**). **64.8**

The emphasis of the CPR is on the encouragement of settlements. Where litigation is continuing, **Part 36** provides incentives to parties who choose to make sensible and reasonable offers to settle at an early stage. The encouragement of the 'serious offer' is the rationale behind the requirement in **r. 36.3(1)** that a defendant who wishes to offer to settle a money claim, after the commencement of proceedings, with the costs and other financial consequences set out in **Part 36**, must demonstrate commitment by supporting the offer with a payment into court (a Part 36 payment). A payment into court is not required to the extent that the offer is already covered by an interim payment (**rr. 36.3(1)** and **36.5(5)**). If a settlement of a money claim would be subject to the Social Security (Recovery of Benefits) Act 1997, payment into court may be delayed until a certificate of recoverable benefit is received (**CPR, rr. 36.3(1)** and **36.23**).

Offers in clinical dispute claims

Under **CPR, r. 36.3(1)**, a defendant's offer to settle a money claim will not have the consequences set out in **Part 36** unless it is made in the form of a Part 36 payment. There are **64.9** three exceptions stated in **r. 36.3(1)**, namely, personal injury claims for future pecuniary loss (**r. 36.2A**), Part 36 offers made by reference to interim payments (**r. 36.5(5)**) and cases where certificates of benefits are awaited (**r. 36.23**). Nevertheless, in *Crouch v King's Healthcare NHS Trust* [2004] EWCA Civ 1332, [2005] 1 WLR 2015, the Court of Appeal approved the practice of NHS trusts making formal offers in clinical dispute claims without making formal payments into court. While there may be public policy reasons for allowing this practice, it is contrary to generally accepted principles of statutory interpretation to give precedence to a general rule (**r. 36.1(2)**) over a specific rule (**r. 36.3(1)**).

The form of offer approved by *Crouch v King's Healthcare NHS Trust* should include wording such as the following:

This offer is open for 21 days from the date you receive this letter, which we calculate as until close of business on [*date*]. Our client also agrees to pay the claimant's standard-basis costs up to acceptance of it on or before that date. Should your client decide to accept this offer after [*date*] then we will agree [*he*] may do so only on the basis that your client will be responsible both for [*his*] own costs and our standard-basis costs thereafter or we otherwise agree liability for costs or with the permission of the court.

Please note that for the following reasons the defendant does not intend to pay the amount offered into court:

1. The defendant is a NHS public authority. You should therefore be in no doubt that its offer is a genuine one that it will pay promptly if the claimant accepts it in accordance with the terms on which we make this offer.
2. As a NHS public authority the defendant respectfully submits that rather than paying NHS funds into court, it is preferable for the amount of its offer (which would be paid out of NHS funds) to continue to be available for the provision of patient services pending resolution of this case either by agreed terms of settlement or court order.
3. As a NHS body, there is no doubt that the defendant will be able to pay the amount of its offer. We respectfully refer you to the National Health Service (Residual Liabilities) Act 1996 which by s. 1 provides that:
   (1) If a National Health Service trust, a Health Authority or a Special Health Authority ceases to exist, the Secretary of State must exercise his statutory powers to transfer property, rights and liabilities of the body so as to secure that all of its liabilities are dealt with.
   (2) For the purposes of subsection (1), a liability is dealt with by being transferred to—
      (a) the Secretary of State;
      (b) a National Health Service trust;
      (c) a Health Authority; or
      (d) a Special Health Authority.

You will appreciate that the court has the power to exercise discretion on the matter of costs in these circumstances and we respectfully refer you to *Crouch v King's Healthcare NHS Trust* [2004] EWCA Civ 1332, [2005] 1 WLR 2015.

Non-money claims

64.10 The effect of **CPR, rr. 36.3(1)** and **36.6**, is that a defendant to a claim for non-monetary relief cannot make a Part 36 payment, but may make an offer to settle in the form of a Part 36 offer. There are obvious difficulties in formulating effective offers in respect of non-monetary relief (such as injunctions and specific performance), but the aim from the defendant's point of view is to formulate an offer which is at least as generous to the claimant as the order which might be made by the court on the final disposal of the claim. Unlike Part 36 payments, Part 36 offers can be made both before (**r. 36.10**) and after (**r. 36.2(4)(a)**) proceedings are issued. Like Part 36 payments, Part 36 offers can be made in appeal proceedings (**r. 36.2(4)(b)**).

Mixed money and non-money claims

64.11 Where a claim includes both a claim for money and a non-money claim, a defendant's offer to settle the whole claim will have the costs and other financial consequences set out in **CPR, Part 36**, only if it is in the form of a Part 36 payment in relation to the money claim together with a Part 36 offer in relation to the non-money claim (**r. 36.4(1) and** (2)). Acceptance by the claimant of the Part 36 payment will then be deemed to be also acceptance of the Part 36 offer in relation to the non-money claim (**r. 36.4(4)**).

Personal injuries claims for future pecuniary loss

Rule 36.2A of the CPR provides for making Part 36 offers in personal injury claims which include claims for future pecuniary loss. All proposals to settle such cases, whether made by defendants or claimants, are made by Part 36 offers (**r. 36.2A(2)**). The offer may deal with the future pecuniary loss in the form of an offer of a lump sum and/or periodical payments, but the other damages should be in the form of a lump-sum offer (**r. 36.2A(4)**). A defendant including a lump sum in an offer must also make a Part 36 payment in the amount of the lump sum (**r. 36.2A(2)**), with the Part 36 offer including details of the Part 36 payment (**r. 36.2A(3)**). **Rule 36.2A(7)** provides that where a defendant makes an offer for both a lump-sum and periodical payment, the claimant may only give notice of acceptance of the offer as a whole. Through a drafting error **r. 36.2A(7)** fails to say that a defendant can likewise only accept a claimant's Part 36 offer as a whole. **64.12**

Any settlement of a claim to which **r. 36.2A** applies must, by **PD 41B, para. 6**, satisfy the requirements of **CPR, rr. 41.8** and **41.9** (for which see **61.24**).

Part 36 and appeals

A Part 36 payment, or a claimant's or defendant's Part 36 offer, made before trial has effect in relation to the costs of the proceedings from the effective date of the offer (21 days from service or receipt, see **CPR, r. 36.8**) up to the final disposal of the proceedings at first instance. A litigant wishing to obtain Part 36 protection for the costs of any appeal must make a further Part 36 payment or offer in respect of the appeal (**r. 36.2(4)(b)**; *P and O Nedlloyd BV v Utaniko Ltd* [2003] EWCA Civ 174, [2003] 1 Lloyd's Rep 265; *Various Claimants v Bryn Alyn Community (Holdings) Ltd* [2003] EWCA Civ 383, LTL 24/3/2003). **64.13**

Payment under court order

Rule 37.1 of the CPR deals with money paid into court by any party under a court order. The payment should be lodged with a copy of the order (**PD 37, para. 1.1**), following the procedure set out in **PD 37, paras 1.2 and 1.3**. It may be in a foreign currency if the order is for payment in that currency (**PD 36, para. 9.1**). Notice must be served by the party making the payment, who must file a certificate of service (**CPR, r. 6.10**) in relation to each notice (**r. 37.1(1)**). **64.14**

A defendant who pays money into court may choose, under **r. 37.2**, to treat the whole or part of it as a Part 36 payment if it was paid following a court order made under **r. 3.1(3)** (payment into court is a condition of the order) or **r. 3.1(5)** (sanction for failing to comply with a rule, practice direction or pre-action protocol). To do this the defendant must file a Part 36 payment notice (**r. 37.3(2)**).

Payment out requires the court's permission, except where the money paid in has been treated as a Part 36 payment and can be accepted by the claimant without needing the court's permission (**r. 37.1(2)**). Permission is obtained by making an application in accordance with **Part 23** (**PD 37, para. 4.2**). The application notice should state the grounds on which the order for payment out is sought, and evidence of any facts on which the applicant relies may also be necessary (**PD 37, para. 4.2**).

Defence of tender before claim

A defendant who wishes to rely on a defence of tender before claim must make a payment into court of the amount said to have been tendered (**CPR, r. 37.3**). The defence of tender before claim will not be available until this is done (**r. 37.3(2)**). The payment should be made at the time of filing the defence and should be accompanied by a notice of payment into court **64.15**

(**PD 37, para. 2.1**; *Greening v Williams* (1999) *The Times*, 10 December 1999). Where the defence is filed in the Royal Courts of Justice, Court Funds Office **form 100** should be used (**PD 37, para. 2**). A defendant who makes a payment into court under **CPR, r. 37.3(1)**, may choose to treat the whole or any part of the money paid into court as a Part 36 payment, for which a Part 36 payment notice must be filed (**r. 37.3(3)**).

MAKING AND ACCEPTING A PART 36 OFFER

Form and content of a Part 36 offer

64.16 A Part 36 offer, whether the offeror is a defendant or a claimant, must:

(a) be in writing (**CPR, r. 36.5(1)**);
(b) state that it is a Part 36 offer (**PD 36, para. 5.1**);
(c) state whether it relates to the whole of the claim or to part of it or to an issue that arises in it and, if so, to which part or issue (**CPR, r. 36.5(3)(a)**);
(d) state whether it takes into account any counterclaim; and
(e) if it is expressed not to be inclusive of interest, give the details relating to interest set out in **r. 36.22(2)**. Unless the contrary is indicated, a Part 36 offer is treated as inclusive of all interest until the last date on which it could be accepted without needing the court's permission (**r. 36.22(1)**).

In addition:

(a) Where a Part 36 offer is made no later than 21 days before the start of the trial, it must be expressed to remain open for acceptance for 21 days from the date it is made and provide that after 21 days the offeree may only accept it if the parties agree liability for costs or the court gives permission (**r. 36.5(6)**). Where a Part 36 offer is made less than 21 days before the start of the trial, it must state that the offeree may only accept it if the parties agree the liability for costs or the court gives permission (**r. 36.5(7)**).
(b) A Part 36 offer must be signed by the offeror or the offeror's legal representative (**PD 36, para. 5.1**). Where a Part 36 offer is made by a company or other corporation, a person holding a senior position in that body may sign the offer on the offeror's behalf, but must state the position he or she holds (**PD 36, para. 5.5**). **Paragraph 5.6 of PD 36** lists persons who are regarded as holding a 'senior position'.

Terms as to costs are not intended to be included in Part 36 offers made after proceedings have commenced (*Mitchell v James* [2002] EWCA Civ 997, [2004] 1 WLR 158). This is because liability for the costs of the claim follow after acceptance by virtue of the rules, see **CPR, rr. 36.13** and **36.14**, so there is no need for costs to be dealt with in the offer. A part 36 offer made before proceedings are commenced must include an offer to pay the costs of the offeree up to the date 21 days after the offer is made (**r. 36.10(2)(b)**). Although claimants' and defendants' Part 36 offers should make provision for interest pursuant to contract or statute on the sum claimed (see (e) above), a claimant's Part 36 offer should not include or make any reference to uplift interest under **r. 36.21**, as this is a discretionary consequence of non-acceptance (*Ali Reza-Delta Transport Co. Ltd v United Arab Shipping Co. SAG (No. 2)* [2003] EWCA Civ 811, [2004] 1 WLR 168).

A Part 36 offer may be made by reference to an interim payment (**CPR, r. 36.5(5)**; see **chapter 36**).

Making a Part 36 offer

64.17 A Part 36 offer, and any improvement in a Part 36 offer, is made when it is received by the offeree (**CPR, rr. 36.8(1), 36.8(3)** and **36.10(5)**). In a decision based on a legalistic interpretation of the rules, the Court of Appeal in *Charles v NTL Group Ltd* [2002] EWCA Civ 2004, LTL 13/12/2002, held that different rules apply to giving notice of Part 36 offers as opposed to

Part 36 payments. The court relied on the difference in wording between **r. 36.8(1) and** (3) (on Part 36 offers) and **r. 36.8(2) and** (4) (on Part 36 payments) to justify the distinction drawn. Regarding Part 36 offers, r. 36.8(1) and (3) provide that Part 36 offers, and improvements on Part 36 offers, are made 'when received by the offeree.' This was interpreted as meaning that the strict rules on service in **Part 6** do not apply at all to Part 36 offers. On the other hand, r. 36.8(2) and (4) provide that Part 36 payments and improvements to Part 36 payments are made 'when written notice of the payment into court is served on the offeree'. This was interpreted as meaning that service in accordance with the rules in **Part 6** is required for Part 36 payments. It is difficult to see any justification for this distinction. It means that if the intended recipient has indicated that it is not willing to accept service by fax, that will not prevent the other side making a Part 36 offer by fax if the claim seeks non-monetary remedies, but will be effective to prevent service of a notice of a Part 36 payment by fax if the claim seeks a monetary remedy. It also means that a party making a Part 36 offer has to prove receipt, whereas a party serving a notice of a Part 36 payment can rely on the irrebuttable presumption of due service in **r. 6.7**.

Withdrawal of Part 36 offers

A Part 36 offer is governed by the usual rules of offer and acceptance in the law of contract, so it can be withdrawn at any stage prior to acceptance, even during the 21-day period after receipt (*Scammell v Dicker* [2001] 1 WLR 631). Making a counter-offer operates as a rejection of a Part 36 offer (*Hawley v Luminar Leisure plc* [2006] EWCA Civ 30, *The Times*, 14 February 2006). **64.18**

If a Part 36 offer is withdrawn, it should not have the costs and other financial consequences set out in **CPR, Part 36** (see **r. 36.5(8)**, but compare *Trustees of Stokes Pension Fund v Western Power Distribution (South West) plc* [2005] EWCA Civ 854, [2005] 1 WLR 3595, discussed at **64.47**). Unlike Part 36 payments, there is no requirement for permission to be sought before a Part 36 offer is withdrawn (*Pitchmastic plc v Birse Construction Ltd* (2000) *The Times*, 21 June 2000). Where an offeror seeks to withdraw a Part 36 offer, and the offeree seeks to accept it, the question whether there is a binding contract of compromise is decided in accordance with the ordinary rules of offer and acceptance.

Acceptance of a Part 36 offer

If a Part 36 offer is accepted within the 21-day period from receipt, a contract results which will bind the offeror (unless there are grounds for impugning the contract, such as fraud or duress). In a number of circumstances, such as where the offeree is a child, permission is necessary to accept a Part 36 offer (see **64.32** to **64.36**). If permission is not required, acceptance must be given in writing to the offeror (**CPR, rr. 36.11(1)** and **36.12(1)**). Acceptance takes place when notice of the acceptance is received by the offeror (**r. 36.8(5)**). Her Majesty's Courts Service has not issued a standard form for a notice of acceptance. **PD 36, para.** 7.7, requires it: **64.19**

(a) to set out the claim number and the title of the proceedings;
(b) to identify the Part 36 offer being accepted; and
(c) to be signed by the offeree or the offeree's legal representative.

If the accepting party is a company or other corporation, the notice can, by **PD 36, para.** 7.7(3), be signed by one of the senior personnel listed in **para. 5.6**, giving his or her position in the organisation.

MAKING AND ACCEPTING A PART 36 PAYMENT

Part 36 payment notice

A defendant who makes a Part 36 payment must file a Part 36 payment notice with the court, in **form N242A** (**CPR, r. 36.6(2)**). The notice must: **64.20**

(a) state the amount of the payment;
(b) state whether the payment relates to the whole claim or to part of it or to any issue that arises in it and if so to which part or issue;
(c) state whether it takes into account any counterclaim;
(d) if an interim payment has been made, state that the defendant has taken the interim payment into account; and
(e) if it is expressed not to be inclusive of interest, give the details relating to interest set out in **r. 36.22(2)**. Unless the contrary is indicated, a Part 36 payment will be treated as inclusive of all interest until the last date on which it could be accepted without needing the court's permission (**r. 36.22(1)**).

A Part 36 payment may be in a foreign currency where the claim itself is in a foreign currency (**PD 36, para. 9.1**).

A Part 36 notice must be signed by the defendant or by the defendant's legal representative (**PD 36, para. 5.1(2)**). If the defendant is a company or other corporation, the notice can, by **PD 36, para. 5.5**, be signed by one of the senior personnel listed in **para. 5.6**, giving his or her position in the organisation (director, treasurer, secretary etc.).

Mixed money and non-money claims

64.21 A defendant to a claim which has both money and non-money parts, who is making money and non-money offers as a proposal to settle the whole claim, must, in the Part 36 payment notice, identify the document which sets out the non-money Part 36 offer (**CPR, r. 36.4(3)(a)**) and state that acceptance of the **Part 36** payment will constitute acceptance of the Part 36 offer as well (**r. 36.4(3)(b)**). It is suggested that the Part 36 payment notice should also expressly state that the Part 36 offer and Part 36 payment together relate to the whole claim.

Provisional damages

64.22 A defendant may make a Part 36 payment in respect of a claim which includes a claim for provisional damages (**CPR, r. 36.7(1)**). If this is done, the Part 36 payment notice must state whether or not the defendant is offering to agree to an award of provisional damages (**r. 36.7(2)**). If so agreeing, the notice must, by **r. 36.7(3)**, also state:

(a) that the payment in is made on the assumption that the claimant will not develop a named disease or deterioration;
(b) that the offer of provisional damages is conditional on the claimant making any claim for further damages within a limited period; and
(c) what that period is.

Deduction of benefits

64.23 Where deduction of social security benefits is relevant, a Part 36 payment notice must include the following statement prescribed by **CPR, r. 36.23**, and **PD 36, para. 10.3**:

1 [*the total amount represented by the Part 36 payment (the gross compensation)*].
2 The defendant has reduced this sum by £ [ ], in accordance with section 8 of and Schedule 2 to the Social Security (Recovery of Benefits) Act 1997, which was calculated as follows:
Name of benefit Amount
3 The amount paid in, being the sum of £ [ ] is the net amount after the deduction of the amount of benefit.

According to the Rules, for the purpose of calculating whether the payment in has been beaten, the payment in is treated as being of the gross sum (**CPR, r. 36.23(4)**). A literal reading of **r. 36.23(4)** was regarded as inconsistent with the Social Security (Recovery of Benefits) Act 1997, s. 8 and sch. 2, in *Williams v Devon County Council* [2003] EWCA Civ 365, [2003] PIQR Q68. To comply with s. 8, a Part 36 notice should go further than **PD 36, para.**

10.3, and give details of how the total sum comprised in the offer is divided between various heads of loss so that the recoverable benefits are only deducted against the appropriate heads of claim. Rather than the issue on costs being whether the total damages award is greater than the gross sum in the Part 36 notice as stated in r. 36.23(4), the issue is (or should be) whether the amount payable to the claimant after deduction of benefits would have been greater on the basis of the award on final disposal of the claim than under the terms of the Part 36 notice. **Rule 36.23** probably needs to be amended.

If the defendant has applied for but is yet to receive the certificate of total recoverable benefits, provided a **Part 36** payment is made within seven days of receipt of the certificate, the defendant can make an offer of settlement taking effect as a **Part 36** payment backdated to the date of the offer (**r. 36.23(2); PD 36, para. 10.2**).

Lodging money in court

A Part 36 payment is made by filing the following, in addition to the Part 36 payment notice (**PD 36, paras 4.1, 10.1(2)** and **11.2**): **64.24**

(a) certificate of service confirming service on the offeree;
(b) certificate of recoverable benefits, if applicable;
(c) where applicable, a notice of a payment to a hospital in respect of a road traffic accident made under the Road Traffic Act 1988, s. 157.

Payment is made by cheque payable to the Accountant General of the Supreme Court and should be accompanied by a sealed copy of the claim form and Court Funds Office **form 100**, all of which should be filed with the Court Funds Office (**PD 36, para. 4.1**). Payments in cash into county court offices or at a district registry are allowed only from litigants in person who do not have a bank account (**para. 4.2**). The Court Funds Office may be willing to accept payment through BACS.

Serving the payment notice

A Part 36 payment is made when it is served, in accordance with **CPR, Part 6**, on the offeree (**CPR, r. 36.8(2)**). The offeror must effect service of the payment notice. When a payment notice is served by the offeror, a certificate of service (**r. 6.10**) must be filed by the offeror (**r. 36.6(4)**). An increase in a Part 36 payment is effective when notice of the increase is served on the offeree (**r. 36.8(4)**). **64.25**

Withdrawal or reduction of a Part 36 payment

Once made, a Part 36 payment may only be withdrawn or reduced with the permission of the court (**CPR, r. 36.6(5)**). Permission is obtained by making an application in accordance with **Part 23**, stating the reasons giving rise to the wish to withdraw or reduce the Part 36 payment (**PD 36, paras 3.4 and 3.5**). **64.26**

Whether to grant permission to withdraw or reduce a Part 36 payment will be considered applying the overriding objective. The court has jurisdiction to allow a Part 36 payment to be withdrawn or reduced even if the application to withdraw is made in the 21-day period after service of the notice of payment in, and even if the claimant serves a notice of acceptance during that 21-day period (*Flynn v Scougall* [2004] EWCA Civ 873, [2004] 1 WLR 3069). In *Flynn v Scougall* May LJ said, at [30] and [34], that the court can entertain a defendant's application to withdraw or reduce a Part 36 payment which is made after the claimant has served notice of acceptance. It is submitted that this is pushing the theory that Part 36 payments are not contractual (see [26], where May LJ quotes Goddard LJ saying this in *Cumper v Pothecary* [1941] 2 KB 58 at p. 67) too far, and that once a Part 36 payment has been accepted the case has been settled. The following factors, if present, are likely, it is submitted, to render it just to allow a defendant to withdraw or reduce a Part 36 payment:

(a) the payment was induced by fraud; or
(b) a mistake affects the payment in; or

(c) the discovery of further evidence puts a wholly different complexion on the case; or
(d) there has been a change in the legal outlook brought about by a judicial decision.

The fact the claimant has given notice of acceptance, if present, is an important factor (*Flynn v Scougall*). Merely receiving an expert's report contradicting the evidence of the claimant's expert is unlikely to be a sufficient change of circumstances to warrant granting permission to the defendant (*Flynn v Scougall*).

Acceptance of a Part 36 payment

64.27 Unless it is necessary to obtain the court's permission to accept a Part 36 payment (see **64.32** to **64.36**) or a court order for payment out (see **64.37** to **64.39**), the claimant can obtain the money by completing **form N243A/form 201** (notice of acceptance and request for payment) and sending one copy to the offeror and filing another copy in court (**CPR, r. 36.16; PD 36, paras 7.6, 7.7, 8.1 and 8.2**). Acceptance takes place when the notice of acceptance is received by the offeror (**CPR, r. 36.8(5)**).

Where a request for payment is made to the Royal Courts of Justice, the claimant should also complete Court Funds Office form 201 and file it in the Court Funds Office (**PD 36, para. 8.3**).

Payment is made by transfer to the bank account nominated on **form N243A/form 201**, which will be that of the claimant's legal representative if there is one (**PD 36, paras 8.4 and 8.5(1)**). To be paid by cheque, a written request must be sent to the Accountant-General (**PD 36, para. 8.4**). If the claimant has filed a notice of being publicly funded, the payment will be made to the Legal Services Commission by direction of the court (**PD 36, para. 8.5(2)**). The court can make payment to an appropriate relative of an intestate deceased claimant if the amount is small (see **PD 36, para. 8.5(3)**).

Interest

64.28 If after 21 days a Part 36 payment has not been accepted, it will be placed in an interest-bearing account in accordance with the Court Funds Office Rules 1987 (**PD 36, para. 11.3**). If the Part 36 payment is in a foreign currency, an application may be made to the court to order that it be placed in an account in that currency (**paras 9.3 and 9.4**). If the payment is subsequently accepted then, unless the parties agree otherwise, interest accrued up to the date of acceptance goes to the offeror, interest after acceptance to the offeree (**para. 7.10**).

Minor defects in Part 36 offers and payments

64.29 An offer that does not comply with the technical requirements of Part 36 can be taken into account for the purposes of costs (**CPR, r. 36.1(2)**). Inadvertent defects in offers and payments may be rectified using the power in **r. 3.10** to cure errors of procedure. **Rule 3.10(a)** provides that errors in procedure do not invalidate steps taken in proceedings unless the court so orders. The jurisdiction under **r. 3.10** is exercised in accordance with the overriding objective, one of the key factors being whether the defect caused any prejudice to the other side. In *Hertsmere Primary Care Trust v Administrators of Balasubramanium's Estate* [2005] EWHC 320 (Ch), [2005] 3 All ER 274, the claimants made a Part 36 offer which failed to state it could be accepted after 21 days only if the parties agreed the liability for costs or the court gave permission. The defendant noticed the defect, informed the claimants that their offer was defective, but declined to explain why. The defect was described by Lightman J as an obvious error and a mere technicality (at [10]), and decided that the defect would be ignored. The parties have a duty to cooperate to rectify technical errors, and it was not open to the defendant to take advantage of its failure to comply with the overriding objective. See also *Mitchell v James* [2002] EWCA Civ 997, [2004] 1 WLR 158, discussed at **64.47**.

CLARIFICATION OF PART 36 OFFERS AND PAYMENT NOTICES

It may happen that a party makes an offer or payment into court in accordance with CPR, **Part 36**, but that its terms are not clear to the offeree. This may occur if the defendant makes a global offer or payment where the claim raises more than one cause of action, or where there are joint claimants. It may also occur where the Part 36 notice of payment or offer fails to make clear what is included. In such cases, the offeree may request the offeror to clarify the offer or payment notice, but the request must be made within seven days of the offer or payment being made (**r. 36.9(1)**). The time when an offer or payment is made is defined in **64.17** and **64.25**. If the offeror fails to give clarification as requested within seven days of receiving the request, the offeree may apply for an order that this be done, unless the trial has started (**r. 36.9(2)**). An application for clarification should be made in accordance with **Part 23** and the application notice should state the respects in which the terms of the Part 36 offer or Part 36 payment notice are said to require clarification (**PD 36, paras 6.2, 6.3**). **64.30**

Where the Part 36 notice of payment or offer fails to make clear what it includes, an order to clarify will almost certainly be made, in accordance with the overriding objective. Cases where the claimant or claimants want a global payment or offer broken down between different causes of action or between the respective claimants are less clear-cut. Under the old rules, the court could order a defendant to break down a global payment in on the ground that it was 'embarrassing'. **Rule 36.9** of the CPR uses the term 'clarification', and is almost certainly intended to lay down a different test. It is arguable that the court only has jurisdiction under **r. 36.9** where the Part 36 offer or payment notice is unclear. This would mean that, provided the offer or notice gives the details required by Part 36, and states clearly whether it covers the whole claim, or which parts, and whether it includes interest and any counterclaim etc., no further breakdown can be ordered. The alternative argument is that **r. 36.9** gives the court a wide discretion to order a more detailed breakdown, for example, into different heads of damages, or to give details of dates and rates applied, whenever the court finds it would be just to give the offeree more information on how the amount offered is calculated.

Where the court does make an order for clarification to be given, the order must specify the date when the Part 36 offer or Part 36 payment is to be treated as having been made (**r. 36.9(3)**). Where clarification is necessary to enable the offeree to consider the offer properly, the date is likely to be the date of the order as opposed to the date the offer was received. This allows the offeree more time in which to accept the offer without requiring the court's permission, and is therefore not necessarily in the interests of the offeror. It is suggested that offers should be suitably and succinctly drafted in order to avoid clarification applications.

The rules contemplate that a Part 36 offer may be improved (**r. 36.8(3)**) and a Part 36 payment increased (**r. 36.8(4)**).

NEED TO APPLY TO THE COURT

In some circumstances (see **64.32** to **64.36**) a Part 36 offer or payment cannot be accepted without the court's permission. In some circumstances (see **64.37** to **64.39**) a Part 36 payment cannot be paid out to the claimant without a court order. An application for permission or for an order should be made using the **Part 23** procedure (**PD 36, para. 7.8**). If the trial has already started, an application for permission should be made to the trial judge (**PD 36, para.** 7.4) and the **Part 23** procedure is not needed. **64.31**

If permission is given, the court's order will direct the payment out of the money in court and the payment of interest (**PD 36, para.** 7.9). The usual rule is that interest is paid to the offeror up to the date of acceptance, but to the offeree thereafter (**para.** 7.10).

Permission to accept a defendant's Part 36 offer or payment

64.32 A defendant's Part 36 offer or payment made 21 or more days before the start of the trial may be accepted by the claimant, without needing the court's permission, provided the claimant gives the defendant written notice of acceptance not later than 21 days after the offer or payment was made (**CPR, r. 36.11(1)**).

If a defendant's Part 36 offer or Part 36 payment is made less than 21 days before trial or the claimant does not accept it within the specified 21-day period, the claimant may accept the offer or payment without needing the permission of the court, provided the parties agree liability for costs (**r. 36.11(2)**). If, however, liability for costs remains in dispute, the offer or payment may only be accepted with the court's permission (**r. 36.11(2)**). Permission to accept a defendant's Part 36 payment more than 21 days after it is made is considered at **64.33** and permission to accept a Part 36 offer is considered at **64.34**. It is suggested that generally permission will be given to accept a Part 36 offer or payment made less than 21 days before the trial, but the court may take into account similar factors to those discussed at **64.33** in refusing permission in an exceptional case. Where permission of the court is required, the court will, if it gives permission, make a costs order (**r. 36.11(3)**). In exercising its discretion on costs, the court is not restricted to considering the circumstances surrounding the offer, and should consider all the circumstances relevant under **r. 44.3**, including the parties' willingness to participate in proposed mediation (*Chaudry v Yap* (2004) LTL 28/10/2004).

Late acceptance of a Part 36 payment

64.33 The principles on which permission for late acceptance of a Part 36 payment may be granted were considered in *Capital Bank plc v Stickland* [2004] EWCA Civ 1677, [2005] 1 WLR 3914. This case concerned purported late acceptance of a claimant's Part 36 offer, but Longmore LJ, at [13], said the same principles apply to Part 36 payments. In the majority of cases permission will be granted, with the only question being as to costs (*Cumper v Pothecary* [1941] 2 KB 58 at p. 67, quoted with approval by Longmore LJ in *Capital Bank plc v Stickland* at [17]). However, the court has a wide discretion in the matter, and may refuse permission, for example, where the acceptance is made very late, where (in relation to a Part 36 offer) there is a doubt about the availability of the money, or where there has been a change of circumstances (at [16]).

If late acceptance is allowed by consent or with the court's permission, the usual rule is that the claimant recovers costs up to the last day for accepting the offer or payment, and the defendant recovers costs thereafter. This is subject to the court's discretion, and there may be reasons for making some other costs order. For example, the claimant may have accepted the offer or payment after late disclosure of evidence or late amendment by the defendant which has had a material effect on the claimant's prospects. If the change is just an excuse for late acceptance, the usual costs rule will be applied, but where the change has had a real impact the court may allow the claimant to recover costs of the claim up to some later point, even the date of acceptance (*Factortame Ltd v Secretary of State for the Environment, Transport and the Regions* [2002] EWCA Civ 22, [2002] 1 WLR 2438).

Permission to accept a claimant's Part 36 offer

64.34 A claimant's Part 36 offer made 21 or more days before the start of the trial may be accepted by the defendant, without requiring the court's permission, provided the defendant gives the claimant written notice of acceptance not later than 21 days after the offer was made (**CPR, r. 36.12(1)**). If a claimant's Part 36 offer is made less than 21 days prior to the start of the trial, or the defendant does not accept the offer within the specified 21 days, the defendant may accept the offer without needing the permission of the court, provided the parties agree liability for costs (**r. 36.12(2)**). If the parties do not agree the liability for costs, the defendant may only accept the offer with the permission of the court (**r. 36.12(2)**).

Where permission of the court is required, if the court gives permission, it will make an order as to costs (**r. 36.12(3)**).

Multiple defendants

Rule 36.17 of the CPR deals with the situation in which there are two or more defendants to a claim and a Part 36 offer or Part 36 payment is made by one or more, but not all defendants. If the defendants are sued jointly or in the alternative, the claimant may accept the offer or payment without requiring the permission of the court, in accordance with **r. 36.11(1)** (see **64.28**), provided (**r. 36.17(2)**): **64.35**

(a) the claimant discontinues the claim against the defendants who have not made the offer or payment; and
(b) those defendants give written consent to the acceptance of the offer or payment.

If the claim alleges several liability the claimant may, under **r. 36.17(3)**:

(a) accept the offer or payment in accordance with **r. 36.11(1)**; and
(b) continue with the claim against the other defendants if entitled to do so.

In all other cases, an application must be made by the claimant to the court for an order permitting a payment out to the claimant of any sum in court and such order as to costs as the court considers appropriate (**r. 36.17(4)**).

Acceptance of Part 36 offer or payment by or on behalf of a child or patient

Rule 36.18 of the CPR deals with offers and payments in proceedings under **r. 21.10**, which deals with compromise by or on behalf of a child or patient. **Rule 36.18(1)** provides that where a Part 36 offer or payment is made in proceedings to which **r. 21.10** applies, no such offer or payment may be accepted without the court's permission and no payment out may be made without a court order. Until a proposed settlement is approved by the court there is no binding agreement, and either party is entitled to repudiate it (*Dietz v Lennig Chemicals Ltd* [1969] 1 AC 170; *Drinkall v Whitwood* [2003] EWCA Civ 1547, [2004] 1 WLR 462). Where the court gives a claimant permission to accept a Part 36 offer or payment after the trial has started, any money in court may only be paid out with a court order, and the court must deal in the order with the entire costs of the proceedings (**r. 36.18(2)**). **64.36**

Provisional damages

A claimant who accepts a Part 36 payment in respect of a claim for provisional damages must, within seven days of acceptance, apply for an award of provisional damages (**CPR, r. 36.7(5)**) and cannot obtain payment out of money in court until this application has been disposed of (**r. 36.7(6)**). **64.37**

Acceptance after a defence of tender before claim

If a claimant accepts a Part 36 payment after a defence of tender before claim has been put forward by the defendant, the money in court may be paid out only after an order of the court (**CPR, r. 36.18(3)**). **64.38**

Apportionment order

It may not be possible to obtain a Part 36 payment until it has been apportioned between various claims by the court. An application for an apportionment order is made in the same way as an application for permission to accept (see **64.29**). **64.39**

Where a claim includes claims arising under the **Fatal Accidents Act 1976** and the **Law Reform (Miscellaneous Provisions) Act 1934** and a single sum of money is paid into court in satisfaction of those claims, which is accepted, the court shall apportion the money between the different claims (**CPR, r. 37.4(1)**). Similarly, it will be for the court to apportion any sum ordered or agreed to be paid in respect of damages or any money accepted in satisfaction of the claim made under the **Fatal Accidents Act 1976** by or behalf of more than one person (**CPR, r. 37.4(3)**).

COSTS CONSEQUENCES

Acceptance of a defendant's Part 36 offer or payment

64.40 Where a defendant's Part 36 offer or Part 36 payment is accepted without requiring the permission of the court, the offeror must pay the claimant's costs of the proceedings up to the date of serving notice of acceptance of the offer (**CPR, r. 36.13(1)**). For the circumstances in which the court's permission is required see **64.32, 64.35** and **64.36**. Where the offer or payment relates only to part of the claim and at the time of serving the notice of acceptance, the claimant abandons the balance of the claim, the offeror must pay the claimant's costs of the proceedings up to the date of serving notice of acceptance, unless the court orders otherwise (**r. 36.13(2)**). The claimant's costs include any costs attributable to the defendant's counterclaim if the Part 36 offer or Part 36 payment notice states that it takes the counterclaim into account (**r. 36.13(3)**). In a defamation claim, the defendant will usually be required to pay the claimant's costs of, and relating to, a statement in open court following the claimant's acceptance of a Part 36 payment (*Phillips v Associated Newspapers Ltd* [2004] EWHC 190 (QB), [2004] 1 WLR 2106). Costs are payable on the standard basis if not agreed (**r. 36.13(4)**). The court has no discretion to award indemnity-basis costs, even if the Part 36 payment is more advantageous to the claimant than a rejected claimant's Part 36 offer (*Dyson Appliances Ltd v Hoover Ltd (No. 3)* [2002] EWHC 2229 (Ch), [2003] FSR 21). A party accepting a Part 36 payment is only entitled to his costs as of right where the acceptance brings the proceedings to an end (*Clark Goldring and Page Ltd v ANC Ltd* (2001) *The Times*, 27 March 2001). Where the Part 36 payment relates to only part of the claim, and the rest is not abandoned, the effect of **rr. 36.13** and **36.15** is that the court has a discretion on the question of costs.

Acceptance in Warsaw Convention cases

64.41 The Warsaw Convention 1929, art. 22(4) (as amended by The Hague Convention 1955), which is set out in the schedule to the Carriage by Air Act 1961, provides:

> The limits prescribed in this article shall not prevent the court from awarding, in accordance with its own law, in addition, the whole or part of the court costs and of the other expenses of the litigation incurred by the plaintiff. The foregoing provision shall not apply if the amount of damages awarded . . . does not exceed the sum which the carrier has offered in writing to the plaintiff within a period of six months from the date of the occurrence causing the damage, or before the commencement of the action, if that is later.

In *GKN Westland Helicopters Ltd v Korean Air Lines Co. Ltd* [2003] EWHC 1120 (Comm), [2003] 2 All ER (Comm) 578, the defendant made an offer within six months of the issue of the claim, then made a Part 36 payment in a slightly larger amount. The Part 36 payment was accepted. It was held that because the Part 36 payment was higher than the Warsaw Convention offer, the normal rule in **CPR, r. 36.13**, applied, and the defendant was liable to pay the claimant's costs of the claim. It was recognised that there is a latent conflict between r. 36.13 and art. 22 of the Convention where a claimant accepts a Part 36 payment which is less than a previous Warsaw Convention offer. The better view is that in such circumstances the Warsaw Convention should prevail, and the defendant should be awarded its costs from the date of the offer.

Acceptance of a claimant's Part 36 offer

64.42 Where a claimant's Part 36 offer is accepted without needing the permission of the court, the offeree must pay the claimant's costs of the proceedings, up to the date upon which notice of acceptance is served (**CPR, r. 36.14**). For the circumstances in which the court's permission is required see **64.34** and **64.36**.

Where claimant fails to do better than a defendant's Part 36 offer or payment

Rule 36.20 of the CPR provides that where the claimant fails to better a Part 36 payment or fails to obtain judgment which is more advantageous than a defendant's Part 36 offer, unless the court considers it unjust to do so, it will order the claimant to pay any costs incurred by the defendant after the latest date on which the payment or offer could have been accepted without needing the permission of the court. For the circumstances in which the court's permission is required see **64.32**, **64.35** and **64.36**. Assuming the claimant has been at least partially successful, the defendant must normally pay the claimant's costs up to that date. Once the date for acceptance has passed, the real issue, so far as costs are concerned, is whether the claimant can do better than the defendant's offer or Part 36 payment. **64.43**

The normal rule, that the claimant recovers costs up to the 21st day after the Part 36 offer or Part 36 payment notice, and the defendant recovers costs thereafter, applies where the award exactly equals or exceeds the offer or payment. Like must be compared with like. Therefore, where a payment in is made some time before trial and includes interest, the court must recalculate its award of interest to the date of the payment in to see whether the trial award exceeds the payment in (*Blackham v Entrepose UK* [2004] EWCA Civ 1109, *The Times*, 28 September 2004).

Claimant fails to exceed payment in, but payment in withdrawn before trial

There are cases where money paid into court under **CPR, Part 36**, is withdrawn (see **64.26**) before trial, and the amount formerly in court exceeds the final judgment obtained by the claimant. According to *Garner v Cleggs* [1983] 1 WLR 862 (approved by Longmore LJ in *Capital Bank plc v Stickland* [2004] EWCA Civ 1677, [2005] 1 WLR 3914, at [21]) in these cases the principled approach (taking into account **r. 36.20(2)**) on costs is: **64.44**

(a) for the claimant to be awarded costs up to the 21st day after being given notice of the payment in;
(b) for the defendant to be awarded costs from the 22nd day after giving notice of payment in through to the date when the defendant could have resisted an application by the claimant to accept the money in court out of time (see **64.33**) (in most cases this will be the date when there was a change in the circumstances); and
(c) for the claimant to be awarded costs thereafter.

Departing from the normal rule on costs

The normal rule on costs described at **64.43** has been departed from where: **64.45**

(a) a party was late in disclosing important evidence (*Ford v GKR Construction Ltd* [2000] 1 WLR 1397);
(b) a party has been unwilling to participate in proposed mediation (*Re Midland Linen Services Ltd* [2004] EWHC 3380 (Ch), LTL 28/10/2004);
(c) a claimant has deliberately exaggerated the claim (*Painting v University of Oxford* [2005] EWCA Civ 161, [2005] PIQR Q5).

Traditionally, the courts have taken a strict line that the normal rule should be followed even when the judge had been considering a slightly higher award (*Wagman v Vare Motors Ltd* [1959] 1 WLR 853). In *Jackson v Ministry of Defence* [2006] EWCA Civ 46, LTL 12/1/2006, the Court of Appeal approved a modest percentage reduction in the costs order to reflect the fact the claimant had only just beaten a payment in. Other factors may persuade a judge to depart from the normal rule, but there is great reluctance in countenancing such departures. Thus, in *Jones v Jones* (1999) *The Times*, 11 November 1999, there had been a payment in of £120,000, and the claimant only recovered damages of £111,000. The amount of damages awarded was probably depressed by a third medical report served by the defendant some six months after the payment in. These events occurred before the CPR came into force. The Court of Appeal held that the judge erred in principle in awarding the claimant costs up to the disclosure of the last medical report. Translated into CPR terms the Court of Appeal's substituted order would mean that the claimant would only recover her costs to the final date for accepting the payment in. This decision may be at variance with the ethos of the CPR, and in particular with **r. 44.3**, which gives the court wide powers to take into account conduct on questions of costs. The case should be contrasted with *Ford v GKR Construction Ltd*, in which the Court of Appeal affirmed a decision to award the entire costs of the claim to the claimant who was awarded £85,000 despite payments in totalling £95,000. This was because her award was depressed below the level of the payments in by virtue of video surveillance evidence introduced in the period of an adjournment between the first and second days of the trial, which was criticised as being late.

In *Painting v University of Oxford* the claimant pleaded loss and damage in excess of £400,000 on the basis that she suffered a long-term debilitating injury, and the defendant made a payment in of £10,000. The judge found that the claimant had intentionally exaggerated her injuries, and awarded her £23,331. The Court of Appeal held that the essential question at trial was whether the claimant was exaggerating her injuries. The claimant's intentional exaggeration, combined with her failure to negotiate, justified making an order for the defendant to pay the claimant's costs to the date of the payment in, and for the claimant to pay the defendant's costs thereafter, despite the judgment exceeding the amount in court. Cases involving exaggeration are very fact-sensitive, as shown by *Allison v Brighton and Hove City Council* [2005] EWCA Civ 548, LTL 22/4/2005. Here the claim was for £45,000, but judgment was for £4,000. The claimant was awarded only 25 per cent of his costs in the period prior to an effective payment in. Percentage costs orders of this type have been increasingly common since the introduction of the CPR.

In *Daniels v Commissioner of Police for the Metropolis* [2005] EWCA Civ 1312, *The Times*, 28 October 2005, the claimant was a serving police officer who was injured when thrown from her horse in a training session. She made a number of claimant's Part 36 offers, but the defendant refused to negotiate. At trial the claim was dismissed. The question on appeal was whether the refusal to negotiate was 'unreasonable' conduct in the *Halsey v Milton Keynes General NHS Trust* [2004] EWCA Civ 576, [2004] 1 WLR 3002, sense (see **66.19**). The Court of Appeal said it was difficult to imagine circumstances where rejecting a Part 36 offer could be characterised as unreasonable if the party who rejected the offer then won the case. That was particularly so on the facts, where the defendant routinely faced unmeritorious claims.

A decision illustrating the point that **r. 44.3** rarely overrides the usual rule where there has been a Part 36 payment exceeding the damages awarded is *Burgess v British Steel* (2000) *The Times*, 29 February 2000. In this case the Court of Appeal overturned a decision to award the claimant costs to the final date for accepting the payment in (which was in the sum of £220,000), and to award no costs thereafter. Before making the payment in the defendant had disclosed a medical report which asserted that the claimant was malingering and which implied the claimant was pursuing a bogus claim. At trial the claimant established that the claim was genuine, but only recovered £161,000. On appeal it was held this did not justify departing from the usual rule, and the second part of the costs order was altered so that the defendant recovered costs from the last date for accepting the Part 36 payment.

Where the award at trial exceeds a Part 36 payment the court should not depart from the usual rule by examining whether the Part 36 payment was reasonable, nor by reason of the claimant having made a claimant's Part 36 offer which was higher than the award at trial (*Quorum AS v Schramm* [2002] CLC 77). In *Johnsey Estates (1990) Ltd v Secretary of State for the Environment* [2001] EWCA Civ 535, LTL 11/4/2001, the defendant made a first Part 36 payment of £200,000, followed by a second Part 36 payment of £250,000. At trial the judge awarded £200,000 plus interest of £36,000 to the date of the first Part 36 payment. The Court of

Appeal overturned the judge's award of costs to the defendant from the date of the first Part 36 payment because this failed to take into account the award of interest, and substituted an award (apart from on one issue) to the claimant of its costs to the date of the second Part 36 payment, with the defendant recovering costs thereafter.

Awarding a defendant indemnity-basis costs

A defendant making a successful Part 36 offer or payment will usually be awarded costs on the standard basis. An award of costs on the indemnity basis is normally reserved to cases where the court wishes to show its disapproval, but may extend to some cases where an offer has been made and rejected. Indemnity-basis costs may be appropriate where the claim is dismissed at trial, if the court also finds that the case was going to fail from the outset of the trial (*Reid Minty v Taylor* [2001] EWCA Civ 1723, [2002] 1 WLR 2800). In *Kiam v MGN Ltd (No. 2)* [2002] EWCA Civ 66, [2002] 1 WLR 2810, the Court of Appeal said that *Reid Minty v Taylor* decided no more than that conduct falling short of conduct deserving moral condemnation could still be so unreasonable as to justify an order of indemnity-basis costs. In *Kiam v MGN Ltd (No. 2)* it was held that such conduct needed to be unreasonable to a high degree, and the refusal of a settlement offer (not being a claimant's Part 36 offer) would rarely attract such an order. **64.46**

Costs where the offer fails to comply with Part 36

By **CPR, r. 36.1(2)**, nothing in **Part 36** prevents a party from making an offer to settle in whatever way he chooses, but if that offer is not made in accordance with **Part 36**, it has the consequences set out in **Part 36** only if the court so orders. It is suspected that the Rule Committee intended this provision to apply to open offers, which can be used at any stage in the trial, and are not subject to the restrictions on disclosure set out in **r. 36.19** (see **64.5**). It may also have been intended to give the court a little leeway where a party had attempted to comply with **Part 36**, but inadvertently made some minor slip in the Part 36 notice or offer. **Rule 36.1(2)** does not say this, and is drafted in general terms. This rule, together with the general discretion on costs given by **r. 44.3**, have as a result generated a contentious body of case law providing instances where the court has given parties the same or similar cost protection following without-prejudice offers which do not, and were never intended to, comply with **Part 36**. **64.47**

An offer which is not in accordance with **Part 36** will be accorded such weight in relation to any issue as to costs as the court thinks appropriate **(PD 36, para. 1.3)**. In *Amber v Stacey* [2001] 1 WLR 1225 the defendant made a written offer that did not comply with **CPR, Part 36**, but which was more generous than the award eventually made by the court. It was held to be wrong in principle to treat the offer in the same way as if it had been a Part 36 payment for the purposes of costs. However, it was taken into account when considering costs, with the result that the defendant was awarded half his costs from the date of the offer, the court being influenced by the claimant's intemperate response to the written offer. In *Mitchell v James* [2002] EWCA Civ 997, [2004] 1 WLR 158, a claimant's Part 36 offer failed to comply with **r. 36.5(6)(b)** in that it did not state that after 21 days the defendant could only accept it if costs liability was agreed or if the court gave permission. It was said that if this had been the only defect in the offer, the court would have waived it as a mere technicality (see **r. 3.10**).

Costs where the offer is not backed by a payment in In *Crouch v King's Healthcare NHS Trust* [2004] EWCA Civ 1332, [2005] 1 WLR 2015, Waller LJ said that **CPR, rr. 36.1(2)** and **44.3**, leave it open to the parties in a money claim to enter into an agreement that the defendant can make a Part 36 offer after proceedings have been issued having the same effect as a Part 36 payment. The Lord Justice also said that it was open to a defendant in a money claim to apply under **r. 36.1(2)** during the currency of the proceedings for an order treating an offer letter as a Part 36 payment. For formal offers to settle in clinical dispute claims, see **64.9**. **64.48**

In *Hardy v Sutherland* [2001] EWCA Civ 976, LTL 13/6/2001, the defendant made a Part 36 offer and, some time later, a Part 36 payment. The claim was for money, so the earlier Part 36 offer did not comply with **r. 36.3**. It was held that proper recognition of the offer would be accorded by depriving the claimant of a percentage of his costs up to the date for acceptance of the Part 36 payment (after which the defendant recovered costs from the claimant).

Perhaps the most radical decision is *Trustees of Stokes Pension Fund v Western Power Distribution (South West) plc* [2005] EWCA Civ 854, [2005] 1 WLR 3595. This was a claim for damages of £780,000. The defendant made a written offer before proceedings of £35,000, but did not pay in after proceedings were started as required by **r. 36.10**. The defendant later paid in £20,000 and informed the claimant that the earlier offer was withdrawn. At trial the claimant recovered £25,000. On appeal the £35,000 written offer was treated as a payment in because the following four conditions were satisfied:

(a) the written offer was expressed in clear terms, stating whether it took into account any counterclaim and interest, in line with **r. 36.5(2)**;
(b) it was expressed to be open for acceptance for at least 21 days and generally accorded with the form of Part 36 offers;
(c) it was a genuine offer, not a sham; and
(d) the defendant was clearly good for the money when the offer was made.

The fact the defendant withdrew the £35,000 offer was held to be irrelevant because there was no evidence the claimant would have accepted the offer at a later stage if it had remained open. The Court of Appeal substituted an order that the claimant had to pay the defendant's costs from 21 days after the written offer. Permission to appeal to the House of Lords was refused ([2005] 1 WLR 3795).

Cases like *Trustees of Stokes Pension Fund v Western Power Distribution (South West) plc* are instances of the court using its discretion under **r. 36.1(2)** to treat offers which do not comply with the strict requirements of **Part 36** as if they were Part 36 offers. Being discretionary, the court has a wide ambit in deciding on the appropriate consequences. It is an error of principle to treat an offer which does not comply with Part 36 as having either full or no effect, without considering intermediate positions (*Codent Ltd v Lyson Ltd* (2005) LTL 8/12/2005). In *Farag v Commissioner of Police of the Metropolis* (2005) LTL 15/12/2005 the claim raised eight causes of action against the police. An offer to settle was refused, then withdrawn two years before the trial. All but one of the causes of action failed. The Court of Appeal took the offer into account in deciding to make no order as to costs. In *Codent Ltd v Lyson Ltd* an offer was made less than 21 days before trial and in the form of a Part 36 offer, whereas it should have been a Part 36 payment. The claimant was awarded 70 per cent of its costs up to the first day of the trial, and the defendant was awarded its costs thereafter.

64.49 **Incomplete or unclear offers** An offer to settle made before the commencement of proceedings in *Phillis Trading Ltd v 86 Lordship Road Ltd* (2001) *The Times*, 16 March 2001, did not refer to costs. Thorpe LJ said that an offeree takes a real risk in rejecting such an offer out of hand, and has an obligation to state what is acceptable and to seek clarification. It was held that the offeree had to pay the costs from the date of the offer. The offer in this case was a *Calderbank* offer rather than an offer under **CPR, r. 36.10**, and was made in proceedings before the Lands Tribunal. It is questionable whether the same decision would be reached where an offer made before the commencement of ordinary litigation, in breach of **r. 36.10(2)(b)**, fails to include an offer to pay costs. In such a case the issue is likely to be whether an offer made without providing for costs was overall more generous than the ultimate result (see *Lindner Ceilings Floors Partitions plc v How Engineering Services Ltd* [2001] BLR 90).

What is required is a 'clear and concise' offer to settle (*Amber v Stacey* [2001] 1 WLR 1225), so the judge is entitled to disregard a letter which is only an offer to negotiate (*Press v Chipperfield*

[2003] EWCA Civ 484, LTL 25/3/2003). There were complex proceedings in *Rio Properties Inc. v Gibson Dunn and Crutcher* [2005] EWCA Civ 534, LTL 22/4/2005. The claimant purported to make a claimant's Part 36 offer in respect of the costs of various interim applications. It was held that it was open to the judge to decide the offer was difficult to evaluate and therefore should be disregarded on the question of costs.

CLAIMANT'S PART 36 OFFER EXCEEDING JUDGMENT

Where the defendant is held liable for more, or the judgment against the defendant is more advantageous to the claimant, than the proposal in the claimant's own offer, **CPR, r. 36.21**, applies. Despite this wording in **r. 36.21**, in *Read v Edmed* (2004) *The Times*, 13 December 2004, it was held **r. 36.21** also applies where a claimant's Part 36 offer is exactly the same as the award at trial. Consistently with the decision in *Mitchell v James* [2002] EWCA Civ 997, [2004] 1 WLR 158, the court should ignore any terms in a claimant's Part 36 offer relating to indemnity-basis costs or enhanced interest rates (as opposed to contractual interest or statutory interest under the **Supreme Court Act 1981, s. 35A**, or the **County Courts Act 1984, s. 69**) in deciding whether the offer exceeds the judgment (*Ali Reza-Delta Transport Co. Ltd v United Arab Shipping Co. SAG (No. 2)* [2003] EWCA Civ 811, [2004] 1 WLR 168). **64.50**

The court may order interest on the whole or any part of any sum of money (excluding interest) awarded to the claimant at a rate not exceeding 10 per cent above base rate for some or all of the period starting with the latest date on which the defendant could have accepted the offer without needing the court's permission to do so (**CPR, r. 36.21(2)**). For the circumstances in which the court's permission is required see **64.34** to **64.36**. Where the court awards interest under **r. 36.21** and also awards interest on the same sum and for the same period under any other power, the total rate of interest may not exceed 10 per cent above base rate (**r. 36.21(6)**). **Rule 36.21** does not apply where judgment is entered otherwise than at trial, such as after an application for summary judgment (*Petrotrade Inc. v Texaco Ltd* [2002] 1 WLR 947). Although the rule does not apply, the court still has jurisdiction to award enhanced interest (Lord Woolf MR indicating he would have awarded 4 per cent above base rate for 12 months) and indemnity-basis costs in such cases. The court should not start from the assumption that it should award the maximum enhanced interest, but must stand back and ensure that the enhanced interest does not provide a disproportionate benefit (*Earl v Cantor Fitzgerald International (No. 2)* (2001) LTL 3/5/2001). Enhanced interest will not be granted in defamation claims, following the usual rule against awarding interest in such cases (*McPhilemy v Times Newspapers Ltd (No. 2)* [2001] EWCA Civ 933, [2002] 1 WLR 934).

The court may also order that the defendant must pay the claimant's costs on an indemnity basis from the latest date on which the defendant could have accepted the offer without requiring the court's permission and interest on those costs at a rate not exceeding 10 per cent above base rate (**r. 36.21(3)**). The court has a discretion not to make the orders set out above where it considers it unjust to do so (**r. 36.21(4)**).

Discretion to make rule 36.21 orders

In deciding whether it would be unjust to make the orders referred to above, the court must, by **CPR, r. 36.21(5)**, take into account all the circumstances of the case, including the following: **64.51**

(a) The terms of any Part 36 offer.
(b) The stage in the proceedings that any Part 36 offer or Part 36 payment was made.
(c) The information available to the parties at the time any Part 36 offer or Part 36 payment was made.
(d) The conduct of the parties with regard to the giving or refusing to give information for

the purposes of enabling the offer or payment into court to be made or evaluated. Conduct includes any failure by the claimant to give adequate disclosure to enable the defendant to assess the validity of the claim (*Mamidoil-Jetoil Greek Petroleum Co. SA v Okta Crude Oil Refinery AD* [2002] EWHC 2462 (Comm), [2003] 1 Lloyd's Rep 42).

(e) Whether it would be unjust to make orders under **r. 36.21** because the defendant had a good reason for rejecting the offer, such as a reasonable belief in its prospects of success based on the law as it then stood (*Mamidoil-Jetoil Greek Petroleum Co. SA v Okta Crude Oil Refinery AD*).

The fact that the offeror is funded under a CFA is irrelevant when deciding whether to make an order under **r. 36.21** (*CEL Group Ltd v Nedlloyd Lines UK Ltd* [2003] EWCA Civ 1871, [2004] 1 Lloyd's Rep 388).

Awarding indemnity-basis costs after a successful claimant's Part 36 offer implies no misconduct on the defendant (*McPhilemy v Times Newspapers Ltd (No. 2)* [2001] EWCA Civ 933, [2002] 1 WLR 934), its practical effect being to ensure that the claimant does not recover any less than the costs he has in fact incurred (*Petrotrade Inc. v Texaco Ltd* [2002] 1 WLR 947). Indemnity costs and enhanced interest on those costs can be awarded even where the claimant is publicly funded (*Earl v Cantor Fitzgerald International (No. 2)* (2001) LTL 3/5/2001). The enhanced rate of interest on indemnity-basis costs runs from the date upon which the work was done or liability for disbursements was incurred, and runs until judgment. Thereafter, interest on costs is payable under the **Judgments Act 1838, s. 17**, in the usual way (*McPhilemy v Times Newspapers Ltd (No. 2)*).

Part 36 offers are not intended to include terms as to costs. Consequently, where it is unclear whether the result at trial is more advantageous to the claimant than the substantive terms of a claimant's Part 36 offer, it is impermissible to refer to any costs terms in the offer to persuade the court that the trial result is more advantageous (*Mitchell v James* [2002] EWCA Civ 997, [2004] 1 WLR 158). In *Huck v Robson* [2002] EWCA Civ 398, [2003] 1 WLR 1340, the claimant in a personal injuries claim made a Part 36 offer to settle a dispute on the basis that the defendant was 95 per cent liable. At trial the judge found for the claimant with no deduction for contributory negligence, and the claimant asked for indemnity-basis costs. It was held that while an offer based on marginally less than full liability might be illusory, that was not so in the present case, and the fact that no trial judge would make a finding of only 5 per cent contributory negligence was irrelevant. It was not unjust for the defendant to have to pay indemnity-basis costs and enhanced interest.

COSTS AFTER COURT'S REFUSAL OF PERMISSION TO ACCEPT CLAIMANT'S PART 36 OFFER

64.52 Cases where the court refuses the defendant permission to accept a claimant's Part 36 offer out of time were considered by Longmore LJ in *Capital Bank plc v Stickland* [2004] EWCA Civ 1677, [2005] 1 WLR 3914, at [23]. Costs remain discretionary, but the following principles, which are based on *Garner v Cleggs* [1983] 1 WLR 862, were laid down:

(a) the claimant should be awarded standard-basis costs up to the 21st day after giving notice to the defendant of the Part 36 offer;

(b) from the 22nd day after making the offer to the date of the defendant's application notice seeking permission to accept the Part 36 offer, the court has a discretion to award the claimant indemnity-basis costs etc. under **CPR, r. 36.21** (see 64.51);

(c) from the date of the defendant's application notice the court should award the claimant standard-basis costs.

RESPONDENT'S PART 36 OFFER ON AN APPEAL

A respondent in an appeal who makes an offer to accept all but a small fraction of the amount awarded by the court below will generally be regarded as having made a genuine offer to settle, and will usually be awarded indemnity costs (and possibly also enhanced interest) under **CPR, r. 36.21**. As discussed in *CEL Group Ltd v Nedlloyd Lines UK Ltd* [2003] EWCA Civ 1871, [2004] 1 Lloyd's Rep 388, a respondent cannot reasonably be expected to give up a substantial part of the judgment under appeal, particularly where the appeal raises an all-or-nothing point. **64.53**

STAY FOLLOWING ACCEPTANCE OF A PART 36 OFFER OR PAYMENT

Under **CPR, r. 36.15**, where a Part 36 offer or payment relates to the whole claim and is accepted, the claim will be stayed. In the case of acceptance of a Part 36 offer, the claim is stayed on the terms of the offer and either party may apply to enforce those terms without the need to institute a new claim (**CPR, r. 36.15(2)**). Where the offer or payment relates to part of a claim and is accepted, that part of the claim will be stayed and unless the parties have agreed liability for costs, the court will determine the costs (**r. 36.15(3)**). **64.54**

If the approval of the court is required before a settlement can be binding, any stay which would otherwise arise on the acceptance of a Part 36 offer or a Part 36 payment will take effect only when court approval is given.

Any stay arising under **r. 36.15** will not affect the court's power to enforce the terms of a Part 36 offer, or to deal with any question of costs relating to the proceedings, or to order payment out of any sum paid into court (**r. 36.15(5)**).

Where a Part 36 offer has been accepted and it is alleged that one party has not honoured the terms of the offer so that another party is entitled to a remedy for breach of contract, that remedy may be claimed by applying to the court without having to begin a new claim, unless the court orders otherwise (**r. 36.15(6)**).

PAYMENTS INTO COURT PURSUANT TO STATUTE

There are special provisions (made under **CPR, r. 37.5**) for payments into court pursuant to: **64.55**

(a) the Life Assurance Companies (Payment into Court) Act 1896 (**PD 37, paras 7** and **8**); and

(b) the Trustee Act 1925, s. 63 (**PD 37, paras 9** and **10**).

Chapter 65 Security for Costs

INTRODUCTION

65.1 Generally, the question of who pays for the costs of a claim is not determined until the claim is finally disposed of, whether by consent, interim process or trial. This is because the usual rule is that the successful party recovers costs from the loser and the outcome on the merits is only known when judgment is obtained. It is for this reason that the parties are not generally allowed to anticipate the eventual costs order by asking for interim orders that their opponents provide funds as security to pay for the costs of the action. Despite this, it is accepted that there have to be exceptions for cases where there is a significant risk of defendants suffering the injustice of having to defend proceedings with no real prospect of being able to recover costs if they are ultimately successful.

An order for security for costs can only be made: (a) before judgment (*Penny v Penny* [1996] 1 WLR 1204), or (b) for the costs of an appellant, or of a respondent to an appeal who also appeals (**CPR, r. 25.15**). Once security is given it may be retained, subject to the court's discretion, pending an appeal. An order for security for costs usually requires the claimant to pay money into court as security for the payment of any costs order that may eventually be made in favour of the defendant, and staying the claim until the security is provided. On the application three matters arise:

(a) whether there are grounds for ordering security for costs;
(b) if so, whether the court's discretion should be exercised in favour of making the order; and
(c) if so, how much security should be provided.

Each of these three matters will be considered after first looking at the procedure for making the application and the capacity of the respondent to the application.

PROCEDURE

A defendant may apply under **CPR, rr. 25.12** to **25.15**, for an order requiring the claimant to give security for costs. It is submitted that, like an application for an interim remedy, an application for security for costs may be made at any time after the defendant has filed an acknowledgment of service or a defence (see **r. 25.2(2)(c)**). The first application for security should normally be made at the first case management conference (see **Admiralty and Commercial Courts Guide, app. 16, para. 1**). It is made using the usual **Part 23** procedure of issuing an application notice supported by written evidence (**r. 25.12(2)**). The written evidence should deal with the grounds on which security is sought, and with any factors relevant to the exercise of the court's discretion. These include the location of the claimant's assets, and any practical difficulties in enforcing any order for costs (see **Admiralty and Commercial Courts Guide, app. 16, para. 3**). It also needs to include an estimate of the defendant's likely costs of defending the claim, which should usually be given in the form of precedent H in the Schedule of Costs Precedents annexed to **PD 43–48** and exhibited to the written evidence. **65.2**

Invariably the application should be made on notice to the claimant, and should be served on the claimant at least three clear days before the day appointed for hearing the application (**CPR, r. 23.7(1)(b)**).

Applications for security for costs will be inappropriate in cases on the small claims track because of the restrictions on the recovery of costs in these claims. In fast track and multi-track claims it is the duty of the parties to make any application that may be appropriate at any hearing that has been fixed (**PD 28, para. 2.5** (fast track); **PD 29, para. 3.5** (multi-track)), so in many cases an application for security for costs should be made at the first case management hearing.

THE RESPONDENT

Claimants

By **CPR, r. 20.3**, the provisions on security for costs in **rr. 25.12** to **25.15** apply to an additional claim as if it were a claim. So a party bringing an additional claim may be ordered to give security for the costs of the additional claim in just the same way as an original claimant may be ordered to give security for the costs of the original claim. Under the old rules it was held that if a defendant makes an additional claim against a person other than the claimant, the defendant to that additional claim cannot obtain an order for security against the original claimant, unless, as a result of directions given in the additional claim (for which see **29.9**), the defendant to the additional claim is given permission to defend jointly with the original defendant (see *Taly NDC International NV v Terra Nova Insurance Co. Ltd* [1985] 1 WLR 1359 per Parker LJ). The question is one of capacity in the main claim. There is therefore no jurisdiction to order a defendant to provide security for the costs of any interim application it may make (*Taly NDC International NV v Terra Nova Insurance Co. Ltd*). **65.3**

With regard to counterclaims, a distinction needs to be drawn between simple counterclaims, where it is possible to obtain orders for security, and set-offs, where it has been held that security will not usually be ordered (*Neck v Taylor* [1893] 1 QB 560). The reason for this distinction is that a set-off, if established, amounts to a defence to the claim, so a defendant raising a set-off is for this purpose regarded as simply defending and not as advancing a claim. The distinction between set-offs and other types of counterclaim was considered at **34.31** and **34.32**. Similarly, it will not be fair or just to order a defendant to provide security for costs of a counterclaim which sets out contentions which are in substance the mirror image of the allegations in the particulars of claim (*Samuel J. Cohl Co. v Eastern Mediterranean Maritime Ltd* [1980] 1 Lloyd's Rep 371; *Aims Asset Management Sdn Bhd v Kazakhstan Investment Fund Ltd* [2002] EWHC 3225 (Ch), LTL 23/5/2002). Where a defendant is counterclaiming, the question to be asked is whether, as a matter of substance, the position of the defendant can fairly be equated with that of a claimant, or whether, in truth, it does not go beyond that of a defendant (*Pimlott v Meregrove Holdings Ltd* [2003] All ER (D) 325 (Jun), in which it was held that the costs of pursuing the counterclaim would not add to the costs of defending the claim so there should be no security). Conversely, in *L/M International Construction Inc. v Circle Partnership Ltd* [1995] CLY 4010 the claimant sued for £1,000,000 and the defendant counterclaimed for £15,000,000. The court found that the defendant was in the position of a claimant and ordered it to give security.

If the issues raised on the counterclaim are wider than those raised by the claim, security for costs may be ordered against the defendant. The amount depends on the facts of the case. In *Petromin SA v Secnav Marine Ltd* [1995] 1 Lloyd's Rep 603 there was a significant claim and counterclaim based on identical facts. The court ordered the defendant to give security for the full amount of the claimant's costs on the counterclaim and not just the increase occasioned by defending the counterclaim. In *Kazakhstan Investment Fund Ltd v Aims Asset Management Sdn Bhd* (2002) LTL 23/5/2002 the court limited the costs to those of defending the counterclaim.

Parties other than claimants

65.4 Security for costs may be ordered against any party in the position of a claimant, even if they are not strictly 'claimants'. An example would be a petitioner on an unfair prejudice petition under the Companies Act 1985 (*Re Unisoft Group Ltd (No. 1)* [1993] BCLC 1292). Another example is an appellant to an appeal (or a respondent who cross-appeals), see **CPR, r. 25.15**. By **r. 25.14**, an order for security for costs may also be made against someone other than a claimant if the court is satisfied that the person against whom the order is sought either:

(a) assigned the claim to the claimant with a view to avoiding the possibility of a costs order being made against him; or
(b) has contributed or agreed to contribute to the claimant's costs in return for a share of any money or property which the claimant may recover in the proceedings.

Foreign governments

65.5 An order for security for costs may be made against a foreign government (*Government of Sierra Leone v Davenport* [2003] EWHC 1913 (Ch), LTL 4/4/2005).

CONDITIONS FOR ORDERING SECURITY FOR COSTS

65.6 Security for costs can only be ordered if one of the conditions set out in **CPR, r. 25.13(2)**, is satisfied. As from 1 April 2003, the conditions are:

(a) the claimant is—
  (i) resident out of the jurisdiction; but
  (ii) not resident in a Brussels Contracting State, a Lugano Contracting State or a Regulation State, as defined in **section 1(3) of the Civil Jurisdiction and Judgments Act 1982**;

[(b) revoked]

(c) the claimant is a company or other body (whether incorporated inside or outside Great Britain) and there is reason to believe that it will be unable to pay the defendant's costs if ordered to do so;
(d) the claimant has changed his address since the claim was commenced with a view to evading the consequences of the litigation;
(e) the claimant failed to give his address in the claim form, or gave an incorrect address in that form;
(f) the claimant is acting as a nominal claimant, other than as a representative claimant under **Part 19**, and there is reason to believe that he will be unable to pay the defendant's costs if ordered to do so;
(g) the claimant has taken steps in relation to his assets that would make it difficult to enforce an order for costs against him.

The condition in **r. 25.13(2)(c)** is derived from the Companies Act 1985, s. 726(1), which provides:

Where in England and Wales a limited company is [the claimant] in an action or other legal proceeding, the court having jurisdiction in the matter may, if it appears by credible testimony that there is reason to believe that the company will be unable to pay the defendant's costs if successful in his defence, require sufficient security to be given for those costs, and may stay all proceedings until the security is given.

Section 726(1) is narrower in scope than **CPR, r. 25.13(2)(c)**, which extends to companies, whether limited or not and wherever incorporated, whereas s. 726(1) applies only to limited companies registered in England and Wales or Scotland.

There are some statutory restrictions on the availability of security for costs. For example, **reg. 6 of the Community Legal Service (Costs) Regulations 2000** (SI 2000/441) provides that where a publicly funded client is required to give security for costs, the amount of security must not exceed the amount, if any, which would be reasonable having regard to all the circumstances, including the client's financial resources and his or her conduct in the proceedings. Security for costs cannot be ordered against a national of a contracting State in proceedings arising out of the Convention on the Contract for the International Carriage of Goods by Road (Carriage of Goods by Road Act 1965, sch., art. 31(5)).

Security for costs as a sanction or condition

The conditions for ordering security for costs in the RSC were regarded as a complete and exhaustive code of circumstances in which security could be ordered (see *Condliffe v Hislop* [1996] 1 WLR 753). The court now has wider powers under the CPR. **65.7**

Under **r. 3.1(5)**, the court may order a party to pay a sum into court where it has failed to comply with a rule, practice direction or pre-action protocol. Under this provision an order may be made which is tantamount to an order for security for costs (*Olatawura v Abiloye* [2002] EWCA Civ 998, [2003] 1 WLR 275).

Under **r. 3.1(3)(a)** any order of the court may be made subject to a condition to pay a sum of money into court, and there is a cross-reference to this provision after **r. 24.6** (court's powers when it determines an application for summary judgment). In *CIBC Mellon Trust Co. v Mora Hotel Corporation NV* [2002] EWCA Civ 1688, [2003] 1 All ER 564, an order for a stay of an application to set aside a default judgment was made subject to a condition that the stay would be lifted if security for the costs of the application was given, and this part of the order was upheld by the Court of Appeal. The **r. 3.1(3)(a)** power cannot be used independently: it can only be used to attach a condition to an order made in the exercise of another power of the court. However, a stay can be ordered under **r. 3.1(2)(f)** 'in any appropriate case' (*CIBC Mellon Trust Co. v Mora Hotel Corporation NV* at [20]) and a condition for security for costs can then be added (at [21]).

The court should exercise its power under **r. 3.1(3)(a) or (5)** to require a payment into court only in limited circumstances, and should only do so in the absence of good faith on the part of the party against whom the order is sought (*CIBC Mellon Trust Co. v Mora Hotel Corporation NV* at [38]). An order for payment in should not be made without first giving the unsuccessful party three days' notice and an opportunity to file evidence as to their means. Such notice can be informal in the form of a letter from one party to another (*Anglo-Eastern Trust Ltd v Kermanshahchi* [2002] EWCA Civ 198, LTL 22/2/2002). An order for security for costs imposed when granting an adjournment at the request of the party obtaining the benefit of the security was set aside in *Dardana Ltd v Yukos Oil Co.* [2002] EWCA Civ 543, [2002] 1 All ER (Comm) 819. See **chapter 46**, especially **46.19**.

Resident outside the jurisdiction

65.8 As from 1 April 2003, condition (a) in **CPR, r. 25.13(2)**, applies to a claimant, whether a natural or legal person, who is resident out of the jurisdiction and outside the States covered by the EU's Jurisdiction and Judgments Regulation and the Brussels and Lugano Conventions (see **16.1**). (Previously, condition (a) dealt with individuals ordinarily resident outside this area and condition (b) — since revoked — dealt with companies and corporations.) In *Levene v Commissioners of Inland Revenue* [1928] AC 217 Viscount Cave LC quoted with approval the *Oxford English Dictionary* definition of 'reside' as 'To dwell permanently or for a considerable time, to have one's settled or usual abode, to live, in or at a particular place'. There is no general principle that a claimant outside the jurisdiction will be ordered to provide security if he fails to disclose where his assets are located (*Somerset-Leeke v Kay Trustees* [2003] EWHC 1243 (Ch), [2004] 3 All ER 406).

Applications for security on the ground of residence outside the jurisdiction almost always turn on the exercise of the court's discretion. The general factors considered are discussed at **65.16** to **65.20**. Factors particularly relevant on this ground are discussed at **65.21** to **65.23**.

65.9 **EU residents** There has been some controversy over whether making an order for security for costs against a national of another EU country on the ground of residence outside the jurisdiction offends against art. 12 of the EC Treaty, which provides: 'Within the scope of application of this Treaty, and without prejudice to any special provisions contained therein, any discrimination on grounds of nationality shall be prohibited'. As nearly all EU nationals protected by art. 12 reside in Regulation or Convention States, this should no longer be a major issue. At one time it was held that there was a valid distinction between residence, which founds the jurisdiction to order security for costs, and nationality (see *Berkeley Administration Inc. v McClelland* [1990] 2 QB 407). This stance is now discredited, and the current approach, based on the ECJ decision of *Mund & Fester v Hatrex Internationaal Transport* (case C-398/92) [1994] ECR I-467, is that an English court should never exercise its discretion to order security for costs against an individual who is a national of and resident in another member State of the EU.

Security for costs can be ordered where the claimant is resident in a State outside the scope of the **Regulation** or the Conventions, even if the claimant has assets within such a State (*De Beer v Kanaar and Co.* [2001] EWCA Civ 1318, [2003] 1 WLR 38).

65.10 **Companies resident outside Great Britain** Although most companies reside in the country where they are incorporated, strictly they reside where their central control and management are. This is a question of fact. In *Re Little Olympian Each Ways Ltd* [1995] 1 WLR 560 Lindsay J identified the following as matters to be considered: the contents of the company's objects clause, its place of incorporation, where its real trade or business is carried on, where its books are kept, where its administrative work is done, where its directors meet or reside, where it 'keeps house', where its chief office is situated, and where its secretary resides.

Impecunious British companies can be ordered to provide security for costs under the Companies Act 1985, s. 726, so ordering an impecunious company registered in another EU country to provide security for costs does not offend against art. 12 of the EC Treaty (*Chequepoint SARL v McClelland* [1997] QB 51).

The Companies Act 1985, s. 726(1), does not apply to companies registered in Northern Ireland (*Wilson Vehicle Distributions Ltd v Colt Car Co. Ltd* [1984] BCLC 93; *DSQ Property Co. Ltd v Lotus Cars Ltd* [1987] 1 WLR 127). However, an impecunious company ordinarily resident in Northern Ireland may be ordered to provide security under **CPR, r. 25.13(2)(c)** (*Re Dynaspan (UK) Ltd* [1995] 1 BCLC 536).

65.11 **Joint claimants** Security for costs may be ordered where there are joint claimants, some of whom are resident outside the jurisdiction. According to Lord Donaldson of Lymington MR in *Corfu Navigation Co. v Mobil Shipping Co. Ltd* [1991] 2 Lloyd's Rep 52 the basic principle underlying **CPR, r. 25.13(2)(a)**, is that it is prima facie unjust for a foreign claimant, who is in practical terms almost immune from the enforcement of any costs order that may be made, to be allowed to proceed with a claim without making funds available within the jurisdiction against which such an order can be enforced. Thus in *Okotcha v Voest Alpine Intertrading GmbH* [1993] BCLC 474 the court ordered security against a Nigerian company even though it was wholly owned by the co-claimant who would proceed with the claim in any event. It would, however, be appropriate to refuse to order security where it is probable that each of the joint claimants will be held to be liable for all the defendant's costs if the action is unsuccessful, provided the English claimants are likely to be able to pay those costs (see *Winthorp v Royal Exchange Assurance Co.* (1755) 1 Dick 282 as explained in *Slazengers Ltd v Seaspeed Ferries International Ltd* [1987] 1 WLR 1197 and in the light of *Corfu Navigation Co. v Mobil Shipping Co. Ltd*). Conversely, security may well be ordered where the English claimants are joined for the purpose of defeating an application for security (*Jones v Gurney* [1913] WN 72), or where it is impossible to predict the likely outcome on costs, or where each claimant is likely to be liable for only a portion of the defendant's costs (*Slazengers Ltd v Seaspeed Ferries International Ltd* [1987] 1 WLR 1197, [1988] 1 WLR 221).

Impecunious limited company

Impecuniosity is no ground for ordering security for costs against an individual claimant, the principle being that individuals should not be prevented from seeking justice through want of means. Companies, being artificial persons, need no such protection. **65.12**

The defendant has the burden of proving that a claimant company will be unable to pay any costs that ultimately may be awarded in the defendant's favour. Proof that the company is in liquidation is prima facie evidence that it will be unable to pay any costs order (*Northampton Coal, Iron and Waggon Co. v Midland Waggon Co.* (1878) 7 ChD 500). The section requires credible testimony of the company's inability to pay. This usually requires a comparison between the company's assets and the likely costs. The crucial question is whether the company will be able to meet the costs order at the time when the order has to be paid (*Re Unisoft Group Ltd (No. 2)* [1993] BCLC 532 at p. 534). A net asset balance is not therefore determinative of whether a company can pay a costs liability when it falls due: the court must consider the nature and liquidity of the company's assets (*Thistle Hotels Ltd v Gamma Four Ltd* [2004] EWHC 322 (Ch), [2004] 2 BCLC 174; *Longstaff International Ltd v Baker and McKenzie* [2004] EWHC 1852 (Ch), [2004] 1 WLR 2917).

Inability to pay may be inferred from evidence that the claimant has declared unusually large dividends after the dispute arose (*Frost Capital Europe Ltd v Gathering of Developers Inc. Ltd* (2002) LTL 20/6/2002). Evidence of these matters should be included in the written evidence in support of the application. For example, in *Cheffick Ltd v JDM Associates* (1988) 43 BLR 52, the company's assets amounted to £1.2 million, and the defendant's costs were assessed at £800,000. Clearly, the claimant also had a large potential liability in costs to its own solicitors. It was held to be wrong in principle to order security against the company in view of its substantial assets. An offer undertaking to pay any costs ordered against the claimant by a related company was treated as a concession that the claimant was unable to pay the defendant's costs in *Longstaff International Ltd v Baker and McKenzie*. It may not be right to order security against a company which has no assets but which can meet the costs out of income (*Kim Barker Ltd v Aegon Insurance Co. (UK) Ltd* (1989) *The Times*, 9 October 1989).

Nominal claimant

The court can order security against a nominal claimant (other than a representative appointed under **CPR, Part 19**) if there is reason to believe that he will be unable to pay the defendant's costs if ordered to do so (**r. 25.13(2)(f)**). The court is required to look at the reality of the situation. The fact that others will benefit from the claim does not render **65.13** the claimant a nominal one. In *Farmer v Moseley (Holdings) Ltd* [2001] 2 BCLC 572 Neuberger J said that, in determining whether a claimant is a nominal claimant, assistance may be gained by looking 'with circumspection' at pre-CPR authorities (see **1.20** to **1.23**). In the 19th century the requirement for a nominal claimant to give security was primarily intended to deal with a claimant who assigned a cause of action to a person of no means, but in fact under the claimant's control, so as to avoid liability for costs (this situation is now specifically provided for in **r. 25.14**). In some cases under the old rules security was ordered when a claimant became insolvent, so that the claimant's creditors would be the recipients of the fruits of the claim (for example, *Lloyd v Hathern Station Brick Co. Ltd* (1901) 85 LT 158; *Semler v Murphy* [1968] Ch 183). In more recent cases it has been stressed that security will not be ordered unless there is something more than the mere existence of others who will benefit from the fruits of the claim but who will not be liable if the claim fails (*Envis v Thakkar* [1997] BPIR 189; *Farmer v Moseley (Holdings) Ltd*). In *Envis v Thakkar* Kennedy LJ said that in his view, 'before a person can be branded as a nominal [claimant] . . . there must be some element of deliberate duplicity or window-dressing which operates and probably was intended to operate to the detriment of the defendant'.

Change of address

65.14 Rule 25.13(2)(d) of the CPR is aimed at the claimant who seeks to go to ground to avoid the possibility of having to pay the defendant's costs (*Aoun v Bahri* [2002] 3 All ER 182). Rule 25.13(2)(d) may be engaged where a claimant changes address more than once, so that the relevant change is not from the address stated on the claim form. In *Aoun v Bahri* the claimant was resident outside the jurisdiction when proceedings were issued, and subsequently moved to an address in England. Doing this to prevent an order for security for costs under r. 25.13(2)(a) would have given grounds for ordering security under r. 25.13(2)(d). On the facts it was held that the move had been for personal reasons.

Taken steps to avoid enforcement

65.15 Rule 25.13(2)(g) of the CPR is not concerned with the claimant's motivation. It does not use the phrase 'with a view to' which can be found in r. 25.13(2)(d), so it is simply a question of whether the effect of the steps taken by the claimant with his assets is to make it more difficult to enforce an order for costs against him (*Aoun v Bahri* [2002] 3 All ER 182). On the facts, the sale of the claimant's home in Australia made it more difficult to enforce a costs order against him, and security was ordered. However, there has to be some connection between the steps alleged to have been taken to avoid enforcement and the proceedings. Examples are *Paragon Investments Inc. v Sharma* (2002) LTL 22/11/2002, where the assets were moved several years before the proceedings, and *Somerset-Leeke v Kay Trustees* [2003] EWHC 1243 (Ch), [2004] 3 All ER 406, where the claimant had moved to Monaco many years before the events involved in the claim.

EXERCISE OF THE COURT'S DISCRETION

Factors to be taken into consideration

65.16 Once it has been established that the case comes within one of the conditions set out in **65.6**, the court has a general discretion whether to grant an order for security. In exercising this discretion the court will have regard to all the circumstances of the case and consider whether it would be just to make the order (see **CPR, rr. 25.13(1)(a)** and **25.14(1)(a)**). There is a conflict in the Court of Appeal authorities on whether it is appropriate to consider the pre-CPR cases on the exercise of the discretion to award security for costs. It is submitted that the better view, which is consistent with the CPR being a new procedural code, is that stated in *Nasser v United Bank of Kuwait* [2001] EWCA Civ 556, [2002] 1 WLR 1868, which is that the substantial body of pre-CPR case law on the subject is consigned to history. Instead, the discretion has to be exercised applying the overriding objective, and by affording a proportionate protection against the difficulty identified by the ground relied upon as justifying security for costs in the case in question. The contrary view is supported by *Vedatech Corporation v Seagate Software Information* [2001] EWCA Civ 1924, LTL 29/11/2001, where an appeal was allowed because the judge had failed to take into account the fact that a Part 36 offer had been made, with particular reliance being placed on pre-CPR cases such as *Sir Lindsay Parkinson and Co. Ltd v Triplan Ltd* [1973] QB 609.

Thus, where security is sought against a claimant outside the EU and Lugano Convention States, the order should reflect the obstacles in the way, or the costs of, enforcing an English judgment for costs against the particular claimant or in the particular country concerned. In the context of applications against impecunious limited liability companies, it is suggested that one of the key factors will be that it is generally unjust for a defendant to have to defend with no realistic prospect of recovering its costs even if successful, but that security should not be in an amount that would stifle an apparently genuine claim. It is further suggested that the following factors should be taken into account:

(a) The risk of not being able to enforce a costs order, and/or the difficulty or expense of being able to enforce a costs order, if the defendant is awarded costs.
(b) The merits of the claim, where this can be investigated without holding a mini-trial (*Porzelack KG v Porzelack (UK) Ltd* [1987] 1 WLR 420; *Swain v Hillman* [2001] 1 All ER 91). This has an impact on the risk of needing to enforce a costs order against the claimant.
(c) Whether the defendant may be able to recover costs from someone other than the claimant.
(d) The impact on the claimant of having to give security. In some cases a substantial order for security will effectively deprive the claimant of the ability to take the claim to trial. Where the claimant is sheltering in a tax haven the court is unlikely to be very sympathetic, but where the claimant's inability to pay has been caused by the defendant's conduct complained of in the claim, a substantial order may unjustly stifle the claim.
(e) Whether the claimant's difficulty (if any) in being able to provide security has been caused by the defendant's activities. If so, security may well be refused (*Interoil Trading SA v Watford Petroleum Ltd* [2003] EWHC 1806 (Ch), LTL 16/7/2003).
(f) Delay in making the application. Generally the application should be made shortly after proceedings are commenced, and delay may be reflected either in refusing the application or reducing the amount of security ordered.
(g) Suspicions about the claimant's financial position if the claim is lost are material (*Frost Capital Europe Ltd v Gathering of Developers Inc. Ltd* (2002) LTL 20/6/2002, where the person in control of the claimant company refused to provide a guarantee for the costs).

Human rights considerations

An order which requires a litigant to pay a sum which the litigant cannot afford may amount to a breach of the right of access to a court guaranteed by the **European Convention on Human Rights, art. 6(1)**. For a full discussion see **97.45**. See also **65.19** on the court's reluctance to make an order for security which would stifle a genuine claim. **65.17**

See also the discussion in **65.22** of potential discrimination contrary to **arts 6(1) and 14 of the Convention** when making orders for security against persons not resident in Regulation or Convention States.

Prospects of success

There is no doubt that the prospect of success at trial is one of the matters that may sometimes be taken into account on the application (*Frost Capital Europe Ltd v Gathering of Developers Inc. Ltd* (2002) LTL 20/6/2002). If this is taken too far, an application for security may be blown up to an investigation similar to a trial. Robert Walker LJ in *Zappia Middle East Construction Co. Ltd v Clifford Chance* [2001] EWCA Civ 946 and also in *Antonelli v Allen* [2001] EWCA Civ 1563 said that evidence as to the merits of the claim or appeal is seldom helpful in an **65.18** application for security for costs, and is rarely decisive unless it makes out an exceptionally strong case that a meritorious claim or appeal is likely to be stifled if security for costs is ordered. In a passage approved by the Court of Appeal in *Trident International Freight Services Ltd v Manchester Ship Canal Co.* [1990] BCLC 263, Browne-Wilkinson V-C in *Porzelack KG v Porzelack (UK) Ltd* [1987] 1 WLR 420 said at p. 423:

> Undoubtedly, if it can clearly be demonstrated that the [claimant] is likely to succeed, in the sense that there is a very high probability of success, then that is a matter that can properly be weighed in the balance. Similarly, if it can be shown that there is a very high probability that the defendant will succeed, that is a matter that can be weighed. But for myself I deplore the attempt to go into the merits of the case, unless it can clearly be demonstrated one way or another that there is a high degree of probability of success or failure.

In the Commercial Court investigation of the merits is strongly discouraged (**Admiralty and Commercial Courts Guide, app. 16, para. 4**). Courts will keep control of applications in the interest of litigants in other actions by excluding evidence and making penal costs orders where the parties transgress the line and seek to delve into the merits in too much detail.

If there is no defence to the claim, it will almost certainly be unjust to order security. In such a case the defendant is highly unlikely to recover costs in any event, and ordering security often has the practical effect of preventing the claimant from proceeding with the claim. Lord Denning MR in *Sir Lindsay Parkinson and Co. Ltd v Triplan Ltd* [1973] QB 609 said at p. 627:

> . . . I am quite clear that a payment into court, or an open offer, is a matter which the court can take into account. It goes to show that there is substance in the claim: and that it would not be right to deprive the company of it by insisting on security for costs.

In *Vedatech Corporation v Seagate Software Information* [2001] EWCA Civ 1924, LTL 29/11/2001, the Court of Appeal set aside an order for security, holding that the judge had been wrong in not taking into account the fact that the defendant had made a substantial Part 36 offer. The decision in *Simaan General Contracting Co. v Pilkington Glass Ltd* [1987] 1 WLR 516, where Judge Newey QC held that the public policy protecting without-prejudice negotiations prevented their use in security for costs applications in assessing the claimant's prospects of success, is inconsistent with *Vedatech Corporation v Seagate Software Information* and (from a different context) *Family Housing Association (Manchester) Ltd v Michael Hyde and Partners* [1993] 1 WLR 354, and it is submitted that Judge Newey's decision should not be followed.

Stifling a genuine claim

65.19 Where the claimant's claim has a good chance of success (there being no need for anything higher), the court will hesitate before making an order which will have the practical effect of preventing the claimant from proceeding. The essential policy is that the need to protect the defendant has to yield to the claimant's right of access to the courts to litigate the dispute if it is a genuine claim (*Hamilton v Al Fayed (No. 2)* [2002] EWCA Civ 665, [2003] QB 1175, a case on costs orders against non-parties, where the importance of the **European Convention on Human Rights, art. 6(1)**, was stressed). If the case is one where the court feels that security should be ordered, it can fix the amount of the security at a level which will not stifle the claimant in proceeding further (*Innovare Displays plc v Corporate Broking Services Ltd* [1991] BCC 174). In deciding whether a claim is likely to be stifled by an order for security for costs, the court is entitled to take into account any ability the claimant might have of raising money from friends, relatives, or if it is a company, its directors, shareholders, or other backers or interested persons. As this information is likely to be entirely within the claimant's knowledge, it is generally for the claimant to satisfy the court that it would be prevented from continuing the litigation by reason of the order (*Flender Werft AG v Aegean Maritime Ltd* [1990] 2 Lloyd's Rep 27), though there are cases where the court will be prepared to infer that the company will be prevented from pursuing its claim if security is ordered (*Trident International Freight Services Ltd v Manchester Ship Canal Co.* [1990] BCLC 263 as interpreted in *Keary Developments Ltd v Tarmac Construction Ltd* [1995] 3 All ER 534).

Delay in applying

Applications for security for costs should be made at an early stage in the proceedings. Lateness may of itself be a reason for refusing an order (*PR Records Ltd v Vinyl 2000 Ltd* (2002) LTL 9/12/2002). There have been cases where security has been refused because the application was made just a few days or even a few hours before the trial. In *Innovare Displays plc v Corporate Broking Services Ltd* [1991] BCC 174 the trial was fixed for 25 January 1991, the application seeking security was issued on 21 December 1990 and was heard on 17 and 24 January 1991. The claimants were in financial difficulties, and throughout had encountered problems in raising money to fight the action. The defendants sought to excuse their late application by saying that it was not until mid December that the claimants confirmed that the action would proceed. They did not want to waste money making applications if there was a chance that the action would not proceed. Once they were told that it would, they acted with proper dispatch. However, their solicitors had written to the claimants' solicitors in November 1990 warning that if agreement to provide security for their costs was not forthcoming by 15 November 1990, an application for security would be made. It was held that they had not acted with all due expedition, but they were not so dilatory that they had to be deprived entirely of security. A reduced order was made. **65.20**

Lateness is regarded even more seriously when the application for security is made in a pending appeal to the Court of Appeal. Thus, an application for security was dismissed solely because of its lateness in *A Co. v K Ltd* [1987] 1 WLR 1655 when it was made 14 days before the hearing. In that case Sir John Donaldson MR mentioned that 'proportionality' may have a bearing on the discretion whether to grant security. The claimants had obtained judgment for $US2.6 million, and it seemed the defendants' only asset in the jurisdiction was $US830,000 which was in court. The costs of the appeal were £20,000, which the Master of the Rolls regarded as quite a tiny sum in proportion to the other sums at stake.

An order for security for costs made shortly before trial may be made in an 'unless' form rather than in the usual form of staying the claim until security is provided (*Vedatech Corporation v Crystal Decisions* (UK) Ltd [2002] EWCA Civ 357, LTL 28/1/2002). Care must be taken that any such order does not act oppressively or disproportionately, and consequently it may not be right to order a large sum to be paid into court within a short period of time.

Claimant resident outside Regulation and Convention States

In *Porzelack KG v Porzelack (UK) Ltd* [1987] 1 WLR 420 Browne-Wilkinson V-C said: **65.21**

> The purpose of ordering security for costs against a [claimant] ordinarily resident outside the jurisdiction is to ensure that a successful defendant will have a fund available within the jurisdiction of this court against which it can enforce the judgment for costs. . . .
>
> [The court has] an entirely general discretion either to award or refuse security, having regard to all the circumstances of the case. . . . The question is what, in all the circumstances of the case, is the just answer.

In *De Bry v Fitzgerald* [1990] 1 WLR 552 Lord Donaldson of Lymington MR said that the rationale of **CPR, r. 25.13(2)(a)**, is that a defendant should be entitled to security if there is reason to believe that, in the event of succeeding and being awarded the costs of the claim, there will be real difficulty in enforcing the order. If the difficulty arises from where the claimant chooses to live and the location of the claimant's assets, so that an order for costs will be unenforceable or only enforceable with a significant expenditure of time or money, the defendant should be entitled to security. It is difficulty in enforcing in the place where the assets are likely to be, rather than enforcement in the country where the respondent happens to live, that has to be considered (*Aims Asset Management Sdn Bhd v Kazakhstan Investment Fund Ltd* [2002] EWHC 3225 (Ch), LTL 23/5/2002).

Country of residence Given that ease of enforcement is an important consideration, much turns on the actual country where the claimant's assets are situated. **65.22**

'Outside the jurisdiction' (in **CPR, r. 25.13(2)(a)(i)**) means outside England and Wales. There is unchallenged authority that security for costs will not be ordered against a resident of another part of the United Kingdom (*Raeburn v Andrews* (1874) LR 9 QB 118), because English judgments can be enforced in Scotland and Northern Ireland by mere registration under the Judgments Extension Act 1868. It is for similar reasons, combined with the effect of the EC Treaty, art. 12, that security for costs will not be granted against a person against whom an English judgment can be enforced under **Council Regulation (EC) No. 44/2001** or the Brussels or Lugano Conventions (**CPR, r. 25.13(2)(a)(ii)**; *Bunzl v Martin Bunzl International Ltd* (2000) *The Times*, 19 September 2000). Security for costs is therefore unavailable on the ground of residence against most claimants living in Europe.

The next category of countries is those with which there is a reciprocal enforcement convention, to which the Foreign Judgments (Reciprocal Enforcement) Act 1933 applies, see **chapter 77**. Denning J rejected an attempt to extend *Raeburn v Andrews* to such cases in *Kohn v Rinson and Stafford (Brod) Ltd* [1948] 1 KB 327. Nevertheless, a claimant can seek to defeat an application for security by adducing written evidence that any order for costs may be cheaply and easily enforced in the claimant's country of residence. The onus is on the claimant. Orders have been refused on account of the ease of enforcement in Monaco (*Somerset-Leeke v Kay Trustees* [2003] EWHC 1243 (Ch), [2004] 3 All ER 406) and the British Virgin Islands (*Longstaff International Ltd v Baker and McKenzie* [2004] EWHC 1852 (Ch), [2004] 1 WLR 2917). Ease of enforcement is not the sole or decisive factor, and may be outweighed by other matters (*Thune v London Properties Ltd* [1990] 1 WLR 562).

The final category comprises the rest of the world. In these cases the court will do what is just in the circumstances (*Leyvand v Barasch* (2000) *The Times*, 23 March 2000). Any order for security for costs must be objectively justified, and not be discriminatory (*Nasser v United Bank of Kuwait* [2001] EWCA Civ 556, [2002] 1 WLR 1868; *Zappia Middle East Construction Co. Ltd v Clifford Chance* [2001] EWCA Civ 946). **Rule 25.13(2)(a)** does not mean that a claimant can be ordered to provide security for costs merely because of not residing in a Regulation or Convention State: that would be discrimination in providing access to the courts, contrary to the **European Convention on Human Rights, arts 6(1)** and **14**. An order for security for costs under **r. 25.13(2)(a)** should reflect the obstacles in the way, or the costs of, enforcing an English judgment for costs against the particular claimant or in the particular country concerned (*Nasser v United Bank of Kuwait*). As Gross J said in *Texuna International Ltd v Cairn Energy Ltd* [2004] EWHC 1102 (Comm), [2005] 1 BCLC 579, the court has to decide whether the claimant's country is:

(a) one where the obstacles to enforcement are so great that the claimant should be required to give security for the whole costs of the claim; or
(b) one where enforcement is simply more expensive than in England and Wales. In these cases the security should reflect the likely additional expense.

Security may be ordered where it is obvious that enforcement will be difficult and costly, particularly where the claimant is a one-ship company resident in, say, Panama or Liberia (see the judgment of Parker LJ in *Berkeley Administration Inc. v McClelland* [1990] 2 QB 407; *Aims Asset Management Sdn Bhd v Kazakhstan Investment Fund Ltd* [2002] EWHC 3225 (Ch), LTL 23/5/2002).

65.23 **Factors where claimant resident outside Regulation and Convention States** Since the effectiveness of enforcement is the most important consideration, the following factors need to be taken into account if present:

(a) Whether the claimant has substantial assets within the jurisdiction. If it has this is a weighty factor against ordering security (*De Bry v Fitzgerald* [1990] 1 WLR 552). Assets within the jurisdiction include damages which the claimant hopes to recover in other proceedings (*Cripps v Heritage Distribution Corporation* (1999) *The Times*, 10 November 1999).

(b) The degree of fixity or permanence of those assets, and whether the claimant has a substantial connection with this country (*Leyvand v Barasch* (2000) *The Times*, 23 March 2000).
(c) Whether the claimant is impecunious. In *Thune v London Properties Ltd* [1990] 1 WLR 562 the bankruptcy of the claimants outweighed the ease of enforcement in Norway, where the claimants were resident.
(d) The ability of the claimant to transfer assets around the world, as in *Berkeley Administration Inc. v McClelland* [1990] 2 QB 407.
(e) Any lack of information, or refusal to provide information, about the claimant's assets (*Paragon Investments Inc. v Sharma* (2002) LTL 22/11/2002; *Zappia Middle East Construction Co. Ltd v Clifford Chance* [2001] EWCA Civ 946).
(f) Any evidence of misapplication of the claimant's assets (*Paragon Investments Inc. v Sharma*).

Claimant an impecunious limited company

As with foreign claimants, the rationale behind ordering security against an impecunious **65.24** company is to safeguard the defendant against the prospect of encountering real difficulty in enforcing any order for the costs of the action. Describing the effects of the Companies Act 1985, s. 726, Megarry V-C in *Pearson v Naydler* [1977] 1 WLR 899 said, at p. 906:

> It is inherent in the whole concept of the section that the court is to have power to order the company to do what it is likely to find difficulty in doing, namely to provide security for the costs which *ex hypothesi* it is likely to be unable to pay. At the same time, the court must not allow the section to be used as an instrument of oppression, as by shutting out a small company from making a genuine claim against a large company.

One factor mentioned by Lord Denning MR in *Sir Lindsay Parkinson and Co. Ltd v Triplan Ltd* [1973] QB 609 is whether the company's want of means has been brought about by any conduct by the defendant, such as, in an action for breach of contract, delay in payment or the defendant's delay in performing its part of the contract.

AMOUNT

Procon (Great Britain) Ltd v Provincial Building Co. Ltd [1984] 1 WLR 557 establishes the principle that **65.25** any security should be such as the court thinks fit in all the circumstances. The court needs assistance on the amount of costs the defendant is likely to incur in the claim, and for this reason it is usual to exhibit a summary statement of costs to the defendant's evidence in support. Security may be ordered for the entire costs of the proceedings, or up to a future point in the claim, and may include past as well as future costs. There is no rule of practice that the court will always reduce the defendant's estimate by a third (*Procon (Great Britain) Ltd v Provincial Building Co. Ltd*), but it is usual to make a deduction from the defendant's costs estimate to take into account any likely reduction on assessment of costs, and also to make an arbitrary discount in respect of future costs to take account of the chances of settling.

In suitable cases the court may sit with a costs officer as an informal assessor (see **Admiralty and Commercial Courts Guide, app. 16, para. 7**).

As was mentioned at **65.19** and **65.20**, relevant factors going to the court's discretion which are in the claimant's favour, but which are not strong enough to deprive the defendant of an order for security, may be taken into account when deciding the amount of security to order. Thus, in *Innovare Displays plc v Corporate Broking Services Ltd* [1991] BCC 174, which was discussed at **65.20**, the lateness of the application and the difficulty faced by the claimants in providing security were taken into account by ordering the claimants to provide security in the sum of £10,000 when the defendant's estimated costs were £147,000. In contrast, it is wrong in principle to order merely nominal security on the ground that the defendant has known all along that the claimant is a company of limited means (*Roburn Construction Ltd v Williams Irwin (South) and Co. Ltd* [1991] BCC 726, where the judge's order for security in the sum of £5,000 out of estimated costs of £150,000 was increased to £40,000).

Security may be ordered in respect of the 'defendant's costs'. This may, according to *Noterise Ltd v Haseltine Lake and Co.* [1992] BCC 497, if the circumstances merit it, include costs the defendant may incur as against a co-defendant in contribution or indemnity proceedings.

Cases dealing with calculating the costs occasioned by bringing a counterclaim are considered at 65.3.

ORDER

65.26 Orders for security for costs should follow form PF 44 (**PD 4, table 2**). It is usual to require security to be given by payment into court, although bonds and guarantees are alternatives, as are solicitors' undertakings. Security for costs will not usually be allowed in the form of a charge on real property. If the property is valuable, there should be no difficulty in obtaining a bank guarantee or money to pay into court. If no bank would lend against the property, it follows that the security is inadequate (*AP (UK) Ltd v West Midlands Fire and Civil Defence Authority* [2001] EWCA Civ 1917, [2002] CPLR 57). Until security is given the claim will be stayed. If the claimant fails to provide security in compliance with the order, the defendant can apply for the action to be struck out (*Speed Up Holdings Ltd v Gough and Co. (Handly) Ltd* [1986] FSR 330), or the order may provide that the claim will be struck out automatically if security for costs is not provided within the time stated in the order (*Zappia Middle East Construction Co. Ltd v Clifford Chance* [2001] EWCA Civ 946; *Antonelli v Allen* [2001] EWCA Civ 1563). If security is provided, the claim continues. After trial, the defendant, if successful, will have a secured fund from which its costs can be paid.

In the Admiralty and Commercial Courts defendants are sometimes required to give undertakings in damages if security is ordered (**Admiralty and Commercial Courts Guide, app. 16, para.** 5), and instead of ordering a stay it is more usual to give a time for providing the security with liberty to apply for dismissal of the claim in the event of default (**para. 6**).

Applications to vary

65.27 An application to vary an order for security for costs may be made if there is a material change in circumstances since the order was made (*Gordano Building Contractors Ltd v Burgess* [1988] 1 WLR 890). An application to vary will be refused if it depends on evidence which was available at the time of the hearing at which the original order was made (*Gordano Building Contractors Ltd v Burgess*).

An agreement on the amount of security is not in itself an agreement not to seek further security at a later stage, so an application to increase the amount of security will be considered on the usual material change of circumstances test (*Kazakhstan v Istil Group Inc.* [2005] EWCA Civ 1468, [2006] 1 WLR 596). An agreement may include a term that the agreed security for costs will not be increased even if there is a material change in circumstances. In such a case the court retains a residual discretion to allow an increase, but only if the circumstances are wholly exceptional (*Kazakhstan v Istil Group Inc.*).

It is common for the court to order security for costs up to a certain stage in the proceedings, for example, a pre-trial review, at which point a further order may be made. Otherwise a party applying for variation of an order must show a relevant change. The courts will be astute to avoid an appeal dressed up as a further application and there will be a heavy burden on a party seeking a further order.

SUCCESS BY THE CLAIMANT

In cases where the claimant is successful, the trial judge will normally accede to an application on the claimant's behalf for the security money in court to be repaid to the claimant, or for the release of any other security. If the defendant wishes to appeal, however, the court has a discretion whether to impose a stay on the release of the security so as to provide continued security for the costs up to trial in the event that the defendant's appeal succeeds (*Stabilad Ltd v Stephens and Carter Ltd* [1999] 1 WLR 1201). The stay is simply to preserve the security for the costs to trial. The respondent to the appeal may make a separate application under **CPR, r. 25.15**, for security for the costs of the appeal. In considering whether to impose such a stay, Auld LJ said that the fact the claimant had succeeded at first instance was irrelevant. Factors to be considered were the risks of the claimant being unable to pay the costs to trial if the security was released, the claimant's need for the money provided as security for fighting the appeal, and the prospects of the appeal succeeding. **65.28**

By a combination of the **Supreme Court Act 1981, s. 15(3)**, and **CPR, rr. 25.12, 25.13** and **52.10**, it was held in *Dar International FEF Co. v Aon Ltd* [2003] EWCA Civ 1833, [2004] 1 WLR 1395, that the Court of Appeal has jurisdiction to order a claimant who was successful at first instance to provide security for the costs of the proceedings in the court below. It will be unusual for such an order to be made, not least because, if the claimant is based overseas, the order may be unenforceable.

Chapter 66 Costs Orders

INTRODUCTION

66.1 Legal costs will be incurred on behalf of a litigant from the time a solicitor is first consulted until the solicitor's retainer is terminated, perhaps after enforcement of any judgment that is obtained. The client (or the Legal Services Commission (LSC) if the client is publicly funded) bears the primary responsibility for paying its own solicitor's bill. The bill comprises the solicitor's remuneration for the work done on the case, together with counsel's and any experts' fees, court fees, and any other charges, expenses and disbursements.

Although each client is primarily responsible for its own solicitor's costs, it is usual for the successful party in an action to be awarded an order for costs against the unsuccessful party. However, there are different bases for assessing, on the one hand, the costs payable by a client to its own solicitor, and, on the other hand, the costs recoverable by a successful litigant from an unsuccessful litigant. The result is that even a successful litigant usually has to pay something to its own solicitor, and an unsuccessful litigant has to pay both its own solicitor's costs and a substantial proportion of the other side's costs.

Orders for costs are made both at the end of the trial and at the end of any interim hearings and enforcement proceedings made in the course of, or after judgment in, the proceedings. The costs of enforcement proceedings are often added to the judgment obtained in the action. The relationship between interim costs orders and the costs in the main action is considered at **66.26**.

CONTENTIOUS AND NON-CONTENTIOUS COSTS

66.2 Solicitors' costs are divided into contentious and non-contentious costs, the distinction being that contentious costs relate to cases where proceedings have been begun before a court (see the **Solicitors Act 1974, s. 87(1)**). Preliminary work in cases where proceedings are not issued and work in proceedings before tribunals and enquiries are regarded as being non-contentious.

When a claim is settled without issuing proceedings, the Court of Appeal in *Callery v Gray* [2001] EWCA Civ 1117, [2001] 1 WLR 2112 interpreted the phrase 'the risk of incurring a liability in those proceedings' in the **Access to Justice Act 1999, s. 29**, as referring to the risk of incurring a liability in proceedings had proceedings been issued (at [44] to [55]). That interpretation was not challenged in the House of Lords (*Callery v Gray (Nos. 1 and 2)* [2002] UKHL 28, [2002] 1 WLR 2000).

The rule dealing with costs-only proceedings (**CPR, r. 47.19**) uses the phrase 'the costs of the proceedings'. Consistently with *Callery v Gray* this was interpreted by *Crosbie v Munroe* [2003] EWCA Civ 350, [2003] 1 WLR 2033, at [34], as covering the costs leading up to the disposal of the substantive claim by a compromise agreement without a claim being issued. At [37] Brooke LJ said the same interpretation should be given to the phrase 'Paragraph 4A. 1 applies to all proceedings' in **PD Protocols, para. 4A. 2**, so the 'proceedings' for the purposes of that paragraph include dealings between solicitors for the parties even if the dispute is settled without the need to issue a claim form.

It is submitted that neither of these authorities alters the position under the **Solicitors Act 1974, s. 87(1)**, where the definition of contentious business refers to 'proceedings begun'. The key word is 'begun'. If a civil dispute is settled without issuing proceedings, the costs of negotiating the dispute are non-contentious under s. 87(1).

The technical position set out above is not changed if costs-only proceedings are issued under **CPR, r. 44.12A**. Rule 44.12A applies where the parties have compromised the substantive dispute and agreed which party is 'to pay the costs', but they have failed to agree 'the amount of those costs'. Nothing is said in r. 44.12A about whether 'the costs' or 'those costs' are contentious or non-contentious. In any event, the Civil Procedure Rule Committee has no power under the **Civil Procedure Act 1997** to make a rule altering a rule of law, and if it purported to do so it would be *ultra vires*. A distinction should be made between the costs of the substantive dispute, which remain non-contentious, and the costs of the Part 8 claim under **r. 44.12A**, which, because proceedings have been begun, will be contentious costs.

Most litigators who negotiate a settlement of a civil dispute without proceedings being issued would regard it as obvious that if they have agreed that one side will pay 'the reasonable' costs of the other side, those costs will be quantified as though they were contentious costs and on the standard basis. Unless there is something very unusual in the circumstances this is likely to be held to be the common intention of both sides, and an implied term will be found to that effect. Cautious litigators may feel it appropriate to set this out expressly, such as by agreeing: '[ ] shall pay the reasonable costs of [ ], to be quantified as if they were contentious costs on the standard basis'.

This chapter is mainly concerned with the rules relating to contentious costs.

GENERAL PRINCIPLES

66.3 The two main principles when it comes to deciding which party should pay the costs of an application or of the whole proceedings are:

(a) the costs payable by one party to another are in the discretion of the court (**Supreme Court Act 1981, s. 51; CPR, r. 44.3(1)**); and

(b) the general rule, as now stated in **r. 44.3(2)**, is that the unsuccessful party will be ordered to pay the costs of the successful party (' costs follow the event' in the old terminology).

Range of possible costs orders

66.4 Under **CPR, r. 44.3(6)**, there are seven possible variations from the main rule that the unsuccessful party should pay the whole of the successful party's costs. These variations are:

(a) that a party must pay only a proportion of another party's costs;
(b) that a party must pay a specified amount in respect of the other side's costs;
(c) that a party must pay costs from or until a certain day only;
(d) that a party must pay costs incurred before proceedings have begun;
(e) that a party must pay costs relating only to certain steps taken in the proceedings, although an order of this type can only be made if an order in either of the forms set out at (a) or (c) would not be practicable (**r. 44.3(7)**);
(f) that a party must pay costs relating only to a certain distinct part of the proceedings;
(g) that a party must pay interest on costs from or until a certain date, including a date before judgment.

All these variations restrict the amount of costs that a winning party may recover from the loser. They would seem appropriate, therefore, to mark the court's displeasure at some conduct on the part of the winning party, or to reflect a partial rather than a full win.

Discretion on costs

66.5 The discretion granted by the **Supreme Court Act 1981, s. 51(1)**, is very wide, and the courts are opposed to limitations being imposed on it by implication or rigid rules of practice (see *Aiden Shipping Co. Ltd v Interbulk Ltd* [1986] AC 965; *Bankamerica Finance Ltd v Nock* [1988] AC 1002). The court has full power to determine by whom and to what extent the costs of an action are to be paid (*Singh v Observer Ltd* [1989] 2 All ER 751). However, like any discretion, it must be exercised judicially and on reasons connected with the case (see *Donald Campbell and Co. Ltd v Pollock* [1927] AC 732, and the speech of Viscount Cave LC, which continues to represent the law after the introduction of the CPR, see *Groupama Insurance Co. Ltd v Aon Ltd* [2003] EWCA Civ 1846, [2004] 1 All ER (Comm) 893).

In exercising its discretion on costs the court is required to have regard to all the circumstances, and in particular to the following matters (**CPR, r. 44.3(4) and (5)**):

(a) the extent to which the parties followed any applicable pre-action protocol;
(b) the extent to which it was reasonable for the parties to raise, pursue or contest each of the allegations or issues;
(c) the manner in which the parties pursued or defended the action or particular allegations or issues;
(d) whether the successful party exaggerated the value of the claim;
(e) whether a party was only partly successful; and
(f) any payment into court or admissible offer to settle.

The first of these factors is one of the methods by which pre-action protocols will be enforced, albeit indirectly (others include a less tolerant attitude on applications by defaulting parties for more time and for relief from sanctions and the interest sanctions discussed in **chapter 46**). **PD Protocols, para. 2.3**, provides that if the court concludes that non-compliance with a pre-action protocol led to the commencement of proceedings which otherwise might not have been commenced, or to costs being incurred which might have been avoided, the court may order the defaulting party to pay all or part of those costs, or to pay those costs on an indemnity basis. Factors (b) and (e) indicate there will be a greater willingness than under the old system to take into account the extent to which the overall winner was in fact successful on the various issues, heads of claim etc. raised in the case, when dealing with costs. This is intended to support the aspects of the overriding objective relating to identifying the real issues in the case, and only pursuing those issues to trial (see **CPR, r. 1.4(2)(b)** and **(c)**). The third factor, which covers unreasonable conduct, could also be used against parties who fail to conduct litigation in accordance with the overriding objective, such as those who are unreasonably uncooperative (see **r. 1.4(2)(a)**). Factors (b) and (c) seem to have been important in justifying reducing the costs ordered against the unsuccessful party in *Mansfield v Wright* (2000) LTL 17/7/2000, where both sides failed to act on an indication by the trial judge to attempt to negotiate a settlement when the trial was adjourned part heard. Exaggeration of the value of a claim (factor (d)) will obviously be relevant where the claim is inflated for the purpose of bringing it in the High Court or to have the case allocated to a higher track than it deserves. It could also be used in cases where exaggeration of the claim makes it difficult for the defendant to assess its true value for the purposes of making an offer to settle or a payment into court.

Shirley v Caswell [2001] Costs LR 1 is a decision on its facts, and does not lay down a principle that orders for payment of a proportion of the other side's costs should not be made in certain circumstances (such as after service of notice of discontinuance). See *Dooley v Parker* [2002] EWCA Civ 1188, LTL 5/7/2002.

Costs follow the event

The rule that costs follow the event generally means that the successful party will obtain a **66.6**
costs order against the loser. So in *Islam v Ali* [2003] EWCA Civ 612, LTL 26/3/2003, the court reversed the trial judge's costs order where he had failed to give due regard to the fact that the defendant had won in principle. See also *Adamson v Halifax plc* [2002] EWCA Civ 1134, [2003] 1 WLR 60. The starting point is that the winner should recover its costs as against the unsuccessful party, although there are factors which may lead to a different order and they are discussed below. In *Scherer v Counting Instruments Ltd* [1986] 1 WLR 615 the Court of Appeal set out the following principles for the award of costs:

(a) The normal rule is that costs follow the event. The party who turns out to have unjustifiably either brought another party before the court, or given another party cause

to have recourse to the court to obtain his rights, is required to recompense that other party in costs; but
(b) The judge has, under the **Supreme Court Act 1981, s. 51**, an unlimited discretion to make what order as to costs he considers that the justice of the case requires.
(c) Consequently a successful party has a reasonable expectation of obtaining an order for his costs to be paid by the opposing party, but has no right to such an order, for it depends upon the exercise of the court's discretion.
(d) This discretion is not one to be exercised arbitrarily; it must be exercised judicially, that is to say, in accordance with established principles and in relation to the facts of the case.
(e) The discretion cannot be well exercised unless there are relevant grounds for its exercise, for its exercise without grounds cannot be a proper exercise of the judge's function.
(f) The grounds must be connected with the case. This may extend to any matter relating to the litigation, but no further. In relation to an interim application, 'the case' is restricted to the application, and does not extend to the whole of the proceedings (see *Hall v Rover Financial Services (GB) Ltd* [2002] EWCA Civ 1514, *The Times*, 8 November 2002).
(g) If a party invokes the jurisdiction of the court to grant him some discretionary relief and establishes the basic grounds therefor, but the relief sought is denied in the exercise of discretion, as in *Dutton v Spink and Beeching (Sales) Ltd* [1977] 1 All ER 287 and *Ottway v Jones* [1955] 1 WLR 706, the opposing party may properly be ordered to pay his costs. But where the party who invokes the court's jurisdiction wholly fails to establish one or more of the ingredients necessary to entitle him to the relief claimed, whether discretionary or not, it is difficult to envisage a ground on which the opposing party could properly be ordered to pay his costs.

Under the CPR, in *Johnsey Estates (1990) Ltd v Secretary of State for the Environment* [2001] EWCA Civ 535, LTL 11/4/2001, the court repeated the above principles but added that:
(a) A judge may make different orders in relation to discrete issues in the case and should do so where a party has been successful in relation to some issues and unsuccessful on others.
(b) A party which has behaved unreasonably in relation to the litigation may be deprived of some or all of its costs.

It is incumbent on a judge to give reasons for departing from the usual rule that costs follow the event (*Brent London Borough Council v Aniedobe (No. 2)* (1999) LTL 23/11/99). See also *Bellamy v Central Sheffield University NHS Trust* [2003] EWCA Civ 1124, LTL 2/7/2003. The approach, stated in *English v Emery Reimbold and Strick Ltd* [2002] EWCA Civ 605, [2002] 1 WLR 2409, to appeals against judgments with inadequate reasons (see **72.8**) applies also in this context (*Gould v Armstrong* [2002] EWCA Civ 1159, LTL 23/7/2002).

A court is not required to order costs. **CPR, r. 44.3(2)**, begins with the words 'If the court decides to make an order for costs'. Where a court feels that the appropriate exercise of the discretion leads to no order for costs, it may decline to make any order (*English v Emery Reimbold and Strick Ltd*).

Re Elgindata Ltd (No. 2) [1992] 1 WLR 1207 is authority for the proposition that a successful party is in normal circumstances entitled to have an order for costs against the loser, subject to limited exceptions such as where a successful party recovers no more than nominal damages or where the successful party has acted improperly or unreasonably. The Court of Appeal interfered with a costs order in *Alpha Chauffeurs Ltd v Citygate Dealership Ltd* [2002] EWCA Civ 207, LTL 21/2/2003, which placed the main burden of the costs on a party which had been broadly successful, and substituted an order complying with the principle that costs follow the event. Although *Re Elgindata Ltd (No. 2)* predates the CPR it has been applied in a number of cases under the CPR (for example, *AEI Rediffusion Music Ltd v Phonographic Performance Ltd* [1999] 1 WLR 1507) and the starting point in most applications for costs is that the loser should pay the winner's costs. *Re Elgindata Ltd (No. 2)* provides a useful guide to the court's approach, but it cannot fetter the general discretion the court has under **r. 44.3**. As Lightman J put it in *Bank* *of Credit and Commerce International SA v Ali (No. 4)* (1999) 149 NLJ 1734, 'The straitjacket imposed on the court by *Re Elgindata Ltd (No. 2)* . . . is gone, and the search for justice is untrammelled by constraints beyond those laid down by the new code [i.e., the CPR] itself'.

Pre-CPR authorities must be treated with caution. The introduction of the CPR has encouraged parties to narrow issues and focus their attention on the points of dispute in a proportionate way. The courts have been encouraged to examine the degree of success and to tailor their orders to reflect that success and the justice of the case. Courts will also consider in detail the conduct of the parties. This has led to courts making issue-based orders and percentage orders (see *Johnsey Estates (1990) Ltd v Secretary of State for the Environment* and *Gwembe Valley Development Co. Ltd v Koshy (No. 2)* (2000) *The Times*, 30 March 2000, though some difficulties in making such orders were identified in *Shirley v Caswell* [2002] Lloyd's Rep PN 955; see **66.11** to **66.14**)

Material change in successful party's case When the basis of a party's case is changed, that party usually has to amend their statement of case, which usually results in an order that they pay the costs of and occasioned by the amendments (see **66.31 and PD 19**). Sometimes the court goes further and makes an order for costs covering all or part of the proceedings (*Beoco Ltd v Alfa Laval Co. Ltd* [1995] QB 137). It is a frequent occurrence that the case that emerges at trial is not exactly the same as that set out in the statements of case. It is a question of degree whether this will require the statements of case to be amended, and in practice it is only substantial changes which justify such a course. Likewise, it is a question of degree whether any difference between the pleaded case and the facts as they emerge at trial justify departing from the general rule that costs follow the event. It is wrong to depart from the general rule where any differences are small (*Alli v Luton and Dunstable NHS Trust* [2005] EWCA Civ 551, LTL 27/4/2005). Where the differences are material, and particularly where the losing party may have been misled, it would be appropriate to deprive the successful party of some or all of their costs. **66.7**

Where there is no 'event' In *Dearling v Foregate Developments (Chester) Ltd* [2003] EWCA Civ 913, LTL 9/6/2003, at the invitation of the judge the parties had negotiated a commercial settlement with the defendant making a modest payment to the claimant. In the circumstances the settlement did not reflect the merits of the case, and it was impractical for the court to look into the facts. It was held that in the absence of any good reason for making some other order, the fall-back position was to make no order as to costs. Contrast *BCT Software Solutions Ltd v C. Brewer and Sons Ltd* [2003] EWCA Civ 939, LTL 11/7/2003, where an apportionment of costs by the trial judge after the claim was compromised, but with costs to be determined by the judge, was upheld on appeal. A judge limited to determine costs may legitimately decide there is no complete agreement to compromise a claim if the parties have not agreed the question of costs (see *BCT Software Solutions Ltd v C. Brewer and Sons Ltd*). **66.8**

Success and State benefits

In *McCaffery v Datta* [1997] 1 WLR 870, the claimant was given judgment in a personal injuries case for £22,373. There had been a payment into court (which, under the CPR, would be a **Part 36** payment) of £2,500 (the maximum exempt sum under the former provisions of the Social Security Administration Act 1992) some time before trial. The amount of recoupable benefits under the Act was £25,419. The effect was that all the damages awarded had to be paid by the defendant to the compensation recovery unit of the Department of Social Security, leaving the claimant with nothing. In those circumstances the defendant contended that it should recover its costs from the date of the payment in. The Court of Appeal held that although the claimant had recovered nothing in the action, it could not be said that the defendant, who had to pay £22,373, was successful. The judge's costs order was therefore varied so as to award the claimant the costs of the action. **66.9**

The general costs rules where there has been a **Part 36** payment are considered at **64.40** to **64.42**. How those rules relate to benefits recoupment was considered in *Bajwa v British Airways plc* [1999] PIQR Q152. In this case the defendant paid into court the sum of £2,500 at a time when the CRU certificate was in the sum of £2,573.34. It was held that the effective payment in was these two sums added together, that is, £5,073.34. At trial the claimant recovered £4,874.43. An appeal against the CRU certificate resulted in the recoupable benefits being reduced to £142.80. The defendant therefore had to pay £142.80 to the Secretary of State and £4,731.63 to the claimant. However, the important figures for costs purposes were the judgment (£4,874.43), which was less than the effective payment in (£5,073.34). The correct order on costs was that the claimant should recover her costs to the last date for accepting the payment in, but had to pay the defendant' s costs thereafter.

Nominal damages

66.10 A claimant who has claimed substantial damages, but has only recovered nominal damages, will normally be ordered to pay the defendant's costs (*Texaco Ltd v Arco Technology Inc.* (1989) *The Times*, 13 October 1989; *Mappouras v Waldrons Solicitors* [2002] EWCA Civ 842, LTL 30/4/2002; for an exceptional case in which no order as to costs was made see *Bank of Credit and Commerce International SA v Ali (No. 4)* (1999) 149 NLJ 1734). Where a claimant recovers more than nominal damages, but only a small proportion of the amount claimed, costs should follow the event unless this conflicts with some other established principle (*Gupta v Klito* (1989) *The Times*, 23 November 1989), for example, that costs will be reduced if a claim has been exaggerated (see **66.15**).

Partial success

66.11 **Partial success to be taken into account** The conduct that has to be taken into account in deciding orders as to costs includes whether the claimant has succeeded in whole or in part (**CPR, r. 44.3(5)(d)**), and also includes whether it was reasonable for a party to raise, pursue or contest a particular allegation or issue (**r. 44.3(5)(b)**). It may therefore be wrong in principle to allow a party all its costs where it has been unsuccessful on some issues, and hence such an order may in some circumstances be overturned on appeal (*Winter v Winter* (2000) LTL 10/11/2000; *Darougar v Belcher* (2002) LTL 25/7/2002). Before the introduction of the CPR, an 'issue' for this purpose was a matter which in itself either gave a right to relief or constituted a defence. Thus, in running-down actions it was held that liability and quantum were separate issues (see *Wagstaffe v Bentley* [1902] 1 KB 124), but negligence and contributory negligence were not (see *Quirk v Thomas* [1916] 1 KB 516). The CPR avoid the word 'issue' and the phrase 'cause of action', and instead refer to a party being successful 'on part of his case' (**r. 44.3(4)(b)**). This is certainly a deliberate move away from the old technical cases (see, by analogy, *Stock v London Underground Ltd* (1999) *The Times*, 13 August 1999, a case dealing with **Part 36** payments). The result is that the court may reflect partial success in the order for costs whenever as a matter of reality the overall winner has not been totally successful, whether or not the partial failure was on a matter constituting of itself a right to relief or defence.

Winter v Winter (2000) LTL 10/11/2000 also made the point that the CPR have changed the position regarding awarding the whole costs to a party meeting with 'substantial success'. In *Stocznia Gdanska SA v Latvian Shipping Co.* (2001) *The Times*, 25 May 2001, Thomas J said that the reasonableness of raising an issue which was lost by the party who was the overall winner is not necessarily relevant to the question of depriving the successful party of part of its costs under **r. 44.3(4)(b)**. In *Carver v Hammersmith and Queen Charlotte's Health Authority* (2000) LTL 7/3/2001 Nelson J held that the appropriate way on the facts for dealing with a claimant who won, but had to abandon a number of issues, and who had been guilty of delay, was to deprive her of 15 per cent of her costs.

66.12 **Principles** It is suggested that the following principles emerge from the authorities:

(a) The courts are likely to concentrate on whether a party was successful on an issue not the reasonableness of raising the issue in the first place (*AEI Rediffusion Music Ltd v Phonographic Performance Ltd* [1999] 1 WLR 1507; *Stocznia Gdanska SA v Latvian Shipping Co. (No. 2)* [1999] 3 All ER 822).
(b) A party which abandons issues, either prior to, or during, a trial, may be taken to have lost on those issues, which may be reflected in the order as to costs (*English v Emery Reimbold and Strick Ltd* [2002] EWCA Civ 605, [2002] 1 WLR 2409; *Carver v Hammersmith and Queen Charlotte's Health Authority* (2000) LTL 7/3/2001).
(c) There will often be an overlap in the evidence relating to issues upon which a party is successful and those upon which it fails. This has to be taken into account. In such circumstances it may be appropriate to award the successful party a proportion of its costs taking into account the fact that the paying party will have to pay its lawyers for the entire costs of the proceedings (*Liverpool City Council v Rosemary Chavasse Ltd* (1999) LTL 19/8/99, in which the court discounted the successful party's costs to 75 per cent).
(d) The award of costs to the successful party may be tempered by the manner in which it took the points, hence late amendment may lead to the loss of some or all of the costs up to the point of amendment and, in extreme cases, the award of the costs of the claim up to amendment against the successful party (for example, *Antonelli v Allen* (2000) *The Times*, 8 December 2000).
(e) Whether the issues on which the successful party lost materially contributed to the costs of the proceedings. If they had a negligible impact on overall costs, it may be appropriate to award the successful party all its costs (*Fleming v Chief Constable of Sussex* [2004] EWCA Civ 643, LTL 5/5/2004).
(f) Where it is clear there has been partial success, but (as happens sometimes when costs are reconsidered on appeal) there is inadequate material on which to decide on an apportionment, no order as to costs may be the appropriate order (*Hackney London Borough Council v Campbell* [2005] EWCA Civ 613, LTL 28/4/2005).

The above points can only represent a guide, and there is a danger that too much can be read into any single case. The courts are anxious to preserve a wide degree of flexibility and discretion in the award of costs. As Lightman J put it in *Bank of Credit and Commerce International SA v Ali (No. 4)* (1999) 149 NLJ 1734:

> My task is . . . to take an overview of the case as a whole . . . and reach a considered conclusion on two questions, first who succeeded in the action, and second (taking into account the answer to the first issue) what order for costs justice requires.

Percentage or issues-based costs orders Where both parties are successful on some, but not all, of the issues in a case, the court may, instead of awarding the whole costs of the action to the ultimately successful party, award the costs of proving some of the issues to the unsuccessful party. The usual approach in the event of partial success is to award the successful party a percentage of its costs rather than an 'issues-based' order (see **CPR, r. 44.3(7)**, which says that an issues-based order should only be made when other forms of order are impracticable). In *English v Emery Reimbold and Strick Ltd* [2002] EWCA Civ 605, [2002] 1 WLR 2409, at [115], Lord Phillips of Worth Matravers MR said that making issues-based orders create difficulties at the stage of assessing costs because the costs judge has to master the issues in detail before determining whether individual items are attributable to issues which have been allowed or disallowed. It is for this reason that percentage orders are generally to be preferred. See also *Budgen v Andrew Gardner Partnership* [2002] EWCA Civ 1125, *The Times*, 9 September 2002. **66.13**

Success on liability, refusal of relief Related problems arise in cases where the claimant succeeds in proving the pleaded cause of action, but is not awarded any relief or remedy. Obviously, if damage is part of the cause of action, as in negligence, then the defendant succeeds and should get the costs of the action. Where, conversely, relief is refused on discretionary grounds, further investigation or analysis may be necessary before the question **66.14**

of costs can be decided. If it should have been clear to the claimant that no relief would be granted, costs should be awarded to the defendant. If the matter preventing the court from granting the remedy sought arose during the course of the litigation, such as the appointment of an administrator preventing the court granting relief under an unfair prejudice petition under the Companies Act 1985, s. 459, probably the best result would be for the claimant to be awarded costs up to the date of the event preventing relief being granted, and for the defendant to be awarded costs thereafter. See *Re a Company (No. 008126 of 1989)* [1992] BCC 542.

66.15 **Opponent's case unclear** In *Sengoz v Secretary of State for the Home Department* [2001] EWCA Civ 1135, *The Times*, 13 August 2001, an appeal from a tribunal was discontinued when the Secretary of State agreed to the matter being reheard before the tribunal. The court accepted that, until the grounds of appeal were fully considered, the Secretary of State was not in a position to decide on the appropriate course to take. In the circumstances there was no order as to costs.

Misconduct by the successful party

66.16 **Principles** Misconduct by the successful party may result in costs not following the event (**CPR, r. 44.3(4)(a)**). Misconduct for this purpose must relate to the proceedings, and exterior dishonest conduct is not a basis for depriving a successful party of its costs (*Hall v Rover Financial Services (GB) Ltd* [2002] EWCA Civ 1514, *The Times*, 8 November 2002, albeit a decision which was regarded as no more than a statement of practice in *Groupama Insurance Co. Ltd v Aon Ltd* [2003] EWCA Civ 1846, [2004] 1 All ER (Comm) 893). The court can take into account conduct before, as well as during, the proceedings, and in particular the extent to which the parties followed any relevant pre-action protocol. It can also take into account the manner in which a party pursued or defended the claim or a particular issue or allegation, and whether the claim was exaggerated by the claimant (**r. 44.3(5)**). In *Hobbs v Marlowe* [1978] AC 16 the successful claimant was deprived of all of his costs apart from the issue fee because he had exaggerated his claim to avoid the action being referred to small-claims arbitration.

A party wishing to raise an issue relating to the conduct of another party should argue the matter before the judge dealing with the costs order (often the trial judge) rather than before the costs judge dealing with any detailed assessment of costs (*Aaron v Shelton* [2004] EWHC 1162 (QB), [2004] 3 All ER 561). Leaving the point until the assessment stage will usually be an abuse of process (see **33.16**). When a conduct point is raised, the trial judge can determine it, or may direct that it be dealt with by the costs judge on assessment (*Aaron v Shelton*). Where a claim or application is disposed of by consent, but the parties cannot agree on costs, because of a dispute about conduct, it is open to the parties to agree to refer the conduct point to a costs judge for determination (*Aaron v Shelton*).

66.17 **Misconduct and final costs orders** Much depends on the nature of the misconduct and its consequences. Misconduct which might justify depriving the successful party of its costs would not necessarily be sufficient to justify an order requiring the successful party to pay the unsuccessful party's costs (see *Scherer v Counting Instruments Ltd* [1986] 1 WLR 615 at p. 622). A successful defendant was deprived of half the costs of the hearing in *Cable v Dallaturca* (1977) 121 SJ 795 for failing to serve an expert's report in accordance with the rules of court. In *Liverpool City Council v Rosemary Chavasse Ltd* (1999) LTL 19/8/99 (discussed at **66.11**) the successful council had acted in flagrant disregard for the approach embodied in the CPR, and left matters to the last minute. This resulted in a costs order being reduced from 75 per cent to 50 per cent. In *Grupo Torras SA v Al-Sabah* (5 July 1999 unreported) a claim had been made against a number of defendants in conspiracy, dishonest assistance in breach of trust and related causes of action. The claims against the fourth, sixth and tenth defendants failed because the claimant failed to prove the essential element of dishonesty as against them. Mance LJ, who was the trial judge, held the fourth defendant would only recover 50 per cent of his costs because, although he did not realise there was a fraud, he was involved in deliberately backdating relevant documentation. The sixth defendant only recovered one third of his costs. He was the finance director of one of the companies, and had deliberately deceived the auditors and gave untrue evidence at trial. The tenth defendant was a professional man who had created false documentation, misled the auditors and gave untruthful evidence at trial. He too only recovered one third of his costs. In *Groupama Insurance Co. Ltd v Aon Ltd* [2003] EWCA Civ 1846, [2004] 1 All ER (Comm) 893, a second defendant which had to some extent brought the proceedings on itself by its conduct, but which succeeded at trial, recovered 90 per cent of its costs from the unsuccessful first defendant.

In *Smiths Ltd v Middleton (No. 2)* [1986] 1 WLR 598 the defendant had made a payment into court exceeding the amount recovered by the claimants, but the judge made no order as to costs after the payment in, because the defendant had brought the action on himself through keeping incomplete accounting records. A claimant who would have lost on the original statements of case, but who won on the basis of an amendment made at a very late stage was ordered to pay the defendant's costs of the action in *Anglo-Cyprian Trade Agencies Ltd v Paphos Wine Industries Ltd* [1951] 1 All ER 873.

Misconduct and interim costs orders A failure to make full and frank disclosure which was **66.18** not sufficiently serious to justify discharging a without notice order was nevertheless used to justify depriving the successful party of 25 per cent of the costs of an interim application to discharge the order in *Re Industrial Services Group Ltd (No. 1)* [2003] BPIR 392. In *R (Teleos plc) v Commissioners of Customs and Excise* [2005] EWCA Civ 200, [2005] 1 WLR 3007, the claimant issued an interim payment application which came on for hearing seven days later. The defendant's evidence was largely an analysis of material supplied by the claimant and was served about the day before the hearing. Skeleton arguments were exchanged on the day before the hearing. The application was dismissed. In those circumstances the Court of Appeal held the judge had been wrong to make no order as to costs. There was insufficient time to negotiate (so as to avoid the need for a hearing), due to the short period secured by the claimant for the hearing. Although the defendant's evidence was technically late, there was no prejudice. An order for costs to follow the event under **CPR, r. 44.3(2)(a)**, was substituted.

In *Jones v University of Warwick* [2003] EWCA Civ 151, [2003] 1 WLR 954, an enquiry agent tricked his way into the claimant's home posing as a market researcher and covertly filmed the claimant carrying out functions inconsistent with her claimed disability. The court allowed the video evidence but ordered the insurer to pay the costs of the admissibility hearing to mark the court's disapproval of the defendant's conduct.

Refusal to participate in ADR A successful party may be deprived of its costs for **66.19** unreasonably refusing to participate in arbitration or mediation procedures. In *Dunnett v Railtrack plc* [2002] EWCA Civ 303, [2002] 1 WLR 2434, a successful appellant was deprived of its costs when it refused mediation because it was not prepared to pay the claimant any further sum and was confident that it would succeed in its appeal. In depriving the successful party of its costs the court stated that parties and their lawyers should ensure that they are aware that it is one of their duties fully to consider ADR, especially when the court has suggested it, and not merely to turn it down flatly. In *Leicester Circuits Ltd v Coates Industries plc* [2003] EWCA 333 Civ, LTL 5/3/2003, a successful appellant was deprived of costs when it withdrew from mediation shortly before the trial.

An order depriving a successful party of its costs is an exception to the rule that costs follow the event. The burden is on the unsuccessful party to establish that the rule should be departed from on the ground of an unreasonable refusal to agree to ADR (*Halsey v Milton Keynes General NHS Trust* [2004] EWCA Civ 576, [2004] 1 WLR 3002). Factors relevant to the question of whether a refusal to agree to ADR was unreasonable include, but according to Dyson LJ are not limited to:

(a) the nature of the dispute;
(b) the merits of the case (it may not be reasonable for a party with a weak case to insist on use of ADR);
(c) the extent to which other settlement methods had been attempted;
(d) whether the costs of the ADR procedure would be disproportionately high;
(e) whether any delay in setting up and attending the ADR procedure would be prejudicial; and
(f) whether it would be just to impose a costs sanction.

There is no presumption in favour of mediation or other forms of ADR. Each case depends on its own circumstances. A public authority is treated in the same way as any other category of party, and is under no additional responsibility to agree to the use of ADR.

Where a party reasonably declines mediation it will not be penalised in costs (*Société Internationale de Télécommunications Aéronautiques SC v Wyatt Co. (UK) Ltd* [2002] EWHC 2401 (Ch), LTL 15/11/2002). In *Hurst v Leeming* [2002] EWHC 1051 (Ch), [2003] 1 Lloyd's Rep 379, Lightman J held that a refusal to mediate was only justified if it would have no reasonable prospect of success. Refusing to negotiate after receiving Part 36 offers is unlikely to be unreasonable, see *Daniels v Commissioner of Police for the Metropolis* [2005] EWCA Civ 1312, *The Times*, 28 October 2005, discussed at **64.50**. Small building disputes are one kind of case for which mediation is suitable (*Burchell v Bullard* [2005] EWCA Civ 358, [2005] BLR 330).

See also **70.13**.

Other costs sanctions

66.20 As well as disallowing costs, the court has various other powers that may be exercised to reflect a finding of misconduct against either party. These powers include:

(a) Ordering costs to be paid on the indemnity basis rather than the standard basis. This is discussed in more detail at **66.20**.
(b) Ordering payment of interim costs forthwith, rather than requiring the party obtaining the costs order to wait until after trial for payment (**CPR, r. 44.3(1)(c)**). Note that an order stating the amount payable in respect of costs (such as a summary assessment) must be complied with within 14 days (**r. 44.8**).
(c) Ordering payment of interest on costs from or until a certain date, including a date before judgment (**r. 44.3(6)(g)**). The normal rule is that **Judgments Act 1838** rate interest (currently 8 per cent a year simple interest) is payable on costs arising from court orders and judgments from the date of the judgment on liability.
(d) Ordering interest on costs at a rate different from the **Judgments Act 1838** rate (e.g., **PD Protocols, para. 2.3(4)**, which allows the court to impose interest on costs at a rate up to 10 per cent above base rate in cases where a protocol has been breached leading to proceedings being commenced which might otherwise have been avoided).

Indemnity-basis costs to reflect misconduct

66.21 One of the circumstances in which the court may order one party to pay another party's costs on the indemnity basis (see **68.37**) is where the court wishes to penalise the paying party for its misconduct in relation to the proceedings. Where the losing party has acted consistently throughout, the absence of proportionality on an indemnity-basis assessment is a factor in favour of awarding costs on the standard basis (*Simms v Law Society* [2005] EWCA Civ 849, [2005] ACD 98).

The Court of Appeal has declined to set out principles on which the discretion to award indemnity-basis costs is to be exercised, beyond stating that an indemnity costs order will be appropriate where the facts of the case or the conduct of the parties removes it from the norm (*Excelsior Commercial and Industrial Holdings Ltd v Salisbury Hamer Aspden and Johnson* [2002] EWCA

Civ 879, *The Independent*, 18 June 2002). It follows that the following list can only be taken as indicative of situations where an indemnity costs order might be made:

(a) Where the claim is an abuse of the court's process. In *R (Taha) v Lambeth London Borough Council* (Administrative Court 7 February 2002), the defendant council had failed to process a housing benefit application for eight months. It then sought possession on the basis of eight weeks' rent arrears. It was ordered to pay the tenant's costs on an indemnity basis. See also *Sodeca SA v NE Investments Inc.* [2002] EWHC 1700 (QB), LTL 27/8/2002.

(b) Where a party is involved in dishonesty, or has acted in such a way as deserves condemnation (*Sea Wanderer Ltd v Nigel Burgess Ltd* (CA 1990 unreported); *Wailes v Stapleton Construction and Commercial Services Ltd* [1997] 2 Lloyd's Rep 112). For example, indemnity-basis costs were ordered in *Somatra Ltd v Sinclair Roche and Temperley* [2002] EWHC 1627 (Comm), LTL 21/10/2002, where a well-known firm of solicitors launched an unjustifiable wholesale attack on a former client and gave unreliable evidence.

(c) Where the party's conduct of the litigation has removed it from the usual and made it appropriate for an indemnity order to be made. In *Cooper v P and O Stena Line Ltd* [1999] 1 Lloyd's Rep 734 the court condemned an allegation of malingering as one of fraud which should be pleaded as such. In fact there was no evidence to support the allegation and indemnity costs were ordered. See also *Craig v Railtrack plc* [2002] EWHC 168 (QB), LTL 18/2/2002, and *Kiam v MGN Ltd (No. 2)* [2002] EWCA Civ 66, [2002] 1 WLR 2810, in which it was said that indemnity-basis costs would be justified if the conduct of the claim was unreasonable to a high degree.

(d) Flagrant breaches of court orders, including unless orders (*Baron v Lovell* [1999] CPLR 630).

(e) Unreasonable pursuit of a weak claim or defence. See, for example, *Amoco (UK) Exploration Co. v British American Offshore Ltd* [2002] BLR 135. There must be something to mark the case out as unusual (*Shaina Investment Corporation v Standard Bank London Ltd* [2002] CPLR 14). Having a weak case does not justify an indemnity basis costs order, but having a case doomed to failure may do so. In *Wates Construction Ltd v HGP Greentree Allchurch Evans Ltd* [2005] EWHC 2174 (TCC), LTL 4/11/2005, an indemnity-basis costs order was made from the point, after the exchange of witness statements, when the claimant knew or ought to have known the case would fail.

(f) Failure to send a letter before claim (*Phoenix Finance Ltd v Fédération Internationale de l'Automobile* [2002] EWHC 1028 (Ch), *The Times*, 27 June 2002).

(g) Where litigation has been pursued for extraneous motives. In *Amoco (UK) Exploration Co. v British American Offshore Ltd* the claimant conducted itself on the basis that its commercial interests took precedence over all other considerations.

The above examples all suggest some degree of turpitude and condemnation from the court, but this is not a necessary prerequisite for an indemnity costs order (*Reid Minty v Taylor* [2001] EWCA Civ 1723, [2002] 1 WLR 2800). Indemnity-basis costs may be awarded, without necessarily being a penalty for misconduct, where a rejected Part 36 offer has turned out to be better than the judgment: see **64.41** and **64.43**. There are other special cases where indemnity-basis costs will be ordered because of the nature of the litigation (see **66.46** and **66.47**).

Indemnity costs in favour of a publicly funded party There has been debate about whether it is appropriate to make an indemnity costs order in favour of a party in receipt of public funding. The award of costs is compensatory and the litigant should not profit from any costs order made. In normal circumstances an indemnity costs order will ensure that the receiving party will receive more of their costs from the paying party (see **68.37**). However, a party in receipt of public funding has no obligation to pay costs. Thus the lawyer may receive a windfall, being the difference between a public funding assessment and an indemnity assessment. This reason for not awarding indemnity costs was rejected in *Brawley v Marczynski* **66.22**

(No. 2) [2002] EWCA Civ 1453, [2003] 1 WLR 813, in which it was held that an indemnity costs order can be made in favour of a publicly funded party where the court intends to mark its disapproval of the paying party's conduct.

Claims wrongly commenced in the High Court

66.23 Where a claim has been commenced in the High Court which should have been commenced in a county court in accordance with the **Courts and Legal Services Act 1990, s. 1**, or any other enactment, the court must take that error into account when quantifying costs (**Supreme Court Act 1981, s. 51(8)**). Usually this will result in a reduction in the costs which would otherwise be allowed, but such reduction must not be in excess of 25 per cent.

Costs of unnecessary attendance

66.24 A party should not be ordered to pay the costs of another party who need not have attended a hearing (*Cullen v Paterson* [2002] EWCA Civ 339, LTL 8/3/2002). Respondents who file written submissions or attend on applications for permission to appeal are in particular danger of being deprived of their costs, even if permission to appeal is refused (*Jolly v Jay* [2002] EWCA Civ 277, *The Times*, 3 April 2002; **PD 52, paras 4.23 and 4.24**).

INFORMING THE CLIENT

66.25 Where a costs order is made against a legally represented client who is not present in court when the order is made, the solicitor representing the client is under a duty to inform the client of the costs liability within seven days of the order being made (**CPR, r. 44.2**). The 'client' includes an insurer, trade union, the LSC or other body which has instructed the solicitor or is liable for the solicitor's fees (**PD 43–48, para. 7.1**). At the same time as informing the client about the order, the solicitor should explain why it was made. The court has the power to order the solicitor to produce evidence that reasonable steps were taken to comply with the duty to notify the client (**PD 43–48, para. 7.3**).

INTERIM COSTS ORDERS

66.26 At the end of almost every interim application, and when almost any interim application is disposed of by consent, an order will be made or agreed declaring which party should pay the costs of that application. Costs of interim applications are in the discretion of the court, but the discretion is usually (but not always) exercised in favour of the party who was successful in the application. Success may be established either by winning a contested application, or by showing that the need to make the application arose through the default of the other party. Other types of application are essentially of a case management nature, so there is no 'winner', and in these applications the costs are usually treated as part of the general costs of the claim. After proceedings have been dismissed the court still has jurisdiction to make an order concerning the costs of an application in the proceedings (*Re Ryan Developments Ltd* [2002] EWHC 1121 (Ch), [2002] 2 BCLC 792). To cater for these various possibilities (and situations where neither party is entirely successful) the courts can resort to a wide selection of different interim costs orders.

PD 43–48, para. 8.3, provides that the court may make an order about costs at any stage in a case, and in particular it may make interim costs orders when it deals with interim applications.

Unless costs are reserved (see term 13 in **table 66.1** below) at the first hearing, the court on a second hearing (unless it is an appeal) in the same claim has no jurisdiction to make a costs order in respect of the first hearing. In *Griffiths v Commissioner of Police of the Metropolis* [2003] EWCA Civ 313, LTL 5/3/2003, there was an interim hearing at which the judge ordered that a wasted costs order (see **66.68**) in respect of the costs of the interim hearing against the claimant and his solicitor be considered at the trial. This order was defective because it made no provision for who should pay the costs of the interim hearing, which meant that each side had to bear its own costs (see term 18 in **table 66.1**), whereas the judge plainly intended the claimant to have to pay the defendant's costs. On appeal it was held that the trial judge had no jurisdiction to make an order as to the costs of the interim hearing.

Summary assessment of interim costs

The costs of an interim hearing which has lasted less than a day ought to be dealt with by way of summary assessment there and then (**PD 43–48, para. 13.2(2)**). There are exceptions where there is good reason not to assess summarily (para. 13.2(3)). These are: **66.27**

(a) where there are substantial grounds for disputing the sum claimed (para. 13.2(3));
(b) where there is insufficient time to carry out the summary assessment (para. 13.2(3));
(c) where there are complex legal arguments (*R v Cardiff City Council, ex parte Browne* (QBD 11 August 1999, unreported));
(d) where the claim is a mortgage possession claim (**para. 13.3**);
(e) where the receiving party (as opposed to the paying party) is publicly funded (**paras 13.9 and 13.10**);
(f) where the receiving party (as opposed to the paying party) is under a disability (**para. 13.11(1) and (2)**);
(g) where there is a conditional fee agreement, the additional liability will not be assessed until the conclusion of the case (**para. 14.2**);
(h) where no statement of costs is served in time (see **32.26**, but see *MacDonald v Taree Holdings Ltd* [2000] CPLR 439, in which it was held that it may be permissible to conduct the summary assessment if time is given to the paying party to consider any schedule produced on short notice).

Where the court makes a summary assessment of interim costs, those costs will be stated in the order made by the court and will be payable in such period as the court decides (**CPR, r. 44.3**). Where the court does not specify a time for the payment of the costs, they are payable within 14 days (**r. 44.8**). Any application for an extension of time in which to pay such costs should be supported by evidence (*Pepin v Watts* [2001] CPLR 9).

Detailed assessment of interim costs

Orders for costs will be treated as requiring detailed assessment unless the order specifies the sum to be paid or states that fixed costs are to be paid (**PD 43–48, para. 12.2**). Detailed assessments generally take place after the proceedings are concluded (**CPR, r. 47.1**). The parties may agree in writing to treat the proceedings as concluded for this purpose (**PD 43–48, para. 28.1(3)**), and the court may make an order allowing detailed assessment proceedings to commence where there is no realistic prospect of the claim proceeding (**para. 28.1(5)**). **66.28**

MEANINGS OF COSTS ORDERS

Various standard forms of wording are regularly used by the courts to express the decision on the incidence of costs. Usually it will be apparent from the whole of the document recording the order whether the costs provision covers the whole proceedings, or just some part of the claim (such as the costs of an interim application). Some of the forms used can apply to both final and interim costs, and some of the commonly occurring decisions can be expressed using more than one form of words, so some care is needed. Table 66.1 sets out the meanings of the most commonly used forms of costs orders. More technical definitions for most of the terms can be found in **PD 43–48, para 8.5**. **66.29**

Table 66.1 Meanings of common costs orders

Term	Meaning
1. Claimant's costs	As a final order, the claimant is entitled to recover its costs of the proceedings from the defendant.
2. Defendant's costs	As a final order, the defendant is entitled to recover its costs of the proceedings from the claimant.
3. Claimant's costs	In an interim application, the claimant is entitled to recover its costs of the application from the defendant.
4. Defendant's costs	In an interim application, the defendant is entitled to recover its costs of the application from the claimant.
5. Claimant's costs in any event	Identical meaning to 1 and 3 above.
6. Defendant's costs in any event	Identical meaning to 2 and 4 above.
7. Costs in the case	This is an order made on interim applications and hearings, often where the court makes case management decisions or otherwise where there is no obvious winner of the interim application. The order means the interim costs form part of the general costs of the proceedings, so the party awarded its costs of the proceedings on the final disposal of the claim will be entitled to be paid its costs of the interim application.
8. Costs in the application	Identical meaning to 7 above.
9. Claimant's costs in the case	This is an order half-way between 3 and 7 above. It is typically used where the claimant has met with partial success on an interim application. It means that if the claimant is awarded its costs of the proceedings on the final disposal of the claim, it will be entitled to be paid its costs of the interim application, but if the defendant is awarded costs on the final disposal of the claim, each party bears its own costs of the interim application.
10. Claimant's costs in the application	Identical meaning to 9 above.
11. Defendant's costs in the case	This is the reverse of 9 above. If the defendant is awarded its costs of the proceedings on the final disposal of the claim, it will be entitled to be paid its costs of the interim application, but if the claimant is awarded costs on the final disposal of the claim, each party bears its own costs of the interim application.
12. Defendant's costs in the application	Identical meaning to 11 above.
13. Costs reserved	This is an interim costs order deferring the decision on costs to a later hearing, when the judge will usually make orders relating to both hearings. If the judge dealing with the second hearing does not make an order relating to the first hearing, the costs of that hearing are treated as being in the case (see 7 above). This form of order should not be used if nothing further can happen at the second hearing (which may be the trial) to affect the costs of the first hearing (*Elvee Ltd v Taylor* [2001] EWCA Civ 1943, [2002] FSR 48).
14. Costs thrown away	Broadly similar to 3 and 4 above. It is typically made when a judgment or order is set aside, such as on a successful application to set aside a default judgment. In such a case the order entitles the claimant to recover from the defendant the costs of: • preparing for and attending any hearing relating to making the original order or judgment that is now being set aside; • preparing for and attending any hearing to set aside the original order or judgment;

Term	Meaning
	• preparing for and attending any adjourned relevant hearing; and • any steps to enforce the original order or judgment.
15. Costs of and occasioned by	This is the usual order made when the court allows an application to amend a statement of case. See further **66.30**. This order requires the party making the amendment to pay the other party's costs of: • preparing for and attending any hearing seeking permission to amend; and • any consequential amendments to its own statement of case.
16. No order as to costs	Each party bears its own costs of the application or proceedings.
17. Each party to pay its own costs	Identical to 16 above.
18. Order silent on costs	The general rule is that neither side can recover costs (**CPR, r. 44.13(1)(a); PD 23, para. 13.2**). Exceptions cover: • trustees and personal representatives who can always recover their costs out of the fund (**CPR, r. 44.13(1)(b)**); • parties entitled to recover costs pursuant to a lease, mortgage or other security, who continue to be entitled to recover their costs under a provision of the contract (**r. 44.13(1)(b)**); and • orders granting permission to appeal, orders granting permission to apply for judicial review, and orders and directions made on applications without notice. These are deemed to include an order for the applicant's costs in the case (**r. 44.13(1A)**). Any party affected by such a deemed order for costs may apply at any time to vary the order (**r. 44.13(1B)**).
19. Costs here and below	This is an order often made on disposal of appeals. The party who is successful on the appeal is by this order entitled to recover its costs both of the appeal and in the court below. See **66.35**.
20. Detailed assessment of the costs of the [Claimant] which are payable out of the Community Legal Service Fund	Order authorising the court to assess the costs payable from public funds of a litigant (whether they are successful or not) with the benefit of public funding. This is the modern form of what used to be called a 'legal aid taxation' (**Supreme Court Costs Office Guide, para. 24.1(c)**).

Fit for counsel

PD 43–48, para. 8.7, allows the court when making a costs order for detailed assessment (including both interim costs orders and final costs orders made at trial) to state an opinion as to whether or not the hearing was fit for representation by one or more counsel. This will generally only be done where the paying party challenges the use of counsel, where the court wishes to record its opinion that the case was not fit for counsel, or where more than one counsel appeared for a party (**para. 8.7(3)**). **66.30**

COSTS OF PARTICULAR TYPES OF PROCEEDINGS

Amendment

The costs of and arising from any amendment to a statements of case are, unless the court orders otherwise, borne by the party making the amendment (see notes to **PD 19**). **66.31**

An order for payment of the costs of an amendment will also require payment of the costs of making consequential amendments to other documents. It is possible to ask for a less onerous costs order where, for example, the need to amend cannot be characterised as being the fault of the party seeking permission. Another point is that if permission is sought at a very late stage to make amendments having a fundamental effect on the way the case is set out, particularly where the other side are prejudiced, such as by being unable to make an effective **Part 36** payment, the court may impose very stringent costs terms when granting permission to amend. Thus in *Beoco Ltd v Alfa Laval Co. Ltd* [1995] QB 137 permission to amend was granted on terms that the claimant paid the defendant's costs up to the date of the amendment, and 85 per cent of the defendant's costs thereafter. Such a penal approach is not always correct. In *Professional Information Technology Consultants Ltd v Jones* (2001) LTL 7/12/2001 the claim succeeded on the basis of a late amendment, but this was reflected by simply reducing the costs of the claim recovered by the claimant by one third.

Costs of pre-commencement disclosure and disclosure against non-parties

66.32 Applications for pre-commencement disclosure and for orders against persons who are not parties for disclosure of documents were considered in **chapter 48**. The general rule is that the court must award the costs of the application to the person against whom the order is sought (**CPR, r. 48.1**). The practice has been to add the costs of the application as a head of damages in the case of pre-commencement disclosure. This may no longer be necessary as under the CPR the pre-commencement application is made in the same action as the main claim, whereas under the old system the application formed a separate action commenced by its own originating process. In the case of disclosure against a non-party the costs will be part of the costs of the claim, and should be dealt with by a specific costs order between the parties. The court retains a discretion to make a different costs order in a particular case, having regard to all the circumstances, including the extent to which it may have been reasonable for the respondent to have opposed the disclosure application (**r. 48.1(3)**). This may be the case where the respondent has failed to honour its obligations under the Access to Health Records Act 1990 (which applies to most medical records compiled since 1 November 1991) or under any applicable pre-action protocol (which will potentially apply to many applications for pre-commencement disclosure against likely defendants).

Costs after transfer

66.33 Subject to any order that may have been made by the original court, once a case is transferred, whether between the High Court and a county court, or between county courts, the new court will deal with all questions as to costs, including the costs incurred before the transfer (**County Courts Act 1984, s. 45; CPR, r. 44.13(3) and (4)**).

Costs before track allocation

66.34 The special rules relating to costs in cases on the small claims track and fast track do not apply until a claim is allocated to one of these tracks (**CPR, r. 44.9(1) and (2); PD 43–48, para. 15.1(1)**). Once a claim is allocated to either of these tracks the special rules relating to that track will apply to work done before as well as after allocation, with the exception that any costs orders made before a claim is allocated to one of these two tracks are not affected by any subsequent allocation (**PD 43–48, para. 15.1(2)**). This means, for example, that where default judgment is entered on a small-value claim, the costs restrictions in **CPR, Part 27**, do not apply, although the fixed costs rules in **Part 45** would be applied instead.

Where a matter has not been allocated to a track the court retains a general discretion as to costs, but will attach considerable weight to the track that the matter would have been allocated to. Thus in *Voice and Script International v Alghafar* [2003] EWCA Civ 736, LTL 8/5/2003, a failure to allocate the case to the small claims track did not preclude the court from awarding the costs as if it had been. Conversely in *Woodings v British Telecommunications plc* (2003) LTL 17/3/2003 several related claims were settled, without issuing proceedings, for less than £1,000 per claimant. Although this would normally have indicated that the claims were small claims, the court was persuaded that, because of the extent of the technical and medical evidence required, they would have been allocated to the multi-track and accordingly costs could be awarded as for that track.

Reallocation from the small claims track

66.35 Before making an order to reallocate a claim from the small claims track to another track, the court must decide whether any party is to pay costs to any other party down to the date of the reallocation order (**PD 43–48, para. 16.2**). Such costs must be those payable under **CPR, Part 27**, which in effect means that they are limited to fixed costs and any further costs which may be ordered for unreasonable behaviour (**r. 27.14**). If a costs order is made on reallocation, the court should make an immediate summary assessment of those costs (**PD 43–48, para. 16.3**). Fast track or multi-track costs rules will apply from the date of reallocation (**CPR, r. 27.15**).

Costs after an appeal

66.36 A court dealing with a case on appeal can make orders relating to the costs of the proceedings giving rise to the appeal as well as the appeal itself (**CPR, r. 44.13(2)**). If an appeal is successful, the appeal court may order the losing party to pay the costs 'here and below', or may make different orders relating to the proceedings at the two levels, or may leave the costs order of the court below undisturbed while making whatever order may be appropriate for the costs of the appeal. It may be appropriate to deprive a party of its costs if the decision on the appeal turned on points not raised bel ow, or on points not rai sed in the notice of appeal, or where the appeal is only partly successful or where the court's time has been wasted.

Wills cases

66.37 In a case involving a disputed will, costs normally follow the event. An alternative costs order may be made where the testator or those interested in the residue of the estate had been the cause of the litigation or if the circumstances led reasonably to an investigation. Applying these principles in *Re Good* [2002] EWHC 640 (Ch), *The Times*, 22 May 2002, Rimer J ordered the unsuccessful parties to pay only half the claimant's costs. In probate claims, a defendant requiring the will to be proved in solemn form (see **CPR, r. 57.7(5)**) will not be ordered to pay costs unless there is no reasonable ground for opposing the will (**Supreme Court Costs Office Guide, para. 2.8(e)**).

Winding-up petitions

66.38 The 'usual compulsory order' on winding-up a company includes provision for the payment of the petitioner's costs and one set of costs for the supporting creditors out of the assets of the company. It is therefore not the practice to ask for costs at the hearing. If there are opposing creditors and the petition succeeds, the costs of the opposing creditors are not paid out of the company's assets unless they are expressly allowed by the court (**Supreme Court Costs Office Guide, para. 2.13**).

Coroners, inferior courts and tribunals

66.39 Whether a coroner, inferior court or tribunal should be ordered to pay or recover its costs in proceedings to challenge its jurisdiction or decision largely depends on the stance it takes in the High Court. In *R (Davies) v HM Deputy Coroner for Birmingham* [2004] EWCA Civ 207, [2004] 1 WLR 2739, the Court of Appeal stated the following principles:

(a) The established practice is to make no order for costs where the inferior court or tribunal does not appear in the High Court (see also *Moore's (Wallisdown) Ltd v Pensions Ombudsman* [2002] 1 WLR 1649), unless there has been a flagrant instance of improper behaviour, or where the court or tribunal unreasonably refuses to sign a consent order.
(b) Where the inferior court or tribunal takes an active part, costs usually follow the event. Where the inferior court or tribunal loses, the costs it is usually ordered to pay are not

limited to the amount by which the costs of other parties were increased by its participation (*Moore's (Wallisdown) Ltd v Pensions Ombudsman*).

(c) Where the inferior court or tribunal plays a neutral role, assisting the High Court on matters of jurisdiction or procedure, the established practice is to make no order for costs for or against it. This is subject to the court's overall discretion on costs, which may make it just for the applicant to be compensated in costs out of public funds through a costs order against the inferior court or tribunal.

MISCELLANEOUS SITUATIONS IN WHICH COSTS DO NOT FOLLOW THE EVENT

66.40 The following are situations where costs orders usually do not follow the event.

(a) The costs of any application to extend time are borne by the party making the application

(b) A party failing to make admissions of facts or in relation to documents after service of a notice to admit facts or documents, or after service of a list of documents, is usually responsible for paying the costs of proving those matters.

(c) In actions under the Slander of Women Act 1891, costs must not exceed the damages awarded, unless the court is satisfied there were reasonable grounds for bringing the action.

(d) If successive actions are brought against persons jointly or otherwise liable for the same damage, costs will be ordered in favour of the claimant in the first action only unless there were reasonable grounds for bringing the later actions (**Civil Liability (Contribution) Act 1978, s. 4**).

MULTIPLE PARTIES AND CLAIMS

Multiple defendants

66.41 Where a claimant succeeds against joint tortfeasors, costs will be ordered against each defendant, and the claimant can then recover costs against any one (or more) of the defendants (*Niru Battery Manufacturing Co. v Milestone Trading Ltd* [2003] EWHC 1032 (Comm)). Any defendant paying such costs can then seek a contribution from the others under the **Civil Liability (Contribution) Act 1978**. If successful defendants are separately represented, the claimant should be liable for any additional costs only if the separate representation was reasonable. An example of what can happen where joint defendants are successful is *Korner v H. Korner and Co. Ltd* [1951] Ch 10. Eight defendants were jointly represented, and seven of them were successful in the action. It was held that generally the defence costs should be regarded as incurred by each defendant equally, which would in this case have resulted in the claimant paying seven eighths of the total defence costs. However, as different defences had been delivered for each defendant, each successful defendant was awarded one eighth of the general costs of the proceedings, together with such costs and counsel's fees as were attributable to their own defence.

Bullock and *Sanderson* orders

66.42 Where a claimant claims against two defendants in the alternative, and succeeds against one only, the court may, in its discretion, make a special order that the unsuccessful defendant must pay the successful defendant's costs (*Irvine v Commissioner of Police for the Metropolis* [2005] EWCA Civ 129, LTL 3/2/2005). It is clear that in this area the court has a wide measure of discretion (*Goldsworthy v Brickell* [1987] Ch 378). That said, from *Besterman v British Motor Cab Co.* [1914] 3 KB 181, it is apparent that, in deciding whether to make a special order, the court must first look at all the facts the claimant knew or could reasonably have discovered as at the date the defendants were joined and consider whether the joinder was reasonable. Factors bearing on this, according to the Court of Appeal in *Irvine v Commissioner of Police for the Metropolis*, include:

(a) whether the claims against the various defendants are made 'in the alternative';
(b) the nature of the evidence and allegations against the defendants who were eventually successful;
(c) whether the causes of action are connected with each other; and
(d) whether the unsuccessful defendant had blamed the other defendants.

If it was not reasonable to join the two defendants, costs should follow the event. In such a case the successful defendant will recover its costs from the claimant and the claimant will recover the costs of the claim against the unsuccessful defendant from the unsuccessful defendant. The unsuccessful defendant is not required to reimburse the claimant for the costs the claimant has to pay to the successful defendant.

If, on the other hand, it was reasonable to join the two defendants, the court has a choice of two special orders, the choice being in the court's discretion (per Lord Brandon of Oakbrook in *Bankamerica Finance Ltd v Nock* [1988] AC 1002). The special orders are known as *Bullock* orders, from *Bullock v London General Omnibus Co.* [1907] 1 KB 264, and *Sanderson* orders, from *Sanderson v Blyth Theatre Co.* [1903] 2 KB 533.

For the purposes of exposition, assume that the claim of the claimant ('C') against the first defendant ('D1') is dismissed, but that C obtains judgment against the second defendant ('D2'). In a *Bullock* order, C would be ordered to pay D1's costs, but would recover its own costs and would be reimbursed in respect of the costs it has had to pay to D1 from D2. The difference between a *Bullock* order and the usual rule that costs follow the event is that if costs followed the event C would not be reimbursed by D2 for the costs C had to pay D1. In a *Sanderson* order, D2 has to pay C's costs, and D2 also has to pay D1's costs direct. C has no liability to pay D1's costs. Provided all parties are solvent, the eventual effect of *Bullock* and *Sanderson* orders is the same. However, the *Bullock* form is more usual because it most closely follows the rule that costs follow the event. Traditionally, the *Sanderson* form has been said to be appropriate where C is either legally aided or insolvent, because in those circumstances only a *Sanderson* order adequately protects the successful D1. Despite the traditional view, a *Sanderson* order was upheld by the House of Lords in *Bankamerica Finance Ltd v Nock* [1988] AC 1002 where D2, not C, was insolvent, the judge having decided to make a *Sanderson* order because it tended to spread the hardship caused by irrecoverable costs most fairly between C and D1, the successful defendant.

Multiple claimants

66.43 Problems are not so likely to be caused through having different judgments in respect of different claimants because actions with joint claimants are only allowed to proceed if the claimants are jointly represented. It is implicit in this that there must be a large degree of identity of interest between the joint claimants, so split judgments must be very rare.

Counterclaims

66.44 Where the claim and counterclaim are unrelated, it may be appropriate to award the winner on the claim the costs of the claim and the winner on the counterclaim the costs of the counterclaim. The effect of this form of order was considered in *Medway Oil and Storage Co. Ltd v Continental Contractors Ltd* [1929] AC 88, where the House of Lords decided that this form of judgment entitled the defendant to all its costs of the action save those costs exclusively referable to the counterclaim. Under this principle there is no apportionment of costs, but items of costs common to both the claim and counterclaim, such as counsel's brief fee, may be divided between the claim and counterclaim. The distinction between apportionment and division is rather technical. The net effect of *Medway Oil and Storage Co. Ltd v Continental Contractors Ltd* is, if the issues on the claim and counterclaim are similar, that the party recovering costs of the claim obtains by far the largest share. Even before the introduction of the CPR it was recognised that this does not always produce a just result (per Denning LJ in *Chell Engineering Ltd v Unit Tool and Engineering Co. Ltd* [1950] 1 All ER 378). While the court continues to have the power to order a party to pay the costs relating to a distinct part of the proceedings (**CPR, r. 44.3(6)(f)**), it should only do so if it is not practicable to make an order for payment of a proportion of the other side's costs or costs from a certain date only (**r. 44.3(7)**). Where the claim and counterclaim are related to each other, the costs order should usually award a percentage of the total costs of claim and counterclaim to the party who has achieved overall success (*English v Emery Reimbold and Strick Ltd* [2002] EWCA Civ 605, [2002] 1 WLR 2409; *Burchell v Bullard* [2005] EWCA Civ 358, [2005] BLR 330).

Another refinement is typified by *Box v Midland Bank Ltd* [1981] 1 Lloyd's Rep 434. The claimant recovered £5,000, and the defendant established a £39,000 equitable set-off. The Court of Appeal held that the judge should have made no order for costs. The approach exemplified by *Medway Oil and Storage Co. Ltd v Continental Contractors Ltd* was recognised by the Court of Appeal in *Universal Cycles plc v Grangebriar Ltd* [2000] CPLR 42 as being the usual form of order where the claimant is successful on the claim and the defendant is successful on a counterclaim. Where there is a set-off, the Court of Appeal in *Universal Cycles plc v Grangebriar Ltd* approved the *Chell Engineering* approach of awarding the overall winner either the entire costs of the claim, or a proportion of those costs. In *Universal Cycles plc v Grangebriar Ltd* itself the claim was for the price of goods sold and delivered, and there was a counterclaim alleging the goods were not of satisfactory quality and not fit for their purpose, it being further alleged that the value of the counterclaim exceeded that of the claim. At trial judgment was given to the claimant for £109,000, and judgment for the defendant on the counterclaim for £25,000. Neither party wanted a costs order in the *Medway Oil* form. The judge awarded the claimant its costs to the date of the defence and counterclaim, and required the claimant to pay half the defendant's costs thereafter. The Court of Appeal held that the judge had erred in placing too much emphasis on the amount of time spent on the substantive issues on which the respective parties had succeeded, and too little emphasis on the fact that the claimant had been the overall winner and on the late service by the defendant of its schedule of loss. Further, the order made by the judge stepped over the well-known line that a successful party should not, in the absence of a **Part 36** offer and save perhaps in very exceptional cases, be ordered to pay any of the losing party's costs. An order was substituted for the defendant to pay all the claimant's costs, apart from the costs of the trial itself. In *Williams Corporate Finance plc v Holland* [2001] EWCA Civ 1526, LTL 22/10/2001, the claim consisted of seven heads, totalling £40,000. Most of the heads of claim were defeated, and the defendant succeeded on his counterclaim, but there was a net finding in favour of the claimant of about £2,500. The judge awarded the claimant its costs, but on appeal no order as to costs was substituted.

Additional claims under Part 20

66.45 Where a claimant succeeds in an action against a defendant, and the defendant successfully claims an indemnity from an additional party under Part 20, here referred to as a third party, the third party should be ordered to pay all the defendant's costs, including the costs the defendant will have been ordered to pay the claimant (*Jablochkoff Co. v McMurdo* [1884] WN 84). In such a case, if the defendant proves to be insolvent, the claimant will be unable to recover its costs from the third party, because it has no direct order against the third party. Therefore, it may, in a proper case, be appropriate to make an order akin to a *Sanderson* order requiring the third party to pay the claimant's costs directly (*Edginton v Clark* [1964] 1 QB 367). If a claimant succeeds against a defendant who succeeds against a third party, but the court considers that the defendant has defended the claim for reasons which provided no benefit to the third party, the third party will be ordered to pay the costs of the additional claim only (*Blore v Ashby* (1889) 42 ChD 682).

It is wrong to order the defendant to pay the third party's costs where the original claim and additional claim are partially successful (*Burchell v Bullard* [2005] EWCA Civ 358, [2005] BLR 330). A percentage order is more appropriate.

When considering costs orders between a defendant and a third party where the main proceedings fail with the result that the additional claim also fails, the usual rule is that costs follow the event under **CPR, r. 44.3(2)(a)**. This means that the court should usually ignore the incidence of costs in the main proceedings. A successful third party should recover its costs from the defendant even if the claimant in the main proceedings is impecunious (*Arkin v Borchard Lines Ltd (Nos. 2 and 3)* [2005] EWCA Civ 655, [2005] 1 WLR 3055, at [77]). As between the claimant and defendant when both the claim and additional claim fail, it may be appropriate to order the claimant to pay the defendant's costs on the claim and to reimburse the defendant in respect of the costs of both sides on the additional claim. This may be appropriate where the nature of the claim made the additional claim both inevitable and reasonable. In an appropriate case the court may make such order as to costs as between claimants, defendants and third parties as may be just in accordance with the overriding objective (see *Arkin v Borchard Lines Ltd (Nos. 2 and 3)* at [75] and [77]). In this case the defendants and third parties were alleged to have collective responsibility for alleged anti-competitive activities. Costs orders were therefore made to share the costs burden equally among them (at [78] and [79]). A claimant who discontinues will normally have to pay the costs both of the defendant and the third party, unless the parties agree that the costs in the additional claim should be considered by the court, and the court finds, for example, that the additional claim would have failed (*Young v J. R. Smart (Builders) Ltd (No. 2)* (2000) LTL 7/2/2000).

Additional claims and Part 36 payments

In *Alpha Chauffeurs Ltd v Citygate Dealership Ltd* [2002] EWCA Civ 207, LTL 21/2/2003, judgment was given for the claimant in the sum of £47,862 against the first defendant. Judgment was given to the first defendant in the sum of £41,219 against the third party, and a counterclaim made by the first defendant against the claimant was dismissed. The third party was also joined as a second defendant, with the claimant recovering nominal damages of £2 against the third party (as a second defendant). The third party had made a Part 36 payment in respect of the sum claimed by the claimant, but no Part 36 offer to the defendant. Applying the rule that costs follow the event: **66.46**

(a) The claimant should have been ordered to pay the third party's costs in its capacity as second defendant, applying the usual rule discussed at **66.10** where nominal damages are recovered.
(b) The first defendant was ordered to pay the claimant's costs of bringing its claim against the first defendant and in defending the first defendant's counterclaim.
(c) The third party was ordered to pay the first defendant's costs of the additional claim and the first defendant's costs of defending the main claim.
(d) The third party was ordered to reimburse the first defendant for the costs it was ordered to pay the claimant under point (b) for bringing the main claim against the first defendant, but not the costs of either the claimant or the first defendant in relation to the counterclaim.

SPECIAL CASES

Litigants under a disability

Generally, where money is ordered or agreed to be paid to, or is ordered to be paid by, a child or patient, the court must order a detailed assessment of the costs payable by that party to his solicitor (**CPR, r. 48.5(1) and (2)**). With effect from 1 October 2005, the obligation to order a detailed assessment under **r. 48.5(2)** is expanded to include costs payable out of money **66.47** belonging to the person under disability. This is a consequential change giving effect to **r. 21.11A** and **PD 21, paras 8A.1** and **8A.2**, which deal in detail with expenses incurred by litigation friends. On an assessment under **CPR, r. 48.5(2)**, the court must also assess any costs payable to the parties under disabilities (**r. 48.5(2)(b)**) unless:

(a) the court has issued a default costs certificate (see **68.14**) in relation to those costs; or
(b) the case is a road traffic accident claim where fixed costs are payable under **Part 45, Section II** (see **67.8** to **67.15**).

Exceptional cases where the court need not order the assessment of the costs payable by a party under a disability to his solicitor are set out in **PD 43–48, para. 51.1**. These cover cases where there is no need to protect the child or patient by ordering an assessment. An example is where another party has agreed to pay a specified sum in respect of the costs of the child or patient and the solicitor waives the right to further costs (**para. 51.1(b)**).

An order for costs can be made against the litigation friend acting for a claimant who is a person under disability by virtue of the undertaking to pay the costs that may be ordered against the person under disability required by **CPR, r. 21.4(3)(c)**. A successful party seeking such an order must apply promptly after judgment. The litigant normally indemnifies the litigation friend, but will not be required to do so where the litigation friend has acted for his or her own personal benefit (*Huxley v Wooton* (1912) 29 TLR 132) or if the litigation friend is guilty of some misconduct in relation to the proceedings.

Trustees and personal representatives

66.48 Trustees and personal representatives are, in so far as costs are not recovered from another party, entitled to recover their costs out of the fund. The court may, however, order otherwise and may do so where the party otherwise entitled to the costs has acted unreasonably. A trustee or personal representative who has acted substantially for his or her own benefit is likely to be treated like any other party. This may be the case where the proceedings are adversarial in nature (see *Holding and Management Ltd v Property Holding and Investment Trust plc* [1989] 1 WLR 1313).

Mortgagees

66.49 It is an established principle that a mortgagee is entitled to add any properly incurred costs, charges or expenses to the secured debt. Many mortgages make express provision for this, but even if they do not such a term will be implied (*Cottrell v Stratton* (1872) LR 8 Ch App 295). A court may disallow any costs, charges or expenses which were not 'properly incurred', unless the mortgage makes express provision to alter this (although a mortgage deed that purported to entitle the mortgagee to add improperly incurred costs might be open to question on public policy grounds: *Gomba Holdings (UK) Ltd v Minories Finance Ltd (No. 2)* [1993] Ch 171).

As an exception to the established principle, a mortgagee will not be permitted to add its costs to the security where a stranger impugns the title to the mortgage, or the enforcement or exercise of some right or power accruing to the mortgagee under the mortgage, even if the costs have been reasonably and properly incurred by the mortgagee (*Parker-Tweedale v Dunbar Bank plc (No. 2)* [1991] Ch 26).

In *Gomba Holdings (UK) Ltd v Minories Finance Ltd (No. 2)* [1993] Ch 171, the Court of Appeal laid down the following principles:

(a) Where there is a contractual right to costs, the discretion in the **Supreme Court Act 1981, s. 51**, should ordinarily be exercised so as to reflect that right.
(b) The power to disallow a mortgagee from adding its costs to the security derives from the power of the courts of equity to fix the terms on which redemption will be allowed.
(c) A decision by the court to refuse costs, in whole or in part, to a mortgagee litigant may be a decision in the exercise of the discretion under the **Supreme Court Act 1981, s. 51**, or

in the exercise of its power to fix the terms on which redemption will be allowed, or a decision on the extent of the mortgagee's contractual right to add its costs to the security or a combination of these.

(d) A mortgagee is not to be deprived of a contractual or equitable right to add costs to the security merely by reason of an order for payment of costs made without reference to the mortgagee's contractual or equitable rights and without any adjudication of whether or not the mortgagee should be deprived of those costs.

(e) The contractual basis of assessing costs under most mortgages will be the indemnity basis (see **68.37**).

The principles laid down in *Gomba Holdings (UK) Ltd v Minories Finance Ltd (No. 2)* are reflected by **PD 43–48, para. 50.1** to **50.4**, which are to the effect that generally the court will not assess a mortgagee's costs, because the mortgagee can simply add its indemnity-basis costs to the security. If the mortgagor wishes to object to the amount added to the security in this way, the mortgagor may apply for the taking of an account as to whether items added to the security were unreasonably incurred or were of an unreasonable amount. If the order is made, the account will be conducted before a costs officer.

Restrictive covenants

A claimant seeking a declaration of freedom from restrictive covenants under the Law of Property Act 1925, s. 84(2), is seeking for his own benefit the protection of a court order against the existence of possible adverse rights. For the declaration to be effective it is necessary for the claimant to join as defendants everyone who might have such an adverse right. The policy adopted by the courts is that defendants joined in this type of claim should be able to participate without risks as to costs until they can make an informed decision on whether to oppose the application. Guidelines laid down by *University of East London Higher Education Corporation v Barking and Dagenham London Borough Council (No. 2)* [2004] EWHC 2908 (Ch), [2005] Ch 354 (applying *Re Jeffkins' Indentures* [1965] 1 WLR 375 and *Re Wembley Park Estate Co. Ltd's Transfer* [1968] Ch 491) are: **66.50**

(a) the claimant must pay each defendant's costs on the indemnity basis up to the point when an informed decision could be made; and

(b) thereafter, any defendant opposing the application unsuccessfully must pay his own costs, but not those of the claimant.

BEDDOE ORDERS

By what is known as a *Beddoe* application, trustees and similar persons may apply to the court in the early stages of litigation for orders that they be indemnified against the costs of and incidental to the claim to be paid out of the trust or other fund. Such an application takes its name from *Re Beddoe* [1893] 1 Ch 547. Such a pre-emptive costs order, made well in advance of the trial, is, of course, of great benefit to trustees who have nothing to gain personally from an action but are under a duty to preserve the funds under their care. Such orders have traditionally been made mainly in favour of trustees and executors, but the discretion is not necessarily restricted to those categories, and orders have been made in favour of a receiver in a company liquidation (*Re Wedstock Realizations Ltd* [1988] BCLC 354) and in favour of employees engaged in hostile litigation against their pension fund trustees (*McDonald v Horn* (1994) *The Times*, 10 August 1994). **66.51**

Where a derivative claim is made on behalf of a company, or other body capable of suing in its own name, that company or body may be ordered, under **CPR, r. 19.9(7)**, to indemnify the claimant against liability for costs. This was first established in *Wallersteiner v Moir (No. 2)* [1975] QB 373 and orders indemnifying claimants in derivative claims are sometimes called *Wallersteiner* orders. When the court is considering making a pre-emptive costs order in favour of a person making a derivative claim for the benefit of a company, it is not an inflexible rule that an order will be refused if the company is jointly owned by the claimant and defendant (*Mumbray v Lapper* [2005] EWHC 1152 (Ch), *The Times*, 31 May 2005). It is better to say that when considering whether to make such an order the court will take into consideration the effect the order would have on the defendant's interests in the company: it may be unfair that a successful defendant who is not required to pay the unsuccessful claimant's costs should nevertheless have to bear a substantial loss in the value of his shares when the company pays the costs (*Halle v Trax BW Ltd* [2000] BCC 1020). Despite *obiter* indications to the contrary in *Halle v Trax BW Ltd*, there is no rule that a successful derivative claimant has a lien, on assets recovered in the claim, for costs (*Qayoumi v Oakhouse Property Holdings plc* [2002] EWHC 2547 (Ch), [2003] 1 BCLC 352).

A liquidator considering bringing proceedings for wrongful trading, preferences or in respect of transactions at an undervalue, is not automatically entitled to the costs of those proceedings from the assets of the company (*Lewis v Commissioner of Inland Revenue* [2001] 3 All ER 499) and should consider making an application for a *Beddoe* order. A pre-emptive costs order was made in *Re Axa Equity and Life Assurance Society plc (No. 1)* (2000) *The Times*, 19 December 2000, in favour of an objector to a scheme of reorganisation of an insurance business which contained novel provisions and where the presence of the objector was necessary to test that the scheme was fair. Such orders will not be made where the litigation is really a hostile claim by one beneficiary against another (*Trustee Corporation Ltd v Nadir* [2001] BPIR 541). Nor will they be made where the litigation can be of no benefit to the trust (*Weth v Attorney-General* [2001] EWCA Civ 263, LTL 23/2/2001).

Where trustees properly exercise a power vested in them to agree the costs of another party in relation to the administration of a trust there is no need for a court order, and the assessment of the costs can be dealt with under **CPR, r. 48.3**. Where the trustees have no such power, or decide against exercising it, an application will be necessary if a prospective costs order is to be made, and Practice Statement (Trust Proceedings: Prospective Costs Orders) [2001] 1 WLR 1082 applies. This sets out a model form of prospective costs order, and provides that in the absence of a dispute as to whether such an order is appropriate most such applications will be dealt with on the papers.

Where the application is made before proceedings are commenced, it is made by application notice in accordance with **CPR, r. 25.2**. Applications made during the course of existing proceedings are also made by application notice. In addition to asking for the indemnity as to costs mentioned above, the application normally also asks for directions whether the applicant should continue or defend the claim, and for any further or other relief. The application, in the usual case, is entirely domestic to the estate or trust concerned, so is often conducted in an informal manner, with material accepted on instructions without formal proof (see *Re Evans* [1986] 1 WLR 101). On the first return day the court may adjourn the application so that letters may be sent to the beneficiaries of the fund informing them of the nature of the application and of their right to file evidence and appear on any further hearing of the application.

Each application depends on its own facts and is essentially a matter for the discretion of the master or judge who hears it. In exercising that discretion the court will take into account the following considerations:

(a) The importance of affording full and proper protection for the costs and expenses of trustees and personal representatives acting properly to protect the fund against adverse claims (*Re Turner* [1907] 2 Ch 126). Conversely, if after trial the court would be unlikely to make an order for payment of the trustee's costs out of the fund it would not be right to make a pre-emptive order (*Re Wedstock Realizations Ltd* [1988] BCLC 354), for example, as in the case of hostile litigation.

(b) The court has to form a view of the prospects of success or failure in the underlying action (*Re Dallaway* [1982] 1 WLR 756). In *National Anti-Vivisection Society Ltd v Duddington* (1989) *The Times*, 23 November 1989 Mummery J said that the fund in dispute should not be used to support contentions which were not made in good faith or on reasonable grounds. Obviously, the court should not be invited to conduct a mini-trial on the merits of the action. A weak claim against the fund would be a powerful reason for making the order (*Re Evans* [1986] 1 WLR 101 per Nourse LJ).
(c) A pre-emptive order should not be made if there is a real possibility of it operating unjustly. Where the beneficiaries are all adult, are not incapacitated and can make up their own minds whether the claim should be resisted or not, there must be countervailing considerations of some weight before it is right for the action to be pursued or defended at the cost of the fund (*Re Evans* [1986] 1 WLR 101).
(d) Occasionally, there may be special factors to be weighed, for example, where it is essential for a company administrator to obtain the court's decision because there is a large class of creditors who may be affected by the decision (*Re Exchange Securities and Commodities Ltd (No. 2)* [1985] BCLC 392).

Protective costs orders

A protective costs order ('PCO') is similar to a *Beddoe* order, but: **66.52**

(a) Under a *Beddoe* order the applicant is given an indemnity for his costs by the company or out of the fund which he is seeking to protect.
(b) Under a PCO the applicant is given an immunity against paying the costs of the defendant. Typically, PCOs are made in judicial review proceedings where the claimant will gain no personal benefit from a successful result.

The procedure for seeking a PCO, according to *R (Corner House Research) v Secretary of State for Trade and Industry* [2005] EWCA Civ 192, [2005] 1 WLR 2600, is that:

(a) the claim form should on its face include the claim for the PCO;
(b) if the defendant intends to resist the application, reasons should be set out in the acknowledgment of service under **CPR, r. 54.8**;
(c) a judge will consider the application on the papers;
(d) if the order is refused, the applicant can ask for a hearing, which should not exceed one hour;
(e) if a PCO is made, unless the applicant's lawyers are acting pro bono, it will be usual to impose a costs budgeting order (see **66.54**).

R (Corner House Research) v Secretary of State for Trade and Industry laid down the following requirements before a PCO can be made (the same requirements apply where a PCO is sought for the first time on an appeal, see *Goodson v Her Majesty's Coroner for Bedfordshire and Luton* [2005] EWCA Civ 1172, *The Times*, 1 November 2005):

(a) The issues raised in the claim must be of general public importance.
(b) The public interest must require the resolution of those issues. It does not necessarily follow that because an issue is of general importance that it is in the public interest to have it resolved (*Goodson v Her Majesty's Coroner for Bedfordshire and Luton*).
(c) The applicant must have no private interest in the outcome of the case. A disqualifying interest need not be financial. In *Goodson v Her Majesty's Coroner for Bedfordshire and Luton* the applicant was disqualified by her interest in seeking a fresh coroner's inquest into her father's death.
(d) Having regard to the financial resources of the applicant and respondent, and to the amount of costs likely to be involved, it must be fair and just to make the order. This is more likely to be satisfied where the applicant's lawyers are acting pro bono.

If the PCO is not made, it was said in *R (Corner House Research) v Secretary of State for Trade and*

Industry that the applicant may well decide to discontinue at that stage. If he does so, he will almost certainly be acting reasonably (and so should not be penalised in costs). In *R (Ministry of Defence) v Wiltshire and Swindon Coroner* [2005] EWHC 889 (Admin), [2006] 1 WLR 134, it was said that a PCO could in theory be ordered in favour of a defendant in judicial review proceedings. The fact that most such defendants are public bodies means that it is rare that they will need such protection.

COSTS LIMITATION ORDERS

66.53 There is jurisdiction to make a pre-emptive order limiting the costs an applicant might be ordered to pay the other side if the litigation is unsuccessful (*R v Lord Chancellor, ex parte Child Poverty Action Group* [1999] 1 WLR 347; *R v Hammersmith and Fulham London Borough Council, ex parte Council for the Protection of Rural England, London Branch (No. 2)* [2000] Env LR 544). A party seeking such an order should say so in the claim form (*R (Campaign for Nuclear Disarmament) v Prime Minister of the United Kingdom* [2002] EWHC 2712 (Admin), *The Times*, 27 December 2002). The discretion to make such an order should be exercised only in the most exceptional cases, and where the court is satisfied:

(a) that the issues raised are truly ones of general importance;
(b) that it has sufficient appreciation of the merits of the claim to conclude it is in the public interest to make an order; and
(c) that the respondent has a clearly superior capacity to bear the costs of the proceedings than the applicant.

COSTS BUDGETING DIRECTIONS

66.54 Some concern has been expressed that the CPR reforms have not had sufficient impact on the costs of litigation. As a reaction to this, some judges are moving towards a costs budgeting regime whereby orders are made at the outset of litigation capping the base costs as between the parties. A typical order is in the following form:

The base costs of the [Claimant/Defendant] shall not without the permission of the court exceed the sum of £____ (save that any costs awarded in favour of a party on any interim application shall not count towards the said £____). Either party may apply without notice to increase the figure of £____ and any such application shall be supported by a statement addressing the need for the increase and a revised costs estimate calculated to trial.

The scheme of the order is to avoid an inflexible cap, while enabling the court to retain control over the amount of costs at any time. The object of the order is to encourage the parties to plan the case in advance so as to ensure that there is a proportionate spend on the case (see *Jefferson v National Freight Carriers plc* [2001] EWCA Civ 2082, LTL 4/10/2001). Either party can apply to increase the cap to accommodate unforeseen developments in the case. The application must be supported by evidence and a revised costs estimate and is made without notice. There is nothing in this form of order to suggest that the application is prospective as opposed to retrospective, although there is a clear risk that a party seeking to recover costs after they have been incurred will fail in the exercise and lose costs.

The order is made under the court's general case management powers (**CPR, r. 3.1(2)(m)**) and is rooted in what was said by the Court of Appeal in *Griffiths v Solutia UK Ltd* [2001] EWCA Civ 736, LTL 26/4/2001. Gage J made such an order to control the costs of the national organ transplant litigation in *A v Leeds Teaching Hospitals NHS Trust* [2003] EWHC 1034 (QB), LTL 8/8/2003 (sub nom. *A v A Teaching Hospitals NHS Trust*), and has provided guidance on applications for cost-capping orders in *Smart v East Cheshire NHS Trust* [2003] EWHC 2806 (QB), LTL 1/12/2003.

It might be appropriate to make a prospective cost-capping order in a case where a claimant may be incurring disproportionate levels of costs in circumstances where the defendant is unlikely to recover its costs if successful. This may happen where the claimant's lawyers are acting under a CFA for a client who has not taken out insurance to cover the costs of the defendant in the event the claim does not succeed (*King v Telegraph Group Ltd* [2004] EWCA Civ 613, [2005] 1 WLR 2282).

GROUP LITIGATION

Where a claim is proceeding under a GLO, there will be 'individual costs' which are specific to that particular claim, and 'common costs', which will be those incurred on the GLO issues, the costs of a claim proceeding as a test claim, and the lead solicitor's costs in administering the group litigants (**CPR, r. 48.6A(2)**). If the group loses, the general rule is that the common costs will be divided equally among group members, who will have several liability for them (**r. 48.6A(3)**). The individual costs of a particular claim will be that claimant's liability. A group litigant who loses will usually be ordered to pay the winning side's costs, and will also be liable for the costs of his own claim and his share of the common costs (**r. 48.6A(4)**). When making costs orders at hearings involving group and individual issues, the court will apportion the costs between the group and individual issues (**r. 48.6A(5)**). Where a party joins the group register late, or leaves early, the court may make an order covering that party's responsibility for the common costs to date (**r. 48.6A(6)** and (7)). **66.55**

The appropriate costs orders to be made in group litigation in respect of the costs of individual claimants who settle or discontinue during the course of the proceedings were considered in *Sayers v Merck SmithKline Beecham plc* [2001] EWCA Civ 2027, [2002] 1 WLR 2274. It might be likely that the costs of common issues will be ordered to follow the determination of those issues rather than awaiting the individual fate of each claimant's claim, it would be wrong to say this is the presumptive position. Claimants who settle should deal with all aspects of costs, including common costs, as part of the settlement negotiations. In relation to discontinuing claimants, the costs of common issues should be determined following the trial of the common issues.

Care needs to be taken to control the costs in group litigation, with one particular concern being the considerable amount of administrative time often expended in these cases (*Solutia UK Ltd v Griffiths* [2001] EWCA Civ 736, [2001] CPLR 419).

PUBLICLY FUNDED LITIGANTS

Successful publicly funded litigants

If an assisted party under the Legal Aid Act 1988 or an LSC funded client (together referred to as 'publicly funded litigants') is successful, the court will make an order for costs on exactly the same principles as apply in unassisted claims. The publicly funded litigant has no beneficial interest in the costs, which must be paid to his or her solicitor to obtain a valid discharge (**Community Legal Service (Costs) Regulations 2000** (SI 2000/441) **reg. 18**). The recovered costs are used to pay the costs incurred under the legal aid or LSC certificate. Any damages or property recovered or preserved in the proceedings will be subject to the LSC's first charge under the Legal Aid Act, 1988, s. 16(6), or the **Access to Justice Act 1999, s. 10**(7), in respect of any shortfall between the solicitor's charges and the costs recovered from the paying party, and contributions from the publicly funded litigant. **66.56**

A problem can arise if another person offers to fund a particular stage in proceedings which are covered by a public funding certificate. Lawyers are not permitted to receive, in addition to public funding (other than Support Funding), any private funding, which must, therefore, be returned. Any breach of the public funding regulations does not prevent the court making a party-and-party costs order in the usual way (*Stacy v Player* [2004] EWCA Civ 241, LTL 16/3/2004).

Costs against a publicly funded litigant

66.57 **Cost protection** Many publicly funded litigants will be protected against adverse costs orders if they are unsuccessful. 'Cost protection' applies to assisted parties under the Legal Aid Act 1988, by virtue of s. 17(1), and to LSC funded clients (see the **Community Legal Service (Costs) Regulations 2000** (SI 2000/441)), other than LSC funded clients receiving assistance by way of:

(a) Help at Court;
(b) Legal Help. Where the client receives Legal Help, but later receives Legal Representation or General Family Help or Help with Mediation (other than in relation to family proceedings as defined by the **Community Legal Service (Cost Protection) Regulations 2002, SI 2002/824, reg. 2(1)**) in respect of the same dispute, cost protection applies both in respect of the costs of the receiving party before the commencement of proceedings while the client had Legal Help, and after the commencement of proceedings while the client had Legal Representation, General Family Help or Help with Mediation;
(c) General Family Help and Help with Mediation in family proceedings; and
(d) Legal Representation in family proceedings.

(See **SI 2000/824, reg. 3**, and the helpful summary of the approach in **PD 43–48, Section 21**.)

Cost protection extends to the work covered by the public funding certificate. A certificate covering a party as the 'appellant' will not afford cost protection for the costs incurred by the other side on a cross-appeal (*Hinde v Harbourne* [2003] EWHC 3109 (Ch), LTL 2/1/2004). The LSC has power to amend a certificate which does not cover all the issues in a case, and a retrospective amendment to a certificate has the effect of conferring cost protection on all the issues covered by the amended certificate. A party likely to be prejudiced by a contemplated retrospective amendment should be allowed to make representations to the LSC as to whether the amendment should be allowed, but will have to demonstrate they would have acted in a significantly different way if the original certificate reflected the LSC's intentions (*Hinde v Harbourne*).

A litigant who obtains public funding by fraud does not obtain cost protection under the **Access to Justice Act 1999, s. 11(1)** (*Jones v Congregational and General Insurance plc* [2003] EWHC 1027 (QB), [2003] 1 WLR 3001).

66.58 **Determining costs payable by assisted party** Where cost protection applies, the Legal Aid Act 1988, s. 17(1), and the **Access to Justice Act 1999, s. 11(1)**, both provide that, except in prescribed circumstances, any costs ordered to be paid by the publicly funded litigant shall not exceed the amount (if any) which is reasonable having regard to all the circumstances including:

(a) the financial resources of all the parties to the proceedings; and
(b) their conduct in connection with the dispute to which the proceedings relate.

Regulation 8 of SI 2000/441 provides that the non-funded party may serve and file a statement of resources, and if this is done at least seven days before the hearing where a s. 11(1) costs order may fall to be determined, the LSC funded client must also make a statement of costs and produce it at the hearing. The financial resources of a litigation friend are not taken into account in assessing the resources of the client (**PD 43–48, para. 21.15(2)**). Unless they have competing interests in the proceedings, the LSC funded client's partner's resources are treated as the resources of the funded party (reg. 7(3)). However, the first £100,000 of the value of the LSC funded client's home is ignored (reg. 7(1)). Also ignored is the value of the LSC funded client's clothes and household furniture, unless the circumstances are exceptional (reg. 7(2)). The court can take into account any damages recovered by a funded party who fails to beat a **Part 36** payment, and any resulting costs liability under s. 11(1) has priority over the Commission's first charge (*Cook v Swinten* [1967] 1 WLR 457).

As from 5 June 2000, regs 9 to 13 of SI 2000/441 apply to legal aid cases as well as LSC funded cases. The court is required to consider whether, but for cost protection, it would have made a costs order against the publicly funded party, and, if so, whether it would have specified the amount payable (reg. 9(1)). If so (or if the court decides to make a reasonably modest order), and if the court considers it has enough information to do so, the court can immediately make an order under s. 11(1) specifying the amount the publicly funded party shall pay (reg. 9(2) and (3)). Usually, the 'reasonable' sum that a publicly funded litigant should pay will be relatively modest, or nothing. It may be a sum payable by instalments (*Williams v Walkett* [1994] CLY 3587) or a set-off against sums awarded in favour of the assisted party. Often the judge will be guided by the level of contribution endorsed on the certificate (*Mercantile Credit Co. Ltd v Cross* [1965] 2 QB 194), but must not follow the certificate blindly, because the test at this stage is not the same as the rules governing the level of contribution (*Gooday v Gooday* [1969] P 1).

If the court does not make an immediate order under s. 11(1), but decides it would have ordered costs against the publicly funded party but for the cost protection rule, the non-funded party has three months to request a hearing to determine the costs payable by the publicly funded party (reg. 10(2)). In respect of applications for funded services made before 3 December 2001, a failure to file a request within three months was an absolute bar under reg. 10(2). For applications for funded services after 3 December 2001 the court may extend the three-month time period, but only if there is a good reason for the delay (this is the effect of an amendment to SI 2000/441, see **PD 43–48, para. 23.4**). Where the paying party was publicly funded for only part of the time, and the receiving party fails to apply within the three-month time limit, the receiving party can still recover his costs for the period when the paying party was not publicly funded (*Re B (Children)* [2005] EWCA Civ 779, LTL 26/5/2005). Regulation 10 lays down a detailed procedure for the determination of the amount, if any, payable in such circumstances.

Form of order Under the Legal Aid Act 1988, it was common to make orders that were colloquially known as 'football pools orders', providing that the assisted party was to pay the other side's costs, not to be enforced without the permission of the court. These were intended to allow the non-assisted party to return to court in the event of the assisted party coming into money at a later date. Under the traditional wording, the non-assisted party could return to court during the six years following the order, but a more sophisticated wording was approved in *Parr v Smith* [1995] 2 All ER 1031, which allowed an indefinite time for the application. Under the **Access to Justice Act 1999**, once a **s. 11(1)** order has been made, the non-funded party should generally apply within the next three months. Any later application can be entertained only up to six years from the order, and only on the grounds of significant change in the funded party's circumstances, or additional information coming to light about the funded party's resources, or other good reasons (SI 2000/441, reg. 12; **PD 43–48, para. 23.16**). **66.59**

A court may make orders in favour of both parties on different issues, even where one party is publicly funded, which will be set off against each other without infringing the principle of cost protection in the **Access to Justice Act 1999, s. 11** (*Hill v Bailey* [2003] EWHC 2835 (Ch), [2004] 1 All ER 1210). In relation to interim costs orders against publicly funded litigants, the court may make an order that the costs (which may be assessed summarily: **PD 43–48, para. 13.10**) shall be set off against any future award in the claim of damages or costs against the non-funded party (*Lockley v National Blood Transfusion Service* [1992] 1 WLR 492; *R (Burkett) v*

Hammersmith and Fulham London Borough Council (No. 2) [2004] EWCA Civ 1342, *The Times*, 20 October 2004).

An unsuccessful party who has been publicly funded for only part of the time during which litigation has been pending obtains the benefit of cost protection (if applicable) only for the period during which public funding was in place (*Dugon v Williamson* [1964] Ch 59). The same result applies where, as in *Turner v Plasplugs Ltd* [1996] 2 All ER 939, proceedings continue beyond a limitation in a certificate without the certificate being amended to cover future stages of the litigation. Cost protection is lost where a certificate is discharged on the date of giving notice of acting in person or change of solicitor (*Burridge v Stafford* (1999) 149 NLJ 1474). The effect of revocation of a certificate is that the party is treated as never having cost protection. In *DEG-Deutsche Investitions- und Entwicklungsgesellschaft mbH v Koshy* [2001] EWCA Civ 79, [2001] 3 All ER 878 the Court of Appeal held that revocation of a certificate is arguably the most significant change that could happen to a person's circumstances, and justified the court varying earlier costs orders previously covered by cost protection.

Costs against the Legal Services Commission

66.60 Under the Legal Aid Act 1988, s. 18, and the **Access to Justice Act 1999, s. 11(4)(d)**, and the **Community Legal Service (Cost Protection) Regulations 2000** (SI 2000/824), a court deciding a claim in favour of a non-publicly funded litigant as against one who is publicly funded may make an order requiring the LSC to pay the non-publicly funded litigant's costs. Before such an order can be made under the **Access to Justice Act 1999**, the following conditions must be satisfied (very similar conditions applied under the Legal Aid Act 1988):

(a) The proceedings must be finally decided in favour of the non-publicly funded litigant. Where an appeal may be brought, any order against the LSC will not take effect until the time limit for seeking permission to appeal has elapsed without permission being granted, or, if no permission is required, no appeal is brought within the time limit for bringing an appeal (**PD 43–48, para. 21.20**). Where an appeal is brought by the LSC funded party, any order against the LSC never takes effect, but a fresh application may be brought in the appeal court.

(b) The non-publicly funded litigant must make the application for a costs order against the LSC within three months of the making of a costs order under the **Access to Justice Act 1999, s. 11(1)** (**Community Legal Service (Costs) Regulations 2000** (SI 2000/441), **reg. 10(3)**). A late application can be made where there is a good reason for the delay (**Community Legal Service (Cost Protection) Regulations 2000 (SI 2000/824), reg. 5(3)**).

(c) The court must be satisfied that it is just and equitable in the circumstances that provision for the costs should be made out of public funds. It will normally be just and equitable that the LSC should stand behind the client unless the costs judge is aware of facts rendering that result unjust or inequitable (*R (Gunn) v Secretary of State for the Home Department* [2001] 1 WLR 1634).

Further, in respect of costs incurred in proceedings at first instance, the following additional conditions must be satisfied:

(d) The proceedings must have been instituted by the publicly funded litigant.

(e) The applicant must be an individual.

(f) It must be shown that the non-publicly funded litigant will suffer financial hardship if the order is not made.

Until an amendment to the regulations came into force on 3 December 2001 (SI 2001/3812, reg. 4), condition (f) required the applicant to show he or she would suffer 'severe' financial hardship. Removal of the word 'severe' was intended to ensure that orders are made in deserving cases. The amendment also restricted applications to individuals (condition (e), which was introduced with effect from 3 December 2001).

Procedure in applications against the Legal Services Commission

A non-publicly funded litigant may make an application for costs to be payable by the LSC at any time within three months of a costs order being made under the **Access to Justice Act 1999, s. 11(1) (Community Legal Service (Costs) Regulations 2000** (SI 2000/441), **reg. 10(2)**). The decision whether to make an order against the LSC is expressly assigned to the costs judge or district judge under the **Community Legal Service (Costs) Regulations 2000, reg. 10(10)**, and should not be exercised by the trial judge (*R (Gunn) v Secretary of State for the Home Department* [2001] 1 WLR 1634). The application (in **form N244**) must be accompanied by the receiving party's bill of costs (unless the full costs have already been determined), a statement of resources, and a notice to the effect that a costs order is being sought against the Commission (**reg. 10(3); PD 43–48, para. 23.3**). All these documents must be served on the publicly funded party and the regional director of the LSC (**reg. 10(4)** and **PD 43–48, para. 23.4**). After being served with the application, the publicly funded litigant must file and serve a statement of resources within 21 days (for the purpose of determining his or her personal liability under the **Access to Justice Act, 1999, s. 11(1)**) and may serve written points of dispute concerning the bill of costs (**PD 43–48, para. 23.5**). If the publicly funded litigant does not provide a statement of resources, the court may make a s. 11(1) determination without a hearing (**PD 43–48, para. 23.6**). Determination hearings are listed giving at least 14 days' notice (**para. 23.7**), and may be heard by a costs judge or district judge (**para. 23.8**). The regional director may appear at the hearing, or may instead rely on a written statement, which should be served and filed seven days before the hearing (**para. 23.10**). **66.61**

Court of first instance Conditions (d), (e) and (f) in **66.60** only apply to costs incurred in a court of first instance. The Divisional Court is not a court of first instance when reviewing the decision of a court or tribunal (*R v Leeds County Court, ex parte Morris* [1990] 1 QB 523), but is a court of first instance when reviewing the decision of a person or body other than a court or tribunal (*R v Greenwich London Borough Council, ex parte Lovelace (No. 2)* [1992] QB 155). **66.62**

Claim finally decided in favour of the assisted person Proceedings are finally decided in favour of an unassisted person (condition (a) in **66.60**) when no appeal lies, or if the time for appealing has expired. In *Kelly v London Transport Executive* [1982] 1 WLR 1055 the unassisted defendant had made a Part 36 payment exceeding the damages awarded to the claimant. The Court of Appeal held that the defendants had been substantially successful and that the action had been finally decided in its favour for these purposes. **66.63**

Financial hardship In *Hanning v Maitland (No. 2)* [1970] 1 QB 580, decided when condition (f) required severe financial hardship, Lord Denning MR said the term should not be restrictively construed 'so as to exclude people of modest income or modest capital who would find it difficult to bear their own costs', but should exclude commercial concerns in a considerable way of business, insurance companies and 'wealthy folk' who would not feel the costs of the litigation. Public bodies, including government departments, could (under the pre-2001 Regulations) suffer severe financial hardship (*R (Gunn) v Secretary of State for the Home Department* [2001] 1 WLR 1634). In *Adams v Riley* [1988] QB 372 it was explained that the unassisted party's spouse's financial resources are not to be aggregated with those of the unassisted party in determining whether the unassisted party will suffer severe financial hardship if an order against what is now the Legal Services Commission is refused, but are to be taken into account in that an unassisted party with a financially independent spouse is better placed than a party with a dependent spouse. In *Adams v Riley* the court determined the amount that the defendant could pay towards his costs without suffering financial hardship, and made an order that what is now the Legal Services Commission should pay the rest. **66.64**

Both parties publicly funded

An order cannot be made against the Legal Services Commission where both parties are **66.65** publicly funded (see condition (a) at **66.60**). This can produce rather harsh results, as in *Almond v Miles* (1992) *The Times*, 4 February 1992. In this case a publicly funded defendant successfully resisted a claim by a publicly funded claimant to a share in the equity of the defendant's flat. Under the Legal Aid Act 1988, s. 16(6), the defendant's costs of £18,000 were a first charge on her flat, which had been 'preserved' in the proceedings. The claimant had the benefit of cost protection, but was required to pay certain instalments towards the defendant's costs. Although the defendant had been financially prejudiced by the proceedings, the court could not make an order against the Legal Aid Board, because the defendant was herself publicly funded.

NON-PARTY COSTS ORDERS

66.66 In *Aiden Shipping Co. Ltd v Interbulk Ltd* [1986] AC 965 the House of Lords decided that the **Supreme Court Act 1981, s. 51**, confers a sufficiently wide discretion on the court on the question of costs to allow it to award costs against non-parties. In the case before the House of Lords two separate sets of proceedings were commenced. In the first, a shipowner made a claim against the charterers of the ship. In the second, essentially the same dispute was litigated between the charterers and their subcharterers. The actions were not consolidated. The House of Lords upheld the judge's order that the unsuccessful shipowner should pay the charterer's costs, such costs to include any costs the charterers had to pay the subcharterers in the second action.

The basic principle is that such an order will only be made where it is in accordance with the requirements of reason and justice. The essential policy is that the need to protect the successful party by granting an effective costs order has to yield to the right of access to the courts to litigate the dispute in the first place (*Hamilton v Al Fayed (No. 2)* [2002] EWCA Civ 665, [2003] QB 1175; **European Convention on Human Rights, art. 6(1)**). It is in the public interest that funding for litigation should be available, provided the real motivation is to enable a party to litigate what the funders perceive to be a genuine case. In *Re Land and Property Trust Co. plc* [1991] 1 WLR 601, Nicholls LJ said '. . . the circumstances in which it will be just to make a costs order against a person who is not a party to the proceedings will be exceptional'. Consequently, a pure funder of litigation should not ordinarily be liable to a non-party costs order, and it is only if there is something exceptional in the circumstances that such an order can be justified (*Gulf Azov Shipping Co Ltd v Idisi* [2004] EWCA Civ 292, LTL 15/3/2004). 'Exceptional' means outside the ordinary run of cases where non-parties pursued or defended claims for their own benefit and at their own expense. Non-parties who substantially control proceedings or who will benefit from them will ordinarily be ordered to pay the successful party's costs (*Dymocks Franchise Systems (NSW) Pty Ltd v Todd* [2004] UKPC 39, [2004] 1 WLR 2807).

Even if there is some exceptional feature present, an order will be refused if there is no causation (*Hamilton v Al Fayed (No. 2)*). Nevertheless, such orders may possibly be made against:

- an outsider who was funding the litigation on behalf of the unsuccessful party (*Singh v Observer Ltd* [1989] 2 All ER 751), doubted in *Symphony Group plc v Hodgson* [1994] QB 179;
- against directors of a company who improperly cause the other side to incur costs in a winding-up petition (*Re a Company (No. 004055 of 1991)* [1991] 1 WLR 1003), although it is not necessary to find impropriety before making a non-party costs order (*BE Studios Ltd v Smith and Williamson Ltd* [2005] EWHC 2730 (Ch), *The Times*, 16 December 2005);
- against a shareholder who was instrumental in commencing or defending proceedings for his own benefit (*CIBC Mellon Trust Co v Stolzenberg (No. 3)* [2005] EWCA Civ 628, *The Times*, 8 June 2005; and
- where the non-party has been found, under the law concerning maintenance and champerty, to have maintained the claim (*McFarlane v E. E. Caledonia Ltd (No. 2)* [1995] 1 WLR 366).

Personal costs orders were made in winding-up proceedings against a director who treated companies as extensions of himself (*Re North West Holdings plc* [2001] 1 BCLC 468), and where a director contested proceedings against the company for his personal reasons (*Re Aurum Marketing Ltd* [2000] 2 BCLC 645). Normally, however, if litigation is conducted in the name of a company in good faith, it is contrary to the principles of separate corporate personality and limited liability to make any person other than the company itself liable to pay another party's costs because the company loses (*Taylor v Pace Developments Ltd* [1991] BCC 406; *Floods of Queensferry Ltd v Shand Construction Ltd* [2002] EWCA Civ 918, in which the circumstances in which a director maintained a company's litigation were described by the trial judge as 'extraordinary').

The motivation of any outside funder will be a relevant consideration. In *Hamilton v Al Fayed (No. 2)* the court drew the distinction between 'pure funders' who fund litigation out of philanthropic or charitable motives and 'professional' funders who are normally contractually bound to fund litigation. The court held that it would be rare for pure funders to be exposed to a costs order where they acted out of altruistic motives and had reasonable grounds for believing that the party was acting properly. If pure funders were regularly exposed to costs orders, there was a real risk that the funds would dry up and that access to justice would be reduced. Regarding professional funders, *Arkin v Borchard Lines Ltd (Nos. 2 and 3)* [2005] EWCA Civ 655, [2005] 1 WLR 3055, said a balance has to be struck between the need not to discourage professional funding of claims brought by persons otherwise unable to afford litigation, and the fair application of the principle that costs follow the event. It was held that the professional funder should ordinarily (in the absence of champerty and unreasonable conduct) be liable up to the amount it contributed to the unsuccessful party's costs.

Non-party costs orders may be made in the case of wanton and officious intermeddling with litigation falling short of champerty in the strict sense (*Nordstern Allgemeine Versicherungs AG v Internav Ltd* [1999] 2 Lloyd's Rep 139). Costs orders against non-parties can be made in cases where there is 'no order as to costs' between claimant and defendant (ibid.). A costs order against a non-party may be made even where the non-party is domiciled outside the jurisdiction, and without the need to comply with the rules in (for example) **Council Regulation (EC) No. 44/2001, art. 2** (see **16.17**) (*National Justice Compania Naviera SA v Prudential Assurance Co. Ltd (No. 2)* [2000] 1 WLR 603). Costs orders against non-parties are, however, unlikely to be made against a liquidator funding litigation in the name of the company (*Eastglen Ltd v Grafton* [1996] 2 BCLC 279).

Procedure on non-party costs applications

An application for a costs order against a non-party follows a summary procedure. The fact **66.67**
that costs proceedings may take some time to determine does not stop them being summary (*Robertson Research International Ltd v ABG Exploration BV* (1999) *The Times*, 3 November 1999, Laddie J). This is a different approach to that adopted in wasted costs applications (see **66.71**). However, if the application is speculative or bound to fail the court should summarily dismiss it (*Bristol and West plc v Bhadresa (No. 2)* [1999] 2 CPLR 209). The person against whom the costs order is sought must be joined as a party for the purposes of costs only, and must be given a reasonable opportunity to attend the hearing to give reasons why the court should not make the order (**CPR, r. 48.2**). The court has a power under the **Supreme Court Act 1981, s. 51(3)**, to determine by whom, and to what extent, costs are to be paid, and it therefore has an ancillary power to order a party to disclose who its funders were (*Raiffeisen Zentralbank Österreich AG v Crossseas Shipping Ltd* [2003] EWHC 1381 (Comm), LTL 13/6/2003, in which the successful claimant found that the defendant was impecunious and was granted an order to discover who was funding the defendant).

The strict rules of evidence will not apply when the court considers whether to make the order. The court should limit the issues to be considered and, if necessary, the length of cross-examination and submissions. An order may accordingly be refused if the non-party against whom the application is made has not been provided with the basic safeguards required by natural justice, such as being informed in advance of the trial that the application will be made, and the issue against the non-party being accurately framed by statements of case (*Symphony Group plc v Hodgson* [1994] QB 179). In *Shah v Karanjia* [1993] 4 All ER 792 an application for costs against a brother of the claimant was refused principally because he had not been separately represented at the trial, the claim against him had not been formulated against him until after the trial, and he had been asked questions in cross-examination at trial with a view to obtaining information for the application for costs against him.

Costs orders against experts

66.68 In *Phillips v Symes (No. 2)* [2004] EWHC 2330 (Ch), [2005] 1 WLR 2043, it was held, by extension of the jurisdiction to order costs against non-parties, that the court has power to order costs to be paid by expert witnesses. Such an order may be made where an expert breaches his or her duties to the court and as a result significant costs are incurred. A similar procedure to that discussed at **66.67** should be followed. The expert should be given a warning, and orders should follow the two-stage process of first considering whether there is a case to answer, followed by a hearing to allow the expert to appear and give reasons why an order should not be made.

Costs order in favour of non-party

66.69 In *J v Oyston* [2002] EWHC 819 (QB), [2002] CPLR 563, an order for costs was made in favour of the Solicitors' Indemnity Fund, a non-party which had taken over conduct of proceedings in the name of the claimant whom it had agreed to indemnify and in which it was successful. Such an order can be made under the **Supreme Court Act 1981, s. 51**, provided the court finds there are exceptional circumstances. The Fund would have been liable for the defendant's costs if he had won, and it would be unreasonable, unjust and extraordinary if the defendant were not to be ordered to pay the Fund's costs if he lost.

WASTED COSTS ORDERS

66.70 The court has a power under the **Supreme Court Act 1981, s. 51(6)**, to make a legal representative liable for any wasted costs. This can take one of two forms:

(a) disallowing the costs of a party and ordering the legal representative to indemnify his or her client against the costs; and/or

(b) ordering the legal representative to pay the costs of another party.

Section 51(6) is supplemented by **CPR, r. 48.7, and PD 43–48, Section 53.**

The term 'wasted costs' is defined in the **Supreme Court Act 1981, s. 51(7)**, to mean any costs incurred by a party:

(a) as a result of any improper, unreasonable or negligent act or omission on the part of any legal or other representative or any employee of such a representative; or

(b) which, in the light of any such act or omission occurring after they were incurred, the court considers it unreasonable to expect that party to pay.

The phrase 'improper, unreasonable or negligent' was considered by the Court of Appeal in *Ridehalgh v Horsefield* [1994] Ch 205, which is the leading authority in this field. Whether an act or omission is 'improper' is to be judged by the standards of the consensus of professional, including judicial, opinion and is not limited to breaches of the professional code. 'Unreasonable' includes behaviour that is:

vexatious, designed to harass the other side rather than advance the resolution of the case, and it makes no difference that the conduct is the product of excessive zeal and not improper motive. . . . The acid test is whether the conduct admits of a reasonable explanation.

'Negligent':

should be understood in an untechnical way to denote failure to act with the competence reasonably to be expected of ordinary members of the profession.

'Negligent' requires something more than mere negligence (*Persaud v Persaud* [2003] EWCA Civ 394, [2003] PNLR 519). Negligent handling of a client's case is not enough: the lawyer's conduct must also be a breach of duty to the court (*Radford and Co. v Charles* (2003) *The Times*, 26 November 2003). A wasted costs order will only be made if there is something akin to a legal representative being guilty of an abuse of process. A failure to address the Bar Council guidance on advising in publicly funded cases was regarded in *Persaud v Persaud* as a breach of duty to the Legal Services Commission and not a breach of duty to the court, and was an insufficient basis for a wasted costs order.

The test to be applied to determine whether an act or omission justifies a wasted costs order is the same whether or not the party is publicly funded (*Filmlab Systems International Ltd v Pennington* [1995] 1 WLR 673). There must be a causal link between the legal representative's behaviour and the waste of costs (**PD 43–48, para. 53.4(2)**; *Ridehalgh v Horsefield*; *Brown v Bennett (No. 2)* [2002] 1 WLR 713).

It is appropriate for the court to make a wasted costs order only if it is just in all the circumstances to make a legal representative compensate a party for wasted costs (**PD 43–48, para. 53.4(3)**).

'Legal representative' includes solicitor and counsel. Acts or omissions by counsel which may lead to costs which may be the subject of a wasted costs order include both pre-trial paperwork and conduct during the trial (*Ridehalgh v Horsefield*; *Brown v Bennett (No. 2)*). Solicitors cannot avoid their responsibility to the parties and the court by slavishly following counsel's advice. It is incumbent on them to exercise an independent judgment (*Davy-Chiesman v Davy-Chiesman* [1984] Fam 48; *Locke v Camberwell Health Authority* (1991) 2 Med LR 249; *Ridehalgh v Horsefield*).

An application for a wasted costs order can be made against one's own legal representative and that of one's opponent (*Medcalf v Mardell* [2002] UKHL 27, [2003] 1 AC 120). An order will not be made against former solicitors who ceased to act before proceedings were issued (*Byrne v Sefton Health Authority* [2001] EWCA Civ 1904, [2002] 1 WLR 775). An application can be made against a non-party (*Lubrizol Ltd v Tyndallwoods Solicitors* (1998) LTL 10/4/98).

The courts must be astute to ensure that wasted costs applications do not become another form of satellite litigation. They will be reserved for exceptional cases where a party was injured by the unjustified behaviour of a legal representative (*Ridehalgh v Horsefield*). They should be confined to matters that are susceptible to summary disposal on agreed facts or after brief investigation. Complex, time-consuming enquiries are to be avoided. Compensation of a party who has suffered at the hand of a legal representative is only one of a number of competing interests to be considered (*Re Merc Property Ltd* [1999] 2 BCLC 286; *Wall v Lefever* [1998] 1 FCR 605; *Medcalf v Mardell*).

The legal representative against whom an application for a wasted costs order is made must be given an opportunity to respond before the court makes the order (**CPR, r. 48.7(2)**; *Re Wiseman Lee (Solicitors) (Wasted Costs Order) (No. 5 of 2000)* [2001] EWCA Crim 707, *The Times*, 5 April 2001). The court should not make an order against the legal representative of a party who is unable or unwilling to waive privilege, unless the court is satisfied that, if unconstrained, the legal representative could say nothing to resist the order and also that it is fair and just to make the order in the circumstances (*Medcalf v Mardell*).

Procedure on wasted costs applications

66.71 An application for a wasted costs order should be made to the judge who tried the matter (*Re P* [2002] 1 Cr App R 207). In certain limited circumstances it is possible for another court to have jurisdiction, such as where it is impracticable for the trial judge to deal with the matter, or where the parties agree to another judge dealing with it. Unless such an exception applies, a district judge has no jurisdiction to make a wasted costs order after a claim has been tried by a circuit judge (*Gray v Going Places Leisure Travel Ltd* (2005) LTL 7/2/2005). The fact that the trial judge has already criticised the conduct complained of will not necessarily mean that the judge is biased and should not hear the application (*Bahai v Rashidian* [1985] 1 WLR 1337).

Although an application can be made at any stage of proceedings, it should normally be made after trial (**PD 43-48, para. 53.1**; *Filmlab Systems International Ltd v Pennington* [1995] 1 WLR 673). An application can be made at any time up to and including the detailed assessment of costs (**PD 43-48, para. 53.1**; *Melchior v Vettivel* [2002] CP Rep 24). It can be made after the main proceedings have been stayed by consent following a Tomlin order (*Wagstaff v Colls* [2003] EWCA Civ 469, [2003] PNLR 561). The award of costs as between the parties and the making of a wasted costs order are two distinct functions (*Melchior v Vettivel*).

A party to proceedings may apply for a wasted costs order either orally or in writing (by application notice under **CPR, Part 23**) (**PD 43–48, para. 53.3**). The court can make an order of its own initiative (**PD 43–48, para. 53.2**). It should be slow to do so as the enquiry will necessarily involve a party in additional expense. Where application is made under Part 23, a copy of the application notice must be served, with a copy of the written evidence and a draft order, at least three days before the application is to be heard (**CPR, r. 23.7**). The application notice and evidence in support must (**PD 43–48, para. 53.8**) identify:

(a) what the legal representative is alleged to have done or failed to do; and
(b) the costs which the legal representative may be ordered to pay or which are sought to be paid.

Where the court initiates the enquiry it is incumbent on the judge to ensure that the order shows clearly the breach alleged so that the legal representative has sufficient information upon which to respond.

The application will generally be considered in two stages (**PD 43–48, para. 53.6**). In the first stage, the court must be satisfied:

(a) that it has before it evidence or other material which, if unanswered, would be likely to lead to a wasted costs order being made; and
(b) the wasted costs proceedings are justified notwithstanding the likely costs involved.

At the second stage (even if the court is satisfied at stage 1) the court will consider, after giving the legal representative an opportunity to give reasons why the court should not make a wasted costs order, whether it is appropriate to make a wasted costs order.

Elaborate proceedings, disclosure or requests for further information are not generally appropriate given the summary nature of the investigation (*Re Merc Property Ltd* [1999] 2 BCLC 286). The court has no power to direct that privileged documents must be disclosed (*General Mediterranean Holdings SA v Patel* [2000] 1 WLR 272; see *Medcalf v Mardell* [2002] UKHL 27, [2003] 1 AC 120, and *Brown v Bennett (No. 2)* [2002] 1 WLR 713 for the consequences of this).

The court will approach the application by considering the three points stated in **PD 43–48, para. 53.4**:

(a) Has the legal representative acted improperly, unreasonably or negligently?
(b) Has the legal representative's conduct caused a party to incur unnecessary costs (see *R v Secretary of State for the Home Department, ex parte Mach* [2001] EWCA Civ 645, LTL 27/4/2001)?

(c) Is it just in all the circumstances to order the legal representative to compensate that party for the whole or part of those costs?

It is submitted that there is no burden on the representative to exculpate him or herself.

The court can direct a costs judge or a district judge to decide the amount of costs to be disallowed or paid (**CPR, r. 48.7**).

Examples of wasted costs

The wasted costs powers against lawyers and other parties are compensatory in nature. **66.72**

Conduct justifying a wasted costs order may include failing to attend an appointment, failing to comply with the court's orders, negligent mispleading of the case, inefficient presentation of the case at trial through being ill-prepared, and pressing on with an action after it has become hopeless (for example, through failing to read the materials disclosed by the other side on disclosure). Pleading an unjustified allegation of fraud in breach of the Bar Code of Conduct may be 'improper' conduct (*Medcalf v Mardell* [2002] UKHL 27, [2003] 1 AC 120, where an order was refused). A solicitor who swears an affidavit in support of a winding-up petition in circumstances where he knows that the petition, if fought on the merits, will fail, acts unreasonably and may be the subject of a wasted costs order (*Re a Company (No. 006798 of 1995)* [1996] 1 WLR 491). A solicitor is not entitled to abdicate all responsibility for a case by instructing counsel, but the more specialist the area the more reasonable it is to follow counsel's advice. Thus in *R v Horsham District Council, ex parte Wenman* [1995] 1 WLR 680 a solicitor was absolved from liability when acting on counsel 's advice in judicial review proceedings. In *Ridehalgh v Horsefield* the Court of Appeal expressed the view that, largely because of the 'cab rank rule' whereby barristers (and to some extent solicitors) are not entitled to pick and choose their clients, it is not improper for a lawyer to represent a client who is bound to lose. However, pursuing a case which amounts to an abuse of process would be 'improper'. The distinction is largely one of degree. The Court of Appeal also made a point of deprecating the practice of making threats to apply for wasted costs orders as a means of unacceptable intimidation, although there is a distinction between that and giving proper notice that an application will be made in the case of persistent improper, unreasonable or negligent conduct.

Chapter 67 Fixed and Predictable Costs on Judgments etc.

INTRODUCTION

67.1 The CPR provide for four main kinds of fixed or predictable costs:

(a) Costs of proceedings where the case is disposed of at an early stage and without substantial dispute by the defendant, the costs of enforcement and other specified miscellaneous costs ('fixed costs').
(b) Predictable costs for certain road traffic claims that settle prior to the issue of proceedings ('predictable costs').
(c) Fixed success fee uplifts for road traffic accident claims and employers' liability claims ('fixed CFA uplifts').
(d) Fixed costs in the fast track.

SOURCES OF THE FIXED COSTS REGIME

67.2 In **Parts 43 to 48** of the CPR the term 'fixed costs' means specifically the fixed costs provided for in **Part 45, Section I (rr. 45.1 to 45.6)**, supplemented by **PD 43–48, Sections 24** and **25 (CPR, r. 43.2(j))**. These fixed costs are adopted by **r. 27.14(2)(a)** for all claims decided on the small claims track. With effect from 1 April 2005 there are five tables in Part 45, Section I, setting out the amounts allowed by way of fixed costs. These are:

Table 1	Fixed costs on commencement of a claim for the recovery of money or goods (**r. 45.2**)
Table 2	Fixed costs on commencement of a claim for recovery of land (**r. 45.2**)
Table 3	Fixed costs on entry of judgment (**r. 45.4A**)
Table 4	Miscellaneous fixed costs (**r. 45.5**)
Table 5	Fixed enforcement costs (**r. 45.6**)

Provisions in the CPR relating to other types of fixed costs are:

(a) Predictable costs in road traffic claims (**rr. 45.7** to **45.14**).
(b) Fixed CFA uplifts in road traffic accident claims and employers' liability and disease claims (**rr. 45.15** to **45.26**).
(c) Fixed costs on issue of a default costs certificate (**r. 47.11** and **PD 43–48, para. 37.8**).
(d) Fixed fast track trial costs (**Part 46** and **PD 43–48, Sections 26** and 27).

Before 1 April 2005 there were fixed costs rules in preserved provisions of RSC, ord. 62, and CCR, ord. 38 (possession of land). These have been revoked by the Civil Procedure (Amendment No. 4) Rules 2004 (SI 2004/3419) and subsumed in **Part 45**.

SITUATIONS WHERE FIXED COSTS APPLY

Part 45 of the CPR and various other provisions lay down the situations where fixed costs apply, broadly as follows: **67.3**

(a) where the only claim is a claim for a specified sum of money which is more than £25 and judgment is given after the defendant admits all or part of the claim (**CPR, r.** 45.1(2)(a)(ii) and (iii));
(b) where the only claim is a claim for a specified sum of money which is more than £25 and judgment is entered by default (**r.** 45.1(2)(a)(i));
(c) where the only claim is a claim for a specified sum of money which is more than £25 and summary judgment is entered (**r.** 45.1(2)(a)(iv));
(d) where the only claim is a claim for a specified sum of money which is more than £25 and the claim succeeds after the defence is struck out as disclosing no reasonable grounds for defending the claim (**r.** 45.1(2)(a)(v));
(e) where the only claim is for a specified sum of money and the defendant pays it together with the fixed commencement costs within 14 days of service of the particulars of claim (**rr.** 45.1(2)(a)(vi) and 45.3(1));
(f) where the only claim is a claim for a specified sum of money and the claimant accepts a Part 36 payment made within 14 days after service of proceedings (**rr.** 45.1(2)(a)(vi) and 45.3(2));
(g) where judgment is given on a fixed date claim (see **r.** 7.9 and **PD 7B**) for delivery of goods, worth more than £25, under a regulated agreement within the meaning of the **Consumer Credit Act 1974 (CPR, rr.** 45.1(2)(b) and 45.4);
(h) in possession claims (with or without a money claim), including claims under **Part 55**, where the defendant gives up possession and pays the amount claimed with fixed commencement costs stated on the claim form (**rr.** 45.1(2)(c) and 45.2A);
(i) in possession claims based on non-payment of rent where the court gives a fixed date for the hearing when it issues the claim and judgment is given without the defendant denying liability (beyond making proposals for paying arrears of rent) (**rr.** 45.1(2)(d) and 45.2A);
(j) in accelerated possession claims of land let on assured shorthold tenancies under **Part 55, Section II**, where possession orders are made without the defendant denying liability (**rr.** 45.1(2)(e) and 45.2A);
(k) in successful demotion claims under **Part 65, Section III (rr.** 45.1(2)(f) and 45.2A);
(l) where a judgment creditor takes steps to enforce a judgment or order under **Parts 70** to 73 (**rr.** 45.1(2)(g) and 45.6);
(m) on the issue of a default costs certificate (**PD 43–48, para.** 25.1); and
(n) on the determination of a small claims track claim (**CPR, r.** 27.14(2)(a)).

The fixed costs regime in **Part 45, Section I (rr.** 45.1 to 45.6), applies unless the court orders otherwise (**r.** 45.1(1)). Except for the fixed costs for acceptance of a Part 36 payment and for enforcement proceedings, the regime does not apply where the value of the claim is £25 or less (**r.** 45.1(2)(a) and (b)). Enforcement proceedings are not subject to a minimum value unless the enforcement is under **r.** 70.5(4) of awards made by tribunals other than the High Court and county courts (**r.** 45.6). In the small claims track, **r.** 27.14(2)(d) permits the court to order further costs to be paid by a party who has behaved unreasonably (see **43.28**).

The scales of fixed costs are intended to deliver a moderate and predictable scheme of costs where there are no unusual factors and no real contest. It follows that the court is likely to depart from this regime where it is clear that it will not deliver proper remuneration for cases outside the norm. It is suggested that the court will have in mind the factors listed in **r. 44.5** (factors to be taken into account in deciding the amount of costs) in deciding whether to depart from fixed costs. For example, the court is unlikely to confine a successful claimant to fixed costs on a contested application for summary judgment, but a court may restrict a claimant to fixed costs on a straightforward rent arrears possession claim.

SUMS INCLUDED IN FIXED COSTS

67.4 Where the fixed costs regime of **CPR, Part 45, Section I (rr. 45.1 to 45.6)**, applies, the costs are incremental, with each increment corresponding to a step in the proceedings:

(a) commencement (Tables 1 and 2);
(b) entry of judgment (Table 3);
(c) exceptional forms of service (Table 4);
(d) enforcement (Table 5).

In addition, the successful litigant is entitled to recover the relevant court fee, for example, the issue fee or (in the case of summary judgment) the application fee (**r. 45.1(3)**).

Because the scheme is incremental, the amount that can be entered or that will be awarded will be the aggregate of the applicable sums.

Amounts allowed

67.5 Table 1 in **CPR, r. 45.2**, sets out the fixed commencement costs in money claims and claims for the delivery of goods.

Table 2 in **r. 45.2A**, sets out the fixed commencement costs for claims for the recovery of land and demotion claims.

Table 3 in **r. 45.4**, sets out the fixed costs for entering judgment recoverable on entering default, summary judgments etc. in money claims and claims for the delivery of goods.

Table 4 in **r. 45.5**, sets out allowances for cases where personal service has been effected by the claimant's solicitor, where defendants have been served by alternative methods, and where defendants have been served outside the jurisdiction.

Table 5 in **r. 45.6** sets out amounts to be allowed for enforcement proceedings.

Rule 45.4A(1) provides for fixed costs under **r. 45.1(2)(d)** and **(f)** of £57.25 for entering judgment in possession claims and demotion claims. Where an order for possession is made in an accelerated possession claim, the fixed costs under **r. 45.1(2)(e)** for preparing and filing the claim form, the documents that accompany the claim form, and the request for possession, total £79.50 (**r. 45.4A(2)**).

PD 43–48, para. 25.1, provides for fixed costs of £80 plus the appropriate court fee to be included in default costs certificates.

ENTERING FIXED COSTS ON THE CLAIM FORM

67.6 Where fixed costs are recoverable they should be inserted on the claim form or application (for example, simple claims for the recovery of money or possession of land, or where the party is seeking to enforce a tribunal award under **CPR, 70.5**) or the request for the enforcement process. At the bottom right-hand corner of the general claim form (N1) there is a box for entering a number of figures, including the issue fee and fixed costs for commencing the proceedings. In claims where fixed costs do not apply (i.e., most damages claims and claims for equitable relief), the relevant box on the claim form should be marked 'to be assessed' (**PD 43–48, para. 24A**).

SMALL CLAIMS TRACK FIXED COSTS

It is provided in **CPR, r. 27.14(2)(a)(ii)**, that the fixed costs payable in small claims track cases are those which are payable under **Part 45**, or would be payable under **Part 45** if that Part applied to the case. This provision is necessary because the fixed costs rules in **Part 45** do not apply, for example, to unspecified money claims (most damages claims), and the plain intention behind **r. 27.14(2)(a)** is that the same fixed costs should be recoverable in all types of small claims track cases. 67.7

PREDICTABLE COSTS IN ROAD TRAFFIC ACCIDENT CLAIMS

Disputes covered by the scheme

CPR, Part 45, Section II (rr. 45.7 to 45.14), which came into force on 6 October 2003, provides a scheme for predictable costs for certain road traffic claims that settle before the issue of proceedings and (from 1 April 2005), proceedings for the approval of a settlement or compromise under **r. 21.10(2)**. The rules are supplemented by **PD 43–48, Section 25A.** 67.8

The provisions apply only to disputes arising out of road traffic accidents occurring on or after 6 October 2003. A road traffic accident is defined as 'an accident resulting in bodily injury to any person or damage to property caused by, or arising out of, the use of a motor vehicle on a road or other public place in England and Wales' (**CPR, r. 45.7(4)(a)**). A motor vehicle is a mechanically propelled vehicle intended for use on roads (**r. 45.7(4)(b)**) and a road is any highway and any other road to which the public has access, including bridges over which a road passes (**r. 45.7(4)(c)**).

The provisions are confined to claims which settle before issue of proceedings (**PD 43–48, para. 25A.1**) for agreed damages which do not exceed £10,000 (**CPR, r. 45.7(2)(c)**) and for which the small claims track would not have been appropriate (**r. 45.7(2)(d)**). The agreed damages must include damages in respect of personal injury and/or damage to property (**r. 45.7(2)(b)**). They must, by **PD 43–48, para. 25A.3**, be calculated including:

(a) general and special damages and interest;
(b) interim payments;

but after deducting:

(c) an amount attributable to agreed contributory negligence;
(d) any amount which the compensating party is required by statute to pay directly to a third party (such as compensation recovery payments and National Health Service expenses).

Provided the above conditions are satisfied, there is no further requirement either that the costs sought fall within the indemnity principle (see **68.29**) or that any uplift sought (see item (c) in the list in **67.9**) is based on an enforceable CFA. It is enough that the conditions are satisfied and that there is a CFA (*Nizami v Butt* [2006] EWHC 159 (QB), [2006] 2 All ER 140).

Amount recoverable

The amount which can be allowed in costs-only proceedings relating to a dispute within **CPR, Part 45, Section II** (see **67.8**), is limited by **r. 45.8** to: 67.9

(a) fixed recoverable costs related to the amount of the agreed damages prescribed by **r. 45.9(1)** (see **67.10**);
(b) VAT on item (a) (**r. 45.9(3)**);
(c) a success fee if the claimant has entered into a CFA or collective CFA which provides for one (**r. 45.11(1)**) — the success fee will be allowed at 12.5 per cent of the fixed recoverable costs calculated under **r. 45.9(1)**, disregarding any additional amount for the London weighting (see **67.12**) (**r. 45.11(2)**);

(d) disbursements (**r. 45.10(1)**), limited to the items listed in **r. 45.10(2)** (see **67.13**). Where there is more than one claimant in relation to a single accident, damages will be agreed in relation to them individually and costs will be calculated in relation to each of them accordingly (**PD 43–48, para. 25A.7**).

Where the costs limit specified in **r. 45.8** is acceptable there is no need for costs-only proceedings. If it is considered that there are exceptional circumstances justifying a greater recovery, costs-only proceedings may be brought under **r. 45.12** (see **67.14**).

Fixed recoverable costs

67.10 The fixed recoverable costs which are to be allowed in relation to a dispute within **CPR, Part 45, Section II** (see **67.8**), are, by **r. 45.9(1)** and **(2)**:

(a) £800, plus
(b) 20 per cent of the damages agreed up to £5,000, plus
(c) 15 per cent of the damages agreed between £5,000 and £10,000, plus
(d) 12.5 per cent London weighting, where available (see **67.12**).

VAT can be added (**r. 45.9(3)**).

If the court considers that there are exceptional circumstances, it may entertain a claim for more than the fixed recoverable costs (**r. 45.12(1)**; see **67.14**).

67.11 **Examples** If agreed damages are £3,500 and no London weighting is available, the fixed recoverable costs are:

£800 + 20% of £3,500 = £800 + £700 = £1,500

If a London weighting is available, the amount is increased by 12.5 per cent (12.5% of £1,500 is £187.50) to £1,687.50.

If agreed damages are £8,500 and no London weighting is available, the fixed recoverable costs are:

£800 + 20% of £5,000 + 15% of £3,500 = £800 + £1,000 + £525 = £2,325

The London weighting on £2,325 is 12.5% of £2,325, which is £290.62, giving a total of £2,615.62.

67.12 **London weighting** The 12.5 per cent London weighting is available under **CPR, r. 45.9(2)**, if the claimant lives or works in the area described by **PD 43–48, para. 25A.6**, and instructs solicitors practising in that area. The designated area consists of the county court districts of: Barnet, Bow, Brentford, Bromley, Central London, Clerkenwell, Croydon, Dartford, Edmonton, Gravesend, Ilford, Lambeth, Mayor's and City of London, Romford, Shoreditch, Uxbridge, Wandsworth, West London, Willesden, and Woolwich.

Disbursements

67.13 By **CPR, r. 45.10**, only the following disbursements can be recovered under the scheme:

(a) the cost of obtaining medical records;
(b) the cost of obtaining a medical report;
(c) the cost of obtaining a police report;
(d) the cost of obtaining an engineer's report;
(e) the cost of a search of the records of the Driver and Vehicle Licensing Agency;
(f) the amount of an ATE insurance premium or the cost of memberhip of an organisation under the **Access to Justice Act 1999, s. 30**, relating to the risk;
(g) where the claimant is a child or patient, necessarily incurred counsels' and court fees for a court application for approval of the settlement;
(h) any other disbursement which has arisen due to a 'particular feature' of the dispute.

Claim for more than the fixed recoverable costs

67.14 If the court considers that there are exceptional circumstances, it may entertain a claim, in costs-only proceedings, for more than the fixed recoverable costs (**CPR, r. 45.12(1)**). If it considers the claim is appropriate, it may either assess the costs or make an order for them to be assessed (**r. 45.12(2)**). However, if the assessed figure is not 20 per cent or more above the fixed costs, the claimant will only be able to recover the fixed costs or, if they are less, the assessed costs (**r. 45.13**). If an application for an assessment is unsuccessful, or results in an assessment which is less than 20 per cent above the fixed costs, the claimant must pay the defendant's costs of defending the costs-only proceedings, and the court cannot make any order in respect of the claimant's costs of those proceedings (**r. 45.14**).

Practical implications

67.15 When a road traffic accident claim is within **CPR, Part 45, Section II**, a solicitor will simply be able to agree the costs set out in **rr. 45.8** to **45.11**, dispensing with any assessment of costs. It is hoped that this will enhance the cash flow for firms representing claimants and provide transparency and predictability for defendant insurers. It should also lead to a reduction in costs-only proceedings for relatively minor cases, as exemplified by the approach in *Nizami v Butt* [2006] EWHC 159 (QB), [2006] 2 All ER 140 (see **67.8**).

Naturally there will be a temptation for the receiving party to bring costs-only proceedings in the hope of achieving a better level of remuneration from a detailed assessment. The scheme therefore places a considerable costs risk on a claimant who seeks to adopt this route (see 67.14). The provisions of **Part 36** and **r. 47.19** concerning offers to settle apply. In addition the assessment must beat the predictable costs by 20 per cent or more before anything extra is payable (**r. 45.13**). This creates something of an anomaly. The costs officer or costs judge will be able to work out from **r. 45.9** the predictable costs and will know when the critical 20 per cent is achieved. It might be suggested that **r. 45.13** is akin to an assessment hearing where the judge knows of an offer under **r. 47.19**. Given the level of costs that can arise on costs-only proceedings, the receiving party will be at significant risk in commencing such proceedings.

The scheme still leaves potential areas for dispute. The level of disbursements and the cost of ATE insurance are not fixed and may be the subject of dispute, which can only be resolved by the court. The authors of the scheme hope that market forces and the duty of solicitors to advise on ATE insurance schemes will prevent these issues arising in practice. Experience since 2000 does not lead to optimism.

FIXED PERCENTAGE INCREASE IN ROAD TRAFFIC ACCIDENT CLAIMS

67.16 With effect from 1 June 2004, Section III of CPR, Part 45 (**rr. 45.15 to 45.19**), provides fixed success-fee percentages for certain road traffic accident CFAs. Section III applies where:

(a) the dispute arises from a road traffic accident; and
(b) the claimant has entered into a funding arrangement of a type specified in **r. 43.2(1)(k)(i)**, which defines a funding arrangement as including an arrangement where a person has entered into a CFA or collective CFA which provides for a success fee.

Section III does not apply:

(a) if the proceedings are costs-only proceedings to which **Section II of Part 45** applies;
(b) to a claim which has been allocated to the small claims track;
(c) to a claim not allocated to a track, but for which the small claims track is the normal track; or

(d) where the road traffic accident which gave rise to the dispute occurred before 6 October 2003.

Fixed road traffic uplift

67.17 By CPR, r. 45.16, the percentage increase which is to be allowed in relation to solicitors' fees in claims to which **Section III of Part 45** applies (see 67.16) is:

(a) 100 per cent where the claim concludes at trial; or
(b) 12.5 per cent where:
  (i) the claim concludes before a trial has commenced; or
  (ii) the dispute is settled before a claim is issued.

By r. 45.17, the percentage uplift to be allowed in relation to counsel's fees is:

(a) 100 per cent where the claim concludes at trial;
(b) 75 per cent if the claim has been allocated to the multi-track and concludes 21 days or less before the day fixed for the commencement of the trial;
(c) 50 per cent if the claim has been allocated to the fast track and concludes 14 days or less before the day fixed for the commencement of the trial;
(d) 12.5 per cent if the claim concludes more than 21 days (multi-track) or 14 days (fast track) before the date fixed for the commencement of the trial, or where the claim has not been allocated to a track or (in costs-only proceedings) if the claim is settled before a claim is issued.

For the purposes of r. 45.17, the first day of a trial window or period is treated as the day fixed for the commencement of the trial, unless an actual fixed date is given before the case concludes (r. 45.17(2) to (4)). The day fixed for the commencement of the trial, or the first day of a trial period, does not count towards the 14 or 21-day period (r. 45.17(5)).

The mandatory language used in **rr. 45.16** and **45.17** means there is a strong argument that the fixed uplifts apply regardless of the agreed uplift in the actual CFA, provided there is a provision for a success fee in the CFA (see r. 45.15 and the reference to r. 43.2(1)(k)(i)).

FIXED PERCENTAGE INCREASE IN EMPLOYERS' LIABILITY CLAIMS

67.18 With effect from 1 October 2004, Section IV of CPR, Part 45 (rr. 45.20 to 45.22), provides fixed success-fee percentages for certain CFAs entered into in employers' liability claims. Section IV applies to CFA agreements in personal injuries claims against employers arising from accidents in the course of an employee's employment. It does not apply to disease cases, or to cases that have been or would be allocated to the small claims track. It only applies to injuries sustained on or after 1 October 2004.

Fixed employers' liability uplift

67.19 Where CPR, Part 45, Section IV, applies the percentage uplift allowed for both solicitors' and counsel's fees is:

(a) 100 per cent where the claim concludes at trial; or
(b) where the claim concludes before a trial has commenced or the dispute is settled before a claim is issued:
  (i) 27.5 per cent if a membership organisation has undertaken to meet the claimant's liabilities for legal costs in accordance with the Access to Justice Act 1999, s. 30; or
  (ii) 25 per cent in any other case.

FIXED PERCENTAGE INCREASE IN EMPLOYERS' LIABILITY DISEASE CLAIMS

With effect from 1 October 2005, a new Section V (**rr.** 45.23 to 45.25) has been added to **CPR, Part** 45, to provide for fixed recoverable success fees in employers' liability disease claims. Section V only applies to diseases contracted on or after 1 October 2005. Where it applies the percentage uplifts allowed are as shown in **Table** 67.1. Uplifts for counsel are divided into claims which are resolved more than 21 days before trial ('>21 days'); less than 21 days before trial ('<21 days'); and at trial. **67.20**

Table 67.1 Percentage uplifts in employers' liability disease claims

	Solicitors		Counsel (multi-track)		
	Before trial	**At trial**	**>21 days**	**<21 days**	**At trial**
Type A (asbestos)	27.5	100	27.5	75	100
Type B (psychiatric/ work related limb)	100	100	100	100	100
Type C (any other)	62.5	100	62.5	75	100

SEEKING AN ALTERNATIVE PERCENTAGE UPLIFT IN RTA AND EMPLOYERS' LIABILITY CLAIMS

It is possible to dispute the fixed percentage increases in **CPR, Part 45, Sections III** to **V**, but there are costs penalties if the court does assess a significantly different percentage. See **rr.** 45.18, 45.19, 45.22 and 45.25 for the detailed requirements. **67.21**

Chapter 68 Assessment of Costs

The following procedural checklist, which is in **appendix 1**, is relevant to this chapter:

Procedural checklist 32 Summary assessment of costs

INTRODUCTION

68.1 Once a costs order has been made, it is necessary to determine how much should be allowed in respect of those costs, that is, how much the paying party must pay to the receiving party. A similar determination must be made when a solicitor bills a client and when a solicitor is seeking to recover costs from the State in a publicly funded claim. In **chapter 67** the system of fixed costs applicable to certain situations in litigation was considered. This chapter will deal with assessment of costs by the courts. As will be seen, there are two methods, summary assessment and detailed assessment.

METHODS OF QUANTIFICATION OF COSTS

Rule 44.7 of the CPR provides that when the court makes a costs order it may either: **68.2**

(a) make a summary assessment of the costs; or
(b) order a detailed assessment by a costs officer.

A 'costs officer' is defined by **CPR, r. 43.2(1)**, to mean a costs judge (which in turn means a taxing master of the Supreme Court), a district judge or an authorised court officer (i.e., a civil servant, in a district registry, the Principal Registry of the Family Division, the Supreme Court Costs Office or a county court, who is authorised by the Lord Chancellor to assess costs).

SUMMARY ASSESSMENT

Summary assessment involves a short assessment of a party's costs. Because it is a summary procedure it will not involve the lengthy consideration of items which is reserved for a detailed assessment. Thus in *Gould v Armstrong* [2002] EWCA Civ 1159, LTL 23/7/2002, the court approved a robust summary assessment as an effective and proportionate means of avoiding the cost and delay associated with a detailed assessment. **68.3**

The procedure for summary assessment of costs is summarised in **procedural checklist** 32, which is in **appendix 1**.

Summary assessment of costs generally arises at the conclusion of a fast track trial or other hearings which do not last more than one day (**PD 43–48, para. 13.2**) (see **32.27, 44.22** and **66.27**). There are situations where it will not be appropriate to conduct a summary assessment of costs even though the conditions of para. 13.2 are met (for a list of these see **66.27**). Conversely there is nothing to prevent the court from summarily assessing the costs even where the conditions in para. 13.2 are not met, for example, when the trial lasts for more than one day (*Q v Q (Family Proceedings: Costs Order)* [2002] 2 FLR 668). Summary assessment is not required where the parties have agreed the amount of the costs (**para. 13.13(a)**).

Summary assessment is preceded by the service of a statement of costs on **form N260** not less than 24 hours before the hearing (**para. 13.5(4)**). At first sight the wording of this provision suggests that the requirement to serve the costs statement is mandatory and that failure would lead to the loss of all costs or alternatively to a detailed assessment. This approach was rejected by the court in *MacDonald v Taree Holdings Ltd* [2000] CPLR 439, where the court made it clear that the loss of all costs was a disproportionate sanction unless the circumstances were exceptional and that the court should consider adjourning to give the paying party time to consider the receiving party's statement. However, any failure to serve the statement of costs without reasonable cause will be taken into account in the summary assessment (**para. 13.6**).

Statement of costs

A statement of costs must be in **form N260** and must, by **PD 43–48, para. 13.5(2)**, address the following matters: **68.4**

(a) The name, status and date of admission of the fee earner. It is important to refer to the four categories of fee earner found at the foot of the form N260 and to appreciate that they are experience-based. Thus the term 'partner' has no place in the form N260, whereas a solicitor with over eight years' post-qualification experience in litigation is an acceptable description.

(b) The number of hours claimed.

(c) The hourly rate claimed. Practitioners may wish to consider **tables 68.1, 68.2** and **68.3**, which set out the guideline rate for each court in the country, based on figures from the Guide to the Summary Assessment of Costs published by the Supreme Court Costs Office (SCCO).

(d) The amount and nature of disbursements. Work which is outsourced should normally appear in the body of the bill as if carried out by the firm (*Smith Graham v Lord Chancellor's Department* (1999) 149 NLJ 1433). There is some concern as to whether a solicitor should be able to recover for work outsourced to agents. While there is no appellate authority on the issue, Judge Michael Cook found that such items could be allowed on an assessment, provided there is sufficient information to allow the judge to ascertain whether they were reasonably incurred and reasonable in amount (*Stringer v Copley* (2002) LTL 17/10/2002).

(e) The solicitor's costs for attending or appearing at the hearing. The court will only allow a sum for attendance at a fast track trial with counsel or another advocate if it is necessary for the representative to be present at trial (**PD 43–48, para. 46(3)**).

(f) Counsel's year of call and fees.

(g) VAT on the above. Practitioners must be vigilant to ensure that VAT is included in the bill only if it is properly claimed. Costs are compensatory and thus VAT can only be charged if the receiving party will lose the VAT. Most VAT registered parties will be able to reclaim VAT and thus it will not represent an overall loss. Hence VAT should not generally be claimed where the party is registered for VAT. (See **PD 43–48, paras 5.3 and 5.4** and **68.59**.)

(h) The schedule must be signed (**PD 43–48, para. 13.5(3)**). The signature is not an empty formality, it is a certificate given by an officer of the court that the schedule is accurate and that there is no infringement of the indemnity principle. It affords a presumption of trust to the paying party (*Bailey v IBC Vehicles Ltd* [1998] 3 All ER 570). Where a solicitor failed to sign a statement of costs the court has been prepared to stay the issue of the costs order (*Wilson v Howard Pawnbrokers* [2002] EWHC 1489 (Ch), LTL 19/8/2002).

Quantifying costs on a summary assessment

68.5 Courts sometimes develop conventional figures for summarily assessed costs for certain types of proceeding, such as the costs awarded for straightforward landlord and tenant possession proceedings. Although this may be acceptable in straightforward possession claims, it is contrary to principle in the majority of claims. On a summary assessment of costs the court must focus on the detailed breakdown of costs actually incurred by the party in question as shown on its statement of costs. The court is entitled to draw on its general experience of costs in comparable cases, and it may be helpful to draw on that experience when comparing the total from its assessment of the costs on the schedule to see whether those costs were reasonable and proportionate. What the court cannot do is to use a judicial tariff for different categories of claims (*1-800 Flowers Inc. v Phonenames Ltd* [2001] EWCA Civ 721, [2001] 2 Costs LR 286). The court can call for whatever evidence is available at the time in deciding on the figure to allow, such as looking at counsel's brief to see the brief fee, as well as looking at the costs statements and hearing the advocates on the work involved in the matter.

In *Edwards v Devon and Cornwall Constabulary* (2001) LTL 13/3/2001, on a summary assessment after a fast track trial, the judge reduced the claimant's costs schedule from £7,500 to £2,500 and did not allow counsel to address him on the reduction. After disbursements this gave the claimant's solicitors £620 in a non-straightforward personal injuries claim. The Court of Appeal substituted its own summary assessment of the claimant's costs. In *Contractreal Ltd v Davies* [2001] EWCA Civ 928, LTL 17/5/2001, the appellant's costs were reduced from £21,000 to £1,750 on a summary assessment. On appeal it was held that the judge had placed too much weight upon the size of the bill in comparison with the amount in issue when considering proportionality, and had failed to distinguish between pre and post-CPR costs (proportionality only applies to the latter), and the court ordered a detailed assessment.

Where costs are assessed summarily they are payable within 14 days unless the court in its discretion thinks fit to order otherwise (**CPR, rr. 44.3** and **44.8**). A party seeking such a direction must apply for it and, where appropriate, must back up the application with evidence. The court can, of its own initiative, postpone the date of payment, where it considers there are appropriate reasons (*Pepin v Watts* [2001] CPLR 9 at [29]).

FAST TRACK TRIAL COSTS

Fixed trial costs

Part of the scheme of the Woolf proposals was that there should be restricted costs recoverable in fast track cases. This has in part been brought into effect by a system of fixed trial costs in fast track claims. **Rule 46.2 of the CPR** provides that advocates' trial fees in fast track cases will be: **68.6**

Value of claim up to £3,000	£350
Value of claim between £3,000 and £10,000	£500
Claims for non-money remedies	£500
Value of claim over £10,000	£750
Additional fee for solicitor attending trial with counsel	£250

For a successful claimant the value of the claim is the amount of the judgment excluding interest, costs and any reduction for contributory negligence, whereas for a successful defendant it is the amount the claimant specified on the claim form (or the maximum amount that could have been recovered on the pleaded case) (**r. 46.2(3)**). If there is a counterclaim and both parties succeed, the relevant amount is the difference between the value of the two claims (**r. 46.3(6)**). If there is a counterclaim with a greater value than the claim, and the claimant succeeds on the claim and defeats the counterclaim, the relevant amount is the value of the counterclaim (**r. 46.2(6)**). There are detailed rules dealing with cases where there are several claimants or several defendants, including whether more than one party can be awarded fast track trial costs, which are set out in **r. 46.4**. For claims for non-monetary remedies the court has a discretion to make some other order, see **r. 46.2(4)**.

The court is not permitted to award more or less than the set figures for trial costs, unless it decides not to award any fast track trial costs or **r. 46.3** applies (**r. 46.2(2)**). Guidance given by the Senior Costs Judge to the Designated Civil Judges Conference on 24 November 2000 is to the effect that this means that unless a **r. 46.3** factor applies, the court must allow the standard trial costs even if the brief fee is lower than the standard amount. This is so notwithstanding the indemnity principle (see **68.29**).

The additional allowance for a solicitor attending with counsel is provided by **r. 46.3**. The allowance of £250 is greater than the £150 suggested in the consultation paper, although the figures for counsel's fast track trial fees are the same as in the paper. The solicitor's attendance fee will only be payable if the court awards fast track trial costs and if the court considers that it was necessary for a legal representative to attend to assist counsel (**r. 46.3(2)**).

Abortive preparation, split trials and misconduct

If a fast track claim settles before the start of the trial, costs may be allowed in respect of the advocate preparing for trial, but the amount allowed cannot be more than the above figures (**CPR, r. 44.10**). In deciding the amount to be allowed for the abortive preparation, the court will take into account when the claim settled and when the court was notified of that fact. **68.7**

If there are split trials, such as on liability and quantum, it is possible to be awarded a second tranche of fast track trial costs, but the second award should not exceed two thirds of the amount payable under the first award, subject to a minimum award of £350 (**r. 46.3(3) and (4)**).

A successful party may, by **r. 46.3(7)**, be awarded less than the above fixed fast track trial costs for unreasonable or improper behaviour during the trial, and the losing party may be ordered to pay an additional amount if it is guilty of behaving improperly during the trial (**r. 46.3(8)**).

INTERIM PAYMENT ON ACCOUNT OF COSTS

68.8 The court has a power to make an order for an amount to be paid on account of costs which will be assessed at some later stage (**CPR, r. 44.3(8)**). In the ordinary course, an order for an interim payment on account will be made if a final costs order has been made, subject to detailed assessment, provided there is no likelihood of an appeal and the paying party is not impecunious (*Soliman v Islington London Borough Council* (2001) LTL 16/10/2001). An order for an interim payment on account of costs may be made even where the receiving party is late in commencing detailed assessment proceedings (*Allason v Random House UK Ltd* (2002) LTL 28/2/2002, where a payment of £140,000 was ordered in respect of costs said to amount to at least £175,000). An interim payment on account of costs may be ordered even where there is no detailed breakdown of the costs (*Simms v Law Society* [2005] EWCA Civ 849, [2005] ACD 98).

Where there has been a full trial, the successful party should normally be awarded an interim payment on account of costs under **r. 44.3(8)** in an amount up to the minimum sum which he will almost certainly be awarded on a detailed assessment (*Mars UK Ltd v Teknowledge Ltd* [1999] IP & T 26). Where there has been no full trial the judge is not constrained by any presumption one way or the other. It is for the successful party to justify the court making an order, and, bearing in mind **r. 47.15**, it may be inappropriate even to make an interim payment in the minimum sum the successful party will inevitably recover in a detailed assessment (*Dyson Ltd v Hoover Ltd (No. 4)* [2003] EWHC 624 (Ch), [2004] 1 WLR 1264).

DETAILED ASSESSMENT

68.9 Unlike summary assessment, a detailed assessment is not generally conducted until the conclusion of the proceedings (**CPR, r. 47.1**). Proceedings are concluded when the court has finally determined the matters in issue in the claim, whether or not there is an appeal (**PD 43–48, para. 28.1(1)**). However, the court retains a power to order an assessment at an earlier stage. An order may be made allowing detailed assessment proceedings to be commenced if there is no realistic prospect of the claim continuing (**PD 43–48, para. 28.1(5)**).

Appropriate office

68.10 All applications and requests in detailed assessment proceedings must be made to or filed at the 'appropriate office' (**CPR, r. 47.4**). In High Court cases this is usually the Supreme Court Costs Office (SCCO). If the court dealing with the case when the judgment or order was made or when the event occurred which gave rise to the right to assessment, or to which the case has subsequently been transferred, is the Principal Registry of the Family Division or a district registry or a county court then that registry or court is the appropriate office (**PD 43–48, para. 31.1**). County courts can specify another county court as the appropriate office for the assessment of costs (**CPR, r. 47.4(3)**). Any court can direct that the SCCO is to be the appropriate office (**CPR, r. 47.4(2)**), but should only do so having regard to the size of the bill of costs, its difficulty, length of hearing and costs to the parties (**PD 43–48, para. 31.2(3)**). An order transferring a bill to another court or to the SCCO can be made on the application of a party or on the court's own initiative. Before making such an order the transferring court must give the parties an opportunity to make representations (**PD 43–48, para.** 13.2(2)).

Detailed assessments in London county courts (Barnet, Bow, Brentford, Central London, Clerkenwell, Croydon, Edmonton, Ilford, Lambeth, Mayor's and City of London, Romford, Shoreditch, Wandsworth, West London, Willesden and Woolwich), where a receiving party is seeking an order specifying costs payable by an LSC-funded client and/or by the LSC, must be commenced and will take place in the SCCO unless the court orders otherwise (PD 43–48, para. 23.2A).

Commencement of detailed assessment proceedings

Detailed assessment proceedings must be commenced within three months of the judgment, order, award or other determination giving rise to the right to costs (**CPR, r.** 47.7). The period may be extended or shortened by agreement between the parties (**PD 43–48, para.** 33.1). A similar three-month period is laid down in respect of cases terminated by discontinuance, dismissal or acceptance of **Part 36** offers and payments (**CPR, r.** 47.7). Detailed assessment proceedings are commenced by serving on the paying party a notice of commencement (**form** N252) together with a copy of the bill of costs (**r.** 47.6(1)). The receiving party is also required to serve copies of counsel's fee notes and experts' fee invoices, written evidence for all disbursements exceeding £250, and a statement giving the name and address for service of any person upon whom the receiving party intends to serve the notice of commencement (**PD 43–48, para.** 32.3). The persons referred to in the previous sentence are known as 'relevant persons', who are defined by **PD 43–48, para.** 32.10, as persons who took part in the proceedings and who are directly liable to pay the costs under a costs order, and also persons who have given notice that they have a financial interest in the outcome of the assessment and any other person the court may direct to be treated as a relevant person. Relevant persons must also be served with the notice of commencement and with the bill of costs (**CPR, r.** 47.6(2)). These additional persons are thereafter regarded as being parties to the assessment proceedings. 68.11

In cases where the costs to be assessed are payable out of the legal aid fund, the assessment is commenced by filing a request for a detailed assessment (**form** N258A), which must be served on the assisted person (**r.** 47.17(3)). Again, this must be done within three months from the date when the right to detailed assessment arose (**r.** 47.17(2)). In assessments of publicly funded costs, in addition to the documents referred to in the previous paragraph, the request for a detailed assessment must, by **PD 43–48, para.** 43.3, be accompanied by the legal aid or LSC certificates, amendments and authorities, and any certificate of discharge or revocation, and also the relevant papers in support of the bill described in **PD 43–48, para.** 40.12, and names and addresses of any person with financial interests in the assessment, and of the assisted person, if he or she wishes to attend.

The effect of failing to commence proceedings for the detailed assessment of costs within the prescribed time limit is considered at **68.24**.

Bill of costs

There are four model forms of bill of costs set out in the schedule to **PD 43–48**. See also the guidance in the **Supreme Court Costs Office Guide, sect. 3. Paragraph 4.1 of PD 43–48** provides that a bill of costs may consist of such of the following sections as may be appropriate: 68.12

(a) a title page;
(b) background information;
(c) items of costs claimed under the following headings:
 (i) attendances on the court and on counsel up to the date of the notice of commencement;

(ii) attendances on and communications with the receiving party;
(iii) attendances on and communications with witnesses including expert witnesses;
(iv) attendances to inspect any property or place for the purposes of the proceedings;
(v) searches and enquiries made at offices of public records, the Companies Registry and similar searches and enquiries;
(vi) attendances on and communications with other persons;
(vii) communications with the court and with counsel;
(viii) work done in connection with arithmetical calculations of compensation and/or interest;
(ix) work done on documents: preparing and considering documentation relevant to the proceedings, including time spent on pre-action protocols and on collating documents;
(x) work done in connection with mediation, ADR and negotiations with a view to settlement if not already covered in the heads listed above;
(xi) attendances on and communications with London and other agents and work done by them;
(xii) other work done which was of or incidental to the proceedings and which is not already covered in the heads listed above.

(d) a summary showing the total costs claimed on each page of the bill;
(e) schedules of time spent on non-routine attendances; and
(f) appropriate certificates as set out in **precedent** F in the schedule to PD 43–48.

The bill may be divided into two or more parts to distinguish between times when the receiving party was acting in person and by different firms of solicitors, and between times before and during the continuance of legal aid (**PD 43–48, para. 4.2**).

Each item in the bill must be consecutively numbered (**PD 43–48, para. 4.9**). The bill may be organised into five columns, headed 'Item', 'Amount claimed', 'VAT', with the last two left blank, but headed 'Amount allowed' and 'VAT' (**PD 43–48, para. 4.1 and precedents A to D**).

Points of dispute

68.13 In a detailed assessment of costs the paying party and others served with the notice of commencement may dispute any item in the bill by serving all the other parties with points of dispute. Points of dispute should be short and to the point, and should follow as closely as possible **precedent C** in the schedule to PD 43–48 (**PD 43–48, para. 35.2; Supreme Court Costs Office Guide, para. 5.2**). They must:

(a) identify each item in the bill of costs which is disputed;
(b) in each case state concisely the nature and grounds of the dispute;
(c) where practicable suggest a figure to be allowed for each item in respect of which a reduction is sought; and
(d) be signed by the party serving them or by the serving party's solicitor.

Copies of the points of dispute should also be served on other persons appearing on the statement of persons whom the receiving party intended to serve with the notice of commencement. These must be served within 21 days after service of the notice of commencement (see **CPR, r. 47.9**).

Default costs certificate

68.14 If the paying party fails to serve points of dispute within the permitted time, the receiving party may, on filing a request (**form N254**), obtain a default costs certificate (**CPR, rr. 47.9(4)** and **47.11; Supreme Court Costs Office Guide, sect. 6**), which means that all the costs in the bill are allowed. A default certificate includes an order to pay the relevant costs (**r. 47.11(2)**; see **forms N255 and N255HC**). The right to a default certificate is lost if the receiving party delays making the request until after the paying party serves points of dispute, albeit late. A party who serves points of dispute late will not be heard on the assessment hearing, unless the court so permits (**r. 47.9(3)**). There is a power to set aside a default costs certificate on the ground of there being good reason to do so. The court will also be concerned to see a draft of the proposed points of dispute and will take into account whether the application to set aside was made promptly (**r. 47.12; PD 43–48, paras 38.1 to 38.4**).

Reply

68.15 The receiving party has the right, but is not obliged, to serve a reply to any points of dispute. Any reply should be served on the party who served the points of dispute within 21 days after service (**CPR, r. 47.13**). A reply may take the form of an annotation of the points of dispute, or may be set out in a separate document (**Supreme Court Costs Office Guide, para 5.3(c)**). Filing a reply does not avoid the receiving party's obligation under **PD 43–48, para 40.2(d)**, when requesting a detailed assessment hearing, to file a copy of the points of dispute annotated to show which items have been agreed and their value and to show the items still in dispute and their value.

Applications within assessment proceedings

68.16 Applications within detailed assessment proceedings, such as for time for commencing the proceedings, for extensions of time for service of points of dispute or replies, or for case management directions, are made under **CPR, Part 23 (Supreme Court Costs Office Guide, sect. 17)**. They therefore require an application notice in **form N244** and written evidence. This can be avoided if there has been a previous order made in the assessment giving 'liberty to apply', in which case it is enough to write to the court requesting the restoration of the previous application (**para. 17.1(c)**).

Assessment hearing

68.17 Once points of dispute have been served the receiving party must, within three months of the expiry of the period for commencing the detailed assessment proceedings, file a request for an assessment hearing (**CPR, r. 47.14**). If the receiving party fails to do so, the paying party may apply under **r. 47.14(3)** for an order that the receiving party must file the request within a specified period, and the court may direct that if there is a breach of that direction, the receiving party will lose all or part of the costs that would otherwise have been recoverable (**r. 47.14(4)**). There will be cases where the receiving party fails to request an assessment hearing within the three-month period, the paying party makes no application requiring a request, and the receiving party then makes a late request for the assessment hearing. In these cases, if the court is minded to impose a sanction to mark the delay in making the request, it will normally be restricted to disallowing interest (**r. 47.14(5)**).

In publicly funded cases, unless the assisted party wishes to attend, the court will provisionally assess the costs without a hearing unless it considers a hearing is necessary. If a bill is provisionally assessed, the solicitor has 14 days after it is returned to request an assessment hearing. In cases where the assisted party wants to attend, the solicitor will certify to this effect, and the court will fix the assessment hearing (**r. 47.17**).

Rights of audience at assessment hearings are considered in the **Supreme Court Costs Office Guide, para. 1.2**. By concession costs draftsmen are treated as if they are in the employ of the firm of solicitors instructing them. The usual reluctance to allow McKenzie friends applies also to assessment hearings (**para. 1.2(g)**). Hearings are in public, although admitting members of the public is often impracticable as hearings are often in district judges' or costs judges' private rooms (**para. 9.1(a)**). Hearings are as informal as is consistent with the need to see that justice is done to all parties (**para. 9.1(c)**). Hearings are usually recorded (**para. 9.2(a)**). The court will usually consider the matters raised by the points of dispute item by item, considering the evidence and argument on an item and giving an oral decision on that item before moving on to the next item (**para. 9.2(b)**). Unless the court otherwise permits, only matters raised in the points of dispute may be raised at the hearing (**CPR, r. 47.14(7)**).

Principles for determining reasonableness

68.18 In deciding whether costs were reasonably incurred or were reasonable and proportionate in amount, the court is to have regard to all the circumstances. Under the old system the court was assisted in this task by what were called the 'seven pillars', which included the complexity of the item or the action, and the difficulty or novelty of the questions involved. The 'seven pillars' were set out in RSC, ord. 62, appendix 2, para. 1. In the **CPR, r. 44.5(3)** provides for eight matters to be taken into account. They echo the former position, but have been expanded to include the conduct of the parties before as well as during the proceedings (and thus take into account compliance, or otherwise, with any applicable pre-action protocol) and their efforts to resolve the dispute. The matters to be taken into account omit the old third pillar, which required the court to have regard to the number and importance of the documents prepared or perused. However, time spent on documentation can still be charged for as is plain from **PD 43–48, para. 4.6(7)**, which includes the time spent on preparing, considering and collating documents. Any costs estimate will be taken into account in determining reasonableness (see **63.19**).

Assessment under the Solicitors Act 1974, part III

68.19 The statutory provisions regulating the remuneration of solicitors in the **Solicitors Act 1974, part III**, including the right to apply for a detailed assessment, are discussed at **63.7** to **63.9**. The principles on which such costs are assessed are considered at **63.18**. A claim for an order under the **Solicitors Act 1974, part III**, can in all cases be issued in the SCCO (**PD 67, para. 2.1(2)**). Alternatively, a claim under **part III** can be made to the relevant county court where the costs relate to contentious business done in a county court or are within the financial limit of the county court's jurisdiction specified in the **Solicitors Act 1974, s. 69(3)** (**CPR, r. 67.3(1)(a)**). In every other case, proceedings under the **Solicitors Act 1974, part III**, must be brought in the High Court (**CPR, r. 67.3(1)(b)**), and, if in London, in the SCCO (**PD 67, para. 2.1(1)**). A claim for an assessment must be brought under **CPR, Part 8**, by issuing a form **N208**, unless the application is made in existing proceedings, when the **Part 23** procedure is used (**r. 67.3(2)**). **Rule 8.5** on filing written evidence does not apply in uncontested cases (**PD 67, para. 4**). By **CPR, r. 67.3(3)**, a claim in the High Court may be determined by:

(a) a High Court judge (though direct application to a judge will be justified only in exceptional circumstances: **PD 67, para. 3.2**), a master, costs judge, or district judge of the Principal Registry of the Family Division, or

(b) a district judge, if the costs are for contentious business in a district registry, contentious business in a county court in the district of a district registry, or non-contentious business (**r. 67.3(3)**).

Within 28 days of an order made under the **Solicitors Act 1974, part III**, for the assessment of costs payable to a solicitor by his or her client, the solicitor must serve the client with a breakdown of the costs (**CPR, r. 48.10(2)**). The client must serve points of dispute within 14 days of service of the breakdown, and the solicitor may serve a reply within 14 days thereafter (**r. 48.10(3)** and **(4)**). When points of dispute have been served, and in any event no later than three months from the date of the original order, either party may file a request for a hearing date. The provisions relating to default costs certificates do not apply to **Solicitors Act 1974** assessments (**PD 43–48, para. 56.7**). Further detailed provisions for these cases can be found in **PD 43–48, paras 56.1** to **56.19**.

The costs of the detailed assessment are paid in accordance with the event (**Solicitors Act 1974, s. 70(9)**). If the bill is reduced by one fifth, the solicitor must pay the costs, but otherwise the party chargeable must pay the costs of the detailed assessment, unless the order for the detailed assessment was made on the application of the solicitor and the party chargeable does not attend the assessment hearing, or the order for the detailed assessment provides otherwise (**s. 70(9)**).

Assessment of Legal Services Commission costs

A publicly funded party will need an order for the 'detailed assessment of [its] costs which are payable out of the Community Legal Service Fund' (**Supreme Court Costs Office Guide, para. 24.1(c)**). **68.20**

Where costs are payable by another person as well as out of the Community Legal Service Fund, the normal rules concerning commencing detailed assessment, points of dispute and replies apply (para. 24.2(a)). There are special forms of bills (PD 43–48, Schedule of Costs Precedents, precedents **C** and **D**). The request for a detailed assessment hearing must be accompanied by the relevant public funding certificates and authorities (**Supreme Court Costs Office Guide, para. 24.2(b)**). The publicly funded party's solicitor prepares a legal aid/ LSC schedule in advance of the hearing. The assessment hearing is conducted in two parts: the first deals with the costs payable between the parties, and the second considers the public funding sections of the bill. The paying party is not normally entitled to remain in attendance for the second part (para. 24.3).

Where costs are payable only out of the Community Legal Service Fund, the publicly funded party's solicitor may request a detailed assessment within three months after the date on which the right to a detailed assessment arose. The request must be in **form N258A**, and must be filed with a copy of the bill of costs and the other documents listed in **PD 43–48, para. 43.3**. There was an unjustifiable delay of four years in lodging a bill for assessment in *Official Receiver v Dobson* (2001) LTL 30/11/2001, which the costs judge penalised under the Civil Legal Aid (General) Regulations 1989 (SI 1989/339), reg. 109, by disallowing 100 per cent of the solicitors' profit costs. On appeal this was held to be disproportionate to the default, and the order was varied by substituting a 30 per cent disallowance.

Costs of assessment

By **PD 43–48, para. 4.18**, a bill of costs may include the reasonable costs of preparing and checking the bill. Generally, by virtue of **CPR, r. 47.18**, the paying party must also pay the receiving party's costs of the assessment proceedings. Normally these will be assessed summarily and added to the bill of costs (**PD 43–48, para. 45.1**). It is not necessary to provide details of these costs in advance unless the court orders this to be done (**Supreme Court Costs Office Guide, para. 11.1**). However, the court may make some other order as to the costs of the assessment having regard to all the circumstances, including: **68.21**

(a) the conduct of all the parties;
(b) the amount, if any, by which the bill of costs is reduced; and
(c) whether it was reasonable for particular items to appear in the bill, or for particular objections to have been taken.

Offers to settle costs

The paying party may make an offer in writing to settle the costs in dispute expressed to be 'without prejudice save as to the costs of the detailed assessment proceedings'. The amount of the offer must not be communicated to the costs officer until the question of the costs of the assessment is to be decided, and at that stage it may be taken into account in deciding who should pay the costs of the assessment proceedings (**CPR, r. 47.19**). Normally, if the offer equals or exceeds the amount allowed, the receiving party should pay the paying party's costs of the assessment proceedings, at least from the date of service of the offer. **68.22**

Normally offers to settle should, if made by the paying party, be made within 14 days of service of the notice of commencement, and if made by the receiving party, within 14 days of service of the points of dispute (**PD 43–48, para. 46.1**). Offers made at a later stage will be given less weight when it comes to costs.

An offer to settle should specify whether or not it is intended to be inclusive of the cost of preparation of the bill, interest and VAT, so that the offeree is clear about the terms of the offer. If no statement is made, the offer will be taken as including all these items (**PD 43–48, para. 46.2**).

When an offer is accepted, an application may be made for a certificate in agreed terms, or the bill may be withdrawn (**PD 43–48, para. 46.3**).

Where the receiving party is an assisted person, an offer to settle will not have any costs consequences unless the court so orders (**PD 43–48, para. 46.4**; *Bufton v Hill* (2002) LTL 7/5/2002).

An offer (in a non-publicly funded case) to pay a fixed sum 'in full settlement of your claim for costs' on an assessment of costs is to be construed as inclusive of the costs in the bill, interest on those costs, and the fee on the assessment (*Morris v Wiltshire* (2001) LTL 6/12/2001, a case under the old rules). In *Crosbie v Munroe* [2003] EWCA Civ 350, [2003] 1 WLR 2033, the claimant issued a costs-only Part 8 claim under **CPR, r. 44.12A** (see **68.59**). The defendant then made an offer to settle costs under **r. 47.19**, which was accepted by the claimant. It was held that the settlement related only to the costs of the substantive claim, which meant the costs of the Part 8 claim were still to be resolved. **CPR, r. 47.18**, raises a rebuttable presumption that the receiving party should recover the costs of an assessment. Launching a successful appeal against a decision not to transfer the assessment to the Supreme Court Costs Office is not a sufficient (or any) ground for depriving the receiving party of some of the costs of an assessment (*Bufton v Hill*).

Interest on costs

68.23 Interest on the costs of the claim normally runs from the date of the judgment or order disposing of the claim (**CPR, rr. 40.8 and 44.3(6)(g)**). Final costs certificates do not record this interest (except where enforcement is to be taken abroad). However, an application using **form N244** can be made seeking a certificate of the interest that has accrued and the daily rate of future interest (**Supreme Court Costs Office Guide, para. 15.2**). Written evidence has to justify the rate and calculation of the interest, explaining the effect of any payments on account.

Interest on the costs of detailed assessment proceedings runs from the date of the default, interim or final costs certificate (**PD 43–48, para. 45.5**).

Failure to adhere to time limits

68.24 There are strict time limits for commencing detailed assessment (see **68.11**). Failure to adhere to the time limits may incur sanctions. These come in two forms. Stage 1 is **CPR, r. 47.8(3)**, which provides that the receiving party's failure to commence the detailed assessment in time may lead to the loss of interest but no other sanction. Stage 2 comes into operation if the paying party seeks an order (on giving seven days' notice) requiring the receiving party to commence the detailed assessment (**PD 43–48, para. 34.1**). Here the sanction is that a failure to commence the proceedings will lead to the loss of some or all of the costs (**CPR, r. 47.8(2)**). The court must adopt a proportionate approach when exercising the power under this provision. Thus in *Q v J* [2003] EWHC 251 (Fam), LTL 14/5/2003, the receiving party failed to commence a detailed assessment but was paid £60,000 on account. After two years the paying party sought and obtained an order that unless the assessment was commenced within seven days, no further sums would be payable to the receiving party. The assessment was not commenced in time. Sumner J overturned the district judge's refusal to allow the receiving party any further costs as being too draconian, and substituted an order that the claimant receive 80 per cent of her assessed costs. (See also *Tanfern Ltd v Cameron-MacDonald* [2000] 1 WLR 1311; *Haji-Ioannou v Frangos* [2006] EWHC 279 (Ch), *The Times*, 7 April 2006.)

Misconduct

68.25 Rule 44.14 of the CPR deals with cases where there has been a failure to conduct detailed assessment proceedings in accordance with the rules, and where the court finds that the conduct of a party or a legal representative before or during the proceedings was unreasonable or improper. Improper conduct includes steps likely to prevent or inhibit the court from furthering the overriding objective (**PD 43–48, para. 18.2**). In any of these cases the court has a power to disallow all or part of the costs being assessed, or to order the party or legal representative in default to pay any other party's costs incurred because of the misconduct. Before making such an order the court must give the party or legal representative a reasonable opportunity to attend a hearing and give reasons why the proposed order should not be made (**PD 43–48, para. 18. 1**). The court's approach can be seen from three cases, *Q v J* [2003] EWHC 251 (Fam), LTL 14/5/2003, *Tanfern Ltd v Cameron-MacDonald* [2000] 1 WLR 1311 and *MacDonald v Taree Holdings Ltd* [2000] CPLR 439. In each case the court was being asked to take action that would have resulted in the successful party being deprived of all or a substantial portion of its costs. Although such an approach may have been within the ambit of the CPR, it was felt that the court had to act proportionately. Dressing up an application complaining of late commencement (see **68.24**) as an application based on misconduct, even after eight years' delay, is unlikely to be successful (*Botham v Niazi* [2004] EWHC 2602 (QB), LTL 18/11/2004). Thus, while it may be possible to deprive a successful party of all of their costs, such orders are likely to be very rare and reserved for the most serious of cases.

Interim costs certificate

Although the court has a general power to order costs on account (see **CPR, rr. 44.3(8)** and **68.26**
68.8), there is also a power to issue an interim costs certificate under **r. 47.15**. This power only arises once the receiving party has lodged a request for a detailed assessment. Generally the order will require that the payment under the interim certificate will be made to the receiving party within 14 days, although there is a power to order the sum to be paid into court. Application is made on notice in the usual way in accordance with **Part 23**. The court has a general discretion and there does not have to be any agreement on the amount to be paid. In practice the court takes into account the matters revealed by the points of dispute and it is good practice to be able to tell the judge the amount that is undisputed.

Final costs certificate

Within 14 days after the end of the detailed assessment hearing the receiving party must **68.27**
complete the bill and return it to the court (**CPR, r. 47.16(2)**) together with receipted fee notes and accounts (**PD 43–48, para. 42.4**). Once the completed bill is filed at the court, a final costs certificate, which includes an order to pay the costs to which it relates, will be served by the court on all the parties to the assessment proceedings (**r. 47.16(3) and (5)**).

Appeals against assessment decisions

There are special rules dealing with appeals from decisions made by authorised court officers **68.28**
in detailed assessment proceedings (see **CPR, rr. 47.20** to **47.24**, and **PD 43–48, paras 47.1 to 48.4**). Appeals from assessment decisions by district judges, masters, costs judges, circuit judges etc. follow the usual rules for appeals described in **chapters 71** and **72**. This paragraph deals with appeals from authorised officers. These appeals are made to a costs judge or a district judge of the High Court (**CPR, r. 47.21**). There is no requirement to seek permission or for written reasons (**PD 43–48, para. 47.2**). The appellant must file an appeal notice in **form N161** within 14 days after the decision appealed against (**CPR, r. 47.22(1)**). The appeal notice should be accompanied by a suitable record of the decision appealed against (**PD 43–48, para. 48.3**), which may be the official transcript, or the officer's comments written on the bill, or the advocates' notes of the reasons given. On receipt of the appeal notice the court will serve copies on the parties together with notice of the appeal hearing (**CPR, r. 47.22(2)**). The appeal takes the form of a rehearing of the assessment proceedings (**r. 47.23**).

INDEMNITY PRINCIPLE

68.29 The 'indemnity principle' is that a party cannot be liable to pay more to the other side in costs than the winner is liable to pay its own lawyers. Thus, if the lawyers representing the successful party have intimated that their client need 'not worry' about paying their fees, there is a prospect that the court will hold the loser has no liability in costs (*British Waterways Board v Norman* (1993) 26 HLR 232). However, this decision has to be compared with *Times Newspapers Ltd v Burstein* [2002] EWCA Civ 139, 28/11/2002. The receiving party's lawyers produced evidence of a valid retainer to pay their fees. In reply the paying party produced evidence to show that the receiving party was impecunious and did not have the wherewithal to pay his solicitors. The receiving party thus argued that the retainer was, in truth, an illegal CFA, that there was no valid retainer and that there was no liability on the paying party to pay his lawyers. The Court of Appeal relied on the fact that there was a retainer in rejecting the receiving party's argument.

For a short time it was thought that the indemnity principle had passed into history after the decision in *Thai Trading Co. v Taylor* [1998] QB 781. However, subsequent developments such as *Hughes v Kingston upon Hull City Council* [1999] QB 1193, *Awwad v Geraghty and Co.* [2001] QB 570, amendments made to the Solicitors' Practice Rules 1990, r. 8(1) (made pursuant to the Solicitors Act 1974, s. 31), and the **Solicitors Act 1974, s. 60(3)** (which provides that a client of a solicitor is not entitled to recover from any other person under an order for the payment of any costs to which a contentious business agreement relates more than the amount payable to the solicitor in respect of those costs under the agreement), have made it clear that the indemnity principle is still adhered to. The **Access to Justice Act 1999, s. 31**, amends the **Supreme Court Act 1981, s. 51(2)**, by adding that rules of court may provide that the amount awarded to a party in respect of costs need not be limited to the amount that would have been payable by the party if costs had not been awarded. This is primarily aimed at enabling the CPR to provide for a losing party to pay all the costs (including any success fee) where the successful party has entered into a conditional fee arrangement (see **r. 44.3A**), but also permits removal of part or even the entire operation of the indemnity principle.

A CFA in the prescribed form (see **6.3**) 'shall not be unenforceable' as being champertous (see **Courts and Legal Services Act 1990, s. 58**). This means that CFAs not in the prescribed form are unenforceable (*Times Newspapers Ltd v Burstein* [2002] EWCA Civ 1739, LTL 28/11/2002). Where a solicitor acts for an impecunious client without a CFA, if it is alleged there has been an infringement of the indemnity principle, it is necessary for the court to determine the true nature of the retainer.

Between 2 June 2003 and 31 October 2005, the **Conditional Fee Agreements Regulations 2000 (SI 2000/692), reg. 3A**, allowed a client to enter into a CFA with a legal representative which provides that the client will be liable to pay the lawyer's fees and expenses only if and to the extent that costs are recovered in the proceedings. This in effect abrogates the indemnity principle for this type of CFA. **CPR, r. 43.2(3)** and **(4)**, provide that costs for legal services provided to a client under a CFA complying with the Regulations are recoverable under **Parts 44 to 48** notwithstanding that the client is liable to pay his legal representative's fees only to the extent that sums are recovered from the other side. Predictable costs under **rr. 45.7** to **45.14** (see **67.8** to **67.15**) are not affected by the indemnity principle (*Nizami v Butt* [2006] EWHC 159 (QB), [2006] 2 All ER 140).

If the arrangement between the solicitor and the client amounts to an unlawful agreement to conduct litigation on a contingency basis, the client will not be entitled to seek an order for costs even if successful (*Hughes v Kingston upon Hull City Council* [1999] QB 1193). In *General of Berne Insurance Co. v Jardine Reinsurance Management Ltd* [1998] 1 WLR 1231 it was held that the indemnity principle has to be applied on an item-by-item basis rather than on a global basis. This means that if the client would not have been liable to pay an individual item in the solicitor's bill, it will be disallowed between the parties simply on the indemnity principle, even if the client is liable to pay the rest of the bill. In *Nederlandse Reassurantie Groep Holding NV v Bacon and Woodrow* (1998) LTL 9/6/98 it was held that the item-by-item approach applies whether or not the receiving party and its solicitor have entered into a contentious business agreement.

In *Bailey v IBC Vehicles Ltd* [1998] 3 All ER 570 it was held that the court has the power to order disclosure of documents and the provision of information to check whether the indemnity principle has been infringed, but went on to say that the jurisdiction to do so should not be over enthusiastically deployed.

For older cases, the principle derived from *R v Miller* [1983] 1 WLR 1056 is that there is a presumption that a solicitor's client is personally liable for the costs incurred by the solicitor. The presumption can be rebutted if it is established that there is a clear express or implied agreement that the client would not have to pay the solicitor's costs in any event. Further, statements of costs and bills of costs have to be signed by the solicitor acting for the receiving party. The signature is no empty formality. It operates as a certificate by an officer of the court that the receiving party's solicitors are not seeking to recover in relation to each item more than they have agreed to charge their client (see per Henry LJ in *Bailey v IBC Vehicles Ltd* [1998] 3 All ER 570 at p. 575).

Since September 1999 there has been a professional requirement that solicitors must provide a client care letter for every case setting out the charging arrangements between them and their client. That letter, or any other written arrangement affecting the costs payable between solicitor and client, must be filed with the court as part of any detailed assessment if liability to pay the receiving party's solicitor is disputed by the receiving party (**PD 43–48, para. 40.2(i)**). Further, the bill of costs used in any detailed assessment must set out a short but adequate explanation of any agreement or arrangement between the solicitor and client which affects the costs claimed against the paying party.

Proving infringement of the indemnity principle

If the issue of whether the indemnity principle has been infringed is raised, the receiving party can ask the costs judge to rule on whether there is a genuine issue. If not, that is the end of the matter. If a genuine issue is raised (or the receiving party accepts that a genuine issue is raised without asking for a ruling on this preliminary point), the costs judge will have to rule on whether the indemnity principle has in fact been infringed. This will almost certainly require the receiving party to adduce documents such as the client care letter, the terms of any retainer contract, and any bills sent to the client. **PD 43–48, para. 40.14**, and the **Supreme Court Costs Office Guide, sect. 10**, provide that the court may direct the receiving party to produce any document which, in the opinion of the court, is necessary to enable it to reach its decision. These documents will in the first instance be produced to the court, but the court may ask the receiving party to elect whether to disclose the particular document to the paying party in order to rely on the contents of the document, or whether to decline disclosure and instead rely on other evidence. **68.30**

Where there is a substantial dispute about whether the indemnity principle has been infringed and/or whether confidential documents should be produced, it may be appropriate to seek directions for split hearing dates or times (**Supreme Court Costs Office Guide, para. 10.5**).

Disclosure of documents to paying party

In *Dickinson v Rushmer* (2002) 152 NLJ 58 it was held that if confidential documents are shown to the costs judge, they should also be disclosed to the paying party. Alternatively, the receiving party can maintain legal professional privilege in these documents, and rely on secondary evidence of the retainer (although this might be difficult or impossible if the assessment **68.31** hearing is being dealt with by a costs draftsman). In *South Coast Shipping Co. Ltd v Havant Borough Council* [2002] 3 All ER 779 Pumfrey J said that in the great majority of cases the paying party would be content to agree that the costs judge alone should see privileged documents, and it is only where it is necessary and proportionate that the receiving party should be put to an election whether to allow privileged documents to be disclosed to the paying party. In *Giambrone v JMC Holidays Ltd* [2002] EWHC 495 (QB), LTL 25/3/2002, it was held the costs judge had been wrong not to follow **PD 43–48, para. 40.14**, the costs judge having ordered the receiving party's solicitor to serve a witness statement on the paying party exhibiting the relevant documents on whether the indemnity principle had been infringed, as this deprived the receiving party of the right to claim privilege in the documents.

CFAs and the indemnity principle

68.32 For CFAs entered into before 1 November 2005, it was frequently argued that even minor infringements of the **Conditional Fee Agreements Regulations 2000** (SI 2000/692, discussed in **chapter 6**) rendered the retainer illegal with the result that there was no payment obligation on the CFA-funded client, and hence no costs liability on the unsuccessful party by reason of the indemnity principle (see **68.29**). Paying parties were therefore anxious to obtain copies of the CFA, in order to scrutinise it for defects. A number of related issues were raised by these arguments, which were brought together in *Hollins v Russell* [2003] EWCA Civ 718, [2003] 1 WLR 2487. The Court of Appeal came to the following conclusions:

(a) The presumption that the bill is accurate and complies with the Regulations afforded by the solicitor's signature on the bill does not apply where the point of substance relates to compliance with the **Conditional Fee Agreements Regulations 2000** (*Bailey v IBC Vehicles Ltd* [1998] 3 All ER 570 distinguished).

(b) The CFA is a privileged document and its production cannot be compelled. However, on a standard-basis assessment, the receiving party will have to show compliance. Thus in practice the CFA will normally be produced, suitably redacted if it contains sensitive commercial information. Other memoranda and documents should not generally be produced. Partial disclosure in accordance with *Hollins v Russell* is difficult to justify, unless it is regarded as a limited waiver (see **48.58**).

(c) Not every breach of the Regulations will lead to a breach of the indemnity principle. The costs judge should ask the following question:

> Has the particular departure from a regulation or requirement in the Courts and Legal Services Act 1990, s. 58, either on its own or in conjunction with any other such departure in this case, had a materially adverse effect either upon the protection afforded to the client or upon the proper administration of justice?

(d) Even where the indemnity principle does work in favour of the paying party, disbursements and any insurance premium will be payable.

(e) Costs officers must be astute to ensure that issues over conditional fees and the indemnity principle do not develop into time-consuming and expensive satellite litigation (*Times Newspapers Ltd v Burstein* [2002] EWCA Civ 139, LTL 28/11/2002).

The process started by *Hollins v Russell* has been completed by the Conditional Fee Agreements (Revocation) Regulations 2005 (SI 2005/2305). The provisions formerly governing the format of CFAs set out in the **Conditional Fee Agreements Regulations 2000** (and related regulations, including those governing collective CFAs) are revoked for CFAs entered into on or after 1 November 2005 (SI 2005/2305, reg. 2). This means that the only formalities governing CFAs entered into on or after 1 November 2005 are those set out in the primary legislation (the **Courts and Legal Services Act 1990, ss. 58, 58A** and, when it is brought into force, **58B**). This means that a CFA entered into on or after 1 November 2005:

(a) has to be in writing (**s. 58(3)(a)**);

(b) must relate to an enforceable and specified type of proceedings (**ss. 58(3)(b), 58A; Conditional Fee Agreements Order 2000 (SI 2000/823), art. 3**);

(c) must state the agreed percentage increase of any success fee (**Courts and Legal Services Act 1990, s. 58(4)(b)**); and
(d) any success fee cannot exceed 100 per cent (**s. 58(4)(c)**; **Conditional Fee Agreements Order 2000, art. 4**).

BASIS OF QUANTIFICATION

The two bases

Costs may be quantified either on the standard or the indemnity basis. Under the old system there was a twofold test to be applied when deciding whether to allow costs on either basis. Costs would only be recoverable if, first, they were reasonably incurred and secondly, to the extent that they were reasonable in amount. These concepts were approached from opposite directions under the two different bases, with doubts resolved in favour of the paying party on the standard basis, and in favour of the receiving party under the indemnity basis. Under the CPR it still is necessary to consider both whether individual items of costs should have been incurred, and whether they should be allowed in full or reduced. However, to tie in with the overriding objective, on an assessment on the standard basis the court is required to consider not only concepts of reasonableness, but also of proportionality. **68.33**

Standard basis

On an assessment on the standard basis, **r. 44.4(2)** of the CPR provides that the court will: **68.34**
(a) only allow costs which are proportionate to the matters in issue; and
(b) resolve any doubt which it may have about whether costs were reasonably incurred or reasonable and proportionate in amount in favour of the paying party.

In applying the test of proportionality on a standard basis assessment, **PD 43–48, para. 11.1**, says that the relationship between the total costs incurred and the financial value of the claim is not always a reliable guide, and still less can the court simply apply a fixed percentage to the value of the claim and say that any costs above that percentage have to be disproportionate. **PD 43–48, para. 11.2**, makes the point that some costs inevitably have to be incurred, or are otherwise necessary, for the successful conduct of a case. It also says that even in smaller cases solicitors are not required to work at uneconomic rates. Consequently, in small cases legal costs may legitimately even equal or exceed the amount in dispute. Further, **PD 43–48, para. 11.3**, says the court should be wary of using the length of the eventual hearing as an accurate guide to the time properly spent by the parties' legal representatives in preparing for the hearing. It is often the case that careful preparation reduces the time taken by hearings in court.

Guidance on the practice to be adopted when deciding whether costs are proportionate on standard basis assessments was given in *Lownds v Home Office* [2002] EWCA Civ 365, [2002] 1 WLR 2450. In a case where proportionality is an issue, a preliminary judgment on the proportionality of the costs as a whole should be made at the outset. This is done having particular regard to the factors in **CPR, r. 44.5(3)** (see **68.17**). If the judge concludes that the costs are not disproportionate, the various items of costs are then considered one by one, applying the reasonableness tests in r. 44.4(2). If the judge concludes that the costs as a whole may be disproportionate, each item will be scrutinised applying both the reasonableness and necessity tests (for the latter, see below). A failure to follow the two-stage process laid down in *Lownds v Home Office* was held to be a serious procedural irregularity in *Lloyds TSB Bank plc v Lampert* [2003] EWHC 249 (Ch), LTL 7/3/2003.

Proportionality

One of the main aims of the CPR is to provide a system of civil justice which is affordable and proportionate to the importance of the claim. The overriding objective requires the court to **68.35** deal with claims in ways that will save expense and which are proportionate to the nature of the case (**CPR, r. 1.1(2)**). The parties are required to cooperate in achieving this aim, which means they must conduct themselves in ways that do not involve unnecessary costs, or costs which are not really justified by the nature or importance of the claim. When assessing costs, even costs which are not disputed by the other side, the court retains the right to reduce or disallow costs which it finds are disproportionate (see **PD 43–48, para. 13.13**).

The key to proportionality, according to the Court of Appeal in *Lownds v Home Office* [2002] EWCA Civ 365, [2002] 1 WLR 2450, at [26] to [28], is to be found in **PD 43–48, para 11.2**, which states that: 'In any proceedings there will be costs which will inevitably be incurred and which are *necessary* for the successful conduct of the case' (emphasis added). If the appropriate conduct of the proceedings made costs necessary then the requirement of proportionality does not prevent recovery of those costs. The threshold required to meet necessity is higher than that of reasonableness, but Lord Woolf CJ in *Lownds v Home Office* at [37] said it was still a standard which a competent solicitor should be able to achieve without undue difficulty, and the courts should be careful not to impose too high a standard with the benefit of hindsight. The court will have regard to whether the appropriate level of fee earner and counsel were employed, whether offers to settle had been made, whether unnecessary experts had been instructed, and the other matters set out in **CPR, r. 44.5(3)**. Regard should also be had to the amount which it was reasonable for the receiving party to believe might be recovered. For a claimant this is the sum it was reasonable for him to believe he might recover at the time the claim was made (*Lownds v Home Office* at [39]). For a defendant this is likely to be the sum claimed. In deciding what is necessary, the paying party's conduct is highly relevant, because cooperation can reduce costs, and being uncooperative can increase costs.

Counsel spending 12 days preparing for a striking-out application was regarded as being disproportionate in *Orwin v British Coal Corporation* [2003] EWHC 757 (Ch), LTL 24/4/2003, and the fee was reduced by two thirds.

Case planning

68.36 Increasingly the courts are expecting to see evidence of case planning. The aspiration was set out in *Jefferson v National Freight Carriers plc* [2001] EWCA Civ 2082, LTL 4/10/2001, when Lord Woolf CJ cited with approval the following extract of the trial judge's comments:

> In modern litigation, with the emphasis on proportionality, it is necessary for parties to make an assessment at the outset of the likely value of the claim and its importance and complexity, and then to plan in advance the necessary work, the appropriate level of person to carry out the work, the overall time that would be necessary and [the] appropriate spend on various stages in bringing the action to trial, and the likely overall cost. While it was not unusual for costs to exceed the amount in issue, it was, in the context of modern litigation such as the present case, one reason for seeking to curb the amount of work done, and the cost by reference to the need for proportionality.

It follows that the courts are increasingly expecting to see evidence that the issue of costs and proportionality was addressed at the outset of the case rather than the amount of costs simply developing as the case progressed. Consideration of the costs estimates and reference to a case plan will begin to illuminate this issue and is likely to assist the judge in deciding whether the costs are proportionate.

Indemnity basis

68.37 On an assessment on the indemnity basis there is no reference to proportionality, and any doubts on whether costs were reasonably incurred or were reasonable in amount is resolved in favour of the receiving party (**CPR, r. 44.4(3)**).

Choice of basis

68.38 Costs orders should identify the intended basis of quantification. Unless the phrase 'indemnity basis' is used, quantification will be on the standard basis (**CPR, r. 44.4(4)**). The usual rule in contentious litigation is that costs are payable on the standard basis. Indemnity basis costs are normally used only where there is some misconduct deserving such a course (*Reid Minty v Taylor* [2001] EWCA Civ 1723, [2002] 1 WLR 2800). Parties who act in the capacity of trustee, personal representative or mortgagee are in general entitled to costs on the indemnity basis, but the court may order otherwise if the party has acted otherwise than for the benefit of the fund (**r. 48.4**).

Assessments between solicitor and own client (other than in publicly funded cases and where there is a conditional fee agreement) are by virtue of **r. 48.8** dealt with on the indemnity basis, but subject to the following presumptions:

(a) that costs were reasonably incurred if they were incurred with the express or implied approval of the client;
(b) that costs were reasonable in amount if the amount was expressly or impliedly approved by the client; and
(c) that costs were unreasonably incurred if they are unusual in nature or amount and the solicitor did not tell the client that for that reason they might not be recoverable from the other side.

AMOUNT TO BE ALLOWED

Hourly rates

Until recently, one of the most common methods for computing the cost of a solicitor's time in conducting litigation was to apply the direct cost to the firm of the fee earner engaged in the matter to the amount of time spent, and then to add a 'mark-up' to reflect imponderable factors, such as general supervision, skill, responsibility and commercial profit. Most county courts developed conventional hourly rates for their courts, which were sometimes refined by applying different hourly rates to different grades of fee earners. It was extremely difficult to persuade a district judge to depart from the conventional figures for his or her court. However, in theory different rates could be applied if an individual firm could show the direct cost for its fee earners was different from the conventional rate. The mark-up percentage could vary for different items on the bill. In *Johnson v Reed Corrugated Cases Ltd* [1992] 1 All ER 169 it was suggested that an uplift starting at 50 per cent was appropriate for ordinary cases, and in *Brush v Bower Cotton and Bower* [1993] 1 WLR 1328 it was suggested that 35 per cent was the appropriate uplift for interim applications where the solicitor sat behind counsel. For more complex cases higher levels of mark-up were appropriate, up to 100 or even 120 per cent for complex commercial or clinical dispute claims. Non-straightforward interim applications dealt with by a solicitor without the assistance of counsel might justify a mark-up of 60 per cent or more. **68.39**

The modern approach is to apply a single hourly rate to the work done by the solicitor. Clients find this less confusing, and, by applying a suitable rate, it is not difficult to find a figure which provides the same rate of remuneration as the old system of direct cost plus mark-up. It is also the modern approach to provide different rates for different grades of fee earner.

Category of fee earner

Her Majesty's Courts Service has published guideline hourly rates for the summary assessment of costs. These provide hourly rates with a built-in 50 per cent uplift (*Various Ledward Claimants v Kent and Medway Health Authority* [2003] EWHC 2551 (QB), LTL 4/11/2003). Various locations in England and Wales have been divided into three bands (see **table 68.1**), and different hourly rates have been laid down (from January 2003, and with inflation-related revisions from January 2005) for four grades of fee-earner (see **table 68.2**). There is a separate table of **68.40** guideline rates for London-based firms (see **table 68.3**). The figures given in **tables 68.2** and **68.3** are guidelines, and it is open to the designated civil judge to lay down more exact guidelines for rates in his area. It is also open for a firm to seek to establish a different rate (either generally or for individual claims where the notional 50 per cent uplift is inappropriate), and for this purpose the costs estimate for the paying party may be relevant evidence (see further at **68.41**).

Table 68.1 Solicitors' hourly rates: areas covered by the three provincial bands

Band one (January 2003)

Aldershot, Farnham, Bournemouth; Birmingham Inner; Cambridge City Centre; Canterbury, Maidstone, Medway and Tunbridge Wells; Cardiff (Inner); Kingston, Guildford, Reigate, Epsom; Leeds Inner (within 1 km of the City Art Gallery); Lewes; Liverpool, Birkenhead; Manchester Central; Newcastle City Centre (within 2 miles of St Nicholas Cathedral); Norwich; Nottingham City; Southampton, Portsmouth; Swindon, Basingstoke.

Band two (January 2003)

Bath, Cheltenham and Gloucester; Bristol; Bury; Chelmsford North, Cambridge County, Peterborough, Bury St Edmunds, Norfolk; Essex and East Suffolk; Lowestoft; Chelmsford South; Hampshire, Dorset, Wiltshire, Isle of Wight; Hull (City); Leeds Outer, Wakefield and Pontefract; Leigh; Luton, Bedford, St Albans, Hitchin and Hertford; Manchester Outer, Oldham, Bolton, Tameside; Milton Keynes and Aylesbury; Oxford (Inner / Outer), Reading, Slough; Sheffield and South Yorkshire; Southport; St Helens; Stockport, Altrincham, Salford; Swansea, Newport, Cardiff (Outer); Watford; Wigan; York, Harrogate.

Band three (January 2003)

Accrington, Burnley, Blackburn, Rawtenstall and Nelson; Birmingham Outer; Bradford (Dewsbury, Halifax, Huddersfield, Keighley and Skipton); Chester and North Wales; Coventry, Rugby, Nuneaton, Stratford and Warwick; Cumbria; Devon, Cornwall, Exeter, Taunton and Yeovil; Grimsby; Hull Outer; Kidderminster; Lincoln; Newcastle (other than City Centre); Northampton and Leicester; Nottingham and Derbyshire; Plymouth; Preston, Lancaster, Blackpool, Chorley; Scarborough and Ripon; South and West Wales; Stafford, Stoke, Tamworth; Teesside; Trowbridge; Weston-super-Mare; Wolverhampton, Walsall, Dudley and Stourbridge; Worcester, Hereford, Evesham and Redditch; Shrewsbury, Telford, Ludlow, Oswestry.

Band one (January 2005)

Aldershot, Farnham, Bournemouth (including Poole); Birmingham Inner; Bristol; Cambridge City, Harlow; Canterbury, Maidstone, Medway and Tunbridge Wells; Cardiff (Inner); Chelmsford South, Essex and East Suffolk; Fareham, Winchester; Hampshire, Dorset, Isle of Wight; Kingston, Guildford, Reigate, Epsom; Leeds Inner (within 2 km of the City Art Gallery); Lewes; Liverpool, Birkenhead; Manchester Central; Newcastle City Centre (within 2 miles of St Nicholas Cathedral); Norwich City; Nottingham City; Oxford, Thames Valley; Southampton, Portsmouth; Swindon, Basingstoke; Watford.

Band two (January 2005)

Bath, Cheltenham and Gloucester, Taunton, Yeovil; Bury; Chelmsford North, Cambridge County, Peterborough, Bury St Edmunds, Norfolk, Lowestoft; Chester and North Wales; Coventry, Rugby, Nuneaton, Stratford and Warwick; Exeter, Plymouth; Hull (City); Leeds Outer, Wakefield and Pontefract; Leigh; Lincoln; Luton, Bedford, St Albans, Hitchin, Hertford; Manchester Outer, Oldham, Bolton, Tameside; Newcastle City Centre (within 2 miles of St Nicholas Cathedral); Nottingham and Derbyshire; Sheffield, Doncaster and South Yorkshire; Southport; St Helens; Stockport, Altrincham, Salford; Swansea, Newport, Cardiff (Outer); Wigan; Wolverhampton, Walsall, Dudley and Stourbridge; York, Harrogate.

Band three (January 2005)

Birmingham Outer; Bradford (Dewsbury, Halifax, Huddersfield, Keighley and Skipton); Cumbria; Devon, Cornwall; Grimsby, Skegness; Hull Outer; Kidderminster; Newcastle (other than City Centre); Northampton and Leicester; Preston, Lancaster, Blackpool, Chorley, Accrington, Burnley, Blackburn, Rawtenstall and Nelson; Scarborough and Ripon; Stafford, Stoke, Tamworth; Teesside; Worcester, Hereford, Evesham and Redditch; Shrewsbury, Telford, Ludlow, Oswestry; South and West Wales.

Table 68.2 Guideline hourly charging rates

	Grade			
	A	B	C	D
Band one				
January 2003	175	155	130	95
January 2005	184	163	137	100
Band two				
January 2003	165	145	120	90
January 2005	173	152	126	95
Band three				
January 2003	150	135	115	85
January 2005	158	142	121	90

Table 68.3 London hourly rates

	Grade			
	A	B	C	D
City of London Jan 2003	342*	247	189	116
City of London Jan 2005 EC1, EC2, EC3, EC4	359	259	198	122
Central London Jan 2003	263	200	163	105
Central London Jan 2005 W1, WC1, WC2, SW1	276	210	171	110
Outer London Jan 2003 (including Bromley, Croydon, Dartford, Gravesend, Uxbridge)	189–221	142–189	137	100
Outer London Jan 2005 (All other London postcodes: W, NW, N, E, SE, SW and Bromley, Croydon, Dartford, Gravesend and Uxbridge)	198–232	149–198	144	105

*Although a guideline figure is given for the top grade of fee earner in the City of London, it is recognised that in certain complex, major litigation the appropriate rate may exceed the guideline by a significant margin.

The four grades of fee earner are:

A Solicitors with over eight years' post-qualification experience including at least eight years' litigation experience.
B Solicitors and legal executives (i.e., fellows of the Institute of Legal Executives) with over four years' post-qualification experience including at least four years' litigation experience.
C Other solicitors and legal executives and fee earners of equivalent experience.
D Trainee solicitors, paralegals and fee earners of equivalent experience.

Fee earners who are not fellows of the Institute of Legal Executives are not entitled to call themselves legal executives. Unqualified clerks may fall into grades B, C or D depending on their experience. Legal executives generally spend two years in a solicitor's office before passing their Part 1 general examinations, then take a further two years before passing their Part 2 specialist examinations, then complete a further two years in practice before being able to become fellows. Unqualified fee earners need to have equivalent experience if they are to be regarded as coming into grades B or C.

Many High Court cases justify category A fee earners, but specific tasks within the proceedings, such as sitting behind counsel at interim hearings, may only justify a fee earner in a lower category. A complex, high-value clinical negligence claim in *Higgs v Camden and Islington Health Authority* [2003] EWHC 15 (QB), LTL 22/1/2003, justified the employment of a senior partner (a category A fee earner), and the client was entitled to expect no less. In the county courts, the nature and complexity of the various items of work will dictate the level of fee earner that will be reasonable. In *Bensusan v Freedman* (2001) LTL 6/11/2001 the work was of a type typically dealt with by grade B fee earners, so the hourly rate was reduced from the amount claimed to the appropriate grade B rate. It is recognised that it is often more economical to brief counsel than for a solicitor to act as the advocate. Where having a solicitor advocate leads to an increase in costs the court will consider whether the increase can be justified.

Exceeding a guideline rate

68.41 The rates in **table 68.2** are no more than a guide and can be exceeded where the nature of the case warrants it. When considering whether the guideline rate provides proper remuneration, the court will take into account the factors set out in **CPR, r. 44.5(3)**, which include the conduct of the parties, the amount involved, any complexity or novelty, the skill, effort and specialist knowledge required, the time spent on the case, and the place where and the circumstances in which the work was done. Thus in *Higgs v Camden and Islington Health Authority* [2003] EWHC 15 (QB), LTL 22/1/2003, the appellate court upheld a rate of £300 per hour where the case involved a child who was brain-damaged from birth. The court indicated that the SCCO guideline figures were not intended to replace the experience and knowledge of those familiar with the local area and with the field generally.

London solicitors

68.42 Whether it is reasonable to instruct expensive London solicitors rather than more economical provincial solicitors involves an objective element of reasonableness which nevertheless has to be considered in the context of the particular circumstances of the particular clients (*Wraith v Sheffield Forgemasters Ltd* [1998] 1 WLR 132; *Truscott v Truscott* [1998] FLR 265). In *Solutia UK Ltd v Griffiths* [2001] EWCA Civ 736, [2001] CPLR 419, it was held to be reasonable to have instructed London solicitors in litigation which could have been handled far more cheaply by provincial solicitors where the London solicitors had previously conducted related, and more complex litigation, arising out of the same facts. In *Ryan v Tretol Group Ltd* (2001) LTL 24/7/2002 it was held to have been reasonable to change from provincial to London solicitors in an asbestosis claim after the fee earner dealing with the claim (who was an asbestosis expert) left the provincial firm. The London firm had been recommended by an asbestosis support organisation, and it was not apparent that there were any firms with experience of asbestosis claims in the local area. In *Gazley v Wade* [2004] EWHC 2675 (QB), LTL 25/11/2004, it was held to have been unreasonable to instruct specialist London solicitors for a libel claim. Although it was not a 'Norfolk case', the claimant was living in Norwich, there was evidence that local non-specialist firms had the necessary competence, and any technical advice could have been sought from specialist members of the Bar.

Correspondence and attendances

68.43 Routine letters (those which by reason of their simplicity should not be regarded as letters of substance) and routine telephone calls (which cannot properly amount to an attendance) will in general be allowed on a unit basis of six minutes each, the charge being calculated by reference to the appropriate hourly rate. The unit charge for letters out will include perusing and considering the relevant letters in, and no separate charge should be made for incoming letters. Emails received will not normally be allowed. The court has a discretion to allow the actual time spent on preparing emails sent, provided the time is recorded or to allow emails on a unit basis. Local travelling expenses incurred by solicitors (normally within 10 miles of the court) will not be allowed. Travelling and waiting time is usually allowed at the rate agreed between solicitor and client. The cost of postage, couriers, outgoing telephone calls, fax and telex messages will in general not be allowed unless unusually heavy. Nor will the cost of making copies normally be allowed, unless the documents to be copied were unusually numerous. Agency charges as between a principal solicitor and his or her agent will be dealt with normally on the basis that the charges form part of the principal solicitor's charges (PD 43–48, para. 4.16).

Counsel's fees

68.44 Counsel's fees are based on a judgment taking into account all the relevant circumstances, including:

(a) the seniority of counsel;
(b) the amount of time reasonably spent on the work;
(c) the number of documents perused and their importance and technicality (even if brief);
(d) the specialist knowledge and skill of counsel;
(e) the complexity of the work undertaken;
(f) the difficulty or novelty of the questions involved;
(g) the value of the claim and its importance;
(h) the responsibility involved;
(i) the place and circumstances where the work is performed; and
(j) whether there is any overlap with other work performed by counsel which reduces the work that would otherwise have been necessary.

Matthews v Dorkin (2000) LTL 10/11/2000 is an interesting example of an appeal dealing with several different fees of counsel of nine years' call in a substantial personal injuries claim. For example, a fee of £875 was allowed for a written advice and schedule of loss and damage reasonably taking seven hours. A fee of £335 was allowed for a 24-minute telephone conference which required two hours and 15 minutes preparation. A fee of £750 was allowed for a 4½ hour conference with experts at the solicitor's office which required three hours' preparation.

In *Matthews v Dorkin* brief fees were allowed of £350 on an application to break a fixture on account of the unavailability of experts, £525 on a 30-minute hearing requiring two and a half hours' preparation, and trial brief fees (at 50 per cent of those of leading counsel) of £4,000 with refreshers of £600 per day. The general approach is that junior counsel are allowed between 50 and 67 per cent of the leader's brief fees. Where there are several counsel on one side, their respective fees should reflect their seniority and responsibility in the conduct of the case (*Loveday v Renton (No. 2)* [1992] 3 All ER 184 at p. 194).

In *Hornsby v Clark Kenneth Leventhal* [2000] 4 All ER 567 it was held, in relation to counsel's fees for an appeal to the Court of Appeal, that the first stage is to assess the fee for the skeleton argument. This is assessed largely by reference to the time reasonably spent in reading the documents, researching the law and drafting the skeleton. Next the brief fee should be assessed applying the guidance in *Loveday v Renton (No. 2)* at p. 194 (which essentially identified the factors set out in points (a) to (j) above). In so far as preparation for the skeleton argument reduced the amount of preparation required for the hearing, that should not be included in the brief fee. The third stage is to aggregate the fees for the skeleton and the brief, to cross-check that the total is not too large or too small, and to adjust accordingly.

The Supreme Court Costs Office has also published figures for counsel's fees based on run-of-the-mill cases in the Queen's Bench and Chancery Divisions. These are set out in **table 68.4**. They are regarded as a useful starting point when assessing counsel's fees. The appropriate figure does not depend wholly on counsel's seniority, but also the level of counsel merited by the application and the circumstances of the individual case.

Disbursements

68.45 Disbursements are payments made by a solicitor for goods or services other than items which enable the solicitor to render its service to the client. Office overheads therefore are not disbursements. Expenses legitimately claimed as disbursements are shown and charged separately on the solicitor's bill, and the client is not charged with VAT on these items. The

Table 68.4 Guidelines for counsel's fees

	Jan 2003, hearings of 1 hour	½ day	Jan 2005, hearings of 1 hour	½ day
Queen's Bench Division				
Junior up to 5 years call	220	385	245	425
Junior 5–10 years call	330	655	365	725
Junior 10+ years call	500	1,000	550	1,100
Chancery Division				
Junior up to 5 years call	250	475	275	525
Junior 5–10 years call	425	800	470	880
Junior 10+ years call	650	1,200	715	1,320
Administrative Court				
Junior up to 5 years call	325	500	360	550
Junior 5–10 years call	600	1,000	660	1,100
Junior 10+ years call	850	1,500	935	1,650

VAT Guide (April 2002) (Her Majesty's Customs and Excise Notice 700) at para. 25.1 sets out eight conditions that must be satisfied if an item is to be treated as a disbursement:

(a) the solicitor must have acted as the agent for the client when paying the third party;
(b) the client must have actually received and used the goods or services provided by the third party (this condition usually prevents the solicitor's travelling and subsistence expenses, telephone bills and postage being treated as disbursements);
(c) the client must be responsible for paying the third party;
(d) the client must have authorised the solicitor to make the payment on the client's behalf;
(e) the client must have known the goods or services would be provided by a third party;
(f) the solicitor's outlay must be separately itemised in the bill (or invoice);
(g) the solicitor can only recover the exact amount paid to the third party; and
(h) the goods or services must be clearly additional to the supplies which the solicitor has made to the client on his own account.

Examples of valid disbursements are court fees, fees on affidavits, estate and stamp duty on contracts made by clients, fees for experts' reports and services such as reproducing photographs. A referral fee paid by a claims handling company to its subsidiary was held not to be a disbursement for the purposes of the Access to Justice Act 1999, s. 29, in *Sharratt v London Central Bus Co. Ltd (No. 2)* [2004] EWCA Civ 575, [2004] 3 All ER 325, because it related to work done before the solicitor's retainer came into existence. Generally, it is only advantageous to treat a payment as a disbursement for VAT purposes where no VAT is chargeable on the supply by the third party, or where the client is not entitled to reclaim the VAT as input tax.

Counsel's fees are not technically disbursements because they are part of the services provided by the solicitor. They should therefore be included in the solicitor's services part of the bill and charged with VAT. This is so even if the barrister is not VAT registered. However, there is a long-standing Customs and Excise concession which allows solicitors to readdress non-VAT-registered barristers' fee notes to the client, who pays counsel directly or provides a separate cheque for the barrister's fees. When this is done, the fees payable to counsel do not appear in the solicitor's bill at all (and are not included in the solicitor's quarterly VAT return).

CONDITIONAL FEE AGREEMENTS

68.46 Where a party is funded under a CFA (a funding arrangement as defined in CPR, r. 43.2), there will be two elements to that party's costs: the 'base costs' and the 'additional liability'. The base costs are those that are charged in the usual way to reflect the solicitor's basic remuneration and are defined as costs other than the amount of any additional liability (**PD 43–48, para. 2.1**). The 'additional liability' means the percentage increase that a lawyer may charge to reflect his or her involvement in the case, any insurance premium charged or any amount in respect of provision made by a membership organisation (**CPR, r. 43.2(1)(o)**). This reflects the three most common forms of funding conditional fee litigation. In some cases the solicitor may charge an uplift expressed as a percentage of the base costs. Either additionally or alternatively the client may insure to cover its own costs, or both sides' costs, or indeed any one of a number of permutations of costs orders that may be made. Subject to the points below, this premium can be charged to the paying party. A litigant may enter into an agreement with one of a number of approved membership organisations (such as trade unions) to meet his legal costs. An amount to secure this benefit may be recovered from the paying party.

While the court may summarily assess base costs at various stages during the case, there will be no assessment of the additional liability until the conclusion of the case or the part of the case to which a funding arrangement relates (**r. 44.3A(1)**). The parties can by agreement provide for an earlier assessment if they so wish.

Procedure for assessing an additional liability

Assessment of an additional liability is commenced in the same way as any other detailed assessment, save that the receiving party has to serve on the paying party and any other relevant persons relevant details of the additional liability (**PD 43–48, para. 32.4**). What constitutes 'relevant details' is set out fully at **para. 32.5**. Otherwise the assessment proceeds in the usual way to assess both base costs and any additional liability. The consideration of each of the two elements must be separate (**para. 11.5**). **68.47**

Recovering additional liabilities from the paying party

A party-and-party costs order in favour of a CFA litigant does not include the following matters (**CPR, r. 44.3B**): **68.48**

(a) any proportion of the percentage increase relating to the cost to the legal representative of the postponement of payment of his fees and expenses;
(b) any provision made by a membership organisation which exceeds the likely cost to the receiving party of the premium of an insurance policy against the risk of incurring a liability to pay the costs of other parties to the proceedings;
(c) any additional liability for any period in the proceedings during which the receiving party failed to provide information about a funding arrangement in accordance with a rule, practice direction or court order;
(d) any percentage increase where a party has failed to comply with:
 (i) a requirement in PD 43–48; or
 (ii) a court order,
 to disclose in any assessment proceedings, the reasons for setting the percentage increase at the level stated in the CFA.

In relation to the last two matters a party who has entered into a funding arrangement is obliged to give notice to its opponents of the fact at the earliest opportunity. This is done by serving a notice in **form N251 (CPR, r. 44.15; PD 43–48, paras 19.1 to 19.5; PD Protocols, para. 4A. 1)**. Where a party has failed to serve the form N251 or otherwise transgressed **CPR, r. 44.3B(1)(d)**, it is precluded from claiming the additional liability for the period when the notice was not served or there was any other default. It is submitted that, like any other sanction, the court has a jurisdiction to disapply the prohibition, but only when application is made on notice and addressing the factors set out in **r. 3.9**.

Assessing the percentage uplift

68.49 Guidance on the court's approach to assessing an additional liability is given in **PD 43–48, section 11**. In respect of any additional liability, the court will view matters as they reasonably appeared to the practitioner at the time that he entered into the agreement (**para. 11.7**). If the success fee was reasonable at that time, the court cannot substitute different rates for different periods of the proceedings as the risks change when more information becomes available (*U v Liverpool City Council* [2005] EWCA Civ 475, [2005] 1 WLR 2657).

In deciding whether a percentage increase is reasonable, relevant factors to be taken into account include (**para. 11.8**):

(a) the risk that the circumstances in which the costs, fees or expenses would be payable might or might not occur;
(b) the legal representative's liability for any disbursements;
(c) what other methods of financing the costs were available to the receiving party.

The costs officer has a power to allow different percentages to cover different items of costs or different periods. So different percentages may be applied for any protocol period, up to the issue of proceedings and for the trial. It is also acceptable to have a particular percentage applicable to one possible outcome (for example, settling within the protocol period) and another to cover a different eventuality (the case being contested to trial). See *Callery v Gray* [2001] EWCA Civ 1117, [2001] 1 WLR 2112.

A percentage increase will not be disallowed on the basis that the total of the additional liability and the base costs seems disproportionate (**PD 43–48, para. 11.9**). Doing so might run the risk of penalising a solicitor for entering into a funding arrangement, by allowing a lesser sum than might be permitted to a non-funded party.

Amounts allowed

68.50 The appellate courts have been reluctant to give guidance on the amount that a court will grant by way of uplift for the good reason that each case will turn on its own facts. The predictable costs rules for road traffic claims in accidents from 6 October 2003 (**CPR, Part 45, Sections II** and **III**), and for employers' liability claims in accidents from 1 October 2004 (**Part 45, Section IV**), lay down fixed success fees for these types of claim. See the discussion at **67.8** to **67.20**. These provide for two-stage success fees. Broadly, 100 per cent uplifts are applied to claims which are taken to trial, but 12.5 per cent (road traffic) and 25 per cent (employers' liability) uplifts apply where the claim is disposed of before trial. These figures should be seen as some guidance for other types of claim. Two-stage success fees are encouraged for all types of case (*Atack v Lee* [2004] EWCA Civ 1712, [2005] 1 WLR 2643). Other categories of case may involve substantially greater risks, and may justify significantly higher success fees for cases which do not go to trial.

Before the introduction of **Part 45, Sections II** to **IV**, there were a number of decisions on rates for success fees, mainly dealing with straightforward road traffic claims. In *Callery v Gray* [2001] EWCA Civ 1117, [2001] 1 WLR 2112, Lord Woolf CJ said that every case has some risk. Experience suggests that at least 90 per cent of straightforward road traffic claims settle without the need to issue proceedings. For this type of claim an uplift of 20 per cent is the maximum that could reasonably be agreed. Naturally if there are other factors then this limit might be exceeded. The court was also of the view that it is permissible to set a success fee on the basis that the matter fought to trial (say 100 per cent) but to rebate that down to 20 per cent if the case settled in the protocol period. The court stressed that this was an indication given on the basis of the present evidence and that it might be appropriate to refine the figures later.

In *Halloran v Delaney* [2002] EWCA Civ 1258, [2003] 1 WLR 28, the court felt that an increase of 5 per cent was appropriate for cases that settled before the issue of proceedings, and that the 5 per cent would be appropriate for any Part 8 costs-only proceedings. In *Re Claims Direct Test Cases* [2003] EWCA Civ 136, [2003] 4 All ER 508, the court said that *Halloran v Delaney* was not a case intended to give general guidance, that it was only intended to refer to the most straightforward of cases where the prospect of success is virtually 100 per cent, and that solicitors would be well advised to adopt the two-tier approach to the success fee advocated in *Callery v Gray*. Faced with these difficult authorities there is still a regrettable lack of certainty about percentage uplifts, even in the most straightforward cases. It is suggested that a case which settles in the protocol period (or before the issue of proceedings) may still attract a 5 per cent success fee or even the 12.5 per cent success fee allowed under the predictable costs regime (see 67.9), provided there is no suggestion to the solicitor that there is anything unusual about the case. To cater for such dangers lurking under the limpid pools of otherwise tranquil litigation a solicitor would be well advised to adopt the two-stage approach outlined in *Callery v Gray*.

It is suggested that it would be wrong in principle to extrapolate from the above cases any general propositions applicable to other areas of litigation. It has to be understood that the cases are predicated on very straightforward litigation where statistics suggest there is a 90 per cent settlement rate. To take this conclusion into another area of litigation, for example, clinical negligence, is to ignore this aspect of the above cases. It is sometimes suggested that *Bensusan v Freedman* (2001) LTL 6/11/2001 is an authority for the contrary proposition. In that case an uplift of 20 per cent was permitted for a case that settled after the defendant had denied liability and asserted contributory negligence. This is a first-instance decision which fails to give due weight to the risks in contested litigation and it is suggested that it may well not be followed.

Assessing an insurance premium

The **Access to Justice Act 1999, s. 29**, enables a successful client to claim the premium from the unsuccessful opponent. It provides: **68.51**

> Where in any proceedings a costs order is made in favour of any party who has taken out an insurance policy against the risk of incurring a liability in those proceedings, the costs payable to him may, subject in the case of court proceedings to rules of court, include costs in respect of the premium of the policy.

In general the same considerations apply to insurance premiums as apply to percentage uplifts. A 'premium' for this purpose is the sum paid by the client to the insurer (*Re Claims Direct Test Cases* [2003] EWCA Civ 136, [2003] 4 All ER 508). A fee charged by a claims handling company for a basket of services is not converted into a 'premium' simply by describing it as such (*Sharratt v London Central Bus Co. Ltd (No. 2)* [2004] EWCA Civ 575, [2004] 3 All ER 325). In this case the Court of Appeal upheld the costs judge's approach of finding how much the company had paid to its underwriters, and making adjustments to that figure to find the premium recoverable under the **Access to Justice Act 1999, s. 29**. The specific considerations relating to insurance cover are in **PD 43–48, para. 11.10**:

> In deciding whether the cost of insurance cover is reasonable, relevant factors to be taken into account include:
> (1) where the insurance cover is not purchased in support of a CFA with a success fee, how its cost compares with the likely cost of funding the case with a CFA with a success fee and supporting insurance cover;
> (2) the level and extent of the cover provided;
> (3) the availability of any pre-existing insurance cover;
> (4) whether any part of the premium would be rebated in the event of early settlement;
> (5) the amount of commission payable to the receiving party or his legal representatives or other agents.

In *Callery v Gray* [2001] EWCA Civ 1117, [2001] 1 WLR 2112, and *Callery v Gray (No. 2)* [2001] EWCA Civ 1246, [2001] 1 WLR 2142, the Court of Appeal considered whether an ATE insurance premium is recoverable in a case that settles prior to the issue of proceedings. The court held that it could be recovered as 'insurance . . . against the risk of incurring a liability' within the **Access to Justice Act 1999, s. 29**. Provided the premium is reasonable, it will usually be recoverable against an unsuccessful defendant even though it is taken out soon after the solicitor is retained, and before the defendant's response is known. On the facts of that decision the premium of £350 was recoverable.

The decisions in *Callery v Gray* and *Callery v Gray (No. 2)* were affirmed by the House of Lords in *Callery v Gray (Nos. 1 and 2)* [2002] UKHL 28, [2002] 1 WLR 2000, in which it was held that it is for the Court of Appeal to lay down principles in this area.

The question of when an ATE insurance policy should be taken out was considered further by the Senior Costs Judge, Chief Master Hurst, in *Re Claims Direct Test Cases* (2002) LTL 29/7/2002. He found that where an incident occurred, particularly a minor road traffic accident causing slight injury, and where liability was accepted at the outset, it would be generally disproportionate and unreasonable to take out an ATE policy. That is likely to have a substantial impact upon the insurance market. Bulk providers generally insist that all cases from panel solicitors are insured, even if liability is, or is very likely to be, accepted. This allows a fixed premium to be set, with the stronger cases subsidising the weaker ones. If the stronger cases are filtered out because the premium is not recoverable, premiums are likely to rise. The Chief Master held that only the insurance element of the package of products included in the Claims Direct contract was recoverable, and allowed £621.13 (against the £1,525 claimed). The claimant's appeal was dismissed (*Re Claims Direct Test Cases* [2003] EWCA Civ 136, [2003] 4 All ER 508).

Some ATE insurers have sought to set their premium by reference to the amount of damages actually awarded. In *Pirie v Ayling* (2003) LTL 5/3/2003 the premium was stated to be 20 per cent of the damages awarded. Chief Master Hurst held that the agreement was not champertous, as there was no real danger that the purity of justice might be offended: the insurance company makes its profit from the insurance not from the litigation, the litigation simply provides the means of satisfying the insured's liability for the premium. However, the effect of the agreement was that the premium was £2,600. That was held not to be reasonable or proportionate in a road traffic accident case worth £13,000. In line with *Callery v Gray (No. 2)* [2001] EWCA Civ 1246, [2001] 1 WLR 2142, the premium allowed was £350.

PD 43–48, para. 11.10, requires the court to consider whether there was an existing policy of insurance (before-the-event or BTE insurance) and whether it would be reasonable for the successful party to have used that policy rather than obtaining fresh ATE insurance. This was considered in *Sarwar v Alam* [2001] EWCA Civ 1401, [2002] 1 WLR 125. The court held that a solicitor is under a duty to make reasonable enquiries to ascertain whether there is a BTE policy. Often such policies are linked to housing or motor insurance. Where there is such a policy, it is unlikely to be reasonable to incur a fresh premium for ATE insurance. However, there may be circumstances where it is inappropriate for the BTE insurance policy to be used. Where, for example, a passenger is covered by the driver's BTE policy, but wants to sue the driver. This might be particularly the case where the policy allows the driver's BTE insurer full control over the claim.

In more complex litigation the courts seem to be taking a more generous stance. In *Ashworth v Peterborough United Football Club Ltd* (2002) LTL 4/7/2002 the Supreme Court Costs Office considered the reasonableness of an ATE insurance premium taken out in a multi-track commercial dispute. By consent the defendant was ordered to pay Mr Ashworth £66,000 in damages plus his costs on the standard basis. The bill of costs came to £104,858, of which £45,937.50 was the ATE premium. The defendant contended that the premium was unreasonable because the insurance could have been taken earlier, that it was disproportionate and excessive and that the claimant did not disclose the amount of the expected premium before it was taken out. The master held that on the evidence available, insurance was probably not available at the outset, and that the defendant could not show that it was disproportionate to the matter in issue (not just as against the sum insured). Further it was not reasonable to have expected the claimant to obtain cover elsewhere given the restrictive market conditions at the time. It was not unlawful for the claimant to obtain retrospective own-cost cover, and the claimant gave as much information to the defendant as he was obliged to give.

In *Inline Logistics Ltd v UCI Logistics Ltd* [2002] EWHC 519 (Ch), *The Times*, 2 May 2002, the amount paid as an ATE premium (£40,000 plus £2,000 tax) was not disputed, though there was an unsuccessful argument that the premium was not recoverable (see **5.11**). Unfortunately the report does not record the level of cover purchased for that sum.

In *Sarwar v Alam* (2003) LTL 23/3/2003 the claimant appealed an important test case to the Court of Appeal having lost before both the district judge and the circuit judge. The claimant took out an ATE policy with a limit of indemnity of £125,000. The premium was £62,500 subject to a 50 per cent no-claims bonus. The full amount was paid in advance. The discount only applied if the paying party made no challenge to the amount of the premium, to the frustration of the defendant. However, Master Rogers allowed the premium in full, saying:

> I have come to the conclusion that although the premium was high, it was unlikely that the claimant's advisers could have obtained an alternative quotation at a lower rate. They tried but were unsuccessful. Law and practice were in a state of flux and insurers were understandably reluctant to commit themselves on a large potential liability.

Assessing a fee to a membership organisation

A court assessing the reasonableness of a fee to a membership organisation has to consider how this form of funding compares with the alternatives. **PD 43–48, para. 11.11**, requires: **68.52**

> Where the court is considering a provision made by a membership organisation, **CPR, r. 44.3B(1)(b)**, provides that any such provision which exceeds the likely cost to the receiving party of the premium of an insurance policy against the risk of incurring a liability to pay the costs of other parties to the proceedings is not recoverable. In such circumstances the court will, when assessing the additional liability, have regard to the factors set out in para. 11.10 [see **68.50**], in addition to the factors set out in r. 44.5.

This will require the court to construe each document as different CFAs may differ in their wording. In *Arkin v Borchard Lines Ltd* (2001) LTL 19/6/2001, interim costs orders had been made in favour of the claimant and the defendant respectively on different interim applications. The claimant had entered into a CFA, and wished to set off the two sets of interim costs. Colman J held that the terms of the CFA in question, which said the lawyers were successful if they 'recover[ed] costs . . . or interim awards during the litigation', meant that the costs award in favour of the claimant did not infringe the indemnity principle (see **68.29** to **68.32**). It was held to be unarguable that the word 'recover' in the CFA meant that actual receipt was necessary. The two costs orders could therefore be set off against each other. Further, where one costs order is summarily assessed, and the competing costs order is directed to be subject to a detailed assessment, the court could legitimately preserve the set-off by varying the time for payment of the summarily assessed costs.

Application to assess

A client who retains a solicitor under a CFA may apply to the court for it to assess the base costs (i.e., the costs other than the percentage increase) or the percentage increase (i.e., the percentage increase pursuant to the CFA either between the solicitor and client or between the solicitor and counsel, and otherwise sometimes known as the success fee) or both (**Solicitors Act 1974, part III; CPR, rr. 48.8 and 48.10; Supreme Court Costs Office Guide, sect. 20**). Base costs are assessed on the indemnity basis as if there was no CFA. The percentage increase may be reduced if the court considers it disproportionate having regard to all the relevant factors as they appeared to the solicitor or counsel when the CFA was entered into. This is discussed in detail at **6.12** to **6.16** and **6.18** to **6.21**. **68.53**

LITIGANTS IN PERSON

68.54 A litigant in person may be awarded costs (Litigants in Person (Costs and Expenses) Act 1975), which may be quantified either by summary or detailed assessment in the court's discretion. When quantifying these costs, **r. 48.6** of the CPR provides that the litigant will not recover more than two thirds of the costs and all the disbursements which would have been allowed if the litigant had been represented by a legal representative. In quantifying the costs for time spent on the litigation, the litigant in person will be allowed his or her financial loss for doing the work on the case. A copy of the evidence proving the financial loss must be served on the paying party at least 24 hours before the assessment hearing (**PD 43–48, para. 52.2**). A litigant who cannot establish any such loss will be allowed an amount in respect of time spent reasonably doing the work at a rate of £9.25 per hour (**PD 43–48, para. 52.4**). A litigant in person is not entitled to a witness allowance for his or her own attendance at court.

By **CPR, r. 48.6(6)**, a company acting without a legal representative is regarded as a litigant in person, as is a barrister, solicitor, solicitor's employee or authorised litigator who is acting for him or herself (*Khan v Lord Chancellor* [2003] EWHC 12 (QB), [2003] 1 WLR 2385; *Boyd and Hutchinson v Joseph* [2003] EWHC 413 (Ch), *The Times*, 28 April 2003). Similarly a qualified barrister as a litigant will have to show good reason for employing another barrister (*Jackson v Lord Chancellor* [2003] EWHC 626 (QB), LTL 31/3/2003). A solicitor who, instead of acting personally, is represented by his or her firm or by him or herself in his or her firm name, is not regarded as a litigant in person (**PD 43–48, para. 52.5**; *Malkinson v Trim* [2002] EWCA Civ 1273, [2003] 1 WLR 463). There is no jurisdiction to allow a party to recover the fees of a person who is not legally qualified who has assisted in the preparation and presentation of a claim (*United Building and Plumbing Contractors v Kajla* [2002] EWCA Civ 628, LTL 26/4/2002).

In a complex case a litigant in person may need to spend an extremely long time researching matters. In *R (Wulfsohn) v Legal Services Commission* [2002] EWCA Civ 250, LTL 8/2/2002, the Court of Appeal accepted that a litigant in person had spent 1,200 hours in preparation for five hearings, and took into account that a firm of solicitors had estimated the costs if they had been retained at £15,000 to £20,000. Applying the cap of two-thirds of the amount which would have been allowed if the client had been represented by lawyers (**CPR, r. 48.6(2)**), the court allowed £10,460. See also the **Supreme Court Costs Office Guide, sect. 22.**

Litigation work done by litigant's employees

68.55 The general rule is that work done by a litigant personally in the course of instructing his solicitor is not recoverable as costs (*Re Nossen's Letter Patent* [1969] 1 WLR 638). The original rule (for which, see *London Scottish Benefit Society v Chorley* (1884) 13 QBD 872) extended to all costs incurred by litigants in person, other than a solicitor acting for himself. As discussed at **68.54**, the old rule has been removed for litigants in person by the Litigants in Person (Costs and Expenses) Act 1975, and for companies acting without legal representatives by **CPR, r. 48.6(6)(a)**. The general rule continues to apply to prevent work done by a litigant in instructing his lawyers from being recoverable as costs (*Admiral Management Services Ltd v Para-Protect Europe Ltd* [2002] EWHC 233 (Ch), [2002] 1 WLR 2722).

By way of exception to the general rule, work done by specialists employed by a litigant may be recoverable as costs, provided:

(a) the staff have a sufficient level of expertise to qualify as experts (*Admiral Management Services Ltd v Para-Protect Europe Ltd*);
(b) the work done was of an expert nature, not merely factual (*Richards and Wallington (Plant Hire) Ltd v Monk and Co. Ltd* (1984) Costs LR (Core Vol) 79); and
(c) the amount recovered is limited to a reasonable sum for the actual and direct costs of the

work done by the specialists, and does not include any element for the general overheads of the business (*Re Nossen's Letter Patent*).

Litigation work done by unauthorised persons

Rights to conduct litigation are governed by the Courts and Legal Services Act 1990, s. 28. Where a client retains an unauthorised person to act on his behalf in litigation, the client is regarded for costs purposes as acting as a litigant in person (*Agassi v Robinson (No. 2)* [2005] EWCA Civ 1507, [2005] NPC 140). A successful party represented by an unauthorised person cannot recover the cost of work which it was not lawful for the unauthorised person to perform. If the unauthorised person is a specialist with expertise in the area, it may be that the expense of some of the work done can be recovered as disbursements under **CPR, r. 48.6(3)(a)(ii)** (*Agassi v Robinson (No. 2)*). **68.56**

COSTS-ONLY PROCEEDINGS

Settling before proceedings are issues

It frequently happens that disputes are resolved before proceedings are issued on the basis that one side shall do or abstain from doing something (often it is simply the payment of compensation) and shall also pay the other side's reasonable costs. Ideally, the parties will at the same time, or soon afterwards, agree the amount of those costs. If they cannot agree the amount of the costs payable, several problems may arise. One analysis of the situation is that there is no complete agreement between the parties. This may be so because a term such as 'reasonable costs' used between the parties may not be sufficiently precise to constitute a contract of compromise. It is submitted that the term 'reasonable costs' has been in use for several decades, and is understood by almost the entire profession as meaning 'standard basis costs, to be agreed between the parties, failing which such amount as would be assessed by the court on a detailed assessment'. However, there are problems. One is that as proceedings have not been issued, the costs of the receiving party are non-contentious costs (**Solicitors Act 1974, s. 87(1)**). Standard basis assessments only arise in the context of contentious costs, so there is a technical problem in the accepted meaning of the term 'reasonable costs' in settlements reached before proceedings are issued. Further, there is scope for disagreement as to what should happen if the parties cannot agree the amount of the receiving party's costs. **68.57**

Assuming the terms of the settlement are held to be sufficiently precise to amount to a contract, the next problem is how to get an adjudication of the amount of costs payable if the parties cannot agree the amount that should be paid. The traditional method, which can still be used (**PD 43–48, para. 17.11**), is for the receiving party to issue proceedings using a **Part 7** claim form for breach of the compromise agreement seeking damages in the amount of their reasonable costs. Assuming liability was not disputed, the court would enter judgment for damages to be assessed, or for a specified sum in respect of costs. If judgment was entered for damages to be assessed, the court would then convene a hearing to assess damages (rather than a hearing for a detailed assessment), at which hearing the court would assess the amount of costs that was reasonable in accordance with the compromise agreement. This in turn would (potentially) raise difficulties as to the intention of the parties on the question of the basis on which the reasonableness of the receiving party's costs should be judged.

Part 8 claim for an order for costs

In an attempt to avoid most of the difficulties identified in **68.56, CPR, r. 44.12A**, provides that where parties to a dispute have a written agreement on all matters in dispute, except the amount of costs to be paid, either party to the compromise agreement may start **Part 8** proceedings seeking an order for costs. If such an order is made, there will then be a court order for costs which can form the basis of detailed assessment proceedings (**PD 43–48,** **68.58**

para. 17.8). For the procedure, see the **Supreme Court Costs Office Guide, sect. 21**. A claim form issued under **r. 44.12A** must identify the claim or dispute giving rise to the compromise, state the date and terms of the compromise, state the amount of costs claimed and whether they are claimed on the standard or indemnity basis, and a draft order (**PD 43–48, para. 17.3**). The written evidence in support has to include a copy of the agreement (or confirmation of the agreement in writing) (**para. 17.4**). However, the court must dismiss the claim if it is opposed (**CPR, r. 44.12A(4)(b)**), which will happen if the paying party files an acknowledgment of service stating an intention to contest the proceedings or to seek a different remedy (**PD 43–48, para. 17.9**). If the claim is not opposed, it will not usually be allocated to a track, despite **CPR, r. 8.9** (**PD 43–48, para. 17.10**). A claim is not treated as opposed merely because the defendant disputes the amount claimed or says the claim has been issued in the wrong court. Once the time for filing an acknowledgment has expired, the claimant should write to the court asking for an order for a detailed assessment, whether to make such an order being the only issue to be decided at this stage. Even if there is a hearing, the judge should not embark on a summary assessment of the costs: only a detailed assessment is possible (*Bensusan v Freedman* (2001) LTL 6/11/2001). If a defendant acts unreasonably in forcing a claimant into using the **Part 7** procedure rather than the procedure under **r. 44.12A**, the court can award costs of the **Part 7** claim on the indemnity basis (*Bensusan v Freedman*).

For offers to settle in costs-only proceedings, see *Crosbie v Munroe* [2003] EWCA Civ 350, [2003] 1 WLR 2033, discussed at **68.22**.

VALUE ADDED TAX

68.59 Every statement, bill of costs, fee sheet, account or voucher on which VAT is included must state the VAT registration number of the provider (**PD 43–48, paras 4.4(3)** and **5.2**). VAT should not be included in a claim for costs if the receiving party is able to recover the VAT as input tax (**para. 5.3**) or if the receiving party is a government department in respect of the costs of services rendered by its legal staff (**para. 5.20**). Where there is a dispute about whether the receiving party is VAT registered, the receiving party's solicitors or auditors must provide a certificate in the form of **precedent F** in the schedule to PD 43-48 (**para. 5.5**).

Whenever there is a dispute about whether a service is zero rated, reference should be made to HM Customs and Excise so that the official view can be made known at the assessment (**para. 5.6**). Medical reports prepared for the purposes of litigation are liable to VAT if the expert is VAT registered (Directive 77/388/EEC; *d'Ambrumenil v Commissioners of Customs and Excise* (case C-307/01) (2003) *The Times,* 27 November 2003). Petty or general disbursements, such as postage, fares, telephone charges and costs of telegraphic transfers are normally treated as part of the solicitor's overheads, included in his profit costs, and charged to VAT (**PD 43–48, paras 5.11** and **5.12**).

The summary in a bill of costs must show the total profit costs and disbursements separately from the total VAT claimed (**para. 4.14**). Where there is a change to the rate of VAT during the course of proceedings, the bill should be divided into separate parts to distinguish work done at the different rates (**para. 4.2(4)**, but see also **paras** 5.7 and 5.8 on electing to charge the lower rate, and **para.** 5.9 on apportionment where there is a lump-sum charge for work spanning both periods).

COURT OF PROTECTION COSTS

68.60 Detailed guidance for the assessment of Court of Protection costs is given in the **Supreme Court Costs Office Guide, sect. 23**.

TRANSITIONAL RULES

Any assessment of costs taking place on or after 26 April 1999 will be in accordance with **CPR, Parts** 43 to 48 (**PD 51, para. 18(1)**). However, there is a general presumption that no costs for work done before 26 April 1999 will be disallowed if those costs would have been allowed in a taxation under the old system. Costs for work done from 26 April 1999 will be considered in accordance with **Parts 43 to 48 (PD 51, para. 18(2) and (3))**. **68.61**

Further transitional provisions dealing with costs are to be found in PD 43–48. These provide for the following:

(a) County court costs orders made before 26 April 1999 allowing costs on scale 1 or the lower scale (the old scales were not carried forward into the CPR) shall be dealt with in assessments after 25 April 1999 with the same limitations as applied in taxations before 26 April 1999 (**PD 43–48, para. 57.3**).
(b) In cases where a bill has been provisionally taxed before 26 April 1999, but the receiving party is unwilling to accept the result of the provisional taxation, the previous rules apply on the question of who can request a hearing and the time limits for doing so, but the CPR will apply on any subsequent hearing in the case (**PD 43–48, para. 57.5**).
(c) In cases where taxation proceedings were commenced and assigned to a taxing master or district judge before 26 April 1999 and were still pending on 26 April 1999, the hearing will be conducted in accordance with the CPR. However, **PD 43–48, para. 57.7(3)**, preserves the right to apply for a review to the same costs judge or district judge who conducted the detailed assessment. The review shall, for procedural purposes, be treated as an appeal from an authorised court officer. The right of review may, however, be removed if the court serves a notice on all the parties at least 28 days before the assessment hearing that their rights of appeal will be governed only by **CPR, Parts 47 and 52** (see **PD 43–48, para. 57.7(4)**).

Chapter 69 Arbitration Claims

The following procedural checklist, which is in **appendix 1**, is relevant to this chapter:
Procedural checklist 33 Arbitration claim

INTRODUCTION

69.1 Arbitration claims are governed by **CPR, Part 62, and PD 62.**

Part 62 of the CPR is part of 'a new procedural code with the overriding objective of enabling the court to deal with cases justly' (**r. 1.1(1)**). However, when dealing with applications under the Arbitration Act 1996, the court must observe the general principles in s. 1 of that Act, which are:

(a) the object of arbitration is to obtain the fair resolution of disputes by an impartial tribunal without unnecessary delay or expense;
(b) the parties should be free to agree how their disputes are resolved, subject only to such safeguards as are necessary in the public interest;
(c) in matters governed by part I of the Act the court should not intervene except as provided by that part.

In *Kalmneft JSC v Glencore International AG* [2002] 1 All ER 76 the Commercial Court heard an application under **CPR, r. 3.1(2)(a)**, to extend the 28-day time limit specified in the Arbitration Act 1996, s. 70(3), for making applications under ss. 67 and 68. Colman J held that, in exercising its discretion under CPR, r. 3.1(2)(a), the court must take into consideration both the general principles of the 1996 Act and the overriding objective of the CPR, and held that the most significant factor is the need, stated in s. 1(a) of the 1996 Act, to avoid unnecessary delay. The application in this case was made before **CPR, Part 62**, came into force, but it is submitted that the replacement of PD 49G by CPR, Part 62, should make no difference to the approach taken by Colman J, given the fundamental importance of the principles in the Arbitration Act 1996, s. 1, to arbitrations in England and Wales.

Part 62 of the CPR is very similar to the old PD 49G. Accordingly, it is likely that case law under PD 49G and its predecessor, RSC, ord. 73, would be considered relevant in determining cases arising out of it. In deciding *Vale do Rio Doce Navegação SA v Shanghai Bao Steel Ocean Shipping Co. Ltd* [2000] 2 Lloyd's Rep 1 Thomas J stated, at p. 8:

It seems to me clear that the principles applicable to the approach to the former RSC, ord. 73, and PD 49G are the same, as the principles are premised on the nature of an arbitration.

Although the judge said that it should generally be unnecessary to consider cases under the old law, he considered previous law extensively when deciding how best to interpret the provisions of what is now **CPR, r. 62.5(1)**. His reason for doing so was that: '. . . the underlying rationale in those cases remains applicable' (at p. 7).

Part 62 is divided into three sections. Section I deals with claims under the Arbitration Act 1996, Section II deals with claims under the old law and Section III applies to all enforcement proceedings other than by an action or claim on the award.

CLAIMS UNDER THE ARBITRATION ACT 1996

Starting the claim

An arbitration claim must be brought using the arbitration claim form, **form N8**. It should be issued using the standard **CPR, Part 8**, procedure (see **chapter 13; CPR, r. 62.3(1); PD 62, para. 2.2**). An application for an interim remedy under the Arbitration Act 1996, s. 4, must be made using an arbitration claim form (**PD 62, para. 8.1**). However, an application to the court to stay legal proceedings in favour of arbitration should be made by application notice to the court dealing with those proceedings (**CPR, r. 62.3(2)**). **69.2**

An arbitration claim form may be issued in one of the following (**PD 62, para. 2.3(1)**):

(a) The Admiralty and Commercial Registry at the Royal Courts of Justice. The arbitration claim will be entered into the Commercial List.
(b) The Technology and Construction Court Registry at St Dunstan's House, London. The arbitration claim will be entered into the TCC List.
(c) A district registry of the High Court where a Mercantile Court has been established (see **2.19**). The arbitration claim will be entered into the list of the Mercantile Court.
(d) A district registry of the High Court with the arbitration claim form marked 'Technology and Construction Court' in the top right-hand corner. The arbitration claim will be entered into the TCC List.
(e) The Central London Civil Justice Centre. The arbitration claim will be entered into the Mercantile List.

However, if the arbitration claim relates to a landlord and tenant or partnership dispute, it must be issued in the Chancery Division of the High Court (**PD 62, para. 2.3(2)**).

A claimant should have regard to the principles set out in the High Court and County Courts (Allocation of Arbitration Proceedings) Order 1996 (SI 1996/3215) in determining where an arbitration claim is to be issued (**PD 62, para. 2.1**). Pursuant to SI 1996/3215, art. 5(4), the following criteria should be taken into account:

(a) the financial substance of the dispute, including the value of any claim or counterclaim;
(b) the nature of the dispute, for example, whether it arises out of a commercial or business transaction or relates to engineering, building or other construction work;
(c) whether the proceedings are otherwise important and, in particular, whether they raise questions of importance to persons who are not parties; and
(d) whether the balance of convenience points to having the proceedings taken in the Central London Civil Justice Centre Mercantile List.

Where the financial substance of the dispute exceeds £200,000, the proceedings are to be taken in the High Court unless they do not raise questions of general importance to persons who are not parties.

The principles contained in **CPR, r. 30.5(3)**, relating to transfer between Divisions and to and from a specialist list apply with the effect that the High Court, or a judge of the Technology and Construction Court, may order arbitration claims to be transferred to another Division or specialist list (**CPR, r. 62.3(4)**).

The **Admiralty and Commercial Courts Guide, para. O19.1**, states that an arbitration claim which raises no significant point of arbitration law or practice will normally be transferred from the Commercial Court:

(a) to the Chancery Division, if it is a rent-review arbitration;
(b) to the Technology and Construction Court, if it is a construction or engineering arbitration;
(c) to the Central London County Civil Justice Centre List, if it is an employment arbitration; or
(d) to the Admiralty Court, if it is a salvage arbitration.

Contents of arbitration claim form

69.3 An arbitration claim form must include a concise statement of the remedy claimed and (where appropriate) the questions on which the claimant seeks the decision of the court (**CPR, r. 62.4(1)(a)**). A reference in the arbitration claim form to a witness statement filed in support of the claim is not sufficient to comply with the requirements of r. 62.4(1)(a) (**Admiralty and Commercial Courts Guide, para. O3.2**)

Where the claimant is challenging an arbitration award, the part or parts of the award being challenged must be identified and the grounds of the challenge must be shown. The claimant must identify the defendants against whom any claim for costs is made. The claimant must also specify the section of the Arbitration Act 1996 under which the application is brought and show that any statutory requirements laid down by the Act for the application being brought have been satisfied (**CPR, r. 62.4(1)(b) to (e)**).

An arbitration claim form must give the names and addresses of the persons on whom it is to be served. It must state their role in the arbitration and whether they are defendants. If the arbitration claim is being made without notice in an urgent application pursuant to the Arbitration Act 1996, s. 44(3) (order for the preservation of evidence or assets), that fact must be stated and the grounds relied upon should be specified (**CPR, r. 62.4(1)(f)**).

Service of arbitration claim form

69.4 Unless the court orders otherwise, the claimant must serve an arbitration claim form within one month from the date of issue (**CPR, r. 62.4(2)**). A claimant may apply to extend the time for service in accordance with the provisions of **r. 7.6** (see **15.7 to 15.10**).

A certificate of service (**r. 6.10**) must be filed within seven days of service of an arbitration claim form by the claimant (**PD 62, para. 3.2**). The court may exercise its powers under CPR, r. 6.8, to permit service of an arbitration claim form at the address of a party's solicitor or representative acting for him in the arbitration (**PD 62, para. 3.1**).

Service of arbitration claim form out of the jurisdiction

69.5 The court may give permission to serve an arbitration claim form out of the jurisdiction in the following circumstances (**CPR, r. 62.5(1)**):

(a) When the claimant seeks to challenge an arbitration award or to appeal to the court on a question of law arising out of an award. For the court to be able to give permission in these circumstances the award must have been made in England and Wales.
(b) If the claim is for an order under the Arbitration Act 1996, s. 44 (court powers exercisable in support of arbitral proceedings). The court may give permission for service out of the jurisdiction notwithstanding that the only remedy sought is in respect of arbitral proceedings which are taking (or will take) place outside of England and Wales.

(c) Any other situation where the claimant seeks a remedy or requires a question to be determined by the court which affects an arbitration (whether pending or anticipated), an arbitration agreement or an arbitration award. However, for this general provision to apply, the seat of the arbitration must be in England and Wales. If this is not the case the court may give permission nonetheless as long as the seat has not been designated or if, by reason of a connection with England and Wales or Northern Ireland, the court is satisfied that it is appropriate to do so.

In *Vale do Rio Doce Navegação SA v Shanghai Bao Steel Ocean Shipping Co. Ltd* [2000] 2 Lloyd's Rep 1 Thomas J decided that these provisions as set out in the former PD 49G only apply to claims brought by and against parties to an arbitration. The court did not consider an application by or against a non-party (e.g., a witness) to be something 'affecting an arbitration'. Accordingly, service of an arbitration claim form outside the jurisdiction would not be permitted in such a case.

An application for the grant of permission must be supported by written evidence stating the grounds on which the application is made. The evidence must also show in what place or country the person to be served is or probably may be found (**r. 62.5(2)**).

The provisions of **rr. 6.24** to **6.29**, which regulate the service of claim forms abroad, apply to the service of arbitration claim forms out of the jurisdiction (**r. 62.5(3)**).

Notice

On an application to remove an arbitrator (Arbitration Act 1996, s. 24), to consider and adjust the amount of fees and expenses for which the parties are liable (s. 28), or to determine the fees and expenses payable to the arbitrators where the arbitrators have withheld the award pending payment (s. 56), the arbitrators concerned must be made defendants to the application (**CPR, r. 62.6(1)**). In this way the statutory requirement for notice is fulfilled by serving the arbitration claim form on them together with any written evidence in support (**r. 62.6(2)**). Where the Arbitration Act 1996 requires an application to the court to be made on notice to any other party to the arbitration, that notice must be given by making that party a defendant (**r. 62.6(3)**). **69.6**

Supply of documents from court records

An arbitration claim form may only be inspected with the permission of the court (**PD 62, para. 5.1** which overrides **CPR, r. 5.4**). In *Glidepath BV v Thompson* [2005] EWHC 818 (Comm), [2005] 2 Lloyd's Rep 549, a third party made an application under **r. 5.4(5)** requesting copies of certain documents on the court file following a successful application for a stay under the Arbitration Act 1996, s. 9. The applicant, to assist him in presenting an employment tribunal case, sought access to the particulars of claim, notices of application in respect of a freezing injunction and a *Norwich Pharmacal* application before the proceedings were stayed. The Commercial Court refused to order production of the documents requested as neither the specific interest of the applicant in establishing his alleged rights before the employment tribunal, nor the interests of justice generally, could justify the granting of access to the documents. The court stated that it must be clearly established that the document sought will play an essential part in establishing the right of defence in question. 'To set the reasonable necessity threshold no higher than a requirement of evidential relevance would represent a most undesirable invasion by the courts of the confidentiality of arbitration in this country' (at [27]). **69.7**

Acknowledgment of service

A defendant to an arbitration application may acknowledge service by completing **form N15** or, as an alternative in the Commercial Court, **form N210(CC)** (**Admiralty and Commercial Courts Guide, para. O5.1(b)**). The general rule is that the defendant must acknowledge service within 14 days after service of the arbitration claim form (**CPR, r. 10.3(1)(b)**). If the **69.8** court authorises service of the arbitration claim form out of the jurisdiction in accordance with r. 62.5(1) (see 69.6), it will set a time limit for acknowledgment of service (**r. 62.5(4)**).

An arbitrator (or ACAS) who is sent a copy of an arbitration claim form for his information may apply to be made a defendant. Such an application must be served on the claimant but need not be served on any other party. Alternatively an arbitrator (or ACAS), without becoming a party to the arbitration claim, may make representations by filing written evidence or in writing to the court (**PD 62, paras 4.1** to **4.3**).

Case management

69.9 All arbitration claims are allocated to the multi-track (although **CPR, Part 29**, does not apply). There is no requirement to file an allocation questionnaire (**CPR, r. 62.7(1)** to **(3)**).

The following directions apply automatically unless the court orders otherwise (**CPR, r. 62.7(4)**; **PD 62, para. 6.1**):

(a) A defendant who wishes to rely on evidence before the court must file and serve his written evidence within 21 days after the date by which he was required to acknowledge service or, if an acknowledgment of service is not required, within 21 days after service of the arbitration claim form (**PD 62, para. 6.2**).
(b) A claimant who wishes to put evidence before the court in reply to written evidence filed under (a) above must file or serve his written evidence within seven days after service of the defendant's evidence (**PD 62, para. 6.3**).
(c) Agreed indexed and paginated bundles of all the evidence and other documents to be used at the hearing must be prepared by the claimant (**PD 62, para. 6.4**).
(d) Not later than five days before the hearing date, estimates for the length of the hearing must be filed together with a complete set of the documents to be used (**PD 62, para. 6.5**).
(e) Not later than two days before the hearing date the claimant must file and serve:
  (i) a chronology of the relevant events cross-referenced to the bundle of documents;
  (ii) where necessary, a list of persons involved; and
  (iii) a skeleton argument which lists succinctly:
    (1) the issues which arise for decision;
    (2) the grounds for relief (or opposing relief) to be relied upon;
    (3) the submissions of fact to be made with references to the evidence; and
    (4) the submissions of law with references to the relevant authorities (**PD 62, para. 6.6**).
(f) Not later than the day before the hearing date the defendant shall file and serve a skeleton argument which lists succinctly:
  (i) the issues which arise for decision;
  (ii) the grounds for relief (or opposing relief) to be relied upon;
  (iii) the submissions of fact to be made with the references to the evidence; and
  (iv) the submissions of law with references to the relevant authorities (**PD 62, para. 6.7**).

The **Admiralty and Commercial Courts Guide, para. O6.2**, states that claimants should apply for a hearing date as soon as possible after issuing an arbitration claim form or, in the case of an appeal, obtaining permission to appeal.

In the Commercial Court an application for directions in a pending arbitration claim should be made by application notice under **CPR, Part 23** (**Admiralty and Commercial Courts Guide, para. O6.5**).

Application for stay of legal proceedings

69.10 An application notice seeking a stay of legal proceedings under the Arbitration Act 1996, s. 9, must be served on all parties to the relevant proceedings who have given an address for service

(**CPR, r. 62.8(1)**). It should also be served on any party to those legal proceedings who has not given an address for service by sending a copy of the application notice to his last known address or at a place where it is likely to come to his attention. This can be done whether or not the party is within the jurisdiction (**r. 62.8(2)**).

On an application for a stay where a question arises as to whether an arbitration agreement has been concluded or as to whether the particular dispute which is the subject matter of the proceedings falls within the terms of an arbitration agreement, the court may determine that question. Alternatively it may give directions for its determination. It may order the court proceedings to be stayed pending its decision (**r. 62.8(3)**).

Securing the attendance of witnesses

The Arbitration Act 1996, s. 43, allows a party to an arbitration to use court proceedings to secure the attendance of witnesses at an arbitration. A party wishing to invoke this procedure may apply for a witness summons in accordance with **CPR, Part 34** (see **chapter 55**) (**PD 62, para.** 7.1). The application should be made to the Admiralty and Commercial Registry, or, if the attendance of the witness is required within the district of a district registry, to that registry (**PD 62, para.** 7.2). This power is only available if the witness is in the United Kingdom and if the arbitral proceedings are being conducted in England and Wales or Northern Ireland (Arbitration Act 1996, s. 43(3)). Section 2(3) gives a discretion to use it in relation to other arbitrations (see *Commerce and Industry Insurance Co. of Canada v Certain Underwriters at Lloyd's of London* [2002] 1 WLR 1323). The applicant must file an affidavit or witness statement showing that the application is made with the permission of the tribunal or the agreement of the other parties (**PD 62, para.** 7.3). **69.11**

This process was used in *Tajik Aluminium Plant v Hydro Aluminium AS* [2005] EWCA Civ 1218, [2006] 1 WLR 767. To ensure the attendance of witnesses at an arbitration, the claimants had obtained the consent of the tribunal to make an application to court under the Arbitration Act 1996, s. 43, to obtain a witness summons to compel third parties to attend the official hearing and to produce documents. The Court of Appeal held that documents so requested had to be specifically identified or at least described in some compendious manner that enabled the individual documents falling within the scope of the witness summons to be clearly identified. The Court of Appeal upheld the order to set aside the witness summonses on the ground that the schedules contained broad descriptions of documents but failed to identify them in a sufficiently certain manner.

Time limit for challenges to or appeals from awards

The Arbitration Act 1996, s. 70(3), provides that any challenge to or appeal from an award brought under ss. 67 to 69 must be brought within 28 days of the date of the award. However, as long as the time limit has not expired, a claimant may apply without notice on a Part 23 application notice for an order extending that time limit (**CPR, r. 62.9(1)** and **(2); PD 62, para. 11.1(1)**). The **Admiralty and Commercial Courts Guide, para. O9.2,** states that any challenge to an award should be made without delay and the court will require cogent reasons for extending time. The court will generally make its decision without a hearing (**PD 62, para. 10.2**). **69.12**

If the time limit has already expired, a claimant is not precluded from applying retrospectively for an extension of time. In such circumstances the claimant must set out in a separately identified part in the arbitration claim form the grounds why an order extending time should be made (**CPR, r. 62.9(3)(a); PD 62, para. 11.1(2)**. Any defendant who wishes to oppose the extension of time application may file written evidence in opposition within seven days after service of the arbitration claim form (**CPR, r. 62.9(3)(b)**). If the court makes an order extending the time limit, each defendant's time for acknowledging service and serving evidence shall start to run as if the arbitration claim form had been served on the date when the court's order is served on that defendant (**r. 62.9(3)(c)**).

In *Kalmneft JSC v Glencore International AG* [2002] 1 All ER 76 Colman J held that applications for an extension of the 28-day time limit provided by the Arbitration Act 1996, s. 70(3), for challenging an award under ss. 67 to 69 are governed by s. 80(5), which provides that such applications are governed by the provisions of the CPR for extending periods of time. Colman J stated that in exercising any discretion available under the CPR, the court should have in mind the general principles set out in the Arbitration Act 1996, s. 1. These differ from the overriding objective of the CPR, because they emphasise the principles of party autonomy and finality of awards and restrict the supervisory role of the courts. Accordingly much weight must be accorded to the avoidance of delay at all stages of an arbitration, both before and after an interim or final award. This was stated to be a distinct public policy factor to be given due weight in the discretionary balance. Other factors emphasised by Colman J were:

(a) whether the claimant had acted reasonably in all the circumstances;
(b) whether the defendant had caused or contributed to the delay;
(c) whether the defendant would suffer irremediable prejudice;
(d) whether the arbitration had proceeded during the period of delay and, if so, what impact on the progress of the arbitration or the costs incurred in respect of it the determination of the application by the court might now have;
(e) the strength of the application; and
(f) whether in the broadest sense it would be unfair to the claimant for him to be denied the opportunity of having the application determined.

The principles laid down in *Kalmneft JSC v Glencore International AG* [2002] 1 All ER 76 were applied by the Court of Appeal in *Nagusina Naviera v Allied Maritime Inc.* [2002] EWCA Civ 1147, LTL 10/7/2002. This approach was endorsed in *Surefire Systems Ltd v Guardian ECL Ltd* [2005] EWHC 1860 (TCC), LTL 9/11/2005. Jackson J accepted the seven relevant considerations in relation to applications for extension of time cited by Coleman J in *Kalmneft JSC v Glencore International AG*. The principles were also applied in *Peoples' Insurance Company of China, Hebei Branch v Vysanthi Shipping Co. Ltd* [2003] EWHC 1655 (Comm), LTL 18/7/2003, with the important gloss that the Arbitration Act 1996, s. 67, expressly draws attention to the fact that parties might lose the right to object if they fail to make a challenge within the requisite time. Thomas J also stated that there may, in certain circumstances, be cases where it is necessary to investigate whether a party seeking a time extension would have a claim against its lawyer.

Permission to appeal against the decision of a court under the Arbitration Act 1996, ss. 67 to 69, can only be granted by the trial judge (*Athletic Union of Constantinople v National Basketball Association (No. 2)* [2002] EWCA Civ 830, [2002] 1 WLR 2863).

Challenging the substantive jurisdiction of the tribunal

69.13 A party may, under the Arbitration Act 1996, s. 67, challenge an award made by an arbitral tribunal on the ground that the tribunal did not have substantive jurisdiction. A court hearing such an arbitration claim may examine the arguments already addressed to the tribunal in a far wider manner than a court hearing a challenge to an award under the Arbitration Act 1996, ss. 68 and 69 (see *Azov Shipping Co. v Baltic Shipping Co.* [1999] 1 All ER 476.

In *Electrosteel Castings Ltd v Scan-Trans Shipping and Chartering Sdn Bhd* [2002] EWHC 1993 (Comm), [2002] 2 All ER (Comm) 1064, Gross J stated that the arbitrator's award as to his jurisdiction was a provisional ruling only. An arbitration claim brought pursuant to the Arbitration Act 1996, s. 67, should thus involve a rehearing rather than simply a review. The parties would be allowed to introduce additional evidence which was not before the arbitrator. Grounds of objection to jurisdiction mixed in an arbitration are not to be examined closely as in a statement of case, so a party may, taking a broad view, be permitted to adduce new evidence in support of a new or different argument, coming within the existing 'grounds of objection', on an appeal under s. 67 (*Primetrade AG v Ythan Ltd* [2005] EWHC 2399 (Comm), [2006] 1 All ER 376).

Challenging an award for serious irregularity

There are directions relating to challenging an award for serious irregularity under the Arbitration Act 1996, s. 68, in the **Admiralty and Commercial Courts Guide, paras O8.6 to O8.10**. Such applications are only appropriate where there are grounds for thinking both: 69.14

(a) that an irregularity has occurred; and
(b) that that irregularity has caused or will cause *substantial* injustice to the party making the challenge (**para. O8.6(a)**, emphasis in original).

An application challenging an award on the grounds of serious irregularity should not therefore be regarded as an alternative to, or as a means of supporting, an application for permission to appeal (**para. O8.6(b)**).

A challenge to an award must be supported by evidence of the circumstances on which the claimant relies as giving rise to the irregularity complained of and the nature of the injustice which has been or will be caused to him (**para. O8.7**). If the nature of the challenge itself or the evidence filed in support of it leads the court to consider that the claim has no real prospect of success, the court may exercise its powers under **CPR, r. 3.3(4)**, to dismiss the application summarily. In such a case the claimant will have the right under **r. 3.3(5)** to apply to the court to set aside the order and to seek directions for the hearing of the claim (**Admiralty and Commercial Courts Guide, para. O8.8**).

If the arbitration claim form includes both a challenge to an award by way of an appeal and a challenge on the grounds of serious irregularity, the applications should be set out in separate sections of the arbitration claim form and the grounds on which they are made should be separately identified (**para. O8.9**). The papers will be placed before a judge to consider how the applications may most appropriately be disposed of. It will usually be more appropriate to dispose of the application to set aside or remit the award before considering the application for permission to appeal (**para. O8.10**).

Applications for permission to appeal

The Arbitration Act 1996, s. 69, provides that in certain circumstances, unless otherwise agreed by the parties, a party to arbitral proceedings may appeal to the court on a question of law arising out of an award. Unless the claimant can obtain the agreement of all the other parties to the proceedings, an appeal cannot be brought without the permission of the court. According to criteria set out in the Arbitration Act 1996, s. 69(3), permission to bring an appeal will only be granted if: 69.15

(a) the determination of the question will substantially affect the rights of one or more of the parties;
(b) the question is one which the tribunal was asked to determine;
(c) on the basis of the findings of fact in the award:
    (i) the decision of the tribunal on the question is obviously wrong; or
    (ii) the question is one of general public importance and the decision of the tribunal is at least open to serious doubt; and
(d) despite the agreement of the parties to resolve the matter by arbitration, it is just and proper in all the circumstances for the court to determine the question.

On an application for permission, the arbitration claim form must identify the question of law and state the grounds on which the claimant alleges that permission should be granted. Any evidence relied upon by the claimants to satisfy the court of the matters set out in s. 69(3), and to satisfy the court that permission should be granted, should be contained in the written evidence in support of the application (**PD 62, paras 12.1 and 12.2**).

Any written evidence filed by the defendant must state the grounds on which the defendant opposes the grant of permission. It should also set out any evidence relied upon relating to the matters set out in the Arbitration Act 1996, s. 69(3). The defendant's written evidence should specify whether the defendant wishes to contend that the award should be upheld for reasons not expressed (or not fully expressed) in it. The reasons for any such contentions should be stated (**PD 62, para. 12.3(3)**). In *CMA CGM SA v Beteiligungs-Kommanditgesellschaft MS 'Northern Pioneer' Schiffahrtsgesellschaft mbH & Co.* [2002] EWCA Civ 1878, [2003] 1 WLR 1015, the Court of Appeal emphasised that the written material should be capable of being read and digested by the judge within 30 minutes.

The judge should give brief reasons on refusing permission to appeal, which need to be sufficient to identify which of the statutory tests has not been met (**PD 62, para. 12. 5**; *North Range Shipping Ltd v Seatrans Shipping Corporation* [2002] EWCA Civ 405, [2002] 1 WLR 2397). It is sufficient to say 'for the reasons given by the arbitrators' if that is the judge's reason. In some cases it is necessary to go further, but reasons should still be brief.

Hearings

69.16 The general rule in **CPR, r. 39.2**, providing for all hearings to be held in public, is displaced in the case of arbitration claims (**r. 62.10(1)**). Although the court has a discretion to order that an arbitration claim be heard either in public or in private, the presumption is that all arbitration claims are to be heard in private. However, arbitration claims concerning the determination of a preliminary point of law under the Arbitration Act 1996, s. 45, or an appeal under s. 69 on a question of law arising out of an award will be heard in public unless the court orders otherwise (**CPR, r. 62.10(3)**). This exception does not apply to hearings to determine the preliminary question of whether the court, on an application to determine a preliminary point of law, is satisfied that the determination of the question is likely to produce substantial savings on costs and was made without delay. It also does not apply to applications for permission to appeal on a point of law.

Rule 62.10 was considered in *Department of Economics, Policy and Development of the City of Moscow v Bankers Trust Co.* [2004] EWCA Civ 314, [2005] QB 207. The Court of Appeal noted that **r. 62.10** introduced a starting point of privacy for arbitration claims which differs from the usual position prevailing under the CPR. However, this is not a blanket rule and in every case, while it is appropriate to start the hearing in private, the court should be ready to hear representations from one or other party that the hearing should continue in public, and should, if appropriate, raise the possibility with the parties. In *Glidepath BV v Thompson* [2005] EWHC 818 (Comm), [2005] 2 Lloyd's Rep 549, the Commercial Court referred to *Bankers Trust* and confirmed, at [17], that the 'character of confidentiality is further reflected in **CPR, r. 62.10**'.

Judgments on arbitration applications are usually made public.

APPLICATIONS UNDER THE OLD LAW

69.17 **Rules 62.11 to 62.16** of the CPR deal with the procedure to be adopted on applications to the court to which the 'old law', as specified in the Arbitration Act 1996, s. 107, applies. These applications are becoming increasingly rare, and will not be considered further.

ENFORCEMENT OF AWARDS

Action on the award

69.18 Part 62 of the CPR does not apply to actions to enforce awards by bringing an action or claim on the award (**r. 62.17**). A party enforcing an award in such a manner, rather than using the simpler statutory methods of enforcement, should commence the claim under **Part 8.**

Such proceedings would not be an arbitration claim and the usual provisions of the CPR would apply.

Statutory enforcement

Applications for permission to enforce awards under the statutory regime (Arbitration Act 1996, ss. 66 and 101; Arbitration Act 1950, s. 26; or Arbitration Act 1975, s. 3(1)(a)) may be made without notice as an arbitration claim using **form N8** (see **69.2**; **CPR, r. 62.18(1)**). **69.19**

On an application for permission to enforce, the court may direct that the arbitration claim form be served on such parties to the arbitration as it may specify (**r. 62.18(2)**). With the permission of the court, the arbitration claim form may be served out of the jurisdiction irrespective of where the award was, or is treated as having been, made (**r. 62.18(4)**). If the court directs that the arbitration form be served on the parties to the arbitration, the parties on whom it is served must acknowledge service and the enforcement proceedings will continue as if they were an arbitration claim governed by all applicable rules of **Part 62** (**r. 62.18(3)**).

On an application for permission to enforce an agreed award (Arbitration Act 1996, s. 51(2)), the arbitration claim form must state that the award is an agreed award. Any order made by the court must also contain such a statement (**CPR, r. 62.18(5)**).

An application for permission to enforce an award must be supported by written evidence exhibiting the arbitration agreement and the original award (or copies thereof). If the application is to enforce a New York Convention award under the Arbitration Act 1996, s. 101, or the Arbitration Act 1975, s. 3(1)(a), the duly authenticated original award and the original arbitration agreement (or duly certified copies) must be exhibited. If the New York Convention award or agreement is in a foreign language, a translation certified by an official or sworn translator or by a diplomat or consular agent must be provided (**CPR, r. 62.18(6)(a)**).

The written evidence must state the name and the usual or last-known place of residence or business of the claimant and of the person against whom it is sought to enforce the award (**r. 62.18(6)(b)**). It must also state that the award has not been complied with or, alternatively, the extent to which it has not been complied with at the date of the application (**r. 62.18(6)(c)**).

The **Admiralty and Commercial Courts Guide, para. O18.4**, states that two copies of the draft order must accompany the application. If the claimant wishes to enter judgment, the form of the judgment must correspond to the form of the award.

The claimant must draw up the order giving permission. It must be served by delivering a copy to the defendant personally or by sending a copy to the defendant's usual or last-known place of residence or business (**CPR, r. 62.18(7)**). The court's permission is not required for the order to be served out of the jurisdiction and any order to be served outside the jurisdiction should be served in accordance with **rr. 6.24** to **6.29** as if the order were an arbitration claim form (**r. 62.18(8)**).

Any application to set aside the order must be brought within 14 days after service and the award cannot be enforced until this period has expired. If the defendant applies within this period, the award cannot be enforced until after the application is finally disposed of. If the order is to be served out of the jurisdiction, the court may fix some other time limit within which the defendant must apply to have it set aside (**r. 62.18(9)**).

The order served on the defendant must contain a statement of the right to make an application to set it aside. It must also state the fact that the award cannot be enforced until after the time limit has expired or until after the application is finally disposed of, should the defendant make an application to set aside the award (**r. 62.18(10)**).

If the defendant is a body corporate, the arbitration claim form and any order giving permission to enforce should be served at its registered or principal address (r. 62.18(11)).

In *Svenska Petroleum Exploration AB v Lithuania* [2005] EWHC 2437 (Comm), LTL 15/11/2005, the claimant applied to enforce an ICC interim award in England under the Arbitration Act 1996, s. 103(1). One of the grounds upon which the respondent objected was that the award was not final and conclusive in this regard. The determination of whether an award was final and binding depended on its status in the country where it was made. The interim award was issued in Denmark. Under Danish law an arbitral award on jurisdiction was reviewable by the Danish courts and so was not final and binding. The enforcement application was thus dismissed.

Interest on award

69.20 An applicant seeking to enforce an award of interest where the whole or any part of the interest relates to a period after the date of the award must file a statement giving the following particulars (CPR, r. 62.19(1)):

(a) whether simple or compound interest was awarded;
(b) the date from which interest was awarded;
(c) whether rests were provided for, in which case they should be specified;
(d) the rate of interest awarded; and
(e) a calculation showing the total amount claimed up to the date of the certificate. Any sums which will become due thereafter should be shown on a daily-rate basis.

Such a statement must be filed whenever the amount of interest has to be quantified for the purpose of obtaining a judgment or order for the enforcement of an award (Arbitration Act 1996, s. 66) or enforcing such a judgment or order (CPR, r. 62.19(2)).

Chapter 70 Alternative Dispute Resolution

INTRODUCTION

The introduction of the CPR began a process designed to reform court procedures to make them more effective and more affordable. However, whatever changes are introduced, a fair trial of complex issues will always be expensive. By its nature, adversarial litigation may not be able to provide a resolution to the parties' dispute which is truly in their best interests. Accordingly, recognising the limits of litigation, Lord Woolf noted in his *Interim Report* (ch. 18, paras 1 and 2) that: **70.1**

> In recent years there has been, both in this country and overseas, a growth in alternative dispute resolution (ADR) and an increasing recognition of its contribution to the fair, appropriate and effective resolution of civil disputes. The fact that litigation is not the only means of achieving this aim, and may not in all cases be the best, is my main reason for including ADR in an Inquiry whose essential focus is on improving access to justice through the courts. My second reason is to increase awareness still further among the legal professional and the general public, of what ADR has to offer . . . From the point of view of the Court Service, ADR has the obvious advantage of saving scarce judicial and other resources. More significantly, in my view, it offers a variety of benefits to litigants or potential litigants.

While the courts were not to become involved in administering ADR, Lord Woolf recommended that the two systems worked together:

> Where there is a satisfactory alternative which offers a prospect of resolving a dispute in a way which is to the advantage of the litigants, then the court should encourage the use of this alternative. This is a responsibility which the courts should accept. It is in their interest that they should do so. (*Interim Report*, ch. 18, para. 31.)

In the past few years the courts have been balancing their support for ADR with the right of access to the courts. The leading case is now the Court of Appeal decision in *Halsey v Milton Keynes General NHS Trust* [2004] EWCA Civ 576, [2004] 1 WLR 3002. The central message of this case (at [11]) is that:

> Parties sometimes need to be encouraged by the court to embark on an ADR. The need for such encouragement should diminish in time if the virtue of ADR in suitable cases is demonstrated even more convincingly than it has been thus far. The value and importance of ADR have been established within a remarkably short time. All members of the legal profession who conduct litigation should now

routinely consider with their clients whether their disputes are suitable for ADR. But we reiterate that the court's role is to encourage, not to compel. The form of encouragement may be robust.

Judicial support for alternative dispute resolution

70.2 In *R (Cowl) v Plymouth City Council* [2001] EWCA Civ 1935, [2002] 1 WLR 803, Lord Woolf restated his support for ADR judicially. He spoke of 'the paramount importance of avoiding litigation whenever this is possible' and how both sides must 'be acutely conscious of the contribution alternative dispute resolution can make to resolving disputes in a manner which both meets the needs of the parties and the public and saves time, expense and stress'.

Judicial support for alternative dispute resolution now extends to holding that agreements to mediate, entered into before a dispute has arisen, are enforceable. This contrasts with the usual English law position that agreements to negotiate are unenforceable. In *Cable and Wireless plc v IBM United Kingdom Ltd* [2002] EWHC 2059 (Comm), [2002] 2 All ER (Comm) 1041, Colman J stated that 'for the courts now to decline to enforce contractual references to ADR on the grounds of intrinsic uncertainty would be to fly in the face of public policy as expressed in the CPR'.

In appropriate circumstances, the courts will impose costs sanctions on parties they perceive to have insufficiently explored the possibilities of alternative dispute resolution (see **70.22**).

There is no official framework or rules for ADR in the CPR. However, the CPR are framed so that ADR is always to be considered as an alternative to pursuing a claim through the courts. There are a number of provisions whereby court proceedings intersect with ADR. These are described at **70.9** to **70.22**.

WHAT IS ADR?

70.3 ADR is understood to mean any alternative process to litigation through the courts. The various types of ADR broadly fall into two main categories. The first category involves processes that are, similar to litigation, adjudicatory. These result in a final and binding determination on the parties. The second category includes procedures that facilitate a negotiated settlement between the disputing parties within a structured framework. These, the non-adjudicative processes, usually involve some kind of third-party involvement.

ADJUDICATIVE ADR

70.4 The adjudicative procedures include such processes as arbitration and expert determination where a final and binding determination is made on the dispute. These types of ADR are widely used in commercial contracts. For example, arbitration is often used for the resolution of rent review disputes under commercial leases while expert determination is included in energy contracts for disputes that relate to specific technical accounting matters. In such cases, an expert accountant will be nominated by the parties to make a determination on the matters in dispute.

Adjudication under the Housing Grants, Construction and Regeneration Act 1996

70.5 In common with certain other jurisdictions, the various United Kingdom jurisdictions have imposed by statute a quasi-judicial process for certain construction disputes. The Housing Grants, Construction and Regeneration Act 1996 came into force on 1 May 1998 and creates a right to refer to adjudication a dispute arising under any agreement which is a construction contract, entered into after that date. The Act applies to England, Wales and Scotland, and there is equivalent legislation for Northern Ireland. To be covered by the Act, a construction contract must be in writing and must comply with certain statutory requirements. Contracts with residential occupiers are not included (s. 106). Certain matters which would normally be called construction work (including most oil and gas, process plant and utility construction work) are outside the scope of statutory adjudication as a result of the detailed definition of 'construction operations' in the Act (s. 105). Other types of contract (including leases, contracts relating to shares and guarantees) are exempted by regulations made by the Secretary of State (the Construction Contracts (England and Wales) Exclusion Order 1998 (SI 1998/648) and its Scottish and Northern Irish counterparts).

In the absence of a compliant adjudication provision in a construction contract a statutory scheme applies as a term of the contract implied by statute. The scheme is set out in sch. 1 to the Scheme for Construction Contracts (England and Wales) Regulations 1998 (SI 1998/649) made under the Act. Under para. 12 of the scheme an adjudicator is obliged to act impartially, reach his decision in accordance with the relevant contract terms and the law applicable to the contract and 'avoid incurring unnecessary expense'. Absent any agreement between the parties on the appointment of an adjudicator, a nominating body, for example, the Royal Institute of Chartered Surveyors (RICS), may make an appointment at the request of one of the parties.

The Act lays down a framework for the conduct of adjudication: for example, the adjudicator must reach a decision within 28 days of the dispute having been referred to him or such longer period as the parties may agree (s. 108(2)). Within this broad outline, the parties are free to agree more detailed express terms, and often do so by reference to published sets of rules.

Adjudication is a fast and often effective mechanism for resolving construction disputes. The adjudicator's decision is binding until 'the dispute is finally determined by legal proceedings, by arbitration . . . or by agreement' (s. 108(3)). The parties can agree that the adjudicator's decision will be final and binding. Enforcement is by way of an application to court for sums owing under the contract. Speed is the critical factor in adjudication proceedings as most parties want to have a determination of the dispute as quickly as possible without having to resort to litigation or arbitration.

Expert determination

Expert determination is where the parties choose to refer a particular type of dispute to an **70.6**
independent third party to decide the matter applying his own expertise. The third party is chosen by the parties and is usually an expert in the subject of the dispute, but may, for example, be a lawyer. It is important that the contract sets out a default appointment process to be used if the parties are unable to agree who is to act as expert. It is usual to provide that an industry body such as the ICAEW or the Law Society is to make the appointment. This type of process is most suitable for determining technical aspects of a complex dispute. Provisions for expert determination, to resolve financial or technical issues, are also common in long-term contracts or where there is an ongoing commercial relationship between the parties. An expert is only vested with the powers prescribed in the relevant contract. It is therefore advisable to set out clearly the manner in which the expert determination should proceed to avoid any delay at the time the dispute arises. There are no procedural restrictions on the parties, although if a speedy outcome is sought a simpler process is preferable. It is useful to include a provision in the contract allowing the parties to agree the procedure for the expert determination. If the parties cannot so agree, a default arrangement should provide for the expert himself to determine the process. This can prevent time being wasted on agreeing a procedure once a dispute has arisen and is referred to expert determination. An expert does not, unless there is a provision to the contrary, have to receive formal submissions from the parties, oral or written. He may reach his final decision based on his own investigations and expertise. However, in practice, it is generally accepted that each party will make at least written submissions on the matters in dispute. The parties and the expert agree terms of reference, setting out the procedure to be followed and the expert's terms of engagement.

Expert determination is particularly useful for resolving technical issues, for example, accounting disputes, valuation of corporate shareholdings and the calculation of sums paid under oil and gas joint operation agreements. The decision of an expert is final and the parties can and usually do expressly agree in the contract to be bound by the decision of the expert. The exceptions to such finality are fraud and manifest error. An expert's determination cannot be enforced in the same way as an arbitration award. The Arbitration Act 1996 does not apply to expert determination so enforcement is a matter of implementing the contract provisions. The English courts will recognise the expert's determination as final and binding save in cases of fraud or if the expert has exceeded his mandate.

An expert differs from an arbitrator in that an expert can be sued for negligence by the parties, though experts usually seek to limit such liability in their terms of reference. An arbitrator is immune under the Arbitration Act 1996, s. 29, unless the alleged act or omission was shown to be committed in bad faith. A clause in a contract may not always be clear as to which type of dispute resolution is being used, expert determination or arbitration. The dispute resolution provision in a contract does not need to refer to an arbitrator or arbitration for it to fall into that category. Accordingly, parties need to be careful when drafting their dispute resolution clause to ensure that their intention is clear. In *David Wilson Homes Ltd v Survey Services Ltd* [2001] EWCA Civ 34, [2001] 1 All ER (Comm) 449, the Court of Appeal confirmed that in interpreting the dispute clause 'the important thing is that there should be an agreement to refer disputes to a person other than the court who is to resolve the dispute in a manner binding on the parties to the agreement' (at [11]). Despite the lack of any reference to arbitration, the Court of Appeal confirmed it was in fact an arbitration clause and not expert determination. Many expert determination clauses clearly state that the expert is acting as an expert and not as an arbitrator to avoid any such confusion. Usually the scope and remit of the expert is narrower than that of an arbitral tribunal and does not involve determinations on questions of law.

Arbitration

70.7 Arbitration is a private, usually contractual, dispute resolution option where an impartial tribunal issues a final and binding award on the matters in dispute. It is consensual in nature and it must be clear from the parties' agreement that they intended to arbitrate. All signatory states to the Convention on the Recognition and Enforcement of Foreign Arbitral Awards 1958 (the New York Convention) will recognise an agreement to arbitrate and stay litigation proceedings. Prima facie evidence of an agreement to arbitrate is required unless the national court finds that the arbitration agreement is 'null and void, inoperative, or incapable of being performed' (art. II(3)). In general, the courts in England and Wales will order a stay of litigation proceedings under the Arbitration Act 1996, s. 9, in the face of an arbitration agreement even if it is unclear and badly drafted (*McNicholas plc v AEI Cables Ltd* (TCC 25 May 1999) www.hmcourts-service.gov.uk/HMCSJudgments; *Sonatrach Petroleum Corporation v Ferrell International Ltd* [2002] 1 All ER (Comm) 627).

The cornerstone of arbitration is party autonomy. The parties are free to agree exactly how any disputes should be resolved in arbitral proceedings. The Arbitration Act 1996 gives effect to this principle by reducing the intervention of the courts to a minimum. They have a purely supportive and supervisory role in arbitration proceedings. The courts can assist the arbitration process, for example, by ordering witnesses to attend hearings, but cannot review the merits of an award. There are limited grounds of appeal should an aggrieved party wish to challenge the tribunal's award.

There are two main options available to commercial entities considering incorporating an arbitration clause into a contract: ad hoc arbitration or institutional arbitration.

In ad hoc arbitration, there is no administering body so the parties are free to agree the type of arbitration procedure that best suits their needs. Should they be unable to do so, the tribunal will determine the process. The parties in ad hoc arbitration only have to pay for the tribunal's costs as there are no additional administrative fees. In reality, it is not unusual for the chairman of an ad hoc tribunal to nominate a secretary to the tribunal to assist in the smooth running of the case. Parties in ad hoc arbitration often apply the UNCITRAL Arbitration Rules which provide some guidance for the tribunal on procedure.

The second option, institutional or administered arbitration, is where the parties incorporate into the contract the rules of a designated international arbitration institution, for example, the LCIA or ICC. Each of the international institutions has its own set of rules and they have varying degrees of regulation. The ICC, for example, has a very supportive secretariat with a high level of regulation throughout the process. This includes scrutiny of an award by the ICC Court before it is issued by the tribunal. In contrast other institutions rely more heavily on the calibre of tribunals to work efficiently and produce well crafted and enforceable awards. Parties often prefer to choose institutional arbitration in their contracts given the level of support and to a certain extent assistance on enforcement.

There are certain types of international disputes that are referred to particular institutions. Investment disputes, for example, between an investor and a host State, are often referred to the International Centre for Settlement of Investment Disputes (ICSID) at the World Bank in Washington. The ICC also has about 10 per cent of its cases each year that involve a State or State entity. Some of these investment disputes arise under concession contracts that have specific arbitration clauses. In other cases, the investor will base its claim on a relevant investment treaty, bilateral or multilateral. These types of international arbitrations are not contractual but rely on the States' standing offer to arbitrate certain types of disputes set out in the relevant treaty.

Domestically, the best-known arbitration institute is the Chartered Institute of Arbitrators. It plays a leading role in training arbitrators and promoting the process generally. It also promulgates arbitration rules and administers more than 100 bespoke arbitration schemes for consumer and commercial markets.

The parties to an arbitration agreement can choose the number of tribunal members, usually three. Although a sole arbitrator is the default position under the Arbitration Act 1996, s. 15(3), parties often prefer to be able to nominate one member each of a three-member tribunal. The parties can also agree the procedure for the arbitration including limiting document production to clear and specific categories. In international arbitration there is usually only limited document disclosure. The IBA Rules on the Taking of Evidence 1999 are often referred to by arbitrators to ensure that full common law style discovery is avoided. Parties can if they so wish expressly include these IBA Rules into their contract, in whole or in part, as a means of eliminating any uncertainty in the procedure to be applied by the tribunal should a dispute arise in the future.

The flexibility and private nature of arbitration makes it a popular option in commercial contracts. In addition, the finality of the award provides commercial certainty. An arbitral award is enforceable in England and Wales under the Arbitration Act 1996, s. 66, as if it was a court judgment. The permission of the court is required (see **CPR, r. 62.18**, and **69.19**). If necessary, it can also be enforced abroad in all of the contracting states to the New York Convention on the Recognition and Enforcement of Foreign Arbitral Awards 1958.

Arbitration is used in a huge range of commercial transactions from sport to construction. Certain types of transactions have given rise to their own specialised arbitration procedures. A good example of this is 'baseball arbitration', or last offer arbitration. This type of arbitration was first used in the United States by sports clubs in negotiations over professional athletes' salaries. It is now more widely used, for example, in reinsurance contracts, and where parties have an ongoing relationship. The arbitrator's ability to determine quantum in the case is restricted. After making their submissions to the tribunal both parties must recommend a figure that they believe would settle the dispute. The arbitrator can only choose the figure which he finds is closest to what he would have awarded. There are therefore only two possible outcomes in a baseball arbitration. Clearly both sides will try to be reasonable in their proposed figure as they would not wish to alienate the tribunal forcing it to choose the other party's suggestion. This type of arbitration is only appropriate where the parties agree sums are due and payable under a contract, but the actual amount is disputed. There are clear risks in this type of arbitration, but as the parties are forced to make reasonable quotes it often encourages a settlement.

Trade arbitration

70.8 London is an international centre for commodity disputes, from maritime to metals. Each commodity association has its own distinct set of arbitration rules, many of which contain an appellate body system. Examples include GAFTA (Grain and Feed Trade Association) and FOSFA (Federation of Oils Seeds and Fats Association). The London Metal Exchange is the world's leading market for base metals. Any disputes arising under a metal contract must be referred to arbitration under the LME Arbitration Rules. The same is true for the Refined Sugar Association (RSA), originally founded in 1891. Although each association has its own rules these arbitrations do add to the jurisprudence under the Arbitration Act 1996. In *Rustal Trading Ltd v Gill & Duffus SA* [2000] 1 Lloyd's Rep 14, for example, the High Court had to decide whether one of the arbitrators in an RSA arbitration was biased as he had been involved in an earlier dispute involving one of the parties. This argument was dismissed as the previous dispute was two years earlier and in any event the court did not find it out of the ordinary that the parties in such trade arbitrations may have had previous experience with each other.

Commodity trade arbitration is a specialist form of arbitration. Nevertheless, maritime arbitration under the LMAA has generated a large number of cases before the English courts. The fundamental principles that govern these arbitrations are the same for general commercial matters, and the Arbitration Act 1996 applies when the seat of the arbitration is in England.

NON-ADJUDICATIVE ADR

70.9 A wide range of processes fall into the category of non-adjudicative ADR. These procedures are often used to assist parties to on-going litigation to reach a settlement away from the courts. They are widely used in England in labour relations and family law disputes, and throughout the commercial sector. They can cut short a dispute and save time and money if an amicable settlement can be agreed. This type of ADR involves the intervention of an independent, neutral third party. The flexibility of procedure and informality allowed lends itself to a positive outcome. Parties can control exactly how the process will take place and can be more forthright in their discussions as non-adjudicative ADR is a confidential process and the result is non-binding and usually unenforceable.

Conciliation/negotiation

70.10 Negotiation is often a useful form of ADR in commercial disputes where the relationship between the parties is ongoing. The parties can use the time of negotiation as a cooling-off period to try to resolve their dispute quickly and cheaply. Negotiation is a precondition in many contracts to arbitration or litigation. The majority of commercial contracts have a multi-tiered dispute resolution clause that will impose an obligation to try to reach an amicable settlement through negotiation. Usually a certain time period is designated for this purpose, for example, seven or 15 days. There does not appear to be the same negative costs implications in failure to engage in pre-agreed forms of ADR followed by arbitration as exist for litigation (see 70.22).

Negotiation can take place with just the parties present or an independent third party can be involved. The role of the negotiator is purely to facilitate the parties in reaching a resolution.

He does not take sides although he can have separate caucus meetings with each side to see if he can bring them any closer to reaching an amicable settlement. A conciliation process takes place in a similar way. A neutral conciliator will also try to assist the parties in finding a mutually satisfactory resolution to the dispute. The procedure in the negotiation or conciliation is driven by the parties and flexibility is essential. It is unlikely there will be any formal written or oral submissions, but it can be a very useful mechanism through which each party gets a better understanding of the subject matter of the dispute.

Negotiation is also successfully used during an on-going arbitration or litigation. The parties may, having commenced formal proceedings, be more willing to reach a compromise solution. Many cases are settled successfully in this way. A party should take care in using arbitration as a tool to force a respondent to negotiate a settlement. Once an arbitration is commenced it cannot be unilaterally withdrawn. The consent of both parties is required. If no negotiated settlement is reached, the arbitration will continue, whether the party chooses to participate or not. It is therefore worth making a genuine attempt to reach a negotiated settlement prior to any formal proceedings being commenced.

Mediation

What kind of cases are suitable for mediation? Virtually all civil disputes can be resolved by mediation. The remedies available in mediation are potentially far wider than those which can be obtained through litigation as the parties to a mediation can agree, or be guided to, any resolution of their dispute which they wish. However, mediation may be less suitable in cases where: **70.11**

(a) a party is contemplating or facing a large number of similar claims for which it seeks to set some kind of legal precedent;
(b) a party is confident it can swiftly vindicate its legal rights and obtain full relief by proceeding to summary judgment; or
(c) a party requires speedy injunctive relief.

The fact that a dispute raises complicated issues of fact or law, involves more than two parties or has given rise to an acrimonious relationship between the litigants, should be no barrier to mediation. In all these cases mediation may ultimately provide the parties with a more satisfactory resolution to their dispute than the courts can provide.

What happens at the mediation? The venue for a mediation will generally consist of one large room where the parties and the mediator can meet together and private rooms for the parties either to meet separately with the mediator or to discuss the matter alone when the mediator is with the other party or parties. **70.12**

At the start of the mediation, the parties will usually meet in the presence of the mediator and briefly explain their case. In some mediations the parties will have had the opportunity, before the mediation meeting begins, to provide the mediator with a written submission outlining their positions and with copies of documents they believe to be relevant.

Having made their opening presentations the parties will retire to their private rooms and the mediator will move between them trying to help them reach an agreement. The mediator will be able to influence the parties during this stage by controlling the flow of information, deciding on how to present a party's evidence to the other side and ultimately by suggesting or influencing the architecture of any settlement.

The mediation can end at any time as the parties and the mediator are under no obligation to remain. If a settlement is reached, it will normally be recorded in writing at the mediation.

The mediation process is confidential and without prejudice. If the mediation does not lead to settlement, a party will not be able to make use of information it obtained during the mediation in the continuing court proceedings.

Unless the parties agree otherwise, the mediator's and mediation institution's fees will be divided equally. Each party will bear its own costs of attending the mediation.

70.13 **Does mediation work?** There is much speculation as to whether mediation does, as its supporters claim, lead to settlements in most cases in which it is used. A report by Professor Hazel Genn, published by the Lord Chancellor's Department in 2002, assessed the impact of ADR orders made in the Commercial Court (*Court-based ADR Initiatives for Non-family Civil Disputes* (Research Paper 1/2002)). The paper is based upon data collected from court files and interviews with solicitors relating to 233 ADR orders made between July 1996 and June 2000.

Professor Genn found that ADR was undertaken in just over half of the cases in which an ADR order was made. However, the figures showed an increasing use of ADR towards the end of her review period. Of the cases in which ADR was attempted, 52 per cent settled through ADR and a further 20 per cent settled some time after the conclusion of the ADR procedure. Only 5 per cent continued to trial. Where ADR was not attempted, 15 per cent went to trial and 63 per cent settled, with about one-fifth of the cases that settled attributing the settlement to the making of an ADR order.

Early neutral evaluation

70.14 Early neutral evaluation aims to provide parties with an early and frank evaluation by an independent party of the merits of their claim. It usually takes place at a much earlier stage than arbitration, although, like negotiation and conciliation, it can be used at any time during a dispute. The concept of early neutral evaluation was conceived in the United States as a mechanism to reduce the costs of litigation. The English courts have encouraged the use of all forms of ADR since the introduction of the CPR in 1999. The Commercial Court offers an early evaluation scheme, where a judge can give an assessment of the merits of the claims (**Admiralty and Commercial Courts Guide, para. G2**). Although this is non-binding it has not been widely used.

The assessment of the judge or third-party evaluator is non-binding on the parties but often works to ensure that the parties reach a settlement before expending time and resources on litigation or arbitration proceedings. The assessment will focus on the central issues involved in the dispute and the relevant law. The evaluation is usually issued in written form to the parties. The costs involved in the process are a lot less than arbitration or litigation and the entire procedure takes place quite quickly. Several ADR centres offer advice on appointing an appropriate evaluator, for example CEDR Solve (www.cedr.co.uk).

Mini-trial or executive trial

70.15 The mini or executive trial is not in reality a trial. It is a structured settlement process where the parties make summary submissions on the particular dispute. The executives of the parties attend the meeting with an independent adviser, often nominated by an appropriate dispute resolution institution. The executives having heard the summary submissions try to reach an agreement. If this is not possible the neutral adviser issues an advisory opinion. This is not binding on the parties, but usually a further meeting between the executives is held after the opinion has been given in a final attempt to reach an amicable settlement. The mini-trial was introduced to meet a business need. It is a fast and efficient means of resolving a dispute where the control rests exclusively with the business executives.

Med-arb

70.16 A hybrid form of dispute resolution is mediation-arbitration or 'med-arb'. Originally conceived in the 1970s med-arb was thought to provide disputing parties with the best of both options. Each stage of the process is kept separate. The mediation process takes place first and if that fails to produce a solution to the dispute, arbitration proceedings will commence. One of the main disadvantages of med-arb is that parties may be less open during the mediation process as they know that if the mediation is unsuccessful they will have the same independent third party acting as an arbitrator with the power to issue a final and binding award. This drawback has given rise to debate on whether the process itself is fundamentally flawed at law. Can a person who has already acted as a mediator and been privy to certain confidential information from the parties in private caucus meetings really be an independent unbiased arbitrator? The Arbitration Act 1996, s. 24(1), requires the tribunal to be impartial and a legitimate concern may be raised as to whether a person who has acted as a mediator first necessarily complies with this obligation. A similar obligation of impartiality and independence exists under the European Convention on Human Rights. In any event, med-arb is used quite extensively throughout Asia, for example in CIETAC and SIAC arbitrations, without any such issues being a problem. Parties seem to be happy that the independent third party is familiar with the dispute from the outset and, if an agreed settlement cannot be reached after the initial mediation, for him to continue to act as arbitrator.

CONTRACT TERMS

The type of dispute resolution clause in any particular contract will depend on the type of transaction, the parties to the contract, the forum and the applicable law. Choice of any form of adjudicative ADR will determine an issue definitively whereas non-adjudicative ADR provides the forum within which the parties can reach an agreed settlement. 70.17

When drafting a contract particular care and attention should be given to the dispute resolution clause. A decision must be made about which type of ADR should be chosen or whether a range of options is required under the contract. Unfortunately, at the time of drafting a contract most parties do not envisage anything going wrong so it can be difficult to discuss in any detail the significance of the type of ADR chosen. It is always essential to consider the preferred dispute resolution option of each client. It is best to explain the implications of each option so that there are no unrealistic expectations should a dispute arise under the contract in the future.

Contract terms should be drafted clearly to avoid any controversy or disagreement as to the scope and extent of the dispute resolution clause. This is particularly true if the contract provides for hybrid or bifurcated dispute resolution provisions, under which different procedures apply to particular types of dispute. For example, technical issues may be referred to an expert accountant, with all other disputes under the contract being referred to arbitration.

It has become quite common to include several different forms of dispute resolution provisions in a multi-tiered clause. In this way, parties seek to minimise their time and costs spent on any future dispute. The options provided in these clauses usually start with mandatory negotiations, move to mediation and then on to arbitration or litigation depending on the will of the parties. The most important consideration for such a multi-tiered clause is to include time limits for each of the non-binding dispute resolution options. Otherwise one party could use them as a mere dilatory tactic rather than a genuine attempt at resolution. Such time limits can range from 15 days to 90 days depending on the type of contract. Clearly the final option of arbitration or litigation cannot be so prescribed. Arbitration can have rigorous time limits imposed in a contract, often referred to as fast-track arbitration. It must, however, be left open to the parties to agree an extension if necessary, otherwise the tribunal could find itself operating *functus officio*.

RELATIONSHIP BETWEEN THE COURTS AND ADR

70.18 In his *Final Report* (ch. 1, para. 7(d)) Lord Woolf stated how ADR should be among the tools used by the court to resolve disputes at an early stage:

> Two other significant aims of my recommendations need to be borne in mind: that of encouraging the resolution of disputes before they come to litigation, for example by greater use of pre-litigation disclosure and of ADR, and that of encouraging settlement, for example by introducing plaintiffs' offers to settle, and by the disposing of issues so as to narrow the dispute. All these are intended to divert cases from the court system or to ensure that those cases which do go through the court system are disposed of as rapidly as possible. I share the view, expressed in the Commercial Court Practice Statement of 10 December 1993, that although the primary role of the court is as a forum for deciding cases it is right that the court should encourage the parties to consider the use of ADR as a means to resolve their dispute. I believe that the same is true of helping the parties to settle a case.

The courts' encouragement of mediation forces litigation practitioners to familiarise themselves with ADR processes. This familiarity leads to an increased demand for mediation. The courts' attitude also goes some way to removing the concern that by suggesting ADR a party could be taken to lack confidence in the strength of its case.

ADR and active case management

70.19 Encouraging ADR is part of the court's active case management role, which in turn is how the court furthers the overriding objective. **Rule 1.4** of the CPR includes 'encouraging the parties to use an alternative dispute resolution procedure if the court considers that appropriate and facilitating the use of such procedure' among the matters expressly included within active case management.

Rule 1.3 of the CPR, which requires the parties to help the court to further the overriding objective, places the parties under a duty in relation to ADR. Practically, this will require the parties to be aware of ADR and to consider seriously the possibility of using it to resolve their dispute.

The extent of a party's obligation to consider ADR was considered in detail by the Court of Appeal in *Halsey v Milton Keynes General NHS Trust* [2004] EWCA Civ 576, [2004] 1 WLR 3002. The court made reference to the judgment of Brooke LJ in *Dunnett v Railtrack plc* [2002] EWCA Civ 303, [2002] 1 WLR 2434, who had emphasised how 'skilled mediators are now able to achieve results satisfactory to both parties in many cases which are quite beyond the power of lawyers and courts to achieve'. However, the court rejected the submission that there should be a presumption in favour of mediation. It also emphasised that any compulsion of ADR would be an unacceptable constraint on the right of access to the court and therefore a violation of the **European Convention on Human Rights, art. 6, in the Human Rights Act 1998, sch. 1.**

In the Glossary to the CPR, 'alternative dispute resolution' is broadly defined as a:

> collective description of methods of resolving disputes otherwise than through the normal trial process.

The well-advised litigant will consider the possibility of resorting to ADR at the earliest possible stage, even before proceedings are initiated. **Practice Direction Protocols, para. 4**, requires all parties, in accordance with the overriding objective, to try to avoid the necessity for starting proceedings. It also requires them to conduct genuine and reasonable negotiations with a view to settling the claim economically.

In certain circumstances the court will use its powers under other provisions of the CPR to assist the parties to mediate. For example, in *Arrow Trading and Investments Est 1920 v Edwardian Group Ltd* [2004] EWHC 1319 (Ch), [2005] 1 BCLC 696, the court granted advance disclosure of documents relating to quantum to put the claimant in a position whereby it could meaningfully mediate the dispute.

The court's encouragement of mediation has even extended to proceedings which the parties have agreed to conduct outside of the usual court processes. In *C v RHL* [2005] EWHC 873 (Comm), LTL 12/5/2005, the court was only asked to issue an anti-suit injunction preventing a party from continuing court proceedings in Russia in breach of an agreement to arbitrate. Instead of issuing the injunction, the court directed the parties to mediate and issued a standard ADR order.

ADR and the allocation questionnaire

Rule 26.4(1) of the CPR provides that a party filing an allocation questionnaire may request the proceedings be stayed while the parties try to settle the case by ADR or other means. Where both parties request a stay or the court of its own initiative considers that a stay would be appropriate, the court will direct the proceedings be stayed for one month (**r. 26.4(2)**). The court may extend the stay for such period as it considers appropriate (**r. 26.4(3)**). **70.20**

In fact, the first question to be addressed by a party completing the allocation questionnaire (**form N150**) relates to ADR. It asks:

> Do you wish there to be a one month stay to attempt to settle the claim, either by informal discussion or by alternative dispute resolution?

If only one party requests a stay, the court is likely to try to ascertain why the other party is refusing (this may be a matter addressed at a case management conference).

ADR and case management conferences

The subject of ADR may be raised at the case management conference, especially if the judge believes that the parties have not previously considered it themselves. The judge may 'invite' the parties to try ADR (see, for example, the **Admiralty and Commercial Courts Guide, paras G1.3** and **G1.6** to **G1.8** and **appendix** 7 for a draft ADR order; **Chancery Guide, para.** 17.3). **70.21**

The draft ADR order set out in **app.** 7 to the **Admiralty and Commercial Courts Guide** provides for the parties to inform the court of the steps they have taken towards ADR, should ADR not be successful. Without prejudice to matters of privilege, they have to inform the court why such steps have failed. Accordingly, while the court cannot ask the parties to provide details of their attempts to settle (questions such as 'How much is between you now?' would be off-limits), the parties can expect to be asked whether they agreed to attend a mediation. If they refused, this may have to be justified. Similarly, a party who did something to frustrate the mediation, such as sending a representative without authority to settle, may have to justify its actions.

Consequences of refusing to consider ADR

A party which does not take its duty to consider ADR seriously is likely to be penalised when the court looks to the question of costs. In exercising its discretion as to the award of costs, the court is obliged to have regard to the conduct of the parties (**CPR, r. 44.3(4)**). This includes considering: **70.22**

> The manner in which a party pursued or defended his case or a particular allegation or issue (**CPR, r. 44.3(5)(c)**).

Accordingly a winning party may find its recovery of costs reduced by reason of a failure to cooperate in relation to ADR. An unsuccessful defendant who refused to consider ADR to try to settle the case before trial could be liable for interest on costs (perhaps running from a date before judgment) (**CPR, r. 44.3(6)(g)**) or indemnity costs.

The Court of Appeal in *Halsey v Milton Keynes General NHS Trust* [2004] EWCA Civ 576, [2004] 1 WLR 3002, stated that a party who refuses even to consider ADR is always at risk of an adverse costs finding. The court set out a number of factors which may be relevant in considering whether a party has acted unreasonably in refusing ADR. These include, but are not limited to:

(a) the nature of the dispute;
(b) the merits of the case (it may not be reasonable for a party with a weak case to insist on the use of ADR);
(c) the extent to which other settlement methods have been attempted;
(d) whether the costs of ADR would be disproportionately high;
(e) whether any delay in setting up and attending the ADR would have been prejudicial; and
(f) whether the ADR had a reasonable prospect of success.

The Court of Appeal also stated that the unsuccessful party should have the burden of showing that mediation would have had a reasonable prospect of success.

The Court of Appeal has subsequently applied the *Halsey* principles both to uphold a party's refusal to mediate (*Reed Executive plc v Reed Business Information Ltd* [2004] EWCA Civ 887, [2004] 1 WLR 3026) and to characterise a refusal as unreasonable (*Burchell v Bullard* [2005] EWCA Civ 358, [2005] BLR 330). In *Reed Executive plc v Reed Business Information Ltd* the court was guided by the fact that the offer to mediate came late and the successful party reasonably believed itself to have a good case. In *Burchell v Bullard* the court favoured mediation in a case where the amounts in dispute were dwarfed by the legal costs. It also stated that a party cannot rely on its own obstinacy to assert that mediation had no reasonable prospect of success.

A further significant holding in *Reed Executive plc v Reed Business Information Ltd* was that the court cannot compel production of without-prejudice material in order to assess whether a failure to mediate was unreasonable. The court would have to base any assessment on material that was either open or marked 'without prejudice subject to costs'.

USEFUL ADDRESSES

70.23 ADR Group
125 High Holborn
London
WC1V 6QA
Tel: 0800 616 130
Email: info@adrgroup.co.uk
Web: www.adrgroup.co.uk

Centre for Effective Dispute Resolution
International Dispute Resolution Centre
70 Fleet Street
London EC4Y 1EU
United Kingdom
Tel: +44 (0)20 7536 6000
Fax: +44 (0)20 7536 6001
Email: info@cedr.co.uk
Web: www.cedr.co.uk

The Chartered Institute of Arbitrators
International Arbitration and Mediation Centre
12 Bloomsbury Square
London WC1A 2LP
Ph: (0) 20 7421 7444
Fax: (0) 20 7404 4023
Website: www.arbitrators.org
Email: info@arbitrators.org

ICC International Chamber of Commerce
38 cours Albert I[er]
75008 Paris
France
Tel: +33 (0)1 49 53 28 28
Fax: +33 (0)1 49 53 29 33
E-mail: arb@iccwbo.org
Web: www.iccwbo.org/index_court.asp

LCIA
The International Dispute Resolution Centre
70 Fleet Street
London
EC4Y 1EU
Great Britain
Tel: +44 (0)20 7936 7007
Fax: +44 (0)20 7936 7008
Email: lcia@lcia-arbtration.com
Web: www.lcia-arbtration.com

RICS
Surveyor Court
Westwood Way
Coventry
CV4 8JE
UK
Tel: +44 (0)870 333 1600
Fax: +44 (0)20 7 334 3811
Email: contactrics@rics.org
Web: www.rics.org

Chapter 71 The Appeals System

The following procedural checklists, which are in **appendix 1**, are relevant to this chapter:

Procedural checklist 34 Appeals within the county courts and High Court
Procedural checklist 35 Appeals to the Court of Appeal

INTRODUCTION

71.1 From time to time decisions are made in error, and the system of appeals is designed to ensure that these are corrected. There is a strong public interest in regarding judicial decisions as final and binding, and an open-ended appeals system would undermine this by encouraging unsuccessful litigants to have 'another bite at the cherry'. Striking a balance between encouraging finality and correcting mistakes is not easy, and explains some of the complications that arise in the area of appeals.

Careful thought must be given before embarking on an appeal. In his annual review of 1989–90, in considering appeals to the Court of Appeal, Lord Donaldson of Lymington MR said:

> The question which the adviser may ask himself is whether, looking at the matter objectively, there are sufficient grounds for believing not only that the case should have been decided differently, but that in all the circumstances it can be demonstrated to the satisfaction of the Court of Appeal that there are grounds for reversing the judge's findings. In considering this question the adviser must never forget the financial risk which an appellant undertakes of having not only to pay his own costs of the appeal, but those of his opponent and, for this purpose, the adviser has two clients if the litigant is [publicly funded]. Nor must he underrate the effect upon his client of the emotional and other consequences of a continued state of uncertainty pending an appeal. In a word, one of the most important duties of a professional legal adviser is to save his clients from themselves and always to remember that, whilst it may well be reasonable to institute or to defend particular proceedings at first instance, a wholly new and different situation arises once the claim has been fully investigated by the court and a decision given.

DECISIONS SUSCEPTIBLE TO APPEAL

The Court of Appeal has jurisdiction to hear appeals from High Court 'judgments' and 'orders' (**Supreme Court Act 1981, s. 16(1)**) and county court 'determinations' (**County Courts Act 1984, s. 77(1)**). This means that a party is not entitled to appeal against the reasons for a decision given in his favour (*Compagnie Noga d'Importation et d'Exportation SA v Australia and New Zealand Banking Group Ltd* [2002] EWCA Civ 1142, [2003] 1 WLR 307). The practice and procedure to be followed in appeals within the county courts and the High Court are governed by the CPR (**Civil Procedure Act 1997, s. 1(1)**). Although the **County Courts Act 1984, s. 77(1A)**, says that such rules may provide for who is to hear any appeal 'from the exercise by a district judge, assistant district judge or deputy district judge of any power' given by any enactment, it is submitted that these appeals are restricted in the same way as appeals to the Court of Appeal. **71.2**

ROUTES OF APPEAL

The basic civil appeals structure is, by the **Access to Justice Act 1999 (Destination of Appeals) Order 2000** (SI 2000/1071) (the Destination of Appeals Order), **PD 52, para. 2A.1**, and the Appellate Jurisdiction Acts 1876 and 1887, as follows: **71.3**

(a) Decisions of county court district judges may be appealed to the county court circuit judge.
(b) Decisions of High Court masters, district judges and registrars may be appealed to a High Court judge.
(c) Decisions of county court circuit judges may be appealed to a High Court judge.
(d) Decisions of High Court judges may be appealed to the Court of Appeal.
(e) Court of Appeal decisions may be appealed to the House of Lords.

See **table 71.1**. These basic routes of appeal also apply in relation to deputy judges and their equivalents, such as recorders sitting as county court circuit judges (for which, see **PD 52, para. 8.13(1A)**). Appeals from county court district judges (category (a) above) are the simplest administratively, with the claim remaining within the same court for the appeal, and simply being listed for the appeal before the judge. Appeals to High Court judges (categories (b) and (c)) may involve the appeal being heard in a new court, see **71.8**. The Court of Appeal is located at the Royal Courts of Justice, and its administrative office is known as the Civil Appeals Office. The Civil Appeals Office staff include a number of lawyers who, among other tasks, ensure that the Court of Appeal has jurisdiction to consider prospective appeals and that permission to appeal is sought where necessary. The Head of the Civil Appeals Office has the title of master when sitting in a judicial capacity and there are a number of deputy masters (**PD 52, para. 15.5**).

By way of exception to the basic routes of appeal, appeals are made to the Court of Appeal rather than to a High Court judge (categories (b) and (c) above) if the hearing in the lower court was either:

(a) a final decision (see 71.5) made in any of the proceedings described in 71.4 (multi-track claims and specialist proceedings) (**Destination of Appeals Order, art. 4**); or
(b) itself an appeal from a county court district judge (in other words, the current appeal is a second appeal, see **Destination of Appeals Order, art. 5**; 71.7).

Table 71.1 Structure of the civil appeals system

Decision appealed from	Appeal to	Period for commencing appeal	Whether permission is required
Magistrates' court licensing matters	Crown Court	21 days from decision (liquor) or notification (others)	No
Magistrates' court Children Act 1989 cases	Family Division single judge	14 days from determination	No
Magistrates' court interim maintenance	Family Division Divisional Court	6 weeks from order	No
Inferior court on point of law or jurisdiction	QBD Divisional Court	21 days after decision	No
Inferior court by way of judicial review	QBD Divisional Court	3 months from ground arising	Yes, from Divisional Court
Statutory appeals	High Court	28 days	Depends on statute
County court district judges	County court circuit judge	21 days from decision	Yes
County court circuit judge final decision in multi-track or specialist claim	Court of Appeal	21 days from decision	Yes
Other decisions of county court circuit judges	High Court judge	21 days from decision	Yes
High Court master, district judge or registrar	High Court judge	21 days from decision	Yes
High Court judge	Court of Appeal	21 days from decision	Yes
Leapfrog appeal from High Court	House of Lords	14 days from judgment	Yes, from both High Court judge and HL
Court of Appeal	House of Lords	1 month from order being made, or 3 months if permission to appeal is granted by the CA	Yes, from CA or HL

Final decisions in specialist and multi-track claims

71.4 Kinds of claims and proceedings in which final appeals are to the Court of Appeal By the **Destination of Appeals Order, art. 4, and PD 52, para. 2A.2**, an appeal against a final decision (see 71.5) of a High Court master, district judge or registrar, or a circuit judge in a county court, is to the Court of Appeal instead of the High Court if it was made in:

(a) a Part 7 claim allocated to the multi-track under the CPR; or
(b) proceedings under the Companies Act 1985 or 1989 (which are allocated to the multi-track by **PD 49B, para. 10**); or
(c) proceedings to which any of the following Parts of the CPR apply (and which are all allocated to the multi-track by those Parts):
   (i) **Part** 57 (probate) (except claims under the Inheritance (Provision for Family and Dependants) Act 1975);
   (ii) **Parts 58** to **63** (Commercial Court, Mercantile Courts, Technology and Construction Court, Admiralty claims, arbitration claims (even though they follow the Part 8 procedure), patents and other intellectual property claims).

An appeal under the **Destination of Appeals Order, art. 4**, is an exception to the usual rule that an appeal is to the next level of judge in the court hierarchy (*Tanfern Ltd v Cameron-MacDonald* [2000] 1 WLR 1311).

If a non-specialist claim has never been allocated to a track, an appeal will not be to the Court of Appeal even if the judge would have allocated the claim to the multi-track had track allocation been considered (*Clark v Perks* [2000] 4 All ER 1). This can arise, for example, if the claim is dealt with as an assessment of damages.

Final decision By the **Destination of Appeals Order, art. 1**(2)(c), and **PD 52, para. 2A.3**, a decision is final, so that an appeal against it is to the Court of Appeal instead of the High Court, if it would determine (subject to any possible appeal or detailed assessment of costs) the entire proceedings whichever way the court decided the issues before it **Destination of Appeals Order, art. 1**(2)(c)). According to *Dooley v Parker* [2002] EWCA Civ 96, [2002] CPLR 251, para. 17 of the judgment in *Tanfern Ltd v Cameron-MacDonald* [2000] 1 WLR 1311 should be taken as saying that a final decision 'does not include a decision only on the detailed assessment of costs'. Consequently, a decision on liability for the costs of a claim is a final decision, which should be appealed to the Court of Appeal if the claim has been allocated to the multi-track. On the other hand, orders on summary and detailed assessments of costs, and on applications to enforce final decisions, are not themselves 'final' (**PD 52, para. 2A.5**). **71.5**

A decision is treated as final where it is made at the conclusion of part of a hearing or trial which has been split into parts, and would, if made at the conclusion of that hearing or trial, be a final decision because it determines the entirety of that part of the claim (**Destination of Appeals Order, art. 1**(3)). This means that if a judge makes a final decision on any aspect of a claim, such as limitation, or on part of a claim which has been directed to be tried separately, this is a final decision within the meaning of the provision (*Tanfern Ltd v Cameron-MacDonald*). In *Roerig v Valiant Trawlers Ltd* [2002] EWCA Civ 21, [2002] 1 WLR 2304, the decision under appeal was made on the trial of a preliminary issue as to whether the Fatal Accidents Act 1976, s. 4, applied to the claim or whether the claimant had to give credit for benefits received if the damages were assessed under Dutch law. It was held that a broad common-sense test should be applied when deciding whether the issue would have formed part of the final trial. On the facts it was, so the decision was final, and the appeal was to the Court of Appeal. On the other hand, orders giving summary judgment (*Scribes West Ltd v Relsa Anstalt* [2004] EWCA Civ 965, [2005] 1 WLR 1839) and orders striking out the proceedings or a statement of case are not final decisions, because they are not decisions that would finally determine the entire proceedings whichever way the court decided the issues before it (*Tanfern Ltd v Cameron-MacDonald*).

The question whether an order is final or not has to be determined by considering the language of the order of the court below. Judges and court staff in the appeal court have to determine whether their court has jurisdiction simply by looking at the face of the order being appealed, and are not required to consider the background of the case or application before deciding whether the decision is final. A party who believes an order has not been drawn up correctly can apply for it to be corrected under the slip rule (see **61.34**). Any refusal to correct the order can itself be a ground of appeal, but does not change the court having jurisdiction to hear the appeal (*Scribes West Ltd v Relsa Anstalt*).

Appeals in Part 8 claims

71.6 Although **Part 8** claims are automatically allocated to the multi-track by **CPR, r. 8.9**(c), the exception laid down in the Destination of Appeals Order, art. 4, does not apply to this category of claim. Therefore appeals in these claims, even from final orders, follow the general routes of appeal. Where the normal appeal court is not the Court of Appeal, a court granting permission to appeal in such a case from a final order should consider whether to order the appeal to be transferred to the Court of Appeal under **CPR, r. 52.14** (see **71.9**). This will often be done where the decision did not involve any substantial dispute of fact (**PD 52, para. 2A.6(2)**).

Second-tier appeals

71.7 The second exception referred to at **71.3** is where the appeal is a second appeal. These appeals are taken to the Court of Appeal, even though the decision being appealed was that made by a circuit judge (**Destination of Appeals Order, art. 5**). Typically this will cover interim applications dealt with by a county court district judge, which are appealed to the circuit judge. If a second appeal is taken, under this exception it must be taken to the Court of Appeal.

In *Southern and District Finance plc v Turner* [2003] EWCA Civ 1574, LTL 7/11/2003, a county court district judge dismissed an application to set aside a possession order. Eight months later the defendant brought an appeal against that decision, but omitted to seek permission to appeal out of time (see **71.20**). The circuit judge dismissed the appeal on the ground that no permission to extend time for appealing had been included in the appellant's notice. An appeal from the circuit judge's refusal to consider extending time (whether this was on the basis of the judge deciding he had no jurisdiction to extend time, or a decision not to extend time) was held to be a first appeal, not a second appeal coming within art. 5, so should have been taken to a High Court judge under **art. 3(1)**. In *Convergence Group plc v Chantrey Vellacott* [2005] EWCA Civ 290, *The Times*, 25 April 2005, there was an application to amend a statement of case. The master refused permission for certain amendments, but did not deal with others through lack of time. The matter was taken to the judge, who refused all the proposed amendments. It was held that an appeal to the Court of Appeal was a first appeal, because the appeal in relation to the amendments which had not been considered by the master was a first appeal, and the others could be regarded as raising common issues. This case must be treated with caution. Its logic could be reversed, producing the opposite result. It also misapplies *Uphill v BRB (Residuary) Ltd* [2005] EWCA Civ 60, [2005] 1 WLR 2070, a case discussed at **71.14**.

An appeal to the Court of Appeal from the Patents Court under the Patents Act 1977, s. 97(3), is a specific procedure for patent appeals, and is not governed by the restrictions on second-tier appeals in the **Access to Justice Act 1999, s. 55**. See *Smith International Inc. v Specialised Petroleum Services Group Ltd* [2005] EWCA Civ 1357, [2006] 1 WLR 252.

The principles governing obtaining permission to appeal in second-tier appeals are considered at **71.14**.

Appeal centres in High Court appeals

71.8 County court and district registry appeals to a High Court judge must be brought in the district registry for an appeal centre on the circuit in which the lower court is situated

(**PD 52, para. 8.4**). There is a list of appeal centres for each of the six circuits in **PD 52, para. 8.2**. On the South Eastern Circuit the appellant's notice must be filed at one of the nine appeal centres listed in **para. 8.2**, but the appeal will be managed and heard at the Royal Courts of Justice (**para. 8.7**).

Transfer of appeals to the Court of Appeal

If the normal route for a first appeal from a decision of a district judge or master would be to a circuit judge or to a High Court judge, either the lower court or the appeal court may order the appeal to be transferred to the Court of Appeal. This may be done if it is considered that the appeal will raise an important point of principle or practice or there is some other compelling reason for the Court of Appeal to hear it (**CPR, r. 52.14(1)**). The Master of the Rolls has a similar power to divert appeals to the Court of Appeal (**Access to Justice Act 1999**, s. 57(1)). **71.9**

Judicial review of county court decisions

There are only very limited circumstances in which a claim may be made for judicial review of a county courts decision, as an appeal court, on an application for permission to appeal. Judicial review is confined to very rare cases where the county court has acted without jurisdiction or failed to afford the appellant a fair hearing (*R (Mahon) v Taunton County Court* (2001) LTL 18/12/2001; *Gregory v Turner* [2003] EWCA Civ 183, [2003] 1 WLR 1149). **71.10**

PERMISSION TO APPEAL

When permission is required

There is a general requirement in **CPR, r. 52.3**, for permission to appeal from any decision of a judge in a county court or the High Court except for appeals against: **71.11**

(a) committal orders (**r. 52.3(1)(a)(i)**);
(b) refusal to grant habeas corpus (**r. 52.3(1)(a)(ii)**);
(c) secure accommodation orders made under the Children Act 1989, s. 25 (**CPR, r. 52.3(1)(a)(iii)**); or
(d) decisions of authorised court officers in detailed assessment proceedings (**rr. 47.21** and **52.1(2)**).

The exceptions set out in **r. 52.3(1)(a)** are cases where the liberty of the subject is in issue, and in these three cases appeals may be brought as of right.

A nominated judge exercising the jurisdiction given by certain statutes, such as the Mental Health Act 1983, part VII, derives his position as a judge of the High Court, but is not sitting in the High Court. As such, **r. 52.3** does not apply, and permission is not required for any appeal to the Court of Appeal (*Re B (A Patient) (Court of Protection: Appeal)* [2005] EWCA Civ 1293, [2006] 1 WLR 278).

Permission to appeal is not required for first appeals from a committal order made by a circuit judge. 'Committal orders' are orders which commit a person to prison. Permission is required for any other order or decision of a circuit judge made in the exercise of the jurisdiction to punish for contempt (*Barnet London Borough Council v Hurst* [2002] EWCA Civ 1009, [2002] 4 All ER 457). Permission is required on appeals by claimants asserting that the lower court was wrong to find that a defendant had purged his contempt, or that the lower court imposed an unduly light penalty for contempt of court (*Government of Sierra Leone v Davenport* [2002] EWCA Civ 230, [2002] CPLR 236). Second appeals in contempt proceedings apparently always require permission, see **r. 52.13** and *Barnet London Borough Council v Hurst*. The guidance given in *Barnet London Borough Council v Hurst* about appeals in contempt proceedings from decisions of district judges is probably wrong as it appears to overlook the fact that the word 'judge' in

r. 52.3 is defined in r. 2.3(1) as meaning, unless the context requires otherwise, a judge, master or district judge or a person authorised as such, and is not restricted to circuit judges.

Seeking permission

71.12 Generally, permission to appeal may be sought either from the lower court at the hearing at which the decision to be appealed was made or from the appeal court (**CPR, r. 52.3(2)**). Permission from the appeal court must be sought within 14 days after the decision of the lower court (**r. 52.4(2)(b)**). This period may be extended either by the lower court or appeal court, see 71.19. However, **r. 52.13(1)** provides that permission is required from the Court of Appeal for all appeals to that court from a decision of a county court or the High Court which was itself made on appeal. Where the lower court refuses an application for permission to appeal, a further application for permission to appeal may be made to the appeal court (**r. 52.3(3)**).

Applications for permission to appeal sought from the lower court are made orally at the end of the hearing, usually as the last item of business after costs have been determined. Permission that is sought from the appeal court is asked for initially by seeking permission in writing in the appeal notice (**r. 52.3(2)(b)**) and is normally considered without a hearing (**PD 52, para. 4.11**). If permission is granted the parties are notified in writing (**para. 4.12**). If permission is refused, the appellant can request the matter to be reconsidered at an oral hearing (see 71.16). Short reasons are usually all that is given on a refusal of permission. Just because they are short does not mean they infringe the requirement for a reasoned decision in the **European Convention on Human Rights, art. 6** (*Hyams v Plender* [2001] 1 WLR 32 at [17]).

Test for granting permission

71.13 **Rule 52.3(6)** of the CPR provides that permission to appeal may be given only where either:

(a) the court considers that the appeal would have a real prospect of success; or
(b) there is some other compelling reason why the appeal should be heard.

Lord Woolf MR said in *Swain v Hillman* [2001] 1 All ER 91 that a 'real' prospect of success means that the prospect of success must be realistic rather than fanciful. The court considering a request for permission is not required to analyse whether the grounds of the proposed appeal will succeed, but merely whether there is a real prospect of success (*Hunt v Peasegood* (2000) *The Times*, 20 October 2000). Even hopeless appeals may be allowed to proceed where the area of law in question is the subject of considerable controversy (*Beedell v West Ferry Printers Ltd* [2001] EWCA Civ 400, [2001] ICR 962). A failure by a judge to address an issue may be a compelling reason within **r. 52.3(6)** (*Sofola v Lloyds TSB Bank* [2005] EWHC 1335 (QB), LTL 5/7/2005). There may be a compelling reason for the appeal where the lower court's decision has been overtaken by a subsequent authority, but there is unlikely to be a compelling reason if the lower court was not informed of a binding authority due to a failure by the appellant's advocate (*Sofola v Lloyds TSB Bank*). Apparently, the court should take into account an appellant's strong feelings of injustice when considering whether to grant permission, at least where those feelings are arguably objectively justified (*Malcolm v MacKenzie* [2004] EWCA Civ 584, LTL 18/5/2004).

There is some reluctance in giving permission to appeal against case management decisions, such as disclosure orders and orders dealing with the timetable of the claim. In these cases the court will also consider whether the issue is of sufficient significance to justify the costs of an appeal; the procedural consequences of an appeal (such as losing a trial date); and whether it would be more convenient to determine the point after trial (**PD 52, para. 4.5**).

Second appeals to the Court of Appeal

71.14 As discussed at 71.12, generally permission to appeal may be sought from either the lower court or from the appeal court. Second appeals are in a different category. The **Access to Justice Act 1999, s. 55(1)**, and the **CPR, r. 52.13(1)**, provide that permission is required from the Court of Appeal (and cannot be given by the lower court) for any appeal to that court from a decision of a county court or the High Court which was itself made on appeal. The question of what amounts to a second-tier appeal is considered at **71.7**. By **r. 52.13(2)**, the Court of Appeal will not give permission unless it considers that either:

(a) the appeal would raise an important point of principle or practice; or
(b) there is some other compelling reason for the Court of Appeal to hear it.

Under **r. 52.13(2)(a)**, the point must be an important one. It is not enough that the grounds of appeal may have a real prospect of success. This is so even if the would-be appellant won in the lower court, but lost on the first appeal. An issue can fall within **r. 52.13(2)(a)** only when it has not yet been determined by previous authority. An appeal based on whether an established point has been correctly applied does not come within the rule (*Uphill v BRB (Residuary) Ltd* [2005] EWCA Civ 60, [2005] 1 WLR 2070). The decision on the first appeal will therefore often be the final decision, with second appeals being something of a rarity (see *Tanfern Ltd v Cameron-MacDonald* [2000] 1 WLR 1311).

Veitch v Avery (2002) LTL 26/7/2002 was an appeal for which permission was granted under **r. 52.13(2)(b)**. No point of practice or principle was raised in the second appeal, but the judge dealing with the first appeal had allowed an appeal from a district judge and struck out the claim based on the original particulars of claim despite there being amended particulars which raised an arguable claim. Conversely, permission was refused in *Uphill v BRB (Residuary) Ltd* where it was emphasised that 'compelling' is a very strong word. Dyson LJ said that even if the prospects of success on the appeal are very high there may not be a compelling reason. However, where there has been a procedural irregularity rendering the first appeal unfair, there may be a compelling reason even if the overall prospects are not very high.

Refusal of permission to appeal

There is no appeal from a decision of the appeal court, made at an oral hearing or on the papers, to allow or refuse permission to appeal to that court (**Access to Justice Act 1999, s. 54(4)**). The ban in s. 54(4) prevents the Court of Appeal from reviewing a High Court judge's refusal of permission to appeal from the decision of a costs judge, and there is no residual inherent jurisdiction to hear such an appeal (*Riniker v University College London* [2001] 1 WLR 13). **71.15**

A judge faced with an application for permission to appeal made out of time may come to the conclusion that the appeal is both weak on the merits and that time should not be extended. By reason of the **Access to Justice Act 1999, s. 54(4)**, refusing permission to appeal will result in an end to the appeal process. Taking the easier course of refusing permission to extend time will not, as the appellant can apply for permission to appeal the refusal of the extension, which can be renewed to the Court of Appeal. This difference should be kept in mind when deciding which course to take (*Foenander v Bond Lewis and Co.* [2001] EWCA Civ 759, [2002] 1 WLR 525).

Reconsideration of whether to grant permission

Where the appeal court, without a hearing, refuses permission to appeal, the person seeking permission may ask for the decision to be reconsidered at a hearing (**CPR, r. 52.3(4)**; *Cassie v Ministry of Defence* [2002] EWCA Civ 838, LTL 17/4/2002). Reconsideration of a refusal is not an appeal against refusal, which is not permitted (see **71.15**). A request for reconsideration of whether to grant permission to appeal must be filed within seven days after service of the notice that permission has been refused (**r. 52.3(5)**). If the appellant is represented, the appellant's advocate must file and serve on the respondent at least four days before the hearing a brief written statement (**PD 52, para. 4.14A**). This must: **71.16**

(a) set out the points he intends to raise at the hearing:
(b) set out his reasons why permission should be granted; and
(c) confirm (if appropriate) that the Legal Services Commission has been sent a copy of the court's reasons for refusing permission on the papers (as required by **para. 4.17**).

Notice of permission hearing to respondent

71.17 A copy of an appellant's request for reconsideration of the question of permission at an oral hearing must be served on the respondent at the same time as it is filed (**PD 52, para. 4.14**). The respondent will also have been served with the appellant's notice and skeleton argument shortly after they were filed (see **71.26**). The court will give notice of the permission hearing to the respondent, but the respondent is not required to attend unless the court requests him to do so (**para. 4.15**).

The purpose of requiring these documents to be served on the respondent is to ensure he is informed of the landmarks in the appeal process. Respondents should not file submissions at the permission stage unless they are addressed to the point that the appeal does not meet the threshold test for permission, or if there is some material inaccuracy in the papers placed before the court, or if the court gives a specific direction (**PD 52, para. 4.22**; *Jolly v Jay* [2002] EWCA Civ 277, *The Times*, 3 April 2002).

If the court requests the respondent's attendance at the permission hearing, the appellant must supply the respondent with a copy of the appeal bundle within seven days of being notified of the request or such other time as the court may direct (**PD 52, para. 4.16**). The costs of providing an appeal bundle under **para. 4.16** are initially borne by the appellant, but will form part of the costs of the permission application. Where the court does not request submissions or attendance by the respondent, costs will not normally be allowed to a respondent who volunteers submissions or attendance (**para. 4.23**). Where the court requests submissions or attendance, normally the respondent will be awarded costs if permission is refused (**para. 4.24**).

Limiting the issues on granting permission

71.18 By **CPR, r. 52.3(7)**, an order giving permission to appeal may limit the issues to be heard and be made subject to conditions. If a court confines its permission to some issues only, it should expressly refuse permission on any remaining issues, or reserve the question of permission on any remaining issues to the appeal court (**PD 52, para. 4.18**). If the question of permission on an issue is reserved to the appeal court, the appellant must, within 14 days after service of the court's order, inform the appeal court and the respondent in writing whether the reserved issue is to be pursued (**para. 4.19**). An appellant can make a request, following the procedure in **71.16**, for the reconsideration of permission on any issues for which permission is refused if the refusal was on the papers (**para. 4.20**), but not if the refusal was at a hearing (**para. 4.21; Access to Justice Act 1999, s. 54(4)**). In **PD 52, para. 4.18** the expression the 'court' is the lower court, so the power to revisit is restricted to situations where the lower court limits the issues on granting permission to appeal. Where the issues are limited by the appeal court on an application for permission, the appeal court cannot revisit the issues to be considered at the final hearing of the appeal (*Fieldman v Markovitch* (2001) *The Times*, 31 July 2001).

TIME FOR APPEALING

Time limits

71.19 An appellant must normally initiate an appeal (by filing an appellant's notice in **form N161**) no later than 21 days from the date of the decision of the lower court (**CPR, r. 52.4(2)(b)**). The lower court may direct some other period for filing a notice of appeal (which may be longer or shorter than 21 days) (**r. 52.4(2)(a)**), but this should not normally be longer than 28 days (**PD 52, para. 5.19**). An extension should be granted by the lower court only in exceptional circumstances (*Aujla v Sanghera* [2004] EWCA Civ 122, LTL 23/1/2004). The reason for this restrictive approach is that the appeal court exercises the main jurisdiction on granting extensions of time in appeals (see **71.20** and **71.21**). This means that stronger grounds are required to justify an enlargement of the usual 21 days than mere pressure on a prospective appellant's solicitors caused by the 21-day time limit (*City Television v Conference and Training Office Ltd* [2001] EWCA Civ 1770, LTL 16/11/2001). Judgments and orders take effect from the date they are given or made, or such other date as the court may specify (**CPR, r. 40.7(1)**). Delays in formally drawing up the order do not, therefore, delay time running for the purposes of appeals. During the course of a detailed assessment of a bill of costs in *Kasir v Darlington and Simpson Rolling Mills Ltd* (2001) LTL 1/5/2001 the costs judge made a number of decisions, which the appellant wished to appeal. He did not appeal until the detailed assessment process was completed five months later. It was held that time started running in respect of each decision when it was made, and permission to appeal was refused.

Where the lower court judge announces a decision and reserves the reasons for the judgment until a later date, the judge should exercise the power under **r. 52.4(2)(a)** in fixing the period for filing a notice of appeal to take account of the delay in giving reasons (**PD 52, para. 5.20**). A lower court judge can exercise the power under **CPR, r. 52.4(2)(a)**, even after the 21-day appeal period has expired, but should not do so after an appellant's notice has been lodged with the appeal court (*Aujla v Sanghera*).

Extending time for appealing

The court may extend or shorten the time for compliance with any rule, practice direction or court order, even if an application for extension is made after the time for compliance has expired (**CPR, r. 3.1(2)(a)**). The time for bringing an appeal may be extended under this power. By **r. 52.6(1)**, an application to vary the time limit for filing an appellant's notice must be made to the appeal court. The parties may not (by **r. 52.6(2)**) agree between themselves to extend any date or time limit for the purposes of appealing. **71.20**

Permission to extend time for appealing is sought by including an application for more time in the appellant's notice (**PD 52, para. 5.2**). The notice should state the reason for the delay and the steps taken prior to the application being made. Bringing an appeal out of time without seeking permission in the appellant's notice to extend time is an irregularity, which the court has jurisdiction to cure under **CPR, r. 3.10** (*Southern and District Finance plc v Turner* [2003] EWCA Civ 1574, LTL 7/11/2003).

Where an extension is sought and permission to appeal is given (as will be seen, usually the respondent is not given an opportunity to make representations on whether permission to appeal should be granted), the respondent has the right to be heard on whether an extension of time should be allowed. However, a respondent who unreasonably opposes an extension of time runs the risk of being ordered to pay the appellant's costs of the application to extend time (**PD 52, para. 5.3**).

Principles for granting extensions of time

The principles laid down in pre-CPR cases on extending time for appealing are no longer good law (*Sayers v Clarke Walker* [2002] EWCA Civ 645, [2002] 1 WLR 3095). In simple cases, it will be enough for the court to consider the matters set out in **PD 52, para. 5.2**, namely, the reason for the delay and the steps taken prior to the application to extend time being made. In more complex cases, the court should apply the factors laid down in **CPR, r. 3.9** (see **46.31**), and should avoid judge-made checklists of matters to consider (*Sayers v Clarke-Walker*). Each application must be viewed by reference to the criterion of justice, and it is important to bear in mind that time limits are there to be observed, and that justice may be seriously defeated if there is any laxity in this regard. In cases where **r. 3.9** is applied, the court should give particular weight to the prospects of success on the appeal (*Southern and District Finance plc v Turner* [2003] EWCA Civ 1574, LTL 7/11/2003). A failure to state reasons for the delay in the appellant's notice, contrary to **PD 52, para. 5.2** (see **71.20**), should not in itself be a reason **71.21** for refusing an extension when there are in fact reasons for the delay (*Hyams v Plender* [2001] 1 WLR 32 at [15]).

APPELLANT'S NOTICE

71.22 An appellant must file an appellant's notice at the appeal court within such period as may be directed by the lower court or, where the court makes no such direction, 21 days after the date of the decision of the lower court that the appellant wishes to appeal (**CPR, r. 52.4(2)**). An appellant's notice must be in **form N161**. It must set out the grounds of the appeal, which should include reasons making it clear why the decision of the lower court is either wrong or unjust through serious procedural or other irregularity (**PD 52, para. 3.2(1)**). Grounds of appeal must identify specific incidents, directions or findings made by the court below which are alleged to be wrong or unjust. Each ground must state in clear terms why the judge below was wrong or why his or her decision was unjust (*Perotti v Collyer-Bristow* [2004] EWCA Civ 639, [2004] 4 All ER 53, at [37] and [40]). Each ground must be stated as an appeal on a point of law or against a finding of fact (**PD, para. 3.2(2)**). Drafting of grounds of appeal is therefore of great importance, because they define the complaints being made against the decision of the court below. It was said in *IS Innovative Software Ltd v Howes* (2004) *The Times*, 10 March 2004, that it is unsatisfactory for counsel to change the basis of a challenge to a finding of the court below from that stated in the appellant's notice. It was said in this case that failing to make clear its real basis for challenging the decision below is unfair on the appeal court (whose pre-reading is wasted) and unfair on respondents, who will not know the case they have to meet. It is submitted that this case should be interpreted as meaning that an appellant cannot change the basis of its case without obtaining permission to amend the grounds of appeal.

The requirement to state whether grounds are on points of law or findings of fact is important when the jurisdiction of the appeal court is limited to appeals on points of law (*Scribes West Ltd v Relsa Anstalt (No. 1)* [2004] EWCA Civ 835, *The Times*, 8 July 2004, at [3]). The distinction is also important because of the reluctance to interfere with decisions on the facts, because it is the trial judge who sees the witnesses (see 72.7).

Points of law include errors concerning the elements of causes of action and defences; errors concerning the standard and burden of proof; evidential errors concerning questions such as the admissibility and relevance of evidence and the effect of presumptions. Points of law can include a failure to deal with an issue in the judgment, and wrongfully withdrawing issues from determination at trial.

Appeals on questions of fact include misstating the facts given in evidence; treating the evidence given by one side unfairly; where there is a jury, summing up the evidence unclearly or illogically or with inappropriate comments (although the judge has a fairly wide area of discretion on the comments that can fairly be made).

Unless permission to appeal is not needed, or has been given by the lower courts an application for permission to appeal must be included in the appellant's notice (**para. 5.1**) with, if necessary, an application for permission to appeal out of time (**para. 5.2**). An appellant's notice may include applications for interim remedies in the course of the appeal (**para. 5.5**). An appellant seeking, for the first time, to rely on any issue or to seek any remedy under the **Human Rights Act 1998** must include information complying with **PD 16, para. 15.1**, in the appellant's notice (**PD 52, para. 5.1A**).

By **CPR, r. 52.11(5)**, an appellant may not rely at the hearing of the appeal on a matter not contained in the appeal notice unless the appeal court gives permission.

LODGING DOCUMENTS

An appellant must lodge the following documents at the appeal court with the appellant's notice (see **PD 52, para. 5.6(2)**): **71.23**

(a) two additional copies of the appellant's notice;
(b) one copy of the appellant's notice for each respondent;
(c) one copy of the appellant's skeleton argument for each copy of the appellant's notice that is filed (see 71.26);
(d) a sealed copy of the order of the lower court;
(e) any order giving or refusing permission to appeal (including such an order from the lower court) together with a copy of the reasons for that decision;
(f) any written evidence in support of any interim application included in the appellant's notice;
(g) an appeal bundle (see 71.24).

Where it is not possible to file all the above documents, the appellant must indicate which documents are not being filed and why, and provide a reasonable estimate of when the missing documents will be filed (**PD 52, para. 5.7**).

Guidance on documentation required for High Court appeals is given in Practice Statement (High Court Appeals: Guidance for Staff and Litigants) (2001) LTL 21/2/2001.

The Civil Appeals Office publishes the following leaflets giving guidance for appellants:

(a) Form 201, Routes of appeal;
(b) Form 202, How to appeal to the Court of Appeal;
(c) Form 203, How to complete an appellant's notice;
(d) Form 205, Sources of help for unrepresented appellants; and
(e) Form 206, Applying for permission to appeal to the Court of Appeal.

Appeal bundles

At the same time as lodging an appellant's notice, an appellant is required to lodge an appeal bundle (**PD 52, para. 6(2)**). The appeal bundle must contain the documents listed in **para. 5.6A(1)**. This sets out a list of 13 categories of document, including a sealed copy of the appellant's notice, a copy of the appellant's skeleton argument, a sealed copy of the order under appeal, relevant statements of case, and other documents which the appellant reasonably considers necessary to enable the appeal court to reach its decision. The key to deciding what to include in the appeal bundle is having a clear grasp of the real issues raised by the appeal. **Paragraph 5.6A(2)** is of the utmost importance, and provides: **71.24**

> All documents that are extraneous to the issues to be considered on the application or the appeal must be excluded. The appeal bundle may include affidavits, witness statements, summaries, experts' reports and exhibits but only where these are directly relevant to the subject matter of the appeal.

Thus, the claim form and statements of case should only be included in the appeal bundle if they are relevant to the subject matter of the appeal (**para. 5.6A(1)(g)**). Application notices and case management documentation relating to the proceedings in the court below likewise should be included only if relevant to the issues raised on the appeal (**para. 5.6A(1)(h)**). What the appeal court does not want is an appeal bundle put together in an unthinking manner, including the whole trial bundle and miscellaneous superfluous documents, such as solicitors' correspondence, unless these materials go to the issues raised by the appeal (**para. 15.4(11)** and *Scribes West Ltd v Relsa Anstalt (No. 1)* [2004] EWCA Civ 835, *The Times*, 8 July 2004, at [11]). No more than a single copy of each document should be included unless there is a good reason for doing so (**para. 15.4(2)**). Where the appellant is represented, the appeal bundle must contain a certificate signed by his solicitor or counsel to the effect he has read and understood **para. 5.6A(2)**, and that the bundle complies with it (**para. 5.6A(3)**).

If permission to appeal is granted, the appellant must add four categories of documents to the appeal bundle as required by **para. 6.3A**. These include the respondent's notice and skeleton argument, the parts of the transcripts of evidence which are directly relevant to the appeal, the order granting permission, and any further documents the parties agree to add to the appeal bundle. Under **para. 7.11**, a respondent who wishes to rely on additional documents which he reasonably considers are necessary to enable the appeal court to decide the appeal is required to make every effort to agree the documents which should be added to the appeal bundle. Where the parties are unable to reach agreement, the respondent is permitted to prepare a supplementary bundle (**para.** 7.12).

Appeal bundles are primarily for use by the judges in the appeal court, particularly to assist them with pre-reading. The ban on thoughtlessly copying trial bundles into appeal bundles does not prevent a party producing a trial bundle at the hearing of the appeal in case it transpires it contains an important document, but the appeal bundle must be limited as required by **para. 5.6A** (*Scribes West Ltd v Relsa Anstalt (No. 1)* at [11]).

Detailed rules for Court of Appeal bundles are laid down in **para. 15.4** (which should be seen as sensible guidance for other appeal courts). Pages in the appeal bundle should be copied in A4 format where possible, must be legible, and copied in colour and transcribed if necessary (**para. 15.4(4)**). They must be copied single-sided, and in exactly the same form with no extra markings other than pagination as those given to the judge at the hearing below (Civil Appeals Form 204, paras 5.5 and 5.6). All staples, clips etc. must be removed (**PD 52, para. 15.4(8)**). Every page in the appeal bundle must be paginated consecutively, in bold figures at the bottom of the page, but differently from the form of pagination used in the hearing below (**para. 15.4(3)**). Statements of case must appear in 'chapter' form, with the claim followed by particulars of claim, and further information following the relevant statement of case. Statements of case overtaken by amendments should be excluded (**para. 15.4(9)**). Documents within categories should appear chronologically. The pages, other than transcripts, must be placed in lever arch files, ring binders or robust plastic folders, filled sensibly (not too many or few pages for the binder), with the Court of Appeal reference and case name appearing clearly on the spine and front of each file (**para. 15.4(5)** and **(7)**). An index must be included at the front of the bundle (**para. 15.4(6)**). Where several files are needed, experience dictates that colour-coded files help at the hearing, but there is no formal requirement for this (*Scribes West Ltd v Relsa Anstalt (No. 1)* at [16]).

Pages sent to the court to be added to the appeal bundle must be sent already punched and paginated for immediate inclusion in the existing binders (**para. 15.4(10)**).

Where bundles include unnecessary documents, or are incomplete, or otherwise do not comply, they may be rejected or made the subject of a special costs sanction (**para. 15.4(1)**). The appeal court may also refer the matter for consideration whether to dismiss the appeal for non-compliance (**para. 15.4(12)**).

Core bundles

71.25 Core bundles are a mandatory requirement only in the Court of Appeal. They are used where the appeal bundles exceed 500 pages, excluding transcripts (**PD 52, para. 15.2**). A core bundle must contain the documents which are central to the appeal, and must not exceed 150 pages (**para. 15.3(2)**). It should be prepared in consultation with the respondent's solicitors, and must be filed within 28 days of receipt of the order giving permission to appeal (**paras 15.2** and **15.3(1)**). Pagination should usually be the same as the main appeal bundle (**para. 15.4(3)**).

Skeleton argument

71.26 Appellants should include skeleton arguments when they first file their appellant's notice (**PD 52, paras 5.6(2)** and **5.9(1)**). It is recognised this may not always be practicable, and

para. 5.9(2) allows an appellant to file and serve his skeleton argument within 14 days after filing the notice. It appears there was a practice in the High Court of construing statements in appellants' notices that they would be filing skeleton arguments within a stated time as undertakings to that effect. There is no basis in law for doing so (*Hyams v Plender* [2001] 1 WLR 32 at [16]). Appellants who are not represented need not file skeleton arguments, although it is helpful if they do (**para.** 5.9(3)).

Form **N163** should be used (or used as a cover sheet) for the skeleton arguments. A skeleton argument should contain a numbered list of points stated in no more than a few sentences, which should both define and confine the areas of controversy. Each point should be followed by references to any documentation on which the appellant proposes to rely (**para. 5.10**(1) and (2)). Points of law should be backed by authorities which should be cited with references to the particular pages or paragraphs where the relevant principles are set out (**para. 5.10(3)**). If more than one authority is cited for a proposition, the skeleton argument must briefly state the reason why this is necessary for the proper presentation of the appeal, and explain the relevance of the authorities to the argument (**para. 5.10**(4) and (5)). In the case of questions of fact, the skeleton should state briefly the basis on which it is contended that the Court of Appeal can interfere with the finding of fact concerned, with cross-references to the passages in the transcript or notes of evidence which bear on the point (see Practice Direction (Court of Appeal: Procedure) [1995] 1 WLR 1191). Skeletons should succinctly identify, not argue, the points raised in the appeal. They should include anything the advocates would expect to be taken down by the court during the hearing. In the past it has been said that for a one-day appeal on a point of law 10 pages should be enough.

Lists of relevant persons, chronologies and glossaries of technical terms are often usefully included with skeleton arguments (**para. 5.11**).

Record of the judgment of the lower court

If the judgment of the lower court was recorded, an approved transcript should accompany the appellant's notice (**PD 52, para.** 5.12). Photocopies are not acceptable. If there is no official transcript, the next best is the lower court judge's written judgment signed by the judge. If the lower court's judgment was oral and not recorded, the advocates should confer and submit, if possible, an agreed note of the judgment to the judge for signature. If the note cannot be agreed, both versions should be submitted with a covering letter explaining the situation. If the appellant was acting in person at the hearing in the lower court, the advocate for the respondent is expected to make his or her notes of judgment available to the appellant (**para.** 5.12(3)). These points are important, because appeals, even from district judges and masters, can only succeed by attacking the decision-making process in some way, and injustice may result if no reliable record is available of what was said in the lower court. **71.27**

A request may be made for the provision of transcripts at the public expense on the ground of poor financial circumstances, and this should wherever possible be made to the lower court when asking for permission to appeal (**paras** 5.17 **and** 5.18). Applications can be made in the Court of Appeal to a deputy master, with a right of review to a judge of the Court of Appeal (see *Hyams v Plender* [2001] 1 WLR 32 at [28], where comments are made by Brooke LJ suggesting that similar arrangements should be made for appeals to the High Court). An order for provision of transcripts at public expense was refused in *Perotti v Westminster City Council* [2005] EWCA Civ 581, *The Times*, 30 May 2005. In this case the litigant said the transcript was needed for formulating his grounds of appeal, but he had tape recorded the judgment, and could have asked for the note of judgment made by the respondent's advocate. See also Practice Statement (High Court Appeals: Guidance for Staff and Litigants) (2001) LTL 21/2/2001.

Transcripts or notes of the evidence (as opposed to the judgment) are not generally needed on applications for permission to appeal, but may become necessary if permission is granted for the purposes of the substantive appeal (**PD 52, para.** 5.15). If so, the transcript must be obtained if the evidence was recorded, otherwise a typed version of the judge's notes must be obtained (**para. 5.16**).

SERVICE ON THE RESPONDENT

71.28 By CPR, r. 52.4(3), unless the appeal court orders otherwise, an appellant's notice must be served on each respondent as soon as practicable, and in any event not later than seven days, after it is filed. A copy of the appellant's skeleton argument should be served at the same time (**PD 52, para. 5.21**) unless this is impracticable, in which case it should be served within 14 days of filing the notice (**para. 5.9(2)**). A certificate of service must be filed (**para. 5.21(2)**). If permission to appeal is not required, or was given by the lower court, a copy of the appeal bundle must be served on each respondent with the appellant's notice (**PD 52, para. 5.24(2)**).

If the appellant is asking the appeal court for permission to appeal, the appeal bundle need not be served on respondents unless the court directs otherwise. No action is required of the respondents until notification is given to them that permission to appeal has been given, unless the court directs otherwise (**PD 52, para. 5.22**).

AFTER PERMISSION TO APPEAL IS GIVEN

Notification

71.29 In cases where permission to appeal has to be obtained from the appeal court, the appeal court will send the parties copies of the order granting permission and any other directions given by the court (**PD 52, para. 6.3(2) and (3)**). The documents specified by **para. 6.3A** (see **71.24**) have to be added to the appeal bundle, which has to be served by the appellant on the respondents within seven days of receiving the order granting permission (**para. 6.2**).

If permission to appeal is granted, and if the appeal court is not the Court of Appeal, the appeal court will send the parties notification of the hearing or the period during which the appeal is likely to be heard ('the listing window'). Appeals in the Court of Appeal are given 'hear-by dates', which are the dates by which the appeal will be heard. Listing in the Court of Appeal is considered at **71.32**.

Service of appeal papers

71.30 The normal rule outside the Court of Appeal is that service is effected by the court unless a party requests otherwise (**CPR, r. 6.3**). However, the Court of Appeal will not effect service of appeal papers, which must be effected by the parties (**PD 52, para. 15.1(2)**).

Appeal questionnaires

71.31 For Court of Appeal cases, at the same time as giving the parties a hear-by date, the Civil Appeals Office will send the appellant an appeal questionnaire. This must be returned within 14 days, and must include the appellant's advocate's time estimate for the hearing, confirmation that the transcript of evidence given at the lower court's hearing has been requested, confirmation that appeal bundles are being prepared (though this should be unnecessary, as appeal bundles should have been filed with the appellant's notice before permission was granted), and confirmation that copies of the questionnaire and appeal bundle have been served on the respondents (**PD 52, para. 6.5**). A respondent who disagrees with the time estimate must inform the court within seven days of receipt of the questionnaire (**para. 6.6**). Where the appeal court is the High Court, use of appeal questionnaires is optional (**para. 8.12**).

Court of Appeal listing

Appeals to the Court of Appeal are divided into seven categories, or lists (**PD 52, para. 15.8**). These are: 71.32

(a) The applications list. This includes all applications for permission to appeal, as well as applications for interim remedies in pending appeals.
(b) The appeals list. These are cases where permission to appeal has been given and cases where an appeal lies without needing permission.
(c) The expedited list. This includes applications and appeals where the Court of Appeal has directed an expedited hearing in accordance with the practice laid down in *Unilever plc v Chefaro Proprietaries Ltd* [1995] 1 WLR 243. Asylum appeals, appeals where rights might be irrevocably conferred on third parties, and cases where unlawful material is about to be published, may typically be allocated to this list.
(d) The stand-out list. This is for appeals and applications which are not ready for hearing and which have, for good reasons, been stood out by judicial direction.
(e) The special fixtures list, which is a subdivision of the appeals list, where there is a need to list cases before particular judges, or in a particular order, or at a particular location or time (see **para. 15.9A**).
(f) The second fixtures list. Appeals designated as 'second fixtures' are given hearing dates on the express basis that the list is fully booked for the period in question, and therefore they will only be heard if a suitable gap occurs in the list.
(g) The short warned list. This is for appeals which the court considers may be prepared for hearing by an advocate other than the one originally instructed on either a half day's notice, or, if the court so directs, 48 hours' notice. An appeal or application on this list may be called on at any time with the appropriate short notice. Further details are given in Practice Note (Court of Appeal: Listing) [2001] 1 WLR 479. An objection to being included in this list may be made to a Lord Justice or the master of the Court of Appeal, but will be granted only for the most compelling reasons. An example would be where the appeal cannot be mastered by a substitute advocate within the contemplated time. If the original advocate cannot deal with the hearing because of prior commitments, he or she is under a professional duty to take all practicable measures to ensure the lay client is represented at the hearing by an advocate who is fully instructed and able to argue the appeal (**PD 52, para. 15.9**). A failure in this duty may be visited by a wasted costs order. There has been a short warned list for many years, and surprisingly few complaints have been made about it despite the fact there are occasions when appeals are handed over to an advocate who has had no prior involvement with the case on very short notice.

Hear-by dates for various categories of appeals to the Court of Appeal are set out in Practice Note (Court of Appeal: Listing Windows) [2003] 1 WLR 838. The longest hear-by date is nine months, and many periods are six months. Arrangements for dealing with applications for expedition and for a hearing beyond a hear-by date are described in Practice Note (Court of Appeal: Listing Windows) [2001] 1 WLR 1517.

SHORT HEARINGS BY VIDEOCONFERENCING

Where appropriate and available, parties should use technology, such as videoconferencing, to reduce costs. In *Black v Pastouna* [2005] EWCA Civ 1389, *The Independent*, 2 December 2005, it was said that the additional costs of travelling a long distance to court may be disallowed on short (up to 30-minute) appeals if videoconferencing facilities are available. 71.33

RESPONDENT'S NOTICE AND OTHER DOCUMENTS

Respondent's notice

71.34 In any appeal a respondent may file and serve a respondent's notice (**CPR, r. 52.5(1)**). By **r. 52.5(2)** a respondent's notice must be filed by a respondent who:

(a) is seeking permission to appeal from the appeal court; or

(b) wishes to ask the appeal court to uphold the order of the lower court for reasons different from or additional to those given by the lower court.

Respondents accordingly fall into three broad categories:

(a) Respondents who simply wish to uphold the decision of the court below for the same reasons as given by the judge below. Such a respondent need not serve a respondent's notice.

(b) Respondents who wish to uphold the decision of the court below for reasons different from or additional to those given by the lower court. Such a respondent is not appealing as such, so there is no question of seeking permission to cross-appeal. However, a respondent's notice is required for the purpose of setting out the different or additional reasons (**PD 52, para. 7.2**). A respondent who does not file a respondent's notice is not entitled to address the appeal court on any reason not relied on in the judgment of the lower court, unless the appeal court gives permission (**para. 7.3(2)**). It is not a legitimate exercise of the lower court judge's discretion to make a declaration in terms of factual findings in order to convert what would otherwise be reasons for the primary decision into 'judgments' or 'orders' or 'determinations' within the meaning of the **Supreme Court Act 1981, s. 16(1)**, or the **County Courts Act 1984, s. 77(1)**, if the only purpose is to force the respondent to seek permission under **CPR, r. 52.3(1)**, for what would otherwise be a purely defensive respondent's notice. See *Compagnie Noga d'Importation et d'Exportation SA v Australia and New Zealand Banking Group Ltd* [2002] EWCA Civ 1142, [2003] 1 WLR 307.

(c) Respondents who wish to ask the appeal court to vary the order of the lower court are cross-appealing, and permission to appeal must be sought on the same basis as for an appellant (**PD 52, para. 7.1**). A respondent's notice is required for setting out the grounds on which it is to be argued that the order of the court below should be varied.

Form of respondent's notice

71.35 A respondent's notice is similar to an appellant's notice (see **71.26**) and must be in **form N162**. Together with appellants' notices they are called 'appeal notices' in the **CPR (r. 52.1(3)(f))**. A respondent who seeks permission to cross-appeal from the appeal court must do so in the respondent's notice (**r. 52.5(3)**).

Filing and serving a respondent's notice

71.36 Generally, a respondent's notice must be filed within such period as may be directed by the lower court. Where the court makes no such direction, the notice must be filed within 14 days after the date laid down by **CPR, r. 52.5(5)**, relevant to the circumstances of the appeal. This date will be either:

(a) the date the respondent was served with the appellant's notice in cases where permission to appeal was given by the lower court, or permission to appeal was not required; or

(b) the date the respondent was served with notification that the appeal court gave the appellant permission to appeal; or

(c) the date the respondent was served with notification that the application for permission to appeal and the appeal itself are to be heard together.

Unless the appeal court orders otherwise, a respondent's notice must be served on the appellant and any other respondent as soon as practicable, and in any event not later than seven days after it is filed (**r. 52.5(6)**). An extension of time for service of a respondent's notice was readily granted in *Bell Electric Ltd v Aweco Appliance Systems GmbH & Co.* [2002] EWCA Civ 1501, [2003] 1 All ER 344.

Respondent's skeleton argument

A respondent who proposes to address arguments to the appeal court must provide a skeleton argument for the court (**PD 52, para. 7.6**). It should conform to the principles applicable to appellants' skeletons (see **71.26**), but should also seek to answer the arguments in the appellants' skeleton (**para. 7.8**). A respondent who does not file a respondent's notice (see **71.33**) must file and serve his skeleton argument at least seven days before the appeal hearing (**para. 7.7(2)**). Where a respondent's notice is used, the respondent's skeleton argument can be included in the respondent's notice (**para. 7.6**), filed with the respondent's notice or within 14 days after filing the notice (**para. 7.7(1)**). An unrepresented respondent need not file a skeleton argument, but is encouraged to do so (**para. 7.7A(2)**). Skeleton arguments must be served on the appellant at the same time as they are filed, and the respondent is required to file a certificate of service (**para. 7.7B**). **71.37**

Respondent's documents

A respondent's notice must, by **PD 52, paras 7.10 to 7.13**, be lodged with: **71.38**

(a) two additional copies of the respondent's notice for the appeal court;
(b) one copy of the respondent's notice for each appellant and any other respondents;
(c) (if filed with the respondent's notice, see **71.37**), two copies of the skeleton argument; and
(d) a supplementary bundle where any additional documents are relied upon that are not included in the appeal bundle.

Supplementary skeleton argument

PD 52, para. 15.11A, lays down a timetable for supplementary skeleton arguments in the Court of Appeal. Supplementary skeleton arguments become necessary sometimes when new advocates are appointed, or when the law has moved on, or where there is a need to respond to a point raised in an opponent's skeleton argument. An appellant in this situation must file and serve its supplementary skeleton argument at least 14 days before the hearing. A respondent must do so at least seven days before the hearing. The court may refuse to hear arguments not contained in skeleton arguments filed within these time limits (**para. 15.11A(4)**). **71.39**

Final deadline

For appeals to the Court of Appeal, all the papers needed for the appeal must be filed at least seven days before the hearing (**PD 52, para. 15.11B(1)**). If the seven-day deadline cannot be met, both the court and the other parties must be informed. Permission to file out of time may be granted if there are exceptional circumstances or an understandable reason for the delay (*Mlauzi v Secretary of State for the Home Department* [2005] EWCA Civ 128, *The Times*, 15 February 2005). Any party who fails to comply may be required to attend before the presiding Lord Justice to explain what is or is not being done, and seek permission to proceed with or to oppose the appeal (**para. 15.11B(2)**; *Jeyapragash v Secretary of State for the Home Department* [2004] EWCA Civ 1260, [2005] 1 All ER 412). The Court of Appeal expects strict compliance with this final deadline, because it is essential for effective pre-reading by the judges. Any party summoned under this provision is advised to ensure that all documents have been filed before attending before the presiding Lord Justice (*Scribes West Ltd v Relsa Anstalt (No. 1)* [2004] EWCA Civ 835, *The Times*, 8 July 2004, at [31]). See also **71.45 to 71.46** for the more general jurisdiction of appeal courts to impose sanctions and to dismiss appeals for non-compliance. **71.40**

APPLICATIONS WITHIN APPEALS

71.41 Notice of an application made to the appeal court for a remedy incidental to the appeal (such as an application for security for costs) may be included in the appeal notice or may be made by an ordinary application notice under **CPR, Part 23 (PD 52, para. 5.5)**.

The applicant must file the following documents with the application (see **PD 52, para. 11.2**):

(a) one additional copy of the application notice for the appeal court and one copy for each of the respondents;
(b) where applicable, a sealed copy of the order which is the subject of the main appeal; and
(c) a bundle of documents, which should include the application notice and any written evidence in support of the application.

In the Court of Appeal, interim applications within appeals are often determined by a single Lord Justice. Short, half-hour, applications to the Court of Appeal may be suitable for hearing through video link. Details can be obtained through the Civil Appeals Office. Costs may be disallowed where counsel travel unnecessary distances instead of using this facility (*Babbings v Kirklees Metropolitan Borough Council* [2004] EWCA Civ 1431, *The Times*, 4 November 2004).

Many interim applications can be determined by the Court of Appeal master (or deputy master). However, masters and deputies cannot give permission to appeal, grant stays (other than temporary stays of the decision of the lower court over a period when the Court of Appeal is not sitting or cannot conveniently be convened) or grant injunctions (**CPR, r. 52.16(3)**). A party is entitled, within seven days of being served with notice of the decision, to request that any decision by a court officer be reviewed by the Court of Appeal (**r. 52.16(5), (6) and (6A)**). A single judge may refer any matter for a decision by a court consisting of two or more judges (**r. 52.16(7)**).

AMENDMENT OF AN APPEAL NOTICE

71.42 An appeal notice (appellant's or respondent's) may be amended with permission (**CPR, r. 52.8**). An application for permission to amend will normally be dealt with at the hearing of the appeal, unless that course would cause unnecessary expense or delay, in which case a request should be made for the application to amend to be heard in advance (**PD 52, para. 5.25**). If skeleton arguments are set out in an appeal notice, it is not necessary to obtain the court's permission to amend them (**PD 52, paras 5.9** and **7.6**).

STAY OF EXECUTION

71.43 Initiating an appeal does not have the automatic effect of staying execution on any judgment obtained in the lower court. By **CPR, r. 52.7**, an appeal will operate as a stay of any order or decision of the lower court only if:

(a) the appeal court or the lower court so orders; or
(b) the appeal is from the Immigration Appeal Tribunal.

For many years the courts have acted on the principle stated in *Atkins v Great Western Railway* (1886) 2 TLR 400 that a stay may be granted where the appellant produces written evidence showing that if the judgment were to be paid, there would be no reasonable prospect of getting it back if the appeal were to succeed. This was regarded as too stringent a test in *Linotype-Hell Finance Ltd v Baker* [1993] 1 WLR 321 by Staughton LJ, who said a stay could be granted if the appellant would face ruin without a stay, provided the appeal had some prospect of success.

Whether the court should exercise its discretion to grant a stay of execution of a judgment pending the hearing of an appeal against the judgment depends upon all the circumstances of the case, but the essential factor is the risk of injustice (*Hammond Suddard Solicitors v Agrichem International Holdings Ltd* [2001] EWCA Civ 1915, LTL 18/12/2001). In particular, if a stay is refused, what are the risks of the appeal being stifled? If a stay is granted and the appeal fails, what are the risks that the respondent will be unable to enforce the judgment? If a stay is refused and the appeal succeeds, and the judgment is enforced in the meantime, what are the risks of the appellant being able to recover what has been paid to the respondent?

Evidence in support of an application for a stay must be full, frank and clear (*Hammond Suddard Solicitors v Agrichem International Holdings Ltd*).

STRIKING OUT OR IMPOSING CONDITIONS

By **CPR, r. 52.9(1)**, an appeal court has the following powers: it may strike out the whole or part of an appeal notice; it may set aside permission to appeal in whole or in part; or it may impose or vary conditions upon which an appeal may be brought. In addition to its powers under **r. 52.9**, an appeal court may impose conditions under its general case management powers in **rr. 2.1** and **3.1**, which can be exercised even after an application to impose conditions has been refused by the judge in the court below (*Contract Facilities Ltd v Rees's Estate* [2003] EWCA Civ 1105, LTL 24/7/2003). Applications to set aside or impose conditions on the grant of permission to appeal should be made within 14 days of service of the order granting permission (*Mamidoil-Jetoil Greek Petroleum Company SA v Okta Crude Oil Refinery AD* [2003] EWCA Civ 808, *The Times*, 19 June 2003). **71.44**

It is recognised that the power to strike out an appeal notice 'is one that is just as capable of abuse as is the power to put in hopeless notices of appeal' (*Burgess v Stafford Hotel Ltd* [1990] 1 WLR 1215 per Glidewell LJ). **Rule 52.9(2)** therefore provides that the court will exercise its powers under **r. 52.9(1)** only where there is a compelling reason for doing so. There may be a compelling reason where the appeal is being brought to secure some collateral advantage, or where the application will achieve a substantial saving of time. This may be so where there are cogent grounds demonstrating the appeal had no prospects of success. Otherwise, in all ordinary circumstances the granting of permission to appeal is conclusive (*Hunt v Peasegood* (2000) *The Times*, 20 October 2000). A party who was present at the hearing at which permission was given may not subsequently apply for an order that the court exercise its powers to set aside permission or to impose conditions (**r. 52.9(3)**).

Sanctions and conditions in appeals

The appeal court has a wholly unfettered discretion under **CPR, r. 52.9(1)(c)**, to impose and vary the conditions upon which an appeal may be brought (*Bell Electric Ltd v Aweco Appliance Systems GmbH & Co.* [2002] EWCA Civ 1501, [2003] 1 All ER 344). In this case the appellant was found to have disregarded the orders of the court below in a deliberate and cynical manner, and ordered that unless the appellant complied with the terms of the order below within the next 14 days the appeal would be stayed. A condition requiring an appellant to pay the costs whether he won or lost was held to be excessive in *King v Daltray* [2003] EWCA Civ 808, LTL 4/6/2003. An order that there be no order as to costs on the appeal was substituted. A condition requiring a payment into court may be varied on the ground that the appellant cannot afford to make the payment, but evidence will be required that the amount is such as to prevent the appellant funding the appeal (*Branch Empire Ltd v Coote* (2003) LTL 16/6/2003). **71.45**

DISMISSAL FOR NON-COMPLIANCE

71.46 Where the rules on lodging documents, skeleton arguments etc. are broken, an appeal may be considered for dismissal. In the Court of Appeal such cases may be considered by the Head of the Civil Appeals Office or by a deputy master. The court sees it as its duty to protect the interests of respondents, who already have a decision of a competent authority in their favour, by insisting on all reasonable expedition and strict compliance with the timetable laid down. See *Hyams v Plender* [2001] 1 WLR 32.

DISPOSAL OF APPEALS BY CONSENT

71.47 Where the parties to an appeal have reached a settlement disposing of the appeal, they may make a joint request asking for the appeal to be dismissed by consent (**PD 52, para. 12.4**). An appellant who does not wish to pursue an appeal may make a request to the appeal court for the appeal to be dismissed. If granted, this will usually be on terms that the appellant pays the costs (**para. 12.2**), but may be on the basis of no order as to costs if the respondent's representative signs a consent to that effect (**para. 12.3**). An appeal may be allowed by consent, but the appeal court must first be satisfied that the lower court's decision was wrong (**para. 13.1**). Appeals and applications settled where one of the parties is under a disability require the court's approval (**para. 13.2**). An amendment made to **para. 13.2** by the 37th update contains a significant drafting flaw. It is intended to say that approval is also required for settlements including periodical payments under the Damages Act 1996, s. 2. In error, its wording is restricted to appeals involving children and patients, and the general words in **para. 13.2(1)** render the specific words in **para. 13.2(2)** redundant. Where one of the parties is a child, the proposed consent order should be supported by an opinion from the advocate acting for the child advising on whether the terms are for the benefit of the child (**para. 13.3**). In the case of patients, an opinion is required and also any relevant reports prepared for the Court of Protection and formal approval by that court where required (**para. 13.4**).

Solicitors and counsel have a duty to inform the court as soon as it is known that an appeal which has been listed for hearing will not proceed. Even if a case settles very late in the day steps must taken through the Royal Courts of Justice switchboard to notify the appeal court judges' clerks, to prevent unnecessary preparation (*Tasyurdu v Immigration Appeal Tribunal* [2003] EWCA Civ 447, [2003] CPLR 343; *Yell Ltd v Garton* [2004] EWCA Civ 87, *The Times*, 26 February 2004).

AUTHORITIES

Cases

71.48 In the High Court lists of authorities should be provided to the Head Usher by 5.30 p.m. on the working day before the appeal hearing. In the county courts it is usually necessary to have photocopies of reports available at the hearing.

For Court of Appeal hearings (only), once the parties have been notified of the date fixed for hearing, the appellant's advocate must file a bundle containing photocopies of the principal authorities each side will be relying upon (**PD 52, para. 15.11**). Obviously, this can only be done after conferring with the advocate for the respondent. There is no need to provide authorities for propositions not in dispute. Normally, the bundle should contain no more than 10 authorities with the relevant passages marked for pre-reading. **Paragraph 15.11(2)(c)** recognises that the scale of the appeal may warrant more extensive citation. The bundle must include a certificate signed by the advocates that the requirements of **para. 5.10(3)** to (5) on citing authorities (see 71.26) has been complied with (**para. 15.11(5)**). The bundle must be filed at least seven days before the hearing (**para. 15.11(3)**). If, through some oversight, a party intends to refer to additional authorities, the parties may agree a second bundle, which the appellant's advocate must file at least 48 hours before the hearing (**para. 15.11(4)**).

The *Law Reports* published by the Incorporated Council of Law Reporting for England and Wales should be cited in preference to other reports, as they contain counsel's arguments and are readily available. Next best are the *Weekly Law Reports* and *All England Law Reports* if a case is not, or not yet, reported in the official *Law Reports.* Other reports, even obscure reports, may be used for sufficient reason, but advocates should provide photocopies (of the title page and relevant pages only). Occasionally it is useful to refer to more than one source if there are discrepancies between reports. There are restrictions on using certain authorities, discussed in Practice Direction (Citation of Authorities) [2001] 1 WLR 1001, see **32.17**. If unreported decisions are relied upon, the official transcript should be produced rather than the handed-down text of the judgment (Practice Direction (Court of Appeal: Citation of Authority) [1995] 1 WLR 1096), and they should only be used if they contain statements of principle not found in reported authorities (Practice Statement (Court of Appeal: Authorities) [1996] 1 WLR 854). Excessive citation of authorities, and reliance on summaries of cases not prepared by a professional lawyer, will not be tolerated (*Hamblin v Field* (2000) *The Times*, 26 April 2000).

Use of *Hansard* extracts

It was decided in *Pepper v Hart* [1993] AC 593 that Parliamentary material may be used as an aid to determining the true intention of the legislature where: **71.49**

(a) the legislation is ambiguous or obscure or the literal meaning leads to an absurdity;
(b) the material relied upon consists of statements by a minister or promoter of the Bill and such other material as is necessary to understand those statements; and
(c) the statements relied on are clear.

It is permissible to have recourse to ministerial statements and explanatory notes prepared by the relevant government department while the Bill was proceeding through Parliament, where doing so complies with the principles in *Pepper v Hart*. However, reference to debates in Parliament is contrary to the Bill of Rights (1688), art. 9, so cannot be justified as an aid to interpretation in court (see *Wilson v First County Trust Ltd (No. 2)* [2003] UKHL 40, [2004] 1 AC 816). Even where use of ministerial statements and explanatory notes is permissible, the court must be careful not to give these documents determinative effect, as members of Parliament may not have generally agreed with the stated reasons or conclusions (*Wilson v First County Trust Ltd (No. 2)*). In *McDonnell v Congregation of Christian Brothers Trustees* [2003] UKHL 63, [2003] 1 AC 1101, Lord Bingham of Cornhill said he would need much persuasion, save possibly in exceptional circumstances, that it is proper to depart from a previous decision of the House of Lords on the basis that the previous decision is inconsistent with the will of Parliament as discovered from *Hansard.* Lord Steyn in the same case said there is a view that *Pepper v Hart* allows the court to treat the intentions of government revealed in debates in Parliament as reflecting the will of Parliament. That view raises serious conceptual and constitutional difficulties. The better view is that it has been decided by *Wilson v First County Trust Ltd (No. 2)* that use of debates from *Hansard* is not permissible.

Any party intending to refer to extracts from *Hansard* in accordance with the principles laid down in *Pepper v Hart* must give reasonable advance notice to the court and other parties. In the Court of Appeal the extracts should be included in the bundle of authorities (see **71.48**).

FORM OF APPEAL ORDERS

The general rules relating to drawing up orders (see **chapter 61**) apply to orders made after **71.50** appeal hearings. However, to assist the Civil Appeals Office in sifting applications for permission to bring a second appeal (see 71.14 for the restrictions on such appeals), orders made on first appeals must (see *Tanfern Ltd v Cameron-MacDonald* [2000] 1 WLR 1311):

(a) state the name and status of the judge in the lower court; and
(b) if it is a final order, state which track (if any) the claim was allocated to, and whether it was a **Part 8** claim.

REOPENING APPEALS

71.51 Confirming the decision in *Taylor v Lawrence* [2002] EWCA Civ 90, [2003] QB 528, it is now provided in **CPR, r. 52.17**, that the Court of Appeal and High Court may reopen an appeal (or application for permission to appeal: **PD 52, para. 25.2**) in exceptional circumstances. This power derives from the court's inherent jurisdiction, and so is not available to a circuit judge in the county court (**CPR, r. 52.17(3)**). A case is exceptional if it is possible a significant injustice will occur and there is no effective alternative remedy (*Re Uddin (A Child)* [2005] EWCA Civ 52, [2005] 1 WLR 2398). This might be found where the integrity of the earlier process has been critically undermined. The admission of fresh evidence (see 72.13) is of an altogether different and less demanding order, and will rarely satisfy the present test given the need for finality in litigation. An appeal may be reopened (see **r. 52.17(1)**) if:

(a) it is necessary to do so to avoid real injustice (such as where new facts come to light after the court makes its decision, as in *Taylor v Lawrence*);
(b) the circumstances are exceptional and make it appropriate to reopen the appeal; and
(c) there is no alternative effective remedy (so if the injustice could be remedied by a readily available further appeal, the court will not reopen the present appeal).

Procedure for reopening appeals

71.52 Permission is required to reopen an appeal, even if permission was not required for the initial appeal (**CPR, r. 52.17(4)**). An application for permission is made by application notice (in **form N244**) supported by written evidence (**PD 52, para. 25.4**), and is made to the court whose decision the applicant wishes to reopen (**para. 25.3**). There is no right to an oral hearing unless the judge so directs (**CPR, r. 52.17(5)**), and the application must not be served on any other party, again unless the court otherwise directs (**PD 52, para. 25.5**). An application cannot be granted unless the judge makes a direction for service on the other party and gives them an opportunity to make representations (**r. 52.17(6)**). The respondent has 14 days from being served to file and serve written evidence in reply (**PD 52, para. 25.6**). There is no right of appeal or review from a decision on an application for permission to reopen, which is final (**r. 52.17(7)**).

STATUTORY APPEALS

71.53 **Paragraph 17 of PD 52** applies to appeals under any enactment to the courts from the decision of a minister of State, government department, tribunal or other person. These appeals are governed by the main provisions of **CPR, Part 52**, but with certain refinements, which include extending the period for filing the appellant's notice to 28 days from the date of the decision of the lower court (**PD 52, para. 17.3**), and a requirement to serve the appellant's notice on the chairman of the tribunal, minister of State, government department or other person from whose decision the appeal is brought, in addition to the respondents (**para. 17.5**). **CPR, Part 52**, and **PD 52** do not impose a requirement for seeking permission to appeal for statutory appeals where otherwise the right of appeal is unrestricted (*Colley v Council for Licensed Conveyancers* (2001) *The Times*, 6 August 2001). The minister or government department is entitled to attend the appeal hearing and to make representations (**para. 17.6**).

For costs against inferior courts, coroners etc. see **66.39**.

Appeals by way of case stated

A number of statutes provide that appeals may be brought to the High Court by way of case stated. Among the most well known are the Magistrates' Courts Act 1980, s. 111, and the **Supreme Court Act 1981, s. 28**. These provide for appeals by case stated from decisions made by magistrates' courts and the Crown Court on the ground they are wrong in law or in excess of jurisdiction. See *Blackstone's Criminal Practice 2006*, paras D27.12 to D27.18 and D27.29. A decision of the High Court on an appeal by case stated under either of these provisions is final, subject to the right of appeal in criminal cases to the House of Lords under the Administration of Justice Act 1960 (see **Supreme Court Act 1981, s. 28A(4)**). Consequently, in a civil case the Court of Appeal has no jurisdiction to entertain a further appeal from the High Court's decision (*Westminster City Council v O'Reilly* [2003] EWCA Civ 1007, [2004] 1 WLR 195). **71.54**

Paragraph 18 of PD 52 applies to cases where enactments provide for appeals to be by way of case stated and to cases where a question of law may be referred to the court by way of case stated. In these cases the general provisions of **CPR, Part 52**, apply, subject to certain amendments. **Paragraphs 18.3 to 18.6** apply to appeals by way of case stated from the Crown Court or magistrates' courts. In these appeals the appellant's notice must be filed in the High Court within 10 days after receipt of the stated case (**para. 18.4**). **Paragraphs 18.7 to 18.20** apply to appeals from ministers, government departments, tribunals and other persons by way of case stated. In these cases the appellant's notice must be filed within 14 days after the stated case is served on the appellant (**para. 18.11**). The minister or government department is entitled to attend the appeal hearing and to make representations (**para. 18.16**).

Special appeal provisions

Section III of **PD 52** contains a large number of special rules applicable to various categories of specialist appeals. These include appeals from various tribunals to the Court of Appeal (such as appeals from the Immigration Appeal Tribunal), and appeals to the High Court under various statutory provisions, most of which are highly specialised. **71.55**

Housing Act 1996, ss. 204 and 204A

Appeals under both ss. 204 and 204A of the Housing Act 1996 should be included in one appellant's notice, unless this is impossible because of urgency (PD 52, para. 24.2). An appeal under s. 204 was held in *Van Aken v Camden London Borough Council* [2002] EWCA Civ 1724, [2003] 1 WLR 684, to have been brought within the 21-day time limit laid down by s. 204(2) where the documents were put through the court's letter box after the court had closed on the twenty-first day. **71.56**

Chapter 72 Hearing of Appeals

INTRODUCTION

72.1 This chapter will discuss the nature of appeal hearings, and the grounds on which an appeal court may overturn the decision of the court below.

COMPOSITION OF THE COURT

72.2 An appeal from a county court district judge will be to a county court circuit judge. An appeal from a High Court master or district judge will be to a High Court judge. The same is true with appeals from county court circuit judges (other than appeals from final decisions in multi-track and specialist jurisdiction proceedings, where the appeal is to the Court of Appeal).

The **Supreme Court Act 1981, s. 54(2)**, provides that the Court of Appeal shall be duly constituted for the purposes of exercising any of its jurisdiction if it consists of one or more judges. Section 54(3) provides that the Master of the Rolls may give directions about the minimum number of judges required for different descriptions of proceedings and, by s. 54(4) the Master of the Rolls or any designated Lord Justice can determine the number of judges who will sit in any particular proceedings. In the absence of special circumstances, there is nothing wrong with a judge who refused permission to appeal on the papers being one of the judges hearing the substantive appeal after permission is granted on a renewed application (*Sengupta v Holmes* [2002] EWCA Civ 1104, *The Times*, 19 August 2002). Normally, two Lords Justices sit on interim appeals, and three sit on final appeals. Where a two-judge court is equally divided, either party may apply for a rehearing before a three-judge court.

Occasionally an appeal court will sit with assessors, as in some appeals on costs issues.

The House of Lords generally sits in five-member courts.

THE HEARING

72.3 Normally it is unnecessary for the advocate for the appellant to open the appeal, as the judges usually do fairly extensive pre-reading. In most cases the judges will have pre-read the appeal bundle and skeleton arguments, and usually will have read the core authorities bundle (if there is one). The judge (or presiding judge in a multi-member court) usually indicates the extent of the pre-reading that has been done. In appeals to the Court of Appeal, if it is felt that it would be helpful for the appellant's advocate to open the appeal, the presiding judge will notify the advocates in advance. The intention is that court time is spent dealing with the substance of the arguments and that time should not be wasted in extensive reading from documents.

PART 36 OFFERS

The fact that a Part 36 offer or Part 36 payment has been made must not be disclosed to the court on any application for permission to appeal or on any appeal until all questions (other than costs) have been determined (**CPR, r. 52.12(1)**). This is for the same reason (the risk of unfairly influencing the court) as applies at trial (see **r. 36.19**). However, the embargo does not apply if the **Part 36** offer or payment is relevant to the substance of the appeal, or if the fact that a **Part 36** offer or payment has been made is properly relevant to the matter to be decided (**r. 52.12(2) and (3)**). **72.4**

REVIEW OF THE DECISION BELOW

Review not rehearing

By **CPR, r. 52.11(1)**, every appeal will be limited to a review of the decision of the lower court unless: **72.5**

(a) a practice direction makes different provision for a particular category of appeal; or

(b) the court considers that in the circumstances of an individual appeal it would be in the interests of justice to hold a rehearing.

There are very few exceptions, and those that exist are of a technical nature (see, e.g., **PD 52, para. 9.1**). The power to conduct an appeal by way of rehearing is to be exercised in rare cases where necessary in order for justice to be done. The fair trial requirements of the **European Convention on Human Rights, art. 6**, do not compel the court to conduct rehearings in appeals from without-notice decisions (*Dyson Ltd v Registrar of Trademarks* [2003] EWHC 1062 (Ch), [2003] 1 WLR 2406). The exceptional nature of holding a rehearing rather than a review on an appeal was stressed in *Lewis v Secretary of State for Trade and Industry* [2001] 2 BCLC 597. It had been submitted that a rehearing was appropriate because the lower court had not stated reasons for its decision. Neuberger J said that even in such cases the appeal should be by way of review unless the court below had been asked to give its reasons and had refused to do so, or there was some good reason for not asking the lower court to give its reasons. The limited circumstances in which an appeal should take the form of a rehearing rather than a review, particularly where the decision appealed against is one based on discretion, were stressed in *Audergon v La Baguette Ltd* [2002] EWCA Civ 10, [2002] CPLR 192. In *Richardson v Ealing London Borough Council* [2005] EWCA Civ 1798, *The Times*, 14 December 2005, the Court of Appeal reiterated the practice requiring an exceptional case before conducting an appeal as a rehearing. The High Court case of *Ansari v Puffin Investment Co. Ltd* [2002] EWHC 1234 (QB), *The Times*, 17 July 2002, should be regarded as wrongly decided. The learned judge disagreed with the restrictive approach to rehearings of appeals, and dealt with an appeal from a summary judgment decision as a rehearing. *Bank of Ireland v Robertson* (2003) LTL 21/2/2003 was an exceptional case where an appeal was conducted by way of rehearing. The appellant was a litigant in person, had been unable to attend the hearing, and this was the first occasion on which he had been able to present his case.

Grounds for allowing appeals

The restriction of an appeal court's function to a review of the lower court's decision means **72.6** that for almost all appeals, the appeal court will allow an appeal only where (**CPR, r. 52.11(3)**) the decision of the lower court was:

(a) wrong; or
(b) unjust because of a serious procedural or other irregularity in the proceedings in the lower court.

'Wrong' means unsustainable (*Abrahams v Lenton* [2003] EWHC 1104 (QB), LTL 20/5/2003). An insubstantial point, even if a technical error, does not render a decision wrong (*Orford v Rasmi Electronics Ltd* [2004] EWCA Civ 809, LTL 4/8/2004). The strength of the other evidence at trial may mean that, despite an error, the decision below was not wrong (*Daly v Sheikh* [2004] EWCA Civ 119, LTL 13/2/2004). In *DEG-Deutsche Investitions- und Entwicklungsgesellschaft mbH v Koshy* [2001] EWCA Civ 79, [2001] 3 All ER 878 Robert Walker LJ at [24] rejected a submission that there is no power to allow an appeal where the lower court's decision was correct on the law and evidence as it stood before the lower court, even though a change in the law, or fresh evidence, or supervening events, show it (with hindsight) to have been wrong. The Court of Appeal seems to have gone even further in *Law v St Margarets Insurance Ltd* [2001] EWCA Civ 30, LTL 18/1/2001, where the appeal was allowed on the basis of furthering the overriding objective rather than holding that the lower court's discretion fell outside the generous ambit given to discretionary decisions. Similarly, in *Ayonrinde v Oyemomilara* [2001] EWCA Civ 1296, LTL 17/7/2001, it was difficult to say that the lower court's decision was wrong on the material before the judge below. However, the decision in the lower court caused injustice to the appellant, and the case was treated as an exceptional case which justified setting aside the decision below.

Questions of fact

72.7 The trial judge sees the demeanour of witnesses, and can assess their intelligence and credibility in a way that an appeal court cannot, even with the benefit of a transcript. It is accordingly very difficult to succeed on an appeal based on arguments that findings of fact by the court below were wrong (*Orford v Rasmi Electronics Ltd* [2004] EWCA Civ 809, LTL 4/8/2004). Appeal courts are more likely to interfere with inferences that may be drawn from the evidence (see 72.10).

The appeal court's function is to review the decision of the court below. It is not to embark on making original findings of fact (*Designer Guild Ltd v Russell Williams (Textiles) Ltd* [2000] 1 WLR 2416). A finding of fact can be upset on appeal if there was no evidence to support that finding, or if the finding was against the weight of the evidence as a whole (*Bank of Credit and Commerce International (Overseas) Ltd v Akindele* [2001] Ch 437). An appeal on a question of fact was allowed in *George Ralph Architects v Lazarowicz* (2000) LTL 27/10/2000, where the judge found an agreement by preferring one side's witnesses, but where the agreement was not referred to in the contemporaneous documents.

Failure to give reasons

72.8 The definition of issues, marshalling of evidence and giving reasons are the building blocks of the reasoned judicial process. An analysis of the judgment in *Glicksman v Redbridge Healthcare NHS Trust* [2001] EWCA Civ 1097, LTL 12/7/2001, showed that the judge below had made findings expressed as conclusions without giving reasons for the implicit rejection of testimony going the other way. Further, there were no findings on the secondary issues on which counsel had relied. The judgment was set aside with an order for a retrial. A judge must address the main evidential conflicts, and identify why (for example) certain witnesses have been found to be truthful and others to be untruthful or inaccurate (*Baird v Thurrock Borough Council* [2005] EWCA Civ 1499, *The Times*, 15 November 2005). Making findings in a column in a Scott schedule is no substitute for a reasoned judgment on the issues (*Habib Bank Ltd v Liverpool Freeport (Electronics) Ltd* [2004] EWCA Civ 1062, LTL 29/7/2004). In *Clifford v Grimley* [2001] EWCA Civ 1658, LTL 23/10/2001, the judge failed to weigh up many of the issues, which were dealt with in a robust manner which was cursory and superficial. Nevertheless, the short analysis did not sufficiently undermine the findings of fact to justify interference on appeal. See also *Flannery v Halifax Estate Agencies Ltd* [2000] 1 WLR 377.

An unsuccessful party should not seek to upset a judgment on the ground of inadequate reasons unless, despite considering the judgment in the light of the evidence and submissions at trial, they are unable to understand why the judge had decided against them (*English v Emery Reimbold and Strick Ltd* [2002] EWCA Civ 605, [2002] 1 WLR 2409). When an application for permission to appeal is made to the trial judge on the ground of inadequate reasons, the trial judge should consider whether his judgment was defective. If so, the judge should seek to remedy this by giving additional reasons, and refuse permission to appeal as the problem is thereby remedied. Where an appeal court finds a renewed application for permission on this ground to be well founded, it should consider adjourning the application and remitting the case to the trial judge with an invitation to provide additional reasons for the decision. If the application proceeds to an appeal hearing, the appeal will only succeed if the reasons cannot be discerned even in the context of the evidence and submissions at the trial (*English v Emery Reimbold and Strick Ltd*). A failure to address an issue was not sufficient to justify interference on appeal where the judgment was otherwise a careful one in *Powell v Pallisers of Hereford Ltd* [2002] EWCA Civ 959, LTL 1/7/2002. The practice of giving no reasons for decisions on costs could only comply with the **European Convention on Human Rights, art. 6(1)**, if the reason for the decision is implicit from the circumstances (*English v Emery Reimbold and Strick Ltd*).

Discretion

The most important statement on the role of an appellate court in a discretionary matter is that of Lord Diplock in *Hadmor Productions Ltd v Hamilton* [1983] 1 AC 191. This was a case dealing with an appeal in respect of an interim injunction, but his lordship's comments are equally applicable in other types of interim appeals. His lordship said, at p. 220: **72.9**

> Upon an appeal from the judge's grant or refusal of an [interim] injunction the function of an appellate court, whether it be the Court of Appeal or your lordships' House, is not to exercise an independent discretion of its own. It must defer to the judge's exercise of his discretion and must not interfere with it merely upon the ground that the members of the appellate court would have exercised the discretion differently. The function of the appellate court is initially one of review only. It may set aside the judge's exercise of his discretion on the ground that it was based upon a misunderstanding of the law or of the evidence before him or upon an inference that particular facts existed or did not exist, which, although it was one that might legitimately have been drawn upon the evidence that was before the judge, can be demonstrated to be wrong by further evidence that has become available by the time of the appeal; or upon the ground that there has been a change of circumstances after the judge made his order that would have justified his acceding to an application to vary it. Since reasons given by judges for granting or refusing [interim] injunctions may sometimes be sketchy, there may also be occasional cases where even though no erroneous assumption of law or fact can be identified the judge's decision to grant or refuse the injunction is so aberrant that it must be set aside upon the ground that no reasonable judge regardful of his duty to act judicially could have reached it. It is only if and after the appellate court has reached the conclusion that the judge's exercise of his discretion must be set aside for one or other of these reasons, that it becomes entitled to exercise an original discretion of its own.

Thus, discretionary decisions may be reversed on appeal where the judge below erred in principle in his approach, or left out of account or took into account some feature he should or should not have considered, or that his decision was wholly wrong because he failed to balance the various factors fairly in the scale (*Adamson v Halifax plc* [2002] EWCA Civ 1134, [2003] 1 WLR 60). The way it was put by Lord Fraser of Tullybelton in *G v G (Minors: Custody Appeal)* [1985] 1 WLR 647 is that the appeal court '. . . should only interfere when it considers that the judge of first instance has not merely preferred an imperfect solution which is different from an alternative imperfect solution which the Court of Appeal might or would have adopted, but has exceeded the generous ambit within which a reasonable disagreement is possible'.

Any conclusion reached at a case management conference is made at the judge's discretion, and, unless the judge has clearly erred by failing to fulfil the overriding objective, there is a distinct reluctance to interfere on an appeal (*Powell v Pallisers of Hereford Ltd* [2002] EWCA Civ 959, LTL 1/7/2002). Costs decisions, being discretionary and turning on the circumstances and conduct of the parties, are notoriously hard to overturn on appeal (*Sullivan v Grout* (2002) LTL 30/4/2002; *Excelsior Commercial and Industrial Holdings Ltd v Salisbury Hamer Aspden and Johnson* [2002] EWCA Civ 879, *The Independent*, 18 June 2002).

Inferences

72.10 An appeal court may draw any inference of fact which it considers justified on the evidence (**CPR, r. 52.11(4)**). This includes inferences to be drawn from the facts found by the judge in the lower court and inferences to be drawn from the documents (*The Mouna* [1991] 2 Lloyd's Rep 221).

Substantial procedural irregularities

72.11 Procedural irregularities include misdirections to the jury (in jury trials) and the improper admission or non-admission of evidence. By **CPR, r. 52.11(3)**, a procedural irregularity is a valid ground for appeal only if it was a serious one and it caused an unjust decision in the lower court (*Tanfern Ltd v Cameron-MacDonald* [2000] 1 WLR 1311). An appeal on this ground is an onerous one, and the procedural irregularity must have caused an injustice to the appellant (*Keith Davy (Crantock) Ltd v Ibatex Ltd* [2001] EWCA Civ 740, LTL 2/5/2001).

Examples of substantial procedural irregularity

72.12 A failure to follow the two-stage process laid down in *Lownds v Home Office* [2002] EWCA Civ 365, [2002] 1 WLR 2450 (see **68.34**), was held to be a serious procedural irregularity in *Lloyds TSB Bank plc v Lampert* [2003] EWHC 249 (Ch), LTL 7/3/2003. Likewise, a failure to consider each of the factors set out in **CPR, r. 3.9**, on an application for relief from sanctions is usually regarded as a sufficiently serious irregularity to justify intervention by the appeal court (see **46.30**).

Allowing one party to adduce additional evidence but not the other, and restricting the cross-examination of a key witness, amounted to a serious procedural irregularity in *Hayes v Transco plc* [2003] EWCA Civ 1261, LTL 17/9/2003). Refusing permission to call a witness who would have made no difference was insufficient in *Wade v Varney* [2003] EWCA Civ 1279, LTL 22/9/2003. In *Aberavon and Port Talbot Rugby Football Club v Welsh Rugby Union Ltd* [2003] EWCA Civ 584, LTL 9/4/2003, it was held that the appellant had been given sufficient opportunity in the court to make representations by being given the opportunity to make written representations.

In *Taylor v Williamsons* [2002] EWCA Civ 1380, *The Times*, 9 August 2002, discussed at **61.35**, an appeal was dismissed despite the judge issuing a written judgment before receiving the submissions from one of the parties. The judge had recalled the judgment, and given a new judgment after hearing submissions. An appeal may be based on excessive delay in delivering judgment, and a lapse of 12 months would be excessive (*Cobham v Frett* [2001] 1 WLR 1775). A delay of three months calls for some explanation (*Habib Bank Ltd v Liverpool Freeport (Electronics) Ltd* [2004] EWCA Civ 1062, LTL 29/7/2004). In appeals based on delay, the appellate court should consider the quality of the judge's notes, and carefully scrutinise the findings of fact and the reasons given by the judge. It is only if there are errors possibly attributable to the delay that an appeal should be allowed on this ground (*Cobham v Frett*).

Fresh evidence

72.13 By **CPR, r. 52.11(2)**, unless it orders otherwise, the appeal court will not receive oral evidence or any evidence which was not before the lower court. Under the old rules a restrictive approach was taken to the introduction of fresh evidence on appeals, the guiding principles being laid down in *Ladd v Marshall* [1954] 1 WLR 1489 (see **72.14**). The rule in *Ladd v Marshall* applied to appeals from trials and final determinations, and reflected the policy of requiring parties to advance their entire case at trial, and not deliberately leaving over points for the purpose of appeals (and thereby obtaining a 'second bite at the cherry'). With the introduction of the CPR, the discretion to admit fresh evidence on an appeal has to be exercised in accordance with the overriding objective (*Evans v Tiger Investments Ltd* [2002] EWCA Civ 161, [2002] 2 BCLC 185). However, the *Ladd v Marshall* principles remain relevant as matters which must necessarily be considered, although not as strict rules (*Banks v Cox* (2000) LTL 17/7/2000). Strong grounds have to be shown before fresh evidence will be admitted, and the *Ladd v Marshall* principles will be looked at with considerable care (*Hertfordshire Investments Ltd v Bubb* [2000] 1 WLR 2318). The Court of Appeal has to be particularly cautious where the appellant seeks to put further questions to witnesses (whether lay or expert) where the witness has been cross-examined at trial (*Riyad Bank SAL v Ahli United Bank (UK) plc* [2005] EWCA Civ 1419, *The Times*, 16 December 2005). It will be a rare case where the *Ladd v Marshall* conditions are not satisfied but the court nevertheless admits fresh evidence on an appeal (*Shaker v Al-Bedrawi* [2002] EWCA Civ 1452, [2003] 1 BCLC 157 at [88]).

Applications for permission to adduce fresh evidence can be made to the master of the Court of Appeal, but they are often directed to be listed for hearing at the same time as the appeal (Practice Direction (Court of Appeal: Procedure) [1995] 1 WLR 1191). A separate bundle should be prepared for the further evidence application, so that it can be kept separate from the main appeal bundles.

Ladd v Marshall principles

Under *Ladd v Marshall* [1954] 1 WLR 1489 fresh evidence would be allowed on an appeal only if the evidence: **72.14**

(a) could not have been obtained with reasonable diligence for use at the hearing in the lower court;
(b) would probably have an important influence on the result; and
(c) was apparently credible.

In considering whether evidence could have been obtained with reasonable diligence, no distinction is to be made between the knowledge of the lay client and that of the solicitor (*Evans v Tiger Investments Ltd* [2002] EWCA Civ 161, [2002] 2 BCLC 185). The *Ladd v Marshall* test will rarely be satisfied where the fresh evidence goes merely to credit (*Hamilton v Al Fayed (No. 1)* [2001] EMLR 394). Where the new evidence is credible and there has been a clear attempt to deceive the court, the requirements of justice would point strongly towards admitting the evidence (*Daly v Sheikh* [2002] EWCA Civ 1630, LTL 24/ 10/2002). Evidence obtained after trial in *Arundel Corporation v Khokher* [2003] EWCA Civ 491, LTL 9/4/2003, from the respondent's solicitor's former employees contradicted evidence given at trial by the respondent and his solicitor. Permission to adduce the evidence was granted, because the evidence was credible and raised a prima facie case that the finding at trial should be reversed. There may be other reasons for refusing permission to adduce new evidence. In *Sadrolashrafi v Marvel International Food Logistics Ltd* [2004] EWHC 777 (Ch), LTL 15/4/2004, permission was refused because the new evidence was entirely contrary to the evidence given by the appellant at the hearing below and which the appellant knew was untrue. Evidence produced at a very late stage (Thursday for an appeal heard the following Monday) was disallowed in *Rakusens Ltd v Baser Ambalaj Plastik Sanayi Ticaret AS* [2001] EWCA Civ 1820, [2002] 1 BCLC 104, on the ground that it was completely unreasonable to expect the other side to deal with the evidence on such short notice.

Judgment obtained by fraud

Where the judge has been wilfully deceived by fraudulent evidence, justice requires a retrial (*Prentice v Hereward Housing Association* [2001] 2 All ER (Comm) 900). Likewise where there is a risk that a fraud has been perpetrated on the court below (*Couwenbergh v Valkova* [2004] EWCA Civ 676, LTL 27/5/2004). Where a House of Lords decision is alleged to have been obtained by fraud, the most appropriate course is to commence fresh proceedings based on that fraud, **72.15** rather than seeking to reverse the original decision by applying back to the House of Lords (*Kuwait Airways Corporation v Iraqi Airways Co.* [2001] 1 WLR 429).

GENERAL POWERS VESTED IN THE APPEAL COURT

72.16 By CPR, r. 52.10(1), in relation to an appeal the appeal court has all the powers of the lower court. In particular, by r. 52.10(2), the appeal court has power to do any of the following things:

(a) Affirm, set aside or vary any order or judgment made or given by the lower court. The power to vary does not extend to making a different type of order from the order the court below had been asked to make (*King v Telegraph Group Ltd* [2004] EWCA Civ 613, [2005] 1 WLR 2282).
(b) Refer any claim or issue for determination by the lower court.
(c) Order a new trial or hearing, which is a last resort (*White v White* [2001] EWCA Civ 955, LTL 21/6/2001). If an appeal court orders a rehearing, it should make it clear on the face of its order whether the rehearing should be at appeal court level, or whether the case should be remitted back to the lower court for the rehearing (*Fowler de Pledge v Smith* [2003] EWCA Civ 703, *The Times*, 27 May 2003).
(d) Make orders for the payment of interest.
(e) Make a costs order.

By r. 52.10(3), in an appeal from a claim tried with a jury, the Court of Appeal may, instead of ordering a new trial, make an order for damages or the award made by the jury. If the appeal court refuses permission to appeal, strikes out an appellant's notice, or dismisses an appeal, and it considers the matter was totally without merit, that fact must be recorded in the court's order, and the court must consider whether to make a civil restraint order (r. 52.10(5); see 14.70).

HANDED-DOWN JUDGMENTS

72.17 Below the Court of Appeal, it is usual for the court to give judgment immediately after the arguments, although occasionally judgment will be reserved. This is rather more common in the Court of Appeal. In the Court of Appeal, if the presiding Lord Justice is satisfied there is no special degree of confidentiality or sensitivity, a copy of the written judgment will be made available to the legal representatives of the parties by 4 p.m. on the second working day before the judgment is due to be pronounced (**PD 52, paras 15.12 and 15.13**, which largely duplicate **PD 40E**, described at **61.28**). This can be shown, in confidence and on the strict condition that it or its effect is not to be disclosed to any other person, to the parties, but only for the purpose of obtaining instructions. Any proposed corrections to the draft judgment must be sent to the clerk to the judge who prepared the draft and to the other parties (**para. 15.18**). This provision is primarily aimed at typing errors, incorrect references and other similar minor corrections (*Perotti v Collyer-Bristow (No. 2)* [2004] EWCA Civ 1019, [2004] 4 All ER 72, at [3], where Brooke LJ said it is not to be used for renewed submissions on the merits). Counsel should only rarely seek to reopen the contentious arguments after receiving the draft judgment (*Gravgaard v Aldridge and Brownlee* (2004) *The Times*, 2 December 2004). As May LJ said in *Robinson v Fernsby* [2003] EWCA Civ 1820, *The Times*, 20 January 2004, at [94]:

> Once a judgment has been handed down or given, there are obvious reasons why the court should hesitate long and hard before making a material alteration to it. . . . there may very occasionally be circumstances in which a judge not only can, but should make a material alteration in the interests of justice. . . . Any attempt to do this is likely to receive summary rejection in most cases.

One of the main reasons for releasing judgments early is to enable counsel to consider and seek to agree with the other side any consequential orders. Where agreement is reached, the parties must fax a copy to the clerk to the presiding Lord Justice and file four copies at the Civil Appeals Office no later than 12 noon on the working day before the judgment is handed down (**para. 15.16**). Where all consequential orders are agreed, advocates need not attend the hearing, and costs are likely to be disallowed if they do (**para. 15.15**). If the parties are not going to attend, the judgment may be handed down by a single member of the court.

COSTS

Under **CPR, r. 52.10(2)(e)**, the appeal court has power to make costs orders in relation to the appeal hearing and for the proceedings in the lower court. **72.18**

Costs of appeals are likely to be summarily assessed (see **PD 52, para. 14.1**) at the following types of hearings:

(a) contested directions hearings;
(b) applications for permission to appeal at which the respondent is present;
(c) dismissal list hearings in the Court of Appeal at which the respondent is present;
(d) appeals from case management decisions; and
(e) appeals listed for one day or less.

Chapter 73 Appeals to the House of Lords

INTRODUCTION

73.1 As the highest appellate court in England and Wales, the House of Lords determines most of the important cases of the day. However, its workload is considerably lower than that of the Court of Appeal, and very few cases are taken as far as the House of Lords. The judicial work of the House of Lords is carried out by 12 Lords of Appeal in Ordinary (law lords) usually sitting as a committee (an appellate committee) of five (occasionally seven or nine). Other members of the House of Lords who hold or have held high judicial office may also take part in its judicial work (Appellate Jurisdiction Act 1876, ss. 5 and 6). From 3 April 2006 the Lord Chancellor ceases to have a judicial role.

The traditional route is for cases to be appealed from courts of first instance to the Court of Appeal and then on to the House of Lords. An alternative 'leapfrog' procedure is available for some High Court cases direct to the House of Lords where the judge at first instance was bound by a previous decision of the Court of Appeal.

SUPREME COURT

73.2 By the Constitutional Reform Act 2005, ss. 23 to 60, a newly constituted Supreme Court of the United Kingdom will replace the House of Lords as the highest court in the land. It is expected that this will come into being in October 2008. The new Supreme Court will have a President, Deputy President, and 10 Justices of the Supreme Court. Appeals from the Court of Appeal will only be available with permission from the Court of Appeal or the Supreme Court (s. 40(6)). It will sit with an uneven number of judges, being at least three in number with a majority being permanent justices (s. 42(1)). Its procedure will be governed by Supreme Court Rules to be made under s. 45.

The existing Supreme Court of England and Wales (High Court, Court of Appeal and Crown Court) will be renamed the 'Senior Courts of England and Wales' (s. 59(1)).

LEAPFROG APPEALS

73.3 Very exceptionally, a direct appeal from the decision of a High Court judge to the House of Lords is possible under the **Administration of Justice Act 1969, ss. 12** to **15**. There are five conditions:

(a) the appeal must involve a point of law of general public importance;
(b) the point of law must either relate to the construction of an Act of Parliament or statutory instrument, or else be a point on which the judge at first instance is bound by a decision of the Court of Appeal or of the House of Lords;
(c) all parties must consent;
(d) the trial judge must certify, either immediately at the end of the trial or within the next 14 days, that the case is a suitable one for a direct appeal to the House of Lords;

(e) the House of Lords must grant permission to bring the appeal direct on an application made by any of the parties within one month of the date of the judge's certificate.

Where a judge issues a certificate for a leapfrog appeal to the House of Lords on two issues, with permission to appeal to the Court of Appeal if the House of Lords refuses leave, and the House of Lords grants leave on only one of the issues, the appellant can appeal on the second issue to the Court of Appeal. See *R (Jones) v Ceredigion County Council* [2005] EWCA Civ 986, [2005] 1 WLR 3626.

APPEALS FROM THE COURT OF APPEAL

An appeal from the Court of Appeal generally lies to the House of Lords. Permission must be obtained either from the Court of Appeal or from the House of Lords (Administration of Justice (Appeals) Act 1934, s. 1). The procedure governing appeals to the House of Lords is largely contained in the **House of Lords Practice Directions and Standing Orders Applicable to Civil Appeals** (the current edition is dated January 2006), referred to in this chapter as 'Dir. [para. number]'. **73.4**

The House of Lords has jurisdiction to hear an appeal from the Court of Appeal where the High Court has refused permission to apply for judicial review because of delay, and the Court of Appeal has granted permission to appeal, but dismissed the appeal (*R (Burkett) v Hammersmith and Fulham London Borough Council* [2002] UKHL 23, [2002] 1 WLR 1593).

Permission to appeal

The initial application for permission to appeal should be made to the Court of Appeal immediately after judgment has been pronounced. The Court of Appeal can deal with an application for permission to appeal by written submissions (**PD 52, para. 15.19**). The parties will usually receive the Court of Appeal judgment in draft two working days in advance (**para. 15.13**). A party seeking to appeal must fax a copy of the written submissions to the clerk to the presiding Lord Justice and file four copies at the Civil Appeals Office no later than 12 noon on the working day before the judgment is handed down (**para. 15.20**). If permission is refused by the Court of Appeal, a petition for leave to appeal may be presented to the House of Lords (Dir. 1.6). A petition for leave to appeal must be lodged in the Judicial Office together with the order being appealed and the order of the Court of Appeal refusing permission (if separate) within one month of the order under appeal (Dirs 2.1 and 3.13). The petition should contain a brief statement of the facts and the points of law involved in the appeal, and a summary of the reasons why permission to appeal should be granted (Dir. 3.1). **73.5**

An appeal committee will consider the papers, and will refuse permission if the petition does not 'raise an arguable point of law of general public importance which ought to be considered by the House at this time, bearing in mind that the matter will already have been the subject of judicial decision and reviewed on appeal' (Dir. 4.7). The need to establish that the point raised by the appeal is one of general public importance is necessary because the House of Lords acts as a supreme court and concentrates its attention on a relatively small number of cases. Its role is not one of correcting errors in the application of settled law, even where errors are shown to exist (*R v Secretary of State for Trade and Industry, ex parte Eastaway* [2000] 1 WLR 2222). There are relatively few appeals 'which ought to be considered by the House'.

A lower court considering whether to give permission to appeal should apply the same criteria as those applied by the House of Lords (*Henry Boot Construction Ltd v Alstom Combined Cycles Ltd* [2005] EWCA Civ 814, [2005] 1 WLR 3850, at [84]).

Permission is also required for the presentation of a cross-appeal by a respondent (Dir. 1.18 and 30.1). A petition for leave to cross-appeal may only be lodged after leave to appeal has been granted to the original petitioner for leave to appeal (Dir. 30.3).

Substantive petition

73.6 If permission is granted, the substantive petition of appeal must be lodged in the Judicial Office within three months of the order being appealed from (Dir. 7.1). The petition must be served on the respondents before being lodged at the Judicial Office, and a signed certificate of service must be endorsed on the back of the original petition (Dir. 9.12). Security for costs in the sum of £25,000 must be paid into the House of Lords Security Fund Account by the appellant within one week of the presentation of an appeal, unless security is waived or unnecessary. Security is unnecessary if the appellant has been granted public funding; is appealing under the Child Abduction and Custody Act 1985; is a cross-appellant; or is a minister or government department. If security is not provided, the appeal will be dismissed (Dirs 10.1 to 10.6).

Further documents

73.7 Three particular forms of document must be prepared:

(a) A statement of the facts and issues involved in the appeal. The front page of this document should indicate the time occupied by the case in the courts below, refer to all law reports of the decisions below and give a headnote summary of the case. The document should be prepared by the appellant, and if possible should be agreed and signed by counsel for both parties (Dirs 11.1 and 11.2).

(b) An appendix containing any documents which are necessary to support and understand the argument when the appeal is heard. Only documents used in the courts below can be included. All documents must be numbered and indexed, and bound with a plastic comb binding with blue covers to indicate a civil appeal. The appendix may be in more than one part where the documents are too numerous for a single binder. The documents in part I must include the originating process; the judgments of the decisions at first instance and on appeal (in the form of an unbound part of the *Law Reports* or, if unreported, a transcript); the relevant statutory provisions; and crucial documents upon which the action is founded (Dirs 12.1 to 12.10).

(c) The appellant's and respondent's cases. A case is the statement of the party's argument, confined to the heads of argument which counsel propose to submit at the hearing (Dirs 15.1 and 15.2). It must conclude with a numbered summary of the reasons upon which the argument is founded, and must be signed by counsel (Dir. 15.7). Its purpose is to enable counsel to concentrate their argument on the real issues in the appeal (*M. V. Yorke Motors v Edwards* [1982] 1 WLR 444). Unreported cases should be cited only if they are binding on the Court of Appeal and if the substance of the decision is not to be found in any fully reported case (*Roberts Petroleum Ltd v Bernard Kenny Ltd* [1983] 2 AC 192). Any intention to invite the House of Lords to depart from one of its own earlier decisions must be clearly stated in a separate paragraph in the case (Dir. 15.5).

Steps after presentation of the appeal

73.8 Within six weeks of presentation, the appellant must lodge the statement and appendix and set the appeal down for hearing (Dirs 13.1 and 14.1). Cases must be lodged by appellants no later than five weeks before the proposed date of the hearing (Dir. 15.3) and by respondents no later than three weeks before the proposed date of the hearing (Dir. 15.14). At least two weeks before the hearing the appellant must lodge 15 bound volumes (Dir. 16.1) containing:

(a) the petition and any cross-petition;
(b) the statement of facts and issues;
(c) Part I of the appendix;
(d) the appellant's and respondent's cases;
(e) case of the advocate to the court or intervener; and
(f) index to the authorities volume(s).

Also at least two weeks before the hearing, 10 comb-bound volumes containing copies of the authorities on which counsel will rely must be delivered to the Judicial Office (Dirs 17.1 to 17.8).

Parties who have lodged cases are entitled to be heard by two counsel, one of whom may be leading counsel (Dir. 15.8). If counsel wish to seek an order other than that the costs be awarded to the successful party, submissions to that effect should be made at the hearing immediately after the conclusion of the argument (Dir. 19.1). Judgment is invariably reserved, and normally only one junior counsel for each party is expected to attend (Dirs 20.1 and 20.2). Judgment is delivered in the Chamber of the House. The final order is sent to the successful party, with prints of the order being sent to the unsuccessful parties (Dirs 21.2 and 21.3).

Chapter 74 Judicial Review

The following procedural checklist, which is in **appendix 1**, is relevant to this chapter:

Procedural checklist 36 Claim for judicial review

INTRODUCTION

74.1 Judicial review is the means by which the courts control administrative action by public bodies (including inferior courts and tribunals). It is a supervisory jurisdiction which reviews administrative action rather than being an appellate jurisdiction.

The principal rules of court governing claims for judicial review are in **CPR, Part 54**, supplemented by **PD 54**. **Rule 54.1(2)(a)** defines a claim for judicial review as:

a claim to review the lawfulness of—

(i) an enactment; or

(ii) a decision, action or failure to act in relation to the exercise of a public function.

Although other remedies may be asked for, the characteristic remedies in judicial review claims are the prerogative mandatory, prohibiting and quashing orders (see **74.48** to **74.55**), which county courts do not have power to grant (**County Courts Act 1984, s. 38(3)(a)**). Judicial review claims are assigned to the Queen's Bench Division in the High Court by the **Supreme Court Act 1981, sch. 1, para. 2(b)**, and are dealt with in the Administrative Court.

BODIES OPEN TO JUDICIAL REVIEW

There are two conditions necessary to determine whether a decision by a body is judicially reviewable: **74.2**

(a) the decision or action must be made by a public body; and
(b) the public body must make a public law decision or take a public law action.

Any body performing public law duties or powers is susceptible to judicial review. Historically, the most important factor considered by the courts in identifying activities subject to judicial review was the source of the power being exercised by the decision-maker whose decision was sought to be challenged. However, the courts have recognised that such an approach is too restrictive and they are now influenced by the type of function performed by the decision-maker (*R v Panel on Take-overs and Mergers, ex parte Datafin plc* [1987] QB 815).

The essential elements which comprise a public law body are (1) a 'public element' (which can take many different forms); and (2) the exclusion of bodies whose sole source of power is consensual submission to their jurisdiction (per Sir John Donaldson MR in *R v Panel on Take-overs and Mergers, ex parte Datafin plc*). Thus, the test of what is a public body is not solely an examination of the source of the regulator's power but also a consideration of the regulator's functions.

Central government and statutory bodies

Central government and bodies which derive authority from statute are susceptible to judicial review. Central government's powers derive from the prerogative (as to which see below) or statute. The range of statutory bodies which have been held to be reviewable also includes inferior courts, local authorities, tribunals and inquiries and regulators with a statutory basis. Ministers acting on behalf of the Crown are also subject to judicial review (*Re M* [1994] 1 AC 377). The Parliamentary Commissioner for Standards has been held not to be reviewable because he or she is one of the means by which the Select Committee on Standards and Privileges carries out its functions, and those functions form part of the proceedings of Parliament (*R v Parliamentary Commissioner for Standards, ex parte Al Fayed* [1998] 1 WLR 669) and the courts will not intervene in the affairs of Parliament. **74.3**

Other courts and tribunals susceptible to judicial review include magistrates' courts, coroners' courts, local election courts (*R v Cripps, ex parte Muldoon* [1984] QB 68 (DC); [1984] QB 686 (CA)), patents appeal tribunals (*Baldwin and Francis Ltd v Patents Appeal Tribunal* [1959] AC 663), county courts (save where they perform the functions of a superior court) and statutory tribunals in certain circumstances (where a High Court judge does not sit, and dependent upon their powers and relationship with the High Court according to its enabling statute) (see *R v Cripps, ex parte Muldoon*). Judicial review does not lie against the High Court or the Court of Appeal, but only against the decisions of inferior courts. Hence the High Court did have jurisdiction to judicially review the decision of a county court refusing permission to appeal (*R (Sivasubramaniam) v Wandsworth County Court* [2002] EWCA Civ 1738, [2003] 1 WLR 475). However, where the applicant had sought judicial review of the original decision, and had not sought permission to appeal it, judicial review was not available since the proper remedy was to seek permission to appeal the decision of the county court in the first instance. It would only be in rare cases that judicial review would be permitted against the decision of a county court to refuse permission to appeal (*Sivasubramaniam*).

Section 29(3) of the Supreme Court Act 1981 enables the High Court to make prerogative orders against the Crown Court to the same extent as it may against an inferior court other than in relation to the Crown Court's jurisdiction in trial on indictment matters.

Nationalised industries are also subject to judicial review. For example, the British Coal Corporation has been held to be reviewable in respect of its decision to close coal pits (*R v British Coal Corporation, ex parte Vardy* [1993] ICR 720).

A person or body exercising prerogative powers (i.e., non-statutory acts of executive government) may be amenable to judicial review (*R v Criminal Injuries Compensation Board, ex parte Lain* [1967] 2 QB 864). In *Council of Civil Service Unions v Minister for the Civil Service* [1985] AC 374 the House of Lords held that prerogative powers were reviewable, but Lord Roskill listed six examples of prerogative powers which he thought would not be reviewable, i.e., treaty making, defence of the realm, prerogative of mercy, grant of honours, dissolution of Parliament and the appointment of ministers. The prerogative of mercy has subsequently been held to be judicially reviewable (*R v Secretary of State for the Home Department, ex parte Bentley* [1994] QB 349).

The High Court has reviewed the exercise of prerogative powers by the Crown in certain instances, including a decision of the Foreign Secretary to refuse to issue an applicant with a passport (*R v Secretary of State for Foreign and Commonwealth Affairs, ex parte Everett* [1989] QB 811) and the residual power of the Home Secretary to depart from immigration rules (*R v Secretary of State for the Home Department, ex parte Beedassee* [1989] COD 525).

It is possible for a statute to confer on a private body public functions and therefore, at least in relation to the performance of those functions, a body could be subject to judicial review. Therefore professional bodies incorporated by royal charter or under the Companies Act 1985 may have statutory powers and duties conferred upon them.

Non-statutory bodies

74.4 Non-statutory bodies which carry out public law functions will also be susceptible to judicial review. Bodies concerned with the regulation of commercial and professional activities to ensure compliance with proper standards, e.g., the Law Society and the Institute of Chartered Accountants, may be susceptible to judicial review whether or not their powers derive from statute or royal charter. Other self-regulating organisations and other private institutions may also perform some types of public function.

The Panel on Takeovers and Mergers was held in *R v Panel on Take-overs and Mergers, ex parte Datafin plc* [1987] QB 815 to be judicially reviewable despite the fact that it had no direct statutory authority. The Court of Appeal was influenced by the fact that the Panel 'oversees and regulates a very important part of the United Kingdom financial market' without any legal support. It considered that if the body in question exercised public law functions or the exercise of its functions had public law consequences, this would be sufficient to make it reviewable. The Panel clearly exercised public functions.

Following *R v Panel on Take-overs and Mergers, ex parte Datafin plc* the Advertising Standards Authority was found to be a public body upon the basis that, in the absence of a self-regulatory body such as the Authority, its function would be exercised by the Director General of Fair Trading (*R v Advertising Standards Authority, ex parte Insurance Service plc* (1990) 2 Admin LR 77). Similarly, although financial services self-regulating organisations lack statutory underpinning (but were contemplated by the Financial Services Act 1986), they have been found to be reviewable (*R v Life Assurance Unit Trust Regulatory Organisation Ltd, ex parte Ross* [1993] QB 17), as has the London Metal Exchange, which is a recognised investment exchange (*R v London Metal Exchange, ex parte Albatros Warehousing BV* (2000) LTL 31/3/2000).

However, the decisions of bodies set up by self-regulating organisations pursuant to regulatory powers are not also automatically reviewable. The Insurance Ombudsman Bureau (a body recognised by LAUTRO as performing a complaints investigation function for the purposes of the Financial Services Act 1986 and with voluntary membership) has been held to possess power over its members which was solely derived from contract and was not therefore regarded as a public body (*R v Insurance Ombudsman Bureau, ex parte Aegon Life Assurance Ltd* [1994] COD 426).

The Court of Appeal has held it arguable that the Press Complaints Commission is a body subject to judicial review (*R v Press Complaints Commission, ex parte Stewart-Brady* (1997) 9 Admin LR 274).

Bodies exercising monopolistic powers may be reviewable. Reviewability was accepted by the Privy Council in the case of a bulk electricity supplier in New Zealand (*Mercury Energy Ltd v Electricity Corporation of New Zealand Ltd* [1994] 1 WLR 521).

However, *R v Panel on Take-overs and Mergers, ex parte Datafin plc* has been interpreted narrowly in some subsequent cases. In *R v Chief Rabbi, ex parte Wachmann* [1992] 1 WLR 1036, Simon Brown J stated that, '[t]o attract the court's supervisory jurisdiction there must be not merely a public but potentially a governmental interest in the decision making power in question'. Subsequently, in *R v Disciplinary Committee of the Jockey Club, ex parte Aga Khan* [1993] 1 WLR 909 the Court of Appeal also took a slightly different approach and required the existence of governmental and not simply 'public' functions and possibly actual (as opposed to potential) governmental intervention. Therefore the Jockey Club was held to fall outside the scope of the court's supervisory jurisdiction because it did not form part of a system of governmental control. The court was also influenced by the fact that the Club's source of power was contractual and that a private law remedy was available to the applicant (see 74.5; see also *R (Mullins) v Appeal Board of the Jockey Club* [2005] EWHC 2197 (Admin), *The Times*, 24 October 2005).

In some instances both public law and private law rights may be protected. For example, the Court of Appeal has accepted that for certain functions the Institute of Chartered Accountants is a public body and that its members might also have contractual rights against it (*Andreou v Institute of Chartered Accountants in England and Wales* [1998] 1 All ER 14).

Sports bodies not backed by statute are generally outside the scope of judicial review, e.g. the Court of Appeal dismissed an application for judicial review of the Jockey Club because of the contractual source of the Club's power over the applicant but held that it was therefore unnecessary to decide whether decisions of the Club could ever be reviewable (*R v Disciplinary Committee of the Jockey Club, ex parte Aga Khan* and see also *R v Football Association Ltd, ex parte Football League Ltd* [1993] 2 All ER 833).

Decisions of leaders of particular faiths on disciplinary issues have consistently been held not to be judicially reviewable (*R v Chief Rabbi, ex parte Wachmann*; *R v Imam of Bury Park Jame Masjid Luton, ex parte Sulaiman Ali* [1994] COD 142; *R v London Beth Din, ex parte Bloom* [1998] COD 131; *R v Provincial Court of the Church in Wales, ex parte Williams* [1999] COD 163). However, the consistory courts of the Church of England have been deemed to be within the jurisdiction of the High Court because of their regulation by measures which have the effect of Acts of Parliament and therefore form part of the fabric of the state (*R v Chancellor of the Chichester Consistory Court, ex parte News Group Newspapers* [1992] COD 48). The position with the Provincial Court of the Church of Wales was held to be different in that, following its disestablishment under the Welsh Church Act 1914, its legal authority arises solely from consensual submission to its jurisdiction and it is therefore analogous to other religious bodies not established as part of the State (*R v Provincial Court of the Church in Wales, ex parte Williams*).

Lloyd's, which has powers derived from a private Act (initially the Lloyd's Act 1871) and which does not extend to any persons other than those who wish to operate in the section of the market governed by Lloyd's and who have to commit themselves by entering into Lloyd's uniform contract, has been held not to be a public body for the purposes of judicial review (*R v Lloyd's of London, ex parte Johnson* (16 August 1996 unreported)). However, certain of Lloyd's functions have been held to be public law functions and amenable to judicial review, although relations between Lloyd's and its names not involving the exercise of regulatory or disciplinary functions are governed by private law (*Doll-Steinberg v Society of Lloyd's* [2002] EWCA Civ 996). Bodies will not be reviewable where their source of authority is contractual or consensual, or if they do not exercise governmental powers (e.g., *R v Association of British Travel Agents, ex parte Sunspell Ltd* [2001] ACD 16) and this can be the case even though in relation to a particular industry or activity the person concerned effectively has no choice other than to sign up to a contract to be bound by a body's rules or regulations, e.g., *R v Panel of the Federation of Communication Services Ltd, ex parte Kubis* (1999) 11 Admin LR 43 concerning dealers in the mobile telephone industry.

The university visitor, whose authority is based upon common law, is subject only to limited review. The House of Lords has held that the jurisdiction of a university visitor is reviewable only in circumstances where the university visitor acts outside his or her jurisdiction or if the university visitor abuses his or her power in a manner wholly incompatible with his or her judicial role or in breach of the rules of natural justice (*Page v Hull University Visitor* [1993] AC 682). Therefore only certain of the visitor's decisions are reviewable on the basis that he or she is in a unique position where it is highly desirable that there should be finality of decisions. This decision has been followed upon the same limited basis (*R v Visitors to the Inns of Court, ex parte Calder* [1994] QB 1). (See also *R (Varma) v Visitor to Cranfield University* [2004] EWHC 1705 (Admin), [2004] ELR 616.)

Decisions concerning pupils made by a non-maintained school for children with special educational needs were not amenable to judicial review even though the school received most of its funding from a local education authority (*R v Muntham House School, ex parte R* [2000] LGR 255).

On the other hand, a decision by managers of a private psychiatric hospital to change the focus of one of its wards is an act of a public nature susceptible to judicial review (*R (A) v Partnerships in Care Ltd* [2002] EWHC 529 (Admin), [2002] 1 WLR 2610).

A defendant private limited company, set up by a local authority to manage local farmers' markets, and having as directors stallholders of those markets, was a public body amenable to judicial review. The defendant owed its existence to the authority, which had set it up using its statutory powers, the defendant had effectively stepped into the authority's shoes and the authority had assisted the defendant in many respects (*R (Beer) v Hampshire Farmers Market Ltd* [2003] EWCA Civ 1056, [2004] 1 WLR 233).

DECISIONS OPEN TO JUDICIAL REVIEW

74.5 Only decisions or actions which are made in a public law context are subject to judicial review. Even if a body may in some circumstances be susceptible to judicial review, not every decision will be reviewable. There must be a decision with a public law element sufficient to justify judicial review (*R v British Broadcasting Corporation, ex parte Lavelle* [1983] 1 WLR 23). Subordinate legislation which has been debated in and approved by affirmative resolution of both Houses of Parliament is susceptible to judicial review (*R (Asif Javed) v Secretary of State for the Home Department* [2001] EWCA Civ 789, [2002] QB 129).

However, even where there is a private law cause of action, judicial review may still be appropriate where there is a sufficiently public issue. For example, judicial review was appropriate where the question was whether the Secretary of State had exceeded his powers in granting consent to a market authority to grant leases (*City of London Corporation v Secretary of State for Environment, Food and Rural Affairs* [2004] EWCA Civ 1765, *The Times*, 27 December 2004).

The existence of a contractual relationship or a decision based upon the consent of the parties will always make it difficult to establish that the decision is amenable to judicial review (*R v Criminal Injuries Compensation Board, ex parte Lain* [1967] 2 QB 864; *R v National Joint Council for the Craft of Dental Technicians (Dispute Committee), ex parte Neate* [1953] 1 QB 704).

Thus ordinary employment cases are generally deemed to be governed by private law. Clearly cases relating purely to the construction of contractual terms and conditions of employment are not reviewable (*McClaren v Home Office* [1990] ICR 808). A disciplinary tribunal set up by the BBC in relation to the dismissal of an employee depended solely upon the contract of employment between the applicant and the BBC and was therefore a procedure of a merely private or domestic character and so not judicially reviewable (*R v British Broadcasting Corporation, ex parte Lavelle* [1983] 1 WLR 23). The terms of a senior nursing officer's employment have been regarded as a matter of private law notwithstanding that they incorporated the NHS Whitley Council agreement on conditions of service, a form of statutory negotiation between employers' and employees' representatives (*R v East Berkshire Health Authority, ex parte Walsh* [1985] QB 152). (See also *R (Tucker) v Director-General of the National Crime Squad* [2003] EWCA Civ 2, [2003] ICR 599; *Skidmore v Dartford and Gravesham NHS Trust* [2003] UKHL 27, [2003] ICR 721.)

However, public law issues may arise where an employer exercises a power which is not wholly contract-based. A decision to suspend an applicant in breach of a code of discipline which had statutory force was reviewable (*R v Secretary of State for the Home Department, ex parte Attard* (1990) 2 Admin LR 641). The employment conditions of police constables are underpinned by statute and accordingly reviewable (*Chief Constable of North Wales Police v Evans* [1982] 1 WLR 1155). A decision is reviewable if it involves a constitutional or public law principle such as the appointment of Crown prosecutors (*R v Crown Prosecution Service, ex parte Hogg* (1994) 6 Admin LR 778). Public law issues arise where the question is whether the public body had authority to enter into the contract, but not where the only issue is whether or not there is a breach by a public authority of its own internal procedures or standing orders (as was the case in *R v Lambeth London Borough Council, ex parte Thompson* [1996] COD 217). The Court of Appeal has left open the question whether a decision of the Civil Service Board that an applicant had not been unfairly dismissed from his position as a civil servant was reviewable on the basis that he had no contract of employment and there was a sufficient public law element involved (*R v Civil Service Appeal Board, ex parte Bruce* [1989] 2 All ER 907).

A body exercising a public function which makes a promise that it would behave in a certain way in the future is making a representation which has the character of a contract, but a breach of that promise may still be amenable to judicial review if the breach amounts to an abuse of power (*R v North and East Devon Health Authority, ex parte Coughlan* [2001] QB 213).

A number of cases establish that public procurement procedures by public authorities can be the subject of judicial review proceedings, e.g., where a local authority boycotted products in order to pressurise companies to withdraw their interests in South Africa (*R v Lewisham London Borough Council, ex parte Shell UK Ltd* [1988] 1 All ER 938; and note *R v Derbyshire County Council, ex parte The Times Supplements Ltd* (1991) 3 Admin LR 241). A more restrictive approach was adopted in relation to tendering for shorthand writers' contracts (*R v Lord Chancellor's Department, ex parte Hibbit and Saunders* [1993] COD 326) and concerning tenders under part II of the Environmental Protection Act 1990 (*Mass Energy Ltd v Birmingham City Council* [1994] Env LR 298).

However, in *R v Legal Aid Board, ex parte Donn and Co.* [1996] 3 All ER 1 the court held that the decision of a Legal Aid Committee, in awarding a contract to solicitors for the conduct of a multi-party action, was justiciable in public law, first, because the nature and purpose of the selection process and its consequences were one indivisible whole and, secondly, in view of the function exercised by the Committee, the purpose for which the Committee was empowered to act, and the consequences of the decision-making process.

The current position in respect of the availability of judicial review in the public procurement context appears to be as follows. First, if it is shown that the tendering process is subject to mandatory statutory provisions, judicial review will be available. Secondly, in order to establish whether the process is subject to statutory requirements, one must look at the wording, scheme and purpose of the relevant statute. Thirdly, in order to allege breach of the principles of natural justice in the tendering process, a claimant must be able to spell out the procedural requirements from the statute by express wording or necessary implication. Finally, even where the tendering process is not carried out pursuant to mandatory statutory provisions, it may still be reviewable provided there is some sufficient public law element to the decision (see *R v Bridgend County Borough Council, ex parte Jones* [2000] 2 LGLR 361 and *Cookson and Clegg Ltd v Ministry of Defence* [2005] EWCA Civ 811, LTL 10/6/2005).

Where the invalidity of a decision arises as a collateral issue in a claim for infringement of a private law right of the claimant, the issue should be resolved as a private law matter (per Lord Diplock in *O'Reilly v Mackman* [1983] 2 AC 237). Consequently, an action for damages against a local planning authority for negligence comprises a private law action (*Davy v Spelthorne Borough Council* [1984] AC 262); a reduction in a general practitioner's practice allowance by a family practitioner committee was a private law issue (*Roy v Kensington and Chelsea and Westminster Family Practitioner Committee* [1992] 1 AC 624); a claim in respect of inordinate delay in paying compensation for handguns surrendered under the Firearms (Amendment) Act 1997 was a private law matter (*Steed v Secretary of State for the Home Department* [2000] 1 WLR 1169); but an action against a local authority in respect of an alleged breach of its duties under the Housing (Homeless Persons) Act 1977 was a public law matter which should have proceeded by way of judicial review (*Cocks v Thanet District Council* [1983] 2 AC 286); a defendant was unable to challenge the validity of an enforcement notice under s. 87 of the Town and Country Planning Act 1971 on the basis that such matters should have been raised by way of judicial review and were not suitable for decision by a criminal court (*R v Wicks* [1998] AC 92); but, subject to clear Parliamentary intention to the contrary, the legality of a decision made pursuant to a by-law could be raised as a defence to a criminal charge (*Boddington v British Transport Police* [1999] 2 AC 143); and an ordinary action was held to be the more appropriate procedure to deal with an action against a local authority to recover sums due under improvement grants (*Trustees of the Dennis Rye Pension Fund v Sheffield City Council* [1998] 1 WLR 840).

Although the courts will not strike out a private law claim simply on the grounds that it would have been more appropriate to use judicial review, they will do so if it amounts to an abuse of process. In deciding whether using a private law claim for a public law issue amounts to an abuse of process the court will consider whether the private law route has been used to take advantage of the longer limitation period, or whether other judicial review rules have been flouted (*Clark v University of Lincolnshire and Humberside* [2000] 1 WLR 1988). It has been held that where a litigant has a claim which could be brought either by judicial review or by an ordinary action the choice of either might amount to an abuse of process. The exercise of the jurisdiction to strike out the claim on this ground would depend on a consideration of all the relevant circumstances, including any matters occurring before the proceedings were instituted and which remedy would be more appropriate (*Phonographic Performance Ltd v Department of Trade and Industry* [2004] EWHC 1795 (Ch), [2004] 1 WLR 2893).

The practical consequences of the choice made between public and private law should be considered rather than merely technical questions concerning the distinction between public and private rights (*Trustees of the Dennis Rye Pension Fund v Sheffield City Council*). A similar approach has been taken where the factual circumstances of cases are such that they may fall into both public law and private law (*Andreou v Institute of Chartered Accountants in England and Wales* [1998] 1 All ER 14 — a finding of the Disciplinary Committee of the Institute of Chartered Accountants).

Decisions taken by the Human Fertilisation and Embryology Authority are open to challenge by way of judicial review only where the Authority exceeds or abuses its powers or responsibilities or if its decision is irrational, on the basis that it is not the function of the court to enter into scientific debate or to adjudicate on the merits of the Authority's decision (*R (Assisted Reproduction and Gynaecology Centre) v Human Fertilisation and Embryology Authority* [2002] EWCA Civ 20, [2002] Lloyd's Rep Med 148).

Judicial review would lie against a refusal of the Foreign Office to render diplomatic assistance to a British national in a foreign State but the expectation which an individual could legitimately hold of a response to a request for assistance would be limited (*R (Abbasi) v Secretary of State for Foreign and Commonwealth Affairs* [2002] EWCA Civ 1598, [2003] UKHRR 76).

GROUNDS OF JUDICIAL REVIEW

Judicial review is not an appeal mechanism, but a review of public law functions (*R v Richmond upon Thames London Borough Council, ex parte JC* (2000) *The Times*, 26 April 2000 (QBD); [2001] LGR 146 (CA)). There are a number of classifications of the grounds upon which a decision by a public authority may be found to be invalid. A commonly used classification is the tripartite distinction in *Council of Civil Service Unions v Minister for the Civil Service* [1985] AC 374 between: **74.6**

(a) illegality,
(b) irrationality, and
(c) procedural impropriety.

This classification is not set in stone. Within each of the three heads are a number of grounds which are capable of being characterised in more than one way. In addition, many factual situations can be analysed in more than one way. For example, where a statute lays down a procedure with which a public authority needs to comply, a failure to follow the wording of the statute could fall under both the illegality head (see **74.7** to **74.10**) and the procedural impropriety head (see **74.21** to **74.26**).

Illegality

Illegality arises where a decision-maker who must understand correctly the law that regulates his or her decision-making power and must give effect to it fails to do so (Lord Diplock in *Council of Civil Service Unions v Minister for the Civil Service* [1985] AC 374). Illegality also includes *ultra vires* acts and errors of law. An error in relation to a precedent (jurisdictional) fact is also often placed under the illegality heading. An action or decision is said to be tainted by illegality if: **74.7**

(a) it was purportedly taken under legislation which does not contain the requisite power; or
(b) it was purportedly taken under legislation which contains precise limits on the circumstances in which a power or duty can be used, and the action or decision in question either exceeds these limits or fails to perform the power or duty in a proper way.

'Illegal' could also be used to describe a statutory instrument which conflicts with primary legislation, or an Act of Parliament which is incompatible with European Community law. One particular aspect of illegality is an allegation of a breach of Convention rights under the **Human Rights Act 1998** (see **chapter 97**).

***Ultra vires* acts** Whether or not a decision is *ultra vires* depends upon the relevant primary or secondary legislation and its interpretation on the particular facts and circumstances of each case. Therefore few general rules can be laid down. Some examples include, however, **74.8**

a refusal to refer a complaint relating to milk price-fixing to a committee of investigation contrary to the policy and objects of the relevant statute (*Padfield v Minister of Agriculture, Fisheries and Food* [1968] AC 997); the destruction of food which was 'unlikely to become' unfit for human consumption (*R v Thames Magistrates' Court, ex parte Clapton Cash and Carry* [1989] COD 518); the removal of school governors because of their failure to support the ILEA's educational policy (*Brunyate v Inner London Education Authority* [1989] 1 WLR 542).

74.9 **Errors of law** An alternative way of analysing illegality is as an error of law. This is where a public body makes a decision based upon an incorrect interpretation of the law. For example, the House of Lords has held that the respondent borough council misinterpreted s. 4(2)(b) of the Housing (Homeless Persons) Act 1977 in holding that the immigrant applicant became 'intentionally homeless' by bringing his homeless family to the United Kingdom to live with him (*Re Islam (Tafazzul)* [1983] 1 AC 688).

74.10 **Precedent (jurisdictional) fact/error of fact** Although error of fact has not historically been regarded as a ground for judicial review (*R v Hillingdon London Borough Council, ex parte Puhlhofer* [1986] AC 484), the courts will review instances where the public body has failed to establish a vital fact which triggers its power and makes the exercise of its powers lawful, e.g. the requirement to establish that a person is an 'illegal entrant' before the power of deportation can lawfully arise under the Immigration Act 1971 (*R v Secretary of State for the Home Department, ex parte Khawaja* [1984] AC 74). Factual aspects of a decision may be reviewed in some limited circumstances (see per Lords Slynn of Hadley, Nolan and Clyde in *R (Alconbury Developments Ltd) v Secretary of State for the Environment, Transport and the Regions* [2001] UKHL 23, [2003] 2 AC 295).

For there to be a sufficient mistake of fact giving rise to unfairness the following criteria need to be fulfilled:

(a) there must be a mistake as to an existing fact, including mistake as to the availability of evidence;
(b) the fact or evidence must now be uncontentious and objectively verifiable;
(c) the appellant or his advisers must not have been responsible for the mistake of fact; and
(d) the mistake must have played a material (but not necessarily decisive) part in the Tribunal's reasoning (*E v Secretary of State for the Home Department* [2004] EWCA Civ 49, [2004] QB 1044).

There is a distinction to be made between cases where an appeal court is satisfied, on new evidence, that a minister or inferior body or tribunal took a decision on the basis of a belief as to the existence of a material fact that has now been demonstrated to be plainly wrong, and cases where it took its decision in the mistaken belief that there was in fact no apparently cogent evidence to refute a material finding it had made (see *Shabana Shaheen v Secretary of State for the Home Department* [2005] EWCA Civ 1294, LTL 2/11/2005, where, on the facts, the Court of Appeal held that the Immigration Appeal Tribunal had not made an error of law).

Irrationality

74.11 A decision may be tainted by irrationality where the decision-making body allegedly:

(a) acted for an improper purpose;
(b) acted with bad faith;
(c) fettered its discretion;
(d) improperly delegated its functions;
(e) reached a conclusion that no body properly directing itself on the relevant law and acting reasonably could have reached;
(f) failed to take into account relevant matters or took into account irrelevant matters;
(g) abused its powers; or, possibly,
(h) acted in a disproportionate manner.

The **Human Rights Act 1998** may also provide a backdrop to claims based upon the ground of irrationality. When scrutinising an executive decision which interferes with human rights, the court will ask, applying an objective test, whether the decision-maker could reasonably have concluded that the interference was necessary to achieve one or more of the legitimate aims recognised by the Convention (*R (Mahmood) v Secretary of State for the Home Department* [2001] 1 WLR 840). The proportionality of any interference will now be an issue in any review by the courts of the decision of a public authority (*R (Daly) v Secretary of State for the Home Department* [2001] 2 AC 532) in a case raising the Human Rights Act 1998.

Improper purpose In cases where a power granted to a public body for one purpose is exercised by it for a different purpose, that power is deemed not to have been validly exercised, e.g., where a local authority decided to avoid the products of a company in order to put pressure upon its parent companies to withdraw their interests from South Africa (*R v Lewisham London Borough Council, ex parte Shell UK Ltd* [1988] 1 All ER 938); where a transaction by a local council was for the improper purpose of circumventing its restrictions on borrowing and spending (*Crédit Suisse v Allerdale Borough Council* [1997] QB 306). **74.12**

Generally the interpretation by the courts of the purpose of a statutory provision involves a search for the 'natural and ordinary meaning' of the word or term. Although reference may be made to parliamentary records to aid the construction of legislation which is ambiguous or obscure (*Pepper v Hart* [1993] AC 593) this principle is not applicable in relation to the determination of the general purpose of a statutory scheme, but only to resolve ambiguity in a statutory provision.

Bad faith A decision is made in bad faith if it has been affected by motives such as fraud, malice, or personal self-interest. A power is deemed to have been exercised fraudulently where the decision-maker had an intention to achieve an object other than that which it claimed to be seeking, e.g., the promotion of another public or private interest. A power is regarded as exercised maliciously if an action or decision is motivated by a personal animosity towards those who are directly affected by its exercise, e.g., the decision by a county council to cease advertising in journals controlled by Times Newspapers (which had written an article criticising a councillor) was explicitly held to be motivated by bad faith and declared invalid (*R v Derbyshire County Council, ex parte The Times Supplements Ltd* (1991) 3 Admin LR 241). **74.13**

Fettering of discretion Where a public body maintains a rigid policy with no exceptions it thereby fetters its discretion. Although a public authority can have a policy, it must consider particular cases rather than fetter its discretion by always following its stated policy blindly. Thus, for example, a rule of the Board of Trade which excluded grants for items costing less than £25 each was only permissible provided that the Board was always willing to listen to anyone with something new to say (*British Oxygen Co. Ltd v Board of Trade* [1971] AC 610); a policy formulated on the premises that amusement arcades would be harmful to young persons was unlawful (*Sagnata Investments Ltd v Norwich Corporation* [1971] 2 QB 614); a policy to restrict access to a solicitor by a person remanded in custody was unlawful (*R v Chief Constable of South Wales, ex parte Merrick* [1994] 1 WLR 663); the policy of a licensing committee which provided that an applicant for a betting office licence must have a legal interest in the premises was unlawful (*R v Forest Betting Licensing Committee, ex parte Noquet* (1988) *The Times*, 21 June 1988). **74.14**

The courts may be prepared to scrutinise closely the conduct of a decision-maker in assessing whether or not he or she has unlawfully fettered his or her discretion, e.g., a course of conduct involving the consistent rejection of applications belonging to a particular class may justify an inference that the public body has adopted a policy to refuse them all. However, it is unlikely that the courts will deem a decision-maker to have fettered his or her discretion in circumstances where he or she afforded those individuals affected the ability to make representations, e.g., decisions of local authorities in relation to the disposition of planning appeals or proposals for the compulsory acquisition of land have been upheld in circumstances where the decision was made after a public inquiry (*Franklin v Minister of Town and Country Planning* [1948] AC 87; *Stringer v Minister of Housing and Local Government* [1970] 1 WLR 1281).

74.15 **Improper delegation** In general a public law function must be exercised only by the body to whom it has been given. When a power is provided to a person in circumstances indicating that trust is being placed in his or her individual judgment and discretion, that person must exercise that power personally unless he or she has been expressly empowered to delegate it to another. Public bodies which exercise functions analogous to the judiciary are precluded from delegating their powers of decision unless there is express authority to that effect (*General Council of Medical Education and Registration of the United Kingdom v Dental Board of the United Kingdom* [1936] Ch 41).

Where an authority vested with discretionary powers affecting private rights then empowers one of its committees, members or officers to exercise those powers independently without any supervisory control, the exercise of those powers is likely to be held invalid. Thus, for example, a delegation by the Director of Public Prosecutions to non-qualified lawyers of the power to review prosecutions in order to decide whether there was sufficient evidence to proceed was held to be unlawful because the statute giving the power to the Director clearly contemplated that it would only be delegated to a member of the Crown Prosecution Service who was a lawyer (*R v Director of Public Prosecutions, ex parte Association of First Division Civil Servants* (1988) *The Times*, 24 May 1988). However, in the case of local authorities, s. 101 of the Local Government Act 1972 expressly permits some delegation.

The degree of control maintained by the delegating authority is an important factor in determining the validity of the delegation. The control must be close enough for the decision to be identified as that of the delegating authority (*Hall v Manchester Corporation* (1915) 84 LJ Ch 732). Clearly it is improper for an authority to delegate wide discretionary powers to another authority over which it is incapable of exercising direct control, unless it is expressly permitted so to delegate. Also relevant to the proper delegation of powers are the nature of the power and the impact of its exercise upon individual interests.

The courts have recognised that duties imposed upon and powers granted to government ministers are normally exercised under the authority of ministers by responsible officials of the department (*Carltona Ltd v Commissioners of Works* [1943] 2 All ER 560). Thus, decisions taken in this manner will not have involved an impermissible delegation. This principle has been applied to the Benefits Agency, which was held to be part of the Department of Social Security, and the Agency staff therefore were regarded as part of the Civil Service (*R v Secretary of State for the Home Department, ex parte Sherwin* (1996) 32 BMLR 1). There may, however, be matters of such importance that the minister is legally required to address them personally. The presumption in relation to ministers may be expressly excluded by legislation (e.g., as in the Immigration Act 1971).

74.16 ***Wednesbury* unreasonableness** Lord Greene MR stated in *Associated Provincial Picture Houses Ltd v Wednesbury Corporation* [1948] 1 KB 223:

> . . . it may be still possible to say that, although the local authority have kept within the four corners of the matters which they ought to consider, they have nevertheless come to a conclusion so unreasonable that no reasonable authority could ever have come to it.

In order to prove '*Wednesbury* unreasonableness' something overwhelming must be proved but this test has been fulfilled in a number of cases, e.g., a local authority resolution to ban a rugby club from its property for not putting pressure upon three of its players not to participate in a tour of South Africa (*Wheeler v Leicester City Council* [1985] AC 1054); a justices' clerk's refusal to supply duplicate legal aid orders (*R v Liverpool Justices, ex parte R. M. Broudie and Co.* (1994) 7 Admin LR 242); and the Lottery Commission's refusal to allow a bidder one month to allay its concerns about the bid (*R v National Lottery Commission, ex parte Camelot Group plc* [2001] EMLR 3).

Failure to take account of relevant considerations A further limb of the ground of irrationality comprises failure to take account of relevant considerations or the taking into account of an irrelevant consideration. For example, the court held that a borough council took into account irrelevant (philanthropic) considerations in deciding to overpay its staff, and also failed to take into account relevant considerations of comparable wages and the costs of living (*Roberts v Hopwood* [1925] AC 578). **74.17**

A statute may expressly or impliedly make clear considerations to which regard must or must not be had. There may also be considerations to which the decision-maker may have regard in the exercise of his discretion (see *CREEDNZ Inc. v Governor-General* [1981] 1 NZLR 172).

The courts may infer either that an extraneous purpose was being pursued or that the exercise of a body's discretion was unreasonable from the surrounding circumstances. It is not necessary to prove that the influence of irrelevant factors was the chief or main influence upon the decision made or action taken. As a general rule it is enough to prove that the influence was material or substantial (*R v Inner London Education Authority, ex parte Westminster City Council* [1986] 1 WLR 28). Where a decision-maker leaves out of account some relevant matter, the legal test is whether that factor might realistically have caused the decision-maker to reach a different conclusion (*W v Special Educational Needs Tribunal* (2000) *The Times*, 12 December 2000).

If the challenge is based upon a claim that relevant considerations were not taken into account, the courts will normally try to assess the actual or potential importance of the factor that was overlooked, even though this may involve a degree of speculation. Examples of decisions challenged under this ground include the unlawful expenditure of public funds by a board of guardians in cancelling a series of loans to miners without taking into account the ability of the debtors to repay their loans (*Attorney-General v Tynemouth Poor Law Union Guardians* [1930] 1 Ch 616) and the decision of a university to refuse to permit a controversial meeting on its premises which had been influenced by an irrelevant consideration, namely, the likelihood of violence outside the premises (*R v University of Liverpool, ex parte Caesar-Gordon* [1991] 1 QB 124).

A number of cases have reviewed the situation where local authorities have sought to use lack of resources as justification for reducing the level of provision of services they are under a statutory duty to provide. For example, a local authority could take into account its resources in assessing 'needs' under s. 2 of the Chronically Sick and Disabled Persons Act 1970 (*R v Gloucestershire County Council, ex parte Barry* [1997] AC 584). However, although a local authority was entitled to have regard to its resources in determining whether claimants were 'in need of care and attention' under s. 21(1) of the National Assistance Act 1948, once a need was established the authority was not then able to take account of its lack of resources in deferring the carrying out of these duties (*R v Sefton Metropolitan Borough Council, ex parte Help the Aged* [1997] 4 All ER 532).

When a local education authority performed its statutory duty under s. 298 of the Education Act 1993 to provide suitable education for children of compulsory school age, it was not entitled to take into account the availability of financial resources when deciding what sort of education was suitable (*R v East Sussex County Council, ex parte Tandy* [1998] AC 714). Similar reasoning has been applied to local authorities in determining whether or not to approve an application for a disabled facilities grant for purposes under s. 23(1) of the Housing Grants, Construction and Regeneration Act 1996 (*R v Birmingham City Council, ex parte Mohammed* [1999] 1 WLR 33) and in determining whether to make a mandatory order under the Housing Act 1996, s. 193, in respect of the provision of suitable accommodation (*R v Newham London Borough Council, ex parte Khan* (2000) 33 HLR 269). However, a Chief Constable's decision to provide policing only two days a week to protect the transport of livestock for shipment to France from animal rights protesters was lawful having regard to the Chief Constable's lack of resources, whether viewed from a domestic or European law perspective (*R v Chief Constable of Sussex, ex parte International Trader's Ferry Ltd* [1999] 2 AC 418). See also *R (Pfizer Ltd) v Secretary of State for Health* [2002] EWCA Civ 1566, *The Times*, 11 November 2002, *R (Haggerty) v St Helens Borough Council* [2003] EWHC 803 (Admin), 74 BMLR 33 and *R (Spink) v Wandsworth London Borough Council* [2005] EWCA Civ 302, [2005] 1 WLR 2884.

74.18 **Abuse of power/substantive legitimate expectation** There is authority that an undertaking or promise by a public authority may lead to a legitimate expectation which must not be thwarted (*R v Liverpool Corporation, ex parte Liverpool Taxi Fleet Operators' Association* [1972] 2 QB 299). The fulfilment of substantive expectations has been upheld, e.g., an expectation contained in the terms of a Home Office circular setting out the conditions for the adoption of children from abroad (*R v Secretary of State for the Home Department, ex parte Asif Mohammed Khan* [1984] 1 WLR 1337). A suggestion that the concept of substantive legitimate expectation is nothing more than a challenge based upon *Wednesbury* unreasonableness grounds (*R v Secretary of State for the Home Department, ex parte Hargreaves* [1997] 1 WLR 906) was effectively circumvented in *R v North and East Devon Health Authority, ex parte Coughlan* [2001] QB 213.

The House of Lords has regarded a case of substantive unfairness, involving failure by the Inland Revenue to comply with a written assurance, as an abuse of power requiring either an improper motive or conduct equivalent to breach of contract or representation (*Re Preston* [1985] AC 835). However, it was not an abuse of power for the Inland Revenue to seek to extract a tax contrary to an advance clearing given by it where there had not been full disclosure by the taxpayer (*R v Inland Revenue Commissioners, ex parte Matrix Securities Ltd* [1994] 1 WLR 334). Nor was it an abuse of power for the Inland Revenue to withdraw tax relief in circumstances where its published documents were not sufficiently clear, unambiguous and devoid of qualification to give rise to a legitimate expectation which a court would protect (*Fletcher v Thompson* [2002] EWHC 1448 (Admin), [2002] STC 1149). There need not be an explicit representation by the public authority. It may be based on a practice established over a number of years, e.g., *R v Inland Revenue Commissioners, ex parte Unilever plc* (1996) 86 TC 205.

The general principles derived from these cases suggest that, in order to qualify for protection under the head of substantive legitimate expectation, the following qualities are necessary:

(a) the representation or expectation sought to be relied upon must be clear, unambiguous and unqualified;
(b) the applicant must be within the class of persons entitled to rely upon the representation or alternatively it must be reasonable for the applicant to rely upon it;
(c) there must usually be reliance upon the representation to the detriment of the applicant, although the claimant need not always demonstrate detriment (*R (Bibi) v Newham London Borough Council* [2001] EWCA Civ 607, [2002] 1 WLR 237); and
(d) there must be no overriding public interest which would entitle the respondent to renege from its representation.

The public law concepts of legitimate expectation and abuse of power, rather than the private law concept of estoppel, have been held to be relevant to planning law. Situations could therefore arise in the planning field where it would be a breach of legitimate expectation and therefore an abuse of power for a public body to act in a particular way (*R (Reprotech (Pebsham) Ltd) v East Sussex County Council* [2002] UKHL 8, [2003] 1 WLR 348), but such situations will be rare (*Henry Boot Homes Ltd v Bassetlaw District Council* [2002] EWCA Civ 983, *The Times*, 16 December 2002).

There can be a legitimate expectation that a policy will be applied even where the claimant was unaware of the policy (*R (Rashid) v Secretary of State for the Home Department* [2005] EWCA Civ 744, *The Times*, 12 July 2005).

74.19 **Proportionality** Proportionality is a concept central both to European Community law and to the European Convention on Human Rights and means that remedies or measures should be proportionate to the legitimate aim that is sought to be achieved or the state of affairs they are intended to redress, and thus the administrative process should be in proportion to the outcome of the process (see **96.13**). The conventional view is that proportionality is simply a facet of irrationality/ *Wednesbury* unreasonableness (see above) and there is no separate ground of proportionality within the domestic context (*R v Secretary of State for the Home Department, ex parte Brind* [1991] 1 AC 696). However, it is clear that the tests of proportionality and *Wednesbury* unreasonableness do not always yield the same results but are moving closer together (*R (Association of British Civilian Internees: Far East Region) v Secretary of State for Defence* [2003] EWCA Civ 473, [2003] QB 1397). Although there is an overlap between the traditional grounds of judicial review and the approach of proportionality, the intensity of review is greater under the proportionality approach (*R (Daly) v Secretary of State for the Home Department* [2001] UKHL 26, [2001] 2 AC 532). Proportionality has been raised in the context of personal liberty (*R v Secretary of State for the Home Department, ex parte Pegg* [1995] COD 84) and has also been applied where a sentencing decision is susceptible to judicial review (*R v Highbury Corner Justices, ex parte Uchendu* (1994) 158 JP 409).

The failure of a decision-maker expressly to refer to proportionality in a decision does not necessarily render the decision liable to be quashed. Where a decision-maker has taken account of all material considerations, there is no 'straitjacket' imposed requiring the presence of the word in the final decision (*Lough v First Secretary of State* [2004] EWCA Civ 905, [2004] 1 WLR 2557).

Administrative consistency There is a general principle that like cases should be treated alike (but clearly where cases are not alike this may justify differential treatment). **74.20**

Where the Agricultural Wages Board established a new category of worker whose minimum wage was lower than that of a standard worker, but excluded mushroom harvesters from those who could be paid this rate, this exclusion was found to infringe the principle of public administration that all persons in a similar situation should be treated similarly (*R (Middlebrook Mushrooms Ltd) v Agricultural Wages Board of England and Wales* [2004] EWHC 1447 (Admin), *The Times*, 15 July 2004).

Similarly, where a policy which applied to Iraqi Kurds was not applied to an applicant who could show a direct comparison with two other Iraqi Kurds who were in precisely the same position as the applicant, and who had both been granted refugee status under this policy, the court found that the application of unequal treatment to refugees in a like position was so unfair as to amount to a misuse of governmental power (*R (Rashid) v Secretary of State for the Home Department* [2005] EWCA Civ 744, *The Times*, 12 July 2005).

Procedural impropriety

Procedural impropriety is concerned with the procedure by which a decision is reached, not the ultimate outcome. In order to prove procedural impropriety the applicant must show that the decision was reached in an unfair manner. If there is no statutory framework which expressly stipulates the relevant procedural requirements, there are two applicable common law rules under this head, namely: **74.21**

(a) the rule against bias, which requires the public body to be impartial and to be seen to be so; and
(b) the right to a fair hearing whereby those affected by a decision of a public body are entitled to know what the case is against them and to have a proper opportunity to put their case forward.

Infringement of express procedural rules

A decision made or action taken by a public body should not infringe express procedural rules outlined in primary or secondary legislation, e.g., a notice of school closure was quashed **74.22** where there was a failure to consult under s. 184 of the Education Act 1993 and a government circular (*R v Lambeth London Borough Council, ex parte N* [1996] ELR 299); procedural codes are laid out in the town and country planning legislation which set out the procedure for an appeal or a full structured inquiry. Courts may be called upon to adjudicate upon the extent to which the statutory procedure is fulfilled. There have also been cases where the courts have supplemented a statutory scheme over and above that which is expressly specified (e.g., *Fairmount Investments Ltd v Secretary of State for the Environment* [1976] 1 WLR 1255). However, it is generally recognised that such supplementation should be exercised only in extreme circumstances where considered necessary to promote the purpose of the legislation (*Wiseman v Borneman* [1971] AC 297).

Implied procedural rules

74.23 The requirement to comply with express procedural rules is supported by the common law obligation to provide a fair hearing. The rules of natural justice embody a duty to act fairly. Whenever a public function is performed there is an inference, in the absence of an express requirement to the contrary, that the function is required to be performed fairly. This is more compelling in the case of any decision which may adversely affect a person's rights or interests (e.g., *R v Liverpool Corporation, ex parte Liverpool Taxi Fleet Operators' Association* [1972] 2 QB 299) but will not apply to situations which are too remote to qualify for a fair hearing.

The two fundamental common law rules set out in **74.21** also apply where there is no statutory procedural code.

Bias

74.24 In cases where the decision-maker has a direct personal or proprietary interest in the outcome of a matter, he or she should always be disqualified from adjudicating upon the issue. However, when the interest is indirect, the courts generally apply the following test. First, the court should ascertain all the circumstances which have a bearing on the suggestion that the tribunal is biased. Secondly, it should ask whether those circumstances would lead a fair-minded and informed observer to conclude that there is a real possibility that the tribunal is biased (*Porter v Magill* [2001] UKHL 67, [2002] 2 AC 357; see also **97.48**).

The House of Lords has held a judge in the House of Lords involved with Amnesty International to be automatically disqualified because his participation in a case where Amnesty was an intervener offended the fundamental principle that a man may not be a judge in his own cause. Although this principle normally applies only in cases where the judge has a pecuniary interest, the court confirmed that it could and did extend to cases where the judge has a non-pecuniary interest (sufficient to amount to an interest in the outcome of the proceedings) in one of the parties thereto (*R v Bow Street Metropolitan Stipendiary Magistrate, ex parte Pinochet Ugarte (No. 2)* [2000] 1 AC 119, subsequently applied in *Locabail (UK) Ltd v Bayfield Properties Ltd* [2000] QB 451 and *Weatherill v Lloyds TSB Bank plc* [2000] CPLR 584).

In considering the question of apparent bias it is necessary to look beyond pecuniary or personal interests and to consider in addition whether, from the point of view of the fair-minded and informed observer, there is a real possibility that the decision-maker is biased in the sense of approaching the decision with a closed mind and without impartial consideration of all relevant issues (*Georgiou v Enfield London Borough* [2004] EWHC 779 (Admin), [2004] LGR 497).

The question of independence should be tested by reference to the fair-minded and informed observer's knowledge of all the information which could have been ascertained by a fair-minded outside observer (*Re P (A Barrister)* [2005] 1 WLR 3019).

A public body should not allow decisions to be made by people who have a financial interest in the decision or a family/business connection with any party. However it has been held that no bias arose in the case of a grant of planning permission to develop a rugby club's land where it was subsequently discovered that the club had an interest in acquiring land belonging to the chairman of the planning authority (*R v Secretary of State for the Environment, ex parte Kirkstall Valley Campaign Ltd* [1996] 3 All ER 304). Bias may also arise because of a personal business relationship between the adjudicator and one of the parties, or because of partisanship by the adjudicator in relation to the issues to be resolved. Where a decision-maker takes part in the determination of an appeal against one of his or her own decisions (unless he or she is expressly authorised to do so by statute) it will be tainted by apparent bias, e.g., a clerk to a statutory tribunal could not act as clerk to the appeal tribunal hearing the appeal against that decision (*R v Salford Assessment Committee, ex parte Ogden* [1937] 2 KB 1). See also *R (Al-Hasan) v Secretary of State for the Home Department* [2005] UKHL 13, [2005] 1 WLR 688.

A party may waive its objections to a decision-maker who may otherwise have been disqualified on the ground of bias (*R (Giant's Causeway etc. Tramway Co.) v Antrim Justices* [1895] 2 IR 603). Any objection may be deemed to have been waived if the party or its legal representative knew of the disqualification and agreed to take part in the proceedings by failing to raise an objection at the earliest opportunity. For example, a claimant waived his right to complain that a decision not to grant him British citizenship was, or appeared to have been, prejudged following a newspaper article reporting that the decision-maker would not grant the application, because he had not objected to that decision-maker continuing to deal with the application and making the decision (*R v Secretary of State for the Home Department, ex parte Al Fayed* [2001] Imm AR 134). Clearly there is no presumption of waiver if there is no complete disclosure of an interest or if the party was not aware of the interest. Statutes may also provide an express exemption in certain instances.

In the absence of bias in respect of an earlier decision which had been remitted, or an expressed view from which it was impossible to depart, a decision-maker could rehear a remitted matter rather than recuse himself and have the matter determined by a different decision-maker (*Jones v Department of Transport Welsh Traffic Office* [2005] EWCA Civ 58, *The Times*, 24 January 2005).

There is no absolute rule that knowledge of prejudicial publicity (such as knowledge of previous convictions) is fatal to the fairness and impartiality of the proceedings (*R (Mahfouz) v Professional Conduct Committee of the General Medical Council* [2004] EWCA Civ 233, [2004] Lloyd's Rep Med 389). Bias or apparent bias is not to be equated with knowledge of inadmissible and potentially prejudicial information. However, the effect of this knowledge has to be considered in the context of the proceedings as a whole, including the likely impact of the oral evidence and the legal advice available. Where the tribunal was made up of experienced and sophisticated members it could be assumed they would understand the proper approach and the need to disregard irrelevant material.

The common law rules on bias are now applied in the context of the requirement in art. 6(1) of the European Convention on Human Rights that civil rights and obligations (and criminal charges) must be determined by 'an independent and impartial tribunal' (see **97.48**).

Right to a fair hearing

The right to a fair hearing embodies the idea of even-handedness between the parties **74.25** in relation to obtaining information which is made available, and the provision of an opportunity to make representations. The concept of a fair hearing varies from case to case. For example, there may be an entitlement to an oral hearing in cases where the livelihood or liberty of the applicant is at stake, whereas such an entitlement will not be deemed necessary in relation to more minor matters with less potentially adverse consequences. The two main elements of procedural fairness are:

(a) the right to know the opposing case; and
(b) a fair opportunity to answer that case.

The overall test is what a reasonable man would consider to be fair in the particular circumstances (*Ridge v Baldwin* [1964] AC 40).

The right to information on the case against an individual includes entitlement to notice of the allegations made against him or her so that the individual has an adequate opportunity to prepare his or her own case, arrange for representation (if necessary) and appear at any hearing. The right to notice includes, by implication, provision of sufficient detail of the opposing case to provide a fair opportunity to prepare one's own case, e.g., a rating assessment which was determined upon a valuer's report which had not been disclosed to the other party was quashed (*R v Westminster Assessment Committee, ex parte Grosvenor House (Park Lane) Ltd* [1941] 1 KB 53). However, the use of anonymous witness statements by a governing body considering whether to exclude a pupil from school was considered to be fair in the particular circumstances of that case (*R (T) v Elliott School Head Teacher* [2002] EWCA Civ 1349, [2003] ELR 160; *R (A) v North Westminster Community School Head Teacher* [2002] EWHC 2351, [2003] ELR 378).

The procedure required to satisfy the requirements of a fair hearing will depend to a large extent on the nature of the decision-making body in question. The necessity for an oral hearing will depend upon the seriousness of the circumstances of the case and the subject matter being dealt with. In many instances an opportunity to make written representations will be sufficient, provided that the demands of fairness are met, e.g., the Army Board of the Defence Council could deal with a complaint of racial discrimination by way of written representations (*R v Army Board of the Defence Council, ex parte Anderson* [1992] QB 169). The exact requirements of a fair hearing will depend on the context. For example, in *R (Smith) v Parole Board (No. 2)* [2005] UKHL 1, [2005] 1 WLR 350, the House of Lords held that, while the common law duty of procedural fairness did not require the Parole Board to hold an oral hearing in every case, the Parole Board's duty was not as constricted as previously assumed. The prisoner should have the benefit of a procedure which fairly reflected, on the facts of his particular case, the importance of what was at stake for him and for society. The Parole Board might be assisted in its task of assessing risk by having some exposure to the prisoner.

On the other hand, where on the facts of the case it is thought that an oral hearing would be a mere formality, there is no absolute right to a public and oral hearing at every stage in proceedings where the prisoner has had a fair and public hearing at his original trial. To provide for oral hearings in every case would cause delay and it has not been shown that any good purpose would be served by adopting such a procedure generally (*R (Dudson) v Secretary of State for the Home Department* [2005] UKHL 52, [2006] 1 All ER 421). It may be sufficient for the prisoner to be given the opportunity to make written representations (*R v Secretary of State for the Home Department ex parte Doody* [1994] 1 AC 531). See also *R (Thompson) v Law Society* [2004] EWCA Civ 167, [2004] 1 WLR 2522; *Naraynsingh v Commissioner of Police* [2004] UKPC 20.

There is no clear entitlement to legal representation. Again, this will depend upon the seriousness or complexity of the charges made. The courts have held that prisoners charged with serious disciplinary offences have no general right to legal representation under the rules of natural justice, but the Boards of prison visitors have a discretion whether to allow it in the individual circumstances of each case (*R v Secretary of State for the Home Department, ex parte Tarrant* [1985] QB 251; *R v Board of Visitors of HM Prison, the Maze, ex parte Hone* [1988] AC 379).

As long as the claimant is given an opportunity to set out his case at some stage during the proceedings, it does not appear to be contrary to the right to a fair hearing for a decision to be made without the claimant or his legal representative being present (e.g., *Auburn Court Ltd v Kingston and Saint Andrew Corporation, Building Surveyor* [2004] UKPC 11).

Practical limitations may be placed upon the right to a fair process. For example, although the presence of an interpreter and/or representative in an interview in respect of an asylum claim provides a practical safeguard against faulty record-keeping and protects the applicant's interests to ensure the requisite standard of fairness, where such a safeguard is no longer practically available due to changes in public funding, a tape recording of the interview would be the only sensible method of redressing the imbalance of the Secretary of State being able to rely on a document without an adequate opportunity for the applicant to refute it (*R (Dirshe) v Secretary of State for the Home Department* [2005] EWCA Civ 421, *The Times*, 5 May 2005).

There is no general duty under English law upon a decision-maker to give reasons for his or her decisions although statute does provide for such a duty in certain instances (e.g., Housing Act 1985, s. 64). However, in *R v Civil Service Appeal Board, ex parte Cunningham* [1992] ICR 816 Lord Donaldson MR stated that:

> I do not accept that, just because Parliament has ruled that some tribunals should be required to give reasons for their decisions, it follows that the common law is unable to impose a similar requirement upon other tribunals, if justice so requires.

The Divisional Court summarised the current position in relation to the existence of a duty to give reasons in *R v Ministry of Defence, ex parte Murray* [1998] COD 134. The court confirmed that although the law did not at present recognise a general duty to give reasons, there was a perceptible trend towards an insistence on greater transparency in decision-making. Where a statute conferred a power to make decisions affecting individuals, the court would readily apply necessary additional procedural safeguards so as to ensure the attainment of fairness. Reasons should therefore be given where either:

(a) a decision without reasons was insufficient to achieve justice; or
(b) the decision appeared aberrant.

In determining whether reasons should be given, relevant considerations include the absence of any right of appeal, the importance of an effective means of detecting the kind of error which would entitle the court to intervene, and whether the body in question exercises a judicial function. Factors which militate against such a duty include the placing of an undue burden on decision-makers, considerations of public interest, or inexpressible value judgments. Therefore the requirement of fairness may require the giving of reasons in circumstances where there is no express statutory authority stipulating this.

Cases suggest that a duty to give reasons arises in cases where the body departs from its usual policy or practice (*R v Islington London Borough Council, ex parte Rixon* [1997] ELR 66), and where a failure to give reasons or the giving of inadequate reasons would lead to the quashing of the decision in question (*R v Westminster City Council, ex parte Ermakov* [1996] 2 All ER 302). Although neither the Medical Act 1983 nor its rules of procedure expressly or impliedly imposed on the Council a duty to state reasons for its decisions, this did not exclude an obligation to give reasons where the common law would require reasons to be given (*Stefan v General Medical Council* [1999] 1 WLR 1293; *Selvanathan v General Medical Council* [2001] Lloyd's Rep Med 1). Although there is no general obligation upon the Director of Public Prosecutions to give reasons for a decision not to prosecute, it has been held that he would, in the absence of compelling reasons to the contrary, be expected to do so where his refusal concerned a death in custody, in respect of which a properly directed jury had returned a verdict of unlawful killing (*R v Director of Public Prosecutions, ex parte Manning* [2001] QB 330). Fairness requires that a decision made by a second opinion appointed doctor the Mental Health Act 1983, s. 58, that an adult patient should be given medication against his will, should be accompanied by written reasons (*R (Wooder) v Feggetter* [2002] EWCA Civ 554, [2003] QB 219). However, an immigration appeal tribunal is not required to give reasons when making a decision to extend the time for giving its decision (*R v Secretary of State for the Home Department, ex parte Berhe* [2000] Imm AR 463). Upon the challenge of a planning decision, a local authority was entitled to repeat its statement of a pure value judgment when an inspector disagreed with that judgment (*Welsh Development Agency v Carmarthenshire County Council* (1999) 80 P & CR 192). The position is influenced by the fact that there is an obligation at common law and also in accordance with art. 6 of the European Convention on Human Rights at least to give a short statement of the reasons for a decision when determining civil rights and obligations or criminal charges.

Where reasons are required they must be clear and adequate and deal with the substantial issues in the case but what are good reasons in any particular case depends on the circumstances of the case (*R v Immigration Appeal Tribunal, ex parte Jebunisha Kharvaleb Patel* [1996] Imm AR 161). An adjudicator refusing permission to appeal against a refusal to grant asylum was not required to address every point raised at length. Rather, sufficient reasons should be given to enable an appellant or other relevant person to see why a claimant had lost on any particular issue. If this test is satisfied, usually a more schematic approach would not be necessary (*R (Bahrami) v Immigration Appeal Tribunal* [2003] EWHC 1453 (Admin), LTL 4/6/2003). See also **97.49**.

Reasons for the decision to grant planning permission need only be intelligible and adequate, and need only refer to the main issues in the dispute and not to every material consideration (*South Bucks District Council v Porter (No. 2)* [2004] UKHL 33, [2004] 1 WLR 1953).

When deciding against an application for a capital grant, the Millennium Commission had only to say that another application was preferred and did not have to elucidate further (*R (Asha Foundation) v Millennium Commission* [2002] EWHC 916 (Admin), [2002] ACD 79; [2003] EWCA Civ 88, *The Times*, 24 January 2003).

Where there is a statutory duty to give reasons as part of the notification of the decision, the court will only accept subsequent evidence of the reasons in exceptional circumstances. In other cases, the court will be cautious about accepting late reasons. Relevant considerations which the court will take into account include: whether the new reasons are consistent with the original reasons, whether the new reasons are the original reasons of the whole tribunal, whether there is a real risk that the later reasons were composed subsequently in order to support the tribunal's decision, and the circumstances in which the later reasons are put forward. The degree of scrutiny and caution to be applied by the court to subsequent reasons is dependent on the subject matter of the administrative decision in question. Furthermore, the court will bear in mind the qualifications and experience of the persons on the tribunal (*R (Nash) v Chelsea College of Art and Design* [2001] EWHC 538 (Admin), *The Times*, 25 July 2001).

Procedural legitimate expectation

74.26 A procedural legitimate expectation arises in circumstances where a decision deprived the applicant of:

> some benefit or advantage which either (i) he had in the past been permitted by the decision-maker to enjoy and which he can legitimately expect to be permitted to continue to do until there has been communicated to him some rational grounds for withdrawing it on which he has been given an opportunity to comment; or (ii) he has received assurance from the decision-maker that it will not be withdrawn without giving him first an opportunity of advancing reasons for contending that they should not be withdrawn. (Lord Diplock in *Council of Civil Service Unions v Minister for the Civil Service* [1985] AC 374.)

The concept of procedural legitimate expectation has been applied to ensure that no adverse decision will be taken without first giving the affected party an opportunity of making representations.

An expectation will be derived from an express promise or representation or an implied representation based upon past actions. In order for a promise to have this effect it must be clear and unambiguous and the applicant must have made full relevant disclosure prior to obtaining it (*R v Inland Revenue Commissioners, ex parte MFK Underwriting Agencies Ltd* [1990] 1 WLR 1545) (see **74.18**). The concept of legitimate expectation will only be protected where there is no contrary public interest.

Examples of legitimate expectations are that taxi drivers had a legitimate expectation of consultation prior to the issue of licences in circumstances where such consultation had been expressly promised (*R v Liverpool Corporation, ex parte Liverpool Taxi Fleet Operators' Association* [1972] 2 QB 299); civil servants had a legitimate expectation of consultation prior to the removal of trade union rights, subject to considerations of national security (*Council of Civil Service Unions v Minister for the Civil Service* [1985] AC 374); coal miners' unions had a legitimate expectation of consultation on pit closures (*R v British Coal Corporation, ex parte Vardy* [1993] ICR 720); illegal immigrants had a legitimate expectation of an opportunity to state their case prior to deportation (*R v Attorney-General of Hong Kong, ex parte Ng Yuen Shiu* [1983] 2 AC 629); residents had a legitimate expectation of being consulted about all the options in respect of a traffic order (*R (Montpeliers and Trevors Association) v City of Westminster* [2005] EWHC 16 (Admin), LTL 14/1/2005).

Although there is a duty to re-consult if the final proposal is significantly different from what has been consulted upon, this duty does not arise if the differences are very slight and clearly not such as to impose a duty of fairness on the body to re-consult, or where the final proposal itself has emerged from the consultation exercise (*R v East Kent Hospital NHS Trust, ex parte Smith* [2002] EWHC 2640 (Admin), LTL 9/12/2002).

ALTERNATIVE REMEDIES TO JUDICIAL REVIEW

Generally, any alternative remedies should be exhausted before resorting to judicial review in **74.27**
cases where the alternative remedy is adequate to resolve the complaint (*R v Sandwell Metropolitan Borough Council, ex parte Wilkinson* (1998) 31 HLR 22). Although the jurisdiction of the court to grant relief by way of judicial review is not ousted by the existence of an alternative remedy, it may exercise its discretion to refuse relief, refuse to grant permission or adjourn the case until after the alternative remedy has been used.

A number of cases have indicated that judicial review is to be regarded as a remedy of last resort. For example, permission to apply for judicial review of a decision of the Law Society was set aside because of the existence of an alternative remedy in the form of an appeal to the Master of the Rolls (*R v Law Society, ex parte Kingsley* [1996] COD 59); permission to apply for judicial review was set aside where a claimant had a statutory right of appeal to the Secretary of State under the Town and Country Planning Act 1990, s. 78, against a grant of planning permission subject to conditions (*R v Secretary of State for the Home Department, ex parte Watts* [1997] COD 152); judicial review of a decision of the Customs and Excise Commissioners was refused because the claimant should have invoked a statutory right of recourse to a value added tax and duties tribunal (*R v Commissioners of Customs and Excise, ex parte Bosworth Beverages Ltd* (2000) *The Times*, 24 April 2000); judicial review of a decision of the Secretary of State for the Home Department to issue a notice of liability to a civil penalty under the Immigration and Asylum Act 1999, s. 35, was refused on the basis that the claimant's remedy was to defend civil proceedings brought by the Home Secretary after the expiry of the time prescribed for payment of the penalty (*R (Balbo B & C Auto Transporti Internazionali) v Secretary of State for the Home Department* [2001] EWHC 195 (Admin), [2001] 1 WLR 1556). A challenge to the service of prohibition notices by the FSA should have been by way of appeal to the Financial Services and Markets Tribunal rather than by way of judicial review (*R (Davies) v Financial Services Authority* [2003] EWCA Civ 1128, [2004] 1 WLR 185). There should not in commercial disputes be two sets of parallel proceedings based on the same facts and seeking the same remedies, with two sets of costs and duplication of the time, effort and resources of both the parties and the court (see *Cookson and Clegg Ltd v Ministry of Defence* [2005] EWCA Civ 811, LTL 10/6/2005, where the judicial review claim was dismissed).

It is possible to depart from this principle in exceptional circumstances, e.g., an urgent case where interim relief is required which would not be available in the appeal or complaint. Factors which the courts have taken into account in order to decide whether the circumstances are exceptional include: the speed of the appeal, whether it is convenient, whether the matter demands a particular or technical knowledge, and whether the alternative remedy is one which the claimant could first be expected to use, e.g., the delay in instituting disciplinary charges against police officers was such a serious breach of police regulations that the officers need not first exercise a right of appeal to the Secretary of State (*R v Chief Constable of Merseyside Police, ex parte Calveley* [1986] QB 424) . However, truly exceptional reasons must be given in order to bypass any statutory appeal procedure in favour of judicial review. Despite the apparent bias of a governing body which decided to exclude two pupils from school, any resulting unfairness could be remedied by the Independent Appeals Panel and any unfairness at an earlier stage in the proceedings was not so serious as to have contaminated an appeal (*R (A) v Kingsmead School Governors* [2002] EWCA Civ 1822, [2003] ELR 104).

Where there is an avenue for an appeal from an inferior court or tribunal to the Court of Appeal or to the High Court, and that avenue has been followed by the claimant and the appeal has been dismissed or the claimant has been refused permission to appeal, the claimant will not normally be permitted to re-litigate the same matter by way of judicial review, because that would be an abuse of the process of the court (see *R (Sivasubramaniam) v Wandsworth County Court* [2002] EWCA Civ 1738, [2003] 1 WLR 475). However, only in the case of the clearest provision will a court conclude that judicial review is excluded (*Leech v Deputy Governor of Parkhurst Prison* [1988] AC 533).

PERMISSION TO PROCEED WITH A CLAIM FOR JUDICIAL REVIEW

Pre-action protocol

74.28 The **Pre-action Protocol for Judicial Review** sets out a code of good practice and contains the steps which the parties should generally follow before making a claim for judicial review. All claimants must consider whether they should follow the protocol, depending upon the circumstances of their case. Where the use of the protocol is appropriate, the court will normally expect all parties to comply with it and will take into account compliance or non-compliance when giving directions for case management proceedings or when making orders for costs (e.g., *Aegis Group plc v Commissioners of Inland Revenue* [2005] EWHC 1468 (Ch), LTL 13/5/2005).

The protocol requires that, before making a claim, the claimant should send a letter to the defendant. The purpose of the letter is to identify the issues in dispute and establish whether litigation can be avoided. The letter should normally contain the details of any interested parties known to the claimant. A copy of the letter before claim should be sent to all interested parties for information. The defendant should normally respond within 14 days to the letter before claim. Failure to do so will be taken into account by the court and sanctions may be imposed unless there are good reasons. The response should be sent to all interested parties identified by the claimant and contain details of any other parties whom the defendant considers also have an interest.

One of the purposes of the protocol is to identify the extent to which the exchange of information can lead to the avoidance of litigation. This links with the recent approach of the Court of Appeal, which has stipulated that courts should ask parties to judicial review proceedings to explain what steps they have taken to resolve the dispute, and why a complaints procedure or some other form of alternative dispute resolution has not been used to resolve or reduce the issues in dispute (*R (Cowl) v Plymouth City Council* [2001] EWCA Civ 1935, [2002] 1 WLR 803; Practice Statement (Administrative Court: Administration of Justice) [2002] 1 WLR 810).

Test for permission

Permission to proceed with a claim for judicial review must be obtained from a High Court judge (usually one of the Queen's Bench Division who has been assigned to hear matters listed in the Administrative Court Office list) (**CPR, r. 54.4; Supreme Court Act 1981, s. 31(3)**). To grant permission the court has to be satisfied that: **74.29**

(a) there is an arguable case for review;
(b) the applicant has a 'sufficient interest' (see 74.32); and
(c) there has not been 'undue delay' (see 74.33).

Traditionally the test for the grant of permission has been that a claimant must demonstrate to the court upon 'a quick perusal of the papers' that there is an arguable case for granting relief (*R v Inland Revenue Commissioners, ex parte National Federation of Self-Employed and Small Businesses Ltd* [1982] AC 617). However, some judges seem to apply more stringent criteria and require a claimant to demonstrate something approaching a reasonable prospect of success or a strong prima facie case.

Permission should be granted if on the material available the court considers, without going into the matter in depth, that there is an arguable case for granting the relief claimed by the claimant. The Court of Appeal has held that the test to be applied in deciding whether to grant permission is whether the judge is satisfied that there is a case fit for further investigation at a full with-notice hearing of a substantive claim for judicial review (*R v Secretary of State for the Home Department, ex parte Begum* [1990] COD 107). The court will generally, in the first instance, consider the question of permission without a hearing (**PD 54, para. 8.4**). In the event of a hearing, neither the defendant nor any other interested party need attend, unless the court directs otherwise (**PD 54, para. 8.5**). If, for example, on considering the papers, the judge cannot decide whether there is an arguable case, he or she may invite the proposed defendant to attend the hearing of the permission application and make representations as to whether permission should be granted.

Permission will be refused where an application is frivolous, vexatious or hopeless; or a claim is made by 'busybodies with misguided or trivial complaints of administrative error' (*R v Inland Revenue Commissioners, ex parte National Federation of Self-Employed and Small Businesses Ltd* [1982] AC 617); or a claim is misconceived, unarguable or groundless. Rigorous examination by the judge is required at the permission stage of a judicial review claim so as to restrict the exploitation of judicial review as a commercial weapon by rival property developers (*R (Noble Organisation Ltd) v Thanet District Council* [2005] EWCA Civ 782, [2006] Env LR 8). Permission will also be refused if there is a more appropriate alternative procedure (see 74.27); or a claim for judicial review is an inappropriate procedure, e.g., because the matter relates to private law and should therefore be commenced by way of a claim form under **CPR, Part** 7.

Procedure on an application for permission

A claimant seeking permission to proceed with a claim for judicial review must, by **PD 54, para. 5.7**, lodge with the Administrative Court Office: **74.30**

(a) a claim form (**form N461**);
(b) written evidence in support of the claim;
(c) a copy of any order that the claimant seeks to have quashed;
(d) where the claim for judicial review relates to a decision of a court or tribunal, an approved copy of the reasons for reaching that decision;
(e) copies of any documents on which the claimant proposes to rely;
(f) copies of any relevant statutory material; and
(g) a list of essential documents for advance reading by the court.

Where it is not possible to file all of these documents, the claimant must indicate which documents have not been filed and the reasons why they are not currently available (**PD 54, para. 5.8**).

The claim form should set out a detailed statement of the claimant's grounds for bringing the claim and the facts which the claimant will seek to rely on (**PD 54, para. 5.6**). It should state the claimant's name and description, the relief sought and the grounds on which it is sought, the name and address of the claimant's solicitor (if any) and the claimant's address for service. The claim form must also include or be accompanied by any application to extend the time limit for filing the claim form and any application for directions (**PD 54, para. 5.6**). The claim form must also state the name and address of any person the claimant considers to be an interested party, that the claimant is requesting permission to proceed with a claim for judicial review, and any remedy (including any interim remedy) sought (**CPR, r. 54.6(1)**). Where the claimant seeks to raise any issue under the **Human Rights Act 1998**, or seeks any remedy available under that Act, the claim form must include the information required by PD 16, para. 16 (**PD 54, para. 5.3**). Where the claimant intends to raise a devolution issue, the claim form must specify that the claimant wishes to raise a devolution issue and identify the relevant provisions of the Government of Wales Act 1998, the Northern Ireland Act 1998 or the Scotland Act 1998, and contain a summary of the facts, circumstances and points of law on the basis of which it is alleged that a devolution issue arises (**PD 54, para. 5.4**).

The written evidence to be filed with the claim form will generally be in witness-statement form. The evidence in support must verify the facts relied upon in support of the application, establish a sufficient interest by the claimant in the subject matter of the claim, exhibit a copy of the decision challenged and make full and frank disclosure of all relevant facts, even those not in the claimant's favour. The witness statement should ideally be signed by someone having first-hand personal knowledge of the facts. If permission is obtained upon the basis of false statements or the suppression of material facts, the court may set aside permission or refuse the relief sought at the substantive hearing (*R v Kensington Income Tax Commissioners, ex parte Princess Edmond de Polignac* [1917] 1 KB 486; *R v Jockey Club Licensing Committee, ex parte Wright* [1991] COD 306). On filing a claim form for judicial review, the claimant's solicitor must also lodge two copies of a paginated indexed bundle containing all the documents referred to above (**PD 54, para. 5.9**) and a further bundle of the relevant legislative provisions and statutory instruments required for the proper consideration of the application (Practice Direction (Crown Office List: Legislation Bundle) [1997] 1 WLR 52).

Urgent cases procedure

74.31 The Administrative Court has issued guidance on the procedure to be followed for cases which are urgent or which include applications for interim injunctions in Practice Statement (Administrative Court: Listing and Urgent Cases) [2002] 1 WLR 810.

A claimant seeking urgent consideration must complete **form N463** stating the reasons for urgency, the proposed timescale for consideration of the permission application, and the date by which the full hearing of the merits should take place if permission is granted. A claimant who applies for an interim injunction must also provide a draft order and a statement of the grounds on which the injunction is sought. The application must be served by fax and post, along with the claim form, on the defendant and interested parties. The defendant and interested parties must be advised that they may make representations on the application.

Each day a judge will act as the 'urgent judge' to hear urgent applications on that day. A judge will consider the application within the time requested, and may order that an oral hearing should take place. The judge will then make such order as is appropriate.

Standing of the claimant

74.32 **Section 31(3) of the Supreme Court Act 1981** provides that the court will not grant permission to proceed with a claim for judicial review 'unless it considers that the [claimant] has a sufficient interest in the matter to which the [claim] relates'.

The phrase 'sufficient interest' has been given a wide interpretation by the courts. They will assess the extent of the claimant's interest against the factual and legal circumstances of the claim. The test for deciding whether a claimant has sufficient interest was considered by the House of Lords in *R v Inland Revenue Commissioners, ex parte National Federation of Self-Employed and Small Businesses Ltd* [1982] AC 617. The court held that not only was standing a ground in itself upon which permission could be refused, it should also be considered at the substantive hearing after the relevant law and facts were examined in full. The court added that there are different tests for standing at the permission and the substantive stages. At the former stage it is merely a 'threshold' question for the court, designed to weed out frivolous or vexatious cases. However, at the substantive hearing the claimant must be able to show a strong case on the merits, judged in relation to the claimant's own concern with the subject matter of the claim (*R v Monopolies and Mergers Commission, ex parte Argyll Group plc* [1986] 1 WLR 763).

Since *R v Inland Revenue Commissioners, ex parte National Federation of Self-Employed and Small Businesses Ltd*, the courts have adopted a broad and flexible approach to this test. The more important the issue and the stronger the merits of the claim, the more ready will the courts be to grant permission, notwithstanding the limited personal involvement of the claimant. Standing will normally extend to individuals affected by the decision or action in question, e.g., a person threatened with deportation, or an individual with a direct financial or legal interest. For example, an elector and taxpayer was deemed to have sufficient standing to claim that a government undertaking to pay a contribution to the European Community was *ultra vires* (*R v Her Majesty's Treasury, ex parte Smedley* [1985] QB 657). Similarly a taxpayer was permitted to challenge a decision of the Inland Revenue on its method of valuation of a rival company's profits (*R v Attorney-General, ex parte Imperial Chemical Industries plc* [1987] 1 CMLR 72). An owner of land within the green belt in the vicinity of a proposed development had sufficient standing, even though not directly affected by the development (*R v Selby District Council, ex parte Samuel Smith Old Breweries* [2001] PLCR 6). Similarly, an inhabitant of Rugby (although temporarily homeless at the time) had standing to challenge the grant of a permit to a cement company with a plant near Rugby town centre because as an inhabitant he would be affected by any adverse impact on the environment (*R (Edwards) v Environment Agency* [2004] EWHC 736 (Admin), [2004] 3 All ER 21). It was not necessary for him to have been active in a campaign on the issue to have an interest. However, the members of a victim's family had no standing to bring a challenge to a decision by the Lord Chief Justice on the appropriate tariff of a juvenile detainee (*R (Bulger) v Secretary of State for the Home Department* [2001] 3 All ER 449).

Standing also extends to representative groups. For example, the Child Poverty Action Group was held to have standing sufficient to commence proceedings relating to the interpretation of social security legislation (*R v Secretary of State for Social Services, ex parte Child Poverty Action Group* [1990] 2 QB 540); the Law Society in a challenge to the Lord Chancellor's cuts to legal aid eligibility (*R v Lord Chancellor, ex parte Law Society (No. 2)* (1994) 6 Admin LR 833); the Royal College of Nursing in a challenge to a government circular advising on abortion-related work for nurses (*Royal College of Nursing of the United Kingdom v Department of Health and Social Security* [1981] AC 800); and the National Union of Mineworkers in relation to the reduction of supplementary benefits to striking workers (*R v Chief Adjudication Officer, ex parte Bland* (1985) *The Times*, 6 February 1985).

Pressure groups acting in the public interest have also been granted standing. For example, Greenpeace were held to have sufficient interest to seek judicial review of the Inspectorate of Pollution's decision to vary authorisations for the discharge of radioactive waste from Sellafield (*R v Inspectorate of Pollution, ex parte Greenpeace Ltd* [1994] 1 WLR 570). The judge was influenced by the fact that, if the claim failed on its merits, the persons whom Greenpeace represented might not have an effective way to bring these issues before the court. He held that the issue of whether an interest group or other representative body had sufficient standing should be decided on the facts of each individual case as a matter of discretion. The World Development Movement was held to have standing to challenge a decision of the Foreign Secretary to use overseas aid money to fund the Pergau Dam project in Malaysia (*R v*

Secretary of State for Foreign and Commonwealth Affairs, ex parte World Development Movement Ltd [1995] 1 WLR 386). The Divisional Court took into account factors such as the importance of the issue raised, the likely absence of any other responsible challenger, and the prominent role of the claimants in giving advice on overseas aid. However, a company set up specifically to save a theatre did not have sufficient standing to challenge the Secretary of State's refusal to list the theatre site as an ancient monument (*R v Secretary of State for the Environment, ex parte Rose Theatre Trust Co.* [1990] 1 QB 504).

It would be misconceived at the permission stage to elevate the question of standing 'above the elementary level of excluding busybodies and troublemakers and to demand something akin to a special private interest in the subject matter' (*R v Somerset County Council, ex parte Dixon* [1997] COD 323). There is no authority for the proposition that a court is compelled to refuse permission where the interest of the claimant is shared with the generality of the public.

The 'sufficient interest' standing test differs from the test under the **Human Rights Act 1998**, which provides that the claimant must be a 'victim' of the alleged violation of the Convention: that is, the claimant must have a personal interest in the claim (**Human Rights Act 1998, s. 7(1)**). Section 7(3) of the Act makes clear that it is the victim test which must prevail in human rights judicial review proceedings. This excludes judicial review challenges by representative bodies or pressure groups on human rights issues which are of general, rather than individual, importance.

Requirement for prompt commencement

74.33 In a claim for judicial review the claim form must be filed promptly, and in any event not later than three months after the grounds to make the claim first arose (**CPR, r. 54.5(1)**). This time limit may not be extended by agreement between the parties (**r. 54.5(2)**). Where the High Court considers that there has been undue delay in making a claim for judicial review, the court may refuse to grant permission or any relief sought in the claim if it considers that the grant of the relief sought would be 'likely to cause substantial hardship to, or substantially prejudice the rights of, any person or would be detrimental to good administration' (**Supreme Court Act 1981, s. 31(6)**).

The wide discretion granted to the courts in relation to the grant or refusal of relief is restricted by the **Supreme Court Act 1981, s. 31**(7), and by **CPR, r. 54.5**(3), which provide that s. 31(6) and **r. 54.5(1)** are without prejudice to any other statutory provisions which have the effect of limiting the time within which a claim for judicial review must be made.

Section 7(5) **of the Human Rights Act 1998** introduces a general time limit of one year for proceedings based upon a Convention right. However, this time limit is expressly stated to be without prejudice to stricter time limits, such as those that usually apply in judicial review proceedings.

A claim form filed after the time limit set by **CPR, r. 54.5(1)**, must be accompanied by an application to extend the limit (**PD 54, para. 5.6**).

A claimant seeking judicial review must file the claim form promptly and is not necessarily entitled to wait up to three months before commencing proceedings. In certain situations the utmost promptitude is expected, particularly where third parties may be adversely affected by the overturning of a decision, e.g., *R v Independent Television Commission, ex parte TVNi* [1996] JR 60. Grounds for a judicial review application in respect of a planning permission first arise for the purposes of **CPR, r. 54.5(1)**, from the date of the grant of permission, not from the earlier date when the planning committee passed a resolution authorising one of the authority's officers to grant outline permission on fulfilment of conditions precedent (*R (Burkett) v Hammersmith and Fulham London Borough Council* [2002] UKHL 23, [2002] 1 WLR 1593). Permission may be granted where a challenged decision was made in circumstances where the claimant for judicial review did not know of its susceptibility to challenge until long after the interveners had incurred most or all of the expense and effort upon which they relied to establish the prejudice in opposition to the grant of permission (*R v Licensing Authority, ex parte Novartis Pharmaceuticals Ltd* [2000] COD 232).

A claimant who has failed to bring proceedings promptly may apply to the court for an extension (under **CPR, r. 3.1(2)(a)**) of the time limit for filing the claim form. The onus is on the claimant to show that there is a good reason for extending time for applying for judicial review (*R v Warwickshire County Council, ex parte Collymore* [1995] ELR 217). Examples of 'good reasons' which have been accepted include:

(a) the claimant's lack of knowledge (it has been held that delay is no bar to relief when material matters were not known to the claimant until a later point in time, e.g., *R v Department of Transport, ex parte Presvac Engineering Ltd* (1992) 4 Admin LR 121);
(b) sensible and reasonable behaviour by the claimant which has caused no prejudice (*R v Commissioner for Local Administration, ex parte Croydon London Borough Council* [1989] 1 All ER 1033);
(c) exhaustion of all alternative remedies by the claimant prior to commencing proceedings (e.g., *R v Rochdale Metropolitan Borough Council, ex parte Cromer Ring Mill Ltd* [1982] 3 All ER 761);
(d) delay by the claimant in securing legal aid — provided that the application for legal aid has been expeditiously pursued on the part of the claimant (e.g., *R v Stratford-on-Avon District Council, ex parte Jackson* [1985] 1 WLR 1319);
(e) issues in the public interest (*R v Secretary of State for the Home Department, ex parte Ruddock* [1987] 1 WLR 1482, which concerned the challenge by a member of CND of the defendant's decision to tap her telephone; *R v Secretary of State for Trade and Industry, ex parte Greenpeace Ltd* [2000] 2 CMLR 94, which related to the incomplete and unlawful implementation by the United Kingdom of an EC Directive and the defendant's legally erroneous approach to the Directive);
(f) ongoing negotiations between the parties (*R v Greenwich London Borough Council, ex parte Patterson* (1994) 26 HLR 159);
(g) poor legal advice — courts have in particular sought to protect the interests of individual claimants in housing and immigration cases where it may not be possible to compensate the claimant by way of a damages award (e.g., *R v Secretary of State for the Home Department, ex parte Oyeleye* [1994] Imm AR 268);
(h) in certain circumstances, awaiting the decision of the Secretary of State on whether to call in a grant of planning permission (*R (Burkett) v Hammersmith and Fulham London Borough Council* [2002] UKHL 23, [2002] 1 WLR 1593).

However, the grant of an extension of time involves an exercise of discretion on the part of the court and there is no guarantee that an extension will be given in any particular case.

The courts have not been persuaded by arguments for an extension of time in circumstances where: there is a risk of prejudice to third parties (e.g., *R v Independent Television Commission, ex parte TVNi* [1996] JR 60); an extension of time would adversely affect market dealings which have been undertaken in good faith (*R v Independent Television, ex parte TVNi*); an intention had been expressed by the claimant to bring proceedings but a significant period of time elapsed before anything was done (*R v Independent Television Commission, ex parte White Rose Television Ltd* (24 January 1992 unreported)).

As to compatibility of the judicial review time limit with the Human Rights Act 1998 see **97.42**.

The claim form must be served on the defendant and any person the claimant considers to be an interested party (unless the court directs otherwise) within seven days after the date of issue (**CPR, r. 54.7**). Where the claim for judicial review relates to proceedings in a court or tribunal, any other parties to those proceedings must be named in the claim form as interested parties and therefore served with the claim form (**PD 54, para. 5.1**).

Acknowledgment of service

74.34 Any person who has been served with a claim form commencing proceedings for judicial review and who wishes to take part in the proceedings must file an acknowledgment of service (**form N462**) (**CPR, r. 54.8(1)**). The acknowledgment of service must be filed not more than 21 days after service of the claim form and must be served on the claimant and any other person named in the claim form as soon as practicable and, in any event, not later than seven days after it is filed (**r. 54.8(2)**). These time limits may not be extended by agreement between the parties (**r. 54.8(3)**).

If the intention is to contest the claim, the acknowledgment of service must set out a summary of the grounds for doing so, and must also state the name and address of any person whom the person filing the acknowledgment considers to be an interested party (**r. 54.8(4)**). The acknowledgment of service may also include or be accompanied by an application for directions. A defendant who succeeds at the substantive hearing is in principle entitled to recover the costs of submitting an acknowledgment of service (*R (Leach) v Local Commissioner for Administration* [2001] EWHC 455 (Admin), [2001] CP Rep 97).

A person served with a judicial review claim form who does not acknowledge service in accordance with **r. 54.8** may not, without the court's permission, take part in the hearing to decide whether permission to proceed should be given (**r. 54.9(1)(a)**). However, if the person complies with **r. 54.14** (filing and service of a response by the defendant or any other person served with the claim form) or any other direction of the court regarding filing and service of detailed grounds for contesting the claim or supporting it on additional grounds, and any written evidence, he may take part in the judicial review hearing (**r. 54.9(1)(b)**).

Where a person takes part in the judicial review hearing, the court may take his failure to file an acknowledgment of service into account when deciding what order to make about costs (**r. 54.9(2)**).

Relevant considerations in deciding whether or not to grant permission

74.35 If the court considers that there has been undue delay in claiming judicial review, permission to proceed with the claim, or relief at the substantive hearing, may be refused if it would be likely to lead to substantial hardship or prejudice or detriment to good administration (**Supreme Court Act 1981, s. 31(6)**). For example, in *R v Secretary of State for Health, ex parte Furneaux* [1994] 2 All ER 652 relief was refused because of prejudice to a rival pharmacy, but in other cases with serious consequences for a party or third party, relief has not been refused, e.g., in *R v Port Talbot Borough Council, ex parte Jones* [1988] 2 All ER 207 the grant of relief required the defendant to leave her home, and in *R v Secretary of State for the Environment, ex parte Chichester District Council* [1993] 2 PLR 1 relief caused a third party to face criminal proceedings.

In *R v Dairy Produce Quota Tribunal, ex parte Caswell* [1990] 2 AC 738 the House of Lords held that matters of particular importance in determining whether or not there is detriment to good administration, apart from the length of time itself, will be the extent of the effect of the relevant decision, and the impact which would be felt if it were to be reopened. **Section 31(6) of the Supreme Court Act 1981** requires affirmative evidence of detriment, i.e., the foreseen consequences of granting the relief sought must be positive harm to good administration, or at least evidence from which it can properly be inferred, and in considering detriment the court can take into account the effect on other potential claimants and the consequences if their claims were successful.

The effect of *R v Criminal Injuries Compensation Board, ex parte A* [1998] QB 659 (CA), [1999] 2 AC 330 (HL), is that permission to proceed and the substantive hearing should be regarded as two distinct stages. Permission should not be granted if:

(a) the claim form for judicial review was not filed promptly and in any event within three months and there is no good reason to extend time (**CPR, rr. 3.1(2)(a) and 54.5(1)**); or

(b) relief would be likely to cause substantial hardship, substantial prejudice or detriment to good administration (**Supreme Court Act 1981, s. 31(6)**).

At the substantive hearing delay may again be considered but the defendant will be permitted to recanvass an issue of promptness which was decided at the permission stage in the claimant's favour only if any of the following conditions are satisfied:

(a) if the judge hearing the original application expressly so indicated;
(b) if new and relevant material was introduced at the substantive hearing;
(c) if, exceptionally, the issues as they had developed at the full hearing put a different aspect on the question of promptness; or
(d) if the first judge had plainly overlooked some relevant matter or otherwise reached a decision *per incuriam.*

See *R (Lichfield Securities Ltd) v Lichfield District Council* [2001] EWCA Civ 304,3 LGLR 35.

It has been held that there is nothing in European Community law which prevents the court from applying the **Supreme Court Act 1981, s. 31(6)**, even in the case of an alleged breach of Community law by the defendant (*R v North West Leicestershire District Council, ex parte Moses* [2000] Env LR 443).

Amendment of application for permission

A judicial review claim form may be amended in accordance with the general principles of **CPR, Part 17**, discussed in **chapter 31**. In general, amendments will be allowed for the purpose of putting the claimant's case fully before the court, provided that the defendant is not unfairly prejudiced as a result. **74.36**

DETERMINATION OF THE APPLICATION FOR PERMISSION

Once a judicial review claim form and supporting evidence have been filed at the Administrative Court Office in the RCJ, the general rule is that, in the first instance, the court will consider the question of permission to proceed with the claim without a hearing (**PD 54, para. 8.4**). Where this rule applies, the papers are passed to a judge to read and to make a decision without hearing oral arguments. **74.37**

If permission to proceed is given, the court may also give directions (**CPR, r. 54.10(1)**), which may include a stay of proceedings to which the claim relates (**r. 54.10(2)**).

The court may give permission to proceed subject to conditions, or on certain grounds only (**r. 54.12(1)**). This was not possible before the CPR (*R v Criminal Injuries Compensation Board, ex parte A* [1998] QB 659).

The court will serve its order giving or refusing permission to proceed with a claim for judicial review, and any directions, on the parties and any other person who filed an acknowledgment of service (**r. 54.11**). The order will be accompanied by the court's reasons if it refuses permission or gives permission to proceed either subject to conditions or on certain grounds only (**r. 54.12(2)**).

The claimant may not appeal against a refusal of permission to proceed, or against permission given subject to conditions or on certain grounds only, but may request that the decision be reconsidered at a hearing (**r. 54.12(3)**). A request for reconsideration of a decision must be filed within seven days after service of the court's reasons for the decision (**r. 54.12(4)**). The parties and any other person who has filed an acknowledgment of service will be given at least two days' notice of the hearing date (**r. 54.12(5)**).

Neither the defendant nor any other person served with the claim form may apply to set aside an order giving permission to proceed with a claim for judicial review (**r. 54.13**).

If, contrary to the general rule, the court, in its discretion, decides that there should be an oral hearing of an application for permission to proceed with a claim for judicial review, the Administrative Court Office will fix a hearing date without any intervening consideration of the papers. The application is made to a judge in open court unless the court directs that it should be made in private or to a divisional court. The defendant and other interested parties are not required to attend, unless the court directs otherwise (**PD 54, para. 8.5**). If the defendant or any other party does attend, the court will not generally order the claimant to pay their costs of doing so (**para. 8.6**) (*R (Mount Cook Land Ltd) v Westminster City Council* [2003] EWCA Civ 1346, *The Times*, 16 October 2003; *Payne v Caerphilly County Borough Council* [2004] EWCA Civ 433, LTL 17/3/2004). In Practice Statement (Judicial Review: Costs) [2004] 2 All ER 994 it was confirmed that a grant of permission to pursue a claim for judicial review would be deemed to contain an order that costs of that application be costs in the case. This was to overcome the problem created by **CPR, r. 44.13**, which is that where no order for costs is made the general rule is that no party is entitled to costs. In the Administrative Court the practice had been to make no order for costs at a permission hearing on the assumption that those costs would be costs in the case. A different costs order can be specifically made by the judge granting permission.

Normally no witnesses attend a permission hearing and the claimant is not required to be there in person. An application for permission to proceed with a claim for judicial review is listed on the basis that the application will take no more than 20 minutes, and any reply by a defendant who attends will take no more than 10 minutes (Practice Direction (Crown Office List) (No. 2) [1991] 1 WLR 280). If permission is granted, any applications for interim relief or special directions are considered. If permission is refused, the decision can be appealed to the Court of Appeal with that court's permission (**CPR, r. 52.15(1)**).

An appeal to the Court of Appeal after permission is refused in an oral application will be heard by a full Court of Appeal (rather than a single Lord Justice). An application for permission to appeal against the High Court's refusal to permit a claim for judicial review to proceed must be made within seven days of the High Court's decision (**r. 52.15(2)**). The appellant's notice must be accompanied by the documents specified in **PD 52, para. 15.4**. A copy of it must be served on all respondents to the appeal in accordance with **CPR, r. 52.4(3)** (**PD 52, paras 5.21** and **15.6**). Instead of granting permission to appeal, the Court of Appeal may proceed directly to give the permission to proceed with the claim which was initially sought (**CPR, r. 52.15(3)**) and the case will be returned to the High Court, unless the Court of Appeal orders otherwise (**r. 52.15(4)**; see *R (Werner) v Commissioners of Inland Revenue* [2002] EWCA Civ 979, [2002] STC 1213 at [30] to [33]). It is likely to be rare for the Court of Appeal to retain the case, but this would be appropriate where, for example, the High Court is bound by authority or, for some other reason, a further appeal to the Court of Appeal would be inevitable (**PD 52, para. 15.3**). If permission has been refused by the Court of Appeal, the court of first instance may, nevertheless, subsequently grant permission if there have been developments of which the Court of Appeal was unaware (*R v Radio Authority, ex parte Wildman* [1999] COD 255). If the Court of Appeal refuses permission there is no appeal or possibility of renewing the application to the House of Lords (*Re Poh* [1983] 1 WLR 2); *R v Secretary of State for Trade and Industry, ex parte Eastaway* [2000] 1 WLR 2222).

A claimant who no longer requires any substantive relief but wishes the claim to go forward to test the lawfulness of the defendant's procedures in general must inform the defendant that he wishes the court to scrutinise the defendant's practices and procedures (*R (Tshikangu) v Newham London Borough Council* [2001] EWHC 92 (Admin), [2001] NPC 33). The parties should consider whether a test case is appropriate, and if so what that case should be. If they are not agreed, application should be made to the court for it to consider the matter before the costs of a substantive hearing are incurred.

PROCEDURE ONCE PERMISSION HAS BEEN GRANTED

Defendant's evidence and evidence in reply

If permission is given to proceed with a claim for judicial review, the order granting permission will be served on the defendant and any other person who filed an acknowledgment of service (**CPR, r. 54.11**). Any of those persons who wish to contest the claim, or to support it on additional grounds, must, within 35 days after service of the permission order, file and serve the detailed grounds for contesting or supporting and their written evidence (**r. 54.14(1)**). If it is intended to rely on documents not already filed, a paginated bundle of the new documents must be filed with the detailed grounds (**PD 54, para. 10.1**). In judicial review proceedings **r. 54.14(1)** applies instead of **r. 8.5(3) to (6)** (**r. 54.14(2)**). The 35-day time limit can be extended or shortened on application to a master of the Administrative Court Office or a High Court judge (**CPR, r. 3.1(2)(a)**). The 35-day time limit applies both to written evidence and to detailed grounds for contesting the claim or supporting it on additional grounds (*R (J) v Newham London Borough Council* [2001] EWHC 992 (Admin), *The Independent*, 10 December 2001). Failure to serve within the time limit may be dealt with by the general discretion of the court to extend time, subject to the overriding objective. Any evidence in reply should include details of the facts which the defendant intends to rely upon, its answers to issues raised by the claimant, a response to the claimant's evidence, and should exhibit all documents relevant to the decision challenged which have not been exhibited with the claimant's evidence and which the defendant wishes to rely upon at the substantive hearing. The written evidence should also make clear if there is any factual conflict between the claimant and the defendant. The written evidence should be filed in the Administrative Court Office. **74.38**

Permission to proceed with a judicial review claim is permission to proceed on specified grounds only. The claimant will not be able to rely on other grounds without further permission from the court (**r. 54.15**). Notice of intention to rely on additional grounds must be given to the court, and to any other person served with the claim form, no later than seven clear days before the hearing (or the warned date if one has been given) (**PD 54, para. 11.1**). Where there is good reason to allow argument on an additional ground, permission should be granted. Each case should be considered on its facts. In exercising discretion, a judge should bear in mind that if permission to rely on a ground is refused, the Court of Appeal on an appeal from the hearing at first instance would not be able to consider it (*R (Smith) v Parole Board* [2003] EWCA Civ 1014, *The Times*, 9 July 2003). Cf. the approach in *Opoku v Principal of Southwark School* [2002] EWHC 2092 (Admin), [2003] 1 WLR 234).

The service of written evidence in reply by the claimant may be considered necessary where there is a factual dispute, where new circumstances have arisen since applying for permission to proceed, or in order to comment upon documents disclosed by the defendant.

Interim remedies

Although most forms of interim remedies are available in judicial review proceedings, obtaining interim remedies is more restricted than in private law actions. Generally the most appropriate time to apply for interim remedies is at the stage of applying for permission but a court may grant interim remedies to any of the parties during the course of judicial review proceedings. (If interim remedies are sought after the substantive application has been dismissed, pending appeal, it will be necessary to show that the appeal has a good prospect of success.) **74.39**

A claim form for judicial review must state any interim remedy which is claimed. In particular, it may ask for the court, when giving permission for the claim to proceed to direct (under **CPR, r. 54.10(2)**) a stay of proceedings to which the claim relates. A stay under **r. 54.10(2)** has the effect that the public body's decision or procedure which is the subject of challenge should not continue or take effect until the judicial review challenge is determined. In considering whether to grant a stay, the court will take into account the effect on third parties and may refuse a stay notwithstanding a grant of permission to proceed with the claim for judicial review, applying balance of convenience considerations. A stay is available as a remedy against all public bodies against whom permission has been granted, including the Crown in the form of a government department or minister (*R v Secretary of State for Education, ex parte Avon County Council* [1991] 1 QB 558). A cross-undertaking for damages to a party to the action may be made a condition of a stay (*R v Inspectorate of Pollution, ex parte Greenpeace Ltd* [1994] 1 WLR 570).

The court may also at any time grant in the proceedings interim remedies in accordance with **CPR, Part 25**. The general principles governing the grant of interim remedies apply also in relation to judicial review proceedings (*R v Ministry of Agriculture, Fisheries and Food, ex parte Monsanto plc* [1999] QB 1161). However, these have to be applied in the context of the public law questions raised in such proceedings (see **74.53**). **Rule 25.1** of the CPR lists the interim remedies which include an interim injunction (**r. 25.1(1)(a)**), interim declaration (**r. 25.1(1)(b)**), freezing injunction (**r. 25.1(f)**), search order (**r. 25.1(1)(h)**), and an order for the detention and inspection of relevant property (**r. 25.1(1)(c)**). Generally, notice of an application for an interim remedy should be given to all parties (**r. 25.3(1)**).

Injunctions are the main type of interim relief ordered in judicial review proceedings. To obtain an interim injunction in a civil case, it must be established that the applicant has a serious issue to be tried on the merits and that the 'balance of convenience' favours the making of an interim order (*American Cyanamid Co. v Ethicon Ltd* [1975] AC 396; see **chapter 37**). The balance of convenience test involves the court considering whether there is an adequate alternative remedy in damages, the interests of the general public to whom the duties are owed, the importance of upholding the law of the land, and the duty upon certain authorities to enforce the law in the public interest. There is a presumption in favour of a cross-undertaking in damages (**PD 25, para. 5.1(1)**). The approach to applications for interim injunctions in judicial review proceedings is similar to that adopted in applications for interim injunctions in private law claims (*R v Kensington and Chelsea Royal London Borough Council, ex parte Hammell* [1989] QB 518). However, where public bodies are concerned the balance of convenience may be more difficult to make out — i.e., ordinary financial considerations may be qualified by recognition of the interests of the general public (*Smith v Inner London Education Authority* [1978] 1 All ER 411). Usually an application is for a prohibitory injunction to prevent a public body from doing something. Where a mandatory injunction is sought, the order will not be granted unless the court has a high degree of assurance of the merits of the case.

An interim injunction is available against a government minister but will only be granted in limited circumstances, i.e., where it is necessary for the court to have power to prevent irreparable harm to the citizen by unauthorised governmental action (*Re M* [1994] 1 AC 377). An interim injunction has been granted against a minister of the Crown to restrain him from implementing a new regime authorised by an Act of Parliament where there was a strong prima facie case that the Act was in breach of European Community law (*R v Secretary of State for Transport, ex parte Factortame Ltd (No. 2)* [1991] 1 AC 603). The Court of Justice of the European Communities ruled that where a national court was seised of a case involving Community law issues and it was necessary to grant interim relief in order to ensure the full effectiveness of the rights claimed under directly applicable Community law, any rule of national law preventing the grant of such interim relief must be set aside. A reference to the European Court of Justice is required to establish whether domestic or Community law is applicable when a domestic court is asked to grant an injunction to restrain the government from making regulations during the implementation period pursuant to an EC Directive (*R v Secretary of State for Health, ex parte Imperial Tobacco Ltd* [2001] 1 WLR 127). Community law permits applications for an injunction in the domestic courts in support of an application to the domestic court challenging the validity of an EC Directive. In order to grant an injunction, serious doubts are required as to the validity of the Community measure and the need to avoid serious and irreparable damage (which is not purely financial) to the party seeking the injunction.

Rule 25.1(1)(b) of the CPR provides for the grant of an interim declaration. Prior to the introduction of the CPR the existence of such a remedy was uncertain. Interim declarations are granted on a similar basis to interim injunctions. The decision whether or not to grant an interim injunction or declaration is a matter of discretion for the court of first instance, with which the Court of Appeal will not interfere unless there is an error of law or plain error of fact or assessment. In deciding whether to grant an interim remedy, the court should have regard to the 'threshold condition' that legislation ought to be fulfilled in all but exceptional cases. Thereafter, considering the balance of convenience, the concurrent elements are the strength of the case and the parties' respective losses if the declaration were granted or refused (*R v Secretary of State for Trade and Industry, ex parte Trades Union Congress* [2000] IRLR 565). An interim declaration of unlawfulness has been granted in respect of arrangements for the control of pesticides made under regulations which were made by statutory instrument, pending determination by the European Court of Justice of a reference made in another case concerning interpretation of the Directive which the regulations were made to implement (*R v Ministry of Agriculture, Fisheries and Food, ex parte British Agrochemicals Association Ltd (No. 2)* [2000] 1 CMLR 826). However, the grant of an interim declaration to render national legislation inoperative pending the decision of the European Court of Justice will be rare, as there is a presumption in favour of the national law being applicable (*R v Secretary of State for Trade and Industry, ex parte Trades Union Congress* [2001] 1 CMLR 8).

Interim applications

An interim application may be made to any judge or to a master of the Queen's Bench **74.40**
Division. Where the application for judicial review is to be heard by a Divisional Court, any appeal from a decision of a master will lie to the Divisional Court itself. Contested interim applications are normally heard by a judge nominated to hear Administrative Court Office list cases.

Part 23 of the CPR and **PD 23** apply to interim applications in judicial review proceedings. **Part 23** requires that all applications are to be made by filing and serving an application notice (**r. 23.3(1)**). An application will not necessarily result in a hearing even if one is requested (**r. 23.8**).

Interim applications may have to be made seeking the exercise of the court's general powers of management under **r. 3.1(2)**, e.g., to extend or shorten the time for compliance with any rule, practice direction or court order (**r. 3.1(2)(a)**), consolidation in order that two or more matters be tried at the same time (**r. 3.1(2)(h)**), or to adjourn or expedite a hearing (**r. 3.1(2)(b)**).

The court has jurisdiction to order cross-examination of witnesses and disclosure in judicial review proceedings but the assumption is that disclosure is not required unless the court orders otherwise (**PD 54, para. 12.1**).

There is no automatic right to disclosure of documents in judicial review proceedings, but this is a context where there is already a separate duty of candour on the part of defendants who must set out fully what they did and why, so far as is necessary, fully and fairly to meet the challenge (*R v Lancashire County Council, ex parte Huddleston* [1986] 2 All ER 941). Disclosure will only be ordered where it is required to ensure the justice of the case and to dispose fairly of the matter (*R v Inland Revenue Commissioners, ex parte J. Rothschild Holdings plc* [1987] STC 163). The courts have held (Lord Scarman in *R v Inland Revenue Commissioners, ex parte National Federation of Self-Employed and Small Businesses Ltd* [1982] AC 617):

Upon general principles, discovery should not be ordered unless or until the court is satisfied that the evidence reveals reasonable grounds for believing that there has been a breach of public duty; and it should be limited strictly to documents relevant to the issue which emerges from the affidavits.

The courts will not permit the claimant to obtain disclosure to go behind an assertion in the defendant's written evidence and check its accuracy unless the claimant has some evidence that the contents are false or not accurate (*R v Secretary of State for the Environment, ex parte Islington London Borough Council* [1992] COD 67). Disclosure and inspection may also be withheld on the grounds of public interest immunity. However, the courts may come under particular pressure to order disclosure in **Human Rights Act 1998** cases, which may involve a factual examination of the merits of a case (see **chapter 97**).

There seems to be no reason in principle why the provisions for pre-action and non-party disclosure (see **48.70** to **48.81**) would not apply to judicial review proceedings but, in practice, it will be very difficult to obtain an order under those provisions in judicial review proceedings. Further, in the case of pre-action disclosure there is the practical issue for a potential claimant of needing to apply for permission to seek judicial review promptly and the timescale may make it impractical to seek pre-action disclosure first.

It is extremely difficult to obtain an order to provide clarification or further information in judicial review proceedings. Claimants who wish defendants to answer a request for further information should first serve them informally, requesting a response within a reasonable time, prior to making an application to the court (**PD 18, para. 1.1**).

Intervening parties

74.41 A claimant seeking judicial review is under a duty to serve a copy of the claim form upon any person the claimant considers to be an interested party, unless the court directs otherwise (**CPR, r. 54.7**). 'Interested party' is defined as any person (other than the claimant and the defendant) who is directly affected by the claim (**r. 54.1(2)(f)**). The meaning of persons 'directly affected' was considered by the House of Lords in *R v Rent Officer Service, ex parte Muldoon* [1996] 1 WLR 1103. It was suggested (per Lord Keith of Kinkel at p. 1105), 'That a person is directly affected by something connotes that he is affected without the intervention of any intermediate agency'. The Secretary of State for Social Security was held to be only indirectly affected by a judicial review claim which challenged a failure to determine claims for housing benefit, as it was the local authority which would have to pay the claimants if the claim were successful. Similarly, the courts have refused to regard tobacco companies as 'directly affected' by a claim for judicial review of a refusal by the Legal Aid Board to grant the claimants legal aid to bring proceedings against the tobacco company (*R v Legal Aid Board, ex parte Megarry* [1994] COD 468).

Any person served with the claim form who wishes to take part in the judicial review must file an acknowledgment of service in accordance with **r. 54.8**. Failure to file an acknowledgment of service means that the permission of the court will be required to take part in a hearing to decide permission to proceed with the claim (**r. 54.9(1)(a)**).

An interested party who has not acknowledged service cannot take part in the substantive hearing without filing and serving detailed grounds for contesting the claim or supporting it on additional grounds, and any written evidence (**r. 54.9(1)(b)**).

Applications to intervene should be made at the earliest reasonable opportunity, since it will usually be essential not to delay the hearing (**PD 54, para. 13.5**). An application for permission to file evidence or make representations at the hearing of the judicial review claim should be made by letter to the Administrative Court Office, identifying the claim, explaining who the applicant is and indicating why and in what form the applicant wants to participate in the hearing (**PD 54, para. 13.3**). If the applicant is seeking a prospective order as to costs, the letter should say what kind of order and on what grounds (**PD 54, para. 13.4**).

Filing an acknowledgment of service entitles an interested party to be served with the court's order giving or refusing permission to proceed and any directions (**r. 54.11**). If the claimant requests that a refusal of permission be reconsidered at a hearing, any person who has filed an acknowledgment of service will be given at least two days' notice of the hearing (**r. 54.12(5)**). Any person served with the claim form may not apply to set aside an order giving permission to proceed (**r. 54.13**).

No interested party need attend a hearing on the question of permission to proceed unless the court directs otherwise (**PD 54, para. 8.5**). Where the defendant or any other party does attend a hearing, the court will not generally make an order for costs against the claimant (**PD 54, para. 8.6**).

Any person served with the claim form who wishes to contest the claim or support it on additional grounds must file and serve detailed grounds for contesting or supporting the claim and any written evidence within 35 days after service of the order giving permission to proceed (**CPR, r. 54.14(1)**).

Any person may apply for permission to file evidence or to make representations at the substantive judicial review hearing (**r. 54.17(1)**). Such an application must be made promptly (**r. 54.17(2)**). Where all the parties consent, the court may deal with such an application without a hearing (**PD 54, para. 13.1**). Where the court gives permission for a person to file evidence or make representations at the substantive hearing, it may do so on conditions and may give case management directions (**PD 54, para. 13.2**).

There is no general right for a third party to be heard on appeal, although the Court of Appeal may exercise its discretion to permit this.

The court will rarely grant two sets of costs in judicial review proceedings to two parties who appear in the same interest (*R v Industrial Disputes Tribunal, ex parte American Express Co. Inc.* [1954] 1 WLR 1118; *Bolton Metropolitan District Council v Secretary of State for the Environment* [1995] 1 WLR 1176). However, in exceptional circumstances the court may grant two sets of costs, e.g., where the issues are complex or important or the interests of the two parties concerned are divergent (*R v Registrar of Companies, ex parte Central Bank of India* [1986] QB 1114).

SUBSTANTIVE HEARING

Listing the hearing

The court may decide a claim for judicial review without a hearing if all the parties agree (**CPR, r. 54.18**). If the parties agree about the final order to be made in a claim for judicial review, the claimant must file at the court two copies of a document signed by all the parties setting out the terms of the proposed agreed order, together with a short statement of the matters relied upon as justifying the proposal and copies of any authorities or statutory provisions relied on (**PD 54, para. 17.1**). The court will consider the documents and will make the order if satisfied that the order should be made (**para. 17.2**). If the court is not satisfied that the order should be made, a hearing date will be set (**para. 17.3**). Where the agreement relates to an order for costs only, the parties need only file a document signed by all the parties setting out the terms of the proposed order (**para. 17.4**). Where a claim is entered for hearing it must be entered in the Administrative Court Office List in accordance with Practice Direction (Crown Office List) [1987] 1 WLR 232. All applications for judicial review are included within the Administrative Court Office List which is divided into five parts. These are: **74.42**

Part A: cases not ready to be heard, i.e., permission has not yet been obtained or the time limits for the filing of evidence have not yet expired.

Part B: cases ready to be heard, i.e., the warned list. All applications are entered in Part B once all relevant time limits have expired, i.e., usually after the 35-day period for service of the defendant's written evidence has ended. When a case enters Part B the claimant or the claimant's solicitors will be informed of this by letter and must duly inform their counsel, the defendant and any other interested parties of the likelihood of the case being listed at short notice. Applications for adjournments will be granted only in exceptional circumstances (Practice Direction (Crown Office List: Preparation for Hearings) [2000] 2 All ER 896).

Part C: cases stood out, i.e., where a case appears in Part B or Part E and any party is not ready to be heard, the case may be stood out of the list into Part C upon application to the master of the court office, and may be appealed to a judge or the divisional court by a court application.

Part D: the expedited list, i.e., cases listed to be heard as soon as practicable. An application to be entered in Part D should initially be made to the master of the Administrative Court Office, and may be appealed to a divisional court or judge by a court application.

Part E: cases listed for hearing, i.e., cases where a date for the substantive hearing has been fixed. When a case is about to be listed under Part E, the Administrative Court Office will send a letter to the claimant's solicitors asking them to confirm that the case is still active and informing them that it will be listed shortly. If the claimant does not confirm within two weeks that the case is still active, the case may be put before the court and struck out for want of prosecution.

Documentation

74.43 Skeleton arguments are mandatory in all cases in the Administrative Court Office List. The claimant's counsel is required to file a skeleton argument with the Administrative Court Office and serve a copy on counsel for the defendant at least 21 working days before the date of the hearing or warned date (**PD 54, para. 15.1**). The defendant and any other party wishing to make representations at the substantive hearing must file and serve a skeleton argument not less than 14 working days before the date of the hearing or the warned date (**para. 15.2**). If the application is to be heard by a divisional court, two copies of the skeleton argument must be lodged. The skeleton arguments may be supplemented up to one working day before the hearing (Practice Direction (Crown Office List: Preparation for Hearings) [1994] 1 WLR 1551). The skeleton arguments must quote the Administrative Court Office reference number and the warned/fixed date, provide a time estimate for the complete hearing (including delivery of judgment), and must also contain a list of issues, a list of the legal points to be taken (together with any relevant authorities with page references to the passages relied on), a chronology of events (with page references to the bundle of documents to be filed), a list of essential documents for the advance reading of the court (with page references to the passages relied on) (if different to that filed with the claim form), a time estimate for that reading, and a list of persons referred to (**PD 54, para. 15.3**). Time estimates will be required from each party once the application is entered in Part B of the List. Great care must be taken by counsel to provide a well-judged and realistic time estimate for the hearing (Practice Direction (Crown Office List: Estimated Length of Hearing) [1987] 1 All ER 1184). The obligations upon counsel in the practice directions apply equally to a solicitor advocate.

For the use of extracts from *Hansard* under the rule in *Pepper v Hart* [1993] AC 593 see the guidance at **71.49**. Where this is permitted, the party must serve upon all other parties and the Administrative Court Office the relevant extract together with a brief summary of the argument based on the extract at least five working days before the hearing (Practice Direction (*Hansard*: Citation) [1995] 1 WLR 192).

The claimant's solicitor is responsible for preparing a paginated and indexed bundle of documents which must be lodged in the Administrative Court Office at the same time as the skeleton argument is filed (**PD 54, para. 16.1**). The bundle must also include documents required by the defendant and any other party who is to make representations at the hearing (**para. 16.2**). If the claim is to be heard by a divisional court, two copies of each bundle must be lodged. The bundles must contain copies of the claim form, the decision complained of (if not separately exhibited), any relevant correspondence between the parties and any orders made in the course of the proceedings, and the written evidence filed by both parties. Where possible, the parties' solicitors should agree the contents of the bundles.

If the obligation to lodge a proper bundle is not complied with, the application for judicial review may be struck out and the costs imposed upon the claimant or the claimant's solicitor (*R v Home Secretary, ex parte Meyer-Wulff* [1986] Imm AR 258).

Oral evidence

In judicial review proceedings the Administrative Court may, either under **CPR, r. 32.1**, or its inherent jurisdiction, hear oral evidence and order the cross-examination of witnesses (*R (G) v Ealing London Borough Council* [2002] EWHC 250 (Admin), [2002] ACD 48). In practice, the courts very rarely allow cross-examination in judicial review cases on the basis that it is not usually required in the interests of justice (*Khera v Secretary of State for the Home Department* [1984] AC 74; *George v Secretary of State for the Environment* (1979) 77 LGR 689). Generally, applications to cross-examine will be successful only where they are necessary in relation to disputes over the factual circumstances, in particular, applications based upon procedural impropriety where there is a material conflict of evidence about the procedure followed by the respondent, or where bad faith and/or bias is alleged against the respondent. **74.44**

A court considering making an order for compulsory treatment of a detained person under the Mental Health Act 1983 which might involve breaches of his rights under the European Convention on Human Rights should fully review the merits of the proposed treatment and, for that purpose, allow cross-examination of the specialists instructed on both sides (*R (Wilkinson) v Responsible Medical Officer Broadmoor Hospital* [2001] EWCA Civ 1545, [2002] 1 WLR 419). However, this approach should not be used as a charter for routine applications to the court for oral evidence in human rights cases generally. The decision whether to allow cross-examination will depend largely on the nature of the right that has allegedly been breached and the nature of the alleged breach. It should not be overlooked that the court's role is essentially one of review (*R (N) v Dr M* [2002] EWCA Civ 1789, [2003] 1 WLR 562).

Expert evidence

The general approach to evidence in judicial review proceedings is that fresh evidence can only be adduced in very limited circumstances (*R v Secretary of State for the Environment, ex parte Powis* [1981] 1 WLR 584). However, in some cases fairness may require that new expert evidence is used, although such cases will be very rare. Expert evidence will be allowed only to explain technical processes, and not to give an opinion on the reasonableness of the expert tribunal's decision, which would amount to an attempt to challenge the technical judgment of the tribunal on the merits of the case (*R (Lynch) v General Dental Council* [2003] EWHC 2987 (Admin), [2004] 1 All ER 1159). **74.45**

Constitution of the court

A claim for judicial review in a civil matter should be made to a judge sitting in open court, unless the court directs that it should be made to a judge in private or to a divisional court of the Queen's Bench Division. **74.46**

Substantive judicial review applications in civil matters are therefore generally heard by a single judge sitting in open court. There may be cases involving regulatory issues in which a private hearing may be ordered in the light of CPR, r. 39.2(3)(a) or (c), in circumstances involving confidential information of significance or where there is a special reason to fear that reporting of the case may be unbalanced (*R (Amvac Chemical UK Ltd) v Secretary State for the Environment, Food and Rural Affairs* [2001] EWHC 1011 (Admin), [2002] ACD 219). A substantive application in a civil case is heard by the divisional court only in exceptional circumstances, such as where the application raises questions of difficulty, complexity or importance. Occasionally, the hearing may be before a judge in chambers. In exceptional cases the Court of Appeal may, where it deals with an appeal against refusal to give permission to proceed with a claim for judicial review (see 74.37), hear the substantive application (e.g., as in *British Airways Board v Laker Airways Ltd* [1984] QB 142). However, usually the substantive hearing is heard by a different judge or court from that which granted permission.

Transfer of proceedings

74.47 Part 30 of the CPR applies to transfers to and from the Administrative Court (**CPR, r. 54.20**). The court may order a claim to continue as if it had not been started under **Part 54**, and where it does so it may give directions about the future management of the claim. **PD 54, para. 14.1** draws attention to **r. 30.5**, which provides that the High Court may order proceedings in any Division of the High Court to be transferred to another Division and to or from a specialist list. An application for the transfer of proceedings to or from a specialist list must be made to a judge dealing with claims in that list (**r. 30.5(3)**).

In deciding whether a claim is suitable for transfer to the Administrative Court, the court will consider whether it raises issues of public law to which **Part 54** should apply (**PD 54, para. 14.2**).

The court may, if it thinks appropriate where a claim for damages is included in an application for judicial review, determine the public law issues and then order issues relating to private law liability to proceed as if commenced under **CPR, Part 7**. Alternatively, the court may award damages at the judicial review hearing and leave quantum to be assessed by the court subsequently. However, it is likely that where the only remedies sought are public law remedies the court will not allow the matter to proceed as if commenced under **Part 7**. In order to permit the transfer of a case under **r. 54.20** it is likely that the court would require that the issues be sufficiently clearly defined, and at least some of the claims that are sought to be pursued in a **Part** 7 action must already be in existence (*R v East Berkshire Health Authority, ex parte Walsh* [1985] QB 152).

A claim in contract will not be struck out because it could more appropriately be made under **Part 54**, unless there is an abuse of process, for example, delay in starting proceedings (*Clark v University of Lincolnshire and Humberside* [2000] 1 WLR 1988).

REMEDIES

74.48 All the remedies available in judicial review proceedings are subject to the discretion of the court, so that even if a case is proved the court may refuse any or all of the remedies sought by the claimant. The High Court may exercise its discretion under the **Supreme Court Act 1981, s. 31**, to make the prerogative mandatory, prohibiting and quashing orders and provide the private law remedies of injunction, declaration, damages, restitution or the recovery of any sum due. The Administrative Court may make a declaration of incompatibility under the **Human Rights Act 1998, s. 4**. These remedies may be sought individually (except that a judicial review claim may not seek a money remedy alone: **r. 54.3(2)**), alternatively or in combination. Declaratory and injunctive relief are obtainable in proceedings for judicial review even when one of the prerogative orders is capable of being granted (*R v Secretary of State for Employment, ex parte Equal Opportunities Commission* [1995] 1 AC 1).

The **CPR, Part 54**, procedure must be used for a judicial review claim seeking a prerogative order or an injunction under the **Supreme Court Act 1981, s. 30**, restraining a person from acting in an office in which he or she is not entitled to act (**CPR, r. 54.2**). It may be used for a judicial review claim seeking a declaration or an injunction, but must be used if a declaration or injunction is sought in addition to a prerogative order or an injunction under the **Supreme Court Act 1981, s. 30 (CPR, r. 54.3(1))**.

The discretionary nature of remedies

74.49 All public law remedies are discretionary, i.e., even though the claimant has standing to commence judicial review proceedings, the decision or action in question is reviewable, and the grounds for review are proved, the court may yet decide not to award the claimant all or part of the remedies requested. The court has withheld remedies on a number of grounds.

The court may refuse to grant the relief requested if suitable alternative remedies have not been pursued (e.g., *R v Secretary of State for the Home Department, ex parte Swati* [1986] 1 WLR 477) (see 74.27).

A court may refuse relief because of the claimant's conduct or motives, for example, where the claimant suppressed or misrepresented material facts in presenting the claim (*R v Kensington Income Tax Commissioners, ex parte Princess Edmond de Polignac* [1917] 1 KB 486), or delayed in commencing proceedings. The time limits set out in **CPR, r. 54.5(1)** and the **Supreme Court Act 1981, s. 31**, must be adhered to strictly and therefore undue delay may result in the refusal of any relief (see 74.33). The court may also refuse to grant relief if it believes the likely effect of a remedy will serve no practical purpose, e.g., in cases where the public body has already remedied its position to meet the claimant's demands (*R v Gloucestershire County Council, ex parte P* [1994] ELR 334) or where a public body shows that it is doing all it can to comply with its statutory duty. Breach of a statutory provision may have such an insignificant effect that the court may refuse relief (as in *R v Dairy Produce Quota Tribunal, ex parte Davies* [1987] 2 CMLR 399). In exercising its discretion, the court will take into account whether others will be directly or indirectly affected by its decision — e.g., a decision which has the potential to affect a large number of individuals such as an inquiry into a new motorway. Therefore reliance upon a decision by third parties may also induce the court not to grant the remedy claimed.

If an issue is theoretical, then in ordinary civil proceedings this may be a compelling factor against the grant of relief. However, the court may occasionally grant an advisory opinion, e.g., in the form of a declaration, where it is desirable that it should do so (*R v Secretary of State for Employment, ex parte Equal Opportunities Commission* [1995] 1 AC 1).

Quashing order

74.50 A quashing order deprives the decision which is being reviewed of all legal effect and the decision challenged is therefore effectively set aside. Until a decision is quashed, it is deemed to possess a 'presumption of validity' and is disobeyed at the claimant's risk pending the substantive judicial review hearing (*F. Hoffmann-La Roche & Co. AG v Secretary of State for Trade and Industry* [1975] AC 295).

A quashing order is available to quash the decisions of inferior courts or tribunals and any other public body 'having legal authority to determine questions affecting the rights of subjects, and having the duty to act judicially' (per Lord Atkin in *R v Electricity Commissioners, ex parte London Electricity Joint Committee Co. (1920) Ltd* [1924] 1 KB 171). The courts have subsequently accepted that a quashing order is not confined to the review of decisions of a judicial nature (*R v Hillingdon London Borough Council, ex parte Royco Homes Ltd* [1974] QB 720). The court will consider the nature of the power exercised in order to determine whether this test has been satisfied. A quashing order may be claimed against a broad range of administrative decision-makers, e.g., local authorities, legal committees and ministers of the Crown and may relate to administrative decisions and delegated legislation.

Where a quashing order is sought and the court is satisfied that there are grounds for quashing the decision it may in addition remit the matter to the decision-maker and 'direct it to reconsider the matter and reach a decision in accordance with the judgment of the court' (**CPR, r. 54.19(2)(b)**). This power may be used to ensure that a decision is reconsidered and a new decision made. However, there is no guarantee that a different result will be reached: the decision-maker is justified in reaching the same result again provided that the matter is reconsidered in accordance with the law. Where the court considers that there is no purpose to be served in remitting the matter to the decision-maker, it may, subject to any statutory provision, take the decision itself (**r. 54.19(3)**). (However, where a power is given by statute to a tribunal, person or other body, it may be the case that the court cannot take the decision itself.)

Prohibiting order

74.51 A prohibiting order prevents the decision-maker from acting or continuing to act in excess of jurisdiction. Therefore, if a public body threatens to make an unlawful decision which could be quashed had it been made, the court may make a prohibiting order to prevent the decision being made. For example, a local council was prohibited from increasing the number of taxi licences in breach of an undertaking to consult the local professional association (*R v Liverpool Corporation, ex parte Liverpool Taxi Fleet Operators' Association* [1972] 2 QB 299).

If a want of jurisdiction is apparent, a prohibiting order may be claimed immediately. If it is not apparent, the claimant must wait until the tribunal has stepped outside its jurisdiction or is undoubtedly about to do so (*Zohrab v Smith* (1848) 17 LJ QB 174). Doubts have been expressed about the power to claim a prohibiting order for an anticipatory excess of jurisdiction (*Re Ashby* [1934] OR 421). A prohibiting order is not granted lightly (*Governors of Queen Anne's Bounty v Pitt-Rivers* [1936] 2 KB 419). A prohibiting order is not available against a public body which has already completed the acts complained of (*Yates v Palmer* (1849) 6 Dowl & L 283). A prohibiting order is also not available to review a finding of fact made by an inferior court for the purpose of assuming jurisdiction (*Joseph v Henry* (1850) 19 LJ QB 369). It may be refused in a case of laches or misconduct by the applicant (*Parochial Church Council of St Magnus-the-Martyr v Chancellor of London* [1923] P 38).

Mandatory order

74.52 A mandatory order requires an inferior court or tribunal or a person or body of persons charged with a public duty to carry out its judicial or other public duty. A mandatory order may compel a court or tribunal to state its case (*R v Watson, ex parte Bretherton* [1945] KB 96) and to give reasons for its decision where it was required to do so by statute (*Brayhead (Ascot) Ltd v Berkshire County Council* [1964] 2 QB 303). This includes the provision of adequately intelligible reasons (*Earl Iveagh v Minister of Housing and Local Government* [1964] 1 QB 395). A mandatory order can compel a public body to exercise its discretion in accordance with the law, though the court is reluctant to use the remedy in this way (e.g., *R v Barnet London Borough Council, ex parte Nilish Shah* [1983] 2 AC 309).

It is preferable that the claimant is able to say that performance of the duty has been demanded and that the performance has been refused by the authority obliged to discharge it (*State (Modern Homes (Ireland) Ltd) v Dublin Corporation* [1953] IR 202). Therefore, before applying for judicial review, a claimant should make a specific demand or request to the authority to perform the duty imposed upon it. This corresponds with the requirement upon a claimant to write an appropriate 'letter before action' prior to claiming judicial review (see 74.28).

The court has a wide discretion to refuse to make a mandatory order. One will not be granted unless the defendant has an absolute duty, or has already decided in the claimant's favour all factors necessary to render it subject to a duty, to do that which the claimant seeks. A mandatory order cannot be made against the Crown (**Crown Proceedings Act 1947, s. 40**) but can be made against ministers.

Injunctions

74.53 Under the **Supreme Court Act 1981, s. 31(2)**, in judicial review proceedings the court may make a declaration or grant an injunction if it considers that it would be just and convenient having regard to:

(a) the nature of the matters in respect of which a remedy may be granted by way of a mandatory, prohibiting or quashing order;
(b) the nature of the persons and bodies against whom a remedy may be granted by way of such an order; and
(c) all the circumstances of the case.

In a claim for judicial review a final injunction can be granted in order to restrain a public body from acting unlawfully, restrain the implementation of an unlawful decision or compel a public authority to comply with its statutory duties. Injunctive relief does not lie against the Crown itself (**Crown Proceedings Act 1947, ss. 21 and 38**) but injunctions can be granted against ministers and other officers of the Crown in their official as well as their private capacities (*Re M* [1994] 1 AC 377) and, in particular, an injunction may be granted against a minister of the Crown in order to give a remedy in favour of a party invoking rights derived from directly applicable Community law (*R v Secretary of State for Transport, ex parte Factortame Ltd (No. 2)* [1991] 1 AC 603).

The discretion conferred upon the court under the conditions stipulated in the **Supreme Court Act 1981, s. 31(2)**, is broad but must be exercised in accordance with recognised principles. An injunction will be refused if the injury complained of is very trivial or if it has ceased and there is no likelihood of its recurrence. Further, a court will not order an injunction to do something which is impossible, or where the grant of an injunction would be oppressive.

A final injunction, although granted at the conclusion of the proceedings, need not be expressed to have perpetual effect, i.e., it may be awarded for a fixed period. However, a mandatory injunction will not be granted to ensure the performance of a continuing series of acts which the court cannot supervise although the court may award a prohibitory injunction to restrain the discontinuance of a public service.

Declarations

A declaration may be granted in judicial review proceedings in the circumstances set out in the **Supreme Court Act 1981, s. 31(2)** (see 74.53). **74.54**

Declaratory relief and any other private law remedy may be granted by a court even if none of the prerogative remedies is available, provided the case is within the realm of public law.

The court has a broad discretion to grant declaratory relief (*Barnard v National Dock Labour Board* [1953] 2 QB 18). Declarations may be sought in order to challenge the legality of decisions taken or policies adopted by a public body, to challenge delegated legislation, to determine the ambit of public law obligations, to pronounce upon questions of law and the compatibility of primary legislation with European Community law (*R v Secretary of State for Employment, ex parte Equal Opportunities Commission* [1995] 1 AC 1).

The court may consider granting relief because of any public interest element involved (*R v Her Majesty's Treasury, ex parte Smedley* [1985] QB 657) or as a means of securing a private law entitlement (*Roy v Kensington and Chelsea and Westminster Family Practitioner Committee* [1992] 1 AC 624). The court may grant a declaration in relation to future rights (*R v Her Majesty's Treasury, ex parte Smedley*). However the circumstances must be appropriate for the grant, e.g., not too complex or uncertain. The courts are also willing to grant a negative declaration, e.g., a declaration of no right or no liability.

There are some limitations upon the scope of declaratory relief. Declaratory relief does not lie in respect of claims which are legally unenforceable (*Mutasa v Attorney-General* [1980] QB 114); *intra vires* errors of law appearing on the face of the record (*Punton v Minister of Pensions and National Insurance (No. 2)* [1964] 1 WLR 226); and matters which are academic or hypothetical. Courts should not make general declarations which are unnecessary and irrelevant for the particular claimant in the case, especially in circumstances where a claimant has been persuaded to bring a claim for judicial review by those who wish to challenge an issue generally (*R (Burke) v General Medical Council* [2005] EWCA Civ 1003, [2005] 2 FLR 1223). The civil courts are also reluctant to grant declaratory relief if a declaration could interfere with criminal proceedings (*R v Medicines Control Agency, ex parte Pharma Nord Ltd* (1997) 10 Admin LR 646).

Damages

74.55 Damages arising from any matter to which a judicial review claim relates may be awarded if the court is satisfied that they would have been awarded in an ordinary claim started at the same time as the judicial review claim (**Supreme Court Act 1981, s. 31(4)**).

A person who has suffered loss as a result of unlawful administrative conduct has to claim and establish liability under a recognised cause of action to claim damages. This will usually be a tort claim, e.g., negligence, negligent misstatement, breach of statutory duty (including breach of Convention rights under the **Human Rights Act 1998**), misfeasance in public office.

There are circumstances in which a public law breach of European Community law gives rise to a claim for damages in judicial review proceedings. The European Court of Justice has held that member States must pay compensation for harm caused to an individual for failure to implement an EU Directive (*Francovich v Italy* (cases C-6 & 9/90) [1991] ECR I-5357). The European Court has subsequently held that a right to compensation from member States is a universal principle and exists where three conditions are met:

(a) the rule of law infringed must be intended to confer rights on individuals;
(b) the breach must be sufficiently serious; and
(c) there must be a direct causal link between the breach and the damage sustained (*Brasserie du Pêcheur SA v Germany* (cases C-46 & 48/93) [1996] QB 404).

Subsequent cases have applied these principles (e.g., *R v Her Majesty's Treasury, ex parte British Telecommunications plc* (case C-392/93) [1996] QB 615; *R v Ministry of Agriculture, Fisheries and Food, ex parte Hedley Lomas (Ireland) Ltd* (case C-5/94) [1997] QB 139; *R v Secretary of State for Transport, ex parte Factortame Ltd (No. 5)* [2000] 1 AC 524).

However, damages are not available simply because an application for judicial review is successful (*R v Metropolitan Borough of Knowsley, ex parte Maguire* [1992] COD 499).

Part 16 of the CPR applies to making a claim for damages in a judicial review claim, i.e., the normal rules as to statements of case apply and the loss or damage suffered must be fully particularised.

APPEALS

74.56 An appeal against the decision of the High Court in a substantive hearing of a judicial review claim lies to the Court of Appeal and thereafter to the House of Lords in the normal way. The procedure for substantive appeals is discussed in **chapters** 72 and 73. Appeals from decisions to refuse permission to apply for judicial review were considered at 74.37.

When considering whether to grant permission to appeal from a substantive hearing for judicial review, the court will consider whether there is a prima facie case that an error has been made; whether there is an issue of legal principle involved (*R v Secretary of State for the Environment, ex parte Kirkstall Valley Campaign Ltd* [1996] 3 All ER 304); whether the issue is one which should be examined by the Court of Appeal in the public interest; and whether the appeal raises an issue where the law requires clarification (*Smith v Cosworth Casting Processes Ltd* [1997] 1 WLR 1538). The task of the Court of Appeal in a judicial review appeal is to resolve genuine questions of law: it does not reconsider the original decision-maker's findings of fact where the original tribunal disbelieved the claimant (*R (Nine Nepalese Asylum Seekers) v Immigration Appeal Tribunal* [2003] EWCA Civ 1892, *The Independent*, 21 January 2004). A further appeal to the House of Lords may be entertained in a public law matter (provided it is otherwise a suitable case for an appeal to the House) even in cases where there is no longer any *lis* between the parties (*R v Secretary of State for the Home Department, ex parte Salem* [1999] 1 AC 450), although academic appeals will only be heard if there are good reasons in the public interest for doing so.

Chapter 75 References to the European Court of Justice

INTRODUCTION

75.1 An English court faced with a question of European Community law may sometimes decide it itself, or may refer it to the European Court of Justice (ECJ) in Luxembourg for a preliminary ruling. If a reference is made, the English proceedings will be stayed pending the ruling of the ECJ. Once it is made, the ruling is binding on the English court, but it is only a preliminary ruling, in that the English court is left to apply the ruling to the facts of the case and to give judgment. The general policy is that Community law should be applied consistently in all member States.

QUESTIONS WHICH MAY BE REFERRED

75.2 References may be made:

(a) under art. 234 of the Treaty establishing the European Community (the 'EC Treaty');
(b) under art. 150 of the Treaty establishing the European Atomic Energy Community; or
(c) on the interpretation of any of the instruments referred to in the **Civil Jurisdiction and Judgments Act 1982, s. 1(1)**, or the Contracts (Applicable Law) Act 1990, s. 1.

Article 234 of the EC Treaty is representative of the various treaties and enactments mentioned above. It provides in its first paragraph:

The Court of Justice shall have jurisdiction to give preliminary rulings concerning:

(a) the interpretation of this Treaty;
(b) the validity and interpretation of acts of the institutions of the Community and of the [European Central Bank];
(c) the interpretation of the statutes of bodies established by an act of the Council, where those statutes so provide.

This includes questions on the amending Treaties and Treaties of Accession, and questions on Regulations, Directives and Decisions of the Council or Commission. Although the ECJ can give rulings on the interpretation of the Brussels Convention and Council Regulation (EC) No. 44/2001 (see **chapter 16**), it cannot do so on the modified versions of those documents governing allocation of jurisdiction within the UK (*Kleinwort Benson Ltd v Glasgow City Council* (case C-346/93) [1996] QB 57).

Questions referred for preliminary rulings must concern only the interpretation or validity of a provision of Community law, since the ECJ does not have jurisdiction to interpret national law or to assess its validity. It is for the referring court to apply the relevant provision of Community law to the case (ECJ Information Note, **PD 68, annex, para. 3**).

REFERRING COURT OR TRIBUNAL

It is a matter for the ECJ to decide whether a body is a court or tribunal for the purposes of art. 234 of the EC Treaty, and the categorisation of that body under national law is not conclusive (*Politi v Italy* (case 43/71) [1971] ECR 1039; *Corbiau v Administration des Contributions* (case C-24/92), [1993] ECR I-1277). The ECJ will take a number of factors into account when making this determination, including: whether the body is established by law, whether it is permanent, whether its jurisdiction is compulsory, whether its procedure is *inter partes*, whether it applies rules of law, and whether it is independent (*Dorsch Consult Ingenieurgesellschaft mbH v Bundesbaugesellschaft Berlin mbH* (case C-54/96) [1997] ECR I-4961; *Denuit v Transorient—Mosaïque Voyages and Culture SA* (case C-125/04) [2005] ECR I-923). For example, a Dutch body, called the Appeals Committee for General Medicine, which operated with the consent of the public authorities and with their cooperation, and which, after an adversarial procedure, delivered decisions, which were recognised as final, was considered as a court or tribunal within the meaning of art. 234 (*Broekmeulen v Huisarts Registratie Commissie* (case 246/80) [1981] ECR 2311). Also, the court or tribunal making the reference must be in a member State. Whether an arbitral court or tribunal can be regarded as an emanation of a member State will depend on the nature of the arbitration in question. The fact that the arbitral body gives a judgment according to law, and that the award is binding between the parties, will not, however, be sufficient. There must be a closer link between the arbitration procedure and the ordinary court system in a member State for the body to be considered as a court or tribunal of a member State (*Nordsee Deutsche Hochseefischerei GmbH v Reederei Mond Hochseefischerei Nordstern AG & Co. KG* (case 102/81) [1982] ECR 1095). 75.3

MANDATORY REFERENCES

Article 234 of the EC Treaty provides: 75.4

> Where any such question is raised in a case pending before a court or tribunal of a member State against whose decisions there is no judicial remedy under national law, that court or tribunal shall bring the matter before the Court of Justice.

Accordingly, references are mandatory in courts of last instance. In England, this is generally the House of Lords, unless by statute or rule some lower court is the final court of appeal. However, even in the House of Lords there must be a 'question' that needs to be referred. If a point is covered by considerable and consistent authority from the ECJ such that its answer is obvious, there is no 'question' within the meaning of art. 234 (per Lord Diplock in *Garland v British Rail Engineering Ltd* [1983] 2 AC 751 at p. 771; *Srl Cilfit v Ministry of Health* (case 283/81) [1982] ECR 3415). If it is not necessary to decide either whether Community law applies or the scope of its application to the present case, the reference procedure is not available even in the House of Lords (*R v Secretary of State for Health, ex parte Imperial Tobacco Ltd* [2001] 1 WLR 127).

DISCRETIONARY REFERENCES

For courts below the House of Lords, art. 234 of the EC Treaty provides: 75.5

> Where such a question is raised before any court or tribunal of a member State, that court or tribunal may, if it considers that a decision on the question is necessary to enable it to give judgment, request the Court of Justice to give a ruling thereon.

Two questions arise in such cases:

(a) whether a decision on the question of Community law is necessary to enable the court to give judgment; and
(b) if so, whether the court should in the exercise of its discretion order that a reference be made.

Guidelines on both questions were given by the Court of Appeal in *H. P. Bulmer Ltd v J. Bollinger SA* [1974] Ch 401 by Lord Denning MR at pp. 422–5. Whether to make a discretionary reference, and the extent of the questions to be posed to the ECJ, are essentially case management matters which are unlikely to be overturned on appeal (*Evans v Secretary of State for the Environment, Transport and the Regions* [2001] EWCA Civ 32, LTL 18/1/2001).

Guidelines for discretionary references

75.6 In *H. P. Bulmer Ltd v J. Bollinger SA* [1974] Ch 401 Lord Denning MR laid down four guidelines as to whether a decision from the European Court is necessary. They are no more than guidelines, and cannot be considered as binding (*Lord Bethell v SABENA* [1983] 3 CMLR 1).

75.7 **Whether the point will be conclusive** Article 234 provides that the court must consider whether 'a decision on the question is necessary to enable it to give judgment'. Lord Denning's view was that the point must be such that, whichever way it is decided, it will be conclusive of the case. This is probably too onerous. Ormrod LJ in *Polydor Ltd v Harlequin Record Shops Ltd* [1982] CMLR 413 said it was sufficient if the point was 'reasonably necessary', and Bingham J in *Customs and Excise Commissioners v ApS Samex* [1983] 1 All ER 1042 said that the question must be substantially, if not quite totally, determinative of the litigation.

75.8 **Previous ruling** As Lord Denning said in *H. P. Bulmer Ltd v J. Bollinger SA* [1974] Ch 401:

> In some cases . . . it may be found that the same point — or substantially the same point — has already been decided by the European Court in a previous case. In that event it is not necessary for the English court to decide it. It can follow the previous decision without troubling the European Court.

This is subject to the proviso that, with changing social and economic factors, the ECJ is not bound by its earlier decisions.

75.9 *Acte claire* Lord Denning MR went on to say:

> In other cases the English court may consider the point is reasonably clear and free from doubt. In that event there is no need to interpret the Treaty but only to apply it.

This should be read in the light of Lord Diplock's comment in *R v Henn* [1981] AC 850 at p. 906 that the court should not be 'too ready to hold that because the meaning of the English text (which is one of [nine] of equal authority) seems plain no question of interpretation can be involved'.

75.10 **Deciding the facts first** In general, it is best to decide the facts before making a reference, because it should then be clear if the question of Community law is necessary, and it enables the ECJ to take into account all the relevant facts when making its ruling. In any event, it is usually best not to make the reference at least until it is possible to define, if only hypothetically, the factual and legal context of the question (ECJ Information Note, **PD 68, annex, para.** 7). It is also usually best not to make a reference until both sides have been heard (*Simmenthal SpA v Amministrazione delle Finanze dello Stato* (case 70/77) [1978] ECR 1453).

Factors relevant to the discretion

75.11 General guidance has been provided by the ECJ on when it is appropriate to refer matters. The following factors were identified by Lord Denning MR in *H. P. Bulmer Ltd v J. Bollinger SA* [1974] Ch 401 as being relevant in the exercise of the court's discretion:

(a) delay in obtaining a ruling from the ECJ. Delays have been reduced in recent years;

(b) the importance of not overloading the ECJ;
(c) expense to the parties;
(d) the wishes of the parties. Although clearly relevant, the court can nevertheless make a reference even if both parties object, and, also, there is no such thing as a reference by consent. Ultimately the decision is that of the judge;
(e) difficulty and importance. Simple points should be decided by the English court;
(f) questions involving the comparison of texts in the different languages of the member States are best decided by the ECJ (*Customs and Excise Commissioners v ApS Samex* [1983] 1 All ER 1042);
(g) questions requiring a panoramic view of the Community and its institutions, the functioning of the Common Market or a broad view of the orderly development of the EU should be decided by the ECJ (*Customs and Excise Commissioners v ApS Samex*);
(h) whether the application for a reference is made in bad faith so as to delay judgment being given (*Customs and Excise Commissioners v ApS Samex*).

Questioning the validity of Community acts

Where a national court intends to question the validity of a Community act, it must refer the question to the ECJ (*Foto-Frost v Hauptzollamt Lübeck-Ost* (case 314/85) [1987] ECR 4199). Where the national court has serious doubts about the validity of a Community act on which a national measure is based, the national court may, in an exceptional case, suspend or grant interim relief in respect of the national measure, but it must refer the question of validity to the ECJ (*Zuckerfabrik Süderdithmarschen AG v Hauptzollamt Itzehoe* (cases C-143/88 and C-92/89) [1991] ECR I-415). **75.12**

PROCEDURE IN ENGLAND

An order referring a question to the ECJ may be made at any stage of the proceedings, and may be made by the court of its own initiative or on an application made by a party in accordance with **CPR, Part 23** (see **r. 68.2(1)**). An order for a reference must be made by a judge, the Court of Appeal or the House of Lords. It cannot be made by consent, or by a master or district judge (**r. 68.2(2)**). Although it can be made at any stage, it is usual for a reference to be made at trial after the facts have been found (see **75.10**). However, once the English court has given final judgment in a claim it is *functus officio* and has no power at that stage to order a reference (*Chiron Corporation v Murex Diagnostics Ltd (No. 8)* [1995] FSR 309). **75.13**

Where the English court decides to make a reference, the request for the preliminary ruling of the ECJ has to be set out in a schedule to the court's order (**r. 68.2(3)**). Often the applicant will prepare a draft, or the court may direct one of the parties to do so, but the order will be settled finally by the court (**PD 68, para. 1.1**). As it will need to be translated into the other official languages, the question on which a ruling is sought must be expressed as clearly and precisely as possible (**PD 68, para. 1.2**), avoiding superfluous detail (ECJ Guidance Note, **PD 68, annex, para.** 21). A precedent reference based on *Garland v British Rail Engineering Ltd* [1983] 2 AC 751 is illustrated at **figure 75.1**. The question should be stated in a general form, and not in a specific form tied to the facts of the case in hand. It should, in a single document scheduled to the order (**PD 68, para. 1.3**):
(a) give the full name of the referring court;
(b) identify the parties;
(c) summarise the nature and history of the proceedings, including the salient facts, indicating whether these have been proved, admitted or assumed;
(d) set out the rules of national law relevant to the dispute;
(e) summarise the relevant contentions of the parties;
(f) explain why a ruling of the ECJ is being sought;
(g) identify the EC provisions the effect of which was in issue.

Unless the court orders otherwise, the English proceedings will be stayed pending the ruling of the ECJ (**CPR, r. 68.4**).

The senior master sends a copy of the order making the reference to the ECJ (**r. 68.3(1)**) at the Registry of Court of Justice of the European Communities, L-2925 Luxembourg. County court references are sent to the senior master by the proper officer of the county court for onward transmission to the ECJ (**r. 68.3(2)**) together with the court file (**PD 68, para. 2.2**). Unless the court orders otherwise, the senior master will not send a copy of the order to the ECJ until the time for appealing has expired, any application for permission to appeal has been refused, or any appeal has been determined (**CPR, r. 68.3(3)**). The order for reference must be succinct, but sufficiently complete, and must set out the matters listed in ECJ Information Note, **PD 68, annex, para. 22**.

Figure 75.1 Order for reference to the ECJ

IN THE HOUSE OF LORDS
ON APPEAL FROM HER MAJESTY'S COURT OF APPEAL (ENGLAND)
BETWEEN

EILEEN MARY GARLAND *Petitioner*

— and —

BRITISH RAIL ENGINEERING LIMITED *Respondents*

It is ordered that the questions set out in the schedule hereto concerning the interpretation of (a) article 141 of the Treaty establishing the European Community ('EC Treaty'), (b) article 1 of Council Directive 75/117/EEC, and (c) article 1 of Council Directive 76/207/EEC be referred to the Court of Justice of the European Communities for a preliminary ruling in accordance with article 234 of the EC Treaty.

And it is ordered that all further proceedings in the above-named cause be stayed until the said Court of Justice has given its ruling on the said questions or until further order.

SCHEDULE
REQUEST FOR PRELIMINARY RULING OF THE COURT OF JUSTICE OF THE EUROPEAN COMMUNITIES

1 The appellant in this appeal is Mrs Eileen Mary Garland of [address] and the respondents are British Rail Engineering Ltd, whose registered office is at [address].

2 Mrs Eileen Mary Garland is a married woman employed by the respondents, British Rail Engineering Limited ('B.R.E.L.'). The whole of the shareholding in B.R.E.L. is held by the British Railways Board which is a public authority charged by statute with the duty of providing railway services in Great Britain.

3 All employees of B.R.E.L. enjoy certain valuable concessionary travel facilities during the period of their employment. These facilities entitle each employee, regardless of sex, to travel free or at a reduced rate on British Rail and certain foreign railways. Such facilities are extended not only to the employee, but to his or her spouse and dependent children.

4 After employees of B.R.E.L. retire from their employment on reaching retiring age (which is earlier for women than for men) there is a difference in their treatment depending on their sex. In the case of former male employees, they continue to be granted (though on a reduced scale) travel facilities for themselves, their wives and dependent children. In the case of former female employees, they receive (on a similarly reduced scale) travel facilities for themselves, but no such facilities are granted in respect of their husbands or dependent children. These facilities are not enjoyed by former employees as a matter of contractual right, but employees have a legitimate expectation that they will enjoy them after retirement and it would be difficult in practice for B.R.E.L. to withdraw them unilaterally without the agreement of the trade unions of which their employees are members.

5 On 25 November 1976, Mrs Garland complained to an industrial tribunal that B.R.E.L. were discriminating against her contrary to the provisions of a United Kingdom Act of Parliament, the Sex Discrimination Act 1975. Her complaint after consideration also by two intermediate appellate courts, the Employment Appeal Tribunal [1978] ICR 495 and the Court of Appeal sub nom. *Roberts v Cleveland Area Health Authority*, [1979] 1 WLR 754 has now reached the House of Lords which is a court against whose decision there is no judicial remedy under United Kingdom law.

The preliminary ruling of the Court of Justice of the European Communities is accordingly requested on the following questions:

1 Where an employer provides (though not bound to do so by contract) special travel facilities for former employees to enjoy after retirement which discriminate against former female employees in the manner described above, is it contrary to:

(a) Article 141 of the EC Treaty?
(b) Article 1 of Council Directive 75/117/EEC?
(c) Article 1 of Council Directive 76/207/EEC?

2 If the answer to questions 1(a), 1(b) or 1(c) is affirmative, is article 141 or either of the Directives directly applicable in member States so as to confer enforceable Community rights upon individuals in the above circumstances?

Dated the 17th day of October 2005.

The domestic court making the reference to the ECJ can request the President of the ECJ to consider whether there are special circumstances which would justify a case being given priority under art. 55 of the Rules of Procedure of the ECJ and whether the case raises matters of exceptional urgency under art. 104A of those Rules. In *R (International Air Transport Association) v Department for Transport* [2004] EWHC 1721 (Admin), LTL 27/7/2004, such a request was made when the Administrative Court found that there was evidence to show a significant risk that low-cost airline operators would suffer serious damage and be liable to criminal proceeding if they became liable to the provisions of a Regulation due to come into force in the next year.

PROCEDURE IN THE EUROPEAN COURT

The registrar of the ECJ notifies the parties, member States and the Commission of any reference filed, and each have two months to submit written observations. A notice is published in the *Official Journal* indicating the names of the parties involved and a summary of the questions on which a preliminary ruling is being sought. The court can make orders for discovery. There may then be a hearing, where interested parties can present oral argument. **75.14**

The case is then adjourned, during which the advocate general delivers an opinion, followed by the judgment of the court. The ECJ Registry stays in contact with the national court until judgment is given, and sends various documents to the national court, including written observations, report of the hearing, opinion of the advocate general, and the judgment of the ECJ. The ruling binds the domestic court on the interpretation of the Community provision in question, but the domestic court has to apply the ruling to the facts of the case in which it arose. It is for the domestic court alone to find the facts, and the domestic court is entitled to disregard any conclusion reached by the ECJ in so far as it is based on a factual background inconsistent with the findings of the domestic court (*Arsenal Football Club plc v Reed* [2003] EWCA Civ 696, [2003] 3 All ER 865). Where the ECJ makes a finding of fact which is not inconsistent with the findings of the domestic court, and which is inevitable in the circumstances, the domestic court should follow the ruling of the ECJ (*Arsenal Football Club plc v Reed*).

Individual concern

75.15 The EC Treaty, art. 230, provides that the ECJ may review the legality of acts adopted by the EU. Such proceedings may be brought by a member State, the Council or the Commission, but may also be brought by a natural or legal person to whom the regulation or decision under review is of direct and individual concern. This is usually interpreted as meaning that the applicant, if not a State or the Council or Commission, must be affected by the measure by reason of certain attributes peculiar to the applicant or a factual situation which differentiated the applicant from all other persons and distinguished it individually (*Plaumann & Co. v Commission* (case 25/62) [1963] ECR 95).

Individuals are therefore not permitted to challenge before the ECJ Community decisions which are not addressed to them personally (*Unión de Pequeños Agricultores v Council of the European Union* (case C-50/00P) [2003] QB 893, where it was held that the ECJ did not have jurisdiction to examine in an individual case whether national procedural rules permitted a challenge to the legality of Community measures). In *Jégo-Quéré et Cie SA v Commission* (case T-177/01) [2003] QB 854 it was held that where there was no other satisfactory means of address *Plaumann & Co. v Commission* would not be followed, and that a natural or legal person would be regarded as individually concerned by a Community measure of general application if it affected his legal position in a definite and immediate manner by restricting his rights or imposing obligations on him.

COSTS

75.16 The costs of the parties in seeking a ruling from the ECJ are always reserved to the domestic court (ECJ Information Note, **PD 68, annex, para.** 27). No order for costs is made in respect of the involvement of member States or the Commission.

Chapter 76 Enforcement

INTRODUCTION

Entering judgment does not provide a litigant with the remedy sought in the proceedings. Parties may well refuse to comply with the judgments and orders of the court. Public confidence in the legal system would be eroded if the courts were without powers to enforce compliance. In fact, a range of enforcement procedures are available, each being designed to deal with different situations. Where a number of procedures are available, a judgment creditor can choose whichever one seems likely to be the most effective. Largely, the procedures are similar in both the High Court and the county courts. The major exception is that attachment of earnings orders (**76.17**) are generally only available in the county courts. One practical difference is that High Court enforcement is carried out by enforcement officers, who are independent of the courts, whereas county court enforcement is carried out by bailiffs, who are employed by Her Majesty's Courts Service. It is often suggested that enforcement officers, who are remunerated by fees and poundage on money they recover, have a greater incentive than bailiffs and hence have a reputation for being more successful. **76.1**

The enforcement system is in the process of transition. Some of the rules on enforcement are in **CPR, Parts 69** to **73**, with the rest being preserved provisions of the old rules to be found in the schedules to the CPR. Further assimilation into the CPR is expected. The legal sources governing the various enforcement procedures are:

(a) General provisions on enforcement: **CPR, Part 70**, and certain surviving provisions of RSC, ord. 45 in CPR, sch. 1, and CCR, ord. 25 in CPR, sch. 2.
(b) General provisions on writs of execution: **RSC, ord. 46** in CPR, sch. 1 (High Court).
(c) Execution by writ of fieri facias: **RSC, ord.** 47 in CPR, sch. 1 (High Court).
(d) Warrants of execution, delivery and possession: **CCR, ord. 26** in CPR, sch. 2 (county court).
(e) Obtaining information from judgment debtors: **CPR, Part 71**.
(f) Attachment of earnings is governed by the **Attachment of Earnings Act 1971**, with procedural rules in **CCR, ord.** 27 in CPR, sch. 2 (county court).
(g) Judgment summonses: **CCR, ord. 28** in CPR, sch. 2.
(h) Committal (see **chapter 78**): **RSC, ord.** 52 in CPR, sch. 1 (High Court), and **CCR, ord. 29** in CPR, sch. 2 (county court);
(i) Third party debt orders: **CPR, Part 72**.
(j) Charging orders are governed by the **Charging Orders Act 1979**. The rules also include stop orders and stop notices. The procedural rules are in **CPR, Part 73**.
(k) Receivers: **CPR, Part 69**.
(l) Administration orders: **CCR, ord. 39** in CPR, sch. 2 (county court).

TRANSFER OF PROCEEDINGS

76.2 A case may need to be transferred before enforcement proceedings are taken:

(a) A county court claim (other than one under the **Consumer Credit Act 1974**) will have to be transferred to the High Court if execution against goods is sought of a judgment exceeding £5,000 (**High Court and County Courts Jurisdiction Order 1991** (SI 1991/724), art. 8(1)(a)).
(b) A High Court claim will have to be transferred to a county court if:
   (i) execution against goods is sought of a judgment under £600 (**High Court and County Courts Jurisdiction Order 1991**, art. 8(1)(b));
   (ii) a charging order is sought where the judgment debt is under £5,000 (**Charging Orders Act 1979, s. 1(2)**); or
   (iii) an attachment of earnings order is sought (**Attachment of Earnings Act 1971, s. 1**).
(c) A county court action will have to be transferred, under **CCR, ord. 25, r. 2** in CPR, sch. 2, to the county court serving the district where the judgment debtor resides or carries on business where the judgment creditor wishes to apply for:
   (i) an oral examination;
   (ii) a charging order;
   (iii) an attachment of earnings order; or
   (iv) a judgment summons.
(d) A possession claim against trespassers (see **CPR, Part 55**, and **chapter 35**) may be enforced either in the High Court or a county court (**High Court and County Courts Jurisdiction Order 1991, art. 8B**).

A judgment creditor seeking to enforce a county court judgment or order in the High Court should issue an application to transfer the claim to the High Court under the **County Courts Act 1984, s. 42**, and should then apply for a certificate of judgment under **CCR, ord. 22, r. 8** in CPR, sch. 2. The request for the certificate is made in writing, must state it is needed for the purpose of enforcement against goods (if this is the case) and confirm that the application to transfer has been made, attaching a copy of the application. Granting the certificate operates as an order to transfer the proceedings to the High Court (**CCR, ord. 25, r. 13** in CPR, sch. 2).

A judgment creditor wishing to enforce a High Court judgment or order in a county court must apply to the High Court for an order transferring the proceedings in accordance with

CPR, r. 70.3. Once a transfer order has been obtained, **PD 70, para.** 3, requires the judgment creditor to file at the county court:

(a) a copy of the judgment or order which is being enforced;
(b) a copy of the order transferring the proceedings;
(c) a certificate verifying the amount due under the judgment or order being enforced;
(d) a copy of any sheriff's return if a writ of execution has been issued; and
(e) an application notice or request for enforcement in the county court.

A judgment creditor needing to transfer proceedings from one county court to another for enforcement must make a request in writing to the court where the claim is presently proceeding for the transfer (**PD 70, para. 2.1**). A court officer will then transfer the proceedings unless a judge orders otherwise (**para. 2.2**), and give notice of the transfer to all parties (para. 2.3).

STAY OF EXECUTION

A judgment debtor who is unable to pay or who alleges that it is otherwise inexpedient to enforce an order may apply for a stay of execution (**RSC, ord. 47, r. 1** in CPR, sch. 1; **CCR, ord. 25, r. 8** in CPR, sch. 2). Such an application must be made in accordance with **CPR, Part 23**, and must be supported by a witness statement or affidavit substantiating the grounds relied on, and usually has to include a full statement of the debtor's means. Often the result of a successful application will be a stay of execution pending payment of the judgment by instalments. **76.3**

ORDERS TO OBTAIN INFORMATION FROM JUDGMENT DEBTORS

Where little is known about a judgment debtor's finances, application may be made without notice for an order to obtain information from the judgment debtor. An application for an order to obtain information from a judgment debtor must be made using the prescribed application notice (**form N316**). This must state the debtor's name and address, identify the judgment and state the amount presently owing under the judgment (**PD 71, para. 1.2**). If the creditor wishes the debtor to be questioned before a judge (which will only be allowed if there are compelling reasons: para. 2.2) or to produce specific documents (such as bank statements and other financial material), these matters must be stated in the application notice (para. 1.2). If the application complies with these requirements, it will be dealt with by a court officer without a hearing (**CPR, r. 71.2**), and the officer will make an order requiring the debtor to attend court, produce documents and answer questions. That order must be served personally on the judgment debtor not less than 14 days before the hearing (**r. 71.3**), with service usually being effected by the creditor rather than the court (**PD 71, para. 3**). Once served, the debtor has seven days to ask the judgment creditor for a reasonable sum to cover the debtor's travelling expenses to court, which must be paid (**r. 71.4**). The judgment creditor must swear an affidavit (a witness statement being insufficient) giving details of service of the order, any request for and payment of travelling expenses, and how much of the judgment remains unpaid. This affidavit must be filed two days before the hearing or produced at the hearing (**r. 71.5**). **76.4**

At the hearing the court officer will ask a set of standard questions which are set out in **form EX140** for the examination of individuals, and **EX141** for officers of companies or corporations. The judgment creditor may ask questions, or may request the court officer to ask additional, written questions (**PD 71, para. 4.2**). If the hearing takes place before a judge, the judgment creditor must attend (**r. 71.6**) and the questioning is conducted by the creditor or the creditor's legal representative (**PD 71, para. 5.1**). 'The examination is not only intended to be an examination, but to be a cross-examination, and that of the severest kind' (per James LJ in *Republic of Costa Rica v Stronsberg* (1880) 16 ChD 8). The basic policy is to prevent a judgment debtor defeating a judgment by dissipating or concealing assets. Accordingly, the debtor is required to answer all questions fairly directed to establishing the debtor's financial circumstances, including amounts, names, account and policy numbers. The evidence is recorded and signed by the debtor.

If the debtor fails to attend or otherwise fails to comply, the court usually makes a suspended committal order, which gives the debtor a second chance to comply (**PD 71, para. 7.1**). If the debtor again fails to comply, a committal order can be made by the judge (**CPR, r. 71.8**).

EXECUTION AGAINST GOODS

Introduction

76.5 Execution against goods is the most common method of enforcement. In the High Court it is effected through the writ of fieri facias, often abbreviated to 'fi. fa.', and in the county courts by warrants of execution.

Issue of writ or warrant of execution

76.6 Issue is usually purely a matter of producing the correct documents and paying a fee. In the High Court the judgment creditor produces a draft writ of fieri facias, a praecipe and the judgment. The writ is issued by being sealed (**RSC, ord. 46, r. 6** in CPR, sch. 1). It is then served on an enforcement officer under the Courts Act 2003. In the county court the judgment creditor simply sends a request for the issue of a warrant of execution to the court, and the court informs its bailiffs.

Enforcement after six years

76.7 Where six years have elapsed since the date of the judgment or order, permission to enforce is required (**RSC, ord. 46, r. 2** in CPR, sch. 1; **CCR, ord. 26, r. 5** in CPR, sch. 2). The six-year period is regarded as a hurdle rather than a limit (*Society of Lloyd's v Longtin* [2005] EWHC 2491 (Comm), [2005] 2 CLC 774). While the exercise of the court's discretion is directed at doing justice between the parties in all the circumstances of the case (*Good Challenger Navegante SA v Metalexportimport SA* [2003] EWCA Civ 1668, [2004] 1 Lloyd's Rep 67), the court will only extend the six-year period where it is demonstrably just to do so. The burden of proof is on the judgment creditor to establish that it is just (*Duer v Frazer* [2001] 1 WLR 919).

Seizing goods

76.8 The enforcement officer or bailiffs (together referred to in this chapter as 'bailiffs') must first gain lawful entry to the debtor's premises. Outer doors must not be broken open, nor is it lawful to place a foot in an open door and push it open against the debtor's attempts to close it. The use of force to gain entry is under review. Once inside, sufficient goods will be seized to satisfy the judgment and the costs of enforcement. 'Goods' includes motor vehicles, money, promissory notes and securities, furniture etc., but excludes, by the **County Courts Act 1984, s. 89(1)**, and the **Supreme Court Act 1981, s. 138(3A)**:

(i) such tools, books, vehicles and other items of equipment as are necessary to [the debtor] for use personally by him in his employment, business or vocation;
(ii) such clothing, bedding, furniture, household equipment and provisions as are necessary for satisfying the basic domestic needs of [the debtor] and his family.

The dividing line is whether such goods are 'necessary'. A debtor claiming the protection of this provision must give notice to the sheriff within five days of the seizure identifying the goods and the grounds for the claim in respect of each item. Further, the goods seized must belong to the debtor. Goods belonging to other members of the debtor's family, a limited company (even if itself owned by the debtor) or a hire-purchase company must not be seized.

If there is doubt about the ownership of goods seized, the bailiff can gain protection by interpleading, see **14.15** to **14.21**.

Once goods have been seized, it is usual for the bailiff to enter into an agreement with some responsible person in the house to take 'walking possession' of the goods. The goods can then remain where they are until payment or sale, the responsible person promising not to remove or damage them without the bailiff's permission, and authorising the bailiff to re-enter the premises at any time to complete the process of enforcement (*National Commercial Bank of Scotland v Arcam Demolition and Construction Ltd* [1966] 2 QB 593). Once walking possession has been taken, the bailiff can use force to retake possession (*McLeod v Butterwick* [1996] 1 WLR 995).

Removal and sale

Often, the threat of sale is sufficient incentive to persuade the debtor to pay. On payment the execution is superseded and the goods are released, see, e.g., the **County Courts Act 1984, s. 87(2)**. Otherwise, the goods will be removed and sold. Usually this is by public auction, but an application may be made for an order under the Courts Act 2002, sch. 7, para. 10, permitting sale otherwise than through auction (see **RSC, ord. 47, r. 6 in CPR, sch. 1**). On removal the debtor must be provided with an inventory, and must be given advance notice of the auction. The auction must be publicly advertised and must be conducted by an appointed broker or appraiser. After the sale the debtor is given a detailed account in writing of the sale and the application of the proceeds. Purchasers of goods sold after execution acquire good title (see, e.g., **County Courts Act 1984, s. 98(1)**). **76.9**

ADMINISTRATION ORDERS

By virtue of the **County Courts Act 1984, s. 112**, a county court has power, of its own initiative or on the application of either the debtor or the creditor, in respect of a debtor who is unable to pay his or her debts to make an administration order in respect of the debtor's estate. Such an order has the immediate effect of restricting creditors named in the order from joining in bankruptcy petitions against the debtor. The order will usually provide for the debtor to make specified payments by instalments, with periodic dividends being paid to the named creditors. Administration orders remain in effect for three years. **76.10**

Sections 112A and 112B, which have yet to be brought into force, confer the following additional powers:

(a) To make an order restricting enforcement against the debtor. A restriction order prevents any creditor named in the order from applying for any remedy against the debtor without the permission of the court. In particular, it restricts suppliers of mains gas, electricity and water from cutting supplies on the ground of past non-payment.

(b) To make an administration order coupled with a composition provision. The composition element of the order has the effect of making a proportionate reduction to the various debts owed by the debtor to the named creditors.

THIRD PARTY DEBT ORDERS

Third party debt orders (formerly called garnishee proceedings) have the effect of transforming a debt payable by a third party (the garnishee under the old terminology) to the judgment debtor into an obligation to pay the debt to the judgment creditor. Third party debt orders are a particularly effective method of enforcement where the debt to be attached is owed by a responsible body, such as a bank or building society. They are not restricted to such **76.11** bodies. A third party debt order was made against a bank account in the name of an unincorporated association in *Huntingdon Life Sciences Group plc v Stop Huntingdon Animal Cruelty* [2005] EWHC 2233 (QB), [2005] 4 All ER 899.

Application for an interim order

76.12 Third party debt orders follow a two-stage process. The first stage is commenced by a without notice application (**CPR, r. 72.3**) verified by a statement of truth in **form N349** containing the information prescribed by **PD 72, para. 1.2**. The required information includes details of the judgment debtor, the judgment, and details of the third party debt. Speculative applications will be rejected, and orders will only be made if there is evidence substantiating a belief that the debtor has (say) an account with a specific bank or building society (**PD 72, para. 1.3**). The application is considered by a judge without a hearing (**CPR, r. 72.4(1)**), and the judge may make an interim third party debt order directing the third party not to make any payment which reduces the amount he owes the judgment debtor to less than the amount specified in the order. The judge will also fix a hearing to consider making the order final. The amount specified will be the total outstanding on the judgment or order being enforced, together with fixed costs (**r. 72.4(3)**).

Service of the interim order

76.13 An interim order must be served on the third party who owes money to the judgment debtor not less than 21 days before the date fixed for the hearing to consider making the order final (**CPR, r. 72.5(1)(a)**), and is binding on the third party when it is served on the third party (r. 72.4(4)). If the third party is a bank or building society it must carry out a search to identify all accounts held by the judgment debtor, and must disclose to the court and the judgment creditor the account numbers, whether they are in credit, and, if so, whether the balance is sufficient to cover the amount specified in the interim order, or the amount in the account if insufficient (**r. 72.6(1) and (2)**). It must also state if it asserts any right to the money in the account, for example, by set-off, giving details of the ground for that assertion (r. 72.6(2)(c)(iii)). A third party which is not a bank or building society has seven days after service to notify the court and the judgment creditor in writing if nothing is owed to the judgment debtor or the amount owed is less than the amount specified in the interim order (**r. 72.6(4)**).

The interim order must also be served on the judgment debtor. This needs to be done not less than seven days after service on the third party, and not less than seven days before the date fixed for the hearing (**r. 72.5(1)(b)**). Where service is effected by the judgment creditor, a certificate of service must be filed not less than two days before the hearing, or must be produced at the hearing (**r. 72.5(2)**). A judgment debtor who is an individual and who is suffering hardship in meeting ordinary living expenses as a result of the interim order may apply for a hardship payment order permitting one or more payments out of the account (**r. 72.7; PD 72, paras 5.1 to 5.6**).

Application for final third party debt order

76.14 The second stage is when the court considers whether to make a final third party debt order on the date fixed when the interim order was made. A judgment debtor or third party objecting to the final order, or who knows or believes someone else has a claim to the money, must file and serve written evidence stating the grounds of any objection or details of the other claim not less than three days before the hearing (**CPR, r. 72.8**). If the court is notified that another person has a claim to the money it will serve notice of the application and the hearing on that person (**r. 72.8(5)**). At the hearing the court may make a final third party debt order, discharge the interim order, decide any issues or direct a trial of any issues (**r. 72.8(6)**). A final third party debt order is enforceable as an order to pay money. By **r. 72.9(2)**, to the extent of the amount paid under the final order, the third party's debt to the judgment debtor is discharged.

Attachable money

It is possible to obtain a third party debt order only over debts due to the judgment debtor. Examples are money in a bank account, trade debts, judgment debts, and rent due to a landlord. Conversely, claims for damages, matrimonial maintenance orders, and salary not presently payable are not attachable. Most conditions imposed by banks and building societies restricting the right to withdraw money from the judgment debtor's account are disregarded once a third party debt order is made (**Supreme Court Act 1981, s. 40; County Courts Act 1984, s. 108; CPR, r. 72.2(3)**). 76.15

Discretion to make third party debt orders

A third party debt order may be refused if it would be inequitable to grant it. It is a fundamental feature of a third party debt order that the third party must be discharged from its liability to the judgment debtor in the amount that the third party pays to the judgment creditor. If the third party is located in a jurisdiction which will not recognise such a discharge, a court in England or Wales should not make a third party debt order (*Société Eram Shipping Co. Ltd v Compagnie Internationale de Navigation* [2003] UKHL 30, [2004] 1 AC 260; *Kuwait Oil Tanker Co. SAK v Qabazard* [2003] UKHL 31, [2004] 1 AC 300). The insolvency of the judgment debtor is a sufficient reason for refusing to make an order, because its effect may be to prefer the judgment creditor over the general body of creditors (*Roberts Petroleum Ltd v Bernard Kenny Ltd* [1983] 2 AC 192). The burden of proof is on the judgment debtor to show why a third party debt order should not be made final. Further, if a judgment creditor secured a charging order or third party debt order in competition with other creditors who had not been so quick off the mark, that should not affect the court's discretion to make the order final (*Reed v Oury* (2000) LTL 12/2/2001). 76.16

ATTACHMENT OF EARNINGS

Where a judgment debtor is employed, but has no other substantial assets, the most effective method of enforcement is by obtaining an attachment of earnings order. Such an order can only be made, unless the application is by the debtor, if the debtor has failed to make one or more payments as required by the relevant adjudication (**Attachment of Earnings Act 1971, s. 3(3)**). The **Attachment of Earnings Act 1971, s. 6(1)**, provides: 76.17

An attachment of earnings order shall be an order directed to a person who appears to the court to have the debtor in his employment and shall operate as an instruction to that person—

(a) to make periodical deductions from the debtor's earnings . . . and
(b) at such times as the order may require, or as the court may allow, to pay the amounts deducted to the collecting officer of the court, as specified in the order.

The High Court has no jurisdiction to make attachment of earnings orders, and High Court actions need to be transferred to a county court for enforcement in this manner. Magistrates' courts have some jurisdiction to make these orders, such as to enforce payment of arrears of council tax.

Earnings attachable

An attachment of earnings order may be made in respect of wages, salaries, fees, bonuses, commission and overtime payable under a contract of service, including occupational pensions and statutory sick pay. An order cannot be made in respect of self-employed income, nor State pensions, benefits or allowances (**Attachment of Earnings Act 1971, s. 24**). 76.18

Procedure for applying for an attachment of earnings order

An application for an attachment of earnings order is made by filing a request in a standard form certifying the amount of money remaining due under the judgment, and paying the fee. 76.19

The court then notifies the debtor of a hearing date at least 21 days in advance, enclosing a questionnaire concerning the debtor's means. The questionnaire should be completed by the debtor and filed at court within eight days after service. A copy of the questionnaire is sent to the judgment creditor. The questionnaire is considered by an administrative officer of the court, who may make an attachment of earnings order if there is sufficient information to do so (**CCR, ord.** 27, **r.** 7(1) in CPR, sch. 1). If either party objects, or if the court officer decides not to make an order, the application is referred to the district judge.

At the hearing the district judge confirms that the debtor is not unemployed or self-employed. Provided the debtor is employed, the district judge will consider the debtor's income and regular outgoings, and will fix:

(a) The debtor's protected earnings rate. This is the amount the debtor is considered to need to maintain his or her family, each week or month, and any deductions made under the order will not reduce the debtor's income below this level.
(b) The debtor's normal deduction rate. This is the amount, subject to the protected earnings rate, which is deducted from the debtor's earnings each week or month.

Normally, the order will then be served on the debtor's employer, who will make the deductions specified and pay the money deducted to the court. Alternatively, the court may make a suspended attachment of earnings order, which will only be served on the employer if the debtor fails to pay agreed instalments promptly. A debtor with several creditors may be ordered to file a list of creditors with a view to making an administration order (76.10) or a consolidated attachment of earnings order.

Supplementary points

76.20 While an attachment of earnings order is in force, permission of the court is required before a warrant of execution will be issued for the judgment debt (**Attachment of Earnings Act 1971, s. 8(2)(b)**). Also, during the currency of the order the debtor is under a duty (enforceable by imprisonment or a fine: **s. 23**) to notify the court of any change in his or her employment (s. 15).

CHARGING ORDERS

76.21 A charging order is defined by the **Charging Orders Act 1979, s. 1(1)**, as an order 'imposing on any such property of the debtor as may be specified in the order a charge for securing the payment of any money due or to become due under [a] judgment or order'. A charging order therefore *secures* a judgment debt: it does not of itself produce any money. By s. 3(4) a charge imposed by a charging order has the same effect, and is enforceable in the same way, 'as an equitable charge created by the debtor by writing under his hand'. Once obtained and registered at the Land Registry, a charging order can give a measure of long-term security, which is necessary if there is no immediate prospect of recovery by other methods. It was held in *Ezekiel v Orakpo* (1994) *The Times*, 8 November 1994, that a charging order extends to cover the judgment debt, interest and costs even if it does not expressly say so. As a charging order is simply security for payment, it is possible to make an order for payment by instalments as well as a charging order, provided the interim charging order is made before the instalment order (*Robaigealach v Allied Irish Bank plc* (2001) LTL 12/11/2001). Exceptionally, it may be possible to enforce the charge by bringing sale proceedings (see 76.25), or the charge may result in the judgment being paid if the charged property is sold by the judgment debtor and the purchaser wishes (as is usual) to purchase it clear of encumbrances.

Chargeable property

76.22 A charge may be imposed by the **Charging Orders Act 1979** only on the types of property listed in s. 2 of the Act. In *Habib Bank Ltd v Ahmed* [2004] EWCA Civ 805, *The Independent*, 30 June 2004, the debtor sought to put real property out of the reach of a charging order by transferring title to members of his family. The transfers were set aside under the Insolvency Act 1986, s. 423, as transactions at an undervalue, and the charging order was made absolute. Likewise, transfers of industrial units from the judgment debtor to related companies, between judgment and the assessment of costs, were set aside under s. 423 so that charging orders could be made in *Beckenham MC Ltd v Centralex Ltd* [2004] EWHC 1287 (Ch), [2004] 2 BCLC 764. In *Walker International Holdings Ltd v Congo* [2005] EWHC 2813 (Comm), LTL 16/12/2005, it was held that shares nominally owned by one company were in reality owned through a second company by the judgment debtor, with the result that an interim charging order was properly made in respect of the shares.

Procedure on applying for a charging order

There is a two-stage process for obtaining charging orders. The first stage is to apply for an interim charging order by issuing an application notice in **form N379** verified by a statement of truth (**CPR, r. 73.3(4)**) containing the information prescribed by **PD 73, para. 1.2**. The required information includes details of the judgment debtor, the judgment, and the property which it is intended to charge. The application is considered, without a hearing, by a judge who will consider making an interim order and fixing a hearing to consider making a final charging order (**CPR, r. 73.4**). If the interim order relates to land, it is usual, as a precaution, to register it as a pending action under the Land Registration Act 1925 or the Land Charges Act 1972 before it is served on the debtor. At least 21 days before the final hearing (which is the second stage) the judgment debtor, such other creditors as the court may direct, and certain other specified persons must be served with the interim charging order, application notice and any supporting documents (**CPR, r. 73.5(1)**). Service of an interim charging order effectively prevents dealings with the assets charged pending the final hearing (**r. 73.6**). **76.23**

The second stage is the hearing to consider making the order final. If service of the interim order was effected by the judgment creditor, a certificate of service must be filed at least two days before the final hearing, or produced at the hearing (**r. 73.5(2)**). Any person objecting to the order being made final must file and serve written evidence setting out the grounds of the objection not less than seven days before the hearing (**r. 73.8**). At the hearing the court may make a final charging order, discharge the interim order, decide any issues or direct a trial of any issues (**r. 73.8(2)**).

Discretion to make a charging order

Particular matters laid down in the **Charging Orders Act 1979, s. 1(5)**, that the court must consider in deciding whether to make a charging order are: **76.24**

(a) the personal circumstances of the debtor; and
(b) whether any other creditor of the debtor would be likely to be unduly prejudiced by the making of the order.

Sale proceedings

Proceedings for the sale of charged property owned by the judgment debtor alone are governed by **CPR, r. 73.10**. Such proceedings are commenced by issuing separate proceedings using a **CPR, Part 8**, claim form, supported by evidence by witness statement or affidavit. The written evidence gives details of the charging order, the property charged, verifies the debtor's title to the property charged, identifies prior encumbrances and persons in possession, certifies the amount outstanding on the judgment, and estimates the price which would be obtained on sale. It is usual to apply for an order that the debtor vacate the premises as well, so that a sale can be made with vacant possession. Such an order can be enforced by writ or warrant of possession, see **76.31**. **76.25**

Sale where more than one person has an interest in the land

76.26 Where the charged property is owned by more than one person, instead of using r. 73.10, any application for an order for sale has to be made under the Trusts of Land and Appointment of Trustees Act 1996, s. 14 (**PD 73, para. 4.5**). The judgment debtor and all other proprietors should be joined as defendants and served with proceedings and notice of the return day. The hearing takes place before a master or district judge. From 1 January 1997 jointly held property (including property previously held on trust for sale) has been held on the trusts of land introduced by the Trusts of Land and Appointment of Trustees Act 1996. By s. 14 any person having an interest in property subject to a trust of land may apply to court for an order relating to the exercise by the trustees of any of their functions. By s. 15, in determining such an application the court must have regard to the intentions of the persons who created the trust, the purposes for which the property is held, the welfare of any child occupying the land as his or her home, and the interests of any secured creditor of any beneficiary. Section 15 does not apply to applications made by trustees in bankruptcy (s. 15(4)). It is clear that these sections have made a fundamental change to the court's function in considering an application for an order for sale by a creditor with the benefit of a charging order. On the question of the exercise of the court's discretion see *Mortgage Corporation v Shaire* [2001] Ch 743, where it is said that the interests of the chargee are just one of the factors to be taken into account, and there is no suggestion in s. 15 that it is to be given more importance than the interests of the family residing in the property. However, in *Bank of Ireland Home Mortgages Ltd v Bell* [2001] 2 All ER (Comm) 920 the Court of Appeal said that a powerful consideration under s. 15 is that a creditor should not be kept out of his money. The fact that the debtor's spouse has children just short of their majority living in the property is a very slight consideration to be weighed against making an order for sale (*Bank of Ireland Home Mortgages Ltd v Bell*).

Standard forms of order for sale following a charging order are in **appendix A of PD 73**.

INSOLVENCY

76.27 Often a failure to pay a judgment debt is evidence that the judgment debtor is insolvent. Consequently, it may be more apt to bring bankruptcy or winding-up proceedings than to apply for enforcement. For further details, see **chapters** 79 and **80**.

JUDGMENT SUMMONSES

76.28 A judgment summons is a procedure for punishing a defaulting judgment debtor who could pay, but has chosen not to, with a period in prison (Debtors Act 1869, s. 5). The punitive nature of the provision was stressed by the Court of Appeal in *Woodley v Woodley* (1993) *The Times*, 15 March 1993. **PD RSC ord. 52** applies equally to judgment summonses, see *Murbarak v Murbarik* [2001] 1 FLR 698. Since the Administration of Justice Act 1970, s. 11, came into force, judgment summonses have only been available for enforcing matrimonial maintenance orders and arrears of some taxes. There are prescribed forms for the request for a judgment summons (**form N342**) and request for a warrant of committal (form N344).

ENFORCEMENT OF JUDGMENTS FOR THE DELIVERY OF GOODS

76.29 Enforcement of judgments for the delivery of goods is by means of warrants (or, in the High Court, writs) of delivery. There are two types, corresponding with the forms of relief stated in the **Torts (Interference with Goods) Act 1977, s. 3**. The first is known as a warrant (or writ) of specific delivery. It requires the bailiff (or enforcement officer) to seize the goods specified in the judgment, with no alternative of seizing other goods up to the assessed value of the goods forming the subject matter of the judgment. The second is known as a warrant (or writ) of delivery. It requires the bailiff (or enforcement officer) to seize either the goods specified in the judgment, or other goods up to the value (specified in the judgment) of the goods forming the subject matter of the judgment.

As with execution against goods (**76.6** and **76.7**), issue is simply a matter of the creditor filing a request (county court) or praecipe, draft writ of delivery and judgment (High Court), and paying the court fee.

ENFORCEMENT OF JUDGMENTS FOR THE POSSESSION OF LAND

Common law

At common law, a claimant who has obtained judgment for the possession of land may enter the land after the judgment has been obtained and take it back, provided no force is used. This right does not apply to land within the scope of the **Rent Act 1977**, **Housing Act 1988**, Landlord and Tenant Act 1954, part I, etc., and see the Protection from Eviction Act 1977. The invariable practice in present times is for enforcement to be effected under warrants (county court) or writs (High Court) of possession. **76.30**

Procedure on writ or warrant of possession

Like execution against goods (**76.6** and **76.7**), issue is simply a matter of filing a request (county court) or a praecipe, draft writ of possession and judgment (High Court) and paying a fee. It is of the utmost importance that the land is adequately described. The police are often informed of the time when possession will be enforced, as entry may be gained by force if necessary. The claimant will also usually need to attend to change the locks and make the premises secure after possession is obtained. **76.31**

When enforcing the warrant or writ, the bailiff or enforcement officer is required to turn out everyone on the premises, even if they are not parties (*R v Wandsworth County Court, ex parte Wandsworth London Borough Council* [1975] 1 WLR 1314). However, there is a divergence of practice regarding goods in the premises. In the High Court, these too must be removed by the enforcement officer, but in the county courts this is unnecessary (**County Courts Act 1984, s. 111(1)**).

Warrants and writs of restitution

It sometimes happens that persons ejected when a warrant or writ of possession is enforced regain entry at some later date. Such persons may be removed a second time under a warrant (county court) or writ (High Court) of restitution. These are a species of warrant (or writ) in aid of a primary warrant (or writ). Permission is required for the issue of such warrants or writs (**RSC, ord. 46, r. 3** in CPR, sch. 1; **CCR, ord. 26, r.** 17(4) in CPR, sch. 2). The application is made using the **CPR, Part 23**, procedure, but the application notice need not be served on the respondent unless the court otherwise directs. The application must be supported by evidence by witness statement or affidavit giving evidence of wrongful re-entry. The court looks for a plain and sufficient nexus between the original recovery of possession and the need to effect further recovery of the same land (*Wiltshire County Council v Frazer (No. 2)* [1986] 1 WLR 109). **76.32**

RECEIVERS BY WAY OF EQUITABLE EXECUTION

Nature of receivership

76.33 Courts are empowered to appoint receivers by the **Supreme Court Act 1981, s. 37** (powers of the High Court regarding receivers), and the **County Courts Act 1984, ss. 38** (remedies available in the county courts) and **107** (receivers by way of equitable execution). A receivership order has the effect of appointing some responsible person to receive rents, profits and moneys receivable in respect of the judgment debtor's interest in certain property, and to apply that income in specified ways, including payment of a judgment debt. According to *Maclaine Watson and Co. Ltd v International Tin Council* [1988] Ch 1, such an order can only be made where:

(a) it is impossible to enforce using any of the other methods of enforcement; and
(b) the appointment of a receiver will be effective.

On the question whether the appointment of a receiver will be effective, the **Supreme Court Act 1981, s. 37(1)**, provides that an appointment can only be made if it is just and convenient. Under **PD 69, para. 5**, when considering an application for the appointment of a receiver as a method of enforcing a judgment, the court must have regard to the amount claimed by the judgment creditor, the amount likely to be obtained by the receiver, and the probable costs of the appointment.

A receiver might be appointed where the judgment debtor has some valuable right not in the nature of a debt (and hence not amenable to a third party debt order). A receiver might also be appointed to receive rents from a number of tenants who are suing their landlord for failing to maintain the premises, and to apply the money in effecting necessary repairs (*Hart v Emelkirk Ltd* [1983] 1 WLR 1289).

Procedure for seeking the appointment of a receiver

76.34 An application for the appointment of a receiver in existing proceedings is made using the **CPR, Part 23**, procedure, and must be supported by two witness statements or affidavits. The first explains the reasons why the appointment is required, gives details of the property which it is proposed that the receiver should get in or manage, estimates the value of the property and amount of income likely to be produced, gives details of the judgment or order being enforced and the extent to which the judgment debtor has failed to comply with it and why judgment cannot be enforced in any other way (**PD 69, para. 4.1**). It should also give the name, address and position of the proposed receiver ('the nominee', para. 4.2(1)). The second witness statement should be by a person who knows the nominee, and needs to state a belief that the nominee is a suitable person to be appointed, and the basis of that belief (para. 4.2(2)). The written evidence must be accompanied by a signed consent from the nominee (para. 4.2(3)).

Order appointing a receiver

76.35 The order appointing a receiver may:

(a) require the receiver to provide security, usually by bond (in the case of insolvency practitioners) or guarantee (**CPR, r. 69.5; PD 69, para. 7.2**) — the security is usually fixed at twice the annual income from the property;
(b) allow the receiver proper remuneration (**CPR, r. 69.7; PD 69, paras 9.1 to 9.6**);
(c) require the receiver to submit periodic accounts (**CPR, r. 69.8; PD 69, paras 10.1 to 10.3**);
(d) require moneys received to be paid into court (**PD 69, para. 6.3(3)**);
(e) authorise the receiver to carry on an activity or incur an expense (**PD 69, para. 6.3(4)**).

ENFORCEMENT AGAINST PARTICULAR TYPES OF PARTY

Partnerships

By **RSC, ord. 81, r.** 5(1) and (2) in CPR, sch. 1, a judgment obtained against a firm name can be enforced without the court's permission only against: **76.36**

(a) partnership property; or
(b) the property of any partner who was served with the claim form, or acknowledged service as a partner, or admitted being a partner in a statement of case or was held by the court to be a partner.

CCR, ord. 25, r. 9(1) in CPR, sch. 2, is in similar terms, save that it makes no provision for enforcing against the property of a partner who acknowledged service. Given that a partner in a firm which is a defendant in a county court claim may now acknowledge service under CPR, r. 10, this is clearly an anomaly.

A judgment may not be enforced without permission against the property of a partner who was out of the jurisdiction when the claim form was issued, unless he or she acknowledged service, was served as a partner within the jurisdiction or was served out of the jurisdiction with the court's permission under **CPR, rr. 6.17** to **6.31** (**RSC, ord. 81, r.** 5(3) in CPR, sch. 1). **CCR, ord. 25, r.** 9(2) in CPR, sch. 2, is in similar terms, save that, like r. 9(1) (see above), it makes no provision for partners who acknowledged service.

Enforcement against the property of any other partner may be made only with the court's permission. Application for permission should be made using the **Part 23** procedure (**RSC, ord. 81, r.** 5(4) in CPR, sch. 1; **CCR, ord. 25, r.** 9(3) in CPR, sch. 2). In both the High Court and the county court, the application notice must be served personally (**RSC, ord. 81, r.** 5(4) in CPR, sch. 1; **CCR, ord. 25, r.** 9(4) in CPR, sch. 2).

Representative parties

If a claim is brought or ordered to be continued against a representative party under **CPR, r. 19.6**(1), any judgment or order given in the claim is binding on all persons represented, unless the court orders otherwise (**r. 19.6**(4)). However, the judgment or order cannot be enforced against a person who is not a party to the claim unless the court gives permission (**r. 19.6**(4)). The same applies to a claim in which the court has, under **r. 19.7**(2), appointed a representative of persons who cannot be ascertained (**r. 19.7**(7)). **76.37**

The Crown

A successful claimant may not enforce a judgment against the Crown by process of execution (**Crown Proceedings Act 1947, s.** 25(4)). None of the provisions of **CPR, Parts 69** to **73**, **RSC, ords 45** to **47** and **52** in CPR, sch. 1, or **CCR, ords 25** to **29** in CPR, sch. 2, apply to the Crown (**CPR, r. 66.6**). The Crown, on the other hand, may enforce a judgment in its favour against a private litigant in the normal way (**Crown Proceedings Act 1947, s.** 26(1)). **76.38**

In order to obtain satisfaction of orders against the Crown, a successful claimant must follow the procedure set out in the **Crown Proceedings Act 1947, s. 25**. It is as follows:

(a) The claimant should apply to the court, at least 21 days after the date of the order, for a certificate in **form No. 95** or **No. 96** in the High Court, or **form N293A** in a county court.
(b) The certificate must set out full particulars of the order made, including, where appropriate, the amount payable by the Crown.
(c) Once obtained, the certificate should be served on the solicitors acting for the Crown.
(d) The Crown will then make payment.

The **Crown Proceedings Act 1947** gives no deadline for payment of the amount due by the Crown. The court may order that payment be suspended pending appeal (**s.** 25(3)).

Attaching Crown debts

76.39 A person who has obtained judgment against a defendant who is owed money by the Crown may obtain an order under the **Crown Proceedings Act 1947, s. 27(1)**, directing payment of the money to the judgment creditor instead of the judgment debtor. The application is made by application notice using the **Part 23** procedure, supported by written evidence setting out the facts giving rise to the application, stating the name and last known address of the person to be restrained, identifying the order to be enforced and the amount outstanding under it, and identifying the debt owed by the Crown in respect of which the application is made **(CPR, r. 66.7)**.

Chapter 77 Enforcement of Foreign Judgments

INTRODUCTION

English law provides for enforcement of foreign judgments under common law and under four different statutory schemes based upon international instruments (Administration of Justice Act 1920, Foreign Judgments (Reciprocal Enforcement) Act 1933, Brussels and Lugano Conventions, **Jurisdiction and Judgments Regulation**). The choice of the appropriate mechanism will depend on the country of origin of the judgment. **77.1**

The common law and the statutory schemes are not mutually exclusive. However, where a statutory scheme is available, it should be preferred because its regime is generally more favourable to the party seeking enforcement.

COMMON LAW

At common law, a foreign judgment creates an implied contract to pay, which can be enforced in England subject to certain defences (*Grant v Eatson* (1883) 13 QBD 302). The party seeking to enforce the foreign judgment must commence proceedings in the appropriate English court based on this implied contract to pay. This party will usually seek to obtain summary judgment on the basis that the defendant has no reasonable prospect of defending the claim. **77.2**

Foreign court must have had jurisdiction over the defendant

The foreign court must have had jurisdiction over the defendant according to English conflict of laws rules (*Sirdar Gurdyal Singh v Rajah of Faridkote* [1894] AC 670). Thus, the defendant, at the date of the commencement of the proceedings, must have been present in the foreign country (*Adams v Cape Industries plc* [1990] Ch 433). Alternatively, the defendant must have submitted, or agreed to submit, to the jurisdiction of the foreign court. Actual submission includes voluntary appearance in the foreign court other than for disputing jurisdiction. Agreement to submit includes contractual non-exclusive and exclusive jurisdiction clauses as well as clauses relating to acceptance of service of process. **77.3**

Conditions relating to the foreign judgment

77.4 To be enforceable at common law, the judgment of the foreign court must be conclusive on its merits. In addition, the foreign court must have ruled it had jurisdiction and accordingly decided on the cause of action, without the possibility of its decision of being varied or reopened (*The Sennar (No. 2)* [1985] 1 WLR 490)). A right to appeal the foreign judgment does not prevent it from being conclusive. However, if a stay of execution has been granted, the judgment may not be enforced (*Carl-Zeiss-Stiftung v Rayner and Keeler Ltd (No. 2)* [1967] 1 AC 853). The claim must be for a definite sum or for a sum ascertainable by a simple calculation (*Beatty v Beatty* [1924] 1 KB 807). Foreign judgments for the enforcement of penal (*United States of America v Inkley* [1989] QB 255) or revenue (*Re State of Norway's Application (Nos. 1 and 2)* [1990] 1 AC 723) laws may not be enforced in the English courts. Revenue debts due in other EU States may be recovered under the Finance Act 2002, s. 134 and sch. 39.

Defences to an enforcement claim

77.5 In addition to the conditions set out at 77.3 and 77.4, a defendant can resist the claim by raising a number of defences. The defendant may argue that the foreign judgment was obtained by fraud (*Jet Holdings Inc. v Patel* [1990] 1 QB 335) whether on the part of the foreign court or the successful party. The defendant may claim that the judgment is contrary to public policy (*Soleimany v Soleimany* [1999] QB 785). The defendant may contend that the proceedings leading to the foreign judgment were contrary to natural or substantive justice (*Adams v Cape Industries plc* [1990] Ch 433). In deciding whether to recognise a foreign judgment, an English court would have regard to its obligation to act in a manner consistent with the right to a fair trial guaranteed by the **European Convention on Human Rights, art. 6, in the Human Rights Act 1998, sch. 1** (*Al-Bassam v Al-Bassam* [2004] EWCA Civ 857, *The Times*, 22 July 2004). For multiple damages see 77.6.

COMMONWEALTH JUDGMENTS

77.6 Under the Administration of Justice Act 1920 (the '1920 Act') an application can be made for the registration of a judgment of a superior court of a Commonwealth country in the High Court within 12 months of the date of the judgment in question. The court has a discretion whether to register the judgment, and the defendant can make use of most of the defences available at common law.

A foreign judgment for multiple damages will not be registered under either the Administration of Justice Act 1920 or the Foreign Judgments (Reciprocal Enforcement) Act 1933, and it is a defence to proceedings at common law for the recovery of any sum payable under such a judgment (Protection of Trading Interests Act 1980, s. 5(1)). A judgment arrived at by multiplying the amount assessed as compensation is a judgment for multiple damages (s. 5(3)). Where a foreign judgment consists of identifiable compensatory damages and multiple damages, it is only the multiple damages part of the judgment which is not enforceable (*Lewis v Eliades* [2003] EWCA Civ 1758, [2004] 1 WLR 692).

RECIPROCAL ENFORCEMENT ARRANGEMENTS

77.7 Under the Foreign Judgments (Reciprocal Enforcement) Act 1933 (the '1933 Act') an application can be made for the registration of judgments of recognised courts and tribunals of States with which this country has entered into reciprocal enforcement arrangements, provided the application is made within six years of the judgment. This Act considerably increased the circumstances in which foreign judgments can be registered, but enforcement is subject to a wide range of defences similar to those available at common law. For multiple damages see 77.6.

BRUSSELS AND LUGANO CONVENTION JUDGMENTS

Under the Civil Jurisdiction and Judgments Act 1982, s. 4, a judgment of a court of another contracting State to the Brussels Convention (i.e., Denmark) or the Lugano Convention (Iceland, Norway and Switzerland) may be registered in the courts of this country. The same applies to a judgment of a Gibraltar court (Civil Jurisdiction and Judgments Act 1982 (Gibraltar) Order 1997 (SI 1997/2602)). When registered, such a judgment has the same force and effect as if the judgment had been given in this country. Articles 27 and 28 of the Conventions set out a number of defences to registration, such as recognition being contrary to public policy, the defendant not having been duly served with the document instituting the foreign proceedings, and the judgment being irreconcilable with another judgment. However, art. 29 provides that there cannot, under any circumstances, be a review of the substance of such a judgment. **77.8**

Third party debt orders are a means of enforcement of a judgment *in rem* against the debt. Accordingly, exclusive jurisdiction for enforcement by this method is given to the courts where the debt is situated by the Lugano Convention, art. 16(5) (*Kuwait Oil Tanker Co. SAK v Qabazard* [2003] UKHL 31, [2004] 1 AC 300).

Recognition of a Dutch judgment which had been obtained in manifest contravention of **art. 6(1) of the European Convention on Human Rights** was refused as being contrary to public policy under art. 27(1) of the Brussels Convention in *Maronier v Larmer* [2002] EWCA Civ 774, [2003] QB 620. *TSN Kunststoffrecycling GmbH v Jurgens* [2002] EWCA Civ 11, [2002] 1 WLR 2459, involved a judgment entered in default in Germany which was registered for enforcement in England. The judgment debtor alleged that the 14-day period for responding to the claim provided by the German rules of procedure was insufficient, and argued that under art. 27(2) the judgment should not be recognised because he had not been served in sufficient time to be able to arrange for his defence. It was held that to do justice both to the judgment debtor's right to a fair trial and to ensure the free movements of judgments, the exception provided by art. 27(2) should not be expanded further than was reasonably necessary to protect the judgment debtor's right to a fair trial. It was found that five weeks had elapsed between service and entry of the default judgment, so registration was not set aside.

JURISDICTION AND JUDGMENTS REGULATION

Since 1 March 2002, Council **Regulation (EC) No. 44/2001**, the 'Jurisdiction and Judgments Regulation', has replaced the provisions on enforcement under the Brussels Convention in all EU countries other than Denmark. The principles are almost identical to those applicable under the Brussels and Lugano Conventions. **77.9**

Conditions for application of the Regulation

To obtain registration, the claimant must show that three conditions are fulfilled: **77.10**

(a) the foreign judgment must fall within the scope of the Regulation, that is, the subject matter of the dispute must be commercial or civil (**Jurisdiction and Judgments Regulation, art. 1(1)** and **(2)**).
(b) The proceedings must have been instituted on or after 1 March 2002. Earlier proceedings will be enforced under the Regulation if instituted after the entry into force of the Brussels and Lugano Conventions in the State of origin and the State of enforcement and if judgment is given on or after 1 March 2002 (**art. 66**). The Regulation will also apply if

the jurisdiction of the court of origin of the foreign judgment was founded upon rules which accorded with those provided for in Chapter II of the Regulation or in a convention concluded between the member State of origin and the member State addressed which was in force when the proceedings were instituted.

(c) The ruling for which enforcement is sought must be a judgment given by a court or tribunal of a member State, whatever the judgment may be called, including a decree, order, decision or writ of execution, as well as the determination of costs or expenses by an officer of the court (**art. 32**).

Authentic instruments and court settlements are also enforceable. A document formally drawn up or registered as an authentic instrument and which is enforceable in one Regulation State must be registered as a foreign judgment (**arts 57 and 58**).

Grounds of defence

77.11 A defendant may raise one of four grounds of defence set out in the **Jurisdiction and Judgments Regulation, art. 34**. Recognition of a foreign judgment may be refused because it is manifestly contrary to public policy of the member State in which recognition is sought (**art. 34(1)**). The judgment will not be recognised where it was given in default of appearance, if the defendant has not been served with the document instituting proceedings in sufficient time and in such a way as to enable him to arrange his defence, unless the defendant failed to commence proceedings to challenge the judgment when it was possible for him to do so (**art. 34(2)**). A judgment will also not be recognised where it is irreconcilable with a judgment given in a dispute between the same parties in the State in which recognition is sought (**art. 34(3)**). The same applies to a judgment that is irreconcilable with an earlier judgment given in another Regulation State or in a third State involving the same cause of action and between the same parties (**art. 34(4)**).

Where an ordinary appeal has been lodged, the court of the country in which recognition is sought may stay the enforcement proceedings (**art. 37**).

NORTHERN IRISH AND SCOTTISH JUDGMENTS

77.12 Under the Civil Jurisdiction and Judgments Act 1982 (the '1982 Act'), s. 18, judgments of the courts of Northern Ireland and Scotland can be enforced in England and Wales by a simple process of registration of a certificate of the judgment in question. The only defences are that the procedure has not been complied with and that there has been an earlier judgment dealing with the same matter. The procedure is set out in **CPR, rr. 74.14 to 74.18**.

REGISTRATION IN ENGLAND AND WALES OF FOREIGN JUDGMENTS

77.13 **Rules** 74.2 to **74.11 of the CPR** set out the procedure for registering judgments under:

(a) the Administration of Justice Act 1920 (the '1920 Act'; see 77.6);
(b) the Foreign Judgments (Reciprocal Enforcement) Act 1933 (the '1933 Act'; see 77.7);
(c) the Civil Jurisdiction and Judgments Act 1982 (the '1982 Act'; see 77.8); and
(d) the **Jurisdiction and Judgments Regulation** (see 77.9).

For this purpose, a 'judgment' means any judgment of a foreign court or tribunal, whatever it may be called, and includes decrees, orders, decisions, writs of execution and costs determinations (CPR, r. 74.2(1)(c)).

Applications for registration must be made to the Queen's Bench Division of the High Court (**r. 74.3(2); PD 74, para. 4.1**). Applications are made without notice (**CPR, r. 74.3(2)**) in accordance with **Part 23** (**PD 74, para. 4.4**) and must be supported by written evidence complying with **CPR, r. 74.4** (see **77.14** to **77.18**).

Common requirements for evidence under the 1920,1933 and 1982 Acts

Applications for registration under the 1920,1933 and 1982 Acts (but not the **Jurisdiction and Judgments Regulation**, for which see **77.18**) must, by **CPR, r. 74.4(1) and** (2), be supported by written evidence which: **77.14**

(a) states the name of the judgment creditor and an address for service within the jurisdiction;
(b) states the name and address of the judgment debtor;
(c) states the grounds on which the judgment creditor is entitled to enforce the judgment;
(d) states the amount outstanding (if a money judgment);
(e) states details of any interest recoverable on the judgment, including the rate, dates and amounts;
(f) exhibits the judgment or a verified or certified or otherwise authenticated copy of the judgment;
(g) exhibits a translation of the judgment (if not in English) into English certified by a notary public or other qualified person, or which is confirmed to be accurate.

Evidence under the 1920 Act

In addition to the matters set out at **77.14**, the evidence in support of an application for registration under the 1920 Act must, by **CPR, r. 74.4(3)**: **77.15**

(a) state that the judgment is not a judgment which under the 1920 Act, s. 9, cannot be registered (**r. 74.4(3)(a)**);
(b) state that the judgment is not one to which the Protection of Trading Interests Act 1980, s. 5, applies (**r. 74.4(3)(b)**).

Evidence under the 1933 Act

In addition to the matters set out at **77.14**, the evidence in support of an application for registration under the 1933 Act must, by **CPR, r. 74.4(4)**, state that it is a money judgment, confirm that it can be enforced by execution in the State of origin, and deal with various other matters, including providing any further evidence required by the relevant Order in Council. **77.16**

Evidence under the 1982 Act

In addition to the matters set out at **77.14**, the evidence in support of an application for registration under the 1982 Act must, by **CPR, r. 74.4(5)**, exhibit documents showing that the judgment is enforceable against the judgment debtor in the State of origin, and, where appropriate, documents proving service of the originating process (if judgment was entered in default) and any legal aid certificate from the State of origin. **77.17**

Evidence under the Jurisdiction and Judgments Regulation

Written evidence in support of applications for registration in the High Court of judgments given in EU States other than Denmark must comply with **CPR, r. 74.4(6)**; **PD 74, paras 6.1** to **6.5**, and the **Jurisdiction and Judgments Regulation, arts** 40, 53, 54 and 55. The evidence must, in particular: **77.18**

(a) state an address for service within the jurisdiction (**Jurisdiction and Judgments Regulation, art. 40(2)**);
(b) state details of any interest recoverable on the judgment, including the rate, dates and amounts (**CPR, r. 74.4(6)**);
(c) exhibit a copy of the judgment in a form establishing its authenticity (**Jurisdiction and Judgments Regulation, art. 53(1)**);

(d) exhibit a certificate in the form set out in Annex V to the **Jurisdiction and Judgments Regulation (art.** 53(2));
(e) exhibit a certified translation of the certificate (**art.** 55(2)); and
(f) exhibit a translation of the judgment (if not in English) into English certified by a notary public or other qualified person, or which is confirmed to be accurate (**CPR, r.** 74.4(6)).

REGISTRATION ORDERS

77.19 An order granting permission to register a judgment must be drawn up by the judgment creditor (**CPR, r.** 74.6(1)). The order must give full particulars of the original judgment, and the name and address for service of the judgment creditor. It must also set out the rights to apply to set aside (under the 1920 and 1933 Acts) or to appeal against the registration (under the 1982 Act and the **Jurisdiction and Judgments Regulation**), the time for making such application or appeal, and that no enforcement measures will be taken until the end of that period (**r.** 74.6(3) and see **r.** 74.9). Registration serves as a decision that the judgment is recognised for the purposes of the 1982 Act and the Jurisdiction and Judgments Regulation (r. 74.10). The Central Office keeps registers of foreign judgments ordered to be enforced under the 1920,1933 and 1982 Acts and the **Jurisdiction and Judgments Regulation (PD 74, para.** 3(1)).

Service of registration orders

77.20 Service must be effected by the judgment creditor on the judgment debtor by delivering the order personally, or by serving a company in accordance with the Companies Act 1985, s. 725, or as directed by the court (**CPR, r.** 74.6(1)). Permission is not required for service outside the jurisdiction (r. 74.6(2)). A party seeking to enforce after registration must file evidence of service of the registration order and any other relevant court order (r. 74.9(2)).

Applications to set aside under the 1920 and 1933 Acts

77.21 Applications to set aside under the 1920 and 1933 Acts must be made within the time allowed in the registration order (**CPR, r.** 74.7(1)). This time limit can be extended (r. 74.7(2)). The court hearing an application may order any issue between the parties to be tried (r. 74.7(3)).

Appeals under the 1982 Act and the Jurisdiction and Judgments Regulation

77.22 Appeals against the granting or refusal of registration under the 1982 Act and the **Jurisdiction and Judgments Regulation** are made in accordance with **CPR, Part** 52, but no permission to appeal is required (r. 74.8(1) and (2)). The appellant's notice must be filed within the period specified in the registration order (**rr.** 52.4(2)(a) and 74.6(3)(d)) or, in the case of an appeal against the refusal of registration, within 14 days of the relevant order (**r.** 52.4(2)(b)). The appellant's notice must be served on the respondent within one month of the order (two months in the case of an appeal against the granting of registration where service is to be effected on a party outside the jurisdiction) (**r.** 74.8(4)).

ENFORCEMENT IN ENGLAND AND WALES OF EUROPEAN COMMUNITY JUDGMENTS

77.23 'Community judgments' are defined by **CPR, r.** 74.19, as judgments, decisions and orders enforceable under:
(a) the Treaty establishing the European Community, arts 244 or 256;
(b) the Euratom Treaty, arts 18, 159 or 164;

(c) the Treaty establishing the European Coal and Steel Community, arts 44 or 92;
(d) Council Regulation (EC) No. 40/94 (on the Community trade mark), art. 82; or
(e) Council Regulation (EC) No. 6/2002 (on Community designs), art. 71.

Enforcement of Community judgments requires an application to the Queen's Bench Division of the High Court (**CPR, r. 74.20; PD 74, para. 4.1**). Written evidence in support must comply with **CPR, r. 74.21**. Any order granting permission to register a Community judgment must be served on every person against whom the judgment was given (**r. 74.22**).

ENFORCEMENT IN ENGLAND AND WALES OF EUROPEAN ENFORCEMENT ORDERS

'European enforcement order' (EEO) is defined, by **CPR, r. 74.27**, as having the meaning given in **Regulation (EC) No. 805/2004** creating a European enforcement order for uncontested claims (the EEO Regulation). For a judgment on an uncontested claim (for payment of a sum of money) to be certified as an EEO, the conditions in **art. 6 of the EEO Regulation** must be fulfilled: **77.24**

(a) the judgment must be enforceable in the member State of origin of the foreign judgment; and
(b) the judgment must not conflict with the rules on jurisdiction in sections 3 and 6 of Chapter II of the **Jurisdiction and Judgments Regulation**.

In addition to the above, where the claim is uncontested as a result of the debtor having never objected to the claim, or where the debtor did not appear or was not represented at the original court hearing:

(a) the court proceedings in the member State of origin must have met minimum procedural standards (laid down in **Chapter III of the EEO Regulation**); and
(b) where the judgment relates to a contract concluded by a consumer (being the debtor) for a purpose outside his trade or profession, the judgment must have been given in the member State of the debtor's domicile.

To enforce an EEO it is necessary, by **CPR, r. 74.31**, to lodge at the court in which enforcement proceedings are to be brought the following documents:

(a) a copy of the judgment;
(b) a copy of the EEO certificate;
(c) where necessary, a transcription or translation of the EEO certificate.

To enforce an EEO expressed in a foreign currency, where an application is made to the High Court (for a charging order, a writ of fieri facias or an attachment of earnings order) or to the county court (for a warrant of execution or an attachment of earnings order), the application must contain a certificate of the sterling equivalent of the judgment sum at the close of business on the date nearest preceding the date of issue of the application (**r. 74.31**).

An application by the judgment debtor that the court should either refuse to enforce an EEO (**r. 74.32**) or stay or limit the enforcement proceedings (**r. 74.33**) must be made in accordance with **Part 23** to the court in which the EEO is being enforced. Any such order made must be served on all other parties to the proceedings and any other person affected by the order and on any court in which enforcement proceedings are pending in England and Wales.

Chapter 78 Committal and Sequestration

CIVIL CONTEMPT OF COURT

Nature of civil contempt

78.1 If one party, A, to civil proceedings obtains a court order (other than for the payment of money) against another party, B, and B disobeys the order, B is said to commit a civil contempt of court and is described as a 'contemnor'. The person who obtained the order, A, may apply to the court for B to be committed to prison (see 78.3) or for B's assets to be sequestrated (seized) by officers of the court (see 78.21 and 78.22).

To show that B is in contempt, it must be established that B's conduct was intentional and that B knew of all the facts which made that conduct a breach of the order, but it is not necessary to prove that B appreciated that the conduct did breach the order (*Heaton's Transport (St Helens) Ltd v Transport and General Workers' Union* [1973] AC 15; *Spectravest Inc. v Aperknit Ltd* [1988] FSR 161 per Millett J at pp. 173–4; see also *Adam Phones Ltd v Goldschmidt* [1999] 4 All ER 486 on the view that it should be necessary to prove intention to breach the order).

Breach of an undertaking is treated in the same way as breach of an order (see 78.19).

An act which contravenes a court order in civil proceedings may be both a civil contempt of court and a criminal offence. There is no abuse of process in bringing both criminal proceedings and proceedings for civil contempt in respect of the same act (*Director of Public Prosecutions v Tweddell* [2001] EWHC 188 (Admin), [2002] 2 FLR 400), though the court hearing the second proceedings should take into account any punishment already imposed (*Lomas v Parle* [2003] EWCA Civ 1804, [2004] 1 WLR 1642).

Punishment for a civil contempt of court is not in itself a remedy: it is a means of enforcing a remedy. A civil contempt of court is prosecuted as a matter between parties to proceedings and is punishable primarily in order to enforce compliance with an order of the court, for the benefit of the party who obtained the order. Enforcing respect for court orders also serves the public interest of promoting respect for the rule of law, which is an essential element of our civil society (*Re S (A Child) (Contact Dispute: Committal)* [2004] EWCA Civ 1790, *The Times*, 9 December 2004). A criminal contempt of court is conduct which frustrates or impedes the due administration of justice and is punishable in the public interest (*Attorney-General v Times Newspapers Ltd* [1992] 1 AC 191). Criminal contempt of court is considered in *Blackstone's Criminal Practice*, paras B14.59 to B14.98.

For contempt of court by making a false statement in a document verified by a statement of truth see **23.13**. For contempt of court by failure to obey a High Court witness summons see **55.8**.

Punishment for civil contempt

A court may commit a contemnor to prison for up to two years (Contempt of Court Act 1981, s. 14(1)). The two-year maximum should not be exceeded on any single occasion, even if the judge is dealing with the activation of a suspended sentence as well as a more recent contempt (*Villiers v Villiers* [1994] 1 WLR 493). **78.2**

A sentence of imprisonment for contempt of court must be for a fixed term (Contempt of Court Act 1981, s. 14(1)), but the court has a power to discharge a committed contemnor (see **78.17**), which will be done on acceptance by the court that the contemnor has purged his or her contempt.

Committal for any period is always a sanction of last resort (*Ansah v Ansah* [1977] Fam 138 per Ormrod LJ at p. 144; *Belgolaise SA v Purchandani* [1999] Lloyd's Rep Bank 116; *Gulf Azov Shipping Co. Ltd v Idisi* [2001] EWCA Civ 21, LTL 16/1/2001, at [70]). It is only appropriate where there is serious, contumacious, flouting of orders of the court (*Gulf Azov Shipping Co. Ltd v Idisi* at [72]). An inadvertent breach of an order or undertaking cannot justify committal (*Gulf Azov Shipping Co. Ltd v Idisi* at [15]). A party applying for committal for a merely technical breach of an order may be ordered to pay the respondent's costs (*Adam Phones Ltd v Goldschmidt* [1999] 4 All ER 486).

A person aged under 21 may not be committed to prison (Powers of Criminal Courts (Sentencing) Act 2000, s. 89(1)(b)). A contemnor who is at least 18 but under 21 may be committed to be detained under s. 108 of the 2000 Act and the Secretary of State will direct where the person is to be detained (s. 108(5)). Committal for detention under s. 108 may not be ordered unless the court is of the opinion that no other method of dealing with the person is appropriate (s. 108(3), which lists matters which the court must take into consideration). The minimum age for imprisonment will be lowered to 18 when the Criminal Justice and Court Services Act 2000, s. 61, is brought into force, and then the provision for committal for detention of persons aged 18 to 20 will be repealed. An injunction should not be made against a person aged under 18, as it cannot be enforced by committal, and the person is unlikely to have assets which could be used to pay a fine or which could be sequestrated (*Wookey v Wookey* [1991] Fam 121; *Harrow London Borough Council v G* [2004] EWHC 17 (QB), LTL 23/1/2004).

If the court grants an injunction against a government minister or other Crown officer in a judicial review claim, it may make a finding of civil contempt, but normally no penalty should be imposed and it is to be expected that the finding would be enough to bring about compliance with the injunction (*Re M* [1994] 1 AC 377). It follows that normally a declaration is sufficient and an injunction is unnecessary.

In addition to, or instead of, committing to prison, the court may impose a fine (Contempt of Court Act 1981, s. 14), take security (a recognisance) for good behaviour, make a summary award of damages (*Midland Marts Ltd v Hobday* [1989] 1 WLR 1148), make a sequestration order or deliver a reprimand.

It is not appropriate to prevent a party to proceedings from taking further part in them as a punishment for not obeying an order made in the course of the proceedings (*Re Swaptronics Ltd* (1998) *The Times*, 17 August 1998), though if a party's disobedience to an order seriously interferes with the fair conduct of the trial, it may be necessary to stay the proceedings or strike out that party's claim or defence (*Arrow Nominees Inc. v Blackledge* [2000] 2 BCLC 167). A party who has been found to be in contempt by failing to comply with an order made in proceedings, and who has made no attempt to purge that contempt, may be prevented from pursuing an appeal in those proceedings: the appellate court should ask whether, in the circumstances of the case, the interests of justice are best served by hearing or by refusing to hear a party in contempt, bearing in mind the paramount importance to be attached to the prompt and unquestioning observance of court orders (*Arab Monetary Fund v Hashim* (1997) LTL 9/6/99; *Raja v Van Hoogstraten* [2004] EWCA Civ 968, [2004] 4 All ER 793, at [82]).

A sequestration order appoints four sequestrators who are empowered to enter the contemnor's land and to seize the contemnor's personal property, which they will hold until the contempt is purged. Sequestration orders are most commonly used against non-natural persons, such as limited liability companies and trade unions.

An employer who is subject to a court order is vicariously liable for any employee's breach of the order and it is no defence to say that all reasonable steps were taken to prevent employees breaching the order (*Director General of Fair Trading v Pioneer Concrete (UK) Ltd* [1995] 1 AC 456). It is not right to qualify an injunction against an employer to state that it does not apply where the employer has exercised due diligence to prevent it being breached by employees: the extent to which steps have been taken to prevent breach by employees may, however, mitigate the penalty for any contempt which does occur (*British Telecommunications plc v Nextcall Telecom plc* [2000] FSR 679).

COMMITTAL FOR DISOBEYING AN ORDER OR JUDGMENT OTHER THAN FOR THE PAYMENT OF MONEY

Rules of court

78.3 RSC, ord. 45, r. 5(1) in CPR, sch. 1, and **CCR, ord. 29, r. 1(1)** in CPR, sch. 2, provide for enforcement of a judgment or order by committal of a person refusing or neglecting to do what the judgment or order requires. The rules apply where:

(a) a person required by a judgment or order to do an act refuses or neglects to do it within the time which is specified in the order (or which is subsequently extended by the court);
(b) a person disobeys a judgment or order requiring the person to abstain from doing an act.

These rules are expressed to be subject to the Debtors Act 1869, the Debtors Act 1878 and the provisions of the CPR. The Debtors Act 1869, s. 4, abolished the power to imprison for default in payment of a sum of money, subject to six exceptions. These include default in paying: non-contractual penalties, sums recoverable before justices of the peace, sums in the hands of trustees or other fiduciaries, sums ordered to be paid by solicitors for misconduct, and income payable by bankrupts. The Debtors Act 1878 creates a wide discretion whether to allow committal in relation to the exceptions dealing with non-payment of sums in the hands of trustees and other fiduciaries and solicitors who have misbehaved. If the court finds that one of the exceptions applies, the committal order must state which exception was found (*Re Wilde* [1910] WN 128), and the period of imprisonment must not exceed one year (Debtors Act 1869, s. 4). Judgments for the recovery of money cannot, therefore, generally be enforced by committal and this position cannot be changed by making a supplementary order fixing a certain date for payment (see *Hulbert v Cathcart* [1894] 1 QB 244 and *Re Oddy* [1906] 1 Ch 93). Money judgments are accordingly usually enforced by the methods described in **chapter 76**.

Need for service of order

78.4 Enforcement of an order or judgment by committal must not take place unless a copy of the order has been served personally on the person required to do or abstain from doing the act in question (**RSC, ord. 45, r. 7(2)** in CPR, sch. 1; **CCR, ord. 29, r. 1(2)** in CPR, sch. 2). In the case of an order requiring a person to do an act, the copy must be served personally before the expiration of the time within which the act was to be done. An order or judgment requiring a body corporate to do or abstain from doing an act shall not be enforced by committal of an officer of the corporation unless (**RSC, ord. 45, r.** 7(3) in CPR, sch. 1; **CCR, ord. 29, r.** 1(2) in CPR, sch. 2):

(a) a copy of the order has also been served personally on the officer against whom an order of committal is sought, and
(b) in the case of an order requiring the body corporate to do an act, the copy has been so served before the expiration of the time within which the body was required to do the act.

An order requiring a person to abstain from doing an act may be enforced before service of the order if the court is satisfied that the person had notice of it, either by being present when it was made or by being notified of it by telephone or otherwise (**RSC, ord. 45, r.** 7(6) in CPR, sch. 1; **CCR, ord. 29, r.** 1(6) in CPR, sch. 2).

The court may dispense with service of an order if it thinks it just to do so (**RSC, ord. 45, r.** 7(7) in CPR, sch. 1; **CCR, ord. 29, r.** 1(7) in CPR, sch. 2). This may be done where it is clear that the contemnor was aware of the order at the time of the breach (*Davy International Ltd v Tazzyman* [1997] 1 WLR 1256).

In the High Court, a penal notice must be prominently displayed on the front of the copy served on the person against whom the order or judgment was made or given (**RSC, ord. 45, r.** 7(4) in CPR, sch. 1). The notice must state that disobedience to the order will be a contempt of court punishable by imprisonment, or (in the case of an order requiring a body corporate to do or abstain from doing an act) punishable by sequestration of the assets of the body corporate and by imprisoning any individual responsible. This notice is not part of the court's order and does not require the judge's sanction: it may be added by the person who makes the copy which is to be served (*Anglo-Eastern Trust Ltd v Kermanshahchi* (2002) *The Times*, 8 November 2002). In county court cases, penal notices will only be endorsed on orders 'in the nature of an injunction' or if the judgment creditor specifically requests this to be done (**CCR, ord. 29, r.** 1(3) in CPR, sch. 2). An order requiring a person to give up possession of land is not an order in the nature of an injunction (*Tuohy v Bell* [2002] EWCA Civ 423, LTL 27/3/2002). Omission of the penal notice is not fatal to enforcement by committal provided that the person sought to be committed was well aware of the consequences of disobedience (*Sofroniou v Szgetti* [1991] FCR 332). The onus is on the applicant to show that no injustice would be done by waiving any defect in the presentation of the penal notice (*Leicester City Council v Saracen Dyers Ltd* [2002] EWHC 2068 (QB), [2003] Env LR 18, in which the court decided that service of an order was not sufficient for the purposes of a committal application because the penal notice was on the last page rather than the front of the order).

APPLICATION FOR A COMMITTAL ORDER

Appropriate court for making the application

Table 78.1 sets out the court which may make committal orders in different circumstances. **78.5**

In insolvency proceedings, applications for committal for contempt must be made direct to the judge (**PD Insolvency Proceedings, paras** 5.1 and 9.1). In other proceedings a master or district judge may not make an order relating to the liberty of the subject (**PD 2B, para.** 3.1(a)).

For appeals in contempt proceedings see 71.11.

Use of application notice or claim form

If a committal application is made in existing proceedings, it may be commenced by filing an **78.6**

Table 78.1 Appropriate court for application for committal for contempt, other than in criminal proceedings

Type of contempt	Appropriate court	Authority
Contempt of the Court of Appeal	Court of Appeal	
Contempt in proceedings in Divisional Court of the Queen's Bench Division.	Divisional Court of the Queen's Bench Division.	RSC, ord. 52, r. 1(2) in CPR, sch. 1.
Contempt in proceedings in the High Court other than in a Divisional Court of the Queen's Bench Division.	Single judge of the Division to which the proceedings were assigned or subsequently transferred.	RSC, ord. 52, r. 1(3) in CPR, sch. 1.
Contempt in proceedings in a county court, including disobedience to an order made in a county court, or breach of an undertaking given to a county court.	The county court in question.	PD RSC ord. 52, para. 1.2.
Statutory power to punish for misconduct as if it were contempt of court.	Single judge of Queen's Bench Division.	RSC, ord. 52, r. 1(4) in CPR, sch. 1.
Contempt committed otherwise than in connection with any proceedings, and not being dealt with under a statutory power to punish misconduct as if it were contempt.	Divisional Court of the Queen's Bench Division.	RSC, ord. 52, r. 1(2) in CPR, sch. 1.

application notice in those proceedings (**PD RSC ord. 52, para. 2.2(1)**). An application to commit for a breach of an undertaking given, or an order made, in proceedings may be commenced by filing an application notice in those proceedings (para. 2.2(2)). The application notice must identify the proceedings in which the application is made and bear the same title and reference number (para. 2.2(3)). **Part 23** of the CPR applies, subject to the provisions of **PD RSC ord. 52** (**PD RSC ord. 52, para. 2.6**).

In other cases, committal applications are commenced by issuing a **Part 8** claim form (para. 2.1) and **Part 8** of the CPR applies, subject to the provisions of **PD RSC ord. 52**. References in **CPR, Part 8**, to the 'claimant' are treated as references to the person making the application, and references to the 'defendant' are treated as references to the person sought to be committed (who, in the practice direction, is referred to as the 'respondent') (**PD RSC ord. 52, para. 2.5**). **Rule 8.4** (court's permission required if respondent is to take part in a hearing after failing to acknowledge service) does not apply (**PD RSC ord. 52, para. 2.5(4)**). The claim form must contain a prominent notice stating the possible consequences if the court makes a committal order or the respondent does not attend the hearing (para. 2.5(5)). A form of notice is annexed to **PD RSC ord. 52**.

Permission to apply to Divisional Court

78.7 An application to a Divisional Court for a committal order cannot be made unless the court gives permission (**RSC, ord. 52, r. 2(1)** in CPR, sch. 1). Permission must be applied for by filing an application notice (**PD RSC ord. 52, para. 2.4(1)**), which need not be served on the respondent (para. 2.4(2)). An application for permission to apply for a committal is made in accordance with **CPR, Part 23**, except that the provisions of **r. 23.9** (service of application made without notice) and **r. 23.10** (application to set aside or vary order made without notice) do not apply (**PD RSC ord. 52, para. 2.4(5)**).

An application for permission is made to a Divisional Court, except during vacation, when it may be made to a judge in chambers (**RSC, ord. 52, r. 2(2)** in CPR, sch. 1). The application must be supported by a statement setting out the name and description of the applicant, the name, description and address of the person sought to be committed and the grounds on which his or her committal is sought (**RSC, ord. 52, r. 2(2)** in CPR, sch. 1). The application must also be supported by an affidavit verifying the facts relied upon, which is to be filed before the application for permission is made (ord. 52, r. 2(2)).

The applicant must, no later than the preceding day, give notice of the application for permission to the Crown Office, and must at the same time lodge copies of the statement and affidavit (ord. 52, r. 2(3)). Where the application for permission is granted, the judge may also give directions, particularly relating to service of the application for an order of committal, and may include a direction that time for service is abridged (**CPR, r. 3.1(2)**). Where a judge in chambers refuses the application for permission, the applicant may make a fresh application for permission to a Divisional Court (**RSC, ord. 52, r. 2(4)** in CPR, sch. 1). A fresh application must be made within eight days after the judge's refusal to give permission or, if a Divisional Court does not sit within that period, on the first day on which it sits thereafter (ord. 52, r. 2(5)).

If permission is given, it expires after 14 days (**RSC, ord. 52, r. 3(2)** in CPR, sch. 1). The application notice or claim form commencing the committal application must contain the date on which, and the name of the judge by whom, the permission was granted (**PD RSC ord. 52, para. 2.4(3)**).

Contents of application and supporting affidavit

An application notice or claim form applying for a committal order must set out in full the grounds on which the committal application is made and should identify, separately and numerically, each alleged act of contempt (**PD RSC ord. 52, paras 2.5(2) and 2.6(2)**; *Dorrell v Dorrell* [1985] FLR 1089). It must be supported by an affidavit (**RSC, ord. 52, r. 4(1)** in CPR, sch. 1; **CCR, ord. 29, r. 1(4A)** in CPR, sch. 2). **78.8**

An application notice or claim form applying for a committal order may be amended only with the permission of the court (**PD RSC ord. 52, paras 2.5(3)** and **2.6(3)**).

Hearing date

When lodging the application notice or claim form with the court for issue or filing, the applicant must obtain a date for the hearing of the application (**PD RSC ord. 52. para. 4.1**). **78.9**

Service

An application notice or claim form applying for a committal order must be served personally on the person sought to be committed (**RSC, ord. 52, rr. 3(3)** and **4(2)** in CPR, sch. 1; **CCR, ord. 29, r. 1(4A)** in CPR, sch. 2), unless the court dispenses with service, which it may if it thinks it just to do so (**RSC, ord. 52, rr. 3(3)** and **4(3)** in CPR, sch. 1; **CCR, ord. 29, r. 1(7)** in CPR, sch. 2). It may be appropriate to dispense with service in cases of urgency, or where there have been persistent breaches of court orders, or the respondent is evading service. **78.10**

There must be at least 14 clear days between the service of the claim form and the date of the hearing, unless the court orders otherwise (**RSC, ord. 52, r. 3(1)** in CPR, sch. 1; **PD RSC ord. 52, para. 4.2**).

When served, the application notice or claim form must be accompanied by a copy of the supporting affidavit (or, in Divisional Court proceedings, a copy of the statement and affidavit in support of the application for permission).

Arrest

The High Court has an inherent power to issue a bench warrant for the arrest of an alleged contemnor to secure his or her attendance in court (*Zakharov v White* [2003] EWHC 2463 (Ch), *The Times*, 13 November 2003). There are also statutory provisions under which a power of arrest can be attached to an injunction, for example, under the **Housing Act 1996, s. 153C** (see **92.5**) and **s. 153D** (see **92.6**), and the Anti-social Behaviour Act 2003, s. 91 (see **92.12**). **78.11**

Evidence

78.12 Written evidence in support of or in opposition to a committal application must be given by affidavit (**PD RSC ord. 52, para. 3.1**) and, unless the court directs otherwise, must be filed (**para. 3.2**). A respondent may give oral evidence at the hearing if he or she expresses a wish to do so, despite not filing or serving any written evidence (**para. 3.3**). A respondent who gives oral evidence may be cross-examined (**para. 3.3**). The respondent may call a witness to give evidence at the hearing even though that witness has not sworn an affidavit, provided the court gives permission (**para. 3.4**).

Orders for further information under **CPR, r. 18.1**, may not be made against a respondent to a committal application (**PD RSC ord. 52, para. 7**). Additional information should not be necessary in committal applications where the breaches are listed in the application notice or claim form and it is a matter for the court to determine whether those breaches are made out. A committal application made in existing proceedings should not be used as a fishing expedition or back-door means of obtaining information. Where the committal application is based on the alleged breach of an order for the respondent to provide further information, the court may, on making the order for committal, direct that the execution of the order be suspended on such terms or conditions as it may specify, such as providing further information (**RSC, ord. 52, r. 7(1)** in CPR, sch. 1; **CPR, r. 3.1(3)**).

Case management

78.13 The court may, at any time, give case management directions, including directions for the service of written evidence by the respondent and written evidence in reply by the applicant (**PD RSC ord. 52, para. 4.3**). The court may also convene and hold a directions hearing (**para. 4.3**). On the hearing date itself, the court may give case management directions with a view to a hearing of the committal application on a future date or if the committal application is ready to be heard, the court may proceed forthwith to hear it (**para. 4.4**).

In general the court must ensure that a committal hearing is conducted in accordance with art. 6 of the European Convention on Human Rights (right to a fair trial) in the **Human Rights Act 1998, sch. 1** (**PD RSC ord. 52, para. 1.4**). Committal proceedings are in the nature of criminal proceedings so that art. 6(3) of the Convention applies (*Berry Trade Ltd v Moussavi* [2002] EWCA Civ 477, [2002] 1 WLR 1910 at [31]). The court must have regard to the need for the respondent to have details of the alleged contempt and an opportunity to respond to the application and prepare a defence (**PD RSC ord. 52, paras 4.5 and 4.6(1)**). The court should ensure that the respondent is aware that assistance may be available from the Community Legal Service (**para. 4.6(2)**) and, if the respondent is unrepresented, should give him or her an opportunity to obtain legal advice (**para. 4.6(3)**; *Berry Trade Ltd v Moussavi*). If the respondent is unable to understand English, the court should assist, if necessary, in finding an interpreter to attend the hearing (**para. 4.6(4)**).

Striking out

78.14 **PD RSC ord. 52, para. 5**, states that the court may, either on the application of the respondent or of its own initiative, strike out a committal application on the following grounds:

(a) The committal application and the evidence served in support of it disclose no reasonable ground for alleging that the respondent is guilty of contempt of court.
(b) The committal application is an abuse of the court's process or, if made in existing proceedings is otherwise likely to obstruct the just disposal of those proceedings.
(c) There has been a failure to comply with a rule, practice direction or court order.

The applicant's failure to comply with a rule or practice direction may not be fatal to the application. **PD RSC ord. 52, para. 10**, provides that any procedural defect in the commencement or conduct by the applicant of a committal application may be waived by the court if the court is satisfied that no injustice has been caused to the respondent by the defect. A committal application may not be discontinued without the permission of the court (**PD RSC ord. 52, para. 8**).

HEARING A COMMITTAL APPLICATION

A committal application commenced in the High Court by application notice cannot be disposed of by the court without a hearing (**PD RSC ord. 52, para. 2.6(4)**). Generally, an application for an order of committal will be heard in public, but under **RSC, ord. 52, r. 6** in CPR, sch. 1, the High Court may hear a committal application in private in the following circumstances: **78.15**

(a) where the application arises out of proceedings relating to the wardship or adoption of a child or wholly or mainly to the guardianship, custody, maintenance or upbringing of an infant or rights of access to a child;
(b) where the application arises out of proceedings relating to a person suffering or appearing to be suffering from mental disorder within the meaning of the Mental Health Act 1983;
(c) where the application arises out of proceedings in which a secret process, discovery or invention was in issue; or
(d) where it appears to the court that in the interests of the administration of justice or for reasons of national security the application should be heard in private.

Where the court does hear the application in private and decides to make an order of committal against the person sought to be committed, it shall in public state:

(a) the name of that person;
(b) in general terms the nature of the contempt of court in respect of which the order of committal is being made; and
(c) the length of the period for which the person is being committed.

The grounds which the applicant may rely upon in support of the application for an order of committal are only the grounds set out in the claim form or application notice: no other grounds may be relied upon at the hearing unless the court gives permission (**RSC, ord. 52, r. 6(3)** in CPR, sch. 1). The person sought to be committed is entitled to give oral evidence on his or her own behalf if he or she wishes to do so (**ord. 52, r. 6(4)**).

For the purposes of the European Convention on Human Rights, art. 6 (right to a fair trial), in the **Human Rights Act 1998, sch. 1**, committal proceedings are of a criminal nature (*Raja v Van Hoogstraten* [2004] EWCA Civ 968, [2004] 4 All ER 793). The court will not commit a person for civil contempt of court unless the allegation of contempt is proved beyond reasonable doubt (**PD RSC ord. 52, para. 1.4**). Where more than one breach is alleged, the court must consider whether each of them has been proved beyond reasonable doubt, but in deciding whether the breaches justify committal, the court must consider the whole picture to see whether it portrays a respondent seeking to comply with the orders of the court or one bent on flouting them (*Gulf Azov Shipping Co. Ltd v Idisi* [2001] EWCA Civ 21, LTL 16/1/2001, at [18]).

In a county court, where service of the application notice or claim form has been dispensed with, and a committal order is made in the absence of the respondent, the judge may, on his or her own initiative, fix a date and time when the person to be committed is to be brought before the judge or before the court (**CCR, ord. 29, r. 1(8)** in CPR, sch. 2).

In a county court, under **CCR, ord. 29, r. 1(5)** in CPR, sch. 2, if a committal order is made, the order shall be for the issue of a warrant of committal and, unless the judge orders otherwise:

(a) a copy of the order shall be served on the person to be committed either before or at the time of the execution of the warrant; or

(b) where the warrant has been signed by the judge, the order for issue of the warrant may be served on the person to be committed at any time within 36 hours after the execution of the warrant.

A committal order will not be set aside for a merely technical error in procedure which has not prejudiced the contemnor (*Nicholls v Nicholls* [1997] 1 WLR 314). For example, in *Re Scriven* [2004] EWCA Civ 683, LTL 14/6/2004, the contemnor's committal was not invalidated by failure to serve the county court's committal order on him, as it was found that he knew the reason for the committal and would not have acted differently, for example, by appealing or purging his contempt, if the order had been served.

There is no jurisdiction to remand a contemnor in custody to await sentencing (*Delaney v Delaney* [1996] QB 387).

POWER TO SUSPEND EXECUTION OF COMMITTAL ORDER

78.16 By **RSC, ord. 52, r. 7** in CPR, sch. 1, the court making an order of committal may, by order, direct that the execution of the committal order shall be suspended for such period, or on such terms or conditions, as it may specify. Where the execution of a committal order is suspended, the applicant for the committal order must, unless the court directs otherwise, serve on the person against whom the order was made, notice informing him or her of the making and terms of the order. In the county court form N79 must be used (**PD 4, Table 3**) and failure to use it is a fundamental defect which will invalidate the order so that it cannot be activated (*Couzens v Couzens* [2001] 2 FLR 701). Care must be taken to distinguish between an allegation that a condition for suspension of committal has been breached and an allegation that there has been a further act of contempt (*Phillips v Symes* [2003] EWCA Civ 1769, LTL 5/12/2003).

DISCHARGE OF CONTEMNOR

78.17 Under **RSC, ord. 52, r. 8(1)** in CPR, sch. 1, the court may discharge a person committed to prison for contempt of court on that person's application. **Rule 8(2)** provides for the discharge of a contemnor who has been committed for failing to comply with a judgment or order requiring him or her to deliver something to some other person, or to deposit it in court or elsewhere, in cases where sequestrators take possession of the item under a writ of sequestration. In these cases the court may give such directions for dealing with the thing taken by the sequestrators as it thinks fit.

A person in custody under a warrant or order, other than a warrant of committal pursuant to an attachment of earnings order or judgment summons, may apply to the court to be discharged. The application is made in writing attested by the governor of the prison (or any other officer of the prison not below the rank of principal officer) showing that the applicant purged or wishes to purge his or her contempt. Not less than one day before the application is made, notice must be served on the party, if any, at whose instance the warrant or order was issued (**CCR, ord. 29, r. 3(1)** in CPR, sch. 2, which, by r. 3(3), does not apply to an application made by the Official Solicitor in his official capacity).

In a county court, if the committal order does not direct that any application for discharge shall be made to a judge, or was made by the district judge under the **County Courts Act 1984, s. 118** (power of judge to commit for contempt), any application for discharge may be made to the district judge (**CCR, ord. 29, r. 3(2)** in CPR, sch. 2).

On hearing an application to be discharged from custody, the court's options are to allow the application to discharge immediately, dismiss it, or adjourn it to be heard on a future date:

there is no jurisdiction to suspend the remainder of the sentence (*Harris v Harris* (2001) *The Times*, 19 November 2001).

FINE OR RECOGNISANCE INSTEAD OF COMMITTAL

Nothing in **RSC, ord.** 52 in CPR, sch. 1, detracts from the court's power to fine a person or require security (a recognisance) for good behaviour, instead of committing to prison (**RSC, ord.** 52, **r.** 9 in CPR, sch. 1). No equivalent provision is made in **CCR, ord.** 29, in CPR, sch. 2, but it is obvious that the county court's powers are just as unaffected by the rules. **78.18**

BREACH OF AN UNDERTAKING

There is a distinction to be drawn between an undertaking to the court, which is given voluntarily, even if unwillingly, by the person concerned, and an order which is imposed by the court. Although an undertaking is often recorded in an order of the court, it is the undertaking, and not the order, which requires the giver of the undertaking to act in accordance with its terms. A failure so to act is a breach of the undertaking, but cannot be called a refusal or neglect to act in accordance with the order which happens to record the undertaking or disobedience of that order (*Hussain v Hussain* [1986] Fam 134). The distinction between an order and an undertaking is, however, of little practical effect, except where there is a statutory power to attach a power of arrest to an order, as such a power cannot be attached to an undertaking. **78.19**

The procedure for committing for breach of undertaking is the same as that relating to breach of court orders and judgments (see **78.3** to **78.18**) with such modifications as are necessary.

In the county courts, a copy of the document recording the undertaking must be delivered by the court officer to the party giving the undertaking:

(a) by handing a copy of the document to that party before he or she leaves the court building; or
(b) where that party's place of residence is known, by posting a copy to that address; or
(c) through that party's solicitor.

Where delivery cannot be effected in this way, the court officer must deliver a copy of the document to the party for whose benefit the undertaking is given, and that party must serve it personally as soon as is practicable (**CCR, ord. 29, r. 1A** in CPR, sch. 2).

There are occasions when a solicitor is required to give an undertaking to the court, for example, when an application is made as a matter of urgency and there has not been time to issue the proceedings in which the application is made. Solicitors' undertakings given in relation to any proceedings in a county court may be enforced, by order of the judge of that court, by committal order against the solicitor (**CCR, ord. 29, r.** 2(1) in CPR, sch. 2). Where it appears to a judge that a solicitor has failed to carry out any such undertaking, the judge may, of his or her own initiative, direct the court officer to issue a notice calling on the solicitor to show cause why he or she should not be committed to prison. Such a notice will also be issued by the court officer where any party to the proceedings desires to have the undertaking enforced by a committal order, provided that the party makes an application supported by an affidavit setting out the facts on which the application is based (**CCR, ord.** 29, **r.** 2(2) and (3) in CPR, sch. 2). This is discussed further in **chapter 21**.

COURT'S POWER TO ORDER COMMITTAL OF ITS OWN INITIATIVE

78.20 Nothing in **RSC, ord.** 52 in CPR, sch. 1, affects the power of the High Court or the Court of Appeal to make an order of committal of its own initiative against a person guilty of contempt of court (**RSC, ord. 52, r.** 5 in CPR, sch. 1). A judge has power to initiate committal proceedings personally for breach of an order of the court, in the absence of an application. However, in these circumstances another judge should try the matter (*Re M (A Minor) (Contempt of Court: Committal of Court's Own Motion)* [1999] Fam 263).

SEQUESTRATION

Nature of sequestration

78.21 A writ of sequestration is one of the 'writs of execution' referred to in **RSC, ord.** 46 in CPR, sch. 1. It is a means of enforcement against the assets of an individual, a body corporate or a trade union. The person in whose favour an order has been made may issue a writ of sequestration requiring the sequestrators named to take possession of all the assets of the person against whom it was made if that person has not complied with the order. It is an appropriate method of enforcement where committal for contempt might be imposed. If a company is found to be in contempt, the court may, in appropriate cases, order sequestration of its assets (*Rose v Laskington Ltd* [1990] 1 QB 562). A judgment or order for the possession of land may be enforced by a writ of sequestration (**RSC, ord. 45, r.** 3(1)(c) in CPR, sch. 1) as may a judgment for delivery of goods (**RSC, ord. 45, r.** 4(1)(c) in CPR, sch. 1). The court may order the sale of sequestrated assets (*Richardson v Richardson* [1989] Fam 95).

For the general rules on issuing writs of execution see 76.6 and 76.7.

Application for permission to issue writ of sequestration

78.22 There are specific rules in **RSC, ord. 46, r.** 5 in CPR, sch. 1, relating to applications for permission to issue writs of sequestration, which are in addition to the general rules regarding writs of execution contained in ord. 46, r. 2. An application for permission to issue a writ of sequestration must be made in accordance with **CPR, Part** 23, and be heard by a judge (r. 5(1)).

The application notice must state the grounds of the application, must be accompanied by a copy of the witness statement or affidavit in support of the application, and must be served personally on the person against whose property it is sought to issue the writ. However, the court has power to dispense with service of the application notice if it thinks it just to do so (r. 5(2) and (3)).

Under r. 5(4), the judge hearing an application for permission to issue a writ of sequestration may sit in private in the circumstances in which an application for committal may be heard in private under **ord. 52, r.** 6 (see 78.14). Otherwise, the application must be heard in public.

Chapter 79 Winding Up and Administration of Registered Companies

The following procedural checklist, which is in **appendix 1**, is relevant to this chapter:

Procedural checklist 37 Application by a creditor whose debt is presently payable to wind up a company incorporated in England and Wales

NATURE OF WINDING UP AND ADMINISTRATION

Winding up

79.1 The Insolvency Act 1986 confers on the High Court and county courts a jurisdiction to order the winding up of virtually any kind of business, other than one conducted by a sole trader. Sole traders are excluded from the winding-up jurisdiction because they are subject to bankruptcy law (see **chapter 80**). The making of a winding-up order is discretionary.

In practice the great majority of applications for winding up are to wind up companies which have been incorporated by registration with the Registrar of Companies in England and Wales under the Companies Act 1985 or its predecessors. These include private limited companies and plcs. They are often referred to as 'registered companies', though in the legislation they are simply called 'companies'.

The winding-up provisions of the Insolvency Act 1986 are primarily drafted to apply to registered companies, which are the subject of part IV of the Act (ss. 73 to 219). Part IV is applied in various ways to other business entities, for example, to societies registered, or deemed to be registered, under the Industrial and Provident Societies Act 1965 (s. 55 of that Act), building societies (Building Societies Act 1986, ss. 86 to 103 and sch. 15), incorporated friendly societies (Friendly Societies Act 1992, ss. 22 and 23 and sch. 10), insolvent partnerships (Insolvent Partnerships Order 1994 (SI 1994/2421)) and limited liability partnerships (Limited Liability Partnerships Regulations 2001 (SI 2001/1090), reg. 5). Part IV of the Insolvency Act 1986 is also extended by part V of the Act to the winding up of what it calls 'unregistered companies', which include companies formed outside England and Wales. The present chapter is concerned only with the winding up of registered companies.

The winding up of a company by order of the court is known as a 'compulsory' winding up to contrast it with a winding up effected without a court order, which is called a 'voluntary' winding up (as in the Insolvency Act 1986, s. 84(2)).

The procedure for compulsory winding up serves three principal purposes:

(a) It enables unsecured creditors of an insolvent company to have it liquidated for their benefit (and in this respect compulsory liquidation has some affinity with bankruptcy, which is discussed in **chapter 80**).
(b) It enables members of a solvent company to have it liquidated for their benefit. (The Insolvency Act 1986 is misleadingly titled: it applies to the winding up of solvent as well as insolvent companies. In the special jargon of insolvency, the members of a company are referred to as 'contributories', see **79.63**.)
(c) It enables the Secretary of State and other public officials to have a company liquidated in the public interest.

The winding up or liquidation (the terms are used interchangeably) of a company is carried out by its liquidator. The provisions of the Insolvency Act 1986, ss. 136 to 140, ensure that a company has a liquidator as from the time that a court makes an order for it to be wound up. Initially the liquidator is the official receiver (see **79.16**), but if the assets are sufficient, an insolvency practitioner, who must be qualified to act in relation to the company (see **79.15**), may be appointed.

The liquidator of a company being wound up by the court entirely displaces the company's directors and performs his or her duties as an officer of the court subject to its control. The task of the liquidator of a company is to remove the company from all its legal relationships. Its contracts must be completed, transferred or otherwise brought to an end; it must cease carrying on its business except so far as may be necessary for its beneficial winding up; its liabilities (including post-liquidation interest) must be paid, as far as possible; and its legal disputes must be settled.

The members are entitled to benefit from any property remaining unless the company's constitution provides otherwise. Surplus non-cash assets may be sold and the proceeds distributed to the members or, if the company's constitution provides, the property may be distributed in kind.

In the compulsory winding up of an insolvent company the official receiver is required to report to the Secretary of State if it appears to the official receiver that the conduct of any person who has been a director of the company makes that person unfit to be concerned in the management of a company, and an application may then be made for a disqualification order (Company Directors Disqualification Act 1986, ss. 6 and 7).

The liquidation of a registered company is completed by dissolving it, which means removing its name from the Register of Companies so that it ceases to exist as a juristic person.

Winding up is a process undertaken for the collective benefit of a company's creditors and members. A winding-up order is said to operate 'in favour of all the creditors and of all contributories of the company' (Insolvency Act 1986, s. 130(4)). Winding up may be contrasted with the appointment of an administrative receiver. Such an appointment is made under the terms of a private contract between a company and one of its creditors, which creates a floating charge as security for the payment of that creditor's debts. An administrative receiver is appointed to take control of a company so as to realise its assets for the benefit of the particular creditor who is entitled to the floating charge. Terms providing for the appointment of administrative receivers in contracts creating floating charges made on or after 15 September 2003 cannot be acted on (Insolvency Act 1986, s. 72A; Insolvency Act 1986, Section 72A (Appointed Date) Order 2003, SI 2003/2095), but the holder of the floating charge can instead appoint an administrator (see **79.2**).

Administration

79.2 For an insolvent registered company, administration is an alternative to both winding up and the appointment of an administrative receiver. An administrator of a company manages its affairs, business and property in accordance with a proposal approved by creditors and usually does so in the interests of all the company's creditors (Insolvency Act 1986, sch. B1, paras 1(1) and 3(2)). The statute law on administration is in the Insolvency Act 1986, part II (s. 8) and sch. B1. These provisions are applied, with modifications, to certain insurance companies and former banking companies specified in sch. B1, para. 9, by the Banks (Administration Proceedings) Order 1989 (SI 1989/1276) and the Financial Services and Markets Act 2000 (Administration Orders Relating to Insurers) Order 2002 (SI 2002/1242) as amended by the Financial Services and Markets Act 2000 (Administration Orders Relating to Insurers) (Amendment) Order 2003 (SI 2003/2134).

A company enters administration when the appointment of an administrator takes effect (Insolvency Act 1986, sch. B1, para. 1(2)). Until 14 September 2003, only the court could appoint an administrator. Now an administrator of a company may be appointed out of court by the company itself or its directors or by the holder of a qualifying floating charge in respect of the company's property (sch. B1, paras 14 and 22), though such an appointment does not take effect until notice of appointment is filed in court (sch. B1, paras 18,19,29 and 31). It is expected that most appointments will in future be made out of court. Persons who are entitled to appoint an administrator out of court may alternatively apply to the court to make an appointment, by means of an administration order under sch. B1, para. 10 (see **79.102** to **79.117**), and in certain circumstances (see **79.103**) must do so. An application for an administration order may also be made by certain persons, such as creditors who do not hold qualifying floating charges, who are not entitled to make an appointment out of court (see **79.103**). The making of an administration order is discretionary.

An administrator of a company is asked to formulate, if possible, proposals for achieving the purpose of administration (see **79.105**). The proposals must be submitted, within 10 weeks of the administrator's appointment, to the company's unsecured creditors for approval (sch. B1, para. 51). If the proposals are approved, the administrator must manage the affairs, business and property of the company in accordance with them (sch. B1, para. 68).

The administrator of a company is required to report to the Secretary of State if it appears to the administrator that the conduct of any person who has been a director of the company makes that person unfit to be concerned in the management of a company, and an application may then be made for a disqualification order (Company Directors Disqualification Act 1986, ss. 6 and 7).

PROCEDURAL RULES

Insolvency Rules 1986

79.3 Applications for winding-up and administration orders are proceedings under the Insolvency Act 1986 and are therefore 'insolvency proceedings' for the purpose of the Insolvency Rules

1986 (SI 1986/1925) (IR 1986), by r. 13.7 of these rules. Rule 7.51(1) of the IR 1986 provides:

The CPR, the practice and procedure of the High Court and of the county court (including any practice direction) apply to insolvency proceedings in the High Court and county court as the case may be, in either case with any necessary modifications, except so far as inconsistent with the [IR 1986].

In fact the IR 1986 are a remarkably self-contained procedural code and insolvency proceedings have as yet been scarcely affected by the revolution in procedure elsewhere in the civil courts. The IR 1986 also govern bankruptcy proceedings, which are considered in **chapter 80**. Applications and appeals in relation to insolvency proceedings are considered in **chapter 81**. The practice direction referred to in r. 7.51(1) is **PD Insolvency Proceedings**, which is printed in **appendix 1**.

The only obvious problem that has arisen from replacing the RSC with the CPR is that the principal method of commencing insolvency proceedings is by petition and it is unclear how petitions are to be treated under the CPR. A petition is not within the definition of a statement of case in **CPR, r. 2.3(1)**, and so is not required by **r. 22.1** to be verified by a statement of truth. Alternative procedures for verifying winding-up petitions and administration applications are provided by IR 1986 (see **79.25** and **79.106**). The provisions of **CPR, Part 17**, permitting amendments to statements of case do not apply to petitions. (In the old RSC there were specific rules on amending petitions in ord. 20, rr. 5 and 7.) It may be that this will not cause too many difficulties in practice, because of the wide powers given to the court by **CPR, r. 1.4**. Allowing amendment of petitions, for example, would be an aspect of 'identifying the issues at an early stage' (**r. 1.4(2)(b)**). As petitions are not statements of case they are apparently not subject to r. 3.4 on striking out, though the court still has an inherent jurisdiction to strike out (*Re Abermeadow Ltd* [2000] 2 BCLC 824). It may be that the simple answer is that the 'necessary modifications' to the CPR authorised by IR 1986, r. 7.51(1), must include treating a petition or an administration application as a statement of case in order to make provisions of the CPR apply to insolvency proceedings.

As the requirement that an application for a winding-up order or bankruptcy order must be made by petition is imposed by statute, the court has no power under the CPR to waive a failure to comply with it (*Re Osea Road Camp Sites Ltd* [2004] EWHC 2437 (Ch), [2005] 1 WLR 760).

Track allocation

All insolvency proceedings, including winding-up and bankruptcy petitions and administration applications, are allocated to the multi-track by IR 1986, r. 7.51(2), and so the provisions of the CPR concerning allocation questionnaires and track allocation do not apply. **79.4**

Forms

The forms contained in sch. 4 to the IR 1986 must be used in and in connection with insolvency proceedings, whether in the High Court or a county court (IR 1986, r. 12.7(1)). The forms must be used with such variations, if any, as the circumstances may require (r. 12.7(2)). **79.5**

Time limits

Where by any provision of the Insolvency Act 1986 or the IR 1986 about winding up, the time for doing anything is limited, the court may extend the time, either before or after it has expired, on such terms, if any, as it thinks fit (IR 1986, r. 4.3). (The same provision is made in relation to bankruptcy proceedings by the Insolvency Act 1986, s. 376.) The court may also, under **CPR, r. 3.1(2)(a)**, as applied by IR 1986, r. 12.9(2), extend or shorten the time for compliance with anything required or authorised to be done by the IR 1986, even if an application for extension is made after the time for compliance has expired. In the High Court, time applications are heard by the court manager of the Companies Court (see **79.8**) in London or by a district judge in a district registry (**PD Insolvency Proceedings, para. 5.4**). **79.6**

Rule 12.9(1) of IR 1986 provides that the provisions of **CPR, r. 2.8** (see **chapter 3**), apply, as regards computation of time, to anything required or authorised to be done by IR 1986.

Meaning of 'business day'

79.7 In IR 1986, 'business day' means (by r. 13.13(1)) any day other than a Saturday, a Sunday, Christmas Day, Good Friday or a day which is a bank holiday in any part of Great Britain under or by virtue of the Banking and Financial Dealings Act 1971. However, in rr. 1.7, 4.10,4.11,4.16,4. 20,5. 10 and 6.23, days which are bank holidays in Scotland but not in England and Wales are counted as business days.

WHICH COURT?

79.8 Subject to Council Regulation (EC) No. 1346/2000, art. 3 (see 79.9), the High Court has jurisdiction to wind up any company incorporated by registration in England and Wales (Insolvency Act 1986, s. 117(1) and (7)).

High Court proceedings under the enactments relating to companies are assigned to the Chancery Division by the **Supreme Court Act 1981, sch. 1, para. 1**. Specific Chancery Division judges are designated to deal with company matters and there is a separate registry for such matters. This administrative arrangement is known as the Companies Court.

Subject to Council Regulation (EC) No. 1346/2000, art. 3 (see **79.9**), if the amount of a registered company's share capital paid up or credited as paid up does not exceed £120,000, the county court which has insolvency jurisdiction for the district in which the company's registered office is situated has concurrent jurisdiction with the High Court to wind up the company (Insolvency Act 1986, s. 117(2) and (7)). If, in the six months immediately preceding presentation of a petition to wind up a company, it has had different addresses for its registered office then it is the place which has longest been its registered office in that period which determines which county court has jurisdiction (s. 117(6)). Under s. 117(4) and the Civil Courts Order 1983 (SI 1983/713), art. 9 and sch. 3, about half of the county courts do not have insolvency jurisdiction: the districts of those courts are attached either to other county courts or, in the London area, to the High Court for the purposes of insolvency jurisdiction. This means that in the London area, only the High Court has insolvency jurisdiction.

A county court has all the powers of the High Court for the purposes of exercising its winding-up jurisdiction (s. 117(5)) and accordingly is not, when exercising those powers, an inferior court subject to supervision by the High Court (*Re New Par Consols Ltd (No. 2)* [1898] 1 QB 669). A question arising in county court winding-up proceedings may be transmitted to the High Court in the form of a special case for the opinion of the High Court, if all the parties to the proceedings, or one of them and the judge, wish to have it determined there (s. 119).

A court in England and Wales does not have jurisdiction to wind up a company registered in Scotland (*Re Scottish Joint Stock Trust* [1900] WN 114; *Re Helene plc* [2000] 2 BCLC 249). A petition to wind up a Scottish registered company must be presented to the Court of Session or a sheriff court.

In relation to a particular company, 'the court' means the court having jurisdiction to wind up the company (Companies Act 1985, s. 744, applied to the Insolvency Act 1986 by s. 251 of the 1986 Act).

Council Regulation (EC) No. 1346/2000

79.9 The jurisdiction of English courts in relation to winding up companies is, by the Insolvency Act 1986, s. 117(7), subject to Council Regulation (EC) No. 1346/2000, art. 3. The same applies to jurisdiction in relation to the bankruptcy of individuals (Insolvency Act 1986, s. 265(3)).

The scheme of the Regulation is that the main insolvency proceedings in the EU (apart from Denmark which has opted out of applying the Regulation) in relation to a debtor should be opened in the EU State where the 'centre of the debtor's main interests' (see **79.10**) is located. Those main insolvency proceedings should be universal, that is, they should deal with all the debtor's assets wherever they are located.

If a debtor with a centre of main interests in one EU State has an establishment (see **79.11**) in another EU State, insolvency proceedings may be opened in that State, but must be limited to dealing with the assets in that State, and are known as 'territorial proceedings' if main proceedings have not been opened or 'secondary proceedings' if main proceedings have been opened.

According to recital 14 in the preamble, the Regulation does not apply to insolvency proceedings relating to a debtor whose centre of main interests is in Denmark or outside the EU. For an example of a case where the Regulation did not apply because the debtor's centre of main interests was outside the EU see *Skjevesland v Geveran Trading Co. Ltd* [2002] EWHC 2898 (Ch), [2003] BCC 391. The Regulation applies to a company whose centre of main interests is in an EU State, even if the company is incorporated outside the EU (*Re BRAC Rent-A-Car International Inc.* [2003] EWHC 128 (Ch), [2003] 1 WLR 1421).

Centre of main interests Recital 13 in the preamble to Council Regulation (EC) No. 1346/ **79.10**
2000 states that the 'centre of main interests' of a debtor should correspond to the place where the debtor conducts the administration of his interests on a regular basis, and asserts that this should be ascertainable by third parties, but the term is left undefined in the body of the Regulation. A debtor can have only one centre of main interests (*Re BRAC Rent-A-Car International Inc.* [2003] EWHC 128 (Ch), [2003] 1 WLR 1421, at [23]). The centre of main interests of a company is presumed to be where its registered office is, in the absence of proof to the contrary (art. 3(1)). The registered office of a company registered in England and Wales must be in England and Wales (Companies Act 1985, s. 10(1)(a)).

Establishment The term 'establishment' is defined in Council Regulation (EC) No. 1346/ **79.11**
2000, art. 2(h), to mean 'any place of operations where the debtor carries out a non-transitory economic activity with human means and goods'. 'With human means and goods' is a literal translation of the French 'avec des moyens humains et des biens', which might be better rendered as 'using human and physical resources'.

Types of enterprise to which the Regulation does not apply By art. 1(2), Council Regulation **79.12**
(EC) No. 1346/2000 does not apply to insolvency proceedings concerning insurance undertakings, credit institutions, investment undertakings which provide services involving the holding of funds or securities for third parties, or collective investment undertakings. These types of enterprise are being dealt with by special rules made under Directives which ensure that such enterprises are wound up in the State where they are primarily regulated. Insurance undertakings are covered by the Insurers (Reorganisation and Winding up) Regulations 2003 (SI 2003/1102); credit institutions are covered by the Credit Institutions (Reorganisation and Winding up) Regulations 2004 (SI 2004/1045).

Effect on winding up of companies registered in England and Wales Article 3 of Council **79.13**
Regulation (EC) No. 1346/2000 affects a company incorporated by registration in England and Wales only if the company's centre of main interests is in another EU State (apart from Denmark). If that is the case, a winding-up order may be made in England and Wales only if the company possesses an establishment here (art. 3(2)) and there are restrictions on who may apply for the order (art. 3(4); see **79.17**). The winding up will be limited to dealing with the company's assets in the United Kingdom.

Effect of proceeding in the wrong court

79.14 By the Insolvency Act 1986, s. 118(1), nothing in s. 117 invalidates a proceeding by reason of its being taken in the wrong court (see, for example, *Re Pleatfine Ltd* [1983] BCLC 102). The winding up of a company by the court, or any proceedings in the winding up, may be retained in the court in which the proceedings were commenced, although it may not be the court in which they ought to have been commenced (s. 118(2); IR 1986, r. 7.12(b)). However, under IR 1986, r. 7.12(a) and (c), where winding-up proceedings are commenced in the wrong court, that court may order the transfer of the proceedings to the court in which they ought to have been commenced or order the proceedings to be struck out. 'Wrong' in these provisions means 'inappropriate': the effect of the provisions is that a county court does not lack jurisdiction to hear a petition concerning a company whose registered office is not in its district (*Re Southsea Garage Ltd* (1911) 27 TLR 295). (The corresponding rules in bankruptcy — in the Insolvency Act 1986, s. 373 — are differently worded and do not have the same effect: *Re Bridgend Goldsmiths Ltd* [1995] 2 BCLC 208.) The court to which the petition was presented may make a winding-up order on the petition before transferring proceedings to a more appropriate court (*Re Milford Haven Shipping Co.* [1895] WN 16). The petitioner must pay the costs incurred by presenting the petition in the wrong court (*Re Buller and Basset Tin and Copper Co. Ltd* (1891) 35 SJ 260).

QUALIFIED INSOLVENCY PRACTITIONERS

79.15 Any person who acts as, among other things, a liquidator or provisional liquidator of a company (known as 'acting as an insolvency practitioner in relation to the company') without being qualified to do so commits an offence punishable by imprisonment for up to two years and/or a fine (IA 1986, s. 389(1) and sch. 10). This does not apply to official receivers (see 79.16) (s. 389(2)). A person can be appointed administrator of a company only if qualified to act as an insolvency practitioner in relation to the company (sch. B1, para. 6).

There are two aspects to being qualified to act as an insolvency practitioner in relation to a company:

(a) qualification to act as an insolvency practitioner generally;
(b) qualification to act in relation to the particular company concerned.

Qualification to act as an insolvency practitioner generally is obtained by being authorised to do so, either by a recognised professional body or by the Secretary of State (s. 390(2)). The recognised professional bodies are specified in the Insolvency Practitioners (Recognised Professional Bodies) Order 1986 (SI 1986/1764).

Qualification to act in relation to a specific company is obtained by posting a bond under which a surety accepts liability for the proper performance of the practitioner's duties in relation to that company (Insolvency Act 1986, s. 390(3); Insolvency Practitioners Regulations 1986 (SI 1986/1995), regs 9 to 12 and sch. 2).

Only an individual can act as an insolvency practitioner (Insolvency Act 1986, s. 390(1)): companies and partnerships are not eligible. An individual cannot act as an insolvency practitioner while an undischarged bankrupt, while subject to a director disqualification order, or while a patient within the meaning of the mental health legislation (s. 390(4)).

OFFICIAL RECEIVERS

79.16 Each court in England and Wales with insolvency jurisdiction has attached to it one or more official receivers who are appointed by, and act under the general authority and directions of, the Secretary of State (Insolvency Act 1986, s. 399(2), (3), (5) and (6) and s. 400(2)). The same official receiver may be attached to two or more different courts (s. 399(5)).

The main tasks of an official receiver are to investigate the causes of insolvencies and to act as trustee in bankruptcy and as liquidator or provisional liquidator in compulsory liquidations of companies. Although the creditors of an insolvent person can put their own appointee (who must be a qualified insolvency practitioner) in place of the official receiver as trustee or liquidator, most insolvent estates are not sufficiently valuable to remunerate an insolvency practitioner.

For the purposes of the Insolvency Act 1986, 'the official receiver', in relation to any winding up, is the person who is authorised under s. 399(4) or (6) to act as the official receiver in relation to that winding up (s. 399(1)).

An official receiver exercises the functions of his or her office as an officer of the court in relation to which those functions are exercised (s. 400(2)).

WHO CAN PETITION FOR WINDING UP?

A person may petition for the compulsory liquidation of a company only if given standing to do so by the legislation that applies to the company (*Mann v Goldstein* [1968] 1 WLR 1091 at p. 1094). The persons who may petition are: **79.17**

(a) any creditor or creditors of the company (including any contingent or prospective creditor or creditors) (Insolvency Act 1986, s. 124(1));
(b) any contributory or contributories of the company (s. 124(1));
(c) the company itself (s. 124(1));
(d) the directors of the company (s. 124(1));
(e) a supervisor of a voluntary arrangement of the company (s. 7(4)(b));
(f) the designated officer for a magistrates' court (if the company has failed to pay a fine) (s. 124(1); Criminal Justice Act 1988, s. 62(2));
(g) a liquidator (within the meaning of Council Regulation (EC) No. 1346/2000, art. 2(b)) appointed in proceedings by virtue of art. 3(1) of the Regulation, or a temporary administrator (within the meaning of art. 38 of the Regulation) (Insolvency Act 1986, s. 124(1));
(h) all or any of the parties listed in (a) to (g) together or separately (s. 124(1));
(i) the Secretary of State (s. 124(4));
(j) an official receiver (though only if the company is already in voluntary liquidation) (s. 124(5));
(k) an administrator of the company (sch. B1, para. 60; sch. 1, para. 21) — an administrator of a company is deemed to act as the company's agent (sch. B1, para. 69);
(l) an administrative receiver of the company (s. 42(1) and (2); sch. 1, para. 21) — an administrative receiver of a company is deemed to act as the company's agent (s. 44(1)).

In addition, various public officials and bodies have statutory powers to petition for the winding up of particular types of company. For example, the Attorney-General may petition for the winding up of a charity (Charities Act 1993, s. 63(1)) as may the Charity Commissioners (s. 63(2)); the Housing Corporation may petition for the winding up of a registered social landlord (Housing Act 1996, sch. 1, para. 14); the Financial Services Authority may petition for the winding up of a company which provides financial services (Financial Services and Markets Act 2000, s. 367).

The Secretary of State may petition for the winding up of a company under the Insolvency Act 1986, s. 124(4)(b), if the case falls within s. 124A. A case falls within s. 124A if the company is not already being wound up by the court (s. 124A(2)) and it appears to the Secretary of State that it is expedient in the public interest that the company should be wound up, this being apparent from a report made or information obtained using various powers of inspection and investigation listed in s. 124A(1). Petitions in cases falling within s. 124A are known as 'public-interest petitions'.

Council Regulation (EC) No. 1346/2000 governs who may apply for a winding-up order in England and Wales in relation to an English company whose centre of main interests is in another EU State (apart from Denmark) (see **79.9** to **79.13**). An application for such a company to be wound up may be made only if the company possesses an establishment in the United Kingdom (art. 3(2)). If insolvency proceedings (main proceedings) have been opened in the State where the company's centre of main interests is located, then, by arts 27 and 29 and the Insolvency Act 1986, s. 124(1), provided the main proceedings are of a type listed in annex A to the Regulation, an application may be made (in secondary proceedings) in England and Wales for a winding-up order by:

(a) the liquidator in the main proceedings (called a 'member State liquidator' in IR 1986: see r. 13.13(11)), or
(b) a temporary administrator (corresponding to an English provisional liquidator) appointed in the main proceedings, or
(c) any other person authorised by s. 124.

If insolvency proceedings have not yet been opened in the State where the company's centre of main interests is located, an application for a winding-up order may be made (in territorial proceedings) in England and Wales only by a creditor who is domiciled or habitually resident in the United Kingdom or has its registered office in the United Kingdom, or a creditor whose claim arises from the operation of the company's establishment in the United Kingdom (Regulation, art. 4(b)). This restriction does not apply if insolvency proceedings cannot be opened in the State where the company's centre of main interests is located, because of the conditions laid down by the law of that State (art. 4(a)).

In practice, the most important classes of petitions are those by creditors and those by contributories (and about 95 per cent of petitions are by creditors). The noticeable difference between these two classes of petitions is that, in general, creditors petition to wind up insolvent companies, whereas contributories petition to wind up solvent companies. The procedure for contributories' petitions is not the same as the procedure on other types of petition and is considered separately in **79.66** to **79.73**. For procedural purposes a petition to wind up a company presented at the instance of the company's administrator or by the supervisor of a voluntary arrangement in force for the company is treated as a contributory's petition.

Effect of voluntary arrangement and administration moratoriums

79.18 A petition for a company to be wound up by the court cannot be presented while a moratorium under the Insolvency Act 1986, s. 1A (moratorium when directors propose a voluntary arrangement), is in force in relation to the company (sch. A1, para. 12(1)(a)).

While a company is in administration, and while an interim moratorium is in force when an administration application has been presented or notice of intention to appoint an administrator out of court has been filed, the court may not make a winding-up order, except on a public-interest petition presented by the Secretary of State or the Financial Services Authority (sch. B1, paras 42 and 44). When the court makes an administration order it must dismiss any outstanding winding-up petition (para. 40(1)(a)).

A petition for the winding up of a company must be 'suspended' while the company is in administration following an appointment out of court by the holder of a floating charge (sch. B1, para. 40(1)(b)), unless it is a public-interest petition (para. 40(2)). During the suspension, s. 127(1) (avoidance of property dispositions) does not apply to anything done by the administrator (s. 127(2)). It is clear that the suspension automatically comes to an end when the administration comes to an end.

FORM AND CONTENTS OF WINDING-UP PETITION

Prescribed form

Under r. 4.7 of the IR 1986 the prescribed form of petition for the winding up of a company, if the petitioner is not a contributory, is **form 4.2** in sch. 4 to the Rules. (Rule 4.7 does not apply to contributories' petitions, by r. 4.2(2).) **79.19**

Heading

A winding-up petition must be entitled, 'In the matter of [the company sought to be wound up] and in the matter of the Insolvency Act 1986' (IR 1986, r. 7.26(1)). **79.20**

A petition can refer to only one company because a winding-up order can refer to only one company (*Re Shields Marine Insurance Co., Lee and Moor's Case* (1867) 17 LT 308). In order to wind up a group of companies it is necessary to present a separate petition for each company in the group (*Re a Company* [1984] BCLC 307). However, the rules permit the petitioner to provide one verifying affidavit or witness statement referring to several petitions (IR 1986, r. 4.12(7); see 79.25).

Prescribed paragraphs

The prescribed paragraphs of a petition (**form 4.2**) to wind up a registered company state: **79.21**

(1) The name and date of incorporation of the company, and which Companies Act it was registered under.
(2) The address of its registered office.
(3) Its nominal capital and how that is divided into shares, and its paid-up capital.
(4) The principal objects of the company.
(5) The 'grounds on which a winding-up order is sought'. In the case of a creditor's petition, this paragraph must state that the company is unable to pay its debts, which is shown by the fact that it has not paid the petitioner's debt. Details should then be given of how that debt arose, including the nature of the transaction, order number and date, invoice number and date, and interest claimed.
(6) A statement of whether the company is or is not one of the types of company to which Council Regulation (EC) No. 1346/2000 does not apply (see **79.12**).
(7) A statement of whether the proceedings will be main, secondary or territorial proceedings (see **79.9**). When petitioning for the winding up of a company registered in England and Wales, we recommend that this paragraph should be completed as follows. If it has been identified in para. (6) that the Regulation does not apply, or if the centre of main interests of the company is in Denmark or is outside the EU, state that the Regulation does not apply. Otherwise, state that the Regulation does apply and identify the proceedings as 'main proceedings', unless the centre of the company's main interests is in another EU State apart from Denmark. If the centre of the company's main interests is in another EU State (apart from Denmark) and main proceedings have not been opened there, identify the petition proceedings as 'territorial proceedings'. If main proceedings have been opened in the State where the centre of main interests is located, identify the petition proceedings as 'secondary proceedings'.
(8) A statement that: 'In the circumstances it is just and equitable that the company should be wound up'.

There is then a prayer that the company named may be wound up by the court under the provisions of the Insolvency Act 1986 or that such other order may be made as the court thinks fit.

It is very important that items (1) to (3) correspond exactly with the data on the company's file at Companies House.

The prescribed form of petition ends with a section headed 'endorsement'. This has spaces to be filled in by a court official with the venue for hearing the petition (see 79.26) and spaces to be filled in with the name, address and telephone number of the petitioner's solicitors and their reference number and equivalent details of their London agents. The information about the petitioner's solicitors must be completed before the petition is filed.

Grounds on which a winding-up order is sought

79.22 A petition for a winding-up order must allege the existence of one or more of the circumstances in which the court may make a winding-up order and state the facts from which it may be concluded that the alleged circumstance or circumstances exist.

The circumstances in which a registered company may be wound up by the court are listed in the Insolvency Act 1986, s. 122(1):

> A company may be wound up by the court if—
> (a) the company has by special resolution resolved that the company be wound up by the court,
> (b) being a public company which was registered as such on its original incorporation, the company has not been issued with a certificate under section 117 of the Companies Act [1985] (public company share capital requirements) and more than a year has expired since it was so registered,
> (c) it is an old public company, within the meaning of the [Companies Consolidation (Consequential Provisions) Act 1985],
> (d) the company does not commence its business within a year from its incorporation or suspends its business for a whole year,
> (e) except in the case of a private company limited by shares or by guarantee, the number of members is reduced below two,
> (f) the company is unable to pay its debts,
> (fa) at the time at which a moratorium for the company under section 1A comes to an end, no voluntary arrangement approved under Part I has effect in relation to the company,
> (g) the court is of the opinion that it is just and equitable that the company should be wound up.

A petition is bound to fail if it does not allege any facts from which it may be concluded that at least one of the prescribed circumstances exists (*Re Wear Engine Works Co.* (1875) LR 10 Ch App 188; *Securum Finance Ltd v Camswell Ltd* [1994] BCC 434, in which it was said that such a petition would be an abuse of process).

Evidence that company is unable to pay its debts

79.23 By far the most common type of petition is a creditor's petition alleging that the company is unable to pay its debts and the Insolvency Act 1986, s. 123, provides several means of proving that circumstance in the case of a registered company:

> (1) A company is deemed unable to pay its debts—
> (a) if a creditor (by assignment or otherwise) to whom the company is indebted in a sum exceeding £750 then due has served on the company, by leaving it at the company's registered office, a written demand (in the prescribed form) requiring the company to pay the sum so due and the company has for three weeks thereafter neglected to pay the sum or to secure or compound for it to the reasonable satisfaction of the creditor, or
> (b) if, in England and Wales, execution or other process issued on a judgment, decree or order of any court in favour of a creditor of the company is returned unsatisfied in whole or in part, or
> (c) if, in Scotland, the inducae of a charge for payment on an extract decree, or an extract registered bond, or an extract registered protest, have expired without payment being made, or
> (d) if, in Northern Ireland, a certificate of unenforceability has been granted in respect of a judgment against the company, or
> (e) if it is proved to the satisfaction of the court that the company is unable to pay its debts as they fall due.
> (2) A company is also deemed unable to pay its debts if it is proved to the satisfaction of the court that the value of the company's assets is less than the amount of its liabilities, taking into account its contingent and prospective liabilities.

Unlike the position in bankruptcy proceedings, it is not necessary for a creditor of a company to present a statutory demand or issue execution before presenting a winding-up petition. In practice, it is common for a creditor petitioner to rely on the fact that the company has not paid a debt owed to the petitioner as proof (under s. 123(1)(e)) of the company's inability to pay its debts (see *Taylors Industrial Flooring Ltd v M and H Plant Hire (Manchester) Ltd* [1990] BCLC 216 at p. 219; *Re a Company (No. 003079 of 1990)* [1991] BCLC 235 at pp. 235–6).

If a statutory demand is used, it must be in the prescribed form, which is **form 4.1** in sch. 4 to the IR 1986. A statutory demand can be served only for an amount due for payment at the time of service: it cannot, for example, be served for a contingent debt where the contingency has not occurred (*JSF Finance and Currency Exchange Co. Ltd v Akma Solutions Inc.* [2001] 2 BCLC 307). Unlike bankruptcy, there is no procedure for obtaining a court order setting aside a statutory demand served on a company.

Only an undisputed creditor of a company has standing to petition for it to be wound up: if there is a substantial dispute about the existence of the petitioner's debt, the petition will be dismissed (see 79.30).

Need to establish case in petition

79.24 In winding-up proceedings the petitioner's case must be stated in the petition: the petitioner cannot leave it to the hearing to establish the ground for the petition. At the hearing the petitioner will be limited to the grounds stated in the petition (*Re Spence's Patent Non-conducting Composition and Cement Co.* (1869) LR 9 Eq 9; *Re Fildes Bros Ltd* [1970] 1 WLR 592; *Re Armvent Ltd* [1975] 1 WLR 1679 at p. 1683).

A petitioner cannot rely on disclosure and inspection of documents (*Re a Company, ex parte Burr* [1992] BCLC 724 per Vinelott J at p. 736 and on appeal sub nom. *Re Saul D. Harrison and Sons plc* [1995] 1 BCLC 14 per Hoffmann LJ at p. 22) or cross-examination of the company's witnesses (*Re a Company* (1917) 34 DLR 396) to reveal facts to support the petition.

The grounds on which a winding up is sought must be stated in the petition itself: it is not sufficient to state them in an accompanying affidavit or witness statement. In *Re a Company (No. 007936 of 1994)* [1995] BCC 705 a statement in a petition that, 'The petitioners will rely on the substantial correspondence exhibited to the affidavit verifying this petition, as the particulars are too numerous to be conveniently set out here' was described by the judge as 'completely unacceptable' (at p. 716).

Verification of the petition

79.25 A petition must be accompanied by an affidavit (known as the 'statutory affidavit') or witness statement verifying the petition (IR 1986, rr. 4.7(1), 4.12(1) and 7.57(5) and (7)). The primary purpose of the verifying affidavit or witness statement is to verify that the statements in the petition are true, or are true to the best of the maker's knowledge, information and belief. The petition must be exhibited to the affidavit or witness statement (r. 4.12(3)). In addition, by r. 4.12(8), the verifying affidavit or witness statement must state:

(a) whether, in the opinion of 'the person making the application' (this is obviously a mistake for 'the person making the affidavit'), Council Regulation (EC) No. 1346/2000 will apply; and
(b) if so, whether the proceedings will be main proceedings or territorial proceedings.

For advice on these statements see the commentary in 79.21 on para. 7 of the prescribed form of petition. That paragraph of the prescribed form of petition states that the verifying affidavit or witness statement states the reasons for these opinions, but r. 4.12(8), which came into force on 1 April 2005, requires only the opinions to be stated.

The statutory affidavit or witness statement, though it may be hearsay, is prima facie evidence of the statements in the petition to which it relates (r. 4.12(6)). The statutory affidavit or witness statement makes the allegations of fact in the petition evidence.

Rule 4.12(4) provides that the affidavit or witness statement must be made by:

(a) the petitioner (or if there are two or more petitioners, any one of them); or
(b) some person such as a director, company secretary or similar company officer, or a solicitor, who has been concerned in the matters giving rise to the presentation of the petition; or
(c) some responsible person who is duly authorised to make the affidavit or witness statement and has the requisite knowledge of those matters.

In cases (b) and (c) the person verifying the petition must state the capacity in which, and the authority by which, he or she does so, and the means of knowing the matters contained in the written evidence (IR 1986, r. 4.12(5)). In r. 4.12(4)(b) 'solicitor' does not include an incorporated solicitors' practice (Solicitors' Incorporated Practices Order 1991 (SI 1991/2684), arts 2(1) and 4(a) and sch. 1).

The court has a discretion to accept a verifying affidavit or witness statement from a person not mentioned in r. 4.12(4) (*Re African Farms Ltd* [1906] 1 Ch 640).

If there are simultaneous petitions to wind up several companies (e.g., all companies in a group), it is permissible to make one affidavit or witness statement referring to all the companies and submit a photocopy with each petition (IR 1986, r. 4.12(7)). There must be a photocopy for each petition and the affidavit or statement must refer to all the companies by name.

FILING OF PETITION AND FIXING OF VENUE

79.26 A petition for the winding up of a company must be filed in court together with copies to be served on the company and sent to other persons. A court officer seals all copies of the petition and fixes a venue for hearing the petition which is endorsed on all copies of the petition (IR 1986, r. 4.7).

Unless the petition is presented by the company itself, it must be accompanied by a copy for service on the company and a copy to be exhibited to the written evidence of service on the company (r. 4.7(3)). (If the company is the petitioner, service on the company is not required.)

Rule 4.7(4) requires additional copies of the petition in the following circumstances:

(a) if the company is in course of being wound up voluntarily, and a liquidator has been appointed, one copy of the petition to be sent to the voluntary liquidator;
(b) if the company is in administration, one copy to be sent to the administrator (the text of the rule states that it is a copy of the administrator's own appointment, rather than of the winding-up petition, which is to be sent, but it is clear that this is not what is intended);
(c) if an administrative receiver has been appointed in relation to the company, one copy to be sent to that administrative receiver;
(d) if there is in force for the company a voluntary arrangement under part I (ss. 1 to 7) of the Insolvency Act 1986, one copy for the supervisor of the arrangement.

If a winding-up petition asks for the opening of secondary proceedings against a company which is already the subject of main insolvency proceedings in another EU State (see **79.9**), a copy of the petition must be provided for service on a member State liquidator (see **79.17**) appointed in the main proceedings (IR 1986, r. 4.7(4)(da)). Rule 4.7(4)(da) does not mention that a copy is not required if the member State liquidator is the petitioner (see r. 4.10(3A)).

There are also special provisions when the company sought to be wound up is a bank (r. 4.7(4)(e)) or insurance company (Financial Services and Markets Act 2000, s. 369(1)).

FEE AND DEPOSIT

On filing a winding-up petition, a court fee of £190 must be paid (**CPFO, fee 3.3**). The petitioner must deposit £655 as security for the administration fee which will become payable to the official receiver if a winding-up order is made and transmitted to the official receiver (Insolvency Act 1986, s. 414(4); Insolvency Proceedings (Fees) Order 2004 (SI 2004/593), art. 6(1)). A petition cannot be filed unless the receipt for the deposit is produced (IR 1986, r. 4.7(2)). The deposit is security for the official receiver's administration fee and must be used to discharge that fee to the extent that the company's assets are insufficient (SI 2004/593, art. 6(2)); the administration fee is £1,950 (SI 2004/593, sch. 2, fee W1). The court must transmit the deposit to its official receiver (SI 2004/593, art. 6(3)). If a winding-up order is made, any part of the deposit which is not required to pay the administration fee must be returned (art. 6(5)). If the petition is dismissed or withdrawn, the whole of the deposit must be repaid (art. 6(4)). The court fee is not repayable. **79.27**

STOPPING PRESENTATION OF, OR PROCEEDING WITH, PETITION

Introduction

Presentation of a petition for the winding up of a company may cause it considerable disruption. The provisions of the Insolvency Act 1986, s. 127, for the control of transactions while a petition is pending mean that the company's bank account will be frozen. Advertisement of the petition is taken up by credit reference agencies and may damage the company's business and reputation. Despite the great inconvenience that can be caused by the presentation of an unsuccessful winding-up petition, a petitioner is never required to give an undertaking in damages unless there is an application for the appointment of a provisional liquidator (*Re Highfield Commodities Ltd* [1985] 1 WLR 149). **79.28**

If the court considers that a petition to wind up a company is an abuse of process, it will:

(a) if the petition has not already been presented, restrain presentation of the petition;

(b) if the petition has been presented, either restrain advertisement of the petition and the taking of further steps to prosecute it or strike out the petition; the usual order is to dismiss the petition.

Applications for orders restraining presentation of petitions must be made to the judge by originating application (**PD Insolvency Proceedings, para. 8**) and, unless otherwise ordered, will be heard in open court (**PD Insolvency Proceedings, para. 5.1**). Applications to stop proceedings on a petition that has already been presented are made by an ordinary application in those proceedings. The procedure on originating and ordinary applications is described in **81.1** to **81.5**.

An order made by the court on an application to restrain presentation of a petition is not made in the exercise of its jurisdiction to wind up companies, and therefore cannot be reviewed, rescinded or varied by it under IR 1986, r. 7.47 (*Re Portedge Ltd* [1997] BCC 23 at p. 27).

In any proceedings to prevent the prosecution of a petition for the compulsory winding up of a company, the company must prove that the petition or proposed petition would constitute an abuse of process by showing, for example:

(a) That it is bound to fail as a matter of law or through lack of evidence (*Charles Forte Investments Ltd v Amanda* [1964] Ch 240), for example, because the petition fails to allege sufficient grounds for the court to make a winding-up order (*Re a Company (No. 00315 of 1973)* [1973] 1 WLR 1566; *Re Saul D. Harrison and Sons plc* [1995] 1 BCLC 14).

(b) That it was presented for an improper purpose (see **79.29**).

(c) That the petitioner is unreasonably seeking to wind up the company instead of pursuing an alternative and more appropriate remedy (*Charles Forte Investments Ltd v Amanda* [1964] Ch 240; *Re Surrey Garden Village Trust Ltd* [1965] 1 WLR 974 per Plowman J at pp. 981–2). This is especially so where the petitioner is actually pursuing alternative and more appropriate legal proceedings (*Re a Company (No. 003028 of 1987)* [1988] BCLC 282).

There is also a practice of preventing further proceedings on a disputed debt petition (see 79.30).

A contractual obligation of a creditor not to apply for winding up (or administration) will be enforced by the court, if necessary by striking out, and is not contrary to public policy (*Re a Company (No. 00928 of 1991)* [1991] BCLC 514; *Re COLT Telecom Group plc* [2002] EWHC 2815 (Ch), LTL 20/12/2002). But a company's articles of association cannot remove its members' statutory right to apply as contributories for it to be wound up (*Re Peveril Gold Mines Ltd* [1898] 1 Ch 122).

Improper purpose

79.29 A winding-up order operates in favour of all creditors and contributories of the company (Insolvency Act 1986, s. 130(4)). It is an abuse of process for a person to petition for a company's compulsory liquidation otherwise than for the purpose of providing for all its creditors and contributories the benefits that the liquidation will produce (though no doubt self-interest will be the petitioner's primary concern) (*Re Wheal Lovell Mining Co.* (1849) 1 Mac & G 1 at p. 22; *Re a Company (No. 001573 of 1983)* [1983] BCLC 492). In *Re Southbourne Sheet Metal Co. Ltd* [1992] BCLC 361 Harman J said, at p. 364:

> . . . a winding-up petition is not a *lis inter partes* [an action between parties] for the benefit of A as against B. It is the invoking by A of a class remedy for the benefit of himself and other members of the class. Nonetheless, it is (a) based upon a commercial interest of the person invoking the remedy, and (b) it is for the benefit of himself, amongst other members of the class.

If other members of the petitioner's class take the view that it is not expedient to pursue the petition, the court will consider their views when deciding whether to exercise its discretion to make a winding-up order. The idea of a petitioner as a representative of a class applies primarily to creditors' petitions.

Disputed debts

79.30 If there is a dispute about the existence of a petitioner's debt then, as a matter of practice, it is usual, on the company's application, to strike out the petition (*Re Gold Hill Mines* (1883) 23 ChD 210; *Re a Company (No. 0013734 of 1991)* [1993] BCLC 59). A disputed debt petition is prevented from proceeding even if the company sought to be wound up is insolvent (*Mann v Goldstein* [1968] 1 WLR 1091; *Re Record Tennis Centres Ltd* [1991] BCC 509 at p. 514; *Re a Company (No. 00212 of 1995)* (1995) *The Times*, 7 April 1995).

A disputed debt petition is prevented from proceeding because, 'the petitioner is not a creditor of the company within the meaning of [the Insolvency Act 1986, s. 124] at all, and the question whether he is or is not a creditor of the company is not appropriate for adjudication in winding-up proceedings' (per Buckley LJ in *Stonegate Securities Ltd v Gregory* [1980] Ch 576 at p. 580). The petition will not be prevented from proceeding if the court decides that it would be proper for the dispute to be determined in the winding-up proceedings (*Re Claybridge Shipping Co. SA* [1997] 1 BCLC 572).

If the fact that a company is indebted to a creditor is not disputed, but the amount to be paid, and/or the time at which it is to be paid, is disputed (in particular, if only part of the petitioner's debt is disputed) then the petitioner's standing is not in question and the petition will not be struck out (*Re Tweeds Garages Ltd* [1962] Ch 406; *Re Claybridge Shipping Co. SA* [1997] 1 BCLC 572 per Lord Denning MR at pp. 574–5; *Re Pendigo Ltd* [1996] 2 BCLC 64; *Corbern v Whatmusic Holdings Ltd* [2003] EWHC 2134 (Ch), LTL 1/10/2003).

If it is found that only part of the debt is disputed and there is no evidence of the company's ability to pay the undisputed part, the petition may be adjourned for a short time to allow the company to pay the undisputed debt if it can (*Re Javelin Promotions Ltd* [2003] EWHC 1932 (Ch), LTL 30/9/2003).

In practice it may be difficult to distinguish between a dispute about existence and a dispute about quantum (see *Re a Company (No. 003729 of 1982)* [1984] 1 WLR 1090; *Re R. A. Foulds Ltd* (1986) 2 BCC 99,269).

It is irrelevant that the company has not paid money to the person who is petitioning or threatening to petition in response to a statutory demand for the disputed amount claimed: the fact that the claim is disputed means that the company has a reasonable excuse for not complying with the statutory demand and so has not 'neglected' to comply with it, and so is not deemed to be unable to pay its debts (*Re London and Paris Banking Corporation* (1874) LR 19 Eq 444; *Re a Company (No. 003729 of 1982)* [1984] 1 WLR 1090).

The court will not prevent a disputed debt petition proceeding unless it is satisfied that 'the debt is disputed on some substantial ground (and not just on some ground which is frivolous or without substance and which the court should, therefore, ignore)' (*Mann v Goldstein* [1968] 1 WLR 1091 per Ungoed-Thomas J at p. 1096). In *Stonegate Securities Ltd v Gregory* [1980] Ch 576 Goff LJ, at p. 589, expressed the court's task as distinguishing 'whether there is a bona fide dispute or whether it is insubstantial or trumped up'.

A bona fide belief that there is a dispute is not enough in itself because it does not prove that there is substance in the dispute (*Re a Company (No. 001946 of 1991)* [1991] BCLC 737, in which Harman J said (at p. 740) that: '"Bona fides", in the sense of good faith, has nothing to do with the matter').

In *Re a Company (No. 0012209 of 1991)* [1992] 1 WLR 351 Hoffmann J said, at p. 354, that a disputed debt petition would be allowed to proceed if the court concluded that the dispute was either not put forward in good faith or that it had no rational prospect of success. In *Re a Company (No. 0013734 of 1991)* [1993] BCLC 59 the court expanded on the second of these alternatives, holding that it is not necessary to decide the arguments over a petitioner's debt: the petition will be allowed to continue if the arguments 'afford the company no really rational prospect of success or . . . the argument of the petitioner cannot be seriously questioned'.

It is for the court hearing the petition to decide whether the dispute is substantial enough to justify dismissing the petition: the question is not decided by the continuance of other proceedings brought by the petitioner to recover the debt, even if an application by the petitioner for summary judgment in those proceedings has failed (*Re Welsh Brick Industries Ltd* [1946] 2 All ER 197). If the court hearing the petition decides there is not a substantial dispute then the petition must continue even if other proceedings are also continuing (*James Dolman and Co. Ltd v Pedley* [2003] EWCA Civ 1686, LTL 25/9/2003).

The fact that a creditor petitioner and the company sought to be wound up have agreed that a court outside England and Wales is to have exclusive jurisdiction to decide disputes about the debt on which the petition is based does not preclude the English court from deciding whether there is a dispute about the debt sufficient to prevent the winding-up petition proceeding (*BST Properties Ltd v Reorg-Aport Pénzügyi Rt* [2001] EWCA Civ 1997, LTL 13/12/2001).

Cross-claim against petitioner

If a creditor of a company presents a petition for the compulsory winding up of the company, but the company claims from the petitioner a sum which is greater than or equal to the petitioner's debt, or falls short of it by £750 or less, the practice is to treat the petition in the same way as a disputed debt petition (*Re Portman Provincial Cinemas Ltd* [1999] 1 WLR 157; *Re LHF* **79.31**

Wools Ltd [1970] Ch 27; *Re Bayoil SA* [1999] 1 WLR 147). Unless there are special circumstances, the petition will be prevented from proceeding.

If the company's cross-claim against the petitioner is less than the petitioner's debt and it is shown that the company is unable to pay its debts, a winding-up order will be made (*Blue Star Security Services (Scotland) Ltd* 1992 SLT (Sh Ct) 80).

The company has the burden of proving:

(a) that its cross-claim is larger than the admitted debt of the petitioner or falls short of it by £750 or less (*Greenacre Publishing Group v The Manson Group* [2000] BCC 11);
(b) that its claim has substance (per Lord Denning MR in *Re Portman Provincial Cinemas Ltd* [1999] 1 WLR 157) or is 'genuine and serious' (*Re Bayoil SA* [1999] 1 WLR 147 per Nourse LJ at p. 155 and Ward LJ at p. 156); provided the cross-claim meets this standard, it does not matter that it is disputed.

In *Re Bayoil SA* Nourse LJ said, *obiter*, that it was also necessary for the company to show that it had been unable to litigate the claim, but it is clear that this is not required (*Montgomery v Wanda Modes Ltd* [2002] 1 BCLC 289).

Costs of proceedings to stop a petition

79.32 Orders as to costs of proceedings for preventing a petition are at the discretion of the court but will normally follow the event (*Cannon Screen Entertainment Ltd v Handmade Films (Distributors) Ltd* (1988) 5 BCC 207). Abuse of process by presenting a petition to put pressure on a solvent company to pay a disputed debt is 'a high risk strategy', and the petitioner may be ordered to pay the company's costs on an indemnity basis (*Re a Company (No. 0012209 of 1991)* [1992] 1 WLR 351).

COMMENCEMENT OF WINDING UP, GOING INTO LIQUIDATION ETC.

79.33 The Insolvency Act 1986, s. 129(2), provides that if an order for the winding up of a company is made on a petition presented when the company was not in voluntary liquidation, the winding up by the court is deemed to have commenced at the time when the petition was presented. This is not at the beginning of the day on which the petition was presented but at the moment of presentation, because s. 129(2) refers to the time rather than the date of presentation of the petition (*Re London and Devon Biscuit Co.* (1871) LR 12 Eq 190; *Re Blackburn Industries Pty Ltd* [1980] QdR 211 per D. M. Campbell J at p. 217 and Dunn J at p. 224; see also the latter case on appeal sub nom. *Wilde v Australian Trade Equipment Co. Pty Ltd* (1981) 145 CLR 590).

If a winding-up order is made on an administration application (see **79.116**), the winding up commences on the making of the order (s. 129(1A)).

If an order for the winding up of a registered company is made on a petition presented after a resolution for voluntary winding up has been adopted, the winding up is deemed to have commenced at the time when that resolution was adopted (s. 129(1)).

The Insolvency Act 1986 also uses the phrase, 'to go into liquidation'. By s. 247(2), a company goes into liquidation when it adopts a resolution for voluntary winding up or when an order for its winding up is made (unless it had already passed a resolution for voluntary winding up, in which case the date of that resolution is the date of going into liquidation). A company subject to compulsory winding up (not preceded by voluntary winding up) 'goes into liquidation' when the winding-up order is made but the winding up 'commenced' when the petition for the order was presented (*Re Walter L. Jacob and Co. Ltd* [1993] BCC 512).

SERVICE OF PETITION

General rule

Unless a petition to wind up a company is presented by the company itself, a copy of the petition must be served on the company (IR 1986, r. 4.8(1)). It must be served at least seven business days *before* it is advertised in the *London Gazette* (see **79.41**), and the advertisement must appear at least seven business days before the hearing date (IR 1986, r. 4.11(2)(b)). 'Business day' is defined in r. 13.13(1) (see **79.7**). In the High Court, service is the responsibility of the petitioner and will not be undertaken by the court (**PD Insolvency Proceedings, para. 1.3**). **79.34**

Service on solicitors

If solicitors are properly instructed, they can accept service on behalf of the company (IR 1986, r. 13.4; *Re Regent United Service Stores* (1878) 8 ChD 75; *Re Fletcher Hunt (Bristol) Ltd* [1989] BCLC 108 per Knox J at p. 113). **79.35**

Service at the registered office

If service of a petition to wind up a registered company is not to be on the company's solicitors, the petition must be served at the company's registered office, if it has one (IR 1986, r. 4.8(2)). 'Registered office' is defined in r. 4.8(2) in the same terms as in the Companies Act 1985, s. 287, but without the provision made by s. 287(4) that when the Registrar of Companies registers a notice of change of situation of a company's registered office, any document may nevertheless be validly served on the company at the previous address for 14 days from the day of registration. **79.36**

A petition may be served at the company's registered office in any of the following ways (IR 1986, r. 4.8(3)):

(a) it may be handed to a person who there and then acknowledges him or herself to be — or to the best of the server's knowledge, information and belief is — a director or other officer, or employee, of the company; or
(b) it may be handed to a person who there and then acknowledges him or herself to be authorised to accept service of documents on the company's behalf; or
(c) in the absence of any such person as is mentioned in (a) or (b), it may be deposited at or about the registered office in such a way that it is likely to come to the notice of a person attending at the office.

It is clear from r. 4.8(6) that service at the registered office may not be effected in any other way (for example, by post) without the court's approval or direction.

Service at principal place of business or on officer of company

Rule 4.8(4) of the IR 1986 specifies methods for serving a winding-up petition on the company sought to be wound up if: **79.37**

(a) service at its registered office is not practicable, or
(b) the company has no registered office.

In either of those cases the petition may be served by:

(a) leaving it at the company's last known principal place of business in such a way that it is likely to come to the attention of a person attending there; or
(b) delivering it to the secretary or some director, manager or principal officer of the company, wherever that person may be found.

Option (a) only authorises service at a place of business within the jurisdiction (*Re Tea Trading Co. K. and C. Popoff Brothers* [1933] Ch 647 at p. 651).

Order for alternative service

79.38 If for any reason it is impracticable to effect service as provided by IR 1986, r. 4.8(2) to (4) (see **79.36** and **79.37**), the petition may be served in such other manner as the court may approve or direct (r. 4.8(6)). An application for the court's approval or direction under r. 4.8(6) should be made by ordinary application (see **81.1** to **81.5**) and may be made without notice to other parties (r. 4.8(7)). An application must be accompanied by a statement of what steps have been taken to comply with r. 4.8(2) to (5) and the reasons why it is impracticable to effect service as provided in those paragraphs (r. 4.8(7)). This statement must be made in an affidavit or by witness statement verified by a statement of truth (r. 7.57(5)). An application in the High Court for alternative service of a winding-up petition is heard by the court manager of the Companies Court in London or by a district judge in a district registry (**PD Insolvency Proceedings, para. 5.4**).

Evidence of service

79.39 Service of a winding-up petition must be proved by affidavit or witness statement, specifying the manner of service (IR 1986, rr. 4.9(1) and 7.57(5)). **Form 4.4** in sch. 4 to the IR 1986 is the form of affidavit of service to be used when a petition for the winding up of a company has been served at the company's registered office. **Form 4.5** is for use otherwise. The affidavit or witness statement must be filed in court immediately after service and must have exhibited to it a sealed copy of the petition (r. 4.9(2)). If alternative service has been ordered, a sealed copy of the order must also be exhibited to the evidence of service (r. 4.9(2)).

Copies for other persons

79.40 If a petition is presented to wind up a company which has a voluntary liquidator, an administrator, a supervisor of a voluntary arrangement and/or an administrative receiver, a copy of the petition must be sent to that officer on the next business day after the petition is served on the company (IR 1986, r. 4.10(1), (2), (3) and (5)). 'Business day' is defined in r. 13.13(1) (see **79.7**). There are special rules for banks (r. 4.10(4) and (5)), insurance companies (Financial Services and Markets Act 2000, s. 369(1)) and railway companies (Railways Act 1993, s. 61(1)). Rule 4.10(4) should have been amended so that it refers to authorised deposit-takers instead of authorised institutions under the Banking Act 1987, but this has not been done.

If a winding-up petition asks for the opening of secondary proceedings against a company which is already the subject of main insolvency proceedings in another EU State (see **79.9**), a copy of the petition must be served on a member State liquidator appointed in the main proceedings (see **79.17**) unless that liquidator is the petitioner (IR 1986, r. 4.10(3A)).

PUBLICISATION OF PETITION

Need for and timing of advertisement

79.41 A winding-up order is a collective remedy and the order operates in favour of all creditors and contributories (Insolvency Act 1986, s. 130(4)), who can all appear at the hearing of the petition to support or oppose it. Therefore a winding-up petition which is not a contributory's petition must, unless the court directs otherwise, be advertised once in the *London Gazette* (IR 1986, r. 4.11(1)). The advertisement serves to invite creditors and contributories to appear on the hearing of the petition and submit their views to the court: the advertisement is a substitute for, and renders unnecessary, service of the petition on them (*Re National Credit and Exchange Co. Ltd* (1862) 7 LT 817; *Re Marlborough Club Co.* (1865) LR 1 Eq 216; *Re New Gas Co.* (1877) 5 ChD 703). The content of the advertisement is specified in r. 4.11(4) of and form 4.6 in sch. 4 to the IR 1986.

The advertisement of a petition must appear at least seven business days *before* the date appointed for the hearing, and, unless the company itself is the petitioner, must not appear until at least seven business days *after* service of the petition on the company (IR 1986, r. 4.11(2)). 'Business day' is defined in r. 13.13(1) (see **79.7**).

If a petition is advertised otherwise than in accordance with the rules, it may be dismissed or the costs of advertisement disallowed, especially if the advertisement is premature (IR 1986, r. 4.11(5); see *Re Signland Ltd* [1982] 2 All ER 609).

The period of seven days between service of the petition on the company and advertisement of the petition is required so that the company may, depending on the circumstances:
(a) apply for the petition to be struck out;
(b) pay the debt on a creditor's petition;
(c) consider its position generally with regard to the petition;
(d) if necessary, make an application under the Insolvency Act 1986, s. 127, for an anticipatory validation order (*Re Signland Ltd* [1982] 2 All ER 609 at p. 609; *Re a Company (No. 0013925 of 1991)* [1992] BCLC 562 at p. 564).

The power to dismiss a prematurely advertised petition to wind up a company is a discretionary disciplinary power and might not be exercised on the company's application if the company does not show that it has been prejudiced, e.g., by showing on a creditor's petition that it could have paid the debt (*Re Roselmar Properties Ltd* (1986) 2 BCC 99,156; *Re Corbenstoke Ltd* [1989] BCLC 496; *Re Garton (Western) Ltd* [1989] BCLC 304).

Equally, the timely advertisement of a creditor's petition is important to ensure that the class remedy of winding up by the court is available to all creditors, and is not used as a means of putting pressure on the company to pay the petitioner's debt (**PD Insolvency Proceedings, para. 2.1**). The court may, under r. 4.11(5), dismiss a petition if there has been a failure to advertise it without good reason accepted by the court (**PD Insolvency Proceedings, para. 2.1**).

A company may apply for a direction that a petition for it to be wound up should not be advertised. It is for the company to show sufficient reason for departure from the normal practice of advertising petitions other than contributories' petitions (*Re a Company (No. 007946 of 1993)* [1994] Ch 198; *Re a Company (No. 007923 of 1994)* [1995] 1 WLR 953), but it is not necessary for the company to show that the petition is bound to fail (*Re a Company (No. 007923 of 1994)* [1995] 1 WLR 953). If the company has not obtained an order under the Insolvency Act 1986, s. 127, validating dispositions in the ordinary course of the company's business, the court will not direct that the petition should not be advertised, other than in exceptional circumstances (*Applied Data Base Ltd v Secretary of State for Trade and Industry* [1995] 1 BCLC 272 at pp. 274–5).

Provision of copies of the petition

When a petition has been presented for the winding up of a company, the petitioner (or the **79.42**
petitioner's solicitor, if there is one) must, on request, supply to any director, contributory or creditor of the company a copy of the petition. A copy must be supplied within two days of being applied for and a fee of 15p per A4 or A5 page (30p per A3 page) may be charged (IR 1986, rr. 4.13 and 13.11(b)). Copies should not be supplied to a person who is not a director, contributory or creditor (*Re Cheltenham and Swansea Railway Carriage and Wagon Co.* (1869) LR 8 Eq 580 per Malins V-C at pp. 582–3).

Other publicisation of the petition

In *Re FSA Business Software Ltd* [1990] BCLC 465 Warner J said, at p. 829: 'It is at least a breach of **79.43**
the spirit of the rules of this court for publicity to be given to a winding-up petition before it has been advertised'.

The court may dismiss a petition if its existence is notified before the expiry of seven business days from service on the company and the notification was designed to put pressure on the company: such conduct is an abuse of process (*Re a Company (No. 0013925 of 1991)* [1992] BCLC 562; *Re a Company (No. 001127 of 1992)* [1992] BCC 477). In *SN Group plc v Barclays Bank plc* [1993] BCC 506 it was found that the publicisation of the petition was not designed to put pressure on the company (which was found to be insolvent) and the company's application to have the petition dismissed was rejected.

Publicity, given otherwise than by an advertisement in the *Gazette*, is not an 'advertisement' for the purposes of IR 1986, r. 4.11, and, in particular, r. 4.11(5) (which provides a power to dismiss a petition for failure to comply with r. 4.11) does not apply (*Re a Company (No. 0013925 of 1991)* [1992] BCLC 562; *SN Group plc v Barclays Bank plc* [1993] BCC 506; *Secretary of State for Trade and Industry v North West Holdings plc* [1999] 1 BCLC 425, overruling *Re a Company (No. 001127 of 1992)* [1992] BCC 477).

Publicisation of an intention to present a petition may be an abuse of process which may be punished by striking out the petition when it is presented (*Re Doreen Boards Ltd* [1996] 1 BCLC 501).

Publication of a winding-up petition may amount to contempt of court because publicity is given to only one side of the case (*Re Cheltenham and Swansea Railway Carriage and Wagon Co.* (1869) LR 8 Eq 580, in which an entire petition by a contributory, containing grave charges of fraud and misconduct against directors, had been published as a news item in a newspaper). See also *Re Crown Bank* (1890) 44 ChD 649, in which the publisher of a newspaper was fined for contempt after publishing articles adopting allegations of fraud made in a contributory's petition while the petition was pending.

Errors in an advertisement

79.44 If there is an error or inaccuracy in an advertisement then, unless the court waives it, the person who was responsible for inserting the advertisement must forthwith have a new advertisement published for the purpose of correcting the error or inaccuracy (IR 1986, r. 12.20(3)). The court has a discretion to waive an error (*Re Worthing Royal Sea House Hotel Co.* [1872] WN 74).

In *Re Vidiofusion Ltd* [1974] 1 WLR 1548 the advertisement incorrectly gave the company's name as 'Videofusion Ltd' ('e' instead of 'i'). Megarry J waived the mistake and said that, normally, an error would be waived if four conditions are satisfied:

(a) There must be no other company on the register with a similar name.
(b) The true name and the misspelt name should have substantially the same pronunciation.
(c) There should be no marked visual difference between the true name and the misspelt name (so that 'Jaxen' for 'Jackson' would not be waived despite the similarity of pronunciation).
(d) The error must not materially affect the alphabetical order of the names.

CONTROL OF TRANSACTIONS AND LITIGATION WHILE PETITION IS PENDING

79.45 If a winding-up order is made against a company, the winding up is deemed to have commenced at the time when the petition was presented, or the time the company went into voluntary liquidation, if earlier (Insolvency Act 1986, s. 129). All claims against the company are fixed as at the commencement of winding up, and it is necessary to prevent specific unsecured creditors recovering payment of debts at the expense of the other unsecured creditors. (The winding up of a company does not, in general, affect security interests in the company's property.) Provision is made for the stay of other proceedings against the company while the petition is pending (Insolvency Act 1986, s. 126, see **81.16**), for all dispositions of the company's property to be invalid unless sanctioned by the court (s. 127), and for avoidance of attachments, sequestrations, distresses and executions against the company's property (s. 128). The company itself and its directors may not appoint an administrator out of court (sch. B1, para. 25(a)), though a holder of a qualifying floating charge may do so unless a provisional liquidator has been appointed (para. 17(a)). The liability of contributories is also fixed as at the commencement of winding up, and so alterations in the status of the company's members cannot be made without the approval of the court (s. 127).

APPOINTMENT OF A PROVISIONAL LIQUIDATOR

Function of a provisional liquidator

A provisional liquidator of a company may be appointed by the court under the Insolvency Act 1986, s. 135. An appointment may be made at any time in the period between presentation of a petition for the compulsory winding up of the company and the court's disposal of the petition (by making a winding-up order, dismissing the petition or striking it out) (Insolvency Act 1986, s. 135(1) and (2); *Re a Company (No. 00315 of 1973)* [1973] 1 WLR 1566). **79.46**

The usual object of the appointment is that an independent person will take charge of the company's affairs, maintain the status quo and prevent prejudice either to those supporting the winding-up petition or to those against it, pending the court's decision on the petition (per Lord President Clyde in *Levy v Napier* 1962 SC 468 at p. 477; per Street J in *Re Carapark Industries Pty Ltd* (1966) 86 WN (Pt 1) (NSW) 165 at p. 171). Provisional liquidators are independent persons operating under the direction of the court for a purpose that is entirely one of preservation during an interim period: a provisional liquidator does not represent any one group of creditors (*Re Bank of Credit and Commerce International SA (No. 2)* [1992] BCLC 579). The name 'provisional liquidator' is misleading because the one thing that a provisional liquidator of a company does not do is carry out the liquidation of the company.

The appointment of a provisional liquidator of a company terminates the powers of the directors as effectively as does the making of a winding-up order (*Re Mawcon Ltd* [1969] 1 WLR 78). The directors do, however, have standing to apply for the provisional liquidator's appointment to be discharged (*Re Union Accident Insurance Co. Ltd* [1972] 1 WLR 640) or apply for an administration order to be made in relation to the company (*Re Gosscott (Groundworks) Ltd* [1988] BCLC 363 per Mervyn Davies J at p. 366).

Who may apply for a provisional liquidator to be appointed

When a petition has been presented for the compulsory liquidation of a company, an application to appoint a provisional liquidator may be made by (IR 1986, r. 4.25(1)): **79.47**

(a) the petitioner,
(b) a creditor of the company,
(c) a contributory of the company,
(d) the company itself,
(e) the Secretary of State,
(f) a temporary administrator (see **79.17**),
(g) a member State liquidator appointed in main proceedings (see **79.17**),
(h) any person who would, under any enactment, be entitled to present a petition to wind up the company.

Application procedure

An application to the court for the appointment of a provisional liquidator of a company is an ordinary application in the winding-up proceedings (see **81.1** to **81.5**). It must be supported by an affidavit or witness statement stating (IR 1986, r. 4.25(2)): **79.48**

(a) The grounds for the appointment.
(b) If the proposed provisional liquidator is not the official receiver, that the person proposed has consented to act and that he or she is, to the best of the applicant's knowledge, a qualified insolvency practitioner.
(c) Whether or not the official receiver has been informed of the application and, if so, whether a copy of the application has been sent to the official receiver. Whether or not it is proposed that the official receiver should be the provisional liquidator, a copy of the application and supporting affidavit must be sent to the official receiver, who may attend the hearing and make representations (r. 4.25(3)). If it is not possible to send these copies, the official receiver must at least be informed of the application in time to attend the hearing (r. 4.25(3)).
(d) Whether, to the applicant's knowledge:
 (i) there has been proposed, or is in force, for the company a voluntary arrangement;
 (ii) an administrator or administrative receiver is acting in relation to the company;
 (iii) a voluntary liquidator has been appointed.
(e) The applicant's estimate of the value of the assets in respect of which the provisional liquidator is to be appointed.

In *Re W. F. Fearman Ltd* (1987) 4 BCC 139, in view of the urgency of the case, Harman J heard, and acceded to, an application to appoint a provisional liquidator which had not been made in writing and did not conform to any of the relevant procedural requirements.

The court may make the appointment applied for, on such terms as it thinks fit, if satisfied that sufficient grounds are shown for the appointment (r. 4.25(4)).

In the High Court, an application for the appointment of a provisional liquidator must be made direct to the judge and, unless otherwise ordered, will be heard in open court (**PD Insolvency Proceedings, para. 5.1**).

An application may be heard in private if it is necessary, in order to protect the company, its creditors and its shareholders, to prevent the appointment of a provisional liquidator becoming known (*Re London and Norwich Investment Services Ltd* [1988] BCLC 226).

The court may make alternative orders instead of appointing a provisional liquidator (*Re a Company (No. 00596 of 1986)* [1987] BCLC 133, in which a receiver was appointed; *Re Senator Hanseatische Verwaltungsgesellschaft mbH* [1996] 2 BCLC 562, in which injunctions were issued to prevent a foreign company which administered a pyramid investment scheme recruiting new members or remitting cash abroad).

Application without notice to other parties

79.49 As it is not inevitable that a winding-up order will be made after the appointment of a provisional liquidator, if an application for such an appointment is made without notice to the company and the court has no opportunity to hear the company's views, the court will not make the appointment unless the applicant gives an undertaking in damages (i.e., undertakes that if winding up is not ordered the applicant will compensate the company for any loss it suffers as a result of the appointment: the company would not be able to sue for damages because the damage would have been caused by court order). However, if an application is made in those circumstances by the Crown in connection with a public-interest winding-up petition, an undertaking in damages will not be required (*Re Highfield Commodities Ltd* [1985] 1 WLR 149). An undertaking in damages is not usually required if the company had an opportunity to give the court its views on the application (ibid. at p. 155).

According to Hoffmann J in *Re First Express Ltd* [1991] BCC 782 at p. 785 and *Re Secure and Provide plc* [1992] BCC 405, an order should not be made without notice to other parties unless:
(a) giving the company an opportunity to be heard appears likely to cause injustice to the applicant, because of:

(i) the delay involved, or
(ii) action which it is likely will be taken before the order can be made; and

(b) the court is satisfied that any damage which the company may suffer from the appointment of the provisional liquidator may be compensated through the applicant's undertaking in damages or that the risk of incompensable loss is clearly outweighed by the risk of injustice to the applicant if the order is not made.

Form of order

The order appointing a provisional liquidator of a company should be in form 4.15 in sch. 4 to the IR 1986 and it must specify the functions to be carried out by the provisional liquidator in relation to the company's affairs (IR 1986, r. 4.26(1)). The appointment of a provisional liquidator may be made on such terms as the court thinks fit (r. 4.25(4)). **79.50**

Transmission of order

Having made an order appointing a provisional liquidator of a company, the court will send a sealed copy of the order to the person appointed as provisional liquidator, and (if the person appointed is not the official receiver) to the official receiver, and to the company's administrative receiver, if there is one (IR 1986, r. 4.26(2) and (3)). Further copies are provided to the provisional liquidator to be sent to the company (or to its voluntary liquidator, if there is one) and to Companies House (r. 4.26(2) and (3)). **79.51**

Public notification

A sealed copy of the order appointing a provisional liquidator must be forwarded by the appointee to Companies House (IR 1986, r. 4.26(2) and (3)). **79.52**

Joint provisional liquidators

If two or more persons are appointed joint provisional liquidators of a company, the order of appointment must state whether any act required or authorised under any enactment to be done by the provisional liquidator is to be done by all or any one or more of the persons for the time being holding the office (Insolvency Act 1986, s. 231). **79.53**

Deposit for the official receiver's remuneration and expenses

On applying for the official receiver to be appointed provisional liquidator of a company, the applicant must deposit with the official receiver such sum as the court directs to cover remuneration and expenses (IR 1986, r. 4.27(1)). Alternatively, security for the amount may be given if the official receiver agrees (r. 4.27(1)). **79.54**

From time to time the official receiver may apply to the court to order a further amount to be deposited or secured, and if the order is not complied with within two days of service, the court may discharge the official receiver's appointment as provisional liquidator (r. 4.27(2)).

Control of litigation after provisional liquidator appointed

Section 130(2) of the Insolvency Act 1986 provides that when a provisional liquidator has been appointed, no action or proceeding shall be proceeded with or commenced against the company or its property, except by permission of the court and subject to such terms as the court may impose. See **81.17**. No one may appoint an administrator out of court (sch. B1, paras 17(a) and 25(a)). **79.55**

CERTIFICATE OF COMPLIANCE

Before the date appointed for the hearing of a winding-up petition, the petitioner or the petitioner's solicitor must file in court a certificate of compliance with the rules relating to **79.56** service and advertisement (IR 1986, r. 4.14(1)). The prescribed form of certificate is form 4.7 in IR 1986, sch. 4. A certificate must (r. 4.14(2)):

(a) state the date of presentation of the petition;
(b) state the date fixed for hearing it;
(c) state the date or dates on which the petition was served and advertised in compliance with the rules;
(d) be accompanied by a copy of the advertisement.

Rule 4.14(1) requires the certificate of compliance to be filed at least five days before the hearing of the petition. In the High Court the latest time for filing a certificate of compliance in relation to a petition is extended by **PD Insolvency Proceedings, para. 3.1**, to 4.30 p.m. on the Friday preceding the day on which the petition is to be heard. An application to file a certificate and copy advertisement after that extended deadline will be allowed only if some good reason is shown for the delay.

Failure to file a certificate of compliance is a ground on which the court may, if it thinks fit, dismiss the petition (r. 4.14(3)). In *Re J. Lang and Co. Ltd* (1892) 36 SJ 271 North J thought that a petition should not be dismissed for failure to file a certificate of compliance unless the failure had caused substantial injustice which could not be remedied by an order of the court.

A copy of the advertisement must be filed with the certificate even if it was defective in some way, for example, because it was published at the wrong time or omitted or misprinted important words (**PD Insolvency Proceedings, para. 2.2**). If the petition has not been advertised because of an order forbidding advertising, the prescribed form of certificate should be adapted to state that the petition was served but that advertisement has been forbidden by the court (see *Re a Company (No. 002791 of 1986)* (1986) 2 BCC 99,281). Non-advertisement of a petition in pursuance of such an order is not in itself a ground for dismissing the petition (*Re Five Oaks Construction Ltd* (1968) 112 SJ 86).

A petitioner who has advertised the petition but has decided not to pursue it should nevertheless file a copy of the advertisement (**PD Insolvency Proceedings, para. 2.2**) and a certificate of compliance so as to be entitled to costs.

PERMISSION TO WITHDRAW A PETITION

79.57 Under IR 1986, r. 4.15, a person petitioning for a company to be wound up may apply to the court without notice to other parties for permission to withdraw the petition. The following conditions must be satisfied:

(a) The petition must not have been advertised and no notices with reference to the petition (whether in support of or in opposition to it) must have been received by the petitioner, either under r. 4.16 (see **79.82**) or otherwise (*Re Wavern Engineering Co. Ltd* (1986) 3 BCC 3).
(b) The company must consent to the court giving permission to withdraw the petition.
(c) The parties must have agreed who is to pay costs. If there has been no agreement, the petition must be heard so that the court can make an order, but then the petition must be advertised (*Re Shusella Ltd* [1983] BCLC 505).
(d) The application must be made at least five days before the day fixed for hearing the petition.

An application is made by ordinary application (see **81.1** to **81.5**). An application in the High Court for permission to withdraw a petition is heard by the court manager of the Companies Court in London or by a district judge in a district registry (**PD Insolvency Proceedings, para. 5.4**). The prescribed form of order for permission to withdraw a petition is form 4.8 in sch. 4 to the IR 1986.

The procedure of r. 4.15 is used when a creditor who has petitioned for winding up is paid the debt before the petition is advertised.

COMPANY'S EVIDENCE IN OPPOSITION

If a petition to wind up a company has been presented and it is to be opposed by the company, the company's affidavit or witness statement in opposition must be filed in court not less than seven days before the day fixed for hearing the petition (IR 1986, r. 4.18(1)). A copy of the written evidence must be sent to the petitioner forthwith after filing (r. 4.18(2)). Written evidence in response to the company's evidence filed under r. 4.18 cannot be filed unless the court directs the filing of further evidence or otherwise gives permission (*Re Multicultural Media Centre for the Millennium Ltd* [2001] EWCA Civ 1687, *The Times*, 16 November 2001). **79.58**

SUBSTITUTION OF PETITIONER

Circumstances in which a substitution may be made

When a winding-up petition is pending, r. 4.19 of IR 1986 permits the substitution of a new petitioner if the original petitioner: **79.59**

(a) is subsequently found not entitled to petition;
(b) fails to advertise the petition, within the time prescribed by IR 1986 (see 79.41) or such extended time as the court may allow;
(c) consents to withdraw the petition;
(d) consents to allow the petition to be dismissed;
(e) consents to an adjournment of the petition;
(f) fails to appear in support of the petition when it is called on in court on the day originally fixed for the hearing or on a day to which it is adjourned; or
(g) appears when the petition is called on in court but does not apply for an order in the terms of the prayer of the petition.

In circumstances (b) and (c), substitution may be ordered at any time (r. 4.19(3)). An application in the High Court for the substitution of a petitioner is heard by the court manager of the Companies Court in London or by a district judge in a district registry (**PD Insolvency Proceedings, para.** 5.4), or may be dealt with at the hearing of the petition.

Who may be substituted?

Any creditor or contributory who, in the court's opinion, would have a right to present a petition, and who is desirous of prosecuting it, may be substituted (IR 1986, r. 4.19(2)). The rule permits the substitution as petitioner of any creditor or contributory with a right to present *a* petition, not *the* petition that is being abandoned by its petitioner. Thus the substituted petitioner may have different grounds for petitioning and need not be from the original petitioner's class. **79.60**

A creditor who is substituted need not have been a creditor at the time the petition was originally presented (*Perak Pioneer Ltd v Petroliam Nasional Bhd* [1986] AC 849; *Re Richbell Strategic Holdings Ltd* [1997] 2 BCLC 429 at p. 455).

If a petitioning creditor's debt is assigned after the petition is presented, the assignee will normally be substituted as petitioner (*Perak Pioneer Ltd v Petroliam Nasional Bhd* [1986] AC 849).

On a petition for the opening of secondary proceedings (see 79.9) the member State liquidator (see 79.17) appointed in the main proceedings may be substituted (IR 1986, r. 4.19(2A)).

Effect of substitution

79.61 If a substitution is ordered, the hearing will be adjourned, the petition will have to be amended and re-verified, and it may need to be re-served and re-advertised. A petition is a single proceeding from presentation to order notwithstanding that there may have been one or more substitutions (*Re Bostels Ltd* [1968] Ch 346 at p. 351). Substitution of petitioner and amendment of the petition does not mean that a new petition is presented (*Re Western Welsh International System Buildings Ltd* (1984) 1 BCC 99,296). This means that if a winding-up order is made, the date of commencement of the winding up is the date the petition was presented by its original petitioner.

FURTHER INFORMATION AND DISCLOSURE

79.62 Any party to insolvency proceedings may apply to the court under IR 1986, r. 7.60, for further information to be given by another party under **CPR, Part 18**, or to obtain disclosure and inspection of documents under **CPR, Part 31**.

Such an application is an ordinary application (see **81.1 to 81.5**) and may be made without notice being served on any other party (IR 1986, r. 7.60(2)). But, on a petition for the winding up of a company the court is very unlikely to order the company to give disclosure to the petitioner (*Re COLT Telecom Group plc* [2002] EWHC 2503 (Ch), [2003] 1 BCLC 290). This is because a petition should not be presented unless it can be supported by evidence which, if accepted at the hearing, would found a claim for relief: it is improper to present a petition in the hope that evidence to support it may be found by disclosure (*Re a Company, ex parte Burr* [1992] BCLC 724 per Vinelott J at p. 736 and on appeal sub nom. *Re Saul D. Harrison and Sons plc* [1995] 1 BCLC 14 per Hoffmann LJ at p. 22).

PROCEEDINGS ON CONTRIBUTORY'S PETITION

Contributories

79.63 **Definition** The Insolvency Act 1986 does not mention members or shareholders of a company as persons entitled to petition for it to be wound up. Instead the legislation uses the term 'contributories', who are the persons who are liable to contribute to the assets of a company in the event of its being wound up (Insolvency Act 1986, s. 79(1)). Section 74(1) provides that 'every present and past member' of a company is liable to contribute to its assets when it is wound up, so every past and present member is a contributory of the company. However, this is subject to the extensive limitations set out in the rest of s. 74, the most significant of which is s. 74(2)(d):

> in the case of a company limited by shares, no contribution is required from any member exceeding the amount (if any) unpaid on the shares in respect of which he is liable as a present or past member.

The emphasis on members as persons contributing to the assets of a company being wound up was very important in the early days of registered companies when shares were usually partly paid. When companies moved to having only fully paid shares the courts took the pragmatic step of deciding that members with fully paid shares are nevertheless contributories for the purposes of the legislation, and have the same rights and duties as other contributories, except that they are not required to contribute anything (*Re National Savings Bank Association* (1866) LR 1 Ch App 547; *Re Anglesea Colliery Co.* (1866) LR 1 Ch App 555; *Re Phoenix Oil and Transport Co. Ltd* [1958] Ch 560).

79.64 **Qualifying period of membership** Standing of a contributory to petition is restricted by the Insolvency Act 1986, s. 124(2), which provides that, unless the number of members of a company has been reduced below two (s. 124(2)(a)), a contributory may petition for its winding up only if:

(a) shares which give the petitioner the status of contributory were originally allotted to the petitioner, or
(b) such shares have been registered in the petitioner's name for at least six of the 18 months preceding presentation of the petition; or
(c) they have devolved on the petitioner through the death of a former holder (s. 124(2)(b)).

Condition (b) is satisfied only if there has been actual registration for six months — an entitlement to be registered is not enough (*Re Gattopardo Ltd* [1969] 1 WLR 619). Registration is sufficient to satisfy condition (b): provided the contributory has been registered as holder of the shares for the requisite period it does not matter that the contributory was not the beneficial owner of them throughout the period (*Re Wala Wynaad Indian Gold Mining Co.* (1882) 21 ChD 849).

Tangible interest A winding-up order will not be made on a contributory's petition unless the petitioner has a sufficient interest (usually described as a 'tangible interest') in having the company wound up (*Re Rica Gold Washing Co.* (1879) 11 ChD 36; *O'Connor v Atlantis Fisheries Ltd* 1998 SCLR 401). **79.65**

A contributory's tangible interest may be an interest in receiving something or an interest in limiting a liability.

It seems that the only tangible interest in receiving something which can be claimed by a contributory of a registered company is the probability of receiving a dividend in the winding up, and it must be shown that more than a negligible amount will be received (*Bryanston Finance Ltd v De Vries (No. 2)* [1976] Ch 63 per Buckley LJ at p. 75).

According to Oliver J in *Re Chesterfield Catering Co. Ltd* [1977] Ch 373, at p. 380, preventing an increase in a contributory petitioner's liability (for example, on partly paid shares) may be enough to satisfy the court that the petitioner has a tangible interest in having the company wound up.

The burden of proving a tangible interest is on the petitioner (*Re Lancashire Brick and Tile Co. Ltd* (1865) 34 LJ Ch 331), and a sufficient interest must be alleged in the petition (*Re W. R. Willcocks and Co. Ltd* [1974] Ch 163).

Procedure on a contributory's petition

Introduction Most of the procedures described in **79.19** to **79.61** do not apply to contributories' petitions. This is because, by IR 1986, r. 4.2(4), the rules in ch. 3 of part 4 of IR 1986 (rr. 4.7 to 4.21A) do not apply to contributories' petitions but instead ch. 4 (rr. 4.22 to 4.24) applies. No certificate of compliance is required for a contributory's petition and there is no provision for substitution of petitioner. **79.66**

In terms of procedure, a petition to wind up a company presented at the instance of the supervisor of a voluntary arrangement in force for the company or by the company's administrator is treated as a contributories' petition (r. 4.7(9)).

Presentation of a petition A contributory's petition for the compulsory liquidation of a company must be in form 4.14 in IR 1986, sch. 4: it must specify the grounds on which it is presented and must be filed in court with one copy for service on the company (IR 1986, r. 4.22(1)). **79.67**

A contributory's petition is required by **PD 49B, para.** 9(2) to (7), to state the petitioner's attitude to validation, under the Insolvency Act 1986, s. 127, of the company's transactions pending hearing of the petition.

A contributory's petition does not have to be verified by affidavit or witness statement, because r. 4.2(4) of the IR 1986 provides that r. 4.12 does not apply to contributories' petitions. However, an affidavit or witness statement is required to provide reasons for the statements made in para. (7) of the petition (see **79.25**) and, if necessary, to provide reasons for the petitioner's objections to a s. 127 order in standard form (PD 49B, para. 9(2) and (3)).

79.68 **Fee and deposit** A court fee and deposit (IR 1986, r. 4.22(1A)) must be paid as for any other petition — see **79.27**.

79.69 **Fixing a return day** The court will fix a hearing for a day (called the 'return day') on which, unless the court otherwise directs, the petitioner and the company must attend for directions to be given in relation to the procedure on the petition (IR 1986, r. 4.22(2)).

79.70 **Service of the petition** The petitioner must, at least 14 days before the return day, serve a sealed copy of the petition on the company (IR 1986, r. 4.22(4)). By r. 13.3(1) and (3) service may be by post under r. 12.10 or personal service under **CPR, r. 6.4.**

79.71 **Directions** Rule 4.23(1) of the IR 1986 requires the court, on the return day, or at any time after it, to give such directions as it thinks appropriate with respect to the following matters:

(a) service of the petition, whether in connection with the venue for a further hearing, or for any other purpose (the court must, by r. 4.23(2), consider whether any of the persons specified in r. 4.10 — see **79.40** — should be served with a copy of the petition);
(b) whether particulars of claim and defence are to be delivered, and generally as to the procedure on the petition;
(c) whether, and if so by what means, the petition is to be advertised;
(d) the manner in which any evidence is to be adduced at any hearing before the judge, including the matters to be dealt with in evidence;
(e) any other matter affecting the procedure on the petition or in connection with the hearing and disposal of the petition.

An application in the High Court for directions on a contributory's petition is heard by the court manager of the Companies Court in London or by a district judge in a district registry **(PD Insolvency Proceedings, para. 5.4).**

The directions may order the petition to stand as particulars of claim (*Re a Company (No. 007936 of 1994)* [1995] BCC 705 at p. 708).

In r. 4.23(1)(c), 'advertised' includes any form of notification: if it is ordered that there is to be no advertisement, mentioning the petition in a letter contravenes the order (*Re a Company (No. 00687 of 1991)* [1992] BCLC 133).

79.72 **Advertisement of petition** A contributory's petition is advertised only if the court directs (IR 1986, r. 4.23(1)(c)). A contributory's petition usually relates to a solvent company whose creditors would be uninterested in appearing at the hearing of the petition but who could be unnecessarily alarmed by the announcement of a petition which they would assume was a creditor's petition on the ground of inability to pay debts.

No publicity may be given to a contributory's petition unless directions for it to be advertised have been given under the IR 1986, r. 4.23(1) (*Re a Company (No. 00687 of 1991)* [1992] BCLC 133; *Re Doreen Boards Ltd* [1996] 1 BCLC 501, in which the petition was struck out after the petitioner had telephoned the company's bank, invoice factors and local Inland Revenue office to inform them of the petition).

79.73 **Appearances** The rules on notices and lists of appearances (see **79.82**) apply to contributories' petition as they do to other petitions (IR 1986, r. 4.24).

Costs of defending a contributory's petition

Where a petition for the compulsory winding up of a company arises from a personal dispute between members of the company, it is a misapplication of the company's money for it to pay any costs of the proceedings (other than as ordered by the court) except for costs necessarily incurred in representing the company as a separate person (*Re A and BC Chewing Gum Ltd* [1975] 1 WLR 579 at p. 592; *Re Kenyon Swansea Ltd* [1987] BCLC 514; *Re Elgindata Ltd* [1991] BCLC 959). **79.74**

HEARING A WINDING-UP PETITION AND MAKING THE ORDER

Judge

A winding-up petition is heard in public (**PD Insolvency Proceedings, para.** 5.3(1)) by the registrar or district judge, who may give any necessary directions and may, in the exercise of his or her discretion, either hear and determine it or refer it to the judge (**PD Insolvency Proceedings, para.** 5.2). If a petition also seeks discharge of an administration order, it must be made direct to the judge and, unless otherwise ordered, will be heard in public (**PD Insolvency Proceedings, para.** 5.1). The registrar exercises the jurisdiction of the High Court, but not as a deputy judge of that court (*Re Calahurst Ltd* [1989] BCLC 140 per Harman J). **79.75**

Who may be heard?

Company as a litigant in person For representation of a company by an employee see **59.28**. **79.76**

Directors As part of their general management powers conferred, for example, by Table A, reg. 70, in the Companies (Tables A to F) Regulations 1985 (SI 1985/805), the directors of a company sought to be wound up have power to instruct solicitors and counsel to appear for the company, even if the company is in administrative receivership (*Re Reprographic Exports (Euromat) Ltd* (1978) 122 SJ 400, but see **79.79**) or a provisional liquidator has been appointed (*Re Union Accident Insurance Co. Ltd* [1972] 1 WLR 640). However, the managing director of a company does not have implied authority to make crucial decisions following the presentation of a petition to wind up the company, and, in particular, does not have implied authority to instruct solicitors to oppose the petition (*Re Qintex Ltd (No. 2)* (1990) 2 ACSR 479; *Nece Pty Ltd v Ritek Incorporation* (1997) 24 ACSR 38). **79.77**

Contributories A person wishing to appear as a contributory must admit to being a contributory (*Re Eastern Counties Junction and Southend Railway Co.* (1850) 14 LT OS 369) and must have a tangible interest (see **79.65**) in the company (*Re Rodencroft Ltd* [2004] EWHC 862 (Ch), [2004] 1 WLR 1566). **79.78**

Administrative receiver By the Insolvency Act 1986, s. 42 and sch. 1, para. 21, an administrative receiver of a company has a power to defend a petition to wind up the company. It may be questioned whether this power is given so that the receiver can represent the company's interests or the interests of the creditor who appointed the receiver. In *Bank of New Zealand v Essington Developments Pty Ltd* (1991) 5 ACSR 86 a similar provision of Australian law was interpreted to mean that the receiver could assume the carriage of the proceedings on the company's behalf but could not actively resist the petition. If the receiver exercised the power then this would supersede the directors' power to defend the petition. Accordingly the receiver should only choose to exercise the power if the purposes of the receivership would be best served by the company going into compulsory liquidation. It is submitted that if an administrative receiver is opposed to a winding-up petition then the creditor who appointed the receiver should appear to state that opposition, not the receiver. In *Re Thames Freightlines Ltd* (1981) 1 NZCLC 98,112 Greig J observed that a receiver appearing to oppose a petition (in **79.79**

that case without statutory power to do so) could either be regarded as representing the creditor by whom he or she was appointed or as a creditor for the costs and expenses of the receivership.

79.80 **Voluntary liquidator** If a petition is presented to wind up a company in voluntary liquidation, the voluntary liquidator should instruct counsel to appear for the company: there should not be separate appearances for the liquidator and the company (*Re A. W. Hall and Co. Ltd* (1885) 53 LT 633; *Re Mont de Piété of England* [1892] WN 166; *Re William Adler and Co. Ltd* [1935] Ch 138). The appearance should be for the purpose of providing information and arguing the company's case: the liquidator should not take sides in an argument among creditors or between contributories and creditors (*Re Roselmar Properties Ltd (No. 2)* (1986) 2 BCC 99,157; *Re Arthur Rathbone Kitchens Ltd* [1997] 2 BCLC 280). If the petition criticises the liquidator's conduct of the voluntary winding up, the liquidator should answer the criticisms fully (*Re Arthur Rathbone Kitchens Ltd*; *Re Leading Guides International Ltd* [1998] 1 BCLC 620).

79.81 **Provisional liquidator** If a provisional liquidator has been appointed then he or she does not, it seems, have a right to appear at the hearing of the winding-up petition (*Re General International Agency Co. Ltd* (1865) 36 Beav 1; *Re Laverton Nickel NL* (1979) 3 ACLR 945 at p. 947) but, if heard as advocate to the court, will be awarded the costs of appearing out of the company's assets (*Re Times Life Assurance and Guarantee Co.* (1869) LR 9 Eq 382; *Re Laverton Nickel NL*).

Notice of appearance

79.82 By IR 1986, r. 4.16, any person wishing to appear on the hearing of a winding-up petition must send notice to the petitioner or the petitioner's solicitor to arrive not later than 4 p.m. on the business day before the date appointed for the hearing (or the date of an adjournment). 'Business day' is defined in r. 13.13(1) (see 79.7).

A notice of appearance must be in form 4.9 in IR 1986, sch. 4, and must state whether the appearance will be to support or oppose the petition (r. 4.16(2)(b)). The notice must also state the name and address of the person giving it, and any telephone number and reference which may be required for communication with that person or with any other person (to be also specified in the notice) authorised to speak or act on behalf of the person giving the notice (r. 4.16(2)(a)). The notice must also state the amount and nature of the debt claimed by the person giving the notice (r. 4.16(2)(c)) — clearly this applies only if the person is a creditor.

The petitioner must prepare for the court a list of persons who have given notice of intention to appear, stating whether they support or oppose the petition, and must hand a copy of the list to the court before the hearing commences (IR 1986, r. 4.17; prescribed form is 4.10 in sch. 4).

A person who has not given notice in accordance with r. 4.16 may appear on the hearing of the petition only with the permission of the court (r. 4.16(5)).

The petitioner must add to the list required by the IR 1986, r. 4.17, the name of anyone given permission by the court to appear without having given proper notice (r. 4.17(4)).

ORDERS THAT THE COURT MAY MAKE

79.83 On hearing a winding-up petition the court has, by virtue of the Insolvency Act 1986, s. 125(1), the following options:

(a) make the winding-up order applied for;
(b) dismiss the petition;
(c) adjourn the hearing conditionally;

(d) adjourn the hearing unconditionally;
(e) make an interim order;
(f) make any other order that it thinks fit.

Form of order

The prescribed form of winding-up order (the usual compulsory order) is form 4.11 in sch. 4 to the IR 1986. **79.84**

The court cannot add to a winding-up order any conditions about how the winding up is to be conducted: 'The court has a discretion in relation to the making of an order, but none as to its operation when made' (per Roxburgh J in *Re Banque des Marchands de Moscou (Koupetschesky)* [1958] Ch 182 at p. 193).

Court's discretion

The fact that one or more of the circumstances in which a company may be compulsorily wound up exists does not mean that a winding-up order will be made as a matter of course (*Re Metropolitan Railway Warehousing Co. Ltd* (1867) 36 LJ Ch 827 per Lord Cairns LJ at p. 829). The court's power to order the winding up of a company is discretionary — the Insolvency Act 1986, s. 122(1), says that a registered company '*may* be wound up by the court' in the circumstances specified in the subsection. In relation to a creditor's petition, even if the creditor's debt is undisputed and unpaid, the court nevertheless has a discretion whether or not to make a winding-up order (*Re P. and J. Macrae Ltd* [1961] 1 WLR 229; *Re Southard and Co. Ltd* [1979] 1 WLR 1198). **79.85**

The basic rule is that where the debt is undisputed and not satisfied and there are no exceptional circumstances, the creditor is entitled to expect the court to exercise its jurisdiction in the way of making a winding-up order (per Buckley LJ in *Re Southard and Co. Ltd* [1979] 1 WLR 1198 at p. 1203). But, as a winding-up order on a creditor's petition should be for the benefit of creditors generally, the court will consider the views of creditors other than the petitioner. In *Re Crigglestone Coal Co. Ltd* [1906] 2 Ch 327 the elder Buckley J said, at pp. 331–2, in relation to a creditor's petition:

> . . . the order which the petitioner seeks is not an order for his benefit, but an order for the benefit of a class of which he is a member. The right *ex debito iustitiae* [by an obligation of justice] is not his individual right, but his representative right. If a majority of the class are opposed to his view, and consider that they have a better chance of getting payment by abstaining from seizing the assets, then, upon general grounds and upon [the Insolvency Act 1986, s. 195], the court gives effect to such right as the majority of the class desire to exercise.

So it may be said that, as between the company and an unpaid admitted creditor, the creditor is entitled to a winding-up order as a matter of course, but, as between the petitioning creditor and the other creditors, the majority's opposition to compulsory liquidation may prevail (see *Re Great Western (Forest of Dean) Coal Consumers' Co.* (1882) 21 ChD 769 at p. 773; *Re Chapel House Colliery Co.* (1883) 24 ChD 259 at pp. 265–6). Those who oppose the petition of an unpaid admitted creditor must produce reasons to persuade the court to vary its normal practice of making a winding-up order on such a petition; the court does not simply abide by a majority decision that there should not be a compulsory liquidation. In *Re J. D. Swain Ltd* [1965] 1 WLR 909 Diplock LJ said, at p. 915:

> . . . if the only circumstances which are available are that the petitioner seeks a compulsory winding up and the majority of the creditors seek that there should be no winding up at all, then prima facie the petitioning creditor is entitled to a winding up unless there are some additional reasons for deciding to the contrary.

The court will not pay so much regard to the views of creditors who are connected with the company — for example, as directors, shareholders or subsidiaries — as to genuine outside creditors, even if the outsiders' debts are smaller (*Re ABC Coupler and Engineering Co. Ltd* [1961]

1 WLR 243 at p. 245; *Re Holiday Stamps Ltd* (1985) 82 LS Gaz 2817; *Re Lowerstoft Traffic Services Ltd* [1986] BCLC 81 at p. 84; *Re Lummus Agricultural Services Ltd* [2001] 1 BCLC 137).

The court will not, unless there are special circumstances, make a winding-up order on a creditor's petition if the amount owed to the creditor is less than the minimum amount for which a statutory demand may be served, currently £750 (*Re Herbert Standring and Co.* [1895] WN 99; *Re Fancy Dress Balls Co.* [1899] WN 109).

Interim or other order; alternative remedies

79.86 The power given to the court by the Insolvency Act 1986, s. 125(1), to make an interim or other order is limited to making ancillary orders in furtherance of or otherwise in connection with a present or prospective winding-up order: the subsection does not empower the court to order some remedy other than winding up. The power to make any other order the court thinks fit is at the end of a list of powers in s. 125(1) and is subject to the *eiusdem generis* rule (*Re Bank of Credit and Commerce International SA (No. 10)* [1997] Ch 213 at p. 239). It does not, for example, empower the court to direct that the company's claim for damages for petitioning maliciously be heard in the winding-up proceedings (*Partizan Ltd v O. J. Kilkenny and Co. Ltd* [1998] 1 BCLC 157). It does not empower the court to direct how the liquidation is to be conducted, for example, by ordering assets to be distributed in kind (*See Teow Guan v Kian Joo Holdings Sdn Bhd* [1995] 3 MLJ 598), by giving a direction disapplying some part of the statutory winding-up scheme (*Re Bank of Credit and Commerce International SA (No. 10)* [1997] Ch 213 at p. 239) or by ordering the liquidator to carry on the company's business and preserve its assets so that they can be handed over to named individuals (*Fairview Schools Bhd v Indrani a/p Rajaratnam (No. 2)* [1998] 1 MLJ 110). The court is, however, empowered to adjourn a winding-up application and give directions and make the adjournment conditional upon compliance with the directions, provided it is contemplated that a winding-up order will be made if the directions are not complied with (so that the order is in connection with a winding up, not a substitute for one) (*Re R. J. Jowsey Mining Co. Ltd* [1969] 2 OR 549).

COSTS

General

79.87 In relation to a winding-up petition, as with any court proceedings, the question of costs is always at the discretion of the court (**Supreme Court Act 1981, s. 51(1); CPR, r. 44.3(1)**). The general rule is that the unsuccessful party will be ordered to pay the costs of the successful party, but the court may make a different order (**CPR, r. 44.3(2)**). The following paragraphs state how the costs of various parties to winding-up proceedings would normally be dealt with by the court.

The petitioner

79.88 **Successful petition** The petitioner's costs of a successful petition are normally ordered to be paid as an expense of the liquidation (*Re Humber Ironworks Co.* (1866) LR 2 Eq 15; *Re Bostels Ltd* [1968] Ch 346 at p. 350). The petitioner is also entitled to the costs of any interim applications, unless there is good reason to the contrary (*Re Ryan Developments Ltd* [2002] EWHC 1121 (Ch), [2002] 2 BCLC 792).

If a petition succeeds after substitution of the petitioner, the original petitioner's costs of presenting and advertising the petition will be ordered to be paid as an expense of the liquidation (*Re Bostels Ltd* [1968] Ch 346), even if the original petitioner does not appear at the hearing as a supporter (*Re Castle Coulson and MacDonald Ltd* [1973] Ch 382).

If the main opposition to a successful petition came from a party other than the company itself then that party may be ordered to pay the petitioner's costs (*Re Worldhams Park Golf Course Ltd* [1998] 1 BCLC 554 (contributory's petition opposed by another contributory)).

Unsuccessful petition Normally, if a petition is unsuccessful, the petitioner must pay the company's costs (see 79.92), one set of costs to opposing creditors and one set to opposing contributories (see 79.96). **79.89**

If the petition of an unpaid creditor whose debt is undisputed is refused only because the court accepts the view of opposing creditors that there should not be a compulsory liquidation, no order as to costs will be made unless the petitioner was acting unreasonably, for example, where the petitioner ought to have known that the petition would fail (*Re Chapel House Colliery Co.* (1883) 24 ChD 259; *Re East Kent Colliery Co. Ltd* (1914) 30 TLR 659; *Re R. W. Sharman Ltd* [1957] 1 WLR 1008; *Re A. E. Hayter and Sons (Porchester) Ltd* [1961] 1 WLR 1008; *Re Sklan Ltd* [1961] 1 WLR 1013; *Re Riviera Pearls Ltd* [1962] 1 WLR 722). In *Re Arrow Leeds Ltd* [1986] BCLC 538 the company was ordered to pay the petitioner's costs because it did not become clear that the majority of creditors opposed winding up until the petition had been adjourned twice.

In some cases, a costs penalty has been imposed on a company for not giving timely information to a petitioner about the circumstances which would lead to dismissal of the petition (*Re M. McCarthy and Co. (Builders) Ltd (No. 2)* [1976] 2 All ER 339; *Re Lanaghan Bros Ltd* [1977] 1 All ER 265).

Creditor's petition achieving payment of the petitioner's debt If a creditor petitioner's debt is paid before the hearing and no winding-up order is asked for at the hearing then, provided the petition has been advertised, the company will be ordered to pay the petitioner's costs (*Re Alliance Contract Co.* [1867] WN 218) even if the company does not appear (*Re Shusella Ltd* [1983] BCLC 505). The petitioner is regarded as having effectively succeeded (*Re Nowmost Co. Ltd* [1996] 2 BCLC 492). However, if the petition was an unnecessarily heavy-handed method of obtaining payment then the court may make no order as to part (*Re Edric Audio Visual Ltd* (1981) 125 SJ 395) or all (*Re Great Barrier Reef Flying Boats Pty Ltd* (1982) 6 ACLR 820; *Re Kingsley Monogramming Ltd* (1985) 2 NZCLC 99,420) of the petitioner's costs. The onus is on the company to show why it should not be ordered to pay the petitioner's costs, but the company's evidence about the circumstances in which the petition was presented may be given to the court informally, unless the petitioner objects, in which case there should be an adjournment (*Re Nowmost Co. Ltd* [1996] 2 BCLC 492). **79.90**

The company

Successful petition The company's costs of preparing for and appearing at the hearing of a successful winding-up petition are normally ordered to be paid as an expense of the liquidation (*Re Humber Ironworks Co.* (1866) LR 2 Eq 15; *Re Bostels Ltd* [1968] Ch 346 at p. 350). However, the company's assets available for distribution to its creditors should not be expended unjustifiably. If the company has unjustifiably opposed the petition or tried to prevent it proceeding, the court may order the person who instigated the company's opposition to pay its costs (*Re a Company (No. 004055 of 1991)* [1991] 1 WLR 1003). There must be an opportunity for the person against whom such a costs order is sought to submit a defence and, if necessary, put in evidence, before the order is made (ibid.). **79.91**

In *Re Gosscott (Groundworks) Ltd* [1988] BCLC 363, after a petition for the winding up of the company was presented by a creditor, the directors of the company presented a petition for an administration order to be made in respect of the company, in good faith and on the advice of competent professionals. The administration petition was abandoned and a winding-up order was made. The company's costs in relation to the administration petition were allowed as costs of the winding up.

Unsuccessful petition The company's costs of opposing an unsuccessful winding-up **79.92**

petition must be paid by the petitioner unless there are exceptional circumstances (*Re Humber Ironworks Co.* (1866) LR 2 Eq 15; *Re Fernforest Ltd* [1990] BCLC 693). The company will be awarded its costs against the petitioner if the petition is dismissed for failure to file a certificate of compliance (*Re Royal Mutual Benefit Building Society* [1960] 1 WLR 1143).

Supporting creditors and contributories

79.93 **Successful petition** When a winding-up order is made, creditors who appeared to support the petition will be awarded one set of costs between them to be paid as an expense of the liquidation, and a second set of costs will be awarded on the same basis to supporting contributories (*Re European Banking Co.* (1866) LR 2 Eq 521; *Re Peckham etc. Tramways Co.* (1888) 57 LJ Ch 462 per Chitty J at p. 463; *Re Bostels Ltd* [1968] Ch 346 at p. 350). It is an invariable rule that only one set of costs is awarded to successful supporting creditors even if several persons legitimately appear to present separate views (*Re Esal (Commodities) Ltd* [1985] BCLC 450). The creditors and contributories must arrange among themselves how to divide up the costs.

Costs ordered to be paid to supporting creditors and contributories rank equally with the petitioner's costs in the order of priority of payments set out in r. 4.218 of the IR 1986 (where they are item (h)).

Supporters who instruct the same solicitors as the petitioner are not allowed separate costs and solicitors instructed in such circumstances should not instruct counsel to represent the supporters in addition to counsel instructed to represent the petitioner (*Re Military and General Tailoring Co. Ltd* (1877) 47 LJ Ch 141; *Re Brighton Marine Palace and Pier Co. Ltd* (1897) 13 TLR 202).

79.94 **Unsuccessful petition** Supporters of an unsuccessful petition are not entitled to costs (*Re Humber Ironworks Co.* (1866) LR 2 Eq 15).

Opposing creditors and contributories

79.95 **Successful petition** Creditors or contributories appearing to oppose a successful petition are not entitled to costs (*Re Humber Ironworks Co.* (1866) LR 2 Eq 15 at p. 18; *Re Criterion Gold Mining Co.* (1889) 41 ChD 146 at p. 149; *Re Bathampton Properties Ltd* [1976] 1 WLR 168 at p. 171).

79.96 **Unsuccessful petition** Creditors who appear to oppose an unsuccessful petition may be given one set of costs between them from the petitioner and so may opposing contributories if their interests are distinct from the company's (*Re European Banking Co.* (1866) LR 2 Eq 521; *Re Anglo-Egyptian Navigation Co.* (1869) LR 8 Eq 660; *Re Heaton's Steel and Iron Co.* [1870] WN 85; *Re Carnarvonshire Slate Co. Ltd* (1879) 40 LT 35; *Re Peckham etc. Tramways Co.* (1888) 57 LJ Ch 462 per Chitty J at p. 463; not following *Re Humber Ironworks Co.* (1866) LR 2 Eq 15). A contributory whose interests are not distinct from the company's will not be awarded costs (*Re Times Life Assurance and Guarantee Co., ex parte Nunneley* (1870) LR 5 Ch App 381).

Opposers who instruct the same solicitors as the company are not allowed separate costs (*Re Brighton Marine Palace and Pier Co. Ltd* (1897) 13 TLR 202).

Assessment

79.97 The court may order costs of proceedings on a winding-up petition to be decided by detailed assessment (IR 1986, r. 7.34(4)). If costs of a successful petition to wind up a company are payable out of the company's assets, the liquidator may agree them with the person entitled to payment or may require them to be decided by detailed assessment by the court which made the order (r. 7.34(1)). The liquidator must require costs to be decided by detailed assessment if instructed to do so by the liquidation committee (r. 7.34(2)).

NOTICE TO OFFICIAL RECEIVER AND PERFECTION OF THE ORDER

When a winding-up order is made the court gives notice to its official receiver forthwith (IR 1986, r. 4.20(1)). **79.98**

The petitioner, and every person who appeared on the hearing of the petition, must, not later than the business day after the order is made, leave at the court all documents necessary to enable the order to be completed (r. 4.20(2)). 'Business day' is defined in r. 13.13(1) (see 79.7). It is not normally necessary to appoint a time for settlement of the order (r. 4.20(3)). The court will draw up the order (**PD Insolvency Proceedings, para. 6**).

When a winding-up order has been made, the court sends three sealed copies to the official receiver (IR 1986, r. 4.21(1)). The official receiver sends one of those copies by post to the company at its registered office (r. 4.21(2)). (If there is no registered office the company's copy may be sent to the company's principal, or last known principal, place of business, or be served on such person or persons as the court directs: r. 4.21(2).) A second copy is forwarded to the registrar of companies (r. 4.21(3)) who must enter it in his records relating to the company (Insolvency Act 1986, s. 130(1)) and officially notify receipt of it in the *London Gazette* (Companies Act 1985, s. 711(1)(p)).

If a winding-up order made against a registered company has been erroneously made against the wrong company, it may be rescinded and the registrar of companies may be ordered to correct the records at Companies House (*Re Calmex Ltd* [1989] 1 All ER 485).

Having received copies of a winding-up order the official receiver must forthwith cause the order to be gazetted and advertise it in a newspaper of his or her choice (IR 1986, r. 4.21(4)). A copy of the newspaper advertisement must be filed in court by the official receiver under r. 7.32.

A copy of the *Gazette* containing the notice of the order may, in any proceedings, be produced as conclusive evidence that the order was made on the date specified in the notice (IR 1986, r. 12.20(2)).

If a winding-up order that has been gazetted is varied by the court, the official receiver must forthwith cause the variation of the order to be gazetted (r. 12.20(3)). If an order has been erroneously or inaccurately gazetted, the official receiver must forthwith cause a further entry to be made in the *Gazette* for the purpose of correcting the error or inaccuracy (r. 12.20(3)).

PERMISSION FOR LITIGATION AGAINST COMPANY IN LIQUIDATION

Section 130(2) of the Insolvency Act 1986 provides that when a winding-up order has been made, no action or proceeding shall be proceeded with or commenced against the company or its property, except by permission of the court and subject to such terms as the court may impose. See **81.18**. **79.99**

CORRECTION OF ERRORS

The court may at any time correct an accidental slip or omission in a judgment or order (**CPR, r. 40.12**). **79.100**

In the High Court in London an application for permission to amend an error in a petition discovered after the winding-up order has been made should be made to the court manager of the Companies Court (**PD Insolvency Proceedings, para. 4.1**). Details of the Companies Court practice are given in **PD Insolvency Proceedings, paras 4.2 to 4.4**.

RESCISSION AND APPEAL

79.101 A winding-up order may be rescinded by the court which made it on the application of an interested party (IR 1986, r. 7.47(1)). See **81.9**.

An appeal against an order made by a court on hearing a winding-up petition is subject to the same rules as any other appeal in insolvency proceedings, for which see **81.10** to **81.14**.

ADMINISTRATION APPLICATIONS

Which court?

79.102 An application for an administration order to be made in respect of a company may be presented to a court which has jurisdiction to order the company to be wound up (see **79.8**). An application must be made by means of an administration application (Insolvency Act 1986, sch. B1, para. 12(1); IR 1986, r. 2.2(1)).

Standing to apply

79.103 An application for an administration order to be made in relation to a company may be made by:

(a) the company itself (Insolvency Act 1986, sch. B1, para. 12(1)(a));
(b) the directors of the company (para. 12(1)(b));
(c) one or more creditors of the company (para. 12(1)(c)) — 'creditor' includes a contingent creditor and a prospective creditor (para. 12(4));
(d) the designated officer for a magistrates' court (if the company has failed to pay a fine) (para. 12(1)(d); Magistrates' Courts Act 1980, s. 87A);
(e) a supervisor of a voluntary arrangement of the company (Insolvency Act 1986, s. 7(4)(b) and sch. B1, para. 12(5));
(f) a combination of persons listed in (a) to (e) (sch. B1, para. 12(1)(e)).

The company, the directors of the company, or a creditor who holds what the legislation calls a 'qualifying floating charge in respect of the company's property', may alternatively appoint an administrator without court proceedings (Insolvency Act 1986, sch. B1, paras 14 and 22), though such an appointment does not take effect until notice of appointment is filed in court (sch. B1, paras 18,19,29 and 31). The wide-ranging definition of 'qualifying floating charge in respect of a company's property' in sch. B1, para. 14, will, in practice, include any floating charge which, alone or in conjunction with other charges, covers the whole or substantially the whole of the company's property.

In the following circumstances persons with the power to appoint an administrator out of court cannot do so and must instead apply to the court for an appointment, if the right to apply is available:

(a) If the company is being wound up voluntarily or by the court, an administrator cannot be appointed out of court and an administration application may be made only by the liquidator (sch. B1, paras 8 and 38) or (if it is a winding up by the court) by the holder of a qualifying floating charge (paras 8 and 37).
(b) If an administrative receiver of the company has been appointed, an administrator cannot be appointed out of court and the court will make an appointment only if the chargee who appointed the receiver consents or the court is satisfied that if an order were made the floating charge under which the receiver was appointed would be discharged or avoided or declared invalid by the court under ss. 238 to 240 (transactions at an undervalue and preferences) or s. 245 (avoidance of floating charges given to secure existing debts) (sch. B1, paras 17(b), 25(c) and 39). The administrative receiver must vacate office if an administrator is appointed (para. 41(1)).

(c) If a petition has been presented asking for the company to be wound up by the court and has not been disposed of, the company itself and its directors may not appoint an administrator out of court (para. 25(a)), though a holder of a qualifying floating charge may do so unless a provisional liquidator has been appointed (para. 17(a)).
(d) If an administration application has been made and has not been disposed of, the company itself and its directors may not appoint an administrator out of court (para. 25(b)), though a holder of a qualifying floating charge may do so.
(e) An appointment may not be made out of court by the company or its directors within 12 months of the ending of a previous administration initiated by it or them (para. 23) or within 12 months of a moratorium under sch. A1 (moratorium to enable preparation of a voluntary arrangement) which failed to produce a workable voluntary arrangement (sch. B1, para. 24).
(f) While a moratorium under sch. A1 is in force, an administrator cannot be appointed out of court, and an administration application cannot be made to the court (sch. A1, para. 12(1)(d)).

Need for insolvency

Unless the administration application is made by the holder of a qualifying floating charge, the court cannot make an administration order in relation to a company unless it is satisfied that the company is, or is likely to become, unable to pay its debts (Insolvency Act 1986, sch. B1, para. 11(a)). To show that a company is likely to become unable to pay its debts it must be shown that it is more probable than not that it will be unable to pay its debts (*Re COLT Telecom Group plc* [2002] EWHC 2815 (Ch), LTL 20/12/2002). **79.104**

If an administration application by the holder of a qualifying floating charge states that it is made in reliance on sch. B1, para. 35, the court may make an administration order without proof of the company's insolvency, but only if satisfied that the conditions for appointing an administrator out of court, under para. 14, are satisfied. The most important of these conditions are that the floating charge must presently be enforceable (para. 16), and the holder of any prior qualifying floating charge must either give written consent or be given at least two business days' notice (para. 15).

Statutory purpose

The court may not make an administration order in relation to a company unless it considers that the order is reasonably likely to achieve the purpose of administration (Insolvency Act 1986, sch. B1, para. 11(b)). The purpose of administration is the objective with which the administrator must perform his or her functions, defined in sch. B1, para. 3(1), as: **79.105**

(a) rescuing the company as a going concern, or
(b) achieving a better result for the company's creditors as a whole than would be likely if the company were wound up (without first being in administration), or
(c) realising property in order to make a distribution to one or more secured or preferential creditors.

Objective (a) must be given priority unless the administrator believes it is not reasonably practicable or that objective (b) would achieve a better result for the company's creditors as a whole (para. 3(3)). Objective (c) may be pursued only if the administrator believes (i) it is not reasonably practicable to achieve either objective (a) or objective (b) and (ii) the interests of the creditors of the company as a whole will not be harmed unnecessarily (para. 3(4)).

Contents of application

The prescribed form of administration application is form 2.1B in sch. 4 to IR 1986. The applicant's address for service must be given in accordance with IR 1986, rr. 2.2(4) and 2.3(1) to (4), the provisions of which are summarised in **table 79.1**. **79.106**

Table 79.1 Address for service of applicant for administration order

Applicant	Address for service
The company, or supervisor of the company's voluntary arrangement	The company's registered office, unless there are special reasons to the contrary.
The company's directors	The company's registered office, unless there are special reasons to the contrary.
One creditor	That creditor's address for service.
Two or more creditors	The address for service of one of the creditors, named in the application as applying on his, her or its behalf and on behalf of the other creditors (who must all be named in the application).

The application must specify the name and address of the person it is proposed should be appointed as administrator (form 2.1B, para. 9), and the nominee's written consent (form 2.2B), stating his or her opinion that the purpose of administration is likely to be achieved, must be attached (r. 2.3(5)).

The application must state:

(a) whether or not the company is one of the types of company to which Council Regulation (EC) No. 1346/2000 does not apply (see 79.12) (form 2.1B, para. 6);

(b) whether the Regulation does apply; and, if it does apply, whether the proceedings will be main or territorial proceedings (administration proceedings cannot be secondary proceedings, because secondary proceedings must be winding-up proceedings: Council Regulation (EC) No. 1346/2000, art. 3(3)) (form 2.1B, para. 7).

The advice on answering these questions given in relation to winding-up petitions (79.21) applies to administration applications.

Supporting affidavit or witness statement

79.107 An administration application must be supported by an affidavit (IR 1986, rr. 2.2 and 2.4) or by a witness statement verified by a statement of truth (r. 7.57(5)), which must be attached to the application (r. 2.4(2)). If the application is presented by the company, its directors or the supervisor of a voluntary arrangement, the supporting affidavit or statement must be made by a director or secretary of the company (r. 2.2(2) and (4)); if presented by creditors, it must be made by a person acting under their authority and must state the nature of that authority and the means of his or her knowledge of the matters stated (r. 2.2(3)). The supporting affidavit or witness statement must state (r. 2.4):

(a) the company's financial position, specifying (to the best of the deponent's knowledge and belief) its assets and liabilities, including contingent and prospective liabilities (r. 2.4(2)(a));

(b) either the reasons for the applicant's belief that the company is, or is likely to become, unable to pay its debts (form 2.1B, para. 8) or, if the application is by the holder of a qualifying floating charge in reliance on the Insolvency Act 1986, sch. B1, para. 35 (see 79.104) or para. 37 (where the company is in liquidation), sufficient details to satisfy the court that the applicant is entitled to appoint an administrator under sch. B1, para. 14 (IR 1986, rr. 2.4(4) and 2.11(2));

(c) details of any securities known or believed to be held by creditors of the company, whether any creditor is entitled to appoint an administrative receiver or administrator and whether an administrative receiver has been appointed (r. 2.4(2)(b));

(d) details of any insolvency proceeding in relation to the company including any winding-up petition that has been presented (r. 2.4(2)(c));

(e) whether, in the opinion of the applicant, Council Regulation (EC) No. 1346/2000 will apply, and the reasons for that opinion, and, if the Regulation will apply, whether the proceedings will be main proceedings or territorial proceedings (r. 2.4(4); form 2.1B, para. 7);

(f) if two or more persons are to be appointed administrators, (i) which functions (if any) are to be exercised by the persons appointed acting jointly, (ii) which functions (if any) are to be exercised by any or all of the persons appointed (r. 2.4(2)(d); Insolvency Act 1986, sch. B1, para. 100(2));

(g) any other information that would assist the court (IR 1986, r. 2.4(2)(e)).

If the company is already in liquidation, the supporting affidavit or witness statement must also, by r. 2.11, contain (i) full details of the proceedings, (ii) the name and address of the liquidator, the date he or she was appointed and by whom, (iii) the reasons why it has subsequently been considered appropriate that an administration application should be made, (iv) all other matters that would, in the opinion of the applicant, assist the court in considering the need to make provisions in respect of matters arising in connection with the liquidation.

Filing of application

Enough copies of the application must be made for service (see **79.109**), and a further copy to be exhibited to the evidence of service. **79.108**

The application and supporting affidavit or witness statement, and the copies for service and exhibition to the evidence of service, must be filed in court for sealing and endorsement with the date and time of filing and with the venue for the hearing (IR 1986, r. 2.5(1) to (3)).

A fee of £150 must be paid (**CPFO, fee 3.2**).

Service of application

As soon as is reasonably practicable, and not less than five days before the date fixed for the hearing, a copy of the application sealed by the court, together with a copy of the supporting affidavit or witness statement and the documents attached to the application, must be served on the following persons (Insolvency Act 1986, sch. B1, para. 12(2); IR 1986, rr. 2.6 and 2.8(1)): **79.109**

(a) any person who has appointed an administrative receiver of the company;
(b) any person who is or may be entitled to appoint an administrative receiver of the company;
(c) any holder of a floating charge who is or may be entitled to appoint an administrator of the company out of court under the Insolvency Act 1986, sch. B1, para. 14;
(d) an administrative receiver of the company, if there is one;
(e) if a petition for the compulsory winding up of the company is pending, the petitioner;
(f) a provisional liquidator of the company, if there is one;
(g) a member State liquidator appointed in main proceedings in relation to the company, if there is one;
(h) the person proposed as administrator;
(i) the company, unless it, or a supervisor of its voluntary arrangement, is the applicant.

Service must be effected by the applicant, or the applicant's solicitor, or a person instructed by either of them (r. 2.8(1)).

Service on the company is by leaving the documents at, or sending them by first-class post to, its registered office or, if that is not practicable, to its last known principal place of business in England and Wales (r. 2.8(2)(a), (3) and (6)). Service on a person other than the company is by leaving the documents at, or sending them by first-class post to, the person's 'proper address' (r. 2.8(2)(b) and (6)).

The proper address of an authorised deposit-taker, which is to be served as a person which has appointed an administrative receiver, or is, or may be, entitled to appoint, an administrative receiver or administrator, is the address of the branch where the company's account is kept, if that is known to the applicant, or the deposit-taker's registered office or usual or last known address (r. 2.8(5)). The proper address of any other person is an address the person has previously notified as an address for service or, if there has been no notification, the person's usual or last known address (r. 2.8(4)).

Alternatively the court may direct the manner of service (r. 2.8(2)(c)).

A document sent by first-class post is treated as served on the second business day after posting, unless the contrary is shown (r. 12.10(2)). 'Business day' is defined in r. 13.13(1) (see 79.7).

Proof of service

79.110 Service of an administration application must be verified by affidavit or witness statement, specifying the date on which, and the manner in which, service was effected (IR 1986, r. 2.9(1)). The prescribed form of affidavit is form 2.3B in sch. 4 to IR 1986. The proof of service, with a sealed copy of the application exhibited to it, must be filed with the court as soon as reasonably practicable after service, and in any event not less than one day before the hearing of the application (r. 2.9(2))

Notice to enforcement officer and distrainors

79.111 Rule 2.7 of IR 1986 requires the applicant, forthwith after filing the application, to give notice of its presentation to:

(a) any enforcement officer or other officer who, to the applicant's knowledge, is charged with an execution or other legal process against the company or its property; and
(b) any person who, to the applicant's knowledge, has distrained against the company or its property.

Notification of other insolvency proceedings

79.112 A person who has filed an administration application in court has a duty to notify the court in writing immediately on becoming aware of the existence of any proceedings under the Insolvency Act 1986, IR 1986 or Council Regulation (EC) No. 1346/2000 (IR 1986, r. 2.5(4)).

Withdrawal

79.113 An administration application may not be withdrawn without the permission of the court (Insolvency Act 1986, sch. B1, para. 12(3)).

Nomination of administrator by holder of qualifying floating charge

79.114 If an administration application is made by a person who does not hold a qualifying floating charge in respect of the company's property (defined in the Insolvency Act 1986, sch. B1, para. 14), the holder of such a charge may apply to have a specified person appointed administrator instead of the person nominated in the application (sch. B1, para. 36). The application (which is an ordinary application, see **81.2**) must, by IR 1986, r. 2.10, be supported by:

(a) the written consent of every holder of a prior qualifying floating charge (defined in the Insolvency Act 1986, sch. B1, para. 15(2));
(b) the consent of the applicant's proposed administrator in form 2.2B;
(c) sufficient evidence to satisfy the court that the applicant is entitled to appoint an administrator under sch. B1, para. 14.

The court must grant the application unless it thinks it right not to do so because of the particular circumstances of the case (sch. B1, para. 36(2)).

Appearance at hearing of the application

By IR 1986, r. 2.12(1), at the hearing of an application to make an administration order in relation to a company, the following may appear or be represented: **79.115**

(a) the applicant;
(b) the company;
(c) one or more of the company's directors;
(d) the company's administrative receiver, if one has been appointed;
(e) any person who has presented a petition for the winding up of the company;
(f) the person proposed for appointment as administrator;
(g) a member State liquidator appointed in main proceedings in relation to the company, if there is one;
(h) any holder of a qualifying floating charge;
(i) a supervisor of a voluntary arrangement, if there is one; and
(j) with the permission of the court, any other person who appears to have an interest justifying appearance.

Court's powers on hearing an application

On hearing an application for an administration order to be made in relation to a company the court may, by the Insolvency Act 1986, sch. B1, para. 13(1), make the order, or dismiss the application, or adjourn the hearing conditionally or unconditionally, or make an interim order, or treat the application as a winding-up petition and make any order which it could make under s. 125 (see **79.83**), or make any other order that it thinks fit. If a winding-up order is made, the winding up commences on the making of the order (s. 129(1A)). **79.116**

If an administration order is made, the costs of the applicant, and of any other person whose costs are allowed by the court, are payable as an expense of the administration (IR 1986, r. 2.12(3)).

An administration order must be in form 2.4B in IR 1986, sch. 4 (r. 2.12(2)). If the company was in liquidation, the order must provide for the transition from liquidation to administration, as specified in the Insolvency Act 1986, sch. B1, paras 37 and 38, and IR 1986, r. 2.13. If a winding-up petition was pending, it must be dismissed (Insolvency Act 1986, sch. B1, para. 40(1)(a)).

An interim order may restrict the exercise of a power of the company or of its directors (sch. B1, para. 13(3)(a)). An interim order may make provision conferring a discretion on the court, or on a qualified insolvency practitioner, in relation to the company (para. 13(3)(b)). The appointment of an insolvency practitioner to supervise under para. 13(3)(b) is analogous to the appointment by the court of a receiver of disputed property that is in jeopardy; such a person is not an administrator, because the appointment is not by an administration order, and so the rights of the holder of a floating charge to intervene (sch. B1, para. 36) or veto the appointment (para. 39) do not arise (*Re a Company (No. 00175 of 1987)* (1987) 3 BCC 124).

The principal question on hearing an administration application is whether the administration order is 'reasonably likely' to achieve the purpose of administration (sch. B1, para. 11(b); see **79.105**). Before amendments were made which came into force on 15 September 2003, the court had to be satisfied that an administration order was 'likely' to achieve the statutory purpose. It was held that, in deciding whether achievement was 'likely' the court had to be satisfied that there was a real prospect of achievement but did not have to be satisfied that achievement was more likely than not (*Re Harris Simons Construction Ltd* [1989] 1 WLR 368; *Re SCL Building Services Ltd* [1990] BCLC 98). As Parliament has not taken the opportunity to change 'likely' to 'more likely than not', it is submitted that the standard of a real prospect of achievement still prevails.

If an administrative receiver of the company has been appointed, and the chargee who made the appointment has not consented to the making of an administration order, and the court is not satisfied that the charge would be discharged or avoided or declared invalid under ss. 238 to 240 or s. 245, the court can only dismiss the application (sch. B1, para. 39; *Re a Company (No. 00175 of 1987)* (1987) 3 BCC 124). This applies whether the administrative receiver was appointed before or after the administration application was made (sch. B1, para. 39(2)).

Notice of court's order

79.117 If an administration order is made, the appointment of the administrator takes effect when the order is made, unless some other time is specified in the order (Insolvency Act 1986, sch. B1, para. 13(2)). The court must, as soon as reasonably practicable, send two sealed copies of the order to the applicant (IR 1986, r. 2.14(1)), who must, as soon as reasonably practicable, send one of them to the person appointed as administrator (r. 2.14(2)).

If the court makes an interim order under the Insolvency Act 1986, sch. B1, para. 13(1)(d), or an order under para. 13(1)(f) (power to make any other order which the court thinks appropriate), the court must give directions as to the persons to whom, and how, notice of that order is to be given (IR 1986, r. 2.14(3)).

Chapter 80 Bankruptcy

The following procedural checklist, which is in **appendix 1**, is relevant to this chapter:

Procedural checklist 38 Application by a creditor whose debt is presently payable for a bankruptcy order

INTRODUCTION

Bankruptcy is a procedure by which an insolvent individual surrenders virtually all of his or her assets to a trustee in bankruptcy for distribution among creditors in return for cancellation of debts. For a period of usually one year, until the discharge of the bankruptcy, all assets acquired by the bankrupt also go to the trustee. Bankruptcy may be achieved only by court order and is an entirely statutory process, governed now by the Insolvency Act 1986. Following amendments made by the Enterprise Act 2002 (including reducing the duration of bankruptcy: s. 256 and sch. 19), the punitive aspects of bankruptcy (such as disqualification from Parliament or the magistracy), which used to apply to all bankrupts, now apply only to those subject to a bankruptcy restrictions order or undertaking (Insolvency Act 1986, s. 281A and sch. 4A). However, it is likely that many bankrupts will still find that the procedure is remarkably costly and often unexpectedly unpleasant for the bankrupt and his or her family. Some of the disadvantages of bankruptcy may be avoided by obtaining the agreement of creditors to an individual voluntary arrangement (IVA), by which an insolvent individual's assets are distributed among creditors outside of bankruptcy (see **80.35** to **80.37**). **80.1**

PROCEDURAL RULES

80.2 An application for an order adjudging an individual bankrupt must be made by petition (a 'bankruptcy petition') presented to the court under the Insolvency Act 1986, s. 264. An individual subject to bankruptcy proceedings is usually referred to as a 'debtor'. As a bankruptcy petition is a proceeding under the Insolvency Act 1986 it is an insolvency proceeding for the purposes of the Insolvency Rules 1986 (SI 1986/1925) (IR 1986), by r. 13.7 of these rules. The scope of the IR 1986 and general rules on track allocation, forms, time limits and the meaning of 'business day' are described in **79.3** to **79.7**.

JURISDICTION

Scope of English bankruptcy law

80.3 Only debtors with a sufficient connection with England and Wales can be made bankrupt under English law. The required connection is specified in the Insolvency Act 1986, s. 265. The debtor must:

(a) be domiciled in England and Wales;
(b) be personally present in England and Wales on the day on which the petition is presented; or
(c) at any time within the three years ending with the day the petition was presented:
(i) have been ordinarily resident, or have had a place of business, in England and Wales; or
(ii) have carried on business in England and Wales.

It is sufficient, for the purposes of condition (c)(ii), that the debtor was a member of a firm or partnership carrying on business, or that an agent or manager carried on the business for the debtor or for a firm or partnership of which the debtor was a member (s. 265(2)).

The scope of English bankruptcy law is, by s. 265(3), subject to Council Regulation (EC) No. 1346/2000, art. 3 (see **79.9**). The effect of art. 3 on bankruptcy jurisdiction is that if the centre of main interests of an individual who would otherwise be covered by the Insolvency Act 1986, s. 265, is in another EU State (apart from Denmark), a bankruptcy order may be made in England and Wales only if the individual possesses an establishment in the United Kingdom (art. 3(2)), and there are restrictions on who may apply for a bankruptcy order here (art. 3(4); see **80.5**). An individual's centre of main interests ought to be the place where he or she can be contacted by creditors (*Skjevesland v Geveran Trading Co. Ltd* [2002] EWHC 2898 (Ch), [2003] BCC 391, at [60]).

Appropriate court

80.4 In general, a bankruptcy petition must be presented to the court which has insolvency jurisdiction for the district in which the debtor resided or carried on business for the longest period during the six months preceding presentation of the petition (IR 1986, r. 6.9(1)(b), (2) and (4) (creditor's petition); r. 6.40(1)(a) and (2) (debtor's petition)). This is the High Court in the London area and a county court elsewhere. Under the Insolvency Act 1986, s. 374, and the Civil Courts Order 1983 (SI 1983/713), art. 9 and sch. 3, about half of county courts do not have insolvency jurisdiction: the districts of those courts are attached either to other county courts or, in the London area, to the High Court for the purposes of insolvency jurisdiction. If, in the six months preceding presentation of the petition, the debtor has carried on business in one insolvency district but resided in another, it is normally the place of business which determines which court has jurisdiction (IR 1986, r. 6.9(3) and (4) (creditor's petition); r. 6.40 (debtor's petition)).

The High Court is the appropriate court if the debtor is not resident in England and Wales (r. 6.9(1)(c) (creditor's petition); r. 6.40(1)(b) (debtor's petition)) or if the petitioner is unable to determine the debtor's place of residence or place of business (r. 6.9(1)(d)). When a petition is presented by a minister of the Crown or a government department, the petitioner may choose to present it to the High Court, and must do so if the petition is based on an unsatisfied execution (r. 6.9(1)(a)).

If the above rules would require a debtor's petition to be presented at a county court with only limited facilities for dealing with insolvency matters, the petition may be presented instead to the nearest full-time court specified in IR 1986, sch. 2 (IR 1986, r. 6.40(3)). Also, where the debtor's residence and business are in different insolvency districts, the debtor may present his or her own petition in the residential district if doing so would expedite the petition (r. 6.40(3)).

A bankruptcy petition which is presented at a time when an IVA is in force for the debtor must be presented to the court in which proceedings relating to the IVA have been taken (r. 6.9(4A) (creditor's petition); r. 6.40(3A) (debtor's petition)).

WHO MAY PRESENT A BANKRUPTCY PETITION?

By the Insolvency Act 1986, s. 264(1), a petition for an order adjudging an individual bankrupt may be presented by: **80.5**

(a) one of the individual's unsecured creditors, or by two or more unsecured creditors jointly (see **80.6** to **80.27**);
(b) the individual personally (see **80.28** to **80.35**);
(c) the supervisor of, or any person (other than the individual) who is for the time being bound by, an approved IVA (see **80.38**).

The Financial Services Authority may petition for an individual's bankruptcy under the Financial Services and Markets Act 2000, s. 372, alleging the individual's inability to pay debts incurred in the course of activities regulated by the 2000 Act. The procedure on such a petition is governed by the Bankruptcy (Financial Services and Markets Act 2000) Rules 2001 (SI 2001/3634).

Council Regulation (EC) No. 1346/2000 governs who may apply for a bankruptcy order in England and Wales in relation to a debtor whose centre of main interests is in another EU State (apart from Denmark) (see **79.9** to **79.12**). An application for a bankruptcy order in respect of such a debtor may be made only if the debtor possesses an establishment in the United Kingdom (art. 3(2)). If insolvency proceedings (main proceedings) have been opened in the State where the debtor's centre of main interests is located, then, by arts 27 and 29 and the Insolvency Act 1986, s. 264(1), provided the main proceedings are of a type listed in annex A to the Regulation, an application may be made (in secondary proceedings) in England and Wales for a bankruptcy order by:

(a) the liquidator in the main proceedings (called a 'member State liquidator' in IR 1986: see r. 13.13(11)), or
(b) a temporary administrator (corresponding to an English interim receiver, see **80.16**) appointed in the main proceedings, or
(c) any other person authorised by s. 264.

If insolvency proceedings have not yet been opened in the State where the debtor's centre of main interests is located, an application for a bankruptcy order may be made (in territorial proceedings) in England and Wales only by a creditor who is domiciled or habitually resident in the United Kingdom or has its registered office in the United Kingdom, or a creditor whose claim arises from the operation of the debtor's establishment in the United Kingdom

(Regulation, art. 4(b)). This restriction does not apply if insolvency proceedings cannot be opened in the State where the debtor's centre of main interests is located, because of the conditions laid down by the law of that State (art. 4(a)).

In *R v Lord Chancellor, ex parte Lightfoot* [2000] QB 597 Simon Brown LJ (with whom Rattee J agreed) held that proceedings on a debtor's petition are not subject to art. 6(1) (fair trial) of the European Convention on Human Rights, because, in his lordship's view, a debtor's petition does not involve a dispute with anyone. It is submitted with respect that it is questionable whether this is the correct test for the application of art. 6(1). The article is concerned with the determination of civil rights and obligations, which is what a court does when making a bankruptcy order (see *R v Davison* (1954) 90 CLR 353, in which the High Court of Australia held that proceedings on a debtor's petition are judicial rather than administrative in character).

CREDITOR'S PETITION

Who may petition as a creditor?

80.6 A creditor can present a petition only in respect of a liquidated debt payable immediately or at some certain, future time (Insolvency Act 1986, s. 267(2)(b)) and the debt must be at least £750 (s. 267(2)(a) and (4)). A secured creditor cannot petition (s. 267(2)(b)) unless the petition states that if a bankruptcy order is made, the creditor will surrender the security for the benefit of all creditors (s. 269(1)(a)). A partially secured creditor may divide the debt into a secured and an unsecured part and petition in respect of the unsecured part (s. 269(1)(b) and (2)).

For restrictions on who may petition as a creditor when the debtor's centre of main interests is in another EU State (other than Denmark) and main insolvency proceedings have not been opened in that State, see **80.5**.

Whether or not a claim is provable in bankruptcy is determined by IR 1986, r. 12.3. Any obligation arising under an order made in family proceedings is not provable (r. 12.3(2)(a)) and this leads to difficult problems in relation to orders made in foreign matrimonial proceedings, see *Cartwright v Cartwright* [2002] EWCA Civ 931, *The Times*, 31 July 2002.

A claim which, though it could be enforced against the debtor in proceedings outside bankruptcy, is not provable in bankruptcy is theoretically sufficient to entitle the claimant to petition for bankruptcy, but in practice the court would not make an order on the petition, because the petitioner would have no interest in the proceedings (*Levy v Legal Services Commission* [2001] 1 All ER 895). It is submitted that a person with a claim against an individual which is wholly unenforceable (for example, because it is statute-barred) is not a creditor and has no standing to petition for bankruptcy.

Service of a statutory demand

80.7 The effect of the Insolvency Act 1986, ss. 267 and 268, is that a creditor who presents a petition in respect of a debt which is payable immediately must prove that the debtor appears to be unable to pay it, and this may be proved only by showing either that a statutory demand for the debt was served on the debtor and not complied with or (if the debt is a judgment debt) that execution issued in respect of it was returned wholly or partly unsatisfied. (Proof of apparent inability to pay a judgment debt may be either by unsatisfied judgment or by failure to comply with a statutory demand.) The demand must be in the prescribed form, which is **form 6.1** in IR 1986, sch. 4 (or **form 6.2** if the debt is a judgment debt). Similarly, a creditor who presents a petition in respect of a debt which is payable at some certain, future time must prove that the debtor appears to have no reasonable prospect of being able to pay the debt, and this may be proved only by showing that a statutory demand for the creditor to establish a reasonable prospect of paying was not complied with. The prescribed form for a statutory demand for a future debt is **form 6.3**.

Where a debt is owed to joint creditors, one of them alone may make a statutory demand for it, provided payment to that one creditor would discharge the debt (*Mahmood v Penrose* [2004] EWHC 1500 (Ch), LTL 13/5/2004).

A statutory demand may be for a sum in a foreign currency: tendering the sterling equivalent of the amount demanded in a foreign currency would be regarded as compounding the debt in a manner which the creditor could not reasonably refuse (*Re a Debtor (No. 51-SD-1991)* [1992] 1 WLR 1294).

The creditor is under an obligation to do all that is reasonable in the circumstances to bring the statutory demand to the debtor's attention (IR 1986, r. 6.3(2)). If practicable in the particular circumstances, there must be personal service of the demand in accordance with **CPR, r. 6.4** (IR 1986, r. 6.3(2)). Where prompt personal service is not possible, service may be effected by other means such as first-class post or insertion through a letter box (**PD Insolvency Proceedings, para. 11.1**). If the debt is a judgment debt, service of the statutory demand may be by newspaper advertisement if the debtor has absconded or is avoiding service and there is no real prospect of recovering the debt by execution (IR 1986, r. 6.3(3); **PD Insolvency Proceedings, para. 11.2**). Information on service abroad (for which court permission is not required) is given in **PD Insolvency Proceedings, para. 10**.

When the petition is filed in court it must be accompanied by written evidence of service in accordance with IR 1986, r. 6.11, and **PD Insolvency Proceedings, para. 13**. The prescribed forms of evidence of service are **form 6.11** and, for substituted service, 6.12, in IR 1986, sch. 4.

Application to set aside a statutory demand

An individual on whom a statutory demand has been served may apply under IR 1986, r. 6.4, **80.8**
to the appropriate court for an order setting the statutory demand aside. Rule 6.4(2) provides that the appropriate court is normally the court to which the debtor may present his or her own petition in accordance with r. 6.40 (see **80.4**), but it is the High Court where the creditor is a minister of the Crown or a government department intending to petition in the High Court under r. 6.9(1)(a) (see **80.4**), which intention must be stated in the statutory demand. An application to set aside a statutory demand must be made within 18 days of service of the demand (r. 6.4(1)). It is made using **form 6.4** in IR 1986, sch. 4, which must be accompanied by written evidence in **form 6.5**. No court fee is charged (**CPFO, note following fee 3.12**). For further details see **PD Insolvency Proceedings, para. 12**, and IR 1986, r. 6.5.

The circumstances in which the court may grant an application to set aside a statutory demand are listed in r. 6.5(4) as follows:

(a) the debtor appears to have a counterclaim, set-off or cross-demand which equals or exceeds the amount of the debt or debts specified in the statutory demand; or
(b) the debt is disputed on grounds which appear to the court to be substantial; or
(c) it appears that the creditor holds some security in respect of the debt claimed by the demand, and either rule 6.1(5) [which requires that the statutory demand must be only for the net amount of the debt after deducting the value of the security] is not complied with in respect of it, or the court is satisfied that the value of the security equals or exceeds the full amount of the debt; or
(d) the court is satisfied, on other grounds, that the demand ought to be set aside.

In r. 6.5(4)(a) the terms 'counterclaim' and 'cross-demand' comprehend counter-claims and cross-demands that are not legal or equitable set-offs, and a statutory demand based on dishonour of a cheque or other bill of exchange may be set aside if the debtor has a counterclaim or cross-demand, even if it would not be a defence to the claim on the bill or cheque (*Hofer v Strawson* [1999] 2 BCLC 336). If a court has already dismissed proceedings brought by the debtor advancing the counterclaim etc. which is said to equal or exceed the debt claimed in a statutory demand, the bankruptcy court may nevertheless set aside the statutory demand if persuaded that an appeal against the first decision has a realistic, as opposed to fanciful, prospect of success (*Society of Lloyd's v Bowman* [2003] EWCA Civ 1886, LTL 19/12/2003).

Under r. 6.5(4)(d) a statutory demand will be set aside if no bankruptcy order would be made on a petition based on not complying with it, for example, because it is for an unprovable debt (*Levy v Legal Services Commission* [2001] 1 All ER 895).

If the amount of the debt is overstated in the demand, the debtor will be deemed to have complied with it if the correct amount is paid within the time allowed (IR 1986, r. 6.25(3)).

A creditor's petition in respect of a debt or debts cannot be presented at a time when there is an outstanding application to set aside a statutory demand served in respect of the debt or any of the debts (Insolvency Act 1986, s. 267(2)(d)). An application made out of time, and for which the court has not extended time, does not count for the purposes of s. 267(2)(d) (*Re Chohan* (2000) LTL 7/11/2000), nor does an appeal against a dismissed application (*Hurst v Bennett* (2001) *The Independent*, 9 April 2001).

Usually, a court's decision to set aside a statutory demand does not determine any substantive dispute about the existence or size of the debt demanded. It follows that on an appeal against a decision to set aside, further evidence concerning that dispute may be admitted even if it does not satisfy the tests established in *Ladd v Marshall* [1954] 1 WLR 1489 (see **72.13** and **72.14**) (*Heavy Duty Parts Ltd v Anelay* [2004] EWHC 960 (Ch), LTL 5/4/2004). The court should consider: (a) the importance of the evidence to the party seeking to adduce it, (b) the reasons for not adducing it in the court below, (c) the extent of any prejudice which its admission would cause the opposing party, and (d) the overriding objective (*Sadrolashrafi v Marvel International Food Logistics Ltd* [2004] EWHC 777 (Ch), LTL 15/4/2004, at [16]).

If the person who served the statutory demand ought to have known of the circumstances which would lead to it being set aside, the costs of applying under r. 6.4 may be awarded on an indemnity basis (*Re Kirkman-Moeller* [2005] EWHC 205 (Ch), LTL 19/1/2005 (sub nom. *Re Moller*)).

Form and contents of creditor's petition

80.9 There are three prescribed forms for a creditor's petition (forms 6.7, 6.8 and 6.9 in IR 1986, sch. 4). **Form 6.7** is used when the petition is based on failure to comply with a statutory demand for a liquidated sum payable immediately. Form 6.8 is used when the petition is based on failure to comply with a statutory demand for a liquidated sum payable at a future date. Form 6.9 is used for a petition based on partially or wholly unsatisfied execution.

There is detailed advice on creditors' bankruptcy petitions in **PD Insolvency Proceedings, paras 15.1** to 15.7.

Verification of creditor's petition

80.10 A creditor's petition must be verified by affidavit or witness statement, using **form 6.13** in IR 1986, sch. 4 (IR 1986, rr. 6.12 and 7.57(5) and (7)). The verification avers that the statements in the petition are true, or are true to the best of the deponent's knowledge, information and belief. If the petition is based on failure to comply with a statutory demand and more than four months have elapsed since the demand was served, the verifying affidavit or witness statement must state the reasons for the delay (r. 6.12(7)).

The verifying affidavit or witness statement, though it may be hearsay, is prima facie evidence of the statements in the petition to which it relates (r. 6.12(6)).

Rule 6.12(4) provides that the verifying affidavit or witness statement must be made by:

(a) the petitioner (or if there are two or more petitioners, any one of them); or

(b) some person such as a director, company secretary or similar company officer, or a solicitor, who has been concerned in the matters giving rise to the presentation of the petition; or

(c) some responsible person who is duly authorised to make the affidavit or witness statement and has the requisite knowledge of those matters.

In cases (b) and (c) the person verifying the petition must state the capacity in which, and the authority by which, he or she does so, and the means of knowing the matters contained in the written evidence (r. 6.12(5)).

Filing of creditor's petition and fixing of venue

A creditor's bankruptcy petition must be filed in court together with one copy for service on the debtor and one copy to be exhibited to the affidavit or witness statement verifying service (IR 1986, r. 6.10(1) and (3)). A court officer seals all copies of the petition and fixes a venue for hearing it, which is endorsed on all copies (r. 6.10(3) and (5)). **80.11**

The court will forthwith send notice of the petition to the Chief Land Registrar to be noted in the register of pending actions (r. 6.13). If the petition is dismissed, or withdrawn with the court's permission, the court will order the registration of the petition as a pending action to be vacated (r. 6.27).

A debtor is allowed three weeks to comply with a statutory demand and normally a petition based on failure to comply with a statutory demand cannot be presented until the three weeks have elapsed. However, the Insolvency Act 1986, s. 270, permits presentation before the three weeks have elapsed if there is a serious possibility that the debtor's property or the value of any of the debtor's property will be significantly diminished during the three weeks, and the petition contains a statement to that effect.

Fee and deposit

On filing a creditor's bankruptcy petition, a court fee of £190 must be paid (**CPFO, fee 3.1(b)**). The petitioner must deposit £390 as security for the administration fee which will become payable to the official receiver if a bankruptcy order is made and transmitted to the official receiver (Insolvency Act 1986, s. 415(3); Insolvency Proceedings (Fees) Order 2004 (SI 2004/593), art. 6(1)). A petition cannot be filed unless the receipt for the deposit is produced (IR 1986, r. 6.10(2)). For details of the payment procedure see **PD Insolvency Proceedings, para. 15.8**. The deposit is security for the official receiver's administration fee and must be used to discharge that fee to the extent that the assets in the bankrupt's estate are insufficient (SI 2004/593, art. 6(2)); the administration fee is £1,625 (SI 2004/593, sch. 2, fee B1). The court must transmit the deposit to its official receiver (SI 2004/593, art. 6(3)). If a bankruptcy order is made, any part of the deposit which is not required to pay the administration fee must be returned (art. 6(5)). If the petition is dismissed or withdrawn, the whole of the deposit must be repaid (art. 6(4)). The court fee is not repayable. **80.12**

Service of creditor's petition

The debtor must be served personally with a sealed copy of a creditor's petition (IR 1986, r. 6.14(1)). If the court is satisfied by written evidence that prompt personal service cannot be effected because the debtor is avoiding service, or for any other cause, it may make an order for substituted service to be effected in such manner as it thinks fit (r. 6.14(2)). **PD Insolvency Proceedings, para. 11.4**, sets out what must normally be done to justify an order for substituted service. If the debtor dies before service of the petition, the court may order it to be served on the deceased's personal representatives, or on such other persons as it thinks fit (IR 1986, r. 6.16). **80.13**

If a bankruptcy petition asks for the opening of secondary proceedings against a debtor who is already the subject of main insolvency proceedings in another EU State (see **80.5**), a copy of the petition must be sent to a member State liquidator appointed in the main proceedings (IR

1986, r. 6.14(5)). Rule 6.14(5) does not make allowance for the member State liquidator being the petitioner.

Proof of service

80.14 Service of a creditor's bankruptcy petition must be proved by written evidence using **form 6.17** (personal service) or form 6.18 (substituted service) in IR 1986, sch. 4, which must be filed in court immediately after service (IR 1986, r. 6.15).

Control of transactions and litigation while petition is pending

80.15 If a bankruptcy order is made, all dispositions of the debtor's property since the bankruptcy petition was presented are void unless made with the consent of the court or subsequently ratified by the court (Insolvency Act 1986, s. 284). For control of litigation while a bankruptcy petition is pending see **81.23**.

Appointment of interim receiver

80.16 At any time after the presentation of a bankruptcy petition, but before a bankruptcy order is made, the court may, under the Insolvency Act 1986, s. 286, appoint the official receiver as interim receiver of the debtor's property. It must be shown that the appointment is necessary for the protection of the debtor's property (s. 286(1)).

An application for the appointment of an interim receiver may be made by the debtor or any creditor, or, if the proceedings are secondary proceedings (see **80.5**), a temporary administrator or member State liquidator appointed in the main proceedings (IR 1986, r. 6.51(1)). It is made by ordinary application (see **81.1** to **81.5**), which must be supported by written evidence showing (r. 6.51(2)):

(a) the grounds for the appointment;
(b) whether or not the official receiver has been informed of the application and has been provided with a copy of it;
(c) whether, to the applicant's knowledge, an IVA has been proposed or is in force;
(d) the applicant's estimate of the value of the property or business in respect of which the interim receiver is to be appointed.

The applicant must send copies of the application and evidence to the official receiver (r. 6.51(4)), who may attend the hearing of the application and make representations (r. 6.51(5)). If it is not possible to send these copies, the official receiver must at least be informed of the application in time to attend the hearing (r. 6.51(4)).

The court may make the appointment applied for, on such terms as it thinks fit, if satisfied that sufficient grounds are shown for the appointment (r. 6.51(6)).

Before an order appointing the official receiver as interim receiver of a debtor may be issued, the applicant must deposit with the official receiver such sum as the court directs to cover remuneration and expenses (r. 6.53(1)). Alternatively, security for the amount may be given if the official receiver agrees (ibid.).

From time to time the official receiver may apply to the court to order a further amount to be deposited or secured, and if the order is not complied with within two days of service, the court may discharge the official receiver's appointment as interim receiver (r. 6.53(2)).

The court's order of appointment must state the nature of and describe the property to which the appointment relates and state what duties are to be performed in relation to the debtor's affairs (IR 1986, r. 6.52(1)). For control of litigation against a debtor when an interim receiver has been appointed see **81.24**.

Permission to withdraw a petition

80.17 A bankruptcy petition cannot be withdrawn without the court's permission (Insolvency Act 1986, s. 266(2)). Permission to withdraw a creditor's petition will not be given until the petition is heard (IR 1986, r. 6.32(3)). An application to withdraw a petition or for it to be dismissed is made by ordinary application (see **81.1** to **81.5**). Unless the court otherwise orders, written evidence must be filed specifying the grounds of the application and the circumstances in which it is made (r. 6.32(1)). If any payment has been made to the petitioner since the petition was filed, the written evidence must include the information set out in r. 6.32(2), which will reveal whether the payment might be avoided under the Insolvency Act 1986, s. 284, if another creditor were to be substituted as petitioner (see **80.20**) and a bankruptcy order made.

Opposition by debtor

80.18 If the debtor intends to oppose a creditor's bankruptcy petition, a notice specifying the grounds of objection must be filed in court at least seven days before the day fixed for the hearing (IR 1986, r. 6.21). A copy must be sent to the petitioner or the petitioner's solicitor (r. 6.21).

Notice of appearance

80.19 By IR 1986, r. 6.23, any creditor wishing to appear on the hearing of a creditor's bankruptcy petition must send notice to the petitioner to arrive not later than 4 p.m. on the business day before the date appointed for the hearing (or the date of an adjournment). 'Business day' is defined in r. 13.13(1) (see **79.7**).

A notice of appearance must be in form 6.20 in IR 1986, sch. 4, and must state whether the appearance will be to support or oppose the petition (r. 6.23(2)(b)). The notice must also state the name and address of the person giving it, and any telephone number and reference which may be required for communication with that person or with any other person (to be also specified in the notice) authorised to speak or act on behalf of the person giving the notice (r. 6.23(2)(a)). The notice must also state the amount and nature of the debt claimed by the person giving the notice (r. 6.23(2)(c)).

The petitioner must prepare for the court a list of persons who have given notice of intention to appear, stating whether they support or oppose the petition, and must hand a copy of the list to the court before the commencement of the hearing (IR 1986, r. 6.24; prescribed form is form 6.21 in sch. 4).

A person who has not given notice in accordance with r. 6.23 may appear on the hearing of the petition only with the permission of the court (r. 6.23(4)).

The petitioner must add to the list required by r. 6.24 the name of anyone given leave by the court to appear without having given proper notice (r. 6.24(4)).

Substitution of petitioner

80.20 When a bankruptcy petition is pending, r. 6.30 of IR 1986 permits the substitution of a new petitioner if the original petitioner:

(a) is subsequently found not entitled to petition;
(b) consents to withdraw the petition;
(c) consents to allow the petition to be dismissed;
(d) consents to an adjournment of the petition;
(e) fails to appear in support of the petition when it is called on in court on the day originally fixed for the hearing or on a day to which it is adjourned; or
(f) appears when the petition is called on in court but does not apply for an order in the terms of the prayer of the petition.

Any creditor who has (a) given notice of intention to appear on the hearing, (b) is desirous of prosecuting the petition, and (c) would have been in a position to petition for the debtor's bankruptcy on the date on which the present petition was presented, may be substituted as petitioner (IR 1986, r. 6.30(2)).

It is clear that it was intended to amend r. 6.30 to provide that if a bankruptcy petition asks for the opening of secondary proceedings (see **80.5**), and the member State liquidator appointed in the main proceedings is not the petitioner, that member State liquidator may be substituted as petitioner if he or she is desirous of prosecuting the petition. This would parallel the provision made in companies winding up (see **79.60**). In fact the amending statutory instrument (the Insolvency (Amendment) Rules 2002 (SI 2002/1307)) only inserts a meaningless reference to 'the member State liquidator' in IR 1986, r. 6.30(2)(c).

It is also possible to make a change of carriage order at the hearing of the petition (see **80.26**).

Change of venue

80.21 **Extension of time for hearing** If a creditor's bankruptcy petition has not been served, the petitioner may apply under IR 1986, r. 6.28, for the court to appoint another venue for the hearing. The application is made by ordinary application (see **81.1** to **81.5**), which must state the reasons why the petition has not been served (r. 6.28(2)). If another date is appointed, the petitioner must forthwith notify any creditor who has given notice of intention to appear on the hearing.

80.22 **Adjournment** If the court adjourns the hearing of a creditor's bankruptcy petition, the petitioner must (unless the court otherwise directs) notify the debtor and any creditor who has given notice of intention to appear on the hearing (IR 1986, r. 6.29).

80.23 **Expedited hearing** Normally the hearing of a creditor's bankruptcy petition cannot take place until 14 days after it was served on the debtor (IR 1986, r. 6.18(1)). However, the court may, under r. 6.18(2), hear the petition at an earlier date if:

(a) it appears that the debtor has absconded;
(b) the court is satisfied that it is a proper case for an expedited hearing; or
(c) the debtor consents.

HEARING A CREDITOR'S PETITION AND MAKING THE ORDER

Orders that the court may make

80.24 On the hearing of a creditor's bankruptcy petition, the court may make a bankruptcy order if satisfied that the statements in the petition are true, and that the debt on which it is founded has not been paid, or secured or compounded for (or, if it is a future debt, that the debtor has no reasonable prospect of being able to pay when it falls due) (Insolvency Act 1986, s. 271(1); IR 1986, r. 6.25(1)). The court will normally be satisfied that a debt has not been paid, or secured or compounded for if a certificate in the form set out in **PD Insolvency Proceedings, para. 15.9**, is provided.

If the petition is in respect of a judgment debt, or a sum ordered to be paid by a court, the court may stay or dismiss the petition if an appeal is pending from the judgment or order, or if execution of the judgment has been stayed (IR 1986, r. 6.25(2)). On a petition in respect of a judgment debt, if there is no appeal against or application to stay judgment, the only grounds on which the correctness of the judgment may be challenged are that: (a) it was obtained fraudulently, (b) it was obtained by collusion between the debtor and the claimant, or (c) there was a miscarriage of justice (*Dawodu v American Express Bank* (2001) LTL 31/5/2001).

A petition will not be dismissed on the ground that the amount of the debt was overstated in a statutory demand, unless the debtor notified the creditor, within the three weeks allowed for complying with the demand, that he or she disputed its validity (r. 6.25(3)).

Ordinarily, a debtor will not be permitted to re-argue, on the hearing of a petition, a contention that the statutory demand was invalid if that contention has already been rejected on a substantive hearing of an application to set aside the statutory demand (*Turner v Royal*

Bank of Scotland plc [2000] BPIR 683). The same applies if a contention advanced in preparation for an application to set aside was abandoned (*Adams v Mason Bullock* [2004] EWHC 2910 (Ch), *The Times*, 6 January 2005).

Non-appearance of creditor

80.25 If the petitioning creditor fails to appear on the hearing of the petition, no subsequent petition against the same debtor may be presented by the same creditor in respect of the same debt, unless the court to which the first petition was presented gives permission (IR 1986, r. 6.26). There is detailed consideration of r. 6.26 in *Omgate Ltd v Gordon* (2001) LTL 24/4/2001.

Change of carriage of creditor's petition

80.26 At the hearing of a creditor's petition, the court may, under IR 1986, r. 6.31, give another creditor carriage of the petition if it appears that the petitioning creditor:

(a) intends by any means to secure the postponement, adjournment or withdrawal of the petition; or
(b) does not intend to prosecute the petition, either diligently or at all.

After a change of carriage order the petition is still based on the original petitioner's debt, unlike the position where there is a substitution of petitioner. This means that the court cannot make a bankruptcy order if the original petitioner's debt has been paid or secured or compounded for (Insolvency Act 1986, s. 271(1)). However, where the original petitioner wishes to withdraw the petition after coming to an arrangement with the debtor, the court can give carriage of the petition to another creditor and adjourn it so that the creditor given carriage can check that the arrangement is carried out and there is no further compromise (*Re Purvis* [1997] 3 All ER 663).

Settlement and transmission of bankruptcy order

80.27 If a bankruptcy order is made on a creditor's petition, the court will settle it (IR 1986, r. 6.33(1)). Two sealed copies will be sent to the official receiver, who will forthwith send one to the bankrupt (r. 6.34(1)).

The official receiver will send a notice to the Chief Land Registrar for registration in the register of writs and orders affecting land, cause the bankruptcy order to be advertised in such newspaper as the official receiver thinks fit, cause the order to be gazetted, and cause prescribed information to be entered in the individual insolvency register (rr. 6.34(2) and 6A.4). However, the bankrupt or a creditor may apply to the court for an order requiring the official receiver not to do these things pending a further order by the court (r. 6.34(3)). An application for such an order is made by ordinary application (see **81.1** to **81.5**) and must be supported by written evidence of the grounds for applying (r. 6.34(3)). If the order is made, the applicant must deliver it forthwith to the official receiver (r. 6.34(4)).

For control of litigation against a bankrupt see **81.25**.

DEBTOR'S PETITION

Form and contents of debtor's petition

80.28 The only ground on which a debtor may petition for his or her own bankruptcy is inability to pay his or her debts (Insolvency Act 1986, s. 272(1)) and that fact must be admitted in the petition (IR 1986, r. 6.39(1)). The prescribed form of petition is **form 6.27** in IR 1986, sch. 4. The petition must be accompanied by a statement of the petitioner's affairs (Insolvency Act 1986, s. 272(2)), which must be in **form 6.28** in IR 1986, sch. 4, and must be verified by affidavit or by witness statement verified by a statement of truth (IR 1986, rr. 6.41(1), 6.68 and 7.57(5) and (7)). The petition itself does not have to be verified.

If a debtor's centre of main interests is in another EU State (apart from Denmark) and insolvency proceedings have not yet been opened in that State, the debtor is not entitled to apply for a bankruptcy order to made here, unless insolvency proceedings cannot be opened in the State where the debtor's centre of main interests is located, because of the conditions laid down by the law of that State (Council Regulation (EC) No. 1346/2000, art. 4).

Filing of petition and fixing of venue

80.29 A debtor's petition and statement of affairs must be filed with three copies of the petition and two copies of the statement (IR 1986, r. 6.42(1)). The court may hear the petition forthwith or fix a venue for the hearing (r. 6.42(2)). If there is an IVA in force for the debtor, the court must fix a venue and give at least 14 days' notice of it to the IVA supervisor, who may appear and be heard on the petition (r. 6.42(2A)). If a venue is fixed, it is endorsed on the copies of the petition. One copy of the petition and of the statement of affairs is sent to the official receiver by the court, unless the court directs the petitioner to deliver it (r. 6.42(3), (4) and (6)). The court will forthwith send notice of the petition to the Chief Land Registrar to be noted in the register of pending actions (IR 1986, r. 6.43).

Fee and deposit

80.30 A court fee and deposit must be paid, as for a creditor's petition (see **80.12**), except that the fee is £150 (**CPFO, fee 3.1(a)**) and the deposit is £325 (Insolvency Proceedings (Fees) Order 2004 (SI 2004/593), art. 6(1)). A petition cannot be filed unless the receipt for the deposit is produced (IR 1986, r. 6.42(1)). Though the court fee may be remitted because of the petitioner's poverty (**CPFO, art. 4**) the deposit will not (*R v Lord Chancellor, ex parte Lightfoot* [2000] QB 597).

Control of transactions and litigation while petition is pending

80.31 The rules on control of transactions and litigation while a petition is pending (see **80.15**) apply to a debtor's petition as well as to a creditor's petition.

Appointment of interim receiver

80.32 During the period when a debtor's petition is pending an interim receiver may be appointed, following the procedure set out in **80.16**.

Investigation of possibility of voluntary arrangement

80.33 Section 273 of the Insolvency Act 1986 provides for special treatment of a debtor's petition where the aggregate amount of the debtor's unsecured debts is less than £40,000 and the debtor has not, within the five years preceding presentation of the present petition:

(a) been adjudged bankrupt; or
(b) made a composition with his or her creditors; or
(c) made a scheme of arrangement of his or her affairs.

If, in such a case, it appears that the debtor's assets are worth at least £4,000, the court may appoint a qualified insolvency practitioner to investigate, under s. 274, whether an IVA can be made. The court will send the appointed practitioner a sealed copy of the order of appointment and copies of the petition and statement of affairs (IR 1986, r. 6.44(1)(a)). It will also fix a venue for the practitioner's report to be considered and send notice of the venue to the practitioner and the debtor (r. 6.44(1)(b) and (c)). The court may also appoint the practitioner interim receiver of the debtor's property (Insolvency Act 1986, s. 286(2)). On receipt of the report, the court will pay the practitioner a fee of £310 out of the petitioner's deposit (see **80.30**) (Insolvency Proceedings (Fees) Order 2004 (SI 2004/593), art. 5). On consideration of the insolvency practitioner's report the court may either make an interim order imposing a moratorium while a proposed IVA is considered (see **80.36**) or, if it seems that an IVA would not succeed, make a bankruptcy order (Insolvency Act 1986, s. 274(3)).

Settlement and transmission of order

The procedures for settlement and transmission of a bankruptcy order made on a debtor's petition are set out in IR 1986, rr. 6.45 and 6.46, and are the same as for an order made on a creditor's petition (see **80.27**). **80.34**

INDIVIDUAL VOLUNTARY ARRANGEMENTS

Nature of voluntary arrangements

An individual who is either an undischarged bankrupt or is able to petition for his or her own bankruptcy may, under part VIII (ss. 252 to 263G) of the Insolvency Act 1986, propose to his or her creditors a composition in satisfaction of their debts or a scheme of arrangement of his or her affairs. A composition or scheme under part VIII is referred to in that part as a 'voluntary arrangement' and in IR 1986 as an individual voluntary arrangement, which is usually abbreviated as IVA. **80.35**

If the procedures of part VIII are followed, a debtor's composition or scheme of arrangement becomes binding on all creditors when it is approved by three quarters of the creditors (by value of their unsecured debts) who vote (Insolvency Act 1986, ss. 260(2) and 263D(2); IR 1986, rr. 5.23 and 5.43). A 'supervisor', who must be a qualified insolvency practitioner or the official receiver, must act in relation to an IVA either as trustee or otherwise for the purpose of supervising its implementation (s. 253(2)).

Undischarged bankrupts may use the procedure for fast-track voluntary arrangement in ss. 263A to 263G (see **80.36**).

As explained in **80.28**, a debtor whose centre of main interests is in another EU State (apart from Denmark) is not usually able to petition for his or her own bankruptcy here if main insolvency proceedings have not been opened in that State (Council Regulation (EC) No. 1346/2000, art. 4). It follows that such a person cannot propose an IVA. If main insolvency proceedings have been opened in the State where the centre of the debtor's main interests is located, the only form of secondary proceedings which may be opened here is bankruptcy and an IVA cannot be proposed (arts 2(c) and 3(3)).

Proposal and interim order

The following procedures do not apply where the court has appointed an insolvency practitioner under the Insolvency Act 1986, s. 273, to investigate the possibility of an IVA in a small bankruptcy (see **80.33**). **80.36**

The first stage in creating an IVA is to prepare a proposal for a composition or scheme and persuade someone to be the debtor's nominee for supervisor if the IVA is approved. The official receiver may be nominated if the debtor is an undischarged bankrupt (Insolvency Act 1986, s. 389B). Otherwise, at present, the nominee must be a qualified insolvency practitioner, who will usually have advised on the preparation of the proposal.

If the official receiver is the nominee, it is likely that the fast-track procedure will be used (s. 263A). In the fast-track procedure the debtor's proposal, conforming with IR 1986, r. 5.37, is submitted to the official receiver with a statement of affairs (Insolvency Act 1986, s. 263B(1)). The official receiver will invite creditors to approve the proposal if he or she considers that it has a reasonable prospect of being approved and implemented (s. 263B(2)).

If the fast-track procedure is not being used, the proposal must conform with IR 1986, r. 5.3, and must be sent to the intended nominee with a notice conforming with r. 5.4. A statement of affairs conforming with r. 5.5 must follow within seven days.

An application may be made to the court under the Insolvency Act 1986, s. 253, for an interim order under s. 252. In the fast-track procedure, the application cannot be made until the official receiver has decided whether or not to invite creditors to approve the proposal (s. 263B(5)). While it is in force, the effect of an interim order is, by s. 252(2), that:

(a) no bankruptcy petition relating to the debtor may be presented or proceeded with;
(b) no other proceedings, and no execution or other legal process, may be commenced or continued against the debtor or his or her property except with the permission of the court.

If the debtor is an undischarged bankrupt, the application for an interim order may be by the debtor, his or her trustee in bankruptcy or the official receiver; in any other case only the debtor may apply (s. 253(3)). If the debtor is an undischarged bankrupt, the application must be made to the court having the conduct of the bankruptcy and is made by ordinary application (see **81.1** to **81.5**) in those bankruptcy proceedings (IR 1986, r. 5.8(3)). Otherwise the application is to a court in which the debtor would be entitled to present his or her own bankruptcy petition (see **80.4**) and is made by originating application (see **81.1** to **81.5**) (r. 5.8(1)). The application must contain sufficient information to establish that it is brought in the appropriate court (r. 5.8(2)). The application must be accompanied by written evidence of the matters listed in r. 5.7(1), a copy of the r. 5.4 notice to the intended nominee endorsed with his or her agreement to act, and a copy of the debtor's proposal (r. 5.7(2)).

On receiving an application for an interim order, the court will fix a venue for hearing it (IR 1986, r. 5.7(3)). If the debtor is an undischarged bankrupt, the applicant must give at least two days' notice of the hearing to the nominee (r. 5.7(4)(c)) and to whichever of the following is not the applicant: the bankrupt, the official receiver, the trustee in bankruptcy (r. 5.7(4)(a)). Otherwise the applicant must give notice to the nominee and to any creditor who has, to the applicant's knowledge, presented a bankruptcy petition against him or her (r. 5.7(4)(b) and (c)). Any of the persons given notice under r. 5.7(4) may appear or be represented at the hearing of the application (r. 5.9(1)) and the court must take account of their representations (r. 5.9(2)).

For control of litigation against the debtor while an application for an interim order is pending see **81.22**.

If the court makes an interim order, it will normally last for only 14 days (Insolvency Act 1986, s. 255(6)). At least two days before the order expires, the nominee must submit a report to the court stating whether, in his or her opinion, a meeting of creditors should be summoned to consider the proposed IVA, and, if so, when (s. 256(1); IR 1986, r. 5.11(1)). On making an interim order the court must fix a venue for consideration of that report (r. 5.9(3)). Any of the persons given notice under r. 5.5(4) may appear or be represented at the hearing to consider the report (r. 5.13(1)).

If there is a proposal prepared in good faith by respected insolvency practitioners and a reputable nominee, the court will usually make an interim order, leaving it to the creditors to decide whether to approve the proposal. However, the court has a discretion to refuse to make an interim order and will refuse one if it is clear that bankruptcy will be preferable to an IVA (*Hurst v Kroll Buchler Phillips Ltd* [2002] EWHC 2688 (Ch), LTL 4/12/2002).

If there is no application for an interim order, and the fast-track procedure is not being used, the nominee reports to the court in accordance with the Insolvency Act 1986, s. 256A, and IR 1986, rr. 5.14 and 5.15.

If the nominee's report to the court under the Insolvency Act 1986, s. 256 (interim order) or s. 256A (no interim order), opines that a creditors' meeting should be held, the nominee will summon one unless the court otherwise directs (s. 257(1)). If an interim order has been made, the court will direct that it shall continue in force to enable the proposal to be considered (s. 256(5)).

In the fast-track procedure, if the official receiver agrees to act as nominee, the proposal is not reported to the court. Instead the official receiver invites creditors to vote by post on the proposal (IR 1986, rr. 5.39 to 5.43).

Approval of voluntary arrangement

If a meeting of creditors is held, its chairman must report the result to the court (Insolvency Act 1986, s. 259(1); IR 1986, r. 5.27). **80.37**

If the result is that the creditors have declined to approve the proposal, the court may discharge any interim order (s. 259(2)).

If the creditors accept the proposal, the IVA will take effect as if made at the meeting (s. 260(1) and (2)) and any interim order will cease to have effect 28 days after the chairman's report is made to the court (s. 260(4)). The chairman must report the approval of the IVA to the Secretary of State for entry in the register of IVAs (IR 1986, rr. 5.28 and 5.29). If a bankruptcy petition is pending against the debtor, it is deemed to have been dismissed when the interim order ceases to have effect, unless the court orders otherwise (Insolvency Act 1986, s. 260(5)). If the debtor is an undischarged bankrupt, the court must annul the bankruptcy order on an application made by the bankrupt or by the official receiver (s. 261; IR 1986, rr. 5.51 to 5.56, 5.60 and 5.61).

It is unnecessary to obtain the court's approval of an IVA which has been approved by a creditors' meeting, but a dissentient creditor may apply to the court under s. 262 to revoke or suspend the approval because the creditor's interests are prejudiced by the IVA and/or the meeting was vitiated by a material irregularity. Such an application is made by ordinary application (see **81.1** to **81.5**) in the IVA proceedings and must be made within 28 days after the chairman's report is made to the court. For the procedure if a revocation or suspension order is made see IR 1986, r. 5.30. An application under the Insolvency Act 1986, s. 262, may also be made by the nominee, the official receiver or the debtor. If the meeting declined to approve the proposal, those persons can also apply under s. 262 for an order directing a further meeting to reconsider the proposal on the ground that there was a material irregularity in the first meeting.

In the fast-track procedure, the official receiver must report to the court whether the proposal has been approved or rejected by the creditors (s. 263C). If the official receiver reports approval, the IVA takes effect (s. 263D(1) and (2)) and the court must annul the bankruptcy order on the application of the official receiver (s. 263D(3); IR 1986, rr. 5.57 to 5.61). Section 263F provides for revocation of a fast-track IVA by the court on an application made within 28 days of delivery of the official receiver's s. 263C report. The procedure if a revocation order is made is in IR 1986, r. 5.46.

BANKRUPTCY PETITION ALLEGING DEFAULT IN CONNECTION WITH VOLUNTARY ARRANGEMENT

A bankruptcy petition may be presented against a debtor who has entered into an approved IVA, but the court will not make a bankruptcy order unless it is satisfied that one of the circumstances listed in the Insolvency Act 1986, s. 276(1), exists. Those circumstances are failure by the debtor to comply with his or her obligations under the IVA, provision of false or misleading information to procure approval of the IVA, and failure of the debtor to co-operate with the IVA supervisor. It is possible to make a bankruptcy order even though a default has been remedied (*Carter-Knight v Peat* (2000) *The Times*, 11 August 2000). A petition may be presented by the supervisor of, or any person (other than the debtor) who is for the time being bound by, the IVA (s. 264(1)(c)) and is subject to the same rules as a creditor's petition (IR 1986, r. 6.6). If the petitioner is not the supervisor of the IVA, an extra copy of the petition must be filed for service on the supervisor (IR 1986, rr. 6.10(3) and 6.14(4)). **80.38**

Chapter 81 Insolvency Applications and Appeals

APPLICATIONS IN INSOLVENCY PROCEEDINGS

Procedural rules

81.1 Applications in insolvency proceedings are governed by rr. 7.1 to 7.10 of the Insolvency Rules 1986 (SI 1986/1925) (IR 1986). Rules 7.1 to 7.10 apply, according to r. 7.1, to any application made to the court under the Insolvency Act 1986 or IR 1986, apart from a petition for a winding-up order or an administration application (see **chapter** 79) and a bankruptcy petition (see **chapter** 80). This chapter outlines the general procedural rules relating to applications in insolvency proceedings and discusses in some detail applications to stay, commence or continue litigation against persons who are the subject of insolvency proceedings.

Originating and ordinary applications

81.2 An originating application is an application under the Insolvency Act 1986 or IR 1986 which is not an application in pending proceedings before the court (IR 1986, r. 7.2(1)). This includes, for example, an application for an order forbidding the presentation of a winding-up petition (see 79.28), an application under the Insolvency Act 1986, s. 252, for an interim order, if the applicant is not an undischarged bankrupt (see **80.36**), an application under s. 35 by a receiver or manager of a company's property, appointed out of court, for directions, and any application in a voluntary winding up (*Re Continental Assurance Co. of London plc (No. 2)* [1998] 1 BCLC 583).

An originating application must be in form 7.1 in sch. 4 to IR 1986 (r. 7.2(2)).

An ordinary application is any application under the Insolvency Act 1986 or the IR 1986 which is not an originating application (IR 1986, r. 7.2(1)). This includes any interim application while a petition for a winding-up, administration or bankruptcy order is pending.

An ordinary application must be in **form 7.2** in sch. 4 to the IR 1986 (r. 7.2(2)).

Filing and fee

An insolvency application must be filed in court, accompanied by one copy in any event, plus enough copies for service on every person who is to be served (IR 1986, r. 7.4(1)). **81.3**

The court fee on an originating application is £130 (**CPFO, fee 3.5**). The court fee on an ordinary application is £30 if it is by consent or without notice (**fee 3.11**), or £60 if it is with notice (**fee 3.12**).

Venue, directions, track allocation

When an insolvency application is filed the court will fix a venue for it to be heard (IR 1986, r. 7.4(2)). Applications concerning matters listed in **PD Insolvency Proceedings, paras 5.1** and **9.1**, must be made to the judge. All other applications are made to a registrar in the RCJ or to a district judge or deputy district judge in a district registry or county court, unless that judicial officer does not have power to make the order required, or the judge has given a general or special direction to the contrary (IR 1986, r. 7.6(2); **PD Insolvency Proceedings, paras** 5.2 and 9.2). In the RCJ a general direction has been given that applications relating to the matters listed in **PD Insolvency Proceedings, paras** 5.4 and **9.5**, are to be heard by the court manager. If the registrar or district judge thinks that the matter should properly be decided by the judge, it may be referred up (r. 7.6(3)). **81.4**

The court may at any time give such directions as it thinks fit concerning service or notice of the application, the procedure on the application, and evidence (rr. 7.4(4) and 7.10).

All insolvency proceedings are allocated to the multi-track by IR 1986, r. 7.51(2), and so the provisions of the CPR concerning allocation questionnaires and track allocation do not apply.

An insolvency application before a registrar, district judge or deputy district judge will be heard in private, and any application before the judge may be heard in private (IR 1986, r. 7.6(1)).

Service

Unless the court directs otherwise, a sealed copy of an insolvency application must be served on the respondent named in it (IR 1986, r. 7.4(3)) at least 14 days before the date fixed for the hearing (r. 7.4(5)). **81.5**

In insolvency proceedings in the High Court service of documents is the responsibility of the parties and will not be undertaken by the court (**PD Insolvency Proceedings, para. 1.3**).

Rule 12.11 of the IR 1986 applies **Part 6** of the CPR as regards any matter relating to the service of documents and the giving of notice in insolvency proceedings. The provisions of **Part 6** are supplemented by IR 1986, rr. 12.4, 12.10, 12.12, 12.14, 13.3, 13.4 and 13.5.

Service may be by post (r. 13.3(1)) and any form of post may be used (r. 13.3(2)). Personal service in accordance with **CPR, r. 6.4**, is also permitted (IR 1986, rr. 12.11 and 13.3(3)).

In order for a document to be properly served by post, it must be contained in an envelope addressed to the person on whom service is to be effected, and prepaid for either first or second-class post (r. 12.10(1)). A document to be served by post may be sent to the last known address of the person to be served (r. 12.10(1A)). Service is deemed to be effected by properly addressing, prepaying and posting a letter containing the document (Interpretation Act 1978, s. 7). A posted document is treated as served on the second business day after the date of posting if first-class post is used, or the fourth business day after posting if second-class post is used, unless the contrary is shown (IR 1986, r. 12.10(2) and (3)). For the meaning of 'business day' in IR 1986 see **79.7**. The date of posting is presumed, unless the contrary is shown, to be the date shown in the postmark on the envelope in which the document is contained (r. 12.10(4)).

A notice or other document which is required or authorised under the Insolvency Act 1986 or IR 1986 to be given to a person may be given instead to a solicitor whom that person has indicated is authorised to accept service on that person's behalf (IR 1986, r. 13.4).

Where two or more persons are acting jointly as the responsible insolvency practitioner in any proceedings, delivery of a document to one of them is to be treated as delivery to them all (r. 13.5).

Where, for the purposes of insolvency proceedings, any process or order of the court, or other document, is required to be served on a person who is not in England and Wales, the court may order service to be effected within such time, on such person, at such place and in such manner as it thinks fit, and may also require such proof of service as it thinks fit (IR 1986, r. 12.12(3)). An application under r. 12.12 must be supported by an affidavit or a witness statement, stating the grounds on which the application is made, and in what place or country the person to be served is, or probably may be, found (rr. 7.57(5) and 12.12(4)). The discretion conferred by r. 12.12 is more extensive than under **CPR, rr. 6.17** to **6.31**, and the practice of the courts in dealing with applications under those provisions is irrelevant to applications under the IR 1986, r. 12.12 (*Re Busytoday Ltd* [1992] 1 WLR 683). In particular, it is not necessary for service in a foreign jurisdiction to be effected in accordance with the law of that jurisdiction (*Re Busytoday Ltd*).

REVIEW, RESCISSION AND VARIATION OF AN ORDER MADE IN INSOLVENCY PROCEEDINGS

Statutory provision

81.6 Rule 7.47(1) of IR 1986 provides:

> Every court having jurisdiction under the [Insolvency Act 1986] to wind up companies may review, rescind or vary any order made by it in the exercise of that jurisdiction.

An equivalent provision in relation to bankruptcy jurisdiction is made by the Insolvency Act 1986, s. 375(1).

The distinction between an appeal and an application to review, rescind or vary is that the question on an appeal against a decision is whether the decision was right or wrong whereas the question on an application to review, rescind or vary is whether the original order ought to remain in force in the light either of changed circumstances or in the light of fresh evidence (per Millett J in *Re a Debtor (No. 32-SD-1991)* [1993] 1 WLR 314 at p. 319).

Jurisdiction

81.7 Any Chancery Division judge may review, rescind or vary an order made by another Chancery Division judge, because the legislation provides that 'the court' may review etc. its decisions (*Re W. and A. Glaser Ltd* [1994] BCC 199 at p. 206), but there has been doubt about who can review etc. a decision of a bankruptcy registrar. Formerly it had been held that the registrars in bankruptcy did not form a separate court within the Chancery Division (*Re Rolls*

Razor Ltd (No. 2) [1970] Ch 576 at pp. 590–1). However, the creation by the 1986 legislation of a procedure for appealing from a registrar to a judge (see **81.12**) appeared to constitute the registrars as a separate court, and it was held in *Re SN Group plc* [1994] 1 BCLC 319 that a decision made by a registrar could be reviewed etc. only by the registrar, though the registrar could adjourn the matter to be heard by the judge (as in *Re Dollar Land (Feltham) Ltd* [1995] 2 BCLC 370). In *Re Piccadilly Property Management Ltd* [1999] 2 BCLC 145, though, Judge Colyer QC, sitting as a High Court judge held, after a thorough review of the authorities, that the registrars are not a separate court and that a decision of a registrar may be reviewed etc. by the registrar or by a judge. This means that when an order has been made by a registrar it is possible both to apply to the judge to rescind or review the order and to appeal against it, though this should be rare (*Re Piccadilly Property Management Ltd*).

In *Re a Debtor (No. 32 of 1991) (No. 2)* [1994] BCC 524 at p. 528 Vinelott J said that the procedure for review etc.:

> should not be resorted to in place of the ordinary process of appeal, save in cases where the court is satisfied that there has been something amounting to a miscarriage of justice which cannot be corrected by the ordinary process of appeal.

An application to review a decision must not be used merely to restate the applicant's case in what is hoped to be a more persuasive way (*RWH Enterprises Ltd v Portedge Ltd* [1998] BCC 556; *Re Thirty-Eight Building Ltd (No. 2)* [2000] 1 BCLC 201).

Fresh evidence

At the discretion of the court, fresh evidence may be adduced on an application to rescind an order, even if it could not have been adduced on an appeal against the order (*Re a Debtor (No. 32-SD-1991)* [1993] 1 WLR 314; *Re Dollar Land (Feltham) Ltd* [1995] 2 BCLC 370) and whether or not that evidence might have been given at the original hearing (*Re a Debtor (No. 32-SD-1991)* [1993] 1 WLR 314). Commenting on this in *RWH Enterprises Ltd v Portedge Ltd* [1998] BCC 556, however, Peter Gibson LJ said, at p. 559: **81.8**

> . . . to my mind the fact that the evidence was available at the earlier hearing is plainly a matter that can properly be taken into account. All the circumstances must be looked at.

RESCISSION OF A WINDING-UP ORDER

An application under IR 1986, r. 7.47(1), for a winding-up order to be rescinded must be made within seven days of the date on which the order was made (r. 7.47(4)) though this time limit may be extended by the court under r. 4.3 as in *Re Calmex Ltd* [1989] 1 All ER 485 and *Re Virgo Systems Ltd* [1990] BCLC 34. An extension of time is unlikely to be granted if liquidators have incurred expense in investigating the company's insolvency (*Re Mid East Trading Ltd* [1997] 3 All ER 481 at p. 489, in which the application was about 14 months late). **81.9**

Applications for rescission of winding-up orders are regulated by **PD Insolvency Proceedings, para.** 7. An application must be accompanied by written evidence of assets and liabilities to demonstrate solvency. An application may be made only by a creditor or a contributory (though the company may join in the application) (*Re Mid East Trading Ltd* [1997] 3 All ER 481) and the costs of an unsuccessful application will be paid by the creditor or contributory applicant even when the company has been joined.

The hearing of an application to rescind a winding-up order is a rehearing of the petition on which the order was made and that petition is restored to the court. Accordingly, any person who might have been heard on the hearing of the petition may appear on the hearing of the application to rescind, and IR 1986, r. 4.16 (which requires notice of intention to appear or the permission of the court — see **79.82**), applies (*Re Dollar Land (Feltham) Ltd* [1995] 2 BCLC 370).

An applicant for rescission of a winding-up order must adduce new material which tends to show that the original order ought not to have been made, and which was not before the court on the making of the order (*Re Mid East Trading Ltd* [1997] 3 All ER 481 at p. 490). If the winding-up order was not opposed and an application to rescind it is made promptly, a statement of the circumstances by the applicant's legal representative may be sufficient, but usually the court will require written evidence (**PD Insolvency Proceedings, para. 7.4**).

APPEALS IN INSOLVENCY PROCEEDINGS

Procedural rules

81.10 The procedure and practice of the Supreme Court relating to appeals to the Court of Appeal apply to appeals in insolvency proceedings (IR 1986, r. 7.49(1)) with some exceptions specified in r. 7.49(2) and **PD Insolvency Proceedings, para. 17**. Practice and procedure of the Supreme Court on appeals are governed by **CPR, Part 52**, and **PD 52**, which are discussed in **chapters** 71 and 72. Allowance is made in **CPR, r. 52.1(4)**, for special provisions in other rules or practice directions for appeals in particular kinds of proceedings.

Tribunal and permission to appeal

81.11 **From a first-instance decision by a High Court judge** An appeal from an order made by a High Court judge is to the Court of Appeal in the normal way, and **CPR, Part 52**, and **PD 52** (see **chapter** 71) apply in full (IR 1986, r. 7.49(1); **PD Insolvency Proceedings, paras 17.3(2)** and 17.4). Permission to appeal must be obtained from the judge or the Court of Appeal (**CPR, r. 52.3; PD Insolvency Proceedings, paras 17.3(2)** and 17.5).

81.12 **From a first-instance decision by a High Court registrar or a county court** An appeal from an order made by a county court or a registrar of the High Court lies to a single judge of the High Court (IR 1986, r. 7.47(2) (winding up); Insolvency Act 1986, s. 375(2), and IR 1986, r. 7.48(2) (bankruptcy); **PD Insolvency Proceedings, para. 17.2(1)**). Such an appeal is called a 'first appeal' in PD Insolvency Proceedings. **Part 52** of the CPR does not apply to a first appeal (**PD Insolvency Proceedings, para. 17.7**), which means, in particular, that permission to appeal is not required (para. 17.6). Permission is required to appeal against a summary assessment of costs in insolvency proceedings (*Hosking v Michaelides* [2003] EWHC 3029 (Ch), *The Times*, 17 December 2003). **PD 52** also does not apply, apart from **paras 5.12** and **5.14** to **5.20** (which concern the record of the judgment being appealed and time limits for appealing) with necessary modifications (**PD Insolvency Proceedings, paras 17.7** and **17.23**). Instead the detailed procedure for a first appeal is set out in **PD Insolvency Proceedings, paras 17.8** to 17.23. **Paragraph 17.8** applies to first appeals three principles which are applied to appeals generally by **CPR, r. 52.11**:

(a) The hearing of a first appeal is limited to a review of the decision made at first instance (**PD Insolvency Proceedings, para. 17.18(1)**).
(b) Oral evidence, and evidence which was not before the court at first instance, will not be received on appeal, unless the court hearing the appeal orders otherwise (**para. 17.18(2)**).
(c) The appeal will be allowed where the first-instance decision was wrong or was unjust because of a serious procedural or other irregularity (**para. 17.18(3)**).

An order made by a district judge sitting in a county court is an order made by the county court and so the only appeal is under IR 1986, r. 7.47(2), or the Insolvency Act 1986, s. 375(2), and IR 1986, r. 7.48(2), to a single judge of the High Court, not to the judge of the county court or to the Court of Appeal under the **Access to Justice Act 1999 (Destination of Appeals) Order 2000** (SI 2000/1071), arts 3(2) and 4(b) (Insolvency Act 1986, s. 375(3); *Re Langley Marketing Services Ltd* [1992] BCC 585).

A decision by a High Court judge on a first appeal may be appealed to the Court of Appeal (a 'second appeal'), but only with the permission of that court (**Access to Justice Act 1999, s. 55; CPR, r. 52.13**). All the provisions of **CPR, Part 52**, and **PD 52** apply to second appeals (**PD Insolvency Proceedings, para. 17.3(3)**).

Appeal against a winding-up order: security for costs

On the petitioner's application, the Court of Appeal will order a person other than the company to give security for the costs of an appeal against a winding-up order. The security should be in the nature of an indemnity. This is because, normally, the costs of an unsuccessful appeal should not be borne by the creditors or contributories of the company but by the person instigating the appeal (*Re Photographic Artists' Co-operative Supply Association* (1883) 23 ChD 370 (creditor's petition); *Re Consolidated South Rand Mines Deep Ltd* [1909] WN 66 (contributory's petition); *Re E. K. Wilson and Sons Ltd* [1972] 1 WLR 791 (contributory's petition)). **81.13**

Stay of proceedings in a winding up pending appeal

It has been said that it is not the practice of the court to stay proceedings in the winding up of a company pending determination of an appeal against the winding-up order (*Re A and BC Chewing Gum Ltd* [1975] 1 WLR 579 at pp. 592–3; *Re Calahurst Ltd* [1989] BCLC 140 at p. 141; **PD Insolvency Proceedings, para. 17.25**). However, there are several reported cases on appeals which incidentally mention that the winding up was stayed, so the practice is not invariable (see, for example, *Re Westbourne Galleries Ltd* [1971] Ch 799 at p. 813 (contributory's petition); *Re Industrial and Commercial Securities plc* (1988) 5 BCC 320 (where the petitioner's debt had been paid after the winding-up order was made and it may be that this payment would, in itself, have justified a stay of proceedings); *Re Dollar Land (Feltham) Ltd* [1995] 2 BCLC 370 at p. 378). **81.14**

LITIGATION AGAINST PERSONS SUBJECT TO INSOLVENCY PROCEEDINGS

Introduction

One of the objectives of winding up a company or administering a debtor's estate in bankruptcy is to distribute the insolvent person's free assets to unsecured creditors equally. The amount of each creditor's claim is to be settled by the liquidator or trustee in bankruptcy, subject to appeal to the court. Accordingly legal proceedings against the estate, including proceedings to execute judgments, must not be taken without the court's permission (see **81.18** and **81.25**), which will always be refused if the proceedings will upset the orderly administration and distribution of the estate (see **81.29**). Similarly the administration of a company is intended to manage the company in accordance with a plan agreed by the majority of unsecured creditors, and so legal proceedings against a company in administration can only be taken with the court's permission or the administrator's consent, so that particular creditors cannot gain any advantage over others (see **81.21**). **81.15**

Litigation against companies and individuals is also controlled while preparations are made for winding up, administration, bankruptcy, and company and individual voluntary arrangements. The different insolvency procedures are subject to two types of control:

(a) An optional power given to an insolvent person and, in the case of companies, to creditors to ask for proceedings to be stayed, either by the court in which the proceedings are pending or by the court controlling the insolvency proceedings. This power is available when:
  (i) a winding-up petition is pending (see **81.16**);
  (ii) a bankruptcy petition is pending (see **81.23**);

(iii) an application for an interim order allowing for preparation of an individual voluntary arrangement is pending (see **81.22**).

(b) A prohibition on proceedings being brought or continued without the permission of the court which is controlling the insolvency procedure. This applies when:

(i) a provisional liquidator has been appointed (see **81.17**);

(ii) an administration application is pending or notice has been filed of the appointment of an administrator out of court (see **81.21**);

(iii) a moratorium is in force allowing preparation of a company voluntary arrangement (see **81.20**);

(iv) an interim order is in force allowing preparation of an individual voluntary arrangement (see **81.22**).

An optional power to ask the court which controls the winding up to stay proceedings is available in the voluntary liquidation of a company (see **81.19**).

There are no provisions for the control of litigation against a company when an administrative receiver is appointed.

While a winding-up petition is pending

81.16 After a petition has been presented asking for the compulsory winding up of a company, but before the final hearing of the petition, an application may be made, by the company, or any creditor or contributory, for any claim or proceeding against the company to be stayed (Insolvency Act 1986, s. 126).

If the claim or proceeding sought to be stayed is in the High Court or Court of Appeal, in England and Wales or Northern Ireland, the application should be made to the court in which the action or proceeding is pending (s. 126(1)(a)) using the **CPR, Part 23**, procedure (see **chapter 32**). An application to stay a proceeding in the High Court must be made to the Division to which the cause or matter is attached, even if the winding-up petition has been presented in the High Court (*Re People's Garden Co.* (1875) 1 ChD 44; *Garbutt v Fawcus* (1875) 1 ChD 155; *Re Morriston Patent Fuel and Brick Co.* [1877] WN 20; *Re Artistic Colour Printing Co.* (1880) 14 ChD 502; *Re General Service Co-operative Stores* [1891] 1 Ch 496).

If the claim or proceeding sought to be stayed is in a county court, the application should be made by ordinary application in the winding-up proceedings (Insolvency Act 1986, s. 126(1)(b)). An order under s. 126(1)(b) may be served by sending a sealed copy to the address for service of the claimant or other party having carriage of the proceedings to be stayed (IR 1986, r. 7.56).

An order under the Insolvency Act 1986, s. 126, will be made on an application made without notice to other parties if the applicant gives an undertaking in damages (see **37.23** to **37.26**) (*Re London and Suburban Bank Ltd* (1871) 25 LT 23; *Masbach v James Anderson and Co. Ltd* (1877) 37 LT 440).

In *Bowkett v Fullers United Electric Works Ltd* [1923] 1 KB 160 Bankes LJ said, at pp. 163–4:

> The general policy of the court in exercising this jurisdiction, when a petition has been presented which may result in a winding-up order or a scheme, is to secure that no creditor shall thenceforward gain priority over others of his class, and when an application is made to stay proceedings under [s. 126] very exceptional circumstances must exist to justify the court in refusing to accede to the application, because if the plaintiff's action is not stayed he will get payment in full while if his action is stayed he will take his place properly among other creditors of his class. . . . No doubt the court has a discretion whether it will stay a plaintiff's action, but it is against the policy of the court to exercise that discretion by allowing a plaintiff to proceed except in very special circumstances.

When a provisional liquidator is appointed

81.17 If, while a winding-up petition is pending against a company, a provisional liquidator is appointed, the effect on claims or proceedings against the company is the same as when a winding-up order is made, that is, they cannot proceed without the permission of the winding-up court (Insolvency Act 1986, s. 130(2); see **81.18**).

When a winding-up order has been made

When a winding-up order has been made against a company no claim or proceeding may be proceeded with or commenced against the company except by permission of the court, and subject to such terms as the court may impose (Insolvency Act 1986, s. 130(2)). **81.18**

The court by which permission must be given under s. 130(2) is the court which made the winding-up order (*Wilson v Natal Investment Co.* (1867) 36 LJ Ch 312; *Thames Plate Glass Co. v Land and Sea Telegraph Construction Co.* (1871) LR 6 Ch App 643). That court will issue an injunction to prevent the continuance of any proceedings which it will not sanction (*Re Waterloo Life etc. Insurance Co. (No. 2)* (1862) 31 Beav 589; *Re International Pulp and Paper Co.* (1876) 3 ChD 594). Any judge of the High Court may exercise its jurisdiction in this respect (*Fabric Sales Ltd v Eratex Ltd* [1984] 1 WLR 863).

Permission is sought by originating application. Permission will not be given on an application made without notice to other parties (*Western and Brazilian Telegraph Co. v Bibby* (1880) 42 LT 821) other than in exceptional cases where permission is urgently required (*Fabric Sales Ltd v Eratex Ltd* [1984] 1 WLR 863 at p. 866).

If a claim has not commenced, the court should be asked for permission to commence it, not to commence and proceed with it, as permission to commence is sufficient to enable the claim to proceed in the usual way (*Steel and Tube Co. of New Zealand Ltd v Barker and Pollock Ltd* [1973] 2 NZLR 30). Any limitation on how far the claim is to go will be expressed as terms to which the permission to commence is subject.

The grant by the winding-up court of permission for a claim to commence or proceed does not make the claim a proceeding in the winding up (*Abitibi Power and Paper Co. Ltd v Montreal Trust Co.* [1943] AC 536).

When a company is in voluntary liquidation

In the voluntary liquidation of a company, an application may be made under the Insolvency Act 1986, s. 112, for the court to exercise its power to restrain or stay proceedings against the company (*Re Keynsham Co.* (1863) 33 Beav 123; *Re Life Association of England Ltd* (1864) 34 LJ Ch 64; *Re Peninsular etc. Banking Co.* (1866) 35 Beav 278; *Re East Kent Shipping Co. Ltd* (1868) 18 LT 748; *Re Paraguassu Steam Tramroad Co., Black and Co.'s Case* (1872) LR 8 Ch App 254 at p. 263). An application may be made by the liquidator or any creditor or contributory (s. 112(1)). If satisfied that it will be just and beneficial to restrain or stay the proceedings, the court may accede wholly or partially to the application on such terms and conditions as it thinks fit, or may make such other order on the application as it thinks just (s. 112(2)). An application under s. 112 concerning the voluntary winding up of a company should be made by originating application to a court having jurisdiction to wind up the company. However, it is not entirely clear whether the statutory power of the court which is invoked by an application to restrain proceedings is the s. 126 or the s. 130 power. Older cases support the view that where a claim is proceeding in the Court of Appeal or the High Court against a company in voluntary liquidation, an application under s. 126, using the **CPR, Part 23**, procedure may be made to the Court of Appeal or the High Court Division in which the claim is proceeding (*Walker v Banagher Distillery Co. Ltd* (1875) 1 QBD 129; *Needham v Rivers Protection and Manure Co.* (1875) 1 ChD 253). **81.19**

Moratorium in force in relation to a company

While a moratorium under the Insolvency Act 1986, s. 1A (moratorium when directors propose a voluntary arrangement), is in force in relation to a company, no proceedings and no execution or other legal process may be commenced or continued against the company or its **81.20** property, except with the permission of the court (sch. A1, para. 12(1)(h)). Permission should be sought by originating application.

While a moratorium is in force in relation to a company no petition for the company to be wound up by the court may be presented, other than by the Secretary of State or the Financial Services Authority (sch. A1, para. 12(1)(a), (4) and (5)), and no administration application may be made (sch. A1, para. 12(1)(d)).

Administration and preparation for administration

81.21 While a company is in administration, no legal process (including legal proceedings, execution and distress) may be instituted against the company or its property except with the consent of the administrator or the permission of the court (Insolvency Act 1986, sch. B1, para. 43(1) and (6)). This protection is known as a moratorium. The same protection applies (except that only the court can give permission) during the following periods of preparation for administration (para. 44):

(a) from when an application is made to the court for an administration order until the court's administration order takes effect or the application is dismissed;
(b) from when the holder of a floating charge files with the court a notice of intention to appoint an administrator until the appointment takes effect, provided this is within five business days;
(c) from when a notice of intention to appoint an administrator is filed with the court by the company or its directors until the appointment takes effect, provided this is within 10 business days.

Protection under para. 44 is known as an interim moratorium. It does not prevent or require the court's permission for (para. 44(7)):

(a) the presentation of a public-interest winding-up petition by the Secretary of State or the Financial Services Authority;
(b) the appointment of an administrator by the holder of a floating charge;
(c) the appointment of an administrative receiver;
(d) the carrying out by an administrative receiver of his or her functions.

Interim order in respect of an individual voluntary arrangement

81.22 While an interim order is in force, under the Insolvency Act 1986, s. 252, in respect of an individual, a moratorium is imposed so that a voluntary arrangement may be prepared for approval by creditors. The effect is that no bankruptcy petition, other proceedings, execution or other legal process may be commenced or continued against the individual, or his or her property, except with the permission of the court (s. 252(2)). Application for permission is by ordinary application in the voluntary arrangement proceedings.

While an application for an interim order in respect of an individual is pending, the court to which the application has been made may stay any action, execution or other legal process against the property or person of the individual (s. 254(1)). An application for a stay should be made by ordinary application in the voluntary arrangement proceedings. Alternatively a court in which other proceedings are pending may stay them, or allow them to continue on such terms as it thinks fit, on proof that an application for an interim order has been made by the defendant (s. 254(2)). An application under s. 254(2) should use the **CPR, Part 23**, procedure.

While a bankruptcy petition is pending

81.23 After a bankruptcy petition has been presented against an individual, but before the final hearing of the petition, the court in which the petition is pending may stay any action, execution or other legal process against the property or person of the individual (Insolvency Act 1986, s. 285(1)). Application for a stay under s. 285(1) is by ordinary application in the bankruptcy proceedings. Alternatively a court in which other proceedings are pending may stay them, or allow them to continue on such terms as it thinks fit, on proof that a bankruptcy petition has been presented against the defendant (s. 285(2)). An application under s. 285(2) should use the **CPR, Part 23**, procedure.

When an interim receiver has been appointed

When an interim receiver of an individual's property has been appointed under the Insolvency Act 1986, s. 286, the effect on other proceedings against the individual is the same as if a bankruptcy order had been made against the individual (s. 286(6); see **81.25**). **81.24**

When a bankruptcy order has been made

After a bankruptcy order has been made against an individual, and before the individual's discharge from bankruptcy, no person who is a creditor in respect of a debt provable in the bankruptcy may commence any claim or other legal proceedings against the bankrupt except with the permission of the court and on such terms as the court may impose (Insolvency Act 1986, s. 285(3)). Application for permission to commence proceedings should be by originating application. In addition the provisions of s. 285(1) and (2) (see **81.23**) continue to apply after a bankruptcy order has been made. **81.25**

General principles governing the exercise of discretion to grant permission

The following paragraphs discuss the general principles which apply when permission is sought to commence or continue proceedings against a defendant who is subject to insolvency proceedings. **81.26**

Existence of discretion Whether or not a claimant is given permission to proceed is a matter for the discretion of the court (*Thames Plate Glass Co. v Land and Sea Telegraph Construction Co.* (1871) LR 6 Ch App 643; *Re Atlantic Computer Systems plc* [1992] Ch 505 at p. 523), which is free to make such order as is 'right and fair in the circumstances' (*Re Aro Co. Ltd* [1980] Ch 196 at p. 209; *Re Exchange Securities and Commodities Ltd* [1983] BCLC 186). **81.27**

Onus The onus is on the applicant to show a case for giving permission (*Re Lancashire Cotton Spinning Co., ex parte Carnelley* (1887) 35 ChD 656; *Re Higginshaw Mills and Spinning Co.* [1896] 2 Ch 544). However, on an application to restrain or stay proceedings against a company in voluntary liquidation the onus is on the applicant to show why the order should be made (*Currie v Consolidated Kent Collieries Corporation Ltd* [1906] 1 KB 134). **81.28**

Purpose of the provisions In *Re David Lloyd and Co.* (1877) 6 ChD 339 James LJ said, at p. 344, that the provisions in winding-up and bankruptcy legislation enabling the court to interfere with claims: **81.29**

> ... were intended, not for the purpose of harassing, or impeding, or injuring third persons, but for the purpose of preserving the limited assets of the company or bankrupt in the best way for distribution among all the persons who have claims upon them. There being only a small fund or a limited fund to be divided among a great number of persons, it would be monstrous that one or more of them should be harassing the company with actions and incurring costs which would increase the claims against the company and diminish the assets which ought to be divided among all the creditors.

See also *Langley Constructions (Brixham) Ltd v Wells* [1969] 1 WLR 503 at p. 508; *Re J. Burrows (Leeds) Ltd* [1982] 1 WLR 1177 at p. 1181.

Substantiality of claim The court should not be asked to order a liquidator or trustee in bankruptcy to waste the assets he or she is administering on defending insubstantial claims (*Re Hartlebury Printers Ltd* [1992] ICR 559). Permission will not be given to commence proceedings if there is no prospect that the court would grant the relief claimed (*Re Polly Peck International plc (No. 2)* [1998] 3 All ER 812). The test is the same as on an application for summary judgment (see **34.10**) (*Enron Metals and Commodity Ltd v HIH Casualty and General Insurance Ltd* [2005] EWHC 485 (Ch), *The Times*, 6 April 2005). The old practice was to require an **81.30**

affidavit from an applicant seeking permission to commence or continue proceedings verifying the claim made in the proceedings (*Re St Cuthbert's Lead Smelting Co. (No. 2)* [1866] WN 154). This practice would seem to be unnecessary now that **CPR, r. 22.1**, requires every statement of case to be verified by a statement of truth. The court does not examine the merits of the applicant's case, provided it is satisfied that the claim is not clearly unsustainable (*Bristol and West Building Society v Trustee of the Property of Back* [1998] 1 BCLC 485). The question of the substantiality of the applicant's case is decided on the material presented by the applicant: the company or debtor or trustee in bankruptcy will not be granted an order for disclosure of documents to test the applicant's case (*Re Bank of Credit and Commerce International SA (No. 4)* [1994] 1 BCLC 419). It is open to the court to limit permission initially to issue of the claim form and particulars of claim and service of defence, after which it can assess the nature of the claim (as in *Thames Plate Glass Co. v Land and Sea Telegraph Co.* (1870) LR 11 Eq 248).

81.31 **Appropriateness of forum** Permission will not be given to bring or continue proceedings if the question at issue can just as well be resolved in the winding-up or bankruptcy proceedings (*Re St Cuthbert Lead Smelting Co.* (1866) 35 Beav 384; *Re Exchange Securities and Commodities Ltd* [1983] BCLC 186). Determining the appropriate method of dealing with the applicant's claim is the essential question on an application for permission to commence or continue proceedings against an insolvent person (*Re Bank of Credit and Commerce International SA (No. 4)* [1994] 1 BCLC 419). In *New Cap Reinsurance Corporation Ltd v HIH Casualty and General Insurance Ltd* [2002] EWCA Civ 300, LTL 20/2/2002, permission was given to continue proceedings against a company in provisional liquidation so that four claims in which a number of parties were involved could be conducted at the same time so as to avoid inconsistent findings.

Proceedings in respect of a claim for which the claimant has already put in a proof in the winding up or bankruptcy will not be allowed to continue because the claimant has elected to have the matter dealt with in the insolvency (*Craven v Blackpool Greyhound Stadium and Racecourse Ltd* [1936] 3 All ER 513).

81.32 **Insolvent person necessary party to proceedings against others or where claim is insured** Permission will normally be given for a claim or proceeding against an insolvent person if that person is a necessary defendant to a claim against another person, or the claim is insured, and the claimant undertakes not to enforce any order obtained in the claim against the insolvent person, without the insolvency court's permission (*McEwen v London Bombay and Mediterranean Bank Ltd* (1866) 15 LT 495; *Re Breech Loading Armoury Co.* [1867] WN 75; *Bristol and West Building Society v Trustee of the Property of Back* [1998] 1 BCLC 485).

Retrospective permission

81.33 A litigant who has, without permission, commenced a claim against a company after a provisional liquidator has been appointed or a winding-up order made, or against an undischarged bankrupt, may be granted retrospective permission, which is sometimes called permission *nunc pro tunc* (now for then) (*Re Marine Investment Co. Ltd* (1868) 17 LT 535; *Re Wanzer Ltd* [1891] 1 Ch 305; *Re Saunders* [1997] Ch 60; *Re Linkrealm Ltd* [1998] BCC 478). (The earlier cases were temporarily forgotten when retrospective permission was said to be beyond the court's powers in *Wilson v Banner Scaffolding Ltd* (1982) *The Times*, 22 June 1982 and *Re National Employers Mutual General Insurance Association Ltd* [1995] 1 BCLC 232.)

In *Re Linkrealm Ltd* [1998] BCC 478 retrospective permission was given to continue a claim which could not have been started again because of the expiry of the limitation period.

Defending claim by the insolvent person

81.34 If a person who has issued a claim pursues it while subject to insolvency proceedings, permission is not required for a counterclaim to the extent that the counterclaim is a defence (*Dominion Trust Co. v Brydges* (1920) 28 BCR 451; *Standard Trust Co. v Turner Crossing Inc.* (1992) 15 CBR (3d) 75), but if judgment is sought on the counterclaim for an amount exceeding the insolvent's claim then permission is required (*Langley Constructions (Brixham) Ltd v Wells* [1969] 1 WLR 503). These rules are derived from *Mersey Steel and Iron Co. v Naylor Benzon and Co.* (1882) 9 QBD 648, (1884) 9 App Cas 434, though the provisions which are now the Insolvency Act 1986, ss. 130(2) and 285(3), were not in issue in that case, and the rules remain questionable.

Permission is not required to pursue an appeal against a judgment in favour of an insolvent person in a claim which that person has proceeded with since a winding-up or bankruptcy order (*Humber and Co. v John Griffiths Cycle Co.* (1901) 85 LT 141).

How does a party 'proceed with' a claim?

In Australia it has been held that 'not everything that happens in litigation involves a person who proceeds with litigation' (*FAI Workers Compensation (NSW) Ltd v Philkor Builders Pty Ltd* (1996) 20 ACSR 592 at p. 595): the test is whether what is done moves the litigation 'from an incipient stage to consummation' (ibid. at p. 596). So a person who has commenced proceedings against an insolvent person does not proceed with them by applying to have them dismissed (ibid.; *Re DIM Furniture Wholesale (NSW) Pty Ltd* (1998) 28 ACSR 407), even though the application may result in the defendant being ordered to pay costs (*FAI Workers Compensation (NSW) Ltd v Philkor Builders Pty Ltd*). An application for permission to proceed with a claim is not itself a 'fresh proceeding' in the claim, because it does not, if successful, advance the claim towards completion: it merely removes a bar against taking further steps (*Re M and M Outdoor Centre Pty Ltd* (1996) 135 FLR 179). **81.35**

Costs

The costs of a successful application to proceed with a claim should be added to the costs of the claim (*Re Aro Co. Ltd* [1980] Ch 196 at p. 211). However, the costs of an application for retrospective permission must normally be paid by the applicant who failed to obtain permission at the proper time (*Re Wanzer Ltd* [1891] 1 Ch 305). **81.36**

If proceedings against a company in liquidation are necessary in order to establish and/or quantify a claim against the company, any costs which the company is ordered to pay must be proved for in the winding up (*Re Poole Firebrick and Blue Clay Co.* (1873) LR 17 Eq 268; *Re Thurso New Gas Co.* (1889) 42 ChD 486; *Re British Gold Fields of West Africa* [1899] 2 Ch 7). But if the company is ordered to pay the costs of proceedings which the liquidator has chosen to carry on in the hope of benefiting the company then the costs are payable in full as an expense of the liquidation (*Re Trent and Humber Ship-building Co., Bailey and Leetham's Case* (1869) LR 8 Eq 94; *Re Wenborn and Co.* [1905] 1 Ch 413). The principles are the same whether the winding up is voluntary or by the court (*Re Pacific Coast Syndicate Ltd* [1913] 2 Ch 26). The costs that are recoverable in full include costs incurred before the commencement of the winding up (*Re London Drapery Stores* [1898] 2 Ch 684; *Norglen Ltd v Reeds Rains Prudential Ltd* [1999] 2 AC 1 at p. 21).

When proceedings by a creditor are halted by the Insolvency Act 1986, s. 130(2), the creditor is entitled to prove for the costs of the proceedings up to the time that s. 130(2) took effect (*Re Welsh Potosi Mining Co., ex parte Tobin* (1858) 28 LJ Ch 44).

Chapter 82 Applications under the Companies Act 1985

INTRODUCTION

Jurisdiction to hear applications under the Companies Act 1985

82.1 The Companies Act 1985, like its predecessors going back to the Joint Stock Companies Act 1856, enables the incorporation of companies by registration with the Registrar of Companies in England and Wales. Companies registered under earlier Acts are governed by the 1985 Act as if registered under it (Companies Act 1985, s. 675).

The 1985 Act has numerous provisions for applications to be made to 'the court' to deal with various types of question relating to the internal affairs of companies registered under the Act. In relation to a particular company, 'the court' means the court which has jurisdiction to order it to be wound up (Companies Act 1985, s. 744). The rules for jurisdiction are set out in 79.8.

It is unfortunate that the rules on jurisdiction over applications under the Companies Act 1985 are expressed in terms of jurisdiction to wind up companies, because the jurisdiction to wind up is now subject to Council Regulation (EC) No. 1346/2000 (see 79.9 to 79.13). If a company registered in England and Wales does not have an establishment within the United Kingdom and its centre of main interests is in another EU State (other than Denmark) then no court in England and Wales has jurisdiction to wind it up. Because the jurisdiction of 'the court' to deal with all other matters relating to a company is defined by the Companies Act 1985 in terms of the jurisdiction to wind up, it seems that, if the English courts do not have jurisdiction to wind up a company then they have no jurisdiction over it at all. This ought to be corrected by amending the Companies Act 1985 so that it defines jurisdiction in matters other than compulsory winding up separately from jurisdiction over winding up.

Purpose of applications under the Companies Act 1985

82.2 Some of the Companies Act 1985 provisions for applications to the court are for the resolution of particular kinds of internal dispute, for example, s. 359 on the rectification of a register of members and ss. 459 to 461 on the relief of unfairly prejudicial conduct of a company's affairs. Others enable a company to obtain court orders to assist in the administration of its affairs, for example, ss. 425 to 427 on court-sanctioned arrangements and reconstructions and s. 216 on freezing orders to enable a public company to discover who has interests in its shares. Some provisions give the court a supervisory power, for example, the requirement that a company cannot reduce its capital without court permission (ss. 135 to

141). Others enable the court to support the Department of Trade and Industry's supervisory and investigatory powers, for example, s. 436 on punishment, for contempt of court, of persons failing to assist investigations.

Procedural rules on litigation concerning the affairs of companies

Applications under any provision of the Companies Act 1985 are governed by the CPR and by **PD 49B**. In addition there are special rules for applications under the Companies Act 1985, ss. 459 to 461 (relief of unfairly prejudicial conduct of a company's affairs) (see **82.9** to **82.18**). There are further rules of practice in the **Chancery Guide, ch. 20**. **82.3**

PD 49B also applies (by **para.** 2(1)) to:

(a) Any application under the Companies Act 1985 as it applies to limited liability partnerships by virtue of the Limited Liability Partnerships Regulations 2001 (SI 2001/1090) (**PD 49B, para.** 1(1)).
(b) Any application under the Financial Services and Markets Act 2000, part VII (transfers of banking and insurance businesses). These applications are the subject of **PD 49B, para. 3A**. They must be made in the High Court (Financial Services and Markets Act 2000, s. 107(4)).
(c) Any application under Council Regulation (EC) No. 2157/2001, art. 25 or art. 26 (scrutiny of legality of merger of companies to form an SE). These applications are the subject of **PD 49B, para. 3B**. They must be made in the High Court (**PD 49B, para. 3B**(1)(a)).
(d) Any application under the Criminal Justice and Police Act 2001, s. 59, for return of property seized in the exercise of the power conferred by the Companies Act 1985, s. 448(3) (warrant to seize documents requisitioned under part XIV of the 1985 Act), either on its own or as extended by s. 50 of the 2001 Act (power to seize material so as to assess whether it is what is sought or which is inseparable from material which is sought). These applications are the subject of **PD 49B, para. 14**. They must be brought in the High Court (**PD 49B, para. 14**(2)).

Lord Woolf's objective of a single claim form for all civil proceedings is very obviously not met in proceedings relating to companies. **PD 49B** divides the applications to which it applies into those which must be commenced by a **Part 8** claim form (**para.** 2; see **82.5**) and those which must be brought by petition (**para.** 4; see **82.4**). Applications for the relief of unfairly prejudicial conduct are required by statute to be brought by petition (Companies Act 1985, s. 459(1)). Applications in relation to companies' affairs are brought not only under the Companies Act 1985, but also under the Insolvency Act 1986 under a completely separate set of rules, which have their own forms of originating process (see **chapters** 79 and **81**). The court's jurisdiction to deal with a company's affairs on an application under the Companies Act 1985 or the Insolvency Act 1986 arises only by virtue of the statute and is limited to the matters mentioned in the various provisions authorising applications to be made. Any claim which is not within those provisions must be pursued by some other form of litigation, such as a claim in equity, contract or tort. Where an application is brought under the Companies Act 1985 and in a related case in the Chancery Division at the same time, special arrangements can be made, on request to the Chancery Judges' Listing Officer, for the applications to be heard by the same judge (**Chancery Guide, para. 20.23**).

PROCEDURE FOR MAKING AN APPLICATION

Commencement by petition

Applications under the provisions of the Companies Act 1985 listed in **PD 49B, para.** 4(1), must be brought by petition (see **table 82.1**). Some of these provisions have hardly ever been used; others are among the most important types of application. A petition under the **82.4**

Table 82.1 Applications which must be brought by petition

Provision		Application for directions
Companies Act 1985		
s. 5,	to cancel an alteration of the statement, in a company's memorandum, of the company's objects.	Required.
s. 17,	to cancel the alteration of a provision in a company's memorandum which could lawfully have been made in its articles.	Required.
s. 54(1),	to cancel a resolution to re-register a public company as private.	Not required.
s. 127,	to cancel a variation of the rights attached to any class of shares in a company whose share capital is divided into shares of different classes.	Required.
s. 136,	to confirm a reduction of a company's share capital, including (by s. 130(3)) a share premium account and (by s. 170(4)) a capital redemption reserve.	Required.
s. 157(2),	to cancel a private company's resolution to give financial assistance for the acquisition of its shares or those of its holding company.	Not required.
s. 176(1),	to cancel a private company's resolution approving a payment out of capital for the redemption or purchase of its shares.	Not required.
s. 425,	to sanction a compromise or arrangement between a company and its creditors, or any class of them, or between a company and its members, or any class of them.	Not required unless there is also an application for an order under s. 427.
s. 653,	to restore to the register of companies a company which was struck off by the registrar as defunct, if the application is made in conjunction with an application for the company to be wound up by the court (which must also be made by petition).	Not required.
s. 690,	to cancel an alteration of the constitution of a company which is registering under the Companies Act 1985, part 22, chapter 2 (registration of companies not formed under the companies legislation).	Required.
s. 727,	for relief from liability of an officer of a company, or of a person employed as an auditor of a company, in respect of negligence, default, breach of duty or breach of trust.	Required.

Companies Act 1985, like a petition under the Insolvency Act 1986 (see 79.3), is not a statement of case under the CPR.

For about half of these types of application (see **table 82.1**), **PD 49B, para.** 5(1), requires the petitioner to apply for directions by filing an application notice after filing the petition. At the directions hearing the court may, by order, give such directions for the hearing of the application as it thinks fit (**PD 49B, para.** 5(3)). In particular the court may direct that an inquiry is to be made or notices are to be published.

A fee of £190 must be paid on filing a petition (**CPFO, fee 3.3**).

Commencement by Part 8 claim form

82.5 Apart from the applications listed in **82.4** and applications under the Companies Act 1985, ss. 459 to 461 (relief of unfairly prejudicial conduct of a company's affairs), which must be brought by petition, all applications to which **PD 49B** applies must be brought by **Part 8** claim form (**PD 49B, para.** 2(1) **and** (4)). In the High Court the claim form must be issued out of the office of the Companies Court Registrar or a Chancery district registry; in the county court it will be issued out of a county court office (**para.** 2(3)).

The court fee for an application under the Companies Act 1985, which is not made in existing proceedings, is £130 (**CPFO, fee 3.5**).

Once properly begun by **Part 8** claim form an application under the Companies Act 1985 follows the procedure of **CPR, Part 8**, except where that procedure is modified by **PD 49B**. This is provided by **PD 49B, para. 2(1)**, which also allows for modification of the **Part 8** procedure by any other practice direction relating to Companies Act 1985 applications, though there are no such practice directions yet.

Title of proceedings

Every claim form or petition by which an application under the Companies Act 1985 or the Financial Services and Markets Act 2000, part VII, is begun must be entitled in the matter of the company in question and in the matter of the relevant Act (**PD 49B, para. 1(3)**). The same applies to all affidavits, witness statements, notices and other documents in the proceedings. **82.6**

Service

If an application to which **PD 49B** applies is made in the High Court, service of documents will be the responsibility of the parties and will not be undertaken by the court (**PD 49B, para. 11**). **82.7**

Track allocation

Every application to which **PD 49B** applies is allocated to the multi-track by **PD 49B, para. 10**, and the provisions of the CPR relating to allocation questionnaires and track allocation are disapplied. **82.8**

UNFAIR PREJUDICE

Statutory provision

Section 459 of the Companies Act 1985 entitles a member of a company to apply to the court by petition for an order giving relief in respect of conduct of the company's affairs which is unfairly prejudicial to the interests of its members generally or of some part of its members (including at least the petitioner), or any actual or proposed act which is or would be so prejudicial. **82.9**

Procedural rules

The Companies (Unfair Prejudice Applications) Proceedings Rules 1986 (SI 1986/2000) apply to all proceedings under the Companies Act 1985, s. 459. The procedure provided by these rules follows the procedure for contributories' petitions for winding up (see **79.66** to **79.74**). A petition under s. 459 may seek a winding up by the court as an alternative remedy, though **PD 49B, para. 9(1)**, says that it is undesirable to do that as a matter of course: 'The petition should not ask for a winding-up order unless that is the relief which the petitioner prefers or it is thought that it may be the only relief to which the petitioner is entitled'. **82.10**

Rule 2(2) of SI 1986/2000 has not been amended to take account of the promulgation of the CPR and still provides that the RSC and the practice of the High Court shall apply to s. 459 petitions in that court, and the CCR and the practice of the county court to petitions in that court, except so far as inconsistent with the Companies Act 1985 and with SI 1986/2000. However, proceedings under s. 459 are not excluded from the application of the CPR by **CPR, r. 2.1(2)** (although SI 1986/2000 was classified by the Statutory Publications Office under 'Insolvency' it is not in fact concerned with insolvency proceedings), so the CPR apply (*Re COLT Telecom Group plc* [2002] EWHC 2503 (Ch), [2003] 1 BCLC 290, at [32]).

The requirement that an application under the Companies Act 1985, s. 459, must be made by petition is imposed by statute and so the court has no power under the CPR to waive a failure to comply with it (*Re Osea Road Camp Sites Ltd* [2004] EWHC 2437 (Ch), [2005] 1 WLR 760).

Form and contents of petition

82.11 The prescribed form for a petition under the Companies Act 1985, s. 459, is set out in the schedule to SI 1986/2000 and is to be used with such variations, if any, as the circumstances may require (SI 1986/2000, r. 3(1)). The petition must specify the grounds on which it is presented and the nature of the relief which is sought by the petitioner (SI 1986/2000, r. 3(2)). The extensive powers of the court to make orders on a s. 459 petition are set out in s. 461. The relief sought must be appropriate to the conduct of which the petition complains (*Re J. E. Cade and Son Ltd* [1992] BCLC 213 at p. 223), though it need not be directed solely towards remedying the particular things that have happened (*Re Hailey Group Ltd* [1993] BCLC 459 at p. 472). The court is required to make the order that is appropriate at the time of the hearing (ibid., loc. cit.).

If a winding-up order is asked for, the petition must comply with **PD 49B, para. 9**, on orders under the Insolvency Act 1986, s. 127, sanctioning transactions by the company while the petition is pending.

The petition must state the names of persons on whom it is intended to serve the petition (known as the 'respondents'), one of whom will be the company itself.

There is no provision for verification of a s. 459 petition by affidavit or statement of truth.

Filing the petition and fixing a return day

82.12 An unfair prejudice petition must be delivered to the court for filing with copies for service on all the respondents (including the company itself) named in the petition (SI 1986/2000, r. 3(2)). The court will fix a hearing for a day (called the 'return day') on which, unless the court otherwise directs, the petitioner and any respondent (including the company) must attend for directions to be given in relation to the procedure on the petition (SI 1986/2000, r. 3(3)).

A fee of £190 must be paid on filing a petition (**CPFO, fee 3.3**).

Service of the petition

82.13 The petitioner must, at least 14 days before the return day, serve a sealed copy of the petition on all respondents named in the petition (including the company itself) (SI 1986/2000, r. 4). The applicable rules on service are those of **CPR, Part 6**. If the petition also prays for a winding up, there must be personal service in accordance with **CPR, r. 6.4** (see **79.70**).

Directions

82.14 Rule 5 of SI 1986/2000 requires the court, on the return day, or at any time after it, to give such directions as it thinks appropriate with respect to the following matters:

(a) service of the petition, whether in connection with the venue for a further hearing, or for any other purpose;
(b) whether particulars of claim and defence are to be delivered, and generally as to the procedure on the petition;
(c) whether, and if so by what means, the petition is to be advertised;
(d) the manner in which any evidence is to be adduced at any hearing before the judge and in particular:
   (i) the taking of evidence wholly or in part by affidavit or orally;
   (ii) the cross-examination of any deponents to affidavits;
   (iii) the matters to be dealt with in evidence;
(e) any other matter affecting the procedure on the petition or in connection with the hearing and disposal of the petition.

The registrar should consider directing the parties and/or their advisers to meet with a view to narrowing the issues, identifying what issues are really important, what issues are really in dispute, how those issues are to be resolved or proved, and resolving and narrowing any other matters which in the context of the particular petition could reasonably be expected to be narrowed (*Re Rotadata Ltd* [2000] 1 BCLC 122 at p. 127).

Interim orders

82.15 It is desirable that the status quo should be preserved between presentation and hearing of a petition under the Companies Act 1985, s. 459, and the court will grant interim injunctions to achieve this (*Re a Company (No. 002612 of 1984)* [1985] BCLC 80; *Re Sticky Fingers Restaurant Ltd* [1992] BCLC 84; *Re a Company (No. 003061 of 1993)* [1994] BCC 883; *Incasep Ltd v Jones* [2002] EWCA Civ 961, LTL 12/7/2002). An interim injunction will not be granted unless the court considers that the petition has a real prospect of success (*Re X Ltd* (2001) *The Times*, 5 June 2001).

In proceedings on an unfair prejudice petition the court does not have jurisdiction to order an interim payment under **CPR, Part 25** (*Re a Company (No. 004175 of 1986)* [1987] 1 WLR 585; *Re a Company (No. 004502 of 1988)* [1991] BCC 234). The court will not make a freezing order against any party to a petition under s. 459, unless the petition alleges what amounts to a cause of action against that party (*Re Premier Electronics (GB) Ltd* [2002] 2 BCLC 634). An interim injunction prohibiting the company from paying a director remuneration which has not been authorised may be made without joining the director as a party (*Riener v Gershinson* [2004] EWHC 76 (Ch), [2004] 2 BCLC 376).

A minority member of a company petitioning under s. 459 may also be frustrating the holding of general meetings, by refusing to attend so that any meeting will be inquorate, so as to prevent prejudicial resolutions being adopted. The majority may apply under s. 317 for an order convening a meeting with the usual quorum rules suspended. The court hearing the s. 317 application will take into account the existence of s. 459 proceedings when deciding whether to make an order under s. 317 (*Re Sticky Fingers Restaurant Ltd*; *Re Whitchurch Insurance Consultants Ltd* [1993] BCLC 1359; *Re Woven Rugs Ltd* [2002] 1 BCLC 324).

Costs

82.16 It is a misapplication of the company's money to pay any costs of proceedings under the Companies Act 1985, s. 459 (other than as ordered by the court), except for those necessarily incurred in representing the company as a separate person (*Re Kenyon Swansea Ltd* [1987] BCLC 514; *Re Elgindata Ltd* [1991] BCLC 959). The court may order the company to indemnify the petitioner for the costs of obtaining an order in favour of the company as a separate person (*Clark v Cutland* [2003] EWCA Civ 810, [2004] 1 WLR 783). The company may provide a qualifying third party indemnity, as permitted by s. 309B, to a director who successfully defends an allegation of negligence, default, breach of duty or breach of trust contained in a s. 459 petition (*Branch v Bagley* [2004] EWHC 426 (Ch), LTL 10/3/2004).

Court's order

82.17 If the court is satisfied that the applicant's petition is well-founded it is empowered by the Companies Act 1985, s. 461(1), to make such order as it thinks fit for giving relief in respect of the matters complained of. More particularly, under s. 461(2), the court may:

(a) regulate the conduct of the company's affairs in the future; this could include ordering an alteration of the company's memorandum or articles or preventing the company from making any, or any specified, alteration to the memorandum or articles without the court's permission;

(b) require the company to refrain from doing or continuing an act complained of by the petitioner or to do an act which the petitioner has complained it has omitted to do;

(c) authorise civil proceedings to be brought in the name and on behalf of the company by such person or persons and on such terms as the court may direct;

(d) provide for the purchase of the shares of any members of the company by other members or by the company itself and, in the case of a purchase by the company itself, the reduction of the company's capital accordingly.

The court has jurisdiction to make orders against persons who are not members of the company or who are not involved in the conduct complained of (provided they have been made parties to the proceedings), but it is inconceivable that the court would order a person who was not a member of the company to buy the petitioner's shares (*Re Little Olympian Each-ways Ltd* [1994] 2 BCLC 420).

The court has a power under s. 461(1) to make such orders as it considers will enable the company, for the future, to be properly run, and for its affairs to be under the conduct of somebody who the shareholders generally can be confident will conduct the affairs of the company properly (*Re a Company (No. 00789 of 1987)* [1990] BCLC 384 per Harman J at p. 395, followed in *Re Hailey Group Ltd* [1993] BCLC 459).

The most common order is that the majority shareholders must buy the petitioner's shares. Exceptionally, in *Re Brenfield Squash Racquets Club Ltd* [1996] 2 BCLC 184 the majority shareholder was ordered to sell its shares to the petitioner.

If it is plain that the appropriate solution to the situation which the petitioner is complaining about is sale of the petitioner's shares, if other members of the company are willing to buy them, and if the articles provide a procedure for determining the price to be paid on a sale from one member to another, that procedure should be adopted, instead of petitioning under s. 459. A petition is appropriate, for the purpose of obtaining the court's valuation of the shares, if there is any risk that the procedure provided by the articles will undervalue them (*Re a Company (No. 00330 of 1991)* [1991] BCLC 597). However, if an offer is made which proposes a genuinely independent valuation, the court will strike out the petition as an abuse of process: the petitioner is not entitled to insist on the court carrying out a valuation which can be performed more cheaply by an accountant (*Re a Company (No. 00836 of 1995)* [1996] 2 BCLC 192).

There is a helpful discussion of what counts as a reasonable offer to purchase a petitioner's shares in *O'Neill v Phillips* [1999] 1 WLR 1092 at pp. 1107–8. An offer is not reasonable if the offeror cannot finance it (*West v Blanchet* [2000] 1 BCLC 795). In many cases the petitioner contends that the value of the shares has been diminished by the conduct complained of in the petition and some way has to be found for a valuer to take this into account. If the value of the shares depends on the answer to a question of law, the question should be left for the court to decide (*North Holdings Ltd v Southern Tropics Ltd* [1999] 2 BCLC 625).

A Tomlin order (see **61.14**) should not be made if the petition asked alternatively for the winding up of the company (*Re a Company (No. 003324 of 1979)* [1981] 1 WLR 1059).

Drawing up and notification of the court's order

82.18 The petitioner, and every person who appeared on the hearing of the petition, must, not later than the business day after the order is made, leave at the court all documents necessary to enable the order to be completed (SI 1986/2000, r. 6(1)). It is not normally necessary to appoint a time for settlement of the order (r. 6(2)). If the court considers that the order should be advertised, it will give directions (r. 6(3)).

Chapter 83 Leases and Licences

INTRODUCTION

The modern decisions of the courts on the distinction between a lease and a licence must be seen in their historical context. The first Rent Act was enacted in 1915 as a temporary measure in response to tenants' protests at rising rents (the Increase of Rent and Mortgage Interest (War Restrictions) Act). Over the next 60 years legislation protecting tenants' rights developed into a comprehensive statutory code culminating in the **Rent Act 1977**. The Rent Acts sought to protect the tenant in two key ways, first by restricting the landlord's right to evict and secondly by restricting his ability to increase rent arbitrarily. As a result many landlords sought different ways to evade the Rent Acts. The most obvious way was to attempt to grant a licence rather than a lease, as licensees were not afforded Rent Act protection. **83.1**

In certain situations the granting of a tenancy resulted in the occupier acquiring a status of virtual irremovability. In marked contrast, the granting of a licence provides the occupier with only minimal security and permits the licensor to regain possession of the premises at short notice and without having to establish reasons before the court.

The situation, from the landlord's point of view, is no longer quite so acute as it was. Since 15 January 1989 it has not been possible (save in certain exceptional circumstances) to create a **Rent Act 1977** protected tenancy. The **Housing Act 1988** removed the **Rent Act 1977**'s system of rent control. It also provided the landlord with several broader grounds of possession than under the old Rent Acts. Most significantly, however, it introduced a means of granting short-term tenancies without security of tenure in the form of assured shorthold tenancies, a type of letting that proved so popular with landlords that its significance was further extended by the **Housing Act 1996** (see **chapter 86**). Thus a landlord of residential property who wishes to avoid the risk of the tenant acquiring substantial protection under a statutory code can now do so without having to claim that the occupier is holding under a licence. This does not mean that there is no longer any distinction between a lease and a licence. It simply means that landlords no longer need to employ the device of granting a licence rather than a tenancy to avoid the consequences of statutory protection.

GRANTING A LICENCE

83.2 Various ingenious attempts to disguise what was effectively a lease under the cloak of a licence culminated in the landmark decision in *Street v Mountford* [1985] AC 809, where the House of Lords finally put paid to the argument that the words used by the parties could negate what would otherwise be the clear legal effect of what they had agreed to do. In the words of Lord Templeman (at p. 819), 'The manufacture of a five pronged implement for manual digging results in a fork, even if the manufacturer, unfamiliar with the English language, insists that he intended to make and has made a spade'.

To see whether an agreement is a tenancy it is necessary to determine whether the effect of the agreement is to confer all the elements of a tenancy on the occupier. In *Street v Mountford* Lord Templeman concentrated primarily on the issue of whether or not exclusive possession has been granted as the test for distinguishing between a lease and a licence.

Thus the general rule is that:

(a) where there is a grant of exclusive possession to an occupier for a definable term at a rent, a tenancy will usually be created (although strictly speaking rent is not an essential characteristic of a tenancy);
(b) where exclusive possession is not granted there cannot be a tenancy;
(c) these principles apply irrespective of the actual intention of the parties.

Exceptions to the general rule

83.3 Although the grant of exclusive possession normally creates a tenancy, there are a number of exceptions to this rule. In certain situations an occupier who has been granted exclusive possession may hold only a licence.

The basis for these exceptions was set out by Denning LJ in *Facchini v Bryson* [1952] 1 TLR 1386 at pp. 1389–90, and is referred to by Lord Templeman in *Street v Mountford* [1985] AC 809:

> In all the cases where an occupier has been held to be a licensee there has been something in the circumstances, such as a family agreement, an act of friendship or generosity, or such like, to negative any intention to create a tenancy.

According to Lord Templeman there are three categories which consist of circumstances of legal significance which would negative a grant of a tenancy:

(a) Where there is no intention to create legal relations (see **83.4**).
(b) Where there is some relationship other than landlord and tenant (see **83.5** to **83.7**).
(c) Where the grantor has no power to grant a tenancy (see **83.8**).

No intention to create legal relations

83.4 In *Booker v Palmer* [1942] 2 All ER 674, the owner allowed a number of evacuees to stay in his cottage rent free for the duration of the war (an act of friendship or generosity). It was held that the parties did not intend to contract at all. 'The law does not impute intention to enter into legal relationships where the circumstances and the conduct of the parties negative any intention of the kind' (per Lord Greene MR at p. 677). Likewise in *Cobb v Lane* [1952] 1 All ER 1199 where the owner of a house allowed his brother to live there rent free (a family arrangement) there was no tenancy because there was no intention to enter into legal relations (see also *Heslop v Burns* [1974] 1 WLR 1241).

The question as to whether the parties entered into a legal relationship is not always straightforward. In *Marcroft Wagons Ltd v Smith* [1951] 2 KB 496, the statutory tenant having died, his daughter upon the death of his widow claimed to be a statutory tenant by succession. The landlords refused to recognise her claim, but accepted payments from her while they considered the matter. The Court of Appeal held that there was no intention to create legal relations and no tenancy had arisen upon the payments made by the daughter. In *Leadenhall Residential 2 Ltd v Stirling* [2001] EWCA Civ 1011, [2002] 1 WLR 499, the landlord had obtained an order for possession of a dwelling-house held on an assured tenancy by Mr Stirling, but had allowed him to remain in occupation on condition that he paid the rent arrears and rent accruing. The Court of Appeal held that there was no intention to affect the legal relations of the parties and that as from the making of the possession order Mr Stirling had occupied the premises as a licensee.

Some other legal relationship

The right to exclusive possession may arise in a legal relationship other than a tenancy. **83.5**

Vendor and purchaser In *Errington v Errington and Woods* [1952] 1 KB 290 a father bought a house by paying £250 in cash and borrowing £500 from the building society. He gave the building society book to his son and daughter-in-law and told them that the £250 was a present, and if they paid the instalments on the loan the house would be theirs. The father died and left the house to his wife who sought to gain possession from the daughter-in-law (the son had moved back to his mother's home). It was held that the daughter-in-law and son were not tenants but licensees, notwithstanding that they had exclusive possession of the property. They were said to be 'in a position analogous to purchasers' (per Denning LJ at p. 154). (The view expressed in this case, that a contractual licence could bind third parties, was overruled in *Ashburn Anstalt v Arnold* [1989] Ch 1.) **83.6**

Employer and employee The fact that an occupier happens to be employed by his or her landlord does not mean that that occupier cannot be a tenant. Where, for example, the owner of a factory also owns housing in the area, it may be convenient for both parties if a worker at the factory lives in a house owned by the factory owner. This is no reason why the worker should not be a tenant; there is no necessity that the worker should live there and not elsewhere. The situation will, however, be different in a case where accommodation 'goes with the job' in that it is necessary for the employee to live in this particular accommodation to perform the duties involved in his or her employment. Such a person is known as a service occupier or a service licensee. **83.7**

Where a person occupies accommodation as a service licensee and has exclusive possession of that accommodation no tenancy will be created. Whether or not a person is a service licensee or a tenant will be a question of fact. If the employee is genuinely required to occupy the premises for the better performance of his or her duties, he or she will be a service licensee (*Norris v Checksfield* [1991] 1 WLR 1241).

No power to grant a tenancy

In *Bruton v London and Quadrant Housing Trust* [2000] 1 AC 406 the House of Lords held that a landlord could grant a tenancy even though it held no proprietary interest in the premises. A charitable housing trust was granted a licence by the local authority to use a block of flats to provide short-term accommodation for homeless persons. It purported to confer a licence on the occupier on a weekly basis. The occupier nevertheless obtained a tenancy, enabling him to enforce the statutorily implied covenant to repair contained in the Landlord and Tenant Act 1985, s. 11, which applies only to tenancies. It is a strange notion that the tenancy identified by the House of Lords in this case had no proprietary effect and was therefore, one presumes, purely contractual. It has since been held that the kind of tenancy held to have been created in *Bruton v London and Quadrant Housing Trust* does not bind the superior landlord and so cannot satisfy the landlord condition which is required to create a secure tenancy of public-sector housing (see **88.2** and **88.3**) (*Kay v Lambeth London Borough Council* [2006] UKHL 10, [2006] 2 WLR 570; *Islington London Borough Council v Green* [2005] EWCA Civ 5, [2005] HLR 35). **83.8**

EXCLUSIVE POSSESSION

83.9 Of course in many cases, as in *Street v Mountford* [1985] AC 809, none of the above exceptions applies, in which case determining whether the occupier has a lease or a licence is decided purely by reference to whether exclusive possession has been granted. Although *Street v Mountford* decided that exclusive possession is the touchstone of a tenancy, the House of Lords failed to provide any in-depth definition or analysis of the concept.

In determining whether exclusive possession has been granted, the decisive consideration appears to be the degree of control over the premises and their use, which is retained by the owner. A number of situations are addressed at **83.10** to **83.19**.

The lodger

83.10 An occupier of residential accommodation for a term at a rent may be a lodger:

> The occupier is a lodger if the landlord provides attendance or services which require the landlord or his servants to exercise unrestricted access to and use of the premises . . . any express reservation to the landlord of limited rights to enter and view the state of the premises and to repair and maintain the premises only serves to emphasise the fact that the grantee is entitled to exclusive possession and is a tenant. (*Street v Mountford* [1985] AC 809, per Lord Templeman at p. 818.)

A lodger is always a licensee, although a licensee is not invariably a lodger. A lodger is an individual who occupies a room in another person's home; he or she has shared use of facilities such as the kitchen and bathroom and traditionally is provided with certain services by the owner, such as breakfast and/or supper, clean linen, and cleaning (see *Marchant v Charters* [1977] 1 WLR 1181). The provision of these services is usually included in the fee paid for the accommodation. It is also common for the owner to impose further restrictions which interfere with the lodger's occupancy of the room, for example, on the number of guests or times during which such guests may enter on the premises.

If attendance and services are provided they indicate that the owner retains a degree of control over the premises which is incompatible with exclusive possession, because they require unrestricted access in order to provide the services which are part of the contract. Whether the rights retained by the owner interfere with the occupancy of the room to such an extent that it cannot be said that the occupier has exclusive possession will often be a question of fact.

Retirement homes and hostels

83.11 The provision of attendance and services is not confined to the traditional lodger. In *Abbeyfield (Harpenden) Society Ltd v Woods* [1968] 1 WLR 374, the occupier of a room in a retirement home was held to be a licensee despite the fact that he had exclusive possession of his room. The elderly person was provided with two meals per day and there was a resident housekeeper. Lord Denning MR decided he was a licensee (despite the fact that the word 'rent' was used to describe his weekly payments) on the basis that the whole agreement was 'personal in nature', not on the grounds that the occupier did not have exclusive possession. Nevertheless Lord Templeman approved of this case in *Street v Mountford* [1985] AC 809 by saying simply that the court came to the conclusion that the occupier was a lodger. He did not explain the reasoning that led him to this conclusion. Following the decision in *Westminster City Council v Clarke* [1992] 2 AC 288, it is probable that if this case was to be decided today it would not be the personal nature of the relationship that was decisive; more likely it would be held that the owner of the retirement home in fact retained a degree of control over the premises such that the occupier could not be said to have exclusive possession.

Retention of keys by the owner

83.12 Whether or not an owner grants exclusive possession is assessed by the courts in a broad way, taking into account not merely the nature of the accommodation provided, but also the surrounding circumstances. A particular example of this is the question of the retention of a key by the owner. It has been argued by many owners in various cases that the retention of a key denies the occupier exclusive possession, but the courts have refused to take such a simple view. Exclusive possession of premises is not to be equated with exclusive possession of the keys to those premises. The retention of a key 'has no magic in itself', what has to be considered is the underlying reason for the retention of the key:

A landlord may well need a key, in order that he may be able to enter quickly in the event of an emergency, fire, burst pipes or whatever. He may need a key to enable him or those authorised by him to read meters or to do repairs which are his responsibility. (*Aslan v Murphy (Nos 1 and 2)* [1989] 3 All ER 130 at p. 135.)

In *Family Housing Association v Jones* [1990] 1 WLR 779, the housing association retained a key in order to inspect the premises and to provide the occupier with help and advice. This was held not to interfere with her exclusive possession of the property. Of course if the key was retained in order for the owner to fulfil an obligation to provide services of some sort, such as to clean the room or to change the sheets, it might well be inferred that the occupier was a licensee and not a tenant.

Sham agreements

The classic definition of a sham comes from *Snook v London and West Riding Investments Ltd* **83.13** [1967] 2 QB 786. In discussing the meaning in law of the word 'sham', Diplock LJ said (at p. 802): '. . . if it has any meaning in law, it means acts done or documents executed by the parties to the "sham" which are intended by them to give to third parties or to the court the appearance of creating between the parties legal rights and obligations different from the actual legal rights and obligations (if any) which the parties intend to create'.

In determining whether the actual legal rights are different from the rights set out in the document the courts must take 'due account of how the parties have acted in performance of their apparent bargain' (*Aslan v Murphy (Nos 1 and 2)* [1989] 3 All ER 130 at p. 133). The starting point, however, will be the document itself. In *Crancour v Da Silvaesa* [1986] 1 EGLR 81 Purchas LJ (at p. 88) set out the correct approach as follows:

. . . to construe the document as a whole in order to determine the nature and quality of the occupancy under the terms of the agreement reached between the parties. To this end the use of the words such as licence or lease in the agreement is not definitive, nor indeed is the *de facto* intention of either or both of the parties. Subject to the agreement on its face appearing to be a sham, the effect in law of the agreement must depend upon its construction in accordance with the normal rules in the context of its factual matrix and genesis.

It is important to note that sham clauses cannot be detected simply by looking at what happened after the grant. It is a combination of looking at the clause itself to see whether it makes sense in the context of a grant of residential accommodation, and looking at the surrounding circumstances for supporting evidence. Subsequent conduct is not relevant as an aid to construction of the document, but it is relevant in determining whether the document gives effect to the true intention of the parties (see *Antoniades v Villiers* [1990] 1 AC 417).

Multiple occupation

Without exclusive possession there can be no tenancy. The occupier of a flat with exclusive **83.14** possession has the right to exclude all others from that flat, including the landlord. However, if an occupier shares that flat with one or more people, the sharers too have a right to be there. The legal position of the individuals within the property will depend on the nature of the agreement between the various parties. Examples are given at **83.15** to **83.18**.

A tenancy is granted of an individual room within a property Each individual is granted a **83.15** tenancy of an individual room, together with the right to share the common areas of the property. Each occupier therefore has exclusive possession of the room allocated. Such an arrangement is almost certain to create a tenancy, in that each tenant has the right to exclude the other sharers from his or her room, and is also only individually liable for the rent. Failure to pay the rent will not render the other tenants liable for the shortfall. Individual tenants have no legal control over the occupancy of the other rooms, and cannot change rooms without entering into a new agreement with the landlord.

83.16 **A joint tenancy of a single property is granted to a group of individuals** A single agreement is signed by all the tenants. There is one rent for which all are jointly and severally liable, as they are for all the other terms and conditions of the agreement. Essentially, the group is treated for legal purposes as if it was a single person. The prerequisites for such an agreement (the 'four unities') are that:

(a) the tenancy must start at the same time for each occupant;
(b) the tenancy must be created by one action or document;
(c) the interest of each sharer must be of the same nature, duration and extent;
(d) each sharer must be equally entitled to possession of the whole.

83.17 **Landlord purports to grant a right to use the property in common with others** Where the landlord purports to grant the occupant the right to use the property in common with others who may from time to time be granted the like right, with the occupant agreeing to share the use of the flat peaceably with, and not to impede the use of the flat by, such persons, the courts will, in determining the relationship between the parties, look to the 'substance and reality of the transaction entered into by the parties' (*AG Securities v Vaughan* [1990] 1 AC 417 per Lord Ackner at p. 466). In *Antoniades v Villiers* (heard together with *AG Securities v Vaughan*), Lord Templeman stated (at p. 458) that surrounding circumstances will include, 'any relationship between the prospective occupiers, the course of negotiations and the nature and extent of the accommodation and the intended and actual mode of occupation of the accommodation'. In the event, for example, that the occupiers in the above example did not know each other before they moved into the property, they entered into agreements with the landlord at various times, the negotiations did not suggest there was any intention to grant a joint tenancy, the situation was clear to each occupier when he or she moved in, the flat being large and suitable for sharing, and other occupiers moving in or being substituted in the course of time, it is probable that the court would see the arrangement as 'a sensible one which suited both the owner of the flat and a shifting population of occupiers' (*Stribling v Wickham* [1989] 2 EGLR 35). The sharers between them would not enjoy exclusive possession of the premises as 'The landlord is not excluded for he continues to enjoy the premises through his invitees, even though he may for the time being have precluded himself by contract with each from withdrawing the invitation' (per Lord Oliver of Aylmerton in *AG Securities v Vaughan* at p. 471). A different approach would be to analyse why such an agreement, if genuine, could *not* be a joint tenancy: each occupant would be liable for no more than his individual payment to the landlord in the event of default by another, and the 'four unities' at **83.16**, would not be satisfied.

83.18 **Landlord purports to grant a licence to a couple who sign separate agreements** The final example is where the landlord purports to grant a licence to occupy to a couple, although individual agreements are signed by each occupant under which they agree to share the rooms in common with the licensor and such other licensees or invitees as the licensor may from time to time permit. Each occupant pays a separate 'licence fee' equivalent to half the agreed rent. As has been discussed earlier, the court will reject any clause it considers to be a sham, by considering whether the clause represented the true bargain between the parties. In the present case, assuming that, during the currency of their occupation, the landlord never sought either to use the rooms himself or herself or to authorise any other person to do so, and that the occupants intended to occupy the property as a couple living together, it is highly probable that the court would hold the agreement to be a sham. In *Antoniades v Villiers* [1990] 1 AC 417 the House of Lords decided, on facts virtually identical to the above, that it was quite implausible that the landlord had ever seriously intended either to move in himself or to authorise a stranger to share the property.

Consequence of deciding that separate agreements to a couple create a lease Nevertheless, one difficulty still remains. The couple, together, have exclusive possession of the flat (the agreement being held to be a sham). If exclusive possession for a term at a rent is granted to a single occupier, that occupier has a tenancy. However, given that the parties have both signed separate agreements which hold them individually liable for half the rent, there appears to be no unity of interest, in that should one party leave, the other would not be liable for the remainder of the rent, it is at first glance hard to see how there could be a valid joint tenancy. **83.19**

This is a difficult question and present authority seems to suggest that without a joint liability to pay the whole of the rent there cannot be a joint tenancy. Consequently it may be the case that a couple can share a flat together under two agreements which entitle them to joint exclusive possession of the flat at a rent for a term but, because each agreement states that each occupier is to pay half the rent, they will not be joint tenants and therefore will not be eligible for statutory protection. It is not possible to argue that they are each individual tenants because they do not individually have exclusive possession of the flat; they hold exclusive possession jointly but not as against each other (see, for example, *Mikeover Ltd v Brady* [1989] 3 All ER 618).

In *Antoniades v Villiers* [1990] 1 AC 417 Lord Templeman avoided this consequence by saying that the two agreements signed were interdependent: 'The grant of a tenancy to two persons jointly cannot be concealed accidentally or by design, by the creation of two documents in the form of licences' (at pp. 458–9). He went on to give the following example:

> If the owner of a one-bedroomed flat granted a licence to a husband to occupy the flat provided he shared the flat with his wife and nobody else and granted a similar licence to the wife provided she shared the flat with the husband and nobody else, the court would be bound to consider the effect of both documents together. If the licence to the husband required him to pay a licence fee of £50 per month and the licence to the wife required her to pay a further licence fee of £50 per month, the two documents read together in the light of the property to be occupied and the obvious intended mode of occupation would confer exclusive occupation on the husband and wife jointly and a tenancy at the rent of £100.

And further, at p. 461:

> A tenancy remains a tenancy even though the landlord may choose to require each of two joint tenants to agree expressly to pay one half of the rent.

Therefore, if one moves out, the other is liable for the full rent.

Summary of principles

The following principles can therefore be drawn: **83.20**

(a) Exclusive possession will not be destroyed by the inclusion of a clause in the agreement entitling an owner to move in another occupier. If it is clear from the surrounding circumstances that the flat is not suitable for multiple occupation, such a clause would not reflect the true nature of the bargain.
(b) If the agreement holds the occupiers separately liable for rent, they will not be joint tenants unless they can show that the conferment of separate liability is a sham.

COMMERCIAL PREMISES

83.21 This chapter has set out the rules distinguishing between leases and licences in relation to agreements for the occupation of residential property. Different factors may affect agreements for the occupation of commercial premises, although for the most part the central principles of *Street v Mountford* [1985] AC 809 have been applied by the courts. This issue is discussed further in 91.3.

Chapter 84 Forfeiture

INTRODUCTION

Forfeiture is not primarily a method of termination, but a remedy. The purpose of the re- **84.1**
entry provision found in most leases is not to enable the fixed term to be ended prematurely for the landlord's own purposes, but rather to provide the landlord with an effective sanction against a defaulting tenant. A landlord who foresees a need to terminate a fixed term early should include a break clause in the tenancy agreement.

However, the result of forfeiture proceedings can be the termination of the tenancy. Of all the remedies a landlord can employ against a defaulting tenant it is the most potent. The landlord could instead pursue a claim for damages for breach of covenant or seek an injunction, but neither of these remedies will be backed by the ultimate sanction of repossession. It is, however, for this very reason that the law seeks to ensure that the landlord cannot use the right of forfeiture inappropriately or capriciously. In the words of Coke (*Duppa v Mayho* (1669) 1 Saund 282 at p. 287), 'The law leans against forfeitures'.

The landlord's right to forfeit is limited in a variety of ways:

(a) It can be used only in situations where the landlord has expressly reserved the right to forfeit in the tenancy agreement.
(b) The landlord must comply with strict procedural requirements.
(c) It is subject to strict rules of waiver.
(d) The tenant has extensive rights to apply to the court for relief from forfeiture.

Who can forfeit?

84.2 Whilst a notice to quit can be served by either the landlord or the tenant, proceedings to forfeit a lease can be brought only by the landlord. A tenant who wishes to end a fixed-term tenancy before the term has expired has very limited options. The only way the tenant can end the tenancy is to try to get the landlord to agree to surrender. This, however, requires the consent of both parties. If the landlord will not voluntarily agree to surrender, the tenant may well be compelled to fulfil the obligations under the lease for the whole of the fixed term.

A tenant does not have a right equivalent to the landlord's right to forfeit. A tenant who wishes to terminate the lease in response to the landlord's breaches of covenant will only be able to do so if the breach is repudiatory, in the sense that it vitiates the central purpose of the contract of letting (*Hussein v Mehlman* [1992] 2 EGLR 87). While the inequity of this situation has not been lost on the Law Commission (see *Forfeiture of Tenancies* (Law Com. No. 142) (1985)), there are no current proposals to mitigate it.

WHEN CAN A LANDLORD FORFEIT?

84.3 A landlord can acquire the right to forfeit a tenancy in only two situations, both of which can be brought about only by some act or omission on the part of the tenant. If the tenant fulfils all the obligations in the lease, the landlord will not acquire any right to forfeit and will be unable to terminate the tenancy before the fixed term has expired.

The landlord will acquire the right to forfeit the lease if the tenant breaches either:

(a) a condition; or

(b) a covenant *and* the lease contains a proviso for re-entry.

Forfeiture for breach of condition is unusual, but may arise, for example, where a lease is made conditional on the performance of an obligation which the tenant breaches, or where the tenant disclaims the landlord's title. In practice virtually every modern lease will contain a re-entry clause. Furthermore, if a tenant holds under an equitable lease a right of re-entry for non-payment of rent and for breach of covenant will be implied as a 'usual covenant'.

Proviso for re-entry

84.4 The proviso for re-entry will set out the circumstances in which the landlord may re-enter the property and terminate the tenancy. Normally the clause permits the landlord to forfeit for any breach of covenant and for non-payment of rent, although a re-entry clause can be drafted to include other circumstances, for example the bankruptcy of the tenant.

The courts will construe any re-entry clause *contra proferentem* (against the person putting it forward) and apply it in favour of the tenant. For example, a clause that reserved the right to re-enter in respect of 'any act matter or thing contrary to and in breach of the covenants' was held not to extend to a breach of the repairing covenant, because to fail to repair was an omission and not an act (*Doe d Abdy v Stevens* (1832) 3 B & Ad 299). A clause which referred to the covenants 'thereinafter contained', when they in fact preceded the clause in the lease, was also held to be ineffective (*Doe d Spencer v Goodwin* (1815) 4 M & S 264).

The landlord must choose to forfeit — an unequivocal act

84.5 If a tenant breaches one of the covenants in the lease, the landlord acquires the right to forfeit, but may choose not to exercise that right and treat the tenancy as continuing. It follows that in order to forfeit, there must be some unequivocal act which demonstrates that the landlord regards the relationship of landlord and tenant as being at an end.

Peaceable re-entry

The most obvious way of showing an intention to end a tenancy is by physically re-entering the premises and recovering possession. Today, however, the landlord would be unwise to take the wording of the forfeiture clause in the lease too literally as the situations in which the landlord can physically re-enter are severely limited by statute (see below) and arise rarely in practice. It is only in the case of unoccupied business premises that peaceable re-entry can be a realistic option for a landlord. Physical re-entry has the advantage that the landlord will not have to wait for the outcome of a possession hearing. **84.6**

Peaceable re-entry has no application with regard to residential tenancies. Section 2 of the Protection from Eviction Act 1977 provides that:

> Where any premises are let as a dwelling on a lease which is subject to a right of re-entry or forfeiture it shall not be lawful to enforce that right otherwise than by proceedings in the court while any person is lawfully residing in the premises or part of them.

A landlord who tries physically to re-enter residential premises may be liable to criminal prosecution for unlawful eviction under this provision if 'any person' (it does not have to be the tenant) is lawfully occupying the premises.

Furthermore, the Criminal Law Act 1977 prohibits anyone using force to re-enter premises. Section 6(1) provides that:

> . . . any person who, without lawful authority, uses or threatens violence for the purpose of securing entry into any premises for himself or for any other person is guilty of an offence, provided that—
> (a) there is someone present on those premises at the time who is opposed to the entry which the violence is intended to secure; and
> (b) the person using or threatening the violence knows that that is the case.

The fact that a person has an interest in or right to possession of the premises does not constitute lawful authority for the purpose of seeking possession (s. 6(2)).

Service of proceedings

The usual way of showing an intention to treat a tenant's breach of a condition or covenant as giving rise to forfeiture is by taking proceedings for possession. (In the majority of cases the landlord will have to give the tenant notice even before issuing proceedings, under s. 146 of the Law of Property Act 1925, see **84.16**.) Serving proceedings upon the tenant is equivalent to the landlord actually re-entering the premises. If the tenant then voluntarily leaves the premises the landlord will be able to regain possession. In practice, however, the service of proceedings upon the tenant is rarely the end of the story. It is by no means a foregone conclusion that the court will make a possession order, and in any case the tenant's right of occupation will continue until such an order is made. **84.7**

If at the hearing the court decides to grant the landlord a possession order, the lease is actually regarded as being forfeited upon the date of the service of the proceedings. This leaves the status of the tenant between service and possession somewhat unclear (see *Liverpool Properties Ltd v Oldbridge Investments Ltd* [1985] 2 EGLR 111). Certainly the tenant possesses some sort of interest, by virtue of having a right to apply for relief from forfeiture; and if doing so can still enforce the landlord's covenants (*Peninsular Maritime Ltd v Padseal Ltd* (1981) 259 EG 860).

On the other hand, having demonstrated an intention to forfeit the lease by serving proceedings, the landlord ceases to be able to enforce any of the covenants in the lease. By forfeiting the lease the landlord treats it as being at an end and the notional date of forfeiture is the date of service of the proceedings. If the landlord issues a claim that assumes the continuation of the lease beyond this notional date of forfeiture — by, for example, seeking an injunction to restrain a future breach — issuing the claim will not be regarded as an unequivocal act and will not give rise to forfeiture (*Moore v Ullcoats Mining Co. Ltd* [1908] 1 Ch 575).

If a claim has been made for relief against forfeiture the status of the tenancy will remain uncertain. Therefore, if the tenant is eventually granted relief, the landlord will be able to claim rent for the entire period up until the final hearing (*Maryland Estates Ltd v Joseph* [1999] 1 WLR 83). This point is of great importance when assessing the amount of arrears of rent that must be paid by a tenant in order to claim relief from forfeiture (see **84.30**). If no application for relief is made, the tenancy will terminate on the date of service of the claim form and the landlord will only be entitled to claim mesne profits (rather than rent) for occupation from that date to the date he or she regains possession.

Mesne profits are a special form of damages payable to the landlord for losses incurred due to a tenant staying in possession after the tenancy has ended.

WAIVER

84.8 Once a tenant has breached an obligation in the lease the landlord must choose whether to forfeit or not. The crucial date, however, is not when the breach itself occurs, but when the landlord first has knowledge of the breach. If the landlord chooses to issue proceedings straightaway, the intention is made clear. However, doing something to indicate that the tenancy is regarded by the landlord as still continuing is deemed to waive the breach. The doctrine of waiver has no application once the landlord has elected to forfeit, either by issuing proceedings or by peaceable re-entry.

The rules of waiver are, however, very strict. For waiver to operate the landlord must:

(a) have knowledge of the breach;
(b) do something which recognises the continuation of the tenancy.

Knowledge of the breach

84.9 Obviously the landlord cannot waive the right to forfeit a lease before knowing that the right has arisen. Establishing knowledge may not always be a straightforward matter, particularly where the landlord rarely visits the property or where it is managed through an agent. The general rule, however, is that where a landlord's agent or other employee knows of a breach of obligation, this knowledge will be imputed to the landlord provided that the employee has had a reasonable amount of time to inform the landlord of the breach. This is based on the principle that an agent or employee is under a duty to communicate information to his or her principal or employer. For example, where a tenant sublets a flat in breach of covenant and the porters in the building are aware that someone else is living in the flat, the landlord is deemed to know of the breach (*Metropolitan Properties Co. Ltd v Cordery* (1979) 39 P & CR 10). However, where a tenant sublet his premises and the landlord became aware that there had been a change of occupation, but accepted the tenant's untruthful explanation that the new tenant was a housekeeper, the landlord did not lose the right to forfeit (*Chrisdell Ltd v Johnson* (1987) 19 HLR 406).

Recognising the continuation of the tenancy

84.10 A landlord who knows of a breach can of course expressly consent to it and thereby waive the right to forfeit. Waiver may also be implied from the landlord's actions and is judged objectively, without regard to the motive or intention of the landlord, or to the actual understanding or belief of the tenant (Buckley LJ in *Central Estates (Belgravia) Ltd v Woolgar (No. 2)* [1972] 1 WLR 1048 at p. 1054, cited in *Expert Clothing Service and Sales Ltd v Hillgate House Ltd* [1986] Ch 340 at p. 360).

84.11 **Accepting rent** The most common way by which a landlord who has knowledge of a breach of obligation by the tenant can recognise the continuation of the tenancy is by accepting or demanding rent which falls due after the breach. To some extent this stands as a special category on its own: the law takes a very strict line and the implication of waiver will be virtually inevitable. To accept rent 'without prejudice' makes no difference, the landlord will still be deemed to have waived the right to forfeit (*Segal Securities Ltd v Thoseby* [1963] 1 QB 887), even if rent is accepted by mistake, for example, where an employee sent out a demand for rent to the tenant (*Central Estates (Belgravia) Ltd v Woolgar (No. 2)* [1972] 1 WLR 1048).

Other acts of waiver If a landlord gives a tenant notice of intention to enter the property to carry out repairs, this will amount to waiver of the right to forfeit for breach of repairing covenant (*Doe d De Rutzen v Lewis* (1836) 5 Ad & El 277). If the landlord serves a notice to quit on the tenant requiring the tenant to give up the tenancy at a date in the future, this will also amount to an act affirming the existence of the tenancy (*Marche v Christodoulakis* (1948) 64 TLR 466). **84.12**

Effect of waiver

The effect of waiver depends upon the nature of the breach of covenant. In the case of a once and for all breach, such as the breach of a covenant against subletting, once the landlord has waived the breach he or she will lose any right to forfeit for that particular breach in the future. The breach of covenant consists of the act of granting the sublease. The fact that the sublease continues to exist after the act of waiver does not give rise to a fresh cause of action. If, however, on the expiry of the sub-tenancy, a fresh subletting took place in breach of covenant, fresh proceedings for forfeiture could then be initiated. **84.13**

LIMITATION

By **s. 15(1) of the Limitation Act 1980**, the limitation period for all proceedings relating to land is 12 years. Once the tenant has breached an obligation in the lease and a cause of action has accrued (which is when the landlord has knowledge of the breach), the landlord must take action to pursue the right to forfeit within 12 years. In practice, because of the strict rules of waiver, it is most unlikely that a landlord will lose a right to forfeit through limitation. **84.14**

FURTHER RESTRICTIONS ON FORFEITURE

Even if a breach of obligation can be established and the landlord does nothing to waive the right to forfeit, it is by no means a foregone conclusion that forfeiture will be the end result of the process. Two further restrictions come into play. First, the landlord must comply with strict procedural rules which give the tenant the opportunity to remedy the breach; and, secondly, the tenant in any case may be granted relief from forfeiture. **84.15**

A certain complexity arises at this point, for the procedural rules relating to forfeiture for non-payment of rent are different to those relating to breach of any other covenant.

Procedure for forfeiture for breaches of covenant other than non-payment of rent

Law of Property Act 1925, s. 146 All breaches of covenant other than non-payment of rent are governed by s. 146 of the Law of Property Act 1925 (apart from a few limited exceptions contained in s. 146(8) and (9) regarding breaches that occurred before the commencement of the Act, mining, agricultural and other specialised leases). The landlord cannot exclude the operation of s. 146 by any contrary provision contained in the lease (s. 146(12)). **84.16**

Section 146 provides that before a right of re-entry can be exercised, whether it is intended to issue proceedings for possession or to re-enter peaceably, the landlord must serve on the tenant a s. 146 notice. A s. 146 notice is a statutory condition precedent to forfeiture proceedings. Any proceedings brought without serving a valid s. 146 notice will be ineffective.

84.17 **Section 146 notices** The s. 146 notice requires the landlord formally to set out the complaint by specifying the breach. For the notice to be valid it also requires the landlord to require the breach to be remedied within a reasonable time, if that breach is capable of remedy. The procedure demanded by statute thus gives the tenant a last chance to remedy the breach once notice has been given of the landlord's complaint. If the breach is capable of remedy, the tenant can avoid forfeiture proceedings altogether by remedying the breach within a reasonable time. The landlord can go on to forfeit only if:

(a) the breach is not capable of remedy within a reasonable time; or
(b) the breach is capable of remedy within a reasonable time and, having been given a reasonable time to do so, the tenant has failed to remedy the breach.

When drafting the s. 146 notice the landlord will have to decide whether the tenant's breach is capable of remedy, for if the landlord fails to require the tenant to remedy a breach that is in fact capable of remedy the notice itself will be invalid. In reality the test is not whether the breach is capable of remedy, but whether the damage caused by the breach is capable of remedy (see *Rugby School v Tannahill* [1935] 1 KB 87).

84.18 **Positive covenants** In *Expert Clothing Service and Sales Ltd v Hillgate House Ltd* [1986] Ch 340 the tenant failed, in breach of covenant, to rebuild the premises within a specified time. This breach was held as being capable of remedy because the rebuilding could be finished late and the landlord could be compensated in money for the delay, in which event the landlord's interest would not be irretrievably damaged. This case laid down a general, if not conclusive, rule that positive covenants are capable of remedy, be they once and for all breaches or continuing breaches.

84.19 **Negative covenants** In the case of continuing breach of a negative covenant, it seems that the breach will also often be remediable. A breach of a covenant not to keep a pet can be remedied by getting rid of the pet without causing significant harm to the landlord. Likewise (as considered by O'Connor LJ in *Expert Clothing Service and Sales Ltd v Hillgate House Ltd* [1986] Ch 340 at p. 362G) the removal of window-boxes and payment for any damage caused by them would remedy a breach of covenant not to have window-boxes. However, the situation may well be different in cases involving immoral user (usually prostitution or gambling), which are dominated by the notion of 'stigma'; and those involving a breach of covenant not to assign or sublet, which turn upon an anomaly which arises when an attempt is made to apply s. 146.

A line of cases (*Egerton v Esplanade Hotels London Ltd* [1947] 2 All ER 88; *Hoffmann v Fineberg* [1949] Ch 245, *Rugby School v Tannahill* [1935] 1 KB 87; *Glass v Kencakes Ltd* [1966] 1 QB 611) involving breach of covenant not to cause or permit immoral user of the premises has established that in general such a breach is not capable of remedy. In *Rugby School v Tannahill* Greer LJ said, at p. 91:

> I cannot conceive how a breach of this kind can be remedied. The result of committing the breach would be known all over the neighbourhood and seriously affect the value of the premises. Even a money payment together with the cessation of the improper use of the house could not be a remedy.

In *Glass v Kencakes Ltd*, however, it was suggested that such a breach could be remediable if prompt action was taken by the tenant to stop the immoral user before the damaging stigma could become established.

In *Scala House and District Property Co. Ltd v Forbes* [1974] QB 575, it was held that a breach of a covenant not to assign or sublet was not capable of remedy.

84.20 **Remediable breaches: conclusion** Thus:

(a) Breaches of positive covenants, whether once and for all or continuing, are capable of remedy (e.g., covenant to repair).

(b) Continuing breaches of negative covenants may be capable of remedy (e.g., user covenants), but not if the breach results in a stigma becoming attached to the property.
(c) Once and for all breaches of negative covenants are not capable of remedy (e.g., assignment, subletting).

If the tenant is unable or unwilling to remedy the breach complained of by the landlord within a reasonable time, or if the breach is of a type not capable of remedy, the statutory condition precedent set by s. 146 will be satisfied and the landlord will be free to re-enter, either by service of proceedings or by peaceable re-entry. The tenant, however, is provided with a further opportunity to avoid forfeiture by applying to the court for relief (see **84.25**).

Procedure for forfeiture for non-payment of rent and sums payable as rent

If the landlord is seeking to forfeit for non-payment of rent, the requirements of the Law of Property Act 1925, s. 146, do not apply (s. 146(11)). A s. 146 notice will be required, however, if a landlord seeks to forfeit a lease for a breach of covenant to pay any sums to the landlord which are not reserved as rent, for example, service charges. To avoid the need to serve s. 146 notices, many leases provide for service charges to be recoverable as 'rent'. **84.21**

Where a tenant is in breach of the covenant to pay rent, no issue arises as to whether the breach is capable of remedy or not; it is clear that here the object of the forfeiture clause is to secure payment. If the tenant pays the arrears, relief will almost certainly be granted (see **84.30**). Forfeiture is only one of a number of remedies available to the landlord, who could also pursue a claim for debt or distrain. Forfeiture is available to the landlord only if a right of re-entry has been reserved in the lease, but most modern leases contain a proviso permitting re-entry if the rent remains unpaid for a specified period (generally 14 or 21 days).

Formal demand At common law the landlord is unable to enforce a right of re-entry for breach of covenant to pay rent until a formal demand has been made for the rent. This must be made by the landlord or the landlord's agent, at the demised premises or at the place specified in the lease for the payment of rent, and must require the exact sum due to be paid before sunset on the last date for due payment (*Duppa v Mayho* (1669) 1 Saund 282 at p. 287). To obviate these inconvenient requirements, virtually all leases now state that the landlord can re-enter once rent is in arrears for a certain period, whether the rent has been formally demanded or not. **84.22**

Even if there are no words in the lease dispensing with the landlord's need to give a formal demand for rent, a formal demand may not be required where more than half a year's rent is in arrears. Section 210 of the Common Law Procedure Act 1852 (for proceedings in the High Court) and **s. 139(1) of the County Courts Act 1984** state that there is no need for a formal demand if at least half a year's rent is in arrears and the goods present on the premises that are available for the purposes of distress are insufficient in value to cover the arrears due.

Forfeiture for breach of repairing covenants

The Leasehold Property (Repairs) Act 1938 applies in relation to the breach of any covenant or agreement to keep or put in repair all or any part of the property let during the currency of the tenancy. It does not apply to agricultural holdings (under the Agricultural Holdings Act 1986) or to tenancies granted for a term of seven years or more of which three years remain at the time of service of notice under the Law of Property Act 1925, s. 146. The landlord's s. 146 notice must inform the tenant that he or she may serve a counter-notice within 28 days. If such a counter-notice is served, the landlord may not proceed by action or otherwise to enforce the forfeiture without the permission of the court. Permission may only be granted on proof (on the balance of probabilities: *Associated British Ports v C. H. Bailey plc* [1990] 2 AC 703) by the landlord of one of five specific grounds set out in s. 1(5) of the 1938 Act. The procedure applies to tenants but not to mortgagees who have no entitlement to be served (*Smith v Spaull*). **84.23**

By the Law of Property Act 1925, s. 147, a tenant on whom a s. 146 notice relating to internal decorative repairs (to a house or other building) has been served may apply to the court for relief from the liability to perform the repairs.

Forfeiture for non-payment of service and administration charges

84.24 A landlord of premises let as a dwelling may not exercise a right of re-entry or forfeiture for failure to pay a service or administration charge unless the amount due has been admitted by the tenant or it has been finally determined by the court, a leasehold valuation tribunal or an arbitral tribunal (Housing Act 1996, s. 81, as amended by the Commonhold and Leasehold Reform Act 2002, sch. 11). This is intended to prevent landlords from seeking to forfeit residential tenancies where the parties are in dispute about a service or administration charge. There are further statutory restrictions, applicable to long leases, on the exercise by the landlord of rights of re-entry or forfeiture for failure to pay rent, service or administration charges (Commonhold and Leasehold Reform Act 2002, ss. 167 to 169). The total amount unpaid must exceed £350 or it must have been payable for longer than three years (Rights of Re-entry and Forfeiture (Prescribed Sum and Period) (England) Regulations 2004 (SI 2004/3086)). More importantly, the landlord is prohibited from serving a notice under the Law of Property Act 1925, s. 146, unless the occurrence of the breach of covenant or condition has been finally determined by the court, a leasehold valuation tribunal or an arbitral tribunal.

RELIEF FROM FORFEITURE

Relief from forfeiture for breaches of covenant other than non-payment of rent

84.25 Once the landlord has served a valid s. 146 notice, avoided the potential pitfalls of the doctrine of waiver and successfully elected to forfeit, there still remains one last barrier between the landlord and forfeiture, which is that the tenant can apply to the court for relief. The Law of Property Act 1925, s. 146(2), states:

> Where a lessor is proceeding, by action or otherwise, to enforce [a right of re-entry or forfeiture under any proviso or stipulation in a lease for a breach of any covenant or condition in the lease], the lessee may, in the lessor's action, if any, or in any action brought by himself, apply to the court for relief; and the court may grant or refuse relief, as the court, having regard to the proceedings and conduct of the parties under the foregoing provisions of this section, and to all the other circumstances, thinks fit; and in case of relief may grant it on such terms, if any, as to costs, expenses, damages, compensation, penalty, or otherwise, including the granting of an injunction to restrain any like breach in the future, as the court, in the circumstances of each case, thinks fit.

Generally the tenant's application will be made by counterclaiming in the landlord's forfeiture proceedings, but it is also possible for the tenant to issue proceedings claiming relief. If the landlord has not issued forfeiture proceedings and is seeking instead to forfeit the tenancy by peaceable re-entry, the tenant will have to issue proceedings to bring the matter before the court.

84.26 **When can the tenant apply for relief?** Section 146(2) of the Law of Property Act 1925 states that a tenant can apply to the court for relief where the landlord 'is proceeding, by action or otherwise' to enforce a right of re-entry. In recent years this phrase has required a certain amount of clarification by the courts. In particular, two questions have needed answering:

(a) When does a landlord start 'proceeding'? Is it when he begins the process of forfeiture by serving a s. 146 notice upon the tenant, or is it when he issues court proceedings?
(b) When does a landlord cease to be 'proceeding'?

In *Pakwood Transport Ltd v 15 Beauchamp Place Ltd* (1977) 36 P & CR 112, the Court of Appeal held that a landlord is 'proceeding' at any time after the s. 146 notice has been served on the tenant, and so application for relief can then be made. After some uncertainty in the lower courts, the House of Lords held in *Billson v Residential Apartments Ltd* [1992] 1 AC 494 that the landlord is 'proceeding' until possession is recovered pursuant to an order of the court. Thus, where the landlord has elected to forfeit by peaceable re-entry, the fact of re-entry does not in itself frustrate the tenant's chances of applying for relief. The tenant's right to apply does not continue indefinitely. In determining the tenant's application for relief, the court will consider the circumstances of the case, including whether the tenant has delayed in making the application.

When will the court grant relief? The Law of Property Act 1925, s. 146(2), gives the court a very wide discretion to grant relief. Relief may be granted subject to terms as to costs, expenses, damages, compensation. The court can also grant an injunction to prevent a future breach of obligation. **84.27**

When it comes to deciding whether or not to grant relief, each case will turn on its own facts. The courts have generally been reluctant to set out anything more than very broad general principles. The courts will take into account all the circumstances of the case, which will include:

(a) the nature of the breach;
(b) the seriousness of the breach;
(c) the conduct of the parties;
(d) the value of the property and the extent of the damage caused by the breach;
(e) the losses that will be suffered by the tenant if relief is not granted.

It should be remembered that the purpose of a forfeiture clause is to act as security for the landlord in the event of a tenant breaching an obligation in the lease. If compliance with the terms of the lease can be achieved without having to resort to forfeiture, the courts will be likely to grant relief.

Breaches of positive covenants are generally regarded as being remediable (*Expert Clothing Service and Sales Ltd v Hillgate House Ltd* [1986] Ch 340, see **84.18**). Thus if a tenant is willing and able to remedy the breach within a reasonable time (the court may well impose a time limit), relief will almost certainly be granted.

Where a breach is irremediable the courts are less likely to grant relief. In cases where the tenant has breached a covenant against immoral user and caused a stigma to become attached to the premises, it is almost certain that relief will not be granted. However, this is not a hard and fast rule: if the damage is slight and the refusal of relief would cause a disproportionate loss to the tenant, relief may be granted. In *Ropemaker Properties Ltd v Noonhaven* [1989] 2 EGLR 50, the judge took into account a variety of factors, including the fact that forfeiture would result in substantial financial loss to the defendants, the fact that the immoral use had already been ended and the fact that any stigma was likely to be short-lived. Relief was granted on condition that the defendants permitted the inclusion of a term in the lease which excluded 'hostesses' from the premises.

The courts may grant relief where there has been a breach of covenant not to assign or sublet. If the subletting or assignment was one to which the landlord would not have been able reasonably to withhold consent had the tenant asked for such consent, it will be more likely that relief will be granted. Likewise if the subletting was unintentional and has caused no damage to the lessor (*Scala House and District Property Co. Ltd v Forbes* [1974] QB 575). If the sub-letting or assignment results in the sub-tenant or assignee acquiring statutory protection that the original tenant would not have had, relief is likely to be refused (*Leeward Securities Ltd v Lilyheath Properties Ltd* (1983) 17 HLR 35).

The conduct of the landlord is also a factor to be taken into account (*Segal Securities Ltd v Thoseby* [1963] 1 QB 887).

Where the tenant's breach is wilful and deliberate it is also less likely that the court will grant relief, although if the breach itself is trivial relief probably will be granted. Clearly great injustice would result if a landlord was able to forfeit a lease for any minor breach of covenant. Long leases commonly contain many detailed but often minor covenants. It would clearly be absurd if the law permitted the freeholder to forfeit a 99-year lease because the tenant kept a goldfish, or failed to clean the windows.

84.28 **Protection of sub-lessees** At common law the rule is that if a lease is successfully forfeited by the landlord any sub-tenancy is also destroyed. This leaves sub-tenants in a particularly vulnerable position.

Sub-tenants are entitled to apply for relief under s. 146(4) of the Law of Property Act 1925. The right of a sub-tenant to apply under this section is in fact broader than the right given to a tenant, for s. 146(4) gives the right to apply when the landlord is seeking to enforce a right of forfeiture under *any* covenant in the lease, including non-payment of rent. A sub-tenant will also be able to apply in situations where a tenant may not be able to apply, for example, where the tenant is bankrupt.

As with tenants, the court has a broad discretion to grant relief. The aim will be to restore the landlord's position to what it would have been prior to forfeiture. This is done by a vesting order. The effect of a vesting order is not, as would be the case if the tenant was granted relief, to continue the original tenancy, but to create a new tenancy which makes the old sub-tenant the tenant of the landlord: the original tenant against whom forfeiture proceedings have successfully been taken drops out of the picture.

The new tenancy will not be for a term exceeding that of the old sub-tenancy and the length of the term granted is generally at the discretion of the court. Section 146(4) does not contain any guidelines as to the level of rent payable under the new tenancy, but the court does have power to vary the rent if it thinks it appropriate (*Ewart v Fryer* [1901] 1 Ch 499). The court can also impose any conditions it thinks fit upon the new tenant (see *Chatham Empire Theatre (1955) Ltd v Ultrans Ltd* [1961] 1 WLR 817 at p. 820). Relief may be granted in respect of part of the premises.

84.29 **Protection of mortgagees** If the tenant has taken out a mortgage on his or her lease, and that lease subsequently is forfeited by the landlord, the mortgage will be destroyed. A mortgagee therefore is able to apply for relief under the Law of Property Act 1925, s. 146(4), in the same way as a sub-tenant. The direct right to claim relief from forfeiture is limited to cases where the person seeking relief is entitled to possession of the land or has a legal estate or equitable interest in it. Indirect relief, in the shoes of the tenant, may be claimed by an equitable chargee, joining the tenant as a defendant (*Bland v Ingrams Estates Ltd* [2001] Ch 767). Relief from forfeiture in favour of chargees would be on condition of payment of arrears and interest accruing under the lease. It is inconsistent with the principle that the right of re-entry is a security for the rent due under the lease to grant relief from forfeiture on terms that enable the lessor to profit from the exercise of the right of re-entry (*Bland v Ingrams Estates Ltd (No. 2)* [2001] EWCA Civ 1088, [2002] Ch 177).

Relief from forfeiture for non-payment of rent

84.30 Two different sets of rules govern the operation of relief from forfeiture for non-payment of rent, depending upon whether the proceedings are being taken in the county court or in the High Court. In general proceedings will be taken in the county court. If a landlord unnecessarily issues proceedings in the High Court, he or she may find himself or herself penalised in costs (*Lircata Properties Ltd v Jones* [1967] 1 WLR 1257 at p. 1261F). (Note that in the case of Rent Act protected tenancies virtually all proceedings will be brought in the county court because, by **s. 141(4) of the Rent Act 1977**, costs are not recoverable in the High Court.)

While the jurisdiction of the High Court to grant relief to the tenant is derived from the High Court's ancient equitable jurisdiction (see *Belgravia Insurance Co. Ltd v Meah* [1964] 1 QB 436 at p. 443), the county court's jurisdiction is contained in the **County Courts Act 1984, s. 138.**

In the High Court Under the Common Law Procedure Act 1852, special procedures apply if the tenant has more than six months' rent arrears. By s. 210 of the 1852 Act the landlord does not need to give formal notice if six months' rent is outstanding. However, if an order for possession is made in such a case it will be stayed for six months to give the tenant time to apply for relief. By s. 212, a tenant who pays off all arrears and costs before the hearing will be automatically entitled to relief. **84.31**

If the tenant falls outside the operation of s. 210 and s. 212 of the 1852 Act, because there are less than six months' arrears or because the landlord has not begun proceedings but has peaceably re-entered, the tenant can apply for relief under **s. 38 of the Supreme Court Act 1981** (formerly the Judicature Act 1925, s. 46). The court's power to grant relief is governed by the old principles of equity, and if the tenant pays off all the arrears and costs before judgment is given relief will almost invariably be granted. The fact that a tenant may have a bad past record of payment will be irrelevant to the question as to whether discretion should be exercised in the tenant's favour. Relief will even be granted after the landlord has re-entered provided the tenant applies within six months and it is equitable to grant such relief. Relief will be refused only in exceptional cases where it would be inequitable to grant it, for example, where the landlord had, after judgment for possession, reasonably let the premises to a new tenant.

In the county court **Section 138 of the County Courts Act 1984** gives the tenant three opportunities of relief from forfeiture. **84.32**

(a) *Relief before the hearing.* Under s. 138(2), if the tenant pays into court or to the lessor all the rent in arrear and the costs of the action five clear days before the date of the hearing, the action will automatically cease and the tenancy will continue as it was.
(b) *Relief after the hearing.* If the tenant fails to pre-empt the hearing under s. 138(2), and at the trial the court is satisfied that the landlord has grounds to enforce forfeiture, the court will order possession. The order for possession must, however, be suspended for a period of at least four weeks (s. 138(3)). If the tenant pays all the arrears and costs within the specified period then the tenant will automatically gain relief and the tenancy will continue as it was. The court may, at its discretion, extend the period of suspension at any time before possession is actually recovered by the landlord (s. 138(4)). The court may also adjourn the hearing to enable enquiries to be made into the tenant's ability to pay, but unless the landlord consents there should not be more than two such adjournments (see *R v A Circuit Judge, ex parte Wathen* (1976) 33 P & CR 423).
(c) *Relief after possession.* Once the court has made an order for possession and the landlord has actually recovered possession, the tenant may still apply to the court for relief at any time within six months of the landlord recovering possession (s. 138(9A)). The court will grant such relief as it thinks fit. If the landlord has sought to forfeit by peaceable re-entry, the tenant can apply for relief under s. 139(2) at any time within six months from the date upon which the landlord re-entered. The court has a discretion to grant the tenant such relief as the High Court could have granted.

Protection for sub-lessees and mortgagees Sub-lessees and mortgagees can apply under the Law of Property Act 1925, s. 146(4), when the landlord is seeking to forfeit both for a breach of covenant and for non-payment of rent (see **84.28** and **84.29**). Difficulties may arise where a mortgagee or sub-tenant finds out about the forfeiture proceedings only after an order for possession has been made. In such a case the landlord is no longer 'proceeding' within the meaning of s. 146(4), and the third party will not be able to apply for relief. Similarly, s. 38 of **84.33**

the Supreme Court Act does not give the court jurisdiction to grant relief to third parties when the landlord seeks to forfeit by peaceable re-entry.

In exceptional cases the court may grant relief by exercising its general equitable jurisdiction (*Abbey National Building Society v Maybeech Ltd* [1985] Ch 190 and *Ladup Ltd v Williams and Glyn's Bank plc* [1985] 1 WLR 851).

However, the **County Courts Act 1984, s. 138(9C)**, provides for relief to be given to those with interests under the lease as if they were the lessee, and for the making of vesting orders on such terms as the court thinks fit. A mortgagee will be entitled to relief on payment of all the arrears (*Escalus Properties Ltd v Robinson* [1996] QB 231). Section 138(9C) may be resorted to even by a creditor having the benefit of a charge under the **Charging Orders Act 1979** (*Croydon (Unique) Ltd v Wright* [2001] Ch 318).

Chapter 85 Introduction to the Statutory Codes

INTRODUCTION

Chapters 86 to **90** consider the statutory codes which, together with the common law principles already covered, serve to regulate the relationship of landlord and tenant. Broadly speaking, all of these statutory codes function in roughly the same way — by restricting a landlord's common law right to terminate a tenancy. However, the means by and the extent to which they do this varies from statute to statute: some simply give a tenant the right to renew the tenancy when it expires; whereas others provide a tenant with a security of tenure so comprehensive that in the absence of a flagrant breach of covenant it can be virtually impossible for a landlord to regain possession. **85.1**

Which code applies to a particular tenancy in question will depend upon a variety of factors: the purpose of the letting (business or residential use?); the length of the lease (is it a long lease at a low rent, a short fixed-term or a periodic tenancy?); the nature of the landlord (public or private?); and the date upon which it was granted. There is no doubt that the present situation is unnecessarily complex and overdue for reform.

The procedure governing possession claims by landlords, mortgages or licensors is in **CPR, Part** 55, and **PD** 55 (see **87.6** to **87.12**). The procedure governing applications under the Landlord and Tenant Acts 1927, 1954 and 1987 is in **CPR, Part** 56, and **PD** 56.

GUIDE TO THE RELEVANT STATUTORY PROVISIONS

Business or residential use

If premises are occupied for the purposes of a business, the tenancy may fall within **part II of the Landlord and Tenant Act 1954** (see **chapter 91**) and the tenant will consequently be excluded from claiming security under any of the codes applying to residential tenancies. Furthermore, all the residential statutory codes require the premises in question to be 'a dwelling-house', thereby excluding many commercial properties. Similarly, most of the residential codes require that the tenant be 'an individual', which prevents companies or other artificial persons from claiming protection. **85.2**

Long leases at a low rent

If the tenancy in question is a long lease which was granted on the payment of a lump sum, and the tenant pays only a minimal 'ground rent' throughout the course of the term, then it will probably be excluded from the operation of the three main codes which apply to residential tenancies (the **Housing Act 1985**, the **Rent Act 1977** and the **Housing Act 1988**). Instead, certain protection is available for the long leaseholder at the end of the term under part I of the Landlord and Tenant Act 1954 or under sch. 10 to the Local Government and Housing Act 1989. **85.3**

Public or private landlord

85.4 The statutory code that applies to a residential tenancy depends to a large extent upon the status of the landlord. If the landlord is a local authority or other public body, the tenancy may be a 'secure tenancy' under **part IV of the Housing Act 1985** (see **chapter 88**). If the landlord is a private individual or other private sector landlord the tenancy will fall under **part I of the Housing Act 1988 (chapters 86** and **87)** or the **Rent Act 1977**. Unfortunately, however, the distinction between public sector and private sector landlords is not always clear-cut. Certain quasi-public bodies which were formerly regarded as belonging to the public sector are now considered to be part of the private sector, in particular registered social landlords (known as housing associations prior to the **Housing Act 1996**). Therefore, the code under which a particular tenant falls may vary depending upon the date of the grant of the tenancy. If the tenancy was granted by a housing association (now 'registered social landlord') prior to 15 January 1989 it will be a secure tenancy under the **Housing Act 1985**. If it was granted after that date it will be an 'assured tenancy' under the **Housing Act 1988** (subject to certain transitional provisions).

Commencement of statutory codes

85.5 The date of the grant of the tenancy is of particular importance in the private rented sector. Statutory protection for tenants of private landlords has a long history stretching back to the First World War and culminating in the **Rent Act 1977**, which consolidated the preceding legislation. For the next 12 years the **Rent Act 1977** remained dominant, providing private sector tenants with both rent control and a high degree of security, until increasing governmental dissatisfaction with a regime that made landlords reluctant to grant new tenancies brought about the **Housing Act 1988**. The 1988 Act removed the system of rent control and reduced the tenant's security of tenure. It also introduced a means by which landlords, if they so chose, could rent property on short fixed-term tenancies with only minimal security. This system of shorthold lettings was extended further by the **Housing Act 1996**, to the extent that now, in the absence of any contrary agreement, a tenant acquires a shorthold tenancy on entering into a tenancy agreement with a private landlord.

Therefore, when considering private sector residential tenancies, there are two dates that need to be borne in mind. The first is 15 January 1989, which is when the **Housing Act 1988** came into force. Broadly speaking, a residential tenancy granted before this date is likely to fall under the **Rent Act 1977** while those granted after that date (but before 1 March 1997) will be assured tenancies under the **Housing Act 1988** (see **chapters 86** and **87**).

The second important date is 28 February 1997, which is when the **Housing Act 1996** came into force. After this date, the vast majority of residential tenancies granted will automatically be 'assured shorthold tenancies' with minimal security of tenure. In practical terms, this is an extremely significant development. Before 28 February 1997, a private sector landlord who wanted to ensure that a tenant did not acquire significant security of tenure had to serve notice on the tenant stating that the tenancy was to be an assured shorthold tenancy. Since 28 February 1997 a new tenant will acquire significant security of tenure only if the landlord positively chooses to confer it.

Although the **Rent Act 1977** continues to apply to tenancies which were granted before 15 January 1989 (and to a small number of tenancies granted subsequently), the number of Rent Act regulated tenancies is now diminishing.

WHICH STATUTORY CODE?

85.6 **Figure 85.1** briefly illustrates under which statutory code a particular tenancy will fall. It is, of course, only an outline and in each case proper reference should be made to the statutory definitions and any relevant transitional provisions.

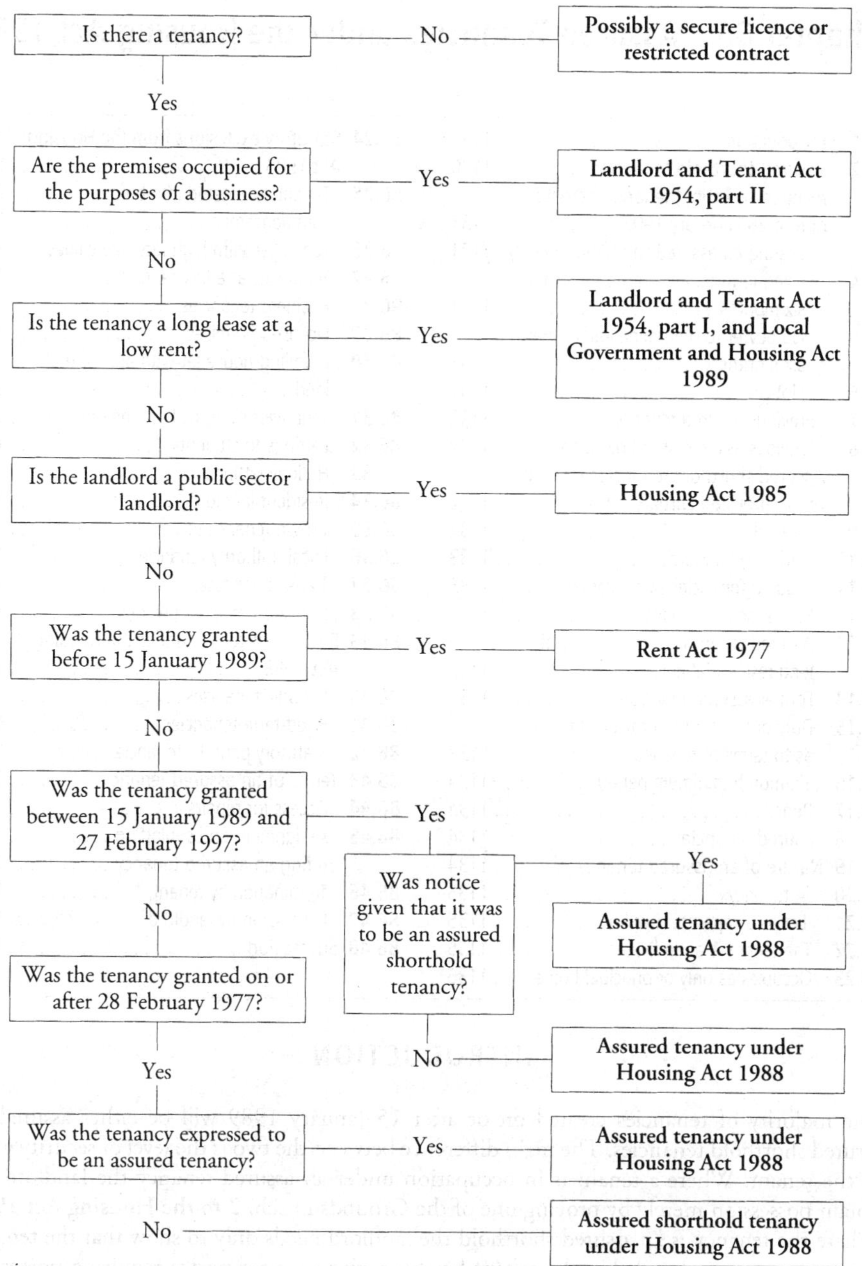

Figure 85.1 Identification of the correct statutory code

Chapter 86 Assured Tenancies under the Housing Act 1988

INTRODUCTION

86.1 The majority of tenancies created on or after 15 January 1989 will be either assured, or assured shorthold tenancies. The main difference between the two is the level of security given to the tenant. Where a tenant is in occupation under an assured tenancy the landlord can obtain possession merely by proving one of the Grounds in **sch. 2 to the Housing Act 1988**. Where the tenancy is an assured shorthold the landlord needs only to show that the tenancy has come to an end and that the tenant has been given proper notice requiring possession before possession will be ordered.

ASSURED SHORTHOLD TENANCIES

86.2 The forerunner to the assured shorthold tenancy was the protected shorthold tenancy, which was introduced by the Housing Act 1980. The protected shorthold tenancy was not a great success — it was procedurally difficult to operate and did not remove the tenant's right to apply for a fair rent. In contrast the assured shorthold tenancy has proved to be very popular with landlords. Under an assured shorthold tenancy a tenant can apply for a rent reduction, but as the tenant will acquire no security of tenure and the landlord is able, under a relatively straightforward system, to regain possession of the premises at short notice, an application is rarely worthwhile. The landlord is of course still obliged to obtain a court order for possession before evicting the tenant where the tenancy is an assured shorthold.

The **Housing Act 1996** has introduced new rules governing the creation of an assured shorthold tenancy. Prior to the commencement of the 1996 Act (28 February 1997) a new tenancy could be a shorthold tenancy only if notice to that effect was given in accordance with the strict guidelines contained in **s. 20 of the Housing Act 1988**. The fact that many landlords were unfamiliar with the procedure, and the rigid application by the courts of the notice provisions, meant that many landlords who intended to create shorthold tenancies found that they had in fact granted an assured tenancy, with the resultant security of tenure. In order to address this problem a new s. 19A was added to the 1988 Act, meaning that most tenancies created after 28 February 1997 will automatically be assured shorthold tenancies.

ASSURED SHORTHOLD TENANCIES CREATED BEFORE 28 FEBRUARY 1997

Creating an assured shorthold tenancy

To be an assured shorthold tenancy the tenancy must first qualify as an assured tenancy. It must therefore satisfy the provisions of the **Housing Act 1988, s. 1**, and must not fall into any of the excluded categories in sch. 1 (see **86.24** to **86.38**). In addition, any tenancy created prior to 28 February 1997 which is to be an assured shorthold tenancy must satisfy the requirements set out in the **Housing Act 1988, s. 20(1)**. It must be a tenancy: **86.3**

(a) which is a fixed-term tenancy granted for a term certain of not less than six months; and
(b) in respect of which there is no power for the landlord to determine the tenancy at any time earlier than six months from the beginning of the tenancy; and
(c) in respect of which a notice was served as mentioned in s. 20(2).

Fixed-term tenancy of not less than six months If it was created prior to 28 February 1997 only a fixed-term tenancy can be an assured shorthold tenancy. The term must be for six months or more, but there is no upper limit on the duration of the term. So despite the name there is no requirement that a shorthold assured tenancy should actually be 'short'. However, given the purpose of the provisions, landlords are unlikely to grant lengthy terms. **86.4**

No power to determine earlier than six months A 'power to determine the tenancy' does not include a power of re-entry or forfeiture for a breach of any term or condition of the tenancy (**Housing Act 1988, s. 45(4)**). Thus the inclusion of a re-entry clause (which is essential if the landlord wishes to retain the right to regain possession in the event of the tenant breaching a term of the lease) does not prevent a tenancy from being an assured shorthold tenancy. If the landlord includes a break clause which can be exercised in the first six months of the tenancy, though, the tenancy cannot be an assured shorthold tenancy and will take effect as an assured tenancy. **86.5**

Notice Prior to 28 February 1997, a landlord who wanted to grant an assured shorthold tenancy had to ensure that the tenant knew, before entering into the agreement, that the tenancy being offered was an assured shorthold tenancy. In order to do this the landlord had to serve notice in accordance with the **Housing Act 1988, s. 20(2)**. Section 20(2) contains the following requirements: **86.6**

(a) The notice must be in the prescribed form (s. 20(2)(a)), which is prescribed in the Assured Tenancies and Agricultural Occupancies (Forms) Regulations 1988 (SI 1988/2203) as amended. The prescribed form gives details of the tenancy, states clearly that the proposed tenancy is to be an assured shorthold tenancy, warns the tenant of the nature of the tenancy, informs the tenant of the right to apply to a rent assessment committee and tells the tenant where to seek advice if he or she does not understand the notice. A form to 'substantially the same effect' will be valid.

(b) The notice must be served before the assured tenancy is entered into (s. 20(2)(b)). Service may be effected on the tenant's agent authorised to accept service (*Yenula Properties Ltd v Naidu* [2002] EWCA Civ 719, [2003] HLR 18).

(c) The notice must be served by the person who is to be the landlord under the assured tenancy on the person who is to be the tenant under that tenancy(s. 20(2)(c)).

(d) The notice must state that the assured tenancy to which it relates is to be a shorthold tenancy (s. 20(2)(d)).

The court has no discretion to dispense with the requirement that a proper notice be served under s. 20(1). But if the notice contains an error which is so obvious or so evident that, read in context, it is sufficiently clear to leave a reasonable recipient in no reasonable doubt as to its terms, the court may overlook the defect (see, e.g., *Andrews v Brewer* (1997) 30 HLR 203; *York v Casey* [1998] 2 EGLR 25 (termination date recorded as being commencement date); *Osborn and Co. Ltd v Dior* [2003] EWCA Civ 281, [2003] HLR 45 (landlord's name omitted or incorrect); cf. *Panayi v Roberts* (1993) 25 HLR 421; *Clickex Ltd v McCann* (1999) 32 HLR 324). It is predominantly a question of fact and degree (*Ravenseft Properties Ltd v Hall* [2002] 1 EGLR 9).

Previous assured tenancy

86.7 Prior to 28 February 1997, if an assured tenant of a tenancy (which was not an assured shorthold tenancy) was granted a new tenancy by the same landlord, the new tenancy could not be an assured shorthold tenancy (**Housing Act 1988, s. 20(3)**). This provision prevented a landlord from depriving an existing tenant of security of tenure by granting the tenant an assured shorthold tenancy when the original tenancy expired. Where the tenancy expires after 28 February 1997 the situation is somewhat different; the landlord may grant a previous assured tenant an assured shorthold tenancy, but only if notice is given that it is to be an assured shorthold tenancy (see **86.14**).

Previous assured shorthold tenancy

86.8 Prior to 28 February 1997, if an assured shorthold tenancy came to an end and a new tenancy of the same (or substantially the same) premises was granted by the same landlord then the new tenancy would also be an assured shorthold tenancy regardless of the fact that no **Housing Act 1988, s. 20**, notice was given (s. 20(4)). In *Lower Street Properties Ltd v Jones* (1996) 28 HLR 877, it was held that a number of tenancies which all succeeded a shorthold tenancy remained shorthold. Similarly, if an assured shorthold tenancy came to an end and no new tenancy was granted but instead a statutory periodic tenancy arose by virtue of s. 5(2) (for an assured shorthold tenancy is an assured tenancy like any other and will be continued by statute, see **86.39**), this statutory periodic tenancy would remain an assured shorthold tenancy.

ASSURED SHORTHOLD TENANCIES CREATED ON OR AFTER 28 FEBRUARY 1997

General

86.9 Any tenancy entered into on or after 28 February 1997 (otherwise than pursuant to a contract made before that date) which qualifies as an assured tenancy under the provisions of the **Housing Act 1988, s. 1** (see **86.19** to **86.23**) will be an assured shorthold tenancy unless it falls within the exceptions set out in the Housing Act 1988, sch. 2A, (s. 19A). Thus, subject to the exceptions considered below, virtually all new tenancies granted by private-sector landlords will be assured shorthold tenancies.

Notice by landlord

It is still possible for a landlord to grant an assured tenancy which is not a shorthold, but to do so the landlord must serve notice on the tenant stating that the tenancy to which it relates is not to be an assured shorthold tenancy. Such notice can be served either before the tenancy is granted (Housing Act 1988, sch. 2A, para. 1) or during the course of the tenancy (in which case the notice will function to convert an assured shorthold tenancy into an assured tenancy: sch. 2A, para. 2). An assured tenancy can also be created if the tenancy contains a provision stating that the tenancy is not to be an assured shorthold tenancy (sch. 2A, para. 3). Effectively these provisions reverse the situation before the amendments made by the **Housing Act 1996** came into force. Prior to 28 February 1997 a tenancy would not be an assured shorthold tenancy unless notice was served stating that it was to be an assured shorthold tenancy. On or after 28 February 1997 it will be an assured tenancy only if notice is served saying it is not to be an assured shorthold tenancy. **86.10**

Assured tenancies by succession

Section 39 of the Housing Act 1988 amended the **Rent Act 1977** to provide that where a family member (but not a spouse) succeeds to a Rent Act tenancy on the first succession, or anyone succeeds on the second succession, that person will acquire an assured tenancy rather than a Rent Act statutory tenancy. Such assured tenancies by succession take effect as assured tenancies, not as assured shorthold tenancies (Housing Act 1988, sch. 2A, para. 4). **86.11**

Former secure tenancies

Where a former secure tenant acquires an assured tenancy (for example, because a local authority landlord transfers part of its housing stock into the private sector) that tenant will acquire an assured tenancy and not an assured shorthold tenancy (Housing Act 1988, sch. 2A, para. 5). **86.12**

Assured tenancies on the expiry of a long residential lease

Under the provisions of sch. 10 to the Local Government and Housing Act 1989, a long leaseholder acquires the right to an assured tenancy at the expiry of his or her leasehold term. Where this occurs the leaseholder will acquire an assured tenancy and not an assured shorthold tenancy (Housing Act 1988, sch. 2A, para. 6). **86.13**

Former assured tenancies

Where an assured tenancy is granted to a tenant who, immediately before the grant, held an assured tenancy which was not an assured shorthold tenancy from the same landlord, that tenant will acquire an assured tenancy. This provision prevents a landlord from depriving an assured tenant of security of tenure by simply granting the tenant a new tenancy. However, the landlord may grant a former assured tenant an assured shorthold tenancy if notice in the prescribed form is served on the tenant stating that the new tenancy is to be an assured shorthold (Housing Act 1988, sch. 2A, para. 7; the prescribed form is No. 8 in the schedule to the Assured Tenancies and Agricultural Occupancies (Forms) Regulations 1997 (SI 1997/194)). This is a considerable change in the law; prior to 28 February 1997 it would not have been possible to grant a former assured tenant an assured shorthold tenancy. **86.14**

The situation is different where a tenant has a fixed-term assured tenancy which is not an assured shorthold tenancy and this tenancy comes to an end. On the expiry of the term a statutory periodic tenancy arises by virtue of s. 5. This statutory periodic tenancy will be an assured tenancy and not an assured shorthold tenancy (sch. 2A, para. 8).

Duty of landlord to provide statement as to terms of tenancy

Prior to 28 February 1997, the strict requirements as to notice and the fact that an assured shorthold tenancy had to be granted for a fixed term meant that virtually all assured shorthold tenancies were entered into by written tenancy agreement. Since 28 February 1997, it has **86.15** been possible to create an assured shorthold tenancy much more informally. Consequently a tenant may not always be fully apprised of the terms of the tenancy. The Housing Act 1988, s. 20A, therefore gives a tenant who has been granted an assured shorthold tenancy under s. 19A the right, on giving written notice to the landlord, to require the landlord to provide a written statement of certain essential terms of the tenancy that have not been evidenced in writing. The landlord must provide information on the following matters:

(a) the date on which the tenancy began;
(b) the rent payable under the tenancy and the dates on which that rent is payable;
(c) any term providing for a review of the rent;
(d) in the case of a fixed-term tenancy, the length of the fixed term.

Six-month minimum period

86.16 In the case of assured shorthold tenancies granted on or after 28 February 1997 there is no requirement that the tenancy be granted for a fixed term of more than six months. A new assured shorthold tenancy can therefore be a periodic tenancy or a fixed-term tenancy granted for less than six months. Despite this, the landlord is prevented from obtaining a court order for possession on the ground that the tenancy has expired until six months after the beginning of that tenancy (**Housing Act 1988, s. 21(5)**). Thus, even if a landlord grants a two-month fixed-term tenancy, the tenant will be able to remain in occupation after the expiry of this term because a statutory periodic tenancy will arise under s. 5 of the 1988 Act; and though the landlord may start proceedings for possession, no order for possession can be made that will take effect earlier than six months after the beginning of the original fixed-term tenancy. However, possession can be recovered within six months if there has been a serious breach of the tenancy agreement (see 87.4).

Rent

86.17 Assured shorthold tenants do benefit from one right that is not available to ordinary assured tenants; they can apply under the Housing Act 1988, s. 22, to a rent assessment committee to have their rent reduced. Rent assessment under s. 22 is different from rent control under the **Rent Act** 1977. The landlord of an assured shorthold tenant is entitled to a market rent. A reduction in rent can be obtained only where the rent exceeds the amount which the landlord might reasonably be expected to obtain.

ASSURED TENANCIES

86.18 The majority of assured tenancies granted on or after 28 February 1997 are assured shorthold tenancies (though there are landlords — particularly in the social sector — who confer full assured status on their tenants by giving notice that the tenancy is not to be an assured shorthold tenancy). Nevertheless, there continue to be a large number of assured tenancies created before this date which are not assured shortholds.

NATURE OF AN ASSURED TENANCY

86.19 Under the **Housing Act 1988, s. 1(1)**, an assured tenancy is defined as follows:

> (1) A tenancy under which a dwelling-house is let as a separate dwelling is for the purposes of this Act an assured tenancy if and so long as —
> (a) the tenant or, as the case may be, each of the joint tenants is an individual; and
> (b) the tenant or, as the case may be, at least one of the joint tenants occupies the dwelling-house as his only or principal home; and
> (c) the tenancy is not one which, by virtue of subsection (2) or subsection (6) below, cannot be an assured tenancy.

'A tenancy'

For a right to occupy premises to fall within **part I of the Housing Act 1988** there must first be a tenancy. A licence will not be eligible for protection under the Act. For the distinction between leases and licences, see **chapter 83**. However, the introduction of the assured shorthold tenancy means that since 15 January 1989 landlords have been able to grant short fixed-term tenancies with no security of tenure, and consequently no longer need to seek to evade statutory protection by attempting to grant a licence rather than a tenancy. **86.20**

'Let as a separate dwelling'

A dwelling-house includes a house or part of a house (**Housing Act 1988, s. 45(1)**). It can be a flat, a single room within a house, or even a caravan provided it has been rendered immobile. **86.21**

The dwelling-house must be let at a quantifiable rent. If no rent is payable, the tenancy will be excluded by sch. 1, para. 3. The dwelling-house must also be let *as* a separate dwelling, and therefore the purpose for which the premises are let at the time of the original letting will be considered rather than the purposes to which the premises are later put. To be a separate dwelling the accommodation must be sufficient for the tenant to carry out the major activities of life, namely sleeping and eating (*Wright v Howell* (1947) 92 SJ 26). The premises do not have to be completely self-contained as long as the tenant has exclusive use of the essential living rooms. Sharing the use of a bathroom or a lavatory will not prevent the tenancy from being protected (*Cole v Harris* [1945] KB 474). Cooking facilities are not an essential feature of a separate dwelling (*Uratemp Ventures Ltd v Collins* [2001] UKHL 43, [2002] 1 AC 301).

There is no reason why a tenant should not have a single assured tenancy of two flats if the two flats are being used together as the tenant's home and are treated as one living unit (*Langford Property Co. Ltd v Goldrich* [1949] 1 KB 511). If, however, the tenant splits his or her living activities between the two properties, for example, by sleeping in one and cooking and eating in the other, it is likely that he or she will not be an assured tenant of either property (*Wimbush v Cibulia* [1949] 2 KB 564; *Hampstead Way Investments Ltd v Lewis-Weare* [1985] 1 WLR 164).

Special provisions are made with regard to tenants who share accommodation. If the tenant has exclusive occupation of some accommodation (the separate accommodation) and shares other accommodation in common with a person or persons other than the landlord, the separate accommodation will be deemed to be a dwelling-house let on an assured tenancy regardless of the fact that the separate accommodation alone may not form a separate dwelling (Housing Act 1988, s. 3). In such a case the tenant does not hold the shared accommodation under an assured tenancy, but the court is prevented from making a possession order in respect of the shared accommodation unless it has already made, or makes at the same time, a possession order in respect of the separate accommodation (s. 10).

The tenant is an individual

This requirement excludes companies and other artificial persons from **Housing Act 1988** protection. If a tenancy is granted to a number of joint tenants and one of these tenants is a company, the tenancy will be excluded from the **Housing Act 1988** since s. 1(1)(a) requires each of the joint tenants to be an individual. **86.22**

The fact that company lets are excluded from **Housing Act 1988** protection has enabled landlords to avoid the consequences of the statute by granting tenancies to companies rather than to individuals. The onus is on an occupier who wishes to argue that the agreement is a sham to establish that it does not reflect the common intention of the parties (see *Hilton v Plustitle Ltd* [1989] 1 WLR 149 and *Kaye v Massbetter Ltd* [1991] 2 EGLR 97).

Occupies as only or principal home

86.23 The **Housing Act 1988** restricts assured tenancy status to the tenant's main residence. A tenant with a house in town and a cottage in the country for use at weekends might be able to establish that the cottage is occupied as a residence, but would probably fail to establish that the cottage was his or her only or principal home.

Whether a tenant is occupying a dwelling-house as his or her only or principal home will in each case be a question of fact. Because of the difference in wording, **Rent Act 1977** authorities should only be used with care. The **Housing Act 1985** employs the same wording, however, and secure tenancy cases may therefore be helpful, as may decisions made under the Leasehold Reform Act 1967.

Where the tenant is absent from the dwelling-house for a prolonged period, such that an inference can be drawn that the tenant has ceased occupation, it will be for the tenant to show that he or she is still in occupation. In determining this question, the court will consider whether the tenant has an intention to return to the property, and whether he or she has left some visible evidence of that intention on the premises (*Crawley Borough Council v Sawyer* (1987) 20 HLR 98). The intention must be 'a real hope coupled with the practical possibility of its fulfilment within a reasonable time' (*Tickner v Hearn* [1960] 1 WLR 1406, per Ormerod LJ at p. 1410). The period of absence may be quite long — six years in *Tickner v Hearn*, 10 years in *Gofor Investments Ltd v Roberts* (1975) 29 P & CR 366. Visible evidence may be provided by the occupation of the house by members of the tenant's family or friends (provided they are preserving it as a residence for the tenant on his or her return) or the presence of the tenant's furniture or other possessions on the premises.

If an assured tenant ceases to occupy the dwelling-house as his or her principal home the tenancy will cease to be assured. The contractual tenancy, however, will continue until it expires or is terminated in accordance with the provisions of the tenancy agreement and the Protection from Eviction Act 1977.

STATUTORY EXCLUSIONS FROM THE HOUSING ACT 1988

86.24 Even if a tenancy satisfies the **Housing Act 1988, s. 1**, it will not be an assured tenancy if it falls within any of the exceptions listed in sch. 1 (see **86.25** to **86.38**).

Tenancies entered into before commencement

86.25 Under the **Housing Act 1988, sch. 1, para. 1**, no tenancy created before 15 January 1989, or a tenancy entered into pursuant to a contract made before 15 January 1989, can be an assured tenancy. The general rule is therefore that tenancies entered into before 15 January 1989 will be **Rent Act 1977** protected tenancies, while those entered into after that date will fall under the **Housing Act 1988**. There are, however, transitional rules set out in s. 34 of the Housing Act 1988 which allow the creation of a **Rent Act 1977** protected tenancy on or after 15 January 1989 in certain limited circumstances.

Tenancies with high rateable values

86.26 The **Housing Act 1988** is not intended to protect the tenants of very high value properties. Under sch. 1, para. 2, a tenancy will not be an assured tenancy if:

(a) the tenancy was entered into on or after 1 April 1990 (otherwise than, where the dwelling-house had a rateable value on 31 March 1990, in pursuance of a contract made before 1 April 1990) and the rent payable is more than £25,000 per annum, or

(b) the tenancy was entered into before 1 April 1990 (or in pursuance of an agreement made before that date) and the rateable value of the premises on 31 March 1990 was over £1,500 in Greater London or £750 elsewhere (sch. 1, para. 2A).

For these purposes 'rent' does not include any sum payable by the tenant which is expressed to be payable in respect of rates, services, management, repairs, maintenance or insurance (sch. 1, para. 2(2)). The court will disregard, as a device, provision in an agreement for payment of a sum which was never expected to be paid (*Bankway Properties Ltd v Pensfold-Dunsford* [2001] 1 WLR 1369).

Tenancies at a low rent

The aim of the **Housing Act 1988, sch. 1, paras 3 to 3C**, is to exclude long tenancies at low rents from the protection of the 1988 Act. A tenancy will not be an assured tenancy if: **86.27**

(a) for the time being no rent is payable; or
(b) the tenancy was entered into before 1 April 1990 (or in pursuance of an agreement made before that date) and the rent payable for the time being is less than two-thirds of the rateable value of the dwelling-house on 31 March 1990; or
(c) the tenancy was entered into on or after 1 April 1990 and the rent payable for the time being is less than £1,000 per annum in Greater London or £250 per annum elsewhere.

As with para. 2, sums expressed to be payable in respect of rates, services, management etc. will not be regarded as rent.

Business tenancies

A business tenancy, that is, a tenancy to which part II of the Landlord and Tenant Act 1954 applies, cannot be an assured tenancy (Housing Act 1988, sch. 1, para. 4). **86.28**

Licensed premises

A tenancy under which the dwelling-house consists of or comprises premises licensed for the sale of intoxicating liquors for consumption on the premises cannot be an assured tenancy (Housing Act 1988, sch. 1, para. 5). **86.29**

Dwelling-house let with agricultural land

A tenancy under which agricultural land exceeding two acres is let together with the dwelling-house cannot be an assured tenancy (Housing Act 1988, sch. 1, para. 6). **86.30**

Tenancies of agricultural holdings etc.

By the Housing Act 1988, sch. 1, para. 7, a tenancy under which the dwelling-house is comprised in an agricultural holding (within the Agricultural Holdings Act 1986) and is occupied by the person responsible for the control of the farming of the holding cannot be an assured tenancy. Nor can a tenancy under which the dwelling-house is comprised in the holding held under a farm business tenancy (within the Agricultural Tenancies Act 1995) and is occupied by the person responsible for the control of the management of the holding. Such tenancies are subject to the statutory regime contained in the relevant Agricultural Act. **86.31**

Lettings to students

A tenancy cannot be an assured tenancy if it is granted to a person who is pursuing, or intends to pursue, a course of study provided by a specified educational institution and is so granted either by that institution or by another specified institution or body or persons (Housing Act 1988, sch. 1, para. 8). An educational institution is specified by the Secretary of State by statutory instrument. A letting by a private landlord to a student is not itself excluded, but it is possible for such a landlord to exclude the operation of the statute by letting to a specified institution which in turn sublets to the student (*St Catherine's College v Dorling* [1980] 1 WLR 66). **86.32**

Holiday lettings

A tenancy the purpose of which is to confer on the tenant a right to occupy the dwelling-house for a holiday cannot be an assured tenancy (Housing Act 1988, sch. 1, para. 9). There is **86.33** no statutory definition of 'holiday'. It has been judicially defined as 'a period of cessation of work or period of recreation' (*Buchmann v May* [1978] 2 All ER 993 at p. 995) and it has been held to include a working holiday, that is 'a temporary suspension of one's normal activity not necessarily implying a period of recreation' (*Franke v Hakmi* [1984] CLY 1906). The court will scrutinise the true purpose of the agreement where the tenant adduces evidence that the holiday letting may be a sham (*Buchmann v May*; *R v Rent Officer for London Borough of Camden, ex parte Plant* (1981) 257 EG 731).

Resident landlord

86.34 Three conditions must be fulfilled before the resident landlord exception, in the Housing Act 1988, sch. 1, para. 10, applies. The conditions differ according to whether or not the dwelling-house let to the tenant forms part of a 'purpose-built block of flats'. To fall within this definition (sch. 1, para. 22), the building must 'as constructed' contain two or more flats. (A 'flat' is a dwelling-house which forms part only of a building which is separated horizontally from another dwelling-house forming part of the same building.) As 'purpose-built' implies, it cannot include buildings which are converted from their former use, typically as a single house, into self-contained flats (see *Barnes v Gorsuch* (1981) 43 P & CR 294).

Where the building in which the tenant lives is a purpose-built block of flats, the three conditions are:

(a) the dwelling-house let to the tenant must form part of one of the flats;
(b) the person who granted the tenancy (the first landlord) must have been an individual (not a company) who occupied another dwelling-house in the same flat as his only or principal home;
(c) subject to certain qualifications, at all times any subsequent landlord must also have been an individual and have occupied another dwelling-house in the flat as his only or principal home.

Where the building in which the tenant lives is not a purpose-built block of flats, the three conditions are:

(a) the dwelling-house let to the tenant must form part only the building;
(b) the first landlord must have been an individual (not a company) who occupied another dwelling-house in the same building as his only or principal home;
(c) subject to certain qualifications, at all times any subsequent landlord must also have been an individual and have occupied another dwelling-house in the same building as his only or principal home.

Whether the dwelling let to the tenant forms part of the same building (or flat) as the dwelling occupied by the landlord is a question of fact and degree (*Bardrick v Haycock* (1976) 31 P & CR 420). The test of occupation to be applied to the landlord is the same as that applied in deciding whether a person is an assured tenant: see **86.23**. The mere retention of a sparsely furnished room in the building, which the landlord sleeps in only occasionally, is unlikely to suffice. Where the landlord's interest is held by more than one person, the occupation of one will be enough (sch. 1, para. 10(2)).

The landlord (for the time being) must in general have occupied throughout the tenancy. Qualifications to this principle arise in circumstances where for some reason it has become difficult for the landlord to satisfy the condition of residence. In some circumstances, the condition is 'deemed to be fulfilled', entitling the landlord to bring possession proceedings on the basis that the tenancy is not assured. In other circumstances, there is a 'period of disregard', during which the landlord's right to recover possession as a resident landlord is suspended, but the landlord can proceed when the condition of residence is once more satisfied (see for the general effect of periods of disregard *Landau v Sloane* [1982] AC 490).

The residence condition will be 'deemed to be fulfilled' in three instances (sch. 1, paras 18 to 20):

(a) where the landlord's interest is vested in trustees on trust for beneficiaries one of whom occupies part of the building (or flat) as his only or principal home;
(b) where the landlord's interest has been so vested in trustees, and the tenancy has come to an end, during the full duration of any new tenancy of the same or substantially the same dwelling-house which the trustees grant to the sitting tenant;
(c) for a period not exceeding two years, throughout which the landlord's interest is vested in personal representatives.

There are four 'periods of disregard' (sch. 1, paras 17 and 18(2)):

(a) for a 28-day period following the vesting of the landlord's interest in an individual who does not occupy the dwelling-house as his or her only or principal home (e.g. following the sale of the reversion);
(b) for a further six-month period following the vesting of the landlord's interest in such an individual, provided that during the 28-day period the individual notifies the tenant in writing of his or her intention to occupy. The six months run from the date of the vesting not the date of the notice;
(c) for a two-year period following the vesting of the landlord's interest in trustees or the Probate judge (e.g. on death intestate);
(d) for a two-year period following the death of a beneficiary whose occupation of the dwelling-house has, until then, led to the condition of residence being fulfilled.

The landlord cannot avoid the complexities of the residence condition by the simple expedient of granting new tenancies. The resident landlord exception will not apply if the tenancy is granted to a person (alone or jointly) who, immediately before it was granted, was a tenant under an assured tenancy of the same dwelling-house or of another dwelling-house which forms part of the building (or flat) in question (sch. 1, para. 10(3)).

Crown tenancies

A tenancy under which the landlord's interest belongs to Her Majesty in right of the Crown (save where it is under the management of the Crown Estate Commissioners), or to a government department, or is held in trust for Her Majesty for the purposes of a government department, cannot be an assured tenancy (Housing Act 1988, sch. 1, para. 11). **86.35**

Local authority tenancies

A tenancy under which the landlord's interest belongs to a local authority, the Commission for New Towns, the Development Board for Rural Wales, an urban development corporation, a development corporation, a waste disposal authority, a residuary body, a fully mutual housing association or a housing action trust, cannot be an assured tenancy (Housing Act 1988, sch. 1, para. 12). Many of these public bodies will let on secure tenancy (see **88.3**). **86.36**

Transitional cases

A tenancy which is a protected tenancy, a housing association tenancy, a secure tenancy or a tenancy by virtue of which a protected occupier under the Rent (Agriculture) Act 1976 occupies a dwelling-house, cannot be an assured tenancy (sch. 1, para. 13). **86.37**

Housing homeless persons

The **Housing Act 1988, s. 1(6)**, provides a further partial exclusion from the protection of the Act. More and more frequently, in the pursuance of their statutory duties to house the homeless, local authorities are making use of private and housing association accommodation. Where a landlord comes to an arrangement with a local housing authority to provide accommodation for the homeless and then in pursuance of this arrangement enters into a tenancy agreement with a person specified by the local housing authority, this tenancy **86.38** cannot be assured until 12 months have expired, unless before the expiry of that period the landlord notifies the tenant that it is to be regarded as an assured tenancy.

SECURITY OF TENURE UNDER THE HOUSING ACT 1988

86.39 The **Housing Act 1988** gives the tenant security of tenure by preventing the exercise of the landlord's common law right to end the tenancy. How the Act operates depends upon whether the tenant holds under a fixed-term or under a periodic tenancy, but in both cases the system is fundamentally the same; the landlord cannot regain possession of the premises without a court order, and a court order will be granted only if the landlord can make out one or more of the grounds contained in sch. 2 to the Act.

Security of tenure is provided for assured tenants by s. 5, which provides that an assured tenancy cannot be brought to an end by the landlord except by obtaining an order of the court in accordance with the Act or, in the case of a fixed-term tenancy which contains power for the landlord to determine the tenancy in certain circumstances, by the exercise of that power. Accordingly, the service by the landlord of a notice to quit shall be of no effect in relation to a periodic assured tenancy. By s. 5(2), if an assured tenancy which is a fixed-term tenancy comes to an end otherwise than by virtue of an order of the court, or a surrender or other action on the part of the tenant, then, subject to any court order for possession, the tenant shall be entitled to remain in possession of the premises. Generally, the tenant's right to possession depends upon a periodic tenancy arising by virtue of s. 5.

An assured tenancy cannot be forfeited. Although s. 5(1) expressly refers to the landlord's reservation and exercise of a power to determine the tenancy in certain circumstances, this is not a reference to forfeiture, as is made clear by s. 45(4). Should the landlord wish to recover possession as a response to tenant default, the proper course is to serve a notice seeking possession on one of the restricted number of grounds which are available during the fixed term (see **86.47**). It follows that the tenant cannot claim relief pursuant to statute or in equity (*Artesian Residential Developments Ltd v Beck* [2000] QB 541).

By s. 7(1), an order for possession of a dwelling-house let on an assured tenancy may only be made on the grounds set out in sch. 2. The grounds of possession are considered in **chapter 87**.

Periodic tenancies

86.40 At common law a landlord wishing to recover possession of premises let under a periodic tenancy would normally terminate the tenancy by serving a notice to quit upon the tenant. The **Housing Act 1988** provides that the service of a notice to quit shall be of no effect. A periodic assured tenancy, therefore, will continue on its original terms even after the landlord serves a notice to quit: it can be terminated only by an order of the court. This way of providing security of tenure is more like the **Housing Act 1985** than the **Rent Act 1977**. Under the **Housing Act 1988** there is no statutory tenancy when the contractual tenancy is brought to an end. Instead the original tenancy simply continues regardless of any attempt at common law to terminate it. A notice to quit served by a tenant upon a landlord, however, will still be effective to end the tenancy.

Fixed-term tenancies

86.41 The position with regard to fixed-term tenancies is somewhat more complicated. Unlike a periodic tenancy, a fixed-term tenancy will come to an end by effluxion of time, and so the **Housing Act 1988** cannot preclude it from coming to an end simply by preventing the parties from taking action. The Act therefore provides that if the tenancy comes to an end in any way other than by an order of the court, or by surrender or other action, a periodic tenancy will arise and thereby continue the tenancy. This statutory periodic tenancy, as with an original periodic tenancy, can be terminated only by an order of the court.

Statutory periodic tenancies

When a fixed-term tenancy comes to an end, either by effluxion of time or by the valid exercise of a power to determine the tenancy (a break clause but not a right of re-entry), a statutory periodic tenancy will automatically arise. The terms of this statutory periodic tenancy are governed by **s. 5(3) of the Housing Act 1988**. **86.42**

However, by s. 5(4), a statutory periodic tenancy shall not arise if, on the coming to an end of the fixed-term tenancy, the tenant is entitled, by virtue of the grant of another tenancy, to possession of the same or substantially the same dwelling-house as was let to him under the fixed-term tenancy.

Either the landlord or the tenant may change the terms of the statutory periodic tenancy by following the procedure set out in s. 6, which applies only to a statutory periodic tenancy arising following a fixed-term tenancy by virtue of s. 5 and cannot be used to alter the terms of any other periodic tenancy or a fixed-term tenancy.

The party wishing to alter the terms must serve notice on the other party in the prescribed form within one year of the date on which the former tenancy came to an end (s. 6(2)). The proposed terms can also include an adjustment in the amount of rent to take account of the proposed terms, but if a party wishes to vary only the rent, a separate procedure must be followed.

TERMS OF AN ASSURED TENANCY

Generally speaking, it is the contractual terms agreed between the parties which govern an assured tenancy. This accords with the basic philosophy of the **Housing Act 1988** that the parties should be free to negotiate and enter into a tenancy on whatever terms they agree. In a limited number of situations, however, the 1988 Act will imply terms into an assured tenancy. It also permits the landlord to apply to a rent assessment committee to increase the rent. **86.43**

Access for repairs

The Housing Act 1988, s. 16, implies into every assured tenancy a term that the tenant will give the landlord access to the dwelling-house let on the tenancy and all reasonable facilities for executing any repairs which the landlord is entitled to execute. **86.44**

Assignment and subletting

The Housing Act 1988, s. 15(1), implies into every periodic assured tenancy (including statutory periodic tenancies) a term that the tenant shall not without the consent of the landlord: **86.45**

(a) assign the tenancy (in whole or in part); or
(b) sublet or part with possession of the whole or any part of the dwelling-house let on the tenancy.

This implied term is not subject to the provisions of s. 19 of the Landlord and Tenant Act 1927 (which provides that a landlord may not unreasonably refuse consent) (Housing Act 1988, s. 15(2)). A landlord therefore is fully entitled to refuse consent to an assignment or a subletting of a periodic assured tenancy even where the refusal of consent is unreasonable.

The aim of this provision is to maintain the landlord's ability to choose who is to occupy the property. Even where the tenant seeks to assign or sublet the tenancy to a seemingly acceptable tenant, the landlord will have the right to refuse (however unreasonably) the assignment or subletting. A tenant who goes ahead and sublets or assigns without consent will be in breach of an obligation in the tenancy (Ground 12, see **87.26**) and the landlord will be entitled to seek a possession order.

Where the assured tenancy is a contractual (as opposed to a statutory) periodic tenancy, the **Housing Act 1988** will not interfere if the parties have already agreed terms dealing with assignment and subletting. By s. 15(3), s. 15 will not apply where the parties have agreed a provision either:

(a) prohibiting or permitting assignment, subletting or parting with possession (whether absolutely or conditionally); or
(b) requiring a premium to be paid on the grant or renewal of the tenancy.

In the case of fixed-term tenancies, no term against assigning and subletting will be implied and it will be for the landlord expressly to include such a term in the tenancy agreement. However, once the fixed term has expired and a statutory periodic tenancy has arisen, s. 15 will apply.

ENDING AN ASSURED TENANCY

Termination by tenant

86.46 The aim of the **Housing Act 1988** is to protect the residential tenant from premature termination by the landlord, not to trap a tenant in a tenancy he or she no longer wants. Section 5(2) of the Act specifically retains the right for the tenant to end a fixed-term tenancy by 'surrender or other action on the part of the tenant'. A tenant may, for example, agree a surrender with the landlord (surrender can also be implied), or exercise a break clause contained in the lease. Likewise, with regard to periodic assured tenancies, s. 5(1) restricts only the landlord's right to serve a notice to quit. A tenant can serve a notice to quit whenever he or she likes, provided the tenant complies with the terms of the tenancy and the Protection from Eviction Act 1977. Where the tenant terminates a tenancy, be that by surrender, exercise of a break clause, or by a notice to quit, the tenant ceases to be an assured tenant and the landlord will be entitled to repossess.

A tenant may also lose assured status by ceasing to qualify as an assured tenant under the **Housing Act 1988, s. 1**, or by changing the use of the premises so as to fall into any of the excluded categories in sch. 1, part I. For example, a tenant may cease to occupy the premises as his or her only or principal home, or may start to use the premises for business purposes. The fact that a tenant ceases to be an assured tenant does not mean that the contractual tenancy is at an end, though. Before the landlord can seek possession the contractual tenancy must be terminated validly (complying with the provisions of the Protection from Eviction Act 1977).

Possession by landlord

86.47 If a landlord wishes to start possession proceedings, the first step is to serve a notice seeking possession upon the tenant in accordance with the **Housing Act 1988, s. 8.** If there are two or more joint landlords, it is sufficient that the notice is served by one of the landlords (s. 8(1)(a)). During the fixed term of an assured tenancy, the only grounds on which the landlord can recover possession are Grounds 2, 8 and 10 to 15, and one of those grounds can be invoked only if the terms of the tenancy provide for it to be brought to an end on that ground (s. 7(6)).

A notice seeking possession must comply with certain requirements:

(a) It must be in the prescribed form (although minor deviations from the prescribed form may not be fatal provided the notice gives the tenant all the information required by statute, see *Mountain v Hastings* (1993) 25 HLR 427; *Tadema Holdings Ltd v Ferguson* (1999) *The Times*, 25 November 1999).
(b) It must inform the tenant that the landlord intends to bring possession proceedings.

(c) It must state on which ground or grounds the landlord intends to rely and also give particulars of the ground or grounds. The grounds specified in the notice may be altered or added to with the leave of the court (s. 8(2)).
(d) The notice must also inform the tenant that proceedings will not be begun earlier than a date specified in the notice (s. 8(3)(b)). In the majority of cases this date should be at least two weeks from the date of the service of the notice. If the landlord specifies an intention to rely upon any of Grounds 1, 2, 5 to 7, 9 and 16 (see **chapter 87**), this date should be at least two months from the date of service of the notice or, if it is longer, the earliest date on which the tenancy could be brought to an end by a notice to quit given by the landlord on the same date as the date of service of the notice (i.e., the contractual period of the tenancy) (s. 8(4A)).
(e) Where the landlord seeks to rely on grounds which include Ground 14 (nuisance, see **87.28**) the date specified in the notice can be any time on or after the date of service of the notice (s. 8(4)). Thus proceedings which include an allegation under Ground 14 may be commenced on the same day that notice is served, thereby speeding up the process of recovery of the property and allowing the landlord to apply for an injunction if necessary. It should be noted, however, that the court cannot order the tenant to give up possession of the property until the earliest day on which the tenancy could be bought to an end by notice to quit. By virtue of s. 5 of the Protection from Eviction Act 1977, the minimum period for a notice to quit is four weeks.
(f) If the landlord is a registered social landlord seeking possession under Ground 14A (domestic violence, see **87.29**) there is an additional notice requirement: the landlord must serve a copy of the s. 8 notice on the partner who has left the dwelling-house or satisfy the court that all reasonable steps have been taken to do so (s. 8A(1)).
(g) It must inform the tenant that those proceedings will not begin later than 12 months from the date of service of the notice (s. 8(3)(c)).

If proceedings are not issued within 12 months a fresh s. 8 notice must be served.

It is important to note that, with the exception of proceedings to recover possession under Ground 8 (three months' rent arrears, see **87.21**), the court has a discretion to dispense with the requirement of notice before commencing possession proceedings if it considers it 'just and equitable' to do so (s. 8(1)(b)). The discretion must be exercised in the light of all material circumstances, taking account of both the landlord and the tenant (*Kelsey Housing Association v King* (1995) 28 HLR 270). The question whether notice should be dispensed with should be dealt with at a hearing (*Knowsley Housing Trust v Revell* [2003] EWCA Civ 496, [2003] HLR 63).

SUCCESSION

Section 17 of the Housing Act 1988 provides a limited system of statutory succession. These **86.48**
provisions do not apply to an assured fixed-term tenancy. If a fixed-term tenant dies, the tenancy forms part of the deceased tenant's estate and will pass according to his or her will or, if there is no will, the rules of intestacy. If a periodic assured tenant dies (whether the tenancy is a statutory periodic tenancy or a contractual periodic tenancy) that tenancy will also pass under the deceased tenant's will or the rules of intestacy unless it falls within s. 17. Where a person inherits a periodic assured tenancy under the deceased tenant's will or the rules of intestacy and occupies the dwelling house in question as his or her only or principal home, the landlord will have the right to recover possession under Ground 7 (see **87.20**).

Under s. 17 of the Act, only the tenant's spouse or civil partner is capable of succeeding to the tenancy, but a person who was living with the tenant as his or her spouse or civil partner is treated as a spouse or civil partner for the purposes of this section (s. 17(4)). Whether a person is to be so treated depends on the relationship being an emotional one of mutual lifetime commitment, not simply one of convenience or friendship (*Nutting v Southern Housing Group* [2004] EWHC 2982, [2005] HLR 25).

Section 17 will apply only where:
(a) the sole tenant under an assured periodic tenancy dies; and
(b) immediately before the tenant's death, the tenant's spouse or civil partner was occupying the dwelling-house as his or her only or principal home; and
(c) the tenant was not himself a successor.

The **Housing Act 1988** therefore provides for only one succession. If the deceased tenant was already a successor, s. 17 will not apply. The deceased tenant will be regarded as a successor if:

(a) the tenancy became vested in the deceased tenant by virtue of s. 17;
(b) the tenancy became vested in the deceased tenant under the will or intestacy of a previous tenant;
(c) the deceased tenant was a joint tenant and had, on the death of the other joint tenant (or tenants), become the sole tenant by the right of survivorship;
(d) the deceased tenant succeeded to an assured tenancy by virtue of the **Rent Act 1977** (see **86.11**).

Even where the tenant, having succeeded to a previous tenancy, has been granted a further tenancy of the same or substantially the same dwelling-house, that tenant will still be regarded as a successor (s. 17(3)).

Chapter 87 Recovering Possession under the Housing Act 1988

POSSESSION OF AN ASSURED SHORTHOLD TENANCY

General

87.1 The main advantage of an assured shorthold tenancy from the landlord's point of view, is that once any fixed term has expired, possession can be recovered without having to establish any of the grounds set out in the **Housing Act 1988, sch. 2.**

Possession on expiry of a fixed-term assured shorthold tenancy

87.2 **Section 21(1) of the Housing Act 1988** provides that on or after the coming to an end of a fixed-term assured shorthold tenancy, the court shall make an order for possession provided it is satisfied that:

(a) the assured shorthold tenancy has come to an end and no further assured tenancy, other than an assured shorthold periodic tenancy, is in existence; and
(b) the tenant has been given not less than two months' notice that possession of the dwelling house is required by the landlord, or by at least one of a number of joint landlords.

The requirement that the notice be in writing was added by the **Housing Act 1996**, which also amended s. 21 to provide that an order for possession of an assured shorthold tenancy granted on or after 28 February 1997 may not be made earlier than six months after the beginning of the tenancy (s. 21(5)(a)). If the shorthold tenancy is a replacement tenancy, possession may be granted after six months from the commencement of the original tenancy

(s. 21(5)(b)). A replacement tenancy is a tenancy which comes into being at the end of an assured shorthold tenancy under which the landlord and tenant are substantially the same as under the earlier tenancy and the premises let are the same or substantially the same as those let under the earlier tenancy (s. 21(7)). These provisions are intended to ensure that shorthold tenancies are granted for a minimum period of six months, since the requirement that an assured shorthold tenancy be granted for a term of not less than six months does not apply to tenancies granted on or after 28 February 1997.

Possession of premises held on a periodic assured shorthold tenancy after expiry of the original term

87.3 In order to recover possession of a dwelling-house which the tenant is holding as an assured periodic shorthold tenant, the landlord must serve notice in accordance with the **Housing Act 1988, s. 21(4)**. This provides that the court must make an order for possession if it is satisfied that the landlord (or at least one of a number of joint landlords) has given the tenant at least two months' written notice specifying a date upon which possession is required. The date specified must be the last day of a period of the tenancy and must be no earlier than the earliest date on which the tenancy could have been brought to an end, apart from s. 5(1), by a notice to quit given by the landlord on the same day as the notice under s. 21(4). If the notice does not give the last day of a period of the tenancy, it will be invalid, even if the day given is the day immediately following the last day of a period (*McDonald v Fernandez* [2003] EWCA 1219, [2003] 4 All ER 1033).

The use of this procedure by a housing association as a public authority under the **Human Rights Act 1998, s. 6**, does not interfere with the tenant's right to respect for his home which is guaranteed by the **European Convention on Human Rights, art. 8** (*Poplar Housing and Regeneration Community Association Ltd v Donoghue* [2001] EWCA Civ 595, [2002] QB 48).

Possession during the fixed term for serious breach

87.4 It is a common misconception to believe that an assured shorthold tenancy cannot be terminated until the fixed term has expired. This is not the case: an assured shorthold tenancy is like any other fixed-term assured tenancy in that it is subject to the provisions of the **Housing Act 1988, s. 7(6)**. Thus, as long as the terms of the tenancy provide for it, the landlord may seek possession on Ground 2, **8**, 10, **11**, **12**, **13**, **14** or **15** (see **87.15**, **87.21**, **87.24** to **87.29**) at any time during the course of the tenancy, even in the first six months.

POSSESSION OF AN ASSURED TENANCY

87.5 Once the landlord has successfully served a notice of intention to bring possession proceedings (or the court has used its discretion to dispense with the requirement of notice) (see **86.47**), one or more of the grounds for possession set out in the **Housing Act 1988, sch. 2**, must be established before the court will grant an order for possession. A mere agreement to give up possession is unenforceable, and a consent order for possession has to indicate (expressly or by necessary implication) the statutory ground on which possession is granted (*Baygreen Properties Ltd v Gil* [2002] EWCA Civ 1340, [2003] HLR 12). If the landlord can establish a mandatory ground (Grounds 1 to 8), the court must grant a possession order (s. 7(3)). If the landlord can establish a discretionary ground (Grounds 9 to 17), the court will grant a possession order only if it considers it reasonable to do so (s. 7(4)).

PROCEDURE FOR POSSESSION CLAIMS

87.6 The procedure for possession claims is governed by **CPR, Part 55**, and **PD 55**. There is now a limited facility operating in specified county courts (where the claim is solely on the ground of rent arrears) for a possession claim to be started online: see **CPR, r. 55.10A**. For possession claims against trespassers see **chapter 35**.

Claim form and particulars of claim

The claim form which must be used for a possession claim is **form N5** (**CPR, r. 55.3(5)**). **87.7**
Particulars of claim (**form N119**) must be filed and served with the claim form (**r. 55.4**). A defence form (**form N11R**) must be served with the particulars of claim.

If the claim includes a claim for non-payment of rent, the particulars of claim must set out (**PD 55, para. 2.3**):

(a) the amount due at the start of the proceedings;
(b) in schedule form, the dates when the arrears of rent arose, all amounts of rent due, the dates and amounts of all payments made and a running total of arrears;
(c) the daily rate of rent;
(d) any previous steps taken to recover the arrears of rent with full details of any court proceedings; and
(e) any relevant information about the defendant's circumstances, in particular:
  (i) whether the defendant is in receipt of social security benefits; and
  (ii) whether any payments are made on the defendant's behalf directly to the claimant under the Social Security Contributions and Benefits Act 1992.

County court or High Court

A possession claim must be started in the county court for the district in which the dwelling-house is situated (**CPR, r. 55.3(1)**), but may be started in the High Court if the claimant files with the claim form a certificate stating the reasons for bringing it in the High Court (**r. 55.3(2)**). The certificate must be verified by a statement of truth (**r. 55.3(2)**). Only exceptional circumstances justify starting a possession claim in the High Court (**PD 55, para. 1.1**). If a possession claim is started in the High Court and that court decides the claim should have been started in the county court, it will either strike out the claim or transfer it to the county court of its own initiative (**para. 1.2**). If this is done, the costs of starting the claim in the High Court and transferring it will normally be disallowed (**para. 1.2**). Circumstances which may justify using the High Court are (**para. 1.3**): **87.8**

(a) there are complicated disputes of fact;
(b) there are points of law of general importance;
(c) the claim is against trespassers and there is a substantial risk of public disturbance or of serious harm to persons or property which properly require immediate determination.

The value of the property and the amount of any financial claim may be relevant circumstances but will not in themselves justify using the High Court (**para. 1.4**).

Hearing date

The court will fix a date for the hearing when it issues the claim form (**CPR, r. 55.5(1)**). This will be not less than 28 days from the date of issue (**r. 55.5(3)(a)**) and usually not more than eight weeks (**r. 55.5(3)(b)**). The court may, under **r. 3.1(2)(a)**, order a hearing in less than 28 days and consideration should be given to the exercise of this power if the tenant is violent or disruptive (**PD 55, para. 3**). On the date fixed for hearing (or any adjournment) the court may either decide the claim or give case management directions (**r. 55.8(1)**). **87.9**

Service and response

The claim form and particulars of claim must be served not less than 21 days before the hearing date (**CPR, r. 55.5(3)(c)**). This time may be shortened by the court under **r. 3.1(2)(a)**. A defence form (**form N11R**) must be served with the particulars of claim. **87.10**

Acknowledgment of service is not required and Part 10 does not apply (**r. 55.7(1)**). Default judgment cannot be given on a possession claim (**r. 55.7(4)**).

If the claimant effects service of the claim form and particulars of claim, a certificate of service must be filed at the hearing and **r. 6.14(2)(a)** does not apply (**r. 55.8(6)**).

Written evidence must be filed and served at least two days before the hearing (**r. 55.8(3) and (4)**). If the maker of a witness statement does not attend the hearing and material points in his or her statement are disputed, the court will normally adjourn the hearing so that oral evidence can be given (**PD 55, para. 5.4**).

If relevant, the claimant's evidence should include the amount of rent arrears, up to the date of the hearing, and this evidence can be brought up to date at the hearing, orally or in writing (**PD 55, para. 5.2**).

If relevant, the defendant should give evidence of relevant outstanding social security or housing benefit payments or pending claims for benefit (**PD 55, para. 5.3**).

Case management

87.11 If the claim is genuinely disputed on grounds which appear to be substantial, the court may allocate the claim to a track or direct how allocation is to be determined (**CPR, r. 55.8(2)**).

A possession claim can be allocated to the small claims track only if all the parties agree (**r. 55.9(2)**). There are special provisions for costs of possession claims on the small claims track in **r. 55.9(3) and (4)**.

In choosing the track for a possession claim the court will, by **r. 55.9(1)**, take into account the matters set out in **r. 26.8** (see **42.14 to 42.19**), but the financial value of the property will not necessarily be the most important factor, so the court may allocate a claim involving property worth more than £15,000 to the fast track (**PD 55, para. 6.1**). The court will also take into account (**CPR, r. 55.9(1)**):

(a) the amount of any arrears of rent;
(b) the importance to the defendant of retaining possession;
(c) the importance of vacant possession to the claimant; and
(d) if applicable, the alleged conduct of the defendant.

ACCELERATED POSSESSION PROCEDURE

87.12 An accelerated procedure may be invoked by landlords seeking to recover possession of property held on assured shorthold tenancy and on assured tenancy where Ground 1,3, 4 or 5 is relied upon. A possession order can be made by the district judge without the need for attendance by either party in what may be little more than 14 days from the date of service of the application on the tenant. The rules, which are in **CPR, rr. 55.11 to 55.19**, and **PD 55, para. 8**, are discussed in **35.15**, and must be strictly adhered to. The accelerated possession procedure cannot be used where the landlord wishes to make any other claim in the proceedings (such as a claim for arrears of rent). It can only be used to recover possession of property held on assured shorthold tenancy where a written agreement was entered into on or after 15 January 1989.

MANDATORY GROUNDS FOR POSSESSION OF DWELLING-HOUSES LET ON ASSURED TENANCIES

87.13 The grounds on which the court must order possession under the **Housing Act 1988, s. 7**, are listed in part I of sch. 2 to the Act and are discussed in **87.14 to 87.21**. Once the court is satisfied that the landlord is entitled to possession on any of these grounds, there is no power to grant an adjournment in any circumstances (s. 9(6)).

Ground 1 — Returning owner-occupier

Not later than the beginning of the tenancy the landlord gave notice in writing to the tenant that possession might be recovered on this ground or the court is of the opinion that it is just and equitable to dispense with the requirement of notice and (in either case) — **87.14**

(a) at some time before the beginning of the tenancy, the landlord who is seeking possession or, in the case of joint landlords seeking possession, at least one of them occupied the dwelling-house as his only or principal home; or

(b) the landlord who is seeking possession or, in the case of joint landlords seeking possession, at least one of them requires the dwelling-house as his or her spouse's or civil partner's only or principal home and neither the landlord (or in the case of joint landlords, any one of them) nor any person who, as landlord, derived title under the landlord who gave the notice mentioned above acquired the reversion on the tenancy for money or money's worth.

To be able to rely upon Ground 1, a landlord must have given written notice to the tenant before the tenancy commenced that possession might be recovered under this ground. The court can, if it considers it just and equitable to do so, dispense with the requirement of notice. If such notice has been given, the landlord can then recover possession in two situations:

(a) Possession of the dwelling-house can be recovered if it was occupied by the landlord as his or her only or principal residence at some time before the grant of the tenancy. The landlord does not have to give any reasons for wanting to recover possession. Neither is it necessary that the landlord occupied the dwelling immediately before the letting to the tenant. In the case of joint landlords, it is sufficient that one of them previously occupied the dwelling-house as his or her only or principal home.

(b) Where the landlord (or in the case of joint landlords, at least one of them) wants to regain possession of the premises for his or her own occupation, or for occupation by his or her spouse. There is no requirement that either the landlord or his or her spouse or civil partner previously occupied the premises. However, a landlord who bought the reversion from the tenant's original landlord cannot use this ground.

Ground 2 — Mortgagees

The dwelling-house is subject to a mortgage granted before the beginning of the tenancy and — **87.15**

(a) the mortgagee is entitled to exercise a power of sale conferred on him by the mortgage or by section 101 of the Law of Property Act 1925; and

(b) the mortgagee requires possession of the dwelling-house for the purpose of disposing of it with vacant possession in exercise of that power; and

(c) either notice was given as mentioned in Ground 1 above or the court is satisfied that it is just and equitable to dispense with the requirement of notice;

and for the purposes of this ground 'mortgage' includes a charge and 'mortgagee' shall be construed accordingly.

The aim of this ground is to enable a landlord to regain possession from the tenant when the bank or building society which lent the landlord the money to purchase the property wants to repossess the property in order to sell it. This will usually be because the landlord has defaulted on the mortgage repayments.

Ground 2 will apply only where:

(a) the mortgage was granted before the beginning of the tenancy; and

(b) the landlord has served notice in accordance with the requirements of Ground 1 (i.e., that the landlord may want possession at a future date because of an intention to occupy the dwelling-house personally), or the court has dispensed with this requirement.

This ground is intended to cover the situation where a landlord is unable to recover possession under Ground 1 when it is not possible to claim that the dwelling-house is required as the landlord's home because the mortgagee intends to sell it. Notice may be dispensed with by the court if it feels it is just and equitable to do so.

The majority of mortgages prohibit the renting out of the property without the mortgagee's consent. If a property is let without consent, the tenant will have no protection (see *Britannia Building Society v Earl* [1990] 1 EGLR 133). This ground can also apply to a fixed-term tenancy before the expiry of the term.

Ground 3 — Holiday lets

87.16 The aim of this provision is to assist a landlord who habitually lets out property on holiday lets during the summer. Holiday lets are, of course, excluded from being assured tenancies (**Housing Act 1988, sch. 1, para. 9**). A landlord who lets out property as a holiday home in season may wish to let it out for a longer period out of season. Such a letting might well not fall within the definition of a holiday letting and be an assured tenancy. Ground 3 enables the landlord to regain possession of the property for use as a holiday home in season. To rely upon this ground:

(a) the tenancy in question must be a fixed-term tenancy for a term not exceeding eight months; and
(b) the landlord must have given written notice to the tenant that possession might be recovered on this ground before the beginning of the tenancy (the court has no discretion under this ground to dispense with the notice requirement); and
(c) at some time within the period of 12 months ending with the beginning of the tenancy the dwelling-house must have been occupied under a right to occupy it for a holiday.

Ground 4 — Student lets

87.17 Ground 4 is similar to Ground 3. Like holiday lettings, lettings to students are precluded from being assured tenancies (**Housing Act 1988, sch. 1, para. 8**). A letting of premises normally used to provide accommodation for students during a vacation period, however, might be capable of being an assured tenancy. Ground 4 therefore enables a landlord to recover possession when the term of the vacation let is over. To rely upon this ground:

(a) the tenancy must be a fixed-term tenancy for a term not exceeding 12 months; and
(b) the landlord must have given written notice to the tenant that possession might be recovered on this ground before the beginning of the tenancy (as with Ground 3 the court has no discretion to dispense with the notice requirement); and
(c) at some time within the period of 12 months ending with the beginning of the tenancy, the dwelling-house was let on a tenancy falling within the **Housing Act 1988, sch. 1, para. 8**.

Ground 5 — Ministers of religion

87.18 To rely upon this ground:

(a) the dwelling-house must be held for the purpose of being available for occupation by a minister of religion as a residence from which to perform the duties of his or her office;
(b) the landlord must have given written notice to the tenant that possession might be recovered on this ground before the beginning of the tenancy (the court has no discretion to dispense with the notice requirement);
(c) the court must be satisfied that the dwelling-house is required for occupation by a minister of religion as a residence from which to perform his or her duties.

Ground 6 — Demolition, reconstruction or substantial works

87.19 This ground is similar to **the Landlord and Tenant Act 1954, s. 30(1)(f)**, with regard to business tenancies, and for public-sector tenancies under the **Housing Act 1985 (sch. 2, Ground 10)**. The inclusion of this ground in the **Housing Act 1988** is no doubt partially due to the fact that the tenants of registered housing associations now derive their protection from the 1988 Act rather than as secure tenants under the 1985 Act.

To rely on this ground the landlord must show the following:

(a) That the landlord intends to demolish or reconstruct the whole or a substantial part of the dwelling-house, or to carry out substantial works on the dwelling-house or any part thereof or any building of which it forms part. There must be a genuine desire to undertake the work and also a reasonable prospect that the work will actually go ahead. Where a landlord had not found a developer to undertake the projected work at the time of the hearing, the landlord was regarded as not having established the necessary intention (*Edwards v Thompson* [1990] 2 EGLR 71; see also *Wansbeck District Council v Marley* (1987) *The Times*, 30 November 1987).

(b) That the work could not reasonably be carried out without the tenant giving up possession of the premises. If the tenant is prepared to agree to a variation of the terms of the tenancy so as to enable the landlord access to undertake the work, possession will not be granted under this ground. Likewise, if the tenant is willing to take a tenancy of a part of the premises so that the landlord can work on the other parts, possession will not be granted under Ground 6. The landlord must show either that the tenant is not willing to agree to such an arrangement (be that a variation of terms or the grant of the tenancy of a part of the premises), or that the nature of the intended work is such that such an arrangement is not possible.

(c) That the landlord's interest in the property was acquired before the tenancy was granted, or, if it was acquired after the grant of the tenancy it was not acquired for money or money's worth (for example, the landlord could have acquired the interest under a will but must not have purchased the interest). The aim of this provision is to prevent speculators from exploiting Ground 6 for commercial gain by purchasing the landlord's reversion with the intention of recovering possession and redeveloping the property.

If a landlord is successful under this ground, s. 11 of the 1988 Act requires the landlord to pay to the tenant a sum equal to the reasonable expenses likely to be incurred by the tenant in removing from the dwelling house. If the landlord and tenant cannot agree on an appropriate sum the amount will be determined by the court.

Ground 7 — Inherited periodic tenancy

Under the **Rent Act 1977**, a statutory tenancy came to an end on the death of the tenant **87.20** unless a person succeeded to that tenancy under the provisions of the Act. Under the **Housing Act 1988**, there is no distinction between the original contractual periodic tenancy and a statutory tenancy. It is therefore possible for an assured tenancy (even a statutorily implied periodic tenancy) to be passed to a third party by the tenant's will. As a result a landlord may find, after the death of an assured periodic tenant, that a third party has inherited the tenant's tenancy and is now occupying the dwelling-house. The landlord has had no say in choosing this new tenant, who may possibly be considered undesirable. This ground therefore provides the landlord with a means of recovering possession in this situation.

Ground 7 applies to periodic tenancies and statutory periodic tenancies only when a tenant has died and the tenancy has been passed to another person by virtue of the deceased tenant's will or intestacy. It does not apply when the deceased tenant's spouse, civil partner or cohabitee has succeeded to the tenancy under s. 17 of the 1988 Act. The landlord has one year from the date of the death of the original tenant, or the date of becoming aware of the death of the tenant, to begin proceedings for possession. Proceedings are begun when the court issues a claim form, not when the landlord serves a notice under s. 8 (*Shepping v Osada* (2000) 33 HLR 146).

This ground also specifically provides that if, after the death of the original tenant, the landlord accepts rent from a new tenant, this will not amount to an implied grant of a new tenancy. (Under common law rules the acceptance of rent by the landlord could well do so.) A new tenancy will be created only if there is a written agreement to vary the terms of the tenancy.

Ground 8 — Serious rent arrears

87.21 Ground 8 gives the landlord a mandatory ground for possession for rent arrears (Grounds 10 and 11 are two further discretionary grounds also dealing with rent arrears). Ground 8 is one of the two exceptional mandatory grounds (along with Ground 2) that can apply to a fixed-term tenancy before the expiry of the contractual term.

To be able to rely upon this ground, the landlord must show that both at the date of service of a s. 8 notice and also at the date of the hearing:

(a) if rent is payable weekly or fortnightly, at least eight weeks' rent is unpaid;
(b) if rent is payable monthly, at least two months' rent is unpaid;
(c) if rent is payable quarterly, at least one quarter's rent is more than three months in arrears; and
(d) if rent is payable yearly, at least three months' rent is more than three months in arrears.

'Rent' here means rent lawfully due from the tenant. The amount of rent arrears for weekly and monthly tenancies was reduced by the Housing Act 1996, s. 101, from 13 weeks and three months respectively.

The tenant who receives a s. 8 notice specifying that the landlord seeks to rely on Ground 8 therefore has a last chance to avoid repossession by paying off some or all of the arrears before the hearing date. Where the landlord accepted an uncleared cheque delivered by the tenant, it was to be treated as payment at the date of delivery provided the cheque was paid at first presentation (*Day v Coltrane* [2003] EWCA Civ 342, [2003] 1 WLR 1379). Most landlords, however, are likely to combine a claim under Ground 8 with a claim under either or both of the discretionary grounds. A tenant may also be able to avoid possession under Ground 8 if able to counterclaim for breach of the landlord's covenant to repair. Any damages awarded on the counterclaim will be set off against the rent arrears and may thereby reduce the outstanding amount below the specified level.

The court does have power, albeit exercisable only in exceptional circumstances, to adjourn a hearing date to enable the tenant to reduce the arrears of rent to below the Ground 8 threshold. Non-receipt of housing benefit cannot, of itself, justify the exercise of the power to adjourn so as to enable the tenant to defeat the landlord's claim. Maladministration on the part of the housing benefit authority is not an exceptional circumstance. See generally *North British Housing Association Ltd v Matthews* [2004] EWCA Civ 1736, [2005] P & CR 13.

DISCRETIONARY GROUNDS FOR POSSESSION OF DWELLING-HOUSES LET ON ASSURED TENANCIES

87.22 The grounds on which the court may order possession under the **Housing Act 1988, s. 7**, if it considers it reasonable to do so are listed in part II of sch. 2 to the Act and are discussed in **87.23 to 87.32**. In considering reasonableness the court should take into account all relevant circumstances as at the date of the hearing and apply a broad, common-sense view (*Cumming v Danson* [1942] 2 All ER 653 per Lord Greene MR at p. 655). The court has a very wide discretion. It may consider virtually any factor which might affect the landlord or the tenant if the order is, or is not, made, and give them such weight as it thinks fit. Reasonableness is a question of fact based upon the particular circumstances of the individual case, and it is therefore difficult for any party dissatisfied with the court's exercise of discretion to appeal unless it can be shown that the court misdirected itself in law. Where a tenant is disabled, the Disability Discrimination Act 1995 may have to be considered: see **88.51**.

Under s. 9 of the 1988 Act the court also has wide powers to:

(a) adjourn the proceedings for such period or periods as it thinks fit (s. 9(1));
(b) if a possession order is made, stay or suspend the execution of that order, or postpone the date of possession for such period or periods as it thinks fit (s. 9(2));
(c) impose other conditions as it thinks fit, provided it considers such conditions would not cause exceptional hardship to the tenant or be otherwise unreasonable.

Ground 9 — Suitable alternative accommodation

Suitable alternative accommodation is available for the tenant or will be available for him when the order for possession takes effect. **87.23**

Part III of sch. 2 to the Housing Act 1988 defines what will be regarded as suitable alternative accommodation. Two possibilities are open to the landlord:

(a) The landlord can produce a certificate of the local housing authority certifying that the authority will provide suitable alternative accommodation for the tenant by a date specified in the certificate (sch. 2, part III, para. 1).
(b) The landlord can seek to establish that suitable alternative accommodation is or will be available. This accommodation may be supplied by the current landlord or by some other landlord.

If the landlord takes the second option, the court will consider the proposed accommodation. It will be deemed suitable for the purposes of Ground 9 if it fulfils two requirements:

(a) The proposed accommodation must, in the opinion of the court, afford to the tenant security of tenure reasonably equivalent to an assured tenancy (e.g., a secure tenancy under the **Housing Act 1985**). An assured shorthold tenancy or an assured tenancy in respect of which notice has been given that possession might be recovered under Grounds 1 to 5 will not be sufficient (sch. 2, part III, para. 2(a)).
(b) The proposed accommodation must be reasonably suitable to the needs of the tenant and his or her family as regards proximity to place of work, and either:
    (i) similar as regards rental and extent to accommodation provided in the neighbourhood by the local housing authority to persons whose needs are similar to those of the tenant and his or her family; or
    (ii) reasonably suitable to the means of the tenant and to the needs of the tenant and his or her family as regards extent and character;

and if furniture was provided under the original assured tenancy, the alternative accommodation should provide furniture which is either similar to that provided under the original tenancy or suitable to the needs of the tenant and his or her family (sch. 2, part III, para. 3).

In determining 'proximity to place of work', the court should consider not simply the distance to be travelled but also the time taken and the means of transport available (*Yewbright Properties Ltd v Stone* (1980) 40 P & CR 402). In determining 'rental and extent', the court may consider that alternative accommodation is suitable even though it is smaller than the current property, and in one case part of the tenanted premises was considered to provide suitable alternative accommodation (*Mykolyshyn v Noah* [1970] 1 WLR 1271). Account should be taken of the tenant's professional needs (an artist's studio: *MacDonnell v Daly* [1969] 1 WLR 1482), the need to entertain business associates (*De Markozoff v Craig* (1949) 93 SJ 693), and the sufficiency of room for lodgers (*Warren v Austen* [1947] 2 All ER 185). Environmental factors affecting the character of the property may also be relevant (*Redspring Ltd v Francis* [1973] 1 WLR 134; *Siddiqui v Rashid* [1980] 1 WLR 1018). As with Ground 2 above, s. 11(1) of the 1988 Act provides that the landlord shall pay to the tenant a sum equal to the reasonable expenses likely to be incurred by the tenant in removing from the dwelling-house.

Ground 10 — Some rent arrears

87.24 Some rent lawfully due from the tenant —

(a) is unpaid on the date on which proceedings for possession are begun; and

(b) except where subsection (1)(b) of section 8 of this Act applies, was in arrears at the date of service of the notice under that section relating to those proceedings.

Ground 10 is notably different from Ground 8 (serious rent arrears). First, all that is required is that the landlord shows that some rent is outstanding: no minimum amount is specified. Secondly, the landlord need show only that rent was outstanding at the date upon which proceedings were issued and at the date of service of the **Housing Act 1988, s. 8,** notice (unless the requirement of notice has been dispensed with by the court). The landlord does not have to show that any rent is outstanding at the date of the hearing. However, this is a discretionary ground and it is unlikely that a court would consider it reasonable to make an order for possession if the tenant has paid off all the arrears by the date of the hearing.

Ground 11 — Persistent rent arrears

87.25 Whether or not any rent is in arrears on the date on which proceedings for possession are begun, the tenant has persistently delayed paying rent which has become lawfully due.

Even when there are no current rent arrears the landlord can rely upon this ground. The aim of this provision is to provide the landlord with a means of regaining possession when a tenant persistently falls into rent arrears but avoids the consequences of Ground 8 by paying off some or all of the outstanding rent after the issue of proceedings but before the date of the hearing.

Ground 12 — Breach of obligation

87.26 Any obligation of the tenancy (other than one related to the payment of rent) has been broken or not performed.

The landlord can seek to rely upon this ground even where there is only a trivial breach, but it is most unlikely that the court will regard it as reasonable to make a possession order unless the breach is serious. In determining the seriousness of the breach an important factor will be whether the breach is remediable and whether it is continuing. If the landlord has waived the breach (see **84.8 to 84.13**) he will not be able to rely upon this ground. If the tenant has remedied the breach, it is unlikely that the court will consider it reasonable to make a possession order.

Ground 13 — Deterioration of the dwelling-house

87.27 The condition of the dwelling-house or any of the common parts has deteriorated owing to acts of waste by, or the neglect or default of, the tenant or any other person residing in the dwelling-house and, in the case of an act of waste by, or the neglect or default of, a person lodging with the tenant or a sub-tenant of his, the tenant has not taken such steps as he ought reasonably to have taken for the removal of the lodger or sub-tenant.

For the purposes of this ground, 'common parts' means any part of a building comprising the dwelling-house and any other premises which the tenant is entitled under the terms of the tenancy to use in common with the occupiers of other dwelling-houses in which the landlord has an estate or interest.

Ground 14 — Nuisance, annoyance or conviction for illegal or immoral user

87.28 The tenant or a person residing in or visiting the dwelling-house—

(a) has been guilty of conduct causing or likely to cause a nuisance or annoyance to a person residing, visiting or otherwise engaging in lawful activity in the locality, or

(b) has been convicted of—
   (i) using the dwelling-house or allowing it to be used for immoral or illegal purposes, or
   (ii) an arrestable offence committed in, or in the locality of the dwelling-house.

This ground is identical to **Ground 2 under the Housing Act 1985** (see **88.31**). It gives the landlord a powerful sanction against anti-social behaviour, not only on the part of the tenant but also on the part of any person residing with or even visiting the tenant. The behaviour does not have to cause actual nuisance, it is sufficient for it merely to be *likely* to cause nuisance or annoyance. Furthermore, the person to whom the nuisance or annoyance is caused does not have to be a neighbour but can be anyone engaging in lawful activity in the locality. Thus, where local residents may be wary of complaining for fear of reprisals, a landlord will be able to rely on evidence from professional witnesses. In deciding whether it is reasonable to make an order for possession, the court must consider the effect of the nuisance or annoyance on other persons (**Housing Act 1988, s. 9A**). Ground 14 will also enable a landlord to seek possession where the tenant, or a person residing with or visiting the tenant, has been convicted not only of using the dwelling-house for immoral or illegal purposes but also of any arrestable offence committed in the locality of the dwelling-house. Where a landlord wishes to rely on Ground 14, court proceedings may be started at the same time that a notice of seeking possession is served (**Housing Act 1988, s. 8(4)**).

Demotion orders

Part 2 of the Anti-Social Behaviour Act 2003 confers additional powers on the court. Where **87.29** the landlord is a registered social landlord, it may apply to the county court for a demotion order terminating the assured tenancy and (where the tenant remains in occupation) replacing it with a demoted tenancy (Housing Act 1988, s. 6A). The only ground for such an application is that the tenant, or a person residing in or visiting the dwelling-house, has engaged, or has threatened to engage in, conduct to which s. 153A or s. 153B of the Housing Act 1996 applies (i.e., anti-social behaviour or use of the premises for unlawful purposes) (Housing Act 1988, s. 6A(4)). The landlord must give the tenant prior notice giving particulars of the conduct relied upon (s. 6A(5) and (6)). The court must not make a demotion order unless it is satisfied that the ground is made out, and that it is reasonable to make an order (s. 6A(4)).

The effect of a demotion order which creates a demoted tenancy is that the former assured tenancy will become an assured shorthold tenancy under the Housing Act 1988, s. 20B. The tenancy will, however, cease to be a shorthold on the expiry of a period of one year after the demotion order takes effect (unless notice of proceedings for possession is given before that period expires), and will convert back into an assured non-shorthold tenancy (s. 20B(2)).

Ground 14A — Domestic violence

The dwelling-house was occupied (whether alone or with others) by a married couple or a couple living **87.30** together as husband and wife and—
(a) one or both of the partners is a tenant of the dwelling-house,
(b) the landlord who is seeking possession is a registered social landlord or charitable housing trust,
(c) one partner has left the dwelling-house because of violence or threats of violence by the other towards—
   (i) that partner, or
   (ii) a member of the family of that partner who was residing with that partner immediately before the partner left, and
(d) the court is satisfied that the partner who has left is unlikely to return.

This ground was introduced by the **Housing Act 1996** primarily to help charitable landlords to obtain possession of family housing from the remaining occupant after his or her partner and children left as a result of that occupant's violence. To be able to rely on Ground 14A the landlord must be a registered social landlord or a charitable housing trust. The landlord must also comply with the additional notice requirements set out in the **Housing Act 1988,**

s. 8A (see 86.47). Ground 14A is identical to **Ground 2A under the Housing Act 1985** (see 88.32).

Ground 15 — Deterioration of furniture

87.31 The condition of any furniture provided for use under the tenancy has, in the opinion of the court, deteriorated owing to ill-treatment by the tenant or any other person residing in the dwelling-house and, in the case of ill-treatment by a person lodging with the tenant or by a sub-tenant of his, the tenant has not taken such steps as he ought reasonably to have taken for the removal of the lodger or sub-tenant.

Ground 16 — Employees

87.32 The dwelling-house was let to the tenant in consequence of his employment by the landlord seeking possession or a previous landlord under the tenancy and the tenant has ceased to be in that employment. . .

The landlord need only prove that the assured tenancy was granted to the tenant in consequence of that tenant's employment by the landlord or a previous landlord and that this employment has now ceased. The landlord does not have to prove that the dwelling-house is required for another employee.

Ground 17 — Grant induced by false statement

87.33 The tenant is the person, or was one of the persons, to whom the tenancy was granted and the landlord was induced to grant the tenancy by a false statement made knowingly or recklessly by—

(a) the tenant, or
(b) a person acting at the tenant's instigation.

This ground was introduced by the **Housing Act 1996**, s. 102. It is identical to **Ground 5 of sch. 2 to the Housing Act 1985** (see **88.35**). Since 15 January 1989 an increasing proportion of housing for the less privileged has been provided on assured tenancies by charitable bodies and registered social landlords. Ground 17 is designed to prevent tenants from acquiring an assured tenancy by falsely representing their circumstances.

Chapter 88 Secure Tenancies under the Housing Act 1985

INTRODUCTION

Given the relatively long history of statutory protection for residential occupiers in the private sector, it is surprising to note that similar statutory protection was introduced into the public sector only in 1980. Before 1980 a public sector tenant had no statutory security of tenure. **88.1**

While it was felt that a private sector tenant needed to be safeguarded against the possibility of exploitation at the hands of landlords renting property for commercial gain, it was generally believed that local authorities, as non profit-making organisations providing housing for the less privileged, could be relied upon to exercise their powers fairly.

Part I of the Housing Act 1980 introduced two very important measures into the public sector. Chapter I introduced the now famous 'right to buy'. For the first time tenants of public sector landlords were able to compel their landlords to sell them the properties in which the tenants were living. Those provisions are outside the scope of this work. Chapter II conferred upon public sector tenants a statutory security of tenure similar to, although not identical with, that already available for tenants in the private sector. These measures are now contained in **parts** IV and V of the Housing Act 1985.

In considering secure tenancies it is important to bear in mind that the aim of the legislation is not so much to protect tenants from unscrupulous landlords but to provide a regime within which the public sector can effectively perform the function of providing housing for the less privileged. As a result, the legislation includes provisions such as those enabling public landlords to keep control of specialised housing for the elderly or disabled.

Over the years the **Housing Act 1985** has been subject to amendment by a variety of statutes, notably the **Housing Act 1988**, which shifted housing associations from the public to the private sector, and most recently the **Housing Act 1996**, which has introduced a new ground for possession and provided a procedure by which tenancies can be granted on a trial basis. The 1996 Act also confers on tenants of registered social landlords a right to acquire their properties. This chapter will discuss the nature of and qualifying conditions for a secure tenancy, security of tenure under the 1985 Act, grounds for possession, and succession.

NATURE OF A SECURE TENANCY

88.2 Security of tenure in the public sector is rooted in the notion of a 'secure tenancy'. The **Housing Act 1985, s. 79(1)**, defines a secure tenancy as follows:

> A tenancy under which a dwelling-house is let as a separate dwelling is a secure tenancy at any time when the conditions described in sections 80 and 81 as the landlord condition and the tenant condition are satisfied.

The initial wording here is the same as that used in the **Rent Act 1977** and also in the **Housing Act 1988**. As with those two statutes there must be 'a tenancy' of 'a dwelling-house' which is 'let as a separate dwelling'. These important phrases have already been considered in **86.20** to **86.21**. There are, however, several notable differences between the public sector legislation and that of the private sector:

(a) Certain licensees obtain statutory protection.
(b) The requirement that the dwelling-house is 'let as a separate dwelling' has harsher consequences within the context of the **Housing Act 1985** than under the **Rent Act 1977** and the **Housing Act 1988**.
(c) The words 'at any time when' mean that it is quite possible for a tenant to move in and out of **Housing Act 1985** protection. The tenant will be a secure tenant at any time when the landlord and tenant conditions (see **88.3** to **88.5**) are satisfied. If one of the conditions ceases to be satisfied (e.g., the tenant ceases to occupy), the tenant loses security, but if at a later date the condition becomes satisfied again (when the tenant moves back in), the tenant will regain security (see *Hussey v Camden London Borough Council* (1995) 27 HLR 5).
(d) Although it is undecided whether a tenancy at will may comprise a secure tenancy, it is clear that a tenant at will cannot invoke the security of tenure provisions of the **Housing Act 1985** (*Banjo v Brent London Borough Council* [2005] EWCA Civ 292, [2005] 1 WLR 2520).

The landlord condition

The key factor that makes a tenancy a secure tenancy is the identity of the landlord. To satisfy the landlord condition the landlord must be one of the prescribed public bodies set out in the list in **s. 80(1) of the Housing Act 1985**. The most common landlord that features on this list is, of course, a local authority. However, the landlord condition will also be satisfied if the landlord is a new town corporation, a housing action trust (a trust which acquires and manages local authority housing under powers contained in part III of the Housing Act 1988), an urban development corporation, the Development Board for Rural Wales, and a certain type of housing cooperative. **88.3**

Registered social landlords A registered social landlord is what was formerly known as a housing association until the advent of the **Housing Act 1996**. For the past 25 years or so they have played an increasing role in the provision of affordable housing. Starting with the Housing Act 1974, various administrations have sought to encourage the development of the voluntary sector, the aim being to permit social landlords to take over from local authorities the responsibility of providing cheaper housing for the less privileged in the community. (This policy has proved so successful that in some areas local authorities have handed over their entire housing stock to registered social landlords.) The **Housing Act 1985, s. 80(1)**, lists bodies which are capable of creating secure tenancies. Amendments to this list were made by the Housing Act 1988, sch. 18, as from 15 January 1989. Before the amendments the list included the Housing Corporation, charitable housing trusts, and housing associations. The amendments removed these bodies from the list so that registered social landlords are now regarded as belonging to the private rather than the public sector. The change in status means that all new tenancies granted by registered social landlords on or after 15 January 1989 are assured rather than secure tenancies. **88.4**

This has the somewhat confusing result that, depending upon the date of the grant of their tenancy, certain tenants of the same registered social landlord may have different types of tenancies. The tenancies granted before 15 January 1989 will be secure tenancies under the **Housing Act 1985**, while those granted on or after 15 January 1989 will be assured tenancies under the **Housing Act 1988**. Anyone seeking to advise a tenant of a registered social landlord should first check to see under which code the tenant falls. In doing so, regard must be had to the transitional provisions contained in the Housing Act 1988, s. 35. This section provides that in certain circumstances a tenancy entered into on or after 15 January 1989 can still be a secure tenancy. The most important of the circumstances in which this can occur are:

(a) if the tenancy was granted pursuant to a contract made before 15 January 1989 (s. 35(4)(c));
(b) if the tenancy was granted to a person who, immediately before the tenancy was entered into, was a secure tenant and the new tenancy was granted by the secure tenant's landlord (s. 35(4)(d));
(c) if the tenancy is granted to a person as 'suitable alternative accommodation' as a result of an order of the court and the court considers that an assured tenancy would not provide sufficient security of tenure (s. 35(4)(e));
(d) if the tenant was previously a private sector protected tenant or statutory tenant and the landlord's interest is transferred to a housing association (s. 35(5)).

The tenant condition

Under the **Housing Act 1985, s. 81**, the tenant condition mentioned in s. 79(1) will be satisfied where: **88.5**

(a) the tenant is an individual and occupies the dwelling-house as his or her only or principal home; or
(b) where the tenancy is a joint tenancy, and each of the joint tenants is an individual and at least one of them occupies the dwelling-house as his or her only or principal home.

This requirement is exactly the same as that demanded for eligibility as an assured tenant under the **Housing Act 1988** (see **86.23**).

Shared accommodation

88.6 To be a 'separate dwelling' the premises need to be sufficient for the occupier to carry out the major activities of life, namely cooking, eating and sleeping. However, under the Rent Act 1977, s. 22, and under the Housing Act 1988, ss. 3 and 10, special allowance is made for tenants who share essential common parts of the premises with others. The **Housing Act 1985** contains no similar provisions with regard to the sharing of accommodation. An occupier who shares a kitchen will not be able to be a secure tenant (*Central YMCA Housing Association Ltd v Saunders* (1990) 23 HLR 212). The sharing of a bathroom, however, will not take a tenant outside of the protection of the **Housing Act 1985**, because a bathroom is not regarded as an essential living room.

Secure licences

88.7 The **Housing Act 1985, s. 79(3)** provides that a licensee may be a secure tenant, but by s. 79(4) this does not apply to a licence granted as a temporary expedient to a person who entered the dwelling-house or any other land as a trespasser (whether or not, before the grant of that licence, another licence to occupy that or another dwelling-house had been granted to him or her).

At first sight s. 79(3) seems to extend statutory protection to a whole class of occupiers (licensees) who previously had no, or very limited, security of tenure.

The significance of s. 79(3), however, has been considerably restricted by the decision of the House of Lords in *Westminster City Council v Clarke* [1992] 2 AC 288 that a licensee could be a secure tenant only if entitled to exclusive possession of a separate dwelling-house. A person who occupied a room in a hostel run by the council was held not to have exclusive possession of any particular room in the hostel and therefore was not a secure tenant. If this decision is considered in the light of *Street v Mountford* [1985] AC 809 (see **83.2**), in which it was held that in the majority of circumstances the presence of exclusive possession would lead to the existence of a tenancy, it becomes clear that the circumstances in which a licensee will be a secure tenant are very limited. An occupier who does not have exclusive possession will be a licensee, and cannot be a secure tenant as a result of *Westminster City Council v Clarke*. An occupier who has exclusive possession will probably be a tenant, and therefore be a secure tenant under s. 79(1). Only if an occupier has exclusive possession but is denied a tenancy (because the circumstances are exceptional, see **83.3**) will s. 79(3) confer a secure tenancy on a licensee.

Introductory tenancies

88.8 Public sector landlords are usually in control of a large housing stock and a large part of their function is to keep existing tenants happy by means of good management. They often provide housing for a wide range of people and frequently, owing to the nature of much public sector housing stock, it is necessary for such tenants to live in close proximity. Public sector landlords, therefore, do not want to find themselves landed with a disruptive, undesirable or anti-social tenant who has security of tenure and cannot be easily removed. As a practical measure the **Housing Act 1996** has introduced a regime whereby it is possible for new tenants to be granted a tenancy on a trial basis: a form of probationary tenancy that at its end, provided the conduct of the tenant is satisfactory, will be converted automatically into a secure tenancy.

The provisions with regard to introductory tenancies are not mandatory. In order to make use of these provisions a local housing authority or housing action trust must first elect to operate an introductory tenancy regime. If they do choose to operate such a scheme then while it is in force every new periodic tenancy entered into or adopted by the authority or trust will be an introductory tenancy and not a secure tenancy. There are only three exceptions to this rule. A new periodic tenancy will not be an introductory tenancy in the following circumstances:

(a) Immediately before the tenancy was entered into the tenant was a secure tenant of the same or another dwelling-house (Housing Act 1996, s. 124(2)(a)). Thus, if a new tenancy is granted to an existing secure tenant (for example, on being rehoused by the local authority), security of tenure will not be lost.
(b) Immediately before the tenancy was entered into the tenant was an assured tenant (but not an assured shorthold tenant) of a registered social landlord in respect of the same or another dwelling-house (s. 124(2)(b)). Thus, a new tenant who was not formerly a local authority tenant but the tenant of a registered social landlord under an assured tenancy will not lose security of tenure and will become a secure tenant of the local authority without having to go through a trial period.
(c) The tenancy was entered into or adopted in pursuance of a contract made before the election was made (s. 124(3)).

What is an introductory tenancy? An introductory tenancy is one which would have been a secure tenancy but for the local housing authority's decision to operate an introductory tenancy regime. Thus it must fulfil the criteria set out earlier in this chapter (i.e., it must be a tenancy under which a dwelling is let as a separate dwelling, and both the landlord condition and the tenant condition must be satisfied). A secure licence may also be an introductory tenancy (Housing Act 1996, s. 126). **88.9**

Where an introductory tenancy is granted or adopted it will remain 'introductory' until the end of a one-year trial period. Tenancies which are granted have a trial period which begins with the date on which the tenancy was entered into or, if later, the date on which the tenant was first entitled to possession under the tenancy (s. 125(2)(a)). If the tenancy was adopted, the trial period begins with the date of adoption (s. 125(2)(b)).

However, where the tenant previously held another introductory tenancy, or held an assured shorthold tenancy from a registered social landlord, any period or periods during which he or she was such a tenant will count towards the trial period, provided:

(a) if there was one such period, it ended immediately before the second introductory tenancy started; and
(b) if there was more than one such period, the most recent period ended immediately before the start of the second tenancy and each period succeeded the other without interruption (s. 125(3)).

During the course of the trial period a tenancy will cease to be an introductory tenancy if:

(a) the circumstances are such that the tenancy would not otherwise be a secure tenancy (for example, if the landlord ceases to satisfy the landlord condition or the tenant ceases to occupy the dwelling as his only or principal home) (s. 125(5)(a));
(b) a person or body other than a local housing authority or housing action trust becomes the landlord under the tenancy (for example, where housing stock is transferred to the private sector) (s. 125(5)(b));
(c) the landlord revokes the election to operate an introductory tenancy regime (s. 125(5)(c)): such an election can be revoked at any time without prejudice to the making of a further election (s. 124(5));
(d) the tenancy ceases to be an introductory tenancy because the tenant has died and there is no one qualified to succeed to the tenancy. Succession to an introductory tenancy is dealt with in s. 133 (see **88.11**).

If the tenancy ceases to be an introductory tenancy it will not end merely because it ceases to be an introductory tenancy; it will continue until it is determined by the usual common law methods, such as by a notice to quit. However, once an introductory tenancy has ceased to be introductory it cannot later become introductory again (s. 125(6)). Thus a tenant under an introductory tenancy cannot move out of the dwelling for a period of time and then rekindle the introductory tenancy by moving back into possession.

88.10 **Seeking possession of an introductory tenancy** If by the end of the trial period the tenant's behaviour has given the landlord no cause for objection then the tenancy will automatically become a secure tenancy. However, the landlord may bring the introductory tenancy to an end at any point during the currency of the trial period if the landlord regards the tenant as unsuitable.

To bring the introductory tenancy to an end the landlord needs only obtain an order of the court for possession (Housing Act 1996, s. 127). The landlord does not have to establish a ground of possession, nor that suitable alternative accommodation is available, nor that it is reasonable to make such an order (as the landlord would if the tenant held under a secure tenancy, see **88.29**). The court, however, will not entertain proceedings for possession unless the landlord has given notice to the tenant in accordance with s. 128. Such notice must include the landlord's reasons for seeking possession (s. 128(3)), specify the date after which possession proceedings may be begun (s. 128(4)) and inform the tenant of the right to request a review of the decision (s. 128(6)). Provided these notice requirements are complied with the court must make an order for possession (*Manchester City Council v Cochrane* [1999] 1 WLR 809). The procedure does not infringe the **European Convention on Human Rights** (*R (McLellan) v Bracknell Forest Borough Council* [2001] EWCA Civ 1510, [2002] QB 1129).

The trial period concludes on the expiry of one year from the date the tenancy was entered into or the tenant was first entitled to possession (if later). Where an introductory tenancy was entered into on 9 November 2001, the trial period ended on 8 November 2002, and as proceedings had not been commenced, by issue of a claim form, on or before that date, the tenancy became a secure tenancy (*Salford City Council v Garner* [2004] EWCA Civ 364, [2004] HLR 35). If a landlord seeks possession towards the end of the trial period and the proceedings are not complete by the date on which the trial period is due to come to an end, the tenancy will not automatically become a secure tenancy; rather, by virtue of s. 130, the tenancy will remain an introductory tenancy until the proceedings are concluded.

The tenant is entitled to seek a review of the landlord's decision. This must be done within 14 days of being served notice (s. 129). The procedures for such a review are set out in the Introductory Tenants (Review) Regulations 1997 (SI 1997/72). There is no prohibition on possession proceedings continuing concurrently with the review process, and a review under s. 129 is not nullified by reason of the review being undertaken after the date specified in the notice of proceedings for possession under s. 128 (*R (McDonagh) v Salisbury District Council* [2001] EWHC Admin 567, *The Times*, 15 August 2001).

The only way of challenging the authority's decision on review is by judicial review. When claiming possession following a review, the authority should provide written evidence of how the procedure was operated, including the degree of independence of the review tribunal from the individuals who took the original decision, the way the review was conducted and the reason for deciding to continue the proceedings (*R (McLellan) v Bracknell Forest Borough Council*). It is not necessary for a second review to be instigated where several months have elapsed before the issue of proceedings (*Cardiff City Council v Stone* [2002] EWCA Civ 298, *The Times*, 19 February 2002). The county court may adjourn the possession claim to await the outcome of judicial review if it is satisfied that permission will be given to proceed with a judicial review claim (*Manchester City Council v Cochrane* [1999] 1 WLR 809).

88.11 **Other rights of an introductory tenant** An introductory tenant may not have security of tenure but, because an introductory tenancy has the potential to become a secure tenancy at the end of the trial period, an introductory tenant will acquire many of the rights that apply to a secure tenant. Sections 132 and 133 of the Housing Act 1996 provide an introductory tenant with a similar right to succession as a secure tenant has under the **Housing Act 1985** (see **88.52** to **88.55**). The Housing Act 1996, s. 134, gives an introductory tenant a limited right to assign, and s. 135 extends the secure tenant's repair scheme to introductory tenancies.

STATUTORY EXCLUSIONS FROM THE HOUSING ACT 1985

Long leases

Under the **Housing Act 1985, sch. 1, para. 1**, a fixed-term tenancy granted for a term certain exceeding 21 years (as defined by s. 115) cannot be a secure tenancy. **88.12**

Introductory tenancies

Introductory tenancies (see **88.8** to **88.11**) are excluded from being secure tenancies by virtue of the **Housing Act 1985, sch. 1, para. 1A.** **88.13**

Premises occupied in connection with employment

Under the **Housing Act 1985, sch. 1, para. 2**, if a tenant is either an employee of the landlord or an employee of one of the public bodies listed in para. 2 (e.g., a local authority), and the tenant's contract of employment requires the tenant to occupy the dwelling-house for the better performance of his or her duties, there cannot be a secure tenancy. **88.14**

It is not necessary that the contract of employment expressly states that the employee must occupy the dwelling-house for the better performance of his or her duties. Such a term will be implied by the court if the landlord can show that, in the particular circumstances of the case, it is essential for the employee to occupy the dwelling-house in order to do the job properly (see *South Glamorgan County Council v Griffiths* (1992) 24 HLR 334; but contrast with *Hughes v Greenwich London Borough Council* [1994] 1 AC 170). If the nature of the occupier's employment changes the occupier may lose secure status. In *Elvidge v Coventry City Council* [1994] QB 241, an employee was originally a secure tenant. He was promoted and his change in duties made it necessary for him to occupy that particular dwelling-house to do his job. The court held that he was no longer a secure tenant. However, if an employee occupying premises for the better performance of his or her duties retires, this does not mean that he or she becomes a secure tenant just because the employment has ceased (see *South Glamorgan County Council v Griffiths*). The purpose of this exception is to enable an employer/landlord to keep control of accommodation that 'goes with the job'. An employee is excluded from protection precisely so that if the employment is ended the landlord/employer will be free to allow a new employee into occupation. If an employee acquired security the moment his or her employment ended, this exception would be rendered ineffective.

It is also open to a landlord, by virtue of sch. 1, para. 2(4), to exclude a tenant from acquiring a secure tenancy by giving the tenant notice that the tenancy in question falls within this exception. Such notice can be given only if, for the three years immediately prior to the grant, the premises in question had been occupied by a tenant in connection with his or her employment (i.e., the previous tenancy or tenancies must have fallen within this exception). If such notice is given and the landlord is a local housing authority the tenancy will not become a secure tenancy unless the landlord notifies the tenant that it is to be a secure tenancy (para. 2(4B)). If the landlord is not a local authority the tenancy will automatically become a secure tenancy if it ceases to be occupied in connection with the tenant's employment for a period of more than three years in total (para. 2(4A)). This somewhat strange distinction, introduced by the **Housing Act 1996**, is presumably intended to give local housing authorities a slightly greater degree of control over their housing stock than other public sector landlords. Quite why a local housing authority should be treated differently from, say, a housing action trust or an urban development corporation is not clear.

Land acquired for development

88.15 A tenancy cannot be a secure tenancy if the dwelling-house is on land which has been acquired for development and the dwelling-house is used by the landlord, pending development of the land, as temporary housing accommodation (**Housing Act 1985, sch. 1, para. 3(1)**). This exception will apply even if the land was acquired for development by the landlord's predecessor in title (*Hyde Housing Association v Harrison* [1991] 1 EGLR 51; also *Attley v Cherwell District Council* (1989) 21 HLR 613). However, if the development is no longer in prospect, the exception will not apply (for example, where the local planning authority has rejected the plans: *Lillieshall Road Housing Co-operative v Brennan* (1992) 24 HLR 195).

Homeless persons

88.16 Part VII of the Housing Act 1996 contains certain provisions that place a duty upon a local authority landlord to provide accommodation for homeless persons. Where a landlord provides accommodation in pursuance of these provisions, namely ss. 63, 65(3) and 68(1), any tenancy granted will not become a secure tenancy until a period of 12 months has expired, unless the landlord gives the tenant notice that the tenancy is to be secure (**Housing Act 1985, sch. 1, para. 4**). The 12-month period runs from the date that the tenant receives notice under the provisions of part VII (*Swansea City Council v Hearn* (1990) 23 HLR 284).

Temporary accommodation for persons taking up employment

88.17 When a person moves into the area in order to take up employment and rents accommodation from a public landlord, that landlord can prevent the tenant from acquiring a secure tenancy (**Housing Act 1985, sch. 1, para. 5**). To do this the landlord must serve notice in writing on the tenant that this exception applies (para. 5(1)(d)). This exclusion will apply only where:

(a) immediately before the grant of the tenancy the person was not resident in the district in which the dwelling-house is situated;
(b) before the grant of the tenancy, the person obtained employment, or an offer of employment, in the district or its surrounding area;
(c) the tenancy was granted to the person for the purposes of meeting his or her need for temporary accommodation in the district or its surrounding area in order to work there, and of enabling him or her to find permanent accommodation there.

If the landlord is a local housing authority, the tenancy will remain excluded until the authority notifies the tenant that the tenancy is to be regarded as a secure tenancy (para. 5(1B)). If the landlord is not a local housing authority, the tenancy will become secure after one year from the date of grant or earlier if the landlord decides to notify the tenant that the tenancy is to be regarded as a secure tenancy before that date (para. 5(1A)).

Short-term arrangements

88.18 The aim of this exclusion under the **Housing Act 1985, sch. 1, para. 6**, is to encourage private-sector landlords to help public sector landlords to provide accommodation. Sub-leasing schemes have been around for a long time. Before the introduction of statutory protection for public sector tenants, it was common for private landlords to let buildings to a local authority who would in turn sublet to residential tenants. Because the local authority was the direct landlord of the tenant, the tenant would not be able to claim Rent Act protection. Schedule 1, para. 6, has enabled this practice to continue even after the introduction of statutory security for public sector tenants by preventing the tenant of a dwelling-house, let on a subletting scheme via a local authority landlord, from being a secure tenant.

This exclusion will apply only if:

(a) the dwelling-house had been leased to the landlord with vacant possession for use as temporary housing accommodation;

(b) the terms on which it has been leased include provision for the lessor to obtain vacant possession from the landlord on the expiry of a specified period or when required by the lessor;
(c) the lessor is not a body which is capable of granting secure tenancies; and
(d) the landlord has no interest in the dwelling-house other than under the lease in question or as a mortgagee.

This exclusion will also operate if the private landlord grants a licence to the local authority to use the dwelling-house as temporary housing accommodation (*Tower Hamlets London Borough Council v Miah* (1991) 24 HLR 199).

Temporary accommodation during works

Under the **Housing Act 1985, sch. 1, para.** 7, a tenancy is not a secure tenancy if: **88.19**

(a) the dwelling-house has been made available for occupation by the tenant (or a predecessor in title of the tenant) while works are carried out on the dwelling-house which he or she previously occupied as his or her home; and
(b) the tenant or predecessor was not a secure tenant of that other dwelling-house at the time of ceasing to occupy it as his or her home.

Thus, if a public landlord provides temporary accommodation for a tenant while works are carried out on his or her home, that tenant will not acquire a secure tenancy of the temporary accommodation.

Agricultural holdings

A tenancy is not a secure tenancy if the dwelling-house is comprised in an agricultural holding (within the meaning of the Agricultural Holdings Act 1986) or in a holding held under a farm business tenancy (within the meaning of the Agricultural Tenancies Act 1995) and is occupied by the person responsible for the control (whether as tenant or as servant or agent of the tenant) of the farming of the holding (**Housing Act 1985, sch. 1, para.** 8). **88.20**

Licensed premises

A tenancy is not a secure tenancy if the dwelling-house consists of or includes premises licensed for the sale of intoxicating liquor for consumption on the premises (**Housing Act 1985, sch. 1, para.** 9). **88.21**

Student lettings

The provisions excluding student lettings from statutory protection are more detailed under the Housing Act 1985 than under the **Rent Act 1977** or the **Housing Act 1988**. Under the **Housing Act 1985, sch. 1, para. 10**, a tenancy of a dwelling-house will not be a secure tenancy if: **88.22**

(a) it is granted for the purpose of enabling the tenant to attend a designated course at an educational establishment; and
(b) before the grant of the tenancy the landlord notifies the tenant in writing of the circumstances in which this exception applies and that in its opinion the proposed tenancy would fall within the exception.

A designated course is defined by the Secure Tenancies (Designated Courses) Regulations 1980 (SI 1980/1407) as amended by the Secure Tenancies (Designated Courses) (Amendment) Regulations 1993 (SI 1993/931). In giving notice the landlord must also specify the educational establishment which the person concerned proposes to attend (**Housing Act 1985, sch. 1, para. 10(2)**). If the landlord is a local housing authority, the exclusion will operate until the authority notifies the tenant that the tenancy is to be regarded as a secure tenancy. If the landlord is not a local housing authority, the exclusion will continue to operate until six months after the tenant ceases to attend a designated course at the educational establishment, or, if the tenant leaves the course earlier, until six months after the grant of the tenancy (sch. 1, para. 10(3)).

Business tenancies

88.23 A tenancy is not a secure tenancy if it is one to which **part II of the Landlord and Tenant Act 1954** applies (tenancies of premises occupied for business purposes) (**Housing Act 1985, sch. 1, para. 11**).

Almshouses

88.24 A licence to occupy an almshouse cannot be a secure tenancy if certain conditions are satisfied (**Housing Act 1985, sch. 1, para. 12**).

SECURITY OF TENURE UNDER THE HOUSING ACT 1985

Termination by the tenant

88.25 The **Housing Act 1985** restricts only the landlord's rights to end a secure tenancy: there is no restriction on the tenant's ability to terminate the tenancy by use of a notice to quit for periodic tenancies or by surrender or exercise of a break clause in the case of fixed-term tenancies.

Termination by the landlord

88.26 Like the **Rent Act 1977** and the **Housing Act 1988** (which largely adopted the system of security of tenure from the 1985 Act), the **Housing Act 1985** provides security of tenure for a secure tenant by preventing the landlord from using the usual common law methods of termination (s. 82(1)). The precise operation of this system depends upon whether the secure tenancy in question is a periodic tenancy or a fixed-term tenancy. If the tenancy in question is a fixed-term tenancy, the procedure will vary depending upon whether the landlord is seeking to terminate the tenancy before the fixed term has expired or whether the term has already expired by effluxion of time. In any event, the landlord will not be able to recover possession of the dwelling-house without obtaining an order for possession from the court. The court will not make an order for possession unless one or more of the grounds set out in sch. 2 to the Act are satisfied (s. 84(1)). If a secure tenancy is a tenancy at will (itself doubtful), issue of possession proceedings will terminate the tenancy, and hence the security of tenure provisions will not apply (*Banjo v Brent London Borough Council* [2005] EWCA Civ 292, [2005] 1 WLR 2520).

88.27 **Fixed-term tenancies** At common law a fixed-term tenancy could come to an end either by effluxion of time or because the landlord had exercised a right of re-entry or forfeiture contained in the lease.

Where the tenancy is a secure tenancy for a term certain and contains a provision enabling the landlord to exercise a right of re-entry on forfeiture, the landlord cannot forfeit the tenancy before the expiry of the term by using the common law forfeiture procedure. Instead the landlord must apply to the court under the **Housing Act 1985, s. 82(3)**, for an order terminating the tenancy (note that to do this the landlord will have to comply with the notice procedure set out in s. 83, see **88.28**). If the landlord can show that, had the tenancy not been secure, the court would have made an order forfeiting the tenancy, the landlord will be entitled to an order terminating the tenancy. Thus, despite the fact that strictly speaking the common law rules of forfeiture do not apply to a secure tenancy, a landlord who wishes to terminate a fixed-term tenancy before the expiry of the term (for, say, a breach of covenant) may do so. Section 82(4) further provides that the normal rules with regard to relief from forfeiture will apply where a landlord seeks to terminate a tenancy under s. 82(3).

At common law, where a fixed-term tenancy comes to an end by effluxion of time it terminates of its own accord and the landlord does not need to apply for an order of the court in order to terminate the tenancy.

When a secure tenancy for a fixed term comes to an end, a statutory periodic tenancy of the same dwelling-house will arise by virtue of the **Housing Act 1985, s. 86(1)**. This statutory periodic tenancy will arise whether the tenancy expired by effluxion of time or was terminated by an order of the court under s. 82(3). The only situation in which it will not arise is where the landlord chooses to grant the tenant a further secure tenancy of the same dwelling-house (whether for a term certain or periodic) to begin when the original tenancy comes to an end.

The terms of the statutory periodic tenancy are determined by s. 86(2) of the 1985 Act. The periods of the tenancy will be the same as those for which rent was last payable under the first tenancy. The parties and the terms of the tenancy will be the same as those at the end of the first tenancy, except that the terms are confined to those which are compatible with a periodic tenancy and do not include any provision for re-entry or forfeiture.

Thus the fact that a fixed-term tenancy has come to an end does not mean that a landlord is entitled to possession. The tenant will now hold on a periodic tenancy and the landlord will have to apply for a court order using the procedure outlined in **88.28**.

Periodic tenancies A secure periodic tenancy, be it the original contractual tenancy or a statutory tenancy, cannot be brought to an end by the landlord by service of a notice to quit. Instead the landlord must follow the notice procedure set out in **ss. 83** and **83A of the Housing Act 1985**. **88.28**

Before proceedings for possession can be started the landlord must serve on the tenant a 'notice seeking possession' in accordance with s. 83. However, the court may, if it considers it just and equitable to do so, dispense with the requirement of such notice (s. 83(1)(b)). This notice must specify a date after which proceedings for the possession of the dwelling-house may be begun (s. 83(4)(a)). This date must not be earlier than the date on which the tenancy could be brought to an end by notice to quit given by the landlord on the same date as the notice under this section (s. 83(5)). Thus possession proceedings cannot be started any earlier than the date on which the tenancy could have been terminated at common law by a notice to quit. Furthermore, the notice will only remain in force for a period of 12 months after the date specified in the notice (s. 83(4)(b)). If the landlord fails to bring proceedings within this time the notice will lapse and it will be necessary for the landlord to serve another notice before proceedings can be taken.

Section 83(2) further provides that a 'notice seeking possession' must:

(a) be in a form prescribed by regulations made by the Secretary of State (currently found in the Secure Tenancies (Notices) Regulations 1987 (SI 1987/755) as amended by the Secure Tenancies (Notices) (Amendment) Regulations 1997 (SI 1997/71));
(b) specify the ground on which the court will be asked to make an order for possession of the dwelling-house or for the termination of the tenancy; and
(c) give particulars of that ground.

The aim of the notice procedure under the **Housing Act 1985** is to give the tenant a chance to avoid possession proceedings by putting right any breaches under the tenancy. Sufficient particulars must therefore be given of the ground on which the landlord intends to seek possession to enable the tenant to correct the breach. For example, if the landlord is alleging a breach of repairing covenant, details must be given of the disrepair; if the landlord is alleging non-payment of rent, the arrears should be specified (see *Torridge District Council v Jones* (1985) 18 HLR 107).

Minor errors in the prescribed form of the notice will not be fatal to the notice provided the notice is substantially to the same effect as that demanded by s. 83 (SI 1987/755, para. 2(1) as amended). Similarly, a mistake in the particulars set out in the notice will not render the notice invalid provided the landlord had a bona fide intention to prove those particulars at the time the notice was served (see *Dudley Metropolitan Borough Council v Bailey* (1990) 22 HLR 424 and *Tadema Holdings Ltd v Ferguson* (1999) *The Times*, 25 November 1999).

The court cannot make an order for possession unless the ground for seeking possession has been specified in the notice, but the landlord may alter or add to the grounds specified with the permission of the court (s. 84(3)).

If the landlord is seeking to recover possession under Ground 2 in sch. 2 (nuisance or other anti-social behaviour, see **88.31**), or Ground 2 is one of the grounds specified by the landlord, then s. 83(3) provides that a slightly different notice is required. Such notice must state that proceedings for possession may be begun immediately and also specify the date sought by the landlord as the date on which the tenant is to give up possession. The reason for this distinction is that where a landlord is taking action against a tenant for anti-social behaviour it may be important to act quickly. If Ground 2A (domestic violence, see **88.32**) is the ground or one of the grounds specified in the notice and the partner who has left the dwelling-house was not a tenant, the landlord must take all reasonable steps to serve a copy of the notice on that partner (s. 83A).

GROUNDS FOR POSSESSION

88.29 Provided a notice seeking possession has been served according to the provisions of the **Housing Act 1985, s. 83**, the landlord may go to court and seek a possession order. A possession order will be granted only if the landlord can make out one or more of the grounds contained in sch. 2. The procedure is in **CPR, Part 55**, and **PD 55** (see **87.6 to 87.11**). In contrast to the **Rent Act 1977** and the **Housing Act 1988**, there are no mandatory grounds as such in the **Housing Act 1985**. Instead the grounds of possession are divided into three categories:

(a) Part I (Grounds 1 to 8) — an order for possession may be made if the court considers it reasonable to make the order.
(b) Part II (Grounds 9 to 11) — the court may make an order for possession if it is satisfied that suitable accommodation will be available for the tenant when the order takes effect.
(c) Part III (Grounds 12 to 16) — the court may make an order for possession if it both considers it reasonable to make the order *and* it is satisfied that suitable accommodation will be available for the tenant when the order takes effect.

Many of the grounds contained in sch. 2 to the 1985 Act are identical or similar to grounds and cases already considered under the **Rent Act 1977** and the **Housing Act 1988**, and in the following discussion, where possible, cross-references have been made.

GROUNDS UNDER PART I

The court may order possession under Grounds 1 to 8 only if it thinks it reasonable.

Ground 1 — Rent arrears or breach of obligation

88.30 Rent lawfully due from the tenant has not been paid or an obligation of the tenancy has been broken or not performed.

This ground is virtually identical to **Case 1 under the Rent Act 1977**. It is a composite ground, permitting the landlord to seek possession for a breach of covenant to pay rent, or for a breach of any other covenant in the tenancy agreement.

With regard to a breach of covenant to pay rent, the landlord must show that some rent is outstanding at the date of the issue of proceedings. If the tenant pays off the arrears by the date of the hearing the court may still make an order for possession, but unless there are special circumstances (e.g., the tenant has a history of late or non-payment of rent) it will generally not be reasonable to make such an order (*Bird v Hillage* [1948] 1 KB 91).

In the case of a breach of an obligation of the tenancy, the court will take into account all the circumstances in determining whether it is reasonable to make the order. Important factors will include, among others, the seriousness of the breach, whether it is capable of remedy, whether there is likelihood of repetition, and whether alternative remedies may be available (e.g., an injunction). In *Wandsworth London Borough Council v Hargreaves* (1994) 27 HLR 142 the tenancy contained a covenant 'not to permit to be done anything which may increase the risk of fire'. A visitor made petrol bombs in the flat and started a fire which caused considerable damage. Nevertheless, the Court of Appeal upheld the county court judge's decision that it was not reasonable to make an order for possession. The tenant had not actually participated in the making of the petrol bombs and there had been no repetition of the breach. On the other hand, where a tenant kept a dog in breach of covenant, the Court of Appeal overturned a county court decision that it could not be reasonable to make an order for possession because the breach was deliberate and persistent (*Sheffield City Council v Jepson* (1993) 25 HLR 299).

Ground 2 — Nuisance, annoyance or conviction

The tenant or a person residing in or visiting the dwelling-house— **88.31**

(a) has been guilty of conduct causing or likely to cause a nuisance or annoyance to a person residing, visiting or otherwise engaging in a lawful activity in the locality, or
(b) has been convicted of—
    (i) using the dwelling-house or allowing it to be used for immoral or illegal purposes, or
    (ii) an arrestable offence committed in, or in the locality of, the dwelling-house.

This ground of possession was amended by the **Housing Act 1996**. It is one of a number of provisions in that Act intended to make it easier for public sector landlords to deal with anti-social behaviour. The ground now has a very wide application. It covers not just the conduct of the tenant and other people residing in the dwelling-house, but also the behaviour of visitors. The conduct itself does not have to amount to actual nuisance or annoyance, it merely has to be *likely* to cause a nuisance or annoyance. The nuisance or annoyance may be caused not only to neighbours but to anyone visiting or carrying out a lawful activity in the locality. This has the advantage of enabling somebody other than the victim of the anti-social behaviour to give evidence — something which might be of considerable practical significance in sensitive cases where an actual neighbour might be wary of giving evidence for fear of reprisals (e.g., evidence could be given by a local authority employee or other professional).

The second limb of Ground 2 also has an extremely broad scope. It similarly applies to visitors as well as to persons actually resident in the dwelling-house, and entitles a landlord to seek possession where such a person has been convicted not just of an offence involving the use of the dwelling-house but also of any arrestable offence that has been committed in the locality of the dwelling-house. Thus a tenant could face possession proceedings under Ground 2 where a visitor to the dwelling-house has been convicted of an arrestable offence committed somewhere in the area.

In any case brought under Ground 2 the court must consider whether it is reasonable to make an order for possession. In doing so, the court must consider the effect of the nuisance or annoyance on other persons (s. 85A). Where the person complained of has little connection to the dwelling-house and is not someone over whom the tenant is able to exercise control, it would be most unlikely that the court would make such an order. However, if there is evidence that the anti-social behaviour is likely to continue it is more probable that a possession order will be made (*Woking Borough Council v Bistram* (1993) 27 HLR 1). There can only be exceptional circumstances in which it is not reasonable to make a possession order where the tenant is guilty of committing a serious offence (*Bristol City Council v Mousah* (1997) 30 HLR 32). A suspended possession order may be in the public interest to assist the tenant's rehabilitation (*Greenwich London Borough Council v Grogan* (2000) 33 HLR 140; see also *Moat Housing Group-South Ltd v Harris* [2005] EWCA Civ 287, [2005] 3 WLR 691). In *Royal London Borough of Kensington and Chelsea Council v Simmonds* (1997) 29 HLR 507 a suspended possession order against a mother was upheld where the conduct complained of (which included racist abuse) was in fact that of her son. But it may be proper to make an immediate order where there is no indication that the tenant can control the behaviour of a third party (*New Charter Housing (North) Ltd v Ashcroft* [2004] EWCA Civ 310, [2004] HLR 36).

Demotion orders

88.32 Seeking possession is not the only weapon in a local authority's armoury. Part 2 of the Anti-social Behaviour Act 2003 (which came into force on 30 June 2004) enables the court to make a demotion order, terminating a secure tenancy and creating in its place a demoted tenancy (Housing Act 1985, s. 82A). The landlord may invoke a statutory procedure to bring a demoted tenancy to an end by obtaining an order for possession following service of notice on the tenant. The notice must set out the reasons for the landlord's application for a possession order, and the tenant's only method of challenge, save on the basis of non-compliance with the procedural requirements, is by requesting a review by the landlord of its decision to seek possession (Housing Act 1996, sch. 1). The procedure for demotion claims and proceedings relating to demoted tenancies is in **CPR, Part 65, Section III.**

Anti-social behaviour injunctions

88.33 Part 2 of the Anti-social Behaviour Act 2003 confers an express power on the court to grant an injunction against anti-social behaviour or against unlawful use of premises, and to support such injunctions with exclusion orders and powers of arrest (**Housing Act 1996, ss. 153A to 153E**). See **91.2 to 91.11**.

Ground 2A — Domestic violence

88.34 The dwelling-house was occupied (whether alone or with others) by a married couple, a couple who are civil partners of each other, a couple living together as husband and wife or a couple living together as if they were civil partners and—

(a) one or both of the partners is a tenant of the dwelling-house,
(b) one partner has left because of violence or threats of violence by the other towards—
  (i) that partner, or
  (ii) a member of the family of that partner who was residing with that partner immediately before the partner left, and
(c) the court is satisfied that the partner who has left is unlikely to return.

This ground, introduced by the **Housing Act 1996**, is designed to counter the situation where a couple separates due to domestic violence, and one partner leaves while the other remains in occupation of the dwelling-house. In such a situation the landlord is often left with a single person occupying family-size accommodation. Ground 2A therefore gives the landlord a ground of possession against such a person.

It remains to be seen how effective this will be in practice. In order to obtain possession on Ground 2A the landlord must establish that the violence (or threatened violence) is the real or effective reason why the partner left (*Camden London Borough Council v Mallett* (2000) 33 HLR 204) and that the departed partner is unlikely to return. The departed partner may well be reluctant to give evidence in open court.

Ground 3 — Deterioration in condition of dwelling-house

88.35 The condition of the dwelling-house or of any of the common parts has deteriorated owing to acts of waste by, or the neglect or default of, the tenant or a person residing in the dwelling-house and, in the case of an act of waste by, or the neglect or default of, a person lodging with the tenant or a sub-tenant of his, the tenant has not taken such steps as he ought reasonably to have taken for the removal of the lodger or sub-tenant.

This ground is not restricted to the dwelling-house itself but extends to the common parts of the building as well. Thus a landlord is able to take action when a tenant residing in a block of flats causes damage to the lifts, hallways, stairwells or other common areas.

Ground 4 — Deterioration in condition of furniture

The condition of furniture provided by the landlord for use under the tenancy, or for use in the common parts, has deteriorated owing to ill-treatment by the tenant or a person residing in the dwelling-house and, in the case of ill-treatment by such a person lodging with the tenant or a sub-tenant of his, the tenant has not taken such steps as he ought reasonably to have taken for the removal of the lodger or sub-tenant. **88.36**

This ground extends to furniture provided by the landlord for use in the common parts of the building. Under both of these grounds a tenant will be able to resist a landlord's claim for possession if the damage was caused by a person living with the tenant and tenant can show that he or she has taken such steps as he or she ought reasonably to have taken to remove the person causing the damage.

Ground 5 — False statement by tenant

The tenant is the person, or one of the persons, to whom the tenancy was granted and the landlord was induced to grant the tenancy by a false statement made knowingly or recklessly by— **88.37**

(a) the tenant, or

(b) a person acting at the tenant's instigation.

Demand for public sector housing is invariably far higher than the amount of accommodation available. Local authorities, housing associations and other bodies try to award housing to the candidates with the greatest need. The purpose of this provision is to prevent people from jumping the queue by falsely representing their circumstances. For example, where a person who was already a secure tenant of a housing association obtained local authority housing by stating in her application form that she was currently living with family and friends (*Rushcliffe Borough Council v Watson* (1991) 24 HLR 124).

To establish this ground the landlord will have to prove not only that a false statement was made, but also that this false statement induced the grant of the tenancy (in other words, how material the false statement was: *Waltham Forest London Borough Council v Roberts* [2004] EWCA Civ 940, [2005] HLR 2). The false statement must be made either by a person to whom the tenancy was granted, or by a person acting at that person's instigation.

Ground 6 — Premium paid on assignment by virtue of exchange

The tenancy was assigned to the tenant, or a predecessor in title of his who is a member of his family and is residing in the dwelling-house, by an assignment made by virtue of section 92 (assignments by virtue of exchange) and a premium was paid either in connection with that assignment or the assignment which the tenant or predecessor himself made by virtue of that section. **88.38**

In this paragraph 'premium' means any fine or other sum and any other pecuniary consideration in addition to rent.

This provision has no counterpart in the private sector. It is designed to prevent tenants exploiting s. 92 of the 1985 Act. Section 92 permits public sector tenants to exchange tenancies. If a tenant (or a predecessor in title who is a member of the tenant's family and still lives in the dwelling-house) obtains a lump sum for exchanging the tenancy, the landlord will be entitled to seek possession under Ground 6.

Ground 7 — Misconduct by employee tenant in certain accommodation

The dwelling-house forms part of, or is within the curtilage of, a building which, or so much of it as is **88.39** held by the landlord, is held mainly for purposes other than housing purposes and consists mainly of accommodation other than housing accommodation, and —

(a) the dwelling-house was let to the tenant or a predecessor in title of his in consequence of the tenant or predecessor being in the employment of the landlord, or of —
    a local authority
    a new town corporation
    a housing action trust
    an urban development corporation
    the development Board for Rural Wales, or
    the governors of an aided school,

and

(b) the tenant or a person residing in the dwelling-house has been guilty of conduct such that, having regard to the purpose for which the building is used, it would not be right for him to continue in occupation of the dwelling-house.

This rather complex ground is again peculiar to the **Housing Act 1985**. It is designed to enable a landlord to regain possession in a specific situation, i.e., where an employee of the landlord (or other body specified in para. (b)) who lives within some non-housing building (for example, a caretaker of a school or hospital) is guilty of misconduct.

Ground 8 — Temporary accommodation while works carried out

88.40 The dwelling-house was made available for occupation by the tenant (or a predecessor in title of his) while works were carried out on the dwelling-house which he previously occupied as his only or principal home and —

(a) the tenant (or predecessor) was a secure tenant of the other dwelling-house at the time when he ceased to occupy it as his home,
(b) the tenant (or predecessor) accepted the tenancy of the dwelling-house of which possession is sought on the understanding that he would give up occupation when, on completion of the works, the other dwelling-house was again available for occupation by him under a secure tenancy, and
(c) the works have been completed and the other dwelling-house is so available.

This ground again enables the landlord to recover possession in a specific situation, namely where a secure tenant is temporarily rehoused by the landlord while works are carried out on the tenant's original dwelling-house, and after completion of the works the tenant refuses to move back to the original dwelling-house. To rely upon Ground 8 the landlord will have to show that when the arrangements for temporary accommodation were made the tenant agreed to move back into the original dwelling-house once the works were completed. As with all of the grounds in part I, Ground 8 is subject to the requirement of reasonableness. Thus if the scheduled works take much longer than expected and the tenant has settled into the alternative accommodation, it may not be reasonable for the landlord to seek possession.

GROUNDS UNDER PART II

Requirements under part II

88.41 A court may order possession under Grounds 9 to 11 only if it is satisfied that suitable alternative accommodation will be available for the tenant when the order takes effect (**Housing Act 1985, s. 84(2)(b)**). There is no requirement under these grounds that ordering possession must be reasonable. The concept of suitable alternative accommodation is considered at 88.40 and Grounds 9 to 11 are considered at **88.41 to 88.44**.

Suitable alternative accommodation

88.42 The requirements regarding suitable accommodation under the **Housing Act 1985, sch. 2, part IV** are very similar to those contained in the **Housing Act 1988** (see 87.23). By the **Housing Act 1985, sch. 2, part IV, para. 1**, accommodation will be suitable if it consists of premises:

(a) which are to be let as a separate dwelling under a secure tenancy; or
(b) which are to be let as a separate dwelling under a protected tenancy, not being a tenancy under which the landlord might recover possession under one of the Cases in **part II of sch. 15 to the Rent Act 1977** (cases where the court must order possession); or
(c) which are to be let as a separate dwelling under an assured tenancy which is neither an assured shorthold tenancy, within the meaning of **part I of the Housing Act 1988**, nor a tenancy under which the landlord might recover possession under any of the Grounds 1 to 5 in sch. 2 to that Act (this was added by the **Housing Act 1988**);

and, in the opinion of the court, the accommodation is reasonably suitable to the needs of the tenant and his family.

In determining whether the alternative accommodation is suitable, a certificate from the local authority stating that it will provide suitable accommodation for the tenant by the date specified in the certificate will be conclusive evidence that suitable accommodation will be available at that date (**Housing Act 1985, sch. 2, part IV, para.** 4(1)). This will not apply when the landlord is itself a local authority (para. 4(3)). If there is no local authority certificate, the court will determine whether the accommodation is suitable to the needs of the tenant having regard to the factors set out in sch. 2, part IV, para. 2:

(a) the nature of the accommodation which it is the practice of the landlord to allocate to persons with similar needs;
(b) the distance of the accommodation available from the place of work or education of the tenant and of any members of his family;
(c) its distance from the home of any members of the tenant's family if proximity to it is essential to that member's or the tenant's well-being;
(d) the needs (as regards extent of accommodation) and means of the tenant and his family;
(e) the terms on which the accommodation is available and the terms of the secure tenancy;
(f) if furniture was provided by the landlord for use under the secure tenancy, whether furniture is to be provided for use in the other accommodation, and if so the nature of the furniture to be provided.

Ground 9 — Dwelling-house overcrowded

The dwelling-house is overcrowded, within the meaning of Part X of the Housing Act 1985, in such circumstances as to render the occupier guilty of an offence. **88.43**

Ground 10 — Landlord intends to demolish or reconstruct dwelling-house

The landlord intends, within a reasonable time of obtaining possession of the dwelling house — **88.44**
(a) to demolish or reconstruct the building or part of the building comprising the dwelling-house, or
(b) to carry out work on that building or on land let together with, and thus treated as part of, the dwelling-house,

and cannot reasonably do so without obtaining possession of the dwelling-house.

Similar provisions, albeit with considerably lengthier wording, have also been included in the **Housing Act 1988, sch. 2** (Ground 6, see 87.19).

Ground 10A — Redevelopment scheme

The dwelling-house is in an area which is the subject of a redevelopment scheme approved by the Secretary of State or the Corporation in accordance with Part V of this Schedule and the landlord intends within a reasonable time of obtaining possession to dispose of the dwelling-house in accordance with the scheme. **88.45**

or

Part of the dwelling-house is in such an area and the landlord intends within a reasonable time of obtaining possession to dispose of that part in accordance with the scheme and for that purpose reasonably requires possession of the dwelling-house.

These provisions were inserted into the **Housing Act 1985** by the Housing and Planning Act 1986 to enable landlords to gain vacant possession of a property in order to sell it for redevelopment. The Housing Act 1985, sch. 2, part V, requires the landlord to consult with tenants before entering into a redevelopment scheme.

Ground 11 — Charitable landlord

88.46 The landlord is a charity and the tenant's continued occupation of the dwelling-house would conflict with the objects of the charity.

GROUNDS UNDER PART III

Requirements under part III

88.47 Possession orders under Grounds 12 to 16 can only be made if the ground is made out, *and* if the court considers it reasonable to make the order (see **87.22**) *and* if it is satisfied that suitable alternative accommodation (see **88.40**) will be available to the tenant when the order takes effect (**Housing Act 1985, s. 84(2)(c)**).

Ground 12 — Certain accommodation required for new employee

88.48 This ground is similar to Ground 7 in that it applies to tenants who are employees of the landlord and are occupying accommodation in a building which is not primarily used for housing purposes (such as school caretakers). However, the aim of this provision is not to enable the landlord to remove the tenant for misconduct but to permit the landlord to release the accommodation for use by a new employee.

Ground 13 — Accommodation required for physically disabled person

88.49 The dwelling-house has features which are substantially different from those of ordinary dwelling-houses and which are designed to make it suitable for occupation by a physically disabled person who requires accommodation of a kind provided by the dwelling-house and —

(a) there is no longer such a person residing in the dwelling-house, and
(b) the landlord requires it for occupation (whether alone or with members of his family) by such a person.

This ground enables a landlord to release accommodation which has been specially adapted or designed for occupation by a physically disabled person when the current tenant does not need such special accommodation.

Ground 14 — Accommodation required for persons in especially difficult circumstances

88.50 Ground 14 contains similar provisions to Ground 13, but with regard to housing provided by a registered social landlord or housing trust which lets accommodation only for occupation by persons whose circumstances make it especially difficult for them to satisfy their need for housing.

Ground 15 — Accommodation required for persons with special needs

88.51 Ground 15 is again a similar provision to Ground 13, but this time dealing with groups of houses let for occupation by people with special needs where a social service or a special facility is provided in close proximity to the group of houses.

Ground 16 — Accommodation too extensive for statutory successor

88.52 The accommodation afforded by the dwelling-house is more extensive than is reasonably required by the tenant and —

(a) the tenancy vested in the tenant by virtue of section 89 (succession to periodic tenancy), the tenant being qualified to succeed by virtue of section 87(b), (members of family other than spouse), and
(b) notice of the proceedings for possession was served under section 83 (or, where no such notice was served, the proceedings for possession were begun) more than six months but less than twelve months after the date of the previous tenant's death.

The matters to be taken into account by the court in determining whether it is reasonable to make an order on this ground include —

(a) the age of the tenant,

(b) the period during which the tenant has occupied the dwelling-house as his only or principal home, and
(c) any financial or other support given by the tenant to the previous tenant

Ground 16 provides that in certain very limited circumstances the landlord may recover possession from a tenant who is 'under-occupying' a dwelling-house. The tenant must have succeeded to the tenancy as a member of the tenant's family, but not as the deceased tenant's spouse. The tenant must have succeeded to a periodic tenancy: this ground will not apply if the tenant acquired a fixed-term tenancy by succession. Furthermore, the notice requirements as set out in s. 83 must be complied with.

EXTENDED DISCRETION AS TO THE TERMS OF ORDERS

In cases where the court must be satisfied that it is reasonable to make a possession order **88.53** under the **Housing Act 1985** (i.e., where the claim is brought under Grounds 1 to 8 or Grounds 12 to 16), the court is given considerable discretion as to the terms of the order by virtue of s. 85. Section 85(1) provides that the court may adjourn the proceedings for such period or periods as it thinks fit. If an order is made the court may stay or suspend the execution of the order or postpone the date of possession for such periods as it thinks fit (s. 85(2); *Manchester City Council v Finn* [2002] EWCA Civ 1998, [2003] HLR 41). This power can be exercised on the making of the order or at any time before the execution of the order (*Dunn v Bradford Metropolitan District Council* [2002] EWCA Civ 1137, [2003] HLR 15). The discretion is wide and the court may give the tenant a considerable period of time in which to pay off the arrears (*Lambeth London Borough Council v Henry* (2000) 32 HLR 874; cf. *Taj v Ali* [2000] 3 EGLR 34).

If the court decides to exercise such powers it must impose conditions with respect to the payment of arrears of rent (if any) or in respect of mesne profits, unless it considers that to do so would cause exceptional hardship to the tenant or would be otherwise unreasonable (s. 85(3)(a)). It may also impose any other conditions as it thinks fit (s. 85(3)(b)). If these conditions are complied with then the court may discharge or rescind the order for possession (s. 85(4)).

Although a possession order is made by the court, the tenant may continue in occupation with the consent of the landlord for some time, and recent case law has discussed the legal consequences of this eventuality. In the absence of special circumstances, the parties to the agreement not to evict the former tenant (against whom the order has been made but not executed) will not be held to have intended to create a new secure tenancy in favour of the former tenant (*Burrows v Brent London Borough Council* [1996] 1 WLR 1448). The former tenant will be a 'tolerated trespasser'. However, application may be made by the former tenant for discharge of the possession order. If it is discharged, the obligations of the lease will be revived, with retrospective effect (*Rogers v Lambeth London Borough Council* (1999) 32 HLR 360).

A warrant of possession will be set aside only if it was obtained by abuse of process or oppression. The fact that the tenant was not expressly advised to apply under s. 85(2) will not in itself justify setting aside. Oppression involves the unfair use of court procedures. Just using a procedure such as the eviction process cannot be oppressive in itself: there must be something about the way it was used that is open to criticism. See *Jephson Homes Housing Association v Moisejevs* [2001] 2 All ER 901. For an unsuccessful challenge of the issue of a warrant on human rights grounds, see *Southwark London Borough Council v St Brice* [2001] EWCA Civ 1138, [2002] 1 WLR 1537.

Recent case law has highlighted the effect of the Disability Discrimination Act 1995 on claims for possession. By s. 22(3) of that Act, it is unlawful for a person managing any premises to discriminate against a disabled person occupying those premises (*inter alia*) by eviction or by subjection to any other detriment. A 'disabled person' is a person with a disability, that is, a physical or mental impairment which has a substantial and long-term adverse effect on the person's ability to carry out normal day-to-day activities (1995 Act, s. 1(1): see sch. 1 for qualifications and exclusions). A person discriminates against such a person if, for a reason relating to that person's disability, he treats that person less favourably than he treats or would treat others to whom that reason does not or would not apply, and he cannot show that the treatment is justified. Treatment is only justified if, in the opinion of the discriminator (for these purposes the landlord), one of the conditions in s. 24(3) of the 1995 Act is satisfied, and it is reasonable, in all the circumstances, for the landlord to hold that opinion. The most relevant condition is that the treatment is necessary in order not to endanger the health or safety of any person (which may include that of the disabled person). In *Manchester City Council v Romano* [2004] EWCA Civ 834, [2004] 4 All ER 21, the Court of Appeal held that where the tenant is a disabled person, to bring possession proceedings is prima facie discriminatory. Not only must the landlord believe that it is justified in taking the action, the landlord's justification must be objectively reasonable. In that case (as in most such cases), the landlord had, therefore, to prove that if it did not take the action to recover possession, the health or safety of someone (usually a neighbour) would be endangered.

SUCCESSION TO SECURE TENANCIES

Who is qualified to succeed?

88.54 The **Housing Act 1985**, s. 87, provides that:

> A person is qualified to succeed the tenant under a secure tenancy if he occupies the dwelling-house as his only or principal home at the time of the tenant's death and either —
> (a) he is the tenant's spouse or civil partner, or
> (b) he is a member of the tenant's family and has resided with the tenant throughout the period of twelve months ending with the tenant's death;
> unless in either case, the tenant was himself a successor, as defined in section 88.

A tenant's spouse or civil partner will therefore be qualified to succeed provided he or she was occupying the dwelling-house as his or her only or principal home when the tenant died.

A member of the tenant's family will be qualified to succeed only if he or she has resided with the tenant for a period of 12 months ending with the tenant's death. Section 113 defines a member of the family as: a spouse, a civil partner, a person who lives together with the tenant as husband and wife or as if they were civil partners, parent, grandparent, child, grandchild, brother, sister, uncle, aunt, nephew and niece. It also provides that 'half-blood' relationships are to be regarded as 'whole-blood' relationships, stepchildren are to be treated as children and illegitimate children are to be treated as legitimate. The statutory list is exhaustive (*Wandsworth London Borough Council v Michalak* [2002] EWCA Civ 271, [2002] 4 All ER 1136). A child may succeed to a secure tenancy (*Kingston upon Thames London Borough Council v Prince* [1999] LGR 333). A de facto spouse or de facto civil partner will count as a member of the family and must therefore have been residing with the tenant for a period of 12 months before the tenant's death.

The residence requirement for family members does not demand that the person living with the tenant lived with the tenant in the property to which that person is seeking to succeed. Where two brothers lived together for more than two and a half years and then moved to a new house, one brother was entitled to succeed to the secure tenancy when the other brother died 10 days after the move (*Waltham Forest London Borough Council v Thomas* [1992] 2 AC 198).

Only one succession

88.55 The **Housing Act 1985** permits only one succession. If the deceased tenant was already a successor, no one will be entitled to succeed to the tenancy. Section 88(1) gives a fairly broad definition of the tenant being 'himself a successor':

The tenant is himself a successor if —
(a) the tenancy vested in him by virtue of section 89 (succession to a periodic tenancy), or
(b) he was a joint tenant and has become a sole tenant, or
(c) the tenancy arose by virtue of section 86 (periodic tenancy arising on the ending of a term certain) and the first tenancy there mentioned was granted to another person or jointly to him and another person, or
(d) he became the tenant on the tenancy being assigned to him (but subject to subsections (2) and (3)), or
(e) he became the tenant on the tenancy being vested in him on the death of the previous tenant, or
(f) the tenancy was previously an introductory tenancy and he was a successor to the introductory tenancy.

Succession to a periodic tenancy under s. 89 is discussed below. A joint tenant who becomes the sole tenant of the dwelling-house by virtue of the right of survivorship will be deemed by s. 88(1)(b) to be a successor and no further succession will be possible — likewise, by s. 88(1)(d), where the tenant has acquired the tenancy by assignment (by s. 88(2) and (3) this will not apply when the assignment was by virtue of s. 23A or 24 of the Matrimonial Causes Act 1973 or if the assignment was by way of exchange). However, if a tenant who is a successor is granted a new tenancy of the same dwelling-house within six months of the end of the periodic tenancy to which he or she was successor, he or she will cease to be regarded as a successor: the new tenancy will 'wipe the slate clean' (**Housing Act 1985, s. 88(4)**).

Periodic tenancies

The succession of periodic tenancies is governed by the **Housing Act 1985, s. 89**. If more than one person is qualified to succeed it is the deceased tenant's spouse or civil partner who takes priority (s. 89(2)(a)). If the deceased tenant had no spouse or civil partner, or the spouse or civil partner is not qualified to succeed, and there are two or more eligible family members, it is for the family members to agree between them who is to succeed. If no agreement can be reached, it is for the landlord to select which of the potential successors is to succeed (s. 89(2)(b)). **88.56**

Where there is no person qualified to succeed, the tenancy will be disposed of according either to the will of the tenant or to the intestacy rules. If this is the case the tenancy will cease to be a secure tenancy unless the vesting or disposal of the tenancy is in pursuance of an order made under s. 23A or 24 of the Matrimonial Causes Act 1973 (**Housing Act 1985, s. 89(3)**). Once a tenancy has ceased to be secure by virtue of this section it cannot subsequently become a secure tenancy (s. 89(4)).

Terms certain

If a secure tenant dies and the tenancy is for a fixed term, it will be disposed of in accordance with the deceased's will or the intestacy rules. Provided the vesting or other disposal of the tenancy is to a person qualified to succeed, it will continue to be a secure tenancy (**Housing Act 1985, s. 90(3)**). It will also (by s. 90(3)) continue to be a secure tenancy if the vesting or other disposal is in pursuance of an order made under the Matrimonial Causes Act 1973, s. 23A or s. 24, the Matrimonial and Family Proceedings Act 1984, s. 17(1), the Children Act 1989, sch. 1, para. 1, or the Civil Partnership Act 2004, sch. 5, part 2. The **Housing Act 1985, s. 90(2)**, provides that while the estate is in course of administration, the tenancy will continue to be a secure tenancy until it is vested or disposed of or until it is known that vesting or disposing of it would end its secure status. If a tenancy ceases to be secure because of this provision, it cannot become secure again (s. 90(4)). **88.57**

Chapter 89 Homelessness and Housing Act 1996 Appeals

INTRODUCTION

89.1 This chapter is concerned with appeals against decisions made by local housing authorities concerning the provision of assistance or accommodation to homeless persons. The duties of local housing authorities towards the homeless are set out in the **Housing Act 1996, part VII**, as amended by the Homelessness Act 2002.

If a decision made by a local housing authority is adverse to an applicant for assistance or accommodation, and is one of the types of decision listed in the **Housing Act 1996, s. 202(1)**, the applicant may require it to be reviewed by the authority. If dissatisfied with the decision on the review, the applicant may appeal to a county court on a point of law (**s. 204**). Any other decision adverse to an applicant may be the subject of a claim for judicial review by the High Court (see **chapter** 74). The appeal to the county court is, in effect, a judicial review, including not only matters of interpretation, but also the full range of issues which would otherwise be the subject of an application to the High Court for judicial review (*Runa Begum v Tower Hamlets London Borough Council* [2003] UKHL 5, [2003] 2 AC 430, per Lord Bingham of Cornhill at [7]).

Summary of local housing authority's duties

89.2 The **Housing Act 1996, part VII**, places an obligation on local housing authorities to secure that suitable accommodation is made available for any person who is:

- homeless (see **89.5** to **89.11**),
- eligible for assistance (see **89.12** and **89.13**),
- in priority need (see **89.14** to **89.16**), and

- who did not become homeless intentionally (see **89.17** to **89.23**).

This obligation is subject to the local connection provisions (see **89.36**). The obligation is commonly referred to as the full housing duty (see **89.36**), as it is the highest duty that can be imposed on an authority under part VII.

Lesser duties are owed to:

(a) persons who are homeless and in priority need but intentionally homeless (see **89.37**);
(b) persons who are not intentionally homeless but have no priority need (see **89.38**).

There is a power to accommodate where no duty arises towards an applicant who is not intentionally homeless but has no priority need. If an applicant is ineligible for assistance but his or her homelessness will mean that a child under 18 will also be homeless, there is a duty to invite the applicant to seek advice and assistance from the social services authority (**s. 213A**).

An authority exercising functions relating to homelessness must have regard to such guidance as may from time to time be given by the Secretary of State (**s. 182**). The current such guidance is the Homelessness Code of Guidance for Local Authorities (July 2002). The Code does not bind an authority: they may depart from its provisions provided they have first had regard to it (*De Falco v Crawley Borough Council* [1980] QB 460).

HOMELESS APPLICATION

If an authority have reason to believe that a person may be homeless or threatened with homelessness, they are under a duty to make such inquiries as are necessary to satisfy themselves whether or not the applicant is eligible for assistance and what, if any, duty is owed to him (**Housing Act 1996, s. 184(1)**). It follows that there is a low threshold before an authority are bound to accept and determine an application under part VII. The authority only need to 'have reason to believe' no more than that the applicant 'may' be homeless or threatened with homelessness. Once an application has been accepted the authority are bound to decide what duty, if any, they owe to the applicant to secure that suitable accommodation is available for the applicant and his or her household to occupy. There may also be a duty to provide interim accommodation pending determination (see **89.35**). **89.3**

Repeat applications

There is no limit to the number of applications a homeless applicant can make (**Housing Act 1996, s. 193(9)**). Where an applicant re-presents himself to an authority after an adverse decision on an earlier application, except where the fresh application is made on exactly the same facts (in which case there is no application before the authority and accordingly there is no duty to carry out inquiries), the authority are under a statutory duty to accept that application and make the necessary further inquiries (*R v Harrow London Borough Council, ex parte Fahia* [1998] 1 WLR 1396). A local housing authority have an obligation to consider a second homelessness application provided there is at least one different factor compared to the previous application (*R (Griffin) v Southwark London Borough Council* [2004] EWHC 2463 (Admin), [2005] HLR 12, at [24]). **89.4**

In *Rikha Begum v Tower Hamlets London Borough Council* [2005] EWCA Civ 340, [2005] 1 WLR 2103, the Court of Appeal held that where an application for housing assistance under part VII is not 'identical' to, or based on 'exactly the same facts' as its predecessor application, the local authority are required to treat the second application as a valid application.

An authority's refusal to accept a fresh application is only challengeable by way of judicial review. The rights of appeal to the county court do not extend to cover an authority's refusal to accept an application (see **89.28**).

HOMELESSNESS

89.5 The **Housing Act 1996, s. 175(1)**, defines a person as homeless if he or she has no accommodation in the UK or elsewhere which is available for his or her occupation which he or she:

(a) is entitled to occupy by virtue of an interest in it or by virtue of an order of a court;
(b) has an express or implied licence to occupy; or
(c) occupies as a residence by virtue of any enactment or rule of law giving him or her the right to remain in occupation or restricting the right of another person to recover possession.

Accommodation available for occupation

89.6 In order for a person to be found to be not homeless because of having accommodation available for his or her occupation, the accommodation must be both physically accessible and legally accessible (*Nipa Begum v Tower Hamlets London Borough Council* [2000] 1 WLR 306).

A person is homeless if he or she 'cannot secure entry to' his or her accommodation (**Housing Act 1996, s. 175(2)**). This covers, for example, persons who have been illegally evicted or who are unable to access their property because of squatters. This seldom causes difficulty as an authority may find that a person who fails to take any action to redress the cause of homelessness is intentionally homeless as opposed to not being homeless.

A person is also homeless if his or her accommodation consists of a movable structure, vehicle or vessel designed for human habitation (for example, a mobile home, caravan or houseboat), and there is no place where the applicant is entitled or permitted to both place it and reside in it (s. 175(2)(b)).

Applicant's family

89.7 By the **Housing Act 1996, s. 176**, accommodation is only to be regarded as available for a person's occupation, for the purposes of the Act, if it is available for occupation by him or her together with:

(a) any other person who normally resides with him or her as a member of his or her family, or
(b) any other person who might reasonably be expected to reside with him or her.

The question of who would reasonably be expected to reside with an applicant is a matter for the authority, challengeable only on conventional public law grounds, not a question of fact which the court on appeal can decide itself (*R v Lambeth London Borough Council, ex parte Ly* (1986) 19 HLR 51; cf. *R v Newham London Borough Council, ex parte Khan* (2000) 33 HLR 29). 'Member of the family' is not defined. The Homelessness Code of Guidance for Local Authorities, at para. 6.3, states that this expression will 'include those with close blood or marital relationships and cohabiting partners', and that 'any other person' might cover a housekeeper or companion for an elderly or disabled person, or children fostered by the applicant or a member of his or her family. The Code concludes that a person who normally lives with an applicant, but is unable to do so because there is no accommodation available for them to live together, 'will normally be included in the assessment' (para. 6.4). This approach reflects the decision of the House of Lords in *Re Islam* [1983] 1 AC 688.

Reasonable to continue to occupy

89.8 A person is to be treated as homeless, even if he or she has accommodation available, if it would not be reasonable for him or her to continue to occupy it (**Housing Act 1996, s. 177**). As there are many reasons why people leave accommodation, there is no simple test of reasonableness. It is for an authority to make a judgment on the facts of each case, taking into account the circumstances of the applicant (Homelessness Code of Guidance for Local Authorities, para. 6.22). The question, however, is not whether it is reasonable to leave accommodation, but whether it is reasonable to continue to occupy it. This is an important distinction. There is no presumption that the current accommodation is unreasonable.

In deciding the question of reasonableness, a local housing authority can have regard to the 'general circumstances prevailing in relation to housing in [their] district' (**s. 177(2)**). The comparison is between current accommodation, wherever it is situated, and conditions in the area of the authority to which the application is made (*R v Tower Hamlets London Borough Council, ex parte Monaf* (1988) 20 HLR 529).

Domestic violence The **Housing Act 1996, s. 177**, provides that it is not reasonable for a person to continue to occupy accommodation if it is probable that this would lead to domestic violence or other violence. It follows that actual violence does not need to have taken place: it just has to be probable. Violence is domestic violence if it is from a person associated with the victim, and a person is associated with another person if, in relation to a child, each of them is a parent or has, or has had, parental responsibility for the child (**ss. 177(1A)** and **178(1)**). **89.9**

Domestic violence is not confined to instances in the home but extends to violence outside the home from a person with whom the applicant is associated. The Homelessness Code of Guidance for Local Authorities advises that the fact that violence has not yet occurred does not, on its own, mean that it is not likely to occur. The authority will have to assess the likelihood of a threat of violence being carried out (para. 6.18). In deciding whether it is reasonable for a person alleging violence to continue to occupy accommodation, the only question an authority may ask is whether it is probable that continued occupation of the accommodation will lead to violence against that person. That is purely a question of fact, devoid of value judgments about what an applicant should or should not do (*Bond v Leicester City Council* [2001] EWCA Civ 1544, [2002] HLR 6). Whether a victim of violence has failed to take steps to prevent it occurring, such as seeking injunctive relief, is irrelevant, but if an applicant does take such steps, the effectiveness of any relief granted may reduce the level of risk to below a probability of it occurring. This is a question for the authority to determine.

Affordability The Homelessness (Suitability of Accommodation) Order 1996 (SI 1996/3204) requires local housing authorities to consider the affordability of an applicant's accommodation when considering the question of reasonableness to continue to occupy. SI 1996/3204 sets out a list of the financial resources and accommodation costs which must be considered. **89.10**

Overcrowding The physical condition of the property and overcrowding, including statutory overcrowding, are also relevant to the assessment of reasonableness (Homelessness Code of Guidance for Local Authorities, para. 6.26). A dwelling is overcrowded for the purposes of the **Housing Act 1985** if the number of persons sleeping is such as to contravene the space standard specified in s. 326 of the 1985 Act. **89.11**

ELIGIBLE FOR ASSISTANCE

An authority owes a duty to an applicant under the **Housing Act 1996, part VII**, only if the applicant is eligible for assistance. An applicant is eligible for assistance if he or she is not excluded by **s. 185**. There are two groups of persons who are not eligible for housing assistance: **89.12**

(a) Persons who are subject to immigration control within the meaning of the Asylum and Immigration Act 1996 unless they are within a class prescribed by regulations made by the Secretary of State (**s. 185(2)**). The relevant regulations are the Homelessness (England) Regulations 2000 (SI 2000/701), reg. 3.
(b) Other persons from abroad not subject to immigration control who are prescribed by regulations (**Housing Act 1996, s. 185(3)**). See **89.13**.

By **s. 185(4)(b)**:

A person from abroad who is not eligible for housing assistance shall be disregarded in determining for the purposes of this Part whether another person—
(a) is homeless or threatened with homelessness, or
(b) has a priority need for accommodation.

This means that an applicant's children can create a priority need of the applicant only if at least one of them is eligible for assistance. In *Westminster City Council v Morris* [2005] EWCA Civ 1184, [2005] HRLR 43, it was declared that this is incompatible with the **European Convention on Human Rights, art. 14**.

Persons not subject to immigration control

89.13 A 'person subject to immigration control' is any person who is not a British citizen, a Commonwealth citizen with a right of abode in the United Kingdom, or a citizen of an EEA State (Asylum and Immigration Act 1996, s. 13).

Regulation 4 of the Homelessness (England) Regulations 2000 (SI 2000/701) provides that a person who is not subject to immigration control, but is not habitually resident in the United Kingdom, the Channel Islands, the Isle of Man or the Republic of Ireland (the 'Common Travel Area'), or whose right to reside in the Common Travel Area is derived solely from Directive 90/364/EEC or Directive 90/365/EEC, is a 'person from abroad' and therefore ineligible for assistance, unless he or she is in any of the categories listed in reg. 4(2). The effect of these provisions is that all persons from abroad who do not have a right to reside in the Common Travel Area are ineligible for housing assistance, and all persons with a right to reside, but who do not fall within the categories of persons specified in reg. 4(2), and who are not habitually resident in the Common Travel Area, will be ineligible.

Habitual residence requires some period of residence, so that a person who arrives in the UK with the intention of settling does not have habitual residence from the moment of arrival (*Nessa v Chief Adjudication Officer* [1999] 1 WLR 1937). The Homelessness Code of Guidance for Local Authorities suggests that an applicant who has two years' continuous residence in the Common Travel Area prior to the application is likely to be habitually resident (para. 5.13). Annex 22 to the Code sets out a number of general principles to be applied in determining habitual residence.

PRIORITY NEED

Priority need categories

89.14 The **Housing Act 1996, s. 189(1)**, provides that a homeless person or a person threatened with homelessness has a priority need if:

(a) she is a pregnant woman, or a person with whom a pregnant woman resides or might reasonably be expected to reside;
(b) he or she is a person with whom dependent children reside or might reasonably be expected to reside;
(c) he or she is a person who is vulnerable as a result of old age, mental illness or handicap or physical disability or other special reason, or is someone with whom such a person resides or might reasonably be expected to reside;
(d) he or she is homeless or threatened with homelessness as a result of an emergency such as a flood, fire or other disaster.

In England the Homelessness (Priority Need for Accommodation) (England) Order 2002 (SI 2002/2051) (there are different provisions in Wales) provides that the following also have a priority need:

(a) any child aged 16 or 17 who is not a 'relevant child' as defined by the Children Act 1989, s. 23A (which generally concerns care-leavers, though not all care-leavers are covered) (SI 2002/2051, reg. 3);
(b) any young person under the age of 21 who, after reaching the age of 16, but while still under 18, was, but no longer is, looked after, accommodated or fostered (reg. 4);
(c) any person who is 21 or over who is vulnerable as a result of being looked after, accommodated or fostered (reg. 5(1));
(d) any person who is vulnerable as a result of having been a member of Her Majesty's regular naval, military or air forces (reg. 5(2));
(e) any person who is vulnerable as a result of being in prison (reg. 5(3));
(f) any person who is vulnerable as a result of ceasing to occupy accommodation by reason of violence from another person, or threats of violence from another person which are likely to be carried out (reg. 5(4)).

Usually, difficulty in determining whether an applicant has a priority need arises mainly when the applicant claims to be vulnerable for the purposes of the **Housing Act 1996, s. 189(1)(c)**, or SI 2002/2051, reg. 5.

Dependent child

Dependent children do not qualify as being in priority need in their own right. They are expected to be provided for by those on whom they are dependent. Dependency connotes a form of parent-child relationship (*Hackney London Borough Council v Ekinci* [2002] EWCA Civ 776, [2002] HLR 2). The child must be 'residing' with an applicant, not merely staying. Further, the child must be dependent. This is not defined in the **Housing Act 1996**, but in *R v Kensington and Chelsea Royal London Borough Council, ex parte Amarfio* (1995) 27 HLR 543 it was held that once a child had gone into full-time employment, he or she could not be dependent. The Homelessness Code of Guidance for Local Authorities provides that children under the age of 16 are dependent, together with those under the age of 19 either receiving full-time education or training or otherwise unable to support themselves (see para. 8.7). **89.15**

Where parents are separated, it is necessary to consider whether the child is dependent on the applicant. This will involve considering whether the child resides with the applicant, or may reasonably be expected to do so. A child may be considered to reside with one parent even though dividing his or her time between both parents. The Homelessness Code of Guidance for Local Authorities says that it is only in very exceptional cases that a child might be considered to reside with both parents (see *R v Port Talbot Borough Council, ex parte McCarthy* (1990) 23 HLR 207). In assessing the question of residence the authority need to ensure that they take into account the future as well as the present arrangements for the child (*R v Kingswood Borough Council, ex parte Smith-Morse* [1995] 2 FLR 137).

Vulnerability

To decide whether an applicant is vulnerable, the local housing authority must undertake a composite assessment of the applicant's needs. The questions for the authority are: **89.16**

(a) whether the applicant is vulnerable, and
(b) if so, did his or her vulnerability arise from any of the matters set out in the **Housing Act 1996, s. 189(1)(c)**, or SI 2002/2051, reg. 5 (*R v Waveney District Council, ex parte Bowers* [1983] QB 238).

In *R v Camden London Borough Council, ex parte Pereira* (1997) 31 HLR 317 the Court of Appeal considered the first of these questions and held, at p. 330, that a person is vulnerable if: when homeless, he is less able to fend for himself than an ordinary homeless person so that injury or detriment to him will result when a less vulnerable man would be able to cope without harmful effect (the *Pereira* test).

In *Osmani v Camden London Borough Council* [2004] EWCA Civ 1706, [2005] HLR 22, Auld LJ said, at [38]:

(4) *Pereira* establishes that a person is vulnerable for the purpose if he has such a lesser ability than that of a hypothetically 'ordinary homeless person' to fend for himself that he would suffer greater harm from homelessness than would such a person. One has only to attempt to apply the *Pereira* test to any particular case by asking the question whether the applicant would, by reason of whatever condition or circumstances assail him, suffer greater harm from homelessness than an 'ordinary homeless person', to see what a necessarily imprecise exercise of comparison it imposes on a local housing authority. Given that each authority is charged with local application of a national scheme of priorities put against its own burden of homeless persons and finite resources, such decisions are often likely to be highly judgmental. In the context of balancing the priorities of such persons a local housing authority is likely to be better placed in most instances for making such a judgment.

(5) In its immediate context, *Pereira* established that a homeless applicant's lesser ability than that of 'an ordinary homeless person' to fend for himself in finding suitable accommodation may, on its own or in combination with other circumstances, amount to vulnerability for this purpose. However, the test does not impose as the sole, or even an integral, requirement of the notion of fending for oneself that an applicant should also be less able than normal to fend for himself in finding accommodation. . . .

(6) Despite some dicta suggesting the contrary, the test is a single one of a homeless person's less than normal ability to fend for himself such that he will suffer more harm than would an ordinary homeless person—a 'composite' assessment, as Hobhouse LJ put it [in *Pereira*]. . . .

(8) Nevertheless, although authorities should look for and pay close regard to medical evidence submitted in support of applicants' claims of vulnerability on account of mental illness or handicap, it is for it, not medical experts, to determine this statutory issue of vulnerability.

In *Bellouti v Wandsworth London Borough Council* [2005] EWCA Civ 602, [2005] HLR 46, Jonathan Parker LJ stated that if there was any room for genuine doubt as to the test to be applied in deciding whether an applicant is vulnerable, Auld LJ's judgment in *Osmani v Camden London Borough Council* had removed it.

INTENTIONAL HOMELESSNESS

Elements of intentionality

89.17 An applicant is intentionally homeless if he has deliberately done or failed to do something in consequence of which he ceases to occupy accommodation that is available for his occupation, and which it would be reasonable for him to continue to occupy (**Housing Act 1996, s. 191(1)**). Therefore:

(a) an applicant must deliberately have done something or failed to do something;
(b) the loss of accommodation must be in consequence of that act or omission;
(c) there must be a cessation of occupation;
(d) that accommodation must have been available to the applicant for the applicant's occupation;
(e) it must have been reasonable for the applicant to continue to occupy that accommodation.

If any one of the above issues is determined in favour of an applicant then it is not open to an authority to find the applicant intentionally homeless. For example, even if the accommodation was lost through a deliberate act and it was available for the applicant's occupation, if it would not have been reasonable for him or her to continue to occupy that accommodation an authority could not find the applicant intentionally homeless.

The first question that has to be asked is: Did the applicant deliberately do or fail to do something, the consequence of which resulted in him or her being homeless from settled accommodation? When considering whether an applicant is intentionally homeless, the authority must look back to the cause of the present homelessness (*Din v Wandsworth London Borough Council* [1983] 1 AC 657). Assessing intentionality requires consideration of the facts that caused the loss of settled, as opposed to temporary, accommodation (see *R v Harrow London Borough Council, ex parte Fahia* [1998] 1 WLR 1396).

Settled accommodation

What amounts to a settled residence is a question of fact and degree depending on the circumstances of the case. In *R v Brent London Borough Council, ex parte Awua* [1996] AC 55 it was held that 'accommodation' in what are now **ss. 175** and **191** of the **Housing Act 1996** means no more than a place which could fairly be described as accommodation and which it would be reasonable, having regard to the general housing conditions in the district, for the person in question to continue to occupy. Where the loss of temporary accommodation takes place, a local housing authority need to look back to the last settled accommodation and determine whether the loss of that accommodation was intentional. **89.18**

Deliberate act or omission

Having determined the settled accommodation from which an applicant is considered to be homeless, that is, disregarding any intervening temporary accommodation, the local housing authority must then determine whether the loss of that accommodation was through a 'deliberate' act or omission. The word 'deliberate' only governs the act or omission (*R v Salford City Council, ex parte Devenport* (1983) 82 LGR 89). There must be a direct link between the act or omission and the homelessness. An applicant whose homelessness is not in consequence of his or her deliberate act cannot be found to be intentionally homeless. There are a large number of decisions on intentionality, such as the loss of accommodation through non-payment of rent, causing nuisance and annoyance, and loss of tied accommodation by leaving a job (see Homelessness Code of Guidance for Local Authorities, paras 7.12 to 7.14). **89.19**

Good faith

'An act or omission in good faith on the part of a person who was unaware of any relevant fact shall not be treated as deliberate' for the purposes of establishing intentional homelessness (**Housing Act 1996, s. 191(2)**; see also Homelessness Code of Guidance for Local Authorities, para. 7.16). This introduces a subjective element into the analysis of intentionality (*R v Exeter City Council, ex parte Tranckle* (1993) 26 HLR 244). The Code states, by way of example, that where there have been 'mistakes of fact' an applicant should not be considered to have lost the accommodation through a deliberate act, but this is qualified so as normally to exclude: **89.20**

> mistakes of judgment based on an unrealistic degree of optimism (for example, where an applicant had used his or her home as surety for a business venture that was not soundly based or which involved a high degree of risk).

In *R v Exeter City Council, ex parte Tranckle* the applicant entered into an imprudent financial arrangement when purchasing a pub, but she had acted in good faith because she was unaware of the (un)reality of the prospects of success, which had been concealed from her by the brewery. Another example of an omission in good faith is where the applicant is unaware of his or her entitlement to housing benefit or other social security benefits (see paras 7.16 to 7.17 of the Code).

Where it is established that an applicant was unaware of a relevant fact, it is not necessary for the ignorance of a relevant fact to be reasonable. A person's ignorance may well be due to unreasonable behaviour but what he does in consequence may still be in good faith. The dividing line is not at the point where an applicant's ignorance of a relevant fact is due to his own unreasonable conduct but at the point where, for example, by shutting his eyes to the obvious he cannot be said to have acted in good faith (*O'Connor v Kensington and Chelsea Royal London Borough Council* [2004] EWCA Civ 394, [2004] HLR 37, at [34]).

Causation

89.21 If there has been a deliberate act or omission by the applicant, the loss of the accommodation must be in consequence of that act or omission. This is a question of 'cause and effect' (*Din v Wandsworth London Borough Council* [1983] 1 AC 657). The authority must look at the original cause of homelessness and determine whether that act was intentional. If the chain of causation is broken, for example, by the applicant enjoying a period of settled accommodation other than temporary accommodation, the authority cannot go back to the original cause of homelessness.

Cease to occupy

89.22 There must be a cessation of occupation as opposed to a failure to take up accommodation. An applicant cannot be intentionally homeless from accommodation that has not been taken up. The accommodation lost can be accommodation abroad and the act causing its loss can be an act abroad (see *De Falco v Crawley Borough Council* [1980] QB 460).

Available for occupation; reasonable to continue to occupy

89.23 The questions of whether accommodation is available for occupation and whether it is reasonable to continue to occupy it are considered in relation to homelessness (see **89.6** to **89.11**).

DECISION

Conduct of inquiries

89.24 Persons or bodies exercising statutory powers must adopt fair procedures when reaching a statutory decision (*Lloyd v McMahon* [1987] AC 625). Procedural fairness encompasses the rules of natural justice, one of which is the right to be heard in advance of the decision being made. This has two elements: first, to inform the party affected about what is being said; and, secondly, to afford him the opportunity to answer it. An applicant for assistance or accommodation under the **Housing Act 1996, part VII**, must be given an opportunity to explain matters which the local housing authority are minded to regard as weighing substantially against him (*R v Hackney London Borough Council, ex parte Decordova* (1994) 27 HLR 108 at p. 113; *Robinson v Brent London Borough Council* (1998) 31 HLR 1015 at p. 1020; see also *R v Newham London Borough Council, ex parte Lumley* (2000) 33 HLR 124 at para. 54).

The proper approach to determining an application is set out in *R v Gravesham Borough Council, ex parte Winchester* (1986) 18 HLR 208. The burden lies upon the local authority to make appropriate inquiries in a caring and sympathetic way. Whilst they are not under a duty to conduct CID-type inquiries, the authority are required to pursue rigorous and fair inquiries and give the applicant an opportunity to comment. If the inquiries suggest that the applicant may have become homeless intentionally, but any doubt or uncertainty remains, the issue is to be resolved in the applicant's favour.

The scope of inquiries is for the authority (*R v Kensington and Chelsea Royal London Borough Council, ex parte Bayani* (1990) 22 HLR 406). The authority can only be criticised for failing to make an inquiry which any reasonable authority would have made (*R v Nottingham City Council, ex parte Costello* (1989) 21 HLR 301). Where—on uncontested facts—an authority take a different view from the applicant, they are not required to inform him of their reasons for rejecting his representations so that he can have an opportunity to deal with them (*Tetteh v Kingston upon Thames London Borough Council* [2004] EWCA Civ 1775, [2005] HLR 21). There may, however, be some cases where in the particular circumstances fairness requires that, before rejecting an application, a local housing authority should indicate to the applicant the reasons for rejecting his representations.

In *R (Amin Begum) v Tower Hamlets London Borough Council* [2002] EWHC 633 (Admin), [2003] HLR 8, Stanley Burnton J said that where, in the course of making inquiries, an authority obtain significant information from a third party which is inconsistent with that provided by the applicant and which would substantially affect their decision, they had to put that information to the applicant and give him an opportunity to comment on it.

Decision-making

Once the authority's inquiries have been completed they will make their decision based on material before them. Matters of fact and weight are for the authority. In *Puhlhofer v Hillingdon London Borough Council* [1986] AC 484 Lord Brightman said, at p. 518: **89.25**

> The plight of the homeless is a desperate one, and the plight of the applicants in the present case commands the deepest sympathy. But it is not, in my opinion, appropriate that the remedy of judicial review, which is discretionary, should be made use of to monitor the actions of local authorities under the Act save in the exceptional case. The ground upon which the courts will review the exercise of an administrative discretion is abuse of power—e.g. bad faith, a mistake in construing the limits of the power, a procedural irregularity, or unreasonableness in the *Wednesbury* sense—unreasonableness verging on an absurdity.

The hurdle to cross in a *Wednesbury* challenge is a high one for any applicant given the latitude of an authority's power.

Notification of decision

On the conclusion of their inquiries, the authority must give the applicant written notification of their decision and, if they decide on any issue against the interests of the applicant, they must also notify him of the reasons for the decision (**Housing Act 1996, s. 184(3)** and **(6)**). **89.26**

Reasons

A decision is unlawful if the authority fail to provide sufficient reasons to enable the court to consider the lawfulness of the decision. In such circumstances the applicant is prima facie entitled to have the decision quashed as unlawful (*R v Croydon London Borough Council, ex parte Graham* (1993) 20 HLR 287; *R v Westminster City Council, ex parte Ermakov* [1996] 2 All ER 302). In *South Bucks District Council v Porter (No. 2)* [2004] UKHL 33, [2004] 1 WLR 1953, Lord Brown of Eaton-under-Heywood gave a broad summary of the authorities governing the proper approach to a reasons challenge in the planning context, which would be applicable in any reasons challenge in a homeless context. He stated, at [36]: **89.27**

> The reasons for a decision must be intelligible and they must be adequate. They must enable the reader to understand why the matter was decided as it was and what conclusions were reached on the 'principal important controversial issues', disclosing how any issue of law or fact was resolved. Reasons can be briefly stated, the degree of particularity required depending entirely on the nature of the issues falling for decision. The reasoning must not give rise to a substantial doubt as to whether the decision-maker erred in law, for example by misunderstanding some relevant policy or some other important matter or by failing to reach a rational decision on relevant grounds. But such adverse inference will not readily be drawn. The reasons need refer only to the main issues in the dispute, not to every material consideration. They should enable disappointed developers to assess their prospects of obtaining some alternative development permission, or, as the case may be, their unsuccessful opponents to understand how the policy or approach underlying the grant of permission may impact upon future such applications. Decision letters must be read in a straightforward manner, recognising that they are addressed to parties well aware of the issues involved and the arguments advanced. A reasons challenge will only succeed if the party aggrieved can satisfy the court that he has genuinely been substantially prejudiced by the failure to provide an adequately reasoned decision.

Review of decision

89.28 On receipt of the authority's decision, if it is adverse to the applicant, he or she has 21 days to request a review (**Housing Act 1996, s. 202(3)**). An applicant has the right, by s. 202(1), to request a review of decisions on any of the following matters:

(a) eligibility;

(b) what duty (if any) is owed under **ss. 190, 191, 192, 193, 195, 196** or **197** (duties to persons found to be homeless or threatened with homelessness);

(c) to make a local connection referral to another authority (there is no right to a review of an authority's decision not to make a local connection referral to another authority (under **s.198 198**): *Sareen v Hackney London Borough Council* [2003] EWCA Civ 351, [2003] HLR 54);

(d) whether the local connection conditions are met;

(e) what duty is owed on referral; and

(f) the suitability of accommodation offered in discharge of (b) or (e) or that offered as a final offer under part VI (allocation of housing accommodation).

On receipt of a request for a review the authority are bound to review their decision and the applicant must be notified of their review decision within eight weeks of the date of request, or such longer period as is agreed between the parties (Allocation of Housing and Homelessness (Review Procedures) Regulations 1999 (SI 1999/71), reg. 5).

The decisions subject to the right to review include an authority's decision that their duty has ceased (*Warsame v Hounslow London Borough Council* [2000] 1 WLR 696). It follows that any challenge as to discharge of a duty under part VII falling within (b) is by way of appeal to the county court, not by judicial review (*R v Merton London Borough Council, ex parte Sembi* (1999) 32 HLR 439).

There is no right to request a review of an earlier review decision (**Housing Act 1996, s.202(2) 202(2)**), though an authority can reconsider it voluntarily.

Conduct of review

89.29 A review must be undertaken by another officer senior to the officer who undertook the original decision (SI 1999/71, reg. 2). If an original decision which has already been reviewed is reconsidered, the officer who reviewed the original decision may also review the reconsidered decision (*Feld v Barnet London Borough Council* [2004] EWCA Civ 1307, [2005] HLR 9). A reviewing officer may seek the views of a superior officer (*Feld v Barnet London Borough Council*).

On review the relevant time for establishing the existence of the facts upon which the review decision is to be based is the date of review (*Mohamed v Hammersmith and Fulham London Borough Council* [2001] UKHL 57, [2002] 1 AC 547, at [23]). The reviewing officer is 'not simply considering whether the initial decision was right on the material before [the authority] at the date it was made. He may have regard to information relevant to the period before the first decision but only obtained thereafter and to matters occurring after the initial decision' (ibid., at [26]).

If the reviewing officer considers there is a deficiency or irregularity in the original decision but is nonetheless minded to uphold the decision on review, the applicant must be notified in writing, with reasons, and must be afforded the opportunity of responding (SI 1999/71, reg. 8(2)). A reviewing officer should treat reg. 8(2) as applicable, not merely when he finds some significant legal or procedural error in the decision, but whenever (looking at the matter broadly and untechnically) he considers that an important aspect of the case was either not addressed, or not addressed adequately, by the original decision-maker. In such a case, if he intends to confirm the decision, he must give notice of the grounds on which he intends to do so, and provide an opportunity for written and (if requested) oral representations (*Hall v Wandsworth London Borough Council* [2004] EWCA Civ 1740, [2005] 2 All ER 192).

Notification of review decision

On completing a review, a local housing authority must notify the applicant of their decision on the review (**Housing Act 1996, s. 203(3)**). If the decision on review is to confirm the original decision, they must set out their reasons for confirming it (**s. 203(4)**). Notification of a decision on review must be in writing (**s. 203(8)**) and must include reasons required by **s. 203(4)** and information about the right to appeal to a county court on a point of law (**s. 203(5)** and **(6)**). **89.30**

RIGHTS OF APPEAL

Appeal to county court

An applicant dissatisfied with a decision on review may appeal to the county court on any point of law arising from the review decision (**Housing Act 1996, s. 204(1)**). District judges have no jurisdiction to hear homelessness appeals (**PD 2B, para. 9**). **89.31**

The right to appeal arises under the **Housing Act 1996, s. 204(1)**, not only where an authority issue an adverse review decision, but also if the authority fail to notify the applicant of their review decision within the prescribed time, which is within eight weeks of the day on which the request for the review was made, unless otherwise extended by the parties (SI 1999/71, reg. 9). Any appeal must be brought within 21 days of notification of the review decision, or the date on which the authority should have notified the applicant of their review decision (**Housing Act 1996, s. 204(2)**).

There is no right to appeal against a reconsidered decision which has already been reviewed, unless the authority have stated that their reconsideration is by way of a fresh review (*Demetri v Westminster City Council* [2000] 1 WLR 772).

An applicant can seek permission to appeal out of time, but the court can only give such permission where there is good reason for the applicant's failure to bring the appeal within time and for any delay in applying for permission (**s. 204(2A)**).

Appeal jurisdiction

An appeal to a county court under the **Housing Act 1996, s. 204**, is, in effect, a judicial review, including not only matters of interpretation, but also the full range of issues which would otherwise be the subject of an application to the High Court for judicial review (*Runa Begum v Tower Hamlets London Borough Council* [2003] UKHL 5, [2003] 2 AC 430, per Lord Bingham of Cornhill at [7]). The grounds for judicial review may be summarised as illegality, irrationality and procedural impropriety (see **chapter 74**). In order to succeed in the county court, an applicant has to satisfy at least one of these grounds. **89.32**

In any appeal the court is only to be concerned with the legitimacy of the decision-making process rather than the decision itself. It is not for the court to impose its decision, only to determine the lawfulness of the authority's decision.

The court has the power to confirm, quash or vary an authority's decision (**s. 204(3)**). The court may refuse to quash the decision, even if the authority acted unlawfully, if the proceedings are pointless (*O'Connor v Kensington and Chelsea Royal London Borough Council* [2004] EWCA Civ 394, [2004] HLR 37). If procedural flaws are identified, a decision may be upheld only if the court is satisfied that a properly directed authority would inevitably have reached the same decision. This is a strict test, and where the possibility exists that a flawless procedure may produce a different result, the authority should be given the opportunity to consider the application again (*Ali v Newham London Borough Council* [2001] EWCA Civ 73, [2002] HLR 20).

On an appeal under **s. 204** the county court can vary the decision. This is a power that the

High Court in a judicial review does not have. A county court can exercise this power where there is no real prospect of the authority finding material that could lead to the conclusion that the applicant had become intentionally homeless (*Ekwuru v Westminster City Council* [2003] EWCA Civ 1293, [2003] HLR 14).

DUTIES AND THEIR DISCHARGE

89.33 The four main duties that may arise under the **Housing Act 1996, part VII**, are:

(a) the duty to provide interim accommodation pending the determination of an application;
(b) the duty to secure the provision of accommodation to those found to be homeless, eligible for assistance, in priority need and not intentionally homeless;
(c) the duty to persons found to be intentionally homeless; and,
(d) the duty to persons not in priority need but who are not intentionally homeless.

There is also a duty towards applicants who are referred to another authority (**s. 200**), and duties that arise when children under the age of 18 are involved (**ss. 213 and 213A**).

On top of these duties, an authority also has the power to provide accommodation pending a review of the original decision (**s. 188(3)**), and pending appeal to the county court (**s. 204(4)**), and to provide accommodation to those not in priority need but found to be unintentionally homeless (**s. 192(3)**).

Suitable accommodation

89.34 Where accommodation is provided the authority must ensure that it is suitable accommodation for the applicant and those who reside or who might reasonably be expected to reside with the applicant. Suitability is governed by the **Housing Act 1996, s. 210**, which identifies considerations which must be taken into account, namely, unfitness, overcrowding and houses in multiple occupation. This list of considerations is not exhaustive: for accommodation to be suitable for the person to whom the duty is owed, local authorities are obliged to have regard to the circumstances of the applicant and his or her family (*R v Brent London Borough Council, ex parte Omar* (1991) 23 HLR 446; *R v Haringey London Borough Council, ex parte Karaman* (1996) 29 HLR 366). For accommodation to be suitable the local authority have to consider the applicant's personal circumstances, which includes the applicant's state of mind (*R v Lambeth London Borough Council, ex parte Woodburne* (1997) 29 HLR 836).

By the Homelessness (Suitability of Accommodation) (England) Order 2003 (SI 2003/3326) B&B accommodation (as defined in art. 2 of the Order) is no longer to be considered suitable, *inter alia*, under the **Housing Act 1996, s. 193(2)**, for an applicant with 'family commitments' (that is, pregnant or living with a pregnant woman or dependent children) for a period of more than six weeks if there is no accommodation available other than B&B: it may still be used for other homeless applicants.

Provision of interim accommodation

89.35 Where an authority accept an application and 'have reason to believe that an applicant may be homeless, eligible for assistance and have a priority need, they shall secure that accommodation is available for his occupation' (**Housing Act 1996, s. 188(1)**). This duty arises irrespective of any possibility that the applicant may be referred to another authority. The duty ceases when the authority's decision is notified to the applicant, even if the applicant requests a review of the decision (**s. 188(3)**).

An authority have a discretion to continue to provide such accommodation pending any review of an adverse decision (**s. 188(3)**). The exercise of the discretion not to accommodate an applicant pending their review can be challenged only in the High Court.

The decision whether to provide an applicant with interim accommodation pending a review is a discretionary power. The underlying requirements in exercising this discretion are:

(a) to keep well in mind the objective of fairness between those who are homeless where the local housing authority have decided that there is no duty to the particular applicant; and
(b) to give proper consideration to the possibility that the applicant might be right, and that to deprive him of accommodation could result in a denial of an entitlement.

In carrying out this balancing exercise the following matters will always require consideration:

(a) the merits of the original decision and the extent to which it could properly be said that it was one which was either contrary to the apparent merits or was one which involved a very fine balance of judgement;
(b) whether consideration was required of new material, information or argument which could have a real effect on the decision under review; and
(c) the personal circumstances of the claimant and the consequences of an adverse decision on the exercise of the discretion.

See *R v Camden London Borough Council, ex parte Mohammed* (1997) 30 HLR 315 at p. 321.

The expression 'the merits of the case' must be taken to mean 'the merits of the applicant's case that the council's original decision was flawed' (*R v Newham London Borough Council, ex parte Lumley* (2000) 33 HLR 124 at para. 54).

Where an authority have taken into account the above factors, and the court is satisfied that they have acted in a principled and fair way in reaching their decision, the court should intervene on judicial review only in an exceptional case (*R v Brighton and Hove Council, ex parte Nacion* (1999) 31 HLR 1095; see also *Francis v Kensington and Chelsea Royal London Borough Council* [2003] EWCA Civ 443, [2004] HLR 32).

On issuing a review decision, a local housing authority have a power to provide accommodation pending any appeal against that decision (**s. 204(4)**). A decision not to exercise this power pending the applicant's appeal to the county court may be challenged in the county court (**s. 204A(2)**). In considering whether to confirm or quash the decision, the county court must apply the same principles applied by the High Court on an application for judicial review (**s. 204A(4)**). In any appeal against a decision refusing to accommodate pending the main appeal, the court may quash the decision, but it may order the provision of accommodation pending appeal only if it is satisfied that failure to provide such accommodation 'would substantially prejudice the applicant's ability to pursue the main appeal' (**s. 204A(6)**). Any order granted cannot extend beyond the final determination of the main appeal.

Discharge of full housing duty

Where a local housing authority are satisfied that an applicant is homeless and eligible for assistance, and that he or she is in priority need and not intentionally homeless, the authority will be under a duty to secure that suitable accommodation is made available for the applicant's occupation, unless they refer him or her to another authority because of a local connection (**Housing Act 1996, s. 193(2)**). **89.36**

The power to refer an applicant to another local housing authority arises only where the conditions for referral are met. Such conditions are not met if the applicant has a local connection with the district of the authority to which the application was made, does not have a local connection with the authority to which the referral is to be made, or will run the risk of violence in the district of the authority to which referral is to be made (**s. 198(2)** and **(2A)**). **Section 199** sets out the circumstances in which an applicant can be found to have a local connection. If an applicant is not satisfied with the authority's decision to accept a duty but refer him to another authority, he can request a review of that decision and appeal any adverse decision. There is, however, no right to appeal against an authority's refusal to refer to another authority (**s. 202(1)(c)**).

Where an authority accept a duty to secure accommodation under **s. 193** they can, under **s. 206(1)** **206(1)**, discharge it in one of three ways:

(a) by securing that suitable accommodation provided by them is available for the applicant;
(b) by securing that the applicant obtains suitable accommodation from some other person; or
(c) by giving the applicant such advice and assistance as will secure that suitable accommodation is available from some other person.

Cessation of duty and discharge are not synonymous. The act of discharging a **s. 193(2)** duty does not necessarily bring that duty to an end. The duty must be performed from time to time as occasion requires (Interpretation Act 1978, s. 12; see also *R v Ealing London Borough Council, ex parte McBain* [1985] 1 WLR 1351 at p. 1356, applying s. 12, where the duty under what is now the **Housing Act 1996, s. 193(2)**, was held to have been revived by reference to the applicant's changed circumstances, notwithstanding an earlier offer that had been rejected and which had entitled the authority to consider that they had—until the change of circumstances—discharged their duty to the applicant).

Prior to the Homelessness Act 2002, it had been established that the **Housing Act 1996, part VII**, did not require the provision of what might be called 'permanent' or 'indefinite' accommodation. Thus in *R v Brent London Borough Council, ex parte Awua* [1996] AC 55, under the Housing Act 1985, part III, Lord Hoffmann said, at p. 72:

> . . . the accommodation must be 'suitable,' but this does not import any requirement of permanence. . . . there is no reason why temporary accommodation should *ipso facto* be unsuitable. . . . the term for which the accommodation is provided is a matter for the council to decide. . . . provided that the decision is not *Wednesbury* unreasonable . . . I do not think that the courts should lay down requirements as to security of tenure.

In *R v Wandsworth London Borough Council, ex parte Mansoor* [1997] QB 953 Bingham MR, considering *Awua*, said:

> The expression 'accommodation' is consistently used without qualification, subject to such indications of duration as are given in defining the interim and the temporary duty. I would add that I find the concept of permanence quite inappropriate in a field such as this.

There is, accordingly, no breach of the duty under **s. 193(2)** in the provision of a series of impermanent accommodation arrangements (that is, temporary or 'staged accommodation'). Discharge of the duty requires the accommodation to be 'suitable' (see **s. 206**), but suitability does not require that the arrangement be indefinite.

The duty ceases, however, in those circumstances for which Parliament has provided. They are to be found in **s. 193**.

The first category is **s. 193**) which refers to the cessation of the duty upon refusal of any offer, whether staged or final. There is no absurdity in its application to a staged offer—it is an instrument through which authorities can encourage applicants to cooperate in their staging towards a permanent or indefinite solution, without being compelled to offer them such at once, for example, when they may not be able to do so. The same would happen in both the private and public sectors. Thus, accommodation provided by an authority under part VII out of their own stock will not normally be secure (**Housing Act 1985, sch. 1, para.** 4). The refusal of such a non-secure, staged offer is plainly governed by the **Housing Act 1996, s. 193(5)**.

Section 193(6)brings the duty to an end if the applicant:

(a) ceases to be eligible for assistance (;**s. 193(6)(a)**;);
(b) becomes homeless intentionally from accommodation made available under part VII (**s. 193(6)(b)**);

(c) accepts an allocation of local authority accommodation (**s. 193(6)(c)**);
(d) accepts a non-shorthold assured tenancy from a private landlord (**s. 193(6)(cc)**); or
(e) ceases to use accommodation made available under part VII as an only or principal home (**s. 193(6)(d)**).

Circumstances (b) and (e) mean that the duty can cease—as it does under **s. 193(5)**—even though what has been lost (through conduct or cessation of use) was not permanent or indefinite accommodation, that is, was temporary or staged. Indeed, it would seem that (a), (b) and (e) are only directed towards staged accommodation, for it is the acceptance of permanent or indefinite accommodation which is the subject of (c) and (d), and of **s. 193(7B)**. Circumstances (b) and (e) are explicitly staged accommodation under part VII. Nor would it be a ground to determine a tenancy allocated under **s. 193(6)(c)** or granted under **s. 193(6)** that the applicant had ceased to be eligible for assistance.

Section 193(7), which is subject to **s. 193(7F)**, deals with the rejection of an offer of accommodation under part VI, being 'a final offer' as defined in **s. 193(7A)**.

Section 193(7B) is therefore directed to the remaining issue, which is the position relating to the offer of an assured shorthold, the acceptance of which is excluded from causing a cessation of duty under **s. 193(6)(cc)**. The offer must be a qualifying offer, as defined in **s. 193(7D)** subject to **s. 193(7)** and **(7F)**. If accepted, the duty ceases; in contrast to a part VI final offer, however, if even a qualifying assured shorthold is refused, the duty will not cease (**s, 193(7C)**).

Duties to persons found to be intentionally homeless

Where a local housing authority's decision is that an applicant is intentionally homeless, as defined above, the duty of the authority, under the **Housing Act 1996, s. 190(2)**, is: **89.37**

(a) to secure that accommodation is available for the applicant's occupation for such period as they consider will give him or her a reasonable opportunity of securing accommodation for his or her occupation; and
(b) to provide the applicant with advice and assistance in any attempts the applicant may make to secure that accommodation becomes available for his or her occupation.

The Homelessness Code of Guidance for Local Authorities suggests 28 days may be adequate, but it warns authorities that they 'will need to take account of local circumstances, including how readily other accommodation is available in the district and have particular regard to the particular circumstances of the applicant', including the resources available to provide rent (para. 9.30). See *R (Conville) v Richmond Upon Thames LBC* [2006] HLR 1. The obligation to provide accommodation runs for the date of the original decision not the review decision.

If the authority are not satisfied that the applicant has a priority need, their duty is limited to providing him with (or securing that he is provided with) advice and assistance in any attempts he may make to secure that accommodation becomes available for his occupation (**s. 190(3)**).

In order to discharge their duty to provide advice and assistance the authority must assess the applicant's housing needs (B). The advice and assistance provided must include information about the likely availability in the authority's district of the types of accommodation appropriate to the applicant's housing needs (including, in particular, the location and sources of such types of accommodation) (**s. 190(5)**).

Duties to persons not in priority need who are not intentionally homeless

The duty towards applicants found not to be intentionally homeless, but not in priority need, is limited to providing advice and assistance in any attempts they may make to secure that accommodation becomes available for their occupation (**Housing Act 1996, s. 192(1)**). The advice and assistance to be given is the same as that to be given to applicants who are in priority need but intentionally homeless. **89.38**

Chapter 90 Protection from Eviction

INTRODUCTION

90.1 Not every residential occupier will fall within the protection of one of the statutory codes discussed in the preceding chapters. The occupier may be a licensee rather than a tenant, or, even if a tenant, he or she may fall within one of the categories excluded from statutory protection. The Protection from Eviction Act 1977 therefore provides a minimum standard of protection for the majority of residential occupiers. This protection is provided in a variety of ways. First, the 1977 Act imposes criminal liability for unlawful eviction and harassment. Secondly, it prevents a landlord from forfeiting a tenancy by peaceable re-entry. Thirdly, it prohibits a landlord or licensor from recovering possession from a residential occupier without taking court proceedings. Lastly where a landlord or licensor seeks to terminate a tenancy or licence by means of a notice to quit, the Act provides that that notice to quit must be in the correct form and must give at least four weeks' notice.

CRIMINAL LIABILITY

90.2 The Protection from Eviction Act 1977, s. 1, creates three offences: one of unlawfully depriving the occupier of occupation of the premises, and two of harassment. These offences may be committed against a 'residential occupier', which term is defined by s. 1(1):

> In this section 'residential occupier', in relation to any premises, means a person occupying the premises as a residence, whether under a contract or by virtue of any enactment or rule of law giving him the right to remain in occupation or restricting the right of any other person to recover possession of the premises.

This is a broad definition. It will include tenants and contractual licensees throughout the currency of the contractual period because they are occupying 'under a contract'. It will include statutory tenants under the **Rent Act 1977** because they are occupying 'by virtue of an enactment'. When read in conjunction with s. 3 (see **90.8**), it will also include certain tenants and licensees even after the contractual period has ended, because s. 3 prevents a landlord or licensor from recovering possession otherwise than by an order of the court. Until such an order is obtained the former tenant or licensee will be occupying by virtue of an enactment 'restricting the right of any other person to recover possession of the premises'.

Section 1 will protect only persons who are occupying the premises as a residence. It will not protect a tenant who has sublet the whole of the premises, neither will it protect a person who is occupying the premises for non-residential purposes. There is, however, no requirement that the premises should be occupied as the occupier's only or principal home.

Unlawful deprivation of occupation

90.3 The Protection from Eviction Act 1977, s. 1(2), provides that:

If any person unlawfully deprives the residential occupier of any premises of his occupation of the premises or any part thereof, or attempts to do so, he shall be guilty of an offence unless he proves that he believed, and had reasonable cause to believe, that the residential occupier had ceased to reside in the premises.

This offence can be committed by 'any person', whether or not that person is the occupier's landlord or licensor. To amount to a deprivation of occupation the act done must have 'the character of an eviction' (*R v Yuthiwattana* (1984) 80 Cr App R 55). Where a person enters the occupier's house while the occupier is out, changes the locks and puts the occupier's belongings on the street, this will almost certainly be a deprivation of occupation. However, where a tenant lost his key and the landlord refused to replace it, with the consequence that the tenant was unable to get back into his flat for a day and a night, the court held that this did not constitute an offence under s. 1(2) (*R v Yuthiwattana*).

The act done must also be unlawful. This will virtually always be the case, because ss. 2 and 3 of the Act (see **90.8**) prohibit a landlord or licensor from seeking to recover possession without a court order.

It is a defence to a charge under s. 1(2) to prove that the accused believed (with reasonable cause) that the residential occupier had ceased to reside in the premises, but the burden of proof is on the accused to establish this belief.

Harassment

Where the acts done by the landlord, licensor or other person do not amount to an unlawful deprivation of occupation, they may still amount to harassment under the Protection from Eviction Act 1977, s. 1(3) or (3A) of the 1977 Act. These subsections provide: **90.4**

(3) If any person with intent to cause the residential occupier of any premises —
  (a) to give up the occupation of the premises or any part thereof; or
  (b) to refrain from exercising any right or pursuing any remedy in respect of the premises or part thereof;

does acts likely to interfere with the peace or comfort of the residential occupier or members of his household, or persistently withdraws or withholds services reasonably required for the occupation of the premises as a residence he shall be guilty of an offence.

(3A) Subject to subsection (3B) below, the landlord of a residential occupier or an agent of the landlord shall be guilty of an offence if —
  (a) he does acts likely to interfere with the peace or comfort of the residential occupier or members of his household, or
  (b) he persistently withdraws or withholds services reasonably required for the occupation of the premises in question as a residence,

and (in either case) he knows or has reasonable cause to believe, that that conduct is likely to cause the residential occupier to give up the occupation of the whole or part of the premises or to refrain from exercising any right or pursuing any remedy in respect of the whole or part of the premises.

Section 1(3B) provides:

A person shall not be guilty of an offence under subsection (3A) above if he proves he had reasonable grounds for doing the acts or withdrawing or withholding the services in question.

The two offences are broadly similar: both will be committed where a person seeks either to get the occupier to give up occupation of the whole or part of the premises, or where a person seeks to prevent the occupier from exercising some right in respect of the property (for example, applying to a rent officer or a rent assessment committee) or pursuing a remedy. In both cases the acts done to achieve these aims can be either acts likely to interfere with the peace or comfort of the occupier (or members of the occupier's household) or persistent withdrawal of services (such as gas, water and electricity). Neither section demands that the acts themselves have to be unlawful (*R v Burke* [1991] 1 AC 135).

The differences between the two sections lie, first, in the identity of the person who can commit the offence and, secondly, in the degree of intention required. Under s. 1(3), 'any person' can commit the offence, while s. 1(3A) applies only to the landlord of the residential occupier or his or her agent. Under s. 1(3), the prosecution must show that the acts or the withdrawal of services were done with intent to cause the occupier to give up occupation or to refrain from exercising a right or pursuing a remedy. Under s. 1(3A), it is necessary to show only that the landlord knew or had reasonable cause to believe that the conduct was likely to have this effect.

Penalties

90.5 A person who is found guilty of any of the three offences contained in s. 1 is liable on summary conviction to a fine not exceeding £2,000, or to imprisonment for up to six months or both. A person convicted on indictment is liable to a fine, or to imprisonment for up to two years or both (s. 1(4)).

Civil remedies

90.6 The fact that criminal proceedings are taken under the Protection from Eviction Act 1977, s. 1, will not prejudice the right of the occupier to seek a civil remedy (s. 1(5)). It is not necessary for an act to be a breach of covenant or a tort for it to amount to an offence under s. 1, but in many cases any attempt by a landlord to deprive a tenant of occupation or to harass a tenant will also be a breach of the covenant for quiet enjoyment. In such a case the tenant will be able to obtain damages and possibly an injunction; in some cases they may even be able to claim exemplary or additional damages. Where, as a result of harassment by the landlord, a tenant gives up occupation of the premises, the landlord will also be liable for the statutory tort of unlawful eviction under s. 27 of the Housing Act 1988.

FORFEITURE UNDER THE PROTECTION FROM EVICTION ACT 1977

90.7 The Protection from Eviction Act 1977, s. 2, requires a landlord of residential premises who has reserved a right of re-entry or forfeiture in the lease to exercise that right by means of proceedings in the court. Section 2 will apply where any person (not necessarily the tenant) is lawfully residing in the premises or part of them. Thus, in the case of residential premises, the landlord is precluded from exercising a right of re-entry or forfeiture by means of peaceable re-entry (see 84.6).

RECOVERY OF POSSESSION UNDER THE PROTECTION FROM EVICTION ACT 1977

90.8 At common law, when a tenancy or a licence comes to an end the landlord or licensor is entitled to re-enter and take possession of the premises. As discussed in the preceding chapters, many occupiers will fall within the protection of a statutory code which will effectively prevent a landlord (and in some cases a licensor) from regaining possession after the original contractual term has come to an end. However, some occupiers, in particular licensees, may find themselves ineligible for statutory protection under one of the codes. In such a case s. 3 of the Protection from Eviction Act 1977 provides a very important, if basic, level of protection. It will not permit the landlord or licensor to recover possession of the premises except by court proceedings.

Section 3 applies where a tenancy or licence has come to an end and the occupier continues to reside in the premises or part of them (s. 3(1)). It will not apply to statutorily protected tenancies (as defined in s. 8), or to tenancies or licences which fall into one of the excluded categories. These excluded categories are contained in s. 3A, which was introduced into the 1977 Act by s. 31 of the Housing Act 1988 which came into force on 15 January 1989.

Section 3 will therefore apply to:

(a) all tenancies entered into before 15 January 1989 (or pursuant to a contract made before that date);
(b) tenancies entered into on or after 15 January 1989 apart from excluded tenancies;
(c) licences, whenever created, apart from excluded licences.

A tenancy or licence will be excluded if:

(a) under its terms the occupier shares any accommodation with the landlord or licensor and immediately before the grant and also at the time it comes to an end the landlord or licensor occupied the shared accommodation as his or her only or principal home (s. 3A(2));
(b) under its terms the occupier shares any accommodation with a member of the landlord's or licensor's family and immediately before the grant and also at the time it comes to an end the member of the landlord's or licensor's family occupied the shared accommodation as his or her only or principal home and immediately before the grant and also at the time it comes to an end the landlord or licensor occupied as his or her only or principal home premises in the same building as the shared accommodation and that building is not a purpose-built block of flats (s. 3A(3));
(c) it was granted as a temporary expedient to a person who entered the premises in question or any other premises as a trespasser (s. 3A(6));
(d) it confers on the tenant or licensee the right to occupy the premises for a holiday only (s. 3A(7)(a));
(e) it is not granted for money or money's worth (s. 3A(7)(b));
(f) it confers rights of occupation in a hostel (as defined by s. 622 of the Housing Act 1985) provided by certain public bodies (s. 3A(8)).

NOTICE TO QUIT

Section 5 of the Protection from Eviction Act 1977 provides that no notice to quit given by either a landlord or tenant will be valid unless: **90.9**

(a) it is in writing and contains such information as may be prescribed (for which see the Notices to Quit (Prescribed Information) Regulations 1988 (SI 1988/2201) as amended), and
(b) it is given not less than four weeks before the date on which it is to take effect.

These provisions will also apply to licensors and licensees (s. 5(1A)). They will not, however, apply to excluded licences or to excluded tenancies made on or after 15 January 1989, unless entered into pursuant to a contract made before that date (s. 5(1B)).

These excluded categories are defined by s. 3A (see **90.8**).

SETTING ASIDE WARRANTS OF EXECUTION: MORTGAGE POSSESSION CLAIMS

The Administration of Justice Act 1970, s. 36 (as amended by the Administration of Justice Act 1973, s. 8), confers on the court a power to suspend a warrant of possession of mortgaged property. See *Refuge Assurance Co. Ltd v Pearlberg* [1938] 3 All ER 231; *Cheltenham and Gloucester plc v Krausz* [1997] 1 WLR 1558; *Scottish and Newcastle plc v Billy Row Working Mens Club and Institute Ltd* (2001) LTL 2/4/2001. **90.10**

Chapter 91 Business Tenancies

INTRODUCTION

91.1 A tenant who uses premises for business purposes may have certain concerns that do not necessarily arise in the case of residential tenancies. First, there is the question of goodwill. When a business owner has spent several years building up a clientele for the business, the location of that business may become very important. Moving the business may lose a good deal of its custom. This will be of particular importance where the tenant relies largely on local customers. Secondly, the tenant may well have expended money on adapting the building for the purposes of the business. Both of these factors mean that when a business tenancy comes to an end the tenant is unlikely to be willing to move. As a result the landlord may be in a position to charge a far higher rent from the existing tenant on the renewal of the tenancy than could be obtained if the premises were let to a new tenant on the open market.

Statutory protection has been given to business tenants by two statutes which will be considered in this chapter. By the Landlord and Tenant Act 1927, a business tenant is entitled to compensation for improvements made by the tenant or the tenant's predecessor in title. By part II of the Landlord and Tenant Act 1954, business tenants are entitled to renewal of their tenancies.

The basic principle of the 1954 Act has been not to interfere directly with the parties' freedom to contract, the presumption being that where two business persons are entering into a commercial arrangement they should be free to arrange it on any terms they can agree between them. During the contractual period the Act does not interfere with the parties' rights or obligations at all; the Act becomes significant only towards the end of the term where the parties may be seeking a renewal of the tenancy or compensation. Even then the objective of the Act is not to push the parties into litigation, but rather to provide a structure within which negotiations can take place.

A business tenant that comes within the protection of the 1954 Act acquires two important rights:

(a) the right to apply for a renewal of the tenancy;
(b) the right to compensation for disturbance if the application for renewal is unsuccessful.

Under the 1927 Act, a business tenant will also acquire the right to compensation for improvements.

These rights are very different to the rights available to a tenant who falls within one of the statutory codes applying to residential tenancies. This can be of particular importance when a tenant lives and works in the same premises. The codes are mutually exclusive. For example, if the tenancy falls under the **Rent Act 1977**, the tenant will acquire far greater security of tenure (and a right to rent control too) than under the 1954 Act.

Significant changes to part II of the Landlord and Tenant Act 1954 have recently been made by the Regulatory Reform (Business Tenancies) (England and Wales) Order 2003 (SI 2003/3096), which came into force on 1 June 2004. The most important changes are:

(a) landlords as well as tenants may apply to the court for the terms of a new tenancy to be settled;
(b) landlords may apply for an order that the tenancy be terminated without renewal if they can make out one of the statutory grounds for opposition;
(c) tenants are no longer required to serve a counter-notice in response to a landlord's s. 25 notice;
(d) there are new time limits for applications to court for renewal of tenancies;
(e) there are amendments to the provisions concerning ownership and control of businesses so that where companies are controlled by individuals the company and the individual are treated as one and the same;
(f) tenants as well as landlords may apply for interim rent, and there are other amendments making the interim rent regime more flexible;
(g) tenants may claim compensation if they are induced not to apply for renewal because of a misrepresentation;

(h) it is no longer necessary for parties, who wish to contract out of the security-of-tenure provisions or to surrender a tenancy, to apply to court for its approval, this requirement being replaced by a new procedure of landlord-notice and tenant-declaration;
(i) the categories of information which may be required to be provided towards the end of the tenancy term are increased;
(j) termination of the tenancy by the tenant following expiry of the contractual term is clarified;
(k) the maximum length of the term of the tenancy that the court may order is increased from 14 to 15 years;
(l) landlords of parts of the same business premises are enabled to make joint use of the procedures contained in part II.

To coincide with implementation of these changes to part II of the 1954 Act, the existing notices regulations have been repealed and replaced by the Landlord and Tenant Act 1954, Part 2 (Notices) Regulations 2004 (SI 2004/1005). These also came into force on 1 June 2004.

NATURE OF A BUSINESS TENANCY

91.2 To be eligible for protection as a business tenant under the **Landlord and Tenant Act 1954**, the occupier must fall within the definition set out in s. 23(1) which provides:

> Subject to the provisions of this Act, this Part of this Act applies to any tenancy where the property comprised in the tenancy is or includes premises which are occupied by the tenant and are so occupied for the purposes of a business carried on by him or for those and other purposes.

A tenancy

91.3 An occupier of premises is not protected by **part II of the Landlord and Tenant Act 1954** unless the occupation is by virtue of a tenancy, which may be either periodic or for a fixed term. A sub-tenancy is just as eligible for protection as a tenancy. In many cases the tenant in occupation will not be renting directly from the freeholder but from an intermediate landlord. Even an unlawful sub-tenancy may fall within the Act (*D'Silva v Lister House Developments Ltd* [1971] Ch 17). An equitable lease is eligible for protection, for example, where the parties entered into an agreement for a lease but the actual lease itself was never created. However, a tenancy at will, whether created by implication or by a written agreement, has been held to fall outside the Act (see *Wheeler v Mercer* [1957] AC 416; *Hagee (London) Ltd v A. B. Erikson and Larson* [1976] QB 209).

An occupier holding under a licence will not come within Part II of the 1954 Act. However, a landlord cannot prevent the acquisition of a business tenancy by the occupier simply by adopting the terminology appropriate to a licence throughout the written agreement. While it has been accepted that the attributes of residential and business premises are often quite different (see *Dresden Estates Ltd v Collinson* [1987] 1 EGLR 45), in general the principles articulated by Lord Templeman in *Street v Mountford* [1985] AC 809 (see **83.2**) will be applied in determining whether the agreement is, as a matter of substance, a tenancy or a licence. See also *Essex Plan Ltd v Broadminster Ltd* [1988] 2 EGLR 72; *Vandersteen v Agius* (1992) 65 P & CR 266; *National Car Parks Ltd v Trinity Development Co. (Banbury) Ltd* [2001] EWCA Civ 1686, [2002] 2 P & CR 18; *Clear Channel UK Ltd v Manchester City Council* [2005] EWCA Civ 1304, [2006] 04 EG 168.

Premises

91.4 The word 'premises' is used in a broad sense. 'Premises' includes a building or part of a building and can also include land, even when the land has no buildings upon it. For example, a tenancy of land used for training horses has been held to be a business tenancy within the 1954 Act (*Bracey v Read* [1963] Ch 88). Even a tenancy of a parking space in a basement garage may constitute a business tenancy (*Harley Queen v Forsyte Kerman* [1983] CLY 2077) as may a tenancy of an advertisement station (*Clear Channel UK Ltd v Manchester City Council* [2005] EWCA Civ 1304, [2006] 04 EG 168). An incorporeal hereditament such as an easement (e.g., a right of way) or a profit à prendre (e.g., fishing rights) will not come within the definition of 'premises' (*Land Reclamation Co. Ltd v Basildon District Council* [1979] 1 WLR 767). However, where the tenant of premises has acquired other rights under his lease (e.g., a right of way, or the right to park a car on adjoining land), these additional rights may be renewed along with the tenancy under **s. 32(3)** or **s. 35** of the 1954 Act (see, for example, *Nevill Long and Co. (Boards) Ltd v Firmenich and Co.* (1983) 47 P & CR 59).

Occupation

In most cases it will be fairly easy to determine whether the tenant is occupying the premises. **91.5**
However, there have been difficulties where the tenant's business has involved allowing others into the premises as sub-tenants or licensees. The leading case is now *Graysim Holdings Ltd v P and O Property Holdings Ltd* [1996] AC 329. A landlord granted a tenancy of a market hall to the tenant company, which in turn sublet the stalls to market traders, retaining the common parts and providing services for the traders. The House of Lords held that the tenant was not in occupation for the purposes of its business. The parts of the premises which had been sublet were occupied by the traders, not by the tenant company. As **part II of the Landlord and Tenant Act 1954** does not allow for the possibility of shared occupation of the same premises by tenant and sub-tenant (as certain previous authorities had indicated), there could only be one business occupier at any one time. An important consideration was that any new tenancy granted pursuant to the statutory procedure would be of 'the holding' (see **91.13**), which term expressly excluded parts of the premises not occupied by the tenant. It would be contrary to the legislative intention of part II of the 1954 Act to grant a new tenancy and yet to deny to the tenant the parts of the premises which rendered the business a going concern. Thus, if the 'holding' consists solely of common parts, as in *Graysim Holdings Ltd v P and O Property Holdings Ltd*, and the remainder of the premises is sublet (or otherwise alienated) such that the tenant is not in occupation, the tenancy will not fall within part II of the 1954 Act (see also *Bagettes Ltd v GP Estates Ltd* [1956] Ch 290; cf. *Lee-Verhulst (Investments) Ltd v Harwood Trust* [1973] 1 QB 204, a decision which must be treated with circumspection and care following *Graysim Holdings Ltd v P and O Property Holdings Ltd*).

Whether a tenant will still fall within the Act if occupation is not continuous will depend upon the facts of the case. The determining criterion is whether the 'thread of continuity' has been broken. In *I. and H. Caplan Ltd v Caplan (No. 2)* [1963] 1 WLR 1247, it was held that where a tenant stopped trading from a shop for a period of seven months it still continued to occupy the premises within the meaning of the Act. Occupation has also been held to be continuous for the purposes of the Act where that occupation was in fact seasonal (*Teasdale v Walker* [1958] 1 WLR 1076).

Section 41 applies where the tenancy is held on trust. **Section 41(1)** provides that:

> Where a tenancy is held on trust, occupation by all or any of the beneficiaries under the trust, and the carrying on of a business by all or any of the beneficiaries, shall be treated for the purposes of section 23 of this Act as equivalent to occupation or the carrying on of a business by the tenant.

There are now two provisions in the Landlord and Tenant Act 1954 that require consideration where the tenant is a company or where, although the tenant is not occupying as such, the premises are being occupied by a company controlled by the tenant.

Section 23(1A) provides that:

> Occupation or the carrying on of a business—
> (a) by a company in which the tenant has a controlling interest; or
> (b) where the tenant is a company, by a person with a controlling interest in the company,

shall be treated for the purposes of this section as equivalent to occupation or, as the case may be, the carrying on of a business by the tenant.

By **s. 46(2)**, a person has a controlling interest in a company if, had he been a company, the other company would have been its subsidiary: 'company' and 'subsidiary' being defined as in the Companies Act 1985, ss. 735 and 736.

Section 42(2) provides that:

Where a tenancy is held by a member of a group, occupation by another member of the group, and the carrying on of a business by another member of the group, shall be treated for the purposes of section 23 of this Act as equivalent to occupation or the carrying on of a business by the member of the group holding the tenancy.

By **s. 42(1)**, two companies are to be taken to be members of the same group if, and only if, one is the subsidiary of the other, or both are subsidiaries of a third company or the same person has a controlling interest in both.

Occupation for the purposes of a business

91.6 To be protected by **part II of the Landlord and Tenant Act 1954** a tenant must occupy the premises for 'the purposes of a business'. 'Business' is given a broad definition for the purposes of the Act by **s. 23(2)**:

In this Part of this Act the expression 'business' includes a trade, profession or employment and includes any activity carried on by a body of persons, whether corporate or unincorporate.

Section 23(2) creates a difference between a tenant who is an individual and a tenant which is a body of persons.

91.7 **Tenant an individual** For an individual to be a business tenant, he or she will have to carry out an activity that can be classed as a trade, profession or employment. In *Lewis v Weldcrest Ltd* [1978] 1 WLR 1107 the Court of Appeal found that a tenant who took in a number of lodgers, but gained no real commercial advantage from doing so, did not carry on a trade. The question of whether the activity is sufficient to comprise a trade will be a question of degree. A common-sense approach should be taken. A person running a seaside boarding house might well be carrying on a trade; a person taking in a few lodgers and making little or no profit would not (see Ormrod LJ at p. 1119). Even where the renting of rooms or property for commercial gain does amount to a business, the tenancy will not fall within the 1954 Act if the tenant is not in occupation of the premises (see **91.5**).

In *Lewis v Weldcrest Ltd* it was also held that the fact that the activity carried on by the individual might be capable of amounting to a breach of covenant against business user, did not mean that the activity would necessarily amount to a trade, profession or employment within the meaning of the 1954 Act.

In *Abernethie v A. M. and J. Kleiman Ltd* [1970] 1 QB 10 the tenant voluntarily conducted a Sunday school on the premises. The tenant was an individual, and the court held that conducting a Sunday school was well outside the definition of a 'trade, profession or employment'.

91.8 **Tenant a body of persons** Where the tenant is a body of persons the Landlord and Tenant Act 1954 seems to indicate that any activity will count as business purposes. Thus where the trustees of a tennis club took a tenancy of tennis courts and a club house, the activity of a tennis club was held to be a business purpose within the 1954 Act (*Addiscombe Garden Estates Ltd v Crabbe* [1958] 1 QB 513). The administration of a hospital by a board of governors, a non profit-making body, has also been held to be a business within the Act (*Hills (Patents) Ltd v University College Hospital Board of Governors* [1956] 1 QB 90). An enterprise that is being carried on by a corporate body commercially, with a view to making a trading surplus, may be a business within **s. 23** even though the surplus cannot be distributed to its shareholders or members (*Hawkesbrook Leisure Ltd v Reece-Jones Partnership* [2003] EWHC 3333 (Ch), [2004]

2 EGLR 61). However, the scope of the word 'activity' should not be regarded as infinite. In *Hillil Property v Naraine Pharmacy* (1980) 39 P & CR 67, Megaw LJ stated, at p. 74:

> Though [an] activity is something that is not strictly a trade, a profession or an employment, nevertheless to be an 'activity' for this purpose it must be something that is correlative to the conceptions involved in those words.

The court held that the use of premises for dumping waste during the renovation of other premises was not an activity.

Mixed business and residential user

The **Landlord and Tenant Act 1954, s. 23,** provides that a tenancy will fall within the Act if the premises are occupied for the purposes of a business carried on by the tenant 'or for those and other purposes'. Where those 'other purposes' are residential an interesting conflict between two statutes can arise. Generally it is unusual to find a tenant arguing that the tenancy does not fall within a statutory code while the landlord seeks to maintain that it does, yet with regard to the 1954 Act this may be worth claiming as under a residential code the tenant is likely to acquire greater security of tenure (and, just possibly, rent control) than under the 1954 Act. **91.9**

The statutory codes applying to business tenancies and the codes applying to residential tenancies are mutually exclusive. If a tenancy falls within the 1954 Act it will be excluded from being a Rent Act tenancy by s. 24(3) of the Rent Act 1977, from being an assured tenancy by the **Housing Act 1988, sch. 1, para.** 4, and from being a secure tenancy by the **Housing Act 1985, sch. 1, para. 11**. Where there is mixed business and residential user the crucial question will therefore be which statutory code should apply.

For the 1954 Act to apply, the business use of the premises must be a significant purpose of the tenant's occupation of the premises. In *Cheryl Investments Ltd v Saldanha* [1978] 1 WLR 1329 business use was held to be a significant purpose for the purposes of occupying the flat when office equipment had been installed, and the business appeared to have no other address. However, in *Royal Life Saving Society v Page* [1978] 1 WLR 1329 (heard together with *Cheryl Investments Ltd v Saldanha*, by the Court of Appeal) it was held on the facts that professional use of a maisonette was only incidental to residential use, notwithstanding that the tenant doctor had been granted permission to carry on his profession in the maisonette as well as in his Harley Street premises. In the event, the tenancy of the maisonette was protected under the **Rent Act** 1977.

Change of user

The use of premises can of course change. If the doctor in the above case gave up his consulting rooms in Harley Street and started seeing his patients at home, he would cease to have a **Rent Act 1977** tenancy and would then fall under the **Landlord and Tenant Act 1954**. However, the converse may not always be true. If the tenant of a shop with a flat above it ceases to trade from the shop but continues to live in the flat, it can no longer be said that the premises are occupied for business purposes. The protection of the 1954 Act will therefore cease. This tenant will, however, not then acquire protection under a residential statutory code. Both the **Rent Act 1977** and the **Housing Act 1988** apply only to 'a dwelling-house' 'let as a separate dwelling'. When the premises were let they were let for business purposes; if the business use ceases, the premises will not come within the residential code unless the landlord agrees to the change of user (see *Pulleng v Curran* (1980) 44 P & CR 58 and *Wagle v Trustees of Henry Smith's Charity Kensington Estate* [1990] 1 QB 42). **91.10**

Providing residential accommodation for employees

A tenant can occupy premises through his or her employees, where, for example, a manager occupies a shop run by the tenant. Here the tenant is clearly occupying the shop, through the manager, for the purposes of a business. However, in *Chapman v Freeman* [1978] 1 WLR 1288, the **91.11** tenant of a cottage used the cottage to provide accommodation for employees who worked at his hotel. The cottage was only 50 yards away from the hotel. It was held that while it was convenient for the employees to reside in the cottage, it was not necessary that they do so for the better performance of their duties. In *Methodist Secondary Schools Trust Deed Trustees v O'Leary* [1993] 1 EGLR 1105, a school caretaker occupied a house adjacent to the school buildings on a service occupancy. The trustees of the school installed a phone and an alarm system in the house connected to the school so that the caretaker would be able to deal with emergencies occurring after normal school hours. In this case the judge was satisfied that it was necessary for the caretaker to occupy the house in order to perform his duties.

In *Groveside Properties Ltd v Westminster Medical School* (1983) 267 EG 593 the medical school rented a flat which was used to provide residential accommodation for students. The medical school retained a degree of control over the premises; it furnished the flat, chose the students who were to live there, kept a set of keys, and the secretary of the medical school visited the flat about once a month to see how the students were getting on. It was held that the medical school was occupying the flat for the purposes of its business (in the broad sense of an 'activity'). The student occupation of the flat was 'not merely to provide a residence but to foster a corporate or collegiate spirit in furtherance of their medical education'.

Business user in breach of covenant

91.12 If the tenant is carrying on a business in the premises in breach of a general covenant against business user, or in breach of a covenant against use for the purposes of a trade, profession or employment, that tenancy will not normally fall within **part II of the Landlord and Tenant Act 1954**. Section 23(4) provides:

> Where the tenant is carrying on a business, in all or any part of the property comprised in a tenancy, in breach of a prohibition (however expressed) of use for business purposes which subsists under the terms of the tenancy and extends to the whole of that property, this Part of this Act shall not apply to the tenancy unless the immediate landlord or his predecessor in title has consented to the breach or the immediate landlord has acquiesced therein.
>
> In this subsection the reference to a prohibition of use for business purposes does not include a prohibition of use for the purposes of a specified business, or of use for purposes of any but a specified business, but save as aforesaid includes a prohibition of use for the purposes of some one or more only of the classes of business specified in the definition of that expression in subsection (2) of this section.

There are, therefore, a number of situations in which the tenancy will still come within the Act even where the tenant's user of the premises is in breach of covenant:

(a) If the covenant extends only to part of the premises.
(b) If the covenant prohibits use only for a specified business (e.g., not to use as a betting shop).
(c) If the covenant prohibits use for any business except a specified business (e.g., not to use except as a betting shop).

A tenancy will also come within the Act if the tenant is in breach of a covenant against business user but either:

(a) the immediate landlord or his predecessor in title has consented to the breach; or
(b) the immediate landlord has acquiesced in the breach.

'Acquiescence' and 'consent' are two distinct concepts. In both cases, however, the landlord must have knowledge of the breach. If, with knowledge of the breach, an immediate landlord takes no action and stands passively by, this can amount to acquiescence. Consent, on the other hand, requires the landlord to take some positive action which indicates consent (see *Bell v Alfred Franks and Bartlett Co. Ltd* [1980] 1 WLR 340).

THE HOLDING

Where a person takes a tenancy of a building, the provisions of **part II of the Landlord and Tenant Act 1954** will not necessarily apply to the whole of the premises let under that tenancy. Many of the provisions in the 1954 Act relate only to 'the holding'. The term 'holding' is defined by s. 23(3): **91.13**

In the following provisions of this Part of this Act the expression 'the holding', in relation to a tenancy to which this Part of this Act applies, means the property comprised in the tenancy, there being excluded any part thereof which is occupied neither by the tenant nor by a person employed by the tenant and so employed for the purposes of a business by reason of which the tenancy is one to which this Part of this Act applies.

'The holding' is of crucial importance, because a tenant who applies for a renewal of the tenancy will be entitled only to a renewal of the tenancy of the holding.

EXCLUSIONS FROM THE LANDLORD AND TENANT ACT 1954

Certain tenancies are expressly excluded from **part II of the Landlord and Tenant Act 1954**: **91.14**

(a) agricultural holdings (**s. 43(1)(a)**);
(b) farm business tenancies (**s. 43(1)(aa)**);
(c) mining leases (**s. 43(1)(b)**);
(d) tenancies of premises licensed to sell alcohol, not including hotels and restaurants and other premises where the sale of alcohol is not the main use of the premises, which were granted before 11 July 1989 (s. 43(1)(d)) — tenancies of premises licensed to sell alcohol granted on or after 11 July 1989 do fall within the 1954 Act (Landlord and Tenant (Licensed Premises) Act 1990, s. 1(1));
(e) service tenancies, i.e., a tenancy granted to a tenant who holds an office, appointment or employment from the landlord and which continues only so long as that employment or appointment continues — if the tenancy was granted after 1 October 1954, the tenancy must have been granted in writing which expresses the purpose for which the tenancy was granted (**s. 43(2)**);
(f) short tenancies, i.e., tenancies granted for a term certain not exceeding six months unless:
    (i) the tenancy contains provision for renewing the term or extending it beyond six months from its beginning, or
    (ii) the tenant, either alone or together with any predecessor in title, has been in occupation for more than 12 months (**s. 43(3)**).

CONTRACTING OUT OF THE LANDLORD AND TENANT ACT 1954

The general rule is that any attempt by a landlord to contract out of the provisions of **part II of the Landlord and Tenant Act 1954** will fall foul of s. 38(1), which renders void any agreement relating to a tenancy to which the Act applies: **91.15**

. . . in so far as it purports to preclude the tenant from making an application or request under this Part of this Act or provides for the termination or the surrender of the tenancy in the event of his making such an application or request or for the imposition of any penalty or disability on the tenant in that event.

However, the strict rules against contracting out were amended by the Law of Property Act 1969 which inserted s. 38(4) into the 1954 Act. It conferred jurisdiction on the court to authorise an agreement excluding a tenancy which was a term of years certain from the security of tenure provisions of the Act (i.e., ss. 24 to 28). This jurisdiction was much used, but following years of doubt concerning the function which the court was being expected to perform, the procedure has now been repealed and replaced by an alternative process which does not involve any application to the court. Agreements authorised by the court prior to 1 June 2004 continue to be governed by the old law: that is, they must satisfy the requirements of s. 38(4) in order to exclude the operation of the Act (see SI 2004/3096, art. 29(2)).

With effect from 1 June 2004, by the **Landlord and Tenant Act 1954, s. 38A(1)**:

The persons who will be the landlord and the tenant in relation to a tenancy to be granted for a term of years certain which will be a tenancy to which this Part of this Act applies may agree that the provisions of sections 24 to 28 of this Act shall be excluded in relation to that tenancy.

A 'term of years certain' includes a fixed term of less than a year (*Re Land and Premises at Liss, Hants* [1971] Ch 986), but not a tenancy for 12 months, to continue thereafter from year to year (*Nicholls v Kinsey* [1994] QB 600). Where the landlord may exercise an option to break during the fixed term, it is nevertheless a term of years certain (*Receiver for the Metropolitan Police District v Palacegate Properties Ltd* [2001] Ch 131).

An agreement under **s. 38A(1)** is void unless it complies with certain conditions. First, the landlord must have served on the tenant a notice in the form (or substantially in the form) set out in SI 2003/3096, sch. 1. Secondly, the requirements of SI 2003/3096, sch. 2, must be met. These may be met in one of two ways:

(a) If the landlord serves the prescribed notice on the tenant not less than 14 days before the tenant enters into the tenancy (or if earlier becomes contractually bound to enter into it), then the tenant must make a declaration in the form (or substantially in the form) in sch. 2, para. 7.
(b) If the landlord serves the prescribed notice on the tenant at a later date, but before the tenant enters into the tenancy (or becomes contractually bound), then the tenant must make a statutory declaration in the form (or substantially in the form) in sch. 2, para. 8.

A reference to the notice, and the declaration or the statutory declaration (which may also be made by a person duly authorised by the tenant), as the case may be, must be contained in or endorsed upon the instrument creating the tenancy. The agreement under **s. 38A(1)**, or a reference to the agreement, must similarly be contained in or endorsed upon the same instrument.

Section 38A(2) enables a landlord and tenant to agree that a tenancy will be surrendered at a specified future date or in specified future circumstances despite the general prohibition contained in s. 38(1). Similar protections are built into the procedure as apply to agreements excluding security of tenure.

SECURITY OF TENURE UNDER THE LANDLORD AND TENANT ACT 1954

91.16 The **Landlord and Tenant Act 1954, s. 24,** contains the core of the security offered by the Act. The basis of this security is automatic continuation. A tenancy which falls within part II of the Act will not come to an end unless it is terminated in one of the ways set out in the Act. This means that a tenancy will not come to an end by effluxion of time (in the case of a fixed-term tenancy), or by the landlord's service of a notice to quit (in the case of a periodic tenancy), which are the two main common law methods by which a landlord can bring a tenancy to an end.

Section 24(1) provides:

A tenancy to which this Part of this Act applies shall not come to an end unless terminated in accordance with the provisions of this Part of this Act; and, subject to the following provisions of this Act either the

tenant or the landlord under such a tenancy may apply to the court for an order for the grant of a new tenancy—
(a) if the landlord has given notice under section 25 of this Act to terminate the tenancy, or
(b) if the tenant has made a request for a new tenancy in accordance with section 26 of this Act.

As a result of amendments made by SI 2003/3096, application to the court for a new tenancy may now be made not only by the tenant (as has always been the case) but also by the landlord. The effect is that, while a tenancy to which the 1954 Act applies will continue beyond its contractual expiry date, either party may take the initiative to have the tenancy replaced by a new tenancy (at the current market rent) by applying to the court. Although the landlord has previously been able to terminate the continuation tenancy by service of a s. 25 notice, the court has only had jurisdiction in such circumstances to grant a new tenancy in place of the old if the tenant responded to the s. 25 notice by applying to the court under s. 24.

It may seem reasonable to ask, if the tenancy automatically continues beyond the expiry date, whether the expiry date has any significance for a tenancy to which the 1954 Act applies. The answer is that the expiry date is of considerable significance, for it is only after the contractual term has expired that the tenant acquires the right to apply to the court for a new tenancy.

TERMINATION OF A BUSINESS TENANCY

The methods of termination available under **part II of the Landlord and Tenant Act 1954** are listed below. They can be divided into two categories: (a) common law methods of termination which are preserved by the Act; and (b) statutory methods of termination which are provided for in the Act. **91.17**

Common law methods of termination

The **Landlord and Tenant Act 1954**, s. 24(2), provides: **91.18**

The last foregoing subsection shall not prevent the coming to an end of a tenancy by notice to quit given by the tenant, by surrender or forfeiture, or by the forfeiture of a superior tenancy, unless—
(a) in the case of a notice to quit, the notice was given before the tenant had been in occupation in right of the tenancy for one month.

Tenant's notice to quit The aim of the 1954 Act is to provide protection for business tenants by preventing the landlord from terminating the tenancy. The tenant's ability to terminate the tenancy by serving a notice to quit on the landlord is unaffected. **91.19**

Surrender As with a notice to quit, the 1954 Act does not prevent a tenant surrendering the tenancy before the expiry of the term. **91.20**

Paragraph (a) of s. 24(2) prevents the tenant from giving a notice to quit before he or she has been in occupation for one month. The aim of this is to prevent landlords from attempting to exclude the operation of the Act by getting a tenant to give a notice to quit when the tenant enters into the tenancy.

Forfeiture The Act does not affect the landlord's right to forfeit the tenancy in the event of the tenant breaching an obligation under the lease. Of course the landlord will be able to forfeit only if a right of re-entry has been reserved in the lease. Likewise, if a landlord forfeits a head tenancy this may also bring a sub-tenancy to an end. Where the landlord seeks to forfeit the tenancy, the tenant, or the sub-tenant, will be able to apply for relief against forfeiture under s. 146 of the Law of Property Act 1925 (see **chapter 84**). **91.21**

Statutory methods of termination

Under the **Landlord and Tenant Act 1954** there are three ways in which a tenancy to which part II of the Act applies can be brought to an end: **91.22**

(a) by the landlord giving notice to terminate the tenancy under **s. 25** (see **91.26** to **91.29**);
(b) by the tenant making an application for a new tenancy under **s. 26** (see **91.30** to **91.32**);
(c) by the tenant giving notice to terminate the tenancy under **s. 27(2)** (see **91.33**).

91.23 **Business use ceasing after the fixed term expires** If a tenant ceases to use the premises for business purposes after the contractual term has expired and while the tenancy is being continued by **s. 24(1)**, the tenancy ceases to be one to which the 1954 Act applies. Such a tenancy will not simply come to an end when the business user ceases, however. **Section 24(3)(a)** provides that the landlord may terminate the tenancy by not less than three nor more than six months' notice given in writing to the tenant (without prejudice to any means of termination contained in the terms of the tenancy).

91.24 **Business use starting after the landlord has served a notice to quit** If a tenancy does not fall within the 1954 Act and the landlord gives the tenant notice to quit, the fact that the tenant may bring the tenancy within the Act before the notice expires (i.e., by starting a business on the premises) will not affect the operation of that notice (**s. 24(3)(b)**).

91.25 **The 'competent landlord'** Negotiation of a new tenancy may not be meaningful if, for example, the immediate landlord is a leaseholder for a term that is only a few days longer than the tenant's interest. The 1954 Act therefore provides a mechanism for identifying one landlord with whom the tenant should deal. This landlord is known as the 'competent landlord'. Only a competent landlord is entitled to serve a notice to terminate on the tenant under s. 25 and the tenant's request under s. 26 for a new tenancy should be served on the competent landlord. Section 44(1) provides that the competent landlord will be either:

(a) the owner of the fee simple; or
(b) the landlord lowest in the chain of tenancies who has a tenancy which will not come to an end within 14 months by effluxion of time, and no notice has been given which will end the tenancy within 14 months.

Where different persons own such interests in different parts of the property, they are considered to be the owner collectively (**s. 44(1A)**).

If the tenant cannot identify the competent landlord, the tenant can serve notice on any landlord above the tenant in the chain requiring that landlord to supply the appropriate information (s. 40(2)). Similarly, a landlord can require information from a tenant under s. 40(1).

Termination by the landlord: s. 25 notices

91.26 In order to terminate a tenancy to which **part II of the Landlord and Tenant Act 1954** applies, the landlord must serve a notice in accordance with **s. 25**. By serving such a notice the landlord puts in motion the mechanism of the renewal procedure. This functions, in essence, by setting out a series of time limits within which both the landlord and tenant must serve their respective notices and replies, and thereby provides a framework for the negotiations.

The landlord's **s. 25** notice must be given in the prescribed form (see the Landlord and Tenant Act 1954, Part 2 (Notices) Regulations 2004 (SI 2004/1005), sch. 1). It must:

(a) specify the date at which the tenancy is to come to an end (the date of termination) (**s. 25(1)**);
(b) state whether the landlord is opposed to the grant of a new tenancy to the tenant (**s. 25(6)**);
(c) where it opposes, it must specify the grounds of opposition in s. 30 relied upon (**s. 25(7)**);
(d) where it does not oppose, it must set out the landlord's proposals as to the property to be comprised in the new tenancy, the rent to be payable, and the other terms (**s. 25(8)**).

A s. 25 notice must be given by the landlord or, if there is more than one, jointly by the landlords in a single notice to the tenant. If there are joint tenants the notice must be served on all of them.

A s. 25 notice must apply to the whole of the demised premises (*Southport Old Links Ltd v Naylor* [1985] 1 EGLR 66). This may prove problematic if the landlord's interest has been severed after the grant of the tenancy. It may be that in such a situation it will not be possible for either of the landlords to serve a valid s. 25 notice (see *Dodson Bull Carpet Co. Ltd v City of London Corporation* [1975] 1 WLR 781; contrast *Skelton and Son v Harrison and Pinder Ltd* [1975] QB 361).

Timing of the notice The notice must be given not more than 12 or less than six months before the date of termination specified in the notice (s. 25(2)). Thus the earliest date that a landlord can give notice, in the case of a fixed-term tenancy, is a year before the tenancy is due to expire. **91.27**

Date of termination A landlord's notice to terminate a business tenancy must specify the date of termination. Calculating the date of termination must be done with care, because if a premature date is given the notice will not be valid. The basic principle behind the 1954 Act is that the date of termination cannot be earlier than the date upon which the tenancy can be terminated at common law. How this date is to be calculated will depend upon whether the tenancy is a periodic or a fixed-term tenancy. **91.28**

(a) *Periodic tenancies* At common law a periodic tenancy is normally brought to an end by means of a notice to quit. Under the 1954 Act the date of termination given in the notice must not be earlier than the earliest date upon which the tenancy could have been brought to an end at common law by a notice to quit (s. 25(3)). At common law it is necessary that the notice to quit expires on the anniversary of the tenancy. Under the 1954 Act the landlord does not have to be so precise, provided that the date of termination given by the landlord is later than the date at which the tenancy could be terminated by a notice to quit (*Commercial Properties Ltd v Wood* [1968] 1 QB 15). The notice, however, must be given not more than 12 and not less than six months before the date of termination specified in the notice (s. 25(2)).
Where the period of notice required to bring a tenancy to an end by a notice to quit is more than six months, the 12-month limit for giving a s. 25 notice no longer applies; instead the limit will be a period six months longer than the length of notice required under the tenancy agreement (s. 25(3)(b)).

(b) *Fixed-term tenancies* With fixed-term tenancies it is easier to calculate the date of termination. The earliest date of termination is the date upon which the tenancy would have come to an end by effluxion of time if it had not been continued by s. 24 of the 1954 Act. Thus the earliest point at which a landlord can serve notice under s. 25 is one year before the tenancy is due to expire. In every case the landlord must give at least six months' notice, even once the contractual tenancy has expired and the tenancy is being continued by s. 24.

A considerable number of business tenancies, however, permit termination before the expiry of the term by incorporating a break clause into the tenancy agreement. What happens then if the landlord wishes to exercise such a break clause? Should the landlord adopt the statutory procedure under s. 25, or follow the contractual provisions set out in the break clause or does the landlord need to serve two notices, one under the Act and one under the contract?

If a s. 25 notice can be served which fulfils both the statutory requirements and the requirements of the contract then one notice will be sufficient (*Scholl Manufacturing Co. Ltd v Clifton (Slim-Line) Ltd* [1967] Ch 41). Achieving this joint goal may not always be easy, and in practice a careful landlord will often serve two notices — one under the break clause and one under s. 25.

If a landlord serves a notice that satisfies **s. 25** but does not fulfil the provisions of the break clause, the **s. 25** notice will be of no effect, for if the break clause is not effectively operated the tenancy will continue under the contract. The landlord will have to wait either until the tenancy expires by effluxion of time, or until the next opportunity at which a break clause can be operated.

If a landlord serves a notice that fulfils the provisions of the break clause but does not comply with **s. 25**, the contractual tenancy will be brought to an end; however, the tenancy will continue under **s. 24** until the landlord complies with the provisions of the Act. Even if a landlord does not wish to terminate the tenancy immediately, it may still be of benefit to operate a break clause.

91.29 **If the tenant does not want to give up possession** It is no longer necessary for the tenant to respond to the landlord's **s. 25** notice by notifying the landlord whether the tenant is willing to give up possession. Once the **s. 25** notice has been served, the tenant may make application to the court for a new tenancy under **s. 24**. For the time limits for such an application, see **91.35**.

Termination by the tenant

91.30 There are two ways in which a tenant can bring a business tenancy to an end under the **Landlord and Tenant Act 1954**:

(a) by requesting a new tenancy under **s. 26**;
(b) by giving notice under **s. 27**.

The first of these options is applicable where the tenant does not wish to give up possession and wants to apply for a new tenancy. The second is applicable where the tenant wants to end the tenancy and give up possession.

In general it is less common for a tenant to request a new tenancy under **s. 26** than it is for a landlord to apply to terminate the tenancy under **s. 25**. Until it is known that the landlord wishes to terminate the tenancy, it will usually not be in the tenant's interest to request a new one. The tenancy will be continued in any event under **s. 24**, and will probably be on terms more favourable to the tenant than those of a new tenancy.

On the other hand, it will often be in the interest of the landlord to terminate the tenancy under **s. 25** even if the landlord does not want to recover possession of the premises, for the landlord will gain an opportunity to renegotiate the terms of the lease and may well be able to obtain a higher rent.

91.31 **Who can request a new tenancy?** Not every tenant can take advantage of **s. 26** of the 1954 Act. First, the tenant must hold a tenancy which is either:

(a) a tenancy granted for a term of years certain exceeding one year (whether or not continued by **s. 24**); or
(b) a tenancy granted for a term of years certain and thereafter from year to year (**s. 26(1)**).

Neither the holder of a periodic tenancy nor the holder of a fixed term of less than one year can request a new tenancy under **s. 26**. Periodic tenants and the holders of terms of less than one year can still apply for a new tenancy if the landlord serves them with a **s. 25** notice. (The holders of fixed terms of less than six months will be excluded from the Act in any case by **s. 43(3)**.)

Secondly, there are provisions designed to prevent the operation of **s. 26** clashing with the operation of **s. 25** and **s. 27**. If the landlord has already served a **s. 25** notice, the tenant cannot then request a new tenancy under **s. 26**. Similarly, a tenant who has already served notice under **s. 27** (see **91.33**) cannot subsequently request a new tenancy under **s. 26** (**s. 26(4)**).

Content of a s. 26 notice A tenant's request for a new tenancy should be served on the competent landlord (see 91.25) and must: **91.32**

(a) be made in the prescribed form (s. 26(3));
(b) set out the tenant's proposals as to —
   (i) the property to be comprised in the new tenancy (being either the whole or part of the property comprised in the current tenancy),
   (ii) the rent payable under the new tenancy,
   (iii) the terms of the new tenancy (s. 26(3));
(c) specify a date for the commencement of the new tenancy.

The date referred to in (c) must not be more than 12 months and not less than six months after the making of the request. The date must not be earlier than the date upon which the current tenancy would come to an end by effluxion of time or could be brought to an end by notice to quit given by the tenant (s. 26(2)). Thus the earliest point at which a tenant could request a new tenancy would be one year before the date on which that tenancy was due to expire by effluxion of time. A tenant cannot invoke a break clause in the lease to terminate the current tenancy and then request a new tenancy under **s. 26** (*Garston v Scottish Widows' Fund and Life Assurance Society* [1998] 1 WLR 1583).

The effect of a **s. 26** request is to terminate the tenant's current tenancy immediately before the date specified in the request for the beginning of the new tenancy (s. 26(5)). Once a tenant has served a request on the landlord, it is essential to comply with the procedure which follows, for if the right to apply for a new tenancy is lost the tenancy will nevertheless terminate and the landlord will be able to regain possession.

A **s. 26** notice, unlike a **s. 25** notice, does not have to relate to the whole of the premises. Once a tenant has served a valid request under **s. 26** it is not possible to withdraw it and serve a second request (which a tenant might want to do, for example, in order to comply with the statutory time limits) (*Polyviou v Seeley* [1980] 1 WLR 55).

The timescale applicable to a **s. 26** request is very similar to that applicable to a **s. 25** notice given by the landlord. Having received the tenant's request, the landlord has two months to serve notice on the tenant that the application to the court for the grant of a new tenancy will be opposed (**s. 26(6)**). There is no prescribed form for the landlord's notice in opposition, but it must state on which of the grounds set out in **s. 30** of the 1954 Act the landlord will oppose the application. The right to oppose the tenant's application for a new tenancy will be lost if no notice of opposition is served.

Termination by tenant's notice under s. 27 This second statutory method of termination applies when the tenant does not wish to apply for a new tenancy. It is applicable only in the case of fixed-term tenancies; a tenant under a periodic tenancy can always terminate the tenancy by means of a notice to quit served on the landlord, this being one of the common law methods of termination preserved by **s. 24(2)** of the Act. **Section 27** can be used only after the tenant has been in occupation in right of the tenancy for one month. This extra provision was added by the Law of Property Act 1969, s. 4(2) to prevent possible evasion of the 1954 Act. **91.33**

Where a fixed-term tenancy is nearing its end and the tenant does not want to continue in occupation after the term has expired, the tenant can give notice under **s. 27(1)**. The tenant must give notice in writing to the immediate landlord not later than three months before the date on which the tenancy would come to an end by effluxion of time. If such notice is given, **s. 24** will not apply to the tenancy and it will come to an end normally by effluxion of time.

It is, however, essential that the tenant continue in occupation up to the contractual term date of the tenancy. If the tenant goes out of occupation before then, the tenancy will not be continued by s. 24 of the 1954 Act and will therefore expire (*Esselte AB v Pearl Assurance plc*

[1997] 1 WLR 891). This will occur even if the tenant has served a counter-notice and made application to the court for a new tenancy, provided the tenant informs the landlord if he ceases to occupy before the term date (*Surrey County Council v Single Horse Properties Ltd* [2002] EWCA Civ 367, [2002] 1 WLR 2106).

Where the tenancy has already passed the date at which it would expire by effluxion of time and is being continued by **s. 24**, the tenant can give notice under **s. 27(2)**. Three months' notice must be given in writing to the immediate landlord and the notice must expire on a quarter day. Rent payable in respect of any period beginning before, and ending after, the tenancy is terminated is to be apportioned and any excess paid by the tenant is recoverable (**s. 27(3)**).

APPLICATION FOR A NEW TENANCY

91.34 A business tenant's right to apply to the court for a new tenancy lies at the core of the 1954 Act. The procedure is in **CPR, Part 56**, and **PD 56**. A new tenancy can be granted only when the current tenancy has been terminated. The right to apply for a new tenancy will therefore arise in only two situations:

(a) where the landlord has terminated the current tenancy by serving a **s. 25** notice and the tenant has given notice to the landlord of unwillingness to give up possession;
(b) where the tenant has terminated the current tenancy by requesting a new tenancy under **s. 26**.

A business tenant will acquire no right to apply for a new tenancy where the landlord seeks to forfeit the tenancy because of the tenant's default, or where the tenant has chosen to give up possession by surrender or by serving notice under **s. 27**.

A business tenant does not need to have a genuine intention to take up a new tenancy when making a request under **s. 26**, and evidence as to the tenant's state of mind is therefore inadmissible (*Sun Life Assurance plc v Thales Tracs Ltd* [2001] EWCA Civ 704, [2001] 1 WLR 1562).

Much of the enduring success of the 1954 Act can be attributed to the way in which it encourages the parties to reach agreement. First, it provides space for the parties to negotiate by continuing a fixed-term tenancy beyond the date on which it would expire by effluxion of time (**s. 24**). During this time the parties have the opportunity to come to agreement without resorting to the statutory provisions. If agreement is not forthcoming then either the landlord or the tenant can serve notice under the Act. By serving notice a statutory framework is brought into play. This framework requires the parties to set out their intentions and reasons within strict time limits (the court has no jurisdiction to extend the time limits but the parties may waive them). The framework itself, by compelling the parties to put their cards on the table, provides a further impetus towards agreement. If agreement is not reached within the specified time limits, either party may then apply to court for the matter to be settled. In the meantime either party may apply to the court for an interim rent to be fixed (see below).

By **s. 28**, if agreement is reached between the parties for the grant of a new tenancy, the current tenancy will continue until the date specified in the agreement for the commencement of the new tenancy and will cease to be a tenancy to which the Act applies (the tenant no longer needs the protection of the Act because he or she will now hold a contract for a lease).

By **s. 29(2)**, the landlord may make application to the court for the termination of the tenancy without the grant of a new tenancy. The landlord may apply if he has given notice under **s. 25** that he is opposed to the grant of a new tenancy, or if the tenant has made a request for a new tenancy under **s. 26** and the landlord has given notice of opposition under **s. 26(6)**. A termination order must be made if the landlord establishes to the satisfaction of the court any of the grounds under s. 30 which he specified in the s. 25 notice or in the s. 26(6) notice.

Time limits for application to court

91.35 Application to the court for the grant of a new tenancy (under s. 24) or for a termination order (under s. 29(2)) must be made within strict time limits ('the statutory period': s. 29A). The statutory period is a period ending:

(a) where the landlord gave a s. 25 notice, on the date specified in the notice; and
(b) where the tenant made a s. 26 request for a new tenancy, immediately before the date specified in the request.

Where the tenant has made a s. 26 request, application under s. 24 must not be entertained by the court if it is made before the end of a two-month period beginning with the date of the request (unless the landlord has given a s. 26(6) notice) (s. 29A(3)).

These time limits may be extended by agreement between the parties (s. 29B). It is open to the court to permit amendment of the claim in order to add or substitute a party after the expiry of the statutory period (*Parsons v George* [2004] EWCA Civ 912, [2004] 1 WLR 3264).

Opposition by landlord

91.36 The **Landlord and Tenant Act 1954**, s. 30 (1), provides seven grounds (91.37 to 91.46) upon which the landlord may oppose a tenant's application for the grant of a new tenancy or make an application under s. 29(2). A landlord must either in the s. 25 notice, or in the landlord's counter-notice to the tenant's s. 26 request, state which of the grounds is to be relied on. Once the landlord has specified a ground or grounds they cannot be changed. If a landlord specifies grounds of opposition and subsequently sells the reversion, the new landlord may rely only on the grounds specified by the original landlord (*Marks v British Waterways Board* [1963] 1 WLR 1008).

Under the 1954 Act, the various grounds of opposition are not grouped separately as mandatory and discretionary grounds as are the grounds of possession under the **Housing Act 1988**. Nevertheless, a similar distinction can be made: grounds (a), (b), (c), and (e) are discretionary in the sense that even if the landlord can establish the ground the court still has to consider whether 'the tenant ought not to be granted a new tenancy'. In the other cases the court must refuse to order the grant if the landlord can establish the ground.

Ground (a) — Tenant's failure to comply with repair obligations

91.37 (a) where under the current tenancy the tenant has any obligations as respects the repair and maintenance of the holding, that the tenant ought not to be granted a new tenancy in view of the state of repair of the holding, being a state resulting from the tenant's failure to comply with the said obligations;

The landlord must establish that the holding is in a state of disrepair as a result of the tenant's failure to comply with the repairing obligations in the lease. However, merely to establish a breach of repairing covenant is not enough; the landlord must also demonstrate that the breaches are such that the court ought not to order the grant of a new tenancy. The court will consider relevant factors such as the severity of the breach, whether the tenant is willing and able to remedy the breach, and the tenant's past conduct (see, for example, *Lyons v Central Commercial Properties Ltd* [1958] 1 WLR 869).

Ground (b) — Tenant's persistent delay in paying rent

91.38 (b) that the tenant ought not to be granted a new tenancy in view of his persistent delay in paying rent which has become due;

The landlord must establish that the tenant has a history of late payment: an occasional delay in payment will not be enough, neither will the fact that there are currently outstanding arrears unless they are long-standing enough to amount to 'persistent delay'. The court will then consider whether the tenant ought not to be granted a new tenancy on this ground. A large range of factors may be taken into account, including:

(a) whether the delay caused the landlord inconvenience and expense;
(b) whether the tenant can offer a good explanation for the delay and show that it was exceptional (*Hurstfell Ltd v Leicester Square Property Co. Ltd* [1988] 2 EGLR 105);
(c) whether the tenant can ensure future payment, e.g., by providing a deposit or by offering to pay interest on any future arrears (*Rawashdeh v Land* [1988] 2 EGLR 109);
(d) whether the landlord (or his predecessors) had allowed the tenant to pay the rent slightly late and had failed to inform the tenant of a change to that practice (*Hazel v Akhtar* [2001] EWCA Civ 1883, [2002] 2 P & CR 17).

Ground (c) — Tenant's breaches of other obligations or use of the holding

91.39 (c) that the tenant ought not to be granted a new tenancy in view of other substantial breaches by him of his obligations under the current tenancy, or for any other reason connected with the tenant's use or management of the holding;

This ground covers breaches of obligation by the tenant other than non-payment of rent and failure to repair. The landlord must show that there is a 'substantial breach'. Ground (c) is not limited to breaches of obligations contained in the lease. It was used, for example, where the tenant's use of the premises contravened a local authority enforcement notice (*Turner and Bell v Searles (Stanford-le-Hope) Ltd* (1977) 33 P & CR 208). However, the landlord must establish some element of fault or mismanagement on the part of the tenant (*John Kay Ltd v Kay* [1952] 2 QB 258). The court must then go on to consider whether the tenant ought not to be granted a tenancy and should take into account all relevant circumstances (see *Eichner v Midland Bank Executor and Trustee Co. Ltd* [1970] 1 WLR 1120).

Ground (d) — Suitable alternative accommodation available

91.40 (d) that the landlord has offered and is willing to provide or secure the provision of alternative accommodation for the tenant, that the terms on which the alternative accommodation is available are reasonable having regard to the terms of the current tenancy and to all other relevant circumstances, and that the accommodation and the time at which it will be available are suitable for the tenant's requirements (including the requirement to preserve goodwill) having regard to the nature and class of his business and to the situation and extent of, and facilities afforded by, the holding;

The court has no discretion when considering this ground: if the landlord can establish it then the tenant's application must be dismissed. If the landlord is unable to satisfy the court that suitable alternative accommodation will be available at the date of termination specified in the landlord's s. 25 notice or the tenant's request for a new tenancy, but can establish that it will be available at a later date, the landlord will still be able to succeed under s. 31(2) (see 91.48).

Ground (e) — Landlord requires whole property for subsequent letting

91.41 (e) where the current tenancy was created by the subletting of part only of the property comprised in a superior tenancy and the landlord is the owner of an interest in reversion expectant on the termination of that superior tenancy, that the aggregate of the rents reasonably obtainable on separate lettings of the holding and the remainder of that property would be substantially less than the rent reasonably obtainable on a letting of that property as a whole, that on the termination of the current tenancy the landlord requires possession of the holding for the purpose of letting or otherwise disposing of the said property as a whole, and that in view thereof the tenant ought not to be granted a new tenancy;

This ground arises only rarely in practice. It applies where a landlord has let premises and the tenant has in turn sublet part of the premises, and the intermediate landlord has less than 14 months of his or her term to run so that the superior landlord is the competent landlord of the sub-tenant under s. 44(1) of the 1954 Act. The landlord has to show:

(a) that the rent obtainable on separate lettings of the two parts of the property would be substantially less than the rent obtainable if he or she let the property as a whole; and
(b) that on the termination of the current tenancy (i.e., the sub-tenancy) the landlord requires possession of the holding for the purposes of letting the property as a whole.

It will be difficult for the landlord to show that possession is required unless the intermediate tenancy is due to come to an end before the sub-tenancy is terminated. This ground is discretionary and **s. 31(2)** (see **91.48**) applies to it.

Ground (f) — Landlord intends to demolish or reconstruct the premises

(f) that on the termination of the current tenancy the landlord intends to demolish or reconstruct the premises comprised in the holding or a substantial part of those premises or to carry out substantial work of construction on the holding or part thereof and that he could not reasonably do so without obtaining possession of the holding; **91.42**

Ground (f) is one of the more popular grounds of opposition employed by landlords.

Landlord's intention In *Cunliffe v Goodman* [1950] 2 KB 237 Asquith LJ said, at p. 253: **91.43**

An 'intention' . . . connotes a state of affairs which the party 'intending' . . . does more than merely contemplate: it connotes a state of affairs which, on the contrary, he decides, so far as in him lies, to bring about, and which, in point of possibility, he has a reasonable prospect of being able to bring about, by his own act of volition.

A landlord seeking to rely on ground (f)must therefore be able to show more than just a vague desire to demolish and reconstruct the premises. In *Cunliffe v Goodman* Asquith LJ expressed this by saying that the project must have 'moved out of the zone of contemplation — out of the sphere of the tentative, the provisional and the exploratory — into the valley of decision'. Whether or not the landlord has a reasonable prospect of bringing about the desired project will be a question of fact. The majority of such projects will require a variety of steps to be taken: planning, financing, planning permission and the employment of a builder. The landlord does not need to show that everything has been arranged, but there should not be too many obstacles left to resolve before the project can be started (*Gregson v Cyril Lord Ltd* [1963] 1 WLR 41; *Westminster City Council v British Waterways Board* [1985] AC 676). Obviously the more a landlord has organised before the hearing, the better will be the chances of success.

The landlord's intention must be established at the time of the hearing (*Betty's Cafes Ltd v Phillips Furnishing Stores Ltd* [1959] AC 20). If the landlord's notice was served by a predecessor in title, the subsequent landlord can rely upon that notice, and the fact that the original landlord had no intention to reconstruct or demolish the premises when the notice was served does not matter (*Marks v British Waterways Board* [1963] 1 WLR 1008). As long as the landlord can establish an intention to demolish or reconstruct at the date of the hearing, it is irrelevant that the landlord may have some ulterior purpose for wanting possession, for example, to occupy the premises after reconstructing them (*Fisher v Taylors Furnishing Stores Ltd* [1956] 2 QB 78); or to incorporate the premises into an agricultural holding after demolition (*Craddock v Hampshire County Council* [1958] 1 WLR 202). A landlord may be required to give an undertaking to the court to carry out the intended works (*Espresso Coffee Machine Co. Ltd v Guardian Assurance Co. Ltd* [1959] 1 WLR 250).

Section 31(2) applies to this ground. If the landlord can satisfy the court that ground (f) would be satisfied at a future date (this must be a date within one year of the date of termination specified in the landlord's **s. 25** notice or the tenant's request for a new tenancy) then the landlord has a second chance to succeed under this ground (see **91.48**).

Demolition, reconstruction or substantial reconstruction As well as establishing an intention to carry out the proposed works to the holding, the landlord must also establish that these works fall within the definition provided by ground (f). This will be a question of fact and will depend upon the nature and extent of the proposed work. In *Joel v Swaddle* [1957] **91.44**

1 WLR 1094, an intention to convert a small shop with two storage rooms into part of a large amusement arcade was held to be within ground (f). On the other hand, where the intended work involved rewiring, re-roofing, redecorating, installing a central heating system and repositioning a staircase, this was not within the ground (*Barth v Pritchard* [1990] 1 EGLR 109). Likewise, an intention to convert three separate floors into one unit by putting in new staircases did not come within ground (f) (*Percy E. Cadle and Co. Ltd v Jacmarch Properties Ltd* [1957] 1 QB 323). For work to be within ground (f) it is not essential that it should involve the demolition or construction of structural or load-bearing features (*Pumperninks of Piccadilly Ltd v Land Securities plc* [2002] EWCA Civ 621, [2002] Ch 332; *Ivorygrove Ltd v Global Grange Ltd* [2003] EWHC 1409 (Ch), [2003] 1 WLR 2090).

91.45 **Work could not reasonably be done without obtaining possession** The landlord needs to establish a need to terminate the tenancy and gain legal possession of the holding in order to carry out the work. If the landlord is able to enter and perform the works under the terms of the lease (i.e., under a covenant that gives the landlord a right of entry to perform alterations and improvements), the landlord will not be able to succeed under this ground because there is no need to terminate the tenancy (see *Heath v Drown* [1973] AC 496; *Pumperninks of Piccadilly Ltd v Land Securities plc* [2002] EWCA Civ 621, [2002] Ch 332).

Even where, under the terms of the current tenancy, the landlord is able to show that possession of the holding is required to carry out the work, the landlord may still fail to succeed under ground (f). **Section 31A** of the 1954 Act provides that in two situations the court will order the tenant to be granted a new tenancy. The court will not hold that the landlord requires possession if:

(a) the tenant agrees to the inclusion in the terms of the new tenancy of terms giving the landlord access and other facilities for carrying out the work intended and, given that access and those facilities, the landlord could reasonably carry out the work without obtaining possession of the holding and without interfering to a substantial extent or for a substantial time with the use of the holding for the purposes of the business carried on by the tenant; or
(b) the tenant is willing to accept a tenancy of an economically separable part of the holding and either paragraph (a) of this section is satisfied with respect to that part or possession of the remainder of the holding would be reasonably sufficient to enable the landlord to carry out the intended work.

Thus if a tenant is prepared to agree to a new tenancy of the holding on terms permitting the landlord to do the work, or to agree to give up part of the holding and take a tenancy of another part of the holding so that the landlord can perform work on the other part, the tenant will succeed in resisting possession under ground (f). All the same, the intended works must not involve interference with the tenant's use of the holding to a substantial extent or for a substantial time. This means interference with the actual use of the holding, not interference with the tenant's business. Thus a tenant who is prepared to move temporarily to an alternative building while the works are carried out will not necessarily be saved by s. 31A (even though the tenant's business may not be unduly affected) if the interference with the holding is to be substantial (see *Redfern v Reeves* (1979) 37 P & CR 364; *Graysim Holdings Ltd v P and O Property Holdings Ltd* [1996] AC 329).

Ground (g) — Landlord intends to occupy the holding

91.46 (g) . . . that on the termination of the current tenancy the landlord intends to occupy the holding for the purposes, or partly for the purposes, of a business to be carried on by him therein, or as his residence.

Section 30(2) provides that a landlord cannot rely upon ground (g) if the landlord's interest 'was purchased or created after the beginning of the period of five years which ends with the termination of the current tenancy'. In other words, the landlord must have owned the interest for five years. The aim of this provision is to prevent someone from buying the landlord's interest with the intention of terminating the tenancy and going into occupation. Where the landlord's interest has itself changed in nature during the five-year period, the landlord may nevertheless be able to rely on ground (g) (*VCS Car Park Ltd v Regional Railways Ltd* [2001] Ch 121).

As with ground (f), the landlord will have to establish a real, fixed and settled intention. It will be a question of fact. Not only must the landlord have a genuine settled commitment to the project, there must also be a reasonable possibility of carrying it into fruition (*Zarvos v Pradhan* [2003] EWCA Civ 208, [2003] 2 EGLR 37). Where a landlord intended to change the use of the land in question from a street-cleaning depot to a marina, and the council indicated that planning permission for this change of use would be refused, this was regarded as a factor that should be taken into account by the court. Ironically, in this case, the council happened to be the tenant and the court held that the landlord had satisfied ground (g) because the council's ground for refusal of planning permission was invalid and a properly considered planning application would have had a reasonable chance of success (*Westminster City Council v British Waterways Board* [1985] AC 676). The landlord does not have to show that on the balance of probabilities planning permission will be granted, but that there is a real chance that it will be (*Gatwick Parking Services Ltd v Sargent* [2000] 2 EGLR 45).

The landlord does not need to show an intention to occupy the premises personally: occupation through an agent or manager will be enough. In *Parkes v Westminster Roman Catholic Diocese Trustee* (1978) 36 P & CR 22 it was held that the trustee company could occupy through the agency of a parish priest. Where the landlord has a controlling interest in a company (see further **s. 46**), either the landlord or the company may have the requisite intention to satisfy **s. 30(1)(g)** (**s. 30(1A)**). Where the landlord is a company and a person has a controlling interest in the company, either the landlord or the controlling person may have the requisite intention (**s. 30(1B)**), unless the controlling interest was acquired in the last five years (before termination of the tenancy) and the holding has since then been comprised in tenancies subject to part II (**s. 30(2A)**).

Effect of opposition

If, on an application for a new tenancy, the landlord successfully establishes any of the grounds in the **Landlord and Tenant Act 1954, s. 30(1)**, to the satisfaction of the court, the court cannot make an order for the grant of a new tenancy (**s. 31(1)**). However, by the time that the court has heard the matter, the termination date specified in the original s. 25 notice or the tenant's request for a new tenancy may have long passed. The question therefore arises as to when the tenancy should actually come to an end. **91.47**

Section 64(1) of the 1954 Act provides that the tenancy will terminate three months after the date on which the application is finally disposed of. The application will be disposed of only once the court process is at an end. Because the tenant has a right to appeal within four weeks of the court's judgment, this means that the tenancy will continue until three months and four weeks after the court's judgment.

Where ground can be satisfied at a future date

Where a landlord seeks to rely on ground (d), (e) or (f) in the **Landlord and Tenant Act 1954, s. 30(1)** (suitable alternative accommodation, uneconomic sub-tenancy, intention to demolish or reconstruct) but fails to establish the ground to the satisfaction of the court, **s. 31(2)** offers a further chance of obtaining possession. **Section 31(2)** provides that if the court would have been satisfied of any of those grounds: **91.48**

> . . . if the date of termination specified in the landlord's notice or, as the case may be, the date specified in the tenant's request for a new tenancy as the date from which the new tenancy is to begin, had been such later date as the court may determine, being a date not more than one year later than the date so specified, —
>
> (a) the court shall make a declaration to that effect, stating on which of the said grounds the court would have been satisfied as aforesaid and specifying the date determined by the court as aforesaid, but shall not make an order for the grant of a new tenancy;

(b) if, within fourteen days after the making of the declaration, the tenant so requires the court shall make an order substituting the said date for the date specified in the said landlord's notice or tenant's request, and thereupon that notice or request shall have effect accordingly.

Tenant's right to compensation

91.49 Where a landlord opposes the tenant's application for the grant of a new tenancy on grounds (a), (b) or (c) in the **Landlord and Tenant Act 1954, s. 30(1)**, the basis of the opposition is that the tenant has breached some obligation in the lease. In the case of ground (d) there is no loss to the tenant because suitable alternative accommodation is provided in exchange for the original tenancy. Grounds (e), (f), and (g), however, are based not on the default of the tenant but on the needs of the landlord. Under these grounds the tenant may have to give up the tenancy through no fault of his or her own. **Section** 37 of the 1954 Act therefore gives the tenant a right to compensation where the landlord has served notice opposing the grant of a new tenancy on ground (e), (f) or (g) ('the compensation grounds'). **Section 37** will apply where:

(a) the tenant has applied for a new tenancy under **s. 24(1)** and the court has been precluded from making an order granting such a tenancy by reason only of any of the compensation grounds (**s. 37(1A)**);
(b) the landlord has made an application under **s. 29(2)** and the court has been precluded from making an order granting a new tenancy by reason only of any of the compensation grounds (**s. 37(1B)**);
(c) the landlord has specified any of the compensation grounds (and no other grounds) in the **s. 25** notice, or the **s. 26(6)** counter-notice, and either the tenant makes no application for a new tenancy, or such an application is made but subsequently withdrawn (**s. 37(1C)**).

The amount of compensation is calculated by multiplying the rateable value of the holding by the appropriate multiplier. The rateable value for these purposes is the rateable value appearing in the valuation list at the date when the landlord served the **s. 25** notice or the tenant served a request for a new tenancy. The appropriate multiplier is fixed by the Secretary of State.

Longer-standing business tenancies attract a higher rate of compensation by virtue of **s. 37(3)**. Where **s. 37(3)** applies, compensation is calculated by multiplying twice the rateable value by the appropriate multiplier (**s. 37(2)(a)**). **Section 37(3)** will apply if:

(a) during the whole of the 14 years immediately preceding the termination of the current tenancy, premises being or comprised in the holding have been occupied for the purposes of a business carried on by the occupier or for those and other purposes;
(b) during those 14 years there was a change in the occupier of the premises, and the person who was the occupier immediately after the change was the successor to the business carried on by the person who was the occupier immediately before the change.

Currently the appropriate multiplier is one, as prescribed by the Landlord and Tenant Act 1954 (Appropriate Multiplier) Order 1990 (SI 1990/363). Prior to 1 April 1990, when the order came into force, the multiplier was three, and for notices served before 1 April 1990 it remains at three.

A tenant may claim compensation where no new tenancy is granted and it subsequently appears that the court was induced not to grant such a tenancy by misrepresentation or the concealment of material facts (**s. 37A(1)**). Compensation is also available where the tenant has quit the holding, having made no application for a new tenancy, or having withdrawn an application, by reason of misrepresentation or the concealment of material facts (**s. 37A(2)**). Compensation is to be quantified as such sum as appears sufficient to compensate for the damage or loss sustained.

WHERE A NEW TENANCY IS GRANTED

Terms of the new tenancy

On a successful application for a new tenancy, the court will determine the terms of the tenancy only where the parties are unable to come to agreement. This can happen where the landlord has opposed the tenant's application for a new tenancy but has failed to establish any of the grounds, and the court has ordered the grant of a new tenancy. In such a case the court is likely to adjourn to give the parties time to negotiate. If they fail to agree, the matter will have to come back before the court. It can also happen where the landlord does not oppose the grant of a new tenancy but the parties are unable to reach agreement as to the terms of the new tenancy. If the parties are able to agree some terms of the tenancy but not others, the court will resolve the unagreed matters but will not interfere with the other terms. **91.50**

The property

If the parties cannot agree what property should be included in the new tenancy, the court will resolve the matter. Normally the new tenancy will be of the holding. If the parties are unable to agree what constitutes the holding then the court will designate the holding by reference to the circumstances existing at the date of the order (**Landlord and Tenant Act 1954, s. 32(1)**). **91.51**

In two situations the tenancy will not be of the holding:

(a) Where the landlord has opposed the grant of a new tenancy on ground (f) in **s. 30(1)** and by virtue of **s. 31A(1)** the tenant has agreed to accept a tenancy of part of the holding, in which case the court will order the grant of a new tenancy of that part only.

(b) Where by virtue of **s. 32(2)** the landlord requires the new tenancy to be a tenancy of the whole of the property comprised in the current tenancy.

Section 32(2) can be of considerable importance to a landlord where the tenant is not occupying the whole of the premises, for example, where the current tenancy is of a shop with a flat above it and the tenant has sublet the flat. Under the 1954 Act the tenant only has a right to a new tenancy of the holding, namely the shop; but in such a situation the landlord may well have no interest in recovering possession of the flat on its own. In this case the landlord can require that all the property comprised in the current tenancy is included in the new tenancy.

Section 32(3) further provides that where the current tenancy includes rights enjoyed by the tenant in connection with the holding, those rights shall be included in the new tenancy unless the parties agree to the contrary. If the parties cannot agree, the court will determine which rights should be included. For example, in *Re No. 1 Albermarle Street W1* [1959] Ch 531 the tenant had the right to display advertising signs on the outside of the premises under his current tenancy and this right was included in the new tenancy.

Duration of the new tenancy

If the parties to a successful application for a new tenancy are unable to agree the length of the new tenancy, the court will determine its duration. The tenancy should be 'such a tenancy as may be determined by the court to be reasonable in all the circumstances' (**Landlord and Tenant Act 1954, s. 33**). The court therefore has a wide discretion. The new tenancy can be a periodic tenancy or for a fixed term, but if it is a fixed-term tenancy the term must not exceed 15 years (**s. 33**). The duration of the old tenancy will be a factor in determining what the length of the new tenancy should be, as will be the nature of the property and the nature of the tenant's business (see *London and Provincial Millinery Stores Ltd v Barclays Bank Ltd* [1962] 1 WLR 510). The court may also take into account the relative hardship caused to both parties. Where a landlord has been able to establish a bona fide intention to redevelop the property **91.52** but has failed to satisfy **s. 30(1)(f)**, the court may grant the tenant a relatively short term (*Reohorn v Barry Corporation* [1956] 1 WLR 845; or, if applicable, the court may order the inclusion of a break clause in the new tenancy (*McCombie v Grand Junction Co. Ltd* [1962] 1 WLR 581).

Rent

91.53 In the majority of cases the most difficult term to settle by agreement between the parties to a successful application for a new tenancy will be the rent. Where the parties fail to reach agreement, the **Landlord and Tenant Act 1954, s. 34(1)**, provides that the rent payable:

> . . . may be determined by the court to be that at which, having regard to the terms of the tenancy (other than those relating to rent), the holding might reasonably be expected to be let in the open market by a willing lessor.

In assessing the open market rent of a property the court has a wide discretion. In practice, however, the evidence of expert witnesses such as surveyors or valuers will be most persuasive, as will evidence of suitable comparables in the area (see *English Exporters (London) Ltd v Eldonwall Ltd* [1973] Ch 415 per Megarry J at p. 423). Where there are no relevant comparables, the court may look more broadly at the general increases of rent in the area (*National Car Parks v Colebrook Estates Ltd* (1982) 266 EG 810).

The court must also have regard to the terms of the tenancy. If any terms of the tenancy have been altered, this may well have consequences for the amount of rent that should be payable. Thus where the court has also to determine other terms of the tenancy, these other terms should be fixed first before the court considers the rent (*Cardshops Ltd v Davies* [1971] 1 WLR 591). The court should not depart from reality and treat the tenancy as including rights which are not enjoyed. Where a property was landlocked, therefore, that should not be disregarded (*J. Murphy and Sons Ltd v Railtrack plc* [2002] EWCA Civ 679, [2002] 2 EGLR 48).

In assessing the rent the court must disregard certain factors (**s. 34(1)**):

(a) Any effect on rent of the fact that the tenant has or his predecessors in title have been in occupation of the holding. Thus the fact that the tenant is already in occupation of the premises does not permit the landlord to charge a rent higher than the market value because the tenancy is of greater value to the current tenant than to a new tenant. Neither is the tenant able to claim that as a sitting tenant the rent payable should be below the market value.

(b) Any goodwill attached to the holding by reason of the carrying on there of the business of the tenant (whether by the tenant or by a predecessor of the tenant in that business). Thus the fact that a tenant has built up goodwill in the current premises does not enable the landlord to charge a rent above the market value.

(c) Any effect on rent of an improvement. By **s. 34(2)**, the improvement must have been carried out by a person who was at that time the tenant and it must not have been carried out in pursuance of an obligation to the current landlord. The improvement must either have been carried out during the current tenancy, or:

  (i) it was completed not more than 21 years before the application for the new tenancy was made; and

  (ii) the holding or any part of it affected by the improvement has at all times since been comprised in tenancies to which part II of the 1954 Act applies; and

  (iii) at the termination of each of those tenancies the tenant did not quit.

(d) In the case of a holding comprising licensed premises, any addition to its value attributable to the licence, if it appears to the court that having regard to the terms of the current tenancy and any other relevant circumstances the benefit of the licence belongs to the tenant (see **s. 34(2A)** for the extended meaning of 'tenant' here).

By **s. 34(3)**, the court may, if it thinks fit, include a provision varying the rent. The court may therefore require a rent review clause to be included in the new tenancy.

Other terms

91.54 Where the parties to a successful application for a new tenancy cannot reach agreement on the terms of the tenancy other than duration and rent then those other terms 'may be determined by the court; and in determining those terms the court shall have regard to the terms of the current tenancy and to all relevant circumstances' (**Landlord and Tenant Act 1954, s. 35**).

Where one party wishes to introduce terms different to those in the current tenancy, the burden is upon that party to establish reasons for the change; and furthermore the proposed change must be fair and reasonable in all the circumstances (*O'May v City of London Real Property Co. Ltd* [1983] 2 AC 726). Where the original tenancy contained a break clause the court permitted the landlord to include a break clause in the new tenancy (*Leslie and Godwin Investments Ltd v Prudential Assurance Co. Ltd* [1987] 2 EGLR 95). However, where the original tenancy contained an option to purchase a similar option was not included in the new tenancy (*Kirkwood v Johnson* (1979) 38 P & CR 392). This was because the option in the original tenancy could be exercised by the tenant serving notice at least three months before the end of the term; so when the tenant applied to the court for a new tenancy the option no longer existed. For discussion of covenants prohibiting alienation subsequent to the Landlord and Tenant (Covenants) Act 1995, see *Wallis Fashion Group Ltd v CGU Life Assurance Ltd* [2000] 2 EGLR 49.

Carrying out the order for a new tenancy

91.55 Where the court makes an order for a new tenancy, the landlord is bound to execute the new tenancy embodying the terms as agreed between the parties or as determined by the court, and the tenant is bound to accept it (**Landlord and Tenant Act 1954, s. 36(1)**). There are two exceptions to this rule. First, the landlord and tenant are free to agree not to act upon the order. Secondly, the tenant may apply to the court within 14 days of the making of the order for the order to be revoked (**s. 36(2)**). This gives the tenant a last chance to back out of the tenancy if the terms are unacceptable. If the tenant applies to revoke the order under **s. 36(2)**, the current tenancy will come to an end at a date agreed or determined by the court so as to give the landlord a reasonable opportunity for reletting or otherwise disposing of the premises.

Interim rent

91.56 Between the time that the landlord gives a **s. 25** notice, or the tenant requests a new tenancy under **s. 26**, and the granting of the new tenancy there may be a considerable delay. Negotiations can take a considerable time, and if they do not result in agreement there will probably be a delay until a trial date can be obtained. Even once the issue is finally resolved by the court it will be three months before the new tenancy starts (s. 64). Throughout this time, the tenancy will be continued by virtue of **s. 24** on the terms of the original tenancy, including the rent payable by the tenant. This may work to the advantage of either party, where the rent under the current tenancy is no longer a market rent. In a buoyant property market, it has traditionally been the tenant who has benefited, being tempted by the favourable rent under the current tenancy to drag out the renewal process as long as possible and thereby obtain a longer period in occupation at a lower rent.

To prevent this possible abuse of the system, the Law of Property Act 1969 conferred power on the court, on application only by the landlord, to determine an 'interim rent' payable while the tenancy is being continued by virtue of **s. 24** of the 1954 Act. The Regulatory Reform (Business Tenancies) (England and Wales) Order 2003 (SI 2003/3096) has now made significant amendments to the interim rent provisions by inserting new **ss. 24A** to **24D** into the 1954 Act.

Both landlords and tenants may now apply to the court for an interim rent following a **s. 25** notice by the landlord or a **s. 26** request by the tenant (**s. 24A(1)**). No application may be entertained if it is made more than six months after termination of the tenancy (**s. 24A(3)**). The rent determined will be payable from the earliest date of termination that could have been specified in the landlord's **s. 25** notice or the earliest date that could have been specified in the tenant's **s. 26** request (**s. 24B**).

Where the landlord does not oppose renewal, the interim rent is set at the same level as the rent for the new tenancy (i.e., normally the open market rent), subject, however, to adjustment where the terms of the new tenancy or its rent differ substantially from those of the old tenancy (**s. 24C**).

In other circumstances, the interim rent is that which it is reasonable for the tenant to pay while the tenancy continues by virtue of **s. 24** (**s. 24D**). In making the determination the court shall have regard to the rent payable under the terms of the tenancy, but otherwise the court should determine the rent as it would under **s. 34(1)** and (2) as if a new periodic yearly tenancy were to be granted of the whole premises (i.e., not just the holding).

The rent will be determined with regard to the current state of repair of the premises, even where the poor state of repair is due to the breach of a repairing obligation by one of the parties (*Fawke v Viscount Chelsea* [1980] QB 441). The court may determine a differential interim rent, so that if the premises are out of repair due to the landlord's failure to repair the rent will increase when the repairs are carried out (*Fawke v Viscount Chelsea*).

The fact that the court is to have regard to the rent under the current tenancy means that where there is a considerable difference between the current rent and the open market rent that would be determined under **s. 34**, the court can determine the interim rent at a level below the current market rent in order to 'cushion the blow' to the tenant. In *Charles Follet Ltd v Cabtell Investment Co. Ltd* (1986) 55 P & CR 36, the judge assessed the market rent as being £80,000; the current rent was £13,500 and the interim rent was fixed at £40,000. A 50 per cent reduction should, however, be regarded as exceptional. A reduction of 10 per cent is likely to be closer to the norm (see *Janes (Gowns) Ltd v Harlow Development Corporation* (1979) 253 EG 799).

COMPENSATION FOR IMPROVEMENTS UNDER THE LANDLORD AND TENANT ACT 1927

91.57 Part I of the Landlord and Tenant Act 1927 gives a tenant the right to claim compensation for improvements made to the premises when quitting them. This right is limited to authorised improvements: and even if the improvements do fall within the Act, the amount of compensation payable is calculated in a way that is generally favourable to landlords. Furthermore, it is generally quite easy for a landlord to avoid the consequences of the 1927 Act by including an express covenant in the lease requiring the tenant to reinstate the premises at the end of the term.

Is the holding within the Act?

91.58 The provisions of the Landlord and Tenant Act 1927 apply only to holdings where the premises are held under a lease and are used wholly or partly for carrying out upon them any trade or business (s. 17(1)). 'Lease' here includes any under-lease (s. 25). In contrast to the 1954 Act, the carrying out of a profession on the premises does not automatically bring the holding within the protection of the 1927 Act. However, any profession regularly conducted on the premises is included as a 'trade or business' so far as part I of the 1927 Act relates to improvements (s. 17(3)). Another difference between the 1927 and 1954 Acts is that under the 1927 Act, 'trade or business' does not include the business of subletting premises as residential flats (s. 17(3)(b)).

The following premises are excluded from the 1927 Act:

(a) premises let under a mining lease (s. 17(1));
(b) agricultural holdings (s. 17(1));
(c) service tenancies (if the service tenancy was created after 24 March 1927, it will be excluded only if the contract is in writing and sets out the purpose for which it was created) (s. 17(2));
(d) premises used to carry on a profession, where the profession is not regularly carried on on the premises (s. 17(3)(a));
(e) premises which are used for the business of subletting as residential flats (s. 17(3)(b)).

Where the premises are used partly for business purposes, and partly for other purposes, compensation for improvements is available only for improvements made in relation to the business purposes (s. 17(4)).

Is the improvement within the Act?

The tenant of a holding to which the Landlord and Tenant Act 1927 applies may claim compensation from the landlord upon quitting the holding at the end of the tenancy for any improvement on the holding made by the tenant or the tenant's predecessors in title (s. 1). The improvement must add to the letting value of the holding at the end of the tenancy. Improvements do not include a trade or other fixture which the tenant is by law entitled to remove. **91.59**

The following improvements do not attract a right to compensation:

(a) improvements made before the commencement of the 1927 Act (25 March 1928) (s. 2(1)(a));
(b) improvements which were begun before 1 October 1954 (when the 1954 Act came into force) and were made in pursuance of a statutory obligation;
(c) improvements which the tenant or his or her predecessors in title were under an obligation to make in pursuance of a contract entered into for valuable consideration (s. 2(1)(b)).

Procedure

The greatest restriction upon the right to claim compensation is the fact that, in order for the improvement to qualify, the tenant must have observed the correct procedure at the time at which the improvement was made. The right to compensation does not arise automatically simply because the tenant has carried out the improvement. The improvement must be an authorised improvement. If the preconditions have not been fulfilled the tenant will not be able to claim compensation at the end of the tenancy. **91.60**

If a tenant wishes to make an improvement, the first step is to serve a notice of intention upon the landlord. This notice should include a specification and a plan showing the proposed improvement and the part of the existing premises affected. Once a notice of intention has been served the landlord has three months in which to serve a notice of objection. If the landlord does not serve a notice of objection within this time the tenant can go ahead and carry out the improvement, which will be authorised and will attract compensation at the end of the tenancy. It is possible, where a lease requires the tenant to obtain the landlord's consent to an improvement, that the obtaining of consent from the landlord within the terms of the lease will amount to compliance with the statutory procedure.

If the landlord does serve a notice of objection, the tenant must apply to court for a certificate authorising the improvement as a 'proper improvement'. The carrying out of an improvement upon a property will, in the long term, affect not only the tenant's immediate landlord, but also, where there is a chain of landlords, any other person with a superior interest in the property. All superior landlords should therefore be notified and are entitled to be heard.

Where there is a chain of landlords it will be the tenant's immediate landlord who has to pay compensation at the end of the tenant's tenancy, for it is the immediate landlord who will then benefit from the improvement. However, at the end of that landlord's term compensation can be claimed from the next landlord up in the chain for the payment made to the original tenant (Landlord and Tenant Act 1927, s. 8).

Where an application is made to the court, the court must give a certificate if it is satisfied that:

(a) the improvement is of such a nature as to be calculated to add to the letting value of the holding at the end of the tenancy;
(b) the improvement is reasonable and suitable to the character of the holding;
(c) the improvement will not diminish the value of any other property belonging to the landlord or to any superior landlord.

The court may also make any modifications to the proposed plans and specifications that it thinks fit and may impose any conditions it thinks reasonable. In carrying out the improvements the tenant must comply with any requirements imposed by the court.

The landlord can prevent a certificate being granted to the tenant if he or she offers to carry out the improvements himself or herself in consideration of a reasonable increase in the rent. No certificate will be granted unless the landlord fails to carry out the proposed undertaking.

When the claim should be made

91.61 The timing of the claim depends upon the way in which the tenancy comes to an end:

(a) If the tenancy is terminated by a notice to quit or by a notice under the **Landlord and Tenant Act 1954, s. 25**, the claim must be made within three months of the service of the notice.
(b) If the tenancy is terminated by a tenant's request for a new tenancy under s. 26 of the 1954 Act, the claim must be made within three months of the service of the landlord's counter-notice or, if no counter-notice is served, within three months of the last date upon which such a notice could have been served (i.e., two months after the service of the tenant's request).
(c) If the tenancy ends by effluxion of time, the claim must be made between three and six months before the term date.
(d) If the tenancy ends by forfeiture or by re-entry, the claim must be made within three months of the date of the possession order, or, if there is no order, within three months of the date of actual re-entry.

The right to compensation arises only when the tenant quits the holding when the tenancy is terminated. The security of tenure offered by s. 24 of the 1954 Act has therefore reduced the significance of the 1927 Act, because the tenancy will automatically be continued and the tenant will be entitled to remain in occupation. All the same, even if the tenant wishes to apply for a new tenancy, it is still sensible to make a claim under the 1927 Act if the right to do so has arisen: first, because the landlord may successfully object to the granting of a new tenancy by establishing one of the grounds contained in s. 30(1) of the 1954 Act; and, secondly, because even if a new tenancy is granted the tenant will then be able to have the increased value of the property disregarded when the rent is determined for the new tenancy under s. 34 of the 1954 Act.

Amount of compensation

91.62 If the amount of compensation cannot be agreed between the parties it will be determined by the court. The Landlord and Tenant Act 1927, s. 1(1) provides that the amount of compensation shall not exceed:

(a) the net addition to the value of the holding as a whole which may be determined to be the direct result of the improvement; or

(b) the reasonable cost of carrying out the improvement at the termination of the tenancy, subject to a deduction of an amount equal to the cost (if any) of putting the works constituting the improvement into a reasonable state of repair, except so far as such cost is covered by the liability of the tenant under any covenant or agreement as to the repair of the premises.

Section 1(2) provides that in determining the amount under item (a), regard shall be had to the purposes for which it is intended that the premises shall be used after the termination of the tenancy. If it is shown that it is intended to demolish, or to make structural alterations to or to change the user of the premises, regard shall be had to the effect of these acts on the additional value attributable to the improvement, and to the length of time likely to elapse between the end of the tenancy and the demolition, alteration or change of use.

Section 2(3) further provides that compensation should be reduced to take into consideration any benefits which the tenant or the tenant's predecessors in title may have received from the landlord or the landlord's predecessors in title in consideration, expressly or impliedly, of the improvement.

The result of these provisions will often be significantly to reduce the amount of compensation payable. If the landlord intends to demolish the premises, it may mean that no compensation is payable at all. However, if the landlord does not carry out the proposals within the time specified the tenant may apply again to the court to vary the amount of compensation determined.

Form of the claim

The claim must be made as prescribed by **PD 56, paras 5.8 and 5.9**. It must be in writing, be signed by the claimant or by the claimant's solicitor or agent, must specify the holding and the business, state the nature of the claim, the cost and particulars of the improvement, the date it was completed and the amount claimed. **91.63**

The Law Commission found that the compensation procedure is little used (*Compensation for Tenants' Improvements* (Law Com. No. 187) (1989), para. 3.3) and recommended its abolition.

Avoiding the effect of the Landlord and Tenant Act 1927

Landlords can avoid the effect of the Landlord and Tenant Act 1927 by: **91.64**

(a) inserting a covenant obliging the tenant to carry out any improvement to which the landlord agrees;

(b) inserting a covenant obliging the tenant to reinstate the premises at the end of the tenancy;

(c) deciding to demolish or change the use of the property at the end of the tenancy.

Chapter 92 Anti-social Behaviour and Harassment

INTRODUCTION

92.1 This chapter deals with the powers of the civil courts to make orders controlling behaviour which causes distress, nuisance or annoyance. The powers considered in this chapter arise under:

(a) the **Housing Act 1996, part V, chapter III** (92.2 to 92.11);
(b) the Anti-social Behaviour Act 2003, s. 91 (92.12);
(c) the Crime and Disorder Act 1998, ss. 1B and 1D (92.13 to 92.18);
(d) the **Protection from Harassment Act 1997, s. 3** (92.19 to 92.21).

Powers (a), (b) and (c) are exercised in the public interest on the application of bodies exercising public functions. Power (d) is a private law remedy, though it can be used to protect large groups of people.

The legal devices employed are injunctions (power (a)), injunctions enhanced by a power of arrest (powers (a) and (b)) and orders of the civil courts which it is a criminal offence to disobey (powers (c) and (d)). Compliance with an injunction may be enforced by committal (see **chapter** 78). Powers of arrest are used to bring to court people who have breached injunctions so that applications to commit them may be heard. If a power of arrest is not attached to an injunction, it may be possible to obtain a warrant for arrest (powers (a) and (d)).

HOUSING ACT 1996 INJUNCTIONS

Types of injunction

92.2 The **Housing Act 1996, part V, chapter III** (ss. 153A to 158), enables landlords of low-cost housing to protect their residents and staff by obtaining injunctions restraining certain behaviour. The following types of injunction are available:

(a) an anti-social behaviour injunction (s. 153A);
(b) an injunction against unlawful use of premises (s. 153B).

These injunctions may also, if the behaviour complained of meets certain criteria of seriousness, exclude the injuncted person from specified premises or a specified area, even from his or her own home (**s. 153C(1)** and (2); see **92.5**). These injunctions can only be obtained on the application of a 'relevant landlord' (**ss. 153A(2)** and **153B(2)**). This means (by **s. 153E(7)**):

(a) a housing action trust (HAT);
(b) a local authority;
(c) a registered social landlord.

Any injunction may be enforced by committal (see **chapter 78**). In addition, if the behaviour complained of meets the seriousness criteria, the court may add to an injunction under **s. 153A** or **s. 153B** a power of arrest (**s. 153C(1)** and (3); see **92.5** and **92.9**).

Under **s. 153D** an exclusion provision and a power of arrest may also be attached to an injunction against breach of a tenancy agreement with a relevant landlord, provided seriousness criteria are met (see **92.6**).

Sections **153A** to **153E** have been inserted by the Anti-social Behaviour Act 2003. They replace similar provisions in ss. 151 and 152 of the 1996 Act, and it is hoped that the wording of the new provisions avoids some problems encountered with the former provisions. For an extended discussion of these problems see Jonathan Manning, Claire-Louise Manning and Victoria Osler, *Blackstone's Guide to the Anti-social Behaviour Act 2003* (Oxford University Press, 2004). The new provisions came into force on 30 June 2004 in England and 30 September 2004 in Wales.

Anti-social behaviour injunction

By the **Housing Act 1996, s. 153A(1)** and (6), an anti-social behaviour injunction prohibits a person from engaging in conduct: **92.3**

(a) which is capable of causing nuisance or annoyance to any person, and
(b) which directly relates or affects the housing management functions of a relevant landlord.

By **s. 153A(2)** the court may make an anti-social behaviour injunction if:

(a) the person against whom the injunction is sought is engaging, has engaged or threatens to engage in such conduct (**s. 153A(2)** and (3)); and
(b) the conduct is capable of causing nuisance or annoyance to any of the persons listed in **s. 153A(4)**, namely:
    (i) a person with a right (of whatever description) to reside in or occupy housing accommodation owned or managed by the relevant landlord;
    (ii) a person with a right (of whatever description) to reside in or occupy other housing accommodation in the neighbourhood of housing accommodation owned or managed by the relevant landlord;
    (iii) a person engaged in lawful activity in or in the neighbourhood of housing accommodation owned or managed by the relevant landlord;
    (iv) a person employed (whether or not by the relevant landlord) in connection with the exercise of the relevant landlord's housing management functions.

By **s. 153A(5)**, 'It is immaterial where conduct to which this section applies occurs'.

'Housing management functions' include functions conferred by or under any enactment, and the powers and duties of the landlord as the holder of an estate or interest in housing accommodation (**s. 153E(11)**). 'Housing accommodation' includes flats, lodging-houses and hostels (**s. 153E(9)(a)**); and the yards, gardens, outhouses and appurtenances belonging to the accommodation and usually enjoyed with it (**s. 153E(9)(b)**). The 'neighbourhood' of housing accommodation owned or managed by a relevant landlord is said, somewhat circularly, by **s. 153E(9)(c)**, to include the neighbourhood of the whole of the housing accommodation owned or managed by the relevant landlord in the neighbourhood and any common areas used in connection with the accommodation.

Injunction against unlawful use of premises

92.4 Under the **Housing Act 1996, s. 153B**, the court may grant an injunction prohibiting a person from engaging in conduct which consists of or involves using or threatening to use housing accommodation owned or managed by a relevant landlord for an unlawful purpose. The concept of ownership of housing accommodation is explained in **s. 153E(10)**.

Exclusion conditions and power of arrest

92.5 Under the **Housing Act 1996, s. 153C**, the court may add to an anti-social behaviour injunction or an injunction against unlawful use of premises:

(a) a provision prohibiting the person in respect of whom it is granted from entering or being in:
 (i) any premises specified in the injunction;
 (ii) any area specified in the injunction.
(b) a power of arrest.

An exclusion provision may have the effect of excluding a person from his or her normal place of residence (**s. 153E(2)(b)**).

These provisions may be added to an anti-social behaviour injunction or an injunction against unlawful use of premises only if the court thinks that:

(a) the conduct consists of or includes the use or threatened use of violence;
(b) there is a significant risk of harm to a person mentioned in **s. 153A(4)** (see 92.3).

'Harm' includes serious ill-treatment or abuse, whether physical or not (**s. 153E(12)**).

Injunction against breach of a tenancy agreement

92.6 Under the **Housing Act 1996, s. 153D**, exclusion provisions and a power of arrest (see 92.5) can be attached to any injunction granted to a relevant landlord against a tenant in respect of the breach or anticipated breach of a tenancy agreement on the grounds that the tenant:

(a) is engaging or threatening to engage in conduct that is capable of causing nuisance or annoyance to any person, or
(b) is allowing, inciting or encouraging any other person to engage or threaten to engage in such conduct.

'Tenancy agreement' includes any agreement for the occupation of residential accommodation owned or managed by a relevant landlord (**s. 153D(5)**). 'Tenancy' includes a licence (**s. 158(1)**). For the purposes of **s. 153**, 'relevant landlord' is extended by **s. 153E(8)** to include a charitable housing trust (defined in **s. 158(1)**) which is not a registered social landlord.

Exclusion and arrest provisions may be attached under **s. 153D** if the court is satisfied:

(a) that the conduct includes the use or threatened use of violence, or
(b) that there is a significant risk of harm to any person.

Application procedure

92.7 An application under the **Housing Act 1996, ss. 153A to 153E**, for an injunction must be commenced in the court for the district in which the defendant resides or the conduct complained of occurred (**CPR, r. 65.3(2)(b)**). An injunction may be granted by the High Court or a county court (**Housing Act 1996, s. 153E(6)**). An application for an injunction must be made as a **CPR, Part 8**, claim (see **chapter 13**), but using form **N16A**, which is treated as the Part 8 claim form (**r. 65.3(1); PD 65, para. 1**). Form **N16A** must state the terms of the injunction applied for (**CPR, r. 65.3(3)**). Each provision of the injunction to which a power of arrest is attached (see 92.5) must be set out in a separate paragraph (r. 65.4(1) and (2)(a)). An application for an injunction must be supported by affidavit evidence, which, as in all Part 8 claims, must be filed with the claim form (r. 65.3(2)(c)).

An application for an injunction may be made without notice (**Housing Act 1996, s. 153E(4)**), but the affidavit in support must state the reasons why notice has not been given (**CPR, r. 65.3(4)(e)**). If an application is made without notice, the rules on acknowledgment of service (**rr. 8.3** and **8.4**) and exchange of evidence (**r. 8.5(2)** to (6)) do not apply, and it is not possible to make an additional claim or for the defendant to object, under **r. 8.8**, to the use of the Part 8 procedure (**r. 65.3(4)(b)**).

In *Moat Housing Group-South Ltd v Harris* [2005] EWCA Civ 287, [2005] 3 WLR 691, at [72], the Court of Appeal stated the following principles governing the making of orders without notice. An order may be made without notice only if there are exceptional circumstances. An example of an exceptional circumstance is that there is a risk of significant harm to some person or persons attributable to the conduct of the defendant if the order is not made immediately. The order must not be wider than is necessary and proportionate as a means of avoiding the apprehended harm. At [80] the Court of Appeal said that a power of arrest should be attached to a provision of an order made without notice only if the court is satisfied:

(a) that the defendant has used or threatened violence against some person or persons mentioned in s. 153A(4) (see 91.3); *and*
(b) that there is a risk of significant harm to one or more of those persons, attributable to the conduct of the defendant, if the power of arrest is not attached immediately.

If an application is made on notice, the claim form and supporting affidavit must be served on the defendant personally (**r. 65.3(5)**). If an application on notice is listed for hearing before the normal time for acknowledging service would expire, the claim form and affidavit must be served on the defendant not less than two days before the hearing, and the defendant may take part in the hearing despite not filing an acknowledgment of service (**r. 65.3(6)**).

An injunction under the **Housing Act 1996, ss. 153A, 153B** or **153D**, may be granted by a district judge (**PD 2B, para. 8.1(d)**).

Duration and variation of injunctions

An injunction granted under the **Housing Act 1996, ss. 153A** to **153D**, may be made for a **92.8**
specified period or until varied or discharged (**s. 153E(2)(a)**). It may be varied or discharge on the application of the injuncted person or the relevant landlord (**s. 153E(3)**).

Power of arrest

If the court grants an injunction with a power of arrest, the claimant must deliver a copy of **92.9**
provisions to which the power is attached (which must be in separate paragraphs) to any police station for the area where the conduct occurred (**CPR, r. 65.4(1)** and (2)). If the injunction was granted without notice, delivery to a police station cannot be done until the injunction has been served on the defendant (**r. 65.4(3)**).

If a provision of an injunction to which a power of arrest is attached is varied or discharged, the claimant must immediately inform the police station to which it delivered the copy of the provision and deliver a copy of the order which varies or discharges it (**r. 65.4(4)**).

If a constable has reasonable cause for suspecting that a person is in breach of provision of an injunction provision to which a power of arrest has been attached, the constable may arrest that person without warrant (**Housing Act 1996, s. 155(1)**). The person who obtained the injunction must be informed of the arrest forthwith (**s. 155(1)**) and the arrestee must be brought before a judge within 24 hours, excluding a Sunday, Christmas Day and Good Friday (**s. 155(2)**). The judge before whom the arrestee must be brought is a judge of the High Court, if that court granted the injunction, or otherwise a judge or district judge of a county court (**s. 158(1)**).

Warrant for arrest

92.10 If an injunction was granted which could have had a power of arrest attached under the **Housing Act 1996, s. 153C(3)** or **153D(4)**, but does not contain one, and the authority which applied for the injunction considers that there is a failure to comply with it, that authority may apply under **s. 155(3)** for a warrant to be issued for the arrest of the injuncted person. An application may also be made under **s. 155(3)** where a power of arrest has not been attached to all provisions of an injunction and there is an apparent failure to comply with provisions to which a power of arrest has not been attached.

An application under **s. 155(3)** must be made under **CPR, Part 23**, and may be made without notice (**r. 65.5(1)**). It must be substantiated on oath (**Housing Act 1996, s. 155(4)(a)**), by either affidavit or oral evidence (**CPR, r. 65.5.(2)**) and the judge may not issue a warrant unless there are reasonable grounds for believing there has been a failure to comply with the injunction (**Housing Act 1996, s. 155(4)(b); PD 65, para. 2.1**).

Dealing with arrestee

92.11 Normally the purpose of a hearing to deal with a person who has failed to comply with an injunction is to consider an application for the person to be committed (see **chapter 78**). Where the person has been arrested under a power of arrest attached to an injunction under the **Housing Act 1996, s. 153C** or **s. 153D**, or a warrant issued under **s. 155(3)**, a district judge has power to make a committal order (**CPR, r. 65.6(6)**). The judge before whom such a person is first brought may deal with the matter or adjourn proceedings (**r. 65.6(2)**). If the matter is not dealt with forthwith, the judge may remand the arrestee (**Housing Act 1996, s. 155(2)(b)** and **(5)**), either in custody or on bail, in accordance with sch. 15. The procedure for applying for bail is in **CPR, r. 65.7** and **PD 65, paras 3.1** to **3.3**. There is also a power under the **Housing Act 1996, s. 156**, to remand for a medical report or a report on mental condition (see **PD 65, para. 4.1**).

An arrestee who is released when proceedings are adjourned must be dealt with (whether by the same or another judge) within 28 days of the first court appearance (**CPR, r. 65.6(4)(a)**) and must be given at least two days' notice of the hearing (**r. 65.6(4)(b)**). 'Must' in **r. 65.6(4)(a)** is directory rather than mandatory, as it is provided in **r. 65.6(5)** that failure to meet the 28-day deadline does not invalidate any application notice seeking committal for contempt.

POWER OF ARREST ADDED TO LOCAL AUTHORITY'S INJUNCTION

92.12 If a local authority is a party (by virtue of the Local Government Act 1972, s. 222) to proceedings in which an injunction is sought to prohibit conduct which is capable of causing nuisance or annoyance to a person (the potential victim), the authority may apply to the court to attach a power of arrest to the injunction (Anti-social Behaviour Act 2003, s. 91). (The Local Government Act 1972, s. 222, enables a local authority to bring, defend or appear in proceedings for the promotion or protection of the interests of inhabitants of its area.) By the Anti-social Behaviour Act 2003, s. 91(3), the court may attach a power of arrest if it thinks that either:

(a) the conduct being prohibited consists of or includes the use or threatened use of violence, or

(b) there is a significant risk of harm to the potential victim — harm being defined in s. 91(4) as including serious ill-treatment or abuse (whether physical or not).

An application under this provision may be made in the claim form, the acknowledgment of service, the defence or counterclaim in a Part 7 claim, or an application under **CPR, Part 23** (**r. 65.9(1)**). It must be supported by written evidence (**r. 65.9(2)**). If the application is made on notice, the local authority must serve it, with a copy of the evidence, personally on the person against whom the injunction is sought, not less than two days before the hearing (r. 65.9(3)).

Rule 65.4 (notification of police, see **91.9**) applies to a power of arrest added under the Anti-social Behaviour Act 2003, s. 91(3) (**CPR, r. 65.10(1)(a)**). When a person arrested under such a power is first brought before a judge, that judge may deal with the matter or adjourn proceedings (**r. 65.6(2)** applied by **r. 65.10(1)(b)**). Paragraphs (4) and (5) of **r. 65.6** (time limit on dealing with arrestee who is released, see **91.11**) apply (**r. 65.10(1)(b)**). Unlike the position in proceedings on a warrant issued under the **Housing Act 1996, s. 155(3)** (see **92.11**), there is no provision for remand, and a district judge does not have power to commit.

ANTI-SOCIAL BEHAVIOUR ORDERS

ASBOs

Provisions for courts to make anti-social behaviour orders (ASBOs) are in the Crime and Disorder Act 1998. Under s. 1(1) the conditions for making an ASBO against a person aged 10 or over are that: **92.13**

(a) the person has acted in an anti-social manner, that is, 'in a manner that has caused or was likely to cause harassment, alarm or distress to one or more persons not of the same household as himself' (s. 1(1)(a)); and
(b) it is necessary to protect relevant persons (defined in s. 1(1B)) from further anti-social acts by the person (s. 1(1)(b)).

Contravention of an ASBO is a criminal offence (s. 1(10)).

The general idea is that ASBOs are made on the application of a local authority, police force, registered social landlord or housing action trust (the 'relevant authorities' listed in s. 1(1A)), after consultation with each other under s. 1E, for the protection of persons in the local area (the 'relevant persons' listed in s. 1(1B)). ASBOs are made principally by magistrates' courts, but provisions which were inserted into the 1998 Act by the Police Reform Act 2002 (which generally revised the ASBO system) enable ASBOs to be made against parties to county court proceedings (see **92.14**): it is envisaged that these will generally be housing claims.

ASBOs incidental to county court proceedings

A county court may make an ASBO against a party to proceedings before it, under the Crime and Disorder Act 1998, s. 1B(4). An order may not be made unless it is proved that the conditions mentioned in s. 1(1) (see **92.13**) are satisfied (s. 1B(4)). An ASBO under s. 1B(4) prohibits a person from doing anything described in the order. The prohibitions which may be imposed are those necessary for the purpose of protecting persons from further anti-social acts by the person against whom the order is made (s. 1(6) applied by s. 1B(7)). The persons to be protected may be the relevant persons (s. 1(1B)) in the local area or persons elsewhere in England and Wales (s. 1(6)). **92.14**

An ASBO must be for a specified period of at least two years or until further notice (s. 1(7) applied by s. 1B(7)). Contravention of an ASBO is a criminal offence (s. 1(10) applied by s. 1B(7)).

A court making an ASBO in respect of a person under the age of 16 must, by s. 9(1B), make a parenting order in respect of that person's parent or guardian if it is satisfied that the relevant condition (in s. 8(6)) is fulfilled. If it is not satisfied that the relevant condition is fulfilled, it must state in open court that it is not and why it is not. The court must obtain and consider information about the person's family circumstances and the likely effect of the order on those circumstances (s. 9(2)). In respect of a young person aged 16 or 17 the court may make a parenting order if satisfied that the relevant condition is fulfilled (s. 8(1)(b) and (2)).

An ASBO under s. 1B(4) may only be made if applied for by a 'relevant authority', which is party to the proceedings: a relevant authority may apply to be joined to enable it to apply for an ASBO (s. 1B(2) and (3)). The relevant authorities are listed in s. 1(1A) and are local authorities, chief officers of police (including the Transport Police), registered social landlords and housing action trusts (HATs).

A relevant authority may apply for an ASBO to be made against a party to county court proceedings (or apply to be joined to proceedings so as to apply for an ASBO) only if it considers that it would be reasonable for it to make an application against that person in the magistrates' court (s. 1B(2) and (3)).

If a relevant authority is already a party to county court proceedings, it may apply for a person to be joined to those proceedings to enable an ASBO to be made against him or her (s. 1B(3A) and (3B)). It must consider that the person has acted in an anti-social manner (s. 1B(3A)(a)), as defined in s. 1(1)(a) (see **92.13**). A person may not be joined to proceedings under s. 1B(3B) unless his or her anti-social acts are material in relation to those proceedings (s. 1B(3C)). No person under 18 may be joined (Anti-social Behaviour Act 2003 (Commencement No. 2) Order 2004 (SI 2004/690), art. 2(b)(ii); **PD 65, para. 13.2**), except under a pilot scheme which is running until 30 September 2006 in the county courts listed in **PD 65, para. 13.3** (Anti-social Behaviour Act 2003 (Commencement No. 4) Order 2004 (SI 2004/2168), art. 4).

Procedure

92.15 Any application for an ASBO to be made under the Crime and Disorder Act 1998, s. 1B(4), must be accompanied by written evidence, which must include evidence that s. 1E (consultation among relevant authorities) has been complied with (**CPR, r. 65.25**). It should be made as soon as possible after the relevant authority becomes aware of the circumstances which lead it to apply for an ASBO (**rr. 65.22(2)**, **65.23(1)(c)** and **65.24(2)(a)**). The application must normally be on notice to the person against whom the ASBO is sought (**rr. 65.22(3)**, **65.23(3)** and **65.24(2)(b)**).

If a relevant authority wishes to apply as a party to county court proceedings for an ASBO to be made under the Crime and Disorder Act 1998, s. 1B(4), against another party, it should make the application in its claim form or, if it is a defendant, in an application notice filed with the defence (**CPR, r. 65.22(1)**). If the relevant authority only becomes aware at a later stage of the need for an ASBO, it must apply for one as soon as possible by application notice (**r. 65.22(2)**).

An application to join a person to county court proceedings so that an ASBO may be made under the Crime and Disorder Act 1998, s. 1B(4), is an application for addition of a party and must be made under **CPR, Part 19, Section I** (see **14.3** to **14.14**) (**r. 65.23(1)(a)**). It should be made in the same application notice as the application for the ASBO (**r. 65.23(1)(b)**). It must contain the authority's reasons for claiming the anti-social acts are material in relation to the proceedings, and details of the anti-social acts alleged (**r. 65.23(2)**).

An application to be joined to county court proceedings so as to apply for an ASBO to be made against one of the existing parties is also an application for addition of a party and so must be made under **CPR, Part 19, Section I** (see **14.3** to **14.14**) (**r. 65.24(1)(a)**). It should be made in the same application notice as the application for the ASBO (**r. 65.24(1)(b)**).

Interim orders

92.16 On an application for an ASBO to be made under the Crime and Disorder Act 1998, s. 1B(4) (see **92.15**), the court may, if it considers it just to do so, make an interim ASBO under s. 1D before determining the main application. An interim order must be for a fixed period (which may be extended) and will automatically cease to have effect on the determination of the main application (s. 1D(4)).

Contravention of an interim order is a criminal offence (s. 1(10) applied by s. 1D(5)).

An application for an interim ASBO is an application for an interim remedy, which must be made in accordance with **CPR, Part 25** (see **chapter 32**) (**r. 65.26(1)**). An application for an interim ASBO should normally be made in the claim form or application notice seeking the final ASBO, and on notice to the person against whom the order is sought (**r. 65.26(2)**).

Service

An ASBO made under the Crime and Disorder Act 1998, s. 1B(4), or an interim order made under s. 1D, must be served personally on the person subject to the order (**PD 65, para. 13.1**). **92.17**

Variation and discharge

A person against whom an ASBO has been made under the Crime and Disorder Act 1998, s. 1B(4), and the authority which applied for the order, may apply to the county court which made the order for it to be varied or discharged (s. 1B(5)). However, unless both those persons consent, an ASBO cannot be discharged less than two years after it is served (s. 1B(6)). **92.18**

A person against whom an interim order has been made under s. 1D, and the authority which applied for the order, may apply to the court which made the order for it to be varied or discharged (s. 1(8) applied by s. 1D(5)). Section 1(8) (which is drafted to apply to magistrates' courts) specifies that such an application is to be by complaint.

PROTECTION FROM HARASSMENT ACT 1997

The **Protection from Harassment Act 1997** prohibits a person knowingly pursuing a course of conduct which amounts to harassment of another (s. 1(1)) and provides both criminal (**ss. 2 and 5**) and civil (**s. 3**) sanctions. The definition of harassment is considered in more detail in **92.20**. Civil proceedings are considered in **92.21** to **92.23**. **92.19**

Definition and prohibition of conduct amounting to harassment

The **Protection from Harassment Act 1997, s. 1(1)**, provides that a person must not pursue a course of conduct which amounts to harassment of another and which he or she knows or ought to know amounts to harassment of the other. By **s. 1(2)**, a person ought to know that conduct amounts to harassment if a reasonable person in possession of the same information would think that the course of conduct amounted to harassment. Whether or not an individual has contravened this prohibition is determined objectively by considering whether a reasonable person would think that what the individual did amounted to harassment (*R v Colohan* [2001] 2 FLR 757). In civil proceedings the standard of proof of contravention of **s. 1(1)** is the civil standard on the balance of probabilities (*Hipgrave v Jones* [2004] EWHC 2901 (QB), [2005] 2 FLR 174). **92.20**

It appears that the definition of harassment has been left deliberately imprecise. The interpretation section (s. 7(2)) defines harassing a person as including 'alarming the person or causing the person distress', but Lord Phillips of Worth Matravers MR said in *Thomas v News Group Newspapers Ltd* [2001] EWCA Civ 1233, [2002] EMLR 4, at [29]–[30]:

> There are many actions that foreseeably alarm or cause a person distress that could not possibly be described as harassment. It seems to me that s. 7 is dealing with that element of the offence which is constituted by the effect of the conduct rather than with the types of conduct that produce that effect. . . .

'Harassment' is . . . a word which has a meaning which is generally understood. It describes conduct targeted at an individual which is calculated to produce the consequences described in s. 7 and which is oppressive and unreasonable.

It is not necessary to prove an intention to alarm or distress: it is sufficient that the conduct is liable to produce those consequences (*Banks v Ablex Ltd* [2005] EWCA Civ 173, [2005] IRLR 357).

By s. 7(4) 'conduct' includes speech, which seems common sense given the nature of the distress which the 1997 Act is intended to relieve.

The prohibition is of a 'course' of conduct, which, by s. 7(3), must involve conduct on at least two occasions. 'The requirement of a course of conduct shows that Parliament was conscious that it might not be in the public interest to allow the law to be set in motion for one boorish incident' (Lord Hoffmann in *Wainwright v Home Office* [2003] UKHL 53, [2004] 2 AC 406, at [46]). The same person must be the victim on each occasion when harassment is alleged to have occurred (*Banks v Ablex Ltd*).

Two separate incidents may amount to a course of conduct, if they are shown to be motivated by a common purpose of harassment (compare *Baron v Crown Prosecution Service* (2000) LTL 13/6/2000, in which two letters, clearly intended as harassment, amounted to a course of conduct, with *Lau v Director of Public Prosecutions* [2000] 1 FLR 799, in which no connection was proved between two incidents six months apart). In *Pratt v Director of Public Prosecutions* (2001) *The Times*, 22 August 2001, the Administrative Court emphasised that the fewer and wider spread the incidents put in evidence, the less likely they would be found to constitute a course of conduct (see also *R v Nitin Patel* [2004] EWCA Crim 3284, [2005] 1 Cr App R 27). A gift of a plant, sending a letter and redirecting a misdirected package could not themselves amount to harassment, but when combined with secretly filming the victim and going through her rubbish, they could (*King v Director of Public Prosecutions* (2000), *The Independent*, 31 July 2000).

Newspaper articles likely to incite racial hatred of an individual may be harassment of that individual (*Thomas v News Group Newspapers Ltd* [2001] EWCA Civ 1233, [2002] EMLR 4). Damage to the claimants' shop windows, obstructing their customers and sending offensive letters and materials constituted harassment in *Silverton v Gravett* (2001) LTL 31/10/2001.

Section 1 does not apply if the person who pursued what would otherwise have been a course of conduct amounting to harassing, shows that it was pursued for the purpose of preventing or detecting crime, or under any enactment or rule of law, or duty imposed by an enactment, or that in the particular circumstances the pursuit of the course of conduct was reasonable. The onus of proof is clearly intended to be on the person accused of the acts, and must, of course, be on the balance of probabilities, for civil purposes (s. 1(3)). It is suggested that the number of instances in which prevention or detection of crime, or statutory authority, could be used as an excuse will (or should) be extremely limited.

Section 1 also does not apply to any act, by a specified person, which is certified by the Secretary of State to have been related to national security, the economic well-being of the United Kingdom, or the prevention or detection of serious crime (s. 12).

Civil proceedings

92.21 **Section 3(1) of the Protection from Harassment Act 1997** provides that an actual or apprehended breach of **s. 1** may be the subject of a claim in civil proceedings by the victim or potential victim. On such a claim, damages may be awarded for (among other things) any anxiety and/or any financial loss caused by the harassment (**s. 3(2)**).

A corporation cannot make a claim under **s. 3** (*Daiichi Pharmaceuticals UK Ltd v Stop Huntingdon Animal Cruelty* [2003] EWHC 2337 (QB), [2004] 1 WLR 1503).

A claim under **s. 3** must use the **CPR, Part 8**, procedure (see **chapter 13**) (**r. 65.28(a)**). In the

High Court it must be commenced in the Queen's Bench Division; otherwise it must be commenced in the county court for the district in which the defendant resides or carries on business, or the court for the district in which the claimant resides or carries on business (r. 65.28(b)).

A civil claim for breach or apprehended breach of the **Protection from Harassment Act 1997, s. 1**, may ask for an injunction to restrain future breach. In a county court an injunction may be granted by a district judge (**PD 2B, para. 8.1(d)**). Contravention of such an injunction without reasonable excuse is a criminal offence (**s. 3(6)** and (9)). Alternatively, breach of an injunction can be punished by committal (see **chapter 78**) and **s. 3** provides for a warrant for arrest to be issued to bring a person who breaches such an injunction to court to consider an application for committal (see **92.22**). Committal for contempt and criminal proceedings are mutually exclusive alternatives (**s. 3(7)** and (8)).

An injunction may create an exclusion zone if that is reasonably necessary for the protection of the claimant's legitimate interests (*Burris v Azadani* [1995] 1 WLR 1372).

If claimant and defendant are within the jurisdiction, an injunction may be granted to restrain harassment of the claimant when abroad (*Potter v Price* [2004] EWHC 781 (QB), LTL 28/7/2004).

Warrant for arrest

Where the court grants an injunction for the purpose of restraining the defendant from pursuing any conduct which amounts to harassment, and the claimant considers that the defendant is in breach, the claimant may apply for a warrant for the defendant's arrest (**Protection from Harassment Act 1997, s. 3(3)**). Such application may be to a High Court judge if the injunction was granted by that court (**s. 3(4)(a)**), or to a judge or district judge of the issuing, or any other, county court (**s. 3(4)(b)**). Such a warrant can only be issued if the application is substantiated on oath (i.e., it must be supported by an affidavit or sworn testimony), and the judge or district judge has reasonable grounds for believing that there may have been a breach of the injunction (**s. 3(5)(a) and (b)**). **92.22**

Dealing with arrestee

Where a person is arrested in execution of a warrant issued under the **Protection from Harassment Act 1997, s. 3(3)**, the judge before whom the person is first brought may deal with the matter or adjourn proceedings (**CPR, r. 65.30(1)**). An arrestee who is released when proceedings are adjourned must be dealt with (whether by the same or another judge) within 28 days of the first court appearance (**r. 65.30(2)(a)**) and must be given at least two days' notice of the hearing (**r. 65.30(2)(b)**). Unlike the position in proceedings on a warrant issued under the **Housing Act 1996, s. 155(3)** (see **92.11**), there is no provision that failure to meet the 28-day deadline does not invalidate any application notice seeking committal for contempt, there is no provision for remand, and a district judge does not have power to commit. **92.23**

Conviction for the offence of doing something prohibited by an anti-harassment injunction precludes punishment of the same act as a civil contempt of court (**Protection from Harassment Act 1997, s. 3(7)**). Conversely, a person cannot be criminally convicted for conduct which has been punished as contempt of court (**s. 3(8)**).

Chapter 93 Sale of Goods

INTRODUCTION

93.1 Most United Kingdom contracts for the sale of goods are governed by the **Sale of Goods Act 1979** (SoGA 1979). A sale of goods contract is one by which the seller transfers or agrees to transfer the property in goods to the buyer for a money consideration called the price (**SoGA 1979, s. 2(1)**). This covers the usual situation where goods are sold and where ownership of the goods is simultaneously transferred to the buyer. The related situation where the transfer of the property in the goods is to take place at a future date, or subject to some condition (such as payment of the price at some time in the future), is called an agreement to sell (**SoGA 1979, s. 2(4)**). Transactions which do not transfer property are not sales of goods.

If a contract is categorised as a sale of goods contract, it will be governed by the general law of contract as modified by the provisions of the SoGA 1979. The modifications made by the Act are in fact wide ranging, covering most aspects of the transaction. The Act lays down general rules governing matters such as the obligations to deliver the goods and pay for them, when property and risk passes from the seller to the buyer, implied terms as to quality and fitness for purpose, and remedies for breach. Many of the general rules set out in the Act are subject to the express or implied intention of the parties, although there are restrictions on contracting out of some provisions.

Major changes have taken place in relation to consumer sales. The Sale of Goods Act 1979 has been amended as from 31 March 2003 to give wide new rights to consumers. New provisions about consumer guarantees have been brought into force. Various provisions of the Enterprise Act 2002 came into force on 20 June 2003 giving wide powers to enforce consumer rights, particularly a new category of 'super-complaint' which permits designated bodies to give notice to the Office of Fair Trading (OFT) of an area of concern and allows the OFT only 90 days in which to publish a response on how the problem will be addressed. There have already been three super-complaints. The power under the Stop Now (EC Directive) Orders Regulations 2001 (SI 2001/1422) has been repealed and replaced by similar powers under the Enterprise Act 2002, part 8. The Law Commission and the Scottish Law Commission have proposed the replacement of the **Unfair Contract Terms Act 1977** and the **Unfair Terms in Consumer Contracts Regulations 1999 (SI 1999/2083)** with a single Act written in plain English (*Unfair Terms in Contracts* (Consultation Paper No. 166) (London: TSO, 2002)).

GENERAL RULES AND DEFINITIONS

Sale of goods or supply of services

In some cases it is difficult to decide whether what is being provided is goods or a service. The distinction is essentially that in a contract for the sale of goods the principal consideration provided by the seller is the transfer of ownership of the goods, whereas in a contract for the supply of services, which could include supplying goods, the principal consideration provided by the supplier is the work done in providing the service, rather than the value of any goods supplied in the course of providing the service. For example, in a building contract the main consideration provided by the builder is usually the value of the work done, rather than the value of the bricks, cement, plaster, wood, nails and other materials supplied. Such a contract is therefore one for the supply of services, but with the incidental supply of goods. It is not a contract for the sale of goods within the meaning of the SoGA 1979. The supply of services aspect of the building contract would, however, be subject to the provisions of the **Supply of Goods and Services Act 1982** (SoGSA 1982), part II (see **94.6**), and the materials supplied under the contract would be subject to the provisions of the SoGSA 1982, part I (see **94.4**). **93.2**

In deciding whether the contract is for the sale of goods or for services, the main tests to be applied can be summarised as follows:

(a) if there is a sale of goods which are later to be fixed to chattels or land as a subsidiary obligation, the contract will be for the sale of goods;
(b) if there is an agreement to fix goods to land or to another chattel to which the sale of the goods is a subsidiary obligation, the contract will be for supply of services;
(c) if the principal obligation is the supply of goods with any work to them being incidental, then the contract will be for sale of goods; and
(d) if the customer supplies materials which are to be worked on (with or without other materials) by the supplier, the contract will be for the supply of services.

The distinction is no longer as important as it once was, as the statutory implied terms about the quality of goods are very similar to those for the quality of services. There are some differences. For example, the property in goods sold under the SoGA 1979 generally passes, in the absence of a term dealing with the matter, in accordance with the rules in **SoGA 1979, s. 18** (see **93.13**). Property often passes in accordance with these rules when the contract for the sale of goods is made. Different considerations apply in contracts for the supply of goods and services, and property in goods supplied may not pass until they are fixed (such as to the land of the customer) or even until the completion of the work of installation (see *Seath v Moore* (1886) 1 App Cas 350 per Lord Watson at p. 381). Another example is the effect of the buyer defaulting at some time after having paid a sum on account. In a contract for the sale of goods, such a sum will usually be recoverable by the defaulting buyer, subject to a set-off by the seller for damages for the buyer's default. In a contract for the supply of goods and services, such an advance may not be recoverable at all by the defaulting buyer (see *Hyundai Heavy Industries Co. Ltd v Papadopolos* [1980] 1 WLR 1129).

Sales distinguished from other contracts

93.3 The concept of 'bailment' covers a number of situations. It includes situations where the owner of goods (the 'bailor') delivers them to another who looks after them for the bailor; where the bailor loans goods to the bailee, either gratuitously or for hire; where the bailor pledges goods by delivering them to another as security for money borrowed by the bailor; where the bailor delivers goods to a carrier for the purpose of having the goods transported somewhere; and where the bailor delivers goods to a tradesman for something to be done to the goods (often repairs or improvements). Bailments are obviously not sales of goods. Even bailments with an option to purchase (such as hire purchase agreements) are not sales of goods (*Helby v Matthews* [1895] AC 471). This is because the hirer under such an agreement has not 'bought or agreed to buy' the goods within the meaning of the **SoGA 1979, s. 25(1)**.

If the contract is intended to operate by way of mortgage, charge, pledge or other security it is not a sale of goods (SoGA 1979, s. 62(4)). A pledge can exist at common law and under the **Consumer Credit Act 1974**, and is an actual or constructive delivery and bailment of the goods by the debtor to the creditor to be kept until the debt has been discharged. Property in the goods does not pass, but the pledgee has a right to sell the goods.

A common form of transaction is a 'sale and lease back' where the owner sells the goods to a finance company and then leases those same goods back. A genuine transaction will be upheld as a sale of the goods rather than a charge over them, the test being the true intention of the parties rather than the legal form (*North Central Wagon Finance Co. v Brailsford* [1962] 1 WLR 1288).

Definition of 'goods'

93.4 The definition of 'goods' appears in **SoGA 1979, s. 61(1)**, and includes all personal chattels other than things in action and money. Things in action are rights to procure the payment of money through court proceedings, such as rights on bills of exchange or on insurance policies. The main definition means that although computer disks, being physical objects, are 'goods', a software programme is not (*St Albans City and District Council v International Computers Ltd* [1996] 4 All ER 481).

Goods may be classified as existing goods or future goods (**SoGA 1979, s. 5(1)**). 'Existing goods' are those already owned or possessed by the seller. 'Future goods' are goods to be manufactured or acquired by the seller after making the contract.

The SoGA 1979 also divides goods into specific goods and unascertained goods. 'Specific goods' are defined as goods identified and agreed on at the time a contract of sale is made and includes an undivided share of goods identified and agreed on (**SoGA 1979, s. 61(1)**). Most everyday sale of goods contracts involve specific existing goods as the buyer selects the product on display which he or she wishes to buy. The definition of specific goods is wide enough to also include identified goods not owned by the seller at the time of the contract but which the seller intends to acquire in order to transfer them to the buyer, and even to a contract for the sale of potatoes to be grown in a particular field (see *Howell v Coupland* (1876) 1 QBD 258). The term 'unascertained goods' is not defined, but means all goods which are not specific goods.

Money consideration

93.5 There must be a money consideration for a contract for the sale of goods. A gift is not provided for money consideration. Promotional gifts are unlikely to give rise to a sale of goods as the consideration is usually the purchase of other goods and not money (*Esso Petroleum Co. Ltd v Customs and Excise Commissioners* [1976] 1 WLR 1). A simple exchange of goods or barter is not a sale of goods. A common difficulty exists when goods (usually motor vehicles) are part exchanged. The court has to decide whether there is an exchange of goods (with or without some balancing payment) or whether there are there two separate, back-to-back, sale of goods transactions with only any credit balance being paid in money. The test is: what is the contractual intention? Each case will turn on its own facts: compare *G. J. Dawson (Clapham) Ltd v H. and G. Dutfield* [1936] 2 All ER 232 and *Forthright Finance Ltd v Ingate* [1997] 4 All ER 99.

Formation of the contract

There must be a binding consensual contract between the buyer and the seller. That is determined applying the usual rules of contract law. Since the abolition in 1954 of the requirement for writing in contracts for the sale of goods over £10, there have been no formalities for a sale of goods contract (see now **SoGA 1979, s. 4**). Capacity to enter into the contract is governed by the general law. A reasonable price must be paid for necessaries sold and delivered to children, or to persons who are incompetent by reason of mental incapacity or drunkenness (**SoGA 1979, s. 3(2)**). **93.6**

Between parties of full capacity, there will be no contract unless the essential terms are agreed (*May and Butcher v R* [1934] 2 KB 17n). This does not preclude there being a valid and binding contract for the sale of goods where no price is agreed for the goods. The price may be fixed in a manner agreed between the parties or may be determined by a course of dealing between the parties (**SoGA 1979, s. 8(1)**). Alternatively, the price may be left unstated and not capable of being determined in accordance with s. 8(1), in which event a reasonable price is payable (s. 8(2)). Finally, s. 9 provides for the unusual cases where the price for the goods is to be fixed by a third party identified in the contract. If the third party does not make the valuation, the contract is avoided, but if any of the goods have been delivered the buyer must pay a reasonable price for them.

MAIN OBLIGATIONS IN A CONTRACT FOR THE SALE OF GOODS

Under a contract for the sale of goods, the seller agrees to transfer ownership in goods to the buyer, and the buyer agrees to accept them and pay the agreed price. The buyer will want to be able to make use of the goods (either personally or by way of resale), and an important question is that of the contractual responsibility for delivering the goods. A related question is the determination of when risk passes to the buyer, which is important if the goods are lost in transit or otherwise before they are received by the buyer. These various matters are discussed at **93.8** to **93.16**. **93.7**

Delivery

The seller's primary obligation is to deliver the goods to the buyer in accordance with the terms of the contract (**SoGA 1979, s. 27(1)**). The contract should define (expressly or by implication) the place where the goods should be delivered. This may be the seller's place of business, or those of the buyer, or some other place (such as a construction site where the goods are to be used, or the place of business of a carrier or a ship to be used to transport the goods to the buyer). The **SoGA 1979, s. 61(1)** defines 'delivery' as the voluntary transfer of possession from one person to another. Often this is done by the seller handing the goods to the buyer, or the buyer selecting them from the stock of the seller, and paying for them. There are more difficult situations. 'Possession', which is a key concept in the definition of delivery, is not defined in the SoGA 1979, and is notoriously difficult to define. A seller may transfer possession, for example, by giving the buyer the means of access to goods, such as by handing over the keys to the warehouse where they are stored (see *Hilton v Tucker* (1888) 39 ChD 669). There are four further common situations that should be noted: **93.8**

(a) Where the goods are in the possession of a third person (such as a warehouseman), delivery takes place when that third person acknowledges to the buyer that the goods are held on behalf of the buyer (**SoGA 1979, s. 29**(4)). This is known as 'attorning'.
(b) A seller can deliver goods for the purposes of a contract for the sale of goods by delivering to the buyer a document of title to the goods. Delivery takes place on delivery of a document of title even if the goods are in the possession of a third person and even if the third person has not attorned to the buyer. This method of delivery is very common in international sales. Documents of title are defined in the Factors Act 1889, s. 1(4), as being any bill of lading, dock warrant, warehouse keeper's certificate, a warrant or order for the delivery of goods, and any other document used in the ordinary course of business as proof of possession or control of goods. Delivery orders, warehouse keepers' receipts and warrants for goods are not, or not always, regarded as documents of title.
(c) Delivery of goods to a carrier for transmission to the buyer is prima facie deemed to be delivery to the buyer (**SoGA 1979, s. 32**(1)).
(d) In a sale and lease-back transaction, the seller makes constructive delivery of the goods to the buyer, which then leases the goods back to the seller, even though the goods never leave the seller's possession (*Michael Gerson (Leasing) Ltd v Wilkinson* [2001] QB 514).

The definition of 'delivery' was extended as from 18 September 1995 by amendments made by the Sale of Goods (Amendment) Act 1995 (SoG(Am)A 1995), s. 2, so that delivery, in relation to sales from a bulk under SoGA 1979, ss. 20A and 20B, includes such appropriation of goods to the contract as results in property in the goods being transferred to the buyer. Sections 20A and 20B are considered at **93.14**.

Delivery is to be distinguished from passing title in the goods, as title can pass before delivery, at the time of delivery or after delivery. The obligation to deliver the goods may be separate from the obligation to pay for them, but in the absence of agreement they are concurrent conditions (**SoGA 1979, s. 28**). The **SoGA 1979, s. 29**, sets out the rules for delivery; s. 30 deals with the quantity to be delivered; s. 31 deals with instalments; and s. 33 deals with deliveries to the buyer at a distant place.

What must be delivered

93.9 The delivery must be of the goods contracted for. This means:
(a) in the case of specific goods, delivery must be of the actual goods agreed upon;
(b) in the case of ascertained goods, delivery must be of the goods ascertained;
(c) in the case of unascertained goods, delivery must be of goods corresponding to the description, since the sale will be by description;
(d) in the case of a sale of goods by sample, delivery must be of goods which correspond to the sample; and
(e) in the case of goods where property passes before delivery, delivery must be of the goods the buyer then owns.

Acceptance

93.10 The buyer's duty is to accept the goods and pay for them in accordance with the terms of the contract (**SoGA 1979, s. 27**). Acceptance is deemed to have occurred when it is intimated by the buyer to the seller, or when the goods have been delivered and the buyer does any act in relation to them which is inconsistent with the seller's ownership (s. 35(1)). Once goods are delivered, if the buyer has not previously examined them, acceptance is not deemed to have occurred until the buyer has had a reasonable opportunity of examining them for the purpose of ascertaining whether they are in conformity with the contract (s. 35(2)(a)). Acceptance is also deemed to have occurred when after a lapse of a reasonable time the buyer retains the goods without intimating to the seller that they have been rejected (s. 35(4)). In determining whether the buyer has had the goods for a reasonable time, the court will take into account whether the buyer has had a reasonable opportunity of examining the goods for the purpose of ascertaining whether they conform with the contract (s. 35(5)).

By **SoGA 1979, s. 35(6)**, a buyer is not deemed to have accepted the goods merely because:

(a) the buyer asks for, or agrees to, their repair by or under an arrangement with the seller; or
(b) the goods are delivered to another under a sub-sale or other disposition.

A buyer does not have to act reasonably in deciding whether to reject goods which are in breach of the implied condition as to quality. The question is whether the buyer has lost the right to reject by acceptance. The notorious decision in *Bernstein v Pamson Motors (Golders Green) Ltd* [1987] 2 All ER 220 (right to reject new car lost after 140 miles' use, and less than four weeks' ownership) has now been expressly stated not to survive the 1995 amendments to SoGA 1979 (*Clegg v Olle Andersson* [2003] EWCA Civ 320, [2003] 1 All ER (Comm) 721).

Payment

The obligation upon the buyer is to make payment in accordance with the terms of the contract between the parties (**SoGA 1979, s. 27**). The price will usually be fixed by the contract, but may be ascertained in a manner agreed by the contract or by a course of dealing between the parties (s. 8(1)). Otherwise the buyer must pay a reasonable price, which is a question of fact depending on all the circumstances of the particular case (s. 8(2) and (3)). **Section 28 of the SoGA 1979** provides that unless otherwise agreed, delivery of the goods and payment of the price are concurrent conditions, and the seller must be ready and willing to give possession of the goods to the buyer in exchange for the price and the buyer must be ready and willing to pay the price in exchange for possession of the goods. **93.11**

Place and method of payment

The place of payment may be specified in the contract in which case the payment must be made at that place. Where there is no express provision in the terms of the contract, the intention of the parties may be determined from the surrounding circumstances, or from the method of payment provided for. If the intention of the parties cannot be ascertained then, by **SoGA 1979, ss. 28** and **29(2)**, the obligation seems to be to make payment at the seller's place of business or residence. **93.12**

In default of agreement between the parties, the manner of payment is cash. Payment by post will be at the seller's risk of loss or delay only if payment by that method is expressly or impliedly authorised by the contract. The defence of tender before claim, which is available to the buyer in an action by the seller for the price, depends upon tender having taken place in cash unless the contract otherwise provides or unless the seller has waived the right to demand cash payment. Tender before claim is a CPR glossary term, and now applies to claims for specified amounts and unspecified amounts. The defence of tender before claim must be included in the statement of case (usually the defence), and the defence is only available if the money is paid into court (**CPR, r. 37.3**).

Passing of property

When goods are sold, three things pass to the buyer: property, possession, and risk. Although they are connected, they are distinct concepts. 'Property' is used in the sense of title or ownership, or a proprietary right in the goods. It may be transferred before delivery, at delivery or after delivery (e.g., on payment). If the contract is clear on this aspect, then property passes in accordance with the terms of the contract (**SoGA 1979, s. 17(2)**). If the intention of the parties is not clear then s. 18 contains five rules to be applied to determine when property is to pass. **93.13**

The five rules in **SoGA 1979, s. 18** are as follows (r. 5 is subdivided into four sub-rules, set out at (e) to (h)):

(a) Where there is an unconditional contract for the sale of specific goods in a deliverable state, the property in the goods passes to the buyer when the contract is made, and it is immaterial whether the time of payment or the time of delivery or both be postponed (**SoGA 1979, s. 18, r. 1**). An 'unconditional' contract is not defined in the SoGA 1979, but means that there are no later conditions which must be fulfilled (e.g., payment of the price) before property passes. Goods will be in a 'deliverable state' if they are in such a condition that the buyer would under the contract be bound to take delivery of them (s. 61(5)). Contracts falling within r. 1 are not common as the courts are very ready to infer that property only passes upon payment (*R. V. Ward Ltd v Bignall* [1967] 1 QB 534).

(b) Where there is a contract for the sale of specific goods and the seller is bound to do something to the goods for the purpose of putting them into a deliverable state, the property does not pass until the thing is done and the buyer has had notice that it has been done (s. 18, r. 2). The key event is that the seller has given notice that the goods are now in a deliverable state.

(c) Where there is a contract for the sale of specific goods in a deliverable state, but the seller is bound to weigh, measure, test, or do some other act or thing with reference to the goods for the purpose of ascertaining the price, the property does not pass until the act or thing is done and the buyer has had notice that it has been done (s. 18, r. 3). The obligation to weigh, measure, test or do some other act must be on the seller, and the act must be for the purpose of ascertaining the price of goods already in the deliverable state. As with r. 2, the key event is that notice must be given to the buyer that the step has been taken.

(d) When goods are delivered to the buyer on approval or on sale or return or other similar terms, the property in the goods passes to the buyer:
   (i) when the buyer signifies approval or acceptance to the seller or does any other act adopting the transaction;
   (ii) if the buyer does not signify approval or acceptance to the seller but retains the goods without giving notice of rejection, then, if a time has been fixed for the return of the goods, on the expiration of that time, and, if no time has been fixed, on the expiration of a reasonable time (s. 18, r. 4).

   Sales on approval and transactions involving sale or return are common, and this rule will govern the passing of title if the parties have not reached some other agreement.

(e) Where there is a contract for the sale of unascertained or future goods by description, and goods of that description and in a deliverable state are unconditionally appropriated to the contract, either by the seller with the assent of the buyer or by the buyer with the assent of the seller, the property in the goods passes to the buyer; and the assent may be express or implied, and may be given either before or after the appropriation is made (s. 18, r. 5(1)).

(f) Where, in pursuance of the contract, the seller delivers the goods to the buyer or to a carrier or other bailee or custodier (whether named by the buyer or not) for the purpose of transmission to the buyer, and does not reserve the right of disposal, the seller is to be taken to have unconditionally appropriated the goods to the contract for the purposes of r. 5(1) so that property passes at that time (s. 18, r. 5(2)).

(g) Where there is a contract for the sale of a specified quantity of unascertained goods in a deliverable state forming part of a bulk which is identified either in the contract or by subsequent agreement between the parties, and the bulk is reduced to (or to less than) that quantity, then, if the buyer under that contract is the only buyer to whom the goods are then due out of the bulk:
   (i) the remaining goods are to be taken as appropriated to that contract at the time when the bulk is so reduced; and
   (ii) the property in those goods then passes to the buyer (s. 18, r. 5(3)).

(h) Rule 5(3) also applies where the bulk is reduced to (or to less than) the aggregate of the quantities due to a single buyer under separate contracts relating to that bulk and that buyer is the only buyer to whom goods are then due out of that bulk (s. 18, r. 5(4)).

Rules 5(1) to 5(4) deal with the unconditional appropriation of deliverable goods to the contract by express or implied agreement. 'Appropriation' is not defined in the SoGA 1979, but means an intention to attach the contract irrevocably to those goods so that those goods and no others are the subject of the sale and become the property of the buyer. Sales of goods forming part of a bulk are now governed by ss. 20A and 20B (**93.14**).

Sales of goods held in bulk

A contract may provide for the sale of (say) 100 tonnes of wheat from a cargo of 2,000 tonnes presently on board a named ship. This would be a sale of a specified quantity of unascertained goods forming part of a bulk which is identified in the agreement between the parties. Once the buyer pays the price for some or all of the 100 tonnes subject to the contract, the SoGA 1979, s. 20A, applies (see s. 20A(1)). If the section applies, by s. 20A(2): **93.14**

(a) property in an undivided share in the bulk is transferred to the buyer; and
(b) the buyer becomes an owner in common of the bulk.

The rest of SoGA 1979, s. 20A, deals with calculating the size of the undivided share of the buyer, particularly where the bulk is insufficient for all the purchasers, and with the situation where a buyer has paid only part of the price. When s. 20A applies, the buyer is deemed to consent to other purchasers taking delivery of their shares out of the bulk, and the section does not impose an obligation on a buyer from the bulk to compensate any other buyer for any shortfall in the goods delivered (s. 20B).

Passing of possession

The concept of possession, and some of the situations encountered in sale contracts, were considered at **93.8**. Normally, possession passes on physically handing over the goods to the buyer. **93.15**

Passing of risk

Risk is important in cases where goods are damaged or lost and in deciding who has an insurable interest in goods. Unless otherwise agreed, risk is presumed to pass with property (SoGA 1979, s. 20(1)). Risk may be transferred to the buyer before delivery if, for example, property passes before delivery. **93.16**

Risk in transit is primarily governed by the contract between the parties. In international sales this is usually provided for expressly, or by reference to well-known forms of international sale agreement — such as cif ('carriage, insurance, freight') and fob ('free on board'), etc. terms. Some aspects of risk in transit are dealt with by ss. 32 and 33. If the seller fails to make a reasonable contract with a carrier having regard to the nature of the goods and the other circumstances of the case, the buyer may decline to treat delivery to the carrier as a delivery to the buyer (s. 32(2)). The result would be that goods damaged in transit would be treated as not delivered to the buyer, so the seller would retain ownership of the goods (presumably lost or damaged), and would be liable to the buyer for non-delivery. Unless otherwise agreed, where goods are sent by the seller by sea transport in circumstances where it is usual to insure, the seller must give the buyer sufficient notice to enable the buyer to insure the goods during transit. If the seller fails to give such notice, the goods remain at the risk of the seller during the transit by sea (s. 32(3)).

In relation to consumer contracts important amendments have been made to s. 20 from 31 March 2003. The goods now remain at the seller's risk until they are delivered (s. 20(4)). Where a carrier is used in a consumer contract, delivery to the carrier is not delivery to the consumer (s. 32(4)).

DETAILED CONTRACTUAL TERMS

93.17 As discussed at **93.6**, there are no legal formalities required for a contract for the sale of goods. A great many contracts for the sale of goods are simply entered into orally, or even without any words being exchanged, such as where uncommunicative customers present goods for payment at a cash till, and the sales assistant simply processes the transaction without saying anything. Usually such a contract will be evidenced by writing in the form of the sales receipt produced by the cash till and handed to the customer. In such contracts the main obligations will take place there and then, with the goods having been selected by the customer, and with delivery, acceptance and payment all taking place on the spot. Where the customer pays in cash, the transaction will be a simple sale of goods governed by the SoGA 1979. Beyond the main obligations just mentioned, the Act will also imply such of the statutory terms discussed at **93.29** to **93.35** as are appropriate into the contract. If the transaction is paid for by credit card and the customer is an individual, the shop in fact looks to the credit card company for payment (see **96.2** (c)), and the transaction has **Consumer Credit Act 1974** ramifications (see, generally, **chapter 96**). Where the customer pays by cheque, the contract will be a simple sale of goods, but with a secondary contract based on the cheque. If the cheque is dishonoured, the shop can take advantage of the simple method of obtaining summary judgment on the cheque discussed at **34.35**.

Although it is possible for detailed contractual terms to be agreed orally, it is far more common for people agreeing oral terms to restrict themselves to matters such as the description of the goods, price, and time and place for delivery. There are plenty of other issues that could be included as terms in a contract of sale. These include insurance of the goods until they are delivered; which party bears the loss if the goods are stolen, damaged or destroyed before delivery; the consequences of minor or major defects in the goods; the arrangements for effecting repairs to rectify defects present when the goods are delivered, including where the repairs should take place; liabilities to third parties arising out of the performance of the contract; limitations in the liability of the parties for consequential losses (particularly loss of profits) in the event of breach and other exclusions of liability; the effect of events outside the control of either party; and choice of law and jurisdiction in the event of litigation. These (and other detailed terms) can often be found in contractual documents. Occasionally, detailed terms will be negotiated between the parties, and reduced to writing in a contract specifically drawn up for the purpose. Far more commonly, detailed terms are found in the small print on the reverse of order forms, confirmation of order forms, invoices, delivery documents and other documents used by the parties. Sometimes such standard terms are simply referred to, such as the quotation form which says it is made on 'our standard terms of trading which are available on request'.

The law relating to the incorporation of express terms into contracts is discussed at **93.18** to **93.20**. The consequences of the classification of different types of terms are discussed at **93.21** to **93.28**. The statutory implied terms in sale of goods contracts are discussed at **93.29** to **93.35**. Breach of the main provisions in sale of goods contracts is discussed at **93.37** to **93.44**.

INCORPORATION OF EXPRESS TERMS INTO CONTRACTS

Signed contracts

93.18 If the contract is in writing and has been signed by a party, that party will be bound by those written terms even if he or she has not read them (*L'Estrange v F. Graucob Ltd* [1934] 2 KB 394), or was unable to understand them (*The Luna* [1920] P 22; *Barclays Bank plc v Schwartz* (1995) *The Times*, 3 August 1995). This clear rule is qualified by the following requirements and exceptions:

(a) The party signing must be aware that the document being signed contains or refers to some written terms.
(b) The terms referred to must actually be present or available so that, for example, where documents sent by facsimile refer to terms stated on the back which are not stated or otherwise communicated that gives rise to a cogent inference that the terms were not intended to apply (*Poseidon Freight Forwarding Co. Ltd v Davies Turner Southern Ltd* [1996] CLC 1264);
(c) The party signing must be given reasonably sufficient notice of the exact terms relied upon by the other side — a concept which the courts apply particularly to unusual or onerous terms (see **93.20**).
(d) Where a complete contract already existed rather than mere negotiations between the parties, subsequent signing of a document including new terms will not bind either party unless there is a variation (for which consideration will be required) or a novation.
(e) Terms cannot be relied upon where the contract is void or unenforceable as a result of a mistake.
(f) An exception exists under the doctrine of *non est factum*, which is a rare and special category of mistake which applies only where a party to the contract has been misled into signing a contract without being negligent (*Saunders v Anglia Building Society* [1971] AC 1004).
(g) Terms cannot be relied on where there has been a misrepresentation of the terms or effect of a clause (*Curtis v Chemical Cleaning and Dyeing Co. Ltd* [1951] 1 KB 805).
(h) Terms cannot be relied on where the contract is voidable as a result of duress (*Atlas Express Ltd v Kafco (Importers and Distributors) Ltd* [1989] QB 833). However, not every form of pressure will amount to duress (*CTN Cash and Carry Ltd v Gallagher Ltd* [1994] 4 All ER 714 and *Alf Vaughan and Co. Ltd v Royscot Trust plc* [1999] 1 All ER (Comm) 856).

The fact that a signed written contract exists will not normally prevent there being other express terms of that contract which have not been put into the signed document, provided they are not inconsistent with the written terms. However, many written contracts contain an 'entire agreement' clause which seeks to exclude the existence of other terms. Such clauses are not always wholly effective, see, for example, *Thomas Witter Ltd v TBP Industries Ltd* [1996] 2 All ER 573, where the claimant was allowed to recover damages for misrepresentation in relation to pre-contract negotiations despite an 'entire agreement' clause partly because a term purporting to confine the parties to the written terms of the contract was insufficiently clear to achieve this end, and partly because the clause was ineffective under the **Misrepresentation Act 1967, s. 1** if the representation had become a warranty of the contract. See also *Deepak Fertilisers and Petrochemicals Ltd v Davy McKee (London) Ltd* [1999] 1 All ER (Comm) 69. There could be a collateral contract between the same parties. If the 'entire agreement' clause excludes misrepresentations or implied terms then it will be subject to the statutory rules limiting the effectiveness of such clauses.

Standard terms of trading

In commercial transactions there is often a dispute as to which set of standard terms applies to **93.19**
the contract. This is usually resolved by examining the events chronologically looking for the offer or counter-offer which has actually been accepted (often by performing the contract) which means that the party firing the last shot in the negotiations will usually succeed in showing that the last terms are the basis for the contract (*British Road Services Ltd v Arthur V. Crutchley and Co. Ltd* [1968] 1 WLR 811). However, sometimes the last shot is construed as an acceptance of the previous terms sent by the other side, with the effect that the other side's standard terms apply to the contract (see *Butler Machine Tool Co. Ltd v Ex-Cell-O Corporation (England) Ltd* [1979] 1 WLR 401). It is also noteworthy that a clause purporting to provide that those standard terms shall prevail over the terms of the other party, is ineffective if the other side then respond by sending their standard terms in the usual situation where this is regarded

as the making of a counter-offer (see *Butler Machine Tool Co. Ltd v Ex-Cell-O Corporation (England) Ltd*).

Onerous or unusual terms

93.20 If a contract contains some particularly onerous or unusual terms the court will look with great care to see whether the onerous term has been incorporated into the contract at all. This approach is at variance with the general approach that a party is bound by the terms which that party is aware are in a written agreement, despite not reading them (see **93.18**). This exception is limited to unusual or onerous terms. The most striking description of this rule is to be found in the judgment of Denning LJ in *J. Spurling Ltd v Bradshaw* [1956] 1 WLR 461 at p. 466, where he said, 'Some clauses I have seen would need to be printed in red ink on the face of the document with a red hand pointing to it before the notice could be held to be sufficient'. The importance of this rule has been slightly reduced by the statutory control of exemption clauses. Nevertheless it remains an important way of challenging onerous or unusual express terms of a written contract. It is still being applied today with important consequences for the parties: see, for example, the decisions of the Court of Appeal in *Interfoto Picture Library Ltd v Stiletto Visual Programmes Ltd* [1989] QB 433 and *AEG (UK) Ltd v Logic Resource Ltd* [1996] CLC 265.

CONSEQUENCES OF CLASSIFICATION OF TERMS

Classification of terms

93.21 Contract terms are usually divided into conditions or warranties. Breach of a condition discharges the innocent party from further performance of the contract and damages may be claimed for loss caused by the breach. Breach of a warranty gives the innocent party only a right to claim damages, the measure of damages being defined in the **SoGA 1979, s. 53**.

A term is a condition if it is expressly made such by statute. What is less clear is the effect of a label given to the obligation in the contract itself. It seems that a term need not be a condition merely because it is so described in the contract (*Wickman Machine Tool Sales Ltd v L. Schuler AG* [1974] AC 235, although contrast *Lombard North Central plc v Butterworth* [1987] QB 527, where the clause provided that terms in the contract had '. . . the property that any breach of them is treated as going to the root of the contract'). Whether a term is a condition (breach of which may give rise to a right to treat the contract as repudiated), or a warranty (breach of which may give rise to a claim for damages but not to a right to reject the goods and treat the contract as repudiated) depends in each case on the construction of the contract and a clause may be a condition, even though called a warranty in the contract (**SoGA 1979, s. 11(3)**).

There is also a further category of terms known as intermediate terms, where the nature and seriousness of the breach will determine whether the innocent party is discharged from further performance or merely entitled to damages.

Construing written contracts

93.22 The object of the rules of construction of written terms is always to discover the intention of the parties from the words used in the contract. There are no special rules for construction of mercantile contracts or business documents. The main rules of construction are:

(a) The ordinary meaning should be given to the words used unless:
   (i) there is some well-known trade custom or trade practice which means that a special meaning is to be given to words (probably the best known example being a 'baker's dozen' meaning 13), or
   (ii) there is some local custom which means words have a particular meaning in that locality, or

(iii) the words are technical words, in which case the normal accepted technical meaning should be applied;

(b) words should be construed so as to avoid absurd or inconsistent provisions as the parties cannot have intended that the contract should be absurd or inconsistent;

(c) the whole contract will be considered so that individual words or phrases are considered in their context, and any recitals may be used as a guide to the interpretation of the operative parts of a contract;

(d) in written contracts, as in statutes, general words which follow several specific words are to be construed in a similar manner — the *eiusdem generis* rule; and

(e) a written contract is construed more strongly against its grantor or maker — the *contra proferentem* rule. This only arises where there remains an ambiguity which has not been resolved by the application of the earlier rules.

The function of the court is to decide the objective intention of the parties. The question is not what the parties understood the words or document to mean but the meaning which the document would convey to a reasonable person having all the background knowledge which would reasonably have been available to the parties in the situation in which they were at the time of the contract (*Investors Compensation Scheme Ltd v West Bromwich Building Society* [1988] 1 WLR 896).

A common problem is the poorly drafted written contract. There are no special rules of construction, but in applying the rules set out above, in *Antaios Compania Naviera SA v Salen Rederierna AB* [1984] AC 676, Lord Diplock said: '. . . if a detailed semantic syntactical analysis of words in a commercial contract is going to lead to a conclusion that flouts business common sense, it must yield to business common sense'. This is an important reflection of the purpose of all rules of construction, namely to ascertain the intention of the parties.

When construing a written contract it is important to remember the effect of the parol evidence rule under which oral evidence cannot be admitted to contradict, vary, add to or subtract from the terms of a written contract. Parol evidence will not even be admitted to establish a mutual but unexpressed intention of both parties to the contract (*New Hampshire Insurance Co. v MGN Ltd* (1995) *The Times*, 25 July 1995). The parol evidence rule applies in most situations, but will not apply if the contract is partly oral and partly in writing, or only evidenced in writing. Evidence of earlier drafts of the contract or negotiations cannot be admitted (save where the court is being asked to rectify the text of the agreement). However, this will not prevent evidence being admitted of the customary meaning of words in a particular trade or of a special technical meaning of words (see **47.31**).

The limits of the role of the court in trying to apply business common sense to a poorly drafted written clause are demonstrated by *Royal and Sun Alliance Insurance plc v Dornoch Ltd* [2005] EWCA Civ 238, [2005] 1 All ER (Comm) 590. The Court of Appeal highlighted the problem for the court where the parties had used a standard term which turned out to be unsuitable and, at [18], held (in construing an exemptions clause) that it is:

> not . . . any part of the court's function to go out of its way to give a purposive or business common-sense construction to one part of a clause in favour of one party and thus enable that party to seek to take advantage of another part of the clause which has draconian consequences for the other party.

Exemption and indemnity clauses

The ordinary rules of construction apply to exemption clauses which exempt one party from the consequences of some breach of contract and to indemnity clauses which require the innocent party to indemnify the party in breach against claims from third parties. The burden of proof is upon the party claiming that some liability is excluded to show that the particular liability falls within the ambit of the particular clause. The party making this claim should therefore set it out in the statement of case (**CPR, r. 16.5(2)(b)**). When ascertaining the intention of the parties: **93.23**

(a) an exemption clause must be clear so that a clause which effectively absolves one party from any performance at all may be held to be meaningless as it could not have been the intention of the parties that there were no mutual obligations (*Tor Line AB v Alltrans Group of Canada Ltd* [1984] 1 WLR 48); and
(b) when considering exemption clauses excluding liability for negligence the three tests in *Canada Steamship Lines Ltd v The King* [1952] AC 192 are applied, namely:
  (i) if the clause plainly excludes such liability then (subject to statutory control) effect will be given to it;
  (ii) if the clause is unclear it will be construed *contra proferentem*; and
  (iii) if the clause covers liabilities other than negligence (e.g., damage by lightning) then it will be held not to cover negligence.

Force majeure clauses

93.24 *Force majeure* clauses are intended to deal with the consequences of one or other of the parties being unable to perform the contract through the intervention of government action or other circumstances outside the party's control. There is no general concept of *force majeure* in English law, and the courts have often seemed reluctant to accept the concept at all. Sale of goods contracts often contain express *force majeure* clauses which limit the seller's liability in circumstances anticipated by the clause with or without provision for notice to be given to the buyer. The true effect of a *force majeure* clause is to limit the seller's obligation to perform and it is not therefore an exemption clause which excludes liability for breach of contract as no breach will have occurred. An important consequence is that such terms may not be required to satisfy the test of reasonableness under the **Unfair Contract Terms Act 1977**. The burden of proving that the clause applies is upon the party seeking to rely upon it, usually the seller. A party making this claim should therefore set it out in its statement of case (**CPR, rr. 16.4** and **16.5**).

Liquidated damages and penalty clauses

93.25 A sum of money which is payable, under a provision of a contract by a party who is in default of contractual obligations in some stated way or ways, may be either liquidated damages or a penalty. Incentives for early performance or payment will not be classified as a penalty. Thus a clause, properly incorporated into the contract, which provides for a 10 per cent discount on the agreed price if it is paid within 28 days will be upheld. Even an acceleration clause, saying that the whole of a sum outstanding shall become due and payable forthwith on default of any payment, is not a penalty (*Wallingford v Mutual Society* (1880) 5 App Cas 685). On the other hand, a clause which provides for a 10 per cent increase in the contract price if the payment is received after 28 days, will be unenforceable as a penalty as it is not (or at least is highly unlikely to be) a genuine pre-estimate of the loss suffered by payment being late. A clause providing for acceleration of payment combined with payment of interest was regarded as a penalty in *The Angelic Star* [1988] 1 Lloyd's Rep 122.

A common problem is 'default interest' payable under a contract. Default interest in regulated agreements is controlled by CCA 1974, s. 93 (see **96.46**). Default interest is also controlled at common law as a possible penalty. In *Patel v Zubowski* [1996] GCCR 2173 interest of 80 per cent which was payable if money owed to a solicitors' firm was not paid on the due date was held to be a penalty and wholly irrecoverable. A provision for 'default interest' in a consumer contract will not necessarily be an unfair contract term, particularly if it is expressed fully, clearly and legibly, and contains no concealed pitfalls or traps (*Director General of Fair Trading v First National Bank plc* [2001] UKHL 52, [2002] 1 AC 481).

A clause which provides for the payment of a sum of money on the happening of a certain event which is not itself a breach of contract by either party will not be a liquidated damages or penalty clause (*Export Credits Guarantee Department v Universal Oil Products Co.* [1983] 1 WLR 399).

There are no special rules of construction for liquidated damages or penalty clauses in contracts, and thus the onerous clauses rule and the *contra proferentem* rule are often of practical importance. If the sum stipulated in the contract is a penalty, the clause will not be enforced. If the sum is a genuine pre-estimate of damage, looked at when the contract was made, it will be a liquidated damages clause and enforceable. The label given by the parties to the clause is a guide, but is not determinative, of whether it is a penalty or a liquidated damages clause (*Dunlop Pneumatic Tyre Co. Ltd v New Garage and Motor Co. Ltd* [1915] AC 79).

Forfeiture clauses

Confusion exists over the effect of forfeiture clauses where a sum, usually the deposit, is forfeited on breach of contract by the buyer. *Workers Trust and Merchant Bank Ltd v Dojap Investments Ltd* [1993] AC 573 suggested that the court can consider the reasonableness of such clauses: contrast *BICC plc v Burndy Corporation* [1985] Ch 232 and *Sport International Bussum BV v InterFootwear Ltd* [1984] 1 WLR 776. **93.26**

Timing of delivery

A common issue is whether the stipulation as to time for delivery is a condition or warranty or intermediate term (see **93.21**). The **SoGA 1979, s. 10(2)**, provides that whether time is of the essence (i.e., is a condition) depends upon the terms of the contract. It is open to the parties to make time of the essence. **93.27**

Time of payment

A further common problem relates to the classification of terms as to the payment of the price. The **SoGA 1979, s. 10(1)**, provides that unless a different intention appears from the terms of the contract, stipulations as to time of payment are not of the essence of the contract (i.e., are not conditions). In effect this creates a statutory presumption for the timing of payment. Section 10(2), mentioned at **93.27**, provides that whether any other stipulation as to time is or is not of the essence of the contract depends on the terms of the contract, the different wording making it plain that the statute is not creating a presumption either way. **93.28**

Where goods are perishable or notice is given of an intention to resell, the SoGA 1979, s. 48(3) provides that if the buyer does not pay or tender the price within a reasonable time, the unpaid seller may resell the goods and recover from the original buyer damages representing any loss occasioned by the buyer's breach.

If the contract does not otherwise provide, the result of these provisions is as follows:

(a) if time for delivery is of the essence then so is the time for payment as they are concurrent obligations;
(b) conversely, if time for delivery is not of the essence then neither is the time of payment; and
(c) if the goods are perishable or if notice of intention to resell has been given by the seller, then payment must be made within a reasonable time and is of the essence.

If the seller has waived or is estopped from relying upon the original date of payment, the buyer may argue that no new date for payment has been agreed and that no reasonable notice has been given (*Charles Rickards Ltd v Oppenheim* [1950] 1 KB 616 and *State Trading Corporation of India Ltd v Compagnie Française d'Importation et de Distribution* [1983] 2 Lloyd's Rep 679).

IMPLIED TERMS

The implied terms of the contract

Terms may be implied into a contract in three main ways: **93.29**

(a) to reflect the actual intention of the parties — the unexpressed terms (*Shirlaw v Southern Foundries (1926) Ltd* [1939] 2 KB 206, affirmed [1940] AC 701);
(b) to give business efficacy to the agreement — the terms which the court presumes the parties would have expressed if they had considered the position (*Luxor (Eastbourne) Ltd v Cooper* [1941] AC 108); and
(c) by law — not as a result of the actual or presumed intention of the parties, but as a result of general considerations of policy (in this context, the statutory implied terms in the **SoGA 1979, ss. 12 to 15**, see **93.30** to **93.35**).

The implication of a term as being the actual intention of the parties can be based on:

(a) custom within the trade or locality, but only if the custom is notorious, certain, legal and reasonable (e.g., *British Crane Hire Corporation Ltd v Ipswich Plant Hire Ltd* [1975] QB 303); or
(b) a previous course of dealing between the parties; or
(c) the circumstances and express obligations of the contract.

There is often an overlap between terms implied because they reflect the intentions of the parties and those which are necessary to give business efficacy to the contract. Terms are implied to give business efficacy when they are required in order to enable the contract to work satisfactorily on the assumption that the parties would have agreed such terms if they had thought about the position. No term will be implied under the first two tests if the suggested term is unreasonable, but the mere fact that the term is reasonable will not mean that it is to be implied into the contract.

The main implied terms imposed by the SoGA 1979 are:

(a) implied terms as to title (s. 12);
(b) implied terms where there has been a sale by description (s. 13);
(c) implied terms as to quality or fitness (s. 14); and,
(d) implied terms where there is a sale by sample (s. 15).

Those implied terms can be varied or excluded by express agreement between the parties, by course of dealings between the parties or by such usage as binds both parties to the contract (**SoGA 1979, s. 55(1)**). These statutory implied terms are considered further at **92.30** to **92.35**.

Implied terms about title

93.30 Section 12(1) of the SoGA 1979 creates an implied condition on the part of the seller that in the case of a sale the seller has the right to sell the goods, and in the case of an agreement to sell the seller will have that right at the time when the property is to pass. By the **Unfair Contract Terms Act 1977, s. 6(1)(a)**, this condition cannot be excluded or restricted by reference to any contract term in either consumer or non-consumer sales. The right to sell involves two concepts. First, the buyer must be able to pass good title. Secondly, the sale must not be unlawful (e.g., an infringement of a trade mark). The **SoGA 1979, s. 12(2)** creates an implied warranty on the part of the seller that:

(a) the goods are free, and will remain free until the time when property is to pass, from any charge or encumbrance not disclosed or known to the buyer before the contract is made; and
(b) the buyer will enjoy quiet possession of the goods except in so far as it may be disturbed by the owner or other person entitled to the benefit of any charge or encumbrance so disclosed or known.

Implied terms in sales by description

93.31 Where there is a contract for sale by description there is an implied term, which is a condition, that the goods will correspond to the description (**SoGA 1979, s. 13(1)**). If the sale is by sample and description, the goods must correspond to the description as well as to the sample (s. 13(2)). A sale is not prevented from being by description merely because being exposed for sale or hire the goods are selected by the buyer (s. 13(3)). In consumer sales the obligations imposed by s. 13 cannot be excluded or restricted by reference to any contract term (**Unfair Contract Terms Act 1977, s. 6(2)(a)**). In non-consumer sales liability can be restricted or excluded only in so far as the term satisfies the test of reasonableness (**Unfair Contract Terms Act 1977, s. 6(3)**).

Sales by description are a common type of contract for the sale of goods. All sales of unascertained goods will be by description, as will all sales of goods which the buyer has not seen at all, and many sales by sample. This implied condition can be extremely important in practice. If the seller is not acting in the course of a business, such as in private sales of second hand cars, the statutory terms as to quality and fitness will not be implied. The only remedy for the buyer may be to rely upon a breach of this condition.

Implied terms about quality and fitness

The **SoGA 1979, s. 14**, implies terms that goods sold should be of satisfactory quality and reasonably fit for their purpose. These are the implied terms which arise in most sale of goods litigation. These implied terms are conditions (**s. 14(6)**). The old standard of merchantable quality has been replaced by the concept of satisfactory quality (see **93.33**). The implied terms apply where the seller sells the goods in the course of a business (s. 14(2)). In consumer sales the obligations imposed by **s. 14** cannot be excluded or restricted by reference to any contract term (**Unfair Contract Terms Act 1977, s. 6(2)(a)**). In non-consumer sales liability can be restricted or excluded only in so far as the term satisfies the test of reasonableness (**Unfair Contract Terms Act 1977, s. 6(3)**). **93.32**

Satisfactory quality

'Satisfactory quality' means the standard that a reasonable person would regard as satisfactory, taking account of any description of the goods, the price (if relevant) and all other relevant circumstances (**SoGA 1979, s. 14(2A)**). Quality of goods includes their state and condition and the following (among others) are in appropriate cases aspects of the quality of goods: **93.33**

(a) fitness for the purpose for which goods of the kind in question are commonly supplied;
(b) appearance and finish;
(c) freedom from minor defects;
(d) safety; and
(e) durability (**s. 14(2B)**).

In consumer contracts made after 31 March 2003, the relevant circumstances also specifically include any public statements on the specific characteristics of the goods made by the seller, the producer or his representative, particularly in advertising or labelling (**s. 14(2D)**) unless one of the limited exceptions applies (**s. 14(2E)**).

The implied term of satisfactory quality does not, by **s. 14(2C)**, extend to any matter making the goods unsatisfactory:

(a) which is specifically drawn to the buyer's attention before the contract is made;
(b) where the buyer examines the goods before the contract is made, which that examination ought to reveal; or
(c) in the case of a contract for sale by sample, which would have been apparent on a reasonable examination of the sample.

Pre-1995 cases need to be read with the slight change in the test from 'merchantable quality' to 'satisfactory quality' in mind. Nevertheless, it has been held that Coalite delivered with an explosive substance accidentally included in the delivery (and which blew up in the claimant's fireplace) was not of merchantable quality (*Wilson v Rickett Cockrell and Co. Ltd* [1954] 1 QB 598). Nor was a bun which contained a stone (*Chaproniere v Mason* (1905) 21 TLR 633). In *Mash and Murrell Ltd v Joseph I. Emmanuel Ltd* [1961] 1 WLR 862 (at first instance, reversed on other grounds) Diplock J held that potatoes were not of merchantable quality as they were not loaded on board a ship for transportation to the buyer in a state that they would endure the normal sea voyage and arrive in a merchantable condition. All of these decisions would be decided the same way under the new test.

There will be a breach of the condition of satisfactory quality when a new car is sold with a number of minor defects (as in a case under the old definition, *Rogers v Parish (Scarborough) Ltd* [1987] QB 933, where the car had minor bodywork defects and also minor mechanical problems that resulted in it misfiring and being excessively noisy). More tolerance is given to sellers of second-hand cars, having regard to the fact they are described as second-hand, and also the fact that prices will be considerably lower than for new vehicles of the same kind. In *Business Appliances Specialists Ltd v Nationwide Credit Corporation Ltd* [1988] RTR 332 it was stressed that merchantability in relation to second-hand goods is not restricted to safety (or in the case of cars, roadworthiness). A second-hand car may of course be sold for ordinary motoring purposes, or for scrap, or as a source for spare parts. More will be expected if the car is bought and sold with the intention that it is still roadworthy. Further, more will be expected of a car that is not very old and with a relatively low mileage, than from a car sold at a lower price near the end of its useful life. The fact that a vehicle breaks down soon after being sold may be evidence that it was defective at the time of purchase (*Crowther v Shannon Motor Co.* [1975] 1 WLR 30).

In *Business Appliances Specialists Ltd v Nationwide Credit Corporation Ltd* the buyer purchased a second-hand Mercedes for £14,850 with 37,000 miles recorded on the clock. After a further 800 miles it broke down with excessive wear evident in its valves (well beyond that expected in a car of that age). It was held there was no breach of the implied term as to merchantability, second-hand cars being expected to have ordinary wear and tear. If the valve defect really was ordinary wear and tear, no doubt this decision would be the same today, but the expert evidence in the case indicated it was worse than that, and it is submitted that the case would be decided differently under the present satisfactory quality test. A second-hand vehicle that was in fact a rebuilt insurance write-off will be sold in breach of the implied condition as to satisfactory quality, even in the absence of any specific defects, if the fact it had been rebuilt was not disclosed (see *Shine v General Guarantee Corporation Ltd* [1988] 1 All ER 911). The description used when the item is sold is of considerable importance. In *Bartlett v Sydney Marcus Ltd* [1965] 1 WLR 1013, a second-hand car was sold with a defective clutch. Before the sale there was a discussion between the buyer and seller, and the seller indicated that if the buyer wanted the seller to repair the clutch the price would be £25 more. The buyer decided to have it repaired elsewhere, and it cost £84. It was held there was no breach of the condition as to merchantable quality, the case really being one where the repairs turned out to be more expensive than anticipated.

The current statutory test of satisfactory quality was considered by the Court of Appeal in *Clegg v Olle Andersson* [2003] EWCA Civ 320, [2003] 1 All ER (Comm) 721. The test is not whether a reasonable person would find the goods acceptable but is an objective comparison of the state of the goods with the standard which a reasonable person would find acceptable. Thus, for a high-priced quality product, the customer may be entitled to expect that it is free from even minor defects, in other words perfect or very nearly so. In consumer contracts made after 31 March 2003, public statements such as advertising can be taken into account in applying this test.

Fitness for purpose

93.34 A term of fitness for a particular purpose is implied where the seller sells in the course of a business and the buyer makes known any particular purpose for which the goods are being bought, except where the circumstances show that the buyer does not rely or that it is unreasonable for the buyer to rely on the skill or judgment of the seller (**SoGA 1979, s. 14(3)**). The particular purpose will not merely be the general purpose for which the goods are designed (*Slater v Finning Ltd* [1997] AC 473). The particular purpose for which goods may have been bought may in fact be the only usual purpose for those goods (see *Priest v Last* [1903] 2 KB 148, where the goods were a hot-water bottle).

The wording of the **s. 14(3)** shows that the burden of proving that the section does not apply on the ground that the buyer has not relied upon the seller's skill or judgment rests on the seller. Normally, it will be taken to be the case that a buyer, simply by going to a retailer to buy something, relies on that retailer to exercise skill and judgment in selecting suitable stock (see *Grant v Australian Knitting Mills Ltd* [1936] AC 85). Where the seller is also the manufacturer, it is nigh on impossible to rebut the presumption of reliance (*Kendall v Lillico* [1969] AC 31). The presumption also applies where both parties are traders, but of course it is easier to rebut it. In cases where a buyer intends to use the goods in another country, it will usually be the case that the presumption will be rebutted in so far as the issue may be whether the goods are reasonably fit for use in that other country, because usually it will be the buyer who will be best placed to know this (see *Teheran-Europe Co. Ltd v S. T. Belton Ltd* [1968] 2 QB 545).

If the buyer has some unusual susceptibility to contaminants found in the goods sold, it is a question of fact and degree whether the goods breach the condition. *Griffiths v Peter Conway Ltd* [1939] 1 All ER 685 has been described as a highly special case (in *Ashington Piggeries Ltd v Christopher Hill Ltd* [1972] AC 441), but in this case it was held that there was no breach of the condition where a buyer contracted dermatitis from a coat sold by the seller, the buyer having an unusually sensitive skin, and the coat not being such as to harm any normal purchaser. On the other hand, in *Ashington Piggeries Ltd v Christopher Hill Ltd* animal meal was contaminated with a trace of a toxic substance that was harmful to many animals, but which was peculiarly harmful to the buyer's mink. It was held there was a breach of the condition.

Sale by sample

The implied conditions in a contract of sale by sample are: **93.35**

(a) that the bulk will correspond to the sample in quality (**SoGA 1979, s. 15(2)(a)**); and
(b) that the goods will be free from any defect making their quality unsatisfactory which would not be apparent on reasonable examination of the sample (s. 15(2)(c)).

In consumer sales the obligations imposed by **SoGA 1979, s. 15**, cannot be excluded or restricted by reference to any contract term (**Unfair Contract Terms Act 1977, s. 6(2)(a)**). In non-consumer sales liability can be restricted or excluded only in so far as the term satisfies the test of reasonableness (**Unfair Contract Terms Act 1977, s. 6(3)**).

BREACH OF THE MAIN PROVISIONS

Breach by the seller

Consumer contracts In consumer contracts made after 31 March 2003, wide new additional remedies for the buyer are contained in **SOGA 1979, ss. 48A to 48F**. If the goods do not conform to the contract at any time within six months after delivery, they must be taken not to have conformed at the date of delivery (**s. 48A(3)**) unless: **93.36**

(a) it is established that they did so conform and the burden of proof must be on the seller, although that is not specified (**s. 48A(4)(a)**) or;
(b) the rule is incompatible with the nature of the goods or the nature of the lack of conformity, which will cover goods such as perishables (**s. 48A(4)(b)**).

Goods do not confirm if there is a breach of an express term of the contract or of **s. 13, 14** or **15**.

There is a new right to require the seller to repair or replace the goods (**s. 48B**) save where that would be impossible, disproportionate to other remedies or disproportionate in comparison to a reduction in purchase price or rescission. The remedy of repair may be important where, for example, the product cannot be repaired by others, because that would breach a warranty, or essential equipment or access codes are required for the repair. The repair or replacement must be within a reasonable time and without significant inconvenience to the buyer and at the cost of the seller.

There is a separate new right to a reduction in the purchase price or rescission of the contract (**s. 48C**). This right can be exercised where the buyer cannot require repair or replacement, or where repair or replacement cannot be done within a reasonable time and without significant inconvenience to the buyer. The reduction in price is 'by an appropriate amount' which is not defined. It will, presumably, be a reduction to the price which would have been paid for the goods in their actual state. This new right to rescind is quite separate from the right to reject goods. There is express power for the reimbursement of the purchase price to be reduced to reflect the use the buyer has had of the goods since delivery.

The court now has express power in these consumer cases (in addition to all existing remedies) to make an order for specific performance or reimbursement unconditionally or on such terms and conditions as to damages, payment of the price and otherwise as it thinks fit (**s. 48E**).

93.37 **Non-delivery** Where the seller fails to deliver in accordance with the contract the recoverable sums are:

(a) damages for non-delivery (**s. 51**); and
(b) any special damages and interest (**s. 54**).

Alternatively, the buyer may sue for specific performance if the goods were specific or ascertained goods (**s. 52**). The damage recoverable under **s. 51** is the estimated loss directly and naturally resulting, in the ordinary course of events, from the seller's breach of contract (**s. 51(2)**). Where there is an available market for the goods the measure of damages is usually the difference between the contract price and the market or current price of the goods at the time or times when they ought to have been delivered (**s. 51(3)**).

An outright refusal by the seller to perform his or her obligations will amount to a repudiatory breach of contract unless the seller's obligations under the contract were limited, or the contract has become frustrated. The ordinary contract law concepts of repudiatory breach, the need for acceptance of that breach, and of anticipatory breach, will apply. If a repudiatory breach exists and is accepted by the buyer, the buyer will have the following remedies:

(a) a claim in restitution for the money paid, on a total failure of consideration; or
(b) a claim for damages for non-delivery; or
(c) a claim for specific performance if the goods are specific goods or are ascertained goods.

93.38 **Wrongful resale by the seller** If the buyer has the right to possession of the goods, a second sale by the seller will amount to a wrongful interference with the buyer's goods. The right to possession is not dependent upon property having passed. A right to possession can only exist where the goods are specific, or have become ascertained goods by the time of the second sale. If the buyer has a right to possession and the seller has sold the goods to someone else, the buyer will have remedies against the seller and may have remedies against the subsequent buyer. The remedies against the seller will be:

(a) a claim in restitution for the money paid, on a total failure of consideration; or
(b) a claim in restitution for the money received by the seller on the subsequent sale; or
(c) a claim for damages for non-delivery; or
(d) a claim for wrongful interference with goods.

If the buyer has no right to possession of the goods, the buyer's remedies will be only against the seller and will be:

(a) a claim in restitution for the money paid, on a total failure of consideration; or
(b) a claim for damages for non-delivery.

Loss of the goods Goods may be lost before the contract is made, partially lost before the contract is made, or may be lost between contract and delivery. If all the goods the seller intended to supply to the buyer are lost before the contract is made, and the contract is for unascertained generic goods, then the goods cannot easily be said to be lost as another source should be available. If the seller does not deliver the buyer will have the following remedies: **93.39**

(a) a claim in restitution for the money paid, on a total failure of consideration; or
(b) a claim for damages for non-delivery.

If all the goods are lost before the contract is made and the contract is for goods from a specific source, or there is only one source, then the contract may be void for mistake (*Bell v Lever Brothers Ltd* [1932] AC 161) or under the **SoGA 1979, s. 6.** The buyer will then be entitled to recover any money paid. Damages will only be awarded to the buyer if the seller has warranted that the goods exist. Similarly, if by the contract the buyer has accepted the risk that the goods may not exist, the contract will not be void for mistake and the buyer will have to pay the contract price notwithstanding the non-existence of the goods.

If there has been only a partial loss of goods before the contract is made the position is that it is a question of construction whether the parties intended that the contract be wholly discharged or not, and if it is not to be wholly discharged the seller must deliver and the buyer must pay for the goods which have not been lost (*H. R. and S. Sainsbury Ltd v Street* [1972] 1 WLR 834). If the seller has warranted the existence of the goods he or she must make delivery of the quantity which is not lost and the ordinary rules applying to delivery of a wrong quantity will apply. If the risk of loss is on the buyer, the seller must deliver the goods which have not been lost and the buyer must pay for them.

If goods are lost after the contract is made a distinction must be drawn between specific and unascertained goods:

(a) Where specific goods perish and:
   (i) property and risk have not vested in the purchaser, and
   (ii) there is no fault by either party,

   the contract will be avoided (**SoGA 1979, s. 7**). Where s. 7 applies, the **Law Reform (Frustrated Contracts) Act 1943** does not apply and the common law rules must be used. This means that if there has been a total failure of consideration any money paid can be recovered and no allowance is made for the seller's expenses. Where s. 7 applies but only part of the specific goods perish, it seems that the seller is not obliged to tender what remains (*Barrow, Lane and Ballard Ltd v Phillip Phillips and Co. Ltd* [1929] 1 KB 574, but contrast *H. R. and S. Sainsbury Ltd v Street* [1972] 1 WLR 834). Where there is a partial failure of consideration on a non-severable contract the common law rules apply: the seller cannot compel payment but the buyer cannot compel the return of money already paid. If the seller has undertaken absolutely to deliver the goods s. 7 will not apply and on a failure to deliver the buyer will have the following remedies:
   (i) a claim in restitution for the money paid, on a total failure of consideration; or
   (ii) a claim for damages for non-delivery.

(b) Where the goods are unascertained goods the seller will only be able to argue that the contract has been frustrated if all sources of supply have been destroyed. In most situations the seller will have to obtain the goods from another source and failure to do so will give the buyer the following remedies:
   (i) a claim in restitution for the money paid, on a total failure of consideration; or
   (ii) a claim for damages for non-delivery.

Delay in delivery If the time for delivery is of the essence, or more than a reasonable **93.40**

time for the delivery has passed and the seller has not delivered the goods, the seller will be in repudiatory breach of contract (*Hartley v Hymans* [1920] 3 KB 475). The buyer will then be able:

(a) to accept the repudiatory breach and claim damages for non-delivery; or
(b) rarely, to seek specific performance of the contract.

Breach by the buyer

93.41 The buyer's duty is to accept the goods and pay for them in accordance with the terms of the contract (see **93.10**). Where the parties have a number of separate contracts it is important to note that (in the absence of express terms in each contract) a claim arising under one contract will not give rise to a defence in another (*B. Hargreaves Ltd v Action 2000 Ltd* [1993] BCLC 1111).

93.42 **Late payment** Many written contracts provide for interest to be charged on late payments. In litigation interest can be claimed under the **Supreme Court Act 1981, s. 35A**, or the County Courts Act 1981, s. 69. In contracts covered by the Late Payment of Commercial Debts (Interest) Act 1998 a statutory implied term is inserted into the contract that the debt carries simple interest at the prescribed statutory rate.

93.43 **Failure to accept goods** If the buyer does not accept the goods, the seller can maintain an action for the price if property in the goods has passed to the buyer or where the price is payable irrespective of delivery (**SOGA 1979, s. 49**). The more usual course is to sue for damages occasioned by the refusal of delivery and a reasonable charge for care of the goods under s. 37. Damages for non-acceptance are governed by s. 50. The measure of damages is the estimated loss directly and naturally resulting from the buyer's breach of contract. If there is an available market for the goods, the seller must resell the goods and the damages will be:

(a) the difference in price; and
(b) the reasonable costs of sale.

If there is no available market for the goods, the seller should resell in order to mitigate the loss and can still claim the costs incurred. An action for the price has obvious advantages where it may be difficult to prove any loss has been suffered, or where arguments over mitigation of loss may arise.

93.44 **Seller's rights in the goods** The seller's rights in the goods can be of particular importance if the buyer is insolvent. Retention of title clauses until payment are now common. Where there are no contract terms, if property has passed, the unpaid seller (defined in the **SoGA 1979, s. 38**) usually has, by virtue of s. 39:

(a) a statutory lien on the goods;
(b) a right of stoppage in transit in case of insolvency; and
(c) a right of resale.

The statutory right of resale arises under s. 48. If property has not passed, the seller may have a claim for delivery up of the goods and damages for wrongful interference with the goods against the buyer and any other person in possession.

SALES BY NON-OWNERS

93.45 The traditional rule remains that no one can pass better title than that person possesses: *nemo dat quod non habet.* There are nine main exceptions to this rule:

(a) Estoppel — where the owner is precluded by conduct from denying the seller's authority to sell (**SoGA 1979, s. 21(1)**).
(b) Sales under the Factors Act 1889 — sales by mercantile agents who are in possession of the goods or documents of title to the goods with the consent of the true owner who sell

in the ordinary course of their business to a person acting in good faith without notice will, pass title (**SoGA 1979, s. 21(2)(a)**; Factors Act 1889).

(c) Sales under special powers — this exception covers a large group of sales such as sales of goods distrained upon, sales by mortgagors, receivers and under bills of sale and sale of uncollected goods under the Torts (Interference with Goods) Act 1977, ss. 12 and 13 (**SoGA 1979, s. 21(2)(b)**).

(d) Sales under voidable title — where a sale of goods contract is voidable (e.g., by misrepresentation, undue influence, mistake or duress), the buyer's title will be voidable and a sale on of the goods to someone in good faith without notice of the defect in title can pass title (**SoGA 1979, s. 23**).

(e) Sales by seller in possession — this is a very similar situation to sales under the Factors Act 1889, s. 8, so that a seller who remains in possession of goods or the documents of title, can sell goods a second time to someone else acting in good faith and without notice of the first sale and will pass title (**SoGA 1979, s. 24**; *Michael Gerson (Leasing) Ltd v Wilkinson* [2001] QB 514).

(f) Sales by buyer in possession — this is similar to the Factors Act 1889, s. 9, and renders valid a sale by the buyer who has possession of the goods or the documents of title and sells on the goods which he or she does not yet own to any person acting in good faith and without notice of a lien or other right of the original seller (**SoGA 1979, s. 25**).

(g) Sales of motor vehicles within part III of the Hire-Purchase Act 1964 — motor vehicles which are hired under hire-purchase agreements or agreed to be sold under conditional sale agreements and are sold by the hirer to a private purchaser in good faith without notice of the hire purchase or conditional sale agreement will pass title in the motor vehicle. Where a fraudster obtains a vehicle from a dealer by purporting to enter into a hire-purchase agreement, the hire-purchase company (which obtains title by buying the vehicle from the dealer) remains the legal owner of the vehicle, and is not defeated by **s. 27**, if the fraudster then sells the car to an innocent purchaser. This is because the fraudster is not a 'debtor' under the hire-purchase agreement within the meaning of **s. 29(4)** (*Shogun Finance Ltd v Hudson* [2003] UKHL 62, [2004] 1 AC 919).

(h) Sales by agents can also pass title under the ordinary rules of agency if the agent has actual or apparent authority to bind his or her principal as the ordinary rules of agency apply (SoGA 1979, s. 62(2)).

(i) Under the **Torts (Interference with Goods) Act 1977** payment of damages under **s. 5** will extinguish the title of the original owner enabling the person paying damages to pass title in those goods.

Chapter 94 Supply of Goods and Services

INTRODUCTION

94.1 Contracts for the sale of goods, which were considered in **chapter 93**, are just one way in which goods are transferred from one person to another. The key distinctions between contracts of sale and other similar types of contracts were considered at **93.2** and **93.3**. Various types of consumer finance contracts, several of which also have as one of their objects the transfer of goods, are considered at **96.2** to **96.11**. Among these are:

(a) hire-purchase agreements, under which a consumer will hire goods from a finance company for a set period, often 24,36 or 60 months, paying a monthly hire charge (which is usually calculated by reference to the cost of financing the price of the goods), with an option to purchase the goods at the end of the hire period;
(b) long-term hire contracts, which are very much like hire-purchase agreements, but without the option to purchase;
(c) conditional sale agreements, where the customer buys goods, but property in the goods does not pass until stated conditions are satisfied (often the payment of agreed instalments of the price);
(d) contracts for the supply of goods and services, such as where a customer commissions a painting or employs a builder to build an extension to a house. In these contracts the main element of the agreement is the provision of services (the work in painting or building), although the provision of the canvas and paints, or building supplies, is also part of the contract.

As discussed at **93.29** to **93.35**, the **SoGA 1979, ss. 12 to 15**, implies various terms for the benefit of buyers into many contracts for the sale of goods. It is the policy of consumer law that similar implied terms apply to other consumer contracts, particularly those mentioned in (a) to (d) above, where customers make use of goods supplied even though the contracts involved do not amount to sales of the goods in question. The statutes achieving this aim are the Supply of Goods (Implied Terms) Act 1973 (SoGITA 1973) and the **Supply of Goods and Services Act 1982** (SoGSA 1982). These Acts have been amended with effect from 31 March 2003 in consumer contracts to give similar new rights to those given in sale of goods contracts (**93.36**).

HIRE-PURCHASE AND CONDITIONAL SALE AGREEMENTS

94.2 The SoGITA 1973 creates implied terms for hire-purchase and conditional sale agreements which are almost identical to those in the SoGA 1979 considered at **93.29** to **93.35**. These rights may be summarised as follows:

(a) Implied terms (both conditions and warranties) about the title of the hirer exist under SoGITA 1973, s. 8, and require the hirer to be able to pass title at the time when title should pass (which can be any time, if the agreement can be brought to an end by the hirer paying the balance due).

(b) Implied conditions in hire-purchase agreements where the goods are hired by description are provided under s. 9, and are very similar to those implied in sales of goods.
(c) Implied conditions about quality and fitness exist under s. 10, which are, again, very similar to those in contracts for the sale of goods. In relation to consumer contacts made after 31 March 2003, SoGITA 1973 has been amended in a similar way to SoGA 1979 so that a relevant circumstance in considering quality is any public statements made about the characteristics of the goods particularly in advertising or labelling.
(d) Implied conditions in relation to hirings under hire-purchase agreements by sample exist under SoGITA 1973, s. 11.

The remedies are modified in non-consumer cases so that the hirer cannot reject the goods if it would be unreasonable to do so (SoGITA 1973, s. 11A).

SUPPLY OF GOODS AND SERVICES ACT 1982

The SoGSA 1982 covers two separate but important areas. Part I covers certain contracts for the supply of goods. Part II covers contracts for the supply of services. The final provision in part I is s. 11 which, together with the **Unfair Contract Terms Act 1977**, restricts the right to contract out of liability. **94.3**

Contracts for work and materials

The first portion of part I of the SoGSA 1982 (ss. 1 to 5A) creates implied terms for contracts under which ownership of goods will pass. The provisions do not (by s. 1(1)) apply to excepted contracts, which are sale of goods contracts (where the position is governed by the SoGA 1979), hire-purchase agreements (where the position is governed by SoGITA 1973), trading stamp redemptions, transfers by deed with no consideration other than that presumed in a deed, and contracts by way of mortgage, pledge, charge or other security (SoGSA 1982, s. 1(2)). The most common contracts to which the provisions do apply are contracts for work and materials. The implied terms are almost identical to those contained in the SoGA 1979, considered at **93.29** to **93.35**. These terms may be summarised as follows: **94.4**

(a) implied terms (conditions and warranties) about title (SoGSA 1982, s. 2);
(b) implied conditions in transfers by description (s. 3);
(c) implied conditions about quality and fitness (s. 4(2)); and
(d) implied conditions in transfers by sample (s. 4(3)).

The remedies are modified in non-consumer cases so that the transferee cannot treat the contract as repudiated if it would be unreasonable to do so (s. 5A).

In relation to consumer contacts made after 31 March 2003, SoGSA 1982 has been amended in a similar way to SoGA 1979. If the goods do not conform to the contract, consumers have new rights to repair or replacement, reduction in price or to rescind the contract (**93.36**). The court has new, additional powers to enforce those rights (SoGSA 1982, s. 11R).

Contracts for the hire of goods

The second portion of part I of the SoGSA 1982 (ss. 6 to 10A) is concerned with implied terms in hire of goods (other than a hire-purchase contract or a trading stamp redemption) (s. 6). The implied terms are almost identical to those contained in the SoGA 1979 considered at **93.29** to **93.35**. These terms may be summarised as follows: **94.5**

(a) implied terms (conditions and warranties) about the right to transfer possession (SoGSA 1982, s. 7);
(b) implied conditions in hire by description (s. 8);
(c) implied conditions about quality and fitness (s. 9); and
(d) implied conditions in hires by sample (s. 10).

The remedies are modified in non-consumer cases so that the transferee cannot treat the contract as repudiated if it would be unreasonable to do so (s. 10A).

Supply of services

94.6 Part II of the SoGSA 1982 covers contracts for the supply of a service (other than a contract of service or apprenticeship) whether or not goods are also transferred or bailed or bailed by way of hire (s. 12). In these contracts, part II implies three sets of implied terms, namely:

(a) An implied term (which is not a condition) that in a contract for the supply of a service where the supplier is acting in the course of a business, the supplier will carry out the service with reasonable care and skill (s. 13).
(b) An implied term that where, under a contract for the supply of a service by the supplier acting in the course of a business, the time for the service to be carried out is not fixed by the contract, left to be fixed in a manner agreed by the contract, or to be determined by the course of dealing between the parties, the supplier will carry out the service within a reasonable time (s. 14(1)). What is a reasonable time is a question of fact (s. 14(2)).
(c) An implied term that where, under a contract for the supply of a service, the consideration for the service is not determined by the contract, left to be determined in a manner agreed by the contract or determined by the course of dealing between the parties, the party contracting with the supplier will pay a reasonable charge (**s. 15(1)**). What is a reasonable charge is a question of fact (s. 15(2)).

The exclusion of these implied terms is governed by **s. 16(1)**, which provides that they may be negatived or varied by express agreement, or by the course of dealing between the parties, or by any usage that binds both parties. An express term will not negative any of the implied terms unless they are inconsistent with each other. The right to negative or vary the statutory implied terms in contracts for the supply of services is subject to the provisions of the **Unfair Contract Terms Act 1977** (see **SoGSA 1982, s. 16(1)**). The 1977 Act in particular restricts the right to exclude liability in consumer contracts and contracts on standard terms of business, such terms being ineffective save in so far as such terms satisfy the requirement of reasonableness (**Unfair Contract Terms Act 1977, s. 3**).

In consumer contacts made after 31 March 2003, SoGSA 1982 has been amended in a similar way to SoGA 1979. If the goods do not conform to the contract, consumers have new rights to repair or replacement, reduction in price or to rescind the contract (**93.36**). The court has new, additional powers to enforce those rights (SoGSA 1982, s. 11R).

Chapter 95 Unfair Contract Terms

INTRODUCTION

Statutory control limiting the normal freedom to contract upon any terms which the parties agree is not new. Even many centuries ago there was legislation, such as the Statute of Frauds (1677) and the usury laws, regulating the formation of binding contracts (e.g., certain contracts had to be in writing or be evidenced in writing) and the content or effectiveness of contract terms (e.g., limits on recoverable interest). Statutory control of contract terms is now of considerable importance. Much of the control which implements European Directives exists in favour of consumers only. Other legislation, notably the **Unfair Contract Terms Act 1977** (UCTA 1977), contains provisions some of which apply to consumers and some of which are of general application. **95.1**

The main policy behind the modern legislation is to provide essential safeguards against the worst excesses of the principle of freedom of contract. The law is particularly concerned to protect consumers as they are often in a weak bargaining position compared to large retailers and other large businesses, and cannot realistically enter into contracts other than on the terms insisted upon by the businesses they are dealing with. The law is also concerned to curb the worst excesses of the use of standard terms of trading. However, the approach is somewhat limited. The legislation is reasonably effective in limiting exclusions of liability (particularly in relation to breaches causing personal injuries or death, and in relation to the statutory implied terms in contracts for the sale of goods and the supply of services), and limiting terms allowing a party to render no performance or a performance substantially different from that reasonably expected. However, there is no general requirement that terms must be fair. Nor does the legislation do anything to protect customers who feel they have been charged an unfair price.

The main statutory provisions are:

(a) The UCTA 1977, which introduced important controls on exclusion clauses and standard terms in contracts, and which limits the right to contract out of the main obligations under the SoGA 1979 (see **chapter 93**) and the SoGITA 1973 (see **chapter 94**). It also controls certain other unfair terms.

(b) The Consumer Protection (Cancellation of Contracts Concluded away from Business Premises) Regulations 1987 (SI 1987/2117) (in this chapter referred to as 'the 1987 Regulations'), which contain important consumer protection provisions and a cooling-off period for doorstep selling. The 1987 Regulations were amended, with effect from 31 December 1998, by the Consumer Protection (Cancellation of Contracts Concluded away from Business Premises) (Amendment) Regulations 1998 (SI 1998/3050).

(c) The **Unfair Terms in Consumer Contracts Regulations 1999** (SI 1999/2083) (in this chapter referred to as 'the 1999 Regulations'), which make consumer contracts subject to a concept of good faith, require written terms to be in plain and intelligible language and give powers of investigation and enforcement to consumer groups.

(d) The Consumer Protection (Distance Selling) Regulations 2000 (SI 2000/2334) came into force on 31 October 2000 to implement Directive 97/7/ EC. Distance selling is any sale where the supplier and consumer are not face to face and covers telephone sales, mail order and e-commerce. A cooling-off period will be introduced which should be similar to the right given under the 1987 Regulations (see **95.13**).

(e) Important changes in relation to consumer contracts made after 31 March 2003 have been enacted, including provisions about consumer guarantees and amendments to the definition of 'consumer' in UCTA 1977.

(f) The Law Commission and the Scottish Law Commission have proposed the replacement of the UCTA 1977 and the 1999 Regulations by a single Act in plain English (*Unfair Terms in Contracts* (Consultation Paper No. 166) (London: TSO, 2002)). That will require a single definition of consumer (95.2).

MEANING OF 'CONSUMER'

95.2 It is unfortunate that the definition of a consumer varies in the legislation. The European concept of a consumer is limited to a natural person who is acting for purposes which can be regarded as outside his or her business. This applies to most of the European Directives and has been retained in the statutory instruments implementing those Directives. A much wider definition of consumer was used in the UCTA 1977, in which there is no requirement that a consumer must be an individual (*R and B Customs Brokers Co. Ltd v United Dominions Trust Ltd* [1988] 1 WLR 321).

For the purposes of the UCTA 1977, the concept of dealing as consumer is defined by s. 12(1), which was amended with effect from 31 March 2003. A person deals as consumer if he neither makes the contract in the course of a business nor holds himself out as doing so, and the other party makes the contract in the course of a business. Further, save where the buyer is an individual, in the case of sales of goods, the goods passing under or in pursuance of the contract must be of a type ordinarily supplied for private use or consumption. A person operating a business may deal as consumer if the transaction is not entered into as an integral part of the business carried on, and is not a transaction carried on with some regularity (*R and B Customs Brokers Co. Ltd v United Dominions Trust Ltd* [1988] 1 WLR 321). Sales at public auction which can be attended in person, where the buyer is an individual and the goods are second-hand goods, are excluded, as are any auction or sale by competitive tender where the buyer is not an individual (s. 12(2)). There is a statutory presumption that a party claiming to do so was dealing as consumer, so the burden of proof is on the other side to show that this was not the case (s. 12(3)).

For the purposes of the 1987 Regulations, a consumer is a person other than a body corporate who is acting for purposes which can be regarded as outside his or her business (SI 1987/2117, reg. 2(1)). A similar definition appears in the **1999 Regulations**, where a 'consumer' is a natural person who in making the contract is acting for purposes which can be regarded as outside his or her business (**SI 1999/2083, reg. 2(1)**).

UNFAIR CONTRACT TERMS ACT 1977

Application of the Act

UCTA 1977 came into force on 1 February 1978. It does not apply to contracts made before that date, but does apply to any loss or damage which is suffered on or after that date (s. 31). The provisions relating to sale and hire-purchase contracts apply to any contract and not only to business contracts. The other provisions apply only to business liability. 'Business' includes a profession and the activities of any government department or local or public authority (s. 14). 'Business liability' is liability for breach of an obligation or duty arising from things done or to be done by a person in the course of a business (whether that person's own or another's) (s. 1(3)). It does not matter whether any breach of duty or obligation is inadvertent or intentional, or whether liability arises directly or vicariously. 'Person' is not defined and so includes a body of persons corporate or unincorporate (Interpretation Act 1978, sch. 1). **95.3**

Negligence liability

By **UCTA 1977, s. 1(1)**, 'negligence' means the breach of: **95.4**

(a) any obligation arising from the express or implied terms of a contract to take reasonable care or exercise reasonable skill in the performance of the contract;
(b) any common law duty to take reasonable care or exercise reasonable skill (but not any stricter duty); and
(c) the duty of care imposed by the **Occupiers' Liability Act 1957**.

UCTA 1977 prevents contract terms or notices which exclude or restrict liability for personal injury or death from being effective at all (s. 2(1)). Loss or damage (other than for personal injury or death) can only be excluded or restricted in so far as a clause satisfies the test of reasonableness (s. 2(2)). Knowledge of or agreement to a contract term or notice which excludes or restricts liability is not of itself to be taken as indicating acceptance of any risk (s. 2(3)).

Contract terms

Before considering whether a purported term may fall foul of **UCTA 1977**, it is first necessary to determine whether it was in fact a term of the contract (see **93.23**: this is a point specifically mentioned also in **UCTA 1977, s. 11(2)**), and secondly whether the term purports to apply on the facts of the case. If the term appears to apply, it will also be necessary to consider whether it may be cut down by **UCTA 1977**. **95.5**

Where one party deals as a consumer or on another's written standard terms of business, there can be no exclusion or restriction of liability in respect of a breach by that other person save where the term satisfies the test of reasonableness (**UCTA 1977, s. 3(2)(a)**). Similarly, a person dealing with a consumer or on standard terms cannot claim to be contractually entitled to render a contractual performance substantially different from that reasonably expected, or no performance at all, unless the contract terms satisfies the test of reasonableness (**s. 3(2)(b)**).

A person dealing as a consumer cannot by reference to a contract term be made to indemnify another person in respect of liability that may be incurred for negligence or breach of contract, except in so far as the contract term satisfies the test of reasonableness (s. 4(1)).

Statutory implied terms

95.6 Prohibitions on excluding liability for breach of the statutory implied terms under **SoGA 1979** and SoGITA 1973 are contained in **UCTA 1977, s. 6**. The restrictions may be summarised as follows:

(a) an absolute prohibition on excluding or restricting the implied terms as to title in **SoGA 1979, s. 12**, and SoGITA 1973, s. 8;

(b) an absolute prohibition in consumer cases on excluding or restricting the implied terms in **SoGA 1979, ss. 13–15**, as to sale by description, quality or fitness, and sale by sample; and in relation to the equivalent provisions in the SoGITA 1973, ss. 9–11; and

(c) a qualified prohibition in non-consumer cases on excluding or restricting the implied terms in **SoGA 1979, ss. 13–15**, and the SoGITA 1973, ss. 9–11, so that to be effective an exclusion or restriction must satisfy the test of reasonableness (which is provided for by **UCTA 1977, s. 11** and **sch. 2**).

Misrepresentations

95.7 Similar protection to that provided under **UCTA 1977** is provided under the **Misrepresentation Act 1967, s. 3**, in relation to the exclusion of liability in respect of misrepresentations. A term purporting to exclude or restrict liability for any misrepresentation made before contract, or to exclude or restrict any remedies available by reason of such misrepresentations, is of no effect except in so far as the term satisfies the test of reasonableness set out in **UCTA 1977, s. 11**.

Reasonableness

95.8 The test of reasonableness is set out in **UCTA 1977, s. 11**. By **s. 11(1)**, the requirement of reasonableness for the purposes of **UCTA 1977** and the **Misrepresentation Act 1967, s. 3**, is that the term must have been a fair and reasonable one to be included having regard to the circumstances which were, or ought reasonably to have been, known to or in the contemplation of the parties when the contract was made. It is for those claiming that a contract term or notice satisfies the test of reasonableness to show that it does (**UCTA 1977, s. 11(5)**). In *Sheffield v Pickfords Ltd* [1997] CLC 648 the Court of Appeal held that any claim concerning standard terms of business implicitly raises the question whether those terms are reasonable, and it is not essential for the party seeking to enforce the terms to assert in a statement of case that they are reasonable. It was also held that particulars of any specific fact or matter relied upon could be given before any issue is raised. It is likely that this approach will be followed under the CPR.

Particular situations are governed by the following additional provisions:

(a) In determining for the purposes of non-consumer contracts governed by **UCTA 1977, s. 6** (sale of goods and hire-purchase) and **s. 7** (miscellaneous contracts, other than sale and hire-purchase, under which ownership or possession of goods passes), whether a contract term satisfies the test of reasonableness, the court must have regard to the matters set out in **sch. 2** to the Act (see **94.9**) (**s. 11(2)**).

(b) In relation to a notice (not being a notice which has contractual effect, such as a notice purporting to restrict or exclude liability in respect of theft), the requirement of reasonableness is that it should be fair and reasonable to allow reliance on it, having regard to all the circumstances obtaining when the liability arose or (but for the notice) would have arisen (**s. 11(3)**).

(c) Where the question arises whether a term or notice seeking to restrict a person's liability to a specified sum or money satisfies the requirement of reasonableness, regard shall be had (in the case of contract terms) to the matters mentioned in (a) above, and in all cases to:

(i) the resources which that person could expect to have available for the purpose of meeting the liability should it arise; and

(ii) how far it was open to that person to obtain insurance cover for the liability (s. 11(4)).

Reasonableness guidelines for non-consumer sales etc.

95.9 The guidelines set out in **UCTA 1977, sch. 2**, need to be considered only in relation to an attempt to exclude or restrict liability for breach of the implied terms as to conformity with description or sample or as to quality or fitness in a sale of goods, hire-purchase or similar transaction with a person who is not acting as a consumer (**UCTA 1977, ss. 6(3)**, 7(3) and (4)). In deciding whether the exclusion or restriction is reasonable in these non-consumer cases, **sch. 2** requires regard to be had to:

(a) the strength of the bargaining position of the parties relative to each other, taking into account (amongst other things) alternative means by which the customer's requirements could have been met;
(b) whether the customer received an inducement to agree to the term, or in accepting it had an opportunity of entering into a similar contract with other persons, but without having to accept such a term;
(c) whether the customer knew or ought reasonably to have known of the existence of the term (having regard, amongst other things, to any custom of the trade and any previous course of dealings between the parties);
(d) where the term excludes or restricts any relevant liability if some condition is not complied with, whether it was reasonable at the time of the contract to expect that compliance with that condition would be practicable;
(e) whether the goods were manufactured, processed or adapted to the special order of the customer.

In *St Albans City and District Council v International Computers Ltd* [1995] FSR 686, the council suffered a £1.3 million loss due to an error made by the computer company. The company sought to rely on a clause in its contract restricting its liability to £100,000. Scott Baker J took into account the following factors: (a) the parties were of unequal bargaining power; (b) the defendant had not justified the figure of £100,000, which was small in relation to the potential risk; (c) the defendant was insured in an aggregate figure of £50 million worldwide; (d) whether it was better for the risk to fall on a council or an international computer company. Despite the facts that both parties were free to make their own bargains, that the council entered into the contract with its eyes open, that such restrictions were commonplace in the computer industry, and that the software involved was a developing technology, it was held that the defendant had failed to discharge its burden of proof. The term was therefore unreasonable and unenforceable.

The fact that a contract is the result of negotiations between substantial companies is likely to indicate that the court should not find that its terms are unreasonable. In *Watford Electronics Ltd v Sanderson CFL Ltd* [2001] 1 All ER (Comm) 696 Peter Gibson LJ quoted with approval the following remarks of Judge Thayne Forbes in *Salvage Association v CAP Financial Services Ltd* [1995] FSR 654:

> Generally speaking, where a party well able to look after itself enters into a commercial contract and, with full knowledge of all relevant circumstances, willingly accepts the terms of the contract which provides for apportionment of the financial risks of that transaction, I think it is very likely that those terms will be held to be fair and reasonable.

In *Watford Electronics Ltd v Sanderson CFL Ltd* Chadwick LJ said, at [55]:

> Where experienced businessmen representing substantial companies of equal bargaining power negotiate an agreement, they may be taken to have had regard to the matters known to them. They should in my view be taken to be the best judge of the commercial fairness of the agreement which they have made; including the fairness of each of the terms in that agreement.

Terms in a standard-form contract are more likely to be held to be reasonable if they were negotiated between trade associations (as opposed to standard terms simply imposed by one party), as in such cases there is no substantial difference in bargaining power (see *R. W. Green Ltd v Cade Bros Farms Ltd* [1978] 1 Lloyd's Rep 602, and compare *George Mitchell (Chesterhall) Ltd v Finney Lock Seeds Ltd* [1983] 2 AC 803, where standard conditions were used by seed merchants without objection from farmers). The guidelines in sch. 2 are not exhaustive of the circumstances that may be considered. So, in *R and B Customs Brokers Co. Ltd v United Dominions Trust Ltd* [1988] 1 WLR 321 it was said that the court could take into account the question whether the party seeking to rely on an exclusion or restriction had an opportunity to discover the defect covered by the term.

Reasonableness in other contracts

95.10 In cases where terms are subject to the test of reasonableness under UCTA 1977, but the guidelines in **sch. 2** (see **95.9**) do not apply (for example, if the term does not purport to restrict the statutory implied terms, or if the dispute concerns the exclusion of liability for misrepresentations, or the contract is not one involving the sale etc. of goods), the court must apply the general test of reasonableness set out at **95.8**. However, the court can apply the sch. 2 guidelines by analogy (see *Singer Co. (UK) Ltd v Tees and Hartlepool Port Authority* [1988] 2 Lloyd's Rep 164).

As regards insurance (**UCTA 1977, s. 11(4)(b)**), the court will consider the availability of insurance rather than the actual insurance cover of the defendant (*Singer Co. (UK) Ltd v Tees and Hartlepool Port Authority*). Limitation of liability may well be reasonable for a person who stores or carries another's goods without being informed of their value, particularly if the goods could be more cheaply insured by the owner (*Singer Co. (UK) Ltd v Tees and Hartlepool Port Authority*).

In *Smith v Eric S. Bush* [1990] 1 AC 831 the question arose as to whether it was reasonable for surveyors instructed by the mortgagee to exclude or restrict liability in relation to their survey reports prepared in connection with the sale of ordinary houses. The House of Lords held, having regard to the relative expense to the purchaser of buying a house, and the high rates of interest charged to borrowers, that it was not reasonable to throw the risk of loss flowing from the incompetence or carelessness of the surveyor on to the purchaser, and exclusion clauses were held to be unenforceable. On the other hand, in relation to very expensive houses, and industrial property, it was said that prudent purchasers would obtain their own survey reports, and it may well be reasonable for surveyors to exclude their liability, or at least to restrict it to the amount of their insurance cover.

Excluded contracts

95.11 Certain contracts are excluded either in whole or in part from the provisions of **UCTA 1977** by **sch. 1**. The provisions on negligence liability (**s. 2**), liability in contract (**s. 3**) and unreasonable indemnity clauses (**s. 4**) do not apply to the types of contract listed in **sch. 1, para. 1**. These exclusions may be summarised as contracts relating to insurance, creation or transfer of an interest in land, intellectual property, formation or dissolution of a company or its constitution, and the creation or transfer of securities. Special provisions exist in relation to certain marine and hovercraft contracts (**paras 2 and 3**). The exclusions of negligence liability in **s. 2(1)** and **(2)** only apply to employment contracts in favour of the employee (**sch. 1, para. 4**).

Practice

95.12 In *Sheffield v Pickfords Ltd* [1997] CLC 648 the Court of Appeal held that it was not essential for a party relying on contract terms or standard terms to assert that those terms are reasonable. That allegation is implicit if a party relies in a statement of case on terms which have to satisfy the test of reasonableness. However, the better practice is to make at least a general assertion of reasonableness of such contract or standard terms in the statement of case. Further information can then be sought or ordered of the facts and matter relied on as showing reasonableness, if necessary. This approach is likely to be followed under the CPR.

CONSUMER PROTECTION (CANCELLATION OF CONTRACTS CONCLUDED AWAY FROM BUSINESS PREMISES) REGULATIONS 1987

Effect of the Regulations

The 1987 Regulations apply to contracts made on or after 1 July 1988 and create a statutory cooling-off period which gives the consumer a right to cancel contracts which are within the scope of the Regulations. The 1987 Regulations impose certain obligations on a trader entering into a cancellable contract with a consumer to give the consumer written information about the consumer's cancellation rights, breach of which makes the contract unenforceable by the trader. Nothing in the 1987 Regulations prevents enforcement of the contract by the consumer against the trader. **95.13**

The 1987 Regulations apply to contracts (other than excepted contracts) for:

(a) the supply of goods or services to a consumer which are made during unsolicited visits by a trader to the consumer's home or to the home of another person, or to the consumer's place of work, i.e., traditional doorstep selling;
(b) contracts made during a visit at the request of the consumer where the goods or services to which the contract relates are other than those concerning which the consumer requested the visit (provided that when the visit was requested the consumer did not know, or could not reasonably have known, that the supply of goods or services formed part of the trader's business activities), i.e., visits at the request of the consumer at which a sale of some unexpected different product is agreed;
(c) contracts made on an excursion organised by the trader away from business premises on which the trader is carrying on any business, i.e., the promotional trip; and
(d) offers to contract made by a consumer to a trader in the circumstances mentioned in (a), (b) or (c) above — this avoids there being any distinction between the situation where the contract is agreed and where the consumer merely offers to make a contract with the contract being formed when that offer is accepted later.

Unsolicited visit

An unsolicited visit is widely defined. Unsolicited visits covered by the 1987 Regulations are those to the consumer's home or to the home of another person and those to the consumer's place of work. Regulation 3(3) defines an unsolicited visit as: **95.14**

a visit by a trader, whether or not he is the trader who supplies the goods or service, which does not take place at the express request of the consumer and includes:
(a) a visit by a trader which takes place after he, or a person acting in his name or on his behalf, telephones the consumer (otherwise that at the consumer's express request) and indicates during the course of the telephone call (either expressly or by implication) that he, or the trader in whose name or on whose behalf he is acting, is willing to visit the consumer, and
(b) a visit by a trader which takes place after he, or a person acting in his name or on his behalf, visits the consumer (otherwise than at the consumer's express request) and indicates during the course of that visit (either expressly or by implication) that he, or the trader in whose name or on whose behalf he is acting, is willing to make a subsequent visit to the consumer.

Excepted contracts

Excepted contracts are defined in reg. 3(2) of the 1987 Regulations, and include transactions relating to land; contracts for sale of food, drink or other goods by regular roundsmen; **95.15** insurance contracts; agreements regulated under the Financial Services and Markets Act 2000; any contract under which the total payments to be made by the consumer do not exceed £35; and any contract under which credit within the meaning of the **Consumer Credit Act 1974** does not exceed £35 (other than a hire-purchase or conditional sale agreement). A further important exempt category exists for contracts which fulfil the following three conditions:

(i) terms of the contract are contained in a trader's catalogue which is readily available to the consumer to read in the absence of the trader or his representative before the conclusion of the contract;

(ii) the parties to the contract intend that there shall be maintained continuity of contact between the trader or his representative and the consumer in relation to the transaction in question or any subsequent transaction; and

(iii) both the catalogue and the contract contain or are accompanied by a prominent notice indicating that the consumer has a right to return to the trader or his representative goods supplied to him within the period of not less than seven days from the day on which the goods are received by the consumer and otherwise to cancel the contract within that period without the consumer incurring any liability, other than any liability which may arise from the failure of the consumer to take reasonable care of the goods while they are in his possession.

Notice of cancellation rights

95.16 If the 1987 Regulations apply, no contract will be enforceable against the consumer unless the trader has delivered to the consumer a notice in writing indicating the right to cancel the contract within seven days. The notice must contain both certain prescribed information and a cancellation form (reg. 4(1)). The notice setting out the right to cancel must be served on the consumer at the time of making the contract or at the time the consumer makes an offer to the trader. There is no saving provision permitting the court to waive any breach (even if it has caused no prejudice), or to grant leave to enforce, or to permit partial enforcement of the contract. In view of the drastic consequences of breach of the 1987 Regulations, it remains surprising that they are so widely ignored by traders.

The information which is required in the notice of cancellation rights is set out in the 1987 Regulations, sch. 1, part I. That notice must contain: (a) the name of the trader; (b) the trader's reference number, code or other details to enable the contract or offer to be identified; (c) a statement that the consumer has the right to cancel the contract if he or she wishes and that this right can be exercised by sending or taking a written notice of cancellation to the person mentioned in the notice within the period of seven days following the making of the contract; (d) the name and address of the person to whom notice of cancellation may be given; and (e) a statement that the consumer can use the cancellation form provided, if he or she wishes.

The cancellation form which must be included in the notice of cancellation rights is set out in part II of the schedule and is as follows:

(Complete and detach and return this form ONLY IF YOU WISH TO CANCEL THE CONTRACT)

To : [*Trader to insert the name and address of the person to whom notice may be given*]

I/We* hereby give notice that I/we* wish to cancel my/our* contract [*Trader to insert reference number, code or other details to enable the contract or offer to be identified. He may also enter the name and address of the consumer*].

Signed

Date

*Delete as appropriate

Cancelling the contract

A consumer wishing to cancel an agreement falling within the 1987 Regulations must serve a notice, which may be informally expressed and need not be on the cancellation form, on the trader within seven days following the making of the contract (reg. 4(5)). If the consumer sends the cancellation form (or other notice stating his or her intention to cancel) by post, it is deemed to have been served at the time of posting whether or not it is actually received (reg. 4(7)). A document to be served under the 1987 Regulations on a person may be served by delivering it to, or by sending it by post to, or by leaving it with the person at the person's proper address, addressed to the person by name (reg. 11). If the consumer does cancel, the contract is treated as if it had never been entered into by the consumer (reg. 4(6)). The 1987 Regulations make detailed provision for return of money paid (reg. 5); repayment of credit (reg. 6); return of the goods (reg. 7, which makes it plain that the duty to return the goods is limited to returning them to the trader at the consumer's own premises); and return or payment for goods part-exchanged (reg. 8). Hardly surprisingly, there is a prohibition on contracting out (reg. 10). **95.17**

Practice

By analogy with the approach to UCTA 1977 adopted in *Sheffield v Pickfords Ltd* [1997] CLC 648 (see **95.12**), it is submitted that any claim concerning a contract to which the 1987 Regulations apply implicitly raises the question whether the contract complies with the Regulations, and it is not essential for the party seeking to enforce the contract to assert in a statement of case that it does comply. **95.18**

If a consumer wishes to allege any breach of the 1987 Regulations, the breach ought to be specifically asserted by the consumer in his or her statement of case. However, a court should refuse to enforce a contract if it becomes aware of a breach of the 1987 Regulations, even if the breach has not been set out in a statement of case because the Regulations absolutely prohibit enforcement. If it is asserted that the contract or offer has been cancelled by giving notice, that fact should be specifically asserted by the consumer, who should also specifically seek any consequential remedies (such as return of money paid or goods).

A consumer who is party to a claim concerning a contract to which the 1987 Regulations apply should consider an application for summary judgment under **CPR, r. 24.2**, and/or to strike out under **r. 3.4** to prevent any enforcement of the contract. In most cases the court can decide without hearing oral evidence whether or not the 1987 Regulations apply and whether or not they have been complied with. If the consumer alleges that he or she returned the cancellation notice by post, it is possible to rely on the deeming provision that it was served when posted whether or not it was actually received (reg. 4(7)).

UNFAIR TERMS IN CONSUMER CONTRACTS REGULATIONS 1999

Scope of the Regulations

The Unfair Terms in Consumer Contracts Regulations 1999 (SI 1999/2083, the 1999 Regulations) came into force on 1 October 1999, replacing the Unfair Terms in Consumer Contracts Regulations 1994 (SI 1994/3159), which applied to contracts made on or after 1 July 1995. The 1999 Regulations differ from UCTA 1977 in that they apply only to consumer contracts. The Arbitration Act 1996 extends the 1999 Regulations to arbitration agreements within s. 89(1) of that Act and, in relation to those agreements only, a consumer does not have to be a natural person. Regulation 3(1) of the 1999 Regulations defines both a 'seller' and a 'supplier' as someone acting for purposes relating to his business and so the Regulations do not apply to non-business transactions. Regulation 6 introduces a *contra proferentem* rule of construction for written terms. **95.19**

The 1999 Regulations lay down two main obligations. First, there is a requirement that written terms be in plain intelligible language (reg. 7). Secondly, there is a requirement of fairness that applies to any term (whether oral or in writing) which is not individually negotiated, other than core terms which are in plain intelligible language (see 95.22). Although there is no specific mention of oral contracts, in the unusual situation of a consumer entering into an oral contract on terms which are not individually negotiated, the Regulations will also apply. The EU Directive on which the 1999 Regulations are based made it plain that the consumer is to receive equal treatment under contracts concluded by word of mouth and written contracts. The 1999 Regulations must be interpreted so as to give full effect to the Directive.

Core terms

95.20 The 1999 Regulations control unfair terms rather than unfair contracts. Provided the contract is in plain and intelligible language, the 1999 Regulations do not (by reg. 6(2)) impeach terms relating to either:

(a) the definition of the subject matter of the contract; or
(b) the adequacy of the price or remuneration.

In this chapter these are referred to as 'core terms'. In the first House of Lords case to consider what is exempted by reg. 6(2) it was held that a default interest provision is not a core term (*Director General of Fair Trading v First National Bank plc* [2001] UKHL 52, [2002] 1 AC 481).

Excluded contracts

95.21 The 1999 Regulations do not apply to contracts of employment; contracts relating to succession rights or rights under family law; contracts relating to the incorporation or organisation of companies or partnerships; nor any term incorporated in order to comply with or which reflects (a) mandatory statutory or regulatory provisions or (b) the provisions or principles of international conventions to which the member States or the Community are party (reg. 4(2)).

Plain and intelligible language test

95.22 Any written term in a contract to which the 1999 Regulations apply must be expressed in plain intelligible language (reg. 7(1)). If there is any doubt about meaning then the *contra proferentem* rule applies (reg. 7(2)). The 1999 Regulations do not specify any burden of proof in showing that the terms are in plain intelligible language as that is a question of law. The 1999 Regulations do not specify any individual remedy for a breach of the requirement to use plain intelligible language. The effect is as follows:

(a) the core terms are excluded from the fairness test only if they are expressed in plain and intelligible language, so that a breach of this requirement would enable the court to consider the fairness of core terms;
(b) a breach of this requirement will have an impact on the test of fairness, as terms which remain unintelligible (even after applying the *contra proferentem* test) are likely to be unfair.

If a term is not plain and intelligible, the Director General of Fair Trading may consider using his powers to prevent its continued use. Unless and until such action is taken, the court simply has to interpret the term, even if it is not plain or intelligible.

Individually negotiated

95.23 The general test of fairness applies only to terms which have not been individually negotiated. There is no definition of individual negotiation. A term which is presented on a 'take it or leave it' basis (whether oral or in writing) is plainly not individually negotiated. Although not a definition, any term shall always be regarded as not having been individually negotiated (i.e., will be covered by the 1999 Regulations) if it is drafted in advance and the consumer has not been able to influence the substance of the term (reg. 5(2)). If certain terms or certain aspects of a contract have been individually negotiated, the 1999 Regulations apply to the rest of the contract if an overall assessment of the contract indicates that it is a pre-formulated standard contract (reg. 5(3)). The burden of showing that the term was individually negotiated is upon the seller or supplier (reg. 5(4)).

Unfairness test

The 1999 Regulations introduce a two-part test for unfairness. The basic test appears in regs 5(1) and 6(1). There is also a non-exhaustive list of terms which may be regarded as unfair (which are set out in sch. 2). Although the burden is upon the seller or supplier to show that the term was individually negotiated, the 1999 Regulations do not indicate who has the burden of proof of the question of unfairness. In order to give purposive effect to the 1999 Regulations and Directive, the burden of proof on fairness should, it is submitted, be regarded as being on the seller or supplier, and not the consumer. **95.24**

The basic test is that a term will be unfair if, 'contrary to the requirement of good faith, it causes a significant imbalance in the parties' rights and obligations under the contract, to the detriment of the consumer' (reg. 5(1)). The assessment of the unfair nature of a term is made taking into account the nature of the goods or services for which the contract was concluded, and referring, as at the time of the conclusion of the contract, to all the circumstances attending the conclusion of the contract or of another contract upon which it is dependent (reg. 6(1)).

Effect of an unfair term

A term which is found to be unfair within the meaning of the 1999 Regulations is not binding on the consumer (reg. 8). The contract will continue to bind the parties if it is capable of continuing in existence without the unfair term (reg. 8(2)). Nothing in the 1999 Regulations prevents enforcement of any term (even an unfair term) by the consumer against the trader. **95.25**

Complaints can be considered by the Director General of Fair Trading or a qualifying body; injunctions can be sought to prevent the use of unfair terms; and documents and information can be sought and publicised (regs 10 to 15). In the first case brought by the Director General he was unsuccessful at first instance, successful on appeal to the Court of Appeal, but eventually lost in the House of Lords (*Director General of Fair Trading v First National Bank plc* [2001] UKHL 52, [2002] 1 AC 481).

Practice

The burden of proof is on the seller or supplier if alleging that a term was individually negotiated (1999 Regulations, reg. 5(4)). Whether or not a term is in plain intelligible language is a matter of law for the court. **95.26**

By analogy with the approach to UCTA 1977 adopted in *Sheffield v Pickfords Ltd* [1997] CLC 648 (see **95.12**), it is submitted that any claim concerning a contract to which the 1999 Regulations apply implicitly raises the question whether the contract complies with the Regulations, and it is not essential for the party seeking to enforce the contract to assert in a statement of case that it does comply.

If a consumer wishes to allege that a term is not in plain intelligible language, that fact ought to be specifically asserted in the consumer's statement of case, particularly if there is to be a challenge to a core term (which can only be challenged if it is not in plain intelligible language). An allegation by a consumer that a term is unfair ought to appear in the consumer's statement of case. However, a mere failure to assert unfairness should not prevent the court refusing to enforce the term, as an unfair term is not binding on the consumer.

If it appears to the court that the 1999 Regulations apply and a term is not in plain intelligible language or a term which is not individually negotiated is unfair, the court should adjudicate on those points whether or not they appear in the statement of case.

CONSUMER PROTECTION (DISTANCE SELLING) REGULATIONS 2000

Scope of the Regulations

95.27 The Consumer Protection (Distance Selling) Regulations 2000 (SI 2000/2334) came into force on 31 October 2000. They apply to any distance contract which is defined as 'any contract concerning goods or services concluded between a supplier and a consumer under an organised distance sales or service provision scheme run by the supplier who, for the purposes of the contract, makes exclusive use of one or more means of distance communication up to and including the moment which the contract is concluded'. Distance communication is defined as any means which, without the simultaneous physical presence of the supplier and the consumer, may be used for the conclusion of a contract between those parties, and an indicative list of such means is contained in sch. 1 to the Regulations.

If the contract is a distance contract then, subject to three qualifications, the regulations will apply:

(a) The first qualification is that certain distance contracts are wholly exempt. Regulation 5 lists the six categories of 'excepted contracts': sale or disposition of land (other than a rental contract); construction of a building where the contract also provides for the sale or other disposition of an interest in land; financial services (a non-exhaustive list of which is contained in sch. 2 to the regulations); automatic vending machines or automated commercial premises; contracts concluded with a telecommunications operator through a public payphone; and auctions.

(b) The second qualification is that certain contracts are partially exempt. Regulation 6 lists the four categories of contract which are partially exempt: timeshare agreements (within the meaning of the Timeshare Act 1992); food, beverages or other goods intended for everyday consumption supplied to the consumer's house or workplace by regular roundsmen; contracts for accommodation, transport, catering or leisure services where the supplier undertakes, when the contract is concluded, to provide the services on a specific date or within a specific period; and package holidays (within the meaning of the Package Travel, Package Holidays and Package Tours Regulations 1992 (SI 1992/3288)) which are sold or offered for sale within a member State.

(c) The third qualification is that the right to cancel will not exist in respect of six categories of contract. Regulation 13 lists these categories: contracts for the supply of services where the supply has started before the end of the cancellation period; contracts for the supply of goods where the price fluctuates in the financial market which cannot be controlled by the supplier; contracts for the supply of goods which are personalised or are liable to deteriorate or expire rapidly; contracts for the supply of audio or video recordings or computer software if they are unsealed by the consumer; contracts for the supply of newspapers, magazines or periodicals; and contracts for the supply of gaming, betting or lottery services.

The European Court of Justice has ruled (on a reference by the Chancery Division) that the exemption relating to 'transport' is to be interpreted as meaning contracts for the provision of transport services and therefore includes car-hire services (*easyCar (UK) Ltd v Office of Fair Trading* (case C-336/03) [2005] ECR I-1947).

Effect of the Regulations

The Regulations require information to be provided to the consumer in good time prior to the conclusion of the contract (reg. 7). Further information is required not later than during performance (in the case of services) and at the time of delivery (in the case of goods, other than goods to be delivered to third parties) (reg. 8). There is then a seven-day cooling-off period in which there is a right to cancel. Detailed provisions about notice of this right and the calculation of the start and end of the seven-day period are in regs 10–12. 95.28

If a distance contract is cancelled, any related credit agreement is automatically cancelled (reg. 15). Detailed provisions are made for the return of money and goods (including goods part-exchanged) in regs 16–18.

If the contract is not cancelled, then (unless there is agreement to the contrary) it must be performed by the supplier within 30 days (reg. 19).

New provision is made to regulate inertia selling (reg. 24). Unsurprisingly, there is a prohibition on contracting out of the Regulations (reg. 25).

Weights and measures authorities and the OFT are charged with enforcing the Regulations. They may apply for injunctions to restrain breaches of the Regulations (reg. 27).

Chapter 96 Consumer Credit

INTRODUCTION

96.1 The Consumer Credit Act 2006 received the Royal Assent on 30 March 2006. It will be brought into force after consultation. The proposal is to introduce the new provisions in three stages. Agreements made before 30 March 2006 will remain largely unaffected, but some provisions will affect agreements made between 30 March 2006 and the date on which the

Act comes into force. The remaining provisions will only apply to agreements made after the Act comes into force. The Act makes major changes to the regulation of consumer credit in the UK, including changes to financial limits, information to be provided to borrowers and the action required where there has been any default. A wholly new concept of unfair relationships is introduced by ss. 19 to 22 of the Act, which will give the court new power to intervene. Detailed new licensing provisions are created, together with an Ombudsman scheme.

Financing of consumer sales and services is a multi-billion-pound industry, and generates a vast number of civil claims each year. Over the years the finance companies have developed a variety of different methods of providing funds to consumers, giving customers a choice of different methods of raising finance. All the different methods are contract based, and their precise effect and legal significance depends in part on the individual terms of the agreement in question, and partly on the general law. In this context, the applicable law is in part the general law of contract, and in part the statutory provisions stemming from the **Consumer Credit Act 1974** (CCA 1974).

It has long been recognised that there is often an imbalance of bargaining power between lenders and borrowers, which can be used unfairly so as to impose onerous terms on the borrower. Irresponsible lending is also regarded as a social evil, with its effect of burdening borrowers and their families with debts they cannot, or can barely, repay. The CCA 1974 seeks to address these problems by:

(a) creating a licensing system for consumer credit businesses (CCA 1974, ss. 21 to 42), with oversight for the whole system in the hands of the Office of Fair Trading (OFT);
(b) imposing restrictions on advertising consumer finance and the canvassing of customers, with criminal sanctions for contravention (CCA 1974, ss. 43 to 54);
(c) regulating the form and content of consumer credit agreements (CCA 1974, ss. 55 to 74);
(d) giving certain rights to customers, including rights to certain types of information (**CCA 1974, ss. 75** to **86**); and
(e) giving protection to customers against the worst excesses of finance companies in the event of default or termination (**CCA 1974, ss. 87** to **144**).

These five areas will be considered, after first discussing, at **96.2** to **96.29**, the nature and definition of various categories of consumer credit transactions.

NATURE AND DEFINITION OF CONSUMER CREDIT TRANSACTIONS

The main classes of consumer credit agreement

Although the exact effect and meaning of a consumer credit agreement will depend on its own wording, several well-known types of agreement have developed. Further, almost all consumer credit agreements are standard form contracts, and many finance companies use agreements that are similar to those used by other companies, or at least which deal with the same issues. **96.2**

Consumer credit agreements may have as their object simply the provision of money to the customer, which may be used for any purpose, or may be designed to enable the customer to obtain some specific item or service. If goods are to be obtained, the customer may simply wish to hire them, or may have in mind acquiring ownership. If ownership is to be acquired by the customer, a further question is when that should take place. The main classes of consumer credit arrangements which have evolved to suit these various situations are described in **96.3** to **96.11**. The descriptions are very general, and there are variations within each category.

96.3 **Loans** These are familiar arrangements whereby a financial institution (often, but not necessarily a High Street bank) lends money to a customer. Often the loan can be used for whatever the customer wants, but many loans are made for specific purposes (such as car purchases or home improvements). The agreement will often provide for repayment (with interest) at a set amount each month for a fixed period (such as 24 months or five years). Some loan agreements provide for fluctuating interest rates varying with the bank's base rate.

96.4 **Overdrafts** These are similar to loans, but tend to be more flexible. Often a bank will give a customer an overdraft limit, allowing the customer to borrow and pay back how much and at such times as the customer chooses, and for the customer to use the money borrowed for whatever purpose the customer chooses, provided the borrowing does not at any stage exceed the limit. The bank's agreement with its customer will usually allow the bank to vary the rate of interest charged from time to time as its basic rates change, and will usually permit the bank to call in the amount overdrawn on demand. A demand does not need to specify how much is owed, and the customer is entitled to no more than a reasonable time to implement the mechanics of repayment, such as delivering a cheque in payment, before the bank becomes entitled to enforce (*Bank of Baroda v Panessar* [1987] Ch 335).

96.5 **Credit cards** In transactions paid for by credit card there are three bilateral contracts. First, there is a contract between the customer and the credit card company under which the customer is usually allowed a credit limit which can be used to buy goods and services as and when the customer chooses. The credit card company will send a monthly account statement to the customer, usually giving the customer a choice of paying off the balance in full or by instalments (often with considerable flexibility about the amount that can be paid each month). The delay between individual purchases by the customer and money becoming due under the monthly statement will often give the customer a short period of interest-free credit. Sums paid off after this period usually attract moderately high rates of interest. The second contract is between the credit card company and the retailer. These contracts usually provide that the credit card company will pay the retailer (say) 95 per cent or 96 per cent of the price charged to the customer. The retailer also gives a period of interest-free credit to the credit card company caused by the delay between the transaction with the customer and payment by the credit card company. Thirdly, there is the contract for the supply of goods or services between the customer and the retailer. It has been held that in credit card transactions the retailer can only look to the credit card company for payment, and not the customer, even if the credit card company becomes insolvent before paying the retailer (*Re Charge Card Services Ltd* [1989] Ch 497). Many credit cards also allow the customer to withdraw money as opposed to being restricted to using it for the payment of goods or services, in which event the transaction is rather like obtaining an overdraft. Further, many large retailers have their own credit cards which can only be used in their own stores. In this event the roles of retailer and credit card company are combined, although not always, because often the credit card business of the retailer will be operated by a separate company within the retailer's group of companies.

96.6 **Charge cards** These may be distinguished from credit cards in that the customer using a charge card will have agreed with the charge card company to repay the whole amount borrowed in a month by a set date after the company renders its account. Note that card companies are not particularly consistent with their use of the terms 'credit card' and 'charge card', with some companies calling their credit cards 'charge cards'.

96.7 **Hiring** A customer who cannot afford to buy an item (or who chooses not to buy it) may instead choose to hire it. As is well known, an item that is hired continues to belong to the hiring company but, during the period of hire, is in the possession of the customer and may be used by the customer. The period of hire may be fixed or indefinite. Fixed hire periods may be short (such as a single day, or a week or two), or any other period, including fixed periods of several years. Hiring companies fall into two main categories. First, there are those who maintain a stock of goods which are hired out to customers, and who will hire out the goods again once a period of hire has expired. Secondly, some hiring companies are really simply finance companies who let out on hire goods which the customer chooses from a retailer, which the hiring company purchases from the retailer after being chosen by the customer, and then lets out to the customer, usually on long-term hire terms. Long-term hire contracts often resemble the credit agreements described below, and the monthly hire charges may not be drastically different from the monthly payments required under equivalent credit agreements for the same goods. The major difference is that under a hire contract ownership of the goods will never be transferred to the hirer. However, even this difference may be more apparent than real, because many hiring companies will sell the goods to the customer at the end of a long-term hiring contract for a nominal sum.

Hire purchase This is rather like a long-term hire contract, but with the addition of giving the customer an option to purchase the goods at the end of the hire period. The purchase fee is usually a nominal sum which is added to the final instalment. In most hire-purchase transactions there are two contracts. A customer will go to a retailer and choose the item in question, but there will be no direct contract between them. Instead, the retailer will arrange for the customer to complete the finance company's proposal forms, which will be sent to the finance company. If the proposal is accepted by the finance company, the retailer will sell the goods to the finance company (the first contract), and the finance company will enter into a hire-purchase agreement with the customer (the second contract). There is nothing to prevent a retailer entering into a hire-purchase agreement directly with a customer, with the retailer also taking the role of the finance company, but this is very unusual. **96.8**

Conditional sale agreements Conditional sales are single-contract transactions between a retailer and a customer under which the passing of property in the goods is postponed until specified conditions are satisfied. The usual conditions include full payment for the goods by stated instalments. They therefore resemble hire-purchase in that they last a stated period of time (often 12,24 or 36 months), during which period the goods do not belong to the customer, but are in the possession of the customer. At the end of the stated period ownership vests in the customer, provided the customer honours the terms of the agreement. Conditional sale agreements may also be made in relation to land (CCA 1974, s. 189(1)). **96.9**

Credit sales Like conditional sales, credit sales are single-contract transactions under which the price is payable by stated instalments (or sometimes at some future date). However, in a credit sale ownership passes to the buyer immediately (see **Sale of Goods Act 1979, s. 18, r. 1**). **96.10**

Mortgages of goods (also known as chattel mortgages) Under these the owner of goods (the customer) agrees to mortgage goods to a finance company in return for money. The goods may have been owned by the customer for some time, or may be those the customer intends to acquire with the finance. The agreement will involve ownership in the goods being vested in the finance company on condition that ownership will be transferred back to the customer when the loan is repaid. Such transactions must comply with the registration and other requirements of the Bills of Sale Acts, which make them highly inconvenient for finance companies, and so this method of finance is extremely rare. **96.11**

Security in consumer credit transactions

A finance company may be prepared to lend money to a customer without taking security. If so, it will usually demand a higher rate of interest to compensate for the risk of default. Security may be provided by: **96.12**

(a) the customer persuading someone else to agree to guarantee the repayments. People standing surety can also be asked to indemnify the finance company in the event of default or other breach by the customer;

(b) the finance company taking a mortgage over the customer's goods. As mentioned at **96.11**, this is rare due to the difficulties caused by the Bills of Sale Acts;
(c) the finance company retaining ownership of the goods acquired in the transaction until the finance has been cleared. This is used particularly in hire purchase, conditional sale and hire agreements. If the customer defaults, the agreement will usually provide that the finance company can repossess the goods and sell them, applying the proceeds of sale against the balance owed by the customer; and
(d) the finance company taking a charge over land or other real property. Often the land in question will be the customer's home, which will frequently already be subject to a mortgage. The finance company accordingly takes a second charge over the property. In times when house prices are increasing this can be a very effective means of securing payment.

Regulated consumer credit agreements

96.13 This chapter is concerned with the law relating to regulated consumer credit agreements. By the **CCA 1974, s. 8**, a 'regulated consumer credit agreement' is an agreement, other than an exempt agreement (see **59.32**), between an individual debtor and a creditor by which credit not exceeding £25,000 is provided (the figure was £15,000 for agreements made before 1 May 1998). Credit agreements exceeding £25,000 are therefore unregulated by the CCA 1974. For the purposes of the definition in s. 8, the word 'credit' includes a cash loan and any other form of financial accommodation (**CCA 1974, s. 9(1)**). The inclusion of the words 'any other form of financial accommodation' makes this a very wide definition. It is not essential that there be a charge for the financial accommodation, although it will often be the case that interest will be charged. The definition is concerned with a contractual deferment of the payment obligation (or part of it). Mere late payment of an invoice will not bring a transaction within the CCA 1974.

Parties to a regulated consumer credit agreement

96.14 In the CCA 1974, the party providing the credit under a consumer credit agreement or the persons to whom his or her rights and duties under the agreement have passed by assignment or operation of law, is called the 'creditor' (CCA 1974, s. 189). In relation to a prospective consumer credit agreement, the definition includes the prospective creditor. The CCA 1974 calls the customer the 'debtor', and by s. 189 defines the term as being the individual receiving credit under a consumer credit agreement, or the persons to whom his or her rights and duties under the agreement have passed by assignment or operation of law, and in relation to a prospective consumer credit agreement, includes the prospective debtor.

Although the creditor under a regulated consumer credit agreement can be, and often is, a limited liability company, an agreement will only be regulated if the debtor is an individual (**CCA 1974, s. 8(1)**). This term includes a partnership or other unincorporated body of persons not consisting entirely of bodies corporate (CCA 1974, s. 189). A credit agreement where the debtor is a company will therefore always be unregulated.

Categorisation of agreements under the CCA 1974

96.15 In addition to the categorisation of consumer credit agreements familiar to the general public, the financial services industry and lawyers (see **96.2** to **96.11**), the CCA 1974 uses its own idiosyncratic categorisation system. The categories used in the Act are set out below (**96.16** to **96.24**).

96.16 **'Running-account credit'** This is defined by CCA 1974, s. 10(1)(a), as a facility under a credit agreement under which the debtor is enabled to receive from time to time from the creditor or a third party cash, goods and services (or any of them) to an amount or value such that, taking into account payments made by or to the credit of the debtor, the credit limit (if any) is not at any time exceeded. The most common examples are authorised bank overdrafts, shop budget accounts and credit cards. A running-account credit agreement will be regulated if the debtor is an individual and the credit limit does not exceed £25,000 (s. 10(3)(a)). If there is no credit limit, or if the limit exceeds £25,000, the agreement may still be regulated by reason of s. 10(3)(b) if, for example, it is probable that the debit balance will never exceed the £25,000 threshold.

'Fixed-sum credit' This is defined by CCA 1974, s. 10(1)(b), to cover all credit agreements to individuals other than running-account credit agreements. An agreement may be for a fixed sum even if the credit is payable by instalments. Most loan agreements will fall within this definition, as will an unauthorised overdraft. If a cheque is presented or debit card transaction takes place which makes an account overdrawn or overdrawn beyond any agreed limit, the transaction constitutes a request to the bank for a fixed-sum loan to cover the transaction which the bank can decide whether to allow. If the transaction is honoured by the bank then fixed-sum credit is provided. **96.17**

'Restricted-use credit' This is dealt with by CCA 1974, s. 11(1), and covers agreements where the creditor can ensure the application of the credit to a particular purchase or other transaction. If the credit agreement is intended for use for a specific purpose, but the mechanics of the transaction leaves the debtor free to use the finance as he or she chooses (even if doing so is a contravention of the agreement), the agreement is not restricted-use credit (s. 11(3)). Three different types of agreement are regarded as restricted-use under s. 11(1): **96.18**

(a) an agreement which finances a transaction between the debtor and the creditor, whether forming part of the agreement or not. This covers the simple situation where the creditor is also the supplier of the goods or services;
(b) an agreement which finances a transaction between the debtor and a person (the 'supplier') other than the creditor. This situation covers purchases of goods made by credit card (but not, of course, cash advances on credit cards). It also covers loan agreements where the supplier is paid directly by the creditor, the most common example of which is the finance for the purchase of goods arranged by a shop. An agreement may fall into this category even if the identity of the supplier is unknown at the time the finance agreement is made (s. 11(4)); and
(c) an agreement which refinances any existing indebtedness of the debtor whether to the creditor or another person. This is restricted-use credit because the money borrowed can only be applied to discharge the existing indebtedness.

'Unrestricted-use credit' This is simply any agreement which is not restricted-use credit (CCA 1974, s. 11(2)). Illustrations include most credit and charge card transactions, and most loan and overdraft arrangements. Even a loan for the purpose of buying (say) a car will be unrestricted use by reason of CCA 1974, s. 11(3), unless the creditor takes some steps to ensure the money is in fact used to buy the intended car. **96.19**

'Debtor-creditor-supplier' (DCS) agreements These are regulated consumer credit agreements where there is a connection between the creditor and the supplier of the goods or services. Typically, but not always, there will be a supplier and someone else who is the creditor. In DCS transactions the policy of the Act is to render both the supplier and the creditor liable for any misrepresentations or breaches of contract in relation to the underlying supply of goods or services. DCS agreements are defined in **CCA 1974, s. 12**, and are of three types: **96.20**

(a) Restricted-use credit agreements within the CCA 1974, s. 11(1)(a), which finance a transaction between the debtor and the creditor whether forming part of that agreement or not (s. 12(a)). This category makes it plain that a DCS agreement does not require three parties. The supplier and the creditor in this category are the same person. Conditional sale and credit sale agreements fall within this definition.

(b) Restricted-use credit agreements within the CCA 1974, s. 11(1)(b), being those made by the creditor under pre-existing arrangements or in contemplation of future arrangements between the creditor and the supplier (s. 12(b)). This category covers transactions where the supplier has arrangements with a finance company. A purchase with a credit card is included, as the arrangement by a shop for acceptance of a credit card constitutes a pre-existing arrangement. Equally, credit agreements arising from the situation where a finance company provides a store with a stock of loan agreement forms which are used to arrange loans to finance purchases, will fall into this category provided the money is paid directly to the supplier so that it is restricted-use credit.

(c) Unrestricted-use credit agreements made by a creditor under pre-existing arrangements between the creditor and the supplier in the knowledge that the credit is to be used to finance a transaction between the debtor and the supplier (s. 12(c)). This covers the more unusual situation where the credit is arranged by the supplier but is unrestricted-use because, for example, the money is not paid directly to the supplier. An example would be where a debtor wants to purchase a car, the car dealer provides the debtor with forms for arranging a loan with the creditor to cover the purchase (which the dealer has under a pre-existing arrangement with the creditor), and when the loan is approved the money lent is paid by the creditor to the debtor who then uses it to buy the car.

96.21 **'Debtor-creditor' (DC) agreements** Any regulated consumer credit agreement that is not a DCS agreement is a DC agreement (**CCA 1974, s. 13**). In effect, this means that DC agreements are those where there is no connection between the creditor and the supplier.

96.22 **'Small agreements'** By CCA 1974, s. 17, regulated consumer credit agreements other than conditional sale and hire-purchase agreements, are regarded as small agreements if they provide for credit not exceeding £50. This definition is simply a drafting device to provide a simple means for exempting small transactions from some of the technical requirements of the Act, such as cancellation rights (see s. 74(2)).

96.23 **'Non-commercial agreements'** These are defined by the CCA 1974, s. 189(1), as consumer credit and consumer hire (see **95.25**) agreements which are not made in the course of a business carried on by the creditor. The word 'business' in this definition has been interpreted as meaning a consumer credit or consumer hire business, so that a car dealer who did not normally sell cars on credit, but who sold one car to a friend on hire-purchase terms, did so under a non-commercial agreement (see *Hare v Schurek* [1993] CCLR 47). Again, this definition is used to exempt these agreements from several of the requirements, particularly the formality and cancellation provisions, of the CCA 1974.

96.24 **Summary** A typical hire-purchase agreement will therefore be a fixed-sum, restricted-use agreement, and almost certainly a DCS agreement. An authorised bank account will be running-account, unrestricted-use credit, and will be a DC agreement. Where a bank provides a loan for home improvements, the money being advanced to the customer, the agreement will be a fixed-sum, unrestricted-use agreement (because the debtor could, in breach of the intended purpose, use the money for anything else), and it will be a DC agreement.

Consumer hire agreements

96.25 The CCA 1974 also regulates consumer hire agreements, other than exempt agreements (see 59.32). A consumer hire agreement, by **CCA 1974, s. 15(1)**, is an agreement between an 'owner' and an individual (the 'hirer') for the bailment of goods to the hirer, being an agreement which:

(a) is not a hire-purchase agreement; and
(b) is capable of subsisting for more than three months; and
(c) does not require the hirer to make payments exceeding £25,000 (£15,000 prior to 20 May 1998).

This definition excludes non-contractual bailments, as a non-contractual bailment does not involve an agreement. The difference between consumer hire and hire-purchase is that in consumer hire there is no provision for the hirer having an option to purchase the goods at the end of the period of the agreement. The wording of s. 15(1)(b) means that short-term hire of items such as DIY tools and cars for periods not exceeding three months are not regulated. Agreements which can be extended or renewed so that they can subsist for more than three months will be covered even if the agreement does not, in fact, subsist for more than three months. This requirement can only be avoided by having separate completely new agreements (not extensions or renewals) each of which cannot subsist for more than three months.

Regulated consumer hire and regulated consumer credit are different creatures. Many provisions in the CCA 1974 apply to both categories, which is indicated by use of phrases such as 'debtor or hirer' and 'creditor or owner'. Other provisions only apply to one of these categories, so that some provisions only apply to regulated consumer credit agreements, while others, such as the termination rights set out in the CCA 1974, s. 101, only apply to regulated consumer hire agreements.

Credit for vehicle hire and repair following road traffic accidents

There is still a large volume of road traffic litigation in which a major issue is the impact of the CCA 1974 on credit provided for the cost of hiring a temporary substitute for a damaged vehicle or for the cost of repairing the damage. In *Dimond v Lovell* [2002] 1 AC 384 the House of Lords decided that credit hire is regulated consumer credit. The particular agreement was not exempt, was improperly executed and could not be enforced at all. As a result most companies in this field now ensure that their agreements are exempt (see **59.32**). In *Wilson v First County Trust Ltd (No. 2)* [2003] UKHL 40, [2004] 1 AC 816, it was held that the complete prohibition in **s. 127(3)** and **(4)** on enforcement of defective agreements is compatible with the European Convention on Human Rights. **96.26**

If a credit hire or credit repair agreement complies with the **CCA 1974** or is exempt, the general rule is that the claimant will recover the spot-market hire charges or repair costs, and not the premium rates usually charged by credit hire and credit repair companies (*Dimond v Lovell*). However, if the claimant is impecunious and unable to afford to pay normal market car hire or repair charges, the premium credit hire or credit repair charges can be recovered in damages from the defendant (*Lagden v O'Connor* [2003] UKHL 64, [2003] 1 AC 1067, overruling *Liesbosch Dredger (Owners of) v Owners of SS Edison* [1933] AC 449 on this point). A claimant is impecunious for this purpose, according to Lord Nicholls of Birkenhead, if he is unable to pay the usual charges without making sacrifices he could not reasonably be expected to make.

Exempt agreements

Exemptions from the controls of the CCA 1974 (other than reopening extortionate credit bargains, for which see **96.65**) are created by s. 16 and the Consumer Credit (Exempt Agreements) Order 1989 (SI 1989/869) as amended. The exemptions relate either to the status of the creditor or to the terms of the agreement. Exempt agreements include: **96.27**

(a) consumer credit agreements secured on land and made by local authorities;
(b) DC agreements financing land purchases and alterations to dwellings etc. secured by land mortgages granted by banks, building societies and various other types of creditor if specified by Order of the Secretary of State;
(c) some fixed-sum DCS agreements where the debtor is to repay in no more than four instalments over a period not exceeding 12 months. A credit hire agreement providing for payment in 12 months 'from the start of the agreement' which also provides for a deferral period 'of no more than 12 months' was held to be exempt in *Thew v Cole* [2003] EWCA Civ 1828, [2004] RTR 410. If a credit extends for the whole of the 12-month period, and is not required to be paid until after it has ended, the agreement is not exempt (*Ketley v Gilbert*

[2001] 1 WLR 986). However, hire-purchase, conditional sale, land purchases and pledges cannot fall into this exemption;

(d) DCS agreements for the purchase of land where the debtor must repay in no more than four instalments;

(e) running-account DCS agreements where the debtor is required to repay the whole sum owing in each accounting period in a single payment. This covers most charge card (as opposed to credit card) agreements, and also things like newspaper bills;

(f) DC agreements where the true annual rate of interest does not exceed 13 per cent or (if higher) 1 per cent above base rate. Few arm's-length consumer credit agreements attract rates as low as this.

Agreements falling into more than one category

96.28 Many individual agreements will fall within more than one category of the CCA 1974. A credit card will create a restricted-use DCS agreement when used to buy goods, but an unrestricted-use DC agreement when the same card is used for a cash advance. The problem of classification of such agreements is resolved by s. 18, which provides that if the terms of the agreement place part of it in one category and another part in a different category, the different parts shall be treated as separate agreements. If the whole of the agreement (or a part of an agreement) falls into more than one category, it is treated as an agreement in each of those categories.

Linked transactions

96.29 Where one transaction is directly or indirectly linked with another there is always the risk that the person entering into the linked transaction could be treated unfairly by the creditor. There are detailed provisions in the CCA 1974, s. 19, and the Consumer Credit (Linked Transactions) (Exemptions) Regulations 1983 (SI 1983/1580) defining the transactions which are linked to the main regulated agreement and those which are exempt. Assuming a transaction is effectively a linked transaction, the consequences are that:

(a) the linked transaction, if made before the main regulated agreement, is of no effect unless and until the regulated agreement is made (CCA 1974, s. 19(3));

(b) if the main regulated agreement is cancelled or if the debtor withdraws, the linked transaction is also cancelled or withdrawn (CCA 1974, s. 69(1)); and

(c) if the debtor is discharged early, the debtor is also discharged from any liability under linked transactions (CCA 1974, s. 96(1)).

REGULATION OF CONSUMER CREDIT BUSINESSES

Licences

96.30 Having discussed the nature and definition of various types of consumer credit transactions, it is now necessary to turn to the regulation of the consumer credit industry. Detailed provisions for licensing traders carrying on a consumer credit business or consumer hire business appear in the CCA 1974, part III (ss. 21 to 42). Different types of licence exist for different areas of business. Any regulated agreement (other than a non-commercial agreement) made when the creditor or owner was unlicensed is enforceable against the debtor only where the OFT has made an order which applies to the agreement. The agreement is not illegal or void but merely unenforceable unless and until an order is made by the OFT (CCA 1974, s. 40(1)). If no order is made, then the claim would have to be dismissed. If an order is made then it takes effect as if the agreement had always been enforceable.

If proceedings are commenced on a regulated agreement (other than a non-commercial agreement), the defendant can properly require the claimant to prove that it was licensed at the date of the agreement either by pleading this in the defence, by requiring disclosure of the licence using **CPR, r. 31.12** or by seeking further information using **CPR, r. 18.1**. If a claimant cannot establish that it is licensed (when that has been made an issue in the case) the court could adjourn the hearing or dismiss the claim, applying s. 40(1). If the claimant is or was unlicensed the court could adjourn the hearing to enable the claimant to seek an order from the OFT or dismiss the claim. There is a strong argument that it would be more appropriate to dismiss the claim, applying the overriding objective.

ENTRY INTO AGREEMENTS

The CCA 1974, part V (ss. 55 to 74), contains detailed provisions relating to the entry into regulated credit or hire agreements. These provisions are designed to protect the debtor by creating rights based on antecedent negotiations, by creating a right to withdraw from prospective agreements, by specifying the form and content of the agreement, by creating limited cancellation rights, and by specifying the consequences of defective agreements and breaches of the CCA 1974. These concepts are considered at **96.32** to **96.36**. Limited exclusions from the effects of part V are set out in s. 74. **96.31**

Antecedent negotiations

For the purposes of the **CCA 1974**, by **s. 56** 'antecedent negotiations' comprise: **96.32**

(a) statements made by the creditor or owner itself (or its employees) to the debtor or hirer in relation to the making of any regulated agreement; or
(b) statements made by a credit-broker to the debtor in relation to goods sold or proposed to be sold by the credit-broker to the creditor before forming the subject matter of a DCS agreement within s. 12(a); or
(c) statements made by a supplier in relation to a DCS agreement within s. 12(b) or (c).

Regulated agreements falling into **CCA 1974, s. 12(a) to (c)**, are described at **96.20**, and cover most hire purchase, conditional sale, credit sale and credit card transactions. Illustrations of antecedent negotiations appear in examples 1 to 4 in sch. 2 to the CCA 1974.

The provision found in the **CCA 1974, s. 56(2)**, is a fundamental protection for debtors, deeming the broker or supplier to have been the agent of the creditor in negotiations preceding an intended DCS agreement (as well as acting in his or her actual capacity of supplier or broker). This avoids the common law approach which (save on very special facts) did not recognise such an agency (*Branwhite v Worcester Works Finance Ltd* [1969] 1 AC 552). This means that the creditor will also be bound by any misrepresentations or contractual promises made by the broker or supplier.

Total charge for credit

One of the core aims of the CCA 1974 was to inform debtors of the true cost of credit. Section 20 of the Act requires regulations to be made. The current regulations are the Consumer Credit (Total Charge for Credit) Regulations 1980 (SI 1980/51), as amended. The regulations specify in great detail how the total charge for credit must be calculated. The most recent amendments, which were made by the Consumer Credit (Total Charge for Credit, Agreements and Advertisements) (Amendment) Regulations 1999 (SI 1999/3177) and apply from 14 April 2000, have scrapped the old APR tables, provided that the calculation is to be rounded to one decimal place, created a new basis for calculating land-related agreement APRs, and addressed the problem of insurance premiums. A document fee which a creditor agrees to treat as an additional loan should be included in the total charge for credit or the agreement will be unenforceable (*Wilson v First County Trust Ltd* [2001] QB 407). **96.33**

The total charge for credit is the true cost to the debtor of the credit. In deciding whether an item forms part of the total charge for credit, or formed part of the credit itself, the court should consider all the circumstances, including the documents relating to the agreement, and it might have to determine the purpose of the borrowing (*Watchtower Investments Ltd v Payne* [2001] EWCA Civ 1159, *The Times*, 22 August 2001).

Withdrawal from prospective agreement

96.34 The right to withdraw from a prospective agreement set out in CCA 1974, s. 57, must not be confused with the separate statutory right to cancel certain agreements contained in CCA 1974, s. 67, although the concepts are similar. The right to withdraw from a prospective regulated agreement is exercised by giving oral or written notice. If notice is given the parties are restored to their pre-contract position. The same approach applies to cancellable agreements. The restoration is effected by applying s. 70 (recovery of money paid), s. 71 (repayment of credit), s. 72 (return of goods) and s. 73 (goods given in part-exchange).

The making of the agreement

96.35 Detailed provisions about the form and content of the documents embodying the agreement are set out in CCA 1974, ss. 60 to 65, in the Consumer Credit (Agreements) Regulations 1983 (SI 1983/1553), as amended and in the Consumer Credit (Cancellation Notices and Copies of Documents) Regulations 1983 (SI 1983/1557), as amended. Different prescribed terms exist according to the type of agreement. If the agreement is not in the prescribed form it is an improperly executed agreement. To ascertain whether the agreement is properly executed, reference should be made to **figure 96.1**.

Cancellable agreements

96.36 The cancellation rights contained in CCA 1974, ss. 67 to 69, are designed to create a cooling-off period during which the debtor can resile from the agreement. An illustration of a cancellable agreement appears as example 4 in CCA 1974, sch. 2. An agreement will be cancellable if:

(a) oral representations were made to the debtor prior to the debtor entering into the contract; and

(b) the contract was signed by the debtor anywhere other than the trade premises of the creditor or owner, any party to a linked transaction or the negotiator.

The typical transaction caught by these provisions is a doorstep sale. The cancellation right can be exercised by the end of the fifth day following receipt of a copy of the agreement under s. 63(2) or notice under s. 64(1). As the crucial date is receipt by the debtor of the agreement or notice, an agreement can remain cancellable indefinitely.

MATTERS ARISING DURING THE CURRENCY OF THE AGREEMENT

96.37 Part VI (ss. 75 to 86) of the CCA 1974 deals with matters arising during an agreement. The main provisions relate to liability of the creditor for breaches by the supplier (s. 75), the duty to give information (ss. 77 to 80), appropriation of payments (s. 81) and the effect of death of the debtor (s. 86). These matters are considered at **96.38** to **96.42**.

Liability for breaches by the supplier

96.38 A core provision of the CCA 1974 is that creditors in DCS agreements (principally hire purchase, conditional sales, credit sales and credit card transactions) should be made jointly liable with suppliers for any misrepresentations or breaches of contract (**CCA 1974, s. 75(1)**). This rule does not apply to non-commercial agreements or to single item claims where the supplier has attached a cash price below £100 or in excess of £30,000 (s. 75(3)). Liability under s. 75 cannot be excluded by a creditor (s. 173(1)). The liability of the creditor will be the same as that of the supplier. If the supplier can rely on a valid exclusion clause (or a valid limit on liability), the creditor will also be able to rely on those clauses. There has long been a dispute between many credit card companies and the OFT concerning the application

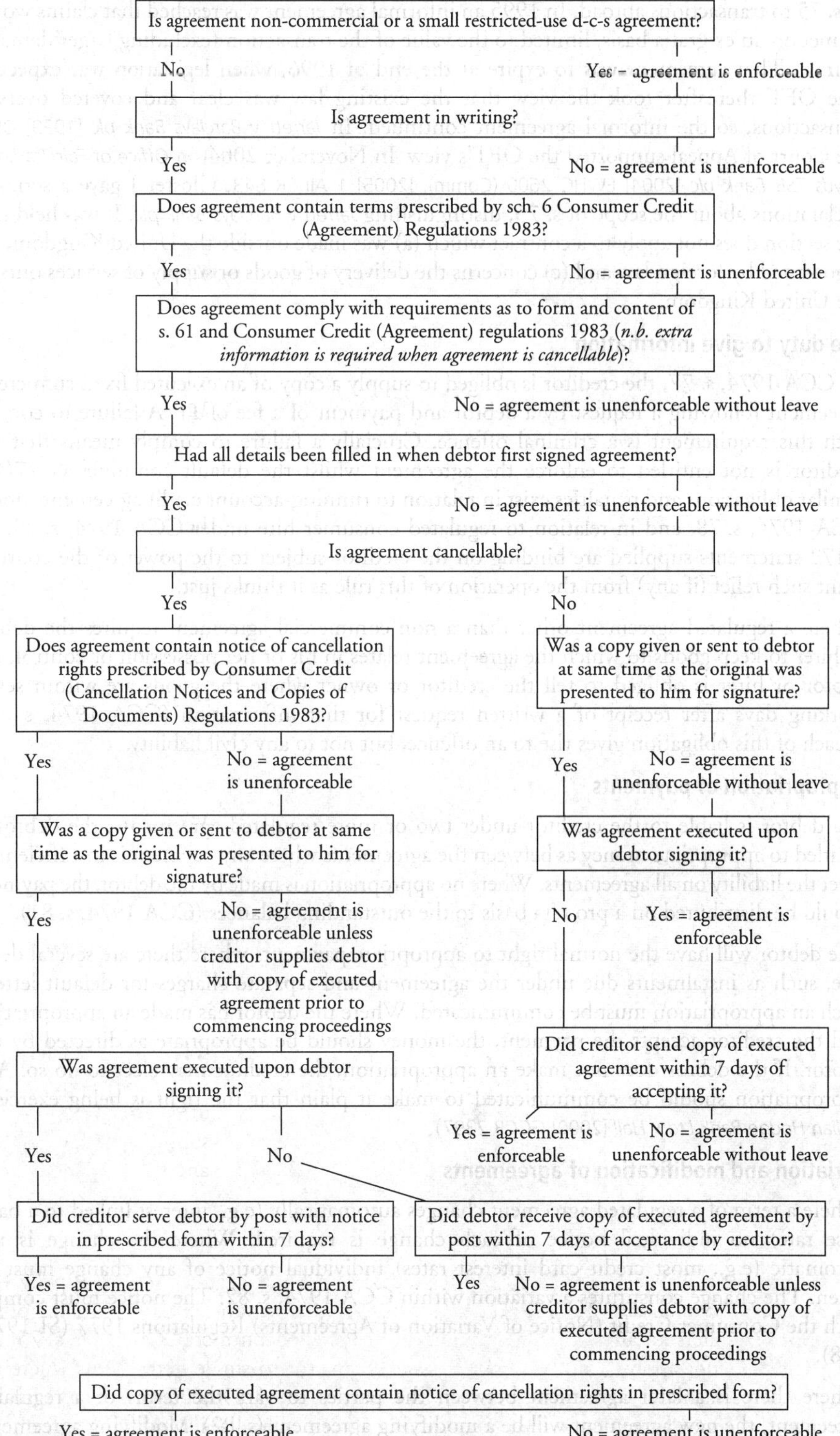

Figure 96.1 Formal requirements for regulated agreements and effect on enforceability

of s. 75 to transactions abroad. In 1995 an informal agreement was reached that claims would be met on an ex gratia basis, limited to the value of the transaction (excluding larger damages claims). That agreement was to expire at the end of 1996, when legislation was expected. The OFT thereafter took the view that the existing law was clear and covered overseas transactions, so the informal agreement continued. In *Jarrett v Barclays Bank plc* [1999] QB 1 the Court of Appeal supported the OFT's view. In November 2004, in *Office of Fair Trading v Lloyds TSB Bank plc* [2004] EWHC 2600 (Comm), [2005] 1 All ER 843, Gloster J gave a series of declarations about the scope of s. 75, distinguishing *Jarrett v Barclays Bank plc*. It was held that the section does not apply to a contract which (a) was made outside the United Kingdom, (b) is governed by foreign law and (c) concerns the delivery of goods or supply of services outside the United Kingdom.

The duty to give information

96.39 By CCA 1974, s. 77, the creditor is obliged to supply a copy of an executed fixed-sum credit agreement following a request by a debtor and payment of a fee of £1. A failure to comply with this requirement is a criminal offence. Crucially a failure to comply means that the creditor is not entitled to enforce the agreement whilst the default continues (s. 77(4)). Similar obligations and penalties exist in relation to running-account credit agreements under CCA 1974, s. 78, and in relation to regulated consumer hire under CCA 1974, s. 79. By s. 172 statements supplied are binding on the creditor subject to the power of the court to grant such relief (if any) from the operation of this rule as it thinks just.

Where a regulated agreement other than a non-commercial agreement requires the debtor or hirer to keep goods to which the agreement relates in his or her possession or control, the debtor or hirer is obliged to tell the creditor or owner where the goods are within seven working days after receipt of a written request for that information (CCA 1974, s. 80). Breach of this obligation gives rise to an offence, but not to any civil liability.

Appropriation of payments

96.40 If a debtor is liable to the creditor under two or more regulated agreements, the debtor is entitled to appropriate money as between the agreements where any payment is insufficient to meet the liability on all agreements. Where no appropriation is made by the debtor, the payment should be distributed on a pro rata basis to the outstanding balances (CCA 1974, s. 81).

The debtor will have the normal right to appropriate payments where there are several debts due, such as instalments due under the agreement and separate charges for default letters. Such an appropriation must be communicated. Where the debtor has made an appropriation and the creditor accepts the payment, the money should be appropriate as directed by the debtor. If the debtor does not make an appropriation, the creditor may elect to do so. Any appropriation should be communicated to make it plain that the right is being exercised (*Julian Hodge Bank Ltd v Hall* [2000] GCCR 2397).

Variation and modification of agreements

96.41 Where a term of a regulated agreement changes automatically (e.g., interest linked to a bank base rate) no individual notice of each change is required. Where the change is not automatic (e.g., most credit card interest rates) individual notice of any change must be given. The change constitutes a variation within CCA 1974, s. 82. The notice must comply with the Consumer Credit (Notice of Variation of Agreements) Regulations 1977 (SI 1977/328).

Where there is a later agreement between the parties to vary the terms of a regulated agreement, the new agreement will be a modifying agreement (s. 82). Modifying agreements are not cancellable agreements unless the initial agreement was cancellable and the period for cancellation had not expired when the modifying agreement was entered into.

Death of debtor or hirer

By CCA 1974, s. 86, the action which can be taken on the death of a debtor or hirer is limited. If the agreement is fully secured the creditor is not allowed by reason of the death to terminate the agreement, demand early payment, recover possession of the goods or land, treat any right as terminated or enforce any security. If the agreement is not fully secured or is not secured at all, an order of the court is necessary (see **96.56**) before any enforcement steps can be taken. 96.42

DEFAULT AND TERMINATION

The **CCA 1974, part VII** (ss. 87 to 104), deals with default and termination. The main provisions relate to default notices (ss. 87 to 89), recovery of goods and land (ss. 90 to 92), default interest (s. 93), early settlement (ss. 94 to 95, 99 to 101), the duty to give information (s. 98), non-default termination (s. 98) and termination statements (s. 103). These matters are dealt with at **96.44** to **96.49**. 96.43

Default notices

Before the creditor can take any action to terminate a regulated agreement, demand early payment of any sum, recover possession of any goods or land, treat any right conferred on the debtor as terminated, restricted or deferred, or enforce any security, service of a default notice complying with the **CCA 1974, s. 88** is necessary (s. 87). A claim only for recovery of arrears under a regulated agreement is not covered by this requirement, nor is a claim for breach of bailment or conversion where goods on hire-purchase, conditional sale or hire have been damaged or disposed of. 96.44

The default notice must be in the form prescribed by the Consumer Credit (Enforcement, Default and Termination) Regulations 1983 (SI 1983/1561) as amended and must contain the information required by s. 88(1) and (4):

(a) the nature of the breach complained of;
(b) if the breach is capable of remedy, the action necessary to remedy it and the date by which it is to be taken. Any date specified in the default notice must be not less than seven full days after service (excluding the day of service);
(c) if the breach is not capable of remedy, the sum required as compensation and the date, not less than seven days after service, by which it is to be paid; and,
(d) information about the consequences of failure to comply with the default notice.

If a default notice is served and complied with, the breach is treated as if it had not occurred and no reliance can be placed on it (s. 89).

If a default notice is required, a breach of s. 87 will exist where no default notice has been served at all, where the notice is defective or where the enforcement action is taken before the expiry of the notice. The consequences will be the same. Any eviction from land will constitute a trespass and possession and damages can be awarded.

Recovery of goods and land

In conditional sale and hire-purchase agreements ownership of the goods usually remains vested in the creditor until all payments have been made. Where ownership remains with the creditor, if the debtor is in breach of a regulated hire-purchase agreement or regulated conditional sale agreement and has paid one third or more of the total purchase price, the creditor can only retake possession with the consent of the debtor or on an order of the court (**CCA 1974, s. 90**). Goods falling within s. 90 are 'protected goods'. Any consent must be genuine (*Mercantile Credit Co. Ltd v Cross* [1965] 2 QB 194). Abandoned goods can be retaken without a court order because recovery is not from the debtor, and consent to the retaking is to be inferred from the abandonment (*Bentinck Ltd v Cromwell Engineering Co.* [1971] QB 324). 96.45

An order from the court authorising the taking of protected goods may be sought using the Consumer Credit Act procedure, see **96.54** and **96.59**. Where such a claim is brought, the debtor may choose to admit the claim and offer terms on which a return order should be suspended under **CCA 1974, s. 135(1)(b)** (this provision gives the court a general power to suspend the operation of any term in any order it might make). The debtor makes such a proposal using **form N9C** (see **PD 7B, paras 8.1** and **8.2**). The creditor may then obtain judgment by filing a request for judgment in **form N228**, which will be entered on the same terms as the debtor's offer, together with costs (**para. 8.6**). Of course the debtor does not have to make such an admission, and the creditor does not have to accept the debtor's terms, and in either event the claim proceeds to a hearing, see **96.59**.

Retaking of protected goods in breach of **CCA 1974, s. 90**, terminates the regulated agreement (if not already terminated), releases the debtor from any further liability under the agreement, and entitles the debtor to recover from the creditor all sums paid by the debtor under the agreement (s. 91). No other claim lies (e.g., damages for wrongful interference with goods) (s. 170(1)). Breach of s. 90 can be raised as a defence to a money claim by the creditor, by a counterclaim for money already paid, or as a claim initiated by the debtor.

Regulated consumer hire agreements are not covered by **CCA 1974, ss. 90** to **91**. However there is statutory power to compensate the hirer where goods are repossessed without a court order in s. 132. An order under s. 132 may release the hirer from future liability and order repayment of all or some money already paid, and is discretionary rather than mandatory. Again, no other claim exists (s. 170(1)).

Equitable relief from forfeiture under a regulated or unregulated agreement may be obtained in the county court under **County Courts Act 1984, s. 38**, and in relation to an unregulated agreement from the High Court (*BICC plc v Burndy Corporation* [1985] Ch 232; *Goker v NWS Bank plc* [1999] GCCR 1507; *Transag Haulage Ltd v Leyland Daf Finance plc* [1994] 2 BCLC 88).

Without a court order, a creditor is not entitled to enter any premises to take possession of goods subject to a regulated hire-purchase agreement, regulated consumer conditional sale agreement or a regulated consumer hire agreement (CCA 1974, s. 92(1)). The restriction applies to any premises and not merely to those of the debtor. Breach of s. 91 is actionable as a breach of statutory duty but no separate measure of damages is specified (s. 92(3)).

Without a court order, the creditor cannot recover possession of land where there is a breach of a conditional sale agreement relating to land (s. 92(2)). Breach of this prohibition is an actionable breach of statutory duty. Conditional sale agreements relating to land are uncommon.

Default interest

96.46 Where a debtor is in arrears under a regulated consumer credit agreement, he or she cannot be required to pay interest at a higher rate than the rate specified in the total charge for credit, or where no rate is specified, the rate charged (excluding certain charges) (CCA 1974, s. 93). Any attempt to contract out of this restriction is void (s. 173(1)). A clause requiring payment of default interest both before and after judgment is not unfair if it does not cause a significant imbalance in the parties' rights and obligations under the contract (*Director General of Fair Trading v First National Bank plc* [2001] UKHL 52, [2002] 1 AC 481).

Early settlement

96.47 A debtor has a right to complete payments due under a regulated consumer credit agreement by giving notice to the creditor and making the necessary payment (CCA 1974, s. 94(1)). Such a notice may also operate as the exercise of any option to purchase the goods, and to determine any linked transaction. The debtor is entitled to a statutory rebate for early settlement (s. 95; Consumer Credit (Rebate on Early Settlement) Regulations 1983 (SI 1983/1562); Consumer Credit (Early Settlement) Regulations 2004 (SI 2004/1483)).

The 1983 Regulations and the 2004 Regulations are quite different. The 2004 Regulations came into force on 31 May 2005. For most debtors, the 2004 Regulations will substantially increase the rebate to be given. However, the 1983 Regulations continue to apply to agreements made before 31 May 2005: (a) until 31 May 2007 for agreements for a term of 10 years or less; and (b) until 31 May 2010, if the agreement was for a term of more than 10 years (reg. 10 of the 2004 Regulations).

When a court gives judgment for money due under a regulated consumer credit agreement, the judgment should be for the full sum due ignoring the rebate which will exist when payment is made (*Forward Trust Ltd v Whymark* [1990] 2 QB 670).

In order that a debtor can exercise the right to early settlement, the creditor is obliged to provide a statement of the sum due on early settlement for regulated consumer credit agreements within seven working days (CCA 1974, s. 97; Consumer Credit (Early Settlement) Regulations 2004). Failure to provide information is a criminal offence and prevents the creditor enforcing the agreement while the default continues (CCA 1974, s. 97(3)).

A right for the debtor to terminate hire-purchase and conditional sale agreements exists under s. 99. The consequences of termination are set out in s. 100 and usually involve bringing the total paid up to half the total hire-purchase price together with any sum due for failing to take reasonable care of the goods. The early settlement rebates for regulated consumer credit agreements do not apply as s. 100 is a complete code for agreements falling within s. 99. A right for the hirer to terminate certain regulated consumer hire agreements by notice is created by s. 101.

Non-default termination

Where the creditor wishes to exercise a contractual right to terminate for an event other than default (e.g., bankruptcy) a notice must be served in the form prescribed by the Consumer Credit (Enforcement, Default and Termination Notices) Regulations 1983 (SI 1983/1561) stating the creditor's intention to terminate the agreement. **96.48**

Termination statements

The debtor or hirer under a regulated agreement has a right to serve a termination statement on the creditor when all payments have been made and the agreement has ceased, requiring the creditor to confirm this or serve counter-notice disputing it (with particulars) (CCA 1974, s. 103). Failure to respond constitutes an offence but does not prevent the creditor enforcing the agreement. **96.49**

SECURITY

The CCA 1974, part VIII, contains detailed provisions relating to security and the provision of information to the surety, debtor or hirer. The main provisions are the restriction on taking negotiable instruments (ss. 123 to 125) and the enforcement of land mortgages (s. 126) (see 96.51 and 96.52). **96.50**

Negotiable instruments

A creditor is not entitled to take a negotiable instrument other than a bank note or cheque in discharge of a sum payable by the debtor under a regulated agreement or any surety, or as security for payment (CCA 1974, s. 123). Contravention means that the creditor can only enforce payment on an order of the court (s. 124). To avoid the normal consequences of transfer of negotiable instruments, the holder of a negotiable instrument taken in contravention of s. 125 will not be a holder in due course and is not entitled to enforce the instrument (s. 125). **96.51**

Enforcement of land mortgages

96.52 A land mortgage securing a regulated agreement is enforceable (so far as provided in relation to the agreement) on an order of the court only (CCA 1974, s. 126).

JUDICIAL CONTROL

96.53 The CCA 1974, **part IX** (ss. 127 to 144), contains detailed provisions creating judicial control of regulated agreements. The main provisions relate to enforcement in cases of infringement (s. 127), time orders (ss. 129 to 130), protection orders (s. 131), hire-purchase (ss. 133 to 134), the power to suspend orders (s. 135), the power to vary agreements (s. 136), and the control of extortionate credit bargains (ss. 137 to 140). These matters are discussed at **96.54** to **96.65**.

Proceedings under the CCA 1974

96.54 The county court has exclusive jurisdiction to hear and determine proceedings to enforce regulated agreements or any security relating to them, or to enforce any linked transaction (**CCA 1974, s. 141**). Proceedings in the High Court must be transferred to the county court. The court also has a statutory power to declare the rights of the parties (s. 142).

Proceedings based on consumer credit agreements have to follow one of three different procedural paths depending on the nature of the claim:

(a) Simple money claims by creditors and owners are brought by issuing an ordinary **Part 7** claim, the special procedure under **PD 7B** not applying (see **PD 7B, para. 3.3**).

(b) There is a special 'Consumer Credit Act procedure' set out in **PD 7B** which must be followed in claims:
   (i) by creditors to enforce regulated agreements relating to goods;
   (ii) by debtors for time orders under s. 129;
   (iii) by creditors for the recovery of protected goods under s. 90;
   (iv) by creditors or owners to enter premises to recover goods under s. 92(1);
   (v) by debtors to reopen extortionate credit bargains under s. 139(1)(a); or
   (vi) by creditors or owners for enforcement orders under ss. 65,86(2), 105(7)(a) or (b), 111(2), or 124(1) or (2).

(c) A claim for recovery of possession of land must follow the procedure in **CPR, Part 55** (see **87.6** to **87.12**). PD 7B does not apply (**PD 7B, para. 3.2**).

Ordinary money claims may be commenced in any county court, but will be transferred to the defendant's home court on filing of a defence under **CPR, r. 26.2**. The appropriate court for claims for the recovery of goods under regulated hire-purchase and regulated conditional sale agreements is the court for the district in which the debtor (or one of the debtors) resides or carries on business or resided or carried on business when the defendant last made a payment under the agreement (**PD 7B, para. 4.1**). In other claims for the recovery of goods the correct court is the court in which the defendant (or one of them) resides or carries on business or in which the goods are situated (**PD 7B, para. 4.2**). Claims for the recovery of land must be brought in the court for the district where the land is situated, unless there are exceptional circumstances justifying proceedings in the High Court (CPR, r. 55.3(1) and (2); see 87.8).

Enforcement by creditors in cases of infringement

96.55 Sections 65, 105, 111 and 124 of **CCA 1974** provide that a creditor who breaches rules in the Act which are intended to protect consumers will not be able to enforce the infringing contract without an order (called an 'enforcement order') of the court. Generally the court has a discretion under **s. 127(1) and (2)** to make an enforcement order if it considers it just to do so, but **s. 127(3) and** (4) preclude the court from making an enforcement order in relation to certain improperly executed agreements. The more draconian approach under **s. 127(3) and** (4) was held not to be incompatible with the European Convention on Human Rights by *Wilson v First County Trust Ltd (No. 2)* [2003] UKHL 40, [2004] 1 AC 816. The Consumer Credit Bill (see **96.1**) proposes abolition of the complete prohibition on enforcement.

The power is discretionary because the court has regard to prejudice, culpability, to its power to suspend or vary the agreement, and to its power to reduce or discharge any sum due. The relevant prejudice is that caused by the breach and not the conduct of the creditor generally or entry into the agreement if that would have happened irrespective of the breach.

In many cases no reduction will be appropriate because there has been no possible prejudice. In *National Guardian Mortgage Corporation v Wilkes* [1993] CCLR 1 enforcement was allowed despite a failure to supply a copy of the agreement. The failure deprived the debtor of the opportunity to find finance at a more favourable rate so compensation in the form of a reduction in arrears was ordered, a time order was made under **CCA 1974, s. 129**, reducing the monthly payments (see **96.60**) and a variation of the interest rate was ordered under s. 136 (see **96.64**). In *Rank Xerox v Hepple* [1994] CCLR 1 enforcement was allowed despite a failure to provide the specified information required by the legislation. This was regarded as a serious breach which prejudiced the debtor who was unaware of an accelerated payment clause which operated on breach. The claim for just over £5,400 was reduced under s. 127 to £500.

Enforcement orders on death of debtor or hirer

After the death of the debtor or hirer in an unsecured (or partly unsecured) regulated **96.56** agreement, an enforcement order is required under CCA 1974, s. 86(2), before enforcement action can be taken by the creditor or owner (see **96.42**). An application for an order under s. 86(2) must be made using the Consumer Credit Act procedure laid down in **PD 7B** (see **para. 3.1(6)(b)** and **96.59**). The personal representatives of the debtor or hirer must be made parties to the proceedings, unless no grant of representation has been made (**PD 7B, para. 9.3**). If no grant of representation has been made, the creditor or owner must make an application in accordance with **CPR, Part 23** (which can be made without notice and before the claim form is issued), for directions as to the persons to be made parties, being persons likely to be affected by enforcement of the agreement (**PD 7B, paras** 9.4 and 9.5).

An enforcement order can only be made if it is proved that the creditor or owner has been unable to be satisfied that the present and future obligations of the debtor or hirer under the agreement are likely to be discharged (CCA 1974, s. 128).

Parties to claims under the CCA 1974

The **CCA 1974, s. 141(5)**, provides that, except as may be provided by rules of court, all the **96.57** parties to a regulated agreement, and any surety, shall be made parties to any proceedings relating to the agreement. Rules relaxing this requirement have been made by **PD 7B, paras 9.1** and **9.2** (although there must be a question whether this is effective as practice directions are not rules of court). These relaxations allow an assignee and a person to whom the creditor's rights and duties have passed by operation of law to bring a claim without joining the original creditor, and also, more generally, allow the court to relax the requirement on an application made between issue and service of the proceedings. The application may be made without notice.

Claims for the recovery of money

As mentioned at **96.54**, claims by creditors for the recovery of money are brought by ordinary **96.58** **Part** 7 claim form. These are claims for arrears of instalments due under regulated agreements, and any other sums due, but which do not seek to enforce any provisions in the agreement relating to recovery of the goods or any land. The procedure to be followed is the same for general form claims under the CPR, except there are some formal requirements for the contents of the particulars of claim set out in **PD 16, para. 6.2**. This requires the particulars of claim to state matters such as the date and parties to the agreement, the identifying number of the agreement, whether the agreement is regulated, and the place where it was signed by the debtor. It must also identify the goods let under the agreement, the total price, the paid-up sum, the amount of any unpaid instalments and the amount and nature of any other claims. These requirements strictly only apply if the consumer credit agreement is one of hire-purchase or conditional sale (**para. 6.1**), but they are a good guide to the basic information that should be given where the agreement is a different form of consumer credit agreement.

Consumer Credit Act procedure

96.59 The types of claim which are governed by the special Consumer Credit Act procedure in **PD 7B** were discussed at **96.54**. These proceedings are commenced by claim form, but the court will fix a hearing date when the claim is issued (**PD 7B, para. 5.1**). Details of the hearing date may be endorsed by the court on the claim form, or may be given in a separate notice. Matters to be included in the particulars of claim are set out in detail in **PD 7B, paras 7.1** to **7.4**. These are similar to the requirements listed in **96.58**, and also include a requirement that the particulars of claim must state that it is a Consumer Credit Act claim. The particulars of claim must be served at the same time as the claim form (**para. 5.2**), and the defendant must be given at least 28 days' notice of the hearing date (**para. 5.6**).

Defendants need not acknowledge service or file defences, although they may do so if they choose to (**PD 7B, para. 5.3**). There is no power to enter default judgment if the defendant decides not to file an acknowledgment or defence (**para. 5.5**). The apparent licence given in **para. 5.3** is tempered by **para. 5.4**, which provides that if the defendant fails to file a defence within 14 days after service of the particulars of claim, the court may take the failure into account when deciding what order to make about costs.

At the hearing fixed when the claim is issued the court may dispose of the claim (**PD 7B, para. 6.1**). The time allocated for this hearing will usually be quite short, and if the claim is too complex to be dealt with on this occasion, by **para. 6.2** the court:

(a) in cases where a defence has been filed, will allocate the claim to a case management track and give directions, or make directions aimed at enabling it to allocate the claim to a track; or

(b) In cases where no defence has been filed, will make such directions and orders as it considers appropriate.

Time orders

96.60 One of the most important powers given to the court is to make a time order under **CCA 1974, s. 129**. By s. 129(2), a time order provides for one or both of the following, as the court considers just:

(a) the payment by the debtor or hirer or any surety of any sum owed under a regulated agreement or a security by such instalments, payable at such times, as the court, having regard to the means of the debtor or hirer and any surety, considers reasonable; and/or

(b) the remedy by the debtor or hirer of any breach of a regulated agreement (other than the non-payment of money) within such period as the court may specify.

By **CCA 1974, s. 130(2)**, in the case of a hire-purchase or conditional sale agreement only, a time order may deal with sums which, although not payable by the debtor at the time the order is made, would if the agreement continued in force, become payable under it subsequently. A time order is not restricted to giving the debtor or hirer time to discharge his or her obligations under the agreement, but may also alter those obligations, including future obligations. The power to alter the terms of the agreement is similar to CCA 1974, s. 136, see **96.64**.

The debtor or hirer can apply for a time order in the following situations:

(a) following service of a default notice under **CCA 1974, s. 87**, a calling-in notice under s. 76 or a termination notice under s. 98;
(b) following issue of proceedings by the creditor to enforce a regulated agreement, security, or to recover possession; and
(c) following an application by the creditor for an enforcement order.

An application for a time order is made using **form N440** (see **PD 7B, para. 3.1(2)**).

In *Southern and District Finance plc v Barnes* (1995) 27 HLR 691 the following principles were laid down: (1) When a time order is applied for, or a possession order is sought in respect of land to which a regulated agreement applies, the court must first consider whether it is just to make a time order. That will involve consideration of all the circumstances of the case and of the position of the creditor as well as of the debtor. (2) When a time order is made, it should normally be made for a stipulated period on account of temporary financial difficulty. If, despite the giving of time, the debtor is unlikely to be able to resume payment of the total indebtedness by at least the amount of the contractual instalments, no time order should be made. In such circumstances it would be more equitable to allow the regulated agreement to be enforced. (3) When a time order is made relating to non-payment of money: (a) the 'sum owed' means every sum which is due and owing under the agreement, but where possession proceedings have been brought by the creditor that will normally comprise the total indebtedness; and (b) the court must consider what instalments would be reasonable both as to amount and timing, having regard to the debtor's means. (4) The court may include in a time order any amendment of the agreement, which it considers just to both parties, and which is a consequence of the order. If the rate of interest is amended, it is relevant that smaller instalments will result both in a liability to pay interest on accumulated arrears and, on the other hand, in an extended period of repayment. But to some extent the high rate of interest usually payable under regulated agreements already takes account of the risk that difficulties in repayment may occur. The practice of amending agreements (including amendment so that no further interest is payable) was approved by the House of Lords in *Director General of Fair Trading v First National Bank plc* [2001] UKHL 52, [2002] 1 AC 481. (5) If a time order is made when the sum owed is the whole outstanding balance due under the loan, there will inevitably be consequences for the term of the loan or for the rate of interest or both. (6) If justice requires the making of a time order, the court may suspend any possession order that it also makes, so long as the terms of the time order are complied with.

Protection orders

A creditor or owner can apply to the court for a order protecting property owned by the creditor or owner or any security from damage or depreciation pending the determination of any proceedings under the CCA 1974, including an order restricting or prohibiting the use of the property or giving directions as to its custody (**CCA 1974, s. 131**). Applications for such orders are made in accordance with **CPR, Part 23**, as they are applications in pending proceedings. **96.61**

Judicial control of hire-purchase and conditional sale

The discretionary power under CCA 1974, s. 132, to order repayment of money paid and to relieve from future liabilities where goods hired under a consumer hire agreement have been retaken without a court order have already been considered (see **96.45**). Additional powers exist in relation to regulated hire-purchase agreements and regulated conditional sale agreements under CCA 1974, s. 133, which permits the court to order that goods be returned to the creditor or a transfer order for goods to be transferred to the debtor. Such orders can be conditional or unconditional, suspended or linked to other orders such as time orders. At common law a party seeking return of goods has to show that possession by another is adverse to his or her rights. In relation to such claims in respect of regulated hire-purchase, **96.62** conditional sale agreements and consumer hire agreements, adverse possession will be presumed in favour of the creditor if a demand for the return of the goods was included in the default notice or in a request to surrender the goods (CCA 1974, s. 134).

Power to impose conditions and suspend orders

96.63 The court has a general power to impose conditions or suspend an order in relation to a regulated agreement by virtue of **CCA 1974, s. 135(1)**. However, the court cannot suspend the operation of a term requiring the delivery of goods unless it is satisfied the goods are in the defendant's possession or control (s. 135(2)).

Variation of agreements

96.64 The court may in an order made by it under the CCA 1974 include such provision as it considers just for amendment of any agreement or security in consequence of a term of the order (CCA 1974, s. 136). This extremely wide power is limited only by the requirement that the variation must be in consequence of an order made under some other power in the CCA 1974. The most common variation will be a reduction in interest rate consequent upon a time order being made.

Extortionate credit

96.65 The court has power to reopen extortionate credit bargains under **CCA 1974, ss. 137** to 140. This is an important power. The court will require evidence of prevailing interest rates, details of the debtor's age, experience, business capacity, state of health and degree of pressure under at the time, and of the degree of risk in view of security provided, the creditor's relationship to the debtor, and whether a colourable (i.e., inflated) price was charged for goods so as to reduce the apparent interest rate. Although each case will turn on its particulars facts, interest rates as high as 48 per cent have been held not to be extortionate for unsecured loans, and rates as high as 44 per cent have been upheld for secure borrowings. If the court concludes that the agreement involved extortionate credit, the court will reduce the rate of interest to an appropriate non-extortionate rate. Once an allegation is made that a bargain is extortionate the burden is upon the creditor to show that it is not (s. 171(7)). In determining whether an agreement is extortionate, the court may only take into account the payments that were quantified when the bargain was made. Unquantified payments which the creditor is allowed to add later, such as under a clause allowing the creditor to vary the rate of interest, are to be disregarded (*Paragon Finance plc v Nash* [2001] EWCA Civ 1466, [2002] 1 WLR 685). Such a contract will have an implied term that a variation must not be made dishonestly, for an improper purpose, capriciously or arbitrarily, and a further implied term that the power to vary will not be used in a way in which no reasonable creditor, acting reasonably, would use it (*Paragon Finance plc v Nash*).

The Court of Appeal reviewed inconsistent decisions on the limitation period for applications to reopen extortionate credit bargains in *Rahman v Sterling Credit Ltd* [2001] 1 WLR 496. The limitation period for claims for return of money paid is six years from the date of the agreement. The limitation period for reopening the agreement is 12 years from the date of the agreement. When a debtor is barred by limitation from seeking repayment of money already paid, it remains to be seen whether the court can take that into account in making any adjustment to the payments. The wide statutory power in **CCA 1974, s. 139**, to do 'justice between the parties' suggests that this could be taken into account.

Applications to reopen extortionate bargains may be made either in proceedings brought for that purpose by the debtor or surety (s. 139(1)(a)), or may be brought within existing proceedings to enforce the agreement or in which the amount paid or payable under the agreement is relevant (s. 139(1)(b) and (c)). An application under s. 139(1)(a) is brought by claim form and must follow the procedure in **PD 7B**. Where the debtor or surety wishes to apply under s. 139(1)(b) or (c), written notice of that intention must be filed and served on every other party within 14 days of service of the claim form (**PD 7B, para. 10.1**). Such a notice is then treated as a defence for the purposes of the proceedings.

MISCELLANEOUS

Four further important provisions in the CCA 1974 should be noted: **96.66**

(a) By CCA 1974, s. 170, a breach of any requirement by or under the CCA 1974 shall incur no civil or criminal sanction as being such a breach, except to the extent (if any) expressly provided by the CCA 1974. Thus, a breach of the Act or the regulations made under it does not give rise to any general plea or defence of illegality, or to a general cause of action for breach of statutory duty.

(b) By CCA 1974, s. 172, the creditor or owner is bound by a statement given under ss. 77(1), 78(1), 79(1), 97(1), 107(1)(c), 108(1)(c) or 109(1)(c). These provisions deal with the provision of information to the debtor. The court has power to direct such relief (if any) to be given from the operation of this rule as the court thinks just (s. 172(3)).

(c) By CCA 1974, s. 173, there is a general prohibition on contracting out of the effect of the CCA 1974. However, by s. 173(3) a provision of the CCA 1974 under which a thing may be done only by order of the court or the Director General of Fair Trading shall not prevent it being done at any time with the other party's consent. This provision is often invoked in relation to the retaking of possession of goods. Even if a court order is required to retake possession, if the hirer consents to removal then there is no breach of the CCA 1974. It is for the creditor to prove on the balance of probabilities that the hirer freely consented (*Mercantile Credit Co. Ltd v Cross* [1965] 2 QB 194).

(d) By CCA 1974, s. 176, detailed general rules for service of documents are created. This section provides, for example, that documents may be served by post to the last known address of the addressee.

Chapter 97 Human Rights and Civil Procedure

INTRODUCTION

97.1 On 2 October 2000 most provisions of the **Human Rights Act 1998** came into force in England and Wales and much of the European Convention on Human Rights was incorporated into English law. As a consequence, public authorities are required to comply with Convention rights such as the right to a fair hearing and freedom of expression. Individuals and companies are able to rely on the Convention directly in cases against the government and other public authorities. Also, courts and tribunals fall within the Act's definition of public authorities and so must comply with the Act.

In 1951, the United Kingdom was amongst the first countries to ratify the European Convention on Human Rights. However, it was not until 2 October 2000 that the Convention could be directly relied upon in the English and Welsh courts. An individual who alleges an infringement of the Convention can still apply to the European Court of Human Rights in Strasbourg notwithstanding the right to rely on the Convention in the domestic courts. However, an application to Strasbourg may only be brought once all domestic remedies, including court and appeal hearings, have been exhausted. Proceedings may then be brought against the United Kingdom government, alleging a failure to ensure that national law is in accordance with the Convention (e.g., *Pretty v United Kingdom* (2002) 35 EHRR 1).

Until the **Human Rights Act 1998** came into force the role of the Convention in the English courts was restricted to, for example, being used to resolve an ambiguity (*R v Secretary of State for the Home Department, ex parte Brind* [1991] 1 AC 696) and being relied upon where the rules of common law or equity were uncertain (*R v Secretary of State for the Environment, ex parte NALGO* (1993) 5 Admin LR 785). Breaches of Convention rights occurring before the coming into force of the 1998 Act will not be entertained by the courts (*R v Lyons (No. 3)* [2002] UKHL 44, [2003] 1 AC 976), though earlier legislation must be interpreted in accordance with the Convention (see **97.3**).

In *Locabail (UK) Ltd v Waldorf Investment Corporation (No. 4)* [2000] UKHRR 592, the applicant applied in the High Court for a stay of execution of a warrant of possession while the European Court of Human Rights considered her complaint that she had been denied her right to a fair trial. The argument that success in Strasbourg would render the initial possession order unlawful did not succeed: the European Court of Human Rights is not a further court of appeal from the domestic courts.

Since the European Court of Human Rights is not an appellate court in the English jurisdiction, the English courts, in deciding whether to enforce their own judgments, do not have to take into account any ruling which the European Court might in the future give on an application regarding the circumstances of liability (*Westminster City Council v Porter* [2002] EWHC 1589 (Ch), [2003] Ch 436).

In relation to overseas territories, the Convention will only apply to nationals of that territory if the governing State has notified the Council of Europe of such intention under art. 56(1). The same principle will apply to protocols enacted under the Convention. Unless there is a specific extension to another territory for whose international relations a contracting State is responsible, actions affecting individuals in that territory will not be subject to the Convention (*R (Quark Fishing Ltd) v Secretary of State for Foreign and Commonwealth Affairs* [2005] UKHL 57, [2005] 3 WLR 837). Furthermore, a national of a contracting State who is outside of the jurisdiction of that State cannot rely on the Convention or the Act if his rights are breached in a non-contracting State (see *R (Abbasi) v Secretary of State for Foreign and Commonwealth Affairs* [2002] EWCA Civ 1598, [2003] UKHRR 76, concerning a British national captured by United States forces in Afghanistan and detained in Guantánamo Bay in Cuba.)

Where the US government sought to have a confiscation order made in the United States registered in the UK so that it could be enforced against the appellant's UK assets, it was accepted that the order would have constituted a breach of **art. 6** if it had taken place in a Convention State. However, given the territorial limitation on the reach of the Convention the House of Lords found that it was difficult to see how registration of the enforcement order in the UK could constitute a breach of the Convention. **Article 6** was therefore not engaged. Only a case of extreme unfairness (which this was not) would justify using the exception to the principle of territoriality so as to give indirect effect to the Convention (*Barnette v United States of America* [2004] UKHL 37, [2004] 1 WLR 2241). See also *United States of America v Montgomery (No. 2)* [2004] UKHL 37, [2004] 1 WLR 2241.

However, actions taken abroad by UK diplomatic or consular officials who exercise the authority of the State will be governed by domestic human rights law and therefore could be the subject of a claim under the **Human Rights Act 1998** (*R (B) v Secretary of State for Foreign and Commonwealth Affairs* [2004] EWCA Civ 1344, [2005] QB 643). This exception also extends to UK vessels, aircraft and even a British military prison operating in Iraq (*R (Al-Skeini) v Secretary of State for Defence* [2004] EWHC 2911 (Admin), *The Times*, 20 December 2004). There is a further exception to the principle of territoriality where the State party has 'effective control' of an area (either lawfully or unlawfully), but this does not apply in territories outside the regional sphere of the party States of the Convention.

MAIN PROVISIONS OF THE HUMAN RIGHTS ACT 1998

Sources of European human rights law

97.2 By virtue of the **Human Rights Act 1998, s. 2(1)**, a court or tribunal determining a question which has arisen in connection with a Convention right must take into account any judgment, decision, declaration or advisory opinion of the European Court of Human Rights. The court or tribunal must also take into account any opinion or decision of the Commission or decision of the Committee of Ministers, whenever made or given, so far as, in the opinion of the court or tribunal, it is relevant to the proceedings in which that question has arisen. The words 'take into account' were chosen deliberately to make it clear that these decisions are to be used as guidance and are not intended to operate as binding precedent. The House of Lords has explained that:

> Under the Convention, the United Kingdom is bound to accept a judgment of the Strasbourg court as binding. But a court adjudicating in litigation in the United Kingdom about a domestic 'Convention right' is not bound by a decision of the Strasbourg court. It must take it into account. (*Re McKerr* [2004] UKHL 12, [2004] 1 WLR 807, per Lord Hoffmann at [66].)

However, Lord Rodger of Earlsferry, also in the House of Lords, has said:

> while the decisions of the European Court of Human Rights on the interpretation of the Convention are not binding, they provide authoritative guidance which courts have to take into account when interpreting the rights in domestic law. (*R (S) v Chief Constable of South Yorkshire* [2004] UKHL 39, [2004] 1 WLR 2196, at [66].)

Where there is a clear and consistent line of Strasbourg authority it would require some special reason to depart from that line of authority. Lord Bingham of Cornhill has commented that:

> This reflects the fact that the Convention is an international instrument, the correct interpretation of which can be authoritatively expounded only by the Strasbourg court. From this it follows that a national court subject to a duty such as that imposed by s. 2 should not without strong reason dilute or weaken the effect of the Strasbourg case law. (*R (Ullah) v Secretary of State for the Home Department* [2004] UKHL 26, [2004] 2 AC 323, at [20].)

Although the non-binding status of Strasbourg authority is accepted, the correct approach seems to be that a clear line of authority is to be treated as so persuasive that only special reasons would justify departure from it.

There may be cases where the Strasbourg jurisprudence is not entirely clear and the domestic courts may have difficulty in identifying clear principles from it. In *N v Secretary of State for the Home Department* [2005] UKHL 31, [2005] 2 AC 296, Lord Hope of Craighead expressed the view, at [25], that:

It is not for us to search for a solution . . . which is not to be found in the Strasbourg case law. It is for the Strasbourg court, not for us, to decide whether its case law is out of touch with modern conditions and to determine what further extensions, if any, are needed to the rights guaranteed by the Convention. We must take the case law as we find it, not as we would like it to be.

Interpretation of legislation

The interpretation of legislation is dealt with in the **Human Rights Act 1998, s. 3(1)**, which provides that so far as it is possible to do so, primary and subordinate legislation must be read and given effect in a way which is compatible with the Convention rights. Section 3 applies to primary and subordinate legislation whenever enacted but does not affect the validity, continuing operation or enforcement of any incompatible primary legislation, or of any incompatible subordinate legislation if primary legislation prevents removal of the incompatibility (s. 3(2)). The courts are free to give a new meaning to legislation which they have interpreted previously where the earlier interpretation was in conflict with a Convention right. However, they will be reluctant to do so if the new interpretation of that legislation would affect transactions that have created rights and obligations on which the parties intend to rely. If interpreting legislation in line with s. 3 would mean that the rights and obligations of the parties to an agreement entered into before 2 October 2000 would be different now to what they were at the time the agreement was entered into then this would result in unfairness to one or another of the parties (*Wilson v First County Trust Ltd (No. 2)* [2003] UKHL 40, [2004] 1 AC 816; *Law v Society of Lloyd's* [2003] EWCA Civ 1887, *The Times*, 23 January 2004). **97.3**

Section 3 will sometimes require the adoption of an interpretation which linguistically may appear strained. The techniques to be used will not only involve the reading down of express language in a statute, but also the implications of provisions (*R v A (No. 2)* [2001] UKHL 25, [2002] 1 AC 45). However, a reading of legislation which 'departs substantially from a fundamental feature of an Act of Parliament is likely to have crossed the boundary between interpretation and amendment' (*Re S (Minors) (Care Order: Implementation of Care Plan)* [2002] UKHL 10, [2002] 2 AC 291, per Lord Nicholls of Birkenhead at [40]). The courts will not interpret legislation in a way which would effectively amend it. It must be possible to give the provision as it stands the Convention-compatible interpretation required by s. 3 (*R (Wilkinson) v Commissioners of Inland Revenue* [2005] UKHL 30, [2005] 1 WLR 1718).

However, the House of Lords has held that the courts have in the past concentrated excessively on the linguistic features of the particular statute. Their lordships rejected a literal approach and instead emphasised a broad approach, which concentrated in a purposive way on the importance of the fundamental right involved (*Ghaidan v Godin-Mendoza* [2004] UKHL 30, [2004] 2 AC 557).

Declaration of incompatibility

Under the **Human Rights Act 1998, s. 4**, where the court is satisfied that a provision in primary legislation is incompatible with a Convention right, it may make a declaration of incompatibility. Such a declaration may also be made in proceedings in which a court considers that a provision of subordinate legislation, made in the exercise of a power conferred by primary legislation, is incompatible. Declarations of incompatibility may only be made in respect of subordinate legislation where the court is satisfied that (disregarding any possibility of revocation) the primary legislation concerned prevents removal of the incompatibility. A person cannot apply for a declaration of incompatibility unless he is adversely affected by the legislation in question (*Taylor v Lancashire County Council* [2005] EWCA Civ 284, [2005] HRLR 17). **97.4**

A declaration of incompatibility may be made only by the High Court, Court of Appeal and House of Lords (s. 4(5)). Such a declaration is not binding on the parties to the proceedings in which it is made and does not affect the validity, continuing operation or enforcement of the provision in respect of which it is given (s. 4(6)). A declaration of incompatibility does, however, enable Parliament to amend the relevant legislation through a fast-track procedure.

The court may not make a declaration of incompatibility unless 21 days' notice, or such other period of notice as the court directs, has been given to the Crown. Where notice has been given to the Crown, a minister or other person permitted by the Act shall be joined as a party on giving notice to the court (**CPR, r. 19.4A**). The Crown should be joined to the proceedings in advance of any appeal hearing in which an issue is raised which might lead the House of Lords to consider making a declaration of incompatibility (*R v A* [2001] 1 WLR 789).

A number of declarations of incompatibility have been made by the courts, including declarations in respect of:

(a) the Mental Health Act 1983, s. 73, which placed the burden of proof on a restricted patient to show that he was no longer suffering from a mental disorder warranting detention in order to satisfy the mental health review tribunal that he was entitled to discharge, contrary to **art. 5 of the Convention** (*R (H) v Mental Health Review Tribunal, North and East Region* [2001] EWCA Civ 415, [2002] QB 1);
(b) part II of the Immigration and Asylum Act 1999, which penalised carriers of illegal immigrants into the United Kingdom, in breach of art. 6 of the Convention (*International Transport Roth GmbH v Secretary of State for the Home Department* [2002] EWCA Civ 158, [2003] QB 728);
(c) the Social Security Contributions and Benefits Act 1992, ss. 36 to 38, which applied a different treatment of benefits as between widows and widowers, contrary to art. 8 of the Convention (*R (Hooper) v Secretary of State for Work and Pensions* [2005] UKHL 29, [2005] 1 WLR 1681);
(d) the Matrimonial Causes Act 1973, s. 11(c), which requires a marriage to be between a man and a woman in order for it to be valid, contrary to arts 8 and 12 of the Convention (in the context of post-operative transsexuals applying for a marriage declaration) (*Bellinger v Bellinger* [2003] UKHL 21, [2003] 2 AC 467);
(e) the Housing Act 1996, s. 185(4), which had the effect that a person who had been subject to immigration control was not afforded the same priority need for accommodation as a comparable person who had not been subject to immigration control, thus infringing **art. 14** in conjunction with **art. 8** (*R (Morris) v Westminster City Council* [2005] EWCA Civ 1184, [2005] HRLR 43).

It appears that the declaration of incompatibility procedure cannot extend to breaches of positive rights. That is, the absence of a provision guaranteeing a particular Convention right in statute does not in itself mean that the statute is incompatible with art. 6(1) of the Convention, but rather signifies at most the existence of a lacuna in the statute (see Lord Nicholls of Birkenhead in *Re S (Minors) (Care Order: Implementation of Care Plan)* [2002] UKHL 10, [2002] 2 AC 291 at p. 322).

Statement of compatibility

97.5 Since 24 November 1998, under the **Human Rights Act 1998, s. 19**, a minister of the Crown in charge of a Bill in either House of Parliament has been required before the second reading of the Bill:

(a) to make a statement to the effect that in his or her view the provisions of the Bill are compatible with Convention rights ('a statement of compatibility'); or
(b) to make a statement to the effect that although he or she is unable to make a statement of compatibility the government nevertheless wishes the House to proceed with the Bill.

This statement must be in writing and be published in such manner as the minister making it considers appropriate. The statement of compatibility is designed to minimise the number of domestic statutes that are incompatible with Convention rights.

Obligations of public authorities

97.6 The **Human Rights Act 1998, s. 6**, requires public authorities to act in a way which is compatible with Convention rights. Section 6(1) provides that: 'It is unlawful for a public authority to act in a way which is incompatible with a Convention right'. An 'act' includes a failure to act but, by s. 6(6), does not include a failure: (a) to introduce in, or lay before, Parliament a proposal for legislation; or (b) to make any primary legislation or remedial order.

The Act provides no exhaustive definition of a public authority. Bodies such as government departments, local authorities, the police and health authorities will clearly be considered public authorities. In addition to these traditional public authorities, the definition of a public authority also includes bodies 'certain of whose functions are functions of a public nature' (s. 6(3)) and these are known as quasi-public authorities. Traditional public organisations must act in accordance with the Convention in respect of all their functions — whether under public or private law — but quasi-public authorities are only required to conform to the Convention in relation to public functions and not private law matters. For example, doctors in general practice will be considered as public authorities in relation to their National Health Service functions, but not in relation to their private patients.

A housing association generally is not a public authority for the purposes of s. 6 (*R (Heather) v Leonard Cheshire Foundation* [2001] EWHC Admin 429, [2002] 2 All ER 936) nor is a private-sector service provider which has a contractual relationship with a local authority to supply residential accommodation (*R (Servite Houses) v Goldsmith* (2001) 33 HLR 35). However, a housing association may be deemed to be a public authority if it was created by a local authority which controls it and has an integrated relationship with it (*Poplar Housing and Regeneration Community Association Ltd v Donoghue* [2001] EWCA Civ 595, [2002] QB 48). Similarly, a private limited company set up by a local authority to manage local farmers' markets and having as directors, stallholders in those markets, was a public authority since the company owed its existence to the authority and initially worked alongside it (*R (Beer) v Hampshire Farmers Market Ltd* [2003] EWCA Civ 1056, [2004] 1 WLR 233).

Bodies which have been held not to be a public authority for the purposes of s. 6 include: a parochial church council in the context of its service of notices on lay rectors, living in church property, requiring them to fund necessary repairs to the chancel (*Aston Cantlow and Wilmcote with Billesley Parochial Church Council v Wallbank* [2003] UKHL 37, [2004] 1 AC 546); the RSPCA in the context of its intention to adopt a policy to exclude from membership persons whose application was for the real or predominant purpose of bringing about a change in RSPCA policy in respect of field sports (*Royal Society for the Prevention of Cruelty to Animals v Attorney-General* [2002] 1 WLR 448); an adjudicator exercising functions under the Housing Grants, Construction and Regeneration Act 1996 (*Austin Hall Building Ltd v Buckland Securities Ltd* [2001] BLR 272); and the Jockey Club (*R (Mullins) v Appeal Board of the Jockey Club* [2005] EWHC 2197 (Admin), *The Times*, 24 October 2005).

Section 6(2) may provide a defence to an allegation of a breach of the Convention under **s. 6(1)** either if the public authority could not have acted differently under the relevant statute **(s. 6(2)(a))** or if the public authority was acting so as to give effect to the relevant legislation **(s. 6(2)(b))** (e.g., *R (Hooper) v Secretary of State for Work and Pensions* [2005] UKHL 29, [2005] 1 WLR 1681).

Section 6(3) expressly includes courts and tribunals as public authorities. Courts and tribunals therefore will be bound to act in a manner that is compatible with the Convention. Unless legislation explicitly states otherwise, judges need to be mindful of the Convention in all proceedings, even those involving only private parties. The Act is therefore developing a degree of *horizontal effect* between private individuals and companies as well as the intended *vertical effect* between public authorities and individuals, both because of s. 6 and because of the Convention's influence on the common law, as in *Douglas v Hello! Ltd* [2001] QB 967.

Both Houses of Parliament, with the exception of the House of Lords acting in its judicial capacity, are outside the definition of public authority (s. 6(4)).

Victims

97.7 Proceedings alleging a breach of Convention rights may only be brought by a 'victim' (**Human Rights Act 1998, s. 7**). The term 'victim' in this context has a more restrictive definition than that used to establish standing in judicial review. Companies and individuals are able to invoke the Convention. Although the point has not been fully argued, it seems that parents of a minor whose human rights have been breached do have standing to complain as victims under s. 7 (*R (Holub) v Secretary of State for the Home Department* [2001] 1 WLR 1359). However, public-interest and pressure groups are unable to bring claims based on the Human Rights Act 1998 unless a 'victim' is found to act as a figurehead applicant (e.g., *Greenpeace Schweiz v Switzerland* (1997) 23 EHRR CD116). A trade association is not a victim for this purpose (*Re Medicaments and Related Classes of Goods (No. 4)* [2001] EWCA Civ 1217, [2002] 1 WLR 269). A local authority cannot be a victim for the purposes of s. 7 (*R (Westminster City Council) v Mayor of London* [2002] EWHC 2440 (Admin), LTL 31/7/2002), nor can an NHS trust (*Grampian University Hospitals NHS Trust v Napier* 2004 JC 117). The expected recipient of a pending decision is not a victim for the purposes of s. 7 because no act or decision capable of being the subject of judicial review has taken place (*R (Hirst) v Secretary of State for the Home Department* [2002] EWHC 1592 (Admin)).

Time limits

97.8 Cases against public bodies alleging a breach of the Convention must be brought within one year of the date on which the relevant act took place (**Human Rights Act 1998, s. 7(5)**). This time limit may be extended where the court considers it equitable so to do, but where another rule imposes a shorter time limit the shorter time limit prevails (e.g., the judicial review time limit) (s. 7(5)).

Remedies

97.9 The **Human Rights Act 1998, s. 8** , provides that in relation to any act (or proposed act) of a public authority which the court finds is (or would be) unlawful, it may grant such relief or remedy or make such order within its powers as it considers just and appropriate. A court may grant any remedy which it deems appropriate provided that it has jurisdiction to grant that remedy (s. 8(11)).

Damages may be awarded only by a court which has power to make such an award, or to order the payment of compensation, in civil proceedings (s. 8(2)). No award may be made unless the court is satisfied that such an award is necessary to 'afford just satisfaction to the person in whose favour it is made' (s. 8(3)) and in considering an award, a court must take into account all the circumstances of the case including:

(a) any other relief or remedy granted, or order made, in relation to the act in question (by that or any other court); and
(b) the consequences of any decision (of that or any other court) in respect of that act.

In determining whether to award damages or the amount of an award, the court must take into account the principles applied by the European Court of Human Rights in relation to the award of compensation under art. 41 of the Convention. Article 41 also proceeds on the basis of affording 'just satisfaction'. There is no automatic entitlement to an award of damages and the Strasbourg court's decision is guided by the particular circumstances of each case having regard to equitable considerations. The European Court of Human Rights often holds that no award of damages should be made since a finding of violation may itself constitute sufficient 'just satisfaction' (e.g., *R (Greenfield) v Secretary of State for the Home Department* [2005] UKHL 14, [2005] 1 WLR 673). Otherwise, the court's awards of damages are usually modest although in some cases, particularly relating to an infringement of property rights, such as expropriation, substantial damages may be awarded. In England, the Administrative Court has suggested that awards by local government ombudsmen for disruption, distress, worry and inconvenience suffered as a result of maladministration are the best available comparable in a housing case (*R (Bernard) v Enfield London Borough Council* [2002] EWHC 2282 (Admin), [2003] HRLR 4). Where an individual was detained under powers conferred by the Mental Health Act 1983, and then later applied for the Mental Health Review Tribunal to review the detention, delays occurring in the hearings of those applications were held to constitute an infringement of art. 5(4) and an award for damages under art. 5(5) would be made 'where necessary' if on the facts the distress and frustration that occurred justified such an award. Damages awarded should so far as possible reflect the English level of damages (*R (KB) v South London and South West Region Mental Health Review Tribunal* [2003] EWHC 193 (Admin), [2004] QB 936). See also *Anufrijeva v Southwark London Borough Council* [2003] EWCA Civ 1406, [2004] QB 1124.

Damages may be awarded for future infringement of rights under the Human Rights Act 1998 (*Marcic v Thames Water Utilities Ltd (No. 2)* [2001] EWHC Technology 394, [2002] QB 1003; although on the facts there was no infringement: *Marcic v Thames Water Utilities Ltd* [2003] UKHL 66, [2004] 2 AC 42).

An individual applicant in judicial review proceedings is not entitled to claim damages under the Human Rights Act 1998 in respect of a local authority's conduct in breach of the European Convention on Human Rights, on the basis that proceedings for judicial review are not brought 'by or at the instigation of a public authority' under the **Human Rights Act 1998, s. 22(4)** (*R (Ben-Abdelaziz) v Haringey London Borough Council* [2001] 1 WLR 1485).

The Strasbourg court also has the power to make a costs order.

Judicial acts

Courts and tribunals are public authorities for the purposes of the **Human Rights Act 1998** (by **s. 6(3)**) but **s. 9** provides that proceedings in respect of a judicial act may be brought only: **97.10**

(a) by exercising a right of appeal;
(b) on an application for judicial review; or
(c) in such other forum as may be prescribed by rules.

Any rule of law which prevents a court from being the subject of judicial review is not affected (s. 9(2)). Where proceedings are brought in respect of a judicial act done in good faith, damages may be awarded to compensate the victim only to the extent required by art. 5(5) of the Convention (which provides that everyone who has been the victim of arrest or detention in contravention of the provisions of art. 5 shall have an enforceable right to compensation). A claim in respect of a judicial act may be brought only in the High Court (**CPR, r. 7.11(1)**). Where a claim is in respect of a judicial act which is alleged to have infringed the claimant's art. 5 rights and which is based on a finding by a court or tribunal that the claimant's Convention rights have been infringed, the court hearing the claim (a) may proceed on the basis of the finding of that other court or tribunal that there has been an infringement but it is not required to do so, and (b) may reach its own conclusion in the light of that finding and of the evidence heard by that other court or tribunal (**CPR, r. 33.9**).

Where a claim is made under the **Human Rights Act 1998** for damages in respect of a judicial act that claim must be set out in the statement of case or the appeal notice; and notice must be given to the Crown. Where the appropriate person has not applied to be joined as a party within 21 days, or such other period as the court directs, after the notice is served, the court may join the appropriate person as a party (**CPR, r. 19.4A**).

Proceedings affecting the right to freedom of expression

The **Human Rights Act 1998, s. 12**, applies where a court (or tribunal) is considering granting relief in civil proceedings which might affect the exercise of the right to freedom of expression (**s. 12(1) and (5)**). The court must not grant such relief if the person against whom the application is made (the respondent) is not present, unless the court is satisfied that the applicant has taken all practicable steps to notify the respondent or there are compelling reasons why the respondent should not be notified (**s. 12(2)**). No relief is to be granted so as **97.11** to restrain publication before trial, unless the court is satisfied that the applicant is likely to establish that publication should not be allowed (**s. 12(3)**). This means that an applicant's prospects of success at trial must be sufficiently favourable to justify an order being made in the particular circumstances of the case and a court will be 'very slow' to make an interim restraint order unless satisfied that the applicant is more likely than not to succeed at trial, but there will be cases where a lesser degree of likelihood will suffice (*Cream Holdings Ltd v Banerjee* [2004] UKHL 44, [2005] 1 AC 253 and see, e.g., *E v Channel Four* [2005] EWHC 1144 (Fam), [2005] 2 FLR 913). The court must have 'particular regard' to the importance of the right of freedom of expression (**s. 12(4)**). If the proceedings relate to journalistic, literary or artistic material the court is required by **s. 12(4)** to have particular regard to two conflicting factors:

(a) the extent to which the material has, or is about to, become available to the public, or it is, or would be, in the public interest for the material to be published; and
(b) any relevant privacy code.

CONVENTION RIGHTS

Derogation from Convention rights

97.12 The Convention rights which are incorporated into domestic law are set out in the **Human Rights Act 1998, sch. 1**. The articles detailing the Convention rights fall into three broad groups: those which are absolute, those which may be derogated from and those which are qualified. Those that are absolute must never be infringed by any of the Convention States. An example is art. 3, which prohibits torture or inhuman or degrading treatment. Some rights may be derogated from, for example, in times of war or other emergency which threatens a State. The United Kingdom entered a derogation, which was set out in sch. 3 to the Act, from **art. 5 of the Convention** (right to liberty and security) so that foreign nationals who were suspected international terrorists thought to be a risk to national security could be detained indefinitely to await deportation but this was held by the House of Lords to be disproportionate and discriminatory (*A (FC) v Secretary of State for the Home Department* [2004] UKHL 56, [2005] 2 AC 68) and has been withdrawn.

Certain rights are qualified in order to balance the competing interests of individuals as against the public interest or, indeed, the interests of other individuals. Qualified rights are, therefore, rights with which a State may legitimately interfere in the interests of the protection of others or of the State itself. Qualified rights are set out in arts 8 to 11, all of which provide that interference with the rights must be in accordance with the law, pursuant to a legitimate aim and necessary in a democratic society.

Any interference with a qualified Convention right must be necessary in a democratic society and consequently 'correspond to a pressing social need' (*Dudgeon v United Kingdom* (1981) 4 EHRR 149) and 'be proportionate to the legitimate aim pursued' (*Silver v United Kingdom* (1983) 5 EHRR 347). State intervention in the lives of individuals should be minimal, and the duty of the State to protect legitimate aims does not permit it to restrict disproportionately the rights of individuals. When considering whether or not a measure is proportionate the court is to conduct a balancing exercise 'between the demands of the general interests of the community and the requirement of the protection of the individual's fundamental rights' (*Soering v United Kingdom* (1989) 11 EHRR 439).

Proportionality

97.13 When considering whether Convention rights have been breached, the European Court of Human Rights has employed the principle of 'proportionality'. A restriction on a freedom guaranteed by the Convention must be 'proportionate to the legitimate aim pursued' (*Handyside v United Kingdom* (1976) 1 EHRR 737). Proportionality is established if the legislative objective is sufficiently important to justify limiting a fundamental right, the measures designed to meet the legislative objective are rationally connected to that objective, and the means used to impair the right are no more than necessary to accomplish the legitimate objective (*De Freitas v Permanent Secretary of Ministry of Agriculture, Fisheries, Lands and Housing* [1999] 1 AC 69; and see, e.g., *R (Countryside Alliance) v Attorney-General* [2005] EWHC 1677 (Admin), [2005] NPC 107).

The proportionality of any interference may now be an issue in any consideration by the courts of certain articles of the Convention. Proportionality has to be considered in two distinct stages, first to ask whether the objective of the measure could be achieved by means involving less interference with an individual's rights, and secondly, to ask whether the measure has an excessive or disproportionate effect on the interests of affected persons. In deciding this last question, the Strasbourg Court assesses whether a fair balance has been struck between the individual's rights and those of the State (*R (Samaroo) v Secretary of State for the Home Department* [2001] UKHRR 1150). See also **74.19**.

Margin of appreciation

When considering whether Convention rights, particularly qualified rights, have been breached, the European Court of Human Rights has employed the concept of the 'margin of appreciation', which permits a State latitude in the manner in which it takes and enforces public policy decisions. This makes allowances for each country's cultural and political identities as it adopts and adapts to this international treaty. For example, what might constitute free speech in one country could be interpreted as an invasion of privacy in another. However, the doctrine cannot directly be applied to cases where United Kingdom courts interpret Convention rights under the **Human Rights Act 1998** because domestic courts can be expected to have a better understanding of domestic UK issues than the Strasbourg court. The domestic application of this doctrine was examined by Lord Hope of Craighead in *R v Director of Public Prosecutions, ex parte Kebilene* [2000] 2 AC 326. He recognised that in certain areas (e.g., economic and social policy) the executive will be given an area of judgment within which the judiciary will defer to the decision in question. **97.14**

ARTICLES OF THE CONVENTION INCORPORATED INTO THE HUMAN RIGHTS ACT 1998

Article 2: right to life

Article 2 establishes a country's positive duty to take steps to safeguard the lives of its citizens, and sets out the limited exceptions to the right to life. These centre on the maintenance of law and order and focus on curbing violence and controlling criminals and prisoners. The overriding objective is to limit the level of permissible force to that which is 'absolutely necessary'. **97.15**

Article 3: prohibition of torture

Article 3 prohibits torture and inhuman or degrading treatment or punishment. This article cannot be derogated from even in times of war and public emergency. **97.16**

Article 4: prohibition of slavery and forced labour

There can be no derogation from this article under any circumstances. **97.17**

Article 5: right to liberty and security of person

Article 5 aims to ensure that no one is deprived of liberty in an arbitrary fashion. It provides that a person can be deprived of liberty only in limited cases. **97.18**

Article 6: right to a fair trial

97.19 Article 6(1) provides:

> In the determination of his civil rights and obligations or of any criminal charge against him, everyone is entitled to a fair and public hearing within a reasonable time by an independent and impartial tribunal established by law. Judgment shall be pronounced publicly but the press and public may be excluded from all or part of the trial in the interest of morals, public order or national security in a democratic society, where the interests of juveniles or the protection of the private life of the parties so require, or to the extent strictly necessary in the opinion of the court in special circumstances where publicity would prejudice the interests of justice.

97.20 **Scope of article 6(1)** In addition to court and arbitration hearings, art. 6(1) will cover other proceedings which determine rights or obligations. For example, art. 6(1) applies to disciplinary proceedings which determine the right of someone to practise a profession (*Le Compte v Belgium* (1981) 4 EHRR 1). On the other hand, a reprimand or the imposition of a fine following a disciplinary hearing held in private by a domestic tribunal of the Law Society does not involve a determination of civil rights and obligations and therefore art. 6 is not engaged (*R (Thompson) v Law Society* [2004] EWCA Civ 167, [2004] 1 WLR 2522). Also art. 6(1) has no relevance to an investigation under the Companies Act 1985 which makes a critical report, as this does not determine the criticised person's rights (*Fayed v United Kingdom* (1994) 18 EHRR 393). If there is no exercisable right in domestic law then there will be no right to a determination under art. 6 (*R (Kehoe) v Secretary of State for Work and Pensions* [2005] UKHL 48, [2006] 1 AC 42).

'Civil rights and obligations' are given an autonomous meaning. For example, the right to practise medicine was held to be a civil right despite its domestic categorisation as public (*König v Germany* (1978) 2 EHRR 170).

The classification of proceedings as 'civil' will not conclusively determine whether a matter should be regarded as civil. When considering whether a matter is civil or criminal (with the additional safeguards which attach to the latter) the European Court of Human Rights looks at three factors: (a) how the proceedings are classified in domestic law; (b) the nature of the offence; and (c) the possible sanctions (*Engel v Netherlands* (1976) 1 EHRR 647). For example, proceedings to obtain an anti-social behaviour order are civil (*Clingham v Kensington and Chelsea Royal London Borough Council* [2002] UKHL 39, [2003] 1 AC 787) as were proceedings before the disciplinary and appeals tribunals of the Securities and Futures Authority (*R (Fleurose) v Securities and Futures Authority* [2002] EWCA Civ 2015, [2002] IRLR 297).

The European Court of Human Rights has held that substantive tax matters are outside the scope of art. 6 (*Ferrazzini v Italy* [2001] STC 1314). Although the imposition of tax surcharges does not determine any civil rights or obligations within art. 6 (*Bancroft v Crutchfield* [2002] STC 347), a VAT assessment has been held to determine a civil right, but not a criminal charge, on the basis that it is civil in nature and there is no penal or deterrent element (*Ali v Commissioners of Customs and Excise* (2002) LTL 15/7/2002). Proceedings brought in a magistrates' court for condemnation of goods seized by customs officers are civil not criminal (*R (Mudie) v Dover Magistrates' Court* [2003] EWCA Civ 237, [2003] QB 1238) and the same classification applies to an application for restoration of goods seized by customs officers (*Gora v Commissioners of Customs and Excise* [2003] EWCA Civ 525, [2004] QB 93). Determinations of penalties by Inland Revenue commissioners (*King v Walden* [2001] STC 822) and the imposition of penalties by Customs and Excise for dishonest evasion of VAT (*Han v Commissioners of Customs and Excise* [2001] EWCA Civ 1040, [2001] 1 WLR 2253) have been held to be criminal but the imposition of a fixed penalty of £50 for a failure to supply documents and information pursuant to a notice was held to be civil (*Sharkey v De Croos* [2005] STC (SCD) 336).

97.21 **Rights protected by article 6** The art. 6(1) requirement to provide a fair hearing breaks down into various rights:

(a) The right of access to a court, which is an integral part of art. 6(1) despite not being expressly set out there (*Jones v Ministry of the Interior of Saudi Arabia* [2004] EWCA Civ 1394, [2005] UKHRR 57). The **Fatal Accidents Act 1976, s. 2(3)** (which provides that not more than one action should lie for and in respect of the same subject matter of complaint), has been construed in such a way as to safeguard the right of access to a court (*Cachia v Faluyi* [2001] 1 WLR 1966).

(b) A hearing in one's own presence. There is a right to an oral hearing although in a civil trial a party has the right to be present only if the tribunal is required to carry out an appraisal of his or her personal character (*Muyldermans v Belgium* (1991) 15 EHRR 204).

(c) Equality of arms. In putting its case, a party must not be put at a substantial disadvantage as regards the opposing party. Thus, for example, each party must have the same opportunity to summon witnesses and each party must have an opportunity to oppose the arguments advanced by the other side. Both the common law and the Convention regard fairness as including the need for the court to know, before it reaches its conclusion, what the parties have to say about the issues and the evidence that the court has before it. Where the judge in an Admiralty claim has sought advice from nautical assessors, for example, that advice should be disclosed to the parties for them to make their own representations as to whether the judge should accept the advice (*Bow Spring (Owners) v Manzanillo II (Owners)* [2004] EWCA Civ 1007, [2005] 1 WLR 144).

(d) Prejudicial publicity. There should be no commentary which prejudges the accused in a criminal trial.

(e) Reasoned judgment. Judgments must be supported by reasoning. The extent and substance of the reasons depend upon the circumstances. They need not be elaborate or lengthy, but they should be such as to tell the parties in broad terms why the decision was reached (*Stefan v General Medical Council* [1999] 1 WLR 1293).

(f) A public hearing. An oral public hearing must be available unless exceptional circumstances dictate otherwise (*Werner v Austria* (1997) 26 EHRR 310). This is not absolute but can be limited only to the extent that is 'strictly necessary . . . in special circumstances'.

(g) A hearing within a reasonable time. Numerous factors will have a bearing on what constitutes a reasonable time from the commencement of proceedings to the final determination of the case, for instance, the importance of the subject matter, the difficulties of the case, whether they be legal or factual, and the behaviour of the individual and the public body (e.g., *EDC v United Kingdom* [1998] BCC 370 concerning the length of time taken to deal with directors disqualification proceedings).

(h) An independent and impartial tribunal. To assess independence, it is necessary to have regard to the manner of appointment of a tribunal's members, their term of office, the existence of guarantees against outside pressures and whether the body presents an appearance of independence (*Bryan v United Kingdom* (1995) 21 EHRR 342). The appearance of independence of any tribunal is to be assessed on an objective basis. 'Impartial' means lack of prejudice or bias (*Piersack v Belgium* (1982) 5 EHRR 169). A tribunal and its members are to be presumed impartial unless proved otherwise (*Le Compte v Belgium* (1981) 4 EHRR 1). The court will examine the actual prejudices, if any, the tribunal holds and also whether undertakings given by the tribunal are sufficient to exclude doubts over impartiality (see further **59.27** and **74.24**).

(i) A tribunal established by law. The de facto doctrine validates the acts as well as the office of a judge, where he mistakenly presides over a court without proper authority, when the world at large believes that he has proper authority (*Coppard v Commissioners of Customs and Excise* [2003] EWCA Civ 511, [2003] QB 1428).

Specific guarantees in criminal cases Article 6(2) preserves the principle that the accused is **97.22** innocent until proved guilty. It does not, however, prevent a burden being placed on the accused to prove a defence. Nor does it prohibit presumptions of law or fact. Strict liability offences are acceptable under art. 6(2) so long as they still require the prosecution to establish the elements of the offence (*Salabiaku v France* (1988) 13 EHRR 379).

Article 6(3) guarantees five further rights in criminal cases. These lay down the minimum requirements for procedural fairness in a criminal trial. They are not exhaustive. Indeed, art. 6(1) may require further protection to be given than is provided for by art. 6(3). The art. 6(3) rights are the right to be informed of a charge, adequate time and facilities for the preparation of a defence, legal representation including legal aid, attendance and examination of witnesses and free translation.

Article 7: no punishment without lawful authority

97.23 Article 7 protects citizens against retrospective criminal laws. A defendant may not be convicted in a criminal case when the relevant action was not illegal at the time it was carried out.

Article 8: right to respect for private and family life

97.24 Article 8(1) provides that 'Everyone has the right to respect for his private and family life, his home and his correspondence'. This article imposes primarily negative obligations on the State not to disclose or delve into personal matters confidential to an individual.

Private life has been held to have a broad definition including the protection of corporeal rights, personal identity, private space, and respect for sexual orientation (*Dudgeon v United Kingdom* (1981) 4 EHRR 149). As a result, for instance, compulsory blood (*X v Austria* (1979) 18 DR 154) and urine (*Peters v Netherlands* (1994) 77-A DR 75) tests and severe corporal punishment (*B v United Kingdom* (1998) 5 BHRC 137) have been found to violate art. 8. Not only does respect for the home include a residence but it can also include an office and business premises (*Niemietz v Germany* (1992) 16 EHRR 97). However, it is unclear whether or not a company can have a right to a private life. In *R v Broadcasting Standards Commission, ex parte British Broadcasting Corporation* [2001] QB 885 it was held that the BBC's actions in surreptitiously filming on a company's premises constituted an unwarranted infringement of the company's privacy under the Broadcasting Act 1996. However, Lord Woolf MR emphasised that the meaning of privacy in this context was not the same as under art. 8 of the Convention. Lord Mustill, whilst concurring on the facts, regarded privacy as an 'essentially human and personal concept' and could not see how it could apply to a company, 'which has no sensitivities to wound, and no selfhood to protect'. A definitive ruling on whether a company can claim under art. 8 is therefore still awaited.

The definition of family life is broad including family relationships between husband and wife and parent and child (*Johansen v Norway* (1996) 23 EHRR 33). Ties between unmarried couples (*Kroon v Netherlands* (1994) 19 EHRR 263), parents and their illegitimate children (*Johnston v Ireland* (1986) 9 EHRR 203) and grandparents and grandchildren (*Marckx v Belgium* (1979) 2 EHRR 330) have also fallen into this category.

Unauthorised settlement on one's own land (in a caravan occupied without planning permission) falls within the concept of 'home' under art. 8 (*Buckley v United Kingdom* (1996) 23 EHRR 101).

Article 8(1) is qualified by art. 8(2). Any interference by a public authority with the exercise of the rights guaranteed by art. 8(1) must both be in accordance with the law and also be necessary in a democratic society in the interests of national security, public safety or the economic well-being of the country, for the prevention of disorder or crime, for the protection of health or morals, or the protection of the rights and freedoms of others. No interference with the right under art. 8(1) may be greater than is necessary to achieve its intended objective.

Rights under art. 8 may be violated when the State obtains personal and private details about an individual without his or her consent and without statutory authority. In *Halford v United*

Kingdom (1997) 24 EHRR 523 it was established that interference with private telephone calls made at work in a private office on a personal line was a breach of art. 8. See also *Khan v United Kingdom* (2000) *The Times*, 23 May 2000, where art. 8 was held to be infringed by the police obtaining evidence using a covertly installed listening device at the applicant's home, and *Armstrong v United Kingdom* (2002) *The Times*, 6 August 2002. A statutory framework for the interception of communications and covert surveillance by security, law enforcement and other public authorities is now provided by the Regulation of Investigatory Powers Act 2000. The government believes that action taken in accordance with that Act will be 'in accordance with the law' for the purposes of art. 8(2).

It appears that art. 8(1) has effectively given rise to a limited cause of action generating rights to equitable remedies and damages for breach of confidence, albeit there is no freestanding cause of action for breach of privacy (see *Wainwright v Home Office* [2003] UKHL 53, [2004] 2 AC 406; see also **97.54**). Article 8 is capable of being infringed by noise resulting from schemes implemented by public authorities if it seriously affects an individual's private life. The absence of any possibility of a grant to help protect against the noise, or any compensation, is capable of negativing any justification for interference with the art. 8 right (*Andrews v Reading Borough Council* [2004] EWHC 970 (Admin), [2004] UKHRR 599).

Article 9: freedom of thought, conscience and religion

Article 9 establishes the right to manifest religion and beliefs, rather than simply to hold particular views. For example, a parent's religious convictions are a relevant consideration for a local education authority when considering the admission of a child to a particular school (*R (K) v Newham London Borough Council* [2002] EWHC 405 (Admin), [2002] ELR 390). Article 9(2) provides that this freedom may be limited by law where necessary in a democratic society in the interests of public safety, for the protection of public order, health or morals or for the protection of the rights and freedoms of others. **97.25**

Article 10: freedom of expression

Article 10(1) provides that: **97.26**

> Everyone has the right to freedom of expression. This right shall include freedom to hold opinions and to receive and impart information and ideas without interference by public authority and regardless of frontiers. This Article shall not prevent States from requiring the licensing of broadcasting, television or cinema enterprises.

The term 'expression' has been given a broad definition and includes words, works of art (*Müller v Switzerland* (1988) 13 EHRR 212), images (*Chorherr v Austria* (1993) 17 EHRR 358) and dress (*Stevens v United Kingdom* (1986) 46 DR 245). The types of expression covered include political, journalistic, artistic and commercial expression. All legal entities including companies are protected by art. 10 (*Autronic AG v Switzerland* (1990) 12 EHRR 485). The right to freedom of expression also includes the right to be provided with information (*Open Door Counselling and Dublin Well Woman v Ireland* (1992) 15 EHRR 244).

Generally, art. 10(1) is qualified by art. 10(2) in that it:

> may be subject to such formalities, conditions, restrictions or penalties as are prescribed by law and are necessary in a democratic society, in the interests of national security, territorial integrity or public safety, for the prevention of disorder or crime, for the protection of health or morals, for the protection of the reputation or rights of others, for preventing the disclosure of information received in confidence, or for maintaining the authority and impartiality of the judiciary.

In practice, commercial and artistic expression have tended to receive less protection from the Strasbourg court than political or journalistic expression, although the court requires a strong justification for interfering with the right to freedom of expression and will need to be satisfied that the restriction is 'prescribed by law' and that a pressing 'social need' is 'convincingly established' (*Handyside v United Kingdom* (1976) 1 EHRR 737). The right to freedom of expression carries with it certain responsibilities which include avoiding expression which does not contribute to public debate and which is gratuitously offensive to others (*Otto-Preminger Institute v Austria* (1994) 19 EHRR 34). Additionally, when an individual agrees or contracts to limit his or her freedom of expression, generally actions by the State will not be interpreted as an interference (*Vereniging Rechtswinkels Utrecht v Netherlands* (1986) 46 DR 200).

Article 11: freedom of assembly and association

97.27 Article 11 provides not only the freedom of peaceful assembly but also guarantees the right to public processions and meetings both in private and in public and includes the right to form and join trade unions. The right in art. 11 can be limited by restrictions prescribed by law which are necessary in a democratic society in the interests of national security or public safety, for the prevention of disorder or crime, for the protection of health or morals or for the protection of the rights and freedoms of others.

Article 12: right to marry

97.28 Article 12 provides the right to marry and found a family. Article 12 rights apply to those already married and those intending to marry. The legislation concerning adoption of children falls within art. 12.

Article 14: prohibition of discrimination in enjoyment of Convention rights

97.29 Article 14 establishes the principle of equality of application of the Convention. The rights and freedoms protected by the Convention must be available to everyone regardless of sex, race, colour, language, religion, political or other opinion, national or social origin, association with a national minority, property, birth or other status. The trigger for the application of art. 14 is whether the facts in issue 'fall within the ambit' of one or more of the other Convention provisions, but the finding of a violation under art. 14 is not dependent on first establishing a violation of some other Convention right (*Michalak v Wandsworth London Borough Council* [2002] EWCA Civ 271, [2003] 1 WLR 617).

The following test is guidance for the application of art. 14:

(a) Do the facts of the case fall within the ambit of one or more of the substantive Convention provisions?
(b) Is there different treatment as respects the Convention right between the complainant on the one hand and other persons put forward by comparison ('the chosen comparators') on the other?
(c) Are the chosen comparators in an analogous situation to the complainant's situation?
(d) If so, does the difference have an objective and reasonable justification, or, otherwise stated, does it pursue a legitimate aim, and does the differential treatment bear a reasonable relationship of proportionality to the aim sought to be achieved?
(e) Is the difference in treatment based on one or more of the grounds prescribed, expressly or by inference, in art. 14?

(See also *Ghaidan v Godin-Mendoza* [2004] UKHL 30, [2004] 2 AC 557; *A v Secretary of State for the Home Department* [2002] EWCA Civ 1502, [2004] QB 335.)

However, it is not always necessary to follow the sequential analysis set out in *Michalak v Wandsworth London Borough Council* (see *R (Carson) v Secretary of State for Work and Pensions* [2005] UKHL 37, [2005] 2 WLR 1369, where the House of Lords recognised that the *Michalak* questions did not suit every case and context, although they may be useful in some cases).

Article 16: restrictions on political activity of aliens

97.30 Article 16 establishes that nothing in arts 10 (freedom of expression), 11 (freedom of assembly and association) and 14 (prohibition against discrimination) shall prevent governments from imposing restrictions on the political activities of aliens (a term which includes stateless persons).

Article 17: prohibition of abuse of rights

Article 17 states that the Convention may not be interpreted as allowing any State, group or person any right to participate in any activities aimed at the destruction of any of the rights and freedoms set out in the Convention. **97.31**

Article 18: limitation on use of restrictions of rights

Article 18 states that restrictions on rights under the Convention cannot be applied for any purposes other than those for which those restrictions have been prescribed. Article 18 (like art. 14) may not be used individually but only in conjunction with a claim for a breach of some other article of the Convention. **97.32**

Article 1 of the First Protocol: protection of property

Article 1 of the First Protocol provides that: **97.33**

> Every natural or legal person is entitled to the peaceful enjoyment of his possessions. No one shall be deprived of his possessions except in the public interest and subject to the conditions provided for by law and by the general principles of international law.

However, this provision does not in any way impair the right of a State to enforce such laws as it deems necessary to control the use of property in accordance with the general interest or to secure the payment of taxes or other contributions or penalties.

A diverse number of economic interests are included within this article, including not only tangible interests such as a house, but shares, patents, the entitlement to a pension, the right to exercise a profession and even a legal claim, so long as it is concrete and adequately specified.

According to the European Court of Human Rights in *Sporrong v Sweden* (1982) 5 EHRR 35, in order to show that art. 1 of the First Protocol has been violated, it must be demonstrated that:

(a) the peaceful enjoyment of the applicant's possessions has been interfered with by the State; or
(b) the applicant has been deprived of possessions by the State; or
(c) the applicant's possessions have been subjected to control by the State.

These rights are to be balanced against the State's rights to interfere with the peaceful enjoyment of property in the public interest or to control use of property in accordance with the general interest. There is a wide margin of appreciation although an interference with property, including raising taxes, must be proportionate.

Any deprivation under art. 1 of the First Protocol must be necessary and proportionate. In the context, necessary means reasonably necessary, rather than strictly or absolutely necessary. The test of what is necessary is driven by a balancing exercise, rather than by a requirement to use the approach which is least intrusive of Convention rights (*R (Clays Lane Housing Co-operative Ltd) v Housing Corporation* [2004] EWCA Civ 1658, [2005] 1 WLR 2229).

Failure by a sewerage undertaker to carry out works to bring an end to repeated flooding to the claimant's property did not constitute an unjustifiable interference with the claimant's rights under art. 1 of the First Protocol and **art. 8 of the Convention** (*Marcic v Thames Water Utilities Ltd* [2003] UKHL 66, [2004] 2 AC 42). The imposition of financial penalties upon lorry drivers and haulage companies under the Immigration and Asylum Act 1999, as persons responsible for clandestine entrants into the United Kingdom, was incompatible with both art. 6 of the Convention and art. 1 of the First Protocol (*International Transport Roth GmbH v Secretary of State for the Home Department* [2002] EWCA Civ 158, [2003] QB 728).

Article 2 of the First Protocol: right to education

97.34 Article 2 of the First Protocol establishes that no one shall be denied the right to education and that the State shall respect the right of parents to ensure such education and teaching is in conformity with their own religious and philosophical convictions. Education has been defined to include primary and secondary education, and the European Commission of Human Rights has accepted that access to university education may be limited. The United Kingdom has made a reservation adopting this Article only 'so far as it is compatible with the provision of efficient instruction and training, and the avoidance of unreasonable public expenditure'.

Article 3 of the First Protocol: right to free elections

97.35 Article 3 of the First Protocol provides that States must hold elections at regular intervals which will allow the free expression of the opinion of the people in choosing the legislature.

Thirteenth Protocol: abolition of the death penalty

97.36 The Thirteenth Protocol abolishes the death penalty and provides that no one shall be condemned to such penalty or executed.

IMPACT OF THE HUMAN RIGHTS ACT 1998 ON CIVIL LITIGATION

97.37 Although **Human Rights Act 1998** points may be raised in civil litigation, they need to be raised carefully and only in appropriate circumstances. There have been a number of cases where bad arguments have been raised and there has been judicial comment about taking a responsible attitude to when it is right to raise a **Human Rights Act 1998** point. For example, Lord Woolf MR was critical of such points being raised in a case management context (*Daniels v Walker* [2000] 1 WLR 1382) and Mummery LJ has also said that the temptation to turn a court hearing into an international human rights seminar should be resisted (*Williams v Cowell* [2000] 1 WLR 187). In instances where the European Convention on Human Rights has been cited in domestic law, judges have been reluctant to accept 'the deployment of generalised propositions from the Convention' (*R v North West Lancashire Health Authority, ex parte A* [2000] 1 WLR 977) and simply referring to the Convention without specific case law is regarded as unhelpful to the court in doing justice to an argument (*Barclays Bank plc v Ellis* (2000) *The Times*, 24 October 2000). However, the Court of Appeal has accepted that the Human Rights Act 1998 provides the courts with an extra tool for interpreting the language of a rule of court so as to produce a just result and avoid any question of the violation of a litigant's right to a fair trial under art. 6 of the Convention (*Goode v Martin* [2001] EWCA Civ 1899, [2002] 1 WLR 1828).

The manner and formalities by which evidence is provided to the court to permit it to take account of European Court judgments, decisions, declarations or opinions are set out in rules which specify the law reports or other versions of cases which may be used and require that parties give the court and other parties three days' notice of the authorities they intend to cite (PD 39, para. 8).

RIGHT TO A FAIR AND PUBLIC HEARING AND CIVIL LITIGATION

Presence of litigant

97.38 In order to comply with the requirements of art. 6 of the Convention, an adjournment will usually have to be granted for a litigant whose presence is needed for the fair trial of a case but who is unable to attend through no fault of his own, although the applicant for the adjournment must be able to demonstrate that the inability to attend is genuine (*Teinaz v Wandsworth London Borough Council* [2002] EWCA Civ 1040, [2002] ICR 1471).

Equality of arms

Courts are bound to give effect to the overriding objective set out in **CPR, r. 1.1(1)**, 'to deal with cases justly' and are given guidelines in **r. 1.1(2)** as to how this might be achieved. Article 6 of the European Convention on Human Rights introduces the principle of equality of arms. It has been held that notwithstanding these principles, the court has no power to veto a party's choice of legal representative. In *Maltez v Lewis* (1999) *The Times*, 4 May 1999, a party who could only afford less experienced representation than her opponent, who had instructed leading counsel, argued that this was against the 'level playing field envisaged by the CPR. As a consequence, it was argued that her opponent should be debarred from instructing such experienced counsel. It was held that the court could not interfere with a party's choice of legal representative, but that any imbalance could be dealt with in other ways, for example, by allowing a smaller firm of solicitors more time to carry out work or requiring a larger firm to prepare bundles for the court. The principle of equality of arms should not affect the approach adopted in *Maltez v Lewis*. In *R v Bow County Court, ex parte Pelling* [1999] 1 WLR 1807 the refusal to allow the claimant to act as a McKenzie friend was held not to contravene art. 6(1). **97.39**

Equality of arms was considered in *R v Secretary of State for the Home Department, ex parte Quaquah* [2000] HRLR 325, in which the Secretary of State was not allowed to remove the claimant from the UK while he was pursuing an outstanding claim for damages for malicious prosecution against the Home Office. The claimant was entitled to have adequate time and facilities to pursue his tort claim.

Limitation periods

Limitation periods must be considered in the light of the right of access to a court. Although the effect of a limitation period is to prevent a claimant having a hearing, this does not infringe art. 6(1) of the European Convention on Human Rights, provided the limitation period is proportionate (*Pérez de Rada Cavanilles v Spain* (1998) 29 EHRR 109). Limitation periods fulfil legitimate aims, including certainty and conclusiveness and prevent courts being forced to consider claims where evidence is either no longer available or not reliable. Where the time limit reflects a proportionate pursuit of these aims, it will be acceptable. However, a particularly strict application of a three-day time limit for requesting a judgment to be set aside was held to be contrary to art. 6 (*Pérez de Rada Cavanilles v Spain* (1998) 29 EHRR 109). Conversely in *Stubbings v United Kingdom* (1997) 23 EHRR 213 the European Court of Human Rights endorsed the application of a six-year limitation period so as to bar a claim arising out of alleged sexual abuse (and see also *A v Hoare* [2005] EWHC 2161 (QB), *The Times*, 27 October 2005). A 14-day time limit to challenge the valuation of livestock was held to be compatible with art. 6 (*J. and P. M. Dockeray v Secretary of State for the Environment, Food and Rural Affairs* [2002] EWHC 420 (Admin), [2002] HRLR 27) and a two-month time limit under **CPR, r. 74.8**, for filing a notice of appeal was held to be compliant with art. 6, notwithstanding that the court had jurisdiction under **r. 3.1(2)(a)** to extend time (*Citibank NA v Rafidian Bank* [2003] EWHC 1950 (QB), [2003] 2 All ER (Comm) 1054). In circumstances where the time limit cannot be extended for good reason or where the ability to extend is extremely limited, issues may arise. **97.40**

There is doubt about whether the obligation to apply 'promptly' in judicial review is sufficiently certain to comply with art. 6 (*R (Burkett) v Hammersmith and Fulham London Borough Council* [2002] UKHL 23, [2002] 1 WLR 1593). However, the European Court of Human Rights has dismissed a complaint that the judicial review time limit of 'promptly and in any event within three months' is misleading and contrary to the principles of legal certainty because of the inconsistent and discretionary views taken by the domestic courts of the applicable time limits. The ECHR regarded the time limit as a strict procedural requirement which served a public-interest purpose, namely, the need to avoid prejudice being caused to third parties who may have altered their situation on the strength of administrative decisions. The time limit is not contrary to art. 6 (*Lam v United Kingdom* (application 41671/98) decision 5 July 2001).

Substitution of parties to a claim so that a new party is being sued may be allowed even after a limitation period has expired. Where the claimant sought to substitute an individual named solicitor for a firm of solicitors as defendant, it was clear that she had always intended to sue this solicitor, indeed he was mentioned by name in her particulars of claim. There was no cause of action against the firm but only against the individual solicitor. The approach to be taken in light of art. 6 was to interpret rules of court so as to produce a just result and avoid unjustifiable infringement of a litigant's right of access to court. Substitution should be allowed even though the limitation period had expired (*Kesslar v Moore and Tibbits* [2004] EWCA Civ 1551, [2005] PNLR 17).

Rule 17.4 of the CPR (which prohibits amendment of a statement of case to include a new claim for which the limitation period has expired if the new claim does not arise out of the same facts as the original claim) has been interpreted broadly in the light of the right of access to a court (*Goode v Martin* [2001] EWCA Civ 1899, [2002] 1 WLR 1828; see **31.16**).

Strike-out applications and default and summary judgment

97.41 The court has a duty actively to manage cases (**CPR, r. 1.4** and **Part 26**). This includes deciding promptly which issues need full investigation and trial and accordingly disposing summarily of the others (**r. 1.4(2)(c)**). The power to make orders for summary disposal of issues includes the power to strike out a statement of case in whole or in part under **r. 3.4**, in addition to the power to give summary judgment under **Part 24**, where a claimant or defendant has no reasonable prospect of success. These powers may be exercised on the court's own initiative, without hearing the parties or giving them an opportunity to make representations (**r. 3.3(4)**).

One issue is whether striking out for failure to comply with procedural rules or orders is a denial of the right of access to a court. In *Canada Trust Co. v Stolzenberg* (14 October 1998 unreported) a party who failed to comply with an unless order unsuccessfully claimed he had been deprived of the right to a fair trial contrary to art. 6 of the European Convention on Human Rights. The court held that he had deprived himself of that right by his own non-compliance. However, in *Re Swaptronics Ltd* (1998) *The Times*, 17 August 1998, and *Arrow Nominees Inc. v Blackledge* [2000] 1 BCLC 709 (point not considered on appeal) it was held that striking out as a penalty for contempt of court could only be consistent with art. 6 if the contempt led to a 'real risk' that a fair trial could not happen.

A defendant's right to a fair trial was not violated by the operation of **CPR, rr. 6.5(6)** and **6.7**, which deemed that the claim form and particulars of claim had been served even though he had not received them (*Akram v Adam* [2004] EWCA Civ 1601, [2005] 1 WLR 2762). The judge had found that the defendant had no defence, and there was therefore no need to set aside the judgment in default and make the claimant apply for summary judgment, with all the time and expense that would involve. Article 6 does not, as of right, entitle the defendant to a trial or oblige the claimant to show on some other occasion that the defendant has no arguable defence.

Refusal to set aside a judgment entered in default of compliance of an unless order raises an art. 6 issue as the losing party would be deprived of a trial of his defence on the merits, but the State can impose restrictions on the right of access to a court provided they serve a legitimate aim, are proportionate and do not destroy the very essence of the right. The legitimate aim of imposing the sanction of judgment in default of compliance is to secure compliance with court orders (*CIBC Mellon Trust Co. v Stolzenberg* [2004] EWCA Civ 827, *The Independent*, 2 July 2004).

The summary judgment procedure has been held to be compliant with art. 6(1) (*Monsanto plc v Tilly* [2000] Env LR 313; *S v Gloucestershire County Council* [2001] Fam 313). Care must be taken where the grant of summary judgment would interfere with the right of a journalist to freedom of expression (*Al Misnad v Azzaman Ltd* [2003] EWHC 1783, LTL 22/7/2003).

Convention rights may also be relevant where claims are struck out on the ground that there is no cause of action. This question has arisen in the context of claims against public authorities in negligence. In *Osman v United Kingdom* (1998) 29 EHRR 245 the European Court of Human Rights held that it was a breach of the applicant's **art. 6(1)** right of access to a court to strike out a negligence claim on the basis that the imposition of a duty of care would not be fair, just or reasonable. However, in its more recent judgments in *TP v United Kingdom* [2001] 2 FLR 549 and *Z v United Kingdom* [2001] 2 FLR 612 the Court effectively overruled *Osman* and held that there was no violation of the right of access to a court in such cases. The Court did, however, hold that in striking out negligence claims arising from local authorities' exercise of their child protection functions, the English courts had denied the claimants an effective remedy for violations of certain substantive Convention rights, contrary to art. 13 of the Convention (which has not been incorporated into United Kingdom law). These decisions might suggest that the courts should not strike out negligence claims which affect substantive Convention rights, but since an apparently effective remedy is now available under the Human Rights Act 1998, the right of access under **art. 6** is likely to have a very limited application to the striking out of negligence claims or other civil claims.

Although *Osman* can no longer be regarded as correct, the effect of English decisions since *Osman* is that some cases which might previously have been the subject of a strike-out application will instead have to proceed to trial (see *Barrett v Enfield London Borough Council* [2001] 2 AC 550). Although Lord Woolf MR held in *Kent v Griffiths* [2001] QB 36, at p. 51, that cases should still be struck out when the position is clear, many English judges now seem to regard questions about the existence of a duty of care in negligence as difficult matters which should generally be decided only after careful consideration of the evidence at trial (e.g., Lord Browne-Wilkinson in *Barrett*; Otton LJ in *L (A Child) v Reading Borough Council* [2001] 1 WLR 1575; and see *JD v East Berkshire Community NHS Trust* [2003] EWCA Civ 1151, [2003] Lloyd's Rep Med 9; note also *Matthews v Ministry of Defence* [2003] UKHL 4, [2003] 1 AC 1163).

Time limits and delay

The CPR aim at dispensing justice without delay and provide sanctions where parties have **97.42** failed to comply with time limits imposed for carrying out steps in litigation (see **r. 3.4(2)** and **chapter 46**). Article 6(1) of the European Convention on Human Rights requires the hearing of the merits of a claim to take place within a reasonable time. It is possible to invoke art. 6(1) when opposing applications for time extensions, although delay in proceedings will not of itself violate art. 6(1), unless the delay is found to be unreasonable (*Darnell v United Kingdom* (1993) 18 EHRR 205; *Re Swaptronics Ltd* (1998) *The Times*, 17 August 1998). Civil proceedings will only be struck out as an abuse of process by reason of the claimant's delay where it would no longer be possible for the defendant to receive a fair trial (*Re McHugh Southern Ltd* (2002) *The Times*, 30 January 2003).

Where criminal proceedings, from the time of the initial arrest to the time when the applicant was finally refused leave to appeal to the House of Lords, lasted eight years and five months, of which there were four years and three months of almost total inactivity, that amounted to breach of art. 6(1), particularly considering that the applicant's liberty was involved. The relevant factors to have regard to are the complexity of the case, the conduct of the applicant and the relevant authorities and the importance of what was at stake for the applicant (*Crowther v United Kingdom* (application 53741/00) judgment of 1 February 2005).

Where it took four years to deal with costs questions there was a violation of art. 6(1) (*Robins v United Kingdom* (1997) 26 EHRR 527). The principle that it is not possible to rebut, by evidence of the actual date of receipt, the presumption that service of a claim form occurred on the day deemed by **CPR, r. 6.7**, is compatible with art. 6 (*Anderton v Clwyd County Council (No. 2)* [2002] EWCA Civ 933, [2002] 1 WLR 3174).

When considering whether to stay proceedings (for example, until the determination of parallel disciplinary proceedings), the court must consider the significance of taking any step which impinges on a litigant's right to have issues determined by a court within a reasonable time under art. 6(1). The burden is on the applicant seeking a stay to demonstrate through cogent evidence that there are sound reasons for granting a stay (*Wakefield v Channel Four Television Corporation* [2005] EWHC 2410 (QB), LTL 4/11/2005).

Directions and evidence

97.43 As part of its case management powers, the court has power to exclude an issue from consideration (**CPR, r. 3.1(2)(k)**) and power to control evidence by giving directions about the issues on which it requires evidence, the nature of the evidence which it requires to decide those issues and the way in which the evidence is to be placed before the court, as well as the power to limit cross-examination (**r. 32.1**).

Receipt of hearsay evidence, consisting of statements made by someone who cannot be cross-examined, does not inevitably prevent a fair trial under **art. 6** (*Clingham v Kensington and Chelsea Royal London Borough Council* [2002] UKHL 39, [2003] 1 AC 787). However, failure by the prosecution to lay evidence before the trial judge and thus permit him to rule on the question of disclosure is contrary to **art. 6** (*Atlan v United Kingdom* (2001) 34 EHRR 33). The court's refusal to permit a party to give evidence by way of video link in order to avoid the risk of being arrested on warrant should he return to the United Kingdom was held not to pay sufficient regard to art. 6 and the need to ensure that the parties were on an equal footing (*Rowland v Bock* [2002] 4 All ER 370). Taking a child's evidence by video link in a criminal case did not contravene the defendant's right to a fair trial under art. 6 (*R (D) v Camberwell Green Youth Court* [2005] UKHL 4, [2005] 1 WLR 393).

The rules on the use of experts encourage the use of a single joint expert and permit the court to control the manner in which the expert investigates the issues as well as limiting the amount which the expert may be paid for his or her services (**r. 35.8(3)(b) and (4)(a)**).

These rules must be seen in the context of the right to a fair trial in art. 6(1) of the European convention on Human Rights. Article 6(1) does not guarantee the right to call expert evidence, save where it is necessary to ensure the fairness of the proceedings. **Rule 35.1** of the CPR requires the court to restrict expert evidence, and **r. 35.7** allows it to direct that evidence shall be given by a single joint expert instructed by both parties. The appointment of a single joint expert will not be contrary to art. 6(1), although the right to a fair trial may demand that the parties participate equally in the preparation of the expert's report, including attending interviews and examining the documents on which the report is based (*Mantovanelli v France* (1997) 24 EHRR 370). In *Daniels v Walker* [2000] 1 WLR 1382 the judge refused to allow a defendant, who was dissatisfied with the instructions to a joint expert and the resulting report, to instruct another expert of his own. Lord Woolf MR accepted that additional questions could be put to the expert, but rejected the defendant's argument that the procedure conflicted with art. 6(1). The overriding objective of the CPR, which requires the court to deal with cases 'justly', enables it to ensure that all CPR procedures operate in accordance with art. 6.

Injunctions

97.44 It is arguable that there are ample safeguards by virtue of the undertakings to be provided by the applicant as set out in the draft orders in the annex to **PD 25** and the normally short return date given by the court to enable the case for the respondent to be put (*Chappell v United Kingdom* (1989) 12 EHRR 1). However, before granting an injunction without notice, the court will have regard to all the circumstances of the case and take account of art. 6(1) of the European Convention on Human Rights. In particular, there may be an issue under art. 6 where an order requires answers to questions. Further, the court has discharged freezing and search orders on the basis of material non-disclosure, namely, failure by the applicant to disclose the fact that evidence relied upon in a without notice application was obtained in breach of **art. 8(1) of the Convention** (*St Merryn Meat Ltd v Hawkins* (2001) LTL 2/7/2001).

It was found to be inconsistent with art. 6(3) rights for a judge to proceed to a hearing on an application to commit for contempt of court for breach of a freezing and disclosure order without giving the breaching party an opportunity to be heard where the judge knew that the absent party wished to be heard in person, but was prevented from being present by matters over which he had no control (*Raja v Van Hoogstraten* [2004] EWCA Civ 968, [2004] 4 All ER 793).

Financial constraints on access to justice

Financial burdens placed on parties to litigation, such as security for costs orders or court fees must be considered in the light of the right of access to a court. **97.45**

The Convention is intended to guarantee practical and effective rights, particularly with regard to the right of access to a court. It is central to the concept of a fair trial, in civil as in criminal proceedings, that a litigant is not denied the opportunity to present his case effectively before the court and that he is able to enjoy equality of arms with the opposing side. However, **art. 6(1)** leaves the State with a free choice as to the means to be used to guarantee litigants these rights. The right of access to a court is not absolute and may be subject to restrictions, provided that they pursue a legitimate aim and are proportionate. Moreover, it is not incumbent on the State to ensure total equality of arms between the assisted party and the opposing side, as long as each side is given a reasonable opportunity to present his case under conditions that do not place him at a substantial disadvantage.

Under **CPR, r. 3.1(5)**, the court may order a party to pay a sum of money into court if that party has, without good reason, failed to comply with a rule, practice direction or a relevant pre-action protocol. Such an order may be made against a claimant or a defendant and the sum of money will be security for any sum payable by that party to any other party in the proceedings (**r. 3.1(6A)**). Before making such an order, the court must have regard to the amount in dispute, the costs incurred and the costs to be incurred (**r. 3.1(6)**).

In deciding whether to require security, the court may anticipate the arguments likely to be put forward on an application under **r. 3.9** for relief from sanctions, including the effect which the granting of relief would have on each party.

The court must, under **art. 6(1) of the European Convention on Human Rights**, take into account inability to pay where that would result in a party being unable to proceed with a claim. In *Tolstoy Miloslavsky v United Kingdom* (1995) 20 EHRR 442, the European Court of Human Rights found that an order for security for costs in relation to appellate proceedings would not infringe **art. 6(1)**, but there could be a violation if an order for security denies access to a court of first instance (*Aït-Mouhoub v France* (1998) 30 EHRR 382). In *Federal Bank of the Middle East Ltd v Hadkinson* [2000] 1 WLR 1695 the Court of Appeal found no contravention of **art. 6(1)** by an order requiring security for the costs of an appeal from a summary judgment. An order for security for costs against a claimant was not upheld where the claimant was not represented at the hearing of the application (*Nasser v United Bank of Kuwait* [2001] EWCA Civ 556, [2002] 1 WLR 1868).

The right to a fair trial pursuant to **art. 6** also requires that a conditional order as to costs, imposed as a condition of defending a claim, should be reasonable on the basis that, in circumstances where a party cannot comply with such an order, the effect of the order extends beyond limiting his right of access to the court and impairs the very essence of the right (*Anglo-Eastern Trust Ltd v Kermanshahchi* [2002] EWCA Civ 198, LTL 22/2/2002).

A litigant who wishes to instruct counsel and solicitors to defend an application in committal proceedings but has insufficient means to do so has a right to apply for public funding which should be respected by the courts (*Berry Trade Ltd v Moussavi* [2002] EWCA Civ 477, [2002] 1 WLR 1910).

It may be possible to argue that there is a breach of **art. 6(1)** if public funding is not available (*Airey v Ireland* (1979) 2 EHRR 305; and see *Re Perotti* [2003] EWCA Civ 1521, The Times, 27 November 2003). The question of whether legal aid is necessary to guarantee a fair hearing must be determined on the particular facts of each case and will depend on the importance of what is at stake for the applicant in the proceedings, the complexity of the relevant law and procedure and the applicant's capacity to represent himself effectively. In unusually lengthy and complicated defamation proceedings, where the applicants were of very limited means and were represented pro bono whereas their opponents were one of the most wealthy companies in the world and employed substantial experienced legal teams, it was found that the denial of legal aid deprived the applicants of the opportunity to present their case effectively and contributed to an unacceptable inequality of arms (*Steel v United Kingdom* (application 68416/01) (2005) 41 EHRR 22). Where legal aid was refused for an appeal on the grounds that there was no reasonable prospect of success and where the costs of the claim would have been disproportionate to the sum at stake, the refusal of legal aid was not contrary to art. 6 (*Stewart-Brady v United Kingdom* (1997) 24 EHRR CD38). However, the withdrawal of a claimant's public funding soon before trial on the basis that it appeared that neither of the defendants had sufficient assets to satisfy any judgment against them was a breach of art. 6(1) (*R (Alliss) v Legal Services Commission* [2002] EWHC 2079 (Admin), LTL 26/9/2002). **Article 6** does not require the Criminal Injuries Compensation Authority to pay a claimant's costs of representation (*C v Secretary of State for the Home Department* [2003] EWHC 1295 (QB), LTL 22/5/2003). Funding for the representation of the family of a deceased person must be provided where an inquiry into the cause of death is required by **art. 2** (*R (Khan) v Secretary of State for Health* [2003] EWCA Civ 1129, [2003] 4 All ER 1239; *R (Amin) v Secretary of State for the Home Department* [2003] UKHL 51, [2004] 1 AC 653).

The scheme chosen by Parliament to allow success fees in CFAs to be recoverable from the losing party in an action for defamation is compatible with **art. 10** and therefore the threat of liability to pay such a sum does not infringe the defendant's right to freedom of expression. It is a proportionate measure chosen by Parliament to provide other litigants access to justice (*Campbell v MGN Ltd (No. 2)* [2005] UKHL 61, [2005] 1 WLR 3394).

Vexatious litigants

97.46 The **Supreme Court Act 1981, s. 42,** which restricts vexatious proceedings, does not infringe the European Convention on Human Rights or the **Human Rights Act 1998** (*Ebert v Official Receiver* [2001] EWCA Civ 340, [2002] 1 WLR 320). Further, a fair and reasonable opportunity to put one's case before the court does not involve an unlimited and uncontrolled opportunity to address the court (*Attorney-General v Covey* [2001] EWCA Civ 254, *The Times*, 2 March 2001). This is on the basis that there is inherent in the Convention the need to balance the interests of the individual against the interests of the community, and if litigants were given unlimited time to make oral submissions, this would prejudice other litigants waiting to have their cases heard, and result in unnecessary expense to the justice system. See also *Attorney-General v D'Souza* (2004) LTL 3/9/2004.

Oral public hearing

97.47 **Rule 39.2(1) of the CPR** provides that, as a general rule, hearings are to be in public. This includes the trial. Article 6(1) of the European Convention on Human Rights provides that every person is entitled to a public hearing, although there are some very limited exceptions. The cases where hearings must be heard in private should be covered by the exceptions in art. 6(1).

Article 6(1) states that judgment should be pronounced publicly, even where the hearing has been in private, and this may cause more difficulty. However, where a hearing in private is strictly necessary because publicity would prejudice the interests of justice, judgment need not be pronounced publicly (*Re Trusts of X Charity* [2003] EWHC 1462 (Ch), [2003] 1 WLR 2751). **Paragraph 1.11 of PD 39** provides that when a hearing takes place in public, members of the public may obtain a transcript of any judgment given or a copy of any order made, upon payment of the appropriate fee. However, where the judgment is given or an order made in private, anyone who seeks a transcript of the judgment or copy order must seek the judge's permission (**PD 39, para. 1.12**).

It is not a requirement of art. 6 that there should be an oral hearing of an application for permission to appeal under the Arbitration Act 1996, s. 69, unless the circumstances are exceptional (*BLCT (13096) Ltd v J. Sainsbury plc* [2003] EWCA Civ 884, LTL 30/6/2003).

Independent and impartial tribunal

The guarantee of a fair hearing in art. 6(1) of the European Convention in Human Rights includes the right to an independent and impartial tribunal. **97.48**

The requirement of an independent and impartial tribunal has already cast doubt on the position of temporary sheriffs in Scotland trying criminal cases, because they do not have sufficient security of tenure (*Starrs v Ruxton* 2000 JC 208). Lack of security of tenure need not be a problem when trying a case to which the State is not a party (*Clancy v Caird* 2000 SC 441).

In *Hoekstra v HM Advocate (No. 2)* 2000 JC 391 it was held that the test of impartiality is both subjective and objective. A judge, who had, with two other judges, just heard an appeal in which issues relating to the application of the Convention were raised, wrote an article for a national newspaper that was highly critical of the Convention and its incorporation into national law. It was held that this did not pass the objective test of impartiality. The judgment in the appeal in question had to be set aside as it had been given by a court which was not properly constituted by three impartial judges.

In the same way the objective test of impartiality may not be fulfilled where a judge is called upon to rule judicially on the effect of legislation that he or she has drafted or promoted during the parliamentary process. The fair-minded and informed observer might conclude that there was a real possibility that the judge would subconsciously strive to avoid reaching a conclusion which would undermine the very clear assurances he had given to Parliament as to the effect of the legislation (*Davidson v Scottish Ministers* [2004] UKHL 34, [2004] HRLR 34).

In some circumstances the requirement of an independent and impartial tribunal can be satisfied by the possibility of a judicial review of a decision of the Secretary of State even when the Secretary of State is not impartial and independent, having formulated the policy which related to the decision under challenge (*R (Alconbury Developments Ltd) v Secretary of State for the Environment, Transport and the Regions* [2001] UKHL 23, [2003] 2 AC 295).

In some cases 'full jurisdiction' would necessitate jurisdiction over findings of primary fact and in others it would not. A local authority's administrative decision that accommodation offered to the homeless claimant was suitable, combined with judicial review, guaranteed compliance with art. 6(1) (*Runa Begum v Tower Hamlets London Borough Council* [2003] UKHL 5, [2003] 2 AC 430). However, the right for asylum seekers to apply for judicial review did not remedy the procedural unfairness of the system operated by the Secretary of State in deciding whether asylum seekers had made their claims as soon as reasonably practicable after arrival in the United Kingdom. Judicial review did not allow sufficiently close review of determinations of fact to satisfy art. 6. However, the Court of Appeal held that if the Secretary of State were to remedy the deficiencies in procedure the combination of his decision-making process and judicial review of that process would then satisfy the requirements of art. 6(1) (*R (Q) v Secretary of State for the Home Department* [2003] EWCA Civ 364, [2004] QB 36; see also *R (Bono) v Harlow District Council* [2002] EWHC 423 (Admin), [2002] 1 WLR 2475; *Adan v Newham London Borough*

Council [2002] EWHC 423 (Admin), [2002] 1 WLR 2475; *R (S) v Brent London Borough Council* [2002] EWCA Civ 693, [2002] ACD 90; *Secretary of State for Health v Personal Representative of Christopher Beeson* [2002] EWCA Civ 1812, [2003] UKHRR 353; *Feld v Barnet London Borough Council* [2004] EWCA Civ 1307, [2005] HLR 9).

The courts have reconciled the domestic law on apparent bias (see 74.24) with the jurisprudence of the European Court of Human Rights by applying the following test. First, the court should ascertain all the circumstances which have a bearing on the suggestion that the judge is biased. Secondly, it should ask whether those circumstances would lead a fair-minded and informed observer to conclude that there is a real possibility that the tribunal is biased (*Porter v Magill* [2001] UKHL 67, [2002] 2 AC 357). The use by a judge of a firm of solicitors for personal services does not give rise to the expectation that the judge would, in his judicial capacity, favour another client of the same firm of solicitors (*Taylor v Lawrence* [2002] EWCA Civ 90, [2003] QB 528). An adjudicator was no longer impartial as a result of his involvement in settlement negotiations (*Glencot Development and Design Co. Ltd v Ben Barrett and Son (Contractors) Ltd* [2001] BLR 207).

There is a real possibility of bias where the adjudicator has had a number of private conversations with one party and thus appears to have taken into account submissions from that party which were not made available to the other party (*Discain Project Services Ltd v Opecprime Development Ltd* [2001] BLR 285); where the judge's brother was chairman of a company with whom the defendant had been in (an unrelated) dispute (*Perot Systems Europe Ltd v Johnson* [2003] EWHC 1635 (QB), LTL 4/6/2003); where a part-time judge of the Employment Appeal Tribunal appeared as an advocate before that Tribunal, chaired by another judge sitting with two lay members, one or both of whom had previously sat with that part-time judge (*Lawal v Northern Spirit Ltd* [2003] UKHL 35, [2003] ICR 856).

There has been held to be no real possibility of bias in the following circumstances: if a judge sits on a substantive appeal after refusing permission to appeal on paper (*Sengupta v Holmes* [2002] EWCA Civ 1104, *The Times*, 19 August 2002); where the judge has an undisclosed acquaintance and association with one of the party's principal witnesses, who was the son of the judge's former employer and long-term partner and the brother of the judge's partner (*Man O'War Station Ltd v Auckland City Council* [2002] UKPC 28, [2002] 3 NZLR 577); where a memory lapse caused a judge to write and circulate his judgment before having the opportunity of considering the closing submissions of the parties' legal advisers, but who had said he would subsequently consider the judgment in the light of the submissions (*Taylor v Williamsons* [2002] EWCA Civ 1380, *The Times*, 9 August 2002); where an employment tribunal indicated to the parties before the evidence was completed that the respondent's treatment of the applicant had been 'appalling', because the views expressed were only preliminary (*Southwark London Borough Council v Jiminez* [2003] EWCA Civ 502, [2003] ICR 1176); where the chairman of an employment tribunal indicated that her husband was a barrister in chambers which did work for the respondent insurance company, there was no presumed bias by way of economic interest, because for this to apply the judge must have a relevant interest in the party whose cause is before him and the case was also not one of apparent bias because a fair-minded observer would conclude that there was no real possibility of bias on the part of the chairman, still less the tribunal (*Jones v DAS Legal Expenses Insurance Co. Ltd* [2003] EWCA Civ 1071, LTL 24/7/2003). Courts should be careful not to accede to applications by people who did not want a case to be heard by a particular judge unless there were sufficient grounds for such recusal (*Phillips v Symes* [2005] EWHC 490 (Ch), LTL 21/3/2005; see also *Dobbs v Triodos Bank NV* [2005] EWCA Civ 630, [2005] 2 Lloyd's Rep 588).

A judge has to be free from any actual or apparent bias, but counsel has no such duty. The court should prevent an advocate from acting only where there is a risk of disclosure of relevant confidential information or in very exceptional circumstances (*Geveran Trading Co. Ltd v Skjevesland* [2002] EWCA Civ 1567, [2003] 1 WLR 912).

Reasoned judgment

Article 6 of the European Convention on Human Rights requires reasons to be given for any decision on the merits and where permission to appeal is not given in order that the parties are aware of the grounds on which the decision was reached. The extent of reasoning required by the European Court of Human Rights does not go any further than that which is required under domestic law (*English v Emery Reimbold and Strick Ltd* [2002] EWCA Civ 605, [2002] 1 WLR 2409). Where there are legitimate restraints on a right of appeal, such as the need for a matter to be of general importance, it is sufficient for the court to refer to those limitations. Article 6 does not require reasons to be given for refusing permission to appeal against arbitral awards (*Mousaka Inc. v Golden Seagull Maritime Inc.* [2002] 1 WLR 395). In refusing leave to appeal under the Arbitration Act 1969, s. 69, adequate reasons would in almost all cases be given by identifying the threshold test or tests which the applicant has failed, without explaining why the relevant test had been failed (*North Range Shipping Ltd v Seatrans Shipping Corporation* [2002] EWCA Civ 405, [2002] 1 WLR 2397). Where the tribunal's decision is not obviously wrong or open to serious doubt, it might not always be enough simply to refer to the statutory test but it would be enough for the judge to uphold the arbitrator's reasons. Otherwise it might be necessary to go further, but any further reasons need only be brief so as to show the losing party why he had lost. **97.49**

Inattentive tribunal

There may not be a fair trial, as required by the **European Convention on Human Rights, art. 6**, if the tribunal does not give full attention to the case. In *Stansby v Datapulse plc* [2003] EWCA Civ 1951, [2004] ICR 523, a hearing by an employment tribunal was unfair because a lay member fell asleep having consumed alcohol. Conversely in *R v Betson* [2004] EWCA Crim 254, *The Times*, 28 January 2004, a criminal trial by jury was not unfair, even though the judge fell asleep during counsel's speeches to the jury, because the judge's summing up could not be criticised and the jury were apparently not influenced by his lapse. **97.50**

Enforcement of foreign judgments and restraining foreign proceedings

Where a party has not received a fair trial in another jurisdiction contrary to art. 6(1) of the Convention, it would be contrary to public policy for the United Kingdom to enforce the judgment (*Maronier v Larmer* [2002] EWCA Civ 774, [2003] QB 620). **97.51**

However, the domestic courts will not refuse to register or enforce a foreign judgment or order just because some aspect constituted a breach of art. 6 where it is not contrary to the overall interests of justice to register the order (*Barnette v United States of America* [2004] UKHL 37, [2004] 1 WLR 2241). Only a flagrant denial of the right to a fair trial would make it contrary to the interests of justice to enforce the foreign order (*United States of America v Montgomery (No. 2)* [2004] UKHL 37, [2004] 1 WLR 2241).

Although a foreign judgment given in proceedings which in the view of an English court do not meet the requirements of a fair trial will not be recognised in England, it is not for the English court to restrain a party in proceedings before it from suing in another jurisdiction where that country is not itself bound by the Convention (*Al-Bassam v Al-Bassam* [2004] EWCA Civ 857, *The Times*, 22 July 2004). The fear as to the fairness of the foreign proceedings and the enforceability of the foreign judgment in England should not be considered until the foreign judgment has been given. Limited interim restraint of the right to sue in another jurisdiction may, however, be necessary to protect the process of the English court from misuse.

RIGHT TO PRIVACY AND CONFIDENTIALITY AND CIVIL LITIGATION

97.52 Article 8 of the European Convention on Human Rights provides a right to confidentiality in communications passing between a lawyer and his or her client. In *General Mediterranean Holdings SA v Patel* [2000] 1 WLR 272 it was contended that **r. 48.7(3)** of the CPR was *ultra vires* the Civil Procedure Rule Committee. provided that for the purposes of determining an application for a wasted costs order, the court could direct the disclosure of privileged documents to the court and, if the court so directed, to the other party to the application. It was held that the general words, 'may modify the rules of evidence' in the **Civil Procedure Act 1997, sch. 1, para.** 4, did not give the rule-makers power to abrogate or limit a person's right to legal confidentiality. To the extent that **r. 48.7(3)** diminished the substantive right to legal confidentiality it was *ultra vires*.

Toulson J also addressed the human rights issue and said that, as a matter of discretion, the court would not have ordered disclosure under **r. 48.7(3)** because the defendants had a right of confidentiality under art. 8 of the European Convention in respect of their communications with their solicitors unless there was justification for the court to interfere with that right under art. 8(2). Adjudicating an application for a wasted costs order did not justify such interference.

Legal professional privilege is not impliedly overridden by the Inland Revenue's power under the Taxes Management Act 1970, s. 20(1), to require delivery of documents in a person's possession or power (*R (Morgan Grenfell and Co. Ltd) v Special Commissioner of Income Tax* [2002] UKHL 21, [2003] 1 AC 563). This decision highlighted the importance of legal professional privilege as 'a fundamental human right long established in the common law' as well as part of the right to privacy guaranteed by art. 8 of the Convention.

Rule 35.10 of the CPR requires an expert's report to state the substance of his or her instructions and effectively removes any privilege which would have attached to those instructions. It is arguable (though not likely) that this requirement might infringe a party's right to privacy under art. 8, although in a case concerning communications with experts who were instructed solely for the purpose of related criminal proceedings, the High Court has held that a witness should neither volunteer, nor be compelled to disclose, such privileged communications unless the privilege has been waived (*S County Council v B* [2000] Fam 76). The without-prejudice rule should be applied with restraint and only in cases in which the public interest plainly justifies its use (*Prudential Assurance Co. Ltd v Prudential Insurance Co. of America* [2002] EWHC 2809 (Ch), LTL 20/12/2002).

When considering a search order, the court ought to have regard to the art. 8 right to respect for home life and this can extend to an individual's office (*Niemietz v Germany* (1992) 16 EHRR 97).

The refusal of the defendant local authority to supply the claimant with confidential information, in order to assist her decision whether to apply to remove the defendant as guardian of a child in care, constituted a breach of the claimant's rights under arts 6 and 8 on the basis that a balance was required to be struck between the public and private interest in maintaining the confidentiality of the information and the public and private interest in permitting its disclosure for certain purposes (*R (Stevens) v Plymouth City Council* [2002] EWCA Civ 388, [2002] 1 WLR 2583).

Other areas where art. 8 might be infringed are:

(a) in applications seeking disclosure of medical records; and
(b) surveillance evidence particularly in personal injury claims and covert videos of employees at work (see *Halford v United Kingdom* (1997) 24 EHRR 523).

However, the actions of the defendant insurers in *Jones v University of Warwick* [2003] EWCA Civ 151, [2003] 1 WLR 954 in filming the claimant covertly at home in order to vitiate her personal injury claim did not necessarily render the evidence inadmissible. The Convention does not decide what is to be the consequence of evidence being obtained in breach of art. 8(1), but rather it is for the domestic court to decide whether or not admitting the evidence would be in keeping with art. 8(2). Such evidence is admissible under art. 8(2), provided that the inquiries made and the surveillance carried out were reasonable and proportionate in the circumstances and necessary in a democratic society (see also *Martin v McGuiness* 2003 SLT 1424).

Admitting as evidence a covert video recording made by a childcare employee, depicting the unwanted sexual advances made towards her by her employer in front of his child, engaged the child's art. 8 rights to respect to his private life. However, where that interference is necessary to protect a claimant's right to a fair trial under art. 6, the court will allow such evidence to be produced. The employment tribunal was directed to view the video in private to protect the child's rights as much as possible (*XXX v YYY* [2004] EWCA Civ 231, [2004] IRLR 471). In contrast where the police covertly filmed a person in a custody suite for identification purposes and used the videotape in the prosecution against him, such interference was not in accordance with the law, because the police had failed to comply with the procedures set out in relevant Codes of Practice under the Police and Criminal Evidence Act 1984, s. 66 (*Perry v United Kingdom* (2003) 39 EHRR 3).

RIGHT TO FREEDOM OF EXPRESSION AND CIVIL LITIGATION

One particular issue concerning the right to freedom of expression is the extent to which it sometimes has to be balanced against conflicting rights, such as whether the right of an individual to a fair trial will be prejudiced by the publication of information about the proceedings (*Observer v United Kingdom* (1991) 14 EHRR 153) and the effect on the right to privacy of others (e.g., *Lingens v Austria* (1986) 8 EHRR 103). Racist material does not enjoy the protection of art. 10 because it breaches the rights of others (*Thomas v News Group Newspapers Ltd* [2001] EWCA Civ 1233, [2002] EMLR 4). **97.53**

Article 10 of the European Convention on Human Rights was cited successfully in reducing excessive damages awarded by a jury in a defamation case (*Tolstoy Miloslavsky v United Kingdom* (1995) 20 EHRR 442), but the article does not affect the principles underlying the defence of justification in the law on defamation (*Chase v News Group Newspapers Ltd* [2002] EWCA Civ 1772, [2003] EMLR 11).

The principle of strict liability for unintentional defamation is an interference with freedom of expression under **art. 10** (*O'Shea v MGN Ltd* [2001] EMLR 943). The repetition and conduct rules in defamation (which deny a defence of justification to a publisher who repeats a libel and require that an allegation of reasonable suspicion be defended by relying on the claimant's conduct) are not incompatible with **arts. 6** and **10** (*Berezovsky v Forbes Inc.* [2001] EWCA Civ 1251, [2001] EMLR 45). For corporate claimants, the principle that libel is actionable without proof of special damage does not infringe **art. 10** (*Jameel v Wall Street Journal Europe Sprl* [2005] EWCA Civ 74, [2005] QB 904). The **Human Rights Act 1998** has rendered the courts more likely to entertain a submission that pursuit of a libel action is an abuse of process, particularly where the publications that took place in England did not amount to a real and substantial tort and the costs of the proceedings would be disproportionate to the damage and vindication that would result from a judgment in the claimant's favour (*Jameel v Dow Jones and Co. Inc.* [2005] EWCA Civ 75, [2005] QB 946).

The High Court has the power to impose a cost-capping regime in appropriate cases, such as defamation cases where extravagant claimant's costs might inhibit the defendant's exercise of his right to freedom of expression (*King v Telegraph Group Ltd* [2004] EWCA Civ 613, [2005] 1 WLR 2282).

The 'public interest' exception to press freedom has been raised in a number of cases concerning protection of a journalist's source. For example, in *Goodwin v United Kingdom* (1996) 22 EHRR 123 the European Court of Human Rights considered that on the facts the case for disclosing a source neither outweighed the need to protect democratic freedoms nor satisfied the requirement of proportionality. In the later case of *Camelot Group plc v Centaur Communications Ltd* [1999] QB 124 the Court of Appeal considered that where there was a continuing threat of leaks the 'interests of justice' as specified in s. 10 of the Contempt of Court Act 1981 outweighed the need to protect press freedoms. The court justified its approach by impliedly equating the 'interests of justice' with the public interest exception in art. 10(2) (see also *John v Express Newspapers* [2000] 1 WLR 1931 and *Ashworth Hospital Authority v MGN Ltd* [2002] UKHL 29, [2002] 1 WLR 2033; cf. *Mersey Care NHS Trust v Ackroyd* [2003] EWCA Civ 663, [2003] Lloyd's Rep Med 379).

The Code of Practice of the Advertising Standards Authority is compliant with the **European Convention on Human Rights, art. 10(2)** (*R v Advertising Standards Authority Ltd, ex parte Matthias Rath BV* [2001] EMLR 22).

PRIVACY, FREEDOM OF EXPRESSION AND INJUNCTIONS

97.54 The key provisions in relation to privacy, freedom of expression and injunctions are **arts 8** and **10 of the European Convention on Human Rights** and **s. 12 of the Human Rights Act 1998** (see 97.11).

Article 8

97.55 **Article 8** informs the right of personal privacy under the equitable doctrine of breach of confidence (*Douglas v Hello! Ltd* [2001] QB 967). It may, for example, be relied upon in order to prevent publication of photographs of the interior of a party's home for security reasons (*Beckham v MGN Ltd* (2001) LTL 30/7/2001; see also *A v B plc* [2002] EWCA Civ 337, [2003] QB 195, and *Douglas v Hello! Ltd (No. 3)* [2003] EWHC 786 (Ch), [2003] 3 All ER 996). However, there is no separate cause of action for invasion of privacy (*Wainwright v Home Office* [2003] UKHL 53, [2004] 2 AC 406).

Article 8 has also been relied upon to prevent the publication of photographs of the claimant, a children's television presenter, visiting a brothel on the basis that freedom of expression was outweighed by the 'peculiar degree of intrusion into the integrity of the claimant's personality' by their publication (*Theakston v MGN Ltd* [2002] EWHC 137 (QB), [2002] EMLR 22). The broad test has been said to be 'whether disclosure of the information about the individual would give substantial offence to a person of ordinary sensibilities assuming that person was placed in similar circumstances' (*Campbell v Mirror Group Newspapers Ltd* [2004] UKHL 22, [2004] 2 AC 457 per Lord Hope of Craighead at [92]). Pictures of the claimant's attendance at Narcotics Anonymous and the details of her treatment were private information and imported a duty of confidence as the claimant had a reasonable expectation that this information would be kept confidential, although it was justifiable to publish the fact that she was misleading the public when she said she did not take drugs. See also *Lady Archer v Williams* [2003] EWHC 1670 (QB), [2003] EMLR 38.

Where the identity of the applicant has already been revealed in local and national media in an unjustified manner, contrary to art. 8, the actions of the applicant in attracting further publicity as the victim of such interference do not nullify his claim. The disclosure by a local authority of closed circuit television footage and photographs of a person during a suicide bid to local and national media without taking adequate steps to ensure that his identity was masked was held to be a disproportionate and therefore unjustified interference with his private life (*Peck v United Kingdom* (application 44647/98) [2003] EMLR 15).

A third party, who knows or ought to be aware that an individual has information which is private or personal to which he can properly deny access to third parties and from which he intends to profit commercially, will be in breach of duty if he uses or publishes the material without authority to the detriment of the owner. However, such material is only protected by the law of confidence and is not treated as property that can be owned or transferred. The publisher who has the right to publish the material has no right of confidence in unauthorised publication of that material by a third party and has no cause of action in that respect (*Douglas v Hello! Ltd* [2005] EWCA Civ 595, *The Times*, 24 May 2005).

Article 10

Injunctions to protect information which might lead to the identification of the claimants have been granted on the basis that the claim fell within the exceptions to the **art. 10(1)** right of freedom of expression on a narrow interpretation of all the criteria within **art. 10(2)** of the Convention. Those criteria were, first, the grant of an injunction had to be in accordance with the law. Secondly, there had to be a strong and pressing need for confidentiality to be protected. Thirdly, the remedy sought had to be proportionate to the legitimate aim pursued (*Venables v News Group Newspapers Ltd* [2001] Fam 430, where **art. 10** was overridden by **arts. 2** and **3**, and see also *X, a Woman Formerly Known as Mary Bell v S* [2003] EWHC 1101 (QB), [2003] FSR 850). However, in criminal proceedings, given the weight traditionally given to the importance of open reporting of criminal proceedings in particular, it is appropriate in carrying out the balancing exercise to begin by acknowledging the force of the argument under art. 10 before considering whether the right under art. 8 is sufficient to outweigh it. Where an injunction was sought to protect the identity of a child who was not itself directly involved in proceedings, but whose mother was the defendant, the art. 8 right was held not to outweigh the strong rule in favour of unrestricted publicity of any proceedings in a criminal trial (*Re S (A Child) (Identification: Restrictions on Publication)* [2004] UKHL 47, [2005] 1 AC 593). **97.56**

However, a local authority was entitled to an injunction restraining the publication of the identity of a defendant and victim in a criminal trial and their HIV status, to protect the privacy of their children who were not involved in the trial but were the subject of care proceedings. In the circumstances knowledge of the identity was not essential in order to give the public an adequate understanding of the issues for the purposes of open justice or general discussion. The naming of the parents was likely to inflict substantial damage on the children's **art. 8** rights (*A Local Authority v W* [2005] EWHC 1564 (Fam), [2006] 1 FLR 1).

A defendant protester's right to freedom of expression under art. 10 would be interfered with in granting an injunction to make him cease his protest and remove placards which encroached on to the public highway but did not interfere with the public's right to pass and repass on the highway (*Westminster City Council v Haw* [2002] EWHC 1885).

The provisions of the Copyright, Designs and Patents Act 1988 fulfil the requirements of **art. 10(2) of the Convention** in that the needs of a democratic society include the recognition and protection of private property including intellectual property. Rare circumstances could arise where the right to freedom of expression under **art. 10** conflicts with the protection afforded by the 1988 Act, notwithstanding the express exceptions in the Act (*Ashdown v Telegraph Group Ltd* [2002] Ch 149). In those circumstances the court is bound to apply the 1988 Act in a manner which accommodates the right of freedom of expression, which requires the court to look closely at the facts of individual cases. Usually this can be achieved by declining the discretionary relief of an injunction.

Interim injunctions

The Human Rights Act 1998 has not substantially altered the test for the grant of interim **97.57** injunctions in *American Cyanamid Co. v Ethicon Ltd* [1975] AC 396. Although the requirement in the **Human Rights Act 1998, s. 12(3)**, that the applicant 'is likely to establish' at trial that publication should not be allowed is slightly higher in the scale of probability than 'a real prospect' of success, the difference between the two is so small that there would not be many, if any, cases that would proceed under *American Cyanamid* but fail under **s. 12(3)** (*Imutran Ltd v Uncaged Campaigns Ltd* [2001] 2 All ER 385).

The right of an author and publisher to freedom of expression under art. 10 is secondary to the countervailing public interest within art. 10(2), namely, the public policy exemplified in the law of contract whereby the courts regularly enforce provisions for the restriction of competition provided they are reasonable and proportionate. Accordingly, an interim injunction was granted to restrain publication until trial of a claim that the defendant publisher had induced or procured a breach of contract between another publisher and the claimant (*Psychology Press Ltd v Flanagan* [2002] EWHC 1205 (QB), LTL 24/6/2002).

Where the potential consequences of not granting injunctive relief may be grave this will be a factor in the court's decision as to whether to grant relief. Where the claimant sought an interim injunction restraining the defendants from pursuing conduct that amounted to harassment of the claimant's employees, the court found that there was a serious likelihood that in the absence of injunctive relief the employees would suffer unlawful harassment of a serious nature and therefore it was just and convenient to afford protection to them when the claimant had established a real prospect of success at trial (*Emerson Developments Ltd v Avery* [2004] EWHC 194 (QB), LTL 26/01/2004).

Where the public interest justifies the publication of information, it is less likely that an injunction will be granted. The public interest justified the disclosure of undercover filming in a food production company that supplied the NHS by an investigative journalist posing as an employee. The public interest in disclosure was not qualified by the need to give the owner of the information a right to respond. Furthermore, the court was not convinced that this was in fact confidential information at all. Mann J stated that there had to be something more than an employee filming the workplace to have the quality of confidential information, and it was not made confidential simply because of the confidentiality provisions in the employee's contract (*Tillery Valley Foods Ltd v Channel Four Television Corporation* [2004] EWHC 1075 (Ch), *The Times*, 21 May 2004).

The body of case law building up under the Human Rights Act 1998 regarding the need to balance the competing interests in art. 8 and art. 10 relates to breach of confidence, and is not equally applicable to interim injunction applications in the law of defamation. Where a claimant sought an interim injunction in libel proceedings and relied on the **Human Rights Act 1998, s. 12(3)**, as interpreted in *Cream Holdings Ltd v Banerjee* [2004] UKHL 44, [2005] 1 AC 253, to argue that the test for restraint of publication should be whether the claimant was able to demonstrate at this stage that she would be more likely than not to establish at trial that publication should not be allowed, the court held that the test to be applied in defamation proceedings is that the claimant must demonstrate that it is clear that the alleged libel is untrue and that the plea of justification is bound to fail (*Bonnard v Perryman* [1891] 2 Ch 269). This test is still good law. The authorities put forward by the claimant dealt with protection of confidential information, and had not changed the law of defamation (*Greene v Associated Newspapers Ltd* [2004] EWCA Civ 1462, [2005] QB 972).

Chapter 98 Changes in Terminology Made by the CPR

The reforms of civil procedure begun by the CPR in 1998 have introduced new terminology. Sometimes this is a straightforward change of name, for example, from plaintiff to claimant. Often the change of terminology reflects a change of procedure, for example, discovery has been replaced by a new procedure for disclosure of documents. Very little legislation dating from before the CPR has been amended to use the new terminology. For example, there are still several references in the **County Courts Act 1984** to 'plaintiffs' and none to 'claimants'. **Table 98.1** is a brief guide to the changes in terminology, which will aid in translating older legislation, cases and textbooks. **98.1**

Table 98.1 New terminology

Old term	New term
action	claim
amicus curiae	advocate to the court
Anton Piller order	search order
assessment (of costs)	summary assessment
Calderbank letter (or offer)	Part 36 offer
certiorari, order of	quashing order
close of pleadings	(no equivalent)
costs in the cause	costs in the case
counterclaim	a counterclaim is an additional claim but the term 'counterclaim' is also still in use
Crown Office	Administrative Court Office
discovery	disclosure
ex parte	without notice (to other parties)
garnishee order	third party debt order
Grepe v Loam order	civil restraint order
guardian *ad litem*	litigation friend
in camera	in private
in open court	in public
inter partes hearing	hearing with notice (or hearing on notice) (to other parties)
interlocutory	interim
interlocutory judgment for damages to be assessed	judgment for an amount to be decided by the court
interrogatory	request for further information
leave	permission
legal aid taxation	detailed assessment of costs payable out of the Community Legal Service Fund
mandamus, order of	mandatory order
Mareva injunction (or order)	freezing injunction
motion (in Chancery)	judge's application
motions day (in Chancery)	applications day
next friend	litigation friend
oral examination	obtaining information from judgment debtor
originating application	Part 8 claim form (but originating applications are still used in insolvency proceedings)
originating summons	Part 8 claim form
plaintiff	claimant
pleading	statement of case
preliminary act (Admiralty proceedings)	collision statement of case
prohibition, order of	prohibiting order
rebutter	(no equivalent)
rejoinder	(no equivalent)

Old term	New term
request for further and better particulars	request for further information
schedule of special damages	schedule of past and future loss and expense
setting down (for trial)	listing (for trial)
small claims arbitration	small claims track
specific discovery	specific disclosure
statement of claim	particulars of claim
subpoena	witness summons
substituted service	alternative service
summons for directions	case management conference
summons (for interim application)	application notice
summons (to commence proceedings in a county court)	claim form
Supreme Court Taxing Office	Supreme Court Costs Office
surrebutter	(no equivalent)
surrejoinder	(no equivalent)
taxation (of costs)	detailed assessment
taxing master	costs judge
third-party proceedings	additional claim
writ (to commence proceedings)	claim form (writs are still used in execution of judgments)

Appendix 1 Procedural Checklists

Procedural checklist 1 Pre-action Protocol for Personal Injury Claims

See **8.7** to **8.21**.

All references are to the Pre-Action Protocol for Personal Injury Claims unless otherwise indicated.

Soon after being retained	Solicitor should consider whether an informal notification of the possible claim should be made to the defendant. This will not start the protocol timetable (para. 2.6).
Letter of claim	This should be sent at least 6 months before the expiry of limitation period to give time for compliance before limitation expires. Two copies of the letter should be sent to the defendant, or one to the defendant and one to the insurer (paras 2.7 and 3.1). For detailed contents of the letter, see paras 3.2 to 3.5 and annex A.
21 days from letter of claim	Defendant should reply with name of insurer, or the insurer should acknowledge (para. 3.6). The period is up to 42 days if the accident was outside England and Wales (para. 3.8).
Failure to acknowledge	If there is no acknowledgment within 21 days, proceedings may be issued (para. 3.6).
3 months from acknowledging letter of claim	Defendant should have completed investigations. Defendant must reply stating if liability is admitted or denied (paras 2.12 and 3.7). If liability is denied or if contributory negligence is alleged, the defendant should give reasons and provide documents on liability (paras 3.7, 3.10 to 3.12). Standard disclosure lists are in annex B. No charge is to be made for providing copy documents (para. 3.13).
Before issuing proceedings	If contributory negligence has been alleged, the claimant should respond to those allegations (para. 3.12).
As soon as possible after defendant's response	Claimant sends defendant a schedule of special damages and documents in support. This is particularly important where liability has been admitted (para. 3.14). Both sides must consider the claimant's rehabilitation needs (para. 4.1).
No time limit, but usually shortly after the defendant's response	Either party may send the other a list of suggested experts for each field of expertise (para. 3.15). The letter should also state the basis of the proposed instruction (otherwise this procedure results in the joint selection of experts rather than joint instruction, see **52.11**).
No time limit	Claimant organises access to relevant medical records (para. 3.16).
14 days after list of experts	Other side may raise objections to the suggested experts (para. 3.17).
Objection to all suggested experts	Both parties are free to instruct their own experts. This may be penalised in costs later if either side has acted unreasonably (para. 3.18).
No complete objection	First party selects an expert from those left, and sends a letter of instruction in accordance with the standard letter (annex C).
Receipt of report	First party decides whether to send copy to the other side (see **52.11**). Both parties consider sending questions to clarify the report to the expert. The second party should send its questions via the first party's solicitors (para. 3.20).
Before proceedings	Both parties should consider sending Part 36 offers to the other side. Both parties should also consider whether mediation or ADR might be appropriate (paras 2.16, 5.2, and 8.7; see **66.10**).
14 days before issue	Claimant should ask the defendant's insurers to nominate solicitors, and both parties should carry out a stocktake of the issues and evidence (para. 2.17).

Procedural checklist 2 Pre-action procedure where no protocol applies

See **8.52** to **8.54**.

All references are to PD Pre-Action Protocols unless otherwise indicated.

First step	Letter of claim is sent to the defendant giving details of the claim and other matters set out in para. 4.3 including time for a detailed response (usually one month), and enclosing copies of the essential documents the claimant relies upon and, if the defendant is not represented, a copy of the PD Pre-action Protocols.
Within next 21 days	Defendant acknowledges letter of claim, stating when a detailed response will be sent, and reasons for any extra time required (para. 4.4).
One month from letter of claim	Defendant provides full written response accepting the claim and making proposals for settlement, or denying the claim with detailed reasons and enclosing essential documents and other matters set out in para. 4.6.
Promptly thereafter	The parties should consider ADR and engage in appropriate genuine and reasonable negotiations with a view to settling the claim economically and without court proceedings (paras 4.2(d), 4.7 and 8.7).
Expert evidence	If expert evidence is required, the parties should if possible engage an agreed expert (paras 4.9 and 4.10).

Procedural checklist 3 Claim under standard Part 8 procedure

See **chapter 13**.

Issue	Issue claim on form N208 (PD 8, para. 2.2). File claimant's notice of funding of claim (form N251), where appropriate (PD 43–48, para. 19.2(2)(a)). At same time, file evidence in support of claim (CPR, r. 8.5(1); PD 8, para. 5.1).
Fee	Part 8 claims are likely to be non-money claims for which the fee is £400 in the High Court, £150 in a county court (CPFO, fee 1.4).
Service	Serve claim form (form N208), form for acknowledging service (form N210), notice of funding of claim (form N251), and evidence in support of claim (CPR, r. 8.5(4)). Forms for defending or admitting the claim are not required (rr. 7.8(2) and 8.9(b)(ii)). Usual rules for service, set out in CPR, Part 6, apply.
Time for service	The claim must be served within four months after issue, if it is served in the jurisdiction, or six months after issue, if it is served out of the jurisdiction (r. 7.5).
Acknowledgment	Defendant should file acknowledgment (form N210), verified by a statement of truth (r. 8.2A) within 14 days after service of claim form, and serve copies of form N210 on other parties at the same time (r. 8.3(1)). Alternatively, the defendant may acknowledge service informally by letter (PD 8, para. 3.2). At the same time the defendant should file and serve notice of funding of claim (form N251), where appropriate (PD 43–48, para. 19.2(3)).
Objecting to Part 8 procedure	At same time as filing acknowledgment, defendant may file and serve statement of reasons for objecting to Part 8 procedure (CPR, r. 8.8(1); PD 8, para. 3.6).
Responding to claim	At the same time as acknowledging service, the defendant should file and serve evidence in opposition to the claim (CPR, r. 8.5(3) and (4)). If he fails to do this, he may participate in the hearing only if the court gives permission. However, judgment in default may not be entered against him (rr. 8.1(5) and 8.4).
Evidence in reply	Within 14 days after service of defendant's evidence, claimant may file and serve evidence in reply (r. 8.5(5) and (6)).
Form of evidence	Evidence may be in the form of an affidavit or witness statement, or in the case of the claimant's evidence in support, in the claim form itself, provided it is verified by a statement of truth (PD 8, para. 5.2).

Extending time for service of evidence	Parties may agree in writing extensions of time for service of the defendant's evidence, and of the claimant's evidence in reply, of up to 14 days. A copy of the agreement to extend time for the defendant's evidence must be filed with his acknowledgment (PD 8, para. 5.6). Any longer extensions may only be granted by the court (PD 8, para. 5.5).
Case management	Part 8 claims are automatically allocated to the multi-track and parties do not need to complete allocation questionnaires (CPR, r. 8.9(c)). No allocation fee is payable in a Part 8 claim (CPFO, notes following fee 2.2). Directions (including fixing a hearing date) will be given by the court either when the claim is issued or after the acknowledgment has been filed (PD 8, para. 4).
Listing fee	A listing fee of £600 (High Court) or £500 (county court) is payable, usually by the claimant on the defendant filing a pre-trial checklist (CPFO, fee 2.2).
Hearing	Most claims will be disposed of with a hearing on the written evidence.

Procedural checklist 4 Modified Part 8 procedure for claims listed in PD 8B, Section B, Table 2

See 13.3.

Issue	Issue claim in form specified in Table 2 of PD 8B. Where no claim specified, issue in form N208 (PD 8B, para. B.8).
Fee	Part 8 claims are likely to be non-money claims for which the fee is £400 in the High Court, £150 in a county court (CPFO, fee 1.4).
Date of hearing	Court will fix hearing date upon issue of claim (PD 8B, para. B.9). A listing fee of £600 (High Court) or £500 (county court) is payable (CPFO, fee 2.2).
Service	Serve claim form, notice of funding of claim (form N251), evidence in support of claim (CPR, r. 8.5(4)), and notice of hearing date (PD 8B, para. B.11). Forms for acknowledging service or for defending or admitting the claim are not required (CPR, rr. 7.8(2) and 8.9(b)(ii); PD 8B, para. B.12). Usual rules for service, set out in CPR, Part 6, apply.
Time for service	The claim form must be served not less than 21 days before the hearing date (PD 8B, para. B.10).
Acknowledgment	The defendant is not required to file or serve an acknowledgment (PD 8B, para. B.12).
Hearing	At the hearing, the court may either dispose of the claim, or give directions, including directions allocating the case to a track (PD 8B, paras B.13 and B.14).

Procedural checklist 5 Application for joinder

See 14.4. to 14.7.

Timing	If joinder is sought before service of claim form, the court's permission is not required. If joinder is sought after service of the claim form, application must be made for the court's permission.
Application notice	Form N244. Apply for new party to be added as Claimant/Defendant, or for new party to be substituted for existing party, or for existing party to be removed and also, in each case, for permission to amend statement of case. Attach draft of order sought and draft of proposed amended statement of case. Set out brief reasons for application.
Consent of new party	Where party to be added or substituted is claimant, file and serve, with the application notice, the signed written consent of the new party (PD 19, para. 2.1).

Evidence	Application to add or substitute a party must be supported by evidence setting out the proposed new party's interest in or connection with the claim (PD 19, para. 1.3). The evidence must be filed and served with the application notice.
Fee	£100 (High Court) or £65 (county court) (CPFO, fee 2.5); for consent application £50 (High Court) or £35 (county court) (CPFO, fee 2.6).
Service	The application notice, attachments and evidence in support must be served on all existing parties and any proposed new party as soon as practicable after filing and at least three clear days before the hearing date (CPR, r. 23.7).
Costs	In contested applications, parties should file and serve costs schedules in form N260 24 hours before hearing (PD 43–48, para. 13.5(4)).
Hearing	Consent applications may be dealt with without a hearing.
After the hearing	Comply with directions. If permission is given, these will normally require the applicant to file the amended claim form and particulars of claim within 14 days of the order (a fee of £50 (High Court) or £35 (county court) is payable (CPFO, fee 1.5)), to serve the new defendant with the existing statements of case, the amended claim form and particulars of claim, a response pack and a copy of the order.
Limitation	A new defendant does not become a party to the proceedings for the purpose of the Limitation Act 1980 until served with the claim form (PD 19, para. 3.3).

Procedural checklist 6 Interpleader proceedings: High Court

See **14.15** to **14.18**.

(a) Sheriff or enforcement officer's interpleader: preliminary steps

Notice to enforcement officer	The person claiming ownership of goods taken or intended to be taken by the enforcement officer should notify the enforcement officer of his claim, and give his address for service (RSC, ord. 17, r. 2(1) in CPR, sch. 1).
Enforcement officer's notice to judgment creditor	Enforcement officer must notify judgment creditor immediately of claim (RSC, ord. 17, r. 2(2) in CPR, sch. 1).
Response from judgment creditor	Within seven days, judgment creditor must inform the enforcement officer whether he admits or disputes the claim (RSC, ord. 17, r. 2(2) in CPR, sch. 1). Where the claim is disputed, the enforcement officer may apply for interpleader relief.

(b) Interpleader application

Application	Application for interpleader relief in existing proceedings is made by application notice (form N244,) and where there are no pending proceedings, by Part 8 claim form (form N208) (RSC, ord. 17, r. 3(1) in CPR, sch. 1).
Fee	£100 where claim is made by application notice (CPFO, fee 2.5); £400 where claim is made by Part 8 claim form (where claim is for goods, not proceeds of sale) (CPFO, fee 1.4).
Evidence in support	Where the enforcement officer is interpleader claimant, no evidence in support is required. Otherwise, evidence must be filed and served showing that the interpleader claimant: • claims no interest in the subject matter in dispute, other than for charges or costs; • does not collude with any of the claimants to the subject matter; and • is willing to pay or transfer that subject matter into court or to dispose of it as the court may direct (RSC, ord. 17, r. 3(4) in CPR, sch. 1).
Service	The claim form or application notice must be served on all persons asserting a claim to the property.

Claimant's response	Where the claim relates to goods seized in execution, the claimant then has 14 days in which to serve a witness statement or affidavit on the enforcement officer and the judgment creditor. This must identify the property claimed and the grounds for asserting rights in the property (RSC, ord. 17, r. 3(6) in CPR, sch. 1).

Procedural checklist 7 Interpleader proceedings: county court

See 14.15 and 14.19 to 14.21.

(a) Bailiff's interpleader

Notice to bailiff	The person claiming ownership of goods taken or intended to be taken in execution (the 'interpleader claimant') should notify the bailiff of his claim, give his address for service, and the grounds for the claim (CCR, ord. 33, r. 1(1) in CPR, sch. 2).
Security	Except where the claim is for the value or proceeds of goods, the interpleader claimant must make a deposit or provide security for the claim (CCR, ord. 33, r. 1(2)(b) in CPR, sch. 2).
Notice to judgment creditor	Court will notify judgment creditor of claim (CCR, ord. 33, r. 1(2)(a) in CPR, sch. 2).
Response from judgment creditor	Within four days, judgment creditor must inform the court whether he admits or disputes the claim (CCR, ord. 33, r. 2 in CPR, sch. 2).
Issue of interpleader proceedings	Where the claim is disputed, the court will issue an interpleader notice (form N88 or N88(1)), fix a date for the hearing and serve the notice on the judgment creditor and the interpleader claimant at least 14 days before the hearing date (CCR, ord. 33, r. 4 in CPR, sch. 2).

(b) Stakeholder's interpleader

Jurisdiction	A person ('the applicant'), who is being, or expects to be, sued by two or more persons (the 'interpleader claimant') making opposing claims to a debt, money or goods for which the applicant is liable, may apply for interpleader relief (CCR, ord. 33, r. 6(1) in CPR, sch. 2).
Application	Application is made by filing a witness statement or affidavit showing that the applicant: • claims no interest in the subject matter in dispute, other than for charges or costs; • does not collude with any of the interpleader claimants; and • is willing to pay or transfer that subject matter into court or to dispose of it as the court may direct (CCR, ord. 33, r. 6(3) in CPR, sch. 2).
Number of copies	One copy of the affidavit or witness statement should be filed for the court together with an additional copy for each competing interpleader claimant (CCR, ord. 33, r. 6(3) in CPR, sch. 2).
Time for application	Where the applicant is a defendant in a pending claim, the application should be filed within 14 days after service of the claim form.
Interpleader notice	Where there are no pending proceedings, the court will issue an interpleader notice (form N89).
Pre-trial review	The court will fix a date for a pre-trial review on receipt of the application.
Service	The court will serve notice of the application, form N89 (where appropriate) and copies of the affidavit or witness statement on all parties and interpleader claimants at least 21 days before the date for the pre-trial review.
Interpleader claimant's response	Within 14 days after service, the interpleader claimant must either file a notice that no interpleader claim is to be made or file particulars of the grounds for a claim. Copies for all parties should be filed. The court will serve the parties (CCR, ord. 33, r. 10 in CPR, sch. 2).

Procedural checklist 8 Approval of settlement or compromise to which a child or patient is party, where sole purpose of claim is to obtain court approval

See 14.38.

Part 8 claim form	Issue Part 8 claim form, including request for approval of the settlement and either set out the terms of the settlement or attach a draft consent order in form N292 (PD 21, para. 6.1).
Contents of Part 8 claim form	The claim form must include the following information (PD 21, para. 6.2): • whether and to what extent the defendant admits liability; • the age and occupation (if any) of the child or patient; • the litigation friend's approval of the proposed settlement; • in a personal injury case only, the circumstances of the accident, any medical reports, a schedule of damages, any evidence or police reports in any related criminal proceedings or inquest and details of any prosecution; • where the settlement provides for periodical payments, the terms of the settlement or compromise. Alternatively the draft consent order should be attached to the claim form.
Part 8 Procedure	See procedural checklist 3.
Opinion on the merits	An opinion on the merits by counsel or solicitor should be supplied to the court (PD 21, para. 6.3).
Hearing	The application will normally be heard by a master or district judge (PD 21, para. 6.5). However, in the Chancery Division the application will be heard by a judge if the amount exceeds £100,000 (PD 2B, para. 5.1(a)).
Privacy	The hearing of the application to approve the settlement may be in private where it involves the interests of a child or patient (CPR, r. 39.2(3)(d); PD 39, para. 1.6).

Procedural checklist 9 Issue and service where service of the claim form is to be effected by the court

See 15.16.

Where the court is to effect service the procedure is as follows:

(a) The claimant sends or takes to court one copy of the claim form and, if necessary, a notice of funding of claim or copy LSC certificate for the court, and a copy for each defendant to be served, together with the issue fee (CPFO, fee 1). Claimants in the RCJ can get the court to seal a 'claimant's copy' claim form, if convenient.

(b) The court issues the claim form by entering the issue date on the claim form, affixing the court seal to the claim form and allocating a number to the claim. It creates a case management file, in which it files its copy of the claim form and, if supplied, notice of funding of claim or LSC certificate. The claimant's copy of the claim form (if any) will be returned.

(c) The court serves the claim form and, if supplied, notice of funding of claim. It is for the court to decide which method of service to choose, although the method will normally be by first-class post (CPR, r. 6.3(2); PD 6, para. 8.1).

(d) Where particulars of claim are contained in the claim form or are to be served with it, court staff will add to the documents for service forms for admitting and for defending the claim and for acknowledging service (CPR, r. 7.8(1)). Where the particulars of claim are to be served later, these documents do not accompany the claim form.

(e) The court will send the claimant a notice of issue (form N205A, N205B or N205C), which will include the date when the claim form is deemed to be served under r. 6.7 (r. 6.14).

(f) Where the court sends the claim form by post and it is returned to the court, or where the court attempts to serve by its bailiff and is unable to do so, it must notify the claimant (rr. 6.11 and 6.11A).

(g) A claimant who receives a notice of ineffectual bailiff service should take steps to effect service of the claim form himself. If the court sent the claim form by first-class post to the correct address for service, there is an irrebuttable presumption of dues service (r. 6.7).

Procedural checklist 10 Issue and service where service of the claim form is to be effected by the claimant

See 15.20.

Where the claimant is to effect service the procedure is as follows:

(a) The claimant sends or takes to court one copy of the claim form for the court, and a copy for each defendant to be served, together with the issue fee. Claimants in the RCJ can get the court to seal a 'claimant's copy' claim form, if convenient. There must be a notification to the court that the claimant wishes to effect service. If necessary, a notice of funding of claim or copy LSC certificate must be filed.

(b) The court issues the claim form by entering the issue date on the claim form, affixing the court seal to the claim form and allocating a number to the claim. It creates a case management file, which will include the court's copy of the claim form and, if supplied, notice of funding of claim or copy LSC certificate.

(c) The claimant's copy of the claim form (if any) and the copies for service on the defendants will be returned.

(d) The claimant will effect service, in one of the ways specified in CPR, r. 6.2. If a notice of funding of claim form N251 was filed, it must be served with the claim form. Where particulars of claim are contained in the claim form or are to be served with it, the claimant must add to the documents for service forms for acknowledging service, for admitting and for defending the claim (r. 7.8(1)). Where the particulars of claim are to be served later, these documents do not accompany the claim form.

(e) The claimant must file a certificate of service (form N215) within seven days of service of the claim form, giving the details set out in table 15.1 (r. 6.14(2)(a)).

Procedural checklist 11 Application to extend time for service of claim form

See 15.7.

Application notice	Form N244. The application is for the period within which the claim form may be served to be extended to a specific date. Brief reasons for the application should be included in form N244.
Evidence in support	Evidence in support must be filed with form N244 and will usually either be set out in the notice of application itself or in a witness statement. The evidence must state all the circumstances relied on; the date of issue of the claim; the expiry date of any extension already granted under CPR, r. 7.6; and a full explanation of why the claim form has not been served (PD 7, para. 8.2). Where the application is without notice, the evidence must also state why notice has not been given (CPR, r. 25.3(3)).
Without notice	Application will usually be made without notice, as the defendant is not yet on the record (CPR, r. 7.6(4)(b)). Because the application is without notice to the defendant, the claimant must make full and frank disclosure of all relevant facts.
Fee	£50 (High Court) or £35 (county court) (CPFO, fee 2.6).
Hearing	As the application is made without notice, there will not normally be a hearing. However, where the application is made shortly before expiry of the period for service of the claim form and where the cause of action has become time-barred since the date of issue of the claim form, it is desirable that the application should be dealt with by an urgent hearing.
Service of order	A copy of any order made without notice to the defendant, whether extending time for service of the claim form or refusing to do so, must be served on the defendant, together with form N244 and any evidence in support. The order should contain a statement of the defendant's right to apply to set aside or vary the order within seven clear days of service of the order (CPR, r. 23.9).

Procedural checklist 12 Application for permission to serve claim form out of jurisdiction

See **16.45**.

Claim form	Claimant has the choice of whether to issue the claim form before seeking permission to serve outside the jurisdiction (see **16.45**).
Application	If a claim form is issued first, the application is for permission to serve outside the jurisdiction, and fee 2.6 (see 'Fee' below) is payable on the application. If a claim form is not issued first, the application is for permission to issue and to serve the claim form, and fee 1.7 (see 'Fee' below) is payable on the application.
Application notice	Form N244. Apply for permission under CPR, r. 6.20, to serve the defendant at his address out of the jurisdiction because [state grounds of r. 6.20 relied on; Claimant believes his claim has a reasonable prospect of success; state Defendant's address, or where it is believed he may be found. Where r. 6.20(3) is relied on state also that it is believed that there is a real issue which it is reasonable for the court to try]. Indicate that the claimant wishes to have the matter dealt with without a hearing, and that no notice should be given to the defendant.
Evidence in support	Evidence in form of witness statement must be filed with form N244. Evidence must show which paragraph of r. 6.20 applies to the claim; that the claimant has a reasonable prospect of success; why England and Wales is the proper place to bring the claim and state the defendant's address, or at least the country in which he may be found. Where r. 6.20(3) is relied on set out evidence for belief that there is a real issue which it is reasonable for the court to try (r. 6.21).
Without notice to defendant	Application will be made without notice to the defendant. In the RCJ, leave the application notice and supporting evidence in the Master's Secretary's Department, room E16.The papers will be placed before a master or district judge, who will note the order on the papers and on the court file. Because the application is made without notice to the defendant, the claimant must make full and frank disclosure of all relevant facts.
Fee	£50 (High Court) or £35 (county court) (CPFO, fees 1.7 and 2.6).
Hearing	As the application is made without notice, there will not normally be a hearing.

Procedural checklist 13 Admitting a claim and requesting time to pay

See **chapter 17**.

Type of claim and admission	Step to be taken by defendant	Step to be taken by claimant where claimant accepts defendant's offer	Step to be taken by claimant where claimant rejects defendant's offer
Specified sum. Admitted in whole; defendant seeking time to pay (CPR, r. 14.9).	Return form N9A to claimant (r. 14.4(2)) within 14 days after service of the particulars of claim (r. 14.2).	File request for judgment, form N225, reflecting defendant's offer for payment. No fee is payable (CPFO, notes to fee 2.6). Court will enter judgment for the amount of the claim and costs, and for payment at the time and rate specified in defendant's request for time to pay (r. 14.9).	File request for judgment form N225, and N9A giving notice that claimant does not accept defendant's offer. No fee is payable (CPFO, notes to fee 2.6). Court will enter judgment for the amount of the claim and decide time and rate for payment (r. 14.10(2) and (4)), and will issue decision on form N30(2). Either party can object to the determination within 14 days after receipt of form N30(2).

Type of claim and admission	Step to be taken by defendant	Step to be taken by claimant where claimant accepts defendant's offer	Step to be taken by claimant where claimant rejects defendant's offer
Specified sum. Admitted in whole; defendant not seeking time to pay (r. 14.4).	Return form N9A to claimant (r. 14.4(2)) within 14 days after service of the particulars of claim (r. 14.2).	Claimant files request for judgment (form N225) and specifies the times and rates for payment. No fee is payable (CPFO, notes to fee 2.6). The court enters judgment as requested by claimant (r. 14.4(4) to (6)).	—
Specified sum. Admitted in part, but defendant seeks time to pay (r. 14.5).	Return forms N9A and N9B to the court (r. 14.5(2)) within 14 days after service of the particulars of claim (r. 14.2). Court sends forms N9A, N9B and N255A to claimant, requiring claimant to notify response to the court within 14 days (r. 14.53)). If defendant does not reply within 14 days, claim stayed (r. 14.5(5)().	Within 14 days of receipt of forms N9A, N9B and N255A, from court, file request for judgment (form N255A), reflecting defendant's offer for payment. Court will enter judgment for the amount admitted and costs, and for payment at the time and rate specified in defendant's request for time to pay (r. 14.9).	Within 14 days of receipt of court notice, file request for judgment (form N255A), giving notice either: • that claimant does not accept defendant's partial admission, in which case the claim will proceed as a defended claim, or • that claimant accepts the partial admission in settlement of the claim but does not accept defendant's proposals for payment. The court will then enter judgment for the amount admitted and will calculate a rate of payment. It will notify the parties of its decision in form N30(2). Either party can object to the determination within 14 days after receipt of form N30(2) (rr. 14.10 to (14.13).
Specified sum. Admitted in part; defendant does not seek time to pay (r. 14.5).	Return forms N9A and N9B to the court (r. 14.5(2)) within 14 days after service of the particulars of claim (r. 14.2). Court sends forms N9A, N9B and N255A, requiring claimant to notify response to court within 14 days (r. 4.5(3)). If defendant does not reply within 14 days, claim stayed (r. 14.5(5)).	Within 14 days of receipt of forms N9A, N9B and N255A, file request for judgment (form N225A), reflecting defendant's offer for payment. No fee is payable (CPFO, notes to fee 2.6). Court enters judgment for amount offered by defendant and costs to be paid by the date or at the rate specified in form N255A (r. 14.5(7) to (9)).	File form N255A at court, indicating that partial admission is rejected and case will proceed as a defended claim.

Type of claim and admission	Step to be taken by defendant	Step to be taken by claimant where claimant accepts defendant's offer	Step to be taken by claimant where claimant rejects defendant's offer
Unspecified sum. Defendant admits liability without saying how much is admitted (r. 14.6).	Return form N9C to court (r. 14.6(2)) within 14 days after service of the particulars of claim (r. 14.2). Court will forward form N9C to claimant, together with form N226 (notice of admission) (r. 14.6(3)). If claimant does not respond within 14 days, claim will be stayed (r. 14.6(5)).	Within 14 days of receipt of forms N9C and N226, file completed N226 asking the court to enter judgment for an amount to be decided by the court and costs. No fee is payable (CPFO, notes to fee 2.6). Court will enter judgment and give directions, either allocating the claim to the small claims track or directing a disposal hearing (r. 14.6(6)).	—
Unspecified sum. Defendant admits liability and offers a fixed sum in settlement of it, without seeking time to pay (r. 14.7).	Return form N9C to court (r. 14.7(2)) within 14 days after service of the particulars of claim (r. 14.2). Court will forward form N9C to claimant, together with form N226 (notice of admission).	Within 14 days of receipt of notice from the court, file form N226, accepting the offer. No fee is payable (CPFO, notes to fee 2.6). Court will enter judgment in accordance with the offer (r. 14.7(6) to (8)). Failing to file N226 results in a stay (r. 14.7(4)).	Within 14 days of receipt of notice from the court, file form N226, notifying court that offer of sum in settlement of claim rejected. No fee is payable (CPFO, notes to fee 2.6). Judgment will be entered for an amount to be decided by the court and costs. The court will give case management directions (r. 14.7(9)).
Unspecified sum. Defendant admits liability, offers a fixed sum in settlement and asks to pay by instalments or at a future date (r. 14.7).	Return form N9C to court (r. 14.7(2)) within 14 days after service of the particulars of claim (r. 14.2). Court will forward form N9C to claimant, together with form N226 (notice of admission). If claimant does not respond within 14 days, claim will be stayed (r. 14.7(4)).	If the offer is accepted in full, including the proposals for payment, file request for payment (form N226) and court will enter judgment for amount offered and costs at the time and rate specified in defendant's request for time to pay (r. 14.9). No fee is payable (CPFO, notes to fee 2.6).	If claimant rejects the amount offered, file request for judgment form N226. No fee is payable (CPFO, notes to fee 2.6). Court enters judgment for an amount to be decided by the court and costs (r. 14.7(9)). If claimant accepts the amount offered, but not the proposals for payment, file form N226. The court will enter judgment and calculate the rate of payment, and will notify the parties of its decision in form N30(2). Either party can object within 14 days after receipt of form N30(2) (r. 14.10).

Procedural checklist 14 Time limits for responding to claim by acknowledging service and/or filing a defence

See chapter 18.

Step to be taken	Place of service of claim form	Time limit
Acknowledgment to be filed at court	Within the jurisdiction.	14 days after service of particulars of claim (whether or not particulars of claim served with claim form) (CPR, r. 10.3(1)).
	Out of the jurisdiction under r. 6.19(1) in Scotland, Northern Ireland, or in a European territory of another contracting State, or under r. 6.19(1A) in another EU State (apart from Denmark).	21 days after service of particulars of claim (r. 6.22(2)).
	Out of the jurisdiction under r. 6.19(1) in any other territory of a contracting State.	31 days after service of particulars of claim (r. 6.22(3)).
	Out of the jurisdiction with permission under r. 6.20.	Court will specify the time for acknowledging service, calculated by reference to the table at the end of PD 6B (r. 6.21(4); PD 6B, paras 7.2(1) and 7.3).
Filing of defence at court, where no acknowledgment filed	Within the jurisdiction.	14 days after service of particulars of claim (CPR, r. 15.4(1)(a)).
	Out of the jurisdiction under r. 6.19(1) in Scotland, Northern Ireland, or in a European territory of another contracting State, or under r. 6.19(1A) in another EU State (apart from Denmark).	21 days after service of particulars of claim (r. 6.23(2)).
	Out of the jurisdiction under r. 6.19(1) in any other territory of a contracting State.	31 days after service of particulars of claim (r. 6.23(3)).
	Out of the jurisdiction with permission under r. 6.20.	Court will specify the time for acknowledging service, calculated by reference to the table at the end of PD 6B (r. 6.21(4) PD 6B, paras 7.2(3) and 7.4(1)).
Filing of defence at court, following filing of acknowledgment	Within the jurisdiction.	28 days after service of particulars of claim (CPR, r. 15.4(1)(b)).
	Out of the jurisdiction under r. 6.19(1) in Scotland, Northern Ireland, or in a European territory of another contracting State, or under r. 6.19(1A) in another EU State (apart from Denmark).	35 days after service of particulars of claim (r. 6.23(2)).
	Out of the jurisdiction under r. 6.19(1) in any other territory of a contracting State.	45 days after service of particulars of claim (r. 6.23(3)).
	Out of the jurisdiction with permission under r. 6.20.	Court will specify the time for acknowledging service, calculated by reference to the table at the end of PD 6B, plus an additional 14 days (PD 6B, paras 7.2(3) and 7.4(2)).

Procedural checklist 15 Procedure for disputing the court's jurisdiction

See chapter 19.

Acknowledgment	File acknowledgment of service within 14 days after service of particulars of claim, if served in the jurisdiction, within 21 days after service of the particulars of claim, if served in Europe under CPR, r. 6.19, or within the period given in the court order, if served out of the jurisdiction with the court's permission, under r. 6.21 (r. 11(2)). Tick only the 'intention to contest the jurisdiction' box. See procedural checklist 14.
Application — time	Within 14 days after filing an acknowledgment make an application under Part 23 for an order that the court has no jurisdiction to try the claim (r. 11(4)).
Extension of time	If more time is needed, apply under r. 3.1(2)(a) for an extension of the time limit laid down in r. 11(4). An extension of time for service of the defence will not carry with it an extension of time for an application to dispute the jurisdiction (*Montrose Investments Ltd v Orion Nominees Ltd* [2001] CP Rep 109).
Application notice	Form N244. Where service out of the jurisdiction is contested, application is for any order giving permission for service out of the jurisdiction under r. 6.20 to be set aside, for service of the claim form to be set aside and for the proceedings to be stayed.
Evidence in support	Must be filed and served with form N244.
Fee	£100 (High Court) or £65 (county court) (CPFO, fee 2.5).
Service	On defendant as soon as practicable after filing application notice, and at least three days before hearing (CPR, r. 23.7(1)).
Costs	Both parties should file and serve costs schedules in form N260 24 hours before hearing (PD 43–48, para. 13.5(4)).
Defence	No need to file defence before hearing (CPR, r. 11(9)(a)). If the application is unsuccessful, the court must give directions for filing and service of the defence (r. 11.7(c)). Claimant cannot enter default judgment (r. 12.3).

Procedural checklist 16 Request for entry of judgment in default

See chapter 20, especially 20.3 to 20.6.

Claim form	Serve claim form on defendant in accordance with CPR, r. 6.2.
Certificate of service of claim form	If claim form is served by claimant rather than court, file certificate of service of claim form, within seven days after service of claim form (r. 6.14(2)).
Particulars of claim	Serve particulars of claim, either with claim form or within 14 days after service of claim form, and within period of validity of the claim form (r. 7.4(1) and (2)).
Certificate of service of particulars of claim	Where the particulars of claim are served separately from the claim form, within seven days of service of the particulars on the defendant, file a copy of the particulars and a certificate that they have been served (rr. 6.10 and (7.4(3)).
Failure to respond: request for judgment	Wait 14 days after service of particulars of claim (whether served with claim form or later) (rr. 10.3 and 15.4). (For time limits where service effected out of the jurisdiction, see procedural checklist 14.) If neither acknowledgment of service nor defence filed by then, file request for default judgment in form N205A or N225 (for specified sum) or N205B or N227 (for unspecified sum) (r. 12.4(1)(a); PD 12, para. 3). No fee is payable (CPFO, notes to fee 2.6).

Failure to file defence: request for judgment	If acknowledgment filed within 14 days after service of particulars of claim, wait until 28 days after service of particulars of claim (CPR, rr. 10.3 and 15.4). (For time limits where service effected out of the jurisdiction, see procedural checklist 14.) If defence not filed by then, file request for default judgment in form N205A or N225 (for specified sum) or N205B or N227 (for unspecified sum) (r. 12.4(1)(b); PD 12, para. 3). No fee is payable (CPFO, notes to fee 2.6).
Calculating time	The periods of 14 and 28 days above should be calculated to exclude the date of service of the particulars of claim but to include the date of filing of the acknowledgment or service of the particulars of claim (CPR, r. 2.8(3)(b)), and must take into account the deemed dates of service in r. 6.7 (see **15.36**).

Procedural checklist 17 Application for entry of judgment in default

See chapter 20, especially **20.8** to **20.9**.

When required	Claims for costs (other than fixed costs); claims for delivery up (where the defendant has not offered the alternative of paying the value of the goods claimed); claims by one spouse or civil partner against the other in tort and claims against children and patients. Also, the following cases where the defendant has not filed an acknowledgment: claims where service has been effected out of the jurisdiction under CPR, r. 6.19, or on a defendant domiciled in a Convention territory or Regulation State; claims against States, diplomats and bodies granted immunity under the International Organisations Acts 1968 and 1981.
Preliminary steps	• Serve claim form and particulars of claim and file certificates of service (procedural checklist 16). • In an application against a child or patient, apply for a litigation friend to be appointed under CPR, r. 21.6.
Time	Wait 14 days after service of particulars of claim (whether served with claim form or later) (rr. 10.3 and 15.4). If neither acknowledgment of service nor defence filed by then, make application under Part 23. If acknowledgment filed within 14 days after service of particulars of claim, wait until 28 days after service of particulars of claim (rr. 10.3 and 15.4) before making application under Part 23. Time limits to be calculated as in procedural checklist 16. (For time limits where service effected out of the jurisdiction, see procedural checklist 14.)
Application notice	Form N244. Application is for judgment to be entered against the defendant on the ground that he has not filed an acknowledgment of service or defence, as the case may be. Where application not on notice, state on form N244 that claimant wishes to have the matter dealt with without a hearing. Where the defendant is an individual, state his/her date of birth, if known.
Evidence in support	An application must be supported by evidence if it is for default judgment • against a child or patient; • in a claim in tort between spouses or civil partners; • against a State; • against a defendant who was served outside the jurisdiction, or inside the jurisdiction when domiciled in a Convention territory or Regulation State, and who has not acknowledged service (see r. 12.11(4)(a)) (r. 12.11(3) and PD 12, para. 4).
Service of evidence	Evidence in support need not be served on defendant who failed to file an acknowledgment of service (CPR, r. 12.11(2)).
Notice	Generally the application is with notice, but will be without notice where the claim was served under the Civil Jurisdiction and Judgments Act 1982 or the Jurisdiction and Judgments Regulation or where application is made against a State and in either case the defendant has failed to file an acknowledgment (CPR, r. 12.11(4) and (5)).

Fee	£100 (High Court); £65 (county court) (CPFO, fee 2.5); £55 (High Court); £35 (county court) where application without notice (CPFO, fee 2.6).
Service of N244	Where application on notice, serve defendant as soon as practicable after filing application notice, and at least three days before hearing (CPR, r. 23.7(1)).
Costs	Where application on notice, both parties should file and serve costs schedules in form N260 24 hours before hearing (PD 43–48, para. 13.5(4)). The court will not summarily assess the costs of a child or patient, unless the solicitor acting or the child or patient has waived the right to further costs (PD 43–48, para. 13.11(1)).
Hearing	Normally before master or district judge. Where the application is made without notice, there will not normally be a hearing.

Procedural checklist 18 Counterclaim (Part 20)

See **chapter 28**.

Timing	Generally, at the same time as filing the defence in order to avoid the need for permission (CPR, r. 20.4(2)). Can be made up to trial, but obtaining permission gets progressively more difficult.
Forms	N211. Simple counterclaims can be made on forms N9B or N9D.
Title	Must comply with PD 20, paras 7.1 to 7.11.
Issue	Issue fee is payable when the counterclaim is filed (CPFO, fees and 1.5 and 1.6).
Pleading	Particulars of the counterclaim, verified by a statement of truth, can be set out in a counterclaim, but if the defendant also intends to defend the main proceedings, the defence and counterclaim should normally form one document with the counterclaim following the defence (PD 20, para. 6.1).
Counterclaim against a person other than the claimant	Most counterclaims are made against the claimant, but it is possible to bring a counterclaim against a person other than a claimant (CPR, r. 20.5). Permission is always required (r. 20.5(1)), and, unless the court otherwise directs, the application is made without notice (r. 20.5(2)). The new party is added as an additional party (r. 20.5(1)).
Permission to issue	Required if a defendant wishes to file a counterclaim after filing a defence (r. 20.4(2)). Issue application notice with written evidence in support: • stating the stage the main proceedings have reached; • stating the nature of the counterclaim; • summarising the facts on which the counterclaim is based; • stating the name and address of the defendant to the counterclaim; • explaining any delay where this is a factor; and • providing a timetable of the steps in the claim to date. As rr. 20.5(2) and 20.7(5) do not apply to this situation, the application is made on notice to the claimant.
Documents to be served	Claim form; counterclaim or defence and counterclaim.
Service	CPR, Part 6, applies (**chapter 15**).
Response	Acknowledgment of service (Part 10) does not apply (r. 20.4(3)). The claimant should file and serve a defence to counterclaim or a reply and defence to counterclaim within 14 days of deemed service of the counterclaim (rr. 15.4(1), 20.3(1); PD 20, para. 6.2).
Default judgment	May be entered (CPR, r. 12.3(2); PD 20, para. 3).
Directions	The effect of rr. 20.3(2)(c) and 20.13, together with PD 20, para. 5.1, is that the relevant directions governing counterclaims are (unless the court gives special directions for the counterclaim) those given in the main proceedings.

Procedural checklist 19 Additional claim (against third party)

See **chapter 29**.

Timing	Generally, before or at the same time as filing the defence in order to avoid the need for permission (CPR, r. 20.7(3)). Can be made up to trial, but obtaining permission gets progressively more difficult.
Form	Additional claim form, form N211.
Title of claim	Must comply with PD 20, paras 7.1 to 7.11.
Issue	Issue fee is the same as for Part 7 claim forms (see CPFO, fee 1). Issue takes place when the claim form is sealed and on the date entered by the court on the claim form (CPR, r. 20.7(2) and r. 7.2(2)).
Pleading	Particulars of the additional claim must be contained in or served with the claim form (r. 20.7(4)), and must be verified by a statement of truth in the form '[I believe] [the defendant believes] that the facts stated in this statement of case are true.' (PD 20, para 4.2).
Permission to issue	Required if a defendant wishes to issue an additional claim after filing a defence (CPR, r. 20.7(3)). Issue application notice (see procedural checklist 20) with written evidence in support: • stating the stage the main proceedings have reached; • stating the nature of the additional claim, question or relief; • summarising the facts on which the additional claim is based; • stating the name and address of the third party; • explaining any delay where this is a factor; and • providing a timetable of the steps in the claim to date. Unless the court otherwise directs, the application is made without notice (r. 20.7(5)).
Documents to be served on third party	Additional claim form (N211); notes for defendant on replying to the additional claim form (N211C); particulars of the additional claim (either contained in or served with the claim form) (r. 20.7(4)); forms for defending and admitting the claim (forms N9A and N9B or N9C and N9D as appropriate); form for acknowledging service (form N213) (r. 20.12(1)); copies of every statement of case previously served (r. 20.12(1)(d)(i)); notice of public funding or of any CFA (form N251); and such other documents as the court may direct (r. 20.12(1)(ii)).
Service	CPR, Part 6, applies (**chapter 15**).
Time to serve	An additional claim issued without permission must be served within 14 days after the additional claim is issued by the court (r. 20.8(1)(b)). Any order for permission will give directions for service (r. 20.8(3)).
Effect of service	Third party becomes a party to the proceedings on being served (r. 20.10(1)).
Service on other parties	Copies of the additional claim form must be served on all existing parties (r. 20.12(2)).
Response	Third party must acknowledge service or file a defence within 14 days of deemed service (r. 6.7, 9.2, 10.3, 14.2, 15.4 and 20.3(1)).
Defence	A defence to the additional claim must be filed within 14 days of deemed service of the additional claim, or within 28 days if an acknowledgment of service is filed (r. 15.4). Time may be extended by consent for up to 28 days (r. 15.5). A copy of the defence to the additional claim must be served on every other party (r. 15.6). It must be verified by a statement of truth (PD 15, paras 2.1, 2.2).

Default judgment	Subject to r. 20.11(2), default judgment is not available (r. 20.3(3)). Instead, if there is no response within the prescribed period, the third party is deemed to admit the additional claim and is bound by any judgment or decision in the main proceedings (r. 20.11(2)(a)). If default judgment is given against the defendant and if the defendant satisfies that judgment, the defendant can enter default judgment for a contribution or indemnity against the third party by filing a request (r. 20.11(3)). Otherwise, default judgment against a third party is possible only with permission (r. 20.11(3), (4)).
Directions	After a defence to an additional claim is filed the court will list the matter for case management directions (r. 20.13(1) and PD 20, para 5.1). The court: • will ensure, so far as practicable, that the main proceedings and additional claim are managed together (r. 20.13(2)); • may treat the hearing as a summary judgment hearing (PD 20, para. 5.3); • may dismiss the additional claim; • may require the additional claim to be dealt with separately from the main proceedings (CPR, r. 20.9(1)(c)); • may give directions about the way the claim should be dealt with (PD 20, para. 5.3); • may give directions as to the third party's involvement at trial; and • may give directions about the extent to which the third party will be bound by any judgment or decision in the main proceedings.

Procedural checklist 20 Interim application without notice

See **chapter 32**, especially **32.7** to **32.9**.

Application notice	Issue and file form N244, stating whether a hearing is sought (CPR, r. 23.6). County court interim injunction applications should be on form N16A.
Evidence in support	Normally required. In addition to covering evidence required for the order sought (PD 25, para. 3.3), written evidence must: • state reasons why notice was not given (CPR, r. 25.3(3)); • where secrecy is not essential, state what steps have been taken to give informal notice to the respondent (PD 25, para. 4.3(3)). Usually in the form of witness statements, but affidavits are required for freezing and search orders (PD 25, para. 3.1). Applicant is under a duty of full and frank disclosure, which includes a duty to disclose adverse matters which could be discovered on making reasonable inquiries.
Fee	£50 (High Court); £35 (county court) (CPFO, fee 2.6).
Draft order	Usually required for without notice applications as most are complex. If application is for an interim injunction, use form PF 39 CH (intended actions) or PF 40 CH (after issue). Freezing and search orders should follow the standard forms in PD 25.
Undertakings	Should be incorporated into the order as required (e.g., to issue and serve a claim form (CPR, r. 25.2(3)), to file and serve written evidence, to pay damages (injunctions)).
Skeleton argument	Required for most High Court applications dealt with by judges. Should state how the requirements for the relief sought are satisfied. File two clear days before the hearing (if possible).
Arrange hearing	Urgent applications: emergency telephone number for the High Court is (020) 7947 6000. See **37.6** and PD 25, para. 4.5.

Hearing	Explain, among other things: • why without notice; • whether any informal notice has been given, and why; • points relevant to the duty of full and frank disclosure; • any variations on standard-form orders.
Note of hearing	Advocate should produce note of the hearing (see **32.8**).
Order	Should include a statement of the respondent's right to apply to set aside (CPR, r. 23.9(3)). It also often provides for listing a hearing to review to be heard on notice. Application notice, evidence in support and note of the hearing should be served with the order (see **32.8**).

Procedural checklist 21 Interim application with notice

See **chapter 32**, especially **32.10** to **32.28**.

Timing	As soon as it becomes apparent that it is desirable or necessary (PD 23, para. 2.7). Other than urgent applications, they can only be made once applicant has come on the record. Applications can be made after judgment (CPR, r. 25.2).
Application notice	Form N244, which must be filed (r. 23.3). It must state the order sought and the reason for applying (r. 23.6) and provide a time estimate. County court interim injunction applications should be on form N16A.
Draft order	Not required for simple applications. Drafts of more complex orders should be brought to the hearing (PD 23, para. 12.1) together with a copy on 3.5 inch disk.
Evidence in support	Consider whether evidence is required. If so, consider whether to use part C of N244, witness statements, affidavits or statements of case. Must be served and filed (if not already done) with the N244.
Combined applications	Are encouraged (CPR, r. 1.4(2)(i)), and should be combined with any existing case management hearing (PD 23, para. 2.8).
Fee	£100 (High Court); £65 (county court) (CPFO, fee 2.5).
Service	On respondent as soon as practicable after N244 is filed, and at least three clear days before hearing (CPR, r. 23.7(1)) (unless some other period is prescribed, such as for summary judgment and interim payments).
Cross-applications	Respondent may issue a cross-application returnable at the same hearing date as the applicant's application. This may require relisting of both applications if the original time estimate is insufficient for both.
Directions	Sometimes directions are made for filing and serving evidence and skeleton arguments in the application (PD 23, para. 9.2).
Respondent's written evidence	Serve and file in accordance with directions, if any, or as soon as possible (PD 23, para. 9.4) and in sufficient time to avoid the need to adjourn.
Applicant's evidence in reply	Serve and file in accordance with directions, if any, or as soon as possible (PD 23, para. 9.5) and in sufficient time to avoid the need to adjourn.
Application bundles	In substantial applications bundles of material documents should be prepared (usually at least two clear days before the hearing, **32.14**).
Skeleton arguments	Not mandatory for applications before circuit judges, masters and district judges, but if used should be served and filed the day before the hearing. Usually required for applications before High Court judges, where they should be filed two clear days before the hearing (see **32.15**)).
Costs schedules	Both parties should file and serve costs schedules in form N260 24 hours before the hearing (PD 43–48, para. 13.5(4)). (But see PD 43–48, paras 13.9 and 13.11, where the receiving party is publicly funded, or a child or patient.)

Hearing	Most applications should be listed for hearing by a master or district judge. Injunctions should usually be heard by judges. Freezing and search orders should normally be dealt with by High Court judges. Most applications are heard in chambers even if technically they are dealt with in public. The court may review the case and give case management directions (PD 23, para. 2.9).
Costs orders	If the hearing is less than a day, usually there will be a summary assessment (PD 43–48, para. 13.2(2)).

Procedural checklist 22 Application for striking out

See **chapter 33**.

General procedure	Follow procedural checklist 21.
Application notice	E.g.: 'for an order that the Particulars of Claim be struck out under CPR, r. 3.4, and judgment be entered for the Defendant with costs because the Particulars of Claim disclose no reasonable grounds for bringing the claim [is an abuse of the court's process] [is likely to obstruct the just disposal of the proceedings]'
Combined application	It is common to combine the various grounds in CPR, r. 3.4 in a single application, and also to seek summary judgment in the alternative.
Fee to costs orders	See procedural checklist 21.
Claim totally without merit	If the court strikes out a claimant's statement of case and considers it is totally without merit, it must record that fact in the order (r. 3.4(5)), and consider making a civil restraint order (see 14.70).

Procedural checklist 23 Application by party for summary judgment

See **chapter 34**.

Timing	After acknowledgment of service or filing defence (**34.2**). Generally before filing allocation questionnaire (PD 26, para. 5.3(1)).
Application notice	Form N244. Apply for 'summary judgment under CPR, Part 24 and costs because the [claimant has no real prospect of succeeding on the claim / issue] or [defendant has no real prospect of successfully defending the claim / issue] and the Applicant knows of no other reason why disposal of the claim or issue should await trial' (PD 24, para. 2(3)). If the application relates to specific issues, these must be identified (CPR, r. 24.4(3)(b)). Also add to the N244: 'Take Notice that if the Respondent wishes to rely on written evidence at the hearing, he must file and serve the written evidence at least 7 days before the summary judgment hearing' (PD 24, para. 2(5)).
Evidence in support	Must be served and filed with the N244.
Combined applications	It is common to combine a summary judgment application with an application for striking out under CPR, r. 3.4, or for interim payment under r. 25.7.
Fee	£100 (High Court); £65 (county court) (CPFO, fee 2.5).
Service	On respondent at least 14 days before hearing (CPR, r. 24.4(3)).
Respondent's written evidence	Serve and file at least seven days before hearing (r. 24.5(2)).
Applicant's evidence in reply	File and serve at least three days before the hearing (r. 24.5(2)).

Main proceedings	No need to file defence (r. 24.4(2)). Claimant cannot enter default judgment if defendant is applying for summary judgment (r. 12.3(3)(a)(ii)). Court will not normally allocate to a track before hearing application to strike out (PD 26, para. 5.3(2)).
Costs	Both parties should file and serve costs schedules in form N260 24 hours before the hearing (PD 43–48, para. 13.5(4)).
Hearing	Normally before master or district judge (PD 24, para. 3(1)). In addition to determining the application, the court usually gives directions (CPR, r. 24.6).

Procedural checklist 24 Proposal by court for order for summary judgment

See **34.5**.

Notice of date for hearing	At least 14 days before the hearing.
Written evidence	Both sides file and (unless the court otherwise orders) serve written evidence at least seven days before the hearing (CPR, r. 24.5(3)(a)).
Evidence in reply	Both sides may file and (unless the court otherwise orders) serve written evidence in reply at least three days before the hearing (r. 24.5(3)(b)).
Costs	Both parties should file and serve costs schedules in form N260 24 hours before the hearing (PD 43–48, para. 13.5(4)).

Procedural checklist 25 Application for an order for interim payment

See **chapter 36**.

Timing	After period for filing acknowledgment of service (CPR, r. 25.6(1)). More than one application can be made (r. 25.6(2)).
Application notice	Form N244. Apply for 'an interim payment under CPR, r. 25.7, and costs because the [defendant has admitted liability] [the claimant has obtained judgment for damages to be assessed] [if the claim went to trial the claimant would obtain judgment for a substantial amount of money (other than costs) against the defendant] [the claim is for possession of land and if the claim went to trial the defendant would be held liable to pay the claimant a sum of money for occupation and use of the land while the claim is pending]'.
Evidence in support	Must be served and filed with the N244. It must deal with the matters set out in PD 25B, para. 2.1, and exhibit all documents in support, including (in personal injuries claims) medical reports (para. 2.2).
Combined applications	Interim payment applications are commonly combined with applications for summary judgment.
Fee	£100 (High Court); £65 (county court) (CPFO, fee 2.5).
Service	On respondent at least 14 days before hearing (CPR, r. 25.6(3)).
Respondent's written evidence	Serve and file at least seven days before hearing (r. 25.6(4)).
Applicant's evidence in reply	File and serve at least three days before the hearing (r. 25.6(5)).
Costs	Both parties should file and serve costs schedules in form N260 24 hours before the hearing (PD 43–48, para. 13.5(4)).
Hearing	Normally before master or district judge (PD 24, para. 3(1)). In addition to determining the application, the court may give directions (PD 23, para. 2.9).

Instalments	If an interim payment is payable by instalments, the order must comply with PD 25B, para. 3.
Trial	The fact that an interim payment has been made should not be mentioned to the trial judge until all questions on liability and quantum have been decided (CPR, r. 25.9), unless the defendant agrees.
Final judgment	Where an interim payment has previously been made, the final judgment must include details in a preamble, deduct the interim payments from the amount of the judgment, and make any necessary adjustments or orders for repayment (PD 25B, para. 5; PD 40B, para. 6).

Procedural checklist 26 Standard disclosure

See **chapter 48**, especially **48.2** to **48.10**.

When first retained	Inform clients of their duty to retain disclosable documents (*Rockwell Machine Tool Co. Ltd v E. P. Barrus (Concessionaires) Ltd* [1968] 1 WLR 693).
Pre-action	Preliminary disclosure of documents should often take place in accordance with PD Protocols and any pre-action protocol applicable to the claim (**chapter 8**). This is not standard disclosure, but a means of providing the other side with the key documents to inform them of the nature and strength of the case.
Timing for standard disclosure	In accordance with directions made by the court. In most fast track and multi-track claims directions are made when the claim is allocated to a track (CPR, rr. 28.2(1), 28.3, 29.2(1)(a) and PD 29, para.4) or at the first case management conference (CPR, r. 29.2(1)(b)) and these typically include directions for standard disclosure.
Normal directions	(1) Standard disclosure by 4 weeks after directions (PD 28, para. 3.12). (2) Requests for inspection of listed documents within 7 days thereafter (CPR, r. 31.15(a)). (3) Inspection of documents, or provision of copies, within 7 days thereafter (r. 31.15(b) and (c)).
Documents to be disclosed	Standard disclosure covers (r. 31.6) documents in a party's control (r. 31.8): (a) on which the disclosing party relies; (b) which adversely affect his own case; (c) which adversely affect another party's case; (d) which support another party's case; and (e) which are specified by a PD (at present there is no relevant PD).
Documents	Anything on which information of any description is recorded (r. 31.4). Includes papers (whether written, pictures or photographs); video and sound recordings; computer records, files, mobile phone texts and emails; metadata; inscriptions on metal, wood and stone.
Control	A document is in a party's control (r. 31.8) if: (a) it is or was in his physical possession; (b) he has or has had a right to possession of it; or (c) he has or has had a right to inspect or take copies of it.
Search	Each party must make a reasonable search for disclosable documents (r. 31.7).
Method of giving disclosure	Usually by serving a list of documents (r. 31.10(2), form N265). Parties may agree in writing to give disclosure without making a list or without a disclosure statement (r. 31.10(8)). Parties may agree in writing, or the court may direct, that disclosure and/or inspection should take place in stages (r. 31.13).
List of documents	The list (N265) must (r. 31.10): (a) Identify the documents concisely and in a convenient order.

	(b) Identify privileged documents, stating the grounds on which it is claimed there is a right or duty to withhold inspection (r. 31.19(3)). (c) Identify documents no longer in the party's control, stating what has happened to them. (d) Include a disclosure statement in the form set out in the annex to PD 31 (PD 31, para. 4.1).
Signing disclosure statement	(a) Should normally be signed by the party (r. 31.10(6): exceptions are set out in r. 31.10(7) to (9)). (b) Legal representative must ensure person signing understands the duty of disclosure in Part 31 (PD 31, para. 4.4). (c) Companies, firms etc. sign by a duly authorised officer. The disclosure statement must include that person's name and address, the office or position held, and explain why he or she is an appropriate person to make the statement (CPR, r. 31.10(7) and PD 31, para. 4.3). (d) An insurer, or the Motor Insurers' Bureau, may sign if they have a financial interest in the claim (PD 31, para. 4.7).
Inspection	The party seeking to inspect must give written notice (by letter) (CPR, r. 31.15(a)), and must be complied with within 7 days. (a) Inspection may take place by attendance at the other side's offices or solicitor's office (r. 31.15(b)). (b) Inspection usually takes place by making a written request for photocopies, with the inspecting party undertaking to pay reasonable copying costs (r. 31.15(c)).
Continuing duty	Each party has a continuing duty to disclose documents subsequently coming into their control. If this happens they must immediately notify the other parties (r. 31.11) by serving a supplemental list (PD 31, para. 3.3).

Procedural checklist 27 Specific disclosure

See **chapter 48**, especially **48.29 and 48.30**.

Timing	After standard disclosure. A request for the documents to be sought in the application should be made first by letter.
Application	Application notice (form N244).Wording for Part A: '. . . intend to apply for an order (a draft of which is attached) that the [claimant/defendant] do give specific disclosure of documents because [the claimant/defendant] [has failed to give full standard disclosure] [further disclosure is necessary in order to investigate this claim fully]'.
Form of order	(1) The [claimant/defendant] do give specific disclosure of documents by filing and serving a supplementary list of documents in form N265 by 4 p.m. on [date] specifying whether each of the [documents] and/or [classes of documents] specified in the schedule to this order are presently in its control, and if not, specifying which of those [documents] and/or [classes of documents] are no longer in its control (and indicating what has happened to such documents), and also specifying which of those [documents] and/or [classes of documents] it claims a right or duty to withhold inspection of. (2) The [claimant/defendant] do make any request for inspection in writing within 7 days after service of the list of documents. (3) The [claimant/defendant] do provide the [claimant/defendant] with copies of the requested documents within 7 days of receipt of the request. A schedule attached to the application, or to a draft order, should set out concisely and in a convenient order the documents and classes of documents sought from the other side.

Written evidence	Is required (PD 31, para. 5.2), and is typically given in a witness statement (although Part C of the N244 can be used). The evidence should: (a) Exhibit the lists of documents provided by the other side. (b) Exhibit relevant correspondence. (c) Deal with each document or class of document in the schedule to the application: (i) Explaining why it is believed to be in the control of the other side; and (ii) Explaining why it should be disclosed (because it is relevant to an issue in the case, and should have been disclosed under standard disclosure, or because it is a 'train of inquiry' document, explaining the value of the document in investigating the claim).
Issue application	See procedural checklist 21, and CPR, Part 23. Fee £100 (High Court); £65 (county court) (CPFO, fee 2.5).
Serve application	At least 3 clear days before the return day (CPR, rr. 23.7(1) and 2.8(3)).

Procedural checklist 28 Non-party disclosure

See **48.70** to **48.82**.

Timing	At any time after proceedings are issued (Supreme Court Act 1981, s. 34(2); County Courts Act 1984, s. 53(2); CPR, r. 31.17(1)). A request for the documents to be sought in the application should be made first by letter.
Application	Application notice (form N244). Wording for Part A: '. . . intend to apply for an order pursuant to the [Supreme Court Act 1981, s. 34(2)] [County Courts Act 1984, s. 53(2)] that [name of person with the documents] give non-party disclosure of documents because it has in its control documents which are likely to support the [claimant's/defendant's] case and disclosure is necessary in order to dispose fairly of the claim or to save costs'.
Form of order	(1) [Name of person with the documents] do by 4 p.m. on [date] serve on the [claimant's/defendant's] solicitors a list of documents in form N265 specifying whether each of the [documents] and / or [classes of documents] specified in the schedule to this order are presently in its control, and if not, specifying which of those [documents] and/or [classes of documents] are no longer in its control (and indicating what has happened to such documents), and also specifying which of those [documents] and/or [classes of documents] it claims a right or duty to withhold inspection of. (2) The [claimant/defendant] do make any request for inspection of the documents disclosed by [name of person with the documents] in writing within 7 days after service of the list of documents. (3) [Name of person with the documents] do provide the [claimant/defendant] with copies of the requested documents within 7 days of receipt of the request. A schedule attached to the application, or to a draft order, should set out concisely and in a convenient order the documents and classes of documents sought from the non-party.
Written evidence	Is required (r. 31.17(2)), and is typically given in a witness statement (although Part C of the N244 can be used). The evidence should: (a) Exhibit relevant correspondence. (b) Deal with each document or class of document in the schedule to the application: (i) explaining why it is believed to be in the control of the non-party; (ii) explaining how it is likely to support the case of the applicant or adversely affect the case of another party (r. 31.17(3)(a));

	(iii) explaining why disclosure is necessary in order to dispose fairly of the claim or to save costs (r. 31.17(3)(b)).
Issue application	See procedural checklist 21, and Part 23. Fee £100 (High Court); £65 (county court) (CPFO, fee 2.5).
Serve application	At least 3 clear days before the return day (rr. 23.7(1) and 2.8(3)).

Procedural checklist 29 Trial preparation

See **chapter 59**.

Item	Timing	Action
Witness availability	Before listing for trial	Communicate with lay and expert witnesses, and also counsel, to obtain available dates (and reasons). See **59.8**.
Witness abroad or incapacitated	Several months before trial	Consider best means of adducing evidence from the witness: (a) Hearsay statement (**chapter 51**). (b) Letter of request **56.8** to **56.12**). (c) Video link (**56.11**). (d) Deposition (**56.2** to **56.7**).
Listing for trial	In accordance with case management directions	See **59.2** to **59.6** and court guides in **appendix 4**.
Inform witnesses	Receipt of trial date or window	Write to lay and expert witnesses confirming trial date or window and seeking confirmation of the witness's availability.
Pre-trial review (if directed in case management directions)	8–10 weeks before trial	Most common in multi-track claims. Brief trial advocate to attend. May result in further directions, settling a statement of issues, and fixing a trial timetable (see **45.21**).
Statement of issues	As directed	May need to be settled and agreed between the parties after a pre-trial review (see **59.13**).
Brief counsel	Sufficient time before trial	Prepare counsel's brief and supporting trial bundles or papers for the trial bundle. Agree fees with counsel's clerk. Even for simple cases counsel should be briefed at least a week in advance because counsel has to prepare a skeleton argument. In complex claims a period of months may be required. Counsel will also often advise on further pre-trial preparation that may be required.
Witness summonses	At least 2 weeks before trial	Issue witness summonses for unwilling witnesses (see **55.2**, form N20). Fee £50 (High Court); £35 (county court) (CPFO, fee 2.7). Serve at least 7 clear days (rr. 2.8(2) and 34.5(1)) before the date the witness is required to attend, bearing in mind deemed dates of service (r. 6.7). Include witness expenses (see **55.6**).
Reading guide and time estimate	Before lodging trial bundle	In QBD and ChD reading lists and time estimates signed by counsel must be lodged with trial bundles (Practice Direction (Royal Courts of Justice: Reading Lists and Time Estimates) [2000] 1 WLR 208), see **57.6**, and see court guides in **appendix 4**.
Trial bundles	c. 14 days before trial	Defendants should notify claimant of documents they wish to be included.

Item	Timing	Action
	3 to 7 days before trial	Copies for judge, witness box and all parties.
	At least 7 days before ChD trials	Paginated and prepared in accordance with PD 39, see **chapter 57** and court guides in **appendix 4**.
Skeleton argument (required in the High Court, often directed or desirable in the county courts)	As directed 2 clear days before HC trials	Usually simultaneous exchange, but directions may provide for sequential exchange (see **32.16 and 59.13**). Lodge at list office (Queen's Bench Guide, para. 7.11.11) or with judge's clerk (Chancery Guide, para. 7.26).
Authorities	4 p.m. day before trial	Advocates should exchange lists of authorities (e.g., Chancery Guide, para. 7.33).
	9 a.m. trial day	Provide usher with list of authorities (Queen's Bench Guide, para. 7.11.8; Chancery Guide, para. 7.32).
Adjournment	As soon as need arises	Immediately inform court and other parties in writing, seeking adjournment. If not dealt with administratively, issue application in accordance with Part 23 (see r. 3.1(2)(b) and **59.7**).
Statement of costs (fast track trials)	24 hours before trial	Form N260. PD 43–48, para. 13.2, see **68.3**.

Procedural checklist 30 Defendant's Part 36 offer

See **chapter 64**.

Timing	Can be made before issue of proceedings. Should be made once an appraisal can be made of the merits and value of the claim. Should be made, if possible, more than 21 days before trial.
Method	Letter written 'Without Prejudice Save as to Costs'.
Form	(a) Must be in writing (CPR, r. 36.5(1)). (b) Must state if it relates to the whole claim or to part, and if to part, it must state to which part or issue (r. 36.5(3)(a)). (c) Must state whether it includes any counterclaim (r. 36.5(3)(b)). (d) May state whether the offer is inclusive of interest. If it is expressed not to be inclusive of interest, the offer must (r. 36.5(3)(c)) state whether interest is offered, and if so, the amount offered, the rates offered and the periods covered (r. 36.22(2)). (e) May be limited to accepting liability up to a specified amount (r. 36.5(4)). (f) May be made by reference to an interim payment (r. 36.5(5)). (g) Must, if made not less than 21 days before trial, be expressed to remain open for acceptance for 21 days from the date it is made, and provide that thereafter the offeree may only accept it if the parties agree liability for costs or the court gives permission (r. 36.5(6)). (h) Must, if made less than 21 days before trial, state the offeree may only accept it if the parties agree liability for costs or the court gives permission (r. 36.5(7)). (i) Must be signed by the offeror or his legal representative (PD 36, para.5.1).
Making a Part 36 offer	A Part 36 offer is made when received by the offeree (r. 36.8(1)).
Clarification	Can be sought, using the Part 23 procedure (see **64.30**). See procedural checklist 21.

Withdrawal	A Part 36 offer can be withdrawn. No permission is required. Once withdrawn it will not have the usual costs consequences (r. 36.5(8)).
Acceptance	By letter (r. 36.11(1)). The notice of acceptance must set out the claim number, title of the proceedings, identify the Part 36 offer and be signed by the offeror or his legal representative (PD 36, para 7.7). If the offer was made less than 21 days before trial, or if the acceptance is more than 21 days after the offer, it may only be accepted if the parties agree liability for costs or if the court gives permission.
Acceptance without permission	The claimant is entitled to costs of the claim up to the date of serving notice of acceptance (r. 36.13(1)).
Trial	Treated as without prejudice save as to costs (r. 36.19(1)).

Procedural checklist 31 Part 36 payment

See **chapter 64**.

Timing	As soon as possible after issue of proceedings. Should be made once an appraisal can be made of the merits and value of the claim. Should be made, if possible, more than 21 days before trial.
Money claims	Part 36 payments can only be made in money claims. In claims seeking money and other types of relief, Part 36 protection may be sought by making a Part 36 payment in respect of the money claim, and a Part 36 offer in respect of the other relief (see **64.11**).
Method	Part 36 notice of payment in, and lodging money in court.
Form	Must be in form N242A, which (CPR, r. 36.6(2)): (a) Must state the amount paid in. (b) Must state if it relates to the whole claim or to part, and if to part, it must state to which part or issue. (c) Must state whether it includes any counterclaim. (d) May be made by reference to an interim payment. (e) May state whether the offer is inclusive of interest. Unless it states to the contrary, the notice will be taken as inclusive of all interest to the last date for acceptance (r. 36.22(1)). If it is expressed not to be inclusive of interest, the offer must (r. 36.22(2)) state whether interest is offered, and if so, the amount offered, the rates offered and the periods covered. (f) In personal injuries claims, the notice should provide a breakdown of the global amount into the amounts allowed for each of the heads of damage (*Williams v Devon County Council* [2003] EWCA Civ 365, [2003] PIQR Q68, considering r.36.23). (g) Must be signed by the offeror or his legal representative (PD 36, para. 5.1).
Service	Is effected by the offeror, who must file a certificate of service (form N215), see CPR, r. 36.6(3).
Making a Part 36 payment	A Part 36 offer is made when written notice of the payment is served on the offeree (r. 36.8(2)).
Clarification	Can be sought, using the Part 23 procedure (see **64.30**). See procedural checklist 21.
Withdrawal or reduction	Requires permission (sought under Part 23). See **64.26**.
Acceptance	Form N243A/Form 201, which is a notice of acceptance and request for payment form.
Acceptance during trial	Permission is sought from the trial judge (**64.29**).
Permission to accept	(1) Part 36 payment made less than 21 days before trial (**64.32**). (2) Acceptance sought more than 21 days after service of Part 36 notice.

	(3) Part 36 payment made on behalf of some only of the defendants. (4) Offeree is a child or a patient. Permission is sought on notice on form N244 with written evidence in support (see Part 23).
Acceptance without permission	The claimant is entitled to costs of the claim up to the date of serving notice of acceptance (r. 36.13(1)).
Trial bundles	No reference to the Part 36 payment must be made in any of the papers in the trial bundles.
Trial	Fact or amount of Part 36 payment not to be referred to until all decisions on liability and quantum have been decided (r. 36.19(2)).
Final order	Should include payment out of the money in court and interest in accordance with the judge's decision.

Procedural checklist 32 Summary assessment of costs

See **68.3** to **68.5**.

When required	Unless the court orders otherwise, costs will be assessed summarily (PD 43–48, para. 13.2): (1) At the conclusion of a trial on the fast track; (2) At the conclusion of an interim hearing lasting no more than one day. In these cases the summary assessment covers the interim costs only, unless the whole proceedings are disposed of, in which event the summary assessment may deal with the costs of the whole claim; and (3) At the conclusion of interim hearings within appeals and appeals listed for one day or less (see also PD 52, para.14).
Statement of costs	Form N260. Should be filed and served 24 hours before the hearing (PD 43–48, para. 13.5(4)).
Failure to serve statement of costs 24 hours in advance	Court may (see **32.27**): (1) give the paying party a brief (minutes or hours) adjournment, and then proceed with the summary assessment; (2) stand over for a detailed assessment; (3) stand over for a summary assessment at a later date; (4) if both sides agree, stand over for a summary assessment to be dealt with in writing.

Procedural checklist 33 Arbitration claim

See **chapter 69**.

Commence an arbitration claim under CPR, Part 62, using arbitration claim form N8.	Claim form must: • include a concise statement of remedy claimed; • include any questions on which the claimant seeks the decision of the court; • give details of any arbitration award challenged by the claimant; • show statutory requirements have been met; • specify under which section of the Arbitration Act 1996 the claim is made; • identify against which (if any) defendants a cost order is sought; • specify either: – the persons on whom the arbitration claim form is to be served; or – that the claim is made without notice. (CPR, r. 62.4(1)). Where required, evidence in support must be filed with the arbitration claim form.

Issue	Claim form may be issued in one of the following courts: • Admiralty and Commercial Registry at the Royal Courts of Justice (Commercial List); • Technology and Construction Court Registry (TCC List); • district registry of the High Court (where a Mercantile Court is established) (Mercantile List); • district registry of the High Court (arbitration claim form must be marked 'Technology and Construction Court' in the top right-hand corner) (TCC List); • Central London Civil Justice Centre (Mercantile List). (PD 62, para. 2.3(1)). Claim form relating to a landlord and tenant or partnership dispute must be issued in the High Court, Chancery Division (PD 62, para. 2.3(2)).
Service	Claim form must be served by the claimant within one month from the date of issue (CPR, r. 62.4(2)). Once served, the claimant must file the certificate of service within seven days of service (PD 62, para. 3.2).
Service out of the jurisdiction	The court can give permission to serve a claim form out of the jurisdiction in the following circumstances: • When a claimant seeks to challenge an arbitration award or appeal on a question of law arising out of an award made within England and Wales. • The claim is for an order under the Arbitration Act 1996, s. 44. The court can give permission for service out of the jurisdiction notwithstanding the only remedy sought is in respect of proceedings taking place outside England and Wales. • Any other situation where the claimant seeks a remedy or requires a question to be determined by the court which affects an arbitration (pending or anticipated), an arbitration agreement or an arbitration award. Seat of the arbitration must be in England and Wales. Where the seat is not in England and Wales the court can still give permission as long as the seat has not been designated or, by reason of connection with England and Wales or Northern Ireland, the court is satisfied it is appropriate to do so. (CPR, r. 62.5(1).) Application must be supported by written evidence and: • state the grounds on which the application is made; • show in what place or country the person to be served is, or probably may be, found (CPR, r. 62.5(2)). CPR, rr. 6.24 to 6.29 (which regulate service of claim forms abroad), apply to the service of arbitration claim forms out of the jurisdiction (r. 62.5(3)). The order giving permission to serve out of the jurisdiction must specify the period within which the defendant has to file the acknowledgment of service (r. 62.5(4)).
Acknowledgment of service	Generally within 14 days after service of the arbitration claim form (r. 10.3(1)(b)) by using form N15 or, alternatively in the commercial court, form N210(CC) (Admiralty and Commercial Courts Guide, para. O5.1(b)).
Defendant's written evidence	Must be filed and served within 21 days after the date by which the defendant is required to acknowledge service or, if not required to file an acknowledgment, within 21 days after the service of the arbitration claim form (PD 62, para. 6.2).
Claimant's written evidence in reply	Evidence in reply to the defendant's written evidence must be filed or served within seven days after service of the defendant's evidence (PD 62, para. 6.3).
Preparation for hearing	Agreed indexed and paginated bundles of all evidence and other documents to be used at the hearing should be prepared by the claimant (PD 62, para 6.4). Estimates for length and a complete set of documents should be filed no later than five days before the hearing date (PD 62, para. 6.5).

Main hearing	The claimant must file and serve no later than 2 days before the hearing: • chronology of relevant events cross-referenced to a bundle of documents; • list of persons involved; and • skeleton argument (PD 62, para. 6.6). The defendant must file and serve its skeleton argument not later than the day before the hearing date. The skeleton argument must list: • issues which arise for decision; • the grounds for relief to be relied upon; • submissions of fact to be made with references to the evidence; and • submissions of law with references to the relevant authorities (PD 62, para. 6.7). Hearing generally in private save for claims to determine a preliminary point of law (Arbitration Act 1996, s. 45) or appeal on a question of law arising out of an award (Arbitration Act 1996, s. 69) (CPR, r. 62.10(3)).

Procedural checklist 34 Appeals within the county courts and High Court

See **chapter** 71.

Timing	At the end of the hearing in the lower court, permission to appeal should be sought (see **71.12**). Any request for the provision of a transcript at public expense (on the ground of poor financial circumstances) should be made at the hearing (PD 52, paras 5.17 and 5.18). An appellant's notice in form N161 must be filed (unless time is extended, see **71.19**) no later than 21 days from the date of the decision of the lower court (CPR, r. 52.4(2)(b)). (Before 6 April 2006 it was 14 days.)
Permission	Required for all civil appeals (r. 52.3) other than those involving personal liberty and from decisions of authorised court officers in detailed assessments (see **71.11**).
Seeking permission	Initially sought orally from the lower court (r. 52.3(2)). If refused, can renew application for permission to the appeal court (r. 52.3(3)). Permission from the appeal court is initially sought in the appellant's notice (form N161), and is normally considered without a hearing (PD 52, para. 4.11).
Reconsideration of permission	Where the appeal court refuses permission without a hearing, it may reconsider granting permission at a hearing (CPR, r. 52.3(4)). If represented, the appellant's advocate must file and serve a brief written statement at least 4 days before the hearing identifying the points proposed to be raised and his reasons why permission should be granted (PD 52, para. 4.14A). There is no jurisdiction to consider an appeal from an appeal court's refusal to grant permission (Access to Justice Act 1999, s. 54(4)).
Appeal court	(1) From county court district judge appeal to circuit judge. (2) From county court circuit judge appeal to High Court judge. (3) From High Court master, district judge or registrar appeal to High Court judge. See **71.3**.The above applies equally to deputies and part-time judges fulfilling the above roles. By way of exceptions to the above (a) Final decisions in multitrack claims are appealed to the Court of Appeal (Destination of Appeals Order, art. 4). (b) Final decisions in specialist claims are appealed to the Court of Appeal (Destination of Appeals Order, art. 4). (c) Second appeals in the county courts are appealed to the Court of Appeal (Destination of Appeals Order, art. 5). This applies where a county court district judge's decision is appealed to the circuit judge, whose decision is subject to a second appeal (which is taken to the Court of Appeal).

Extending time to appeal	Can only be granted by the appeal court (not by consent) (CPR, r. 52.6), although the lower court can direct some period other than 21 days for filing the appellant's notice (r. 52.4(2)(a)). Applications to extend time are made in the appellant's notice (PD 52, para. 5.2).
Appellant's notice	Form N161. Must be filed with the appeal court no more than 21 days after the decision of the lower court (or as directed or extended) (CPR, r. 52.4(2)(b)). It must: (a) set out the grounds of the appeal; (b) give reasons why the lower court's decision is wrong or unjust through serious procedural or other irregularity and state whether each ground is on a point of law or against a finding of fact (PD 52, para. 3.2); (c) include any application for permission to appeal (para. 5.1); (d) include any application to appeal out of time (para. 5.2); (e) include information about any issue raised or remedy sought under the Human Rights Act 1998 (para. 5.1A). The N161 may include applications for interim relief (para. 5.5), including any stay of execution.
Fee	£100 for small claims appeal; £120 for other appeals in the county courts (CPFO, fee 2.4); £200 for appeals in the High Court (CPFO, fee 2.3).
Documents to be filed	At the same time as filing the appellant's notice, the appellant must file (PD 52, para. 5.6): (a) two additional copies of the appellant's notice for the court and one for each respondent; (b) the same number of copies of the appellant's skeleton argument; (c) a sealed copy of the order of the court below; (d) any orders giving or refusing permission to appeal together with the reasons for each decision; (e) any written evidence in support of any interim application within the appeal; (f) a paginated appeal bundle complying with PD 52, para. 5.6A; and (g) a transcript (or agreed note, see **71.25**) of the judgment under appeal (PD 52, para. 5.12). Where it is not possible to file any of the above, the appellant must state which items are not being filed and why (PD 52, para. 5.7). For small claims appeals, see PD 52, para. 5.8.
Skeleton argument	Form N163. Should be filed with the appellant's notice, or, if impractical, within 14 days of filing the notice (PD 52, para. 5.9).
Transcripts of evidence	Are requested, if required, after permission to appeal is granted (see **71.25**). Transcripts of judgments are required before permission.
Service of appellant's notice	As soon as practicable, and within 7 days of being filed the appellant must serve the appellant's notice and skeleton argument on the respondents (CPR, r. 52.4(3); PD 52, para. 5.21). The appellant must then file a certificate of service (form N215).
Service of skeleton argument	With appellant's notice, unless impracticable, when within 14 days of filing appellant's notice (PD 52, para. 5.9(2)).
Service of supporting documents	Appeal bundles, orders in the court below and for permission etc.: (a) where permission to appeal is being sought, need not be served unless and until permission is given; (b) where permission is granted by the lower court (or not required), supporting documents must be served with the appellant's notice (PD 52, para. 5.24). Where permission is granted by the appeal court, service is required within 7 days of receiving the order granting permission (para. 6.2).

Permission granted	Court sends order and any directions to the parties (PD 52, para. 6.3(2)) together with date for the appeal hearing or listing window. The appellant must add the order and other documents to the appeal bundle (para. 6.3A). Appeal questionnaires are optional in the High Court.
Respondent's notice	Respondent's notice (form N162) is required (r. 52.5(2)) where the respondent: (a) seeks permission to appeal against the decision in the court below; (b) wishes the appeal court to uphold the decision of the court below for different or additional reasons to those given by the court below. In circumstances (a) and (b), there is a fee of £100 for a small claims appeal or £120 for any other appeal in the county court (CPFO, fee 2.4); £200 in the High Court (CPFO, fee 2.3).
Filing respondent's notice	As directed, otherwise within 14 days of: (a) service of appellant's notice if permission to appeal was not required or if permission was given to the appellant by the court below; (b) service of notification of permission to appeal; or (c) service of notification that permission and the substantive appeal are to be heard together. With the respondent's notice, the respondent must file two additional copies of the notice for the court and one for every other party (PD 52, para. 7.10).
Additional documents	The respondent must make every effort to agree any additional documents for the appeal bundle with the appellant. If they cannot agree, the respondent should prepare a supplementary bundle, to be served and filed with the respondent's notice (PD 52, paras. 7.11 and 7.12).
Service of respondent's notice	As soon as practicable, and within 7 days of being filed (r. 52.5(6)).
Respondent's skeleton argument	May be included in the respondent's notice, or served within 14 days of filing the respondent's notice (PD 52, para. 7.7).
Authorities	In the county court authorities must be brought to the hearing. In the High Court lists of authorities must be provided to the head usher by 5.30 p.m. on the working day before the hearing (see **71.48**) or copies should be included in the appeal bundles (Queen's Bench Guide, para. 7.11.9).
Summary assessment of costs	In appeals from case management decisions and appeals listed for one day or less, statements of costs should be filed 24 hours before the appeal hearing (PD 52, para. 14.1).

Procedural checklist 35 Appeals to the Court of Appeal

See **chapter** 71.

Timing	At the end of the hearing in the lower court, permission to appeal should be sought (see **71.12**). Any request for the provision of a transcript at public expense (on the ground of poor financial circumstances) should be made at the hearing (PD 52, paras 5.17 and 5.18). An appellant's notice in form N161 must be filed (unless time is extended, see **71.18**) no later than 21 days from the date of the decision of the lower court (CPR, r. 52.4(2)(b)). (Before 6 April 2006 it was 14 days.)
Permission	Required for all civil appeals (r. 52.3) other than those involving personal liberty and from decisions of authorised court officers in detailed assessments (see **71.11**).
Fee	£200 if permission or an extension of time is required (CPFO, fee 12.1(a)); £400 if permission is not required or was granted by the lower court (CPFO, fee 12.1(b)).

Seeking permission	Initially sought orally from the lower court (r. 52.3(2)). If refused, can renew application for permission to the appeal court (r. 52.3(3)). Except that in second appeals to the Court of Appeal permission can only be sought from the Court of Appeal (r. 52.13(1)(c)). Permission from the Court of Appeal is initially sought in the appellant's notice (form N161), and is normally considered without a hearing (PD 52, para. 4.11).
Reconsideration of permission	Where the Court of Appeal refuses permission without a hearing, it may reconsider granting permission at a hearing (CPR, r. 52.3(4)). If represented, the appellant's advocate must file and serve a brief written statement at least 4 days before the hearing identifying the points proposed to be raised and his reasons why permission should be granted (PD 52, para. 4.14A). There is no jurisdiction to consider an appeal from a refusal by the Court of Appeal to grant permission (Access to Justice Act 1999, s. 54(4)).
Appeals taken to the Court of Appeal	(a) Final decisions in multi-track claims (Destination of Appeals Order, art. 4). (b) Final decisions in specialist claims (Destination of Appeals Order, art. 4). (c) Second appeals in the county courts (Destination of Appeals Order, art. 5). This applies where a county court district judge's decision is appealed to the circuit judge, whose decision is subject to a second appeal (which is taken to the Court of Appeal). See **71.17**. (d) Appeals from High Court judges.
Extending time to appeal	Can only be granted by the appeal court (not by consent) (CPR, r. 52.6), although the lower court can direct some period other than 21 days for filing the appellant's notice (r. 52.4(2)(a)). Applications to extend time are made in the appellant's notice (PD 52, para. 5.2).
Appellant's notice	Form N161. Must be filed with the appeal court no more than 21 days after the decision of the lower court (or as directed or extended) (CPR, r. 52.4(2)(b)). It must: (a) set out the grounds of the appeal; (b) give reasons why the lower court's decision is wrong or unjust through serious procedural or other irregularity and state whether each ground is on a point of law or against a finding of fact (PD 52, para. 3.2); (c) include any application for permission to appeal (para. 5.1); (d) include any application to appeal out of time (para. 5.2); (e) include information about any issue raised or remedy sought under the Human Rights Act 1998 (para. 5.1A). The N161 may include applications for interim relief (para. 5.5), including any stay of execution.
Documents to be filed	At the same time as filing the appellant's notice, the appellant must file (PD 52, para. 5.6): (a) two additional copies of the appellant's notice for the court and one for each respondent; (b) the same number of copies of the appellant's skeleton argument; (c) a sealed copy of the order of the court below; (d) any orders giving or refusing permission to appeal together with the reasons for each decision; (e) any written evidence in support of any interim application within the appeal; and (f) a paginated appeal bundle complying with PD 52, para. 5.6A. Where it is not possible to file any of the above, the appellant must state which items are not being filed and why (PD 52, para. 5.7). If the bundles exceed 500 pages, a core bundle not exceeding 150 pages must be filed and served (PD 52, para. 15.2) within 28 days of receipt of the order granting permission to appeal.
Skeleton argument	Form N163. Should be filed with the appellant's notice.
Transcripts	Transcripts of evidence are requested, if required, after permission to appeal is granted (see **71.27**). Transcripts of judgments are required before permission.

Service of appellant's notice	As soon as practicable, and within 7 days of being filed (CPR, r. 52.4(3)). Served by the appellant (PD 52, para. 15.1(2)), who must file a certificate of service (para. 5.21(2)).
Service of skeleton argument	With appellant's notice, unless impracticable, when within 14 days of filing appellant's notice (PD 52, para. 5.9(2)).
Service of supporting documents	Appeal bundles, orders in the court below and for permission etc.: (a) where permission to appeal is being sought, need not be served unless and until permission is given; (b) where permission is granted by the lower court (or not required), supporting document must be served with the appellant's notice (PD 52, para. 5.24). Where permission is granted by the appeal court, service is required within 7 days of receiving the order granting permission (para. 6.2).
Permission granted	Court sends order and any directions to the parties (PD 52, para. 6.3(2)) together with listing details and an appeal questionnaire to the appellant.
Appeal questionnaires	Must be returned to court within 14 days together with £400 fee, unless fee 12.1(b) has been paid (CPFO, fee 12.1(c)). Must include: (a) appellant's advocate's time estimate; (b) confirmation that lower court transcript has been requested; (c) confirmation that appeal bundles are being prepared; (d) confirmation that copies of the questionnaire have been sent to the respondents; and (e) confirmation that appeal bundles have been served on the respondents.
Listing	See **71.32**.
Respondent's notice	Form N162. Is required (r. 52.5(2)) where the respondent: (a) seeks permission to appeal against the decision in the court below; (b) wishes the appeal court to uphold the decision of the court below for different or additional reasons to those given by the court below. In circumstances (a) and (b), there is a fee of £200 (CPFO, fee 12.2).
Filing respondent's notice	As directed, otherwise within 14 days of: (a) service of appellant's notice if permission to appeal was not required or if permission was given to the appellant by the court below; (b) service of notification of permission to appeal; or (c) service of notification that permission and the substantive appeal are to be heard together. With the respondent's notice, the respondent must file two additional copies of the notice for the court and one for every other party (PD 52, para. 7.10).
Additional documents	The respondent must make every effort to agree any additional documents for the appeal bundle with the appellant. If they cannot agree, the respondent should prepare a supplementary bundle, to be served and filed with the respondent's notice (PD 52, para. 7.11 and 7.12).
Service of respondent's notice	As soon as practicable, and within 7 days of being filed (r. 52.5(6)).
Respondent's skeleton argument	May be included in the respondent's notice, or served within 14 days of filing the respondent's notice (PD 52, para. 7.7).
Authorities	When notified of the date fixed for the hearing, the appellant's advocate must file a bundle containing copies of the principal authorities relied upon by both sides (PD 52, para. 15.11).
Final deadline	All the documents needed for an appeal must be filed at least 7 days before the hearing (PD 52, para. 15.11B(1)). A party failing to comply may be summoned before the presiding lord justice.
Summary assessment of costs	In appeals from case management decisions and appeals listed for one day or less, statements of costs (form N260) should be filed 24 hours before the appeal hearing (PD 52, para. 14.1).

Procedural checklist 36 Claim for judicial review

See **chapter 74**.

Pre-action protocol	The Pre-action Protocol for Judicial Review requires that, before making a claim, the claimant should send a letter to the defendant identifying issues in dispute and establishing whether litigation can be avoided. Copies of the letter should be sent to all interested parties for information. Defendant should normally respond within 14 days to the letter before claim. Response should be sent to all interested parties identified by claimant and contain details of any other parties who the defendant considers also have an interest.
Timing	Claim form must be filed promptly and in any event not later than three months after the grounds to make the claim first arose (CPR, r. 54.5(1)). There must be good reason before this time limit will be extended. This time limit may not be extended by agreement between the parties (r. 54.5(2)).
Claim form	Form N461. The claim form must specify: • the name and address of any person considered to be an interested party, • that permission is sought to proceed with a judicial review claim, and • any remedy (including any interim remedy) being claimed. The claim form must include or be accompanied by: • a detailed statement of the claimant's grounds for bringing the claim, • a statement of facts relied on, • any application to extend the time limit for filing the claim form, and • any application for directions (PD 54, para. 5.6). In addition the claim form must be accompanied by: • any written evidence in support of the claim or application to extend time, • a copy of any order that the claimant seeks to have quashed, • where the claim relates to a decision of a court or tribunal, an approved copy of the reasons for reaching that decision, • copies of any relevant statutory material, and • a list of essential documents for advance reading by the court (with page references to the passages relied on) (PD 54, para. 5.7). Where it is not possible to file all the above documents, the claimant must indicate which documents have not been filed and the reasons why they are not currently available (PD 54, para. 5.8).
Urgent procedure	Form N463. Claimant must state the reasons for urgency, the proposed timescale for consideration of the permission application, and the date by which the full hearing of the merits should take place if permission is granted. A claimant who applies for an interim injunction must also provide a draft order and a statement of the grounds on which the injunction is sought. The application must be served by fax and post, along with the claim form, on the defendant and interested parties. The defendant and interested parties must be advised that they may make representations on the application.
Fee	£50 when claim form is issued and a further £180 if permission to proceed is granted (CPFO, fee 1.8).
Service	The claim form must be served on the defendant and any person the claimant considers to be an interested party within seven days of issue (CPR, r. 54.7).
Acknowledgment of service	Form N462. Any person served with the claim form must file an acknowledgment of service (A/S) in the Administrative Court Office within 21 days after service of the claim form. Where person filing A/S intends to contest the claim, the A/S must set out a summary of his grounds for doing so. The A/S must also be served on the claimant and interested persons not later than seven days after it is filed (CPR, r. 54.8).

Permission	The court's permission to proceed is required in a judicial review claim (CPR, r. 54.4). If permission is granted, the court may give directions (r. 54.10). The court will serve the permission decision on the claimant and defendant and on any other person who filed an A/S (r. 54.11).
Defendant's and other interested parties' detailed grounds of opposition/support	The defendant and any other interested person has 35 days after service of the permission order to file detailed grounds for contesting the claim or supporting it on additional grounds (CPR, r. 54.14).
Skeleton arguments	The claimant must file and serve a skeleton argument not less than 21 working days before the date of the hearing (or the warned date) (PD 54, para. 15.1). The defendant and other relevant parties wishing to make representations must file and serve a skeleton argument not less than 14 working days before the hearing (or warned date) (PD 54, para. 15.2).
Substantive hearing	Substantive judicial review applications in civil matters are generally heard by a single judge sitting in open court. The court may determine the claim without a hearing where all parties agree (CPR, r. 54.18).

Procedural checklist 37 Application by a creditor whose debt is presently payable to wind up a company incorporated in England and Wales

See **chapter** 79.

Pre-action	Check that the amount of the creditor's claim is at least £750 and that there is no substantial dispute about the amount or about whether it is due and payable. Check that there is no substantial cross-claim which would reduce the balance owed to the creditor to less than £750. Check that an appropriately clear demand for payment has been made and that no payment has been received. Consider whether serving a statutory demand (form 4.1) or other action short of petitioning might induce payment.
Preparation	Check the company's correct name and details required for the petition (form 4.2) at Companies House. Check at the Central Registry of Winding-up Petitions that no other petition has been presented (go to the RCJ Companies Court General Office or telephone (020) 7947 7328). If a petition has already been presented, do not present a second petition, but notify the existing petitioner of intention to support. In order to complete the petition and verifying evidence, ascertain whether the company appears to be an insurance undertaking, credit institution, investment undertaking providing services involving the holding of funds or securities for third parties, or a collective investment undertaking, and ascertain whether the company's centre of main interests is outside the United Kingdom.
Appropriate court	High Court, or, if company's paid-up capital is £120,000 or less, the county court with insolvency jurisdiction for the district where the company's registered office is located. In the London area only the High Court has jurisdiction. If the company's centre of main interests is in another EU State and it has no establishment in the United Kingdom (see **79.9 to 79.13**), proceedings must be started in the country where the centre of main interests is located, not in England and Wales.
Form of petition	Form 4.2, which must be verified by witness statement or affidavit complying with IR 1986, r. 4.12. For details see **79.19 to 79.25**. At least three copies will be required for filing (one for the court, one for service on the company, one to be exhibited to the affidavit of service). Extra copies are required if the company has a liquidator in a voluntary winding up, an administrator, an administrative receiver or a supervisor of a voluntary arrangement.

Fees	A court fee of £190 and a deposit of £655 for the official receiver's fee must be paid when filing.
Filing	All required copies are sealed and endorsed with the venue for hearing the petition. One copy is retained by the court, the others are returned to the petitioner.
Service	On the company at its registered office: • by handing it to a person who there and then acknowledges him or herself to be, or to the best of the server's knowledge, information and belief is, a director or other officer, or employee, of the company, or • by handing it to a person who there and then acknowledges him or herself to be authorised to accept service on the company's behalf, or • if no individual meeting these criteria is available, by depositing it at or about the registered office in such a way that it is likely to come to the notice of a person attending at the office. If service at the registered office is not practicable, see **79.37** and 79.38. Copies of the petition must also be sent (by post) to the company's voluntary liquidator, administrator, supervisor of a voluntary arrangement or administrative receiver.
Evidence of service	Evidence of service on the company (form 4.4 if service was at registered office, form 4.5 otherwise) must be filed immediately after service exhibiting a sealed copy of petition.
Advertisement	Petition must be advertised in the *London Gazette* (fee £30 + VAT), but not until seven business days after service on the company. There must be no other publicity for the petition until this advertisement appears. Advertisement must appear at least seven days before the date appointed for hearing the petition.
Track	Automatically multi-track.
Provisional liquidator	An application may be made for the appointment of a provisional liquidator (see **79.46** to **79.55**).
Evidence	The petition and verifying affidavit are evidence, and will usually be the only evidence in the case. The company may file evidence in opposition, a copy of which must be sent to the petitioner, not less than seven days before the hearing. No further evidence may be filed unless the court directs.
Certificate of compliance	Certificate of compliance (form 4.7) must be filed, with a copy of the advertisement, by 4.30 p.m. on Friday before hearing (at least five days before hearing in county courts).
List of persons appearing	Form 4.10 must be completed and handed to the court before the hearing commences.
Heard by	Registrar or district judge in public.
Decision	Court may make order applied for, dismiss the petition, adjourn (conditionally or unconditionally), make an interim order, or any other order it thinks fit. Registrar or district judge may refer case to judge.
Perfection	If court makes winding-up order, it will notify the official receiver, who becomes liquidator. All documents necessary to enable the order to be completed must be left at the court by the next business day. Court draws up the order. Official receiver notifies the order in the *London Gazette*.

Procedural checklist 38 Application by a creditor whose debt is presently payable for a bankruptcy order

See **chapter 80**.

Pre-action	Check that the amount of the creditor's claim is at least £750 and that there is no substantial dispute about the amount. Check that the claim is unsecured and is for a liquidated debt payable immediately and there is no substantial dispute that it is due and payable. Check that there is no substantial cross-claim which would reduce the balance owed to the creditor to less than £750. Check that an appropriately clear demand for payment has been made and that no payment has been received. If judgment has been obtained for the debt, consider whether to execute: partly or wholly unsatisfied execution is a ground for a bankruptcy petition.
Statutory demand	Unless there is a partly or wholly unsatisfied execution for the debt, a statutory demand must be served on the debtor. Prescribed form is form 6.1, or form 6.2 if the debt is a judgment debt for which execution has not been issued. If practicable, there must be personal service of a statutory demand, by leaving it with the debtor (CPR, r. 6.4(3)). If prompt personal service is not possible, service may be by first-class post or insertion through a letter box. If the debt is a judgment debt, service may be by newspaper advertisement if the debtor has absconded or is avoiding service and there is no real prospect of successful execution. Evidence of service, using form 6.11 or, for substituted service, 6.12, must be filed with the petition. The debtor has three weeks to comply with the statutory demand and may apply for it to be set aside, see **80.8**. A petition may be presented before the three weeks expire if there is a serious possibility that the debtor's property or the value of any of it will be significantly diminished during the three weeks. The petition must state that possibility.
Preparation	In order to complete the petition, ascertain whether the debtor appears to be carrying on business as an insurance undertaking, credit institution, investment undertaking providing services involving the holding of funds or securities for third parties, or a collective investment undertaking, and ascertain whether the debtor's centre of main interests is outside the United Kingdom.
Appropriate court	County court which has insolvency jurisdiction for the district in which the debtor resided or carried on business in the previous six months. In the London area, the High Court. If residence and business are in different districts, jurisdiction is normally determined by place of business (see **80.4**). If the debtor's centre of main interests is in another EU State and the debtor has no establishment in the United Kingdom (see **79.9 to 79.12**), proceedings must be started in the country where the centre of main interests is located, not in England and Wales.
Form of petition	Form 6.7, or form 6.9 if the petition is based on partially or wholly unsatisfied execution. The petition must be verified by witness statement or affidavit in form 6.13. See **80.9 and 80.10**. Three copies will be required for filing (one for the court, one for service on the debtor, one to be exhibited to the affidavit of service).
Fees	A court fee of £190 and a deposit of £390 for the official receiver's fee must be paid when filing.
Filing	Three copies of the petition must be filed and, if the petition relies on non-compliance with a statutory demand, written evidence of service of the demand. All three copies of the petition are sealed and endorsed with the venue for hearing the petition. One copy is retained by the court, the others are returned to the petitioner.

Service	Personal service of the petition by leaving it with the debtor (CPR, r. 6.4(3)) is required. PD Insolvency Proceedings, para. 11.4, sets out the steps which should be taken before concluding that personal service cannot be effected so that an application for substituted service is justified. Application for substituted service is by ordinary application (see **81.1** to **81.5**).
Evidence of service	Evidence of service on the debtor (form 6.17 for personal service; form 6.18 for substituted service) must be filed immediately after service exhibiting a sealed copy of the petition.
Track	Automatically multi-track.
Interim receiver	An application may be made by the debtor or any creditor for the appointment of an interim receiver (see **80.16**).
Evidence	The petition and verifying affidavit are evidence, and will usually be the only evidence in the case. If the debtor intends to oppose the petition, he or she must, not later than seven days before the hearing, file in court a notice specifying the grounds of objection and send a copy to the petitioner.
List of persons appearing	Form 6.20 must be completed and handed to the court before the hearing commences.
Decision	Court may make order applied for if satisfied that the statements in the petition are true, and that the debt on which it is founded has not been paid, or secured or compounded for.
Perfection	The court settles a bankruptcy order. Two sealed copies are sent to the official receiver, who sends one to the bankrupt. Official receiver notifies the order in the *London Gazette*.

Appendix 2 Civil Procedure Rules 1998 and Practice Directions

* Most of the forms listed in this practice direction are in the CD-ROM version of *Blackstone's Civil Practice.*

Civil Procedure Rules & Practice Directions

Civil Procedure Rules & Practice Directions

CCR Orders

The following item is on the CD-ROM version of *Blackstone's Civil Practice.* Click on the title of the item to open it.

Introduction

What is in Appendix 2
Civil Procedure Rules 1998 preamble
Introduction to the practice directions

What Is in Appendix 2

This appendix contains the text of the Civil Procedure Rules 1998 (SI 1998/3132) as amended, with the text of all supplementing practice directions. Each practice direction has been placed after the Part of the CPR which it supplements. Practice Direction — Protocols is in **appendix** 3. The text of the rules and practice directions incorporates all amendments in force on 6 April 2006.

To clarify the headings, we have inserted 'CPR' at the beginning of the heading of each Part of the CPR, and 'PD' and the relevant Part number at the beginning of the heading of each practice direction.

In SI 1998/3132 there is a contents list at the beginning of each Part of the CPR (except Parts 4, 49, 50 and 51). We have updated those contents lists to reflect subsequent amendments to the CPR.

In this appendix, unless otherwise stated, a reference to a Part or rule is a reference to a Part or rule of the CPR. A footnote in square brackets is editorial.

The places where a Part of the CPR is referred to in chapters 1 to 98 of *Blackstone's Civil Practice* are listed under the title of the Part. The places where a rule is referred to are listed under the title of the rule. And similarly for practice directions and their paragraphs.

There is a list of amendments to the CPR, the dates they came into force and transitional provisions in Notes on text of the CPR starting on page 2254.

Civil Procedure Rules 1998 Preamble

The Civil Procedure Rule Committee, having power under section 2 of the Civil Procedure Act 1997 to make rules of court under section 1 of that Act, make the following rules which may be cited as the Civil Procedure Rules 1998.

Introduction to the Practice Directions

1 The practice directions to the Civil Procedure Rules apply to civil litigation in the Queen's Bench Division and the Chancery Division of the High Court and to litigation in the county courts other than family proceedings. Where relevant they also apply to appeals to the Civil Division of the Court of Appeal.

2 The practice directions are made:
(1) for the Queen's Bench Division by the Lord Chief Justice as president of that Division;
(2) for the Civil Division of the Court of Appeal by the Master of the Rolls as president of that Division;
(3) for the Chancery Division by the Vice-Chancellor as vice-president of that Division; and
(4) for the county courts by the Lord Chancellor or a person authorised to act on his behalf under s. 74A of the County Courts Act 1984.

3 From April 1999 to July 2000 the Lord Chancellor authorised the Vice-Chancellor, Sir Richard Scott (as he then was) under s. 74A of the 1984 Act. The Vice-Chancellor made all practice directions for county courts during that time.

4 From July 2000 to September 2003 the Lord Chancellor authorised Lord Justice May to make these practice directions. Lord Justice May made all practice directions for county courts during that time.

5 From September 2003 the Lord Chancellor has authorised Lord Justice Dyson to make practice directions for the county courts.

CPR Part 1 Overriding Objective

Part 1 **30.2, 33.1, 58.4, 59.31** [For commentary on a specific rule, please refer to the cross-references after the title of the rule.]

1.1 The Overriding Objective

r.1.1 **1.10, 1.11, 1.12, 1.20, 23.15, 46.5, 46.6, 47.7, 57.3**
r.1.1(1) **1.10, 69.1, 97.39**
r.1.1(2) **1.27, 15.9, 15.13, 42.1, 47.7, 68.35, 97.39**
r.1.1(2)(a) **8.52**
r.1.1(2)(b) **1.14, 8.52, 37.10**
r.1.1(2)(c) **1.31, 8.52, 44.1**
r.1.1(2)(c)(i)–(iii) **1.27**
r.1.1(2)(d) **1.31, 32.6, 45.27**
r.1.1(2)(e) **1.27, 37.10**

(1) These Rules are a new procedural code with the overriding objective of enabling the court to deal with cases justly.
(2) Dealing with a case justly includes, so far as is practicable—
 (a) ensuring that the parties are on an equal footing;
 (b) saving expense;
 (c) dealing with the case in ways which are proportionate—
  (i) to the amount of money involved;
  (ii) to the importance of the case;
  (iii) to the complexity of the issues; and
  (iv) to the financial position of each party;
 (d) ensuring that it is dealt with expeditiously and fairly; and
 (e) allotting to it an appropriate share of the court's resources, while taking into account the need to allot resources to other cases.

1.2 Application by the Court of the Overriding Objective

r.1.2 **1.11, 1.12, 47.71**

The court must seek to give effect to the overriding objective when it—
 (a) exercises any power given to it by the Rules; or
 (b) interprets any rule,
subject to rule 76.2.

1.3 Duty of the Parties

r.1.3 **1.11, 1.37, 1.38, 21.2, 41.2, 44.15, 46.9, 70.19**

The parties are required to help the court to further the overriding objective.

1.4 Court's Duty to Manage Cases

r.1.4 **47.71, 70.19, 79.3, 97.41**
r.1.4(1) **42.1**
r.1.4(2)(a) **44.15, 46.1, 46.9, 66.5**
r.1.4(2)(b) **33.6, 66.5, 79.3**
r.1.4(2)(c) **33.1, 33.6, 34.5, 59.17, 59.35, 66.5, 97.41**
r.1.4(2)(d) **59.17**
r.1.4(2)(e) **42.24**
r.1.4(2)(f) **42.24**
r.1.4(2)(h) **32.1**
r.1.4(2)(i) **32.1, 37.10**
r.1.4(2)(j) **13.15, 32.22, 59.19**
r.1.4(2)(k) **32.22**

(1) The court must further the overriding objective by actively managing cases.
(2) Active case management includes—
 (a) encouraging the parties to co-operate with each other in the conduct of the proceedings;
 (b) identifying the issues at an early stage;

(c) deciding promptly which issues need full investigation and trial and accordingly disposing summarily of the others;
(d) deciding the order in which issues are to be resolved;
(e) encouraging the parties to use an alternative dispute resolution(GL) procedure if the court considers that appropriate and facilitating the use of such procedure;
(f) helping the parties to settle the whole or part of the case;
(g) fixing timetables or otherwise controlling the progress of the case;
(h) considering whether the likely benefits of taking a particular step justify the cost of taking it;
(i) dealing with as many aspects of the case as it can on the same occasion;
(j) dealing with the case without the parties needing to attend at court;
(k) making use of technology; and
(l) giving directions to ensure that the trial of a case proceeds quickly and efficiently.

CPR Part 2 Application and Interpretation of the Rules

Part 2 **23.1** [For commentary on a specific rule, please refer to the cross-references after the title of the rule.]

2.1 Application of the Rules

r.2.1 **47.71, 71.44**
r.2.1(2) **13.3, 82.10**

(1) Subject to paragraph (2), these Rules apply to all proceedings in—
  (a) county courts;
  (b) the High Court; and
  (c) the Civil Division of the Court of Appeal.

(2) These Rules do not apply to proceedings of the kinds specified in the first column of the following table (proceedings for which rules may be made under the enactments specified in the second column) except to the extent that they are applied to those proceedings by another enactment—

	Proceedings	Enactments
1.	Insolvency proceedings	Insolvency Act 1986, ss. 411 and 412
2.	Non-contentious or common form probate proceedings	Supreme Court Act 1981, s. 127
3.	Proceedings in the High Court when acting as a Prize Court	Prize Courts Act 1894, s. 3
4.	Proceedings before the judge within the meaning of Part VII of the Mental Health Act 1983	Mental Health Act 1983, s. 106
5.	Family proceedings	Matrimonial and Family Proceedings Act 1984, s. 40
6.	Adoption proceedings	Adoption Act 1976, s. 66 or Adoption and Children Act 2002, s. 141
7.	Election petitions in the High Court	Representation of the People Act 1983, s. 182

2.2 The Glossary

(1) The glossary at the end of these Rules is a guide to the meaning of certain legal expressions used in the Rules, but is not to be taken as giving those expressions any meaning in the Rules which they do not have in the law generally.

(2) Subject to paragraph (3), words in these Rules 1 which are included in the glossary are followed by '(GL)'.

(3) The words 'counterclaim', 'damages', 'practice form' and 'service', which appear frequently in the Rules, are included in the glossary but are not followed by '(GL)'.

2.3 Interpretation

r.2.3 **23.11**
r. 2.3(1) **14.1, 14.68, 14.70, 15.14, 20.18, 23.1, 23.10, 26.22, 49.12, 71.11, 79.3**

(1) In these Rules—
'child' has the meaning given by rule 21.1(2);

Civil Procedure Rules & Practice Directions

'civil restraint order' means an order restraining a party—
(a) from making any further applications in current proceedings (a limited civil restraint order);
(b) from issuing certain claims or making certain applications in specified courts (an extended civil restraint order); or
(c) from issuing any claim or making any application in specified courts (a general civil restraint order).
'claim for personal injuries' means proceedings in which there is a claim for damages in respect of personal injuries to the claimant or any other person or in respect of a person's death, and
'personal injuries' includes any disease and any impairment of a person's physical or mental condition;
'claimant' means a person who makes a claim;
'CCR' is to be interpreted in accordance with Part 50;
'court officer' means a member of the court staff,
'defendant' means a person against whom a claim is made;
'defendant's home court' means—
(a) if the claim is proceeding in a county court, the county court for the district in which the defendant resides or carries on business; and
(a) if the claim is proceeding in the High Court, the district registry for the district in which the defendant resides or carries on business or, where there is no such district registry, the Royal Courts of Justice;
(Rule 6.5 provides for a party to give an address for service)
'filing', in relation to a document, means delivering it, by post or otherwise, to the court office;
'judge' means, unless the context otherwise requires, a judge, Master or district judge or a person authorised to act as such;
'jurisdiction' means, unless the context requires otherwise, England and Wales and any part of the territorial waters of the United Kingdom adjoining England and Wales;
'legal representative' means a barrister or a solicitor, solicitor's employee or other authorised litigator (as defined in the Courts and Legal Services Act 1990) who has been instructed to act for a party in relation to a claim.
'litigation friend' has the meaning given by Part 21;
'patient' has the meaning given by rule 21.1(2);
'RSC' is to be interpreted in accordance with Part 50;
'statement of case'—
(a) means a claim form, particulars of claim where these are not included in a claim form, defence, Part 20 claim, or reply to defence; and
(a) includes any further information given in relation to them voluntarily or by court order under rule 18.1;
'statement of value' is to be interpreted in accordance with rule 16.3;
'summary judgment' is to be interpreted in accordance with Part 24.
(2) A reference to a 'specialist list' is a reference to a list[(GL)] that has been designated as such by a rule or practice direction.
(3) Where the context requires, a reference to 'the court' means a reference to a particular county court, a district registry, or the Royal Courts of Justice.

2.4 Power of Judge, Master or District Judge to Perform Functions of the Court

r.2.4 **32.3, 40.3, 42.2**

Where these Rules provide for the court to perform any act then, except where an enactment, rule or practice direction provides otherwise, that act may be performed—
(a) in relation to proceedings in the High Court, by any judge, Master or district judge of that Court; and
(b) in relation to proceedings in a county court, by any judge or district judge.

2.5 Court Staff

(1) Where these Rules require or permit the court to perform an act of a formal or administrative character, that act may be performed by a court officer.

(2) A requirement that a court officer carry out any act at the request of a party is subject to the payment of any fee required by a fees order for the carrying out of that act.
(Rule 3.2 allows a court officer to refer to a judge before taking any step)

2.6 Court Documents to Be Sealed

r.2.6(1)–(2) **12.3**
r.2.6(3) **47.76, 49.6**

(1) The court must seal(GL) the following documents on issue—
  (a) the claim form; and
  (b) any other document which a rule or practice direction requires it to seal.
(2) The court may place the seal(GL) on the document—
  (a) by hand; or
  (b) by printing a facsimile of the seal on the document whether electronically or otherwise.
(3) A document purporting to bear the court's seal(GL) shall be admissible in evidence without further proof.

2.7 Court's Discretion as to Where It Deals With Cases

r.2.7 **32.2**

The court may deal with a case at any place that it considers appropriate.

2.8 Time

r.2.8 **3.1, 32.20, 79.6**
r.2.8(1) **15.37**
r.2.8(2) **3.2, 15.37**
r.2.8(3) **3.2**
r.2.8(4) **3.3, 15.37**
r.2.8(4)(b) **3.3**
r.2.8(5) **3.5**

(1) This rule shows how to calculate any period of time for doing any act which is specified—
  (a) by these Rules;
  (b) by a practice direction; or
  (c) by a judgment or order of the court.
(2) A period of time expressed as a number of days shall be computed as clear days.
(3) In this rule 'clear days' means that in computing the number of days—
  (a) the day on which the period begins; and
  (b) if the end of the period is defined by reference to an event, the day on which that event occurs are not included.

Examples
  (i) Notice of an application must be served at least 3 days before the hearing.
  An application is to be heard on Friday 20 October.
  The last date for service is Monday 16 October.
  (ii) The court is to fix a date for a hearing.
  The hearing must be at least 28 days after the date of notice.
  If the court gives notice of the date of the hearing on 1 October, the earliest date for the hearing is 30 October.
  (iii) Particulars of claim must be served within 14 days of service of the claim form.
  The claim form is served on 2 October.
  The last day for service of the particulars of claim is 16 October.

(4) Where the specified period—
  (a) is 5 days or less; and
  (b) includes—
    (i) a Saturday or Sunday; or
    (ii) a Bank Holiday, Christmas Day or Good Friday, that day does not count.

Examples
Notice of an application must be served at least 3 days before the hearing.
An application is to be heard on Monday 20 October.
The last date for service is Tuesday 14 October.

(5) When the period specified—

(a) by these Rules or a practice direction; or
(b) by any judgment or court order,

for doing any act at the court office ends on a day on which the office is closed, that act shall be in time if done on the next day on which the court office is open.

2.9 Dates for Compliance to Be Calendar Dates and to Include Time of Day

r.2.9 **3.1, 46.28** r.2.9(1) **3.6, 32.29, 42.27, 61.8**

(1) Where the court gives a judgment, order or direction which imposes a time limit for doing any act, the last date for compliance must, wherever practicable—
(a) be expressed as a calendar date; and
(b) include the time of day by which the act must be done.

(2) Where the date by which an act must be done is inserted in any document, the date must, wherever practicable, be expressed as a calendar date.

2.10 Meaning of 'Month' in Judgments, etc.

r.2.10 **3.1, 3.4**

Where 'month' occurs in any judgment, order, direction or other document, it means a calendar month.

2.11 Time Limits May Be Varied by Parties

r.2.11 **3.1, 3.7, 46.1**

Unless these Rules or a practice direction provide otherwise or the court orders otherwise, the time specified by a rule or by the court for a person to do any act may be varied by the written agreement of the parties.

(Rules 3.8 (sanctions have effect unless defaulting party obtains relief), 28.4 (variation of case management timetable — fast track) and 29.5 (variation of case management timetable — multi-track) provide for time limits that cannot be varied by agreement between the parties)

PD 2 Practice Direction — Court Offices

This practice direction supplements CPR Part 2

[For commentary on a specific paragraph, please refer to the cross-references after the title of the paragraph.]

Central Office of the High Court at the Royal Courts of Justice

1 The Central Office shall be divided into such departments, and the business performed in the Central Office shall be distributed among the departments in such manner, as is set out in the Queen's Bench Division Guide.

Business in the Offices of the Supreme Court

para.2.1(1)–(3) **2.7**

2.1 (1) The offices of the Supreme Court shall be open on every day of the year except:
(a) Saturdays and Sundays,
(b) Good Friday and the day after Easter Monday,
(c) Christmas Day and, if that day is a Friday or Saturday, then 28 December,
(d) Bank Holidays in England and Wales under the Banking and Financial Dealings Act 1971, and
(e) such other days as the Lord Chancellor, with the concurrence of the Lord Chief Justice, the Master of the Rolls, the President of the Family Division and the Vice-Chancellor ('the Heads of Division') may direct.

(2) The hours during which the offices of the Supreme Court at the Royal Courts of Justice and at the Principal Registry of the Family Division at First Avenue House, 42–49 High Holborn, London WC1V 6NP shall be open to the public shall be as follows:
(a) from 10 a.m. to 4.30 p.m.;
(b) such other hours as the Lord Chancellor, with the concurrence of the Heads of Division, may from time to time direct.

(3) Every district registry shall be open on the days and during the hours that the Lord Chancellor from time to time directs and, in the absence of any such directions, shall be open on the same days and during the same hours as the county court offices of which it forms part are open.

2.2 One of the masters of the Queen's Bench Division (the 'Practice Master') shall be present at the Central Office on every day on which the office is open for the purpose of superintending the business performed there and giving any directions which may be required on questions of practice and procedure.

County Courts

para.3.2 **2.2, 3.5** para.3.3 **3.5**

3.1 Every county court shall have an office or, if the Lord Chancellor so directs, two or more offices, situated at such place or places as he may direct, for the transaction of the business of the court.

3.2 (1) Every county court office, or if a court has two or more offices at least one of those offices, shall be open on every day of the year except:
(a) Saturdays and Sundays,
(b) the day before Good Friday from noon onwards and Good Friday,
(c) the Tuesday after the Spring bank holiday,
(d) Christmas Day and, if that day is a Friday or Saturday, then 28 December,
(e) bank holidays and
(f) such other days as the Lord Chancellor may direct.

(2) In this paragraph 'bank holiday' means a bank holiday in England and Wales under the Banking and Financial Dealings Act 1971 and 'Spring bank holiday' means the bank holiday on the last Monday in May or any day appointed instead of that day under section 1(2) of that Act.

3.3 Subject to para. 3.2(1)(b), the hours during which any court office is open to the public shall be from 10 a.m. to 4 p.m. or such other hours as the Lord Chancellor may from time to time direct.

PD 2B Practice Direction — Allocation of Cases to Levels of Judiciary

PD 2B **2.8, 37.2, 40.3, 45.1** [For commentary on a specific paragraph, please refer to the cross-references after the title of the paragraph.]

para.1.1 42.2

1.1 Rule 2.4 provides that judges, masters and district judges may exercise any function of the court except where an enactment, rule or practice direction provides otherwise. This practice direction sets out the matters over which masters and district judges do not have jurisdiction or which they may deal with only on certain conditions. It does not affect jurisdiction conferred by other enactments. Reference should also be made to other relevant practice directions (e.g. PD 24, para. 3, and PD 26, paras 12.1–10). References to circuit judges include recorders and assistant recorders and references to masters and district judges include deputies.

1.2 Wherever a master or district judge has jurisdiction, he may refer the matter to a judge instead of dealing with it himself.

THE HIGH COURT

Injunctions

para.2 **2.8, 32.3**
para.2.1 **40.3**
para.2.3 **2.10, 41.4**

2.1 Search orders (r. 25.1(1)(h)), freezing orders (r. 25.1(1)(f)), an ancillary order under r. 25.1(1)(g) and orders authorising a person to enter land to recover, inspect or sample property (r. 25.1(1)(d)) may only be made by a judge.

2.2 Except where paras 2.3 and 2.4 apply, injunctions and orders relating to injunctions, including orders for specific performance where these involve an injunction, must be made by a judge.

2.3 A master or a district judge may only make an injunction:

(a) in terms agreed by the parties;

(b) in connection with or ancillary to a charging order;

(c) in connection with or ancillary to an order appointing a receiver by way of equitable execution; or

(d) in proceedings under [r. 66.7(3)*] (order restraining person from receiving sum due from the Crown).

2.4 A master or district judge may make an order varying or discharging an injunction or undertaking given to the court if all parties to the proceedings have consented to the variation or discharge.

Other Pre-trial Orders and Interim Remedies

para.3.1 **2.10, 42.2**
para.3.1(a) **78.5**
para.3.2 **2.8**

3.1 A master or district judge may not make orders or grant interim remedies:

(a) relating to the liberty of the subject;

(b) relating to criminal proceedings or matters except procedural applications in appeals to the High Court (including appeals by case stated) under any enactment;

(c) relating to a claim for judicial review, except that interim applications in claims for judicial review may be made to masters of the Queen's Bench Division;

(d) relating to appeals from masters or district judges;

(e) in appeals against costs assessment under Parts 43 to 48, except on an appeal under r. 47.20 against the decision of an authorised court officer;

(f) in applications under s. 42 of the Supreme Court Act 1981 by a person subject to a civil or a criminal or an all proceedings order (vexatious litigant) for permission to start or continue proceedings;

[* The text issued by the Department for Constitutional Affairs refers to an earlier version of this provision.]

(g) in applications under the Mental Health Act 1983, s. 139, for permission to bring proceedings against a person.

3.2 This practice direction is not concerned with family proceedings. It is also not concerned with proceedings in the Family Division except to the extent that such proceedings can be dealt with in the Chancery Division or the Family Division e.g. proceedings under the Inheritance (Provision for Family and Dependants) Act 1975 or under s. 14 of the Trusts of Land and Appointment of Trustees Act 1996. District judges (including district judges of the Principal Registry of the Family Division) have jurisdiction to hear such proceedings, subject to any direction given by the President of the Family Division.

Trials and Assessments of Damages

paras.4.1–4.2 **2.9, 59.26**

4.1 A master or district judge may, subject to any practice direction, try a case which is treated as being allocated to the multi-track because it is proceeding under Part 8 (see r. 8.9(c)). He may try a case which has been allocated to the multi-track under Part 26 only with the consent of the parties. Restrictions on the trial jurisdiction of masters and district judges do not prevent them from hearing applications for summary judgment or, if the parties consent, for the determination of a preliminary issue.

4.2 A master or a district judge may assess the damages or sum due to a party under a judgment without limit as to the amount.

Chancery Proceedings

para.5.1 **2.11, 42.2** para.5.1(d) **2.9**
para.5.1(a) **14.38**

5.1 In proceedings in the Chancery Division, a master or a district judge may not deal with the following without the consent of the [Chancellor of the High Court†]:

(a) approving compromises (other than applications under the Inheritance (Provision for Family and Dependants) Act 1975) (i) on behalf of a person under disability where that person's interest in a fund, or if there is no fund, the maximum amount of the claim, exceeds £100,000 and (ii) on behalf of absent, unborn and unascertained persons;

(b) making declarations, except in plain cases;

(c) making final orders under s. 1(1) of the Variation of Trusts Act 1958, except for the removal of protective trusts where the interest of the principal beneficiary has not failed or determined;

(d) where the proceedings are brought by a Part 8 claim form in accordance with PD 8B, para. A.1(2) or (3) (statutory or other requirement to use originating summons), determining any question of law or as to the construction of a document which is raised by the claim form;

(e) giving permission to executors, administrators and trustees to bring or defend proceedings or to continue the prosecution or defence of proceedings, and granting an indemnity for costs out of the trust estate, except in plain cases;

(f) granting an indemnity for costs out of the assets of a company on the application of minority shareholders bringing a derivative [claim], except in plain cases;

(g) making an order for rectification, except for:

(i) rectification of the register under the Land Registration Act 1925; or

(ii) alteration or rectification of the register under the Land Registration Act 2002, in plain cases;

(h) making orders to vacate entries in the register under the Land Charges Act 1972, except in plain cases;

(i) making final orders on applications under s. 19 of the Leasehold Reform Act 1967, s. 48 of the Administration of Justice Act 1985 and ss. 21 and 25 of the Law of Property Act 1969;

(j) making final orders under the Landlord and Tenant Acts 1927 and 1954, except (i) by consent, and (ii) orders for interim rents under ss. 24A to 24D of the 1954 Act;

[† The text issued by the Department for Constitutional Affairs refers to the Vice-Chancellor.]

(k) making orders in proceedings in the Patents Court except (i) by consent, (ii) to extend time, (iii) on applications for permission to serve out of the jurisdiction and (iv) on applications for security for costs.

5.2 A master or district judge may only give directions for early trial after consulting the judge in charge of the relevant list.

5.3 Where a winding-up order has been made against a company, any proceedings against the company by or on behalf of debenture holders may be dealt with, at the Royal Courts of Justice, by a registrar and, in a district registry with insolvency jurisdiction, by a district judge.

Assignment of Claims to Masters and Transfer between Masters

para.6 **2.8, 2.12** para.6.2 **32.3**
para.6.1 **42.2**

6.1 The Senior Master and the Chief Master will make arrangements for proceedings to be assigned to individual masters. They may vary such arrangements generally or in particular cases, for example, by transferring a case from a master to whom it had been assigned to another master.

6.2 The fact that a case has been assigned to a particular master does not prevent another master from dealing with that case if circumstances require, whether at the request of the assigned master or otherwise.

Freezing Orders: Cross-examination of Deponents about Assets

para.7 **2.8, 2.10, 38.27**

7 Where the court has made a freezing order under r. 25.1(1)(f) and has ordered a person to make a witness statement or affidavit about his assets and to be cross-examined on its contents, unless the judge directs otherwise, the cross-examination will take place before a master or a district judge, or if the master or district judge directs, before an examiner of the court.

Human Rights

para.7A **2.8, 2.9**

7A A deputy High Court judge, a master or district judge may not try:
(1) a case in a claim made in respect of a judicial act under the Human Rights Act 1998; or
(2) a claim for a declaration of incompatibility in accordance with s. 4 of the Human Rights Act 1998.

COUNTY COURTS

Injunctions, Anti-social Behaviour Orders and Committal

para.8 **42.2** para.8.3 **2.4**

8.1 Injunctions which a county court has jurisdiction to make may only be made by a circuit judge, except:
(a) where the injunction is to be made in proceedings which a district judge otherwise has jurisdiction to hear (see para. 11.1 below);
(b) where the injunction is sought in a money claim which has not yet been allocated to a track, where the amount claimed does not exceed the fast track financial limit;
(c) in the circumstances provided by para. 2.3.
(d) where the injunction is to be made under any of the following provisions:
(i) the Housing Act 1996, s. 153A, 153B or 153D; or
(ii) the Protection from Harassment Act 1997, s. 3.

8.2 A district judge may make orders varying or discharging injunctions in the circumstances provided by para. 2.4.

8.3 A district judge may not make an order committing a person to prison except where an enactment authorises this: see s. 23 of the Attachment of Earnings Act 1971, ss. 14 and 118 of the County Courts Act 1984, ss. 152–157 of the Housing Act 1996, and the relevant rules.

Homelessness Appeals

para.9 **42.2, 89.31**

9 A district judge may not hear appeals under s. 204 or s. 204A of the Housing Act 1996.

Other Pre-trial Orders and Interim Remedies

10.1 In addition to the restrictions on jurisdiction mentioned at paras 8.1–3, para. 3.1(d) and (e) above applies.

Trials and Assessments of Damages

para.11.1 **2.3, 2.4, 32.3, 42.2, 42.23, 59.26**
para.11.1(a) **2.3, 31.12**
para.11.1(d) **2.3, 31.12**
para.11.2 **2.3, 43.19**

11.1 A district judge has jurisdiction to hear the following:
- (a) any claim which has been allocated to the small claims track or fast track or which is treated as being allocated to the multi-track under r. 8.9(c) and Table 2 of PD 8B, except claims:
  - (i) under the Landlord and Tenant Act 1927, part I;
  - (ii) for a new tenancy under the Landlord and Tenant Act 1954, s. 24, or for the termination of a tenancy under s. 29(2);
  - (iii) for an order under the Landlord and Tenant Act 1987, s. 38 or 40;
  - (iv) under the Agricultural Holdings Act 1986, s. 27, or sch. 11, para. 26 or 27;
  - (v) under the Matrimonial Causes Act 1973, s. 45(2), for a declaration of legitimation by virtue of the Legitimacy Act 1976;
  - (vi) under the Fair Trading Act 1973, s. 35,38 or 40;
  - (vii) under the Mental Health Act 1983, part II;
- (b) proceedings for the recovery of land, proceedings under the Housing Act 1985, s. 82A(2), or the Housing Act 1988, s. 6A(2) (demotion claims), or proceedings in a county court under the Housing Act 1996, part 5, chapter 1A (demoted tenancies);
- (c) the assessment of damages or other sum due to a party under a judgment without any financial limit;
- (d) with the permission of the designated civil judge in respect of that case, any other proceedings.

11.2 A case allocated to the small claims track may only be assigned to a circuit judge to hear with his consent.

Freezing Orders: Cross-examination of Deponents about Assets

12 To the extent that a county court has power to make a freezing order, para. 7 applies as appropriate.

Distribution of Business between Circuit Judge and District Judge

para.13 **2.5**
para.14 **2.5**

13 Where both the circuit judge and the district judge have jurisdiction in respect of any proceedings, the exercise of jurisdiction by the district judge is subject to any arrangements made by the designated civil judge for the proper distribution of business between circuit judges and district judges.

14.1 In district registries of the High Court and in the county court, the designated civil judge may make arrangements for proceedings to be assigned to individual district judges. He may vary such arrangements generally or in particular cases.

14.2 The fact that a case has been assigned to a particular district judge does not prevent another district judge from dealing with the case if the circumstances require.

Human Rights

para.15 2.3

15 A district judge may not try a case in which an allegation of indirect discrimination is made against a public authority that would, if the court finds that it occurred, be unlawful under the Race Relations Act 1976, s. 19B.

CPR Part 3 The Court's Case Management Powers

Part 3 **46.13** [For commentary on a specific rule, please refer to the cross-references after the title of the rule.]

3.1 The Court's General Powers of Management

r.3.1 **15.11, 46.21, 46.22, 71.44**
r.3.1(2) **14.2, 20.19, 32.29, 42.27,45.13, 59.53, 74.40, 78.7**
r.3.1(2)(a) **1.23, 1.26, 15.11, 15.13, 18.7, 19.3, 26.5, 35.7, 42.27, 44.15, 46.21, 64.7, 69.1, 71.20, 74.33, 74.35, 74.38, 74.40, 79.6, 87.9, 87.10, 97.40**
r.3.1(2)(b) **32.38, 35.7, 44.11, 59.7, 59.9, 74.40**
r.3.1(2)(d) **32.22**
r.3.1(2)(e) **28.1, 29.7, 59.17**
r.3.1(2)(f) **54.1, 65.7**
r.3.1(2)(g) **14.58**
r.3.1(2)(h) **74.40**
r.3.1(2)(i) **59.17**
r.3.1.2(j) **28.1, 59.17**
r.3.1(2)(k) **97.43**
r.3.1(2)(l) **59.17**
r.3.1(2)(ll) **5.10, 63.19**
r.3.1(2)(m) **32.24**
r.3.1(3) **20.11, 20.19, 32.29, 46.21, 61.8, 64.14, 78.12**
r.3.1(3)(a) **15.13, 65.7**
r.3.1(4) **1.7, 8.4**
r.3.1(5) **1.7, 8.4, 64.14, 65.7, 97.45**
r.3.1(6) **97.45**
r. 3.1(6A) **97.45**

(1) The list of powers in this rule is in addition to any powers given to the court by any other rule or practice direction or by any other enactment or any powers it may otherwise have.
(2) Except where these Rules provide otherwise, the court may—
  (a) extend or shorten the time for compliance with any rule, practice direction or court order (even if an application for extension is made after the time for compliance has expired);
  (b) adjourn or bring forward a hearing;
  (c) require a party or a party's legal representative to attend the court;
  (d) hold a hearing and receive evidence by telephone or by using any other method of direct oral communication;
  (e) direct that part of any proceedings (such as a counterclaim) be dealt with as separate proceedings;
  (f) stay(GL) the whole or part of any proceedings or judgment either generally or until a specified date or event;
  (g) consolidate proceedings;
  (h) try two or more claims on the same occasion;
  (i) direct a separate trial of any issue;
  (j) decide the order in which issues are to be tried;
  (k) exclude an issue from consideration;
  (l) dismiss or give judgment on a claim after a decision on a preliminary issue;
  (ll) order any party to file and serve an estimate of costs;
  (m) take any other step or make any other order for the purpose of managing the case and furthering the overriding objective.
(3) When the court makes an order, it may—
  (a) make it subject to conditions, including a condition to pay a sum of money into court; and
  (b) specify the consequence of failure to comply with the order or a condition.
(4) Where the court gives directions it may take into account whether or not a party has complied with any relevant pre-action protocol(GL).
(5) The court may order a party to pay a sum of money into court if that party has, without good reason, failed to comply with a rule, practice direction or a relevant pre-action protocol.

(6) When exercising its power under paragraph (5) the court must have regard to—
   (a) the amount in dispute; and
   (b) the costs which the parties have incurred or which they may incur.

(6A) Where a party pays money into court following an order under paragraph (3) or (5), the money shall be security for any sum payable by that party to any other party in the proceedings, subject to the right of a defendant under rule 37.2 to treat all or part of any money paid into court as a Part 36 payment.
(Rule 36.2 explains what is meant by a Part 36 payment)

(7) A power of the court under these Rules to make an order includes a power to vary or revoke the order.

3.2 Court Officer's Power to Refer to a Judge

r.3.2 33.5

Where a step is to be taken by a court officer—
   (a) the court officer may consult a judge before taking that step;
   (b) the step may be taken by a judge instead of the court officer.

3.3 Court's Power to Make Order of Its Own Initiative

r.3.3 **54.7, 59.35**
r.3.3(1) **32.24, 46.38**
r.3.3(2) **32.24**
r.3.3(3) **32.25, 45.8**
r.3.3(4) **32.38, 69.14, 97.41**
r.3.3(5) **32.38, 44.15, 69.14**
r.3.3(5)(a) **32.21**
r.3.3(5)(b) **32.21, 32.24**
r.3.3(6) **32.21, 32.24**

(1) Except where a rule or some other enactment provides otherwise, the court may exercise its powers on an application or of its own initiative.
(Part 23 sets out the procedure for making an application)

(2) Where the court proposes to make an order of its own initiative—
   (a) it may give any person likely to be affected by the order an opportunity to make representations; and
   (b) where it does so it must specify the time by and the manner in which the representations must be made.

(3) Where the court proposes—
   (a) to make an order of its own initiative; and
   (b) to hold a hearing to decide whether to make the order,
   it must give each party likely to be affected by the order at least 3 days' notice of the hearing.

(4) The court may make an order of its own initiative, without hearing the parties or giving them an opportunity to make representations.

(5) Where the court has made an order under paragraph (4)—
   (a) a party affected by the order may apply to have it set aside varied or stayed [(GL)]; and
   (b) the order must contain a statement of the right to make such an application.

(6) An application under paragraph (5)(a) must be made—
   (a) within such period as may be specified by the court; or
   (b) if the court does not specify a period, not more than 7 days after the date on which the order was served on the party making the application.

(7) If the court of its own initiative strikes out a statement of case or dismisses an application (including an application for permission to appeal or for permission to apply for judicial review), and it considers that the claim or application is totally without merit—
   (a) the court's order must record that fact; and
   (b) the court must at the same time consider whether it is appropriate to make a civil restraint order.

3.4 Power to Strike Out a Statement of Case

r.3.4 **26.3, 31.16, 33.1, 33.5, 33.6, 79.3, 95.18, 97.41**
r.3.4(1) **33.2**
r.3.4(2) **33.2, 97.42**
r.3.4(2)(a) **33.7, 33.8**
r.3.4(2)(b) **33.2, 33.12, 33.22**
r.3.4(2)(c) **42.1, 46.1, 46.14**
r.3.4(3) **33.24**
r.3.4(4) **33.23, 54.4**
r.3.4(5) **33.2, 46.38**

(1) In this rule and rule 3.5, reference to a statement of case includes reference to part of a statement of case.
(2) The court may strike out(GL) a statement of case if it appears to the court—
  (a) that the statement of case discloses no reasonable grounds for bringing or defending the claim;
  (b) that the statement of case is an abuse of the court's process or is otherwise likely to obstruct the just disposal of the proceedings; or
  (c) that there has been a failure to comply with a rule, practice direction or court order.
(3) When the court strikes out a statement of case it may make any consequential order it considers appropriate.
(4) Where—
  (a) the court has struck out a claimant's statement of case;
  (b) the claimant has been ordered to pay costs to the defendant; and
  (c) before the claimant pays those costs, he starts another claim against the same defendant, arising out of facts which are the same or substantially the same as those relating to the claim in which the statement of case was struck out,

  the court may, on the application of the defendant, stay(GL) that other claim until the costs of the first claim have been paid.
(5) Paragraph (2) does not limit any other power of the court to strike out(GL) a statement of case.
(6) If the court strikes out a claimant's statement of case and it considers that the claim is totally without merit—
  (a) the court's order must record that fact; and
  (b) the court must at the same time consider whether it is appropriate to make a civil restraint order.

3.5 Judgment without Trial after Striking Out

r.3.5 **46.28, 46.29, 46.30** r.3.5(2)(a)–(b) **46.30**
r.3.5(3)–(4) **46.30**

(1) This rule applies where—
  (a) the court makes an order which includes a term that the statement of case of a party shall be struck out if the party does not comply with the order; and
  (b) the party against whom the order was made does not comply with it.
(2) A party may obtain judgment with costs by filing a request for judgment if—
  (a) the order referred to in paragraph (1)(a) relates to the whole of a statement of case; and
  (b) where the party wishing to obtain judgment is the claimant, the claim is for—
    (i) a specified amount of money;
    (ii) an amount of money to be decided by the court;
    (iii) delivery of goods where the claim form gives the defendant the alternative of paying their value; or
    (iv) any combination of these remedies.
(3) Where judgment is obtained under this rule in a case to which paragraph (2)(b)(iii) applies, it will be judgment requiring the defendant to deliver the goods, or (if he does not do so) pay the value of the goods as decided by the court (less any payments made).
(4) The request must state that the right to enter judgment has arisen because the court's order has not been complied with.
(5) A party must make an application in accordance with Part 23 if he wishes to obtain judgment under this rule in a case to which paragraph (2) does not apply.

3.6 Setting Aside Judgment Entered after Striking Out

(1) A party against whom the court has entered judgment under rule 3.5 may apply to the court to set the judgment aside.
(2) An application under paragraph (1) must be made not more than 14 days after the judgment has been served on the party making the application.

(3) If the right to enter judgment had not arisen at the time when judgment was entered, the court must set aside(GL) the judgment.
(4) If the application to set aside(GL) is made for any other reason, rule 3.9 (relief from sanctions) shall apply.

3.7 Sanctions for Non-payment of Certain Fees

r.3.7 **14.70, 42.12, 44.10, 45.16, 46.11** r.3.7(7)–(8) **42.12**

(1) This rule applies where—
(a) an allocation questionnaire or a pre-trial checklist (listing questionnaire) is filed without payment of the fee specified by the relevant Fees Order;
(b) the court dispenses with the need for an allocation questionnaire or a pre-trial checklist or both;
(c) these Rules do not require an allocation questionnaire or a pre-trial checklist to be filed in relation to the claim in question; or
(d) the court has made an order giving permission to proceed with a claim for judicial review.

(Rule 26.3 provides for the court to dispense with the need for an allocation questionnaire and rules 28.5 and 29.6 provide for the court to dispense with the need for a pre-trial checklist)

(Rule 54.12 provides for the service of the order giving permission to proceed with a claim for judicial review)

(2) The court will serve a notice on the claimant requiring payment of the fee specified in the relevant Fees Order if, at the time the fee is due, the claimant has not paid it or made an application for exemption or remission.
(3) The notice will specify the date by which the claimant must pay the fee.
(4) If the claimant does not—
(a) pay the fee; or
(b) make an application for an exemption from or remission of the fee,

by the date specified in the notice—
(i) the claim will automatically be struck out without further order of the court; and
(ii) the claimant shall be liable for the costs which the defendant has incurred unless the court orders otherwise.

(Rule 44.12 provides for the basis of assessment where a right to costs arises under this rule)

(5) Where an application for exemption from or remission of a fee is refused, the court will serve notice on the claimant requiring payment of the fee by the date specified in the notice.
(6) If the claimant does not pay the fee by the date specified in the notice—
(a) the claim will automatically be struck out without further order of the court; and
(b) the claimant shall be liable for the costs which the defendant has incurred unless the court orders otherwise.
(7) If—
(a) a claimant applies to have the claim reinstated; and
(b) the court grants relief,

the relief shall be conditional on the claimant either paying the fee or filing evidence of exemption from payment or remission of the fee within the period specified in paragraph (8).
(8) The period referred to in paragraph (7) is—
(a) if the order granting relief is made at a hearing at which a claimant is present or represented, 2 days from the date of the order;
(b) in any other case, 7 days from the date of service of the order on the claimant.

3.7A

r.3.7A **28.3, 42.12** r.3.7B **42.12**

(1) This rule applies where a defendant files a counterclaim without—
(a) payment of the fee specified by the relevant Fees Order; or
(b) making an application for an exemption from or remission of the fee.
(2) The court will serve a notice on the defendant requiring payment of the fee specified in the relevant Fees Order if, at the time the fee is due, the defendant has not paid it or made an application for exemption or remission.

(3) The notice will specify the date by which the defendant must pay the fee.
(4) If the defendant does not—
(a) pay the fee, or
(b) make an application for an exemption from or remission of the fee,
by the date specified in the notice, the counterclaim will automatically be struck out without further order of the court.
(5) Where an application for exemption from or remission of a fee is refused, the court will serve notice on the defendant requiring payment of the fee by the date specified in the notice.
(6) If the defendant does not pay the fee by the date specified in the notice, the counterclaim will automatically be struck out without further order of the court.
(7) If—
(a) the defendant applies to have the counterclaim reinstated; and
(b) the court grants relief,
the relief will be conditional on the defendant either paying the fee or filing evidence of exemption from payment or remission of the fee within the period specified in paragraph (8).
(8) The period referred to in paragraph (7) is—
(a) if the order granting relief is made at a hearing at which the defendant is present or represented, 2 days from the date of the order;
(b) in any other case, 7 days from the date of service of the order on the defendant.

3.7B Sanctions for Dishonouring Cheque

(1) This rule applies where any fee is paid by cheque and that cheque is subsequently dishonoured.
(2) The court will serve a notice on the paying party requiring payment of the fee which will specify the date by which the fee must be paid.
(3) If the fee is not paid by the date specified in the notice—
(a) where the fee is payable by the claimant, the claim will automatically be struck out without further order of the court;
(b) where the fee is payable by the defendant, the defence will automatically be struck out without further order of the court,
and the paying party shall be liable for the costs which any other party has incurred unless the court orders otherwise.
(Rule 44.12 provides for the basis of assessment where a right to costs arises under this rule)
(4) If—
(a) the paying party applies to have the claim or defence reinstated; and
(b) the court grants relief,
the relief shall be conditional on that party paying the fee within the period specified in paragraph (5).
(5) The period referred to in paragraph (4) is—
(a) if the order granting relief is made at a hearing at which the paying party is present or represented, 2 days from the date of the order;
(b) in any other case, 7 days from the date of service of the order on the paying party.
(6) For the purposes of this rule, 'claimant' includes a Part 20 claimant and 'claim form' includes a Part 20 claim.

3.8 Sanctions have Effect Unless Defaulting Party Obtains Relief

r.3.8 **8.4, 46.29** r.3.8(3) **3.7, 46.29**
r.3.8(1) **46.29, 46.31**

(1) Where a party has failed to comply with a rule, practice direction or court order, any sanction for failure to comply imposed by the rule, practice direction or court order has effect unless the party in default applies for and obtains relief from the sanction.
(Rule 3.9 sets out the circumstances which the court may consider on an application to grant relief from a sanction)
(2) Where the sanction is the payment of costs, the party in default may only obtain relief by appealing against the order for costs.
(3) Where a rule, practice direction or court order—
(a) requires a party to do something within a specified time, and
(b) specifies the consequence of failure to comply,

the time for doing the act in question may not be extended by agreement between the parties.

3.9 Relief from Sanctions

r.3.9 **6.17, 8.4, 15.11, 15.13, 15.26, 42.12, 42.27, 46.1, 46.13, 46.22, 46.23, 46.32, 46.35, 68.48, 71.20, 71.21, 72.12, 97.45**
r.3.9(1) **8.4, 46.31, 54.7**
r.3.9(1)(e) **1.7, 8.4**
r.3.9(1)(f) **46.8**

(1) On an application for relief from any sanction imposed for a failure to comply with any rule, practice direction or court order the court will consider all the circumstances including—
(a) the interests of the administration of justice;
(b) whether the application for relief has been made promptly;
(c) whether the failure to comply was intentional;
(d) whether there is a good explanation for the failure;
(e) the extent to which the party in default has complied with other rules, practice directions, court orders and any relevant pre-action protocol[(GL)];
(f) whether the failure to comply was caused by the party or his legal representative;
(g) whether the trial date or the likely trial date can still be met if relief is granted;
(h) the effect which the failure to comply had on each party; and
(i) the effect which the granting of relief would have on each party.
(2) An application for relief must be supported by evidence.

3.10 General Power of the Court to Rectify Matters Where There Has Been an Error of Procedure

r.3.10 **2.2, 15.9, 15.11, 23.12, 29.9, 35.7, 37.17, 42.27, 46.27, 64.29, 64.47, 71.20**
r.3.10(a) **64.29**
r.3.10(b) **46.27**

Where there has been an error of procedure such as a failure to comply with a rule or practice direction—
(a) the error does not invalidate any step taken in the proceedings unless the court so orders; and
(b) the court may make an order to remedy the error.

3.11 Power of the Court to Make Civil Restraint Orders

A practice direction may set out—
(a) the circumstances in which the court has the power to make a civil restraint order against a party to proceedings;
(b) the procedure where a party applies for a civil restraint order against another party; and
(c) the consequences of the court making a civil restraint order.

PD 3 Practice Direction — Striking Out a Statement of Case

This practice direction supplements CPR rule 3.4.

[For commentary on a specific paragraph, please refer to the cross-references after the title of the paragraph.]

Introductory

para.1.2 **33.1**
para.1.5 **33.2, 33.22**
para.1.7 **33.1, 33.3, 34.1**
para.1.9 **46.29**

1.1 Rule 1.4(2)(c) includes as an example of active case management the summary disposal of issues which do not need full investigation at trial.

1.2 The rules give the court two distinct powers which may be used to achieve this. Rule 3.4 enables the court to strike out the whole or part of a statement of case which discloses no reasonable grounds for bringing or defending a claim (rule 3.4(2)(a)), or which is an abuse of the process of the court or otherwise likely to obstruct the just disposal of the proceedings (rule 3.4(2)(b)). Rule 24.2 enables the court to give summary judgment against a claimant or defendant where that party has no real prospect of succeeding on his claim or defence. Both those powers may be exercised on an application by a party or on the court's own initiative.

1.3 This practice direction sets out the procedure a party should follow if he wishes to make an application for an order under rule 3.4.

1.4 The following are examples of cases where the court may conclude that particulars of claim (whether contained in a claim form or filed separately) fall within rule 3.4(2)(a):

(1) those which set out no facts indicating what the claim is about, for example 'Money owed £5000',

(2) those which are incoherent and make no sense,

(3) those which contain a coherent set of facts but those facts, even if true, do not disclose any legally recognisable claim against the defendant.

1.5 A claim may fall within rule 3.4(2)(b) where it is vexatious, scurrilous or obviously ill-founded.

1.6 A defence may fall within rule 3.4(2)(a) where:

(1) it consists of a bare denial or otherwise sets out no coherent statement of facts, or

(2) the facts it sets out, while coherent, would not even if true amount in law to a defence to the claim.

1.7 A party may believe he can show without a trial that an opponent's case has no real prospect of success on the facts, or that the case is bound to succeed or fail, as the case may be, because of a point of law (including the construction of a document). In such a case the party concerned may make an application under rule 3.4 or Part 24 (or both) as he thinks appropriate.

1.8 The examples set out above are intended only as illustrations.

1.9 Where a rule, practice direction or order states 'shall be struck out or dismissed' or 'will be struck out or dismissed' this means that the striking out or dismissal will be automatic and that no further order of the court is required.

Claims Which Appear to Fall within Rule 3.4(2)(a) or (b)

para.2.1 **33.5**
paras.2.3–2.6 **33.5**

2.1 If a court officer is asked to issue a claim form which he believes may fall within rule 3.4(2)(a) or (b) he should issue it, but may then consult a judge (under rule 3.2) before returning the claim form to the claimant or taking any other step to serve the defendant. The judge may on his own initiative make an immediate order designed to ensure that the claim is disposed of or (as the case may be) proceeds in a way that accords with the rules.

2.3 The judge may allow the claimant a hearing before deciding whether to make such an order.

2.4 Orders the judge may make include:

(1) an order that the claim be stayed until further order,

(2) an order that the claim form be retained by the court and not served until the stay is lifted,

(3) an order that no application by the claimant to lift the stay be heard unless he files such further documents (for example a witness statement or an amended claim form or particulars of claim) as may be specified in the order.

2.5 Where the judge makes any such order or, subsequently, an order lifting the stay he may give directions about the service on the defendant of the order and any other documents on the court file.

2.6 The fact that a judge allows a claim referred to him by a court officer to proceed does not prejudice the right of any party to apply for any order against the claimant.

Defences Which Appear to Fall within Rule 3.4(2)(a) or (b)

para.3 **33.5**

3.1 A court officer may similarly consult a judge about any document filed which purports to be a defence and which he believes may fall within rule 3.4(2)(a) or (b).

3.2 If the judge decides that the document falls within rule 3.4(2)(a) or (b) he may on his own initiative make an order striking it out. Where he does so he may extend the time for the defendant to file a proper defence.

3.3 The judge may allow the defendant a hearing before deciding whether to make such an order.

3.4 Alternatively the judge may make an order under rule 18.1 requiring the defendant within a stated time to clarify his defence or to give additional information about it. The order may provide that the defence will be struck out if the defendant does not comply.

3.5 The fact that a judge does not strike out a defence on his own initiative does not prejudice the right of the claimant to apply for any order against the defendant.

General Provisions

para.4.2 **33.24**

4.1 The court may exercise its powers under rule 3.4(2)(a) or (b) on application or on its own initiative at any time.

4.2 Where a judge at a hearing strikes out all or part of a party's statement of case he may enter such judgment for the other party as that party appears entitled to.

Applications for Orders under Rule 3.4(2)

para.5.1 **33.3**
para.5.2 **33.3, 33.7**

5.1 Attention is drawn to Part 23 (General Rules about Applications) and to the practice direction that supplements it. The practice direction requires all applications to be made as soon as possible and before allocation if possible.

5.2 While many applications under rule 3.4(2) can be made without evidence in support, the applicant should consider whether facts need to be proved and, if so, whether evidence in support should be filed and served.

Applications for Summary Judgment

para.6.1 **33.1**

6.1 Applications for summary judgment may be made under Part 24. Attention is drawn to that Part and to the practice direction that supplements it.

Vexatious Litigants

para.7 **14.69** para.7.9 **14.69**

7.1 This practice direction applies where a 'civil proceedings order' or an 'all proceedings order' (as respectively defined under section 42(1A) of the Supreme Court Act 1981) is in force against a person ('the litigant').

7.2 An application by the litigant for permission to begin or continue, or to make any application in, any civil proceedings shall be made by application notice issued in the High Court and signed by the litigant.

7.3 The application notice must state:

(1) the title and reference number of the proceedings in which the civil proceedings order or the all proceedings order, as the case may be, was made,

(2) the full name of the litigant and his address,
(3) the order the applicant is seeking, and
(4) briefly, why the applicant is seeking the order.

7.4 The application notice must be filed together with any written evidence on which the litigant relies in support of his application.

7.5 Either in the application notice or in written evidence filed in support of the application, the previous occasions on which the litigant made an application for permission under section 42(1A) of the said Act must be listed.

7.6 The application notice, together with any written evidence, will be placed before a High Court judge who may:
(1) without the attendance of the applicant make an order giving the permission sought;
(2) give directions for further written evidence to be supplied by the litigant before an order is made on the application;
(3) make an order dismissing the application without a hearing; or
(4) give directions for the hearing of the application.

7.7 Directions given under paragraph 7.6(4) may include an order that the application notice be served on the Attorney-General and on any person against whom the litigant desires to bring the proceedings for which permission is being sought.

7.8 Any order made under paragraphs 7.6 or 7.7 will be served on the litigant at the address given in the application notice. CPR Part 6 will apply.

7.9 A person may apply to set aside the grant of permission if:
(1) the permission allowed the litigant to bring or continue proceedings against that person or to make any application against him, and
(2) the permission was granted other than at a hearing of which that person was given notice under paragraph 7.7.

7.10 Any application under paragraph 7.9 must be made in accordance with CPR Part 23.

PD 3B Practice Direction — Sanctions for Non-payment of Fees

This practice direction supplements CPR rule 3.7

PD 3B **42.12**

1 If a claim is struck out under rule 3.7, the court will send notice that it has been struck out to the defendant.

2 The notice will also explain the effect of rule 25.11. This provides that any interim injunction will cease to have effect 14 days after the date the claim is struck out under rule 3.7. Paragraph (2) provides that if the claimant applies to reinstate the claim before the interim injunction ceases to have effect, the injunction will continue until the hearing of the application unless the court orders otherwise. If the claimant makes such an application, the defendant will be given notice in the ordinary way under rule 23.4.

PD 3C Practice Direction — Civil Restraint Orders

This practice direction supplements r. 3.11

Introduction

1 This practice direction applies where the court is considering whether to make:
(a) a limited civil restraint order;
(b) an extended civil restraint order; or
(c) a general civil restraint order,
against a party who has issued claims or made applications which are totally without merit.

(Rules 3.3(7), 3.4(6) and 23.12 provide that where a statement of case or application is struck out or dismissed and is totally without merit, the court order must specify that fact and the court must consider whether to make a civil restraint order. Rule 52.10(6) makes similar provision where the appeal court refuses an application for permission to appeal, strikes out an appellant's notice or dismisses an appeal.)

Limited Civil Restraint Orders

para.2.1 **14.71**
para.2.2(1)–(3) **14.71**
para.2.3(1)–(2) **14.71**
paras.2.6–2.9 **14.71**

2.1 A limited civil restraint order may be made by a judge of any court where a party has made two or more applications which are totally without merit.

2.2 Where the court makes a limited civil restraint order, the party against whom the order is made:
(1) will be restrained from making any further applications in the proceedings in which the order is made without first obtaining the permission of a judge identified in the order;
(2) may apply for amendment or discharge of the order provided he has first obtained the permission of a judge identified in the order; and
(3) may apply for permission to appeal the order and if permission is granted, may appeal the order.

2.3 Where a party who is subject to a limited civil restraint order:
(1) makes a further application in the proceedings in which the order is made without first obtaining the permission of a judge identified in the order, such application will automatically be dismissed:
(a) without the judge having to make any further order; and
(b) without the need for the other party to respond to it;
(2) repeatedly makes applications for permission pursuant to that order which are totally without merit, the court may direct that if the party makes any further application for permission which is totally without merit, the decision to dismiss the application will be final and there will be no right of appeal, unless the judge who refused permission grants permission to appeal.

2.4 A party who is subject to a limited civil restraint order may not make an application for permission under para. 2.2(1) or (2) without first serving notice of the application on the other party in accordance with para. 2.5.

2.5 A notice under para. 2.4 must:
(1) set out the nature and grounds of the application; and
(2) provide the other party with at least seven days within which to respond.

2.6 An application for permission under para. 2.2(1) or (2):
(1) must be made in writing;
(2) must include the other party's written response, if any, to the notice served under para. 2.4; and
(3) will be determined without a hearing.

2.7 An order under para. 2.3(2) may only be made by:
(1) a Court of Appeal judge;
(2) a High Court judge or master; or
(3) a designated civil judge or his appointed deputy.

2.8 Where a party makes an application for permission under para. 2.2(1) or (2) and permission is refused, any application for permission to appeal:

(1) must be made in writing; and
(2) will be determined without a hearing.

2.9 A limited civil restraint order:
(1) is limited to the particular proceedings in which it is made;
(2) will remain in effect for the duration of the proceedings in which it is made, unless the court otherwise orders; and
(3) must identify the judge or judges to whom an application for permission under paras 2.2(1), 2.2(2) or 2.8 should be made.

Extended Civil Restraint Orders

para.3.1 3B **14.72**
para.3.2(1)–(3) **14.72**
para.3.3(1)–(2) **14.72**
paras.3.6–3.11 **14.72**

3.1 An extended civil restraint order may be made by:
(1) a judge of the Court of Appeal;
(2) a judge of the High Court; or
(3) a designated civil judge or his appointed deputy in the county court,
where a party has persistently issued claims or made applications which are totally without merit.

3.2 Unless the court otherwise orders, where the court makes an extended civil restraint order, the party against whom the order is made:
(1) will be restrained from issuing claims or making applications in:
(a) any court if the order has been made by a judge of the Court of Appeal;
(b) the High Court or any county court if the order has been made by a judge of the High Court; or
(c) any county court identified in the order if the order has been made by a designated civil judge or his appointed deputy,
concerning any matter involving or relating to or touching upon or leading to the proceedings in which the order is made without first obtaining the permission of a judge identified in the order;
(2) may apply for amendment or discharge of the order provided he has first obtained the permission of a judge identified in the order; and
(3) may apply for permission to appeal the order and if permission is granted, may appeal the order.

3.3 Where a party who is subject to an extended civil restraint order:
(1) issues a claim or makes an application in a court identified in the order concerning any matter involving or relating to or touching upon or leading to the proceedings in which the order is made without first obtaining the permission of a judge identified in the order, the claim or application will automatically be struck out or dismissed:
(a) without the judge having to make any further order; and
(b) without the need for the other party to respond to it;
(2) repeatedly makes applications for permission pursuant to that order which are totally without merit, the court may direct that if the party makes any further application for permission which is totally without merit, the decision to dismiss the application will be final and there will be no right of appeal, unless the judge who refused permission grants permission to appeal.

3.4 A party who is subject to an extended civil restraint order may not make an application for permission under para. 3.2(1) or (2) without first serving notice of the application on the other party in accordance with para. 3.5.

3.5 A notice under para. 3.4 must:
(1) set out the nature and grounds of the application; and
(2) provide the other party with at least seven days within which to respond.

3.6 An application for permission under para. 3.2(1) or (2):
(1) must be made in writing;
(2) must include the other party's written response, if any, to the notice served under para. 3.4; and
(3) will be determined without a hearing.

3.7 An order under para. 3.3(2) may only be made by:
(1) a Court of Appeal judge;

(2) a High Court judge; or
(3) a designated civil judge or his appointed deputy.

3.8 Where a party makes an application for permission under para. 3.2(1) or (2) and permission is refused, any application for permission to appeal:
(1) must be made in writing; and
(2) will be determined without a hearing.

3.9 An extended civil restraint order:
(1) will be made for a specified period not exceeding two years;
(2) must identify the courts in which the party against whom the order is made is restrained from issuing claims or making applications; and
(3) must identify the judge or judges to whom an application for permission under paras 3.2(1), 3.2(2) or 3.8 should be made.

3.10 The court may extend the duration of an extended civil restraint order, if it considers it appropriate to do so, but it must not be extended for a period greater than two years on any given occasion.

3.11 If he considers that it would be appropriate to make an extended civil restraint order:
(1) a master or a district judge in a district registry of the High Court must transfer the proceedings to a High Court judge; and
(2) a circuit judge or a district judge in a county court must transfer the proceedings to the designated civil judge.

General Civil Restraint Orders

para.4.1 **14.73**
para.4.2(1)–(3) **14.73**
para.4.3(1)–(2) **14.73**
paras.4.6–4.11 **14.73**

4.1 A general civil restraint order may be made by:
(1) a judge of the Court of Appeal;
(2) a judge of the High Court; or
(3) a designated civil judge or his appointed deputy in a county court,
where the party against whom the order is made persists in issuing claims or making applications which are totally without merit, in circumstances where an extended civil restraint order would not be sufficient or appropriate.

4.2 Unless the court otherwise orders, where the court makes a general civil restraint order, the party against whom the order is made:
(1) will be restrained from issuing any claim or making any application in:
(a) any court if the order has been made by a judge of the Court of Appeal;
(b) the High Court or any county court if the order has been made by a judge of the High Court; or
(c) any county court identified in the order if the order has been made by a designated civil judge or his appointed deputy,
without first obtaining the permission of a judge identified in the order;
(2) may apply for amendment or discharge of the order provided he has first obtained the permission of a judge identified in the order; and
(3) may apply for permission to appeal the order and if permission is granted, may appeal the order.

4.3 Where a party who is subject to a general civil restraint order:
(1) issues a claim or makes an application in a court identified in the order without first obtaining the permission of a judge identified in the order, the claim or application will automatically be struck out or dismissed:
(a) without the judge having to make any further order; and
(b) without the need for the other party to respond to it;
(2) repeatedly makes applications for permission pursuant to that order which are totally without merit, the court may direct that if the party makes any further application for permission which is totally without merit, the decision to dismiss that application will be final and there will be no right of appeal, unless the judge who refused permission grants permission to appeal.

4.4 A party who is subject to a general civil restraint order may not make an application for permission under para. 4.2(1) or (2) without first serving notice of the application on the other party in accordance with para. 4.5.

4.5 A notice under para. 4.4 must:
(1) set out the nature and grounds of the application; and
(2) provide the other party with at least seven days within which to respond.

4.6 An application for permission under para. 4.2(1) or (2):
(1) must be made in writing;
(2) must include the other party's written response, if any, to the notice served under paragraph 4.4; and
(3) will be determined without a hearing.

4.7 An order under para. 4.3(2) may only be made by:
(1) a Court of Appeal judge;
(2) a High Court judge; or
(3) a designated civil judge or his appointed deputy.

4.8 Where a party makes an application for permission under para. 4.2(1) or (2) and permission is refused, any application for permission to appeal:
(1) must be made in writing; and
(2) will be determined without a hearing.

4.9 A general civil restraint order:
(1) will be made for a specified period not exceeding two years;
(2) must identify the courts in which the party against whom the order is made is restrained from issuing claims or making applications; and
(3) must identify the judge or judges to whom an application for permission under paras 4.2(1), 4.2(2) or 4.8 should be made.

4.10 The court may extend the duration of a general civil restraint order, if it considers it appropriate to do so, but it must not be extended for a period greater than two years on any given occasion.

4.11 If he considers that it would be appropriate to make a general civil restraint order:
(1) a master or a district judge in a district registry of the High Court must transfer the proceedings to a High Court judge; and
(2) a circuit judge or a district judge in a county court must transfer the proceedings to the designated civil judge.

General

5.1 The other party or parties to the proceedings may apply for any civil restraint order.

5.2 An application under para. 5.1 must be made using the Part 23 procedure unless the court otherwise directs and the application must specify which type of civil restraint order is sought.

5.3 Examples of a limited civil restraint order, an extended civil restraint order and a general civil restraint order are annexed to this practice direction. These examples may be modified as appropriate in any particular case.

[The forms annexed to PD 3C are on the CD-ROM version of *Blackstone's Civil Practice*. Click on the number of a form to open it.

Form N19 Limited civil restraint order

Form N19A Extended civil restraint order

Form N19B General civil restraint order]

CPR Part 4 Forms

4—(1) The forms set out in a practice direction shall be used in the cases to which they apply.

(2) A form may be varied by the court or a party if the variation is required by the circumstances of a particular case.

(3) A form must not be varied so as to leave out any information or guidance which the form gives to the recipient.

(4) Where these Rules require a form to be sent by the court or by a party for another party to use, it must be sent without any variation except such as is required by the circumstances of the particular case.

(5) Where the court or a party produces a form shown in a practice direction with the words 'Royal Arms', the form must include a replica of the Royal Arms at the head of the first page.

PD 4 Practice Direction — Forms*

This practice direction supplements CPR Part 4

[For commentary on a specific paragraph, please refer to the cross-references after the title of the paragraph.]

Scope of This Practice Direction

1.1 This practice direction lists the forms to be used in civil proceedings on or after 26 April 1999, when the Civil Procedure Rules (CPR) came into force.

1.2 The forms may be modified as the circumstances require, provided that all essential information, especially information or guidance which the form gives to the recipient, is included.

1.3 This practice direction contains 3 tables—

- Table 1 lists forms required by CPR, Parts 1 to 75
- Table 2 lists High Court forms in use before 26 April 1999 which have remained in use on or after that date (see para. 4 below)
- Table 3 lists county court forms in use before 26 April 1999 that will remain in use on or after that date (see para. 5 below)

1.4 Former prescribed forms are shown as 'No. 00'. The former practice forms where they are appropriate for use in either the Chancery or Queen's Bench Division (or where no specific form is available for use in the county court, in that court also) are prefixed 'PF' followed by the number. Where the form is used mainly in the Chancery or Queen's Bench Division, the suffix CH or QB follows the form number.

Other Forms

2.1 Other forms may be authorised by practice directions. For example the forms relating to Part 61 Admiralty claims are authorised by, and annexed to, PD 61.

Table 1 'N' Forms

Contents

3.1 This table lists the forms that are referred to and required to be used by rules or practice directions supplementing particular Parts of the CPR. For ease of reference, forms required for claims in the Commercial Court, Technology and Construction Court and for Admiralty claims and arbitration claims, are separately listed.

No.	Title
N1	Part 7 (general) claim form (PD 7, para. 3.1)
N1CPC	Claim Production Centre ('CPC') claim form (r. 7.10)
N1A	Notes for claimant
N1C	Notes for defendant
N1(FD)	Notes for defendant (Consumer Credit Act cases)
N2	Claim form (probate claim) (PD 57, para. 2.1)
N2A	Claimant's notes for guidance (probate claim)
N2B	Defendant's notes for guidance (probate claim)
N3	Acknowledgment of service (probate claim) (r. 57.4(1))
N5	Claim form for possession of property (PD 55, para. 1.5)
N5A	Claim form for relief against forfeiture (PD 55, para. 1.5)
N5B	Claim form for possession of property (accelerated procedure) (assured shorthold tenancy) (PD 55, para. 1.5)
N5C	Notes for the claimant (accelerated possession procedure)
N6	Claim form for demotion of tenancy (PD 65, para. 5.2)
N7	Notes for defendant (mortgaged residential premises)
N7A	Notes for defendant (rented residential premises)

[* Most of the forms listed in this practice direction are in the CD-ROM version of *Blackstone's Civil Practice.* In the CD-ROM version a click on a form number which is in red will open the form. For more information on forms in the CD-ROM version, see **appendix 5**.]

No.	Title
N7B	Notes for defendant — forfeiture of the lease (residential premises)
N7D	Notes for defendant — demotion/suspension claim
N8	Claim form (arbitration)
N8A	Arbitration claim (notes for claimant)
N8B	Arbitration claim (notes for defendant)
N9	Acknowledgment of service/response pack (PD 10, para.2)
N9A	Admission and statement of means (specified amount) (PD 14, para. 2.1)
N9B	Defence and counterclaim (specified amount) (PD 15, para. 1.3)
N9C	Admission and statement of means (unspecified amount and non money claims) (PD 14, para. 2.1)
N9D	Defence and counterclaim (unspecified amount and non money claims) (PD 15, para. 1.3)
N10	Notice that acknowledgment of service has been filed (r. 10.4)
N11	Defence form (PD 55, para. 1.5)
N11B	Defence form (accelerated possession procedure) (assured shorthold tenancy) (PD 55, para. 1.5)
N11D	Defence form (demotion of tenancy) (PD 65, para. 5.2)
N11M	Defence form (mortgaged residential premises) (PD 55, para. 1.5)
N11R	Defence form (rented residential premises) (PD 55, para. 1.5)
N15	Acknowledgment of service (arbitration)
N16	General form of injunction
N16(1)	General form of injunction (formal parts only)
N16A	General form of application for injunction
N17	Judgment for claimant (amount to be decided by court)
N19	Limited civil restraint order
N19A	Extended civil restraint order
N19B	General civil restraint order
N20	Witness summons (PD 34, para. 1.2)
N21	Order for examination of deponent before the hearing (PD 34, para. 4.1)
N24	Blank form of order or judgment
N26	Order for possession
N26A	Order for possession (accelerated possession procedure) (assured shorthold tenancy)
N27	Order for possession on forfeiture (for rent arrears)
N27(2)	Order for possession on forfeiture (for rent arrears) (suspended)
N28	Order for possession (rented premises) (suspended)
N30	Judgment for claimant (default HC)
N30	Judgment for claimant (default CC)
N30(1)	Judgment for claimant (acceptance HC)
N30(1)	Judgment for claimant (acceptance CC)
N30(2)	Judgment for claimant (after determination HC)
N30(2)	Judgment for claimant (after determination CC)
N30(3)	Judgment for claimant (after redetermination HC)
N30(3)	Judgment for claimant (after redetermination CC)
N31	Order for possession (mortgaged premises) (suspended)
N32	Judgment for return of goods
N32(1) HP/CCA	Judgment for delivery of goods
N32(2) HP/CCA	Judgment for delivery of goods (suspended)
N32(3) HP/CCA	Judgment for delivery of goods
N32(4)	Variation order (return of goods)
N32(5) HP/CCA	Order for balance of purchase price
N33	Judgment for delivery of goods
N34	Judgment for claimant (after amount decided by court HC)
N34	Judgment for claimant (after amount decided by court CC)
N37	Hardship payment order
N39	Order to attend court for questioning
N40A(CC)	Warrant of arrest
N40A(HC)	Warrant of arrest

No.	Title
N40B(CC)	Warrant of committal
N40B(HC)	Warrant of committal
N54	Notice of eviction
N79A	Suspended committal order (for disobedience)
N84	Interim third party debt order
N85	Final third party debt order
N86	Interim charging order
N87	Final charging order
N110A	Anti-social behaviour injunction — power of arrest (Housing Act 1996, ss. 153C and 153D)
N113	Anti-social behaviour order under the Crime and Disorder Act 1998, s. 1B(4)
N119	Particulars of claim for possession (rented residential premises) (PD 55, para. 2.1)
N119A	Notes for guidance on completing particulars of claim form (rented residential premises)
N120	Particulars of claim for possession (mortgaged residential premises) (PD 55, para. 2.1)
N121	Particulars of claim for possession (trespassers) (PD 55, para. 2.1)
N122	Particulars of claim for demotion of tenancy (PD 65, para. 5.2)
N130	Application for an interim possession order
N133	Witness statement of the defendant to oppose the making of an interim possession order
N134	Interim possession order
N136	Order for possession
N142	Guardianship order (Housing Act 1996, Mental Health Act 1983)
N143	(Interim) Hospital order (Housing Act 1996, Mental Health Act 1983)
N144	Recognisance of defendant (Housing Act 1996)
N145	Recognisance of surety (Housing Act 1996)
N147	Remand order (Housing Act 1996) (bail granted)
N148	Remand order (Housing Act 1996) (bail not granted)
N149	Allocation questionnaire (small claims track) (PD 2B, para. 2.1)
N150	Allocation questionnaire (PD 26, para. 2.1)
N150A	Master/DJ's directions on allocation
N151	Allocation questionnaire (amount to be decided by court)
N151A	Master/DJ's directions on allocation
N152	Notice that [defence] [counterclaim] has been filed (PD 26, para. 2.5)
N153	Notice of allocation or listing hearing (PD 26, para. 6.2)
N154	Notice of allocation to fast track (PD 26, paras 4.2 and 9)
N155	Notice of allocation to multi-track (PD 26, paras 4.2 and 10)
N156	Order for further information (for allocation) (PD 26, para. 4.22))
N157	Notice of allocation to small claims track (PD 26, paras 4.2 and 8)
N158	Notice of allocation to small claims track (preliminary hearing) (PD 26, paras 4.2 and 8)
N159	Notice of allocation to small claims track (no hearing) (PD 26, paras 4.2 and 8)
N160	Notice of allocation to small claims track (with parties' consent) (PD 26, paras 4.2 and 8)
N161	Appellant's notice (PD 52, para. 5.1)
N161A	Guidance notes on completing the appellant's notice
N161B	Important notes for respondent
N162	Respondent's notice (PD 52, para. 7.3)
N162A	Guidance notes on completing the respondent's notice
N163	Skeleton argument (PD 52, paras 5.9 and 7.10)
N164	Appellant's notice (small claims track only) (PD 52, para. 5.8(1A))
N170	Listing questionnaire (pre-trial checklist) (PD 28, para. 6.1)
N171	Notice of date for return of listing questionnaire (PD 26, para. 6.1 and PD 28, para. 8.1)
N172	Notice of trial date
N173	Notice of non-payment of fee (r. 3.7)
N205A	Notice of issue (specified amount)

No.	Title
N205B	Notice of issue (unspecified amount)
N205C	Notice of issue (non-money claim)
N205D	Notice of issue (probate claim)
N206A	Notice of issue (accelerated possession procedure) (assured shorthold tenancy)
N206B	Notice of issue (possession claim)
N206D	Notice of issue (demotion claim)
N208	Part 8 claim form (PD 8, para. 2.2)
N208A	Part 8 notes for claimant
N208C	Part 8 notes for defendant
N209	Part 8 notice of issue
N210	Part 8 acknowledgment of service (PD 8, para. 3.2)
N210A	Part 8 acknowledgment of service (costs-only claim) (PD 43–48, para. 17.9)
N211	Part 20 claim form (r. 20.7)
N211A	Part 20 notes for claimant
N211C	Part 20 notes for defendant
N212	Part 20 notice of issue
N213	Part 20 acknowledgment of service (r. 20.12)
N215	Certificate of service (r. 6.10)
N216	Notice of returned document (r. 6.11)
N217	Order for substituted service (r. 6.8)
N218	Notice of service on a partner (PD 6, para. 4.2)
N225	Request for judgment and reply to admission (specified amount) (PD 12, para. 3)
N225A	Notice of part admission (specified amount) (r. 14.5)
N226	Notice of admission (unspecified amount) (r. 14.7)
N227	Request for judgment by default (amount to be decided by the court) (r. 12.5)
N228	Notice of admission (return of goods) (PD 7B, para. 8.5)
N235	Certificate of suitability of litigation friend (PD 21, para. 2.3)
N236	Notice of defence that amount claimed has been paid (r. 15.10)
N242	Notice of payment into court (under order—Part 37)
N242A	Notice of payment into court (in settlement — Part 36)
N243A	Notice of acceptance of payment into court (PD 36, para. 7.7)
N244	Application notice (PD 23, para. 2.1)
N244A	Notice of hearing of application (PD 23, para. 2.2)
N251	Notice of funding of case or claim
N252	Notice of commencement of assessment (PD 43–48, para. 2.3)
N253	Notice of amount allowed on provisional assessment (PD 43–48, para. 6.5)
N254	Request for default costs certificate (PD 43–48, para. 3.1)
N255	Default costs certificate HC (PD 43–48, para. 3.3)
N255	Default costs certificate CC (PD 43–48, para. 3.3)
N256	Final costs certificate HC (PD 43–48, para. 5.11)
N256	Final costs certificate CC (PD 43–48, para. 5.11)
N257	Interim costs certificate (PD 43–48, para. 5.11)
N258	Request for detailed assessment hearing (non-legal aid) (PD 43–48, para. 4.3)
N258A	Request for detailed assessment hearing (legal aid only)
N258B	Request for detailed assessment (costs payable out of a fund other than the Community Legal Service Fund)
N258C	Request for detailed assessment hearing pursuant to an order under part III of the Solicitors Act 1974
N259	Notice of appeal (PD 43–48, para. 48.1)
N260	Statement of costs (summary assessment) (PD 43–48, para. 3.2)
N265	List of documents (PD 31, para. 3.1)
N266	Notice to admit facts/admission of facts (r. 32.18)
N268	Notice to prove documents at trial (r. 32.19)
N271	Notice of transfer of proceedings (r. 30)
N279	Notice of discontinuance (r. 38.3)
N292	Order on settlement on behalf of child or patient (PD 21, para. 11.3)
N294	Claimant's application for a variation order

No.	Title
N316	Application for order that debtor attend court for questioning (PD 71, para. 1.1)
N316A	Application that an officer of a company attend court for questioning (PD 71, para. 1.1)
N322	Order for recovery of an award
N322A	Application to enforce an award (PD 70, para. 4.1)
N322H	Request to register a High Court judgment or order for enforcement
N349	Application for third party debt order (PD 72, para. 1.1)
N367	Notice of hearing to consider why fine should not be imposed (r. 34.10)
N379	Application for charging order on land or property (PD 73, para. 1.1)
N380	Application for charging order on securities (PD 73, para. 1.1)
N434	Notice of change of solicitor (rule 42.2)
N446	Request for reissue of enforcement or an order to obtain information from a judgment debtor (not warrant)
N460	Reasons for allowing or refusing permission to appeal
N461	Judicial review claim form (PD 54)
N461 (notes)	Guidance notes on completing the judicial review claim form
N462	Judicial review acknowledgment of service (PD 54)
N463	Judicial review — application for urgent consideration
No. 32	Order for examination within jurisdiction of witness before trial (r. 34.8)
No. 33	Application for issue of letter of request to judicial authority out of jurisdiction (r. 34.13)
No. 34	Order for issue of letter of request to judicial authority out of jurisdiction (r. 34.13)
No. 35	Letter of request for examination of witness out of jurisdiction (r. 34.13)
No. 37	Order for appointment of examiner to take evidence of witness out of jurisdiction (r. 34.13(4))
No. 41	Default judgment in claim relating to detention of goods (r. 12.4(1)(c))
No. 44	Part 24 judgment for claimant
No. 44A	Part 24 judgment for defendant
No. 45	Judgment after trial before judge without jury (PD 40B, para. 14)
No. 46	Judgment after trial before judge with jury (PD 40B, para. 14)
No. 47	Judgment after trial before a judge of the Technology and Construction Court or a master or district judge (PD 40B, para. 14)
No. 48	Order after trial of issue directed to be tried under r. 3.1(2)(i)
No. 49	Judgment against personal representatives (PD 40B, para. 14.3)
No. 52	Notice of claim (r. 19.8A(4)(a))
No. 52A	Notice of judgment or order to an interested party
No. 82	Application for appointment of a receiver
No. 83	Order directing application for appointment of receiver and granting injunction meanwhile
No. 84	Order for appointment of receiver by way of equitable execution (Supreme Court Act 1981, s. 37)
No. 93	Order under the Evidence (Proceedings in Other Jurisdictions) Act 1975
No. 94	Order for production of documents in marine insurance action [r. 58.14*]
No. 109	Order for reference to the European Court
No. 111	Certificate of money provisions contained in a judgment for registration in another part of the United Kingdom (Civil Jurisdiction and Judgments Act 1982, sch. 6)
No. 112	Certificate issued under the Civil Jurisdiction and Judgments Act 1982, sch. 7, in respect of non-money provisions for registration in another part of the United Kingdom
PF 1	Application for time (r. 3.1(2)(a))
PF 2	Order for time (r. 3.1(2)(a))
PF 3	Application for an extension of time for serving a claim form (r. 7.6)
PF 4	Order for an extension of time for serving a claim form (r. 7.6)
PF 6(A)	Application for permission to serve claim form out of jurisdiction (r. 6.21)
PF 6(B)	Order for service out of the jurisdiction (r. 6.21(4))
PF 7 QB	Request for service of document abroad (rr. 6.26(2)(a) and 6.27(2)(a))
PF 8	Standard 'unless' order (r. 26.5(5, PD 26, para. 2.5 and N150A)

[* The reference in the text issued by the Department for Constitutional Affairs is to a superseded practice direction.]

No.	Title
PF 11	Application for Part 24 judgment (whole claim) (r. 24.2)
PF 12	Application for Part 24 judgment (one or some of several claims) (r. 24.2)
PF 13	Order under Part 24 (No. 1)
PF 14	Order under Part 24 (No. 2)
PF 15	Order under Part 24 for amount found due upon detailed assessment of solicitor's bill of costs
PF 16	Notice of court's intention to make an order of its own initiative (r. 3.3(2) and (3))
PF 17	Order made on court's own initiative without a hearing (r. 3.3(4) and (5))
PF 19	Group Litigation Order (r. 19.1)
PF 20	Application for Part 20 directions
PF 21	Order for Part 20 directions
PF 21A	Order to add person as defendant to counterclaim (r. 20.5)
PF 22	Notice claiming contribution or indemnity against another defendant (r. 20.6)
PF 43	Application for security for costs (r. 25.12, also Companies Act 1985, s. 726)
PF 44	Order for security for costs (r. 25.12, also Companies Act 1985, s. 726)
PF 48	Court record available for use before and at hearing
PF 49	Request to parties to state convenient dates for hearing of 1st CMC
PF 50	Application for directions (Part 29)
PF 52	Order for case management directions in the multi-track (Part 29)
PF 53	Order for separate trial of an issue (r. 3.1(2)(i))
PF 56	Request for further information or clarification with provision for response (PD 18, para. 1.6(2))
PF 57	Application for further information or clarification (PD 18, para.5)
PF 58	Order for further information or clarification (r. 18.1)
PF 63	Interim order for receiver in pending claim
PF 67	Evidence in support of application to make order of House of Lords an order of the High Court (PD 40B, para. 13.2)
PF 68	Order making an order of the House of Lords an order of the High Court (PD 40B, para. 13.3)
PF 72	List of exhibits handed in at trial (PD 39, para.7)
PF 74	Order for trial of whole claim or of an issue by master or district judge (PD 2B, para. 4.1)
PF 78 QB	Solicitor's undertaking as to expenses (re letter of request) (r. 34.13(6)(b) and PD 34, para. 5.3(5))
PF 83	Judgment (non-attendance of party) (r. 39.3)
PF 84A	Order on application arising from a failure to comply with an order or condition (r. 3.13)
PF 84B	Judgment on application arising from a failure to comply with an order (r. 3.5(1) and (4))
PF 85A	Request for judgment (r. 3.5(2))
PF 85B	Judgment on request arising from a failure to comply with an order (r. 3.52)
PF 113	Evidence in support of application for service by an alternative method (PD 6, para. 9.1)
PF 130	Form of advertisement (r. 6.8)
PF 147	Application for order declaring solicitor ceased to act (death etc.)
PF 148	Order declaring solicitor has ceased to act
PF 149	Application by solicitor that he has ceased to act
PF 150	Order that solicitor has ceased to act
PF 152 QB	Evidence in support of application for examination of witness under the Evidence (Proceedings in Other Jurisdictions) Act 1975
PF 153 QB	Certificate witness under the Evidence (Proceedings in Other Jurisdictions) Act 1975
PF 154 QB	Order for registration of foreign judgment under the Foreign Judgments (Reciprocal Enforcement) Act 1933
PF 155	Certificates under s. 10 of the Foreign Judgments (Reciprocal Enforcement) Act 1933
PF 156 QB	Evidence in support of application for registration of a Community judgment
PF 157 QB	Order for registration of a Community judgment
PF 158 QB	Notice of registration of a Community judgment

No.	Title
PF 159 QB	Evidence in support of application for registration of a judgment of another Contracting State or Regulation State
PF 160 QB	Order for registration of a judgment of another Contracting State or Regulation State under the Civil Jurisdiction and Judgments Act 1982, s. 4
PF 161 QB	Notice of registration of a judgment of another Contracting State or Regulation State
PF 163 QB	Evidence in support of application for certified copy of a judgment for enforcement in another Contracting State or Regulation State
PF 164	Evidence in support of application for certificate as to money provisions of a judgment of the High Court for registration elsewhere in the United Kingdom
PF 165	Evidence in support of application for registration of a judgment of a court in another part of the United Kingdom containing non-money provisions
PF 166 QB	Certificate as to finality etc. of arbitration award for enforcement abroad (Arbitration Act 1996, s. 58)
PF 167 QB	Order to stay proceedings under the Arbitration Act 1996, s. 9 [r. 62.8*]
PF 168	Order to transfer claim from the High Court to county court (County Courts Act 1984, s. 40; High Court and County Courts Jurisdiction Order 1991; r. 30.3)
PF 170A	Application for child or patient's settlement in personal injury or Fatal Accidents Act claims before proceedings begun (r. 21.10(2); PD 21, paras 6 and 7)
PF 170B	Application for child or patient's settlement in personal injury or fatal accident claims in existing proceedings (r. 21.10(2); PD 21, paras 6 and 7)
PF 172 QB	Request for directions in respect of funds in court or to be brought into court (r. 21.11)
PF 197	Application for order for transfer from the Royal Courts of Justice to a district registry or vice versa or from one district registry to another (r. 30.2(4))
PF 198	Order under PF 197
PF 205	Evidence in support of application for permission to execute for earlier costs of enforcement under the Courts and Legal Services Act 1990, s. 15(3) and (4)
PF 244 RCJ	Application notice
PF 12 CH	Advertisement for creditors (PD 40, para 10)
PF 13 CH	Advertisement for claimants other than creditors
PF 14 CH	[Witness statement] [Affidavit] verifying list of creditors' claims
PF 15 CH	List of claims by persons claiming to be creditors following advertisement (Exhibit A referred to in [witness statement] [affidavit] in PF 14 CH)
PF 16 CH	List of claims by persons claiming to be creditors other than those sent in following advertisement (Exhibit B referred to in [witness statement] [affidavit] in PF 14 CH)
PF 17 CH	List of sums of money which may be due in respect of which no claim has been received (Exhibit C referred to in [witness statement] [affidavit] in PF 14 CH)
PF 18 CH	Notice to creditor to prove claim
PF 19 CH	Notice to creditor or other claimant to produce documents or particulars in support of claim
PF 20 CH	Notice to creditor of allowance of claim
PF 21 CH	Notice to creditor of disallowance of claim in whole or in part
PF 22 CH	Order for administration: beneficiaries' action reconstituted as creditors' claim (Van Oppen order)
PF 23 CH	[Witness statement] [Affidavit] verifying list of claims other than creditors' claims
PF 24 CH	List of claims not being creditors' claims sent following advertisement (Exhibit D referred to in [witness statement] [affidavit] in PF 23 CH)
PF 25 CH	List of claims not being creditors' claims other than those sent in following advertisement (Exhibit E referred to in [witness statement] [affidavit] in PF 23 CH)
PF 26 CH	Notice to claimant other than a creditor to prove claim
PF 27 CH	[Witness statement] [Affidavit] verifying accounts and answering usual enquiries in administration claim (rr. 32.8 and 32.16)
PF 28 CH	Executors' [or administrators'] account (account A in PF 27 CH)

[* The reference in the text issued by the Department for Constitutional Affairs is to a superseded practice direction.]

No.	Title
PF 29 CH	Master's order stating the results of proceedings before him on the usual accounts and inquiries in an administration claim
PF 30 CH	Security of receiver or administrator pending determination of a probate claim (PD 44)
PF 31 CH	Consent to act as trustee (r. 33.8)
PF 32 CH	[Witness statement] [Affidavit] in support of application for appointment of new litigation friend of child claimant
PF 33 CH	Order for distribution of a Lloyd's estate
PF 34 CH	Order in inquiry as to title in proceedings to enforce charging order where the defendant's title is not disclosed
PF 36 CH	Order appointing administrator pending determination of probate claim (PD 44)
PF 38 CH	Order in probate claim approving compromise (PD 44)
Commercial Court forms (Part 58)	
N1(CC)	Claim form (PD 58, para. 2.4)
N1C(CC)	Notes for the defendant
N9(CC)	Acknowledgment of service (PD 58, para. 5.1)
N208(CC)	Claim form (Part 8) (PD 58, para. 2.4)
N208C(CC)	Notes for the defendant
N210(CC)	Acknowledgment of service (Part 8) (PD 58, para. 5.2)
N211(CC)	Claim form (Part 20) (PD 58, para. 12)
N211C(CC)	Notes for defendant (Part 20)
N213(CC)	Acknowledgment of service (Part 20)
N244(C)	Application notice (PD 58, para. 10.7(2))
N265(CC)	List of documents
Technology and Construction forms (Part 60)	
TCC/CM1	Case management information sheet (PD 60, para. 8.2)
TCC/PTR1	Pre-trial review questionnaire (PD 60, para. 9.1)
Admiralty forms (Part 61)	
ADM1	Claim form (Admiralty claim *in rem*) (PD 61, para. 3.1)
ADM1A	Claim form (Admiralty claim) (PD 61, para. 12.3)
ADM1C	Notes for the defendant on replying to an *in rem* claim form
ADM2	Acknowledgment of service for Admiralty claims *in rem* (PD 61, para. 3.4)
ADM3	Collision statement of case (PD 61, para. 4.1)
ADM4	Application and undertaking for arrest and custody (PD 61, para. 5.1(1))
ADM5	Declaration in support of an application for warrant of arrest (PD 61, para. 5.1(2))
ADM6	Notice to consular officer of intention to apply for warrant of arrest (PD 61, para. 5.4)
ADM7	Request for caution against arrest (PD 61, para. 6.2)
ADM9	Warrant of arrest (PD 61, para. 5.5(1))
ADM10	Standard directions to Admiralty Marshal (PD 61, para. 5.6)
ADM11	Request for caution against release (PD 61, para. 7.1)
ADM12	Request for undertaking for release (PD 61, para. 7.4)
ADM12A	Request for withdrawal and caution against release (PD 61, para. 7.5)
ADM13	Application for judgment in default (PD 61, para. 8.1)
ADM14	Order for sale of a ship (PD 61, para. 9.2)
ADM15	Claim form (Admiralty limitation claim) (PD 61, para. 10.1(1))
ADM15B	Notes for defendant on replying to an Admiralty limitation claim
ADM16	Notice of admission of right of claimant to limit liability (PD 61, para. 10.3))
ADM16A	Defence to Admiralty limitation claim (PD 61, para. 10.2)
ADM16B	Acknowledgment of service (Admiralty limitation claim) (PD 61, para. 10.4)
ADM17	Application for restricted limitation decree (PD 61, para. 10.5)
ADM17A	Application for general limitation decree (PD 61, para. 10.6)
ADM18	Restricted limitation decree (PD 61, para. 10.5)
ADM19	General limitation decree
ADM20	Defendant's claim in limitation (PD 61, para. 10.14)
ADM21	Declaration as to liability of a defendant to file and serve statement of case under a decree of limitation (PD 61, para. 10.16)

No.	Title
Arbitration forms (Part 62)	
N8	Claim form (arbitration) (PD 62, para. 2.1)
N8A	Notes for claimant (arbitration)
N8B	Notes for defendant (arbitration)
N15	Acknowledgment of service (arbitration claim)

Table 2 Practice Forms

table 2 **65.26**

Contents

4.1 This table lists the practice forms that may be used under this practice direction. It contains forms that were previously:

- Prescribed forms contained in Appendix A to the Rules of the Supreme Court 1965
- Queen's Bench masters' practice forms
- Chancery masters' practice forms

4.2 Where a rule permits, a party intending to use a witness statement as an alternative to an affidavit should amend any form in this Table to be used in connection with that rule so that 'witness statement' replaces 'affidavit' wherever it appears in the form.

4.3 The forms in this list are reproduced in [*Practice Forms for Use in Proceedings in the High Court* (London: Royal Courts of Justice, 2000)], in practitioners' textbooks, and on Her Majesty's Courts Service website (www.hmcourts-service.gov.uk).

No.	Title
No. 53	Writ of fieri facias (sch. 1, RSC, ord. 45, r. 12)
No. 54	Writ of fieri facias on order for costs (sch. 1, RSC, ord. 45, r. 12)
No. 55	Notice of seizure (sch. 1, RSC, ord. 45, r. 2)
No. 56	Writ of fieri facias after levy of part (sch. 1, RSC, ord. 45, r. 12)
No. 57	Writ of fieri facias against personal representatives (sch. 1, RSC, ord. 45, r. 12)
No. 58	Writ of fieri facias de bonis ecclesiasticis (sch. 1, RSC, ord. 45, r. 12)
No. 59	Writ of sequestrari de bonis ecclesiasticis (sch. 1, RSC, ord. 45, r. 12)
No. 62	Writ of fieri facias to enforce Northern Irish or Scottish judgment (sch. 1, RSC, ord. 45, r. 12)
No. 63	Writ of fieri facias to enforce foreign registered judgment (sch. 1, RSC, ord. 45, r. 12)
No. 64	Writ of delivery: delivery of goods, damages and costs (sch. 1, RSC, ord. 45, r. 4)
No. 65	Writ of delivery: delivery of goods or value, damages and costs (sch. 1, RSC, ord. 45, r. 12(2))
No. 66	Writ of possession (sch. 1, RSC, ord. 45, r. 12(3))
No. 66A	Writ of possession (sch. 1, RSC, ord. 113, r. 7)
No. 67	Writ of sequestration (sch. 1, RSC, ord. 45, r. 12(4), and ord. 46, r. 5)
No. 68	Writ of restitution (sch. 1, RSC, ord. 46, rr. 1 and 3)
No. 69	Writ of assistance (sch. 1, RSC, ord. 46, rr. 1 and 3)
No. 71	Notice of renewal of writ of execution (sch. 1, RSC, ord. 46, r. 8)
No. 85	Order of committal or other penalty upon finding of contempt of court (sch. 1, RSC, ord. 52)
No. 87	Claim form for writ of habeas corpus ad subjiciendum
No. 88	Notice of adjourned application for writ of habeas corpus
No. 89	Writ of habeas corpus ad subjiciendum
No. 90	Notice to be served with writ of habeas corpus ad subjiciendum
No. 91	Writ of habeas corpus ad testificandum
No. 92	Writ of habeas corpus ad respondendum
No. 95	Certificate of order against the Crown (sch. 1, RSC, ord. 77, r. 15, and Crown Proceedings Act 1947, s. 25)
No. 96	Certificate of order against the Crown (sch. 1, RSC, ord. 77, r. 15, and Crown Proceedings Act 1947, s. 25)

No.	Title
No. 97	Claim form to grant bail (criminal proceedings) (sch. 1, RSC, ord. 79, r. 9(1)))
No. 97A	Claim form to vary arrangements for bail (criminal proceedings) (sch. 1, RSC, ord. 79, r. 9(1)))
No. 98	Order to release prisoner on bail (sch. 1, RSC, ord. 79, r. 9(6), (6A) and (6B))
No. 98A	Order varying arrangements for bail (sch. 1, RSC, ord. 79, r. 9(10)
No. 99	Order of Court of Appeal to admit prisoner to bail
No. 100	Notice of bail (sch. 1, RSC, ord. 79, r. 9(7)
No. 101	Witness summons — Crown Court
No. 103	Witness summons — Crown Court
No. 104	Attachment of earnings order (Attachment of Earnings Act 1971)
No. 105	Notice under the Attachment of Earnings Act 1971, s. 10(2)
No. 110	Certificate under s. 12 of the Civil Jurisdiction and Judgments Act 1982
PF 23 QB	Notice by sheriff of claim to goods taken in execution (sch. 1, RSC, ord. 17, r. 22)
PF 24 QB	Notice by execution creditor of admission or dispute of title of interpleader claimant
PF 25 QB	Interpleader application (sch. 1, RSC, ord. 17, r. 3)
PF 26 QB	Interpleader application by an enforcement officer
PF 27 QB	Evidence in support of interpleader application (sch. 1, RSC, ord. 17, r. 34)
PF 28 QB	Interpleader order (1) claim barred where an enforcement officer interpleads
PF 29 QB	Interpleader order (1a) enforcement officer to withdraw
PF 30 QB	Interpleader order (2) interpleader claimant substituted as defendant (sch. 1, RSC, ord. 17)
PF 31 QB	Interpleader order (3) trial of issue
PF 32 QB	Interpleader order (4) conditional order for an enforcement officer to withdraw and trial of issue
PF 34 QB	Interpleader order (6) summary disposal
PF 86	Praecipe for writ of fieri facias (sch. 1, RSC, ord. 45, r. 121) and ord. 46, r. 6)
PF 87	Praecipe for writ of sequestration (sch. 1, RSC, ord. 45, r. 124) and ord. 46, r. 6)
PF 88	Praecipe for writ of possession (sch. 1, RSC, ord. 45, r. 12(3; ord. 46, r. 6 and ord. 113, r. 7)
PF 89	Praecipe for writ of possession and fieri facias combined (sch. 1, RSC, ord. 45, r. 12 and ord. 46, r. 6)
PF 90	Praecipe for writ of delivery (sch. 1, RSC, ord. 45, r. 122) and ord. 46, r. 6)
PF 97 QB	Order for sale by an enforcement officer by private contract
PF 102	Bench warrant (sch. 1, RSC, ord. 52)
PF 103	Warrant of committal (general) (sch. 1, RSC, ord. 52) (not for orders to obtain information — use forms N40A and N40B)
PF 104	Warrant of committal (contempt in face of court) (sch. 1, RSC, ord. 52)
PF 105	Warrant of committal (failure of witness to attend) (sch. 1, RSC, ord. 52)
PF 106	Warrant of committal (of prisoner) (sch. 1, RSC, ord. 52)
PF 141	Witness statement/affidavit of personal service of judgment or order (sch. 1, RSC, ord. 45, r. 7)
PF 177	Order for written statement as to partners in firm (sch. 1, RSC, ord. 81, r. 2)
PF 179 QB	Evidence on registration of a bill of sale (Bills of Sale Act 1878; sch. 1, RSC, ord. 95)
PF 180 QB	Evidence on registration of an absolute bill of sale, settlement and deed of gift (sch. 1, RSC, ord. 95)
PF 181 QB	Evidence in support of an application for re-registration of a bill of sale (Bills of Sale Act 1878, s. 11; sch. 1, RSC, ord. 95)
PF 182 QB	Order for extension of time to register or re-register a bill of sale (Bills of Sale Act 1878, s. 14; sch. 1, RSC, ord. 95)
PF183 QB	Evidence for permission to enter a memorandum of satisfaction on a bill of sale (Bills of Sale Act 1878, s. 15; sch. 1, RSC, ord. 95; PD RSC Ord. 95, para. 1)
PF 184 QB	Claim form for entry of satisfaction on a registered bill of sale (Bills of Sale Act 1878, s. 15; sch. 1, RSC, ord. 95, r. 2; PD RSC Ord. 95, para. 3)
PF 185 QB	Order for entry of satisfaction on a registered bill of sale (Bills of Sale Act 1878, s. 14; sch. 1, RSC, ord. 95, r. 2)
PF 186 QB	Evidence on registration of assignment of book debts (Insolvency Act 1986, s. 344; sch. 1, RSC, ord. 95, r. 62)

No.	Title
PF 187	Claim form for solicitor's charging order (Solicitors Act 1974, s. 73; sch. 1, RSC, ord. 106, r. 2)
PF 188	Charging order: solicitor's costs (Solicitors Act 1974, s. 73; sch. 1, RSC, ord. 106, r. 2)
	PF 6 CH Certificate on application for permission to issue execution on suspended order for possession where defendant in default of acknowledgment of service (sch. 1, RSC, ord. 46, rr. 2 and 4 and CPR, Part 23)
PF 7 CH	Inquiry for persons entitled to the property of an intestate (sch. 1, RSC, ord. 85)
PF 8 CH	Application notice after master's findings on kin enquiry (*Re Benjamin* order) giving permission to distribute estate upon footing (sch. 1, RSC, ord. 85)
PF 9 CH	Order giving leave to distribute estate upon footing (*Re Benjamin*) (sch. 1, RSC, ord. 85)
PF 10 CH	Judgment in beneficiaries' administration claim (sch. 1, RSC, ord. 85)
PF 11 CH	Judgment in creditors' administration claim (sch. 1, RSC, ord. 85)

Table 3

table 3 **78.16**

Contents

5.1 This table lists county court forms in use before 26 April 1999 that have continued to be used on or after that date.

5.2 Where a rule permits, a party intending to use a witness statement as an alternative to an affidavit should amend any form in this Table to be used in connection with that rule so that 'witness statement' replaces 'affidavit' wherever it appears in the form.

No.	Title
N16	General form of injunction
N16(1)	General form of injunction (formal parts only)
N16A	General form of application for injunction
N27	Judgment for claimant in action of forfeiture for non-payment of rent
N35	Variation order
N35A	Variation order (determination)
N41	Order suspending judgment or order, and/or warrant of execution/committal
N41A	Order suspending warrant (determination)
N42	Warrant of execution
N46	Warrant of delivery and execution for damages and costs
N48	Warrant of delivery, where, if goods are not returned, levy is to be made for their value
N49	Warrant for possession of land
N50	Warrant of restitution (CCR, ord. 26, r. 17)
N51	Warrant of restitution (CCR, ord. 24, r. 6(1))
N52	Warrant of possession under CCR, ord. 24
N53	Warrant of execution or committal to district judge of foreign court
N55	Notice of application for attachment of earnings order
N55A	Notice of application for attachment of earnings order (maintenance)
N56	Form for replying to an attachment of earnings application (statement of means)
N58	Order for defendant's attendance at an adjourned hearing of an attachment of earnings application (maintenance)
N59	Warrant of committal under the (Attachment of Earnings Act 1971, s. 231)
N60	Attachment of earnings order (judgment debt)
N61	Order for production of statement of means
N61A	Order to employer for production of statement of earnings
N62	Summons for offence under Attachment of Earnings Act 1971
N63	Notice to show cause (Attachment of Earnings Act 1971, s. 23)
N64	Suspended attachment of earnings order
N64A	Suspended attachment of earnings order (maintenance)
N65	Attachment of earnings order (priority maintenance)

No.	Title
N65A	Attachment of earnings arrears order
N66	Consolidated attachment of earnings order
N66A	Notice of application for consolidated attachment of earnings order
N67	Judgment summons under the Debtors Act 1869
N68	Certificate of service (judgment summons)
N69	Order for debtor's attendance at an adjourned hearing of judgment summons
N70	Order of commitment under the County Courts Act 1984, s. 110
N71	Order revoking an order of commitment under the County Courts Act 1984, s. 110
N72	Notice to defendant where a committal order made but directed to be suspended under Debtors Act 1869
N73	New order on judgment summons
N74	Warrant of committal on a judgment summons under the Debtors Act 1869
N75	Endorsement on a warrant of committal sent to a foreign court
N76	Certificate to be endorsed on duplicate warrant of committal issued for rearrest of debtor
N77	Notice as to consequences of disobedience to court order
N78	Notice to show good reason why an order for your committal to prison should not be made (family proceedings only)
N79	Committal of other order, upon proof of disobedience of a court order or breach of undertaking
N80	Warrant for committal to prison
N81	Notice to solicitor to show cause why an undertaking should not be enforced by committal to prison
N82	Order for committal for failure by solicitor to carry out undertaking
N83	Order for discharge from custody under warrant of committal
N88	Interpleader summons to execution creditor
N88(1)	Interpleader summons to claimant claiming goods or rent under an execution
N89	Interpleader summons to persons making adverse claims to debt
N90	Summons for assaulting an officer of the court or rescuing goods
N91	Order of commitment and/or imposing a fine for assaulting an officer of the court or rescuing goods
N92	Request for administration order
N93	List of creditors furnished under the Attachment of Earnings Act 1971
N94	Administration order
N95	Order revoking an administration order
N95A	Order suspending or varying an administration order
N110	Power of arrest attached to injunction under the Domestic Violence and Matrimonial Proceedings Act 1976, s. 2
N110A	Antisocial behaviour injunction — power of arrest Housing Act 1996, s. 152/153
N112	Order for Arrest under the County Courts Act 1984, s. 110
N112A	Power of arrest, Attachment of Earnings Act 1971, s. 23
N117	General form of undertaking
N118	Notice to defendant where committal order made but directed to be suspended
N130	Application for possession including application for interim possession order
N133	Affidavit to occupier to oppose the making of an interim possession order
N134	Interim possession order
N136	Order for possession
N138	Injunction order
N139	Application for warrant of arrest
N140	Warrant of arrest
N200	Petition — Note old number was N208
N201	Request for entry of appeal — Note old number was N209
N202	Order for party to sue or defend on behalf of others having the same interest — Note old number was N210
N203	Notice to persons on whose behalf party has obtained leave to sue or defend — Note old number was N211

Civil Procedure Rules & Practice Directions

No.	Title
N204	Notice to person against whom party has obtained leave to sue or defend on behalf of others — Note old number was N212
N206	Notice of issue of fixed date claim
N207	Plaint note (adoption freeing for adoption)
N224	Request for service out of England and Wales through the court
N245	Application for suspension of a warrant and/or variation of an instalment order
N246	Claimant's reply to defendant's application to vary instalment order
N246A	Claimant's reply to defendant's application to suspend warrant of execution
N270	Notes for guidance (application for administration order)
N276	Notice of hearing of interpleader proceedings transferred from High Court
N277	Notice of pre-trial review of interpleader proceedings transferred from the High Court
N280	Order of reference of proceedings or questions for inquiry and report
N285	General form of affidavit
N288	Order to produce prisoner
N289	Judgment for defendant
N293	Certificate of judgment or order
N293A	Combined certificate of judgment and request for writ of fieri facias
N295	Order for sale of land
N296	Notice of judgment or order to party directed to be served with notice
N297	Order for accounts and inquiries in creditors' administration action
N298	Order for administration
N299	Order for foreclosure nisi of legal mortgage of land
N300	Order for sale in action by equitable mortgagee
N302	Judgment in action for specific performance (vendor's action, title accepted)
N303	Order for dissolution of partnership
N304	Notice to parties to attend upon taking accounts
N305	Notice to creditor to prove his claim
N306	Notice to creditor of determination of claim
N307	District judge's order (accounts and inquiries)
N309	Order for foreclosure absolute
N310	Partnership order on further consideration
N311	Administrative action order on further consideration
N313	Endorsement on certificate of judgment (transfer)
N317	Bailiff's report
N317A	Bailiff's report to the claimant
N319	Notice of execution of warrant of committal
N320	Request for return of, or to, warrant
N322	Order for recovery of money awarded by tribunal
N323	Request for warrant of execution
N324	Request for warrant of goods
N325	Request for warrant for possession of land
N326	Notice of issue of warrant of execution
N327	Notice of issue of warrant of execution to enforce a judgment or order
N328	Notice of transfer of proceedings to the High Court
N329	Notes for guidance on completion of N79
N330	Notice of sale or payment under execution in respect of a judgment for a sum exceeding £500
N331	Notice of withdrawal from possession or payment of moneys on notice of receiving or winding-up order
N332	Inventory of goods removed
N333	Notice of time when and where goods will be sold
N334	Request to hold walking possession and authority to re-enter
N336	Request and result of search in the attachment of earnings index
N337	Request for attachment of earnings order
N338	Request for statement of earnings
N339	Discharge of attachment of earnings order
N340	Notice as to payment under attachment of earnings order made by the High Court

No.	Title
N341	Notice of intention to vary attachment of earnings order under the Attachment of Earnings Act 1971, s. 10(2)
N342	Request for judgment summons
N343	Notice of result of hearing of a judgment summons issued on a judgment or order of the High Court
N344	Request for warrant of committal on judgment summons
N345	Certificate of payment under the Debtors Act 1869
N353	Order appointing receiver of real and personal property
N354	Order appointing receiver of partnership
N355	Interim order for appointment of receiver
N356	Order for appointment of receiver by way of equitable execution
N358	Notice of claim to goods taken in execution
N359	Notice to claimant to goods taken in execution to make deposit or give security
N360	Affidavit in support of interpleader summons other than an execution
N361	Notice of application for relief in pending action
N362	Order on interpleader summons under an execution where the claim is not established
N363	Order on interpleader summons under an execution where the claim is established
N364	Order on interpleader summons (other than execution) where there is an action
N365	Order on interpleader summons (other than execution) where there is no action
N366	Summons for neglect to levy execution
N368	Order fining a witness for non-attendance
N370	Order of commitment or imposing a fine for insult or misbehaviour
N372	Order for rehearing
N373	Notice of application for an administration order
N374	Notice of intention to review an administration order
N374A	Notice of intention to revoke an administration order
N375	Notice of further creditors' claim
N376	Notice of hearing administration order (by direction of the court)
N377	Notice of dividend
N388	Notice to probate registry to produce documents
N390	Notice that a claim has been entered against the Crown
N391	Crown Proceedings Act 1947 affidavit in support of application directing payment by Crown to judgment creditor
N392	Crown Proceedings Act 1947 notice of application for order directing payment by the Crown to the judgment creditor
N432	Affidavit on payment into court under the Trustee Act 1925, s. 63
N436	Order for sale of land under charging order
N437	District judge's report
N438	Notice to charge holder under Matrimonial Homes Act 1983
N440	Notice of application for time order by debtor or hirer — Consumer Credit Act 1974
N441	Notification of request for certificate of satisfaction or cancellation
N441A	Certificate of satisfaction or cancellation of judgment debt
N444	Details of sale under a warrant of execution
N445	Request for reissue of warrant
N447	Notice to claimant of date fixed for adjourned hearing
N448	Request to defendant for employment details, attachment of earnings
N449	Notice to employer, failure to make deductions under attachment of earnings order

CPR Part 5 Court Documents

[For commentary on a specific rule, please refer to the cross-references after the title of the rule.]

5.1 Scope of this Part

This part contains general provisions about—

(a) documents used in court proceedings; and

(b) the obligations of a court officer in relation to those documents.

5.2 Preparation of Documents

(1) Where under these Rules, a document is to be prepared by the court, the document may be prepared by the party whose document it is, unless—

(a) a court officer otherwise directs; or

(b) it is a document to which—

(ii) CCR Order 25, rule 8(9) (reissue of warrant where condition upon which warrant was suspended has not been complied with); or

(iii) CCR Order 28, rule 11(1) (issue of warrant of committal), applies.

(2) Nothing in this rule shall require a court officer to accept a document which is illegible, has not been duly authorised, or is unsatisfactory for some other similar reason.

5.3 Signature of Documents by Mechanical Means

r.5.3 **23.12**

Where any of these Rules or any practice direction requires a document to be signed, that requirement shall be satisfied if the signature is printed by computer or other mechanical means.

5.4 Supply of Documents from Court Records — General

r.5.4 **15.15, 15.17, 69.7**
r.5.4(1) **12.3, 15.15**
r.5.4(2)–(3) **15.15**
r.5.4(4) **15.17**
r.5.4(5)(a)–(b) **15.15**
r.5.4(7) **15.17**
r.5.4(7)(a)–(c) **15.15**
r.5.4(8)(a) **15.17**
r.5.4(9)–(10) **15.17**

(1) A court or court office may keep a publicly accessible register of claims which have been issued out of that court or court office.

(2) Any person who pays the prescribed fee may, during office hours, search any available register of claims.

(The practice direction contains details of available registers)

(3) A party to proceedings may, unless the court orders otherwise, obtain from the records of the court a copy of any document listed in paragraph 4.2A of the Practice Direction.

(4) A party to proceedings may, if the court gives permission, obtain from the records of the court a copy of any other document filed by a party or communication between the court and a party or another person.

(5) Any other person may—

(a) unless the court orders otherwise, obtain from the records of the court a copy of—

(i) a claim form, but not any documents filed with or attached to or intended by the claimant to be served with such claim form, subject to paragraph (6) and to any order of the court under paragraph (7);

(ii) a judgment or order given or made in public (whether made at a hearing or without a hearing), subject to paragraph (6); and

(b) if the court gives permission, obtain from the records of the court a copy of any other document filed by a party, or communication between the court and a party or another person.

(6) A person may obtain a copy of a claim form or a judgment or order under paragraph (5)(a) only if—

(a) where there is one defendant, the defendant has filed an acknowledgment of service or a defence;

(b) where there is more than one defendant, either—

(i) all the defendants have filed an acknowledgment of service or a defence;

(ii) at least one defendant has filed an acknowledgment of service or a defence, and the court gives permission;

(c) the claim has been listed for a hearing; or

(d) judgment has been entered in the claim.

(7) The court may, on the application of a party or of any person identified in the claim form—

(a) restrict the persons or classes of persons who may obtain a copy of the claim form;

(b) order that persons or classes of persons may only obtain a copy of the claim form if it is edited in accordance with the directions of the court; or

(c) make such other order as it thinks fit.

(8) A person wishing to obtain a copy of a document under paragraph (3), (4) or (5) must pay any prescribed fee and—

(a) if the court's permission is required, file an application notice in accordance with Part 23; or

(b) if permission is not required, file a written request for the document.

(9) An application for permission to obtain a copy of a document, or for an order under paragraph (7), may be made without notice, but the court may direct notice to be given to any person who would be affected by its decision.

(10) Paragraphs (3) to (9) of this rule do not apply in relation to any proceedings in respect of which a rule or practice direction makes different provision.

5.4A Supply of Documents to Attorney-General from Court Records

(1) The Attorney-General may search for, inspect and take a copy of any documents within a court file for the purpose of preparing an application or considering whether to make an application under section 42 of the Supreme Court Act 1981 or section 33 of the Employment Tribunals Act 1996 (restriction of vexatious proceedings).

(2) The Attorney-General must, when exercising the right under paragraph (1)—

(a) pay any prescribed fee; and

(b) file a written request, which must—

(i) confirm that the request is for the purpose of preparing an application or considering whether to make an application mentioned in paragraph (1); and

(ii) name the person who would be the subject of the application.

5.5 Filing and Sending Documents

r.5.5 **15.14**

(1) A practice direction may make provision for documents to be filed or sent to the court by—

(a) facsimile; or

(b) other electronic means.

(2) Any such practice direction may—

(a) provide that only particular categories of documents may be filed or sent to the court by such means;

(b) provide that particular provisions only apply in specific courts; and

(c) specify the requirements that must be fulfilled for any document filed or sent to the court by such means.

PD 5 Practice Direction — Court Documents

This practice direction supplements CPR Part 5

[For commentary on a specific paragraph, please refer to the cross-references after the title of the paragraph.]

Signature of Documents by Mechanical Means

1 Where, under rule 5.3, a replica signature is printed electronically or by other mechanical means on any document, the name of the person whose signature is printed must also be printed so that the person may be identified. This paragraph does not apply to claim forms issued through the Claims Production Centre.

Form of Documents

para.2.1 **24.4**

2.1 Statements of case and other documents drafted by a legal representative should bear his/her signature and if they are drafted by a legal representative as a member or employee of a firm they should be signed in the name of the firm.

2.2 Every document prepared by a party for filing or use at the court must:

(1) Unless the nature of the document renders it impracticable, be on A4 paper of durable quality having a margin, not less than 3.5 centimetres wide,

(2) be fully legible and should normally be typed,

(3) where possible be bound securely in a manner which would not hamper filing or otherwise each page should be endorsed with the case number,

(4) have the pages numbered consecutively,

(5) be divided into numbered paragraphs,

(6) have all numbers, including dates, expressed as figures, and

(7) give in the margin the reference of every document mentioned that has already been filed.

2.3 A document which is a copy produced by a colour photostat machine or other similar device may be filed at the court office provided that the coloured date seal of the court is not reproduced on the copy.

Supply of Documents to New Parties

3.1 Where a party is joined to existing proceedings, the party joined shall be entitled to require the party joining him to supply, without charge, copies of all statements of case, written evidence and any documents appended or exhibited to them which have been served in the proceedings by or upon the joining party which relate to any issues between the joining party and the party joined, and copies of all orders made in those proceedings. The documents must be supplied within 48 hours after a written request for them is received.

3.2 If the party joined is not supplied with copies of the documents requested under paragraph 3.1 within 48 hours, he may apply under Part 23 for an order that they be supplied.

3.3 The party by whom a copy is supplied under paragraph 3.1 or, if he is acting by a solicitor, his solicitor, shall be responsible for it being a true copy.

Supply of Documents from Court Records

paras.4.1–4.2 **15.15**
para.4.2A **15.16**
paras.4.3–4.4 **15.17**
paras.5.1–5.3 **15.14**

4.1 Registers of claims which have been issued are available for inspection at the following offices of the High Court at the Royal Courts of Justice:

(1) the Central Office of the Queen's Bench Division;

(2) Chancery Chambers;

(3) the Admiralty and Commercial Court Registry.

4.2 No registers of claims are at present available for inspection in county courts or in district registries or other offices of the High Court.

4.2A A party to proceedings may, unless the court orders otherwise, obtain from the records of the court a copy of:

(a) a certificate of suitability of a litigation friend;

(b) a notice of funding;
(c) a claim form or other statement of case together with any documents filed with or attached to or intended by the claimant to be served with such claim form;
(d) an acknowledgment of service together with any documents filed with or attached to or intended by the party acknowledging service to be served with such acknowledgement of service;
(e) a certificate of service, other than a certificate of service of an application notice or order in relation to a type of application mentioned in sub-paragraph (h)(i) or (ii);
(f) a notice of non-service;
(g) an allocation questionnaire;
(h) an application notice, other than in relation to:
  (i) an application by a solicitor for an order declaring that he has ceased to be the solicitor acting for a party; or
  (ii) an application for an order that the identity of a party or witness should not be disclosed;
(i) any written evidence filed in relation to an application, other than a type of application mentioned in sub-paragraph (h)(i) or (ii);
(j) a judgment or order given or made in public (whether made at a hearing or without a hearing);
(k) a statement of costs;
(l) a list of documents;
(m) a notice of payment into court;
(n) a notice of discontinuance;
(o) a notice of change; or
(p) an appellant's or respondent's notice of appeal.

4.3 An application under r. 5.4(4), (5)(b) or (6)(b)(ii) for permission to obtain a copy of a document, even if made without notice, must be made under Part 23 and the application notice must identify the document or class of document in respect of which permission is sought and the grounds relied upon.

4.4 An application under r. 5.4(7) by a party or a person identified in a claim form must be made:
(1) under Part 23; and
(2) to a master or district judge, unless the court directs otherwise.

Documents for Filing at Court

paras.5.1–5.3 **15.14**

5.1 The date on which a document was filed at court must be recorded on the document. This may be done by a seal or a receipt stamp.

5.2 Particulars of the date of delivery at a court office of any document for filing and the title of the proceedings in which the document is filed shall be entered in court records, on the court file or on a computer kept in the court office for the purpose. Except where a document has been delivered at the court office through the post, the time of delivery should also be recorded.

5.3 Filing by Facsimile
(1) Subject to paragraph (6) below, a party may file a document at court by sending it by facsimile ('fax').
(2) Where a party files a document by fax, he must not send a hard copy in addition.
(3) A party filing a document by fax should be aware that the document is not filed at court until it is delivered by the court's fax machine, whatever time it is shown to have been transmitted from the party's machine.
(4) The time of delivery of the faxed document will be recorded on it in accordance with paragraph 5.2.
(5) It remains the responsibility of the party to ensure that the document is delivered to the court in time.
(6) If a fax is delivered after 4 p.m. it will be treated as filed on the next day the court office is open.
(7) If a fax relates to a hearing, the date and time of the hearing should be prominently displayed.

(8) Fax should not be used to send letters or documents of a routine or non-urgent nature.
(9) Fax should not be used, except in an unavoidable emergency, to deliver:
(a) a document which attracts a fee;
(b) a Part 36 payment notice;
(c) a document relating to a hearing less than two hours ahead;
(d) trial bundles or skeleton arguments.
(10) Where (9)(a) or (b) applies, the fax should give an explanation for the emergency and include an undertaking that the fee or money has been dispatched that day by post or will be paid at the court office counter the following business day.
(11) Where courts have several fax machines, each allocated to an individual section, fax messages should only be sent to the machine of the section for which the message is intended.

5.4 Where the court orders any document to be lodged in court, the document must, unless otherwise directed, be deposited in the office of that court.

5.5 A document filed, lodged or held in any court office shall not be taken out of that office without the permission of the court unless the document is to be sent to the office of another court (for example, under CPR Part 30 (transfer)), except in accordance with CPR rule 39.7 (impounded documents) or in accordance with paragraph 5.6 below.

5.6 (1) Where a document filed, lodged or held in a court office is required to be produced to any court, tribunal or arbitrator, the document may be produced by sending it by registered post (together with a certificate as in paragraph 5.6(8)(b)) to the court, tribunal or arbitrator in accordance with the provisions of this paragraph.
(2) Any court, tribunal or arbitrator or any party requiring any document filed, lodged or held in any court office to be produced must apply to that court office by sending a completed request (as in paragraph 5.6(8)(a)), stamped with the prescribed fee.
(3) On receipt of the request the court officer will submit the same to a master in the Royal Courts of Justice or to a district judge elsewhere, who may direct that the request be complied with. Before giving a direction the master or district judge may require to be satisfied that the request is made in good faith and that the document is required to be produced for the reasons stated. The master or district judge giving the direction may also direct that, before the document is sent, an official copy of it is made and filed in the court office at the expense of the party requiring the document to be produced.
(4) On the direction of the master or district judge the court officer shall send the document by registered post addressed to the court, tribunal or arbitrator, with:
(a) an envelope stamped and addressed for use in returning the document to the court office from which it was sent;
(b) a certificate as in paragraph 5.6(8)(b);
(c) a covering letter describing the document, stating at whose request and for what purpose it is sent, referring to this paragraph of the practice direction and containing a request that the document be returned to the court office from which it was sent in the enclosed envelope as soon as the court or tribunal no longer requires it.
(5) It shall be the duty of the court, tribunal or arbitrator to whom the document was sent to keep it in safe custody, and to return it by registered post to the court office from which it was sent, as soon as the court, tribunal or arbitrator no longer requires it.
(6) In each court office a record shall be kept of each document sent and the date on which it was sent and the court, tribunal or arbitrator to whom it was sent and the date of its return. It shall be the duty of the court officer who has signed the certificate referred to in para. 5.6(8)(b) below to ensure that the document is returned within a reasonable time and to make inquiries and report to the master or district judge who has given the direction under paragraph (3) above if the document is not returned, so that steps may be taken to secure its return.
(7) Notwithstanding the preceding paragraphs, the master or district judge may direct a court officer to attend the court, tribunal or arbitrator for the purpose of producing the document.
(8) (a) I, of , an officer of the Court/Tribunal at /an arbitrator of /the Claimant/Defendant/Solicitor for the

Claimant/Defendant *[describing the Applicant so as to show that he is a proper person to make the request]* in the case of v. [19 No.] REQUEST that the following document [or documents] be produced to the Court/ Tribunal/arbitrator on the day of 19 [and following days] and I request that the said document [or documents] be sent by registered post to the proper officer of the Court/ Tribunal/arbitrator for production to that Court/Tribunal/arbitrator on that day.
(Signed).
Dated the day of 1999/2

(b) I, A. B., an officer of the Court of certify that the document sent herewith for production to the Court/Tribunal/arbitrator on the day of 1999/2 in the case of v. and marked 'A.B.' is the document requested on the day of 1999/2 and I FURTHER CERTIFY that the said document has been filed in and is produced from the custody of the Court.
(Signed)
Dated the day of 1999/2

Enrolment of Deeds and Other Documents

6.1 (1) Any deed or document which by virtue of any enactment is required or authorised to be enrolled in the Supreme Court may be enrolled in the Central Office of the High Court.

(2) Attention is drawn to the Enrolment of Deeds (Change of Name) Regulations 1994 which are reproduced in the appendix to this practice direction.

6.2 The following paragraph of the practice direction describes the practice to be followed in any case in which a child's name is to be changed and to which the 1994 Regulations apply.

6.3 (1) Where a person has by any order of the High Court, county court or Family Proceedings Court been given parental responsibility for a child and applies to the Central Office, Filing Department, for the enrolment of a deed poll to change the surname (family name) of a child who is under the age of 18 years (unless a child who is or has been married or has formed a civil partnership), the application must be supported by the production of the consent in writing of every other person having parental responsibility.

(2) In the absence of that consent, the application will be adjourned generally unless and until permission is given in the proceedings, in which the said order was made, to change the surname of the child and the permission is produced to the Central Office.

(3) Where an application is made to the Central Office by a person who has not been given parental responsibility for a child by any order of the High Court, county court or Family Proceedings Court for the enrolment of a deed poll to change the surname of the child who is under the age of 18 years (unless the child is or has been married or has formed a civil partnership), permission of the court to enrol the deed will be granted if the consent in writing of every person having parental responsibility is produced or if the person (or, if more than one, persons) having parental responsibility is dead or overseas or despite the exercise of reasonable diligence it has not been possible to find him or her for other good reason.

(4) In cases of doubt the Senior Master or, in his absence, the practice master will refer the matter to the Master of the Rolls.

(5) In the absence of any of the conditions specified above the Senior Master or the Master of the Rolls, as the case may be, may refer the matter to the Official Solicitor for investigation and report.

APPENDIX

Regulations made by the Master of the Rolls, Sir Thomas Bingham MR, on 3 March 1994 (SI 1994/604) under the Supreme Court Act 1981, s. 133(1).

1 (1) These regulations may be cited as the Enrolment of Deeds (Change of Name) Regulations 1994 and shall come into force on 1 April 1994.

(2) These Regulations shall govern the enrolment in the Central Office of the Supreme Court of deeds evidencing change of name (referred to in these Regulations as 'deeds poll').

2 (1) A person seeking to enrol a deed poll ('the applicant') must be a Commonwealth citizen as defined by section 37(1) of the British Nationality Act 1981.

(2) If the applicant is a British citizen, a British Dependent Territories citizen or a British Overseas citizen, he must be described as such in the deed poll, which must also specify the section of the British Nationality Act under which the relevant citizenship was acquired.

(3) In any other case, the applicant must be described as a Commonwealth citizen.

(4) The applicant must be described in the deed poll as single, married, widowed, divorced, a civil partner or former civil partner and, if a former civil partner, whether the civil partnership ended on death or dissolution.

3 (1) As proof of the citizenship named in the deed poll, the applicant must produce

(a) a certificate of birth; or

(b) a certificate of citizenship by registration or naturalisation or otherwise; or

(c) some other document evidencing such citizenship.

(2) In addition to the documents set out in paragraph (1), an applicant who is married or a civil partner must—

(a) produce his certificate of marriage or a civil partnership certificate; and

(b) show that the notice of his intention to apply for the enrolment of the deed poll has been given to his spouse or civil partner by delivery or by post to his spouse's or civil partner's last known address; and

(c) show that he has obtained the consent of his spouse or civil partner to the proposed change of name or that there is good reason why such consent should be dispensed with.

4 (1) The deed poll and the documents referred to in regulation 3 must be exhibited to a statutory declaration by a Commonwealth citizen who is a householder in the United Kingdom and who must declare that he is such in the statutory declaration.

(2) The statutory declaration must state the period, which should ordinarily not be less than 10 years, during which the householder has known the applicant and must identify the applicant as the person referred to in the documents exhibited to the statutory declaration.

(3) Where the period mentioned in paragraph (2) is stated to be less than 10 years, the Master of the Rolls, may, in his absolute discretion decide whether to permit the deed poll to be enrolled and may require the applicant to provide more information before so deciding.

5 If the applicant is resident outside the United Kingdom, he must provide evidence that such residence is not intended to be permanent and the applicant may be required to produce a certificate by a solicitor or as to the nature and probable duration of such residence.

6 The applicant must sign the deed poll in both his old and new names.

7 Upon enrolment the deed poll shall be advertised in the London Gazette by the clerk in charge for the time being of the Filing and Record Department at the Central Office of the Supreme Court.

8 (1) Subject to the following provisions of this regulation, these Regulations shall apply in relation to a deed poll evidencing the change of name of a child as if the child were the applicant.

(2) Paragraphs (3) to (8) shall not apply to a child who has attained the age of 16 and is or has been married or a civil partner.

(3) If the child is under the age of 16, the deed poll must be executed by a person having parental responsibility for him.

(4) If the child has attained the age of 16, the deed poll must, except in the case of a person mentioned in paragraph (2), be executed by a person having parental responsibility for the child and be endorsed with the child's consent signed in both his old and new names and duly witnessed.

(5) The application for enrolment must be supported—

(a) by a witness statement showing that the change of name is for the benefit of the child, and

(i) that the application is submitted by all persons having parental responsibility for the child; or

(ii) that it is submitted by one person having parental responsibility for the child with the consent of every other person; or

(iii) that it is submitted by one person having parental responsibility for the child

without the consent of every other such person, or by some other person whose name and capacity are given, for reasons set out in the affidavit;
and

(b) by such other evidence, if any, as the Master of the Rolls may require in the particular circumstances of the case.

(6) Regulation 4(2) shall not apply but the statutory declaration mentioned in regulation 4(1) shall state how long the householder has known the deponent under paragraph (5)(a) and the child respectively.

(7) Regulation 6 shall not apply to a child who has not attained the age of 16.

(8) In this regulation 'parental responsibility' has the meaning given in section 3 of the Children Act 1989.

9 The Enrolment of Deeds (Change of Name) Regulations 1983 and the Enrolment of Deeds (Change of Name) (Amendment) Regulations 1990 are hereby revoked.

[The text of the appendix incorporates amendments made by the Enrolment of Deeds (Change of Name) (Amendment) Regulations 2005 (SI 2005/2056).]

PD 5B Practice Direction — Pilot Scheme for Communication and Filing of Documents by Email

This practice direction supplements CPR rule 5.5

General

1.1 Section I of this practice direction provides for parties to claims in specified courts to:
(1) communicate with the court by email; and
(2) file specified documents by email.

1.2 Section II of this practice direction provides for parties to claims in specified courts to file specified documents electronically via an online forms service.

1.3 Section III of this practice direction contains general provisions which apply to both Section I and Section II.

1.4 This practice direction does not allow:
(1) communication with the court or the filing of documents by email; or
(2) use of the online forms service,
in proceedings to which the Civil Procedure Rules do not apply.

I COMMUNICATION AND FILING OF DOCUMENTS BY EMAIL

Interpretation

2.1 For the purposes of this Section:
(1) a specified court is a court or court office which has published an email address for the filing of documents on Her Majesty's Courts Service website www.hmcourts-service.gov.uk ('the Court Service website'); and
(2) a specified document is a document listed on the Court Service website as a document that may be sent to or filed in that court by email.

Communications and Documents Which May Be Sent by Email

3.1 Subject to para. 3.2, a party to a claim in a specified court may send a specified document to the court by email.

3.2 Subject to para. 3.2A, a party must not use email to take any step in a claim for which a fee is payable.

3.2A A party may make an application using email in the Preston Combined Court, where he is permitted to do so by PREMA (Preston Email Application Service) User Guide and Protocols.

3.3 Subject to para. 3.3A and PD 52, para. 15.1A, if:
(a) a fee is payable on the filing of a particular document; and
(b) a party purports to file that document by email,
the court shall treat the document as not having been filed.

3.3A A party may file by email an application notice by email in the Preston Combined Court where he is permitted to do so by PREMA (Preston Email Application Service) User Guide and Protocols.

(PD 52, para. 15.1A, provides for filing by email an appeal notice or application notice in proceedings in the Court of Appeal, Civil Division.)

(Rule 6.2(1)(e) permits service by email in accordance with the relevant practice direction. PD 6, para. 3 sets out the circumstances in which a party may serve a document by email.)

Technical Specifications of Email

4.1 The email message must contain the name, telephone number and email address of the sender and should be in plain text or rich text format rather than HTML.

4.2 Correspondence and documents may be sent as either text in the body of the email, or as attachments, except as mentioned in para. 4.3.

4.3 Documents required to be in a practice form must be sent in that form as attachments.

4.4 Court forms may be downloaded from the Court Service website.

4.5 Attachments must be sent in a format supported by the software used by the specified court to which it is sent. The format or formats which may be used in sending attachments to a particular specified court are listed on the Court Service website.

4.6 An attachment which is sent to a specified court in a format not listed on the Court Service website as appropriate for that court will be treated as not having been received by the court.

4.7 The length of attachments and total size of email must not exceed the maximum which a particular specified court has indicated that it can accept. This information is listed on the Court Service website.

4.8 Where proceedings have been commenced, the subject line of the email must contain the following information:
(1) the case number;
(2) the parties' names (abbreviated if necessary); and
(3) the date and time of any hearing to which the email relates.

II ONLINE FORMS SERVICE

Scope and Interpretation

5.1 Reference to an online forms service is reference to a service available at www.courtservice.gov.uk ('the forms website'). The forms website contains certain documents which a user may complete online and then submit electronically to a specified court.

5.2 For the purposes of this Section:
(1) a specified court is a court or court office listed on the Court Service website as able to receive documents filed electronically via the online forms service; and
(2) a specified document is a document which is available for completion on the forms website.

Filing of Documents Online

6.1 A party to a claim in a specified court may send a specified document to the court using the online forms service.

6.2 A party may use the online forms service to take a step in a claim for which a fee is payable. The fee must be paid, using the facilities available at the online forms service, before the application, or other document attracting a fee, is forwarded to the specified court.

6.3 The online forms service will assist the user in completing a document accurately but the user is responsible for ensuring that the rules and practice directions relating to the document have been complied with. Transmission by the service does not guarantee that the document will be accepted by the specified court.

III GENERAL PROVISIONS

Interpretation

7 In this Section:
(1) filing or sending a document 'electronically', means filing or sending it in accordance with Section I or Section II; and
(2) a reference to 'transmission' means, unless the context otherwise requires:
(a) in relation to Section I, the email sent by the party to the court; and
(b) in relation to Section II, the electronic transmission of the form by the online forms service to the court.

Provisions Relating to the Filing of Documents Electronically

8.1 Where a party files a document electronically, he must not send a hard copy of that document to the court.

8.2 A document is not filed until the transmission is received by the court, whatever time it is shown to have been sent.

8.3 The time of receipt of a transmission will be recorded electronically on the transmission as it is received.

8.4 If a transmission is received after 4 p.m.:
(1) the transmission will be treated as received; and
(2) any document attached to the transmission will be treated as filed,
on the next day the court office is open.

8.5 A party:
(1) sending an email in accordance with Section I; or
(2) using the online forms service in accordance with Section II,
is responsible for ensuring that the transmission or any document attached to it is filed within any relevant time limits.

8.6 The court will normally reply by email where:
(1) the response is to a message transmitted electronically; and
(2) the sender has provided an email address.

8.7 Parties are advised not to transmit electronically any correspondence or documents of a confidential or sensitive nature, as security cannot be guaranteed.

8.8 If a document transmitted electronically requires urgent attention, the sender should contact the court by telephone.

Statement of Truth in Documents Filed Electronically

9 Where a party wishes to file a document containing a statement of truth electronically, that party should retain the document containing the original signature and file with the court a version of the document satisfying one of the following requirements:
(1) the name of the person who has signed the statement of truth is typed underneath the statement;
(2) the person who has signed the statement of truth has applied a facsimile of his signature to the statement in the document by mechanical means; or
(3) the document that is filed is a scanned version of the document containing the original signature to the statement of truth.

CPR Part 6 Service of Documents

Part 6 **1.17, 13.6, 15.12, 15.21, 15.27, 15.30, 15.31, 16.1, 16.47, 16.61, 22.2, 60.2, 81.5, 82.13** [For commentary on a specific rule, please refer to the cross-references after the title of the rule.]

I GENERAL RULES ABOUT SERVICE

6.1 Part 6 Rules about Service Apply Generally

The rules in this Part apply to the service of documents, except where—

(a) any other enactment, a rule in another Part, or a practice direction makes a different provision; or

(b) the court orders otherwise.

(For service in possession claims, see Part 55)

6.2 Methods of Service — General

r.6.2 **15.12, 15.20, 15.21, 15.40, 16.61, 20.20** r.6.2(1)(a)–(e) **15.24**
r.6.2(1) **15.21, 15.24, 15.32, 15.33** r.6.2(2) **15.30, 15.31**

(1) A document may be served by any of the following methods—

(a) personal service, in accordance with rule 6.4;

(b) first class post (or an alternative service which provides for delivery on the next working day);
(c) leaving the document at a place specified in rule 6.5;
(d) through a document exchange in accordance with the relevant practice direction; or
(e) by fax or other means of electronic communication in accordance with the relevant practice direction.

(Rule 6.8 provides for the court to permit service by an alternative method)

(2) A company may be served by any method permitted under this Part as an alternative to the methods of service set out in—
(a) section 725 of the Companies Act 1985 (service by leaving a document at or posting it to an authorised place);
(b) section 695 of that Act (service on overseas companies); and
(c) section 694Aof that Act (service of documents on companies incorporated outside the UK and Gibraltar and having a branch in Great Britain).

6.3 Who is to Serve

r.6.3 **32.20, 32.35, 61.30, 71.30**
r.6.3(1) **15.18, 32.1**
r.6.3(1)(b) **15.20**
r.6.3(2) **15.19**
r.6.3(3) **15.19**

(b) first class post (For service in possession claims, see Part 55);

(1) The court will serve a document which it has issued or prepared except where—
(a) a rule provides that a party must serve the document in question;
(b) the party on whose behalf the document is to be served notifies the court that he wishes to serve it himself;
(c) a practice direction provides otherwise;
(d) the court orders otherwise; or
(e) the court has failed to serve and has sent a notice of non-service to the party on whose behalf the document is to be served in accordance with rule 6.11.

(2) Where the court is to serve a document, it is for the court to decide which of the methods of service specified in rule 6.2 is to be used.

(3) Where a party prepares a document which is to be served by the court, that party must file a copy for the court, and for each party to be served.

6.4 Personal Service

r.6.4 **15.21, 15.22, 15.24, 79.70, 80.7, 81.5, 82.13**
r.6.4(2) **15.24**
r.6.4(2A) **15.34**
r.6.4(3) **15.22**
r.6.4(4) **15.30, 15.32, 23.11**
r.6.4(5) **15.33**

(1) A document to be served may be served personally, except as provided in paragraphs (2) and (2A).

(2) Where a solicitor—
(a) is authorised to accept service on behalf of a party; and
(b) has notified the party serving the document in writing that he is so authorised,
a document must be served on the solicitor, unless personal service is required by an enactment, rule, practice direction or court order.

(2A) In civil proceedings by or against the Crown, as defined in rule 66.1(2), documents required to be served on the Crown may not be served personally.

(3) A document is served personally on an individual by leaving it with that individual.

(4) A document is served personally on a company or other corporation by leaving it with a person holding a senior position within the company or corporation.

(The service practice direction sets out the meaning of 'senior position')

(5) A document is served personally on a partnership where partners are being sued in the name of their firm by leaving it with—
(a) a partner; or
(b) a person who, at the time of service, has the control or management of the partnership business at its principal place of business.

6.5 Address for Service

r.6.5 **15.21, 15.23, 15.24, 23.3**
r.6.5(1) **15.2, 15.38**
r.6.5(2) **15.23, 15.26, 15.30, 15.32, 15.33, 16.62, 21.3, 22.2, 26.12, 29.11**
r.6.5(3) **15.23, 22.2, 22.4**
r.6.5(4) **15.23**
r.6.5(5) **15.24, 21.3, 22.2**
r.6.5(6) **15.23, 15.24, 15.30, 15.31, 15.32, 15.33, 96.41**
r.6.5(8) **15.34, 20.7**

(1) Except as provided by Section III of this Part (service out of the jurisdiction) a document must be served within the jurisdiction.

('Jurisdiction' is defined in rule 2.3)

(2) A party must give an address for service within the jurisdiction. Such address must include a full postcode, unless the court orders otherwise.

(Paragraph 2.4 of the Practice Direction to Part 16 contains provision about the content of an address for service)

(3) Where a party—
 (a) does not give the business address of his solicitor as his address for service; and
 (b) resides or carries on business within the jurisdiction,
 he must give his residence or place of business as his address for service.

(4) Any document to be served—
 (a) by first class post (or an alternative service which provides for delivery on the next working day);
 (b) by leaving it at the place of service;
 (c) through a document exchange; or
 (d) by fax or by other means of electronic communication,
 must be sent or transmitted to, or left at, the address for service given by the party to be served.

(5) Where—
 (a) a solicitor is acting for the party to be served; and
 (b) the document to be served is not the claim form;
 the party's address for service is the business address of his solicitor.

(Rule 6.13 specifies when the business address of a defendant's solicitor may be the defendant's address for service in relation to the claim form)

(6) Where—
 (a) no solicitor is acting for the party to be served; and
 (b) the party has not given an address for service,
 the document must be sent or transmitted to, or left at, the place shown in the following table.

(Rule 6.2(2) sets out the statutory methods of service on a company)

Nature of party to be served	Place of service
Individual	• Usual or last known residence.
Proprietor of a business	• Usual or last known residence; or • Place of business or last known place of business.
Individual who is suing or being sued in the name of a firm	• Usual or last known residence; or • Principal or last known place of business of the firm.
Corporation incorporated in England and Wales other than a company	• Principal office of the corporation; or • Any place within the jurisdiction where the corporation carries on its activities and which has a real connection with the claim.
Company registered in England and Wales	• Principal office of the company; or • Any place of business of the company within the jurisdiction which has a real connection with the claim.
Any other company or corporation	• Any place within the jurisdiction where the corporation carries on its activities; or • Any place of business of the company within the jurisdiction.

(7) This rule does not apply where an order made by the court under rule 6.8 (service by an alternative method) specifies where the document in question may be served.

(Rule 42.1 provides that if the business address of his solicitor is given that solicitor will be treated as acting for that party)

(8) In civil proceedings by or against the Crown, as defined in rule 66.1(2)—
(a) service on the Attorney General must be effected on the Treasury Solicitor;
(b) service on a government department must be effected on the solicitor acting for that department as required by section 18 of the Crown Proceedings Act 1947.

(The practice direction to Part 66 gives the list published under section 17 of that Act of the solicitors acting for the different government departments on whom service is to be effected, and of their addresses)

6.6 Service of Documents on Children and Patients

r.6.6 **14.35, 15.24**
r.6.6(1)–(2) **15.29**
r.6.6(4)–(5) **15.29**

(1) The following table shows the person on whom a document must be served if it is a document which would otherwise be served on a child or a patient—

Type of document	Nature of party	Person to be served
Claim form	Child who is not also a patient	• One of the child's parents or guardians; or • If there is no parent or guardian, the person with whom the child resides or in whose care the child is.
Claim form	Patient	• The person authorised under Part VII of the Mental Health Act 1983 to conduct the proceedings in the name of the patient or on his behalf; or • If there is no person so authorised, the person with whom the patient resides or in whose care the patient is.
Application for an order appointing a litigation friend, where a child or patient has no litigation friend	Child or patient	See rule 21.8.
Any other document	Child or patient	The litigation friend who is conducting proceedings on behalf of the child or patient.

(2) The court may make an order permitting a document to be served on the child or patient, or on some person other than the person specified in the table in this rule.
(3) An application for an order under paragraph (2) may be made without notice.
(4) The court may order that, although a document has been served on someone other than the person specified in the table, the document is to be treated as if it had been properly served.
(5) This rule does not apply where the court has made an order under rule 21.2(3) allowing a child to conduct proceedings without a litigation friend.

(Part 21 contains rules about the appointment of a litigation friend)

6.7 Deemed Service

r.6.7 **1.17, 3.3, 15.3, 15.19, 15.20, 15.26, 15.27, 15.37, 20.14, 20.20, 32.20, 64.17, 97.41, 97.42**
r.6.7(1) **15.36, 15.37, 16.61**
r.6.7(2) **15.37**
r.6.7(3) **3.3, 15.37**

(1) A document which is served in accordance with these rules or any relevant practice direction shall be deemed to be served on the day shown in the following table—

Method of Service	Deemed day of service
First class post (or an alternative service which provides for delivery on the next working day)	The second day after it was posted.
Document exchange	The second day after it was left at the document exchange.
Delivering the document to or leaving it at a permitted address	The day after it was delivered to or left at the permitted address.
Fax	• If it is transmitted on a business day before 4 p.m., on that day; or • In any other case, on the business day after the day on which it is transmitted.
Other electronic method	The second day after the day on which it is transmitted.

(2) If a document is served personally—
(a) after 5 p.m., on a business day; or
(b) at any time on a Saturday, Sunday or a Bank Holiday,
it will be treated as being served on the next business day.
(3) In this rule—
'business day' means any day except Saturday, Sunday or a bank holiday; and
'bank holiday' includes Christmas Day and Good Friday.

6.8 Service by an Alternative Method

r.6.8 **15.11, 15.21, 15.23, 15.26, 15.38, 16.54, 16.61, 20.12, 69.4**
r.6.8(1) **15.38**
r.6.8(2)(a)–(b) **15.39**
r.6.8(3) **15.39**

(1) Where it appears to the court that there is a good reason to authorise service by a method not permitted by these Rules, the court may make an order permitting service by an alternative method.
(2) An application for an order permitting service by an alternative method—
(a) must be supported by evidence; and
(b) may be made without notice.
(3) An order permitting service by an alternative method must specify—
(a) the method of service; and
(b) the date when the document will be deemed to be served.

6.9 Power of Court to Dispense with Service

r.6.9 **12.11, 15.12, 15.41, 16.54, 20.12**
r.6.9(1) **15.12, 15.41**
r.6.9(2) **15.41**

(1) The court may dispense with service of a document.
(2) An application for an order to dispense with service may be made without notice.

6.10 Certificate of Service

r.6.10 **15.20, 64.14, 64.25, 69.4**

Where a rule, practice direction or court order requires a certificate of service, the certificate must state the details set out in the following table—

Method of service	Details to be certified
Post	Date of posting
Personal	Date of personal service
Document exchange	Date of delivery to the document exchange
Delivery of document to or leaving it at a permitted place	Date when the document was delivered to or left at the permitted place
Fax	Date and time of transmission
Method of service	Details to be certified
Other electronic means	Date of transmission and the means used
Alternative method permitted by the court	As required by the court

6.11 Notification of Outcome of Postal Service by the Court

Where—
(a) a document to be served by the court is served by post; and
(b) such document is returned to the court,
the court must send notification to the party who requested service stating that the document has been returned.

6.11A Notice of Non-service by Bailiff

r.6.11A **15.19**

Where—
(a) the court bailiff is to serve a document; and
(b) the bailiff is unable to serve it,
the court must send notification to the party who requested service.

II SPECIAL PROVISIONS ABOUT SERVICE OF THE CLAIM FORM

6.12 General Rules about Service Subject to Special Rules about Service of Claim Form

The general rules about service are subject to the special rules about service contained in rules 6.13 to 6.16.

6.13 Service of Claim Form by the Court — Defendant's Address for Service

r.6.13 **15.24, 15.30, 15.32, 15.33**

(1) Where a claim form is to be served by the court, the claim form must include the defendant's address for service.
(2) For the purposes of paragraph (1), the defendant's address for service may be the business address of the defendant's solicitor if he is authorised to accept service on the defendant's behalf but not otherwise.

(Rule 6.5 contains general provisions about the address for service)

(Paragraph 2.4 of the Practice Direction to Part 16 contains provision about the content of an address for service)

6.14 Certificate of Service Relating to the Claim Form

r.6.14 **15.19** r.6.14(2)(b) **15.20**
r.6.14(2)(a) **87.10**

(1) Where a claim form is served by the court, the court must send the claimant a notice which will include the date when the claim form is deemed to be served under rule 6.7.
(2) Where the claim form is served by the claimant—
(a) he must file a certificate of service within 7 days of service of the claim form; and
(b) he may not obtain judgment in default under Part 12 unless he has filed the certificate of service.

(Rule 6.10 specifies what a certificate of service must show)

6.15 Service of Claim Form by Contractually Agreed Method

r.6.15(1)–(2) **15.28**

(1) Where—
(a) a contract contains a term providing that, in the event of a claim being issued in relation to the contract, the claim form may be served by a method specified in the contract; and
(b) a claim form containing only a claim in respect of that contract is issued,
the claim form shall, subject to paragraph (2), be deemed to be served on the defendant if it is served by a method specified in the contract.
(2) Where the claim form is served out of the jurisdiction in accordance with the contract, it shall not be deemed to be served on the defendant unless—
(a) permission to serve it out of the jurisdiction has been granted under rule 6.20; or
(b) it may be served without permission under rule 6.19.

6.16 Service of Claim Form on Agent of Principal Who Is Overseas

r.6.16 **17.4, 18.2** r.6.16(4) **15.35, 18.2, 18.5, 26.3**
r.6.16(1)–(3) **15.35** r.6.16(6) **15.35**

(1) Where—
 (a) the defendant is overseas; and
 (b) the conditions specified in paragraph (2) are satisfied,
 the court may, on an application only, permit a claim form relating to a contract to be served on a defendant's agent.
(2) The court may not make an order under this rule unless it is satisfied that—
 (a) the contract to which the claim relates was entered into within the jurisdiction with or through the defendant's agent; and
 (b) at the time of the application either the agent's authority has not been terminated or he is still in business relations with his principal.
(3) An application under this rule—
 (a) must be supported by evidence; and
 (b) may be made without notice.
(4) An order under this rule must state a period within which the defendant must respond to the particulars of claim.
(Rule 9.2 sets out how a defendant may respond to particulars of claim)
(5) The power conferred by this rule is additional to the power conferred by rule 6.8 (service by an alternative method).
(6) Where the court makes an order under this rule, the claimant must send to the defendant copies of—
 (a) the order; and
 (b) the claim form.

III SPECIAL PROVISIONS ABOUT SERVICE OUT OF THE JURISDICTION

6.17 Scope of This Section

r.6.17 **15.2, 76.36, 81.5**

This Section contains rules about—
(a) service out of the jurisdiction;
(b) how to obtain the permission of the court to serve out of the jurisdiction; and
(c) the procedure for serving out of the jurisdiction.
(Rule 2.3 defines 'jurisdiction')

6.18 Definitions

r.6.18 **15.2, 76.36, 81.5**
r.6.18(g) **16.47**

For the purposes of this Part—
(a) 'the 1982 Act' means the Civil Jurisdiction and Judgments Act 1982;
(b) 'the Hague Convention' means the Convention on the service abroad of judicial and extra-judicial documents in civil or commercial matters signed at the Hague on November 15, 1965;
(c) 'Contracting State' has the meaning given by section 1(3) of the 1982 Act;
(d) 'Convention territory' means the territory or territories of any Contracting State to which the Brussels or Lugano Conventions (as defined in section 1(1) of the 1982 Act) apply;
(e) 'Civil Procedure Convention' means the Brussels and Lugano Conventions and any other Convention entered into by the United Kingdom regarding service outside the jurisdiction;
(ea) 'the Service Regulation' means Council Regulation (EC) No 1348/2000 of 29 May 2000 on the service in the Member States of judicial and extrajudicial documents in civil or commercial matters;
(f) 'United Kingdom Overseas Territory' means those territories as set out in the relevant practice direction.
(g) 'domicile' is to be determined—
 (i) in relation to a Convention territory, in accordance with sections 41 to 46 of the 1982 Act;

(ii) in relation to a Regulation State, i n accordance with the Judgments Regulation and paragraphs 9 to 12 of Schedule 1 to the Civil Jurisdiction and Judgments Order 2001;

(h) 'claim form' includes petition and application notice; and

(i) 'claim' includes petition and application.

(j) 'the Judgments Regulation' means Council Regulation (EC) No. 44/2001 of 22nd December 2000 on jurisdiction and the recognition and enforcement of judgments in civil and commercial matters; and

(k) 'Regulation State' has the same meaning as 'Member State' in the Judgments Regulation, that is all Member States except Denmark.

(Rule 6.30 provides that where an application notice is to be served out of the jurisdiction under this Part, rules 6.21(4), 6.22 and 6.23 do not apply)

6.19 Service Out of the Jurisdiction Where the Permission of the Court Is Not Required

r.6.19 **15.2, 15.28, 16.42, 16.64, 18.2, 18.5, 20.8, 20.9, 38.5, 76.36, 81.5**
r.6.19(1) **16.18, 16.42, 20.8**
r.6.19(1A) **16.18, 16.42, 20.8**
r.6.19(2) **16.42**
r.6.19(3) **16.42**

(1) A claim form may be served on a defendant out of the jurisdiction where each claim included in the claim form made against the defendant to be served is a claim which the court as power to determine under the 1982 Act and—

(a) no proceedings between the parties concerning the same claim are pending in the courts of any other part of the United Kingdom or any other Convention territory; and

(b) (i) the defendant is domiciled in the United Kingdom or in any Convention territory;

(ii) Article 16 of Schedule 1 or 3C to the 1982 Act, or paragraph 11 of Schedule 4 to that Act, refers to the proceedings; or

(iii) the defendant is a party to an agreement conferring jurisdiction to which Article 17 of Schedule 1 or 3C to the 1982 Act, or paragraph 12 of Schedule 4 to that Act, refers.

(1A) A claim form may be served on a defendant out of the jurisdiction where each claim included in the claim form made against the defendant to be served is a claim which the court has power to determine under the Judgments Regulation and—

(a) no proceedings between the parties concerning the same claim are pending in the courts of any other part of the United Kingdom or any other Regulation State; and

(b) (i) the defendant is domiciled in the United Kingdom or in any Regulation State;

(ii) Article 22 of the Judgments Regulation refers to the proceedings; or

(iii) the defendant is a party to an agreement conferring jurisdiction to which Article 23 of the Judgments Regulation refers.

(2) A claim form may be served on a defendant out of the jurisdiction where each claim included in the claim form made against the defendant to be served is a claim which, under any other enactment, the court has power to determine, although—

(a) the person against whom the claim is made is not within the jurisdiction; or

(b) the facts giving rise to the claim did not occur within the jurisdiction.

(3) Where a claim form is to be served out of the jurisdiction under this rule, it must contain a statement of the grounds on which the claimant is entitled to serve it out of the jurisdiction.

6.20 Service Out of the Jurisdiction Where the Permission of the Court Is Required

r.6.20 **15.2, 15.4, 15.28, 16.1, 16.44, 16.45, 16.46, 16.65, 38.5, 76.36, 81.5**
r.6.20(1) **16.47**
r.6.20(2) **16.48**
r.6.20(3) **16.45, 16.49**
r.6.20(3)(b) **16.53**
r.6.20(3A) **16.49**
r.6.20(4) **16.48**
r.6.20(5) **16.50**
r.6.20(5)(a)–(d) **16.50**
r.6.20(6) **16.50**
r.6.20(7) **16.50**
r.6.20(8) **16.51**
r.6.20(11) **16.52**

In any proceedings to which rule 6.19 does not apply, a claim form may be served out of the jurisdiction with the permission of the court if—

General grounds

(1) a claim is made for a remedy against a person domiciled within the jurisdiction;

(2) a claim is made for an injunction[GL] ordering the defendant to do or refrain from doing an act within the jurisdiction;

(3) a claim is made against someone on whom the claim form has been or will be served (otherwise than in reliance on this paragraph) and—
   (a) there is between the claimant and that person a real issue which it is reasonable for the court to try; and
   (b) the claimant wishes to serve the claim form on another person who is a necessary or proper party to that claim;

(3A) a claim is a Part 20 claim and the person to be served is a necessary or proper party to the claim against the Part 20 claimant;

Claims for interim remedies

(4) a claim is made for an interim remedy under section 25(1) of the 1982 Act;

Claims in relation to contracts

(5) a claim is made in respect of a contract where the contract—
   (a) was made within the jurisdiction;
   (b) was made by or through an agent trading or residing within the jurisdiction;
   (c) is governed by English law; or
   (d) contains a term to the effect that the court shall have jurisdiction to determine any claim in respect of the contract;

(6) a claim is made in respect of a breach of contract committed within the jurisdiction;

(7) a claim is made for a declaration that no contract exists where, if the contract was found to exist, it would comply with the conditions set out in paragraph (5);

Claims in tort

(8) a claim is made in tort where—
   (a) damage was sustained within the jurisdiction; or
   (b) the damage sustained resulted from an act committed within the jurisdiction;

Enforcement

(9) a claim is made to enforce any judgment or arbitral award;

Claims about property within the jurisdiction

(10) the whole subject matter of a claim relates to property located within the jurisdiction;

Claims about trusts etc.

(11) a claim is made for any remedy which might be obtained in proceedings to execute the trusts of a written instrument where—
   (a) the trusts ought to be executed according to English law; and
   (b) the person on whom the claim form is to be served is a trustee of the trusts;

(12) a claim is made for any remedy which might be obtained in proceedings for the administration of the estate of a person who died domiciled within the jurisdiction;

(13) a claim is made in probate proceedings which includes a claim for the rectification of a will;

(14) a claim is made for a remedy against the defendant as constructive trustee where the defendant's alleged liability arises out of acts committed within the jurisdiction;

(15) a claim is made for restitution where the defendant's alleged liability arises out of acts committed within the jurisdiction;

Claims by HM Revenue and Customs

(16) a claim is made by the Commissioners for HM Revenue and Customs relating to duties or taxes against a defendant not domiciled in Scotland or Northern Ireland;

Claim for costs order in favour of or against third parties

(17) a claim is made by a party to proceedings for an order that the court exercise its power under section 51 of the Supreme Court Act 1981 to make a costs order in favour of or against a person who is not a party to those proceedings;

(Rule 48.2 sets out the procedure where the court is considering whether to exercise its discretion to make a costs order in favour of or against a non-party)

Admiralty claims

(17A) a claim is—

(a) in the nature of salvage and any part of the services took place within the jurisdiction; or

(b) to enforce a claim under section 153, 154 or 175 of the Merchant Shipping Act 1995.

Claims under various enactments

(18) a claim is made under an enactment specified in the relevant practice direction.

6.21 Application for Permission to Serve Claim Form Out of Jurisdiction

r.6.21 **15.2, 16.45, 16.46, 76.36, 81.5**
r.6.21(1)(b) **16.44**
r.6.21(2A) **16.53**
r.6.21(4) **17.4, 18.2, 18.5**

(1) An application for permission under rule 6.20 must be supported by written evidence stating—

(a) the grounds on which the application is made and the paragraph or paragraphs of rule 6.20 relied on;

(b) that the claimant believes that his claim has a reasonable prospect of success; and

(c) the defendant's address or, if not known, in what place or country the defendant is, or is likely, to be found.

(2) Where the application is made in respect of a claim referred to in rule 6.20(3), the written evidence must also state the grounds on which the witness believes that there is between the claimant and the person on whom the claim form has been, or will be served, a real issue which it is reasonable for the court to try.

(2A) The court will not give permission unless satisfied that England and Wales is the proper place in which to bring the claim.

(3) Where—

(a) the application is for permission to serve a claim form in Scotland or Northern Ireland; and

(b) it appears to the court that the claimant may also be entitled to a remedy there, the court, in deciding whether to give permission, shall—

(i) compare the cost and convenience of proceeding there or in the jurisdiction; and

(ii) (where relevant) have regard to the powers and jurisdiction of the Sheriff court in Scotland or the county courts or courts of summary jurisdiction in Northern Ireland.

(4) An order giving permission to serve a claim form out of the jurisdiction must specify the periods within which the defendant may—

(a) file an acknowledgment of service;

(b) file or serve an admission; and

(c) file a defence.

(The second practice direction to this Part [PD 6B] sets out how the periods referred to in paragraphs (a), (b) and (c) are calculated)

(Part 11 sets out the procedure by which a defendant may dispute the court's jurisdiction)

6.22 Period for Acknowledging Service or Admitting the Claim Where the Claim Form Is Served Out of the Jurisdiction under Rule 6.19

r.6.22 **15.2, 17.4, 18.2, 19.2, 76.36, 81.5**
r.6.22(2) **16.62**
r.6.22(3) **16.62**

(1) This rule sets out the period for filing an acknowledgment of service or filing or serving an admission where a claim form has been served out of the jurisdiction under rule 6.19. (Part 10 contains rules about the acknowledgment of service and Part 14 contains rules about admissions)

(2) If the claim form is to be served under rule 6.19(1) or (1A) in Scotland, Northern Ireland or in the European territory of another Contracting State or Regulation State the period is—

(a) where the defendant is served with a claim form which states that particulars of claim are to follow, 21 days after the service of the particulars of claim; and

(b) in any other case, 21 days after service of the claim form.

(3) If the claim form is to be served under rule 6.19(1) in any other territory of a Contracting State the period is—

(a) where the defendant is served with a claim form which states that particulars of claim are to follow, 31 days after the service of the particulars of claim; and

(b) in any other case, 31 days after service of the claim form.

(4) If the claim form is to be served under—
(a) rule 6.19(1) or (1A) in a country not referred to in paragraphs (2) or (3); or
(b) rule 6.19(2),
the period is set out in the relevant practice direction.

6.23 Period for Filing a Defence Where the Claim Form Is Served Out of the Jurisdiction under Rule 6.19

r.6.23 **15.2, 18.5, 76.36, 81.5**

(1) This rule sets out the period for filing a defence where a claim form has been served out of the jurisdiction under rule 6.19.
(Part 15 contains rules about the defence)
(2) If the claim form is to be served under rule 6.19(1) or (1A) in Scotland, Northern Ireland or in the European territory of another Contracting State or Regulation State the period is—
(a) 21 days after service of the particulars of claim; or
(b) if the defendant files an acknowledgment of service, 35 days after service of the particulars of claim.
(3) If the claim form is to be served under rule 6.19(1) in any other territory of a Contracting State the period is—
(a) 31 days after service of the particulars of claim; or
(b) if the defendant files an acknowledgment of service, 45 days after service of the particulars of claim.
(4) If the claim form is to be served under—
(a) rule 6.19(1) or (1A) in a country not referred to in paragraphs (2) or (3); or
(b) rule 6.19(2),
the period is set out in the relevant practice direction.

6.24 Method of Service — General Provisions

r.6.24 **15.2, 16.54, 16.61, 69.5, 69.19, 76.36, 81.5**

(1) Where a claim form is to be served out of the jurisdiction, it may be served by any method—
(a) permitted by the law of the country in which it is to be served;
(b) provided for by—
(i) rule 6.25 (service through foreign governments, judicial authorities and British Consular authorities);
(ii) rule 6.26A (service in accordance with the Service Regulation); or
(iii) rule 6.27 (service on a State); or
(c) permitted by a Civil Procedure Convention.
(2) Nothing in this rule or in any court order shall authorise or require any person to do anything in the country where the claim form is to be served which is against the law of that country.

6.25 Service through Foreign Governments, Judicial Authorities and British Consular Authorities

r.6.25 **15.2, 69.5, 69.19, 76.36, 81.5**
r.6.25(1) **16.57**
r.6.25(2) **16.58**
r.6.25(3)–(4) **16.60**

(1) Where a claim form is to be served on a defendant in any country which is a party to the Hague Convention, the claim form may be served—
(a) through the authority designated under the Hague Convention in respect of that country; or
(b) if the law of that country permits—
(i) through the judicial authorities of that country, or
(ii) through a British Consular authority in that country.
(2) Where—
(a) paragraph (4) (service in Scotland etc., other than under the Hague Convention) does not apply; and
(b) a claim form is to be served on a defendant in any country which is a party to a Civil Procedure Convention (other than the Hague Convention) providing for service in that country,

the claim form maybe served, if the law of that country permits—
- (i) through the judicial authorities of that country; or
- (ii) through a British Consular authority in that country (subject to any provisions of the applicable convention about the nationality of persons who may be served by such a method).

(3) Where—
- (a) paragraph (4) (service in Scotland etc., other than under the Hague Convention) does not apply; and
- (b) a claim form is to be served on a defendant in any country with respect to which there is no Civil Procedure Convention providing for service in that country,

the claim form may be served, if the law of that country so permits—
- (i) through the government of that country, where that government is willing to serve it; or
- (ii) through a British Consular authority in that country.

(4) Except where a claim form is to be served in accordance with paragraph (1) (service under the Hague Convention), the methods of service permitted by this rule are not available where the claim form is to be served in—
- (a) Scotland, Northern Ireland, the Isle of Man or the Channel Islands;
- (b) any Commonwealth State; or
- (c) any United Kingdom Overseas Territory.

(5) This rule does not apply where service is to be effected in accordance with the Service Regulation.

6.26 Procedure Where Service Is to Be through Foreign Governments, Judicial Authorities and British Consular Authorities

r.6.26 **15.2, 69.5, 69.19, 76.36, 81.5** r.6.26(2) **16.57**

(1) This rule applies where the claimant wishes to serve the claim form through—
- (a) the judicial authorities of the country where the claim form is to be served;
- (b) a British Consular authority in that country;
- (c) the authority designated under the Hague Convention in respect of that country; or
- (d) the government of that country.

(2) Where this rule applies, the claimant must file—
- (a) a request for service of the claim form by the method in paragraph (1) that he has chosen;
- (b) a copy of the claim form;
- (c) any translation required under rule 6.28; and
- (d) any other documents, copies of documents or translations required by the relevant practice direction.

(3) When the claimant files the documents specified in paragraph (2), the court officer will—
- (a) seal[(GL)] the copy of the claim form; and
- (b) forward the documents to the Senior Master.

(4) The Senior Master will send documents forwarded under this rule—
- (a) where the claim form is being served through the authority designated under the Hague Convention, to that authority; or
- (b) in any other case, to the Foreign and Commonwealth Office with a request that it arranges for the claim to be served by the method indicated in the request for service filed under paragraph (2) or, where that request indicates alternative methods, by the most convenient method.

(5) An official certificate which—
- (a) states that the claim form has been served in accordance with this rule either personally, or in accordance with the law of the country in which service was effected;
- (b) specifies the date on which the claim form was served; and
- (c) is made by—
  - (i) a British Consular authority in the country where the claim form was served;
  - (ii) the government or judicial authorities in that country; or
  - (iii) any other authority designated in respect of that country under the Hague Convention,

shall be evidence of the facts stated in the certificate.

(6) A document purporting to be an official certificate under paragraph (5) shall be treated as such a certificate, unless it is proved not to be.
(7) This rule does not apply where service is to be effected in accordance with the Service Regulation.

6.26A Service in Accordance with the Service Regulation

r.6.26A(2) **16.59**
r.6.26A(3) **16.59**
r.6.26A(4) **16.64**

(1) This rule applies where a claim form is to be served in accordance with the Service Regulation.
(2) The claimant must file the claim form and any translations or other documents required by the Service Regulation.
(3) When the claimant files the documents referred to in paragraph (2), the court officer will—
  (a) seal(GL) the copy of the claim form; and
  (b) forward the documents to the Senior Master.
(4) Rule 6.31 does not apply.
(The Service Regulation is annexed to the relevant practice direction)

6.27 Service of Claim Form on State Where Court Permits Service Out of the Jurisdiction

r.6.27 **15.2, 16.54, 16.56, 69.5, 69.19,**
r.6.27(6) **16.56**

(1) This rule applies where a claimant wishes to serve the claim form on a State.
(2) The claimant must file in the Central Office of the Royal Courts of Justice—
  (a) a request for service to be arranged by the Foreign and Commonwealth Office;
  (b) a copy of the claim form; and
  (c) any translation required under rule 6.28.
(3) The Senior Master will send documents filed under this rule to the Foreign and Commonwealth Office with a request that it arranges for the claim form to be served.
(4) An official certificate by the Foreign and Commonwealth Office stating that a claim form has been duly served on a specified date in accordance with a request made under this rule shall be evidence of that fact.
(5) A document purporting to be such a certificate shall be treated as such a certificate, unless it is proved not to be.
(6) Where—
  (a) section 12(6) of the State Immunity Act 1978 applies; and
  (b) the State has agreed to a method of service other than through the Foreign and Commonwealth Office,

the claim may be served either by the method agreed or in accordance with this rule.
(Section 12(6) of the State Immunity Act 1978 provides that section 12(1) of that Act, which prescribes a method for serving documents on a State, does not prevent the service of a claim form or other document in a manner to which the State has agreed)
(7) In this rule 'State' has the meaning given by section 14 of the State Immunity Act 1978.

6.28 Translation of Claim Form

r.6.28 **15.2, 16.57, 69.5, 69.19, 76.36, 81.5**

(1) Except where paragraph (4) or (5) applies, every copy of the claim form filed under rule 6.26 (service through judicial authorities, foreign governments etc.) or 6.27 (service on State) must be accompanied by a translation of the claim form.
(2) The translation must be—
  (a) in the official language of the country in which it is to be served; or
  (b) if there is more than one official language of that country, in any official language which is appropriate to the place in the country where the claim form is to be served.
(3) Every translation filed under this rule must be accompanied by a statement by the person making it that it is a correct translation, and the statement must include—
  (a) the name of the person making the translation;

(b) his address; and
(c) his qualifications for making a translation.

(4) The claimant is not required to file a translation of a claim form filed under rule 6.26 (service through judicial authorities, foreign governments etc.) where the claim form is to be served—
(a) in a country of which English is an official language; or
(b) on a British subject,
unless a Civil Procedure Convention expressly requires a translation.

(5) The claimant is not required to file a translation of a claim form filed under rule 6.27 (service on State) where English is an official language of the State where the claim form is to be served.

6.29 Undertaking to be Responsible for Expenses of the Foreign and Commonwealth Office

Every request for service filed under rule 6.26 (service through judicial authorities, foreign governments etc.) or rule 6.27 (service on State) must contain an undertaking by the person making the request—
(a) to be responsible for all expenses incurred by the Foreign and Commonwealth Office or foreign judicial authority; and
(b) to pay those expenses to the Foreign and Commonwealth Office or foreign judicial authority on being informed of the amount.

6.30 Service of Documents Other than the Claim Form

r.6.30 **15.2, 76.36, 81.5**

(1) Where an application notice is to be served out of the jurisdiction under this Section of this Part—
(a) rules 6.21(4), 6.22 and 6.23 do not apply; and
(b) where the person on whom the application notice has been served is not a party to proceedings in the jurisdiction in which the application is made, that person may make an application to the court under rule 11(1) as if he were a defendant and rule 11(2) does not apply.

(Rule 6.21(4) provides that an order giving permission to serve a claim form out of the jurisdiction must specify the periods within which the defendant may (a) file an acknowledgment of service, (b) file or serve an admission, and (c) file a defence)

(Rule 6.22 provides rules for the period for acknowledging service or admitting the claim where the claim form is served out of the jurisdiction under rule 6.19)

(Rule 6.23 provides rules for the period for filing a defence where the claim form is served out of the jurisdiction under rule 6.19)

(The practice direction supplementing this Section of this Part [PD 6B] provides that where an application notice is to be served out of the jurisdiction in accordance with this Section of this Part, the court must have regard to the country in which the application notice is to be served in setting the date for the hearing of the application and giving any direction about service of the respondent's evidence)

(Rule 11(1) provides that a defendant may make an application to the court to dispute the court's jurisdiction to try the claim or argue that the court should not exercise its jurisdiction. Rule 11(2) provides that a defendant who wishes to make such an application must first file an acknowledgment of service in accordance with Part 10)

(2) Unless paragraph (3) applies, where the permission of the court is required for a claim form to be served out of the jurisdiction the permission of the court must also be obtained for service out of the jurisdiction of any other document to be served in the proceedings.

(3) Where—
(a) the court gives permission for a claim form to be served out of the jurisdiction; and
(b) the claim form states that particulars of claim are to follow,
the permission of the court is not required to serve the particulars of claim out of the jurisdiction.

6.31 Proof of Service

r.6.31 **15.2, 16.64, 76.36, 81.5**

Where—
(a) a hearing is fixed when the claim is issued;
(b) the claim form is served on a defendant out of the jurisdiction; and
(c) that defendant does not appear at the hearing,
the claimant may take no further steps against that defendant until the claimant files written evidence showing that the claim form has been duly served.

IV SERVICE OF FOREIGN PROCESS

6.32 Scope and Definitions

(1) This Section of this Part—
  (a) applies to the service in England or Wales of any court process in connection with civil or commercial proceedings in a foreign court or tribunal; but
  (b) does not apply where the Service Regulation applies.
(The Service Regulation is annexed to the relevant practice direction)
(2) In this Section—
  (a) 'convention country'—
    (i) means a foreign country in relation to which there is a civil procedure convention providing for service in that country of process of the High Court; and
    (ii) includes a country which is a party to the Convention on the Service Abroad of Judicial and Extra Judicial Documents in Civil or Commercial Matters signed at the Hague on 15 November 1965; and
  (b) 'process server' means—
    (i) a process server appointed by the Lord Chancellor to serve documents to which this Section applies, or
    (ii) his authorised agent.

6.33 Request for Service

Process will be served where the Senior Master receives—
(a) a written request for service—
  (i) where the foreign court or tribunal is in a convention country, from a consular or other authority of that country; or
  (ii) from the Secretary of State for Foreign and Commonwealth Affairs, with a recommendation that service should be effected;
(b) a translation of that request into English;
(c) two copies of the process to be served; and
(d) unless the foreign court or tribunal certifies that the person to be served understands the language of the process, two copies of a translation of it into English.

6.34 Method of Service

The process must be served as directed by the Senior Master.

6.35 After Service

(1) The process server must—
  (a) send the Senior Master a copy of the process, and
    (i) proof of service; or
    (ii) a statement why the process could not be served; and
  (b) if the Senior Master directs, specify the costs incurred in serving or attempting to serve the process.
(2) The Senior Master will send the following documents to the person who requested service—
  (a) a certificate, sealed with the seal of the Supreme Court for use out of the jurisdiction, stating—
    (i) when and how the process was served or the reason why it has not been served; and

(ii) where appropriate, an amount certified by a costs judge to be the costs of serving or attempting to serve the process; and

(b) a copy of the process.

PD 6 Practice Direction — Service

This practice direction supplements CPR Part 6

PD 6 **23.11** [For commentary on a specific paragraph, please refer to the cross-references after the title of the paragraph.]

Methods of Service

1.1 The various methods of service are set out in rule 6.2.

1.2 The following provisions apply to the specific methods of service referred to.

Service by Non-electronic Means

para.2 **15.21, 15.25**

Service by document exchange

2.1 Service by document exchange (DX) may take place only where:

(1) the party's address for service[1] includes a numbered box at a DX, or

(2) the writing paper of the party who is to be served or of his legal representative[2] sets out the DX box number, and

(3) the party or his legal representative has not indicated in writing that they are unwilling to accept service by DX.

2.2 Service by DX is effected by leaving the document addressed to the numbered box:

(1) at the DX of the party who is to be served, or

(2) at a DX which sends documents to that party's DX every business day.

Service by Electronic Means

para.3 **15.21**
para.3.1(1) **15.26**
para.3.1(2) **15.26**
para.3.2 **15.26**

Service by facsimile

3.1 Subject to the provisions of para. 3.3 below, where a document is to be served by electronic means:

(1) the party who is to be served or his legal representative must previously have expressly indicated in writing to the party serving:

(a) that he is willing to accept service by electronic means; and

(b) the fax number, email address or electronic identification to which it should be sent; and

(2) the following shall be taken as sufficient written indication for the purposes of para. 3.1(1):

(a) a fax number set out on the writing paper of the legal representative of the party who is to be served; or

(b) a fax number, email address or electronic identification set out on a statement of case or a response to a claim filed with the court.

3.2 Where a party seeks to serve a document by electronic means he should first seek to clarify with the party who is to be served whether there are any limitations to the recipient's agreement to accept service by such means including the format in which documents are to be sent and the maximum size of attachments that may be received.

3.3 An address for service given by a party must be within the jurisdiction and any fax number must be at the address for service. Where an email address or electronic identification is given in conjunction with an address for service, the email address or electronic identification will be deemed to be at the address for service.

---

[1] See rule 6.5.

[2] See rule 2.3 for the definition of legal representative.

3.4 Where a document is served by electronic means, the party serving the document need not in addition send a hard copy by post or document exchange.

Service on Certain Individuals

para.4.2 **15.33**

Personal service on partners

4.1 Where partners are sued in the name of a partnership, service should be in accordance with rule 6.4(5) and the table set out in rule 6.5(5) where it refers to an 'individual who is suing or being sued in the name of a firm'.

4.2 A claim form or particulars of claim which are served by leaving them with a person at the principal or last known place of business of the partnership, must at the same time have served with them a notice as to whether that person is being served:

(1) as a partner,
(2) as a person having control or management of the partnership business, or
(3) as both.

Service on members of HM Forces and United States Air Force

5 The Lord Chancellor's Office issued a memorandum on 26 July 1979 as to service on members of HM Forces and guidance notes as to service on members of the United States Air Force. The provisions annexed to this practice direction are derived from that memorandum and guidance notes.

Service Generally

para.6.1 **15.32**
para.6.2 **15.32, 23.11**
para.6.2(1) **15.30**

Personal service on a company or other corporation

6.1 Personal service on a registered company or corporation in accordance with rule 6.4(4) service is effected by leaving a document with 'a person holding a senior position'.

6.2 Each of the following persons is a person holding a senior position:

(1) in respect of a registered company or corporation, a director, the treasurer, secretary, chief executive, manager or other officer of the company or corporation, and
(2) in respect of a corporation which is not a registered company, in addition to those persons set out in (1), the mayor, chairman, president, town clerk or similar officer of the corporation.

Change of Address

para.7 **22.2**

7 A party or his legal representative who changes his address for service shall give notice in writing of the change as soon as it has taken place to the court and every other party.

Service by the Court

para.8.1 **15.19, 32.20**

8.1 Where the court effects service of a document in accordance with rule 6.3(1) and (2), the method will normally be by first class post.

8.2 [*deleted*]

8.3 Where the court effects service of a claim form, delivers a defence to a claimant or notifies a claimant that the defendant has filed an acknowledgment of service, the court will also serve or deliver a copy of any notice of funding that has been filed provided:

(a) it was filed at the same time as the claim form, defence or acknowledgment of service, and
(b) copies were provided for service.

Content of Evidence

para.9.1 **15.39** para.9.2 **15.35**

The following applications relating to service require evidence in support

9.1 An application for an order for service by an alternative method[3] should be supported by evidence stating:
   (1) the reason an order for an alternative method of service is sought, and
   (2) what steps have been taken to serve by other permitted means.

9.2 An application for service of a claim form relating to a contract on the agent of a principal who is overseas should be supported by evidence setting out:
   (1) full details of the contract and that it was entered into within the jurisdiction with or through an agent who is either an individual residing or carrying on business within the jurisdiction, or a registered company or corporation having a registered office or a place of business within the jurisdiction,
   (2) that the principal for whom the agent is acting was, at the time the contract was entered into and is at the time of making the application, neither an individual, registered company or corporation as described in (1) above, and
   (3) why service out of the jurisdiction cannot be effected.

ANNEX SERVICE ON MEMBERS OF HM FORCES

1. The following information is for litigants and legal representatives who wish to serve legal documents in civil proceedings in the courts of England and Wales on parties to the proceedings who are (or who, at the material time, were) regular members of Her Majesty's Forces.
2. The proceedings may take place in the county court or the High Court, and the documents to be served may be both originating claims, interim applications and pre-action applications. Proceedings for divorce or maintenance and proceedings in the Family Courts generally are subject to special rules as to service which are explained in a practice direction issued by the Senior District Judge of the Principal Registry on 26 June 1979.
3. In these instructions, the person wishing to effect service is referred to as the 'claimant' and the person to be served is referred to as the 'serviceman'; the expression 'overseas' means outside the United Kingdom.

Enquiries as to Address

4. As a first step, the claimant's legal representative will need to find out where the serviceman is serving, if he does not already know. For this purpose he should write to the appropriate officer of the Ministry of Defence as specified in paragraph 10 below.
5. The letter of enquiry should in every case show that the writer is a legal representative and that the enquiry is made solely with a view to the service of legal documents in civil proceedings.
6. In all cases the letter should give the full name, service number, rank or rating, and Ship, Arm or Trade, Regiment or Corps and Unit or as much of this information as is available. Failure to quote the service number and the rank or rating may result either in failure to identify the serviceman or in considerable delay.
7. The letter should contain an undertaking by the legal representative that, if the address is given, it will be used solely for the purpose of issuing and serving documents in the proceedings and that so far as is possible the legal representative will disclose the address only to the court and not to his client or to any other person or body. A legal representative in the service of a public authority or private company should undertake that the address will be used solely for the purpose of issuing and serving documents in the proceedings and that the address will not be disclosed so far as is possible to any other part of his employing organisation or to any other person but only to the court. Normally on receipt of the required information and undertaking the appropriate office will give the service address.

[3] See rule 6.8.

8. If the legal representative does not give the undertaking, the only information he will receive will be whether the serviceman is at that time serving in England or Wales, Scotland, Northern Ireland or overseas.
9. It should be noted that a serviceman's address which ends with a British Forces Post Office address and reference (BFPO) will nearly always indicate that he is serving overseas.
10. The letter of enquiry should be addressed as follows:
    (a) *Royal Navy Officers*
    The Naval Secretary
    Room 161
    Victory Building
    HM Naval Base
    Portsmouth Hants PO1 3LS
    RN Ratings
    Commodore Naval Drafting
    Centurion Building
    Grange Road
    Gosport
    Hants PO13 9XA
    RN Medical and Dental Officers
    The Medical Director General
    (Naval)
    Room 114 Victory Building
    HM Naval Base
    Portsmouth Hants PO1 3LS
    Officers of Queen Alexandra's Royal Naval Nursing Service
    The Matron-in-Chief
    QARNNS
    Room 129
    Victory Building
    HM Naval Base
    Portsmouth
    Hants PO1 3LS
    Naval Chaplains
    Director General Naval
    Chaplaincy Service
    Room 201
    Victory Building
    HM Naval Base
    Portsmouth
    Hants PO1 3LS
    (b) *Royal Marine Officers and Ranks*
    Personnel section
    West Battery
    Whale Island
    Portsmouth
    Hants PO2 8DX
    RM Ranks HQRM
    (DRORM)
    West Battery
    Whale Island
    Portsmouth
    Hants PO2 8DX

(c) *Army Officers and Other Ranks*
Ministry of Defence
Army Personnel Centre
Secretariat, Public Enquiries
RM CD424
Kentigern House
65 Brown Street
Glasgow G2 8EH

(d) *Royal Air Force Officers and Other Ranks*
Personnel Management Agency (RAF)
Building 248
RAF Innsworth
Gloucester GL3 1EZ

Assistance in Serving Documents on Servicemen

11. Once the claimant's legal representative has learnt the serviceman's address he may use that address as the address for service by post, in cases where this method of service is allowed by the Civil Procedure Rules. There are, however, some situations in which service of the proceedings, whether in the High Court or in the county court, has to be effected personally; in these cases an appointment will have to be sought, through the Commanding Officer of the Unit, Establishment or Ship concerned, for the purpose of effecting service. The procedure for obtaining an appointment is described below, and it applies whether personal service is to be effected by the claimant's legal representative or his agent or by a court bailiff, or, in the case of proceedings served overseas (with the leave of the court) through the British Consul or the foreign judicial authority.
12. The procedure for obtaining an appointment to effect personal service is by application to the Commanding Officer of the Unit, Establishment or Ship in which the serviceman is serving. The Commanding Officer may grant permission for the document server to enter the Unit, Establishment or Ship but if this is not appropriate he may offer arrangements for the serviceman to attend at a place in the vicinity of the Unit, Establishment or Ship in order that he may be served. If suitable arrangements cannot be made the legal representative will have evidence that personal service is impracticable, which may be useful in an application for service by an alternative method.

General

13. Subject to the procedure outlined in paragraphs 11 and 12, there are no special arrangements to assist in the service of process when a serviceman is outside the United Kingdom. The appropriate office will however give an approximate date when the serviceman is likely to return to the United Kingdom.
14. It sometimes happens that a serviceman has left the service by the time that the enquiry is made. If the claimant's legal representative confirms that the proceedings result from an occurrence when the serviceman was in the Forces and he gives the undertaking referred to in paragraph 7, the last known private address after discharge will normally be provided. In no other case however will the Department disclose the private address of a member of HM Forces.

Service on Members of United States Air Force

15. In addition to the information contained in the memorandum of 26 July 1979, the Lord Chancellor's Office, some doubts having been expressed as to the correct procedure to be followed by persons having civil claims against members of the United States Air Force in this country, issued the following notes for guidance with the approval of the appropriate United States authorities:
16. Instructions have been issued by the U.S. authorities to the commanding officers of all their units in this country that every facility is to be given for the service of documents in civil proceedings on members of the U.S. Air Force. The proper course to be followed by a creditor or other person having a claim against a member of the U.S. Air Force is for him to communicate

with the commanding officer or, where the unit concerned has a legal officer, with the legal officer of the defendant's unit requesting him to provide facilities for the service of documents on the defendant. It is not possible for the U.S. authorities to act as arbitrators when a civil claim is made against a member of their forces. It is, therefore, essential that the claim should either be admitted by the defendant or judgment should be obtained on it, whether in the High Court or a county court. If a claim has been admitted or judgment has been obtained and the claimant has failed to obtain satisfaction within a reasonable period, his proper course is then to write to: Office of the Staff Judge Advocate, Headquarters, Third Air Force, R.A.F. Mildenhall, Suffolk, enclosing a copy of the defendant's written admission of the claim or, as the case may be, a copy of the judgment. Steps will then be taken by the Staff Judge Advocate to ensure that the matter is brought to the defendant's attention with a view to prompt satisfaction of the claim.

PD 6B Practice Direction — Service Out of the Jurisdiction

This practice direction supplements Section III of CPR Part 6

PD 6B **16.42, 16.64** [For commentary on a specific paragraph, please refer to the cross-references after the title of the paragraph.]

Service in Other Member States of the European Union

A1.1 Where service is to be effected in another Member of State of the European Union, Council Regulation (EC) No. 1348/2000 of 29 May 2000 on the service in the Member States of judicial and extrajudicial documents in civil or commercial matters ('the Service Regulation') applies.

A1.2 The Service Regulation is [on the CD-ROM version of *Blackstone's Civil Practice*].

(Article 20(1) of the Service Regulation provides that the Regulation prevails over other provisions contained in bilateral or multilateral agreements or arrangements concluded by the Member States and in particular art. IV of the protocol to the Brussels Convention of 1968 and the Hague Convention of 15 November 1965.)

Service Out of the Jurisdiction Where Permission of the Court Is Not Required

paras.1.1–1.3C **16.42** para.1.5 **16.57**
para.1.4 **16.2, 16.42, 16.43**

1.1 The usual form of words of the statement required by r. 6.19(3) where the court has power to determine the claim under the 1982 Act should be:

I state that the High Court of England and Wales has power under the Civil Jurisdiction and Judgments Act 1982 to hear this claim and that no proceedings are pending between the parties in Scotland, Northern Ireland or another Convention territory of any contracting State as defined by section 1(3) of the Act.

1.2 However, in proceedings to which r. 6.19(1)(b)(ii) applies, the statement should be:

I state that the High Court of England and Wales has power under the Civil Jurisdiction and Judgments Act 1982, the claim having as its object rights *in rem* in immovable property or tenancies in immovable property (or otherwise in accordance with the provisions of Article 16 of Schedule 1 or 3C to that Act, or paragraph 11 of Schedule 4 to that Act) to which Article 16 of Schedule 1,3C or 4 to that Act applies, to hear the claim and that no proceedings are pending between the parties in Scotland, Northern Ireland or another Convention territory of any contracting State as defined by section 1(3) of the Act.

1.3 And in proceedings to which r. 6.19(1)(b)(iii) applies, the statement should be:

I state that the High Court of England and Wales has power under the Civil Jurisdiction and Judgments Act 1982, the defendant being a party to an agreement conferring jurisdiction to which Article 17 of Schedule 1 or 3C to that Act or paragraph 12 of Schedule 4 to that Act applies, to hear the claim and that no proceedings are pending between the parties in Scotland, Northern Ireland or another Convention territory of any contracting State as defined by section 1(3) of the Act.

1.3A The usual form of words of the statement required by r. 6.19(3) where the Judgments Regulation applies should be:

I state that the High Court of England and Wales has power under Council Regulation (EC) No. 44/2001 of 22 December 2000 (on jurisdiction and the recognition and enforcement of judgments in civil and commercial matters) to hear this claim and that no proceedings are pending between the parties in Scotland, Northern Ireland or any other Regulation State as defined by section 1(3) of the Civil Jurisdiction and Judgments Act 1982.

1.3B However, in proceedings to which r. 6.19(1A)(b)(ii) applies, the statement should be:

I state that the High Court of England and Wales has power under Council Regulation (EC) No. 44/2001 of 22 December 2000 (on jurisdiction and the recognition and enforcement of judgments in civil and commercial matters), the claim having as its object rights *in rem* in immovable property or tenancies in immovable property (or otherwise in accordance with the provisions of Article 22 of that Regulation) to which Article 22 of that Regulation applies, to hear this claim and that no proceedings are pending between the parties in Scotland, Northern Ireland or any other Regulation State as defined by section 1(3) of the Civil Jurisdiction and Judgments Act 1982.

1.3C And in proceedings to which r. 6.19(1A)(b)(iii) applies, the statement should be:
I state that the High Court of England and Wales has power under Council Regulation (EC) No. 44/2001 of 22 December 2000 (on jurisdiction and the recognition and enforcement of judgments in civil and commercial matters), the defendant being a party to an agreement conferring jurisdiction to which Article 23 of that Regulation applies, to hear this claim and that no proceedings are pending between the parties in Scotland, Northern Ireland or any other Regulation State as defined by section 1(3) of the Civil Jurisdiction and Judgments Act 1982.

1.3D In proceedings to which r. 6.19(2) applies, the statement should be:
I state that the High Court of England and Wales has power to hear this claim under [*state the provisions of the relevant enactment*] which satisfies the requirements of rule 6.19(2), and that no proceedings are pending between the parties in Scotland or Northern Ireland, or in another Contracting State or Regulation State as defined by section 1(3) of the Civil Jurisdiction and Judgments Act 1982.

1.4 A claim form appearing to be for service on a defendant under the provisions of r. 6.19 which does not include a statement in the form of 1.1, 1.2, 1.3, 1.3A, 1.3B, 1.3C or 1.3D above will be marked on issue 'Not for service out of the jurisdiction'.

1.5 Where a claim form is served without particulars of claim, it must be accompanied by a copy of form N1C (notes for defendants).

Service Out of the Jurisdiction Where Permission Is Required

para.2 **16.57**

Documents to be filed under rule 6.26(2)(d)

2.1 A complete set of the following documents must be provided for each party to be served out of the jurisdiction:
(1) a copy of particulars of claim if not already incorporated in or attached to the claim;
(2) a duplicate of the claim form of the particulars of claim and of any documents accompanying the claim and of any translation required by r. 6.28;
(3) forms for responding to the claim;
(4) any translation required under r. 6.28 and paras 4.1 and 4.2, in duplicate.

2.2 The documents to be served in certain countries require legalisation and the Foreign Process Section (Room E02), Royal Courts of Justice will advise on request. Some countries require legalisation and some require a formal letter of request, see form No. 34 which must be signed by the Senior Master of the Queen's Bench Division irrespective of the Division of the High Court or any county court in which the order was made.

Service in Scotland, Northern Ireland, the Channel Islands, the Isle of Man, Commonwealth Countries and United Kingdom Overseas Territories

paras.3.1–3.2 **16.60**

3.1 Where r. 6.25(4) applies service should be effected by the claimant or his agent direct except in the case of a Commonwealth State where the judicial authorities have required service to be in accordance with r. 6.24(1)(b)(i). These are presently Malta and Singapore.

3.2 For the purposes of r. 6.25(4)(c), the following countries are United Kingdom Overseas Territories:
(a) Anguilla;
(b) Bermuda;
(c) British Antarctic Territory;
(d) British Indian Ocean Territory;
(e) Cayman Islands;
(f) Falkland Islands;
(g) Gibraltar;
(h) Montserrat;

(i) Pitcairn, Henderson, Ducie and Oeno;
(j) St Helena and Dependencies;
(k) South Georgia and the South Sandwich Islands;
(l) Sovereign Base Areas of Akrotiri and Dhekelia;
(m) Turks and Caicos Islands; and
(n) Virgin Islands.

Translations

para.4 **16.57**

4.1 Rule 6.28 applies to particulars of claim not included in a claim form as well as to claim forms.

4.2 Where a translation of a claim form is required under r. 6.28, the claimant must also file a translation of all the forms that will accompany the claim form.

(It should be noted that English is not an official language in the Province of Quebec.)

Service with the Permission of the Court under Certain Acts

5.1 Rule 6.20(18) provides that a claim form may be served out of the jurisdiction with the court's permission if the claim is made under an enactment specified in the relevant practice direction.

5.2 These enactments are:
(1) the Nuclear Installations Act 1965;
(2) the Social Security Contributions and Benefits Act 1992;
(3) the Directive of the Council of the European Communities dated 15 March 1976 No. 76/308/EEC, where service is to be effected in a member State of the European Union;
(4) the Drug Trafficking Offences Act 1994;
(7) Part VI of the Criminal Justice Act 1988;
(8) the Inheritance (Provision for Family and Dependants) Act 1975;
(9) Part II of the Immigration and Asylum Act 1999;
(10) Schedule 2 to the Immigration Act 1971;
(11) the Financial Services and Markets Act 2000;
(12) the Pensions Act 1995;
(13) the Pensions Act 2004.

5.3 Under the State Immunity Act 1978, the foreign State being served is allowed an additional two months over the normal period for filing an acknowledgment of service or defence or for filing or serving an admission allowed under paras 7.3 and 7.4.

Service of Petitions, Application Notices and Orders

6.1 The provisions of Section III of Part 6 (special provisions about service out of the jurisdiction) apply to service out of the jurisdiction of a petition, application notice or order. (Rule 6.30(1) contains special provisions relating to application notices.)

6.2 Where an application notice is to be served out of the jurisdiction in accordance with Section III of Part 6 the court must have regard to the country in which the application notice is to be served in setting the date for the hearing of the application and giving any direction about service of the respondents evidence.

6.3 Where the permission of the court is required for a claim form to be served out of the jurisdiction the permission of the court, unless r. 6.30(3) applies, must also be obtained for service out of the jurisdiction of any other document to be served in the proceedings and the provisions of this practice direction will, so far as applicable to that other document, apply.

6.4 When particulars of claim are served out of the jurisdiction any statement as to the period for responding to the claim contained in any of the forms required by r. 7.8 to accompany the particulars of claim must specify the period prescribed under r. 6.22 or 6.23 or (as the case may be) by the order permitting service out of the jurisdiction (see r. 6.21(4)).

Period for Responding to a Claim Form

para.7.2 **17.4, 18.2, 18.5**
para.7.3 **18.2, 18.5, 19.2**
para.7.4 **18.5**
para.7.4(2) **16.62**

7.1 Where a claim has been served out of the jurisdiction without permission under r. 6.19:

(1) r. 6.22 sets out the period for filing an acknowledgment of service or filing or serving an admission; and where r. 6.22(4) applies, the period will be calculated in accordance with para. 7.3 having regard to the Table below;
(2) r. 6.23 sets out the period for filing a defence and where r. 6.23(4) applies, the period will be calculated in accordance with para. 7.4 having regard to the Table below.

7.2 Where an order grants permission to serve a claim form out of the jurisdiction, the periods within which the defendant may:
(1) file an acknowledgment of service;
(2) file or serve an admission;
(3) file a defence,
will be calculated in accordance with paras 7.3 and 7.4 having regard to the table below.
(Rule 6.21(4) requires an order giving permission for a claim form to be served out of the jurisdiction to specify the period within which the defendant may respond to the claim form)

7.3 The period for filing an acknowledgment of service under Part 10 or filing or serving an admission under Part 14 is:
(1) where the defendant is served with a claim form which states that particulars of claim are to follow, the number of days listed in the table after service of the particulars of claim; and
(2) in any other case, the number of days listed in the table after service of the claim form.
For example: where a defendant has been served with a claim form (accompanied by particulars of claim) in the Bahamas, the period for acknowledging service or admitting the claim is 22 days after service.

7.4 The period for filing a defence under Part 15 is:
(1) the number of days listed in the table after service of the particulars of claim; or
(2) where the defendant has filed an acknowledgment of service, the number of days listed in the table plus an additional 14 days after the service of the particulars of claim.
For example, where a defendant has been served with particulars of claim in Gibraltar and has acknowledged service, the period for filing a defence is 45 days after service of the particulars of claim.

Period for Responding to an Application Notice

para.8.1 **16.62**

8.1 Where an application notice or order needs to be served out of the jurisdiction, the period for responding to service is seven days less than the number of days listed in the table.

Address for Service and Further Information

10.1 A defendant is required by r. 6.5(2) to give an address for service within the jurisdiction.

10.2 Further information concerning service out of the jurisdiction can be obtained from the Foreign Process Section, Room E02, Royal Courts of Justice, Strand, London WC2A 2LL (telephone (020)79476691).

Table

table **16.62, 17.4, 18.2, 18.5**

Place or country	Number of days
Abu Dhabi	22
Afghanistan	23
Albania	25
Algeria	22
Angola	22
Anguilla	31
Antigua	23
Antilles (Netherlands)	31

Place or country	Number of days
Argentina	22
Armenia	21
Ascension	31
Australia	25
Austria	21
Azores	23
Bahamas	22
Bahrain	22
Balearic Islands	21
Bangladesh	23
Barbados	23
Belarus	21
Belgium	21
Belize	23
Benin	25
Bermuda	31
Bhutan	28
Bolivia	23
Bosnia-Hercegovina	21
Botswana	23
Brazil	22
Brunei	25
Bulgaria	23
Burkina Faso	23
Burma	23
Burundi	22
Cameroon	22
Canada	22
Canary Islands	22
Cape Verde Islands	25
Caroline Islands	31
Cayman Islands	31
Central African Republic	25
Chad	25
Chile	22
China	24
Christmas Island	27
Cocos (Keeling) Islands	41
Colombia	22
Comoros	23
Congo (People's Republic)*	25
Corsica	21
Costa Rica	23
Croatia	21
Cuba	24
Cyprus	31
Cyrenaica (see Libya)	21
Czech Republic	21
Denmark	21
Djibouti	22
Dominica	23
Dominican Republic	23
Dubai	22
Ecuador	22
Egypt (Arab Republic)	22
El Salvador (Republic of)	25

[* Now Republic of Congo.]

Place or country	Number of days
Equatorial Guinea	23
Estonia	21
Ethiopia	22
Falkland Islands and Dependencies	31
Faroe Islands	31
Fiji	23
Finland	24
France	21
French Guiana	31
French Polynesia	31
French West Indies	31
Gabon	25
Gambia	22
Georgia	21
Germany	21
Ghana	22
Gibraltar	31
Greece	21
Greenland	31
Grenada	24
Guatemala	24
Guernsey	18
Guyana	22
Haiti	23
Holland (Netherlands)	21
Honduras	24
Hong Kong	31
Hungary	22
Iceland	22
India	23
Indonesia	22
Iran	22
Iraq	22
Ireland (Republic of)	21
Ireland (Northern)	21
Isle of Man	18
Israel	22
Italy	21
Ivory Coast	22
Jamaica	22
Japan	23
Jersey	18
Jordan	23
Kampuchea	38
Kazakhstan	21
Kenya	22
Kirgizstan	21
Korea (North)	28
Korea (South)	24
Kuwait	22
Laos	30
Latvia	21
Lebanon	22
Lesotho	23
Liberia	22
Libya	21
Liechtenstein	21

Place or country	Number of days
Lithuania	21
Luxembourg	21
Macau	31
Macedonia	21
Madagascar	
Madeira	31
Malawi	23
Malaya	24
Maldive Islands	26
Mali	25
Malta	21
Mariana Islands	26
Marshall Islands	32
Mauritania	23
Mauritius	22
Mexico	23
Moldova	21
Monaco	21
Montserrat	31
Morocco	22
Mozambique	23
Nauru Island	36
Nepal	23
Netherlands	21
Nevis	24
New Caledonia	31
New Hebrides (now Vanuatu)	29
New Zealand	26
New Zealand Island Territories	50
Nicaragua	24
Niger (Republic of)	25
Nigeria	22
Norfolk Island	31
Norway	21
Oman (Sultanate of)	22
Pakistan	23
Panama (Republic of)	26
Papua New Guinea	26
Paraguay	22
Peru	22
Philippines	23
Pitcairn Island	31
Poland	21
Portugal	21
Portuguese Timor	31
Puerto Rico	23
Qatar	23
Reunion	31
Romania	22
Russia	21
Rwanda	23
Sabah	23
St Helena	31
St Kitts–Nevis	24
St Lucia	24
St Pierre and Miquelon	31
St Vincent and the Grenadines	24

Place or country	Number of days
Samoa (USA Territory) (see also Western Samoa)	30
Sarawak	28
Saudi Arabia	24
Scotland	21
Senegal	22
Seychelles	22
Sharjah	24
Sierra Leone	22
Singapore	22
Slovakia	21
Slovenia	21
Society Islands (French Polynesia)	31
Solomon Islands	29
Somali Democratic Republic*	22
South Africa (Republic of)	22
South Georgia (Falkland Island Dependencies)	31
South Orkneys	21
South Shetlands	21
Spain	21
Spanish Territories of North Africa	31
Sri Lanka	23
Sudan	22
Suriname	22
Swaziland	22
Sweden	21
Switzerland	21
Syria	23
Taiwan	23
Tajikistan	21
Tanzania	22
Thailand	23
Tibet	34
Tobago	23
Togo	22
Tonga	30
Tortola	31
Trinidad and Tobago	23
Tristan da Cunha	31
Tunisia	22
Turkey	21
Turkmenistan	21
Turks and Caicos Islands	31
Uganda	22
Ukraine	21
United States of America	22
Uruguay	22
Uzbekistan	21
Vanuatu	29
Vatican City State	21
Venezuela	22
Vietnam	28
Virgin Islands — British (Tortola)	31
Virgin Islands — USA	24
Wake Island	25
Western Samoa	34
Yemen (Republic of)	30

[* At present, this country is generally referred to as Somalia.]

Place or country	Number of days
Yugoslavia (except for Bosnia-Hercegovina, Croatia, Macedonia and Slovenia)*	21
Zaire†	25
Zambia	23
Zimbabwe	22

[* The country referred to in this entry is now Serbia and Montenegro. It includes Kosovo (which is under United Nations administration) and the autonomous province of Vojvodina. There are separate entries in this table for Bosnia-Hercegovina, Croatia, Macedonia and Slovenia.]
[† Now Democratic Republic of the Congo.]

[COUNCIL REGULATION (EC) NO. 1348/2000

This Regulation, which is annexed to PD 6B, is on the CD-ROM version of *Blackstone's Civil Practice.* Click on the title of the Regulation to open it.]

CPR Part 7 How to Start Proceedings — The Claim Form

Part 7 **13.6, 48.71, 68.58, 71.4, 74.29, 74.47, 74.47, 95.54, 95.58** [For commentary on a specific rule, please refer to the cross-references after the title of the rule.]

7.1 Where to Start Proceedings

Restrictions on where proceedings may be started are set out in the relevant practice direction.

7.2 How to Start Proceedings

r.7.2 **15.2**   r.7.2(1) **12.3, 12.5**

(1) Proceedings are started when the court issues a claim form at the request of the claimant.
(2) A claim form is issued on the date entered on the form by the court.
(A person who seeks a remedy from the court before proceedings are started or in relation to proceedings which are taking place, or will take place, in another jurisdiction must make an application under Part 23)
(Part 16 sets out what the claim form must include)
(The costs practice direction sets out the information about a funding arrangement to be provided with the claim form where the claimant intends to seek to recover an additional liability)
('Funding arrangement' and 'additional liability' are defined in rule 43.2)

7.3 Right to Use One Claim Form to Start Two or More Claims

r.7.3 **14.2, 16.36**

A claimant may use a single claim form to start all claims which can be conveniently disposed of in the same proceedings.

7.4 Particulars of Claim

r.7.4 **18.5**   r.7.4(2) **15.13**
r.7.4(1) **15.13, 24.1**   r.7.4(3) **15.13, 15.20**

(1) Particulars of claim must—
  (a) be contained in or served with the claim form; or
  (b) subject to paragraph (2) be served on the defendant by the claimant within 14 days after service of the claim form.
(2) Particulars of claim must be served on the defendant no later than the latest time for serving a claim form.
(Rule 7.5 sets out the latest time for serving a claim form)
(3) Where the claimant serves particulars of claim separately from the claim form in accordance with paragraph (1)(b), he must, within 7 days of service on the defendant, file a copy of the particulars together with a certificate of service.
(Part 16 sets out what the particulars of claim must include)
(Part 22 requires particulars of claim to be verified by a statement of truth)
(Rule 6.10 makes provision for a certificate of service)

7.5 Service of a Claim Form

r.7.5 **13.7, 15.2, 15.3**
r.7.5(2) **15.12, 16.2**
r.7.5(3) **15.4, 16.2**

(1) After a claim form has been issued, it must be served on the defendant.
(2) The general rule is that a claim form must be served within 4 months after the date of issue.
(3) The period for service is 6 months where the claim form is to be served out of the jurisdiction.

7.6 Extension of Time for Serving a Claim Form

r.7.6 **1.26, 13.7, 15.7, 15.41, 42.27, 69.4**
r.7.6(2) **15.9, 15.10**
r.7.6(3) **15.4, 15.9, 15.10, 15.11, 15.12, 15.13, 15.41, 16.46**
r.7.6(3)(b) **15.10, 15.12**
r.7.6(4) **15.10, 32.7**
r.7.6(4)(a)–(b) **15.7**

(1) The claimant may apply for an order extending the period within which the claim form may be served.
(2) The general rule is that an application to extend the time for service must be made—
    (a) within the period for serving the claim form specified by rule 7.5; or
    (b) where an order has been made under this rule, within the period for service specified by that order.
(3) If the claimant applies for an order to extend the time for service of the claim form after the end of the period specified by rule 7.5 or by an order made under this rule, the court may make such an order only if—
    (a) the court has been unable to serve the claim form; or
    (b) the claimant has taken all reasonable steps to serve the claim form but has been unable to do so; and
    (c) in either case, the claimant has acted promptly in making the application.
(4) An application for an order extending the time for service—
    (a) must be supported by evidence; and
    (b) may be made without notice.

7.7 Application by Defendant for Service of Claim Form

r.7.7 **15.42**

(1) Where a claim form has been issued against a defendant, but has not yet been served on him, the defendant may serve a notice on the claimant requiring him to serve the claim form or discontinue the claim within a period specified in the notice.
(2) The period specified in a notice served under paragraph (1) must be at least 14 days after service of the notice.
(3) If the claimant fails to comply with the notice, the court may, on the application of the defendant—
    (a) dismiss the claim; or
    (b) make any other order it thinks just.

7.8 Form for Defence etc. Must Be Served with Particulars of Claim

r.7.8(1) **15.6, 17.4, 18.1**
r.7.8(2) **13.6, 15.6**
r.7.8(2)(b) **18.1**

(1) When particulars of claim are served on a defendant, whether they are contained in the claim form, served with it or served subsequently, they must be accompanied by—
    (a) a form for defending the claim;
    (b) a form for admitting the claim; and
    (c) a form for acknowledging service.
(2) Where the claimant is using the procedure set out in Part 8 (alternative procedure for claims)—
    (a) paragraph (1) does not apply; and
    (b) a form for acknowledging service must accompany the claim form.

7.9 Fixed Date and Other Claims

r.7.9 **12.9, 67.3**

A practice direction—

(a) may set out the circumstances in which the court may give a fixed date for a hearing when it issues a claim;
(b) may list claims in respect of which there is a specific claim form for use and set out the claim form in question; and
(c) may disapply or modify these Rules as appropriate in relation to the claims referred to in paragraphs (a) and (b).

7.10 Production Centre for Claims

(1) There shall be a Production Centre for the issue of claim forms and other related matters.
(2) The relevant practice direction makes provision for—
  (a) which claimants may use the Production Centre;
  (b) the type of claims which the Production Centre may issue;
  (c) the functions which are to be discharged by the Production Centre;
  (d) the place where the Production Centre is to be located; and
  (e) other related matters.
(3) The relevant practice direction may disapply or modify these Rules as appropriate in relation to claims issued by the Production Centre.

7.11 Human Rights

r.7.11 **11.2** r.7.11(1) **96.10**

(1) A claim under section 7(1)(a) of the Human Rights Act 1998 in respect of a judicial act may be brought only in the High Court.
(2) Any other claim under section 7(1)(a) of that Act may be brought in any court.

7.12 Electronic Issue of Claims

r.7.12 **12.10**

(1) A practice direction may make provision for a claimant to start a claim by requesting the issue of a claim form electronically.
(2) The practice direction may, in particular—
  (a) specify—
    (i) the types of claim which may be issued electronically; and
    (ii) the conditions which a claim must meet before it may be issued electronically;
  (b) specify—
    (i) the court where the claim will be issued; and
    (ii) the circumstances in which the claim will be transferred to another court;
  (c) provide for the filing of other documents electronically where a claim has been started electronically;
  (d) specify the requirements that must be fulfilled for any document filed electronically; and
  (e) provide how a fee payable on the filing of any document is to be paid where that document is filed electronically.
(3) The practice direction may disapply or modify these Rules as appropriate in relation to claims started electronically.

PD 7 Practice Direction — How to Start Proceedings — The Claim Form

This practice direction supplements CPR Part 7

PD 7 **24.9** [For commentary on a specific paragraph, please refer to the cross-references after the title of the paragraph.]

General

1 Subject to the following provisions of this practice direction, proceedings which both the High Court and the county courts have jurisdiction to deal with may be started in the High Court or in a county court.

Where to Start Proceedings

paras.2.1–2.4 **11.4**
para.2.5 **11.6**
para.2.6 **11.2, 11.5**
para.2.8 **11.5**
para.2.9 **11.2**

2.1 Proceedings (whether for damages or for a specified sum) may not be started in the High Court unless the value of the claim is more than £15,000.

2.2 Proceedings which include a claim for damages in respect of personal injuries must not be started in the High Court unless the value of the claim is £50,000 or more (art. 9 of the High Court and County Courts Jurisdiction Order 1991 (SI 1991/724 as amended) describes how the value of a claim is to be determined).

2.3 A claim must be issued in the High Court or a county court if an enactment so requires.

2.4 Subject to paragraphs 2.1 and 2.2 above, a claim should be started in the High Court if by reason of:

(1) the financial value of the claim and the amount in dispute, and/or
(2) the complexity of the facts, legal issues, remedies or procedures involved, and/or
(3) the importance of the outcome of the claim to the public in general,

the claimant believes that the claim ought to be dealt with by a High Court judge.

(CPR Part 30 and PD 30 contain provisions relating to the transfer to the county court of proceedings started in the High Court and vice versa.)

2.5 A claim relating to Chancery business (which includes any of the matters specified in the Supreme Court Act 1981, sch. 1, para. 1) may, subject to any enactment, rule or practice direction, be dealt with in the High Court or in a county court. The claim form should, if issued in the High Court, be marked in the top right-hand corner 'Chancery Division' and, if issued in the county court, be marked 'Chancery Business'. (For the equity jurisdiction of county courts, see the County Courts Act 1984, s. 23.)

2.6 A claim relating to any of the matters specified in the Supreme Court Act 1981, sch. 1, para. 2(a) and (b) must be dealt with in the High Court and will be assigned to the Queen's Bench Division.

2.7 Practice directions applying to particular types of proceedings, or to proceedings in particular courts, will contain provisions relating to the commencement and conduct of those proceedings.

2.8 A claim in the High Court for which a jury trial is directed will, if not already being dealt with in the Queen's Bench Division, be transferred to that Division.

2.9 The following proceedings may not be started in a county court unless the parties have agreed otherwise in writing:

(1) a claim for damages or other remedy for libel or slander, and
(2) a claim in which the title to any toll, fair, market or franchise is in question.

2.10 (1) The normal rules apply in deciding in which court and specialist list a claim that includes issues under the Human Rights Act 1998 should be started. They also apply in deciding which procedure to use to start the claim: Part 7, Part 8 or Part 54 (judicial review).

(2) The exception is a claim for damages in respect of a judicial act, which should be commenced in the High Court, If the claim is made in a notice of appeal then it will be dealt with according to the normal rules governing where that appeal is heard.

(A county court cannot make a declaration of incompatibility in accordance with s. 4 of the Human Rights Act 1998. Legislation may direct that such a claim is to be brought before a specified tribunal.)

The Claim Form

para.3 **23.6**
para.3.5 **1.15, 37.17**
para.3.5A **1.15, 23.17, 24.6, 37.17**
paras.3.8–3.9 **23.6**

3.1 A claimant must use form N1 or form N208 (the Part 8 claim form) to start a claim (but see paragraphs 3.2 and 3.4 below).

3.2 Rule 7.9 deals with fixed date claims and rule 7.10 deals with the Production Centre for the issue of claims; there are separate practice directions supplementing rules 7.9 and 7.10.

3.3 If a claimant wishes his claim to proceed under Part 8, or if the claim is required to proceed under Part 8, the claim form should so state. Otherwise the claim will proceed under Part 7. But note that in respect of claims in specialist proceedings (listed in Part 49) and claims brought under the RSC or CCR set out in the schedules to the CPR (see Part 50) the CPR will apply only to the extent that they are not inconsistent with the rules and practice directions that expressly apply to those claims.

3.4 Other practice directions may require special forms to be used to commence particular types of proceedings, or proceedings in particular courts.

3.5 Where a claim which is to be served out of the jurisdiction is one which the court has power to deal with under the Civil Jurisdiction and Judgments Act 1982, the claim form and, when they are contained in a separate document, the particulars of claim should be endorsed with a statement that the court has power under that Act to deal with the claim and that no proceedings based on the same claim are pending between the parties in Scotland, Northern Ireland or another Convention territory.[1]

3.5A Where a claim which is to be served out of jurisdiction is one which the court has power to deal with under Council Regulation (EC) No. 44/2001 of 22 December 2000 on jurisdiction and the recognition and enforcement of judgments in civil and commercial matters, the claim form and, when they are contained in a separate document, the particulars of claim must be endorsed with a statement that the court has power under that Regulation to deal with the claim and that no proceedings based on the same claim are pending between the parties in Scotland, Northern Ireland or another Regulation State.[2]

3.6 If a claim for damages or for an unspecified sum is started in the High Court, the claim form must:

(1) state that the claimant expects to recover more than £15,000 (or £50,000 or more if the claim is for personal injuries) or

(2) state that some enactment provides that the claim may only be commenced in the High Court and specify that enactment or

(3) state that the claim is to be in one of the specialist High Court lists (see CPR Parts 49 and 58 to 62) and specify that list.

3.7 If the contents of a claim form commencing specialist proceedings complies with the requirements of the specialist list in question the claim form will also satisfy paragraph 3.6 above.

3.8 If a claim for damages for personal injuries is started in the county court, the claim form must state whether or not the claimant expects to recover more than £1000 in respect of pain, suffering and loss of amenity.

[1] 'Convention territory' means the territory or territories of any Contracting State as defined by s. 1(3) of the Civil Jurisdiction and Judgments Act 1982, to which the Brussels Convention or Lugano Convention apply.

[2] 'Regulation State' means all member States except Denmark.

3.9 If a claim for housing disrepair which includes a claim for an order requiring repairs or other work to be carried out by the landlord is started in the county court, the claim form must state:
(1) whether or not the cost of the repairs or other work is estimated to be more than £1000, and
(2) whether or not the claimant expects to recover more than £1000 in respect of any claim for damages.[3]
If either of the amounts mentioned in (1) and (2) is more than £1000, the small claims track will not be the normal track for that claim.
(PD 43–48 contains details of the information required to be filed with a claim form to comply with r. 44.15 (providing information about funding arrangements).)

Title of Proceedings

para.4 **49.4**
para.4.1 **14.27, 24.9, 37.17**
para.4.2 **24.9**

4.1 The claim form and every other statement of case, must be headed with the title of the proceedings. The title should state:
(1) the number of proceedings,
(2) the court or division in which they are proceeding,
(3) the full name of each party,
(4) his status in the proceedings (i.e. claimant/defendant).
(PD 16, para. 2.6, sets out what is meant by a full name in respect of each type of claimant.)
4.2 Where there is more than one claimant and/or more than one defendant, the parties should be described in the title as follows:
(1) AB
(2) CD
(3) EF *Claimants*
and
(1) GH
(2) IJ
(3) KL *Defendants*

Start of Proceedings

para.5.1 **10.32, 12.5**
para.5.2 **10.32, 12.5**
para.5.3 **10.32**
para.5.4 **10.32, 12.5**
para.5.5 **14.29**

5.1 Proceedings are started when the court issues a claim form at the request of the claimant (see rule 7.2) but where the claim form as issued was received in the court office on a date earlier than the date on which it was issued by the court, the claim is 'brought' for the purposes of the Limitation Act 1980 and any other relevant statute on that earlier date.
5.2 The date on which the claim form was received by the court will be recorded by a date stamp either on the claim form held on the court file or on the letter that accompanied the claim form when it was received by the court.
5.3 An enquiry as to the date on which the claim form was received by the court should be directed to a court officer.
5.4 Parties proposing to start a claim which is approaching the expiry of the limitation period should recognise the potential importance of establishing the date the claim form was received by the court and should themselves make arrangements to record the date.
5.5 Where it is sought to start proceedings against the estate of a deceased defendant where probate or letters of administration have not been granted, the claimant should issue the claim against 'the personal representatives of A.B. deceased'. The claimant should then, before the expiry of the period for service of the claim form, apply to the court for the appointment of a person to represent the estate of the deceased.

[3] See rules 16.3(4) and 26.6.

Particulars of Claim

para.6.2 **15.13**

6.1 Where the claimant does not include the particulars of claim in the claim form, particulars of claim may be served separately:

(1) either at the same time as the claim form, or

(2) within 14 days after service of the claim form[4] provided that the service of the particulars of claim is within four months after the date of issue of the claim form[5] (or six months where the claim form is to be served out of the jurisdiction).[6]

6.2 If the particulars of claim are not included in or have not been served with the claim form, the claim form must contain a statement that particulars of claim will follow.[7]

(These paragraphs do not apply where the Part 8 procedure is being used. For information on matters to be included in the claim form or the particulars of claim, see Part 16 (statements of case) and PD 16.)

Statement of Truth

7.1 Part 22 requires the claim form and, where they are not included in the claim form, the particulars of claim, to be verified by a statement of truth.

7.2 The form of the statement of truth is as follows:

'[I believe] [the claimant believes] that the facts stated in [this claim form] [these particulars of claim] are true.'

7.3 Attention is drawn to rule 32.14 which sets out the consequences of verifying a statement of case containing a false statement without an honest belief in its truth.

(For information regarding statements of truth see Part 22 and PD 22.)

Extension of Time

para.8.2 **15.7, 15.9**

8.1 An application under rule 7.6 (for an extension of time for serving a claim form under rule 7.6(1)) must be made in accordance with Part 23 and supported by evidence.

8.2 The evidence should state:

(1) all the circumstances relied on,

(2) the date of issue of the claim,

(3) the expiry date of any rule 7.6 extension, and

(4) a full explanation as to why the claim has not been served.

(For information regarding (1) written evidence see Part 32 and PD 32 and (2) service of the claim form see Part 6 and PD 6.)

---

[4] See rule 7.4(1)(b).

[5] See rules 7.4(2) and 7.5(2).

[6] See rule 7.5(3).

[7] See rule 16.2(2).

PD 7B Practice Direction — Consumer Credit Act Claim

This practice direction supplements CPR rule 7.9

PD 7B **12.9, 23.17, 24.1, 95.54, 95.59, 95.65** [For commentary on a specific paragraph, please refer to the cross-references after the title of the paragraph.]

1.1 In this practice direction 'the Act' means the Consumer Credit Act 1974, a section referred to by number means the section with that number in the Act, and expressions which are defined in the Act have the same meaning in this practice direction as they have in the Act.

1.2 'Consumer Credit Act procedure' means the procedure set out in this practice direction.

When to Use the Consumer Credit Act Procedure

2.1 A claimant must use the Consumer Credit Act procedure where he makes a claim under a provision of the Act to which paragraph 3 of this practice direction applies.

2.2 Where a claimant is using the Consumer Credit Act procedure the CPR are modified to the extent that they are inconsistent with the procedure set out in this practice direction.

2.3 The court may at any stage order the claim to continue as if the claimant had not used the Consumer Credit Act procedure, and if it does so the court may give any directions it considers appropriate.

2.4 This practice direction also sets out matters which must be included in the particulars of claim in certain types of claim, and restrictions on where certain types of claim may be started.

The Provisions of the Act

para.3 **12.9**
para.3.1(2) **96.60**
para.3.1(6)(b) **96.56**
para.3.2 **96.54**
para.3.3 **96.54**

3.1 Subject to paragraph 3.2 and 3.3 this practice direction applies to claims made under the following provisions of the Act:

(1) section 141 (claim by the creditor to enforce regulated agreement relating to goods etc.),
(2) section 129 (claim by debtor or hirer for a time order),
(3) section 90 (creditor's claim for an order for recovery of protected goods),
(4) section 92(1) (creditor's or owner's claim to enter premises to take possession of goods),
(5) section 139(1)(a) (debtor's claim for a credit agreement to be reopened as extortionate), and
(6) creditor's or owner's claim for a court order to enforce a regulated agreement relating to goods or money where the court order is required by—
  (a) section 65(1) (improperly-executed agreement),
  (b) section 86(2) of the Act (death of debtor or hirer where agreement is partly secured or unsecured),
  (c) section 111(2) (default notice etc. not served on surety),
  (d) section 124(1) or (2) (taking of a negotiable instrument in breach of terms of section 123), or
  (e) section 105(7)(a) or (b) (security not expressed in writing, or improperly executed).

3.2 This practice direction does not apply to any claim made under the provisions listed in paragraph 3.1 above if that claim relates to the recovery of land.

3.3 This practice direction also does not apply to a claim made by the creditor under section 141 of the Act to enforce a regulated agreement where the agreement relates only to money. Such a claim must be started by the issue of a Part 7 claim form.

Restrictions on Where to Start Some Consumer Credit Act Claims

para.4 **11.3**
paras.4.1–4.2 **96.54**

4.1 Where the claim includes a claim to recover goods to which a regulated hire purchase agreement or conditional sale agreements relates, it may only be started in the county court for the district in which the debtor, or one of the debtors:

(1) resides or carries on business, or

(2) resided or carried on business at the date when the defendant last made a payment under the agreement.

4.2 In any other claim to recover goods, the claim may only be started in the court for the district:

(1) in which the defendant, or one of the defendants, resides or carries on business, or

(2) in which the goods are situated.

4.3 A claim of a debtor or hirer for an order under section 129(1)(b) of the Act (a time order) may only be started in the court where the claimant resides or carries on business.

(Costs rule 45.1(2)(b) allows the claimant to recover fixed costs in certain circumstances where such a claim is made.)

(Paragraph 7 sets out the matters the claimant must include in his particulars of claim where he is using the Consumer Credit Act procedure.)

The Consumer Credit Act Procedure

para.5 **12.9** para.5.2 **24.1, 96.59**
para.5.1 **96.59** paras.5.3–5.6 **96.59**

5.1 In the types of claim to which paragraph 3 applies the court will fix a hearing date on the issue of the claim form.

5.2 The particulars of claim must be served with the claim form.

5.3 Where a claimant is using the Consumer Credit Act procedure, the defendant to the claim is not required to:

(1) serve an acknowledgment of service, or

(2) file a defence, although he may choose to do so.

5.4 Where a defendant intends to defend a claim, his defence should be filed within 14 days of service of the particulars of claim. If the defendant fails to file a defence within this period, but later relies on it, the court may take such a failure into account as a factor when deciding what order to make about costs.

5.5 Part 12 (default judgment) does not apply where the claimant is using the Consumer Credit Act procedure.

5.6 Each party must be given at least 28 days' notice of the hearing date.

5.7 Where the claimant serves the claim form, he must serve notice of the hearing date at the same time, unless the hearing date is specified in the claim form.

Powers of the Court at the Hearing

para.6.1–6.2 **96.59**

6.1 On the hearing date the court may dispose of the claim.

6.2 If the court does not dispose of the claim on the hearing date:

(1) if the defendant has filed a defence, the court will:

(a) allocate the claim to a track and give directions about the management of the case, or

(b) give directions to enable it to allocate the claim to a track,

(2) if the defendant has not filed a defence, the court may make any order or give any direction it considers appropriate.

6.3 Rule 26.5(3) to (5) and rules 26.6 to 26.10 apply to the allocation of a claim under paragraph 6.2.

Matters Which Must Be Included in the Particulars of Claim

para.7 **24.6** paras.7.1–7.4 **96.59**

7.1 Where the Consumer Credit Act procedure is used, the claimant must state in his particulars of claim that the claim is a Consumer Credit Act claim.

7.2 A claimant making a claim for the delivery of goods to enforce a hire purchase agreement or conditional sale agreement which is:

(1) a regulated agreement for the recovery of goods, and

(2) let to a person other than a company or other corporation,

must also state (in this order) in his particulars of claim:

(a) the date of the agreement,

(b) the parties to the agreement,

(c) the number or other identification of the agreement (with enough information to allow the debtor to identify the agreement),

(d) where the claimant was not one of the original parties to the agreement, the means by which the rights and duties of the creditor passed to him,
(e) the place where the agreement was signed by the defendant (if known),
(f) the goods claimed,
(g) the total price of the goods,
(h) the paid up sum,
(i) the unpaid balance of the total price,
(j) whether a default notice or a notice under section 76(1) or section 88(1) of the Act has been served on the defendant, and, if it has, the date and the method of service,
(k) the date on which the right to demand delivery of the goods accrued,
(l) the amount (if any) claimed as an alternative to the delivery of goods, and
(m) the amount (if any) claimed in addition to:
  (i) the delivery of the goods, or
  (ii) any claim under sub paragraph (l) above with the grounds of each such claim.

7.3 A claimant who is a debtor or hirer making a claim for an order under section 129(1)(b) of the Act (a time order) must state (in the following order) in his particulars of claim:
(1) the date of the agreement,
(2) the parties to the agreement,
(3) the number or other means of identifying the agreement,
(4) details of any sureties,
(5) if the defendant is not one of the original parties to the agreement then the name of the original party to the agreement,
(6) the names and addresses of the persons intended to be served with the claim form,
(7) the place where the claimant signed the agreement,
(8) details of the notice served by the creditor or owner giving rise to the claim for the time order,
(9) the total unpaid balance the claimant admits is due under the agreement, and:
  (a) the amount of any arrears (if known), and
  (b) the amount and frequency of the payments specified in the agreement,
(10) the claimant's proposals for payments of any arrears and of future instalments together with details of his means,
(11) where the claim relates to a breach of the agreement other than for the payment of money the claimant's proposals for remedying it.

7.4 (1) This paragraph applies where a claimant is required to obtain a court order to enforce a regulated agreement by:
  (a) section 65(1) (improperly-executed agreement),
  (b) section 105(7)(a) or (b) (security not expressed in writing, or improperly executed),
  (c) section 111(2) (default notice etc. not served on surety),
  (d) section 124(1) or (2) (taking of a negotiable instrument in breach of terms of section 123), or
  (e) section 86(2) of the Act (death of debtor or hirer where agreement is partly secured or unsecured).
(2) The claimant must state in his particulars of claim what the circumstances are that require him to obtain a court order for enforcement.

Admission of Certain Claims for Recovery of Goods under Regulated Agreements

paras.8.1–8.2 **96.45**

8.1 In a claim to recover goods to which section 90(1)[1] applies:

[1] Section 90(1) provides that:
'At any time when—
(a) the debtor is in breach of a regulated hire-purchase or a regulated conditional sale agreement relating to goods, and
(b) the debtor has paid to the creditor one-third or more of the total price of the goods, and
(c) the property in the goods remains in the creditor, the creditor is not entitled to recover possession of the goods from the debtor except on an order of the court.'

(1) the defendant may admit the claim, and
(2) offer terms on which a return order should be suspended under section 135(1)(b).

8.2 He may do so by filing a request in form N9C.

8.3 He should do so within the period for making an admission specified in rule 14.2(b). If the defendant fails to file his request within this period, and later makes such a request, the court may take the failure into account as a factor when deciding what order to make about costs.

8.4 On receipt of the admission, the court will serve a copy on the claimant.

8.5 The claimant may obtain judgment by filing a request in form N228.

8.6 On receipt of the request for judgment, the court will enter judgment in the terms of the defendant's admission and offer and for costs.

8.7 If:
(1) the claimant does not accept the defendant's admission and offer, and
(2) the defendant does not appear on the hearing date fixed when the claim form was issued,

the court may treat the defendant's admission and offer as evidence of the facts stated in it for the purposes of sections 129(2)(a)[2] and 135(2).[3]

Additional Requirements about Parties to the Proceedings

paras.9.1–9.2 **96.57** paras.9.3–9.5 **96.56**

9.1 The court may dispense with the requirement in section 141(5) (all parties to a regulated agreement and any surety to be parties to any proceedings) in any claim relating to the regulated agreement, if:
(1) the claim form has not been served on the debtor or the surety, and
(2) the claimant either before or at the hearing makes an application (which may be made without notice) for the court to make such an order.

9.2 In a claim relating to a regulated agreement where:
(1) the claimant was not one of the original parties to the agreement, and
(2) the former creditor's rights and duties under the agreement have passed to him by:
(a) operation of law, or
(b) assignment,

the requirement of section 141(5) (all parties to a regulated agreement and any surety to be parties to any proceedings) does not apply to the former creditor, unless the court otherwise orders.

9.3 Where a claimant who is a creditor or owner makes a claim for a court order under section 86(2) (death of debtor or hirer where agreement is partly secured or unsecured) the personal representatives of the deceased debtor or hirer must be parties to the proceedings in which the order is sought, unless no grant of representation has been made to the estate.

9.4 Where no grant of representation has been made to the estate of the deceased debtor or hirer, the claimant must make an application in accordance with Part 23 for directions about which persons (if any) are to be made parties to the claim as being affected or likely to be affected by the enforcement of the agreement.

9.5 The claimant's application under paragraph 9.4:
(a) may be made without notice, and
(b) should be made before the claim form is issued.

---

2 Section 129(2) provides that:
'A time order shall provide for one or both of the following, as the court considers just—
(a) the payment by the debtor or hirer or any surety of any sum owed under a regulated agreement or a security by such instalments, payable at such times, as the court, having regard to the means of the debtor or hirer and any surety, considers reasonable;
(b) the remedying by the debtor or hirer of any breach of a regulated agreement (other than non-payment of money) within such period as the court may specify.'

3 Section 135(2) provides that:
'The court shall not suspend the operation of a term [in an order relating to a regulated agreement] requiring the delivery up of goods by any person unless satisfied that the goods are in his possession or control.'

Notice to Be Given to Reopen a Consumer Credit Agreement

para.10.1 **96.65**

10.1 Where a debtor or any surety intends to apply for a consumer credit agreement to be reopened after a claim on or relating to the agreement has already begun, and:
(1) section 139(1)(b);[4] or
(2) section 139(1)(c),
applies, the debtor or surety must serve written notice of his intention on the court and every other party to the proceedings within 14 days of the service of the claim form on him.

10.2 If the debtor or surety (as the case may be) serves a notice under paragraph 10.1 he will be treated as having filed a defence for the purposes of the Consumer Credit Act procedure.

[4] Section 139(1) provides that:
'(1) A credit agreement may, if the court thinks just, be reopened on the ground that the credit bargain is extortionate—
(a) on an application for the purpose made by the debtor or any surety to the High Court, county court or sheriff court; or
(b) at the instance of the debtor or a surety in any proceedings to which the debtor and creditor are parties, being proceedings to enforce the credit agreement, any security relating to it or any linked transaction; or
(c) at the instance of the debtor or a surety in other proceedings in any court where the amount paid or payable under the credit agreement is relevant.'

PD 7C Practice Direction — Production Centre

This practice direction supplements CPR rule 7.10

PD 7C **12.8** [For commentary on a specific paragraph, please refer to the cross-references after the title of the paragraph.]

General

para.1.3(2)(e) **12.8** para.1.4(4) **24.3**

1.1 In this Practice Direction

'the Centre' means the Production Centre,

'Centre user' means a person who is for the time being permitted to issue claims through the Centre, and includes a solicitor acting for such a person,

'officer' means the officer in charge of the Centre or another officer of the Centre acting on his behalf,

'national creditor code' means the number or reference allotted to a Centre user by the officer,

'Code of Practice' means any code of practice which may at any time be issued by Her Majesty's Courts Service relating to the discharge by the Centre of its functions and the way in which a Centre user is to conduct business with the Centre,

'data' means any information which is required to be given to the court or which is to be contained in any document to be sent to the court or to any party.

1.2 For any purpose connected with the exercise of its functions, the Centre will be treated as part of the office of the court whose name appears on the claim form to which the functions relate, or in whose name the claim form is requested to be issued and, the officer will be treated as an officer of that court.

1.3 (1) The functions of the Centre include the provision of a facility which, through the use of information technology, enables a Centre user to have claim forms issued and served, whether or not those claim forms are to be treated as issued in the Northampton County Court or in another county court.

(2) If a Centre user issues claim forms in the name of Northampton County Court, the functions of the Centre also include:

(a) the handling of defences and admissions,

(b) the entry of judgment in default, on admission, on acceptance, or on determination,

(c) the registration of judgments,

(d) the issue of warrants of execution,

(e) where the defendant is an individual, the transfer to the defendant's home court of any case that is to continue following the filing of a defence or where a hearing is required before judgment; or, where the defendant is not an individual, the transfer to the court for the area of the claimant's, or where he is represented, his solicitor's, address, and

(f) the transfer to the defendant's home court of any case for an oral examination or where enforcement of a judgment (other than by warrant of execution, charging order or third party debt order) is to follow.

1.4 (1) Where the officer is to take any step, any rule or practice direction which requires a document to be filed before he does so will be treated as complied with if the data which that document would contain is delivered to the Centre in computer readable form in accordance with the Code of Practice.

(2) Data relating to more than one case may be included in a single document or delivery of data.

(3) Rule 6.3(3) (copies of documents to be served by court) does not apply to any document which is to be produced by electronic means from data supplied by a Centre user.

(4) PD 16, para. 7.3, which requires documentation to be attached to the particulars of contract claims, does not apply to claims to be issued by the Centre.

(5) PD 22 (statements of truth) is modified as follows:

(a) a single statement of truth may accompany each batch of requests to issue claim forms and may be in electronic form,

(b) the form of such a statement should be as follows: 'I believe that the facts stated in the attached claim forms are true.', and
(c) the signature of the appropriate person (as to which see PD 22, para. 3) may be in electronic form.

Claims Which May Not Be issued through the Centre

para.2.3(2) **23.17, 24.1**

2.1 The Centre will not issue any claim form which is to be issued in the High Court.
2.2 The Centre will only issue a claim form if the claim is for a specified sum of money less than £100,000.
2.3 The Centre will not issue any of the following types of claim:
(1) a claim against more than two defendants,
(2) a claim against two defendants where a different sum is claimed against each of them,
(3) a claim where particulars of claim separate from the claim form are required,
(4) a claim against the Crown,
(5) a claim for an amount in a foreign currency,
(6) a claim where either party is known to be a child or patient within Part 21 of the Civil Procedure Rules,
(7) a claim where the claimant is a legally assisted person within the meaning of the Legal Aid Act 1988,
(8) a claim where the defendant's address for service as it appears on the claim form is not in England or Wales.
(9) a claim which is to be issued under Part 8 of the Civil Procedure Rules.

Centre Users

3.1 Only a Centre user may issue or conduct claims through the Centre.
3.2 The officer may permit any person to be a Centre user.
3.3 The officer may withdraw the permission for any person to be a Centre user.
3.4 A Centre user must comply with the provisions of the Code of Practice in his dealings with the Centre.
3.5 The officer will allot a national creditor code to each Centre user.

The Code of Practice

4.1 The Code of Practice will contain provisions designed to ensure that the Centre can discharge its functions efficiently, and it may in particular provide for:
(1) the forms of magnetic media that may be used,
(2) the circumstances in which data may or must be supplied in magnetic form,
(3) the circumstances in which data may or must be supplied in a document and the form that such a document must take,
(4) how often data may be supplied,
(5) the numbering of cases and data relating to cases,
(6) data to be given to the Centre by the Centre user about cases which have been settled or paid or are otherwise not proceeding, and
(7) accounting arrangements and the method of payment of fees.
4.2 Her Majesty's Courts Service may change the Code of Practice from time to time.

Other Modifications to the Civil Procedure Rules

para.5.2 **12.8**

Powers of the officer to make orders
5.1 The officer may make the following orders:
(1) an order to set aside a default judgment where, after that judgment has been entered, the claim form in the case is returned by the Post Office as undelivered,
(2) an order to set aside a judgment on application by a Centre user,
(3) an order to transfer a case to another county court for enforcement or for a judgment debtor to attend court for questioning.

Procedure on the filing of a defence

5.2 (1) This paragraph applies where a Centre user has issued a claim in the Northampton County Court and the defendant has filed a defence to the claim or to part of the claim.

(2) On the filing of the defence the officer will serve a notice on the Centre user requiring the Centre user to notify him within 28 days whether he wishes the claim to proceed.

(3) If the Centre user does not notify the officer within the time specified in the notice that he wishes the claim to proceed the claim will be stayed, and the officer will notify the parties accordingly.

(4) The proceedings will not be transferred as provided by para. 1.3(2)(e) until the Centre user notifies the officer that he wishes the claim to continue.

PD 7D Practice Direction — Claims for the Recovery of Taxes

PD 7D **23.17**

This practice direction supplements CPR rule 7.9

Scope

1.1 This practice direction applies to claims by HM Revenue and Customs for the recovery of:
   (a) income tax,
   (b) corporation tax,
   (c) capital gains tax,
   (d) interest, penalties and surcharges on income tax, corporation tax or capital gains tax which by virtue of the Taxes Management Act 1970, s. 69, are to be treated as if they are taxes due and payable,
   (e) national insurance contributions and interest, penalties and surcharges thereon.

Procedure

2.1 If a defence is filed, the court will fix a date for the hearing.

2.2 Part 26 (case management — preliminary stage) apart from r. 26.2 (automatic transfer) does not apply to claims to which this practice direction applies.

At the Hearing

3.1 On the hearing date the court may dispose of the claim.
(The Taxes Management Act 1970, s. 70, and the Social Security Administration Act 1992, s. 118, provide that a certificate of an officer of the Commissioners for HM Revenue and Customs is sufficient evidence that a sum mentioned in such a certificate is unpaid and due to the Crown)

3.2 But exceptionally, if the court does not dispose of the claim on the hearing date it may give case management directions, which may, if the defendant has filed a defence, include allocating the case.

PD 7E Practice Direction — Money Claim Online

PD 7E **15.14** [For commentary on a specific paragraph, please refer to the cross-references after the title of the paragraph.]

General

para.1.2 **12.10**
para.1.2(2) **12.10**
para.1.4 **12.10**

1.1 This practice direction provides for a scheme in which, in the circumstances set out in this practice direction, a request for a claim form to be issued and other specified documents may be filed electronically ('Money Claim Online').

1.2 This practice direction enables claimants and their representatives:

(1) to start certain types of county court claims by requesting the issue of a claim form electronically via Her Majesty's Courts Service website; and

(2) where a claim has been started electronically:

(a) to file electronically a request for:

(i) judgment in default:

(ii) judgment on acceptance of an admission of the whole of the amount claimed; or

(iii) the issue of a warrant of execution; and

(b) to view an electronic record of the progress of the claim.

1.3 This practice direction also enables defendants and their representatives:

(1) to file electronically:

(a) an acknowledgment of service;

(b) a part admission;

(c) a defence; or

(d) a counterclaim (if filed together with a defence).

(2) to view an electronic record of the progress of the claim.

1.4 Claims started using Money Claim Online will be issued by Northampton County Court and will proceed in that court unless they are transferred to another court. The address for filing any document, application or request (other than one which is filed electronically in accordance with this practice direction) is Northampton County Court, St Katharine's House, 21–27 St Katharine's Street, Northampton NN1 2LH, DX 702885 Northampton 7, fax No. 0845 6015889.

Security

2. Her Majesty's Courts Service will take such measures as it thinks fit to ensure the security of steps taken or information stored electronically. These may include requiring users of Money Claim Online:

(1) to enter a customer identification and password;

(2) to provide personal information for identification purposes; and

(3) to comply with any other security measures,

before taking any of the steps mentioned in para. 1.2 or 1.3.

Fees

3.1 Where this practice direction provides for a fee to be paid electronically, it may be paid by:

(1) credit card;

(2) debit card; or

(3) any other method which Her Majesty's Courts Service may permit.

3.2 A step may only be taken using Money Claim Online on payment of the prescribed fee. The County Court Fees Order 1999 provides that parties may, in certain circumstances, be exempt from payment of fees, or may be entitled to apply for fees to be remitted or reduced. Her Majesty's Courts Service website contains guidance as to when this entitlement arises. A claimant who wishes to claim exemption from payment of fees, or to apply for remission or reduction of fees, may not use Money Claim Online and should issue his claim at a court office.

Types of Claims Which May Be Started Using Money Claim Online

para.4 **12.10**

4. A claim may be started using Money Claim Online if it meets all the following conditions:
   (1) the only remedy claimed is a specified amount of money:
      (a) less than £100,000 (excluding any interest or costs claimed); and
      (b) in sterling;
   (2) the procedure under Part 7 is used;
   (3) the claimant is not:
      (a) a child or patient; or
      (b) funded by the Legal Services Commission;
   (4) the claim is against:
      (a) a single defendant; or
      (b) two defendants, if the claim is for a single amount against each of them;
   (5) the defendant is not:
      (a) the Crown; or
      (b) a person known to be a child or patient; and
   (6) the defendant's address for service is within England and Wales.

Starting a Claim

para.5.1 **12.10**
para. 5.2(1) **23.17, 24.1**
para.5.3 **24.3**
paras.5.5–5.7 **12.10**

5.1 A claimant may request the issue of a claim form by:
   (1) completing and sending an online claim form; and
   (2) electronically paying the appropriate issue fee,
   at www.moneyclaim.gov.uk.

5.2 The particulars of claim:
   (1) must be included in the online claim form and may not be filed separately; and
   (2) must be limited in size to not more than 1080 characters (including spaces).

5.3 PD 16, para. 7.3, which requires documents to be filed with the particulars of claim in contract claims, does not apply to claims started using an online claim form.

5.4 When an online claim form is received by the Money Claim Online website, an acknowledgment of receipt will automatically be sent to the claimant. The acknowledgment of receipt does not constitute a notice that the claim form has been issued.

5.5 When the court issues a claim form following the submission of an online claim form, the claim is 'brought' for the purposes of the Limitation Act 1980 and any other enactment on the date on which the online claim form is received by the court's computer system. The court will keep a record, by electronic or other means, of when online claim forms are received.

5.6 When the court issues a claim form, it will:
   (1) serve a printed version of the claim form on the defendant; and
   (2) send the claimant notice of issue by post.

5.7 The claim form shall have printed on it a unique customer identification number or a password by which the defendant may access the claim on Her Majesty's Courts Service website.

5.8 The claim form shall be deemed to be served on the fifth day after the claim was issued irrespective of whether that day is a business day or not.

5.9 Where a period of time within which an acknowledgment of service or a defence must be filed ends on a day when the court is closed, the defendant may file his acknowledgment or defence on the next day that the court is open.

Online Response

para.6.1 **12.10**

6.1 A defendant wishing to file:
   (1) an acknowledgment of service of the claim form under Part 10;
   (2) a part admission under r. 14.5;
   (3) a defence under Part 15; or
   (4) a counterclaim (to be filed together with a defence),

may, instead of filing a written form, do so by completing and sending the relevant online form at www.moneyclaim.gov.uk.

6.2 Where a defendant files an online form:

(1) he must not send a hard copy in addition;

(2) the form is not filed until it is received by the court, whatever time it is shown to have been sent;

(3) an online form received after 4 p.m. will be treated as filed on the next day the court office is open; and

(4) where a time limit applies, it remains the responsibility of the defendant to ensure that the online form is filed in time.

Acknowledgment of Service

7.1 Attention is drawn to Part 10 and PD 10, which contain rules about acknowledgment of service.

Admission

8.1 Attention is drawn to Part 14 and PD 14, which contain rules about admissions.

Defence

9.1 Attention is drawn to Part 15 and PD 15, which contain rules about defences.

Counterclaim

10.1 Where a counterclaim is filed using an online form, any fee payable shall be taken by the court to which the claim is transferred under para. 14.1.

10.2 Attention is drawn to Part 20 and PD 20, which contain provisions about counterclaims.

Statement of Truth

11.1 Part 22 requires any statement of case to be verified by a statement of truth. This applies to any online forms.

11.2 The statement of truth in an online statement of case must be in the form:

[I believe] [The claimant believes] that the facts stated in this claim form are true.

or

[I believe] [The defendant believes] that the facts stated in this defence are true.

as appropriate.

11.3 Attention is drawn to:

(1) PD 22, para. 3, which provides who may sign a statement of truth; and

(2) r. 32.14, which sets out the consequences of making, or causing to be made, a false statement in a document verified by a statement of truth, without an honest belief in its truth.

Signature

12.1 Any provision of the CPR which requires a document to be signed by any person is satisfied by that person entering his name on an online form.

Request for Judgment or Issue of Warrant

para.13 **12.10**

13.1 If, in a claim started using Money Claim Online:

(1) the claimant wishes to apply for judgment in default in accordance with Part 12; or

(2) the defendant has filed or served an admission of the whole of the claim in accordance with r. 14.4,

the claimant may request judgment to be entered in default or on the admission (as the case may be) by completing and sending an online request form at: www.moneyclaim.gov.uk.

13.2 Where:

(1) judgment has been entered following a request under para. 13.1; and

(2) the claimant is entitled to the issue of a warrant of execution without requiring the permission of the court,

the claimant may request the issue of a warrant of execution by:

(a) completing and sending an online request form; and

(b) electronically paying the appropriate fee,

at www.moneyclaim.gov.uk.

(CCR, ord. 26 in CPR, sch. 2, contains rules about warrants of execution. Among other matters, CCR, ord. 26, r. 1, contains restrictions on when a warrant of execution may be issued if the court has made an order for payment of a sum of money by instalments, and CCR, ord. 26, r. 5, sets out certain circumstances in which a warrant of execution may not be issued without the permission of the court.)

13.3 A request under para. 13.1 or 13.2 will be treated as being filed:

(1) on the day the court receives the request, if it receives it before 10 a.m. on a working day; and

(2) otherwise, on the next working day after the court receives the request.

Transfer of Claim

para.14 **12.10**

14.1 Where the defendant is an individual and Northampton County Court is not his home court, the court will transfer the claim to the defendant's home court:

(1) under r. 13.4, if the defendant applies to set aside or vary judgment;

(2) under r. 14.12, if there is to be a hearing for a judge to determine the time and rate of payment;

(3) under r. 26.2, if a defence is filed to all or part of the claim; or

(4) if either party makes an application which cannot be dealt with without a hearing.

14.2 Where the defendant is not an individual, if:

(1) the claimant's address for service on the claim form is not within the district of Northampton County Court; and

(2) one of the events mentioned in para. 14.1 arises,

the court will transfer the claim to the county court for the district in which the claimant's address for service on the claim form is situated.

Viewing the Case Record

para.15.2 **12.10**

15.1 A facility will be provided for parties or their representatives to view an electronic record of the status of claims started using Money Claim Online.

15.2 The record of each claim will be reviewed and, if necessary, updated at least once each day until the claim is transferred from Northampton County Court.

CPR Part 8 Alternative Procedure for Claims

Part 8 **1.31, 12.1, 13.1, 13.4, 13.7, 13.14, 14.38, 18.3, 23.2, 34.18, 48.71, 50.1, 76.25, 78.6, 82.3, 82.5, 92.21** [For commentary on a specific rule, please refer to the cross-references after the title of the rule.]

8.1 Types of Claim in Which Part 8 Procedure May Be Followed

r.8.1(2) **13.1**
r.8.1(3) **13.2, 13.12, 42.6**
r.8.1(5) **13.9**
r.8.1(6) **13.1**

(1) The Part 8 procedure is the procedure set out in this Part.
(2) A claimant may use the Part 8 procedure where—
   (a) he seeks the court's decision on a question which is unlikely to involve a substantial dispute of fact; or
   (b) paragraph (6) applies.
(3) The court may at any stage order the claim to continue as if the claimant had not used the Part 8 procedure and, if it does so, the court may give any directions it considers appropriate.
(4) Paragraph (2) does not apply if a practice direction provides that the Part 8 procedure may not be used in relation to the type of claim in question.
(5) Where the claimant uses the Part 8 procedure he may not obtain default judgment under Part 12.
(6) A rule or practice direction may, in relation to a specified type of proceedings—
   (a) require or permit the use of the Part 8 procedure; and
   (b) disapply or modify any of the rules set out in this Part as they apply to those proceedings.

(Rule 8.9 provides for other modifications to the general rules where the Part 8 procedure is being used)

8.2 Contents of the Claim Form

r.8.2 **13.7**

Where the claimant uses the Part 8 procedure the claim form must state—
(a) that this Part applies;
(b) (i) the question which the claimant wants the court to decide; or
   (ii) the remedy which the claimant is seeking and the legal basis for the claim to that remedy;
(c) if the claim is being made under an enactment, what that enactment is;
(d) if the claimant is claiming in a representative capacity, what that capacity is; and
(e) if the defendant is sued in a representative capacity, what that capacity is.

(Part 22 provides for the claim form to be verified by a statement of truth)
(Rule 7.5 provides for service of the claim form)
(The costs practice direction [PD 43–48] sets out the information about a funding arrangement to be provided with the claim form where the claimant intends to seek to recover an additional liability)
('Funding arrangement' and 'additional liability' are defined in rule 43.2)

8.2A Issue of Claim Form without Naming Defendants

r.8.2A **13.7**

(1) A practice direction may set out the circumstances in which a claim form may be issued under this Part without naming a defendant.

(2) The practice direction may set out those cases in which an application for permission must be made by application notice before the claim form is issued.
(3) The application notice for permission—
  (a) need not be served on any other person; and
  (b) must be accompanied by a copy of the claim form that the applicant proposes to issue.
(4) Where the court gives permission it will give directions about the future management of the claim.

8.3 Acknowledgment of Service

r.8.3 **13.8, 18.1, 92.7**
r.8.3(1) **13.8**
r.8.3(2)(a)–(b) **13.8**

(1) The defendant must—
  (a) file an acknowledgment of service in the relevant practice form not more than 14 days after service of the claim form; and
  (b) serve the acknowledgment of service on the claimant and any other party.
(2) The acknowledgment of service must state—
  (a) whether the defendant contests the claim; and
  (b) if the defendant seeks a different remedy from that set out in the claim form, what that remedy is.
(3) The following rules of Part 10 (acknowledgment of service) apply—
  (a) rule 10.3(2) (exceptions to the period for filing an acknowledgment of service); and
  (b) rule 10.5 (contents of acknowledgment of service).

(The costs practice direction [PD 43–48] sets out the information about a funding arrangement to be provided with the acknowledgment of service where the defendant intends to seek to recover an additional liability)
('Funding arrangement' and 'additional liability' are defined in rule 43.2)

8.4 Consequence of Not Filing an Acknowledgment of Service

r.8.4 **13.9, 78.6, 92.7**

(1) This rule applies where—
  (a) the defendant has failed to file an acknowledgment of service; and
  (b) the time period for doing so has expired.
(2) The defendant may attend the hearing of the claim but may not take part in the hearing unless the court gives permission.

8.5 Filing and Serving Written Evidence

r.8.5 **13.15**
r.8.5(1) **13.7, 15.6**
r.8.5(2) **13.7, 15.6, 92.7**
r.8.5(3)–(4) **13.10, 74.38, 92.7**
r.8.5(5)–(6) **13.13, 74.38, 92.7**

(1) The claimant must file any written evidence on which he intends to rely when he files his claim form.
(2) The claimant's evidence must be served on the defendant with the claim form.
(3) A defendant who wishes to rely on written evidence must file it when he files his acknowledgment of service.
(4) If he does so, he must also, at the same time, serve a copy of his evidence on the other parties.
(5) The claimant may, within 14 days of service of the defendant's evidence on him, file further written evidence in reply.
(6) If he does so, he must also, within the same time limit, serve a copy of his evidence on the other parties.
(7) The claimant may rely on the matters set out in his claim form as evidence under this rule if the claim form is verified by a statement of truth.

8.6 Evidence — General

r.8.6(1) **13.13**
r.8.6(1)(b) **13.10, 13.13, 13.15**
r.8.6(2) **13.15**
r.8.6(3) **13.15**

(1) No written evidence may be relied on at the hearing of the claim unless—

Civil Procedure Rules & Practice Directions

(a) it has been served in accordance with rule 8.5; or
(b) the court gives permission.

(2) The court may require or permit a party to give oral evidence at the hearing.
(3) The court may give directions requiring the attendance for cross-examination[(GL)] of a witness who has given written evidence.

(Rule 32.1 contains a general power for the court to control evidence)

8.7 Part 20 Claims

r.8.7 **13.16**

Where the Part 8 procedure is used, Part 20 (counterclaims and other additional claims) applies except that a party may not make a Part 20 claim (as defined by rule 20.2) without the court's permission.

8.8 Procedure Where Defendant Objects to Use of the Part 8 Procedure

r.8.8(1)–(2) **13.12**

(1) Where the defendant contends that the Part 8 procedure should not be used because—
(a) there is a substantial dispute of fact; and
(b) the use of the Part 8 procedure is not required or permitted by a rule or practice direction,
he must state his reasons when he files his acknowledgment of service.

(Rule 8.5 requires a defendant who wishes to rely on written evidence to file it when he files his acknowledgment of service)

(2) When the court receives the acknowledgment of service and any written evidence it will give directions as to the future management of the case.

(Rule 8.1(3) allows the court to make an order that the claim continue as if the claimant had not used the Part 8 procedure)

8.9 Modifications to the General Rules

r.8.9(a)(i) **13.1, 13.7, 24.1**
r.8.9(a)(ii) **13.1, 13.8**
r.8.9(b)(i) **13.8**
r.8.9(b)(ii) **13.6**
r.8.9(c) **13.1, 13.14, 42.6, 71.6**

Where the Part 8 procedure is followed—
(a) provision is made in this Part for the matters which must be stated in the claim form and the defendant is not required to file a defence and therefore—
(i) Part 16 (statements of case) does not apply;
(ii) Part 15 (defence and reply) does not apply;
(iii) any time limit in these Rules which prevents the parties from taking a step before a defence is filed does not apply;
(iv) the requirement under rule 7.8 to serve on the defendant a form for defending the claim does not apply;
(b) the claimant may not obtain judgment by request on an admission and therefore—
(i) rules 14.4 to 14.7 do not apply; and
(ii) the requirement under rule 7.8 to serve on the defendant a form for admitting the claim does not apply; and
(c) the claim shall be treated as allocated to the multi-track and therefore Part 26 does not apply.

PD 8 Practice Direction — Alternative Procedure for Claims

This practice direction supplements CPR Part 8

[For commentary on a specific paragraph, please refer to the cross-references after the title of the paragraph.]

Types of Claim in Which Part 8 Procedure May Be Used

paras.1.1–1.2 **13.1** paras.1.4–1.5 **13.2**

1.1 A claimant may use the Part 8 procedure where he seeks the court's decision on a question which is unlikely to involve a substantial dispute of fact.

1.2 A claimant may also use the Part 8 procedure if a practice direction permits or requires its use for the type of proceedings in question.

1.3 The practice directions referred to in para. 1.2 above may in some respects modify or disapply the Part 8 procedure and, where that is so, it is those practice directions that must be complied with.

1.4 The types of claim for which the Part 8 procedure may be used include:

(1) a claim by or against a child or patient which has been settled before the commencement of proceedings and the sole purpose of the claim is to obtain the approval of the court to the settlement,

(2) a claim for provisional damages which has been settled before the commencement of proceedings and the sole purpose of the claim is to obtain a consent judgment, and

(3) provided there is unlikely to be a substantial dispute of fact, a claim for a summary order for possession against named or unnamed defendants occupying land or premises without the licence or consent of the person claiming possession.

1.5 Where it appears to a court officer that a claimant is using the Part 8 procedure inappropriately, he may refer the claim to a judge for the judge to consider the point.

1.6 The court may at any stage order the claim to continue as if the claimant had not used the Part 8 procedure and, if it does so, the court will allocate the claim to a track and give such directions as it considers appropriate.[1]

Issuing the Claim

2.1 Part 7 and PD 7 contain a number of rules and directions applicable to all claims, including those to which Part 8 applies. Those rules and directions should be applied where appropriate.

2.2 Where a claimant uses the Part 8 procedure, the claim form (form N208) should be used and must state the matters set out in r. 8.2 and, if paras 1.2 or 1.3 apply, must comply with the requirements of the practice direction in question. In particular, the claim form must state that Part 8 applies; a Part 8 claim form means a claim form which so states.

(PD 43–48 contains details of the information required to be filed with a claim form to comply with r. 44.15 (providing information about funding arrangements).)

Responding to the Claim

para.3.2 **13.8** para.3.6 **13.12**

3.1 The provisions of Part 15 (defence and reply) do not apply where the claim form is a Part 8 claim form.

3.2 Where a defendant who wishes to respond to a Part 8 claim form is required to file an acknowledgment of service, that acknowledgment of service should be in form N210[2] but can, alternatively, be given in an informal document such as a letter.

3.3 Rule 8.3 sets out provisions relating to an acknowledgment of service of a Part 8 claim form.

3.4 Rule 8.4 sets out the consequence of failing to file an acknowledgment of service.

---

[1] Rule 8.1(3).

[2] Rule 8.3(1)(a).

3.5 The provisions of Part 12 (obtaining default judgment) do not apply where the claim form is a Part 8 claim form.

3.6 Where a defendant believes that the Part 8 procedure should not be used because there is a substantial dispute of fact or, as the case may be, because its use is not authorised by any rule or practice direction, he must state his reasons in writing when he files his acknowledgment of service.[3] If the statement of reasons includes matters of evidence it should be verified by a statement of truth.

Managing the Claim

para.4.1 **13.14**

4.1 The court may give directions immediately a Part 8 claim form is issued either on the application of a party or on its own initiative. The directions may include fixing a hearing date where:

(1) there is no dispute, such as in child and patient settlements, or

(2) where there may be a dispute, such as in claims for mortgage possession or appointment of trustees, but a hearing date could conveniently be given.

4.2 Where the court does not fix a hearing date when the claim form is issued, it will give directions for the disposal of the claim as soon as practicable after the defendant has acknowledged service of the claim form or, as the case may be, after the period for acknowledging service has expired.

4.3 Certain applications may not require a hearing.

4.4 The court may convene a directions hearing before giving directions.

Evidence

para.5.2 **13.7, 13.10**
para.5.5 **13.10, 13.13**
para.5.6 **13.10, 13.13**

5.1 A claimant wishing to rely on written evidence should file it when his Part 8 claim form is issued[4] (unless the evidence is contained in the claim form itself).

5.2 Evidence will normally be in the form of a witness statement or an affidavit but a claimant may rely on the matters set out in his claim form provided that it has been verified by a statement of truth.

(For information about (1) statements of truth see Part 22 and PD 22, and (2) written evidence see Part 32 and PD 32.)

5.3 A defendant wishing to rely on written evidence, should file it with his acknowledgment of service.[5]

5.4 Rule 8.5 sets out the times and provisions for filing and serving written evidence.

5.5 A party may apply to the court for an extension of time to serve and file evidence under r. 8.5 or for permission to serve and file additional evidence under r. 8.6(1).

(For information about applications see Part 23 and PD 23.)

5.6 (1) The parties may, subject to the following provisions, agree in writing on an extension of time for serving and filing evidence under r. 8.5(3) or r. 8.5(5).

(2) An agreement extending time for a defendant to file evidence r. 8.5(3):

(a) must be filed by the defendant at the same time as he files his acknowledgment of service; and

(b) must not extend time by more than 14 days after the defendant files his acknowledgment of service.

(3) An agreement extending time for a claimant to file evidence in reply under r. 8.5(5) must not extend time to more than 28 days after service of the defendant's evidence on the claimant.

[3] Rule 8.8(1).
[4] Rule 8.5.
[5] Rule 8.5(3).

PD 8B Practice Direction — Part 8

This practice direction supplements CPR Part 8, and Schedule 1 and Schedule 2 to the CPR

PD 8B **1.5, 13.3** [For commentary on a specific paragraph, please refer to the cross-references after the title of the paragraph.]

Terminology

1.1 In this practice direction 'Schedule rules' means provisions contained in the Schedules to the CPR, which were previously contained in the Rules of the Supreme Court (1965) or the County Court Rules (1981).

Contents of This Practice Direction

2.1 This practice direction explains:

(1) how to start the claims referred to in Sections A and B;

(2) which form to use as the claim form; and

(3) the procedure which those claims will follow.

(Further guidance about forms other than claim forms can be found in PD 4.)

(Form 87 (modified as necessary) should be used when making an application for a writ of habeas corpus under RSC, ord. 54 in sch. 1. Attention is drawn to the relevant existing Administrative Court practice directions for further guidance.)

How to Use This Practice Direction

3.1 This practice direction is divided into sections A and B. Only one section will be relevant to how to make a particular claim or appeal.

3.2 If the claim is described in paragraph A. 1 — use section A.

3.3 If the claim is described in paragraph B. 1 — use section B.

SECTION A

section A **13.3**

Application

para.A. 1 **13.3** para.A. 1(2) **2.11**

A.1 Section A applies if:

(1) the claim is listed in Table 1 below;

(2) an Act provides that a claim or application in the High Court is to be brought by originating summons; or

(3) before 26 April 1999, a claim or application in the High Court would have been brought by originating summons, and

no other method for bringing the claim or application on and after 26 April 1999 is specified in a rule or practice direction.

A.2 (1) The claimant must use the Part 8 procedure unless an Act, rule, or practice direction, makes any additional or contrary provision.

(2) Where such additional or contrary provision is made the claimant must comply with it and modify the Part 8 procedure accordingly.

Claim Form

A.3 The claimant must use the Part 8 claim form.

Table 1

Table 1 **13.3**

RSC, ord. 17, r. 3(1)	Interpleader (Mode of application)
RSC, ord. 77, r. 11	Proceedings by and against the Crown (Interpleader: Application for order against Crown)
RSC, ord. 77, r. 16(2)	Proceedings by and against the Crown (Attachment of debts, etc.)
RSC, ord. 77, r. 17(1)	Proceedings by and against the Crown (Proceedings relating to postal packets)
RSC, ord. 77, r. 18(1)	Proceedings by and against the Crown (Applications under sections 17 and 29 of Crown Proceedings Act 1947)
RSC, ord. 79, r. 8(2)	Criminal Proceedings (Estreat of recognisances)
RSC, ord. 79, r. 9(2)	Criminal Proceedings (Bail)
RSC, ord. 81, r. 10(1)	Partners (Applications for orders charging partner's interest in partnership property)
RSC, ord. 93, r. 5(2)	Applications and Appeals to High Court under Various Acts: Chancery Division (Applications under section 2(3) of the Public Order Act 1936)
RSC, ord. 93, r. 18(2)	Applications and Appeals to High Court under Various Acts: Chancery Division (Proceedings under section 86 of the Civil Aviation Act 1982)
RSC, ord. 94, r. 5	Applications and Appeals to High Court under Various Acts: Queen's Bench Division (Exercise of jurisdiction under Representation of the People Acts)
RSC, ord. 95, r. 2(1)	Bills of Sale Acts 1878 and 1882 and the Industrial and Provident Societies Act 1967 (Entry of satisfaction)
RSC, ord. 95, r. 3	Bills of Sale Acts 1878 and 1882 and the Industrial and Provident Societies Act 1967 (Restraining removal on sale of goods seized)
RSC, ord. 96, r. 1	The Mines (Working Facilities and Support) Act 1966 etc. (Assignment to Chancery Division)
RSC, ord. 96, r. 3	The Mines (Working Facilities and Support) Act 1966 etc. (Issue of claim form)
RSC, ord. 109, r. 1(3)	Administration of Justice Act 1960 (Applications under Act)

SECTION B

section B **13.3, 13.5, 13.6, 13.7, 13.8, 13.14, 14.69**

Application

para.B.1(3) **13.3**

B.1 Section B applies if the claim:
- (1) is listed in Table 2;
- (3) would have been brought before 26 April 1999:
  - (a) in the High Court, by originating motion;
  - (b) in the county court:
    - (i) by originating application; or
    - (ii) by petition, and

no other procedure is prescribed in an Act, a rule or a practice direction.

Table 2

Table 2 **13.3, 13.6, 14.69**

Schedule rule	Claim form
RSC, ord. 77, r. 8(2)[1]	Proceedings by and against the Crown (Summary applications to the court in certain revenue matters)
RSC, ord. 93, r. 19(1)	Applications and Appeals to High Court under Various Acts: (Proceedings under section 85(7) of the Fair Trading Act 1973 and the Control of Misleading Advertisements Regulations 1988)
RSC, ord. 93, r. 22(3)	Applications and Appeals to High Court under Various Acts: Chancery Division (Proceedings under the Financial Services Act and Markets Act 2000)
RSC, ord. 94, r. 1(2)	Applications and Appeals to High Court under Various Acts: Queen's Bench Division (Jurisdiction of High Court to Quash Certain Orders, Schemes etc.)
RSC, ord. 94, r. 7(2)*	Applications and Appeals to High Court under Various Acts: Queen's Bench Division (Reference of Question of Law by Agricultural Land Tribunal)
RSC, ord. 94, r. 11(4)*	Applications and Appeals to High Court under Various Acts: Queen's Bench Division (Case stated by Mental Health Review Tribunal)
RSC, ord. 94, r. 12(5)(c)	Applications and Appeals to High Court r. 12(5)(c) under Various Acts: Queen's Bench Division Applications for permission under section 289(6) of the Town and Country Planning Act 1990 and section 65(5) of the Planning (Listed Buildings and Conservation Areas) Act 1990
RSC, ord. 94, r. 13(5)	Applications and Appeals to High Court under Various Acts: Queen's Bench Division Proceedings under sections 289 and 290 of the Town and Country Planning Act 1990 and under section 65 of the Planning (Listed Buildings and Conservation Areas) Act 1990
RSC, ord. 94, r. 14(2)	Applications and Appeals to High Court under Various Acts: Queen's Bench Division Applications under section 13 of the Coroners Act 1988
RSC, ord. 94, r. 15(2)	Applications and Appeals to High Court under Various Acts: Queen's Bench Division Applications under section 42 of the Supreme Court Act 1981
RSC, ord. 109, r. 2(4)	Administration of Justice Act 1960 (Appeals under section 13 of Act)
RSC, ord. 115, r. 2B(1)	Confiscation and Forfeiture in Connection with Criminal Proceedings (I. Drug Trafficking Act 1994 and Criminal Justice (International Co-operation) Act 1990 — Application for confiscation order)
RSC, ord. 115, r. 3(1)	Confiscation and Forfeiture in Connection with Criminal Proceedings (I. Drug Trafficking Act 1994 and Criminal Justice (International Co-operation) Act 1990 — Application for restraint order or charging order)
RSC, ord. 115, r. 7(1)	Confiscation and Forfeiture in Connection with Criminal Proceedings (I. Drug Trafficking Act 1994 and Criminal Justice (International Co-operation) Act 1990 — Realisation of property)
RSC, ord. 115, r. 26(1)	Confiscation and Forfeiture in Connection with Criminal Proceedings (III. Prevention of Terrorism (Temporary Provisions) Act 1989 — Application for restraint order)
RSC, ord. 116, r. 5(1)	The Criminal Procedure and Investigations Act 1996 (Application under section 54(3)).

[1] This type of claim may also be brought by the Part 8 procedure
[* This rule has been revoked.]

Schedule rule		Claim form
CCR, ord. 44, r. 1(1)	The Agricultural Holdings Act 1986 (Special case stated by arbitrator)	
CCR, ord. 44, r. 3(1)	The Agricultural Holdings Act 1986 (Removal of arbitrator or setting aside award)	
CCR, ord. 45, r. 1(1)	The Representation of the People Act 1983 (Application for detailed assessment of returning officer's account)	N408
CCR, ord. 46, r. 1(1)	The Legitimacy Act 1976 (Manner of application)	
CCR, ord. 49, r. 7(2)	Miscellaneous Statutes: Injunctions to Prevent Environmental Harm: Town and Country Planning Act 1990 etc. (Application for injunction)	
CCR, ord. 49, r. 12(2)	Miscellaneous Statutes: Mental Health Act 1983 (Application)	
CCR, ord. 49, r. 15(1)	Miscellaneous Statutes: Post Office Act 1969 (Application under section 30(5))	

The Local Government Act 1972 (claims under s. 92 — proceedings for disqualification)

Special Provisions Take Precedence

para.B.2–B. 5 **13.3**

B.2 The claimant must first comply with any special provision set out in the Schedule rules, practice direction or any Act relating to the claim.

(Special provisions are made in CCR, ord. 6 in CPR, sch. 2, about particulars of claim for certain types of claim.)

B.3 Special provisions contained in Schedule rules or an Act may set out:

(1) where the claim may be started;
(2) the contents of the claim form;
(3) whether a hearing is required;
(4) the nature of evidence required in support of the claim, and when it must be filed or served;
(5) the method of service of the claim form and evidence;
(6) persons on whom service must or may be effected;
(7) the form and content of notices, and when they must or may be filed, and on whom served;
(8) the form and content of any affidavit, answer, or reply and when they must or may be filed or served;
(9) persons who may apply to be joined as parties to the claim;
(10) minimum periods of notice before the hearing date.

B.4 Where a Schedule rule makes special provision for the contents of particulars of claim, those particulars must be attached to the claim form and served with it.

B.5 Subject to any special or contrary provision in an Act or Schedule rule, the claimant must use the procedure set out in the remainder of this section.

Restrictions on Where to Start the Claim

B.6 Where the claimant is bringing a claim in a county court that claim may only be started:

(1) in the county court for the district in which:
  (a) the defendants or one of the defendants lives or carries on business; or
  (b) the subject matter of the claim is situated; or
(2) if there is no defendant named in the claim form, in the county court for the district in which the claimant or one of the claimants lives or carries on business.

B.7 Where the claimant is making a claim in the county court for:

(1) enforcing any charge or lien on land;
(2) the recovery of moneys secured by a mortgage or charge on land,

the claim must be started in the court for the district in which the land, or any part of it, is situated.

Claim Form

B.8 This paragraph sets out which form is to be used as the claim form:

(1) where a claim form number is listed against a particular claim in Table 2, the claimant must use that numbered form as the claim form;

(2) in every other claim, the claimant must use the Part 8 claim form.

Court Will Fix a Date

para.B.9 **13.3, 13.6**

B.9 When the court issues the claim form it will:

(1) fix a date for the hearing; and

(2) prepare a notice of the hearing date for each party.

Service of the Claim Form

para.B.10 **13.3, 13.7** para.B.11 **13.3, 13.6**

B.10 The claim form must be served not less than 21 days before the hearing date.

B.11 Where the claimant serves the claim form, he must serve notice of the hearing date at the same time, unless the hearing date is specified in the claim form.

(CPR, r. 3.1(2)(a) and (b) provide for the court to extend or shorten the time for compliance with any rule or practice direction, and to adjourn or bring forward a hearing.)

Defendant is Not Required to Respond

para.B.12 **13.3, 13.6, 13.8**

B.12 The defendant is not required to serve an acknowledgment of service.

At the Hearing

para.B.13 **13.3, 13.14** para.B.15 **13.3, 13.14**
para.B.14 **13.3, 13.14, 42.6**

B.13 The court may on the hearing date:

(1) proceed to hear the case and dispose of the claim; or

(2) give case management directions.

B.14 Case management directions given under paragraph B.13 will, if the defendant has filed a defence, include the allocation of a case to a track, or directions to enable the case to be allocated.

(A defended county court claim for possession of land, where it has been allocated to the multi-track, will not normally be transferred to the Civil Trial Centre: see PD 26, para. 10.1(1).)

B.15 CPR, rr. 26.5(3) to (5) and 26.6 to 26.10, apply to the allocation of a claim under para. B.14.

CPR Part 9 Responding to Particulars of Claim — General

Part 9 **17.1**

9.1 Scope of this Part

(1) This Part sets out how a defendant may respond to particulars of claim.
(2) Where the defendant receives a claim form which states that particulars of claim are to follow, he need not respond to the claim until the particulars of claim have been served on him.

9.2 Defence, Admission or Acknowledgment of Service

When particulars of claim are served on a defendant, the defendant may—

(a) file or serve an admission in accordance with Part 14;
(b) file a defence in accordance with Part 15,
(or do both, if he admits only part of the claim); or
(c) file an acknowledgment of service in accordance with Part 10.

(Paragraph 10.6 of the Practice Direction to Part 16 contains provision about the content of the admission, defence or acknowledgment of service)

CPR Part 10 Acknowledgment of Service

[For commentary on a specific rule, please refer to the cross-references after the title of the rule.]

10.1 Acknowledgment of Service

r.10 **15.33, 76.36** r.10.1(3) **18.1**

(1) This Part deals with the procedure for filing an acknowledgment of service.
(2) Where the claimant uses the procedure set out in Part 8 (alternative procedure for claims) this Part applies subject to the modifications set out in rule 8.3.
(3) A defendant may file an acknowledgment of service if—
 (a) he is unable to file a defence within the period specified in rule 15.4; or
 (b) he wishes to dispute the court's jurisdiction.

(Part 11 sets out the procedure for disputing the court's jurisdiction)

10.2 Consequence of Not Filing an Acknowledgment of Service

If—
(a) a defendant fails to file an acknowledgment of service within the period specified in rule 10.3; and
(b) does not within that period file a defence in accordance with Part 15 or serve or file an admission in accordance with Part 14,

the claimant may obtain default judgment if Part 12 allows it.

10.3 The Period for Filing an Acknowledgment of Service

r.10.3(1) **18.2** r.10.3(2) **13.8**
r.10.3(1)(b) **69.8** r.10.3(2)(a)–(b) **18.2**

(1) The general rule is that the period for filing an acknowledgment of service is—
 (a) where the defendant is served with a claim form which states that particulars of claim are to follow, 14 days after service of the particulars of claim; and
 (b) in any other case, 14 days after service of the claim form.
(2) The general rule is subject to the following rules—
 (a) Rule 6.22 (which specifies how the period for filing an acknowledgment of service is calculated where the claim form is served out of the jurisdiction);
 (b) rule 6.16(4) (which requires the court to specify the period for responding to the particulars of claim when it makes an order under that rule); and
 (c) rule 6.21(4) (which requires the court to specify the period within which the defendant may file an acknowledgment of service calculated by reference to Practice Direction 6B when it makes an order giving permission to serve a claim form out of the jurisdiction).

10.4 Notice to Claimant That Defendant Has Filed an Acknowledgment of Service

r.10.4 **18.2**

On receipt of an acknowledgment of service, the court must notify the claimant in writing.

10.5 Contents of Acknowledgment of Service

r.10.5 **13.8** r.10.5(a)–(b) **18.3**

An acknowledgment of service must—
(a) be signed by the defendant or his legal representative; and
(b) include the defendant's address for service.

(Rule 6.5 provides that an address for service must be within the jurisdiction)
(Rule 19.8A modifies this Part where a notice of claim is served under that rule to bind a person not a party to the claim)

PD 10 Practice Direction — Acknowledgment of Service

This practice direction supplements CPR Part 10

[For commentary on a specific paragraph, please refer to the cross-references after the title of the paragraph.]

Responding to the Claim

1.1 Part 9 sets out how a defendant may respond to a claim.

1.2 Part 10 sets out the provisions for acknowledging service (but see rule 8.3 for information about acknowledging service of a claim under the Part 8 procedure).

The Form of Acknowledgment of Service

2 A defendant who wishes to acknowledge service of a claim should do so by using form N9.

Address for Service

para.3.2 **18.3**

3.1 The defendant must include in his acknowledgment of service an address for the service of documents.[1]

3.2 Where the defendant is represented by a legal representative[2] and the legal representative has signed the acknowledgment of service form, the address must be the legal representative's business address; otherwise the address for service that is given should be as set out in rule 6.5 and the practice direction which supplements Part 6.

Signing the Acknowledgment of Service

para.4.2 **13.8**
para.4.3 **13.8, 18.3**
para.4.4 **13.8, 15.33, 18.3**
para.4.5 **18.3**

4.1 An acknowledgment of service must be signed by the defendant or by his legal representative.

4.2 Where the defendant is a company or other corporation, a person holding a senior position in the company or corporation may sign the acknowledgment of service on the defendant's behalf, but must state the position he holds.

4.3 Each of the following persons is a person holding a senior position:

(1) in respect of a registered company or corporation, a director, the treasurer, secretary, chief executive, manager or other officer of the company or corporation, and

(2) in respect of a corporation which is not a registered company, in addition to those persons set out in (1), the mayor, chairman, president, town clerk or similar officer of the corporation.

4.4 Where the defendant is a partnership, the acknowledgment of service may be signed by:

(1) any of the partners, or

(2) a person having the control or management of the partnership business.

4.5 Children and patients may acknowledge service only by their litigation friend or his legal representative unless the court otherwise orders.[3]

General

para.5.3 **18.3, 22.2**
para.5.4 **18.3**

5.1 The defendant's name should be set out in full on the acknowledgment of service.

5.2 Where the defendant's name has been incorrectly set out in the claim form, it should be correctly set out on the acknowledgment of service followed by the words 'described as' and the incorrect name.

5.3 If two or more defendants to a claim acknowledge service of a claim through the same legal representative at the same time, only one acknowledgment of service need be used.

---

[1] See rule 6. 5.

[2] See rule 2.3 for the definition of legal representative.

[3] See Part 21.

5.4 An acknowledgment of service may be amended or withdrawn only with the permission of the court.

5.5 An application for permission under paragraph 5.4 must be made in accordance with Part 23 and supported by evidence.

(Paragraph 8.3 of PD 6 (service of documents) makes provision for the service on the claimant of any notice of funding filed with an acknowledgment of service.)

CPR Part 11 Disputing the Court's Jurisdiction

Part 11 **13.11, 14.81, 16.3, 19.1, 19.4, 26.3** [For commentary on a specific rule, please refer to the cross-references after the title of the rule.]

11 Procedure for Disputing the Court's Jurisdiction

r.11(2) **19.2**
r.11(3) **18.1, 19.4**
r.11(4) **19.3**
r.11(4)(a) **13.11, 19.3**
r.11(4)(b) **19.3**
r.11(5)(b) **19.3**
r.11(6) **19.6**
r.11(7) **19.7**
r.11(7)(c) **19.7**
r.11(8) **19.7**
r.11(9) **18.5, 19.3, 26.3**
r.11(9)(a)–(b) **19.5**

(1) A defendant who wishes to—
  (a) dispute the court's jurisdiction to try the claim; or
  (b) argue that the court should not exercise its jurisdiction,
may apply to the court for an order declaring that it has no such jurisdiction or should not exercise any jurisdiction which it may have.

(2) A defendant who wishes to make such an application must first file an acknowledgment of service in accordance with Part 10.

(3) A defendant who files an acknowledgment of service does not, by doing so, lose any right that he may have to dispute the court's jurisdiction.

(4) An application under this rule must—
  (a) be made within 14 days after filing an acknowledgment of service; and
  (b) be supported by evidence.

(5) If the defendant—
  (a) files an acknowledgment of service; and
  (b) does not make such an application within the period specified in paragraph (4), he is to be treated as having accepted that the court has jurisdiction to try the claim.

(6) An order containing a declaration that the court has no jurisdiction or will not exercise its jurisdiction may also make further provision including—
  (a) setting aside the claim form;
  (b) setting aside service of the claim form;
  (c) discharging any order made before the claim was commenced or before the claim form was served; and
  (d) staying(GL) the proceedings.

(7) If on an application under this rule the court does not make a declaration—
  (a) the acknowledgment of service shall cease to have effect;
  (b) the defendant may file a further acknowledgment of service within 14 days or such other period as the court may direct; and
  (c) the court shall give directions as to the filing and service of the defence in a claim under Part 7 or the filing of evidence in a claim under Part 8 in the event that a further acknowledgment of service is filed.

(8) If the defendant files a further acknowledgment of service in accordance with paragraph (7)(b) he shall be treated as having accepted that the court has jurisdiction to try the claim.

(9) If a defendant makes an application under this rule, he must file and serve his written evidence in support with the application notice, but he need not before the hearing of the application file—
  (a) in a Part 7 claim, a defence; or
  (b) in a Part 8 claim, any other written evidence.

CPR Part 12 Default Judgment

Part 12 **12.9, 13.9, 15.20, 18.6, 20.1, 26.2, 26.5, 28.6, 29.9, 29.10** [For commentary on a specific rule, please refer to the cross-references after the title of the rule.]

12.1 Meaning of 'Default Judgment'

r.12.1 **18.6**

In these Rules, 'default judgment' means judgment without trial where a defendant—

(a) has failed to file an acknowledgment of service; or

(b) has failed to file a defence.

(Part 10 contains provisions about filing an acknowledgment of service and Part 15 contains provisions about filing a defence)

12.2 Claims in Which Default Judgment May Not Be Obtained

r.12.2 **20.2** r.12.2(h) **13.1**

A claimant may not obtain a default judgment—

(a) on a claim for delivery of goods subject to an agreement regulated by the Consumer Credit Act 1974;

(b) where he uses the procedure set out in Part 8 (alternative procedure for claims); or

(c) in any other case where a practice direction provides that the claimant may not obtain default judgment.

12.3 Conditions to Be Satisfied

r.12.3 **20.3** r.12.3(3)(a) **26.3, 34.6**

r.12.3(3) **33.4**

(1) The claimant may obtain judgment in default of an acknowledgment of service only if—

(a) the defendant has not filed an acknowledgment of service or a defence to the claim (or any part of the claim); and

(b) the relevant time for doing so has expired.

(2) Judgment in default of defence may be obtained only—

(a) where an acknowledgment of service has been filed but a defence has not been filed;

(b) in a counterclaim made under rule 20.4, where a defence has not been filed,

and, in either case, the relevant time limit for doing so has expired.

(Rules 10.3 and 15.4 deal respectively with the period for filing an acknowledgment of service and the period for filing a defence)

(Rule 20.4 makes general provision for a defendant's counterclaim against a claimant, and rule 20.4(3) provides that Part 10 (acknowledgment of service) does not apply to a counterclaim made under that rule)

(3) The claimant may not obtain a default judgment if—

(a) the defendant has applied—

(i) to have the claimant's statement of case struck out under rule 3.4; or

(ii) for summary judgment under Part 24,

and, in either case, that application has not been disposed of;

(b) the defendant has satisfied the whole claim (including any claim for costs) on which the claimant is seeking judgment; or

(c) (i) the claimant is seeking judgment on a claim for money; and
(ii) the defendant has filed or served on the claimant an admission under rule 14.4 or 14.7 (admission of liability to pay all of the money claimed) together with a request for time to pay.

(Part 14 sets out the procedure where a defendant admits a money claim and asks for time to pay)

(Rule 6.14 provides that, where the claim form is served by the claimant, he may not obtain default judgment unless he has filed a certificate of service)

(Article 19(1) of Council Regulation (EC) No. 1348/2000 of 29 May 2000 on the service in the Member States of judicial and extrajudicial documents in civil or commercial matters applies in relation to judgment in default where the claim form is served in accordance with that Regulation)

12.4 Procedure for Obtaining Default Judgment

r.12.4 **20.4** r.12.4(2) **20.9**
r.12.4(1) **20.1** r.12.4(3) **20.4**

(1) Subject to paragraph (2), a claimant may obtain a default judgment by filing a request in the relevant practice form where the claim is for—
(a) a specified amount of money;
(b) an amount of money to be decided by the court;
(c) delivery of goods where the claim form gives the defendant the alternative of paying their value; or
(d) any combination of these remedies.

(2) The claimant must make an application in accordance with Part 23 if he wishes to obtain a default judgment—
(a) on a claim which consists of or includes a claim for any other remedy; or
(b) where rule 12.9 or rule 12.10 so provides,

and where the defendant is an individual, the claimant must provide the defendant's date of birth (if known) in Part C of the application notice.

(3) Where a claimant—
(a) claims any other remedy in his claim form in addition to those specified in paragraph (1); but
(b) abandons that claim in his request for judgment,

he may still obtain a default judgment by filing a request under paragraph (1).

(4) In civil proceedings against the Crown, as defined in rule 66.1(2), a request for a default judgment must be considered by a Master or district judge, who must in particular be satisfied that the claim form and particulars of claim have been properly served on the Crown in accordance with section 18 of the Crown Proceedings Act 1947 and rule 6.5(8).

12.5 Nature of Judgment Where Default Judgment Obtained by Filing a Request

r.12.5 **20.5** r.12.5(3) **20.6**

(1) Where the claim is for a specified sum of money, the claimant may specify in a request filed under rule 12.4(1)—
(a) the date by which the whole of the judgment debt is to be paid; or
(b) the times and rate at which it is to be paid by instalments.

(2) Except where paragraph (4) applies, a default judgment on a claim for a specified amount of money obtained on the filing of a request, will be judgment for the amount of the claim (less any payments made) and costs—
(a) to be paid by the date or at the rate specified in the request for judgment; or
(b) if none is specified, immediately.

(Interest may be included in a default judgment obtained by filing a request if the conditions set out in Rule 12.6 are satisfied)

(Rule 45.4 provides for fixed costs on the entry of a default judgment)

(3) Where the claim is for an unspecified amount of money a default judgment obtained on the filing of a request will be for an amount to be decided by the court and costs.

(4) Where the claim is for delivery of goods and the claim form gives the defendant the alternative of

paying their value, a default judgment obtained on the filing of a request will be judgment requiring the defendant to—
(a) deliver the goods or (if he does not do so) pay the value of the goods as decided by the court (less any payments made); and
(b) pay costs.

(Rule 12.7 sets out the procedure for deciding the amount of a judgment or the value of the goods)

(5) The claimant's right to enter judgment requiring the defendant to deliver goods is subject to rule 40.14 (judgment in favour of certain part owners relating to the detention of goods).

12.6 Interest

r.12.6 **20.5** r.12.6(2) **20.5**

(1) A default judgment on a claim for a specified amount of money obtained on the filing of a request may include the amount of interest claimed to the date of judgment if—
(a) the particulars of claim include the details required by rule 16.4;
(b) where interest is claimed under section 35A of the Supreme Court Act 1981 or section 69 of the County Courts Act 1984, the rate is no higher than the rate of interest payable on judgment debts at the date when the claim form was issued; and
(c) the claimant's request for judgment includes a calculation of the interest claimed for the period from the date up to which interest was stated to be calculated in the claim form to the date of the request for judgment.

(2) In any case where paragraph (1) does not apply, judgment will be for an amount of interest to be decided by the court.

(Rule 12.7 sets out the procedure for deciding the amount of interest)

12.7 Procedure for Deciding an Amount or Value

r.12.7 **20.6** r.12.7(2)(b) **42.6**

(1) This rule applies where the claimant obtains a default judgment on the filing of a request under rule 12.4(1) and judgment is for—
(a) an amount of money to be decided by the court;
(b) the value of goods to be decided by the court; or
(c) an amount of interest to be decided by the court.

(2) Where the court enters judgment it will—
(a) give any directions it considers appropriate; and
(b) if it considers it appropriate, allocate the case.

12.8 Claim against More Than One Defendant

r.12.8(1)–(3) **20.10**

(1) A claimant may obtain a default judgment on request under this Part on a claim for money or a claim for delivery of goods against one of two or more defendants, and proceed with his claim against the other defendants.

(2) Where a claimant applies for a default judgment against one of two or more defendants—
(a) if the claim can be dealt with separately from the claim against the other defendants—
(i) the court may enter a default judgment against that defendant; and
(ii) the claimant may continue the proceedings against the other defendants;
(b) if the claim cannot be dealt with separately from the claim against the other defendants—
(i) the court will not enter default judgment against that defendant; and
(ii) the court must deal with the application at the same time as it disposes of the claim against the other defendants.

(3) A claimant may not enforce against one of two or more defendants any judgment obtained under this Part for possession of land or for delivery of goods unless—
(a) he has obtained a judgment for possession or delivery (whether or not obtained under this Part) against all the defendants to the claim; or
(b) the court gives permission.

12.9 Procedure for Obtaining a Default Judgment for Costs Only

r.12.9(1)(b) **20.8**

(1) Where a claimant wishes to obtain a default judgment for costs only—
 (a) if the claim is for fixed costs, he may obtain it by filing a request in the relevant practice form;
 (b) if the claim is for any other type of costs, he must make an application in accordance with Part 23.
(2) Where an application is made under this rule for costs only, judgment shall be for an amount to be decided by the court.

(Part 45 sets out when a claimant is entitled to fixed costs)

12.10 Default Judgment Obtained by Making an Application

r.12.10 **20.1, 20.8**
r.12.10(a)(i) **14.33**
r.12.10(b)(i) **16.64**

The claimant must make an application in accordance with Part 23 where—
(a) the claim is—
 (i) a claim against a child or patient; or
 (ii) a claim in tort by one spouse or civil partner against the other.
(b) he wishes to obtain a default judgment where the defendant has failed to file an acknowledgment of service—
 (i) against a defendant who has been served with the claim out of the jurisdiction under rule 6.19(1) or (1A) (service without leave);
 (ii) against a defendant domiciled in Scotland or Northern Ireland or in any other Convention territory or Regulation State;
 (iii) against a State;
 (iv) against a diplomatic agent who enjoys immunity from civil jurisdiction by virtue of the Diplomatic Privileges Act 1964; or
 (v) against persons or organisations who enjoy immunity from civil jurisdiction pursuant to the provisions of the International Organisations Acts 1968 and 1981.

12.11 Supplementary Provisions Where Applications for Default Judgment Are Made

r.12.11 **20.9**
r.12.11(1) **20.1, 20.9**
r.12.11(4) **20.9**

(1) Where the claimant makes an application for a default judgment, judgment shall be such judgment as it appears to the court that the claimant is entitled to on his statement of case.
(2) Any evidence relied on by the claimant in support of his application need not be served on a party who has failed to file an acknowledgment of service.
(3) An application for a default judgment on a claim against a child or patient or a claim in tort between spouses or civil partners must be supported by evidence.
(4) An application for a default judgment may be made without notice if—
 (a) the claim under the Civil Jurisdiction and Judgments Act 1982 or the Judgments Regulation, was served in accordance with rules 6.19(1) or 6.19(1A) as appropriate;
 (b) the defendant has failed to file an acknowledgment of service; and
 (c) notice does not need to be given under any other provision of these Rules.
(5) Where an application is made against a State for a default judgment where the defendant has failed to file an acknowledgment of service—
 (a) the application may be made without notice, but the court hearing the application may direct that a copy of the application notice be served on the State;
 (b) if the court—
  (i) grants the application; or
  (ii) directs that a copy of the application notice be served on the State,
  the judgment or application notice (and the evidence in support) may be served out of the jurisdiction without any further order;
 (c) where paragraph (5)(b) permits a judgment or an application notice to be served out of the jurisdiction, the procedure for serving the judgment or the application notice is the same as for serving a claim form under Section III of Part 6 except where an alternative method of service has been agreed under section 12(6) of the State Immunity Act 1978.

(Rule 23.1 defines 'application notice')

(6) For the purposes of this rule and rule 12.10—
   (a) 'domicile' is to be determined—
      (i) in relation to a Convention territory, in accordance with sections 41 to 46 of the Civil Jurisdiction and Judgments Act 1982;
      (ii) in relation to a Regulation State, in accordance with the Judgments Regulation and paragraphs 9 to 12 of Schedule 1 to the Civil Jurisdiction and Judgments Order 2001;
   (b) 'Convention territory' means the territory or territories of any Contracting State, as defined by section 1(3) of the Civil Jurisdiction and Judgments Act 1982, to which the Brussels Conventions or Lugano Convention apply;
   (c) 'State' has the meaning given by section 14 of the State Immunity Act 1978; and
   (d) 'Diplomatic agent' has the meaning given by Article 1(e) of Schedule 1 to the Diplomatic Privileges Act 1964.
   (e) 'the Judgments Regulation' means Council Regulation (EC) No. 44/2001 of 22nd December 2000 on jurisdiction and the recognition and enforcement of judgments in civil and commercial matters; and
   (f) 'Regulation State' has the same meaning as 'Member State' in the Judgments Regulation, that is all Member States except Denmark.

PD 12 Practice Direction — Default Judgment

This practice direction supplements CPR Part 12

[For commentary on a specific paragraph, please refer to the cross-references after the title of the paragraph.]

Default Judgment

para.1.1 **20.3** para.1.2 **20.2**

1.1 A default judgment is judgment without a trial where a defendant has failed to file either:
(1) an acknowledgment of service, or
(2) a defence.
For this purpose a defence includes any document purporting to be a defence.
(See Part 10 and PD 10 for information about the acknowledgment of service, and Parts 15 and 16, PD 15 and PD 16 for information about the defence and what it should contain.)

1.2 A claimant may not obtain a default judgment under Part 12 (notwithstanding that no acknowledgment of service or defence has been filed) if:
(1) the procedure set out in Part 8 (alternative procedure for claims) is being used, or
(2) the claim is for delivery of goods subject to an agreement regulated by the Consumer Credit Act 1974.

1.3 Other rules and practice directions provide that default judgment under Part 12 cannot be obtained in particular types of proceedings. Examples are:
(1) admiralty proceedings;
(2) arbitration proceedings;
(3) contentious probate proceedings;
(4) claims for provisional damages;
(5) possession claims.

Obtaining Default Judgment

para.2.3 **20.8**

2.1 Rules 12.4(1) and 12.9(1) describe the claims in respect of which a default judgment may be obtained by filing a request in the appropriate practice form.

2.2 A default judgment on:
(1) the claims referred to in rules 12.9(1)(b) and 12.10, and
(2) claims other than those described in rule 12.4(1),
can only be obtained if an application for default judgment is made and cannot be obtained by filing a request.

2.3 The following are some of the types of claim which require an application for a default judgment:
(1) against children and patients,[1]
(2) for costs (other than fixed costs) only,[2]
(3) by one spouse against the other[3] on a claim in tort,[4]
(4) for delivery up of goods where the defendant will not be allowed the alternative of paying their value,
(5) [deleted], and
(6) against persons or organisations who enjoy immunity from civil jurisdiction under the provisions of the International Organisations Acts 1968 and 1981.

[1] See rule 12.10(a)(i).
[2] See rule 12.9(b).
[3] See rule 12.10(a)(ii).
[4] Tort may be defined as an act or a failure to do an act which causes harm or damage to another person and which gives the other person a right to claim compensation without having to rely on a contract with the person who caused the harm or damage.

Default Judgment by Request

3.1 Requests for default judgment:
(1) in respect of a claim for a specified amount of money or for the delivery of goods where the defendant will be given the alternative of paying a specified sum representing their value, or for fixed costs only, must be in form N205A or N225, and
(2) in respect of a claim where an amount of money (including an amount representing the value of goods) is to be decided by the court, must be in form N205B or N227.
3.2 The forms require the claimant to provide the date of birth (if known) of the defendant where the defendant is an individual.

Evidence

para.4.1 **20.3**
para.4.2 **20.9**
para.4.3 **20.9**
para.4.4 **20.9**
para.4.5 **20.9, 50.7**

4.1 Both on a request and on an application for default judgment the court must be satisfied that:
(1) the particulars of claim have been served on the defendant (a certificate of service on the court file will be sufficient evidence),
(2) either the defendant has not filed an acknowledgment of service or has not filed a defence and that in either case the relevant period for doing so has expired,
(3) the defendant has not satisfied the claim, and
(4) the defendant has not returned an admission to the claimant under rule 14.4 or filed an admission with the court under rule 14.6.
4.2 On an application against a child or patient:[5]
(1) a litigation friend[6] to act on behalf of the child or patient must be appointed by the court before judgment can be obtained, and
(2) the claimant must satisfy the court by evidence that he is entitled to the judgment claimed.
4.3 On an application where the defendant was served with the claim either:
(1) outside the jurisdiction[7] without leave under the Civil Jurisdiction and Judgments Act 1982, or
(2) within the jurisdiction but when domiciled[8] in Scotland or Northern Ireland or in any other Convention territory[9] or Regulation State,
and the defendant has not acknowledged service, the evidence must establish that:
(a) the claim is one that the court has power to hear and decide,
(b) no other court has exclusive jurisdiction under the Act or Jurisdiction and Judgments Regulation to hear and decide the claim, and
(c) the claim has been properly served in accordance with art. 20 of sch. 1 or 3C to the Act, para. 15 of sch. 4 to the Act, or art. 26 of the Jurisdiction and Judgments Regulation.
4.4 On an application against a State[10] the evidence must:
(1) set out the grounds of the application,
(2) establish the facts proving that the State is excepted from the immunity conferred by s. 1 of the State Immunity Act 1978,
(3) establish that the claim was sent through the Foreign and Commonwealth Office to the Ministry of Foreign Affairs of the State or, where the State has agreed to another form of service, that the claim was served in the manner agreed, and
(4) establish that the time for acknowledging service (which is extended to two months by s. 12(2) of the Act when the claim is sent through the Foreign and Commonwealth Office to the Ministry of Foreign Affairs of the State) has expired.
(See rule [40.10*] for when default judgment against a State takes effect.)

[5] As defined in rule 21.1(2).
[6] As defined in PD 21.
[7] As defined in rule 2. 3.
[8] As determined in accordance with the provisions of ss. 41 to 46 of the Civil Jurisdiction and Judgments Act 1982.
[9] Means the territory of a Contracting State as defined in s. 1(3) of the Civil Jurisdiction and Judgments Act 1982.
[10] As defined in s. 14 of the State Immunity Act 1978.
[*The text issued by the Department for Constitutional Affairs mistakenly refers to r. 40.8.]

4.5 Evidence in support of an application referred to in paragraphs 4.3 and 4.4 above must be by affidavit.

4.6 On an application for judgment for delivery up of goods where the defendant will not be given the alternative of paying their value, the evidence must identify the goods and state where the claimant believes the goods to be situated and why their specific delivery up is sought.

General

para.5.1 **20.9**

5.1 On all applications to which this practice direction applies, other than those referred to in paragraphs 4.3 and 4.4 above,[11] notice should be given in accordance with Part 23.

5.2 Where default judgment is given on a claim for a sum of money expressed in a foreign currency, the judgment should be for the amount of the foreign currency with the addition of 'or the sterling equivalent at the time of payment'.

[11] See rule 12.11(4) and (5).

CPR Part 13 Setting Aside or Varying Default Judgment

Part 13 **1.15, 18.6, 20.11, 60.2, 61.1** [For commentary on a specific rule, please refer to the cross-references after the title of the rule.]

13.1 Scope of this Part

The rules in this Part set out the procedure for setting aside or varying judgment entered under Part 12 (default judgment).

(CCR Order 22, r. 10 sets out the procedure for varying the rate at which a judgment debt must be paid)

13.2 Cases Where the Court Must Set Aside Judgment Entered under Part 12

r.13.2 **1.15, 16.54, 16.64, 20.1, 20.12, 60.2** r.13.2(a)–(c) **20.12**

The court must set aside a judgment entered under Part 12 if judgment was wrongly entered because—

(a) in the case of a judgment in default of an acknowledgment of service, any of the conditions in rule 12.3(1) and 12.3(3) was not satisfied;
(b) in the case of a judgment in default of a defence, any of the conditions in rule 12.3(2) and 12.3(3) was not satisfied; or
(c) the whole of the claim was satisfied before judgment was entered.

13.3 Cases Where the Court May Set Aside or Vary Judgment Entered under Part 12

r.13.3 **1.15, 20.16, 60.2** r.13.3(1)(b) **20.13, 20.14**
r.13.3(1) **20.13, 20.14** r.13.3(2) **20.13**
r.13.3(1)(a) **20.13, 20.15**

(1) In any other case, the court may set aside(GL) or vary a judgment entered under Part 12 if—
 (a) the defendant has a real prospect of successfully defending the claim; or
 (b) it appears to the court that there is some other good reason why—
  (i) the judgment should be set aside or varied; or
  (ii) the defendant should be allowed to defend the claim.
(2) In considering whether to set aside(GL) or vary a judgment entered under Part 12, the matters to which the court must have regard include whether the person seeking to set aside the judgment made an application to do so promptly.

(Rule 3.1(3) provides that the court may attach conditions when it makes an order)

(Article 19(4) of Council Regulation (EC) No. 1348/2000 of 29 May 2000 on the service in the Member States of judicial and extrajudicial documents in civil or commercial matters applies to applications to appeal a judgment in default when the time limit for appealing has expired)

13.4 Application to Set Aside or Vary Judgment — Procedure

r.13.4 **12.10** r.13.4(3) **20.18**
r.13.4(1) **20.18**

(1) Where—
 (a) the claim is for a specified amount of money;
 (b) the judgment was obtained in a court which is not the defendant's home court;
 (c) the claim has not been transferred to another defendant's home court under rule 14.12 (admission— determination of rate of payment by judge) or rule 26.2 (automatic transfer); and

(d) the defendant is an individual

the court will transfer an application by a defendant under this Part to set aside[(GL)] or vary judgment to the defendant's home court.

(2) Paragraph (1) does not apply where the claim was commenced in a specialist list.

(3) An application under rule 13.3 (cases where the court may set aside[(GL)] or vary judgment) must be supported by evidence.

13.5 [*Revoked*]

13.6 Abandoned Claim Restored Where Default Judgment Set Aside

r.13.6 **20.4**

Where—

(a) the claimant claimed a remedy in addition to one specified in rule 12.4(1) (claims in respect of which the claimant may obtain default judgment by filing a request);

(b) the claimant abandoned his claim for that remedy in order to obtain default judgment on request in accordance with rule 12.4(3); and

(c) that default judgment is set aside[(GL)] under this Part,

the abandoned claim is restored when the default judgment is set aside.

CPR Part 14 Admissions

Part 14 **17.2, 20.2, 26.6, 29.9, 42.15** [For commentary on a specific rule, please refer to the cross-references after the title of the rule.]

14.1 Making an Admission

r.14.1(1)–(2) **17.2, 29.9, 47.8**
r.14.1(4) **17.4**
r.14.1(4)(a)–(b) **14.33**
r.14.1(5) **17.3, 47.8**

(1) A party may admit the truth of the whole or any part of another party's case.
(2) He may do this by giving notice in writing (such as in a statement of case or by letter).
(3) Where the only remedy which the claimant is seeking is the payment of money, the defendant may also make an admission in accordance with—
  (a) rule 14.4 (admission of whole claim for specified amount of money);
  (b) rule 14.5 (admission of part of claim for specified amount of money);
  (c) rule 14.6 (admission of liability to pay whole of claim for unspecified amount of money); or
  (d) rule 14.7 (admission of liability to pay claim for unspecified amount of money where defendant offers a sum in satisfaction of the claim).
(4) Where the defendant makes an admission as mentioned in paragraph (3), the claimant has a right to enter judgment except where—
  (a) the defendant is a child or patient; or
  (b) the claimant is a child or patient and the admission is made under rule 14.5 or 14.7.

(Rule 21.10 provides that, where a claim is made by or on behalf of a child or patient or against a child or patient, no settlement, compromise or payment shall be valid, so far as it relates to that person's claim, without the approval of the court)

(5) The court may allow a party to amend or withdraw an admission.

(Rule 3.1(3) provides that the court may attach conditions when it makes an order)

14.2 Period for Making an Admission

r.14.2 **12.10, 17.4**
r.14.2(2)–(3) **17.4**

(1) The period for returning an admission under rule 14.4 or for filing it under rules 14.5, 14.6 or 14.7 is—
  (a) where the defendant is served with a claim form which states that particulars of claim will follow, 14 days after service of the particulars; and
  (b) in any other case, 14 days after service of the claim form.
(2) Paragraph (1) is subject to the following rules—
  (a) rule 6.22 (which specifies how the period for filing or returning an admission is calculated where the claim form is served out of the jurisdiction); and
  (b) rule 6.16(4) (which requires the court to specify the period for responding to the particulars of claim when it makes an order under that rule).

(3) A defendant may return an admission under rule 14.4 or file it under rules 14.5, 14.6 or 14.7 after the end of the period for returning or filing it specified in paragraph (1) if the claimant has not obtained default judgment under Part 12.
(4) If he does so, this Part shall apply as if he had made the admission within that period.

14.3 Admission by Notice in Writing — Application for Judgment

r.14.3 **29.9** r.14.3(1)–(2) **17.2**

(1) Where a party makes an admission under rule 14.1(2) (admission by notice in writing), any other party may apply for judgment on the admission.
(2) Judgment shall be such judgment as it appears to the court that the applicant is entitled to on the admission.

14.4 Admission of Whole of Claim for Specified Amount of Money

r.14.4 **13.8, 17.4, 17.5** r.14.4(2)–(6) **17.5**

(1) This rule applies where—
  (a) the only remedy which the claimant is seeking is the payment of a specified amount of money; and
  (b) the defendant admits the whole of the claim.
(2) The defendant may admit the claim by returning to the claimant an admission in the relevant practice form.
(3) The claimant may obtain judgment by filing a request in the relevant practice form and, if he does so—
  (a) if the defendant has not requested time to pay, the procedure in paragraphs (4) to (6) will apply;
  (b) if the defendant has requested time to pay, the procedure in rule 14.9 will apply.
(4) The claimant may specify in his request for judgment—
  (a) the date by which the whole of the judgment debt is to be paid; or
  (b) the times and rate at which it is to be paid by instalments.
(5) On receipt of the request for judgment the court will enter judgment.
(6) Judgment will be for the amount of the claim (less any payments made) and costs—
  (a) to be paid by the date or at the rate specified in the request for judgment; or
  (b) if none is specified, immediately.

(Rule 14.14 deals with the circumstances in which judgment under this rule may include interest)

14.5 Admission of Part of a Claim for a Specified Amount of Money

r.14.5 **13.8, 14.33, 17.4, 17.6** r.14.5(4)–(5) **17.6**

(1) This rule applies where—
  (a) the only remedy which the claimant is seeking is the payment of a specified amount of money; and
  (b) the defendant admits part of the claim.
(2) The defendant may admit part of the claim by filing an admission in the relevant practice form.
(3) On receipt of the admission, the court will serve a notice on the claimant requiring him to return the notice stating that—
  (a) he accepts the amount admitted in satisfaction of the claim;
  (b) he does not accept the amount admitted by the defendant and wishes the proceedings to continue; or
  (c) if the defendant has requested time to pay, he accepts the amount admitted in satisfaction of the claim, but not the defendant's proposals as to payment.
(4) The claimant must—
  (a) file the notice; and
  (b) serve a copy on the defendant,
  within 14 days after it is served on him.
(5) If the claimant does not file the notice within 14 days after it is served on him, the claim is stayed[(GL)] until he files the notice.
(6) If the claimant accepts the amount admitted in satisfaction of the claim, he may obtain judgment by filing a request in the relevant practice form and, if he does so—

(a) if the defendant has not requested time to pay, the procedure in paragraphs (7) to (9) will apply;
(b) if the defendant has requested time to pay, the procedure in rule 14.9 will apply.
(7) The claimant may specify in his request for judgment—
(a) the date by which the whole of the judgment debt is to be paid; or
(b) the time and rate at which it is to be paid by instalments.
(8) On receipt of the request for judgment, the court will enter judgment.
(9) Judgment will be for the amount admitted (less any payments made) and costs—
(a) to be paid by the date or at the rate specified in the request for judgment; or
(b) if none is specified, immediately.
(If the claimant files notice under paragraph (3) that he wishes the proceedings to continue, the procedure which then follows is set out in Part 26)

14.6 Admission of Liability to Pay Whole of Claim for Unspecified Amount of Money

r.14.6 **13.8, 17.4, 17.7** r.14.6(5) **17.7**

(1) This rule applies where—
(a) the only remedy which the claimant is seeking is the payment of money;
(b) the amount of the claim is not specified; and
(c) the defendant admits liability but does not offer to pay a specified amount of money in satisfaction of the claim.
(2) The defendant may admit the claim by filing an admission in the relevant practice form.
(3) On receipt of the admission, the court will serve a copy on the claimant.
(4) The claimant may obtain judgment by filing a request in the relevant practice form.
(5) If the claimant does not file a request for judgment within 14 days after service of the admission on him, the claim is stayed[(GL)] until he files the request.
(6) On receipt of the request for judgment the court will enter judgment.
(7) Judgment will be for an amount to be decided by the court and costs.

14.7 Admission of Liability to Pay Claim for Unspecified Amount of Money Where Defendant Offers a Sum in Satisfaction of the Claim

r.14.7 **13.8, 14.33, 17.4, 17.8**

(1) This rule applies where—
(a) the only remedy which the claimant is seeking is the payment of money;
(b) the amount of the claim is not specified; and
(c) the defendant—
(i) admits liability; and
(ii) offers to pay a specified amount of money in satisfaction of the claim.
(2) The defendant may admit the claim by filing an admission in the relevant practice form.
(3) On receipt of the admission, the court will serve a notice on the claimant requiring him to return the notice stating whether or not he accepts the amount in satisfaction of the claim.
(4) If the claimant does not file the notice within 14 days after it is served on him, the claim is stayed[(GL)] until he files the notice.
(5) If the claimant accepts the offer he may obtain judgment by filing a request in the relevant practice form and if he does so—
(a) if the defendant has not requested time to pay, the procedure in paragraphs (6) to (8) will apply;
(b) if the defendant has requested time to pay, the procedure in rule 14.9 will apply.
(6) The claimant may specify in his request for judgment—
(a) the date by which the whole of the judgment debt is to be paid; or
(b) the times and rate at which it is to be paid by instalments.
(7) On receipt of the request for judgment, the court will enter judgment.
(8) Judgment will be for the amount offered by the defendant (less any payments made) and costs—
(a) to be paid on the date or at the rate specified in the request for judgment; or
(b) if none is specified, immediately.

(9) If the claimant does not accept the amount offered by the defendant, he may obtain judgment by filing a request in the relevant practice form.
(10) Judgment under paragraph (9) will be for an amount to be decided by the court and costs.

14.8 Allocation of Claims in Relation to Outstanding Matters

r.14.8 **17.7, 42.6**

Where the court enters judgment under rule 14.6 or 14.7 for an amount to be decided by the court it will—
(a) give any directions it considers appropriate; and
(b) if it considers it appropriate, allocate the case.

14.9 Request for Time to Pay

r.14.9 **17.5** r.14.9(4)–(5) **17.5**

(1) A defendant who makes an admission under rules 14.4, 14.5 or 14.7 (admission relating to a claim for a specified amount of money or offering to pay a specified amount of money) may make a request for time to pay.
(2) A request for time to pay is a proposal about the date of payment or a proposal to pay by instalments at the times and rate specified in the request.
(3) The defendant's request for time to pay must be served or filed (as the case may be) with his admission.
(4) If the claimant accepts the defendant's request, he may obtain judgment by filing a request in the relevant practice form.
(5) On receipt of the request for judgment, the court will enter judgment.
(6) Judgment will be—
  (a) where rule 14.4 applies, for the amount of the claim (less any payments made) and costs;
  (b) where rule 14.5 applies, for the amount admitted (less any payments made) and costs; or
  (c) where rule 14.7 applies, for the amount offered by the defendant (less any payments made) and costs; and

  (in all cases) will be for payment at the time and rate specified in the defendant's request for time to pay.

(Rule 14.10 sets out the procedure to be followed if the claimant does not accept the defendant's request for time to pay)

14.10 Determination of Rate of Payment

r.14.10(2) **17.5** r.14.10(4) **17.5**

(1) This rule applies where the defendant makes a request for time to pay under rule 14.9.
(2) If the claimant does not accept the defendant's proposals for payment, he must file a notice in the relevant practice form.
(3) Where the defendant's admission was served direct on the claimant, a copy of the admission and the request for time to pay must be filed with the claimant's notice.
(4) When the court receives the claimant's notice, it will enter judgment for the amount admitted (less any payments made) to be paid at the time and rate of payment determined by the court.

14.11 Determination of Rate of Payment by Court Officer

(1) A court officer may exercise the powers of the court under rule 14.10(4) where the amount outstanding (including costs) is not more than £50,000.
(2) Where a court officer is to determine the time and rate of payment, he must do so without a hearing.

14.12 Determination of Rate of Payment by Judge

(1) Where a judge is to determine the time and rate of payment, he may do so without a hearing.
(2) Where a judge is to determine the time and rate of payment at a hearing, the proceedings must be transferred automatically to the defendant's home court if—
  (a) the only claim is for a specified amount of money;
  (b) the defendant is an individual;

(c) the claim has not been transferred to another defendant's home court under rule 13.4 (application to set aside[(GL)] or vary default judgment — procedure) or rule 26.2 (automatic transfer);
(d) the claim was not started in the defendant's home court; and
(e) the claim was not started in a specialist list.

(Rule 2.3 explains which court is a defendant's home court)

(3) If there is to be a hearing to determine the time and rate of payment, the court must give each party at least 7 days' notice of the hearing.

14.13 Right of Redetermination

(1) Where—
(a) a court officer has determined the time and rate of payment under rule 14.11; or
(b) a judge has determined the time and rate of payment under rule 14.12 without a hearing,
either party may apply for the decision to be redetermined by a judge.

(2) An application for redetermination must be made within 14 days after service of the determination on the applicant.

(3) Where an application for redetermination is made, the proceedings must be transferred to the defendant's home court if—
(a) the only claim (apart from a claim for interest or costs) is for a specified amount of money;
(b) the defendant is an individual;
(c) the claim has not been transferred to another defendant's home court under rule 13.4 (application to set aside[(GL)] or vary default judgment — procedure) or rule 26.2 (automatic transfer);
(d) the claim was not started in the defendant's home court; and
(e) the claim was not started in a specialist list.

(Rule 2.3 explains which court is a defendant's home court)

14.14 Interest

(1) Judgment under rule 14.4 (admission of whole of claim for specified amount of money) shall include the amount of interest claimed to the date of judgment if—
(a) the particulars of claim include the details required by rule 16.4;
(b) where interest is claimed under section 35A of the Supreme Court Act 1981 or section 69 of the County Courts Act 1984, the rate is no higher than the rate of interest payable on judgment debts at the date when the claim form was issued; and
(c) the claimant's request for judgment includes a calculation of the interest claimed for the period from the date up to which interest was stated to be calculated in the claim form to the date of the request for judgment.

(2) In any case where judgment is entered under rule 14.4 and the conditions in paragraph (1) are not satisfied judgment shall be for an amount of interest to be decided by the court.

(3) Where judgment is entered for an amount of interest to be decided by the court, the court will give directions for the management of the case.

PD 14 Practice Direction — Admissions

This practice direction supplements CPR Part 14

[For commentary on a specific paragraph, please refer to the cross-references after the title of the paragraph.]

Admissions Generally

1.1 Rules 14.1 and 14.2 deal with the manner in which a defendant may make an admission of a claim or part of a claim.

1.2 Rules 14.3, 14.4, 14.5, 14.6 and 14.7 set out how judgment may be obtained on a written admission.

Forms

para.2.1 **17.4**

2.1 When particulars of claim are served on a defendant the forms for responding to the claim that will accompany them will include a form[1] for making an admission.

2.2 If the defendant is requesting time to pay he should complete as fully as possible the statement of means contained in the admission form, or otherwise give in writing the same details of his means as could have been given in the admission form.

Returning or Filing the Admission

3.1 If the defendant wishes to make an admission in respect of the whole of a claim for a specified amount of money, the admission form or other written notice of the admission should be completed and returned to the claimant within 14 days of service of the particulars of claim.[2]

3.2 If the defendant wishes to make an admission in respect of a part of a claim for a specified amount of money, or in respect of a claim for an unspecified amount of money, the admission form or other written notice of admission should be completed and filed with the court within 14 days of service of the particulars of claim.[3]

3.3 The defendant may also file a defence under rule 15.2.

Request for Time to Pay

4.1 A defendant who makes an admission in respect of a claim for a specified sum of money or offers to pay a sum of money in respect of a claim for an unspecified sum may, in the admission form, make a request for time to pay.[4]

4.2 If the claimant accepts the defendant's request, he may obtain judgment by filing a request for judgment contained in form N225A;[5] the court will then enter judgment for payment at the time and rate specified in the defendant's request.[6]

4.3 If the claimant does not accept the request for time to pay, he should file notice to that effect by completing form N225A; the court will then enter judgment for the amount of the admission (less any payments made) at a time and rate of payment decided by the court (see rule 14.10).

Determining the Rate of Payment

5.1 In deciding the time and rate of payment the court will take into account:

(1) the defendant's statement of means set out in the admission form or in any other written notice of the admission filed,

(2) the claimant's objections to the defendant's request set out in the claimant's notice,[7] and

---

[1] form N9A (specified amount) or N9C (unspecified amount).

[2] Rules 14.2 and 14.4.

[3] Rules 14.2, 14.5, 14.6 and 14.7.

[4] Rule 14. 9.

[5] Rule 14.9(4).

[6] Rule 14.9(5) and (6).

[7] Form N225A.

(3) any other relevant factors.

5.2 The time and rate of payment may be decided:
(1) by a judge with or without a hearing, or
(2) by a court officer without a hearing provided that:
(a) the only claim is for a specified sum of money, and
(b) the amount outstanding is not more than £50,000 (including costs).

5.3 Where a decision has been made without a hearing whether by a court officer or by a judge, either party may apply for the decision to be redetermined by a judge.[8]

5.4 If the decision was made by a court officer the redetermination may take place without a hearing, unless a hearing is requested in the application notice.

5.5 If the decision was made by a judge the redetermination must be made at a hearing unless the parties otherwise agree.

5.6 Rule 14.13(2) describes how to apply for a redetermination.

Varying the Rate of Payment

6.1 Either party may, on account of a change in circumstances since the date of the decision (or redetermination as the case may be) apply to vary the time and rate of payment of instalments still remaining unpaid.

6.2 An application to vary under paragraph 6.1 above should be made in accordance with Part 23.

[8] Rule 14.13(1).

CPR Part 15 Defence and Reply

[For commentary on a specific rule, please refer to the cross-references after the title of the rule.]

15.1 Part Not to Apply Where Claimant Uses Part 8 Procedure

r.15.1 **13.1, 18.4**

This Part does not apply where the claimant uses the procedure set out in Part 8 (alternative procedure for claims).

15.2 Filing a Defence

r.15.2 **18.4, 26.2, 35.8**

A defendant who wishes to defend all or part of a claim must file a defence.

(Part 14 contains further provisions which apply where the defendant admits a claim)

15.3 Consequence of Not Filing a Defence

r.15.3 **18.4, 18.6, 26.2**

If a defendant fails to file a defence, the claimant may obtain default judgment if Part 12 allows it.

15.4 The Period for Filing a Defence

r.15.4 **19.3, 26.3**
r.15.4(1)(a)–(b) **18.5, 26.3**
r.15.4(2) **28.8**
r.15.4(2)(a) **26.3**

(1) The general rule is that the period for filing a defence is—
   (a) 14 days after service of the particulars of claim; or
   (b) if the defendant files an acknowledgment of service under Part 10, 28 days after service of the particulars of claim.

(Rule 7.4 provides for the particulars of claim to be contained in or served with the claim form or served within 14 days of service of the claim form)

(2) The general rule is subject to the following rules—
   (a) rule 6.23 (which specifies how the period for filing a defence is calculated where the claim form is served out of the jurisdiction);
   (b) rule 11 (which provides that, where the defendant makes an application disputing the court's jurisdiction, he need not file a defence before the hearing);
   (c) rule 24.4(2) (which provides that, if the claimant applies for summary judgment before the defendant has filed a defence, the defendant need not file a defence before the summary judgment hearing); and
   (d) rule 6.16(4) (which requires the court to specify the period for responding to the particulars of claim when it makes an order under that rule).

15.5 Agreement Extending the Period for Filing a Defence

r.15.5 **18.7, 26.4** r.15.5(2) **18.7, 26.4**
r.15.5(1) **3.7**

(1) The defendant and the claimant may agree that the period for filing a defence specified in rule 15.4 shall be extended by up to 28 days.

(2) Where the defendant and the claimant agree to extend the period for filing a defence, the defendant must notify the court in writing.

15.6 Service of Copy of Defence

r.15.6 **18.4, 26.2**

A copy of the defence must be served on every other party.
(Part 16 sets out what a defence must contain)
(The costs practice direction sets out the information about a funding arrangement to be provided with the defence where the defendant intends to seek to recover an additional liability)
('Funding arrangement' and 'additional liability' are defined in rule 43.2)

15.7 Making a Counterclaim

Part 20 applies to a defendant who wishes to make a counterclaim.

15.8 Reply to Defence

r.15.8 **27.1**

If a claimant files a reply to the defence, he must—
(a) file his reply when he files his allocation questionnaire; and
(b) serve his reply on the other parties at the same time as he files it.
(Rule 26.3(6) requires the parties to file allocation questionnaires and specifies the period for doing so)
(Part 22 requires a reply to be verified by a statement of truth)

15.9 No Statement of Case after a Reply to be Filed without Court's Permission

r.15.9 **27.3**

A party may not file or serve any statement of case after a reply without the permission of the court.

15.10 Claimant's Notice Where Defence Is That Money Claimed Has Been Paid

r.15.10 **26.10**

(1) Where—
(a) the only claim (apart from a claim for costs and interest) is for a specified amount of money; and
(b) the defendant states in his defence that he has paid to the claimant the amount claimed,
the court will send notice to the claimant requiring him to state in writing whether he wishes the proceedings to continue.

(2) When the claimant responds, he must serve a copy of his response on the defendant.

(3) If the claimant fails to respond under this rule within 28 days after service of the court's notice on him the claim shall be stayed(GL).

(4) Where a claim is stayed under this rule any party may apply for the stay(GL) to be lifted.
(If the claimant files notice under this rule that he wishes the proceedings to continue, the procedure which then follows is set out in Part 26)

15.11 Claim Stayed If It Is Not Defended or Admitted

r.15.11 **26.5**

(1) Where—
(a) at least 6 months have expired since the end of the period for filing a defence specified in rule 15.4;
(b) no defendant has served or filed an admission or filed a defence or counterclaim; and
(c) the claimant has not entered or applied for judgment under Part 12 (default judgment), or Part 24 (summary judgment),
the claim shall be stayed(GL).

(2) Where a claim is stayed(GL) under this rule any party may apply for the stay to be lifted.

PD 15 Practice Direction — Defence and Reply

This practice direction supplements CPR Part 15

[For commentary on a specific paragraph, please refer to the cross-references after the title of the paragraph.]

Defending the Claim

para.1.3 **26.1**

1.1 The provisions of Part 15 do not apply to claims in respect of which the Part 8 procedure is being used.

1.2 In relation to specialist proceedings (see Part 49) in respect of which special provisions for defence and reply are made by the rules and practice directions applicable to those claims, the provisions of Part 15 apply only to the extent that they are not inconsistent with those rules and practice directions.

1.3 Form N9B (specified amount) or N9D (unspecified amount or non-money claims) may be used for the purpose of defence and is included in the response pack served on the defendant with the particulars of claim.

1.4 Attention is drawn to r. 15.3 which sets out a possible consequence of not filing a defence.

(Part 16 (statements of case) and PD 16 contain rules and directions about the contents of a defence.)

(PD 43–48 contains details of the information required to be filed with a defence to comply with r. 44.15 (providing information about funding arrangements).)

Statement of Truth

2.1 Part 22 requires a defence to be verified by a statement of truth.

2.2 The form of the statement of truth is as follows:

'[I believe] [the defendant believes] that the facts stated in this defence are true.'

2.3 Attention is drawn to r. 32.14 which sets out the consequences of verifying a statement of case containing a false statement without an honest belief in its truth.

(For information about statements of truth see Part 22 and PD 22.)

General

para.3.1 **28.3** para.3.4 **26.5**

3.1 Where a defendant to a claim serves a counterclaim under Part 20, the defence and counterclaim should normally form one document with the counterclaim following on from the defence.

3.2 Where a claimant serves a reply and a defence to counterclaim, the reply and defence to counterclaim should normally form one document with the defence to counterclaim following on from the reply.

3.3 Where a claim has been stayed under r. 15.10(3) or 15.11(1) any party may apply for the stay to be lifted.[1]

3.4 The application should be made in accordance with Part 23 and should give the reason for the applicant's delay in proceeding with or responding to the claim.

(Paragraph 8.3 of PD 6 (service of documents) makes provision for the service on the claimant of any notice of funding filed with a defence.)

[1] Rules 15.10(4) and 15.11(2).

CPR Part 16 Statements of Case

Part 16 **13.7, 74.55** [For commentary on a specific rule, please refer to the cross-references after the title of the rule.]

16.1 Part Not to Apply Where Claimant Uses Part 8 Procedure

r.16.1 **13.1**

This Part does not apply where the claimant uses the procedure set out in Part 8 (alternative procedure for claims).

16.2 Contents of the Claim Form

r.16.2(1) **24.18**
r.16.2(1)(a) **23.4, 24.18, 31.19**
r.16.2(1)(b) **4.1, 23.5, 61.6**
r.16.2(1)(c) **23.6**
r.16.2(1)(d) **23.17**
r.16.2(1A) **23.17**
r.16.2(3)–(4) **23.3**
r16.2(5) **4.1, 23.5**

(1) The claim form must—
(a) contain a concise statement of the nature of the claim;
(b) specify the remedy which the claimant seeks;
(c) where the claimant is making a claim for money, contain a statement of value in accordance with rule 16.3;
(cc) where the claimant's only claim is for a specified sum, contain a statement of the interest accrued on that sum; and
(d) contain such other matters as may be set out in a practice direction.
(1A) In civil proceedings against the Crown, as defined in rule 66.1(2), the claim form must also contain—
(a) the names of the government departments and officers of the Crown concerned; and
(b) brief details of the circumstances in which it is alleged that the liability of the Crown arose.
(2) If the particulars of claim specified in rule 16.4 are not contained in, or are not served with the claim form, the claimant must state on the claim form that the particulars of claim will follow.
(3) If the claimant is claiming in a representative capacity, the claim form must state what that capacity is.
(4) If the defendant is sued in a representative capacity, the claim form must state what that capacity is.
(5) The court may grant any remedy to which the claimant is entitled even if that remedy is not specified in the claim form.

(Part 22 requires a claim form to be verified by a statement of truth)
(The costs practice direction [PD 43–48] sets out the information about a funding arrangement to be provided with the statement of case where the defendant intends to seek to recover an additional liability)
('Funding arrangement' and 'additional liability' are defined in rule 43.2)

16.3 Statement of Value to Be Included in the Claim Form

r.16.3 **23.6, 24.14, 26.9**
r.16.3(2)–(4) **23.6**
r.16.3(5) **23.7**
r.16.3(6) **11.4, 23.8**
r.16.3(7) **23.6**

(1) This rule applies where the claimant is making a claim for money.

(2) The claimant must, in the claim form, state—
  (a) the amount of money which he is claiming;
  (b) that he expects to recover—
    (i) not more than £5,000;
    (ii) more than £5,000 but not more than £15,000; or
    (iii) more than £15,000; or
  (c) that he cannot say how much he expects to recover.

(3) In a claim for personal injuries, the claimant must also state in the claim form whether the amount which he expects to recover as general damages for pain, suffering and loss of amenity is—
  (a) not more than £1,000; or
  (b) more than £1,000.

(4) In a claim which includes a claim by a tenant of residential premises against his landlord where the tenant is seeking an order requiring the landlord to carry out repairs or other work to the premises, the claimant must also state in the claim form—
  (a) whether the estimated costs of those repairs or other work is—
    (i) not more than £1,000; or
    (ii) more than £1,000; and
  (b) whether the financial value of any other claim for damages is—
    (i) not more than £1,000; or
    (ii) more than £1,000.

(5) If the claim form is to be issued in the High Court it must, where this rule applies—
  (a) state that the claimant expects to recover more than £15,000;
  (b) state that some other enactment provides that the claim may be commenced only in the High Court and specify that enactment;
  (c) if the claim is a claim for personal injuries state that the claimant expects to recover £50,000 or more; or
  (d) state that the claim is to be in one of the specialist High Court lists and state which list.

(6) When calculating how much he expects to recover, the claimant must disregard any possibility—
  (a) that he may recover—
    (i) interest;
    (ii) costs;
  (b) that the court may make a finding of contributory negligence against him;
  (c) that the defendant may make a counterclaim or that the defence may include a set-off; or
  (d) that the defendant may be liable to pay an amount of money which the court awards to the claimant to the Secretary of State for Social Security under section 6 of the Social Security (Recovery of Benefits) Act 1997.

(7) The statement of value in the claim form does not limit the power of the court to give judgment for the amount which it finds the claimant is entitled to.

16.4 Contents of the Particulars of Claim

r.16.4 **24.1, 93.24**
r.16.4(1) **47.2**
r.16.4(1)(a) **24.3, 24.18, 33.1**
r.16.4(1)(b) **24.3**
r.16.4(1)(c) **4.9, 4.10, 24.3, 24.14**
r.16.4(1)(d)–(e) **24.3**
r.16.4(2) **24.3, 24.14, 62.11**
r.16.4(2)(a)–(b) **24.3**

(1) Particulars of claim must include—
  (a) a concise statement of the facts on which the claimant relies;
  (b) if the claimant is seeking interest, a statement to that effect and the details set out in paragraph (2);
  (c) if the claimant is seeking aggravated damages(GL) or exemplary damages(GL), a statement to that effect and his grounds for claiming them;
  (d) if the claimant is seeking provisional damages, a statement to that effect and his grounds for claiming them; and
  (e) such other matters as may be set out in a practice direction.

(2) If the claimant is seeking interest he must—
  (a) state whether he is doing so—
    (i) under the terms of a contract;

Civil Procedure Rules & Practice Directions

(ii) under an enactment and if so which; or
(iii) on some other basis and if so what that basis is; and
(b) if the claim is for a specified amount of money, state—
(i) the percentage rate at which interest is claimed;
(ii) the date from which it is claimed;
(iii) the date to which it is calculated, which must not be later than the date on which the claim form is issued;
(iv) the total amount of interest claimed to the date of calculation; and
(v) the daily rate at which interest accrues after that date.

(Part 22 requires particulars of claim to be verified by a statement of truth)

16.5 Contents of Defence

r.16.5 **26.13, 93.24**	r.16.5(2)(b) **93.23**
r.16.5(1) **26.6, 47.2**	r.16.5(3)–(4) **26.6, 47.2**
r.16.5(1)(b) **26.6**	r.16.5(5) **26.6, 47.2, 47.8**
r.16.5(1)(c) **47.8**	r.16.5(6) **26.9**
r.16.5(2) **26.6, 26.22**	r.16.5(7) **26.11**
r.16.5(2)(a) **33.1**	r.16.5(8) **26.12**

(1) In his defence, the defendant must state—
(a) which of the allegations in the particulars of claim he denies;
(b) which allegations he is unable to admit or deny, but which he requires the claimant to prove; and
(c) which allegations he admits.

(2) Where the defendant denies an allegation—
(a) he must state his reasons for doing so; and
(b) if he intends to put forward a different version of events from that given by the claimant, he must state his own version.

(3) A defendant who—
(a) fails to deal with an allegation; but
(b) has set out in his defence the nature of his case in relation to the issue to which that allegation is relevant, shall be taken to require that allegation to be proved.

(4) Where the claim includes a money claim, a defendant shall be taken to require that any allegation relating to the amount of money claimed be proved unless he expressly admits the allegation.

(5) Subject to paragraphs (3) and (4), a defendant who fails to deal with an allegation shall be taken to admit that allegation.

(6) If the defendant disputes the claimant's statement of value under rule 16.3 he must—
(a) state why he disputes it; and
(b) if he is able, give his own statement of the value of the claim.

(7) If the defendant is defending in a representative capacity, he must state what that capacity is.

(8) If the defendant has not filed an acknowledgment of service under Part 10, he must give an address for service.

(Part 22 requires a defence to be verified by a statement of truth)
(Rule 6.5 provides that an address for service must be within the jurisdiction)

16.6 Defence of Set-off

r.16.6 **4.6, 26.20**

Where a defendant—
(a) contends he is entitled to money from the claimant; and
(b) relies on this as a defence to the whole or part of the claim,
the contention may be included in the defence and set off against the claim, whether or not it is also a Part 20 claim.

16.7 Reply to Defence

r.16.7(1) **27.1**

(1) A claimant who does not file a reply to the defence shall not be taken to admit the matters raised in the defence.

(2) A claimant who—

(a) files a reply to a defence; but

(b) fails to deal with a matter raised in the defence,

shall be taken to require that matter to be proved.

(Part 22 requires a reply to be verified by a statement of truth)

16.8 Court's Power to Dispense with Statements of Case

r.16.8 **24.2**

If a claim form has been—

(a) issued in accordance with rule 7.2; and

(b) served in accordance with rule 7.5,

the court may make an order that the claim will continue without any other statement of case.

PD 16 Practice Direction — Statements of Case

This practice direction supplements CPR Part 16

[For commentary on a specific paragraph, please refer to the cross-references after the title of the paragraph.]

General

para.1.4 **23.4**

1.1 The provisions of Part 16 do not apply to claims in respect of which the Part 8 procedure is being used.

1.2 Where special provisions about statements of case are made by the rules and practice directions applying to particular types of proceedings, the provisions of Part 16 and of this practice direction apply only to the extent that they are not inconsistent with those rules and practice directions.

1.3 Examples of types of proceedings with special provisions about statements of case include:
(1) defamation claims (Part 53);
(2) possession claims (Part 55); and
(3) probate claims (Part 57).

1.4 If exceptionally a statement of case exceeds 25 pages (excluding schedules) an appropriate short summary must also be filed and served.

The Claim Form

para.2.2 **23.3**
para.2.3 **23.3**
para.2.5 **23.3**
para.2.6 **14.1, 23.3, 24.9**
para.2.6(a) **14.1**

2.1 Rule 16.2 refers to matters which the claim form must contain. Where the claim is for money, the claim form must also contain the statement of value referred to in r. 16.3.

2.2 The claim form must include an address at which the claimant resides or carries on business. This paragraph applies even though the claimant's address for service is the business address of his solicitor.

2.3 Where the defendant is an individual, the claimant should (if he is able to do so) include in the claim form an address at which the defendant resides or carries on business. This paragraph applies even though the defendant's solicitor have agreed to accept service on the defendant's behalf.

2.4 Any address which is provided for the purpose of these provisions must include a postcode, unless the court orders otherwise. Postcode information may be obtained from www.royalmail.com or the Royal Mail Address Management Guide.

2.5 If the claim form does not show a full address, including postcode, at which the claimant(s) and defendant(s) reside or carry on business, the claim form will be issued but will be retained by the court and will not be served until the claimant has supplied a full address, including postcode, or the court has dispensed with the requirement to do so. The court will notify the claimant.

2.6 The claim form must be headed with the title of the proceedings, including the full name of each party. The full name means, in each case where it is known:
(a) in the case of an individual, his full unabbreviated name and title by which he is known;
(b) in the case of an individual carrying on business in a name other than his own name, the full unabbreviated name of the individual, together with the title by which he is known, and the full trading name (for example, John Smith 'trading as' or 'T/as' 'JS Autos');
(c) in the case of a partnership (other than a limited liability partnership (LLP)):
  (i) where partners are being sued in the name of the partnership, the full name by which the partnership is known, together with the words '(A Firm)'; or
  (ii) where partners are being sued as individuals, the full unabbreviated name of each partner and the title by which he is known;
(d) in the case of a company or limited liability partnership registered in England and Wales, the full registered name, including suffix (plc, limited, LLP, etc.), if any;
(e) in the case of any other company or corporation, the full name by which it is known, including suffix where appropriate.

(RSC, ord. 81 in CPR, sch. 1, contains rules about claims made by or against partners in their firm name.)

(For information about how and where a claim may be started see Part 7 and PD 7.)

Particulars of Claim

para.3.1 **15.13, 24.1**
para.3.6(2) **24.3**
para.3.8 **24.3**

3.1 If practicable, the particulars of claim should be set out in the claim form.

3.2 Where the claimant does not include the particulars of claim in the claim form, particulars of claim may be served separately:
(1) either at the same time as the claim form, or
(2) within 14 days after service of the claim form[1] provided that the service of the particulars of claim is not later than four months from the date of issue of the claim form[2] (or six months where the claim form is to be served out of the jurisdiction[3]).

3.3 If the particulars of claim are not included in or have not been served with the claim form, the claim form must also contain a statement that particulars of claim will follow.[4]

3.4 Particulars of claim which are not included in the claim form must be verified by a statement of truth, the form of which is as follows:
[I believe] [the claimant believes] that the facts stated in these particulars of claim are true.

3.5 Attention is drawn to r. 32.14 which sets out the consequences of verifying a statement of case containing a false statement without an honest belief in its truth.

3.6 The full particulars of claim must include:
(1) the matters set out in r. 16.4, and
(2) where appropriate, the matters set out in practice directions relating to specific types of claims.

3.7 Attention is drawn to the provisions of r. 16.4(2) in respect of a claim for interest.

3.8 Particulars of claim served separately from the claim form must also contain:
(1) the name of the court in which the claim is proceeding,
(2) the claim number,
(3) the title of the proceedings, and
(4) the claimant's address for service.

Matters Which Must Be Included in the Particulars of Claim in Certain Types of Claim

para.4 **24.6**
para.4.2 **4.12, 15.6, 24.13**
para.4.3 **15.6, 24.13**

Personal injury claims

4.1 The particulars of claim must contain:
(1) the claimant's date of birth, and
(2) brief details of the claimant's personal injuries.

4.2 The claimant must attach to his particulars of claim a schedule of details of any past and future expenses and losses which he claims.

4.3 Where the claimant is relying on the evidence of a medical practitioner the claimant must attach to or serve with his particulars of claim a report from a medical practitioner about the personal injuries which he alleges in his claim.

4.4 In a provisional damages claim the claimant must state in his particulars of claim:
(1) that he is seeking an award of provisional damages under either the Supreme Court Act 1981, s. 32A or the County Courts Act 1984, s. 51,
(2) that there is a chance that at some future time the claimant will develop some serious disease or suffer some serious deterioration in his physical or mental condition, and
(3) specify the disease or type of deterioration in respect of which an application may be made at a future date.

(Part 41 and PD 41 contain information about awards for provisional damages.)

[1] See r. 7.4(1)(b).
[2] See r. 7.4(2) and 7.5(2).
[3] See r. 7.5(3).
[4] See r. 16.2(2).

Fatal accident claims

para.5 **24.6**

5.1 In a fatal accident claim the claimant must state in his particulars of claim:
(1) that it is brought under the Fatal Accidents Act 1976,
(2) the dependants on whose behalf the claim is made,
(3) the date of birth of each dependant, and
(4) details of the nature of the dependency claim.

5.2 A fatal accident claim may include a claim for damages for bereavement.

5.3 In a fatal accident claim the claimant may also bring a claim under the Law Reform (Miscellaneous Provisions) Act 1934 on behalf of the estate of the deceased.
(For information on apportionment under the Law Reform (Miscellaneous Provisions) Act 1934 and the Fatal Accidents Act 1976 or between dependants see Part 37 and PD 37.)

Hire-purchase claims

para.6 **24.6** para.6.1–6.2 **96.58**

6.1 Where the claim is for the delivery of goods let under a hire-purchase agreement or conditional sale agreement to a person other than a company or other corporation, the claimant must state in the particulars of claim:
(1) the date of the agreement,
(2) the parties to the agreement,
(3) the number or other identification of the agreement,
(4) where the claimant was not one of the original parties to the agreement, the means by which the rights and duties of the creditor passed to him,
(5) whether the agreement is a regulated agreement, and if it is not a regulated agreement, the reason why,
(6) the place where the agreement was signed by the defendant,
(7) the goods claimed,
(8) the total price of the goods,
(9) the paid-up sum,
(10) the unpaid balance of the total price,
(11) whether a default notice or a notice under s. 76(1) or 98(1) of the Consumer Credit Act 1974 has been served on the defendant, and if it has, the date and method of service,
(12) the date when the right to demand delivery of the goods accrued,
(13) the amount (if any) claimed as an alternative to the delivery of goods, and
(14) the amount (if any) claimed in addition to:
(a) the delivery of the goods, or
(b) any claim under (13) above, with the grounds of each claim.
(If the agreement is a regulated agreement the procedure set out in PD 7B should be used.)

6.2 Where the claim is not for the delivery of goods, the claimant must state in his particulars of claim:
(1) the matters set out in para. 6.1(1) to (6) above,
(2) the goods let under the agreement,
(3) the amount of the total price,
(4) the paid-up sum,
(5) the amount (if any) claimed as being due and unpaid in respect of any instalment or instalments of the total price, and
(6) the nature and amount of any other claim and how it arises.

Other Matters to Be Included in Particulars of Claim

para.7.1 **24.6** para.7.3 **15.6, 24.3**
para.7.2 **24.3, 24.6** para.7.4–7.6 **24.3**

7.1 Where a claim is made for an injunction or declaration in respect of or relating to any land or the possession, occupation, use or enjoyment of any land the particulars of claim must:
(1) state whether or not the injunction or declaration relates to residential premises, and
(2) identify the land (by reference to a plan where necessary).

7.2 Where a claim is brought to enforce a right to recover possession of goods the particulars of claim must contain a statement showing the value of the goods.

7.3 Where a claim is based upon a written agreement:

(1) a copy of the contract or documents constituting the agreement should be attached to or served with the particulars of claim and the original(s) should be available at the hearing, and

(2) any general conditions of sale incorporated in the contract should also be attached (but where the contract is or the documents constituting the agreement are bulky this practice direction is complied with by attaching or serving only the relevant parts of the contract or documents).

7.4 Where a claim is based upon an oral agreement, the particulars of claim should set out the contractual words used and state by whom, to whom, when and where they were spoken.

7.5 Where a claim is based upon an agreement by conduct, the particulars of claim must specify the conduct relied on and state by whom, when and where the acts constituting the conduct were done.

7.6 In a claim issued in the High Court relating to a consumer credit agreement, the particulars of claim must contain a statement that the action is not one to which the Consumer Credit Act 1974, s. 141, applies.

Matters Which Must Be Specifically Set Out In the Particulars of Claim If Relied On

para.8.1 **24.6, 47.93, 47.95** para.8.2 **24.3**

8.1 A claimant who wishes to rely on evidence:

(1) under the Civil Evidence Act 1968, s. 11 of a conviction of an offence, or

(2) under s. 12 of the above mentioned Act of a finding or adjudication of adultery or paternity,

must include in his particulars of claim a statement to that effect and give the following details:

(1) the type of conviction, finding or adjudication and its date,

(2) the court or court martial which made the conviction, finding or adjudication, and

(3) the issue in the claim to which it relates.

8.2 The claimant must specifically set out the following matters in his particulars of claim where he wishes to rely on them in support of his claim:

(1) any allegation of fraud,

(2) the fact of any illegality,

(3) details of any misrepresentation,

(4) details of all breaches of trust,

(5) notice or knowledge of a fact,

(6) details of unsoundness of mind or undue influence,

(7) details of wilful default, and

(8) any facts relating to mitigation of loss or damage.

General

para.9.1 **23.9, 61.16** para.9.3 **23.3**
para.9.2 **27.2**

9.1 Where a claim is for a sum of money expressed in a foreign currency it must expressly state:

(1) that the claim is for payment in a specified foreign currency,

(2) why it is for payment in that currency,

(3) the sterling equivalent of the sum at the date of the claim, and

(4) the source of the exchange rate relied on to calculate the sterling equivalent.

9.2 A subsequent statement of case must not contradict or be inconsistent with an earlier one; for example a reply to a defence must not bring in a new claim. Where new matters have come to light the appropriate course may be to seek the court's permission to amend the statement of case.

9.3 In clinical negligence claims, the words 'clinical negligence' should be inserted at the top of every statement of case.

The Defence

para.10.2 **26.6** para.10.7 **26.6**
para.10.4 **26.6**

General

10.1 Rule 16.5 deals with the contents of the defence.

10.2 A defendant should deal with every allegation in accordance with r. 16.5(1) and (2).

10.3 Rule 16.5(3), (4) and (5) sets out the consequences of not dealing with an allegation.

10.4 Where the defendant is an individual, and the claim form does not contain an address at which he resides or carries on business, or contains an incorrect address, the defendant must provide such an address in the defence.

10.5 Where the defendant's address for service is not where he resides or carries on business, he must still provide the address required by [para. 10.4*].

10.6 Any address which is provided for the purpose of these provisions must include a postcode, unless the court orders otherwise. Postcode information may be obtained from www.royalmail.com or the Royal Mail Address Management Guide.

10.7 Where a defendant to a claim or counterclaim is an individual, he must provide his date of birth (if known) in the acknowledgment of service, admission, defence, defence and counterclaim, reply or other response.

Statement of truth

para.11.2 **26.21**

11.1 Part 22 requires a defence to Be verified by a statement of truth.

11.2 The form of the statement of truth is as follows:

[I believe] [the defendant believes] that the facts stated in the defence are true.

11.3 Attention is drawn to r. 32.14 which sets out the consequences of verifying a statement of case containing a false statement without an honest belief in its truth.

Matters Which Must Be Included in the Defence

para.12.1 **26.13** para.12.1(2)–(3) **26.13**
para.12.1(1)(c) **26.13** para.12.2(1)–(2) **26.13**

Personal injury claims

12.1 Where the claim is for personal injuries and the claimant has attached a medical report in respect of his alleged injuries, the defendant should:

(1) state in his defence whether he:
  (a) agrees,
  (b) disputes, or
  (c) neither agrees nor disputes but has no knowledge of,

  the matters contained in the medical report,

(2) where he disputes any part of the medical report, give in his defence his reasons for doing so, and

(3) where he has obtained his own medical report on which he intends to rely, attach it to his defence.

12.2 Where the claim is for personal injuries and the claimant has included a schedule of past and future expenses and losses, the defendant should include in or attach to his defence a counter-schedule stating:

(1) which of those items he:
  (a) agrees,
  (b) disputes, or
  (c) neither agrees nor disputes but has no knowledge of, and

(2) where any items are disputed, supplying alternative figures where appropriate.

(PD 43–48 contains details of the information required to be filed with certain statements of case to comply with r. 44.15 (providing information about funding arrangements).)

[* The text issued by the Department for Constitutional Affairs mistakenly refers to para. 11.4.]

Other matters

para.13.1 **10.1, 26.15** para.13.3 **24.7**
para.13.2 **26.18**

13.1 The defendant must give details of the expiry of any relevant limitation period relied on.
13.2 Rule 37.3 and PD 37, para. 2, contain information about a defence of tender.
13.3 A party may:
(1) refer in his statement of case to any point of law on which his claim or defence, as the case may be, is based,
(2) give in his statement of case the name of any witness he proposes to call, and
(3) attach to or serve with this statement of case a copy of any document which he considers is necessary to his claim or defence, as the case may be (including any expert's report to be filed in accordance with Part 35).

Competition Act 1998

para.14 **23.17, 24.6, 26.19**

14 A party who wishes to rely on a finding of the Office of Fair Trading as provided by the Competition Act 1998, s. 58, must include in his statement of case a statement to that effect and identify the Office's finding on which he seeks to rely.

Human Rights

para.15 **23.17, 24.6** para.15.1 **24.3, 26.16, 71.22**

15.1 A party who seeks to rely on any provision of or right arising under the Human Rights Act 1998 or seeks a remedy available under that Act:
(1) must state that fact in his statement of case; and
(2) must in his statement of case:
(a) give precise details of the Convention right which it is alleged has been infringed and details of the alleged infringement;
(b) specify the relief sought;
(c) state if the relief sought includes:
(i) a declaration of incompatibility in accordance with s. 4 of that Act, or
(ii) damages in respect of a judicial act to which s. 9(3) of that Act applies;
(d) where the relief sought includes a declaration of incompatibility in accordance with s. 4 of that Act, give precise details of the legislative provision alleged to be incompatible and details of the alleged incompatibility;
(e) where the claim is founded on a finding of unlawfulness by another court or tribunal, give details of the finding; and
(f) where the claim is founded on a judicial act which is alleged to have infringed a Convention right of the party as provided by the Human Rights Act 1998, s. 9, the judicial act complained of and the court or tribunal which is alleged to have made it.

(PD 19 provides for notice to be given and parties joined in the circumstances referred to in (c), (d) and (f).)

15.2 A party who seeks to amend his statement of case to include the matters referred to in para. 15.1 must, unless the court orders otherwise, do so as soon as possible.
(Part 17 provides for the amendment of a statement of case.)

CPR Part 17 Amendments to Statements of Case

Part 17 **31.14**, **74.36**, **79.3** [For commentary on a specific rule, please refer to the cross-references after the title of the rule.]

17.1 Amendments to Statements of Case

r.17.1(1) **31.2, 31.10**
r.17.1(2)(a) **31.2, 31.14**
r.17.1(2)(b) **31.3**

(1) A party may amend his statement of case at any time before it has been served on any other party.

(2) If his statement of case has been served, a party may amend it only—

(a) with the written consent of all the other parties; or

(b) with the permission of the court.

(3) If a statement of case has been served, an application to amend it by removing, adding or substituting a party must be made in accordance with rule 19.4.

(Part 22 requires amendments to a statement of case to be verified by a statement of truth unless the court orders otherwise)

17.2 Power of Court to Disallow Amendments Made without Permission

r.17.2 **31.14**
r.17.2(1)–(2) **31.2**

(1) If a party has amended his statement of case where permission of the court was not required, the court may disallow the amendment.

(2) A party may apply to the court for an order under paragraph (1) within 14 days of service of a copy of the amended statement of case on him.

17.3 Amendments to Statements of Case with the Permission of the Court

r.17.3(1)–(2) **31.3**

(1) Where the court gives permission for a party to amend his statement of case, it may give directions as to—

(a) amendments to be made to any other statement of case; and

(b) service of any amended statement of case.

(2) The power of the court to give permission under this rule is subject to—

(a) rule 19.1 (change of parties — general);

(b) rule 19.4 (special provisions about adding or substituting parties after the end of a relevant limitation period[(GL)]); and

(c) rule 17.4 (amendments of statement of case after the end of a relevant limitation period).

17.4 Amendments to Statements of Case after the End of a Relevant Limitation Period

r.17.4 **1.18, 14.9, 31.3, 31.14, 97.40**
r.17.4(1) **31.14**
r.17.4(2) **31.17, 31.18**
r.17.4(3) **14.9**
r.17.4(4) **14.12, 31.14**

(1) This rule applies where—

(a) a party applies to amend his statement of case in one of the ways mentioned in this rule; and

(b) a period of limitation has expired under—

(i) the Limitation Act 1980;

(ii) the Foreign Limitation Periods Act 1984; or

(iii) any other enactment which allows such an amendment, or under which such an amendment is allowed.

(2) The court may allow an amendment whose effect will be to add or substitute a new claim, but only if the new claim arises out of the same facts or substantially the same facts as a claim in respect of which the party applying for permission has already claimed a remedy in the proceedings.

(3) The court may allow an amendment to correct a mistake as to the name of a party, but only where the mistake was genuine and not one which would cause reasonable doubt as to the identity of the party in question.

(4) The court may allow an amendment to alter the capacity in which a party claims if the new capacity is one which that party had when the proceedings started or has since acquired.

(Rule 19.5 specifies the circumstances in which the court may allow a new party to be added or substituted after the end of a relevant limitation period[GL])

PD 17 Practice Direction — Amendments to Statements of Case

This practice direction supplements CPR Part 17

[For commentary on a specific paragraph, please refer to the cross-references after the title of the paragraph.]

A party applying for an amendment will usually be responsible for the costs of and arising from the amendment.

Applications to Amend Where the Permission of the Court Is Required

paras.1.1–1.3 **31.3**
para.1.4 **31.10**
para.1.5 **31.3**

1.1 The application may be dealt with at a hearing or, if rule 23.8 applies, without a hearing.

1.2 When making an application to amend a statement of case, the applicant should file with the court:

(1) the application notice, and

(2) a copy of the statement of case with the proposed amendments.

1.3 Where permission to amend has been given, the applicant should within 14 days of the date of the order, or within such other period as the court may direct, file with the court the amended statement of case.

1.4 If the substance of the statement of case is changed by reason of the amendment, the statement of case should be re-verified by a statement of truth.[1]

1.5 A copy of the order and the amended statement of case should be served on every party to the proceedings, unless the court orders otherwise.

General

para.2 **14.7**
para.2.1(1) **31.3**
para.2.1(2) **31.2**
para.2.2 **31.3, 31.10**
paras.2.3–2.4 **31.10**

2.1 The amended statement of case and the court copy of it should be endorsed as follows:

(1) where the court's permission was required:

'Amended [Particulars of Claim *or as may be*] by Order of [Master ....] [District Judge .... *or as may be*] dated .... '

(2) Where the court's permission was not required:

'Amended [Particulars of Claim *or as may be*] under CPR [rule 17.1(1) or (2)(a)] dated .... '

2.2 The statement of case in its amended form need not show the original text. However, where the court thinks it desirable for both the original text and the amendments to be shown, the court may direct that the amendments should be shown either:

(1) by coloured amendments, either manuscript or computer generated, or

(2) by use of a numerical code in a monochrome computer generated document.

2.3 Where colour is used, the text to be deleted should be struck through in colour and any text replacing it should be inserted or underlined in the same colour.

2.4 The order of colours to be used for successive amendments is: (1) red, (2) green, (3) violet and (4) yellow.

(For information about changes to parties see Part 19 and PD 19.)

[1] See Part 22 for information about the statement of truth.

CPR Part 18 Further Information

Part 18 **14.18, 26.6, 30.1, 30.3, 43.6, 43.15, 48.27, 79.62** [For commentary on a specific rule, please refer to the cross-references after the title of the rule.]

18.1 Obtaining Further Information

r.18.1 **23.1, 30.1, 30.2, 30.6, 47.8, 78.12, 96.30** r.18.1(3) **30.6**

(1) The court may at any time order a party to—
 (a) clarify any matter which is in dispute in the proceedings; or
 (b) give additional information in relation to any such matter, whether or not the matter is contained or referred to in a statement of case.
(2) Paragraph (1) is subject to any rule of law to the contrary.
(3) Where the court makes an order under paragraph (1), the party against whom it is made must—
 (a) file his response; and
 (b) serve it on the other parties,
within the time specified by the court.

(Part 22 requires a response to be verified by a statement of truth)

(Part 53 (defamation) restricts requirements for providing further information about sources of information in defamation claims)

18.2 Restriction on the Use of Further Information

r.18.2 **30.6, 30.7**

The court may direct that information provided by a party to another party (whether given voluntarily or following an order made under rule 18.1) must not be used for any purpose except for that of the proceedings in which it is given.

PD 18 Practice Direction — Further Information

This practice direction supplements CPR Part 18

PD 18 **30.1**, **47.8** [For commentary on a specific paragraph, please refer to the cross-references after the title of the paragraph.]

Attention is also drawn to Part 22 (statements of truth).

Preliminary Request for Further Information or Clarification

para.1.1 **30.2**, **74.40**
para.1.2 **26.8**, **30.2**
para.1.3 **30.2**
paras.1.4–1.5 **30.3**
para.1.6 **30.3**
para.1.6(1) **30.3**
para.1.6(2) **30.3**, **30.4**

1.1 Before making an application to the court for an order under Part 18, the party seeking clarification or information (the first party) should first serve on the party from whom it is sought (the second party) a written request for that clarification or information (a Request) stating a date by which the response to the Request should be served. The date must allow the second party a reasonable time to respond.

1.2 A Request should be concise and strictly confined to matters which are reasonably necessary and proportionate to enable the first party to prepare his own case or to understand the case he has to meet.

1.3 Requests must be made as far as possible in a single comprehensive document and not piecemeal.

1.4 A Request may be made by letter if the text of the Request is brief and the reply is likely to be brief; otherwise the Request should be made in a separate document.

1.5 If a Request is made in a letter, the letter should, in order to distinguish it from any other that might routinely be written in the course of a case,
(1) state that it contains a Request made under Part 18, and
(2) deal with no matters other than the Request.

1.6 (1) A Request (whether made by letter or in a separate document) must—
(a) be headed with the name of the court and the title and number of the claim,
(b) in its heading state that it is a Request made under Part 18, identify the first party and the second party and state the date on which it is made,
(c) set out in a separate numbered paragraph each request for information or clarification,
(d) where a Request relates to a document, identify that document and (if relevant) the paragraph or words to which it relates,
(e) state the date by which the first party expects a response to the Request,
(2) (a) A Request which is not in the form of a letter may, if convenient, be prepared in such a way that the response may be given on the same document.
(b) To do this the numbered paragraphs of the Request should appear on the left hand half of each sheet so that the paragraphs of the response may then appear on the right.
(c) Where a Request is prepared in this form an extra copy should be served for the use of the second party.

1.7 Subject to the provisions of PD 6, paras 3.1 to 3.3, a request should be served by email if reasonably practicable.

Responding to a Request

para.2.1 **30.4**
para.2.2(1)–(2) **30.4**
para.2.3(1) **30.4**
para.2.3(1)(c) **30.3**
para.2.3(2) **30.4**
para.2.4 **30.4**

2.1 A response to a Request must be in writing, dated and signed by the second party or his legal representative.

2.2 (1) Where the Request is made in a letter the second party may give his response in a letter or in a formal reply.
(2) Such a letter should identify itself as a response to the Request and deal with no other matters than the response.

2.3 (1) Unless the Request is in the format described in paragraph 1.6(2) and the second party uses the document supplied for the purpose, a response must:
(a) be headed with the name of the court and the title and number of the claim,
(b) in its heading identify itself as a response to that Request,
(c) repeat the text of each separate paragraph of the Request and set out under each paragraph the response to it,
(d) refer to and have attached to it a copy of any document not already in the possession of the first party which forms part of the response.
(2) A second or supplementary response to a Request must identify itself as such in its heading.
2.4 The second party must when he serves his response on the first party serve on every other party and file with the court a copy of the Request and of his response.

Statements of Truth

para.3 **30.3, 30.4**

3 Attention is drawn to Part 22 and to the definition of a statement of case in Part 2 of the rules; a response should be verified by a statement of truth.

General Matters

para.4.1(1)–(2) **30.5** para.4.2(1)–(2) **30.5**

4.1 (1) If the second party objects to complying with the Request or part of it or is unable to do so at all or within the time stated in the Request he must inform the first party promptly and in any event within that time.
(2) He may do so in a letter or in a separate document (a formal response), but in either case he must give reasons and, where relevant, give a date by which he expects to be able to comply.
4.2 (1) There is no need for a second party to apply to the court if he objects to a Request or is unable to comply with it at all or within the stated time. He need only comply with paragraph 4.1(1) above.
(2) Where a second party considers that a Request can only be complied with at disproportionate expense and objects to comply for that reason he should say so in his reply and explain briefly why he has taken that view.

Applications for Orders under Part 18

paras.5.2–5.7 **30.6** para.5.8(2) **30.6**
para.5.8 **30.6**

5.1 Attention is drawn to Part 23 (applications) and to PD 23.
5.2 An application notice for an order under Part 18 should set out or have attached to it the text of the order sought and in particular should specify the matter or matters in respect of which the clarification or information is sought.
5.3 (1) If a Request under paragraph 1 for the information or clarification has not been made, the application notice should, in addition, explain why not.
(2) If a Request for clarification or information has been made, the application notice or the evidence in support should describe the response, if any.
5.4 Both the first party and the second party should consider whether evidence in support of or in opposition to the application is required.
5.5 (1) Where the second party has made no response to a Request served on him, the first party need not serve the application notice on the second party, and the court may deal with the application without a hearing.
(2) Sub-paragraph (1) above only applies if at least 14 days have passed since the Request was served and the time stated in it for a response has expired.
5.6 Unless paragraph 5.5 applies the application notice must be served on the second party and on all other parties to the claim.
5.7 An order made under Part 18 must be served on all parties to the claim.
5.8 Costs:
(1) Attention is drawn to PD 43–48 and in particular the court's power to make a summary assessment of costs.
(2) Attention is also drawn to rule 44.13(1) which provides that the general rule is that if an order does not mention costs no party is entitled to costs relating to that order.

CPR Part 19 Parties and Group Litigation

Part 19 **14.64, 65.6, 65.13** [For commentary on a specific rule, please refer to the cross-references after the title of the rule.]

19.1 Parties — General

r.19.1 **14.2, 14.9**

Any number of claimants or defendants may be joined as parties to a claim.

I ADDITION AND SUBSTITUTION OF PARTIES

19.2 Change of Parties — General

r.19.2 **14.3, 16.49, 31.3**
r.19.2(2) **14.3, 38.31**
r.19.2(2)(a) **9.6, 14.3**
r.19.2(2)(b) **29.12**
r.19.2(3) **14.3**
r.19.2(4) **14.3, 14.26, 14.30**

(1) This rule applies where a party is to be added or substituted except where the case falls within rule 19.5 (special provisions about changing parties after the end of a relevant limitation period[(GL)]).

(2) The court may order a person to be added as a new party if—
  (a) it is desirable to add the new party so that the court can resolve all the matters in dispute in the proceedings; or
  (b) there is an issue involving the new party and an existing party which is connected to the matters in dispute in the proceedings, and it is desirable to add the new party so that the court can resolve that issue.

(3) The court may order any person to cease to be a party if it is not desirable for that person to be a party to the proceedings.

(4) The court may order a new party to be substituted for an existing one if—
  (a) the existing party's interest or liability has passed to the new party; and
  (b) it is desirable to substitute the new party so that the court can resolve the matters in dispute in the proceedings.

19.3 Provisions Applicable Where Two or More Persons Are Jointly Entitled to a Remedy

r.19.3 **14.2**
r.19.3(1)–(3) **14.2**

(1) Where a claimant claims a remedy to which some other person is jointly entitled with him, all persons jointly entitled to the remedy must be parties unless the court orders otherwise.

(2) If any person does not agree to be a claimant, he must be made a defendant, unless the court orders otherwise.
(3) This rule does not apply in probate proceedings.

19.4 Procedure for Adding and Substituting Parties

r.19.4 **31.2, 35.9**
r.19.4(1) **14.4**
r.19.4(2) **14.3**
r.19.4(3) **14.26**
r.19.4(4) **14.3, 14.26**
r.19.4(4A) **14.3, 14.76**
r.19.4(5) **14.7, 14.26**
r.19.5(2)(a) **14.9**
r.19.4(6) **14.7**

(1) The court's permission is required to remove, add or substitute a party, unless the claim form has not been served.
(2) An application for permission under paragraph (1) may be made by—
(a) an existing party; or
(b) a person who wishes to become a party.
(3) An application for an order under rule 19.2(4) (substitution of a new party where existing party's interest or liability has passed)—
(a) may be made without notice; and
(b) must be supported by evidence.
(4) Nobody may be added or substituted as a claimant unless—
(a) he has given his consent in writing; and
(b) that consent has been filed with the court.
(4A) The Commissioners for HM Revenue and Customs may be added as a party to proceedings only if they consent in writing.
(5) An order for the removal, addition or substitution of a party must be served on—
(a) all parties to the proceedings; and
(b) any other person affected by the order.
(6) When the court makes an order for the removal, addition or substitution of a party, it may give consequential directions about—
(a) filing and serving the claim form on any new defendant;
(b) serving relevant documents on the new party; and
(c) the management of the proceedings.

19.4A Human Rights

r.19.4A **14.78, 97.4, 97.10**
r.19.4A(1) **14.78**
r.19.4A(3)–(4) **14.78**

Section 4 of the Human Rights Act 1998
(1) The court may not make a declaration of incompatibility in accordance with section 4 of the Human Rights Act 1998 unless 21 days' notice, or such other period of notice as the court directs, has been given to the Crown.
(2) Where notice has been given to the Crown a Minister, or other person permitted by that Act, shall be joined as a party on giving notice to the court.
(Only courts specified in section 4 of the Human Rights Act 1998 can make a declaration of incompatibility)

Section 9 of the Human Rights Act 1998
(3) Where a claim is made under that Act for damages in respect of a judicial act—
(a) that claim must be set out in the statement of case or the appeal notice; and
(b) notice must be given to the Crown.
(4) Where paragraph (3) applies and the appropriate person has not applied to be joined as a party within 21days, or such other period as the court directs, after the notice is served, the court may join the appropriate person as a party.
(A practice direction makes provision for these notices)

19.5 Special Provisions about Adding or Substituting Parties after the End of a Relevant Limitation Period

r.19.5 **14.8, 14.9, 31.3, 31.5**
r.19.5(2) **14.9**
r.19.5(3) **14.9**
r.19.5(3)(a) **14.9**
r.19.5(3)(b) **14.10**
r.19.5(4) **14.13**

(1) This rule applies to a change of parties after the end of a period of limitation under—
(a) the Limitation Act 1980;
(b) the Foreign Limitation Periods Act 1984; or
(c) any other enactment which allows such a change, or under which such a change is allowed.
(2) The court may add or substitute a party only if—
(a) the relevant limitation period[(GL)] was current when the proceedings were started; and
(b) the addition or substitution is necessary.
(3) The addition or substitution of a party is necessary only if the court is satisfied that—
(a) the new party is to be substituted for a party who was named in the claim form in mistake for the new party;
(b) the claim cannot properly be carried on by or against the original party unless the new party is added or substituted as claimant or defendant; or
(c) the original party has died or had a bankruptcy order made against him and his interest or liability has passed to the new party.
(4) In addition, in a claim for personal injuries the court may add or substitute a party where it directs that—
(a) (i) section 11 (special time limit for claims for personal injuries); or
(ii) section 12 (special time limit for claims under fatal accidents legislation),
of the Limitation Act 1980 shall not apply to the claim by or against the new party; or
(b) the issue of whether those sections apply shall be determined at trial.
(Rule 17.4 deals with other changes after the end of a relevant limitation period[(GL)])

19.5A Special Rules about Parties in Claims for Wrongful Interference with Goods

r.19.5A **14.14**
r.19.5A(1) **24.3**

(1) A claimant in a claim for wrongful interference with goods must, in the particulars of claim, state the name and address of every person who, to his knowledge, has or claims an interest in the goods and who is not a party to the claim.
(2) A defendant to a claim for wrongful interference with goods may apply for a direction that another person be made a party to the claim to establish whether the other person—
(a) has a better right to the goods than the claimant; or
(b) has a claim which might render the defendant doubly liable under section 7 of the Torts (Interference with Goods) Act 1977.
(3) Where the person referred to in paragraph (2) fails to attend the hearing of the application, or comply with any directions, the court may order that he is deprived of any claim against the defendant in respect of the goods.
(Rule 3.1(3) provides that the court may make an order subject to conditions)
(4) The application notice must be served on all parties and on the person referred to in paragraph (2).

II REPRESENTATIVE PARTIES

19.6 Representative Parties with Same Interest

r.19.6 **14.55, 14.56, 14.61**
r.19.6(1) **14.55, 76.37**
r.19.6(2) **14.56**
r.19.6(4) **14.56, 76.37**

(1) Where more than one person has the same interest in a claim—
(a) the claim may be begun; or
(b) the court may order that the claim be continued,
by or against one or more of the persons who have the same interest as representatives of any other persons who have that interest.
(2) The court may direct that a person may not act as a representative.
(3) Any party may apply to the court for an order under paragraph (2).

(4) Unless the court otherwise directs any judgment or order given in a claim in which a party is acting as a representative under this rule—
  (a) is binding on all persons represented in the claim; but
  (b) may only be enforced by or against a person who is not a party to the claim with the permission of the court.

(5) This rule does not apply to a claim to which rule 19.7 applies.

19.7 Representation of Interested Persons Who Cannot Be Ascertained etc.

r.19.7 **14.55, 14.57, 14.60, 14.61** r.19.7(7) **14.57, 76.37**
r.19.7(2) **76.37**

(1) This rule applies to claims about—
  (a) the estate of a deceased person;
  (b) property subject to a trust; or
  (c) the meaning of a document, including a statute.

(2) The court may make an order appointing a person to represent any other person or persons in the claim where the person or persons to be represented—
  (a) are unborn;
  (b) cannot be found;
  (c) cannot easily be ascertained; or
  (d) are a class of persons who have the same interest in a claim and—
    (i) one or more members of that class are within sub-paragraphs (a), (b) or (c); or
    (ii) to appoint a representative would further the overriding objective.

(3) An application for an order under paragraph (2)—
  (a) may be made by—
    (i) any person who seeks to be appointed under the order; or
    (ii) any party to the claim; and
  (b) may be made at any time before or after the claim has started.

(4) An application notice for an order under paragraph (2) must be served on—
  (a) all parties to the claim, if the claim has started;
  (b) the person sought to be appointed, if that person is not the applicant or a party to the claim; and
  (c) any other person as directed by the court.

(5) The court's approval is required to settle a claim in which a party is acting as a representative under this rule.

(6) The court may approve a settlement where it is satisfied that the settlement is for the benefit of all the represented persons.

(7) Unless the court otherwise directs, any judgment or order given in a claim in which a party is acting as a representative under this rule—
  (a) is binding on all persons represented in the claim; but
  (b) may only be enforced by or against a person who is not a party to the claim with the permission of the court.

19.7A Representation of Beneficiaries by Trustees etc.

r.19.7A **14.54**

(1) A claim may be brought by or against trustees, executors or administrators in that capacity without adding as parties any persons who have a beneficial interest in the trust or estate ('the beneficiaries').

(2) Any judgment or order given or made in the claim is binding on the beneficiaries unless the court orders otherwise in the same or other proceedings.

19.7B Postal Services Act 2000 (c. 26)

r.19.7B **13.4**

(1) An application under section 92 of the Postal Services Act 2000 for permission to bring proceedings in the name of the sender or addressee of a postal packet or his personal representative is made in accordance with Part 8.

(2) A copy of the application notice must be served on the universal service provider and on the person in whose name the applicant seeks to bring the proceedings.

19.8 Death

r.19.8 **14.61**
r.19.8(1) **14.30**
r.19.8(1)(b) **14.30**
r.19.8(2) **14.29**
r.19.8(2)(b)(i)–(ii) **14.29**
r.19.8(3)(a)–(b) **14.29**
r.19.8(4) **14.30**
r.19.8(5) **14.30**

(1) Where a person who had an interest in a claim has died and that person has no personal representative the court may order—
 (a) the claim to proceed in the absence of a person representing the estate of the deceased; or
 (b) a person to be appointed to represent the estate of the deceased.
(2) Where a defendant against whom a claim could have been brought has died and
 (a) a grant of probate or administration has been made, the claim must be brought against the persons who are the personal representatives of the deceased;
 (b) a grant of probate or administration has not been made—
  (i) the claim must be brought against 'the estate of' the deceased; and
  (ii) the claimant must apply to the court for an order appointing a person to represent the estate of the deceased in the claim.
(3) A claim shall be treated as having been brought against 'the estate of' the deceased in accordance with paragraph (2)(b)(i) where—
 (a) the claim is brought against the 'personal representatives' of the deceased but a grant of probate or administration has not been made; or
 (b) the person against whom the claim was brought was dead when the claim was started.
(4) Before making an order under this rule, the court may direct notice of the application to be given to any other person with an interest in the claim.
(5) Where an order has been made under paragraphs (1) or (2)(b)(ii) any judgment or order made or given in the claim is binding on the estate of the deceased.

19.8A Power to Make Judgments Binding on Non-parties

r.19.8A **14.31, 14.54**
r.19.8A(8)(b) **14.31**

(1) This rule applies to any claim relating to—
 (a) the estate of a deceased person;
 (b) property subject to a trust; or
 (c) the sale of any property.
(2) The court may at any time direct that notice of—
 (a) the claim; or
 (b) any judgment or order given in the claim,
 be served on any person who is not a party but who is or may be affected by it.
(3) An application under this rule—
 (a) may be made without notice; and
 (b) must be supported by written evidence which includes the reasons why the person to be served should be bound by the judgment in the claim.
(4) Unless the court orders otherwise—
 (a) a notice of a claim or of a judgment or order under this rule must be—
  (i) in the form required by the practice direction;
  (ii) issued by the court; and
  (iii) accompanied by a form of acknowledgment of service with any necessary modifications;
 (b) a notice of a claim must also be accompanied by—
  (i) a copy of the claim form; and
  (ii) such other statements of case, witness statements or affidavits as the court may direct; and
 (c) a notice of a judgment or order must also be accompanied by a copy of the judgment or order.
(5) If a person served with notice of a claim files an acknowledgment of service of the notice within 14 days he will become a party to the claim.

(6) If a person served with notice of a claim does not acknowledge service of the notice he will be bound by any judgment given in the claim as if he were a party.
(7) If, after service of a notice of a claim on a person, the claim form is amended so as substantially to alter the remedy claimed, the court may direct that a judgment shall not bind that person unless a further notice, together with a copy of the amended claim form, is served on him.
(8) Any person served with a notice of a judgment or order under this rule—
 (a) shall be bound by the judgment or order as if he had been a party to the claim; but
 (b) may, provided he acknowledges service—
  (i) within 28 days after the notice is served on him, apply to the court to set aside or vary the judgment or order; and
  (ii) take part in any proceedings relating to the judgment or order.
(9) The following rules of Part 10 (acknowledgment of service) apply—
 (a) rule 10.4; and
 (b) rule 10.5, subject to the modification that references to the defendant are to be read as references to the person served with the notice.
(10) A notice under this rule is issued on the date entered on the notice by the court.

19.9 Derivative Claims

r.19.9 **14.61** r.19.9(2)–(6) **14.42**

(1) This rule applies where a company, other incorporated body or trade union is alleged to be entitled to claim a remedy and a claim is made by one or more members of the company, body or trade union for it to be given that remedy (a 'derivative claim').
(2) The company, body or trade union for whose benefit a remedy is sought must be a defendant to the claim.
(3) After the claim form has been issued the claimant must apply to the court for permission to continue the claim and may not take any other step in the proceedings except—
 (a) as provided by paragraph (5); or
 (b) where the court gives permission.
(4) An application in accordance with paragraph (3) must be supported by written evidence.
(5) The—
 (a) claim form;
 (b) application notice; and
 (c) written evidence in support of the application,
 must be served on the defendant within the period within which the claim form must be served and, in any event, at least 14 days before the court is to deal with the application.
(6) If the court gives the claimant permission to continue the claim, the time within which the defence must be filed is 14 days after the date on which the permission is given or such period as the court may specify.
(7) The court may order the company, body or trade union to indemnify the claimant against any liability in respect of costs incurred in the claim.

III GROUP LITIGATION

19.10 Definition

A Group Litigation Order ('GLO') means an order made under rule 19.11 to provide for the case management of claims which give rise to common or related issues of fact or law (the 'GLO issues').

19.11 Group Litigation Order

r.19.11 **14.60** r.19.11(3) **14.65**
r.19.11(2) **14.63**

(1) The court may make a GLO where there are or are likely to be a number of claims giving rise to the GLO issues.
(The practice direction provides the procedure for applying for a GLO)

(2) A GLO must—
(a) contain directions about the establishment of a register (the 'group register') on which the claims managed under the GLO will be entered;
(b) specify the GLO issues which will identify the claims to be managed as a group under the GLO; and
(c) specify the court (the 'management court') which will manage the claims on the group register.

(3) A GLO may—
(a) in relation to claims which raise one or more of the GLO issues—
(i) direct their transfer to the management court;
(ii) order their stay(GL) until further order; and
(iii) direct their entry on the group register;
(b) direct that from a specified date claims which raise one or more of the GLO issues should be started in the management court and entered on the group register; and
(c) give directions for publicising the GLO.

19.12 Effect of the GLO

r.19.12(1)(a)–(b) **14.66** r.19.12(3) **14.66**
r.19.12(2) **14.66** r.19.12(4) **14.66**

(1) Where a judgment or order is given or made in a claim on the group register in relation to one or more GLO issues—
(a) that judgment or order is binding on the parties to all other claims that are on the group register at the time the judgment is given or the order is made unless the court orders otherwise; and
(b) the court may give directions as to the extent to which that judgment or order is binding on the parties to any claim which is subsequently entered on the group register.

(2) Unless paragraph (3) applies, any party who is adversely affected by a judgment or order which is binding on him may seek permission to appeal the order.

(3) A party to a claim which was entered on the group register after a judgment or order which is binding on him was given or made may not—
(a) apply for the judgment or order to be set aside(GL), varied or stayed(GL); or
(b) appeal the judgment or order,

but may apply to the court for an order that the judgment or order is not binding on him.

(4) Unless the court orders otherwise, disclosure of any document relating to the GLO issues by a party to a claim on the group register is disclosure of that document to all parties to claims—
(a) on the group register; and
(b) which are subsequently entered on the group register.

19.13 Case Management

Directions given by the management court may include directions—
(a) varying the GLO issues;
(b) providing for one or more claims on the group register to proceed as test claims;
(c) appointing the solicitor of one or more parties to be the lead solicitor for the claimants or defendants;
(d) specifying the details to be included in a statement of case in order to show that the criteria for entry of the claim on the group register have been met;
(e) specifying a date after which no claim may be added to the group register unless the court gives permission; and
(f) for the entry of any particular claim which meets one or more of the GLO issues on the group register.

(Part 3 contains general provisions about the case management powers of the court)

19.14 Removal from the Register

r.19.14 **14.64**

(1) A party to a claim entered on the group register may apply to the management.

(2) If the management court orders the claim to be removed from the register it may give directions about the future management of the claim.

19.15 Test Claims

(1) Where a direction has been given for a claim on the group register to proceed as a test claim and that claim is settled, the management court may order that another claim on the group register be substituted as the test claim.
(2) Where an order is made under paragraph (1), any order made in the test claim before the date of substitution is binding on the substituted claim unless the court orders otherwise.

PD 19 Practice Direction — Addition and Substitution of Parties

This practice direction supplements CPR Part 19

PD 19 **14.30**, **66.7**, **66.31** [For commentary on a specific paragraph, please refer to the cross-references after the title of the paragraph.]

A party applying for an amendment will usually be responsible for the costs of and arising from the amendment.

Changes of Parties

para.1.1 **14.3**
para.1.2 **14.6**
para.1.3 **14.5**
para.1.4 **14.4, 14.5, 35.9**
para.1.5 **14.7**

General

1.1 Parties may be removed, added or substituted in existing proceedings either on the court's own initiative or on the application of either an existing party or a person who wishes to become a party.

1.2 The application may be dealt with without a hearing where all the existing parties and the proposed new party are in agreement.

1.3 The application to add or substitute a new party should be supported by evidence setting out the proposed new party's interest in or connection with the claim.

1.4 The application notice should be filed in accordance with rule 23.3 and, unless the application is made under rule 19.2(4),[1] be served in accordance with rule 23.4.

1.5 An order giving permission to amend will, unless the court orders otherwise, be drawn up. It will be served by the court unless the parties wish to serve it or the court orders them to do so.

Addition or substitution of claimant

para.2.1 **14.5**
para.2.2 **14.3**
para.2.3(1)–(3) **14.7**

2.1 Where an application is made to the court to add or to substitute a new party to the proceedings as claimant, the party applying must file:
(1) the application notice,
(2) the proposed amended claim form and particulars of claim, and
(3) the signed, written consent of the new claimant to be so added or substituted.

2.2 Where the court makes an order adding or substituting a party as claimant but the signed, written consent of the new claimant has not been filed:
(1) the order, and
(2) the addition or substitution of the new party as claimant,
will not take effect until the signed, written consent of the new claimant is filed.

2.3 Where the court has made an order adding or substituting a new claimant, the court may direct:
(1) a copy of the order to be served on every party to the proceedings and any other person affected by the order,
(2) copies of the statements of case and of documents referred to in any statement of case to be served on the new party,
(3) the party who made the application to file within 14 days an amended claim form and particulars of claim.

Addition or substitution of defendant

para.3.2(1)–(3) **14.7**
para.3.3 **14.7**

3.1 The Civil Procedure Rules apply to a new defendant who has been added or substituted as they apply to any other defendant (see in particular the provisions of Parts 9, 10, 11 and 15).

[1] See rule 19.4(3)(a).

3.2 Where the court has made an order adding or substituting a defendant whether on its own initiative or on an application, the court may direct:

(1) the claimant to file with the court within 14 days (or as ordered) an amended claim form and particulars of claim for the court file,

(2) a copy of the order to be served on all parties to the proceedings and any other person affected by it,

(3) the amended claim form and particulars of claim, forms for admitting, defending and acknowledging the claim and copies of the statements of case and any other documents referred to in any statement of case to be served on the new defendant.

(4) unless the court orders otherwise, the amended claim form and particulars of claim to be served on any other defendants.

3.3 A new defendant does not become a party to the proceedings until the amended claim form has been served on him.[2]

Removal of party

para.4 **14.7**

4 Where the court makes an order for the removal of a party from the proceedings:

(1) the claimant must file with the court an amended claim form and particulars of claim, and

(2) a copy of the order must be served on every party to the proceedings and on any other person affected by the order.

Transfer of interest or liability

para.5.2 **14.5, 14.26**

5.1 Where the interest or liability of an existing party has passed to some other person, application should be made to the court to add or substitute that person.[3]

5.2 The application must be supported by evidence showing the stage the proceedings have reached and what change has occurred to cause the transfer of interest or liability.

(For information about making amendments generally, see PD 17.)

Human Rights, Joining the Crown

para.6.2 **14.78**
para.6.4(1) **14.78**
para.6.6 **14.78**

Section 4 of the Human Rights Act 1998

6.1 Where a party has included in his statement of case:

(1) a claim for a declaration of incompatibility in accordance with s. 4 of the Human Rights Act 1998, or

(2) an issue for the court to decide which may lead to the court considering making a declaration,

then the court may at any time consider whether notice should be given to the Crown as required by that Act and give directions for the content and service of the notice. The rule [i.e., r. 19.4A] allows a period of 21 days before the court will make the declaration but the court may vary this period of time.

6.2 The court will normally consider the issues and give the directions referred to in para. 6.1 at the case management conference.

6.3 Where a party amends his statement of case to include any matter referred to in para. 6.1, then the court will consider whether notice should be given to the Crown and give directions for the content and service of the notice.

(PD 16 requires a party to include issues under the Human Rights Act 1998 in his statement of case)

6.4 (1) The notice given under r. 19.4A must be served on the person named in the list published under s. 17 of the Crown Proceedings Act 1947.

(The list, made by the Minister for the Civil Service, [follows the text of the Crown Proceedings Act 1947 in **appendix** 7].)

---

[2] *Ketteman v Hansel Properties Ltd* [1987] AC 189, HL.

[3] See rule 19.2(4).

(2) The notice will be in the form directed by the court but will normally include the directions given by the court and all the statements of case in the claim. The notice will also be served on all the parties.

(3) The court may require the parties to assist in the preparation of the notice.

(4) In the circumstances described in the National Assembly for Wales (Transfer of Functions) (No. 2) Order 2000 the notice must also be served on the National Assembly for Wales.

(Section 5(3) of the Human Rights Act 1998 provides that the Crown may give notice that it intends to become a party at any stage in the proceedings once notice has been given.)

6.5 Unless the court orders otherwise, the minister or other person permitted by the Human Rights Act 1998 to be joined as a party must, if he wishes to be joined, give notice of his intention to be joined as a party to the court and every other party. Where the minister has nominated a person to be joined as a party the notice must be accompanied by the written nomination.

(Section 5(2)(a) of the Human Rights Act 1998 permits a person nominated by a minister of the Crown to be joined as a party. The nomination may be signed on behalf of the minister.)

Section 9 of the Human Rights Act 1998

6.6 (1) The procedure in paras 6.1 to 6.5 also applies where a claim is made under ss. 7(1)(a) and 9(3) of the Human Rights Act 1998 for damages in respect of a judicial act.

(2) Notice must be given to the Lord Chancellor and should be served on the Treasury Solicitor on his behalf, except where the judicial act is of a court martial when the appropriate person is the Secretary of State for Defence and the notice must be served on the Treasury Solicitor on his behalf.

(3) The notice will also give details of the judicial act, which is the subject of the claim for damages, and of the court or tribunal that made it.

(Section 9(4) of the Human Rights Act 1998 provides that no award of damages may be made against the Crown as provided for in s. 9(3) unless the appropriate person is joined in the proceedings. The appropriate person is the minister responsible for the court concerned or a person or department nominated by him (s. 9(5) of the Act))

[The annex to this practice direction is not reproduced here, because it consists of the list of authorised government departments, which is set out after the text of the Crown Proceedings Act 1947 in **appendix** 7.]

PD 19B Practice Direction — Group Litigation

This practice direction supplements Section III of CPR Part 19

PD 19B **14.60** [For commentary on a specific paragraph, please refer to the cross-references after the title of the paragraph.]

Introduction

1 This practice direction deals with group litigation where the multiple parties are claimants. Section III of Part 19 (group litigation orders) also applies where the multiple parties are defendants. The court will give such directions in such a case as are appropriate.

Preliminary Steps

paras 2.1–2.3 **14.61**

2.1 Before applying for a group litigation order ('GLO') the solicitor acting for the proposed applicant should consult the Law Society's Multi-Party Actions Information Service in order to obtain information about other cases giving rise to the proposed GLO issues.

2.2 It will often be convenient for the claimants' solicitors to form a solicitors' group and to choose one of their number to take the lead in applying for the GLO and in litigating the GLO issues. The lead solicitor's role and relationship with the other members of the solicitors' group should be carefully defined in writing and will be subject to any directions given by the court under r. 19.13(c).

2.3 In considering whether to apply for a GLO, the applicant should consider whether any other order would be more appropriate. In particular he should consider whether, in the circumstances of the case, it would be more appropriate for:
(1) the claims to be consolidated; or
(2) the rules in Section II of Part 19 (representative parties) to be used.

Application for a GLO

para.3.1 **14.60, 14.62** paras 3.2–3.8 **14.62**

3.1 An application for a GLO must be made in accordance with CPR, Part 23, may be made at any time before or after any relevant claims have been issued and may be made either by a claimant or by a defendant.

3.2 The following information should be included in the application notice or in written evidence filed in support of the application:
(1) a summary of the nature of the litigation;
(2) the number, and nature of claims already issued;
(3) the number of parties likely to be involved;
(4) the common issues of fact or law (the 'GLO issues') that are likely to arise in the litigation; and
(5) whether there are any matters that distinguish smaller groups of claims within the wider group.

3.3 A GLO may not be made:
(1) in the Queen's Bench Division, without the consent of the Lord Chief Justice;
(2) in the Chancery Division, without the consent of the Vice-Chancellor; or
(3) in a county court, without the consent of the Head of Civil Justice.

3.4 The court to which the application for a GLO is made will, if minded to make the GLO, send to the Lord Chief Justice, the Vice-Chancellor, or the Head of Civil Justice, as appropriate:
(1) a copy of the application notice;
(2) a copy of any relevant written evidence; and
(3) a written statement as to why a GLO is considered to be desirable.

These steps may be taken either before or after a hearing of the application.

High Court in London

3.5 The application for the GLO should be made to the Senior Master in the Queen's Bench Division or the Chief Chancery Master in the Chancery Division. For claims that are proceeding or are likely to proceed in a specialist list, the application should be made to the senior judge of that list.

High Court outside London

3.6 Outside London, the application should be made to a presiding judge or a Chancery supervising judge of the circuit in which the district registry which has issued the application notice is situated.

County courts

3.7 The application should be made to the designated civil judge for the area in which the county court which has issued the application notice is situated.

3.8 The applicant for a GLO should request the relevant court to refer the application notice to the judge by whom the application will be heard as soon as possible after the application notice has been issued. This is to enable the judge to consider whether to follow the practice set out in para. 3.4 above prior to the hearing of the application.

3.9 The directions under paras 3.5, 3.6 and 3.7 above do not prevent the judges referred to from making arrangements for other judges to hear applications for GLOs when they themselves are unavailable.

GLO Made by Court of Its Own Initiative

para.4 **14.60**

4 Subject to obtaining the appropriate consent referred to in para. 3.3 and the procedure set out in para. 3.4, the court may make a GLO of its own initiative.

(Rule 3.3 deals with the procedure that applies when a court proposes to make an order of its own initiative.)

The GLO

5 Paragraphs 2 and (3) of r. 19.11 set out rules relating to the contents of GLOs.

The Group Register

paras 6.2–6.5 **14.64** para.6.6(2) **14.64**

6.1 Once a GLO has been made a group register will be established on which will be entered such details as the court may direct of the cases which are to be subject to the GLO.

6.1A A claim must be issued before it can be entered on a group register.

6.2 An application for details of a case to be entered on a group register may be made by any party to the case.

6.3 An order for details of the case to be entered on the group register will not be made unless the case gives rise to at least one of the GLO issues.

(Rule 19.10 defines GLO issues.)

6.4 The court, if it is not satisfied that a case can be conveniently case managed with the other cases on the group register, or if it is satisfied that the entry of the case on the group register would adversely affect the case management of the other cases, may refuse to allow details of the case to be entered on the group register, or order their removal from the register if already entered, although the case gives rise to one or more of the Group issues.

6.5 The group register will normally be maintained by and kept at the court but the court may direct this to be done by the solicitor for one of the parties to a case entered on the register.

6.6 (1) Rule 5.4 (supply of documents from court records) applies where the register is maintained by the court. A party to a claim on the group register may request documents relating to any other claim on the group register in accordance with r. 5.4(1) as if he were a party to those proceedings.

(2) Where the register is maintained by a solicitor, any person may inspect the group register during normal business hours and upon giving reasonable notice to the solicitor; the solicitor may charge a fee not exceeding the fee prescribed for a search at the court office.

6.7 In this paragraph, 'the court' means the management court specified in the GLO.

Allocation to Track

paras.7–9 **14.65**

7 Once a GLO has been made and unless the management court directs otherwise:
(1) every claim in a case entered on the group register will be automatically allocated, or reallocated (as the case may be), to the multi-track;
(2) any case management directions that have already been given in any such case otherwise than by the management court will be set aside; and
(3) any hearing date already fixed otherwise than for the purposes of the group litigation will be vacated.

Managing Judge

8 A judge ('the managing judge') will be appointed for the purpose of the GLO as soon as possible. He will assume overall responsibility for the management of the claims and will generally hear the GLO issues. A master or a district judge may be appointed to deal with procedural matters, which he will do in accordance with any directions given by the managing judge. A costs judge may be appointed and may be invited to attend case management hearings.

Claims to Be Started in Management Court

9.1 The management court may order that as from a specified date all claims that raise one or more of the GLO issues shall be started in the management court.

9.2 Failure to comply with an order made under para. 9.1 will not invalidate the commencement of the claim but the claim should be transferred to the management court and details entered on the group register as soon as possible. Any party to the claim may apply to the management court for an order under r. 19.14 removing the case from the register or, as the case may be, for an order that details of the case be not entered on the register.

Transfer

10 Where the management court is a county court and a claim raising one or more of the GLO issues is proceeding in the High Court, an order transferring the case to the management court and directing the details of the case to be entered on the group register can only be made in the High Court.

Publicising the GLO

para.11 **14.63**

11 After a GLO has been made, a copy of the GLO should be supplied:
(1) to the Law Society, 113 Chancery Lane, London WC2A 1PL; and
(2) to the Senior Master, Queen's Bench Division, Royal Courts of Justice, Strand, London WC2A 2LL.

Case Management

para.12 **14.65** para.12.2 **14.63**

12.1 The management court may give case management directions at the time the GLO is made or subsequently. Directions given at a case management hearing will generally be binding on all claims that are subsequently entered on the group register (see r. 19.12(1)).

12.2 Any application to vary the terms of the GLO must be made to the management court.

12.3 The management court may direct that one or more of the claims are to proceed as test claims.

12.4 The management court may give directions about how the costs of resolving common issues or the costs of claims proceeding as test claims are to be borne or shared as between the claimants on the group register.

Cut-off Dates

para.13 **14.64**

13 The management court may specify a date after which no claim may be added to the group register unless the court gives permission. An early cut-off date may be appropriate in the case of

'instant disasters' (such as transport accidents). In the case of consumer claims, and particularly pharmaceutical claims, it may be necessary to delay the ordering of a cut-off date.

Statements of Case

para.14 **14.65** para.14.3 **14.65**
para.14.1 **14.65**

14.1 The management court may direct that the GLO claimants serve 'group particulars of claim' which set out the various claims of all the claimants on the group register at the time the particulars are filed. Such particulars of claim will usually contain:

(1) general allegations relating to all claims; and

(2) a schedule containing entries relating to each individual claim specifying which of the general allegations are relied on and any specific facts relevant to the claimant.

14.2 The directions given under para. 14.1 should include directions as to whether the group particulars should be verified by a statement or statements of truth and, if so, by whom.

14.3 The specific facts relating to each claimant on the group register may be obtained by the use of a questionnaire. Where this is proposed, the management court should be asked to approve the questionnaire. The management court may direct that the questionnaires completed by individual claimants take the place of the schedule referred to in para. 14.1(2).

14.4 The management court may also give directions about the form that particulars of claim relating to claims which are to be entered on the group register should take.

The Trial

paras 15.1–15.2 **14.65**

15.1 The management court may give directions:

(1) for the trial of common issues; and

(2) for the trial of individual issues.

15.2 Common issues and test claims will normally be tried at the management court. Individual issues may be directed to be tried at other courts whose locality is convenient for the parties.

Costs

16.1 Part 48 contains rules about costs where a GLO has been made.

16.2 Where the court has made an order about costs in relation to any application or hearing which involved both:

(1) one or more of the GLO issues; and

(2) an issue or issues relevant only to individual claims;

and the court has not directed the proportion of the costs that is to relate to common costs and the proportion that is to relate to individual costs in accordance with r. 48.6A(5), the costs judge will make a decision as to the relevant proportions at or before the commencement of the detailed assessment of costs.

CPR Part 20 Counterclaims and Other Additional Claims

Part 20 **10.32, 12.1, 14.1, 16.37, 23.1, 26.20, 28.1, 28.2, 28.6, 28.8, 29.1, 31.16, 36.4, 42.23, 48.71, 54.7, 65.3, 66.45** [For commentary on a specific rule, please refer to the cross-references after the title of the rule.]

20.1 Purpose of This Part

The purpose of this Part is to enable counterclaims and other additional claims to be managed in the most convenient and effective manner.

20.2 Scope and Interpretation

r.20.2(2) **28.1**

(1) This Part applies to—
  (a) a counterclaim by a defendant against the claimant or against the claimant and some other person;
  (b) an additional claim by a defendant against any person (whether or not already a party) for contribution or indemnity or some other remedy; and
  (c) where an additional claim has been made against a person who is not already a party, any additional claim made by that person against any other person (whether or not already a party).
(2) In these Rules—
  (a) 'additional claim' means any claim other than the claim by the claimant against the defendant; and
  (b) unless the context requires otherwise, references to a claimant or defendant include a party bringing or defending an additional claim.

20.3 Application of These Rules to Additional Claims

r.20.3 **18.4, 64.1, 65.3**
r.20.3(2) **28.6**
r.20.3(3)–(4) **29.9**

(1) An additional claim shall be treated as if it were a claim for the purposes of these Rules, except as provided by this Part.
(2) The following rules do not apply to additional claims—
  (a) rules 7.5 and 7.6 (time within which a claim form may be served);
  (b) rule 16.3(5) (statement of value where claim to be issued in the High Court); and
  (c) Part 26 (case management—preliminary stage).
(3) Part 12 (default judgment) applies to a counterclaim but not to other additional claims.
(4) Part 14 (admissions) applies to a counterclaim, but only—
  (a) rules 14.1(1) and 14.1(2) (which provide that a party may admit the truth of another party's case in writing); and

(b) rule 14.3 (admission by notice in writing—application for judgment),

apply to other additional claims.

(Rule 12.3(2) sets out how to obtain judgment in default of defence for a counterclaim against the claimant, and rule 20.11 makes special provision for default judgment for some additional claims)

20.4 Defendant's Counterclaim against the Claimant

r.20.4(1) **28.3**
r.20.4(2)(a) **28.2**
r.20.4(2)(b) **28.2**
r.20.4(3) **28.6**

(1) A defendant may make a counterclaim against a claimant by filing particulars of the counterclaim.

(2) A defendant may make a counterclaim against a claimant—

(a) without the court's permission if he files it with his defence; or

(b) at any other time with the court's permission.

(Part 15 makes provision for a defence to a claim and applies to a defence to a counterclaim by virtue of rule 20.3)

(3) Part 10 (acknowledgment of service) does not apply to a claimant who wishes to defend a counterclaim.

20.5 Counterclaim against a Person Other than the Claimant

r.20.5(1) **28.2, 29.4**
r.20.5(2)–(3) **28.2**

(1) A defendant who wishes to counterclaim against a person other than the claimant must apply to the court for an order that that person be added as an additional party.

(2) An application for an order under paragraph (1) may be made without notice unless the court directs otherwise.

(3) Where the court makes an order under paragraph (1), it will give directions as to the management of the case.

20.6 Defendant's Additional Claim for Contribution or Indemnity from Another Party

r.20.6 **16.37, 29.4, 29.11**

(1) A defendant who has filed an acknowledgment of service or a defence may make an additional claim for contribution or indemnity against a person who is already a party to the proceedings by—

(a) filing a notice containing a statement of the nature and grounds of his additional claim; and

(b) serving the notice on that party.

(2) A defendant may file and serve a notice under this rule—

(a) without the court's permission, if he files and serves it—

(i) with his defence; or

(ii) if his additional claim for contribution or indemnity is against a party added to the claim later, within 28 days after that party files his defence; or

(b) at any other time with the court's permission.

20.7 Procedure for Making Any Other Additional Claim

r.20.7 **29.8, 29.11**
r.20.7(1) **29.4, 29.8**
r.20.7(3) **28.4, 29.4, 29.9**
r.20.7(3)(a) **29.4**
r.20.7(4) **29.8**
r.20.7(5) **29.6, 32.7**

(1) This rule applies to any additional claim except—

(a) a counterclaim only against an existing party; and

(b) a claim for contribution or indemnity made in accordance with rule 20.6.

(2) An additional claim is made when the court issues the appropriate claim form.

(Rule 7.2(2) provides that a claim form is issued on the date entered on the form by the court)

(3) A defendant may make an additional claim—

(a) without the court's permission if the additional claim is issued before or at the same time as he files his defence;

(b) at any other time with the court's permission.

(Rule 15.4 sets out the period for filing a defence)

(4) Particulars of an additional claim must be contained in or served with the additional claim.

(5) An application for permission to make an additional claim may be made without notice, unless the court directs otherwise.

20.8 Service of Claim Form

r.20.8 **29.11**
r.20.8(1) **29.5**
r.20.8(1)(a) **28.2, 28.3**
r.20.8(1)(b) **28.3, 29.5**
r.20.8(2) **29.5**
r.20.8(3) **28.3, 29.9**
r.20.9 **28.1**

(1) Where an additional claim may be made without the court's permission, any claim form must—
  (a) in the case of a counterclaim against an additional party only, be served on every other party when a copy of the defence is served;
  (b) in the case of any other additional claim, be served on the person against whom it is made within 14 days after the date on which the additional claim is issued by the court.
(2) Paragraph (1) does not apply to a claim for contribution or indemnity made in accordance with rule 20.6.
(3) Where the court gives permission to make an additional claim it will at the same time give directions as to its service.

20.9 Matters Relevant to Question of Whether an Additional Claim Should Be Separate from the Claim

r.20.9 **28.1, 29.11**
r.20.9(2) **29.7**

(1) This rule applies where the court is considering whether to—
  (a) permit an additional claim to be made;
  (b) dismiss an additional claim; or
  (c) require an additional claim to be dealt with separately from the claim by the claimant against the defendant.

(Rule 3.1(2)(e) and (j) deal respectively with the court's power to order that part of proceedings be dealt with as separate proceedings and to decide the order in which issues are to be tried)

(2) The matters to which the court may have regard include—
  (a) the connection between the additional claim and the claim made by the claimant against the defendant;
  (b) whether the additional claimant is seeking substantially the same remedy which some other party is claiming from him; and
  (c) whether the additional claimant wants the court to decide any question connected with the subject matter of the proceedings—
    (i) not only between existing parties but also between existing parties and a person not already a party; or
    (ii) against an existing party not only in a capacity in which he is already a party but also in some further capacity.

20.10 Effect of Service of an Additional Claim

r.20.10 **29.9, 29.11**

(1) A person on whom an additional claim is served becomes a party to the proceedings if he is not a party already.
(2) When an additional claim is served on an existing party for the purpose of requiring the court to decide a question against that party in a further capacity, that party also becomes a party in the further capacity specified in the additional claim.

20.11 Special Provisions Relating to Default Judgment on an Additional Claim Other than a Counterclaim or a Contribution or Indemnity Notice

r.20.11 **29.9, 29.10, 29.11**
r.20.11(1)(a) **20.10, 29.9**
r.20.11(2)(b) **29.10**
r.20.11(3) **29.10**
r.20.11(3)(b) **29.10**
r.20.11(4)–(5) **29.10**

(1) This rule applies if—
  (a) the additional claim is not—
    (i) a counterclaim; or
    (ii) a claim by a defendant for contribution or indemnity against another defendant under rule 20.6; and

(b) the party against whom an additional claim is made fails to file an acknowledgment of service or defence in respect of the additional claim.

(2) The party against whom the additional claim is made—

(a) is deemed to admit the additional claim, and is bound by any judgment or decision in the proceedings in so far as it is relevant to any matter arising in the additional claim;

(b) subject to paragraph (3), if default judgment under Part 12 is given against the additional claimant, the additional claimant may obtain judgment in respect of the additional claim by filing a request in the relevant practice form.

(3) An additional claimant may not enter judgment under paragraph (2)(b) without the court's permission if—

(a) he has not satisfied the default judgment which has been given against him; or

(b) he wishes to obtain judgment for any remedy other than a contribution or indemnity.

(4) An application for the court's permission under paragraph (3) may be made without notice unless the court directs otherwise.

(5) The court may at any time set aside or vary a judgment entered under paragraph (2)(b).

20.12 Procedural Steps on Service of an Additional Claim Form on a Non-party

r.20.12 **29.8, 29.11** r.20.12(1)–(2) **28.3, 29.5, 29.9**

(1) Where an additional claim form is served on a person who is not already a party it must be accompanied by—

(a) a form for defending the claim;

(b) a form for admitting the claim;

(c) a form for acknowledging service; and

(d) a copy of—

(i) every statement of case which has already been served in the proceedings; and

(ii) such other documents as the court may direct.

(2) A copy of the additional claim form must be served on every existing party.

20.13 Case Management Where a Defence to an Additional Claim Is Filed

r.20.13 **29.9** r.20.13(1)–(2) **29.9**

(1) Where a defence is filed to an additional claim the court must consider the future conduct of the proceedings and give appropriate directions.

(2) In giving directions under paragraph (1) the court must ensure that, so far as practicable, the original claim and all additional claims are managed together.

(CCR Order 42, in Schedule 2, makes provision for an additional claim against the Crown where the Crown is not a party.*)

PD 20 Practice Direction — Counterclaims and Other Additional Claims

PD20 **28.1, 28.2, 28.5** [For commentary on a specific paragraph, please refer to the cross-references after the title of the paragraph.]

This practice direction supplements CPR Part 20

An additional claim is any claim other than the claim by the claimant against the defendant.

Claims under this Part were formerly known as 'Part 20 claims'. As a result of the amendments to Part 20, introduced by Civil Procedure (Amendment No. 4) Rules 2005 (SI 2005/3515), they are now called 'additional claims'.

However, they are described as 'Part 20 claims' on a number of court forms. For the present, some of those forms will continue to refer to Part 20 claims. These references should be construed as being additional claims under this Part. Any reference to a Part 20 claimant or a Part 20 defendant means a claimant or defendant in an additional claim under this Part.

Cases Where Court's Permission to Make an Additional Claim Is Required

para.1.2 **28.2, 29.6**

1.1 Rules 20.4(2)(b), 20.5(1) and 20.7(3)(b) set out the circumstances in which the court's permission will be needed for making an additional claim.

1.2 Where an application is made for permission to make an additional claim the application notice should be filed together with a copy of the proposed additional claim.

Applications for Permission to Issue an Additional Claim

para.2.1 **28.2, 29.6**

2.1 An application for permission to make an additional claim must be supported by evidence stating:
  (1) the stage which the proceedings have reached,
  (2) the nature of the additional claim to be made or details of the question or issue which needs to be decided,
  (3) a summary of the facts on which the additional claim is based, and
  (4) the name and address of any proposed additional party.

  (For further information regarding evidence see PD 32).

2.2 Where delay has been a factor contributing to the need to apply for permission to make an additional claim an explanation of the delay should be given in evidence.

2.3 Where possible the applicant should provide a timetable of the proceedings to date.

2.4 Rules 20.5(2) and 20.7(5) allow applications to be made to the court without notice unless the court directs otherwise.

General

para.3 **28.6**

3. The CPR apply generally to additional claims as if they were claims. Parties should be aware that the provisions relating to failure to respond to a claim will apply.

Statement of Truth

paras.4.1–4.2 **28.4, 29.8**

4.1 The contents of an additional claim should be verified by a statement of truth. Part 22 requires a statement of case to be verified by a statement of truth.

4.2 The form of the statement of truth should be as required by PD 22, para. 2.1.

4.3 Attention is drawn to r. 32.14 which sets out the consequences of verifying a statement of case containing a false statement without an honest belief in its truth.

Case Management Where There Is a Defence to an Additional Claim

para.5.1 **28.8, 29.6** paras.5.2–5.4 **29.9**

5.1 Where the defendant to an additional claim files a defence, other than to a counterclaim, the court will arrange a hearing to consider case management of the additional claim. This will normally be at the same time as a case management hearing for the original claim and any other additional claims.

5.2 The court will give notice of the hearing to each party likely to be affected by any order made at the hearing.

5.3 At the hearing the court may:

(1) treat the hearing as a summary judgment hearing,

(2) order that the additional claim be dismissed,

(3) give directions about the way any claim, question or issue set out in or arising from the additional claim should be dealt with,

(4) give directions as to the part, if any, the additional defendant will take at the trial of the claim,

(5) give directions about the extent to which the additional defendant is to be bound by any judgment or decision to be made in the claim.

5.4 The court may make any of the orders in para. 5.3(1) to (5) either before or after any judgment in the claim has been entered by the claimant against the defendant.

Form of Counterclaim

para.6.1 **28.3** para.6.2 **28.8**

6.1 Where a defendant to a claim serves a counterclaim, the defence and counterclaim should normally form one document with the counterclaim following on from the defence.

6.2 Where a claimant serves a reply and a defence to counterclaim, the reply and the defence to counterclaim should normally form one document with the defence to counterclaim following on from the reply.

Titles of Proceedings Where There Are Additional Claims

para.7.2 **28.4, 29.8**
para.7.3 **14.1, 28.4, 28.5, 29.8**
para.7.4(c) **28.5**
para.7.5 **28.4, 29.8**
para.7.9 **29.8**
para.7.10 **28.5**
para.7.11 **29.8**

7.1 PD 7, para. 4, contains directions regarding the title to proceedings.

7.2 Where there are additional claims which add parties, the title to the proceedings should comprise a list of all parties describing each by giving them a single identification. Subject to para. 7.11, this identification should be used throughout.

7.3 Claimants and defendants in the original claim should always be referred to as such in the title to the proceedings, even if they subsequently acquire an additional procedural status.

7.4 Additional parties should be referred to in the title to the proceedings in accordance with the order in which they are joined to the proceedings, for example 'Third Party' or 'Fourth Party', whatever their actual procedural status.

Examples:

(a) If the defendant makes an additional claim against a single additional party, the additional party should be referred to in the title as 'Third Party'.

(b) If the defendant makes separate additional claims against two additional parties, the additional parties should be referred to in the title as 'Third Party' and 'Fourth Party'.

(c) If the defendant makes a counterclaim against the claimant and an additional party, the claimant should remain as 'Claimant' and the additional party should be referred to in the title as 'Third Party'.

(d) If the Third Party in example (b) makes an additional claim against a further additional party, that additional party should be referred to in the title as 'Fifth Party'.

7.5 If an additional claim is brought against more than one party jointly, they should be referred to in the title to the proceedings as, for example, 'First Named Third Party' and 'Second Named Third Party'.

7.6 In group litigation, the court should give directions about the designation of parties.

7.7 All parties should cooperate to ensure that two parties each making additional claims do not attribute the same nominal status to more than one party.

7.8 In proceedings with numerous parties, the court will if necessary give directions as to the preparation and updating of a list of parties giving their roles in the claim and each additional claim.

7.9 If an additional party ceases to be a party to the proceedings, for example because the claim against that party is discontinued or dismissed, all other additional parties should retain their existing nominal status.

7.10 In proceedings where there are additional parties, the description of all statements of case or other similar documents should clearly identify the nature of the document with reference to each relevant party.
Examples:
(e) In example (a), the defendant's additional claim should be headed 'Defendant's Additional Claim against Third Party' and the Third Party's defence to it should be headed 'Third Party's Defence to Defendant's Additional Claim'.
(f) In example (c), the defendant's counterclaim should be headed 'Defendant's Counterclaim against Claimant and Third Party' and the Third Party's defence to it should be headed 'Third Party's Defence to Defendant's Counterclaim'.

7.11 In proceedings where there are fourth or subsequent parties, additional parties should be referred to in the text of statements of case or other similar documents by name, suitably abbreviated if appropriate. If parties have similar names, suitable distinguishing abbreviations should be used.

CPR Part 21 Children and Patients

Part 21 **6.23** [For commentary on a specific rule, please refer to the cross-references after the title of the rule.]

21.1 Scope of this Part

r.21.1(2)(a)–(b) **14.32**

(1) This Part—
 (a) contains special provisions which apply in proceedings involving children and patients; and
 (b) sets out how a person becomes a litigation friend.

(2) In this Part—
 (a) 'child' means a person under 18; and
 (b) 'patient' means a person who by reason of mental disorder within the meaning of the Mental Health Act 1983 is incapable of managing and administering his property and affairs.

(Rule 6.6 contains provisions about the service of documents on children and patients)
(Rule 48.5 deals with costs where money is payable by or to a child or patient)

21.2 Requirement for Litigation Friend in Proceedings by or against Children and Patients

r.21.2 **14.33** r.21.2(3)–(5) **14.36**

(1) A patient must have a litigation friend to conduct proceedings on his behalf.

(2) A child must have a litigation friend to conduct proceedings on his behalf unless the court makes an order under paragraph (3).

(3) The court may make an order permitting the child to conduct proceedings without a litigation friend.

(4) An application for an order under paragraph (3)—
 (a) may be made by the child;
 (b) if the child already has a litigation friend, must be made on notice to the litigation friend; and
 (c) if the child has no litigation friend, may be made without notice.

(5) Where—
 (a) the court has made an order under paragraph (3); and
 (b) it subsequently appears to the court that it is desirable for a litigation friend to conduct the proceedings on behalf of the child,

the court may appoint a person to be the child's litigation friend.

21.3 Stage of Proceedings at Which a Litigation Friend Becomes Necessary

r.21.3(2) **14.33, 20.8** r.21.3(4) **14.33**
r.21.3(3) **14.33**

(1) This rule does not apply where the court has made an order under rule 21.2(3).

(2) A person may not, without the permission of the court—

(a) make an application against a child or patient before proceedings have started; or
(b) take any step in proceedings except—
(i) issuing and serving a claim form; or
(ii) applying for the appointment of a litigation friend under rule 21.6,
until the child or patient has a litigation friend.

(3) If a party becomes a patient during proceedings, no party may take any step in the proceedings without the permission of the court until the patient has a litigation friend.

(4) Any step taken before a child or patient has a litigation friend shall be of no effect unless the court otherwise orders.

21.4 Who May Be a Litigation Friend without a Court Order

r.21.4(1)–(2) **14.34** r.21.4(3)(c) **66.47**
r.21.4(3) **14.34, 14.35, 14.37**

(1) This rule does not apply if the court has appointed a person to be a litigation friend.

(2) A person authorised under Part VII of the Mental Health Act 1983 to conduct legal proceedings in the name of a patient or on his behalf is entitled to be the litigation friend of the patient in any proceedings to which his authority extends.

(3) If nobody has been appointed by the court or, in the case of a patient, authorised under Part VII, a person may act as a litigation friend if he—
(a) can fairly and competently conduct proceedings on behalf of the child or patient;
(b) has no interest adverse to that of the child or patient; and
(c) where the child or patient is a claimant, undertakes to pay any costs which the child or patient may be ordered to pay in relation to the proceedings, subject to any right he may have to be repaid from the assets of the child or patient.

21.5 How a Person Becomes a Litigation Friend without a Court Order

r.21.5 **14.33, 14.35** r.21.5(6) **14.35**

(1) If the court has not appointed a litigation friend, a person who wishes to act as a litigation friend must follow the procedure set out in this rule.

(2) A person authorised under Part VII of the Mental Health Act 1983 must file an official copy[(GL)] of the order or other document which constitutes his authorisation to act.

(3) Any other person must file a certificate of suitability stating that he satisfies the conditions specified in rule 21.4(3).

(4) A person who is to act as a litigation friend for a claimant must file—
(a) the authorisation; or
(b) the certificate of suitability,
at the time when the claim is made.

(5) A person who is to act as a litigation friend for a defendant must file—
(a) the authorisation; or
(b) the certificate of suitability,
at the time when he first takes a step in the proceedings on behalf of the defendant.

(6) The litigation friend must—
(a) serve the certificate of suitability on every person on whom, in accordance with rule 6.6 (service on parent, guardian etc.), the claim form should be served; and
(b) file a certificate of service when he files the certificate of suitability.

(Rule 6.10 sets out the details to be contained in a certificate of service)

21.6 How a Person Becomes a Litigation Friend by Court Order

r.21.6 **14.34, 14.35, 20.8** r.21.6(2) **14.35**

(1) The court may make an order appointing a litigation friend.

(2) An application for an order appointing a litigation friend may be made by—
(a) a person who wishes to be the litigation friend; or
(b) a party.

(3) Where—
(a) a person makes a claim against a child or patient;
(b) the child or patient has no litigation friend;

(c) the court has not made an order under rule 21.2(3) (order that a child can act without a litigation friend); and
(d) either—
(i) someone who is not entitled to be a litigation friend files a defence; or
(ii) the claimant wishes to take some step in the proceedings,
the claimant must apply to the court for an order appointing a litigation friend for the child or patient.
(4) An application for an order appointing a litigation friend must be supported by evidence.
(5) The court may not appoint a litigation friend under this rule unless it is satisfied that the person to be appointed complies with the conditions specified in rule 21.4(3).

21.7 Court's Power to Change Litigation Friend and to Prevent Person Acting as Litigation Friend

r.21.7 **14.37** r.21.7(3) **14.37**

(1) The court may—
(a) direct that a person may not act as a litigation friend;
(b) terminate a litigation friend's appointment;
(c) appoint a new litigation friend in substitution for an existing one.
(2) An application for an order under paragraph (1) must be supported by evidence.
(3) The court may not appoint a litigation friend under this rule unless it is satisfied that the person to be appointed complies with the conditions specified in rule 21.4(3).

21.8 Appointment of Litigation Friend by Court Order — Supplementary

r.21.8(1) **14.35, 14.37** r.21.8(3) **14.37**
r.21.8(2) **14.35** r.21.8(4) **14.35, 14.37**

(1) An application for an order under rule 21.6 or 21.7 must be served on every person on whom, in accordance with rule 6.6 (service on parent, guardian etc.), the claim form should be served.
(2) Where an application for an order under rule 21.6 is in respect of a patient, the application must also be served on the patient unless the court orders otherwise.
(3) An application for an order under rule 21.7 must also be served on—
(a) the person who is the litigation friend, or who is purporting to act as the litigation friend, when the application is made; and
(b) the person who it is proposed should be the litigation friend, if he is not the applicant.
(4) On an application for an order under rule 21.6 or 21.7, the court may appoint the person proposed or any other person who complies with the conditions specified in rule 21.4(3).

21.9 Procedure Where Appointment of Litigation Friend Ceases

r.21.9(1)–(2) **14.37**

(1) When a child who is not a patient reaches the age of 18, a litigation friend's appointment ceases.
(2) When a party ceases to be a patient, the litigation friend's appointment continues until it is ended by a court order.
(3) An application for an order under paragraph (2) may be made by—
(a) the former patient;
(b) the litigation friend; or
(c) a party.
(4) The child or patient in respect of whom the appointment to act has ceased must serve notice on the other parties—
(a) stating that the appointment of his litigation friend to act has ceased;
(b) giving his address for service; and
(c) stating whether or not he intends to carry on the proceedings.
(5) If he does not do so within 28 days after the day on which the appointment of the litigation friend ceases the court may, on application, strike out[(GL)] any claim or defence brought by him.
(6) The liability of a litigation friend for costs continues until—
(a) the person in respect of whom his appointment to act has ceased serves the notice referred to in paragraph (4); or
(b) the litigation friend serves notice on the parties that his appointment to act has ceased.

21.10 Compromise etc. by or on Behalf of Child or Patient

r.21.10 **53.4, 64.36** r.21.10(1)–(2) **14.38**

(1) Where a claim is made—
 (a) by or on behalf of a child or patient; or
 (b) against a child or patient,
 no settlement, compromise or payment and no acceptance of money paid into court shall be valid, so far as it relates to the claim by, on behalf of or against the child or patient, without the approval of the court.
(2) Where—
 (a) before proceedings in which a claim is made by or on behalf of, or against a child or patient (whether alone or with any other person) are begun, an agreement is reached for the settlement of the claim; and
 (b) the sole purpose of proceedings on that claim is to obtain the approval of the court to a settlement or compromise of the claim,
 the claim must—
  (i) be made using the procedure set out in Part 8 (alternative procedure for claims); and
  (ii) include a request to the court for approval of the settlement or compromise.
(3) In proceedings to which Section II of Part 45 applies, the court shall not make an order for detailed assessment of the costs payable to the child or patient but shall assess the costs in the manner set out in that Section.

(Rule 48.5 contains provisions about costs where money is payable to a child or patient)

21.11 Control of Money Recovered by or on Behalf of Child or Patient

r.21.11 **14.39**

(1) Where in any proceedings—
 (a) money is recovered by or on behalf of or for the benefit of a child or patient; or
 (b) money paid into court is accepted by or on behalf of a child or patient, the money shall be dealt with in accordance with directions given by the court under this rule and not otherwise.
(2) Directions given under this rule may provide that the money shall be wholly or partly paid into court and invested or otherwise dealt with.

21.11A Expenses Incurred by a Litigation Friend

r.21.11A **14.34, 66.47**

(1) In proceedings to which rule 21.11 applies, a litigation friend who incurs expenses on behalf of a child or patient in any proceedings is entitled to recover the amount paid or payable out of any money recovered or paid into court to the extent that it—
 (a) has been reasonably incurred; and
 (b) is reasonable in amount.
(2) Expenses may include all or part of—
 (a) an insurance premium, as defined by rule 43.2(1)(m); or
 (b) interest on a loan taken out to pay an insurance premium or other recoverable disbursement.
(3) No application may be made under this rule for expenses that—
 (a) are of a type that may be recoverable on an assessment of costs payable by or out of money belonging to a child or patient; but
 (b) are disallowed in whole or in part on such an assessment.

(Expenses which are also 'costs' as defined in rule 43.2(1)(a) are dealt with under rule 48.5(2))

(4) In deciding whether the expense was reasonably incurred and reasonable in amount, the court must have regard to all the circumstances of the case including the factors set out in rule 44.5(3).
(5) When the court is considering the factors to be taken into account in assessing the reasonableness of expenses incurred by the litigation friend on behalf of a child or patient, it will have regard to the facts and circumstances as they reasonably appeared to the litigation friend or child's or patient's legal representative when the expense was incurred.
(6) Where the claim is settled or compromised, or judgment is given, on terms that an amount not exceeding £5,000 is paid to the child or patient, the total amount the litigation friend may recover under paragraph (1) of this rule shall not exceed 25% of the sum so agreed or awarded,

unless the Court directs otherwise. Such total amount shall not exceed 50% of the sum so agreed or awarded.

21.12 Appointment of Guardian of Child's Estate

r.21.12 **14.39**

(1) The court may appoint the Official Solicitor to be a guardian of a child's estate where—
  (a) money is paid into court on behalf of the child in accordance with directions given under rule 21.11 (control of money received by a child or patient);
  (b) the Criminal Injuries Compensation Board or the Criminal Injuries Compensation Authority notifies the court that it has made or intends to make an award to the child;
  (c) a court or tribunal outside England and Wales notifies the court that it has ordered or intends to order that money be paid to the child;
  (d) the child is absolutely entitled to the proceeds of a pension fund; or
  (e) in any other case, such an appointment seems desirable to the court.

(2) The court may not appoint the Official Solicitor under this rule unless—
  (a) the persons with parental responsibility (within the meaning of section 3 of the Children Act 1989) agree; or
  (b) the court considers that their agreement can be dispensed with.

(3) The Official Solicitor's appointment may continue only until the child reaches 18.

PD 21 Practice Direction — Children and Patients

This practice direction supplements CPR Part 21

[For commentary on a specific paragraph, please refer to the cross-references after the title of the paragraph.]

General

para.1.3 **14.33** para.1.5(2) **14.36**
para.1.5 **14.33**

1.1 In this practice direction 'child' means a person under 18 years old and 'patient' means a person who by reason of mental disorder within the meaning of the Mental Health Act 1983 is incapable of managing and administering his property and affairs.[1]

1.2 A patient must bring or defend proceedings by a litigation friend (see para. 2 below for the definition of a litigation friend).

1.3 In the proceedings referred to in para. 1.2 above the patient should be referred to in the title as 'A. B. (by C. D. his litigation friend)'.

1.4 A child must bring or defend proceedings by a litigation friend unless the court has made an order permitting the child to do so on his own behalf.[2]

1.5 Where:

(1) the child has a litigation friend, the child should be referred to in the title to proceedings as 'A. B. (a child by C. D. his litigation friend)', and

(2) the child is conducting proceedings on his own behalf, the child should be referred to in the title as 'A. B. (a child)'.

1.6 The approval of the court must be obtained if a settlement of a claim by or against a child or patient is to be valid. A settlement includes an agreement on a sum to be apportioned to a dependent child under the Fatal Accidents Act 1976.

1.7 The approval of the court must also be obtained before making a voluntary interim payment to a child or patient.

(Rule 39.2(3) provides for a hearing or part of a hearing to be in private.)

The Litigation Friend

para.2.1 **14.34** para.2.3(2) **14.35**

2.1 It is the duty of a litigation friend fairly and competently to conduct proceedings on behalf of a child or patient. He must have no interest in the proceedings adverse to that of the child or patient and all steps and decisions he takes in the proceedings must be taken for the benefit of the child or patient.

2.2 A person may become a litigation friend:

(1) of a child:

(a) without a court order under the provisions of r. 21.5, or

(b) by a court order under r. 21.6, and

(2) of a patient:

(a) by authorisation under Part VII of the Mental Health Act 1983, or

(b) by a court order under r. 21.6.

2.3 In order to become a litigation friend without a court order the person who wishes to act as litigation friend must:

(1) if he wishes to act on behalf of a patient, file an official copy of the order or other document which constitutes the authorisation referred to in para. 2.2(2)(a) above, or

(2) if he wishes to act on behalf of a child, or on behalf of a patient without the authorisation referred to in (1) above, file a certificate of suitability:[3]

(a) stating that he consents to act,

[1] See r. 21.1(2).
[2] See r. 21.2(3).
[3] See r. 21.5(3).

Civil Procedure Rules & Practice Directions

(b) stating that he knows or believes that the [claimant] [defendant] is a [child] [patient],
(c) in the case of a patient, stating the grounds of his belief and if his belief is based upon medical opinion attaching any relevant document to the certificate,
(d) stating that he can fairly and competently conduct proceedings on behalf of the child or patient and has no interest adverse to that of the child or patient,
(e) where the child or patient is a claimant, undertaking to pay any costs which the child or patient may be ordered to pay in relation to the proceedings, subject to any right he may have to be repaid from the assets of the child or patient, and
(f) which he has signed in verification of its contents.

2.4 The litigation friend must serve a certificate of suitability:[4]
(1) in the case of a child (who is not also a patient) on one of the child's parents or guardians or if there is no parent or guardian, on the person with whom the child resides or in whose care the child is, and
(2) in the case of a patient on the person authorised under Part VII of the Mental Health Act 1983 to conduct proceedings on behalf of the patient or if there is no person so authorised, on the person with whom the patient resides or in whose care the patient is.

2.4A The litigation friend is not required to serve the documents referred to in para. 2.3(2)(c) when he serves a certificate of suitability on the person to be served under para. 2.4.

2.5 The litigation friend must file either the certificate of suitability together with a certificate of service[5] of it, or the authorisation referred to in paragraph 2.31(1) above:
(1) where the litigation friend is acting on behalf of a claimant, when the claim form is issued, and
(2) where the litigation friend is acting on behalf of a defendant, when he first takes a step in the action.

Application for a Court Order Appointing a Litigation Friend

para.3.4 **14.35**

3.1 Rule 21.6 sets out who may apply for an order appointing a litigation friend.

3.2 An application should be made in accordance with Part 23 and must be supported by evidence.[6]

3.3 The application notice must be served:
(1) on the persons referred to in para. 2.4 above, and
(2) where the application is in respect of a patient, on the patient unless the court orders otherwise.

3.4 The evidence in support must satisfy the court that the proposed litigation friend:
(1) consents to act,
(2) can fairly and competently conduct proceedings on behalf of the child or patient,
(3) has no interest adverse to that of the child or patient, and
(4) where the child or patient is a claimant, undertakes to pay any costs which the child or patient may be ordered to pay in relation to the proceedings, subject to any right he may have to be repaid from the assets of the child or patient.

3.5 Where a claimant wishes to take a step in proceedings against a child or patient who does not have a litigation friend he must apply to the court for an order appointing a litigation friend.

3.6 The proposed litigation friend must satisfy the conditions in para. 3.4(1), (2) and (3) above and may be one of the persons referred to in para. 2.4 above where appropriate, or otherwise may be the Official Solicitor. Where it is sought to appoint the Official Solicitor, provision should be made for payment of his charges.

Change of Litigation Friend and Prevention of Person Acting as Litigation Friend

para.4 **14.37**

4.1 Rule 21.7(1) states that the court may:
(1) direct that a person may not act as a litigation friend,

[4] See r. 21.5(6) and r. 6.9 (service).

[5] See r. 6.10 for the certificate of service.

[6] See r. 21.6(4).

(2) terminate a litigation friend's appointment,
(3) substitute a new litigation friend for an existing one.

4.2 Where an application is made for an order under r. 21.7(1), the application notice must set out the reasons for seeking it. The application must be supported by evidence.

4.3 If the order sought is the substitution of a new litigation friend for an existing one, the evidence must satisfy the court of the matters set out in para. 3.4 above.

4.4 The application notice must be served:
(1) on the persons referred to in para. 2.4 above, and
(2) on the litigation friend or person purporting to act as litigation friend.

Procedure Where the Need for a Litigation Friend Has Come to an End

paras.5.2–5.3 **14.37** paras.5.7–5.8 **14.37**

5.1 Rule 21.9 deals with the situation where the need for a litigation friend comes to an end during the proceedings because either:
(1) a child who is not also a patient reaches the age of 18 (full age) during the proceedings, or
(2) a patient ceases to be a patient (recovers).

5.2 A child on reaching full age must serve on the other parties to the proceedings and file with the court a notice:
(1) stating that he has reached full age,
(2) stating that his litigation friend's appointment has ceased,[7]
(3) giving an address for service,[8] and
(4) stating whether or not he intends to carry on with or continue to defend the proceedings.

5.3 If the notice states that the child intends to carry on with or continue to defend the proceedings he shall subsequently be described in the proceedings as:
'A. B. (formerly a child but now of full age)'

5.4 Whether or not a child having reached full age serves a notice in accordance with r. 21.9(4)(a) and para. 5.2(2) above, a litigation friend may at any time after the child has reached full age serve a notice on the other parties that his appointment has ceased.

5.5 The liability of a litigation friend for costs continues until a notice that his appointment to act has ceased is served on the other parties.[9]

5.6 Where a patient recovers, an application under r. 21.9(3) must be made for an order under r. 21.9(2) that the litigation friend's appointment has ceased.

5.7 The application must be supported by the following evidence:
(1) a medical report indicating that the patient has recovered and that he is capable of managing and administering his property and affairs,
(2) where the patient's affairs were under the control of the Court of Protection, a copy of the order or notice discharging the receiver, and
(3) if the application is made by the patient, a statement whether or not he intends to carry on with or continue to defend the proceedings.

5.8 An order under r. 21.9(2) must be served on the other parties to the proceedings. The patient must file with the court a notice:
(1) stating that his litigation friend's appointment has ceased,
(2) giving an address for service,[10] and
(3) stating whether or not he intends to carry on with or continue to defend the proceedings.

Settlement or Compromise by or on Behalf of a Child or Patient Prior to the Start of Proceedings

para.6.1–6.2 **14.38** para.6.4A **14.38, 61.25**
para.6.3 **61.25** paras.6.5–6.9 **61.25**
para.6.4 **14.38, 61.25**

6.1 Where a claim by or on behalf of a child or patient has been dealt with by agreement prior to the start of proceedings and only the approval of the court to the agreement is sought, the claim:

[7] Rule 21.9(4)(a).
[8] See r. 6.5.
[9] Rule 21.9(6).
[10] See r. 6.5.

Civil Procedure Rules & Practice Directions

(1) must be made using the Part 8 procedure,
(2) must include a request for approval of the settlement or compromise, and
(3) subject to para. 6.4 in addition to the details of the claim, must set out the terms of the settlement or compromise or have attached to it a draft consent order in form N292.

6.2 In order to approve the settlement or compromise, the information concerning the claim that the court will require will include:
(1) whether and to what extent the defendant admits liability,
(2) the age and occupation (if any) of the child or patient,
(3) the litigation friend's approval of the proposed settlement or compromise, and
(4) in a personal injury case arising from an accident:
(a) the circumstances of the accident,
(b) any medical reports,
(c) where appropriate, a schedule of any past and future expenses and losses claimed and any other relevant information relating to personal injury as set out in PD 16, and
(d) where considerations of liability are raised:
(i) any evidence or police reports in any criminal proceedings or in an inquest, and
(ii) details of any prosecution brought.

6.3 (1) An opinion on the merits of the settlement or compromise given by counsel or solicitor acting for the child or patient should, except in very clear cases, be obtained.
(2) A copy of the opinion and, unless the instructions on which it was given are sufficiently set out in it, a copy of the instructions, must also be supplied to the court.
(3) A copy or record of any financial advice must also be supplied to the court.

6.4 Where in any personal injury case a claim for damages for future pecuniary loss is settled, the provisions in paras 6.4A and 6.4B must in addition be complied with.

6.4A The court must be satisfied that the parties have considered whether the damages should wholly or partly take the form of periodical payments.

6.4B Where the settlement includes provision for periodical payments, the claim must:
(1) set out the terms of the settlement or compromise; or
(2) have attached to it a draft consent order,
which must satisfy the requirements of rr. 41.8 and 41.9 as appropriate.

6.5 Applications for the approval of a settlement or compromise will normally be heard by a master or district judge.
(For information about provisional damages claims see Part 41 and PD 41.)

Settlement or compromise by or on behalf of a child or patient after proceedings have been commenced

6.6 Where in any personal injury case a claim for damages for future pecuniary loss, by or on behalf of a child or patient, is dealt with by agreement after proceedings have been commenced, an application should be made for the court's approval of the agreement.

6.7 The court must be satisfied that the parties have considered whether the damages should wholly or partly take the form of periodical payments.

6.8 Where the settlement includes provision for periodical payments, an application under para. 6.6 must:
(1) set out the terms of the settlement or compromise; or
(2) have attached to it a draft consent order,
which must include the requirements of rr. 41.8 and 41.9 as appropriate.

6.9 The court must be supplied with:
(1) an opinion on the merits of the settlement or compromise given by counsel or solicitor acting for the child or patient, except in very clear cases; and
(2) a copy or record of any financial advice.

Apportionment under the Fatal Accidents Act 1976

para.7 **14.39**

7.1 A judgment on or settlement in respect of a claim under the Fatal Accidents Act 1976 must be apportioned between the persons by or on whose behalf the claim has been brought.

7.2 Where a claim is brought on behalf of a dependent child or children, the money apportioned to any child must be invested on his behalf in accordance with rr. 21.10 and 21.11 and paras 8 and 9 below.

7.3 In order to approve an apportionment of money to a dependent child, the court will require the following information:

(1) the matters set out in para. 6.2(1) and (2) above, and

(2) in respect of the deceased:

(a) where death was caused by an accident, the matters set out in para. 6.2(3)(a), (b) and (c) above, and

(b) his future loss of earnings, and

(3) the extent and nature of the dependency.

Control of Money Recovered by or on Behalf of a Child or Patient

para.8 **14.39**

8.1 Money recovered or paid into court on behalf of or for the benefit of a child or patient shall be dealt with in accordance with directions of the court under r. 21.11.

8.2 The court:

(1) may direct the money to be paid into the High Court for investment,

(2) may also direct that certain sums be paid direct to the child or patient, his litigation friend or his legal representative[11] for the immediate benefit of the child or patient or for expenses incurred on his behalf, and

(3) may direct the applications in respect of the investment of the money be transferred to a local district registry.

8.3 The master or district judge will consider the general aims to be achieved for the money in court (the fund) by investment and will give directions as to the type of investment.

8.4 Where a child is also a patient, and likely to remain so on reaching full age, his fund should be administered as a patient's fund.

8.5 Where a child or patient is legally aided the fund will be subject to a first charge under s. 16 of the Legal Aid Act 1988 (the legal aid charge) and an order for the investment of money on the child or patient's behalf must contain a direction to that effect.

Expenses Incurred by Litigation Friend

para.8A.1 **66.47** para.8A.2 **14.34, 66.47**

8A.1 A litigation friend may make a claim for expenses under r. 21.11A(1):

(a) where the court has ordered an assessment of costs under r. 48.5(2), at the detailed assessment hearing;

(b) where the litigation friend's expenses are not of a type which would be recoverable as costs on an assessment of costs between the parties, to the master or district judge at the hearing to approve the settlement or compromise under Part 21 (the master or district judge may adjourn the matter to the costs judge); or

(c) where an assessment of costs under r. 48.5(2) is not required, and no approval under Part 21 is necessary, by a Part 23 application supported by a witness statement to a costs judge or district judge as appropriate.

8A.2 In all circumstances, the litigation friend shall support a claim for expenses by filing a witness statement setting out:

(i) the nature and amount of the expense;

(ii) the reason the expense was incurred.

Guardian's Accounts

paras.9–12 **14.39**

9 Paragraph 8 of PD 40 deals with the approval of the accounts of a guardian of assets of a child.

[11] See r. 2.3 for a definition of legal representative.

Investment on Behalf of a Child

10.1 At the hearing of the application for the approval of the agreement the litigation friend or his legal representative should provide a CFO form 320 (request for investment) for completion by the master or district judge.

10.2 On receipt of that form in the Court Funds Office the investment managers of the Public Trust Office will make the appropriate investment.

10.3 Where an award of damages for a child is made at trial the trial judge may direct:

(1) the money to be paid into court and placed in the special investment account, and

(2) the litigation friend to make an application to a master or district judge for further investment directions.

10.4 If the money to be invested is very small the court may order it to be paid direct to the litigation friend to be put into a building society account (or similar) for the child's use.

10.5 If the money is invested in court it must be paid out to the child when he reaches full age.

Investment on Behalf of a Patient

11.1 The Court of Protection is responsible for protecting the property of patients and is given extensive powers to do so under the Mental Health Act 1983. Fees are charged for the administration of funds by the Court of Protection and these should be provided for in any settlement.

11.2 Where the sum to be administered is:

(1) over £30,000, the order approving the settlement will contain a direction to the litigation friend to apply to the Court of Protection for the appointment of a receiver, after which the fund will be transferred to the Court of Protection,

(2) under £20,000, it may be retained in court and invested in the same way as the fund of a child, or

(3) in intermediate cases the advice of the Master of the Court of Protection should be sought.

11.3 A form of order transferring the fund to the Court of Protection is set out in form N292.

11.4 In order for the Court Funds Office to release a fund which is subject to the legal aid charge to the Court of Protection the litigation friend or his legal representative should provide the appropriate area office of the Legal Aid Board with an undertaking in respect of a sum to cover their costs, following which the area office will advise the Court Funds Office in writing of that sum, enabling them to transfer the balance to the Court of Protection on receipt of a CFO form 200 payment schedule authorised by the court.

11.5 The CFO form 200 should be completed and presented to the court where the settlement or trial took place for authorisation, subject to paras 11.6 and 11.7 below.

11.6 Where the settlement took place in the Royal Courts of Justice the CFO form 200 should be completed and presented for authorisation:

(1) on behalf of a child, in the Masters' Secretary's Office, Room E214, and

(2) on behalf of a patient, in the Action Department, Room E15.

11.7 Where the trial took place in the Royal Courts of Justice the CFO form 200 is completed and authorised by the court officer.

Payment Out of Funds in Court

12.1 Applications to a master or district judge:

(1) for payment out of money from the fund for the benefit of the child, or

(2) to vary an investment strategy,

may be dealt with without a hearing unless the court directs otherwise.

12.2 When the child reaches full age, his fund in court:

(1) where it is a sum of money will be paid out to him, and

(2) where it is in the form of investments other than money (for example shares or unit trusts), will be transferred into his name.

12.3 An application for payment out of funds being administered by the Court of Protection must be made to the Court of Protection.

(For further information on payments into and out of court see PD 36 and PD 37.)

CPR Part 22 Statements of Truth

Part 22 **13.7** [For commentary on a specific rule, please refer to the cross-references after the title of the rule.]

22.1 Documents to Be Verified by a Statement of Truth

r.22.1 **79.3, 81.30**
r.22.1(1)(a) **23.10, 24.5, 27.2, 28.7, 29.8, 30.3, 30.4**
r.22.1(d) **13.8, 18.3**
r.22.1(3) **32.13**
r.22.1(4) **23.10, 32.13**
r.22.1(5) **23.13**
r.22.1(6) **23.10, 23.12**
r.22.1(6)(a)(i)–(ii) **23.11**

(1) The following documents must be verified by a statement of truth—
  (a) a statement of case;
  (b) a response complying with an order under rule 18.1 to provide further information;
  (c) a witness statement;
  (d) an acknowledgment of service in a claim begun by way of the Part 8 procedure;
  (e) a certificate stating the reasons for bringing a possession claim or a landlord and tenant claim in the High Court in accordance with rules 55.3(2) and 56.2(2);
  (f) a certificate of service; and
  (g) any other document where a rule or practice direction requires.
(2) Where a statement of case is amended, the amendments must be verified by a statement of truth unless the court orders otherwise.
(Part 17 provides for amendments to statements of case)
(3) If an applicant wishes to rely on matters set out in his application notice as evidence, the application notice must be verified by a statement of truth.
(4) Subject to paragraph (5), a statement of truth is a statement that—
  (a) the party putting forward the document;
  (b) in the case of a witness statement, the maker of the witness statement; or
  (c) in the case of a certificate of service, the person who signs the certificate,
  believes the facts stated in the document are true.
(5) If a party is conducting proceedings with a litigation friend, the statement of truth in—
  (a) a statement of case;
  (b) a response; or
  (c) an application notice,
  is a statement that the litigation friend believes the facts stated in the document being verified are true.
(6) The statement of truth must be signed by—
  (a) in the case of a statement of case, a response or an application—
    (i) the party or litigation friend; or
    (ii) the legal representative on behalf of the party or litigation friend; and
  (b) in the case of a witness statement, the maker of the statement.
(7) A statement of truth which is not contained in the document which it verifies, must clearly identify that document.
(8) A statement of truth in a statement of case may be made by—
  (a) a person who is not a party; or
  (b) by two parties jointly,
  where this is permitted by a relevant practice direction.

22.2 Failure to Verify a Statement of Case

r.22.2(1) **23.12, 23.16** r.22.2(2) **23.16**

(1) If a party fails to verify his statement of case by a statement of truth—
  (a) the statement of case shall remain effective unless struck out; but
  (b) the party may not rely on the statement of case as evidence of any of the matters set out in it.
(2) The court may strike out(GL) a statement of case which is not verified by a statement of truth.
(3) Any party may apply for an order under paragraph (2).

22.3 Failure to Verify a Witness Statement

If the maker of a witness statement fails to verify the witness statement by a statement of truth the court may direct that it shall not be admissible as evidence.

22.4 Power of the Court to Require a Document to Be Verified

r.22.4 **23.16**

(1) The court may order a person who has failed to verify a document in accordance with rule 22.1 to verify the document.
(2) Any party may apply for an order under paragraph (1).

PD 22 Practice Direction — Statements of Truth

This practice direction supplements CPR Part 22

[For commentary on a specific paragraph, please refer to the cross-references after the title of the paragraph.]

Documents to Be Verified by a Statement of Truth

para.1.5 **23.10**

1.1 Rule 22.1(1) sets out the documents which must be verified by a statement of truth. The documents include:
(1) a statement of case,
(2) a response complying with an order under r. 18.1 to provide further information,
(3) a witness statement,
(4) an acknowledgment of service in a claim begun by the Part 8 procedure,
(5) a certificate stating the reasons for bringing a possession claim or a landlord and tenant claim in the High Court in accordance with rr. 55.3(2) and 56.2(2),
(6) a certificate of service.

1.2 If an applicant wishes to rely on matters set out in his application notice as evidence, the application notice must be verified by a statement of truth.[1]

1.3 An expert's report should also be verified by a statement of truth. For the form of the statement of truth verifying an expert's report (which differs from that set out below) see PD 35.

1.4 In addition, the following documents must be verified by a statement of truth:
(1) an application notice for:
(a) a third party debt order (r. 72.3),
(b) a hardship payment order (r. 72.7), or
(c) a charging order (r. 73.3);
(2) a notice of objections to an account being taken by the court, unless verified by an affidavit or witness statement;
(3) a schedule or counter-schedule of expenses and losses in a personal injury claim, and any amendments to such a schedule or counter-schedule, whether or not they are contained in a statement of case.

1.5 The statement of truth may be contained in the document it verifies or it may be in a separate document served subsequently, in which case it must identify the document to which it relates.

1.6 Where the form to be used includes a jurat for the content to be verified by an affidavit then a statement of truth is not required in addition.

Form of the Statement of Truth

para.2.1 **23.10, 32.13** para.2.3 **23.10**

2.1 The form of the statement of truth verifying a statement of case, a response, an application notice or a notice of objections should be as follows:
'[I believe] [the (claimant or as may be) believes] that the facts stated in this [*name document being verified*] are true.'

2.2 The form of the statement of truth verifying a witness statement should be as follows:
'I believe that the facts stated in this witness statement are true.'

2.3 Where the statement of truth is contained in a separate document, the document containing the statement of truth must be headed with the title of the proceedings and the claim number. The document being verified should be identified in the statement of truth as follows:
(1) claim form: 'the claim form issued on [*date*]',
(2) particulars of claim: 'the particulars of claim issued on [*date*]',
(3) statement of case: 'the [*defence or as may be*] served on the [*name of party*] on [*date*]',
(4) application notice: 'the application notice issued on [*date*] for [*set out the remedy sought*]',
(5) witness statement: 'the witness statement filed on [*date*] or served on [*party*] on [*date*]'.

[1] See r. 22.1(3) .

Who May Sign the Statement of Truth

3.1 In a statement of case, a response or an application notice, the statement of truth must be signed by:
(1) the party or his litigation friend,[2] or
(2) the legal representative[3] of the party or litigation friend.

3.2 A statement of truth verifying a witness statement must be signed by the witness.

3.3 A statement of truth verifying a notice of objections to an account must be signed by the objecting party or his legal representative.

3.4 Where a document is to be verified on behalf of a company or other corporation, subject to para. 3.7 below, the statement of truth must be signed by a person holding a senior position[4] in the company or corporation. That person must state the office or position he holds.

3.5 Each of the following persons is a person holding a senior position:
(1) in respect of a registered company or corporation, a director, the treasurer, secretary, chief executive, manager or other officer of the company or corporation, and
(2) in respect of a corporation which is not a registered company, in addition to those persons set out in (1), the mayor, chairman, president or town clerk or other similar officer of the corporation.

3.6 Where the document is to be verified on behalf of a partnership, those who may sign the statement of truth are:
(1) any of the partners, or
(2) a person having the control or management of the partnership business.

3.6A An insurer or the Motor Insurers' Bureau may sign a statement of truth in a statement of case on behalf of a party where the insurer or the Motor Insurers' Bureau has a financial interest in the result of proceedings brought wholly or partially by or against that party.

3.6B If insurers are conducting proceedings on behalf of many claimants or defendants a statement of truth in a statement of case may be signed by a senior person responsible for the case at a lead insurer, but:
(1) the person signing must specify the capacity in which he signs;
(2) the statement of truth must be a statement that the lead insurer believes that the facts stated in the document are true; and
(3) the court may order that a statement of truth also be signed by one or more of the parties.

3.7 Where a party is legally represented, the legal representative may sign the statement of truth on his behalf. The statement signed by the legal representative will refer to the client's belief, not his own. In signing he must state the capacity in which he signs and the name of his firm where appropriate.

3.8 Where a legal representative has signed a statement of truth, his signature will be taken by the court as his statement:
(1) that the client on whose behalf he has signed had authorised him to do so,
(2) that before signing he had explained to the client that in signing the statement of truth he would be confirming the client's belief that the facts stated in the document were true, and
(3) that before signing he had informed the client of the possible consequences to the client if it should subsequently appear that the client did not have an honest belief in the truth of those facts (see r. 32.14).

3.9 The individual who signs a statement of truth must print his full name clearly beneath his signature.

3.10 A legal representative who signs a statement of truth must sign in his own name and not that of his firm or employer.

2 See Part 21 (children and patients).
3 See r. 2.3 for the definition of legal representative.
4 See r. 6.4(4) .

3.11 The following are examples of the possible application of this practice direction describing who may sign a statement of truth verifying statements in documents other than a witness statement. These are only examples and not an indication of how a court might apply the practice direction to a specific situation.

Managing agent	An agent who manages property or investments for the party cannot sign a statement of truth. It must be signed by the party or by the legal representative of the party.
Trusts	Where some or all of the trustees comprise a single party one, some or all of the trustees comprising the party may sign a statement of truth. The legal representative of the trustees may sign it.
Insurers and the Motor Insurers' Bureau	If an insurer has a financial interest in a claim involving its insured then, if the insured is the party, the insurer may sign a statement of truth in a statement of case for the insured party. Paragraphs 3.4 and 3.5 apply to the insurer if it is a company. The claims manager employed by the insurer responsible for handling the insurance claim or managing the staff handling the claim may sign the statement of truth for the insurer (see next example). The position for the Motor Insurers' Bureau is similar.
Companies	Paragraphs 3.4 and 3.5 apply. The word manager will be construed in the context of the phrase 'a person holding a senior position' which it is used to define. The court will consider the size of the company and the size and nature of the claim. It would expect the manager signing the statement of truth to have personal knowledge of the content of the document or to be responsible for managing those who have that knowledge of the content. A small company may not have a manager, apart from the directors, who holds a senior position. A large company will have many such managers. In a larger company with specialist claims, insurance or legal departments the statement may be signed by the manager of such a department if he or she is responsible for handling the claim or managing the staff handling it.
In-house legal representatives	Legal representative is defined in r. 2.3(1). A legal representative employed by a party may sign a statement of truth. However a person who is not a solicitor, barrister or other authorised litigator, but who is employed by the company and is managed by such a person, is not employed by that person and so cannot sign a statement of truth. (This is unlike the employee of a solicitor in private practice who would come within the definition of legal representative.) However such a person may be a manager and able to sign the statement on behalf of the company in that capacity.

Inability of Persons to Read or Sign Documents to Be Verified by a Statement of Truth

3A.1 Where a document containing a statement of truth is to be signed by a person who is unable to read or sign the document, it must contain a certificate made by an authorised person.

3A.2 An authorised person is a person able to administer oaths and take affidavits but need not be independent of the parties or their representatives.

3A.3 The authorised person must certify:

(1) that the document has been read to the person signing it;

(2) that that person appeared to understand it and approved its content as accurate;

(3) that the declaration of truth has been read to that person;

(4) that that person appeared to understand the declaration and the consequences of making a false declaration; and

(5) that that person signed or made his mark in the presence of the authorised person.

3A.4 The form of the certificate is set out at annex 1 to this practice direction.

Consequences of Failure to Verify

para.4.2 **23.16** para.4.3 **23.16**

4.1 If a statement of case is not verified by a statement of truth, the statement of case will remain effective unless it is struck out,[5] but a party may not rely on the contents of a statement of case as evidence until it has been verified by a statement of truth.

[5] See r. 22.2(1).

4.2 Any party may apply to the court for an order that unless within such period as the court may specify the statement of case is verified by the service of a statement of truth, the statement of case will be struck out.

4.3 The usual order for the costs of an application referred to in para. 4.2 will be that the costs be paid by the party who had failed to verify in any event and forthwith.

Penalty

5 Attention is drawn to r. 32.14 which sets out the consequences of verifying a statement of case containing a false statement without an honest belief in its truth, and to the procedures set out in PD 32, para. 28.

ANNEX 1

annex 1 **49.10**

CERTIFICATE TO BE USED WHERE A PERSON IS UNABLE TO READ OR SIGN A DOCUMENT TO BE VERIFIED BY A STATEMENT OF TRUTH

I certify that I [*name and address of authorised person*] have read over the contents of this document and the declaration of truth to the person signing the document [*if there are exhibits, add* and explained the nature and effect of the exhibits referred to in it] who appeared to understand (a) the document and approved its content as accurate and (b) the declaration of truth and the consequences of making a false declaration, and made his mark in my presence.

CPR Part 23 General Rules about Applications for Court Orders

Part 23 **14.4, 14.17, 14.37, 14.38, 14.42, 15.7, 15.17, 15.35, 18.7, 19.3, 20.1, 20.2, 20.8, 20.9, 22.6, 30.6, 33.3, 35.9, 38.31, 40.3, 46.30, 48.76, 54.7, 56.10, 61.25, 64.14, 64.26, 64.30, 64.31, 65.2, 66.71, 68.16, 68.19, 68.26, 69.9, 71.41, 74.40, 75.13, 76.3, 76.32, 76.34, 76.36, 76.37, 77.24, 78.6, 78.7, 78.22, 81.16, 81.19, 81.22, 81.23, 92.10, 92.12, 96.56, 96.61**

[For commentary on a specific rule, please refer to the cross-references after the title of the rule.]

23.1 Meaning of 'Application Notice' and 'Respondent'

r.23.1 **14.1**

In this Part—

'application notice' means a document in which the applicant states his intention to seek a court order; and

'respondent' means—

(a) the person against whom the order is sought; and

(b) such other person as the court may direct.

23.2 Where to Make an Application

r.23.2(1)–(3) **32.2, 37.10**
r.23.2(4) **11.8, 32.2, 37.5**
r.23.2(5) **32.2, 37.10**

(1) The general rule is that an application must be made to the court where the claim was started.

(2) If a claim has been transferred to another court since it was started, an application must be made to the court to which the claim has been transferred.

(3) If the parties have been notified of a fixed date for the trial, an application must be made to the court where the trial is to take place.

(4) If an application is made before a claim has been started, it must be made to the court where it is likely that the claim to which the application relates will be started unless there is good reason to make the application to a different court.

(5) If an application is made after proceedings to enforce judgment have begun, it must be made to any court which is dealing with the enforcement of the judgment unless any rule or practice direction provides otherwise.

23.3 Application Notice to Be Filed

r.23.3 **14.5**
r.23.3(1) **32.8, 32.11, 37.5, 74.40**
r.23.3(2)(b) **37.5**

(1) The general rule is that an applicant must file an application notice.

(2) An applicant may make an application without filing an application notice if—

(a) this is permitted by a rule or practice direction; or

(b) the court dispenses with the requirement for an application notice.

23.4 Notice of an Application

r.23.4 **14.5** r.23.4(2) **32.7**
r.23.4(1) **32.7, 32.10, 48.76**

(1) The general rule is that a copy of the application notice must be served on each respondent.
(2) An application may be made without serving a copy of the application notice if this is permitted by—
 (a) a rule;
 (b) a practice direction; or
 (c) a court order.
(Rule 23.7 deals with service of a copy of the application notice)

23.5 Time When an Application Is Made

Where an application must be made within a specified time, it is so made if the application notice is received by the court within that time.

23.6 What an Application Notice Must Include

r.23.6 **32.8, 32.11, 37.5**

An application notice must state—
(a) what order the applicant is seeking; and
(b) briefly, why the applicant is seeking the order.
(Part 22 requires an application notice to be verified by a statement of truth if the applicant wishes to rely on matters set out in his application notice as evidence)

23.7 Service of a Copy of an Application Notice

r.23.7 **37.5, 66.71** r.23.7(3) **32.13, 32.20**
r.23.7(1) **32.10, 32.11, 32.20** r.23.7(5) **32.13, 32.20**
r.23.7(1)(b) **65.2**

(1) A copy of the application notice—
 (a) must be served as soon as practicable after it is filed; and
 (b) except where another time limit is specified in these Rules or a practice direction, must in any event be served at least 3 days before the court is to deal with the application.
(2) If a copy of the application notice is to be served by the court, the applicant must, when he files the application notice, file a copy of any written evidence in support.
(3) When a copy of an application notice is served it must be accompanied by—
 (a) a copy of any written evidence in support; and
 (b) a copy of any draft order which the applicant has attached to his application.
(4) If—
 (a) an application notice is served; but
 (b) the period of notice is shorter than the period required by these Rules or a practice direction, the court may direct that, in the circumstances of the case, sufficient notice has been given and hear the application.
(5) This rule does not require written evidence—
 (a) to be filed if it has already been filed; or
 (b) to be served on a party on whom it has already been served.
(Part 6 contains the general rules about service of documents including who must serve a copy of the application notice)

23.8 Applications Which May Be Dealt with without a Hearing

r.23.8 **32.21, 37.5, 74.40** r.23.8(c) **15.7, 32.11, 32.38**
r.23.8(a) **32.30**

The court may deal with an application without a hearing if—
(a) the parties agree as to the terms of the order sought;
(b) the parties agree that the court should dispose of the application without a hearing, or
(c) the court does not consider that a hearing would be appropriate.

23.9 Service of Application Where Application Made without Notice

r.23.9 **15.8, 33.5, 37.8, 37.12, 78.7** r.23.9(3) **15.8, 32.8**
r.23.9(2) **32.8**

(1) This rule applies where the court has disposed of an application which it permitted to be made without service of a copy of the application notice.
(2) Where the court makes an order, whether granting or dismissing the application, a copy of the application notice and any evidence in support must, unless the court orders otherwise, be served with the order on any party or other person—
 (a) against whom the order was made; and
 (b) against whom the order was sought.
(3) The order must contain a statement of the right to make an application to set aside[(GL)] or vary the order under rule 23.10.

23.10 Application to Set Aside or Vary Order Made without Notice

r.23.10 **15.7, 15.8, 33.5, 35.12, 37.8, 37.12, 61.1, 78.7**

(1) A person who was not served with a copy of the application notice before an order was made under rule 23.9, may apply to have the order set aside [(GL)] or varied.
(2) An application under this rule must be made within 7 days after the date on which the order was served on the person making the application.

23.11 Power of the Court to Proceed in the Absence of a Party

r.23.11(1) **32.28, 60.1**
r.23.11(2) **60.1**

(1) Where the applicant or any respondent fails to attend the hearing of an application, the court may proceed in his absence.
(2) Where—
 (a) the applicant or any respondent fails to attend the hearing of an application; and
 (b) the court makes an order at the hearing,
 the court may, on application or of its own initiative, relist the application.

(Part 40 deals with service of orders)

23.12 Dismissal of Totally without Merit Applications

r.23.12 **32.29, 61.7**

If the court dismisses an application (including an application for permission to appeal or for permission to apply for judicial review) and it considers that the application is totally without merit—
(a) the court's order must record that fact; and
(b) the court must at the same time consider whether it is appropriate to make a civil restraint order.

PD 23 Practice Direction — Applications

This practice direction supplements CPR Part 23

PD 23 **32.19, 74.40** [For commentary on a specific paragraph, please refer to the cross-references after the title of the paragraph.]

Reference to a Judge

para.1 **32.3**

1 A master or district judge may refer to a judge any matter which he thinks should properly be decided by a judge, and the judge may either dispose of the matter or refer it back to the master or district judge.

Application Notices

para.2.1 **32.8, 32.11, 37.5**
para.2.1(5) **15.7**
para.2.1(4) **32.11**
para.2.3 **32.11**
para.2.7 **32.1, 32.4, 33.3, 34.2, 37.9**
para.2.8 **32.1, 37.9, 37.10**
para.2.9 **32.26, 37.11**
para.2.10 **32.7, 45.13**

2.1 An application notice must, in addition to the matters set out in r. 23.6, be signed and include:
(1) the title of the claim,
(2) the reference number of the claim,
(3) the full name of the applicant,
(4) where the applicant is not already a party, his address for service, including a postcode (postcode information may be obtained from www.royalmail.com or the Royal Mail Address Management Guide), and
(5) either a request for a hearing or a request that the application be dealt with without a hearing.
(Form N244 may be used.)

2.2 On receipt of an application notice containing a request for a hearing the court will notify the applicant of the time and date for the hearing of the application.

2.3 On receipt of an application notice containing a request that the application be dealt with without a hearing, the application notice will be sent to a master or district judge so that he may decide whether the application is suitable for consideration without a hearing.

2.4 Where the master or district judge agrees that the application is suitable for consideration without a hearing, the court will so inform the applicant and the respondent and may give directions for the filing of evidence. (Rules 23.9 and 23.10 enable a party to apply for an order made without a hearing to be set aside or varied.)

2.5 Where the master or district judge does not agree that the application is suitable for consideration without a hearing, the court will notify the applicant and the respondent of the time, date and place for the hearing of the application and may at the same time give directions as to the filing of evidence.

2.6 If the application is intended to be made to a judge, the application notice should so state. In that case, paragraphs 2.3, 2.4 and 2.5 will apply as though references to the master or district judge were references to a judge.

2.7 Every application should be made as soon as it becomes apparent that it is necessary or desirable to make it.

2.8 Applications should wherever possible be made so that they can be considered at any other hearing for which a date has already been fixed or for which a date is about to be fixed. This is particularly so in relation to case management conferences, allocation and listing hearings and pre-trial reviews fixed by the court.

2.9 The parties must anticipate that at any hearing the court may wish to review the conduct of the case as a whole and give any necessary case management directions. They should be ready to assist the court in doing so and to answer questions the court may ask for this purpose.

2.10 Where a date for a hearing has been fixed and a party wishes to make an application at that hearing but he does not have sufficient time to serve an application notice he should inform the other party and the court (if possible in writing) as soon as he can of the nature of the application and the reason for it. He should then make the application orally at the hearing.

Applications without Service of Application Notice

3 An application may be made without serving an application notice only:
(1) where there is exceptional urgency,
(2) where the overriding objective is best furthered by doing so,
(3) by consent of all parties,
(4) with the permission of the court,
(5) where para. 2.10 above applies, or
(6) where a court order, rule or practice direction permits.

Giving Notice of an Application

para.4.2 **32.7**

4.1 Unless the court otherwise directs or para. 3 of this practice direction applies the application notice must be served as soon as practicable after it has been issued and, if there is to be a hearing, at least three clear days before the hearing date (r. 23.7(1)(b)).

4.2 Where an application notice should be served but there is not sufficient time to do so, informal notification of the application should be given unless the circumstances of the application require secrecy.

Pre-action Applications

para.5 **37.3**

5 All applications made before a claim is commenced should be made under Part 23. Attention is drawn in particular to r. 23.2(4).

Telephone Hearings

para.6 **32.22**
para.6.1 **37.11**
para.6.1A **32.11**
para.6.2 **32.22**
para.6.3(1)–(2) **32.22**

6.1 The court may order that an application or part of an application be dealt with by a telephone hearing.

6.1A The applicant should indicate on his application notice if he seeks a court order under para. 6.1. Where he has not done so but nevertheless wishes to seek an order the request should be made as early as possible.

6.2 An order under para. 6.1 will not normally be made unless every party entitled to be given notice of the application and to be heard at the hearing has consented to the order.

6.3 (1) Where a party entitled to be heard at the hearing of the application is acting in person, the court:
(a) may not make an order under para. 6.1 except on condition that arrangements will be made for the party acting in person to be attended at the telephone hearing by a responsible person to whom the party acting in person is known and who can confirm to the court the identity of the party; and
(b) may not give effect to an order under para. 6.1 unless the party acting in person is accompanied by a responsible person who at the commencement of the hearing confirms to the court the identity of the party.
(2) The 'responsible person' may be a barrister, solicitor, legal executive, doctor, clergyman, police officer, prison officer or other person of comparable status.
(3) If the court makes an order under para. 6.1 it will give any directions necessary for the telephone hearing.

6.4 No representative of a party to an application being heard by telephone may attend the judge in person while the application is being heard unless the other party to the application has agreed that he may do so.

6.5 If an application is to be heard by telephone the following directions will apply, subject to any direction to the contrary:
(1) The applicant's legal representative must arrange the telephone conference for precisely the

Civil Procedure Rules & Practice Directions

time fixed by the court. The telecommunications provider must be capable of connecting the parties and the court.

(2) He must tell the operator the telephone numbers of all those participating in the conference call and the sequence in which they are to be called.

(3) It is the responsibility of the applicant's legal representative to ascertain from all the other parties whether they have instructed counsel and, if so the identity of counsel, and whether the legal representative and counsel will be on the same or different telephone numbers.

(4) The sequence in which they are to be called will be:
(a) the applicant's legal representative and (if on a different number) his counsel,
(b) the legal representative (and counsel) for all other parties, and
(c) the judge.

(5) The applicant's legal representative must arrange for the conference to be recorded on tape by the telecommunications provider whose system is being used and must send the tape to the court.

(6) Each speaker is to remain on the line after being called by the operator setting up the conference call. The call may be two or three minutes before the time fixed for the application.

(7) When the judge has been connected the applicant's legal representative (or his counsel) will introduce the parties in the usual way.

(8) If the use of a 'speakerphone' by any party causes the judge or any other party any difficulty in hearing what is said the judge may require that party to use a hand-held telephone.

(9) The telephone charges debited to the account of the party initiating the conference call will be treated as part of the costs of the application.

Videoconferencing

para.7 **37.11**

7 Where the parties to a matter wish to use videoconferencing facilities, and those facilities are available in the relevant court, they should apply to the master or district judge for directions. (PD 32, para. 29.1 and annex 3, provide guidance on the use of videoconferencing in the civil courts.)

Note of Proceedings

para.8 **32.26**

8 The procedural judge should keep, either by way of a note or a tape recording, brief details of all proceedings before him, including the dates of the proceedings and a short statement of the decision taken at each hearing.

Evidence

para.9.1 **32.13**
para.9.4 **32.13, 37.13**
para.9.6 **32.13**

9.1 The requirement for evidence in certain types of applications is set out in some of the rules and practice directions. Where there is no specific requirement to provide evidence it should be borne in mind that, as a practical matter, the court will often need to be satisfied by evidence of the facts that are relied on in support of or for opposing the application.

9.2 The court may give directions for the filing of evidence in support of or opposing a particular application. The court may also give directions for the filing of evidence in relation to any hearing that it fixes on its own initiative. The directions may specify the form that evidence is to take and when it is to be served.

9.3 Where it is intended to rely on evidence which is not contained in the application itself, the evidence, if it has not already been served, should be served with the application.

9.4 Where a respondent to an application wishes to rely on evidence which has not yet been served he should serve it as soon as possible and in any event in accordance with any directions the court may have given.

9.5 If it is necessary for the applicant to serve any evidence in reply it should be served as soon as possible and in any event in accordance with any directions the court may have given.

9.6 Evidence must be filed with the court as well as served on the parties. Exhibits should not be filed unless the court otherwise directs.

9.7 The contents of an application notice may be used as evidence (otherwise than at trial) provided the contents have been verified by a statement of truth.[1]

Consent Orders

para.10.2 **32.34, 61.32** para.10.3 **61.32**

10.1 Rule 40.6 sets out the circumstances where an agreed judgment or order may be entered and sealed.

10.2 Where all parties affected by an order have written to the court consenting to the making of the order a draft of which has been filed with the court, the court will treat the draft as having been signed in accordance with r. 40.6(7).

10.3 Where a consent order must be made by a judge (i.e. r. 40.6(2) does not apply) the order must be drawn so that the judge's name and judicial title can be inserted.

10.4 The parties to an application for a consent order must ensure that they provide the court with any material it needs to be satisfied that it is appropriate to make the order. Subject to any rule or practice direction a letter will generally be acceptable for this purpose.

10.5 Where a judgment or order has been agreed in respect of an application or claim where a hearing date has been fixed, the parties must inform the court immediately. (Note that parties are reminded that under rr. 28.4 and 29.5 the case management timetable cannot be varied by written agreement of the parties.)

Other Applications Considered without a Hearing

11.1 Where r. 23.8(b) applies the parties should so inform the court in writing and each should confirm that all evidence and other material on which he relies has been disclosed to the other parties to the application.

11.2 Where r. 23.8(c) applies the court will treat the application as if it were proposing to make an order on its own initiative.

Applications to Stay Claim Where Related Criminal Proceedings

para.11A. 1 **54.5** para.11A. 3 **54.5**

11A.1 An application for the stay of civil proceedings pending the determination of related criminal proceedings may be made by any party to the civil proceedings or by the prosecutor or any defendant in the criminal proceedings.

11A.2 Every party to the civil proceedings must, unless he is the applicant, be made a respondent to the application.

11A.3 The evidence in support of the application must contain an estimate of the expected duration of the stay and must identify the respects in which the continuance of the civil proceedings may prejudice the criminal trial.

11A.4 In order to make an application under para. 11A. 1, it is not necessary for the prosecutor or defendant in the criminal proceedings to be joined as a party to the civil proceedings.

Miscellaneous

para.12.1 **32.19**

12.1 Except in the most simple application the applicant should bring to any hearing a draft of the order sought. If the case is proceeding in the Royal Courts of Justice and the order is unusually long or complex it should also be supplied on disk for use by the court office.

12.2 Where r. 23.11 applies, the power to relist the application in r. 23.11(2) is in addition to any other powers of the court with regard to the order (for example, to set aside, vary, discharge or suspend the order).

Costs

para.13.2 **66.29**

13.1 Attention is drawn to PD 43–48 and, in particular, to the court's power to make a summary assessment of costs.

13.2 Attention is also drawn to r. 44.13(1) which provides that if an order makes no mention of costs, none are payable in respect of the proceedings to which it relates.

[1] See Part 22.

PD 23B Practice Direction — Pilot Scheme for Telephone Hearings

This practice direction supplements CPR Part 23

PD 23B **32.23**

General

1.1 This practice direction is made under r. 51.2. It provides for a pilot scheme ('the Telephone Hearings Pilot Scheme') to operate at the courts specified in the appendix between the dates specified for each court in the appendix. The purpose of the Telephone Hearings Pilot Scheme is to extend the scope of hearings which may be conducted by telephone.

1.2 During the operation of the Telephone Hearings Pilot Scheme:

(1) paras 6.1 to 6.3 of PD 23 do not apply to hearings conducted under the Telephone Hearings Pilot Scheme; but

(2) paras 6.4 and 6.5 do apply and where:

(a) the hearing is an allocation hearing, a listing hearing, a case management conference or a pre-trial review; or

(b) the court of its own initiative orders a telephone hearing,

references in para. 6.5 to the applicant are to be read as references to the claimant or such other party as the court directs to arrange the telephone hearing; and

(3) para. 6.4 is modified so that it also applies to unrepresented parties.

Hearings to Be Conducted by Telephone

2.1 Subject to para. 2.2, the following hearings will be conducted by telephone unless the court otherwise orders:

(1) allocation hearings;

(2) listing hearings;

(3) interim applications, case management conferences or pre-trial reviews with a time estimate of no more than one hour; and

(4) any other application with the consent of the parties and the court's agreement.

2.2 Paragraph 2.1 does not apply where:

(1) all the parties are unrepresented;

(2) more than four parties may wish to make representations at the hearing (for this purpose where two or more parties are represented by the same person, they are to be treated as one party);

(3) the hearing could result in the final determination of the whole or part of the proceedings.

2.3 An application for an order that a hearing under para. 2.1(1), (2) or (3) should not be conducted by telephone:

(1) must be made at least seven days before the hearing; and

(2) may be made by letter,

and the court shall determine such application without requiring the attendance of the parties.

2.4 The claimant's legal representative (if any), or the legal representative of such other party as the court directs, shall be responsible for arranging the telephone hearing.

Documents

3.1 The legal representative responsible for arranging the telephone hearing must file and serve a case summary and draft order no later than 4 p.m. on the last working day before the hearing:

(1) if the claim has been allocated to the multi-track; and

(2) in any other case, if the court so directs.

3.2 Where a party seeks to rely on any other document at the hearing, he must file and serve the document no later than 4 p.m. on the last working day before the hearing.

APPENDIX

Newcastle Combined Court Centre	1 September 2003 — 1 October 2006
Bedford County Court	1 February 2004 — 1 October 2006
Luton County Court	1 February 2004 — 1 October 2006
Any county court specified on Her Majesty's Courts Service website at www.hmcourts-service.gov.uk as one in which telephone hearings are available	1 April 2006 — 1 October 2006

CPR Part 24 Summary Judgment

Part 24 **26.3, 26.5, 33.1, 97.41** [For commentary on a specific rule, please refer to the cross-references after the title of the rule.]

24.1 Scope of this Part

This Part sets out a procedure by which the court may decide a claim or a particular issue without a trial.

(Part 53 makes special provision about summary disposal of defamation claims in accordance with the Defamation Act 1996)

24.2 Grounds for Summary Judgment

r.24.2 **33.1, 34.9, 34.10, 34.11, 95.18** r.24.2(b) **34.42**

The court may give summary judgment against a claimant or defendant on the whole of a claim or on a particular issue if—

(a) it considers that—
   (i) that claimant has no real prospect of succeeding on the claim or issue; or
   (ii) that defendant has no real prospect of successfully defending the claim or issue; and
(b) there is no other compelling reason why the case or issue should be disposed of at a trial.

(Rule 3.4 makes provision for the court to strike out(GL) a statement of case or part of a statement of case if it appears that it discloses no reasonable grounds for bringing or defending a claim)

24.3 Types of Proceedings in Which Summary Judgment Is Available

r.24.3(1)–(2) **34.7**

(1) The court may give summary judgment against a claimant in any type of proceedings.
(2) The court may give summary judgment against a defendant in any type of proceedings except—
   (a) proceedings for possession of residential premises against—
      (i) a mortgagor; or
      (ii) a tenant or person holding over after the end of his tenancy, whose occupancy is protected within the meaning of the Rent Act 1977, or the Housing Act 1988; and
   (b) proceedings for an admiralty claim in rem.

24.4 Procedure

r.24.4(1) **1.16, 32.6, 34.2** r.24.4(3) **34.5, 34.8, 59.35**
r.24.4(2) **18.5, 26.3, 34.3** r.24.4(4) **34.8**

(1) A claimant may not apply for summary judgment until the defendant against whom the application is made has filed—
   (a) an acknowledgment of service; or
   (b) a defence,
   unless—
      (i) the court gives permission; or
      (ii) a practice direction provides otherwise.

(Rule 10.3 sets out the period for filing an acknowledgment of service and rule 15.4 the period for filing a defence)

(1A) In civil proceedings against the Crown, as defined in rule 66.1(2), a claimant may not apply for summary judgment until after expiry of the period for filing a defence specified in rule 15.4.

(2) If a claimant applies for summary judgment before a defendant against whom the application is made has filed a defence, that defendant need not file a defence before the hearing.
(3) Where a summary judgment hearing is fixed, the respondent (or the parties where the hearing is fixed of the court's own initiative) must be given at least 14 days' notice of—
   (a) the date fixed for the hearing; and
   (b) the issues which it is proposed that the court will decide at the hearing.
(4) A practice direction may provide for a different period of notice to be given.
(Part 23 contains the general rules about how to make an application)
(Rule 3.3 applies where the court exercises its powers of its own initiative)

24.5 Evidence for the Purposes of a Summary Judgment Hearing

r.24.5(1)–(3) **34.8**

(1) If the respondent to an application for summary judgment wishes to rely on written evidence at the hearing, he must—
   (a) file the written evidence; and
   (b) serve copies on every other party to the application,
   at least 7 days before the summary judgment hearing.
(2) If the applicant wishes to rely on written evidence in reply, he must—
   (a) file the written evidence; and
   (b) serve a copy on the respondent,
   at least 3 days before the summary judgment hearing.
(3) Where a summary judgment hearing is fixed by the court of its own initiative—
   (a) any party who wishes to rely on written evidence at the hearing must—
      (i) file the written evidence; and
      (ii) unless the court orders otherwise, serve copies on every other party to the proceedings,
      at least 7 days before the date of the hearing;
   (b) any party who wishes to rely on written evidence at the hearing in reply to any other party's written evidence must—
      (i) file the written evidence in reply; and
      (ii) unless the court orders otherwise serve copies on every other party to the proceedings,
      at least 3 days before the date of the hearing.
(4) This rule does not require written evidence—
   (a) to be filed if it has already been filed; or
   (b) to be served on a party on whom it has already been served.

24.6 Court's Powers When It Determines a Summary Judgment Application

r.24.6 **34.42, 65.7**

When the court determines a summary judgment application it may—
(a) give directions as to the filing and service of a defence;
(b) give further directions about the management of the case.
(Rule 3.1(3) provides that the court may attach conditions when it makes an order)

PD 24 Practice Direction — The Summary Disposal of Claims

This practice direction supplements CPR Part 24

[For commentary on a specific paragraph, please refer to the cross-references after the title of the paragraph.]

Applications for Summary Judgment under Part 24

1.1 Attention is drawn to Part 24 itself and to:
Part 3, in particular rule 3.1(3) and (5),
Part 22,
Part 23, in particular rule 23.6,
Part 32, in particular rule 32.6(2).

1.2 In this paragraph, where the context so admits, the word 'claim' includes:
(1) a part of a claim, and
(2) an issue on which the claim in whole or part depends.

1.3 An application for summary judgment under rule 24.2 may be based on:
(1) a point of law (including a question of construction of a document),
(2) the evidence which can reasonably be expected to be available at trial or the lack of it, or
(3) a combination of these.

1.4 Rule 24.4(1) deals with the stage in the proceedings at which an application under Part 24 can be made (but see paragraph 7.1 below).

Procedure for Making an Application

para.2(5) **34.8** para.2(6) **34.2**

2 (1) Attention is drawn to rules 24.4(3) and 23.6.
(2) The application notice must include a statement that it is an application for summary judgment made under Part 24.
(3) The application notice or the evidence contained or referred to in it or served with it must:
(a) identify concisely any point of law or provision in a document on which the applicant relies, and/or
(b) state that it is made because the applicant believes that on the evidence the respondent has no real prospect of succeeding on the claim or issue or (as the case may be) of successfully defending the claim or issue to which the application relates,
and in either case state that the applicant knows of no other reason why the disposal of the claim or issue should await trial.
(4) Unless the application notice itself contains all the evidence (if any) on which the applicant relies, the application notice should identify the written evidence on which the applicant relies. This does not affect the applicant's right to file further evidence under rule 24.5(2).
(5) The application notice should draw the attention of the respondent to rule 24.5(1).
(6) Where the claimant has failed to comply with any relevant pre-action protocol, an application for summary judgment will not normally be entertained before the defence has been filed or, alternatively, the time for doing so has expired.

The Hearing

3 (1) The hearing of the application will normally take place before a master or a district judge.
(2) The master or district judge may direct that the application be heard by a High Court judge (if the case is in the High Court) or a circuit judge (if the case is in a county court).

The Court's Approach

para.4 **34.29** para.4.1(1) **34.11**
para. 4.1 **34.11** para. 4.2 **34.11**

4 Where it appears to the court possible that a claim or defence may succeed but improbable that it will do so, the court may make a conditional order, as described below.

Orders the Court May Make

para.5.1 **34.9** para. 5.2 **34.29**

5.1 The orders the court may make on an application under Part 24 include:
(1) judgment on the claim,
(2) the striking out or dismissal of the claim,
(3) the dismissal of the application,
(4) a conditional order.

5.2 A conditional order is an order which requires a party:
(1) to pay a sum of money into court, or
(2) to take a specified step in relation to his claim or defence, as the case may be,
and provides that that party's claim will be dismissed or his statement of case will be struck out if he does not comply.
(Note — the court will not follow its former practice of granting leave to a defendant to defend a claim, whether conditionally or unconditionally.)

Accounts and Inquiries

6 If a remedy sought by a claimant in his claim form includes, or necessarily involves, taking an account or making an inquiry, an application can be made under Part 24 by any party to the proceedings for an order directing any necessary accounts or inquiries to be taken or made.
(PD 40 contains further provisions as to orders for accounts and inquiries.)

Specific Performance

para.7 **34.43**

7.1 (1) If a remedy sought by a claimant in his claim form includes a claim—
(a) for specific performance of an agreement (whether in writing or not) for the sale, purchase, exchange, mortgage or charge of any property, or for the grant or assignment of a lease or tenancy of any property, with or without an alternative claim for damages, or
(b) for rescission of such an agreement, or
(c) for the forfeiture or return of any deposit made under such an agreement,
the claimant may apply under Part 24 for judgment.
(2) The claimant may do so at any time after the claim form has been served, whether or not the defendant has acknowledged service of the claim form, whether or not the time for acknowledging service has expired and whether or not any particulars of claim have been served.

7.2 The application notice by which an application under paragraph 7.1 is made must have attached to it the text of the order sought by the claimant.

7.3 The application notice and a copy of every affidavit or witness statement in support and of any exhibit referred to therein must be served on the defendant not less than 4 days before the hearing of the application. (Note — the 4 days replaces for these applications the 14 days specified in rule 24.4(3). Rule 24.5 cannot, therefore, apply.)
(This paragraph replaces RSC, ord. 86, rr. 1 and 2, but applies to county court proceedings as well as to High Court proceedings.)

Setting Aside Order for Summary Judgment

8.1 If an order for summary judgment is made against a respondent who does not appear at the hearing of the application, the respondent may apply for the order to be set aside or varied (see also rule 23.11).

8.2 On the hearing of an application under paragraph 8.1 the court may make such order as it thinks just.

Costs

9.1 Attention is drawn to Part 45 (fixed costs).

9.2 Attention is drawn to PD 43–48 and in particular to the court's power to make a summary assessment of costs.

9.3 Attention is also drawn to rule 44.13(1) which provides that if an order does not mention costs no party is entitled to costs relating to that order.

Case Management

para.10 **34.42**

10 Where the court dismisses the application or makes an order that does not completely dispose of the claim, the court will give case management directions as to the future conduct of the case.

CPR Part 25 Interim Remedies and Security for Costs

Part 25 **24.18, 43.6, 65.2, 74.39, 82.15, 92.16** [For commentary on a specific rule, please refer to the cross-references after the title of the rule.]

I INTERIM REMEDIES

25.1 Orders for Interim Remedies

r.25.1 **36.3, 74.39**
r.25.1(1) **32.29, 42.27**
r.25.1(1)(a) **74.39**
r.25.1(1)(b) **4.18, 4.19, 74.39**
r.25.1(1)(c) **40.3, 41.1, 41.2, 74.39**
r.25.1(1)(c)(v)–(vi) **41.9**
r.25.1(1)(d) **41.1, 41.2**
r.25.1(1)(e) **40.2**
r.25.1(1)(f) **38.1, 74.39**
r.25.1(1)(g) **38.25**
r.25.1(1)(h) **39.1, 74.39**
r.25.1(1)(k) **36.1, 36.4**
r.25.1(1)(m) **32.29**
r.25.1(1)(n) **32.29**
r.25.1(1)(o) **32.29, 34.44, 61.29**
r.25.1(1)(p) **32.29**
r.25.1(2) **41.2, 41.3, 41.9**
r.25.1(4) **37.1**

(1) The court may grant the following interim remedies—
(a) an interim injunction(GL);
(b) an interim declaration;
(c) an order—
(i) for the detention, custody or preservation of relevant property;
(ii) for the inspection of relevant property;
(iii) for the taking of a sample of relevant property;
(iv) for the carrying out of an experiment on or with relevant property;
(v) for the sale of relevant property which is of a perishable nature or which for any other good reason it is desirable to sell quickly; and
(vi) for the payment of income from relevant property until a claim is decided;
(d) an order authorising a person to enter any land or building in the possession of a party to the proceedings for the purposes of carrying out an order under sub-paragraph (c);
(e) an order under section 4 of the Torts (Interference with Goods) Act 1977 to deliver up goods;
(f) an order (referred to as a 'freezing injunction(GL)')—
(i) restraining a party from removing from the jurisdiction assets located there; or
(ii) restraining a party from dealing with any assets whether located within the jurisdiction or not;
(g) an order directing a party to provide information about the location of relevant property or assets or to provide information about relevant property or assets which are or may be the subject of an application for a freezing injunction(GL);
(h) an order (referred to as a 'search order') under section 7 of the Civil Procedure Act 1997

(order requiring a party to admit another party to premises for the purpose of preserving evidence etc.);

(i) an order under section 33 of the Supreme Court Act 1981 or section 52 of the County Courts Act 1984 (order for disclosure of documents or inspection of property before a claim has been made);

(j) an order under section 34 of the Supreme Court Act 1981 or section 53 of the County Courts Act 1984 (order in certain proceedings for disclosure of documents or inspection of property against a non-party);

(k) an order (referred to as an order for interim payment) under rule 25.6 for payment by a defendant on account of any damages, debt or other sum (except costs) which the court may hold the defendant liable to pay;

(l) an order for a specified fund to be paid into court or otherwise secured, where there is a dispute over a party's right to the fund;

(m) an order permitting a party seeking to recover personal property to pay money into court pending the outcome of the proceedings and directing that, if he does so, the property shall be given up to him;

(n) an order directing a party to prepare and file accounts relating to the dispute;

(o) an order directing any account to be taken or inquiry to be made by the court; and

(p) an order under Article 9 of Council Directive (EC) 2004/48 on the enforcement of intellectual property rights (order in intellectual property proceedings making the continuation of an alleged infringement subject to the lodging of guarantees).

(Rule 34.2 provides for the court to issue a witness summons requiring a witness to produce documents to the court at the hearing or on such date as the court may direct)

(2) In paragraph (1)(c) and (g), 'relevant property' means property (including land) which is the subject of a claim or as to which any question may arise on a claim.

(3) The fact that a particular kind of interim remedy is not listed in paragraph (1) does not affect any power that the court may have to grant that remedy.

(4) The court may grant an interim remedy whether or not there has been a claim for a final remedy of that kind.

25.2 Time When an Order for an Interim Remedy May Be Made

r.25.2 **66.51**	r.25.2(2)(b) **32.5, 37.13**
r.25.2(1) **37.3**	r.25.2(2)(c) **34.2, 37.9, 65.2**
r.25.2(1)(b) **32.6**	r.25.2(3) **32.5, 37.7, 41.6, 53.8**
r.25.2(2) **32.4, 37.3, 37.9**	r.25.2(4) **32.5, 41.6**

(1) An order for an interim remedy may be made at any time, including—

(a) before proceedings are started; and

(b) after judgment has been given.

(Rule 7.2 provides that proceedings are started when the court issues a claim form)

(2) However—

(a) paragraph (1) is subject to any rule, practice direction or other enactment which provides otherwise;

(b) the court may grant an interim remedy before a claim has been made only if—

(i) the matter is urgent; or

(ii) it is otherwise desirable to do so in the interests of justice; and

(c) unless the court otherwise orders, a defendant may not apply for any of the orders listed in rule 25.1(1) before he has filed either an acknowledgment of service or a defence.

(Part 10 provides for filing an acknowledgment of service and Part 15 for filing a defence)

(3) Where it grants an interim remedy before a claim has been commenced, the court should give directions requiring a claim to be commenced.

(4) In particular, the court need not direct that a claim be commenced where the application is made under section 33 of the Supreme Court Act 1981 or section 52 of the County Courts Act 1984 (order for disclosure, inspection etc. before commencement of a claim).

25.3 How to Apply for an Interim Remedy

r.25.3(1) **37.5, 74.39**
r.25.3(2) **32.1, 32.11, 32.13, 33.7, 34.8, 37.5, 37.13, 40.3, 41.4, 46.30**
r.25.3(3) **32.8, 37.13**

(1) The court may grant an interim remedy on an application made without notice if it appears to the court that there are good reasons for not giving notice.
(2) An application for an interim remedy must be supported by evidence, unless the court orders otherwise.
(3) If the applicant makes an application without giving notice, the evidence in support of the application must state the reasons why notice has not been given.
(Part 3 lists general powers of the court)
(Part 23 contains general rules about making an application)

25.4 Application for an Interim Remedy Where There Is No Related Claim

(1) This rule applies where a party wishes to apply for an interim remedy but—
  (a) the remedy is sought in relation to proceedings which are taking place, or will take place, outside the jurisdiction; or
  (b) the application is made under section 33 of the Supreme Court Act 1981or section 52 of the County Courts Act 1984 (order for disclosure, inspection etc. before commencement) before a claim has been commenced.
(2) An application under this rule must be made in accordance with the general rules about applications contained in Part 23.
(The following provisions are also relevant—
- Rule 25.5 (inspection of property before commencement or against a non-party)
- Rule 31.16 (orders for disclosure of documents before proceedings start)
- Rule 31.17 (orders for disclosure of documents against a person not a party))

25.5 Inspection of Property before Commencement or against a Non-party

r.25.5(2)–(3) **41.6, 41.8**

(1) This rule applies where a person makes an application under—
  (a) section 33(1) of the Supreme Court Act 1981 or section 52(1) of the County Courts Act 1984 (inspection etc. of property before commencement);
  (b) section 34(3) of the Supreme Court Act 1981 or section 53(3) of the County Courts Act 1984 (inspection etc. of property against a non-party).
(2) The evidence in support of such an application must show, if practicable by reference to any statement of case prepared in relation to the proceedings or anticipated proceedings, that the property—
  (a) is or may become the subject matter of such proceedings; or
  (b) is relevant to the issues that will arise in relation to such proceedings.
(3) A copy of the application notice and a copy of the evidence in support must be served on—
  (a) the person against whom the order is sought; and
  (b) in relation to an application under section 34(3) of the Supreme Court Act 1981 or section 53(3) of the County Courts Act 1984, every party to the proceedings other than the applicant.

25.6 Interim Payments — General Procedure

r.25.6 **59.56**
r.25.6(1) **32.6, 36.4, 36.5**
r.25.6(2) **36.5, 36.17**
r.25.6(3)–(5) **36.6**
r.25.6(7) **36.15**

(1) The claimant may not apply for an order for an interim payment before the end of the period for filing an acknowledgment of service applicable to the defendant against whom the application is made.
(Rule 10.3 sets out the period for filing an acknowledgment of service)
(Rule 25.1(1)(k) defines an interim payment)
(2) The claimant may make more than one application for an order for an interim payment.

(3) A copy of an application notice for an order for an interim payment must—
(a) be served at least 14 days before the hearing of the application; and
(b) be supported by evidence.

(4) If the respondent to an application for an order for an interim payment wishes to rely on written evidence at the hearing, he must—
(a) file the written evidence; and
(b) serve copies on every other party to the application,
at least 7 days before the hearing of the application.

(5) If the applicant wishes to rely on written evidence in reply, he must—
(a) file the written evidence; and
(b) serve a copy on the respondent,
at least 3 days before the hearing of the application.

(6) This rule does not require written evidence—
(a) to be filed if it has already been filed; or
(b) to be served on a party on whom it has already been served.

(7) The court may order an interim payment in one sum or in instalments.

(Part 23 contains general rules about applications)

25.7 Interim Payments — Conditions to Be Satisfied and Matters to Be Taken into Account

r.25.7 **36.7, 36.8, 59.56**
r.25.7(1) **36.7**
r.25.7(1)(a)–(b) **36.7**
r.25.7(1)(c) **36.7, 36.9, 36.10, 36.11, 36.12, 36.15**
r.25.7(1)(d) **36.7, 36.9**
r.25.7(2) **36.8**
r.25.7(2)(a)–(c) **36.8**
r.25.7(3) **36.11**
r.25.7(4) **36.15**
r.25.7(5) **36.12, 36.15**

(1) The court may only make an order for an interim payment where any of the following conditions are satisfied—
(a) the defendant against whom the order is sought has admitted liability to pay damages or some other sum of money to the claimant;
(b) the claimant has obtained judgment against that defendant for damages to be assessed or for a sum of money (other than costs) to be assessed;
(c) it is satisfied that, if the claim went to trial, the claimant would obtain judgment for a substantial amount of money (other than costs) against the defendant from whom he is seeking an order for an interim payment whether or not that defendant is the only defendant or one of a number of defendants to the claim;
(d) the following conditions are satisfied—
(i) the claimant is seeking an order for possession of land (whether or not any other order is also sought); and
(ii) the court is satisfied that, if the case went to trial, the defendant would be held liable (even if the claim for possession fails) to pay the claimant a sum of money for the defendant's occupation and use of the land while the claim for possession was pending; or
(e) in a claim in which there are two or more defendants and the order is sought against any one or more of those defendants, the following conditions are satisfied—
(i) the court is satisfied that, if the claim went to trial, the claimant would obtain judgment for a substantial amount of money (other than costs) against at least one of the defendants (but the court cannot determine which); and
(ii) all the defendants are either—
(a) a defendant that is insured in respect of the claim;
(b) a defendant whose liability will be met by an insurer under section 151 of the Road Traffic Act 1988 or an insurer acting under the Motor Insurers Bureau Agreement, or the Motor Insurers Bureau where it is acting itself; or
(c) a defendant that is a public body.

(2) [*revoked*]

(3) [*revoked*]

(4) The court must not order an interim payment of more than a reasonable proportion of the likely amount of the final judgment.
(5) The court must take into account—
 (a) contributory negligence; and
 (b) any relevant set-off or counterclaim.

25.8 Powers of Court Where It Has Made an Order for Interim Payment

r.25.8 **36.19, 59.56** r.25.8(2) **61.19**

(1) Where a defendant has been ordered to make an interim payment, or has in fact made an interim payment (whether voluntarily or under an order), the court may make an order to adjust the interim payment.
(2) The court may in particular—
 (a) order all or part of the interim payment to be repaid;
 (b) vary or discharge the order for the interim payment;
 (c) order a defendant to reimburse, either wholly or partly, another defendant who has made an interim payment.
(3) The court may make an order under paragraph (2)(c) only if—
 (a) the defendant to be reimbursed made the interim payment in relation to a claim in respect of which he has made a claim against the other defendant for a contribution(GL), indemnity(GL) or other remedy; and
 (b) where the claim or part to which the interim payment relates has not been discontinued or disposed of, the circumstances are such that the court could make an order for interim payment under rule 25.7.
(4) The court may make an order under this rule without an application by any party if it makes the order when it disposes of the claim or any part of it.
(5) Where—
 (a) a defendant has made an interim payment; and
 (b) the amount of the payment is more than his total liability under the final judgment or order,
 the court may award him interest on the overpaid amount from the date when he made the interim payment.

25.9 Restriction on Disclosure of an Interim Payment

r.25.9 **36.18, 59.56**

The fact that a defendant has made an interim payment, whether voluntarily or by court order, shall not be disclosed to the trial judge until all questions of liability and the amount of money to be awarded have been decided unless the defendant agrees.

25.10 Interim Injunction to Cease If Claim Is Stayed

r.25.10 **37.60**

If—
(a) the court has granted an interim injunction(GL) other than a freezing injunction; and
(b) the claim is stayed(GL) other than by agreement between the parties,
the interim injunction(GL) shall be set aside(GL) unless the court orders that it should continue to have effect even though the claim is stayed.

25.11 Interim Injunction to Cease after 14 Days If Claim Struck Out

r.25.11 **37.60, 42.12**

(1) If—
 (a) the court has granted an interim injunction(GL); and
 (b) the claim is struck out under rule 3.7 (sanction for non-payment of certain fees),
 the interim injunction shall cease to have effect 14 days after the date that the claim is struck out unless paragraph (2) applies.
(2) If the claimant applies to reinstate the claim before the interim injunction ceases to have effect under paragraph (1), the injunction shall continue until the hearing of the application unless the court orders otherwise.

II SECURITY FOR COSTS

25.12 Security for Costs

r.25.12 **65.2, 65.3, 65.28** r.25.12(2) **65.2**

(1) A defendant to any claim may apply under this Section of this Part for security for his costs of the proceedings.

(Part 3 provides for the court to order payment of sums into court in other circumstances. Rule 20.3 provides for this Section of this Part to apply to Part 20 claims)

(2) An application for security for costs must be supported by written evidence.

(3) Where the court makes an order for security for costs, it will—
 (a) determine the amount of security; and
 (b) direct—
  (i) the manner in which; and
  (ii) the time within which
 the security must be given.

25.13 Conditions to Be Satisfied

r.25.13 **59.21, 65.2, 65.3, 65.28** r.25.13(2)(c) **65.6, 65.10**
r.25.13(1)(a) **65.16** r.25.13(2)(d) **65.14, 65.15**
r.25.13(2) **65.6, 65.8** r.25.13(2)(f) **65.13**
r.25.13(2)(a) **65.11, 65.14, 65.21, 65.22** r.25.13(2)(g) **65.15**
r.25.13(2)(a)(i)–(ii) **65.22**

(1) The court may make an order for security for costs under rule 25.12 if—
 (a) it is satisfied, having regard to all the circumstances of the case, that it is just to make such an order; and
 (b) (i) one or more of the conditions in paragraph (2) applies, or
  (ii) an enactment permits the court to require security for costs.

(2) The conditions are—
 (a) The claimant is—
  (i) resident out of the jurisdiction; but
  (ii) not resident in a Brussels Contracting State, a Lugano Contracting State or a Regulation State, as defined in section 1(3) of the Civil Jurisdiction and Judgments Act 1982;
 [*(b) revoked*]
 (c) the claimant is a company or other body (whether incorporated inside or outside Great Britain) and there is reason to believe that it will be unable to pay the defendant's costs if ordered to do so;
 (d) the claimant has changed his address since the claim was commenced with a view to evading the consequences of the litigation;
 (e) the claimant failed to give his address in the claim form, or gave an incorrect address in that form;
 (f) the claimant is acting as a nominal claimant, other than as a representative claimant under Part 19, and there is reason to believe that he will be unable to pay the defendant's costs if ordered to do so;
 (g) the claimant has taken steps in relation to his assets that would make it difficult to enforce an order for costs against him.

(Rule 3.4 allows the court to strike out a statement of case and Part 24 for it to give summary judgment)

25.14 Security for Costs Other than from the Claimant

r.25.14 **65.2, 65.3, 65.4, 65.13** r.25.14(1)(a) **65.16**

(1) The defendant may seek an order against someone other than the claimant, and the court may make an order for security for costs against that person if—
 (a) it is satisfied, having regard to all the circumstances of the case, that it is just to make such an order; and
 (b) one or more of the conditions in paragraph (2) applies.

(2) The conditions are that the person—
  (a) has assigned the right to the claim to the claimant with a view to avoiding the possibility of a costs order being made against him; or
  (b) has contributed or agreed to contribute to the claimant's costs in return for a share of any money or property which the claimant may recover in the proceedings; and

is a person against whom a costs order may be made.
(Rule 48.2 makes provision for costs orders against non-parties)

25.15 Security for Costs of an Appeal

r.25.15 **65.1, 65.2, 65.3, 65.4, 65.28**

(1) The court may order security for costs of an appeal against—
  (a) an appellant;
  (b) a respondent who also appeals,

on the same grounds as it may order security for costs against a claimant under this Part.
(2) The court may also make an order under paragraph (1) where the appellant, or the respondent who also appeals, is a limited company and there is reason to believe it will be unable to pay the costs of the other parties to the appeal should its appeal be unsuccessful.

PD 25 Practice Direction — Interim Injunctions

This practice direction supplements CPR Part 25

PD25 **32.13**, **38.3**, **38.10**, **38.25**, **38.28**, **38.29**, **61.7** [For commentary on a specific paragraph, please refer to the cross-references after the title of the paragraph.]

Jurisdiction

para.1.1–1.2 **37.2**
para.1.3 **32.3, 37.2**
para.1.4 **37.2**

1.1 High Court judges and any other judge duly authorised may grant 'search orders'[1] and 'freezing injunctions'.[2]

1.2 In a case in the High Court, masters and district judges have the power to grant injunctions:
(1) by consent,
(2) in connection with charging orders and appointments of receivers,
(3) in aid of execution of judgments.

1.3 In any other case any judge who has jurisdiction to conduct the trial of the action has the power to grant an injunction in that action.

1.4 A master or district judge has the power to vary or discharge an injunction granted by any judge with the consent of all the parties.

Making an Application

para.2.1 **37.5**
para.2.3 **37.10**
para.2.4 **37.5, 38.29**

2.1 The application notice must state:
(1) the order sought, and
(2) the date, time and place of the hearing.

2.2 The application notice and evidence in support must be served as soon as practicable after issue and in any event not less than three days before the court is due to hear the application.[3]

2.3 Where the court is to serve, sufficient copies of the application notice and evidence in support for the court and for each respondent should be filed for issue and service.

2.4 Whenever possible a draft of the order sought should be filed with the application notice and a disk containing the draft should also be available to the court in a format compatible with the word processing software used by the court. This will enable the court officer to arrange for any amendments to be incorporated and for the speedy preparation and sealing of the order.

Evidence

para.3.1 **38.3, 39.3**
para. 3.2 **37.13**
para. 3.3 **37.13, 37.61**
para. 3.4 **37.13**

3.1 Applications for search orders and freezing injunctions must be supported by affidavit evidence.

3.2 Applications for other interim injunctions must be supported by evidence set out in either:
(1) a witness statement, or
(2) a statement of case provided that it is verified by a statement of truth,[4] or
(3) the application provided that it is verified by a statement of truth,
unless the court, an Act, a rule or a practice direction requires evidence by affidavit.

3.3 The evidence must set out the facts on which the applicant relies for the claim being made against the respondent, including all material facts of which the court should be made aware.

3.4 Where an application is made without notice to the respondent, the evidence must also set out why notice was not given.
(See Part 32 and PD 32 for information about evidence.)

---

[1] Rule 25.2(3).
[2] Rule 25.1(1)(f).
[3] Rule 23.7(1) and (2) and see rule 23.7(4) (short service).
[4] See Part 22.

Urgent Applications and Applications without Notice

para.4.2 **37.6**
para. 4.3(1) **37.11, 38.3**
para.4.3(2)–(3) **37.11**
para.4.4(2) **37.8**
para.4.4(3) **37.52**
para.4.5(1) **37.6**
para.4.5(5) **37.6**

4.1 These fall into two categories:
(1) applications where a claim form has already been issued, and
(2) applications where a claim form has not yet been issued,
and, in both cases, where notice of the application has not been given to the respondent.

4.2 These applications are normally dealt with at a court hearing but cases of extreme urgency may be dealt with by telephone.

4.3 Applications dealt with at a court hearing after issue of a claim form:
(1) the application notice, evidence in support and a draft order (as in para. 2.4 above) should be filed with the court two hours before the hearing wherever possible,
(2) if an application is made before the application notice has been issued, a draft order (as in para. 2.4 above) should be provided at the hearing, and the application notice and evidence in support must be filed with the court on the same or next working day or as ordered by the court, and
(3) except in cases where secrecy is essential, the applicant should take steps to notify the respondent informally of the application.

4.4 Applications made before the issue of a claim form:
(1) in addition to the provisions set out at para. 4.3 above, unless the court orders otherwise, either the applicant must undertake to the court to issue a claim form immediately or the court will give directions for the commencement of the claim,[5]
(2) where possible the claim form should be served with the order for the injunction,
(3) an order made before the issue of a claim form should state in the title after the names of the applicant and respondent 'the Claimant and Defendant in an Intended Action'.

4.5 Applications made by telephone:
(1) where it is not possible to arrange a hearing, application can be made between 10.00 a.m. and 5.00 p.m. weekdays by telephoning the Royal Courts of Justice on (020) 7947 6000 and asking to be put in contact with a High Court judge of the appropriate Division available to deal with an emergency application in a High Court matter. The appropriate district registry may also be contacted by telephone. In county court proceedings, the appropriate county court should be contacted,
(2) where an application is made outside those hours the applicant should either:
(a) telephone the Royal Courts of Justice on (020)79476000 where he will be put in contact with the clerk to the appropriate duty judge in the High Court (or the appropriate area circuit judge where known), or
(b) the Urgent Court Business Officer of the appropriate circuit who will contact the local duty judge,
(3) where the facility is available it is likely that the judge will require a draft order to be faxed to him,
(4) the application notice and evidence in support must be filed with the court on the same or next working day or as ordered, together with two copies of the order for sealing,
(5) injunctions will be heard by telephone only where the applicant is acting by counsel or solicitors.

Orders for Injunctions

para.5.1 **40.5, 41.1**
para.5.1(1) **37.53, 74.39**
para.5.1(2)–(3) **37.7**
para.5.1(4) **37.5**
para.5.1(5) **37.7**
para.5.2–5.3 **37.54, 40.5, 41.1**

5.1 Any order for an injunction, unless the court orders otherwise, must contain:
(1) an undertaking by the applicant to the court to pay any damages which the respondent(s) (or any other party served with or notified of the order) sustain which the court considers the applicant should pay,

[5] Rule 25.2(3).

(2) if made without notice to any other party, an undertaking by the applicant to the court to serve on the respondent the application notice, evidence in support and any order made as soon as practicable,
(3) if made without notice to any other party, a return date for a further hearing at which the other party can be present,
(4) if made before filing the application notice, an undertaking to file and pay the appropriate fee on the same or next working day, and
(5) if made before issue of a claim form:
(a) an undertaking to issue and pay the appropriate fee on the same or next working day, or
(b) directions for the commencement of the claim.

5.2 An order for an injunction made in the presence of all parties to be bound by it or made at a hearing of which they have had notice, may state that it is effective until trial or further order.

5.3 Any order for an injunction must set out clearly what the respondent must do or not do.

Freezing Injunctions

Orders to restrain disposal of assets worldwide and within England and Wales

6.1 An example of a freezing injunction is annexed to this practice direction.

6.2 This example may be modified as appropriate in any particular case. In particular, the court may if it considers it appropriate, require the applicant's solicitors, as well as the applicant, to give undertakings.

Search Orders

para.7.1 **40.5, 41.1**	para.7.5 **40.5, 41.1**
para.7.2 **39.5, 40.5, 41.1**	para.7.5(2)–(10) **39.13**
para.7.3 **39.4, 40.5, 41.1**	para.7.5(11)–(13) **39.14**
para. 7.3(2) **39.9**	paras.7.6–7.7 **39.5, 40.5, 41.1**
para.7.4 **40.5, 41.1**	para.7.8 **39.12, 40.5, 41.1**
para.7.4(1)–(2) **39.11**	para.7.9 **39.10, 39.16, 40.5, 41.1**
para.7.4(4) **39.11**	para.7.10 **40.5, 41.1**
para.7.4(5)–(6) **39.11**	para.7.11 **39.10, 40.5, 41.1**

7.1 The following provisions apply to search orders in addition to those listed above.

The Supervising Solicitor

7.2 The Supervising Solicitor must be experienced in the operation of search orders. A Supervising Solicitor may be contacted either through the Law Society or, for the London area, through the London Solicitors Litigation Association.

7.3 Evidence:
(1) the affidavit must state the name, firm and its address, and experience of the Supervising Solicitor, also the address of the premises and whether it is a private or business address, and
(2) the affidavit must disclose very fully the reason the order is sought, including the probability that relevant material would disappear if the order were not made.

7.4 Service:
(1) the order must be served personally by the Supervising Solicitor, unless the court otherwise orders, and must be accompanied by the evidence in support and any documents capable of being copied,
(2) confidential exhibits need not be served but they must be made available for inspection by the respondent in the presence of the applicant's solicitors while the order is carried out and afterwards be retained by the respondent's solicitors on their undertaking not to permit the respondent:
(a) to see them or copies of them except in their presence, and
(b) to make or take away any note or record of them,
(3) the Supervising Solicitor may be accompanied only by the persons mentioned in the order,
(4) the Supervising Solicitor must explain the terms and effect of the order to the respondent in everyday language and advise him:
(a) of his right to take legal advice and to apply to vary or discharge the order; and
(b) that he may be entitled to avail himself of:
(i) legal professional privilege; and
(ii) the privilege against self-incrimination,

(5) where the Supervising Solicitor is a man and the respondent is likely to be an unaccompanied woman, at least one other person named in the order must be a woman and must accompany the Supervising Solicitor, and
(6) the order may only be served between 9.30 a.m. and 5.30 p.m. Monday to Friday unless the court otherwise orders.

7.5 Search and custody of materials:
(1) no material shall be removed unless clearly covered by the terms of the order,
(2) the premises must not be searched and no items shall be removed from them except in the presence of the respondent or a person who appears to be a responsible employee of the respondent,
(3) where copies of documents are sought, the documents should be retained for no more than two days before return to the owner,
(4) where material in dispute is removed pending trial, the applicant's solicitors should place it in the custody of the respondent's solicitors on their undertaking to retain it in safe-keeping and to produce it to the court when required,
(5) in appropriate cases the applicant should insure the material retained in the respondent's solicitors' custody,
(6) the Supervising Solicitor must make a list of all material removed from the premises and supply a copy of the list to the respondent,
(7) no material shall be removed from the premises until the respondent has had reasonable time to check the list,
(8) if any of the listed items exists only in computer-readable form, the respondent must immediately give the applicant's solicitors effective access to the computers, with all necessary passwords, to enable them to be searched, and cause the listed items to be printed out,
(9) the applicant must take all reasonable steps to ensure that no damage is done to any computer or data,
(10) the applicant and his representatives may not themselves search the respondent's computers unless they have sufficient expertise to do so without damaging the respondent's system,
(11) the Supervising Solicitor shall provide a report on the carrying out of the order to the applicant's solicitors,
(12) as soon as the report is received the applicant's solicitors shall:
(a) serve a copy of it on the respondent, and
(b) file a copy of it with the court, and
(13) where the Supervising Solicitor is satisfied that full compliance with para. 7.5(7) and (8) above is impracticable, he may permit the search to proceed and items to be removed without compliance with the impracticable requirements.

7.6 General:
The Supervising Solicitor must not be an employee or member of the applicant's firm of solicitors.

7.7 If the court orders that the order need not be served by the Supervising Solicitor, the reason for so ordering must be set out in the order.

7.8 The search order must not be carried out at the same time as a police search warrant.

7.9 There is no privilege against self incrimination in:
(1) intellectual property cases in respect of a 'related offence' or for the recovery of a 'related penalty' as defined in the Supreme Court Act 1981, s. 72;
(2) proceedings for the recovery or administration of any property, for the execution of any trust or for an account of any property or dealings with property in relation to offences under the Theft Act 1968 (see the Theft Act 1968, s. 31); or
(3) proceedings in which a court is hearing an application for an order under part IV or part V of the Children Act 1989 (see the Children Act 1989, s. 98).

However, the privilege may still be claimed in relation to material or information required to be disclosed by an order, as regards potential criminal proceedings outside those statutory provisions.

7.10 Applications in intellectual property cases should be made in the Chancery Division.

7.11 An example of a search order is annexed to this practice direction. This example may be modified as appropriate in any particular case.

Delivery-up Orders

para.8.2 **40.5, 41.1**

8.1 The following provisions apply to orders, other than search orders, for delivery up or preservation of evidence or property where it is likely that such an order will be executed at the premises of the respondent or a third party.

8.2 In such cases the court shall consider whether to include in the order for the benefit or protection of the parties similar provisions to those specified above in relation to injunctions and search orders.

Injunctions against third parties

para.9.2 **37.55, 38.3, 39.6**

9.1 The following provisions apply to orders which will affect a person other than the applicant or respondent, who:

(1) did not attend the hearing at which the order was made; and

(2) is served with the order.

9.2 Where such a person served with the order requests:

(1) a copy of any materials read by the judge, including material prepared after the hearing at the direction of the judge or in compliance with the order; or

(2) a note of the hearing,

the applicant, or his legal representative, must comply promptly with the request, unless the court orders otherwise.

ANNEX

annex **1.9, 37.52, 38.3, 97.44**

Freezing injunction

IN THE HIGH COURT OF JUSTICE
[ ] DIVISION

Before The Honourable Mr Justice [ ]

Claim No.
Dated

Applicant

Seal

Respondent

Name, address and reference of Respondent

PENAL NOTICE

IF YOU [ ][6] DISOBEY THIS ORDER YOU MAY BE HELD TO BE IN CONTEMPT OF COURT AND MAY BE IMPRISONED, FINED OR HAVE YOUR ASSETS SEIZED

ANY OTHER PERSON WHO KNOWS OF THIS ORDER AND DOES ANYTHING WHICH HELPS OR PERMITS THE RESPONDENT TO BREACH THE TERMS OF THIS ORDER MAY ALSO BE HELD TO BE IN CONTEMPT OF COURT AND MAY BE IMPRISONED, FINED OR HAVE THEIR ASSETS SEIZED.

THIS ORDER

1. This is a Freezing Injunction made against [ ] ('the Respondent') on [ ] by Mr Justice [ ] on the application of [ ] ('the Applicant'). The Judge read the Affidavits listed in Schedule A and accepted the undertakings set out in Schedule B at the end of this Order.
2. This order was made at a hearing without notice to the Respondent. The Respondent has a right to apply to the court to vary or discharge the order — see paragraph 13 below.
3. There will be a further hearing in respect of this order on [ ] ('the return date').
4. If there is more than one Respondent:

[6] Insert name of Respondent.

(a) unless otherwise stated, references in this order to 'the Respondent' mean both or all of them; and
(b) this order is effective against any Respondent on whom it is served or who is given notice of it.

FREEZING INJUNCTION

[For injunction limited to assets in England and Wales]

5. Until the return date or further order of the court, the Respondent must not remove from England and Wales or in any way dispose of, deal with or diminish the value of any of his assets which are in England and Wales up to the value of £ .

[For worldwide injunction]

5. Until the return date or further order of the court, the Respondent must not:
(1) remove from England and Wales any of his assets which are in England and Wales up to the value of £ ; or
(2) in any way dispose of, deal with or diminish the value of any of his assets whether they are in or outside England and Wales up to the same value.

[For either form of injunction]

6. Paragraph 5 applies to all the Respondent's assets whether or not they are in his own name and whether they are solely or jointly owned. For the purpose of this order the Respondent's assets include any asset which he has the power, directly or indirectly, to dispose of or deal with as if it were his own. The Respondent is to be regarded as having such power if a third party holds or controls the asset in accordance with his direct or indirect instructions.
7. This prohibition includes the following assets in particular:
(a) the property known as [title/address] or the net sale money after payment of any mortgages if it has been sold;
(b) the property and assets of the Respondent's business [known as [name]] [carried on at [address]] or the sale money if any of them have been sold; and
(c) any money standing to the credit of any bank account including the amount of any cheque drawn on such account which has not been cleared.

[For injunction limited to assets in England and Wales]

8. If the total value free of charges or other securities ('unencumbered value') of the Respondent's assets in England and Wales exceeds £ , the Respondent may remove any of those assets from England and Wales or may dispose of or deal with them so long as the total unencumbered value of his assets still in England and Wales remains above £ .

[For worldwide injunction]

8. (1) If the total value free of charges or other securities ('unencumbered value') of the Respondent's assets in England and Wales exceeds £ , the Respondent may remove any of those assets from England and Wales or may dispose of or deal with them so long as the total unencumbered value of the Respondent's assets still in England and Wales remains above £ .
(2) If the total unencumbered value of the Respondent's assets in England and Wales does not exceed £ , the Respondent must not remove any of those assets from England and Wales and must not dispose of or deal with any of them. If the Respondent has other assets outside England and Wales, he may dispose of or deal with those assets outside England and Wales so long as the total unencumbered value of all his assets whether in or outside England and Wales remains above £ .

PROVISION OF INFORMATION

9. (1) Unless paragraph (2) applies, the Respondent must [immediately] [within hours of service of this order] and to the best of his ability inform the Applicant's solicitors of all his assets [in England and Wales] [worldwide] [exceeding £ in value] whether in his own name or not and whether solely or jointly owned, giving the value, location and details of all such assets.
(2) If the provision of any of this information is likely to incriminate the Respondent, he may be entitled to refuse to provide it, but is recommended to take legal advice before refusing to provide the information. Wrongful refusal to provide the information is contempt

of court and may render the Respondent liable to be imprisoned, fined or have his assets seized.

10. Within [ ] working days after being served with this order, the Respondent must swear and serve on the Applicant's solicitors an affidavit setting out the above information.

EXCEPTIONS TO THIS ORDER

11. (1) This order does not prohibit the Respondent from spending £ a week towards his ordinary living expenses and also £ [or a reasonable sum] on legal advice and representation. [But before spending any money the Respondent must tell the Applicant's legal representatives where the money is to come from.]

[(2) This order does not prohibit the Respondent from dealing with or disposing of any of his assets in the ordinary and proper course of business.]

(3) The Respondent may agree with the Applicant's legal representatives that the above spending limits should be increased or that this order should be varied in any other respect, but any agreement must be in writing.

(4) The order will cease to have effect if the Respondent:

(a) provides security by paying the sum of £ into court, to be held to the order of the court; or

(b) makes provision for security in that sum by another method agreed with the Applicant's legal representatives.

COSTS

12. The costs of this application are reserved to the judge hearing the application on the return date.

VARIATION OR DISCHARGE OF THIS ORDER

13. Anyone served with or notified of this order may apply to the court at any time to vary or discharge this order (or so much of it as affects that person), but they must first inform the Applicant's solicitors. If any evidence is to be relied upon in support of the application, the substance of it must be communicated in writing to the Applicant's solicitors in advance.

INTERPRETATION OF THIS ORDER

14. A Respondent who is an individual who is ordered not to do something must not do it himself or in any other way. He must not do it through others acting on his behalf or on his instructions or with his encouragement.

15. A Respondent which is not an individual which is ordered not to do something must not do it itself or by its directors, officers, partners, employees or agents or in any other way.

PARTIES OTHER THAN THE APPLICANT AND RESPONDENT EFFECT OF THIS ORDER

16. It is a contempt of court for any person notified of this order knowingly to assist in or permit a breach of this order. Any person doing so may be imprisoned, fined or have their assets seized.

SET-OFF BY BANKS

17. This injunction does not prevent any bank from exercising any right of set-off it may have in respect of any facility which it gave to the respondent before it was notified of this order.

WITHDRAWALS BY THE RESPONDENT

18. No bank need enquire as to the application or proposed application of any money withdrawn by the Respondent if the withdrawal appears to be permitted by this order.

[For worldwide injunction]

PERSONS OUTSIDE ENGLAND AND WALES

19. (1) Except as provided in paragraph (2) below, the terms of this order do not affect or concern anyone outside the jurisdiction of this court.

(2) The terms of this order will affect the following persons in a country or State outside the jurisdiction of this court:

(a) the Respondent or his officer or agent appointed by power of attorney;

(b) any person who:

(i) is subject to the jurisdiction of this court;
(ii) has been given written notice of this order at his residence or place of business within the jurisdiction of this court; and
(iii) is able to prevent acts or omissions outside the jurisdiction of this court which constitute or assist in a breach of the terms of this order; and
(c) any other person, only to the extent that this order is declared enforceable by or is enforced by a court in that country or State.

[For worldwide injunction]

ASSETS LOCATED OUTSIDE ENGLAND AND WALES

20. Nothing in this order shall, in respect of assets located outside England and Wales, prevent any third party from complying with:
(1) what it reasonably believes to be its obligations, contractual or otherwise, under the laws and obligations of the country or State in which those assets are situated or under the proper law of any contract between itself and the Respondent; and
(2) any orders of the courts of that country or State, provided that reasonable notice of any application for such an order is given to the Applicant's solicitors.

COMMUNICATIONS WITH THE COURT

All communications to the court about this order should be sent to:

[Insert the address and telephone number of the appropriate court office]

If the order is made at the Royal Courts of Justice, communications should be addressed as follows:

Where the order is made in the Chancery Division:
Room TM 505, Royal Courts of Justice, Strand, London WC2A 2LL quoting the case number. The telephone number is (020) 7947 6754.

Where the order is made in the Queen's Bench Division:
Room WG034, Royal Courts of Justice, Strand, London WC2A 2LL quoting the case number. The telephone number is (020) 7947 6009.

Where the order is made in the Commercial Court
Room E201, Royal Courts of Justice, Strand, London WC2A 2LL quoting the case number. The telephone number is (020) 7947 6826.

The offices are open between 10 a.m. and 4.30 p.m. Monday to Friday.

SCHEDULE A AFFIDAVITS

The Applicant relied on the following affidavits:
[name] [number of affidavit] [date sworn]
[filed on behalf of]
(1)
(2)

SCHEDULE B UNDERTAKINGS GIVEN TO THE COURT BY THE APPLICANT

(1) If the court later finds that this order has caused loss to the Respondent, and decides that the Respondent should be compensated for that loss, the Applicant will comply with any order the court may make.
[(2) The Applicant will:
(a) on or before [date] cause a written guarantee in the sum of £ to be issued from a bank with a place of business within England or Wales, in respect of any order the court may make pursuant to paragraph (1) above; and
(b) immediately upon issue of the guarantee, cause a copy of it to be served on the Respondent.]
(3) As soon as practicable the Applicant will issue and serve a claim form [in the form of the draft produced to the court] [claiming the appropriate relief].
(4) The Applicant will [swear and file an affidavit] [cause an affidavit to be sworn and filed] [substantially in the terms of the draft affidavit produced to the court] [confirming the substance of what was said to the court by the Applicant's counsel/solicitors].
(5) The Applicant will serve upon the Respondent [together with this order] [as soon as practicable]:

(i) copies of the affidavits and exhibits containing the evidence relied upon by the Applicant, and any other documents provided to the court on the making of the application;
(ii) the claim form; and
(iii) an application notice for continuation of the order.

[(6) Anyone notified of this order will be given a copy of it by the Applicant's legal representatives.]

(7) The Applicant will pay the reasonable costs of anyone other than the Respondent which have been incurred as a result of this order including the costs of finding out whether that person holds any of the Respondent's assets and if the court later finds that this order has caused such person loss, and decides that such person should be compensated for that loss, the Applicant will comply with any order the court may make.

(8) If this order ceases to have effect (for example, if the Respondent provides security or the Applicant does not provide a bank guarantee as provided for above) the Applicant will immediately take all reasonable steps to inform in writing anyone to whom he has given notice of this order, or who he has reasonable grounds for supposing may act upon this order, that it has ceased to have effect.

[(9) The Applicant will not without the permission of the court use any information obtained as a result of this order for the purpose of any civil or criminal proceedings, either in England and Wales or in any other jurisdiction, other than this claim.]

[(10) The Applicant will not without the permission of the court seek to enforce this order in any country outside England and Wales [or seek an order of a similar nature including orders conferring a charge or other security against the Respondent or the Respondent's assets].]

NAME AND ADDRESS OF APPLICANT'S LEGAL REPRESENTATIVES

The Applicant's legal representatives are:

[Name, address, reference, fax and telephone numbers both in and out of office hours and email]

Search order

IN THE HIGH COURT OF JUSTICE
[ ] DIVISION

Before The Honourable Mr Justice [ ]

Claim No.
Dated

Applicant

Seal

Respondent

Name, address and reference of Respondent

PENAL NOTICE

IF YOU [ ][7] DISOBEY THIS ORDER YOU MAY BE HELD TO BE IN CONTEMPT OF COURT AND LIABLE TO IMPRISONMENT OR FINED OR HAVE OR YOUR ASSETS SEIZED

ANY OTHER PERSON WHO KNOWS OF THIS ORDER AND DOES ANYTHING WHICH HELPS OR PERMITS THE RESPONDENT TO BREACH THE TERMS OF THIS ORDER MAY ALSO BE HELD TO BE IN CONTEMPT OF COURT AND MAY BE IMPRISONED, FINED OR HAVE THEIR ASSETS SEIZED.

THIS ORDER

1. This is a Search Order made against [ ] ('the Respondent') on [ ] by Mr Justice [ ] on the application of [ ] ('the Applicant'). The Judge read the Affidavits listed in Schedule F and accepted the undertakings set out in Schedules C, D and E at the end of this order.

[7] Insert name of Respondent.

2. This order was made at a hearing without notice to the Respondent. The Respondent has a right to apply to the court to vary or discharge the order — see paragraph 27 below.
3. There will be a further hearing in respect of this order on [ ] ('the return date').
4. If there is more than one Respondent:
   (a) unless otherwise stated, references in this order to 'the Respondent' mean both or all of them; and
   (b) this order is effective against any Respondent on whom it is served or who is given notice of it.
5. This order must be complied with by:
   (a) the Respondent;
   (b) any director, officer, partner or responsible employee of the Respondent; and
   (c) if the Respondent is an individual, any other person having responsible control of the premises to be searched.

THE SEARCH

6. The Respondent must permit the following persons:[8]
   (a) [ ] ('the Supervising Solicitor');
   (b) [ ], a solicitor in the firm of [ ], the Applicant's solicitors; and
   (c) up to [ ] other persons[9] being [their identity or capacity] accompanying them,

   (together 'the search party'), to enter the premises mentioned in Schedule A to this order and any other premises of the Respondent disclosed under paragraph 18 below and any vehicles under the Respondent's control on or around the premises ('the premises') so that they can search for, inspect, photograph or photocopy, and deliver into the safe keeping of the Applicant's solicitors all the documents and articles which are listed in Schedule B to this order ('the listed items').
7. Having permitted the search party to enter the premises, the Respondent must allow the search party to remain on the premises until the search is complete. In the event that it becomes necessary for any of those persons to leave the premises before the search is complete, the Respondent must allow them to re-enter the premises immediately upon their seeking re-entry on the same or the following day in order to complete the search.

RESTRICTIONS ON SEARCH

8. This order may not be carried out at the same time as a police search warrant.
9. Before the Respondent allows anybody on to the premises to carry out this order, he is entitled to have the Supervising Solicitor explain to him what it means in everyday language.
10. The Respondent is entitled to seek legal advice and to ask the court to vary or discharge this order. Whilst doing so, he may ask the Supervising Solicitor to delay starting the search for up to 2 hours or such other longer period as the Supervising Solicitor may permit. However, the Respondent must:
    (a) comply with the terms of paragraph 27 below;
    (b) not disturb or remove any listed items; and
    (c) permit the Supervising Solicitor to enter, but not start to search.
11. (1) Before permitting entry to the premises by any person other than the Supervising Solicitor, the Respondent may, for a short time (not to exceed two hours, unless the Supervising Solicitor agrees to a longer period):
    (a) gather together any documents he believes may be incriminating or privileged; and
    (b) hand them to the Supervising Solicitor for him to assess whether they are incriminating or privileged as claimed.

    (2) If the Supervising Solicitor decides that the Respondent is entitled to withhold production of any of the documents on the ground that they are privileged or incriminating, he will exclude them from the search, record them in a list for inclusion in his report and return them to the Respondent.

    (3) If the Supervising Solicitor believes that the Respondent may be entitled to withhold production of the whole or any part of a document on the ground that it or part of it may be

[8] Where the premises are likely to be occupied by an unaccompanied woman and the Supervising Solicitor is a man, at least one of the persons accompanying him should be a woman.

[9] None of these persons should be people who could gain personally or commercially from anything they might read or see on the premises, unless their presence is essential.

privileged or incriminating, or if the Respondent claims to be entitled to withhold production on those grounds, the Supervising Solicitor will exclude it from the search and retain it in his possession pending further order of the court.

12. If the Respondent wishes to take legal advice and gather documents as permitted, he must first inform the Supervising Solicitor and keep him informed of the steps being taken.
13. No item may be removed from the premises until a list of the items to be removed has been prepared, and a copy of the list has been supplied to the Respondent, and he has been given a reasonable opportunity to check the list.
14. The premises must not be searched, and items must not be removed from them, except in the presence of the Respondent.
15. If the Supervising Solicitor is satisfied that full compliance with paragraphs 13 or 14 is not practicable, he may permit the search to proceed and items to be removed without fully complying with them.

DELIVERY UP OF ARTICLES/DOCUMENTS

16. The Respondent must immediately hand over to the Applicant's solicitors any of the listed items, which are in his possession or under his control, save for any computer or hard disk integral to any computer. Any items the subject of a dispute as to whether they are listed items must immediately be handed over to the Supervising Solicitor for safe keeping pending resolution of the dispute or further order of the court.
17. The Respondent must immediately give the search party effective access to the computers on the premises, with all necessary passwords, to enable the computers to be searched. If they contain any listed items the Respondent must cause the listed items to be displayed so that they can be read and copied.[11] The Respondent must provide the Applicant's Solicitors with copies of all listed items contained in the computers. All reasonable steps shall be taken by the Applicant and the Applicant's solicitors to ensure that no damage is done to any computer or data. The Applicant and his representatives may not themselves search the Respondent's computers unless they have sufficient expertise to do so without damaging the Respondent's system.

PROVISION OF INFORMATION

18. The Respondent must immediately inform the Applicant's Solicitors (in the presence of the Supervising Solicitor) so far as he is aware:
    (a) where all the listed items are;
    (b) the name and address of everyone who has supplied him, or offered to supply him, with listed items;
    (c) the name and address of everyone to whom he has supplied, or offered to supply, listed items; and
    (d) full details of the dates and quantities of every such supply and offer.
19. Within [ ] working days after being served with this order the Respondent must swear and serve an affidavit setting out the above information.[12]

PROHIBITED ACTS

20. Except for the purpose of obtaining legal advice, the Respondent must not directly or indirectly inform anyone of these proceedings or of the contents of this order, or warn anyone that proceedings have been or may be brought against him by the Applicant until 4.30 p.m. on the return date or further order of the court.
21. Until 4.30 p.m. on the return date the Respondent must not destroy, tamper with, cancel or part with possession, power, custody or control of the listed items otherwise than in accordance with the terms of this order.
22. [Insert any negative injunctions.]
23. [Insert any further order]

[11] If it is envisaged that the Respondent's computers are to be imaged (i.e. the hard drives are to be copied wholesale, thereby reproducing listed items and other items indiscriminately), special provision needs to be made and independent computer specialists need to be appointed, who should be required to give undertakings to the court.

[12] The period should ordinarily be longer than the period in paragraph (2) of Schedule D, if any of the information is likely to be included in listed items taken away of which the Respondent does not have copies.

COSTS

24. The costs of this application are reserved to the judge hearing the application on the return date.

RESTRICTIONS ON SERVICE

25. This order may only be served between [ ] a.m./ p.m. and [ ] a.m./ p.m. [and on a weekday].[13]

26. This order must be served by the Supervising Solicitor, and paragraph 6 of the order must be carried out in his presence and under his supervision.

VARIATION AND DISCHARGE OF THIS ORDER

27. Anyone served with or notified of this order may apply to the court at any time to vary or discharge this order (or so much of it as affects that person), but they must first inform the Applicant's solicitors. If any evidence is to be relied upon in support of the application, the substance of it must be communicated in writing to the Applicant's solicitors in advance.

INTERPRETATION OF THIS ORDER

28. Any requirement that something shall be done to or in the presence of the Respondent means:
    (a) if there is more than one Respondent, to or in the presence of any one of them; and
    (b) if a Respondent is not an individual, to or in the presence of a director, officer, partner or responsible employee.

29. A Respondent who is an individual who is ordered not to do something must not do it himself or in any other way. He must not do it through others acting on his behalf or on his instructions or with his encouragement.

30. A Respondent which is not an individual which is ordered not to do something must not do it itself or by its directors, officers, partners, employees or agents or in any other way.

COMMUNICATIONS WITH THE COURT

All communications to the court about this order should be sent to:

[Insert the address and telephone number of the appropriate court office]

If the order is made at the Royal Courts of Justice, communications should be addressed as follows:

Where the order is made in the Chancery Division:

Room TM 505, Royal Courts of Justice, Strand, London WC2A 2LL quoting the case number. The telephone number is (020) 7947 6754.

Where the order is made in the Queen's Bench Division:

Room WG034, Royal Courts of Justice, Strand, London WC2A 2LL quoting the case number. The telephone number is (020) 7947 6009.

Where the order is made in the Commercial Court:

Room E201, Royal Courts of Justice, Strand, London WC2A 2LL quoting the case number. The telephone number is (020) 7947 6826.

The offices are open between 10 a.m. and 4.30 p.m. Monday to Friday.

SCHEDULE A THE PREMISES

SCHEDULE B THE LISTED ITEMS

SCHEDULE C UNDERTAKINGS GIVEN TO THE COURT BY THE APPLICANT

(1) If the court later finds that this order or carrying it out has caused loss to the Respondent, and decides that the Respondent should be compensated for that loss, the Applicant will comply with any order the court may make. Further if the carrying out of this order has been in breach of the terms of this order or otherwise in a manner inconsistent with the Applicant's solicitors' duties as officers of the court, the Applicant will comply with any order for damages the court may make.

[(2) As soon as practicable the Applicant will issue a claim form [in the form of the draft produced to the court] [claiming the appropriate relief].]

(3) The Applicant will [swear and file an affidavit] [cause an affidavit to be sworn and filed]

[13] Normally, the order should be served in the morning (not before 9.30 a.m.) and on a weekday to enable the Respondent more readily to obtain legal advice.

[substantially in the terms of the draft affidavit produced to the court] [confirming the substance of what was said to the court by the Applicant's counsel/solicitors].

(4) The Applicant will not, without the permission of the court, use any information or documents obtained as a result of carrying out this order nor inform anyone else of these proceedings except for the purposes of these proceedings (including adding further Respondents) or commencing civil proceedings in relation to the same or related subject matter to these proceedings until after the return date.

[(5) The Applicant will maintain pending further order the sum of £ in an account controlled by the Applicant's solicitors.]

[(6) The Applicant will insure the items removed from the premises.]

SCHEDULE D UNDERTAKINGS GIVEN BY THE APPLICANT'S SOLICITORS

(1) The Applicant's solicitors will provide to the Supervising Solicitor for service on the Respondent:
   (i) a service copy of this order;
   (ii) the claim form (with defendant's response pack) or, if not issued, the draft produced to the court;
   (iii) an application for hearing on the return date;
   (iv) copies of the affidavits [or draft affidavits] and exhibits capable of being copied containing the evidence relied upon by the applicant;
   (v) a note of any allegation of fact made orally to the court where such allegation is not contained in the affidavits or draft affidavits read by the judge; and
   (vi) a copy of the skeleton argument produced to the court by the Applicant's [counsel/solicitors].

(2) The Applicant's solicitors will answer at once to the best of their ability any question whether a particular item is a listed item.

(3) Subject as provided below the Applicant's solicitors will retain in their own safe keeping all items obtained as a result of this order until the court directs otherwise.

(4) The Applicant's solicitors will return the originals of all documents obtained as a result of this order (except original documents which belong to the Applicant) as soon as possible and in any event within [2] working days of their removal.

SCHEDULE E UNDERTAKINGS GIVEN BY THE SUPERVISING SOLICITOR

(1) The Supervising Solicitor will use his best endeavours to serve this order upon the Respondent and at the same time to serve upon the Respondent the other documents required to be served and referred to in paragraph (1) of Schedule D.

(2) The Supervising Solicitor will offer to explain to the person served with the order its meaning and effect fairly and in everyday language, and to inform him of his right to take legal advice (including an explanation that the Respondent may be entitled to avail himself of the privilege against self-incrimination and legal professional privilege) and to apply to vary or discharge this order as mentioned in paragraph 27 above.

(3) The Supervising Solicitor will retain in the safe keeping of his firm all items retained by him as a result of this order until the court directs otherwise.

(4) Unless and until the court otherwise orders, or unless otherwise necessary to comply with any duty to the court pursuant to this order, the Supervising Solicitor shall not disclose to any person any information relating to those items, and shall keep the existence of such items confidential.

(4) Within [48] hours of completion of the search the Supervising Solicitor will make and provide to the Applicant's solicitors, the Respondent or his solicitors and to the judge who made this order (for the purposes of the court file) a written report on the carrying out of the order.

SCHEDULE F AFFIDAVITS

The Applicant relied on the following affidavits:
[name] [number of affidavit] [date sworn] [filed on behalf of]
(1)
(2)

NAME AND ADDRESS OF APPLICANT'S SOLICITORS

The Applicant's solicitors are:
[Name, address, reference, fax and telephone numbers both in and out of office hours.]

PD 25B Practice Direction — Interim Payments

This practice direction supplements CPR Part 25

PD 25B **61.19** [For commentary on a specific paragraph, please refer to the cross-references after the title of the paragraph.]

General

para.1.2 **36.2**

1.1 Rule 25.7 sets out the conditions to be satisfied and matters to be taken into account before the court will make an order for an interim payment.

1.2 The permission of the court must be obtained before making a voluntary interim payment in respect of a claim by a child or patient.

Evidence

para.2.1 **36.6** para.2.1(2) **36.15**

2.1 An application for an interim payment of damages must be supported by evidence dealing with the following:

(1) the sum of money sought by way of an interim payment,
(2) the items or matters in respect of which the interim payment is sought,
(3) the sum of money for which final judgment is likely to be given,
(4) the reasons for believing that the conditions set out in r. 25.7 are satisfied,
(5) any other relevant matters,
(6) in claims for personal injuries, details of special damages and past and future loss, and
(7) in a claim under the Fatal Accidents Act 1976, details of the person(s) on whose behalf the claim is made and the nature of the claim.

2.2 Any documents in support of the application should be exhibited, including, in personal injuries claims, the medical report(s).

2.3 If a respondent to an application for an interim payment wishes to rely on written evidence at the hearing he must comply with the provisions of r. 25.6(4).

2.4 If the applicant wishes to rely on written evidence in reply he must comply with the provisions of r. 25.6(5).

Interim Payment Where Account to Be Taken

2A.1 This section of this practice direction applies if a party seeks an interim payment under r. 25.7(b) [*sic*] where the court has ordered an account to be taken.

2A.2 If the evidence on the application for interim payment shows that the account is bound to result in a payment to the applicant the court will, before making an order for interim payment, order that the liable party pay to the applicant 'the amount shown by the account to be due'.

Instalments

para.3 **36.15**

3 Where an interim payment is to be paid in instalments the order should set out:

(1) the total amount of the payment,
(2) the amount of each instalment,
(3) the number of instalments and the date on which each is to be paid, and
(4) to whom the payment should be made.

Compensation Recovery Payments

paras.4.1–4.4 **36.15**

4.1 Where in a claim for personal injuries there is an application for an interim payment of damages:

(1) which is other than by consent,

(2) which falls under the heads of damage set out in column 1 of sch. 2 to the Social Security (Recovery of Benefits) Act 1997 in respect of recoverable benefits received by the claimant set out in column 2 of that schedule, and
(3) where the defendant is liable to pay recoverable benefits to the Secretary of State, the defendant should obtain from the Secretary of State a certificate of recoverable benefits.

4.2 A copy of the certificate should be filed at the hearing of the application for an interim payment.

4.3 The order will set out the amount by which the payment to be made to the claimant has been reduced according to the Act and the Social Security (Recovery of Benefits) Regulations 1997.

4.4 The payment made to the claimant will be the net amount but the interim payment for the purposes of para. 5 below will be the gross amount.

Adjustment of Final Judgment Figure

para.5 **36.19**

5.1 In this paragraph 'judgment' means:
(1) any order to pay a sum of money,
(2) a final award of damages,
(3) an assessment of damages.

5.2 In a final judgment where an interim payment has previously been made which is less than the total amount awarded by the judge, the order should set out in a preamble:
(1) the total amount awarded by the judge, and
(2) the amounts and dates of the interim payment(s).

5.3 The total amount awarded by the judge should then be reduced by the total amount of any interim payments, and an order made for entry of judgment and payment of the balance.

5.4 In a final judgment where an interim payment has previously been made which is more than the total amount awarded by the judge, the order should set out in a preamble:
(1) the total amount awarded by the judge, and
(2) the amounts and dates of the interim payment(s).

5.5 An order should then be made for repayment, reimbursement, variation or discharge under r. 25.8(2) and for interest on an overpayment under r. 25.8(5).

5.6 PD 40B provides further information concerning adjustment of the final judgment sum.

CPR Part 26 Case Management — Preliminary Stage

Part 26 **28.3, 97.41** [For commentary on a specific rule, please refer to the cross-references after the title of the rule.]

26.1 Scope of This Part

(1) This Part provides for—
  (a) the automatic transfer of some defended cases between courts; and
  (b) the allocation of defended cases to case management tracks.
(2) There are three tracks—
  (a) the small claims track;
  (b) the fast track; and
  (c) the multi-track.

(Rule 26.6 sets out the normal scope of each track. Part 27 makes provision for the small claims track. Part 28 makes provision for the fast track. Part 29 makes provision for the multi-track)

26.2 Automatic Transfer

r.26.2 **12.10, 42.3, 96.54**

(1) This rule applies to proceedings where—
  (a) the claim is for a specified amount of money;
  (b) the claim was commenced in a court which is not the defendant's home court;
  (c) the claim has not been transferred to another defendant's home court under rule 13.4 (application to set aside[GL] or vary default judgment — procedure) or rule 14.12 (admission — determination of rate of payment by judge); and
  (d) the defendant is an individual.
(2) This rule does not apply where the claim was commenced in a specialist list[GL].
(3) Where this rule applies, the court will transfer the proceedings to the defendant's home court when a defence is filed, unless paragraph (4) applies.

(Rule 2.3 defines 'defendant's home court')

(4) Where the claimant notifies the court under rule 15.10 or rule 14.5 that he wishes the proceedings to continue, the court will transfer the proceedings to the defendant's home court when it receives that notification from the claimant.

(Rule 15.10 deals with a claimant's notice where the defence is that money claimed has been paid)

(Rule 14.5 sets out the procedure where the defendant admits part of a claim for a specified amount of money)

(5) Where—
  (a) the claim is against two or more defendants with different home courts; and
  (b) the defendant whose defence is filed first is an individual,

proceedings are to be transferred under this rule to the home court of that defendant.

(6) The time when a claim is automatically transferred under this rule may be varied by a practice direction in respect of claims issued by the Production Centre.

(Rule 7.10 makes provision for the Production Centre)

26.3 Allocation Questionnaire

r.26.3(1)–(2) **42.7** r.26.3(6A) **3.7, 42.7, 44.15, 46.1**
r.26.3(6) **27.1**

(1) When a defendant files a defence the court will serve an allocation questionnaire on each party unless—
  (a) rule 15.10 or rule 14.5 applies; or
  (b) the court dispenses with the need for a questionnaire.
(2) Where there are two or more defendants and at least one of them files a defence, the court will serve the allocation questionnaire under paragraph (1)—
  (a) when all the defendants have filed a defence; or
  (b) when the period for the filing of the last defence has expired, whichever is the sooner.
(Rule 15.4 specifies the period for filing a defence)
(3) Where proceedings are automatically transferred to the defendant's home court under rule 26.2, the court in which the proceedings have been commenced will serve an allocation questionnaire before the proceedings are transferred.
(4) Where—
  (a) rule 15.10 or 14.5 applies; and
  (b) the proceedings are not automatically transferred to the defendant's home court under rule 26.2,
  the court will serve an allocation questionnaire on each party when the claimant files a notice indicating that he wishes the proceedings to continue.
(5) The court may, on the application of the claimant, serve an allocation questionnaire earlier than it would otherwise serve it under this rule.
(6) Each party must file the completed allocation questionnaire no later than the date specified in it, which shall be at least 14 days after the date when it is deemed to be served on the party in question.
(6A) The date for filing the completed allocation questionnaire may not be varied by agreement between the parties.
(7) The time when the court serves an allocation questionnaire under this rule may be varied by a practice direction in respect of claims issued by the Production Centre.
(Rule 7.10 makes provision for the Production Centre)
(Rule 6.7 specifies when a document is deemed to be served)

26.4 Stay to Allow for Settlement of the Case

r.26.4 **54.3** r.26.4(2)–(3) **42.24, 70.20**
r.26.4(1) **70.20** r.26.4(4)–(5) **42.24**

(1) A party may, when filing the completed allocation questionnaire, make a written request for the proceedings to be stayed(GL) while the parties try to settle the case by alternative dispute resolution(GL) or other means.
(2) Where—
  (a) all parties request a stay(GL) under paragraph (1); or
  (b) the court, of its own initiative, considers that such a stay would be appropriate,
  the court will direct that the proceedings, either in whole or in part, be stayed for one month, or for such specified period as it considers appropriate.
(3) The court may extend the stay(GL) until such date or for such specified period as it considers appropriate.
(4) Where the court stays(GL) the proceedings under this rule, the claimant must tell the court if a settlement is reached.
(5) If the claimant does not tell the court by the end of the period of the stay(GL) that a settlement has been reached, the court will give such directions as to the management of the case as it considers appropriate.

26.5 Allocation

r.26.5(1) **42.6**
r.26.5(2) **42.6, 42.24**
r.26.5(3) **13.14, 42.10, 45.5, 47.8**
r.26.5(4) **13.14, 42.13**
r.26.5(5) **13.14, 42.11**

(1) The court will allocate the claim to a track—
(a) when every defendant has filed an allocation questionnaire, or
(b) when the period for filing the allocation questionnaires has expired,
whichever is the sooner, unless it has—
(i) stayed(GL) the proceedings under rule 26.4; or
(ii) dispensed with the need for allocation questionnaires.

(Rules 12.7 and 14.8 provide for the court to allocate a claim to a track where the claimant obtains default judgment on request or judgment on admission for an amount to be decided by the court)

(2) If the court has stayed(GL) the proceedings under rule 26.4, it will allocate the claim to a track at the end of the period of the stay.

(3) Before deciding the track to which to allocate proceedings or deciding whether to give directions for an allocation hearing to be fixed, the court may order a party to provide further information about his case.

(4) The court may hold an allocation hearing if it thinks it is necessary.

(5) If a party fails to file an allocation questionnaire, the court may give any direction it considers appropriate.

26.6 Scope of Each Track

r.26.6(1) **42.16**
r.26.6(1)(a)–(b) **23.6, 42.15**
r.26.6(2) **42.15, 42.16**
r.26.6(3) **42.15, 42.16**
r.26.6(4) **42.16**
r.26.6(4)(b) **2.4**
r.26.6(5) **42.16, 44.6**
r.26.6(6) **42.17**

(1) The small claims track is the normal track for—
(a) any claim for personal injuries where—
(i) the financial value of the claim is not more than £5,000; and
(ii) the financial value of any claim for damages for personal injuries is not more than £1,000;
(b) any claim which includes a claim by a tenant of residential premises against his landlord where—
(i) the tenant is seeking an order requiring the landlord to carry out repairs or other work to the premises (whether or not the tenant is also seeking some other remedy);
(ii) the cost of the repairs or other work to the premises is estimated to be not more than £1,000; and
(iii) the financial value of any other claim for damages is not more than £1,000.

(Rule 2.3 defines 'claim for personal injuries' as proceedings in which there is a claim for damages in respect of personal injuries to the claimant or any other person or in respect of a person's death)

(2) For the purposes of paragraph (1) 'damages for personal injuries' means damages claimed as compensation for pain, suffering and loss of amenity and does not include any other damages which are claimed.

(3) Subject to paragraph (1), the small claims track is the normal track for any claim which has a financial value of not more than £5,000.

(Rule 26.7(4) provides that the court will not allocate to the small claims track certain claims in respect of harassment or unlawful eviction)

(4) Subject to paragraph (5), the fast track is the normal track for any claim—
(a) for which the small claims track is not the normal track; and
(b) which has a financial value of not more than £15,000.

(5) The fast track is the normal track for the claims referred to in paragraph (4) only if the court considers that—
(a) the trial is likely to last for no longer than one day; and
(b) oral expert evidence at trial will be limited to—

(i) one expert per party in relation to any expert field; and
(ii) expert evidence in two expert fields.

(6) The multi-track is the normal track for any claim for which the small claims track or the fast track is not the normal track.

26.7 General Rule for Allocation

r.26.7(2) **42.18** r.26.7(4) **42.15**
r.26.7(3) **42.14, 42.15**

(1) In considering whether to allocate a claim to the normal track for that claim under rule 26.6, the court will have regard to the matters mentioned in rule 26.8(1).

(2) The court will allocate a claim which has no financial value to the track which it considers most suitable having regard to the matters mentioned in rule 26.8(1).

(3) The court will not allocate proceedings to a track if the financial value of the claim, assessed by the court under rule 26.8, exceeds the limit for that track unless all the parties consent to the allocation of the claim to that track.

(4) The court will not allocate a claim to the small claims track, if it includes a claim by a tenant of residential premises against his landlord for a remedy in respect of harassment or unlawful eviction.

26.8 Matters Relevant to Allocation to a Track

r.26.8 **42.14, 42.19, 42.23, 87.11** r.26.8(2) **42.14**

(1) When deciding the track for a claim, the matters to which the court shall have regard include—
(a) the financial value, if any, of the claim;
(b) the nature of the remedy sought;
(c) the likely complexity of the facts, law or evidence;
(d) the number of parties or likely parties;
(e) the value of any counterclaim or other Part 20 claim and the complexity of any matters relating to it;
(f) the amount of oral evidence which may be required;
(g) the importance of the claim to persons who are not parties to the proceedings;
(h) the views expressed by the parties; and
(i) the circumstances of the parties.

(2) It is for the court to assess the financial value of a claim and in doing so it will disregard—
(a) any amount not in dispute;
(b) any claim for interest;
(c) costs; and
(d) any contributory negligence.

(3) Where—
(a) two or more claimants have started a claim against the same defendant using the same claim form; and
(b) each claimant has a claim against the defendant separate from the other claimants,

the court will consider the claim of each claimant separately when it assesses financial value under paragraph (1).

26.9 Notice of Allocation

r.26.9 **42.21**

(1) When it has allocated a claim to a track, the court will serve notice of allocation on every party.

(2) When the court serves notice of allocation on a party, it will also serve—
(a) a copy of the allocation questionnaires filed by the other parties; and
(b) a copy of any further information provided by another party about his case (whether by order or not).

(Rule 26.5 provides that the court may, before allocating proceedings, order a party to provide further information about his case)

26.10 Reallocation

r.26.10 **42.23**

The court may subsequently reallocate a claim to a different track.

26.11 Trial with a Jury

r.26.11 **58.3**

An application for a claim to be tried with a jury must be made within 28 days of service of the defence.
(Section 69 of the Supreme Court Act 1981 and section 66 of the County Courts Act 1984 specify when a claim may be tried with a jury)

PD 26 Practice Direction — Case Management — Preliminary Stage: Allocation and Reallocation

This practice direction supplements CPR Part 26

[For commentary on a specific paragraph, please refer to the cross-references after the title of the paragraph.]

Reminders of Important Rule Provisions Other than Parts 26–29

Attention is drawn in particular to the following provisions of the Civil Procedure Rules:

Part 1 The Overriding Objective (defined in Rule 1.1).
The duty of the court to further that objective by actively managing cases (set out in Rule 1.4).
The requirement that the parties help the court to further that objective (set out in Rule 1.3).

Part 3 The court's case management powers (which may be exercised on application or on its own initiative) and the sanctions which it may impose.

Part 24 The court's power to grant summary judgment.

Parts 32– 35 Evidence, especially the court's power to control evidence.
Attention is also drawn to the practice directions which supplement those Parts and Parts 27–29, and to those which relate to the various specialist jurisdictions.

The Allocation Questionnaire

Form

2.1 (1) The allocation questionnaire referred to in Part 26 will be in form N149 or form N150.

(2) (a) Attention is drawn to Section 6 of PD 43–48, which requires an estimate of costs to be filed and served when an allocation questionnaire is filed by a party to a claim which is outside the limits of the small claims track.

(b) A party will comply with that obligation if the costs estimate he files and serves states the figures for the base costs, incurred and to be incurred, which he expects, if he is successful, to recover from the other party. The estimate should show an itemised breakdown of how it is calculated, showing separately the amounts included for profit costs, disbursements and VAT. It should be substantially in the form illustrated in precedent H in the schedule to PD 43–48.
(Paragraph 2.2 of PD 43–48 defines 'base costs'.)

(c) Any party who has entered into a funding arrangement need not reveal the amount of any additional liability.
(Rule 43.2 defines 'funding arrangement' and 'additional liability'.)

(d) No later than when he files the estimate the solicitor acting for that party must deliver a copy to his client.

Provision of extra information

para.2.2 **32.6**
para.2.2(2) **42.9, 45.4**
para.2.2(3)(a) **33.4**
para.2.2(3)(d) **41.4**

2.2 (1) This paragraph sets out what a party should do when he files his allocation questionnaire if he wishes to give the court information about matters which he believes may affect its decision about allocation or case management.

(2) The general rule is that the court will not take such information into account unless the document containing it either:

(a) confirms that all parties have agreed that the information is correct and that it should be put before the court, or

(b) confirms that the party who has sent the document to the court has delivered a copy to all the other parties.

(3) The following are examples of information which will be likely to help the court:

(a) a party's intention to apply for summary judgment or some other order that may dispose of the case or reduce the amount in dispute or the number of issues remaining to be decided,

(b) a party's intention to issue a Part 20 claim or to add another party,
(c) the steps the parties have taken in the preparation of evidence (in particular expert evidence), the steps they intend to take and whether those steps are to be taken in cooperation with any other party,
(d) the directions the party believes will be appropriate to be given for the management of the case,
(e) about any particular facts that may affect the timetable the court will set,
(f) any facts which may make it desirable for the court to fix an allocation hearing or a hearing at which case management directions will be given.

Consultation

para.2.3 **42.7**

2.3 (1) The parties should consult one another and cooperate in completing the allocation questionnaires and giving other information to the court.
(2) They should try to agree the case management directions which they will invite the court to make. Further details appear in the PD 28 and PD 29.
(3) The process of consultation must not delay the filing of the allocation questionnaires.

Hearings before allocation

para.2.4 **33.4, 33.24, 37.11, 42.7**

2.4 Where a court hearing takes place (for example on an application for an interim injunction or for summary judgment under Part 24) before the claim is allocated to a track, the court may at that hearing:
(1) dispense with the need for the parties to file allocation questionnaires, treat the hearing as an allocation hearing, make an order for allocation and give directions for case management, or
(2) fix a date for allocation questionnaires to be filed and give other directions.

Consequences of failure to file an allocation questionnaire

para.2.5(1) **42.11** para.2.5(2)(b) **42.11**

2.5 (1) If no party files an allocation questionnaire within the time specified by form N152, the court will order that unless an allocation questionnaire is filed within seven days from service of that order, the claim, defence and any counterclaim will be struck out without further order of the court.
(2) Where a party files an allocation questionnaire but another party does not, the file will be referred to a judge for his directions and the court may:
(a) allocate the claim to a track if it considers that it has enough information to do so, or
(b) order that an allocation hearing is listed and that all or any parties must attend.

Stay to Allow for Settlement of the Case

para.3.1(1) **42.24**

Procedure for the parties to apply to extend the stay

3.1 (1) (a) The court will generally accept a letter from any party or from the solicitor for any party as an application to extend the stay under rule 26.4.
(b) The letter should—
(i) confirm that the application is made with the agreement of all parties, and
(ii) explain the steps being taken and identify any mediator or expert assisting with the process.
(2) (a) An order extending the stay must be made by a judge.
(b) The extension will generally be for no more than 4 weeks unless clear reasons are given to justify a longer time.
(3) More than one extension of the stay may be granted.

3.2 Position at the end of the stay if no settlement is reached
(1) At the end of the stay the file will be referred to a judge for his directions.
(2) He will consider whether to allocate the claim to a track and what other directions to give, or may require any party to give further information or fix an allocation hearing.

3.3 Any party may apply for a stay to be lifted.

Position where settlement is reached during a stay

3.4 Where the whole of the proceedings are settled during a stay, the taking of any of the following steps will be treated as an application for the stay to be lifted:

(1) an application for a consent order (in any form) to give effect to the settlement,

(2) an application for the approval of a settlement where a party is a person under a disability,

(3) giving notice of acceptance of money paid into court in satisfaction of the claim or applying for money in court to be paid out.

Allocation, Reallocation and Case Management

The court's general approach

4.1 The Civil Procedure Rules lay down the overriding objective, the powers and duties of the court and the factors to which it must have regard in exercising them. The court will expect to exercise its powers as far as possible in cooperation with the parties and their legal representatives so as to deal with the case justly in accordance with that objective.

Allocation to track

para.4.2(2) **42.10**

4.2 (1) In most cases the court will expect to have enough information from the statements of case and allocation questionnaires to be able to allocate the claim to a track and to give case management directions.

(2) If the court does not have enough information to allocate the claim it will generally make an order under rule 26.5(3) requiring one or more parties to provide further information within 14 days.

(3) Where there has been no allocation hearing the notice of allocation will be in forms N154 (fast track), N155 (multi-track) or N157, N158, N159 or N160 (small claims).

(4) (a) The general rule is that the court will give brief reasons for its allocation decision, and these will be set out in the notice of allocation.

(b) The general rule does not apply where all the allocation questionnaires which have been filed have expressed the wish for the claim to be allocated to the track to which the court has allocated it.

(5) Paragraph 6 of this practice direction deals with allocation hearings and paragraph 7 deals with allocation principles.

(6) Paragraph 11 of this practice direction deals with reallocation.

4.3 PD 27, PD 28 and PD 29 contain further information about the giving of case management directions at the allocation stage.

Summary Judgment or Other Early Termination

para.5.2 **33.1**
para.5.3(1) **32.6, 33.3, 34.2, 43.2**
para.5.3(2)–(4) **33.4, 34.4**
para.5.4 **34.5**

5.1 Part of the court's duty of active case management is the summary disposal of issues which do not need full investigation and trial (rule 1.4(2)(c)).

5.2 The court's powers to make orders to dispose of issues in that way include:

(a) under rule 3.4, striking out a statement of case, or part of a statement of case, and

(b) under Part 24, giving summary judgment where a claimant or a defendant has no reasonable prospect of success.

The court may use these powers on an application or on its own initiative. PD 24 contains further information.

5.3 (1) A party intending to make such an application should do so before or when filing his allocation questionnaire.

(2) Where a party makes an application for such an order before a claim has been allocated to a track the court will not normally allocate the claim before the hearing of the application.

(3) Where a party files an allocation questionnaire stating that he intends to make such an application but has not done so, the judge will usually direct that an allocation hearing is listed.

(4) The application may be heard at that allocation hearing if the application notice has been issued and served in sufficient time.

5.4 (1) This paragraph applies where the court proposes to make such an order of its own initiative.
(2) The court will not allocate the claim to a track but instead it will either:
(a) fix a hearing, giving the parties at least 14 days notice of the date of the hearing and of the issues which it is proposed that the court will decide, or
(b) make an order directing a party to take the steps described in the order within a stated time and specifying the consequence of not taking those steps.

5.5 Where the court decides at the hearing of an application or a hearing fixed under paragraph 5.4(2)(a) that the claim (or part of the claim) is to continue it may:
(1) treat that hearing as an allocation hearing, allocate the claim and give case management directions, or
(2) give other directions.

Allocation Hearings

General principle

6.1 The court will only hold an allocation hearing on its own initiative if it considers that it is necessary to do so.

Procedure

6.2 Where the court orders an allocation hearing to take place:
(1) it will give the parties at least seven days' notice of the hearing in form N153, and
(2) form N153 will give a brief explanation of the decision to order the hearing.

6.3 Power to treat another hearing as an allocation hearing
Where the court may treat another hearing as an allocation hearing it does not need to give notice to any party that it proposes to do so.

6.4 The notice of allocation after an allocation hearing will be in forms N154, N155 or N157.

Representation

para.6.5 **42.13**

6.5 A legal representative who attends an allocation hearing should, if possible, be the person responsible for the case and must in any event be familiar with the case, be able to provide the court with the information it is likely to need to take its decisions about allocation and case management, and have sufficient authority to deal with any issues that are likely to arise.

Sanctions

para.6.6(2) **42.11** para.6.6(3) **42.13**

6.6 (1) This paragraph sets out the sanctions that the court will usually impose for default in connection with the allocation procedure, but the court may make a different order.
(2) (a) Where an allocation hearing takes place because a party has failed to file an allocation questionnaire or to provide further information which the court has ordered, the court will usually order that party to pay on the indemnity basis the costs of any other party who has attended the hearing, summarily assess the amount of those costs, and order them to be paid forthwith or within a stated period.
(b) The court may order that if the party does not pay those costs within the time stated his statement of case will be struck out.
(3) Where a party whose default has led to a fixing of an allocation hearing is still in default and does not attend the hearing the court will usually make an order specifying the steps he is required to take and providing that unless he takes them within a stated time his statement of case will be struck out.

Allocation Principles

Rules 26.6, 26.7 and 26.8

7.1 (1) Rule 26.6 sets out the scope of each track,
(2) Rule 26.7 states the general rule for allocation, and
(3) Rule 26.8 sets out the matters relevant to allocation to a track.

Objective of this paragraph

7.2 The object of this paragraph is to explain what will be the court's general approach to some of the matters set out in rule 26.8.

'the financial value of the claim'

7.3 (1) Rule 26.8(2) provides that it is for the court to assess the financial value of a claim.
(2) Where the court believes that the amount the claimant is seeking exceeds what he may reasonably be expected to recover it may make an order under rule 26.5(3) directing the claimant to justify the amount.

'any amount not in dispute'

para.7.4 **42.14, 42.15**

7.4 In deciding, for the purposes of rule 26.8(2), whether an amount is in dispute the court will apply the following general principles:
(1) Any amount for which the defendant does not admit liability is in dispute,
(2) Any sum in respect of an item forming part of the claim for which judgment has been entered (for example a summary judgment) is not in dispute,
(3) Any specific sum claimed as a distinct item and which the defendant admits he is liable to pay is not in dispute,
(4) Any sum offered by the defendant which has been accepted by the claimant in satisfaction of any item which forms a distinct part of the claim is not in dispute.

It follows from these provisions that if, in relation to a claim the value of which is above the small claims track limit of £5,000, the defendant makes, before allocation, an admission that reduces the amount in dispute to a figure below £5,000 (see CPR Part 14), the normal track for the claim will be the small claims track. As to recovery of pre-allocation costs, the claimant can, before allocation, apply for judgment with costs on the amount of the claim that has been admitted (see CPR rule 14.3 but see also PD 43–48, para. 15.1(3), under which the court has a discretion to allow pre-allocation costs).

'the views expressed by the parties'

para.7.5 **42.19**

7.5 The court will treat these views as an important factor, but the allocation decision is one for the court, to be taken in the light of all the circumstances, and the court will not be bound by any agreement or common view of the parties.

'the circumstances of the parties'

7.6 See paragraph 8.

'the value of any counterclaim or other Part 20 claim'

para.7.7 **42.19**

7.7 Where the case involves more than one money claim (for example where there is a Part 20 claim or there is more than one claimant each making separate claims) the court will not generally aggregate the claims. Instead it will generally regard the largest of them as determining the financial value of the claims.

The Small Claims Track — Allocation and Case Management

para.8.1(1)(c)–(d) **42.15** para.8.1(2)(b)–(c) **42.15**

Allocation

8.1 (1) (a) The small claims track is intended to provide a proportionate procedure by which most straightforward claims with a financial value of not more than £5,000 can be decided, without the need for substantial pre-hearing preparation and the formalities of a traditional trial, and without incurring large legal costs. (Rule 26.6 provides for a lower financial value in certain types of case.)
(b) The procedure laid down in Part 27 for the preparation of the case and the conduct of the hearing are designed to make it possible for a litigant to conduct his own case without legal representation if he wishes.
(c) Cases generally suitable for the small claims track will include consumer disputes, accident claims, disputes about the ownership of goods and most disputes between a landlord and tenant other than opposed claims under Part 56, disputed claims for possession under Part 55 and demotion claims whether in the alternative to possession claims or under Part 65.

(d) A case involving a disputed allegation of dishonesty will not usually be suitable for the small claims track.

(2) Rule 26.7(3) and rule 27.14(5)

(a) These rules allow the parties to consent to the allocation to the small claims track of a claim the value of which is above the limits mentioned in rule 26.6(2) and, in that event, the rules make provision about costs.

(b) The court will not allocate such a claim to the small claims track, notwithstanding that the parties have consented to the allocation, unless it is satisfied that it is suitable for that track.

(c) The court will not normally allow more than one day for the hearing of such a claim.

(d) The court will give case management directions to ensure that the case is dealt with in as short a time as possible. These may include directions of a kind that are not usually given in small claim cases, for example, for Scott Schedules.

Case management

8.2 (1) Directions for case management of claims allocated to the small claims track will generally be given by the court on allocation.

(2) Rule 27.4 contains further provisions about directions and PD 27 sets out the standard directions which the court will usually give.

The Fast Track

para.9.1(3)(b) **42.25** para.9.1(3)(c) **42.16**

Allocation

9.1 (1) Where the court is to decide whether to allocate to the fast track or the multi-track a claim for which the normal track is the fast track, it will allocate the claim to the fast track unless it believes that it cannot be dealt with justly on that track.

(2) The court will, in particular, take into account the limits likely to be placed on disclosure, the extent to which expert evidence may be necessary and whether the trial is likely to last more than a day.

(3) (a) When it is considering the likely length of the trial the court will regard a day as being a period of 5 hours, and will consider whether that is likely to be sufficient time for the case to be heard.

(b) The court will also take into account the case management directions (including the fixing of a trial timetable) that are likely to be given and the court's powers to control evidence and to limit cross-examination.

(c) The possibility that a trial might last longer than one day is not necessarily a conclusive reason for the court to allocate or to reallocate a claim to the multi-track.

(d) A claim may be allocated to the fast track or ordered to remain on that track although there is to be a split trial.

(e) Where the case involves a counterclaim or other Part 20 claim that will be tried with the claim and as a result the trial will last more than a day, the court may not allocate it to the fast track.

Case management

9.2 (1) Directions for the case management of claims which have been allocated to the fast track will be given at the allocation stage or at the listing stage (in either case with or without a hearing) or at both, and if necessary at other times. The trial judge may, at or before the trial, give directions for its conduct.

(2) PD 28 contains further provisions and contains standard directions which the court may give.

The Multi-track

para.10.2(5)–(6) **42.4** para.10.2(8)–(10) **42.4**

10.1 Paragraph 10.2 does not apply to:

(1) a claim for possession of land in the county court or a demotion claim whether in the alternative to a possession claim or under Part 65;

(2) any claim which is being dealt with at the Royal Courts of Justice.

Venue for allocation and case management

10.2 (1) The case management of a claim which is allocated to the multi-track will normally be dealt with at a Civil Trial Centre.

(2) In the case of a claim to which any of Parts 49 or 58 to 62 apply, case management must be dealt with at a Civil Trial Centre. Sub-paragraphs (4) to (10) do not apply to such a claim. The claim will be allocated to the multi-track irrespective of its value, and must be transferred to a Civil Trial Centre for allocation and case management if not already there.

(3) Where a claim is issued in or automatically transferred to a Civil Trial Centre it will be allocated and managed at that court.

(4) The following sub-paragraphs apply to a claim which is issued in or automatically transferred to a court which is not a Civil Trial Centre. Such a court is referred to as a 'feeder court'.

(5) Where a judge sitting at a feeder court decides, on the basis of the allocation questionnaires and any other documents filed by the parties, that the claim should be dealt with on the multi-track he will normally make an order:

(a) allocating the claim to that track,

(b) giving case management directions, and

(c) transferring the claim to a Civil Trial Centre.

(6) If he decides that an allocation hearing or some pre-allocation hearing is to take place (for example to strike out a statement of case under Part 3 of the Rules) that hearing will take place at the feeder court.

(7) If, before allocation, a hearing takes place at a feeder court and in exercising his powers under paragraph 2.4(1) above the judge allocates the claim to the multi-track, he will also normally make an order transferring the claim to a Civil Trial Centre.

(8) A judge sitting at a feeder court may, rather than making an allocation order himself, transfer the claim to a Civil Trial Centre for the decision about allocation to be taken there.

(9) When, following an order for transfer, the file is received at the Civil Trial Centre, a judge sitting at that Centre will consider it and give any further directions that appear necessary or desirable.

(10) Where there is reason to believe that more than one case management conference may be needed and the parties or their legal advisers are located inconveniently far from the Civil Trial Centre, a judge sitting at a feeder court may, with the agreement of the Designated Civil Judge and notwithstanding the allocation of the case to the multi-track, decide that in the particular circumstances of the case it should not be transferred to a Civil Trial Centre, but should be case managed for the time being at the feeder court.

(11) A Designated Civil Judge may at any time make an order transferring a claim from a feeder court to a Civil Trial Centre and he may do so irrespective of the track, if any, to which it has been allocated. He may also permit a feeder court to keep for trial a claim or (subject to review from time to time) a category of claims. Any such permission should take into account the ability of the feeder court in relation to the Civil Trial Centre to provide suitable and effective trial within an appropriate trial period.

(12) No order will be made by a feeder court fixing a date for a hearing at a Civil Trial Centre unless that date has been given or confirmed by a judge or listing officer of that Centre.

Case management

10.3 Part 29 of the Rules and PD 29 set out the procedure to be adopted.

Reallocation of Claims and the Variation of Directions

para.11.1 **42.23** para.11.2 **42.23**
para.11.1(1) **42.23**

11.1 (1) Where a party is dissatisfied with an order made allocating the claim to a track he may appeal or apply to the court to reallocate the claim.

(2) He should appeal if the order was made at a hearing at which he was present or represented, or of which he was given due notice.

(3) In any other case he should apply to the court to reallocate the claim.

11.2 Where there has been a change in the circumstances since an order was made allocating the claim to a track the court may reallocate the claim. It may do so on application or on its own initiative.

PD 28 and PD 29 contain provisions about the variation of case management directions.

Determining the Amount to Be Paid under a Judgment or Order

para.12 **20.6**
para.12.1 **36.13**
para.12.1(1)–(2) **42.28**

Scope

12.1 (1) In the following paragraphs:
(a) a 'relevant order' means a judgment or order of the court which requires the amount of money to be paid by one party to another to be decided by the court; and
(b) a 'disposal hearing' means a hearing in accordance with para. 12.4.
(2) A relevant order may have been obtained:
(a) by a judgment in default under Part 12;
(b) by a judgment on an admission under Part 14;
(c) on the striking out of a statement of case under Part 3;
(d) on a summary judgment application under Part 24;
(e) on the determination of a preliminary issue or on a trial as to liability; or
(f) at trial.
(3) A relevant order includes any order for the amount of a debt, damages or interest to be decided by the court (including an order for the taking of an account or the making of an inquiry as to any sum due, and any similar order), but does not include an order for the assessment of costs.

Directions

para.12.2 **20.6**
para.12.2(1) **42.28, 42.30**
para.12.2(2) **42.31**
para.12.2(3) **42.30**

12.2 (1) When the court makes a relevant order it will give directions, which may include:
(a) listing the claim for a disposal hearing;
(b) allocating or reallocating the claim (but see para. 12.3);
(c) directing the parties to file allocation questionnaires by a specified date; and
(d) staying the claim while the parties try to settle the case by alternative dispute resolution or other means.
(2) Directions may specify the level or type of judge before whom a hearing or a further hearing will take place and the nature and purpose of that hearing.
(3) Where the parties apply for a relevant order by consent, they should if possible file with their draft consent order agreed directions for the court's approval.

Allocation

para.12.3 **20.6, 42.28, 42.30**
para.12.3(2) **20.6**

12.3 (1) If, when the court makes a relevant order:
(a) the claim has not previously been allocated to a track; and
(b) the financial value of the claim (determined in accordance with Part 26) is such that the claim would, if defended be allocated to the small claims track,
the court will normally allocate it to that track.
(2) Where para. (1)(b) does not apply, the court will not normally allocate the claim to a track (other than the small claims track) unless:
(a) the amount payable appears to be genuinely disputed on substantial grounds; or
(b) the dispute is not suitable to be dealt with at a disposal hearing.

Disposal hearings

para.12.4(1) **42.29**
para.12.4(1)(h) **42.29**
para.12.4(2)–(4) **42.29**

12.4 (1) A disposal hearing is a hearing:
(a) which will not normally last longer than 30 minutes, and
(b) at which the court will not normally hear oral evidence.

(2) At a disposal hearing the court may:
(a) decide the amount payable under or in consequence of the relevant order and give judgment for that amount; or
(b) give directions as to the future conduct of the proceedings.
(3) If the claim has been allocated to the small claims track, or the court decides at the disposal hearing to allocate it to that track, the court may treat the disposal hearing as a final hearing in accordance with Part 27.
(4) Rule 32.6 applies to evidence at a disposal hearing unless the court directs otherwise.
(5) Except where the claim has been allocated to the small claims track, the court will not exercise its power under sub-paragraph (2)(a) unless any written evidence on which the claimant relies has been served on the defendant at least three days before the disposal hearing.

Costs

12.5 (1) Attention is drawn to:
(a) PD 43–48 and in particular to the court's power to make a summary assessment of costs;
(b) r. 44.13(1) which provides that if an order makes no mention of costs, none are payable in respect of the proceedings to which it relates; and
(c) r. 27.14 (special rules about costs in cases allocated to the small claims track).
(2) Part 46 (fast track trial costs) will not apply to a case dealt with at a disposal hearing whatever the financial value of the claim. So the costs of a disposal hearing will be in the discretion of the court.

Jurisdiction of masters and district judges

para.12.6 **42.31**

12.6 Unless the court otherwise directs, a master or a district judge may decide the amount payable under a relevant order irrespective of the financial value of the claim and of the track to which the claim may have been allocated.

PD 26B Practice Direction — Pilot Scheme for Mediation in Central London County Court

PD 26B **70.21**

This practice direction supplements Part 26

General

1.1 This practice direction provides for a pilot scheme to operate from 1 April 2004 to 31 March 2005 in relation to claims in the Central London County Court.

1.2 This practice direction enables the Central London County Court to:
  (1) require the parties to certain types of claims either to attend a mediation appointment or to give reasons for objecting to doing so; and
  (2) stay the claim until such an appointment takes place.

1.3 Cases in which a notice of referral to mediation has been served under para. 3.1 prior to 31 March 2005 shall remain subject to this practice direction until either:
  (1) a mediation appointment has taken place; or
  (2) any stay of execution imposed under para. 5 has expired or been lifted by the court,
whichever shall be the sooner.

Types of Claims to Which This Practice Direction Applies

2. This practice direction applies to a claim if it meets all the following conditions:
  (1) the small claims track is not the normal track for the claim;
  (2) no party to the claim is:
    (a) a child or patient; or
    (b) exempt from payment of court fees; and
  (3) the court has not granted an interim injunction in the proceedings.

Service of Mediation Notice

3.1 The court may, when it serves the allocation questionnaire under r. 26.3, serve a notice of referral to mediation on each party:
  (1) notifying them that the claim is to be referred to mediation; and
  (2) requiring them, within 14 days after service of the notice on them, to file and serve a reply to the notice in which they must:
    (a) state whether they agree or object to mediation;
    (b) specify any dates within three months of the date of filing the response on which they would not be able to attend a mediation appointment; and
    (c) if they object to mediation, set out their reasons for doing so.

3.2 The cases where a notice of referral to mediation is served on the parties will be chosen at random from those that meet the criteria set out in para. 2.

3.3 A party who receives a notice of referral to mediation need not complete and file an allocation questionnaire unless or until directed to do so by the court.

Objection to Mediation

4.1 If one or more of the parties states in his reply that he objects to mediation, the case will be referred to a district judge who may:
  (1) direct the case to be listed for a hearing of the objections to mediation;
  (2) direct that a mediation appointment should proceed;
  (3) order the parties to file and serve completed allocation questionnaires; or
  (4) give such directions as to the management of the case as he considers appropriate.

4.2 If a party does not file a reply within the time specified in the notice of referral to mediation, the court and all other parties may proceed as if that party has no objection to the use of mediation in the case.

Mediation Appointment

5.1 If no party objects to mediation, or the court directs that mediation should proceed, the court will direct that the proceedings be stayed for an initial period of two months.

5.2 In accordance with the existing Central London County Court Mediation Scheme, the court will fix a date, time and place for the mediation appointment and notify the parties accordingly once all the parties have paid the mediator's charges.

5.3 When the court fixes a mediation appointment it will if necessary extend the stay of proceedings until the date of the appointment.

Mediator's Charges

6.1 A mediator's charge is payable by each party who is to attend a mediation appointment. The court will notify each party of the amount of the charge and request payment of that amount in the notice of referral to mediation.

6.2 A party must pay the mediator's charge to the court within 14 days of being requested to do so or such other period as the court may direct. Any request for further time in which to pay the mediator's charge may be made by letter.

6.3 If any party fails to pay the mediator's charge the court will refer the case to a district judge for directions.

Unsuccessful Mediation

7 If the mediation does not proceed or does not fully resolve the dispute, the mediator will notify the court and the court will:

(1) either:

  (a) allocate the claim to a track; or

  (b) order the parties to file and serve completed allocation questionnaires (if not already filed); and

(2) give such directions for the further management of the case as it considers appropriate.

CPR Part 27 The Small Claims Track

Part 27 **42.27**, **66.34**, **66.35** [For commentary on a specific rule, please refer to the cross-references after the title of the rule.]

27.1 Scope of This Part

(1) This Part—
  (a) sets out the special procedure for dealing with claims which have been allocated to the small claims track under Part 26; and
  (b) limits the amount of costs that can be recovered in respect of a claim which has been allocated to the small claims track.

(Rule 27.14 deals with costs on the small claims track)

(2) A claim being dealt with under this Part is called a small claim.

(Rule 26.6 provides for the scope of the small claims track. A claim for a remedy for harassment or unlawful eviction relating, in either case, to residential premises shall not be allocated to the small claims track whatever the financial value of the claim. Otherwise, the small claims track will be the normal track for—

- any claim which has a financial value of not more than £5,000 subject to the special provisions about claims for personal injuries and housing disrepair claims;
- any claim for personal injuries which has a financial value of not more than £5,000 where the claim for damages for personal injuries is not more than £1,000; and
- any claim which includes a claim by a tenant of residential premises against his landlord for repairs or other work to the premises where the estimated cost of the repairs or other work is not more than £1,000 and the financial value of any other claim for damages in respect of those repairs or other work is not more than £1,000)

27.2 Extent to Which Other Parts Apply

r.27.2 **43.6, 64.1**
r.27.2(1) **37.1, 47.7**
r.27.2(1)(b) **43.16, 48.2**
r.27.2(1)(c) **43.17, 49.17**
r.27.2(1)(e) **43.18**
r.27.2(1)(f) **43.15**
r.27.2(1)(g) **43.28**
r.27.2(1)(h) **43.25**
r.27.2(3) **43.15**

(1) The following Parts of these Rules do not apply to small claims—
  (a) Part 25 (interim remedies) except as it relates to interim injunctions(GL);
  (b) Part 31 (disclosure and inspection);
  (c) Part 32 (evidence) except rule 32.1 (power of court to control evidence);
  (d) Part 33 (miscellaneous rules about evidence);
  (e) Part 35 (experts and assessors) except rules 35.1 (duty to restrict expert evidence), 35.3 (experts — overriding duty to the court), 35.7 (court's power to direct that evidence is to be given by single joint expert) and 35.8 (instructions to a single joint expert);
  (f) subject to paragraph (3), Part 18 (further information);
  (g) Part 36 (offers to settle and payments into court); and
  (h) Part 39 (hearings) except rule 39.2 (general rule — hearing to be in public).

(2) The other Parts of these Rules apply to small claims except to the extent that a rule limits such application.

(3) The court of its own initiative may order a party to provide further information if it considers it appropriate to do so.

27.3 Court's Power to Grant a Final Remedy

r.27.3 **43.4, 43.17**

The court may grant any final remedy in relation to a small claim which it could grant if the proceedings were on the fast track or the multi-track.

27.4 Preparation for the Hearing

r.27.4 **43.7, 43.11**
r.27.4(1)(a) **43.8**
r.27.4(1)(b) **43.10**
r.27.4(1)(c) **43.9**
r.27.4(1)(d) **43.11**
r.27.4(3)(a) **43.8, 43.16, 48.2**
r.27.4(3)(b) **43.10**

(1) After allocation the court will—
   (a) give standard directions and fix a date for the final hearing;
   (b) give special directions and fix a date for the final hearing;
   (c) give special directions and direct that the court will consider what further directions are to be given no later than 28 days after the date the special directions were given;
   (d) fix a date for a preliminary hearing under rule 27.6; or
   (e) give notice that it proposes to deal with the claim without a hearing under rule 27.10 and invite the parties to notify the court by a specified date if they agree the proposal.
(2) The court will—
   (a) give the parties at least 21 days' notice of the date fixed for the final hearing, unless the parties agree to accept less notice; and
   (b) inform them of the amount of time allowed for the final hearing.
(3) In this rule—
   (a) 'standard directions' means—
      (i) a direction that each party shall, at least 14 days before the date fixed for the final hearing, file and serve on every other party copies of all documents (including any expert's report) on which he intends to rely at the hearing; and
      (ii) any other standard directions set out in the relevant practice direction; and
   (b) 'special directions' means directions given in addition to or instead of the standard directions.

27.5 Experts

r.27.5 **42.15, 43.17, 43.18, 43.19**

No expert may give evidence, whether written or oral, at a hearing without the permission of the court.

(Rule 27.14(3)(d) provides for the payment of an expert's fees)

27.6 Preliminary Hearing

r.27.6 **43.11**
r.27.6(4)–(5) **43.11**

(1) The court may hold a preliminary hearing for the consideration of the claim, but only—
   (a) where—
      (i) it considers that special directions, as defined in rule 27.4, are needed to ensure a fair hearing; and
      (ii) it appears necessary for a party to attend at court to ensure that he understands what he must do to comply with the special directions; or
   (b) to enable it to dispose of the claim on the basis that one or other of the parties has no real prospect of success at a final hearing; or
   (c) to enable it to strike out(GL) a statement of case or part of a statement of case on the basis that the statement of case, or the part to be struck out, discloses no reasonable grounds for bringing or defending the claim.
(2) When considering whether or not to hold a preliminary hearing, the court must have regard to the desirability of limiting the expense to the parties of attending court.
(3) Where the court decides to hold a preliminary hearing, it will give the parties at least 14 days' notice of the date of the hearing.

(4) The court may treat the preliminary hearing as the final hearing of the claim if all the parties agree.
(5) At or after the preliminary hearing the court will—
 (a) fix the date of the final hearing (if it has not been fixed already) and give the parties at least 21 days' notice of the date fixed unless the parties agree to accept less notice;
 (b) inform them of the amount of time allowed for the final hearing; and
 (c) give any appropriate directions.

27.7 Power of Court to Add to, Vary or Revoke Directions

r.27.7 **43.7**

The court may add to, vary or revoke directions.

27.8 Conduct of the Hearing

r.27.8 **43.19, 43.22** r.27.8(4) **47.49**
r.27.8(6) **43.24**

(1) The court may adopt any method of proceeding at a hearing that it considers to be fair.
(2) Hearings will be informal.
(3) The strict rules of evidence do not apply.
(4) The court need not take evidence on oath.
(5) The court may limit cross-examination(GL).
(6) The court must give reasons for its decision.

27.9 Non-attendance of Parties at a Final Hearing

r.27.9 **43.26** r.27.9(1)(b) **43.23**
r.27.9(1) **43.23, 43.24, 43.25** r.27.9(2)–(4) **43.23**

(1) If a party who does not attend a final hearing—
 (a) has given written notice to the court and the other party at least 7 days before the hearing date that he will not attend;
 (b) has served on the other party at least 7 days before the hearing date any other documents which he has filed with the court; and
 (c) has, in his written notice, requested the court to decide the claim in his absence and has confirmed his compliance with paragraphs (a) and (b) above,

 the court will take into account that party's statement of case and any other documents he has filed and served when it decides the claim.
(2) If a claimant does not—
 (a) attend the hearing; and
 (b) give the notice referred to in paragraph (1),

 the court may strike out(GL) the claim.
(3) If—
 (a) a defendant does not—
  (i) attend the hearing; or
  (ii) give the notice referred to in paragraph (1); and
 (b) the claimant either—
  (i) does attend the hearing; or
  (ii) gives the notice referred to in paragraph (1),

 the court may decide the claim on the basis of the evidence of the claimant alone.
(4) If neither party attends or gives the notice referred to in paragraph (1), the court may strike out(GL) the claim and any defence and counterclaim.

27.10 Disposal without a Hearing

r.27.10 **43.12, 43.24, 43.25, 43.26**

The court may, if all parties agree, deal with the claim without a hearing.

27.11 Setting Judgment Aside and Rehearing

r.27.11 **43.25**
r.27.11(1)–(4) **43.25**
r.27.11(4)(a)–(b) **43.25**
r.27.11(5) **43.25**

(1) A party—
(a) who was neither present nor represented at the hearing of the claim; and
(b) who has not given written notice to the court under rule 27.9(1),
may apply for an order that a judgment under this Part shall be set aside[(GL)] and the claim reheard.
(2) A party who applies for an order setting aside a judgment under this rule must make the application not more than 14 days after the day on which notice of the judgment was served on him.
(3) The court may grant an application under paragraph (2) only if the applicant—
(a) had a good reason for not attending or being represented at the hearing or giving written notice to the court under rule 27.9(1); and
(b) has a reasonable prospect of success at the hearing.
(4) If a judgment is set aside[(GL)]—
(a) the court must fix a new hearing for the claim; and
(b) the hearing may take place immediately after the hearing of the application to set the judgment aside and may be dealt with by the judge who set aside[(GL)] the judgment.
(5) A party may not apply to set aside[(GL)] a judgment under this rule if the court dealt with the claim without a hearing under rule 27.10.

27.12 *[Revoked]*

27.13 *[Revoked]*

27.14 Costs on the Small Claims Track

r.27.14 **43.28, 66.35**
r.27.14(2) **43.27**
r.27.14(2)(a) **67.2, 67.3, 67.7**
r.27.14(2)(a)(ii) **67.7**
r.27.14(2)(d) **43.28, 64.1, 67.3**
r.27.14(2A) **43.28, 64.1**
r.27.14(3) **43.27**
r.27.14(3)(a)–(d) **43.27**
r.27.14(5) **42.14, 42.15, 43.31**
r.27.14(6) **43.31**

(1) This rule applies to any case which has been allocated to the small claims track unless paragraph (5) applies.
(Rules 44.9 and 44.11 make provision in relation to orders for costs made before a claim has been allocated to the small claims track)
(2) The court may not order a party to pay a sum to another party in respect of that other party's costs except—
(a) the fixed costs attributable to issuing the claim which—
(i) are payable under Part 45; or
(ii) would be payable under Part 45 if that Part applied to the claim;
(b) in proceedings which included a claim for an injunction[(GL)] or an order for specific performance a sum not exceeding the amount specified in the relevant practice direction for legal advice and assistance relating to that claim;
(c) costs assessed by the summary procedure in relation to an appeal; and
(d) such further costs as the court may assess by the summary procedure and order to be paid by a party who has behaved unreasonably.
(2A) A party's rejection of an offer in settlement will not of itself constitute unreasonable behaviour under paragraph (2)(d) but the court may take it into consideration when it is applying the unreasonableness test.
(Rule 36.2(5) allows the court to order Part 36 costs consequences in a small claim)
(3) The court may also order a party to pay all or part of—
(a) any court fees paid by another party;
(b) expenses which a party or witness has reasonably incurred in travelling to and from a hearing or in staying away from home for the purposes of attending a hearing;
(c) a sum not exceeding the amount specified in the relevant practice direction for any loss of earnings or loss of leave by a party or witness due to attending a hearing or to staying away from home for the purpose of attending a hearing; and

(d) a sum not exceeding the amount specified in the relevant practice direction for an expert's fees.

(4) The limits on costs imposed by this rule also apply to any fee or reward for acting on behalf of a party to the proceedings charged by a person exercising a right of audience by virtue of an order under section 11 of the Courts and Legal Services Act 1990 (a lay representative).

(5) Where—

(a) the financial value of a claim exceeds the limit for the small claims track; but

(b) the claim has been allocated to the small claims track in accordance with rule 26.7(3),

the small claims track costs provisions will apply unless the parties agree that the fast track costs provisions are to apply.

(6) Where the parties agree that the fast track costs provisions are to apply, the claim will be treated for the purposes of costs as if it were proceeding on the fast track except that trial costs will be in the discretion of the court and will not exceed the amount set out for the value of claim in rule 46.2 (amount of fast track trial costs).

27.15 Claim Reallocated from the Small Claims Track to Another Track

r.27.15 **42.23, 43.29, 66.35**

Where a claim is allocated to the small claims track and subsequently reallocated to another track, rule 27.14 (costs on the small claims track) will cease to apply after the claim has been reallocated and the fast track or multi-track costs rules will apply from the date of reallocation.

PD 27 Practice Direction — Small Claims Track

This practice direction supplements CPR Part 27

For commentary on a specific paragraph, please refer to the cross-references after the title of the paragraph.]

Judges

para.1 **43.19**

1 The functions of the court described in Part 27 which are to be carried out by a judge will generally be carried out by a district judge but may be carried out by a circuit judge.

Case Management Directions

para.2.2 **43.8**
para.2.3 **42.10, 43.17**
para.2.4 **43.7**
para.2.5 **43.17**

2.1 Rule 27.4 explains how directions will be given, and r. 27.6 contains provisions about the holding of a preliminary hearing and the court's powers at such a hearing.

2.2 Appendix A sets out details of the case that the court usually needs in the type of case described. Appendix B sets out the standard directions that the court may give. Appendix C sets out special directions that the court may give.

2.3 Before allocating the claim to the small claims track and giving directions for a hearing the court may require a party to give further information about that party's case.

2.4 A party may ask the court to give particular directions about the conduct of the case.

2.5 In deciding whether to make an order for exchange of witness statements the court will have regard to the following:
(a) whether either or both the parties are represented;
(b) the amount in dispute in the proceedings;
(c) the nature of the matters in dispute;
(d) whether the need for any party to clarify his case can better be dealt with by an order under para. 2.3;
(e) the need for the parties to have access to justice without undue formality, cost or delay.

Representation at a Hearing

para.3.2(1)–(4) **43.20**

3.1 In this paragraph:
(1) a lawyer means a barrister, a solicitor or a legal executive employed by a solicitor, and
(2) a lay representative means any other person.

3.2 (1) A party may present his own case at a hearing or a lawyer or lay representative may present it for him.
(2) The Lay Representatives (Rights of Audience) Order 1999 (SI 1999/1225) provides that a lay representative may not exercise any right of audience:
(a) where his client does not attend the hearing,
(b) at any stage after judgment, or
(c) on any appeal brought against any decision made by the district judge in the proceedings.
(3) However the court, exercising its general discretion to hear anybody, may hear a lay representative even in circumstances excluded by the Order.
(4) Any of its officers or employees may represent a corporate party.

Small Claim Hearing

paras.4.1–4.2 **43.21**
para.4.3 **43.22**

4.1 (1) The general rule is that a small claim hearing will be in public.
(2) The judge may decide to hold it in private if:
(a) the parties agree, or
(b) a ground mentioned in r. 39.2(3) applies.
(3) A hearing or part of a hearing which takes place other than at the court, for example at the home or business premises of a party, will not be in public.

4.2 A hearing that takes place at the court will generally be in the judge's room but it may take place in a courtroom.

4.3 Rule 27.8 allows the court to adopt any method of proceeding that it considers to be fair and to limit cross-examination. The judge may in particular:
(1) ask questions of any witness himself before allowing any other person to do so,
(2) ask questions of all or any of the witnesses himself before allowing any other person to ask questions of any witnesses,
(3) refuse to allow cross-examination of any witness until all the witnesses have given evidence-in-chief,
(4) limit cross-examination of a witness to a fixed time or to a particular subject or issue, or both.

Recording Evidence and the Giving of Reasons

para.5.1 **43.24** para.5.4 **43.24**
para.5.3(1)–(2) **43.24**

5.1 A hearing that takes place at the court will be tape-recorded by the court. A party may obtain a transcript of such a recording on payment of the proper transcriber's charges.

5.2 Attention is drawn to the Contempt of Court Act 1981, s. 9 (which deals with the unauthorised use of tape recorders in court), and to Practice Direction (Tape Recorders) [1981] 1 WLR 1526 which relates to it.

5.3 (1) The judge may give reasons for his judgment as briefly and simply as the nature of the case allows.
(2) He will normally do so orally at the hearing, but he may give them later at a hearing either orally or in writing.

5.4 Where the judge decides the case without a hearing under r. 27.10 or a party who has given notice under r. 27.9(1) does not attend the hearing, the judge will prepare a note of his reasons and the court will send a copy to each party.

5.5 Nothing in this practice direction affects the duty of a judge at the request of a party to make a note of the matters referred to in the County Courts Act 1984, s. 80.

Non-attendance of a Party at a Hearing

6.1 Attention is drawn to r. 27.9 (which enables a party to give notice that he will not attend a final hearing and sets out the effect of his giving such notice and of not doing so), and to para. 3 above.

6.2 Nothing in those provisions affects the general power of the court to adjourn a hearing, for example where a party who wishes to attend a hearing on the date fixed cannot do so for a good reason.

Costs

para.7.2 **43.27** para.7.3(1) **43.27**
para.7.3 **43.27** para.7.3(2) **42.15, 43.27**

7.1 Attention is drawn to r. 27.14 which contains provisions about the costs which may be ordered to be paid by one party to another.

7.2 The amount which a party may be ordered to pay under r. 27.14(2)(b) (for legal advice and assistance in claims including an injunction or specific performance) is a sum not exceeding £260.

7.3 The amounts which a party may be ordered to pay under r. 27.14(3)(c) (loss of earnings) and (d) (experts' fees) are:
(1) for the loss of earnings or loss of leave of each party or witness due to attending a hearing or staying away from home for the purpose of attending a hearing, a sum not exceeding £50 per day for each person, and
(2) for expert's fees, a sum not exceeding £200 for each expert.
(As to recovery of pre-allocation costs in a case in which an admission by the defendant has reduced the amount in dispute to a figure below £5,000, reference should be made to PD 26, para. 7.4 and to [PD 43–48, para. 15.1(3)*].)

[* The text issued by the Department for Constitutional Affairs refers to an earlier version of this practice direction.]

Appeals

para.8A **43.26** paras.8.2–8.3 **43.26**

8.1 Part 52 deals with appeals and attention is drawn to that Part and the accompanying practice direction.

8A An appellant's notice in small claims must be filed and served in form N164.

8.2 Where the court dealt with the claim to which the appellant is a party:

(1) under r. 27.10 without a hearing; or

(2) in his absence because he gave notice under r. 27.9 requesting the court to decide the claim in his absence,

an application for permission to appeal must be made to the appeal court.

8.3 Where an appeal is allowed the court will if possible, dispose of the case at the same time without referring the claim to the lower court or ordering a new hearing. It may do so without hearing further evidence.

8.7 The circuit judge will give any necessary directions:

(1) about the filing of any evidence concerning any allegation of serious irregularity, and

(2) about the supply to the parties of copies of any document (including any note made by the judge who heard the case) which he has taken or may have taken into account in dealing with the appeal.

8.8 Where the circuit judge dismisses the appeal without a hearing his order will contain brief reasons for his decision.

8.9 Where the circuit judge directs that the appeal is to be listed for hearing the court will give at least seven days notice of the hearing to all parties.

8.10 If the appeal is allowed, the circuit judge will if possible dispose of the case at the same time without ordering the claim to be reheard. He may do so without hearing further evidence.

APPENDIX A INFORMATION AND DOCUMENTATION THE COURT USUALLY NEEDS IN PARTICULAR TYPES OF CASE

appendix A **42.1, 43.10, 43.13, 43.16, 43.17**

Road Accident Cases (Where the Information or Documentation Is Available)

- witness statements (including statements from the parties themselves);
- invoices and estimates for repairs;
- agreements and invoices for any car hire costs;
- the Police accident report;
- sketch plan which should wherever possible be agreed;
- photographs of the scene of the accident and of the damage.

Building Disputes, Repairs, Goods Sold and Similar Contractual Claims (Where the Information or Documentation Is Available)

- any written contract;
- photographs;
- any plans;
- a list of works complained of;
- a list of any outstanding works;
- any relevant estimate, invoice or receipt including any relating to repairs to each of the defects;
- invoices for work done or goods supplied;
- estimates for work to be completed;
- a valuation of work done to date.

Landlord and Tenant Claims (Where the Information or Documentation Is Available)

- a calculation of the amount of any rent alleged to be owing, showing amounts received;
- details of breaches of an agreement which are said to justify withholding any deposit itemised showing how the total is made up and with invoices and estimates to support them.

Breach of Duty Cases (Negligence, Deficient Professional Services and the Like)

Details of the following:

- what it is said by the claimant was done negligently by the defendant;
- why it is said that the negligence is the fault of the defendant;
- what damage is said to have been caused;
- what injury or losses have been suffered and how any (and each) sum claimed has been calculated;
- the response of the defendant to each of the above.

APPENDIX B STANDARD DIRECTIONS

appendix B **43.8, 43.9**

(*For use where the district judge specifies no other directions*)

THE COURT DIRECTS:

1 Each party must deliver to every other party and to the court office copies of all documents on which he intends to rely at the hearing no later than [ ] [14 days before the hearing]. (These should include the letter making the claim and the reply.)

2 The original documents must be brought to the hearing.

3 [Notice of hearing date and time allowed.]

4 The parties are encouraged to contact each other with a view to trying to settle the case or narrow the issues. However the court must be informed immediately if the case is settled by agreement before the hearing date.

5 No party may rely at the hearing on any report from an expert unless express permission has been granted by the court beforehand. Anyone wishing to rely on an expert must write to the court immediately on receipt of this Order and seek permission, giving an explanation why the assistance of an expert is necessary.

NOTE: Failure to comply with the directions may result in the case being adjourned and in the party at fault having to pay costs. The parties are encouraged always to try to settle the case by negotiating with each other. The court must be informed immediately if the case is settled before the hearing.

APPENDIX C SPECIAL DIRECTIONS

appendix C **43.14, 43.18**

The must clarify his case.

He must do this by delivering to the court office and to the no later than [a list of] [details of]

The must allow the to inspect by appointment within days of receiving a request to do so.

The hearing will not take place at the court but at .

The must bring to court at the hearing the .

Signed statements setting out the evidence of all witnesses on whom each party intends to rely must be prepared and copies included in the documents mentioned in paragraph 1. This includes the evidence of the parties themselves and of any other witness, whether or not he is going to come to court to give evidence.

The court may decide not to take into account a document [or video] or the evidence of a witness if these directions have not been complied with.

If he does not [do so] [ ] his [Claim] [Defence] [and Counterclaim] will be struck out and (*specify consequence*).

It appears to the court that expert evidence is necessary on the issue of and that that evidence should be given by a single expert to be instructed by the parties jointly. If the parties cannot agree about who to choose and what arrangements to make about paying his fee, either party MUST apply to the court for further directions. The evidence is to be given in the form of a written report. Either party may ask the expert questions and must then send copies of the questions and replies to the other party and to the court. Oral expert evidence may be allowed in exceptional circumstances but only after a further order of the court. Attention is drawn to the limit of £200 on expert's fees that may be recovered.

If either party intends to show a video as evidence he must:

(a) contact the court at once to make arrangements for him to do so, because the court may not have the necessary equipment, and

(b) provide the other party with a copy of the video or the opportunity to see it at least days before the hearing.

CPR Part 28 The Fast Track

[For commentary on a specific rule, please refer to the cross-references after the title of the rule.]

28.1 Scope of This Part

This Part contains general provisions about management of cases allocated to the fast track and applies only to cases allocated to that track.

(Part 27 sets out the procedure for claims allocated to the small claims track)

(Part 29 sets out the procedure for claims allocated to the multi-track)

28.2 General Provisions

r.28.2(1) **44.3, 48.1**
r.28.2(2) **44.3, 44.12**
r.28.2(3) **44.12**
r.28.2(4) **44.12, 59.1**
r.28.2(5) **44.22**

(1) When it allocates a case to the fast track, the court will give directions for the management of the case and set a timetable for the steps to be taken between the giving of the directions and the trial.

(2) When it gives directions, the court will—
   (a) fix the trial date; or
   (b) fix a period, not exceeding 3 weeks, within which the trial is to take place.

(3) The trial date or trial period will be specified in the notice of allocation.

(4) The standard period between the giving of directions and the trial will be not more than 30 weeks.

(5) The court's power to award trial costs is limited in accordance with Part 46.

28.3 Directions

r.28.3 **44.3, 48.1, 48.25**
r.28.3(2) **44.4, 48.25**

(1) The matters to be dealt with by directions under rule 28.2(1) include—
   (a) disclosure of documents;
   (b) service of witness statements; and
   (c) expert evidence.

(2) If the court decides not to direct standard disclosure, it may—
   (a) direct that no disclosure take place; or
   (b) specify the documents or the classes of documents which the parties must disclose.

(Rule 31.6 explains what is meant by standard disclosure)

(Rule 26.6(5) deals with limitations in relation to expert evidence and the likely length of trial in fast track cases)

28.4 Variation of Case Management Timetable

r.28.4 **3.7, 46.1**
r.28.4(1)–(2) **44.15**

(1) A party must apply to the court if he wishes to vary the date which the court has fixed for—
   (a) the return of a pre-trial checklist under rule 28.5;
   (b) the trial; or
   (c) the trial period.

(2) Any date set by the court or these Rules for doing any act may not be varied by the parties if the variation would make it necessary to vary any of the dates mentioned in paragraph (1).

(Rule 2.11 allows the parties to vary a date by written agreement except where the rules provide otherwise or the court orders otherwise)

28.5 Pre-trial Checklist (Listing Questionnaire)

r.28.5(2) **44.3, 44.10** r.28.5(4) **42.1, 44.3, 44.11**
r.28.5(3) **44.3, 44.11**

(1) The court will send the parties a pre-trial checklist (listing questionnaire) for completion and return by the date specified in the notice of allocation unless it considers that the claim can proceed to trial without the need for a pre-trial checklist.
(2) The date specified for filing a pre-trial checklist will not be more than 8 weeks before the trial date or the beginning of the trial period.
(3) If no party files the completed pre-trial checklist by the date specified, the court will order that unless a completed pre-trial checklist is filed within 7 days from service of that order, the claim, defence and any counterclaim will be struck out without further order of the court.
(4) If—
(a) a party files a completed pre-trial checklist but another party does not;
(b) a party has failed to give all the information requested by the pre-trial checklist; or
(c) the court considers that a hearing is necessary to enable it to decide what directions to give in order to complete preparation of the case for trial,
the court may give such directions as it thinks appropriate.

28.6 Fixing or Confirming the Trial Date and Giving Directions

r.28.6 **59.16** r.28.6(1)(b) **44.18**
r.28.6(1) **44.3, 44.16, 59.16** r.28.6(2) **44.12**

(1) As soon as practicable after the date specified for filing a completed pre-trial checklist the court will—
(a) fix the date for the trial (or, if it has already done so, confirm that date);
(b) give any directions for the trial, including a trial timetable, which it considers appropriate; and
(c) specify any further steps that need to be taken before trial.
(2) The court will give the parties at least 3 weeks' notice of the date of the trial unless, in exceptional circumstances, the court directs that shorter notice will be given.

28.7 Conduct of Trial

r.28.7 **59.16**

Unless the trial judge otherwise directs, the trial will be conducted in accordance with any order previously made.

PD 28 Practice Direction — The Fast Track

This practice direction supplements CPR Part 28

PD 28 **52.5** [For commentary on a specific paragraph, please refer to the cross-references after the title of the paragraph.]

General

1.1 Attention is drawn in particular to the following Parts of the Civil Procedure Rules:

Part 1	The overriding objective
Part 3	The court's case management powers
Part 26	Case management — preliminary stage
Part 31	Disclosure and inspection of documents
Parts 32–34	Evidence
Part 35	Experts and assessors

and to the practice directions which relate to those Parts.

1.2 Attention is also drawn to:

Rule 26.6(5) — which makes provision about limitations on expert evidence and the length of trial in fast track cases.

Part 46 — Fast Track Trial Costs

Rule 19.4A and PD 19, para. 6, on joining the Crown in certain cases raising Convention rights issues.

Case Management

para.2.3 **41.4, 44.3** para.2.8 **44.3**
para.2.5 **32.1, 44.3, 65.2**

2.1 Case management of cases allocated to the fast track will generally be by directions given at two stages in the case:
(1) at allocation to the track, and
(2) on the filing of pre-trial checklists (listing questionnaires).

2.2 The court will seek whenever possible to give directions at those stages only and to do so without the need for a hearing to take place. It will expect to do so with the cooperation of the parties.

2.3 The court will however hold a hearing to give directions whenever it appears necessary or desirable to do so, and where this happens because of the default of a party or his legal representative it will usually impose a sanction.

2.4 The court may give directions at any hearing on the application of a party or on its own initiative.

2.5 When any hearing has been fixed it is the duty of the parties to consider what directions the court should be asked to give and to make any application that may be appropriate to be dealt with at that hearing.

2.6 When the court fixes a hearing to give directions it will give the parties at least 3 days' notice of the hearing.

2.7 Appendix A contains forms of directions. When making an order the court will as far as possible base its order on those forms. Agreed directions which the parties file and invite the court to make should also be based on those forms.

2.8 Where a party needs to apply for a direction of a kind not included in the case management timetable which has been set (for example to amend his statement of case or for further information to be given by another party) he must do so as soon as possible so as to minimise the need to change that timetable.

2.9 Courts will make arrangements to ensure that applications and other hearings are listed promptly to avoid delay in the conduct of cases.

Directions on Allocation

3.1 Attention is drawn to the court's duty under rule 28.2(2) to set a case management timetable and to fix a trial date or a trial period, and to the matters which are to be dealt with by directions under Rule 28.3(1).

3.2 The court will seek to tailor its directions to the needs of the case and the steps of which it is aware that the parties have already taken to prepare the case. In particular it will have regard to the extent to which any pre-action protocol has or (as the case may be) has not been complied with.

3.3 At this stage the court's first concern will be to ensure that the issues between the parties be identified and that the necessary evidence is prepared and disclosed.

3.4 The court may have regard to any document filed by a party with his allocation questionnaire containing further information provided that the document states either that its contents have been agreed with every other party or that it has been served on every other party and when it was served.

3.5 If:

(1) the parties have filed agreed directions for the management of the case, and

(2) the court considers that the proposals are suitable,

it may approve them and give directions in the terms proposed.

3.6 (1) To obtain the court's approval the agreed directions must:

(a) set out a timetable by reference to calendar dates for the taking of steps for the preparation of the case,

(b) include a date or a period (the trial period) when it is proposed that the trial will take place,

(c) include provision about disclosure of documents, and

(d) include provision about both factual and expert evidence.

(2) The latest proposed date for the trial or the end of the trial period must be not later than 30 weeks from the date the directions order is made.

(3) The trial period must not be longer than 3 weeks.

(4) The provision in (1)(c) above may:

(a) limit disclosure to standard disclosure between all parties or to less than that, and/or

(b) direct that disclosure will take place by the supply of copy documents without a list, but it must in that case either direct that the parties must serve a disclosure statement with the copies or record that they have agreed to disclose in that way without such a statement.

(5) The provision in (1)(d) may be to the effect that no expert evidence is required.

3.7 Directions agreed by the parties should also where appropriate contain provisions about:

(1) the filing of any reply or amended statement of case that may be required,

(2) dates for the service of requests for further information under the practice direction supplementing Part 18 and questions to experts under rule 35.6 and when they are to be dealt with,

(3) the disclosure of evidence,

(4) the use of a single joint expert, or in cases where the use of a single expert has not been agreed the exchange and agreement of expert evidence (including whether exchange is to be simultaneous or sequential) and without-prejudice discussions of the experts.

3.8 If the court does not approve the agreed directions filed by the parties but decides that it will give directions on its own initiative without a hearing, it will take them into account in deciding what directions to give.

3.9 Where the court is to give directions on its own initiative and it is not aware of any steps taken by the parties other than the service of statements of case, its general approach will be:

(1) to give directions for the filing and service of any further information required to clarify either party's case,

(2) to direct standard disclosure between the parties,
(3) to direct the disclosure of witness statements by way of simultaneous exchange,
(4) to give directions for a single joint expert unless there is good reason not to do so,
(5) in cases where directions for a single expert are not given:
 (a) to direct disclosure of experts' reports by way of simultaneous exchange, and
 (b) if experts' reports are not agreed, to direct a discussion between the experts for the purpose set out in rule 35.12(1) and the preparation of a report under rule 35.12(3).

3.10 (1) If it appears to the court that the claim is one which will be allocated to the fast track but that it cannot properly give directions on its own initiative or approve agreed directions that have been filed, the court may either:
 (a) allocate the claim to the fast track, fix a trial date or trial period and direct that a case management hearing is to be listed and give directions at that hearing, or
 (b) direct that an allocation hearing is to be listed and give directions at that hearing.
(2) In either case the hearing will be listed as promptly as possible.

3.11 Where the court is proposing on its own initiative to make an order under rule 35.15 (which gives the court power to appoint an assessor), the court must, unless the parties have consented in writing to the order, list a directions hearing.

3.12 The table set out below contains a typical timetable the court may give for the preparation of the case.

Disclosure	4 weeks
Exchange of witness statements	10 weeks
Exchange of experts' reports	14 weeks
Sending of pre-trial checklists (listing questionnaires) by the court	20 weeks
Filing of completed pre-trial checklists	22 weeks
Hearing	30 weeks

These periods will run from the date of the notice of allocation.

3.13 (1) Where it considers that some or all of the steps in that timetable are not necessary the court may omit them and direct an earlier trial.
(2) This may happen where the court is informed that a pre-action protocol has been complied with or that steps which it would otherwise order to be taken have already been taken.
(3) It may also happen where an application (for example for summary judgment or for an injunction) has been heard before allocation and little or no further preparation is required. In such a case the court may dispense with the need for a pre-trial checklist.

Variation of Directions

para.4.2(1) **44.15** para.4.5 **3.7**
para.4.2(2) **32.24, 44.15, 46.2** para.4.5(1) **44.15**

4.1 This paragraph deals with the procedure to be adopted:
(1) where a party is dissatisfied with a direction given by the court,
(2) where the parties agree about changes they wish made to the directions given, or
(3) where a party wishes to apply to vary a direction.

4.2 (1) It is essential that any party who wishes to have a direction varied takes steps to do so as soon as possible.
(2) The court will assume for the purposes of any later application that a party who did not appeal and who made no application to vary within 14 days of service of the order containing the directions was content that they were correct in the circumstances then existing.

4.3 (1) Where a party is dissatisfied with a direction given or other order made by the court he may appeal or apply to the court for it to reconsider its decision.
(2) He should appeal if the direction was given or the order was made at a hearing at which he was present or represented, or of which he had due notice.
(3) In any other case he should apply to the court to reconsider its decision.
(4) If an application is made for the court to reconsider its decision:
 (a) it will usually be heard by the judge who gave the directions or another judge of the same level,

(b) the court will give all parties at least 3 days' notice of the hearing, and
(c) the court may confirm its decision or make a different order.

4.4 Where there has been a change in the circumstances since the order was made the court may set aside or vary any direction it has given. It may do so on application or on its own initiative.

4.5 Where the parties agree about changes to be made to the directions given:
(1) If r. 2.11 (variation by agreement of a date set by the court for doing any act other than those stated in the note to that rule) or r. 31.5, 31.10(8) or 31.13 (agreements about disclosure) applied the parties need not file the written agreement.
(2) (a) In any other case the parties must apply for an order by consent.
(b) The parties must file a draft of the order sought and an agreed statement of the reasons why the variation is sought.
(c) The court may make an order in the agreed terms or in other terms without a hearing, but it may direct that a hearing is to be listed.

Failure to Comply with Case Management Directions

paras.5.1–5.3 **46.3** para.5.4(4) **44.15**
para.5.4 **46.5, 59.11** para.5.4(6) **44.15, 56.1**
para.5.4(1) **42.22**

5.1 Where a party has failed to comply with a direction given by the court any other party may apply for an order to enforce compliance or for a sanction to be imposed or both of these.

5.2 The party entitled to apply for such an order must do so without delay but should first warn the other party of his intention to do so.

5.3 The court may take any such delay into account when it decides whether to make an order imposing a sanction or whether to grant relief from a sanction imposed by the rules or any practice direction.

5.4 (1) The court will not allow a failure to comply with directions to lead to the postponement of the trial unless the circumstances of the case are exceptional.
(2) If it is practicable to do so the court will exercise its powers in a manner that enables the case to come on for trial on the date or within the period previously set.
(3) In particular the court will assess what steps each party should take to prepare the case for trial, direct that those steps are taken in the shortest possible time and impose a sanction for non-compliance. Such a sanction may, for example, deprive a party of the right to raise or contest an issue or to rely on evidence to which the direction relates.
(4) Where it appears that one or more issues are or can be made ready for trial at the time fixed while others cannot, the court may direct that the trial will proceed on the issues which are or will then be ready, and order that no costs will be allowed for any later trial of the remaining issues or that those costs will be paid by the party in default.
(5) Where the court has no option but to postpone the trial it will do so for the shortest possible time and will give directions for the taking of the necessary steps in the meantime as rapidly as possible.
(6) Litigants and lawyers must be in no doubt that the court will regard the postponement of a trial as an order of last resort. The court may exercise its power to require a party as well as his legal representative to attend court at a hearing where such an order is to be sought.

Pre-trial Checklists (Listing Questionnaires)

para.6.3 **44.11, 44.16** para.6.5 **44.11**

6.1 (1) The pre-trial checklist (listing questionnaire) will be in form N170.
(2) Unless it has dispensed with listing questionnaires, the court will send forms N170 and N171 (notice of date for return of the listing questionnaire) to each party no later than two weeks before the date specified in the notice of allocation or in any later direction of the court for the return of the completed questionnaires.
(3) When all the pre-trial checklists have been filed or when the time for filing them has expired and where a party has filed a pre-trial checklist but another party has not done so, the file will be placed before a judge for his directions.
(4) Although the CPR do not require the parties to exchange copies of the checklists before they are filed they are encouraged to do so to avoid the court being given conflicting or incomplete information.

Attention is drawn to PD 43–48, Section 6, which requires a costs estimate to be filed and served at the same time as the pre-trial checklist is filed.

6.2 Attention is drawn to r. 28.6(1) (which sets out the court's duty at the pre-trial checklist stage) and to r. 28.5(4) (which sets out circumstances in which the court may decide to hold a hearing).

6.3 Where the judge decides to hold a hearing under r. 28.5(4) the court will fix a date which is as early as possible and the parties will be given at least three days' notice of the date.

The notice of such a hearing will be in form N153.

6.4 The court's general approach will be as set out in the following paragraphs. The court may however decide to make other orders, and in particular the court will take into account the steps, if any, which the parties have taken to prepare the case for trial.

6.5 (1) Where no party files a pre-trial checklist the court will order that unless a completed pre-trial checklist is filed within seven days from service of that order, the claim, defence and any counterclaim will be struck out.

(2) Where a party files a pre-trial checklist but another party does not do so, the court normally will give directions. These will usually fix or confirm the trial date and provide for steps to be taken to prepare the case for trial.

Directions the Court Will Give on Listing

para.7.2(1) **44.16** para.7.2(4) **44.17**

7.1 Directions the court must give:

(1) The court must confirm or fix the trial date, specify the place of trial and give a time estimate. The trial date must be fixed and the case listed on the footing that the hearing will end on the same calendar day as that on which it commenced.

(2) The court will serve a notice of hearing on the parties at least three weeks before the hearing unless they agree to accept shorter notice or the court authorises shorter service under r. 28.6(2), and

(3) The notice of hearing will be in form N172.

7.2 Other directions:

(1) The parties should seek to agree directions and may file the proposed order. The court may make an order in those terms or it may make a different order.

(2) Agreed directions should include provision about:

(a) evidence,

(b) a trial timetable and time estimate,

(c) the preparation of a trial bundle,

(d) any other matter needed to prepare the case for trial.

(3) The court will include such of these provisions as are appropriate in any order that it may make, whether or not the parties have filed agreed directions.

(4) (a) A direction giving permission to use expert evidence will say whether it gives permission for oral evidence or reports or both and will name the experts concerned.

(b) The court will not make a direction giving permission for an expert to give oral evidence unless it believes it is necessary in the interests of justice to do so.

(c) Where no 'without prejudice' meeting or other discussion between experts has taken place the court may grant that permission conditionally on such a discussion taking place and a report being filed before the trial.

7.3 The principles set out in para. 4 of this practice direction about the variation of directions apply also to directions given at this stage.

The Trial

para.8.1 **59.25** para.8.3 **44.21, 59.16**

para.8.2 **59.39** para.8.6 **44.21**

8.1 The trial will normally take place at the court where the case is being managed, but it may be at another court if it is appropriate having regard to the needs of the parties and the availability of court resources.

8.2 The judge will generally have read the papers in the trial bundle and may dispense with an opening address.

8.3 The judge may confirm or vary any timetable given previously, or if none has been given set his own.

8.4 Attention is drawn to the provisions in Part 32 and the following parts of the Rules about evidence, and in particular—
(1) to rule 32.1 (court's power to control evidence and to restrict cross-examination), and
(2) to rule 32.5(2) (witness statements to stand as evidence-in-chief).

8.5 At the conclusion of the trial the judge will normally summarily assess the costs of the claim in accordance with rule 44.7 and Part 46 (fast track trial costs). Attention is drawn to the steps the practice directions about costs require the parties to take.

8.6 Where a trial is not finished on the day for which it is listed the judge will normally sit on the next court day to complete it.

APPENDIX FAST TRACK STANDARD DIRECTIONS

app. **42.1, 42.22, 44.16, 44.19**

Further Statements of Case

The must file a and serve a copy on no later than .

Requests for Further Information

Any request for clarification or further information based on another party's statement of case shall be served no later than .
[Any such request shall be dealt with no later than].

Disclosure of Documents

[No disclosure of documents is required].
[[Each party] [The]
shall give [to the]
[to every other party] standard disclosure of documents
[relating to]
by serving copies together with a disclosure statement no later than].
[Disclosure shall take place as follows:
[Each party shall give standard discovery to every other party by list]
[Disclosure is limited to [standard] [disclosure by the to the]
[of documents relating to damage]
[the following documents].
[The latest date for delivery of the lists is]
[The latest date for service of any request to inspect or for a copy of a document is]].

Witnesses of Fact

Each party shall serve on every other party the witness statements of all witnesses of fact on whom he intends to rely.
There shall be simultaneous exchange of such statements no later than .

Expert Evidence

[No expert evidence being necessary, no party has permission to call or rely on expert evidence].
[On it appearing to the court that expert evidence is necessary on the issue of
[ ]
and that that evidence should be given by the report of a single expert instructed jointly by the parties, the shall no later than inform the court whether or not such an expert has been instructed].
[The expert evidence on the issue of
shall be limited to a single expert jointly instructed by the parties.

If the parties cannot agree by who that expert is to be and about the payment of his fees either party may apply for further directions.
Unless the parties agree in writing or the court orders otherwise, the fees and expenses of such an expert shall be paid to him [by the parties equally]
[ ] and be limited to £ .
[The report of the expert shall be filed at the court no later than].
[No party shall be entitled to recover by way of costs from any other party more than £ for the fees or expenses of an expert].
The parties shall exchange reports setting out the substance of any expert evidence on which they intend to rely.
[The exchange shall take place simultaneously no later than].
[The shall serve his report(s) no later than the and the shall serve his reports no later than the].
[The exchange of reports relating to [causation] [ ] shall take place simultaneously no later than .
The shall serve his report(s) relating to [damage] [ ] no later than
and the shall serve his reports relating to it no later than].
Reports shall be agreed if possible no later than [days after service] [ ].
[If the reports are not agreed within that time there shall be a without prejudice discussion between the relevant experts no later than
to identify the issues between them and to reach agreement if possible.
The experts shall prepare for the court a statement of the issues on which they agree and on which they disagree with a summary of their reasons, and that statement shall be filed with the court [no later than] [with] [no later than the date for filing] [the listing questionnaire].
[Each party has permission to use [ ] as expert witness(es) to give [oral] evidence [in the form of a report] at the trial in the field of provided that the substance of the evidence to be given has been disclosed as above and has not been agreed].
[Each party has permission to use in evidence experts' report(s) [and the court will consider when the claim is listed for trial whether expert oral evidence will be allowed].]

Questions to Experts

The time for service on another party of any question addressed to an expert instructed by that party is not later than days after service of that expert's report.
Any such question shall be answered within days of service.

Requests for Information etc.

Each party shall serve any request for clarification or further information based on any document disclosed or statement served by another party no later than days after disclosure or service.
Any such request shall be dealt with within days of service.

Documents to be Filed with Pre-trial Checklists

The parties must file with their listing questionnaires* copies of [their experts' reports] [witness statements] [replies to requests for further information]

Dates for Filing Pre-trial Checklists and the Trial

Each party must file a completed pre-trial checklist no later than .
The trial of this case will take place [on][on a date to be fixed between and].

[* In the text issued by the Department for Constitutional Affairs the old term 'listing questionnaires' has not been changed to 'pre-trial checklists'.]

Directions Following Filing of Pre-trial Checklist

Expert evidence

The parties have permission to rely at the trial on expert evidence as follows:

The claimant:	Oral evidence— Written evidence—
The defendant:	Oral evidence— Written evidence—

Trial timetable

The time allowed for the trial is

[The timetable for the trial may be agreed by the parties, subject to the approval of the trial judge].

[The timetable for the trial (subject to the approval of the trial judge) will be that].

[The evidence-in-chief for each party will be contained in witness statements and reports, the time allowed for cross-examination by the defendant is limited to

and the time allowed for cross-examination by the claimant is limited to].

[The time allowed for the claimant's evidence is . The time allowed for the defendant's evidence is].

The time allowed for the submissions on behalf of each party is

The remainder of the time allowed for the trial (being) is reserved for the judge to consider and give the judgment and to deal with costs].

Trial bundle etc.

The claimant shall lodge an indexed bundle of documents contained in a ring binder and with each page clearly numbered at the court not more than 7 days and not less than 3 days before the start of the trial.

[A case summary (which should not exceed 250 words) outlining the matters still in issue, and referring where appropriate to the relevant documents shall be included in the bundle for the assistance of the judge in reading the papers before the trial].

[The parties shall seek to agree the contents of the trial bundle and the case summary].

Settlement

Each party must inform the court immediately if the claim is settled whether or not it is then possible to file a draft consent order to give effect to their agreement.

CPR Part 29 The Multi-track

Part 29 **13.14, 69.9** [For commentary on a specific rule, please refer to the cross-references after the title of the rule.]

29.1 Scope of This Part

This Part contains general provisions about management of cases allocated to the multi-track and applies only to cases allocated to that track.
(Part 27 sets out the procedure for claims allocated to the small claims track)
(Part 28 sets out the procedure for claims allocated to the fast track)

29.2 Case Management

r.29.2 **48.25**
r.29.2(1) **45.3**
r.29.2(1)(a)–(b) **48.1**
r.29.2(2) **45.12, 45.15, 59.1, 59.4**
r.29.2(3) **45.15**

(1) When it allocates a case to the multi-track, the court will—
 (a) give directions for the management of the case and set a timetable for the steps to be taken between the giving of directions and the trial; or
 (b) fix—
  (i) a case management conference; or
  (ii) a pre-trial review,
 or both, and give such other directions relating to the management of the case as it sees fit.
(2) The court will fix the trial date or the period in which the trial is to take place as soon as practicable.
(3) When the court fixes the trial date or the trial period under paragraph (2), it will—
 (a) give notice to the parties of the date or period; and
 (b) specify the date by which the parties must file a pre-trial checklist.

29.3 Case Management Conference and Pre-trial Review

r.29.3(2) **1.39, 45.9, 59.8**

(1) The court may fix—
 (a) a case management conference; or
 (b) a pre-trial review,
 at any time after the claim has been allocated.
(2) If a party has a legal representative, a representative—
 (a) familiar with the case; and
 (b) with sufficient authority to deal with any issues that are likely to arise,
 must attend case management conferences and pre-trial reviews.
(Rule 3.1(2)(c) provides that the court may require a party to attend the court)

29.4 Steps Taken by the Parties

r.29.4 **45.6**

If—
(a) the parties agree proposals for the management of the proceedings (including a proposed trial date or period in which the trial is to take place); and
(b) the court considers that the proposals are suitable,
it may approve them without a hearing and give directions in the terms proposed.

29.5 Variation of Case Management Timetable

r.29.5 **3.7, 46.1** r.29.5(1) **45.28**

(1) A party must apply to the court if he wishes to vary the date which the court has fixed for—
- (a) a case management conference;
- (b) a pre-trial review;
- (c) the return of a pre-trial checklist under rule 29.6;
- (d) the trial; or
- (e) the trial period.

(2) Any date set by the court or these Rules for doing any act may not be varied by the parties if the variation would make it necessary to vary any of the dates mentioned in paragraph (1).

(Rule 2.11 allows the parties to vary a date by written agreement except where the rules provide otherwise or the court orders otherwise)

29.6 Pre-trial Checklist (Listing Questionnaire)

r.29.6 **45.16** r.29.6(3) **45.19**
r.29.6(1) **45.15** r.29.6(4) **42.1, 45.19**

(1) The court will send the parties a pre-trial checklist (listing questionnaire) for completion and return by the date specified in directions given under rule 29.2(3) unless it considers that the claim can proceed to trial without the need for a pre-trial checklist.

(2) Each party must file the completed pre-trial checklist by the date specified by the court.

(3) If no party files the completed pre-trial checklist by the date specified, the court will order that unless a completed pre-trial checklist is filed within 7 days from service of that order, the claim, defence and any counterclaim will be struck out without further order of the court.

(4) If—
- (a) a party files a completed pre-trial checklist but another party does not;
- (b) a party has failed to give all the information requested by the pre-trial checklist; or
- (c) the court considers that a hearing is necessary to enable it to decide what directions to give in order to complete preparation of the case for trial,

the court may give such directions as it thinks appropriate.

29.7 Pre-trial Review

r.29.7 **45.22**

If, on receipt of the parties' pre-trial checklists, the court decides—
- (a) to hold a pre-trial review; or
- (b) to cancel a pre-trial review which has already been fixed,

it will serve notice of its decision at least 7 days before the date fixed for the hearing or, as the case may be, the cancelled hearing.

29.8 Setting a Trial Timetable and Fixing or Confirming the Trial Date or Week

r.29.8 **59.16** r.29.8(ii) **44.12, 59.4**
r.29.8(i) **59.16**

As soon as practicable after—
- (a) each party has filed a completed pre-trial checklist;
- (b) the court has held a listing hearing under rule 29.6(3); or
- (c) the court has held a pre-trial review under rule 29.7,

the court will—
- (i) set a timetable for the trial unless a timetable has already been fixed, or the court considers that it would be inappropriate to do so;
- (ii) fix the date for the trial or the week within which the trial is to begin (or, if it has already done so, confirm that date); and
- (iii) notify the parties of the trial timetable (where one is fixed under this rule) and the date or trial period.

29.9 Conduct of Trial

r.29.9 **59.16**

Unless the trial judge otherwise directs, the trial will be conducted in accordance with any order previously made.

PD 29 Practice Direction — The Multi-track

This practice direction supplements CPR Part 29

PD 29 **52.5** [For commentary on a specific paragraph, please refer to the cross-references after the title of the paragraph.]

General

1.1 Attention is drawn in particular to the following Parts of the Civil Procedure Rules:

Part 1	The overriding objective
Part 3	The court's case management powers
Part 26	Case management — preliminary stage
Part 31	Disclosure and inspection of documents
Parts 32 to 34	Evidence
Part 35	Experts and assessors

and to the practice directions which relate to those Parts.

Case Management in the Royal Courts of Justice

para.2 **45.1**
para.2.2 **11.4, 42.20**
para.2.6 **11.4**

2.1 This part of the practice direction applies to claims begun by claim form issued in the Central Office or Chancery Chambers in the Royal Courts of Justice.

2.2 A claim with an estimated value of less than £50,000 will generally, unless:
(a) it is required by an enactment to be tried in the High Court,
(b) it falls within a specialist list, or
(c) it falls within one of the categories specified in 2.6 below or is otherwise within the criteria of article 7(5) of the High Court and County Courts Jurisdiction Order 1991,
be transferred to a county court.

2.3 Paragraph 2.2 is without prejudice to the power of the court in accordance with Part 30 to transfer to a county court a claim with an estimated value that exceeds £50,000.

2.4 The decision to transfer may be made at any stage in the proceedings but should, subject to paragraph 2.5, be made as soon as possible and in any event not later than the date for the filing of pre-trial checklists (listing questionnaires).

2.5 If an application is made under rule 3.4 (striking out) or under Part 24 (summary judgment) or under Part 25 (interim remedies), it will usually be convenient for the application to be dealt with before a decision to transfer is taken.

2.6 Each party should state in his allocation questionnaire whether he considers the claim should be managed and tried at the Royal Courts of Justice and, if so, why. Claims suitable for trial in the Royal Courts of Justice include:
(1) professional negligence claims,
(2) Fatal Accident Act claims,
(3) fraud or undue influence claims,
(4) defamation claims,
(5) claims for malicious prosecution or false imprisonment,
(6) claims against the police,
(7) contentious probate claims.
Such claims may fall within the criteria of article 7(5) of the High Court and County Courts Jurisdiction Order 1991.

2.7 Attention is drawn to PD 30

Civil Procedure Rules & Practice Directions

Case Management — General Provisions

para.3.1 **45.1**
para.3.2(2) **45.1**
para.3.4 **45.26, 45.30**
para.3.5 **32.1, 45.1, 45.26, 65.2**
para.3.6 **41.4, 45.26, 46.11**
para.3.7 **45.8**
para.3.8 **32.6, 45.26**
para.3.10 **2.6, 2.13, 42.2**

3.1 (1) Case management of a claim which is proceeding at the Royal Courts of Justice will be undertaken there.

(2) (a) Case management of any other claim which has been allocated to the multi-track will normally be undertaken at a Civil Trial Centre.

(b) The practice direction supplementing Part 26 provides for what will happen in the case of a claim which is issued in or transferred to a court which is not a Civil Trial Centre.

3.2 The hallmarks of the multi-track are:

(1) the ability of the court to deal with cases of widely differing values and complexity, and

(2) the flexibility given to the court in the way it will manage a case in a way appropriate to its particular needs.

3.3 (1) On allocating a claim to the multi-track the court may give directions without a hearing, including fixing a trial date or a period in which the trial will take place,

(2) Alternatively, whether or not it fixes a trial date or period, it may either—

(a) give directions for certain steps to be taken and fix a date for a case management conference or a pre-trial review to take place after they have been taken, or

(b) fix a date for a case management conference.

(3) Attention is drawn to rule 29.2(2) which requires the court to fix a trial date or period as soon as practicable.

3.4 The court may give or vary directions at any hearing which may take place on the application of a party or of its own initiative.

3.5 When any hearing has been fixed it is the duty of the parties to consider what directions the court should be asked to give and to make any application that may be appropriate to be dealt with then.

3.6 The court will hold a hearing to give directions whenever it appears necessary or desirable to do so, and where this happens because of the default of a party or his legal representative it will usually impose a sanction.

3.7 When the court fixes a hearing to give directions it will give the parties at least 3 days' notice of the hearing unless rule 29.7 applies (7 days' notice to be given in the case of a pre-trial review).

3.8 Where a party needs to apply for a direction of a kind not included in the case management timetable which has been set (for example to amend his statement of case or for further information to be given by another party) he must do so as soon as possible so as to minimise the need to change that timetable.

3.9 Courts will make arrangements to ensure that applications and other hearings are listed promptly to avoid delay in the conduct of cases.

3.10 (1) Case management will generally be dealt with by:

(a) a master in cases proceeding in the Royal Courts of Justice,

(b) a district judge in cases proceeding in a district registry of the High Court, and

(c) a district judge or a circuit judge in cases proceeding in a county court.

(2) A master or a district judge may consult and seek the directions of a judge of a higher level about any aspect of case management.

(3) A member of the court staff who is dealing with the listing of a hearing may seek the directions of any judge about any aspect of that listing.

Case Management: Consideration of Periodical Payments

3A Attention is drawn to PD 41B and in particular to the direction that in a personal injury claim the court should consider and indicate to the parties as soon as practicable whether periodical payments or a lump sum is likely to be the more appropriate form for all or part of an award of damages for future pecuniary loss.

Directions on Allocation

4.1 Attention is drawn to the court's duties under Rule 29.2.

4.2 The court will seek to tailor its directions to the needs of the case and the steps which the parties have already taken to prepare the case of which it is aware. In particular it will have regard to the extent to which any pre-action protocol has or (as the case may be) has not been complied with.

4.3 At this stage the court's first concern will be to ensure that the issues between the parties are identified and that the necessary evidence is prepared and disclosed.

4.4 The court may have regard to any document filed by a party with his allocation questionnaire containing further information, provided that the document states either that its contents has been agreed with every other party or that it has been served on every other party, and when it was served.

4.5 On the allocation of a claim to the multi-track the court will consider whether it is desirable or necessary to hold a case management conference straight away, or whether it is appropriate instead to give directions on its own initiative.

4.6 The parties and their advisers are encouraged to try to agree directions and to take advantage of rule 29.4 which provides that if:
(1) the parties agree proposals for the management of the proceedings (including a proposed trial date or period in which the trial is to take place), and
(2) the court considers that the proposals are suitable,
it may approve them without a hearing and give directions in the terms proposed.

4.7 (1) To obtain the court's approval the agreed directions must:
(a) set out a timetable by reference to calendar dates for the taking of steps for the preparation of the case,
(b) include a date or a period (the trial period) when it is proposed that the trial will take place,
(c) include provision about disclosure of documents, and
(d) include provision about both factual and expert evidence.
(2) The court will scrutinise the timetable carefully and in particular will be concerned to see that any proposed date or period for the trial and (if provided for) for a case management conference is no later than is reasonably necessary.
(3) The provision in (1)(c) above may:
(a) limit disclosure to standard disclosure or less than that, and/or
(b) direct that disclosure will take place by the supply of copy documents without a list, but it must in that case say either that the parties must serve a disclosure statement with the copies or that they have agreed to disclose in that way without such a statement.
(4) The provision in (1)(d) about expert evidence may be to the effect that none is required.

4.8 Directions agreed by the parties should also where appropriate contain provisions about:
(1) the filing of any reply or amended statement of case that may be required,
(2) dates for the service of requests for further information under the practice direction supplementing Part 18 and of questions to experts under rule 35.6 and by when they are to be dealt with,
(3) the disclosure of evidence,
(4) the use of a single joint expert, or in cases where it is not agreed, the exchange of expert evidence (including whether exchange is to be simultaneous or sequential) and without prejudice discussions between experts.

4.9 If the court does not approve the agreed directions filed by the parties but decides that it will give directions of its own initiative without fixing a case management conference, it will take them into account in deciding what directions to give.

4.10 Where the court is to give directions on its own initiative without holding a case management conference and it is not aware of any steps taken by the parties other than the exchange of statements of case, its general approach will be:
(1) to give directions for the filing and service of any further information required to clarify either party's case,
(2) to direct standard disclosure between the parties,
(3) to direct the disclosure of witness statements by way of simultaneous exchange,
(4) to give directions for a single joint expert on any appropriate issue unless there is a good reason not to do so,
(5) unless para. 4.11 (below) applies, to direct disclosure of experts' reports by way of simultaneous exchange on those issues where a single joint expert is not directed,
(6) if experts' reports are not agreed, to direct a discussion between experts for the purpose set out in r. 35.12(1) and the preparation of a statement under r. 35.12(3),
(7) to list a case management conference to take place after the date for compliance with those directions,
(8) to specify a trial period, and
(9) in such cases as the court thinks appropriate, the court may give directions requiring the parties to consider ADR. Such directions may be, for example, in the following terms:
'The parties shall by [date] consider whether the case is capable of resolution by ADR. If any party considers that the case is unsuitable for resolution by ADR, that party shall be prepared to justify that decision at the conclusion of the trial, should the judge consider that such means of resolution were appropriate, when he is considering the appropriate costs order to make.
The party considering the case unsuitable for ADR shall, not less than 28 days before the commencement of the trial, file with the court a witness statement without prejudice save as to costs, giving reasons upon which they rely for saying that the case was unsuitable.'

4.11 If it appears that expert evidence will be required both on issues of liability and on the amount of damages, the court may direct that the exchange of those reports that relate to liability will be exchanged simultaneously but that those relating to the amount of damages will be exchanged sequentially.

4.12 (1) If it appears to the court that it cannot properly give directions on its own initiative and no agreed directions have been filed which it can approve, the court will direct a case management conference to be listed.
(2) The conference will be listed as promptly as possible.

4.13 Where the court is proposing on its own initiative to make an order under r. 35.7 (which gives the court power to direct that evidence on a particular issue is to be given by a single expert) or under r. 35.15 (which gives the court power to appoint an assessor), the court must, unless the parties have consented in writing to the order, list a case management conference.

Case Management Conferences

para.5.1 **45.10**
para.5.2(3) **45.9**
paras.5.3–5.4 **45.12**
para.5.6 **45.10, 45.11, 59.17**
para.5.7 **45.11, 59.17**
para.5.8 **32.6, 45.13**
para.5.9 **45.12**

5.1 The court will at any case management conference:
(1) review the steps which the parties have taken in the preparation of the case, and in particular their compliance with any directions that the court may have given,
(2) decide and give directions about the steps which are to be taken to secure the progress of the claim in accordance with the overriding objective, and
(3) ensure as far as it can that all agreements that can be reached between the parties about the matters in issue and the conduct of the claim are made and recorded.

5.2 (1) Rule 29.3(2) provides that where a party has a legal representative, a representative familiar with the case and with sufficient authority to deal with any issues that are likely to arise must attend case management conferences and pre-trial reviews.
(2) That person should be someone who is personally involved in the conduct of the case, and who has the authority and information to deal with any matter which may reasonably be

expected to be dealt with at such a hearing, including the fixing of the timetable, the identification of issues and matters of evidence.

(3) Where the inadequacy of the person attending or of his instructions leads to the adjournment of a hearing, the court will expect to make a wasted costs order.

5.3 The topics the court will consider at a case management conference are likely to include:

(1) whether the claimant has made clear the claim he is bringing, in particular the amount he is claiming, so that the other party can understand the case he has to meet,

(2) whether any amendments are required to the claim, a statement of case or any other document,

(3) what disclosure of documents, if any, is necessary,

(4) what expert evidence is reasonably required in accordance with rule 35.1 and how and when that evidence should be obtained and disclosed,

(5) what factual evidence should be disclosed,

(6) what arrangements should be made about the giving of clarification or further information and the putting of questions to experts, and

(7) whether it will be just and will save costs to order a split trial or the trial of one or more preliminary issues.

5.4 In all cases the court will set a timetable for the steps it decides are necessary to be taken. These steps may include the holding of a case management conference or a pre-trial review, and the court will be alert to perform its duty to fix a trial date or period as soon as it can.

5.5 (1) The court will not at this stage give permission to use expert evidence unless it can identify each expert by name or field in its order and say whether his evidence is to be given orally or by the use of his report.

(2) A party who obtains expert evidence before obtaining a direction about it does so at his own risk as to costs, except where he obtained the evidence in compliance with a pre-action protocol.

5.6 To assist the court, the parties and their legal advisers should:

(1) ensure that all documents that the court is likely to ask to see (including witness statements and experts' reports) are brought to the hearing,

(2) consider whether the parties should attend,

(3) consider whether a case summary will be useful, and

(4) consider what orders each wishes to be made and give notice of them to the other parties.

5.7 (1) A case summary:

(a) should be designed to assist the court to understand and deal with the questions before it,

(b) should set out a brief chronology of the claim, the issues of fact which are agreed or in dispute and the evidence needed to decide them,

(c) should not normally exceed 500 words in length, and

(d) should be prepared by the claimant and agreed with the other parties if possible.

5.8 (1) Where a party wishes to obtain an order not routinely made at a case management conference and believes that his application will be opposed, he should issue and serve the application in time for it to be heard at the case management conference.

(2) If the time allowed for the case management conference is likely to be insufficient for the application to be heard he should inform the court at once so that a fresh date can be fixed.

(3) A costs sanction may be imposed on a party who fails to comply with sub-paragraph (1) or (2).

5.9 At a case management conference the court may also consider whether the case ought to be tried by a High Court judge or by a judge who specialises in that type of claim and how that question will be decided. In that case the claim may need to be transferred to another court.

Variation of Directions

para.6 **45.24**
para.6.2 **32.6, 45.27**
para.6.2(2) **32.24, 45.5, 46.2**
para.6.3 **45.31**
para.6.3(2) **45.32**
para.6.4 **45.30**
para.6.5(1) **45.28**
para.6.5(2) **45.29**

6.1 This paragraph deals with the procedure to be adopted:

(1) where a party is dissatisfied with a direction given by the court,

(2) where the parties have agreed about changes they wish made to the directions given, or
(3) where a party wishes to apply to vary a direction.

6.2 (1) It is essential that any party who wishes to have a direction varied takes steps to do so as soon as possible.
(2) The court will assume for the purposes of any later application that a party who did not appeal, and who made no application to vary within 14 days of service of the order containing the directions, was content that they were correct in the circumstances then existing.

6.3 (1) Where a party is dissatisfied with a direction given or other order made by the court he may appeal or apply to the court for it to reconsider its decision.
(2) Unless paragraph 6.4 applies, a party should appeal if the direction was given or the order was made at a hearing at which he was present, or of which he had due notice.
(3) In any other case he should apply to the court to reconsider its decision.
(4) If an application is made for the court to reconsider its decision:
(a) it will usually be heard by the judge who gave the directions or another judge of the same level,
(b) the court will give all parties at least 3 days' notice of the hearing, and
(c) the court may confirm its directions or make a different order.

6.4 Where there has been a change in the circumstances since the order was made the court may set aside or vary a direction it has given. It may do so on application or on its own initiative.

6.5 Where the parties agree about changes they wish made to the directions given:
(1) If rule 2.11 (variation by agreement of a date set by the court for doing any act other than those stated in the note to that rule) or rule 31.5, 31.10(8) or 31.13 (agreements about disclosure) applies the parties need not file the written agreement.
(2) (a) In any other case the parties must apply for an order by consent.
(b) The parties must file a draft of the order sought and an agreed statement of the reasons why the variation is sought.
(c) The court may make an order in the agreed terms or in other terms without a hearing, but it may direct that a hearing is to be listed.

Failure to Comply with Case Management Directions

para.7 **46.5**
paras.7.1–7.3 **46.3**
para.7.4 **46.5, 59.11**
para.7.4(6) **56.1**

7.1 Where a party fails to comply with a direction given by the court any other party may apply for an order that he must do so or for a sanction to be imposed or both of these.

7.2 The party entitled to apply for such an order must do so without delay but should first warn the other party of his intention to do so.

7.3 The court may take any such delay into account when it decides whether to make an order imposing a sanction or to grant relief from a sanction imposed by the rules or any other practice direction.

7.4 (1) The court will not allow a failure to comply with directions to lead to the postponement of the trial unless the circumstances are exceptional.
(2) If it is practical to do so the court will exercise its powers in a manner that enables the case to come on for trial on the date or within the period previously set.
(3) In particular the court will assess what steps each party should take to prepare the case for trial, direct that those steps are taken in the shortest possible time and impose a sanction for non-compliance. Such a sanction may, for example, deprive a party of the right to raise or contest an issue or to rely on evidence to which the direction relates.
(4) Where it appears that one or more issues are or can be made ready for trial at the time fixed while others cannot, the court may direct that the trial will proceed on the issues which are then ready, and direct that no costs will be allowed for any later trial of the remaining issues or that those costs will be paid by the party in default.
(5) Where the court has no option but to postpone the trial it will do so for the shortest possible time and will give directions for the taking of the necessary steps in the meantime as rapidly as possible.
(6) Litigants and lawyers must be in no doubt that the court will regard the postponement of a trial as an order of last resort. Where it appears inevitable the court may exercise its power to

require a party as well as his legal representative to attend court at the hearing where such an order is to be sought.

(7) The court will not postpone any other hearing without a very good reason, and for that purpose the failure of a party to comply on time with directions previously given will not be treated as a good reason.

Pre-trial Checklists (Listing Questionnaires)

para.8.1(2) **45.15**
para.8.1(5) **45.18**
para.8.5(1) **45.19**
para.8.3(1) **45.19**
para.8.3(2) **45.20**
para.8.5 **45.19**

8.1 (1) The pre-trial checklist (listing questionnaire) will be in form N170.

(2) Unless it dispenses with pre-trial checklist and orders an early trial on a fixed date, the court will specify the date for filing completed pre-trial checklist when it fixes the trial date or trial period under r. 29.2(2).

(3) The date for filing the completed pre-trial checklist will be not later than eight weeks before the trial date or the start of the trial period.

(4) The court will serve the pre-trial checklist on the parties at least 14 days before that date.

(5) Although the rules do not require the parties to exchange copies of the checklists before they are filed they are encouraged to do so to avoid the court being given conflicting or incomplete information.

(6) The file will be placed before a judge for his directions when all the checklists have been filed or when the time for filing them has expired and where a party has filed a checklist but another party has not done so.

8.2 The court's general approach will be as set out in the following paragraphs. The court may however decide to make other orders, and in particular the court will take into account the steps, if any, of which it is aware which the parties have taken to prepare the case for trial.

8.3 (1) Where no party files a pre-trial checklist the court will order that unless a completed pre-trial checklist is filed within seven days from service of that order, the claim, defence and any counterclaim will be struck out without further order of the court.

(2) Where a party files a pre-trial checklist but another party (the defaulting party) does not do so, the court will fix a hearing under r. 29.6(4). Whether or not the defaulting party attends the hearing, the court will normally fix or confirm the trial date and make other orders about the steps to be taken to prepare the case for trial.

8.4 Where the court decides to hold a hearing under r. 29.6(4) the court will fix a date which is as early as possible and the parties will be given at least three days' notice of the date.

8.5 Where the court decides to hold a pre-trial review (whether or not this is in addition to a hearing under r. 29.6(4)) the court will give the parties at least seven days' notice of the date.

Directions the Court Will Give on Listing

Directions the court must give

9.1 The court must fix the trial date or week, give a time estimate and fix the place of trial.

Other directions

para.9.2 **45.25**
para.9.3 **45.24**

9.2 (1) The parties should seek to agree directions and may file an agreed order. The court may make an order in those terms or it may make a different order.

(2) Agreed directions should include provision about:

(a) evidence especially expert evidence,
(b) a trial timetable and time estimate,
(c) the preparation of a trial bundle, and
(d) any other matter needed to prepare the case for trial.

(3) The court will include such of these provisions as are appropriate in any order that it may make, whether or not the parties have filed agreed directions.

(4) Unless a direction doing so has been given before, a direction giving permission to use expert evidence will say whether it gives permission to use oral evidence or reports or both and will name the experts concerned.

9.3 The principles set out in para. 6 of this practice direction about variation of directions applies equally to directions given at this stage.

The Trial

para.10.1 **45.24, 59.25** para.10.3 **59.16**
para.10.2 **59.39**

10.1 The trial will normally take place at a civil trial centre but it may be at another court if it is appropriate having regard to the needs of the parties and the availability of court resources.

10.2 The judge will generally have read the papers in the trial bundle and may dispense with an opening address.

10.3 The judge may confirm or vary any timetable given previously, or if none has been given set his own.

10.4 Attention is drawn to the provisions in Part 32 and the following parts of the Rules about evidence, and in particular:

(1) to rule 32.1 (court's power to control evidence and to restrict cross-examination), and

(2) to rule 32.5(2) statements and reports to stand as evidence-in-chief.

10.5 In an appropriate case the judge may summarily assess costs in accordance with rule 44.7. Attention is drawn to the practice directions about costs and the steps the parties are required to take.

10.6 Once the trial of a multi-track claim has begun, the judge will normally sit on consecutive court days until it has been concluded.

CPR Part 30 Transfer

Part 30 **11.9**, **42.3**, **74.47** [For commentary on a specific rule, please refer to the cross-references after the title of the rule.]

30.1 Scope of This Part

(1) This Part deals with the transfer of proceedings between county courts, between the High Court and the county courts and within the High Court.
(2) The practice direction may make provision about the transfer of proceedings between the court and a tribunal.
(Rule 26.2 provides for automatic transfer in certain cases)

30.2 Transfer between County Courts and within the High Court

(1) A county court may order proceedings before that court, or any part of them (such as a counterclaim or an application made in the proceedings), to be transferred to another county court if it is satisfied that—
 (a) an order should be made having regard to the criteria in rule 30.3; or
 (b) proceedings for—
  (i) the detailed assessment of costs; or
  (ii) the enforcement of a judgment or order, could be more conveniently or fairly taken in that other county court.
(2) If proceedings have been started in the wrong county court, a judge of the county court may order that the proceedings—
 (a) be transferred to the county court in which they ought to have been started;
 (b) continue in the county court in which they have been started; or
 (c) be struck out.
(3) An application for an order under paragraph (1) or (2) must be made to the county court where the claim is proceeding.
(4) The High Court may, having regard to the criteria in rule 30.3, order proceedings in the Royal Courts of Justice or a district registry, or any part of such proceedings (such as a counterclaim or an application made in the proceedings), to be transferred—
 (a) from the Royal Courts of Justice to a district registry; or
 (b) from a district registry to the Royal Courts of Justice or to another district registry.
(5) A district registry may order proceedings before it for the detailed assessment of costs to be transferred to another district registry if it is satisfied that the proceedings could be more conveniently or fairly taken in that other district registry.
(6) An application for an order under paragraph (4) or (5) must, if the claim is proceeding in a district registry, be made to that registry.
(7) Where some enactment, other than these Rules, requires proceedings to be started in a particular county court, neither paragraphs (1) nor (2) give the court power to order proceedings to be transferred to a county court which is not the court in which they should have been started or to order them to continue in the wrong court.
(8) Probate proceedings may only be transferred under paragraph (4) to the Chancery Division at the Royal Courts of Justice or to one of the Chancery district registries.

30.3 Criteria for a Transfer Order

r.30.3(2)(h) **14.75**

(1) Paragraph (2) sets out the matters to which the court must have regard when considering whether to make an order under—
   (a) section 40(2), 41(1) or 42(2) of the County Courts Act 1984 (transfer between the High Court and a county court);
   (b) rule 30.2(1) (transfer between county courts); or
   (c) rule 30.2(4) (transfer between the Royal Courts of Justice and the district registries).
(2) The matters to which the court must have regard include—
   (a) the financial value of the claim and the amount in dispute, if different;
   (b) whether it would be more convenient or fair for hearings (including the trial) to be held in some other court;
   (c) the availability of a judge specialising in the type of claim in question;
   (d) whether the facts, legal issues, remedies or procedures involved are simple or complex;
   (e) the importance of the outcome of the claim to the public in general;
   (f) the facilities available at the court where the claim is being dealt with and whether they may be inadequate because of any disabilities of a party or potential witness;
   (g) whether the making of a declaration of incompatibility under section 4 of the Human Rights Act 1998 has arisen or may arise;
   (h) in the case of civil proceedings by or against the Crown, as defined in rule 66.1(2), the location of the relevant government department or officers of the Crown and, where appropriate, any relevant public interest that the matter should be tried in London.

30.4 Procedure

(1) Where the court orders proceedings to be transferred, the court from which they are to be transferred must give notice of the transfer to all the parties.
(2) An order made before the transfer of the proceedings shall not be affected by the order to transfer.

30.5 Transfer between Divisions and to and from a Specialist List

r.30.5 **74.47**
r.30.5(2) **42.3**
r.30.5(3) **69.2, 74.47**

(1) The High Court may order proceedings in any Division of the High Court to be transferred to another Division.
(2) A judge dealing with claims in a specialist list may order proceedings to be transferred to or from that list.
(3) An application for the transfer of proceedings to or from a specialist list must be made to a judge dealing with claims in that list.

30.6 Power to Specify Place Where Hearings Are to Be Held

The court may specify the place (for instance, a particular county court) where the trial or some other hearing in any proceedings is to be held and may do so without ordering the proceedings to be transferred.

30.7 Transfer of Control of Money in Court

The court may order that control of any money held by it under rule 21.11 (control of money recovered by or on behalf of a child or patient) be transferred to another court if that court would be more convenient.

30.8 Transfer of Competition Law Claims

r.30.8 **2.14, 11.6**
r.30.8(4) **11.6**

(1) This rule applies if, in any proceedings in the Queen's Bench Division (other than proceedings in the Commercial or Admiralty Courts), a district registry of the High Court or a county court, a party's statement of case raises an issue relating to the application of—
   (a) Article 81 or Article 82 of the Treaty establishing the European Community; or
   (b) Chapter I or II of Part I of the Competition Act 1998.
(2) Rules 30.2 and 30.3 do not apply.

(3) The court must transfer the proceedings to the Chancery Division of the High Court at the Royal Courts of Justice.

(4) If any such proceedings which have been commenced in the Queen's Bench Division or a Mercantile Court fall within the scope of rule 58.1(2), any party to those proceedings may apply for the transfer of the proceedings to the Commercial Court, in accordance with rule 58.4(2) and rule 30.5(3). If the application is refused, the proceedings must be transferred to the Chancery Division of the High Court at the Royal Courts of Justice.

PD 30 Practice Direction — Transfer

This practice direction supplements CPR Part 30

Value of a Case and Transfer

1 In addition to the criteria set out in r. 30.3(2) attention is drawn to the financial limits set out in the High Court and County Courts Jurisdiction Order 1991, as amended.

2 Attention is also drawn to PD 29, para. 2.

Date of Transfer

3 Where the court orders proceedings to be transferred, the order will take effect from the date it is made by the court.

Procedure on Transfer

4.1 Where an order for transfer has been made the transferring court will immediately send notice of the transfer to the receiving court. The notice will contain:
(1) the name of the case, and
(2) the number of the case.

4.2 At the same time as the transferring court notifies the receiving court it will also notify the parties of the transfer under r. 30.4(1) .

Procedure for an Appeal against Order of Transfer

5.1 Where a district judge orders proceedings to be transferred and both the transferring and receiving courts are county courts, any appeal against that order should be made in the receiving court.

5.2 The receiving court may, if it is more convenient for the parties, remit the appeal to the transferring court to be dealt with there.

Applications to Set Aside

6.1 Where a party may apply to set aside an order for transfer (e.g. under r. 23.10) the application should be made to the court which made the order.

6.2 Such application should be made in accordance with Part 23 of the Rules and PD 23.

Transfer on the Criterion in Rule 30.3(2)(g)

7 A transfer should only be made on the basis of the criterion in r. 30.3(2)(g) where there is a real prospect that a declaration of incompatibility will be made.

Enterprise Act 2002

8.1 In this paragraph:
(1) 'the 1998 Act' means the Competition Act 1998;
(2) 'the 2002 Act' means the Enterprise Act 2002; and
(3) 'the CAT' means the Competition Appeal Tribunal.

8.2 Rules 30.1, 30.4 and 30.5 and paras 3 and 6 apply.

Transfer from the High Court or a county court to the Competition Appeal Tribunal under the Enterprise Act 2002, s. 16(4)

8.3 The High Court or a county court may pursuant to s. 16(4) of the 2002 Act, on its own initiative or on application by the claimant or defendant, order the transfer of any part of the proceedings before it, which relates to a claim to which s. 47A of the 1998 Act applies, to the CAT.

8.4 When considering whether to make an order under para. 8.3 the court shall take into account whether:

(1) there is a similar claim under s. 47A of the 1998 Act based on the same infringement currently before the CAT;
(2) the CAT has previously made a decision on a similar claim under s. 47A of the 1998 Act based on the same infringement; or
(3) the CAT has developed considerable expertise by previously dealing with a significant number of cases arising from the same or similar infringements.

8.5 Where the court orders a transfer under para. 8.3 it will immediately:
(1) send to the CAT:
(a) a notice of the transfer containing the name of the case; and
(b) all papers relating to the case; and
(2) notify the parties of the transfer.

8.6 An appeal against a transfer order made under para. 8.3 must be brought in the court which made the transfer order.

Transfer from the Competition Appeal Tribunal to the High Court under the Enterprise Act 2002, s. 16(5)

8.7 Where the CAT pursuant to s. 16(5) of the 2002 Act directs transfer of a claim made in proceedings under s. 47A of the 1998 Act to the High Court, the claim should be transferred to the Chancery Division of the High Court at the Royal Courts of Justice.

8.8 As soon as a claim has been transferred under para. 8.7, the High Court must:
(1) allocate a case number; and
(2) list the case for a case management hearing before a judge.

8.9 A party to a claim which has been transferred under para. 8.7 may apply to transfer it to the Commercial Court if it otherwise falls within the scope of r. 58.2(1), in accordance with the procedure set out in rr. 58.4(2) and 30.5(3).

CPR Part 31 Disclosure and Inspection of Documents

Part 31 **14.18, 43.6, 45.14, 47.10, 47.83, 48.1, 48.16, 48.2, 48.9, 48.31, 48.82, 79.62** [For commentary on a specific rule, please refer to the cross-references after the title of the rule.]

31.1 Scope of This Part

(1) This Part sets out rules about the disclosure and inspection of documents.
(2) This Part applies to all claims except a claim on the small claims track.

31.2 Meaning of Disclosure

r.31.2 **48.5** r.31.2(2) **48.21**

A party discloses a document by stating that the document exists or has existed.

31.3 Right of Inspection of a Disclosed Document

r.31.3 **48.6, 48.21, 48.24** r.31.3(2) **48.19, 48.23, 48.24**
r.31.3(1)(b) **48.37**

(1) A party to whom a document has been disclosed has a right to inspect that document except where—
   (a) the document is no longer in the control of the party who disclosed it;
   (b) the party disclosing the document has a right or a duty to withhold inspection of it; or
   (c) paragraph (2) applies.

(Rule 31.8 sets out when a document is in the control of a party)
(Rule 31.19 sets out the procedure for claiming a right or duty to withhold inspection)

(2) Where a party considers that it would be disproportionate to the issues in the case to permit inspection of documents within a category or class of document disclosed under rule 31.6(b)—
   (a) he is not required to permit inspection of documents within that category or class; but
   (b) he must state in his disclosure statement that inspection of those documents will not be permitted on the grounds that to do so would be disproportionate.

(Rule 31.6 provides for standard disclosure)
(Rule 31.10 makes provision for a disclosure statement)
(Rule 31.12 provides for a party to apply for an order for specific inspection of documents)

31.4 Meaning of Document

r.31.4 **48.1, 48.9, 48.10**

In this Part—

'document' means anything in which information of any description is recorded; and

'copy', in relation to a document, means anything onto which information recorded in the document has been copied, by whatever means and whether directly or indirectly.

31.5 Disclosure Limited to Standard Disclosure

r.31.5 **48.25**
r.31.5(1) **48.4**
r.31.5(2)–(3) **48.25**

(1) An order to give disclosure is an order to give standard disclosure unless the court directs otherwise.
(2) The court may dispense with or limit standard disclosure.
(3) The parties may agree in writing to dispense with or to limit standard disclosure.

(The court may make an order requiring standard disclosure under rule 28.3 which deals with directions in relation to cases on the fast track and under rule 29.2 which deals with case management in relation to cases on the multi-track)

31.6 Standard Disclosure — What Documents Are to Be Disclosed

r.31.6 **48.4, 48.5, 48.6, 48.13, 48.14, 48.16, 48.71**
r.31.6(a) **48.4**
r.31.6(b) **48.4, 48.19, 48.21**
r.31.6(c) **48.4, 48.19**

Standard disclosure requires a party to disclose only—
(a) the documents on which he relies; and
(b) the documents which—
  (i) adversely affect his own case;
  (ii) adversely affect another party's case; or
  (iii) support another party's case; and
(c) the documents which he is required to disclose by a relevant practice direction.

31.7 Duty of Search

r.31.7 **48.4, 48.13**
r.31.7(2) **48.13**
r.31.7(3) **48.13, 48.19**

(1) When giving standard disclosure, a party is required to make a reasonable search for documents falling within rule 31.6(b) or (c).
(2) The factors relevant in deciding the reasonableness of a search include the following—
  (a) the number of documents involved;
  (b) the nature and complexity of the proceedings;
  (c) the ease and expense of retrieval of any particular document; and
  (d) the significance of any document which is likely to be located during the search.
(3) Where a party has not searched for a category or class of document on the grounds that to do so would be unreasonable, he must state this in his disclosure statement and identify the category or class of document.

(Rule 31.10 makes provision for a disclosure statement)

31.8 Duty of Disclosure Limited to Documents Which Are or Have Been in a Party's Control

r.31.8 **48.1, 48.6**
r.31.8(1) **48.11**
r.31.8(2) **48.6**
r.31.8(3) **48.11**

(1) A party's duty to disclose documents is limited to documents which are or have been in his control.
(2) For this purpose a party has or has had a document in his control if—
  (a) it is or was in his physical possession;
  (b) he has or has had a right to possession of it; or
  (c) he has or has had a right to inspect or take copies of it.

31.9 Disclosure of Copies

r.31.9 **48.12** r.31.9(1) **48.12**

(1) A party need not disclose more than one copy of a document.
(2) A copy of a document that contains a modification, obliteration or other marking or feature—
(a) on which a party intends to rely; or
(b) which adversely affects his own case or another party's case or supports another party's case;
shall be treated as a separate document.
(Rule 31.4 sets out the meaning of a copy of a document)

31.10 Procedure for Standard Disclosure

r.31.10 **48.18** r.31.10(6) **1.36, 48.14, 48.18, 48.19**
r.31.10(2) **48.5** r.31.10(6)(b)–(c) **48.14**
r.31.10(3) **48.5** r.31.10(7) **48.18**
r.31.10(4) **48.5** r.31.10(8) **48.5**
r.31.10(5) **48.14, 48.18** r.31.10(9) **48.18**

(1) The procedure for standard disclosure is as follows.
(2) Each party must make and serve on every other party, a list of documents in the relevant practice form.
(3) The list must identify the documents in a convenient order and manner and as concisely as possible.
(4) The list must indicate—
(a) those documents in respect of which the party claims a right or duty to withhold inspection; and
(b) (i) those documents which are no longer in the party's control; and
(ii) what has happened to those documents.
(Rule 31.19(3) and (4) require a statement in the list of documents relating to any documents inspection of which a person claims he has a right or duty to withhold)
(5) The list must include a disclosure statement.
(6) A disclosure statement is a statement made by the party disclosing the documents—
(a) setting out the extent of the search that has been made to locate documents which he is required to disclose;
(b) certifying that he understands the duty to disclose documents; and
(c) certifying that to the best of his knowledge he has carried out that duty.
(7) Where the party making the disclosure statement is a company, firm, association or other organisation, the statement must also—
(a) identify the person making the statement; and
(b) explain why he is considered an appropriate person to make the statement.
(8) The parties may agree in writing—
(a) to disclose documents without making a list; and
(b) to disclose documents without the disclosing party making a disclosure statement.
(9) A disclosure statement may be made by a person who is not a party where this is permitted by a relevant practice direction.

31.11 Duty of Disclosure Continues during Proceedings

r.31.11(2) **48.32**

(1) Any duty of disclosure continues until the proceedings are concluded.
(2) If documents to which that duty extends come to a party's notice at any time during the proceedings, he must immediately notify every other party.

31.12 Specific Disclosure or Inspection

r.31.12 **48.21, 48.22, 48.29, 96.30** r.31.12(3) **48.6**

(1) The court may make an order for specific disclosure or specific inspection.
(2) An order for specific disclosure is an order that a party must do one or more of the following things—
(a) disclose documents or classes of documents specified in the order;

(b) carry out a search to the extent stated in the order;
(c) disclose any documents located as a result of that search.

(3) An order for specific inspection is an order that a party permit inspection of a document referred to in rule 31.3(2).

(Rule 31.3(2) allows a party to state in his disclosure statement that he will not permit inspection of a document on the grounds that it would be disproportionate to do so)

31.13 Disclosure in Stages

r.31.13 **48.26**

The parties may agree in writing, or the court may direct, that disclosure or inspection or both shall take place in stages.

31.14 Documents Referred to in Statements of Case etc.

r.31.14 **48.22**
r.31.14(1) **48.22**
r.31.14(2) **48.22**

(1) A party may inspect a document mentioned in—
(a) a statement of case;
(b) a witness statement;
(c) a witness summary; or
(d) an affidavit[(GL)].

(2) Subject to rule 35.10(4), a party may apply for an order for inspection of any document mentioned in an expert's report which has not already been disclosed in the proceedings.

(Rule 35.10(4) makes provision in relation to instructions referred to in an expert's report)

31.15 Inspection and Copying of Documents

r.31.15(a)–(b) **48.21**
r.31.15(c) **48.21, 57.3**

Where a party has a right to inspect a document—
(a) that party must give the party who disclosed the document written notice of his wish to inspect it;
(b) the party who disclosed the document must permit inspection not more than 7 days after the date on which he received the notice; and
(c) that party may request a copy of the document and, if he also undertakes to pay reasonable copying costs, the party who disclosed the document must supply him with a copy not more than 7 days after the date on which he received the request.

(Rule[s] 31.3 and 31.14 deal with the right of a party to inspect a document)

31.16 Disclosure before Proceedings Start

r.31.16 **48.70, 48.73, 48.81**
r.31.16(2) **48.74**
r.31.16(3)(a)–(d) **48.71**
r.31.16(4)(a)–(b) **48.74**
r.31.16(5) **48.74**

(1) This rule applies where an application is made to the court under any Act for disclosure before proceedings have started.
(2) The application must be supported by evidence.
(3) The court may make an order under this rule only where—
(a) the respondent is likely to be a party to subsequent proceedings;
(b) the applicant is also likely to be a party to those proceedings;
(c) if proceedings had started, the respondent's duty by way of standard disclosure, set out in rule 31.6, would extend to the documents or classes of documents of which the applicant seeks disclosure; and
(d) disclosure before proceedings have started is desirable in order to—
(i) dispose fairly of the anticipated proceedings;
(ii) assist the dispute to be resolved without proceedings; or
(iii) save costs.
(4) An order under this rule must—
(a) specify the documents or the classes of documents which the respondent must disclose; and
(b) require him, when making disclosure, to specify any of those documents—

Civil Procedure Rules & Practice Directions

(i) which are no longer in his control; or
(ii) in respect of which he claims a right or duty to withhold inspection.

(5) Such an order may—
(a) require the respondent to indicate what has happened to any documents which are no longer in his control; and
(b) specify the time and place for disclosure and inspection.

31.17 Orders for Disclosure against a Person Not a Party

r.31.17 **48.3, 48.22, 48.70, 48.78, 48.81, 55.6** r.31.17(2) **48.76** r.31.17(3) **48.77** r.31.17(4)–(5) **48.79**

(1) This rule applies where an application is made to the court under any Act for disclosure by a person who is not a party to the proceedings.
(2) The application must be supported by evidence.
(3) The court may make an order under this rule only where—
(a) the documents of which disclosure is sought are likely to support the case of the applicant or adversely affect the case of one of the other parties to the proceedings; and
(b) disclosure is necessary in order to dispose fairly of the claim or to save costs.
(4) An order under this rule must—
(a) specify the documents or the classes of documents which the respondent must disclose; and
(b) require the respondent, when making disclosure, to specify any of those documents—
(i) which are no longer in his control; or
(ii) in respect of which he claims a right or duty to withhold inspection.
(5) Such an order may—
(a) require the respondent to indicate what has happened to any documents which are no longer in his control; and
(b) specify the time and place for disclosure and inspection.

31.18 Rules Not to Limit Other Powers of the Court to Order Disclosure

r.31.18 **48.81**

Rules 31.16 and 31.17 do not limit any other power which the court may have to order—
(a) disclosure before proceedings have started; and
(b) disclosure against a person who is not a party to proceedings.

31.19 Claim to Withhold Inspection or Disclosure of a Document

r.31.19 **48.68** r.31.19(1) **48.23, 48.68** r.31.19(2) **48.68** r.31.19(3) **48.23, 48.37** r.31.19(4) **48.5, 48.23, 48.37, 48.68** r.31.19(5) **48.23** r.31.19(6) **48.23, 48.67**

(1) A person may apply, without notice, for an order permitting him to withhold disclosure of a document on the ground that disclosure would damage the public interest.
(2) Unless the court orders otherwise, an order of the court under paragraph (1)—
(a) must not be served on any other person; and
(b) must not be open to inspection by any person.
(3) A person who wishes to claim that he has a right or a duty to withhold inspection of a document, or part of a document, must state in writing—
(a) that he has such a right or duty; and
(b) the grounds on which he claims that right or duty.
(4) The statement referred to in paragraph (3) must be made—
(a) in the list in which the document is disclosed; or
(b) if there is no list, to the person wishing to inspect the document.
(5) A party may apply to the court to decide whether a claim made under paragraph (3) should be upheld.
(6) For the purpose of deciding an application under paragraph (1) (application to withhold disclosure) or paragraph (3) (claim to withhold inspection) the court may—
(a) require the person seeking to withhold disclosure or inspection of a document to produce that document to the court; and
(b) invite any person, whether or not a party, to make representations.

(7) An application under paragraph (1) or paragraph (5) must be supported by evidence.
(8) This Part does not affect any rule of law which permits or requires a document to be withheld from disclosure or inspection on the ground that its disclosure or inspection would damage the public interest.

31.20 Restriction on Use of a Privileged Document Inspection of Which Has Been Inadvertently Allowed

r.31.20 **48.63**

Where a party inadvertently allows a privileged document to be inspected, the party who has inspected the document may use it or its contents only with the permission of the court.

31.21 Consequence of Failure to Disclose Documents or Permit Inspection

r. 31.21 **48.28**

A party may not rely on any document which he fails to disclose or in respect of which he fails to permit inspection unless the court gives permission.

31.22 Subsequent Use of Disclosed Documents

r.31.22 **48.33, 48.35, 52.25**
r.31.22(1) **48.34**
r.31.22(1)(a) **48.34**
r.31.22(1)(b) **48.35**
r.31.22(2)–(3) **48.33**

(1) A party to whom a document has been disclosed may use the document only for the purpose of the proceedings in which it is disclosed, except where—
(a) the document has been read to or by the court, or referred to, at a hearing which has been held in public;
(b) the court gives permission; or
(c) the party who disclosed the document and the person to whom the document belongs agree.
(2) The court may make an order restricting or prohibiting the use of a document which has been disclosed, even where the document has been read to or by the court, or referred to, at a hearing which has been held in public.
(3) An application for such an order may be made—
(a) by a party; or
(b) by any person to whom the document belongs.

31.23 False Disclosure Statements

(1) Proceedings for contempt of court may be brought against a person if he makes, or causes to be made, a false disclosure statement, without an honest belief in its truth.
(2) Proceedings under this rule may be brought only—
(a) by the Attorney General; or
(b) with the permission of the court.

PD 31 Practice Direction — Disclosure and Inspection

This practice direction supplements CPR Part 31

PD 31 **48.18** [For commentary on a specific paragraph, please refer to the cross-references after the title of the paragraph.]

General

para.1.4 **48.5, 48.25, 48.26**

1.1 The normal order for disclosure will be an order that the parties give standard disclosure.

1.2 In order to give standard disclosure the disclosing party must make a reasonable search for documents falling within the paragraphs of rule 31.6.

1.3 Having made the search the disclosing party must (unless rule 31.10(8) applies) make a list of the documents of whose existence the party is aware that fall within those paragraphs and which are or have been in the party's control (see rule 31.8).

1.4 The obligations imposed by an order for standard disclosure may be dispensed with or limited either by the court or by written agreement between the parties. Any such written agreement should be lodged with the court.

The Search

para.2 **48.4**

2 The extent of the search which must be made will depend upon the circumstances of the case including, in particular, the factors referred to in rule 31.7(2). The parties should bear in mind the overriding principle of proportionality (see rule 1.1(2)(c)). It may, for example, be reasonable to decide not to search for documents coming into existence before some particular date, or to limit the search to documents in some particular place or places, or to documents falling into particular categories.

Electronic Disclosure

para.2A.1 **48.10, 48.13**
para.2A.2 **48.10**
para.2A.3 **48.21.**
paras.2A.4–2A.5 **48.13**

2A.1 Rule 31.4 contains a broad definition of a document. This extends to electronic documents, including email and other electronic communications, word-processed documents and databases. In addition to documents that are readily accessible from computer systems and other electronic devices and media, the definition covers those documents that are stored on servers and back-up systems and electronic documents that have been 'deleted'. It also extends to additional information stored and associated with electronic documents known as metadata.

2A.2 The parties should, prior to the first case management conference, discuss any issues that may arise regarding searches for and the preservation of electronic documents. This may involve the parties providing information about the categories of electronic documents within their control, the computer systems, electronic devices and media on which any relevant documents may be held, the storage systems maintained by the parties and their document retention policies. In the case of difficulty or disagreement, the matter should be referred to a judge for directions at the earliest practical date, if possible at the first case management conference.

2A.3 The parties should cooperate at an early stage as to the format in which electronic copy documents are to be provided on inspection. In the case of difficulty or disagreement, the matter should be referred to a judge for directions at the earliest practical date, if possible at the first case management conference.

2A.4 The existence of electronic documents impacts upon the extent of the reasonable search required by r. 31.7 for the purposes of standard disclosure. The factors that may be relevant in deciding the reasonableness of a search for electronic documents include (but are not limited to) the following:

(a) The number of documents involved.

(b) The nature and complexity of the proceedings.

(c) The ease and expense of retrieval of any particular document. This includes:

(i) The accessibility of electronic documents or data including email communications on computer systems, servers, back-up systems and other electronic devices or media that may contain such documents taking into account alterations or developments in hardware or software systems used by the disclosing party and/or available to enable access to such documents.

(ii) The location of relevant electronic documents, data, computer systems, servers, back-up systems and other electronic devices or media that may contain such documents.

(iii) The likelihood of locating relevant data.

(iv) The cost of recovering any electronic documents.

(v) The cost of disclosing and providing inspection of any relevant electronic documents.

(vi) The likelihood that electronic documents will be materially altered in the course of recovery, disclosure or inspection.

(d) The significance of any document which is likely to be located during the search.

2A.5 It may be reasonable to search some or all of the parties' electronic storage systems. In some circumstances, it may be reasonable to search for electronic documents by means of keyword searches (agreed as far as possible between the parties) even where a full review of each and every document would be unreasonable. There may be other forms of electronic search that may be appropriate in particular circumstances.

The List

para.3.1 **48.5** para.3.3 **48.32**
para.3.2 **48.5**

3.1 The list should be in **form N265**.

3.2 In order to comply with rule 31.10(3) it will normally be necessary to list the documents in date order, to number them consecutively and to give each a concise description (e.g. letter, claimant to defendant). Where there is a large number of documents all falling into a particular category the disclosing party may list those documents as a category rather than individually e.g. 50 bank statements relating to account number _ at _ Bank, _ 20 _ to _ 20 _; or, 35 letters passing between _ and _ between _ 20 _ and _ 20 _.

3.3 The obligations imposed by an order for disclosure will continue until the proceedings come to an end. If, after a list of documents has been prepared and served, the existence of further documents to which the order applies comes to the attention of the disclosing party, the party must prepare and serve a supplemental list.

Disclosure Statement

para.4.2 **48.19** para.4.4 **48.14, 48.19**
para.4.2(2) **48.19** paras.4.5–4.6 **48.5**
para.4.3 **48.18** para.4.7 **48.18**

4.1 A list of documents must (unless rule 31.10(8)(b) applies) contain a disclosure statement complying with rule 31.10. The form of disclosure statement is set out in the Annex to this practice direction.

4.2 The disclosure statement should:

(1) expressly state that the disclosing party believes the extent of the search to have been reasonable in all the circumstances, and

(2) in setting out the extent of the search (see rule 31.10(6)) draw attention to any particular limitations on the extent of the search which were adopted for proportionality reasons and give the reasons why the limitations were adopted, e.g. the difficulty or expense that a search not subject to those limitations would have entailed or the marginal relevance of categories of documents omitted from the search.

4.3 Where rule 31.10(7) applies, the details given in the disclosure statement about the person making the statement must include his name and address and the office or position he holds in the disclosing party or the basis upon which he makes the statement on behalf of the party.

4.4 If the disclosing party has a legal representative acting for him, the legal representative must endeavour to ensure that the person making the disclosure statement (whether the disclosing party or, in a case to which rule 31.10(7) applies, some other person) understands the duty of disclosure under Part 31.

4.5 If the disclosing party wishes to claim that he has a right or duty to withhold a document, or part of a document, in his list of documents from inspection (see rule 31.19(3)), he must state in writing:
(1) that he has such a right or duty, and
(2) the grounds on which he claims that right or duty.
4.6 The statement referred to in paragraph 4.5 above should normally be included in the disclosure statement and must identify the document, or part of a document, to which the claim relates.
4.7 An insurer or the Motor Insurers' Bureau may sign a disclosure statement on behalf of a party where the insurer or the Motor Insurers' Bureau has a financial interest in the result of proceedings brought wholly or partially by or against that party. Rule 31.10(7) and paragraph 4.3 above shall apply to the insurer or the Motor Insurers' Bureau making such a statement.

Specific Disclosure

paras.5.1–5.3 **48.29** para.5.4 **48.17, 48.30**

5.1 If a party believes that the disclosure of documents given by a disclosing party is inadequate he may make an application for an order for specific disclosure (see rule 31.12).
5.2 The application notice must specify the order that the applicant intends to ask the court to make and must be supported by evidence (see rule 31.12(2) which describes the orders the court may make).
5.3 The grounds on which the order is sought may be set out in the application notice itself but if not there set out must be set out in the evidence filed in support of the application.
5.4 In deciding whether or not to make an order for specific disclosure the court will take into account all the circumstances of the case and, in particular, the overriding objective described in Part 1. But if the court concludes that the party from whom specific disclosure is sought has failed adequately to comply with the obligations imposed by an order for disclosure (whether by failing to make a sufficient search for documents or otherwise) the court will usually make such order as is necessary to ensure that those obligations are properly complied with.
5.5 An order for specific disclosure may in an appropriate case direct a party to:
(1) carry out a search for any documents which it is reasonable to suppose may contain information which may:
(a) enable the party applying for disclosure either to advance his own case or to damage that of the party giving disclosure; or
(b) lead to a train of enquiry which has either of those consequences; and
(2) disclose any documents found as a result of that search.

Claims to Withhold Disclosure or Inspection of a Document

para.6.1 **48.23**

6.1 A claim to withhold inspection of a document, or part of a document, disclosed in a list of documents does not require an application to the court. Where such a claim has been made, a party who wishes to challenge it must apply to the court (see rule 31.19(5)).
6.2 Rule 31.19(1) and (6) provide a procedure enabling a party to apply for an order permitting disclosure of the existence of a document to be withheld.

Inspection of Documents Mentioned in Expert's Report (Rule 31.14(2))

7.1 If a party wishes to inspect documents referred to in the expert report of another party, before issuing an application he should request inspection of the documents informally, and inspection should be provided by agreement unless the request is unreasonable.
7.2 Where an expert report refers to a large number or volume of documents and it would be burdensome to copy or collate them, the court will only order inspection of such documents if it is satisfied that it is necessary for the just disposal of the proceedings and the party cannot reasonably obtain the documents from another source.
8 Attention is drawn to r. 31.23 which sets out the consequences of making a false disclosure statement without an honest belief in its truth, and to the procedures set out in PD 32, paras 28.1 to 28.3.

ANNEX DISCLOSURE STATEMENT

annex **48.19**

I, the above-named claimant [or defendant] [*if party making disclosure is a company, firm or other organisation identify here who the person making the disclosure statement is and why he is the appropriate person to make it*] state that I have carried out a reasonable and proportionate search to locate all the documents which I am required to disclose under the order made by the court on day of . I did not search:

(1) for documents predating ,
(2) for documents located elsewhere than ,
(3) for documents in categories other than .
(4) for electronic documents.]

[I carried out a search for electronic documents contained on or created by the following: [*list what was searched and extent of search*] I did not search for the following:

(1) documents created before ,
(2) documents contained on or created by the [Claimant's] [Defendant's] PCs/portable data storage media/databases/servers/back-up tapes/off-site storage/mobile phones/laptops/note-books/handheld devices/PDA devices (*delete as appropriate*),
(3) documents contained on or created by the [Claimant's] [Defendant's] mail files/document files/calendar files/spreadsheet files/graphic and presentation files/web-based applications (*delete as appropriate*),
(4) documents other than by reference to the following keyword(s)/concept(s): (*delete if your search was not confined to specific keywords or concepts*).]

I certify that I understand the duty of disclosure and to the best of my knowledge I have carried out that duty. I certify that the list above is a complete list of all documents which are or have been in my control and which I am obliged under the said order to disclose.

CPR Part 32 Evidence

Part 32 **43.6, 46.11, 49.17** [For commentary on a specific rule, please refer to the cross-references after the title of the rule.]

32.1 Power of Court to Control Evidence

r.32.1 **39.19, 42.22, 42.25, 43.6, 47.2, 47.70, 47.71, 49.13, 74.44, 96.43**
r.32.1(1) **47.7, 47.51**
r.32.1(1)(a)–(c) **59.13**
r.32.1(2) **42.22, 47.7, 47.51, 48.61**
r.32.1(3) **47.7, 47.70**

(1) The court may control the evidence by giving directions as to—
  (a) the issues on which it requires evidence;
  (b) the nature of the evidence which it requires to decide those issues; and
  (c) the way in which the evidence is to be placed before the court.
(2) The court may use its power under this rule to exclude evidence that would otherwise be admissible.
(3) The court may limit cross-examination^(GL).

32.2 Evidence of Witnesses — General Rule

r.32.2 **43.17, 47.50**
r.32.2(1) **32.13**
r.32.2(2) **47.50**

(1) The general rule is that any fact which needs to be proved by the evidence of witnesses is to be proved—
  (a) at trial, by their oral evidence given in public; and
  (b) at any other hearing, by their evidence in writing.
(2) This is subject—
  (a) to any provision to the contrary contained in these Rules or elsewhere; or
  (b) to any order of the court.

32.3 Evidence by Video Link or Other Means

r.32.3 **47.50, 56.11**

The court may allow a witness to give evidence through a video link or by other means.

32.4 Requirement to Serve Witness Statements for Use at Trial

r.32.(4) **43.17**
r.32.4(1) **49.1**
r.32.4(2)–(3) **49.17**

(1) A witness statement is a written statement signed by a person which contains the evidence which that person would be allowed to give orally.
(2) The court will order a party to serve on the other parties any witness statement of the oral evidence which the party serving the statement intends to rely on in relation to any issues of fact to be decided at the trial.

(3) The court may give directions as to—
  (a) the order in which witness statements are to be served; and
  (b) whether or not the witness statements are to be filed.

32.5 Use at Trial of Witness Statements Which Have Been Served

r.32.(5) **43.17**
r.32.5(1) **49.20**
r.32.5(2) **49.20, 51.7, 59.41**
r.32.5(3) **49.20, 59.41**
r.32.5(4) **44.5, 49.20, 59.41**
r.32.5(5) **1.16, 49.22, 51.12**

(1) If—
  (a) a party has served a witness statement; and
  (b) he wishes to rely at trial on the evidence of the witness who made the statement,
  he must call the witness to give oral evidence unless the court orders otherwise or he puts the statement in as hearsay evidence.
(Part 33 contains provisions about hearsay evidence)
(2) Where a witness is called to give oral evidence under paragraph (1), his witness statement shall stand as his evidence-in-chief[(GL)] unless the court orders otherwise.
(3) A witness giving oral evidence at trial may with the permission of the court—
  (a) amplify his witness statement; and
  (b) give evidence in relation to new matters which have arisen since the witness statement was served on the other parties.
(4) The court will give permission under paragraph (3) only if it considers that there is good reason not to confine the evidence of the witness to the contents of his witness statement.
(5) If a party who has served a witness statement does not—
  (a) call the witness to give evidence at trial; or
  (b) put the witness statement in as hearsay evidence,
  any other party may put the witness statement in as hearsay evidence.

32.6 Evidence in Proceedings Other than at Trial

r.32.6 **14.17, 15.7, 42.29, 43.17**
r.32.6(1) **32.13**
r.32.6(2) **23.14, 23.16, 26.3**
r.32.6(2)(a)–(b) **32.13**

(1) Subject to paragraph (2), the general rule is that evidence at hearings other than the trial is to be by witness statement unless the court, a practice direction or any other enactment requires otherwise.
(2) At hearings other than the trial, a party may rely on the matters set out in—
  (a) his statement of case; or
  (b) his application notice,
  if the statement of case or application notice is verified by a statement of truth.

32.7 Order for Cross-examination

r.32.7 **43.17**

(1) Where, at a hearing other than the trial, evidence is given in writing, any party may apply to the court for permission to cross-examine the person giving the evidence.
(2) If the court gives permission under paragraph (1) but the person in question does not attend as required by the order, his evidence may not be used unless the court gives permission.

32.8 Form of Witness Statement

r.32.8 **43.17**

A witness statement must comply with the requirements set out in the relevant practice direction.
(Part 22 requires a witness statement to be verified by a statement of truth)

32.9 Witness Summaries

r.32.9 **43.17, 47.62, 49.18**
r.32.9(1) **44.5**

(1) A party who—
  (a) is required to serve a witness statement for use at trial; but
  (b) is unable to obtain one,
  may apply, without notice, for permission to serve a witness summary instead.
(2) A witness summary is a summary of—
  (a) the evidence, if known, which would otherwise be included in a witness statement; or

(b) if the evidence is not known, the matters about which the party serving the witness summary proposes to question the witness.

(3) Unless the court orders otherwise, a witness summary must include the name and address of the intended witness.

(4) Unless the court orders otherwise, a witness summary must be served within the period in which a witness statement would have had to be served.

(5) Where a party serves a witness summary, so far as practicable rules 32.4 (requirement to serve witness statements for use at trial), 32.5(3) (amplifying witness statements), and 32.8 (form of witness statement) shall apply to the summary.

32.10 Consequence of Failure to Serve Witness Statement or Summary

r.32.10 **43.17, 49.19**

If a witness statement or a witness summary for use at trial is not served in respect of an intended witness within the time specified by the court, then the witness may not be called to give oral evidence unless the court gives permission.

32.11 Cross-examination on a Witness Statement

r.32.11 **43.17, 49.21, 59.42**

Where a witness is called to give evidence at trial, he may be cross-examined on his witness statement whether or not the statement or any part of it was referred to during the witness's evidence-in-chief(GL).

32.12 Use of Witness Statements for Other Purposes

r.32.12 **43.17** r.32.12(1) **49.24**

(1) Except as provided by this rule, a witness statement may be used only for the purpose of the proceedings in which it is served.

(2) Paragraph (1) does not apply if and to the extent that—

(a) the witness gives consent in writing to some other use of it;

(b) the court gives permission for some other use; or

(c) the witness statement has been put in evidence at a hearing held in public.

32.13 Availability of Witness Statements for Inspection

r.32.13 **15.15, 43.17, 49.23, 56.6** r.32.13(4) **49.23**

(1) A witness statement which stands as evidence-in-chief(GL) is open to inspection during the course of the trial unless the court otherwise directs.

(2) Any person may ask for a direction that a witness statement is not open to inspection.

(3) The court will not make a direction under paragraph (2) unless it is satisfied that a witness statement should not be open to inspection because of—

(a) the interests of justice;

(b) the public interest;

(c) the nature of any expert medical evidence in the statement;

(d) the nature of any confidential information (including information relating to personal financial matters) in the statement; or

(e) the need to protect the interests of any child or patient.

(4) The court may exclude from inspection words or passages in the statement.

32.14 False Statements

r.32.14 **49.9** r.32.14(2) **23.13**

r.32.14(1) **23.1, 23.13** r.32.14(2)(b) **23.15**

(1) Proceedings for contempt of court may be brought against a person if he makes, or causes to be made, a false statement in a document verified by a statement of truth without an honest belief in its truth.

(Part 22 makes provision for a statement of truth)

(2) Proceedings under this rule may be brought only—

(a) by the Attorney General; or

(b) with the permission of the court.

32.15 Affidavit Evidence

r.32.15 **14.17, 43.17** r.32.15(2) **15.7, 32.13**

(1) Evidence must be given by affidavit(GL) instead of or in addition to a witness statement if this is required by the court, a provision contained in any other rule, a practice direction or any other enactment.

(2) Nothing in these Rules prevents a witness giving evidence by affidavit(GL) at a hearing other than the trial if he chooses to do so in a case where paragraph (1) does not apply, but the party putting forward the affidavit(GL) may not recover the additional cost of making it from any other party unless the court orders otherwise.

32.16 Form of Affidavit

r.32.16 **43.17, 50.2**

An affidavit(GL) must comply with the requirements set out in the relevant practice direction.

32.17 Affidavit Made outside the Jurisdiction

r.32.17 **43.17**

A person may make an affidavit(GL) outside the jurisdiction in accordance with—

(a) this Part; or
(b) the law of the place where he makes the affidavit(GL).

32.18 Notice to Admit Facts

r.32.18 **43.17, 47.8**

(1) A party may serve notice on another party requiring him to admit the facts, or the part of the case of the serving party, specified in the notice.

(2) A notice to admit facts must be served no later than 21 days before the trial.

(3) Where the other party makes any admission in response to the notice, the admission may be used against him only—
  (a) in the proceedings in which the notice to admit is served; and
  (b) by the party who served the notice.

(4) The court may allow a party to amend or withdraw any admission made by him on such terms as it thinks just.

32.19 Notice to Admit or Produce Documents

r.32.19 **32.15, 43.17, 48.31** r.32.19(2) **48.31**
r.32.19(1) **47.83**

(1) A party shall be deemed to admit the authenticity of a document disclosed to him under Part 31 (disclosure and inspection of documents) unless he serves notice that he wishes the document to be proved at trial.

(2) A notice to prove a document must be served—
  (a) by the latest date for serving witness statements; or
  (b) within 7 days of disclosure of the document,
whichever is later.

32.20 Notarial Acts and Instruments

r.32.20 **51.18**

A notarial act or instrument may be received in evidence without further proof as duly authenticated in accordance with the requirements of law unless the contrary is proved.

PD 32 Practice Direction — Evidence

This practice direction supplements CPR Part 32

PD 32 **32.13**, **46.11**, **50.7** [For commentary on a specific paragraph, please refer to the cross-references after the title of the paragraph.]

Evidence in General

para.1.4 **50.7** para.1.7 **32.13**

1.1 Rule 32.2 sets out how evidence is to be given and facts are to be proved.

1.2 Evidence at a hearing other than the trial should normally be given by witness statement[1] (see para. 17 onwards). However, a witness may give evidence by affidavit if he wishes to do so[2] (and see para. 1.4 below).

1.3 Statements of case (see para. 26 onwards) and application notices[3] may also be used as evidence provided that their contents have been verified by a statement of truth.[4]

(For information regarding evidence by deposition see Part 34 and PD 34.)

1.4 Affidavits must be used as evidence in the following instances:

(1) where sworn evidence is required by an enactment,[5] rule, order or practice direction,

(2) in any application for a search order, a freezing injunction, or an order requiring an occupier to permit another to enter his land, and

(3) in any application for an order against anyone for alleged contempt of court.

1.5 If a party believes that sworn evidence is required by a court in another jurisdiction for any purpose connected with the proceedings, he may apply to the court for a direction that evidence shall be given only by affidavit on any pre-trial applications.

1.6 The court may give a direction under r. 32.15 that evidence shall be given by affidavit instead of or in addition to a witness statement or statement of case:

(1) on its own initiative, or

(2) after any party has applied to the court for such a direction.

1.7 An affidavit, where referred to in the Civil Procedure Rules or a practice direction, also means an affirmation unless the context requires otherwise.

Affidavits

paras.2–16 **50.2**

Deponent

2 A deponent is a person who gives evidence by affidavit or affirmation.

Heading

para.3.2 **50.2**

3.1 The affidavit should be headed with the title of the proceedings (see PD 7, para. 4, and PD 20, para. 7); where the proceedings are between several parties with the same status it is sufficient to identify the parties as follows:

	Number:
A.B. (and others)	Claimants/Applicants
C.D. (and others)	Defendants/Respondents
	(as appropriate)

3.2 At the top right-hand corner of the first page (and on the backsheet) there should be clearly written:

(1) the party on whose behalf it is made,

(2) the initials and surname of the deponent,

[1] See rule 32.6(1).

[2] See rule 32.15(2).

[3] See Part 23 for information about making an application.

[4] Rule 32.6(2) and see Part 22 for information about the statement of truth.

[5] See, e.g., s. 3(5)(a) of the Protection from Harassment Act 1997.

(3) the number of the affidavit in relation to that deponent,
(4) the identifying initials and number of each exhibit referred to, and
(5) the date sworn.

Body of affidavit

paras.4.1–4.2 **50.2**

4.1 The affidavit must, if practicable, be in the deponent's own words, the affidavit should be expressed in the first person and the deponent should:
(1) commence 'I (*full name*) of (*address*) state on oath . . . ',
(2) if giving evidence in his professional, business or other occupational capacity, give the address at which he works in (1) above, the position he holds and the name of his firm or employer,
(3) give his occupation or, if he has none, his description, and
(4) state if he is a party to the proceedings or employed by a party to the proceedings, if it be the case.

4.2 An affidavit must indicate:
(1) which of the statements in it are made from the deponent's own knowledge and which are matters of information or belief, and
(2) the source for any matters of information or belief.

4.3 Where a deponent:
(1) refers to an exhibit or exhibits, he should state 'there is now shown to me marked ". . ." the (*description of exhibit*) ', and
(2) makes more than one affidavit (to which there are exhibits) in the same proceedings, the numbering of the exhibits should run consecutively throughout and not start again with each affidavit.

Jurat

para.5 **50.2**

5.1 The jurat of an affidavit is a statement set out at the end of the document which authenticates the affidavit.

5.2 It must:
(1) be signed by all deponents,
(2) be completed and signed by the person before whom the affidavit was sworn whose name and qualification must be printed beneath his signature,
(3) contain the full address of the person before whom the affidavit was sworn, and
(4) follow immediately on from the text and not be put on a separate page.

Format of affidavits

para.6.1(1)–(2) **50.2**
para.6.1(4) **50.2**
para.6.1(7) **50.2**

6.1 An affidavit should:
(1) be produced on durable quality A4 paper with a 3.5 cm margin,
(2) be fully legible and should normally be typed on one side of the paper only,
(3) where possible, be bound securely in a manner which would not hamper filing, or otherwise each page should be endorsed with the case number and should bear the initials of the deponent and of the person before whom it was sworn,
(4) have the pages numbered consecutively as a separate document (or as one of several documents contained in a file),
(5) be divided into numbered paragraphs,
(6) have all numbers, including dates, expressed in figures, and
(7) give the reference to any document or documents mentioned either in the margin or in bold text in the body of the affidavit.

6.2 It is usually convenient for an affidavit to follow the chronological sequence of events or matters dealt with; each paragraph of an affidavit should as far as possible be confined to a distinct portion of the subject.

Inability of deponent to read or sign affidavit

para.7.1(1)–(3) **50.5** para.7.2 **50.5**

7.1 Where an affidavit is sworn by a person who is unable to read or sign it, the person before whom the affidavit is sworn must certify in the jurat that:
(1) he read the affidavit to the deponent,
(2) the deponent appeared to understand it, and
(3) the deponent signed or made his mark, in his presence.

7.2 If that certificate is not included in the jurat, the affidavit may not be used in evidence unless the court is satisfied that it was read to the deponent and that he appeared to understand it. Two versions of the form of jurat with the certificate are set out at Annex 1 to this practice direction.

Alterations to affidavits

para.8.1 **50.2**

8.1 Any alteration to an affidavit must be initialled by both the deponent and the person before whom the affidavit was sworn.

8.2 An affidavit which contains an alteration that has not been initialled may be filed or used in evidence only with the permission of the court.

Who may administer oaths and take affidavits

para.9 **50.3**

9.1 Only the following may administer oaths and take affidavits:
(1) commissioners for oaths,[6]
(2) practising solicitors,[7]
(3) other persons specified by statute,[8]
(4) certain officials of the Supreme Court,[9]
(5) a circuit judge or district judge,[10]
(6) any justice of the peace,[11] and
(7) certain officials of any county court appointed by the judge of that court for the purpose.[12]

9.2 An affidavit must be sworn before a person independent of the parties or their representatives.

Filing of affidavits

para.10 **50.6** para.10.2 **50.7**

10.1 If the court directs that an affidavit is to be filed,[13] it must be filed in the court or Division, or office or registry of the court or Division where the action in which it was or is to be used, is proceeding or will proceed.

10.2 Where an affidavit is in a foreign language:
(1) the party wishing to rely on it:
(a) must have it translated, and
(b) must file the foreign-language affidavit with the court, and
(2) the translator must make and file with the court an affidavit verifying the translation and exhibiting both the translation and a copy of the foreign-language affidavit.

Exhibits

paras.11.3–11.4 **49.6**

Manner of exhibiting documents

11.1 A document used in conjunction with an affidavit should be:
(1) produced to and verified by the deponent, and remain separate from the affidavit, and

---

[6] Commissioners for Oaths Acts 1889 and 1891.
[7] Section 81 of the Solicitors Act 1974.
[8] Section 65 of the Administration of Justice Act 1985, s. 113 of the Courts and Legal Services Act 1990 and the Commissioners for Oaths (Prescribed Bodies) Regulations 1994 and 1995.
[9] Section 2 of the Commissioners for Oaths Act 1889.
[10] Section 58 of the County Courts Act 1984.
[11] Section 58 as above.
[12] Section 58 as above.
[13] Rules 32.1(3) and 32.4(3)(b).

(2) identified by a declaration of the person before whom the affidavit was sworn.

11.2 The declaration should be headed with the name of the proceedings in the same way as the affidavit.

11.3 The first page of each exhibit should be marked:

(1) as in para. 3.2 above, and

(2) with the exhibit mark referred to in the affidavit.

Letters

12.1 Copies of individual letters should be collected together and exhibited in a bundle or bundles. They should be arranged in chronological order with the earliest at the top, and firmly secured.

12.2 When a bundle of correspondence is exhibited, the exhibit should have a front page attached stating that the bundle consists of original letters and copies. They should be arranged and secured as above and numbered consecutively.

Other documents

paras.13.1–13.2 **49.6**

13.1 Photocopies instead of original documents may be exhibited provided the originals are made available for inspection by the other parties before the hearing and by the judge at the hearing.

13.2 Court documents must not be exhibited (official copies of such documents prove themselves).

13.3 Where an exhibit contains more than one document, a front page should be attached setting out a list of the documents contained in the exhibit; the list should contain the dates of the documents.

Exhibits other than documents

para.14 **49.6**

14.1 Items other than documents should be clearly marked with an exhibit number or letter in such a manner that the mark cannot become detached from the exhibit.

14.2 Small items may be placed in a container and the container appropriately marked.

General provisions

para.15.1(1) **49.6** para.15.4 **49.7**
para.15.3 **49.16, 50.6**

15.1 Where an exhibit contains more than one document:

(1) the bundle should not be stapled but should be securely fastened in a way that does not hinder the reading of the documents, and

(2) the pages should be numbered consecutively at bottom centre.

15.2 Every page of an exhibit should be clearly legible; typed copies of illegible documents should be included, paginated with 'a' numbers.

15.3 Where affidavits and exhibits have become numerous, they should be put into separate bundles and the pages numbered consecutively throughout.

15.4 Where on account of their bulk the service of exhibits or copies of exhibits on the other parties would be difficult or impracticable, the directions of the court should be sought as to arrangements for bringing the exhibits to the attention of the other parties and as to their custody pending trial.

Affirmations

para.16 **50.4**

16 All provisions in this or any other practice direction relating to affidavits apply to affirmations with the following exceptions:

(1) the deponent should commence 'I (*name*) of (*address*) do solemnly and sincerely affirm . . .', and

(2) in the jurat the word 'sworn' is replaced by the word 'affirmed'.

Witness Statements

para.17.1 **49.4** para.17.2 **49.3**

Heading

17.1 The witness statement should be headed with the title of the proceedings (see PD 7, para. 4, and PD 20, para. 7); where the proceedings are between several parties with the same status it is sufficient to identify the parties as follows:

Number:
A.B. (and others) Claimants/Applicants
C.D. (and others) Defendants/Respondents
(as appropriate)

17.2 At the top right-hand corner of the first page there should be clearly written:
(1) the party on whose behalf it is made,
(2) the initials and surname of the witness,
(3) the number of the statement in relation to that witness,
(4) the identifying initials and number of each exhibit referred to, and
(5) the date the statement was made.

Body of witness statement

para.18.1 **49.1, 49.5** para.18.5 **49.6, 49.16**
para.18.2 **49.5** para.18.6 **49.3**

18.1 The witness statement must, if practicable, be in the intended witness's own words, the statement should be expressed in the first person and should also state:
(1) the full name of the witness,
(2) his place of residence or, if he is making the statement in his professional, business or other occupational capacity, the address at which he works, the position he holds and the name of his firm or employer,
(3) his occupation, or if he has none, his description, and
(4) the fact that he is a party to the proceedings or is the employee of such a party if it be the case.

18.2 A witness statement must indicate:
(1) which of the statements in it are made from the witness's own knowledge and which are matters of information or belief, and
(2) the source for any matters of information or belief.

18.3 An exhibit used in conjunction with a witness statement should be verified and identified by the witness and remain separate from the witness statement.

18.4 Where a witness refers to an exhibit or exhibits, he should state 'I refer to the (*description of exhibit*) marked "..."'.

18.5 The provisions of paras 11.3 to 15.4 (exhibits) apply similarly to witness statements as they do to affidavits.

18.6 Where a witness makes more than one witness statement to which there are exhibits, in the same proceedings, the numbering of the exhibits should run consecutively throughout and not start again with each witness statement.

Format of witness statement

para.19.1(1)–(4) **49.2** para.19.1(7) **49.8**
para.19.1(5)–(6) **49.5** para.19.2 **49.5**

19.1 A witness statement should:
(1) be produced on durable quality A4 paper with a 3.5 cm margin,
(2) be fully legible and should normally be typed on one side of the paper only,
(3) where possible, be bound securely in a manner which would not hamper filing, or otherwise each page should be endorsed with the case number and should bear the initials of the witness,
(4) have the pages numbered consecutively as a separate statement (or as one of several statements contained in a file),
(5) be divided into numbered paragraphs,
(6) have all numbers, including dates, expressed in figures, and
(7) give the reference to any document or documents mentioned either in the margin or in bold text in the body of the statement.

19.2 It is usually convenient for a witness statement to follow the chronological sequence of the events or matters dealt with, each paragraph of a witness statement should as far as possible be confined to a distinct portion of the subject.

Statement of truth

para.20.1 **56.11** para.20.2 **49.9**

20.1 A witness statement is the equivalent of the oral evidence which that witness would, if called, give in evidence; it must include a statement by the intended witness that he believes the facts in it are true.[14]

20.2 To verify a witness statement the statement of truth is as follows:

'I believe that the facts stated in this witness statement are true'

20.3 Attention is drawn to r. 32.14 which sets out the consequences of verifying a witness statement containing a false statement without an honest belief in its truth.

(PD 22, para. 3A, sets out the procedure to be followed where the person who should sign a document which is verified by a statement of truth is unable to read or sign the document.)

21 [*deleted*]

Alterations to witness statements

paras.22.1–22.2 **49.11**

22.1 Any alteration to a witness statement must be initialled by the person making the statement or by the authorised person where appropriate (see para. 21).

22.2 A witness statement which contains an alteration that has not been initialled may be used in evidence only with the permission of the court.

Filing of witness statements

para.23.1 **49.14** para.23.2 **49.15, 50.7**

23.1 If the court directs that a witness statement is to be filed,[15] it must be filed in the court or Division, or office or registry of the court or Division where the action in which it was or is to be used, is proceeding or will proceed.

23.2 Where the court has directed that a witness statement in a foreign language is to be filed:

(1) the party wishing to rely on it must:

(a) have it translated, and

(b) file the foreign-language witness statement with the court, and

(2) the translator must make and file with the court an affidavit verifying the translation and exhibiting both the translation and a copy of the foreign-language witness statement.

Certificate of court officer

24.1 Where the court has ordered that a witness statement is not to be open to inspection by the public[16] or that words or passages in the statement are not to be open to inspection[17] the court officer will so certify on the statement and make any deletions directed by the court under r. 32.13(4).

Defects in affidavits, witness statements and exhibits

para.25 **46.11, 50.6** para.25.1 **49.12**

25.1 Where:

(1) an affidavit,

(2) a witness statement, or

(3) an exhibit to either an affidavit or a witness statement

does not comply with Part 32 or this practice direction in relation to its form, the court may refuse to admit it as evidence and may refuse to allow the costs arising from its preparation.

25.2 Permission to file a defective affidavit or witness statement or to use a defective exhibit may be obtained from a judge[18] in the court where the case is proceeding.

---

[14] See Part 22 for information about the statement of truth.

[15] Rule 32.4(3)(b).

[16] Rule 32.13(2).

[17] Rule 32.13(4).

[18] Rule 2.3(1); definition of judge.

Statements of Case

26.1 A statement of case may be used as evidence in an interim application provided it is verified by a statement of truth.[19]

26.2 To verify a statement of case the statement of truth should be set out as follows:

'[I believe] [the (*party on whose behalf the statement of case is being signed*) believes] that the facts stated in the statement of case are true'.

26.3 Attention is drawn to rule 32.14 which sets out the consequences of verifying a witness statement containing a false statement without an honest belief in its truth.

(For information regarding statements of truth see Part 22 and PD 22.)

(Practice directions supplementing Parts 7, 9 and 17 provide further information concerning statements of case.*)

Agreed Bundles for Hearings

para.27.2 **57.5**

27.1 The court may give directions requiring the parties to use their best endeavours to agree a bundle or bundles of documents for use at any hearing.

27.2 All documents contained in bundles which have been agreed for use at a hearing shall be admissible at that hearing as evidence of their contents, unless:
(1) the court orders otherwise; or
(2) a party gives written notice of objection to the admissibility of particular documents.

Penalty

para.28 **49.9**
paras.28.1–28.4 **23.13**

28.1 (1) Where a party alleges that a statement of truth or a disclosure statement is false the party shall refer that allegation to the court dealing with the claim in which the statement of truth or disclosure statement has been made.
(2) The court may:
(a) exercise any of its powers under the CPR;
(b) initiate steps to consider if there is a contempt of court and, where there is, to punish it; (PD RSC Ord. 52 makes provision where committal to prison is a possibility if contempt is proved.)
(c) direct the party making the allegation to refer the matter to the Attorney-General with a request to him to consider whether he wishes to bring proceedings for contempt of court.

28.2 (1) An application to the Attorney-General should be made to his chambers at 9 Buckingham Gate, London SW1E 6JP in writing. The Attorney-General will initially require a copy of the order recording the direction of the judge referring the matter to him and information which:
(a) identifies the statement said to be false; and
(b) explains:
(i) why it is false, and
(ii) why the maker knew it to be false at the time he made it; and
(c) explains why contempt proceedings would be appropriate in the light of the overriding objective in Part 1.
(2) The practice of the Attorney-General is to prefer an application that comes from the court, and so has received preliminary consideration by a judge, to one made direct to him by a party to the claim in which the alleged contempt occurred without prior consideration by the court. An application to the Attorney-General is not a way of appealing against, or reviewing, the decision of the judge.

28.3 Where a party makes an application to the court for permission for that party to commence proceedings for contempt of court, it must be supported by written evidence containing the information specified in para. 28.2(1) and the result of the application to the Attorney-General made by the applicant.

[19] See r. 32.6(2)(a).
[* In fact no practice direction supplementing Part 9 has been issued.]

28.4 The rules do not change the law of contempt or introduce new categories of contempt. A person applying to commence such proceedings should consider whether the incident complained of does amount to contempt of court and whether such proceedings would further the overriding objective in Part 1.

Videoconferencing

29.1 Guidance on the use of videoconferencing in the civil courts is set out at Annex 3 to this practice direction. A list of the sites which are available for videoconferencing can be found on Her Majesty's Courts Service website at www.hmcourts-service.gov.uk.

ANNEX 1

annex 1 **50.5**

Certificate to Be Used Where a Deponent to an Affidavit is Unable to Read or Sign it

Sworn at ...... this ...... day of ...... Before me, I having first read over the contents of this affidavit to the deponent [*if there are exhibits, add* 'and explained the nature and effect of the exhibits referred to in it'] who appeared to understand it and approved its content as accurate, and made his mark on the affidavit in my presence.

Or, (after, *Before me*) the witness to the mark of the deponent having been first sworn that he had read over etc. (*as above*) and that he saw him make his mark on the affidavit. (*Witness must sign*).

Certificate to Be Used Where a Deponent to an Affirmation is Unable to Read or Sign it

Affirmed at ...... this ...... day of ...... Before me, I having first read over the contents of this affirmation to the deponent [*if there are exhibits, add* 'and explained the nature and effect of the exhibits referred to in it'] who appeared to understand it and approved its content as accurate, and made his mark on the affirmation in my presence.

Or, (after, *Before me*) the witness to the mark of the deponent having been first sworn that he had read over etc. (*as above*) and that he saw him make his mark on the affirmation. (*Witness must sign*).

ANNEX 2

[*deleted*]

ANNEX 3

annex 3 **56.11**

Videoconferencing Guidance

This guidance is for the use of videoconferencing (VCF) in civil proceedings. It is in part based, with permission, upon the protocol of the Federal Court of Australia. It is intended to provide a guide to all persons involved in the use of VCF, although it does not attempt to cover all the practical questions which might arise.

Videoconferencing Generally

1. The guidance covers the use of VCF equipment both (a) in a courtroom, whether via equipment which is permanently placed there or via a mobile unit, and (b) in a separate studio or conference room. In either case, the location at which the judge sits is referred to as the 'local site'. The other site or sites to and from which transmission is made are referred to as the 'remote site' and in any particular case any such site may be another courtroom. The guidance applies to cases where VCF is used for the taking of evidence and also to its use for other parts of any legal proceedings (for example, interim applications, case management conferences, pre-trial reviews).
2. VCF may be a convenient way of dealing with any part of proceedings: it can involve considerable savings in time and cost. Its use for the taking of evidence from overseas witnesses will, in particular, be likely to achieve a material saving of costs, and such savings may also be achieved by its use for taking domestic evidence. It is, however, inevitably not as ideal as having the witness physically present in court. Its convenience should not therefore be allowed to dictate its use. A judgment must be made in every case in which the use of VCF is being considered not only as to whether it will achieve an overall cost saving but as to whether its use will be likely to

be beneficial to the efficient, fair and economic disposal of the litigation. In particular, it needs to be recognised that the degree of control a court can exercise over a witness at the remote site is or may be more limited than it can exercise over a witness physically before it.

3. When used for the taking of evidence, the objective should be to make the VCF session as close as possible to the usual practice in a trial court where evidence is taken in open court. To gain the maximum benefit, several differences have to be taken into account. Some matters, which are taken for granted when evidence is taken in the conventional way, take on a different dimension when it is taken by VCF: for example, the administration of the oath, ensuring that the witness understands who is at the local site and what their various roles are, the raising of any objections to the evidence and the use of documents.
4. It should not be presumed that all foreign governments are willing to allow their nationals or others within their jurisdiction to be examined before a court in England or Wales by means of VCF. If there is any doubt about this, enquiries should be directed to the Foreign and Commonwealth Office (International Legal Matters Unit, Consular Division) with a view to ensuring that the country from which the evidence is to be taken raises no objection to it at diplomatic level. The party who is directed to be responsible for arranging the VCF (see para. 8 below) will be required to make all necessary inquiries about this well in advance of the VCF and must be able to inform the court what those inquiries were and of their outcome.
5. Time zone differences need to be considered when a witness abroad is to be examined in England or Wales by VCF. The convenience of the witness, the parties, their representatives and the court must all be taken into account. The cost of the use of a commercial studio is usually greater outside normal business hours.
6. Those involved with VCF need to be aware that, even with the most advanced systems currently available, there are the briefest of delays between the receipt of the picture and that of the accompanying sound. If due allowance is not made for this, there will be a tendency to 'speak over' the witness, whose voice will continue to be heard for a millisecond or so after he or she appears on the screen to have finished speaking.
7. With current technology, picture quality is good, but not as good as a television picture. The quality of the picture is enhanced if those appearing on VCF monitors keep their movements to a minimum.

Preliminary Arrangements

8. The court's permission is required for any part of any proceedings to be dealt with by means of VCF. Before seeking a direction, the applicant should notify the listing officer, diary manager or other appropriate court officer of the intention to seek it, and should enquire as to the availability of court VCF equipment for the day or days of the proposed VCF. The application for a direction should be made to the master, district judge or judge, as may be appropriate. If all parties consent to a direction, permission can be sought by letter, fax or email, although the court may still require an oral hearing. All parties are entitled to be heard on whether or not such a direction should be given and as to its terms. If a witness at a remote site is to give evidence by an interpreter, consideration should be given at this stage as to whether the interpreter should be at the local site or the remote site. If a VCF direction is given, arrangements for the transmission will then need to be made. The court will ordinarily direct that the party seeking permission to use VCF is to be responsible for this. That party is hereafter referred to as the 'VCF arranging party'.
9. Subject to any order to the contrary, all costs of the transmission, including the costs of hiring equipment and technical personnel to operate it, will initially be the responsibility of, and must be met by, the VCF arranging party. All reasonable efforts should be made to keep the transmission to a minimum and so keep the costs down. All such costs will be considered to be part of the costs of the proceedings and the court will determine at such subsequent time as is convenient or appropriate who, as between the parties, should be responsible for them and (if appropriate) in what proportions.
10. The local site will, if practicable, be a courtroom but it may instead be an appropriate studio or conference room. The VCF arranging party must contact the listing officer, diary manager or other appropriate officer of the court which made the VCF direction and make arrangements for the VCF transmission. Details of the remote site, and of the equipment to be used both at the local site (if not being supplied by the court) and the remote site (including the number of ISDN

lines and connection speed), together with all necessary contact names and telephone numbers, will have to be provided to the listing officer, diary manager or other court officer. The court will need to be satisfied that any equipment provided by the parties for use at the local site and also that at the remote site is of sufficient quality for a satisfactory transmission. The VCF arranging party must ensure that an appropriate person will be present at the local site to supervise the operation of the VCF throughout the transmission in order to deal with any technical problems. That party must also arrange for a technical assistant to be similarly present at the remote site for like purposes.

11. It is recommended that the judge, practitioners and witness should arrive at their respective VCF sites about 20 minutes prior to the scheduled commencement of the transmission.
12. If the local site is not a courtroom, but a conference room or studio, the judge will need to determine who is to sit where. The VCF arranging party must take care to ensure that the number of microphones is adequate for the speakers and that the panning of the camera for the practitioners' table encompasses all legal representatives so that the viewer can see everyone seated there.
13. The proceedings, wherever they may take place, form part of a trial to which the public is entitled to have access (unless the court has determined that they should be heard in private). If the local site is to be a studio or conference room, the VCF arranging party must ensure that it provides sufficient accommodation to enable a reasonable number of members of the public to attend.
14. In cases where the local site is a studio or conference room, the VCF arranging party should make arrangements, if practicable, for the royal coat of arms to be placed above the judge's seat.
15. In cases in which the VCF is to be used for the taking of evidence, the VCF arranging party must arrange for recording equipment to be provided by the court which made the VCF direction so that the evidence can be recorded. An associate will normally be present to operate the recording equipment when the local site is a courtroom. The VCF arranging party should take steps to ensure that an associate is present to do likewise when it is a studio or conference room. The equipment should be set up and tested before the VCF transmission. It will often be a valuable safeguard for the VCF arranging party also to arrange for the provision of recording equipment at the remote site. This will provide a useful back-up if there is any reduction in sound quality during the transmission. A direction from the court for the making of such a back-up recording must, however, be obtained first. This is because the proceedings are court proceedings and, save as directed by the court, no other recording of them must be made. The court will direct what is to happen to the back-up recording.
16. Some countries may require that any oath or affirmation to be taken by a witness accord with local custom rather than the usual form of oath or affirmation used in England and Wales. The VCF arranging party must make all appropriate prior inquiries and put in place all arrangements necessary to enable the oath or affirmation to be taken in accordance with any local custom. That party must be in a position to inform the court what those inquiries were, what their outcome was and what arrangements have been made. If the oath or affirmation can be administered in the manner normal in England and Wales, the VCF arranging party must arrange in advance to have the appropriate holy book at the remote site. The associate will normally administer the oath.
17. Consideration will need to be given in advance to the documents to which the witness is likely to be referred. The parties should endeavour to agree on this. It will usually be most convenient for a bundle of the copy documents to be prepared in advance, which the VCF arranging party should then send to the remote site.
18. Additional documents are sometimes quite properly introduced during the course of a witness's evidence. To cater for this, the VCF arranging party should ensure that equipment is available to enable documents to be transmitted between sites during the course of the VCF transmission. Consideration should be given to whether to use a document camera. If it is decided to use one, arrangements for its use will need to be established in advance. The panel operator will need to know the number and size of documents or objects if their images are to be sent by document camera. In many cases, a simpler and sufficient alternative will be to ensure that there are fax transmission and reception facilities at the participating sites.

The Hearing

19. The procedure for conducting the transmission will be determined by the judge. He will determine who is to control the cameras. In cases where the VCF is being used for an application in the course of the proceedings, the judge will ordinarily not enter the local site until both sites are on line. Similarly, at the conclusion of the hearing, he will ordinarily leave the local site while both sites are still on line. The following paragraphs apply primarily to cases where the VCF is being used for the taking of the evidence of a witness at a remote site. In all cases, the judge will need to decide whether court dress is appropriate when using VCF facilities. It might be appropriate when transmitting from courtroom to courtroom. It might not be when a commercial facility is being used.
20. At the beginning of the transmission, the judge will probably wish to introduce himself and the advocates to the witness. He will probably want to know who is at the remote site and will invite the witness to introduce himself and anyone else who is with him. He may wish to give directions as to the seating arrangements at the remote site so that those present are visible at the local site during the taking of the evidence. He will probably wish to explain to the witness the method of taking the oath or of affirming, the manner in which the evidence will be taken, and who will be conducting the examination and cross-examination. He will probably also wish to inform the witness of the matters referred to in paras 6 and 7 above (coordination of picture with sound, and picture quality).
21. The examination of the witness at the remote site should follow as closely as possible the practice adopted when a witness is in the courtroom. During examination, cross-examination and re-examination, the witness must be able to see the legal representative asking the question and also any other person (whether another legal representative or the judge) making any statements in regard to the witness's evidence. It will in practice be most convenient if everyone remains seated throughout the transmission.

CPR Part 33 Miscellaneous Rules about Evidence

Part 33 **43.6**, **51.9** [For commentary on a specific rule, please refer to the cross-references after the title of the rule.]

33.1 Introductory

In this Part—

(a) 'hearsay' means a statement made, otherwise than by a person while giving oral evidence in proceedings, which is tendered as evidence of the matters stated; and

(b) references to hearsay include hearsay of whatever degree.

33.2 Notice of Intention to Rely on Hearsay Evidence

r.33.2(1) **49.5, 51.9**
r.33.2(2) **49.5, 51.9**
r.33.2(3)–(4) **51.9**

(1) Where a party intends to rely on hearsay evidence at trial and either—
   (a) that evidence is to be given by a witness giving oral evidence; or
   (b) that evidence is contained in a witness statement of a person who is not being called to give oral evidence;

   that party complies with section 2(1)(a) of the Civil Evidence Act 1995 by serving a witness statement on the other parties in accordance with the court's order.

(2) Where paragraph (1)(b) applies, the party intending to rely on the hearsay evidence must, when he serves the witness statement—
   (a) inform the other parties that the witness is not being called to give oral evidence; and
   (b) give the reason why the witness will not be called.

(3) In all other cases where a party intends to rely on hearsay evidence at trial, that party complies with section 2(1)(a) of the Civil Evidence Act 1995 by serving a notice on the other parties which—
   (a) identifies the hearsay evidence;
   (b) states that the party serving the notice proposes to rely on the hearsay evidence at trial; and
   (c) gives the reason why the witness will not be called.

(4) The party proposing to rely on the hearsay evidence must—
   (a) serve the notice no later than the latest date for serving witness statements; and
   (b) if the hearsay evidence is to be in a document, supply a copy to any party who requests him to do so.

33.3 Circumstances in Which Notice of Intention to Rely on Hearsay Evidence is Not Required

r.33.3 **51.11**
r.33.3(a) **49.5**

Section 2(1) of the Civil Evidence Act 1995 (duty to give notice of intention to rely on hearsay evidence) does not apply—

(a) to evidence at hearings other than trials;

(aa) to an affidavit or witness statement which is to be used at trial but which does not contain hearsay evidence;

(b) to a statement which a party to a probate action wishes to put in evidence and which is alleged to have been made by the person whose estate is the subject of the proceedings; or
(c) where the requirement is excluded by a practice direction.

33.4 Power to Call Witness for Cross-examination on Hearsay Evidence

r.33.4 **51.12** r.33.4(2) **51.12**

(1) Where a party—
(a) proposes to rely on hearsay evidence; and
(b) does not propose to call the person who made the original statement to give oral evidence,
the court may, on the application of any other party, permit that party to call the maker of the statement to be cross-examined on the contents of the statement.
(2) An application for permission to cross-examine under this rule must be made not more than 14 days after the day on which a notice of intention to rely on the hearsay evidence was served on the applicant.

33.5 Credibility

r.33.5 **51.14**

(1) Where a party—
(a) proposes to rely on hearsay evidence; but
(b) does not propose to call the person who made the original statement to give oral evidence; and
(c) another party wishes to call evidence to attack the credibility of the person who made the statement,
the party who so wishes must give notice of his intention to the party who proposes to give the hearsay statement in evidence.
(2) A party must give notice under paragraph (1) not more than 14 days after the day on which a hearsay notice relating to the hearsay evidence was served on him.

33.6 Use of Plans, Photographs and Models as Evidence

r.33.6 **47.87, 47.91, 57.2** r.33.6(6) **47.91, 51.16**
r.33.6(2)–(3) **51.16** r.33.6(7) **47.91**
r.33.6(4) **45.14, 51.16** r.33.6(8) **51.16**
r.33.6(5) **47.91**

(1) This rule applies to evidence (such as a plan, photograph or model) which is not—
(a) contained in a witness statement, affidavit(GL) or expert's report;
(b) to be given orally at trial; or
(c) evidence of which prior notice must be given under rule 33.2.
(2) This rule includes documents which may be received in evidence without further proof under section 9 of the Civil Evidence Act 1995.
(3) Unless the court orders otherwise the evidence shall not be receivable at a trial unless the party intending to put it in evidence has given notice to the other parties in accordance with this rule.
(4) Where the party intends to use the evidence as evidence of any fact then, except where paragraph (6) applies, he must give notice not later than the latest date for serving witness statements.
(5) He must give notice at least 21 days before the hearing at which he proposes to put in the evidence, if—
(a) there are not to be witness statements; or
(b) he intends to put in the evidence solely in order to disprove an allegation made in a witness statement.
(6) Where the evidence forms part of expert evidence, he must give notice when the expert's report is served on the other party.
(7) Where the evidence is being produced to the court for any reason other than as part of factual or expert evidence, he must give notice at least 21 days before the hearing at which he proposes to put in the evidence.
(8) Where a party has given notice that he intends to put in the evidence, he must give every other party an opportunity to inspect it and to agree to its admission without further proof.

33.7 Evidence of Finding on Question of Foreign Law

r.33.7 **47.98**

(1) This rule sets out the procedure which must be followed by a party who intends to put in evidence a finding on a question of foreign law by virtue of section 4(2) of the Civil Evidence Act 1972.
(2) He must give any other party notice of his intention.
(3) He must give the notice—
  (a) if there are to be witness statements, not later than the latest date for serving them; or
  (b) otherwise, not less than 21 days before the hearing at which he proposes to put the finding in evidence.
(4) The notice must—
  (a) specify the question on which the finding was made; and
  (b) enclose a copy of a document where it is reported or recorded.

33.8 Evidence of Consent of Trustee to Act

r.33.8 **47.99**

A document purporting to contain the written consent of a person to act as trustee and to bear his signature verified by some other person is evidence of such consent.

33.9 Human Rights

r.33.9 **97.10**

(1) This rule applies where a claim is—
  (a) for a remedy under section 7 of the Human Rights Act 1998 in respect of a judicial act which is alleged to have infringed the claimant's Article 5 Convention rights; and
  (b) based on a finding by a court or tribunal that the claimant's Convention rights have been infringed.
(2) The court hearing the claim—
  (a) may proceed on the basis of the finding of that other court or tribunal that there has been an infringement but it is not required to do so; and
  (b) may reach its own conclusion in the light of that finding and of the evidence heard by that other court or tribunal.

PD 33 Practice Direction — Civil Evidence Act 1995

This practice direction supplements CPR Part 33

PD 33 **47.76** [For commentary on a specific paragraph, please refer to the cross-references after the title of the paragraph.]

1. Section 16(3A) of the Civil Evidence Act 1995 (as amended) provides that transitional provisions for the application of the provisions of the Civil Evidence Act 1995 to proceedings begun before 31 January 1997 may be made by practice direction.
2. Except as provided for by para. 3, the provisions of the Civil Evidence Act 1995 apply to claims commenced before 31 January 1997.
3. The provisions of the Civil Evidence Act 1995 do not apply to claims commenced before 31 January 1997 if, before 26 April 1999:
   (a) directions were given, or orders were made, as to the evidence to be given at the trial or hearing; or
   (b) the trial or hearing had begun.

CPR Part 34 Witnesses, Depositions and Evidence for Foreign Courts

Part 34 **55.1, 55.2, 56.14, 69.11** [For commentary on a specific rule, please refer to the cross-references after the title of the rule.]

I WITNESSES AND DEPOSITIONS

34.1 Scope of This Section

(1) This Section of this Part provides—
  (a) for the circumstances i n which a person may be required to attend court to give evidence or to produce a document; and
  (b) for a party to obtain evidence before a hearing to be used at the hearing.
(2) In this Section, reference to a hearing includes a reference to the trial.

34.2 Witness Summonses

r.34.2 **47.78, 47.79**
r.34.2(1)–(3) **55.1**
r.34.2(4)–(5) **48.22, 55.1**

(1) A witness summons is a document issued by the court requiring a witness to—
  (a) attend court to give evidence; or
  (b) produce documents to the court.
(2) A witness summons must be in the relevant practice form.
(3) There must be a separate witness summons for each witness.
(4) A witness summons may require a witness to produce documents to the court either—
  (a) on the date fixed for a hearing; or
  (b) on such date as the court may direct.
(5) The only documents that a summons under this rule can require a person to produce before a hearing are documents which that person could be required to produce at the hearing.

34.3 Issue of a Witness Summons

r.34.3(1)–(3) **55.2**
r.34.3(4) **55.9**

(1) A witness summons is issued on the date entered on the summons by the court.
(2) A party must obtain permission from the court where he wishes to—

(a) have a summons issued less than 7 days before the date of the trial;
(b) have a summons issued for a witness to attend court to give evidence or to produce documents on any date except the date fixed for the trial; or
(c) have a summons issued for a witness to attend court to give evidence or to produce documents at any hearing except the trial.

(3) A witness summons must be issued by—
(a) the court where the case is proceeding; or
(b) the court where the hearing in question will be held.

(4) The court may set aside(GL) or vary a witness summons issued under this rule.

34.4 Witness Summons in Aid of Inferior Court or of Tribunal

r.34.4(1)–(2) **55.3**

(1) The court may issue a witness summons in aid of an inferior court or of a tribunal.
(2) The court which issued the witness summons under this rule may set it aside.
(3) In this rule, 'inferior court or tribunal' means any court or tribunal that does not have power to issue a witness summons in relation to proceedings before it.

34.5 Time for Serving a Witness Summons

r.34.5 **55.4** r.34.5(1)–(3) **55.4**

(1) The general rule is that a witness summons is binding if it is served at least 7 days before the date on which the witness is required to attend before the court or tribunal.
(2) The court may direct that a witness summons shall be binding although it will be served less than 7 days before the date on which the witness is required to attend before the court or tribunal.
(3) A witness summons which is—
(a) served in accordance with this rule; and
(b) requires the witness to attend court to give evidence,
is binding until the conclusion of the hearing at which the attendance of the witness is required.

34.6 Who is to Serve a Witness Summons

r.34.6(2) **55.6**

(1) A witness summons is to be served by the court unless the party on whose behalf it is issued indicates in writing, when he asks the court to issue the summons, that he wishes to serve it himself.
(2) Where the court is to serve the witness summons, the party on whose behalf it is issued must deposit, in the court office, the money to be paid or offered to the witness under rule 34.7.

34.7 Right of Witness to Travelling Expenses and Compensation for Loss of Time

r.34.7 **55.6**

At the time of service of a witness summons the witness must be offered or paid—
(a) a sum reasonably sufficient to cover his expenses in travelling to and from the court; and
(b) such sum by way of compensation for loss of time as may be specified in the relevant practice direction.

34.8 Evidence by Deposition

r.34.8 **48.22, 56.2, 56.6** r.34.8(6)–(7) **56.2**
r.34.8(3)–(4) **56.2**

(1) A party may apply for an order for a person to be examined before the hearing takes place.
(2) A person from whom evidence is to be obtained following an order under this rule is referred to as a 'deponent' and the evidence is referred to as a 'deposition'.
(3) An order under this rule shall be for a deponent to be examined on oath before—
(a) a judge;
(b) an examiner of the court; or
(c) such other person as the court appoints.

(Rule 34.15 makes provision for the appointment of examiners of the court)

(4) The order may require the production of any document which the court considers is necessary for the purposes of the examination.
(5) The order must state the date, time and place of the examination.
(6) At the time of service of the order the deponent must be offered or paid—
(a) a sum reasonably sufficient to cover his expenses in travelling to and from the place of examination; and
(b) such sum by way of compensation for loss of time as may be specified in the relevant practice direction.
(7) Where the court makes an order for a deposition to be taken, it may also order the party who obtained the order to serve a witness statement or witness summary in relation to the evidence to be given by the person to be examined.
(Part 32 contains the general rules about witness statements and witness summaries)

34.9 Conduct of Examination

r.34.9 **56.3, 56.12, 56.13** r.34.9(1)–(6) **56.3**

(1) Subject to any directions contained in the order for examination, the examination must be conducted in the same way as if the witness were giving evidence at a trial.
(2) If all the parties are present, the examiner may conduct the examination of a person not named in the order for examination if all the parties and the person to be examined consent.
(3) The examiner may conduct the examination in private if he considers it appropriate to do so.
(4) The examiner must ensure that the evidence given by the witness is recorded in full.
(5) The examiner must send a copy of the deposition—
(a) to the person who obtained the order for the examination of the witness; and
(b) to the court where the case is proceeding.
(6) The party who obtained the order must send each of the other parties a copy of the deposition which he receives from the examiner.

34.10 Enforcing Attendance of Witness

r.34.10 **56.12, 56.13** r.34.10(1)–(2) **56.4**

(1) If a person served with an order to attend before an examiner—
(a) fails to attend; or
(b) refuses to be sworn for the purpose of the examination or to answer any lawful question or produce any document at the examination,
a certificate of his failure or refusal, signed by the examiner, must be filed by the party requiring the deposition.
(2) On the certificate being filed, the party requiring the deposition may apply to the court for an order requiring that person to attend or to be sworn or to answer any question or produce any document, as the case may be.
(3) An application for an order under this rule may be made without notice.
(4) The court may order the person against whom an order is made under this rule to pay any costs resulting from his failure or refusal.

34.11 Use of Deposition at a Hearing

r.34.11(1)–(4) **56.6**

(1) A deposition ordered under rule 34.8 may be given in evidence at a hearing unless the court orders otherwise.
(2) A party intending to put in evidence a deposition at a hearing must serve notice of his intention to do so on every other party.
(3) He must serve the notice at least 21 days before the day fixed for the hearing.
(4) The court may require a deponent to attend the hearing and give evidence orally.
(5) Where a deposition is given in evidence at trial, it shall be treated as if it were a witness statement for the purposes of rule 32.13 (availability of witness statements for inspection).

34.12 Restrictions on Subsequent Use of Deposition Taken for the Purpose of Any Hearing Except the Trial

r.34.12 **56.7**

(1) Where the court orders a party to be examined about his or any other assets for the purpose of any hearing except the trial, the deposition may be used only for the purpose of the proceedings in which the order was made.
(2) However, it may be used for some other purpose—
(a) by the party who was examined;
(b) if the party who was examined agrees; or
(c) if the court gives permission.

34.13 Where a Person to Be Examined Is out of the Jurisdiction — Letter of Request

r.34.13 **47.77, 56.10** r.34.13(2)–(6) **56.10**

(1) This rule applies where a party wishes to take a deposition from a person who is—
(a) out of the jurisdiction; and
(b) not in a Regulation State within the meaning of Section III of this Part.
(1A) The High Court may order the issue of a letter of request to the judicial authorities of the country in which the proposed deponent is.
(2) A letter of request is a request to a judicial authority to take the evidence of that person, or arrange for it to be taken.
(3) The High Court may make an order under this rule in relation to county court proceedings.
(4) If the government of a country allows a person appointed by the High Court to examine a person in that country, the High Court may make an order appointing a special examiner for that purpose.
(5) A person may be examined under this rule on oath or affirmation or in accordance with any procedure permitted in the country in which the examination is to take place.
(6) If the High Court makes an order for the issue of a letter of request, the party who sought the order must file—
(a) the following documents and, except where paragraph (7) applies, a translation of them—
(i) a draft letter of request;
(ii) a statement of the issues relevant to the proceedings;
(iii) a list of questions or the subject matter of questions to be put to the person to be examined; and
(b) an undertaking to be responsible for the Secretary of State's expenses.
(7) There is no need to file a translation if—
(a) English is one of the official languages of the country where the examination is to take place; or
(b) a practice direction has specified that country as a country where no translation is necessary.

34.13A Letter of Request — Proceeds of Crime Act 2002

(1) This rule applies where a party to existing or contemplated proceedings in—
(a) the High Court; or
(b) a magistrates' court,
under Part 5 of the Proceeds of Crime Act 2002 (civil recovery of the proceeds etc. of unlawful conduct) wishes to take a deposition from a person who is out of the jurisdiction.
(2) The High Court may, on the application of such a party, order the issue of a letter of request to the judicial authorities of the country in which the proposed deponent is.
(3) Paragraphs (4) to (7) of rule 34.13 shall apply irrespective of where the proposed deponent is, and rule 34.23 shall not apply in cases where the proposed deponent is in a Regulation State within the meaning of Section III of this Part.

34.14 Fees and Expenses of Examiner of the Court

r.34.14(1)–(5) **56.5**

(1) An examiner of the court may charge a fee for the examination.
(2) He need not send the deposition to the court unless the fee is paid.

(3) The examiner's fees and expenses must be paid by the party who obtained the order for examination.
(4) If the fees and expenses due to an examiner are not paid within a reasonable time, he may report that fact to the court.
(5) The court may order the party who obtained the order for examination to deposit in the court office a specified sum in respect of the examiner's fees and, where it does so, the examiner will not be asked to act until the sum has been deposited.
(6) An order under this rule does not affect any decision as to the party who is ultimately to bear the costs of the examination.

34.15 Examiners of the Court

r.34.15 **56.2**

(1) The Lord Chancellor shall appoint persons to be examiners of the court.
(2) The persons appointed shall be barristers or solicitor-advocates who have been practising for a period of not less than three years.
(3) The Lord Chancellor may revoke an appointment at any time.

II EVIDENCE FOR FOREIGN COURTS

34.16 Scope and Interpretation

r.34.16 **56.12**

(1) This Section applies to an application for an order under the 1975 Act for evidence to be obtained, other than an application made as a result of a request by a court in another Regulation State.
(2) In this Section—
  (a) 'the 1975 Act' means the Evidence (Proceedings in Other Jurisdictions) Act 1975; and
  (b) 'Regulation State' has the same meaning as in Section III of this Part.

34.17 Application for Order

r.34.17 **56.12** r.34.17(b) **56.12**

An application for an order under the 1975 Act for evidence to be obtained—
(a) must be—
  (i) made to the High Court;
  (ii) supported by written evidence; and
  (iii) accompanied by the request as a result of which the application is made, and where appropriate, a translation of the request into English; and
(b) may be made without notice.

34.18 Examination

r.34.18 **56.12, 56.13**

(1) The court may order an examination to be taken before—
  (a) any fit and proper person nominated by the person applying for the order;
  (b) an examiner of the court; or
  (c) any other person whom the court considers suitable.
(2) Unless the court orders otherwise—
  (a) the examination will be taken as provided by rule 34.9; and
  (b) rule 34.10 applies.
(3) The court may make an order under rule 34.14 for payment of the fees and expenses of the examination.

34.19 Dealing with Deposition

r.34.19 **56.12**

(1) The examiner must send the deposition of the witness to the Senior Master unless the court orders otherwise.
(2) The Senior Master will—
  (a) give a certificate sealed with the seal of the Supreme Court for use out of the jurisdiction identifying the following documents—

(i) the request;
(ii) the order of the court for examination; and
(iii) the deposition of the witness; and
(b) send the certificate and the documents referred to in paragraph (a) to—
(i) the Secretary of State; or
(ii) where the request was sent to the Senior Master by another person in accordance with a Civil Procedure Convention, to that other person,

for transmission to the court or tribunal requesting the examination.

34.20 Claim to Privilege

r.34.20 **56.12**

(1) This rule applies where—
(a) a witness claims to be exempt from giving evidence on the ground specified in section 3(1)(b) of the 1975 Act; and
(b) that claim is not supported or conceded as referred to in section 3(2) of that Act.
(2) The examiner may require the witness to give the evidence which he claims to be exempt from giving.
(3) Where the examiner does not require the witness to give that evidence, the court may order the witness to do so.
(4) An application for an order under paragraph (3) may be made by the person who obtained the order under section 2 of the 1975 Act.
(5) Where such evidence is taken—
(a) it must be contained in a document separate from the remainder of the deposition;
(b) the examiner will send to the Senior Master—
(i) the deposition; and
(ii) a signed statement setting out the claim to be exempt and the ground on which it was made.
(6) On receipt of the statement referred to in paragraph (5)(b)(ii), the Senior Master will—
(a) retain the document containing the part of the witness's evidence to which the claim to be exempt relates; and
(b) send the statement and a request to determine that claim to the foreign court or tribunal together with the documents referred to in rule 34.17.
(7) The Senior Master will—
(a) if the claim to be exempt is rejected by the foreign court or tribunal, send the document referred to in paragraph (5)(a) to that court or tribunal;
(b) if the claim is upheld, send the document to the witness; and
(c) in either case, notify the witness and person who obtained the order under section 2 of the foreign court or tribunal's decision.

34.21 Order under 1975 Act as Applied by Patents Act 1977

r.34.21 **56.12**

Where an order is made for the examination of witnesses under section 1 of the 1975 Act as applied by section 92 of the Patents Act 1977 the court may permit an officer of the European Patent Office to—
(a) attend the examination and examine the witnesses; or
(b) request the court or the examiner before whom the examination takes place to put specified questions to them.

III TAKING OF EVIDENCE — MEMBER STATES OF THE EUROPEAN UNION

34.22 Interpretation

In this Section—
(a) 'designated court' has the meaning given in the relevant practice direction;
(b) 'Regulation State' has the same meaning as 'Member State' in the Taking of Evidence Regulation, that is all Member States except Denmark;
(c) 'the Taking of Evidence Regulation' means Council Regulation (EC) No. 1206/2001 of 28 May 2001 on cooperation between the courts of the Member States in the taking of evidence in civil and commercial matters.

(The Taking of Evidence Regulation is annexed to the relevant practice direction)

34.23 Where a Person to Be Examined Is in Another Regulation State

r.34.23(2) **56.8**
r.34.23(3) **56.8**
r.34.23(5) **56.9**
r.34.23(6)(b) **56.9**
r.34.23(6)(c) **56.9**

(1) Subject to rule 34.13A, this rule applies where a party wishes to take a deposition from a person who is in another Regulation State.
(2) The court may order the issue of a request to a designated court ('the requested court') in the Regulation State in which the proposed deponent is.
(3) If the court makes an order for the issue of a request, the party who sought the order must file—
   (a) a draft Form A as set out in the annex to the Taking of Evidence Regulation (request for the taking of evidence);
   (b) except where paragraph (4) applies, a translation of the form;
   (c) an undertaking to be responsible for costs sought by the requested court in relation to—
      (i) fees paid to experts and interpreters; and
      (ii) where requested by that party, the use of special procedures or communications technology; and
   (d) an undertaking to be responsible for the court's expenses.
(4) There is no need to file a translation if—
   (a) English is one of the official languages of the Regulation State where the examination is to take place; or
   (b) the Regulation State has indicated, in accordance with the Taking of Evidence Regulation, that English is a language which it will accept.
(5) Where article 17 of the Taking of Evidence Regulation (direct taking of evidence by the requested court) allows evidence to be taken directly in another Regulation State, the court may make an order for the submission of a request in accordance with that article.
(6) If the court makes an order for the submission of a request under paragraph (5), the party who sought the order must file—
   (a) a draft Form I as set out in the annex to the Taking of Evidence Regulation (request for direct taking of evidence);
   (b) except where paragraph (4) applies, a translation of the form; and
   (c) an undertaking to be responsible for the court's expenses.

34.24 Evidence for Courts of Other Regulation States

r.34.24(2) **56.13**
r.34.24(2)(c) **56.13**
r.34.24(3)–(4) **56.13**

(1) This rule applies where a court in another Regulation State ('the requesting court') issues a request for evidence to be taken from a person who is in the jurisdiction.
(2) An application for an order for evidence to be taken—
   (b) must be accompanied by—
      (i) the form of request for the taking of evidence as a result of which the application is made; and
      (ii) where appropriate, a translation of the form of request; and
   (c) may be made without notice.
(3) Rule 34.18(1) and (2) apply.
(4) The examiner must send—
   (a) the deposition to the court for transmission to the requesting court; and
   (b) a copy of the deposition to the person who obtained the order for evidence to be taken.

Civil Procedure Rules & Practice Directions

PD 34 Practice Direction — Depositions and Court Attendance by Witnesses

This practice direction supplements CPR Part 34.

[For commentary on a specific paragraph, please refer to the cross-references after the title of the paragraph.]

WITNESS SUMMONSES

para.1.2 **55.1**

Issue of Witness Summons

1.1 A witness summons may require a witness to:
(1) attend court to give evidence,
(2) produce documents to the court, or
(3) both,
on either a date fixed for the hearing or such date as the court may direct.[1]

1.2 Two copies of the witness summons[2] should be filed with the court for sealing, one of which will be retained on the court file.

1.3 A mistake in the name or address of a person named in a witness summons may be corrected if the summons has not been served.

1.4 The corrected summons must be re-sealed by the court and marked 'Amended and Re-sealed'.

Witness Summons Issued in Aid of an Inferior Court or Tribunal

paras.2.3–2.4 **55.3**

2.1 A witness summons may be issued in the High Court or a county court in aid of a court or tribunal which does not have the power to issue a witness summons in relation to the proceedings before it.[3]

2.2 A witness summons referred to in paragraph 2.1 may be set aside by the court which issued it.[4]

2.3 An application to set aside a witness summons referred to in paragraph 2.1 will be heard:
(1) in the High Court by a master at the Royal Courts of Justice or by a district judge in a District Registry, and
(2) in a county court by a district judge.

2.4 Unless the court otherwise directs, the applicant must give at least 2 days' notice to the party who issued the witness summons of the application, which will normally be dealt with at a hearing.

Travelling Expenses and Compensation for Loss of Time

paras.3.1–3.4 **55.6**

3.1 When a witness is served with a witness summons he must be offered a sum to cover his travelling expenses to and from the court and compensation for his loss of time.[5]

3.2 If the witness summons is to be served by the court, the party issuing the summons must deposit with the court:
(1) a sum sufficient to pay for the witness's expenses in travelling to the court and in returning to his home or place of work, and
(2) a sum in respect of the period during which earnings or benefit are lost, or such lesser sum as it may be proved that the witness will lose as a result of his attendance at court in answer to the witness summons.

---

[1] Rule 34.2(4).
[2] In form N20.
[3] Rule 34.4(1).
[4] Rule 34.4(2).
[5] Rule 34.7.

3.3 The sum referred to in 3.2(2) is to be based on the sums payable to witnesses attending the Crown Court.[6]

3.4 Where the party issuing the witness summons wishes to serve it himself,[7] he must:
(1) notify the court in writing that he wishes to do so, and
(2) at the time of service offer the witness the sums mentioned in paragraph 3.2 above.

DEPOSITIONS

para.4.1 **56.10**
paras.4.2 **56.2, 56.10, 56.12**
paras.4.3–4.4 **56.3, 56.10, 56.12**
para.4.5 **56.4, 56.10, 56.12**
paras.4.6–4.11 **56.10, 56.12**
paras.4.12 **56.3, 56.10, 56.12**
paras.4.12(4) **56.3**

To Be Taken in England and Wales for Use as Evidence in Proceedings in Courts in England and Wales

4.1 A party may apply for an order for a person to be examined on oath before:
(1) a judge,
(2) an examiner of the court, or
(3) such other person as the court may appoint.[8]

4.2 The party who obtains an order for the examination of a deponent[9] before an examiner of the court[10] must:
(1) apply to the Foreign Process Section of the Masters' Secretary's Department at the Royal Courts of Justice for the allocation of an examiner,
(2) when allocated, provide the examiner with copies of all documents in the proceedings necessary to inform the examiner of the issues, and
(3) pay the deponent a sum to cover his travelling expenses to and from the examination and compensation for his loss of time.[11]

4.3 In ensuring that the deponent's evidence is recorded in full, the court or the examiner may permit it to be recorded on audiotape or videotape, but the deposition[12] must always be recorded in writing by him or by a competent shorthand writer or stenographer.

4.4 If the deposition is not recorded word for word, it must contain, as nearly as may be, the statement of the deponent; the examiner may record word for word any particular questions and answers which appear to him to have special importance.

4.5 If a deponent objects to answering any question or where any objection is taken to any question, the examiner must:
(1) record in the deposition or a document attached to it:
(a) the question,
(b) the nature of and grounds for the objection, and
(c) any answer given, and
(2) give his opinion as to the validity of the objection and must record it in the deposition or a document attached to it.

The court will decide as to the validity of the objection and any question of costs arising from it.

4.6 Documents and exhibits must:
(1) have an identifying number or letter marked on them by the examiner, and
(2) be preserved by the party or his legal representative[13] who obtained the order for the examination, or as the court or the examiner may direct.

[6] Fixed pursuant to the Prosecution of Offences Act 1985 and the Costs in Criminal Cases (General) Regulations 1986 (SI 1986/1335).
[7] Rule 34.6(1).
[8] Rule 34.8(3).
[9] See rule 34.8(2) for explanation of 'deponent' and 'deposition'.
[10] For the appointment of examiners of the court see rule 34.15.
[11] Rule 34.8(6).
[12] See rule 34.8(2) for explanation of 'deponent' and 'deposition'.
[13] For the definition of legal representative see rule 2. 3.

4.7 The examiner may put any question to the deponent as to:
(1) the meaning of any of his answers, or
(2) any matter arising in the course of the examination.

4.8 Where a deponent:
(1) fails to attend the examination, or
(2) refuses to:
(a) be sworn, or
(b) answer any lawful question, or
(c) produce any document,
the examiner will sign a certificate[14] of such failure or refusal and may include in his certificate any comment as to the conduct of the deponent or of any person attending the examination.

4.9 The party who obtained the order for the examination must file the certificate with the court and may apply for an order that the deponent attend for examination or as may be.[15] The application may be made without notice.[16]

4.10 The court will make such order on the application as it thinks fit including an order for the deponent to pay any costs resulting from his failure or refusal.[17]

4.11 A deponent who wilfully refuses to obey an order made against him under Part 34 may be proceeded against for contempt of court.

4.12 A deposition must:
(1) be signed by the examiner,
(2) have any amendments to it initialled by the examiner and the deponent,
(3) be endorsed by the examiner with:
(a) a statement of the time occupied by the examination, and
(b) a record of any refusal by the deponent to sign the deposition and of his reasons for not doing so, and
(4) be sent by the examiner to the court where the proceedings are taking place for filing on the court file.

4.13 Rule 34.14 deals with the fees and expenses of an examiner.

Depositions to Be Taken Abroad for Use as Evidence in Proceedings before Courts in England and Wales Where the Taking of Evidence Regulation Does Not Apply

paras.5.2–5.3 **56.10** paras.5.8–5.9 **56.10**

5.1 Where a party wishes to take a deposition from a person outside the jurisdiction, the High Court may order the issue of a letter of request to the judicial authorities of the country in which the proposed deponent is.[18]

5.2 An application for an order referred to in paragraph 5.1 should be made by application notice in accordance with Part 23.

5.3 The documents which a party applying for an order for the issue of a letter of request must file with his application notice are set out in rule 34.13(6). They are as follows:
(1) a draft letter of request is set out in Annex A to this practice direction,
(2) a statement of the issues relevant to the proceedings,
(3) a list of questions or the subject matter of questions to be put to the proposed deponent,
(4) a translation of the documents in (1), (2) and (3) above unless the proposed deponent is in a country of which English is an official language, and
(5) an undertaking to be responsible for the expenses of the Secretary of State.
In addition to the documents listed above the party applying for the order must file a draft order.

5.4 The above documents should be filed with the Masters' Secretary in Room E214, Royal Courts of Justice, Strand, London WC2A 2LL.

---

[14] Rule 34.10.
[15] Rule 34.10(2) and (3).
[16] Rule 34.10(3).
[17] Rule 34.10(4).
[18] Rule 34.13(1).

5.5 The application will be dealt with by the Senior Master of the Queen's Bench Division of the High Court who will, if appropriate, sign the letter of request.

5.6 Attention is drawn to the provisions of rule 23.10 (application to vary or discharge an order made without notice).

5.7 If parties are in doubt as to whether a translation under paragraph 5.3(4) above is required, they should seek guidance from the Foreign Process Section of the Masters' Secretary's Department.

5.8 A special examiner appointed under rule 34.13(4) may be the British consul or the consul-general or his deputy in the country where the evidence is to be taken if:

(1) there is in respect of that country a Civil Procedure Convention providing for the taking of evidence in that country for the assistance of proceedings in the High Court or other court in this country, or

(2) with the consent of the Secretary of State.

5.9 The provisions of paragraphs 4.1 to 4.12 above apply to the depositions referred to in this paragraph.

Depositions to Be Taken in England and Wales for Use as Evidence in Proceedings before Courts Abroad Pursuant to Letters of Request Where the Taking of Evidence Regulation Does Not Apply

paras.6.1–6.8 **56.12**

6.1 Section II of Part 34 relating to obtaining evidence for foreign courts and should be read in conjunction with this part of the practice direction.

6.2 The Evidence (Proceedings in Other Jurisdictions) Act 1975 applies to these depositions.

6.3 The written evidence supporting an application under r. 34.17 (which should be made by application notice: see Part 23) must include or exhibit:

(1) a statement of the issues relevant to the proceedings;

(2) a list of questions or the subject matter of questions to be put to the proposed deponent;

(3) a draft order; and

(4) a translation of the documents in (1) and (2) into English, if necessary.

6.4 (1) The Senior Master will send to the Treasury Solicitor any request:

(a) forwarded by the Secretary of State with a recommendation that effect should be given to the request without requiring an application to be made; or

(b) received by him in pursuance of a civil procedure convention providing for the taking of evidence of any person in England and Wales to assist a court or tribunal in a foreign country where no person is named in the document as the applicant.

(2) In relation to such a request, the Treasury Solicitor may, with the consent of the Treasury:

(a) apply for an order under the 1975 Act; and

(b) take such other steps as are necessary to give effect to the request.

6.5 The order for the deponent to attend and be examined together with the evidence upon which the order was made must be served on the deponent.

6.6 Attention is drawn to the provisions of r. 23.10 (application to vary or discharge an order made without notice).

6.7 Arrangements for the examination to take place at a specified time and place before an examiner of the court or such other person as the court may appoint shall be made by the applicant for the order and approved by the Senior Master.

6.8 The provisions of paragraphs 4.2 to 4.12 apply to the depositions referred to in this paragraph, except that the examiner must send the deposition to the Senior Master.

(For further information about evidence see Part 32 and PD 32.)

TAKING OF EVIDENCE BETWEEN EU MEMBER STATES

Taking of Evidence Regulation

7.1 Where evidence is to be taken:

(a) from a person in another Member State of the European Union for use as evidence in proceedings before courts in England and Wales; or

(b) from a person in England and Wales for use as evidence in proceedings before a court in another Member State,

Civil Procedure Rules & Practice Directions

Council Regulation (EC) No. 1206/2001 of 28 May 2001 on cooperation between the courts of the Member States in the taking of evidence in civil or commercial matters ('the Taking of Evidence Regulation') applies.

7.2 The Taking of Evidence Regulation is [on the CD-ROM version of *Blackstone's Civil Practice*].

7.3 The Taking of Evidence Regulation does not apply to Denmark. In relation to Denmark, therefore, r. 34.13 and Section II of Part 34 will continue to apply.

(Article 21(1) of the Taking of Evidence Regulation provides that the Regulation prevails over other provisions contained in bilateral or multilateral agreements or arrangements concluded by the Member States and in particular the Hague Convention of 1 March 1954 on Civil Procedure and the Hague Convention of 18 March 1970 on the Taking of Evidence Abroad in Civil or Commercial Matters.)

Meaning of 'Designated Court'

8.1 In accordance with the Taking of Evidence Regulation, each Regulation State has prepared a list of courts competent to take evidence in accordance with the Regulation indicating the territorial and, where appropriate, special jurisdiction of those courts.

8.2 Where Part 34, Section III, refers to a 'designated court' in relation to another Regulation State, the reference is to the court, referred to in the list of competent courts of that State, which is appropriate to the application in hand.

8.3 Where the reference is to the 'designated court' in England and Wales, the reference is to the appropriate competent court in the jurisdiction. The designated courts for England and Wales are listed in Annex C to this practice direction.

Central Body

para.9.2 **56.8**

9.1 The Taking of Evidence Regulation stipulates that each Regulation State must nominate a Central Body responsible for:

(a) supplying information to courts;

(b) seeking solutions to any difficulties which may arise in respect of a request; and

(c) forwarding, in exceptional cases, at the request of a requesting court, a request to the competent court.

9.2 The United Kingdom has nominated the Senior Master, Queen's Bench Division, to be the Central Body for England and Wales.

9.3 The Senior Master, as Central Body, has been designated responsible for taking decisions on requests pursuant to art. 17 of the Regulation. Article 17 allows a court to submit a request to the Central Body or a designated competent authority in another Regulation State to take evidence directly in that State.

Evidence to Be Taken in Another Regulation State for Use in England and Wales

10.1 Where a person wishes to take a deposition from a person in another Regulation State, the court where the proceedings are taking place may order the issue of a request to the designated court in the Regulation State (r. 34.23(2)). The form of request is prescribed as form A in the Taking of Evidence Regulation.

10.2 An application to the court for an order under r. 34.23(2) should be made by application notice in accordance with Part 23.

10.3 Rule 34.23(3) provides that the party applying for the order must file a draft form of request in the prescribed form. Where completion of the form requires attachments or documents to accompany the form, these must also be filed.

10.4 If the court grants an order under r. 34.23(2), it will send the form of request directly to the designated court.

10.5 Where the taking of evidence requires the use of an expert, the designated court may require a deposit in advance towards the costs of that expert. The party who obtained the order is responsible for the payment of any such deposit which should be deposited with the court for onward transmission. Under the provisions of the Taking of Evidence Regulation, the designated court is not required to execute the request until such payment is received.

10.6 Article 17 permits the court where proceedings are taking place to take evidence directly from a deponent in another Regulation State if the conditions of the article are satisfied. Direct taking of evidence can only take place if evidence is given voluntarily without the need for coercive measures. Rule 34.23(5) provides for the court to make an order for the submission of a request to take evidence directly. The form of request is form I annexed to the Taking of Evidence Regulation and r. 34.23(6) makes provision for a draft of this form to be filed by the party seeking the order. An application for an order under r. 34.23(5) should be by application notice in accordance with Part 23.

10.7 Attention is drawn to the provisions of r. 23.10 (application to vary or discharge an order made without notice).

Evidence to Be Taken in England and Wales for Use in Another Regulation State

paras.11.2–7 **56.13**

11.1 Where a designated court in England and Wales receives a request to take evidence from a court in a Regulation State, the court will send the request to the Treasury Solicitor.

11.2 On receipt of the request, the Treasury Solicitor may, with the consent of the Treasury, apply for an order under r. 34.24.

11.3 An application to the court for an order must be accompanied by the form of request to take evidence and any accompanying documents, translated if required under para. 11.4.

11.4 The United Kingdom has indicated that, in addition to English, it will accept French as a language in which documents may be submitted. Where the form or request and any accompanying documents are received in French they will be translated into English by the Treasury Solicitor.

11.5 The order for the deponent to attend and be examined together with the evidence on which the order was made must be served on the deponent.

11.6 Arrangements for the examination to take place at a specified time and place shall be made by the Treasury Solicitor and approved by the court.

11.7 The court shall send details of the arrangements for the examination to such of:
(a) the parties and, if any, their representatives; or
(b) the representatives of the foreign court,
who have indicated, in accordance with the Taking of Evidence Regulation, that they wish to be present at the examination.

11.8 The provisions of para. 4.3 to 4.12 apply to the depositions referred to in this paragraph.

ANNEX A

Draft Letter of Request (Where the Taking of Evidence Regulation Does Not Apply)

To the Competent Judicial Authority of
in the of
I [name] Senior Master of the Queen's Bench Division of the Supreme Court of England and Wales respectfully request the assistance of your court with regard to the following matters.

1. A claim is now pending in the Division of the High Court of Justice in England and Wales entitled as follows
[*set out full title and claim number*]
in which [*name*] of [*address*] is the claimant and [*name*] of [*address*] is the defendant.
2. The names and addresses of the representatives or agents of [*set out names and addresses of representatives of the parties*].
3. The claim by the claimant is for:—
(a) [*set out the nature of the claim*]
(b) [*the relief sought, and*]
(c) [*a summary of the facts.*]
4. It is necessary for the purposes of justice and for the due determination of the matters in dispute between the parties that you cause the following witnesses, who are resident within your jurisdiction, to be examined. The names and addresses of the witnesses are as follows:—

Civil Procedure Rules & Practice Directions

5. The witnesses should be examined on oath or if that is not possible within your laws or is impossible of performance by reason of the internal practice and procedure of your court or by reason of practical difficulties, they should be examined in accordance with whatever procedure your laws provide for in these matters.
6. Either/
   The witnesses should be examined in accordance with the list of questions annexed hereto.
   Or/
   The witnesses should be examined regarding [*set out full details of evidence sought*]
   N.B. Where the witness is required to produce documents, these should be clearly identified.
7. I would ask that you cause me, or the agents of the parties (if appointed), to be informed of the date and place where the examination is to take place.
8. Finally, I request that you will cause the evidence of the said witnesses to be reduced into writing and all documents produced on such examinations to be duly marked for identification and that you will further be pleased to authenticate such examinations by the seal of your court or in such other way as is in accordance with your procedure and return the written evidence and documents produced to me addressed as follows:—
   Senior Master of the Queen's Bench Division
   Royal Courts of Justice
   Strand
   London WC2A 2LL
   England

[ANNEX B

Council Regulation (EC) No. 1206/2001

This Regulation is on the CD-ROM version of *Blackstone's Civil Practice.* Please click on the title of the Regulation to open it.]

ANNEX C

annex C **56.8, 56.13**

Designated courts in England and Wales under the Taking of Evidence Regulation (see para. 8 above)

Area	Designated court
London and South Eastern Circuit	Royal Courts of Justice (Queen's Bench Division)
Midland Circuit	Birmingham Civil Justice Centre
Western Circuit	Bristol County Court
Wales and Chester Circuit	Cardiff Civil Justice Centre
Northern Circuit	Manchester County Court
North Eastern Circuit	Leeds County Court

PD 34B Practice Direction — Fees for Examiners of the Court

This practice direction supplements CPR Part 34

Scope

1.1 This practice direction sets out:
   (1) how to calculate the fees an examiner of the court ('an examiner') may charge; and
   (2) the expenses he may recover.
   (Rule 34.8(3)(b) provides that the court may make an order for evidence to be obtained by the examination of a witness before an examiner of the court.)

1.2 The party who obtained the order for the examination must pay the fees and expenses of the examiner.
   (Rule 34.14 permits an examiner to charge a fee for the examination and contains other provisions about his fees and expenses, and r. 34.15 provides who may be appointed as an examiner of the court.)

The Examination Fee

2.1 An examiner may charge an hourly rate for each hour (or part of an hour) that he is engaged in examining the witness.

2.2 The hourly rate is to be calculated by reference to the formula set out in para. 3.

2.3 The examination fee will be the hourly rate multiplied by the number of hours the examination has taken. For example:

Examination fee = hourly rate × number of hours.

How to Calculate the Hourly Rate — The Formula

3.1 Divide the amount of the minimum annual salary of a post within Group 7 of the judicial salary structure as designated by the Review Body on Senior Salaries,[1] by 220 to give 'x'; and then divide 'x' by 6 to give **the hourly rate**.
   For example:

$$\frac{\text{minimum annual salary}}{220} = x$$

$$\frac{x}{6} = \text{hourly rate}$$

Single Fee Chargeable on Making the Appointment for Examination

4.1 An examiner of court is also entitled to charge a single fee of twice the hourly rate (calculated in accordance with para. 3 above) as 'the appointment fee' when the appointment for the examination is made.

4.2 The examiner is entitled to retain the appointment fee where the witness fails to attend on the date and time arranged.

4.3 Where the examiner fails to attend on the date and time arranged he may not charge a further appointment fee for arranging a subsequent appointment.
   (The examiner need not send the deposition to the court until his fees are paid — see r. 34.14(2).)

Examiners' Expenses

5.1 The examiner of court is also entitled to recover the following expenses:

[1] The Report of the Review Body on Senior Salaries is published annually by the Stationery Office.

Civil Procedure Rules & Practice Directions

(1) all reasonable travelling expenses;
(2) any other expenses reasonably incurred; and
(3) subject to para. 5.2, any reasonable charge for the room where the examination takes place.

5.2 No expenses may be recovered under para. 5.1(3) above if the examination takes place at the examiner's usual business address.

(If the examiner's fees and expenses are not paid within a reasonable time he may report the fact to the court, see r. 34.14(4) and (5).)

CPR Part 35 Experts and Assessors

Part 35 **24.7, 43.6, 44.7, 52.5** [For commentary on a specific rule, please refer to the cross-references after the title of the rule.]

35.1 Duty to Restrict Expert Evidence

r.35.1 **43.6, 43.18, 52.4, 97.43**

Expert evidence shall be restricted to that which is reasonably required to resolve the proceedings.

35.2 Interpretation

A reference to an 'expert' in this Part is a reference to an expert who has been instructed to give or prepare evidence for the purpose of court proceedings.

35.3 Experts — Overriding Duty to the Court

r.35.3 **43.6, 43.18, 52.4, 52.10, 52.24** r.35.3(1) **52.1**

(1) It is the duty of an expert to help the court on the matters within his expertise.
(2) This duty overrides any obligation to the person from whom he has received instructions or by whom he is paid.

35.4 Court's Power to Restrict Expert Evidence

r.35.4 **52.4** r.35.4(2)–(3) **52.4**
r.35.4(1) **52.1, 52.4, 52.5** r.35.4(4) **8.16, 42.15, 52.4**

(1) No party may call an expert or put in evidence an expert's report without the court's permission.
(2) When a party applies for permission under this rule he must identify—
  (a) the field in which he wishes to rely on expert evidence; and
  (b) where practicable the expert in that field on whose evidence he wishes to rely.
(3) If permission is granted under this rule it shall be in relation only to the expert named or the field identified under paragraph (2).
(4) The court may limit the amount of the expert's fees and expenses that the party who wishes to rely on the expert may recover from any other party.

35.5 General Requirement for Expert Evidence to Be Given in a Written Report

r.35.5(1) **52.19** r.35.5(2) **44.6, 52.6, 52.19**

(1) Expert evidence is to be given in a written report unless the court directs otherwise.
(2) If a claim is on the fast track, the court will not direct an expert to attend a hearing unless it is necessary to do so in the interests of justice.

35.6 Written Questions to Experts

r.35.6 **44.7, 52.15, 52.23**
r.35.6(2)(a)–(c) **52.23**
r.35.6(3)–(4) **52.23**

(1) A party may put to—
 (a) an expert instructed by another party; or
 (b) a single joint expert appointed under rule 35.7, written questions about his report.
(2) Written questions under paragraph (1)—
 (a) may be put once only;
 (b) must be put within 28 days of service of the expert's report; and
 (c) must be for the purpose only of clarification of the report,
 unless in any case—
  (i) the court gives permission; or
  (ii) the other party agrees.
(3) An expert's answers to questions put in accordance with paragraph (1) shall be treated as part of the expert's report.
(4) Where—
 (a) a party has put a written question to an expert instructed by another party in accordance with this rule; and
 (b) the expert does not answer that question,
 the court may make one or both of the following orders in relation to the party who instructed the expert—
  (i) that the party may not rely on the evidence of that expert; or
  (ii) that the party may not recover the fees and expenses of that expert from any other party.

35.7 Court's Power to Direct that Evidence Is to Be Given by a Single Joint Expert

r.35.7 **8.16, 43.6, 43.18, 44.6, 52.10, 52.18, 97.43**

(1) Where two or more parties wish to submit expert evidence on a particular issue, the court may direct that the evidence on that issue is to given [*sic*] by one expert only.
(2) The parties wishing to submit the expert evidence are called 'the instructing parties'.
(3) Where the instructing parties cannot agree who should be the expert, the court may—
 (a) select the expert from a list prepared or identified by the instructing parties; or
 (b) direct that the expert be selected in such other manner as the court may direct.

35.8 Instructions to a Single Joint Expert

r.35.8 **43.6, 43.18**
r.35.8(1)–(2) **52.18**
r.35.8(3) **52.10**
r.35.8(3)(b) **97.43**
r.35.8(4) **52.10**
r.35.8(4)(a) **97.43**
r.35.8(5) **52.10**

(1) Where the court gives a direction under rule 35.7 for a single joint expert to be used, each instructing party may give instructions to the expert.
(2) When an instructing party gives instructions to the expert he must, at the same time, send a copy of the instructions to the other instructing parties.
(3) The court may give directions about—
 (a) the payment of the expert's fees and expenses; and
 (b) any inspection, examination or experiments which the expert wishes to carry out.
(4) The court may, before an expert is instructed—
 (a) limit the amount that can be paid by way of fees and expenses to the expert; and
 (b) direct that the instructing parties pay that amount into court.
(5) Unless the court otherwise directs, the instructing parties are jointly and severally liable[(GL)] for the payment of the expert's fees and expenses.

35.9 Power of Court to Direct a Party to Provide Information

r.35.9 **52.18**

Where a party has access to information which is not reasonably available to the other party, the court may direct the party who has access to the information to—
(a) prepare and file a document recording the information; and
(b) serve a copy of that document on the other party.

35.10 Contents of Report

r.35.10 **7.52**
r.35.10(2) **52.20**
r.35.10(3) **48.22, 52.21, 52.29**
r.35.10(4) **48.22, 52.21, 52.29**

(1) An expert's report must comply with the requirements set out in the relevant practice direction.
(2) At the end of an expert's report there must be a statement that—
 (a) the expert understands his duty to the court; and
 (b) he has complied with that duty.
(3) The expert's report must state the substance of all material instructions, whether written or oral, on the basis of which the report was written.
(4) The instructions referred to in paragraph (3) shall not be privileged[(GL)] against disclosure but the court will not, in relation to those instructions—
 (a) order disclosure of any specific document; or
 (b) permit any questioning in court, other than by the party who instructed the expert,
 unless it is satisfied that there are reasonable grounds to consider the statement of instructions given under paragraph (3) to be inaccurate or incomplete.

35.11 Use by One Party of Expert's Report Disclosed by Another

r.35.11 **52.19**

Where a party has disclosed an expert's report, any party may use that expert's report as evidence at the trial.

35.12 Discussions between Experts

r.35.12 **44.6, 52.22**
r.35.12(1) **52.6**
r.35.12(2) **52.22**
r.35.12(3) **52.6, 52.22**
r.35.12(4)–(5) **52.22**

(1) The court may, at any stage, direct a discussion between experts for the purpose of requiring the experts to—
 (a) identify and discuss the expert issues in the proceedings; and
 (b) where possible, reach an agreed opinion on those issues.
(2) The court may specify the issues which the experts must discuss.
(3) The court may direct that following a discussion between the experts they must prepare a statement for the court showing—
 (a) those issues on which they agree; and
 (b) those issues on which they disagree and a summary of their reasons for disagreeing.
(4) The content of the discussion between the experts shall not be referred to at the trial unless the parties agree.
(5) Where experts reach agreement on an issue during their discussions, the agreement shall not bind the parties unless the parties expressly agree to be bound by the agreement.

35.13 Consequence of Failure to Disclose Expert's Report

r.35.13 **46.11, 52.19**

A party who fails to disclose an expert's report may not use the report at the trial or call the expert to give evidence orally unless the court gives permission.

35.14 Expert's Right to Ask Court for Directions

r.35(14) **44.7, 52.17, 52.24**
r.35.14(2) **52.24**
r.35.14(3) **52.24**

(1) An expert may file a written request for directions to assist him in carrying out his function as an expert.
(2) An expert must, unless the court orders otherwise, provide a copy of any proposed request for directions under paragraph (1)—
 (a) to the party instructing him, at least 7 days before he files the request; and
 (b) to all other parties, at least 4 days before he files it.
(3) The court, when it gives directions, may also direct that a party be served with a copy of the directions.

35.15 Assessors

r.35.15 **52.30**
r.35.15(3) **52.30**
r.35.15(5)–(7) **52.30**

(1) This rule applies where the court appoints one or more persons (an 'assessor') under section 70 of the Supreme Court Act 1981 or section 63 of the County Courts Act 1984.

(2) The assessor shall assist the court in dealing with a matter in which the assessor has skill and experience.
(3) An assessor shall take such part in the proceedings as the court may direct and in particular the court may—
  (a) direct the assessor to prepare a report for the court on any matter at issue in the proceedings; and
  (b) direct the assessor to attend the whole or any part of the trial to advise the court on any such matter.
(4) If the assessor prepares a report for the court before the trial has begun—
  (a) the court will send a copy to each of the parties; and
  (b) the parties may use it at trial.
(5) The remuneration to be paid to the assessor for his services shall be determined by the court and shall form part of the costs of the proceedings.
(6) The court may order any party to deposit in the court office a specified sum in respect of the assessor's fees and, where it does so, the assessor will not be asked to act until the sum has been deposited.
(7) Paragraphs (5) and (6) do not apply where the remuneration of the assessor is to be paid out of money provided by Parliament.

PD 35 Practice Direction — Experts and Assessors

This practice direction supplements CPR Part 35

PD 35 **43.18**, **46.25**, **47.7** [For commentary on a specific paragraph, please refer to the cross-references after the title of the paragraph.]

Part 35 is intended to limit the use of oral expert evidence to that which is reasonably required. In addition, where possible, matters requiring expert evidence should be dealt with by a single expert. Permission of the court is always required either to call an expert or to put an expert's report in evidence. There is annexed to this practice direction a protocol for the instruction of experts to give evidence in civil claims. Experts and those instructing them are expected to have regard to the guidance contained in the protocol.

Expert Evidence — General Requirements

1.1 It is the duty of an expert to help the court on matters within his own expertise (r. 35.3(1)). This duty is paramount and overrides any obligation to the person from whom the expert has received instructions or by whom he is paid (r. 35.3(2)).

1.2 Expert evidence should be the independent product of the expert uninfluenced by the pressures of litigation.

1.3 An expert should assist the court by providing objective, unbiased opinion on matters within his expertise, and should not assume the role of an advocate.

1.4 An expert should consider all material facts, including those which might detract from his opinion.

1.5 An expert should make it clear:
- (a) when a question or issue falls outside his expertise; and
- (b) when he is not able to reach a definite opinion, for example because he has insufficient information.

1.6 If, after producing a report, an expert changes his view on any material matter, such change of view should be communicated to all the parties without delay, and when appropriate to the court.

Form and Content of Experts' Reports

para.2 **52.20**
para.2.1 **52.20**
para.2.2 **52.20**
para.2.2(5) **52.25**
para.2.3 **52.20**
para.2.4 **52.20**

2.1 An expert's report should be addressed to the court and not to the party from whom the expert has received his instructions.

2.2 An expert's report must:
- (1) give details of the expert's qualifications;
- (2) give details of any literature or other material which the expert has relied on in making the report;
- (3) contain a statement setting out the substance of all facts and instructions given to the expert which are material to the opinions expressed in the report or upon which those opinions are based;
- (4) make clear which of the facts stated in the report are within the expert's own knowledge;
- (5) say who carried out any examination, measurement, test or experiment which the expert has used for the report, give the qualifications of that person, and say whether or not the test or experiment has been carried out under the expert's supervision;
- (6) where there is a range of opinion on the matters dealt with in the report:
  - (a) summarise the range of opinion, and
  - (b) give reasons for his own opinion;
- (7) contain a summary of the conclusions reached;
- (8) if the expert is not able to give his opinion without qualification, state the qualification; and
- (9) contain a statement that the expert understands his duty to the court, and has complied and will continue to comply with that duty.

2.3 An expert's report must be verified by a statement of truth as well as containing the statements required in para. 2.2(8) and (9) above.

2.4 The form of the statement of truth is as follows:
I confirm that in so far as the facts stated in my report are within my own knowledge I have made clear which they are and I believe them to be true, and that the opinions I have expressed represent my true and complete professional opinion.

2.5 Attention is drawn to r. 32.14 which sets out the consequences of verifying a document containing a false statement without an honest belief in its truth.
(For information about statements of truth see Part 22 and PD 22.)

Information

para.3 **52.18**

3 Under r. 35.9 the court may direct a party with access to information which is not reasonably available to another party to serve on that other party a document which records the information. The document served must include sufficient details of all the facts, tests, experiments and assumptions which underlie any part of the information to enable the party on whom it is served to make, or to obtain, a proper interpretation of the information and an assessment of its significance.

Instructions

para.4 **52.29**

4 The instructions referred to in para. 2.2(3) will not be protected by privilege (see r. 35.10(4)). But cross-examination of the expert on the contents of his instructions will not be allowed unless the court permits it (or unless the party who gave the instructions consents to it). Before it gives permission the court must be satisfied that there are reasonable grounds to consider that the statement in the report of the substance of the instructions is inaccurate or incomplete. If the court is so satisfied, it will allow the cross-examination where it appears to be in the interests of justice to do so.

Questions to Experts

para.5.1 **44.7** paras.5.2–5.3 **52.23**

5.1 Questions asked for the purpose of clarifying the expert's report (see r. 35.6) should be put, in writing, to the expert not later than 28 days after receipt of the expert's report (see paras [2.3 to 2.5*] above as to verification).

5.2 Where a party sends a written question or questions direct to an expert, a copy of the questions should, at the same time, be sent to the other party or parties.

5.3 The party or parties instructing the expert must pay any fees charged by that expert for answering questions put under r. 35.6. This does not affect any decision of the court as to the party who is ultimately to bear the expert's costs.

Single Expert

para.6 **52.10**

6 Where the court has directed that the evidence on a particular issue is to be given by one expert only (r. 35.7) but there are a number of disciplines relevant to that issue, a leading expert in the dominant discipline should be identified as the single expert. He should prepare the general part of the report and be responsible for annexing or incorporating the contents of any reports from experts in other disciplines.

Orders

para.6A **44.7, 52.5**

6A Where an order requires an act to be done by an expert, or otherwise affects an expert, the party instructing that expert must serve a copy of the order on the expert instructed by him. In the case of a jointly instructed expert, the claimant must serve the order.

Assessors

para.7.1–7.4 **52.30**

7.1 An assessor may be appointed to assist the court under r. 35.15. Not less than 21 days before making any such appointment, the court will notify each party in writing of the name of the proposed assessor, of the matter in respect of which the assistance of the assessor will be sought and of the qualifications of the assessor to give that assistance.

7.2 Where any person has been proposed for appointment as an assessor, objection to him, either personally or in respect of his qualification, may be taken by any party.

7.3 Any such objection must be made in writing and filed with the court within seven days of receipt of the notification referred to in para. [7.1*] and will be taken into account by the court in deciding whether or not to make the appointment (County Courts Act 1984, s. 63(5)).

7.4 Copies of any report prepared by the assessor will be sent to each of the parties but the assessor will not give oral evidence or be open to cross-examination or questioning.

ANNEX
PROTOCOL FOR THE INSTRUCTION OF EXPERTS TO GIVE EVIDENCE IN CIVIL CLAIMS

June 2005

1 Introduction

Expert witnesses perform a vital role in civil litigation. It is essential that both those who instruct experts and experts themselves are given clear guidance as to what they are expected to do in civil proceedings. The purpose of this protocol is to provide such guidance. It has been drafted by the Civil Justice Council and reflects the rules and practice directions current in June 2005, replacing the Code of Guidance on Expert Evidence. The authors of the protocol wish to acknowledge the valuable assistance they obtained by drawing on earlier documents produced by the Academy of Experts and the Expert Witness Institute, as well as suggestions made by the Clinical Dispute Forum. The protocol has been approved by the Master of the Rolls.

2 Aims of Protocol

2.1 This protocol offers guidance to experts and to those instructing them in the interpretation of and compliance with Part 35 and PD 35 and to further the objectives of the CPR in general. It is intended to assist in the interpretation of those provisions in the interests of good practice but it does not replace them. It sets out standards for the use of experts and the conduct of experts and those who instruct them. The existence of this protocol does not remove the need for experts and those who instruct them to be familiar with Part 35 and PD 35.

2.2 Experts and those who instruct them should also bear in mind Practice Direction Protocols, para. 1.4, which contains the following objectives, namely to:

(a) encourage the exchange of early and full information about the expert issues involved in a prospective legal claim;

(b) enable the parties to avoid or reduce the scope of litigation by agreeing the whole or part of an expert issue before commencement of proceedings; and

(c) support the efficient management of proceedings where litigation cannot be avoided.

3 Application

3.1 This protocol applies to any steps taken for the purpose of civil proceedings by experts or those who instruct them on or after 5 September 2005.

3.2 It applies to all experts who are, or who may be, governed by Part 35 and to those who instruct them. Experts are governed by Part 35 if they are or have been instructed to give or prepare evidence for the purpose of civil proceedings in a court in England and Wales (r. 35.2).

3.3 Experts, and those instructing them, should be aware that some cases may be 'specialist proceedings' (Part 49) where there are modifications to the CPR. Proceedings may also be governed by other protocols. Further, some courts have published their own guides which supplement the CPR for proceedings in those courts. They contain provisions affecting expert evidence. Expert witnesses and those instructing them should be familiar with them when they are relevant.

[* In the text issued by the Department for Constitutional Affairs this cross-reference was not updated when the paragraphs of the practice direction were renumbered.]

3.4 Courts may take into account any failure to comply with this protocol when making orders in relation to costs, interest, time limits, the stay of proceedings and whether to order a party to pay a sum of money into court.

Limitation

3.5 If, as a result of complying with any part of this protocol, claims would or might be time barred under any provision in the Limitation Act 1980, or any other legislation that imposes a time limit for bringing an action, claimants may commence proceedings without complying with this protocol. In such circumstances, claimants who commence proceedings without complying with all, or any part, of this protocol must apply, giving notice to all other parties, to the court for directions as to the timetable and form of procedure to be adopted, at the same time as they request the court to issue proceedings. The court may consider whether to order a stay of the whole or part of the proceedings pending compliance with this protocol and may make orders in relation to costs.

4 Duties of Experts

para.4.3 **52.3**

4.1 Experts always owe a duty to exercise reasonable skill and care to those instructing them, and to comply with any relevant professional code of ethics. However when they are instructed to give or prepare evidence for the purpose of civil proceedings in England and Wales they have an overriding duty to help the court on matters within their expertise (r. 35.3). This duty overrides any obligation to the person instructing or paying them. Experts must not serve the exclusive interest of those who retain them.

4.2 Experts should be aware of the overriding objective that courts deal with cases justly. This includes dealing with cases proportionately, expeditiously and fairly (r. 1.1). Experts are under an obligation to assist the court so as to enable them to deal with cases in accordance with the overriding objective. However, the overriding objective does not impose on experts any duty to act as mediators between the parties or require them to trespass on the role of the court in deciding facts.

4.3 Experts should provide opinions which are independent, regardless of the pressures of litigation. In this context, a useful test of 'independence' is that the expert would express the same opinion if given the same instructions by an opposing party. Experts should not take it upon themselves to promote the point of view of the party instructing them or engage in the role of advocates.

4.4 Experts should confine their opinions to matters which are material to the disputes between the parties and provide opinions only in relation to matters which lie within their expertise. Experts should indicate without delay where particular questions or issues fall outside their expertise.

4.5 Experts should take into account all material facts before them at the time that they give their opinion. Their reports should set out those facts and any literature or any other material on which they have relied in forming their opinions. They should indicate if an opinion is provisional, or qualified, or where they consider that further information is required or if, for any other reason, they are not satisfied that an opinion can be expressed finally and without qualification.

4.6 Experts should inform those instructing them without delay of any change in their opinions on any material matter and the reason for it.

4.7 Experts should be aware that any failure by them to comply with the CPR or court orders or any excessive delay for which they are responsible may result in the parties who instructed them being penalised in costs and even, in extreme cases, being debarred from placing the experts' evidence before the court. In *Phillips v Symes* [2004] EWHC 2330 (Ch), [2005] 1 WLR 2043, Peter Smith J held that courts may also make orders for costs (under the Supreme Court Act 1981, s. 51) directly against expert witnesses who by their evidence cause significant expense to be incurred, and do so in flagrant and reckless disregard of their duties to the court.

5 Conduct of Experts Instructed Only to Advise

paras.5.1–5.2 **52.14**

5.1 Part 35 only applies where experts are instructed to give opinions which are relied on for the purposes of court proceedings. Advice which the parties do not intend to adduce in litigation is likely to be confidential; the protocol does not apply in these circumstances (*Carlson v Townsend* [2001] EWCA Civ 511, [2001] 1 WLR 2415; *Jackson v Marley Davenport Ltd* [2004] EWCA Civ 1225, [2004] 1 WLR 2926).

5.2 The same applies where, after the commencement of proceedings, experts are instructed only to advise (e.g. to comment upon a single joint expert's report) and not to give or prepare evidence for use in the proceedings.

5.3 However, this protocol does apply if experts who were formerly instructed only to advise are later instructed to give or prepare evidence for the purpose of civil proceedings.

6 The Need for Experts

6.1 Those intending to instruct experts to give or prepare evidence for the purpose of civil proceedings should consider whether expert evidence is appropriate, taking account of the principles set out in Parts 1 and 35, and in particular whether:
- (a) it is relevant to a matter which is in dispute between the parties;
- (b) it is reasonably required to resolve the proceedings (r. 35.1);
- (c) the expert has expertise relevant to the issue on which an opinion is sought;
- (d) the expert has the experience, expertise and training appropriate to the value, complexity and importance of the case; and whether
- (e) these objects can be achieved by the appointment of a single joint expert (see section 17 below).

6.2 Although the court's permission is not generally required to instruct an expert, the court's permission is required before experts can be called to give evidence or their evidence can be put in (r. 35.4).

7 The Appointment of Experts

paras.7.1–7.2 **52.16** paras.7.6–7.7 **52.16**

7.1 Before experts are formally instructed or the court's permission to appoint named experts is sought, the following should be established:
- (a) that they have the appropriate expertise and experience;
- (b) that they are familiar with the general duties of an expert;
- (c) that they can produce a report, deal with questions and have discussions with other experts within a reasonable time and at a cost proportionate to the matters in issue;
- (d) a description of the work required;
- (e) whether they are available to attend the trial, if attendance is required; and
- (f) there is no potential conflict of interest.

7.2 Terms of appointment should be agreed at the outset and should normally include:
- (a) the capacity in which the expert is to be appointed (e.g. party appointed expert, single joint expert or expert advisor);
- (b) the services required of the expert (e.g. provision of expert's report, answering questions in writing, attendance at meetings and attendance at court);
- (c) time for delivery of the report;
- (d) the basis of the expert's charges (either daily or hourly rates and an estimate of the time likely to be required, or a total fee for the services);
- (e) travelling expenses and disbursements;
- (f) cancellation charges;
- (g) any fees for attending court;
- (h) time for making the payment;
- (i) whether fees are to be paid by a third party; and
- (j) if a party is publicly funded, whether or not the expert's charges will be subject to assessment by a costs officer.

7.3 As to the appointment of single joint experts, see section 17 below.

7.4 When necessary, arrangements should be made for dealing with questions to experts and discussions between experts, including any directions given by the court, and provision should be made for the cost of this work.

7.5 Experts should be informed regularly about deadlines for all matters concerning them. Those instructing experts should promptly send them copies of all court orders and directions which may affect the preparation of their reports or any other matters concerning their obligations.

Conditional and contingency fees

7.6 Payments contingent upon the nature of the expert evidence given in legal proceedings, or upon the outcome of a case, must not be offered or accepted. To do so would contravene experts' overriding duty to the court and compromise their duty of independence.

7.7 Agreement to delay payment of experts' fees until after the conclusion of cases is permissible as long as the amount of the fee does not depend on the outcome of the case.

8 Instructions

para.8.1 **52.17**

8.1 Those instructing experts should ensure that they give clear instructions, including the following:
(a) basic information, such as names, addresses, telephone numbers, dates of birth and dates of incidents;
(b) the nature and extent of the expertise which is called for;
(c) the purpose of requesting the advice or report, a description of the matter(s) to be investigated, the principal known issues and the identity of all parties;
(d) the statement(s) of case (if any), those documents which form part of standard disclosure and witness statements which are relevant to the advice or report;
(e) where proceedings have not been started, whether proceedings are being contemplated and, if so, whether the expert is asked only for advice;
(f) an outline programme, consistent with good case management and the expert's availability, for the completion and delivery of each stage of the expert's work; and
(g) where proceedings have been started, the dates of any hearings (including any case management conferences and/or pre-trial reviews), the name of the court, the claim number and the track to which the claim has been allocated.

8.2 Experts who do not receive clear instructions should request clarification and may indicate that they are not prepared to act unless and until such clear instructions are received.

8.3 As to the instruction of single joint experts, see section 17 below.

9 Experts' Acceptance of Instructions

para.9.1 **52.17**

9.1 Experts should confirm without delay whether or not they accept instructions. They should also inform those instructing them (whether on initial instruction or at any later stage) without delay if:
(a) instructions are not acceptable because, for example, they require work that falls outside their expertise, impose unrealistic deadlines, or are insufficiently clear;
(b) they consider that instructions are or have become insufficient to complete the work;
(c) they become aware that they may not be able to fulfil any of the terms of appointment;
(d) the instructions and/or work have, for any reason, placed them in conflict with their duties as an expert; or
(e) they are not satisfied that they can comply with any orders that have been made.

9.2 Experts must neither express an opinion outside the scope of their field of expertise, nor accept any instructions to do so.

10 Withdrawal

para.10.1 **52.17**

10.1 Where experts' instructions remain incompatible with their duties, whether through incompleteness, a conflict between their duty to the court and their instructions, or for any other substantial and significant reason, they may consider withdrawing from the case. However, experts should not withdraw without first discussing the position fully with those who instruct them and considering carefully whether it would be more appropriate to make a written request for directions from the court. If experts do withdraw, they must give formal written notice to those instructing them.

11 Experts' Right to Ask Court for Directions

11.1 Experts may request directions from the court to assist them in carrying out their functions as experts. Experts should normally discuss such matters with those who instruct them before making any such request. Unless the court otherwise orders, any proposed request for directions should be copied to the party instructing the expert at least seven days before filing any request to the court, and to all other parties at least four days before filing it (r. 35.14).

11.2 Requests to the court for directions should be made by letter, containing:
(a) the title of the claim;
(b) the claim number of the case;
(c) the name of the expert;
(d) full details of why directions are sought; and
(e) copies of any relevant documentation.

12 Power of the Court to Direct a Party to Provide Information

12.1 If experts consider that those instructing them have not provided information which they require, they may, after discussion with those instructing them and giving notice, write to the court to seek directions (r. 35.14).

12.2 Experts and those who instruct them should also be aware of r. 35.9. This provides that where one party has access to information which is not readily available to the other party, the court may direct the party who has access to the information to prepare, file and copy to the other party a document recording the information. If experts require such information which has not been disclosed, they should discuss the position with those instructing them without delay, so that a request for the information can be made, and, if not forthcoming, an application can be made to the court. Unless a document appears to be essential, experts should assess the cost and time involved in the production of a document and whether its provision would be proportionate in the context of the case.

13 Contents of Experts' Reports

paras.13.1–13.15 **52.20**

13.1 The content and extent of experts' reports should be governed by the scope of their instructions and general obligations, the contents of Part 35 and PD 35 and their overriding duty to the court.

13.2 In preparing reports, experts should maintain professional objectivity and impartiality at all times.

13.3 PD 35, para. 2, provides that experts' reports should be addressed to the court and gives detailed directions about the form and content of such reports. All experts and those who instruct them should ensure that they are familiar with these requirements.

13.4 Model forms of experts' reports are available from bodies such as the Academy of Experts or the Expert Witness Institute.

13.5 Experts' reports must contain statements that they understand their duty to the court and have complied and will continue to comply with that duty (PD 35, para. 2.2(9)). They must also be verified by a statement of truth. The form of the statement of truth is as follows:

> I confirm that in so far as the facts stated in my report are within my own knowledge I have made clear which they are and I believe them to be true, and that the opinions I have expressed represent my true and complete professional opinion.

This wording is mandatory and must not be modified.

Qualifications

13.6 The details of experts' qualifications to be given in reports should be commensurate with the nature and complexity of the case. It may be sufficient merely to state academic and professional qualifications. However, where highly specialised expertise is called for, experts should include the detail of particular training and/or experience that qualifies them to provide that highly specialised evidence.

Tests

13.7 Where tests of a scientific or technical nature have been carried out, experts should state:
(a) the methodology used; and
(b) by whom the tests were undertaken and under whose supervision, summarising their respective qualifications and experience.

Reliance on the work of others

13.8 Where experts rely in their reports on literature or other material and cite the opinions of others without having verified them, they must give details of those opinions relied on. It is likely to assist the court if the qualifications of the originator(s) are also stated.

Facts

13.9 When addressing questions of fact and opinion, experts should keep the two separate and discrete.

13.10 Experts must state those facts (whether assumed or otherwise) upon which their opinions are based. They must distinguish clearly between those facts which experts know to be true and those facts which they assume.

13.11 Where there are material facts in dispute experts should express separate opinions on each hypothesis put forward. They should not express a view in favour of one or other disputed version of the facts unless, as a result of particular expertise and experience, they consider one set of facts as being improbable or less probable, in which case they may express that view, and should give reasons for holding it.

Range of opinion

13.12 If the mandatory summary of the range of opinion is based on published sources, experts should explain those sources and, where appropriate, state the qualifications of the originator(s) of the opinions from which they differ, particularly if such opinions represent a well-established school of thought.

13.13 Where there is no available source for the range of opinion, experts may need to express opinions on what they believe to be the range which other experts would arrive at if asked. In those circumstances, experts should make it clear that the range that they summarise is based on their own judgment and explain the basis of that judgment.

Conclusions

13.14 A summary of conclusions is mandatory. The summary should be at the end of the report after all the reasoning. There may be cases, however, where the benefit to the court is heightened by placing a short summary at the beginning of the report whilst giving the full conclusions at the end. For example, it can assist with the comprehension of the analysis and with the absorption of the detailed facts if the court is told at the outset of the direction in which the report's logic will flow in cases involving highly complex matters which fall outside the general knowledge of the court.

Basis of report: material instructions

13.15 The mandatory statement of the substance of all material instructions should not be incomplete or otherwise tend to mislead. The imperative is transparency. The term 'instructions' includes all material which solicitors place in front of experts in order to gain advice. The omission from the statement of 'off-the-record' oral instructions is not permitted. Courts may allow cross-examination about the instructions if there are reasonable grounds to consider that the statement may be inaccurate or incomplete.

14 After Receipt of Experts' Reports

14.1 Following the receipt of experts' reports, those instructing them should advise the experts as soon as reasonably practicable whether, and if so when, the report will be disclosed to other parties; and, if so disclosed, the date of actual disclosure.

14.2 If experts' reports are to be relied upon, and if experts are to give oral evidence, those instructing them should give the experts the opportunity to consider and comment upon other reports within their area of expertise and which deal with relevant issues at the earliest opportunity.

14.3 Those instructing experts should keep experts informed of the progress of cases, including amendments to statements of case relevant to experts' opinion.

14.4 If those instructing experts become aware of material changes in circumstances or that relevant information within their control was not previously provided to experts, they should without delay instruct experts to review, and if necessary, update the contents of their reports.

15 Amendment of Reports

para.15.2 **52.20**

15.1 It may become necessary for experts to amend their reports:

(a) as a result of an exchange of questions and answers;

(b) following agreements reached at meetings between experts; or

(c) where further evidence or documentation is disclosed.

15.2 Experts should not be asked to, and should not, amend, expand or alter any parts of reports in a manner which distorts their true opinion, but may be invited to amend or expand reports to ensure accuracy, internal consistency, completeness and relevance to the issues and clarity. Although experts should generally follow the recommendations of solicitors with regard to the form of reports, they should form their own independent views as to the opinions and contents expressed in their reports and exclude any suggestions which do not accord with their views.

15.3 Where experts change their opinion following a meeting of experts, a simple signed and dated addendum or memorandum to that effect is generally sufficient. In some cases, however, the benefit to the court of having an amended report may justify the cost of making the amendment.

15.4 Where experts significantly alter their opinion, as a result of new evidence or because evidence on which they relied has become unreliable, or for any other reason, they should amend their reports to reflect that fact. Amended reports should include reasons for amendments. In such circumstances those instructing experts should inform other parties as soon as possible of any change of opinion.

15.5 When experts intend to amend their reports, they should inform those instructing them without delay and give reasons. They should provide the amended version (or an addendum or memorandum) clearly marked as such as quickly as possible.

16 Written Questions to Experts

16.1 The procedure for putting written questions to experts (r. 35.6) is intended to facilitate the clarification of opinions and issues after experts' reports have been served. Experts have a duty to provide answers to questions properly put. Where they fail to do so, the court may impose sanctions against the party instructing the expert, and, if, there is continued non-compliance, debar a party from relying on the report. Experts should copy their answers to those instructing them.

16.2 Experts' answers to questions automatically become part of their reports. They are covered by the statement of truth and form part of the expert evidence.

16.3 Where experts believe that questions put are not properly directed to the clarification of the report, or are disproportionate, or have been asked out of time, they should discuss the questions with those instructing them and, if appropriate, those asking the questions. Attempts should be made to resolve such problems without the need for an application to the court for directions.

Written requests for directions in relation to questions

16.4 If those instructing experts do not apply to the court in respect of questions, but experts still believe that questions are improper or out of time, experts may file written requests with the court for directions to assist in carrying out their functions as experts (r. 35.14). See Section 11 above.

17 Single Joint Experts

paras.17.4–17.5 **52.14** para.17.8 **10.52**
paras.17.6–17.7 **52.18** paras.17.10–17.11 **52.18**

17.1 Part 35 and PD 35 deal extensively with the instruction and use of joint experts by the parties and the powers of the court to order their use (see rr. 35.7 and 35.8; PD 35, para. 5).

17.2 The CPR encourage the use of joint experts. Wherever possible a joint report should be obtained. Consideration should therefore be given by all parties to the appointment of single joint experts in all cases where a court might direct such an appointment. Single joint experts are the norm in cases allocated to the small claims track and the fast track.

17.3 Where, in the early stages of a dispute, examinations, investigations, tests, site inspections, experiments, preparation of photographs, plans or other similar preliminary expert tasks are necessary, consideration should be given to the instruction of a single joint expert, especially where such matters are not, at that stage, expected to be contentious as between the parties. The objective of such an appointment should be to agree or to narrow issues.

17.4 Experts who have previously advised a party (whether in the same case or otherwise) should only be proposed as single joint experts if other parties are given all relevant information about the previous involvement.

17.5 The appointment of a single joint expert does not prevent parties from instructing their own experts to advise (but the costs of such expert advisers may not be recoverable in the case).

Joint instructions

17.6 The parties should try to agree joint instructions to single joint experts, but, in default of agreement, each party may give instructions. In particular, all parties should try to agree what documents should be included with instructions and what assumptions single joint experts should make.

17.7 Where the parties fail to agree joint instructions, they should try to agree where the areas of disagreement lie and their instructions should make this clear. If separate instructions are given, they should be copied at the same time to the other instructing parties.

17.8 Where experts are instructed by two or more parties, the terms of appointment should, unless the court has directed otherwise, or the parties have agreed otherwise, include:

(a) a statement that all the instructing parties are jointly and severally liable to pay the experts' fees and, accordingly, that experts' invoices should be sent simultaneously to all instructing parties or their solicitors (as appropriate); and

(b) a statement as to whether any order has been made limiting the amount of experts' fees and expenses (r. 35.8(4)(a)).

17.9 Where instructions have not been received by the expert from one or more of the instructing parties the expert should give notice (normally at least seven days) of a deadline to all instructing parties for the receipt by the expert of such instructions. Unless the instructions are received within the deadline the expert may begin work. In the event that instructions are received after the deadline but before the signing off of the report the expert should consider whether it is practicable to comply with those instructions without adversely affecting the timetable set for delivery of the report and in such a manner as to comply with the proportionality principle. An expert who decides to issue a report without taking into account instructions received after the deadline should inform the parties who may apply to the court for directions. In either event the report must show clearly that the expert did not receive instructions within the deadline, or, as the case may be, at all.

Conduct of the single joint expert

17.10 Single joint experts should keep all instructing parties informed of any material steps that they may be taking by, for example, copying all correspondence to those instructing them.

17.11 Single joint experts are Part 35 experts and so have an overriding duty to the court. They are the parties' appointed experts and therefore owe an equal duty to all parties. They should maintain independence, impartiality and transparency at all times.

17.12 Single joint experts should not attend any meeting or conference which is not a joint one, unless all the parties have agreed in writing or the court has directed that such a meeting may be held (*Peet v Mid Kent Area Healthcare Trust* [2001] EWCA Civ 1703, [2002] 1 WLR 2104) and who is to pay the experts' fees for the meeting.

17.13 Single joint experts may request directions from the court—see Section 11 above.

17.14 Single joint experts should serve their reports simultaneously on all instructing parties. They should provide a single report even though they may have received instructions which contain areas of conflicting fact or allegation. If conflicting instructions lead to different opinions (for example, because the instructions require experts to make different assumptions of fact), reports may need to contain more than one set of opinions on any issue. It is for the court to determine the facts.

Cross-examination

17.15 Single joint experts do not normally give oral evidence at trial but if they do, all parties may cross-examine them. In general written questions (r. 35.6) should be put to single joint experts before requests are made for them to attend court for the purpose of cross-examination (*Daniels v Walker* [2000] 1 WLR 1382).

18 Discussions between Experts

18.1 The court has powers to direct discussions between experts for the purposes set out in the CPR (r. 35.12). Parties may also agree that discussions take place between their experts.

18.2 Where single joint experts have been instructed but parties have, with the permission of the court, instructed their own additional Part 35 experts, there may, if the court so orders or the parties agree, be discussions between the single joint experts and the additional Part 35 experts.

Such discussions should be confined to those matters within the remit of the additional Part 35 experts or as ordered by the court.

18.3 The purpose of discussions between experts should be, wherever possible, to:
(a) identify and discuss the expert issues in the proceedings;
(b) reach agreed opinions on those issues, and, if that is not possible, to narrow the issues in the case;
(c) identify those issues on which they agree and disagree and summarise their reasons for disagreement on any issue; and
(d) identify what action, if any, may be taken to resolve any of the outstanding issues between the parties.

Arrangements for discussions between experts

18.4 Arrangements for discussions between experts should be proportionate to the value of cases. In small claims and fast-track cases there should not normally be meetings between experts. Where discussion is justified in such cases, telephone discussion or an exchange of letters should, in the interests of proportionality, usually suffice. In multi-track cases, discussion may be face to face, but the practicalities or the proportionality principle may require discussions to be by telephone or videoconference.

18.5 The parties, their lawyers and experts should cooperate to produce the agenda for any discussion between experts, although primary responsibility for preparation of the agenda should normally lie with the parties' solicitors.

18.6 The agenda should indicate what matters have been agreed and summarise concisely those which are in issue. It is often helpful for it to include questions to be answered by the experts. If agreement cannot be reached promptly or a party is unrepresented, the court may give directions for the drawing up of the agenda. The agenda should be circulated to experts and those instructing them to allow sufficient time for the experts to prepare for the discussion.

18.7 Those instructing experts must not instruct experts to avoid reaching agreement (or to defer doing so) on any matter within the experts' competence. Experts are not permitted to accept such instructions.

18.8 The parties' lawyers may only be present at discussions between experts if all the parties agree or the court so orders. If lawyers do attend, they should not normally intervene except to answer questions put to them by the experts or to advise about the law (*Hubbard v Lambeth, Southwark and Lewisham Health Authority* [2001] EWCA Civ 1455, [2002] Lloyd's Rep Med 8).

18.9 The content of discussions between experts should not be referred to at trial unless the parties agree (r. 35.12(4)). It is good practice for any such agreement to be in writing.

18.10 At the conclusion of any discussion between experts, a statement should be prepared setting out:
(a) a list of issues that have been agreed, including, in each instance, the basis of agreement;
(b) a list of issues that have not been agreed, including, in each instance, the basis of disagreement;
(c) a list of any further issues that have arisen that were not included in the original agenda for discussion;
(d) a record of further action, if any, to be taken or recommended, including as appropriate the holding of further discussions between experts.

18.11 The statement should be agreed and signed by all the parties to the discussion as soon as may be practicable.

18.12 Agreements between experts during discussions do not bind the parties unless the parties expressly agree to be bound by the agreement (r. 35.12(5)). However, in view of the overriding objective, parties should give careful consideration before refusing to be bound by such an agreement and be able to explain their refusal should it become relevant to the issue of costs.

19 Attendance of Experts at Court

para.19.2(a) **56.11**

19.1 Experts instructed in cases have an obligation to attend court if called upon to do so and accordingly should ensure that those instructing them are always aware of their dates to be avoided and take all reasonable steps to be available.

19.2 Those instructing experts should:
(a) ascertain the availability of experts before trial dates are fixed;

(b) keep experts updated with timetables (including the dates and times experts are to attend) and the location of the court;
(c) give consideration, where appropriate, to experts giving evidence via a video-link;
(d) inform experts immediately if trial dates are vacated.

19.3 Experts should normally attend court without the need for the service of witness summonses, but on occasion they may be served to require attendance (Part 34). The use of witness summonses does not affect the contractual or other obligations of the parties to pay experts' fees.

CPR Part 36 Offers to Settle and Payments into Court

Part 36 **1.17, 1.20, 43.6, 43.28, 45.11, 54.2, 59.8, 64.1, 64.2, 64.5, 64.9, 64.32, 64.44, 67.15** [For commentary on a specific rule, please refer to the cross-references after the title of the rule.]

36.1 Scope of This Part

r.36.1(2) **64.1, 64.9, 64.29, 64.47, 64.48**

(1) This Part contains rules about—
  (a) offers to settle and payments into court; and
  (b) the consequences where an offer to settle or payment into court is made in accordance with this Part.
(2) Nothing in this Part prevents a party making an offer to settle in whatever way he chooses, but if that offer is not made in accordance with this Part, it will only have the consequences specified in this Part if the court so orders.

(Part 36 applies to Part 20 claims by virtue of rule 20.3)

36.2 Part 36 Offers and Part 36 Payments — General Provisions

r.36.2 **64.3**
r.36.2(2)–(3) **64.2**
r.36.2(4) **64.8**
r.36.2(4)(a) **64.10**
r.36.2(4)(b) **64.10, 64.13**
r.36.2(5) **43.28, 61.1**

(1) An offer made in accordance with the requirements of this Part is called—
  (a) if made by way of a payment into court, 'a Part 36 payment';
  (b) otherwise 'a Part 36 offer'.
  (Rule 36.3 sets out when an offer has to be made by way of a payment into court)
(2) The party who makes an offer is the 'offeror'.
(3) The party to whom an offer is made is the 'offeree'.
(4) A Part 36 offer or a Part 36 payment—
  (a) may be made at any time after proceedings have started; and

Civil Procedure Rules & Practice Directions

(b) may be made in appeal proceedings.

(5) A Part 36 offer or a Part 36 payment shall not have the consequences set out in this Part while the claim is being dealt with on the small claims track unless the court orders otherwise.

(Part 26 deals with allocation to the small claims track)

(Rule 27.2 provides that Part 36 does not apply to small claims)

36.2A Personal Injury Claims for Future Pecuniary Loss

para.36.2A(7) **64.12**

(1) This rule applies to a claim for damages for personal injury which is or includes a claim for future pecuniary loss.

(2) An offer to settle such a claim will not have the consequences set out in this Part unless it is made by way of a Part 36 offer under this rule, and where such an offer is or includes an offer to pay the whole or part of any damages in the form of a lump sum, it will not have the consequences set out in this Part unless a Part 36 payment of the amount of the lump sum offer is also made.

(3) Where both a Part 36 offer and a Part 36 payment are made under this rule—
  (a) the offer must include details of the payment, and
  (b) rules 36.11(1) and (2) and 36.13(1) and (2) apply as if there were only a Part 36 offer.

(4) A Part 36 offer to which this rule applies may contain an offer to pay, or an offer to accept—
  (a) the whole or part of the damages for future pecuniary loss in the form of—
    (i) either a lump sum or periodical payments, or
    (ii) both a lump sum and periodical payments,
  (b) the whole or part of any other damages in the form of a lump sum.

(5) A Part 36 offer to which this rule applies—
  (a) must state the amount of any offer to pay the whole or part of any damages in the form of a lump sum;
  (b) may state what part of the offer relates to damages for future pecuniary loss to be accepted in the form of a lump sum;
  (c) may state, where part of the offer relates to other damages to be accepted in the form of a lump sum, what amounts are attributable to those other damages;
  (d) must state what part of the offer relates to damages for future pecuniary loss to be paid or accepted in the form of periodical payments and must specify—
    (i) the amount and duration of the periodical payments,
    (ii) the amount of any payments for substantial capital purchases and when they are to be made, and
    (iii) that each amount is to vary by reference to the retail prices index (or to some other named index, or that it is not to vary by reference to any index); and
  (e) must state either that any damages which take the form of periodical payments will be funded in a way which ensures that the continuity of payment is reasonably secure in accordance with section 2(4) of the Damages Act 1996 or how such damages are to be paid and how the continuity of their payment is to be secured.

(6) Where a Part 36 payment includes a lump sum for damages for future pecuniary loss, the Part 36 payment notice may state the amount of that lump sum.

(7) Where the defendant makes a Part 36 offer to which this rule applies and which offers to pay damages in the form of both a lump sum and periodical payments, the claimant may only give notice of acceptance of the offer as a whole.

36.3 A Defendant's Offer to Settle a Money Claim Requires a Part 36 Payment

r.36.3 **64.48** r.36.3(2) **64.2, 64.3, 64.8**
r.36.3(1) **64.2, 64.8, 64.9, 64.10**

(1) Subject to rules 36.2A(2), 36.5(5) and 36.23, an offer by a defendant to settle a money claim will not have the consequences set out in this Part unless it is made by way of a Part 36 payment.

(2) A Part 36 payment may only be made after proceedings have started.

(Rule 36.5(5) permits a Part 36 offer to be made by reference to an interim payment) (Rule 36.10 makes provision for an offer to settle a money claim before the commencement of proceedings)

(Rule 36.23 makes provision for where benefit is recoverable under the Social Security (Recovery of Benefits) Act 1997)

36.4 Defendant's Offer to Settle the Whole of a Claim Which Includes Both a Money Claim and a Non-money Claim

r.36.4 **64.10**
r.36.4(1)–(2) **64.11**
r.36.4(3)(a)–(b) **64.21**
r.36.4(4) **64.11**

(1) This rule applies where a defendant to a claim which includes both a money claim and a non-money claim wishes—
 (a) to make an offer to settle the whole claim which will have the consequences set out in this Part; and
 (b) to make a money offer in respect of the money claim and a non-money offer in respect of the non-money claim.
(2) The defendant must—
 (a) make a Part 36 payment or Part 36 offer made under rule 36.2A in relation to the money claim; and
 (b) make a Part 36 offer in relation to the non-money claim.
(3) The Part 36 payment notice or Part 36 offer made under rule 36.2A must—
 (a) identify the document which sets out the terms of the Part 36 offer made under this rule; and
 (b) state that if the claimant gives notice of acceptance of the Part 36 payment or Part 36 offer made under rule 36.2A he will be treated as also accepting the Part 36 offer made under this rule.
(Rule 36.6 makes provision for a Part 36 payment notice)
(4) If the claimant gives notice of acceptance of the Part 36 payment, he shall also be taken as giving notice of acceptance of the Part 36 offer in relation to the non-money claim.

36.5 Form and Content of a Part 36 Offer

r.36.5(1) **64.16**
r.36.5(2) **64.3, 64.48**
r.36.5(3)(a) **64.16**
r.36.5(5) **64.8, 64.9, 64.16**
r.36.5(6) **64.2, 64.16**
r.36.5(6)(b) **64.47**
r.36.5(7) **64.2, 64.16**
r.36.5(8) **64.18**

(1) A Part 36 offer must be in writing.
(2) A Part 36 offer may relate to the whole claim or to part of it or to any issue that arises in it.
(3) A Part 36 offer must—
 (a) state whether it relates to the whole of the claim or to part of it or to an issue that arises in it and if so to which part or issue;
 (b) state whether it takes into account any counterclaim; and
 (c) if it is expressed not to be inclusive of interest, give the details relating to interest set out in rule 36.22(2).
(4) A defendant may make a Part 36 offer limited to accepting liability up to a specified proportion.
(5) A Part 36 offer may be made by reference to an interim payment.
(Part 25 contains provisions relating to interim payments)
(6) A Part 36 offer made not less than 21 days before the start of the trial must—
 (a) be expressed to remain open for acceptance for 21 days from the date it is made; and
 (b) provide that after 21 days the offeree may only accept it if—
  (i) the parties agree the liability for costs; or
  (ii) the court gives permission.
(7) A Part 36 offer made less than 21 days before the start of the trial must state that the offeree may only accept it if—
 (a) the parties agree the liability for costs; or
 (b) the court gives permission.
(Rule 36.8 makes provision for when a Part 36 offer is treated as being made)
(8) If a Part 36 offer is withdrawn it will not have the consequences set out in this Part.

36.6 Notice of a Part 36 Payment

r.36.6(1) **64.3** r.36.6(4) **64.25**
r.36.6(2) **64.20** r.36.6(5) **64.26**

(1) A Part 36 payment may relate to the whole claim or part of it or to an issue that arises in it.
(2) A defendant who makes a Part 36 payment must file with the court a notice ('Part 36 payment notice') which—
  (a) states the amount of the payment;
  (b) states whether the payment relates to the whole claim or to part of it or to any issue that arises in it and if so to which part or issue;
  (c) states whether it takes into account any counterclaim;
  (d) if an interim payment has been made, states that the defendant has taken into account the interim payment; and
  (e) if it is expressed not to be inclusive of interest, gives the details relating to interest set out in rule 36.22(2).

(Rule 25.6 makes provision for an interim payment)
(Rule 36.4 provides for further information to be included where a defendant wishes to settle the whole of a claim which includes a money claim and a non-money claim)
(Rule 36.23 makes provision for extra information to be included in the payment notice in a case where benefit is recoverable under the Social Security (Recovery of Benefits) Act 1997)
(3) The offeror must—
  (a) serve the Part 36 payment notice on the offeree; and
  (b) file a certificate of service of the notice.

(Rule 6.10 specifies what must be contained in a certificate of service)
(5) A Part 36 payment may be withdrawn or reduced only with the permission of the court.

36.7 Offer to Settle a Claim for Provisional Damages

r.36.7(1)–(3) **64.22** r.36.7(5)–(6) **64.37**

(1) A defendant may make a Part 36 payment in respect of a claim which includes a claim for provisional damages.
(2) Where he does so, the Part 36 payment notice must specify whether or not the defendant is offering to agree to the making of an award of provisional damages.
(3) Where the defendant is offering to agree to the making of an award of provisional damages the payment notice must also state—
  (a) that the sum paid into court is in satisfaction of the claim for damages on the assumption that the injured person will not develop the disease or suffer the type of deterioration specified in the notice;
  (b) that the offer is subject to the condition that the claimant must make any claim for further damages within a limited period; and
  (c) what that period is.
(4) Where a Part 36 payment is—
  (a) made in accordance with paragraph (3); and
  (b) accepted within the relevant period in rule 36.11,

  the Part 36 payment will have the consequences set out in rule 36.13, unless the court orders otherwise.
(5) If the claimant accepts the Part 36 payment he must, within 7 days of doing so, apply to the court for an order for an award of provisional damages under rule 41.2.

(Rule 41.2 provides for an order for an award of provisional damages)
(6) The money in court may not be paid out until the court has disposed of the application made in accordance with paragraph (5).

36.8 Time When a Part 36 Offer or a Part 36 Payment Is Made and Accepted

r.36.8 **64.13** r.36.8(3) **1.17, 15.27, 64.17, 64.30**
r.36.8(1) **1.17, 15.27, 64.2, 64.17** r.36.8(4) **1.17, 15.27, 64.17, 64.25, 64.30**
r.36.8(2) **1.17, 15.27, 64.17, 64.25** r.36.8(5) **64.19, 64.27**

(1) A Part 36 offer is made when received by the offeree.

(2) A Part 36 payment is made when written notice of the payment into court is served on the offeree.
(3) An improvement to a Part 36 offer will be effective when its details are received by the offeree.
(4) An increase in a Part 36 payment will be effective when notice of the increase is served on the offeree.
(5) A Part 36 offer or Part 36 payment is accepted when notice of its acceptance is received by the offeror.

36.9 Clarification of a Part 36 Offer or a Part 36 Payment Notice

r.36.9 **64.30** r.36.9(1)–(3) **64.30**

(1) The offeree may, within 7 days of a Part 36 offer or payment being made, request the offeror to clarify the offer or payment notice.
(2) If the offeror does not give the clarification requested under paragraph (1) within 7 days of receiving the request, the offeree may, unless the trial has started, apply for an order that he does so.
(3) If the court makes an order under paragraph (2), it must specify the date when the Part 36 offer or Part 36 payment is to be treated as having been made.

36.10 Court to Take into Account Offer to Settle Made before Commencement of Proceedings

r.36.10 **64.2, 64.7, 64.10, 64.48, 64.49**
r.36.10(1) **64.7**
r.36.10(2) **64.7**
r.36.10(2)(b) **64.16, 64.49**
r.36.10(2)(c) **64.7**
r.36.10(3) **64.7**
r.36.10(3)(a) **46.21**
r.36.10(4) **64.7**
r.36.10(5) **64.7, 64.17**

(1) If a person makes an offer to settle before proceedings are begun which complies with the provisions of this rule, the court will take that offer into account when making any order as to costs.
(2) The offer must—
(a) be expressed to be open for at least 21 days after the date it was made;
(b) if made by a person who would be a defendant were proceedings commenced, include an offer to pay the costs of the offeree incurred up to the date 21 days after the date it was made; and
(c) otherwise comply with this Part.
(3) Subject to paragraph (3A), if the offeror is a defendant to a money claim—
(a) he must make a Part 36 payment within 14 days of service of the claim form; and
(b) the amount of the payment must be not less than the sum offered before proceedings began.
(3A) In a claim to which rule 36.2A applies, if the offeror is a defendant who wishes to offer to pay the whole or part of any damages in the form of a lump sum—
(a) he must make a Part 36 payment within 14 days of service of the claim form; and
(b) the amount of the payment must be not less than the lump sum offered before proceedings began.
(4) An offeree may not, after proceedings have begun, accept—
(a) an offer made under paragraph (2); or
(b) a Part 36 payment made under paragraph (3) or (3A),
without the permission of the court.
(5) An offer under this rule is made when it is received by the offeree.

36.11 Time for Acceptance of a Defendant's Part 36 Offer or Part 36 Payment

r.36.11(1) **64.19, 64.32, 64.35** r.36.11(2)–(3) **64.32**

(1) A claimant may accept a Part 36 offer or a Part 36 payment made not less than 21 days before the start of the trial without needing the court's permission if he gives the defendant written notice of acceptance not later than 21 days after the offer or payment was made.

(Rule 36.13 sets out the costs consequences of accepting a defendant's offer or payment without needing the permission of the court)

(2) If—
   (a) a defendant's Part 36 offer or Part 36 payment is made less than 21 days before the start of the trial; or
   (b) the claimant does not accept it within the period specified in paragraph (1)—
      (i) if the parties agree the liability for costs, the claimant may accept the offer or payment without needing the permission of the court;
      (ii) if the parties do not agree the liability for costs the claimant may only accept the offer or payment with the permission of the court.

(3) Where the permission of the court is needed under paragraph (2) the court will, if it gives permission, make an order as to costs.

36.12 Time for Acceptance of a Claimant's Part 36 Offer

r.36.12(1) **64.19, 64.34** r.36.12(2)–(3) **64.34**

(1) A defendant may accept a Part 36 offer made not less than 21 days before the start of the trial without needing the court's permission if he gives the claimant written notice of acceptance not later than 21 days after the offer was made.

(Rule 36.14 sets out the costs consequences of accepting a claimant's offer without needing the permission of the court)

(2) If—
   (a) a claimant's Part 36 offer is made less than 21 days before the start of the trial; or
   (b) the defendant does not accept it within the period specified in paragraph (1)—
      (i) if the parties agree the liability for costs, the defendant may accept the offer without needing the permission of the court;
      (ii) if the parties do not agree the liability for costs the defendant may only accept the offer with the permission of the court.

(3) Where the permission of the court is needed under paragraph (2) the court will, if it gives permission, make an order as to costs.

36.13 Costs Consequences of Acceptance of a Defendant's Part 36 Offer or Part 36 Payment

r.36.13 **64.16, 64.40, 64.41** r.36.13(2) **64.2, 64.40**
r.36.13(1) **46.21, 64.7, 64.40** r.36.13(3)–(4) **64.40**

(1) Where a
Part 36 offer or a Part 36 payment is accepted without needing the permission of the court the claimant will be entitled to his costs of the proceedings up to the date of serving notice of acceptance.

(2) Where—
   (a) a Part 36 offer or a Part 36 payment relates to part only of the claim; and
   (b) at the time of serving notice of acceptance the claimant abandons the balance of the claim,

the claimant will be entitled to his costs of the proceedings up to the date of serving notice of acceptance, unless the court orders otherwise.

(3) The claimant's costs include any costs attributable to the defendant's counterclaim if the Part 36 offer or the Part 36 payment notice states that it takes into account the counter-claim.

(4) Costs under this rule will be payable on the standard basis if not agreed.

36.14 Costs Consequences of Acceptance of a Claimant's Part 36 Offer

r.36.14 **64.2, 64.16, 64.42**

Where a claimant's Part 36 offer is accepted without needing the permission of the court the claimant will be entitled to his costs of the proceedings up to the date upon which the defendant serves notice of acceptance.

36.15 The Effect of Acceptance of a Part 36 Offer or a Part 36 Payment

r.36.15 **64.5, 64.40, 64.54** r.36.15(5)–(6) **64.54**
r.36.15(2)–(3) **64.54**

(1) If a Part 36 offer or Part 36 payment relates to the whole claim and is accepted, the claim will be stayed[(GL)].

(2) In the case of acceptance of a Part 36 offer which relates to the whole claim—

(a) the stay[(GL)] will be upon the terms of the offer; and
(b) either party may apply to enforce those terms without the need for a new claim.

(3) If a Part 36 offer or a Part 36 payment which relates to part only of the claim is accepted—
(a) the claim will be stayed[(GL)] as to that part; and
(b) unless the parties have agreed costs, the liability for costs shall be decided by the court.

(4) If the approval of the court is required before a settlement can be binding, any stay[(GL)] which would otherwise arise on the acceptance of a Part 36 offer or a Part 36 payment will take effect only when that approval has been given.

(5) Any stay[(GL)] arising under this rule will not affect the power of the court—
(a) to enforce the terms of a Part 36 offer;
(b) to deal with any question of costs (including interest on costs) relating to the proceedings;
(c) to order payment out of court of any sum paid into court.

(6) Where—
(a) a Part 36 offer has been accepted; and
(b) a party alleges that—
(i) the other party has not honoured the terms of the offer; and
(ii) he is therefore entitled to a remedy for breach of contract,

the party may claim the remedy by applying to the court without the need to start a new claim unless the court orders otherwise.

36.16 Payment Out of a Sum in Court on the Acceptance of a Part 36 Payment

r.36.16 **64.27**

Where a Part 36 payment is accepted the claimant obtains payment out of the sum in court by making a request for payment in the practice form.

36.17 Acceptance of a Part 36 Offer or a Part 36 Payment Made by One or More, But Not All, Defendants

r.36.17 **64.35** r.36.17(2)–(4) **64.35**

(1) This rule applies where the claimant wishes to accept a Part 36 offer or a Part 36 payment made by one or more, but not all, of a number of defendants.

(2) If the defendants are sued jointly or in the alternative, the claimant may accept the offer or payment without needing the permission of the court in accordance with rule 36.11(1) if—
(a) he discontinues his claim against those defendants who have not made the offer or payment; and
(b) those defendants give written consent to the acceptance of the offer or payment.

(3) If the claimant alleges that the defendants have a several liability[(GL)] to him the claimant may—
(a) accept the offer or payment in accordance with rule 36.11(1); and
(b) continue with his claims against the other defendants if he is entitled to do so.

(4) In all other cases the claimant must apply to the court for—
(a) an order permitting a payment out to him of any sum in court; and
(b) such order as to costs as the court considers appropriate.

36.18 Other Cases Where a Court Order is Required to Enable Acceptance of a Part 36 Offer or a Part 36 Payment

r.36.18 **64.36** r.36.18(2) **64.36**
r.36.18(1) **64.36** r.36.18(3) **64.38**

(1) Where a Part 36 offer or a Part 36 payment is made in proceedings to which rule 21.10 applies—
(a) the offer or payment may be accepted only with the permission of the court; and
(b) no payment out of any sum in court shall be made without a court order.

(Rule 21.10 deals with compromise etc. by or on behalf of a child or patient)

(2) Where the court gives a claimant permission to accept a Part 36 offer or payment after the trial has started—

(a) any money in court may be paid out only with a court order; and
(b) the court must, in the order, deal with the whole costs of the proceedings.
(3) Where a claimant accepts a Part 36 payment after a defence of tender before claim (GL) has been put forward by the defendant, the money in court may be paid out only after an order of the court.

(Rule 37.3 requires a defendant who wishes to rely on a defence of tender before claim(GL) to make a payment into court)

36.19 Restriction on Disclosure of a Part 36 Offer or a Part 36 Payment

r.36.19 **45.7, 64.44, 72.4** r.36.19(2) **64.5, 64.6**
r.36.19(1) **64.5** r.36.19(3) **64.5**

(1) A Part 36 offer will be treated as 'without prejudice(GL) except as to costs'.
(2) The fact that a Part 36 payment has been made shall not be communicated to the trial judge until all questions of liability and the amount of money to be awarded have been decided.
(3) Paragraph (2) does not apply—
(a) where the defence of tender before claim(GL) has been raised;
(b) where the proceedings have been stayed(GL) under rule 36.15 following acceptance of a Part 36 offer or Part 36 payment; or
(c) where—
(i) the issue of liability has been determined before any assessment of the money claimed; and
(ii) the fact that there has or has not been a Part 36 payment may be relevant to the question of the costs of the issue of liability.

36.20 Costs Consequences Where Claimant Fails to Do Better Than a Part 36 Offer or a Part 36 Payment

r.36.20 **64.43** r.36.20(2) **64.44**

(1) This rule applies where at trial a claimant—
(a) fails to better a Part 36 payment;
(b) fails to obtain a judgment which is more advantageous than a defendant's Part 36 offer; or
(c) in a claim to which rule 36.2A applies, fails to obtain a judgment which is more advantageous than the Part 36 offer made under that rule.
(2) Unless it considers it unjust to do so, the court will order the claimant to pay any costs incurred by the defendant after the latest date on which the payment or offer could have been accepted without needing the permission of the court.

(Rule 36.11 sets out the time for acceptance of a defendant's Part 36 offer or Part 36 payment)

36.21 Costs and Other Consequences Where Claimant Does Better than He Proposed in His Part 36 Offer

r.36.21 **64.16, 64.50, 64.51, 64.52, 64.53** r.36.21(5) **64.51**
r.36.21(2) **62.12, 64.50** r.36.21(6) **64.50**
r.36.21(3)–(4) **64.50**

(1) This rule applies where at trial—
(a) a defendant is held liable for more; or
(b) the judgment against a defendant is more advantageous to the claimant,
than the proposals contained in a claimant's Part 36 offer (including a Part 36 offer made under rule 36.2A).
(2) The court may order interest on the whole or part of any sum of money (excluding interest) awarded to the claimant at a rate not exceeding 10% above base rate(GL) for some or all of the period starting with the latest date on which the defendant could have accepted the offer without needing the permission of the court.
(3) The court may also order that the claimant is entitled to—
(a) his costs on the indemnity basis from the latest date when the defendant could have accepted the offer without needing the permission of the court; and

(b) interest on those costs at a rate not exceeding 10% above base rate(GL).

(4) Where this rule applies, the court will make the orders referred to in paragraphs (2) and (3) unless it considers it unjust to do so.

(Rule 36.12 sets out the latest date when the defendant could have accepted the offer)

(5) In considering whether it would be unjust to make the orders referred to in paragraphs (2) and (3) above, the court will take into account all the circumstances of the case including—
 (a) the terms of any Part 36 offer;
 (b) the stage in the proceedings when any Part 36 offer or Part 36 payment was made;
 (c) the information available to the parties at the time when the Part 36 offer or Part 36 payment was made; and
 (d) the conduct of the parties with regard to the giving or refusing to give information for the purposes of enabling the offer or payment into court to be made or evaluated.

(6) Where the court awards interest under this rule and also awards interest on the same sum and for the same period under any other power, the total rate of interest may not exceed 10% above base rate(GL).

36.22 Interest

r.36.22(1)–(2) **64.16, 64.20**

(1) Unless—
 (a) a claimant's Part 36 offer which offers to accept a sum of money; or
 (b) a Part 36 payment notice,
 indicates to the contrary, any such offer or payment will be treated as inclusive of all interest until the last date on which it could be accepted without needing the permission of the court.

(2) Where a claimant's Part 36 offer or Part 36 payment notice is expressed not to be inclusive of interest, the offer or notice must state—
 (a) whether interest is offered; and
 (b) if so, the amount offered, the rate or rates offered and the period or periods for which it is offered.

36.23 Deduction of Benefits

r.36.23 **64.8, 64.9, 64.23**
r.36.23(2) **64.2, 64.23**
r.36.23(4) **64.23**

(1) This rule applies where a payment to a claimant following acceptance of a Part 36 offer or Part 36 payment into court would be a compensation payment as defined in section 1 of the Social Security (Recovery of Benefits) Act 1997.

(2) A defendant to a money claim may make an offer to settle the claim which will have the consequences set out in this Part, without making a Part 36 payment if—
 (a) at the time he makes the offer he has applied for, but not received, a certificate of recoverable benefit; and
 (b) he makes a Part 36 payment not more than 7 days after he receives the certificate.

(Section 1 of the 1997 Act defines 'recoverable benefit')

(3) A Part 36 payment notice must state—
 (a) the amount of gross compensation;
 (b) the name and amount of any benefit by which that gross amount is reduced in accordance with section 8 and Schedule 2 to the 1997 Act; and
 (c) that the sum paid in is the net amount after deduction of the amount of benefit.

(4) For the purposes of rule 36.20(1)(a), a claimant fails to better a Part 36 payment if he fails to obtain judgment for more than the gross sum specified in the Part 36 payment notice.

(4A) For the purposes of rule 36.20(1)(c), where the court is determining whether the claimant has failed to obtain a judgment which is more advantageous than the Part 36 offer made under rule 36.2A, the amount of any lump sum paid into court which it takes into account is to be the amount of the gross sum specified in the Part 36 payment notice.

(5) Where—
 (a) a Part 36 payment has been made; and

(b) application is made for the money remaining in court to be paid out,

the court may treat the money in court as being reduced by a sum equivalent to any further recoverable benefits paid to the claimant since the date of payment into court and may direct payment out accordingly.

PD 36 Practice Direction — Offers to Settle and Payments into Court

This practice direction supplements CPR Part 36

[For commentary on a specific paragraph, please refer to the cross-references after the title of the paragraph.]

Part 36 Offers and Part 36 Payments

para.1.3 **64.47**

1.1 A written offer to settle a claim[1] or part of a claim or any issue that arises in it made in accordance with the provisions of Part 36 is called:
(1) if made by way of a payment into court, a Part 36 payment,[2] or
(2) if made otherwise, a Part 36 offer[3] (including an offer under r. 36.2A).

1.2 A Part 36 offer or Part 36 payment has the costs and other consequences set out in rules 36.13,36.14,36.20 and 36.21.

1.3 An offer to settle which is not made in accordance with Part 36 will only have the consequences specified in that Part if the court so orders and will be given such weight on any issue as to costs as the court thinks appropriate.[4]

Parties and Part 36 Offers

2.1 A Part 36 offer, subject to paragraph 3 below, may be made by any party.

2.2 The party making an offer is the 'offeror' and the party to whom it is made is the 'offeree'.

2.3 A Part 36 offer may consist of a proposal to settle for a specified sum or for some other remedy.

2.4 A Part 36 offer is made when received by the offeree.[5]

2.5 An improvement to a Part 36 offer is effective when its details are received by the offeree.[6]

Parties and Part 36 Payments

para.3.4–3.5 **64.26**

3.1 An offer to settle for a specified sum made by a defendant[7] must, in order to comply with Part 36, be made by way of a Part 36 payment into court.[8]

3.2 A Part 36 payment is made when the Part 36 payment notice is served on the claimant.[9]

3.3 An increase to a Part 36 payment will be effective when notice of the increase is served on the claimant.[10]
(For service of the Part 36 payment notice see rule 36.6(3) and (4).)

3.4 A defendant who wishes to withdraw or reduce a Part 36 payment must obtain the court's permission to do so.

3.5 Permission may be obtained by making an application in accordance with Part 23 stating the reasons giving rise to the wish to withdraw or reduce the Part 36 payment.

Making a Part 36 Payment

para.4.1 **64.24**

[1] Includes Part 20 claims.
[2] See rule 36.2(1)(a).
[3] See rule 36.2(1)(b).
[4] See rule 36.1(2).
[5] See rule 36.8(1).
[6] See rule 36.8(3).
[7] Includes a respondent to a claim or issue.
[8] See rule 36.3(1).
[9] See rule 36.8(2).
[10] See rule 36.8(4).

4.1 Except where para. 4.2 applies, to make a Part 36 payment in any court the defendant must:
(1) serve the Part 36 payment notice on the offeree;
(2) file at the court:
(a) a copy of the payment notice; and
(b) a certificate of service confirming service on the offeree; and
(3) send to the Court Funds Office:
(a) the payment, usually a cheque made payable to the Accountant General of the Supreme Court;
(b) a sealed copy of the claim form; and
(c) Court Funds Office form 100.

4.2 A litigant in person without a current account may, in a claim proceeding in a county court or district registry, make a Part 36 payment by:
(1) lodging the payment in cash with the court;
(2) filing at the court:
(a) the Part 36 payment notice; and
(b) Court Funds Office form 100.

Part 36 Offers and Part 36 Payments — General Provisions

para.5.1 **64.16**
para. 5.1(2) **64.20**
para.5.5 **64.16, 64.20**
para. 5.6 **64.16, 64.19, 64.20**

5.1 A Part 36 offer or a Part 36 payment notice must:
(1) state that it is a Part 36 offer or that the payment into court is a Part 36 payment, and
(2) be signed by the offeror or his legal representative.[11]

5.2 The contents of a Part 36 offer must also comply with the requirements of rule 36.5(3), (5) and (6).

5.3 The contents of a Part 36 payment notice must comply with rule 36.6(2) and, if rule 36.23 applies, with rule 36.23(3).

5.3A The contents of a Part 36 offer to which r. 36.2A applies must comply with the requirements of r. 36.2A(5).

5.4 A Part 36 offer or Part 36 payment will be taken to include interest unless it is expressly stated in the offer or the payment notice that interest is not included, in which case the details set out in rule 36.22(2) must be given.

5.5 Where a Part 36 offer is made by a company or other corporation, a person holding a senior position in the company or corporation may sign the offer on the offeror's behalf, but must state the position he holds.

5.6 Each of the following persons is a person holding a senior position:
(1) in respect of a registered company or corporation, a director, the treasurer, secretary, chief executive, manager or other officer of the company or corporation, and
(2) in respect of a corporation which is not a registered company, in addition to those persons set out in (1), the mayor, chairman, president, town clerk or similar officer of the corporation.

Clarification of Part 36 Offer or Payment

paras.6.2–6.3 **64.30**

6.1 An offeree may apply to the court for an order requiring the offeror to clarify the terms of a Part 36 offer or Part 36 payment notice (a clarification order) where the offeror has failed to comply within seven days with a request for clarification.[12]

6.2 An application for a clarification order should be made in accordance with Part 23.

6.3 The application notice should state the respects in which the terms of the Part 36 offer or Part 36 payment notice, as the case may be, are said to need clarification.

[11] For the definition of legal representative see rule 2. 3.
[12] See rule 36.9(1) and (2).

Acceptance of a Part 36 Offer or Payment

7.1 The times for accepting a Part 36 offer or a Part 36 payment are set out in rules 36.11 and 36.12.

7.2 The general rule is that a Part 36 offer or Part 36 payment made more than 21 days before the start of the trial may be accepted within 21 days after it was made without the permission of the court. The costs consequences set out in rules 36.13 and 36.14 will then come into effect.

7.2A Where a Part 36 payment is made as part of a Part 36 offer made under r. 36.2A, the payment is ignored for the purposes of determining the times set out in rr. 36.11 and 36.13.

7.3 A Part 36 offer or Part 36 payment made less than 21 days before the start of the trial cannot be accepted without the permission of the court unless the parties agree what the costs consequences of acceptance will be.

7.4 The permission of the court may be sought:
(1) before the start of the trial, by making an application in accordance with Part 23, and
(2) after the start of the trial, by making an application to the trial judge.

7.5 If the court gives permission it will make an order dealing with costs and may order that, in the circumstances, the costs consequences set out in rules 36.13 and 36.14 will apply.

7.6 Where a Part 36 offer or Part 36 payment is accepted in accordance with rule 36.11(1) or rule 36.12(1) the notice of acceptance must be sent to the offeror and filed with the court.

7.7 The notice of acceptance:
(1) must set out:
(a) the claim number, and
(b) the title of the proceedings,
(2) must identify the Part 36 offer or Part 36 payment notice to which it relates, and
(3) must be signed by the offeree or his legal representative (see paragraphs 5.5 and 5.6 above).

7.8 Where:
(1) the court's approval, or
(2) an order for payment of money out of court, or
(3) an order apportioning money in court:
(a) between the Fatal Accidents Act 1976 and the Law Reform (Miscellaneous Provisions) Act 1934, or
(b) between the persons entitled to it under the Fatal Accidents Act 1976,
is required for acceptance of a Part 36 offer or Part 36 payment, application for the approval or the order should be made in accordance with Part 23.

7.9 The court will include in any order made under paragraph 7.8 above a direction for:
(1) the payment out of the money in court, and
(2) the payment of interest.

7.10 Unless the parties have agreed otherwise:
(1) interest accruing up to the date of acceptance will be paid to the offeror, and
(2) interest accruing as from the date of acceptance until payment out will be paid to the offeree.

7.11 A claimant may not accept a Part 36 payment or Part 36 offer made under r. 36.2A which is part of a defendant's offer to settle the whole of a claim consisting of both a money and a non-money claim unless at the same time he accepts the offer to settle the whole of the claim. Therefore:
(1) if a claimant accepts a Part 36 payment which is part of a defendant's offer to settle the whole of the claim, or
(2) if a claimant accepts a Part 36 offer which is part of a defendant's offer to settle the whole of the claim,
the claimant will be deemed to have accepted the offer to settle the whole of the claim.[13]
(See paragraph 8 below for the method of obtaining money out of court.)

[13] See rule 36. 4.

Payment Out of Court

paras.8.1–8.4 **64.27** para. 8.5(1)–(3) **64.27**

8.1 To obtain money out of court following acceptance of a Part 36 payment, the claimant should:
(1) file a request for payment in Court Funds Office form 201 with the Court Funds Office; and
(2) file a copy of form 201 at the court.

8.2 The request for payment should contain the following details:
(1) where the party receiving the payment:
(a) is legally represented:
(i) the name, business address and reference of the legal representative, and
(ii) the name of the bank and the sort code number, the title of the account and the account number where the payment is to be transmitted, and
(2) where the party is acting in person:
(a) his name and address, and
(b) his bank account details as in (ii) above.

8.3 Where a trial is to take place at a different court to that where the case is proceeding, the claimant must also file notice of request for payment with the court where the trial is to take place.

8.4 Subject to paragraph 8.5(1) and (2), if a party does not wish the payment to be transmitted into his bank account or if he does not have a bank account, he may send a written request to the Accountant-General for the payment to be made to him by cheque.

8.5 Where a party seeking payment out of court has provided the necessary information, the payment:
(1) where a party is legally represented, must be made to the legal representative,
(2) if the party is not legally represented but is, or has been, in receipt of legal aid in respect of the proceedings and a notice to that effect has been filed, should be made to the Legal Aid Board by direction of the court,
(3) where a person entitled to money in court dies without having made a will and the court is satisfied:
(a) that no grant of administration of his estate has been made, and
(b) that the assets of his estate, including the money in court, do not exceed in value the amount specified in any order in force under section 6 of the Administration of Estates (Small Payments) Act 1965,

may be ordered to be made to the person appearing to have the prior right to a grant of administration of the estate of the deceased, e.g. a widower, widow, child, father, mother, brother or sister of the deceased.

Foreign Currency

para.9.1 **64.14, 64.20** para.9.3–9.4 **64.28**

9.1 Money may be paid into court in a foreign currency:
(1) where it is a Part 36 payment and the claim is in a foreign currency, or
(2) under a court order.

9.2 The court may direct that the money be placed in an interest bearing account in the currency of the claim or any other currency.

9.3 Where a Part 36 payment is made in a foreign currency and has not been accepted within 21 days, the defendant may apply for an order that the money be placed in an interest bearing account.

9.4 The application should be made in accordance with Part 23 and should state:
(1) that the payment has not been accepted in accordance with rule 36.11, and
(2) the type of currency on which interest is to accrue.

Compensation Recovery

para.10.1(2) **64.24** para.10.2–10.3 **64.23**

10.1 Where a defendant makes a Part 36 payment in respect of a claim for a sum or part of a sum:
(1) which fails under the heads of damage set out in column 1 of sch. 2 to the Social Security (Recovery of Benefits) Act 1997 in respect of recoverable benefits received by the claimant as set out in column 2 of that schedule, and
(2) where the defendant is liable to pay recoverable benefits to the Secretary of State,

the defendant should obtain from the Secretary of State a certificate of recoverable benefits and file the certificate with the Part 36 payment notice.

10.2 If a defendant wishes to offer to settle a claim where he has applied for but not yet received a certificate of recoverable benefits, he may, provided that he makes a Part 36 payment not more than 7 days after he has received the certificate, make a Part 36 offer which will have the costs and other consequences set out in rules 36.13 and 36.20.

10.3 The Part 36 payment notice should state in addition to the requirements set out in rule 36.6(2):

(1) the total amount represented by the Part 36 payment (the gross compensation),

(2) that the defendant has reduced this sum by £ , in accordance with s. 8 of and sch. 2 to the Social Security (Recovery of Benefits) Act 1997, which was calculated as follows:

Name of benefit Amount

and

(3) that the amount paid in, being the sum of £ is the net amount after the deduction of the amount of benefit.

10.4 On acceptance of a Part 36 payment to which this paragraph relates, a claimant will receive the sum in court which will be net of the recoverable benefits.

10.5 In establishing at trial whether a claimant has bettered or obtained a judgment more advantageous than a Part 36 payment to which this paragraph relates, the court will base its decision on the gross sum specified in the Part 36 payment notice.

General

para.11.2 **64.24** para.11.3 **64.28**

11.1 Where a party on whom a Part 36 offer, a Part 36 payment notice or a notice of acceptance is to be served is legally represented, the Part 36 offer, Part 36 payment notice and notice of acceptance must be served on the legal representative.

11.2 In a claim arising out of an accident involving a motor vehicle on a road or in a public place:

(1) where the damages claimed include a sum for hospital expenses, and

(2) the defendant or his insurer pays that sum to the hospital under section 157 of the Road Traffic Act 1988,

the defendant must give notice of that payment to the court and all the other parties to the proceedings.

11.3 Money paid into court:

(1) as a Part 36 payment which is not accepted by the claimant, or

(2) under a court order,

will be placed after 21 days in a basic account[14] (subject to paragraph 11.4 below) for interest to accrue.

11.4 Where money referred to in paragraph 11.3 above is paid in in respect of a child or patient it will be placed in a special investment account[15] for interest to accrue.

(PD 21 contains information about the investment of money in court in respect of a child or patient.)

(PD 40B and PD 40C contain information about adjustment of the judgment sum in respect of recoverable benefits, and about structured settlements.)

(PD 41 contains information about provisional damages awards.)

Personal Injury Claims for Future Pecuniary Loss

12.1 A Part 36 offer to settle a claim for damages (whether in the form of a lump sum, periodical payments or both) for personal injury which includes a claim for future pecuniary loss must contain the details of the offer which are set out in r. 36.2A.

12.2 The Damages Act 1996, s. 2(4), sets out the circumstances in which the continuity of periodical payments will be taken to be secure. Section 2(8) and (9) of the Act deal with the index-linking of periodical payments.

12.3 Except where otherwise stated in this practice direction, the rules in Part 36 will apply to offers to settle made under r. 36.2A as they apply to other Part 36 payments and to Part 36 offers.

[14] See rule 26 of the Court Funds Office Rules 1987.

[15] See rule 26 as above.

CPR Part 37 Miscellaneous Provisions about Payments into Court

[For commentary on a specific rule, please refer to the cross-references after the title of the rule.]

37.1 Money Paid into Court under a Court Order — General

r.37.1 **64.14** r.37.1(1)–(2) **64.14**

(1) A party who makes a payment into court under a court order must—
 (a) serve notice of the payment on every other party; and
 (b) in relation to each such notice, file a certificate of service.

(2) Money paid into court under a court order may not be paid out without the court's permission except where—
 (a) the defendant treats the money as a Part 36 payment under rule 37.2; and
 (b) the claimant accepts the Part 36 payment without needing the permission of the court.

(Rule 36.11 sets out when the claimant can accept a Part 36 payment without needing the permission of the court)

37.2 Money Paid into Court May Be Treated as a Part 36 Payment

r.37.2 **64.14**

(1) Where a defendant makes a payment into court following an order made under rule 3.1(3) or 3.1(5) he may choose to treat the whole or any part of the money paid into court as a Part 36 payment.

(Rule 36.2 defines a Part 36 payment)

(2) To do this he must file a Part 36 payment notice.

(Rule 36.6 sets out what a Part 36 payment notice must contain and provides for the court to serve it on the other parties)

(3) If he does so Part 36 applies to the money as if he had paid it into court as a Part 36 payment.

37.3 Money Paid into Court Where Defendant Wishes to Rely on Defence of Tender before Claim

r.37.3 **26.18, 64.15, 93.12** r.37.3(2) **64.14, 64.15**
r.37.3(1) **64.15** r.37.3(3) **64.15**

(1) Where a defendant wishes to rely on a defence of tender before claim[(GL)] he must make a payment into court of the amount he says was tendered.

(2) If the defendant does not make a payment in accordance with paragraph (1) the defence of tender before claim[(GL)] will not be available to him until he does so.

(3) Where the defendant makes such payment into court—
 (a) he may choose to treat the whole or any part of the money paid into court as a Part 36 payment; and
 (b) if he does so, he must file a Part 36 payment notice.

37.4 Proceedings under Fatal Accidents Act 1976 and Law Reform (Miscellaneous Provisions) Act 1934 — Apportionment by Court

r.37.4(1) **64.39** r.37.4(3) **64.39**

(1) Where—
   (a) a claim includes claims arising under—
      (i) the Fatal Accidents Act 1976; and
      (ii) the Law Reform (Miscellaneous Provisions) Act 1934;
   (b) a single sum of money is paid into court in satisfaction of those claims; and
   (c) the money is accepted,
   the court shall apportion the money between the different claims.
(2) The court shall apportion money under paragraph (1)—
   (a) when it gives directions under rule 21.11 (control of money received by a child or patient); or
   (b) if rule 21.11 does not apply, when it gives permission for the money to be paid out of court.
(3) Where, in an action in which a claim under the Fatal Accidents Act 1976 is made by or on behalf of more than one person—
   (a) a sum in respect of damages is ordered or agreed to be paid in satisfaction of the claim; or
   (b) a sum of money is accepted in satisfaction of the claim,
   the court shall apportion it between the persons entitled to it unless it has already been apportioned by the court, a jury, or agreement between the parties.

37.5 Payment into Court under Enactments

r.37.5 **64.55**

A practice direction may set out special provisions with regard to payments into court under various enactments.

PD 37 Practice Direction — Miscellaneous Provisions about Payments into Court

This practice direction supplements CPR Part 37

[For commentary on a specific paragraph, please refer to the cross-references after the title of the paragraph.]

For information about payments into and out of court in relation to offers to settle see Part 36 and PD 36.

Payment into Court under an Order

paras.1.1–1.3 **64.14**

1.1 Except where paragraph 1.2 applies a party paying money into any court under an order must:
(1) send to the Court Funds Office:
(a) the payment, usually a cheque made payable to the Accountant General of the Supreme Court;
(b) a sealed copy of the order; and
(c) a completed Court Funds Office form 100;
(2) serve notice of payment on the other parties; and
(3) file at the court:
(a) a copy of the notice of payment; and
(b) a certificate of service confirming service of the notice on each party served.

1.2 A litigant in person without a current account may, in a claim proceeding in a county court or district registry, make a payment into court by:
(1) lodging the payment in cash with the court; and
(2) filing at the court:
(a) a notice of payment; and
(b) Court Funds Office form 100.

Defence of Tender

para.2 **26.18, 64.15** para.2.1 **64.15**

2.1 Except where paragraph 2.1A applies, a defendant who wishes to pay a sum of money into court in support of a defence of tender should:
(1) send to the Court Funds Office:
(a) the payment, usually a cheque made payable to the Accountant General of the Supreme Court;
(b) a sealed copy of the claim form; and
(c) a completed Court Funds Office form 100;
(2) file at the court with his defence:
(a) a notice of payment into court; and
(b) a certificate of service confirming service of the notice on the claimant and his defence; and
(3) serve a copy of the notice of payment into court on the claimant.

2.1A A litigant in person without a current account may, in a claim proceeding in a county court or district registry, pay a sum of money into court in support of a defence of tender by:
(1) lodging the payment in cash with the court; and
(2) filing with the court:
(a) a notice of payment with his defence; and
(b) Court Funds Office form 100.

2.2 A defence of tender will not be available to a defendant until he has complied with para. 2.1.

General

3.1 Where money is paid into court:
(1) under an order permitting a defendant to defend or to continue to defend under r. 37.2(1), or

(2) in support of a defence of tender under r. 37.3,
the party making the payment may, if a defendant, choose to treat the whole or any part of the money as a Part 36 payment.[1]

3.2 In order to do so the defendant must file a Part 36 payment notice in accordance with r. 36.6 (see also PD 36, para. [5*]).

3.3 Rule 37.4 deals with the apportionment of money paid into court in respect of claims arising under:
(1) the Fatal Accidents Act 1976, and
(2) the Law Reform (Miscellaneous Provisions) Act 1934.
(See also PD 36, para. 7.8.)

Payment Out of Court

para.4.2 **64.14**

4.1 Except where money which has been paid into court is treated as a Part 36 payment and can be accepted by the claimant without needing the court's permission, the court's permission is required to take the money out of court.

4.2 Permission may be obtained by making an application in accordance with Part 23. The application notice must state the grounds on which the order for payment out is sought. Evidence of any facts on which the applicant relies may also be necessary.

4.3 To obtain the money out of court the applicant must comply with the provisions of PD 36, para. 8, where they apply.

Foreign Currency

5 For information on payments into court made in a foreign currency, see PD 36, para. 9.

Applications Relating to Funds in Court

6.1 Subject to para. 6.2, any application relating to money or securities which have been paid into court, other than an application for the payment out of the money or securities (for example, an application for money to be invested, or for payment of interest to any person):
(1) must be made in accordance with Part 23; and
(2) may be made without notice, but the court may direct notice to be served on any person.

6.2 Where money paid into court is accepted by or on behalf of a child or patient, r. 21.11(1)(b) provides that the money shall be dealt with in accordance with directions given by the court under that rule and not otherwise. In relation to such cases, reference should be made to PD 21, paras 8 to 12.

Payment into Court by Life Assurance Company

para.7 **64.55** para.7.3(2) **43.18**

7.1 A company wishing to make a payment into court under the Life Assurance Companies (Payment into Court) Act 1896 ('the 1896 Act') must file a witness statement or an affidavit setting out:
(1) a short description of the policy under which money is payable;
(2) a statement of the persons entitled under the policy, including their names and addresses so far as known to the company;
(3) a short statement of:
(a) the notices received by the company making any claim to the money assured, or withdrawing any such claim;
(b) the dates of receipt of such notices; and
(c) the names and addresses of the persons by whom they were given;
(4) a statement that, in the opinion of the board of directors of the company, no sufficient discharge can be obtained for the money which is payable, other than by paying it into court under the 1896 Act;

[1] Rules 37.2(2) and 37.3(3).
[* The text issued by the Department for Constitutional Affairs mistakenly refers to para. 6.]

(5) a statement that the company agrees to comply with any order or direction the court may make:
(a) to pay any further sum into court; or
(b) to pay any costs;
(6) an undertaking by the company immediately to send to the Accountant General at the Court Funds Office any notice of claim received by the company after the application notice has been filed, together with a letter referring to the Court Funds Office reference number; and
(7) the company's address for service.

7.2 The witness statement or affidavit must be filed at:
(1) Chancery Chambers at the Royal Courts of Justice, or
(2) a Chancery district registry of the High Court.

7.3 The company must not deduct from the money payable by it under the policy any costs of the payment into court, except for any court fee.

7.4 If the company is a party to any proceedings issued in relation to the policy or the money assured by it, it may not make a payment into court under the 1896 Act without the permission of the court in those proceedings.

7.5 If a company pays money into court under the 1896 Act, unless the court orders otherwise it must immediately serve notice of the payment on every person who is entitled under the policy or has made a claim to the money assured.

Application for Payment Out of Money Paid into Court by Life Assurance Company

para.8 **64.55**

8.1 Any application for the payment out of money which has been paid into court under the 1896 Act must be made in accordance with para. 4.2 of this practice direction.

8.2 The application must be served on:
(1) every person stated in the written evidence of the company which made the payment to be entitled to or to have an interest in the money;
(2) any other person who has given notice of a claim to the money; and
(3) the company which made the payment, if an application is being made for costs against it, but not otherwise.

Payment into Court under Trustee Act 1925

para.9 **64.55**

9.1 A trustee wishing to make a payment into court under the Trustee Act 1925, s. 63, must file a witness statement or an affidavit setting out:
(1) a short description of:
(a) the trust; and
(b) the instrument creating the trust, or the circumstances in which the trust arose;
(2) the names of the persons interested in or entitled to the money or securities to be paid into court, with their address so far as known to him;
(3) a statement that he agrees to answer any inquiries which the court may make or direct relating to the application of the money or securities; and
(4) his address for service.

9.2 The witness statement or affidavit must be filed at:
(1) Chancery Chambers at the Royal Courts of Justice;
(2) a Chancery district registry of the High Court; or
(3) a county court.

9.3 If a trustee pays money or securities into court, unless the court orders otherwise he must immediately serve notice of the payment into court on every person interested in or entitled to the money or securities.

Application for Payment Out of Funds Paid into Court by Trustee

para.10 **64.55**

10.1 An application for the payment out of any money or securities paid into court under the Trustee Act 1925, s. 63, must be made in accordance with para. 4.2 of this practice direction.

10.2 The application may be made without notice, but the court may direct notice to be served on any person.

Payment into Court under Vehicular Access across Common and Other Land (England) Regulations 2002

11.1 In this Section of this practice direction:
- (1) expressions used have the meanings given by the Vehicular Access across Common and Other Land (England) Regulations 2002 (SI 2002/1711); and
- (2) a regulation referred to by number alone means the regulation so numbered in those Regulations.

11.2 Where the applicant wishes to pay money into a county court under reg. 14 he must file a witness statement or an affidavit when he lodges the money.

11.3 The witness statement or affidavit must:
- (1) state briefly why the applicant is making the payment into court; and
- (2) be accompanied by copies of:
  - (a) the notice served under reg. 6;
  - (b) any counter-notice served under reg. 8;
  - (c) any amended notice or counter-notice served under reg. 9;
  - (d) any determination of the Lands Tribunal of a matter referred to it under reg. 10; and
  - (e) any determination of the value of the premises by a chartered surveyor following the service of a valuation notice under reg. 12.

11.4 If an applicant pays money into court under reg. 14, he must immediately serve notice of the payment and a copy of the witness statement or affidavit on the landowner.

11.5 An application for payment out of the money must be made in accordance with para. 4 of this practice direction.

CPR Part 38 Discontinuance

[For commentary on a specific rule, please refer to the cross-references after the title of the rule.]

38.1 Scope of This Part

r.38.1(1) **53.3** r.38.1(2) **53.2**

(1) The rules in this Part set out the procedure by which a claimant may discontinue all or part of a claim.

(2) A claimant who—

(a) claims more than one remedy; and

(b) subsequently abandons his claim to one or more of the remedies but continues with his claim for the other remedies,

is not treated as discontinuing all or part of a claim for the purposes of this Part.

(The procedure for amending a statement of case, set out in Part 17, applies where a claimant abandons a claim for a particular remedy but wishes to continue with his claim for other remedies)

38.2 Right to Discontinue Claim

r.38.2(1) **53.4** r.38.2(3) **53.3**
r.38.2(2)(a)–(c) **53.4**

(1) A claimant may discontinue all or part of a claim at any time.

(2) However—

(a) a claimant must obtain the permission of the court if he wishes to discontinue all or part of a claim in relation to which—

(i) the court has granted an interim injunction[GL]; or

(ii) any party has given an undertaking to the court;

(b) where the claimant has received an interim payment in relation to a claim (whether voluntarily or pursuant to an order under Part 25), he may discontinue that claim only if—

(i) the defendant who made the interim payment consents in writing; or

(ii) the court gives permission;

(c) where there is more than one claimant, a claimant may not discontinue unless—

(i) every other claimant consents in writing; or

(ii) the court gives permission.

(3) Where there is more than one defendant, the claimant may discontinue all or part of a claim against all or any of the defendants.

38.3 Procedure for Discontinuing

r.38.3(2)–(4) **53.5**

(1) To discontinue a claim or part of a claim, a claimant must—

(a) file a notice of discontinuance; and

(b) serve a copy of it on every other party to the proceedings.

(2) The claimant must state in the notice of discontinuance which he files that he has served notice of discontinuance on every other party to the proceedings.

(3) Where the claimant needs the consent of some other party, a copy of the necessary consent must be attached to the notice of discontinuance.

(4) Where there is more than one defendant, the notice of discontinuance must specify against which defendants the claim is discontinued.

38.4 Right to Apply to Have Notice of Discontinuance Set Aside

r.38.4 **53.6**

(1) Where the claimant discontinues under rule 38.2(1) the defendant may apply to have the notice of discontinuance set aside[(GL)].

(2) The defendant may not make an application under this rule more than 28 days after the date when the notice of discontinuance was served on him.

38.5 When Discontinuance Takes Effect Where Permission of the Court Is Not Needed

r.38.5 **53.7**

(1) Discontinuance against any defendant takes effect on the date when notice of discontinuance is served on him under rule 38.3(1).

(2) Subject to rule 38.4, the proceedings are brought to an end as against him on that date.

(3) However, this does not affect proceedings to deal with any question of costs.

38.6 Liability for Costs

r.38.6(1)–(3) **53.7**

(1) Unless the court orders otherwise, a claimant who discontinues is liable for the costs which a defendant against whom he discontinues incurred on or before the date on which notice of discontinuance was served on him.

(2) If proceedings are only partly discontinued—
   (a) the claimant is liable under paragraph (1) for costs relating only to the part of the proceedings which he is discontinuing; and
   (b) unless the court orders otherwise, the costs which the claimant is liable to pay must not be assessed until the conclusion of the rest of the proceedings.

(3) This rule does not apply to claims allocated to the small claims track.

(Rule 44.12 provides for the basis of assessment where right to costs arises on discontinuance)

38.7 Discontinuance and Subsequent Proceedings

r.38.7 **53.8**

A claimant who discontinues a claim needs the permission of the court to make another claim against the same defendant if—

(a) he discontinued the claim after the defendant filed a defence; and

(b) the other claim arises out of facts which are the same or substantially the same as those relating to the discontinued claim.

38.8 Stay of Remainder of Partly Discontinued Proceedings Where Costs Not Paid

r.38.8 **53.7**

(1) This rule applies where—
   (a) proceedings are partly discontinued;
   (b) a claimant is liable to pay costs under rule 38.6; and
   (c) the claimant fails to pay those costs within 14 days of—
      (i) the date on which the parties agreed the sum payable by the claimant; or
      (ii) the date on which the court ordered the costs to be paid.

(2) Where this rule applies, the court may stay[(GL)] the remainder of the proceedings until the claimant pays the whole of the costs which he is liable to pay under rule 38.6.

CPR Part 39 Miscellaneous Provisions Relating to Hearings

Part 39 **14.18, 43.6** [For commentary on a specific rule, please refer to the cross-references after the title of the rule.]

39.1 Interpretation

In this Part, reference to a hearing includes a reference to the trial.

39.2 General Rule — Hearing to be in Public

r.39.2 **32.8, 32.26, 37.11, 43.6, 69.16**
r.39.2(1) **59.20, 97.47**
r.39.2(3) **43.21, 59.20**
r.39.2(3)(a) **32.8, 74.46**
r.39.2(3)(c) **74.46**
r.39.2(3)(d) **59.21**
r.39.2(3)(e) **32.8**
r.39.2(4) **59.20**

(1) The general rule is that a hearing is to be in public.
(2) The requirement for a hearing to be in public does not require the court to make special arrangements for accommodating members of the public.
(3) A hearing, or any part of it, may be in private if—
  (a) publicity would defeat the object of the hearing;
  (b) it involves matters relating to national security;
  (c) it involves confidential information (including information relating to personal financial matters) and publicity would damage that confidentiality;
  (d) a private hearing is necessary to protect the interests of any child or patient;
  (e) it is a hearing of an application made without notice and it would be unjust to any respondent for there to be a public hearing;
  (f) it involves uncontentious matters arising in the administration of trusts or in the administration of a deceased person's estate; or
  (g) the court considers this to be necessary, in the interests of justice.
(4) The court may order that the identity of any party or witness must not be disclosed if it considers non-disclosure necessary in order to protect the interests of that party or witness.

39.3 Failure to Attend the Trial

r.39.3 **60.2**
r.39.3(1)–(4) **60.2**
r.39.3(5) **43.25, 60.2**
r.39.3(5)(b) **60.2**

(1) The court may proceed with a trial in the absence of a party but—
  (a) if no party attends the trial, it may strike out[(GL)] the whole of the proceedings;
  (b) if the claimant does not attend, it may strike out his claim and any defence to counterclaim; and
  (c) if a defendant does not attend, it may strike out his defence or counterclaim (or both).
(2) Where the court strikes out proceedings, or any part of them, under this rule, it may subsequently restore the proceedings, or that part.
(3) Where a party does not attend and the court gives judgment or makes an order against him, the party who failed to attend may apply for the judgment or order to be set aside.[(GL)]
(4) An application under paragraph (2) or paragraph (3) must be supported by evidence.
(5) Where an application is made under paragraph (2) or (3) by a party who failed to attend the trial, the court may grant the application only if the applicant—
  (a) acted promptly when he found out that the court had exercised its power to strike out[(GL)] or to enter judgment or make an order against him;

(b) had a good reason for not attending the trial; and
(c) has a reasonable prospect of success at the trial.

39.4 Timetable for Trial

r.39.4 **44.18, 59.16**

When the court sets a timetable for a trial in accordance with rule 28.6 (fixing or confirming the trial date and giving directions — fast track) or rule 29.8 (setting a trial timetable and fixing or confirming the trial date or week — multi-track) it will do so in consultation with the parties.

39.5 Trial Bundles

r.39.5(1) **57.3** r.39.5(2) **57.1**

(1) Unless the court orders otherwise, the claimant must file a trial bundle containing documents required by—
(a) a relevant practice direction; and
(b) any court order.
(2) The claimant must file the trial bundle not more than 7 days and not less than 3 days before the start of the trial.

39.6 Representation at Trial of Companies or Other Corporations

r.39.6 **59.33**

A company or other corporation may be represented at trial by an employee if—
(a) the employee has been authorised by the company or corporation to appear at trial on its behalf; and
(b) the court gives permission.

39.7 Impounded Documents

(1) Documents impounded by order of the court must not be released from the custody of the court except in compliance—
(a) with a court order; or
(b) with a written request made by a Law Officer or the Director of Public Prosecutions.
(2) A document released from the custody of the court under paragraph (1)(b) must be released into the custody of the person who requested it.
(3) Documents impounded by order of the court, while in the custody of the court, may not be inspected except by a person authorised to do so by a court order.

39.8 Claims under the Race Relations Act 1976

r.39.8 **59.21**

In a claim brought under section 57(1) of the Race Relations Act 1976, the court may, where it considers it expedient in the interests of national security—
(a) exclude from all or part of the proceedings—
(i) the claimant;
(ii) the claimant's representatives; or
(iii) any assessors appointed under section 67(4) of that Act;
(b) permit a claimant or representative to make a statement to the court before the start of the proceedings (or part of the proceedings) from which he is to be excluded; or
(c) take steps to keep secret all or part of the reasons for its decision in the claim.
(Section 67A(2) of the Race Relations Act 1976 provides that the Attorney General may appoint a person to represent the interests of a claimant in any proceedings from which he and his representatives are excluded)

PD 39 Practice Direction — Miscellaneous Provisions Relating to Hearings

This practice direction supplements CPR Part 39

[For commentary on a specific paragraph, please refer to the cross-references after the title of the paragraph.]

Hearings

para.1.4A **59.20**
para.1.5 **59.21**
para.1.6 **59.21**
para.1.10 **32.26**
para.1.11 **97.47**
para.1.12 **59.21, 97.47**
para.1.15 **59.23**

1.1 In Part 39, reference to a hearing includes reference to the trial.[1]

1.2 The general rule is that a hearing is to be in public.[2]

1.3 Rule 39.2(3) sets out the type of proceedings which may be dealt with in private.

1.4 The decision as to whether to hold a hearing in public or in private must be made by the judge conducting the hearing having regard to any representations which may have been made to him.

1.4A The judge should also have regard to Article 6(1) of the European Convention on Human Rights. This requires that, in general, court hearings are to be held in public, but the press and public may be excluded in the circumstances specified in that Article. Article 6(1) will usually be relevant, for example, where a party applies for a hearing which would normally be held in public to be held in private as well as where a hearing would normally be held in private. The judge may need to consider whether the case is within any of the exceptions permitted by Article 6(1).

1.5 The hearings set out below shall in the first instance be listed by the court as hearings in private under rule 39.2(3)(c), namely:

(1) a claim by a mortgagee against one or more individuals for an order for possession of land,
(2) a claim by a landlord against one or more tenants or former tenants for the repossession of a dwelling house based on the non-payment of rent,
(3) an application to suspend a warrant of execution or a warrant of possession or to stay execution where the court is being invited to consider the ability of a party to make payments to another party,
(4) a redetermination under rule 14.13 or an application to vary or suspend the payment of a judgment debt by instalments,
(5) an application for a charging order (including an application to enforce a charging order), third party debt order, attachment of earnings order, administration order, or the appointment of a receiver,
(6) an order to attend court for questioning,
(7) the determination of an LSC funded client under regulations 9 and 10 of the Community Legal Service (Costs) Regulations 2000, or of an assisted person's liability for costs under regulation 127 of the Civil Legal Aid (General) Regulations 1989,
(8) an application for security for costs under section 726(1) of the Companies Act 1985, and
(9) proceedings brought under the Consumer Credit Act 1974, the Inheritance (Provision for Family and Dependants) Act 1975 or the Protection from Harassment Act 1997,
(10) an application by a trustee or personal representative for directions as to bringing or defending legal proceedings.

1.6 Rule 39.2(3)(d) states that a hearing may be in private where it involves the interests of a child or patient. This includes the approval of a compromise or settlement on behalf of a child or patient or an application for the payment of money out of court to such a person.

---

[1] Rule 39.1.
[2] Rule 39.2(1).

1.7 Attention is drawn to PD 27, para. [4.1*] (relating to the hearing of claims in the small claims track), which provides that the judge may decide to hold a small claim hearing in private if the parties agree or if a ground mentioned in rule 39.2(3) applies. A hearing of a small claim in premises other than the court will not be a hearing in public.

1.8 Nothing in this practice direction prevents a judge ordering that a hearing taking place in public shall continue in private, or vice versa.

1.9 If the court or judge's room in which the proceedings are taking place has a sign on the door indicating that the proceedings are private, members of the public who are not parties to the proceedings will not be admitted unless the court permits.

1.10 Where there is no such sign on the door of the court or judge's room, members of the public will be admitted where practicable. The judge may, if he thinks it appropriate, adjourn the proceedings to a larger room or court.

1.11 When a hearing takes place in public, members of the public may obtain a transcript of any judgment given or a copy of any order made, subject to payment of the appropriate fee.

1.12 When a judgment is given or an order is made in private, if any member of the public who is not a party to the proceedings seeks a transcript of the judgment or a copy of the order, he must seek the leave of the judge who gave the judgment or made the order.

1.13 A judgment or order given or made in private, when drawn up, must have clearly marked in the title:

'Before [*title and name of judge*] sitting in Private'

1.14 References to hearings being in public or private or in a judge's room contained in the Civil Procedure Rules (including the Rules of the Supreme Court and the County Court Rules scheduled to Part 50) and the practice directions which supplement them do not restrict any existing rights of audience or confer any new rights of audience in respect of applications or proceedings which under the rules previously in force would have been heard in court or in chambers respectively.

1.15 Where the court lists a hearing of a claim by a mortgagee for an order for possession of land under para. 1.5(1) above to be in private, any fact which needs to be proved by the evidence of witnesses may be proved by evidence in writing.

(CPR, r. 32.2, sets out the general rule as to how evidence is to be given and facts are to be proved.)

Failure to Attend the Trial

2.1 Rule 39.3 sets out the consequences of a party's failure to attend the trial.

2.2 The court may proceed with a trial in the absence of a party.[3] In the absence of:

(1) the defendant, the claimant may:
  (a) prove his claim at trial and obtain judgment on his claim and for costs, and
  (b) seek the striking out of any counterclaim,

(2) the claimant, the defendant may:
  (a) prove any counterclaim at trial and obtain judgment on his counterclaim and for costs, and
  (b) seek the striking out of the claim, or

(3) both parties, the court may strike out the whole of the proceedings.

2.3 Where the court has struck out proceedings, or any part of them, on the failure of a party to attend, that party may apply in accordance with Part 23 for the proceedings, or that part of them, to be restored and for any judgment given against that party to be set aside.[4]

2.4 The application referred to in paragraph 2.3 above must be supported by evidence giving reasons for the failure to attend court and stating when the applicant found out about the order against him.

[* The text issued by the Department for Constitutional Affairs mistakenly refers to para. 5.1.]

[3] Rule 39.3(1).

[4] Rule 39.3(2) and (3).

Bundles of Documents for Hearings or Trial

para.3 **57.2** para.3.9 **57.2**
para.3.3 **57.3** para.3.10 **57.3**

3.1 Unless the court orders otherwise, the claimant must file the trial bundle not more than seven days and not less than three days before the start of the trial.

3.2 Unless the court orders otherwise, the trial bundle should include a copy of:
(1) the claim form and all statements of case,
(2) a case summary and/or chronology where appropriate,
(3) requests for further information and responses to the requests,
(4) all witness statements to be relied on as evidence,
(5) any witness summaries,
(6) any notices of intention to rely on hearsay evidence under rule [33.2*],
(7) any notices of intention to rely on evidence (such as a plan, photograph etc.) under rule 33.6 which is not:
(a) contained in a witness statement, affidavit or expert's report,
(b) being given orally at trial,
(c) hearsay evidence under rule 33.2,
(8) any medical reports and responses to them,
(9) any experts' reports and responses to them,
(10) any order giving directions as to the conduct of the trial, and
(11) any other necessary documents.

3.3 The originals of the documents contained in the trial bundle, together with copies of any other court orders should be available at the trial.

3.4 The preparation and production of the trial bundle, even where it is delegated to another person, is the responsibility of the legal representative[5] who has conduct of the claim on behalf of the claimant.

3.5 The trial bundle should be paginated (continuously) throughout, and indexed with a description of each document and the page number. Where the total number of pages is more than 100, numbered dividers should be placed at intervals between groups of documents.

3.6 The bundle should normally be contained in a ring binder or lever arch file. Where more than one bundle is supplied, they should be clearly distinguishable, for example, by different colours or letters. If there are numerous bundles, a core bundle should be prepared containing the core documents essential to the proceedings, with references to the supplementary documents in the other bundles.

3.7 For convenience, experts' reports may be contained in a separate bundle and cross referenced in the main bundle.

3.8 If a document to be included in the trial bundle is illegible, a typed copy should be included in the bundle next to it, suitably cross-referenced.

3.9 The contents of the trial bundle should be agreed where possible. The parties should also agree where possible:
(1) that the documents contained in the bundle are authentic even if not disclosed under Part 31, and
(2) that documents in the bundle may be treated as evidence of the facts stated in them even if a notice under the Civil Evidence Act 1995 has not been served.

Where it is not possible to agree the contents of the bundle, a summary of the points on which the parties are unable to agree should be included.

3.10 The party filing the trial bundle should supply identical bundles to all the parties to the proceedings and for the use of the witnesses.

Settlement or Discontinuance after the Trial Date Is Fixed

para.4.1 **59.15** para.4.2 **61.3**

4.1 Where:
(1) an offer to settle a claim is accepted,

[* The text issued by the Department for Constitutional Affairs refers, mistakenly, to rule 32.2.]
[5] For the definition of legal representative see rule 2.3.

(2) or a settlement is reached, or
(3) a claim is discontinued,

which disposes of the whole of a claim for which a date or 'window' has been fixed for the trial, the parties must ensure that the listing officer for the trial court is notified immediately.

4.2 If an order is drawn up giving effect to the settlement or discontinuance, a copy of the sealed order should be filed with the listing officer.

Representation at Hearings

para.5.1 **59.33, 59.34** paras.5.2–5.6 **59.33**

5.1 At any hearing, a written statement containing the following information should be provided for the court:
(1) the name and address of each advocate,
(2) his qualification or entitlement to act as an advocate, and
(3) the party for whom he so acts.

5.2 Where a party is a company or other corporation and is to be represented at a hearing by an employee the written statement should contain the following additional information:
(1) The full name of the company or corporation as stated in its certificate of registration.
(2) The registered number of the company or corporation.
(3) The position or office in the company or corporation held by the representative.
(4) The date on which and manner in which the representative was authorised to act for the company or corporation, e.g. —— 20 —— : written authority from managing director; or —— 20 —— : Board resolution dated —— 20 —— .

5.3 Rule 39.6 is intended to enable a company or other corporation to represent itself as a litigant in person. Permission under rule 39.6(b) should therefore be given by the court unless there is some particular and sufficient reason why it should be withheld. In considering whether to grant permission the matters to be taken into account include the complexity of the issues and the experience and position in the company or corporation of the proposed representative.

5.4 Permission under rule 39.6(b) should be obtained in advance of the hearing from, preferably, the judge who is to hear the case, but may, if it is for any reason impracticable or inconvenient to do so, be obtained from any judge by whom the case could be heard.

5.5 The permission may be obtained informally and without notice to the other parties. The judge who gives the permission should record in writing that he has done so and supply a copy to the company or corporation in question and to any other party who asks for one.

5.6 Permission should not normally be granted under Rule 39.6:
(a) in jury trials;
(b) in contempt proceedings.

Recording of Proceedings

para.6.1 **59.51** paras.6.3–6.5 **59.51**

6.1 At any hearing, whether in the High Court or a county court, the proceedings will be tape-recorded unless the judge directs otherwise.

6.2 No party or member of the public may use unofficial recording equipment in any court or judge's room without the permission of the court. To do so without permission constitutes a contempt of court.[6]

6.3 Any party or person may require a transcript or transcripts of the recording of any hearing to be supplied to him, upon payment of the charges authorised by any scheme in force for the making of the recording or the transcript.

6.4 Where the person requiring the transcript or transcripts is not a party to the proceedings and the hearing or any part of it was held in private under CPR rule 39.2, paragraph 6.3 does not apply unless the court so orders.

6.5 Attention is drawn to [PD 52, paras 5.17 and 5.18* which deal] with the provision of transcripts for use in the Court of Appeal at public expense.

[6] Section 9 of the Contempt of Court Act 1981.

[* The text issued by the Department for Constitutional Affairs refers to an earlier practice direction.]

Exhibits at Trial

para.7 **59.40**

7 Exhibits which are handed in and proved during the course of the trial should be recorded on an exhibit list and kept in the custody of the court until the conclusion of the trial, unless the judge directs otherwise. At the conclusion of the trial it is the parties' responsibility to obtain the return of those exhibits which they handed in and to preserve them for the period in which any appeal may take place.

Citation of Authorities Human Rights

para.8 **97.37**

8.1 If it is necessary for a party to give evidence at a hearing of an authority referred to in s. 2 of the Human Rights Act 1998:

(1) the authority to be cited should be an authoritative and complete report; and

(2) the party must give to the court and any other party a list of the authorities he intends to cite and copies of the reports not less than three days before the hearing. (Section 2(1) of the Human Rights Act 1998 requires the court to take into account the authorities listed there.)

(3) Copies of the complete original texts issued by the European Court and Commission either paper based or from the Court's judgment database (HUDOC), which is available on the Internet, may be used.

PD 39B Practice Direction — Court Sittings

This practice direction supplements CPR Part 39

PD 39B **59.24** [For commentary on a specific paragraph, please refer to the cross-references after the title of the paragraph.]

Court Sittings

1.1 (1) The sittings of the Court of Appeal and of the High Court shall be four in every year, that is to say:
(a) the Michaelmas sittings which shall begin on 1 October and end on 21 December;
(b) the Hilary sittings which shall begin on 11 January and end on the Wednesday before Easter Sunday;
(c) the Easter sittings which shall begin on the second Tuesday after Easter Sunday and end on the Friday before the spring holiday; and
(d) the Trinity sittings which shall begin on the second Tuesday after the spring holiday and end on 31 July.
(2) In the above paragraph 'spring holiday' means the bank holiday falling on the last Monday in May or any day appointed instead of that day under the Banking and Financial Dealings Act 1971, s. 1(2).

Vacations: The High Court

para.2.1(2) **59.24**
para.2.2 **59.24**
para.2.3(2)–(3) **59.24**
para.2.4–2.5 **59.24**

2.1 (1) One or more judges of each Division of the High Court shall sit in vacation on such days as the senior judge of that Division may from time to time direct, to hear such cases, claims, matters or applications as require to be immediately or promptly heard and to hear other cases, claims, matters or applications if the senior judge of that Division determines that sittings are necessary for that purpose.
(2) Any party to a claim or matter may at any time apply to the court for an order that such claim or matter be heard in vacation and, if the court is satisfied that the claim or matter requires to be immediately or promptly heard, it may make an order accordingly and fix a date for the hearing.
(3) Any judge of the High Court may hear such other cases, claims, matters or applications in vacation as the court may direct.

2.2 The directions in para. [2.1*] shall not apply in relation to the trial or hearing of cases, claims, matters or applications outside the Royal Courts of Justice but the senior presiding judge of each circuit, with the concurrence of the senior presiding judge, and the Vice-Chancellor of the County Palatine of Lancaster and the Chancery supervising judge for Birmingham, Bristol and Cardiff, with the concurrence of the Vice-Chancellor, may make such arrangements for vacation sittings in the courts for which they are respectively responsible as they think desirable.

2.3 (1) Subject to the discretion of the judge, any appeal and any application normally made to a judge may be made in the month of September.
(2) In the month of August, save with the permission of a judge or under arrangements for vacation sittings in courts outside the Royal Courts of Justice, appeals to a judge will be limited to the matters set out in para. [2.5†] below, and only applications of real urgency will be dealt with, for example, urgent applications in respect of injunctions or for possession under RSC, ord. 113 in CPR, sch. 1.
(3) It is desirable, where this is practical, that applications or appeals are submitted to a master, district judge or judge prior to the hearing of the application or appeal so that they can be marked 'fit for August' or 'fit for vacation'. If they are so marked, then normally the judge will be prepared to hear the application or appeal in August, if marked 'fit for August' or in

[* The text issued by the Department for Constitutional Affairs mistakenly refers to para. 3.1.]
[† The text issued by the Department for Constitutional Affairs mistakenly refers to para. 3.5.]

September if marked 'fit for vacation'. A request to have the papers so marked should normally be made in writing, shortly setting out the nature of the application or appeal and the reasons why it should be dealt with in August or in September, as the case may be.

Chancery masters

2.4 There is no distinction between term time and vacation so far as business before the Chancery masters is concerned. The masters will deal with all types of business throughout the year, and when a master is on holiday his list will normally be taken by a deputy master.

Queen's Bench masters

2.5 (1) An application notice may, without permission, be issued returnable before a master in the month of August for any of the following purposes:

to set aside a claim form or particulars of claim, or service of a claim form or particulars of claim;

to set aside judgment; for stay of execution;

for any order by consent;

for judgment or permission to enter judgment;

for approval of settlements or for interim payment;

for relief from forfeiture; for charging order; for garnishee order;

for appointment or discharge of a receiver;

for relief by way of interpleader by a sheriff or High Court enforcement officer;

for transfer to a county court or for trial by master;

for time where time is running in the month of August;

(2) In any case of urgency any other type of application notice (that is, other than those for the purposes in (1) above), may, with the permission of a master be issued returnable before a master during the month of August.

PD 39C Practice Direction — Claims under the Race Relations Act 1976 (National Security)

PD 39C **59.21**

This practice direction supplements r. 39.8

PD 39C **59.20** [For commentary on a specific paragraph, please refer to the cross-references after the title of the paragraph.]

1.1 Where a claimant and his representatives have been excluded from all or part of the proceedings under r. 39.8(a), the court will inform the Attorney-General of the proceedings.

1.2 The Attorney-General may appoint a person (a 'special advocate') under the Race Relations Act 1976, s. 67A(2), to represent the claimant in respect of those parts of the proceedings from which he and his representative have been excluded.

1.3 In exercise of its powers under r. 39.8(c), the court may order the special advocate not to communicate (directly or indirectly) with any persons (including the excluded claimant):

(1) on any matter discussed or referred to, or

(2) with regard to any material disclosed,

during or with reference to any part of the proceedings from which the claimant and his representative are excluded.

1.4 Where the court makes an order referred to in para. 1.3 (or any similar order), the special advocate may apply to the court for directions enabling him to seek instructions from, or otherwise to communicate with an excluded person.

CPR Part 40 Judgments, Orders, Sale of Land etc.

[For commentary on a specific rule, please refer to the cross-references after the title of the rule.]

I JUDGMENTS AND ORDERS

40.1 Scope of This Section

This Section sets out rules about judgments and orders which apply except where any other of these Rules or a practice direction makes a different provision in relation to the judgment or order in question.

40.2 Standard Requirements

r.40.2(1)–(2) **32.35, 61.7, 61.30** r.40.2(4) **61.7**

(1) Every judgment or order must state the name and judicial title of the person who made it, unless it is—
   (a) default judgment entered under rule 12.4(1) (entry of default judgment where judgment is entered by a court officer) or a default costs certificate obtained under rule 47.11;
   (b) judgment entered under rule 14.4, 14.5, 14.6, 14.7 and 14.9 (entry of judgment on admission where judgment is entered by a court officer);
   (c) a consent order under rule 40.6(2) (consent orders made by court officers);
   (d) an order made by a court officer under rule 70.5 (orders to enforce awards as if payable under a court order); or
   (e) an order made by a court officer under rule 71.2 (orders to obtain information from judgment debtors).
(2) Every judgment or order must—
   (a) bear the date on which it is given or made; and
   (b) be sealed(GL) by the court.
(3) Paragraph (4) applies where a party applies for permission to appeal against a judgment or order at the hearing at which the judgment or order was made.
(4) Where this paragraph applies, the judgment or order shall state—
   (a) whether or not the judgment or order is final;
   (b) whether an appeal lies from the judgment or order and, if so, to which appeal court;
   (c) whether the court gives permission to appeal; and
   (d) if not, the appropriate appeal court to which any further application for permission may be made.

(Paragraph 4.3B of the Practice Direction supplementing Part 52 deals with the court's power to adjourn a hearing where a judgment or order is handed down and no application for permission to appeal is made at that hearing)

40.3 Drawing up and Filing of Judgments and Orders

r.40.3(1) **61.30** r.40.3(3) **32.35, 61.30**
r.40.3(1)(c) **32.35**

(1) Except as is provided at paragraph (4) below or by any Practice Direction, every judgment or order will be drawn up by the court unless—
(a) the court orders a party to draw it up;
(b) a party, with the permission of the court, agrees to draw it up;
(c) the court dispenses with the need to draw it up; or
(d) it is a consent order under rule 40.6.
(2) The court may direct that—
(a) a judgment or an order drawn up by a party must be checked by the court before it is sealed(GL); or
(b) before a judgment or an order is drawn up by the court, the parties must file an agreed statement of its terms.
(3) Where a judgment or an order is to be drawn up by a party—
(a) he must file it no later than 7 days after the date on which the court ordered or permitted him to draw it up so that it can be sealed(GL) by the court; and
(b) if he fails to file it within that period, any other party may draw it up and file it.
(4) Except for orders made by the court of its own initiative and unless the court otherwise orders, every judgment or order made in claims proceeding in the Queen's Bench Division at the Royal Courts of Justice, other than in the Administrative Court, will be drawn up by the parties, and rule 40.3 is modified accordingly.

40.4 Service of Judgments and Orders

r.40.4(1)–(2) **32.35, 61.30**

(1) Where a judgment or an order has been drawn up by a party and is to be served by the court—
(a) the party who drew it up must file a copy to be retained at court and sufficient copies for service on him and on the other parties; and
(b) once it has been sealed(GL), the court must serve a copy of it on each party to the proceedings.
(2) Unless the court directs otherwise, any order made otherwise than at trial must be served on—
(a) the applicant and the respondent; and
(b) any other person on whom the court orders it to be served.
(Rule 6.3 specifies who must serve judgments and orders)

40.5 Power to Require Judgment or Order to Be Served on a Party as Well as His Solicitor

r.40.5 **1.36, 32.35, 61.30**

Where the party on whom a judgment or order is to be served is acting by a solicitor, the court may order the judgment or order to be served on the party as well as on his solicitor.

40.6 Consent Judgments and Orders

r.40.6 **61.31** r.40.6(5)–(6) **61.32**
r.40.6(2)(b) **32.31, 61.31** r.40.6(7) **32.34**
r.40.6(3) **32.31** r.40.6(7)(b) **61.11**

(1) This rule applies where all the parties agree the terms in which a judgment should be given or an order should be made.
(2) A court officer may enter and seal(GL) an agreed judgment or order if—
(a) the judgment or order is listed in paragraph (3);
(b) none of the parties is a litigant in person; and
(c) the approval of the court is not required by these Rules, a practice direction or any enactment before an agreed order can be made.
(3) The judgments and orders referred to in paragraph (2) are—
(a) a judgment or order for—
(i) the payment of an amount of money (including a judgment or order for damages or the value of goods to be decided by the court); or
(ii) the delivery up of goods with or without the option of paying the value of the goods or the agreed value.

(b) an order for—
   (i) the dismissal of any proceedings, wholly or in part;
   (ii) the stay(GL) of proceedings on agreed terms, disposing of the proceedings, whether those terms are recorded in a schedule to the order or elsewhere;
   (iii) the stay(GL) of enforcement of a judgment, either unconditionally or on condition that the money due under the judgment is paid by instalments specified in the order;
   (iv) the setting aside under Part 13 of a default judgment which has not been satisfied;
   (v) the payment out of money which has been paid into court;
   (vi) the discharge from liability of any party;
   (vii) the payment, assessment or waiver of costs, or such other provision for costs as may be agreed.

(4) Rule 40.3 (drawing up and filing of judgments and orders) applies to judgments and orders entered and sealed(GL) by a court officer under paragraph (2) as it applies to other judgments and orders.

(5) Where paragraph (2) does not apply, any party may apply for a judgment or order in the terms agreed.

(6) The court may deal with an application under paragraph (5) without a hearing.

(7) Where this rule applies—
   (a) the order which is agreed by the parties must be drawn up in the terms agreed;
   (b) it must be expressed as being 'By Consent';
   (c) it must be signed by the legal representative acting for each of the parties to whom the order relates or, where paragraph (5) applies, by the party if he is a litigant in person.

40.7 When Judgment or Order Takes Effect

r.40.7 **32.35, 48.32, 61.36** r.40.7(1) **4.2, 61.1, 71.19**

(1) A judgment or order takes effect from the day when it is given or made, or such later date as the court may specify.

(2) This rule applies to all judgments and orders except those to which rule 40.10 (judgment against a State) applies.

40.8 Time from Which Interest Begins to Run

r.40.8 **62.17, 68.23**

(1) Where interest is payable on a judgment pursuant to section 17 of the judgments Act 1838 or section 74 of the County Courts Act 1984, the interest shall begin to run from the date that judgment is given unless—
   (a) a rule in another Part or a practice direction makes different provision; or
   (b) the court orders otherwise.

(2) The court may order that interest shall begin to run from a date before the date that judgment is given.

40.9 Who May Apply to Set Aside or Vary a Judgment or Order

r.40.9 **4.2**

A person who is not a party but who is directly affected by a judgment or order may apply to have the judgment or order set aside or varied.

40.10 Judgment against a State in Default of Acknowledgment of Service

r.40.10 **4.2**

(1) Where the claimant obtains default judgment under Part 12 on a claim against a State where the defendant has failed to file an acknowledgment of service, the judgment does not take effect until 2 months after service on the State of—
   (a) a copy of the judgment; and
   (b) a copy of the evidence in support of the application for permission to enter default judgment (unless the evidence has already been served on the State in accordance with an order made under Part 12).

(2) In this rule, 'State' has the meaning given by section 14 of the State Immunity Act 1978.

40.11 Time for Complying with a Judgment or Order

r.40.11 **61.15**

A party must comply with a judgment or order for the payment of an amount of money (including costs) within 14 days of the date of the judgment or order, unless—
(a) the judgment or order specifies a different date for compliance (including specifying payment by instalments);
(b) any of these Rules specifies a different date for compliance; or
(c) the court has stayed the proceedings or judgment.
(Parts 12 and 14 specify different dates for complying with certain default judgments and judgments on admissions)

40.12 Correction of Errors in Judgments and Orders

r.40.12 **4.2, 37.53, 79.100** r.40.12(1) **42.27, 61.35**

(1) The court may at any time correct an accidental slip or omission in a judgment or order.
(2) A party may apply for a correction without notice.

40.13 Cases Where Court Gives Judgment Both on Claim and Counterclaim

r.40.13(2)–(3) **61.17**

(1) This rule applies where the court gives judgment for specified amounts both for the claimant on his claim and against the claimant on a counterclaim.
(2) If there is a balance in favour of one of the parties, it may order the party whose judgment is for the lesser amount to pay the balance.
(3) In a case to which this rule applies, the court may make a separate order as to costs against each party.

40.14 Judgment in Favour of Certain Part Owners Relating to the Detention of Goods

r.40.14 **61.26**

(1) In this rule 'part owner' means one of two or more persons who have an interest in the same goods.
(2) Where—
(a) a part owner makes a claim relating to the detention of the goods; and
(b) the claim is not based on a right to possession,
any judgment or order given or made in respect of the claim is to be for the payment of damages only, unless the claimant had the written authority of every other part owner of the goods to make the claim on his behalf as well as for himself.
(3) This rule applies notwithstanding anything in subsection (3) of section 3 of the Torts (Interference with Goods) Act 1977, but does not affect the remedies and jurisdiction mentioned in subsection (8) of that section.

II SALE OF LAND ETC. AND CONVEYANCING COUNSEL

40.15 Scope of This Section

(1) This Section—
(a) deals with the court's power to order the sale, mortgage, partition or exchange of land; and
(b) contains provisions about conveyancing counsel.
(Section 131 of the Supreme Court Act 1981 provides for the appointment of the conveyancing counsel of the Supreme Court)
(2) In this Section 'land' includes any interest in, or right over, land.

40.16 Power to Order Sale etc.

In any proceedings relating to land, the court may order the land, or part of it, to be—
(a) sold;
(b) mortgaged;
(c) exchanged; or
(d) partitioned.

40.17 Power to Order Delivery Up of Possession etc.

Where the court has made an order under rule 40.16, it may order any party to deliver up to the purchaser or any other person—
(a) possession of the land;
(b) receipt of rents or profits relating to it; or
(c) both.

40.18 Reference to Conveyancing Counsel

(1) The court may direct conveyancing counsel to investigate and prepare a report on the title of any land or to draft any document.
(2) The court may take the report on title into account when it decides the issue in question.
(Provisions dealing with the fees payable to conveyancing counsel are set out in the practice direction relating to Part 44 [PD 43–48, para. 8.8])

40.19 Party May Object to Report

(1) Any party to the proceedings may object to the report on title prepared by conveyancing counsel.
(2) Where there is an objection, the issue will be referred to a judge for determination.
(Part 23 contains general rules about making an application)

III DECLARATORY JUDGMENTS

40.20

r.40.20 **4.1, 4.18**

The court may make binding declarations whether or not any other remedy is claimed.

PD 40 Practice Direction — Accounts, Inquiries etc.

This practice direction supplements CPR Part 40

PD 40 **34.44, 61.28** [For commentary on a specific paragraph, please refer to the cross-references after the title of the paragraph.]

Accounts and Inquiries: General

para.1.1 **34.44, 61.29** para.1.2 **34.44, 61.29**

1.1 Where the court orders any account to be taken or any inquiry to be made, it may, by the same or a subsequent order, give directions as to the manner in which the account is to be taken and verified or the inquiry is to be conducted.

1.2 In particular, the court may direct that in taking an account, the relevant books of account shall be evidence of their contents but that any party may take such objections to the contents as he may think fit.

1.3 Any party may apply to the court in accordance with CPR Part 23 for directions as to the taking of an account or the conduct of an inquiry or for the variation of directions already made.

1.4 Every direction for the taking of an account or the making of an inquiry shall be numbered in the order so that, as far as possible, each distinct account and inquiry is given its own separate number.

Verifying the Account

para.2(1) **34.44, 61.29**

2. Subject to any order to the contrary:
   (1) the accounting party must make out his account and verify it by an affidavit or witness statement to which the account is exhibited,
   (2) the accounting party must file the account with the court and at the same time notify the other parties that he has done so and of the filing of any affidavit or witness statement verifying or supporting the account.

Objections

para.3.1 **34.44, 61.29**

3.1 Any party who wishes to contend:
   (a) that an accounting party has received more than the amount shown by the account to have been received, or
   (b) that the accounting party should be treated as having received more than he has actually received, or
   (c) that any item in the account is erroneous in respect of amount, or
   (d) that in any other respect the account is inaccurate,

   must, unless the court directs otherwise, give written notice to the accounting party of his objections.

3.2 The written notice referred to in paragraph 3.1 must, so far as the objecting party is able to do so:
   (a) state the amount by which it is contended that the account understates the amount received by the accounting party,
   (b) state the amount which it is contended that the accounting party should be treated as having received in addition to the amount he actually received,
   (c) specify the respects in which it is contended that the account is inaccurate, and
   (d) in each case, give the grounds on which the contention is made.

3.3 The contents of the written notice must, unless the notice contains a statement of truth, be verified by either an affidavit or a witness statement to which the notice is an exhibit.

(Part 22 and PD 22 contain provisions about statements of truth.)

Allowances

4. In taking any account all just allowances shall be made without any express direction to that effect.

Management of Proceedings

para.5 **34.44, 61.29**

5. The court may at any stage in the taking of an account or in the course of an inquiry direct a hearing in order to resolve an issue that has arisen and for that purpose may order that points of claim and points of defence be served and give any necessary directions.

Delay

6.1 If it appears to the court that there is undue delay in the taking of any account or the progress of any inquiry the court may require the accounting party or the party with the conduct of the inquiry, as the case may be, to explain the delay and may then make such order for the management of the proceedings (including a stay) and for costs as the circumstances may require.

6.2 The directions the court may give under para. 6.1 include a direction that the Official Solicitor take over the conduct of the proceedings and directions providing for the payment of the Official Solicitor's costs.

Distribution

7. Where some of the persons entitled to share in a fund are known but there is, or is likely to be, difficulty or delay in ascertaining other persons so entitled, the court may direct, or allow, immediate payment of their shares to the known persons without reserving any part of those shares to meet the subsequent costs of ascertaining the other persons.

Guardian's Accounts

8. The accounts of a person appointed guardian of the property of a child (defined in CPR, r. 21.1(2)) must be verified and approved in such manner as the court may direct.

Accounts and Inquiries to be Conducted before Master or District Judge

para.9 **34.44, 61.29**

9. Unless the court orders otherwise, an account or inquiry will be taken or made:
   (1) by a master or district judge, if the proceedings are in the High Court; and
   (2) by a district judge, if the proceedings are in a county court.

Advertisements

para.10 **34.44, 61.29**

10. The court may:
   (1) direct any necessary advertisement; and
   (2) fix the time within which the advertisement should require a reply.

Examination of Claims

para.11 **34.44**
para.11.1(1) **61.29**
para.11.1(3) **61.29**

11.1 Where the court orders an account of debts or other liabilities to be taken, it may direct any party, within a specified time, to:
   (1) examine the claims of persons claiming to be owed money out of the estate or fund in question.
   (2) determine, so far as he is able, which of them are valid; and
   (3) file written evidence:
      (a) stating his findings and his reasons for them; and
      (b) listing any other debts which are or may be owed out of the estate or fund.

11.2 Where the court orders an inquiry for next of kin or other unascertained claimants to an estate or fund, it may direct any party, within a specified time, to:
   (1) examine the claims that are made;
   (2) determine, so far as he is able, which of them are valid; and
   (3) file written evidence stating his findings and his reasons for them.

11.3 If the personal representatives or trustees concerned are not the parties directed by the court to examine claims, the court may direct them to join with the party directed to examine claims in producing the written evidence required by this rule.

Consideration of Claims by the Court

para.12 **34.44, 61.29**

12. For the purpose of considering a claim the court may:
(1) direct it to be investigated in any manner;
(2) direct the person making the claim to give further details of it; and
(3) direct that person to:
(a) file written evidence; or
(b) attend court to give evidence,
to support his claim.

Notice of Decision

para.13 **34.44**

13. If:
(1) the court has allowed or disallowed any claim or part of a claim; and
(2) the person making the claim was not present when the decision was made,
the court will serve on that person a notice informing him of its decision.

Interest on Debts

para.14 **34.44**

14. (1) Where an account of the debts of a deceased person is directed by any judgment, unless the deceased's estate is insolvent or the court orders otherwise, interest shall be allowed:
(a) on any debt which carries interest, at the rate it carries, and
(b) on any other debt, from the date of the judgment, at the rate payable on judgment debts at that date.
(2) Where interest on a debt is allowed under para. (1)(b), it shall be paid out of any assets of the estate which remain after payment of:
(a) any costs of the proceedings directed to be paid out of the estate;
(b) all the debts which have been established; and
(c) the interest on such of those debts as by law carry interest.
(3) For the purpose of this rule:
(a) 'debt' includes funeral, testamentary or administration expenses; and
(b) in relation to any expenses incurred after the judgment, para. (1)(b) applies as if, instead of the date of the judgment, it referred to the date when the expenses became payable.

Interest on Legacies

para.15 **34.44**

15. Where an account of legacies is directed by any judgment, then, subject to:
(a) any directions contained in the will or codicil in question; and
(b) any order made by the court,
interest shall be allowed on each legacy at the basic rate payable for the time being on funds in court or at such other rate as the court shall direct, beginning one year after the testator's death.

PD 40B Practice Direction — Judgments and Orders

This practice direction supplements CPR Part 40

[For commentary on a specific paragraph, please refer to the cross-references after the title of the paragraph.]

Drawing Up and Filing of Judgments and Orders

1.1 Rule 40.2 sets out the standard requirements for judgments and orders and rule 40.3 deals with how judgments and orders should be drawn up.

1.2 A party who has been ordered or given permission to draw up an order must file it for sealing within seven days of being ordered or permitted to do so.[1] If he falls to do so, any other party may draw it up and file it.[2]

1.3 If the court directs that a judgment or order which is being drawn up by a party must be checked by the court before it is sealed, the party responsible must file the draft within seven days of the date the order was made with a request that the draft be checked before it is sealed.

1.4 If the court directs the parties to file an agreed statement of terms of an order which the court is to draw up,[3] the parties must do so no later than seven days from the date the order was made, unless the court directs otherwise.

1.5 If the court requires the terms of an order which is being drawn up by the court to be agreed by the parties the court may direct that a copy of the draft order is to be sent to all the parties:

(1) for their agreement to be endorsed on it and returned to the court before the order is sealed, or

(2) with notice of an appointment to attend before the court to agree the terms of the order.

Preparation of Deeds or Documents under an Order

2.1 Where a judgment or order directs any deed or document to be prepared, executed or signed, the order will state:

(1) the person who is to prepare the deed or document, and

(2) if the deed or document is to be approved, the person who is to approve it.

2.2 If the parties are unable to agree the form of the deed or document, any party may apply in accordance with Part 23 for the form of the deed or document to be settled.

2.3 In such case the judge may:

(1) settle the deed or document himself, or

(2) refer it to

(a) a master, or

(b) a district judge, or

(c) a conveyancing counsel of the Supreme Court to settle.

(See also PD 40D.)

Consent Orders

para.3.4 **61.11** para.3.5 **61.14, 61.31**

3.1 Rule 40.6(3) sets out the types of consent judgments and orders which may be entered and sealed by a court officer. The court officer may do so in those cases provided that:

(1) none of the parties is a litigant in person, and

(2) the approval of the court is not required by the Rules, a practice direction or any enactment.[4]

3.2 If a consent order filed for sealing appears to be unclear or incorrect the court officer may refer it to a judge for consideration.[5]

---

[1] Rule 40.3(3)(a)

[2] Rule 40.3(3)(b)

[3] Rule 40.3(2)(b)

[4] Rule 40.6(2)

[5] Rule 3.2

3.3 Where a consent judgment or order does not come within the provisions of rule 40.6(2):
(1) an application notice requesting a judgment or order in the agreed terms should be filed with the draft judgment or order to be entered or sealed, and
(2) the draft judgment or order must be drawn so that the judge's name and judicial title can be inserted.

3.4 A consent judgment or order must:
(1) be drawn up in the terms agreed,
(2) bear on it the words 'By Consent', and
(3) be signed by
(a) solicitors or counsel acting for each of the parties to the order, or
(b) where a party is a litigant in person, the litigant.[6]

3.5 Where the parties draw up a consent order in the form of a stay of proceedings on agreed terms, disposing of the proceedings,[7] and where the terms are recorded in a schedule to the order, any direction for:
(1) payment of money out of court, or
(2) payment and assessment of costs
should be contained in the body of the order and not in the schedule.

Correction of Errors in Judgments and Orders

paras.4.1–4.5 **61.35**

4.1 Where a judgment or order contains an accidental slip or omission a party may apply for it to be corrected.[8]

4.2 The application notice (which may be an informal document such as a letter) should describe the error and set out the correction required. An application may be dealt with without a hearing:
(1) where the applicant so requests,
(2) with the consent of the parties, or
(3) where the court does not consider that a hearing would be appropriate.

4.3 The judge may deal with the application without notice if the slip or omission is obvious or may direct notice of the application to be given to the other party or parties.

4.4 If the application is opposed it should, if practicable, be listed for hearing before the judge who gave the judgment or made the order.

4.5 The court has an inherent power to vary its own orders to make the meaning and intention of the court clear.

Adjustment of Final Judgment Figure in Respect of Compensation Recovery Payments

para.5.1 **61.18**

5.1 In a final judgment[9] where some or all of the damages awarded:
(2) fall under the heads of damage set out in column 1 of sch. 2 to the Social Security (Recovery of Benefits) Act 1997 in respect of recoverable benefits received by the claimant set out in column 2 of that schedule and
(3) where the defendant has paid to the Secretary of State the recoverable benefits in accordance with the certificate of recoverable benefits,
there should be stated in a preamble to the judgment or order the amount awarded under each head of damage and the amount by which it has been reduced in accordance with s. 8 of and sch. 2 to the Social Security (Recovery of Benefits) Act 1997.

5.2 The judgment or order should then provide for entry of judgment and payment of the balance.

[6] Rule 40.6(7)
[7] Rule 40.6(3)(b)(ii)
[8] Rule [40.12]. [The text issued by the Department for Constitutional Affairs mistakenly refers to r. 40.10.]
[9] In this paragraph final 'judgment' includes any order to pay a sum of money, a final award of damages and an assessment of damages.

Adjustment of Final Judgment Figure in Respect of an Interim Payment

para.6 **36.19**

6.1 In a final judgment[10] where an interim payment has previously been made which is less than the total amount awarded by the judge, the judgment or order should set out in a preamble:
(1) the total amount awarded by the judge, and
(2) the amount and date of the interim payment(s).

6.2 The total amount awarded by the judge should then be reduced by the total amount of any interim payments, and the judgment or order should then provide for entry of judgment and payment of the balance.

6.3 In a final judgment where an interim payment has previously been made which is more than the total amount awarded by the judge, the judgment or order should set out in a preamble:
(1) the total amount awarded by the judge, and
(2) the amount and date of the interim payment(s).

6.4 An order should then be made for repayment, reimbursement, variation or discharge under rule 25.8(2) and for interest on an overpayment under rule 25.8(5).

Statement as to Service of a Claim Form

7.1 Where a party to proceedings which have gone to trial requires a statement to be included in the judgment as to where, and by what means the claim form issued in those proceedings was served, application should made to the trial judge when judgment is given.

7.2 If the judge so orders, the statement will be included in a preamble to the judgment as entered.

Orders Requiring an Act to be Done

para.8.1 **61.9** para.8.2 **46.28, 61.9**

8.1 An order which requires an act to be done (other than a judgment or order for the payment of an amount of money) must specify the time within which the act should be done.

8.2 The consequences of failure to do an act within the time specified may be set out in the order. In this case the wording of the following examples suitably adapted must be used:
(1) Unless the [claimant] [defendant] serves his list of documents by 4.00 p.m. on Friday, January 22, 1999 his [claim] [defence] will be struck out and judgment entered for the [defendant] [claimant], or
(2) Unless the [claimant] [defendant] serves his list of documents within 14 days of service of this order his [claim] [defence] will be struck out and judgment entered for the [defendant] [claimant].

Example (1) should be used wherever possible.

Non-compliance with a Judgment or Order

para.9.1 **37.42, 61.10** para.9.3 **61.10**

9.1 An order which restrains a party from doing an act or requires an act to be done should, if disobedience is to be dealt with by an application to bring contempt of court proceedings, have a penal notice endorsed on it as follows:

'If you the within-named [ ] do not comply with this order you may be held to be in contempt of court and imprisoned or fined, or [in the case of a company or corporation] your assets may be seized.'

9.2 The provisions of paragraph [9.1*] above also apply to an order which contains an undertaking by a party to do or not do an act, subject to paragraph 9.3 below.

9.3 The court has the power to decline to:
(1) accept an undertaking, and
(2) deal with disobedience in respect of an undertaking by contempt of court proceedings,
unless the party giving the undertaking has made a signed statement to the effect that he understands the terms of his undertaking and the consequences of failure to comply with it.

[10] As in note 9 above.

[* The text issued by the Department for Constitutional Affairs mistakenly refers to para. 8.1.]

9.4 The statement may be endorsed on the [court copy of the] order containing the undertaking or may be filed in a separate document such as a letter.

Foreign Currency

para.10 **61.16, 61.27**

10. Where judgment is ordered to be entered in a foreign currency, the order should be in the following form:

'It is ordered that the defendant pay the claimant (*state the sum in the foreign currency)* or the sterling equivalent at the time of payment.'

Costs

11.1 Attention is drawn to the costs practice direction and, in particular, to the court's power to make a summary assessment of costs and the provisions relating to interest in detailed assessment proceedings.

11.2 Attention is also drawn to r. 44.13(1) which provides that if an order makes no mention of costs, none are payable in respect of the proceedings to which it relates.

Judgments Paid by Instalments

para.12 **61.15**

12. Where a judgment is to be paid by instalments, the judgment should set out:
(1) the total amount of the judgment,
(2) the amount of each instalment,
(3) the number of instalments and the date on which each is to be paid, and
(4) to whom the instalments should be paid.

Order to Make an Order of the House of Lords an Order of the High Court

13.1 Application may be made in accordance with Part 23 for an order to make an order of the House of Lords an order of the High Court. The application should be made to the procedural judge of the Division, District Registry or court in which the proceedings are taking place and may be made without notice unless the court directs otherwise.

13.2 The application must be supported by the following evidence:
(1) details of the order which was the subject of the appeal to the House of Lords,
(2) details of the order of the House of Lords, with a copy annexed, and
(3) a copy annexed of the certificate of the Clerk of Parliaments of the assessment of the costs of the appeal to the House of Lords in the sum of £ ....

13.3 The order to make an order of the House of Lords an order of the High Court should be in form PF 68.

Examples of Forms of Trial Judgment

14.1 The following general forms may be used:
(1) judgment after trial before judge without jury — form No. 45,
(2) judgment after trial before judge with jury — form No. 46,
(3) judgment after trial before a Master or district judge — form No. 47,
(4) judgment after trial before a judge of the Technology and Construction court — form No. 47 but with any necessary modifications.

14.2 A trial judgment should, in addition to the matters set out in paragraphs 5, 6 and 7 above, have the following matters set out in a preamble:
(1) the questions put to a jury and their answers to those questions,
(2) the findings of a jury and whether unanimous or by a majority,
(3) any order made during the course of the trial concerning the use of evidence,
(4) any matters that were agreed between the parties prior to or during the course of the trial in respect of
(a) liability,
(b) contribution,
(c) the amount of the damages or part of the damages, and
(5) the findings of the judge in respect of each head of damage in a personal injury case.

14.3 Form No. 49 should be used for a trial judgment against an estate.
The forms referred to in this practice direction are listed in PD 4.

14.4 On any application or appeal concerning:
(i) a committal order;
(ii) a refusal to grant habeas corpus; or
(iii) a secure accommodation order made under s. 25 of the Children Act 1998,
if the court ordering the release of the person concludes that his Convention rights have been infringed by the making of the order to which the application or appeal relates, the judgment or order should so state. If the court does not do so, that failure will not prevent another court from deciding the matter.

For Information About

(1) Orders for provisional damages: see Part 41 and PD 41.
(2) Orders in respect of children and patients: see Part [21 and PD 21*].
(3) Orders containing directions for payment of money out of court: see Parts 36 and 37 and PD 36 and 37.
(4) Structured settlement orders: see the separate practice direction supplementing Part 40.†
(5) Taking accounts and conducting inquiries under a judgment or order: see PD 40.

[* The text issued by the Department for Constitutional Affairs mistakenly refers to Part 22.
† Structured settlement orders have been replaced by orders for periodical payments under the Damages Act 1996, for which the relevant practice direction is PD 41B. The practice direction relating to structured settlements is no longer in force.]

PD 40D Practice Direction — 1 Court's Powers in Relation to Land 2 Conveyancing Counsel of the Court

This practice direction supplements CPR Part 40

PART 1 COURT'S POWERS IN RELATION TO LAND

Application to the Court Where Land Subject to an Encumbrance

1.1 In this paragraph 'encumbrance' has the same meaning as it has in s. 205(1) of the Law of Property Act 1925.

1.2 Where land subject to any encumbrance is sold or exchanged any party to the sale or exchange may apply to the court for a direction under s. 50 of the Law of Property Act 1925 (discharge of encumbrances by the court on sales or exchanges).

1.3 The directions a court may give on such an application include a direction for the payment into court of a sum of money that the court considers sufficient to meet:

(1) the value of the encumbrance; and

(2) further costs, expenses and interest that may become due on or in respect of the encumbrance.

(Section 50(1) of the Law of Property Act 1925 contains provisions relating to the calculation of these amounts.)

1.4 Where a payment into court has been made in accordance with a direction under s. 50(1) the court may:

(1) declare the land to be freed from the encumbrance; and

(2) make any order it considers appropriate for giving effect to an order made under r. 40.16 or relating to the money in court and the income thereof.

1.5 An application under s. 50 should:

(1) if made in existing proceedings, be made in accordance with CPR, Part 23;

(2) otherwise, be made by claim form under CPR, Part 8.

Directions about the Sale etc.

2 Where the court has made an order under r. 40.16 it may give any other directions it considers appropriate for giving effect to the order. In particular the court may give directions:

(1) appointing a party or other person to conduct the sale;

(2) for obtaining evidence of the value of the land;

(3) as to the manner of sale;

(4) settling the particulars and conditions of the sale;

(5) fixing a minimum or reserve price;

(6) as to the fees and expenses to be allowed to an auctioneer or estate agent;

(7) for the purchase money to be paid

(a) into court;

(b) to trustees; or

(c) to any other person;

(8) for the result of a sale to be certified;

(9) under r. 40.18.

Application for Permission to Bid

3.1 Where:

(1) the court has made an order under r. 40.16 for land to be sold; and

(2) a party wishes to bid for land,

he should apply to the court for permission to do so.

3.2 An application for permission to bid must be made before the sale takes place.

3.3 If the court gives permission to all the parties to bid, it may appoint an independent person to conduct the sale.

3.4 'Bid' in this paragraph includes submitting a tender or other offer to buy.

Certifying Sale Result

4.1 If:

(1) the court has directed the purchase money to be paid into court; or

(2) the court has directed that the result of the sale be certified,

the result of the sale must be certified by the person having conduct of the sale.

4.2 Unless the court directs otherwise, the certificate must give details of:

(1) the amount of the purchase price;

(2) the amount of the fees and expenses payable to any auctioneer or estate agent;

(3) the amount of any other expenses of the sale;

(4) the net amount received in respect of the sale;

and must be verified by a statement of truth.

(Part 22 sets out requirements about statements of truth.)

4.3 The certificate must be filed:

(1) if the proceedings are being dealt with in the Royal Courts of Justice, in Chancery Chambers;

(2) if the proceedings are being dealt with anywhere else, in the court where the proceedings are being dealt with.

Fees and Expenses of Auctioneers and Estate Agents

5.1 (1) Where the court has ordered the sale of land under r. 40.16, auctioneer's and estate agent's charges may, unless the court orders otherwise, include:

(a) commission;

(b) fees for valuation of the land;

(c) charges for advertising the land;

(2) The court's authorisation is required for charges relating to surveys.

5.2 If the total amount of the auctioneer's and estate agent's charges authorised under para. 5.1(1):

(1) does not exceed 2.5 per cent of the sale price; and

(2) does not exceed the rate of commission that that agent would normally charge on a sole agency basis,

the charges may, unless the court orders otherwise and subject to para. 5.3(3) and (4), be met by deduction of the amount of the charges from the proceeds of sale without the need for any further authorisation from the court.

5.3 If:

(1) a charge made by an auctioneer or estate agent (whether in respect of fees or expenses or both) is not authorised under para. 5.1(1);

(2) the total amount of the charges so authorised exceeds the limits set out in para. 5.2;

(3) the land is sold in lots or by valuation; or

(4) the sale is of investment property, business property or farm property,

an application must be made to the court for approval of the fees and expenses to be allowed.

5.4 An application under para. 5.3 may be made by any party or, if he is not a party, by the person having conduct of the sale, and may be made either before or after the sale has taken place.

PART 2 CONVEYANCING COUNSEL OF THE COURT

Reference to Conveyancing Counsel

6.1 When the court refers a matter under r. 40.18, the court may specify a particular conveyancing counsel.

6.2 If the court does not specify a particular conveyancing counsel, references will be distributed among conveyancing counsel in accordance with arrangements made by the Chief Chancery Master.

6.3 Notice of every reference under r. 40.18 must be given to the Chief Chancery Master.

6.4 The court will send a copy of the order, together with all other necessary documents, to conveyancing counsel.

6.5 A court order sent to conveyancing counsel under para. 6.4 will be sufficient authority for him to prepare his report or draft the document.

6.6 (1) An objection under r. 40.19 to a report on title prepared by conveyancing counsel must be made by application notice.

(2) The application notice must state:

(a) the matters the applicant objects to; and

(b) the reason for the objection.

PD 40E Practice Direction — Reserved Judgments

This practice direction supplements Part 40.

Scope and Interpretation

para.1.1 **61.28**

1.1 This practice direction applies to all judgments given in:
(a) the Court of Appeal (Civil Division); and
(b) the Queen's Bench Division and Chancery Division of the High Court at the Royal Courts of Justice,
including judgments given by masters, registrars and costs judges.

1.2 In this practice direction:
(a) 'relevant court office' means the office of the court in which judgment is to be given; and
(b) 'working day' means any day on which the relevant court office is open.

Availability of Reserved Judgments before Handing Down

paras.2.3–2.4 **61.28**

2.1 Where judgment is to be reserved the judge (or presiding judge) may, at the conclusion of the hearing, invite the views of the parties' legal representatives as to the arrangements to be made for the handing down of the judgment.

2.2 Unless the court directs otherwise, the following provisions of this paragraph apply where the judge or presiding judge is satisfied that the judgment will attract no special degree of confidentiality or sensitivity.

2.3 The court will provide a copy of the draft judgment to the parties' legal representatives by 4 p.m. on the second working day before handing down, or at such other time as the court may direct.

2.4 A copy of the draft judgment may be shown, in confidence, to the parties provided that:
(a) neither the judgment nor its substance is disclosed to any other person or used in the public domain; and
(b) no action is taken (other than internally) in response to the judgment, before the judgment is handed down.

2.5 Any breach of the obligation of confidentiality prescribed by para. 2.4 may be treated as contempt of court.

2.6 The case will be listed for judgment, and the judgment handed down at the appropriate time.

Attendance at Handing Down

paras.3.1–3.2 **61.28**

3.1 Where any consequential orders are agreed, the parties' advocates need not attend on the handing down.

3.2 Where an advocate does attend the court may, if it considers such attendance was unnecessary, disallow the costs of the attendance.

3.3 If the parties do not indicate that they intend to attend, the judgment may be handed down by a single member of the court.

Agreed Orders Following Judgment

para.4.1 **61.28**

4.1 Unless the parties or their legal representatives are told otherwise when the draft judgment is circulated, the parties must, in respect of any draft agreed order:
(a) fax or email a copy to the clerk to the judge or presiding judge (together with any proposed corrections or amendments to the draft judgment); and
(b) file four copies (with completed backsheets) in the relevant court office, by 12 noon on the working day before handing down.

4.2 A copy of a draft order must bear the case reference, the date of handing down and the name of the judge or presiding judge.

Corrections to the Draft Judgment

para.5 **61.28**

5 Unless the parties or their legal representatives are told otherwise when the draft judgment is circulated, any proposed corrections to the draft judgment should be sent to the clerk to the judge who prepared the draft with a copy to any other party.

(Paragraphs 15.12 to 15.21 of PD 52 contain provision about the handing down of reserved judgments in appeals.)

CPR Part 41 Damages

[For commentary on a specific rule, please refer to the cross-references after the title of the rule.]

I PROCEEDINGS TO WHICH SECTION 32A OF THE SUPREME COURT ACT 1981 OR SECTION 51 OF THE COUNTY COURTS ACT 1984 APPLIES

41.1 Application and Definitions

(1) This Part applies to proceedings to which SCA s. 32A or CCA s. 51 applies.
(2) In this Part—
 (a) 'SCA s. 32A' means section 32A of the Supreme Court Act 1981;
 (b) 'CCA s. 51' means section 51 of the County Courts Act 1984; and
 (c) 'award of provisional damages' means an award of damages for personal injuries under which
  (i) damages are assessed on the assumption referred to in SCA s. 32A or CCA s. 51 that the injured person will not develop the disease or suffer the deterioration; and
  (ii) the injured person is entitled to apply for further damages at a future date if he develops the disease or suffers the deterioration.

41.2 Order for an Award of Provisional Damages

r.41.2(1)(a) **61.21**

(1) The court may make an order for an award of provisional damages if—
 (a) the particulars of claim include a claim for provisional damages; and
 (b) the court is satisfied that SCA s. 32A or CCA s. 51 applies.

(Rule 16.4(1)(d) sets out what must be included in the particulars of claim where the claimant is claiming provisional damages)

(2) An order for an award of provisional damages—
 (a) must specify the disease or type of deterioration in respect of which an application may be made at a future date;
 (b) must specify the period within which such an application may be made; and
 (c) may be made in respect of more than one disease or type of deterioration and may, in respect of each disease or type of deterioration, specify a different period within which a subsequent application may be made.
(3) The claimant may make more than one application to extend the period specified under paragraph (2)(b) or (2)(c).

41.3 Application for Further Damages

r.41.3(6) **61.24**

(1) The claimant may not make an application for further damages after the end of the period specified under rule 41.2(2), or such period as extended by the court.

(2) Only one application for further damages may be made in respect of each disease or type of deterioration specified in the award of provisional damages.
(3) The claimant must give at least 28 days' written notice to the defendant of his intention to apply for further damages.
(4) If the claimant knows—
   (a) that the defendant is insured in respect of the claim; and
   (b) the identity of the defendant's insurers,
   he must also give at least 28 days' written notice to the insurers.
(5) Within 21 days after the end of the 28 day notice period referred to in paragraphs (3) and (4), the claimant must apply for directions.

II PERIODICAL PAYMENTS UNDER THE DAMAGES ACT 1996

41.4 Scope and Interpretation

(1) This Section of this Part contains rules about the exercise of the court's powers under section 2(1) of the 1996 Act to order that all or part of an award of damages in respect of personal injury is to take the form of periodical payments.
(2) In this Section—
   (a) 'the 1996 Act' means the Damages Act 1996;
   (b) 'damages' means damages for future pecuniary loss; and
   (c) 'periodical payments' means periodical payments under section 2(1) of the 1996 Act.

41.5 Statement of Case

r.41.5 **61.25**

(1) In a claim for damages for personal injury, each party in its statement of case may state whether it considers periodical payments or a lump sum is the more appropriate form for all or part of an award of damages and where such statement is given must provide relevant particulars of the circumstances which are relied on.
(2) Where a statement under paragraph (1) is not given, the court may order a party to make such a statement.
(3) Where the court considers that a statement of case contains insufficient particulars under paragraph (1), the court may order a party to provide such further particulars as it considers appropriate.

41.6 Court's Indication to Parties

r.41.6 **61.25**

The court shall consider and indicate to the parties as soon as practicable whether periodical payments or a lump sum is likely to be the more appropriate form for all or part of an award of damages.

41.7 Factors to Be Taken into Account

r.41.7 **61.25**

When considering—
(a) its indication as to whether periodical payments or a lump sum is likely to be the more appropriate form for all or part of an award of damages under rule 41.6; or
(b) whether to make an order under section 2(1)(a) of the 1996 Act,
the court shall have regard to all the circumstances of the case and in particular the form of award which best meets the claimant's needs, having regard to the factors set out in the practice direction.

41.8 The Award

r.41.8 **61.25, 64.12** r.41.8(1)–(4) **61.25**

(1) Where the court awards damages in the form of periodical payments, the order must specify—
   (a) the annual amount awarded, how each payment is to be made during the year and at what intervals;
   (b) the amount awarded for future—
      (i) loss of earnings and other income; and
      (ii) care and medical costs and other recurring or capital costs;
   (c) that the claimant's annual future pecuniary losses, as assessed by the court, are to be paid for the duration of the claimant's life, or such other period as the court orders; and

(d) that the amount of the payments shall vary annually by reference to the retail prices index, unless the court orders otherwise under section 2(9) of the 1996 Act.

(2) Where the court orders that any part of the award shall continue after the claimant's death, for the benefit of the claimant's dependants, the order must also specify the relevant amount and duration of the payments and how each payment is to be made during the year and at what intervals.

(3) Where an amount awarded under paragraph (1)(b) is to increase or decrease on a certain date, the order must also specify—

(a) the date on which the increase or decrease will take effect; and

(b) the amount of the increase or decrease at current value.

(4) Where damages for substantial capital purchases are awarded under paragraph (1)(b)(ii), the order must also specify—

(a) the amount of the payments at current value;

(b) when the payments are to be made; and

(c) that the amount of the payments shall be adjusted by reference to the retail prices index, unless the court orders otherwise under section 2(9) of the 1996 Act.

41.9 Continuity of Payment

r.41.9 **61.25, 64.12**

(1) An order for periodical payments shall specify that the payments must be funded in accordance with section 2(4) of the 1996 Act, unless the court orders an alternative method of funding.

(2) Before ordering an alternative method of funding, the court must be satisfied that—

(a) the continuity of payment under the order is reasonably secure; and

(b) the criteria set out in the practice direction are met.

(3) An order under paragraph (2) must specify the alternative method of funding.

41.10 Assignment or Charge

r.41.10 **61.25**

Where the court under section 2(6)(a) of the 1996 Act is satisfied that special circumstances make an assignment or charge of periodical payments necessary, it shall, in deciding whether or not to approve the assignment or charge, also have regard to the factors set out in the practice direction.

PD 41 Practice Direction — Provisional Damages

This practice direction supplements CPR Part 41

PD 41 **61.23** [For commentary on a specific paragraph, please refer to the cross-references after the title of the paragraph.]

Claims for Provisional Damages

1.1 CPR Part 16 and PD 16 set out information which must be included in the particulars of claim if a claim for provisional damages is made.

Judgment for an Award of Provisional Damages

2.1 When giving judgment at trial the judge will:
(1) specify the disease or type of deterioration, or diseases or types of deterioration, which
(a) for the purpose of the award of immediate damages it has been assumed will not occur, and
(b) will entitle the claimant to further damages if it or they do occur at a future date,
(2) give an award of immediate damages,
(3) specify the period or periods within which an application for further damages may be made in respect of each disease or type of deterioration, and
(4) direct what documents are to be filed and preserved as the case file in support of any application for further damages.

2.2 The claimant may make an application or applications to extend the periods referred to in paragraph 2.1(3) above.[1]

2.3 A period specified under paragraph 2.1(3) may be expressed as being for the duration of the life of the claimant.

2.4 The documents to be preserved as the case file ('the case file documents') referred to in paragraph 2.1(4) will be set out in a schedule to the judgment as entered.

2.5 Causation of any further damages within the scope of the order shall be determined when any application for further damages is made.

2.6 A form for a provisional damages judgment is set out in the Annex to this practice direction.

The Case File

para.3.2 **61.23**

3.1 The case file documents must be preserved until the expiry of the period or periods specified or of any extension of them.

3.2 The case file documents will normally include:
(1) the judgment as entered,
(2) the statements of case,
(3) a transcript of the judge's oral judgment,
(4) all medical reports relied on, and
(5) a transcript of any parts of the claimant's own evidence which the judge considers necessary.

3.3 The associate/court clerk will:
(1) ensure that the case file documents are provided by the parties where necessary and filed on the court file,
(2) endorse the court file
(a) to the effect that it contains the case file documents, and
(b) with the period during which the case file documents must be preserved, and
(3) preserve the case file documents in the court office where the proceedings took place.

3.4 Any subsequent order:
(1) extending the period within which an application for further damages may be made, or

[1] See CPR rule 41.2(3).

Civil Procedure Rules & Practice Directions

(2) of the Court of Appeal discharging or varying the provisions of the original judgment or of any subsequent order under sub-paragraph (1) above,

will become one of the case file documents and must be preserved accordingly and any variation of the period within which an application for further damages may be made should be endorsed on the court file containing the case file documents.

3.5 On an application to extend the periods referred to in paragraph 2.1(3) above a current medical report should be filed.

3.6 Legal representatives are reminded that it is their duty to preserve their own case file.

Consent Orders

paras.4–5 **61.23**

4.1 An application to give effect to a consent order for provisional damages should be made in accordance with CPR Part 23. If the claimant is a child or patient[2] the approval of the court must also be sought and the application for approval will normally be dealt with at a hearing.

4.2 The order should be in the form of a consent judgment and should contain;

(1) the matters set out in paragraph 2.1(1) to (3) above, and

(2) a direction as to the documents to be preserved as the case file documents, which will normally be

(a) the consent judgment,

(b) any statements of case,

(c) an agreed statement of facts, and

(d) any agreed medical report(s).

4.3 The claimant or his legal representative must lodge the case file documents in the court office where the proceedings are taking place for inclusion in the court file. The court file should be endorsed as in paragraph 3.3(2) above, and the case file documents preserved as in paragraph 13(3) above.

Default Judgment

para.5.1 **21.3**, **22.2**

5.1 Where a defendant:

(1) fails to file an acknowledgment of service in accordance with CPR Part 10, and

(2) fails to file a defence in accordance with CPR Part 15,

within the time specified for doing so, the claimant may not, unless he abandons his claim for provisional damages, enter judgment in default but should make an application in accordance with CPR Part 23 for directions.

5.2 The Master or district judge will normally direct the following issues to be decided:

(1) whether the claim is an appropriate one for an award of provisional damages and if so, on what terms, and

(2) the amount of immediate damages.

5.3 If the judge makes an award of provisional damages, the provisions of paragraph 3 above apply.

ANNEX

Example of an Award of Provisional Damages after Trial

Title of proceedings

THIS CLAIM having been tried before [*title and name of judge*] without a jury at [the Royal Courts of Justice *or as may be*] and [*title and name of judge*] having ordered that judgment as set out below be entered for the claimant

IT IS ORDERED:

(1) that the defendant pay the claimant by way of immediate damages the sum of £.............. (being (i) £.............. for special damages and £.............. [agreed interest] [interest at the rate of .... from .... to .... (ii) £.............. for general damages and £.............. [agreed interest] [interest at the rate of 2% from .... to ....] and (iii) £.............. for loss of future earnings and/or earning capacity) on the assumption that the claimant would not

[2] See CPR Part 21 for the definitions of child and patient.

at a future date as a result of the act or omission giving rise to the claim develop the following disease/type of deterioration namely [set out disease or type of deterioration] [*set out disease or type of deterioration*]

(2) that if the claimant at a further date does develop that [disease] [type of deterioration] he should be entitled to apply for further damages provided that the application is made on or before [*set out period*]

(3) that the documents set out in the schedule to this order be filed on the court file and preserved as the case file until the expiry of the period set out in paragraph (2) above or of any extension of that period which has been ordered

(4) (costs)

Schedule

[*list documents referred to in paragraph (3)*]

PD 41B Practice Direction — Periodical Payments under the Damages Act 1996

This practice direction supplements Part 41

Factors to Be Taken into Account (Rule 41.7)

para.1 **61.25**

1. The factors which the court shall have regard to under r. 41.7 include:
   (1) the scale of the annual payments taking into account any deduction for contributory negligence;
   (2) the form of award preferred by the claimant including:
      (a) the reasons for the claimant's preference; and
      (b) the nature of any financial advice received by the claimant when considering the form of award; and
   (3) the form of award preferred by the defendant including the reasons for the defendant's preference.

The Award (Rule 41.8)

para.2 **61.25**

2.1 An order may be made under r. 41.8(2) where a dependant would have had a claim under the Fatal Accidents Act 1976, s. 1, if the claimant had died at the time of the accident.

2.2 Examples of circumstances which might lead the court to order an increase or decrease under r. 41.8(3) are where the court determines that:
   (1) the claimant's condition will change leading to an increase or reduction in his or her need to incur care, medical or other recurring or capital costs;
   (2) gratuitous carers will no longer continue to provide care;
   (3) the claimant's educational circumstances will change;
   (4) the claimant would have received a promotional increase in pay;
   (5) the claimant will cease earning.

Continuity of Payment (Rule 41.9)

para.3 **61.25**

3. Before ordering an alternative method of funding under r. 41.9(1), the court must be satisfied that the following criteria are met:
   (1) that a method of funding provided for under s. 2(4) of the 1996 Act is not possible or there are good reasons to justify an alternative method of funding;
   (2) that the proposed method of funding can be maintained for the duration of the award or for the proposed duration of the method of funding; and
   (3) that the proposed method of funding will meet the level of payment ordered by the court.

Assignment or Charge (Rule 41.10)

para.4 **61.25**

4. The factors which the court shall have regard to under r. 41.10 include:
   (1) whether the capitalised value of the assignment or charge represents value for money;
   (2) whether the assignment or charge is in the claimant's best interests, taking into account whether these interests can be met in some other way; and
   (3) how the claimant will be financially supported following the assignment or charge.

Variation

5. The Damages (Variation of Periodical Payments) Order 2005 (SI 2005/841) sets out provisions which enable the court in certain circumstances to provide in an order for periodical payments that it may be varied.

Settlement

para.6 **61.25**

6. Where the parties settle a claim to which r. 36.2A applies, any consent order, whether made under r. 40.6 or on an application under Part 23, must satisfy the requirements of rr. 41.8 and 41.9.

Settlement or Compromise on Behalf of Child or Patient

7. Where a claim for damages for personal injury is made by or on behalf of a child or patient and is settled prior to the start of proceedings or before trial, the provisions of PD 21 must be complied with.

CPR Part 42 Change of Solicitor

Part 42 **21.3, 22.2** [For commentary on a specific rule, please refer to the cross-references after the title of the rule.]

42.1 Solicitor Acting for a Party

r.42.1 **21.3, 22.3**

Where the address for service of a party is the business address of his solicitor, the solicitor will be considered to be acting for that party until the provisions of this Part have been complied with.

(Part 6 contains provisions about the address for service)

42.2 Change of Solicitor — Duty to Give Notice

r.42.2 **22.4**
r.42.2(5) **21.3, 22.3**
r.42.2(6)(a) **22.5**
r.42.2(6)(b) **22.5**
r.42.2(6)(b)(i) **22.5**

(1) This rule applies where—
 (a) a party for whom a solicitor is acting wants to change his solicitor;
 (b) a party, after having conducted the claim in person, appoints a solicitor to act on his behalf (except where the solicitor is appointed only to act as an advocate for a hearing); or
 (c) a party, after having conducted the claim by a solicitor, intends to act in person.
(2) Where this rule applies, the party or his solicitor (where one is acting) must—
 (a) file notice of the change; and
 (b) serve notice of the change on every other party and, where paragraph (1)(a) or (c) applies, on the former solicitor.
(3) The notice must state the party's new address for service.
(4) The notice filed at court must state that notice has been served as required by paragraph (2)(b).
(5) Subject to paragraph (6), where a party has changed his solicitor or intends to act in person, the former solicitor will be considered to be the party's solicitor unless and until—
 (a) notice is filed and served in accordance with paragraph (2); or
 (b) the court makes an order under rule 42.3 and the order is served as required by paragraph (3) of that rule.
(6) Where the certificate of a LSC funded client or an assisted person is revoked or discharged—
 (a) the solicitor who acted for that person will cease to be the solicitor acting in the case as soon as his retainer is determined—
  (i) under regulation 4 of the Community Legal Service (Costs) Regulations 2000; or
  (ii) under regulation 83 of the Civil Legal Aid (General) Regulations 1989; and
 (b) if that person wishes to continue—
  (i) where he appoints a solicitor to act on his behalf, paragraph (2) will apply as if he had previously conducted the claim in person; and
  (ii) where he wants to act in person, he must give an address for service.

(Rule 6.5 deals with a party's address for service)

(' LSC funded client' and 'assisted person' are defined in rule 43.2)

(7) 'Certificate' in paragraph (6) means—
 (a) in the case of a LSC funded client, a certificate issued under the Funding Code (approved under section 9 of the Access to Justice Act 1999), or
 (b) in the case of an assisted person, a certificate within the meaning of the Civil Legal Aid (General) Regulations 1989.

42.3 Order That a Solicitor Has Ceased to Act

r.42.3 **22.6** r.42.3(2)–(3) **22.6**

(1) A solicitor may apply for an order declaring that he has ceased to be the solicitor acting for a party.
(2) Where an application is made under this rule—
  (a) notice of the application must be given to the party for whom the solicitor is acting, unless the court directs otherwise; and
  (b) the application must be supported by evidence.
(3) Where the court makes an order that a solicitor has ceased to act—
  (a) a copy of the order must be served on every party to the proceedings; and
  (b) if it is served by a party or the solicitor, the party or the solicitor (as the case may be) must file a certificate of service.

42.4 Removal of Solicitor Who Has Ceased to Act on Application of Another Party

r.42.4 **22.7** r.42.4(3) **22.7**
r.42.4(1) **22.7**

(1) Where—
  (a) a solicitor who has acted for a party—
    (i) has died;
    (ii) has become bankrupt;
    (iii) has ceased to practise; or
    (iv) cannot be found; and
  (b) the party has not given notice of a change of solicitor or notice of intention to act in person as required by rule 42.2(2),

  any other party may apply for an order declaring that the solicitor has ceased to be the solicitor acting for the other party in the case.
(2) Where an application is made under this rule, notice of the application must be given to the party to whose solicitor the application relates unless the court directs otherwise.
(3) Where the court makes an order made under this rule—
  (a) a copy of the order must be served on every other party to the proceedings; and
  (b) where it is served by a party, that party must file a certificate of service.

PD 42 Practice Direction — Change of Solicitor

This practice direction supplements CPR Part 42

[For commentary on a specific paragraph, please refer to the cross-references after the title of the paragraph.]

Solicitor Acting for a Party

para.1.2 **22.4** para.1.3 **22.3**

1.1 Rule 42.1 states that where the address for service of a party is the business address[1] of his solicitor, the solicitor will be considered to be acting for that party until the provisions of Part 42 have been complied with.

1.2 Subject to r. 42.2(6) (where the certificate of a LSC funded client or assisted person is revoked or discharged), where a party has changed his solicitor or intends to act in person, the former solicitor will be considered to be the party's solicitor unless or until:

(1) a notice of the change is
 (a) filed with the court,[2] and
 (b) served on every other party,[3] or

(2) the court makes an order under r. 42.3 and the order is served on every other party.[4]

The notice should not be filed until every other party has been served.

1.3 A solicitor appointed to represent a party only as an advocate at a hearing will not be considered to be acting for that party within the meaning of Part 42.

Notice of Change of Solicitor

para.2.2 **22.5** para.2.7 **22.4**
para. 2.5 **22.4**

2.1 Rule 42.2(1) sets out the circumstances following which a notice of the change must be filed and served.

2.2 A notice of the change giving the last known address of the former assisted person must also be filed and served on every party where, under r. 42.2(6):

(1) the certificate of a LSC funded client or assisted person is revoked or discharged,

(2) the solicitor who acted for that person has ceased to act on determination of his retainer under reg. 83 of [the Civil Legal Aid (General) Regulations 1989], and

(3) the assisted person wishes either to act in person or appoint another solicitor to act on his behalf.

2.3 In addition, where a party or solicitor changes his address for service, a notice of that change should be filed and served on every party.

2.4 A party who, having conducted a claim by a solicitor, intends to act in person must give in his notice an address for service that is within the jurisdiction.[5]

2.5 Form N434 should be used to give notice of any change. The notice should be filed in the court office in which the claim is proceeding.

2.6 Where the claim is proceeding in the High Court the notice should be filed either in the appropriate district registry or if the claim is proceeding in the Royal Courts of Justice, as follows:

(1) a claim proceeding in the Queen's Bench Division — in the Action Department of the Central Office,

(2) a claim proceeding in the Chancery Division — in Chancery Chambers,

(3) a claim proceeding in the Administrative Court — in the Administrative Court Office,

(4) a claim proceeding in the Admiralty and Commercial Registry — in the Admiralty and Commercial Registry, and

---

1 Rule 6.5 and PD 6 contain information about the business address.

2 Rule 42.2(2)(a).

3 Rule 42.2(2)(b).

4 Rule 42.2(5).

5 See r. 6.5(3).

(5) a claim proceeding in the Technology and Construction Court — in the Registry of the Technology and Construction Court.

2.7 Where the claim is the subject of an appeal to the Court of Appeal, the notice should also be filed in the Civil Appeals Office.
(PD 43–48 contains details of the information required to be included when the funding arrangements for the claim change.)

Application for an Order That a Solicitor Has Ceased to Act

3.1 A solicitor may apply under r. 42.3 for an order declaring that he has ceased to be the solicitor acting for a party.

3.2 The application should be made in accordance with Part 23[6] and must be supported by evidence.[7] Unless the court directs otherwise the application notice must be served on the party.[8]

3.3 An order made under r. 42.3 must be served on every party and takes effect when it is served. Where the order is not served by the court, the person serving must file a certificate of service in form N215.

Application by Another Party to Remove a Solicitor

para.4.2 **22.7**

4.1 Rule 42.4 sets out circumstances in which any other party may apply for an order declaring that a solicitor has ceased to be the solicitor acting for another party in the proceedings.

4.2 The application should be made in accordance with Part 23 and must be supported by evidence. Unless the court directs otherwise the application notice must be served on the party to whose solicitor the application relates.

4.3 An order made under r. 42.4 must be served on every other party to the proceedings. Where the order is not served by the court, the person serving must file a certificate of service in form N215.

New Address for Service Where Order Made under Rules 42.3 or 42.4

5.1 Where the court has made an order under r. 42.3 that a solicitor has ceased to act or under r. 42.4 declaring that a solicitor has ceased to be the solicitor for a party, the party for whom the solicitor was acting must give a new address for service to comply with r. 6.5(2).
(Rule 6.5(2) provides that a party must give an address for service within the jurisdiction.)
(Until such time as a new address for service is given r. 6.5(6) will apply.)

[6] See Part 23 and PD 23.
[7] See Part 32 and PD 32 for information about evidence.
[8] Rule 42.3(2).

CPR Part 43 Scope of Cost Rules and Definitions

Part 43 **67.2, 68.61** [For commentary on a specific rule, please refer to the cross-references after the title of the rule.]

43.1 Scope of This Part

This Part contains definitions and interpretation of certain matters set out in the rules about costs contained in Parts 44 to 48.

(Part 44 contains general rules about costs; Part 45 deals with fixed costs; Part 46 deals with fast track trial costs; Part 47 deals with the detailed assessment of costs and related appeals and Part 48 deals with costs payable in special cases)

43.2 Definitions and Application

r.43.2 **68.46**
r.43.2(1) **6.26, 68.2**
r.43.2(1)(j) **67.2**
r.43.2(1)(k) **12.3, 13.6, 13.8, 18.3, 18.4, 20.18, 23.17**
r.43.2(1)(o) **68.46**
r.43.2(3) **6.7, 14.23, 68.29**
r.43.2(4) **68.29**

(1) In Parts 44 to 48, unless the context otherwise requires—
  (a) 'costs' includes fees, charges, disbursements, expenses, remuneration, reimbursement allowed to a litigant in person under rule 48.6, any additional liability incurred under a funding arrangement and any fee or reward charged by a lay representative for acting on behalf of a party in proceedings allocated to the small claims track;
  (b) 'costs judge' means a taxing master of the Supreme Court;
  (c) 'costs officer' means—
    (i) a costs judge;
    (ii) a district judge; and
    (iii) an authorised court officer;
  (d) 'authorised court officer' means any officer of—
    (i) a county court;
    (ii) a district registry;
    (iii) the Principal Registry of the Family Division; or
    (iv) the Supreme Court Costs Office, whom the Lord Chancellor has authorised to assess costs.
  (e) 'fund' includes any estate or property held for the benefit of any person or class of person and any fund to which a trustee or personal representative is entitled in his capacity as such;
  (f) 'receiving party' means a party entitled to be paid costs;
  (g) 'paying party' means a party liable to pay costs;
  (h) 'assisted person' means an assisted person within the statutory provisions relating to legal aid;
  (i) 'LSC funding client' means an individual who receives services funded by the Legal Service Commission as part of the Community Legal Service within the meaning of Part I of the Access to Justice Act 1999;
  (j) 'fixed costs' means the amounts which are to be allowed in respect of solicitors' charges in the circumstances set out in section I of Part 45.
  (k) 'funding arrangement' means an arrangement where a person has—
    (i) entered into a conditional fee agreement or a collective conditional fee agreement which provides for a success fee within the meaning of section 58(2) of the Courts and Legal Services Act 1990;

(ii) taken out an insurance policy to which section 29 of the Access to Justice Act 1999 (recovery of insurance premiums by way of costs) applies; or
(iii) made an agreement with a membership organisation to meet his legal costs;

(l) 'percentage increase' means the percentage by which the amount of a legal representative's fee can be increased in accordance with a conditional fee agreement which provides for a success fee;

(m) 'insurance premium' means a sum of money paid or payable for insurance against the risk of incurring a costs liability in the proceedings, taken out after the event that is the subject matter of the claim;

(n) 'membership organisation' means a body prescribed for the purposes of section 30 of the Access to Justice Act 1999 (recovery where body undertakes to meet costs liabilities); and

(o) 'additional liability' means the percentage increase, the insurance premium, or the additional amount in respect of provision made by a membership organisation, as the case may be.

(2) The costs to which Parts 44 to 48 apply include—
(a) the following costs where those costs may be assessed by the court—
(i) costs of proceedings before an arbitrator or umpire;
(ii) costs of proceedings before a tribunal or other statutory body; and
(iii) costs payable by a client to his solicitor; and
(b) costs which are payable by one party to another party under the terms of a contract, where the court makes an order for an assessment of those costs.

(3) Where advocacy or litigation services are provided to a client under a conditional fee agreement, costs are recoverable under Parts 44 to 48 notwithstanding that the client is liable to pay his legal representative's fees and expenses only to the extent that sums are recovered in respect of the proceedings, whether by way of costs or otherwise.

(4) In paragraph (3), the reference to a conditional fee agreement is to an agreement which satisfies all the conditions applicable to it by virtue of section 58 of the Courts and Legal Services Act 1990.

43.3 Meaning of Summary Assessment

'Summary assessment' means the procedure by which the court, when making an order about costs, orders payment of a sum of money instead of fixed costs or 'detailed assessment'.

43.4 Meaning of Detailed Assessment

'Detailed assessment' means the procedure by which the amount of costs is decided by a costs officer in accordance with Part 47.

[PD 43–48 is positioned after CPR 48.]

CPR Part 44 General Rules about Costs

Part 44 **52.4, 67.2, 68.29, 68.61** [For commentary on a specific rule, please refer to the cross-references after the title of the rule.]

44.1 Scope of This Part

This Part contains general rules about costs and entitlement to costs.
(The definitions contained in Part 43 are relevant to this Part)

44.2 Solicitor's Duty to Notify Client

r.44.2 **1.36, 66.25**

Where—

(a) the court makes a costs order against a legally represented party; and
(b) the party is not present when the order is made,

the party's solicitor must notify his client in writing of the costs order no later than 7 days after the solicitor receives notice of the order.

44.3 Court's Discretion and Circumstances to Be Taken into Account When Exercising its Discretion as to Costs

r.44.3 **64.32, 64.45, 64.47, 64.48, 66.6, 66.27, 68.5**
r.44.3(1) **64.1, 66.3, 79.87**
r.44.3(1)(c) **66.20**
r.44.3(2) **5.3, 66.3, 66.6, 79.87**
r.44.3(2)(a) **64.1, 66.18, 66.45**
r.44.3(4) **1.36, 8.5, 66.5, 70.22**
r.44.3(4)(a) **66.16**
r.44.3(4)(b) **66.11**
r.44.3(4)(c) **64.1**
r.44.3(5) **1.36, 8.5, 66.5, 66.16**
r.44.3(5)(a) **1.7, 8.4**
r.44.3(5)(b) **66.11**
r.44.3(5)(c) **70.22**
r.44.3(5)(d) **66.11**
r.44.3(6) **66.4**
r.44.3(6)(f) **66.4**
r.44.3(6)(g) **62.17, 66.20, 68.23, 70.22**
r.44.3(7) **66.4, 66.13, 66.44**
r.44.3(8) **68.8, 68.26**

(1) The court has discretion as to—
  (a) whether costs are payable by one party to another;
  (b) the amount of those costs; and
  (c) when they are to be paid.
(2) If the court decides to make an order about costs—
  (a) the general rule is that the unsuccessful party will be ordered to pay the costs of the successful party; but
  (b) the court may make a different order.

(3) The general rule does not apply to the following proceedings—
 (a) proceedings in the Court of Appeal on an application or appeal made in connection with proceedings in the Family Division; or
 (b) proceedings in the Court of Appeal from a judgment, direction, decision or order given or made in probate proceedings or family proceedings.

(4) In deciding what order (if any) to make about costs, the court must have regard to all the circumstances, including—
 (a) the conduct of all the parties;
 (b) whether a party has succeeded on part of his case, even if he has not been wholly successful; and
 (c) any payment into court or admissible offer to settle made by a party which is drawn to the court's attention (whether or not made in accordance with Part 36).

(Part 36 contains further provisions about how the court's discretion is to be exercised where a payment into court or an offer to settle is made under that Part)

(5) The conduct of the parties includes—
 (a) conduct before, as well as during, the proceedings and in particular the extent to which the parties followed any relevant pre-action protocol;
 (b) whether it was reasonable for a party to raise, pursue or contest a particular allegation or issue;
 (c) the manner in which a party has pursued or defended his case or a particular allegation or issue; and
 (d) whether a claimant who has succeeded in his claim, in whole or in part, exaggerated his claim.

(6) The orders which the court may make under this rule include an order that a party must pay—
 (a) a proportion of another party's costs;
 (b) a stated amount in respect of another party's costs;
 (c) costs from or until a certain date only;
 (d) costs incurred before proceedings have begun;
 (e) costs relating to particular steps taken in the proceedings;
 (f) costs relating only to a distinct part of the proceedings; and
 (g) interest on costs from or until a certain date, including a date before judgment.

(7) Where the court would otherwise consider making an order under paragraph (6)(f), it must instead, if practicable, make an order under paragraph (6)(a) or (c).

(8) Where the court has ordered a party to pay costs, it may order an amount to be paid on account before the costs are assessed.

(9) Where a party entitled to costs is also liable to pay costs the court may assess the costs which that party is liable to pay and either—
 (a) set off the amount assessed against the amount the party is entitled to be paid and direct him to pay any balance; or
 (b) delay the issue of a certificate for the costs to which the party is entitled until he has paid the amount which he is liable to pay.

44.3A Costs Orders Relating to Funding Arrangements

r.44.3A **6.18, 6.20, 6.22, 68.29** r.44.3A(1) **66.46**

(1) The court will not assess any additional liability until the conclusion of the proceedings, or the part of the proceedings, to which the funding arrangement relates.

('Funding arrangement' and 'additional liability' are defined in rule 43.2)

(2) At the conclusion of the proceedings, or the part of the proceedings, to which the funding arrangement relates the court may—
 (a) make a summary assessment of all the costs, including any additional liability;
 (b) make an order for detailed assessment of the additional liability but make a summary assessment of the other costs; or
 (c) make an order for detailed assessment of all the costs.

(Part 47 sets out the procedure for the detailed assessment of costs)

44.3B Limits on Recovery under Funding Arrangements

r.44.3B **6.18, 6.20, 68.48**
r.44.3B(1)(b) **68.52**
r.44.3B(1)(c) **5.10, 6.17**
r.44.3B(1)(d) **68.48**

(1) A party may not recover as an additional liability—
   (a) any proportion of the percentage increase relating to the cost to the legal representative of the postponement of the payment of his fees and expenses;
   (b) any provision made by a membership organisation which exceeds the likely cost to that party of the premium of an insurance policy against the risk of incurring a liability to pay the costs of other parties to the proceedings;
   (c) any additional liability for any period in the proceedings during which he failed to provide information about a funding arrangement in accordance with a rule, practice direction or court order;
   (d) any percentage increase where a party has failed to comply with—
      (i) a requirement in the costs practice direction; or
      (ii) a court order,

   to disclose in any assessment proceedings the reasons for setting the percentage increase at the level stated in the conditional fee agreement.
(2) This rule does not apply in an assessment under rule 48.9 (assessment of a solicitor's bill to his client).

(Rule 3.9 sets out the circumstances the court will consider on an application for relief from a sanction for failure to comply with any rule, practice direction or court order)

44.4 Basis of Assessment

r.44.4 **5.10**
r.44.4(2) **1.28, 68.34**
r.44.4(3) **68.37**
r.44.4(4) **68.38**

(1) Where the court is to assess the amount of costs (whether by summary or detailed assessment) it will assess those costs—
   (a) on the standard basis; or
   (b) on the indemnity basis,

   but the court will not in either case allow costs which have been unreasonably incurred or are unreasonable in amount.

   (Rule 48.3 sets out how the court decides the amount of costs payable under a contract)
(2) Where the amount of costs is to be assessed on the standard basis, the court will—
   (a) only allow costs which are proportionate to the matters in issue; and
   (b) resolve any doubt which it may have as to whether costs were reasonably incurred or reasonable and proportionate in amount in favour of the paying party.

(Factors which the court may take into account are set out in rule 44.5)

(3) Where the amount of costs is to be assessed on the indemnity basis, the court will resolve any doubt which it may have as to whether costs were reasonably incurred or were reasonable in amount in favour of the receiving party.
(4) Where—
   (a) the court makes an order about costs without indicating the basis on which the costs are to be assessed; or
   (b) the court makes an order for costs to be assessed on a basis other than the standard basis or the indemnity basis,

   the costs will be assessed on the standard basis.
(5) [*revoked*]
(6) Where the amount of a solicitor's remuneration in respect of non-contentious business is regulated by any general orders made under the Solicitors Act 1974, the amount of the costs to be allowed in respect of any such business which falls to be assessed by the court will be decided in accordance with those general orders rather than this rule and rule 44.5.

44.5 Factors to Be Taken into Account in Deciding the Amount of Costs

r.44.5 **5.10, 67.3, 68.52**
r.44.5(3) **42.15, 68.18, 68.34, 68.35, 68.41**

(1) The court is to have regard to all the circumstances in deciding whether costs were—
   (a) if it is assessing costs on the standard basis—

(i) proportionately and reasonably incurred; or
(ii) were proportionate and reasonable in amount, or
(b) if it is assessing costs on the indemnity basis—
(i) unreasonably incurred; or
(ii) unreasonable in amount.
(2) In particular the court must give effect to any orders which have already been made.
(3) The court must also have regard to—
(a) the conduct of all the parties, including in particular—
(i) conduct before, as well as during, the proceedings; and
(ii) the efforts made, if any, before and during the proceedings in order to try to resolve the dispute;
(b) the amount or value of any money or property involved;
(c) the importance of the matter to all the parties;
(d) the particular complexity of the matter or the difficulty or novelty of the questions raised;
(e) the skill, effort, specialised knowledge and responsibility involved;
(f) the time spent on the case; and
(g) the place where and the circumstances in which work or any part of it was done.
(Rule 35.4(4) gives the court power to limit the amount that a party may recover with regard to the fees and expenses of an expert)

44.6 Fixed Costs

A party may recover the fixed costs specified in Part 45 in accordance with that Part.

44.7 Procedure for Assessing Costs

r.44.7 **68.2**

Where the court orders a party to pay costs to another party (other than fixed costs) it may either—
(a) make a summary assessment of the costs; or
(b) order detailed assessment of the costs by a costs officer,
unless any rule, practice direction or other enactment provides otherwise.
(The costs practice direction [PD 43–48] sets out the factors which will affect the court's decision under this rule)

44.8 Time for Complying with an Order for Costs

r.44.8 **32.27, 66.20, 66.27, 68.5**

A party must comply with an order for the payment of costs within 14 days of—
(a) the date of the judgment or order if it states the amount of those costs;
(b) if the amount of those costs (or part of them) is decided later in accordance with Part 47, the date of the certificate which states the amount; or
(c) in either case, such later date as the court may specify.
(Part 47 sets out the procedure for detailed assessment of costs)

44.9 Costs on the Small Claims Track and Fast Track

r.44.9(1)–(2) **66.34**

(1) Part 27 (small claims) and Part 46 (fast track trial costs) contain special rules about—
(a) liability for costs;
(b) the amount of costs which the court may award; and
(c) the procedure for assessing costs.
(2) Once a claim is allocated to a particular track, those special rules shall apply to the period before, as well as after, allocation except where the court or a practice direction provides otherwise.

44.10 Limitation on Amount Court May Allow Where a Claim Allocated to the Fast Track Settles before Trial

r.44.10 **68.7**

(1) Where the court—
(a) assesses costs in relation to a claim which—

(i) has been allocated to the fast track; and
(ii) settles before the start of the trial; and

(b) is considering the amount of costs to be allowed in respect of a party's advocate for preparing for the trial,

it may not allow, in respect of those advocate's costs, an amount that exceeds the amount of fast track trial costs which would have been payable in relation to the claim had the trial taken place.

(2) When deciding the amount to be allowed in respect of the advocate's costs, the court shall have regard to—

(a) when the claim was settled; and
(b) when the court was notified that the claim had settled.

(3) In this rule, 'advocate' and 'fast track trial costs' have the meanings given to them by Part 46.

(Part 46 sets out the amount of fast track trial costs which may be awarded)

44.11 Costs Following Allocation and Reallocation

r.44.11(2) **43.30**

(1) Any costs orders made before a claim is allocated will not be affected by allocation.

(2) Where—

(a) a claim is allocated to a track; and
(b) the court subsequently reallocates that claim to a different track,

then unless the court orders otherwise, any special rules about costs applying—

(i) to the first track, will apply to the claim up to the date of reallocation; and
(ii) to the second track, will apply from the date of reallocation.

(Part 26 deals with the allocation and reallocation of claims between tracks)

44.12 Cases Where Costs Orders Deemed to Have Been Made

r.44.12 **62.17**

(1) Where a right to costs arises under—

(a) rule 3.7 (defendant's right to costs where claim struck out for non-payment of fees);
(b) rule 36.13(1) (claimant's right to costs where he accepts defendant's Part 36 offer or Part 36 payment);
(c) rule 36.14 (claimant's right to costs where defendant accepts the claimant's Part 36 offer); or
(d) rule 38.6 (defendant's right to costs where claimant discontinues),

a costs order will be deemed to have been made on the standard basis.

(2) Interest payable pursuant to section 17 of the Judgments Act 1838 or section 74 of the County Courts Act 1984 on the costs deemed to have been ordered under paragraph (1) shall begin to run from the date on which the event which gave rise to the entitlement to costs occurred.

44.12A Costs-only Proceedings

r.44.12A **66.2, 68.22, 68.58** r.44.12A(4)(b) **68.58**

(1) This rule sets out a procedure which may be followed where—

(a) the parties to a dispute have reached an agreement on all issues (including which party is to pay the costs) which is made or confirmed in writing; but
(b) they have failed to agree the amount of those costs; and
(c) no proceedings have been started.

(2) Either party to the agreement may start proceedings under this rule by issuing a claim form in accordance with Part 8.

(3) The claim form must contain or be accompanied by the agreement or confirmation.

(4) Except as provided in paragraph (4A), in proceedings to which this rule applies the court—

(a) may—
(i) make an order for costs to be determined by detailed assessment; or
(ii) dismiss the claim; and
(b) must dismiss the claim if it is opposed.

(4A) In proceedings to which Section II of Part 45 applies, the court shall assess the costs in the manner set out in that Section.

(5) Rule 48.3 (amount of costs where costs are payable pursuant to a contract) does not apply to claims started under the procedure in this rule.

(Rule 7.2 provides that proceedings are started when the court issues a claim form at the request of the claimant)
(Rule 8.1(6) provides that a practice direction may modify the Part 8 procedure)

44.13 Special Situations

r.44.13(1) **66.29**
r.44.13(1)(a)–(b) **66.29**
r.44.13(1A)–(1B) **66.29**
r.44.13(2) **66.36**
r.44.13(3)–(4) **66.33**

(1) Where the court makes an order which does not mention costs—
  (a) subject to paragraphs (1A) and (1B), the general rule is that no party is entitled to costs in relation to that order; but
  (b) this does not affect any entitlement of a party to recover costs out of a fund held by him as trustee or personal representative, or pursuant to any lease, mortgage or other security.
(1A) Where the court makes—
  (a) an order granting permission to appeal;
  (b) an order granting permission to apply for judicial review; or
  (c) any other order or direction sought by a party on an application without notice,
  and its order does not mention costs, it will be deemed to include an order for applicant's costs in the case.
(1B) Any party affected by a deemed order for costs under paragraph (1A) may apply at any time to vary the order.
(2) The court hearing an appeal may, unless it dismisses the appeal, make orders about the costs of the proceedings giving rise to the appeal as well as the costs of the appeal.
(3) Where proceedings are transferred from one court to another, the court to which they are transferred may deal with all the costs, including the costs before the transfer.
(4) Paragraph (3) is subject to any order of the court which ordered the transfer.

44.14 Court's Powers in Relation to Misconduct

r.44.14 **68.25**

(1) The court may make an order under this rule where—
  (a) a party or his legal representative in connection with a summary or detailed assessment, fails to comply with a rule, practice direction or court order; or
  (b) it appears to the court that the conduct of a party or his legal representative, before or during the proceedings which gave rise to the assessment proceedings, was unreasonable or improper.
(2) Where paragraph (1) applies, the court may—
  (a) disallow all or part of the costs which are being assessed; or
  (b) order the party at fault or his legal representative to pay costs which he has caused any other party to incur.
(3) Where—
  (a) the court makes an order under paragraph (2) against a legally represented party; and
  (b) the party is not present when the order is made,
  the party's solicitor must notify his client in writing of the order no later than 7 days after the solicitor receives notice of the order.

44.15 Providing Information about Funding Arrangements

r.44.15 **6.6, 68.48**
r.44.15(1) **6.17**
r.44.15(2) **6.17, 63.19**
r.44.15(3) **6.17**

(1) A party who seeks to recover an additional liability must provide information about the funding arrangement to the court and to other parties as required by a rule, practice direction or court order.
(2) Where the funding arrangement has changed, and the information a party has previously provided in accordance with paragraph (1) is no longer accurate, that party must file notice of the change and serve it on all other parties within 7 days.
(3) Where paragraph (2) applies, and a party has already filed—
  (a) an allocation questionnaire; or

(b) a pre-trial checklist (listing questionnaire),

he must file and serve a new estimate of costs with the notice.

(The costs practice direction [PD 43–48] sets out—

- the information to be provided when a party issues or responds to a claim form, files an allocation questionnaire, a pre-trial checklist, and a claim for costs;
- the meaning of estimate of costs and the information required in it)

(Rule 44.3B sets out situations where a party will not recover a sum representing any additional liability)

44.16 Adjournment Where Legal Representative Seeks to Challenge Disallowance of Any Amount of Percentage Increase

r.44.16 **6.21**

(1) This rule applies where the Conditional Fee Agreements Regulations 2000 or the Collective Conditional Fee Agreements Regulations 2000 continues [*sic*] to apply to an agreement which provides for a success fee.

(2) Where—

(a) the court disallows any amount of a legal representative's percentage increase in summary or detailed assessment proceedings; and

(b) the legal representative applies for an order that the disallowed amount should continue to be payable by his client,

the court may adjourn the hearing to allow the client to be—

(i) notified of the order sought; and

(ii) separately represented.

(Regulation 3(2)(b) of the Conditional Fee Agreements Regulations 2000, which applies to Conditional Fee Agreements entered into before 1st November 2005, provides that a conditional fee agreement which provides for a success fee must state that any amount of a percentage increase disallowed on assessment ceases to be payable unless the court is satisfied that it should continue to be so payable. Regulation 5(2)(b) of the Collective Conditional Fee Agreements Regulations 2000, which applies to Collective Conditional Fee Agreements entered into before 1st November 2005, makes similar provision in relation to collective conditional fee agreements.)

44.17 Application of Costs Rules

This Part and Part 45 (fixed costs), Part 46 (fast track trial costs), Part 47 (procedure for detailed assessment of costs and default provisions) and Part 48 (special cases), do not apply to the assessment of costs in proceedings to the extent that—

(a) section 11 of the Access to Justice Act 1999, and provisions made under that Act, or

(b) regulations made under the Legal Aid Act 1988,

make different provision.

(The costs practice direction [PD 43–48] sets out the procedure to be followed where a party was wholly or partially funded by the Legal Services Commission)

[PD 43–48 is positioned after CPR 48.]

CPR Part 45 Fixed Costs

Part 45 **43.27, 66.34, 66.47, 67.2, 67.7, 67.20, 68.61** [For commentary on a specific rule, please refer to the cross-references after the title of the rule.]

I FIXED COSTS

45.1 Scope of This Section

r.45.1 **67.2, 67.3, 67.4**
r.45.1(1) **67.3**
r.45.1(2)(a) **67.3**
r.45.1(2)(a)(i)–(vi) **67.3**
r.45.1(2)(b)–(c) **67.3**
r.45.1(2)(d)–(f) **67.3, 67.5**
r.45.1(2)(g) **67.3**
r.45.1(3) **67.4**

(1) This Section sets out the amounts which, unless the court orders otherwise, are to be allowed in respect of solicitors' charges in the cases to which this Section applies.

(2) This Section applies where—

(a) the only claim is a claim for a specified sum of money where the value of the claim exceeds £25 and—

(i) judgment in default is obtained under rule 12.4(1);

(ii) judgment on admission is obtained under rule 14.4(3);

(iii) judgment on admission on part of the claim is obtained under rule 14.5(6);

(iv) summary judgment is given under Part 24;

(v) the court has made an order to strike out[(GL)] a defence under rule 3.4(2)(a) as disclosing no reasonable grounds for defending the claim; or

(vi) rule 45.3 applies;

(b) the only claim is a claim where the court gave a fixed date for the hearing when it issued the claim and judgment is given for the delivery of goods and the value of the claim exceeds £25;

(c) the claim is for the recovery of land, including a possession claim under Part 55, whether or not the claim includes a claim for a sum of money and the defendant gives up possession, pays the amount claimed, if any, and the fixed commencement costs stated in the claim form;

(d) the claim is for the recovery of land, including a possession claim under Part 55, where one of the grounds for possession is arrears of rent, for which the court gave a fixed date for the hearing when it issued the claim and judgment is given for the possession of land (whether or not the order for possession is suspended on terms) and the defendant—
 (i) has neither delivered a defence, or counterclaim, nor otherwise denied liability; or
 (ii) has delivered a defence which is limited to specifying his proposals for the payment of arrears of rent;

(e) the claim is a possession claim under Section II of Part 55 (accelerated possession claims of land let on an assured shorthold tenancy) and a possession order is made where the defendant has neither delivered a defence, or counterclaim, nor otherwise denied liability;

(f) the claim is a demotion claim under Section III of Part 65 or a demotion claim is made in the same claim form in which a claim for possession is made under Part 55 and that demotion claim is successful; or

(g) a judgment creditor has taken steps under Parts 70 to 73 to enforce a judgment or order.

(The practice direction supplementing rule 7.9 [PD 7D] sets out the types of case where a court may give a fixed date for a hearing when it issues a claim)

(3) Any appropriate court fee will be allowed in addition to the costs set out in this Section.

(4) The claim form may include a claim for fixed commencement costs.

45.2 Amount of Fixed Commencement Costs in a Claim for the Recovery of Money or Goods

r.45.2 **67.2, 67.3, 67.4, 67.5**

(1) The amount of fixed commencement costs in a claim to which rule 45.1(2)(a) or (b) applies—
(a) shall be calculated by reference to Table 1; and
(b) the amount claimed, or the value of the goods claimed if specified, in the claim form is to be used for determining the band in Table 1 that applies to the claim.

(2) The amounts shown in Table 4 are to be allowed in addition, if applicable.

Table 1 Fixed costs on commencement of a claim for the recovery of money or goods

Table 1 –Table 4 **67.4**

Relevant band	Where the claim form is served by the court or by any method other than personal service by the claimant	Where • the claim form is served personally by the claimant; and • there is only one defendant	Where there is more than one defendant, for each additional defendant personally served at separate addresses by the claimant
Where— • the value of the claim exceeds £25 but does not exceed £500	£50	£60	£15
Where— • the value of the claim exceeds £500 but does not exceed £1,000	£70	£80	£15
Where— • the value of the claim exceeds £1,000 but does not exceed £5,000; or • the only claim is for delivery of goods and no value is specified or stated on the claim form	£80	£90	£15
Where— • the value of the claim exceeds £5,000	£100	£110	£15

45.2A Amount of Fixed Commencement Costs in a Claim for the Recovery of Land or a Demotion Claim

r.45.2A **67.3, 67.5**

(1) The amount of fixed commencement costs in a claim to which rule 45.1(2)(c), (d) or (f) applies shall be calculated by reference to Table 2.
(2) The amounts shown in Table 4 are to be allowed in addition, if applicable.

Table 2 Fixed costs on commencement of a claim for the recovery of land or a demotion claim

Where the claim form is served by the court or by any method other than personal service by the claimant	£69.50
Where— • the claim form is served personally by the claimant; and • there is only one defendant	£77.00
Where there is more than one defendant, for each additional defendant personally served at separate addresses by the claimant	£15.00

45.3 When Defendant Only Liable for Fixed Commencement Costs

r.45.3 **67.2, 67.3, 67.4** r.45.3(1)–(2) **67.3**

(1) Where—
    (a) the only claim is for a specified sum of money; and
    (b) the defendant pays the money claimed within 14 days after service of particulars of claim on him, together with the fixed commencement costs stated in the claim form,
  the defendant is not liable for any further costs unless the court orders otherwise.
(2) Where—
    (a) the claimant gives notice of acceptance of a payment into court in satisfaction of the whole claim;
    (b) the only claim is for a specified sum of money; and
    (c) the defendant made the payment into court within 14 days after service of the particulars of claim on him, together with the fixed costs stated in the claim form,
  the defendant is not liable for any further costs unless the court orders otherwise.

45.4 Costs on Entry of Judgment in a Claim for the Recovery of Money or Goods

r.45.4 **20.5, 67.2, 67.3, 67.4, 67.5**

Where—
(a) the claimant has claimed fixed commencement costs under rule 45.2; and
(b) judgment is entered in a claim to which rule 45.1(2)(d) or (f) applies, the amount to be included in the judgment for the claimant's solicitor's charges is the total of—
    (i) the fixed commencement costs; and
    (ii) the relevant amount shown in Table 3.

45.4A Costs on Entry of Judgment in a Claim for the Recovery of Land or a Demotion Claim

r.45.4A(1)–(2) **67.5**

(1) Where—
    (a) the claimant has claimed fixed commencement costs under rule 45.2A; and
    (b) judgment is entered in a claim to which rule 45.1(2)(d) or (f) applies, the amount to be included in the judgment for the claimant's solicitor's charges is the total of—
        (i) the fixed commencement costs; and
        (ii) the sum of £57.25.

Table 3 Fixed costs on entry of judgment in a claim for the recovery of money or goods

	Where the amount of the judgment exceeds £25 but does not exceed £5,000	Where the amount of the judgment exceeds £5,000
Where judgment in default of an acknowledgment of service is entered under rule 12.4(1) (entry of judgment by request on claim for money only)	£22	£30
Where judgment in default of a defence is entered under rule 12.4(1) (entry of judgment by request on claim for money only)	£25	£35
Where judgment is entered under rule 14.4 (judgment on admission), or rule 14. 5(judgment on admission of part of claim) and claimant accepts the defendant's proposal as to the manner of payment	£40	£55
Where judgment is entered under rule 14.4 (judgment on admission), or rule 14. 5(judgment on admission of part of claim) and court decides the date or time of payment	£55	£70
Where summary judgment is given under Part 24 or the court strikes out a defence under rule 3.4(2)(a), in either case, on application by a party	£175	£210
Where judgment is given on a claim for delivery of goods under a regulated agreement within the meaning of the Consumer Credit Act 1974 and no other entry in this table applies	£60	£85

(2) Where an order for possession is made in a claim to which rule 45.1(2)(e) applies, the amount allowed for the claimant's solicitor's charges for preparing and filing—
   (a) the claim form;
   (b) the documents that accompany the claim form; and
   (c) the request for possession,
   is £79.50.

45.5 Miscellaneous Fixed Costs

r.45.5 **67.2, 67.3, 67.4, 67.5**

The table in this rule (Table 4) shows the amount to be allowed in respect of solicitor's charges in the circumstances mentioned.

Table 4 Miscellaneous fixed costs

For service by a party of any document required to be served personally including preparing and copying a certificate of service for each individual served	£15.00
Where service by an alternative method is permitted by an order under rule 6.8 for each individual served	£53.25
Where a document is served out of the jurisdiction—	
(a) in Scotland, Northern Ireland, the Isle of Man or the Channel Islands;	£68.25
(b) in any other place	£77.00

45.6 Fixed Enforcement Costs

r.45.6 **67.2, 67.3, 67.4, 67.5**

Table 5 shows the amount to be allowed in respect of solicitors' costs in the circumstances mentioned. The amounts shown in Table 4 are to be allowed in addition, if applicable.

Table 5 Fixed enforcement costs

For an application under rule 70.5(4) that an award may be enforced as if payable under a court order, where the amount outstanding under the award:	
exceeds £25 but does not exceed £250	£30.75
exceeds £250 but does not exceed £600	£41.00
exceeds £600 but does not exceed £2,000	£69.50
exceeds £2,000	£75.50
On attendance to question a judgment debtor (or officer of a company or other corporation) who has been ordered to attend court under rule 71.2 where the questioning takes place before a court officer, including attendance by a responsible representative of the solicitor:	for each half hour or part, £15.00 (When the questioning takes place before a judge, he may summarily assess any costs allowed.)
On the making of a final third party debt order under rule 72.8(6)(a) or an order for the payment to the judgment creditor of money in court under rule 72.10(1)(b):	
if the amount recovered is less than £150	one-half of the amount recovered
otherwise	£98.50
On the making of a final charging order under rule 73.8(2)(a):	£110.00 The court may also allow reasonable disbursements in respect of search fees and the registration of the order.
Where a certificate is issued and registered under Schedule 6 to the Civil Jurisdiction and Judgments Act 1982, the costs of registration	£39.00
Where permission is given under RSC Order 45, rule 3 to enforce a judgment or order giving possession of land and costs are allowed on the judgment or order, the amount to be added to the judgment or order for costs—	
(a) basic costs	£42.50
(b) where notice of the proceedings is to be to more than one person, for each additional person	£2.75
Where a writ of execution as defined in the RSC Order 46, rule 1, is issued against any party	£51.75
Where a request is filed for the issue of a warrant of execution under CCR Order 26, rule 1, for a sum exceeding £25	£2.25
Where an application for an attachment of earnings order is made and costs are allowed under CCR Order 27, rule 9 or CCR Order 28, rule 10, for each attendance on the hearing of the application	£8.50

II ROAD TRAFFIC ACCIDENTS — FIXED RECOVERABLE COSTS

45.7 Scope and Interpretation

(1) This Section sets out the costs which are to be allowed in—
  (a) costs-only proceedings under the procedure set out in rule 44.12A; or
  (b) proceedings for approval of a settlement or compromise under rule 21.10(2),
  in cases to which this Section applies.
(2) This Section applies where—
  (a) the dispute arises from a road traffic accident;
  (b) the agreed damages include damages in respect of personal injury, damage to property, or both;

(c) the total value of the agreed damages does not exceed £10,000; and
(d) if a claim had been issued for the amount of the agreed damages, the small claims track would not have been the normal track for that claim.

(3) This Section does not apply where the claimant is a litigant in person.

(Rule 2.3 defines 'personal injuries' as including any disease and any impairment of a person's physical or mental condition)

(Rule 26.6 provides for when the small claims track is the normal track)

(4) In this Section—
(a) 'road traffic accident' means an accident resulting in bodily injury to any person or damage to property caused by, or arising out of, the use of a motor vehicle on a road or other public place in England and Wales;
(b) 'motor vehicle' means a mechanically propelled vehicle intended for use on roads; and
(c) 'road' means any highway and any other road to which the public has access and includes bridges over which a road passes.

45.8 Application of Fixed Recoverable Costs

r.45.8 **67.9, 67.15**

Subject to rule 45.12, the only costs which are to be allowed are—
(a) fixed recoverable costs calculated in accordance with rule 45.9;
(b) disbursements allowed in accordance with rule 45.10; and
(c) a success fee allowed in accordance with rule 45.11.

(Rule 45.12 provides for where a party issues a claim for more than the fixed recoverable costs).

45.9 Amount of Fixed Recoverable Costs

r.45.9 **67.15**
r.45.9(1) **67.9, 67.10**
r.45.9(2) **67.10, 67.12**
r.45.9(3) **67.9, 67.10**

(1) Subject to paragraphs (2) and (3), the amount of fixed recoverable costs is the total of—
(a) £800;
(b) 20% of the damages agreed up to £5,000; and
(c) 15% of the damages agreed between £5,000 and £10,000.

(2) Where the claimant—
(a) lives or works in an area set out in the relevant practice direction; and
(b) instructs a solicitor or firm of solicitors who practise in that area,

the fixed recoverable costs shall include, in addition to the costs specified in paragraph (1), an amount equal to 12.5% of the costs allowable under that paragraph.

(3) Where appropriate, value added tax (VAT) may be recovered in addition to the amount of fixed recoverable costs and any reference in this Section to fixed recoverable costs is a reference to those costs net of any such VAT.

45.10 Disbursements

r.45.10 **67.13, 67.15**
r.45.10(1)–(2) **67.9**

(1) The court—
(a) may allow a claim for a disbursement of a type mentioned in paragraph (2); but
(b) must not allow a claim for any other type of disbursement.

(2) The disbursements referred to in paragraph (1) are—
(a) the cost of obtaining—
(i) medical records;
(ii) a medical report;
(iii) a police report;
(iv) an engineer's report; or
(v) a search of the records of the Driver Vehicle Licensing Authority;
(b) the amount of an insurance premium or, where a membership organisation undertakes to meet liabilities incurred to pay the costs of other parties to proceedings, a sum not exceeding such additional amount of costs as would be allowed under section 30 in respect of provision made against the risk of having to meet such liabilities;

('membership organisation' is defined in rule 43.2(1)(n))

(c) where they are necessarily incurred by reason of one or more of the claimants being a child or patient as defined in Part 21—
  (i) fees payable for instructing counsel, or
  (ii) court fees payable on an application to the court;
(d) any other disbursement that has arisen due to a particular feature of the dispute.
('insurance premium' is defined in rule 43.2)

45.11 Success Fee

r.45.11 **67.15** r.45.11(2) **67.9**
r.45.11(1) **67.9**

(1) A claimant may recover a success fee if he has entered into a funding arrangement of a type specified in rule 43.2(k)(i).
(2) The amount of the success fee shall be 12.5% of the fixed recoverable costs calculated in accordance with rule 45.9(1), disregarding any additional amount which may be included in the fixed recoverable costs by virtue of rule 45.9(2).

(Rule 43.2(k)(i) defines [a] funding arrangement as including a conditional fee agreement or collective conditional fee agreement which provides for a success fee)

45.12 Claims for an Amount of Costs Exceeding Fixed Recoverable Costs

r.45.12 **67.9** r.45.12(2) **67.14**
r.45.12(1) **67.10, 67.14**

(1) The court will entertain a claim for an amount of costs (excluding any success fee or disbursements) greater than the fixed recoverable costs but only if it considers that there are exceptional circumstances making it appropriate to do so.
(2) If the court considers such a claim appropriate, it may—
  (a) assess the costs; or
  (b) make an order for the costs to be assessed.
(3) If the court does not consider the claim appropriate, it must make an order for fixed recoverable costs only.

45.13 Failure to Achieve Costs Greater Than Fixed Recoverable Costs

r.45.13 **67.14, 67.15**

(1) This rule applies where—
  (a) costs are assessed in accordance with rule 45.12(2); and
  (b) the court assesses the costs (excluding any VAT) as being an amount which is less than 20% greater than the amount of the fixed recoverable costs.
(2) The court must order the defendant to pay to the claimant the lesser of—
  (a) the fixed recoverable costs; and
  (b) the assessed costs.

45.14 Costs of the Costs-only Proceedings or the Detailed Assessment

r.45.14 **67.14**

Where—
(a) the court makes an order for fixed recoverable costs in accordance with rule 45.12(3); or
(b) rule 45.13 applies, the court must—
  (i) make no award for the payment of the claimant's costs in bringing the proceedings under rule 44.12A; and
  (ii) order that the claimant pay the defendant's costs of defending those proceedings.

III FIXED PERCENTAGE INCREASE IN ROAD TRAFFIC ACCIDENT CLAIMS

45.15 Scope and Interpretation

r.45.15 **5.5, 6.14, 67.16, 67.17** r.45.15(4)(c) **6.14**

(1) This Section sets out the percentage increase which is to be allowed in the cases to which this Section applies.

(Rule 43.2(1)(l) defines 'percentage increase' as the percentage by which the amount of a legal representative's fee can be increased in accordance with a conditional fee agreement which provides for a success fee)

(2) This Section applies where—
(a) the dispute arises from a road traffic accident; and
(b) the claimant has entered into a funding arrangement of a type specified in rule [43.2(1)(k)(i)*].

(Rule [43.2(1)(k)(i)*] defines a funding arrangement as including an arrangement where a person has entered into a conditional fee agreement or collective conditional fee agreement which provides for a success fee)

(3) This Section does not apply if the proceedings are costs only proceedings to which Section II of this Part applies.
(4) This Section does not apply—
(a) to a claim which has been allocated to the small claims track;
(b) to a claim not allocated to a track, but for which the small claims track is the normal track; or
(c) where the road traffic accident which gave rise to the dispute occurred before 6th October 2003.
(5) The definitions in rule 45.7(4) apply to this Section as they apply to Section II.
(6) In this Section—
(a) a reference to 'fees' is a reference to fees for work done under a conditional fee agreement or collective conditional fee agreement;
(b) a reference to 'trial' is a reference to the final contested hearing or to the contested hearing of any issue ordered to be tried separately;
(c) a reference to a claim concluding at trial is a reference to a claim concluding by settlement after the trial has commenced or by judgment; and
(d) 'trial period' means a period of time fixed by the court within which the trial is to take place and where the court fixes more than one such period in relation to a claim, means the most recent period to be fixed.

45.16 Percentage Increase of Solicitors' Fees

r.45.16 **5.5, 6.14, 67.2, 67.16, 67.17**

Subject to rule 45.18, the percentage increase which is to be allowed in relation to solicitors' fees is—
(a) 100% where the claim concludes at trial; or
(b) 12.5% where—
(i) the claim concludes before a trial has commenced; or
(ii) the dispute is settled before a claim is issued.

45.17 Percentage Increase of Counsel's Fees

r.45.17 **5.5, 6.14, 67.2, 67.16, 67.17** r.45.17(2)–(5) **67.17**

(1) Subject to rule 45.18, the percentage increase which is to be allowed in relation to counsel's fees is—
(a) 100% where the claim concludes at trial;
(b) if the claim has been allocated to the fast track—
(i) 50% if the claim concludes 14 days or less before the date fixed for the commencement of the trial; or
(ii) 12.5% if the claim concludes more than 14 days before the date fixed for the commencement of the trial or before any such date has been fixed;
(c) if the claim has been allocated to the multi-track—
(i) 75% if the claim concludes 21 days or less before the date fixed for the commencement of the trial; or
(ii) 12.5% if the claim concludes more than 21 days before the date fixed for the commencement of the trial or before any such date has been fixed;
(d) 12.5% where—
(i) the claim has been issued but concludes before it has been allocated to a track; or
(ii) in relation to costs-only proceedings, the dispute is settled before a claim is issued.
(2) Where a trial period has been fixed, if—
(a) the claim concludes before the first day of that period; and
(b) no trial date has been fixed within that period before the claim concludes,

[* In the Queen's Printer's copy this is 43.2(k)(i).]

the first day of that period is treated as the date fixed for the commencement of the trial for the purposes of paragraph (1).

(3) Where a trial period has been fixed, if—
 (a) the claim concludes before the first day of that period; but
 (b) before the claim concludes, a trial date had been fixed within that period,
 the trial date is the date fixed for the commencement of the trial for the purposes of paragraph (1).

(4) Where a trial period has been fixed and the claim concludes—
 (a) on or after the first day of that period; but
 (b) before commencement of the trial, the percentage increase in paragraph (1)(b)(i) or (1)(c)(i) shall apply as appropriate, whether or not a trial date has been fixed within that period.

(5) For the purposes of this rule, in calculating the periods of time, the day fixed for the commencement of the trial (or the first day of the trial period, where appropriate) is not included.

45.18 Application for an Alternative Percentage Increase Where the Fixed Increase Is 12.5%

r.45.18 **5.5, 6.14, 67.2, 67.16, 67.21**

(1) This rule applies where the percentage increase to be allowed—
 (a) in relation to solicitors' fees under the provisions of rule 45.16; or
 (b) in relation to counsel's fees under rule 45.17,
 is 12.5%.

(2) A party may apply for a percentage increase greater or less than that amount if—
 (a) the parties agree damages of an amount greater than £500,000 or the court awards damages of an amount greater than £500,000; or
 (b) the court awards damages of £500,000 or less but would have awarded damages greater than £500,000 if it had not made a finding of contributory negligence; or
 (c) the parties agree damages of £500,000 or less and it is reasonable to expect that if the court had made an award of damages, it would have awarded damages greater than £500,000, disregarding any reduction the court may have made in respect of contributory negligence.

(3) In paragraph (2), a reference to a lump sum of damages includes a reference to periodical payments of equivalent value.

(4) If the court is satisfied that the circumstances set out in paragraph (2) apply it must—
 (a) assess the percentage increase; or
 (b) make an order for the percentage increase to be assessed.

45.19 Assessment of Alternative Percentage Increase

r.45 **5.5, 6.14, 67.2, 67.16, 67.21**

(1) This rule applies where the percentage increase of fees is assessed under rule 45.18(4).

(2) If the percentage increase is assessed as greater than 20% or less than 7.5%, the percentage increase to be allowed shall be that assessed by the court.

(3) If the percentage increase is assessed as no greater than 20% and no less than 7.5%—
 (a) the percentage increase to be allowed shall be 12.5%; and
 (b) the costs of the application and assessment shall be paid by the applicant.

IV FIXED PERCENTAGE INCREASE IN EMPLOYERS' LIABILITY CLAIMS

45.20 Scope and Interpretation

r.45 **5.5, 6.14, 67.2, 67.18** r.45.20(2)(b) **6.14**
r.45.20(2)(a)(i)–(iii) **6.14**

(1) Subject to paragraph (2), this Section applies where—
 (a) the dispute is between an employee and his employer arising from a bodily injury sustained by the employee in the course of his employment; and
 (b) the claimant has entered into a funding arrangement of a type specified in rule 43.2(1)(k)(i).

(2) This Section does not apply—
 (a) where the dispute—
  (i) relates to a disease;
  (ii) relates to an injury sustained before 1st October 2004; or

(iii) arises from a road traffic accident (as defined in rule 45.7(4)(a)); or
(iv) relates to an injury to which Section V of this Part applies; or
(b) to a claim—
(i) which has been allocated to the small claims track; or
(ii) not allocated to a track, but for which the small claims track is the normal track.

(3) For the purposes of this Section—
(a) 'employee' has the meaning given to it by section 2(1) of the Employers' Liability (Compulsory Insurance) Act 1969; and
(b) a reference to 'fees' is a reference to fees for work done under a conditional fee agreement or collective conditional fee agreement.

45.21 Percentage Increase of Solicitors' and Counsel's Fees

r.45.21 **5.5, 6.14, 67.2, 67.18**

In the cases to which this Section applies, subject to rule 45.22 the percentage increase which is to be allowed in relation to solicitors' and counsel's fees is to be determined in accordance with rules 45.16 and 45.17, subject to the modifications that—
(a) the percentage increase which is to be allowed in relation to solicitors' fees under rule 45.16(b) is—
(i) 27.5% if a membership organisation has undertaken to meet the claimant's liabilities for legal costs in accordance with section 30 of the Access to Justice Act 1999; and
(ii) 25% in any other case; and
(b) the percentage increase which is to be allowed in relation to counsel's fees under rule 45.17(1)(b)(ii), (1)(c)(ii) or (1)(d) is 25%.

('membership organisation' is defined in rule 43.2(1)(n))

45.22 Alternative Percentage Increase

r.45.22 **5.5, 6.14, 67.2, 67.18, 67.21**

(1) In the cases to which this Section applies, rule 45.18(2)–(4) applies where—
(a) the percentage increase of solicitors' fees to be allowed in accordance with rule 45.21 is 25% or 27.5%; or
(b) the percentage increase of counsel's fees to be allowed is 25%.

(2) Where the percentage increase of fees is assessed by the court under rule 45.18(4) as applied by paragraph (1) above—
(a) if the percentage increase is assessed as greater than 40% or less than 15%, the percentage increase to be allowed shall be that assessed by the court; and
(b) if the percentage increase is assessed as no greater than 40% and no less than 15%—
(i) the percentage increase to be allowed shall be 25% or 27.5% (as the case may be); and
(ii) the costs of the application and assessment shall be paid by the applicant.

V FIXED RECOVERABLE SUCCESS FEES IN EMPLOYER'S LIABILITY DISEASE CLAIMS

45.23 Scope and Interpretation

r.45.23 **67.20**

(1) Subject to paragraph (2), this Section applies where—
(a) the dispute is between an employee (or, if the employee is deceased, the employee's estate or dependants) and his employer (or a person alleged to be liable for the employer's alleged breach of statutory or common law duties of care); and
(b) the dispute relates to a disease with which the employee is diagnosed that is alleged to have been contracted as a consequence of the employer's alleged breach of statutory or common law duties of care in the course of the employee's employment; and
(c) the claimant has entered into a funding arrangement of a type specified in rule 43.2(1)(k)(i).

(2) This Section does not apply where—
(a) the claimant sent a letter of claim to the defendant containing a summary of the facts on which the claim is based and main allegations of fault before 1st October 2005; or
(b) rule 45.20(2)(b) applies.

(3) For the purposes of this Section—
(a) rule 45.15(6) applies;

(b) 'employee' has the meaning given to it by section 2(1) of the Employers' Liability (Compulsory Insurance) Act 1969;
(c) 'Type A claim' means a claim relating to a disease or physical injury alleged to have been caused by exposure to asbestos;
(d) 'Type B claim' means a claim relating to—
  (i) a psychiatric injury alleged to have been caused by work-related psychological stress;
  (ii) a work-related upper limb disorder which is alleged to have been caused by physical stress or strain, excluding hand/arm vibration injuries; and
(e) 'Type C claim' means a claim relating to a disease not falling within either type A or type B.

(The Table annexed to the Practice Direction supplementing Part 45 contains a non-exclusive list of diseases within Type A and Type B)

45.24 Percentage Increase of Solicitors' Fees

r.45.24 **67.20**

(1) In the cases to which this Section applies, subject to rule 45.26, the percentage increase which is to be allowed in relation to solicitors' fees is—
  (a) 100% if the claim concludes at trial; or
  (b) where—
    (i) the claim concludes before a trial has commenced; or
    (ii) the dispute is settled before a claim is issued,
  to be determined by rule 45.24(2).
(2) Where rule 45.24(1)(b) applies, the percentage increase which is to be allowed in relation to solicitors' fees is—
  (a) in type A claims—
    (i) 30% if a membership organisation has undertaken to meet the claimant's liabilities for legal costs in accordance with section 30 of the Access to Justice Act 1999; and
    (ii) 27.5% in any other case;
  (b) in type B claims, 100%; and
  (c) in type C claims—
    (i) 70% if a membership organisation has undertaken to meet the claimant's liabilities for legal costs in accordance with section 30 of the Access to Justice Act 1999; and
    (ii) 62.5% in any other case.

('Membership organisation' is defined in rule 43.2(1)(n))

45.25 Percentage Increase of Counsel's Fees

r.45.24 **67.20**

(1) In the cases to which this Section applies, subject to rule 45.26, the percentage increase which is to be allowed in relation to counsel's fees is—
  (a) 100% if the claim concludes at trial; or
  (b) where—
    (i) the claim concludes before a trial has commenced; or
    (ii) the dispute is settled before a claim is issued,
  to be determined by rule 45.25(2).
(2) Where rule 45.25(1)(b) applies, the percentage increase which is to be allowed in relation to counsel's fees is—
  (a) if the claim has been allocated to the fast track, the amount shown in Table 6; and
  (b) if the claim has been allocated to the multi-track, the amount shown in Table 7.
(3) Where a trial period has been fixed, rules 45.17(2) to 45.17(5) apply for the purposes of determining the date fixed for the commencement of the trial.

Table 6 Claims allocated to the fast track

	If the claim concludes 14 days or less before the date fixed for commencement of the trial	**If the claim concludes more than 14 days before the date fixed for commencement of the trial or before any such date has been fixed**
Type A claim	50%	27.5%
Type B claim	100%	100%
Type C claim	62.5%	62.5%

Table 7 **Claims allocated to the multi-track**

	If the claim concludes 21 days or less before the date fixed for commencement of the trial	If the claim concludes more than 21 days before the date fixed for commencement of the trial or before any such date has been fixed
Type A claim	75%	27.5%
Type B claim	100%	100%
Type C claim	75%	62.5%

45.26 Alternative Percentage Increase

(1) In cases to which this Section applies and subject to paragraph (2) below, rules 45.18(2) to (4) apply where the percentage increase is the amount allowed under rules 45.24 and 45.25.
(2) For the purposes of this section, the sum of £250,000 shall be substituted for the sum of £500,000 in rules 45.18(2)(a) to (c).
(3) Where the percentage increase of fees is assessed by the court under rule 45.18(4), as applied by paragraph 1 above, the percentage increase to be allowed shall be the amount shown in Table 8.
(4) The percentage increase cannot be varied where the case concludes at trial.

Table 8

Type of claim	Amount allowed	
A	If the percentage increase is assessed as greater than 40% or less than 15%, the percentage increase that is assessed by the court.	If the percentage increase is assessed as no greater than 40% and no less than 15%— (i) 27.5%; and (ii) the costs of the application and assessment shall be paid by the applicant.
B	If the percentage increase is assessed as less than 75%, the percentage increase that is assessed by the court.	If the percentage increase is assessed as no less than 75%— (i) 100%; and (ii) the costs of the application and assessment shall be paid by the applicant.
C	If the percentage increase is assessed as greater than 75% or less than 50%, the percentage increase that is assessed by the court.	If the percentage increase is assessed as no greater than 75% and no less than 50%— (i) 62.5%; and (ii) the costs of the application and assessment shall be paid by the applicant.

[PD 43–48 is positioned after CPR 48.]

CPR Part 46 Fast Track Trial Costs

Part 46 **67.2, 68.29, 68.61** [For commentary on a specific rule, please refer to the cross-references after the title of the rule.]

46.1 Scope of This Part

(1) This Part deals with the amount of costs which the court may award as the costs of an advocate for preparing for and appearing at the trial of a claim in the fast track (referred to in this rule as 'fast track trial costs').

(2) For the purposes of this Part—
  (a) 'advocate' means a person exercising a right of audience as a representative of, or on behalf of, a party;
  (b) 'fast track trial costs' means the costs of a party's advocate for preparing for and appearing at the trial, but does not include—
    (i) any other disbursements; or
    (ii) any value added tax payable on the fees of a party's advocate; and
  (c) 'trial' includes a hearing where the court decides an amount of money or the value of goods following a judgment under Part 12 (default judgment) or Part 14 (admissions) but does not include—
    (i) the hearing of an application for summary judgment under Part 24; or
    (ii) the court's approval of a settlement or other compromise under rule 21.10. (Part 21 deals with claims made by or on behalf of, or against, children and patients)

46.2 Amount of Fast Track Trial Costs

r.46.2 **42.15, 68.6**
r.46.2(2)–(4) **68.6**
r.46.2(6) **68.6**

(1) The following table shows the amount of fast track trial costs which the court may award (whether by summary or detailed assessment).

Value of the claim	Amount of fast track trial costs which the court may award
Up to £3,000	£350
More than £3,000 but not more than £10,000	£500
More than £10,000	£750

(2) The court may not award more or less than the amount shown in the table except where—
  (a) it decides not to award any fast track trial costs; or
  (b) rule 46.3 applies,

but the court may apportion the amount awarded between the parties to reflect their respective degrees of success on the issues at trial.

(3) Where the only claim is for the payment of money—
  (a) for the purpose of quantifying fast track trial costs awarded to a claimant, the value of the claim is the total amount of the judgment excluding—
    (i) interest and costs; and
    (ii) any reduction made for contributory negligence.
  (b) for the purpose of the quantifying fast track trial costs awarded to a defendant, the value of the claim is—

(i) the amount specified in the claim form (excluding interest and costs);
(ii) if no amount is specified, the maximum amount which the claimant reasonably expected to recover according to the statement of value included in the claim form under rule 16.3; or
(iii) more than £10,000, if the claim form states that the claimant cannot reasonably say how much he expects to recover.

(4) Where the claim is only for a remedy other than the payment of money the value of the claim is deemed to be more than £3,000 but not more than £10,000, unless the court orders otherwise.

(5) Where the claim includes both a claim for the payment of money and for a remedy other than the payment of money, the value of the claim is deemed to be the higher of—
(a) the value of the money claim decided in accordance with paragraph (3); or
(b) the deemed value of the other remedy decided in accordance with paragraph (4), unless the court orders otherwise.

(6) Where—
(a) a defendant has made a counterclaim against the claimant;
(b) the counterclaim has a higher value than the claim; and
(c) the claimant succeeds at trial both on his claim and the counterclaim,

for the purpose of quantifying fast track trial costs awarded to the claimant, the value of the claim is the value of the defendant's counterclaim calculated in accordance with this rule.

(Rule 20.4 sets out how a defendant may make a counterclaim)

46.3 Power to Award More or Less Than the Amount of Fast Track Trial Costs

r.46.3 **68.6**
r.46.3(2) **68.6**
r.46.3(3)–(4) **68.7**
r.46.3(6) **68.6**
r.46.3(7)–(8) **68.7**

(1) This rule sets out when a court may award—
(a) an additional amount to the amount of fast track trial costs shown in the table in rule 46.2(1); and
(b) less than those amounts.

(2) If—
(a) in addition to the advocate, a party's legal representative attends the trial;
(b) the court considers that it was necessary for a legal representative to attend to assist the advocate; and
(c) the court awards fast track trial costs to that party, the court may award an additional £250 in respect of the legal representative's attendance at the trial.

(Legal representative is defined in rule 2.3)

(2A) The court may in addition award a sum representing an additional liability.

(The requirements to provide information about a funding arrangement where a party wishes to recover any additional liability under a funding arrangement are set out in the costs practice direction)

('Additional liability' is defined in rule 43.2)

(3) If the court considers that it is necessary to direct a separate trial of an issue then the court may award an additional amount in respect of the separate trial but that amount is limited in accordance with paragraph (4) of this rule.

(4) The additional amount the court may award under paragraph 3 must not exceed two-thirds of the amount payable for that claim, subject to a minimum award of £350.

(5) Where the party to whom fast track trial costs are to be awarded is a litigant in person, the court will award—
(a) if the litigant in person can prove financial loss, two-thirds of the amount that would otherwise be awarded; or
(b) if the litigant in person fails to prove financial loss, an amount in respect of the time spent reasonably doing the work at the rate specified in the costs practice direction.

(6) Where a defendant has made a counterclaim against the claimant, and—
(a) the claimant has succeeded on his claim; and
(b) the defendant has succeeded on his counterclaim,

the court will quantify the amount of the award of fast track trial costs to which—

(i) but for the counterclaim, the claimant would be entitled for succeeding on his claim; and

(ii) but for the claim, the defendant would be entitled for succeeding on his counterclaim,

and make one award of the difference, if any, to the party entitled to the higher award of costs.

(7) Where the court considers that the party to whom fast track trial costs are to be awarded has behaved unreasonably or improperly during the trial, it may award that party an amount less than would otherwise be payable for that claim, as it considers appropriate.

(8) Where the court considers that the party who is to pay the fast track trial costs has behaved improperly during the trial the court may award such additional amount to the other party as it considers appropriate.

46.4 Fast Track Trial Costs Where There Is More Than One Claimant or Defendant

r.46.4 **68.6**

(1) Where the same advocate is acting for more than one party—

(a) the court may make only one award in respect of fast track trial costs payable to that advocate; and

(b) the parties for whom the advocate is acting are jointly entitled to any fast track trial costs awarded by the court.

(2) Where—

(a) the same advocate is acting for more than one claimant; and

(b) each claimant has a separate claim against the defendant,

the value of the claim, for the purpose of quantifying the award in respect of fast track trial costs is to be ascertained in accordance with paragraph (3).

(3) The value of the claim in the circumstances mentioned in paragraph (2) is—

(a) where the only claim of each claimant is for the payment of money—

(i) if the award of fast track trial costs is in favour of the claimants, the total amount of the judgment made in favour of all the claimants jointly represented; or

(ii) if the award is in favour of the defendant, the total amount claimed by the claimants,

and in either case, quantified in accordance with rule 46.2(3);

(b) where the only claim of each claimant is for a remedy other than the payment of money, deemed to be more than £3,000 but not more than £10,000; and

(c) where claims of the claimants include both a claim for the payment of money and for a remedy other than the payment of money, deemed to be—

(i) more than £3,000 but not more than £10,000; or

(ii) if greater, the value of the money claims calculated in accordance with sub-paragraph (a) above.

(4) Where—

(a) there is more than one defendant; and

(b) any or all of the defendants are separately represented,

the court may award fast track trial costs to each party who is separately represented.

(5) Where—

(a) there is more than one claimant; and

(b) a single defendant,

the court may make only one award to the defendant of fast track trial costs, for which the claimants are jointly and severally liable[(GL)].

(6) For the purpose of quantifying the fast track trial costs awarded to the single defendant under paragraph (5), the value of the claim is to be calculated in accordance with paragraph (3) of this rule.

[PD 43–48 is positioned after CPR 48.]

CPR Part 47 Procedure for Detailed Assessment of Costs and Default Provisions

Part 47 **67.2, 68.29, 68.61** [For commentary on a specific rule, please refer to the cross-references after the title of the rule.]

(The definitions contained in Part 43 are relevant to this Part)

I GENERAL RULES ABOUT DETAILED ASSESSMENT

47.1 Time When Detailed Assessment May Be Carried Out

r.47.1 **66.28, 68.9**

The general rule is that the costs of any proceedings or any part of the proceedings are not to be assessed by the detailed procedure until the conclusion of the proceedings but the court may order them to be assessed immediately.

(The costs practice direction [PD 43–48] gives further guidance about when proceedings are concluded for the purpose of this rule)

47.2 No Stay of Detailed Assessment Where There Is an Appeal

Detailed assessment is not stayed pending an appeal unless the court so orders.

47.3 Powers of an Authorised Court Officer

(1) An authorised court officer has all the powers of the court when making a detailed assessment, except—

(a) power to make a wasted costs order as defined in rule 48.7;
(b) power to make an order under—
  (i) rule 44.14 (powers in relation to misconduct);
  (ii) rule 47.8 (sanction for delay in commencing detailed assessment proceedings);
  (iii) paragraph (2) (objection to detailed assessment by authorised court officer); and
(c) power to make a detailed assessment of costs payable to a solicitor by his client, unless the costs are being assessed under rule 48.5 (costs where money is payable to a child or patient).

(2) Where a party objects to the detailed assessment of costs being made by an authorised court officer, the court may order it to be made by a costs judge or a district judge.

(The costs practice direction [PD 43–48] sets out the relevant procedure)

47.4 Venue for Detailed Assessment Proceedings

r.47.4 **68.10** r.47.4(2)–(3) **68.10**

(1) All applications and requests in detailed assessment proceedings must be made to or filed at the appropriate office.
(The costs practice direction sets out the meaning of 'appropriate office' in any particular case)

(2) The court may direct that the appropriate office is to be the Supreme Court Costs Office.

(3) A county court may direct that another county court is to be the appropriate office.

(4) A direction under paragraph (3) may be made without proceedings being transferred to that court.

(Rule 30.2 makes provision for any county court to transfer the proceedings to another county court for detailed assessment of costs)

II COSTS PAYABLE BY ONE PARTY TO ANOTHER — COMMENCEMENT OF DETAILED ASSESSMENT PROCEEDINGS

47.5 Application of This Section

This section of Part 47 applies where a costs officer is to make a detailed assessment of costs which are payable by one party to another.

47.6 Commencement of Detailed Assessment Proceedings

r.47.6(1)–(2) **68.11**

(1) Detailed assessment proceedings are commenced by the receiving party serving on the paying party—
  (a) notice of commencement in the relevant practice form; and
  (b) a copy of the bill of costs.

(Rule 47.7 sets out the period for commencing detailed assessment proceedings)

(2) The receiving party must also serve a copy of the notice of commencement and the bill on any other relevant persons specified in the costs practice direction.

(3) A person on whom a copy of the notice of commencement is served under paragraph (2) is a party to the detailed assessment proceedings (in addition to the paying party and the receiving party).

(The costs practice direction [PD 43–48] deals with—
- other documents which the party must file when he requests detailed assessment;
- the court's powers where it considers that a hearing may be necessary;
- the form of a bill; and
- the length of notice which will be given if a hearing date is fixed)

47.7 Period for Commencing Detailed Assessment Proceedings

r.47.7 **68.11**

The following table shows the period for commencing detailed assessment proceedings.

Source of right to detailed assessment	Time by which detailed assessment proceedings must be commenced
Judgment, direction, order, award or other determination	3 months after the date of the judgment etc. Where detailed assessment is stayed pending an appeal, 3 months after the date of the order lifting the stay
Discontinuance under Part 38	3 months after the date of service of notice of discontinuance under rule 38.3; or 3 months after the date of the dismissal of application to set the notice of discontinuance aside under rule 38.4
Acceptance of an offer to settle or a payment into court under Part 36	3 months after the date when the right to costs arose

47.8 Sanction for Delay in Commencing Detailed Assessment Proceedings

r.47.8(2)–(3) **68.24**

(1) Where the receiving party fails to commence detailed assessment proceedings within the period specified—
  (a) in rule 47.7; or
  (b) by any direction of the court,
the paying party may apply for an order requiring the receiving party to commence detailed assessment proceedings within such time as the court may specify.

(2) On an application under paragraph (1), the court may direct that,
unless the receiving party commences detailed assessment proceedings within the time specified by the court, all or part of the costs to which the receiving party would otherwise be entitled will be disallowed.

(3) If—
  (a) the paying party has not made an application in accordance with paragraph (1); and
  (b) the receiving party commences the proceedings later than the period specified in rule 47.7,
the court may disallow all or part of the interest otherwise payable to the receiving party under—
    (i) section 17 of the Judgments Act 1838; or
    (ii) section 74 of the County Courts Act 1984,
but must not impose any other sanction except in accordance with rule 44.14 (powers in relation to misconduct).

(4) Where the costs to be assessed in a detailed assessment are payable out of the Community Legal Service Fund, this rule applies as if the receiving party were the solicitor to whom the costs are payable and the paying party were the Legal Services Commission.

47.9 Points of Dispute and Consequence of Not Serving

r.47.9 **68.13** r.47.9(3)–(4) **68.14**

(1) The paying party and any other party to the detailed assessment proceedings may dispute any item in the bill of costs by serving points of dispute on—
  (a) the receiving party; and
  (b) every other party to the detailed assessment proceedings.

(2) The period for serving points of dispute is 21 days after the date of service of the notice of commencement.

(3) If a party serves points of dispute after the period set out in paragraph (2), he may not be heard further in the detailed assessment proceedings unless the court gives permission.

(The costs practice direction [PD 43–48] sets out requirements about the form of points of dispute)

(4) The receiving party may file a request for a default costs certificate if—
  (a) the period set out in rule 47.9(2) for serving points of dispute has expired; and
  (b) he has not been served with any points of dispute.

(5) If any party (including the paying party) serves points of dispute before the issue of a default costs certificate the court may not issue the default costs certificate.

(Section IV of this Part sets out the procedure to be followed after points of dispute have been filed)

47.10 Procedure Where Costs Are Agreed

(1) If the paying party and the receiving party agree the amount of costs, either party may apply for a costs certificate (either interim or final) in the amount agreed.

(Rule 47.15 and rule 47.16 contain further provisions about interim and final costs certificates respectively)

(2) An application for a certificate under paragraph (1) must be made to the court which would be the venue for detailed assessment proceedings under rule 47.4.

III COSTS PAYABLE BY ONE PARTY TO ANOTHER — DEFAULT PROVISIONS

47.11 Default Costs Certificate

r.47.11 **67.2, 68.14** r.47.11(2) **68.14**

(1) Where the receiving party is permitted by rule 47.9 to obtain a default costs certificate, he does so by filing a request in the relevant practice form.

(The costs practice direction [PD 43–48] deals with the procedure by which the receiving party may obtain a default costs certificate)

(2) A default costs certificate will include an order to pay the costs to which it relates.

(3) Where a receiving party obtains a default costs certificate, the costs payable to him for the commencement of detailed assessment proceedings shall be the sum set out in the costs practice direction.

47.12 Setting Aside Default Costs Certificate

r.47.12 **68.14**

(1) The court must set aside a default costs certificate if the receiving party was not entitled to it.

(2) In any other case, the court may set aside or vary a default costs certificate if it appears to the court that there is some good reason why the detailed assessment proceedings should continue.

(3) Where—
   (a) the receiving party has purported to serve the notice of commencement on the paying party;
   (b) a default costs certificate has been issued; and
   (c) the receiving party subsequently discovers that the notice of commencement did not reach the paying party at least 21 days before the default costs certificate was issued,

the receiving party must—
   (i) file a request for the default costs certificate to be set aside; or
   (ii) apply to the court for directions.

(4) Where paragraph (3) applies, the receiving party may take no further step in—
   (a) the detailed assessment proceedings; or
   (b) the enforcement of the default costs certificate,

until the certificate has been set aside or the court has given directions.

(The costs practice direction [PD 43–48] contains further details about the procedure for setting aside a default costs certificate and the matters which the court must take into account)

IV COSTS PAYABLE BY ONE PARTY TO ANOTHER — PROCEDURE WHERE POINTS OF DISPUTE ARE SERVED

47.13 Optional Reply

r.47.13 **68.15**

(1) Where any party to the detailed assessment proceedings serves points of dispute, the receiving party may serve a reply on the other parties to the assessment proceedings.

(2) He may do so within 21 days after service on him of the points of dispute to which his reply relates.

(The costs practice direction [PD 43–48] sets out the meaning of reply)

47.14 Detailed Assessment Hearing

r.47.14 **68.17** r.47.14(5) **68.17**
r.47.14(3) **68.17** r.47.14(7) **68.17**
r.47.14(4) **68.17**

(1) Where points of dispute are served in accordance with this Part, the receiving party must file a request for a detailed assessment hearing.
(2) He must file the request within 3 months of the expiry of the period for commencing detailed assessment proceedings as specified—
  (a) in rule 47.7; or
  (b) by any direction of the court.
(3) Where the receiving party fails to file a request in accordance with paragraph (2), the paying party may apply for an order requiring the receiving party to file the request within such time as the court may specify.
(4) On an application under paragraph (3), the court may direct that, unless the receiving party requests a detailed assessment hearing within the time specified by the court, all or part of the costs to which the receiving party would otherwise be entitled will be disallowed.
(5) If—
  (a) the paying party has not made an application in accordance with paragraph (3); and
  (b) the receiving party files a request for a detailed assessment hearing later than the period specified in paragraph (2),

the court may disallow all or part of the interest otherwise payable to the receiving party under—
    (i) section 17 of the Judgments Act 1838; or
    (ii) section 74 of the County Courts Act 1984,

but must not impose any other sanction except in accordance with rule 44.14 (powers in relation to misconduct).
(6) No party other than—
  (a) the receiving party;
  (b) the paying party; and
  (c) any party who has served points of dispute under rule 47.9,

may be heard at the detailed assessment hearing unless the court gives permission.
(7) Only items specified in the points of dispute may be raised at the hearing, unless the court gives permission.

(The costs practice direction [PD 43–48] specifies other documents which must be filed with the request for hearing and the length of notice which the court will give when it fixes a hearing date.)

V INTERIM COSTS CERTIFICATE AND FINAL COSTS CERTIFICATE

47.15 Power to Issue an Interim Certificate

r.47.15 **68.8, 68.26**

(1) The court may at any time after the receiving party has filed a request for a detailed assessment hearing—
  (a) issue an interim costs certificate for such sum as it considers appropriate;
  (b) amend or cancel an interim certificate.
(2) An interim certificate will include an order to pay the costs to which it relates, unless the court orders otherwise.
(3) The court may order the costs certified in an interim certificate to be paid into court.

47.16 Final Costs Certificate

r.47.16(2)–(3) **68.27** r.47.16(5) **68.27**

(1) In this rule a completed bill means a bill calculated to show the amount due following the detailed assessment of the costs.
(2) The period for filing the completed bill is 14 days after the end of the detailed assessment hearing.
(3) When a completed bill is filed the court will issue a final costs certificate and serve it on the parties to the detailed assessment proceedings.
(4) Paragraph (3) is subject to any order made by the court that a certificate is not to be issued until other costs have been paid.

(5) A final costs certificate will include an order to pay the costs to which it relates, unless the court orders otherwise.

(The costs practice direction [PD 43–48] deals with the form of a final costs certificate)

VI DETAILED ASSESSMENT PROCEDURE FOR COSTS OF AN ASSISTED PERSON WHERE COSTS ARE PAYABLE OUT OF THE LEGAL AID FUND

47.17 Detailed Assessment Procedure for Costs of a LSC Funded Client or an Assisted Person Where Costs Are Payable Out of the Community Legal Service Fund

r.47.17 **68.17** r.47.17(3) **68.11**
r.47.17(2) **68.11**

(1) Where the court is to assess costs of a LSC funded client or an assisted person which are payable out of the Community Legal Service Fund, that person's solicitor may commence detailed assessment proceedings by filing a request in the relevant practice form.

(2) A request under paragraph (1) must be filed within 3 months after the date when the right to detailed assessment arose.

(3) The solicitor must also serve a copy of the request for detailed assessment on the LSC funded client or the assisted person, if notice of that person's interest has been given to the court in accordance with community legal service or legal aid regulations.

(4) Where the solicitor has certified that the LSC funded client or the assisted person wishes to attend an assessment hearing, the court will, on receipt of the request for assessment, fix a date for the assessment hearing.

(5) Where paragraph (3) does not apply, the court will, on receipt of the request for assessment provisionally assess the costs without the attendance of the solicitor, unless it considers that a hearing is necessary.

(6) After the court has provisionally assessed the bill, it will return the bill to the solicitor.

(7) The court will fix a date for an assessment hearing if the solicitor informs the court, within 14 days after he receives the provisionally assessed bill, that he wants the court to hold such a hearing.

47.17A Detailed Assessment Procedure Where Costs Are Payable Out of a Fund Other Than the Community Legal Service Fund

(1) Where the court is to assess costs which are payable out of a fund other than the Community Legal Service Fund, the receiving party may commence detailed assessment proceedings by filing a request in the relevant practice form.

(2) A request under paragraph (1) must be filed within 3 months after the date when the right to detailed assessment arose.

(3) The court may direct that the party seeking assessment serve a copy of the request on any person who has a financial interest in the outcome of the assessment.

(4) The court will, on receipt of the request for assessment, provisionally assess the costs without the attendance of the receiving party, unless it considers that a hearing is necessary.

(5) After the court has provisionally assessed the bill, it will return the bill to the receiving party.

(6) The court will fix a date for an assessment hearing if the party informs the court, within 14 days after he receives the provisionally assessed bill, that he wants the court to hold such a hearing.

VII COSTS OF DETAILED ASSESSMENT PROCEEDINGS

47.18 Liability for Costs of Detailed Assessment Proceedings

r.47.18 **68.21, 68.22**

(1) The receiving party is entitled to his costs of the detailed assessment proceedings except where—
   (a) the provisions of any Act, any of these Rules or any relevant practice direction provide otherwise; or
   (b) the court makes some other order in relation to all or part of the costs of the detailed assessment proceedings.

(2) In deciding whether to make some other order, the court must have regard to all the circumstances, including—
  (a) the conduct of all the parties;
  (b) the amount, if any, by which the bill of costs has been reduced; and
  (c) whether it was reasonable for a party to claim the costs of a particular item or to dispute that item.

47.19 Offers to Settle without Prejudice Save as to Costs of the Detailed Assessment Proceedings

r.47.19 **66.2, 67.15, 68.22**

(1) Where—
  (a) a party (whether the paying party or the receiving party) makes a written offer to settle the costs of the proceedings which gave rise to the assessment proceedings; and
  (b) the offer is expressed to be without prejudice(GL) save as to the costs of the detailed assessment proceedings,

  the court will take the offer into account in deciding who should pay the costs of those proceedings.

(2) The fact of the offer must not be communicated to the costs officer until the question of costs of the detailed assessment proceedings falls to be decided.

(The costs practice direction [PD 43–48] provides that rule 47.19 does not apply where the receiving party is a LSC funded client or an assisted person, unless the court orders otherwise)

VIII APPEALS FROM AUTHORISED COURT OFFICERS IN DETAILED ASSESSMENT PROCEEDINGS

47.20 Right to Appeal

r.47.20 **68.28**

(1) Any party to detailed assessment proceedings may appeal against a decision of an authorised court officer in those proceedings.

(2) For the purposes of this Section, a LSC funded client or an assisted person is not a party to detailed assessment proceedings.

(Part 52 sets out general rules about appeals)

47.21 Court to Hear Appeal

r.47.21 **68.28, 71.11**

An appeal against a decision of an authorised court officer is to a costs judge or a district judge of the High Court.

47.22 Appeal Procedure

r.47.22 **68.28** r.47.22(2) **68.28**
r.47.22(1) **68.28**

(1) The appellant must file an appeal notice within 14 days after the date of the decision he wishes to appeal against.

(2) On receipt of the appeal notice, the court will—
  (a) serve a copy of the notice on the parties to the detailed assessment proceedings; and
  (b) give notice of the appeal hearing to those parties.

47.23 Powers of the Court on Appeal

r.47.23 **68.28**

On an appeal from an authorised court officer the court will—
(a) rehear the proceedings which gave rise to the decision appealed against; and
(b) make any order and give any directions as it considers appropriate.

[PD 43–48 is positioned after CPR 48.]

CPR Part 48 Costs — Special Cases

Part 48 **48.75, 67.2, 68.29, 68.61** [For commentary on a specific rule, please refer to the cross-references after the title of the rule.]

(The definitions contained in Part 43 are relevant to this Part)

I COSTS PAYABLE BY OR TO PARTICULAR PERSONS

48.1 Pre-commencement Disclosure and Orders for Disclosure against a Person Who Is Not a Party

r.48.1 **48.80, 66.32**
r.48.1(2) **48.75, 48.80, 55.6**
r.48.1(3) **48.75, 48.80, 66.32**

(1) This paragraph applies where a person applies—
  (a) for an order under—
    (i) section 33 of the Supreme Court Act 1981; or
    (ii) section 52 of the County Courts Act 1984,
  (which give the court powers exercisable before commencement of proceedings); or
  (b) for an order under—
    (i) section 34 of the Supreme Court Act 1981; or
    (ii) section 53 of the County Courts Act 1984,
  (which give the court power to make an order against a non-party for disclosure of documents, inspection of property etc.).
(2) The general rule is that the court will award the person against whom the order is sought his costs—
  (a) of the application; and
  (b) of complying with any order made on the application.
(3) The court may however make a different order, having regard to all the circumstances, including—
  (a) the extent to which it was reasonable for the person against whom the order was sought to oppose the application; and
  (b) whether the parties to the application have complied with any relevant pre-action protocol.

48.2 Costs Orders in Favour of or against Non-parties

r.48.2 **6.19, 66.67**

(1) Where the court is considering whether to exercise its power under section 51 of the Supreme Court Act 1981 (costs are in the discretion of the court) to make a costs order in favour of or against a person who is not a party to proceedings—
  (a) that person must be added as a party to the proceedings for the purposes of costs only; and

(b) he must be given a reasonable opportunity to attend a hearing at which the court will consider the matter further.

(2) This rule does not apply—

(a) where the court is considering whether to—

(i) make an order against the Legal Services Commission;

(ii) make a wasted costs order (as defined in 48.7); and

(b) in proceedings to which rule 48.1 applies (pre-commencement disclosure and orders for disclosure against a person who is not a party).

48.3 Amount of Costs Where Costs Are Payable Pursuant to a Contract

r.48.3 **66.51**

(1) Where the court assesses (whether by the summary or detailed procedure) costs which are payable by the paying party to the receiving party under the terms of a contract, the costs payable under those terms are, unless the contract expressly provides otherwise, to be presumed to be costs which—

(a) have been reasonably incurred; and

(b) are reasonable in amount,

and the court will assess them accordingly.

(The costs practice direction [PD 43–48] sets out circumstances where the court may order otherwise)

(2) This rule does not apply where the contract is between a solicitor and his client.

48.4 Limitations on Court's Power to Award Costs in Favour of Trustee or Personal Representative

r.48.4 **68.38**

(1) This rule applies where—

(a) a person is or has been a party to any proceedings in the capacity of trustee or personal representative; and

(b) rule 48.3 does not apply.

(2) The general rule is that he is entitled to be paid the costs of those proceedings, in so far as they are not recovered from or paid by any other person, out of the relevant trust fund or estate.

(3) Where he is entitled to be paid any of those costs out of the fund or estate, those costs will be assessed on the indemnity basis.

48.5 Costs Where Money Is Payable by or to a Child or Patient

r.48.5(1) **66.47** r.48.5(2)(b) **66.47**
r.48.5(2) **66.47**

(1) This rule applies to any proceedings where a party is a child or patient and—

(a) money is ordered or agreed to be paid to, or for the benefit of, that party; or

(b) money is ordered to be paid by him or on his behalf.

('Child' and 'patient' are defined in rule 2.3)

(2) The general rule is that—

(a) the court must order a detailed assessment of the costs payable by, or out of money belonging to, any party who is a child or patient; and

(b) on an assessment under paragraph (a), the court must also assess any costs payable to that party in the proceedings, unless—

(i) the court has issued a default costs certificate in relation to those costs under rule 47.11; or

(ii) the costs are payable in proceedings to which Section II of Part 45 applies.

(3) The court need not order detailed assessment of costs in the circumstances set out in the costs practice direction.

(4) Where—

(a) a claimant is a child or patient; and

(b) a detailed assessment has taken place under paragraph (2)(a),

the only amount payable by the child or patient is the amount which the court certifies as payable.

(This rule applies to a counterclaim by or on behalf of a child or patient by virtue of rule 20.3)

48.6 Litigants in Person

r.48.6 **68.54** r.48.6(6) **68.54**
r.48.6(2) **68.54** r.48.6(6)(a) **68.55**
r.48.6(3)(a)(ii) **68.56**

(1) This rule applies where the court orders (whether by summary assessment or detailed assessment) that the costs of a litigant in person are to be paid by any other person.
(2) The costs allowed under this rule must not exceed, except in the case of a disbursement, two-thirds of the amount which would have been allowed if the litigant in person had been represented by a legal representative.
(3) The litigant in person shall be allowed—
   (a) costs for the same categories of—
      (i) work; and
      (ii) disbursements,
   which would have been allowed if the work had been done or the disbursements had been made by a legal representative on the litigant in person's behalf;
   (b) the payments reasonably made by him for legal services relating to the conduct of the proceedings; and
   (c) the costs of obtaining expert assistance in assessing the costs claim.

(The costs practice direction [PD 43–48] deals with who may be an expert for the purpose of paragraph [(3)(c)*])

(4) The amount of costs to be allowed to the litigant in person for any item of work claimed shall be—
   (a) where the litigant can prove financial loss, the amount that he can prove he has lost for time reasonably spent on doing the work; or
   (b) where the litigant cannot prove financial loss, an amount for the time reasonably spent on doing the work at the rate set out in the practice direction.
(5) A litigant who is allowed costs for attending at court to conduct his case is not entitled to a witness allowance in respect of such attendance in addition to those costs.
(6) For the purposes of this rule, a litigant in person includes—
   (a) a company or other corporation which is acting without a legal representative; and
   (b) a barrister, solicitor, solicitor's employee or other authorised litigator (as defined in the Courts and Legal Services Act 1990) who is acting for himself.

48.6A Costs Where the Court Has Made a Group Litigation Order

r.48.6A **14.67** r.48.6A(2)–(7) **66.55**

(1) This rule applies where the court has made a Group Litigation Order (GLO).
(2) In this rule—
   (a) 'individual costs' means costs incurred in relation to an individual claim on the group register;
   (b) 'common costs' means—
      (i) costs incurred in relation to the GLO issues;
      (ii) individual costs incurred in a claim while it is proceeding as a test claim, and
      (iii) costs incurred by the lead solicitor in administering the group litigation; and
   (c) 'group litigant' means a claimant or defendant, as the case may be, whose claim is entered on the group register.
(3) Unless the court orders otherwise, any order for common costs against group litigants imposes on each group litigant several liability[(GL)] for an equal proportion of those common costs.
(4) The general rule is that where a group litigant is the paying party, he will, in addition to any costs he is liable to pay to the receiving party, be liable for—
   (a) the individual costs of his claim; and
   (b) an equal proportion, together with all the other group litigants, of the common costs.
(5) Where the court makes an order about costs in relation to any application or hearing which involved—
   (a) one or more GLO issues; and
   (b) issues relevant only to individual claims,

[* The text in the statutory instrument erroneously refers to paragraph (2)(c).]

the court will direct the proportion of the costs that is to relate to common costs and the proportion that is to relate to individual costs.

(6) Where common costs have been incurred before a claim is entered on the group register, the court may order the group litigant to be liable for a proportion of those costs.

(7) Where a claim is removed from the group register, the court may make an order for costs in that claim which includes a proportion of the common costs incurred up to the date on which the claim is removed from the group register.

(Part 19 sets out rules about group litigation)

II COSTS RELATING TO SOLICITORS AND OTHER LEGAL REPRESENTATIVES

48.7 Personal Liability of Legal Representative for Costs — Wasted Costs Orders

r.48.7 **66.70, 66.71** r.48.7(3) **97.52**
r.48.7(2) **66.70**

(1) This rule applies where the court is considering whether to make an order under section 51(6) of the Supreme Court Act 1981 (court's power to disallow or (as the case may be) order a legal representative to meet, 'wasted costs').

(2) The court must give the legal representative a reasonable opportunity to attend a hearing to give reasons why it should not make such an order.

(3) [*Revoked*]

(4) When the court makes a wasted costs order, it must—
  (a) specify the amount to be disallowed or paid; or
  (b) direct a costs judge or a district judge to decide the amount of costs to be disallowed or paid.

(5) The court may direct that notice must be given to the legal representative's client, in such manner as the court may direct—
  (a) of any proceedings under this rule; or
  (b) of any order made under it against his legal representative.

(6) Before making a wasted costs order, the court may direct a costs judge or a district judge to inquire into the matter and report to the court.

(7) The court may refer the question of wasted costs to a costs judge or a district judge, instead of making a wasted costs order.

48.8 Basis of Detailed Assessment of Solicitor and Client Costs

r.48.8 **63.18, 68.38, 68.53** r.48.8(2) **6.19, 63.18**
r.48.8(1) **6.19** r.48.8(3) **6.18, 6.21, 6.23**
r.48.8(1A) **6.19** r.48.8(4) **6.18, 6.21**

(1) This rule applies to every assessment of a solicitor's bill to his client except a bill which is to be paid out of the Community Legal Service Fund under the Legal Aid Act 1988 or the Access to Justice Act 1999.

(1A) Section 74(3) of the Solicitors Act 1974 applies unless the solicitor and client have entered into a written agreement which expressly permits payment to the solicitor of an amount of costs greater than that which the client could have recovered from another party to the proceedings.

(2) Subject to paragraph (1A), costs are to be assessed on the indemnity basis but are to be presumed—
  (a) to have been reasonably incurred if they were incurred with the express or implied approval of the client;
  (b) to be reasonable in amount if their amount was expressly or impliedly approved by the client;
  (c) to have been unreasonably incurred if—
    (i) they are of an unusual nature or amount; and
    (ii) the solicitor did not tell his client that as a result he might not recover all of them from the other party.

(3) Where the court is considering a percentage increase, whether on the application of the legal representative under rule 44.16 or on the application of the client, the court will have regard to all the relevant factors as they reasonably appeared to the solicitor or counsel when the conditional fee agreement was entered into or varied.

(4) In paragraph (3), 'conditional fee agreement' means an agreement enforceable under section 58 of the Courts and Legal Services Act 1990 at the date on which that agreement was entered into or varied.

48.9 [*Revoked*]

48.10 Assessment Procedure

r.48.10 **63.9, 63.18, 68.53** r.48.10(2)–(4) **68.19**

(1) This rule sets out the procedure to be followed where the court has made an order under Part III of the Solicitors Act 1974 for the assessment of costs payable to a solicitor by his client.
(2) The solicitor must serve a breakdown of costs within 28 days of the order for costs to be assessed.
(3) The client must serve points of dispute within 14 days after service on him of the breakdown of costs.
(4) If the solicitor wishes to serve a reply, he must do so within 14 days of service on him of the points of dispute.
(5) Either party may file a request for a hearing date—
(a) after points of dispute have been served; but
(b) no later than 3 months after the date of the order for the costs to be assessed.
(6) This procedure applies subject to any contrary order made by the court.

PD 43–48 Practice Direction about Costs

This practice direction supplements CPR Parts 43 to 48

PD 43–48 **63.19**, **65.2**, **68.48** [For commentary on a specific paragraph, please refer to the cross-references after the title of the paragraph.]

PD 43–48 (Practice Direction about Costs supplementing CPR, Parts 43–48) **5.12, 63.19, 68.48, 68.58**

Section 1 Introduction

1.1 This practice direction supplements Parts 43 to 48 of the Civil Procedure Rules. It applies to all proceedings to which those Parts apply.

1.2 Paragraphs 57.1 to 57.9 of this practice direction deal with various transitional provisions affecting proceedings about costs.

1.3 Attention is drawn to the powers to make orders about costs conferred on the Supreme Court and any county court by the Supreme Court Act 1981, s. 51.

1.4 In these directions:

'counsel' means a barrister or other person with a right of audience in relation to proceedings in the High Court or in the county courts in which he is instructed to act;

'LSC' means Legal Services Commission;

'solicitor' means a solicitor of the Supreme Court or other person with a right of audience in relation to proceedings, who is conducting the claim or defence (as the case may be) on behalf of a party to the proceedings and, where the context admits, includes a patent agent.

1.5 In respect of any document which is required by these directions to be signed by a party or his legal representative PD 22 will apply as if the document in question was a statement of truth. (PD 22 makes provision for cases in which a party is a child, a patient or a company or other corporation and cases in which a document is signed on behalf of a partnership.)

Section 2 Scope of Costs Rules and Definitions

Rule 43.2 definitions and application

para.2.1 **68.46**

2.1 Where the court makes an order for costs and the receiving party has entered into a funding arrangement as defined in r. 43.2, the costs payable by the paying party include any additional liability (also defined in r. 43.2) unless the court orders otherwise.

2.2 In the following paragraphs—

'funding arrangement', 'percentage increase', 'insurance premium', 'membership organisation' and 'additional liability' have the meanings given to them by r. 43.2;

a 'conditional fee agreement' is an agreement with a person providing advocacy or litigation services which provides for his fees and expenses, or part of them, to be payable only in specified circumstances, whether or not it provides for a success fee as mentioned in the Courts and Legal Services Act 1990, s. 58(2)(b);

'base costs' means costs other than the amount of any additional liability.

2.3 Rule 44.3A(1) provides that the court will not assess any additional liability until the conclusion of the proceedings or the part of the proceedings to which the funding arrangement relates. (As to the time when detailed assessment may be carried out see para. 27.1 below.)

2.4 For the purposes of the following paragraphs of this practice direction and r. 44.3A proceedings are concluded when the court has finally determined the matters in issue in the claim, whether or not there is an appeal. The making of an award of provisional damages under Part 41 will also be treated as a final determination of the matters in issue.

2.5 The court may order or the parties may agree in writing that, although the proceedings are continuing, they will nevertheless be treated as concluded.

Section 3 Model Forms for Claims for Costs

Rule 43.3 meaning of summary assessment

3.1 Rule 43.3 defines summary assessment. When carrying out a summary assessment of costs where there is an additional liability the court may assess the base costs alone, or the base costs and the additional liability.

3.2 Form N260 is a model form of statement of costs to be used for summary assessments.

3.3 Further details about statements of costs are given in para. 13.5 below.

Rule 43.4 meaning of detailed assessment

3.4 Rule 43.4 defines detailed assessment. When carrying out a detailed assessment of costs where there is an additional liability the court will assess both the base costs and the additional liability, or, if the base costs have already been assessed, the additional liability alone.

3.5 Precedents A, B, C and D in the Schedule of Costs Precedents annexed to this practice direction are model forms of bills of costs to be used for detailed assessments.

3.6 Further details about bills of costs are given in the next section of these directions and in para. 28.1 to 49.1 below.

3.7 Precedents A, B, C and D in the Schedule of Costs Precedents and the next section of this practice direction all refer to a model form of bill of costs. The use of a model form is not compulsory, but is encouraged. A party wishing to rely upon a bill which departs from the model forms should include in the background information of the bill an explanation for that departure.

3.8 In any order of the court (whether made before or after 26 April 1999) the word 'taxation' will be taken to mean 'detailed assessment' and the words 'to be taxed' will be taken to mean 'to be decided by detailed assessment' unless in either case the context otherwise requires.

Section 4 Form and Contents of Bills of Costs

para.4.1 **68.12**
para.4.2 **68.12**
para.4.2(4) **68.59**
para.4.4(3) **68.59**
para.4.6(7) **68.18**
para.4.9 **68.12**
para.4.14 **68.59**
para.4.16 **68.43**

4.1 A bill of costs may consist of such of the following sections as may be appropriate:
(1) title page;
(2) background information;
(3) items of costs claimed under the headings specified in para. 4.6;
(4) summary showing the total costs claimed on each page of the bill;
(5) schedules of time spent on non-routine attendances; and
(6) the certificates referred to in para. 4.15.

4.2 Where it is necessary or convenient to do so, a bill of costs may be divided into two or more parts, each part containing sections (2), (3) and (4) above. A division into parts will be necessary or convenient in the following circumstances:

(1) Where the receiving party acted in person during the course of the proceedings (whether or not he also had a legal representative at that time) the bill should be divided into different parts so as to distinguish between;
(a) the costs claimed for work done by the legal representative; and
(b) the costs claimed for work done by the receiving party in person.
(2) Where the receiving party was represented by different solicitors during the course of the proceedings, the bill should be divided into different parts so as to distinguish between the costs payable in respect of each solicitor.
(3) Where the receiving party obtained legal aid or LSC funding in respect of all or part of the proceedings the bill should be divided into separate parts so as to distinguish between:
(a) costs claimed before legal aid or LSC funding was granted;
(b) costs claimed after legal aid or LSC funding was granted; and
(c) any costs claimed after legal aid or LSC funding ceased.
(4) Where value added tax (VAT) is claimed and there was a change in the rate of VAT during the course of the proceedings, the bill should be divided into separate parts so as to distinguish between:
(a) costs claimed at the old rate of VAT; and
(b) costs claimed at the new rate of VAT.
(5) Where the bill covers costs payable under an order or orders under which there are different paying parties the bill should be divided into parts so as to deal separately with the costs payable by each paying party.
(6) Where the bill covers costs payable under an order or orders, in respect of which the receiving party wishes to claim interest from different dates, the bill should be divided to enable such interest to be calculated.

4.3 Where a party claims costs against another party and also claims costs against the LSC only for work done in the same period, the costs claimed against the LSC only can be claimed either in a separate part of the bill or in additional columns in the same part of the bill. Precedents C and D in the Schedule of Costs Precedents annexed to this practice direction show how bills should be drafted when costs are claimed against the LSC only.

4.4 The title page of the bill of costs must set out:
(1) the full title of the proceedings;
(2) the name of the party whose bill it is and a description of the document showing the right to assessment (as to which see para. 40.4 below);
(3) if VAT is included as part of the claim for costs, the VAT number of the legal representative or other person in respect of whom VAT is claimed;
(4) details of all legal aid certificates, LSC certificates and relevant amendment certificates in respect of which claims for costs are included in the bill.

4.5 The background information included in the bill of costs should set out:
(1) a brief description of the proceedings up to the date of the notice of commencement;
(2) a statement of the status of the solicitor or solicitor's employee in respect of whom costs are claimed and (if those costs are calculated on the basis of hourly rates) the hourly rates claimed for each such person.
It should be noted that 'legal executive' means a Fellow of the Institute of Legal Executives. Other clerks, who are fee earners of equivalent experience, may be entitled to similar rates. It should be borne in mind that Fellows of the Institute of Legal Executives will have spent approximately six years in practice, and taken both general and specialist examinations. The Fellows have therefore acquired considerable practical and academic experience. Clerks without the equivalent experience of legal executives will normally be treated as being the equivalent of trainee solicitors and paralegals.
(3) a brief explanation of any agreement or arrangement between the receiving party and his solicitors, which affects the costs claimed in the bill.

4.6 The bill of costs may consist of items under such of the following heads as may be appropriate:
(1) attendance on the court and counsel up to the date of the notice of commencement;
(2) attendances on and communications with the receiving party;
(3) attendances on and communications with witnesses including any expert witness;
(4) attendances to inspect any property or place for the purposes of the proceedings;

(5) attendances on and communications with other persons, including offices of public records;
(6) communications with the court and with counsel;
(7) work done on documents: preparing and considering documentation, including documentation relating to pre-action protocols where appropriate, work done in connection with arithmetical calculations of compensation and/or interest and time spent collating documents;
(8) work done in connection with negotiations with a view to settlement if not already covered in the heads listed above;
(9) attendances on and communications with London and other agents and work done by them;
(10) other work done which was of or incidental to the proceedings and which is not already covered in the heads listed above.

4.7 In respect of each of the heads of costs:
(1) 'communications' means letters out and telephone calls;
(2) communications, which are not routine communications, must be set out in chronological order;
(3) routine communications should be set out as a single item at the end of each head;

4.8 Routine communications are letters out, emails out and telephone calls which because of their simplicity should not be regarded as letters or emails of substance or telephone calls which properly amount to an attendance.

4.9 Each item claimed in the bill of costs must be consecutively numbered.

4.10 In each part of the bill of costs which claims items under head (1) (attendances on court and counsel) a note should be made of:
(1) all relevant events, including events which do not constitute chargeable items;
(2) any orders for costs which the court made (whether or not a claim is made in respect of those costs in this bill of costs).

4.11 The numbered items of costs may be set out on paper divided into columns. Precedents A, B, C and D in the Schedule of Costs precedents annexed to this practice direction illustrate various model forms of bills of costs.

4.12 In respect of heads (2) to (10) in para. 4.6 above, if the number of attendances and communications other than routine communications is 20 or more, the claim for the costs of those items in that section of the bill of costs should be for the total only and should refer to a schedule in which the full record of dates and details is set out. If the bill of costs contains more than one schedule each schedule should be numbered consecutively.

4.13 The bill of costs must not contain any claims in respect of costs or court fees which relate solely to the detailed assessment proceedings other than costs claimed for preparing and checking the bill.

4.14 The summary must show the total profit costs and disbursements claimed separately from the total VAT claimed. Where the bill of costs is divided into parts the summary must also give totals for each part. If each page of the bill gives a page total the summary must also set out the page totals for each page.

4.15 The bill of costs must contain such of the certificates, the texts of which are set out in Precedent F of the Schedule of Costs Precedents annexed to this practice direction, as are appropriate.

4.16 The following provisions relate to work done by solicitors:
(1) Routine letters out and routine telephone calls will in general be allowed on a unit basis of 6 minutes each, the charge being calculated by reference to the appropriate hourly rate. The unit charge for letters out will include perusing and considering the relevant letters in and no separate charge should be made for incoming letters.
(2) Emails received by solicitors will not normally be allowed. The court may, in its discretion, allow an actual time charge for preparation of emails sent by solicitors, which properly amount to attendances provided that the time taken has been recorded. The court may also, in its discretion allow a sum in respect of routine emails sent to the client or others on a unit basis of 6 minutes each, the charge being calculated by reference to the appropriate hourly rate.
(3) Local travelling expenses incurred by solicitors will not be allowed. The definition of 'local' is a matter for the discretion of the court. While no absolute rule can be laid down, as a

matter of guidance, 'local' will, in general, be taken to mean within a radius of 10 miles from the court dealing with the case at the relevant time. Where travelling and waiting time is claimed, this should be allowed at the rate agreed with the client unless this is more than the hourly rate on the assessment.

(4) The cast of postage, couriers, outgoing telephone calls, fax and telex messages will in general not be allowed but the court may exceptionally in its discretion allow such expenses in unusual circumstances or where the cost is unusually heavy.

(5) The cost of making copies of documents will not in general be allowed but the court may exceptionally in its discretion make an allowance for copying in unusual circumstances or where the documents copied are unusually numerous in relation to the nature of the case. Where this discretion is invoked the number of copies made, their purpose and the costs claimed for them must be set out in the bill.

(6) Agency charges as between a principal solicitor and his agent will be dealt with on the principle that such charges, where appropriate, form part of the principal solicitor's charges. Where these charges relate to head (1) in para. 4.6 (attendances at court and on counsel) they should be included in their chronological order in that head. In other cases they should be included in head (9) (attendances on London and other agents).

4.17 (1) Where a claim is made for a percentage increase in addition to an hourly rate or base fee, the amount of the increase must be shown separately, either in the appropriate arithmetic column or in the narrative column. (For an example see Precedent A or Precedent B.)

(2) Where a claim is made against the LSC only and includes enhancement and where a claim is made in family proceedings and includes a claim for uplift or general care and conduct, the amount of enhancement uplift and general care and conduct must be shown, in respect of each item upon which it is claimed, as a separate amount either in the appropriate arithmetic column or in the narrative column. (For an example, see Precedent C.)

'Enhancement' means the increase in prescribed rates which may be allowed by a costs officer in accordance with the Legal Aid in Civil Proceedings (Remuneration) Regulations 1994 or the Legal Aid in Family Proceedings Regulations 1991.

Costs of preparing the bill

para.4.18 **68.21**

4.18 A claim may be made for the reasonable costs of preparing and checking the bill of costs.

Section 5 Special Provisions Relating to VAT

5.1 This section deals with claims for value added tax (VAT) which are made in respect of costs being dealt with by way of summary assessment or detailed assessment.

VAT registration number

para.5.2 **68.59**

5.2 The number allocated by HM Revenue and Customs to every person registered under the Value Added Tax Act 1994* (except a government department) must appear in a prominent place at the head of every statement, bill of costs, fee sheet, account or voucher on which VAT is being included as part of a claim for costs.

Entitlement to VAT on costs

para.5.3 **68.4, 68.59** para.5.5 **68.59**
para.5.4 **68.4** para.5.6 **68.59**

5.3 VAT should not be included in a claim for costs if the receiving party is able to recover the VAT as input tax. Where the receiving party is able to obtain credit from HM Revenue and Customs for a proportion of the VAT as input tax, only that proportion which is not eligible for credit should be included in the claim for costs.

5.4 The receiving party has responsibility for ensuring that VAT is claimed only when the receiving party is unable to recover the VAT or a proportion thereof as input tax.

5.5 Where there is a dispute as to whether VAT is properly claimed the receiving party must provide a certificate signed by the solicitors or the auditors of the receiving party substantially

[* The text issued by the Department for Constitutional Affairs mistakenly refers to the Value Added Tax Act 1983.]

in the form illustrated in precedent F in the Schedule of Costs Precedents annexed to this practice direction. Where the receiving party is a litigant in person who is claiming VAT, reference should be made by him to HM Revenue and Customs and wherever possible a statement to similar effect produced at the hearing at which the costs are assessed.

5.6 Where there is a dispute as to whether any service in respect of which a charge is proposed to be made in the bill is zero rated or exempt, reference should be made to HM Customs and Excise and wherever possible the view of HM Revenue and Customs obtained and made known at the hearing at which the costs are assessed. Such application should be made by the receiving party. In the case of a bill from a solicitor to his own client, such application should be made by the client.

Form of bill of costs where VAT rate changes

para.5.7 **68.59** para.5.8 **68.59**

5.7 Where there is a change in the rate of VAT, suppliers of goods and services are entitled ss. 88(1) and (2) of the Value Added Tax Act 1994 in most circumstances to elect whether the new or the old rate of VAT should apply to a supply where the basic and actual tax points span a period during which there has been a change in VAT rates.

5.8 It will be assumed, unless a contrary indication is given in writing, that an election to take advantage of the provisions mentioned in para. 5.7 above and to charge VAT at the lower rate has been made. In any case in which an election to charge at the lower rate is not made, such a decision must be justified to the court assessing the costs.

Apportionment

para.5.9 **68.59**

5.9 All bills of costs, fees and disbursements on which VAT is included must be divided into separate parts so as to show work done before, on and after the date or dates from which any change in the rate of VAT takes effect. Where, however, a lump-sum charge is made for work which spans a period during which there has been a change in VAT rates, and paras 5.7 and 5.8 above do not apply, reference should be made to paras 8 and 9 of Appendix F of Customs and Excise Notice 700 (or any revised edition of that notice),* a copy of which should be in the possession of every registered trader. If necessary, the lump sum should be apportioned. The totals of profit costs and disbursements in each part must be carried separately to the summary.

5.10 Should there be a change in the rate between the conclusion of a detailed assessment and the issue of the final costs certificate, any interested party may apply for the detailed assessment to be varied so as to take account of any increase or reduction in the amount of tax payable. Once the final costs certificate has been issued, no variation under this paragraph will be permitted.

Disbursements

para.5.11 **68.59** para.5.12 **68.59**

5.11 Petty (or general) disbursements such as postage, fares etc. which are normally treated as part of a solicitor's overheads and included in his profit costs should be charged with VAT even though they bear no tax when the solicitor incurs them. The cost of travel by public transport on a specific journey for a particular client where it forms part of the service rendered by a solicitor to his client and is charged in his bill of costs, attracts VAT.

5.12 Reference is made to the criteria set out in the VAT Guide (Customs and Excise Notice 700,1 August 1991 ed., para. 83, or any revised edition of that notice)† as to expenses which are not subject to VAT. Charges for the cost of travel by public transport, postage, telephone calls and telegraphic transfers where these form part of the service rendered by the solicitor to his client are examples of charges which do not satisfy these criteria and are thus liable to VAT at the standard rate.

Legal aid/LSC funding

5.13 (1) VAT will be payable in respect of every supply made pursuant to a legal aid/LSC certificate where:

[* A revised version of Notice 700 was issued in April 2002. In the revised version, changes in VAT rates are dealt with in section 30.]

[† A revised version of Notice 700 was issued in April 2002.]

(a) the person making the supply is a taxable person; and
(b) the assisted person/LSC funded client:
(i) belongs in the United Kingdom or another member State of the European Union; and
(ii) is a private individual or receives the supply for non-business purposes.

(2) Where the assisted person/LSC funded client belongs outside the European Union, VAT is generally not payable unless the supply relates to land in the United Kingdom.

(3) For the purpose of sub-paragraphs (1) and (2), the place where a person belongs is determined by the Value Added Tax Act 1994, s. 9.

(4) Where the assisted person/LSC funded client is registered for VAT and the legal services paid for by the LSC are in connection with that person's business, the VAT on those services will be payable by the LSC only.

5.14 Any summary of costs payable by the LSC must be drawn so as to show the total VAT on counsel's fees as a separate item from the VAT on other disbursements and the VAT on profit costs.

Tax invoice

5.15 A bill of costs filed for detailed assessment is always retained by the court. Accordingly if a solicitor waives his solicitor and client costs and accepts the costs certified by the court as payable by the unsuccessful party in settlement, it will be necessary for a short statement as to the amount of the certified costs and the VAT thereon to be prepared for use as the tax invoice.

Vouchers

5.16 Where receipted accounts for disbursements made by the solicitor or his client are retained as tax invoices a photostat copy of any such receipted account may be produced and will be accepted as sufficient evidence of payment when disbursements are vouched.

Certificates

5.17 In a costs certificate payable by the LSC, the VAT on solicitor's costs, counsel's fees and disbursements will be shown separately.

Litigants acting in person

5.18 Where a litigant acts in litigation on his own behalf he is not treated for the purposes of VAT as having supplied services and therefore no VAT is chargeable in respect of work done by that litigant (even where, for example, that litigant is a solicitor or other legal representative).

5.19 Consequently in the circumstances described in the preceding paragraph, a bill of costs presented for agreement or assessment should not claim any VAT which will not be allowed on assessment.

Government departments

para.5.20 **68.59**

5.20 On an assessment between parties, where costs are being paid to a government department in respect of services rendered by its legal staff, VAT should not be added.

Section 6 Estimates of Costs

para.6.2 **44.10, 63.19**
para.6.3 **63.19**
para.6.4(1) **42.5, 63.19**
para.6.4(2) **45.16, 63.19**
para.6.5 **63.19**
para.65A **63.19**
para.6.5A(2) **63.19**
para.6.6 **63.19**
para.6.6(2) **63.19**

6.1 This section sets out certain steps which parties and their legal representatives must take in order to keep the parties informed about their potential liability in respect of costs and in order to assist the court to decide what, if any, order to make about costs and about case management.

6.2 (1) In this section an 'estimate of costs' means:
(a) an estimate of base costs (including disbursements) already incurred; and
(b) an estimate of base costs (including disbursements) to be incurred,

which a party intends to seek to recover from any other party under an order for costs if he is successful in the case. ('Base costs' are defined in para. 2.2 of this practice direction.)

(2) A party who intends to recover an additional liability (defined in r. 43.2) need not reveal the amount of that liability in the estimate.

6.3 The court may at any stage in a case order any party to file an estimate of base costs and to serve copies of the estimate on all other parties. The court may direct that the estimate be prepared in such a way as to demonstrate the likely effects of giving or not giving a particular case management direction which the court is considering, for example, a direction for a split trial or for the trial of a preliminary issue. The court may specify a time limit for filing and serving the estimate. However, if no time limit is specified the estimate should be filed and served within 28 days of the date of the order.

6.4 (1) When:
(a) a party to a claim which is outside the financial scope of the small claims track files an allocation questionnaire; or
(b) a party to a claim which is being dealt with on the fast track or the multi track, or under Part 8, files a pre-trial checklist (listing questionnaire),

he must also file an estimate of costs and serve a copy of it on every other party, unless the court otherwise directs. Where a party is represented, the legal representative must in addition serve an estimate on the party he represents.

(2) Where a party is required to file and serve a new estimate of costs in accordance with r. 44.15(3), if that party is represented the legal representative must in addition serve the new estimate on the party he represents.

(3) This paragraph does not apply to litigants in person.

6.5 An estimate of base costs should be substantially in the form illustrated in Precedent H in the Schedule of Costs Precedents annexed to this practice direction.

6.5A (1) If there is a difference of 20% or more between the base costs claimed by a receiving party on detailed assessment and the costs shown in an estimate of costs filed by that party, the receiving party must provide a statement of the reasons for the difference with his bill of costs.

(2) If a paying party:
(a) claims that he reasonably relied on an estimate of costs filed by a receiving party; or
(b) wishes to rely upon the costs shown in the estimate in order to dispute the reasonableness or proportionality of the costs claimed,

the paying party must serve a statement setting out his case in this regard in his points of dispute.

('Relevant person' is defined in para. 32.10(1) of this practice direction.)

6.6 (1) On an assessment of the costs of a party, the court may have regard to any estimate previously filed by that party, or by any other party in the same proceedings. Such an estimate may be taken into account as a factor among others, when assessing the reasonableness and proportionality of any costs claimed.

(2) In particular, where:
(a) there is a difference of 20% or more between the base costs claimed by a receiving party and the costs shown in an estimate of costs filed by that party; and
(b) it appears to the court that:
(i) the receiving party has not provided a satisfactory explanation for that difference; or
(ii) the paying party reasonably relied on the estimate of costs;

the court may regard the difference between the costs claimed and the costs shown in the estimate as evidence that the costs claimed are unreasonable or disproportionate.

DIRECTIONS RELATING TO PART 44 — GENERAL RULES ABOUT COSTS

Section 7 Solicitor's Duty to Notify Client: Rule 44.2

para.7.1 **66.25** para.7.3 **66.25**

7.1 For the purposes of r. 44.2 'client' includes a party for whom a solicitor is acting and any other person (for example, an insurer, a trade union or the LSC) who has instructed the solicitor to act or who is liable to pay his fees.

7.2 Where a solicitor notifies a client of an order under that rule, he must also explain why the order came to be made.

7.3 Although r. 44.2 does not specify any sanction for breach of the rule the court may, either in the order for costs itself or in a subsequent order, require the solicitor to produce to the court evidence showing that he took reasonable steps to comply with the rule.

Section 8 Court's Discretion and Circumstances to Be Taken into Account When Exercising Its Discretion as to Costs: Rule 44.3

para.8.3 **66.26** para.8.5 **66.29**

8.1 Attention is drawn to the factors set out in this rule which may lead the court to depart from the general rule stated in r. 44.3(2) and to make a different order about costs.

8.2 In a probate claim where a defendant has in his defence given notice that he requires the will to be proved in solemn form (see [r. 57.7(5)*]), the court will not make an order for costs against the defendant unless it appears that there was no reasonable ground for opposing the will. The term 'probate claim' is defined in r. 57.1(2).

8.3 (1) The court may make an order about costs at any stage in a case.

(2) In particular the court may make an order about costs when it deals with any application, makes any order or holds any hearing and that order about costs may relate to the costs of that application, order or hearing.

(3) Rule 44.3A(1) provides that the court will not assess any additional liability until the conclusion of the proceedings or the part of the proceedings to which the funding arrangement relates. (Paragraphs 2.4 and 2.5 above explain when proceedings are concluded. As to the time when detailed assessment may be carried out see para. 28.1, below.)

8.4 In deciding what order to make about costs the court is required to have regard to all the circumstances including any payment into court or admissible offer to settle made by a party which is drawn to the court's attention (whether or not it is made in accordance with Part 36). Where a claimant has made a Part 36 offer and fails to obtain a judgment which is more advantageous than that offer, that circumstance alone will not lead to a reduction in the costs awarded to the claimant under this rule.

8.5 There are certain costs orders which the court will commonly make in proceedings before trial. The following table sets out the general effect of these orders. The table is not an exhaustive list of the orders which the court may make.

Term	Effect
• Costs • Costs in any event	The party in whose favour the order is made is entitled to the costs in respect of the part of the proceedings to which the order relates, whatever other costs orders are made in the proceedings.
• Costs in the case • Costs in the application	The party in whose favour the court makes an order for costs at the end of the proceedings is entitled to his costs of the part of the proceedings to which the order relates.
• Costs reserved	The decision about costs is deferred to a later occasion, but if no later order is made the costs will be costs in the case.
• Claimant's/Defendant's costs in the case/ application	If the party in whose favour the costs order is made is awarded costs at the end of the proceedings, that party is entitled to his costs of the part of the proceedings to which the order relates. If any other party is awarded costs at the end of the proceedings, the party in whose favour the final costs order is made is not liable to pay the costs of any other party in respect of the part of the proceedings to which the order relates.
• Costs thrown away	Where, for example, a judgment or order is set aside, the party in whose favour the costs order is made is entitled to the costs which have been incurred as a consequence. This includes the costs of: (a) preparing for and attending any hearing at which the judgment or order which has been set aside was made; (b) preparing for and attending any hearing to set aside the judgment or order in question; (c) preparing for and attending any hearing at which the court orders the proceedings or the part in question to be adjourned; (d) any steps taken to enforce a judgment or order which has subsequently been set aside.

[* The text issued by the Department for Constitutional Affairs mistakenly refers to PD 57, para. 8.3.]

Term	Effect
• Costs of and caused by	Where, for example, the court makes this order on an application to amend a statement of case, the party in whose favour the costs order is made is entitled to the costs of preparing for and attending the application and the costs of any consequential amendment to his own statement of case.
• Costs here and below	The party in whose favour the costs order is made is entitled not only to his costs in respect of the proceedings in which the court makes the order but also to his costs of the proceedings in any lower court. In the case of an appeal from a Divisional Court the party is not entitled to any costs incurred in any court below the Divisional Court.
• No order as to costs • Each party to pay his own costs	Each party is to bear his own costs of the part of the proceedings to which the order relates whatever costs order the court makes at the end of the proceedings.

8.6 Where, under r. 44.3(8) , the court orders an amount to be paid before costs are assessed:
(1) the order will state that amount, and
(2) if no other date for payment is specified in the order r. 44.8 (time for complying with an order for costs) will apply.

Fees of counsel

para.8.7 **66.30** para.8.7(3) **66.30**

8.7 (1) This paragraph applies where the court orders the detailed assessment of the costs of a hearing at which one or more counsel appeared for a party.
(2) Where an order for costs states the opinion of the court as to whether or not the hearing was fit for the attendance of one or more counsel, a costs officer conducting a detailed assessment of costs to which that order relates will have regard to the opinion stated.
(3) The court will generally express an opinion only where:
(a) the paying party asks it to do so;
(b) more than one counsel appeared for a party; or
(c) the court wishes to record its opinion that the case was not fit for the attendance of counsel.

Fees payable to conveyancing counsel appointed by the court to assist it

8.8 (1) Where the court refers any matter to the conveyancing counsel of the court the fees payable to counsel in respect of the work done or to be done will be assessed by the court in accordance with r. 44.3.
(2) An appeal from a decision of the court in respect of the fees of such counsel will be dealt with under the general rules as to appeals set out in Part 52. If the appeal is against the decision of an authorised costs officer, it will be dealt with in accordance with rr. 47.20 to 47.23.

Section 9 Costs Orders Relating to Funding Arrangements: Rule 44.3A

9.1 Under an order for payment of 'costs' the costs payable will include an additional liability incurred under a funding arrangement.

9.2 (1) If before the conclusion of the proceedings the court carries out a summary assessment of the base costs it may identify separately the amount allowed in respect of: solicitor's charges; counsel's fees; other disbursements; and any value added tax (VAT). (Sections 13 and 14 of this practice direction deal with summary assessment.)
(2) If an order for the base costs of a previous application or hearing did not identify separately the amounts allowed for solicitor's charges, counsel's fees and other disbursements, a court which later makes an assessment of an additional liability may apportion the base costs previously ordered.

Section 10 Limits on Recovery under Funding Arrangements: Rule 44.3B

10.1 In a case to which r. 44.3B(1)(c) or (d) applies the party in default may apply for relief from the sanction. He should do so as quickly as possible after he becomes aware of the default. An application, supported by evidence, should be made under Part 23 to a costs judge or district judge of the court which is dealing with the case. (Attention is drawn to rr. 3.8 and 3.9 which deal with sanctions and relief from sanctions.)

10.2 Where the amount of any percentage increase recoverable by counsel may be affected by the outcome of the application, the solicitor issuing the application must serve on counsel a copy of the application notice and notice of the hearing as soon as practicable and in any event at least two days before the hearing. Counsel may make written submissions or may attend and make oral submissions at the hearing. (Paragraph 1.4 contains definitions of the terms 'counsel' and 'solicitor'.)

Section 11 Factors to Be Taken into Account in Deciding the Amount of Costs: Rule 44.5

para.11.1 **68.34**
para.11.2 **68.35**
para.11.3 **68.34**
para.11.4 **6.18, 6.20**
para.11.5 **6.18, 6.20, 68.47**
para.11.6 **6.18, 6.20**
paras.11.7–11.9 **6.12, 6.18, 6.20, 68.49**
para.11.10 **6.12, 6.18, 6.20, 68.51, 68.52**
para.11.11 **68.52**

11.1 In applying the test of proportionality the court will have regard to r. 1.1(2)(c). The relationship between the total of the costs incurred and the financial value of the claim may not be a reliable guide. A fixed percentage cannot be applied in all cases to the value of the claim in order to ascertain whether or not the costs are proportionate.

11.2 In any proceedings there will be costs which will inevitably be incurred and which are necessary for the successful conduct of the case. Solicitors are not required to conduct litigation at rates which are uneconomic. Thus in a modest claim the proportion of costs is likely to be higher than in a large claim, and may even equal or possibly exceed the amount in dispute.

11.3 Where a trial takes place, the time taken by the court in dealing with a particular issue may not be an accurate guide to the amount of time properly spent by the legal or other representatives in preparation for the trial of that issue.

11.4 Where a party has entered into a funding arrangement the costs claimed may, subject to r. 44.3B include an additional liability.

11.5 In deciding whether the costs claimed are reasonable and (on a standard basis assessment) proportionate, the court will consider the amount of any additional liability separately from the base costs.

11.6 In deciding whether the base costs are reasonable and (if relevant) proportionate the court will consider the factors set out in r. 44.5.

11.7 Subject to para. 17.8(2), when the court is considering the factors to be taken into account in assessing an additional liability, it will have regard to the facts and circumstances as they reasonably appeared to the solicitor or counsel when the funding arrangement was entered into and at the time of any variation of the arrangement.

11.8 (1) In deciding whether a percentage increase is reasonable relevant factors to be taken into account may include:

(a) the risk that the circumstances in which the costs, fees or expenses would be payable might or might not occur;

(b) the legal representative's liability for any disbursements;

(c) what other methods of financing the costs were available to the receiving party.

(2) *[deleted]*

11.9 A percentage increase will not be reduced simply on the ground that, when added to base costs which are reasonable and (where relevant) proportionate, the total appears disproportionate.

11.10 In deciding whether the cost of insurance cover is reasonable, relevant factors to be taken into account include:

(1) where the insurance cover is not purchased in support of a conditional fee agreement with a success fee, how its cost compares with the likely cost of funding the case with a conditional fee agreement with a success fee and supporting insurance cover;

(2) the level and extent of the cover provided;
(3) the availability of any pre-existing insurance cover;
(4) whether any part of the premium would be rebated in the event of early settlement;
(5) the amount of commission payable to the receiving party or his legal representatives or other agents.

11.11 Where the court is considering a provision made by a membership organisation, r. 44.3B(1)(b) provides that any such provision which exceeds the likely cost to the receiving party of the premium of an insurance policy against the risk of incurring a liability to pay the costs of other parties to the proceedings is not recoverable. In such circumstances the court will, when assessing the additional liability, have regard to the factors set out in para. 11.10 above, in addition to the factors set out in r. 44.5.

Section 12 Procedure for Assessing Costs: Rule 44.7

para.12.2 **66.28**

12.1 Where the court does not order fixed costs (or no fixed costs are provided for) the amount of costs payable will be assessed by the court. This rule allows the court making an order about costs either:
(a) to make a summary assessment of the amount of the costs, or
(b) to order the amount to be decided in accordance with Part 47 (a detailed assessment).

12.2 An order for costs will be treated as an order for the amount of costs to be decided by a detailed assessment unless the order otherwise provides.

12.3 Whenever the court awards costs to be assessed by way of detailed assessment it should consider whether to exercise the power in r. 44.3(8) (court's discretion as to costs) to order the paying party to pay such sum of money as it thinks just on account of those costs.

Section 13 Summary Assessment: General Provisions

para.13.2 **32.27, 44.22, 68.3**
para.13.2(2) **66.27, 68.10**
para.13.2(3) **66.27**
para.13.3 **66.27**
para.13.4 **32.27, 32.33, 68.3**
para.13.5 **32.27**
para.13.5(2) **44.22, 68.4**
para.13.5(3) **68.4**
para.13.5(5) **6.22**
para.13.6 **32.27, 44.22, 68.3**
para.13.8 **32.27**
para.13.9 **32.27, 44.22, 66.27**
para.13.10 **32.27, 66.27, 66.59**
para.13.11 **44.22**
para.13.11(1) **32.27, 66.27**
para.13.11(2) **32.27, 66.27**
para.13.13 **44.22, 68.35**
para.13.13(a) **68.3**

13.1 Whenever a court makes an order about costs which does not provide for fixed costs to be paid the court should consider whether to make a summary assessment of costs.

13.2 The general rule is that the court should make a summary assessment of the costs:
(1) at the conclusion of the trial of a case which has been dealt with on the fast track, in which case the order will deal with the costs of the whole claim, and
(2) at the conclusion of any other hearing, which has lasted not more than one day, in which case the order will deal with the costs of the application or matter to which the hearing related. If this hearing disposes of the claim, the order may deal with the costs of the whole claim;
(3) in hearings in the Court of Appeal to which PD 52, para. 14, applies, unless there is good reason not to do, for example, where the paying party shows substantial grounds for disputing the sum claimed for costs that cannot be dealt with summarily or there is insufficient time to carry out a summary assessment.

13.3 The general rule in para. 13.2 does not apply to a mortgagee's costs incurred in mortgage possession proceedings or other proceedings relating to a mortgage unless the mortgagee asks the court to make an order for his costs to be paid by another party. Paragraphs 50.3 and 50.4 deal in more detail with costs relating to mortgages.

13.4 Where an application has been made and the parties to the application agree an order by consent without any party attending, the parties should agree a figure for costs to be inserted in the consent order or agree that there should be no order for costs. If the parties cannot agree the costs position, attendance on the appointment will be necessary but, unless good reason can be shown for the failure to deal with costs as set out above, no costs will be allowed for that attendance.

13.5 (1) It is the duty of the parties and their legal representatives to assist the judge in making a summary assessment of costs in any case to which para. 13.2 above applies, in accordance with the following paragraphs.

(2) Each party who intends to claim costs must prepare a written statement of the costs he intends to claim showing separately in the form of a schedule:

(a) the number of hours to be claimed,

(b) the hourly rate to be claimed,

(c) the grade of fee earner,

(d) the amount and nature of any disbursement to be claimed, other than counsel's fee for appearing at the hearing,

(e) the amount of solicitor's costs to be claimed for attending or appearing at the hearing,

(f) the fees of counsel to be claimed in respect of the hearing, and

(g) any value added tax (VAT) to be claimed on these amounts.

(3) The statement of costs should follow as closely as possible form N260 and must be signed by the party or his legal representative. Where a litigant is an assisted person or is a LSC funded client or is represented by a solicitor in the litigant's employment the statement of costs need not include the certificate appended at the end of form N260.

(4) The statement of costs must be filed at court and copies of it must be served on any party against whom an order for payment of those costs is intended to be sought. The statement of costs should be filed and the copies of it should be served as soon as possible and in any event not less than 24 hours before the date fixed for the hearing.

(5) Where the litigant is or may be entitled to claim an additional liability the statement filed and served need not reveal the amount of that liability.

13.6 The failure by a party, without reasonable excuse, to comply with the foregoing paragraphs will be taken into account by the court in deciding what order to make about the costs of the claim, hearing or application, and about the costs of any further hearing or detailed assessment hearing that may be necessary as a result of that failure.

13.7 If the court makes a summary assessment of costs at the conclusion of proceedings the court will specify separately:

(1) the base costs, and if appropriate, the additional liability allowed as solicitor's charges, counsel's fees, other disbursements and any VAT; and

(2) the amount which is awarded under Part 46 (fast track trial costs).

13.8 The court awarding costs cannot make an order for a summary assessment of costs by a costs officer. If a summary assessment of costs is appropriate but the court awarding costs is unable to do so on the day, the court must give directions as to a further hearing before the same judge.

13.9 The court will not make a summary assessment of the costs of a receiving party who is an assisted person or LSC funded client.

13.10 A summary assessment of costs payable by an assisted person or LSC funded client is not by itself a determination of that person's liability to pay those costs (as to which see r. 44.17 and paras 21.1 to 23.17 of this practice direction).

13.11 (1) The court will not make a summary assessment of the costs of a receiving party who is a child or patient within the meaning of Part 21 unless the solicitor acting for the child or patient has waived the right to further costs (see para. 51.1 below).

(2) The court may make a summary assessment of costs payable by a child or patient.

13.12 (1) Attention is drawn to r. 44.3A which prevents the court from making a summary assessment of an additional liability before the conclusion of the proceedings or the part of the proceedings to which the funding arrangement relates. Where this applies, the court should nonetheless make a summary assessment of the base costs of the hearing or application unless there is a good reason not to do so.

(2) Where the court makes a summary assessment of the base costs all statements of costs and costs estimates put before the judge will be retained on the court file.

13.13 The court will not give its approval to disproportionate and unreasonable costs. Accordingly:

(a) When the amount of the costs to be paid has been agreed between the parties the order for costs must state that the order is by consent.

(b) If the judge is to make an order which is not by consent, the judge will, so far as possible, ensure that the final figure is not disproportionate and/or unreasonable having regard to Part 1 of the CPR. The judge will retain this responsibility notwithstanding the absence of challenge to individual items in the make-up of the figure sought. The fact that the paying party is not disputing the amount of costs can however be taken as some indication that the amount is proportionate and reasonable. The judge will therefore intervene only if satisfied that the costs are so disproportionate that it is right to do so.

Section 14 Summary Assessment Where Costs Claimed Include an Additional Liability

para.14.1 **6.22** paras.14.3–14.4 **6.22**
para.14.2 **6.22, 66.27**

Orders made before the conclusion of the proceedings

14.1 The existence of a conditional fee agreement or other funding arrangement within the meaning of r. 43.2 is not by itself a sufficient reason for not carrying out a summary assessment.

14.2 Where a legal representative acting for the receiving party has entered into a conditional fee agreement the court may summarily assess all the costs (other than any additional liability).

14.3 Where costs have been summarily assessed an order for payment will not be made unless the court has been satisfied that in respect of the costs claimed, the receiving party is at the time liable to pay to his legal representative an amount equal to or greater than the costs claimed. A statement in the form of the certificate appended at the end of form N260 may be sufficient proof of liability. The giving of information under r. 44.15 (where that rule applies) is not sufficient.

14.4 The court may direct that any costs, for which the receiving party may not in the event be liable, shall be paid into court to await the outcome of the case, or shall not be enforceable until further order, or it may postpone the receiving party's right to receive payment in some other way.

Orders made at the conclusion of the proceedings

14.5 Where there has been a trial of one or more issues separately from other issues, the court will not normally order detailed assessment of the additional liability until all issues have been tried unless the parties agree.

14.6 Rule 44.3A(2) sets out the ways in which the court may deal with the assessment of the costs where there is a funding arrangement. Where the court makes a summary assessment of the base costs:

(1) The order may state separately the base costs allowed as (a) solicitor's charges, (b) counsel's fees, (c) any other disbursements and (d) any VAT;

(2) the statements of costs upon which the judge based his summary assessment will be retained on the court file.

14.7 Where the court makes a summary assessment of an additional liability at the conclusion of proceedings, that assessment must relate to the whole of the proceedings; this will include any additional liability relating to base costs allowed by the court when making a summary assessment on a previous application or hearing.

14.8 Paragraph 13.13 applies where the parties are agreed about the total amount to be paid by way of costs, or are agreed about the amount of the base costs that will be paid. Where they disagree about the additional liability the court may summarily assess that liability or make an order for a detailed assessment.

14.9 In order to facilitate the court in making a summary assessment of any additional liability at the conclusion of the proceedings the party seeking such costs must prepare and have available for the court a bundle of documents which must include:

(1) a copy of every notice of funding arrangement (form N251) which has been filed by him;

(2) a copy of every estimate and statement of costs filed by him;

(3) a copy of the risk assessment prepared at the time any relevant funding arrangement was entered into and on the basis of which the amount of the additional liability was fixed.

Section 15 Costs on the Small Claims Track and Fast Track: Rule 44.9

paras.15.1(1)–(2) **66.34**

15.1 (1) Before a claim is allocated to one of those tracks the court is not restricted by any of the special rules that apply to that track.

(2) Where a claim has been allocated to one of those tracks, the special rules which relate to that track will apply to work done before as well as after allocation save to the extent (if any) that an order for costs in respect of that work was made before allocation.

(3) (i) This paragraph applies where a claim, issued for a sum in excess of the normal financial scope of the small claims track, is allocated to that track only because an admission of part of the claim by the defendant reduces the amount in dispute to a sum within the normal scope of that track.
(See also PD 26, para. 7.4)

(ii) On entering judgment for the admitted part before allocation of the balance of the claim the court may allow costs in respect of the proceedings down to that date.

Section 16 Costs Following Allocation and Reallocation: Rule 44.11

paras.16.2–16.3 **66.35**

16.1 This paragraph applies where the court is about to make an order to reallocate a claim from the small claims track to another track.

16.2 Before making the order to reallocate the claim, the court must decide whether any party is to pay costs to any other party down to the date of the order to reallocate in accordance with the rules about costs contained in Part 27 (the small claims track).

16.3 If it decides to make such an order about costs, the court will make a summary assessment of those costs in accordance with that Part.

Section 17 Costs-only Proceedings: Rule 44.12A

paras.17.3–17.4 **68.58** para.17.11 **68.56**
paras.17.8–17.10 **68.58**

17.1 A claim form under this rule should not be issued in the High Court unless the dispute to which the agreement relates was of such a value or type that had proceedings been begun they would have been commenced in the High Court.

17.2 A claim form which is to be issued in the High Court at the Royal Courts of Justice will be issued in the Supreme Court Costs Office.

17.3 Attention is drawn to r. 8.2 (in particular to para. (b)(ii)) and to r. 44.12A(3). The claim form must:

(1) identify the claim or dispute to which the agreement to pay costs relates;
(2) state the date and terms of the agreement on which the claimant relies;
(3) set out or have attached to it a draft of the order which the claimant seeks;
(4) state the amount of the costs claimed; and,
(5) state whether the costs are claimed on the standard or indemnity basis. If no basis is specified the costs will be treated as being claimed on the standard basis.

17.4 The evidence to be filed and served with the claim form under r. 8.5 must include copies of the documents on which the claimant relies to prove the defendant's agreement to pay costs.

17.5 A costs judge or a district judge has jurisdiction to hear and decide any issue which may arise in a claim issued under this rule irrespective of the amount of the costs claimed or of the value of the claim to which the agreement to pay costs relates. A costs officer may make an order by consent under para. 17.7, or an order dismissing a claim under para. 17.9 below.

17.6 When the time for filing the defendant's acknowledgment of service has expired, the claimant may by letter request the court to make an order in the terms of his claim, unless the defendant has filed an acknowledgment of service stating that he intends to contest the claim or to seek a different order.

17.7 Rule 40.6 applies where an order is to be made by consent. An order may be made by consent in terms which differ from those set out in the claim form.

17.8 (1) An order for costs made under this rule will be treated as an order for the amount of costs to be decided by a detailed assessment to which Part 47 and the practice directions

Civil Procedure Rules & Practice Directions

relating to it apply. Rule 44.4(4) (determination of basis of assessment) also applies to the order.

(2) In cases in which an additional liability is claimed, the costs judge or district judge should have regard to the time when and the extent to which the claim has been settled and to the fact that the claim has been settled without the need to commence proceedings.

17.9 (1) For the purposes of r. 44.12A(4)(b):

(a) a claim will be treated as opposed if the defendant files an acknowledgment of service stating that he intends to contest the making of an order for costs or to seek a different remedy; and

(b) a claim will not be treated as opposed if the defendant files an acknowledgment of service stating that he disputes the amount of the claim for costs.

(2) An order dismissing the claim will be made as soon as an acknowledgment of service opposing the claim is filed. The dismissal of a claim under r. 44.12A(4) does not prevent the claimant from issuing another claim form under Part 7 or Part 8 based on the agreement or alleged agreement to which the proceedings under this rule related.

17.10 (1) Rule 8.9 (which provides that claims issued under Part 8 shall be treated as allocated to the multi-track) shall not apply to claims issued under this rule. A claim issued under this rule may be dealt with without being allocated to a track.

(2) Rule 8.1(3) and Part 24 do not apply to proceedings brought under r. 44.12A.

17.11 Nothing in this rule prevents a person from issuing a claim form under Part 7 or Part 8 to sue on an agreement made in settlement of a dispute where that agreement makes provision for costs, nor from claiming in that case an order for costs or a specified sum in respect of costs.

Section 18 Court's Powers in Relation to Misconduct: Rule 44.14

paras.18.1–18.2 **68.25**

18.1 Before making an order under r. 44.14 the court must give the party or legal representative in question a reasonable opportunity to attend a hearing to give reasons why it should not make such an order.

18.2 Conduct before or during the proceedings which gave rise to the assessment which is unreasonable or improper includes steps which are calculated to prevent or inhibit the court from furthering the overriding objective.

18.3 Although r. 44.14(3) does not specify any sanction for breach of the obligation imposed by the rule the court may, either in the order under paragraph (2) or in a subsequent order, require the solicitor to produce to the court evidence that he took reasonable steps to comply with the obligation.

Section 19 Providing Information about Funding Arrangements: Rule 44.15

para.19 **5.10** para.19.1(1) **5.10**
para.19.1 **68.48**

19.1 (1) A party who wishes to claim an additional liability in respect of a funding arrangement must give any other party information about that claim if he is to recover the additional liability. There is no requirement to specify the amount of the additional liability separately nor to state how it is calculated until it falls to be assessed. That principle is reflected in rr. 44.3A and 44.15, in the following paragraphs and in sections 6,13,14 and 31 of this practice direction. Section 6 deals with estimates of costs, sections 13 and 14 deal with summary assessment and section 31 deals with detailed assessment.

(2) In the following paragraphs a party who has entered into a funding arrangement is treated as a person who intends to recover a sum representing an additional liability by way of costs.

(3) Attention is drawn to para. 57.9 of this practice direction which sets out time limits for the provision of information where a funding arrangement is entered into between 31 March and 2 July 2000 and proceedings relevant to that arrangement are commenced before 3 July 2000.

Method of giving information

para.19.2 **6.17, 6.20, 68.48**
para.19.2(2) **15.6, 23.17**
para. 19.2(2)(a) **12.3**
para. 19.2(2)(b) **13.6, 15.1**
para.19.2(3) **13.8, 18.3, 18.4, 20.18**
para.19.2(4) **6.17**

19.2 (1) In this paragraph, 'claim form' includes petition and application notice, and the notice of funding to be filed or served is a notice containing the information set out in form N251.

(2) (a) A claimant who has entered into a funding arrangement before starting the proceedings to which it relates must provide information to the court by filing the notice when he issues the claim form.

(b) He must provide information to every other party by serving the notice. If he serves the claim form himself he must serve the notice with the claim form. If the court is to serve the claim form, the court will also serve the notice if the claimant provides it with sufficient copies for service.

(3) A defendant who has entered into a funding arrangement before filing any document:

(a) must provide information to the court by filing notice with his first document. A 'first document' may be an acknowledgment of service, a defence, or any other document, such as an application to set aside a default judgment.

(b) must provide information to every party by serving notice. If he serves his first document himself he must serve the notice with that document. If the court is to serve his first document the court will also serve the notice if the defendant provides it with sufficient copies for service.

(4) In all other circumstances a party must file and serve notice within seven days of entering into the funding arrangement concerned.

(5) There is no requirement in this practice direction for the provision of information about funding arrangements before the commencement of proceedings. Such provision is however recommended and may be required by a pre-action protocol.

Notice of change of information

para.19.3 **68.48**

19.3 (1) Rule 44.15 imposes a duty on a party to give notice of change if the information he has previously provided is no longer accurate. To comply he must file and serve notice containing the information set out in form N251. Rule 44.15(3) may impose other duties in relation to new estimates of costs.

(2) Further notification need not be provided where a party has already given notice:

(a) that he has entered into a conditional fee agreement with a legal representative and during the currency of that agreement either of them enters into another such agreement with an additional legal representative; or

(b) of some insurance cover, unless that cover is cancelled or unless new cover is taken out with a different insurer.

(3) Part 6 applies to the service of notices.

(4) The notice must be signed by the party or by his legal representative.

Information which must be provided

para.19.4 **68.48**
para.19.5 **68.48**

19.4 (1) Unless the court otherwise orders, a party who is required to supply information about a funding arrangement must state whether he has:

(a) entered into a conditional fee agreement which provides for a success fee within the meaning of section 58(2) of the Courts and Legal Services Act 1990;

(b) taken out an insurance policy to which section 29 of the Access to Justice Act 1999 applies;

(c) made an arrangement with a body which is prescribed for the purpose of section 30 of that Act;

or more than one of these.

(2) Where the funding arrangement is a conditional fee agreement, the party must state the date of the agreement and identify the claim or claims to which it relates (including Part 20 claims if any).

(3) Where the funding arrangement is an insurance policy, the party must state the name of the insurer, the policy number and the date of the policy, and must identify the claim or claims to which it relates (including Part 20 claims if any).

(4) Where the funding arrangement is by way of an arrangement with a relevant body the party must state the name of the body and set out the date and terms of the undertaking it has given and must identify the claim or claims to which it relates (including Part 20 claims if any).

(5) Where a party has entered into more than one funding arrangement in respect of a claim, for example, a conditional fee agreement and an insurance policy, a single notice containing the information set out in form N251 may contain the required information about both or all of them.

19.5 Where the court makes a Group Litigation Order, the court may give directions as to the extent to which individual parties should provide information in accordance with r. 44.15. (Part 19 deals with Group Litigation Orders.)

Section 20 Procedure Where Legal Representative Wishes to Recover from His Client an Agreed Percentage Increase Which Has Been Disallowed or Reduced on Assessment: Rule 44.16

20.1 (1) Attention is drawn to the Conditional Fee Agreements Regulations 2000, reg. 3(2)(b), and to the Collective Conditional Fee Agreements Regulations 2000, reg. 5(2)(b), which provide that some or all of a success fee ceases to be payable in certain circumstances. Both sets of regulations were revoked by the Conditional Fee Agreements (Revocation) Regulations 2005 (SI 2005/2305) but continue to have effect in relation to conditional fee agreements and collective conditional fee agreements entered into before 1 November 2005.

(2) Rule 44.16 allows the court to adjourn a hearing at which the legal representative acting for the receiving party applies for an order that a disallowed amount should continue to be payable under the agreement.

20.2 In the following paragraphs 'counsel' means counsel who has acted in the case under a conditional fee agreement which provides for a success fee. A reference to counsel includes a reference to any person who appeared as an advocate in the case and who is not a partner or employee of the solicitor or firm which is conducting the claim or defence (as the case may be) on behalf of the receiving party.

Procedure following summary assessment

20.3 (1) If the court disallows any amount of a legal representative's percentage increase, the court will, unless sub-para. (2) applies, give directions to enable an application to be made by the legal representative for the disallowed amount to be payable by his client, including, if appropriate, a direction that the application will be determined by a costs judge or district judge of the court dealing with the case.

(2) The court that has made the summary assessment may then and there decide the issue whether the disallowed amount should continue to be payable, if:

(a) the receiving party and all parties to the relevant agreement consent to the court doing so;

(b) the receiving party (or, if corporate, an officer) is present in court; and

(c) the court is satisfied that the issue can be fairly decided then and there.

Procedure following detailed assessment

para.20.4(3) **6.24**

20.4 (1) Where detailed assessment proceedings have been commenced, and the paying party serves points of dispute (as to which see section 34 of this practice direction), which show that he is seeking a reduction in any percentage increase charged by counsel on his fees, the solicitor acting for the receiving party must within three days of service deliver to counsel a copy of the relevant points of dispute and the bill of costs or the relevant parts of the bill.

(2) Counsel must within 10 days thereafter inform the solicitor in writing whether or not he will accept the reduction sought or some other reduction. Counsel may state any points he

wishes to have made in a reply to the points of dispute, and the solicitor must serve them on the paying party as or as part of a reply.

(3) Counsel who fails to inform the solicitor within the time limits set out above will be taken to accept the reduction unless the court otherwise orders.

20.5 Where the paying party serves points of dispute seeking a reduction in any percentage increase charged by a legal representative acting for the receiving party, and that legal representative intends, if necessary, to apply for an order that any amount of the percentage disallowed as against the paying party shall continue to be payable by his client, the solicitor acting for the receiving party must, within 14 days of service of the points of dispute, give to his client a clear written explanation of the nature of the relevant point of dispute and the effect it will have if it is upheld in whole or in part by the court, and of the client's right to attend any subsequent hearings at court when the matter is raised.

20.6 Where the solicitor acting for a receiving party files a request for a detailed assessment hearing it must if appropriate, be accompanied by a certificate signed by him stating:

(1) that the amount of the percentage increase in respect of counsel's fees or solicitor's charges is disputed;

(2) whether an application will be made for an order that any amount of that increase which is disallowed should continue to be payable by his client;

(3) that he has given his client an explanation in accordance with para. 20.5; and

(4) whether his client wishes to attend court when the amount of any relevant percentage increase may be decided.

20.7 (1) The solicitor acting for the receiving party must within seven days of receiving from the court notice of the date of the assessment hearing, notify his client, and if appropriate, counsel in writing of the date, time and place of the hearing.

(2) Counsel may attend or be represented at the detailed assessment hearing and may make oral or written submissions.

20.8 (1) At the detailed assessment hearing, the court will deal with the assessment of the costs payable by one party to another, including the amount of the percentage increase, and give a certificate accordingly.

(2) The court may decide the issue whether the disallowed amount should continue to be payable under the relevant conditional fee agreement without an adjournment if:

(a) the receiving party and all parties to the relevant agreement consent to the court deciding the issue without an adjournment,

(b) the receiving party (or, if corporate, an officer or employee who has authority to consent on behalf of the receiving party) is present in court, and

(c) the court is satisfied that the issue can be fairly decided without an adjournment.

(3) In any other case the court will give directions and fix a date for the hearing of the application.

Section 21 Application of Costs Rules: Rule 44.17

para.21 **66.57** para.21.6 **12.3**

21.1 Rule 44.17(b) excludes the costs rules to the extent that regulations under the Legal Aid Act 1988 make different provision. The primary examples of such regulations are the regulations providing prescribed rates (with or without enhancement).

21.2 Rule 44.17(a) provides that the procedure for detailed assessment does not apply to the extent that the Access to Justice Act 1999, s. 11, and provisions made under that Act make different provision.

21.3 Section 11 of the Access to Justice Act 1999 provides special protection against liability for costs for litigants who receive funding by the LSC (Legal Services Commission) as part of the Community Legal Service. Any costs ordered to be paid by a LSC funded client must not exceed the amount which is reasonable for him to pay having regard to all the circumstances including:

(a) the financial resources of all the parties to the proceedings, and

(b) their conduct in connection with the dispute to which the proceedings relate.

21.4 In this practice direction:

'cost protection' means the limit on costs awarded against a LSC funded client set out in s. 11(1) of the Access to Justice Act 1999;

'partner' has the meaning given by the Community Legal Service (Costs) Regulations 2000 (SI 2000/441).

21.5 Whether or not cost protection applies depends upon the 'level of service' for which funding was provided by the LSC in accordance with the Funding Code approved under s. 9 of the Access to Justice Act 1999. The levels of service referred to are:

(1) Legal Help — advice and assistance about a legal problem, not including representation or advocacy in proceedings.
(2) Help at Court — advocacy at a specific hearing, where the advocate is not formally representing the client in the proceedings.
(3) Family Mediation.
(4) Legal Representation — representation in actual or contemplated proceedings. Legal Representation can take the form of Investigative Help (limited to investigating the merits of a potential claim) or Full Representation.
(5) General Family Help and Help with Mediation.

21.6 Levels of service (4) and (5) are provided under a certificate (similar to a legal aid certificate). The certificate will state which level of service is covered. Where there are proceedings, a copy of the certificate will be lodged with the court.

21.7 Cost protection does not apply where:

(1) the LSC funded client receives Help at Court;
(2) the LSC funded client receives Legal Help only i.e. where the solicitor is advising, but not representing a litigant in person. However, where the LSC funded client receives Legal Help e.g. to write a letter before action, but later receives Legal Representation or General Family Help or Help with Mediation in respect of the same dispute, other than in family proceedings, cost protection does apply to all costs incurred by the receiving party in the funded proceedings or prospective proceedings;
(3) the LSC funded client receives General Family Help or Help with Mediation in family proceedings;
(4) the LSC funded client receives Legal Representation in family proceedings.

21.8 Where cost protection does not apply, the court may award costs in the normal way.

21.9 Where work is done before the issue of a certificate, cost protection does not apply to those costs, except where:

(1) pre-action Legal Help is given and the LSC funded client subsequently receives Legal Representation or General Family Help or Help with Mediation in respect of the same dispute, other than in family proceedings; or
(2) where urgent work is undertaken immediately before the grant of an emergency certificate, other than in family proceedings, when no emergency application could be made as the LSC's offices were closed, provided that the solicitor seeks an emergency certificate at the first available opportunity and the certificate is granted.

21.10 If a LSC funded client's certificate is revoked, costs protection does not apply to work done before or after revocation.

21.11 If a LSC funded client's certificate is discharged, costs protection only applies to costs incurred before the date on which funded services ceased to be provided under the certificate. This may be a date before the date on which the certificate is formally discharged by the LSC (*Burridge v Stafford* [2000] 1 WLR 927, [1999] 4 All ER 660, CA).

21.11A Where an LSC funded client has cost protection, the procedure described in sections 22 and 23 of this practice direction applies, However, that procedure does not apply in relation to costs claimed during any periods in the proceedings when the LSC funded client did not have cost protection, and the procedure set out in Parts 45 to 47 will apply (as appropriate) in relation to those periods.

Assessing a LSC funded client's resources

21.12 The first £100,000 of the value of the LSC funded client's interest in the main or only home is disregarded when assessing his or her financial resources for the purposes of s. 11 and cannot be the subject of any enforcement process by the receiving party. The receiving party cannot apply for an order to sell the LSC funded client's home, but could secure the debt against any value exceeding £100,000 by way of a charging order.

21.13 The court may only take into account the value of the LSC funded client's clothes, household furniture, tools and implements of trade to the extent that it considers that having regard to the quantity or value of the items, the circumstances are exceptional.

21.14 The LSC funded client's resources include the resources of his partner, unless the partner has a contrary interest in the dispute in respect of which funded services are provided.

Party acting in a representative, fiduciary or official capacity

para.21.15(2) **66.58**

21.15 (1) Where a LSC funded client is acting in a representative, fiduciary or official capacity, the court shall not take the personal resources of the party into account for the purposes of either a s. 11 order or costs against the Commission, but shall have regard to the value of any property or estate or the amount of any fund out of which the party is entitled to be indemnified, and may also have regard to the resources of any persons who are beneficially interested in the property, estate or fund.

(2) Similarly, where a party is acting as a litigation friend to a client who is a child or a patient, the court shall not take the personal resources of the litigation friend into account in assessing the resources of the client.

(3) The purpose of this provision is to ensure that any liability is determined with reference to the value of the property or fund being used to pay for the litigation, and the financial position of those who may benefit from or rely on it.

Costs against the LSC

21.16 Regulation 5 of the Community Legal Service (Cost Protection) Regulations 2000 (SI 2000/824) governs when costs can be awarded against the LSC. This provision only applies where cost protection applies and the costs ordered to be paid by the LSC funded client do not fully meet the costs that would have been ordered to be paid by him if cost protection did not apply.

21.17 In this section and the following two sections of this practice direction 'non-funded party' means a party to proceedings who has not received LSC funded services in relation to these proceedings under a legal aid certificate or a certificate issued under the LSC Funding Code other than a certificate which has been revoked.

21.18 The following criteria set out in reg. 5 must be satisfied before the LSC can be ordered to pay the whole or any part of the costs incurred by a non-funded party:

(1) the proceedings are finally decided in favour of a non-funded party;

(2) unless there is good reason for delay the non-funded party provides written notice of intention to seek an order against the LSC within three months of the making of the s. 11(1) costs order;

(3) the court is satisfied that it is just and equitable in the circumstances that provision for the costs should be made out of public funds; and

(4) where costs are incurred in a court of first instance, the following additional criteria must also be met:

(i) the proceedings were instituted by the LSC funded client;

(ii) the non-funded party is an individual; and

(iii) the non-funded party will suffer financial hardship unless the order is made.

('Section 11(1) costs order' is defined in para. 22.1 below.)

21.19 In determining whether conditions (3) and (4) are satisfied, the court shall take into account the resources of the non-funded party and his partner, unless the partner has a contrary interest.

21.19A An order under reg. 5 may be made in relation to proceedings in the Court of Appeal, High Court or a county court, by a costs judge or a district judge.

Effect of appeals

para.21.20 **66.60**

21.20 (1) An order for costs can only be made against the LSC when the proceedings (including any appeal) are finally decided. Therefore, where a court of first instance decides in favour of a non-funded party and an appeal lies, any order made against the LSC shall not take effect unless:

(a) where permission to appeal is required, the time limit for permission to appeal expires, without permission being granted;

(b) where permission to appeal is granted or is not required, the time limit for appeal expires without an appeal being brought.

(2) Accordingly, if the LSC funded client appeals, any earlier order against the LSC can never take effect. If the appeal is unsuccessful, an application can be made to the appeal court for a fresh order.

Section 22 Orders for Costs to Which Section 11 of the Access to Justice Act 1999 Applies

22.1 In this practice direction:

'order for costs to be determined' means an order for costs to which s. 11 of the Access to Justice Act 1999 applies under which the amount of costs payable by the LSC funded client is to be determined by a costs judge or district judge under section 23 of this practice direction.

'order specifying the costs payable' means an order for costs to which s. 11 of the Act applies and which specifies the amount which the LSC funded client is to pay.

'full costs' means, where an order to which s. 11 of the Act applies is made against a LSC funded client, the amount of costs which that person would, had cost protection not applied, have been ordered to pay.

'determination proceedings' means proceedings to which paras 22.1 to 22.10 apply.

's. 11(1) costs order' means an order for costs to be determined or an order specifying the costs payable other than an order specifying the costs payable which was made in determination proceedings.

'statement of resources' means:

(1) a statement, verified by a statement of truth, made by a party to proceedings setting out:

(a) his income and capital and financial commitments during the previous year and, if applicable, those of his partner;

(b) his estimated future financial resources and expectations and, if applicable, those of his partner ('partner' is defined in para. 21.4, above);

(c) a declaration that he and, if applicable, his partner, has not deliberately forgone or deprived himself of any resources or expectations;

(d) particulars of any application for funding made by him in connection with the proceedings; and

(e) any other facts relevant to the determination of his resources; or

(2) a statement, verified by a statement of truth, made by a client receiving funded services, setting out the information provided by the client under reg. 6 of the Community Legal Service (Financial) Regulations 2000 (SI 2000/516), and stating that there has been no significant change in the client's financial circumstances since the date on which the information was provided or, as the case may be, details of any such change.

'regional director' means any regional director appointed by the LSC and any member of his staff authorised to act on his behalf.

22.2 Regulations 8 to 13 of the Community Legal Service (Costs) Regulations 2000 (SI 2000/441) as amended set out the procedure for seeking costs against a funded client and the LSC. The effect of these Regulations is set out in this section and the next section of this practice direction.

22.3 As from 5 June 2000, regs 9 to 13 of the Community Legal Service (Costs) Regulations 2000 as amended also apply to certificates issued under the Legal Aid Act 1988 where costs against the assisted person fall to be assessed under reg. 124 of the Civil Legal Aid (General) Regulations 1989. In this section and the next section of this practice direction the expression 'LSC funded client' includes an assisted person (defined in r. 43.2).

22.4 Regulation 8 of the Community Legal Service (Costs) Regulations 2000 as amended provides that a party intending to seek an order for costs against a LSC funded client may at any time file and serve on the LSC funded client a statement of resources. If that statement is served seven or more days before a date fixed for a hearing at which an order for costs may be made, the LSC funded client must also make a statement of resources and produce it at the hearing.

22.5 If the court decides to make an order for costs against a LSC funded client to whom cost protection applies it may either:

(1) make an order for costs to be determined, or

(2) make an order specifying the costs payable.

22.6 If the court makes an order for costs to be determined it may also:
(1) state the amount of full costs, or
(2) make findings of facts, e.g., concerning the conduct of all the parties which are to be taken into account by the court in the subsequent determination proceedings.

22.7 The court will not make an order specifying the costs payable unless:
(1) it considers that it has sufficient information before it to decide what amount is a reasonable amount for the LSC funded client to pay in accordance with s. 11 of the Act, and
(2) either:
(a) the order also states the amount of full costs, or
(b) the court considers that it has sufficient information before it to decide what amount is a reasonable amount for the LSC funded client to pay in accordance with s. 11 of the Act and is satisfied that, if it were to determine the full costs at that time, they would exceed the amounts specified in the order.

22.8 Where an order specifying the costs payable is made and the LSC funded client does not have cost protection in respect of all of the costs awarded in that order, the order must identify the sum payable (if any) in respect of which the LSC funded client has cost protection and the sum payable (if any) in respect of which he does not have cost protection.

22.9 The court cannot make an order under regs 8 to 13 of the Community Legal Service (Costs) Regulations 2000 as amended except in proceedings to which the next section of this practice direction applies.

Section 23 Determination Proceedings and Similar Proceedings under the Community Legal Service (Costs) Regulations 2000

para.23.2A **68.10**
para.23.3 **66.61**
para.23.4 **66.58**, **66.61**
paras.23.5–23.8 **66.61**
para.23.10 **66.61**

23.1 This section of this practice direction deals with:
(1) proceedings subsequent to the making of an order for costs to be determined,
(2) variations in the amount stated in an order specifying the amount of costs payable, and
(3) the late determination of costs under an order for costs to be determined.

23.2 In this section of this practice direction 'appropriate court office' means:
(1) the district registry or county court in which the case was being dealt with when the s. 11(1) order was made, or to which it has subsequently been transferred; or
(2) in all other cases, the Supreme Court Costs Office.

23.2A (1) This paragraph applies where the appropriate office is any of the following county courts: Barnet, Bow, Brentford, Bromley, Central London, Clerkenwell, Croydon, Edmonton, Ilford, Kingston, Lambeth, Mayor's and City of London, Romford, Shoreditch, Uxbridge, Wandsworth, West London, Willesden and Woolwich.
(2) Where this paragraph applies:
(i) a receiving party seeking an order specifying costs payable by an LSC funded client and/or by the Legal Services Commission under this section must file his application in the Supreme Court Costs Office and, for all purposes relating to that application, the Supreme Court Costs Office will be treated as the appropriate office in that case; and
(ii) unless an order is made transferring the application to the Supreme Court Costs Office as part of the High Court, an appeal from any decision made by a costs judge shall lie to the designated civil judge for the London Group of County Courts or such judge as he shall nominate. The appeal notice and any other relevant papers should be lodged at the Central London Civil Justice Centre.

23.3 (1) A receiving party seeking an order specifying costs payable by a LSC funded client and/or by the LSC may within three months of an order for costs to be determined, file in the appropriate court office an application in form N244 accompanied by:
(a) the receiving party's bill of costs (unless the full costs have already been determined);
(b) the receiving party's statement of resources (unless the court is determining an application against a costs order against the LSC and the costs were not incurred in the court of first instance); and
(c) if the receiving party intends to seek costs against the LSC, written notice to that effect.

(2) If the LSC funded client's liability has already been determined and is less than the full costs, the application will be for costs against the LSC only. If the LSC funded client's liability has not yet been determined, the receiving party must indicate if costs will be sought against the LSC if the funded client's liability is determined as less than the full costs.

(The LSC funded client's certificate will contain the addresses of the LSC funded client, his solicitor, and the relevant regional office of the LSC.)

23.4 The receiving party must file the above documents in the appropriate court office and (where relevant) serve copies on the LSC funded client and the regional director. In respect of applications for funded services made before 3 December 2001 a failure to file a request within the three-month time limit specified in reg. 10(2) is an absolute bar to the making of a costs order against the LSC. Where the application for funded services was made on or after 3 December 2001 the court does have power to extend the three-month time limit, but only if the applicant can show good reason for the delay.

23.5 On being served with the application, the LSC funded client must respond by filing a statement of resources and serving a copy of it on the receiving party (and the regional director where relevant) within 21 days. The LSC funded client may also file and serve written points disputing the bill within the same time limit. (Under r. 3.1 the court may extend or shorten this time limit.)

23.6 If the, LSC funded client fails to file a statement of resources without good reason, the court will determine his liability (and the amount of full costs if relevant) and need not hold an oral hearing for such determination.

23.7 When the LSC funded client files a statement or the 21 day period for doing so expires, the court will fix a hearing date and give the relevant parties at least 14 days notice. The court may fix a hearing without waiting for the expiry of the 21day period if the application is made only against the LSC.

23.8 Determination proceedings will be listed for hearing before a costs judge or district judge. The determination of the liability on the LSC funded client will be listed as a private hearing.

23.9 Where the LSC funded client does not have cost protection in respect of all of the costs awarded, the order made by the costs judge or district judge must in addition to specifying the costs payable, identify the full costs in respect of which cost protection applies and the full costs in respect of which cost protection does not apply.

23.10 The regional director may appear at any hearing at which a costs order may be made against the LSC. Instead of appearing, he may file a written statement at court and serve a copy on the receiving party. The written statement should be filed and a copy served, not less than seven days before the hearing.

Variation of an order specifying the costs payable

para.23.16 **66.59**

23.11 (1) This paragraph applies where the amount stated in an order specifying the costs payable plus the amount ordered to be paid by the LSC is less than the full costs to which cost protection applies.

(2) The receiving party may apply to the court for a variation of the amount which the LSC funded client is required to pay on the ground that there has been a significant change in the client's circumstances since the date of the order.

23.12 On an application under para. 23.11, where the order specifying the costs payable does not state the full costs:

(1) the receiving party must file with his application the receiving party's statement of resources and bill of costs and copies of these documents should be served with the application.

(2) The LSC funded client must respond to the application by making a statement of resources which must be filed at court and served on the receiving party within 21 days thereafter. The LSC funded client may also file and serve written points disputing the bill within the same time limit.

(3) The court will, when determining the application assess the full costs identifying any part of them to which cost protection does apply and any part of them to which cost protection does not apply.

23.13 On an application under para. 23.11 the order specifying the costs payable may be varied as the court thinks fit. That variation must not increase:
(1) the amount of any costs ordered to be paid by the LSC, and
(2) the amount payable by the LSC funded client, to a sum which is greater than the amount of the full costs plus the costs of the application.

23.14 (1) Where an order for costs to be determined has been made but the receiving party has not applied, within the three month time limit under para. 23.2, the receiving party may apply on any of the following grounds for a determination of the amount which the funded client is required to pay:
(a) there has been a significant change in the funded client's circumstances since the date of the order for costs to be determined; or
(b) material additional information about the funded client's financial resources is available which could not with reasonable diligence have been obtained by the receiving party at the relevant time; or
(c) there were other good reasons for the failure by the receiving party to make an application within the time limit.
(2) An application for costs payable by the LSC cannot be made under this paragraph.

23.15 (1) Where the receiving party has received funded services in relation to the proceedings, the LSC may make an application under paras 23.11 and 23.14 above.
(2) In respect of an application under para. 23.11 made by the LSC, the LSC must file and serve copies of the documents described in para. 23.12(1).

23.16 An application under para. 23.11,23.14 and 23.15 must be commenced before the expiration of six years from the date on which the court made the order specifying the costs payable, or (as the case may be) the order for costs to be determined.

23.17 Applications under paras 23.11,23.14 and 23.15 should be made in the appropriate court office and should be made in form N244 to be listed for a hearing before a costs judge or district judge.

Appeals

23.18 (1) Save as mentioned above any determination made under the Community Legal Service (Costs) Regulations 2000 (SI 2000/441), reg. 9 or 10, is final (reg. 11(1)). Any party with a financial interest in the assessment of the full costs, other than a funded party, may appeal against that assessment in accordance with CPR, Part 52 (SI 2000/441, reg. 11(2); CPR, r. 47.20).
(2) The receiving party or the Commission may appeal on a point of law against the making of a costs order against the Commission, against the amount of costs the Commission is required to pay or against the court's refusal to make such an order (SI 2000/441, reg. 11(4)).

DIRECTIONS RELATING TO PART 45 — FIXED COSTS

Section 24 Fixed Costs in Small Claims

para.24 **67.2**

24.1 Under r. 27.14 the costs which can be awarded to a claimant in a small claims track case include the fixed costs payable under Part 45 attributable to issuing the claim.

24.2 Those fixed costs shall be the sum of:
(a) the fixed commencement costs calculated in accordance with Table 1 of r. 45.2; and
(b) the appropriate court fee or fees paid by the claimant.

Section 24A Claims to Which Part 45 Does Not Apply

para.24A **23.17**

24A In a claim to which Part 45 does not apply, no amount shall be entered on the claim form for the charges of the claimant's solicitor, but the words 'to be assessed' shall be inserted.

Section 25 Fixed Costs on the Issue of a Default Costs Certificate

para.25 **67.2** para.25.1 **67.3, 67.5**

25.1 Unless [para. 25.2*] applies or unless the court orders otherwise, the fixed costs to be included

[* The text issued by the Department for Constitutional Affairs mistakenly refers to para. 24.2.]

in a default costs certificate are £80 plus a sum equal to any appropriate court fee payable on the issue of the certificate.

25.2 The fixed costs included in a certificate must not exceed the maximum sum specified for costs and court fee in the notice of commencement.

Section 25A Road Traffic Accidents: Fixed Recoverable Costs in Costs-only Proceedings

Scope

para.25A.1 **67.8** para.25A.3 **67.8**

25A.1 Section II of Part 45 ('the Section') provides for certain fixed costs to be recoverable between parties in respect of costs incurred in disputes which are settled prior to proceedings being issued. The Section applies to road traffic accident disputes as defined in r. 45.7(4)(a), where the accident which gave rise to the dispute occurred on or after 6 October 2003.

25A.2 The Section does not apply to disputes where the total agreed value of the damages is within the small claims limit or exceeds £10,000. Rule 26.8(2) sets out how the financial value of a claim is assessed for the purposes of allocation to track.

25A.3 Fixed recoverable costs are to be calculated by reference to the amount of agreed damages which are payable to the receiving party. In calculating the amount of these damages:
(a) account must be taken of both general and special damages and interest;
(b) any interim payments made must be included;
(c) where the parties have agreed an element of contributory negligence, the amount of damages attributed to that negligence must be deducted;
(d) any amount required by statute to be paid by the compensating party directly to a third party (such as sums paid by way of compensation recovery payments and National Health Service expenses) must not be included.

25A.4 The Section applies to cases which fall within the scope of the Uninsured Drivers Agreement dated 13 August 1999. The Section does not apply to cases which fall within the scope of the Untraced Drivers Agreement dated 14 February 2003.

Fixed recoverable costs formula

25A.5 The amount of fixed costs recoverable is calculated by totalling the following:
(a) £800;
(b) 20% of the agreed damages up to £5,000; and
(c) 15% of the agreed damages between £5,000 and £10,000.

For example, agreed damages of £7,523 would result in recoverable costs of £2,178.45, i.e.: £800 + (20% of £5,000) + (15% of £2,523).

Additional costs for work in specified areas

para.25A.6 **67.12**

25A.6 The area referred to in r. 45.9(2) consists of (within London) the county court districts of Barnet, Bow, Brentford, Central London, Clerkenwell, Edmonton, Ilford, Lambeth, Mayor's and City of London, Romford, Shoreditch, Wandsworth, West London, Willesden and Woolwich and (outside London) the county court districts of Bromley, Croydon, Dartford, Gravesend and Uxbridge.

Multiple claimants

para.25A.7 **67.9**

25A.7 Where there is more than one potential claimant in relation to a dispute and two or more claimants instruct the same solicitor or firm of solicitors, the provisions of the section apply in respect of each claimant.

Information to be included in the claim form

25A.8 Costs only proceedings are commenced using the procedure set out in r. 44.12A. A claim form should be issued in accordance with Part 8. Where the claimant is claiming an amount of costs which exceed the amount of the fixed recoverable costs he must include on the claim form details of the exceptional circumstances which he considers justifies the additional costs.

25A.9 The claimant must also include on the claim form details of any disbursements or success fee he wishes to claim. The disbursements that may be claimed are set out in r. 45.10(1). If the disbursement falls within r. 45.10(2)(d) (disbursements that have arisen due to a particular feature of the dispute) the claimant must give details of the particular feature of the dispute and why he considers the disbursement to be necessary.

Disbursements and success fee

25A.10 If the parties agree the amount of the fixed recoverable costs and the only dispute is as to the payment of, or amount of, a disbursement or as to the amount of a success fee, then proceedings should be issued under r. 44.12A in the normal way and not by reference to Section II of Part 45.

Section 25B Fixed Recoverable Success Fees in Employer's Liability Disease Claims

25.1 The following table is a non-exclusive list of the conditions that will fall within Type A and Type B claims for the purposes of r. 45.23.

Claim type	Description
A	Asbestosis Mesothelioma Bilateral pleural thickening Pleural plaques
B	Repetitive strain injury / WRULD Carpal tunnel syndrome caused by repetitive strain injury Occupational stress

DIRECTIONS RELATING TO PART 46 — FAST TRACK TRIAL COSTS

Section 26 Scope of Part 46: Rule 46.1

para.26 **67.2**

26.1 Part 46 applies to the costs of an advocate for preparing for and appearing at the trial of a claim in the fast track.

26.2 It applies only where, at the date of the trial, the claim is allocated to the fast track. It does not apply in any other case, irrespective of the final value of the claim.

26.3 In particular it does not apply to:

(a) the hearing of a claim which is allocated to the small claims track with the consent of the parties given under r. 26.7(3); or

(b) a disposal hearing at which the amount to be paid under a judgment or order is decided by the court (see PD 26, para. 12.8).

Cases which settle before trial

26.4 Attention is drawn to r. 44.10 (limitation on amount court may award where a claim allocated to the fast track settles before trial).

Section 27 Power to Award More or Less Than the Amount of Fast Track Trial Costs: Rule 46.3

para.27 **67.2**

27.1 Rule 44.15 (providing information about funding arrangements) sets out the requirement to provide information about funding arrangements to the court and other parties. Section 19 of this practice direction sets out the information to be provided and when this is to be done.

27.2 Section 11 of this practice direction explains how the court will approach the question of what sum to allow in respect of additional liability.

27.3 The court has the power, when considering whether a percentage increase is reasonable, to allow different percentages for different items of costs or for different periods during which costs were incurred.

DIRECTIONS RELATING TO PART 47 — PROCEDURE FOR DETAILED ASSESSMENT OF COSTS AND DEFAULT PROVISIONS

Section 28 Time When Assessment May Be Carried Out: Rule 47.1

para.28.1(1) **68.9** para.28.1(5) **66.28, 68.9**
para.28.1(3) **66.28**

28.1 (1) For the purposes of r. 47.1, proceedings are concluded when the court has finally determined the matters in issue in the claim, whether or not there is an appeal.
(2) For the purposes of this rule, the making of an award of provisional damages under Part 41 will be treated as a final determination of the matters in issue.
(3) The court may order or the parties may agree in writing that, although the proceedings are continuing, they will nevertheless be treated as concluded.
(4) (a) A party who is served with a notice of commencement (see para. 32.3 below) may apply to a costs judge or a district judge to determine whether the party who served it is entitled to commence detailed assessment proceedings.
(b) On hearing such an application the orders which the court may make include: an order allowing the detailed assessment proceedings to continue, or an order setting aside the notice of commencement.
(5) A costs judge or a district judge may make an order allowing detailed assessment proceedings to be commenced where there is no realistic prospect of the claim continuing.

Section 29 No Stay of Detailed Assessment Where There Is an Appeal: Rule 47.2

29.1 (1) Rule 47.2 provides that detailed assessment is not stayed pending an appeal unless the court so orders.
(2) An application to stay the detailed assessment of costs pending an appeal may be made to the court whose order is being appealed or to the court who will hear the appeal.

Section 30 Powers of an Authorised Court Officer: Rule 47.3

30.1 (1) The court officers authorised by the Lord Chancellor to assess costs in the Supreme Court Costs Office and the Principal Registry of the Family Division are authorised to deal with claims for costs not exceeding £30,000 (excluding VAT) in the case of senior executive officers, or their equivalent, and £75,000 (excluding VAT) in the case of principal officers.
(2) In calculating whether or not a bill of costs is within the authorised amounts, the figure to be taken into account is the total claim for costs including any additional liability.
(3) Where the receiving party, paying party and any other party to the detailed assessment proceedings who has served points of dispute are agreed that the assessment should not be made by an authorised court officer, the receiving party should so inform the court when requesting a hearing date. The court will then list the hearing before a costs judge or a district judge.
(4) In any other case a party who objects to the assessment being made by an authorised court officer must make an application to the costs judge or district judge under Part 23 setting out the reasons for the objection and if sufficient reason is shown the court will direct that the bill be assessed by a costs judge or district judge.

Section 31 Venue for Detailed Assessment Proceedings: Rule 47.4

paras 31.1 **68.10** paras.31.2(3) **68.11**

31.1 For the purposes of r. 47.4(1) the 'appropriate office' means:
(1) the district registry or county court in which the case was being dealt with when the judgment or order was made or the event occurred which gave rise to the right to assessment, or to which it has subsequently been transferred; or
(2) in all other cases, including Court of Appeal cases, the Supreme Court Costs Office.

31.2 (1) A direction under r. 47.4(2) or (3) specifying a particular court, registry or office as the appropriate office may be given on application or on the court's own initiative.

(2) Before making such a direction on its own initiative the court will give the parties the opportunity to make representations.
(3) Unless the Supreme Court Costs Office is the appropriate office for the purposes of r. 47.4(1) an order directing that an assessment is to take place at the Supreme Court Costs Office will be made only if it is appropriate to do so having regard to the size of the bill of costs, the difficulty of the issues involved, the likely length of the hearing, the cost to the parties and any other relevant matter.

Section 32 Commencement of Detailed Assessment Proceedings: Rule 47.6

para.32.3 **68.11**
para.32.4 **68.47**
para.32.5 **68.47**
para.32.10 **68.11**

32.1 Precedents A, B, C and D in the Schedule of Costs Precedents annexed to this practice direction are model forms of bills of costs for detailed assessment. Further information about bills of costs is set out in section 4.

32.2 A detailed assessment may be in respect of:
(1) base costs, where a claim for additional liability has not been made or has been agreed;
(2) a claim for additional liability only, base costs having been summarily assessed or agreed; or
(3) both base costs and additional liability.

32.3 If the detailed assessment is in respect of costs without any additional liability, the receiving party must serve on the paying party and all the other relevant persons the following documents:
(a) a notice of commencement;
(b) a copy of the bill of costs;
(c) copies of the fee notes of counsel and of any expert in respect of fees claimed in the bill;
(d) written evidence as to any other disbursement which is claimed and which exceeds £250;
(e) a statement giving the name and address for service of any person upon whom the receiving party intends to serve the notice of commencement.

32.4 If the detailed assessment is in respect of an additional liability only, the receiving party must serve on the paying party and all other relevant persons the following documents:
(a) a notice of commencement;
(b) a copy of the bill of costs;
(c) the relevant details of the additional liability;
(d) a statement giving the name and address of any person upon whom the receiving party intends to serve the notice of commencement.

32.5 The relevant details of an additional liability are as follows:
(1) In the case of a conditional fee agreement with a success fee:
(a) a statement showing the amount of costs which have been summarily assessed or agreed, and the percentage increase which has been claimed in respect of those costs;
(b) a statement of the reasons for the percentage increase given in accordance with the Conditional Fee Agreements Regulations 2000, reg. 3(1)(a), or the Collective Conditional Fee Agreements Regulations 2000, reg. 5(1)(c). Both sets of regulations were revoked by the Conditional Fee Agreements (Revocation) Regulations 2005 (SI 2005/2305) but continue to have effect in relation to conditional fee agreements and collective conditional fee agreements entered into before 1 November 2005.
(2) If the additional liability is an insurance premium: a copy of the insurance certificate showing whether the policy covers the receiving party's own costs; his opponents costs; or his own costs and his opponent's costs; and the maximum extent of that cover, and the amount of the premium paid or payable.
(3) If the receiving party claims an additional amount under s. 30 of the Access to Justice Act 1999: a statement setting out the basis upon which the receiving party's liability for the additional amount is calculated.

32.6 Attention is drawn to the fact that the additional amount recoverable pursuant to s. 30 of the Access to Justice Act 1999 in respect of a membership organisation must not exceed the likely cost of the premium of an insurance policy against the risk of incurring a liability to pay the costs of other parties to the proceedings as provided by the Access to Justice (Membership Organisations) Regulations 2000 (SI 2000/693), reg. 4 (for the purposes of arrangements entered into before 1 November 2005) and the Access to Justice (Membership Organisation) Regulations 2005 (SI 2005/2306), reg. 5 (for the purposes of arrangements entered into on or after 1 November 2005).

32.7 If a detailed assessment is in respect of both base costs and an additional liability, the receiving party must serve on the paying party and all other relevant persons the documents listed in para. 32.3 and the documents giving relevant details of an additional liability listed in para. 32.5.

32.8 (1) The notice of commencement should be in form N252.
(2) Before it is served, it must be completed to show as separate items:
(a) the total amount of the costs claimed in the bill;
(b) the extra sum which will be payable by way of fixed costs and court fees if a default costs certificate is obtained.

32.9 (1) This paragraph applies where the notice of commencement is to be served outside England and Wales.
(2) The date to be inserted in the notice of commencement for the paying party to send points of dispute is a date (not less than 21 days from the date of service of the notice) which must be calculated by reference to Part 6, Section III, as if the notice were a claim form and as if the date to be inserted was the date for the filing of a defence.

32.10 (1) For the purposes of r. 47.6(2) a 'relevant person' means:
(a) any person who has taken part in the proceedings which gave rise to the assessment and who is directly liable under an order for costs made against him;
(b) any person who has given to the receiving party notice in writing that he has a financial interest in the outcome of the assessment and wishes to be a party accordingly;
(c) any other person whom the court orders to be treated as such.
(2) Where a party is unsure whether a person is or is not a relevant person, that party may apply to the appropriate office for directions.
(3) The court will generally not make an order that the person in respect of whom the application is made will be treated as a relevant person, unless within a specified time he applies to the court to be joined as a party to the assessment proceedings in accordance with Part 19 (parties and group litigation).

32.11 (1) This paragraph applies in cases in which the bill of costs is capable of being copied on to a computer disk.
(2) If, before the detailed assessment hearing, a paying party requests a disk copy of a bill to which this paragraph applies, the receiving party must supply him with a copy free of charge not more than seven days after the date on which he received the request.

Section 33 Period for Commencing Detailed Assessment Proceedings: Rule 47.7

para.33.1 **68.11**

33.1 The parties may agree under r. 2.11 (time limits may be varied by parties) to extend or shorten the time specified by r. 47.7 for commencing the detailed assessment proceedings.

33.2 A party may apply to the appropriate office for an order under r. 3.1(2)(a) to extend or shorten that time.

33.3 Attention is drawn to r. 47.6(1). The detailed assessment proceedings are commenced by service of the documents referred to.

33.4 Permission to commence assessment proceedings out of time is not required.

Section 34 Sanction for Delay in Commencing Detailed Assessment Proceedings: Rule 47.8

para.34.1 **68.24**

34.1 (1) An application for an order under r. 47.8 must be made in writing and be issued in the appropriate office.
(2) The application notice must be served at least seven days before the hearing.

Section 35 Points of Dispute and Consequences of Not Serving: Rule 47.9

para.35.2 **68.13**

35.1 The parties may agree under r. 2.11 (time limits may be varied by parties) to extend or shorten the time specified by r. 47.9 for service of points of dispute. A party may apply to the appropriate office for an order under r. 3.1(2)(a) to extend or shorten that time.

35.2 Points of dispute should be short and to the point and should follow as closely as possible Precedent G of the Schedule of Costs Precedents annexed to this practice direction.

35.3 Points of dispute must:
(1) identify each item in the bill of costs which is disputed,
(2) in each case, state concisely the nature and grounds of dispute,
(3) where practicable suggest a figure to be allowed for each item in respect of which a reduction is sought, and
(4) be signed by the party serving them or his solicitor.

35.4 (1) The normal period for serving points of dispute i s 21 days after the date of service of the notice of commencement.
(2) Where a notice of commencement is served on a party outside England and Wales the period within which that party should serve points of dispute is to be calculated by reference to Part 6, Section III, as if the notice of commencement was a claim form and as if the period for serving points of dispute were the period for filing a defence.

35.5 A party who serves points of dispute on the receiving party must at the same time serve a copy on every other party to the detailed assessment proceedings, whose name and address for service appears on the statement served by the receiving party in accordance with para. 32.3 or 32.4 above.

35.6 (1) This paragraph applies in cases in which points of dispute are capable of being copied on to a computer disk.
(2) If, within 14 days of the receipt of the points of dispute, the receiving party requests a disk copy of them, the paying party must supply him with a copy free of charge not more than seven days after the date on which he received the request.

35.7 (1) Where the receiving party claims an additional liability, a party who serves points of dispute on the receiving party may include a request for information about other methods of financing costs which were available to the receiving party.
(2) Part 18 (further information) and PD 18 apply to such a request.

Section 36 Procedure Where Costs Are Agreed: Rule 47.10

36.1 Where the parties have agreed terms as to the issue of a costs certificate (either interim or final) they should apply under r. 40.6 (consent judgments and orders) for an order that a certificate be issued in terms set out in the application. Such an application may be dealt with by a court officer, who may issue the certificate.

36.2 Where in the course of proceedings the receiving party claims that the paying party has agreed to pay costs but that he will neither pay those costs nor join in a consent application under para. 36.1, the receiving party may apply under Part 23 (general rules about applications for court orders) for a certificate either interim or final to be issued.

36.3 An application under para. 36.2 must be supported by evidence and will be heard by a costs judge or a district judge. The respondent to the application must file and serve any evidence he relies on at least two days before the hearing date.

36.4 Nothing in r. 47.10 prevents parties who seek a judgment or order by consent from including in the draft a term that a party shall pay to another party a specified sum in respect of costs.

36.5 (1) The receiving party may discontinue the detailed assessment proceedings in accordance with Part 38 (discontinuance).
(2) Where the receiving party discontinues the detailed assessment proceedings before a detailed assessment hearing has been requested, the paying party may apply to the appropriate office for an order about the costs of the detailed assessment proceedings.
(3) Where a detailed assessment hearing has been requested the receiving party may not discontinue unless the court gives permission.
(4) A bill of costs may be withdrawn by consent whether or not a detailed assessment hearing has been requested.

Section 37 Default Costs Certificate: Rule 47.11

para.37.8 **67.2**

37.1 (1) A request for the issue of a default costs certificate must be made in form N254 and must be signed by the receiving party or his solicitor.

(2) The request must be accompanied by a copy of the document giving the right to detailed assessment. (Paragraph 40.4 identifies the appropriate documents.)

37.2 The request must be filed at the appropriate office.

37.3 A default costs certificate will be in form N255.

37.4 Attention is drawn to r. 40.3 (drawing up and filing of judgments and orders) and r. 40.4 (service of judgments and orders) which apply to the preparation and service of a default costs certificate. The receiving party will be treated as having permission to draw up a default costs certificate by virtue of this practice direction.

37.5 The issue of a default costs certificate does not prohibit, govern or affect any detailed assessment of the same costs which are payable out of the Community Legal Service Fund.

37.6 An application for an order staying enforcement of a default costs certificate may be made either:

(1) to a costs judge or district judge of the court office which issued the certificate; or

(2) to the court (if different) which has general jurisdiction to enforce the certificate.

37.7 Proceedings for enforcement of default costs certificates may not be issued in the Supreme Court Costs Office.

37.8 The fixed costs payable in respect of solicitor's charges on the issue of the default costs certificate are £80.

Section 38 Setting Aside Default Costs Certificate: Rule 47.12

paras 38.1–38.4 **68.14**

38.1 (1) A court officer may set aside a default costs certificate at the request of the receiving party under r. 47.12(3).

(2) A costs judge or a district judge will make any other order or give any directions under this rule.

38.2 (1) An application for an order under r. 47.12(2) to set aside or vary a default costs certificate must be supported by evidence.

(2) In deciding whether to set aside or vary a certificate under r. 47.12(2) the matters to which the court must have regard include whether the party seeking the order made the application promptly.

(3) As a general rule a default costs certificate will be set aside under r. 47.12(2) only if the applicant shows a good reason for the court to do so and if he files with his application a copy of the bill and a copy of the default costs certificate, and a draft of the points of dispute he proposes to serve if his application is granted.

a copy of the bill and a copy of the default costs certificate, and a draft of the points of dispute he proposes to serve if his application is granted.

38.3 (1) Attention is drawn to r. 3.1(3) (which enables the court when making an order to make it subject to conditions) and to r. 44.3(8) (which enables the court to order a party whom it has ordered to pay costs to pay an amount on account before the costs are assessed).

(2) A costs judge or a district judge may exercise the power of the court to make an order under r. 44.3(8) although he did not make the order about costs which led to the issue of the default costs certificate.

38.4 If a default costs certificate is set aside the court will give directions for the management of the detailed assessment proceedings.

Section 39 Optional Reply: Rule 47.13

39.1 (1) Where the receiving party wishes to serve a reply, he must also serve a copy on every other party to the detailed assessment proceedings. The time for doing so is within 21 days after service of the points of dispute.

(2) A reply means:

(i) a separate document prepared by the receiving party; or
(ii) his written comments added to the points of dispute.
(3) A reply must be signed by the party serving it or his solicitor.

Section 40 Detailed Assessment Hearing: Rule 47.14

para.40.2(d) **68.15**
para.40.2(i) **63.3**, **68.29**
para.40.12 **68.11**
para.40.14 **68.30**, **68.31**

40.1 The time for requesting a detailed assessment hearing is within three months of the expiry of the period for commencing detailed assessment proceedings.

40.2 The request for a detailed assessment hearing must be in form N258. The request must be accompanied by:

(a) a copy of the notice of commencement of detailed assessment proceedings;
(b) a copy of the bill of costs,
(c) the document giving the right to detailed assessment (see para. 40.4 below);
(d) a copy of the points of dispute, annotated as necessary in order to show which items have been agreed and their value and to show which items remain in dispute and their value;
(e) as many copies of the points of dispute so annotated as there are persons who have served points of dispute;
(f) a copy of any replies served;
(g) a copy of all orders made by the court relating to the costs which are to be assessed;
(h) copies of the fee notes and other written evidence as served on the paying party in accordance with para. 32.3 above;
(i) where there is a dispute as to the receiving party's liability to pay costs to the solicitors who acted for the receiving party, any agreement, letter or other written information provided by the solicitor to his client explaining how the solicitor's charges are to be calculated;
(j) a statement signed by the receiving party or his solicitor giving the name, address for service, reference and telephone number and fax number, if any, of:
  (i) the receiving party;
  (ii) the paying party;
  (iii) any other person who has served points of dispute or who has given notice to the receiving party under para. 32.10(1)(b) above;

  and giving an estimate of the length of time the detailed assessment hearing will take;
(k) where the application for a detailed assessment hearing is made by a party other than the receiving party, such of the documents set out in this paragraph as are in the possession of that party;
(l) where the court is to assess the costs of an assisted person or LSC funded client:
  (i) the legal aid certificate, LSC certificate and relevant amendment certificates, any authorities and any certificates of discharge or revocation;
  (ii) a certificate, in Precedent F(3) of the Schedule of Costs Precedents;
  (iii) if the assisted person has a financial interest in the detailed assessment hearing and wishes to attend, the postal address of that person to which the court will send notice of any hearing;
  (iv) if the rates payable out of the LSC fund are prescribed rates, a schedule to the bill of costs setting out all the items in the bill which are claimed against other parties calculated at the legal aid prescribed rates with or without any claim for enhancement (further information as to this schedule is set out in section 48 of this practice direction);
  (v) a copy of any default costs certificate in respect of costs claimed in the bill of costs.

40.3 (1) This paragraph applies to any document described in para. 40.2(i) above which the receiving party has filed in the appropriate office. The document must be the latest relevant version and in any event have been filed not more than two years before filing the request for a detailed assessment hearing.

(2) In respect of any documents to which this paragraph applies, the receiving party may, instead of filing a copy of it, specify in the request for a detailed assessment hearing the case number under which a copy of the document was previously filed.

40.4 'The document giving the right to detailed assessment' means such one or more of the following documents as are appropriate to the detailed assessment proceedings:

(a) a copy of the judgment or order of the court giving the right to detailed assessment;
(b) a copy of the notice served under r. 3.7 (sanctions for non-payment of certain fees) where a claim is struck out under that rule;
(c) a copy of the notice of acceptance where an offer to settle is accepted under Part 36 (offers to settle and payments into court);
(d) a copy of the notice of discontinuance in a case which is discontinued under Part 38 (discontinuance);
(e) a copy of the award made on an arbitration under any Act or pursuant to an agreement, where no court has made an order for the enforcement of the award;
(f) a copy of the order, award or determination of a statutorily constituted tribunal or body;
(g) in a case under the Sheriffs Act 1887, the sheriff's bill of fees and charges, unless a court order giving the right to detailed assessment has been made;
(h) a notice of revocation or discharge under reg. 82 of the Civil Legal Aid (General) Regulations 1989.
(j) In the county courts certain Acts and Regulations provide for costs incurred in proceedings under those Acts and Regulations to be assessed in the county court if so ordered on application. Where such an application is made, a copy of the order.

40.5 On receipt of the request for a detailed assessment hearing the court will fix a date for the hearing, or, if the costs officer so decides, will give directions or fix a date for a preliminary appointment.

40.6 (1) The court will give at least 14 days' notice of the time and place of the detailed assessment hearing to every person named in the statement referred to in para. 40.2(j) above.

(2) The court will when giving notice, give each person who has served points of dispute a copy of the points of dispute annotated by the receiving party in compliance with para. 40.2(d) above.

(3) Attention is drawn to r. 47.14(6) and (7): apart from the receiving party, only those who have served points of dispute may be heard on the detailed assessment unless the court gives permission, and only items specified in the points of dispute may be raised unless the court gives permission.

40.7 (1) If the receiving party does not file a request for a detailed assessment hearing within the prescribed time, the paying party may apply to the court to fix a time within which the receiving party must do so. The sanction, for failure to commence detailed assessment proceedings within the time specified by the court, is that all or part of the costs may be disallowed (see r. 47.8(2)).

(2) Where the receiving party commences detailed assessment proceedings after the time specified in the rules but before the paying party has made an application to the court to specify a time, the only sanction which the court may impose is to disallow all or part of the interest which would otherwise be payable for the period of delay, unless the court exercises its powers under r. 44.14 (court's powers in relation to misconduct).

40.8 If either party wishes to make an application in the detailed assessment proceedings the provisions of Part 23 (general rules about applications for court orders) apply.

40.9 (1) This paragraph deals with the procedure to be adopted where a date has been given by the court for a detailed assessment hearing and:

(a) the detailed assessment proceedings are settled; or
(b) a party to the detailed assessment proceedings wishes to apply to vary the date which the court has fixed; or
(c) the parties to the detailed assessment proceedings agree about changes they wish to make to any direction given for the management of the detailed assessment proceedings.

(2) If detailed assessment proceedings are settled, the receiving party must give notice of that fact to the court immediately, preferably by fax.

(3) A party who wishes to apply to vary a direction must do so in accordance with Part 23 (general rules about-applications for court orders).

(4) If the parties agree about changes they wish to make to any direction given for the management of the detailed assessment proceedings:
(a) they must apply to the court for an order by consent; and
(b) they must file a draft of the directions sought and an agreed statement of the reasons why the variation is sought; and
(c) the court may make an order in the agreed terms or in other terms without a hearing, but it may direct that a hearing is to be listed.

40.10 (1) If a party wishes to vary his bill of costs, points of dispute or a reply, an amended or supplementary document must be filed with the court and copies of it must be served on all other relevant parties.
(2) Permission is not required to vary a bill of costs, points of dispute or a reply but the court may disallow the variation or permit it only upon conditions, including conditions as to payment of any costs caused or wasted by the variation.

40.11 Unless the court directs otherwise the receiving party must file with the court the papers in support of the bill not less than seven days before the date for the detailed assessment hearing and not more than 14 days before that date.

40.12 The following provisions apply in respect of the papers to be filed in support of the bill:
(a) If the claim is for costs only without any additional liability the papers to be filed, and the order in which they are to be arranged are as follows:
(i) instructions and briefs to counsel arranged in chronological order together with all advices, opinions and drafts received and response to such instructions;
(ii) reports and opinions of medical and other experts;
(iii) any other relevant papers;
(iv) a full set of any relevant pleadings to the extent that they have not already been filed in court.
(v) correspondence, files and attendance notes;
(b) where the claim is in respect of an additional liability only, such of the papers listed at (a) above, as are relevant to the issues raised by the claim for additional liability.
(c) where the claim is for both base costs and an additional liability, the papers listed at (a) above, together with any papers relevant to the issues raised by the claim for additional liability.

40.13 The provisions set out in section 20 of this practice direction apply where the court disallows any amount of a legal representative's percentage increase, and the legal representative applies for an order that the disallowed amount should continue to be payable by the client in accordance with r. 44.16.

40.14 The court may direct the receiving party to produce any document which in the opinion of the court is necessary to enable it to reach its decision. These documents will in the first instance be produced to the court, but the court may ask the receiving party to elect whether to disclose the particular document to the paying party in order to rely on the contents of the document, or whether to decline disclosure and instead rely on other evidence.

40.15 Costs assessed at a detailed assessment at the conclusion of proceedings may include an assessment of any additional liability in respect of the costs of a previous application or hearing.

40.16 Once the detailed assessment hearing has ended it is the responsibility of the legal representative appearing for the receiving party or, as the case may be, the receiving party in person to remove the papers filed in support of the bill.

Section 41 Power to Issue an Interim Certificate: Rule 47.15

41.1 (1) A party wishing to apply for an interim certificate may do so by making an application in accordance with Part 23 (general rules about applications for court orders).
(2) Attention is drawn to the fact that the court's power to issue an interim certificate arises only after the receiving party has filed a request for a detailed assessment hearing.

Section 42 Final Costs Certificate: Rule 47.16

para.42.4 **68.27**

42.1 At the detailed assessment hearing the court will indicate any disallowance or reduction in the sums claimed in the bill of costs by making an appropriate note on the bill.

42.2 The receiving party must, in order to complete the bill after the detailed assessment hearing make clear the correct figures agreed or allowed in respect of each item and must recalculate the summary of the bill appropriately.

42.3 The completed bill of costs must be filed with the court no later than 14 days after the detailed assessment hearing.

42.4 At the same time as filing the completed bill of costs, the party whose bill it is must also produce receipted fee notes and receipted accounts in respect of all disbursements except those covered by a certificate in Precedent F(5) in the Schedule of Costs Precedents annexed to this practice direction.

42.5 No final costs certificate will be issued until all relevant court fees payable on the assessment of costs have been paid.

42.6 If the receiving party fails to file a completed bill in accordance with r. 47.16 the paying party may make an application under Part 23 (general rules about applications for court orders) seeking an appropriate order under r. 3.1 (the court's general powers of management).

42.7 A final costs certificate will show:

(a) the amount of any costs which have been agreed between the parties or which have been allowed on detailed assessment;

(b) where applicable the amount agreed or allowed in respect of VAT on the costs agreed or allowed.

This provision is subject to any contrary provision made by the statutory provisions relating to costs payable out of the Community Legal Service Fund.

42.8 A final costs certificate will include disbursements in respect of the fees of counsel only if receipted fee notes or accounts in respect of those disbursements have been produced to the court and only to the extent indicated by those receipts.

42.9 Where the certificate relates to costs payable between parties a separate certificate will be issued for each party entitled to costs.

42.10 Form N257 is a model form of interim costs certificate and forms N256 and N256HC are model forms of final costs certificate.

42.11 An application for an order staying enforcement of an interim costs certificate or final costs certificate may be made either:

(1) to a costs judge of district judge of the court office which issued the certificate; or

(2) to the court (if different) which has general jurisdiction to enforce the certificate.

42.12 Proceedings for enforcement of interim costs certificates or final costs certificates may not be issued in the Supreme Court Costs Office.

Section 43 Detailed Assessment Procedure Where Costs Are Payable Out of the Community Legal Service Fund: Rule 47.17

para.43.3 **68.11, 68.20**

43.1 The provisions of this section apply where the court is to assess costs which are payable only out of the community legal service fund. Paragraphs 39.1 to 40.16 and 49.1 to 49.8 apply in cases involving costs payable by another person as well as costs payable only out of the community legal service fund.

43.2 The time for requesting a detailed assessment under r. 47.17 is within three months after the date when the right to detailed assessment arose.

43.3 The request for a detailed assessment of costs must be in form N258A. The request must be accompanied by:

(a) a copy of the bill of costs;

(b) the document giving the right to detailed assessment (for further information as to this document, see para. 40.4 above);

(c) a copy of all orders made by the court relating to the costs which are to be assessed;

(d) copies of any fee notes of counsel and any expert in respect of fees claimed in the bill;

(e) written evidence as to any other disbursement which is claimed and which exceeds £250;
(f) the legal aid certificates, LSC certificates, any relevant amendment certificates, any authorities and any certificates of discharge or revocation;
(g) In the Supreme Court Costs Office the relevant papers in support of the bill as described in para. 40.12 above; in cases proceeding in district registries and county courts this provision does not apply and the papers should only be lodged if requested by the costs officer;
(h) a statement signed by the solicitor giving his name, address for service, reference, telephone number, fax number and, if the assisted person has a financial interest in the detailed assessment and wishes to attend, giving the postal address of that person, to which the court will send notice of any hearing.

43.4 Rule 47.17 provides that the court will hold a detailed assessment hearing if the assisted person has a financial interest in the detailed assessment and wishes to attend. The court may also hold a detailed assessment hearing in any other case, instead of provisionally assessing a bill of costs, where it considers that a hearing is necessary. Before deciding whether a hearing is necessary under this rule, the court may require the solicitor whose bill it is, to provide further information relating to the bill.

43.5 Where the court has provisionally assessed a bill of costs it will send to the solicitor a notice, in form N253 annexed to this practice direction, of the amount of costs which the court proposed to allow together with the bill itself. The legal representative should, if the provisional assessment is to be accepted, then complete the bill.

43.6 The court will fix a date for a detailed assessment hearing if the solicitor informs the court within 14 days after he receives the notice of the amount allowed on the provisional assessment that he wants the court to hold such a hearing.

43.7 The court will give at least 14 days' notice of the time and place of the detailed assessment hearing to the solicitor and, if the assisted person has a financial interest in the detailed assessment and wishes to attend, to the assisted person.

43.8 If the solicitor whose bill it is, or any other party wishes to make an application in the detailed assessment proceedings, the provisions of Part 23 (general rules about applications for court orders) applies.

43.9 It is the responsibility of the legal representative to complete the bill by entering in the bill the correct figures allowed in respect of each item, recalculating the summary of the bill appropriately and completing the Community Legal Service assessment certificate (form EX80A).

Section 44 Costs of Detailed Assessment Proceedings Where Costs Are Payable Out of a Fund Other than the Community Legal Service Fund: Rule 47.17A

44.1 Rule 47.17A provides that the court will make a provisional assessment of a bill of costs payable out of a fund (other than the Community Legal Service Fund) unless it considers that a hearing is necessary. It also enables the court to direct under r. 47.17A(3) that the receiving party must serve a copy of the request for assessment and copies of the documents which accompany it, on any person who has a financial interest in the outcome of the assessment.
(a) A person has a financial interest in the outcome of the assessment if the assessment will or may affect the amount of money or property to which he is or may become entitled out of the fund.
(b) Where an interest in the fund is itself held by a trustee for the benefit of some other person, that trustee will be treated as the person having such a financial interest.
(c) 'Trustee' includes a personal representative, receiver or any other person acting in a fiduciary capacity.

44.3 The request for a detailed assessment of costs out of the fund should be in form N258B, be accompanied by the documents set out at para. 43.3(a) to (e) and (g) above and the following:
(a) a statement signed by the receiving party giving his name, address for service, reference, telephone number, fax number; and
(b) a statement of the postal address of any person who has a financial interest in the outcome of the assessment, to which the court may send notice of any hearing; and

Civil Procedure Rules & Practice Directions

(c) in respect of each person stated to have such an interest if such person is a child or patient, a statement to that effect.

44.4 The court will decide, having regard to the amount of the bill, the size of the fund and the number of persons who have a financial interest, which of those persons should be served. The court may dispense with service on all or some of them.

44.5 Where the court makes an order dispensing with service on all such persons it may proceed at once to make a provisional assessment, or, if it decides that a hearing is necessary, give appropriate directions. Before deciding whether a hearing is necessary under this rule, the court may require the receiving party to provide further information relating to the bill.

44.6 (1) Where the court has provisionally assessed a bill of costs, it will send to the receiving party, a notice in form N253 of the amount of costs which the court proposes to allow together with the bill itself. If the receiving party is legally represented the legal representative should, if the provisional assessment is to be accepted, then complete the bill.

(2) The court will fix a date for a detailed assessment hearing, if the receiving party informs the court within 14 days after he receives the notice in form N253 of the amount allowed on the provisional assessment, that he wants the court to hold such a hearing.

44.7 Where the court makes an order that a person who has a financial interest is to be served with a copy of the request for assessment, it may give directions about service and about the hearing.

44.8 The court will give at least 14 days' notice of the time and place of the detailed assessment hearing to the receiving party and to any person who has a financial interest in the outcome of the assessment and has been served with a copy of the request for assessment.

44.9 If the receiving party, or any other party or any person who has a financial interest in the outcome of assessment, wishes to make an application in the detailed assessment proceedings, the provisions of Part 23 (general rules about applications for court orders) applies.

44.10 If the receiving party is legally represented the legal representative must in order to complete the bill after the assessment make clear the correct figures allowed in respect of each item and must recalculate the summary of the bill if appropriate.

Section 45 Liability for Costs of Detailed Assessment Proceedings: Rule 47.18

para.45.1 **68.21** para.45.5 **68.23**

45.1 As a general rule the court will assess the receiving party's costs of the detailed assessment

45.2 proceedings and add them to the bill of costs. If the costs of the detailed assessment proceedings are awarded to the paying party, the court will either assess those costs by summary assessment or make an order for them to be decided by detailed assessment.

45.3 No party should file or serve a statement of costs of the detailed assessment proceedings unless the court orders him to do so.

45.4 Attention is drawn to the fact that in deciding what order to make about the costs of detailed assessment proceedings the court must have regard to the conduct of all parties, the amount by which the bill of costs has been reduced and whether it was reasonable for a party to claim the costs of a particular item or to dispute that item.

45.5 (1) In respect of interest on the costs of detailed assessment proceedings, the interest shall begin to run from the date of the default, interim or final costs certificate as the case may be.

(2) This provision applies only to the costs of the detailed assessment proceedings themselves. The costs of the substantive proceedings are governed by r. 40.8(1).

Section 46 Offers to Settle without Prejudice Save as to the Costs of the Detailed Assessment Proceedings: Rule 47.19

paras 46.1–46.2 **68.22** paras 46.4 68.22
paras 46.3 **68.4, 68.22**

46.1 Rule 47.19 allows the court to take into account offers to settle, without prejudice save as to the costs of detailed assessment proceedings, when deciding who is liable for the costs of those proceedings. The rule does not specify a time within which such an offer should be made. An offer made by the paying party should usually be made within 14 days after service of the notice of commencement on that party. If the offer is made by the receiving party, it should normally be made within 14 days after the service of points of dispute by the paying party. Offers made after these periods are likely to be given less weight by the court in deciding what order as to costs to make unless there is good reason for the offer not being made until the later time.

46.2 Where an offer to settle is made it should specify whether or not it is intended to be inclusive of the cost of preparation of the bill, interest and value added tax (VAT). The offer may include or exclude some or all of these items but the position must be made clear on the face of the offer so that the offeree is clear about the terms of the offer when it is being considered. Unless the offer states otherwise, the offer will be treated as being inclusive of all these items.

46.3 Where an offer to settle is accepted, an application may be made for a certificate in agreed terms, or the bill of costs may be withdrawn, in accordance with r. 47.10 (procedure where costs are agreed).

46.4 Where the receiving party is an assisted person or a LSC funded client, an offer to settle without prejudice save as to the costs of the detailed assessment proceedings will not have the consequences specified under r. 47.19 unless the court so orders.

Section 47 Appeals from Authorised Court Officers in Detailed Assessment Proceedings: Right to Appeal: Rule 47.20

paras 47.1–48.4 **68.28**

47.1 This section and the next section of this practice direction relate only to appeals from authorised court officers in detailed assessment proceedings. All other appeals arising out of detailed assessment proceedings (and arising out of summary assessments) are dealt with in accordance with Part 52 and PD 52. The destination of appeals is dealt with in accordance with the Access to Justice Act 1999 (Destination of Appeals) Order 2000.
with Part 52 and PD 52. The destination of appeals is dealt with in accordance with the Access to Justice Act 1999 (Destination of Appeals) Order 2000.

47.2 In respect of appeals from authorised court officers, there is no requirement to obtain permission, or to seek written reasons.

Section 48 Procedure on Appeal from Authorised Court Officers: Rule 47.22

48.1 The appellant must file a notice which should be in form N161 (an appellant's notice).

48.2 The appeal will be heard by a costs judge or a district judge of the High Court, and is a rehearing.

48.3 The appellant's notice should, if possible, be accompanied by a suitable record of the judgment appealed against. Where reasons given for the decision have been officially recorded by the court an approved transcript of that record should accompany the notice. Photocopies will not be accepted for this purpose. Where there is no official record the following documents will be acceptable:

(1) The officers comments written on the bill.

(2) Advocates' notes of the reasons agreed by the respondent if possible and approved by the authorised court officer.

When the appellant was unrepresented before the authorised court officer, it is the duty of any advocate for the respondent to make his own note of the reasons promptly available, free of charge to the appellant where there is no official record or if the court so directs. Where the appellant was represented before the authorised court officer, it is the duty of his/her own former advocate to make his/her notes available. The appellant should submit the note of the reasons to the costs judge or district judge hearing the appeal.

48.4 The appellant may not be able to obtain a suitable record of the authorised court officers decision within the time in which the appellant's notice must be filed. In such cases, the appellant's notice must still be completed to the best of the appellant's ability. It may however be amended subsequently with the permission of the costs judge or district judge hearing the appeal.

Section 49 Costs Payable by the LSC at Prescribed Rates

49.1 This section applies to a bill of costs of an assisted person or LSC funded client which is payable by another person where the costs which can be claimed against the LSC are restricted to prescribed rates (with or without enhancement).

49.2 Where this section applies, the solicitor of the assisted person or LSC funded client must file a legal aid/LSC schedule in accordance with para. 40.2(l) above. The schedule should follow as closely as possible Precedent E of the Schedule of Costs Precedents annexed to this practice direction.

49.3 The schedule must set out by reference to the item numbers in the bill of costs, all the costs claimed as payable by another person, but the arithmetic in the schedule should claim those items at prescribed rates only (with or without any claim for enhancement).

49.4 Where there has been a change in the prescribed rates during the period covered by the bill of costs, the schedule (as opposed to the bill) should be divided into separate parts, so as to deal separately with each change of rate. The schedule must also be divided so as to correspond with any divisions in the bill of costs.

49.5 If the bill of costs contains additional columns setting out costs claimed against the LSC only, the schedule may be set out in a separate document or, alternatively, may be included in the additional columns of the bill.

49.6 The detailed assessment of the legal aid/LSC schedule will take place immediately after the detailed assessment of the bill of costs.

49.7 Attention is drawn to the possibility that, on occasions, the court may decide to conduct the detailed assessment of the legal aid/LSC schedule separately from any detailed assessment of the bill of costs. This will occur, for example, where a default costs certificate is obtained as between the parties but that certificate is not set aside at the time of the detailed assessment pursuant to the Legal Aid Act 1988 or regulations thereunder.

49.8 Where costs have been assessed at prescribed rates it is the responsibility of the legal representative to enter the correct figures allowed in respect of each item and to recalculate the summary of the legal aid/LSC schedule.

Section 49A Costs Payable by the Trustee for Civil Recovery under a Recovery Order

49A.1 In this section:

'the Act' means the Proceeds of Crime Act 2002;

'the Order in Council' means the Proceeds of Crime Act 2002 (External Requests and Orders) Order 2005 (SI 2005/3181); and

'the Regulations' means the Proceeds of Crime Act 2002 (Legal Expenses in Civil Recovery Proceedings) Regulations 2005 (SI 2005/3382).

49A.2 This section applies to the assessment of costs where the court has made a recovery order which provides for the payment by the trustee for civil recovery of a person's reasonable legal costs in respect of civil recovery proceedings. Such an order may be made under s. 266(8A) of the Act or art. 177(10) of the Order in Council. The procedure for obtaining a recovery order is set out in the Act and Order in Council, together with the Civil Recovery Proceedings Practice Direction.

49A.3 Where this section applies, costs are to be assessed in accordance with the procedure for detailed assessment under Part 47, subject to the modifications set out in parts 4 and 5 of the Regulations.

49A.4 The detailed assessment will normally be made by a costs judge, even if the costs are within the authorised amounts specified in para. 30.1(1). The appropriate office for the purpose of r. 47.4(1) is the Supreme Court Costs Office.

49A.5 In detailed assessment proceedings to which this section applies:

(1) the paying party is the trustee for civil recovery;

(2) the receiving party is the person whose reasonable legal costs are payable pursuant to provision made in the recovery order under s. 266(8A) of the Act or art. 177(10) of the Order in Council; and

(3) the relevant persons for the purpose of r. 47.6(2) include the Director of the Assets Recovery Agency in addition to the persons referred to in para. 32.10.

49A.6 On commencing detailed assessment proceedings, the receiving party must, in addition to serving the documents listed in para. 32.3 on the paying party and all other relevant persons, serve a statement giving the date, amount and source of all interim payments which have been released in respect of any of those costs under part 3 of the Regulations.

49A.7 By virtue of reg. 13(2) of the Regulations, detailed assessment proceedings must be commenced not later than two months after the date of the recovery order, and a request for a detailed assessment hearing must be filed not later than two months after the expiry of the period for commencing the detailed assessment proceedings.

49A.8 The documents which must accompany the request for a detailed assessment hearing shall include copies of all exclusions from property freezing orders or interim receiving orders made by the court for the purpose of enabling the receiving party to meet the costs which are to be assessed, and of every estimate of costs filed by the receiving party in support of an application for such an exclusion.

49A.9 The receiving party's costs will be assessed on the standard basis, subject to part 5 of the Regulations (and in particular reg. 17, which specifies the hourly rates which may be allowed). Attention is also drawn to reg. 14, which provides that the amounts of any interim payments released in respect of the receiving party's costs will be deducted from the costs allowed in accordance with part 5 of the Regulations.

DIRECTIONS RELATING TO PART 48 — COSTS — SPECIAL CASES

Section 50 Amount of Costs Where Costs Are Payable Pursuant to Contract: Rule 48.3

paras 50.1–50.4 **66.49**

50.1 Where the court is assessing costs payable under a contract, it may make an order that all or part of the costs payable under the contract shall be disallowed if it is satisfied by the paying party that costs have been unreasonably incurred or are unreasonable in amount.

50.2 Rule 48.3 only applies if the court is assessing costs payable under a contract. It does not:

(1) require the court to make an assessment of such costs; or

(2) require a mortgagee to apply for an order for those costs that he has a contractual right to recover out of the mortgage funds.

50.3 The following principles apply to costs relating to a mortgage:

(1) An order for the payment of costs of proceedings by one party to another is always a discretionary order (Supreme Court Act 1981, s. 51).

(2) Where there is a contractual right to the costs the discretion should ordinarily be exercised so as to reflect that contractual right.

(3) The power of the court to disallow a mortgagee's costs sought to be added to the mortgage security is a power that does not derive from s. 51, but from the power of the courts of equity to fix the terms on which redemption will be allowed.

(4) A decision by a court to refuse costs in whole or in part to a mortgagee litigant may be:

(a) a decision in the exercise of the s. 51 discretion;

(b) a decision in the exercise of the power to fix the terms on which redemption will be allowed;

(c) a decision as to the extent of a mortgagee's contractual right to add his costs to the security; or

(d) a combination of two or more of these things.

The statements of case in the proceedings or the submissions made to the court may indicate which of the decisions has been made.

(5) A mortgagee is not to be deprived of a contractual or equitable right to add costs to the security merely by reason of an order for payment of costs made without reference to the mortgagee's contractual or equitable rights, and without any adjudication as to whether or not the mortgagee should be deprived of those costs.

50.4 (1) Where the contract entitles a mortgagee to:

(a) add the costs of litigation relating to the mortgage to the sum secured by it;

(b) require a mortgagor to pay those costs; or

(c) both,

the mortgagor may make an application for the court to direct that an account of the mortgagee's costs be taken.

(Rule 25.1(1)(n) provides that the court may direct that a party file an account.)

(2) The mortgagor may then dispute an amount in the mortgagee's account on the basis that is has been unreasonably incurred or is unreasonable in amount.

(3) Where a mortgagor disputes an amount, the court may make an order that the disputed costs are assessed under r. 48.3.

Section 50A Limitation on Court's Power to Award Costs in Favour of Trustee or Personal Representative: Rule 48.4

50A.1 A trustee or personal representative is entitled to an indemnity out of the relevant trust fund or estate for costs properly incurred, which may include costs awarded against the trustee or personal representative in favour of another party.

50A.2 Whether costs were properly incurred depends on all the circumstances of the case, and may, for example, depend on:

(1) whether the trustee or personal representative obtained directions from the court before bringing or defending the proceedings;

(2) whether the trustee or personal representative acted in the interests of the fund or estate or in substance for a benefit other than that of the estate, including his own; and

(3) whether the trustee or personal representative acted in some way unreasonably in bringing or defending, or in the conduct of, the proceedings.

50A.3 The trustee or personal representative is not to be taken to have acted in substance for a benefit other than that of the fund by reason only that he has defended a claim in which relief is sought against him personally.

Section 51 Costs Where Money Is Payable by or to a Child or Patient: Rule 48.5

para.51.1 **66.47** para.51.1(b) **66.47**

51.1 The circumstances in which the court need not order the assessment of costs under r. 48.5(3) are as follows:

(a) where there is no need to do so to protect the interests of the child or patient or his estate;

(b) where another party has agreed to pay a specified sum in respect of the costs of the child or patient and the solicitor acting for the child or patient has waived the right to claim further costs;

(c) where the court has decided the costs payable to the child or patient by way of summary assessment and the solicitor acting for the child or patient has waived the right to claim further costs;

(d) where an insurer or other person is liable to discharge the costs which the child or patient would otherwise be liable to pay to his solicitor and the court is satisfied that the insurer or other person is financially able to discharge those costs.

Section 52 Litigants in Person: Rule 48.6

para.52.2 **68.54** paras.52.4–52.5 **68.54**

52.1 In order to qualify as an expert for the purpose of r. 48.6(3)(c) (expert assistance in connection with assessing the claim for costs), the person in question must be a:

(1) barrister,

(2) solicitor,

(3) Fellow of the Institute of Legal Executives,

(4) Fellow of the Association of Law Costs Draftsmen,

(5) law costs draftsman who is a member of the Academy of Experts,

(6) law costs draftsman who is a member of the Expert Witness Institute.

52.2 Where a litigant in person wishes to prove that he has suffered financial loss he should produce to the court any written evidence he relies on to support that claim, and serve a copy of that evidence on any party against whom he seeks costs at least 24 hours before the hearing at which the question may be decided.

52.3 Where a litigant in person commences detailed assessment proceedings under r. 47.6 he should serve copies of that written evidence with the notice of commencement.

52.4 The amount, which may be allowed to a litigant in person under r. 46.3(5)(b) and r. 48.6(4), is £9.25 per hour.

52.5 Attention is drawn to r. 48.6(6)(b). A solicitor who, instead of acting for himself, is represented in the proceedings by his firm or by himself in his firm name, is not, for the purpose of the Civil Procedure Rules, a litigant in person.

Section 53 Personal Liability of Legal Representative for Costs — Wasted Costs Orders: Rule 48.7

para.53.1–53.2 **66.71**
para.53.4 **66.71**
para. 53.4(2)–(3) **66.70**
para.53.5 **66.71**
para.53.6 **66.71**
para.53.8 **66.71**

53.1 Rule 48.7 deals with wasted costs orders against legal representatives. Such orders can be made at any stage in the proceedings up to and including the proceedings relating to the detailed assessment of costs. In general, applications for wasted costs are best left until after the end of the trial.

53.2 The court may make a wasted costs order against a legal representative on its own initiative.

53.3 A party may apply for a wasted costs order:
(1) by filing an application notice in accordance with Part 23; or
(2) by making an application orally in the course of any hearing.

53.4 It is appropriate for the court to make a wasted costs order against a legal representative, only if:
(1) the legal representative has acted improperly, unreasonably or negligently;
(2) his conduct has caused a party to incur unnecessary costs; and
(3) it is just in all the circumstances to order him to compensate that party for the whole or part of those costs.

53.5 The court will give directions about the procedure that will be followed in each case in order to ensure that the issues are dealt with in a way which is fair and as simple and summary as the circumstances permit.

53.6 As a general rule the court will consider whether to make a wasted costs order in two stages:
(1) in the first stage, the court must be satisfied:
(a) that it has before it evidence or other material which, if unanswered, would be likely to lead to a wasted costs order being made; and
(b) the wasted costs proceedings are justified notwithstanding the likely costs involved.
(2) at the second stage (even if the court is satisfied under sub-para. (1)) the court will consider, after giving the legal representative an opportunity to give reasons why the court should not make a wasted costs order, whether it is appropriate to make a wasted costs order in accordance with para. 53.4 above.

53.7 On an application for a wasted costs order under Part 23 the court may proceed to the second stage described in para. 53.6 without first adjourning the hearing if it is satisfied that the legal representative has already had a reasonable opportunity to give reasons why the court should not make a wasted costs order. In other cases the court will adjourn the hearing before proceeding to the second stage.

53.8 On an application for a wasted costs order under Part 23 the application notice and any evidence in support must identify:
(1) what the legal representative is alleged to have done or failed to do; and
(2) the costs that he may be ordered to pay or which are sought against him.

53.9 A wasted costs order is an order:
(1) that the legal representative pay a specified sum in respect of costs to a party; or
(2) for costs relating to a specified sum or items of work to be disallowed.

53.10 Attention is drawn to r. 44.3A(1) and (2) which respectively prevent the court from assessing any additional liability until the conclusion of the proceedings (or the part of the proceedings) to which the funding arrangement relates, and set out the orders the court may make at the conclusion of the proceedings.

Section 54 Basis of Detailed Assessment of Solicitor and Client Costs: Rule 48.8

paras 54.4–54.6 **6.18**
paras.54.7 **6.18, 6.21**
para.54.8 **6.18**

54.1 A client and his solicitor may agree whatever terms they consider appropriate about the payment of the solicitor's charges for his services. If however, the costs are of an unusual nature (either in amount or in the type of costs incurred) those costs will be presumed to have been unreasonably incurred unless the solicitor satisfies the court that he informed the client that they were unusual and, where the costs relate to litigation, that he informed the client

Civil Procedure Rules & Practice Directions

they might not be allowed on an assessment of costs between the parties. That information must have been given to the client before the costs were incurred.

54.2 (1) Costs as between a solicitor and client are assessed on the indemnity basis as defined by r. 44.4.

(2) Attention is drawn to the presumptions set out in r. 48.8(2). These presumptions may be rebutted by evidence to the contrary.

54.3 Rule 48.10 and section 56 of this practice direction deal with the procedure to be followed for obtaining the assessment of a solicitor's bill pursuant to an order under Part III of the Solicitors Act 1974.

54.4 If a party fails to comply with the requirements of r. 48.10 concerning the service of a breakdown of costs or points of dispute, any other party may apply to the court in which the detailed assessment hearing should take place for an order requiring compliance with r. 48.10. If the court makes such an order, it may:

(a) make it subject to conditions including a condition to pay a sum of money into court; and
(b) specify the consequence of failure to comply with the order or a condition.

54.5 (1) A client who has entered into a conditional fee agreement with a solicitor may apply for assessment of the base costs (which is carried out in accordance with r. 48.8(2) as if there were no conditional fee agreement) or for assessment of the percentage increase (success fee) or both.

(2) Where the court is to assess the percentage increase the court will have regard to all the relevant factors as they appeared to the solicitor or counsel when the conditional fee agreement was entered into.

54.6 Where the client applies to the court to reduce the percentage increase which the solicitor has charged the client under the conditional fee agreement, the client must set out in his application notice:

(a) the reasons why the percentage increase should be reduced; and
(b) what the percentage increase should be.

54.7 The factors relevant to assessing the percentage increase include:

(a) the risk that the circumstances in which the fees or expenses would be payable might not occur;
(b) the disadvantages relating to the absence of payment on account;
(c) whether there is a conditional fee agreement between the solicitor and counsel;
(d) the solicitor's liability for any disbursements.

54.8 When the court is considering the factors to be taken into account, it will have regard to the circumstances as they reasonably appeared to the solicitor or counsel when the conditional fee agreement was entered into.

Section 56 Procedure on Assessment of Solicitor and Client Costs: Rule 48.10

para.56.1–56.19 **63.9, 68.19**

56.1 The paragraphs in this section apply to orders made under Part III of the Solicitors Act 1974 for the assessment of costs. In these paragraphs 'client' includes any person entitled to make an application under Part III of that Act.

56.2 The procedure for obtaining an order under Part III of the Solicitors Act 1974 is by the alternative procedure for claims under Part 8, as modified by r. 67.3 and PD 67. Precedent J of the Schedule of Costs Precedents annexed to this practice direction is a model form of claim form. The application must be accompanied by the bill or bills in respect of which assessment is sought, and, if the claim concerns a conditional fee agreement, a copy of that agreement. If the original bill is not available a copy will suffice.

56.3 Model forms of order, which the court may make, are set out in Precedents K, L and M of the Schedule of Costs Precedents annexed to this practice direction.

56.4 Attention is drawn to the time limits within which the required steps must be taken: i.e. the solicitor must serve a breakdown of costs within 28 days of the order for costs to be assessed, the client must serve points of dispute within 14 days after service on him of the breakdown, and any reply must be served within 14 days of service of the points of dispute.

56.5 The breakdown of costs referred to in r. 48.10 is a document which contains the following information:

(a) details of the work done under each of the bills sent for assessment; and

(b) in applications under the Solicitors Act 1974, s. 70, an account showing money received by the solicitor to the credit of the client and sums paid out of that money on behalf of the client but not payments out which were made in satisfaction of the bill or of any items which are claimed in the bill.

56.6 Precedent P of the Schedule of Costs Precedents annexed to this practice direction is a model form of breakdown of costs. A party who is required to serve a breakdown of costs must also serve:

(1) copies of the fee notes of counsel and of any expert in respect of fees claimed in the breakdown, and

(2) written evidence as to any other disbursement which is claimed in the breakdown and which exceeds £250.

56.7 The provisions relating to default costs certificates (r. 47.11) do not apply to cases to which r. 48.10 applies.

56.8 Points of dispute should, as far as practicable, be in the form complying with paras 35.1 to 35.7.

56.9 The time for requesting a detailed assessment hearing is within three months after the date of the order for the costs to be assessed.

56.10 The form of request for a hearing date must be in form N258C. The request must be accompanied by copies of:

(a) the order sending the bill or bills for assessment;

(b) the bill or bills sent for assessment;

(c) the solicitor's breakdown of costs and any invoices or accounts served with that breakdown;

(d) a copy of the points of dispute, annotated as necessary in order to show which items have been agreed and their value and to show which items remain in dispute;

(e) as many copies of the points of dispute so annotated as there are other parties to the proceedings to whom the court should give details of the assessment hearing requested;

(f) a copy of any replies served;

(g) a statement signed by the party filing the request or his legal representative giving the names and addresses for service of all parties to the proceedings.

56.11 The request must include an estimate of the length of time the detailed assessment hearing will take.

56.12 On receipt of the request for a detailed assessment hearing the court will fix a date for the hearing or if the costs judge or district judge so decides, will give directions or fix a date for a preliminary appointment.

56.13 (1) The court will give at least 14 days' notice of the time and place of the detailed assessment hearing to every person named in the statement referred to in para. 56.10(g) above.

(2) The court will when giving notice, give all parties other than the party who requested the hearing a copy of the points of dispute annotated by the party requesting the hearing in compliance with para. 56.10(e) above.

(3) Attention is drawn to r. 47.14(6) and (7): apart from the solicitor whose bill it is, only those parties who have served points of dispute may be heard on the detailed assessment unless the court gives permission, and only items specified in the points of dispute may be raised unless the court gives permission.

56.14 (1) If a party wishes to vary his breakdown of costs, points of dispute or reply, an amended or supplementary document must be filed with the court and copies of it must be served on all other relevant parties.

(2) Permission is not required to vary a breakdown of costs, points of dispute or a reply but the court may disallow the variation or permit it only upon conditions, including conditions as to the payment of any costs caused or wasted by the variation.

56.15 Unless the court directs otherwise the solicitor must file with the court the papers in support of the bill not less than seven days before the date for the detailed assessment hearing and not more than 14 days before that date.

56.16 Once the detailed assessment hearing has ended it is the responsibility of the legal representative appearing for the solicitor or, as the case may be, the solicitor in person to remove the papers filed in support of the bill.

56.17 (1) Attention is drawn to r. 47.15 (power to issue an interim certificate).

(2) If, in the course of a detailed assessment hearing of a solicitor's bill to his client, it appears to the costs judge or district judge that in any event the solicitor will be liable in connection with that bill to pay money to the client, he may issue an interim certificate specifying an amount which in his opinion is payable by the solicitor to his client. Such a certificate will include an order to pay the sum it certifies unless the court orders otherwise.

56.18 (1) Attention is drawn to r. 47.16 which requires the solicitor to file a completed bill within 14 days after the end of the detailed assessment hearing. The court may dispense with the requirement to file a completed bill.

(2) After the detailed assessment hearing is concluded the court will:

(a) complete the court copy of the bill so as to show the amount allowed;

(b) determine the result of the cash account;

(c) award the costs of the detailed assessment hearing in accordance with the Solicitors Act 1974, s. 70(8); and

(d) issue a final costs certificate showing the amount due following the detailed assessment hearing.

56.19 A final costs certificate will include an order to pay the sum it certifies unless the court orders otherwise.

Section 57 Transitional Arrangements:

57.1 In this section 'the previous rules' means the Rules of the Supreme Court 1965 ('RSC') or County Court Rules 1981 ('CCR'), as appropriate.

General scheme of transitional arrangements concerning costs proceedings

57.2 (1) Paragraph 18 of PD 51 (transitional arrangements) provides that the CPR govern any assessments of costs which take place on or after 26 April 1999 and states a presumption to be applied in respect of costs for work undertaken before 26 April 1999.

(2) The following paragraphs provide five further transitional arrangements:

(a) to provide an additional presumption to be applied when assessing costs which were awarded by an order made in a county court before 26 April 1999 which allowed costs 'on Scale 1' to be determined in accordance with CCR, Appendix A, or 'on the lower scale' to be determined in accordance with CCR, Appendix C.

(b) to preserve the effect of CCR, Appendix B, Part III, para. 2;

(c) to clarify the approach to be taken where a bill of costs was provisionally taxed before 26 April 1999 and the receiving party is unwilling to accept the result of the provisional taxation.

(d) to preserve the right to carry in objections or apply for a reconsideration in all taxation proceedings commenced before 26 April 1999.

(e) to deal with funding arrangements made before 3 July 2000.

Scale 1 or lower scale costs

para.57.3 **68.61**

57.3 Where an order was made in county court proceedings before 26 April 1999 under which the costs were allowed on Scale 1 or the lower scale, the general presumption is that no costs will be allowed under that order which would not have been allowed in a taxation before 26 April 1999.

Fixed costs on the lower scale

57.4 The amount to be allowed as fixed costs for making or opposing an application for a rehearing to set aside a judgment given before 26 April 1999 where the costs are on lower scale is £11.25.

Bills provisionally taxed before 26 April 1999

para.57.5 **68.61**

57.5 In respect of bills of costs provisionally taxed before 26 April 1999:

(1) the previous rules apply on the question who can request a hearing and the time limits for doing so; and

(2) the CPR govern any subsequent hearing in that case.

Bills taxed before 26 April 1999

57.6 Where a bill of costs was taxed before 26 April 1999, the previous rules govern the steps which can be taken to challenge that taxation.

Other taxation proceedings

para.57.7(3)–(4) **68.61**

57.7 (1) This paragraph applies to taxation proceedings which were commenced before 26 April 1999, were assigned for taxation to a taxing master or district judge, and which were still pending on 26 April 1999.

(2) Any assessment of costs that takes place in cases to which this paragraph applies which is conducted on or after 26 April 1999, will be conducted in accordance with the CPR.

(3) In addition to the possibility of appeal under rr. 47.20 to 47.23 and Part 52 any party to a detailed assessment who is dissatisfied with any decision on a detailed assessment made by a costs judge or district judge may apply to that costs judge or district judge for a review of the decision. The review shall, for procedural purposes, be treated as if it were an appeal from an authorised court officer.

(4) The right of review provided by sub-para. (3) above, will not apply in cases in which, at least 28 days before the date of the assessment hearing, all parties were served with notice that the rights of appeal in respect of that hearing would be governed by Part 47, Section VIII (appeals from authorised court officers in detailed assessment proceedings) and Part 52 (appeals).

(5) An order for the service of notice under sub-para. (4) above may be made on the application of any party to the detailed assessment proceedings or may be made by the court of its own initiative.

Transitional provisions concerning the Access to Justice Act 1999, sections 28 to 31

57.8 (1) Sections 28 to 31 of the Access to Justice Act 1999, the Conditional Fee Agreements Regulations 2000 (SI 2000/692), the Access to Justice (Membership Organisations) Regulations 2000 (SI 2000/693), and the Access to Justice Act 1999 (Transitional Provisions) Order 2000 (SI 2000/900) came into force on 1 April 2000. The Civil Procedure (Amendment No. 3) Rules 2000 (SI 2000/1317) came into force on 3 July 2000. The Conditional Fee Agreements Regulations 2000 were revoked by the Conditional Fee Agreements (Revocation) Regulations 2005 (SI 2005/2305) but continue to have effect in relation to conditional fee agreements entered into before 1 November 2005. The Access to Justice (Membership Organisations) Regulations 2000 were revoked by the Access to Justice (Membership Organisation) Regulations 2005 (SI 2005/2306) but continue to have effect in relation to arrangements entered into before 1 November 2005.

(2) The Access to Justice Act 1999 (Transitional Provisions) Order 2000 provides that no conditional fee agreement or other arrangement about costs entered into before 1 April 2000 can be a funding arrangement, as defined in r. 43.2. The order also has the effect that where a conditional fee agreement or other funding arrangement has been entered into before 1 April 2000 and a second or subsequent funding arrangement of the same type is entered into on or after 1 April 2000, the second or subsequent funding arrangement does not give rise to a liability which is recoverable from a paying party.

(3) The Collective Conditional Fee Agreements Regulations 2000 came into force on 30 November 2000. The Regulations apply to agreements entered into from 30 November 2000 to 31 October 2005. Agreements entered into before 30 November 2000 are treated as if the Regulations had not come into force. The Regulations do not apply to collective conditional fee agreements entered into on or after 1 November 2005.

57.9 (1) Rule 39 of the Civil Procedure (Amendment No. 3) Rules 2000 applies where between 1 April and 2 July 2000 (including both dates):

(a) a funding arrangement is entered into, and

(b) proceedings are started in respect of a claim which is the subject of that agreement.

(2) Attention is drawn to the need to act promptly so as to comply with the requirements of the rules and the practice directions by 31 July 2000 (i.e. within the 28 days from 3 July 2000 permitted by r. 39) if that compliance is to be treated as compliance with the relevant provision. Attention is drawn in particular to r. 44.15 (providing information about funding arrangements) and section 19 of this practice direction.

(3) Nothing in the legislation referred to above makes provision for a party who has entered into a funding arrangement to recover from another party any amount of an additional liability which relates to anything done or any costs incurred before the arrangement was entered into.

SCHEDULE OF COSTS PRECEDENTS

[The following precedents are on the CD-ROM version of *Blackstone's Civil Practice*. Click on the title of a precedent to open it.

A: Model form of bill of costs (receiving party's solicitor and counsel on CPA terms)

B: Model form of bill of costs (detailed assessment of additional liability only)

C: Model form of bill of costs (payable by defendant and the LSC)

D: Model form of bill of costs (alternative form, single column for amounts claimed, separate parts for costs payable by the LSC only)

E: Legal Aid/LSC schedule of costs

F: Certificates for inclusion in bill of costs

G. Points of dispute

H: Estimate of costs served on other parties

J: Solicitors Act 1974: Part 8 claim form under Part III of the Act

K: Solicitors Act 1974: order for delivery of bill

L: Solicitors Act 1974: order for detailed assessment (client)

M: Solicitors Act 1974: order for detailed assessment (solicitors)

P: Solicitors Act 1974: breakdown of costs]

CPR Part 49 Specialist Proceedings

49

(1) These Rules shall apply to the proceedings listed in paragraph (2) subject to the provisions of the relevant practice direction which applies to those proceedings.
(2) The proceedings referred to in paragraph (1) are—
  (f) proceedings under the Companies Act 1985 and the Companies Act 1989.

PD 49B Practice Direction — Applications under the Companies Act 1985 and Other Legislation Relating to Companies

This practice direction supplements CPR Part 49 and replaces, with modifications, RSC Order 102 and CCR Order 49 rule 3

PD 49B **11.7**, **82.3**, **82.5**, **82.7**, **82.8** [For commentary on a specific paragraph, please refer to the cross-references after the title of the paragraph.]

General

para.1(3) **82.6**

1 (1) In this practice direction:
'the Act' means the Companies Act 1985 and includes the Act as applied to limited liability partnerships by the Limited Liability Partnerships Regulations 2001 (SI 2001/1090);
'the CJPA' means the Criminal Justice and Police Act 2001;
'the Companies Court registrar' means any officer of the High Court who is a registrar within the meaning of any rules for the time being in force relating to the winding-up of companies;
'the court' includes the Companies Court registrar;
'the EC Regulation' means Council Regulation (EC) No. 2157/2001 of 8 October 2001 on the statute for a European company (SE);
'the ICA' means the Insurance Companies Act 1982;
'Part VII FISMA' means Part VII of the Financial Services and Markets Act 2000;
'the Rules' means the Civil Procedure Rules 1998;
'SE' means a European public limited-liability company (societas europaea) within the meaning of art. 1 of the EC Regulation.

(2) Applications under the Act may be made in the county court if the county court would have jurisdiction to wind up the company in question (see the definition of 'the court' in section 744 of the Act). A company can be wound up in the county court if its paid-up capital is not more than £120,000 (Insolvency Act 1986, s. 117(2)).

(3) Every claim form or petition by which an application under the Act, Part VII FISMA or the ICA is begun and all affidavits, witness statements, notices and other documents in those proceedings must be entitled in the matter of the company in question and in the matter of the Act, Part VII FISMA or the ICA as the case may be.

Commencement of Proceedings

para.2 **82.3**
para.2(1) **13.4, 82.3, 82.5**
para.2(3)–(4) **82.5**
para.3A **82.3**

2 (1) Except in the case of the applications mentioned in sub-paragraph (4) below:
(a) every application under the Act, whether made in the High Court or in the county court;
(b) every application under Part VII FISMA;
(c) every application under arts 25 and 26 of the EC Regulation; and
(d) every application under s. 59 of the CJPA,
must be made by the issue of a claim form and the use of the procedure set out in CPR, Part 8, subject to any modification of that procedure under this practice direction or any other practice direction relating to applications under the Act.

(2) Notice of an application under section 721 of the Act need not be given to the respondent and the claim form need not be served on him.

(3) A claim form issued under this paragraph must, in the High Court, be issued out of the office of the Companies Court registrar or a Chancery district registry or, in the county court, out of a county court office.

(4) This paragraph does not apply to applications under sections 459 or 460 of the Act or to any of the applications specified in paragraph 4(1) of this practice direction.

3 All High Court applications to which this practice direction applies shall be assigned to the Chancery Division.

3A (1) From 1 December 2001 applications to sanction insurance business transfer schemes or banking business transfer schemes must be made under Part VII FISMA. Schedule 2C to the ICA, subject to minor modifications, will continue to apply to applications to sanction or approve transfers of insurance business which are made up to and including 30 November 2001 (see the Financial Services and Markets Act 2000 (Transitional Provisions and Savings) (Business Transfers) Order 2001 (SI 2001/3639)).

(2) Any application under Part VII FISMA must comply with the requirements of the Financial Services and Markets Act 2000 (Control of Business Transfers) (Requirements on Applicants) Regulations 2001 (SI 2001/3625).

(3) In relation to insurance business transfer schemes, the Supervision Manual of the Financial Services Authority (FSA), available on the FSA's website (http://www.fsa.gov.uk), contains rules and guidance with regard to the operation of Part VII FISMA and the FSA's role thereunder which should be referred to before any application under Part VII FISMA is made.

(4) Paragraphs 10 to 13 of this practice direction apply to applications under Part VII FISMA.

Applications under the EC Regulation

para.3B(1)(a) **82.3**

3B (1) An application for a certificate under art. 25(2) of the EC Regulation must:

(a) be issued in the Chancery Division of the High Court;

(b) identify the pre-merger acts and formalities applicable to the applicant company, and be accompanied by evidence that those acts and formalities have been completed;

(c) be accompanied by copies of:

(i) the draft terms of merger as provided for in art. 20 of the EC Regulation;

(ii) the entry in the *Gazette* containing the particulars specified in art. 21 of the EC Regulation;

(iii) a report drawn up and adopted by the directors of the applicant company containing the same information as would be required by para. 4 of sch. 15B to the Act if there were to be a scheme of arrangement under ss. 425 and 427A of the Act;

(iv) the expert's report to the members of the applicant company drawn up in accordance with para. 5 of sch. 15B to the Act or art. 22 of the EC Regulation; and

(v) the resolution of the applicant company approving the draft terms of merger in accordance with art. 23 of the EC Regulation.

(2) Attention is drawn to art. 26(2) of the EC Regulation. Where it is proposed that the registered office of an SE should be in England or Wales, each of the merging companies is required, within six months after a certificate is issued in respect of that company under art. 25(2), to submit the certificate to the High Court in order that it may scrutinise the legality of the merger.

(3) Where a merging company is required to submit a certificate to the High Court under art. 26(2) of the EC Regulation, if no other merging company has commenced proceedings under art. 26, that company shall commence such proceedings by issuing a claim form in the Chancery Division.

(4) The claim form must:

(a) identify the SE and all of the merging companies;

(b) be accompanied by the documents referred to in para. 3B(6); and

(c) be served on each of the other merging companies.

(5) Where a merging company is required to submit a certificate to the High Court under art. 26(2) of the EC Regulation and proceedings under art. 26 have already been commenced, that company shall:

(a) file an acknowledgment of service not more than 14 days after service of the claim form, and serve the acknowledgment of service on each of the other merging companies; and

(b) file the documents referred to in para. 3B(6) within the time limit specified in art. 26(2), and serve copies of those documents on each of the other merging companies.

(6) Each merging company must file and serve the following documents in proceedings under art. 26 of the EC Regulation:

(a) the certificate issued under art. 25(2) in respect of that company;

(b) a copy of the draft terms of merger approved by that company;

(c) evidence that arrangements for employee involvement have been determined by that company pursuant to Council Directive 2001/86/EC of 8 October 2001 supplementing the statute for a European company with regard to the involvement of employees; and

(d) evidence that the SE has been formed in accordance with the requirements of art. 26(4) of the EC Regulation.

(7) Proceedings under art. 25 and art. 26 of the EC Regulation will be heard by a High Court judge.

(8) Paragraphs 10 to 13 of this practice direction apply to proceedings under art. 25 and 26 of the EC Regulation.

Applications Made by Petition

para.4 **82.3**
para.4(1) **82.4**
para.5(1) **82.4**
para.5(3) **82.4**

4 (1) The following applications under the Act in addition to applications under sections 459 and 460 of the Act and applications under the ICA must be made by petition, namely, applications:

(a) under section 5 to cancel the alteration of a company's objects,

(b) under section 17 to cancel the alteration of a condition contained in a company's memorandum,

(c) under section 130 to confirm a reduction of the share premium account of a company,

(d) under section 136 to confirm a reduction of the share capital of a company,

(e) under section 127 to cancel any variation or abrogation of the rights attached to any class of shares in a company,

(f) under section 425 to sanction a compromise or arrangement between a company and its creditors or any class of them or between a company and its members or any class of them,

(g) under section 653 for an order restoring the name of a company to the register, where the application is made in conjunction with an application for the winding up of the company,

(h) under section 690 to cancel the alteration of the form of a company's constitution,

(i) under section 727 for relief from liability of an officer of a company or a person employed by a company as auditor,

(j) under section 54(1) to cancel a special resolution to which that section applies,

(k) under sections 157(2) or 176(1) to cancel a special resolution to which either of those sections applies, and

(l) under section 170 in relation to the reduction of capital redemption reserve.

(2) Paragraphs 5 to 14 of this practice direction apply to the applications specified in sub-paragraph (1).

5 (1) After the presentation of a petition by which any application mentioned in paragraph 4 is made, the petitioner, except where his application is one of those mentioned in sub-paragraph (2), must apply for directions by filing an application notice.

(2) The exceptions referred to in sub-paragraph (1) are:

(a) an application under section 425 of the Act to sanction a compromise or arrangement unless there is included in the petition for such sanction an application for an order under section 427 of the Act,

(b) an application under section 653 of the Act for an order restoring the name of a company to the register,

(c) an application under section 54(1) of the Act for an order cancelling a special resolution to which that section applies, and

(d) an application under section 157(2) or 176(1) of the Act for an order cancelling a special resolution to which those sections apply.

(3) At the directions hearing the court may by order give such directions for the hearing of the application as it thinks fit including, in particular, directions for the publication of notices and the making of any inquiry.

(4) Where the application made by the petition is to confirm a reduction of the share capital, the share premium account, or the capital redemption reserve, of a company the court may give directions:

(a) for an inquiry to be made as to the debts of, and claims against, the company or as to any class or classes of such debts or claims,

(b) as to the proceedings to be taken for settling the list of creditors entitled to object to the reduction and fixing the date by reference to which the list is to be made,

and the power of the court under section 136(6) of the Act to direct that section 136(3) to (5) thereof shall not apply as regards any class of creditors may be exercised at any directions hearing.

Reduction of Capital and Schemes of Arrangement

6 (1) The consent of a creditor to such reduction as is mentioned in paragraph 5(4) may be proved in such manner as the court thinks sufficient.

(2) The evidence in support of a petition to confirm a reduction of capital need not show as regards any issue of shares made since 1900 for a consideration other than cash that the statutory requirements as to registration were complied with. It is sufficient to state in the petition the extent to which any issued shares (other than shares issued otherwise than for cash before 1901) are or are deemed to be paid up.

(3) The existing practice will remain unaltered in respect of issues of shares otherwise than for cash made before 1901 whilst s. 25 of the Companies Act 1867 remained in operation.

7 (1) This paragraph applies to:

(a) schemes of arrangement under ss. 425 to 427A of the Companies Act 1985, whether made with creditors or members,

(b) schemes for the transfer of the whole or part of the long-term business of an insurance company to which sch. 2C to the ICA applies, and

(c) reductions of capital, share premium account or capital redemption reserve.

References in this and subsequent paragraphs to 'schemes' are to schemes failing within (a) or (b) above, and references to 'reductions' are to reductions failing within (c) above.

(2) Petitions to sanction schemes will be heard by the Companies Court judge.

(3) Petitions to confirm reductions will be heard by the Companies Court Registrar unless otherwise ordered. The Registrar will hear petitions to confirm reductions in open court on a Wednesday each week after completion of the list of winding-up petitions.

Schemes and Reductions in the Long Vacation

para.9 **82.11** para.9(2)–(7) **79.67**
para.9(1) **82.10**

8 (1) The following requirements must be satisfied for a hearing to be fixed to sanction a scheme and/or confirm a reduction in the Long Vacation:

(a) The application is one in which for financial, commercial or economic reasons a hearing before the end of the Long Vacation is desirable. This category will include cases of mergers and takeovers which arise in the summer and are likely to be affected by market fluctuations.

(b) The application is one which could not with reasonable diligence have been made and prosecuted in time to be heard before the Long Vacation begins.

(2) An informal application in chambers, to the Court Manager, accompanied by an advocate's certificate that requirements (a) and (b) are satisfied, must be made as soon as possible so that a suitable timetable may be settled, including a date for hearing.

(3) In the case of reductions to be heard by the Registrar, certain applications which do not fall within the above categories will be heard provided (i) that there is an urgent need for a hearing or (ii) that there is sufficient time available after the Registrar has disposed of the urgent applications.

(4) Applications to the Registrar in chambers for orders convening meetings to consider schemes and for directions on reduction applications will continue to be heard during the Long Vacation. Provided notice is given to the court before the Long Vacation begins, a timetable will be fixed which will enable any necessary documents to be settled in chambers and enable the Registrar to hear the application.

(5) The Vacation Judge will be available to hear petitions to sanction schemes and any petitions to confirm reductions which require to be heard by a judge on one Wednesday in August and two Wednesdays in September on dates to be arranged and subsequently notified in the Long Vacation Notice which is printed in the Daily Cause List.

(6) The Vacation Judge may also hear petitions to sanction schemes or confirm reductions on other days if he thinks fit.

9 (1) Attention is drawn to the undesirability of asking as a matter of course for a winding-up order as an alternative to an order under s. 459 of the Companies Act 1985. The petition should not ask for a winding up order unless that is the relief which the petitioner prefers or it is thought that it may be the only relief to which the petitioner is entitled.

(2) Whenever a winding-up order is asked for in a contributory's petition, the petition must state whether the petitioner consents or objects to an order under s. 127 of the Act in the standard form. If he objects, the written evidence in support must contain a short statement of his reasons.

(3) If the petitioner objects to a s. 127 order in the standard form but consents to such an order in a modified form, the petition must set out the form of order to which he consents, and the written evidence in support must contain a short statement of his reasons for seeking the modification.

(4) If the petition contains a statement that the petitioner consents to a s. 127 order, whether in the standard or a modified form, but the petitioner changes his mind before the first hearing of the petition, he must notify the respondents and may apply on notice to a judge for an order directing that no s. 127 order or a modified order only (as the case may be) shall be made by the Registrar, but validating dispositions made without notice of the order made by the judge.

(5) If the petition contains a statement that the petitioner consents to a s. 127 order, whether in the standard or a modified form, the Registrar shall without further enquiry make an order in such form at the first hearing unless an order to the contrary has been made by the judge in the meantime.

(6) If the petition contains a statement that the petitioner objects to a s. 127 order in the standard form, the company may apply (in the case of urgency, without notice) to the judge for an order.

(7) Section 127 Order — Standard Form:

(Title etc.)

ORDER that notwithstanding the presentation of the said Petition

(1) payments made into or out of the bank accounts of the Company in the ordinary course of the business of the Company and

(2) dispositions of the property of the Company made in the ordinary course of its business for proper value

between the date of presentation of the Petition and the date of judgment on the Petition or further order in the meantime shall not be void by virtue of the provisions of section 127 of the Insolvency Act 1986 in the event of an Order for the winding up of the Company being made on the said Petition Provided that (the relevant bank) shall be under no obligation to verify for itself whether any transaction through the company's bank accounts is in the ordinary course of business, or that it represents full market value for the relevant transaction.

This form of Order may be departed from where the circumstances of the case require.

Case Management

para.10 **42.6, 42.8, 71.4, 82.8**

10 Every application to which this practice direction applies shall be allocated to the multi-track and the CPR relating to allocation questionnaires and track allocation will not apply.

Service

para.11 **15.18, 82.7**

11 Service of documents in proceedings in the High Court to which this practice direction applies will be the responsibility of the parties and will not be undertaken by the court. Subject to that CPR Part 6 applies.

Filing of Documents

12 (1) Where an application to which this practice direction relates is proceeding in any Chancery district registry, all affidavits and witness statements made in connection with the application must be filed in that registry.
(2) Where an application to which this practice direction relates is proceeding in any county court, all affidavits and witness statements made in connection with the application must be filed in the office of that county court.

Drawing Up of Orders

13 The court will draw up all orders with the following exceptions:
(a) orders by the Registrar on the application of the Official Receiver or for which the Treasury Solicitor is responsible under the existing practice,
(b) orders by the court in relation to reductions or schemes.

Applications under Section 59 of the CJPA

para.14 **82.3** para.14(2) **69.5**

14 (1) This paragraph applies to applications under s. 59 of the CJPA in respect of property seized in the exercise of the power conferred by s. 448(3) of the Act (including any additional powers of seizure conferred by s. 50 of the CJPA which are exercisable by reference to that power).
(2) An application to which this paragraph applies should be made to a judge of the Chancery Division.
(3) The defendant to an application under s. 59(2) or 59(5)(c) of the CJPA shall be the person for the time being having possession of the property to which the application relates.
(4) On an application under s. 59(2) or 59(5)(c) of the CJPA, the claim form and the claimant's evidence must be served on:
(a) the person for the time being having possession of the property to which the application relates;
(b) in the case of an application under s. 59(2) for the return of seized property, the person specified as the person to whom notice of such an application should be given by any notice served under s. 52 of the CJPA when the property was seized;
(c) in the case of an application under s. 59(5)(c), the person from whom the property was seized (if not the claimant); and
(d) in all cases, any other person appearing to have a relevant interest in the property within the meaning of s. 59(11) of the CJPA.
(5) An application under s. 59(2) or 59(5)(c) of the CJPA must be supported by evidence:
(a) that the claimant has a relevant interest in the property to which the application relates within the meaning of s. 59(11) of the CJPA; and
(b) in the case of an application under s. 59(2), that one or more of the grounds set out in s. 59(3) of the CJPA is satisfied in relation to the property.
(6) The defendants to an application under s. 59(5)(b) of the CJPA by a person for the time being in possession of seized property shall be:
(a) the person from whom the property was seized; and
(b) any other person appearing to have a relevant interest in the property to which the application relates within the meaning of s. 59(11) of the CJPA.

(7) If an application to which this paragraph applies would not otherwise be served on the person who seized the property, and the identity of that person is known to the applicant, notice of the application shall be given to the person who seized the property.

(8) In all applications to which this paragraph applies, when the court issues the claim form it will fix a date for the hearing.

CPR Part 50 Application of the Schedules

Part 50 **1.5** [For commentary on a specific rule, please refer to the cross-references after the title of the rule.]

r.50(2) **1.5** r.50(3)(c) **15.33**

50

(1) The Schedules to these Rules set out, with modifications, certain provisions previously contained in the Rules of the Supreme Court 1965 and the County Court Rules 1981.
(2) These Rules apply in relation to the proceedings to which the Schedules apply subject to the provisions in the Schedules and the relevant practice directions.
(3) A provision previously contained in the Rules of the Supreme Court 1965—
  (a) is headed 'RSC';
  (b) is numbered with the Order and rule numbers it bore as part of the RSC; and
  (c) unless otherwise stated in the Schedules or the relevant practice direction, applies only to proceedings in the High Court.
(4) A provision previously contained in the County Court Rules 1981—
  (a) is headed 'CCR';
  (b) is numbered with the Order and rule numbers it bore as part of the CCR; and
  (c) unless otherwise stated in the Schedules or the relevant practice direction, applies only to proceedings in the county court.
(5) A reference in a Schedule to a rule by number alone is a reference to the rule so numbered in the Order in which the reference occurs.
(6) A reference in a Schedule to a rule by number prefixed by 'CPR' is a reference to the rule with that number in these Rules.
(7) In the Schedules, unless otherwise stated, 'the Act' means—
  (a) in a provision headed 'RSC', the Supreme Court Act 1981; and
  (b) in a provision headed 'CCR', the County Courts Act 1984.

CPR Part 51 Transitional Arrangements and Pilot Schemes

51.1

A practice direction shall make provision for the extent to which these Rules shall apply to proceedings issued before 26 April 1999.

51.2

Practice directions may modify or disapply any provision of these Rules—
(a) for specified periods; and
(b) in relation to proceedings in specified courts,
during the operation of pilot schemes for assessing the use of new practices and procedures in connection with proceedings.

PD 51 Practice Direction — Transitional Arrangements

This practice direction supplements CPR Part 51

[For commentary on a specific paragraph, please refer to the cross-references after the title of the paragraph.]

Contents of This Practice Direction

1 (1) This Practice Direction deals with the application of the Civil Procedure Rules ('CPR') to proceedings issued before 26 April 1999 ('existing proceedings').

(2) In this Practice Direction 'the previous rules' means, as appropriate the Rules of the Supreme Court 1965 ('RSC') or County Court Rules 1981 ('CCR') in force immediately before 26 April 1999.

General Scheme of Transitional Arrangements

2 The general scheme is:

(a) to apply the previous rules to undefended cases, allowing them to progress to their disposal, but

(b) to apply the CPR to defended cases so far as is practicable.

Where the Previous Rules Will Normally Apply

General principle

3 Where an initiating step has been taken in a case before 26 April 1999, in particular one that uses forms or other documentation required by the previous rules, the case will proceed in the first instance under the previous rules. Any step which a party must take in response to something done by another party in accordance with the previous rules must also be in accordance with those rules.

Responding to old process

4 A party who is served with an old type of originating process (writ, summons etc.) on or after 26 April 1999 is required to respond in accordance with the previous rules and the instructions on any forms received with the originating process.

Filing and service of pleadings where old process served

5 Where a case has been begun by an old type of originating process (whether served before or after 26 April 1999), filing and service of pleadings will continue according to the previous rules.

Automatic Directions/Discovery

High Court

6 (1) Where the timetable for automatic directions under RSC Order 25, rule 8 or automatic discovery under RSC Order 24 has begun to apply to proceedings before 26 April 1999, those directions will continue to have effect on or after 26 April 1999.

County court

(2) Where automatic directions under CCR Order 17, rule 11 have begun to apply to existing proceedings before 26 April 1999 or the court has sent out notice that automatic directions under CCR Order 17, rule 11 (Form N. 450) will apply (even if the timetable will not begin until 26 April 1999 or after), those directions will continue to have effect on or after 26 April 1999.

(3) However CCR Order 17, rule 11(9) will not apply and therefore proceedings will not be struck out where there has been no request for a hearing to be fixed within 15 months of the date when pleadings were deemed to close. (But see paragraph 19.)

High Court and county court

(4) However, if the case comes before the court on or after 26 April 1999, the new rules may apply. (See paragraph 15.)

Default judgment

7 (1) If a party wishes default judgment to be entered in existing proceedings, he must do so in accordance with the previous rules.

(2) Where default judgment has been entered and there are outstanding issues to be resolved (e.g. damages to be assessed), the court officer may refer the proceedings to the judge, so that case management decisions about the proceedings and the conduct of the hearing can be made in accordance with the practice set out in paragraph 15.

(3) If a party needs to apply for permission to enter default judgment, he must make that application under CPR Part 23 (general rules about applications for court orders).

(4) An application to set aside judgment entered in default must be made under CPR Part 23 (general rules about applications for court orders) and CPR Part 13 (setting aside or varying default judgment) will apply to the proceedings as it would apply to default judgment entered under the CPR.

(5) CPR rule 15.11 (claims stayed if it is not defended or admitted) applies to these proceedings.

Judgment on admission in the county court

8 (1) If a party to existing proceedings in the county court wishes to request judgment to be entered on an admission, he must do so in accordance with the previous rules.

(2) Where judgment has been entered and there are outstanding issues to be resolved (e.g. damages to be assessed), the court officer may refer the proceedings to the judge, so that case management decisions about the proceedings and the conduct of the hearing can be made in accordance with the practice set out in paragraph 15.

(3) If a party needs to apply for permission to enter judgment, he must make that application under CPR Part 23 (general rules about applications for court orders).

Order inconsistent with CPR

9 Where a court order has been made before 26 April 1999, that order must still be complied with on or after 26 April 1999.

Steps taken before 26 April 1999

10 (1) Where a party has taken any step in the proceedings in accordance with the previous rules that step will remain valid on or after 26 April 1999.

(2) A party will not normally be required to take any action that would amount to taking that step again under the CPR. For example if discovery has been given, a party will not normally be required to provide disclosure under CPR Part 31.

Where the CPR Will Normally Apply

General principle

11 Where a new step is to be taken in any existing proceedings on or after 26 April 1999, it is to be taken under the CPR.

Part 1 (overriding objective) to apply

12 Part 1 (overriding objective) will apply to all existing proceedings from 26 April 1999 onwards.

Originating process

13 (1) Only claim forms under the CPR will be issued by the court on or after 26 April 1999.

(2) If a request to issue an old type of originating process (writ, summons etc.) is received at the court on or after 26 April 1999 it will be returned unissued.

(3) An application made on or after 26 April 1999 to extend the validity of originating process issued before 26 April 1999 must be made in accordance with CPR Part 23 (general rules about applications for court orders), but the court will decide whether to allow the application in accordance with the previous law.

Application to the court

14 (1) Any application to the court made on or after 26 April 1999 must be made in accordance with CPR Part 23 (general rules about applications for court orders).

(2) Any other relevant CPR will apply to the substance of the application, unless this practice direction provides otherwise. (See paragraphs 13(3) (application to extend the validity of originating process) and 18(2) (costs)).

(3) For example, a party wishing to apply for summary judgment must do so having regard to the test in CPR Part 24. A party wishing to apply for an interim remedy must do so under CPR Part 25 etc.

(4) Any other CPR will apply as necessary. For example, CPR Part 4 will apply as to forms and CPR Part 6 will apply to service of documents.

(5) If the pleadings have not been filed at court, the applicant must file all pleadings served when he files his application notice.

First time before a judge on or after 26 April 1999

15 (1) When proceedings come before a judge (whether at a hearing or on paper) for the first time on or after 26 April 1999, he may direct how the CPR are to apply to the proceedings and may disapply certain provisions of the CPR. He may also give case management directions (which may include allocating the proceedings to a case management track).

(2) The general presumption will be that the CPR will apply to the proceedings from then on unless the judge directs or this practice direction provides otherwise. (See paragraphs 13(3) (application to extend the validity of originating process) and 18(2) (costs).)

(3) If an application has been issued before 26 April 1999 and the hearing of the application has been set for a date on or after 26 April 1999, the general presumption is that the application will be decided having regard to the CPR. (For example an application for summary judgment issued before 26 April 1999, with a hearing date set for 1 May 1999, will be decided having regard to the test in CPR Part 24 (summary judgment).)

(4) When the first occasion on which existing proceedings are before a judge on or after 26 April 1999 is a trial or hearing of a substantive issue, the general presumption is that the trial or hearing will be conducted having regard to the CPR.

Where pleadings deemed to close on or after 26 April 1999

16 (1) This paragraph applies to existing proceedings where pleadings are deemed to close on or after 26 April 1999. However, this paragraph does not apply to those county court proceedings where notice that automatic directions apply (Form N. 450) has been sent (in which case the automatic directions will apply — see paragraph 6).

(2) CPR Part 26 (case management — preliminary stage) applies to these proceedings.

(3) If a defence is filed at court on or after 26 April 1999, the court will serve an allocation questionnaire where CPR rule 26.3 would apply, unless it dispenses with the need for one.

(4) If pleadings have not been filed at court (this will normally be the case in the Queen's Bench Division) the claimant must file copies of all the pleadings served within 14 days of the date that pleadings are deemed to close.

(5) Unless it dispenses with the need for one, the court will then serve an allocation questionnaire.

(6) In the previous rules pleadings are deemed to close:

(a) High court:

(i) 14 days after service of any reply, or

(ii) if there is no reply, 14 days after service of the defence to counterclaim, or

(iii) if there is no reply or defence to counterclaim, 14 days after the service of the defence.

(b) County court:

14 days after the delivery of a defence or, where a counterclaim is served with the defence, 28 days after the delivery of the defence.

(7) Where there are 2 or more defendants the court will normally wait until the claimant has filed copies of all the pleadings before serving an allocation questionnaire. However, the court may (in cases where there is a delay) serve allocation questionnaires despite the fact that pleadings have not closed in respect of any other defendant.

(8) The court will then allocate the proceedings in accordance with CPR rule 26.5.

(9) The CPR will then apply generally to the proceedings.

Agreement to apply the CPR

17 The parties may agree in writing that the CPR will apply to any proceedings from the date of the agreement. When they do so:

(a) all those who are parties at that time must agree,

(b) the CPR must apply in their entirety,
(c) the agreement is irrevocable,
(d) the claimant must file a copy of the agreement at court.

Costs

para.18(1)–(3) **68.61**

18 (1) Any assessment of costs that takes place on or after 26 April 1999 will be in accordance with CPR Parts 43 to 48.
(2) However, the general presumption is that no costs for work undertaken before 26 April 1999 will be disallowed if those costs would have been allowed in a costs taxation before 26 April 1999.
(3) The decision as to whether to allow costs for work undertaken on or after 26 April will generally be taken in accordance with CPR Parts 43 to 48.

(PD 43–48 contains more information on the operation of the transitional arrangements in relation to costs.)

Existing proceedings after one year

para.19 **54.7**
para.19(1) **54.7**
para. 19(2) **54.7**
para.19(3)(b) **54.3**

19 (1) If any existing proceedings have not come before a judge, at a hearing or on paper, between 26 April 1999 and 25 April 2000, those proceedings shall be stayed.
(2) Any party to those proceedings may apply for the stay to be lifted.
(3) Proceedings of the following types will not be stayed as a result of this provision:
(a) where the case has been given a fixed trial date which is after 25 April 2000,
(b) personal injury cases where there is no issue on liability but the proceedings have been adjourned by court order to determine the prognosis,
(c) where the court is dealing with the continuing administration of an estate or a trust or a receivership,
(d) applications relating to funds in court.
(4) For the purposes of this paragraph proceedings will not be 'existing proceedings' once final judgment has been given.

CPR Part 52 Appeals

Part 52 **71.54, 77.22, 81.10, 81.11, 81.12** [For commentary on a specific rule, please refer to the cross-references after the title of the rule.]

I GENERAL RULES ABOUT APPEALS

52.1 Scope and Interpretation

r.52.1(2) **71.11** r.52.1(4) **81.10**

(1) The rules in this Part apply to appeals to—
  (a) the civil division of the Court of Appeal;
  (b) the High Court; and
  (c) a county court.
(2) This Part does not apply to an appeal in detailed assessment proceedings against a decision of an authorised court officer.

(Rules 47.20 to 47.23 deal with appeals against a decision of an authorised court officer in detailed assessment proceedings)

(3) In this Part—
  (a) 'appeal' includes an appeal by way of case stated;
  (b) 'appeal court' means the court to which an appeal is made;
  (c) 'lower court' means the court, tribunal or other person or body from whose decision an appeal is brought;
  (d) 'appellant' means a person who brings or seeks to bring an appeal;
  (e) 'respondent' means—
    (i) a person other than the appellant who was a party to the proceedings in the lower court and who is affected by the appeal; and
    (ii) a person who is permitted by the appeal court to be a party to the appeal; and
  (f) 'appeal notice' means an appellant's or respondent's notice.
(4) This Part is subject to any rule, enactment or practice direction which sets out special provisions with regard to any particular category of appeal.

52.2 Parties to Comply with the Practice Direction

All parties to an appeal must comply with the relevant practice direction.

52.3 Permission

(1) An appellant or respondent requires permission to appeal—
  (a) where the appeal is from a decision of a judge in a county court or the High Court, except where the appeal is against—
    (i) a committal order;
    (ii) a refusal to grant habeas corpus; or
    (iii) a secure accommodation order made under section 25 of the Children Act 1989; or
  (b) as provided by the relevant practice direction.

(Other enactments may provide that permission is required for particular appeals)

(2) An application for permission to appeal may be made—
  (a) to the lower court at the hearing at which the decision to be appealed was made; or
  (b) to the appeal court in an appeal notice.

(Rule 52.4 sets out the time limits for filing an appellant's notice at the appeal court. Rule 52.5 sets out the time limits for filing a respondent's notice at the appeal court. Any application for permission to appeal to the appeal court must be made in the appeal notice (see rules 52.4(1) and 52.5(3))

(Rule 52.13(1) provides that permission is required from the Court of Appeal for all appeals to that court from a decision of a county court or the High Court which was itself made on appeal)

(3) Where the lower court refuses an application for permission to appeal, a further application for permission to appeal may be made to the appeal court.

(4) Where the appeal court, without a hearing, refuses permission to appeal, the person seeking permission may request the decision to be reconsidered at a hearing.

(5) A request under paragraph (4) must be filed within 7 days after service of the notice that permission has been refused.

(6) Permission to appeal may be given only where—
  (a) the court considers that the appeal would have a real prospect of success; or
  (b) there is some other compelling reason why the appeal should be heard.

(7) An order giving permission may—
  (a) limit the issues to be heard; and
  (b) be made subject to conditions.

(Rule 3.1(3) also provides that the court may make an order subject to conditions)

(Rule 25.15 provides for the court to order security for costs of an appeal)

52.4 Appellant's Notice

(1) Where the appellant seeks permission from the appeal court it must be requested in the appellant's notice.

(2) The appellant must file the appellant's notice at the appeal court within—
  (a) such period as may be directed by the lower court (which may be longer or shorter than the period referred to in sub-paragraph (b)); or
  (b) where the court makes no such direction, 21 days after the date of the decision of the lower court that the appellant wishes to appeal.

(3) Unless the appeal court orders otherwise, an appellant's notice must be served on each respondent—
  (a) as soon as practicable; and
  (b) in any event not later than 7 days,

after it is filed.

52.5 Respondent's Notice

(1) A respondent may file and serve a respondent's notice.
(2) A respondent who—
  (a) is seeking permission to appeal from the appeal court; or
  (b) wishes to ask the appeal court to uphold the order of the lower court for reasons different from or additional to those given by the lower court,
must file a respondent's notice.
(3) Where the respondent seeks permission from the appeal court it must be requested in the respondent's notice.
(4) A respondent's notice must be filed within—
  (a) such period as may be directed by the lower court; or
  (b) where the court makes no such direction, 14 days, after the date in paragraph (5).
(5) The date referred to in paragraph (4) is—
  (a) the date the respondent is served with the appellant's notice where—
    (i) permission to appeal was given by the lower court; or
    (ii) permission to appeal is not required;
  (b) the date the respondent is served with notification that the appeal court has given the appellant permission to appeal; or
  (c) the date the respondent is served with notification that the application for permission to appeal and the appeal itself are to be heard together.
(6) Unless the appeal court orders otherwise a respondent's notice must be served on the appellant and any other respondent—
  (a) as soon as practicable; and
  (b) in any event not later than 7 days,
after it is filed.

52.6 Variation of Time

r.52.6(1)–(2) **71.20**

(1) An application to vary the time limit for filing an appeal notice must be made to the appeal court.
(2) The parties may not agree to extend any date or time limit set by—
  (a) these Rules;
  (b) the relevant practice direction; or
  (c) an order of the appeal court or the lower court.

(Rule 3.1(2)(a) provides that the court may extend or shorten the time for compliance with any rule, practice direction or court order (even if an application for extension is made after the time for compliance has expired))
(Rule 3.1(2)(b) provides that the court may adjourn or bring forward a hearing)

52.7 Stay(GL)

r.52.7 **71.43**

Unless—
(a) the appeal court or the lower court orders otherwise; or
(b) the appeal is from the Immigration Appeal Tribunal,
an appeal shall not operate as a stay of any order or decision of the lower court.

52.8 Amendment of Appeal Notice

r.52.8 **71.42**

An appeal notice may not be amended without the permission of the appeal court.

52.9 Striking Out(GL) Appeal Notices and Setting Aside or Imposing Conditions on Permission to Appeal

r.52.9 **71.44**
r.52.9(1) **71.44**
r.52.9(1)(c) **71.45**
r.52.9(2)–(3) **71.44**

(1) The appeal court may—
  (a) strike out the whole or part of an appeal notice;
  (b) set aside(GL) permission to appeal in whole or in part;
  (c) impose or vary conditions upon which an appeal may be brought.

(2) The court will only exercise its powers under paragraph (1) where there is a compelling reason for doing so.
(3) Where a party was present at the hearing at which permission was given he may not subsequently apply for an order that the court exercise its powers under sub-paragraphs (1)(b) or (1)(c).

52.10 Appeal Court's Powers

r.52.10 **65.28**
r.52.10(1)–(2) **72.16**
r.52.10(2)(e) **72.18**
r.52.10(3) **72.16**
r.52.10(5) **72.16**
r.52.10(6) **14.70, 61.7**

(1) In relation to an appeal the appeal court has all the powers of the lower court.
(Rule 52.1(4) provides that this Part is subject to any enactment that sets out special provisions with regard to any particular category of appeal — where such an enactment gives a statutory power to a tribunal, person or other body it may be the case that the appeal court may not exercise that power on an appeal)
(2) The appeal court has power to—
(a) affirm, set aside or vary any order or judgment made or given by the lower court;
(b) refer any claim or issue for determination by the lower court;
(c) order a new trial or hearing;
(d) make orders for the payment of interest;
(e) make a costs order.
(3) In an appeal from a claim tried with a jury the Court of Appeal may, instead of ordering a new trial—
(a) make an order for damages(GL); or
(b) vary an award of damages made by the jury.
(4) The appeal court may exercise its powers in relation to the whole or part of an order of the lower court.
(Part 3 contains general rules about the court's case management powers)
(5) If the appeal court—
(a) refuses an application for permission to appeal;
(b) strikes out an appellant's notice; or
(c) dismisses an appeal,
and it considers that the application, the appellant's notice or the appeal is totally without merit, the provisions of paragraph (6) must be complied with.
(6) Where paragraph (5) applies—
(a) the court's order must record the fact that it considers the application, the appellant's notice or the appeal to be totally without merit; and
(b) the court must at the same time consider whether it is appropriate to make a civil restraint order.

52.11 Hearing of Appeals

r.52.11 **81.12**
r.52.11(1) **72.5**
r.52.11(2) **72.13**
r.52.11(3) **72.6, 72.11**
r.52.11(4) **72.10**
r.52.11(5) **71.22**

(1) Every appeal will be limited to a review of the decision of the lower court unless—
(a) a practice direction makes different provision for a particular category of appeal; or
(b) the court considers that in the circumstances of an individual appeal it would be in the interests of justice to hold a rehearing.
(2) Unless it orders otherwise, the appeal court will not receive—
(a) oral evidence; or
(b) evidence which was not before the lower court.
(3) The appeal court will allow an appeal where the decision of the lower court was—
(a) wrong; or
(b) unjust because of a serious procedural or other irregularity in the proceedings in the lower court.
(4) The appeal court may draw any inference of fact which it considers justified on the evidence.

(5) At the hearing of the appeal a party may not rely on a matter not contained in his appeal notice unless the appeal court gives permission.

52.12 Non-disclosure of Part 36 Offers and Payments

r.52.12(1) **64.5, 72.4** r.52.12(2)–(3) **72.4**

(1) The fact that a Part 36 offer or Part 36 payment has been made must not be disclosed to any judge of the appeal court who is to hear or determine—
   (a) an application for permission to appeal; or
   (b) an appeal,
   until all questions (other than costs) have been determined.
(2) Paragraph (1) does not apply if the Part 36 offer or Part 36 payment is relevant to the substance of the appeal.
(3) Paragraph (1) does not prevent disclosure in any application in the appeal proceedings if disclosure of the fact that a Part 36 offer or Part 36 payment has been made is properly relevant to the matter to be decided.

II SPECIAL PROVISIONS APPLYING TO THE COURT OF APPEAL

52.13 Second Appeals to the Court

r.52.13 **71.11, 81.12,**
r.52.13(1) **71.12, 71.14**
r.52.13(2) **71.14**
r.52.13(2)(a)–(b) **71.14**

(1) Permission is required from the Court of Appeal for any appeal to that court from a decision of a county court or the High Court which was itself made on appeal.
(2) The Court of Appeal will not give permission unless it considers that—
   (a) the appeal would raise an important point of principle or practice; or
   (b) there is some other compelling reason for the Court of Appeal to hear it.

52.14 Assignment of Appeals to the Court of Appeal

r.52.14 **71.6** r.52.14(1) **71.9**

(1) Where the court from or to which an appeal is made or from which permission to appeal is sought ('the relevant court') considers that—
   (a) an appeal which is to be heard by a county court or the High Court would raise an important point of principle or practice; or
   (b) there is some other compelling reason for the Court of Appeal to hear it,
   the relevant court may order the appeal to be transferred to the Court of Appeal.

(The Master of the Rolls has the power to direct that an appeal which would be heard by a county court or the High Court should be heard instead by the Court of Appeal — see section 57 of the Access to Justice Act 1999)

(2) The Master of the Rolls or the Court of Appeal may remit an appeal to the court in which the original appeal was or would have been brought.

52.15 Judicial Review Appeals

r.52.15(1)–(4) **74.37**

(1) Where permission to apply for judicial review has been refused at a hearing in the High Court, the person seeking that permission may apply to the Court of Appeal for permission to appeal.
(2) An application in accordance with paragraph (1) must be made within 7 days of the decision of the High Court to refuse to give permission to apply for judicial review.
(3) On an application under paragraph (1), the Court of Appeal may, instead of giving permission to appeal, give permission to apply for judicial review.
(4) Where the Court of Appeal gives permission to apply for judicial review in accordance with paragraph (3), the case will proceed in the High Court unless the Court of Appeal orders otherwise.

52.16 Who May Exercise the Powers of the Court of Appeal

r.52.16(3) **71.41**
r.52.16(5) **71.41**
r.52.16(6) **71.41**
r.52.16(6A) **71.41**
r.52.16(7) **71.41**

(1) A court officer assigned to the Civil Appeals Office who is—
(a) a barrister; or
(b) a solicitor
may exercise the jurisdiction of the Court of Appeal with regard to the matters set out in paragraph (2) with the consent of the Master of the Rolls.

(2) The matters referred to in paragraph (1) are—
(a) any matter incidental to any proceedings in the Court of Appeal;
(b) any other matter where there is no substantial dispute between the parties; and
(c) the dismissal of an appeal or application where a party has failed to comply with any order, rule or practice direction.

(3) A court officer may not decide an application for—
(a) permission to appeal;
(b) bail pending an appeal;
(c) an injunction(GL);
(d) a stay(GL) of any proceedings, other than a temporary stay of any order or decision of the lower court over a period when the Court of Appeal is not sitting or cannot conveniently be convened.

(4) Decisions of a court officer may be made without a hearing.

(5) A party may request any decision of a court officer to be reviewed by the Court of Appeal.

(6) At the request of a party, a hearing will be held to reconsider a decision of—
(a) a single judge; or
(b) a court officer,
made without a hearing.

(6A) A request under paragraph (5) or (6) must be filed within 7 days after the party is served with notice of the decision.

(7) A single judge may refer any matter for a decision by a court consisting of two or more judges.

(Section 54(6) of the Supreme Court Act 1981 provides that there is no appeal from the decision of a single judge on an application for permission to appeal)

(Section 58(2) of the Supreme Court Act 1981 provides that there is no appeal to the House of Lords from decisions of the Court of Appeal that—
(a) are taken by a single judge or any officer or member of staff of that court in proceedings incidental to any cause or matter pending before the civil division of that court; and
(b) do not involve the determination of an appeal or of an application for permission to appeal,
and which may be called into question by rules of court. Rules 52.16(5) and (6) provide the procedure for the calling into question of such decisions)

III PROVISIONS ABOUT REOPENING APPEALS

52.17 Reopening of Final Appeals

r.52.17 **61.36, 71.51**
r.52.17(1) **71.51**
r.52.17(3) **61.39, 71.51**
r.52.17(4)–(6) **71.52**
r.52.17(7) **61.39, 71.52**

(1) The Court of Appeal or the High Court will not reopen a final determination of any appeal unless—
(a) it is necessary to do so in order to avoid real injustice;
(b) the circumstances are exceptional and make it appropriate to reopen the appeal; and
(c) there is no alternative effective remedy.

(2) In paragraphs (1), (3), (4) and (6), 'appeal' includes an application for permission to appeal.

(3) This rule does not apply to appeals to a county court.

(4) Permission is needed to make an application under this rule to reopen a final determination of an appeal even in cases where under rule 52.3(1) permission was not needed for the original appeal.

(5) There is no right to an oral hearing of an application for permission unless, exceptionally, the judge so directs.

(6) The judge will not grant permission without directing the application to be served on the other party to the original appeal and giving him an opportunity to make representations.

(7) There is no right of appeal or review from the decision of the judge on the application for permission, which is final.

(8) The procedure for making an application for permission is set out in the practice direction.

PD 52 Practice Direction — Appeals

This practice direction supplements CPR Part 52

PD 52 **71.53**, **81.10**, **81.11**, **81.12** [For commentary on a specific paragraph, please refer to the cross-references after the title of the paragraph.]

Contents of this Practice Direction

1.1 This practice direction is divided into four Sections:
- Section I — General provisions about appeals.
- Section II — General provisions about statutory appeals and appeals by way of cased stated.
- Section III — Provisions about specific appeals.
- Section IV — Provisions about reopening appeals.

SECTION I — GENERAL PROVISIONS ABOUT APPEALS

2.1 This practice direction applies to all appeals to which Part 52 applies except where specific provision is made for appeals to the Court of Appeal.

2.2 For the purpose only of appeals to the Court of Appeal from cases in family proceedings this practice direction will apply with such modifications as may be required.

Routes of Appeal

para.2A.1 **43.26, 71.3**
para.2A.2 **71.4**
para.2A.3 **71.5**
para.2A.5 **71.5**
para.2A.6(2) **71.6**

2A.1 The court or judge to which an appeal is to be made (subject to obtaining any necessary permission) is set out in the tables below:

Table 1[1] addresses appeals in cases other than insolvency proceedings and those cases to which Table 3 applies;

Table 2 addresses insolvency proceedings; and

Table 3 addresses certain family cases to which Part 52 may apply.

The tables do not include so-called 'leapfrog' appeals either to the Court of Appeal pursuant to the Access to Justice Act 1999, s. 57, or to the House of Lords pursuant to the Administration of Justice Act 1969, s. 13.

(An interactive routes of appeal guide can be found on the Court of Appeal's website at www.hmcourts-service.gov.uk/infoabout/coa_civil/routes_app/index.htm.)

Table 1

In this Table references to a 'circuit judge' include a recorder or a district judge who is exercising the jurisdiction of a circuit judge with the permission of the designated civil judge in respect of that case (see PD 2B, para. 11.1(d)).

For the meaning of 'final decision' for the purposes of this table see paras 2A.2 and 2A.3 below.

Court	Track/nature of claim	Judge who made decision	Nature of decision under appeal	Appeal court
County	Unallocated Small Fast	District judge	Any	Circuit judge in county court
County	Part 8 (if not allocated to any track or if simply treated as allocated to the multi-track under r. 8.9(c))	District judge	Final	Circuit judge in county court

[1] Reproduced with the kind permission of Tottel Publishing, publisher of *Manual of Civil Appeals.*

Court	Track/nature of claim	Judge who made decision	Nature of decision under appeal	Appeal court
County	Multi-track	District judge	Any decision other than a final decision	Circuit judge in county court
County	Multi-track	District judge	Final decision	Court of Appeal
County	Specialist proceedings (under the Companies Acts 1985 or 1989 or to which Sections I, II or III of Part 57 or any of Parts 59, 60, 62 or 63 apply)	District judge	Any decision other than a final decision	Circuit judge in county court
County	Specialist proceedings (under the Companies Acts 1985 or 1989 or to which Sections I, II or III of Part 57 or any of Parts 59, 60, 62 or 63 apply)	District judge	Final decision	Court of Appeal
County	Unallocated Small Fast	Circuit judge	Any (except final decision in specialist proceedings; see below)	Single judge of the High Court
County	Multi-track	Circuit judge	Any decision other than a final decision	Single judge of the High Court
County	Part 8 (if not allocated to any track or if simply treated as allocated to the multi-track under r. 8.9(c))	Circuit judge	Final	Single judge of the High Court
County	Specialist proceedings (under the Companies Acts 1985 or 1989 or to which Sections I, II or III of Part 57 or any of Parts 59, 60, 62 or 63 apply)	Circuit judge	Final	Court of Appeal
County	Multi-track	Circuit judge	Final decision	Court of Appeal
High Court	Multi-track	Master or district judge sitting in a district registry	Any decision other than a final decision	Single judge of the High Court
High Court	Part 8 (if not allocated to any track or if simply treated as allocated to the multi-track under r. 8.9(c))	Master or district judge sitting in a district registry	Final	Single judge of the High Court
High Court	Multi-track	Master or district judge sitting in a district registry	Final	Court of Appeal
High Court	Specialist proceedings (under the Companies Acts 1985 or 1989 or to which Sections I, II or III of Part 57 or any of Parts 58 to 63 apply)	Master or district judge sitting in a district registry	Any decision other than a final decision	High Court

Civil Procedure Rules & Practice Directions

Court	Track/nature of claim	Judge who made decision	Nature of decision under appeal	Appeal court
High Court	Specialist proceedings (under the Companies Acts 1985 or 1989 or to which Sections I, II or III of Part 57 or any of Parts 58 to 63 apply)	Master or district judge sitting in a district registry	Final decision	Court of Appeal
High Court	Any	High Court judge	Any	Court of Appeal

Table 2 Insolvency proceedings

In this Table references to a 'circuit judge' include a recorder or a district judge who is exercising the jurisdiction of a circuit judge with the permission of the designated civil judge in respect of that case (see PD 2B, para. 11.1(d)).

Court	Track/nature of claim	Judge who made decision	Nature of decision under appeal	Appeal court
County	Insolvency	District judge or circuit judge	Any	Single judge of the High Court
High Court	Insolvency	Registrar	Any	Single judge of the High Court
High Court	Insolvency	High Court judge	Any	Court of Appeal

Table 3: Proceedings which may be heard in the Family Division of the High Court and to which the CPR may apply

The proceedings to which this table will apply include proceedings under the Inheritance (Provision for Family and Dependants) Act 1975 and proceedings under the Trusts of Land and Appointment of Trustees Act 1996.

For the meaning of 'final decision' for the purposes of this table see paras 2A.2 and 2A.3 below.

Court	Judge who made decision	Track/nature of claim	Nature of decision under appeal	Appeal court
High Court Principal Registry of the Family Division	District judge	Proceedings under Part 8 (if not allocated to any track or if simply treated as allocated to the multi-track under r. 8.9(c))	Any decision	High Court judge of the Family Division
High Court Principal Registry of the Family Division	District judge	Proceedings under Part 8 specifically allocated to the multi-track by an order of the court.	Any decision	High Court judge of the Family Division
High Court Principal Registry of the Family Division	District judge	Proceedings under Part 7	Any decision other than a final decision	High Court judge of the Family Division
High Court Principal Registry of the Family Division	District judge	Proceedings under Part 7 and allocated to the multi-track	Final decision	Court of Appeal

Court	Judge who made decision	Track/nature of claim	Nature of decision under appeal	Appeal court
High Court Family Division	High Court Judge	Proceedings under Part 7 or 8	Any	Court of Appeal

2A.2 A 'final decision' is a decision of a court that would finally determine (subject to any possible appeal or detailed assessment of costs) the entire proceedings whichever way the court decided the issues before it. Decisions made on an application to strike out or for summary judgment are not final decisions for the purpose of determining the appropriate route of appeal (Access to Justice Act 1999 (Destination of Appeals) Order 2000 (SI 2000/1071), art. 1). Accordingly:

(1) a case management decision;
(2) the grant or refusal of interim relief;
(3) a summary judgment;
(4) a striking out,

are not final decisions for this purpose.

2A.3 A decision of a court is to be treated as a final decision for routes of appeal purposes where it:

(1) is made at the conclusion of part of a hearing or trial which has been split into parts; and
(2) would, if it had been made at the conclusion of that hearing or trial, have been a final decision.

Accordingly, a judgment on liability at the end of a split trial is a 'final decision' for this purpose and the judgment at the conclusion of the assessment of damages following a judgment on liability is also a 'final decision' for this purpose.

2A.4 An order made:

(1) on a summary or detailed assessment of costs; or
(2) on an application to enforce a final decision,

is not a 'final decision' and any appeal from such an order will follow the routes of appeal set out in the tables above.

(The Supreme Court Act 1981, s. 16(1), the County Courts Act 1984, s. 77(1), and the Access to Justice Act 1999 (Destination of Appeals) Order 2000 set out the provisions governing routes of appeal.)

2A.5 (1) Where an applicant attempts to file an appellant's notice and the appeal court does not have jurisdiction to issue the notice, a court officer may notify the applicant in writing that the appeal court does not have jurisdiction in respect of the notice.

(2) Before notifying a person under para. (1) the court officer must confer:

(a) with a judge of the appeal court; or,
(b) where the Court of Appeal, Civil Division is the appeal court, with a court officer who exercises the jurisdiction of that court under r. 52.16.

(3) Where a court officer in the Court of Appeal, Civil Division notifies a person under para. (1), r. 52.16(5) shall not apply.

Grounds for Appeal

para.3.2 **71.22**

3.1 Rule 52.11(3)(a) and (b) sets out the circumstances in which the appeal court will allow an appeal.

3.2 The grounds of appeal should:

(1) set out clearly the reasons why r. 52.11(3)(a) or (b) is said to apply; and
(2) specify, in respect of each ground, whether the ground raises an appeal on a point of law or is an appeal against a finding of fact.

Permission to Appeal

4.1 Rule 52.3 sets out the circumstances when permission to appeal is required.

4.2 The permission of:

(1) the Court of Appeal; or
(2) where the lower court's rules allow, the lower court,

is required for all appeals to the Court of Appeal except as provided by statute or r. 52.3. (The requirement of permission to appeal may be imposed by a practice direction — see r. 52.3(b).)

4.3 Where the lower court is not required to give permission to appeal, it may give an indication of its opinion as to whether permission should be given.
(Rule 52.1(3)(c) defines 'lower court'.)

4.3A (1) This paragraph applies where a party applies for permission to appeal against a decision at the hearing at which the decision was made.
(2) Where this paragraph applies, the judge making the decision shall state:
(a) whether or not the judgment or order is final;
(b) whether an appeal lies from the judgment or order and, if so, to which appeal court;
(c) whether the court gives permission to appeal; and
(d) if not, the appropriate appeal court to which any further application for permission may be made.
(Rule 40.2(4) contains requirements as to the contents of the judgment or order in these circumstances.)

4.3B Where no application for permission to appeal has been made in accordance with r. 52.3(2)(a) but a party requests further time to make such an application, the court may adjourn the hearing to give that party the opportunity to do so.

Appeals from case management decisions

para.4.5 **71.13**

4.4 Case management decisions include decisions made under r. 3.1(2) and decisions about:
(1) disclosure;
(2) filing of witness statements or experts' reports;
(3) directions about the timetable of the claim;
(4) adding a party to a claim;
(5) security for costs.

4.5 Where the application is for permission to appeal from a case management decision, the court dealing with the application may take into account whether:
(1) the issue is of sufficient significance to justify the costs of an appeal;
(2) the procedural consequences of an appeal (e.g. loss of trial date) outweigh the significance of the case management decision;
(3) it would be more convenient to determine the issue at or after trial.

Court to which permission to appeal application should be made

4.6 An application for permission should be made orally at the hearing at which the decision to be appealed against is made.

4.7 Where:
(a) no application for permission to appeal is made at the hearing; or
(b) the lower court refuses permission to appeal,
an application for permission to appeal may be made to the appeal court in accordance with r. 52.3(2) and (3).

4.8 There is no appeal from a decision of the appeal court to allow or refuse permission to appeal to that court (although where the appeal court, without a hearing, refuses permission to appeal, the person seeking permission may request that decision to be reconsidered at a hearing). See the Access to Justice Act 1999, s. 54(4), and r. 52.3(2), (3), (4) and (5).

Second appeals

4.9 An application for permission to appeal from a decision of the High Court or a county court which was itself made on appeal must be made to the Court of Appeal.

4.10 If permission to appeal is granted the appeal will be heard by the Court of Appeal.

Consideration of permission without a hearing

paras 4.11–4.12 **71.12**
paras 4.14 **71.16**
para.4.14A **71.16**
paras 4.15–4.16 **71.17**

4.11 Applications for permission to appeal may be considered by the appeal court without a hearing.

4.12 If permission is granted without a hearing the parties will be notified of that decision and the procedure in paras 6.1 to 6.6 will then apply.

4.13 If permission is refused without a hearing the parties will be notified of that decision with the reasons for it. The decision is subject to the appellant's right to have it reconsidered at an oral hearing. This may be before the same judge.

4.14 A request for the decision to be reconsidered at an oral hearing must be filed at the appeal court within seven days after service of the notice that permission has been refused. A copy of the request must be served by the appellant on the respondent at the same time.

Permission hearing

4.14A (1) This paragraph applies where an appellant, who is represented, makes a request for a decision to be reconsidered at an oral hearing.

(2) The appellant's advocate must, at least four days before the hearing, in a brief written statement:

(a) inform the court and the respondent of the points which he proposes to raise at the hearing;

(b) set out his reasons why permission should be granted notwithstanding the reasons given for the refusal of permission; and

(c) confirm, where applicable, that the requirements of para. 4.17 have been complied with (appellant in receipt of services funded by the Legal Services Commission).

4.15 Notice of a permission hearing will be given to the respondent but he is not required to attend unless the court requests him to do so.

4.16 If the court requests the respondent's attendance at the permission hearing, the appellant must supply the respondent with a copy of the appeal bundle (see para. 5.6A) within seven days of being notified, or such other period as the court may direct. The costs of providing that bundle shall be borne by the appellant initially, but will form part of the costs of the permission application.

Appellants in receipt of services funded by the Legal Services Commission applying for permission to appeal

para.4.17 **71.16**

4.17 Where the appellant is in receipt of services funded by the Legal Services Commission (or legally aided) and permission to appeal has been refused by the appeal court without a hearing, the appellant must send a copy of the reasons the appeal court gave for refusing permission to the relevant office of the Legal Services Commission as soon as it has been received from the court. The court will require confirmation that this has been done if a hearing is requested to reconsider the question of permission.

Limited permission

para.4.18 **71.18**
para.4.19–4.21 **71.18**
para.4.23 **66.24, 71.17**
para.4.24 **66.24, 71.17**

4.18 Where a court under r. 52.3(7) gives permission to appeal on some issues only, it will:

(1) refuse permission on any remaining issues; or

(2) reserve the question of permission to appeal on any remaining issues to the court hearing the appeal.

4.19 If the court reserves the question of permission under para. 4.18(2), the appellant must, within 14 days after service of the court's order, inform the appeal court and the respondent in writing whether he intends to pursue the reserved issues. If the appellant does intend to pursue the reserved issues, the parties must include in any time estimate for the appeal hearing, their time estimate for the reserved issues.

4.20 If the appeal court refuses permission to appeal on the remaining issues without a hearing and the applicant wishes to have that decision reconsidered at an oral hearing, the time limit in r. 52.3(5) shall apply. Any application for an extension of this time limit should be made promptly. The court hearing the appeal on the issues for which permission has been granted will not normally grant, at the appeal hearing, an application to extend the time limit in r. 52.3(5) for the remaining issues.

4.21 If the appeal court refuses permission to appeal on remaining issues at or after an oral hearing, the application for permission to appeal on those issues cannot be renewed at the appeal hearing. See the Access to Justice Act 1999, s. 54(4).

Respondents' costs of permission applications

4.22 In most cases, applications for permission to appeal will be determined without the court requesting:
(1) submissions from, or
(2) if there is an oral hearing, attendance by,
the respondent.

4.23 Where the court does not request submissions from or attendance by the respondent, costs will not normally be allowed to a respondent who volunteers submissions or attendance.

4.24 Where the court does request:
(1) submissions from; or
(2) attendance by the respondent,
the court will normally allow the respondent his costs if permission is refused.

Appellant's Notice

para.5.1 **71.22**

5.1 An appellant's notice (N161) must be filed and served in all cases. Where an application for permission to appeal is made to the appeal court it must be applied for in the appellant's notice.

Human rights

para.5.1A **71.22**

5.1A (1) This paragraph applies where the appellant seeks:
(a) to rely on any issue under the Human Rights Act 1998; or
(b) a remedy available under that Act,
for the first time in an appeal.
(2) The appellant must include in his appeal notice the information required by PD 16, para. 15.1.
(3) PD 16, para. 15.2, applies as if references to a statement of case were to the appeal notice.

5.1B Rule 19.4A and PD 19 shall apply as if references to the case management conference were to the application for permission to appeal.
(PD 19 provides for notice to be given and parties joined in certain circumstances to which this paragraph applies.)

Extension of time for filing appellant's notice

para.5.2 **71.20, 71.21, 71.22** para.5.3 **71.20**
para.5.2(2) **71.28**

5.2 Where the time for filing an appellant's notice has expired, the appellant must:
(a) file the appellant's notice; and
(b) include in that appellant's notice an application for an extension of time.
The appellant's notice should state the reason for the delay and the steps taken prior to the application being made.

5.3 Where the appellant's notice includes an application for an extension of time and permission to appeal has been given or is not required the respondent has the right to be heard on that application. He must be served with a copy of the appeal bundle (see para. 5.6A). However, a respondent who unreasonably opposes an extension of time runs the risk of being ordered to pay the appellant's costs of that application.

5.4 If an extension of time is given following such an application the procedure at paras 6.1 to 6.6 applies.

Applications

para.5.5 **71.22, 71.41**

5.5 Notice of an application to be made to the appeal court for a remedy incidental to the appeal (e.g. an interim remedy under r. 25.1 or an order for security for costs) may be included in the appeal notice or in a Part 23 application notice.
(Rule 25.15 deals with security for costs of an appeal.)
(Paragraph 11 of this practice direction contains other provisions relating to applications.)

Documents

5.6 (1) This paragraph applies to every case except where the appeal:
(a) relates to a claim allocated to the small claims track; and
(b) is being heard in a county court or the High Court.
(Paragraph 5.8 applies where this paragraph does not apply.)
(2) The appellant must file the following documents together with an appeal bundle (see para. 5.6A) with his appellant's notice:
(a) two additional copies of the appellant's notice for the appeal court; and
(b) one copy of the appellant's notice for each of the respondents;
(c) one copy of his skeleton argument for each copy of the appellant's notice that is filed (see para. 5.9);
(d) a sealed copy of the order being appealed;
(e) a copy of any order giving or refusing permission to appeal, together with a copy of the judge's reasons for allowing or refusing permission to appeal;
(f) any witness statements or affidavits in support of any application included in the appellant's notice;
(g) a copy of the order allocating a case to a track (if any).

5.6A (1) An appellant must include in his appeal bundle the following documents:
(a) a sealed copy of the appellant's notice;
(b) a sealed copy of the order being appealed;
(c) a copy of any order giving or refusing permission to appeal, together with a copy of the judge's reasons for allowing or refusing permission to appeal;
(d) any affidavit or witness statement filed in support of any application included in the appellant's notice;
(e) a copy of his skeleton argument;
(f) a transcript or note of judgment (see para. 5.12), and in cases where permission to appeal was given by the lower court or is not required those parts of any transcript of evidence which are directly relevant to any question at issue on the appeal;
(g) the claim form and statements of case (where relevant to the subject of the appeal);
(h) any application notice (or case management documentation) relevant to the subject of the appeal;
(i) in cases where the decision appealed was itself made on appeal (e.g. from district judge to circuit judge), the first order, the reasons given and the appellant's notice used to appeal from that order;
(j) in the case of judicial review or a statutory appeal, the original decision which was the subject of the application to the lower court;
(k) in cases where the appeal is from a tribunal, a copy of the tribunal's reasons for the decision, a copy of the decision reviewed by the tribunal and the reasons for the original decision and any document filed with the tribunal setting out the grounds of appeal from that decision;
(l) any other documents which the appellant reasonably considers necessary to enable the appeal court to reach its decision on the hearing of the application or appeal; and
(m) such other documents as the court may direct.
(2) All documents that are extraneous to the issues to be considered on the application or the appeal must be excluded. The appeal bundle may include affidavits, witness statements, summaries, experts' reports and exhibits but only where these are directly relevant to the subject matter of the appeal.
(3) Where the appellant is represented, the appeal bundle must contain a certificate signed by his solicitor, counsel or other representative to the effect that he has read and understood sub-paragraph (2) above and that the composition of the appeal bundle complies with it.

5.7 Where it is not possible to file all the above documents, the appellant must indicate which documents have not yet been filed and the reasons why they are not currently available. The appellant must then provide a reasonable estimate of when the missing document or documents can be filed and file them as soon as reasonably practicable.

Small claims

para.5.8 **43.26** paras.5.8(4)–(5) **43.26**
para.5.8(1A) **43.26**

5.8 (1) This paragraph applies where:
(a) the appeal relates to a claim allocated to the small claims track; and
(b) the appeal is being heard in a county court or the High Court.
(1A) An appellant's notice must be filed and served in form N164.
(2) The appellant must file the following documents with his appellant's notice:
(a) a sealed copy of the order being appealed; and
(b) any order giving or refusing permission to appeal, together with a copy of the reasons for that decision.
(3) The appellant may, if relevant to the issues to be determined on the appeal, file any other document listed in para. 5.6 or 5.6A in addition to the documents referred to in sub-paragraph (2).
(4) The appellant need not file a record of the reasons for judgment of the lower court with his appellant's notice unless sub-paragraph (5) applies.
(5) The court may order a suitable record of the reasons for judgment of the lower court (see para. 5.12) to be filed:
(a) to enable it to decide if permission should be granted; or
(b) if permission is granted to enable it to decide the appeal.

Skeleton arguments

para.5.9 **71.26, 71.42** para.5.9(2) **71.26, 71.28**
para.5.9(1) **71.26** para.5.9(3) **71.26**

5.9 (1) The appellant's notice must, subject to (2) and (3) below, be accompanied by a skeleton argument. Alternatively the skeleton argument may be included in the appellant's notice. Where the skeleton argument is so included it will not form part of the notice for the purposes of r. 52.8.
(2) Where it is impracticable for the appellant's skeleton argument to accompany the appellant's notice it must be lodged and served on all respondents within 14 days of filing the notice.
(3) An appellant who is not represented need not lodge a skeleton argument but is encouraged to do so since this will be helpful to the court.

Content of skeleton arguments

para.5.10–5.11 **71.26**

5.10 (1) A skeleton argument must contain a numbered list of the points which the party wishes to make. These should both define and confine the areas of controversy. Each point should be stated as concisely as the nature of the case allows.
(2) A numbered point must be followed by a reference to any document on which the party wishes to rely.
(3) A skeleton argument must state, in respect of each authority cited:
(a) the proposition of law that the authority demonstrates; and
(b) the parts of the authority (identified by page or paragraph references) that support the proposition.
(4) If more than one authority is cited in support of a given proposition, the skeleton argument must briefly state the reason for taking that course.
(5) The statement referred to in sub-paragraph (4) should not materially add to the length of the skeleton argument but should be sufficient to demonstrate, in the context of the argument:
(a) the relevance of the authority or authorities to that argument; and
(b) that the citation is necessary for a proper presentation of that argument.
(6) The cost of preparing a skeleton argument which:
(a) does not comply with the requirements set out in this paragraph; or
(b) was not filed within the time limits provided by this practice direction (or any further time granted by the court),
will not be allowed on assessment except to the extent that the court otherwise directs.

5.11 The appellant should consider what other information the appeal court will need. This may include a list of persons who feature in the case or glossaries of technical terms. A chronology of relevant events will be necessary in most appeals.

Suitable record of the judgment

para.5.12 **71.27, 81.12** para.5.12(3) **71.27**

5.12 Where the judgment to be appealed has been officially recorded by the court, an approved transcript of that record should accompany the appellant's notice. Photocopies will not be accepted for this purpose. However, where there is no officially recorded judgment the following documents will be acceptable:

Written judgments

(1) Where the judgment was made in writing a copy of that judgment endorsed with the judge's signature.

Note of judgment

(2) When judgment was not officially recorded or made in writing a note of the judgment (agreed between the appellant's and respondent's advocates) should be submitted for approval to the judge whose decision is being appealed. If the parties cannot agree on a single note of the judgment, both versions should be provided to that judge with an explanatory letter. For the purpose of an application for permission to appeal the note need not be approved by the respondent or the lower court judge.

Advocates' notes of judgments where the appellant is unrepresented

(3) When the appellant was unrepresented in the lower court it is the duty of any advocate for the respondent to make his/her note of judgment promptly available, free of charge to the appellant where there is no officially recorded judgment or if the court so directs. Where the appellant was represented in the lower court it is the duty of his/her own former advocate to make his/her note available in these circumstances. The appellant should submit the note of judgment to the appeal court.

Reasons for judgment in tribunal cases

(4) A sealed copy of the tribunal's reasons for the decision.

5.13 An appellant may not be able to obtain an official transcript or other suitable record of the lower court's decision within the time within which the appellant's notice must be filed. In such cases the appellant's notice must still be completed to the best of the appellant's ability on the basis of the documentation available. However it may be amended subsequently with the permission of the appeal court.

Advocates' notes of judgment

para.5.14 **81.12**

5.14 Advocates' brief (or, where appropriate, refresher) fee includes:

(1) remuneration for taking a note of the judgment of the court;
(2) having the note transcribed accurately;
(3) attempting to agree the note with the other side if represented;
(4) submitting the note to the judge for approval where appropriate;
(5) revising it if so requested by the judge;
(6) providing any copies required for the appeal court, instructing solicitors and lay client; and
(7) providing a copy of his note to an unrepresented appellant

Transcripts or notes of evidence

paras 5.15–5.17 **71.27, 81.12**

5.15 When the evidence is relevant to the appeal an official transcript of the relevant evidence must be obtained. Transcripts or notes of evidence are generally not needed for the purpose of determining an application for permission to appeal.

Notes of evidence

5.16 If evidence relevant to the appeal was not officially recorded, a typed version of the judge's notes of evidence must be obtained.

Transcripts at public expense

para.5.18 **71.27**

Civil Procedure Rules & Practice Directions

5.17 Where the lower court or the appeal court is satisfied:
(1) that an unrepresented appellant; or
(2) an appellant whose legal representation is provided free of charge to the appellant and not funded by the Community Legal Service,
is in such poor financial circumstances that the cost of a transcript would be an excessive burden the court may certify that the cost of obtaining one official transcript should be borne at public expense.

5.18 In the case of a request for an official transcript of evidence or proceedings to be paid for at public expense, the court must also be satisfied that there are reasonable grounds for appeal. Whenever possible a request for a transcript at public expense should be made to the lower court when asking for permission to appeal.

Filing and service of appellant's notice

paras 5.19–5.20 **71.19, 81.12**
para.5.21 **71.28, 74.37**
para.5.21(2) **71.28**
para.5.22 **71.28**
para.5.24 **71.28, 71.29**
para.5.25 **71.42**

5.19 Rule 52.4 sets out the procedure and time limits for filing and serving an appellant's notice. The appellant must file the appellant's notice at the appeal court within such period as may be directed by the lower court which should not normally exceed 28 days or, where the lower court directs no such period, within 14 days of the date of the decision that the appellant wishes to appeal.
(Rule 52.15 sets out the time limit for filing an application for permission to appeal against the refusal of the High Court to grant permission to apply for judicial review.)

5.20 Where the lower court judge announces his decision and reserves the reasons for his judgment or order until a later date, he should, in the exercise of powers under r. 52.4(2)(a), fix a period for filing the appellant's notice at the appeal court that takes this into account.

5.21 (1) Except where the appeal court orders otherwise a sealed copy of the appellant's notice, including any skeleton arguments must be served on all respondents in accordance with the timetable prescribed by r. 52.4(3) except where this requirement is modified by para. 5.9(2) in which case the skeleton argument should be served as soon as it is filed.
(2) The appellant must, as soon as practicable, file a certificate of service of the documents referred to in paragraph (1).

5.22 Unless the court otherwise directs a respondent need not take any action when served with an appellant's notice until such time as notification is given to him that permission to appeal has been given.

5.23 The court may dispense with the requirement for service of the notice on a respondent. Any application notice seeking an order under r. 6.9 to dispense with service should set out the reasons relied on and be verified by a statement of truth.

5.24 (1) Where the appellant is applying for permission to appeal in his appellant's notice, he must serve on the respondents his appellant's notice and skeleton argument (but not the appeal bundle), unless the appeal court directs otherwise.
(2) Where permission to appeal:
(a) has been given by the lower court; or
(b) is not required,
the appellant must serve the appeal bundle on the respondents with the appellant's notice.

Amendment of appeal notice

para.5.25 **71.42**

5.25 An appeal notice may be amended with permission. Such an application to amend and any application in opposition will normally be dealt with at the hearing unless that course would cause unnecessary expense or delay in which case a request should be made for the application to amend to be heard in advance.

Procedure after Permission Is Obtained

para.6.2 **71.24, 71.29**
para.6.3(2)–(3) **71.29**
para.6.3A **71.24, 71.29**

6.1 This paragraph sets out the procedure where:
(1) permission to appeal is given by the appeal court; or

(2) the appellant's notice is filed in the appeal court and:
 (a) permission was given by the lower court; or
 (b) permission is not required.

6.2 If the appeal court gives permission to appeal, the appeal bundle must be served on the respondents within seven days of receiving the order giving permission to appeal.
(Part 6 (service of documents) provides rules on service.)

6.3 The appeal court will send the parties:
 (1) notification of:
  (a) the date of the hearing or the period of time (the 'listing window') during which the appeal is likely to be heard; and
  (b) in the Court of Appeal, the date by which the appeal will be heard (the 'hear-by date');
 (2) where permission is granted by the appeal court a copy of the order giving permission to appeal; and
 (3) any other directions given by the court.

6.3A (1) Where the appeal court grants permission to appeal, the appellant must add the following documents to the appeal bundle:
  (a) the respondent's notice and skeleton argument (if any);
  (b) those parts of the transcripts of evidence which are directly relevant to any question at issue on the appeal;
  (c) the order granting permission to appeal and, where permission to appeal was granted at an oral hearing, the transcript (or note) of any judgment which was given; and
  (d) any document which the appellant and respondent have agreed to add to the appeal bundle in accordance with para. 7.11.
 (2) Where permission to appeal has been refused on a particular issue, the appellant must remove from the appeal bundle all documents that are relevant only to that issue.

Appeal questionnaire in the Court of Appeal

paras 6.5–6.6 **71.31**

6.4 The Court of Appeal will send an appeal questionnaire to the appellant when it notifies him of the matters referred to in para. 6.3.

6.5 The appellant must complete and lodge the appeal questionnaire within 14 days of the date of the letter of notification of the matters in para. 6.3. The appeal questionnaire must contain:
 (1) if the appellant is legally represented, the advocate's time estimate for the hearing of the appeal;
 (2) where a transcript of evidence is relevant to the appeal, confirmation as to what parts of a transcript of evidence have been ordered where this is not already in the bundle of documents;
 (3) confirmation that copies of the appeal bundle are being prepared and will be held ready for the use of the Court of Appeal and an undertaking that they will be supplied to the court on request. For the purpose of these bundles photocopies of the transcripts will be accepted;
 (4) confirmation that copies of the appeal questionnaire and the appeal bundle have been served on the respondents and the date of that service.

Time estimates

6.6 The time estimate included in an appeal questionnaire must be that of the advocate who will argue the appeal. It should exclude the time required by the court to give judgment. If the respondent disagrees with the time estimate, the respondent must inform the court within seven days of receipt of the appeal questionnaire. In the absence of such notification the respondent will be deemed to have accepted the estimate proposed on behalf of the appellant.

Respondent

paras 7.1–7.2 **71.33** paras.7.3(2) **71.34**

7.1 A respondent who wishes to ask the appeal court to vary the order of the lower court in any way must appeal and permission will be required on the same basis as for an appellant.
(Paragraph 3.2 applies to grounds of appeal by a respondent.)

7.2 A respondent who wishes only to request that the appeal court upholds the judgment or order of the lower court whether for the reasons given in the lower court or otherwise does not make an appeal and does not therefore require permission to appeal in accordance with r. 52.3(1).

(Paragraph 7.6 requires a respondent to file a skeleton argument where he wishes to address the appeal court.)

7.3 (1) A respondent who wishes to appeal or who wishes to ask the appeal court to uphold the order of the lower court for reasons different from or additional to those given by the lower court must file a respondent's notice.

(2) If the respondent does not file a respondent's notice, he will not be entitled, except with the permission of the court, to rely on any reason not relied on in the lower court.

7.3A Paragraphs 5.1A, 5.1B and 5.2 of this practice direction (human rights and extension for time for filing appellant's notice) also apply to a respondent and a respondent's notice.

Time limits

7.4 The time limits for filing a respondent's notice are set out in r. 52.5(4) and (5).

7.5 Where an extension of time is required the extension must be requested in the respondent's notice and the reasons why the respondent failed to act within the specified time must be included.

Respondent's skeleton argument

para.7.6 **71.37, 71.42**
para.7.7 **71.37**
para.7.7(1)–(2) **71.37**
para.7.7A(2) **71.37**
para.7.7B **71.37**

7.6 Except where para. 7.7A applies, the respondent must provide a skeleton argument for the court in all cases where he proposes to address arguments to the court. The respondent's skeleton argument may be included within a respondent's notice. Where a skeleton argument is included within a respondent's notice it will not form part of the notice for the purposes of r. 52.8.

7.7 (1) A respondent who:

(a) files a respondent's notice; but

(b) does not include his skeleton argument within that notice,

must file and serve his skeleton argument within 14 days of filing the notice.

(2) A respondent who does not file a respondent's notice but who files a skeleton argument must file and serve that skeleton argument at least seven days before the appeal hearing.

(Rule 52.5(4) sets out the period for filing and serving a respondent's notice.)

7.7A (1) Where the appeal relates to a claim allocated to the small claims track and is being heard in a county court or the High Court, the respondent may file a skeleton argument but is not required to do so.

(2) A respondent who is not represented need not file a skeleton argument but is encouraged to do so in order to assist the court.

7.7B The respondent must:

(1) serve his skeleton argument on:

(a) the appellant; and

(b) any other respondent,

at the same time as he files it at the court; and

(2) file a certificate of service.

Content of skeleton arguments

para.57.8 **71.37**

7.8 A respondent's skeleton argument must conform to the directions at paras 5.10 and 5.11 with any necessary modifications. It should, where appropriate, answer the arguments set out in the appellant's skeleton argument.

Applications within respondent's notices

7.9 A respondent may include an application within a respondent's notice in accordance with para. 5.5 above.

Filing respondent's notices and skeleton arguments

para.7.10 **71.38**
paras 7.11–7.12 **71.24, 71.38**
para.7.13 **71.38**

7.10 (1) The respondent must lodge the following documents with his respondent's notice in every case:

(a) two additional copies of the respondent's notice for the appeal court; and

(b) one copy each for the appellant and any other respondents.

(2) The respondent may file a skeleton argument with his respondent's notice and:
(a) where he does so he must file two copies; and
(b) where he does not do so he must comply with para. 7.7.

7.11 If the respondent wishes to rely on any documents which he reasonably considers necessary to enable the appeal court to reach its decision on the appeal in addition to those filed by the appellant, he must make every effort to agree amendments to the appeal bundle with the appellant.

7.12 (1) If the representatives for the parties are unable to reach agreement, the respondent may prepare a supplemental bundle.
(2) If the respondent prepares a supplemental bundle he must file it, together with the requisite number of copies for the appeal court, at the appeal court:
(a) with the respondent's notice; or
(b) if a respondent's notice is not filed, within 21 days after he is served with the appeal bundle.

7.13 The respondent must serve:
(1) the respondent's notice;
(2) his skeleton argument (if any); and
(3) the supplemental bundle (if any),
on:
(a) the appellant; and
(b) any other respondent,
at the same time as he files them at the court.

Appeals to the High Court

para.8.2 **71.8** para.8.7 **71.8**
para.8.4 **71.8**

Application

8.1 This paragraph applies where an appeal lies to a High Court judge from the decision of a county court or a district judge of the High Court.

8.2 The following table sets out the following venues for each circuit:
(a) Appeal centres —court centres where appeals to which this paragraph applies may be filed, managed and heard. Paragraphs 8.6 to 8.8 provide for special arrangements in relation to the South Eastern Circuit.
(b) Hearing-only centres — court centres where appeals to which this paragraph applies may be heard by order made at an appeal centre (see para. 8.10).

Circuit	Appeal centres	Hearing-only centres
Midland Circuit	Birmingham Nottingham	Lincoln Leicester Northampton Stafford
North Eastern Circuit	Leeds Newcastle Sheffield	Teesside
Northern Circuit	Manchester Liverpool Preston	Carlisle
Wales and Chester Circuit	Cardiff Swansea Chester	
Western Circuit	Bristol Exeter Winchester	Truro Plymouth

Circuit	Appeal centres	Hearing-only centres
South Eastern Circuit	Royal Courts of Justice Lewes Luton Norwich Reading Chelmsford St Albans Maidstone Oxford	

Venue for appeals and filing of notices on circuits other than the South Eastern Circuit

8.3 Paragraphs 8.4 and 8.5 apply where the lower court is situated on a circuit other than the South Eastern Circuit.

8.4 The appellant's notice must be filed at an appeal centre on the circuit in which the lower court is situated. The appeal will be managed and heard at that appeal centre unless the appeal court orders otherwise.

8.5 A respondent's notice must be filed at the appeal centre where the appellant's notice was filed unless the appeal has been transferred to another appeal centre, in which case it must be filed at that appeal centre.

Venue for appeals and filing of notices on the South Eastern Circuit

para.8.7 **71.8**

8.6 Paragraphs 8.7 and 8.8 apply where the lower court is situated on the South Eastern Circuit.

8.7 The appellant's notice must be filed at an appeal centre on the South Eastern Circuit. The appeal will be managed and heard at the Royal Courts of Justice unless the appeal court orders otherwise. An order that an appeal is to be managed or heard at another appeal centre may not be made unless the consent of the presiding judge of the circuit in charge of civil matters has been obtained.

8.8 A respondent's notice must be filed at the Royal Courts of Justice unless the appeal has been transferred to another appeal centre, in which case it must be filed at that appeal centre.

General provisions

para.8.12 **71.31** para.8.13(1A) **71.3**

8.9 The appeal court may transfer an appeal to another appeal centre (whether or not on the same circuit). In deciding whether to do so the court will have regard to the criteria in r. 30.3 (criteria for a transfer order). The appeal court may do so either on application by a party or of its own initiative. Where an appeal is transferred under this paragraph, notice of transfer must be served on every person on whom the appellant's notice has been served. An appeal may not be transferred to an appeal centre on another circuit, either for management or hearing, unless the consent of the presiding judge of that circuit in charge of civil matters has been obtained.

8.10 Directions may be given for:
(a) an appeal to be heard at a hearing-only centre; or
(b) an application in an appeal to be heard at any other venue,
instead of at the appeal centre managing the appeal.

8.11 Unless a direction has been made under para. 8.10, any application in the appeal must be made at the appeal centre where the appeal is being managed.

8.12 The appeal court may adopt all or any part of the procedure set out in paras 6.4 to 6.6.

8.13 Where the lower court is a county court:
(1) subject to sub-para. (1A), appeals and applications for permission to appeal will be heard by a High Court judge or by a person authorised under paras (1), (2) or (4) of the Table in the Supreme Court Act 1981, s. 9(1), to act as a judge of the High Court; and
(1A) an appeal or application for permission to appeal from the decision of a recorder in the county court may be heard by a designated civil judge who is authorised under para. (5) of the Table in the Supreme Court Act 1981, s. 9(1), to act as a judge of the High Court; and
(2) other applications in the appeal may be heard and directions in the appeal may be given either by a High Court judge or by any person authorised under the Supreme Court Act 1981, s. 9, to act as a judge of the High Court.

8.14 In the case of appeals from masters or district judges of the High Court, appeals, applications for permission and any other applications in the appeal may be heard and directions in the appeal may be given by a High Court judge or by any person authorised under the Supreme Court Act 1981, s. 9, to act as a judge of the High Court.

Appeals to a Judge of a County Court from a District Judge

8A.1 The designated civil judge in consultation with his presiding judges has responsibility for allocating appeals from decisions of district judges to circuit judges.

Rehearings

para.9.1 **72.5**

9.1 The hearing of an appeal will be a rehearing (as opposed to a review of the decision of the lower court) if the appeal is from the decision of a minister, person or other body and the minister, person or other body:
(1) did not hold a hearing to come to that decision; or
(2) held a hearing to come to that decision, but the procedure adopted did not provide for the consideration of evidence.

Appeals Transferred to the Court of Appeal

10.1 Where an appeal is transferred to the Court of Appeal under r. 52.14 the Court of Appeal may give such additional directions as are considered appropriate.

Applications

para.11.2 **71.41**

11.1 Where a party to an appeal makes an application whether in an appeal notice or by Part 23 application notice, the provisions of Part 23 will apply.
11.2 The applicant must file the following documents with the notice:
(1) one additional copy of the application notice for the appeal court and one copy for each of the respondents;
(2) where applicable a sealed copy of the order which is the subject of the main appeal;
(3) a bundle of documents in support which should include:
(a) the Part 23 application notice;
(b) any witness statements and affidavits filed in support of the application notice.

Disposing of Applications or Appeals by Consent

Dismissal of applications or appeals by consent

paras 12.2–12.4 **71.47**

12.1 These paragraphs do not apply where any party to the proceedings is a child or patient.
12.2 Where an appellant does not wish to pursue an application or an appeal, he may request the appeal court for an order that his application or appeal be dismissed. Such a request must contain a statement that the appellant is not a child or patient. If such a request is granted it will usually be on the basis that the appellant pays the costs of the application or appeal.
12.3 If the appellant wishes to have the application or appeal dismissed without costs, his request must be accompanied by a consent signed by the respondent or his legal representative stating that the respondent is not a child or patient and consents to the dismissal of the application or appeal without costs.
12.4 Where a settlement has been reached disposing of the application or appeal, the parties may make a joint request to the court stating that none of them is a child or patient, and asking that the application or appeal be dismissed by consent. If the request is granted the application or appeal will be dismissed.

Allowing unopposed appeals or applications on paper

para.13.1–13.4 **71.47**

13.1 The appeal court will not normally make an order allowing an appeal unless satisfied that the decision of the lower court was wrong, but the appeal court may set aside or vary the order of the lower court with consent and without determining the merits of the appeal, if it is satisfied that there are good and sufficient reasons for doing so. Where the appeal court is requested by all parties to allow an application or an appeal the court may consider the request on the papers. The request should state that none of the parties is a child or patient and set out the relevant history of the proceedings and the matters relied on as justifying the proposed order and be accompanied by a copy of the proposed order.

Procedure for consent orders and agreements to pay periodical payments involving a child or patient

13.2 Where one of the parties is a child or patient:
(1) a settlement relating to an appeal or application; or
(2) in a personal injury claim for damages for future pecuniary loss, an agreement reached at the appeal stage to pay periodical payments,

requires the court's approval.

Child

para.13.3–13.4 **71.47**

13.3 In cases involving a child a copy of the proposed order signed by the parties' solicitors should be sent to the appeal court, together with an opinion from the advocate acting on behalf of the child.

Patient

13.4 Where a party is a patient the same procedure will be adopted, but the documents filed should also include any relevant reports prepared for the Court of Protection and a document evidencing formal approval by that court where required.

Periodical payments

13.5 Where periodical payments for future pecuniary loss have been negotiated in a personal injury case which is under appeal, the documents filed should include those which would be required in the case of a personal injury claim for damages for future pecuniary loss dealt with at first instance. Details can be found in PD 21.

Summary Assessment of Costs

para.14.1 **72.18**

14.1 Costs are likely to be assessed by way of summary assessment at the following hearings:
(1) contested directions hearings;
(2) applications for permission to appeal at which the respondent is present;
(3) dismissal list hearings in the Court of Appeal at which the respondent is present;
(4) appeals from case management decisions; and
(5) appeals listed for one day or less.

14.2 Parties attending any of the hearings referred to in para. 14.1 should be prepared to deal with the summary assessment.

Other Special Provisions Regarding the Court of Appeal

para.15.1(2) **71.30**
para.15.2 **57.4, 71.25**
para.15.3 **74.37**
para.15.3(1)–(2) **71.25**

Filing of documents

15.1 (1) The documents relevant to proceedings in the Court of Appeal, Civil Division must be filed in the Civil Appeals Office Registry, Room E307, Royal Courts of Justice, Strand, London WC2A 2LL.
(2) The Civil Appeals Office will not serve documents and where service is required by the CPR or this practice direction it must be effected by the parties.

15.1A (1) A party may file by email:
(a) an appellant's notice;
(b) a respondent's notice;
(c) an application notice,

in the Court of Appeal, Civil Division, using the email account specified in the 'Guidelines for filing by email' which appear on the Court of Appeal, Civil Division website at www.civilappeals.gov.uk.

(2) A party may only file a notice in accordance with para. (1) where he is permitted to do so by the 'Guidelines for filing by email'.

15.2 In cases where the appeal bundle comprises more than 500 pages, exclusive of transcripts, the appellant's solicitors must, after consultation with the respondent's solicitors, also prepare and file with the court, in addition to copies of the appeal bundle (as amended in accordance with para. 7.11) the requisite number of copies of a core bundle.

15.3 (1) The core bundle must be filed within 28 days of receipt of the order giving permission to appeal or, where permission to appeal was granted by the lower court or is not required, within 28 days of the date of service of the appellant's notice on the respondent.

(2) The core bundle:

(a) must contain the documents which are central to the appeal; and

(b) must not exceed 150 pages.

Preparation of bundles

para.15.4 **57.4, 71.24, 74.37** para.15.4(3) **71.24, 71.25**
para.15.4(1)–(2) **71.24** para.15.4(4)–(12) **71.24**

15.4 The provisions of this paragraph apply to the preparation of appeal bundles, supplemental respondents' bundles where the parties are unable to agree amendments to the appeal bundle, and core bundles.

(1) *Rejection of bundles.* Where documents are copied unnecessarily or bundled incompletely, costs may be disallowed. Where the provisions of this practice direction as to the preparation or delivery of bundles are not followed the bundle may be rejected by the court or be made the subject of a special costs order.

(2) *Avoidance of duplication.* No more than one copy of any document should be included unless there is a good reason for doing otherwise (such as the use of a separate core bundle: see para. 15.2).

(3) *Pagination*

(a) Bundles must be paginated, each page being numbered individually and consecutively. The pagination used at trial must also be indicated. Letters and other documents should normally be included in chronological order. (An exception to consecutive page numbering arises in the case of core bundles where it may be preferable to retain the original numbering.)

(b) Page numbers should be inserted in bold figures at the bottom of the page and in a form that can be clearly distinguished from any other pagination on the document.

(4) *Format and presentation*

(a) Where possible the documents should be in A4 format. Where a document has to be read across rather than down the page, it should be so placed in the bundle as to ensure that the text starts nearest the spine.

(b) Where any marking or writing in colour on a document is important, the document must be copied in colour or marked up correctly in colour.

(c) Documents which are not easily legible should be transcribed and the transcription marked and placed adjacent to the document transcribed.

(d) Documents in a foreign language should be translated and the translation marked and placed adjacent to the document translated. The translation should be agreed or, if it cannot be agreed, each party's proposed translation should be included.

(e) The size of any bundle should be tailored to its contents. A large lever arch file should not be used for just a few pages nor should files of whatever size be overloaded.

(f) Where it will assist the Court of Appeal, different sections of the file may be separated by cardboard or other tabbed dividers so long as these are clearly indexed. Where, for example, a document is awaited when the appeal bundle is filed, a single sheet of paper can be inserted after a divider, indicating the nature of the document awaited. For example, 'Transcript of evidence of Mr J Smith (to follow)'.

(5) *Binding*

(a) All documents, with the exception of transcripts, must be bound together. This may be in a lever arch file, ring-binder or plastic folder. Plastic sleeves containing loose documents must not be used. Binders and files must be strong enough to withstand heavy use.

(b) Large documents such as plans should be placed in an easily accessible file. Large documents which will need to be opened up frequently should be inserted in a file larger than A4 size.

(6) *Indices and labels*

(a) An index must be included at the front of the bundle listing all the documents and providing the page references for each. In the case of documents such as letters, invoices or bank statements, they may be given a general description.

(b) Where the bundles consist of more than one file, an index to all the files should be included in the first file and an index included for each file. Indices should, if possible, be on a single sheet. The full name of the case should not be inserted on the index if this would waste space. Documents should be identified briefly but properly.

(7) *Identification*

(a) Every bundle must be clearly identified, on the spine and on the front cover, with the name of the case and the Court of Appeal's reference. Where the bundle consists of more than one file, each file must be numbered on the spine, the front cover and the inside of the front cover.

(b) Outer labels should use large lettering e.g. 'Appeal Bundle A' or 'Core Bundle'. The full title of the appeal and solicitors' names and addresses should be omitted. A label should be used on the front as well as on the spine.

(8) *Staples etc.* All staples, heavy metal clips etc., must be removed.

(9) *Statements of case*

(a) Statements of case should be assembled in 'chapter' form: i.e. claim followed by particulars of claim, followed by further information, irrespective of date.

(b) Redundant documents, e.g. particulars of claim overtaken by amendments, requests for further information recited in the answers given, should generally be excluded.

(10) *New documents*

(a) Before a new document is introduced into bundles which have already been delivered to the court, steps should be taken to ensure that it carries an appropriate bundle/page number so that it can be added to the court documents. It should not be stapled and it should be prepared with punch holes for immediate inclusion in the binders in use.

(b) If it is expected that a large number of miscellaneous new documents will from time to time be introduced, there should be a special tabbed empty loose-leaf file for that purpose. An index should be produced for this file, updated as necessary.

(11) *Inter-solicitor correspondence.* Since inter-solicitor correspondence is unlikely to be required for the purposes of an appeal, only those letters which will need to be referred to should be copied.

(12) *Sanctions for non-compliance.* If the appellant fails to comply with the requirements as to the provision of bundles of documents, the application or appeal will be referred for consideration to be given as to why it should not be dismissed for failure to so comply.

Master in the Court of Appeal, Civil Division

para.15.5 **71.3, 74.37**

15.5 When the Head of the Civil Appeals Office acts in a judicial capacity pursuant to r. 52.16, he shall be known as master. Other eligible officers may also be designated by the Master of the Rolls to exercise judicial authority under r. 52.16 and shall then be known as deputy masters.

Respondent to notify Civil Appeals Office whether he intends to file respondent's notice

15.6 A respondent must, no later than 21 days after the date he is served with notification that:

(1) permission to appeal has been granted; or

(2) the application for permission to appeal and the appeal are to be heard together,

inform the Civil Appeals Office and the appellant in writing whether:

(a) he proposes to file a respondent's notice appealing the order or seeking to uphold the order for reasons different from, or additional to, those given by the lower court; or

(b) he proposes to rely on the reasons given by the lower court for its decision.

(Paragraph 15.11B requires all documents needed for an appeal hearing, including a respondent's skeleton argument, to be filed at least seven days before the hearing.)

Listing and hear-by dates

paras 15.8–15.9 **71.32**

15.7 The management of the list will be dealt with by the listing officer under the direction of the master.

15.8 The Civil Appeals List of the Court of Appeal is divided as follows:

- *The applications list* — applications for permission to appeal and other applications.
- *The appeals list* — appeals where permission to appeal has been given or where an appeal lies without permission being required where a hearing date is fixed in advance. (Appeals in this list which require special listing arrangements will be assigned to the special fixtures list.)
- *The expedited list* — appeals or applications where the Court of Appeal has directed an expedited hearing. The current practice of the Court of Appeal is summarised in *Unilever plc v Chefaro Proprietaries Ltd* [1995] 1 WLR 243.
- *The stand-out list* — appeals or applications which, for good reason, are not at present ready to proceed and have been stood out by judicial direction.
- *The special fixtures list* — see para. 15.9A(1).
- *The second fixtures list* — if an appeal is designated as a 'second fixture' it means that a hearing date is arranged in advance on the express basis that the list is fully booked for the period in question and therefore the case will be heard only if a suitable gap occurs in the list.
- *The short warned list* — appeals which the court considers may be prepared for the hearing by an advocate other than the one originally instructed with a half day's notice, or such other period as the court may direct.

Special provisions relating to the short warned list

para.15.9 **71.32**

15.9 (1) Where an appeal is assigned to the short warned list, the Civil Appeals Office will notify the parties' solicitors in writing. The court may abridge the time for filing any outstanding bundles in an appeal assigned to this list.

(2) The solicitors for the parties must notify their advocate and their client as soon as the Civil Appeals Office notifies them that the appeal has been assigned to the short warned list.

(3) The appellant may apply in writing for the appeal to be removed from the short warned list within 14 days of notification of its assignment. The application will be decided by a Lord Justice, or the master, and will only be granted for the most compelling reasons.

(4) The Civil Appeals Listing Officer may place an appeal from the short warned list 'on call' from a given date and will inform the parties' advocates accordingly.

(5) An appeal which is 'on call' may be listed for hearing on half a day's notice or such longer period as the court may direct.

(6) Once an appeal is listed for hearing from the short warned list it becomes the immediate professional duty of the advocate instructed in the appeal, if he is unable to appear at the hearing, to take all practicable measures to ensure that his lay client is represented at the hearing by an advocate who is fully instructed and able to argue the appeal.

Special provisions relating to the special fixtures list

para.15.9A **71.32**

15.9A (1) The special fixtures list is a subdivision of the appeals list and is used to deal with appeals that may require special listing arrangements, such as the need to list a number of cases before the same constitution, in a particular order, during a particular period or at a given location.

(2) The Civil Appeals Office will notify the parties' representatives, or the parties if acting in person, of the particular arrangements that will apply. The notice:

(a) will give details of the specific period during which a case is scheduled to be heard; and

(b) may give directions in relation to the filing of any outstanding documents.

(3) The listing officer will notify the parties' representatives of the precise hearing date as soon as practicable. While every effort will be made to accommodate the availability of counsel, the requirements of the court will prevail.

Requests for directions

15.10 To ensure that all requests for directions are centrally monitored and correctly allocated, all requests for directions or rulings (whether relating to listing or any other matters) should be made to the Civil Appeals Office. Those seeking directions or rulings must not approach the supervising lord justice either directly, or via his or her clerk.

Bundles of authorities

para.15.11 **57.4, 71.48** para.15.11(3)–(5) **71.48**
para.15.11(2)(c) **71.48**

15.11 (1) Once the parties have been notified of the date fixed for the hearing, the appellant's advocate must, after consultation with his opponent, file a bundle containing photocopies of the authorities upon which each side will rely at the hearing.

(2) The bundle of authorities should, in general:

(a) have the relevant passages of the authorities marked;

(b) not include authorities for propositions not in dispute; and

(c) not contain more than 10 authorities unless the scale of the appeal warrants more extensive citation.

(3) The bundle of authorities must be filed:

(a) at least seven days before the hearing; or

(b) where the period of notice of the hearing is less than seven days, immediately.

(4) If, through some oversight, a party intends, during the hearing, to refer to other authorities the parties may agree a second agreed bundle. The appellant's advocate must file this bundle at least 48 hours before the hearing commences.

(5) A bundle of authorities must bear a certification by the advocates responsible for arguing the case that the requirements of sub-paragraphs (3) to (5) of para. 5.10 have been complied with in respect of each authority included.

Supplementary skeleton arguments

para.15.11A **71.39** para.15.11A(4) **71.39**

15.11A (1) A supplementary skeleton argument on which the appellant wishes to rely must be filed at least 14 days before the hearing.

(2) A supplementary skeleton argument on which the respondent wishes to rely must be filed at least seven days before the hearing.

(3) All supplementary skeleton arguments must comply with the requirements set out in para. 5.10.

(4) At the hearing the court may refuse to hear argument from a party not contained in a skeleton argument filed within the relevant time limit set out in this paragraph.

Papers for the appeal hearing

para.15.11B(1)–(2) **71.40**

15.11B (1) All the documents which are needed for the appeal hearing must be filed at least seven days before the hearing. Where a document has not been filed 10 days before the hearing a reminder will be sent by the Civil Appeals Office.

(2) Any party who fails to comply with the provisions of sub-paragraph (1) may be required to attend before the presiding Lord Justice to seek permission to proceed with, or to oppose, the appeal.

Disposal of bundles of documents

15.11C (1) Where the court has determined a case, the official transcriber will retain one set of papers. The Civil Appeals Office will destroy any remaining sets of papers not collected within 21 days of:

(a) where one or more parties attend the hearing, the date of the court's decision;

(b) where there is no attendance, the date of the notification of court's decision.

(2) The parties should ensure that bundles of papers supplied to the court do not contain original documents (other than transcripts). The parties must ensure that they:

(a) bring any necessary original documents to the hearing; and

(b) retrieve any original documents handed up to the court before leaving the court.

(3) The court will retain application bundles where permission to appeal has been granted. Where permission is refused the arrangements in sub-paragraph (1) will apply.

(4) Where a single Lord Justice has refused permission to appeal on paper, application bundles will not be destroyed until after the time limit for seeking a hearing has expired.

Availability of reserved judgments before hand-down

para.15.12 **72.17** para.15.13 **72.17, 73.5**

15.12 This section applies where the presiding Lord Justice is satisfied that the result of the appeal will attract no special degree of confidentiality or sensitivity.

15.13 A copy of the written judgment will be made available to the parties' legal advisers by 4 p.m. on the second working day before judgment is due to be pronounced or such other period as the court may direct. This can be shown, in confidence, to the parties but only for the purpose of obtaining instructions and on the strict understanding that the judgment, or its effect, is not to be disclosed to any other person. A working day is any day on which the Civil Appeals Office is open for business.

15.14 The appeal will be listed for judgment in the cause list and the judgment handed down at the appropriate time.

Attendance of advocates on the handing down of a reserved judgment

para.15.15 **72.17**

15.15 Where any consequential orders are agreed, the parties' advocates need not attend on the handing down of a reserved judgment. Where an advocate does attend the court may, if it considers such attendance unnecessary, disallow the costs of the attendance. If the parties do not indicate that they intend to attend, the judgment may be handed down by a single member of the court.

Agreed orders following judgment

para.15.16 **72.17**

15.16 The parties must, in respect of any draft agreed orders:
(a) fax a copy to the clerk to the presiding Lord Justice; and
(b) file four copies in the Civil Appeals Office,
no later than 12 noon on the working day before the judgment is handed down.

15.17 A copy of a draft order must bear the Court of Appeal case reference, the date the judgment is to be handed down and the name of the presiding Lord Justice.

Corrections to the draft judgment

paras.15.18 **72.17**

15.18 Any proposed correction to the draft judgment should be sent to the clerk to the judge who prepared the draft with a copy to any other party.

Application for leave to appeal

para.15.19–15.20 **73.5**

15.19 Where a party wishes to apply for leave to appeal to the House of Lords under the Administration of Justice (Appeals) Act 1934, s. 1, the court may deal with the application on the basis of written submissions.

15.20 A party must, in relation to his submission:
(a) fax a copy to the clerk to the presiding Lord Justice; and
(b) file four copies in the Civil Appeals Office,
no later than 12 noon on the working day before the judgment is handed down.

15.21 A copy of a submission must bear the Court of Appeal case reference, the date the judgment is to be handed down and the name of the presiding Lord Justice.

SECTION II — GENERAL PROVISIONS ABOUT STATUTORY APPEALS AND APPEALS BY WAY OF CASE STATED

section II **71.53**

16.1 This Section of this practice direction contains general provisions about statutory appeals (paras 17.1–17.6) and appeals by way of case stated (paras 18.1–18.20).

16.2 Where any of the provisions in this section provide for documents to be filed at the appeal court, these documents are in addition to any documents required under Part 52 or Section I of this practice direction.

Statutory Appeals

para.17 **71.53**

17.1 This part of this section:
(1) applies where under any enactment an appeal (other than by way of case stated) lies to

the court from a minister of State, government department, tribunal or other person ('statutory appeals'); and

(2) is subject to any provision about a specific category of appeal in any enactment or Section III of this practice direction.

Part 52

17.2 Part 52 applies to statutory appeals with the following amendments.

Filing of appellant's notice

para.17.3 **71.53**

17.3 The appellant must file the appellant's notice at the appeal court within 28 days after the date of the decision of the lower court he wishes to appeal.

17.4 Where a statement of the reasons for a decision is given later than the notice of that decision, the period for filing the appellant's notice is calculated from the date on which the statement is received by the appellant.

Service of appellant's notice

para.17.5–17.6 **71.53**

17.5 In addition to the respondents to the appeal, the appellant must serve the appellant's notice in accordance with r. 52.4(3) on the chairman of the tribunal, minister of State, government department or other person from whose decision the appeal is brought.

Right of minister etc. to be heard on the appeal

17.6 Where the appeal is from an order or decision of a minister of State or government department, the minister or department, as the case may be, is entitled to attend the hearing and to make representations to the court.

Appeals by Way of Case Stated

18.1 This part of this Section:

(1) applies where under any enactment:

(a) an appeal lies to the court by way of case stated; or

(b) a question of law may be referred to the court by way of case stated; and

(2) is subject to any provision about to a specific category of appeal in any enactment or Section III of this practice direction.

Part 52

18.2 Part 52 applies to appeals by way of case stated subject to the following amendments.

Case stated by Crown Court or magistrates' court

para.18.3–18.20 **71.54**

Application to state a case

para.18.3 **71.54**

18.3 The procedure for applying to the Crown Court or a magistrates' court to have a case stated for the opinion of the High Court is set out in the Crown Court Rules 1982 and the Magistrates' Courts Rules 1981 respectively.

Filing of appellant's notice

para.18.4 **71.54**

18.4 The appellant must file the appellant's notice at the appeal court within 10 days after he receives the stated case.

Documents to be lodged

para.18.5 **71.54**

18.5 The appellant must lodge the following documents with his appellant's notice:

(1) the stated case;

(2) a copy of the judgment, order or decision in respect of which the case has been stated; and

(3) where the judgment, order or decision in respect of which the case has been stated was itself given or made on appeal, a copy of the judgment, order or decision appealed from.

Service of appellant's notice

para.18.6 **71.54**

18.6 The appellant must serve the appellant's notice and. accompanying documents on all respondents within four days after they are filed or lodged at the appeal court.

Case stated by minister, government department, tribunal or other person

Application to state a case

para.18.7 **71.54**

18.7 The procedure for applying to a minister, government department, tribunal or other person ('minister or tribunal etc.') to have a case stated for the opinion of the court may be set out in:
(1) the enactment which provides for the right of appeal; or
(2) any rules of procedure relating to the minister or tribunal etc.

Signing of stated case by minister or tribunal etc.

para.18.8 **71.54**

18.8 A case stated by a tribunal must be signed by the chairman or president of the tribunal. A case stated by any other person must be signed by that person or by a person authorised to do so.

Service of stated case by minister or tribunal etc.

paras 8.9–8.10 **71.54**

18.9 The minister or tribunal etc. must serve the stated case on:
(1) the party who requests the case to be stated; or
(2) the party as a result of whose application to the court, the case was stated.

18.10 Where an enactment provides that a minister or tribunal etc. may state a case or refer a question of law to the court by way of case stated without a request being made, the minister or tribunal etc. must:
(1) serve the stated case on those parties that the minister or tribunal etc. considers appropriate; and
(2) give notice to every other party to the proceedings that the stated case has been served on the party named and on the date specified in the notice.

Filing and service of appellant's notice

paras 18.11–18.14 **71.54**

18.11 The party on whom the stated case was served must file the appellant's notice and the stated case at the appeal court and serve copies of the notice and stated case on:
(1) the minister or tribunal etc. who stated the case; and
(2) every party to the proceedings to which the stated case relates,
within 14 days after the stated case was served on him.

18.12 Where para. 18.10 applies the minister or tribunal etc. must:
(1) file an appellant's notice and the stated case at the appeal court; and
(2) serve copies of those documents on the persons served under para. 18.10,
within 14 days after stating the case.

18.13 Where:
(1) a stated case has been served by the minister or tribunal etc. in accordance with para. 18.9; and
(2) the party on whom the stated case was served does not file an appellant's notice in accordance with para. 18.11,
any other party may file an appellant's notice with the stated case at the appeal court and serve a copy of the notice and the case on the persons listed in para. 18.11 within the period of time set out in para. 18.14.

18.14 The period of time referred to in para. 18.13 is 14 days from the last day on which the party on whom the stated case was served may file an appellant's notice in accordance with para. 18.11.

Amendment of stated case

para.18.15 **71.54**

18.15 The court may amend the stated case or order it to be returned to the minister or tribunal etc. for amendment and may draw inferences of fact from the facts stated in the case.

Right of minister etc. to be heard on the appeal

para.18.16 **71.54**

18.16 Where the case is stated by a minister or government department, that minister or department, as the case may be, is entitled to appear on the appeal and to make representations to the court.

Application for order to state a case

paras 18.17–18.20 **71.54**

18.17 An application to the court for an order requiring a minister or tribunal etc. to state a case for the decision of the court, or to refer a question of law to the court by way of case stated must be made to the court which would be the appeal court if the case were stated.

18.18 An application to the court for an order directing a minister or tribunal etc. to:
(1) state a case for determination by the court; or
(2) refer a question of law to the court by way of case stated,
must be made in accordance with CPR, Part 23.

18.19 The application notice must contain:
(1) the grounds of the application;
(2) the question of law on which it is sought to have the case stated; and
(3) any reasons given by the minister or tribunal etc. for his or its refusal to state a case.

18.20 The application notice must be filed at the appeal court and served on:
(1) the minister, department, secretary of the tribunal or other person as the case may be; and
(2) every party to the proceedings to which the application relates,
within 14 days after the appellant receives notice of the refusal of his request to state a case.

SECTION III — PROVISIONS ABOUT SPECIFIC APPEALS

section III **71.55**

20.1 This section of this practice direction provides special provisions about the appeals to which the following table refers. This Section is not exhaustive and does not create, amend or remove any right of appeal.

20.2 Part 52 applies to all appeals to which this Section applies subject to any special provisions set out in this Section.

20.3 Where any of the provisions in this Section provide for documents to be filed at the appeal court, these documents are in addition to any documents required under Part 52 or Sections I or II of this practice direction.

	Paragraph
Appeals to the Court of Appeal	
Articles 81 and 82 of the EC Treaty and chapters I and II of part I of the Competition Act 1998	21.10A
Civil partnership—conditional order for dissolution or nullity	21.1
Competition Appeal Tribunal	21.10
Contempt of court	21.4
Decree nisi of divorce	21.1
Immigration Appeal Tribunal	21.7
Lands Tribunal	21.9
Nullity of marriage	21.1
Patents Court on appeal from Comptroller	21.3
Revocation of patent	21.2
Social Security Commissioners	21.5
Special commissioner (where the appeal is direct to the Court of Appeal)	21.8
Value added tax and duties tribunals (where the appeal is direct to the Court of Appeal)	21.6
Appeals to the High Court	
Agricultural Land Tribunal	22.7
Architects Act 1997, s. 22	22.3
Charities Act 1993	23.8
Chiropractors Act 1994, s. 31	22.3
Clergy Pensions Measure 1961, s. 38(3)	23.2
Commons Registration Act 1965	23.9
Consumer Credit Act 1974	22.4
Dentists Act 1984, s. 20 or s. 44	22.3
Extradition Act 2003	22.6A
Friendly Societies Act 1974	23.7

	Paragraph
Friendly Societies Act 1992	23.7
Industrial and Provident Societies Act 1965	23.2, 23.7
Industrial Assurance Act 1923	23.2, 23.7
Industrial Assurance Act 1923, s. 17	23.6
Inheritance Tax Act 1984, s. 222	23.3
Inheritance Tax Act 1984, s. 225	23.5
Inheritance Tax Act 1984, ss. 249(3) and 251	23.4
Land Registration Act 1925	23.2
Land Registration Act 2002	23.2, 23.8B
Law of Property Act 1922, sch. 15, para. 16	23.2
Medical Act 1983, s. 40	22.3
Medicines Act 1968, ss. 82(3) and 83(2)	22.3
Mental Health Review Tribunal	22.8
Merchant Shipping Act 1995	22.2
Nurses, Midwives and Health Visitors Act 1997, s. 12	22.3
Nursing and Midwifery Order 2001 (SI 2002/253), art. 38	22.3
Opticians Act 1989, s. 23	22.3
Osteopaths Act 1993, s. 31	22.3
Pension Schemes Act 1993, ss. 151 and 173	23.2
Pensions Act 1995, s. 97	23.2
Pensions Appeal Tribunals Act 1943	22.5
Pharmacy Act 1954	22.3
Social Security Administration Act 1992	22.6
Stamp Duty Reserve Tax Regulations 1986, reg. 10	23.5
Taxes Management Act 1970, ss. 53 and 100C(4)	23.4
Taxes Management Act 1970, s. 56A	23.5
Value added tax and duties tribunal	23.8
Water Resources Act 1991, s. 205(4)	23.2
Appeals to County Court	
Local Government (Miscellaneous Provisions) Act 1976	24.1
Housing Act 1996, ss. 204 and 204A	24.2
Immigration and Asylum Act 1999, part II	24.3

Appeals to the Court of Appeal

Appeal against decree nisi of divorce or nullity of marriage or conditional dissolution or nullity order in relation to civil partnership

21.1 (1) The appellant must file the appellant's notice at the Court of Appeal within 28 days after the date on which the decree was pronounced or conditional order made.

(2) The appellant must file the following documents with the appellant's notice:
(a) the decree or conditional order; and
(b) a certificate of service of the appellant's notice.

(3) The appellant's notice must be served on the appropriate district judge (see sub-para. (6)) in addition to the persons to be served under r. 52.4(3) and in accordance with that rule.

(4) The lower court may not alter the time limits for filing of the appeal notices.

(5) Where an appellant intends to apply to the Court of Appeal for an extension of time for serving or filing the appellant's notice he must give notice of that intention to the appropriate district judge (see sub-para. (6)) before the application is made.

(6) In this paragraph 'the appropriate district judge' means where the lower court is:
(a) a county court, the district judge of that court;
(b) a district registry, the district judge of that registry;
(c) the Principal Registry of the Family Division, the senior district judge of that division.

Appeal against order for revocation of patent

21.2 (1) This paragraph applies where an appeal lies to the Court of Appeal from an order for the revocation of a patent.

(2) The appellant must serve the appellant's notice on the Comptroller-General of Patents,

Designs and Trade Marks (the 'Comptroller') in addition to the persons to be served under r. 52.4(3) and in accordance with that rule.

(3) Where, before the appeal hearing, the respondent decides not to oppose the appeal or not to attend the appeal hearing, he must immediately serve notice of that decision on:
(a) the Comptroller; and
(b) the appellant

(4) Where the respondent serves a notice in accordance with sub-para. (3), he must also serve copies of the following documents on the Comptroller with that notice:
(a) the petition;
(b) any statements of claim;
(c) any written evidence filed in the claim.

(5) Within 14 days after receiving the notice in accordance with sub-para. (3), the Comptroller must serve on the appellant a notice stating whether or not he intends to attend the appeal hearing.

(6) The Comptroller may attend the appeal hearing and oppose the appeal:
(a) in any case where he has given notice under sub-para. (5) of his intention to attend; and
(b) in any other case (including, in particular, a case where the respondent withdraws his opposition to the appeal during the hearing) if the Court of Appeal so directs or permits.

Appeal from Patents Court on appeal from Comptroller

21.3 Where the appeal is from a decision of the Patents Court which was itself made on an appeal from a decision of the Comptroller-General of Patents, Designs and Trade Marks, the appellant must serve the appellant's notice on the Comptroller in addition to the persons to be served under r. 52.4(3) and in accordance with that rule.

Appeals in cases of contempt of court

21.4 In an appeal under the Administration of Justice Act 1960, s. 13 (appeals in cases of contempt of court), the appellant must serve the appellant's notice on the court from whose order or decision the appeal is brought in addition to the persons to be served under r. 52.4(3) and in accordance with that rule.

Appeals from Social Security or Child Support Commissioners

21.5 (1) This paragraph applies to appeals under the following provisions (appeals from the decision of a Social Security Commissioner or a Child Support Commissioner on a question of law):
(a) the Pensions Appeal Tribunals Act 1943, s. 6C;
(b) the Child Support Act 1991, s. 25;
(c) the Social Security Act 1998, s. 15;
(d) the Child Support, Pensions and Social Security Act 2000, sch. 7, para. 9.

(2) The appellant must file the appellant's notice within six weeks after the date on which the Commissioner's decision on permission to appeal to the Court of Appeal was given in writing to the appellant.

(3) In an appeal brought under the Child Support, Pensions and Social Security Act 2000, sch. 7, para. 9, by a party other than the Secretary of State, the appellant must serve the appellant's notice on the Secretary of State in addition to the persons to be served under r. 52.4(3) and in accordance with that rule.

(4) Where, after a Commissioner has given a decision, responsibility for the subject matter of the appeal has been transferred from a government department or the Commissioners of HM Revenue and Customs or a local authority ('the first body') to another such body ('the second body') and an appeal is brought by a party other than the second body:
(a) the second body shall be a respondent in place of the first body and the second body shall notify the court accordingly;
(b) if the appellant serves the appellant's notice or any other document on the first body, or if the court sends to the first body any communication in relation to the appeal, the first body shall forthwith send the notice, document or communication to the second body and the date on which the appellant's notice or other document was served on the first body shall be treated as the date on which it was served on the second body.

(5) This sub-paragraph applies where the appellant is the Secretary of State, the Commissioners of HM Revenue and Customs or a local authority. The appellant must serve the appellant's notice on any person appointed by the appellant to proceed with a claim, or an appeal arising out of a claim, in addition to the persons to be served under r. 52.4(3) and in accordance with that rule.

(Sub-paragraph (5) applies where the Secretary of State, the Commissioners of HM Revenue and Customs or a local authority is the appellant and that appellant appoints a person to proceed, in effect, on behalf of a respondent who is not himself able to proceed. An example is the Social Security (Claims and Payments) Regulations 1987 (SI 1987/1968), reg. 33, which authorises the Secretary of State to appoint a person to proceed with the claim of another person who is unable for the time being to act.)

Appeals from value added tax and duties tribunals

21.6 (1) An application to the Court of Appeal for permission to appeal from a value added tax and duties tribunal direct to that court must be made within 28 days after the date on which the tribunal certifies that its decision involves a point of law relating wholly or mainly to the construction of:

(a) an enactment or of a statutory instrument; or

(b) any of the Community treaties or any Community instrument,

which has been fully argued before and fully considered by it.

(2) The application must be made by the parties jointly filing at the Court of Appeal an appellant's notice that:

(a) contains a statement of the grounds for the application; and

(b) is accompanied by a copy of the decision to be appealed, endorsed with the certificate of the tribunal.

(3) The court will notify the appellant of its decision and:

(a) where permission to appeal to the Court of Appeal is given, the appellant must serve the appellant's notice on the chairman of the tribunal in addition to the persons to be served under r. 52.4(3) within 14 days after that notification.

(b) where permission to appeal to the Court of Appeal is refused, the period for appealing to the High Court is to be calculated from the date of the notification of that refusal.

Appeals from Immigration Appeal Tribunal

21.7 (1) This paragraph applies to appeals under the Nationality, Immigration and Asylum Act 2002, s. 103(1) (appeal on a point of law from a determination of the Immigration Appeal Tribunal).

(2) The appellant's notice must be filed at the Court of Appeal within 14 days after the appellant is served in accordance with the Immigration and Asylum Appeals (Procedure) Rules 2003 with written notice of the Tribunal's decision to grant or refuse permission to appeal.

(3) The appellant must serve the appellant's notice in accordance with CPR, r. 52.4(3) , on:

(a) the persons to be served under that rule; and

(b) the President of the Tribunal.

21.7A (1) This paragraph applies to appeals from the Asylum and Immigration Tribunal referred to the Court of Appeal under the Nationality, Immigration and Asylum Act 2002, s. 103C.

(2) On making an order referring an appeal to the Court of Appeal, the High Court shall send to the Court of Appeal copies of:

(a) that order and any other order made in relation to the application for reconsideration; and

(b) the application notice, written submissions and other documents filed under r. 54.29.

(3) Unless the court directs otherwise, the application notice filed under r. 54.29 shall be treated as the appellant's notice.

(4) The respondent may file a respondent's notice within 14 days after the date on which the respondent is served with the order of the High Court referring the appeal to the Court of Appeal.

(5) The Court of Appeal may give such additional directions as are appropriate.

Appeal from special commissioners

21.8 (1) An application to the Court of Appeal for permission to appeal from the special commissioners direct to that court under s. 56A of the Taxes Management Act 1970 must be made within 28 days after the date on which the special commissioners certify that their decision involves a point of law relating wholly or mainly to the construction of an enactment which has been fully argued before and fully considered before them.

(2) The application must be made by the parties jointly filing at the Court of Appeal an appellant's notice that:

(a) contains a statement of the grounds for the application; and

(b) is accompanied by a copy of the decision to be appealed, endorsed with the certificate of the tribunal.

(3) The court will notify the parties of its decision and:

(a) where permission to appeal to the Court of Appeal is given, the appellant must serve the appellant's notice on the Clerk to the Special Commissioners in addition to the persons to be served under r. 52.4(3) within 14 days after that notification.

(b) where permission to appeal to the Court of Appeal is refused, the period for appealing to the High Court is to be calculated from the date of the notification of that refusal.

Appeal from Lands Tribunal

21.9 The appellant must file the appellant's notice at the Court of Appeal within 28 days after the date of the decision of the tribunal.

Appeal from Competition Appeal Tribunal

21.10 (1) Where the appellant applies for permission to appeal at the hearing at which the decision is delivered by the tribunal and:

(a) permission is given; or

(b) permission is refused and the appellant wishes to make an application to the Court of Appeal for permission to appeal,

the appellant's notice must be filed at the Court of Appeal within 14 days after the date of that hearing.

(2) Where the appellant applies in writing to the registrar of the tribunal for permission to appeal and:

(a) permission is given; or

(b) permission is refused and the appellant wishes to make an application to the Court of Appeal for permission to appeal,

the appellant's notice must be filed at the Court of Appeal within 14 days after the date of receipt of the tribunal's decision on permission.

(3) Where the appellant does not make an application to the tribunal for permission to appeal, but wishes to make an application to the Court of Appeal for permission, the appellant's notice must be filed at the Court of Appeal within 14 days after the end of the period within which he may make a written application to the registrar of the tribunal.

Appeals relating to the application of Articles 81 and 82 of the EC Treaty and Chapters I and II of Part I of the Competition Act 1998

21.10A (1) This paragraph applies to any appeal to the Court of Appeal relating to the application of:

(a) art. 81 or art. 82 of the Treaty Establishing the European Community; or

(b) chapter I or chapter II of part I of the Competition Act 1998.

(2) In this paragraph:

(a) 'the Act' means the Competition Act 1998;

(b) 'the Commission' means the European Commission;

(c) 'the Competition Regulation' means Council Regulation (EC) No. 1/2003 of 16 December 2002 on the implementation of the rules on competition laid down in arts 81 and 82 of the Treaty;

(d) 'national competition authority' means:

(i) the Office of Fair Trading; and

(ii) any other person or body designated pursuant to art. 35 of the Competition Regulation as a national competition authority of the United Kingdom;

(e) 'the Treaty' means the Treaty Establishing the European Community.

(3) Any party whose appeal notice raises an issue relating to the application of art. 81 or 82 of the Treaty, or chapter I or II of part I of the Act, must:
(a) state that fact in his appeal notice; and
(b) serve a copy of the appeal notice on the Office of Fair Trading at the same time as it is served on the other party to the appeal (addressed to the Director of Competition Policy Coordination, Office of Fair Trading, Fleetbank House, 2–6 Salisbury Square, London EC4Y 8JX).

(4) Attention is drawn to the provisions of the Competition Regulation, art. 15.3, which entitles competition authorities and the Commission to submit written observations to national courts on issues relating to the application of art. 81 or 82 of the Treaty and, with the permission of the court in question, to submit oral observations to the court.

(5) A national competition authority may also make written observations to the Court of Appeal, or apply for permission to make oral observations, on issues relating to the application of chapter I or II of part I of the Act.

(6) If a national competition authority or the Commission intends to make written observations to the Court of Appeal, it must give notice of its intention to do so by letter to the Civil Appeals Office at the earliest opportunity.

(7) An application by a national competition authority or the Commission for permission to make oral representations at the hearing of an appeal must be made by letter to the Civil Appeals Office at the earliest opportunity, identifying the appeal and indicating why the applicant wishes to make oral representations.

(8) If a national competition authority or the Commission files a notice under sub-paragraph (6) or an application under sub-paragraph (7), it must at the same time serve a copy of the notice or application on every party to the appeal.

(9) Any request by a national competition authority or the Commission for the court to send it any documents relating to an appeal should be made at the same time as filing a notice under sub-paragraph (6) or an application under sub-paragraph (7).

(10) When the Court of Appeal receives a notice under sub-paragraph (6) it may give case management directions to the national competition authority or the Commission, including directions about the date by which any written observations are to be filed.

(11) The Court of Appeal will serve on every party to the appeal a copy of any directions given or order made:
(a) on an application under sub-paragraph (7); or
(b) under sub-paragraph (10).

(12) Every party to an appeal which raises an issue relating to the application of art. 81 or 82 of the Treaty, and any national competition authority which has been served with a copy of a party's appeal notice, is under a duty to notify the Court of Appeal at any stage of the appeal if they are aware that:
(a) the Commission has adopted, or is contemplating adopting, a decision in relation to proceedings which it has initiated; and
(b) the decision referred to in (a) above has or would have legal effects in relation to the particular agreement, decision or practice in issue before the court.

(13) Where the Court of Appeal is aware that the Commission is contemplating adopting a decision as mentioned in sub-paragraph (12)(a), it shall consider whether to stay the appeal pending the Commission's decision.

(14) Where any judgment is given which decides on the application of art. 81 or 82, the court shall direct that a copy of the transcript of the judgment shall be sent to the Commission.
Judgments may be sent to the Commission electronically to comp-amicus@cec.eu.int or by post to the European Commission — DG Competition, B-1049, Brussels.

Appeal from Proscribed Organisations Appeal Commission

21.11 (1) The appellant's notice must be filed at the Court of Appeal within 14 days after the date when the Proscribed Organisations Appeal Commission:
(a) granted; or
(b) where the Terrorism Act 2000, s. 6(2)(b), applies, refused
permission to appeal.

Appeals to the High Court — Queen's Bench Division

22.1 The following appeals are to be heard in the Queen's Bench Division.

Statutory appeals

Appeals under the Merchant Shipping Act 1995

22.2 (1) This paragraph applies to appeals under the Merchant Shipping Act 1995 and for this purpose a rehearing and an application under s. 61 of the Merchant Shipping Act 1995 are treated as appeals.

(2) The appellant must file any report to the Secretary of State containing the decision from which the appeal is brought with the appellant's notice.

(3) Where a rehearing by the High Court is ordered under ss. 64 or 269 of the Merchant Shipping Act 1995, the Secretary of State must give reasonable notice to the parties whom he considers to be affected by the rehearing.

Appeal where court's decision is final

22.3 (1) This paragraph applies to an appeal to the High Court under:

(a) the Architects Act 1997, s. 22;
(b) the Medicines Act 1968, s. 82(3) and 83(2);
(c) the Nurses, Midwives and Health Visitors Act 1997, s. 12;
(cc) the Nursing and Midwifery Order 2001 (SI 2002/253), art. 38;
(d) the Pharmacy Act 1954, s. 10;
(e) the Medical Act 1983, s. 40;
(f) the Dentists Act 1984, s. 29 or s. 44;
(g) the Opticians Act 1989, s. 23;
(h) the Osteopaths Act 1993, s. 31; and
(i) the Chiropractors Act 1994, s. 31.

(2) Every appeal to which this paragraph applies must be supported by written evidence and, if the court so orders, oral evidence and will be by way of rehearing.

(3) The appellant must file the appellant's notice within 28 days after the decision that the appellant wishes to appeal.

(4) In the case of an appeal under an enactment specified in column 1 of the following table, the persons to be made respondents are the persons specified in relation to that enactment in column 2 of the table and the person to be served with the appellant's notice is the person so specified in column 3.

1 Enactment	2 Respondent	3 Person to be served
Architects Act 1997, s. 22	The Architects' Registration Council of the United Kingdom	The Registrar of the Council
Chiropractors Act 1994, s. 31	The General Chiropractic Council	The Registrar of the Council
Dentists Act 1984, s. 29 or s. 44	The General Dental Council	The Registrar of the Council
Medical Act 1983, s. 40	The General Medical Council	The Registrar of the Council
Medicines Act 1968, s. 82(3) and s. 83(2)	The Pharmaceutical Society of Great Britain	The Registrar of the Society
Nurses, Midwives and Health Visitors Act 1997, s. 12; Nursing and Midwifery Order 2001 (SI 2002/253), art. 38	The United Kingdom Central Council for Nursing, Midwifery and Health Visiting	The Registrar of the Council
Opticians Act 1989, s. 23	The General Optical Council	The Registrar of the Council
Osteopaths Act 1993, s. 31	The General Osteopathic Council	The Registrar of the Council
Pharmacy Act 1954, s. 10	The Pharmaceutical Society of Great Britain	The Registrar of the Society

Consumer Credit Act 1974: appeal from Secretary of State

22.4 (1) A person dissatisfied in point of law with a decision of the Secretary of State on an appeal under s. 41 of the Consumer Credit Act 1974 from a determination of the Office of Fair Trading who had a right to appeal to the Secretary of State, whether or not he exercised that right, may appeal to the High Court.

(2) The appellant must serve the appellant's notice on:

(a) the Secretary of State;

(b) the original applicant if any, where the appeal is by a licensee under a group licence against compulsory variation, suspension or revocation of that licence; and

(c) any other person as directed by the court.

(3) The appeal court may remit the matter to the Secretary of State to the extent necessary to enable him to provide the court with such further information as the court may direct

(4) If the appeal court allows the appeal, it shall not set aside or vary the decision but shall remit the matter to the Secretary of State with the opinion of the court for hearing and determination by him.

The Pensions Appeal Tribunals Act 1943

22.5 (1) In this paragraph 'the judge' means the judge nominated by the Lord Chancellor under s. 6(2) of the Pensions Appeal Tribunals Act 1943 ('the Act').

(2) An application to the judge for permission to appeal against a decision of a Pensions Appeal Tribunal:

(a) may not be made unless an application was made to the tribunal and was refused; and

(b) must be made within 28 days after the date of the tribunal's refusal.

(3) The appellant's notice seeking permission to appeal from the judge must contain:

(a) the point of law as respects which the appellant alleges that the tribunal's decision was wrong; and

(b) the date of the tribunal's decision refusing permission to appeal.

(4) The court officer shall request the chairman of the tribunal to give the judge a written statement of the reasons for the tribunal's decision to refuse permission to appeal, and within seven days after receiving the request, the chairman must give the judge such a statement.

(5) Where permission to appeal was given by:

(a) the tribunal, the appellant must file and serve the appellant's notice;

(b) the judge, the appellant must serve the appellant's notice,

within 28 days after permission to appeal was given.

(6) Within 28 days after service of the notice of appeal on him, the chairman of the tribunal must:

(a) state a case selling out the facts on which the decision appealed against was based;

(b) file the case stated at the court; and

(c) serve a copy of the case stated on the appellant and the respondent.

(7) A copy of the judge's order on the appeal must be sent by the court officer to the appellant, the respondent and the chairman of the tribunal.

The Social Security Administration Act 1992

22.6 (1) Any person who by virtue of s. 18 or 58(8) of the Social Security Administration Act 1992 ('the Act') is entitled and wishes to appeal against a decision of the Secretary of State on a question of law must within the prescribed period, or within such further time as the Secretary of State may allow, serve on the Secretary of State a notice requiring him to state a case setting out:

(a) his decision; and

(b) the facts on which his decision was based.

(2) Unless paragraph (3) applies the prescribed period is 28 days after receipt of the notice of the decision.

(3) Where, within 28 days after receipt of notice of the decision, a request is made to the Secretary of State in accordance with regulations made under the Act to furnish a statement of the grounds of the decision, the prescribed period is 28 days after receipt of that statement.

(4) Where under s. 18 or s. 58(8) of the Act the Secretary of State refers a question of law to the court, he must state that question together with the relevant facts in a case.

(5) The appellant's notice and the case stated must be filed at the appeal court and a copy of the notice and the case stated served on:
(a) the Secretary of State; and
(b) every person as between whom and the Secretary of State the question has arisen,
within 28 days after the case stated was served on the party at whose request, or as a result of whose application to the court, the case was stated.
(6) Unless the appeal court otherwise orders, the appeal or reference shall not be heard sooner than 28 days after service of the appellant's notice.
(7) The appeal court may order the case stated by the Secretary of State to be returned to the Secretary of State for him to hear further evidence.

Appeals under the Extradition Act 2003

22.6A (1) In this paragraph, 'the Act' means the Extradition Act 2003.
(2) Appeals to the High Court under the Act must be brought in the Administrative Court of the Queen's Bench Division.
(3) Where an appeal is brought under section 26 or 28 of the Act:
(a) the appellant's notice must be filed and served before the expiry of seven days, starting with the day on which the order is made;
(b) the appellant must endorse the appellant's notice with the date of the person's arrest;
(c) the High Court must begin to hear the substantive appeal within 40 days of the person's arrest; and
(d) the appellant must serve a copy of the appellant's notice on the Crown Prosecution Service, if they are not a party to the appeal, in addition to the persons to be served under rule 52.4(3) and in accordance with that rule.
(4) The High Court may extend the period of 40 days under paragraph (3)(c) if it believes it to be in the interests of justice to do so.
(5) Where an appeal is brought under section 103 of the Act, the appellant's notice must be filed and served before the expiry of 14 days, starting with the day on which the Secretary of State informs the person under section 100(1) or (4) of the Act of the order he has made in respect of the person.
(6) Where an appeal is brought under section 105 of the Act, the appellant's notice must be filed and served before the expiry of 14 days, starting with the day on which the order for discharge is made.
(7) Where an appeal is brought under section 108 of the Act the appellant's notice must be filed and served before the expiry of 14 days, starting with the day on which the Secretary of State informs the person that he has ordered his extradition.
(8) Where an appeal is brought under section 110 of the Act the appellant's notice must be filed and served before the expiry of 14 days, starting with the day on which the Secretary of State informs the person acting on behalf of a category 2 territory, as defined in section 69 of the Act, of the order for discharge.
(Section 69 of the Act provides that a category 2 territory is that designated for the purposes of Part 2 of the Act.)
(9) Subject to paragraph (10), where an appeal is brought under section 103, 105, 108 or 110 of the Act, the High Court must begin to hear the substantive appeal within 76 days of the appellant's notice being filed.
(10) Where an appeal is brought under section 103 of the Act before the Secretary of State has decided whether the person is to be extradited:
(a) the period of 76 days does not start until the day on which the Secretary of State informs the person of his decision; and
(b) the Secretary of State must, as soon as practicable after he informs the person of his decision, inform the High Court:
(i) of his decision; and
(ii) of the date on which he informs the person of his decision.
(11) The High Court may extend the period of 76 days if it believes it to be in the interests of justice to do so.
(12) Where an appeal is brought under section 103, 105, 108 or 110 of the Act, the appellant must serve a copy of the appellant's notice on:
(a) the Crown Prosecution Service; and

(b) the Home Office,

if they are not a party to the appeal, in addition to the persons to be served under rule 52.4(3) and in accordance with that rule.

Appeals under section 49 of the Solicitors Act 1974

22.6B (1) This paragraph applies to appeals from the Solicitors Disciplinary Tribunal ('the Tribunal') to the High Court under the Solicitors Act 1974 ('the Act'), s. 49(1)(b). The procedure for appeals to the Master of the Rolls under s. 49(1)(a) of the Act is set out in the Master of the Rolls (Appeals and Applications) Regulations 2001.

(2) Appeals to the High Court under s. 49(1)(b) of the Act must be brought in the Administrative Court of the Queen's Bench Division.

(3) The appellant's notice:

(a) must state in the heading that the appeal relates to a solicitor, or a solicitor's clerk, and is made under s. 49 of the Act;

(b) must be filed within 14 days after the date on which the Tribunal's statement of its findings was filed with the Law Society in accordance with s. 48(1) of the Act; and

(c) must be accompanied by copies of the order appealed against and the statement of the Tribunal's findings required by s. 48(1) of the Act; and

(d) unless the court orders otherwise, must be served by the appellant on:

(i) every party to the proceedings before the Tribunal; and

(ii) the Law Society.

(4) The court:

(a) may order an appellant to give security for the costs of an appeal only if he was the applicant in the proceedings before the Tribunal; and

(b) may not order any other party to give security for costs.

(5) The court may direct the Tribunal to provide it with a written statement of their opinion on the case, or on any question arising in it. If the court gives such a direction, the clerk to the Tribunal must as soon as possible:

(a) file the statement; and

(b) serve a copy on each party to the appeal.

(6) The court may give permission for any person to intervene to be heard in opposition to the appeal.

(7) An appellant may at any time discontinue his appeal by:

(a) serving notice of discontinuance on the clerk to the Tribunal and every other party to the appeal; and

(b) filing a copy of the notice.

(8) Unless the court orders otherwise, an appellant who discontinues is liable for the costs of every other party to the appeal.

Appeals by way of case stated

Reference of question of law by Agricultural Land Tribunal

22.7 (1) A question of law referred to the High Court by an Agricultural Land Tribunal under s. 6 of the Agriculture (Miscellaneous Provisions) Act 1954 shall be referred by way of case stated by the tribunal.

(2) Where the proceedings before the tribunal arose on an application under s. 11 of the Agricultural Holdings Act 1986, an:

(a) application notice for an order under s. 6 that the tribunal refers a question of law to the court; and

(b) appellant's notice by which an appellant seeks the courts determination on a question of law,

must be served on the authority having power to enforce the statutory requirement specified in the notice in addition to every other party to those proceedings and on the secretary of the tribunal.

(3) Where, in accordance with paragraph (2), a notice is served on the authority mentioned in that paragraph, that authority may attend the appeal hearing and make representations to the court.

Case stated by Mental Health Review Tribunal

22.8 (1) In this paragraph 'the Act' means the Mental Health Act 1983 and 'party to proceedings' means:

(a) the person who initiated the proceedings; and

(b) any person to whom, in accordance with rules made under s. 78 of the Act, the tribunal sent notice of the application or reference or a request instead notice of reference.

(2) A party to proceedings shall not be entitled to apply to the High Court for an order under s. 78(8) of the Act directing the tribunal to state a case for determination by court unless:

(a) within 21 days after the decision of the tribunal was communicated to him in accordance with rules made under s. 78 of the Act he made a written request to the tribunal to state a case; and

(b) either the tribunal:

(i) failed to comply with that request within 21 days after it was made; or

(ii) refused to comply with it.

(3) The period for filing the application notice for an order under s. 78(8) of the Act is:

(a) where the tribunal failed to comply with the applicant's request to state a case within the period mentioned in sub-para. (2)(b)(i), 14 days after the expiration of that period;

(b) where the tribunal refused that request, 14 days after receipt by the applicant of notice of the refusal of his request.

(4) A Mental Health Review Tribunal by whom a case is stated shall be entitled to attend the proceedings for the determination of the case and make representations to the court.

(5) If the court allows the appeal, it may give any direction which the tribunal ought to have given under Part V of the Act.

Appeals to the High Court — Chancery Division

23.1 The following appeals are to be heard in the Chancery Division

Determination of appeal or case stated under various Acts

23.2 Any appeal to the High Court, and any case stated or question referred for the opinion of that court under any of the following enactments shall be heard in the Chancery Division:

(1) the Law of Property Act 1922, sch. 15, para. 16;

(2) the Industrial Assurance Act 1923;

(3) the Land Registration Act 1925;

(4) the Water Resources Act 1991, s. 205(4);

(5) the Clergy Pensions Measure 1961, s. 38(3);

(6) the Industrial and Provident Societies Act 1965;

(7) the Pension Schemes Act 1993, s. 151;

(8) the Pension Schemes Act 1993, s. 173;

(9) the Pensions Act 1995, s. 97;

(10) the Charities Act 1993;

(11) the Stamp Act 1891, ss. 13 and 13B;

(12) the Income and Corporation Taxes Act 1988, s. 705A;

(13) the General Commissioners (Jurisdiction and Procedure) Regulations 1994, reg. 22;

(14) the Taxes Management Act 1970, ss. 53, 56A or 100C(4);

(15) the Inheritance Tax Act 1984, ss. 222(3), 225, 249(3) or 251;

(16) the Stamp Duty Reserve Tax Regulations 1986, regs 8(3) or 10;

(17) the Land Registration Act 2002;

(18) the European Public Limited-Liability Company Regulations 2004 (SI 2004/2326), reg. 74.

(This list is not exhaustive.)

Statutory appeals

Appeal under s. 222 of the Inheritance Tax Act 1984

23.3 (1) This paragraph applies to appeals to the High Court under s. 222(3) of the Inheritance Tax

Act 1984 (the '1984 Act') and reg. 8(3) of the Stamp Duty Reserve Tax Regulations 1986 (the '1986 Regulations').

(2) The appellant's notice must:

(a) state the date on which the Commissioners of HM Revenue and Customs (the 'Board') gave notice to the appellant under s. 221 of the 1984 Act or reg. 6 of the 1986 Regulations of the determination that is the subject of the appeal;

(b) state the date on which the appellant gave to the Board notice of appeal under s. 222(1) of the 1984 Act or reg. 8(1) of the 1986 Regulations and, if notice was not given within the time permitted, whether the Board or the Special Commissioners have given their consent to the appeal being brought out of time, and, if they have, the date they gave their consent; and

(c) either state that the appellant and the Board have agreed that the appeal may be to the High Court or contain an application for permission to appeal to the High Court.

(3) The appellant must file the, following documents with the appellant's notice:

(a) two copies of the notice referred to in sub-para. 2(a);

(b) two copies of the notice of appeal (under s. 222(1) of the 1984 Act or reg. 8(1) of the 1986 Regulations) referred to in sub-para. 2(b); and

(c) where the appellant's notice contains an application for permission to appeal, written evidence setting out the grounds on which it is alleged that the matters to be decided on the appeal are likely to be substantially confined to questions of law.

(4) The appellant must:

(a) file the appellant's notice at the court; and

(b) serve the appellant's notice on the Board,

within 30 days of the date on which the appellant gave to the Board notice of appeal under s. 222(1) of the 1984 Act or reg. 8(1) of the 1986 Regulations or, if the Board or the Special Commissioners have given consent to the appeal being brought out of time, within 30 days of the date on which such consent was given.

(5) The court will set a date for the hearing of not less than 40 days from the date that the appellant's notice was filed.

(6) Where the appellant's notice contains an application for permission to appeal:

(a) a copy of the written evidence filed in accordance with para. (3)(c) must be served on the Board with the appellant's notice; and

(b) the Board:

(i) may file written evidence; and

(ii) if it does so, must serve a copy of that evidence on the appellant,

within 30 days after service of the written evidence under para. (6)(a).

(7) The appellant may not rely on any grounds of appeal not specified in the notice referred to in para. (2)(b) on the hearing of the appeal without the permission of the court.

Appeals under s. 53 and 100C(4) of the Taxes Management Act 1970 and s. 249(3) or 251 of the Inheritance Tax Act 1984

23.4 (1) The appellant must serve the appellant's notice on:

(a) the General or Special Commissioners against whose decision, award or determination the appeal is brought; and

(b) (i) in the case of an appeal brought under s. 100C(4) of the Taxes Management Act 1970 or s. 249(3) of the Inheritance Tax Act 1984 by any party other than the defendant in the proceedings before the Commissioners, that defendant; or

(ii) in any other case, the Commissioners of Inland Revenue.

(2) The appellant must file the appellant's notice at the court within 30 days after the date of the decision, award or determination against which the appeal is brought.

(3) Within 30 days of the service on them of the appellant's notice, the general or special commissioners, as the case may be, must:

(a) file two copies of a note of their findings and of the reasons for their decision, award or determination at the court; and

(b) serve a copy of the note on every other party to the appeal.

(4) Any document to be served on the general or special commissioners may be served by delivering or sending it to their clerk.

Appeals under s. 56A of the Taxes Management Act 1970, s. 225 of the Inheritance Tax Act 1984 and reg. 10 of the Stamp Duty Reserve Tax Regulations 1986

23.5 (1) The appellant must file the appellant's notice:
(a) where the appeal is made following the refusal of the special commissioners to issue a certificate under s. 56A(2)(b) of the Taxes Management Act 1970, within 28 days from the date of the release of the decision of the special commissioners containing the refusal;
(b) where the appeal is made following the refusal of permission to appeal to the Court of Appeal under s. 56A(2)(c) of that Act, within 28 days from the date when permission is refused; or
(c) in all other cases within 56 days after the date of the decision or determination that the appellant wishes to appeal.

Appeal under s. 17 of the Industrial Assurance Act 1923

23.6 The appellant must file the appellant's notice within 21 days after the date of the Commissioner's refusal or direction under s. 17(3) of the Industrial Assurance Act 1923.

Appeals affecting industrial and provident societies etc.

23.7 (1) This paragraph applies to all appeals under:
(a) the Friendly Societies Act 1974;
(b) the Friendly Societies Act 1992;
(c) the Industrial Assurance Act 1923; and
(d) the Industrial and Provident Societies Act 1965.
(2) At any stage on an appeal, the court may:
(a) direct that the appellant's notice be served on any person;
(b) direct that notice be given by advertisement or otherwise of:
(i) the bringing of the appeal;
(ii) the nature of the appeal; and
(iii) the time when the appeal will or is likely to be heard; or
(c) give such other directions as it thinks proper to enable any person interested in:
(i) the society, trade union, alleged trade union or industrial assurance company; or
(ii) the subject matter of the appeal,
to appear and be heard at the appeal hearing.

Appeal from value added tax and duties tribunal

23.8 (1) A party to proceedings before a value added tax and duties tribunal who is dissatisfied in point of law with a decision of the tribunal may appeal under s. 11(1) of the Tribunals and Inquiries Act 1992 to the High Court.
(2) The appellant must file the appellant's notice:
(a) where the appeal is made following the refusal of the value added tax and duties tribunal to grant a certificate under art. 2(b) of the Value Added Tax and Duties Tribunal Appeals Order 1986, within 28 days from the date of the release of the decision containing the refusal;
(b) in all other cases within 56 days after the date of the decision or determination that the appellant wishes to appeal.

Appeal against an order or decision of the Charity Commissioners

23.8A (1) In this paragraph:
'the Act' means the Charities Act 1993; and
'the Commissioners' means the Charity Commissioners for England and Wales.
(2) The Attorney-General, unless he is the appellant, must be made a respondent to the appeal.
(3) The appellant's notice must state the grounds of the appeal, and the appellant may not rely on any other grounds without the permission of the court.
(4) Sub-paragraphs (5) and (6) apply, in addition to the above provisions, where the appeal is made under s. 16(12) of the Act.
(5) If the Commissioners have granted a certificate that it is a proper case for an appeal, a copy of the certificate must be filed with the appellant's notice.
(6) If the appellant applies in the appellant's notice for permission to appeal under s. 16(13) of the Act:

(a) the appellant's notice must state:
   (i) that the appellant has requested the Commissioners to grant a certificate that it is a proper case for an appeal, and they have refused to do so,
   (ii) the date of such refusal;
   (iii) the grounds on which the appellant alleges that it is a proper case for an appeal; and
   (iv) if the application for permission to appeal is made with the consent of any other party to the proposed appeal, that fact;
(b) if the Commissioners have given reasons for refusing a certificate, a copy of the reasons must be attached to the appellant's notice;
(c) the court may, before determining the application, direct the Commissioners to file a written statement of their reasons for refusing a certificate;
(d) the court will serve on the appellant a copy of any statement filed under sub-paragraph (c).

Appeal against a decision of the adjudicator under the Land Registration Act 2002, s. 111

23.8B (1) A person who is aggrieved by a decision of the adjudicator and who wishes to appeal that decision must obtain permission to appeal.

(2) The appellant must serve on the adjudicator a copy of the appeal court's decision on a request for permission to appeal as soon as reasonably practicable and in any event within 14 days of receipt by the appellant of the decision on permission.

(3) The appellant must serve on the adjudicator and the Chief Land Registrar a copy of any order by the appeal court to stay a decision of the adjudicator pending the outcome of the appeal as soon as reasonably practicable and in any event within 14 days of receipt by the appellant of the appeal court's order to stay.

(4) The appellant must serve on the adjudicator and the Chief Land Registrar a copy of the appeal court's decision on the appeal as soon as reasonably practicable and in any event within 14 days of receipt by the appellant of the appeal court's decision.

Appeals under regulation 74 of the European Public Limited-Liability Company Regulations 2004

23.8C (1) In this paragraph:
(a) 'the 2004 Regulations' means the European Public Limited-Liability Company Regulations 2004 (SI 2004/2326);
(b) 'the EC Regulation' means Council Regulation (EC) No. 2157/2001 of 8 October 2001 on the Statute for a European company (SE);
(c) 'SE' means a European public limited-liability company (societas europaea) within the meaning of art. 1 of the EC Regulation.

(2) This paragraph applies to appeals under reg. 74 of the 2004 Regulations against the opposition:
(a) of the Secretary of State or national financial supervisory authority to the transfer of the registered office of an SE under art. 8(14) of the EC Regulation; and
(b) of the Secretary of State to the participation by a company in the formation of an SE by merger under art. 19 of the EC Regulation.

(3) Where an SE seeks to appeal against the opposition of the national financial supervisory authority to the transfer of its registered office under art. 8(14) of the EC Regulation, it must serve the appellant's notice on both the national financial supervisory authority and the Secretary of State.

(4) The appellant's notice must contain an application for permission to appeal.

(5) The appeal will be a review of the decision of the Secretary of State and not a rehearing. The grounds of review are set out in reg. 74(2) of the 2004 Regulations.

(6) The appeal will be heard by a High Court judge.

Appeals by way of case stated

Proceedings under the Commons Registration Act 1965

23.9 A person aggrieved by the decision of a Commons Commissioner who requires the Commissioner to state a case for the opinion of the High Court under s. 18 of the Commons Registration Act 1965 must file the appellant's notice within 42 days from the date on which notice of the decision was sent to the aggrieved person.

Appeals to a County Court

Local Government (Miscellaneous Provisions) Act 1976

para.24.2 **71.56**

24.1 Where one of the grounds upon which an appeal against a notice under ss. 21, 23 or 35 of the Local Government (Miscellaneous Provisions) Act 1976 is brought is that:
(a) it would have been fairer to serve the notice on another person; or
(b) that it would be reasonable for the whole or part of the expenses to which the appeal relates to be paid by some other person,
that person must be made a respondent to the appeal, unless the court, on application of the appellant made without notice, otherwise directs.

Appeals under sections 204 and 204A of the Housing Act 1996

para.24.2 **71.56**

24.2 (1) An appellant should include appeals under s. 204 and s. 204A of the Housing Act 1996 in one appellant's notice.
(2) If it is not possible to do so (for example because an urgent application under s. 204A is required) the appeals may be included in separate appellant's notices.
(3) An appeal under s. 204A may include an application for an order under s. 204A(4)(a) requiring the authority to secure that accommodation is available for the applicant's occupation.
(4) If, exceptionally, the court makes an order under s. 204A(4)(a) without notice, the appellant's notice must be served on the authority together with the order. Such an order will normally require the authority to secure that accommodation is available until a hearing date when the authority can make representations as to whether the order under s. 204A(4)(a) should be continued.

Appeal under part II of the Immigration and Asylum Act 1999 (carriers' liability)

24.3 (1) A person appealing to a county court under s. 35A or s. 40B of the Immigration and Asylum Act 1999 ('the Act') against a decision by the Secretary of State to impose a penalty under s. 32 or a charge under s. 40 of the Act must, subject to sub-paragraph (2), file the appellant's notice within 28 days after receiving the penalty notice or charge notice.
(2) Where the appellant has given notice of objection to the Secretary of State under s. 35(4) or s. 40A(3) of the Act within the time prescribed for doing so, he must file the appellant's notice within 28 days after receiving notice of the Secretary of State's decision in response to the notice of objection.
(3) Sections 35A and 40B of the Act provide that any appeal under those sections shall be a rehearing of the Secretary of State's decision to impose a penalty or charge, and therefore r. 52.11(1) does not apply.

SECTION IV — PROVISIONS ABOUT REOPENING APPEALS

Reopening of Final Appeals

para.25.2 **71.51** para.25.3–25.6 **71.52**

25.1 This paragraph applies to applications under r. 52.17 for permission to reopen a final determination of an appeal.
25.2 In this paragraph, 'appeal' includes an application for permission to appeal.
25.3 Permission must be sought from the court whose decision the applicant wishes to reopen.
25.4 The application for permission must be made by application notice and supported by written evidence, verified by a statement of truth.
25.5 A copy of the application for permission must not be served on any other party to the original appeal unless the court so directs.
25.6 Where the court directs that the application for permission is to be served on another party, that party may within 14 days of the service on him of the copy of the application file and serve a written statement either supporting or opposing the application.
25.7 The application for permission, and any written statements supporting or opposing it, will be considered on paper by a single judge, and will be allowed to proceed only if the judge so directs.

CPR Part 53 Defamation Claims

53.1 Scope of This Part

This Part contains rules about defamation claims.

53.2 Summary Disposal under the Defamation Act 1996

(1) This rule provides for summary disposal in accordance with the Defamation Act 1996 ('the Act').
(2) In proceedings for summary disposal under sections 8 and 9 of the Act, rules 24.4 (procedure), 24.5 (evidence) and 24.6 (directions) apply.
(3) An application for summary judgment under Part 24 may not be made if—
  (a) an application has been made for summary disposal in accordance with the Act, and that application has not been disposed of; or
  (b) summary relief has been granted on an application for summary disposal under the Act.
(4) The court may on any application for summary disposal direct the defendant to elect whether or not to make an offer to make amends under section 2 of the Act.
(5) When it makes a direction under paragraph (4), the court will specify the time by which and the manner in which—
  (a) the election is to be made; and
  (b) notification of it is to be given to the court and the other parties.

53.3 Sources of Information

Unless the court orders otherwise, a party will not be required to provide further information about the identity of the defendant's sources of information.

(Part 18 provides for requests for further information)

PD 53 Practice Direction — Defamation Claims

This practice direction supplements CPR Part 53

[For commentary on a specific paragraph, please refer to the cross-references after the title of the paragraph.]

General

1 This practice direction applies to defamation claims.

Statements of Case

para.2 **24.6, 26.17**

2.1 Statements of case should be confined to the information necessary to inform the other party of the nature of the case he has to meet. Such information should be set out concisely and in a manner proportionate to the subject matter of the claim.

2.2 (1) In a claim for libel the publication the subject of the claim must be identified in the claim form.

(2) In a claim for slander the claim form must so far as possible contain the words complained of, and identify the person to whom they were spoken and when.

2.3 (1) The claimant must specify in the particulars of claim the defamatory meaning which he alleges that the words or matters complained of conveyed, both:

(a) as to their natural and ordinary meaning; and

(b) as to any innuendo meaning (that is a meaning alleged to be conveyed to some person by reason of knowing facts extraneous to the words complained of).

(2) In the case of an innuendo meaning, the claimant must also identify the relevant extraneous facts.

2.4 In a claim for slander the precise words used and the names of the persons to whom they were spoken and when must, so far as possible, be set out in the particulars of claim, if not already contained in the claim form.

2.5 Where a defendant alleges that the words complained of are true he must:

(1) specify the defamatory meanings he seeks to justify; and

(2) give details of the matters on which he relies in support of that allegation.

2.6 Where a defendant alleges that the words complained of are fair comment on a matter of public interest he must:

(1) specify the defamatory meaning he seeks to defend as fair comment on a matter of public interest; and

(2) give details of the matters on which he relies in support of that allegation.

2.7 Where a defendant alleges that the words complained of were published on a privileged occasion he must specify the circumstances he relies on in support of that contention.

2.8 Where a defendant alleges that the words complained of are true, or are fair comment on a matter of public interest, the claimant must serve a reply specifically admitting or denying the allegation and giving the facts on which he relies.

2.9 If the defendant contends that any of the words or matters are fair comment on a matter of public interest, or were published on a privileged occasion, and the claimant intends to allege that the defendant acted with malice, the claimant must serve a reply giving details of the facts or matters relied on.

2.10 (1) A claimant must give full details of the facts and matters on which he relies in support of his claim for damages.

(2) Where a claimant seeks aggravated or exemplary damages he must provide the information specified in r. 16.4(1)(c).

2.11 A defendant who relies on an offer to make amends under s. 2 of the Defamation Act 1996, as his defence must:

(1) state in his defence:

(a) that he is relying on the offer in accordance with s. 4(2) of the Defamation Act 1996; and

(b) that it has not been withdrawn by him or been accepted, and
(2) attach a copy of the offer he made with his defence.

Court's Powers in Connection with an Offer of Amends

3.1 Sections 2 to 4 of the Defamation Act 1996 make provision for a person who has made a statement which is alleged to be defamatory to make an offer to make amends. Section 3 provides for the court to assist in the process of making amends.

3.2 A claim under s. 3 of the Defamation Act 1996 made other than in existing proceedings may be made under CPR Part 8:
(1) where the parties agree on the steps to make amends, and the sole purpose of the claim is for the court to make an order under s. 3(3) for an order that the offer be fulfilled; or
(2) where the parties do not agree:
(a) on the steps to be taken by way of correction, apology and publication (see s. 3(4));
(b) on the amount to be paid by way of compensation (see s. 3(5)); or
(c) on the amount to be paid by way of costs (see s. 3(6)).

(Applications in existing proceedings made under s. 3 of the Defamation Act 1996 must be made in accordance with CPR Part 23.)

3.3 (1) A claim or application under s. 3 of the Defamation Act 1996 must be supported by written evidence.
(2) The evidence referred to in para. (1) must include:
(a) a copy of the offer of amends;
(b) details of the steps taken to fulfil the offer of amends;
(c) a copy of the text of any correction and apology;
(d) details of the publication of the correction and apology;
(e) a statement of the amount of any sum paid as compensation;
(f) a statement of the amount of any sum paid for costs;
(g) why the offer is unsatisfactory.
(3) Where any step specified in s. 2(4) of the Defamation Act 1996 has not been taken, then the evidence referred to in sub-para. (2)(c) to (f) must state what steps are proposed by the party to fulfil the offer of amends and the date or dates on which each step will be fulfilled and, if none, that no proposal has been made to take that step.

Ruling on Meaning

4.1 At any time the court may decide:
(1) whether a statement complained of is capable of having any meaning attributed to it in a statement of case;
(2) whether the statement is capable of being defamatory of the claimant;
(3) whether the statement is capable of bearing any other meaning defamatory of the claimant.

4.2 An application for a ruling on meaning may be made at any time after the service of particulars of claim. Such an application should be made promptly.

(This provision disapplies for these applications the usual time restriction on making applications in r. 24.4(1).)

4.3 Where an application is made for a ruling on meaning, the application notice must state that it is an application for a ruling on meaning made in accordance with this practice direction.

4.4 The application notice or the evidence contained or referred to in it, or served with it, must identify precisely the statement, and the meaning attributed to it, that the court is being asked to consider.

(Rule 3.3 applies where the court exercises its powers of its own initiative.)
(Following a ruling on meaning the court may exercise its power under r. 3.4.)
(Section 7 of the Defamation Act 1996 applies to rulings on meaning.)

Summary Disposal

5.1 Where an application is made for summary disposal, the application notice must state:
(1) that it is an application for summary disposal made in accordance with s. 8 of the Defamation Act 1996.

(2) the matters set out in para. 2(3) of PD 24; and
(3) whether or not the defendant has made an offer to make amends under s. 2 of the Act and whether or not it has been withdrawn.

5.2 An application for summary disposal may be made at any time after the service of particulars of claim.

(This provision disapplies for these applications the usual time restriction on making applications in r. 24.4(1).)

5.3 (1) This paragraph applies where:
(a) the court has ordered the defendant in defamation proceedings to agree and publish a correction and apology as summary relief under s. 8(2) of the Defamation Act 1996; and
(b) the parties are unable to agree its content within the time specified in the order.
(2) Where the court grants this type of summary relief under the Act, the order will specify the date by which the parties should reach agreement about the content, time, manner, form and place of publication of the correction and apology.
(3) Where the parties cannot agree the content of the correction and apology by the date specified in the order, then the claimant must prepare a summary of the judgment given by the court and serve it on all the other parties within three days following the date specified in the order.
(4) Where the parties cannot agree the summary of the judgment prepared by the claimant they must within three days of receiving the summary:
(a) file with the court and serve on all the other parties a copy of the summary showing the revisions they wish to make to it; and
(b) apply to the court for the court to settle the summary.
(5) The court will then itself settle the summary and the judge who delivered the judgment being summarised will normally do this.

Statements in Open Court

6.1 This paragraph only applies where a party wishes to accept a Part 36 offer, Part 36 payment or other offer of settlement in relation to a claim for:
(1) libel;
(2) slander.

6.2 A party may apply for permission to make a statement in open court before or after he accepts the Part 36 offer or the Part 36 payment in accordance with r. 36.8(5) or other offer to settle the claim.

6.3 The statement that the applicant wishes to make must be submitted for the approval of the court and must accompany the notice of application.

6.4 The court may postpone the time for making the statement if other claims relating to the subject matter of the statement are still proceeding.

(Applications must be made in accordance with Part 23.)

Transitional Provision Relating to Section 4 of the Defamation Act 1952

7 Paragraph 3 of this practice direction applies, with any necessary modifications to an application to the court to determine any question as to the steps to be taken to fulfil an offer made under s. 4 of the Defamation Act 1952.

(Section 4 of the Defamation Act 1952 is repealed by the Defamation Act 1996. The commencement order bringing in the repeal makes transitional provision for offers which have been made at the date the repeal came into force.)

CPR Part 54 Judicial Review and Statutory Review

Part 54 **2.22, 74.33, 74.47, 74.48** [For commentary on a specific rule, please refer to the cross-references after the title of the rule.]

I JUDICIAL REVIEW

54.1 Scope and Interpretation

r.54.1(2)(a) **74.1** r.54.1(2)(f) **74.41**

(1) This Section of this Part contains rules about judicial review.
(2) In this Section—
  (a) a 'claim for judicial review' means a claim to review the lawfulness of—
    (i) an enactment; or
    (ii) a decision, action or failure to act in relation to the exercise of a public function.
  (e) 'the judicial review procedure' means the Part 8 procedure as modified by this Section;
  (f) 'interested party' means any person (other than the claimant and defendant) who is directly affected by the claim; and
  (g) 'court' means the High Court, unless otherwise stated.

(Rule 8.1(6)(b) provides that a rule or practice direction may, in relation to a specified type of proceedings, disapply or modify any of the rules set out in Part 8 as they apply to those proceedings)

54.2 When This Section Must Be Used

r.54.2 **74.48**

The judicial review procedure must be used in a claim for judicial review where the claimant is seeking—
(a) a mandatory order;

(b) a prohibiting order;
(c) a quashing order; or
(d) an injunction under section 30 of the Supreme Court Act 1981 (restraining a person from acting in any office in which he is not entitled to act).

54.3 When This Section May Be Used

r.54.3(1)–(2) **74.48**

(1) The judicial review procedure may be used in a claim for judicial review where the claimant is seeking—
(a) a declaration; or
(b) an injunction(GL).
(Section 31(2) of the Supreme Court Act 1981 sets out the circumstances in which the court may grant a declaration or injunction in a claim for judicial review)
(Where the claimant is seeking a declaration or injunction in addition to one of the remedies listed in rule 54.2, the judicial review procedure must be used)
(2) A claim for judicial review may include a claim for damages, restitution or the recovery of a sum due but may not seek such a remedy alone.
(Section 31(2) of the Supreme Court Act sets out the circumstances in which the court may award damages, restitution or the recovery of a sum due on a claim for judicial review)

54.4 Permission Required

r.54.4 **74.29**

The court's permission to proceed is required in a claim for judicial review whether started under this Section or transferred to the Administrative Court.

54.5 Time Limit for Filing Claim Form

r.54.5 **10.2**
r.54.5(1) **74.33, 74.35, 74.49**
r.54.5(2)–(3) **74.33**

(1) The claim form must be filed—
(a) promptly; and
(b) in any event not later than 3 months after the grounds to make the claim first arose.
(2) The time limit in this rule may not be extended by agreement between the parties.
(3) This rule does not apply when any other enactment specifies a shorter time limit for making the claim for judicial review.

54.6 Claim Form

r.54.6(1) **74.30**

(1) In addition to the matters set out in rule 8.2 (contents of the claim form) the claimant must also state—
(a) the name and address of any person he considers to be an interested party;
(b) that he is requesting permission to proceed with a claim for judicial review; and
(c) any remedy (including any interim remedy) he is claiming.
(Part 25 sets out how to apply for an interim remedy)
(2) The claim form must be accompanied by the documents required by the relevant practice direction.

54.7 Service of Claim Form

r.54.7 **74.33, 74.41**

The claim form must be served on—
(a) the defendant; and
(b) unless the court otherwise directs, any person the claimant considers to be an interested party,
within 7 days after the date of issue.

54.8 Acknowledgment of Service

r.54.8 **66.52, 74.41**
r.54.8(1) **74.34**
r.54.8(2) **18.2, 74.34**
r.54.8(3)–(4) **74.34**

(1) Any person served with the claim form who wishes to take part in the judicial review must file an

acknowledgment of service in the relevant practice form in accordance with the following provisions of this rule.
(2) Any acknowledgment of service must be
(a) filed not more than 21 days after service of the claim form; and
(b) served on—
(i) the claimant; and
(ii) subject to any direction under rule 54.7(b), any other person named in the claim form,
as soon as practicable and, in any event, not later than 7 days after it is filed.
(3) The time limits under this rule may not be extended by agreement between the parties.
(4) The acknowledgment of service—
(a) must—
(i) where the person filing it intends to contest the claim, set out a summary of his grounds for doing so; and
(ii) state the name and address of any person the person filing it considers to be an interested party; and
(b) may include or be accompanied by an application for directions.
(5) Rule 10.3(2) does not apply.

54.9 Failure to File Acknowledgment of Service

r.54.9(1)(a)–(b) **74.34, 74.41** r.54.9(2) **74.34**

(1) Where a person served with the claim form has failed to file an acknowledgment of service in accordance with rule 54.8, he—
(a) may not take part in a hearing to decide whether permission should be given unless the court allows him to do so; but
(b) provided he complies with rule 54.14 or any other direction of the court regarding the filing and service of—
(i) detailed grounds for contesting the claim or supporting it on additional grounds; and
(ii) any written evidence,
may take part in the hearing of the judicial review.
(2) Where that person takes part in the hearing of the judicial review, the court may take his failure to file an acknowledgment of service into account when deciding what order to make about costs.
(3) Rule 8.4 does not apply.

54.10 Permission Given

r.54.10(1) **74.37** r.54.10(2) **74.37, 74.39**

(1) Where permission to proceed is given the court may also give directions.
(2) Directions under paragraph (1) may include a stay[(GL)] of proceedings to which the claim relates.
(Rule 3.7 provides a sanction for the non-payment of the fee payable when permission to proceed has been given)

54.11 Service of Order Giving or Refusing Permission

r.54.11 **74.37, 74.38, 74.41**

The court will serve—
(a) the order giving or refusing permission; and
(b) any directions,
on—
(i) the claimant;
(ii) the defendant; and
(iii) any other person who filed an acknowledgment of service.

54.12 Permission Decision without a Hearing

r.54.12(1)–(4) **74.37** r.54.12(5) **74.37, 74.41**

(1) This rule applies where the court, without a hearing—
(a) refuses permission to proceed; or
(b) gives permission to proceed—

(i) subject to conditions; or
(ii) on certain grounds only.

(2) The court will serve its reasons for making the decision when it serves the order giving or refusing permission in accordance with rule 54.11.
(3) The claimant may not appeal but may request the decision to be reconsidered at a hearing.
(4) A request under paragraph (3) must be filed within 7 days after service of the reasons under paragraph (2).
(5) The claimant, defendant and any other person who has filed an acknowledgment of service will be given at least 2 days' notice of the hearing date.

54.13 Defendant etc. May Not Apply to Set Aside(GL)

r.54.13 **74.37, 74.41**

Neither the defendant nor any other person served with the claim form may apply to set aside(GL) an order giving permission to proceed.

54.14 Response

r.54.14 **74.34** r.54.14(2) **74.38**
r.54.14(1) **74.38, 74.41**

(1) A defendant and any other person served with the claim form who wishes to contest the claim or support it on additional grounds must file and serve—
(a) detailed grounds for contesting the claim or supporting it on additional grounds; and
(b) any written evidence,
within 35 days after service of the order giving permission.
(2) The following rules do not apply—
(a) rule 8.5(3) and 8.5(4) (defendant to file and serve written evidence at the same time as acknowledgment of service); and
(b) rule 8.5(5) and 8.5(6) (claimant to file and serve any reply within 14 days).

54.15 Where Claimant Seeks to Rely on Additional Grounds

r.54.15 **74.38**

The court's permission is required if a claimant seeks to rely on grounds other than those for which he has been given permission to proceed.

54.16 Evidence

(1) Rule 8.6(1) does not apply.
(2) No written evidence may be relied on unless—
(a) it has been served in accordance with any—
(i) rule under this Section; or
(ii) direction of the court; or
(b) the court gives permission.

54.17 Court's Powers to Hear Any Person

r.54.17(1)–(2) **74.41**

(1) Any person may apply for permission—
(a) to file evidence; or
(b) make representations at the hearing of the judicial review.
(2) An application under paragraph (1) should be made promptly.

54.18 Judicial Review May Be Decided Without a Hearing

r.54.18 **74.42**

The court may decide the claim for judicial review without a hearing where all the parties agree.

54.19 Court's Powers in Respect of Quashing Orders

r.54.19(2)(b) **74.50** r.54.19(3) **74.50**

(1) This rule applies where the court makes a quashing order in respect of the decision to which the claim relates.

(2) The court may—
 (a) remit the matter to the decision-maker; and
 (b) direct it to reconsider the matter and reach a decision in accordance with the judgment of the court.
(3) Where the court considers that there is no purpose to be served in remitting the matter to the decision-maker it may, subject to any statutory provision, take the decision itself.

(Where a statutory power is given to a tribunal, person or other body it may be the case that the court cannot take the decision itself.)

54.20 Transfer

r.54.20 74.47

The court may—
(a) order a claim to continue as if it had not been started under this Section; and
(b) where it does so, give directions about the future management of the claim.

(Part 30 (transfer) applies to transfers to and from the Administrative Court)

II STATUTORY REVIEW UNDER THE NATIONALITY, IMMIGRATION AND ASYLUM ACT 2002

54.21 Scope and Interpretation

(1) This Section of this Part contains rules about applications to the High Court under section 101(2) of the Nationality, Immigration and Asylum Act 2002 for a review of a decision of the Immigration Appeal Tribunal on an application for permission to appeal from an adjudicator.
(2) In this Section—
 (a) 'the Act' means the Nationality, Immigration and Asylum Act 2002;
 (b) 'adjudicator' means an adjudicator appointed for the purposes of Part 5 of the Act;
 (c) 'applicant' means a person applying to the High Court under section 101(2) of the Act;
 (d) 'other party' means the other party to the proceedings before the Tribunal; and
 (e) 'Tribunal ' means the Immigration Appeal Tribunal.

54.22 Application for Review

(1) An application under section 101(2) of the Act must be made to the Administrative Court.
(2) The application must be made by filing an application notice.
(3) The applicant must file with the application notice—
 (a) the immigration or asylum decision to which the proceedings relate, and any document giving reasons for that decision;
 (b) the grounds of appeal to the adjudicator;
 (c) the adjudicator's determination;
 (d) the grounds of appeal to the Tribunal together with any documents sent with them;
 (e) the Tribunal's determination on the application for permission to appeal; and
 (f) any other documents material to the application which were before the adjudicator.
(4) The applicant must also file with the application notice written submissions setting out—
 (a) the grounds upon which it is contended that the Tribunal made an error of law; and
 (b) reasons in support of those grounds.

54.23 Time Limit for Application

(1) The application notice must be filed not later than 14 days after the applicant is deemed to have received notice of the Tribunal's decision in accordance with rules made under section 106 of the Act.
(2) The court may extend the time limit in paragraph (1) in exceptional circumstances.
(3) An application to extend the time limit must be made in the application notice and supported by written evidence verified by a statement of truth.

54.24 Service of Application

(1) The applicant must serve on the Asylum and Immigration Tribunal copies of the application notice and written submissions.

(2) Where an application is for review of a decision by the Tribunal to grant permission to appeal, the applicant must serve on the other party copies of—
(a) the application notice;
(b) the written submissions; and
(c) all the documents filed in support of the application, except for documents which come from or have already been served on that party.
(3) Where documents are required to be served under paragraphs (1) and (2), they must be served as soon as practicable after they are filed.

54.25 Determining the Application

(1) The application will be determined by a single judge without a hearing, and by reference only to the written submissions and the documents filed with them.
(2) If the applicant relies on evidence which was not submitted to the adjudicator or the Tribunal, the court will not consider that evidence unless it is satisfied that there were good reasons why it was not submitted to the adjudicator or the Tribunal.
(3) The court may—
(a) affirm the Tribunal's decision to refuse permission to appeal;
(b) reverse the Tribunal's decision to grant permission to appeal; or
(c) order the Asylum and Immigration Tribunal to reconsider the adjudicator's decision on the appeal.
(4) Where the Tribunal refused permission to appeal, the court will order the Asylum and Immigration Tribunal to reconsider the adjudicator's decision on the appeal only if it is satisfied that—
(a) the Tribunal may have made an error of law; and
(b) there is a real possibility that the Asylum and Immigration Tribunal would make a different decision from the adjudicator on reconsidering the appeal (which may include making a different direction under section 87 of the 2002 Act).
(5) Where the Tribunal granted permission to appeal, the court will reverse the Tribunal's decision only if it is satisfied that there is no real possibility that the Asylum and Immigration Tribunal, on reconsidering the adjudicator's decision on the appeal, would make a different decision from the adjudicator.
(6) The court's decision shall be final and there shall be no appeal from that decision or renewal of the application.

54.26 Service of Order

(1) The court will send copies of its order to—
(a) the applicant, except where paragraph (2) applies;
(b) the other party; and
(c) the Asylum and Immigration Tribunal.
(2) Where—
(a) the application relates, in whole or in part, to a claim for asylum;
(b) the Tribunal refused permission to appeal; and
(c) the court affirms the Tribunal's decision,
the court will send a copy of its order to the Secretary of State, who must serve the order on the applicant.
(3) Where the Secretary of State has served an order in accordance with paragraph (2), he must notify the court on what date and by what method the order was served.
(4) If the court issues a certificate under section 101(3)(d) of the Act, it will send a copy of the certificate together with the order to—
(a) the persons to whom it sends the order under paragraphs (1) and (2); and
(b) if the applicant is in receipt of public funding, the Legal Services Commission.

54.27 Costs

The court may reserve the costs of the application to be determined by the Asylum and Immigration Tribunal.

III APPLICATIONS FOR STATUTORY REVIEW UNDER SECTION 103A OF THE NATIONALITY, IMMIGRATION AND ASYLUM ACT 2002

54.28 Scope and Interpretation

(1) This Section of this Part contains rules about applications to the High Court under section 103A of the Nationality, Immigration and Asylum Act 2002 for an order requiring the Asylum and Immigration Tribunal to reconsider its decision on an appeal.
(2) In this Section—
  (a) 'the 2002 Act' means the Nationality, Immigration and Asylum Act 2002;
  (b) 'the 2004 Act' means the Asylum and Immigration (Treatment of Claimants, etc.) Act 2004;
  (c) 'appellant' means the appellant in the proceedings before the Tribunal;
  (d) 'applicant' means a person applying to the High Court under section 103A;
  (e) 'asylum claim' has the meaning given in section 113(1) of the 2002 Act;
  (ea) 'fast track case' means any case in relation to which an order made under section 26(8) of the 2004 Act provides that the time period for making an application under section 103A(1) of the 2002 Act or giving notification under paragraph 30(5) of Schedule 2 to the 2004 Act is less than 5 days;
  (f) 'filter provision' means paragraph 30 of Schedule 2 to the 2004 Act;
  (g) 'order for reconsideration' means an order under section 103A(1) requiring the Tribunal to reconsider its decision on an appeal;
  (h) 'section 103A' means section 103A of the 2002 Act;
  (i) 'Tribunal' means the Asylum and Immigration Tribunal.
(3) Any reference in this Section to a period of time specified in—
  (a) section 103A(3) for making an application for an order under section 103A(1); or
  (b) paragraph 30(5)(b) of Schedule 2 to the 2004 Act for giving notice under that paragraph,

  includes a reference to that period as varied by any order under section 26(8) of the 2004 Act.
(4) Rule 2.8 applies to the calculation of the periods of time specified in—
  (a) section 103A(3); and
  (b) paragraph 30(5)(b) of Schedule 2 to the 2004 Act.
(5) Save as provided otherwise, the provisions of this Section apply to an application under section 103A regardless of whether the filter provision has effect in relation to that application.

54.28A Representation of Applicants while Filter Provision Has Effect

(1) This rule applies during any period in which the filter provision has effect.
(2) An applicant may, for the purpose of taking any step under rule 54.29 or 54.30, be represented by any person permitted to provide him with immigration advice or immigration services under section 84 of the Immigration and Asylum Act 1999.
(3) A representative acting for an applicant under paragraph (2) shall be regarded as the applicant's legal representative for the purpose of rule 22.1 (Documents to be verified by a statement of truth) regardless of whether he would otherwise be so regarded.

54.28B Service of Documents on Appellants within the Jurisdiction

(1) In proceedings under this Section, rules 6.4(2) and 6.5(5) do not apply to the service of documents on an appellant who is within the jurisdiction.
(2) Where a representative is acting for an appellant who is within the jurisdiction, a document must be served on the appellant by—
  (a) serving it on his representative; or
  (b) serving it on the appellant personally or sending it to his address by first class post,

  but if the document is served on the appellant under sub-paragraph (b), a copy must also at the same time be sent to his representative.

54.29 Application for Review

(1) Subject to paragraph (5), an application for an order for reconsideration must be made by filing an application notice—

(a) during a period in which the filter provision has effect, with the Tribunal at the address specified in the relevant practice direction; and
(b) at any other time, at the Administrative Court Office.

(2) During any period in which the filter provision does not have effect, the applicant must file with the application notice—
(a) the notice of the immigration, asylum or nationality decision to which the appeal related;
(b) any other document which was served on the appellant giving reasons for that decision;
(c) the grounds of appeal to the Tribunal;
(d) the Tribunal's determination on the appeal; and
(e) any other documents material to the application which were before the Tribunal.

(2A) During any period in which the filter provision has effect, the applicant must file with the application notice a list of the documents referred to in paragraph (2)(a) to (e).

(3) The applicant must also file with the application notice written submissions setting out—
(a) the grounds upon which it is contended that the Tribunal made an error of law which may have affected its decision; and
(b) reasons in support of those grounds.

(4) Where the applicant –
(a) was the respondent to the appeal; and
(b) was required to serve the Tribunal's determination on the appellant,
the application notice must contain a statement of the date on which, and the means by which, the determination was served.

(5) Where the applicant is in detention under the Immigration Acts, the application may be made either—
(a) in accordance with paragraphs (1) to (3); or
(b) by serving the documents specified in paragraphs (1) to (3) on the person having custody of him.

(6) Where an application is made in accordance with paragraph (5)(b), the person on whom the application notice is served must—
(a) endorse on the notice the date that it is served on him;
(b) give the applicant an acknowledgment in writing of receipt of the notice; and
(c) forward the notice and documents within 2 days—
(i) during a period in which the filter provision has effect, to the Tribunal; and
(ii) at any other time, to the Administrative Court Office.

54.30 Application to Extend Time Limit

An application to extend the time limit for making an application under section 103A(1) must—
(a) be made in the application notice;
(b) set out the grounds on which it is contended that the application notice could not reasonably practicably have been filed within the time limit; and
(c) be supported by written evidence verified by a statement of truth.

54.31 Procedure While Filter Provision Has Effect

(1) This rule applies during any period in which the filter provision has effect.

(2) Where the applicant receives notice from the Tribunal that it—
(a) does not propose to make an order for reconsideration; or
(b) does not propose to grant permission for the application to be made outside the relevant time limit,
and the applicant wishes the court to consider the application, the applicant must file a notice in writing at the Administrative Court Office in accordance with paragraph 30(5)(b) of Schedule 2 to the 2004 Act.

(3) Where the applicant—
(a) was the respondent to the appeal; and
(b) was required to serve the notice from the Tribunal mentioned in paragraph (2) on the appellant,
the notice filed in accordance with paragraph 30(5)(b) of Schedule 2 to the 2004 Act must

contain a statement of the date on which, and the means by which, the notice from the Tribunal was served.

(4) A notice which is filed outside the period specified in paragraph 30(5)(b) must—
 (a) set out the grounds on which it is contended that the notice could not reasonably practicably have been filed within that period; and
 (b) be supported by written evidence verified by a statement of truth.

(5) If the applicant wishes to respond to the reasons given by the Tribunal for its decision that it—
 (a) does not propose to make an order for reconsideration; or
 (b) does not propose to grant permission for the application to be made outside the relevant time limit,

the notice filed in accordance with paragraph 30(5)(b) of Schedule 2 to the 2004 Act must be accompanied by written submissions setting out the grounds upon which the applicant disputes any of the reasons given by the Tribunal and giving reasons in support of those grounds.

54.32 Procedure in Fast Track Cases While Filter Provision Does Not Have Effect

(1) This rule applies only during a period in which the filter provision does not have effect.

(2) Where a party applies for an order for reconsideration in a fast track case—
 (a) the court will serve copies of the application notice and written submissions on the other party to the appeal; and
 (b) the other party to the appeal may file submissions in response to the application not later than 2 days after being served with the application.

(3) [*revoked*]

54.33 Determination of the Application by the Administrative Court

(1) This rule, and rules 54.34 and 54.35, apply to applications under section 103A which are determined by the Administrative Court.

(2) The application will be considered by a single judge without a hearing.

(3) Unless it orders otherwise, the court will not receive evidence which was not submitted to the Tribunal.

(4) Subject to paragraph (5), where the court determines an application for an order for reconsideration, it may—
 (a) dismiss the application;
 (b) make an order requiring the Tribunal to reconsider its decision on the appeal under section 103A(1) of the 2002 Act; or
 (c) refer the appeal to the Court of Appeal under section 103C of the 2002 Act.

(5) The court will only make an order requiring the Tribunal to reconsider its decision on an appeal if it thinks that –
 (a) the Tribunal may have made an error of law; and
 (b) there is a real possibility that the Tribunal would make a different decision on reconsidering the appeal (which may include making a different direction under section 87 of the 2002 Act).

(6) Where the Court of Appeal has restored the application to the court under section 103C(2)(g) of the 2002 Act, the court may not refer the appeal to the Court of Appeal.

(7) The court's decision shall be final and there shall be no appeal from that decision or renewal of the application.

54.34 Service of Order

(1) The court will send copies of its order to—
 (a) the applicant and the other party to the appeal, except where paragraph (2) applies; and
 (b) the Tribunal.

(2) Where the appellant is within the jurisdiction and the application relates, in whole or in part, to an asylum claim, the court will send a copy of its order to the Secretary of State.

(2A) Paragraph (2) does not apply in a fast track case.

(3) Where the court sends an order to the Secretary of State under paragraph (2), the Secretary of State must—

(a) serve the order on the appellant; and
(b) immediately after serving the order, notify—
(i) the court; and
(ii) where the order requires the Tribunal to reconsider its decision on the appeal, the Tribunal,

on what date and by what method the order was served.

(4) The Secretary of State must provide the notification required by paragraph (3)(b) no later than 28 days after the date on which the court sends him a copy of its order.

(5) If, 28 days after the date on which the court sends a copy of its order to the Secretary of State in accordance with paragraph (2), the Secretary of State has not provided the notification required by paragraph (3)(b)(i), the court may serve the order on the appellant.

(5A) Where the court serves an order for reconsideration under paragraph (5), it will notify the Tribunal of the date on which the order was served.

(6) If the court makes an order under section 103D(1) of the 2002 Act, it will send copies of that order to—
(a) the appellant's legal representative; and
(b) the Legal Services Commission.

(7) Where paragraph (2) applies, the court will not serve copies of an order under section 103D(1) of the 2002 Act until either—
(a) the Secretary of State has provided the notification required by paragraph (3)(b); or
(b) 28 days after the date on which the court sent a copy of its order to the Secretary of State,

whichever is the earlier.

54.35 Costs

The court shall make no order as to the costs of an application under this Section except, where appropriate, an order under section 103D(1) of the 2002 Act.

PD 54 Practice Direction — Judicial Review

This practice direction supplements CPR Part 54

PD 54 **2.22, 74.38** [For commentary on a specific paragraph, please refer to the cross-references after the title of the paragraph.]

1.1 In addition to Part 54 and this practice direction attention is drawn to:

- s. 31 of the Supreme Court Act 1981; and
- the Human Rights Act 1998

The Court

para.2.1 **11.2**

2.1 Part 54 claims for judicial review are dealt with in the Administrative Court.

2.2 Where the claim is proceeding in the Administrative Court in London, documents must be filed at the Administrative Court Office, the Royal Courts of Justice, Strand, London WC2A 2LL.

2.3 Where the claim is proceeding in the Administrative Court in Wales (see para. 3.1), documents must be filed at the Civil Justice Centre, 2 Park Street, Cardiff CF10 1ET.

Urgent applications

2.4 Where urgency makes it necessary for the claim for judicial review to be made outside London or Cardiff, the Administrative Court Office in London should be consulted (if necessary, by telephone) prior to filing the claim form.

Judicial Review Claims in Wales

3.1 A claim for judicial review may be brought in the Administrative Court in Wales where the claim or any remedy sought involves:

(1) a devolution issue arising out of the Government of Wales Act 1998; or

(2) an issue concerning the National Assembly for Wales, the Welsh executive, or any Welsh public body (including a Welsh local authority) (whether or not it involves a devolution issue).

3.2 Such claims may also be brought in the Administrative Court at the Royal Courts of Justice.

Time Limit for Filing Claim Form: Rule 54.5

4.1 Where the claim is for a quashing order in respect of a judgment, order or conviction, the date when the grounds to make the claim first arise, for the purposes of r. 54.5(1)(b), is the date of that judgment, order or conviction.

Claim Form: Rule 54.6

Interested parties

para.5.1 **74.33**

5.1 Where the claim for judicial review relates to proceedings in a court or tribunal, any other parties to those proceedings must be named in the claim form as interested parties under r. 54.6(1)(a) (and therefore served with the claim form under r. 54.7(b)).

5.2 For example, in a claim by a defendant in a criminal case in the magistrates' or Crown Court for judicial review of a decision in that case, the prosecution must always be named as an interested party.

Human rights

paras.5.3–5.4 **74.30**

5.3 Where the claimant is seeking to raise any issue under the Human Rights Act 1998, or seeks a remedy available under that Act, the claim form must include the information required by PD 16, para. 15.

Devolution issues

5.4 Where the claimant intends to raise a devolution issue, the claim form must:
(1) specify that the applicant wishes to raise a devolution issue and identify the relevant provisions of the Government of Wales Act 1998, the Northern Ireland Act 1998 or the Scotland Act 1998; and
(2) contain a summary of the facts, circumstances and points of law on the basis of which it is alleged that a devolution issue arises.

5.5 In this practice direction 'devolution issue' has the same meaning as in the Government of Wales Act 1998, sch. 8, para. 1; the Northern Ireland Act 1998, sch. 10, para. 1; and the Scotland Act 1998, sch. 6, para. 1.

Claim form

para.5.6 **57.4, 74.30, 74.33**
para.5.7 **57.4, 74.30**
para.5.8 **57.4, 74.30**

5.6 The claim form must include or be accompanied by:
(1) a detailed statement of the claimant's grounds for bringing the claim for judicial review;
(2) a statement of the facts relied on;
(3) any application to extend the time limit for filing the claim form;
(4) any application for directions.

5.7 In addition, the claim form must be accompanied by:
(1) any written evidence in support of the claim or application to extend time;
(2) a copy of any order that the claimant seeks to have quashed;
(3) where the claim for judicial review relates to a decision of a court or tribunal, an approved copy of the reasons for reaching that decision;
(4) copies of any documents on which the claimant proposes to rely;
(5) copies of any relevant statutory material;
(6) a list of essential documents for advance reading by the court (with page references to the passages relied on); and

5.8 Where it is not possible to file all the above documents, the claimant must indicate which documents have not been filed and the reasons why they are not currently available.

Bundle of documents

para.5.9 **57.4, 74.30**

5.9 The claimant must file two copies of a paginated and indexed bundle containing all the documents referred to in paras 5.6 and 5.7.

5.10 Attention is drawn to r. 8.5(1) and (7).

Service of Claim Form: Rule 54.7

6.1 Except as required by r. 54.11 or 54.12(2), the Administrative Court will not serve documents and service must be effected by the parties.

Acknowledgment of Service: Rule 54.8

7.1 Attention is drawn to r. 8.3(2) and PD 8 and to r. 10.5.

Permission Given: Rule 54.10

Directions

8.1 Case management directions under r. 54.10(1) may include directions about serving the claim form and any evidence on other persons.

8.2 Where a claim is made under the Human Rights Act 1998, a direction may be made for giving notice to the Crown or joining the Crown as a party. Attention is drawn to r. 19.4A and PD 19, para. 6.

8.3 A direction may be made for the hearing of the claim for judicial review to be held outside London or Cardiff. Before making any such direction the judge will consult the judge in charge of the Administrative Court as to its feasibility.

Permission without a hearing

para.8.4 **74.29, 74.37**

8.4 The court will generally, in the first instance, consider the question of permission without a hearing.

Permission hearing

para.8.5 **74.29, 74.37, 74.41** para.8.6 **74.37, 74.41**

8.5 Neither the defendant nor any other interested party need attend a hearing on the question of permission unless the court directs otherwise.

8.6 Where the defendant or any party does attend a hearing, the court will not generally make an order for costs against the claimant.

Service of Order Giving or Refusing Permission: Rule 54.11

9.1 An order refusing permission or giving it subject to conditions or on certain grounds only must set out or be accompanied by the court's reasons for coming to that decision.

Response: Rule 54.14

para.10.1 **74.38**

10.1 Where the party filing the detailed grounds intends to rely on documents not already filed, he must file a paginated bundle of those documents when he files the detailed grounds.

Where Claimant Seeks to Rely on Additional Grounds: Rule 54.15

para.11.1 **74.38**

11.1 Where the claimant intends to apply to rely on additional grounds at the hearing of the claim for judicial review, he must give notice to the court and to any other person served with the claim form no later than seven clear days before the hearing (or the warned date where appropriate).

Evidence: Rule 54.16

para.12.1 **74.40**

12.1 Disclosure is not required unless the court orders otherwise.

Court's Powers to Hear Any Person: Rule 54.17

paras.13.1–13.5 **74.41**

13.1 Where all the parties consent, the court may deal with an application under r. 54.17 without a hearing.

13.2 Where the court gives permission for a person to file evidence or make representations at the hearing of the claim for judicial review, it may do so on conditions and may give case management directions.

13.3 An application for permission should be made by letter to the Administrative Court office, identifying the claim, explaining who the applicant is and indicating why and in what form the applicant wants to participate in the hearing.

13.4 If the applicant is seeking a prospective order as to costs, the letter should say what kind of order and on what grounds.

13.5 Applications to intervene must be made at the earliest reasonable opportunity, since it will usually be essential not to delay the hearing.

Transfer: Rule 54.20

para.14.1 **74.47** para.14.2 **74.47**

14.1 Attention is drawn to r. 30.5.

14.2 In deciding whether a claim is suitable for transfer to the Administrative Court, the court will consider whether it raises issues of public law to which Part 54 should apply.

Skeleton arguments

para.15.1 **74.43** para.15.3 **74.43**

15.1 The claimant must file and serve a skeleton argument not less than 21 working days before the date of the hearing of the judicial review (or the warned date).

15.2 The defendant and any other party wishing to make representations at the hearing of the judicial review must file and serve a skeleton argument not less than 14 working days before the date of the hearing of the judicial review (or the warned date).

15.3 Skeleton arguments must contain:
(1) a time estimate for the complete hearing, including delivery of judgment;
(2) a list of issues;
(3) a list of the legal points to be taken (together with any relevant authorities with page references to the passages relied on);
(4) a chronology of events (with page references to the bundle of documents (see para. 16.1);
(5) a list of essential documents for the advance reading of the court (with page references to the passages relied on) (if different from that filed with the claim form) and a time estimate for that reading; and
(6) a list of persons referred to.

Bundle of Documents to Be Filed

para.16.1 **74.43** para.16.2 **74.43**

16.1 The claimant must file a paginated and indexed bundle of all relevant documents required for the hearing of the judicial review when he files his skeleton argument.

16.2 The bundle must also include those documents required by the defendant and any other party who is to make representations at the hearing.

Agreed Final Order

para.17.1–17.4 **74.42**

17.1 If the parties agree about the final order to be made in a claim for judicial review, the claimant must file at the court a document (with two copies) signed by all the parties setting out the terms of the proposed agreed order together with a short statement of the matters relied on as justifying the proposed agreed order and copies of any authorities or statutory provisions relied on.

17.2 The court will consider the documents referred to in para. 17.1 and will make the order if satisfied that the order should be made.

17.3 If the court is not satisfied that the order should be made, a hearing date will be set.

17.4 Where the agreement relates to an order for costs only, the parties need only file a document signed by all the parties setting out the terms of the proposed order.

PD 54B Practice Direction — Applications for Statutory Review under Section 103A of the Nationality, Immigration and Asylum Act 2002

This practice direction supplements Section III of Part 54

1 Attention is drawn to:
(1) the Nationality, Immigration and Asylum Act 2002, ss. 103A, 103C and 103D (inserted by the Asylum and Immigration (Treatment of Claimants, etc.) Act 2004, s. 26(6)); and
(2) para. 30 of sch. 2 to the 2004 Act.

The Court

2.1 Applications for review under s. 103A(1) of the 2002 Act are dealt with in the Administrative Court, subject to the transitional filter provision in para. 30 of sch. 2 to the 2004 Act which provides that they shall initially be considered by a member of the Tribunal.

2.2 During any period in which the filter provision has effect, the address for filing s. 103A applications shall be the Asylum and Immigration Tribunal, PO Box 6987, Leicester LE1 6ZX.

2.3 Where a fast track order within the meaning of r. 54.32(3) applies to a s. 103A application, para. 2.2 shall not apply and the address for filing the application shall be the address specified in the Tribunal's determination of the appeal.

Access to Court Orders Served on the Appellant by the Secretary of State

3.1 Where the court sends a copy of its order on a s. 103A application to the Secretary of State but not the appellant in accordance with r. 54.34(2), then r. 5.4(3)(b) and r. 5.4(5)(a)(ii) are modified as follows.

3.2 Neither the appellant nor any other person may obtain from the records of the court a copy of the court's order on the s. 103A application, or of any order made under s. 103D(1) of the 2002 Act in relation to that application, until either the Secretary of State has given the court the notification required by r. 54.34(3)(b) or 28 days after the date on which the court sent a copy of the order to the Secretary of State, whichever is the earlier.

Referral to Court of Appeal

4.1 Where the court refers an appeal to the Court of Appeal, its order will set out the question of law raised by the appeal which is of such importance that it should be decided by the Court of Appeal.

4.2 PD 52, para. 21.7A, makes provision about appeals which are referred to the Court of Appeal.

CPR Part 55 Possession Claims

Part 55 **15.21, 20.2, 35.1, 35.14, 67.3, 76.2, 85.1, 87.6, 88.29, 96.54** [For commentary on a specific rule, please refer to the cross-references after the title of the rule.]

55.1 Interpretation

r.55.1(b) **35.3, 35.4**

In this Part—
(a) 'a possession claim' means a claim for the recovery of possession of land (including buildings or parts of buildings);
(b) 'a possession claim against trespassers' means a claim for the recovery of land which the claimant alleges is occupied only by a person or persons who entered or remained on the land without the consent of a person entitled to possession of that land but does not include a claim against a tenant or sub-tenant whether his tenancy has been terminated or not;
(c) 'mortgage' includes a legal or equitable mortgage and a legal or equitable charge and 'mortgagee' is to be interpreted accordingly;
(d) 'the 1985 Act' means the Housing Act 1985;
(e) 'the 1988 Act' means the Housing Act 1988;
(f) 'a demotion claim' means a claim made by a landlord for an order under section 82A of the 1985 Act or section 6A of the 1988 Act ('a demotion order');
(g) 'a demoted tenancy' means a tenancy created by virtue of a demotion order; and
(h) 'a suspension claim' means a claim made by a landlord for an order under section 121A of the 1985 Act.

I GENERAL RULES

55.2 Scope

(1) The procedure set out in this Section of this Part must be used where the claim includes—
  (a) a possession claim brought by a—
    (i) landlord (or former landlord);
    (ii) mortgagee; or
    (iii) licensor (or former licensor);
  (b) a possession claim against trespassers; or
  (c) a claim by a tenant seeking relief from forfeiture.

(Where a demotion claim or a suspension claim (or both) is made in the same claim form in which a possession claim is started, this Section of this Part applies as modified by rule 65.12. Where the claim is a demotion claim or a suspension claim only, or a suspension claim made in addition to a demotion claim, Section III of Part 65 applies)

(2) This Section of this Part—
  (a) is subject to any enactment or practice direction which sets out special provisions with regard to any particular category of claim;
  (b) does not apply where the claimant uses the procedure set out in Section II of this Part; and
  (c) does not apply where the claimant seeks an interim possession order under Section III of this Part except where the court orders otherwise or that Section so provides.

55.3 Starting the Claim

r.55.3(1) **35.5, 87.8, 96.54**
r.55.3(2) **87.8, 96.54**
r.55.3(5) **87.7**

(1) The claim must be started in the county court for the district in which the land is situated unless paragraph (2) applies or an enactment provides otherwise.
(2) The claim may be started in the High Court if the claimant files with his claim form a certificate stating the reasons for bringing the claim in that court verified by a statement of truth in accordance with rule 22.1(1).
(3) The practice direction refers to circumstances which may justify starting the claim in the High Court.
(4) Where, in a possession claim against trespassers, the claimant does not know the name of a person in occupation or possession of the land, the claim must be brought against 'persons unknown' in addition to any named defendants.
(5) The claim form and form of defence sent with it must be in the forms set out in the relevant practice direction.

55.4 Particulars of Claim

r.55.4 **35.6, 87.7**

The particulars of claim must be filed and served with the claim form.
(The relevant practice direction and Part 16 provide details about the contents of the particulars of claim)

55.5 Hearing Date

r.55.5(1) **87.9**
r.55.5(2) **35.7**
r.55.5(3)(a)–(b) **87.9**
r.55.5(3)(c) **87.10**

(1) The court will fix a date for the hearing when it issues the claim form.
(2) In a possession claim against trespassers the defendant must be served with the claim form, particulars of claim and any witness statements—
  (a) in the case of residential property, not less than 5 days; and
  (b) in the case of other land, not less than 2 days,
  before the hearing date.
(3) In all other possession claims—
  (a) the hearing date will be not less than 28 days from the date of issue of the claim form;
  (b) the standard period between the issue of the claim form and the hearing will be not more than 8 weeks; and
  (c) the defendant must be served with the claim form and particulars of claim not less than 21 days before the hearing date.

(Rule 3.1(2)(a) provides that the court may extend or shorten the time for compliance with any rule)

55.6 Service of Claims against Trespassers

r.55.6 **35.7**

Where, in a possession claim against trespassers, the claim has been issued against 'persons unknown', the claim form, particulars of claim and any witness statements must be served on those persons by—
(a) (i) attaching copies of the claim form, particulars of claim and any witness statements to the main door or some other part of the land so that they are clearly visible; and

(ii) if practicable, inserting copies of those documents in a sealed transparent envelope addressed to 'the occupiers' through the letter box; or

(b) placing stakes in the land in places where they are clearly visible and attaching to each stake copies of the claim form, particulars of claim and any witness statements in a sealed transparent envelope addressed to 'the occupiers'.

55.7 Defendant's Response

r.55.7(1) **35.7, 87.10** r.55.7(4) **20.2, 35.8, 87.10**
r.55.7(2) **35.8**

(1) An acknowledgment of service is not required and Part 10 does not apply.

(2) In a possession claim against trespassers rule 15.2 does not apply and the defendant need not file a defence.

(3) Where, in any other possession claim, the defendant does not file a defence within the time specified in rule 15.4, he may take part in any hearing but the court may take his failure to do so into account when deciding what order to make about costs.

(4) Part 12 (default judgment) does not apply in a claim to which this Part applies.

55.8 The Hearing

r.55.8(1) **87.9** r.55.8(4) **87.10**
r.55.8(2) **35.14, 87.11** r.55.8(5) **35.6**
r.55.8(3) **35.10, 87.10** r.55.8(6) **35.10, 87.10**

(1) At the hearing fixed in accordance with rule 55.5(1) or at any adjournment of that hearing, the court may—
 (a) decide the claim; or
 (b) give case management directions.

(2) Where the claim is genuinely disputed on grounds which appear to be substantial, case management directions given under paragraph (1)(b) will include the allocation of the claim to a track or directions to enable it to be allocated.

(3) Except where—
 (a) the claim is allocated to the fast track or the multi-track; or
 (b) the court orders otherwise,

any fact that needs to be proved by the evidence of witnesses at a hearing referred to in paragraph (1) may be proved by evidence in writing.

(Rule 32.2(1) sets out the general rule about evidence. Rule 32.2(2) provides that rule 32.2(1) is subject to any provision to the contrary)

(4) Subject to paragraph (5), all witness statements must be filed and served at least 2 days before the hearing.

(5) In a possession claim against trespassers all witness statements on which the claimant intends to rely must be filed and served with the claim form.

(6) Where the claimant serves the claim form and particulars of claim, he must produce at the hearing a certificate of service of those documents and rule 6.14(2)(a) does not apply.

55.9 Allocation

r.55.9(1)–(4) **87.11**

(1) When the court decides the track for a possession claim, the matters to which it shall have regard include—
 (a) the matters set out in rule 26.8 as modified by the relevant practice direction;
 (b) the amount of any arrears of rent or mortgage instalments;
 (c) the importance to the defendant of retaining possession of the land;
 (d) the importance of vacant possession to the claimant; and
 (e) if applicable, the alleged conduct of the defendant.

(2) The court will only allocate possession claims to the small claims track if all the parties agree.

(3) Where a possession claim has been allocated to the small claims track the claim shall be treated, for the purposes of costs, as if it were proceeding on the fast track except that trial costs shall be in the discretion of the court and shall not exceed the amount that would be recoverable under rule 46.2 (amount of fast track costs) if the value of the claim were up to £3,000.

(4) Where all the parties agree the court may, when it allocates the claim, order that rule 27.14 (costs on the small claims track) applies and, where it does so, paragraph (3) does not apply.

55.10 Possession Claims Relating to Mortgaged Residential Property

(1) This rule applies where a mortgagee seeks possession of land which consists of or includes residential property.
(2) Not less than 14 days before the hearing the claimant must send a notice to the property addressed to 'the occupiers'.
(3) The notice referred to in paragraph (2) must—
  (a) state that a possession claim for the property has started;
  (b) show the name and address of the claimant, the defendant and the court which issued the claim form; and
  (c) give details of the hearing.
(4) The claimant must produce at the hearing—
  (a) a copy of the notice; and
  (b) evidence that he has served it.

55.10A Electronic Issue of Certain Possession Claims

r.55.10A **87.6**

(1) A practice direction may make provision for a claimant to start certain types of possession claim in certain courts by requesting the issue of a claim form electronically.
(2) The practice direction may, in particular—
  (a) provide that only particular provisions apply in specific courts;
  (b) specify—
    (i) the type of possession claim which may be issued electronically;
    (ii) the conditions that a claim must meet before it may be issued electronically;
  (c) specify the court where the claim may be issued;
  (d) enable the parties to make certain applications or take further steps in relation to the claim electronically;
  (e) specify the requirements that must be fulfilled in relation to such applications or steps;
  (f) enable the parties to correspond electronically with the court about the claim;
  (g) specify the requirements that must be fulfilled in relation to electronic correspondence;
  (h) provide how any fee payable on the filing of any document is to be paid where the document is filed electronically.
(3) The Practice Direction may disapply or modify these Rules as appropriate in relation to possession claims started electronically.

II ACCELERATED POSSESSION CLAIMS OF PROPERTY LET ON AN ASSURED SHORTHOLD TENANCY

55.11 When This Section May Be Used

r.55.11 **35.15, 87.12**

(1) The claimant may bring a possession claim under this Section of this Part where—
  (a) the claim is brought under section 21 of the 1988 Act to recover possession of residential property let under an assured shorthold tenancy; and
  (b) subject to rule 55.12(2), all the conditions listed in rule 55.12(1) are satisfied.
(2) The claim must be started in the county court for the district in which the property is situated.
(3) In this Section of this Part, a 'demoted assured shorthold tenancy' means a demoted tenancy where the landlord is a registered social landlord.

(By virtue of section 20B of the 1988 Act, a demoted assured shorthold tenancy is an assured shorthold tenancy)

55.12 Conditions

r.55.12 **35.15, 87.12**

(1) The conditions referred to in rule 55.11(1)(b) are that—

(a) the tenancy and any agreement for the tenancy were entered into on or after 15 January 1989;
(b) the only purpose of the claim is to recover possession of the property and no other claim is made;
(c) the tenancy did not immediately follow an assured tenancy which was not an assured shorthold tenancy;
(d) the tenancy fulfilled the conditions provided by section 19A or 20(1)(a) to (c) of the 1988 Act;
(e) the tenancy—
  (i) was the subject of a written agreement;
  (ii) arises by virtue of section 5 of the 1988 Act but follows a tenancy that was the subject of a written agreement; or
  (iii) relates to the same or substantially the same property let to the same tenant and on the same terms (though not necessarily as to rent or duration) as a tenancy which was the subject of a written agreement; and
(f) a notice in accordance with sections 21(1) or 21(4) of the 1988 Act was given to the tenant in writing.

(2) If the tenancy is a demoted assured shorthold tenancy, only the conditions in paragraph (1)(b) and (f) need be satisfied.

55.13 Claim Form

r.55.13 **35.15, 87.12**

(1) The claim form must—
(a) be in the form set out in the relevant practice direction; and
(b) (i) contain such information; and
  (ii) be accompanied by such documents, as are required by that form.
(2) All relevant sections of the form must be completed.
(3) The court will serve the claim form by first class post (or an alternative service which provides for delivery on the next working day).

55.14 Defence

r.55.14 **35.15, 87.12**

(1) A defendant who wishes to—
(a) oppose the claim; or
(b) seek a postponement of possession in accordance with rule 55.18,
must file his defence within 14 days after service of the claim form.
(2) The defence should be in the form set out in the relevant practice direction.

55.15 Claim Referred to Judge

r.55.15 **35.15, 87.12**

(1) On receipt of the defence the court will—
(a) send a copy to the claimant; and
(b) refer the claim and defence to a judge.
(2) Where the period set out in rule 55.14 has expired without the defendant filing a defence—
(a) the claimant may file a written request for an order for possession; and
(b) the court will refer that request to a judge.
(3) Where the defence is received after the period set out in rule 55.14 has expired but before a request is filed in accordance with paragraph (2), paragraph (1) will still apply.
(4) Where—
(a) the period set out in rule 55.14 has expired without the defendant filing a defence; and
(b) the claimant has not made a request for an order for possession under paragraph (2) within 3 months after the expiry of the period set out in rule 55.14,
the claim will be stayed.

55.16 Consideration of the Claim

r.55.16 **35.15, 87.12** r.55.16(1)(c) **35.15**

(1) After considering the claim and any defence, the judge will—
(a) make an order for possession under rule 55.17;
(b) where he is not satisfied as to any of the matters set out in paragraph (2)—
(i) direct that a date be fixed for a hearing; and
(ii) give any appropriate case management directions; or
(c) strike out the claim if the claim form discloses no reasonable grounds for bringing the claim.
(2) The matters referred to in paragraph (1)(b) are that—
(a) the claim form was served; and
(b) the claimant has established that he is entitled to recover possession under section 21 of the 1988 Act against the defendant.
(3) The court will give all parties not less than 14 days' notice of a hearing fixed under paragraph (1)(b)(i).
(4) Where a claim is struck out under paragraph (1)(c)—
(a) the court will serve its reasons for striking out the claim with the order; and
(b) the claimant may apply to restore the claim within 28 days after the date the order was served on him.

55.17 Possession Order

r.55.17 **35.15, 87.12**

Except where rules 55.16(1)(b) or (c) apply, the judge will make an order for possession without requiring the attendance of the parties.

55.18 Postponement of Possession

r.55.18 **35.15, 87.12**

(1) Where the defendant seeks postponement of possession on the ground of exceptional hardship under section 89 of the Housing Act 1980, the judge may direct a hearing of that issue.
(2) Where the judge directs a hearing under paragraph (1)—
(a) the hearing must be held before the date on which possession is to be given up; and
(b) the judge will direct how many days' notice the parties must be given of that hearing.
(3) Where the judge is satisfied, on a hearing directed under paragraph (1), that exceptional hardship would be caused by requiring possession to be given up by the date in the order of possession, he may vary the date on which possession must be given up.

55.19 Application to Set Aside or Vary

r.55.19 **35.15, 87.12**

The court may—
(a) on application by a party within 14 days of service of the order; or
(b) of its own initiative,
set aside or vary any order made under rule 55.17.

III INTERIM POSSESSION ORDERS

55.20 When This Section May Be Used

r.55.20 **35.13**

(1) This Section of this Part applies where the claimant seeks an Interim Possession Order.
(2) In this Section—
(a) 'IPO' means Interim Possession Order; and
(b) 'premises' has the same meaning as in section 12 of the Criminal Law Act 1977.
(3) Where this Section requires an act to be done within a specified number of hours, rule 2.8(4) does not apply.

55.21 Conditions for IPO Application

r.55.21 **35.13**

(1) An application for an IPO may be made where the following conditions are satisfied—
(a) the only claim made is a possession claim against trespassers for the recovery of premises;
(b) the claimant—
(i) has an immediate right to possession of the premises; and
(ii) has had such a right throughout the period of alleged unlawful occupation; and
(c) the claim is made within 28 days of the date on which the claimant first knew, or ought reasonably to have known, that the defendant (or any of the defendants), was in occupation.
(2) An application for an IPO may not be made against a defendant who entered or remained on the premises with the consent of a person who, at the time consent was given, had an immediate right to possession of the premises.

55.22 The Application

r.55.22 **35.13**

(1) Rules 55.3(1) and (4) apply to the claim.
(2) The claim form and the defendant's form of witness statement must be in the form set out in the relevant practice direction.
(3) When he files his claim form, the claimant must also file—
(a) an application notice in the form set out in the relevant practice direction; and
(b) written evidence.
(4) The written evidence must be given—
(a) by the claimant personally; or
(b) where the claimant is a body corporate, by a duly authorised officer.

(Rule 22.1(6)(b) provides that the statement of truth must be signed by the maker of the witness statement)

(5) The court will—
(a) issue—
(i) the claim form; and
(ii) the application for the IPO; and
(b) set a date for the hearing of the application.
(6) The hearing of the application will be as soon as practicable but not less than 3 days after the date of issue.

55.23 Service

r.55.23 **35.13**

(1) Within 24 hours of the issue of the application, the claimant must serve on the defendant—
(a) the claim form;
(b) the application notice together with the written evidence in support; and
(c) a blank form for the defendant's witness statement (as set out in the relevant practice direction) which must be attached to the application notice.
(2) The claimant must serve the documents listed in paragraph (1) in accordance with rule 55.6(a).
(3) At or before the hearing the claimant must file a certificate of service in relation to the documents listed in paragraph (1) and rule 6.14(2)(a) does not apply.

55.24 Defendant's Response

r.55.24 **35.13**

(1) At any time before the hearing the defendant may file a witness statement in response to the application.
(2) The witness statement should be in the form set out in the relevant practice direction.

55.25 Hearing of the Application

r.55.25 **35.13** r.55.25(3) **35.13**
r.55.25(1) **35.13**

(1) In deciding whether to grant an IPO, the court will have regard to whether the claimant has given, or is prepared to give, the following undertakings in support of his application—
  (a) if, after an IPO is made, the court decides that the claimant was not entitled to the order to—
    (i) reinstate the defendant if so ordered by the court; and
    (ii) pay such damages as the court may order; and
  (b) before the claim for possession is finally decided, not to—
    (i) damage the premises;
    (ii) grant a right of occupation to any other person; and
    (iii) damage or dispose of any of the defendant's property.
(2) The court will make an IPO if—
  (a) the claimant has—
    (i) filed a certificate of service of the documents referred to in rule 55.23(1); or
    (ii) proved service of those documents to the satisfaction of the court; and
  (b) the court considers that—
    (i) the conditions set out in rule 55.21(1) are satisfied; and
    (ii) any undertakings given by the claimant as a condition of making the order are adequate.
(3) An IPO will be in the form set out in the relevant practice direction and will require the defendant to vacate the premises specified in the claim form within 24 hours of the service of the order.
(4) On making an IPO the court will set a date for the hearing of the claim for possession which will be not less than 7 days after the date on which the IPO is made.
(5) Where the court does not make an IPO—
  (a) the court will set a date for the hearing of the claim;
  (b) the court may give directions for the future conduct of the claim; and
  (c) subject to such directions, the claim shall proceed in accordance with Section I of this Part.

55.26 Service and Enforcement of the IPO

r.55.26 **35.13**

(1) An IPO must be served within 48 hours after it is sealed.
(2) The claimant must serve the IPO on the defendant together with copies of—
  (a) the claim form; and
  (b) the written evidence in support,
  in accordance with rule 55.6(a).
(3) CCR Order 26, rule 17 does not apply to the enforcement of an IPO.
(4) If an IPO is not served within the time limit specified by this rule, the claimant may apply to the court for directions for the claim for possession to continue under Section I of this Part.

55.27 After IPO Made

r.55.27 **35.13**

(1) Before the date for the hearing of the claim, the claimant must file a certificate of service in relation to the documents specified in rule 55.26(2).
(2) The IPO will expire on the date of the hearing of the claim.
(3) At the hearing the court may make any order it considers appropriate and may, in particular—
  (a) make a final order for possession;
  (b) dismiss the claim for possession;
  (c) give directions for the claim for possession to continue under Section I of this Part; or
  (d) enforce any of the claimant's undertakings.
(4) Unless the court directs otherwise, the claimant must serve any order or directions in accordance with rule 55.6(a).
(5) CCR Order 24, rule 6 applies to the enforcement of a final order for possession.

55.28 Application to Set Aside IPO

r.55.28 **35.13**

(1) If the defendant has left the premises, he may apply on grounds of urgency for the IPO to be set aside before the date of the hearing of the claim.
(2) An application under paragraph (1) must be supported by a witness statement.
(3) On receipt of the application, the court will give directions as to—
  (a) the date for the hearing; and
  (b) the period of notice, if any, to be given to the claimant and the method of service of any such notice.
(4) No application to set aside an IPO may be made under rule 39.3.
(5) Where no notice is required under paragraph (3)(b), the only matters to be dealt with at the hearing of the application to set aside are whether—
  (a) the IPO should be set aside; and
  (b) any undertaking to reinstate the defendant should be enforced,
  and all other matters will be dealt with at the hearing of the claim.
(6) The court will serve on all the parties—
  (a) a copy of the order made under paragraph (5); and
  (b) where no notice was required under paragraph (3)(b), a copy of the defendant's application to set aside and the witness statement in support.
(7) Where notice is required under paragraph (3)(b), the court may treat the hearing of the application to set aside as the hearing of the claim.

PD 55 Practice Direction — Possession Claims

This practice direction supplements CPR Part 55

PD 55 **35.14, 85.1, 87.6, 88.29** [For commentary on a specific paragraph, please refer to the cross-references after the title of the paragraph.]

SECTION I GENERAL RULES

Starting the Claim: Rule 55.3

para.1 **11.3**
para.1.1 **87.8**
para.1.2 **35.5, 87.8**
para.1.3 **35.5, 87.8**
para.1.4 **87.8**

1.1 Except where the county court does not have jurisdiction, possession claims should normally be brought in the county court. Only exceptional circumstances justify starting a claim in the High Court.

1.2 If a claimant starts a claim in the High Court and the court decides that it should have been started in the county court, the court will normally either strike the claim out or transfer it to the county court on its own initiative. This is likely to result in delay and the court will normally disallow the costs of starting the claim in the High Court and of any transfer.

1.3 Circumstances which may, in an appropriate case, justify starting a claim in the High Court are if:

(1) there are complicated disputes of fact;
(2) there are points of law of general importance; or
(3) the claim is against trespassers and there is a substantial risk of public disturbance or of serious harm to persons or property which properly require immediate determination.

1.4 The value of the property and the amount of any financial claim may be relevant circumstances, but these factors alone will not normally justify starting the claim in the High Court.

1.5 The claimant must use the appropriate claim form and particulars of claim form set out in Table 1 to PD 4. The defence must be in form N11, N11B, N11M or N11R, as appropriate.

1.6 High Court claims for the possession of land subject to a mortgage will be assigned to the Chancery Division.

1.7 A claim which is not a possession claim may be brought under the procedure set out in Section I of Part 55 if it is started in the same claim form as a possession claim which, by virtue of r. 55.2(1) must be brought in accordance with that Section.

(Rule 7.3 provides that a claimant may use a single claim form to start all claims which can be conveniently disposed of in the same proceedings.)

1.8 For example a claim under the Mobile Homes Act 1983, sch. 1, part 1, paras 4,5 or 6, may be brought using the procedure set out in Section I of CPR, Part 55, if the claim is started in the same claim form as a claim enforcing the rights referred to in the Caravan Sites Act 1968, s. 3(1)(b) (which, by virtue of CPR, r. 55.2(1), must be brought under Section I of Part 55).

1.9 Where the claim form includes a demotion claim, the claim must be started in the county court for the district in which the land is situated.

Particulars of Claim: Rule 55.4

para.2 **24.14**
para.2.1 **24.6, 35.6**

2.1 In a possession claim the particulars of claim must:

(1) identify the land to which the claim relates;
(2) state whether the claim relates to residential property;
(3) state the ground on which possession is claimed;
(4) give full details about any mortgage or tenancy agreement; and
(5) give details of every person who, to the best of the claimant's knowledge, is in possession of the property.

Civil Procedure Rules & Practice Directions

Residential property let on a tenancy

para.2.3 **24.6, 87.7**

2.2 Paragraphs 2.3, 2.4 and 2.4A apply if the claim relates to residential property let on a tenancy.

2.3 If the claim includes a claim for non-payment of rent the particulars of claim must set out:

(1) the amount due at the start of the proceedings;

(2) in schedule form, the dates and amounts of all payments due and payments made under the tenancy agreement for a period of two years immediately preceding the date of issue, or if the first date of default occurred less than two years before the date of issue from the first date of default and a running total of the arrears;

(3) the daily rate of any rent and interest;

(4) any previous steps taken to recover the arrears of rent with full details of any court proceedings; and

(5) any relevant information about the defendant's circumstances, in particular:

(a) whether the defendant is in receipt of social security benefits; and

(b) whether any payments are made on his behalf directly to the claimant under the Social Security Contributions and Benefits Act 1992.

2.3A If the claimant wishes to rely on a history of arrears which is longer than two years, he should state this in his particulars and exhibit a full (or longer) schedule to a witness statement.

2.4 If the claimant knows of any person (including a mortgagee) entitled to claim relief against forfeiture as underlessee under s. 146(4) of the Law of Property Act 1925 (or in accordance with s. 38 of the Supreme Court Act 1981, or s. 138(9C) of the County Courts Act 1984):

(1) the particulars of claim must state the name and address of that person; and

(2) the claimant must file a copy of the particulars of claim for service on him.

2.4A If the claim for possession relates to the conduct of the tenant, the particulars of claim must state details of the conduct alleged.

Land subject to a mortgage

para.2.5 **24.6**

2.5 If the claim is a possession claim by a mortgagee, the particulars of claim must also set out:

(1) if the claim relates to residential property whether:

(a) a land charge of Class F has been registered under s. 2(7) of the Matrimonial Homes Act 1967;

(b) a notice registered under s. 2(8) or 8(3) of the Matrimonial Homes Act 1983 has been entered and on whose behalf; or

(c) a notice under s. 31(10) of the Family Law Act 1996 has been registered and on whose behalf; and

if so, that the claimant will serve notice of the claim on the persons on whose behalf the land charge is registered or the notice or caution entered;

(2) the state of the mortgage account by including:

(a) the amount of:

(i) the advance;

(ii) any periodic repayment; and

(iii) any payment of interest required to be made;

(b) the amount which would have to be paid (after taking into account any adjustment for early settlement) in order to redeem the mortgage at a stated date not more than 14 days after the claim started specifying the amount of solicitor's costs and administration charges which would be payable;

(c) if the loan which is secured by the mortgage is a regulated consumer credit agreement, the total amount outstanding under the terms of the mortgage; and

(d) the rate of interest payable:

(i) at the commencement of the mortgage;

(ii) immediately before any arrears referred to in sub-paragraph (3) accrued;

(iii) at the commencement of the proceedings;

(3) if the claim is brought because of failure to pay the periodic payments when due:

(a) in schedule form, the dates and amounts of all payments due and payments made under the mortgage agreement or mortgage deed for a period of two years immediately preceding the date of issue, or if the first date of default occurred less than two years before the date of issue from the first date of default and a running total of the arrears;

(b) give details of:
   (i) any other payments required to be made as a term of the mortgage (such as for insurance premiums, legal costs, default interest, penalties, administrative or other charges);
   (ii) any other sums claimed and stating the nature and amount of each such charge; and
   (iii) whether any of these payments is in arrears and whether or not it is included in the amount of any periodic payment;

(4) whether or not the loan which is secured by the mortgage is a regulated consumer credit agreement and, if so, specify the date on which any notice required by ss. 76 or 87 of the Consumer Credit Act 1974 was given;
(5) if appropriate details that show the property is not one to which s. 141 of the Consumer Credit Act 1974 applies;
(6) any relevant information about the defendant's circumstances, in particular:
   (a) whether the defendant is in receipt of social security benefits; and
   (b) whether any payments are made on his behalf directly to the claimant under the Social Security Contributions and Benefits Act 1992;
(7) give details of any tenancy entered into between the mortgagor and mortgagee (including any notices served); and
(8) state any previous steps which the claimant has taken to recover the money secured by the mortgage or the mortgaged property and, in the case of court proceedings, state:
   (a) the dates when the claim started and concluded; and
   (b) the dates and terms of any orders made.

2.5A If the claimant wishes to rely on a history of arrears which is longer than two years, he should state this in his particulars and exhibit a full (or longer) schedule to a witness statement.

Possession claim against trespassers

para.2.6 **24.6, 35.6**

2.6 If the claim is a possession claim against trespassers, the particulars of claim must state the claimant's interest in the land or the basis of his right to claim possession and the circumstances in which it has been occupied without licence or consent.

Possession claim in relation to a demoted tenancy by a housing action trust or a local housing authority

2.7 If the claim is a possession claim under the Housing Act 1996, s. 143D (possession claim in relation to a demoted tenancy where the landlord is a housing action trust or a local housing authority), the particulars of claim must have attached to them a copy of the notice to the tenant served under s. 143E of the 1996 Act.

Hearing Date: Rule 55.5

para.3 **87.9** para.3.2 **35.7**

3.1 The court may exercise its powers under r. 3.1(2)(a) and (b) to shorten the time periods set out in r. 55.5(2) and (3).

3.2 Particular consideration should be given to the exercise of this power if:
(1) the defendant, or a person for whom the defendant is responsible, has assaulted or threatened to assault:
   (a) the claimant;
   (b) a member of the claimant's staff; or
   (c) another resident in the locality;
(2) there are reasonable grounds for fearing such an assault; or
(3) the defendant, or a person for whom the defendant is responsible, has caused serious damage or threatened to cause serious damage to the property or to the home or property of another resident in the locality.

3.3 Where para. 3.2 applies but the case cannot be determined at the first hearing fixed under r. 55.5, the court will consider what steps are needed to finally determine the case as quickly as reasonably practicable.

Service in Claims against Trespassers: Rule 55.6

para.4.1 **35.7**

4.1 If the claim form is to be served by the court and in accordance with r. 55.6(b) the claimant must provide sufficient stakes and transparent envelopes.

The Hearing: Rule 55.8

para.5.2 **87.10**
para.5.3 **87.10**
para.5.4 **35.10, 87.10**

5.1 Attention is drawn to r. 55.8(3) . Each party should wherever possible include all the evidence he wishes to present in his statement of case, verified by a statement of truth.

5.2 If relevant the claimant's evidence should include the amount of any rent or mortgage arrears and interest on those arrears. These amounts should, if possible, be up to date to the date of the hearing (if necessary by specifying a daily rate of arrears and interest). However, r. 55.8(4) does not prevent such evidence being brought up to date orally or in writing on the day of the hearing if necessary.

5.3 If relevant the defendant should give evidence of:

(1) the amount of any outstanding social security or housing benefit payments relevant to rent or mortgage arrears; and

(2) the status of:

(a) any claims for social security or housing benefit about which a decision has not yet been made; and

(b) any applications to appeal or review a social security or housing benefit decision where that appeal or review has not yet concluded.

5.4 If:

(1) the maker of a witness statement does not attend a hearing; and

(2) the other party disputes material evidence contained in his statement,

the court will normally adjourn the hearing so that oral evidence can be given.

Consumer Credit Act Claims Relating to the Recovery of Land

7.1 Any application by the defendant for a time order under s. 129 of the Consumer Credit Act 1974 may be made:

(1) in his defence; or

(2) by application notice in the proceedings.

Enforcement of Charging Order by Sale

7.2 A party seeking to enforce a charging order by sale should follow the procedure set out in r. 73.10 and the Part 55 procedure should not be used.

SECTION II ACCELERATED POSSESSION CLAIMS OF PROPERTY LET ON AN ASSURED SHORTHOLD TENANCY

Postponement of Possession: Rule 55.18

para.8 **87.12**

8.1 If the judge is satisfied as to the matters set out in r. 55.16(2), he will make an order for possession in accordance with r. 55.17, whether or not the defendant seeks a postponement of possession on the ground of exceptional hardship under s. 89 of the Housing Act 1980.

8.2 In a claim in which the judge is satisfied that the defendant has shown exceptional hardship, he will only postpone possession without directing a hearing under r. 55.18(1) if:

(1) he considers that possession should be given up six weeks after the date of the order or, if the defendant has requested postponement to an earlier date, on that date; and

(2) the claimant indicated on his claim form that he would be content for the court to make such an order without a hearing.

8.3 In all other cases if the defendant seeks a postponement of possession under s. 89 of the Housing Act 1980, the judge will direct a hearing under r. 55.18(1).

8.4 If, at that hearing, the judge is satisfied that exceptional hardship would be caused by requiring possession to be given up by the date in the order of possession, he may vary that order under r. 55.18(3) so that possession is to be given up at a later date. That later date may be no later than six weeks after the making of the order for possession on the papers (see s. 89 of the Housing Act 1980).

SECTION III INTERIM POSSESSION ORDERS

9.1 The claim form must be in **form N5**, the application notice seeking the interim possession order must be in **form N130** and the defendant's witness statement must be in **form N133**.

9.2 The IPO will be in **form N134**.

PD 55B Practice Direction — Possession Claims Online

This practice direction supplements r. 55.10A.

Scope of This Practice Direction

1.1 This practice direction provides for a scheme ('Possession Claims Online') to operate in specified county courts:

(1) enabling claimants and their representatives to start certain possession claims under Part 55 by requesting the issue of a claim form electronically via the PCOL website; and

(2) where a claim has been started electronically, enabling the claimant or defendant and their representatives to take further steps in the claim electronically as specified below.

1.2 In this practice direction:

(1) 'PCOL website' means the website www.possessionclaim.gov.uk which may be accessed via Her Majesty's Courts Service website (www.hmcourts-service.gov.uk) and through which Possession Claims Online will operate; and

(2) 'specified court' means a county court specified on the PCOL website as one in which Possession Claims Online is available.

Information on the PCOL Website

2.1 The PCOL website contains further details and guidance about the operation of Possession Claims Online.

2.2 In particular the PCOL website sets out:

(1) the specified courts; and

(2) the dates from which Possession Claims Online will be available in each specified court.

2.3 The operation of Possession Claims Online in any specified court may be restricted to taking certain of the steps specified in this practice direction, and in such cases the PCOL website will set out the steps which may be taken using Possession Claims Online in that specified court.

Security

3.1 Her Majesty's Courts Service will take such measures as it thinks fit to ensure the security of steps taken or information stored electronically. These may include requiring users of Possession Claims Online:

(1) to enter a customer identification number or password;

(2) to provide personal information for identification purposes; and

(3) to comply with any other security measures,

before taking any step online.

Fees

4.1 A step may only be taken using Possession Claims Online on payment of the prescribed fee where a fee is payable. Where this practice direction provides for a fee to be paid electronically, it may be paid by:

(1) credit card;

(2) debit card; or

(3) any other method which Her Majesty's Courts Service may permit.

4.2 A defendant who wishes to claim exemption from payment of fees must do so through an organisation approved by Her Majesty's Courts Service before taking any step using PCOL which attracts a fee. If satisfied that the defendant is entitled to fee exemption, the organisation will submit the fee exemption form through the PCOL website to Her Majesty's Courts Service. The defendant may then use PCOL to take such a step.

(Her Majesty's Courts Service website contains guidance as to when the entitlement to claim an exemption from payment of fees arises. The PCOL website will contain a list of organisations through which the defendant may claim an exemption from fees.)

Claims Which May Be Started Using Possession Claims Online

5.1 A claim may be started online if:

(1) it is brought under Section I of Part 55;

(2) it includes a possession claim for residential property by:

(a) a landlord against a tenant, solely on the ground of arrears of rent (but not a claim for forfeiture of a lease); or

(b) a mortgagee against a mortgagor, solely on the ground of default in the payment of sums due under a mortgage,

relating to land within the district of a specified court;

(3) it does not include a claim for any other remedy except for payment of arrears of rent or money due under a mortgage, interest and costs;

(4) the defendant has an address for service in England and Wales; and

(5) the claimant is able to provide a postcode for the property.

5.2 A claim must not be started online if a defendant is known to be a child or patient.

Starting a Claim

6.1 A claimant may request the issue of a claim form by:

(1) completing an online claim form at the PCOL website;

(2) paying the appropriate issue fee electronically at the PCOL website or by some other means approved by Her Majesty's Courts Service.

6.2 The particulars of claim must be included in the online claim form and may not be filed separately. It is not necessary to file a copy of the tenancy agreement, mortgage deed or mortgage agreement with the particulars of claim.

6.3 The particulars of claim must include a history of the rent or mortgage account, in schedule form setting out:

(1) the dates and amounts of all payments due and payments made under the tenancy agreement, mortgage deed or mortgage agreement either from the first date of default if that date occurred less than two years before the date of issue or for a period of two years immediately preceding the date of issue; and

(2) a running total of the arrears.

6.4 If the claimant wishes to rely on a history of arrears which is longer than two years, he should state this in his particulars and exhibit a full (or longer) schedule to a witness statement.

6.5 When an online claim form is received, an acknowledgment of receipt will automatically be sent to the claimant. The acknowledgment does not constitute notice that the claim form has been issued or served.

6.6 When the court issues a claim form following the submission of an online claim form, the claim is 'brought' for the purposes of the Limitation Act 1980 and any other enactment on the date on which the online claim form is received by the court's computer system. The court will keep a record, by electronic or other means, of when online claim forms are received.

6.7 When the court issues a claim form it will:

(1) serve a printed version of the claim form and a defence form on the defendant; and

(2) send the claimant notice of issue by post or, where the claimant has supplied an email address, by electronic means.

6.8 The claim shall be deemed to be served on the fifth day after the claim was issued irrespective of whether that day is a business day or not.

6.9 Where the period of time within which a defence must be filed ends on a day when the court is closed, the defendant may file his defence on the next day that the court is open.

6.10 The claim form shall have printed on it a unique customer identification number or a password by which the defendant may access the claim on the PCOL website.

6.11 PCOL will issue the proceedings in the appropriate county court by reference to the postcode provided by the claimant and that court shall have jurisdiction to hear and determine the claim and to carry out enforcement of any judgment irrespective of whether the property is within or outside the jurisdiction of that court.

(Rule 30.2(1) authorises proceedings to be transferred from one county court to another.)

Civil Procedure Rules & Practice Directions

Defence

7.1 A defendant wishing to file:
(1) a defence; or
(2) a counterclaim (to be filed together with a defence) to a claim which has been issued through the PCOL system,
may, instead of filing a written form, do so by:
(a) completing the relevant online form at the PCOL website; and
(b) if the defendant is making a counterclaim, paying the appropriate fee electronically at the PCOL website or by some other means approved by Her Majesty's Courts Service.

7.2 Where a defendant files a defence by completing the relevant online form, he must not send the court a hard copy.

7.3 When an online defence form is received, an acknowledgment of receipt will automatically be sent to the defendant. The acknowledgment does not constitute notice that the defence has been served.

7.4 The online defence form will be treated as being filed:
(1) on the day the court receives it, if it receives it before 4 p.m. on a working day; and
(2) otherwise, on the next working day after the court receives the online defence form.

7.5 A defence is filed when the online defence form is received by the court's computer system. The court will keep a record, by electronic or other means, of when online defence forms are received.

Statement of Truth

8.1 Part 22 requires any statement of case to be verified by a statement of truth. This applies to any online claims and defences and application notices.

8.2 Part 22 also requires that if an applicant wishes to rely on matters set out in his application notice as evidence, the application notice must be verified by a statement of truth. This applies to any application notice completed online that contains matters on which the applicant wishes to rely as evidence.

8.3 Attention is drawn to:
(1) PD 22, para. 2, which stipulates the form of the statement of truth; and
(2) PD 22, para. 3, which provides who may sign a statement of truth; and
(3) r. 32.14, which sets out the consequences of making, or causing to be made, a false statement in a document verified by a statement of truth, without an honest belief in its truth.

Signature

9.1 Any provision of the CPR which requires a document to be signed by any person is satisfied by that person entering his name on an online form.

Communication with the Court Electronically by the Messaging Service

10.1 If the PCOL website specifies that a court accepts electronic communications relating to claims brought using Possession Claims Online the parties may communicate with the court using the messaging service facility, available on the PCOL website ('the messaging service').

10.2 The messaging service is for brief and straightforward communications only. The PCOL website contains a list of examples of when it will not be appropriate to use the messaging service.

10.3 Parties must not send to the court forms or attachments via the messaging service.

10.4 The court shall treat any forms or attachments sent via the messaging service as not having been filed or received.

10.5 The court will normally reply via the messaging service where:
(1) the response is to a message transmitted via the messaging service; and
(2) the sender has provided an email address.

Electronic Applications

11.1 Certain applications in relation to a possession claim started online may be made electronically ('online applications'). An online application may be made if a form for that application is published on the PCOL website ('online application form') and the application is made at least five clear days before the hearing.

11.2 If a claim for possession has been started online and a party wishes to make an online application, he may do so by:
(1) completing the appropriate online application form at the PCOL website; and
(2) paying the appropriate fee electronically at the PCOL website or by some other means approved by Her Majesty's Courts Service.

11.3 When an online application form is received, an acknowledgment of receipt will automatically be sent to the applicant. The acknowledgment does not constitute a notice that the online application form has been issued or served.

11.4 Where an application must be made within a specified time, it is so made if the online application form is received by the court's computer system within that time. The court will keep a record, by electronic or other means, of when online application forms are received.

11.5 When the court receives an online application form it shall:
(1) serve a copy of the online application endorsed with the date of the hearing by post on the claimant at least two clear days before the hearing; and
(2) send the defendant notice of service and confirmation of the date of the hearing by post; provided that
(3) where either party has provided the court with an email address for service, service of the application and/or the notice of service and confirmation of the hearing date may be effected by electronic means.

Request for Issue of Warrant

12.1 Where:
(1) the court has made an order for possession in a claim started online; and
(2) the claimant is entitled to the issue of a warrant of possession without requiring the permission of the court,

the claimant may request the issue of a warrant by completing an online request form at the PCOL website and paying the appropriate fee electronically at the PCOL website or by some other means approved by Her Majesty's Courts Service.

12.2 A request under para. 12.1 will be treated as being filed:
(1) on the day the court receives the request, if it receives it before 4 p.m. on a working day; and
(2) otherwise, on the next working day after the court receives the request.

(CCR, ord. 26, r. 5, sets out certain circumstances in which a warrant of execution may not be issued without the permission of the court. CCR, ord. 26, r. 17(6), applies r. 5 of that Order with necessary modifications to a warrant of possession.)

Application to Suspend Warrant of Possession

13.1 Where the court has issued a warrant of possession, the defendant may apply electronically for the suspension of the warrant, provided that:
(1) the application is made at least five clear days before the appointment for possession; and
(2) the defendant is not prevented from making such an application without the permission of the court.

13.2 The defendant may apply electronically for the suspension of the warrant, by:
(1) completing an online application for suspension at the PCOL website; and
(2) paying the appropriate fee electronically at the PCOL website or by some other means approved by Her Majesty's Courts Service.

13.3 When an online application for suspension is received, an acknowledgment of receipt will automatically be sent to the defendant. The acknowledgment does not constitute a notice that the online application for suspension has been served.

13.4 Where an application must be made within a specified time, it is so made if the online application for suspension is received by the court's computer system within that time. The court will keep a record, by electronic or other means, of when online applications for suspension are received.

13.5 When the court receives an online application for suspension it shall:
(1) serve a copy of the online application for suspension endorsed with the date of the hearing by post on the claimant at least two clear days before the hearing; and

(2) send the defendant notice of service and confirmation of the date of the hearing by post; provided that

(3) where either party has provided the court with an email address for service, service of the application and/or the notice of service and confirmation of the hearing date may be effected by electronic means.

Viewing the Case Record

14.1 A facility will be provided on the PCOL website for parties or their representatives to view:

(1) an electronic record of the status of claims started online, which will be reviewed and, if necessary, updated at least once each day; and

(2) all information relating to the case that has been filed by the parties electronically.

14.2 In addition, where the PCOL website specifies that the court has the facility to provide viewing of such information by electronic means, the parties or their representatives may view the following information electronically:

(1) court orders made in relation to the case; and

(2) details of progress on enforcement and subsequent orders made.

CPR Part 56 Landlord and Tenant Claims and Miscellaneous Provisions about Land

Part 56 **42.15**, **85.1**, **91.34** [For commentary on a specific rule, please refer to the cross-references after the title of the rule.]

I LANDLORD AND TENANT CLAIMS

56.1 Scope and Interpretation

(1) In this Section of this Part 'landlord and tenant claim' means a claim under—
  (a) the Landlord and Tenant Act 1927;
  (b) the Leasehold Property (Repairs) Act 1938;
  (c) the Landlord and Tenant Act 1954;
  (d) the Landlord and Tenant Act 1985; or
  (e) the Landlord and Tenant Act 1987.
(2) A practice direction may set out special provisions with regard to any particular category of landlord and tenant claim.

56.2 Starting the Claim

(1) The claim must be started in the county court for the district in which the land is situated unless paragraph (2) applies or an enactment provides otherwise.
(2) The claim may be started in the High Court if the claimant files with his claim form a certificate stating the reasons for bringing the claim in that court verified by a statement of truth in accordance with rule 22.1(1).
(3) The practice direction refers to circumstances which may justify starting the claim in the High Court.

56.3 Claims for a New Tenancy under Section 24 and for the Termination of a Tenancy under Section 29(2) of the Landlord and Tenant Act 1954

(1) This rule applies to a claim for a new tenancy under section 24 and to a claim for the termination of a tenancy under section 29(2) of the 1954 Act.
(2) In this rule—
  (a) 'the 1954 Act' means the Landlord and Tenant Act 1954;
  (b) 'an unopposed claim' means a claim for a new tenancy under section 24 of the 1954 Act in circumstances where the grant of a new tenancy is not opposed;
  (c) 'an opposed claim' means a claim for—
    (i) a new tenancy under section 24 of the 1954 Act in circumstances where the grant of a new tenancy is opposed; or
    (ii) the termination of a tenancy under section 29(2) of the 1954 Act.
(3) Where the claim is an unopposed claim—
  (a) the claimant must use the Part 8 procedure, but the following rules do not apply—
    (i) rule 8.5; and
    (ii) rule 8.6;
  (b) the claim form must be served within 2 months after the date of issue and rules 7.5 and 7.6 are modified accordingly; and

(c) the court will give directions about the future management of the claim following receipt of the acknowledgment of service.

(4) Where the claim is an opposed claim—

(a) the claimant must use the Part 7 procedure; but

(b) the claim form must be served within 2 months after the date of issue, and rules 7.5 and 7.6 are modified accordingly.

(The practice direction to this Part contains provisions about evidence, including expert evidence in opposed claims)

II MISCELLANEOUS PROVISIONS ABOUT LAND

56.4 Scope

A practice direction may set out special provisions with regard to claims under the following enactments—

(a) the Chancel Repairs Act 1932;
(b) the Leasehold Reform Act 1967;
(c) the Access to Neighbouring Land Act 1992;
(d) the Leasehold Reform, Housing and Urban Development Act 1993; and
(e) the Commonhold and Leasehold Reform Act 2002.

PD 56 Practice Direction — Landlord and Tenant Claims and Miscellaneous Provisions about Land

This practice direction supplements CPR Part 56

PD 56 **85.1, 91.34** [For commentary on a specific paragraph, please refer to the cross-references after the title of the paragraph.]

SECTION I LANDLORD AND TENANT CLAIMS

1.1 In this section of this practice direction:
'the 1927 Act' means the Landlord and Tenant Act 1927;
'the 1954 Act' means the Landlord and Tenant Act 1954;
'the 1985 Act' means the Landlord and Tenant Act 1985; and
'the 1987 Act' means the Landlord and Tenant Act 1987.

Starting the Claim: Rule 56.2

2.1 Subject to para. 2.1A, the claimant in a landlord and tenant claim must use the Part 8 procedure as modified by Part 56 and this practice direction.

2.1A Where the landlord and tenant claim is a claim for:
(1) a new tenancy under s. 24 of the 1954 Act in circumstances where the grant of a new tenancy is opposed; or
(2) the termination of a tenancy under s. 29(2) of the 1954 Act,
the claimant must use the Part 7 procedure as modified by Part 56 and this practice direction.

2.2 Except where the county court does not have jurisdiction, landlord and tenant claims should normally be brought in the county court. Only exceptional circumstances justify starting a claim in the High Court.

2.3 If a claimant starts a claim in the High Court and the court decides that it should have been started in the county court, the court will normally either strike the claim out or transfer it to the county court on its own initiative. This is likely to result in delay and the court will normally disallow the costs of starting the claim in the High Court and of any transfer.

2.4 Circumstances which may, in an appropriate case, justify starting a claim in the High Court are if:
(1) there are complicated disputes of fact; or
(2) there are points of law of general importance.

2.5 The value of the property and the amount of any financial claim may be relevant circumstances, but these factors alone will not normally justify starting the claim in the High Court.

2.6 A landlord and tenant claim started in the High Court must be brought in the Chancery Division.

Claims for a New Tenancy under Section 24 and Termination of a Tenancy under Section 29(2) of the 1954 Act

3.1 This paragraph applies to a claim for a new tenancy under s. 24 and termination of a tenancy under s. 29(2) of the 1954 Act where r. 56.3 applies and in this paragraph:
(1) 'an unopposed claim' means a claim for a new tenancy under s. 24 of the 1954 Act in circumstances where the grant of a new tenancy is not opposed;
(2) 'an opposed claim' means a claim for:
(a) a new tenancy under s. 24 of the 1954 Act in circumstances where the grant of a new tenancy is opposed; or
(b) the termination of a tenancy under s. 29(2) of the 1954 Act; and
(3) 'grounds of opposition' means:
(a) the grounds specified in s. 30(1) of the 1954 Act on which a landlord may oppose an application for a new tenancy under s. 24(1) of the 1954 Act or make an application under s. 29(2) of the 1954 Act; or

Civil Procedure Rules & Practice Directions

(b) any other basis on which the landlord asserts that a new tenancy ought not to be granted.

Precedence of claim forms where there is more than one application to the court under s. 24(1) or s. 29(2) of the 1954 Act

3.2 Where more than one application to the court under s. 24(1) or s. 29(2) of the 1954 Act is made, the following provisions shall apply:

(1) once an application to the court under s. 24(1) of the 1954 Act has been served on a defendant, no further application to the court in respect of the same tenancy whether under s. 24(1) or s. 29(2) of the 1954 Act may be served by that defendant without the permission of the court;

(2) if more than one application to the court under s. 24(1) of the 1954 Act in respect of the same tenancy is served on the same day, any landlord's application shall stand stayed until further order of the court;

(3) if applications to the court under both s. 24(1) and s. 29(2) of the 1954 Act in respect of the same tenancy are served on the same day, any tenant's application shall stand stayed until further order of the court; and

(4) if a defendant is served with an application under s. 29(2) of the 1954 Act ('the s. 29(2) application') which was issued at a time when an application to the court had already been made by that defendant in respect of the same tenancy under s. 24(1) of the 1954 Act ('the s. 24(1) application'), the service of the s. 29(2) application shall be deemed to be a notice under r. 7.7 requiring service or discontinuance of the s. 24(1) application within a period of 14 days after the service of the s. 29(2) application.

Defendant where the claimant is the tenant making a claim for a new tenancy under s. 24 of the 1954 Act

3.3 Where a claim for a new tenancy under s. 24 of the 1954 Act is made by a tenant, the person who, in relation to the claimant's current tenancy, is the landlord as defined in s. 44 of the 1954 Act must be a defendant.

Contents of the claim form in all cases

3.4 The claim form must contain details of:

(1) the property to which the claim relates;

(2) the particulars of the current tenancy (including date, parties and duration), the current rent (if not the original rent) and the date and method of termination;

(3) every notice or request given or made under ss. 25 or 26 of the 1954 Act; and

(4) the expiry date of:

(a) the statutory period under s. 29A(2) of the 1954 Act; or

(b) any agreed extended period made under s. 29B(1) or 29B(2) of the 1954 Act.

Claim form where the claimant is the tenant making a claim for a new tenancy under s. 24 of the 1954 Act

3.5 Where the claimant is the tenant making a claim for a new tenancy under s. 24 of the 1954 Act, in addition to the details specified in para. 3.4, the claim form must contain details of:

(1) the nature of the business carried on at the property;

(2) whether the claimant relies on s. 23(1A), 41 or 42 of the 1954 Act and, if so, the basis on which he does so;

(3) whether the claimant relies on s. 31A of the 1954 Act and, if so, the basis on which he does so;

(4) whether any, and if so what part, of the property comprised in the tenancy is occupied neither by the claimant nor by a person employed by the claimant for the purpose of the claimant's business;

(5) the claimant's proposed terms of the new tenancy; and

(6) the name and address of:

(a) anyone known to the claimant who has an interest in the reversion in the property (whether immediate or in not more than 15 years) on the termination of the claimant's current tenancy and who is likely to be affected by the grant of a new tenancy; or

(b) if the claimant does not know of anyone specified by sub-paragraph (6)(a), anyone who has a freehold interest in the property.

3.6 The claim form must be served on the persons referred to in para. 3.5(6)(a) or (b) as appropriate.

Claim form where the claimant is the landlord making a claim for a new tenancy under s. 24 of the 1954 Act

3.7 Where the claimant is the landlord making a claim for a new tenancy under s. 24 of the 1954 Act, in addition to the details specified in para. 3.4, the claim form must contain details of:

(1) the claimant's proposed terms of the new tenancy;

(2) whether the claimant is aware that the defendant's tenancy is one to which s. 32(2) of the 1954 Act applies and, if so, whether the claimant requires that any new tenancy shall be a tenancy of the whole of the property comprised in the defendant's current tenancy or just of the holding as defined by s. 23(3) of the 1954 Act; and

(3) the name and address of:

(a) anyone known to the claimant who has an interest in the reversion in the property (whether immediate or in not more than 15 years) on the termination of the claimant's current tenancy and who is likely to be affected by the grant of a new tenancy; or

(b) if the claimant does not know of anyone specified by sub-paragraph (3)(a), anyone who has a freehold interest in the property.

3.8 The claim form must be served on the persons referred to in para. 3.7(3)(a) or (b) as appropriate.

Claim form where the claimant is the landlord making an application for the termination of a tenancy under s. 29(2) of the 1954 Act

3.9 Where the claimant is the landlord making an application for the termination of a tenancy under s. 29(2) of the 1954 Act, in addition to the details specified in para. 3.4, the claim form must contain:

(1) the claimant's grounds of opposition;

(2) full details of those grounds of opposition; and

(3) the terms of a new tenancy that the claimant proposes in the event that his claim fails.

Acknowledgment of service where the claim is an unopposed claim and where the claimant is the tenant

3.10 Where the claim is an unopposed claim and the claimant is the tenant, the acknowledgment of service is to be in form N210 and must state with particulars:

(1) whether, if a new tenancy is granted, the defendant objects to any of the terms proposed by the claimant and if so:

(a) the terms to which he objects; and

(b) the terms that he proposes in so far as they differ from those proposed by the claimant;

(2) whether the defendant is a tenant under a lease having less than 15 years unexpired at the date of the termination of the claimant's current tenancy and, if so, the name and address of any person who, to the knowledge of the defendant, has an interest in the reversion in the property expectant (whether immediate or in not more than 15 years from that date) on the termination of the defendant's tenancy;

(3) the name and address of any person having an interest in the property who is likely to be affected by the grant of a new tenancy; and

(4) if the claimant's current tenancy is one to which s. 32(2) of the 1954 Act applies, whether the defendant requires that any new tenancy shall be a tenancy of the whole of the property comprised in the claimant's current tenancy.

Acknowledgment of service where the claim is an unopposed claim and the claimant is the landlord

3.11 Where the claim is an unopposed claim and the claimant is the landlord, the acknowledgment of service is to be in form N210 and must state with particulars:

(1) the nature of the business carried on at the property;

(2) if the defendant relies on s. 23(1A), 41 or 42 of the 1954 Act, the basis on which he does so;

(3) whether any, and if so what part, of the property comprised in the tenancy is occupied neither by the defendant nor by a person employed by the defendant for the purpose of the defendant's business;

(4) the name and address of:

(a) anyone known to the defendant who has an interest in the reversion in the property (whether immediate or in not more than 15 years) on the termination of the defendant's current tenancy and who is likely to be affected by the grant of a new tenancy; or
(b) if the defendant does not know of anyone specified by sub-paragraph (4)(a), anyone who has a freehold interest in the property; and
(5) whether, if a new tenancy is granted, the defendant objects to any of the terms proposed by the claimant and, if so:
(a) the terms to which he objects; and
(b) the terms that he proposes in so far as they differ from those proposed by the claimant.

Acknowledgment of service and defence where the claim is an opposed claim and where the claimant is the tenant

3.12 Where the claim is an opposed claim and the claimant is the tenant:
(1) the acknowledgment of service is to be in form N9; and
(2) in his defence the defendant must state with particulars:
(a) the defendant's grounds of opposition;
(b) full details of those grounds of opposition;
(c) whether, if a new tenancy is granted, the defendant objects to any of the terms proposed by the claimant and if so:
(i) the terms to which he objects; and
(ii) the terms that he proposes in so far as they differ from those proposed by the claimant;
(d) whether the defendant is a tenant under a lease having less than 15 years unexpired at the date of the termination of the claimant's current tenancy and, if so, the name and address of any person who, to the knowledge of the defendant, has an interest in the reversion in the property expectant (whether immediately or in not more than 15 years from that date) on the termination of the defendant's tenancy;
(e) the name and address of any person having an interest in the property who is likely to be affected by the grant of a new tenancy; and
(f) if the claimant's current tenancy is one to which s. 32(2) of the 1954 Act applies, whether the defendant requires that any new tenancy shall be a tenancy of the whole of the property comprised in the claimant's current tenancy.

Acknowledgment of service and defence where the claimant is the landlord making an application for the termination of a tenancy under s. 29(2) of the 1954 Act

3.13 Where the claim is an opposed claim and the claimant is the landlord:
(1) the acknowledgment of service is to be in form N9; and
(2) in his defence the defendant must state with particulars:
(a) whether the defendant relies on s. 23(1A), 41 or 42 of the 1954 Act and, if so, the basis on which he does so;
(b) whether the defendant relies on s. 31A of the 1954 Act and, if so, the basis on which he does so; and
(c) the terms of the new tenancy that the defendant would propose in the event that the claimant's claim to terminate the current tenancy fails.

Evidence in an unopposed claim

3.14 Where the claim is an unopposed claim, no evidence need be filed unless and until the court directs it to be filed.

Evidence in an opposed claim

3.15 Where the claim is an opposed claim, evidence (including expert evidence) must be filed by the parties as the court directs and the landlord shall be required to file his evidence first.

Grounds of opposition to be tried as a preliminary issue

3.16 Unless in the circumstances of the case it is unreasonable to do so, any grounds of opposition shall be tried as a preliminary issue.

Applications for interim rent under s. 24A to 24D of the 1954 Act

3.17 Where proceedings have already been commenced for the grant of a new tenancy or the termination of an existing tenancy, the claim for interim rent under s. 24A of the 1954 Act shall be made in those proceedings by:
(1) the claim form;
(2) the acknowledgment of service or defence; or
(3) an application on notice under Part 23.

3.18 Any application under s. 24D(3) of the 1954 Act shall be made by an application on notice under Part 23 in the original proceedings.

3.19 Where no other proceedings have been commenced for the grant of a new tenancy or termination of an existing tenancy or where such proceedings have been disposed of, an application for interim rent under s. 24A of the 1954 Act shall be made under the procedure in Part 8 and the claim form shall include details of:
(1) the property to which the claim relates;
(2) the particulars of the relevant tenancy (including date, parties and duration) and the current rent (if not the original rent);
(3) every notice or request given or made under ss. 25 or 26 of the 1954 Act;
(4) if the relevant tenancy has terminated, the date and mode of termination; and
(5) if the relevant tenancy has been terminated and the landlord has granted a new tenancy of the property to the tenant:
(a) particulars of the new tenancy (including date, parties and duration) and the rent; and
(b) in a case where s. 24C(2) of the 1954 Act applies but the claimant seeks a different rent under s. 24C(3) of that Act, particulars and matters on which the claimant relies as satisfying s. 24C(3).

Other Claims under Part II of the 1954 Act

4.1 The mesne landlord to whose consent a claim for the determination of any question arising under para. 4(3) of sch. 6 to the 1954 Act shall be made a defendant to the claim.

4.2 If any dispute as to the rateable value of any holding has been referred under s. 37(5) of the 1954 Act to the Commissioners for HM Revenue and Customs for decision by a valuation officer, any document purporting to be a statement of the valuation officer of his decision is admissible as evidence of the matters contained in it.

Claim for Compensation for Improvements under Part I of the 1927 Act

5.1 This paragraph applies to a claim under Part I of the 1927 Act.

The claim form

5.2 The claim form must include details of:
(1) the nature of the claim or the matter to be determined;
(2) the property to which the claim relates;
(3) the nature of the business carried on at the property;
(4) particulars of the lease or agreement for the tenancy including:
(a) the names and addresses of the parties to the lease or agreement;
(b) its duration;
(c) the rent payable;
(d) details of any assignment or other devolution of the lease or agreement;
(5) the date and mode of termination of the tenancy;
(6) if the claimant has left the property, the date on which he did so;
(7) particulars of the improvement or proposed improvement to which the claim relates; and
(8) if the claim is for payment of compensation, the amount claimed;

5.3 The court will fix a date for a hearing when it issues the claim form.

Defendant

5.4 The claimant's immediate landlord must be a defendant to the claim.

5.5 The defendant must immediately serve a copy of the claim form and any document served with it and of his acknowledgment of service on his immediate landlord. If the person so served is not the freeholder, he must serve a copy of these documents on his landlord and so on from landlord to landlord.

Evidence

5.6 Evidence need not be filed — with the claim form or acknowledgment of service.

Certification under section 3 of the 1927 Act

5.7 If the court intends to certify under s. 3 of the 1927 Act that an improvement is a proper improvement or has been duly executed, it shall do so by way of an order.

Compensation under section 1 or 8 of the 1927 Act

para.5.8 **91.63** para.5.9 **91.63**

5.8 A claim under s. 1(1) or 8(1) of the 1927 Act must be in writing, signed by the claimant, his solicitor or agent and include details of:
(1) the name and address of the claimant and of the landlord against whom the claim is made;
(2) the property to which the claim relates;
(3) the nature of the business carried on at the property;
(4) a concise statement of the nature of the claim;
(5) particulars of the improvement, including the date when it was completed and costs; and
(6) the amount claimed.

5.9 A mesne landlord must immediately serve a copy of the claim on his immediate superior landlord. If the person so served is not the freeholder, he must serve a copy of the document on his landlord and so on from landlord to landlord.

(Paragraphs 5.8 and 5.9 provide the procedure for making claims under s. 1(1) and 8(1) of the 1927 Act — these 'claims' do not, at this stage, relate to proceedings before the court.)

Transfer to Leasehold Valuation Tribunal under 1985 Act

6.1 If a question is ordered to be transferred to a leasehold valuation tribunal for determination under s. 31C of the 1985 Act the court will:
(1) send notice of the transfer to all parties to the claim; and
(2) send to the leasehold valuation tribunal:
(a) copies certified by the district judge of all entries in the records of the court relating to the question;
(b) the order of transfer; and
(c) all documents filed in the claim relating to the question.

(Paragraph 6.1 no longer applies to proceedings in England but continues to apply to proceedings in Wales.)

Claim to Enforce Obligation under Part I of the 1987 Act

7.1 A copy of the notice served under s. 19(2)(a) of the 1987 Act must accompany the claim form seeking an order under s. 19(1) of that Act.

Claim for Acquisition Order under Section 28 of the 1987 Act

8.1 This paragraph applies to a claim for an acquisition order under s. 28 of the 1987 Act.

Claim form

8.2 The claim form must:
(1) identify the property to which the claim relates and give details to show that s. 25 of the 1987 Act applies;
(2) give details of the claimants to show that they constitute the requisite majority of qualifying tenants;
(3) state the names and addresses of the claimants and of the landlord of the property, or, if the landlord cannot be found or his identity ascertained, the steps taken to find him or ascertain his identity;
(4) state the name and address of:
(a) the person nominated by the claimants for the purposes of part III of the 1987 Act; and
(b) every person known to the claimants who is likely to be affected by the application, including (but not limited to), the other tenants of flats contained in the property

(whether or not they could have made a claim), any mortgagee or superior landlord of the landlord, and any tenants' association (within the meaning of s. 29 of the 1985 Act); and

(5) state the grounds of the claim.

Notice under section 27

8.3 A copy of the notice served on the landlord under s. 27 of the 1987 Act must accompany the claim form unless the court has dispensed with the requirement to serve a notice under s. 27(3) of the 1987 Act.

Defendants

8.4 The landlord of the property (and the nominated person, if he is not a claimant) must be defendants.

Service

8.5 A copy of the claim form must be served on each of the persons named by the claimant under para. 8.2(4)(b) together with a notice that he may apply to be made a party.

Payment into court by nominated person

8.6 If the nominated person pays money into court in accordance with an order under s. 33(1) of the 1987 Act, he must file a copy of the certificate of the surveyor selected under s. 33(2)(a) of that Act.

Claim for an Order Varying Leases under the 1987 Act

9.1 This paragraph applies to a claim for an order under s. 38 or s. 40 of the 1987 Act.

Claim form

9.2 The claim form must state:

(1) the name and address of the claimant and of the other current parties to the lease or leases to which the claim relates;

(2) the date of the lease or leases, the property to which they relate, any relevant terms and the variation sought;

(3) the name and address of every person known to the claimant who is likely to be affected by the claim, including (but not limited to), the other tenants of flats contained in premises of which the relevant property forms a part, any previous parties to the lease, any mortgagee or superior landlord of the landlord, any mortgagee of the claimant and any tenants' association (within the meaning of s. 29 of the 1985 Act); and

(4) the grounds of the claim.

Defendants

9.3 The other current parties to the lease must be defendants.

Service

9.4 A copy of the claim form must be served on each of the persons named under para. 9.2(3).

9.5 If the defendant knows of or has reason to believe that another person or persons are likely to be affected by the variation, he must serve a copy of the claim form on those persons, together with a notice that they may apply to be made a party.

Defendant's application to vary other leases

9.6 If a defendant wishes to apply to vary other leases under s. 36 of the 1987 Act:

(1) he must make the application in his acknowledgment of service;

(2) paras 9.2 to 9.5 apply as if the defendant were the claimant; and

(3) Part 20 does not apply.

(Paragraphs 9.1 to 9.6 no longer apply to proceedings in England but continue to apply to proceedings in Wales.)

Service of Documents in Claims under the 1987 Act

10.1 All documents must be served by the parties.

10.2 If a notice is to be served in or before a claim under the 1987 Act, it must be served:

(1) in accordance with s. 54, and

(2) in the case of service on a landlord, at the address given under s. 48(1).

SECTION II MISCELLANEOUS PROVISIONS ABOUT LAND

Access to Neighbouring Land Act 1992

11.1 The claimant must use the Part 8 procedure.

11.2 The claim form must set out:

(1) details of the dominant and servient land involved and whether the dominant land includes or consists of residential property;

(2) the work required;

(3) why entry to the servient land is required with plans (if applicable);

(4) the names and addresses of the persons who will carry out the work;

(5) the proposed date when the work will be carried out; and

(6) what (if any) provision has been made by way of insurance in the event of possible injury to persons or damage to property arising out of the proposed work.

11.3 The owner and occupier of the servient land must be defendants to the claim.

Chancel Repairs Act 1932

12.1 The claimant in a claim to recover the sum required to put a chancel in proper repair must use the Part 8 procedure.

12.2 A notice to repair under s. 2 of the Chancel Repairs Act 1932 must:

(1) state:

(a) the responsible authority by whom the notice is given;

(b) the chancel alleged to be in need of repair;

(c) the repairs alleged to be necessary; and

(d) the grounds on which the person to whom the notice is addressed is alleged to be liable to repair the chancel; and

(2) call upon the person to whom the notice is addressed to put the chancel in proper repair.

12.3 The notice must be served in accordance with Part 6.

Leasehold Reform Act 1967

13.1 In this paragraph a section or schedule referred to by number means the section or schedule so numbered in the Leasehold Reform Act 1967.

13.2 If a tenant of a house and premises wishes to pay money into court under ss. 11(4), 13(1) or 13(3):

(1) he must file in the office of the appropriate court an application notice containing or accompanied by evidence stating:

(a) the reasons for the payment into court,

(b) the house and premises to which the payment relates;

(c) the name and address of the landlord; and

(d) so far as they are known to the tenant, the name and address of every person who is or may be interested in or entitled to the money;

(2) on the filing of the witness statement the tenant must pay the money into court and the court will send notice of the payment to the landlord and every person whose name and address are given in the witness statement;

(3) any subsequent payment into court by the landlord under s. 11(4) must be made to the credit of the same account as the payment into court by the tenant and sub-paras (1) and (2) will apply to the landlord as if he were a tenant;

(4) the appropriate court for the purposes of sub-para. (1)(a) is the county court for the district in which the property is situated or, if the payment into court is made by reason of a notice under s. 13(3), any other county court as specified in the notice.

13.3 If an order is made transferring an application to a leasehold valuation tribunal under s. 21(3), the court will:

(1) send notice of the transfer to all parties to the application; and

(2) send to the tribunal copies of the order of transfer and all documents filed in the proceedings.

(Paragraph 13.3 no longer applies to proceedings in England but continues to apply to proceedings in Wales.)

13.4 A claim under s. 17 or 18 for an order for possession of a house and premises must be made in accordance with Part 55.

13.5 In a claim under s. 17 or 18, the defendant must:

(1) immediately after being served with the claim form, serve on every person in occupation of the property or part of it under an immediate or derivative subtenancy, a notice informing him of the claim and of his right under para. 3(4) of sch. 2 [to] take part in the hearing of the claim with the permission of the court; and

(2) within 14 days after being served with the claim form, file a defence stating the ground, if any, on which he intends to oppose the claim and giving particulars of every such sub-tenancy.

13.6 An application made to the High Court under s. 19 or 27 shall be assigned to the Chancery Division.

Leasehold Reform, Housing and Urban Development Act 1993

14.1 In this paragraph:

(1) 'the 1993 Act' means the Leasehold Reform, Housing and Urban Development Act 1993; and

(2) a section or schedule referred to by number means the section or schedule so numbered in the 1993 Act.

14.2 If a claim is made under s. 23(1) by a person other than the reversioner:

(1) on the issue of the claim form in accordance with Part 8, the claimant must send a copy to the reversioner; and

(2) the claimant must promptly inform the reversioner either:

(a) of the court's decision; or

(b) that the claim has been withdrawn.

14.3 Where an application is made under s. 26(1) or (2) or s. 50(1) or (2):

(1) it must be made by the issue of a claim form in accordance with the Part 8 procedure which need not be served on any other party; and

(2) the court may grant or refuse the application or give directions for its future conduct, including the addition as defendants of such persons as appear to have an interest in it.

14.4 An application under s. 26(3) must be made by the issue of a claim form in accordance with the Part 8 procedure and:

(1) the claimants must serve the claim form on any person who they know or have reason to believe is a relevant landlord, giving particulars of the claim and the hearing date and informing that person of his right to be joined as a party to the claim;

(2) the landlord whom it is sought to appoint as the reversioner must be a defendant, and must file an acknowledgment of service;

(3) a person on whom notice is served under sub-para. (1) must be joined as a defendant to the claim if he gives notice in writing to the court of his wish to be added as a party, and the court will notify all other parties of the addition.

14.5 If a person wishes to pay money into court under s. 27(3), s. 51(3) or para. 4 of sch. 8:

(1) he must file in the office of the appropriate court an application notice containing or accompanied by evidence stating:

(a) the reasons for the payment into court,

(b) the interest or interests in the property to which the payment relates or where the payment into court is made under s. 51(3), the flat to which it relates;

(c) details of any vesting order;

(d) the name and address of the landlord; and

(e) so far as they are known to the tenant, the name and address of every person who is or may be interested in or entitled to the money;

(2) on the filing of the witness statement the money must be paid into court and the court will send notice of the payment to the landlord and every person whose name and address are given in the witness statement;

(3) any subsequent payment into court by the landlord must be made to the credit of the same account as the earlier payment into court;

(4) the appropriate court for the purposes of sub-para. (1) is:

(a) where a vesting order has been made, the county court that made the order; or

(b) where no such order has been made, the county court in whose district the property is situated.

14.6 If an order is made transferring an application to a leasehold valuation tribunal under s. 91(4), the court will:

(1) send notice of the transfer to all parties to the application; and

(2) send to the tribunal copies of the order of transfer and all documents filed in the proceedings.

(Paragraph 14.6 no longer applies to proceedings in England but continues to apply to proceedings in Wales.)

14.7 If a relevant landlord acts independently under sch. 1, para. 7, he is entitled to require any party to claims under the 1993 Act (as described in para. 7(1)(b) of sch. 1) to supply him, on payment of the reasonable costs of copying, with copies of all documents which that party has served on the other parties to the claim.

Transfer to Leasehold Valuation Tribunal under the Commonhold and Leasehold Reform Act 2002

15.1 If a question is ordered to be transferred to a leasehold valuation tribunal for determination under the Commonhold and Leasehold Reform Act 2002, sch. 12, para. 3, the court will:

(1) send notice of the transfer to all parties to the claim; and

(2) send to the leasehold valuation tribunal:

(a) the order of transfer; and

(b) all documents filed in the claim relating to the question.

(Paragraph 15.1 applies to proceedings in England but does not apply to proceedings in Wales.)

CPR Part 57 Probate and Inheritance

Part 57 **11.7, 71.4** [For commentary on a specific rule, please refer to the cross-references after the title of the rule.]

57.1 Scope of This Part and Definitions

(1) This Part contains rules about—
  (a) probate claims;
  (b) claims for the rectification of wills;
  (c) claims and applications to—
    (i) substitute another person for a personal representative; or
    (ii) remove a personal representative; and
  (d) claims under the Inheritance (Provision for Family and Dependants) Act 1975.

(2) In this Part:
  (a) 'probate claim' means a claim for—
    (i) the grant of probate of the will, or letters of administration of the estate, of a deceased person;
    (ii) the revocation of such a grant; or
    (iii) a decree pronouncing for or against the validity of an alleged will;

  not being a claim which is non-contentious (or common form) probate business;

(Section 128 of the Supreme Court Act 1981 defines non-contentious (or common form) probate business.)

  (b) 'relevant office' means—
    (i) in the case of High Court proceedings in a Chancery district registry, that registry;
    (ii) in the case of any other High Court proceedings, Chancery Chambers at the Royal Courts of Justice, Strand, London, WC2A 2LL; and
    (iii) in the case of county court proceedings, the office of the county court in question;
  (c) 'testamentary document' means a will, a draft of a will, written instructions for a will made by or at the request of, or under the instructions of, the testator, and any document purporting to be evidence of the contents, or to be a copy, of a will which is alleged to have been lost or destroyed;
  (d) 'will' includes a codicil.

I PROBATE CLAIMS

57.2 General

r.57.2(3) **11.6, 11.7**

(1) This Section contains rules about probate claims.
(2) Probate claims in the High Court are assigned to the Chancery Division.
(3) Probate claims in the county court must only be brought in—

(a) a county court where there is also a Chancery district registry; or
(b) the Central London County Court.

(4) All probate claims are allocated to the multi-track.

57.3 How to Start a Probate Claim

A probate claim must be commenced—
(a) in the relevant office; and
(b) using the procedure in Part 7.

57.4 Acknowledgment of Service and Defence

r.57.4 **18.2** r.57.4(3) **18.2**

(1) A defendant who is served with a claim form must file an acknowledgment of service.

(2) Subject to paragraph (3), the period for filing an acknowledgment of service is—
(a) if the defendant is served with a claim form which states that particulars of claim are to follow, 28 days after service of the particulars of claim; and
(b) in any other case, 28 days after service of the claim form.

(3) If the claim form is served out of the jurisdiction under rule 6.19, the period for filing an acknowledgment of service is 14 days longer than the relevant period specified in rule 6.22 or the practice direction supplementing Section 3 of Part 6.

(4) Rule 15.4 (which provides the period for filing a defence) applies as if the words 'under Part 10' were omitted from rule 15.4(1)(b).

57.5 Lodging of Testamentary Documents and Filing of Evidence about Testamentary Documents

r.57.5(5) **15.17**

(1) Any testamentary document of the deceased person in the possession or control of any party must be lodged with the court.

(2) Unless the court directs otherwise, the testamentary documents must be lodged in the relevant office—
(a) by the claimant when the claim form is issued; and
(b) by a defendant when he acknowledges service.

(3) The claimant and every defendant who acknowledges service of the claim form must in written evidence—
(a) describe any testamentary document of the deceased of which he has any knowledge or, if he does not know of any such testamentary document, state that fact, and
(b) if any testamentary document of which he has knowledge is not in his possession or under his control, give the name and address of the person in whose possession or under whose control it is or, if he does not know the name or address of that person, state that fact.

(A specimen form for the written evidence about testamentary documents is annexed to the practice direction.)

(4) Unless the court directs otherwise, the written evidence required by paragraph (3) must be filed in the relevant office—
(a) by the claimant, when the claim form is issued; and
(b) by a defendant when he acknowledges service.

(5) Except with the permission of the court, a party shall not be allowed to inspect the testamentary documents or written evidence lodged or filed by any other party until he himself has lodged his testamentary documents and filed his evidence.

(6) The provisions of paragraphs (2) and (4) may be modified by a practice direction under this Part.

57.6 Revocation of Existing Grant

(1) In a probate claim which seeks the revocation of a grant of probate or letters of administration every person who is entitled, or claims to be entitled, to administer the estate under that grant must be made a party to the claim.

(2) If the claimant is the person to whom the grant was made, he must lodge the probate or letters of administration in the relevant office when the claim form is issued.

(3) If a defendant has the probate or letters of administration under his control, he must lodge it in the relevant office when he acknowledges service.

(4) Paragraphs (2) and (3) do not apply where the grant has already been lodged at the court, which in this paragraph includes the Principal Registry of the Family Division or a district probate registry.

57.7 Contents of Statements of Case

r.57.7(5) **66.37**

(1) The claim form must contain a statement of the nature of the interest of the claimant and of each defendant in the estate.
(2) If a party disputes another party's interest in the estate he must state this in his statement of case and set out his reasons.
(3) Any party who contends that at the time when a will was executed the testator did not know of and approve its contents must give particulars of the facts and matters relied on.
(4) Any party who wishes to contend that—
  (a) a will was not duly executed;
  (b) at the time of the execution of a will the testator was not of sound mind, memory and understanding; or
  (c) the execution of a will was obtained by undue influence or fraud,
must set out the contention specifically and give particulars of the facts and matters relied on.
(5) (a) A defendant may give notice in his defence that he does not raise any positive case, but insists on the will being proved in solemn form and, for that purpose, will cross-examine the witnesses who attested the will.
  (b) If a defendant gives such a notice, the court will not make an order for costs against him unless it considers that there was no reasonable ground for opposing the will.

57.8 Counterclaim

(1) A defendant who contends that he has any claim or is entitled to any remedy relating to the grant of probate of the will, or letters of administration of the estate, of the deceased person must serve a counterclaim making that contention.
(2) If the claimant fails to serve particulars of claim within the time allowed, the defendant may, with the permission of the court, serve a counterclaim and the probate claim shall then proceed as if the counterclaim were the particulars of claim.

57.9 Probate Counterclaim in Other Proceedings

(1) In this rule 'probate counterclaim' means a counterclaim in any claim other than a probate claim by which the defendant claims any such remedy as is mentioned in rule 57.1(2)(a).
(2) Subject to the following paragraphs of this rule, this Part shall apply with the necessary modifications to a probate counterclaim as it applies to a probate claim.
(3) A probate counterclaim must contain a statement of the nature of the interest of each of the parties in the estate of the deceased to which the probate counterclaim relates.
(4) Unless an application notice is issued within 7 days after the service of a probate counterclaim for an order under rule 3.1(2)(e) or 3.4 for the probate counterclaim to be dealt with in separate proceedings or to be struck out, and the application is granted, the court shall order the transfer of the proceedings to either—
  (a) the Chancery Division (if it is not already assigned to that Division) and to either the Royal Courts of Justice or a Chancery district registry (if it is not already proceeding in one of those places); or
  (b) if the county court has jurisdiction, to a county court where there is also a Chancery district registry or the Central London County Court.
(5) If an order is made that a probate counterclaim be dealt with in separate proceedings, the order shall order the transfer of the probate counterclaim as required under paragraph (4).

57.10 Failure to Acknowledge Service or to File a Defence

r.57.10(1) **20.2**

(1) A default judgment cannot be obtained in a probate claim and rule 10.2 and Part 12 do not apply.
(2) If any of several defendants fails to acknowledge service the claimant may—

(a) after the time for acknowledging service has expired; and
(b) upon filing written evidence of service of the claim form and (if no particulars of claim were contained in or served with the claim form) the particulars of claim on that defendant;

proceed with the probate claim as if that defendant had acknowledged service.

(3) If no defendant acknowledges service or files a defence then, unless on the application of the claimant the court orders the claim to be discontinued, the claimant may, after the time for acknowledging service or for filing a defence (as the case may be) has expired, apply to the court for an order that the claim is to proceed to trial.

(4) When making an application under paragraph (3) the claimant must file written evidence of service of the claim form and (if no particulars of claim were contained in or served with the claim form) the particulars of claim on each of the defendants.

(5) Where the court makes an order under paragraph (3), it may direct that the claim be tried on written evidence.

57.11 Discontinuance and Dismissal

(1) Part 38 does not apply to probate claims.

(2) At any stage of a probate claim the court, on the application of the claimant or of any defendant who has acknowledged service, may order that—

(a) the claim be discontinued or dismissed on such terms as to costs or otherwise as it thinks just; and
(b) a grant of probate of the will, or letters of administration of the estate, of the deceased person be made to the person entitled to the grant.

II RECTIFICATION OF WILLS

57.12

(1) This Section contains rules about claims for the rectification of a will.

(Section 20 of the Administration of Justice Act 1982 provides for rectification of a will. Additional provisions are contained in rule 55 of the Non-Contentious Probate Rules 1987.)

(2) Every personal representative of the estate shall be joined as a party.

(3) The practice direction makes provision for lodging the grant of probate or letters of administration with the will annexed in a claim under this Section.

III SUBSTITUTION AND REMOVAL OF PERSONAL REPRESENTATIVES

57.13

(1) This Section contains rules about claims and applications for substitution or removal of a personal representative.

(2) Claims under this Section must be brought in the High Court and are assigned to the Chancery Division.

(Section 50 of the Administration of Justice Act 1985 gives the High Court power to appoint a substitute for, or to remove, a personal representative.)

(3) Every personal representative of the estate shall be joined as a party.

(4) The practice direction makes provision for lodging the grant of probate or letters of administration in a claim under this Section.

(5) If substitution or removal of a personal representative is sought by application in existing proceedings, this rule shall apply with references to claims being read as if they referred to applications.

IV CLAIMS UNDER THE INHERITANCE (PROVISION FOR FAMILY AND DEPENDANTS) ACT 1975

57.14 Scope of This Section

This Section contains rules about claims under the Inheritance (Provision for Family and Dependants) Act 1975 ('the Act').

57.15 Proceedings in the High Court

(1) Proceedings in the High Court under the Act shall be issued in either—
  (a) the Chancery Division; or
  (b) the Family Division.

(2) The Civil Procedure Rules apply to proceedings under the Act which are brought in the Family Division, except that the provisions of the Family Proceedings Rules 1991 relating to the drawing up and service of orders apply instead of the provisions in Part 40 and its practice direction.

57.16 Procedure for Claims under Section 1 of the Act

r.57.16(1) **13.4**

(1) A claim under section 1 of the Act must be made by issuing a claim form in accordance with Part 8.

(2) Rule 8.3 (acknowledgment of service) and rule 8.5 (filing and serving written evidence) apply as modified by paragraphs (3) to (5) of this rule.

(3) The written evidence filed and served by the claimant with the claim form must have exhibited to it an official copy of—
  (a) the grant of probate or letters of administration in respect of the deceased's estate; and
  (b) every testamentary document in respect of which probate or letters of administration were granted.

(4) Subject to paragraph (4A), the time within which a defendant must file and serve—
  (a) an acknowledgment of service; and
  (b) any written evidence,

is not more than 21 days after service of the claim form on him.

(4A) If the claim form is served out of the jurisdiction under rule 6.19, the period for filing an acknowledgment of service and any written evidence is 7 days longer than the relevant period specified in rule 6.22 or the practice direction supplementing Section III of Part 6.

(5) A defendant who is a personal representative of the deceased must file and serve written evidence, which must include the information required by the practice direction.

PD 57 Practice Direction — Probate

This practice direction supplements CPR Part 57

PD 57 **11.7**

I PROBATE CLAIMS

General

1.1 This Section of this practice direction applies to contentious probate claims.

1.2 The rules and procedure relating to non-contentious probate proceedings (also known as 'common form') are the Non-Contentious Probate Rules 1987 (SI 1987/2024) as amended.

How to Start a Probate Claim

2.1 A claim form and all subsequent court documents relating to a probate claim must be marked at the top 'In the estate of [name] deceased (Probate)'.

2.2 The claim form must be issued out of:

(1) Chancery Chambers at the Royal Courts of Justice; or

(2) one of the Chancery district registries; or

(3) if the claim is suitable to be heard in the county court:

(a) a county court in a place where there is also a Chancery district registry; or

(b) the Central London County Court.

There are Chancery district registries at Birmingham, Bristol, Cardiff, Leeds, Liverpool, Manchester, Newcastle upon Tyne and Preston.

(Section 32 of the County Courts Act 1984 identifies which probate claims may be heard in a county court.)

2.3 When the claim form is issued, the relevant office will send a notice to Leeds District Probate Registry, Coronet House, Queen Street, Leeds LS1 2BA, DX 26451 Leeds (Park Square), telephone (0113)2431505, requesting that all testamentary documents, grants of representation and other relevant documents currently held at any probate registry are sent to the relevant office.

2.4 The commencement of a probate claim will, unless a court otherwise directs, prevent any grant of probate or letters of administration being made until the probate claim has been disposed of. (Rule 45 of the Non-Contentious Probate Rules 1987 makes provision for notice of the probate claim to be given, and s. 117 of the Supreme Court Act 1981 for the grant of letters of administration pending the determination of a probate claim. Paragraph 8 of this practice direction makes provision about an application for such a grant.)

Testamentary Documents and Evidence about Testamentary Documents

3.1 Unless the court orders otherwise, if a testamentary document is held by the court (whether it was lodged by a party or it was previously held at a probate registry) when the claim has been disposed of the court will send it to the Leeds District Probate Registry.

3.2 The written evidence about testamentary documents required by this Part:

(1) should be in the form annexed to this practice direction; and

(2) must be signed by the party personally and not by his solicitor or other representative (except that if the party is a child or patient the written evidence must be signed by his litigation friend).

3.3 In a case in which there is urgent need to commence a probate claim (for example, in order to be able to apply immediately for the appointment of an administrator pending the determination of the claim) and it is not possible for the claimant to lodge the testamentary documents or to file the evidence about testamentary documents in the relevant office at the same time as the claim form is to be issued, the court may direct that the claimant shall be allowed to issue the claim form upon his giving an undertaking to the court to lodge the documents and file the evidence within such time as the court shall specify.

Case Management

4 In giving case management directions in a probate claim the court will give consideration to the questions:
(1) whether any person who may be affected by the claim and who is not joined as a party should be joined as a party or given notice of the claim, whether under r. 19.8A or otherwise; and
(2) whether to make a representation order under r. 19.6 or r. 19.7.

Summary Judgment

5.1 If an order pronouncing for a will in solemn form is sought on an application for summary judgment, the evidence in support of the application must include written evidence proving due execution of the will.

5.2 If a defendant has given notice in his defence under r. 57.7(5) that he raises no positive case but:
(1) he insists that the will be proved in solemn form; and
(2) for that purpose he will cross-examine the witnesses who attested the will,
any application by the claimant for summary judgment is subject to the right of that defendant to require those witnesses to attend court for cross-examination.

Settlement of a Probate Claim

6.1 If at any time the parties agree to settle a probate claim, the court may:
(1) order the trial of the claim on written evidence, which will lead to a grant in solemn form;
(2) order that the claim be discontinued or dismissed under r. 57.11, which will lead to a grant in common form; or
(3) pronounce for or against the validity of one or more wills under s. 49 of the Administration of Justice Act 1985.

(For a form of order which is also applicable to discontinuance and which may be adapted as appropriate, see PF 38 CH.)

(Section 49 of the Administration of Justice Act 1985 permits a probate claim to be compromised without a trial if every 'relevant beneficiary', as defined in that section, has consented to the proposed order. It is only available in the High Court.)

6.2 Applications under s. 49 of the Administration of Justice Act 1985 may be heard by a master or district judge and must be supported by written evidence identifying the relevant beneficiaries and exhibiting the written consent of each of them. The written evidence of testamentary documents required by r. 57.5 will still be necessary.

Application for an Order to Bring in a Will, etc.

7.1 Any party applying for an order under s. 122 of the Supreme Court Act 1981 ('the 1981 Act') must serve the application notice on the person against whom the order is sought. (Section 122 of the 1981 Act empowers the court to order a person to attend court for examination, and to answer questions and bring in documents, if there are reasonable grounds for believing that such person has knowledge of a testamentary document. Rule 50(1) of the Non-Contentious Probate Rules 1987 makes similar provision where a probate claim has not been commenced.)

7.2 An application for the issue of a witness summons under s. 123 of the 1981 Act:
(1) may be made without notice; and
(2) must be supported by written evidence setting out the grounds of the application.

(Section 123 of the 1981 Act empowers the court, where it appears that any person has in his possession, custody or power a testamentary document, to issue a witness summons ordering such person to bring in that document. Rule 50(2) of the Non-Contentious Probate Rules makes similar provision where a probate claim has not been commenced.)

7.3 An application under s. 122 or 123 of the 1981 Act should be made to a master or district judge.

7.4 A person against whom a witness summons is issued under s. 123 of the 1981 Act who denies that the testamentary document referred to in the witness summons is in his possession or under his control may file written evidence to that effect.

Administration Pending the Determination of a Probate Claim

8.1 An application under s. 117 of the Supreme Court Act 1981 for an order for the grant of administration pending the determination of a probate claim should be made by application notice in the probate claim.

8.2 If an order for a grant of administration is made under s. 117 of the 1981 Act:

(1) Rules 69.4 to 69.7 shall apply as if the administrator were a receiver appointed by the court;

(2) if the court allows the administrator remuneration under r. 69.7, it may make an order under s. 117(3) of the 1981 Act assigning the remuneration out of the estate of the deceased; and

(3) every application relating to the conduct of the administration shall be made by application notice in the probate claim.

8.3 An order under s. 117 may be made by a master or district judge.

8.4 If an order is made under s. 117 an application for the grant of letters of administration should be made to the Principal Registry of the Family Division, First Avenue House, 42–49 High Holborn, London WC1V 6NP.

8.5 The appointment of an administrator to whom letters of administration are granted following an order under s. 117 will cease automatically when a final order in the probate claim is made but will continue pending any appeal.

II RECTIFICATION OF WILLS

Scope of This Section

9 This Section of this practice direction applies to claims for the rectification of a will.

Lodging the Grant

10.1 If the claimant is the person to whom the grant was made in respect of the will of which rectification is sought, he must, unless the court orders otherwise, lodge the probate or letters of administration with the will annexed with the court when the claim form is issued.

10.2 If a defendant has the probate or letters of administration in his possession or under his control, he must, unless the court orders otherwise, lodge it in the relevant office within 14 days after the service of the claim form on him.

Orders

11 A copy of every order made for the rectification of a will shall be sent to the Principal Registry of the Family Division for filing, and a memorandum of the order shall be endorsed on, or permanently annexed to, the grant under which the estate is administered.

III SUBSTITUTION AND REMOVAL OF PERSONAL REPRESENTATIVES

Scope of This Section

12 This Section of this practice direction applies to claims and applications for substitution or removal of a personal representative. If substitution or removal of a personal representative is sought by application in existing proceedings, this Section shall apply with references to the claim, claim form and claimant being read as if they referred to the application, application notice and applicant respectively.

Starting the Claim

13.1 The claim form must be accompanied by:

(1) a sealed or certified copy of the grant of probate or letters of administration; and

(2) written evidence containing the grounds of the claim and the following information so far as it is known to the claimant:

(a) brief details of the property comprised in the estate, with an approximate estimate of its capital value and any income that is received from it;

(b) brief details of the liabilities of the estate;

(c) the names and addresses of the persons who are in possession of the documents relating to the estate;

(d) the names of the beneficiaries and their respective interests in the estate; and
(e) the name, address and occupation of any proposed substituted personal representative;

13.2 If the claim is for the appointment of a substituted personal representative, the claim form must be accompanied by:
(1) a signed or (in the case of the Public Trustee or a corporation) sealed consent to act; and
(2) written evidence as to the fitness of the proposed substituted personal representative, if an individual, to act.

Production of the Grant

14.1 On the hearing of the claim the personal representative must produce to the court the grant of representation to the deceased's estate.

14.2 If an order is made substituting or removing the personal representative, the grant (together with a sealed copy of the order) must be sent to and remain in the custody of the Principal Registry of the Family Division until a memorandum of the order has been endorsed on or permanently annexed to the grant.

IV CLAIMS UNDER THE INHERITANCE (PROVISION FOR FAMILY AND DEPENDANTS) ACT 1975

Acknowledgment of Service by Personal Representatives: Rule 57.16(4)

15 Where a defendant who is a personal representative wishes to remain neutral in relation to the claim, and agrees to abide by any decision which the court may make, he should state this in Section A of the acknowledgment of service form.

Written Evidence of Personal Representative: Rule 57.16(5)

16 The written evidence filed by a defendant who is a personal representative must state to the best of that person's ability:
(1) full details of the value of the deceased's net estate, as defined in s. 25(1) of the Act;
(2) the person or classes of persons beneficially interested in the estate, and:
(a) the names and (unless they are parties to the claim) addresses of all living beneficiaries; and
(b) the value of their interests in the estate so far as they are known.
(3) whether any living beneficiary (and if so, naming him) is a child or patient within the meaning of r. 21.1(2); and
(4) any facts which might affect the exercise of the court's powers under the Act.

Separate Representation of Claimants

17 If a claim is made jointly by two or more claimants, and it later appears that any of the claimants have a conflict of interests:
(1) any claimant may choose to be represented at any hearing by separate solicitors or counsel, or may appear in person; and
(2) if the court considers that claimants who are represented by the same solicitors or counsel ought to be separately represented, it may adjourn the application until they are.

Production of the Grant

18.1 On the hearing of a claim the personal representative must produce to the court the original grant of representation to the deceased's estate.

18.2 If the court makes an order under the Act, the original grant (together with a sealed copy of the order) must be sent to the Principal Registry of the Family Division for a memorandum of the order to be endorsed on or permanently annexed to the grant in accordance with s. 19(3) of the Act.

18.3 Every final order embodying terms of compromise made in proceedings under the Act, whether made with or without a hearing, must contain a direction that a memorandum of the order shall be endorsed on or permanently annexed to the probate or letters of administration and a copy of the order shall be sent to the Principal Registry of the Family Division with the relevant grant of probate or letters of administration for endorsement.

ANNEX

A FORM OF WITNESS STATEMENT OR AFFIDAVIT ABOUT TESTAMENTARY DOCUMENTS (CPR, RULE 57.5)

[*Title of the claim*]

I [*name and address*] the claimant/defendant in this claim state [on oath] that I have no knowledge of any document:

(1) being or purported to be or having the form or effect of a will or codicil of [*name of deceased*] whose estate is the subject of this claim;

(2) being or purporting to be a draft or written instructions for any such will or codicil made by or at the request of or under the instructions of the deceased;

(3) being or purporting to be evidence of the contents or a copy of any such will or codicil which is alleged to have been lost or destroyed, except [*describe any testamentary document of the deceased, and if any such document is not in your control, give the name and address of the person who you believe has possession or control of it, or state that you do not know the name and address of that person*].

[I believe that the facts stated in this witness statement are true] [*or jurat for affidavit*]

[*NOTE: 'testamentary document' is defined in CPR, r. 57.1.*]

CPR Part 58 Commercial Court

Part 58 **2.17, 2.18, 11.7, 42.6, 71.4** [For commentary on a specific rule, please refer to the cross-references after the title of the rule.]

58.1 Scope of This Part and Interpretation

r.58.1 **2.17** r.58.1(2) **11.6, 11.7**

(1) This Part applies to claims in the Commercial Court of the Queen's Bench Division.
(2) In this Part and its practice direction, 'commercial claim' means any claim arising out of the transaction of trade and commerce and includes any claim relating to—
  (a) a business document or contract;
  (b) the export or import of goods;
  (c) the carriage of goods by land, sea, air or pipeline;
  (d) the exploitation of oil and gas reserves or other natural resources;
  (e) insurance and re-insurance;
  (f) banking and financial services;
  (g) the operation of markets and exchanges;
  (h) the purchase and sale of commodities;
  (i) the construction of ships;
  (j) business agency; and
  (k) arbitration.

58.2 Specialist List

r.58.2(1) **11.4**

(1) The commercial list is a specialist list for claims proceeding in the Commercial Court.
(2) One of the judges of the Commercial Court shall be in charge of the commercial list.

58.3 Application of the Civil Procedure Rules

These Rules and their practice directions apply to claims in the commercial list unless this Part or a practice direction provides otherwise.

58.4 Proceedings in the Commercial List

(1) A commercial claim may be started in the commercial list.
(2) Rule 30.5 applies to claims in the commercial list, except that a Commercial Court judge may order a claim to be transferred to any other specialist list.

(Rule 30.5(3) provides that an application for the transfer of proceedings to or from a specialist list must be made to a judge dealing with claims in that list)

58.5 Claim Form and Particulars of Claim

(1) If, in a Part 7 claim, particulars of claim are not contained in or served with the claim form—
  (a) the claim form must state that, if an acknowledgment of service is filed which indicates an intention to defend the claim, particulars of claim will follow;
  (b) when the claim form is served, it must be accompanied by the documents specified in rule 7.8(1);

(c) the claimant must serve particulars of claim within 28 days of the filing of an acknowledgment of service which indicates an intention to defend; and
(d) rule 7.4(2) does not apply.

(2) A statement of value is not required to be included in the claim form.
(3) If the claimant is claiming interest, he must—
(a) include a statement to that effect; and
(b) give the details set out in rule 16.4(2),
in both the claim form and the particulars of claim.

58.6 Acknowledgment of Service

r.58.6(1)–(3) **18.1**

(1) A defendant must file an acknowledgment of service in every case.
(2) Unless paragraph (3) applies, the period for filing an acknowledgment of service is 14 days after service of the claim form.
(3) Where the claim form is served out of the jurisdiction, or on the agent of a defendant who is overseas, the time periods provided by rules 6.16(4), 6.21(4) and 6.22 apply after service of the claim form.

58.7 Disputing the Court's Jurisdiction

r.58.7 **19.3, 19.5**

(1) Part 11 applies to claims in the commercial list with the modifications set out in this rule.
(2) An application under rule 11(1) must be made within 28 days after filing an acknowledgment of service.
(3) If the defendant files an acknowledgment of service indicating an intention to dispute the court's jurisdiction, the claimant need not serve particulars of claim before the hearing of the application.

58.8 Default Judgment

r.58.8 **20.3**

(1) If, in a Part 7 claim in the commercial list, a defendant fails to file an acknowledgment of service, the claimant need not serve particulars of claim before he may obtain or apply for default judgment in accordance with Part 12.
(2) Rule 12.6(1) applies with the modification that paragraph (a) shall be read as if it referred to the claim form instead of the particulars of claim.

58.9 Admissions

(1) Rule 14.5 does not apply to claims in the commercial list.
(2) If the defendant admits part of a claim for a specified amount of money, the claimant may apply under rule 14.3 for judgment on the admission.
(3) Rule 14.14(1) applies with the modification that paragraph (a) shall be read as if it referred to the claim form instead of the particulars of claim.

58.10 Defence and Reply

(1) Part 15 (defence and reply) applies to claims in the commercial list with the modification to rule 15.8 that the claimant must—
(a) file any reply to a defence; and
(b) serve it on all other parties,
within 21 days after service of the defence.

(2) Rule 6.23 (period for filing a defence where the claim form is served out of the jurisdiction) applies to claims in the commercial list, except that if the particulars of claim are served after the defendant has filed an acknowledgment of service the period for filing a defence is 28 days from service of the particulars of claim.

58.11 Statements of Case

The court may at any time before or after the issue of the claim form order a claim in the commercial list to proceed without the filing or service of statements of case.

58.12 Part 8 Claims

Part 8 applies to claims in the commercial list, with the modification that a defendant to a Part 8 claim who wishes to rely on written evidence must file and serve it within 28 days after filing an acknowledgment of service.

58.13 Case Management

r.58.13(1) **2.17, 42.6**

(1) All proceedings in the commercial list are treated as being allocated to the multi-track and Part 26 does not apply.
(2) The following parts only of Part 29 apply—
   (a) rule 29.3(2) (legal representative to attend case management conferences and pre-trial reviews);
   (b) rule 29.5 (variation of case management timetable) with the exception of rule 29.5(1)(c).
(3) As soon as practicable the court will hold a case management conference which must be fixed in accordance with the practice direction.
(4) At the case management conference or at any hearing at which the parties are represented the court may give such directions for the management of the case as it considers appropriate.

58.14 Disclosure — Ships Papers

(1) If, in proceedings relating to a marine insurance policy, the underwriters apply for specific disclosure under rule 31.12, the court may—
   (a) order a party to produce all the ships papers; and
   (b) require that party to use his best endeavours to obtain and disclose documents which are not or have not been in his control.
(2) An order under this rule may be made at any stage of the proceedings and on such terms, if any, as to staying the proceedings or otherwise, as the court thinks fit.

58.15 Judgments and Orders

(1) Except for orders made by the court on its own initiative and unless the court orders otherwise, every judgment or order will be drawn up by the parties, and rule 40.3 is modified accordingly.
(2) An application for a consent order must include a draft of the proposed order signed on behalf of all the parties to whom it relates.
(3) Rule 40.6 (consent judgments and orders) does not apply.

PD 58 Practice Direction — Commercial Court

This practice direction supplements CPR Part 58

PD 58 **2.17**, **11.7** [For commentary on a specific paragraph, please refer to the cross-references after the title of the paragraph.]

General

para.1.3 **2.17**

1.1 This practice direction applies to commercial claims proceeding in the commercial list of the Queen's Bench Division. It supersedes all previous practice directions and practice statements in the Commercial Court.

1.2 All proceedings in the commercial list, including any appeal from a judgment, order or decision of a master or district judge before the proceedings were transferred to the Commercial Court, will be heard or determined by a Commercial Court judge, except that:

(1) another judge of the Queen's Bench Division or Chancery Division may hear urgent applications if no Commercial Court judge is available; and

(2) unless the court otherwise orders, any application relating to the enforcement of a Commercial Court judgment or order for the payment of money will be dealt with by a master of the Queen's Bench Division or a district judge.

1.3 Provisions in other practice directions which refer to a master or district judge are to be read, in relation to claims in the commercial list, as if they referred to a Commercial Court judge.

1.4 The Admiralty and Commercial Registry in the Royal Courts of Justice is the administrative office of the court for all proceedings in the commercial list.

Starting Proceedings in the Commercial Court

para.2.2 **23.3**
para.2.3 **2.17, 23.3**
para.2.4 **13.6**

2.1 Claims in the Commercial Court must be issued in the Admiralty and Commercial Registry.

2.2 When the Registry is closed, a request to issue a claim form may be made by fax, using the procedure set out in Appendix A to this practice direction. If a request is made which complies with that procedure, the claim form is issued when the fax is received by the Registry.

2.3 The claim form must be marked in the top right hand corner 'Queen's Bench Division, Commercial Court'.

2.4 A claimant starting proceedings in the commercial list, other than an arbitration claim, must use form N1(CC) for Part 7 claims or form N208(CC) for Part 8 claims.

Applications before Proceedings Are Issued

3.1 A party who intends to bring a claim in the commercial list must make any application before the claim form is issued to a Commercial Court judge.

3.2 The written evidence in support of such an application must state that the claimant intends to bring proceedings in the commercial list.

3.3 If the Commercial Court judge hearing the application considers that the proceedings should not be brought in the commercial list, he may adjourn the application to be heard by a master or by a judge who is not a Commercial Court judge.

Transferring Proceedings to or from the Commercial Court

4.1 If an application is made to a court other than the Commercial Court to transfer proceedings to the commercial list, the other court may:

(1) adjourn the application to be heard by a Commercial Court judge; or

(2) dismiss the application.

4.2 If the Commercial Court orders proceedings to be transferred to the commercial list:

(1) it will order them to be transferred to the Royal Courts of Justice; and

(2) it may give case management directions.

4.3 An application by a defendant, including a Part 20 defendant, for an order transferring proceedings from the commercial list should be made promptly and normally not later than the first case management conference.

4.4 A party applying to the Commercial Court to transfer a claim to the commercial list must give notice of the application to the court in which the claim is proceeding, and the Commercial Court will not make an order for transfer until it is satisfied that such notice has been given.

Acknowledgment of Service

para.5.2 **13.6**

5.1 For Part 7 claims, a defendant must file an acknowledgment of service using form N9(CC).

5.2 For Part 8 claims, a defendant must file an acknowledgment of service using form N210(CC).

Default Judgment and Admissions

6. PD 12 and PD 14 apply with the following modifications:
   (1) PD 12, para. 4.1(1), is to be read as referring to the service of the claim form; and
   (2) the references to 'particulars of claim' in PD 14, paras 2.1, 3.1 and 3.2, are to be read as referring to the claim form.

Variation of Time Limits

7.1 If the parties, in accordance with r. 2.11, agree in writing to vary a time limit, the claimant must notify the court in writing, giving brief written reasons for the agreed variation.

7.2 The court may make an order overriding an agreement by the parties varying a time limit.

Amendments

8. PD 17, para. 2.2, is modified so that amendments to a statement of case must show the original text, unless the court orders otherwise.

Service of Documents

para.9 **15.18**

9. Unless the court orders otherwise, the Commercial Court will not serve documents or orders and service must be effected by the parties.

Case Management

para.10.2 **42.8**
para.10.7–10.8 **42.7**
para.10.9 **45.22**

10.1 The following parts only of PD 29 apply:
   (1) para. 5 (case management conferences), excluding para. 5.9 and modified so far as is made necessary by other specific provisions of this practice direction; and
   (2) para. 7 (failure to comply with case management directions).

10.2 If the proceedings are started in the commercial list, the claimant must apply for a case management conference:
   (a) for a Part 7 claim, within 14 days of the date when all defendants who intend to file and serve a defence have done so; and
   (b) for a Part 8 claim, within 14 days of the date when all defendants who intend to serve evidence have done so.

10.3 If the proceedings are transferred to the commercial list, the claimant must apply for a case management conference within 14 days of the date of the order transferring them, unless the judge held, or gave directions for, a case management conference when he made the order transferring the proceedings.

10.4 Any party may, at a time earlier than that provided in paras 10.2 or 10.3, apply in writing to the court to fix a case management conference.

10.5 If the claimant does not make an application in accordance with paras 10.2 or 10.3, any other party may apply for a case management conference.

10.6 The court may fix a case management conference at any time on its own initiative. If it does so, the court will give at least seven days' notice to the parties, unless there are compelling reasons for a shorter period of notice.

10.7 Not less than seven days before a case management conference, each party must file and serve:
(1) a completed case management information sheet; and
(2) an application notice for any order which that party intends to seek at the case management conference, other than directions referred to in the case management information sheet.

10.8 Unless the court orders otherwise, the claimant, in consultation with the other parties, must prepare:
(1) a case memorandum, containing a short and uncontroversial summary of what the case is about and of its material case history;
(2) a list of issues, with a section listing important matters which are not in dispute; and
(3) a case management bundle containing:
(a) the claim form;
(b) all statements of case (excluding schedules), except that, if a summary of a statement of case has been filed, the bundle should contain the summary, and not the full statement of case;
(c) the case memorandum;
(d) the list of issues;
(e) the case management information sheets and, if a pre-trial timetable has been agreed or ordered, that timetable;
(f) the principal orders of the court; and
(g) any agreement in writing made by the parties as to disclosure,

and provide copies of the case management bundle for the court and the other parties at least seven days before the first case management conference or any earlier hearing at which the court may give case management directions.

10.9 The claimant, in consultation with the other parties, must revise and update the documents referred to in para. 10.8 appropriately as the case proceeds. This must include making all necessary revisions and additions at least seven days before any subsequent hearing at which the court may give case management directions.

Pre-trial Review

para.11.3 **45.22**

11.1 At any pre-trial review or case management hearing, the court will ensure that case management directions have been complied with and give any further directions for the trial that are necessary.

11.2 Advocates who are to represent the parties at the trial should represent them at the pre-trial review and any case management hearing at which arrangements for the trial are to be discussed.

11.3 Before the pre-trial review, the parties must discuss and, if possible, agree a draft written timetable for the trial.

11.4 The claimant must file a copy of the draft timetable for the trial at least two days before the hearing of the pre-trial review. Any parts of the timetable which are not agreed must be identified and short explanations of the disagreement must be given.

11.5 At the pre-trial review, the court will set a timetable for the trial, unless a timetable has already been fixed or the court considers that it would be inappropriate to do so or appropriate to do so at a later time.

Case Management Where There Is a Part 20 Claim

12. PD 20, para. 5, applies, except that, unless the court otherwise orders, the court will give case management directions for Part 20 claims at the same case management conferences as it gives directions for the main claim.

Evidence for Applications

13.1 The general requirement is that, unless the court orders otherwise:
(1) evidence in support of an application must be filed and served with the application (see r. 23.7(3));

(2) evidence in answer must be filed and served within 14 days after the application is served; and

(3) evidence in reply must be filed and served within seven days of the service of evidence in answer.

13.2 In any case in which the application is likely to require an oral hearing of more than half a day the periods set out in paras 13.1(2) and (3) will be 28 days and 14 days respectively.

13.3 If the date fixed for the hearing of an application means that the times in paras 13.1(2) and (3) cannot both be achieved, the evidence must be filed and served:

(1) as soon as possible; and

(2) in sufficient time to ensure that the application may fairly proceed on the date fixed.

13.4 The parties may, in accordance with r. 2.11, agree different periods from those in paras 13.1(2) and (3) provided that the agreement does not affect the date fixed for the hearing of the application.

Judgments and Orders

14.1 An application for a consent order must include a draft of the proposed order signed on behalf of all parties to whom it relates (see PD 23, para. 10.4).

14.2 Judgments and orders are generally drawn up by the parties (see r. 58.15). The parties are not therefore required to supply draft orders on disk (see PD 23, para. 12.1).

APPENDIX A PROCEDURE FOR ISSUE OF CLAIM FORM WHEN REGISTRY IS CLOSED — PARAGRAPH 2.2

appendix A **12.7**

1. A request to issue a claim form may be made by fax when the Registry is closed, provided that:
   (a) the claim form is signed by a solicitor acting on behalf of the claimant; and
   (b) it does not require the permission of the court for its issue (unless such permission has already been given).
2. The solicitor requesting the issue of the claim form ('the issuing solicitor') must:
   (a) endorse on the claim form and sign the endorsement set out below;
   (b) send a copy of the claim form so endorsed to the Registry by fax for issue under para. 2.2 of this practice direction; and
   (c) complete and sign a certificate in the form set out below, certifying that he has received a transmission report confirming that the fax has been transmitted in full, and stating the time and date of transmission.
3. When the Registry is next open to the public after the issue of a claim form in accordance with this procedure, the issuing solicitor or his agent must attend and deliver to the Registry:
   (a) the original of the claim form which was sent by fax (including the endorsement and the certificate) or, if the claim form has been served, a true and certified copy of it;
   (b) as many copies of the claim form as the Registry requires; and
   (c) the transmission report.
4. When a court officer at the Registry has checked that:
   (a) the claim form delivered under para. 3 matches the claim form received by fax; and
   (b) the correct issue fee has been paid,

   he will allocate a number to the case, and seal, mark as 'original' and date the claim form with the date of issue (being the date when the fax is recorded at the Registry as having been received).
5. If the issuing solicitor has served the unsealed claim form on any person, he must as soon as practicable:
   (a) inform that person of the case number; and
   (b) if requested, serve him with a copy of the sealed and dated claim form at any address in England and Wales.
6. Any person served with a claim form issued under this procedure may, without paying a fee, inspect and take copies of the documents lodged at the Registry under paras 2 and 3 above.
7. The issue of a claim form in accordance with this procedure takes place when the fax is recorded at the Registry as having been received, and the claim form has the same effect for all purposes as a claim form issued under Part 7 or 8. Unless the court otherwise orders, the sealed version of the

claim form retained by the Registry is conclusive proof that the claim form was issued at the time and on the date stated.

8. If the procedure set out in this Appendix is not complied with, the court may declare that a claim form shall be treated as not having been issued.

Endorsement

A claim form issued pursuant to a request by fax must be endorsed as follows:

(1) This claim form is issued under paragraph 2.2 of the Commercial Court practice direction and may be served notwithstanding that it does not bear the seal of the Court.

(2) A true copy of this claim form and endorsement has been sent to the Admiralty and Commercial Registry, Royal Courts of Justice, Strand, London WC2A 2LL, at the time and date certified below by the solicitor whose name appears below (' the issuing solicitor').

(3) It is the duty of the issuing solicitor or his agent to attend at the Registry when it is next open to the public for the claim form to be sealed.

(4) Any person served with this unsealed claim form:
 (a) will be notified by the issuing solicitor of the case number;
 (b) may require the issuing solicitor to serve him with a copy of the sealed claim form at an address in England and Wales; and
 (c) may inspect without charge the documents lodged at the Registry by the issuing solicitor.

(5) I, the issuing solicitor, undertake [to the Court, to the defendants named in this claim form, and to any other person served with this claim form]:
 (a) that the statement in paragraph 2 above is correct;
 (b) that the time and date given in the certificate with this endorsement are correct;
 (c) that this claim form is a claim form which may be issued under paragraph 2.2 of and Appendix A to the Commercial Court practice direction;
 (d) that I will comply in all respects with the requirements of Appendix A of the Commercial Court practice direction; and
 (e) that I will indemnify any person served with the claim form before it is sealed against any loss suffered as a result of the claim form being or becoming invalid as a result of any failure to comply with Appendix A of the Commercial Court practice direction.

(Signed)
Solicitor for the claimant

Note: the endorsement may be signed in the name of the firm of solicitors rather than an individual solicitor, or by solicitors' agents in their capacity as agents acting on behalf of their professional clients.

Certificate

The issuing solicitor must sign a certificate in the following form:

I certify that I have received a transmission report confirming that the transmission of a copy of this claim form to the Registry by fax was fully completed and that the time and date of transmission to the Registry were [enter the time and date shown on the transmission report].

Dated

(Signed)
Solicitor for the claimant

Note: the certificate must be signed in the name of the firm of solicitors rather than an individual solicitor, or by solicitors' agents in their capacity as agents acting on behalf of their professional clients.

[The following forms are annexed to PD 58:

N1(CC) Claim form (CPR, Part 7)
N1C(CC) Notes for defendant on replying to the Part 7 claim form (Commercial Court)
N9(CC) Acknowledgment of service
N208(CC) Claim form (CPR, Part 8)
N208C(CC) Notes for defendant on replying to the Part 8 claim form

N210(CC)	Acknowledgment of service (Part 8) claim
N211(CC)	Claim form (additional claims — CPR, Part 20)
N211C(CC)	Notes for Part 20 defendant on replying to the Part 20 claim form (Commercial Court)
N213(CC)	Acknowledgment of service (Part 20 claim)

These forms are on the CD-ROM version of *Blackstone's Civil Practice*. Click on the number of a form to open it.]

CPR Part 59 Mercantile Courts

Part 59 **2.19, 11.7, 71.4** [For commentary on a specific rule, please refer to the cross-references after the title of the rule.]

59.1 Scope of This Part and Interpretation

r.59.1(2) **2.19, 11.7**
r.59.1(3) **2.19**
r.59.1(3)(a) **11.4**

(1) This Part applies to claims in Mercantile Courts.
(2) A claim may only be started in a Mercantile Court if it—
   (a) relates to a commercial or business matter in a broad sense; and
   (b) is not required to proceed in the Chancery Division or in another specialist list.
(3) In this Part and its practice direction—
   (a) 'Mercantile Court' means a specialist list established within—
      (i) the district registries listed in the practice direction; and
      (ii) the Central London County Court,
   to hear mercantile claims;
   (b) 'mercantile claim' means a claim proceeding in a Mercantile Court; and
   (c) 'Mercantile judge' means a judge authorised to sit in a Mercantile Court.

59.2 Application of the Civil Procedure Rules

These Rules and their practice directions apply to mercantile claims unless this Part or a practice direction provides otherwise.

59.3 Transfer of Proceedings

Rule 30.5 applies with the modifications that—
(a) a Mercantile judge may transfer a mercantile claim to another Mercantile Court; and
(b) a Commercial Court judge may transfer a claim from the Commercial Court to a Mercantile Court.
(Rule 30.5(3) provides that an application for the transfer of proceedings to or from a specialist list must be made to a judge dealing with claims in that list)

59.4 Claim Form and Particulars of Claim

(1) If particulars of claim are not contained in or served with the claim form—
   (a) the claim form must state that, if an acknowledgment of service is filed which indicates an intention to defend the claim, particulars of claim will follow;
   (b) when the claim form is served, it must be accompanied by the documents specified in rule 7.8(1);
   (c) the claimant must serve particulars of claim within 28 days of the filing of an acknowledgment of service which indicates an intention to defend; and
   (d) rule 7.4(2) does not apply.
(2) If the claimant is claiming interest, he must—
   (a) include a statement to that effect; and
   (b) give the details set out in rule 16.4(2),
   in both the claim form and the particulars of claim.

(3) Rules 12.6(1)(a) and 14.14(1)(a) apply with the modification that references to the particulars of claim shall be read as if they referred to the claim form.

59.5 Acknowledgment of Service

r.59.5(1)–(3) **18.1**

(1) A defendant must file an acknowledgment of service in every case.
(2) Unless paragraph (3) applies, the period for filing an acknowledgment of service is 14 days after service of the claim form.
(3) Where the claim form is served out of the jurisdiction, or on the agent of a defendant who is overseas, the time periods provided by rules 6.16(4), 6.21(4) and 6.22 apply after service of the claim form.

59.6 Disputing the Court's Jurisdiction

r.59.6 **19.3, 19.5**

(1) Part 11 applies to mercantile claims with the modifications set out in this rule.
(2) An application under rule 11(1) must be made within 28 days after filing an acknowledgment of service.
(3) If the defendant files an acknowledgment of service indicating an intention to dispute the court's jurisdiction, the claimant need not serve particulars of claim before the hearing of the application.

59.7 Default Judgment

r.59.7 **20.3**

(1) Part 12 applies to mercantile claims, except that rules 12.10 and 12.11 apply as modified by paragraphs (2) and (3) of this rule.
(2) If, in a Part 7 claim—
    (a) the claim form has been served but no particulars of claim have been served; and
    (b) the defendant has failed to file an acknowledgment of service,
    the claimant must make an application if he wishes to obtain a default judgment.
(3) The application may be made without notice, but the court may direct it to be served on the defendant.

59.8 Admissions

(1) Rule 14.5 does not apply to mercantile claims.
(2) If the defendant admits part of a claim for a specified amount of money, the claimant may apply under rule 14.3 for judgment on the admission.

59.9 Defence and Reply

(1) Part 15 (defence and reply) applies to mercantile claims with the modification to rule 15.8 that the claimant must—
    (a) file any reply to a defence; and
    (b) serve it on all other parties,
    within 21 days after service of the defence.
(2) Rule 6.23 (period for filing a defence where the claim form is served out of the jurisdiction) applies to mercantile claims, except that if the particulars of claim are served after the defendant has filed an acknowledgment of service the period for filing a defence is 28 days from service of the particulars of claim.

59.10 Statements of Case

The court may at any time before or after issue of the claim form order a mercantile claim to proceed without the filing or service of statements of case.

59.11 Case Management

r.59.11(1) **42.6**

(1) All mercantile claims are treated as being allocated to the multi-track, and Part 26 does not apply.
(2) The following parts only of Part 29 apply—

(a) rule 29.3(2) (appropriate legal representative to attend case management conferences and pre-trial reviews); and
(b) rule 29.5 (variation of case management timetable) with the exception of rule 29.5(1)(c).

(3) As soon as practicable the court will hold a case management conference which must be fixed in accordance with the practice direction.

(4) At the case management conference or at any hearing at which the parties are represented the court may give such directions for the management of the case as it considers appropriate.

59.12 Judgments and Orders

(1) Except for orders made by the court of its own initiative and unless the court otherwise orders every judgment or order will be drawn up by the parties, and rule 40.3 is modified accordingly.

(2) An application for a consent order must include a draft of the proposed order signed on behalf of all the parties to whom it relates.

(3) Rule 40.6 (consent judgments and orders) does not apply.

PD 59 Practice Direction — Mercantile Courts

This practice direction supplements CPR Part 59

PD 59 **2.19**, **11.7** [For commentary on a specific paragraph, please refer to the cross-references after the title of the paragraph.]

General

1.1 This practice direction applies to mercantile claims.

1.2 Mercantile Courts are established in:

(1) the following district registries of the High Court: Birmingham, Bristol, Cardiff, Chester, Leeds, Liverpool, Manchester and Newcastle; and

(2) the Central London County Court (previously called the Business List and now called the Mercantile List).

1.3 All mercantile claims will be heard or determined by a mercantile judge, except that:

(1) an application may be heard and determined by any other judge who, if the claim were not a mercantile claim, would have jurisdiction to determine it, if:

(a) the application is urgent and no mercantile judge is available to hear it; or

(b) a mercantile judge directs it to be heard by another judge; and

(2) unless the court otherwise orders, all proceedings for the enforcement of a Mercantile Court judgment or order for the payment of money will be dealt with by a district judge.

1.4 Provisions in other practice directions which refer to a master or district judge are to be read, in relation to mercantile claims, as if they referred to a mercantile judge.

Starting Proceedings in a Mercantile Court

para.2.1 **2.19** para.2.3 **11.7**
para.2.2 **23.3**

2.1 A claim should only be started in a Mercantile Court if it will benefit from the expertise of a mercantile judge.

2.2 The claim form must be marked in the top right hand corner 'Queen's Bench Division, __________ District Registry, Mercantile Court' or 'Central London County Court, Mercantile List' as appropriate.

2.3 A claim having a value less than £15,000 may not be issued in the Mercantile List at the Central London County Court without permission of the court.

2.4 A claim may be issued in the Mercantile List at the Central London County Court provided it has some connection with the South Eastern Circuit, for example, because:

(1) it is convenient for the claim to be dealt with in that court;

(2) the claim arises out of a transaction which took place within that circuit; or

(3) one of the parties resides or carries on business within that circuit.

Applications before Proceedings Are Issued

3.1 A party who intends to bring a claim in a Mercantile Court must make any application before the claim form is issued to a judge of that court.

3.2 The written evidence in support of such an application should show why the claim is suitable to proceed as a mercantile claim.

Transfer of Proceedings to or from a Mercantile Court

4.1 If a claim which has not been issued in a Mercantile Court is suitable to continue as a mercantile claim:

(1) any party wishing the claim to be transferred to a Mercantile Court may make an application for transfer to the court to which transfer is sought;

(2) if all parties consent to the transfer, the application may be made by letter to the mercantile listing officer of the court to which transfer is sought, stating why the case is suitable to be transferred to that court and enclosing the written consents of the parties, the claim form and statements of case.

4.2 If an application for transfer is made to a court which does not have power to make the order, that court may:
(1) adjourn the application to be heard by a mercantile judge; or
(2) dismiss the application.

4.3 A mercantile judge may make an order under r. 59.3 of his own initiative.

Default Judgment and Admissions

5. PD 12 and PD 14 apply with the following modifications:
(1) PD 12, para. 4.1(1), is to be read as referring to the service of the claim form; and
(2) the references to 'particulars of claim' in PD 14, paras 2.1, 3.1 and 3.2, are to be read as referring to the claim form.

Variation of Time Limits by Agreement

6.1 If the parties, in accordance with r. 2.11, agree in writing to vary a time limit, the claimant must notify the court in writing, giving brief written reasons for the agreed variation.

6.2 The court may make an order overriding an agreement by the parties varying a time limit.

Case Management

7.1 The following parts only of PD 29 apply:
(1) para. 5 (case management conferences), excluding para. 5.9 and modified so far as is made necessary by other specific provisions of this practice direction; and
(2) para. 7 (failure to comply with case management directions).

7.2 If proceedings are started in a Mercantile Court, the claimant must apply for a case management conference:
(1) for a Part 7 claim, within 14 days of the date when all defendants who intend to file and serve a defence have done so; and
(2) for a Part 8 claim, within 14 days of the date when all defendants who intend to serve evidence have done so.

7.3 If proceedings are transferred to a Mercantile Court, the claimant must apply for a case management conference within 14 days of receiving an acknowledgment of the transfer from the receiving court, unless the judge held, or gave directions for, a case management conference when he made the order transferring the proceedings.

7.4 Any party may, at a time earlier than that provided in paras 7.2 or 7.3, apply in writing to the court to fix a case management conference.

7.5 If the claimant does not make an application in accordance with paras 7.2 or 7.3, any other party may apply for a case management conference.

7.6 The court may fix a case management conference at any time on its own initiative. If it does so, the court will give at least seven days' notice to the parties, unless there are compelling reasons for a shorter period of notice.

7.7 Not less than seven days before a case management conference:
(1) each party shall file and serve:
(a) a case management information sheet substantially in the form set out at Appendix A to this practice direction; and
(b) an application notice for any order which that party intends to seek at the case management conference, other than directions referred to in the case management information sheet; and
(2) the claimant (or other party applying for the conference) shall in addition file and serve:
(a) a case management file containing:
— the claim form;
— the statements of case (excluding schedules of more than 15 pages);
— any orders already made;
— the case management information sheets; and
— a short list of the principal issues to be prepared by the claimant; and
(b) a draft order substantially in the form set out at Appendix B to this practice direction, setting out the directions which that party thinks appropriate.

7.8 In appropriate cases:
(1) the parties may, not less than seven days before the date fixed for the case management conference, submit agreed directions for the approval of the judge;
(2) the judge will then either:
(a) make the directions proposed; or
(b) make them with alterations; or
(c) require the case management conference to proceed; but
(3) the parties must assume that the conference will proceed until informed to the contrary.

7.9 If the parties submit agreed directions and the judge makes them with alterations, any party objecting to the alterations may, within seven days of receiving the order containing the directions, apply to the court for the directions to be varied.

7.10 The directions given at the case management conference:
(1) will normally cover all steps in the case through to trial, including the fixing of a trial date or window, or directions for the taking of steps to fix the trial date or window; and
(2) may include the fixing of a progress monitoring date or dates, and make provision for the court to be informed as to the progress of the case at the date or dates fixed.

7.11 If the court fixes a progress monitoring date, it may after that date fix a further case management conference or a pre-trial review on its own initiative if:
(1) no or insufficient information is provided by the parties; or
(2) it is appropriate in view of the information provided.

Pre-trial Review and Questionnaire

8.1 The court may order a pre-trial review at any time.

8.2 Each party must file and serve a completed pre-trial checklist substantially in the form set out in Appendix C to this practice direction:
(1) if a pre-trial review has been ordered, not less than seven days before the date of the review; or
(2) if no pre-trial review has been ordered, not less than six weeks before the trial date.

8.3 When pre-trial checklists are filed under para. 8.2(2):
(1) the judge will consider them and decide whether to order a pre-trial review; and
(2) if he does not order a pre-trial review, he may on his own initiative give directions for the further preparation of the case or as to the conduct of the trial.

8.4 At a pre-trial review:
(1) the parties should if possible be represented by the advocates who will be appearing at the trial;
(2) any representatives appearing must be fully informed and authorised for the purposes of the review; and
(3) the court will give such directions for the conduct of the trial as it sees fit.

Evidence for Applications

9.1 The general requirement is that, unless the court orders otherwise:
(1) evidence in support of an application must be filed and served with the application: see r. 23.7(3);
(2) evidence in answer must be filed and served within 14 days after the application is served;
(3) evidence in reply must be filed and served within seven days of the service of the evidence in answer.

9.2 In any case in which the application is likely to require an oral hearing of more than half a day the periods set out in paras 9.1(2) and (3) will be 28 days and 14 days respectively.

9.3 If the date fixed for the hearing of the application means that the times in paras 9.1(2) and (3) cannot both be achieved, the evidence must be filed and served:
(1) as soon as possible; and
(2) in sufficient time to ensure that the application may fairly proceed on the date fixed.

9.4 The parties may, in accordance with r. 2.11, agree different periods from those provided above, provided that the agreement does not affect the ability to proceed on the date fixed for the hearing of the application.

Files for Applications

10. Before the hearing of any application, the applicant must:
    (1) provide to the court and each other party an appropriate indexed file for the application with consecutively numbered pages; and
    (2) attach to the file an estimate of the reading time required by the judge.

Judgments and Orders

11.1 After any hearing the claimant must draw up a draft order, unless the decision was made on the application of another party in which case that party must do so.

11.2 A draft order must be submitted by the party responsible for drawing it up within three clear days of the decision, with sufficient copies for each party and for one to be retained by the court.

11.3 The sealed orders will be returned to the party submitting them, who will be responsible for serving the order on the other parties.

11.4 Orders must be dated with the date of the decision, except for consent orders submitted for approval, which must be left undated.

ANNEX A CASE MANAGEMENT INFORMATION SHEET MERCANTILE COURTS

[Title of case]

This information sheet must be filed with Mercantile Listing at least seven days before the case management conference, and copies served on all other parties: see PD 59, para. 7.7.

Party filing:
Solicitors:
Advocate(s) for trial:
Date:

Substance of case

1. What in about 20 words maximum is the case about? Please provide a separate concise list of issues in a complex case.

Parties

2. Are all parties still effective?
3. Do you intend to add any further party?

Statements of case

4. Do you intend to amend your statement of case?
5. Do you require any 'further information' see CPR, Part 18?

Disclosure

6. By what date can you give standard disclosure?
7. Do you contend that to search for any type of document falling within r. 31.6(b) would be unreasonable within r. 31.7(2); if so, what type and on what grounds?
8. Is any specific disclosure required (r. 31.12)?
9. Is a full disclosure order appropriate?
10. By what dates could you give:
    (i) any specific disclosure referred to at 8; and
    (ii) full disclosure?

Admissions

11. Can you make any additional admissions?

Preliminary issues

12. Are any issues suitable for trial as preliminary issues? If yes, which?

Witnesses of fact

13. On how many witnesses of fact do you intend to rely at the trial (subject to the court's direction)?

14. Please name them, or explain why you do not.
15. Which of them will be called to give oral evidence?
16. When can you serve their witness statements?
17. Will any require an interpreter?

Expert evidence
18. Are there issues requiring expert evidence?
19. If yes, what issues?
20. Might a single joint expert be suitable on any issues (see r. 35.7)?
21. What experts do you intend (subject to the court's direction) to call? Please give the number, their names and expertise.
22. By what date can you serve signed expert reports?
23. Should there be meetings of experts of like disciplines, of all disciplines? By when?
24. Which experts, if any, do you intend not to call at the trial?
25. Will any require an interpreter?

Trial
26. What are the advocates' present estimates of the length of the trial?
27. What is the earliest date that you think the case can be ready for trial?
28. Where should the trial be held?
29. Is a pre-trial review advisable?

ADR
30. Might some form of alternative dispute resolution assist to resolve the dispute or some part of it?
31. Has this been considered with the client?
32. Has this been considered with the other parties?
33. Do you want the case to be stayed pending ADR or other means of settlement (r. 26.4); or any other directions relating to ADR?

Other applications
34. What applications, if any, not covered above, will you be making at the conference? Costs
35. What, do you estimate, are your costs to date?
36. What, do you estimate, will be your costs to end of trial?

[Signature of party/solicitor]

ANNEX B STANDARD DIRECTIONS IN MERCANTILE COURTS

[Title of case with judge's name]
Order for directions
made on [ ]

1. Standard disclosure is to be made by [ ]. Inspection on 48 hours' notice to be completed by [ ].
2. Signed statements of witnesses of fact, and hearsay notices when required by r. 33.2, are to be exchanged not later than [ ]. Unless otherwise ordered, the witness statements are to stand as the evidence-in-chief of the witnesses at trial.
3. Each party has permission to call at the trial expert witnesses as follows:

Number *Expertise* *Issue(s) to be covered*

whose reports are to be exchanged by [ ].
4. Experts of like disciplines are to:
   (i) meet without prejudice by [ ] to identify the issues between them and to attempt to reach agreement on such issues, and
   (ii) prepare a joint statement pursuant to r. 35.12(3), by [ ].

or

3. Expert evidence in the following field(s) of expertise is limited to a written report by a single expert jointly instructed by the parties:

Expertise *Issue(s) to be covered*

4. (i) The report of the single joint expert is to be produced by [ ].
   (ii) Any questions to the expert are to be presented to him by [ ] and answered by [ ].
   (iii) Any party may apply not later than [ ] for an order that the expert witness shall give oral evidence at the trial.
5. The case will be tried in [ ] by judge alone, estimated length of trial [ ] days, [commencing on] [not before]. [The claimant is to apply to the mercantile listing officer to fix a date for the trial, not later than [ ], specifying dates which any party wishes to avoid.]
6. [The progress monitoring date is [ ]. Each party is to notify the court in writing by that date (with a copy to all other parties) of the progress of the case, including:
   (i) whether the directions have been complied with in all respects;
   (ii) if any directions are outstanding, which of them and why; and
   (iii) whether a further case management conference or a pre-trial review is required.]
7. There will be a pre-trial review on [ ]. [In the event of both parties notifying the court in writing not less than [ ] days before the pre-trial review that it is not required, then it will be vacated.]
8. Signed pre-trial checklists are to be filed and served by [ ] [not less than seven days before the pre-trial review] [not less than six weeks before the trial date].
9. Trial bundles must be agreed, prepared and delivered to counsel not less than [ ] days before the trial date, and to the court not less than [ ] days before the trial date.
10. Costs in the case.

DATED

ANNEX C PRE-TRIAL CHECKLIST MERCANTILE COURTS

[Title of case]

Where a pre-trial review has been ordered, this checklist must be filed with Mercantile Listing not less than seven days before the pre-trial review, and copies served on all other parties. Where a pre-trial review has not been ordered, it must be filed and served not less than six weeks before the trial date. See PD 59, para. 8.2.

a. Trial date:
b. Whether pre-trial review ordered:
c. Date of review:
d. Party lodging:
e. Solicitors:
f. Advocate(s) for trial:
g. Date lodged:

[Note: this checklist should normally be completed with the involvement of the advocate(s) instructed for trial.]

1. Have all the directions made to date been carried out?
2. If not, what remains to be carried out? When will it be carried out?
3. Do you intend to take any further steps regarding:
   (i) statements of case?
   (ii) disclosure?
   (iii) witnesses and witness statements?
   (iv) experts and expert reports?
   If yes in any case, what and by when?
4. Will the preparation of trial bundles be completed not later than three weeks before the date fixed for trial? If not, what is the position?
5. What witnesses of fact do you intend to call?
6. (Where directions for expert evidence have been given) what experts do you intend to call?
7. Is any interpreter needed: for whom?
8. If a pre-trial review has not been ordered, do you think one would be useful?

9. What are the advocate(s)' confirmed estimates of the minimum and maximum lengths of the trial? A confirmed estimate signed by the advocate(s) and dated must be attached.
10. (i) Might some form of alternative dispute resolution now assist?
 (ii) Has the question been considered with the client?
 (iii) Has the question been explored with the other parties to the case?

[Signature of party/solicitor]

CPR Part 60 Technology and Construction Court Claims

Part 60 **2.16**, **11.7**, **71.4** [For commentary on a specific rule, please refer to the cross-references after the title of the rule.]

60.1 General

r.60.1 **2.16**

(1) This Part applies to Technology and Construction Court claims ('TCC claims').
(2) In this Part and its practice direction—
  (a) 'TCC claim' means a claim which—
    (i) satisfies the requirements of paragraph (3); and
    (ii) has been issued in or transferred into the specialist list for such claims;
  (b) 'Technology and Construction Court' means any court in which TCC claims are dealt with in accordance with this Part or its practice direction; and
  (c) 'TCC judge' means any judge authorised to hear TCC claims.
(3) A claim may be brought as a TCC claim if—
  (a) it involves issues or questions which are technically complex; or
  (b) a trial by a TCC judge is desirable.

(The practice direction gives examples of types of claims which it may be appropriate to bring as TCC claims.)

(4) TCC claims include all official referees' business referred to in section 68(1)(a) of the Supreme Court Act 1981.
(5) TCC claims will be dealt with—
  (a) in a Technology and Construction Court; and
  (b) by a TCC judge, unless—
    (i) this Part or its practice direction permits otherwise; or
    (ii) a TCC judge directs otherwise.

60.2 Specialist List

r.60.2(1) **42.8**

(1) TCC claims form a specialist list.
(2) A judge will be appointed to be the judge in charge of the TCC specialist list.

60.3 Application of the Civil Procedure Rules

These Rules and their practice directions apply to TCC claims unless this Part or a practice direction provides otherwise.

60.4 Issuing a TCC Claim

A TCC claim must be issued in—
(a) the High Court in London;
(b) a district registry of the High Court; or
(c) a county court specified in the practice direction.

60.5 Reply

Part 15 (defence and reply) applies to TCC claims with the modification to rule 15.8 that the claimant must—
(a) file any reply to a defence; and

(b) serve it on all other parties,

within 21 days after service of the defence.

60.6 Case Management

r.60.6 **42.8** r.60.6(1) **42.6**

(1) All TCC claims are treated as being allocated to the multi-track and Part 26 does not apply.

(2) Part 29 and its practice direction apply to the case management of TCC claims, except where they are varied by or inconsistent with the practice direction to this Part.

60.7 Judgments and Orders

r.60.7 **61.30**

(1) Except for orders made by the court of its own initiative and unless the court otherwise orders, every judgment or order made in claims proceeding in the Technology and Construction Court will be drawn up by the parties, and rule 40.3 is modified accordingly.

(2) An application for a consent order must include a draft of the proposed order signed on behalf of all the parties to whom it relates.

(3) Rule 40.6 (consent judgments and orders) does not apply.

PD 60 Practice Direction — Technology and Construction Court Claims

This practice direction supplements CPR Part 60

PD 60 **2.16**, **11.7** [For commentary on a specific paragraph, please refer to the cross-references after the title of the paragraph.]

General

1 This practice direction applies to Technology and Construction Court claims ('TCC claims').

TCC Claims

2.1 The following are examples of the types of claim which it may be appropriate to bring as TCC claims:

(a) building or other construction disputes, including claims for the enforcement of the decisions of adjudicators under the Housing Grants, Construction and Regeneration Act 1996;
(b) engineering disputes;
(c) claims by and against engineers, architects, surveyors, accountants and other specialised advisers relating to the services they provide;
(d) claims by and against local authorities relating to their statutory duties concerning the development of land or the construction of buildings;
(e) claims relating to the design, supply and installation of computers, computer software and related network systems;
(f) claims relating to the quality of goods sold or hired, and work done, materials supplied or services rendered;
(g) claims between landlord and tenant for breach of a repairing covenant;
(h) claims between neighbours, owners and occupiers of land in trespass, nuisance etc.;
(i) claims relating to the environment (for example, pollution cases);
(j) claims arising out of fires;
(k) claims involving taking of accounts where these are complicated; and
(l) challenges to decisions of arbitrators in construction and engineering disputes including applications for permission to appeal and appeals.

2.2 A claim given as an example in para. 2.1 will not be suitable for this specialist list unless it demonstrates the characteristics in r. 60.1(3). Similarly, the examples are not exhaustive and other types of claim may be appropriate to this specialist list.

How to Start a TCC Claim

para.3.2 **23.3** para.3.3–3.4 **2.16, 11.7**

3.1 TCC claims must be issued in the High Court or in a county court specified in this practice direction.

3.2 The claim form must be marked in the top right-hand corner 'Technology and Construction Court' below the words 'The High Court, Queen's Bench Division' or 'The ____ County Court'.

3.3 TCC claims brought in the High Court outside London may be issued in any District Registry, but it is preferable that wherever possible they should be issued in one of the following district registries, in which a TCC judge will usually be available: Birmingham, Bristol, Cardiff, Chester, Exeter, Leeds, Liverpool, Newcastle, Nottingham and Salford.

3.4 The county courts in which a TCC claim may be issued are the following: Birmingham, Bristol, Cardiff, Central London, Chester, Exeter, Leeds, Liverpool, Newcastle, Nottingham and Salford.

Applications before Proceedings Are Issued

4.1 A party who intends to issue a TCC claim must make any application before the claim form is issued to a TCC judge.

4.2 The written evidence in support of such an application must state that the proposed claim is a TCC claim.

Transfer of Proceedings

5.1 Where no TCC judge is available to deal with a claim which has been issued in a High Court District Registry or one of the county courts listed in para. 3.4 above, the claim may be transferred:
(1) if it has been issued in a district registry, to another district registry or to the High Court in London; or
(2) if it has been issued in a county court, to another county court where a TCC judge would be available.

5.2 Paragraph 5.1 is without prejudice to the court's general powers to transfer proceedings under Part 30.
(Rule 30.5(3) provides that an application for the transfer of proceedings to or from a specialist list must be made to a judge dealing with claims in that list.)

5.3 A party applying to a TCC judge to transfer a claim to the TCC specialist list must give notice of the application to the court in which the claim is proceeding, and a TCC judge will not make an order for transfer until he is satisfied that such notice has been given.

Assignment of Claim to a TCC Judge

para.6.1 **2.16**

6.1 When a TCC claim is issued or an order is made transferring a claim to the TCC specialist list, the court will assign the claim to a named TCC judge ('the assigned TCC judge') who will have the primary responsibility for the case management of that claim.

6.2 All documents relating to the claim must be marked in similar manner to the claim form with the words 'Technology and Construction Court' and the name of the assigned TCC judge.

Applications

7.1 An application should normally be made to the assigned TCC judge. If the assigned TCC judge is not available, or the court gives permission, the application may be made to another TCC judge.

7.2 If an application is urgent and there is no TCC judge available to deal with it, the application may be made to any judge who, if the claim were not a TCC claim, would be authorised to deal with the application.

Case Management Conference

para.8.1 **45.11**
para.8.2 **42.8, 45.11**
para.8.3 **45.11**
para.8.6 **45.15**

8.1 The court will fix a case management conference within 14 days of the earliest of these events:
(1) the filing of an acknowledgment of service;
(2) the filing of a defence; or
(3) the date of an order transferring the claim to a TCC.

8.2 When the court notifies the parties of the date and time of the case management conference, it will at the same time send each party a case management information sheet and a case management directions form.
(The case management information sheet and the case management directions form are in the form set out in Appendices A and B to this practice direction.)

8.3 Not less than two days before the case management conference, each party must file and serve on all other parties:
(1) completed copies of the case management information sheet and case management directions form; and
(2) an application notice for any order which that party intends to seek at the case management conference, other than directions referred to in the case management directions form.

8.4 The parties are encouraged to agree directions to propose to the court by reference to the case management directions form.

8.5 If any party fails to file or serve the case management information sheet and the case management directions form by the date specified, the court may:
(1) impose such sanction as it sees fit; and
(2) either proceed with or adjourn the case management conference.

8.6 The directions given at the case management conference will normally include the fixing of dates for:
(1) any further case management conferences;
(2) a pre-trial review;
(3) the trial of any preliminary issues that it orders to be tried; and
(4) the trial.

Pre-trial Review

9.1 When the court fixes the date for a pre-trial review it will send each party a pre-trial review questionnaire and a pre-trial review directions form.
(The pre-trial review questionnaire is in the form set out in Appendix C to this practice direction.)

9.2 Each party must file and serve on all other parties completed copies of the questionnaire not less than two days before the date fixed for the pre-trial review.

9.3 The parties are encouraged to agree directions to propose to the court.

9.4 If any party fails to return or exchange the questionnaire by the date specified the court may:
(1) impose such sanction as it sees fit; and
(2) either proceed with or adjourn the pre-trial review.

9.5 At the pre-trial review, the court will give such directions for the conduct of the trial as it sees fit.

Listing

10 The provisions about listing questionnaires and listing in Part 29 and PD 29 do not apply to TCC claims.

Trial

para.11.1 **2.16**

11.1 Whenever possible the trial of a claim will be heard by the assigned TCC judge.

11.2 A TCC claim may be tried at any place where there is a TCC judge available to try the claim.

app.A **42.8, 45.11** app.B **42.8, 45.11**

[The following forms are appended to PD 60:

Appendix A TCC/CM1 Case management information sheet
Appendix B TCC/CMD Case management directions form
Appendix C TCC/PTR1 Pre-trial review questionnaire

These forms are on the CD-ROM version of *Blackstone's Civil Practice*. Click on a form or appendix number to open it.]

CPR Part 61 Admiralty Claims

Part 61 **2.18**, **11.7**, **71.4** [For commentary on a specific rule, please refer to the cross-references after the title of the rule.]

61.1 Scope and Interpretation

r.61.1(3) **42.6**

(1) This Part applies to admiralty claims.
(2) In this Part—
  (a) 'admiralty claim' means a claim within the Admiralty jurisdiction of the High Court as set out in section 20 of the Supreme Court Act 1981;
  (b) 'the Admiralty Court' means the Admiralty Court of the Queen's Bench Division of the High Court of Justice;
  (c) 'claim in rem' means a claim in an admiralty action in rem;
  (d) 'collision claim' means a claim within section 20(3)(b) of the Supreme Court Act 1981;
  (e) 'limitation claim' means a claim under the Merchant Shipping Act 1995 for the limitation of liability in connection with a ship or other property;
  (f) 'salvage claim' means a claim—
    (i) for or in the nature of salvage;
    (ii) for special compensation under Article 14 of Schedule 11 to the Merchant Shipping Act 1995;
    (iii) for the apportionment of salvage; and
    (iv) arising out of or connected with any contract for salvage services;
  (g) 'caution against arrest' means a caution entered in the Register under rule 61.7;
  (h) 'caution against release' means a caution entered in the Register under rule 61.8;
  (i) 'the Register' means the Register of cautions against arrest and release which is open to inspection as provided by the practice direction;
  (j) 'the Marshal' means the Admiralty Marshal;
  (k) 'ship' includes any vessel used in navigation; and
  (l) 'the Registrar' means the Queen's Bench Master with responsibility for Admiralty claims.
(3) Part 58 (Commercial Court) applies to claims in the Admiralty Court except where this Part provides otherwise.
(4) The Registrar has all the powers of the Admiralty judge except where a rule or practice direction provides otherwise.

61.2 Admiralty Claims

r.61.2 **11.2**
r.61.2(1) **11.7**
r.61.2(3) **2.18**

(1) The following claims must be started in the Admiralty Court—
  (a) a claim—
    (i) in rem;
    (ii) for damage done by a ship;
    (iii) concerning the ownership of a ship;

(iv) under the Merchant Shipping Act 1995;
(v) for loss of life or personal injury specified in section 20(2)(f) of the Supreme Court Act 1981;
(vi) by a master or member of a crew for wages;
(vii) in the nature of towage; or
(viii) in the nature of pilotage;
(b) a collision claim;
(c) a limitation claim; or
(d) a salvage claim.

(2) Any other admiralty claim may be started in the Admiralty Court.
(3) Rule 30.5 applies to claims in the Admiralty Court except that the Admiralty Court may order the transfer of a claim to—
(a) the Commercial list;
(b) a Mercantile Court;
(c) the Mercantile list at the Central London County Court; or
(d) any other appropriate court.

61.3 Claims in Rem

r.61.3 **18.1**

(1) This rule applies to claims in rem.
(2) A claim in rem is started by the issue of an in rem claim form as set out in the practice direction.
(3) Subject to rule 61.4, the particulars of claim must—
(a) be contained in or served with the claim form; or
(b) be served on the defendant by the claimant within 75 days after service of the claim form.
(4) An acknowledgment of service must be filed within 14 days after service of the claim form.
(5) The claim form must be served—
(a) in accordance with the practice direction; and
(b) within 12 months after the date of issue and rules 7.5 and 7.6 are modified accordingly.
(6) If a claim form has been issued (whether served or not), any person who wishes to defend the claim may file an acknowledgment of service.

61.4 Special Provisions Relating to Collision Claims

r.61.4 **18.1**

(1) This rule applies to collision claims.
(2) A claim form need not contain or be followed by particulars of claim and rule 7.4 does not apply.
(3) An acknowledgment of service must be filed.
(4) A party who wishes to dispute the court's jurisdiction must make an application under Part 11 within 2 months after filing his acknowledgment of service.
(5) Every party must—
(a) within 2 months after the defendant files the acknowledgment of service; or
(b) where the defendant applies under Part 11, within 2 months after the defendant files the further acknowledgment of service,

file at the court a completed collision statement of case in the form specified in the practice direction.
(6) A collision statement of case must be—
(a) in the form set out in the practice direction; and
(b) verified by a statement of truth.
(7) A claim form in a collision claim may not be served out of the jurisdiction unless—
(a) the case falls within section 22(2)(a), (b) or (c) of the Supreme Court Act 1981; or
(b) the defendant has submitted to or agreed to submit to the jurisdiction; and the court gives permission in accordance with Section III of Part 6.
(8) Where permission to serve a claim form out of the jurisdiction is given, the court will specify the period within which the defendant may file an acknowledgment of service and, where appropriate, a collision statement of case.
(9) Where, in a collision claim in rem ('the original claim')—
(a) (i) a Part 20 claim; or
(ii) a cross-claim in rem

arising out of the same collision or occurrence is made; and

(b) (i) the party bringing the original claim has caused the arrest of a ship or has obtained security in order to prevent such arrest; and
(ii) the party bringing the Part 20 claim or cross-claim is unable to arrest a ship or otherwise obtain security,

the party bringing the Part 20 claim or cross-claim may apply to the court to stay the original claim until sufficient security is given to satisfy any judgment that may be given in favour of that party.

(10) The consequences set out in paragraph (11) apply where a party to a claim to establish liability for a collision claim (other than a claim for loss of life or personal injury)—
(a) makes an offer to settle in the form set out in paragraph (12) not less than 21 days before the start of the trial;
(b) that offer is not accepted; and
(c) the maker of the offer obtains at trial an apportionment equal to or more favourable than his offer.

(11) Where paragraph (10) applies the parties will, unless the court considers it unjust, be entitled to the following costs—
(a) the maker of the offer will be entitled to—
(i) all his costs from 21 days after the offer was made; and
(ii) his costs before then in the percentage to which he would have been entitled had the offer been accepted; and
(b) all other parties to whom the offer was made—
(i) will be entitled to their costs up to 21 days after the offer was made in the percentage to which they would have been entitled had the offer been accepted; but
(ii) will not be entitled to their costs thereafter.

(12) An offer under paragraph (10) must be in writing and must contain—
(a) an offer to settle liability at stated percentages;
(b) an offer to pay costs in accordance with the same percentages;
(c) a term that the offer remain open for 21 days after the date it is made; and
(d) a term that, unless the court orders otherwise, on expiry of that period the offer remains open on the same terms except that the offeree should pay all the costs from that date until acceptance.

61.5 Arrest

(1) In a claim in rem—
(a) a claimant; and
(b) a judgment creditor

may apply to have the property proceeded against arrested.

(2) The practice direction sets out the procedure for applying for arrest.

(3) A party making an application for arrest must—
(a) request a search to be made in the Register before the warrant is issued to determine whether there is a caution against arrest in force with respect to that property; and
(b) file a declaration in the form set out in the practice direction.

(4) A warrant of arrest may not be issued as of right in the case of property in respect of which the beneficial ownership, as a result of a sale or disposal by any court in any jurisdiction exercising admiralty jurisdiction in rem, has changed since the claim form was issued.

(5) A warrant of arrest may not be issued against a ship owned by a State where by any convention or treaty, the United Kingdom has undertaken to minimise the possibility of arrest of ships of that State until—
(a) notice in the form set out in the practice direction has been served on a consular officer at the consular office of that State in London or the port at which it is intended to arrest the ship; and
(b) a copy of that notice is attached to any declaration under paragraph (3)(b).

(6) Except—
(a) with the permission of the court; or
(b) where notice has been given under paragraph (5),

a warrant of arrest may not be issued in a claim in rem against a foreign ship belonging to a port of a State in respect of which an order in council has been made under section 4 of the Consular Relations Act 1968, until the expiration of 2 weeks from appropriate notice to the consul.

(7) A warrant of arrest is valid for 12 months but may only be executed if the claim form—
(a) has been served; or
(b) remains valid for service at the date of execution.

(8) Property may only be arrested by the Marshal or his substitute.

(9) Property under arrest—
(a) may not be moved unless the court orders otherwise; and
(b) may be immobilised or prevented from sailing in such manner as the Marshal may consider appropriate.

(10) Where an in rem claim form has been issued and security sought, any person who has filed an acknowledgment of service may apply for an order specifying the amount and form of security to be provided.

61.6 Security Claim in Rem

(1) This rule applies if, in a claim in rem, security has been given to—
(a) obtain the release of property under arrest; or
(b) prevent the arrest of property.

(2) The court may order that the—
(a) amount of security be reduced and may stay the claim until the order is complied with; or
(b) claimant may arrest or re-arrest the property proceeded against to obtain further security.

(3) The court may not make an order under paragraph (2)(b) if the total security to be provided would exceed the value of the property at the time—
(a) of the original arrest; or
(b) security was first given (if the property was not arrested).

61.7 Cautions against Arrest

(1) Any person may file a request for a caution against arrest.

(2) When a request under paragraph (1) is filed the court will enter the caution in the Register if the request is in the form set out in the practice direction and—
(a) the person filing the request undertakes—
(i) to file an acknowledgment of service; and
(ii) to give sufficient security to satisfy the claim with interest and costs; or
(b) where the person filing the request has constituted a limitation fund in accordance with Article 11 of the Convention on Limitation of Liability for Maritime Claims 1976 he—
(i) states that such a fund has been constituted; and
(ii) undertakes that the claimant will acknowledge service of the claim form by which any claim may be begun against the property described in the request.

(3) A caution against arrest—
(a) is valid for 12 months after the date it is entered in the Register; but
(b) may be renewed for a further 12 months by filing a further request.

(4) Paragraphs (1) and (2) apply to a further request under paragraph (3)(b).

(5) Property may be arrested if a caution against arrest has been entered in the Register but the court may order that—
(a) the arrest be discharged; and
(b) the party procuring the arrest pays compensation to the owner of or other persons interested in the arrested property.

61.8 Release and Cautions against Release

(1) Where property is under arrest—
(a) an in rem claim form may be served upon it; and
(b) it may be arrested by any other person claiming to have an in rem claim against it.

(2) Any person who—
(a) claims to have an in rem right against any property under arrest; and

(b) wishes to be given notice of any application in respect of that property or its proceeds of sale,

may file a request for a caution against release in the form set out in the practice direction.

(3) When a request under paragraph (2) is filed, a caution against release will be entered in the Register.

(4) Property will be released from arrest if—

(a) it is sold by the court;

(b) the court orders release on an application made by any party;

(c) (i) the arresting party; and

(ii) all persons who have entered cautions against release

file a request for release in the form set out in the practice direction; or

(d) any party files—

(i) a request for release in the form set out in the practice direction (containing an undertaking); and

(ii) consents to the release of the arresting party and all persons who have entered cautions against release.

(5) Where the release of any property is delayed by the entry of a caution against release under this rule any person who has an interest in the property may apply for an order that the person who entered the caution pay damages for losses suffered by the applicant because of the delay.

(6) The court may not make an order under paragraph (5) if satisfied that there was good reason to—

(a) request the entry of; and

(b) maintain

the caution.

(7) Any person—

(a) interested in property under arrest or in the proceeds of sale of such property; or

(b) whose interests are affected by any order sought or made,

may be made a party to any claim in rem against the property or proceeds of sale.

(8) Where—

(a) (i) a ship is not under arrest but cargo on board her is; or

(ii) a ship is under arrest but cargo on board her is not; and

(b) persons interested in the ship or cargo wish to discharge the cargo,

they may, without being made parties, request the Marshal to authorise steps to discharge the cargo.

(9) If—

(a) the Marshal considers a request under paragraph (8) reasonable; and

(b) the applicant gives an undertaking in writing acceptable to the Marshal to pay—

(i) his fees; and

(ii) all expenses to be incurred by him or on his behalf

on demand,

the Marshal will apply to the court for an order to permit the discharge of the cargo.

(10) Where persons interested in the ship or cargo are unable or unwilling to give an undertaking as referred to in paragraph (9)(b), they may—

(a) be made parties to the claim; and

(b) apply to the court for an order for—

(i) discharge of the cargo; and

(ii) directions as to the fees and expenses of the Marshal with regard to the discharge and storage of the cargo.

61.9 Judgment in Default

r.61.9 **20.2**

(1) In a claim in rem (other than a collision claim) the claimant may obtain judgment in default of—

(a) an acknowledgment of service only if—

(i) the defendant has not filed an acknowledgment of service; and

(ii) the time for doing so set out in rule 61.3(4) has expired; and

(b) defence only if—
(i) a defence has not been filed; and
(ii) the relevant time limit for doing so has expired.

(2) In a collision claim, a party who has filed a collision statement of case within the time specified by rule 61.4(5) may obtain judgment in default of a collision statement of case only if—
(a) the party against whom judgment is sought has not filed a collision statement of case; and
(b) the time for doing so set out in rule 61.4(5) has expired.

(3) An application for judgment in default—
(a) under paragraph (1) or paragraph (2) in an in rem claim must be made by filing—
(i) an application notice as set out in the practice direction;
(ii) a certificate proving service of the claim form; and
(iii) evidence proving the claim to the satisfaction of the court; and
(b) under paragraph (2) in any other claim must be made in accordance with Part 12 with any necessary modifications.

(4) An application notice seeking judgment in default and, unless the court orders otherwise, all evidence in support, must be served on all persons who have entered cautions against release on the Register.

(5) The court may set aside or vary any judgment in default entered under this rule.

(6) The claimant may apply to the court for judgment against a party at whose instance a notice against arrest was entered where—
(a) the claim form has been served on that party;
(b) the sum claimed in the claim form does not exceed the amount specified in the undertaking given by that party in accordance with rule 61.7(2)(a)(ii); and
(c) that party has not fulfilled that undertaking within 14 days after service on him of the claim form.

61.10 Sale by the Court, Priorities and Payment Out

(1) An application for an order for the survey, appraisement or sale of a ship may be made in a claim in rem at any stage by any party.

(2) If the court makes an order for sale, it may—
(a) set a time within which notice of claims against the proceeds of sale must be filed; and
(b) the time and manner in which such notice must be advertised.

(3) Any party with a judgment against the property or proceeds of sale may at any time after the time referred to in paragraph (2) apply to the court for the determination of priorities.

(4) An application notice under paragraph (3) must be served on all persons who have filed a claim against the property.

(5) Payment out of the proceeds of sale will be made only to judgment creditors and—
(a) in accordance with the determination of priorities; or
(b) as the court orders.

61.11 Limitation Claims

(1) This rule applies to limitation claims.

(2) A claim is started by the issue of a limitation claim form as set out in the practice direction.

(3) The—
(a) claimant; and
(b) at least one defendant
must be named in the claim form, but all other defendants may be described.

(4) The claim form—
(a) must be served on all named defendants and any other defendant who requests service upon him; and
(b) may be served on any other defendant.

(5) The claim form may not be served out of the jurisdiction unless—
(a) the claim falls within section 22(2)(a), (b) or (c) of the Supreme Court Act 1981;
(b) the defendant has submitted to or agreed to submit to the jurisdiction of the court; or
(c) the Admiralty Court has jurisdiction over the claim under any applicable Convention; and
the court grants permission in accordance with Section III of Part 6.

(6) An acknowledgment of service is not required.
(7) Every defendant upon whom a claim form is served must—
  (a) within 28 days of service file—
    (i) a defence; or
    (ii) a notice that he admits the right of the claimant to limit liability; or
  (b) if he wishes to—
    (i) dispute the jurisdiction of the court; or
    (ii) argue that the court should not exercise its jurisdiction,
  file within 14 days of service (or where the claim form is served out of the jurisdiction, within the time specified in rule 6.22) an acknowledgment of service as set out in the practice direction.
(8) If a defendant files an acknowledgment of service under paragraph (7)(b) he will be treated as having accepted that the court has jurisdiction to hear the claim unless he applies under Part 11 within 14 days after filing the acknowledgment of service.
(9) Where one or more named defendants admits the right to limit—
  (a) the claimant may apply for a restricted limitation decree in the form set out in the practice direction; and
  (b) the court will issue a decree in the form set out in the practice direction limiting liability only against those named defendants who have admitted the claimant's right to limit liability.
(10) A restricted limitation decree—
  (a) may be obtained against any named defendant who fails to file a defence within the time specified for doing so; and
  (b) need not be advertised, but a copy must be served on the defendants to whom it applies.
(11) Where all the defendants upon whom the claim form has been served admit the claimant's right to limit liability—
  (a) the claimant may apply to the Admiralty Registrar for a general limitation decree in the form set out in the practice direction; and
  (b) the court will issue a limitation decree.
(12) Where one or more of the defendants upon whom the claim form has been served do not admit the claimant's right to limit, the claimant may apply for a general limitation decree in the form set out in the practice direction.
(13) When a limitation decree is granted the court—
  (a) may—
    (i) order that any proceedings relating to any claim arising out of the occurrence be stayed;
    (ii) order the claimant to establish a limitation fund if one has not been established or make such other arrangements for payment of claims against which liability is limited; or
    (iii) if the decree is a restricted limitation decree, distribute the limitation fund; and
  (b) will, if the decree is a general limitation decree, give directions as to advertisement of the decree and set a time within which notice of claims against the fund must be filed or an application made to set aside the decree.
(14) When the court grants a general limitation decree the claimant must—
  (a) advertise it in such manner and within such time as the court directs; and
  (b) file—
    (i) a declaration that the decree has been advertised in accordance with paragraph (a); and
    (ii) copies of the advertisements.
(15) No later than the time set in the decree for filing claims, each of the defendants who wishes to assert a claim must file and serve his statement of case on—
  (a) the limiting party; and
  (b) all other defendants except where the court orders otherwise.
(16) Any person other than a defendant upon whom the claim form has been served may apply to the court within the time fixed in the decree to have a general limitation decree set aside.
(17) An application under paragraph (16) must be supported by a declaration—
  (a) stating that the applicant has a claim against the claimant arising out of the occurrence; and

(b) setting out grounds for contending that the claimant is not entitled to the decree, either in the amount of limitation or at all.

(18) The claimant may constitute a limitation fund by making a payment into court.

(19) A limitation fund may be established before or after a limitation claim has been started.

(20) If a limitation claim is not commenced within 75 days after the date the fund was established—
(a) the fund will lapse; and
(b) all money in court (including interest) will be repaid to the person who made the payment into court.

(21) Money paid into court under paragraph (18) will not be paid out except under an order of the court.

(22) A limitation claim for—
(a) a restricted decree may be brought by counterclaim; and
(b) a general decree may only be brought by counterclaim with the permission of the court.

61.12 Stay of Proceedings

Where the court orders a stay of any claim in rem—
(a) any property under arrest in the claim remains under arrest; and
(b) any security representing the property remains in force,
unless the court orders otherwise.

61.13 Assessors

The court may sit with assessors when hearing—
(a) collision claims; or
(b) other claims involving issues of navigation or seamanship, and
the parties will not be permitted to call expert witnesses unless the court orders otherwise.

PD 61 Practice Direction — Admiralty Claims

This practice direction supplements CPR Part 61

PD 61 **2.18**, **11.7** [For commentary on a specific paragraph, please refer to the cross-references after the title of the paragraph.]

Scope: Rule 61.1

1.1 PD 58 (commercial claims) also applies to Admiralty claims except where it is inconsistent with Part 61 or this practice direction.

Case Management

2.1 After a claim form is issued the Registrar will issue a direction in writing stating:
  (1) whether the claim will remain in the Admiralty Court or be transferred to another court; and
  (2) if the claim remains in the Admiralty Court:
    (a) whether it will be dealt with by:
      (i) the Admiralty judge; or
      (ii) the Registrar; and
    (b) whether the trial will be in London or elsewhere.

2.2 In making these directions the Registrar will have regard to:
  (1) the nature of the issues and the sums in dispute; and
  (2) the criteria set in r. 26.8 so far as they are applicable.

2.3 Where the Registrar directs that the claim will be dealt with by the Admiralty judge, case management directions will be given and any case management conference or pre-trial review will be heard by the Admiralty judge.

Claims *In Rem*: Rule 61.3

3.1 A claim form *in rem* must be in form ADM1.

3.2 The claimant in a claim *in rem* may be named or may be described, but if not named in the claim form must identify himself by name if requested to do so by any other party.

3.3 The defendant must be described in the claim form.

3.4 The acknowledgment of service must be in form ADM2. The person who acknowledges service must identify himself by name.

3.5 The period for acknowledging service under r. 61.3(4) applies irrespective of whether the claim form contains particulars of claim.

3.6 A claim form *in rem* may be served in the following ways:
  (1) on the property against which the claim is brought by fixing a copy of the claim form:
    (a) on the outside of the property in a position which may reasonably be expected to be seen; or
    (b) where the property is freight, either:
      (i) on the cargo in respect of which the freight was earned; or
      (ii) on the ship on which the cargo was carried;
  (2) if the property to be served is in the custody of a person who will not permit access to it, by leaving a copy of the claim form with that person;
  (3) where the property has been sold by the Marshal, by filing the claim form at the court;
  (4) where there is a notice against arrest, on the person named in the notice as being authorised to accept service;
  (5) on any solicitor authorised to accept service;
  (6) in accordance with any agreement providing for service of proceedings; or
  (7) in any other manner as the court may direct under r. 6.8 provided that the property against which the claim is brought or part of it is within the jurisdiction of the court.

3.7 In claims where the property:

(1) is to be arrested; or
(2) is already under arrest in current proceedings,

the Marshal will serve the *in rem* claim form if the claimant requests the court to do so.

3.8 In all other cases *in rem* claim forms must be served by the claimant.

3.9 Where the defendants are described and not named on the claim form (for example as 'the Owners of the Ship X'), any acknowledgment of service in addition to stating that description must also state the full names of the persons acknowledging service and the nature of their ownership.

3.10 After the acknowledgment of service has been filed, the claim will follow the procedure applicable to a claim proceeding in the Commercial list except that the claimant is allowed 75 days to serve the particulars of claim.

3.11 A defendant who files an acknowledgment of service to an *in rem* claim does not lose any right he may have to dispute the jurisdiction of the court (see r. 10.1(3)(b) and Part 11).

3.12 Any person who pays the prescribed fee may, during office hours, search for, inspect and take a copy of any claim form *in rem* whether or not it has been served.

Collision Claims: Rule 61.4

4.1 A collision statement of case must be in form ADM3.

4.2 A collision statement of case must contain:
(1) in part 1 of the form, answers to the questions set out in that part; and
(2) in part 2 of the form, a statement:
(a) of any other facts and matters on which the party filing the collision statement of case relies;
(b) of all allegations of negligence or other fault which the party filing the collision statement of case makes; and
(c) of the remedy which the party filing the collision statement of case claims.

4.3 When he files his collision statement of case each party must give notice to every other party that he has done so.

4.4 Within 14 days after the last collision statement of case is filed each party must serve a copy of his collision statement of case on every other party.

4.5 Before the coming into force of Part 61, a collision statement of case was known as a preliminary act and the law relating to preliminary acts will continue to apply to collision statements of case.

Arrest: Rule 61.5

5.1 An application for arrest must be:
(1) in form ADM4 (which must also contain an undertaking); and
(2) accompanied by a declaration in form ADM5.

5.2 When it receives an application for arrest that complies with the rules and the practice direction the court will issue an arrest warrant.

5.3 The declaration required by r. 61.5(3)(b) must be verified by a statement of truth and must state:
(1) in every claim:
(a) the nature of the claim or counterclaim and that it has not been satisfied and if it arises in connection with a ship, the name of that ship;
(b) the nature of the property to be arrested and, if the property is a ship, the name of the ship and her port of registry; and
(c) the amount of the security sought, if any;
(2) in a claim against a ship by virtue of the Supreme Court Act 1981, s. 21(4):
(a) the name of the person who would be liable on the claim if it were not commenced *in rem*;
(b) that the person referred to in sub-paragraph (a) was, when the right to bring the claim arose:
(i) the owner or charterer of; or
(ii) in possession or in control of,
the ship in connection with which the claim arose; and
(c) that at the time the claim form was issued the person referred to in sub-paragraph (a) was either:

(i) the beneficial owner of all the shares in the ship in respect of which the warrant is required; or
(ii) the charterer of it under a charter by demise;
(3) in the cases set out in rr. 61.5(5) and (6) that the relevant notice has been sent or served, as appropriate; and
(4) in the case of a claim in respect of liability incurred under the Merchant Shipping Act 1995, s. 153, the facts relied on as establishing that the court is not prevented from considering the claim by reason of s. 166(2) of that Act.

5.4 The notice required by r. 61.5(5)(a) must be in form ADM6.
5.5 Property is arrested:
(1) by service on it of an arrest warrant in form ADM9 in the manner set out at para. 3.6(1); or
(2) where it is not reasonably practicable to serve the warrant, by service of a notice of the issue of the warrant:
(a) in the manner set out in para. 3.6(1) on the property; or
(b) by giving notice to those in charge of the property.

5.6 When property is arrested the Registrar will issue standard directions in form ADM10.
5.7 The Marshal does not insure property under arrest.

Cautions against Arrest: Rule 61.7

6.1 The entry of a caution against arrest is not treated as a submission to the jurisdiction of the court.
6.2 The request for a caution against arrest must be in form ADM7.
6.3 On the filing of such a request, a caution against arrest will be entered in the Register.
6.4 The Register is open for inspection when the Admiralty and Commercial Registry is open.

Release and Cautions against Release: Rule 61.8

7.1 The request for a caution against release must be in form ADM11.
7.2 On the filing of such a request, a caution against release will be entered in the Register.
7.3 The Register is open for inspection when the Admiralty and Commercial Registry is open.
7.4 A request for release under r. 61.8(4)(c) and (d) must be in form ADM12.
7.5 A withdrawal of a caution against release must be in form ADM12A.

Judgment in Default: Rule 61.9

para.8.1 **20.2**

8.1 An application notice for judgment in default must be in form ADM13.

Sale by the Court and Priorities: Rule 61.10

9.1 Any application to the court concerning:
(1) the sale of the property under arrest; or
(2) the proceeds of sale of property sold by the court
will be heard in public and the application notice served on:
(a) all parties to the claim;
(b) all persons who have requested cautions against release with regard to the property or the proceeds of sale; and
(c) the Marshal.

9.2 Unless the court orders otherwise an order for sale will be in form ADM14.
9.3 An order for sale before judgment may only be made by the Admiralty judge.
9.4 Unless the Admiralty judge orders otherwise, a determination of priorities may only be made by the Admiralty judge.
9.5 When:
(1) proceeds of sale are paid into court by the Marshal; and
(2) such proceeds are in a foreign currency,
the funds will be placed on one-day-call interest-bearing account unless the court orders otherwise.

9.6 Unless made at the same time as an application for sale, or other prior application, an application to place foreign currency on longer-term deposit may be made to the Registrar.

Civil Procedure Rules & Practice Directions

9.7 Notice of the placement of foreign currency in an interest-bearing account must be given to all parties interested in the fund by the party who made the application under para. 9.6.

9.8 Any interested party who wishes to object to the mode of investment of foreign currency paid into court may apply to the Registrar for directions.

Limitation Claims: Rule 61.11

10.1 The claim form in a limitation claim must be:

(1) in form ADM15; and

(2) accompanied by a declaration:

(a) setting out the facts upon which the claimant relies; and

(b) stating the names and addresses (if known) of all persons who, to the knowledge of the claimant, have claims against him in respect of the occurrence to which the claim relates (other than named defendants),

verified by a statement of truth.

10.2 A defence to a limitation claim must be in form ADM16A.

10.3 A notice admitting the right of the claimant to limit liability in a limitation claim must be in form ADM16.

10.4 An acknowledgment of service in a limitation claim must be in form ADM16B.

10.5 An application for a restricted limitation decree must be in form ADM17 and the decree issued by the court on such an application must be in form ADM18.

10.6 An application for a general limitation decree must be in form ADM17A.

10.7 Where:

(1) the right to limit is not admitted; and

(2) the claimant seeks a general limitation decree in form ADM17A,

the claimant must, within seven days after the date of the filing of the defence of the defendant last served or the expiry of the time for doing so, apply for an appointment before the Registrar for a case management conference.

10.8 On an application under r. 61.11(12) the Registrar may:

(1) grant a general limitation decree; or

(2) if he does not grant a decree:

(a) order service of a defence;

(b) order disclosure by the claimant; or

(c) make such other case management directions as may be appropriate.

10.9 The fact that a limitation fund has lapsed under r. 61.11(20)(a) does not prevent the establishment of a new fund.

10.10 Where a limitation fund is established, it must be:

(1) the sterling equivalent of the number of special drawing rights to which the claimant claims to be entitled to limit his liability under the Merchant Shipping Act 1995; together with

(2) interest from the date of the occurrence giving rise to his liability to the date of payment into court.

10.11 Where the claimant does not know the sterling equivalent referred to in para. 10.10(1) on the date of payment into court he may:

(1) calculate it on the basis of the latest available published sterling equivalent of a special drawing right as fixed by the International Monetary Fund; and

(2) in the event of the sterling equivalent of a special drawing right on the date of payment into court being different from that used for calculating the amount of that payment into court the claimant may:

(a) make up any deficiency by making a further payment into court which, if made within 14 days after the payment into court, will be treated, except for the purpose of the rules relating to the accrual of interest on money paid into court, as if made on the date of that payment into court; or

(b) apply to the court for payment out of any excess amount (together with any interest accrued) paid into court.

10.12 An application under para. 10.11(2)(b):

(1) may be made without notice to any party; and

(2) must be supported by evidence proving, to the satisfaction of the court, the sterling equivalent of the appropriate number of special drawing rights on the date of payment into court.

10.13 The claimant must give notice in writing to every named defendant of:
(1) any payment into court specifying:
(a) the date of the payment in;
(b) the amount paid in;
(c) the amount and rate of interest included; and
(d) the period to which it relates; and
(2) any excess amount (and interest) paid out to him under para. 10.11(2)(b).

10.14 A claim against the fund must be in form ADM20.

10.15 A defendant's statement of case filed and served in accordance with r. 61.11(15) must contain particulars of the defendant's claim.

10.16 Any defendant who is unable to file and serve a statement of case in accordance with r. 61.11(15) and para. 10.15 must file a declaration, verified by a statement of truth, in form ADM21 stating the reason for his inability.

10.17 No later than seven days after the time for filing claims or declarations, the Registrar will fix a date for a case management conference at which directions will be given for the further conduct of the proceedings.

10.18 Nothing in r. 61.11 prevents limitation being relied on by way of defence.

Proceeding against or Concerning the International Oil Pollution Compensation Fund

11.1 For the purposes of s. 177 of the Merchant Shipping Act 1995 ('the Act') and the corresponding provision of sch. 4 to the Act, the Fund may be given notice of proceedings by any party to a claim against an owner or guarantor in respect of liability under:
(1) s. 153 or s. 154 of the Act; or
(2) the corresponding provisions of sch. 4 to the Act,
by that person serving a notice in writing on the Fund together with copies of the claim form and any statements of case served in the claim.

11.2 The Fund may intervene in any claim to which para. 11.1 applies, (whether or not served with the notice), by serving notice of intervention on the:
(1) owner;
(2) guarantor; and
(3) court.

11.3 Where a judgment is given against the Fund in any claim under:
(1) s. 175 of the Act; or
(2) the corresponding provisions of sch. 4 to the Act,
the Registrar will arrange for a stamped copy of the judgment to be sent to the Fund by post.

11.4 Notice to the Registrar of the matters set out in:
(1) s. 176(3)(b) of the Act; or
(2) the corresponding provisions of sch. 4 to the Act,
must be given by the Fund in writing and sent to the court.

Other Claims

12.1 This section applies to Admiralty claims which, before the coming into force of Part 61, would have been called claims *in personam*. Subject to the provisions of Part 61 and this practice direction relating to limitation claims and to collision claims, the following provisions apply to such claims.

12.2 All such claims will proceed in accordance with Part 58 (Commercial Court).

12.3 The claim form must be in form ADM1A and must be served by the claimant.

12.4 The claimant may be named or may be described, but if not named in the claim form must identify himself by name if requested to do so by any other party.

12.5 The defendant must be named in the claim form.

12.6 Any person who files a defence must identify himself by name in the defence.

References to the Registrar

13.1 The court may at any stage in the claim refer any question or issue for determination by the Registrar (a 'reference').

13.2 Unless the court orders otherwise, where a reference has been ordered:

(1) if particulars of claim have not already been served, the claimant must file and serve particulars of claim on all other parties within 14 days after the date of the order; and

(2) any party opposing the claim must file a defence to the claim within 14 days after service of the particulars of claim on him.

13.3 Within seven days after the defence is filed, the claimant must apply for an appointment before the Registrar for a case management conference.

Undertakings

14.1 Where, in Part 61 or this practice direction, any undertaking to the Marshal is required it must be given:

(1) in writing and to his satisfaction; or

(2) in accordance with such other arrangements as he may require.

14.2 Where any party is dissatisfied with a direction given by the Marshal in this respect he may apply to the Registrar for a ruling.

[The following forms are annexed to PD 61:

ADM1	Claim form (Admiralty claim *in rem*)
ADM1A	Claim form (Admiralty claim)
ADM1C	Notes for defendant
ADM2	Acknowledgment of service
ADM3	Collision statement of case
ADM4	Application and undertaking for arrest and custody
ADM5	Declaration in support of application for warrant of arrest
ADM6	Notice to consular officer of intention to apply for warrant of arrest
ADM7	Request for caution against arrest
ADM9	Warrant of arrest
ADM10	Standard directions to the Admiralty Marshal
ADM11	Request for caution against release
ADM12	Request and undertaking for release
ADM12A	Request for withdrawal of caution against release
ADM13	Application for judgment in default of filing an acknowledgment of service and/or defence or collision statement of case
ADM14	Order for sale of a ship
ADM15	Claim form (Admiralty limitation claim)
ADM15B	Notes for defendant (Admiralty limitation claim)
ADM16	Notice of admission of right of claimant to limit liability
ADM16A	Defence to Admiralty limitation claim
ADM16B	Acknowledgment of service (Admiralty limitation claim)
ADM17	Application for restricted limitation decree
ADM17A	Application for general limitation decree
ADM18	Restricted limitation decree
ADM19	General limitation decree
ADM20	Defendant's claim in a limitation claim
ADM21	Declaration as to inability of a defendant to file and serve statement of case under a decree of limitation

These forms are on the CD-ROM version of *Blackstone's Civil Practice.* Click on a form number to open it.]

CPR Part 62 Arbitration Claims

Part 62 **20.2, 69.1, 69.18, 71.4** [For commentary on a specific rule, please refer to the cross-references after the title of the rule.]

62.1 Scope of This Part and Interpretation

(1) This Part contains rules about arbitration claims.
(2) In this Part—
   (a) 'the 1950 Act' means the Arbitration Act 1950;
   (b) 'the 1975 Act' means the Arbitration Act 1975;
   (c) 'the 1979 Act' means the Arbitration Act 1979;
   (d) 'the 1996 Act' means the Arbitration Act 1996;
   (e) references to—
      (i) the 1996 Act; or
      (ii) any particular section of that Act
   include references to that Act or to the particular section of that Act as applied with modifications by the ACAS Arbitration Scheme (England and Wales) Order 2001; and
   (f) 'arbitration claim form' means a claim form in the form set out in the practice direction.
(3) Part 58 (Commercial Court) applies to arbitration claims in the Commercial Court, Part 59 (Mercantile Court) applies to arbitration claims in the Mercantile Court and Part 60 (Technology and Construction Court claims) applies to arbitration claims in the Technology and Construction Court, except where this Part provides otherwise.

I CLAIMS UNDER THE 1996 ACT

62.2 Interpretation

(1) In this Section of this Part 'arbitration claim' means—
   (a) any application to the court under the 1996 Act;
   (b) a claim to determine—
      (i) whether there is a valid arbitration agreement;
      (ii) whether an arbitration tribunal is properly constituted; or
   what matters have been submitted to arbitration in accordance with an arbitration agreement;
   (c) a claim to declare that an award by an arbitral tribunal is not binding on a party; and
   (d) any other application affecting—
      (i) arbitration proceedings (whether started or not); or
      (ii) an arbitration agreement.

(2) This Section of this Part does not apply to an arbitration claim to which Sections II or III of this Part apply.

62.3 Starting the Claim

r.62.3(1) **13.4, 20.2, 69.2** r.62.3(4) **69.2**
r.62.3(2) **69.2**

(1) Except where paragraph (2) applies an arbitration claim must be started by the issue of an arbitration claim form in accordance with the Part 8 procedure.
(2) An application under section 9 of the 1996 Act to stay legal proceedings must be made by application notice to the court dealing with those proceedings.
(3) The courts in which an arbitration claim may be started are set out in the practice direction.
(4) Rule 30.5 applies with the modification that a judge of the Technology and Construction Court may transfer the claim to any other court or specialist list.

62.4 Arbitration Claim Form

r.62.4(1)(a)–(f) **69.3** r.62.4(2) **69.4**

(1) An arbitration claim form must—
  (a) include a concise statement of—
    (i) the remedy claimed; and
    (ii) any questions on which the claimant seeks the decision of the court;
  (b) give details of any arbitration award challenged by the claimant, identifying which part or parts of the award are challenged and specifying the grounds for the challenge;
  (c) show that any statutory requirements have been met;
  (d) specify under which section of the 1996 Act the claim is made;
  (e) identify against which (if any) defendants a costs order is sought; and
  (f) specify either—
    (i) the persons on whom the arbitration claim form is to be served, stating their role in the arbitration and whether they are defendants; or
    (ii) that the claim is made without notice under section 44(3) of the 1996 Act and the grounds relied on.
(2) Unless the court orders otherwise an arbitration claim form must be served on the defendant within 1 month from the date of issue and rules 7.5 and 7.6 are modified accordingly.
(3) Where the claimant applies for an order under section 12 of the 1996 Act (extension of time for beginning arbitral proceedings or other dispute resolution procedures), he may include in his arbitration claim form an alternative application for a declaration that such an order is not needed.

62.5 Service Out of the Jurisdiction

r.62.5(1) **69.1, 69.5, 69.8** r.62.5(4) **69.8**
r.62.5(2)–(3) **69.5**

(1) The court may give permission to serve an arbitration claim form out of the jurisdiction if—
  (a) the claimant seeks to—
    (i) challenge; or
    (ii) appeal on a question of law arising out of,
  an arbitration award made within the jurisdiction;

(The place where an award is treated as made is determined by section 53 of the 1996 Act.)
  (b) the claim is for an order under section 44 of the 1996 Act; or
  (c) the claimant—
    (i) seeks some other remedy or requires a question to be decided by the court affecting an arbitration (whether started or not), an arbitration agreement or an arbitration award; and
    (ii) the seat of the arbitration is or will be within the jurisdiction or the conditions in section 2(4) of the 1996 Act are satisfied.
(2) An application for permission under paragraph (1) must be supported by written evidence—
  (a) stating the grounds on which the application is made; and
  (b) showing in what place or country the person to be served is, or probably may be found.
(3) Rules 6.24 to 6.29 apply to the service of an arbitration claim form under paragraph (1).

(4) An order giving permission to serve an arbitration claim form out of the jurisdiction must specify the period within which the defendant may file an acknowledgment of service.

62.6 Notice

r.62.6(1)–(3) **69.6**

(1) Where an arbitration claim is made under section 24,28 or 56 of the 1996 Act, each arbitrator must be a defendant.
(2) Where notice must be given to an arbitrator or any other person it may be given by sending him a copy of—
 (a) the arbitration claim form; and
 (b) any written evidence in support.
(3) Where the 1996 Act requires an application to the court to be made on notice to any other party to the arbitration, that notice must be given by making that party a defendant.

62.7 Case Management

r.62.7(1) **69.9**
r.62.7(2) **42.6, 69.9**
r.62.7(3)–(4) **69.9**

(1) Part 26 and any other rule that requires a party to file an allocation questionnaire does not apply.
(2) Arbitration claims are allocated to the multi-track.
(3) Part 29 does not apply.
(4) The automatic directions set out in the practice direction apply unless the court orders otherwise.

62.8 Stay of Legal Proceedings

r.62.8(1)–(3) **69.10**

(1) An application notice seeking a stay of legal proceedings under section 9 of the 1996 Act must be served on all parties to those proceedings who have given an address for service.
(2) A copy of an application notice under paragraph (1) must be served on any other party to the legal proceedings (whether or not he is within the jurisdiction) who has not given an address for service, at—
 (a) his last known address; or
 (b) a place where it is likely to come to his attention.
(3) Where a question arises as to whether—
 (a) an arbitration agreement has been concluded; or
 (b) the dispute which is the subject-matter of the proceedings falls within the terms of such an agreement,

 the court may decide that question or give directions to enable it to be decided and may order the proceedings to be stayed pending its decision.

62.9 Variation of Time

r.62.9(1)–(2) **69.12**
r.62.9(3)(a)–(c) **69.12**

(1) The court may vary the period of 28 days fixed by section 70(3) of the 1996 Act for—
 (a) challenging the award under section 67 or 68 of the Act; and
 (b) appealing against an award under section 69 of the Act.
(2) An application for an order under paragraph (1) may be made without notice being served on any other party before the period of 28 days expires.
(3) After the period of 28 days has expired—
 (a) an application for an order extending time under paragraph (1) must—
  (i) be made in the arbitration claim form; and
  (ii) state the grounds on which the application is made;
 (b) any defendant may file written evidence opposing the extension of time within 7 days after service of the arbitration claim form; and
 (c) if the court extends the period of 28 days, each defendant's time for acknowledging service and serving evidence shall start to run as if the arbitration claim form had been served on the date when the court's order is served on that defendant.

62.10 Hearings

r.62.10 **59.21, 69.16** r.62.10(3) **69.16**
r.62.10(1) **69.16**

(1) The court may order that an arbitration claim be heard either in public or in private.
(2) Rule 39.2 does not apply.
(3) Subject to any order made under paragraph (1)—
(a) the determination of—
(i) a preliminary point of law under section 45 of the 1996 Act; or
(ii) an appeal under section 69 of the 1996 Act on a question of law arising out of an award,
will be heard in public; and
(b) all other arbitration claims will be heard in private.
(4) Paragraph (3)(a) does not apply to—
(a) the preliminary question of whether the court is satisfied of the matters set out in section 45(2)(b); or
(b) an application for permission to appeal under section 69(2)(b).

II OTHER ARBITRATION CLAIMS

62.11 Scope of This Section

r.62.11 **69.17**

(1) This Section of this Part contains rules about arbitration claims to which the old law applies.
(2) In this Section—
(a) 'the old law' means the enactments specified in Schedules 3 and 4 of the 1996 Act as they were in force before their amendment or repeal by that Act; and
(b) 'arbitration claim' means any application to the court under the old law and includes an appeal (or application for permission to appeal) to the High Court under section 1(2) of the 1979 Act.
(3) This Section does not apply to—
(a) a claim to which Section III of this Part applies; or
(b) a claim on the award.

62.12 Applications to Judge

r.62.12 **69.17**

A claim—
(a) seeking permission to appeal under section 1(2) of the 1979 Act;
(b) under section 1(5) of that Act (including any claim seeking permission); or
(c) under section 5 of that Act,
must be made in the High Court and will be heard by a judge of the Commercial Court unless any such judge directs otherwise.

62.13 Starting the Claim

r.62.13 **69.17** r.62.13(1) **13.4, 20.2**

(1) Except where paragraph (2) applies an arbitration claim must be started by the issue of an arbitration claim form in accordance with the Part 8 procedure.
(2) Where an arbitration claim is to be made in existing proceedings—
(a) it must be made by way of application notice; and
(b) any reference in this Section of this Part to an arbitration claim form includes a reference to an application notice.
(3) The arbitration claim form in an arbitration claim under section 1(5) of the 1979 Act (including any claim seeking permission) must be served on—
(a) the arbitrator or umpire; and
(b) any other party to the reference.

62.14 Claims in District Registries

r.62.14 **69.17**

If—

(a) a claim is to be made under section 12(4) of the 1950 Act for an order for the issue of a witness summons to compel the attendance of the witness before an arbitrator or umpire; and
(b) the attendance of the witness is required within the district of a District Registry,

the claim may be started in that Registry.

62.15 Time Limits and Other Special Provisions about Arbitration Claims

r.62.15 **69.17**

(1) An arbitration claim to—
 (a) remit an award under section 22 of the 1950 Act;
 (b) set aside an award under section 23(2) of that Act or otherwise; or
 (c) direct an arbitrator or umpire to state the reasons for an award under section 1(5) of the 1979 Act,

 must be made, and the arbitration claim form served, within 21 days after the award has been made and published to the parties.
(2) An arbitration claim to determine any question of law arising in the course of a reference under section 2(1) of the Arbitration Act 1979 must be made, and the arbitration claim form served, within 14 days after—
 (a) the arbitrator or umpire gave his consent in writing to the claim being made; or
 (b) the other parties so consented.
(3) An appeal under section 1(2) of the 1979 Act must be filed, and the arbitration claim form served, within 21 days after the award has been made and published to the parties.
(4) Where reasons material to an appeal under section 1(2) of the 1979 Act are given on a date subsequent to the publication of the award, the period of 21 days referred to in paragraph (3) will run from the date on which reasons are given.
(5) In every arbitration claim to which this rule applies—
 (a) the arbitration claim form must state the grounds of the claim or appeal;
 (b) where the claim or appeal is based on written evidence, a copy of that evidence must be served with the arbitration claim form; and
 (c) where the claim or appeal is made with the consent of the arbitrator, the umpire or the other parties, a copy of every written consent must be served with the arbitration claim form.
(6) In an appeal under section 1(2) of the 1979 Act—
 (a) a statement of the grounds for the appeal specifying the relevant parts of the award and reasons; and
 (b) where permission is required, any written evidence in support of the contention that the question of law concerns—
  (i) a term of a contract; or
  (ii) an event,

  which is not a 'one-off' term or event,

 must be filed and served with the arbitration claim form.
(7) Any written evidence in reply to written evidence under paragraph (6)(b) must be filed and served on the claimant not less than 2 days before the hearing.
(8) A party to a claim seeking permission to appeal under section 1(2) of the 1979 Act who wishes to contend that the award should be upheld for reasons not expressed or fully expressed in the award and reasons must file and serve on the claimant, a notice specifying the grounds of his contention not less than 2 days before the hearing.

62.16 Service Out of the Jurisdiction

r.62.16 **69.17**

(1) Subject to paragraph (2)—
 (a) any arbitration claim form in an arbitration claim under the 1950 Act or the 1979 Act; or
 (b) any order made in such a claim,

 may be served out of the jurisdiction with the permission of the court if the arbitration to which the claim relates—

(i) is governed by the law of England and Wales; or
(ii) has been, is being, or will be, held within the jurisdiction.

(2) An arbitration claim form seeking permission to enforce an award may be served out of the jurisdiction with the permission of the court whether or not the arbitration is governed by the law of England and Wales.

(3) An application for permission to serve an arbitration claim form out of the jurisdiction must be supported by written evidence—
(a) stating the grounds on which the application is made; and
(b) showing in what place or country the person to be served is, or probably may be found.

(4) Rules 6.24 to 6.29 apply to the service of an arbitration claim form under paragraph (1).

(5) An order giving permission to serve an arbitration claim form out of the jurisdiction must specify the period within which the defendant may file an acknowledgment of service.

III ENFORCEMENT

62.17 Scope of This Section

This Section of this Part applies to all arbitration enforcement proceedings other than by a claim on the award.

62.18 Enforcement of Awards

r.62.18 **70.7**
r.62.18(1)–(5) **69.19**
r.62.18(6)(a)–(c) **69.19**
r.62.18(7)–(11) **69.19**

(1) An application for permission under—
(a) section 66 of the 1996 Act;
(b) section 101 of the 1996 Act;
(c) section 26 of the 1950 Act; or
(d) section 3(1)(a) of the 1975 Act,
to enforce an award in the same manner as a judgment or order may be made without notice in an arbitration claim form.

(2) The court may specify parties to the arbitration on whom the arbitration claim form must be served.

(3) The parties on whom the arbitration claim form is served must acknowledge service and the enforcement proceedings will continue as if they were an arbitration claim under Section I of this Part.

(4) With the permission of the court the arbitration claim form may be served out of the jurisdiction irrespective of where the award is, or is treated as, made.

(5) Where the applicant applies to enforce an agreed award within the meaning of section 51(2) of the 1996 Act—
(a) the arbitration claim form must state that the award is an agreed award; and
(b) any order made by the court must also contain such a statement.

(6) An application for permission must be supported by written evidence—
(a) exhibiting—
(i) where the application is made under section 66 of the 1996 Act or under section 26 of the 1950 Act, the arbitration agreement and the original award (or copies);
(ii) where the application is under section 101 of the 1996 Act, the documents required to be produced by section 102 of that Act; or
(iii) where the application is under section 3(1)(a) of the 1975 Act, the documents required to be produced by section 4 of that Act;
(b) stating the name and the usual or last known place of residence or business of the claimant and of the person against whom it is sought to enforce the award; and
(c) stating either—
(i) that the award has not been complied with; or
(ii) the extent to which it has not been complied with at the date of the application.

(7) An order giving permission must—
(a) be drawn up by the claimant; and
(b) be served on the defendant by—

(i) delivering a copy to him personally; or
(ii) sending a copy to him at his usual or last known place of residence or business.

(8) An order giving permission may be served out of the jurisdiction—
(a) without permission; and
(b) in accordance with rules 6.24 to 6.29 as if the order were an arbitration claim form.

(9) Within 14 days after service of the order or, if the order is to be served out of the jurisdiction, within such other period as the court may set—
(a) the defendant may apply to set aside the order; and
(b) the award must not be enforced until after—
(i) the end of that period; or
(ii) any application made by the defendant within that period has been finally disposed of.

(10) The order must contain a statement of—
(a) the right to make an application to set the order aside; and
(b) the restrictions on enforcement under rule 62.18(9)(b).

(11) Where a body corporate is a party any reference in this rule to place of residence or business shall have effect as if the reference were to the registered or principal address of the body corporate.

62.19 Interest on Awards

r.62.19(1)–(2) **69.20**

(1) Where an applicant seeks to enforce an award of interest the whole or any part of which relates to a period after the date of the award, he must file a statement giving the following particulars—
(a) whether simple or compound interest was awarded;
(b) the date from which interest was awarded;
(c) where rests were provided for, specifying them;
(d) the rate of interest awarded; and
(e) a calculation showing—
(i) the total amount claimed up to the date of the statement; and
(ii) any sum which will become due on a daily basis.

(2) A statement under paragraph (1) must be filed whenever the amount of interest has to be quantified for the purpose of—
(a) obtaining a judgment or order under section 66 of the 1996 Act (enforcement of the award); or
(b) enforcing such a judgment or order.

62.20 Registration in High Court of Foreign Awards

(1) Where—
(a) an award is made in proceedings on an arbitration in any part of a United Kingdom Overseas Territory (within the meaning of rule 6.18(f)) or other territory to which Part I of the Foreign Judgments (Reciprocal Enforcement) Act 1933 ('the 1933 Act') extends;
(b) Part II of the Administration of Justice Act 1920 extended to that part immediately before Part I of the 1933 Act was extended to that part; and
(c) an award has, under the law in force in the place where it was made, become enforceable in the same manner as a judgment given by a court in that place, rules 74.1 to 74.7 and 74.9 apply in relation to the award as they apply in relation to a judgment given by the court subject to the modifications in paragraph (2).

(2) The modifications referred to in paragraph (1) are as follows—
(a) for references to the State of origin are substituted references to the place where the award was made; and
(b) the written evidence required by rule 74.4 must state (in addition to the matters required by that rule) that to the best of the information or belief of the maker of the statement the award has, under the law in force in the place where it was made, become enforceable in the same manner as a judgment given by a court in that place.

62.21 Registration of Awards under the Arbitration (International Investment Disputes) Act 1966

(1) In this rule—
  (a) 'the 1966 Act' means the Arbitration (International Investment Disputes) Act 1966;
  (b) 'award' means an award under the Convention;
  (c) 'the Convention' means the Convention on the settlement of investment disputes between States and nationals of other States which was opened for signature in Washington on 18th March 1965;
  (d) 'judgment creditor' means the person seeking recognition or enforcement of an award; and
  (e) 'judgment debtor' means the other party to the award.

(2) Subject to the provisions of this rule, the following provisions of RSC Order 71 apply with such modifications as may be necessary in relation to an award as they apply in relation to a judgment to which Part II of the Foreign Judgments (Reciprocal Enforcement) Act 1933 applies—
  (a) rule 74.1;
  (b) rule 74.3;
  (c) rule 74.4(1), (2)(a) to (d), and (4)
  (d) rule 74.6 (except paragraph (3)(c) to (e)); and
  (e) rule 74.9(2).

(3) An application to have an award registered in the High Court under section 1 of the 1966 Act must be made in accordance with the Part 8 procedure.

(4) The written evidence required by rule 74.4 in support of an application for registration must—
  (a) exhibit the award certified under the Convention instead of the judgment (or a copy of it); and
  (b) in addition to stating the matters referred to in rule 74.4(2)(a) to (d), state whether—
    (i) at the date of the application the enforcement of the award has been stayed (provisionally or otherwise) under the Convention; and
    (ii) any, and if so what, application has been made under the Convention, which, if granted, might result in a stay of the enforcement of the award.

(5) Where, on granting permission to register an award or an application made by the judgment debtor after an award has been registered, the court considers—
  (a) that the enforcement of the award has been stayed (whether provisionally or otherwise) under the Convention; or
  (b) that an application has been made under the Convention which, if granted, might result in a stay of the enforcement of the award,

the court may stay the enforcement of the award for such time as it considers appropriate.

PD 62 Practice Direction — Arbitration

This practice direction supplements CPR Part 62

PD 62 **69.1** [For commentary on a specific paragraph, please refer to the cross-references after the title of the paragraph.]

SECTION I

1.1 This Section of this practice direction applies to arbitration claims to which Section I of Part 62 applies.

1.2 In this Section 'the 1996 Act' means the Arbitration Act 1996.

1.3 Where a rule provides for a document to be sent, it may be sent:

(1) by first-class post;

(2) through a document exchange; or

(3) by fax, electronic mail or other means of electronic communication.

Starting the Claim: Rule 62.3

paras.2.1–2.2 **69.2** para.2.3(1)–(2) **69.2**

2.1 An arbitration claim under the 1996 Act (other than under s. 9) must be started in accordance with the High Court and County Courts (Allocation of Arbitration Proceedings) Order 1996 (SI 1996/3215) by the issue of an arbitration claim form.

2.2 An arbitration claim form must be substantially in [**form N8**].

2.3 Subject to para. 2.1, an arbitration claim form:

(1) may be issued at the courts set out in column 1 of the table below and will be entered in the list set out against that court in column 2;

(2) relating to a landlord and tenant or partnership dispute must be issued in the Chancery Division of the High Court.

Court	List
Admiralty and Commercial Registry at the Royal Courts of Justice, London	Commercial list
Technology and Construction Court Registry, St Dunstan's House, London	TCC list
District Registry of the High Court (where mercantile court established)	Mercantile list
District Registry of the High Court (where arbitration claim form marked 'Technology and Construction Court' in top right-hand corner)	TCC list
Central London County Court	Mercantile list

2.3A An arbitration claim form must, in the case of an appeal, or application for permission to appeal, from a judge-arbitrator, be issued in the Civil Division of the Court of Appeal. The judge hearing the application may adjourn the matter for oral argument before two judges of that court.

Arbitration Claim Form: Rule 62.4

paras.3.1–3.2 **69.4**

Service

3.1 The court may exercise its powers under r. 6.8 to permit service of an arbitration claim form at the address of a party's solicitor or representative acting for him in the arbitration.

3.2 Where the arbitration claim form is served by the claimant he must file a certificate of service within seven days of service of the arbitration claim form.

(Rule 6.10 specifies what a certificate of service must show.)

Acknowledgment of Service or Making Representations by Arbitrator or ACAS

paras.4.1–4.3 **69.8**

4.1 Where:

(1) an arbitrator; or

(2) ACAS (in a claim under the 1996 Act as applied with modifications by the ACAS Arbitration Scheme (England and Wales) Order 2001 (SI 2001/1185)),

is sent a copy of an arbitration claim form (including an arbitration claim form sent under r. 62.6(2)), that arbitrator or ACAS (as the case may be) may:

(a) apply to be made a defendant; or

(b) make representations to the court under para. 4.3.

4.2 An application under para. 4.1(2)(a) to be made a defendant:

(1) must be served on the claimant; but

(2) need not be served on any other party.

4.3 An arbitrator or ACAS may make representations by filing written evidence or in writing to the court.

Supply of Documents from Court Records

para.5.1 **15.17, 69.7**

5.1 An arbitration claim form may only be inspected with the permission of the court.

Case Management: Rule 62.7

paras.6.1–6.7 **69.9**

6.1 The following directions apply unless the court orders otherwise.

6.2 A defendant who wishes to rely on evidence before the court must file and serve his written evidence:

(1) within 21 days after the date by which he was required to acknowledge service; or,

(2) where a defendant is not required to file an acknowledgment of service, within 21 days after service of the arbitration claim form.

6.3 A claimant who wishes to rely on evidence in reply to written evidence filed under para. 6.2 must file and serve his written evidence within seven days after service of the defendant's evidence.

6.4 Agreed indexed and paginated bundles of all the evidence and other documents to be used at the hearing must be prepared by the claimant.

6.5 Not later than five days before the hearing date estimates for the length of the hearing must be filed together with a complete set of the documents to be used.

6.6 Not later than two days before the hearing date the claimant must file and serve:

(1) a chronology of the relevant events cross-referenced to the bundle of documents;

(2) (where necessary) a list of the persons involved; and

(3) a skeleton argument which lists succinctly:

(a) the issues which arise for decision;

(b) the grounds of relief (or opposing relief) to be relied upon;

(c) the submissions of fact to be made with the references to the evidence; and

(d) the submissions of law with references to the relevant authorities.

6.7 Not later than the day before the hearing date the defendant must file and serve a skeleton argument which lists succinctly:

(1) the issues which arise for decision;

(2) the grounds of relief (or opposing relief) to be relied upon;

(3) the submissions of fact to be made with the references to the evidence; and

(4) the submissions of law with references to the relevant authorities.

Securing the Attendance of Witnesses

paras.7.1–7.3 **69.11**

7.1 A party to arbitral proceedings being conducted in England or Wales who wishes to rely on s. 43 of the 1996 Act to secure the attendance of a witness must apply for a witness summons in accordance with Part 34.

7.2 If the attendance of the witness is required within the district of a district registry, the application may be made at that registry.

7.3 A witness summons will not be issued until the applicant files written evidence showing that the application is made with:

(1) the permission of the tribunal; or

(2) the agreement of the other parties.

Interim Remedies

para.8.1 **69.2**

8.1 An application for an interim remedy under s. 44 of the 1996 Act must be made in an arbitration claim form.

Applications under Sections 32 and 45 of the 1996 Act

9.1 This paragraph applies to arbitration claims for the determination of:
(1) a question as to the substantive jurisdiction of the arbitral tribunal under s. 32 of the 1996 Act; and
(2) a preliminary point of law under s. 45 of the 1996 Act.

9.2 Where an arbitration claim is made without the agreement in writing of all the other parties to the arbitral proceedings but with the permission of the arbitral tribunal, the written evidence or witness statements filed by the parties must set out any evidence relied on by the parties in support of their contention that the court should, or should not, consider the claim.

9.3 As soon as practicable after the written evidence is filed, the court will decide whether or not it should consider the claim and, unless the court otherwise directs, will so decide without a hearing.

Decisions without a Hearing

para.10.2 **69.12**

10.1 Having regard to the overriding objective the court may decide particular issues without a hearing. For example, as set out in para. 9.3, the question whether the court is satisfied as to the matters set out in s. 32(2)(b) or s. 45(2)(b) of the 1996 Act.

10.2 The court will generally decide whether to extend the time limit under s. 70(3) of the 1996 Act without a hearing. Where the court makes an order extending the time limit, the defendant must file his written evidence within 21 days from service of the order.

Variation of Time: Rule 62.9

para.11.1(1)–(2) **69.12**

11.1 An application for an order under r. 62.9(1):
(1) before the period of 28 days has expired, must be made in a Part 23 application notice; and
(2) after the period of 28 days has expired, must be set out in a separately identified part in the arbitration claim form.

Applications for Permission to Appeal

paras.12.1–12.2 **69.15**
para.12.3(3) **69.15**
para.12.5 **69.15**

12.1 Where a party seeks permission to appeal to the court on a question of law arising out of an arbitration award, the arbitration claim form must:
(1) identify the question of law; and
(2) state the grounds
on which the party alleges that permission should be given.

12.2 The written evidence in support of the application must set out any evidence relied on by the party for the purpose of satisfying the court:
(1) of the matters referred to in s. 69(3) of the 1996 Act; and
(2) that permission should be given.

12.3 The written evidence filed by the respondent to the application must:
(1) state the grounds on which the respondent opposes the grant of permission;
(2) set out any evidence relied on by him relating to the matters mentioned in s. 69(3) of the 1996 Act; and
(3) specify whether the respondent wishes to contend that the award should be upheld for reasons not expressed (or not fully expressed) in the award and, if so, state those reasons.

12.4 The court will normally determine applications for permission to appeal without an oral hearing.

12.5 Where the court refuses an application for permission to appeal without an oral hearing, it must provide brief reasons.

12.6 Where the court considers that an oral hearing is required, it may give such further directions as are necessary.

SECTION II

13.1 This Section of this practice direction applies to arbitration claims to which Section II of Part 62 applies.

Starting the Claim: Rule 62.13

14.1 An arbitration claim must be started in the Commercial Court and, where required to be heard by a judge, be heard by a judge of that court unless he otherwise directs.

SECTION III

15.1 This Section of this practice direction applies to enforcement proceedings to which Section III of Part 62 applies.

Registration of Awards under the Arbitration (International Investment Disputes) Act 1966: Rule 62.21

16.1 Awards ordered to be registered under the 1966 Act and particulars will be entered in the Register kept for that purpose at the Admiralty and Commercial Registry.

[The following forms are annexed to PD 62:

N8 Claim form (arbitration)
N8A Arbitration claim — notes for the claimant
N8B Arbitration claim — notes for the defendant
N15 Acknowledgment of service (arbitration claim)

These forms are on the CD-ROM of *Blackstone's Civil Practice.* Click on a form number to open it.]

CPR Part 63 Patents and Other Intellectual Property Claims

Part 63 **2.21, 11.17, 71.4** [For commentary on a specific rule, please refer to the cross-references after the title of the rule.]

63.1 Scope of This Part and Interpretation

(1) This Part applies to all intellectual property claims including—
- (a) registered intellectual property rights such as—
  - (i) patents;
  - (ii) registered designs; and
  - (iii) registered trade marks; and
- (b) unregistered intellectual property rights such as—
  - (i) copyright;
  - (ii) design right;
  - (iii) the right to prevent passing off; and
  - (iv) the other rights set out in the practice direction.

(2) In this Part—
- (a) 'the 1977 Act' means the Patents Act 1977;
- (b) 'the 1988 Act' means the Copyright, Designs and Patents Act 1988;
- (c) 'the 1994 Act' means the Trade Marks Act 1994;
- (d) 'the Comptroller' means the Comptroller General of Patents, Designs and Trade Marks;
- (e) 'patent' means a patent under the 1977 Act and includes any application for a patent or supplementary protection certificate granted under—
  - (i) the Patents (Supplementary Protection Certificates) Rules 1997;
  - (ii) the Patents (Supplementary Protection Certificate for Medicinal Products) Regulations 1992; and
  - (iii) the Patents (Supplementary Protection Certificate for Plant Protection Products) Regulations 1996;
- (f) 'Patents Court' means the Patents Court of the High Court constituted as part of the Chancery Division by section 6(1) of the Supreme Court Act 1981;
- (g) 'Patents County Court' means a county court designated as a Patents County Court under section 287(1) of the 1988 Act;
- (gg) 'patents judge' means a person nominated under section 291(1) of the 1988 Act as the patents judge of a patents county court;
- (h) 'the register' means whichever of the following registers is appropriate—
  - (i) patents maintained by the Comptroller under section 32 of the 1977 Act;
  - (ii) designs maintained by the registrar under section 17 of the Registered Designs Act 1949;

(iii) trade marks maintained by the registrar under section 63 of the 1994 Act;
(iv) Community trade marks maintained by the Office for Harmonisation in the Internal Market under Article 83 of Council Regulation (EC) 40/94; and
(v) Community designs maintained by the Office for Harmonisation in the Internal Market under Article 72 of Council Regulation (EC) 6/2002; and

(i) 'the registrar' means—
(i) the registrar of trade marks; or
(ii) the registrar of registered designs,
whichever is appropriate.

(3) Claims to which this Part applies are allocated to the multi-track.

63.2 Application of the Civil Procedure Rules

These Rules and their practice directions apply to intellectual property claims unless this Part or a practice direction provides otherwise.

I PATENTS AND REGISTERED DESIGNS

63.3 Scope of Section I

(1) This Section of this Part applies to claims in—
(a) the Patents Court; and
(b) a Patents County Court.

(2) Claims in the court include any claim relating to matters arising out of—
(a) the 1977 Act;
(b) the Registered Designs Act 1949; and
(c) the Defence Contracts Act 1958.

63.4 Specialist List

r.63.4 **11.4**

Claims in the Patents Court and a Patents County Court form specialist lists for the purpose of rule 30.5.

63.4A Patents Judge

(1) Subject to paragraph (2), proceedings in the patents county court shall be dealt with by the patents judge.

(2) When a matter needs to be dealt with urgently and it is not practicable or appropriate for the patents judge to deal with such matter, the matter may be dealt with by another judge with appropriate specialist experience who shall be nominated by the Vice-Chancellor.

63.5 Starting the Claim

Claims to which this Section of this Part applies must be started—
(a) by issuing a Part 7 claim form; or
(b) in existing proceedings under Part 20.

63.6 Defence and Reply

Part 15 applies with the modification—
(a) to rule 15.4 that in a claim for infringement under rule 63.9, the defence must be filed within 42 days of service of the claim form; and
(b) to rule 15.8 that the claimant must—
(i) file any reply to a defence; and
(ii) serve it on all other parties,
within 21 days of service of the defence.

63.7 Case Management

r.63.7 **42.6**

(1) [*revoked*]

(2) Part 26 and any other rule that requires a party to file an allocation questionnaire do not apply.

(3) The following provisions only of Part 29 apply—
   (a) rule 29.3(2) (legal representatives to attend case management conferences);
   (b) rule 29.4 (the court's approval of agreed proposals for the management of proceedings); and
   (c) rule 29.5 (variation of case management timetable) with the exception of paragraph (1)(b) and (c).

(4) As soon as practicable the court will hold a case management conference which must be fixed in accordance with the practice direction.

63.8 Disclosure and Inspection

Part 31 is modified to the extent set out in the practice direction.

63.9 Claim for Infringement and Challenge to Validity

(1) In a claim for infringement or an application in which the validity of a patent or registered design is challenged, the statement of case must contain particulars as set out in the practice direction.

(2) In a claim for infringement, the period for service of the defence or Part 20 claim is 42 days after service of the claim form.

63.10 Application to Amend a Patent Specification in Existing Proceedings

(1) An application under section 75 of the 1977 Act for permission to amend the specification of a patent by the proprietor of the patent must be made by application notice.

(2) The application notice must—
   (a) give particulars of—
      (i) the proposed amendment sought; and
      (ii) the grounds upon which the amendment is sought;
   (b) state whether the applicant will contend that the claims prior to amendment are valid; and
   (c) be served by the applicant on all parties and the Comptroller within 7 days of its issue.

(3) The application notice must, if it is reasonably possible, be served on the Comptroller electronically.

(4) Unless the court otherwise orders, the Comptroller will forthwith advertise the application to amend in the journal.

(5) The advertisement will state that any person may apply to the Comptroller for a copy of the application notice.

(6) Within 14 days of the first appearance of the advertisement any person who wishes to oppose the application must file and serve on all parties and the Comptroller a notice opposing the application which must include the grounds relied on.

(7) Within 28 days of the first appearance of the advertisement the applicant must apply to the court for directions.

(8) Unless the court otherwise orders, the applicant must within 7 days serve on the Comptroller any order of the court on the application.

(9) In this rule, 'the journal' means the journal published pursuant to rules made under section 123(6) of the 1977 Act.

63.11 Court's Determination of Question or Application

Where the Comptroller—
(a) declines to deal with a question under section 8(7), 12(2), 37(8) or 61(5) of the 1977 Act;
(b) declines to deal with an application under section 40(5) of the 1977 Act; or
(c) certifies under section 72(7)(b) of the 1977 Act that the court should determine the question whether a patent should be revoked,

any person seeking the court's determination of that question or application must issue a claim form within 14 days of the Comptroller's decision.

63.12 Application by Employee for Compensation

(1) An application by an employee for compensation under section 40(1) or (2) of the 1977 Act must be made—

(a) in a claim form; and
(b) within the period prescribed by paragraphs (2) and (3).

(2) The prescribed period begins on the date of the grant of the patent and ends one year after the patent has ceased to have effect.

(3) Where a patent has ceased to have effect as a result of failure to pay the renewal fees within the period prescribed under rule 39 of the Patents Rules 1995, and an application for restoration is made to the Comptroller under section 28 of the 1977 Act, the period prescribed under paragraph (2)—
(a) if restoration is ordered, continues as if the patent had remained continuously in effect; or
(b) if restoration is refused, is treated as expiring one year after the patent ceased to have effect, or six months after the refusal, whichever is the later.

II REGISTERED TRADE MARKS AND OTHER INTELLECTUAL PROPERTY RIGHTS

63.13 Allocation

r.63.13 **11.6**

(1) This Section of this Part applies to—
(a) claims relating to matters arising out of the 1994 Act; and
(b) other intellectual property rights as set out in the practice direction.

(2) [*revoked*]

(3) Claims to which this Section of this Part applies must be brought in—
(a) the Chancery Division;
(b) a Patents County Court; or
(c) a county court where there is also a Chancery district registry.

63.14 Claims under the 1994 Act

In a claim under the 1994 Act, the claim form or application notice must be served on the registrar where the relief sought would, if granted, affect an entry in the United Kingdom register.

63.15 Claim for Infringement of Registered Trade Mark

(1) In a claim for infringement of a registered trade mark the defendant may—
(a) in his defence, challenge the validity of the registration of the trade mark; and
(b) apply by Part 20 claim for—
(i) revocation of the registration;
(ii) a declaration that the registration is invalid; or
(iii) rectification of the register.

(2) Where a defendant applies under paragraph (1)(b) and the relief sought would, if granted, affect an entry in the United Kingdom register, he must serve on the registrar a copy of his claim form.

III SERVICE

63.16 Service

(1) Subject to paragraph (2), Part 6 applies to service of a claim form and any document under this Part.

(2) A claim form relating to a registered right may be served—
(a) on a party who has registered the right at the address for service given for that right in the United Kingdom Patent Office register, provided the address is within the jurisdiction; or
(b) in accordance with rule 6.19(1) or (1A) on a party who has registered the right at the address for service given for that right in the appropriate register at—
(i) the United Kingdom Patent Office; or
(ii) the Office for Harmonisation in the Internal Market.

IV APPEALS

63.17 Appeals from the Comptroller

(1) Part 52 applies to appeals from the Comptroller.
(2) Patent appeals are to be made to the Patents Court, and other appeals to the Chancery Division.
(3) Where Part 52 requires a document to be served, it must also be served on the Comptroller or registrar, as appropriate.

PD 63 Practice Direction — Patents and Other Intellectual Property Claims

This practice direction supplements CPR, Part 63

PD 63 **2.21, 11.7**

Contents of this Practice Direction

1.1 This practice direction is divided into three sections:
Section I — Provisions about patents and registered designs
Section II — Provisions about registered trade marks and other intellectual property rights
Section III — Provisions about appeals

I PROVISIONS ABOUT PATENTS AND REGISTERED DESIGNS

2.1 This Section of this practice direction applies to claims in the Patents Court and a Patents County Court.

2.2 The following claims must be dealt with in the court:
(1) any matter arising out of the 1977 Act, including:
(a) infringement actions;
(b) revocation actions;
(c) threats under s. 70 of the 1977 Act; and
(d) disputes as to ownership;
(2) registered designs;
(3) Community registered designs; and
(4) semiconductor topography rights.

Starting the Claim (Rule 63.5)

para.3.1 **23.3**

3.1 A claim form to which this Section of this practice direction applies must be marked in the top right-hand corner 'Patents Court' below the title of the court in which it is issued.

Case Management (Rule 63. 7)

4.1 The following parts only of PD 29 apply:
(1) para. 5 (case management conferences):
(a) excluding para. 5.9; and
(b) modified so far as is made necessary by other specific provisions of this practice direction; and
(2) para. 7 (failure to comply with case management directions).

4.2 Case management shall be dealt with by:
(1) a judge of the court; or
(2) a master or district judge where a judge of the court so directs.

4.3 The claimant must apply for a case management conference within 14 days of the date when all defendants who intend to file and serve a defence have done so.

4.4 Where the claim has been transferred, the claimant must apply for a case management conference within 14 days of the date of the order transferring the claim, unless the court:
(1) held; or
(2) gave directions for
a case management conference, when it made the order transferring the claim.

4.5 Any party may, at a time earlier than that provided in paras 4.3 and 4.4, apply in writing to the court to fix a case management conference.

4.6 If the claimant does not make an application in accordance with paras 4.3 and 4.4, any other party may apply for a case management conference.

4.7 The court may fix a case management conference at any time on its own initiative.

4.8 Not less than four days before a case management conference, each party must file and serve an application notice for any order which that party intends to seek at the case management conference.

4.9 Unless the court orders otherwise, the claimant, or the party who makes an application under para. 4.6, in consultation with the other parties, must prepare a case management bundle containing:

(1) the claim form;

(2) all statements of case (excluding schedules), except that, if a summary of a statement of case has been filed, the bundle should contain the summary, and not the full statement of case;

(3) a pre-trial timetable, if one has been agreed or ordered;

(4) the principal orders of the court; and

(5) any agreement in writing made by the parties as to disclosure,

and provide copies of the case management bundle for the court and the other parties at least four days before the first case management conference or any earlier hearing at which the court may give case management directions.

4.10 At the case management conference the court may direct that:

(1) a scientific adviser under the Supreme Court Act 1981, s. 70(3), be appointed; and

(2) a document setting out basic undisputed technology should be prepared.

(Rule 35.15 applies to scientific advisers.)

4.11 Where a trial date has not been fixed by the court, a party may apply for a trial date by filing a certificate which must:

(1) state the estimated length of the trial, agreed if possible by all parties;

(2) detail the time required for the judge to consider the documents;

(3) identify the area of technology; and

(4) assess the complexity of the technical issues involved by indicating the complexity on a scale of 1 to 5 (with 1 being the least and 5 the most complex).

4.12 The claimant, in consultation with the other parties, must revise and update the documents referred to in para. 4.9 appropriately as the case proceeds. This must include making all necessary revisions and additions at least seven days before any subsequent hearing at which the court may give case management directions.

Disclosure and Inspection (Rule 63.8)

5.1 Standard disclosure does not require the disclosure of documents where the documents relate to:

(1) the infringement of a patent by a product or process if, before or at the same time as serving a list of documents, the defendant has served on the claimant and any other party:

(a) full particulars of the product or process alleged to infringe; and

(b) drawings or other illustrations, if necessary;

(2) any ground on which the validity of a patent is put in issue, except documents which came into existence within the period:

(a) beginning two years before the earliest claimed priority date; and

(b) ending two years after that date; and

(3) the issue of commercial success.

5.2 Where the issue of commercial success arises, the patentee must, within such time limit as the court may direct, serve a schedule containing:

(1) where the commercial success relates to an article or product:

(a) an identification of the article or product (for example by product code number) which the patentee asserts has been made in accordance with the claims of the patent;

(b) a summary by convenient periods of sales of any such article or product;

(c) a summary for the equivalent periods of sales, if any, of any equivalent prior article or product marketed before the article or product in sub-paragraph (a); and

(d) a summary by convenient periods of any expenditure on advertising and promotion which supported the marketing of the articles or products in sub-paragraphs (a) and (c); or

Civil Procedure Rules & Practice Directions

(2) where the commercial success relates to the use of a process:
(a) an identification of the process which the patentee asserts has been used in accordance with the claims of the patent;
(b) a summary by convenient periods of the revenue received from the use of such process;
(c) a summary for the equivalent periods of the revenues, if any, received from the use of any equivalent prior art process; and
(d) a summary by convenient periods of any expenditure which supported the use of the process in sub-paragraphs (a) and (c).

Short Applications

6.1 Where any application is listed for a short hearing, the parties must file all necessary documents, skeleton arguments and drafts of any orders sought, by no later than 3.00 p.m. on the preceding working day.

6.2 A short hearing is any hearing which is listed for no more than one hour.

Timetable for a Trial

7.1 Not less than one week before the beginning of the trial, each party must inform the court in writing of the estimated length of its:
(1) oral submissions;
(2) examination-in-chief, if any, of its own witnesses; and
(3) cross-examination of witnesses of any other party.

7.2 At least four days before the date fixed for the trial, the claimant must file:
(1) the trial bundle; and
(2) a reading guide for the judge.

7.3 The reading guide filed under para. 7.2 must:
(1) be short and, if possible, agreed;
(2) set out the issues, the parts of the documents that need to be read on each issue and the most convenient order that they should be read;
(3) identify the relevant passages in textbooks and cases, if appropriate; and
(4) not contain argument.

Jurisdiction of Masters

8.1 A master may deal with:
(1) orders by way of settlement, except settlement of procedural disputes;
(2) orders on applications for extension of time;
(3) applications for leave to serve out of the jurisdiction;
(4) applications for security for costs;
(5) other matters as directed by a judge of the court; and
(6) enforcement of money judgments.

Experiments

9.1 Where a party seeks to establish any fact by experimental proof conducted for the purpose of litigation he must, at least 21 days before service of the application notice for directions under para. 9.3, or within such other time as the court may direct, serve on all parties a notice:
(1) stating the facts which he seeks to establish; and
(2) giving full particulars of the experiments proposed to establish them.

9.2 A party served with notice under para. 9.1:
(1) must within 21 days after such service, serve on the other party a notice stating whether or not he admits each fact; and
(2) may request the opportunity to inspect a repetition of all or a number of the experiments identified in the notice served under para. 9.1.

9.3 Where any fact which a party seeks to establish by experimental proof is not admitted, he must apply to the court for permission and directions by application notice.

Use of Models or Apparatus

10.1 Where a party intends to rely on any model or apparatus, he must apply to the court for directions at the first case management conference.

Claim for Infringement and Challenge to Validity: Rule 63.9

11.1 In a claim for infringement of a patent:
  (1) the statement of case must:
    (a) show which of the claims in the specification of the patent are alleged to be infringed; and
    (b) give at least one example of each type of infringement alleged; and
  (2) a copy of each document referred to in the statement of case, and where necessary a translation of the document, must be served with the statement of case.

11.2 Where the validity of a patent or registered design is challenged:
  (1) the statement of case must contain particulars of:
    (a) the relief sought; and
    (b) the issues except those relating to validity of the patent or registered design;
  (2) the statement of case must have a separate document annexed to it headed 'Grounds of Invalidity' specifying the grounds on which validity of the patent is challenged;
  (3) a copy of each document referred to in the grounds of invalidity, and where necessary a translation of the document, must be served with the grounds of invalidity; and
  (4) the Comptroller must be sent a copy of the grounds of invalidity and where any such grounds of invalidity are amended, a copy of the amended document, at the same time as the grounds of invalidity are served or amended.

11.3 Where, in an application in which validity of a patent or a registered design is challenged, the grounds of invalidity include an allegation:
  (1) that the invention is not a patentable invention because it is not new or does not involve an inventive step, the particulars must specify such details of the matter in the state of art relied on, as set out in para. 11.4;
  (2) that the specification of the patent does not disclose the invention clearly enough and completely enough for it to be performed by a person skilled in the art, the particulars must state, if appropriate, which examples of the invention cannot be made to work and in which respects they do not work or do not work as described in the specification; or
  (3) that the registered design is not new, the particulars must specify such details of the matter in the state of art relied on, as set out in para. 11.4.

11.4 The details required under para. 11.3(1) and (3) are:
  (1) in the case of matter or a design made available to the public by written description the date on which and the means by which it was so made available, unless this is clear from the face of the matter; and
  (2) in the case of matter or a design made available to the public by use:
    (a) the date or dates of such use;
    (b) the name of all persons making such use;
    (c) any written material which identifies such use;
    (d) the existence and location of any apparatus employed in such use; and
    (e) all facts and matters relied on to establish that such matter was made available to the public.

11.5 In any proceedings in which the validity of a patent is challenged:
  (1) on the ground that the invention did not involve an inventive step, a party who wishes to rely on the commercial success of the patent must state the grounds on which he so relies in his statement of case; and
  (2) the court may order inspection of machinery or apparatus where a party alleges such machinery or apparatus was used before the priority date of the claim.

Application to Amend a Patent Specification in Existing Proceedings: Rule 63.10

12.1 Not later than two days before the first hearing date the applicant, the Comptroller if he wishes to be heard, the parties to the proceedings and any other opponent, must file and serve a document stating the directions sought.

12.2 Where the application notice is served on the Comptroller electronically under r. 63.10(3), it must comply with any requirements for the sending of electronic communications to the Comptroller.

Application by Employee for Compensation: Rule 63.12

13.1 Where an employee applies for compensation under s. 40(1) or (2) of the 1977 Act, the court must at the case management conference give directions as to:

(1) the manner in which the evidence, including any accounts of expenditure and receipts relating to the claim, is to be given at the hearing of the claim and if written evidence is to be given, specify the period within which witness statements or affidavits must be filed; and

(2) the provision to the claimant by the defendant or a person deputed by him, of reasonable facilities for inspecting and taking extracts from the accounts by which the defendant proposes to verify the accounts in sub-paragraph (1) or from which those accounts have been derived.

Communication of Information to the European Patent Office

14.1 The court may authorise the communication of any such information in the court files as the court thinks fit to:

(1) the European Patent Office; or

(2) the competent authority of any country which is a party to the European Patent Convention.

14.2 Before authorising the disclosure of information under para. 14.1, the court shall permit any party who may be affected by the disclosure to make representations, in writing or otherwise, on the question of whether the information should be disclosed.

Order Affecting Entry in the Register of Patents or Designs

15.1 Where any order of the court affects the validity of an entry in the register, the court and the party in whose favour the order is made, must serve a copy of such order on the Comptroller within 14 days.

15.2 Where the order is in favour of more than one party, a copy of the order must be served by such party as the court directs.

Claim for Rectification of the Register of Patents or Designs

16.1 Where a claim is made for the rectification of the register of patents or designs, the claimant must at the same time as serving the other parties, serve a copy of:

(1) the claim form; and

(2) accompanying documents

on the Comptroller or registrar, as appropriate.

16.2 Where documents under para. 16.1 are served on the Comptroller or registrar, he shall be entitled to take part in the proceedings.

European Community Designs

17.1 The Patents Court and the Central London County Court are the designated Community design courts under Council Regulation (EC) 6/2002, art. 80(5).

17.2 Where a counterclaim is filed at the Community design court, for a declaration of invalidity of a registered Community design, the Community design court shall inform the Office for Harmonisation in the Internal Market of the date on which the counterclaim was filed, in accordance with Council Regulation (EC) 6/2002, art. 86(2).

17.3 On filing a counterclaim under para. 17.2, the party filing it must inform the Community design court in writing that it is a counterclaim to which para. 17.2 applies and that the Office for Harmonisation in the Internal Market needs to be informed of the date on which the counterclaim was filed.

17.4 Where a Community design court has given a judgment which has become final on a counter-claim for a declaration of invalidity of a registered Community design, the Community design court shall send a copy of the judgment to the Office for Harmonisation in the Internal Market, in accordance with Council Regulation (EC) 6/2002, art. 86(4).

17.5 The party in whose favour judgment is given under para. 17.4 must inform the Community design court at the time of judgment that para. 17.4 applies and that the Office for Harmonisation in the Internal Market needs to be sent a copy of the judgment.

II PROVISIONS ABOUT REGISTERED TRADE MARKS AND OTHER INTELLECTUAL PROPERTY RIGHTS

Allocation: Rule 63.13

para.18 **11.6**

18.1 Any of the following claims must be brought in the Chancery Division, a Patents County Court or a county court where there is also a Chancery district registry:
(1) copyright;
(2) rights in performances;
(3) rights conferred under part VII of the 1988 Act;
(4) design right;
(5) Community design right;
(6) Olympic symbols;
(7) plant varieties;
(8) moral rights;
(9) database rights;
(10) unauthorised decryption rights;
(11) hallmarks;
(12) technical trade secrets litigation;
(13) passing off;
(14) geographical indications;
(15) registered trade marks; and
(16) Community registered trade marks.

18.2 There are Chancery district registries at Birmingham, Bristol, Cardiff, Leeds, Liverpool, Manchester and Newcastle upon Tyne.

Starting the Claim

19.1 A claim form to which this Section of this practice direction applies must be marked in the top right-hand corner 'Chancery Division, Intellectual Property' below the title of the court in which it is issued.

Claims Under the 1994 Act: Rule 63.14

20.1 Where the registrar refers to the court an application made to him under the 1994 Act, then unless within one month of receiving notification of the decision to refer, the applicant makes the application to the court, he shall be deemed to have abandoned it.

20.2 The period prescribed under para. 20.1 may be extended by:
(1) the registrar; or
(2) the court,
where a party so applies, even if such application is not made until after the expiration of the period prescribed.

20.3 Where an application is made under s. 19 of the 1994 Act, the applicant must serve his claim form or application notice on all identifiable persons having an interest in the goods, materials or articles within the meaning of s. 19 of the 1994 Act.

Claim for Infringement of Registered Trade Mark: Rule 63.15

21.1 Where a document under r. 63.15(2) is served on the registrar, he:
(1) may take part in the proceedings; and
(2) need not serve a defence or other statement of case, unless the court otherwise orders.

Order Affecting Entry in the Register of Trade Marks

22.1 Where any order of the court affects the validity of an entry in the register, the provisions of paras 15.1 and 15.2 shall apply.

Claim for Rectification of the Register of Trade Marks

23.1 Where a claim is made for the rectification of the register of trade marks, the provisions of paras 16.1 and 16.2 shall apply.

European Community Trade Marks

24.1 The Chancery Division of the High Court, a Patents County Court or a county court where there is also a Chancery district registry are designated Community trade mark courts under Council Regulation (EC) 40/94, art. 91(1).

24.2 Where a counterclaim is filed at the Community trade mark court, for revocation or for a declaration of invalidity of a Community trade mark, the Community trade mark court shall inform the Office for Harmonisation in the Internal Market of the date on which the counterclaim was filed, in accordance with Council Regulation (EC) 40/94, art. 96(4).

24.3 On filing a counterclaim under para. 24.2, the party filing it must inform the Community trade mark court in writing that it is a counterclaim to which para. 24.2 applies and that the Office for Harmonisation in the Internal Market needs to be informed of the date on which the counterclaim was filed.

24.4 Where the Community trade mark court has given a judgment which has become final on a counterclaim for revocation or for a declaration of invalidity of a Community trade mark, the Community trade mark court shall send a copy of the judgment to the Office for Harmonisation in the Internal Market, in accordance with Council Regulation (EC) 40/94, art. 96(6).

24.5 The party in whose favour judgment is given under para. 24.4 must inform the Community trade mark court at the time of judgment that para. 24.4 applies and that the Office for Harmonisation in the Internal Market needs to be sent a copy of the judgment.

Claim for Additional Damages under Section 97(2) or Section 229(3) of the 1988 Act

25.1 Where a claimant seeks to recover additional damages under s. 97(2) or s. 229(3) of the 1988 Act, the particulars of claim must include:
(1) a statement to that effect; and
(2) the grounds for claiming them.

Application for Delivery Up or Forfeiture under the 1988 Act

26.1 Where a claimant applies under ss. 99, 114, 195, 204, 230 or 231 of the 1988 Act for delivery up or forfeiture he must serve:
(1) the claim form; or
(2) application notice, where appropriate,
on all identifiable persons who have an interest in the goods, material or articles within the meaning of ss. 114 or 204 of the 1988 Act.

Olympic Symbols

27.1 In this practice direction 'the Olympic Symbol Regulations' means the Olympics Association Right (Infringement Proceedings) Regulations 1995 (SI 1995/3325).

27.2 Where an application is made under reg. 5 of the Olympic Symbol Regulations, the applicant must serve his claim form or application notice on all identifiable persons having an interest in the goods, materials or articles within the meaning of reg. 5 of the Olympic Symbol Regulations.

III PROVISIONS ABOUT APPEALS

Appeals and References from the Comptroller: Rule 63.17

28.1 Where:

(1) a person appointed by the Lord Chancellor to hear and decide appeals under s. 77 of the 1994 Act, refers an appeal to the Chancery Division of the High Court under s. 76(3) of the 1994 Act; or

(2) the Comptroller refers the whole proceedings or a question or issue to the Chancery Division of the High Court under s. 251(1) of the 1988 Act,

the appeal or reference must be brought within 14 days of the reference.

IV PROVISIONS ABOUT FINAL ORDERS

29.1 Where the court makes an order for delivery up or destruction of infringing goods, or articles designed or adapted to make such goods, the defendant will pay the costs of complying with that order unless the court orders otherwise.

29.2 Where the court finds that an intellectual property right has been infringed, the court may, at the request of the applicant, order appropriate measures for the dissemination and publication of the judgment to be taken at the defendant's expense.

CPR Part 64 Estates, Trusts and Charities

64.1 General

(1) This Part contains rules—
   (a) in Section I, about claims relating to—
      (i) the administration of estates of deceased persons, and
      (ii) trusts; and
   (b) in Section II, about charity proceedings.

(2) In this Part and its practice directions, where appropriate, references to trustees include executors and administrators.

(3) All proceedings in the High Court to which this Part applies must be brought in the Chancery Division.

I CLAIMS RELATING TO THE ADMINISTRATION OF ESTATES AND TRUSTS

64.2 Scope of this Section

This Section of this Part applies to claims—

(a) for the court to determine any question arising in—
   (i) the administration of the estate of a deceased person; or
   (ii) the execution of a trust;

(b) for an order for the administration of the estate of a deceased person, or the execution of a trust, to be carried out under the direction of the court ('an administration order');

(c) under the Variation of Trusts Act 1958; or

(d) under section 48 of the Administration of Justice Act 1985.

64.3 Claim Form

A claim to which this Section applies must be made by issuing a Part 8 claim form.

64.4 Parties

(1) In a claim to which this Section applies, other than an application under section 48 of the Administration of Justice Act 1985—
   (a) all the trustees must be parties;
   (b) if the claim is made by trustees, any of them who does not consent to being a claimant must be made a defendant; and
   (c) the claimant may make parties to the claim any persons with an interest in or claim against the estate, or an interest under the trust, who it is appropriate to make parties having regard to the nature of the order sought.

(2) In addition, in a claim under the Variation of Trusts Act 1958, unless the court directs otherwise any person who—
   (a) created the trust; or
   (b) provided property for the purposes of the trust,

   must, if still alive, be made a party to the claim.

(The court may, under rule 19.2, order additional persons to be made parties to a claim)

II CHARITY PROCEEDINGS

64.5 Scope of this Section and Interpretation

(1) This Section applies to charity proceedings.
(2) In this Section—
   (a) 'the Act' means the Charities Act 1993;
   (b) 'charity proceedings' has the same meaning as in section 33(8) of the Act; and
   (c) 'the Commissioners' means the Charity Commissioners for England and Wales.

64.6 Application for Permission to Take Charity Proceedings

(1) An application to the High Court under section 33(5) of the Act for permission to start charity proceedings must be made within 21 days after the refusal by the Commissioners of an order authorising proceedings.
(2) The application must be made by issuing a Part 8 claim form, which must contain the information specified in the practice direction.
(3) The Commissioners must be made defendants to the claim, but the claim form need not be served on them or on any other person.
(4) The judge considering the application may direct the Commissioners to file a written statement of their reasons for their decision.
(5) The court will serve on the applicant a copy of any statement filed under paragraph (4).
(6) The judge may either—
   (a) give permission without a hearing; or
   (b) fix a hearing.

PD 64 Practice Direction — Estates, Trusts and Charities

This practice direction supplements CPR Part 64

I CLAIMS RELATING TO THE ADMINISTRATION OF ESTATES AND TRUSTS

Examples of Claims under Rule 64.2(a)

1 The following are examples of the types of claims which may be made under r. 64.2(a):
(1) a claim for the determination of any of the following questions:
(a) any question as to who is included in any class of persons having:
(i) a claim against the estate of a deceased person;
(ii) a beneficial interest in the estate of such a person; or
(iii) a beneficial interest in any property subject to a trust;
(b) any question as to the rights or interests of any person claiming:
(i) to be a creditor of the estate of a deceased person;
(ii) to be entitled under a will or on the intestacy of a deceased person; or
(iii) to be beneficially entitled under a trust;
(2) a claim for any of the following remedies:
(a) an order requiring a trustee:
(i) to provide and, if necessary, verify accounts;
(ii) to pay into court money which he holds in that capacity; or
(iii) to do or not to do any particular act;
(b) an order approving any sale, purchase, compromise or other transaction by a trustee; or
(c) an order directing any act to be done which the court could order to be done if the estate or trust in question were being administered or executed under the direction of the court.

Applications by Trustees for Directions

2 A separate practice direction (PD 64B) contains guidance about applications by trustees for directions.

Administration Orders: Rule 64.2(b)

3.1 The court will only make an administration order if it considers that the issues between the parties cannot properly be resolved in any other way.

3.2 If, in a claim for an administration order, the claimant alleges that the trustees have not provided proper accounts, the court may:
(1) stay the proceedings for a specified period, and order them to file and serve proper accounts within that period; or
(2) if necessary to prevent proceedings by other creditors or persons claiming to be entitled to the estate or fund, make an administration order and include in it an order that no such proceedings are to be taken without the court's permission.

3.3 Where an administration order has been made in relation to the estate of a deceased person, and a claim is made against the estate by any person who is not a party to the proceedings:
(1) no party other than the executors or administrators of the estate may take part in any proceedings relating to the claim without the permission of the court; and
(2) the court may direct or permit any other party to take part in the proceedings, on such terms as to costs or otherwise as it thinks fit.

3.4 Where an order is made for the sale of any property vested in trustees, those persons shall have the conduct of the sale unless the court directs otherwise.

Applications under the Variation of Trusts Act 1958: Rule 64.2(c)

4.1 Where children or unborn beneficiaries will be affected by a proposed arrangement under the Act, the evidence filed in support of the application must:

(1) show that their litigation friends or the trustees support the arrangements as being in the interests of the children or unborn beneficiaries; and

(2) unless para. 4.3 applies or the court orders otherwise, be accompanied by a written opinion to this effect by the advocate who will appear on the hearing of the application.

4.2 A written opinion filed under para. 4.1(2) must:

(1) if it is given on formal instructions, be accompanied by a copy of those instructions; or

(2) otherwise, state fully the basis on which it is given.

4.3 No written opinion needs to be filed in support of an application to approve an arrangement under s. 1(1)(d) of the Act (discretionary interests under protective trusts).

4.4 Where the interests of two or more children, or two or more of the children and unborn beneficiaries, are similar, only a single written opinion needs to be filed.

Applications under Section 48 of the Administration of Justice Act 1985: Rule 64.2(d)

5 A Part 8 claim form for an application by trustees under s. 48 of the Administration of Justice Act 1985 (power of High Court to authorise action to be taken in reliance on legal opinion) may be issued without naming a defendant, under r. 8.2A. No separate application for permission under r. 8.2A need be made.

Prospective Costs Orders

6.1 These paragraphs are about the costs of applications under r. 64.2(a).

6.2 Where trustees have power to agree to pay the costs of a party to such an application, and exercise such a power, r. 48.3 applies. In such a case, an order is not required and the trustees are entitled to recover out of the trust fund any costs which they pay pursuant to the agreement made in the exercise of such power.

6.3 Where the trustees do not have, or decide not to exercise, a power to make such an agreement, the trustees or the party concerned may apply to the court at any stage of proceedings for an order that the costs of any party (including the costs of the trustees) shall be paid out of the fund (a 'prospective costs order').

6.4 The court, on an application for a prospective costs order, may:

(a) in the case of the trustees' costs, authorise the trustees to raise and meet such costs out of the fund;

(b) in the case of the costs of any other party, authorise or direct the trustees to pay such costs (or any part of them, or the costs incurred up to a particular time) out of the trust fund to be assessed, if not agreed by the trustees, on the indemnity basis or, if the court directs, on the standard basis, and to make payments from time to time on account of such costs. A model form of order is annexed to this practice direction.

6.5 The court will always consider whether it is possible to deal with the application for a prospective costs order on paper without a hearing and in an ordinary case would expect to be able to do so. The trustees must consider whether a hearing is needed for any reason. If they consider that it is they should say so and explain why in their evidence. If any party to the application referred to in para. 6.1 above (or any other person interested in the trust fund) considers that a hearing is necessary (for instance because he wishes to oppose the making of a prospective costs order) this should be stated, and the reasons explained, in his evidence, if any, or otherwise in a letter to the court.

6.6 If the court would be minded to refuse the application on a consideration of the papers alone, the parties will be notified and given the opportunity, within a stated time, to ask for a hearing.

6.7 The evidence in support of an application for a prospective costs order should be given by witness statement. The trustees and the applicant (if different) must ensure full disclosure of the relevant matters to show that the case is one which falls within the category of case where a prospective costs order can properly be made.

6.8 The model form of order is designed for use in the more straightforward cases, where a question needs to be determined which has arisen in the administration of the trust, whether the claimants are the trustees or a beneficiary. The form may be adapted for use in less straightforward cases, in particular where the proceedings are hostile, but special factors may also have to be reflected in the terms of the order in such a case.

II CHARITY PROCEEDINGS

Role of Attorney-General

7 The Attorney-General is a necessary party to all charity proceedings, other than any commenced by the Charity Commissioners, and must be joined as a defendant if he is not a claimant.

Service on Charity Commissioners or Attorney-General

8 Any document required or authorised to be served on the Commissioners or the Attorney-General must be served on the Treasury Solicitor in accordance with RSC, ord. 77, r. 4(2) in CPR, sch. 1.

Applications for Permission to Take Charity Proceedings: Rule 64.6

9.1 The claim form for an application under s. 33(5) of the Act must state:
(1) the name, address and description of the applicant;
(2) details of the proceedings which he wishes to take;
(3) the date of the Commissioners' refusal to grant an order authorising the taking of proceedings;
(4) the grounds on which the applicant alleges that it is a proper case for taking proceedings; and
(5) if the application is made with the consent of any other party to the proposed proceedings, that fact.

9.2 If the Commissioners have given reasons for refusing to grant an order, a copy of their reasons must be filed with the claim form.

Appeals against Orders of the Charity Commissioners

10 Part 52 applies to any appeal against an order of the Charity Commissioners. Section III of PD 52 contains special provisions about such appeals.

Model form of prospective costs order

UPON THE APPLICATION etc.
AND UPON HEARING etc.
AND UPON READING etc.
AND UPON the Solicitors for the . . . . Defendant undertaking to make the repayments mentioned in paragraph 2 below in the circumstances there mentioned
IT IS [BY CONSENT] ORDERED THAT:

1. The Claimants as trustees of . . . . ('the [Settlement/Scheme]') do—
(a) pay from the assets of the [Settlement/Scheme] the costs of and incidental to these proceedings incurred by the . . . . Defendant such costs to be subject to a detailed assessment on the indemnity basis if not agreed and (for the avoidance of doubt) to—
(i) include costs incurred by the . . . . Defendant from and after [*date*] in anticipation of being appointed to represent any class of persons presently or formerly beneficially interested under the trusts of the [Settlement/Scheme] irrespective of whether [he/she] is in fact so appointed; and
(ii) exclude (in the absence of any further order) costs incurred in prosecuting any Part 20 claim or any appeal;
(b) indemnify the . . . . Defendant in respect of any costs which he may be ordered to pay to any other party to these proceedings in connection therewith.

2. Until the outcome of the detailed assessment (or the agreement regarding costs) contemplated in paragraph 1 above, the Claimants as trustees do pay from the assets of the [Settlement/Scheme] to the Solicitors for the . . . . Defendant monthly (or at such other intervals as may be agreed) such sums on account of the costs referred to in paragraph 1(a) of this Order as the Solicitors for the . . . . Defendant shall certify—
(i) to have been reasonably and property incurred and not to exceed such amount as is likely in their opinion to be allowed on a detailed assessment on the indemnity basis; and

(ii) to have accrued on account of the present proceedings in the period prior to the date of such certificate and not to have been previously provided for under this Order.

PROVIDED ALWAYS that the Solicitors for the . . . . Defendant shall repay such sums (if any) as, having been paid to them on account, are disallowed on a detailed assessment or are otherwise agreed to be repaid and any such sums shall be repaid together with interest at 1% above the base rate for the time being of [Barclays] Bank plc from and including the date of payment to those Solicitors up to and including the date of repayment, such interest to accrue daily.

3. Any party may apply to vary or discharge paragraphs 1 and 2 of this Order but only in respect of costs to be incurred after the date of such application.

Note: this form of order assumes that the trustees are the claimants. If the claimant is a beneficiary and the trustees are defendants, references to the parties need to be adapted accordingly.

PD 64B Practice Direction — Applications to the Court for Directions by Trustees in Relation to the Administration of the Trust

This practice direction supplements Section I of CPR Part 64

1 This practice direction is about applications to the court for directions by trustees in relation to the administration of the trust.

Contents of the Claim Form

2 If confidentiality of the directions sought is important (for example, where the directions relate to actual or proposed litigation with a third party who could find out what directions the trustees are seeking through access to the claim form under r. 5.4) the statement of the remedy sought, for the purposes of r. 8.2(b), may be expressed in general terms. The trustees must, in that case, state specifically in the evidence what it is that they seek to be allowed to do.

Proceedings in Private

3 The proceedings will in the first instance be listed in private (see PD 39, para. 1.5, and r. 39.2(3)(f)). Accordingly the order made, as well as the other documents among the court records (apart from a claim form which has been served), will not be open to inspection by third parties without the court's permission (r. 5.4(2)). If the matter is disposed of without a hearing, the order made will be expressed to have been made in private.

Joining Defendants or Giving Notice to Those Interested

4.1 Rule 64.4(1)(c) deals with the joining of beneficiaries as defendants. Often, especially in the case of a private trust, it will be clear that some, and which, beneficiaries need to be joined as defendants. Sometimes, if there are only two views of the appropriate course, and one is advocated by one beneficiary who will be joined, it may not be necessary for other beneficiaries to be joined since the trustees may be able to present the other arguments. Equally, in the case of a pension trust, it may not be necessary for a member of every possible different class of beneficiaries to be joined.

4.2 In some cases the court may be able to assess whether or not to give the directions sought, or what directions to give, without hearing from any party other than the trustees. If the trustees consider that their case is in that category they may apply to the court to issue the claim form without naming any defendants under r. 8.2A. They must apply to the court before the claim form is issued (r. 8.2A(2)) and include a copy of the claim form that they propose to issue (r. 8.2A(3)(b)).

4.3 In other cases the trustees may know that beneficiaries need to be joined as defendants, or to be given notice, but may be in doubt as to which. Examples could include a case concerning a pension scheme with many beneficiaries and a number of different categories of interest, especially if they may be differently affected by the action for which directions are sought, or a private trust with a large class of discretionary beneficiaries. In those cases the trustees may apply to issue the claim form without naming any defendants under r. 8.2A. The application may be combined with an application to the court for directions as to which persons to join as parties or to give notice to under r. 19.8A.

4.4 In the case of a charitable trust the Attorney-General is always the appropriate defendant, and almost always the only one.

Case Management Directions

5.1 The claim will be referred to the master or district judge once a defendant has acknowledged service, or otherwise on expiry of the period for acknowledgment of service (or, if no defendant is named, as soon as the claimants' evidence has been filed), to consider directions for the management of the case. Such directions may be given without a hearing in some cases; these might include directions as to parties or as to notice of proceedings, as mentioned in para. 4 above.

Proceeding without a Hearing

6.1 The court will always consider whether it is possible to deal with the application on paper without a hearing. The trustees must always consider whether a hearing is needed for any reason. If they consider that it is they should say so and explain why in their evidence. If a defendant considers that a hearing is needed, this should be stated, and the reasons explained, in his evidence, if any, or otherwise in a letter to the court.

6.2 If the court would be minded to refuse to give the directions asked for on a consideration of the papers alone, the parties will be notified and given the opportunity, within a stated time, to ask for a hearing.

6.3 In charity cases, the master or district judge may deal with the case without a hearing on the basis of a letter by or on behalf of the Attorney-General that sets out his attitude to the application.

Evidence

7.1 The trustees' evidence should be given by witness statement. In order to ensure that, if directions are given, the trustees are properly protected by the order, they must ensure full disclosure of relevant matters, even if the case is to proceed with the participation of beneficiaries as defendants.

7.2 Applications for directions whether or not to take or defend or pursue litigation should be supported by evidence including the advice of an appropriately qualified lawyer as to the prospects of success and other matters relevant to be taken into account, including a cost estimate for the proceedings and any known facts concerning the means of the opposite party to the proceedings, and a draft of any proposed statement of case. There are cases in which it is likely to be so clear that the trustees ought to proceed as they wish that the costs of making the application, even on a simplified procedure without a hearing and perhaps without defendants, are not justified in comparison with the size of the fund or the matters at issue.

7.3 References in this practice direction to an appropriately qualified lawyer mean one whose qualifications and experience are appropriate to the circumstances of the case. The qualifications should be stated. If the advice is given on formal instructions, the instructions should always be put in evidence as well, so that the court can see the basis on which the advice was given. If it is not, the advice must state fully the basis on which it is given.

7.4 All applications for directions should be supported by evidence showing the value of the trust assets, the significance of the proposed litigation or other course of action for the trust, and why the court's directions are needed. In the case of a pension trust the evidence should include the latest actuarial valuation, and should describe the membership profile and, if a deficit on winding up is likely, the priority provisions and their likely effect.

7.5 On an application for directions about actual or possible litigation the evidence should also state whether (i) any relevant pre-action protocol has been followed; and (ii) the trustees have proposed or undertaken, or intend to propose, mediation by ADR, and (in each case) if not why not.

7.6 If a beneficiary of the trust is a party to the litigation about which directions are sought, with an interest opposed to that of the trustees, that beneficiary should be a defendant to the trustees' application, but any material which would be privileged as regards that beneficiary in the litigation should be put in evidence as exhibits to the trustees' witness statement, and should not be served on the beneficiary. However if the trustees' representatives consider that no harm would be done by the disclosure of all or some part of the material, then that material should be served on that defendant. That defendant may also be excluded from part of the hearing, including that which is devoted to discussion of the material withheld.

Consultation with beneficiaries

7.7 The evidence must explain what, if any, consultation there has been with beneficiaries, and with what result. In preparation for an application for directions in respect of litigation, the following guidance is to be followed:

(1) If the trust is a private trust where the beneficiaries principally concerned are not numerous and are all or mainly adult, identified and traceable, the trustees will be expected to have canvassed with all the adult beneficiaries the proposed or possible courses of action before applying for directions.

(2) If it is a private trust with a larger number of beneficiaries, including those not yet born or identified, or children, it is likely that there will nevertheless be some adult beneficiaries principally concerned, with whom the trustees must consult.

(3) In relation to a charitable trust the trustees must have consulted the Attorney-General, through the Treasury Solicitor, as well as the Charity Commissioners whose consent to the application will have been needed under the Charities Act 1993, s. 33.

(4) In relation to a pension trust, unless the members are very few in number, no particular steps by way of consultation with beneficiaries (including, where relevant, employers) or their representatives are required in preparation for the application, though the trustees' evidence should describe any consultation that has in fact taken place. If no consultation has taken place, the court could in some cases direct that meetings of one or more classes of beneficiaries be held to consider the subject matter of the application, possibly as a preliminary to deciding whether a member of a particular class ought to be joined as a defendant, though in a case concerning actual or proposed litigation, steps would need to be considered to protect privileged material from too wide disclosure.

7.8 (1) If the court gives directions allowing the trustees to take, defend or pursue litigation it may do so up to a particular stage in the litigation, requiring the trustees, before they carry on beyond that point, to renew their application to the court. What stage that should be will depend on the likely management of the litigation under the CPR. If the application is to be renewed after disclosure of documents, and disclosed documents need to be shown to the court, it may be necessary to obtain permission to do this from the court in which the other litigation is proceeding.

(2) In such a case the court may sometimes direct that the case be dealt with at that stage without a hearing if the beneficiaries obtain and lodge the written advice of an appropriately qualified lawyer stating that he or they support the continuation of the directions. Any such advice will be considered by the court and, if thought fit, the trustees will be given a direction allowing them to continue pursuing the proceedings without a hearing.

7.9 In a case of urgency, such as where a limitation period or period for service of proceedings is about to expire, the court may be able to give directions on a summary consideration of the evidence to cover the steps which need to be taken urgently, but limiting those directions so that the application needs to be renewed on fuller consideration at an early stage.

7.10 In any application for directions where a child is a defendant, the court will expect to have put before it the instructions to and advice of an appropriately qualified lawyer as to the benefits and disadvantages of the proposed, and any other relevant, course of action from the point of view of the child beneficiary.

7.11 The master or district judge may give the directions sought though, if the directions relate to actual or proposed litigation, only if it is a plain case, and therefore the master or district judge may think it appropriate to give the directions without a hearing: see PD 2B, paras 4.1 and 5.1(e), and see also para. 6 above. Otherwise the case will be referred to the judge.

7.12 Where a hearing takes place, if the advice of a lawyer has been put in evidence in accordance with para. 7.2 or 7.10, that lawyer should if possible appear on the hearing.

CPR Part 65 Proceedings Relating to Anti-social Behaviour and Harassment

65.1 Scope of This Part

This Part contains rules—

(a) in Section I, about injunctions under the Housing Act 1996;
(b) in Section II, about applications by local authorities under section 91(3) of the Anti-social Behaviour Act 2003 for a power of arrest to be attached to an injunction;
(c) in Section III, about claims for demotion orders under the Housing Act 1985 and Housing Act 1988 and proceedings relating to demoted tenancies;
(d) in Section IV, about anti-social behaviour orders under the Crime and Disorder Act 1998;
(e) in Section V, about claims under section 3 of the Protection from Harassment Act 1997.

I HOUSING ACT 1996 INJUNCTIONS

65.2 Scope of This Section and Interpretation

(1) This Section applies to applications for an injunction and other related proceedings under Chapter III of Part V of the Housing Act 1996 (injunctions against anti-social behaviour).
(2) In this Section 'the 1996 Act' means the Housing Act 1996.

65.3 Applications for an Injunction

r.65.3(1) **92.7**
r.65.3(2)(b)–(c) **92.7**
r.65.3(4)(b) **92.7**
r.65.3(4)(e) **92.7**
r.65.3(5)–(6) **92.7**

(1) An application for an injunction under Chapter III of Part V of the 1996 Act shall be subject to the Part 8 procedure as modified by this rule and the relevant practice direction.
(2) The application must be—
   (a) made by a claim form in accordance with the relevant practice direction;

(b) commenced in the court for the district in which the defendant resides or the conduct complained of occurred; and
(c) supported by a witness statement which must be filed with the claim form.

(3) The claim form must state—
(a) the matters required by rule 8.2; and
(b) the terms of the injunction applied for.

(4) An application under this rule may be made without notice and where such an application without notice is made—
(a) the witness statement in support of the application must state the reasons why notice has not been given; and
(b) the following rules do not apply—
(i) 8.3;
(ii) 8.4;
(iii) 8.5(2) to (6);
(iv) 8.6(1);
(v) 8.7; and
(vi) 8.8.

(5) In every application made on notice, the application notice must be served, together with a copy of the witness statement, by the claimant on the defendant personally.

(6) An application made on notice may be listed for hearing before the expiry of the time for the defendant to file an acknowledgment of service under rule 8.3, and in such a case—
(a) the claimant must serve the application notice and witness statement on the defendant not less than two days before the hearing; and
(b) the defendant may take part in the hearing whether or not he has filed an acknowledgment of service.

65.4 Injunction Containing Provisions to which a Power of Arrest Is Attached

r.65.4 **92.12**
r.65.4(1) **92.7, 92.9**
r.65.4(2) **92.9**
r.65.4(2)(a) **92.7**
r.65.4(3)–(4) **92.9**

(1) In this rule 'relevant provision' means a provision of an injunction to which a power of arrest is attached.

(Sections 153C(3) and 153D(4) of the 1996 Act confer powers to attach a power of arrest to an injunction)

(2) Where an injunction contains one or more relevant provisions—
(a) each relevant provision must be set out in a separate paragraph of the injunction; and
(b) subject to paragraph (3), the claimant must deliver a copy of the relevant provisions to any police station for the area where the conduct occurred.

(3) Where the injunction has been granted without notice, the claimant must not deliver a copy of the relevant provisions to any police station for the area where the conduct occurred before the defendant has been served with the injunction containing the relevant provisions.

(4) Where an order is made varying or discharging any relevant provision, the claimant must—
(a) immediately inform the police station to which a copy of the relevant provisions was delivered under paragraph (2)(b); and
(b) deliver a copy of the order to any police station so informed.

65.5 Application for Warrant of Arrest under Section 155(3) of the 1996 Act

r.65.5(1)–(2) **92.10**

(1) An application for a warrant of arrest under section 155(3) of the 1996 Act must be made in accordance with Part 23 and may be made without notice.

(2) An applicant for a warrant of arrest under section 155(3) of the 1996 Act must—
(a) file an affidavit setting out grounds for the application with the application notice; or
(b) give oral evidence as to the grounds for the application at the hearing.

65.6 Proceedings following Arrest

r.65.6(2) **92.11, 92.12**
r.65.6(4) **92.12**
r.65.6(4)(a)–(b) **92.11**
r.65.6(5) **92.11, 92.12**
r.65.6(6) **2.4, 92.11**

(1) This rule applies where a person is arrested pursuant to—
 (a) a power of arrest attached to a provision of an injunction; or
 (b) a warrant of arrest.

(2) The judge before whom a person is brought following his arrest may—
 (a) deal with the matter; or
 (b) adjourn the proceedings.

(3) Where the proceedings are adjourned the judge may remand the arrested person in accordance with section 155(2)(b) or (5) of the 1996 Act.

(4) Where the proceedings are adjourned and the arrested person is released—
 (a) the matter must be dealt with (whether by the same or another judge) within 28 days of the date on which the arrested person appears in court; and
 (b) the arrested person must be given not less than 2 days' notice of the hearing.

(5) An application notice seeking the committal for contempt of court of the arrested person may be issued even if the arrested person is not dealt with within the period mentioned in paragraph (4)(a).

(6) CCR Order 29, rule 1 shall apply where an application is made in a county court to commit a person for breach of an injunction, as if references in that rule to the judge included references to a district judge.

(For applications in the High Court for the discharge of a person committed to prison for contempt of court see RSC Order 52, rule 8. For such applications in the county court see CCR Order 29, rule 3)

65.7 Recognisance

r.65.7 **92.11**

(1) Where, in accordance with paragraph 2(2)(b) of Schedule 15 to the 1996 Act, the court fixes the amount of any recognisance with a view to it being taken subsequently, the recognisance may be taken by—
 (a) a judge;
 (b) a justice of the peace;
 (c) a justices' clerk;
 (d) a police officer of the rank of inspector or above or in charge of a police station; or
 (e) where the arrested person is in his custody, the governor or keeper of a prison,

with the same consequences as if it had been entered into before the court.

(2) The person having custody of an applicant for bail must release him if satisfied that the required recognisances have been taken.

II APPLICATIONS BY LOCAL AUTHORITIES FOR POWER OF ARREST TO BE ATTACHED TO AN INJUNCTION

65.8 Scope of This Section and Interpretation

(1) This Section applies to applications by local authorities under section 91(3) of the Anti-social Behaviour Act 2003 for a power of arrest to be attached to an injunction.

(Section 91 of the 2003 Act applies to proceedings in which a local authority is a party by virtue of section 222 of the Local Government Act 1972 (power of local authority to bring, defend or appear in proceedings for the promotion or protection of the interests of inhabitants in their area))

(2) In this Section 'the 2003 Act' means the Anti-social Behaviour Act 2003.

65.9 Applications under Section 91(3) of the 2003 Act for a Power of Arrest to Be Attached to any Provision of an Injunction

r.65.9(1)–(3) **92.2**

(1) An application under section 91(3) of the 2003 Act for a power of arrest to be attached to any provision of an injunction must be made in the proceedings seeking the injunction by—
 (a) the claim form;

(b) the acknowledgment of service;
(c) the defence or counterclaim in a Part 7 claim; or
(d) application under Part 23.

(2) Every application must be supported by written evidence.

(3) Every application made on notice must be served personally, together with a copy of the written evidence, by the local authority on the person against whom the injunction is sought not less than 2 days before the hearing.

(Attention is drawn to rule 25.3(3) — applications without notice)

65.10 Injunction Containing Provisions to which a Power of Arrest Is Attached

r.65.10(1)(a)–(b) **92.12**

(1) Where a power of arrest is attached to a provision of an injunction on the application of a local authority under section 91(3) of the 2003 Act, the following rules in Section I of this Part shall apply—
(a) rule 65.4; and
(b) paragraphs (1), (2), (4) and (5) of rule 65.6.

(2) CCR Order 29, rule 1 shall apply where an application is made in a county court to commit a person for breach of an injunction.

III DEMOTION CLAIMS, PROCEEDINGS RELATING TO DEMOTED TENANCIES AND APPLICATIONS TO SUSPEND THE RIGHT TO BUY

65.11 Scope of This Section and Interpretation

(1) This Section applies to—
(a) claims by a landlord for an order under section 82A of the Housing Act 1985 or under section 6A of the Housing Act 1988 ('a demotion order');
(aa) claims by a landlord for an order under section 121A of the Housing Act 1985 ('a suspension order'); and
(b) proceedings relating to a tenancy created by virtue of a demotion order.

(2) In this Section—
(a) 'a demotion claim' means a claim made by a landlord for a demotion order;
(b) 'a demoted tenancy' means a tenancy created by virtue of a demotion order;
(c) 'suspension claim' means a claim made by a landlord for a suspension order; and
(d) 'suspension period' means the period during which the suspension order suspends the right to buy in relation to the dwelling house.

65.12 Demotion Claims or Suspension Claims Made in the Alternative to Possession Claims

Where a demotion order or suspension order (or both) is claimed in the alternative to a possession order, the claimant must use the Part 55 procedure and Section I of Part 55 applies, except that the claim must be made in the county court for the district in which the property to which the claim relates is situated.

65.13 Other Demotion or Suspension Claims

Where a demotion claim or suspension claim (or both) is made other than in a possession claim, rules 65.14 to 65.19 apply.

65.14 Starting a Demotion or Suspension Claim

(1) The claim must be made in the county court for the district in which the property to which the claim relates is situated.

(2) The claim form and form of defence sent with it must be in the forms set out in the relevant practice direction.

(The relevant practice direction and Part 16 provide details about the contents of the particulars of claim)

65.15 Particulars of Claim

The particulars of claim must be filed and served with the claim form.

65.16 Hearing Date

(1) The court will fix a date for the hearing when it issues the claim form.
(2) The hearing date will be not less than 28 days from the date of issue of the claim form.
(3) The standard period between the issue of the claim form and the hearing will be not more than 8 weeks.
(4) The defendant must be served with the claim form and the particulars of claim not less than 21 days before the hearing date.

(Rule 3.1(2)(a) provides that the court may extend or shorten the time for compliance with any rule and rule 3.1(2)(b) provides that the court may adjourn or bring forward a hearing)

65.17 Defendant's Response

(1) An acknowledgment of service is not required and Part 10 does not apply.
(2) Where the defendant does not file a defence within the time specified in rule 15.4 he may take part in any hearing but the court may take his failure to do so into account when deciding what order to make about costs.
(3) Part 12 (default judgment) does not apply.

65.18 The Hearing

(1) At the hearing fixed in accordance with rule 65.16(1) or at any adjournment of that hearing the court may—
   (a) decide the claim; or
   (b) give case management directions.
(2) Where the claim is genuinely disputed on grounds which appear to be substantial, case management directions given under paragraph (1)(b) will include the allocation of the claim to a track or directions to enable it to be allocated.
(3) Except where—
   (a) the claim is allocated to the fast track or the multi-track; or
   (b) the court directs otherwise,

   any fact that needs to be proved by the evidence of witnesses at a hearing referred to in paragraph (1) may be proved by evidence in writing.

(Rule 32.2(1) sets out the general rule about evidence. Rule 32.2(2) provides that rule 32.2(1) is subject to any provision to the contrary)

(4) All witness statements must be filed and served at least two days before the hearing.
(5) Where the claimant serves the claim form and particulars of claim, he must produce at the hearing a certificate of service of those documents and rule 6.14(2)(a) does not apply.

65.19 Allocation

When the court decides the track for the claim, the matters to which it shall have regard include—
   (a) the matters set out in rule 26.8; and
   (b) the nature and extent of the conduct alleged.

65.20 Proceedings Relating to Demoted Tenancies

A practice direction may make provision about proceedings relating to demoted tenancies.

IV ANTI-SOCIAL BEHAVIOUR ORDERS UNDER THE CRIME AND DISORDER ACT 1998

65.21 Scope of This Section and Interpretation

(1) This Section applies to applications in proceedings in a county court under sub-sections (2), (3) or (3B) of section 1B of the Crime and Disorder Act 1998 by a relevant authority, and to applications for interim orders under section 1D of that Act.
(2) In this Section—
   (a) 'the 1998 Act' means the Crime and Disorder Act 1998;

(b) 'relevant authority' has the same meaning as in section 1(1A) of the 1998 Act; and
(c) 'the principal proceedings' means any proceedings in a county court.

65.22 Application Where the Relevant Authority is a Party in Principal Proceedings

r.65.22(1)–(3) **92.15**

(1) Subject to paragraph (2)—
(a) where the relevant authority is the claimant in the principal proceedings, an application under section 1B(2) of the 1998 Act for an order under section 1B(4) of the 1998 Act must be made in the claim form; and
(b) where the relevant authority is a defendant in the principal proceedings, an application for an order must be made by application notice which must be filed with the defence.
(2) Where the relevant authority becomes aware of the circumstances that lead it to apply for an order after its claim is issued or its defence filed, the application must be made by application notice as soon as possible thereafter.
(3) Where the application is made by application notice, it should normally be made on notice to the person against whom the order is sought.

65.23 Application by a Relevant Authority to Join a Person to the Principal Proceedings

r.65.23(1)(a)–(b) **92.15** r.65.23(2)–(3) **92.15**

(1) An application under section 1B(3B) of the 1998 Act by a relevant authority which is a party to the principal proceedings to join a person to the principal proceedings must be made—
(a) in accordance with Section I of Part 19;
(b) in the same application notice as the application for an order under section 1B(4) of the 1998 Act against the person; and
(c) as soon as possible after the relevant authority considers that the criteria in section 1B(3A) of the 1998 Act are met.
(2) The application notice must contain—
(a) the relevant authority's reasons for claiming that the person's anti-social acts are material in relation to the principal proceedings; and
(b) details of the anti-social acts alleged.
(3) The application should normally be made on notice to the person against whom the order is sought.

65.24 Application Where the Relevant Authority is Not Party in Principal Proceedings

r.65.24(1)(a)–(b) **92.15** r.65.24(2)(a) **92.15**

(1) Where the relevant authority is not a party to the principal proceedings—
(a) an application under section 1B(3) of the 1998 Act to be made a party must be made in accordance with Section I of Part 19; and
(b) the application to be made a party and the application for an order under section 1B(4) of the 1998 Act must be made in the same application notice.
(2) The applications—
(a) must be made as soon as possible after the authority becomes aware of the principal proceedings; and
(b) should normally be made on notice to the person against whom the order is sought.

65.25 Evidence

r.65.25 **92.15**

An application for an order under section 1B(4) of the 1998 Act must be accompanied by written evidence, which must include evidence that section 1E of the 1998 Act has been complied with.

65.26 Application for an Interim Order

r.65.26(1)–(2) **92.16**

(1) An application for an interim order under section 1D of the 1998 Act must be made in accordance with Part 25.
(2) The application should normally be made—
(a) in the claim form or application notice seeking the order; and
(b) on notice to the person against whom the order is sought.

V PROCEEDINGS UNDER THE PROTECTION FROM HARASSMENT ACT 1997

65.27 Scope of this Section

This Section applies to proceedings under section 3 of the Protection from Harassment Act 1997 ('the 1997 Act').

65.28 Claims under Section 3 of the 1997 Act

r.65.28(a)–(b) **92.21**

A claim under section 3 of the 1997 Act—
(a) shall be subject to the Part 8 procedure; and
(b) must be commenced—
 (i) if in the High Court, in the Queen's Bench Division;
 (ii) if in the county court, in the court for the district in which the defendant resides or carries on business or the court for the district in which the claimant resides or carries on business.

65.29 Applications for Issue of a Warrant of Arrest under Section 3(3) of the 1997 Act

(1) An application for a warrant of arrest under section 3(3) of the 1997 Act—
 (a) must be made in accordance with Part 23; and
 (b) may be made without notice.
(2) The application notice must be supported by affidavit evidence which must—
 (a) set out the grounds for the application;
 (b) state whether the claimant has informed the police of the conduct of the defendant as described in the affidavit; and
 (c) state whether, to the claimant's knowledge, criminal proceedings are being pursued.

65.30 Proceedings Following Arrest

r.65.30(1) **92.23** r.65.30(2)(a)–(b) **92.23**

(1) The judge before whom a person is brought following his arrest may—
 (a) deal with the matter; or
 (b) adjourn the proceedings.
(2) Where the proceedings are adjourned and the arrested person is released—
 (a) the matter must be dealt with (whether by the same or another judge) within 28 days of the date on which the arrested person appears in court; and
 (b) the arrested person must be given not less than 2 days' notice of the hearing.

PD 65 Practice Direction — Anti-social Behaviour and Harassment

This practice direction supplements Part 65

I HOUSING ACT 1996 INJUNCTIONS

Issuing the Claim

para.1 **92.7**

1.1 An application for an injunction under chapter III of part V of the 1996 Act must be made by form N16A and for the purposes of applying PD 8 to applications under Section I of Part 65, form N16A shall be treated as the Part 8 claim form.

Warrant of Arrest on an Application under Section 155(3) of the 1996 Act

para.2.1 **92.10**

2.1 In accordance with s. 155(4) of the 1996 Act, a warrant of arrest on an application under s. 155(3) of that Act shall not be issued unless:
(1) the application is substantiated on oath; and
(2) the judge has reasonable grounds for believing that the defendant has failed to comply with the injunction.

Application for Bail

paras.3.1–3.3 **92.11**

3.1 An application for bail by a person arrested under:
(1) a power of arrest attached to an injunction under chapter III of part V of the 1996 Act; or
(2) a warrant of arrest issued on an application under s. 155(3) of that Act,
may be made either orally or in an application notice.

3.2 An application notice seeking bail must contain:
(1) the full name of the person making the application;
(2) the address of the place where the person making the application is detained at the time when the application is made;
(3) the address where the person making the application would reside if he were to be granted bail;
(4) the amount of the recognisance in which he would agree to be bound; and
(5) the grounds on which the application is made and, where previous application has been refused, full details of any change in circumstances which has occurred since that refusal.

3.3 A copy of the application notice must be served on the person who obtained the injunction.

Remand for Medical Examination and Report

para.4.1 **92.11**

4.1 Section 156(4) of the 1996 Act provides that the judge has power to make an order under the Mental Health Act 1983, s. 35, in certain circumstances. If he does so attention is drawn to s. 35(8) of that Act, which provides that a person remanded to hospital under that section may obtain at his own expense an independent report on his mental condition from a registered medical practitioner chosen by him and apply to the court on the basis of it for his remand to be terminated under s. 35(7).

II DEMOTION OR SUSPENSION CLAIMS

(Suspension claims may be made in England, but may not be made in Wales.)

Demotion Claims Made in the Alternative to Possession Claims

5.1 If the claim relates to residential property let on a tenancy and if the claim includes a demotion claim, the particulars of claim must:

(1) state whether the demotion claim is a claim under s. 82A(2) of the 1985 Act or under s. 6A(2) of the 1988 Act;
(2) state whether the claimant is a local housing authority, a housing action trust or a registered social landlord;
(3) provide details of any statement of express terms of the tenancy served on the tenant under s. 82A(7) of the 1985 Act or under s. 6A(10) of the 1988 Act, as applicable; and
(4) state details of the conduct alleged.

Suspension Claims Made in the Alternative to Possession Claims

5A.1 If the claim relates to a residential property let on a tenancy and if the claim includes a suspension claim, the particulars of claim must:
(1) state that the suspension claim is a claim under s. 121A of the 1985 Act;
(2) state which of the bodies the claimant's interest belongs to in order to comply with the landlord condition under s. 80 of the 1985 Act;
(3) state details of the conduct alleged; and
(4) explain why it is reasonable to make the suspension order, having regard in particular to the factors set out in s. 121A(4) of the 1985 Act.

Other Demotion or Suspension Claims

6.1 Demotion claims, other than those made in the alternative to possession claims, must be made in the county court for the district in which the property to which the claim relates is situated.
6.2 The claimant must use the appropriate claim form and particulars of claim form set out in Table 1 of PD 4. The defence must be in form N11D as appropriate.
6.3 The claimant's evidence should include details of the conduct alleged, and any other matters relied upon.

Particulars of Claim

7.1 In a demotion claim the particulars of claim must:
(1) state whether the demotion claim is a claim under s. 82A(2) of the 1985 Act or under s. 6A(2) of the 1988 Act;
(2) state whether the claimant is a local housing authority, a housing action trust or a registered social landlord;
(3) identify the property to which the claim relates;
(4) provide the following details about the tenancy to which the demotion claim relates:
(a) the parties to the tenancy;
(b) the period of the tenancy;
(c) the amount of the rent;
(d) the dates on which the rent is payable; and
(e) any statement of express terms of the tenancy served on the tenant under s. 82A(7) of the 1985 Act or under s. 6A(10) of the 1988 Act, as applicable; and
(5) state details of the conduct alleged.

Hearing Date

8.1 The court may use its powers under r. 3.1(2)(a) and (b) to shorten the time periods set out in r. 65.16(2), (3) and (4).
8.2 Particular consideration should be given to the exercise of this power if:
(1) the defendant, or a person for whom the defendant is responsible, has assaulted or threatened to assault:
(a) the claimant;
(b) a member of the claimant's staff; or
(c) another resident in the locality;
(2) there are reasonable grounds for fearing such an assault; or
(3) the defendant, or a person for whom the defendant is responsible, has caused serious damage or threatened to cause serious damage to the property or to the home or property of another resident in the locality.
8.3 Where para. 8.2 applies but the case cannot be determined at the first hearing fixed under

r. 65.16, the court will consider what steps are needed to finally determine the case as quickly as reasonably practicable.

The Hearing

9.1 Attention is drawn to r. 65.18(3). Each party should wherever possible include all the evidence he wishes to present in his statement of case, verified by a statement of truth.

9.2 The claimant's evidence should include details of the conduct to which s. 153A or 153B of the 1996 Act applies and in respect of which the demotion claim is made.

9.3 If:
(1) the maker of a witness statement does not attend a hearing; and
(2) the other party disputes material evidence contained in the statement,
the court will normally adjourn the hearing so that oral evidence can be given.

III PROCEEDINGS RELATING TO DEMOTED TENANCIES

Proceedings for the Possession of a Demoted Tenancy

10.1 Proceedings against a tenant of a demoted tenancy for possession must be brought under the procedure in Part 55 (possession claims).

Proceedings in Relation to a Written Statement of Demoted Tenancy Terms

11.1 Proceedings as to whether a statement supplied in pursuance to s. 143M(4)(b) of the 1996 Act (written statement of certain terms of tenancy) is accurate must be brought under the procedure in Part 8.

Recovery of Costs

12.1 Attention is drawn to s. 143N(4) of the 1996 Act which provides that if a person takes proceedings under chapter 1A of the 1996 Act in the High Court which he could have taken in the county court, he is not entitled to recover any costs.

IV ANTI-SOCIAL BEHAVIOUR ORDERS UNDER THE CRIME AND DISORDER ACT 1998

Service of an Order under Sections 1B(4) or 1D of the 1998 Act

para.13.1 **92.17**

13.1 An order under s. 1B(4) or an interim order under s. 1D of the 1998 Act must be served personally on the defendant.

Application to join a person to the principal proceedings

para.13.2 **92.14**

13.2 Except as provided in para. 13.3, an application by a relevant authority under s. 1B(3B) of the 1998 Act to join a person to the principal proceedings may only be made against a person aged 18 or over.

Pilot scheme: application to join a child to the principal proceedings

para.13.3 **92.14**

13.3 (1) A pilot scheme shall operate from 1 October 2004 to 30 September 2006 in the county courts specified below, under which a relevant authority may:
(a) apply under s. 1B(3B) of the 1998 Act to join a child to the principal proceedings; and
(b) if that child is so joined, apply for an order under s. 1B(4) of the 1998 Act against him.
(2) In this paragraph, 'child' means a person aged under 18.
(3) The county courts in which the pilot scheme shall operate are Bristol, Central London, Clerkenwell, Dewsbury, Huddersfield, Leicester, Manchester, Oxford, Tameside, Wigan and Wrexham.
(4) Attention is drawn to the provisions of Part 21 and PD 21: in particular as to the requirement for a child to have a litigation friend unless the court makes an order under

r. 21.2(3), and as to the procedure for appointment of a litigation friend. The Official Solicitor may be invited to act as litigation friend where there is no other willing and suitable person.

(5) Rule 21.3(2)(b) shall not apply to an application under the pilot scheme, and sub-para. (6) shall apply instead.

(6) A relevant authority may not, without the permission of the court, take any step in an application to join a child to the principal proceedings, except:
(a) filing and serving its application notice; and
(b) applying for the appointment of a litigation friend under r. 21.6,
unless the child has a litigation friend.

V PROCEEDINGS UNDER THE PROTECTION FROM HARASSMENT ACT 1997

Warrant of Arrest on Application under Section 3(3) of the 1997 Act

14.1 In accordance with s. 3(5) of the 1997 Act, a warrant of arrest on an application under s. 3(3) of that Act may only be issued if:
(1) the application is substantiated on oath; and
(2) the judge has reasonable grounds for believing that the defendant has done anything which he is prohibited from doing by the injunction.

CPR Part 66 Crown Proceedings

66.1 Scope of This Part and Interpretation

(1) This Part contains rules for civil proceedings by or against the Crown, and other civil proceedings to which the Crown is a party.
(2) In this Part—
(a) 'the Act' means the Crown Proceedings Act 1947;
(b) 'civil proceedings by the Crown' means the civil proceedings described in section 23(1) of the Act, but excluding the proceedings described in section 23(3);
(c) 'civil proceedings against the Crown' means the civil proceedings described in section 23(2) of the Act, but excluding the proceedings described in section 23(3);
(d) 'civil proceedings to which the Crown is a party' has the same meaning as it has for the purposes of Parts III and IV of the Act by virtue of section 38(4).

66.2 Application of the Civil Procedure Rules

These Rules and their practice directions apply to civil proceedings by or against the Crown and to other civil proceedings to which the Crown is a party unless this Part, a practice direction or any other enactment provides otherwise.

66.3 Action on Behalf of the Crown

(1) Where by reason of a rule, practice direction or court order the Crown is permitted or required—
(a) to make a witness statement,
(b) to swear an affidavit,
(c) to verify a document by a statement of truth;
(d) to make a disclosure statement; or
(e) to discharge any other procedural obligation,
that function shall be performed by an appropriate officer acting on behalf of the Crown.
(2) The court may if necessary nominate an appropriate officer.

66.4 Counterclaims, Other Part 20 Claims, and Set-off

r.66.4(1)–(2) **28.3** r.66.4(3)–(4) **28.2**

(1) In a claim by the Crown for taxes, duties or penalties, the defendant cannot make a counterclaim or other Part 20 claim or raise a defence of set-off.
(2) In any other claim by the Crown, the defendant cannot make a counterclaim or other Part 20 claim or raise a defence of set-off which is based on a claim for repayment of taxes, duties or penalties.
(3) In proceedings by or against the Crown in the name of the Attorney-General, no counterclaim or other Part 20 claim can be made or defence of set-off raised without the permission of the court.
(4) In proceedings by or against the Crown in the name of a government department, no counterclaim or other Part 20 claim can be made or defence of set-off raised without the permission of the court unless the subject-matter relates to that government department.

66.5 Applications in Revenue Matters

(1) This rule sets out the procedure under section 14 of the Act, which allows the Crown to make summary applications in the High Court in certain revenue matters.

(2) The application must be made in the High Court using the Part 8 procedure.
(3) The title of the claim form must clearly identify the matters which give rise to the application.

66.6 Enforcement against the Crown

r.66.6 **76.38**

(1) The following rules do not apply to any order against the Crown—
  (a) Parts 69 to 73;
  (b) RSC Orders 45 to 47 and 52; and
  (c) CCR Orders 25 to 29.
(2) In paragraph (1), 'order against the Crown' means any judgment or order against the Crown, a government department, or an officer of the Crown as such, made—
  (a) in civil proceedings by or against the Crown;
  (b) in proceedings in the Administrative Court;
  (c) in connection with an arbitration to which the Crown is a party; or
  (d) in other civil proceedings to which the Crown is a party.
(3) An application under section 25(1) of the Act for a separate certificate of costs payable to the applicant may be made without notice.

66.7 Money Due from the Crown

r.66.7 **76.39** r.66.7(3) **2.10**

(1) None of the following orders—
  (a) a third party debt order under Part 72;
  (b) an order for the appointment of a receiver under Part 69; or
  (c) an order for the appointment of a sequestrator under RSC Order 45,
  may be made or have effect in respect of any money due from the Crown.
(2) In paragraph (1), 'money due from the Crown' includes money accruing due, and money alleged to be due or accruing due.
(3) An application for an order under section 27 of the Act—
  (a) restraining a person from receiving money payable to him by the Crown; and
  (b) directing payment of the money to the applicant or another person,
  may be made under Part 23.
(4) The application must be supported by written evidence setting out the facts on which it is based, and in particular identifying the debt from the Crown.
(5) Where the debt from the Crown is money in a National Savings Bank account, the witness must if possible identify the number of the account and the name and address of the branch where it is held.
(6) Notice of the application, with a copy of the written evidence, must be served—
  (a) on the Crown, and
  (b) on the person to be restrained,
  at least 7 days before the hearing.
(7) Rule 72.8 applies to an application under this rule as it applies to an application under rule 72.2 for a third party debt order, except that the court will not have the power to order enforcement to issue against the Crown.

PD 66 Practice Direction — Crown Proceedings

This practice direction supplements Part 66.

PD 66 **14.75, 15.34, 42.3**

Transfer

1.1 Rule 30.3(2) sets out the circumstances to which the court must have regard when considering whether to make an order under the County Courts Act 1984, s. 40(2), 41(1) or 42(2) (transfer between the High Court and County Court), CPR, r. 30.2(1) (transfer between county courts) or r. 30.2(4) (transfer between the Royal Courts of Justice and the district registries).

1.2 From time to time the Attorney-General will publish a note concerning the organisation of the Government Legal Service and matters relevant to the venue of Crown proceedings, for the assistance of practitioners and judges. When considering questions of venue under r. 30.3(2), the court should have regard to the Attorney-General's note in addition to all the other circumstances of the case.

Service of Documents

2.1 In civil proceedings by or against the Crown, documents required to be served on the Crown must be served in accordance with r. 6.5(8).

(The list published under the Crown Proceedings Act 1947, s. 17, of the solicitors acting for the different government departments on whom service is to be effected, and of their addresses [follows the text of the Crown Proceedings Act 1947 in **appendix** 7].)

CROWN PROCEEDINGS

DISPUTES AS TO VENUE — FACTORS TO BE TAKEN INTO CONSIDERATION

Note to supplement PD 66 (Crown proceedings).

Introduction

Until the recent rule changes, the Crown was entitled in High Court matters to insist that venue was the Royal Courts of Justice in London (RCJ) (RSC, ord. 77, r. 2). This rule has now been revoked. A new r. 30.3(2)(h) of the CPR provides that in cases involving civil proceedings by or against the Crown, when considering whether to order a transfer of those proceedings, the court must have regard to, 'the location of the relevant government department or officers of the Crown and, where appropriate, any relevant public interest that the matter should be tried in London'.

PD 66, para. 2, provides that the Attorney-General will publish a note concerning the organisation of the Government Legal Service and matters relevant to the venue of Crown proceedings, for the assistance of practitioners and judges. When considering questions of venue under CPR, r. 30.3(2), the court should have regard to the Attorney-General's note in addition to all the other circumstances of the case.

This note sets out the further factors to be taken into consideration where there is a dispute as to venue between a claimant and a government department. Where there is such a dispute, it should be dealt with at a case management conference.

Organisation of the Government Legal Service

The Government Legal Service (GLS) has the responsibility for advising the Government about its legal affairs and has the conduct of civil litigation on its behalf. The Treasury Solicitor conducts this litigation for the majority of Government Departments but lawyers in HM Revenue and Customs, the Department for the Environment, Food and Rural Affairs and the Department for Work and Pensions (which also acts for the Department of Health and the Food Standards Agency) have the conduct of litigation for their Departments. All Government litigation lawyers are based in the London [*sic*] with the exception of HM Revenue and Customs, whose personal injury lawyers are in Manchester. A full list of addresses for service [follows the Crown Proceedings Act 1947 in **appendix** 7].

Factors to Be Taken into Account Generally

Location

Whilst a number of government departments have offices outside London, central government bodies are based in London and the GLS is geared towards processing claims in the RCJ (see above). Where there is a High Court claim, many witnesses as well as lawyers and officials are London based and there may be a disproportionate cost in transferring them to a venue outside London. That is not to say, bearing in mind the overriding objective, that the Crown would oppose transfer away from the RCJ where it was appropriate, for example in personal injury disputes.

Precedent value

Some cases have important precedent value or are of general importance to the public, which may make them more suitable for being heard in the RCJ.

Special Considerations in Relation to HM Revenue and Customs

HM Revenue and Customs has no lawyers outside London, except for those personal injury lawyers based in Manchester.

The work of HM Revenue and Customs is very specialised, needing in many cases to be dealt with by specialist judges in the Chancery Division familiar, for example, with tax work.

There is also the public interest to consider. All revenue cases (including those of HM Revenue and Customs) have important precedent value that applies across the entire tax system, with implications for the Exchequer.

CPR Part 67 Proceedings Relating to Solicitors

Part 67 **63.9**

67.1 Scope and Interpretation

(1) This Part contains rules about the following types of proceedings relating to solicitors—
- (a) proceedings to obtain an order for a solicitor to deliver a bill or cash account and proceedings in relation to money or papers received by a solicitor (rule 67.2);
- (b) proceedings under Part III of the Solicitors Act 1974 relating to the remuneration of solicitors (rule 67.3); and
- (c) proceedings under Schedule 1 to the Solicitors Act 1974 arising out of the Law Society's intervention in a solicitor's practice (rule 67.4).

(2) In this Part—
'the Act' means the Solicitors Act 1974; and
'LLP' means limited liability partnership.

(Part 48 and Section 56 of the Costs Practice Direction [PD 43–48] contain provisions about the procedure and basis for the detailed assessment of solicitor and client costs under Part III of the Act)

(The practice direction supplementing Part 52 [PD 52] contains provisions about appeals to the High Court from the Solicitors Disciplinary Tribunal under section 49 of the Act)

67.2 Power to Order Solicitor to Deliver Cash Account etc.

(1) Where the relationship of solicitor and client exists or has existed, the orders which the court may make against the solicitor, on the application of the client or his personal representatives, include any of the following—
- (a) to deliver a bill or cash account;
- (b) to pay or deliver up any money or securities;
- (c) to deliver a list of the moneys or securities which the solicitor has in his possession or control on behalf of the applicant;
- (d) to pay into or lodge in court any such money or securities.

(2) An application for an order under this rule must be made—
- (a) by Part 8 claim form; or
- (b) if the application is made in existing proceedings, by application notice in accordance with Part 23.

(3) If the solicitor alleges that he has a claim for costs against the applicant, the court may make an order for—
- (a) the detailed assessment and payment of those costs; and
- (b) securing the payment of the costs, or protecting any solicitor's lien.

67.3 Proceedings under Part III of the Act

r.67.3(1)(a)–(b) **68.19** r.67.3(2)–(3) **68.19**

(1) A claim for an order under Part III of the Act for the assessment of costs payable to a solicitor by his client—
- (a) which—
  - (i) relates to contentious business done in a county court; and
  - (ii) is within the financial limit of the county court's jurisdiction specified in section 69(3) of the Act,

  may be made in that county court;
- (b) in every other case, must be made in the High Court.

(Rule 30.2 makes provision for any county court to transfer the proceedings to another county court for detailed assessment of costs)

(Provisions about the venue for detailed assessment proceedings are contained in rule 47.4, Section 31 of the Costs Practice Direction [PD 43–48] and the Costs Pilot Scheme Practice Direction supplementing Part 47 [PD 43–48B])

(2) A claim for an order under Part III of the Act must be made—
- (a) by Part 8 claim form; or
- (b) if the claim is made in existing proceedings, by application notice in accordance with Part 23.

(A model form of claim form is annexed to the Costs Practice Direction)

(3) A claim in the High Court under Part III of the Act may be determined by—
- (a) a High Court judge;
- (b) a Master, a costs judge or a district judge of the Principal Registry of the Family Division; or
- (c) a district judge, if the costs are for—
  - (i) contentious business done in proceedings in the district registry of which he is the district judge;
  - (ii) contentious business done in proceedings in a county court within the district of that district registry; or
  - (iii) non-contentious business.

67.4 Proceedings under Schedule 1 to the Act

(1) Proceedings in the High Court under Schedule 1 to the Act must be brought—
- (a) in the Chancery Division; and
- (b) by Part 8 claim form, unless paragraph (4) below applies.

(2) The heading of the claim form must state that the claim relates to a solicitor and is made under Schedule 1 to the Act.

(3) Where proceedings are brought under paragraph 6(4) or 9(8) of Schedule 1 to the Act, the court will give directions and fix a date for the hearing immediately upon issuing the claim form.

(4) If the court has made an order under Schedule 1 to the Act, any subsequent application for an order under that Schedule which has the same parties may be made by a Part 23 application in the same proceedings.

(5) The table below sets out who must be made a defendant to each type of application under Schedule 1.

Defendants to applications under Schedule 1 to the Act

Paragraph of Schedule 1 under which the application is made	Defendant to application
Paragraph 5	if the application relates to money held on behalf of an individual solicitor, the solicitor if the application relates to money held on behalf of a firm, every partner in the firm if the application relates to money held on behalf of a LLP or other corporation, the LLP or other corporation
Paragraph 6(4) or 9(8)	the Law Society
Paragraph 8, 9(4), 9(5) or 9(6)	the person against whom the Law Society is seeking an order
Paragraph 9(10)	the person from whom the Law Society took possession of the documents which it wishes to dispose of or destroy
Paragraph 10	if the application relates to postal packets addressed to an individual solicitor, the solicitor if the application relates to postal packets addressed to a firm, every partner in the firm if the application relates to postal packets addressed to a LLP or other corporation, the LLP or other corporation
Paragraph 11	the trustee whom the Law Society is seeking to replace and, if he is a co-trustee, the other trustees of the trust

(6) At any time after the Law Society has issued an application for an order under paragraph 5 of Schedule 1 to the Act, the court may, on an application by the Society—
   (a) make an interim order under that paragraph to have effect until the hearing of the application; and
   (b) order the defendant, if he objects to the order being continued at the hearing, to file and serve written evidence showing cause why the order should not be continued.

PD 67 Practice Direction — Proceedings Relating to Solicitors

This practice direction supplements Part 67

General

1 This practice direction applies to proceedings under r. 67.2 and to the following types of claim under r. 67.3 and part III of the Solicitors Act 1974 ('the Act'):

(1) an application under s. 57(5) of the Act for a costs officer to enquire into the facts and certify whether a non-contentious business agreement should be set aside or the amount payable under it reduced;

(2) a claim under s. 61(1) of the Act for the court to enforce or set aside a contentious business agreement and determine questions as to its validity and effect;

(3) a claim by a client under s. 61(3) of the Act for a costs officer to examine a contentious business agreement as to its fairness and reasonableness;

(4) where the amount agreed under a contentious business agreement has been paid, a claim under s. 61(5) of the Act for the agreement to be reopened and the costs assessed;

(5) proceedings under s. 62 of the Act for the examination of a contentious business agreement, where the client makes the agreement as a representative of a person whose property will be chargeable with the amount payable;

(6) proceedings under s. 63 of the Act where, after some business has been done under a contentious business agreement, but before the solicitor has wholly performed it:

(a) the solicitor dies or becomes incapable of acting; or

(b) the client changes solicitor;

(7) where an action is commenced on a gross sum bill, an application under s. 64(3) of the Act for an order that the bill be assessed;

(8) a claim under s. 68 of the Act for the delivery by a solicitor of a bill of costs and for the delivery up of, or otherwise in relation to, any documents;

(9) an application under s. 69 of the Act for an order that the solicitor be at liberty to commence an action to recover his costs within one month of delivery of the bill;

(10) a claim under s. 70(1) of the Act, by the party chargeable with the solicitor's bill, for an order that the bill be assessed and that no action be taken on the bill until the assessment is completed;

(11) a claim under s. 70(2) of the Act, by either party, for an order that the bill be assessed and that no action be commenced or continued on the bill until the assessment is completed;

(12) a claim under s. 70(3) of the Act, by the party chargeable with the bill, for detailed assessment showing special circumstances;

(13) a claim under s. 71(1) of the Act, by a person other than the party chargeable with the bill, for detailed assessment;

(14) a claim under s. 71(3) of the Act, by any person interested in any property out of which a trustee, executor or administrator has paid or is entitled to pay a solicitor's bill, for detailed assessment; and

(15) a claim by a solicitor under s. 73 of the Act for a charging order.

Proceedings in the Supreme Court Costs Office

para.2.1(1)–(2) **68.19**

2.1 Where a claim to which this practice direction applies is made by Part 8 claim form in the High Court in London:

(1) if the claim is of a type referred to in para. 1(1) to (5), it must be issued in the Supreme Court Costs Office;

(2) in any other case, the claim may be issued in the Supreme Court Costs Office.

2.2 A claim which is made by Part 8 claim form in a district registry or by Part 23 application notice in existing High Court proceedings may be referred to the Supreme Court Costs Office.

Jurisdiction and Allocation of Claims between Judiciary

3.1 Rule 67.3(3) makes provision about jurisdiction to determine claims under part III of the Act.

3.2 Claims for any of the orders listed in para. 1 should normally be made to a master, costs judge or district judge. Only exceptional circumstances will justify making the claim directly to a High Court judge.

3.3 PD 23, para. 1, sets out the circumstances in which a matter may be referred to a judge.

Evidence in Proceedings for Order for Detailed Assessment

para.4 **68.19**

4 Where a Part 8 claim is brought for an order for the detailed assessment of a solicitor's bill of costs, the parties are not required to comply with r. 8.5 unless:

(1) the claim will be contested; or

(2) the court directs that the parties should comply with r. 8.5.

Drawing Up and Service of Orders

5 Unless the court orders otherwise, an order in proceedings in the Supreme Court Costs Office to which this practice direction applies shall be drawn up and served by the party who made the relevant claim or application.

CPR Part 68 References to the European Court

[For commentary on a specific rule, please refer to the cross-references after the title of the rule.]

68.1 Interpretation

In this Part—

(a) 'the court' means the court making the order;

(b) 'the European Court' means the Court of Justice of the European Communities;

(c) 'order' means an order referring a question to the European Court for a preliminary ruling under—

(i) article 234 of the Treaty establishing the European Community;

(ii) article 150 of the Euratom Treaty;

(iii) article 41 of the ECSC Treaty;

(iv) the Protocol of 3 June 1971 on the interpretation by the European Court of the Convention of 27 September 1968 on Jurisdiction and the Enforcement of Judgments in Civil and Commercial Matters; or

(v) the Protocol of 19 December 1988 on the interpretation by the European Court of the Convention of 19 June 1980 on the Law applicable to Contractual Obligations.

68.2 Making Order of Reference

r.68.2(1)–(3) **75.13**

(1) An order may be made at any stage of the proceedings—

(a) by the court of its own initiative; or

(b) on an application by a party in accordance with Part 23.

(2) An order may not be made—

(a) in the High Court, by a Master or district judge;

(b) in a county court, by a district judge.

(3) The request to the European Court for a preliminary ruling must be set out in a schedule to the order, and the court may give directions on the preparation of the schedule.

68.3 Transmission to the European Court

r.68.3(1)–(3) **75.13**

(1) The Senior Master will send a copy of the order to the Registrar of the European Court.

(2) Where an order is made by a county court, the proper officer will send a copy of it to the Senior Master for onward transmission to the European Court.

(3) Unless the court orders otherwise, the Senior Master will not send a copy of the order to the European Court until—

(a) the time for appealing against the order has expired; or

(b) any application for permission to appeal has been refused, or any appeal has been determined.

68.4 Stay of Proceedings

r.68.4 **75.13**

Where an order is made, unless the court orders otherwise the proceedings will be stayed until the European Court has given a preliminary ruling on the question referred to it.

PD 68 Practice Direction — References to the European Court

This practice direction supplements CPR Part 68

[For commentary on a specific paragraph, please refer to the cross-references after the title of the paragraph.]

Wording of References

paras.1.1–1.3 **75.13**

1.1 Where the court intends to refer a question to the European Court it will welcome suggestions from the parties for the wording of the reference. However the responsibility for settling the terms of the reference lies with the English court and not with the parties.

1.2 The reference should identify as clearly and succinctly as possible the question on which the court seeks the ruling of the European Court. In choosing the wording of the reference, it should be remembered that it will need to be translated into many other languages.

1.3 The court will incorporate the reference in its order. Scheduled to the order should be a document:

(1) giving the full name of the referring court;
(2) identifying the parties;
(3) summarising the nature and history of the proceedings, including the salient facts, indicating whether these are proved or admitted or assumed;
(4) setting out the relevant rules of national law;
(5) summarising the relevant contentions of the parties;
(6) explaining why a ruling of the European Court is sought; and
(7) identifying the provisions of Community law which it is being requested to interpret.

1.4 Where, as will often be convenient, some of these matters are in the form of a judgment, passages of the judgment not relevant to the reference should be omitted.

Transmission to the European Court

para.2.2 **75.13**

2.1 The order containing the reference, and the document scheduled to it, should be sent to The Senior Master, Room E115, Queen's Bench Division, Royal Courts of Justice, Strand, London WC2A 2LL, for onward transmission to the European Court.

2.2 The relevant court file should also be sent to the Senior Master at the above address.

European Court Information Note

3 There is annexed to this practice direction an Information Note issued by the European Court.

ANNEX

COURT OF JUSTICE OF THE EUROPEAN COMMUNITIES INFORMATION NOTE ON REFERENCES FROM NATIONAL COURTS FOR A PRELIMINARY RULING

annex
para.3 **75.2**
para.6 **75.13**
para.7 **75.10**
para.21 **75.13**
para.27 **75.16**

1 The preliminary ruling system is a fundamental mechanism of European Union law aimed at enabling national courts to ensure uniform interpretation and application of that law in all the member States.

2 The Court of Justice of the European Communities has jurisdiction to give preliminary rulings on the interpretation of the law of the European Union and on the validity of acts of secondary legislation. That general jurisdiction is conferred on it by art. 234 of the EC Treaty and, in certain specific cases, by other provisions.

3 The preliminary ruling procedure being based on cooperation between the Court and national courts, it may be helpful, in order to ensure that that cooperation is effective, to provide the national courts with the following information.

4 This practical information, which is in no way binding, is intended to provide guidance to national courts as to whether it is appropriate to make a reference for a preliminary ruling and, should they proceed, to help them formulate and submit questions to the Court.

The Role of the Court in the Preliminary Ruling Procedure

5 Under the preliminary ruling procedure, the Court's role is to give an interpretation of Community law or to rule on its validity, not to apply that law to the factual situation underlying the main proceedings, which is the task of the national court. It is not for the Court to decide issues of fact raised in the main proceedings or to resolve differences of opinion on the interpretation or application of rules of national law.

6 In ruling on the interpretation or validity of Community law, the Court makes every effort to give a reply which will be of assistance in resolving the dispute, but it is for the referring court to draw the appropriate conclusions from that reply, if necessary by disapplying the rule of national law in question.

The Decision to Submit a Question to the Court

The originator of the question

7 Under art. 234 of the EC Treaty and art. 150 of the EAEC Treaty, any court or tribunal of a Member State, in so far as it is called upon to give a ruling in proceedings intended to arrive at a decision of a judicial nature, may as a rule refer a question to the Court for a preliminary ruling. The status of that court or tribunal is interpreted by the Court as a self-standing concept of Community law.

8 However, in the specific sphere of acts of the institutions in Title IV of Part Three of the EC Treaty on visa, asylum, immigration and other policies related to free movement of persons—in particular jurisdiction and the recognition and enforcement of judicial decisions—a reference may be made only by courts or tribunals against the decisions of which there is no appeal, in accordance with art. 68 of the EC Treaty.

9 Likewise, under art. 35 of the Treaty on European Union, acts of the institutions in the area of police and judicial cooperation in criminal matters may be the subject of a reference for a preliminary ruling only from courts in the Member States which have accepted the jurisdiction of the Court, each Member State specifying whether that right of referral to the Court applies to any court or tribunal of that State or only to those against the decisions of which there is no appeal.

10 It is not necessary for the parties in the case to raise the question; the national court may do so of its own motion.

References on interpretation

11 Any court or tribunal *may* refer a question to the Court on the interpretation of a rule of Community law if it considers it necessary to do so in order to resolve a dispute brought before it.

12 However, courts or tribunals against whose decisions there is no judicial remedy under national law *must*, as a rule, refer such a question to the Court, unless the Court has already ruled on the point (and there is no new context that raises any serious doubt as to whether that case-law may be applied), or unless the correct interpretation of the rule of Community law is obvious.

13 Thus, a court or tribunal against whose decisions there is a judicial remedy may, in particular when it considers that sufficient clarification is given by the case-law of the Court, itself decide on the correct interpretation of Community law and its application to the factual situation before it. However, a reference for a preliminary ruling may prove particularly useful, at an appropriate stage of the proceedings, when there is a new question of interpretation of general interest for the uniform application of Community law throughout the Union, or where the existing case-law does not appear to be applicable to a new set of facts.

14 It is for the national court to explain why the interpretation sought is necessary to enable it to give judgment.

References on determination of validity

15 Although national courts may reject pleas raised before them challenging the validity of Community acts, the Court has exclusive jurisdiction to declare such acts invalid.

Civil Procedure Rules & Practice Directions

16 All national courts *must* therefore refer a question to the Court when they have doubts about the validity of a Community act, stating the reasons for which they consider that the Community act may be invalid.

17 If a national court has serious doubts about the validity of a Community act on which a national measure is based, it may exceptionally suspend application of that measure temporarily or grant other interim relief with respect to it. It must then refer the question of validity to the Court of Justice, stating the reasons for which it considers the Community act to be invalid.

The Stage at Which to Submit a Question for a Preliminary Ruling

18 A national court or tribunal may refer a question to the Court of Justice for a preliminary ruling as soon as it finds that a ruling on the point or points of interpretation or validity is necessary to enable it to give judgment; it is the national court which is in the best position to decide at what stage of the proceedings such a question should be referred.

19 It is, however, desirable that a decision to seek a preliminary ruling should be taken when the proceedings have reached a stage at which the national court is able to define the factual and legal context of the question, so that the Court has available to it all the information necessary to check, where appropriate, that Community law applies to the main proceedings. It may also be in the interests of justice to refer a question for a preliminary ruling only after both sides have been heard.

The Form of the Reference for a Preliminary Ruling

20 The decision by which a national court or tribunal refers a question to the Court of Justice for a preliminary ruling may be in any form allowed by national law as regards procedural steps. It must however be borne in mind that it is that document which serves as the basis of the proceedings before the Court and that it must therefore contain such information as will enable the latter to give a reply which is of assistance to the national court. Moreover, it is only the actual reference for a preliminary ruling which is notified to the parties entitled to submit observations to the Court, in particular the Member States and the institutions, and which is translated.

21 Owing to the need to translate the reference, it should be drafted simply, clearly and precisely, avoiding superfluous detail.

22 A maximum of about 10 pages is often sufficient to set out in a proper manner the context of a reference for a preliminary ruling. The order for reference must be succinct but sufficiently complete and must contain all the relevant information to give the Court and the parties entitled to submit observations a clear understanding of the factual and legal context of the main proceedings. In particular, the order for reference must:

- include a brief account of the subject matter of the dispute and the relevant findings of fact, or, at least, set out the factual situation on which the question referred is based;
- set out the tenor of any applicable national provisions and identify, where necessary, the relevant national case-law, giving in each case precise references (e.g. page of an official journal or specific law report, with any internet reference);
- identify the Community provisions relevant to the case as accurately as possible;
- explain the reasons which prompted the national court to raise the question of the interpretation or validity of the Community provisions, and the relationship between those provisions and the national provisions applicable to the main proceedings;
- include, where appropriate, a summary of the main arguments of the parties.

In order to make it easier to read and refer to the document, it is helpful if the different points or paragraphs of the order for reference are numbered.

23 Finally, the referring court may, if it considers itself to be in a position to do so, briefly state its view on the answer to be given to the questions referred for a preliminary ruling.

24 The question or questions themselves should appear in a separate and clearly identified section of the order for reference, generally at the beginning or the end. It must be possible to understand them without referring to the statement of the grounds for the reference, which however provides the necessary background for a proper assessment.

The Effects of the Reference for a Preliminary Ruling on the National Proceedings

25 A reference for a preliminary ruling in general calls for the national proceedings to be stayed until the Court has given its ruling.

26 However, the national court may still order protective measures, particularly in a reference on determination of validity (see point 17 above).

Costs and Legal Aid

27 Proceedings for a preliminary ruling before the Court are free of charge and the Court does not rule on the costs of the parties to the main proceedings; it is for the national court to rule on those costs.

28 If a party has insufficient means and where possible under national rules, the national court may grant that party legal aid to cover the costs, including those of lawyers' fees, which it incurs before the Court. The Court itself may also grant legal aid.

Communication between the National Court and the Court of Justice

29 The order for reference and the relevant documents (including, where applicable, the case file or a copy of the case file) are to be sent by the national court directly to the Court of Justice, by registered post (addressed to the Registry of the Court of Justice of the European Communities, L-2925 Luxembourg, telephone +352-4303-1).

30 The Court Registry will stay in contact with the national court until a ruling is given, and will send it copies of the procedural documents.

31 The Court will send its ruling to the national court. It would welcome information from the national court on the action taken upon its ruling in the national proceedings and, where appropriate, a copy of the national court's final decision.

CPR Part 69 Court's Power to Appoint a Receiver

Part 69 **76.1**, **76.38** [For commentary on a specific rule, please refer to the cross-references after the title of the rule.]

69.1 Scope of This Part

(1) This Part contains provisions about the court's power to appoint a receiver.
(2) In this Part 'receiver' includes a manager.

69.2 Court's Power to Appoint Receiver

(1) The court may appoint a receiver—
  (a) before proceedings have started;
  (b) in existing proceedings; or
  (c) on or after judgment.
(2) A receiver must be an individual.
(3) The court may at any time—
  (a) terminate the appointment of a receiver; and
  (b) appoint another receiver in his place.

(The practice direction [PD 69] describes the powers for the court to appoint a receiver)

69.3 How to Apply for the Appointment of a Receiver

An application for the appointment of a receiver—
(a) may be made without notice; and
(b) must be supported by written evidence.

69.4 Service of Order Appointing Receiver

An order appointing a receiver must be served by the party who applied for it on—
(a) the person appointed as receiver;
(b) unless the court orders otherwise, every other party to the proceedings; and
(c) such other persons as the court may direct.

69.5 Security

r.69.5 **76.35**

(1) The court may direct that before a receiver begins to act or within a specified time he must either—
  (a) give such security as the court may determine; or
  (b) file and serve on all parties to the proceedings evidence that he already has in force sufficient security,

  to cover his liability for his acts and omissions as a receiver.
(2) The court may terminate the appointment of the receiver if he fails to—
  (a) give the security; or
  (b) satisfy the court as to the security he has in force,

  by the date specified.

69.6 Receiver's Application for Directions

(1) The receiver may apply to the court at any time for directions to assist him in carrying out his function as a receiver.
(2) The court, when it gives directions, may also direct the receiver to serve on any person—
 (a) the directions; and
 (b) the application for directions.
(The practice direction [PD 69] makes provision for the form of applications by, and directions to, a receiver)

69.7 Receiver's Remuneration

r.69.7 **76.35**

(1) A receiver may only charge for his services if the court—
 (a) so directs; and
 (b) specifies the basis on which the receiver is to be remunerated.
(2) The court may specify—
 (a) who is to be responsible for paying the receiver; and
 (b) the fund or property from which the receiver is to recover his remuneration.
(3) If the court directs that the amount of a receiver's remuneration is to be determined by the court—
 (a) the receiver may not recover any remuneration for his services without a determination by the court; and
 (b) the receiver or any party may apply at any time for such a determination to take place.
(4) Unless the court orders otherwise, in determining the remuneration of a receiver the court shall award such sum as is reasonable and proportionate in all the circumstances and which takes into account—
 (a) the time properly given by him and his staff to the receivership;
 (b) the complexity of the receivership;
 (c) any responsibility of an exceptional kind or degree which falls on the receiver in consequence of the receivership;
 (d) the effectiveness with which the receiver appears to be carrying out, or to have carried out, his duties; and
 (e) the value and nature of the subject matter of the receivership.
(5) The court may refer the determination of a receiver's remuneration to a costs judge.

69.8 Accounts

r.69.8 **76.35**

(1) The court may order a receiver to prepare and serve accounts.
(The practice direction [PD 69] contains provisions about directions for the preparation and service of accounts)
(2) A party served with such accounts may apply for an order permitting him to inspect any document in the possession of the receiver relevant to those accounts.
(3) Any party may, within 14 days of being served with the accounts, serve notice on the receiver—
 (a) specifying any item in the accounts to which he objects;
 (b) giving the reason for such objection; and
 (c) requiring the receiver, within 14 days of receipt of the notice, either—
  (i) to notify all the parties who were served with the accounts that he accepts the objection; or
  (ii) if he does not accept the objection, to apply for an examination of the accounts in relation to the contested item.
(4) When the receiver applies for the examination of the accounts he must at the same time file—
 (a) the accounts; and
 (b) a copy of the notice served on him under this rule.
(5) If the receiver fails to comply with paragraph (3)(c) of this rule, any party may apply to the court for an examination of the accounts in relation to the contested item.
(6) At the conclusion of its examination of the accounts the court will certify the result.
(The practice direction supplementing Part 40 [PD 40] provides for inquiries into accounts)

69.9 Non-compliance by Receiver

(1) If a receiver fails to comply with any rule, practice direction or direction of the court the court may order him to attend a hearing to explain his non-compliance.

(2) At the hearing the court may make any order it considers appropriate, including—
 (a) terminating the appointment of the receiver;
 (b) reducing the receiver's remuneration or disallowing it altogether; and
 (c) ordering the receiver to pay the costs of any party.

(3) Where—
 (a) the court has ordered a receiver to pay a sum of money into court; and
 (b) the receiver has failed to do so,

the court may order him to pay interest on that sum for the time he is in default at such rate as it considers appropriate.

69.10 Application for Discharge of Receiver

(1) A receiver or any party may apply for the receiver to be discharged on completion of his duties.

(2) The application notice must be served on the persons who were required under rule 69.4 to be served with the order appointing the receiver.

69.11 Order Discharging or Terminating Appointment of Receiver

(1) An order discharging or terminating the appointment of a receiver may—
 (a) require him to pay into court any money held by him; or
 (b) specify the person to whom he must pay any money or transfer any assets still in his possession; and
 (c) make provision for the discharge or cancellation of any guarantee given by the receiver as security.

(2) The order must be served on the persons who were required under rule 69.4 to be served with the order appointing the receiver.

PD 69 Practice Direction — Court's Power to Appoint a Receiver

This practice direction supplements CPR Part 69

[For commentary on a specific paragraph, please refer to the cross-references after the title of the paragraph.]

Court's Power to Appoint Receiver

1.1 The court's powers to appoint a receiver are set out in:
  (1) the Supreme Court Act 1981, s. 37 (powers of the High Court with respect to injunctions and receivers);
  (2) the County Courts Act 1984, s. 38 (remedies available in county courts); and
  (3) the County Courts Act 1984, s. 107 (receivers by way of equitable execution.

Applications before Proceedings Are Started — Rule 69.2(1)(a)

2.1 The court will normally only consider an application for the appointment of a receiver before proceedings are started after notice of the application has been served.

2.2 Rule 25.2(2) contains provisions about the grant of an order before proceedings are started.

Related Injunctions

3.1 If a person applies at the same time for:
  (1) the appointment of a receiver; and
  (2) a related injunction,

he must use the same claim form or application notice for both applications.

3.2 PD 2B sets out who may grant injunctions. Among other things, it provides that a master or a district judge may grant an injunction related to an order appointing a receiver by way of equitable execution.

Evidence in Support of an Application: Rule 69.3

para.4.1 **76.34** para.4.2(1)–(3) **76.34**

4.1 The written evidence in support of an application for the appointment of a receiver must:
  (1) explain the reasons why the appointment is required;
  (2) give details of the property which it is proposed that the receiver should get in or manage, including estimates of:
    (a) the value of the property; and
    (b) the amount of income it is likely to produce;
  (3) if the application is to appoint a receiver by way of equitable execution, give details of:
    (a) the judgment which the applicant is seeking to enforce;
    (b) the extent to which the debtor has failed to comply with the judgment;
    (c) the result of any steps already taken to enforce the judgment; and
    (d) why the judgment cannot be enforced by any other method; and
  (4) if the applicant is asking the court to allow the receiver to act:
    (a) without giving security; or
    (b) before he has given security or satisfied the court that he has security in place,

  explain the reasons why that is necessary.

4.2 In addition, the written evidence should normally identify an individual whom the court is to be asked to appoint as receiver ('the nominee'), and should:
  (1) state the name, address and position of the nominee;
  (2) include written evidence by a person who knows the nominee, stating that he believes the nominee is a suitable person to be appointed as receiver, and the basis of that belief; and
  (3) be accompanied by written consent, signed by the nominee, to act as receiver if appointed.

4.3 If the applicant does not nominate a person to be appointed as receiver, or if the court decides not to appoint the nominee, the court may:

(1) order that a suitable person be appointed as receiver; and
(2) direct any party to nominate a suitable individual to be appointed.

4.4 A party directed to nominate a person to be appointed as receiver must file written evidence containing the information required by para. 4.2 and accompanied by the written consent of the nominee.

Appointment of Receiver to Enforce a Judgment

para.5 **76.33**

5 Where a judgment creditor applies for the appointment of a receiver as a method of enforcing a judgment, in considering whether to make the appointment the court will have regard to:
(1) the amount claimed by the judgment creditor;
(2) the amount likely to be obtained by the receiver; and
(3) the probable costs of his appointment.

Court's Directions

para.6.3(3)–(4) **76.35**

6.1 The court may give directions to the receiver when it appoints him or at any time afterwards.

6.2 The court will normally, when it appoints a receiver, give directions in relation to security — see para. 7 below.

6.3 Other matters about which the court may give directions include:
(1) whether, and on what basis, the receiver is to be remunerated for carrying out his functions;
(2) the preparation and service of accounts — see r. 69.8(1) and para. 10 below;
(3) the payment of money into court; and
(4) authorising the receiver to carry on an activity or incur an expense.

Directions Relating to Security: Rule 69.5

para.7.2 **76.35**

7.1 An order appointing a receiver will normally specify the date by which the receiver must:
(1) give security; or
(2) file and serve evidence to satisfy the court that he already has security in force.

7.2 Unless the court directs otherwise, security will be given:
(1) if the receiver is a licensed insolvency practitioner, by the bond provided by him under the Insolvency Practitioners Regulations 1990 (SI 1990/439) extended to cover appointment as a court-appointed receiver; or
(2) in any other case, by a guarantee.

7.3 Where the court has given directions about giving security, then either:
(1) written evidence of the bond, the sufficiency of its cover and that it includes appointment as a court-appointed receiver must be filed at court; or
(2) a guarantee should be prepared in a form, and entered into with a clearing bank or insurance company, approved by the court.

Receiver's Application for Directions: Rule 69.6

8.1 An application by a receiver for directions may be made by filing an application notice in accordance with Part 23.

8.2 If the directions sought by the receiver are unlikely to be contentious or important to the parties, he may make the application by letter, and the court may reply by letter. In such cases the receiver need not serve his letter or the court's reply on the parties, unless the court orders him to do so.

8.3 Where a receiver applies for directions by letter, the court may direct him to file and serve an application notice.

Receiver's Remuneration: Rule 69.7

para.9.1–9.6 **76.35**

9.1 A receiver may only charge for his services if the court gives directions permitting it and specifying how the remuneration is to be determined.

9.2 The court will normally determine the amount of the receiver's remuneration on the basis of the criteria in r. 69.7(4). Parts 43 to 48 (costs) do not apply to the determination of the remuneration of a receiver.

9.3 Unless the court orders otherwise, the receiver will only be paid or be able to recover his remuneration after the amount of it has been determined.

9.4 An application by a receiver for the amount of his remuneration to be determined must be supported by:
(1) written evidence showing:
(a) on what basis the remuneration is claimed; and
(b) that it is justified and in accordance with Part 69; and
(2) a certificate signed by the receiver that he considers that the remuneration he claims is reasonable and proportionate.

9.5 The court may, before determining the amount of a receiver's remuneration:
(1) require the receiver to provide further information in support of his claim; and
(2) appoint an assessor under r. 35.15 to assist the court.

9.6 Paragraphs 9.1 to 9.5 do not apply to expenses incurred by a receiver in carrying out his functions. These are accounted for as part of his account for the assets he has recovered, and not dealt with as part of the determination of his remuneration.

Accounts: Rule 69.8

para.10.1–10.3 **76.35**

10.1 When the court gives directions under r. 69.8(1) for the receiver to prepare and serve accounts, it may:
(1) direct the receiver to prepare and serve accounts either by a specified date or at specified intervals; and
(2) specify the persons on whom he must serve the accounts.

10.2 A party should not apply for an order under r. 69.8(2) permitting him to inspect documents in the possession of the receiver, without first asking the receiver to permit such inspection without an order.

10.3 Where the court makes an order under r. 69.8(2), it will normally direct that the receiver must:
(1) permit inspection within seven days after being served with the order; and
(2) provide a copy of any documents the subject of the order within seven days after receiving a request for a copy from the party permitted to inspect them, provided that party has undertaken to pay the reasonable cost of making and providing the copy.

CPR Part 70 General Rules about Enforcement of Judgments and Orders

Part 70 **76.1, 76.38** [For commentary on a specific rule, please refer to the cross-references after the title of the rule.]

70.1 Scope of This Part and Interpretation

(1) This Part contains general rules about enforcement of judgments and orders.

(Rules about specific methods of enforcement are contained in Parts 71 to 73, Schedule 1 RSC Orders 45 to 47 and 52 and Schedule 2 CCR Orders 25 to 29)

(2) In this Part and in Parts 71 to 73—

(a) 'judgment creditor' means a person who has obtained or is entitled to enforce a judgment or order;

(b) 'judgment debtor' means a person against whom a judgment or order was given or made;

(c) 'judgment or order' includes an award which the court has—

(i) registered for enforcement;

(ii) ordered to be enforced; or

(iii) given permission to enforce

as if it were a judgment or order of the court, and in relation to such an award, 'the court which made the judgment or order' means the court which registered the award or made such an order; and

(d) 'judgment or order for the payment of money' includes a judgment or order for the payment of costs, but does not include a judgment or order for the payment of money into court.

70.2 Methods of Enforcing Judgments or Orders

(1) The relevant practice direction sets out methods of enforcing judgments or orders for the payment of money.

(2) A judgment creditor may, except where an enactment, rule or practice direction provides otherwise—

(a) use any method of enforcement which is available; and

(b) use more than one method of enforcement, either at the same time or one after another.

70.3 Transfer of Proceedings for Enforcement

r.70.3 **76.2**

(1) A judgment creditor wishing to enforce a High Court judgment or order in a county court must apply to the High Court for an order transferring the proceedings to that county court.

(2) A practice direction may make provisions about the transfer of proceedings for enforcement.

(CCR Order 25 rule 13 contains provisions about the transfer of county court proceedings to the High Court for enforcement.)

70.4 Enforcement of Judgment or Order by or against Non-party

If a judgment or order is given or made in favour of or against a person who is not a party to proceedings, it may be enforced by or against that person by the same methods as if he were a party.

70.5 Enforcement of Awards of Bodies Other Than the High Court and County Courts

r.70.5 **61.30** r.70.5(4) **67.3**

(1) This rule applies, subject to paragraph (2), if—
  (a) an award of a sum of money or other decision is made by any court, tribunal, body or person other than the High Court or a county court; and
  (b) an enactment provides that the award may be enforced as if payable under a court order, or that the decision may be enforced as if it were a court order.
(2) This rule does not apply to—
  (a) any judgment to which Part 74 applies;
  (b) arbitration awards; or
  (c) any order to which RSC Order 115 applies.

(Part 74 provides for the registration in the High Court for the purposes of enforcement of judgments from other jurisdictions and European Community judgments)

(**RSC Order 115** provides for the registration in the High Court for the purposes of enforcement of certain orders made in connection with criminal proceedings and investigations)

(3) If the enactment provides that an award of a sum of money is enforceable if a court so orders, an application for such an order must be made in accordance with paragraphs (4) to (7) of this rule.
(4) An application for an order that an award may be enforced as if payable under a court order—
  (a) may be made without notice; and
  (b) must be made to the court for the district where the person against whom the award was made resides or carries on business, unless the court otherwise orders.
(5) The application notice must—
  (a) be in the form; and
  (b) contain the information

  required by the relevant practice direction.
(6) A copy of the award must be filed with the application notice.
(7) The application may be dealt with by a court officer without a hearing.
(8) If an enactment provides that an award or decision may be enforced in the same manner as an order of the High Court if it is registered, any application to the High Court for registration must be made in accordance with the relevant practice direction.

70.6 Effect of Setting Aside Judgment or Order

If a judgment or order is set aside, any enforcement of the judgment or order shall cease to have effect unless the court otherwise orders.

Civil Procedure Rules & Practice Directions

PD 70 Practice Direction — Enforcement of Judgments and Orders

This practice direction supplements CPR Part 70

[For commentary on a specific paragraph, please refer to the cross-references after the title of the paragraph.]

Methods of Enforcing Money Judgments: Rule 70.2

1.1 A judgment creditor may enforce a judgment or order for the payment of money by any of the following methods:
   (1) a writ of fieri facias or warrant of execution (see RSC, ord. 46 and ord. 47 in CPR, sch. 1; CCR, ord. 26 in CPR, sch. 2);
   (2) a third party debt order (see Part 72);
   (3) a charging order, stop order or stop notice (see Part 73);
   (4) in a county court, an attachment of earnings order (see CCR, ord. 27 in CPR, sch. 2);
   (5) the appointment of a receiver (see Part 69).

1.2 In addition the court may make the following orders against a judgment debtor:
   (1) an order of committal, but only if permitted by:
      (a) a rule; and
      (b) the Debtors Acts 1869 and 1878;[1] and
   (2) in the High Court, a writ of sequestration, but only if permitted by RSC, ord. 45, r. 5 in CPR, sch. 1.

1.3 The enforcement of a judgment or order may be affected by:
   (1) the enactments relating to insolvency; and
   (2) county court administration orders.

Transfer of County Court Proceedings to Another County Court for Enforcement: Rule 70.3

para. 2.1–2.3 **76.2**

2.1 If a judgment creditor is required by a rule or practice direction to enforce a judgment or order of one county court in a different county court, he must first make a request in writing to the court in which the case is proceeding to transfer the proceedings to that other court.

2.2 On receipt of such a request, a court officer will transfer the proceedings to the other court unless a judge orders otherwise.

2.3 The court will give notice of the transfer to all the parties.

2.4 When the proceedings have been transferred, the parties must take any further steps in the proceedings in the court to which they have been transferred, unless a rule or practice direction provides otherwise.

(Part 52 and PD 52 provide to which court or judge an appeal against the judgment or order, or an application for permission to appeal, must be made.)

Enforcement of High Court Judgment or Order in a County Court: Rule 70.3

para.3 **76.2**

3.1 If a judgment creditor wishes to enforce a High Court judgment or order in a county court, he must file the following documents in the county court with his application notice or request for enforcement:
   (1) a copy of the judgment or order;
   (2) a certificate verifying the amount due under the judgment or order;
   (3) if a writ of execution has previously been issued in the High Court to enforce the judgment or order, a copy of the relevant enforcement officer's return to the writ; and

---

[1] See RSC, ord. 45, r. 5 in CPR, sch. 1, and CCR, ord. 28 in CPR, sch. 2. PD RSC Ord. 52 applies to an application for committal of a judgment debtor.

(4) a copy of the order transferring the proceedings to the county court.

3.2 In this paragraph and para. 7:

(1) 'enforcement officer' means an individual who is authorised to act as an enforcement officer under the Courts Act 2003; and

(2) 'relevant enforcement officer' means:

(a) in relation to a writ of execution which is directed to a single enforcement officer, that officer;

(b) in relation to a writ of execution which is directed to two or more enforcement officers, the officer to whom the writ is allocated.

Enforcement of Awards of Bodies Other than the High Court or a County Court: Rule 70.5

4.1 An application under r. 70.5 for an order to enforce an award as if payable under a court order must be made by filing an application notice in form N322A.

4.2 The application notice must state:

(1) the name and address of the person against whom it is sought to enforce the award; and

(2) how much of the award remains unpaid.

4.3 Rule 70.5(6) provides that a copy of the award must be filed with the application notice.

Registration of Awards and Decisions in the High Court for Enforcement: Rule 70.5(8)

5.1 An application to the High Court under an enactment to register a decision for enforcement must be made in writing to the head clerk of the Action Department at the Royal Courts of Justice, Strand, London WC2A 2LL.

5.2 The application must:

(1) specify the statutory provision under which the application is made;

(2) state the name and address of the person against whom it is sought to enforce the decision;

(3) if the decision requires that person to pay a sum of money, state the amount which remains unpaid.

Interest on Judgment Debts

6. If a judgment creditor is claiming interest on a judgment debt, he must include in his application or request to issue enforcement proceedings in relation to that judgment details of:

(1) the amount of interest claimed and the sum on which it is claimed;

(2) the dates from and to which interest has accrued; and

(3) the rate of interest which has been applied and, where more than one rate of interest has been applied, the relevant dates and rates.

(Interest may be claimed on High Court judgment debts under the Judgments Act 1838, s. 17. The County Courts (Interest on Judgment Debts) Order 1991 specifies when interest may be claimed on county court judgment debts.)

Payment of Debt after Issue of Enforcement Proceedings

7.1 If a judgment debt or part of it is paid:

(1) after the judgment creditor has issued any application or request to enforce it; but

(2) before:

(a) any writ or warrant has been executed; or

(b) in any other case, the date fixed for the hearing of the application,

the judgment creditor must, unless para. 7.2 applies, immediately notify the court in writing.

7.2 If a judgment debt or part of it is paid after the judgment creditor has applied to the High Court for a writ of execution, para. 7.1 does not apply, and the judgment creditor must instead immediately notify the relevant enforcement officer in writing.

CPR Part 71 Orders to Obtain Information from Judgment Debtors

Part 71 **76.1, 76.38** [For commentary on a specific rule, please refer to the cross-references after the title of the rule.]

71.1 Scope of This Part

This Part contains rules which provide for a judgment debtor to be required to attend court to provide information, for the purpose of enabling a judgment creditor to enforce a judgment or order against him.

71.2 Order to Attend Court

r.71.2 **61.30, 76.4**

(1) A judgment creditor may apply for an order requiring—
  (a) a judgment debtor; or
  (b) if a judgment debtor is a company or other corporation, an officer of that body, to attend court to provide information about—
    (i) the judgment debtor's means; or
    (ii) any other matter about which information is needed to enforce a judgment or order.

(2) An application under paragraph (1)—
  (a) may be made without notice; and
  (b) (i) must be issued in the court which made the judgment or order which it is sought to enforce, except that
    (ii) if the proceedings have since been transferred to a different court, it must be issued in that court.

(3) The application notice must—
  (a) be in the form; and
  (b) contain the information

  required by the relevant practice direction.

(4) An application under paragraph (1) may be dealt with by a court officer without a hearing.

(5) If the application notice complies with paragraph (3), an order to attend court will be issued in the terms of paragraph (6).

(6) A person served with an order issued under this rule must—
  (a) attend court at the time and place specified in the order;
  (b) when he does so, produce at court documents in his control which are described in the order; and
  (c) answer on oath such questions as the court may require.

(7) An order under this rule will contain a notice in the following terms—

'You must obey this order. If you do not, you may be sent to prison for contempt of court.'

71.3 Service of Order

r.71.3–71.6 **76.4**

(1) An order to attend court must, unless the court otherwise orders, be served personally on the person ordered to attend court not less than 14 days before the hearing.

(2) If the order is to be served by the judgment creditor, he must inform the court not less than 7 days before the date of the hearing if he has been unable to serve it.

71.4 Travelling Expenses

(1) A person ordered to attend court may, within 7 days of being served with the order, ask the judgment creditor to pay him a sum reasonably sufficient to cover his travelling expenses to and from court.
(2) The judgment creditor must pay such a sum if requested.

71.5 Judgment Creditor's Affidavit

(1) The judgment creditor must file an affidavit(GL) or affidavits—
  (a) by the person who served the order (unless it was served by the court) giving details of how and when it was served;
  (b) stating either that—
    (i) the person ordered to attend court has not requested payment of his travelling expenses; or
    (ii) the judgment creditor has paid a sum in accordance with such a request; and
  (c) stating how much of the judgment debt remains unpaid.
(2) The judgment creditor must either—
  (a) file the affidavit(GL) or affidavits not less than 2 days before the hearing; or
  (b) produce it or them at the hearing.

71.6 Conduct of the Hearing

(1) The person ordered to attend court will be questioned on oath.
(2) The questioning will be carried out by a court officer unless the court has ordered that the hearing shall be before a judge.
(3) The judgment creditor or his representative—
  (a) may attend and ask questions where the questioning takes place before a court officer; and
  (b) must attend and conduct the questioning if the hearing is before a judge.

71.7 Adjournment of the Hearing

If the hearing is adjourned, the court will give directions as to the manner in which notice of the new hearing is to be served on the judgment debtor.

71.8 Failure to Comply with Order

r.71.8 **76.4**

(1) If a person against whom an order has been made under rule 71.2—
  (a) fails to attend court;
  (b) refuses at the hearing to take the oath or to answer any question; or
  (c) otherwise fails to comply with the order,

  the court will refer the matter to a High Court judge or circuit judge.
(2) That judge may, subject to paragraphs (3) and (4), make a committal order against the person.
(3) A committal order for failing to attend court may not be made unless the judgment creditor has complied with rules 71.4 and 71.5.
(4) If a committal order is made, the judge will direct that—
  (a) the order shall be suspended provided that the person—
    (i) attends court at a time and place specified in the order; and
    (ii) complies with all the terms of that order and the original order; and
  (b) if the person fails to comply with any term on which the committal order is suspended, he shall be brought before a judge to consider whether the committal order should be discharged.

PD 71 Practice Direction — Orders to Obtain Information from Judgment Debtors

This practice direction supplements CPR Part 71

[For commentary on a specific paragraph, please refer to the cross-references after the title of the paragraph.]

Application Notice: Rule 71.2

para.1.2 **76.4**

1.1 An application by a judgment creditor under r. 71.2(1) must be made by filing an application notice in form N316 if the application is to question an individual judgment debtor, or N316A if the application is to question an officer of a company or other corporation.

1.2 The application notice must:

(1) state the name and address of the judgment debtor;

(2) identify the judgment or order which the judgment creditor is seeking to enforce;

(3) if the application is to enforce a judgment or order for the payment of money, state the amount presently owed by the judgment debtor under the judgment or order;

(4) if the judgment debtor is a company or other corporation, state:

(a) the name and address of the officer of that body whom the judgment creditor wishes to be ordered to attend court; and

(b) his position in the company;

(5) if the judgment creditor wishes the questioning to be conducted before a judge, state this and give his reasons;

(6) if the judgment creditor wishes the judgment debtor (or other person to be questioned) to be ordered to produce specific documents at court, identify those documents; and

(7) if the application is to enforce a judgment or order which is not for the payment of money, identify the matters about which the judgment creditor wishes the judgment debtor (or officer of the judgment debtor) to be questioned.

1.3 The court officer considering the application notice:

(1) may, in any appropriate case, refer it to a judge (r. 3.2); and

(2) will refer it to a judge for consideration, if the judgment creditor requests the judgment debtor (or officer of the judgment debtor) to be questioned before a judge.

Order to Attend Court: Rule 71.2

para.2.2 **76.4**

2.1 The order will provide for the judgment debtor (or other person to be questioned) to attend the county court for the district in which he resides or carries on business, unless a judge decides otherwise.

2.2 The order will provide for questioning to take place before a judge only if the judge considering the request decides that there are compelling reasons to make such an order.

Service of Order to Attend Court: Rule 71.3

para.3 **76.4**

3. Service of an order to attend court for questioning must be carried out by the judgment creditor (or someone acting on his behalf), except that in county court proceedings if the judgment creditor is an individual litigant in person the order will be served by the court bailiff.

Attendance at Court: Normal Procedure: Rule 71.6

para.4.2 **76.4**

4.1 The court officer will ask a standard series of questions, as set out in the forms in Appendices A and B to this practice direction. The form in Appendix A will be used if the person being questioned is the judgment debtor, and the form in Appendix B will be used if the person is an officer of a company or other corporation.

4.2 The judgment creditor or his representative may either:
(1) attend court and ask questions himself; or
(2) request the court officer to ask additional questions, by attaching a list of proposed additional questions to his application notice.

4.3 The court officer will:
(1) make a written record of the evidence given, unless the proceedings are tape-recorded;
(2) at the end of the questioning, read the record of evidence to the person being questioned and ask him to sign it; and
(3) if the person refuses to sign it, note that refusal on the record of evidence.

Attendance at Court: Procedure Where the Order is to Attend before a Judge: Rule 71.6

para.5.1 **76.4**

5.1 Where the hearing takes places before a judge, the questioning will be conducted by the judgment creditor or his representative, and the standard questions in the forms in Appendices A and B will not be used.

5.2 The proceedings will be tape-recorded and the court will not make a written record of the evidence.

Failure to Comply with Order: Reference to Judge: Rule 71.8(1)

6. If a judge or court officer refers to a High Court judge or circuit judge the failure of a judgment debtor to comply with an order under r. 71.2, he shall certify in writing the respect in which the judgment debtor failed to comply with the order.

Suspended Committal Order: Rule 71.8(2) and (4)(a)

para.7.1 **76.4**

7.1 A committal order will be suspended provided that the person attends court at a time and place specified in the order (r. 71.8(4)(a)(i)). The appointment specified will be:
(1) before a judge, if:
(a) the original order under r. 71.2 was to attend before a judge; or
(b) the judge making the suspended committal order so directs; and
(2) otherwise, before a court officer.

7.2 Rule 71.3 and para. 3 of this practice direction (service of order), and r. 71.5(1)(a) and (2) (affidavit of service), apply with the necessary changes to a suspended committal order as they do to an order to attend court.

Breach of Terms on Which Committal Order Is Suspended: Rule 71.8(4)(b)

8.1 If:
(1) the judgment debtor fails to attend court at the time and place specified in the suspended committal order; and
(2) it appears to the judge or court officer that the judgment debtor has been duly served with the order,
the judge or court officer will certify in writing the debtor's failure to attend.

8.2 If the judgment debtor fails to comply with any other term on which the committal order was suspended, the judge or court officer will certify in writing the non-compliance and set out details of it.

8.3 A warrant to bring the judgment debtor before a judge may be issued on the basis of a certificate under para. 8.1 or 8.2.

8.4 The hearing under r. 71.8(4)(b) may take place before a master or district judge.

8.5 At the hearing the judge will discharge the committal order unless he is satisfied beyond reasonable doubt that:
(1) the judgment debtor has failed to comply with:
(a) the original order to attend court; and
(b) the terms on which the committal order was suspended; and
(2) both orders have been duly served on the judgment debtor.

8.6 If the judge decides that the committal order should not be discharged, a warrant of committal shall be issued immediately.

[The following forms are appended to PD 71:
Appendix A EX140 Record of examination (individual)
Appendix B EX141 Record of examination (officer of company or corporation)

These forms are on the CD-ROM version of *Blackstone's Civil Practice*. Click on a form number to open the form.]

CPR Part 72 Third Party Debt Orders

Part 72 **76.1**, **76.38** [For commentary on a specific rule, please refer to the cross-references after the title of the rule.]

72.1 Scope of This Part and Interpretation

(1) This Part contains rules which provide for a judgment creditor to obtain an order for the payment to him of money which a third party who is within the jurisdiction owes to the judgment debtor.
(2) In this Part, 'bank or building society' includes any person carrying on a business in the course of which he lawfully accepts deposits in the United Kingdom.

72.2 Third Party Debt Order

r.72.2(3) **76.15**

(1) Upon the application of a judgment creditor, the court may make an order (a 'final third party debt order') requiring a third party to pay to the judgment creditor—
 (a) the amount of any debt due or accruing due to the judgment debtor from the third party; or
 (b) so much of that debt as is sufficient to satisfy the judgment debt and the judgment creditor's costs of the application.
(2) The court will not make an order under paragraph 1 without first making an order (an 'interim third party debt order') as provided by rule 72.4(2).
(3) In deciding whether money standing to the credit of the judgment debtor in an account to which section 40 of the Supreme Court Act 1981 or section 108 of the County Courts Act 1984 relates may be made the subject of a third party debt order, any condition applying to the account that a receipt for money deposited in the account must be produced before any money is withdrawn will be disregarded.

(Section 40(3) of the Supreme Court Act 1981 and section 108(3) of the County Courts Act 1984 contain a list of other conditions applying to accounts that will also be disregarded.)

72.3 Application for Third Party Debt Order

r.72.3 **76.12**

(1) An application for a third party debt order—
 (a) may be made without notice; and
 (b) (i) must be issued in the court which made the judgment or order which it is sought to enforce; except that
  (ii) if the proceedings have since been transferred to a different court, it must be issued in that court.
(2) The application notice must—
 (a) (i) be in the form; and
  (ii) contain the information
 required by the relevant practice direction; and
 (b) be verified by a statement of truth.

72.4 Interim Third Party Debt Order

r.72.4(1) **76.12** r.72.4(4) **76.13**
r.72.4(3) **76.12**

(1) An application for a third party debt order will initially be dealt with by a judge without a hearing.
(2) The judge may make an interim third party debt order—
  (a) fixing a hearing to consider whether to make a final third party debt order; and
  (b) directing that until that hearing the third party must not make any payment which reduces the amount he owes the judgment debtor to less than the amount specified in the order.
(3) An interim third party debt order will specify the amount of money which the third party must retain, which will be the total of—
  (a) the amount of money remaining due to the judgment creditor under the judgment or order; and
  (b) an amount for the judgment creditor's fixed costs of the application, as specified in the relevant practice direction.
(4) An interim third party debt order becomes binding on a third party when it is served on him.
(5) The date of the hearing to consider the application shall be not less than 28 days after the interim third party debt order is made.

72.5 Service of Interim Order

r.72.5(1)(a)–(b) **76.13** r.72.5(2) **76.13**

(1) Copies of an interim third party debt order, the application notice and any documents filed in support of it must be served—
  (a) on the third party, not less than 21 days before the date fixed for the hearing; and
  (b) on the judgment debtor not less than—
    (i) 7 days after a copy has been served on the third party; and
    (ii) 7 days before the date fixed for the hearing.
(2) If the judgment creditor serves the order, he must either—
  (a) file a certificate of service not less than 2 days before the hearing; or
  (b) produce a certificate of service at the hearing.

72.6 Obligations of Third Parties Served with Interim Order

r.72.6(1)–(2) **76.13** r.72.6(4) **76.13**
r.72.6(2)(c)(iii) **76.13**

(1) A bank or building society served with an interim third party debt order must carry out a search to identify all accounts held with it by the judgment debtor.
(2) The bank or building society must disclose to the court and the creditor within 7 days of being served with the order, in respect of each account held by the judgment debtor—
  (a) the number of the account;
  (b) whether the account is in credit; and
  (c) if the account is in credit—
    (i) whether the balance of the account is sufficient to cover the amount specified in the order;
    (ii) the amount of the balance at the date it was served with the order, if it is less than the amount specified in the order; and
    (iii) whether the bank or building society asserts any right to the money in the account, whether pursuant to a right of set-off or otherwise, and if so giving details of the grounds for that assertion.
(3) If—
  (a) the judgment debtor does not hold an account with the bank or building society; or
  (b) the bank or building society is unable to comply with the order for any other reason (for example, because it has more than one account holder whose details match the information contained in the order, and cannot identify which account the order applies to),

the bank or building society must inform the court and the judgment creditor of that fact within 7 days of being served with the order.

(4) Any third party other than a bank or building society served with an interim third party debt order must notify the court and the judgment creditor in writing within 7 days of being served with the order, if he claims—
   (a) not to owe any money to the judgment debtor; or
   (b) to owe less than the amount specified in the order.

72.7 Arrangements for Debtors in Hardship

r.72.7 **76.13**

(1) If—
   (a) a judgment debtor is an individual;
   (b) he is prevented from withdrawing money from his account with a bank or building society as a result of an interim third party debt order; and
   (c) he or his family is suffering hardship in meeting ordinary living expenses as a result,
   the court may, on an application by the judgment debtor, make an order permitting the bank or building society to make a payment or payments out of the account ('a hardship payment order').
(2) An application for a hardship payment order may be made—
   (a) in High Court proceedings, at the Royal Courts of Justice or to any district registry; and
   (b) in county court proceedings, to any county court.
(3) A judgment debtor may only apply to one court for a hardship payment order.
(4) An application notice seeking a hardship payment order must—
   (a) include detailed evidence explaining why the judgment debtor needs a payment of the amount requested; and
   (b) be verified by a statement of truth.
(5) Unless the court orders otherwise, the application notice—
   (a) must be served on the judgment creditor at least 2 days before the hearing; but
   (b) does not need to be served on the third party.
(6) A hardship payment order may—
   (a) permit the third party to make one or more payments out of the account; and
   (b) specify to whom the payments may be made.

72.8 Further Consideration of the Application

r.72.8 **76.14** r.72.8(5)–(6) **76.14**

(1) If the judgment debtor or the third party objects to the court making a final third party debt order, he must file and serve written evidence stating the grounds for his objections.
(2) If the judgment debtor or the third party knows or believes that a person other than the judgment debtor has any claim to the money specified in the interim order, he must file and serve written evidence stating his knowledge of that matter.
(3) If—
   (a) the third party has given notice under rule 72.6 that he does not owe any money to the judgment debtor, or that the amount which he owes is less than the amount specified in the interim order; and
   (b) the judgment creditor wishes to dispute this,
   the judgment creditor must file and serve written evidence setting out the grounds on which he disputes the third party's case.
(4) Written evidence under paragraphs (1), (2) or (3) must be filed and served on each other party as soon as possible, and in any event not less than 3 days before the hearing.
(5) If the court is notified that some person other than the judgment debtor may have a claim to the money specified in the interim order, it will serve on that person notice of the application and the hearing.
(6) At the hearing the court may—
   (a) make a final third party debt order;
   (b) discharge the interim third party debt order and dismiss the application;
   (c) decide any issues in dispute between the parties, or between any of the parties and any other person who has a claim to the money specified in the interim order; or
   (d) direct a trial of any such issues, and if necessary give directions.

72.9 Effect of Final Third Party Order

r.72.9(2) **76.14**

(1) A final third party debt order shall be enforceable as an order to pay money.
(2) If—
  (a) the third party pays money to the judgment creditor in compliance with a third party debt order; or
  (b) the order is enforced against him,
  the third party shall, to the extent of the amount paid by him or realised by enforcement against him, be discharged from his debt to the judgment debtor.
(3) Paragraph (2) applies even if the third party debt order, or the original judgment or order against the judgment debtor, is later set aside.

72.10 Money in Court

(1) If money is standing to the credit of the judgment debtor in court—
  (a) the judgment creditor may not apply for a third party debt order in respect of that money; but
  (b) he may apply for an order that the money in court, or so much of it as is sufficient to satisfy the judgment or order and the costs of the application, be paid to him.
(2) An application notice seeking an order under this rule must be served on—
  (a) the judgment debtor; and
  (b) the Accountant General at the Court Funds Office.
(3) If an application notice has been issued under this rule, the money in court must not be paid out until the application has been disposed of.

72.11 Costs

If the judgment creditor is awarded costs on an application for an order under rule 72.2 or 72.10—
(a) he shall, unless the court otherwise directs, retain those costs out of the money recovered by him under the order; and
(b) the costs shall be deemed to be paid first out of the money he recovers, in priority to the judgment debt.

PD 72 Practice Direction — Third Party Debt Orders

This practice direction supplements CPR Part 72

[For commentary on a specific paragraph, please refer to the cross-references after the title of the paragraph.]

Application Notice: Rule 72.3

paras.1.2–1.3 **76.12**

1.1 An application for a third party debt order must be made by filing an application notice in form N349.

1.2 The application notice must contain the following information:
- (1) the name and address of the judgment debtor;
- (2) details of the judgment or order sought to be enforced;
- (3) the amount of money remaining due under the judgment or order;
- (4) if the judgment debt is payable by instalments, the amount of any instalments which have fallen due and remain unpaid;
- (5) the name and address of the third party;
- (6) if the third party is a bank or building society:
  - (a) its name and the address of the branch at which the judgment debtor's account is believed to be held; and
  - (b) the account number;

  or, if the judgment creditor does not know all or part of this information, that fact;
- (7) confirmation that to the best of the judgment creditor's knowledge or belief the third party:
  - (a) is within the jurisdiction; and
  - (b) owes money to or holds money to the credit of the judgment debtor;
- (8) if the judgment creditor knows or believes that any person other than the judgment debtor has any claim to the money owed by the third party:
  - (a) his name and (if known) his address; and
  - (b) such information as is known to the judgment creditor about his claim;
- (9) details of any other applications for third party debt orders issued by the judgment creditor in respect of the same judgment debt; and
- (10) the sources or grounds of the judgment creditor's knowledge or belief of the matters referred to in (7), (8) and (9).

1.3 The court will not grant speculative applications for third party debt orders, and will only make an interim third party debt order against a bank or building society if the judgment creditor's application notice contains evidence to substantiate his belief that the judgment debtor has an account with the bank or building society in question.

Interim Third Party Debt Order: Rule 72.4

2. An interim third party debt order will specify the amount of money which the third party must retain (r. 72.4(3)). This will include, in respect of the judgment creditor's fixed costs of the application, the amount which would be allowed to the judgment creditor under r. 45.6 if the whole balance of the judgment debt were recovered.

Interim Orders Relating to Bank or Building Society Accounts: Rule 72.6(1)–(3)

3.1 A bank or building society served with an interim third party debt order is only required by r. 72.6, unless the order states otherwise:
- (1) to retain money in accounts held solely by the judgment debtor (or, if there are joint judgment debtors, accounts held jointly by them or solely by either or any of them); and
- (2) to search for and disclose information about such accounts.

3.2 The bank or building society is not required, for example, to retain money in, or disclose information about:

(1) accounts in the joint names of the judgment debtor and another person; or
(2) if the interim order has been made against a firm, accounts in the names of individual members of that firm.

Transfer

4. The court may, on an application by a judgment debtor who wishes to oppose an application for a third party debt order, transfer it to the court for the district where the judgment debtor resides or carries on business, or to another court.

Applications for Hardship Payment Orders: Rule 72.7

paras.5.1–5.6 **76.13**

5.1 The court will treat an application for a hardship payment order as being made:
(1) in the proceedings in which the interim third party debt order was made; and
(2) under the same claim number,
regardless of where the judgment debtor makes the application.

5.2 An application for a hardship payment order will be dealt with by the court to which it is made. (Rule 72.7(2) provides that an application may be made:
- in High Court proceedings, in the Royal Courts of Justice or to any district registry; and
- in county court proceedings, to any county court.)

5.3 If the application is made to a different court from that dealing with the application for a third party debt order:
(1) the application for a third party debt order will not be transferred; but
(2) the court dealing with that application will send copies of:
(a) the application notice; and
(b) the interim third party debt order
to the court hearing the application for a hardship payment order

5.4 Rule 72.7(3) requires an application for a hardship payment order to be served on the judgment creditor at least two days before the court is to deal with the application, unless the court orders otherwise. In cases of exceptional urgency the judgment debtor may apply for a hardship payment order without notice to the judgment creditor and a judge will decide whether to:
(1) deal with the application without it being served on the judgment creditor; or
(2) direct it to be served.

5.5 If the judge decides to deal with the application without it being served on the judgment creditor, where possible he will normally:
(1) direct that the judgment creditor be informed of the application; and
(2) give him the opportunity to make representations,
by telephone, fax or other appropriate method of communication.

5.6 The evidence filed by a judgment debtor in support of an application for a hardship payment order should include documentary evidence, for example (if appropriate) bank statements, wage slips and mortgage statements, to prove his financial position and need for the payment.

Final Orders Relating to Building Society Accounts

6. A final third party debt order will not require a payment which would reduce to less than £1 the amount in a judgment debtor's account with a building society or credit union.

CPR Part 73 Charging Orders, Stop Orders and Stop Notices

Part 73 **76.1, 76.23, 76.38** [For commentary on a specific rule, please refer to the cross-references after the title of the rule.]

73.1 Scope of This Part and Interpretation

(1) This Part contains rules which provide for a judgment creditor to enforce a judgment by obtaining—
  (a) a charging order (Section I);
  (b) a stop order (Section II); or
  (c) a stop notice (Section III),
over or against the judgment debtor's interest in an asset.

(2) In this Part—
  (a) 'the 1979 Act' means the Charging Orders Act 1979;
  (b) 'the 1992 Regulations' means the Council Tax (Administration & Enforcement) Regulations 1992;
  (c) 'funds in court' includes securities held in court;
  (d) 'securities' means securities of any of the kinds specified in section 2(2)(b) of the 1979 Act.

I CHARGING ORDERS

73.2 Scope of This Section

This Section applies to an application by a judgment creditor for a charging order under—
(a) section 1 of the 1979 Act; or
(b) regulation 50 of the 1992 Regulations.

73.3 Application for Charging Order

r.73.3(4) **76.23**

(1) An application for a charging order may be made without notice.

(2) An application for a charging order must be issued in the court which made the judgment or order which it is sought to enforce, unless—
  (a) the proceedings have since been transferred to a different court, in which case the application must be issued in that court;
  (b) the application is made under the 1992 Regulations, in which case it must be issued in the county court for the district in which the relevant dwelling (as defined in regulation 50(3)(b) of those Regulations) is situated;
  (c) the application is for a charging order over an interest in a fund in court, in which case it must be issued in the court in which the claim relating to that fund is or was proceeding; or

Civil Procedure Rules & Practice Directions

(d) the application is to enforce a judgment or order of the High Court and it is required by section 1(2) of the 1979 Act to be made to a county court.

(3) Subject to paragraph (2), a judgment creditor may apply for a single charging order in respect of more than one judgment or order against the same debtor.

(4) The application notice must—

(a) (i) be in the form; and

(ii) contain the information,

required by the relevant practice direction; and

(b) be verified by a statement of truth.

73.4 Interim Charging Order

r.73.4 **76.23**

(1) An application for a charging order will initially be dealt with by a judge without a hearing.

(2) The judge may make an order (an 'interim charging order')—

(a) imposing a charge over the judgment debtor's interest in the asset to which the application relates; and

(b) fixing a hearing to consider whether to make a final charging order as provided by rule 73.8(2)(a).

73.5 Service of Interim Order

r.73.5(1)–(2) **76.23**

(1) Copies of the interim charging order, the application notice and any documents filed in support of it must, not less than 21 days before the hearing, be served on the following persons—

(a) the judgment debtor;

(b) such other creditors as the court directs;

(c) if the order relates to an interest under a trust, on such of the trustees as the court directs;

(d) if the interest charged is in securities other than securities held in court, then—

(i) in the case of stock for which the Bank of England keeps the register, the Bank of England;

(ii) in the case of government stock to which (i) does not apply, the keeper of the register;

(iii) in the case of stock of any body incorporated within England and Wales, that body;

(iv) in the case of stock of any body incorporated outside England and Wales or of any state or territory outside the United Kingdom, which is registered in a register kept in England and Wales, the keeper of that register;

(v) in the case of units of any unit trust in respect of which a register of the unit holders is kept in England and Wales, the keeper of that register; and

(e) if the interest charged is in funds in court, the Accountant General at the Court Funds Office.

(2) If the judgment creditor serves the order, he must either—

(a) file a certificate of service not less than 2 days before the hearing; or

(b) produce a certificate of service at the hearing.

73.6 Effect of Interim Order in Relation to Securities

r.73.6 **76.23**

(1) If a judgment debtor disposes of his interest in any securities, while they are subject to an interim charging order which has been served on him, that disposition shall not, so long as that order remains in force, be valid as against the judgment creditor.

(2) A person served under rule 73.5(1)(d) with an interim charging order relating to securities must not, unless the court gives permission—

(a) permit any transfer of any of the securities; or

(b) pay any dividend, interest or redemption payment relating to them.

(3) If a person acts in breach of paragraph (2), he will be liable to pay to the judgment creditor—

(a) the value of the securities transferred or the amount of the payment made (as the case may be); or

(b) if less, the amount necessary to satisfy the debt in relation to which the interim charging order was made.

73.7 Effect of Interim Order in Relation to Funds in Court

If a judgment debtor disposes of his interest in funds in court while they are subject to an interim charging order which has been served on him and on the Accountant General in accordance with rule 73.5(1), that disposition shall not, so long as that order remains in force, be valid as against the judgment creditor.

73.8 Further Consideration of the Application

r.73.8 **76.23** r.73.8(2) **76.23**

(1) If any person objects to the court making a final charging order, he must—
(a) file; and
(b) serve on the applicant;
written evidence stating the grounds of his objections, not less than 7 days before the hearing.
(2) At the hearing the court may—
(a) make a final charging order confirming that the charge imposed by the interim charging order shall continue, with or without modification;
(b) discharge the interim charging order and dismiss the application;
(c) decide any issues in dispute between the parties, or between any of the parties and any other person who objects to the court making a final charging order; or
(d) direct a trial of any such issues, and if necessary give directions.
(3) If the court makes a final charging order which charges securities other than securities held in court, the order will include a stop notice unless the court otherwise orders.
(Section III of this Part contains provisions about stop notices.)
(4) Any order made at the hearing must be served on all the persons on whom the interim charging order was required to be served.

73.9 Discharge or Variation of Order

(1) Any application to discharge or vary a charging order must be made to the court which made the charging order.
(Section 3(5) of the 1979 Act and regulation 51(4) of the 1992 Regulations provide that the court may at any time, on the application of the debtor, or of any person interested in any property to which the order relates, or (where the 1992 Regulations apply) of the authority, make an order discharging or varying the charging order.)
(2) The court may direct that—
(a) any interested person should be joined as a party to such an application; or
(b) the application should be served on any such person.
(3) An order discharging or varying a charging order must be served on all the persons on whom the charging order was required to be served.

73.10 Enforcement of Charging Order by Sale

r.73.10 **76.25, 76.26**

(1) Subject to the provisions of any enactment, the court may, upon a claim by a person who has obtained a charging order over an interest in property, order the sale of the property to enforce the charging order.
(2) A claim for an order for sale under this rule should be made to the court which made the charging order, unless that court does not have jurisdiction to make an order for sale.
(A claim under this rule is a proceeding for the enforcement of a charge, and section 23(c) of the County Courts Act 1984 provides the extent of the county court's jurisdiction to hear and determine such proceedings.)
(3) The claimant must use the Part 8 procedure.
(4) A copy of the charging order must be filed with the claim form.
(5) The claimant's written evidence must include the information required by the relevant practice direction.

II STOP ORDERS

73.11 Interpretation

In this Section, 'stop order' means an order of the High Court not to take, in relation to funds in court or securities specified in the order, any of the steps listed in section 5(5) of the 1979 Act.

73.12 Application for Stop Order

r.73.12(2) **13.4**

(1) The High Court may make—
  (a) a stop order relating to funds in court, on the application of any person—
    (i) who has a mortgage or charge on the interest of any person in the funds; or
    (ii) to whom that interest has been assigned; or
    (iii) who is a judgment creditor of the person entitled to that interest; or
  (b) a stop order relating to securities other than securities held in court, on the application of any person claiming to be beneficially entitled to an interest in the securities.

(2) An application for a stop order must be made—
  (a) by application notice in existing proceedings; or
  (b) by Part 8 claim form if there are no existing proceedings in the High Court.

(3) The application notice or claim form must be served on—
  (a) every person whose interest may be affected by the order applied for; and
  (b) either—
    (i) the Accountant General at the Court Funds Office, if the application relates to funds in court; or
    (ii) the person specified in rule 73.5(1)(d), if the application relates to securities other than securities held in court.

73.13 Stop Order Relating to Funds in Court

A stop order relating to funds in court shall prohibit the transfer, sale, delivery out, payment or other dealing with—
(a) the funds or any part of them; or
(b) any income on the funds.

73.14 Stop Order Relating to Securities

(1) A stop order relating to securities other than securities held in court may prohibit all or any of the following steps—
  (a) the registration of any transfer of the securities;
  (b) the making of any payment by way of dividend, interest or otherwise in respect of the securities; and
  (c) in the case of units of a unit trust, any acquisition of or other dealing with the units by any person or body exercising functions under the trust.

(2) The order shall specify—
  (a) the securities to which it relates;
  (b) the name in which the securities stand;
  (c) the steps which may not be taken; and
  (d) whether the prohibition applies to the securities only or to the dividends or interest as well.

73.15 Variation or Discharge of Order

(1) The court may, on the application of any person claiming to have a beneficial interest in the funds or securities to which a stop order relates, make an order discharging or varying the order.

(2) An application notice seeking the variation or discharge of a stop order must be served on the person who obtained the order.

III STOP NOTICES

73.16 General

In this Section—

(a) 'stop notice' means a notice issued by the court which requires a person or body not to take, in relation to securities specified in the notice, any of the steps listed in section 5(5) of the 1979 Act, without first giving notice to the person who obtained the notice; and
(b) 'securities' does not include securities held in court.

73.17 Request for Stop Notice

(1) The High Court may, on the request of any person claiming to be beneficially entitled to an interest in securities, issue a stop notice.
(A stop notice may also be included in a final charging order, by either the High Court or a county court, under rule 73.8(3).)
(2) A request for a stop notice must be made by filing—
  (a) a draft stop notice; and
  (b) written evidence which—
    (i) identifies the securities in question;
    (ii) describes the applicant's interest in the securities; and
    (iii) gives an address for service for the applicant.
(A sample form of stop notice is annexed to the relevant practice direction.)
(3) If a court officer considers that the request complies with paragraph (2), he will issue a stop notice.
(4) The applicant must serve copies of the stop notice and his written evidence on the person to whom the stop notice is addressed.

73.18 Effect of Stop Notice

(1) A stop notice—
  (a) takes effect when it is served in accordance with rule 73.17(4); and
  (b) remains in force unless it is withdrawn or discharged in accordance with rule 73.20 or 73.21.
(2) While a stop notice is in force, the person on whom it is served—
  (a) must not—
    (i) register a transfer of the securities described in the notice; or
    (ii) take any other step restrained by the notice,
  without first giving 14 days' notice to the person who obtained the stop notice; but
  (b) must not, by reason only of the notice, refuse to register a transfer or to take any other step, after he has given 14 days' notice under paragraph (2)(a) and that period has expired.

73.19 Amendment of Stop Notice

(1) If any securities are incorrectly described in a stop notice which has been obtained and served in accordance with rule 73.17, the applicant may request an amended stop notice in accordance with that rule.
(2) The amended stop notice takes effect when it is served.

73.20 Withdrawal of Stop Notice

(1) A person who has obtained a stop notice may withdraw it by serving a request for its withdrawal on—
  (a) the person or body on whom the stop notice was served; and
  (b) the court which issued the stop notice.
(2) The request must be signed by the person who obtained the stop notice, and his signature must be witnessed by a practising solicitor.

73.21 Discharge or Variation of Stop Notice

(1) The court may, on the application of any person claiming to be beneficially entitled to an interest in the securities to which a stop notice relates, make an order discharging or varying the notice.
(2) An application to discharge or vary a stop notice must be made to the court which issued the notice.
(3) The application notice must be served on the person who obtained the stop notice.

PD 73 Practice Direction — Charging Orders, Stop Orders and Stop Notices

This practice direction supplements CPR Part 73

[For commentary on a specific paragraph, please refer to the cross-references after the title of the paragraph.]

I CHARGING ORDERS

Application Notice: Rule 73.3

para.1.2 **76.23**

1.1 An application for a charging order must be made by filing an application notice in form N379 if the application relates to land, or N380 if the application relates to securities.

1.2 The application notice must contain the following information:
- (1) the name and address of the judgment debtor;
- (2) details of the judgment or order sought to be enforced;
- (3) the amount of money remaining due under the judgment or order;
- (4) if the judgment debt is payable by instalments, the amount of any instalments which have fallen due and remain unpaid;
- (5) if the judgment creditor knows of the existence of any other creditors of the judgment debtor, their names and (if known) their addresses;
- (6) identification of the asset or assets which it is intended to charge;
- (7) details of the judgment debtor's interest in the asset; and
- (8) the names and addresses of the persons on whom an interim charging order must be served under r. 73.5(1).

1.3 A judgment creditor may apply in a single application notice for charging orders over more than one asset, but if the court makes interim charging orders over more than one asset, it will draw up a separate order relating to each asset.

High Court and County Court Jurisdiction

2. The jurisdiction of the High Court and the county court to make charging orders is set out in the Charging Orders Act 1979, s. 1(2).

Transfer

3. The court may, on an application by a judgment debtor who wishes to oppose an application for a charging order, transfer it to the court for the district where the judgment debtor resides or carries on business, or to another court.

Enforcement of Charging Orders by Sale: Rule 73.10

para.4.5 **76.26**

4.1 A county court has jurisdiction to determine a claim under r. 73.10 for the enforcement of a charging order if the amount owing under the charge does not exceed the county court limit.

4.2 A claim in the High Court for an order for sale of land to enforce a charging order must be started in Chancery Chambers at the Royal Courts of Justice, or a Chancery district registry. (There are Chancery district registries at Birmingham, Bristol, Cardiff, Leeds, Liverpool, Manchester, Newcastle upon Tyne and Preston.)

4.3 The written evidence in support of a claim under r. 73.10 must:
- (1) identify the charging order and the property sought to be sold;
- (2) state the amount in respect of which the charge was imposed and the amount due at the date of issue of the claim;
- (3) verify, so far as known, the debtor's title to the property charged;
- (4) state, so far as the claimant is able to identify:

(a) the names and addresses of any other creditors who have a prior charge or other security over the property; and
(b) the amount owed to each such creditor; and

(5) give an estimate of the price which would be obtained on sale of the property;
(6) if the claim relates to land, give details of every person who to the best of the claimant's knowledge is in possession of the property; and
(7) if the claim relates to residential property:
(a) state whether:
(i) a land charge of Class F; or
(ii) a notice under the Family Law Act 1996, s. 31(10), or under any provision of an Act which preceded that section,
has been registered; and
(b) if so, state:
(i) on whose behalf the land charge or notice has been registered; and
(ii) that the claimant will serve notice of the claim on that person.

4.4 The claimant must take all reasonable steps to obtain the information required by para. 4.3(4) before issuing the claim.

4.5 Sample forms of orders for sale are set out in Appendix A to this practice direction for guidance. These are not prescribed forms of order and they may be adapted or varied by the court to meet the requirements of individual cases.

II STOP NOTICES

5. A sample form of stop notice is set out in Appendix B to this practice direction.
appendix.A **76.26**

[PD 73 has the following appendices:
Appendix A Sample forms of order for sale following a charging order
Appendix B Sample form of stop notice
These appendices are on the CD-ROM version of *Blackstone's Civil Practice.* Click on the title of an appendix to open it.]

CPR Part 74 Enforcement of Judgments in Different Jurisdictions

[For commentary on a specific rule, please refer to the cross-references after the title of the rule.]

74.1 Scope of this Part and Interpretation

(1) Section I of this Part applies to the enforcement in England and Wales of judgments of foreign courts.
(2) Section II applies to the enforcement in foreign countries of judgments of the High Court and of county courts.
(3) Section III applies to the enforcement of United Kingdom judgments in other parts of the United Kingdom.
(4) Section IV applies to the enforcement in England and Wales of European Community judgments and Euratom inspection orders.
(4A) Section V applies to—
  (a) the certification of judgments and court settlements in England and Wales as European Enforcement Orders; and
  (b) the enforcement in England and Wales of judgments, court settlements and authentic instruments certified as European Enforcement Orders by other Member States.
(5) In this Part:
  (a) 'the 1920 Act' means the Administration of Justice Act 1920;
  (b) 'the 1933 Act' means the Foreign Judgments (Reciprocal Enforcement) Act 1933;
  (c) 'the 1982 Act' means the Civil Jurisdiction and Judgments Act 1982;
  (d) 'the Judgments Regulation' means Council Regulation (EC) No. 44/2001 of 22nd

December 2000 on jurisdiction and the recognition and enforcement of judgments in civil and commercial matters;

(e) 'the EEO Regulation' means Council Regulation (EC) No. 805/2004 creating a European Enforcement Order for uncontested claims.

(A copy of the EEO Regulation is annexed to Practice Direction 74B European Enforcement Orders and can be found at http://europa.eu.int/eur-lex/pri/en/oj/dat/2004/l_143/l_14320040430en00150039.pdf)

I ENFORCEMENT IN ENGLAND AND WALES OF JUDGMENTS OF FOREIGN COURTS

74.2 Interpretation

r.74.2 **77.13** r.74.2(1)(c) **77.13**

(1) In this Section:
   (a) 'Contracting State' has the meaning given in section 1(3) of the 1982 Act;
   (b) 'Regulation State' has the same meaning as 'Member State' in the Judgments Regulation, that is all Member States except Denmark;
   (c) 'judgment' means, subject to any other enactment, any judgment given by a foreign court or tribunal, whatever the judgment may be called, and includes—
      (i) a decree;
      (ii) an order;
      (iii) a decision;
      (iv) a writ of execution; and
      (v) the determination of costs by an officer of the court;
   (d) 'State of origin', in relation to any judgment, means the State in which that judgment was given.

(2) For the purposes of this Section, 'domicile' is to be determined—
   (a) in an application under the 1982 Act, in accordance with sections 41 to 46 that Act;
   (b) in an application under the Judgments Regulation, in accordance with paragraphs 9 to 12 of Schedule 1 to the Civil Jurisdiction and Judgments Order 2001.

74.3 Applications for Registration

r.74(3) **77.13** r.74.3(2) **77.13**

(1) This Section provides rules about applications under—
   (a) section 9 of the 1920 Act, in respect of judgments to which Part II of that Act applies;
   (b) section 2 of the 1933 Act, in respect of judgments to which Part I of that Act applies;
   (c) section 4 of the 1982 Act; and
   (d) the Judgments Regulation,

   for the registration of foreign judgments for enforcement in England and Wales.

(2) Applications—
   (a) must be made to the High Court; and
   (b) may be made without notice.

74.4 Evidence in Support

r.74.4 **77.13**
r.74.4(1)–(2) **77.14**
r.74.4(3) **77.15**
r.74.4(3)(a)–(b) **77.15**
r.74.4(4) **77.16**
r.74.4(5) **77.17**
r.74.4(6) **77.18**

(1) An application for registration of a judgment under the 1920, 1933 or 1982 Act must be supported by written evidence exhibiting—
   (a) the judgment or a verified or certified or otherwise authenticated copy of it; and
   (b) where the judgment is not in English, a translation of it into English—
      (i) certified by a notary public or other qualified person; or
      (ii) accompanied by written evidence confirming that the translation is accurate.

(2) The written evidence in support of the application must state—
   (a) the name of the judgment creditor and his address for service within the jurisdiction;

Civil Procedure Rules & Practice Directions

(b) the name of the judgment debtor and his address or place of business, if known;
(c) the grounds on which the judgment creditor is entitled to enforce the judgment;
(d) in the case of a money judgment, the amount in respect of which it remains unsatisfied; and
(e) where interest is recoverable on the judgment under the law of the State of origin—
(i) the amount of interest which has accrued up to the date of the application, or
(ii) the rate of interest, the date from which it is recoverable, and the date on which it ceases to accrue.

(3) Written evidence in support of an application under the 1920 Act must also state that the judgment is not a judgment—
(a) which under section 9 of that Act may not be ordered to be registered; or
(b) to which section 5 of the Protection of Trading Interests Act 1980 applies.

(4) Written evidence in support of an application under the 1933 Act must also—
(a) state that the judgment is a money judgment;
(b) confirm that it can be enforced by execution in the State of origin;
(c) confirm that the registration could not be set aside under section 4 of that Act;
(d) confirm that the judgment is not a judgment to which section 5 of the Protection of Trading Interests Act 1980 applies;
(e) where the judgment contains different provisions, some but not all of which can be registered for enforcement, set out those provisions in respect of which it is sought to register the judgment; and
(f) be accompanied by any further evidence as to—
(i) the enforceability of the judgment in the State of origin, and
(ii) the law of that State under which any interest has become due under the judgment,
which may be required under the relevant Order in Council extending Part I of the 1933 Act to that State.

(5) Written evidence in support of an application under the 1982 Act must also exhibit—
(a) documents which show that, under the law of the State of origin, the judgment is enforceable on the judgment debtor and has been served;
(b) in the case of a judgment in default, a document which establishes that the party in default was served with the document instituting the proceedings or with an equivalent document; and
(c) where appropriate, a document showing that the judgment creditor is in receipt of legal aid in the State of origin.

(6) An application for registration under the Judgments Regulation must, in addition to the evidence required by that Regulation, be supported by the evidence required by paragraphs (1)(b) and (2)(e) of this rule.

74.5 Security for Costs

r.74.5 **77.13**

(1) Subject to paragraphs (2) and (3), section II of Part 25 applies to an application for security for the costs of—
(a) the application for registration;
(b) any proceedings brought to set aside the registration; and
(c) any appeal against the granting of the registration,
as if the judgment creditor were a claimant.

(2) A judgment creditor making an application under the 1982 Act or the Judgments Regulation may not be required to give security solely on the ground that he is resident out of the jurisdiction.

(3) Paragraph (1) does not apply to an application under the 1933 Act where the relevant Order in Council otherwise provides.

74.6 Registration Orders

r.74.6 **77.13**
r.74.6(1) **77.19, 77.20**
r.74.6(2) **77.20**
r.74.6(3) **77.19**
r.74.6(3)(d) **77.22**

(1) An order granting permission to register a judgment ('registration order') must be drawn up by the judgment creditor and served on the judgment debtor—
  (a) by delivering it to him personally;
  (b) as provided by section 725 of the Companies Act 1985; or
  (c) in such other manner as the court may direct.
(2) Permission is not required to serve a registration order out of the jurisdiction, and rules 6.24, 6.25, 6.26 and 6.29 apply to such an order as they apply to a claim form.
(3) A registration order must state—
  (a) full particulars of the judgment registered;
  (b) the name of the judgment creditor and his address for service within the jurisdiction;
  (c) the right of the judgment debtor—
    (i) in the case of registration following an application under the 1920 or the 1933 Act, to apply to have the registration set aside;
    (ii) in the case of registration following an application under the 1982 Act or under the Judgments Regulation, to appeal against the registration order;
  (d) the period within which such an application or appeal may be made; and
  (e) that no measures of enforcement will be taken before the end of that period, other than measures ordered by the court to preserve the property of the judgment debtor.

74.7 Applications to Set Aside Registration

r.74.7 **77.13**
r.74.7(1)–(3) **77.21**

(1) An application to set aside registration under the 1920 or the 1933 Act must be made within the period set out in the registration order.
(2) The court may extend that period; but an application for such an extension must be made before the end of the period as originally fixed or as subsequently extended.
(3) The court hearing the application may order any issue between the judgment creditor and the judgment debtor to be tried.

74.8 Appeals

r.74.8 **77.13, 97.40**
r.74.8(1)–(2) **77.22**
r.74.8(4) **77.22**

(1) An appeal against the granting or the refusal of registration under the 1982 Act or the Judgments Regulation must be made in accordance with Part 52, subject to the following provisions of this rule.
(2) Permission is not required—
  (a) to appeal; or
  (b) to put in evidence.
(3) If—
  (a) the judgment debtor is not domiciled within a Contracting State or a Regulation State, as the case may be, and
  (b) an application to extend the time for appealing is made within two months of service of the registration order,

  the court may extend the period for filing an appellant's notice against the order granting registration, but not on grounds of distance.
(4) The appellant's notice must be served—
  (a) where the appeal is against the granting of registration, within —
    (i) one month; or
    (ii) where service is to be effected on a party not domiciled within the jurisdiction, two months, of service of the registration order;
  (b) where the appeal is against the refusal of registration, within one month of the decision on the application for registration.

74.9 Enforcement

r.74.9 **77.13, 77.19** r.74.9(2) **77.20**

(1) No steps may be taken to enforce a judgment—
 (a) before the end of the period specified in accordance with rule 74.6(3)(d), or that period as extended by the court; or
 (b) where there is an application under rule 74.7 or an appeal under rule 74.8, until the application or appeal has been determined.
(2) Any party wishing to enforce a judgment must file evidence of the service on the judgment debtor of—
 (a) the registration order; and
 (b) any other relevant order of the court.
(3) Nothing in this rule prevents the court from making orders to preserve the property of the judgment debtor pending final determination of any issue relating to the enforcement of the judgment.

74.10 Recognition

r.74.10 **77.13, 77.19**

(1) Registration of a judgment serves as a decision that the judgment is recognised for the purposes of the 1982 Act and the Judgments Regulation.
(2) An application for recognition of a judgment is governed by the same rules as an application for registration of a judgment under the 1982 Act or under the Judgments Regulation, except that rule 74.4(5)(a) and (c) does not apply.

74.11 Authentic Instruments and Court Settlements

r.74.11 **77.13**

The rules governing the registration of judgments under the 1982 Act or under the Judgments Regulation apply as appropriate and with any necessary modifications for the enforcement of—
(a) authentic instruments which are subject to—
 (i) article 50 of Schedule 1 to the 1982 Act;
 (ii) article 50 of Schedule 3C to the 1982 Act; and
 (iii) article 57 of the Judgments Regulation; and
(b) court settlements which are subject to—
 (i) article 51 of Schedule 1 to the 1982 Act;
 (ii) article 51 of Schedule 3C to the 1982 Act; and
 (iii) article 58 of the Judgments Regulation.

II ENFORCEMENT IN FOREIGN COUNTRIES OF JUDGMENTS OF THE HIGH COURT AND COUNTY COURTS

74.12 Application for a Certified Copy of a Judgment

(1) This Section applies to applications—
 (a) to the High Court under section 10 of the 1920 Act;
 (b) to the High Court or to a county court under section 10 of the 1933 Act;
 (c) to the High Court or to a county court under section 12 of the 1982 Act; or
 (d) to the High Court or to a county court under article 54 of the Judgments Regulation.
(2) A judgment creditor who wishes to enforce in a foreign country a judgment obtained in the High Court or in a county court must apply for a certified copy of the judgment.
(3) The application may be made without notice.

74.13 Evidence in Support

(1) The application must be supported by written evidence exhibiting copies of—
 (a) the claim form in the proceedings in which judgment was given;
 (b) evidence that it was served on the defendant;
 (c) the statements of case; and

(d) where relevant, a document showing that for those proceedings the applicant was an assisted person or an LSC funded client, as defined in rule 43.2(1)(h) and (i).

(2) The written evidence must—

(a) identify the grounds on which the judgment was obtained;

(b) state whether the defendant objected to the jurisdiction and, if he did, the grounds of his objection;

(c) show that the judgment—

(i) has been served in accordance with Part 6 and rule 40.4, and

(ii) is not subject to a stay of execution;

(d) state—

(i) the date on which the time for appealing expired or will expire;

(ii) whether an appeal notice has been filed;

(iii) the status of any application for permission to appeal; and

(iv) whether an appeal is pending;

(e) state whether the judgment provides for the payment of a sum of money, and if so, the amount in respect of which it remains unsatisfied;

(f) state whether interest is recoverable on the judgment, and if so, either—

(i) the amount of interest which has accrued up to the date of the application, or

(ii) the rate of interest, the date from which it is recoverable, and the date on which it ceases to accrue.

III ENFORCEMENT OF UNITED KINGDOM JUDGMENTS IN OTHER PARTS OF THE UNITED KINGDOM

74.14 Interpretation

r.74.14 **77.12**

In this Section—

(a) 'money provision' means a provision for the payment of one or more sums of money in a judgment whose enforcement is governed by section 18 of, and Schedule 6 to, the 1982 Act; and

(b) 'non-money provision' means a provision for any relief or remedy not requiring payment of a sum of money in a judgment whose enforcement is governed by section 18 of, and Schedule 7 to, the 1982 Act.

74.15 Registration of Money Judgments in the High Court

r.74.15 **77.12**

(1) This rule applies to applications to the High Court under paragraph 5 of Schedule 6 to the 1982 Act for the registration of a certificate for the enforcement of the money provisions of a judgment—

(a) which has been given by a court in another part of the United Kingdom, and

(b) to which section 18 of that Act applies.

(2) The certificate must within six months of the date of its issue be filed in the Central Office of the Supreme Court, together with a copy certified by written evidence to be a true copy.

74.16 Registration of Non-money Judgments in the High Court

r.74.16 **77.12**

(1) This rule applies to applications to the High Court under paragraph 5 of Schedule 7 to the 1982 Act for the registration for enforcement of the non-money provisions of a judgment—

(a) which has been given by a court in another part of the United Kingdom, and

(b) to which section 18 of that Act applies.

(2) An application under paragraph (1) may be made without notice.

(3) An application under paragraph (1) must be accompanied—

(a) by a certified copy of the judgment issued under Schedule 7 to the 1982 Act; and

(b) by a certificate, issued not more than six months before the date of the application, stating that the conditions set out in paragraph 3 of Schedule 7 are satisfied in relation to the judgment.

(4) Rule 74.6 applies to judgments registered under Schedule 7 to the 1982 Act as it applies to judgments registered under section 4 of that Act.
(5) Rule 74.7 applies to applications to set aside the registration of a judgment under paragraph 9 of Schedule 7 to the 1982 Act as it applies to applications to set aside registrations under the 1920 and 1933 Acts.

74.17 Certificates of High Court and County Court Money Judgments

r.74.17 **77.12**

(1) This rule applies to applications under paragraph 2 of Schedule 6 to the 1982 Act for a certificate to enable the money provisions of a judgment of the High Court or of a county court to be enforced in another part of the United Kingdom.
(2) The judgment creditor may apply for a certificate by filing at the court where the judgment was given or has been entered written evidence stating—
 (a) the name and address of the judgment creditor and, if known, of the judgment debtor;
 (b) the sums payable and unsatisfied under the money provisions of the judgment;
 (c) where interest is recoverable on the judgment, either—
  (i) the amount of interest which has accrued up to the date of the application, or
  (ii) the rate of interest, the date from which it is recoverable, and the date on which it ceases to accrue;
 (d) that the judgment is not stayed;
 (e) the date on which the time for appealing expired or will expire;
 (f) whether an appeal notice has been filed;
 (g) the status of any application for permission to appeal; and
 (h) whether an appeal is pending.

74.18 Certified Copies of High Court and County Court Non-money Judgments

r.74.18 **77.12**

(1) This rule applies to applications under paragraph 2 of Schedule 7 to the 1982 Act for a certified copy of a judgment of the High Court or of a county court to which section 18 of the Act applies and which contains non-money provisions for enforcement in another part of the United Kingdom.
(2) An application under paragraph (1) may be made without notice.
(3) The applicant may apply for a certified copy of a judgment by filing at the court where the judgment was given or has been entered written evidence stating—
 (a) full particulars of the judgment;
 (b) the name and address of the judgment creditor and, if known, of the judgment debtor;
 (c) that the judgment is not stayed;
 (d) the date on which the time for appealing expired or will expire;
 (e) whether an appeal notice has been filed;
 (f) the status of any application for permission to appeal; and
 (g) whether an appeal is pending.

IV ENFORCEMENT IN ENGLAND AND WALES OF EUROPEAN COMMUNITY JUDGMENTS

74.19 Interpretation

r.74.19 **77.23**

In this Section—
(a) 'Community judgment' means any judgment, decision or order which is enforceable under—
 (i) article 244 or 256 of the Treaty establishing the European Community;
 (ii) article 18,159 or 164 of the Euratom Treaty;
 (iii) article 44 or 92 of the ECSC Treaty;
 (iv) article 82 of Council Regulation (EC) 40/94 of 20 December 1993 on the Community trade mark; or
 (v) article 71 of Council Regulation (EC) 6/2002 of 12 December 2001 on Community designs;

(b) 'Euratom inspection order' means an order made by the President of the European Court, or a decision of the Commission of the European Communities, under article 81 of the Euratom Treaty;
(c) 'European Court' means the Court of Justice of the European Communities;
(d) 'order for enforcement' means an order under the authority of the Secretary of State that the Community judgment to which it is appended is to be registered for enforcement in the United Kingdom.

74.20 Application for Registration of a Community Judgment

r.74.20 **77.23**

An application to the High Court for the registration of a Community judgment may be made without notice.

74.21 Evidence in Support

r.74.21 **77.23**

(1) An application for registration must be supported by written evidence exhibiting—
  (a) the Community judgment and the order for its enforcement, or an authenticated copy; and
  (b) where the judgment is not in English, a translation of it into English—
    (i) certified by a notary public or other qualified person; or
    (ii) accompanied by written evidence confirming that the translation is accurate.
(2) Where the application is for registration of a Community judgment which is a money judgment, the evidence must state—
  (a) the name of the judgment creditor and his address for service within the jurisdiction;
  (b) the name of the judgment debtor and his address or place of business, if known;
  (c) the amount in respect of which the judgment is unsatisfied; and
  (d) that the European Court has not suspended enforcement of the judgment.

74.22 Registration Orders

r.74.22 **77.23**

(1) A copy of the order granting permission to register a Community judgment ('the registration order') must be served on every person against whom the judgment was given.
(2) The registration order must state the name and address for service of the person who applied for registration, and must exhibit—
  (a) a copy of the registered Community judgment; and
  (b) a copy of the order for its enforcement.
(3) In the case of a Community judgment which is a money judgment, the registration order must also state the right of the judgment debtor to apply within 28 days for the variation or cancellation of the registration under rule 74.23.

74.23 Application to Vary or Cancel Registration

(1) An application to vary or cancel the registration of a Community judgment which is a money judgment on the ground that at the date of registration the judgment had been partly or wholly satisfied must be made within 28 days of the date on which the registration order was served on the judgment debtor.
(2) The application must be supported by written evidence.

74.24 Enforcement

No steps may be taken to enforce a Community judgment which is a money judgment—
(a) before the end of the period specified in accordance with rule 74.23(1); or
(b) where an application is made under that rule, until it has been determined.

74.25 Application for Registration of Suspension Order

(1) Where the European Court has made an order that the enforcement of a registered Community judgment should be suspended, an application for the registration of that order in the High Court is made by filing a copy of the order in the Central Office of the Supreme Court.
(2) The application may be made without notice.

74.26 Registration and Enforcement of a Euratom Inspection Order

(1) Rules 74.20, 74.21(1), and 74.22(1) and (2), which apply to the registration of a Community judgment, also apply to the registration of a Euratom inspection order but with the necessary modifications.

(2) An application under article 6 of the European Communities (Enforcement of Community Judgments) Order 1972 to give effect to a Euratom inspection order may be made on written evidence, and—
   (a) where the matter is urgent, without notice;
   (b) otherwise, by claim form.

V EUROPEAN ENFORCEMENT ORDERS

74.27 Interpretation

r.74.27 **77.24**

In this Section—

(a) 'European Enforcement Order' has the meaning given in the EEO Regulation;
(b) 'EEO' means European Enforcement Order;
(c) 'judgment', 'authentic instrument', 'member state of origin', 'member state of enforcement', and 'court of origin' have the meanings given by Article 4 of the EEO Regulation; and
(d) 'Regulation State' has the same meaning as 'Member State' in the EEO Regulation, that is all Member States except Denmark.

74.28 Certification of Judgments of the Courts of England and Wales

An application for an EEO certificate must be made by filing the relevant practice form in accordance with Article 6 of the EEO Regulation.

74.29 Applications for a Certificate of Lack or Limitation of Enforceability

An application under Article 6(2) of the EEO Regulation for a certificate indicating the lack or limitation of enforceability of an EEO certificate must be made to the court of origin by application in accordance with Part 23.

74.30 Applications for Rectification or Withdrawal

An application under Article 10 of the EEO Regulation for rectification or withdrawal of an EEO certificate must be made to the court of origin and may be made by application in accordance with Part 23.

74.31 Enforcement of European Enforcement Orders in England and Wales

r.74.31 **77.24**

(1) A person seeking to enforce an EEO in England and Wales must lodge at the court in which enforcement proceedings are to be brought the documents required by Article 20 of the EEO Regulation.

(2) Where a person applies—
   (a) to the High Court for a charging order, a writ of fieri facias or an attachment of earnings order; or
   (b) to the county court for a warrant of execution or an attachment of earnings order,

   to enforce an EEO expressed in a foreign currency, the application must contain a certificate of the sterling equivalent of the judgment sum at the close of business on the date nearest preceding the date of issue of the application.

(Section 1 of the Charging Orders Act 1979 provides that the High Court only has jurisdiction to make a charging order where the amount of the original judgment exceeds the county court limit)

(Article 8 of the High Court and County Courts Jurisdiction Order 1991 provides that (1) judgments in excess of £5,000 shall only be enforced by execution against goods in the High Court (2) those in excess of £600 may be enforced in the High Court and (3) those for less than £600 shall only be enforced in the county court)

74.32 Refusal of Enforcement

r.74.32 **77.24**

(1) An application under Article 21 of the EEO Regulation that the court should refuse to enforce an EEO must be made by application in accordance with Part 23 to the court in which the EEO is being enforced.
(2) The judgment debtor must, as soon as practicable, serve copies of any order made under Article 21(1) on—
    (a) all other parties to the proceedings and any other person affected by the order; and
    (b) any court in which enforcement proceedings are pending in England and Wales.
(3) Upon service of the order on those persons all enforcement proceedings in England and Wales under the EEO, in respect of those persons upon whom, and those courts at which, the order has been served in accordance with paragraph (2), will cease.

74.33 Stay or Limitation of Enforcement

r.74.33 **77.23**

(1) Where an EEO certificate has been lodged and the judgment debtor applies to stay or limit the enforcement proceedings under Article 23 of the EEO Regulation, such application must be made by application in accordance with Part 23 to the court in which the EEO is being enforced.
(2) The judgment debtor shall, as soon as practicable, serve a copy of any order made under the Article on—
    (a) all other parties to the proceedings and any other person affected by the order; and
    (b) any court in which enforcement proceedings are pending in England and Wales;
    and the order will not have effect on any person until it has been served in accordance with this rule and they have received it.

PD 74 Practice Direction — Enforcement of Judgments in Different Jurisdictions

This practice direction supplements CPR Part 74

[For commentary on a specific paragraph, please refer to the cross-references after the title of the paragraph.]

1 This practice direction is divided into two sections:
(1) Section I — Provisions about the enforcement of judgments
(2) Section II — The Merchant Shipping (Liner Conferences) Act 1982

I ENFORCEMENT OF JUDGMENTS

Meaning of 'Judgment'

2 In r. 74.2(1)(c), the definition of 'judgment' is 'subject to any other enactment'. Such provisions include:
(1) s. 9(1) of the 1920 Act, which limits enforcement under that Act to judgments of superior courts;
(2) s. 1(1) of the 1933 Act, which limits enforcement under that Act to judgments of those courts specified in the relevant Order in Council;
(3) s. 1(2) of the 1933 Act, which limits enforcement under that Act to money judgments.

Registers

para.3.1 **77.19**

3 There will be kept in the Central Office of the Supreme Court at the Royal Courts of Justice, under the direction of the Senior Master:
(1) registers of foreign judgments ordered by the High Court to be enforced following applications under:
(a) s. 9 of the 1920 Act;
(b) s. 2 of the 1933 Act;
(c) s. 4 of the 1982 Act; or
(d) the Judgments Regulation;
(2) registers of certificates issued for the enforcement in foreign countries of High Court judgments under the 1920,1933 and 1982 Acts, and under art. 54 of the Judgments Regulation;
(3) a register of certificates filed in the Central Office of the High Court under r. 74.15(2) for the enforcement of money judgments given by the courts of Scotland or Northern Ireland;
(4) a register of certificates issued under r. 74.16(3) for the enforcement of non-money judgments given by the courts of Scotland or Northern Ireland;
(5) registers of certificates issued under rr. 74.17 and 74.18 for the enforcement of High Court judgments in Scotland or Northern Ireland under sch. 6 or sch. 7 to the 1982 Act; and
(6) a register of Community judgments and Euratom inspection orders ordered to be registered under art. 3 of the European Communities (Enforcement of Community Judgments) Order 1972 (SI 1972/1590).

Making an Application

para.4.1 **77.13, 77.23** para.4.4 **77.13**

4.1 Applications for the registration for enforcement in England and Wales of:
(1) foreign judgments under r. 74.3;
(2) judgments of courts in Scotland or Northern Ireland under r. 74.15 or 74.16; and
(3) European Community judgments under r. 74.20,
are assigned to the Queen's Bench Division and may be heard by a master.

4.2 An application under r. 74.12 for a certified copy of a High Court or county court judgment for enforcement abroad must be made:

(1) in the case of a judgment given in the Chancery Division or the Queen's Bench Division of the High Court, to a Master or district judge;
(2) in the case of a judgment given in the Family Division of the High Court, to a district judge of that Division;
(3) in the case of a county court judgment, to a district judge.

4.3 An application under r. 74.17 or 74.18 for a certificate or a certified copy of a High Court or county court judgment for enforcement in Scotland or Northern Ireland must be made:
(1) in the case of a judgment given in the Chancery Division or the Queen's Bench Division of the High Court, to a Master or district judge;
(2) in the case of a judgment given in the Family Division of the High Court, to a district judge of that Division;
(3) in the case of a county court judgment, to a district judge.

4.4 The following applications must be made under Part 23:
(1) applications under r. 74.3 for the registration of a judgment;
(2) applications under r. 74.7 to set aside the registration of a judgment;
(3) applications under r. 74.12 for a certified copy of a judgment;
(4) applications under section III for a certificate for enforcement of a judgment;
(5) applications under r. 74.20 for the registration of a Community judgment;
(6) applications under r. 74.23 to vary or cancel the registration of a Community judgment; and
(7) applications under r. . 74.25 for the registration of an order of the European Court that the enforcement of a registered Community judgment should be suspended.

Applications under the 1933 Act

5 Foreign judgments are enforceable in England and Wales under the 1933 Act where there is an agreement on the reciprocal enforcement of judgments between the United Kingdom and the country in which the judgment was given. Such an agreement may contain particular provisions governing the enforcement of judgments (for example limiting the categories of judgments which are enforceable, or the courts whose judgments are enforceable). Any such specific limitations will be listed in the Order in Council giving effect in the United Kingdom to the agreement in question, and the rules in Section I of Part 74 will take effect subject to such limitations.

Evidence in Support of an Application under the Judgments Regulation: Rule 74.4(6)

para.6.1–6.5 **77.18**

6.1 Where a judgment is to be recognised or enforced in a Regulation State, Council Regulation (EC) No. 44/2001 of 22 December 2000 on jurisdiction and the recognition and enforcement of judgments in civil and commercial matters applies.

6.2 As a consequence of art. 38(2) of the Judgments Regulation, the provisions in Chapter III of that Regulation relating to declaring judgments enforceable are the equivalent, in the United Kingdom, of provisions relating to registering judgments for enforcement.

6.3 Chapter III of, and Annex V to, the Judgments Regulation are annexed to this practice direction. They were originally published in the official languages of the European Community in the *Official Journal of the European Communities* by the Office for Official Publications of the European Communities.

6.4 Sections 2 and 3 of Chapter III of the Judgments Regulation (in particular articles 40, 53, 54 and 55, and Annex V) set out the evidence needed in support of an application.

6.5 The Judgments Regulation is supplemented by the Civil Jurisdiction and Judgments Order 2001 (SI 2001/3929). The Order also makes amendments, in respect of that Regulation, to the Civil Jurisdiction and Judgments Act 1982.

Certified Copies of Judgments Issued under Rule 74.12

7.1 In an application by a judgment creditor under r. 74.12 for the enforcement abroad of a High Court judgment, the certified copy of the judgment will be an office copy, and will be accompanied by a certificate signed by a judge. The judgment and certificate will be sealed with the seal of the Supreme Court.

7.2 In an application by a judgment creditor under r. 74.12 for the enforcement abroad of a county court judgment, the certified copy will be a sealed copy, and will be accompanied by a certificate signed by a judge.

7.3 In applications under the 1920,1933 or 1982 Acts, the certificate will be in form No. 110, and will have annexed to it a copy of the claim form by which the proceedings were begun.

7.4 In an application under the Judgments Regulation, the certificate will be in the form of Annex V to the Regulation.

Certificates under Section III of Part 74

8.1 A certificate of a money judgment of a court in Scotland or Northern Ireland must be filed for enforcement under r. 74.15(2) in the Action Department of the Central Office of the Supreme Court, Royal Courts of Justice, Strand, London WC2A 2LL. The copy will be sealed by a court officer before being returned to the applicant.

8.2 A certificate issued under r. 74.17 for the enforcement in Scotland or Northern Ireland of a money judgment of the High Court or of a county court will be in form No. 111.

8.3 In an application by a judgment creditor under r. 74.18 for the enforcement in Scotland or Northern Ireland of a non-money judgment of the High Court or of a county court, the certified copy of the judgment will be a sealed copy to which will be annexed a certificate in form No. 112.

Material Additional to Section IV of Part 74

9.1 Enforcement of Community judgments and of Euratom inspection orders is governed by the European Communities (Enforcement of Community Judgments) Order 1972 (SI 1972/1590).

9.2 The Treaty establishing the European Community is the Treaty establishing the European Economic Community (Rome, 1957); relevant amendments are made by the Treaty of Amsterdam (1997, Cm 3780).

9.3 The text of the Protocol of 3 June 1971 on the interpretation by the European Court of the Convention of 27 September 1968 on Jurisdiction and the Enforcement of Judgments in Civil and Commercial Matters is set out in the Civil Jurisdiction and Judgments Act 1982, sch. 2.

9.4 The text of the Protocol of 19 December 1988 on the interpretation by the European Court of the Convention of 19 June 1980 on the Law applicable to Contractual Obligations is set out in the Contracts (Applicable Law) Act 1990, sch. 3.

II THE MERCHANT SHIPPING (LINER CONFERENCES) ACT 1982

Content of This Section

10 The Merchant Shipping (Liner Conferences) Act 1982 ('the Act') contains provisions for the settlement of disputes between liner conferences, shipping lines and shippers. This Section of this practice direction deals with the enforcement by the High Court under s. 9 of the Act of recommendations of conciliators, and determinations and awards of costs.

Exercise of Powers under the Act

11 The powers of the High Court under the Act are exercised by the Commercial Court.

Applications for Registration

12.1 An application under s. 9 of the Act for the registration of a recommendation, determination or award is made under Part 23.

12.2 An application for the registration of a recommendation must be supported by written evidence exhibiting:

(1) a verified or certified or otherwise authenticated copy of:

(a) the recommendation;

(b) the reasons for it; and

(c) the record of settlement;

(2) where any of those documents is not in English, a translation of it into English:

(a) certified by a notary public or other qualified person; or
(b) accompanied by written evidence confirming that the translation is accurate; and
(3) copies of the acceptance of the recommendation by the parties on whom it is binding, or otherwise verifying the acceptance where it is not in writing.

12.3 The evidence in support of the application must:
(1) give particulars of the failure to implement the recommendation; and
(2) confirm that none of the grounds which would render it unenforceable is applicable.

12.4 An application for the registration of a determination of costs or an award of costs must be supported by written evidence:
(1) exhibiting a verified or certified or otherwise authenticated copy of the recommendation or other document containing the determination or award; and
(2) stating that the costs have not been paid.

Order for Registration

13.1 The applicant must draw up the order giving permission to register the recommendation, determination or award.

13.2 The order must include a provision that the reasonable costs of the registration should be assessed.

Register of Recommendations

14 There will be kept in the Admiralty and Commercial Registry at the Royal Courts of Justice, under the direction of the Senior Master, a register of the recommendations, determinations and awards ordered to be registered under s. 9 of the Act, with particulars of enforcement.

APPENDIX

[The appendix is not printed here, because it consists of extracts from Regulation (EC) No. 44/2001, which is printed in full in **appendix** 7.]

PD 74B Practice Direction — European Enforcement Orders

This practice direction supplements Section V of Part 74.

Council Regulation

1.1 Certification and enforcement of European Enforcement Orders is governed by Council Regulation (EC) No. 805/2004 creating a European Enforcement Order for uncontested claims.

1.2 The EEO Regulation is annexed to this practice direction and can be found at http://europa.eu.int/eur-lex/pri/en/oj/dat/2004/l_143/l_14320040430en00150039.pdf. It was originally published in the official languages of the European Community in the *Official Journal of the European Communities* by the Office for Official Publications of the European Communities.

1.3 Section V of Part 74 sets out the procedure for enforcement under the EEO Regulation. A claim that does not meet the requirements of the EEO Regulation, or which the judgment creditor does not wish to enforce using the EEO Regulation, may be enforceable using another method of enforcement.

Certification of Judgments of the Courts of England and Wales (Rule 74.28)

2.1 An application under r. 74.28 for a certificate of a High Court or county court judgment for enforcement in another Regulation State must be made using form N219 or form N219A:

(1) in the case of a judgment given in the Chancery or Queen's Bench Division of the High Court, or in a district registry, to a master or district judge; or

(2) in the case of a county court judgment, to a district judge.

2.2 Where the application is granted, the court will send the EEO certificate and a sealed copy of the judgment to the person making the application. Where the court refuses the application, the court will give reasons for the refusal and may give further directions.

Applications for a Certificate of Lack of Enforceability (Rule 74.29)

3.1 An application must be supported by written evidence in support of the grounds on which the judgment has ceased to be enforceable or its enforceability has been suspended or limited.

Application for Rectification or Withdrawal (Rule 74.30)

4.1 An application must be supported by written evidence in support of the grounds on which it is contended that the EEO should be rectified or withdrawn.

Enforcement of European Enforcement Orders in England and Wales (Rule 74.31)

5.1 When an EEO is lodged at the court in which enforcement proceedings are to be brought, it will be assigned a case number.

5.2 A copy of a document will satisfy the conditions necessary to establish its authenticity if it is an official copy of the courts of the member State of origin.

5.3 The judgment creditor must notify all courts in which enforcement proceedings are pending in England and Wales under the EEO if judgment is set aside in the court of origin, as soon as reasonably practicable after the order is served on the judgment creditor. Notification may be by any means available including fax, email, post or telephone.

Refusal of Enforcement (Rule 74.32)

6.1 An application must be accompanied by an official copy of the earlier judgment, any other documents relied upon and any translations required by the EEO Regulation and supported by written evidence stating:

(1) why the earlier judgment is irreconcilable; and

(2) why the irreconcilability was not, and could not have been, raised as an objection in the proceedings in the court of origin.

Stay or Limitation of Enforcement (Rule 74.33)

7.1 An application must, unless the court orders otherwise, be accompanied by evidence of the application in the court of origin, including:
(1) the application (or equivalent foreign process) or a copy of the application (or equivalent foreign process) certified by an appropriate officer of the court of origin; and
(2) where that document is not in English, a translation of it into English:
(a) certified by a notary public or person qualified to certify a translation in the member State of the court of origin under art. 20(2)(c) of the EEO Regulation; or
(b) accompanied by written evidence confirming that the translation is accurate.

7.2 The written evidence in support of the application must state:
(1) that an application has been brought in the member State of origin;
(2) the nature of that application, including the grounds on which the application is made and the order sought; and
(3) the date on which the application was filed, the state of the proceedings and the date by which it is believed that the application will be determined.

7.3 If on the application of a debtor under r. 74.32 the court makes a conditional order under art. 23(b), the order shall be effective to bar enforcement until the creditor has lodged evidence at court that he has complied with such conditions. In cases other than where the order is conditional upon the creditor making a payment into court, the evidence lodged should be referred to the master or district judge.

ANNEX

[The annex is Regulation (EC) No. 805/2004, which is on the CD-ROM version of *Blackstone's Civil Practice.* Click on the title of the Regulation to open it. In the first paragraph of art. 33, '21 January 2004' should be '21 January 2005' ([2005] OJ L97/64).]

CPR Part 75 Traffic Enforcement

[For commentary on a specific rule, please refer to the cross-references after the title of the rule.]

75.1 Scope and Interpretation

(1) The practice direction—
(a) sets out the proceedings to which this Part applies; and
(b) may apply this Part with modifications in relation to any particular category of those proceedings.

(2) In this Part—
(a) 'the Centre' means the Traffic Enforcement Centre established under the direction of the Lord Chancellor;
(b) 'no relevant return to the warrant' means that—
(i) the bailiff has been unable to seize goods because he has been denied access to premises occupied by the defendant or because the goods have been removed from those premises;
(ii) any goods seized under a warrant of execution are insufficient to satisfy the debt and the cost of execution; or
(iii) the goods are insufficient to cover the cost of their removal and sale.
(c) 'the 1993 Order' means the Enforcement of Road Traffic Debts Order 1993;
(d) 'relevant period', in relation to any particular case, means—
(i) the period allowed for serving a statutory declaration under any enactment which applies to that case; or
(ii) where an enactment permits the court to extend that period, the period as extended;
(e) 'specified debts' means the debts specified in article 2 of the 1993 Order or treated as so specified by any other enactment; and
(f) 'the authority', 'notice of the amount due', 'order' and 'the respondent' have the meaning given by the practice direction.

75.2 The Centre

(1) Proceedings to which this Part applies must be started in the Centre.

(2) For any purpose connected with the exercise of the Centre's functions—
(a) the Centre shall be deemed to be part of the office of the court whose name appears on the documents to which the functions relates or in whose name the documents are issued; and
(b) any officer of the Centre, in exercising its functions, is deemed to act as an officer of that court.

75.3 Request

r.75.3 **12.1**

(1) The authority must file a request in the appropriate form scheduling the amount claimed to be due.

(2) The authority must, in that request or in another manner approved by the court officer—
(a) certify—
(i) that 14 days have elapsed since service of the notice of the amount due;

(ii) the date of such service;
(iii) the number of the notice of the amount due; and
(iv) that the amount due remains unpaid;

(b) specify the grounds (whether by reference to the appropriate code or otherwise), as stated in the notice, on which the authority claims to be entitled to claim that amount; and

(c) state—
(i) the name, title and address of the respondent;
(ii) the registration number of the vehicle concerned;
(iii) the authority's address for service;
(iv) the court fee; and
(v) such other matters as required by the practice direction.

(3) On receipt of a request that meets the requirements of paragraphs (1) and (2), the court officer will order that the amount due may be recovered as if it were payable under a county court order by sealing the request and returning it to the authority.

(4) On receipt of a sealed request the authority may draw up an order and must attach to it a form of statutory declaration for the respondent's use.

(5) Within 14 days of receipt of the sealed request, the authority must serve the order (and the form of statutory declaration) on the respondent in accordance with Part 6.

(6) Where an order is served by first class post (or an alternative service which provides for delivery on the next working day) rule 6.7 is modified so that the date of service will be deemed to be the seventh day after the date on which the order was sent to the respondent.

75.4 Electronic Delivery of Documents

(1) Where the authority is required to file any document other than the request, that requirement is satisfied if the information which would be contained in the document is delivered in computer-readable form.

(2) For the purposes of paragraph (1), information which would be contained in a document relating to one case may be combined with information of the same nature relating to another case.

(3) Where a document is required to be produced, that requirement will be satisfied if a copy of the document is produced from computer records.

75.5 Functions of Court Officer

(1) The practice direction sets out circumstances in which a court officer may exercise the functions of the court or a district judge.

(2) Any party may request any decision of a court officer to be reviewed by a district judge.

(3) Such a request must be made within 14 days of service of the decision.

75.6 Enforcement of Orders

Subject to the 1993 Order and this rule the following rules apply to the enforcement of specified debts—

(a) Parts 70 to 73;
(b) CCR Order 25, rules 1 and 9;
(c) CCR Order 26, rule 5; and
(d) CCR Order 27, rules 1 to 7,7A, 7B, 9 to 16 and 18 to 22.

(Rule 30.2 provides for the transfer between courts in order to enforce a judgment.)

75.7 Warrant of Execution

(1) An authority seeking the issue of a warrant of execution must file a request—
(a) certifying the amount remaining due under the order;
(b) specifying the date of service of the order on the respondent; and
(c) certifying that the relevant period has elapsed.

(2) The court will seal the request and return it to the authority.

(3) Within 7 days of the sealing of the request the authority must prepare the warrant in the appropriate form.

(4) No payment under a warrant will be made to the court.

(5) For the purposes of execution a warrant will be valid for 12 months beginning with the date of its issue.

(6) An authority may not renew a warrant issued in accordance with this Part.

75.8 Revocation of Order

Where, in accordance with any enactment, an order is deemed to have been revoked following the filing of a statutory declaration—

(a) the court will serve a copy of the statutory declaration on the authority;

(b) any execution issued on the order will cease to have effect; and

(c) if appropriate, the authority must inform any bailiff instructed to levy execution of the withdrawal of the warrant as soon as possible.

75.9 Transfer for Enforcement

If an authority requests the transfer of proceedings to another county court for enforcement, the request must—

(a) where the authority has not attempted to enforce by execution, give the reason why no such attempt was made;

(b) certify that there has been no relevant return to the warrant of execution;

(c) specify the date of service of the order on the respondent; and

(d) certify that the relevant period has elapsed.

75.10 Further Information Required

An application for—

(a) an attachment of earnings order;

(b) an order to obtain information from a debtor;

(c) a third party debt order; or

(d) a charging order,

must, in addition to the requirements of Parts 71, 72 or 73 or CCR Order 27—

(i) where the authority has not attempted to enforce by execution, give the reasons no such attempt was made;

(ii) certify that there has been no relevant return to the warrant of execution;

(iii) specify the date of service of the order on the respondent; and

(iv) certify that the relevant period has elapsed.

75.11 Combining Requests

If the court officer allows, an authority may combine information relating to different orders against the same defendant in any request or application made under rules 75.9 or 75.10.

PD 75 Practice Direction — Traffic Enforcement

This practice direction supplements CPR Part 75

Interpretation and Scope

1.1 In this Practice Direction:
(1) 'the 1991 Act' means the Road Traffic Act 1991;
(2) 'the 1996 Act' means the London Local Authorities Act 1996;
(3) 'the Road User Charging Regulations' means the Road User Charging (Enforcement and Adjudication) (London) Regulations 2001 (SI 2001/2313);
(4) 'the Vehicle Emissions (England) Regulations' means the Road Traffic (Vehicle Emissions) (Fixed Penalty) (England) Regulations 2002 (SI 2002/1808);
(5) 'the Vehicle Emissions (Wales) Regulations' means the Road Traffic (Vehicle Emissions) (Fixed Penalty) (Wales) Regulations 2003 (SI 2003/300);
(6) 'the 2003 Act' means the London Local Authorities and Transport for London Act 2003.

1.2 Part 75 applies to proceedings for the recovery of:
(1) increased penalty charges provided for in parking charge certificates issued under para. 6 of Schedule 6 to the 1991 Act;
(2) amounts payable by a person other than an authority under an adjudication of a parking adjudicator pursuant to s. 73 of the 1991 Act;
(3) increased penalty charges provided for in a charge certificate issued under para. 8 of sch. 1 to the 1996 Act (relating to a contravention or failure to comply with an order made under a provision referred to in s. 4(2) of that Act reserving all or part of a carriageway of a road as a bus lane);
(4) increased fixed penalties to which reg. 17(6) of the Vehicle Emissions (England) Regulations refers;
(5) amounts payable by a person other than an authority under an adjudication of an adjudicator pursuant to the schedule to the Road User Charging Regulations;
(6) increased penalty charges provided for in charge certificates issued under reg. 17 of the Road User Charging Regulations; and
(7) increased fixed penalties to which reg. 17(6) of the Vehicle Emissions (Wales) Regulations refers.

1.3 In Part 75 and this practice direction:
(1) 'authority' means the authority entitled to recover amounts due under the enactments referred to in para. 1.2;
(2) 'notice of the amount due' means, as the case may be:
(a) a parking charge certificate issued under para. 6 of sch. 6 to the 1991 Act;
(b) a charge certificate issued under para. 8 of sch. 1 to the 1996 Act;
(c) a fixed penalty notice issued under reg. 10 or reg. 13 of the Vehicle Emissions (England) Regulations;
(d) a charge certificate issued under reg. 17 of the Road User Charging Regulations; or
(e) a fixed penalty notice issued under reg. 10 or reg. 13 of the Vehicle Emissions (Wales) Regulations.
(3) 'order' means an order made under:
(a) para. 7 of sch. 6 to the 1991 Act;
(b) para. 9 of sch. 1 to the 1996 Act;
(c) s. 73(15) of the 1991 Act;
(d) reg. 21 of the Vehicle Emissions (England) Regulations;
(e) reg. 7 of the Road User Charging Regulations;
(f) reg. 18 of the Road User Charging Regulations; or
(g) reg. 21 of the Vehicle Emissions (Wales) Regulations;
(4) 'respondent' means:
(a) the person on whom the notice of the amount due was served; or

(b) the person (other than an authority) by whom the amount due under an adjudication is payable.

Traffic Enforcement Centre

2.1 All claims to which Part 75 applies must be started in the Traffic Enforcement Centre ('the Centre') at Northampton County Court.

Request

3.1 Where an order in respect of amounts payable by a person other than an authority under an adjudication pursuant to s. 73 of the 1991 Act or the schedule to the Road User Charging Regulations is sought, r. 75.3 applies with the necessary modifications and, in addition, the request must:
(1) state the date on which the adjudication was made;
(2) provide details of the order made on the adjudication; and
(3) certify the amount awarded by way of costs and that the amount remains unpaid.

Functions of Court Officer

4.1 A court officer may exercise the functions of:
(1) the district judge under:
(a) para. 8(4) and (5)(d) of sch. 6 to the 1991 Act;
(b) para. 10(4) and (5)(d) of sch. 1 to the 1996 Act; and
(c) reg. 19(4) and (5)(d) of the Road User Charging Regulations; and
(2) the court under:
(a) reg. 23(3) of the Vehicle Emissions (England) Regulations; and
(b) reg. 23(3) of the Vehicle Emissions (Wales) Regulations.

Application for Longer Period for Filing of Statutory Declaration

5.1 Paragraphs 5.2 to 5.5 apply where the respondent applies under:
(1) para. 8(3) of sch. 6 to the Road Traffic Act 1991;
(2) para. 10(3) of sch. 1 to the London Local Authorities Act 1996;
(3) reg. 23(3) of the Vehicle Emissions (England) Regulations;
(4) reg. 19(3) of the Road User Charging Regulations; or
(5) reg. 23(3) of the Vehicle Emissions (Wales) Regulations,
for an order allowing a longer period than 21 days for service of the statutory declaration.

5.2 The respondent must send to the Centre:
(1) a completed application notice (form PE 2 may be used); and
(2) a completed statutory declaration in form PE 3.
(Forms PE 2 and PE 3 can be obtained from the Centre at Northampton County Court, Bulk Centre, 21/27 St Katharine's Street, Northampton NN1 2LH. Telephone number: 08457 045007.)

5.3 The court will serve a copy of the application notice and a copy of the statutory declaration on the authority that obtained the court order seeking representations on the application.

5.4 A court officer will deal with the application without a hearing. The matter will not be dealt with until at least 14 days after the date on which the application notice and statutory declaration were served on the authority.

5.5 If the proceedings have been transferred to another court the Centre will transfer the application to that court.

5.6 Paragraphs 5.3 to 5.5 shall not apply where the court receives an application notice that is accompanied by a statutory declaration that is invalid by virtue of para. 8(2A) of sch. 6 to the 1991 Act as inserted by s. 15 of the 2003 Act.

Application to Review Order Made by Court Officer

6.1 Where any order is made by a court officer it will contain a statement of the right of either party to request a review of the decision by a district judge at a hearing.

6.2 Attention is drawn to r. 75.5(2) and (3).

Hearing

7.1 When a hearing is to be held, the proceedings will be transferred to the county court for the district in which the respondent's address for service is situated. This transfer is only for the purposes of holding the hearing and serving any orders made as a result of the hearing.

7.2 The respondent's address for service is his address for service shown on the last of the following documents filed at court by the respondent:
(1) the application notice or, if more than one, the latest application notice; and
(2) the appellant's notice.

7.3 The court where the hearing is held will serve any orders made as a result of the hearing before returning the papers to the Centre, or, if the proceedings have been transferred, to the court where the proceedings have been transferred.

7.4 Evidence at any hearing may be given orally or by witness statement.

Applications to Suspend a Warrant of Execution

8.1 Where:
(1) the respondent makes an application under para. 5; and
(2) before that application is determined, a warrant of execution is issued,
the local authority must suspend enforcement of the warrant of execution until the application for an extension order is determined.
(Rule 75.7(b) provides that, where a court order is revoked because a statutory declaration has been served, any execution issued on the order will cease to have effect.)

CPR Part 76 Proceedings under the Prevention of Terrorism Act 2005

1 APPLICATION OF THIS PART

76.1 Scope and Interpretation

r.76.1(4) **1.11**

(1) This Part contains rules about—
  (a) control order proceedings in the High Court; and
  (b) appeals to the Court of Appeal against an order of the High Court in such proceedings.

(2) In the case of proceedings brought by virtue of section 11(2) of the Act, the rules in this Part shall apply with any modification which the court considers necessary.

(3) In this Part—
  (a) 'the Act' means the Prevention of Terrorism Act 2005;
  (b) 'closed material' means any relevant material that the Secretary of State objects to disclosing to a relevant party;
  (c) 'control order proceedings' has the same meaning as in section 11(6) of the Act;
  (d) 'controlled person', has the same meaning as in section 15(1) of the Act;
  (e) 'legal representative' is to be construed in accordance with paragraph 11 of the Schedule to the Act;
  (f) 'open material' means any relevant material that the Secretary of State does not object to disclosing to a relevant party;
  (g) 'relevant law officer' has the same meaning as in paragraph 7(6) of the Schedule to the Act;
  (h) 'relevant material' has the same meaning as in paragraph 4(5) of the Schedule to the Act;
  (i) 'relevant party' has the same meaning as in paragraph 11 of the Schedule to the Act;
  (j) 'special advocate' means a person appointed under paragraph 7 of the Schedule to the Act.

(4) For the purposes of this Part, disclosure is contrary to the public interest if it is made contrary to the interests of national security, the international relations of the United Kingdom, the detection and prevention of crime, or in any other circumstances where disclosure is likely to harm the public interest.

76.2 Modification to the Overriding Objective

r.76.2 **1.11, 1.12**

(1) Where this Part applies, the overriding objective in Part 1, and so far as relevant any other rule, must be read and given effect in a way which is compatible with the duty set out in paragraph (2).
(2) The court must ensure that information is not disclosed contrary to the public interest.
(3) Subject to paragraph (2), the court must satisfy itself that the material available to it enables it properly to determine proceedings.

2 APPLICATIONS TO THE HIGH COURT RELATING TO DEROGATING CONTROL ORDERS

76.3 Scope of This Section

(1) This Section of this Part contains rules about applications relating to derogating control orders.
(2) Part 23 does not apply to an application made under this Section of this Part.

76.4 Applications for the Making of a Derogating Control Order

An application for the making of a derogating control order under section 4(1) of the Act must be made by the Secretary of State by filing with the court—
- (a) a statement of reasons to support the application for—
  - (i) making such an order, and
  - (ii) imposing each of the obligations to be imposed by that order;
- (b) all relevant material;
- (c) any written submissions; and
- (d) a draft of the order sought.

76.5 Directions for a Full Hearing on Notice

(1) When the court makes a derogating control order under section 4(3) of the Act, it must—
- (a) immediately fix a date, time and place for a further hearing at which the controlled person, his legal representative and a special advocate (if one has been appointed) can be present; and
- (b) unless the court otherwise directs, that date must be no later than 7 days from the date that the order is made.

(2) At the hearing referred to in paragraph (1)(a) the court must give directions—
- (a) for the holding of a full hearing under section 4(1)(b) of the Act to determine whether to confirm the control order (with or without modifications) or to revoke it; and
- (b) specifying the date and time by which the parties and special advocate must file and serve any written evidence or written submissions in accordance with rule 76.30.

(3) When giving directions under paragraph (2), the court must have regard to the need to expedite the full hearing.

76.6 Applications on Notice

(1) An application under section 4(9) for the renewal, or under section 7(4) of the Act, for the revocation of a control order or for the modification of obligations imposed by such an order, must be made in accordance with this rule.
(2) An application by the Secretary of State must be made by—
- (a) filing with the court—
  - (i) a statement of reasons to support the application,
  - (ii) all relevant material,
  - (iii) any written submissions, and
  - (iv) a draft of the order sought; and

(b) serving on the controlled person or his legal representative any open material.

(3) An application by the controlled person must be made by filing with the court and serving on the Secretary of State—
   (a) a statement of reasons to support the application;
   (b) any written evidence upon which he relies;
   (c) any written submissions; and
   (d) where appropriate, a draft of the order sought.

(4) If the controlled person wishes to oppose an application made under this rule, he must as soon as practicable file with the court, and serve on the Secretary of State, any written evidence and any written submissions upon which he relies.

(5) If the Secretary of State wishes to oppose an application made under this rule, he must as soon as practicable—
   (a) file with the court—
      (i) all relevant material, and
      (ii) any written submissions; and
   (b) serve on the controlled person any open material.

(Attention is drawn to rule 76.18 relating to the address for issuing proceedings in the High Court. Rules 76.28 and 76.29 will apply where any closed material is filed by the Secretary of State)

3 PERMISSION APPLICATIONS, REFERENCES AND APPEALS TO THE HIGH COURT RELATING TO NON-DEROGATING CONTROL ORDERS

76.7 Scope of This Section

This Section of this Part contains rules about—
   (a) applications under section 3(1)(a) of the Act (application for permission to make a non-derogating control order);
   (b) references under section 3(3) of the Act (reference of a non-derogating control order made without permission); and
   (c) appeals to the High Court under section 10 of the Act (appeals relating to non-derogating control orders).

76.8 Application for Permission to Make Non-derogating Control Order

An application under section 3(1)(a) for permission to make a non-derogating control order must be made by the Secretary of State by filing with the court—
   (a) a statement of reasons to support the application;
   (b) all relevant material;
   (c) any written submissions; and
   (d) the proposed control order.

76.9 References under Section 3(3) of the Act

(1) This rule applies where the Secretary of State makes a reference under section 3(3) of the Act (reference of a non-derogating control order).

(2) The Secretary of State must promptly file with the court—
   (a) a statement of the reasons for—
      (i) making the control order,
      (ii) imposing the obligations imposed by that order;
   (b) all relevant material; and
   (c) any written submissions.

76.10 Directions for Hearing on Application for Permission or on a Reference

(1) This rule applies where the court gives directions under section 3(2)(c) or (6)(b) or (c) of the Act.

(2) The court must immediately—
   (a) fix a date, time and place for a further hearing at which the controlled person, his legal representative and a special advocate (if one has been appointed) can be present; and

(b) unless the court otherwise directs, that date must be no later than 7 days from the date that the order is made.

(3) At the hearing referred to in paragraph (2), the court must give directions—
(a) for a hearing under section 3(10); and
(b) specifying the date and time by which the parties and special advocate must file and serve any written evidence or written submissions in accordance with rule 76.30.

(4) When giving directions under paragraph (3), the court must have regard to the need to expedite that hearing.

(Rules 76.28 and 76.29 will apply where any closed material is filed by the Secretary of State)

76.11 Appeals under Section 10 of the Act

This rule and rules 76.12 to 76.15 apply to an appeal under section 10 of the Act (appeals relating to a non-derogating control order).

76.12 Modification of Part 52 (Appeals)

(1) Part 52 (appeals) applies to an appeal under section 10 of the Act, subject to—
(a) rule 76.2;
(b) the rules in Section 5 of this Part; and
(c) the modifications set out in paragraphs (2) and (3) of this rule.

(2) The following rules do not apply to appeals under section 10 of the Act—
(a) rule 52.3 (permission);
(b) rule 52.4 (appellant's notice);
(c) rule 52.5 (respondent's notice); and
(d) rule 52.11 (hearing of appeals).

(3) Rule 52.2 (all parties to comply with the practice direction) applies, but the parties shall not be required to comply with paragraphs 5.6, 5.6A, 5.7, 5.9 and 5.10 of that practice direction.

76.13 Notice of Appeal

(1) The controlled person must give notice of appeal by—
(a) filing it with the court; and
(b) serving a copy of the notice and any accompanying documents on the Secretary of State.

(2) The notice of appeal must—
(a) set out the grounds of the appeal; and
(b) state the name and address of—
(i) the controlled person, and
(ii) any legal representative of that person.

(3) A notice of appeal may include an application for an order under rule 76.19 requiring anonymity.

(4) The notice of appeal must be filed with—
(a) a copy of the order that is the subject of the appeal;
(b) a copy of the Secretary of State's decision on an application for the revocation of the control order, or for the modification of an obligation imposed by such an order.

(Attention is drawn to rule 76.18 relating to the address for issuing proceedings in the High Court)

76.14 Time Limit for Appealing

(1) Subject to paragraph (2), the controlled person must give notice of appeal no later than 28 days after receiving notice of—
(a) the order that is the subject of the appeal; or
(b) the decision by the Secretary of State on an application for the revocation of the control order, or for the modification of an obligation imposed by such an order.

(2) In a case where the Secretary of State has failed to determine an application for the revocation of the control order, or for the modification of an obligation imposed by such an order, the controlled person must file the notice of appeal—
(a) no earlier than 28 days; and
(b) no later than 42 days;
after the date the application was made.

76.15 Secretary of State's Reply

If the Secretary of State wishes to oppose an appeal made under section 10 of the Act, he must no later than 14 days after he is served with the notice of appeal—
- (a) file with the court—
  - (i) all relevant material, and
  - (ii) any written submissions; and
- (b) serve on the controlled person any open material.

4 APPEALS TO THE COURT OF APPEAL

76.16 Modification of Part 52 (Appeals)

(1) Part 52 (appeals) applies to an appeal to the Court of Appeal against an order of the High Court in control order proceedings, subject to—
- (a) rule 76.2;
- (b) the rules in Section 5 of this Part; and
- (c) paragraphs (2) and (3) of this rule.

(2) The following rules do not apply to appeals to the Court of Appeal—
- (a) rule 52.4(1) (appellant's notice); and
- (b) rule 52.5 (respondent's notice); but

the provisions of rules 76.13 and 76.15 shall apply with appropriate modifications.

(3) Rule 52.2 (all parties to comply with the practice direction) applies, but the parties shall not be required to comply with paragraphs 5.6, 5.6A, 5.7, 6.3A, 15.2, 15.3, 15.4 and 15.6 of that practice direction.

5 GENERAL PROVISIONS

76.17 Scope of This Section

This Section of this Part applies to—
- (a) control order proceedings in the High Court; and
- (b) appeals to the Court of Appeal against an order of the High Court in such proceedings.

76.18 Address for Issuing Proceedings in the High Court

Any control order proceedings must be issued at the Administrative Court Office, Room C315, Royal Courts of Justice, Strand, London, WC2A 2LL.

76.19 Applications for Anonymity

(1) The controlled person or the Secretary of State may apply for an order requiring the anonymity of the controlled person.

(2) An application under paragraph (1) may be made at any time, irrespective of whether any control order proceedings have been commenced.

(3) An application may be made without notice to the other party.

(4) References in this rule to an order requiring anonymity for the controlled person are to be construed in accordance with paragraph 5(3) of the Schedule to the Act.

76.20 Notification of Hearing

Unless the court orders otherwise, it must serve notice of the date, time and place fixed for any hearing on—
- (a) every party, whether or not entitled to attend that hearing; and
- (b) if one has been appointed for the purposes of the hearing, the special advocate or those instructing him.

76.21 Hearings

(1) The following proceedings must be determined at a hearing—
- (a) a hearing pursuant to directions given under section 4(1)(b) of the Act (derogating control orders);

(b) a hearing pursuant to directions given under sections 3(2)(c) or (6)(b) or (c) of the Act (non-derogating control orders);
(c) an appeal under section 10 of the Act (appeal relating to a non-derogating control order);
(d) an appeal to the Court of Appeal from an order of the High Court made in any of the above proceedings; and
(e) a hearing under rule 76.29(2) (consideration of Secretary of State's objection).

(2) Paragraph (1)(c) and (d) do not apply where—
(a) the appeal is withdrawn by the controlled person;
(b) the Secretary of State consents to the appeal being allowed; or
(c) the controlled person is outside the United Kingdom or it is impracticable to give him notice of a hearing and, in either case, he is unrepresented.

76.22 Hearings in Private

(1) If the court considers it necessary for any relevant party and his legal representative to be excluded from a hearing or part of a hearing in order to secure that information is not disclosed contrary to the public interest, it must—
(a) direct accordingly; and
(b) conduct the hearing, or that part of it from which the relevant party and his legal representative are excluded, in private.

(2) The court may conduct a hearing or part of a hearing in private for any other good reason.

76.23 Appointment of a Special Advocate

(1) Subject to paragraph (2), the Secretary of State must immediately give notice of the proceedings to the relevant law officer upon—
(a) making an application under section 4(1) of the Act (relating to a derogating control order);
(b) making an application under section 3(1)(a) of the Act (application for permission to make a non-derogating control order);
(c) making a reference under section 3(3) of the Act (reference of a non-derogating control order made without permission); or
(d) being served with a copy of any application, claim, or notice of appeal in proceedings to which this Part applies.

(2) Paragraph (1) applies unless—
(a) the Secretary of State does not intend to—
(i) oppose the appeal or application; or
(ii) withhold closed material from a relevant party; or
(b) a special advocate has already been appointed to represent the interests of the relevant party in the proceedings and that special advocate is not prevented from communicating with that party by virtue of rule 76.25.

(3) Where notice is given to the relevant law officer under paragraph (1), the relevant law officer may appoint a special advocate to represent the interests of the relevant party in the proceedings.

(4) Where any proceedings to which this Part apply are pending but no special advocate has been appointed, a relevant party or the Secretary of State may request the relevant law officer to appoint a special advocate.

76.24 Functions of Special Advocate

The functions of a special advocate are to represent the interests of a relevant party by—
(a) making submissions to the court at any hearings from which the relevant party and his legal representatives are excluded;
(b) cross-examining witnesses at any such hearings; and
(c) making written submissions to the court.

76.25 Special Advocate: Communicating about Proceedings

(1) The special advocate may communicate with the relevant party or his legal representative at any time before the Secretary of State serves closed material on him.

(2) After the Secretary of State serves closed material on the special advocate, the special advocate must not communicate with any person about any matter connected with the proceedings,

except in accordance with paragraph (3) or a direction of the court pursuant to a request under paragraph (4).

(3) The special advocate may, without directions from the court, communicate about the proceedings with—
- (a) the court;
- (b) the Secretary of State, or any person acting for him;
- (c) the relevant law officer, or any person acting for him; or
- (d) any other person, except for the relevant party or his legal representative, with whom it is necessary for administrative purposes for him to communicate about matters not connected with the substance of the proceedings.

(4) The special advocate may request directions from the court authorising him to communicate with the relevant party or his legal representative or with any other person.

(5) Where the special advocate makes a request for directions under paragraph (4)—
- (a) the court must notify the Secretary of State of the request; and
- (b) the Secretary of State must, within a period specified by the court, file with the court and serve on the special advocate notice of any objection which he has to the proposed communication, or to the form in which it is proposed to be made.

(6) Paragraph (2) does not prohibit the relevant party from communicating with the special advocate after the Secretary of State has served material on him as mentioned in paragraph (1), but—
- (a) the relevant party may only communicate with the special advocate through a legal representative in writing; and
- (b) the special advocate must not reply to the communication other than in accordance with directions of the court, except that he may without such directions send a written acknowledgment of receipt to the legal representative of the relevant party.

76.26 Modification of the General Rules of Evidence and Disclosure

(1) Part 31 (disclosure and inspection of documents), Part 32 (evidence) and Part 33 (miscellaneous rules about evidence) do not apply to any proceedings to which this Part applies.

(2) Subject to the other rules in this Part, the evidence of a witness may be given either—
- (a) orally, before the court; or;
- (b) in writing, in which case it shall be given in such manner and at such time as the court directs.

(3) The court may also receive evidence in documentary or any other form.

(4) The court may receive evidence that would not, but for this rule, be admissible in a court of law.

(5) Every party shall be entitled to adduce evidence and to cross-examine witnesses during any part of a hearing from which he and his legal representative are not excluded.

(6) The court may require a witness to give evidence on oath.

76.27 Filing and Service of Relevant Material

The Secretary of State is required to make a reasonable search for relevant material and to file and serve that material in accordance with the rules in this Part.

76.28 Closed Material

(1) The Secretary of State—
- (a) must apply to the court for permission to withhold closed material from a relevant party or his legal representative in accordance with this rule; and
- (b) may not rely on closed material at a hearing on notice unless a special advocate has been appointed to represent the interests of the relevant party.

(2) The Secretary of State must file with the court and serve, at such time as the court directs, on the special advocate—
- (a) the closed material;
- (b) a statement of his reasons for withholding that material from the relevant party; and
- (c) if he considers it possible to summarise that material without disclosing information contrary to the public interest, a summary of that material in a form which can be served on the relevant party.

(3) The Secretary of State may at any time amend or supplement material filed under this rule, but only with—
   (a) the agreement of the special advocate; or
   (b) the permission of the court.

76.29 Consideration of Secretary of State's Objection

(1) This rule applies where the Secretary of State has—
   (a) objected under rule 76.25(5)(b) to a proposed communication by the special advocate; or
   (b) applied under rule 76.28 for permission to withhold closed material.
(2) The court must fix a hearing for the Secretary of State and the special advocate to make oral representations, unless—
   (a) the special advocate gives notice to the court that he does not challenge the objection or application;
   (b) the court has previously considered—
      (i) an objection under rule 76.25(5)(b), or
      (ii) an application under rule 76.28(1) for permission to withhold the same or substantially the same material, and
      is satisfied that it would be just to uphold that objection or to give permission without a hearing; or
   (c) the Secretary of State and the special advocate consent to the court deciding the issue without a hearing.
(3) If the special advocate does not challenge the objection or the application, he must give notice of that fact to the court and the Secretary of State within 14 days, or such other period as the court may direct, after the Secretary of State serves on him a notice under rule 76.25(5)(b) or material under rule 76.28(2).
(4) Where the court fixes a hearing under this rule, the Secretary of State and the special advocate must before the hearing file with the court a schedule identifying the issues which cannot be agreed between them, which must—
   (a) list the items or issues in dispute;
   (b) give brief reasons for their contentions on each; and
   (c) set out any proposals for the court to resolve the issues in contention.
(5) A hearing under this rule shall take place in the absence of the relevant party and his legal representative.
(6) Where the court gives permission to the Secretary of State to withhold closed material, the court must—
   (a) consider whether to direct the Secretary of State to serve a summary of that material on the relevant party or his legal representative; but
   (b) ensure that no such summary contains information or other material the disclosure of which would be contrary to the public interest.
(7) Where the court has not given permission to the Secretary of State to withhold closed material from, or has directed the Secretary of State to serve a summary of that material on, a relevant party or his legal representative—
   (a) the Secretary of State shall not be required to serve that material or summary; but
   (b) if he does not do so, at a hearing on notice the court may—
      (i) if it considers that the material or anything that is required to be summarised might be of assistance to the relevant party in relation to a matter under consideration by the court, direct that the matter be withdrawn from its consideration, and
      (ii) in any other case, direct that the Secretary of State shall not rely in the proceedings on that material or (as the case may be) on what is required to be summarised.
(8) The court must give permission to the Secretary of State to withhold closed material where it considers that the disclosure of that material would be contrary to the public interest.

76.30 Order of Filing and Serving Material and Written Submissions

Subject to any directions given by the court, the parties must file and serve any material and written submissions, and the special advocate must file and serve any written submissions, in the following order—

(a) the Secretary of State must file with the court all relevant material;
(b) the Secretary of State must serve on—
 (i) the relevant party or his legal representative; and
 (ii) the special advocate (as soon as one is appointed) or those instructing him,
 any open material;
(c) the relevant party must file with the court and serve on the Secretary of State and special advocate (if one is appointed) or those instructing him any written evidence which he wishes the court to take into account at the hearing;
(d) the Secretary of State must file with the court any further relevant material;
(e) the Secretary of State must serve on—
 (i) the relevant party or his legal representative, and
 (ii) the special advocate (as soon as one is appointed) or those instructing him,
 any open material filed with the court under paragraph (d);
(f) the Secretary of State must serve on the special advocate (if one has been appointed) any closed material;
(g) the parties and the special advocate (if one has been appointed) must file and serve any written submissions as directed by the court.

(Rules 76.28 and 76.29 will apply where any closed material is filed by the Secretary of State)

76.31 Failure to Comply with Directions

(1) Where a party or the special advocate fails to comply with a direction of the court, the court may serve on him a notice which states—
 (a) the respect in which he has failed to comply with the direction;
 (b) a time limit for complying with the direction; and
 (c) that the court may proceed to determine the proceedings before it, on the material available to it, if the party or the special advocate fails to comply with the relevant direction within the time specified.
(2) Where a party or special advocate fails to comply with such a notice, the court may proceed in accordance with paragraph (1)(c).

76.32 Judgments

(1) When the court gives judgment in any proceedings to which this Part applies, it may withhold any or part of its reasons if and to the extent that it is not possible to give reasons without disclosing information contrary to the public interest.
(2) Where the judgment of the court does not include the full reasons for its decision, the court must serve on the Secretary of State and the special advocate a separate written judgment including those reasons.

76.33 Application by Secretary of State for Reconsideration of Decision

(1) This rule applies where the court proposes, in any proceedings to which this Part applies, to serve notice on a relevant party of any—
 (a) order or direction made or given in the absence of the Secretary of State; or
 (b) any judgment.
(2) Before the court serves any such notice on the relevant party, it must first serve notice on the Secretary of State of its intention to do so.
(3) The Secretary of State may, within 5 days of being served with notice under paragraph (2), apply to the court to reconsider the terms of the order or direction or to review the terms of the proposed judgment if he considers that—
 (a) his compliance with the order or direction; or
 (b) the notification to the relevant party of any matter contained in the judgment, order or direction;
 would cause information to be disclosed contrary to the public interest.
(4) Where the Secretary of State makes an application under paragraph (3), he must at the same time serve a copy of it on the special advocate, if one has been appointed.
(5) Rule 76.29 (except for paragraphs (6) and (7)) shall, if a special advocate has been appointed,

apply with any necessary modifications to the consideration of an application under paragraph (3) of this rule.

(6) The court must not serve notice on the relevant party as mentioned in paragraph (1) before the time for the Secretary of State to make an application under paragraph (3) has expired.

76.34 Supply of Court Documents

Unless the court otherwise directs, rule 5.4 (supply of court documents — general) does not apply to any proceedings to which this Part applies.

Glossary

Scope

This glossary is a guide to the meaning of certain legal expressions as used in these Rules, but it does not give the expressions any meaning in the Rules which they do not otherwise have in the law.

Expression	Meaning
Affidavit	A written, sworn statement of evidence.
Alternative dispute resolution	Collective description of methods of resolving disputes otherwise than through the normal trial process.
Base rate	The interest rate set by the Bank of England which is used as the basis for other banks' rates.
Contribution	A right of someone to recover from a third person all or part of the amount which he himself is liable to pay.
Counterclaim	A claim brought by a defendant in response to the claimant's claim, which is included in the same proceedings as the claimant's claim.
Cross-examination (and see 'evidence-in-chief')	Questioning of a witness by a party other than the party who called the witness.
Damages	A sum of money awarded by the court as compensation to the claimant.
• aggravated damages	Additional damages which the court may award as compensation for the defendant's objectionable behaviour.
• exemplary damages	Damages which go beyond compensating for actual loss and are awarded to show the court's disapproval of the defendant's behaviour.
Defence of tender before claim	A defence that, before the claimant started proceedings, the defendant unconditionally offered to the claimant the amount due or, if no specified amount is claimed, an amount sufficient to satisfy the claim.
Evidence-in-chief (and see 'cross-examination')	The evidence given by a witness for the party who called him.
Indemnity	A right of someone to recover from a third party the whole amount which he himself is liable to pay.
Injunction	A court order prohibiting a person from doing something or requiring a person to do something.
Joint liability (and see 'several liability')	Parties who are jointly liable share a single liability and each party can be held liable for the whole of it.
Limitation period	The period within which a person who has a right to claim against another person must start court proceedings to establish that right. The expiry of the period may be a defence to the claim.
List	Cases are allocated to different lists depending on the subject matter of the case. The lists are used for administrative purposes and may also have their own procedures and judges.
Official copy	A copy of an official document, supplied and marked as such by the office which issued the original.
Practice form	Form to be used for a particular purpose in proceedings, the form and purpose being specified by a practice direction.
Pre-action protocol	Statements of understanding between legal practitioners and others about pre-action practice and which are approved by a relevant practice direction.

Expression	Meaning
Privilege	The right of a party to refuse to disclose a document or produce a document or to refuse to answer questions on the ground of some special interest recognised by law.
Seal	A seal is a mark which the court puts on a document to indicate that the document has been issued by the court.
Service	Steps required by rules of court to bring documents used in court proceedings to a person's attention.
Set aside	Cancelling a judgment or order or a step taken by a party in the proceedings.
Several liability (and see 'joint liability')	A person who is severally liable with others may remain liable for the whole claim even where judgment has been obtained against the others.
Stay	A stay imposes a halt on proceedings, apart from taking any steps allowed by the Rules or the terms of the stay. Proceedings can be continued if a stay is lifted.
Strike out	Striking out means the court ordering written material to be deleted so that it may no longer be relied upon.
Without prejudice	Negotiations with a view to a settlement are usually conducted 'without prejudice', which means that the circumstances in which the content of those negotiations may be revealed to the court are very restricted.

CPR Schedule 1

sch. 1 **1.5, 12.1** [For commentary on a specific RSC order, please refer to the cross-references after the title of the RSC rule.]

RSC ORDER 17 — INTERPLEADER

ord. 17 **14.15**

Rule 1 Entitlement to Relief by Way of Interpleader

(1) Where–
  (a) a person is under a liability in respect of a debt or in respect of any money, goods or chattels and he is, or expects to be, sued for or in respect of that debt or money or those goods or chattels by two or more persons making adverse claims thereto; or
  (b) claim is made to any money, goods or chattels taken or intended to be taken by a sheriff in execution under any process, or to the proceeds or value of any such goods or chattels, by a person other than the person against whom the process is issued,

the person under liability as mentioned in sub-paragraph (a) or (subject to rule 2) the sheriff, may apply to the court for relief by way of interpleader.

(2) References in this Order to a sheriff shall be construed as including references to—
  (a) an individual authorised to act as an enforcement officer under the Courts Act 2003; and
  (b) any other officer charged with the execution of process by or under the authority of the High Court.

Rule 2 Claim to Goods, etc., Taken in Execution

r.2(1)–(4) **14.16**

(1) Any person making a claim to or in respect of any money, goods or chattels taken or intended to be taken in execution under process of the court, or to the proceeds or value of any such goods or chattels, must give notice of his claim to the sheriff charged with the execution of the process and must include in his notice a statement of his address, and that address shall be his address for service.

(2) On receipt of a claim made under this rule the sheriff must forthwith give notice thereof to the execution creditor and the execution creditor must, within seven days after receiving the notice, give notice to the sheriff informing him whether he admits or disputes the claim. An execution creditor who gives notice in accordance with this paragraph admitting a claim shall only be liable to the sheriff for any fees and expenses incurred by the sheriff before receipt of that notice.

(3) Where—
  (a) the sheriff receives a notice from an execution creditor under paragraph (2) disputing a claim, or the execution creditor fails, within the period mentioned in that paragraph, to give the required notice; and
  (b) the claim made under this rule is not withdrawn,

the sheriff may apply to the court for relief under this order.

(4) A sheriff who receives a notice from an execution creditor under paragraph (2) admitting a claim made under this rule shall withdraw from possession of the money, goods or chattels claimed and may apply to the court for relief under this order of the following kind, that is to say, an order restraining the bringing of a claim against him for or in respect of his having taken possession of that money or those goods or chattels.

Rule 2A Claim in Respect of Goods Protected from Seizure

(1) Where a judgment debtor whose goods have been seized, or are intended to be seized, by a sheriff under a writ of execution claims that such goods are not liable to execution by virtue of section 138(3A) of the Act, he must within 5 days of the seizure give notice in writing to the sheriff identifying all those goods in respect of which he makes such a claim and the grounds of such claim in respect of each item.

(2) Upon receipt of a notice of claim under paragraph (1), the sheriff must forthwith give notice thereof to the execution creditor and to any person who has made a claim to, or in respect of, the goods under rule 2(1) and the execution creditor and any person who has made claim must, within 7 days of receipt of such notice, inform the sheriff in writing whether he admits or disputes the judgment debtor's claim in respect of each item.

(3) The sheriff shall withdraw from possession of any goods in respect of which the judgment debtor's claim is admitted or if the execution creditor or any person claiming under rule 2(1) fails to notify him in accordance with paragraph (2) and the sheriff shall so inform the parties in writing.

(4) Where the sheriff receives notice from—
 (a) the execution creditor; or
 (b) any such person to whom notice was given under paragraph (2),
 that the claim or any part thereof is disputed, he must forthwith seek the directions of the court and may include therein an application for an order restraining the bringing of any claim against him for, or in respect of, his having seized any of those goods or his having failed so to do.

(5) The sheriff's application for directions under paragraph (4) shall be made by an application in accordance with CPR Part 23 and, on the hearing of the application, the court may—
 (a) determine the judgment debtor's claim summarily; or
 (b) give such directions for the determination of any issue raised by such claim as may be just.

(6) A Master and a district judge of a district registry shall have power to make an order of the kind referred to in paragraph (4) and the reference to Master shall be construed in accordance with rule 4.

Rule 3 Mode of Application

r.3(1)–(2) **14.17** r.3(6) **14.17**
r.3(4) **14.17**

(1) An application for relief under this order must be made by claim form unless made in an existing claim, in which case it must be made by accordance with CPR Part 23.

(2) Where the applicant is a sheriff who has withdrawn from possession of money, goods or chattels taken in execution and who is applying for relief under rule 2(4) the claim form must be served on any person who made a claim under that rule to or in respect of that money or those goods or chattels, and that person may attend the hearing of the application.

(4) Subject to paragraph (5) a claim form or application notice under this rule must be supported by evidence that the applicant—
 (a) claims no interest in the subject-matter in dispute other than for charges or costs;
 (b) does not collude with any of the claimants to that subject-matter; and
 (c) is willing to pay or transfer that subject-matter into court or to dispose of it as the court may direct.

(5) Where the applicant is a sheriff, he shall not provide such evidence as is referred to in paragraph (4) unless directed by the court to do so.

(6) Any person who makes a claim under rule 2 and who is served with a claim form under this rule shall within 14 days serve on the execution creditor and the sheriff a witness statement or affidavit specifying any money and describing any goods and chattels claimed and setting out the grounds upon which such claim is based.

(7) Where the applicant is a sheriff a claim form under this rule must give notice of the requirement in paragraph (6).

Rule 4 To Whom Sheriff May Apply for Relief

r.4 **14.16**

An application to the court for relief under this order may, if the applicant is a sheriff, be made—
(a) where the claim in question is proceeding in the Royal Courts of Justice, to a Master or, if the execution to which the application relates has been or is to be levied in the district of a District Registry, either to a Master or to the district judge of that Registry;
(b) where the claim in question is proceeding in a District Registry, to the district judge of that Registry or, if such execution has been or is to be levied in the district of some other District

Registry or outside the district of any District Registry, either to the said district judge or to the district judge of that other registry or to a Master as the case may be.

Where the claim in question is proceeding in the Admiralty Court or the Family Division, references in this rule to a Master shall be construed as references to the Admiralty Registrar or to a Registrar of that Division.

Rule 5 Powers of Court Hearing Claim

r.5(1)(a) **14.18** r.5(2)–(3) **14.18**

(1) Where on the hearing of a claim under this order all the persons by whom adverse claims to the subject-matter in dispute (hereafter in this Order referred to as 'the interpleader claimants') appear, the court may order—
   (a) that any interpleader claimant be made a defendant in any claim pending with respect to the subject-matter in dispute in substitution for or in addition to the applicant for relief under this order; or
   (b) that an issue between the interpleader claimants be stated and tried and may direct which of the interpleader claimants is to be claimant and which defendant.

(2) Where—
   (a) the applicant under this order is a sheriff; or
   (b) all the interpleader claimants consent or any of them so requests; or
   (c) the question at issue between the interpleader claimants is a question of law and the facts are not in dispute,

   the court may summarily determine the question at issue between the interpleader claimants and make an order accordingly on such terms as may be just.

(3) Where an interpleader claimant, having been duly served with a claim form under this order, does not appear at the hearing or, having appeared, fails or refuses to comply with an order made in the proceedings, the court may make an order declaring the interpleader claimant, and all persons claiming under him, for ever barred from prosecuting his claim against the applicant for such relief and all persons claiming under him, but such an order shall not affect the rights of the interpleader claimants as between themselves.

Rule 6 Power to Order Sale of Goods Taken in Execution

r.6–r. 11 **14.18**

Where an application for relief under this order is made by a sheriff who has taken possession of any goods or chattels in execution under any process, and an interpleader claimant alleges that he is entitled, under a bill of sale or otherwise. to the goods or chattels by way of security for debt, the court may order those goods or chattels or any part thereof to be sold and may direct that the proceeds of sale be applied in such manner and on such terms as may be just and as may be specified in the order.

Rule 7 Power to Stay Proceedings

Where a defendant to a claim applies for relief under this Order in the claim, the court may by order stay all further proceedings in the claim.

Rule 8 Other Powers

(1) Subject to the foregoing rules of this Order, the court may in or for the purposes of any interpleader proceedings make such order as to costs or any other matter as it thinks just.

(2) Where the interpleader claimant fails to appear at the hearing, the Court may direct that the sheriff's and execution creditor's costs shall be assessed by a master or, where the hearing was heard in a district registry, by a district judge of that registry and the following CPR rules shall apply—
   (a) 44.4 (basis of assessment);
   (b) 44.5 (factors to be taken into account in deciding the amount of costs);
   (c) 48.4 (limitations on court's power to award costs in favour of trustee or personal representative); and
   (d) 48.6 (litigants in person).

(3) Where the claim in question is proceeding in the Admiralty Court or the Family Division, references in this rule to a Master shall be construed as references to the Admiralty Registrar or to a Registrar of that Division.

Rule 9 One Order in Several Proceedings

Where the Court considers it necessary or expedient to make an order in any interpleader proceedings in several proceedings pending in several Divisions, or before different judges of the same Division, the court may make such an order; and the order shall be entitled in all those causes or matters and shall be binding on all the parties to them.

Rule 10 Disclosure

CPR Parts 31 and 18 shall, with the necessary modifications, apply in relation to an interpleader issue as they apply in relation to any other proceedings.

Rule 11 Trial of Interpleader Issue

r.11(1) **14.18**

(1) CPR Part 39 shall, with the necessary modifications, apply to the trial of an interpleader issue as it applies to the trial of a claim.
(2) The court by whom an interpleader issue is tried may give such judgment or make such order as finally to dispose of all questions arising in the interpleader proceedings.

RSC ORDER 45 — ENFORCEMENT OF JUDGMENTS AND ORDERS: GENERAL

ord. 45 **76.1**, **76.38**

Rule 1 Enforcement of Judgment, etc., for Payment of Money

(4) In this Order references to any writ shall be construed as including references to any further writ in aid of the first mentioned writ.

Rule 1A Interpretation

In this Order, and in RSC Orders 46 and 47—
(a) 'enforcement officer' means an individual who is authorised to act as an enforcement officer under the Courts Act 2003; and
(b) 'relevant enforcement officer' means—
 (i) in relation to a writ of execution which is directed to a single enforcement officer, that officer;
 (ii) in relation to a writ of execution which is directed to two or more enforcement officers, the officer to whom the writ is allocated.

Rule 2 Notice of Seizure

When first executing a writ of fieri facias, the Sheriff or his officer or the relevant enforcement officer shall deliver to the debtor or leave at each place where execution is levied a notice in Form No. 55 in the relevant Practice Direction informing the debtor of the execution.

Rule 3 Enforcement of Judgment for Possession of Land

r.3(1)(c) **78.21**

(1) Subject to the provisions of these rules, a judgment or order for the giving of possession of land may be enforced by one or more of the following means, that is to say—
 (a) writ of possession;
 (b) in a case in which rule 5 applies, an order of committal;
 (c) in such a case, writ of sequestration.
(2) A writ of possession to enforce a judgment or order for the giving of possession of any land shall not be issued without the permission of the court except where the judgment or order was given or made in proceedings by a mortgagee or mortgagor or by any person having the right to foreclose or redeem any mortgage, being proceedings in which there is a claim for—
 (a) payment of moneys secured by the mortgage;
 (b) sale of the mortgaged property;

(c) foreclosure;
(d) delivery of possession (whether before or after foreclosure or without foreclosure) to the mortgagee by the mortgagor or by any other person who is alleged to be in possession of the property;
(e) redemption;
(f) reconveyance of the land or its release from the security; or
(g) delivery of possession by the mortgagee.

(2A) In paragraph (2) 'mortgage' includes a legal or equitable mortgage and a legal or equitable charge, and reference to a mortgagor, a mortgagee and mortgaged land is to be interpreted accordingly.

(3) Such permission as is referred to in paragraph (2) shall not be granted unless it is shown—
(a) that every person in actual possession of the whole or any part of the land has received such notice of the proceedings as appears to the court sufficient to enable him to apply to the court for any relief to which he may be entitled; and
(b) if the operation of the judgment or order is suspended by subsection (2) of section 16 of the Landlord and Tenant Act, 1954, that the applicant has not received notice in writing from the tenant that he desires that the provisions of paragraphs (a) and (b) of that subsection shall have effect.

(4) A writ of possession may include provision for enforcing the payment of any money adjudged or ordered to be paid by the judgment or order which is to be enforced by the writ.

Rule 4 Enforcement of Judgment for Delivery of Goods

r.4(1)(c) **78.21**

(1) Subject to the provisions of these rules, a judgment or order for the delivery of any goods which does not give a person against whom the judgment is given or order made the alternative of paying the assessed value of the goods may be enforced by one or more of the following means, that is to say—
(a) writ of delivery to recover the goods without alternative provision for recovery of the assessed value thereof (hereafter in this rule referred to as a 'writ of specific delivery');
(b) in a case in which rule 5 applies, an order of committal;
(c) in such a case, writ of sequestration.

(2) Subject to the provisions of these rules, a judgment or order for the delivery of any goods or payment of their assessed value may be enforced by one or more of the following means, that is to say—
(a) writ of delivery to recover the goods or their assessed value;
(b) by order of the court, writ of specific delivery;
(c) in a case in which rule 5 applies, writ of sequestration.

An application for an order under sub-paragraph (b) shall be made in accordance with CPR Part 23, which must be served on the defendant against whom the judgment or order sought to be enforced was given or made.

(3) A writ of specific delivery, and a writ of delivery to recover any goods or their assessed value, may include provision for enforcing the payment of any money adjudged or ordered to be paid by the judgment or order which is to be enforced by the writ.

(4) A judgment or order for the payment of the assessed value of any goods may be enforced by the same means as any other judgment or order for the payment of money.

Rule 5 Enforcement of Judgment to Do or Abstain from Doing Any Act

r.5(1) **78.3**

(1) Where—
(a) a person required by a judgment or order to do an act within a time specified in the judgment or order refuses or neglects to do it within that time or, as the case may be, within that time as extended or abridged under a court order or CPR rule 2.11; or
(b) a person disobeys a judgment or order requiring him to abstain from doing an act,

then, subject to the provisions of these rules, the judgment or order may be enforced by one or more of the following means, that is to say—

(i) with the permission of the court, a writ of sequestration against the property of that person;
(ii) where that person is a body corporate, with the permission of the court, a writ of sequestration against the property of any director or other officer of the body;
(iii) subject to the provisions of the Debtors Act 1869 and 1878, an order of committal against that person or, where that person is a body corporate, against any such officer.

(2) Where a judgment or order requires a person to do an act within a time therein specified and an order is subsequently made under rule 6 requiring the act to be done within some other time, references in paragraph (1) of this rule to a judgment or order shall be construed as references to the order made under rule 6.

(3) Where under any judgment or order requiring the delivery of any goods the person liable to execution has the alternative of paying the assessed value of the goods, the judgment or order shall not be enforceable by order of committal under paragraph (1), but the court may, on the application of the person entitled to enforce the judgment or order, make an order requiring the first mentioned person to deliver the goods to the applicant within a time specified in the order, and that order may be so enforced.

Rule 6 Judgment, etc. Requiring Act to Be Done: Order Fixing Time for Doing It

(1) Notwithstanding that a judgment or order requiring a person to do an act specifies a time within which the act is to be done, the court shall have power to make an order requiring the act to be done within another time, being such time after service of that order, or such other time, as may be specified therein.

(2) Where a judgment or order requiring a person to do an act does not specify a time within which the act is to be done, the court shall have power subsequently to make an order requiring the act to be done within such time after service of that order, or such other time, as may be specified therein.

(3) An application for an order under this rule must be made in accordance with CPR Part 23 and the application notice must, be served on the person required to do the act in question.

Rule 7 Service of Copy of Judgment, etc., Prerequisite to Enforcement under Rule 5

r.7(2)–(4) **78.4** r.7(6)–(7) **78.4**

(1) In this rule references to an order shall be construed as including references to a judgment.

(2) Subject to paragraphs (6) and (7) of this rule, an order shall not be enforced under rule 5 unless—
(a) a copy of the order has been served personally on the person required to do or abstain from doing the act in question; and
(b) in the case of an order requiring a person to do an act, the copy has been so served before the expiration of the time within which he was required to do the act.

(3) Subject as aforesaid, an order requiring a body corporate to do or abstain from doing an act shall not be enforced as mentioned in rule 5(1)(b)(ii) or (iii) unless—
(a) a copy of the order has also been served personally on the officer against whose property permission is sought to issue a writ of sequestration or against whom an order of committal is sought; and
(b) in the case of an order requiring the body corporate to do an act, the copy has been so served before the expiration of the time within which the body was required to do the act.

(4) There must be prominently displayed on the front of the copy of an order served under this rule a warning to the person on whom the copy is served that disobedience to the order would be a contempt of court punishable by imprisonment, or (in the case of an order requiring a body corporate to do or abstain from doing an act) punishable by sequestration of the assets of the body corporate and by imprisonment of any individual responsible.

(5) With the copy of an order required to be served under this rule, being an order requiring a person to do an act, there must also be served a copy of any order or agreement under CPR rule 2.11 extending or abridging the time for doing the act and, where the first-mentioned order was made under rule 5(3) or 6 of this Order, a copy of the previous Order requiring the act to be done.

(6) An order requiring a person to abstain from doing an act may be enforced under rule 5 notwithstanding that service of a copy of the order has not been effected in accordance with this rule if the court is satisfied that pending such service, the person against whom or against whose property is sought to enforce the order has had notice thereof either—
(a) by being present when the order was made; or
(b) by being notified of the terms of the order, whether by telephone, telegram or otherwise.

(7) The court may dispense with service of a copy of an order under this rule if it thinks it just to do so.

Rule 8 Court May Order Act to Be Done at Expense of Disobedient Party

If a mandatory order, an injunction or a judgment or order for the specific performance of a contract is not complied with, then, without prejudice to its powers under section 39 of the Act and its powers to punish the disobedient party for contempt, the court may direct that the act required to be done may, so far as practicable, be done by the party by whom the order or judgment was obtained or some other person appointed by the court, at the cost of the disobedient party, and upon the act being done the expenses incurred may be ascertained in such manner as the court may direct and execution may issue against the disobedient party for the amount so ascertained and for costs.

Rule 11 Matters Occurring after Judgment: Stay of Execution, etc.

Without prejudice to Order 47, rule 1, a party against whom a judgment has been given or an order made may apply to the court for a stay of execution of the judgment or order or other relief on the ground of matters which have occurred since the date of the judgment or order, and the court may by order grant such relief, and on such terms, as it thinks just.

Rule 12 Forms of Writs

(1) A writ of fieri facias must be in such of the Forms Nos. 53 to 63 in the relevant practice direction as is appropriate in the particular case.

(2) A writ of delivery must be in Form No. 64 or 65 in the relevant practice direction, whichever is appropriate.

(3) A writ of possession must be in Form No. 66 or 66A in the relevant practice direction, whichever is appropriate.

(4) A writ of sequestration must be in Form No. 67 in the relevant practice direction.

RSC ORDER 46 — WRITS OF EXECUTION: GENERAL

ord.46 **76.1, 76.38, 78.21**

Rule 1 Definition

In this Order, unless the context otherwise requires, 'writ of execution' includes a writ of fieri facias, a writ of possession, a writ of delivery, a writ of sequestration and any further writ in aid of any of the aforementioned writs.

Rule 2 When Permission to Issue Any Writ of Execution Is Necessary

r.2 **76.7, 78.22**

(1) A writ of execution to enforce a judgment or order may not issue without the permission of the court in the following cases, that is to say—
(a) where 6 years or more have elapsed since the date of the judgment or order;
(b) where any change has taken place, whether by death or otherwise, in the parties entitled or liable to execution under the judgment or order;
(c) where the judgment or order is against the assets of a deceased person coming to the hands of his executors or administrators after the date of the judgment or order, and it is sought to issue execution against such assets;
(d) where under the judgment or order any person is entitled to a remedy subject to the fulfilment of any condition which it is alleged has been fulfilled;
(e) where any goods sought to be seized under a writ of execution are in the hands of a receiver appointed by the court or a sequestrator.

(2) Paragraph (1) is without prejudice to section 2 of the Reserve and Auxiliary Forces (Protection of Civil Interests) Act 1951, or any other enactment or rule by virtue of which a person is required to obtain the permission of the court for the issue of a writ of execution or to proceed to execution on or otherwise to the enforcement of a judgment or order.
(3) Where the court grants permission, whether under this rule or otherwise, for the issue of a writ of execution and the writ is not issued within one year after the date of the order granting such permission, the order shall cease to have effect, without prejudice, however, to the making of a fresh order.

Rule 3 Permission Required for Issue of Writ in Aid of Other Writ

r.3 **76.32**

A writ of execution in aid of any other writ of execution shall not issue without the permission of the court.

Rule 4 Application for Permission to Issue Writ

(1) An application for permission to issue a writ of execution may be made in accordance with CPR Part 23 but the application notice need not be served on the respondent unless the court directs.
(2) Such an application must be supported by a witness statement or affidavit—
  (a) identifying the judgment or order to which the application relates and, if the judgment or order is for the payment of money, stating the amount originally due thereunder and the amount due thereunder at the date the application notice is filed;
  (b) stating, where the case falls within rule 2(1)(a), the reasons for the delay in enforcing the judgment or order;
  (c) stating, where the case falls within rule 2(1)(b), the change which has taken place in the parties entitled or liable to execution since the date of the judgment or order;
  (d) stating, where the case falls within rule 2(1)(c) or (d), that a demand to satisfy the judgment or order was made on the person liable to satisfy it and that he has refused or failed to do so;
  (e) giving such other information as is necessary to satisfy the court that the applicant is entitled to proceed to execution on the judgment or order in question and that the person against whom it is sought to issue execution is liable to execution on it.
(3) The court hearing such application may grant permission in accordance with the application or may order that any issue or question, a decision on which is necessary to determine the rights of the parties, be tried in any manner in which any question of fact or law arising in proceedings may be tried and, in either case, may impose such terms as to costs or otherwise as it thinks just.

Rule 5 Application for Permission to Issue Writ of Sequestration

r.5(1)–(4) **78.22**

(1) Notwithstanding anything in rules 2 and 4, an application for permission to issue a writ of sequestration must be made in accordance with CPR Part 23 and be heard by a judge.
(2) Subject to paragraph (3), the application notice, stating the grounds of the application and accompanied by a copy of the witness statement or affidavit in support of the application, must be served personally on the person against whose property it is sought to issue the writ.
(3) The court may dispense with service of the application notice under this rule if it thinks it just to do so.
(4) The judge hearing an application for permission to issue a writ of sequestration may sit in private in any case in which, if the application were for an order of committal, he would be entitled to do so by virtue of Order 52, rule 6 but, except in such a case, the application shall be heard in public.

Rule 6 Issue of Writ of Execution

r.6 **76.6**

(1) Issue of a writ of execution takes place on its being sealed by a court officer of the appropriate office.
(2) Before such a writ is issued, a praecipe for its issue must be filed.
(3) The praecipe must be signed by or on behalf of the solicitor of the person entitled to execution or, if that person is acting in person, by him.

(4) No such writ shall be sealed unless at the time of the tender thereof for sealing—
(a) the person tendering it produces—
(i) the judgment or order on which the writ is to issue, or an office copy thereof,
(ii) where the writ may not issue without the permission of the court, the order granting such permission or evidence of the granting of it;
(iii) where judgment on failure to acknowledge service has been entered against a State, as defined in section 14 of the State Immunity Act 1978, evidence that the State has been served in accordance with CPR rule 40.10 and that the judgment has taken effect; and
(b) the court officer authorised to seal it is satisfied that the period, if any, specified in the judgment or order for the payment of any money or the doing of any other act thereunder has expired.
(5) Every writ of execution shall bear the date of the day on which it is issued.
(6) In this rule 'the appropriate office' means—
(a) where the proceedings in which execution is to issue are in a District Registry, that Registry;
(b) where the proceedings are in the Principal Registry of the Family Division, that Registry;
(c) where the proceedings are Admiralty proceedings or commercial proceedings which are not in a District Registry, the Admiralty and Commercial Registry;
(ca) where the proceedings are in the Chancery Division, Chancery Chambers;
(d) in any other case, the Central Office of the Supreme Court.

Rule 8 Duration and Renewal of Writ of Execution

(1) For the purpose of execution, a writ of execution is valid in the first instance for 12 months beginning with the date of its issue.
(2) Where a writ has not been wholly executed the court may by order extend the validity of the writ from time to time for a period of 12 months at any one time beginning with the day on which the order is made, if an application for extension is made to the court before the day next following that on which the writ would otherwise expire or such later day, if any, as the court may allow.
(3) Before a writ the validity of which had been extended under paragraph (2) is executed either the writ must be sealed with the seal of the office out of which it was issued showing the date on which the order extending its validity was made or the applicant for the order must serve a notice (in Form No. 71 in the relevant practice direction) sealed as aforesaid, on the sheriff to whom the writ is directed or the relevant enforcement officer informing him of the making of the order and the date thereof.
(4) The priority of a writ, the validity of which has been extended under this rule, shall be determined by reference to the date on which it was originally delivered to the sheriff or the relevant enforcement officer.
(5) The production of a writ of execution, or of such a notice as is mentioned in paragraph (3) purporting in either case to be sealed as mentioned in that paragraph, shall be evidence that the validity of that writ, or, as the case may be, of the writ referred to in that notice, has been extended under paragraph (2).
(6) If, during the validity of a writ of execution, an interpleader summons is issued in relation to an execution under that writ, the validity of the writ shall be extended until the expiry of 12 months from the conclusion of the interpleader proceedings.

Rule 9 Return to Writ of Execution

(1) Any party at whose instance or against whom a writ of execution was issued may serve a notice on the sheriff to whom the writ was directed or the relevant enforcement officer requiring him, within such time as may be specified in the notice, to indorse on the writ a statement of the manner in which he has executed it and to send to that party a copy of the statement.
(2) If a sheriff or enforcement officer on whom such a notice is served fails to comply with it the party by whom it was served may apply to the court for an order directing the sheriff or enforcement officer to comply with the notice.

RSC ORDER 47 — WRITS OF FIERI FACIAS

ord.47 **76.1**, **76.38**

Rule 1 Power to Stay Execution by Writ of Fieri Facias

r.1 **76.3**

(1) Where a judgment is given or an order made for the payment by any person of money, and the court is satisfied, on an application made at the time of the judgment or order, or at any time thereafter, by the judgment debtor or other party liable to execution—
  (a) that there are special circumstances which render it inexpedient to enforce the judgment or order; or
  (b) that the applicant is unable from any cause to pay the money,
 then, notwithstanding anything in rule 2 or 3, the court may by order stay the execution of the judgment or order by writ of fieri facias either absolutely or for such period and subject to such conditions as the court thinks fit.

(2) An application under this rule, if not made at the time the judgment is given or order made, must be made in accordance with CPR Part 23 and may be so made notwithstanding that the party liable to execution did not acknowledge service of the claim form or serve a defence or take any previous part in the proceedings.

(3) The grounds on which an application under this rule is made must be set out in the application notice and be supported by a witness statement or affidavit made by or on behalf of the applicant substantiating the said grounds and, in particular, where such application is made on the grounds of the applicant's inability to pay, disclosing his income, the nature and value of any property of his and the amount of any other liabilities of his.

(4) The application notice and a copy of the supporting witness statement or affidavit must, not less than 4 clear days before the hearing, be served on the party entitled to enforce the judgment or order.

(5) An order staying execution under this rule may be varied or revoked by a subsequent order.

Rule 3 Separate Writs to Enforce Payment of Costs, etc.

(1) Where only the payment of money, together with costs to be assessed in accordance with CPR Part 47 (detailed costs assessment), is adjudged or ordered, then, if when the money becomes payable under the judgment or order the costs have not been assessed, the party entitled to enforce that judgment or order may issue a writ of fieri facias to enforce payment of the sum (other than for costs) adjudged or ordered and, not less than 8 days after the issue of that writ, he may issue a second writ to enforce payment of the assessed costs.

(2) A party entitled to enforce a judgment or order for the delivery of possession of any property (other than money) may, if he so elects, issue a separate writ of fieri facias to enforce payment of any damages or costs awarded to him by that judgment or order.

Rule 4 No Expenses of Execution in Certain Cases

Where a judgment or order is for less than £600 and does not entitle the claimant to costs against the person against whom the writ of fieri facias to enforce the judgment or order is issued, the writ may not authorise the sheriff or enforcement officer to whom it is directed to levy any fees, poundage or other costs of execution.

Rule 5 Writ of Fieri Facias De Bonis Ecclesiasticis, etc.

(1) Where it appears upon the return of any writ of fieri facias that the person against whom the writ was issued has no goods or chattels in the county of the sheriffs to whom the writ was directed or the district of the relevant enforcement officer but that he is the incumbent of a benefice named in the return, then, after the writ and return have been filed, the party by whom the writ of fieri facias was issued may issue a writ of fieri facias de bonis ecclesiasticis or a writ of sequestrari de bonis ecclesiasticis directed to the bishop of the diocese within which that benefice is.

(2) Any such writ must be delivered to the bishop to be executed by him.

(3) Only such fees for the execution of any such writ shall be taken by or allowed to the bishop or any diocesan officer as are for the time being authorised by or under any enactment, including any measure of the General Synod.

Rule 6 Order for Sale Otherwise than by Auction

r.6 **76.9**

(1) An order of the court under paragraph 10 of Schedule 7 to the Courts Act 2003 that a sale of goods seized under an execution may be made otherwise than by public auction may be made on the application of—
   (a) the person at whose instance the writ of execution under which the sale is to be made was issued;
   (b) the person against whom that writ was issued (in this rule referred to as 'the judgment debtor');
   (c) if the writ was directed to a sheriff, that sheriff; and
   (d) if the writ was directed to one or more enforcement officers, the relevant enforcement officer.
(2) Such an application must be made in accordance with CPR Part 23 and the application notice must contain a short statement of the grounds of the application.
(3) Where the applicant for an order under this rule is not the sheriff or enforcement officer, the sheriff or enforcement officer must, on the demand of the applicant, send to the applicant a list stating—
   (a) whether he has notice of the issue of another writ or writs of execution against the goods of the judgment debtor; and
   (b) so far as is known to him, the name and address of every creditor who has obtained the issue of another such writ of execution,

   and where the sheriff or enforcement officer is the applicant, he must prepare such a list.
(4) Not less than 4 clear days before the hearing the applicant must serve the application notice on each of the other persons by whom the application might have been made and on every person named in the list under paragraph (3).
(5) Service of the application notice on a person named in the list under paragraph (3) is notice to him for the purpose of paragraph 10(3) of Schedule 7 to the Courts Act 2003.

   (Paragraph 10(3) provides that if the person who seized the goods has notice of another execution or other executions, the court must not consider an application for leave to sell privately until the notice prescribed by Civil Procedure Rules has been given to the other execution creditor or creditors)
(6) The applicant must produce the list under paragraph (3) to the court on the hearing of the application.
(7) Every person on whom the application notice was served may attend and be heard on the hearing of the application.

RSC ORDER 52 — COMMITTAL

ord.52 **76.1, 76.38, 78.18, 78.20**

Rule 1 Committal for Contempt of Court

r.1(2)–(4) **78.5**

(1) The power of the High Court or Court of Appeal to punish for contempt of court may be exercised by an order of committal.
(2) Where contempt of court—
   (a) is committed in connection with—
      (i) any proceedings before a Divisional Court of the Queen's Bench Division; or
      (ii) criminal proceedings, except where the contempt is committed in the face of the court or consists of disobedience to an order of the court or a breach of an undertaking to the court; or
      (iii) proceedings in an inferior court; or
   (b) is committed otherwise than in connection with any proceedings, then, subject to paragraph (4), an order of committal may be made only by a Divisional Court of the Queen's Bench Division.

   This paragraph shall not apply in relation to contempt of the Court of Appeal.

(3) Where contempt of court is committed in connection with any proceedings in the High Court, then, subject to paragraph (2), an order of committal may be made by a single judge of the Queen's Bench Division except where the proceedings were assigned or subsequently transferred to some other Division, in which case the order may be made only by a single judge of that other Division.

The reference in this paragraph to a single judge of the Queen's Bench Division shall, in relation to proceedings in any court the judge or judges of which are, when exercising the jurisdiction of that court, deemed by virtue of any enactment to constitute a court of the High Court, be construed as a reference to a judge of that court.

(4) Where by virtue of any enactment the High Court has power to punish or take steps for the punishment of any person charged with having done anything in relation to a court, tribunal or person which would, if it had been done in relation to the High Court, have been a contempt of that court, an order of committal may be made—

(a) on an application under section 88 of the Charities Act 1993, by a single judge of the Chancery Division; and

(b) in any other case, by a single judge of the Queen's Bench Division.

Rule 2 Application to Divisional Court

r.2(1)–(5) **78.7**

(1) No application to a Divisional Court for an order of committal against any person may be made unless permission to make such an application has been granted in accordance with this rule.

(2) An application for such permission must be made without notice to a Divisional Court, except in vacation when it may be made to a judge in chambers and must be supported by a statement setting out the name and description of the applicant, the name, description and address of the person sought to be committed and the grounds on which his committal is sought, and by an affidavit, to be filed before the application is made, verifying the facts relied on.

(3) The applicant must give notice of the application for permission not later than the preceding day to the Crown Office and must at the same time lodge in that office copies of the statement and affidavit.

(4) Where an application for permission under this rule is refused by a judge in chambers, the applicant may make a fresh application for such permission to a Divisional Court.

(5) An application made to a Divisional Court by virtue of paragraph (4) must be made within 8 days after the judge's refusal to give permission or, if a Divisional Court does not sit within that period, on the first day on which it sits thereafter.

Rule 3 Application for Order after Leave to Apply Granted

r.3(1) **78.10**
r.3(2) **78.7**
r.3(3) **78.10**

(1) When permission has been granted under rule 2 to apply for an order of committal, the application for the order must be made to a Divisional Court and, unless the court or judge granting permission has otherwise directed, there must be at least 14 clear days between the service of the claim form and the day named therein for the hearing.

(2) Unless within 14 days after such permission was granted, the claim form is issued the permission shall lapse.

(3) Subject to paragraph 4, the claim form, accompanied by a copy of the statement and affidavit in support of the application for permission, must be served personally on the person sought to be committed.

(4) Without prejudice to the powers of the court or judge under Part 6 of the CPR, the court or judge may dispense with service under this rule if it or he thinks it just to do so.

Rule 4 Application to Court Other than Divisional Court

r.4(1) **78.8**
r.4(2)–(3) **78.10**

(1) Where an application for an order of committal may be made to a court other than a Divisional Court, the application must be made by claim form or application notice and be supported by an affidavit.

(2) Subject to paragraph (3) the claim form or application notice, stating the grounds of the application and accompanied by a copy of the affidavit in support of the application, must be served personally on the person sought to be committed.
(3) Without prejudice to its powers under Part 6 of the CPR, the court may dispense with service under this rule if it thinks it just to do so.
(4) This rule does not apply to committal applications which under rules 1(2) and 3(1) should be made to a Divisional Court but which, in vacation, have been properly made to a single judge in accordance with RSC Order 64, rule 4.

Rule 5 Saving for Power to Commit without Application For Purpose

r.5 **78.20**

Nothing in the foregoing provisions of this Order shall be taken as affecting the power of the High Court or Court of Appeal to make an order of committal of its own initiative against a person guilty of contempt of court.

Rule 6 Provisions as to Hearing

s.6 **78.14, 78.22** r.6(3)–(4) **78.14**

(1) Subject to paragraph (2), the court hearing an application for an order of committal may sit in private in the following cases, that is to say—
(a) where the application arises out of proceedings relating to the wardship or adoption of an infant or wholly or mainly to the guardianship, custody, maintenance or upbringing of an infant, or rights of access to an infant;
(b) where the application arises out of proceedings relating to a person suffering or appearing to be suffering from mental disorder within the meaning of the Mental Health Act 1983;
(c) where the application arises out of proceedings in which a secret process, discovery or invention was in issue;
(d) where it appears to the court that in the interests of the administration of justice or for reasons of national security the application should be heard in private;
but, except as aforesaid, the application shall be heard in public.
(2) If the court hearing an application in private by virtue of paragraph (1) decides to make an order of committal against the person sought to be committed, it shall in public state—
(a) the name of that person;
(b) in general terms the nature of the contempt of court in respect of which the order of committal is being made; and
(c) the length of the period for which he is being committed.
(3) Except with the permission of the court hearing an application for an order of committal, no grounds shall be relied upon at the hearing except the grounds set out in the statement under rule 2 or, as the case may be, in the claim form or application notice under rule 4.
(4) If on the hearing of the application the person sought to be committed expresses a wish to give oral evidence on his own behalf, he shall be entitled to do so.

Rule 7 Power to Suspend Execution of Committal Order

r.7 **78.16** r.7(1) **78.12**

(1) The court by whom an order of committal is made may by order direct that the execution of the order of committal shall be suspended for such period or on such terms or conditions as it may specify.
(2) Where execution of an order of committal is suspended by an order under paragraph (1), the applicant for the order of committal must, unless the court otherwise directs, serve on the person against whom it was made a notice informing him of the making and terms of the order under that paragraph.

Rule 7A Warrant for Arrest

A warrant for the arrest of a person against whom an order of committal has been made shall not, without further order of the court, be enforced more than 2 years after the date on which the warrant is issued.

Rule 8 Discharge of Person Committed

r.8(1)–(2) **78.17**

(1) The court may, on the application of any person committed to prison for any contempt of court, discharge him.

(2) Where a person has been committed for failing to comply with a judgment or order requiring him to deliver any thing to some other person or to deposit it in court or elsewhere, and a writ of sequestration has also been issued to enforce that judgment or order, then, if the thing is in the custody or power of the person committed, the commissioners appointed by the writ of sequestration may take possession of it as if it were the property of that person and, without prejudice to the generality of paragraph (1), the court may discharge the person committed and may give such directions for dealing with the thing taken by the commissioners as it thinks fit.

(RSC Order 46, rule 5 contains rules relating to writs of sequestration)

Rule 9 Saving for Other Powers

r.9 **78.18**

Nothing in the foregoing provisions of this Order shall be taken as affecting the power of the court to make an order requiring a person guilty of contempt of court, or a person punishable by virtue of any enactment in like manner as if he had been guilty of contempt of the High Court, to pay a fine or to give security for his good behaviour, and those provisions, so far as applicable, and with the necessary modifications, shall apply in relation to an application for such an order as they apply in relation to an application for an order of committal.

RSC ORDER 54 — APPLICATIONS FOR WRIT OF HABEAS CORPUS

Rule 1 Application for Writ of Habeas Corpus Ad Subjiciendum

(1) Subject to rule 11, an application for a writ of habeas corpus ad subjiciendum shall be made to a judge in court, except that—
   (a) it shall be made to a Divisional Court of the Queen's Bench Division if the court so directs;
   (b) it may be made to a judge otherwise than in court at any time when no judge is sitting in court; and
   (c) any application on behalf of a child must be made in the first instance to a judge otherwise than in court.

(2) An application for such writ may be made without notice being served on any other party and, subject to paragraph (3) must be supported by a witness statement or affidavit by the person restrained showing that it is made at his instance and setting out the nature of the restraint.

(3) Where the person restrained is unable for any reason to make the witness statement or affidavit required by paragraph (2) the witness statement or affidavit may be made by some other person on his behalf and that witness statement or affidavit must state that the person restrained is unable to make the witness statement or affidavit himself and for what reason.

Rule 2 Power of Court to Whom Application Made without Notice Being Served on Any Other Party

(1) The court or judge to whom an application under rule 1 is made without notice being served on any other party may make an order forthwith for the writ to issue, or may—
   (a) where the application is made to a judge otherwise than in court, direct the issue of a claim form seeking the writ, or that an application therefor be made by claim form to a Divisional Court or to a judge in court;
   (b) where the application is made to a judge in court, adjourn the application so that notice thereof may be given, or direct that an application be made by claim form to a Divisional Court;
   (c) where the application is made to a Divisional Court, adjourn the application so that notice thereof may be given.

(2) The claim form must be served on the person against whom the issue of the writ is sought and on such other persons as the court or judge may direct, and, unless the court or judge otherwise directs, there must be at least 8 clear days between the service of the claim form and the date named therein for the hearing of the application.

Rule 3 Copies of Witness Statements or Affidavits to Be Supplied

Every party to an application under rule 1 must supply to every other party on demand and on payment of the proper charges copies of the witness statements or affidavits which he proposes to use at the hearing of the application.

Rule 4 Power to Order Release of Person Restrained

(1) Without prejudice to rule 2(1), the court or judge hearing an application for a writ of habeas corpus ad subjiciendum may in its or his discretion order that the person restrained be released, and such order shall be a sufficient warrant to any governor of a prison, constable or other person for the release of the person under restraint.
(2) Where such an application in criminal proceedings is heard by a judge and the judge does not order the release of the person restrained, he shall direct that the application be made by claim form to a Divisional Court of the Queen's Bench Division.

Rule 5 Directions as to Return to Writ

Where a writ of habeas corpus ad subjiciendum is ordered to issue, the court or judge by whom the order is made shall give directions as to the court or judge before whom, and the date on which, the writ is returnable.

Rule 6 Service of Writ and Notice

(1) Subject to paragraphs (2) and (3), a writ of habeas corpus ad subjiciendum must be served personally on the person to whom it is directed.
(2) If it is not possible to serve such writ personally, or if it is directed to a governor of a prison or other public official, it must be served by leaving it with a servant or agent of the person to whom the writ is directed at the place where the person restrained is confined or restrained.
(3) If the writ is directed to more than one person, the writ must be served in manner provided by this rule on the person first named in the writ, and copies must be served on each of the other persons in the same manner as the writ.
(4) There must be served with the writ a notice (in Form No. 90 in the relevant practice direction) stating the court or judge before whom and the date on which the person restrained is to be brought and that in default of obedience proceedings for committal of the party disobeying will be taken.

Rule 7 Return to the Writ

(1) The return to a writ of habeas corpus ad subjiciendum must be indorsed on or annexed to the writ and must state all the causes of the detainer of the person restrained.
(2) The return may be amended, or another return substituted therefor, by permission of the court or judge before whom the writ is returnable.

Rule 8 Procedure at Hearing of Writ

When a return to a writ of habeas corpus ad subjiciendum is made, the return shall first be read, and motion then made for discharging or remanding the person restrained or amending or quashing the return, and where that person is brought up in accordance with the writ, his counsel shall be heard first, then the counsel for the Crown, and then one counsel for the person restrained in reply.

Rule 9 Bringing Up Prisoner to Give Evidence, etc.

(1) An application for a writ of habeas corpus ad testificandum or of habeas corpus ad respondendum must be made on witness statement or affidavit to a judge.
(2) An application for an order to bring up a prisoner, otherwise than by writ of habeas corpus, to give evidence in any proceedings, civil or criminal, before any court, tribunal or justice, must be made on witness statement or affidavit to a judge.

Rule 10 Form of Writ

A writ of habeas corpus must be in Form No. 89, 91 or 92 in the relevant practice direction, whichever is appropriate.

Rule 11 Applications Relative to the Custody, etc., of Child

r.11 **11.2**

An application by a parent or guardian of a child for a writ of habeas corpus ad subjiciendum relative to the custody, care or control of the child must be made in the Family Division, and this Order shall accordingly apply to such applications with the appropriate modifications.

RSC ORDER 64 — SITTINGS, VACATIONS AND OFFICE HOURS

Rule 4 Divisional Court Business during Vacation

Proceedings which require to be immediately or promptly heard and which by virtue of the following provisions must be brought in a Divisional Court may, in vacation, be brought before a single judge:
(a) Order 52, rules 1(2) and 3(1).

RSC ORDER 79 — CRIMINAL PROCEEDINGS

Rule 8 Estreat of Recognisances

(1) No recognisance acknowledged in or removed into the Queen's Bench Division shall be estreated without the order of a judge.
(2) Every application to estreat a recognisance in the Queen's Bench Division must be made by claim form and will be heard by a judge and must be supported by a witness statement or affidavit showing in what manner the breach has been committed and proving that the claim form was duly served.
(2A) When it issues the claim form the court will fix a date for the hearing of the application.
(3) A claim form under this rule must be served at least 2 clear days before the day named therein for the hearing.
(4) On the hearing of the application the judge may, and if requested by any party shall, direct any issue of fact in dispute to be tried by a jury.
(5) If it appears to the judge that a default has been made in performing the conditions of the recognisance, the judge may order the recognisance to be estreated.

Rule 9 Bail

(1) Subject to the provisions of this rule, every application to the High Court in respect of bail in any criminal proceeding—
  (a) where the defendant is in custody, must be made by claim form to a judge to show cause why the defendant should not be granted bail;
  (b) where the defendant has been admitted to bail, must be made by claim form to a judge to show cause why the variation in the arrangements for bail proposed by the applicant should not be made.
(2) Subject to paragraph (5), the claim form (in Form No. 97 or 97A in the relevant practice direction) must, at least 24 hours before the day named therein for the hearing, be served—
  (a) where the application was made by the defendant, on the prosecutor and on the Director of Public Prosecutions, if the prosecution is being carried on by him;
  (b) where the application was made by the prosecutor or a constable under section 3(8) of the Bail Act 1976, on the defendant.
(3) Subject to paragraph (5), every application must be supported by witness statement or affidavit.
(4) Where a defendant in custody who desires to apply for bail is unable through lack of means to instruct a solicitor, he may give notice in writing to the court stating his desire to apply for bail and requesting that the Official Solicitor shall act for him in the application, and the court may assign the Official Solicitor to act for the applicant accordingly.
(5) Where the Official Solicitor has been so assigned the court may dispense with the requirements of paragraphs (1) to (3) and deal with the application in a summary manner.
(6) Where the court grants the defendant bail, the order must be in Form No. 98 in the relevant practice direction and a copy of the order shall be transmitted forthwith—
  (a) where the proceedings in respect of the defendant have been transferred to the Crown

Civil Procedure Rules & Practice Directions

Court for trial or where the defendant has been committed to the Crown Court to be sentenced or otherwise dealt with, to the appropriate officer of the Crown Court;

(b) in any other case, to the designated officer for the court which committed the defendant.

(6A) The recognisance of any surety required as a condition of bail granted as aforesaid may, where the defendant is in a prison or other place of detention, be entered into before the governor or keeper of the prison or place as well as before the persons specified in section 8(4) of the Bail Act 1976.

(6B) Where under section 3(5) or (6) of the Bail Act 1976 the court imposes a requirement to be complied with before a person's release on bail, it may give directions as to the manner in which and the person or persons before whom the requirement may be complied with.

(7) A person who in pursuance of an order for the grant of bail made by the court under this rule proposes to enter into a recognisance or give security must, unless the court otherwise directs, give notice (in Form No. 100 in the relevant practice direction) to the prosecutor at least 24 hours before he enters into the recognisance or complies with the requirements as aforesaid.

(8) Where in pursuance of such an order as aforesaid a recognisance is entered into or requirement complied with before any person, it shall be the duty of that person to cause the recognisance or, as the case may be, a statement of the requirement complied with to be transmitted forthwith—

(a) where the proceedings in respect of the defendant have been transferred to the Crown Court for trial or where the defendant has been committed to the Crown Court to be sentenced or otherwise dealt with, to the appropriate officer of the Crown Court;

(b) in any other case, to the designated officer for the court which committed the defendant,

and a copy of such recognisance or statement shall at the same time be sent to the governor or keeper of the prison or other place of detention in which the defendant is detained, unless the recognisance was entered into or the requirement complied with before such governor or keeper.

(10) An order varying the arrangements under which the defendant has been granted bail shall be in Form 98A in the relevant practice direction and a copy of the order shall be transmitted forthwith—

(a) where the proceedings in respect of the defendant have been transferred to the Crown Court for trial or where the defendant has been committed to the Crown Court to be sentenced or otherwise dealt with, to the appropriate officer of the Crown Court;

(b) in any other case, to the designated officer for the court which committed the defendant.

(11) Where in pursuance of an order of the High Court or the Crown Court a person is released on bail in any criminal proceeding pending the determination of an appeal to the High Court or House of Lords or an application for a quashing order, then, upon the abandonment of the appeal or application, or upon the decision of the High Court or House of Lords being given, any justice (being a justice acting for the same petty sessions area as the magistrates' court by which that person was convicted or sentenced) may issue process for enforcing the decision in respect of which such appeal or application was brought or, as the case may be, the decision of the High Court or House of Lords.

(12) If an applicant to the High Court in any criminal proceedings is refused bail, the applicant shall not be entitled to make a fresh application for bail to any other judge or to a Divisional Court.

(13) The record required by section 5 of the Bail Act 1976 to be made by the High Court shall be made by including in the file relating to the case in question a copy of the relevant order of the Court and shall contain the particulars set out in Form No. 98 or 98A in the relevant practice direction, whichever is appropriate, except that in the case of a decision to withhold bail the record shall be made by inserting a statement of the decision on the court's copy of the relevant claim form and including it in the file relating to the case in question.

(14) In the case of a person whose return or surrender is sought under the Extradition Act 1989, this rule shall apply as if references to the defendant were references to that person and references to the prosecutor were references to the state seeking the return or surrender of that person.

RSC ORDER 81 — PARTNERS

Rule 1 Claims by and against Firms within Jurisdiction

r.1 **14.44**

Subject to the provisions of any enactment, any two or more persons claiming to be entitled, or alleged to be liable, as partners in respect of a cause of action and carrying on business within the jurisdiction may sue, or be sued, in the name of the firm (if any) of which they were partners at the time when the cause of action accrued.

Rule 2 Disclosure of Partners' Names

r.2 **14.45, 14.46, 54.4**

(1) Any defendant to a claim brought by partners in the name of a firm may serve on the claimants or their solicitor a notice requiring them or him forthwith to furnish the defendant with a written statement of the names and places of residence of all the persons who were partners in the firm at the time when the cause of action accrued; and if the notice is not complied with the court may order the claimants or their solicitor to furnish the defendant with such a statement and to verify it on oath or otherwise as may be specified in the order, or may order that further proceedings in the claim be stayed on such terms as the court may direct.

(2) When the names of the partners have been declared in compliance with a notice or order given or made under paragraph (1) the proceedings shall continue in the name of the firm but with the same consequences as would have ensued if the persons whose names have been so declared had been named as claimants in the claim form.

(3) Paragraph (1) shall have effect in relation to a claim brought against partners in the name of a firm as it has effect in relation to a claim brought by partners in the name of a firm but with the substitution, for references to the defendant and the claimants, of references to the claimant and the defendants respectively, and with the omission of the words 'or may order' to the end.

Rule 4 Acknowledgment of Service in a Claim against Firm

r.4(1)–(2) **15.33**

(1) Where persons are sued as partners in the name of their firm, service may not be acknowledged in the name of the firm but only by the partners thereof in their own names, but the claim shall nevertheless continue in the name of the firm.

(2) Where in a claim against a firm the claim form by which the claim is begun is served on a person as a partner, that person, if he denies that he was a partner or liable as such at any material time, may acknowledge service of the claim form and state in his acknowledgment that he does so as a person served as a partner in the defendant firm but who denies that he was a partner at any material time.

An acknowledgment of service given in accordance with this paragraph shall, unless and until it is set aside, be treated as an acknowledgment by the defendant firm.

(3) Where an acknowledgment of service has been given by a defendant in accordance with paragraph (2) then—

(a) the claimant may either apply to the court to set it aside on the ground that the defendant was a partner or liable as such at a material time or may leave that question to be determined at a later stage of the proceedings;

(b) the defendant may either apply to the court to set aside the service of the claim form on him on the ground that he was not a partner or liable as such at a material time or may at the proper time serve a defence on the claimant denying in respect of the claimant's claim either his liability as a partner or the liability of the defendant firm or both.

(4) The court may at any stage of the proceedings in a claim in which a defendant has acknowledged service in accordance with paragraph (2) on the application of the claimant or of that defendant, order that any question as to the liability of that defendant or as to the liability of the defendant firm be tried in such manner and at such time as the court directs.

Rule 5 Enforcing Judgment or Order against Firm

r.5(1)–(4) **76.36**

(1) Where a judgment is given or order made against a firm, execution to enforce the judgment or order may, subject to rule 6, issue against any property of the firm within the jurisdiction.

(2) Where a judgment is given or order made against a firm, execution to enforce the judgment or order may, subject to rule 6 and to the next following paragraph, issue against any person who—

(a) acknowledged service of the claim form as a partner; or

(b) having been served as a partner with the claim form, failed to acknowledge service of it; or

(c) admitted in his statement of case that he is a partner; or

(d) was adjudged to be a partner.

(3) Execution to enforce a judgment or order given or made against a firm may not issue against a member of the firm who was out of the jurisdiction when the claim form was issued unless he—

(a) acknowledged service of the claim form as a partner; or

(b) was served within the jurisdiction with the claim form as a partner; or

(c) was, with the permission of the court given under Section III of CPR Part 6, served out of the jurisdiction with the claim form, as a partner,

and, except as provided by paragraph (1) and by the foregoing provisions of this paragraph, a judgment or order given or made against a firm shall not render liable, release or otherwise affect a member of the firm who was out of the jurisdiction when the claim form was issued.

(4) Where a party who has obtained a judgment or order against a firm claims that a person is liable to satisfy the judgment or order as being a member of the firm, and the foregoing provisions of this rule do not apply in relation to that person, that party may apply to the court for permission to issue execution against that person, the application to be made in accordance with CPR Part 23 and the application notice must be served personally on that person.

(5) Where the person against whom an application under paragraph (4) is made does not dispute his liability, the court hearing the application may, subject to paragraph (3) give permission to issue execution against that person, and, where that person disputes his liability, the court may order that the liability of that person be tried and determined in any manner in which any issue or question in a claim may be tried and determined.

Rule 6 Enforcing Judgment or Order in Actions between Partners, etc.

(1) Execution to enforce a judgment or order given or made in—

(a) a claim by or against a firm in the name of the firm against or by a member of the firm; or

(b) a claim by a firm in the name of the firm against a firm in the name of the firm where those firms have one or more members in common,

shall not issue except with the permission of the court.

(2) The court hearing an application under this rule may give such directions, including directions as to the taking of accounts and the making of inquiries, as may be just.

Rule 7 Attachment of Debts Owed by Firm

(1) An order may be made under CPR rule 72.2 in relation to debts due or accruing due from a firm carrying on business within the jurisdiction notwithstanding that one or more members of the firm is resident out of the jurisdiction.

(2) An interim third party debt order under CPR rule 72.4(2) relating to such debts as aforesaid must be served on a member of the firm within the jurisdiction or on some other person having the control or management of the partnership business.

(3) Where an order made under the said rules 72.2 or 72.4(2) requires a firm to appear before the court, an appearance by a member of the firm constitutes a sufficient compliance with the order.

Rule 9 Application to Person Carrying On Business in Another Name

r.9 **14.46**

An individual carrying on business within the jurisdiction in a name or style other than his own name, may whether or not he is within the jurisdiction be sued in that name or style as if it were the name of a firm, and rules 2 to 8 shall, so far as applicable, apply as if he were a partner and the name in which he carries on business were the name of his firm.

Rule 10 Applications for Orders Charging Partner's Interest in Partnership Property, etc.

(1) Every application to the court by a judgment creditor of a partner for an order under section 23 of the Partnership Act 1890 (which authorises the High Court or a judge thereof to make certain orders on the application of a judgment creditor of a partner, including an order charging the partner's interest in the partnership property) and every application to the court by a partner of the judgment debtor made in consequence of the first mentioned application must be made in accordance with CPR Part 23.

(2) A Master or the Admiralty Registrar or a district judge may exercise the powers conferred on a judge by the said section 23.

(3) Every application notice issued by a judgment creditor under this rule, and every order made on such an application, must be served on the judgment debtor and on such of his partners as are within the jurisdiction or, if the partnership is a cost book company, on the judgment debtor and the purser of the company.

(4) Every application notice issued by a partner of a judgment debtor under this rule, and every order made on such an application, must be served—

  (a) on the judgment creditor; and
  (b) on the judgment debtor; and
  (c) on such of the other partners of the judgment debtor as do not join in the application and are within the jurisdiction or, if the partnership is a cost book company, on the purser of the company.

(5) An application notice or order served in accordance with this rule on the purser of a cost book company or, in the case of a partnership not being such a company, on some only of the partners thereof, shall be deemed to have been served on that company or on all the partners of that partnership, as the case may be.

RSC ORDER 93 — APPLICATIONS AND APPEALS TO HIGH COURT UNDER VARIOUS ACTS: CHANCERY DIVISION

ord.93 **1.5**

Rule 1 Notice of Petition under Section 55 of the National Debt Act 1870

Where a petition is presented under section 55 of the National Debt Act 1870, the petitioner must, before the petition is heard, apply to a judge of the Chancery Division for directions with respect to giving notice of the claim to which the petition relates, and the judge may direct that notice thereof be given by advertisement or in such other manner as he may direct or may dispense with the giving of such notice.

Rule 2 Application under the Public Trustee Act 1906

Without prejudice to sections 10(2) and 13(7) of the Public Trustee Act, 1906, the jurisdiction of the High Court under that Act shall be exercised by a judge of the Chancery Division sitting in private.

Rule 4 Proceedings under the Trustee Act 1925

All proceedings brought in the High Court under the Trustee Act 1925, shall be assigned to the Chancery Division.

Rule 5 Application under Section 2(3) of the Public Order Act 1936

(1) Proceedings by which an application is made to the High Court under section 2(3) of the Public Order Act 1936, shall be assigned to the Chancery Division.

(2) Such an application shall be made by claim form and the persons to be made defendants to the claim shall be such persons as the Attorney-General may determine.

(3) In the absence of other sufficient representation the court may appoint the Official Solicitor to represent any interests which in the opinion of the court ought to be represented on any inquiry directed by the court under the said section 2(3).

Rule 9 Right of Appeal under the Law of Property Act

An appeal shall lie to the High Court against a decision of the Minister of Agriculture, Fisheries and Food under paragraph 16 of Schedule 15 to the Law of Property Act 1922.

Rule 10 Determination of Appeal or Case Stated under Various Acts

(1) An appeal to the High Court against an order of a county court made under the Land Registration Act 1925 shall be heard and determined by a Divisional Court of the Chancery Division.

Rule 16 Proceedings under the Commons Registration Act 1965

(1) Proceedings in the High Court under section 14 or 18 of the Commons Registration Act 1965 shall be assigned to the Chancery Division.

Rule 17 Proceedings under Section 21 or 25 of the Law of Property Act 1969

Proceedings in the High Court under section 21 or 25 of the Law of Property Act 1969 shall be assigned to the Chancery Division.

Rule 18 Proceedings under Section 86 of the Civil Aviation Act 1982

(1) Proceedings in the High Court for the amendment of any register of aircraft mortgages kept pursuant to an Order in Council made under section 86 of the Civil Aviation Act 1982 shall be assigned to the Chancery Division.
(2) Such proceedings shall be brought by claim form and every person, other than the claimant, appearing in the register as mortgagee or mortgagor of the aircraft in question shall be made a defendant to the claim.
(3) A copy of the claim form shall also be sent to the Civil Aviation Authority and the Authority shall be entitled to be heard in the proceedings.

Rule 19 Proceedings under Section 85(7) of the Fair Trading Act 1973 and the Control of Misleading Advertisements Regulations 1988

(1) Proceedings to which this rule applies shall be assigned to the Chancery Division and may be begun by claim form.
(2) This rule applies to any application to the High Court for an order under section 85(7) of the Fair Trading Act 1973, or under any provision to which that section applies or under the Control of Misleading Advertisements Regulations 1988.

Rule 22 Proceedings under the Financial Services and Markets Act 2000

(1) In this rule 'the Act' means the Financial Services and Markets Act 2000 and a section referred to by number means the section so numbered in that Act.
(2) Proceedings in the High Court under the Act (other than applications for a mandatory order) and actions for damages for breach of a statutory duty imposed by the Act shall be assigned to the Chancery Division.
(3) Such proceedings and actions shall be begun by claim form except for applications by petition by the Financial Services Authority under section 367.
(4) Where there is a question of the construction of any rule or other instrument made by or with the approval or consent of the Financial Services Authority under the Act, that Authority may make representations to the court.

RSC ORDER 94 — APPLICATIONS AND APPEALS TO HIGH COURT UNDER VARIOUS ACTS: QUEEN'S BENCH DIVISION

ord.94 **1.5**, **46.21**

Rule 1 Jurisdiction of High Court to Quash Certain Orders, Schemes, etc.

(1) Where by virtue of any enactment the High Court has jurisdiction, on the application of any person, to quash or prohibit any order, scheme, certificate or plan, any amendment or approval

of a plan, any decision of a Minister or government department or any action on the part of a Minister or government department, the jurisdiction shall be exercisable by a single judge of the Queen's Bench Division.

(2) The application must be made by claim form which must state the grounds of the application.

Rule 2 Filing and Service of Claim Form

(1) A claim form under rule 1 must be filed at the Crown Office, and served, within the time limited by the relevant enactment for making the application.

(2) Subject to paragraph (4) the claim form must be served on the appropriate Minister or government department, and—

(a) if the application relates to a compulsory purchase order made by an authority other than the appropriate Minister or government department, or to a clearance order under the Housing Act 1985, on the authority by whom the order was made;

(b) if the application relates to a scheme or order to which Schedule 2 to the Highways Act 1980, applies made by an authority other than the Secretary of State, on that authority;

(c) if the application relates to a structure plan, local plan or other development plan within the meaning of the Town and Country Planning Act 1990, on the local planning authority who prepared the plan;

(d) if the application relates to any decision or order, or any action on the part of a Minister of the Crown to which section 21 of the Land Compensation Act 1961, or section 288 of the Town and Country Planning Act 1990, applies, on the authority directly concerned with such decision, order or action or, if that authority is the applicant, on every person who would, if he were aggrieved by the decision, order or action, be entitled to apply to the High Court under the said section 21 or the said section 245, as the case may be;

(e) if the application relates to a scheme to which Schedule 32 to the Local Government, Planning and Land Act 1980 applies, on the body which adopted the scheme.

(3) In paragraph (2) 'the appropriate Minister or government department' means the Minister of the Crown or government department by whom the order, scheme, certificate, plan, amendment, approval or decision in question was or may be made, authorised, confirmed, approved or given or on whose part the action in question was or may be taken.

(4) Where the application relates to an order made under the Road Traffic Regulation Act 1984, the claim form must be served—

(a) if the order was made by a Minister of the Crown, on that Minister;

(b) if the order was made by a local authority with the consent, or in pursuance of a direction, of a Minister of the Crown, on that authority and also on that Minister;

(c) in any other case, on the local authority by whom the order was made.

Rule 3 Filing of Witness Statement or Affidavits, etc.

(1) Evidence at the hearing of an application under rule 1 shall be by witness statement or affidavit.

(2) Any witness statement or affidavit in support of the application must be filed by the applicant in the Crown Office within 14 days after service of the claim form and the applicant must, at the time of filing, serve a copy of the witness statement or affidavit and of any exhibit thereto on the respondent.

(3) Any witness statement or affidavit in opposition to the application must be filed by the respondent in the Crown Office within 21 days after the service on him under paragraph (2) of the applicant's witness statement or affidavit and the respondent must, at the time of filing, serve a copy of his witness statement or affidavit and of any exhibit thereto on the applicant.

(4) When filing a witness statement or affidavit under this rule a party must leave a copy thereof and of any exhibit thereto at the Crown Office for the use of the court.

(5) Unless the court otherwise orders, an application under rule 1 shall not be heard earlier than 14 days after the time for filing a witness statement or affidavit by the respondent has expired.

Rule 4 Rectification of Register of Deeds of Arrangement

r.4(1) **12.1**

(1) Every application to the Court under section 7 of the Deeds of Arrangement Act 1914, for an order—

(a) that any omission to register a deed of arrangement within the time prescribed by that Act be rectified by extending the time for such registration; or

(b) that any omission or misstatement of the name, residence or description of any person be rectified by the insertion in the register of his true name, residence or description,

must be made by witness statement or affidavit without notice being served on any other party to a master of the Queen's Bench Division.

(2) The witness statement or affidavit must set out particulars of the deed of arrangement and of the omission or misstatement in question and must state the grounds on which the application is made.

Rule 5 Exercise of Jurisdiction under Representation of the People Acts

(1) Proceedings in the High Court under the Representation of the People Acts shall be assigned to the Queen's Bench Division.

(2) Subject to paragraphs (3) and (4) the jurisdiction of the High Court under the said Acts in matters relating to parliamentary and local government elections shall be exercised by a Divisional Court.

(3) Paragraph (2) shall not be construed as taking away from a single judge or a Master any jurisdiction under the said Acts which, but for that paragraph, would be exercisable by a single judge or, as the case may be, by a Master.

(4) Where the jurisdiction of the High Court under the said Acts is by a provision of any of those Acts made exercisable in matters relating to parliamentary elections by a single judge, that jurisdiction in matters relating to local government elections shall also be exercisable by a single judge.

Rule 8 Tribunals and Inquiries Act 1992: Appeal from Tribunal

(1) A person who was a party to proceedings before any such tribunal as is mentioned in section 11(1) of the Tribunals and Inquiries Act 1992 and is dissatisfied in point of law with the decision of the tribunal may appeal to the High Court.

(2) The appellant's notice must be served—

(a) on the chairman of the tribunal;

(b) in the case of a tribunal which has no chairman or member who acts as a chairman, on the member or members of that tribunal; or

(c) in the case of any such tribunal as is specified in paragraph 16 of Schedule 1 to the said Act of 1992, on the secretary of the tribunal.

(3) Where an appeal is against the decision of the tribunal constituted under section 46 of the National Health Service Act 1977 the appellant's notice must be filed at the High Court within 14 days after the date of that decision.

(4) Where an appeal is against the decision of a tribunal established under section 1 of the Employment Tribunals Act 1996 the appellant's notice must be filed at the High Court within 42 days after the date of that decision.

Rule 9 Tribunals and Inquiries Act 1992: Case Stated by Tribunal

(1) Any such tribunal as is mentioned in section 11(1) of the Tribunals and Inquiries Act 1992 may, of its own initiative or at the request of any party to proceedings before it, state in the course of proceedings before it in the form of a special case for the decision of the High Court any question of law arising in the proceedings.

(2) Any party to proceedings before any such tribunal who is aggrieved by the tribunal's refusal to state such a case may apply to the High Court for an order directing the tribunal to do so.

(3) A case stated by any such tribunal which has no chairman or member who acts as a chairman must be signed by the member or members of the tribunal.

Rule 12 Applications for Permission under Section 289(6) of the Town and Country Planning Act 1990 and Section 65(5) of the Planning (Listed Buildings and Conservation Areas) Act 1990

(1) An application for permission to appeal to the High Court under section 289 of the Town and Country Planning Act 1990 or section 65 of the Planning (Listed Buildings and Conservation

Areas) Act 1990 shall be made within 28 days after the date on which notice of the decision was given to the applicant.

(2) An application shall—
   (a) include, where necessary, any application to extend the time for applying;
   (b) be in writing setting out the reasons why permission should be granted, and if the time for applying has expired, the reasons why the application was not made within that time;
   (c) be made by filing it in the Crown Office together with the decision, a draft claim form, and a witness statement or affidavit verifying any facts relied on;
   (d) before being filed under sub-paragraph (c), be served together with the draft appellant's notice and a copy of the witness statement or affidavit to be filed with the application, upon the persons who are referred to in rule 13(5); and
   (e) be accompanied by a witness statement or affidavit giving the names and addresses of, and the places and dates of service on, all persons who have been served with the application and, if any person who ought to be served has not been served, the witness statement or affidavit must state that fact and the reason for it.

(3) An application shall be heard—
   (a) by a single judge;
   (b) unless the court otherwise orders, not less than 21 days after it was filed at the Crown Office.

   Any person served with the application shall be entitled to appear and be heard.

(4) If on the hearing of an application the court is of opinion that any person who ought to have been served has not been served, the court may adjourn the hearing on such terms (if any) as it may direct in order that the application may be served on that person.

(5) If the court grants permission—
   (a) it may impose such terms as to costs and as to giving security as it thinks fit;
   (b) it may give directions; and
   (c) the appellant's notice by which the appeal is to be brought shall be served and filed within 7 days of the grant.

(6) Any respondent who intends to use a witness statement or affidavit at the hearing shall file it in the Crown Office and serve a copy thereof on the applicant as soon as is practicable and in any event, unless the court otherwise allows, at least 2 days before the hearing.

   The court may allow the applicant to use a further witness statement or affidavit.

Rule 13 Proceedings under Sections 289 and 290 of the Town and Country Planning Act 1990 and under Section 65 of the Planning (Listed Buildings and Conservation Areas) Act 1990

(1) In this rule a reference to 'section 65' is a reference to section 65 of the Planning (Listed Buildings and Conservation Areas) Act 1990, but, save as aforesaid, a reference to a section by number is a reference to the section so numbered in the Town and Country Planning Act 1990.

(2) An appeal shall lie to the High Court on a point of law against a decision of the Secretary of State under subsection (1) or (2) of section 289 or under subsection (1) of section 65 at the instance of any person or authority entitled to appeal under any of those subsections respectively.

(3) In the case of a decision to which section 290 applies, the person who made the application to which the decision relates, or the local planning authority, if dissatisfied with the decision in point of law, may appeal against the decision to the High Court.

(4) Any appeal under section 289(1) or (2), section 65(1) or section 290, and any case stated under section 289(3) or section 65(2), shall be heard and determined by a single judge unless the court directs that the matter shall be heard and determined by a Divisional Court.

(5) The persons to be served with the appellant's notice by which an appeal to the High Court is brought by virtue of section 289(1) or (2), section 65(1) or section 290 are—
   (a) the Secretary of State;
   (b) the local planning authority who served the notice or gave the decision, as the case may be, or, where the appeal is brought by that authority, the appellant or applicant in the proceedings in which the decision appealed against was given;

(c) in the case of an appeal brought by virtue of section 289(1) or section 65(1), any other person having an interest in the land to which the notice relates, and;
(d) in the case of an appeal brought by virtue of section 289(2), any other person on whom the notice to which those proceedings related was served.

(6) The court hearing any such appeal may remit the matter to the Secretary of State to the extent necessary to enable him to provide the court with such further information in connection with the matter as the court may direct.

(7) Where the court is of opinion that the decision appealed against was erroneous in point of law, it shall not set aside or vary that decision but shall remit the matter to the Secretary of State with the opinion of the court for re-hearing and determination by him.

(9) The court may give directions as to the exercise, until an appeal brought by virtue of section 289(1) is finally concluded and any rehearing and determination by the Secretary of State has taken place, of the power to serve, and institute proceedings (including criminal proceedings) concerning—
(a) a stop notice under section 183; and
(b) a breach of condition notice under section 187A.

Rule 14 Applications under Section 13 of the Coroners Act 1988

(1) Any application under section 13 of the Coroners Act 1988 shall be heard and determined by a Divisional Court.

(2) The application must be made by claim form and the claim form must state the grounds of the application and, unless the application is made by the Attorney-General, shall be accompanied by his fiat.

(3) The claim form must be filed in the Crown Office and served upon all persons directly affected by the application within six weeks after the grant of the fiat.

Rule 15 Applications under Section 42 of the Supreme Court Act 1981

r.15 **14.69**

(1) Every application to the High Court by the Attorney-General under section 42 of the Supreme Court Act 1981 shall be heard and determined by a Divisional Court.

(2) The application must be made by claim form which, together with a witness statement or affidavit in support, shall be filed in the Crown Office and served on the person against whom the order is sought.

RSC ORDER 95 — BILLS OF SALE ACTS 1878 AND 1882 AND THE INDUSTRIAL AND PROVIDENT SOCIETIES ACT 1967

ord.95 **1.5**

Rule 1 Rectification of Register

(1) Every application to the court under section 14 of the Bills of Sale Act 1878, for an order—
(a) that any omission to register a bill of sale or a witness statement or affidavit of renewal thereof within the time prescribed by that Act be rectified by extending the time for such registration; or
(b) that any omission or misstatement of the name, residence or occupation of any person be rectified by the insertion in the register of his true name, residence or occupation,
must be made by witness statement or affidavit to a Master of the Queen's Bench Division, and a copy of the witness statement or affidavit need not be served on any other person.

(2) Every application for such an order as is described in paragraph (1) shall be supported by a witness statement or affidavit setting out particulars of the bill of sale and of the omission or misstatement in question and stating the grounds on which the application is made.

Rule 2 Entry of Satisfaction

(1) Every application under section 15 of the Bills of Sale Act 1878, to a Master of the Queen's Bench Division for an order that a memorandum of satisfaction be written on a registered copy of a bill of sale must be made by claim form.

(1A) If a consent to the satisfaction signed by the person entitled to the benefit of the bill of sale can be obtained, the claim form and the documents set out in paragraph (2) must not be served on any other person.

(2) Where paragraph (1A) applies, the claim form must be supported by—
 (a) particulars of the consent referred to in that paragraph; and
 (b) a witness statement or affidavit by a witness who attested the consent verifying the signature on it.

(3) Where paragraph (1A) does not apply, the cl aim form must be served on the person entitled to the benefit of the bill of sale and must be supported by evidence that the debt (if any) for which the bill of sale was made has been satisfied or discharged.

Rule 3 Restraining Removal on Sale of Goods Seized

An application to the court under the proviso to section 7 of the Bills of Sale Act (1878) Amendment Act 1882 must be made by the issue of a claim form.

Rule 4 Search of Register

Any Master of the Queen's Bench Division shall, on a request in writing giving sufficient particulars, and on payment of the prescribed fee, cause a search to be made in the register of bills of sale and issue a certificate of the result of the search.

Rule 5 Application under Section 1(5) of the Industrial and Provident Societies Act 1967

Every application to the court under section 1(5) of the Industrial and Provident Societies Act 1967 for an order—
(a) that the period for making an application for recording a charge be extended; or
(b) that any omission from or misstatement in such an application be rectified,
must be made to a Master of the Queen's Bench Division by witness statement or affidavit setting out particulars of the charge and of the omission or misstatement in question and stating the grounds of the application, and need not be served on any other person.

Rule 6 Assignment of Book Debts

(1) There shall continue to be kept in the Central Office, under the supervision of the registrar, a register of assignments of book debts.

(2) Every application for registration of an assignment of a book debt under section 344 of the Insolvency Act 1986 shall be made by producing at the Filing and Record Department of the Central Office—
 (a) a true copy of the assignment, and of every schedule thereto; and
 (b) a witness statement or affidavit verifying the date and the time, and the due execution of the assignment in the presence of the witness, and setting out the particulars of the assignment and the parties thereto.

(3) On an application being made in accordance with the preceding paragraph, the documents there referred to shall be filed, and the particulars of the assignment, and of the parties to it, shall be entered in the register.

(4) In this rule, 'the registrar' has the meaning given in section 13 of the Bills of Sale Act 1878.

RSC ORDER 96 — THE MINES (WORKING FACILITIES AND SUPPORT) ACT 1966, ETC.

ord.96 **1.5**

Rule 1 Assignment to Chancery Division

Any proceedings in which the jurisdiction conferred on the High Court by section 1 of the Railway and Canal Commission (Abolition) Act 1949 is invoked shall be assigned to the Chancery Division and be begun by claim form which need not be served on any other party.

Rule 2 Reference by Secretary of State of Certain Applications

Where under any provision of the Mines (Working Facilities and Support) Act 1966, the Secretary of State refers any application to the High Court, he shall—

(a) file the reference, signed by him or by an officer authorised by him for the purpose, in Chancery Chambers, together with all documents and plans deposited with him by the applicant; and

(b) within 3 days after doing so give notice to the applicant of the filing of the reference.

Rule 3 Issue of Claim Form

Within 10 days after receipt of the notice mentioned in rule 2(b) the applicant must issue a claim form which need not be served on any other party which must state the application of the applicant under the said Act of 1966 and any other relief sought.

Rule 4 Appointment for Directions

(1) Within 7 days after issue of the claim form the applicant, having applied at Chancery Chambers for the name of the Master assigned to hear the claim, must take an appointment before that Master for the hearing of the claim and must forthwith serve notice of the appointment on the Secretary of State.

(2) Not less than 2 clear days before the day appointed for the first hearing of the claim, the applicant must leave at Chancery Chambers—

  (a) a witness statement or affidavit of facts in support of the claim, giving particulars of all persons known to the applicant to be interested in or affected by the application; and

  (b) a draft of any proposed advertisement or notice of the application.

(3) On the appointment the master shall—

  (a) fix a time within which any notice of objection under rule 5 must be given;

  (b) fix a date for the further hearing of the claim; and

  (c) direct what, if any, advertisements and notices of the application and of the date fixed for the further hearing of the claim are to be inserted and given, and what persons, if any, are to be served with a copy of the application and of any other document in the proceedings.

(4) Any such advertisement or notice must include a statement of the effect of rule 5.

Rule 5 Objections to Application

(1) Any person wishing to oppose the application must, within the time fixed by the Master under rule 4 (3), serve on the applicant a notice of objection stating—

  (a) his name and address and the name and address of his solicitor, if any;

  (b) the grounds of his objection and any alternative methods of effecting the objects of the application which he alleges may be used; and

  (c) the facts on which he relies.

(2) Any notice required to be served on a person who has given notice of objection (hereafter in this Order referred to as 'the objector') may be served by delivering it or sending it by prepaid post—

  (a) where the name and address of a solicitor is stated in the notice of objection, to the solicitor at that address; and

  (b) in any other case, to the objector at his address stated in the notice of objection.

(3) An objector shall be entitled to appear in person or by a solicitor or counsel at the further hearing of the claim and to take such part in the proceedings as the Master or judge thinks fit; but if he does not so appear his notice of objection shall be of no effect and he shall not be entitled to take any part in the proceedings unless the Master or judge otherwise orders.

Rule 6 List of Objectors

Not less than 2 clear days before the day fixed for the further hearing of the claim, the applicant must leave at Chancery Chambers any notices of objection served on the applicant together with a list arranged in 3 columns stating—

(a) in column 1, the names and addresses of the objectors;

(b) in column 2, the names and addresses of their respective solicitors, if any; and

(c) in column 3, short summaries of their respective grounds of objection.

Rule 7 Directions on Further Hearing

At the further hearing of the claim the Master shall—

(a) give directions as to the procedure to be followed before the claim is set down for hearing, including, if he thinks fit, a direction—
  (i) that further particulars be given of any of the grounds or facts relied on in support of or in opposition to the application made by the claim;
  (ii) that the applicant may serve a reply to any notice of objection;
  (iii) that any particular fact be proved by witness statement or affidavit;
  (iv) that statements of case or points of claim or defence be served; and
(b) adjourn the claim for hearing before the judge in such manner as he shall think best adapted to secure the just, expeditious and economical disposal of the proceedings.

Rule 8 Other Applications

Rules 2 to 7 shall, so far as applicable and with the necessary adaptations, apply in relation to any other application to the High Court falling within rule 1 as they apply in relation to an application under the Mines (Working Facilities and Support) Act 1966.

RSC ORDER 109 — THE ADMINISTRATION OF JUSTICE ACT 1960

ord.109 **1.5**

Rule 1 Applications under Act

(1) Any of the following applications, that is to say—
  (a) an application under section 2 of the Administration of Justice Act 1960, or under that section as applied by section 13 of that Act, to extend the time within which an application may be made to a Divisional Court for permission to appeal to the House of Lords under section 1 of that Act, or section 13 thereof, from an order or decision of that court, and
  (b) an application by a defendant under section 9(3) of that Act to a Divisional Court for permission to be present on the hearing of any proceedings preliminary or incidental to an appeal to the House of Lords under section 1 of that Act from a decision of that court

must be made to a Divisional Court except in vacation when it may be made to a judge.

(2) Any such application to a Divisional Court, if not made in the proceedings before the Divisional Court from whose order or decision the appeal in question is brought, must be made by the issue of a claim form.

(3) Any such application to a judge must, in the case of such an application as is referred to in paragraph (1)(a) be made by the issue of a claim form and, in the case of such an application as is referred to in paragraph (1)(b) need not be served on any other person unless, in the latter case, the judge otherwise directs.

(4) No application notice or copy of the claim form (as the case may be) by which such an application as is referred to in paragraph (1)(b) is made, need be given to any party affected thereby unless the Divisional Court otherwise directs.

(5) Where any application to which this rule applies is made in vacation to a single judge and the judge refuses the application, the applicant shall be entitled to have the application determined by a Divisional Court.

Rule 2 Appeals under Section 13 of Act

(1) An appeal to a Divisional Court of the High Court under section 13 of the Administration of Justice Act 1960, shall be heard and determined by a Divisional Court of the Queen's Bench Division.

(4) Unless the court gives permission, there shall be not more than 4 clear days between the date on which the order or decision appealed against was made and the day named in the notice of appeal for the hearing of the appeal.

(5) The notice must be served, and the appeal entered, not less than one clear day before the day named in the notice for the hearing of the appeal.

Rule 3 Release of Appellant on Bail

(1) Where, in the case of an appeal under section 13 of the Administration of justice Act 1960, to a Divisional Court or to the House of Lords from a Divisional Court, the appellant is in custody, the High Court may order his release on his giving security (whether by recognisance, with or without sureties, or otherwise and for such reasonable sum as the court may fix) for his appearance, within 10 days after the judgment of the Divisional Court or, as the case may be, of the House of Lords, on the appeal before the court from whose order or decision the appeal is brought unless the order or decision is reversed by that judgment.

(2) Order 79, rule 9(1) to (6) and (8) shall apply in relation to an application to the High Court for bail pending an appeal under the said section 13 to which this rule applies, and to the admission of a person to bail in pursuance of an order made on the application, as they apply in relation to an application to that court for bail in criminal proceedings, and to the admission of a person to bail in pursuance of an order made on the application, but with the substitution, for references to the defendant, of references to the appellant, and, for references to the prosecutor, of references to the court officer of the court from whose order or decision the appeal is brought and to the parties to the proceedings in that court who are directly affected by the appeal.

Rule 4 Release of Appellant on Bail by the Court of Appeal

(1) Where, in the case of an appeal under section 13 of the Administration of Justice Act 1960 to the Court of Appeal or to the House of Lords from the Court of Appeal, the appellant is in custody, the Court of Appeal may order his release on his giving security (whether by recognisance, with or without sureties, or otherwise and for such reasonable sum as that court may fix) for his appearance within 10 days after the judgment of the Court of Appeal or, as the case may be, of the House of Lords on the appeal shall have been given, before the court from whose order or decision the appeal is brought unless the order or decision is reversed by that judgment.

(2) An application for the release of a person under paragraph (1) pending an appeal to the Court of Appeal or House of Lords under the said section 13 must be made in accordance with CPR Part 23, and the application notice must, at least 24 hours before the day named therein for the hearing, be served on the court from whose order or decision the appeal is brought and on all parties to the proceedings in that court who are directly affected by the appeal.

(3) Order 79, rules 9(6), (6A), (6B) and (8) shall apply in relation to the grant of bail under this rule by the Court of Appeal in a case of criminal contempt of court as they apply in relation to the grant of bail in criminal proceedings by the High Court, but with the substitution for references to a judge of references to the Court of Appeal and for references to the defendant of references to the appellant.

(4) When granting bail under this rule in a case of civil contempt of court, the Court of Appeal may order that the recognisance or other security to be given by the appellant or the recognisance of any surety shall be given before any person authorised by virtue of section 119(1) of the Magistrates' Courts Act 1980 to take a recognisance where a magistrates' court having power to take it has, instead of taking it, fixed the amount in which the principal and his sureties, if any, are to be bound. An order by the Court of Appeal granting bail as aforesaid must be in Form 98 in the relevant Practice Direction with the necessary adaptations.

(5) Where in pursuance of an order of the Court of Appeal under paragraph (4) of this rule a recognisance is entered into or other security given before any person, it shall be the duty of that person to cause the recognisance of the appellant or any surety or, as the case may be, a statement of the other security given, to be transmitted forthwith to the designated officer for the court which committed the appellant; and a copy of such recognisance or statement shall at the same time be sent to the governor or keeper of the prison or other place of detention in which the appellant is detained, unless the recognisance or security was given before such governor or keeper.

(6) The powers conferred on the Court of Appeal by paragraphs (1), (3) and (4) of this rule may be exercised by a single judge.

RSC ORDER 110 — ENVIRONMENTAL CONTROL PROCEEDINGS

ord.110 **1.5**

Rule 1 Injunctions to Prevent Environmental Harm

(1) An injunction under—
   (a) section 187B or 214A of the Town and Country Planning Act 1990;
   (b) section 44A of the Planning (Listed Buildings and Conservation Areas) Act 1990; or
   (c) section 26AA of the Planning (Hazardous Substances) Act 1990
   may be granted against a person whose identity is unknown to the applicant; and in the following provisions of this rule such an injunction against such a person is referred to as 'an injunction under paragraph (1) ' and the person against whom it is sought is referred to as 'the defendant'.
(2) An applicant for an injunction under paragraph (1) shall, in the claim form, describe the defendant by reference to—
   (a) a photograph,
   (b) a thing belonging to or in the possession of the defendant, or
   (c) any other evidence,
   with sufficient particularity to enable service to be effected.
(3) An applicant for an injunction under paragraph (1) shall file in support of the application evidence by witness statement or affidavit—
   (a) verifying that he was unable to ascertain, within the time reasonably available to him, the defendant's identity,
   (b) setting out the action taken to ascertain the defendant's identity, and
   (c) verifying the means by which the defendant has been described in the application and that the description is the best that the applicant is able to provide.
(4) Paragraph (2) is without prejudice to the power of the Court to make an order for service by an alternative method or dispensing with service.

RSC ORDER 112 — APPLICATIONS FOR USE OF SCIENTIFIC TESTS IN DETERMINING PARENTAGE

ord.112 **1.5**

Rule 1 Interpretation

In this Order—
   'the Act' means Part III of the Family Law Reform Act 1969;
   'bodily samples' and 'scientific tests' have the meanings assigned to them by section 25 of the Act;
   'direction' means a direction for the use of scientific tests under section 20(1) of the Act;
   'the court officer' means the officer of the court who draws up a direction.

Rule 2 Application for Direction

(1) Except with the permission of the court, an application in any proceedings for a direction shall be in accordance with CPR Part 23 and a copy of the application notice shall be served on every party to the proceedings (other than the applicant) and to any other person from whom the direction involves the taking of bodily samples.
(3) Any notice required by this rule to be served on a person who is not a party to the proceedings shall be served on him personally.

Rule 3 Applications Involving Children under 16 and Patients

Where an application is made for a direction in respect of a person who is either—
(a) under 16; or
(b) suffering from a mental disorder within the meaning of the Mental Health Act 1983 and incapable of understanding the nature and purpose of scientific tests,
the application notice shall state the name and address of the person having the care and control of the person under disability and shall be served on him instead of on the person under disability.

Rule 4 Addition as a Party of Person to be Tested

Where an application is made for a direction involving the taking of bodily samples from a person who is not a party to the proceedings in which the application is made, the court may at any time direct that person to be made a party to the proceedings.

Rule 5 Service of Direction and Adjournment of Proceedings

Where the court gives a direction in any proceedings, the court officer shall send a copy to every party to the proceedings and to every other person from whom the direction involves the taking of bodily samples and, unless otherwise ordered, further consideration of the proceedings shall be adjourned until the court receives a report pursuant to the direction.

Rule 6 Service of Copy Report

On receipt by the court of a report made pursuant to a direction, the proper officer shall send a copy to every party to the proceedings and to every other person from whom the direction involved the taking of bodily samples.

RSC ORDER 113 — SUMMARY PROCEEDINGS FOR POSSESSION OF LAND

ord.113 **1.5**

Rule 7 Writ of Possession

(1) Order 45, rule 3(2) shall not apply in relation to an order for possession in a possession claim against trespassers under Part 55 but no writ of possession to enforce such an order shall be issued after the expiry of three months from the date of the order without the permission of the court.
An application for permission may be made without notice being served on any other party unless the court otherwise directs.

(2) The writ of possession shall be in Form No. 66A.

RSC ORDER 115 — CONFISCATION AND FORFEITURE IN CONNECTION WITH CRIMINAL PROCEEDINGS

ord.115 **1.5**

I Drug Trafficking Act 1994 and Criminal Justice (International Co-operation) Act 1990

Rule 1 Interpretation

(1) In this Part of this Order, 'The Act' means the Drug Trafficking Act 1994 and a section referred to by number means the section so numbered in the Act.

(2) Expressions used in this Part of this Order which are used in the Act have the same meanings in this Part of this Order as in the Act and include any extended meaning given by the Criminal Justice (Confiscation) (Northern Ireland) Order 1990.

Rule 2 Assignment of Proceedings

Subject to rule 12, the jurisdiction of the High Court under the Act shall be exercised by a judge of the Chancery Division or of the Queen's Bench Division.

Rule 2A Title of Proceedings

An application made in accordance with CPR Part 23, or a claim form issued in relation to proceedings under this Part of this Order shall be entitled in the matter of the defendant, naming him, and in the matter of the Act, and all subsequent documents in the matter shall be so entitled.

Rule 2B Application for Confiscation Order

(1) An application by the prosecutor for a confiscation order under section 19 shall be made in accordance with CPR Part 23 where there have been proceedings against the defendant in the High Court, and shall otherwise be made by the issue of a claim form.

(2) The application shall be supported by a witness statement or affidavit giving full particulars of the following matters—

(a) the grounds for believing that the defendant has died or absconded;

(b) the date or approximate date on which the defendant died or absconded;

(c) where the application is made under section 19(2), the offence or offences of which the defendant was convicted, and the date and place of conviction;

(d) where the application is made under section 19(4), the proceedings which have been initiated against the defendant (including particulars of the offence and the date and place of institution of those proceedings); and

(e) where the defendant is alleged to have absconded, the steps taken to contact him.

(3) The prosecutor's statement under section 11 shall be exhibited to the witness statement or affidavit and shall include the following particulars—

(a) the name of the defendant;

(b) the name of the person by whom the statement is given;

(c) such information known to the prosecutor as is relevant to the determination whether the defendant has benefited from drug trafficking and to the assessment of the value of his proceeds of drug trafficking.

(4) Unless the court otherwise orders, a witness statement or affidavit under paragraph (2) may contain statements of information and belief, with their sources and grounds.

(5) The application and the witness statement or affidavit in support shall be served not less than 7 days before the date fixed for the hearing of the application on—

(a) the defendant (or on the personal representatives of a deceased defendant);

(b) any person who the prosecutor reasonably believes is likely to be affected by the making of a confiscation order; and

(c) the receiver, where one has been appointed in the matter.

Rule 3 Application for Restraint Order or Charging Order

(1) An application for a restraint order under section 26 or for a charging order under section 27 (to either of which may be joined an application for the appointment of a receiver) may be made by the prosecutor by the issue of a claim form notice of which need not be served on any other party.

(2) An application under paragraph (1) shall be supported by a witness statement or affidavit, which shall—

(a) give the grounds for the application; and

(b) to the best of the witness's ability, give full particulars of the realisable property in respect of which the order is sought and specify the person or persons holding such property.

(3) Unless the court otherwise directs, a witness statement or affidavit under paragraph (2) may contain statements of information or belief with the sources and grounds thereof.

Rule 4 Restraint Order and Charging Order

(1) A restraint order may be made subject to conditions and exceptions, including but not limited to conditions relating to the indemnifying of third parties against expenses incurred in complying with the order, and exceptions relating to living expenses and legal expenses of the defendant, but the prosecutor shall not be required to give an undertaking to abide by any order as to damages sustained by the defendant as a result of the restraint order.

(2) Unless the court otherwise directs, a restraint order made where notice of it has not been served on any person shall have effect until a day which shall be fixed for the hearing where all parties may attend on the application and a charging order shall be an order to show cause, imposing the charge until such day.

(3) Where a restraint order is made the prosecutor shall serve copies of the order and of the witness statement or affidavit in support on the defendant and on all other named persons restrained by the order and shall notify all other persons or bodies affected by the order of its terms.

(4) Where a charging order is made the prosecutor shall serve copies of the order and of the witness statement or affidavit in support on the defendant and, where the property to which the order relates is held by another person, on that person and shall serve a copy of the order on such of the persons or bodies specified in CPR rule 73.5(1)(c) to (e) as shall be appropriate.

Rule 5 Discharge or Variation of Order

(1) Any person or body on whom a restraint order or a charging order is served or who is notified of such an order may make an application in accordance with CPR Part 23 to discharge or vary the order.

(2) The application notice and any witness statement or affidavit in support shall be lodged with the court and served on the prosecutor and, where he is not the applicant, on the defendant, not less than two clear days before the date fixed for the hearing of the application.

(3) Upon the court being notified that proceedings for the offences have been concluded or that the amount, payment of which is secured by a charging order has been paid into court, any restraint order or charging order, as the case may be, shall be discharged.

(4) The court may also discharge a restraint order or a charging order upon receiving notice from the prosecutor that it is no longer appropriate for the restraint order or the charging order to remain in place.

Rule 6 Further Application by Prosecutor

(1) Where a restraint order or a charging order has been made the prosecutor may apply by an application in accordance with CPR Part 23 with notice or, where the case is one of urgency or the giving of notice would cause a reasonable apprehension of dissipation of assets, without notice—

(a) to vary such order; or

(b) for a restraint order or a charging order in respect of other realisable property; or

(c) for the appointment of a receiver.

(2) An application under paragraph (1) shall be supported by a witness statement or affidavit which, where the application is for a restraint order or a charging order, shall to the best of the witness's ability give full particulars of the realisable property in respect of which the order is sought and specify the person or persons holding such property.

(3) The application and witness statement or affidavit in support shall be lodged with the court and served on the defendant and, where one has been appointed in the matter, on the receiver, not less than two clear days before the date fixed for the hearing of the application.

(4) Rule 4(3) and (4) shall apply to the service of restraint orders and charging orders respectively made under this rule on persons other than the defendant.

Rule 7 Realisation of Property

(1) An application by the prosecutor under section 29 shall, where there have been proceedings against the defendant in the High Court, be made by an application in accordance with CPR Part 23 and shall otherwise be made by the issue of a claim form

(2) The application notice or claim form, as the case may be, shall be served with the evidence in support not less than 7 days before the date fixed for the hearing of the application or claim on—

(a) the defendant;

(b) any person holding any interest in the realisable property to which the application relates; and

(c) the receiver, where one has been appointed in the matter.

(3) The application shall be supported by a witness statement or affidavit, which shall, to the best of the witness's ability, give full particulars of the realisable property to which it relates and specify the person or persons holding such property, and a copy of the confiscation order, of any certificate issued by the Crown Court under section 5(2) and of any charging order made in the matter shall be exhibited to such witness statement or affidavit.

(4) The Court may, on an application under section 29—

(a) exercise the power conferred by section 30(2) to direct the making of payments by a receiver;

(b) give directions in respect of the property interests to which the application relates; and

(c) make declarations in respect of those interests.

Rule 8 Receivers

(1) Subject to the provisions of this rule, the provisions of CPR Part 69 shall apply where a receiver is appointed in pursuance of a charging order or under sections 26 or 29.
(2) Where the receiver proposed to be appointed has been appointed receiver in other proceedings under the Act, it shall not be necessary for a witness statement or affidavit of fitness to be sworn or for the receiver to give security, unless the court otherwise orders.
(3) Where a receiver has fully paid the amount payable under the confiscation order and any sums remain in his hands, he shall make an application to the court for directions in accordance with CPR Part 23, as to the distribution of such sums.
(4) An application under paragraph (3) shall be served with any evidence in support not less than 7 days before the date fixed for the hearing of the application on—
 (a) the defendant; and
 (b) any other person who held property realised by the receiver.
(5) A receiver may apply for an order to discharge him from his office by making an application in accordance with CPR Part 23, which shall be served, together with any evidence in support, on all persons affected by his appointment not less than 7 days before the day fixed for the hearing of the application.

Rule 9 Certificate of Inadequacy

(1) The defendant or a receiver appointed under section 26 or 29 or in pursuance of a charging order may apply in accordance with CPR Part 23 for a certificate under section 17(1).
(2) An application under paragraph (1) shall be served with any supporting evidence not less than 7 days before the date fixed for the hearing of the application on the prosecutor and, as the case may be, on either the defendant or the receiver (where one has been appointed).

Rule 9A Certificate under Section 16

An application under section 16(2) (increase in realisable property) shall be served with any supporting evidence not less than 7 days before the date fixed for the hearing of the application on the defendant and, as the case may be, on either the prosecutor or (where one has been appointed in the matter) on the receiver.

Rule 10 Compensation

An application for an order under section 18 shall be made in accordance with CPR Part 23, which shall be served, with any supporting evidence, on the person alleged to be in default and on the relevant authority under section 18(5) not less than 7 days before the date fixed for the hearing of the application.

Rule 11 Disclosure of Information

(1) An application by the prosecutor under section 59 shall be made in accordance with CPR Part 23 and the application notice shall state the nature of the order sought and whether material sought to be disclosed is to be disclosed to a receiver appointed under section 26 or 29 or in pursuance of a charging order or to a person mentioned in section 59(8).
(2) The application notice and witness statement or affidavit in support shall be served on the authorised Government Department in accordance with Order 77, rule 4 not less than 7 days before the date fixed for the hearing of the application.
(3) The witness statement or affidavit in support of an application under paragraph (1) shall state the grounds for believing that the conditions in section 59(4) and, if appropriate, section 59(7) are fulfilled.

Rule 11A Compensation for, Discharge and Variation of Confiscation Order

(1) An application under section 21, 22 or 23 shall be made in accordance with CPR Part 23 which, together with any evidence in support, shall be lodged with the court and served on the prosecutor not less than 7 days before the day fixed for the hearing of the application.
(2) Notice shall also be served on any receiver appointed in pursuance of a charging order or under section 26 or 29.

(3) An application for an order under section 22 shall be supported by a witness statement or affidavit giving details of—
   (a) the confiscation order made under section 19(4);
   (b) the acquittal of the defendant;
   (c) the realisable property held by the defendant; and
   (d) the loss suffered by the applicant as a result of the confiscation order.

(4) An application for an order under section 23 shall be supported by a witness statement or affidavit giving details of—
   (a) the confiscation order made under section 19(4);
   (b) the date on which the defendant ceased to be an absconder;
   (c) the date on which proceedings against the defendant were instituted and a summary of the steps taken in the proceedings since then; and
   (d) any indication given by the prosecutor that he does not intend to proceed against the defendant.

(5) An application made under section 21 shall be supported by a witness statement or affidavit giving details of—
   (a) the confiscation order made under section 19(4);
   (b) the circumstances in which the defendant ceased to be an absconder; and
   (c) the amounts referred to in section 21(2).

(6) Where an application is made for an order under section 23(3) or 24(2)(b), the witness statement or affidavit shall also include—
   (a) details of the realisable property to which the application relates; and
   (b) details of the loss suffered by the applicant as a result of the confiscation order.

(7) Unless the court otherwise orders, a witness statement or affidavit under paragraphs (3) to (6) may contain statements of information and belief, with the sources and grounds thereof.

Rule 12 Exercise of Powers under Sections 37 and 40

The powers conferred on the High Court by sections 37 and 40 may be exercised by a judge or a Master of the Queen's Bench Division.

Rule 13 Application for Registration

An application for registration of an order specified in an Order in Council made under section 37 or of an external confiscation order under section 40(1) must be made in accordance with CPR Part 23, and may be made without notice.

Rule 14 Evidence in Support of Application under Section 37

An application for registration of an order specified in an Order in Council made under section 37 must be made in accordance with CPR Part 23, and be supported by a witness statement or affidavit—

(i) exhibiting the order or a certified copy thereof; and
(ii) stating, to the best of the witness's knowledge, particulars of what property the person against whom the order was made holds in England and Wales, giving the source of the witness's knowledge.

Rule 15 Evidence in Support of Application under Section 40(1)

(1) An application for registration of an external confiscation order must be made in accordance with CPR Part 23, and be supported by a witness statement or affidavit—
   (a) exhibiting the order or a verified or certified or otherwise duly authenticated copy thereof and, where the order is not in the English language, a translation thereof into English certified by a notary public or authenticated by witness statement or affidavit; and
   (b) stating—
      (i) that the order is in force and is not subject to appeal;
      (ii) where the person against whom the order was made did not appear in the proceedings, that he received notice thereof in sufficient time to enable him to defend them;
      (iii) in the case of money, either that at the date of the application the sum payable under the order has not been paid or the amount which remains unpaid, as may be appropriate, or, in the case of other property, the property which has not been recovered; and

(iv) to the best of the witness's knowledge, particulars of what property the person against whom the order was made holds in England and Wales, giving the source of the witness's knowledge.

(2) Unless the court otherwise directs, a witness statement or affidavit for the purposes of this rule may contain statements of information or belief with the sources and grounds thereof.

Rule 16 Register of Orders

(1) There shall be kept in the Central Office under the direction of the Master of the Crown Office a register of the orders registered under the Act.

(2) There shall be included in such register particulars of any variation or setting aside of a registration and of any execution issued on a registered order.

Rule 17 Notice of Registration

(1) Notice of the registration of an order must be served on the person against whom it was obtained by delivering it to him personally or by sending it to him at his usual or last known address or place of business or in such other manner as the court may direct.

(2) Permission is not required to serve such a notice out of the jurisdiction and CPR rules 6.24, 6.25 and 6.29 shall apply in relation to such notice as they apply in relation to a claim form.

Rule 18 Application to Vary or Set Aside Registration

An application made in accordance with CPR Part 23 by the person against whom an order was made to vary or set aside the registration of an order must be made to a judge and be supported by witness statement or affidavit.

Rule 19 Enforcement of Order

(2) If an application is made under rule 18, an order shall not be enforced until after such application is determined.

Rule 20 Variation, Satisfaction and Discharge of Registered Order

Upon the court being notified by the applicant for registration that an order which has been registered has been varied, satisfied or discharged, particulars of the variation, satisfaction or discharge, as the case may be, shall be entered in the register.

Rule 21 Rules to Have Effect Subject to Orders in Council

Rules 12 to 20 shall have effect subject to the provisions of the Order in Council made under section 37 or, as the case may be, of the Order in Council made under section 39.

Rule 21A Criminal Justice (International Co-operation) Act 1990: External Forfeiture Orders

The provisions of this Part of this Order shall, with such modifications as are necessary and subject to the provisions of any Order in Council made under section 9 of the Criminal Justice (International Cooperation) Act 1990, apply to proceedings for the registration and enforcement of external forfeiture orders as they apply to such proceedings in relation to external confiscation orders.

For the purposes of this rule, an external forfeiture order is an order made by a court in a country or territory outside the United Kingdom which is enforceable in the United Kingdom by virtue of any such Order in Council.

II Part VI of the Criminal Justice Act 1988

Rule 22 Interpretation

(1) In this Part of this Order, 'the 1988 Act' means the Criminal Justice Act 1988 and a section referred to by number means the section so numbered in that Act.

(2) Expressions which are used in this Part of this Order which are used in the 1988 Act have the same meanings in this Part of this Order as in the 1988 Act and include any extended meaning given by the Criminal Justice (Confiscation) (Northern Ireland) Order 1990.

Rule 23 Application of Part I of Order 115

Part I of Order 115 (except rule 11) shall apply for the purposes of proceedings under Part VI of the 1988 Act with the necessary modifications and, in particular—

(a) references to drug trafficking offences and to drug trafficking shall be construed as references to offences to which Part VI of the 1988 Act applies and to committing such an offence;

(b) references to the Drug Trafficking Act 1994 shall be construed as references to the 1988 Act and references to sections 5(2), 26, 27, 29, 30(2), 17(1), 18, 18(5), 39 and 40 of the 1994 Act shall be construed as references to sections 73(6), 77, 78, 80, 81, 81(1), 83(1), 89, 89(5), 96 and 97 of the 1988 Act respectively;

(c) rule 3(2) shall have effect as if the following sub-paragraphs were substituted for sub-paragraphs (a) and (b)—

'(a) state, as the case may be, either that proceedings have been instituted against the defendant for an offence to which Part VI of the 1988 Act applies (giving particulars of the offence) and that they have not been concluded or that, whether by the laying of an information or otherwise, a person is to be charged with such an offence;

(b) state, as the case may be, either that a confiscation order has been made or the grounds for believing that such an order may be made;'

(d) rule 7(3) shall have effect as if the words 'certificate issued by a magistrates' court or the Crown Court' were substituted for the words 'certificate issued by the Crown Court';

(e) rule 8 shall have effect as if the following paragraph were added at the end—

'(6) Where a receiver applies in accordance with CPR Part 23 for the variation of a confiscation order, the application notice shall be served, with any supporting evidence, on the defendant and any other person who may be affected by the making of an order under section 83 of the 1988 Act, not less than 7 days before the date fixed for the hearing of the application.';

(f) rule 11 shall apply with the necessary modifications where an application is made under section 93J of the 1988 Act for disclosure of information held by government departments.

III Terrorism Act 2000

Rule 24 Interpretation

In this Part of this Order—

(a) 'the Act' means the Terrorism Act 2000;

(b) 'Schedule 4' means Schedule 4 to the Act;

(ba) 'the prosecutor' means the person with conduct of proceedings which have been instituted in England and Wales for an offence under any of sections 15 to 18 of the Act, or the person who the High Court is satisfied will have the conduct of any proceedings for such an offence; and

(c) other expressions used have the same meanings as they have in Schedule 4 to the Act.

Rule 25 Assignment of Proceedings

(1) Subject to paragraph (2), the jurisdiction of the High Court under the Act shall be exercised by a judge of the Queen's Bench Division or of the Chancery Division sitting in private.

(2) The jurisdiction conferred on the High Court by paragraph 9 of Schedule 4 may also be exercised by a Master of the Queen's Bench Division.

Rule 26 Application for Restraint Order

(1) An application for a restraint order under paragraph 5 of Schedule 4 may be made by the prosecutor by a claim form, which need not be served on any person.

(2) An application under paragraph (1) shall be supported by a witness statement or affidavit, which shall—

(a) state, as the case may be, either—

(i) that proceedings have been instituted against a person for an offence under any of sections 15 to 18 of the Act and that they have not been concluded; or

(ii) that a criminal investigation has been started in England and Wales with regard to such an offence, and in either case give details of the alleged or suspected offence and of the defendant's involvement;

(b) where proceedings have been instituted, state, as the case may be, that a forfeiture order has been made in the proceedings or the grounds for believing that such an order may be made;

(ba) where proceedings have not been instituted—

(i) indicate the state of progress of the investigation and when it is anticipated that a decision will be taken on whether to institute proceedings against the defendant;

(ii) state the grounds for believing that a forfeiture order may be made in any proceedings against the defendant; and

(iii) verify that the prosecutor is to have the conduct of any such proceedings;

(c) to the best of the witness's ability, give full particulars of the property in respect of which the order is sought and specify the person or persons holding such property and any other persons having an interest in it.

(3) A claim form under paragraph (1) shall be entitled in the matter of the defendant, naming him, and in the matter of the Act, and all subsequent documents in the matter shall be so entitled.

(4) Unless the court otherwise directs, a witness statement or affidavit under paragraph (2) may contain statements of information or belief with the sources and grounds thereof.

Rule 27 Restraint Order

(1) A restraint order may be made subject to conditions and exceptions, including but not limited to conditions relating to the indemnifying of third parties against expenses incurred in complying with the order, and exceptions relating to living expenses and legal expenses of the defendant; but the prosecutor shall not be required to give an undertaking to abide by any order as to damages sustained by the defendant as a result of the restraint order.

(2) Unless the court otherwise directs, the application for it being served on any person shall have effect until a day which shall be fixed for the hearing where all parties may attend on the application.

(3) Where a restraint order is made the prosecutor shall serve copies of the order and, unless the court otherwise orders, of the witness statement or affidavit in support on the defendant and on all other persons affected by the order.

Rule 28 Discharge or Variation of Order

(1) Subject to paragraph (2), an application to discharge or vary a restraint order shall be made in accordance with CPR Part 23.

(2) Where the case is one of urgency, an application under this rule by the prosecutor may be made without notice.

(3) The application and any witness statement or affidavit in support shall be lodged with the court and, where the application is made in accordance with CPR Part 23 the application notice shall be served on the following persons (other than the applicant)—

(a) the prosecutor;

(b) the defendant; and

(c) all other persons restrained or otherwise affected by the order;

not less than two clear days before the date fixed for the hearing of the application.

(4) Where a restraint order has been made and has not been discharged, the prosecutor shall notify the court when proceedings for the offence have been concluded, and the court shall thereupon discharge the restraint order.

(5) Where an order is made discharging or varying a restraint order, the applicant shall serve copies of the order of discharge or variation on all persons restrained by the earlier order and shall notify all other persons affected of the terms of the order of discharge or variation.

Rule 29 Compensation

An application for an order under paragraph 9 or 10 of Schedule 4 shall be made in accordance with CPR Part 23, and the application notice, shall be served, with any supporting evidence, on the person alleged to be in default and on the person or body by whom compensation, if ordered, will be payable under paragraph 9(6) or 10(4) not less than 7 days before the date fixed for the hearing of the application.

Rule 30 Application for Registration

An application for registration of a Scottish order, a Northern Ireland order or an Islands order must be made in accordance with CPR Part 23 and may be made without notice.

Rule 31 Evidence in Support of Application

(1) An application for registration of any such order as is mentioned in rule 30 must be supported by a witness statement or affidavit—
  (a) exhibiting the order or a certified copy thereof; and
  (b) which shall, to the best of the witness's ability, give particulars of such property in respect of which the order was made as is in England and Wales, and specify the person or persons holding such property.

(2) Unless the court otherwise directs, a witness statement or affidavit for the purposes of this rule may contain statements of information or belief with the sources and grounds thereof.

Rule 32 Register of Orders

(1) There shall be kept in the Central Office under the direction of the Master of the Administrative Court a register of the orders registered under the Act.

(2) There shall be included in such register particulars of any variation or setting aside of a registration, and of any execution issued on a registered order.

Rule 33 Notice of Registration

(1) Notice of the registration of an order must be served on the person or persons holding the property referred to in rule 3 1 (1)(b) and any other persons appearing to have an interest in that property.

(2) Permission is not required to serve such a notice out of the jurisdiction and CPR rules 6.24, 6.25 and 6.29 shall apply in relation to such notice as they apply in relation to a claim form.

Rule 34 Application to Vary or Set Aside Registration

An application to vary or set aside the registration of an order must be made to a judge in accordance with CPR Part 23 and be supported by a witness statement or affidavit.

This rule does not apply to a variation or cancellation under rule 36.

Rule 35 Enforcement of Order

(2) If an application is made under rule 34, an order shall not be enforced until after such application is determined.

(3) This rule does not apply to the taking of steps under paragraph 7 or 8 of Schedule 4, as applied by paragraph 13(6) of that Schedule.

Rule 36 Variation and Cancellation of Registration

If effect has been given (whether in England or Wales or elsewhere) to a Scottish, Northern Ireland or Islands order, or if the order has been varied or discharged by the court by which it was made, the applicant for registration shall inform the court and—

(a) if such effect has been given in respect of all the money or other property to which the order applies, or if the order has been discharged by the court by which it was made, registration of the order shall be cancelled;

(b) if such effect has been given in respect of only part of the money or other property, or if the order has been varied by the court by which it was made, registration of the order shall be varied accordingly.

IV International Criminal Court Act 2001: Fines, Forfeitures and Reparation Orders

Rule 37 Interpretation

In this Part of this Order—

(a) 'the Act' means the International Criminal Court Act 2001;

(b) 'the ICC' means the International Criminal Court;
(c) 'an order of the ICC' means—
(i) a fine or forfeiture ordered by the ICC; or
(ii) an order by the ICC against a person convicted by the ICC specifying a reparation to, or in respect of, a victim.

Rule 38 Registration of ICC Orders for Enforcement

(1) An application to the High Court to register an order of the ICC for enforcement, or to vary or set aside the registration of an order, may be made to a judge or a Master of the Queen's Bench Division.
(2) Rule 13 and rules 15 to 20 in Part I of this Order shall, with such modifications as are necessary and subject to the provisions of any regulations made under section 49 of the Act, apply to the registration for enforcement of an order of the ICC as they apply to the registration of an external confiscation order.

RSC ORDER 116 — THE CRIMINAL PROCEDURE AND INVESTIGATIONS ACT 1996

ord.116 **1.5**

Rule 1 Application

This Order shall apply in relation to acquittals in respect of offences alleged to be committed on or after 15th April 1997.

Rule 2 Interpretation

In this Order, unless the context otherwise requires—
'the Act' means the Criminal Procedure and Investigations Act 1996;
'acquitted person' means a person whose acquittal of an offence is the subject of a certification under section 54(2) of the Act, and 'acquittal' means the acquittal of that person of that offence;
'magistrates' court' has the same meaning as in section 148 of the Magistrates' Courts Act 1980;
'prosecutor' means the individual or body which acted as prosecutor in the proceedings which led to the acquittal;
'record of court proceedings' means—
(a) (where the proceedings took place in the Crown Court) a transcript of the evidence, or
(b) a note of the evidence made by the justices' clerk,
in the proceedings which led to the conviction for the administration of justice offence referred to in section 54(1)(b) of the Act or, as the case may be, the proceedings which led to the acquittal;

'single judge' means a judge of the Queen's Bench Division;
'witness' means a witness whose evidence is contained in a witness statement or affidavit filed under rule 5, 7, 8 or 9.

Rule 3 Assignment of Proceedings

The jurisdiction of the High Court under section 54(3) of the Act shall be exercised by a single judge.

Rule 4 Time Limit for Making Application

An application under section 54(3) of the Act shall be made not later than 28 days after—
(a) the expiry of the period allowed for appealing (whether by case stated or otherwise), or making an application for leave to appeal, against the conviction referred to in section 54(1)(b) of the Act; or
(b) where notice of appeal or application for leave to appeal against the conviction is given, the determination of the appeal or application for leave to appeal and, for this purpose, 'determination' includes abandonment (within the meaning of rule 10 of the Criminal Appeal Rules 1968 or, as the case may be, rule 11 of the Crown Court Rules 1982).

Rule 5 Application

(1) An application under section 54(3) of the Act shall be made by claim form which shall be issued out of the Crown Office by the prosecutor.
(2) The application shall be accompanied by—
   (a) a witness statement or affidavit which deals with the conditions in section 55(1), (2) and (4) of the Act and which exhibits any relevant documents (which may include a copy of any record of court proceedings);
   (b) a copy of the certification under section 54(2) of the Act.

Rule 6 Notice to the Acquitted Person

(1) The prosecutor shall, within 4 days of the issue of the application, serve written notice on the acquitted person that the application has been issued.
(2) The notice given under paragraph (1) shall—
   (a) specify the date on which the application was issued;
   (b) be accompanied by a copy of the application and of the documents which accompanied it;
   (c) inform the acquitted person that—
      (i) the result of the application may be the making of an order by the High Court quashing the acquittal, and
      (ii) if he wishes to respond to the application, he must, within 28 days of the date of service on him of the notice, file in the Crown Office any witness statement or affidavit on which he intends to rely.

Rule 7 Witness Statement or Affidavit of Service on an Acquitted Person

The prosecutor shall, as soon as practicable after service of the notice under rule 6, file at the Crown Office a witness statement or affidavit of service which exhibits a copy of the notice.

Rule 8 Response of Acquitted Person

(1) If the acquitted person wishes to respond to the application, he shall, within 28 days of service on him of notice under rule 6, file in the Crown Office a witness statement or affidavit which—
   (a) deals with the conditions in section 55(1), (2) and (4) of the Act; and
   (b) exhibits any relevant documents (which may include a copy of any record of court proceedings).
(2) The acquitted person shall, within 4 days of the filing of the documents mentioned in paragraph (1), serve copies of them on the prosecutor.

Rule 9 Evidence

(1) A witness statement or affidavit filed under rule 5, 7, 8 or this rule may contain statements of information or belief with the sources and grounds thereof.
(2) The prosecutor may, not later than 10 days after expiry of the period allowed under rule 8(1), apply for an order granting permission to file further evidence without notice being served on any other party.
(3) If the single judge grants permission, the order shall specify a period within which further evidence or records are to be filed, and the Crown Office shall serve a copy of the order on the prosecutor and on the acquitted person.
(4) The prosecutor shall, within 4 days of filing further evidence in the Crown Office, serve a copy of that evidence on the acquitted person.

Rule 10 Determination of the Application

(1) Subject to paragraph (3), the single judge shall determine whether or not to make an order under section 54(3) of the Act on the basis of the written material provided under rules 5, 7, 8 and 9 in the absence of the prosecutor, the acquitted person, or of any witness.
(2) The determination shall not be made, and any hearing under paragraph (3) shall not take place, before the expiry of—

(a) 10 days after the expiry of the period allowed under rule 8(1), or
(b) 10 days after the expiry of the period allowed by any order made under rule 9(3).

(3) The single judge may, of his own initiative or on the application of the prosecutor or acquitted person, order a hearing of the application if he thinks fit.

(4) An application under paragraph (3) shall state whether a hearing is desired in order for a deponent for the other party to attend and be cross-examined, and, if so, the reasons for wishing the witness to attend.

(5) An application under paragraph (3) shall be made no later than 7 days after the expiry of the period allowed—
(a) under rule 8(1), or
(b) by any order made under rule 9(3).

(6) Where a hearing is ordered, the single judge may, of his own initiative or on the application of the prosecutor or acquitted person, order a witness to attend in order to be cross-examined.

(7) The prosecutor or the acquitted person, as the case may be, shall within 4 days after filing the application under paragraph (3), serve a copy of it on the other party, and file in the Crown Office a witness statement or affidavit of service.

(8) A party served under paragraph (7) shall, within 5 days of service, file any representations he wishes to make as to whether or not a hearing should be ordered.

(9) Subject to paragraph (10) below—
(a) the single judge shall not determine an application for a hearing under paragraph (3) unless—
(i) a witness statement or affidavit of service has been filed as required by paragraph (7), and
(ii) the period for filing representations allowed under paragraph (8) has elapsed, or
(iii) representations have been filed under paragraph (8).
(b) The requirements imposed by sub-paragraph (a)(i) and (iii) are satisfied even though the witness statement or affidavit of service or, as the case may be, the representations are filed outside the time limits allowed.

(10) Where after an application for a hearing has been made—
(a) no witness statement or affidavit or service has been filed, and
(b) no representations under paragraph (8) have been received after the expiry of 7 days from the filing of the application,
the single judge may reject the application.

(11) Where after a hearing is ordered, either the prosecutor or the acquitted person desires a witness for the other party to attend the hearing in order to be cross-examined, he must apply for an order under paragraph (5) giving his reasons without notice being served on any other party.

(12) The Crown Office shall serve notice on the prosecutor and the acquitted person of any order made under the foregoing paragraphs of this rule and, where a hearing is ordered, the notice shall—
(a) set out the date, time and place of the hearing, and
(b) give details of any witness ordered to attend for cross-examination.

(13) A hearing ordered under paragraph (3) above shall be in public unless the single judge otherwise directs.

(14) The Crown Office shall serve notice of any order made under section 54(3) of the Act quashing the acquittal or of a decision not to make such an order on the prosecutor, the acquitted person and—
(a) where the court before which the acquittal or conviction occurred was a magistrates' court, on the designated officer;
(b) where the court before which the acquittal or conviction occurred was the Crown Court, on the appropriate officer of the Crown Court sitting at the place where the acquittal or conviction occurred.

PD RSC Ord. 46 Practice Direction — Execution

This practice direction supplements RSC Order 46 (Schedule 1 to the CPR) and CCR Order 26 (Schedule 2 to the CPR)

Levying Execution on Certain Days

1.1 Unless the Court orders otherwise, a writ of execution or a warrant of execution to enforce a judgment or order must not be executed on a Sunday, Good Friday or Christmas Day.

1.2 Paragraph 1.1 does not apply to an Admiralty claim *in rem*.

PD RSC Ord. 52 Practice Direction — Committal Applications

PD ord. 52 **76.28, 78.6**

This practice direction is supplemental to RSC Order 52 (Schedule 1 to the CPR) and CCR Order 29 (Schedule 2 to the CPR)

PD RSC ord. 52 **78.6** [For commentary on a specific paragraph, please refer to the cross-references after the title of the paragraph.]

General

para.1.2 **78.5**
para.1.4 **78.2, 78.13**

1.1 Part I of this practice direction applies to any application for an order for committal of a person to prison for contempt of court (a 'committal application'). Part II makes additional provision where the committal application relates to a contempt in the face of the court.

1.2 Where the alleged contempt of court consists of or is based upon disobedience to an order made in a county court or breach of an undertaking given to a county court or consists of an act done in the course of proceedings in a county court, or where in any other way the alleged contempt is a contempt which the county court has power to punish, the committal application may be made in the county court in question.

1.3 In every other case (other than one within Part II of this practice direction), a committal application must be made in the High Court.

1.4 In all cases the Convention rights of those involved should particularly be borne in mind. It should be noted that the burden of proof, having regard to the possibility that a person may be sent to prison, is that the allegation be proved beyond reasonable doubt. (Section 1 of the Human Rights Act 1998 defines 'the Convention rights'.)

PART I

Commencement of Committal Proceedings

para.2.1 **78.6**
para.2.2(1)–(3) **78.6**
para.2.4(1)–(3) **78.7**
para.2.4(5) **78.7**
para.2.5 **78.6**
para.2.5(4) **78.6**
para.2.5(5) **78.6**
para.2.6 **78.5**
para.2.6(2)–(3) **78.8**
para.2.6(4) **78.15**

2.1 A committal application must, subject to para. 2.2, be commenced by the issue of a Part 8 claim form (see para. 2.5).

2.2 (1) If the committal application is made in existing proceedings it must be commenced by the filing of an application notice in those proceedings.

(2) An application to commit for breach of an undertaking or order must be commenced by the filing of an application notice in the proceedings in which the undertaking was given or the order was made.

(3) The application notice must state that the application is made in the proceedings in question and its title and reference number must correspond with the title and reference number of those proceedings.

2.3 If the committal application is one which cannot be made without permission, the claim form or application notice, as the case may be, may not be issued or filed until the requisite permission has been granted.

2.4 If the permission of the court is needed in order to make a committal application:

(1) the permission must be applied for by filing an application notice (see r. 23.2(4));

(2) the application notice need not be served on the respondent;

(3) the date on which and the name of the judge by whom the requisite permission was granted must be stated on the claim form or application notice by which the committal application is commenced;

(4) the permission may only be granted by a judge who, under para. 11, would have power to hear the committal application if permission were granted; and

(5) rr. 23.9 and 23.10 do not apply.

2.5 If the committal application is commenced by the issue of a claim form, Part 8 shall, subject to the provisions of this practice direction, apply as though references to 'claimant' were references to the person making the committal application and references to 'defendant' were references to the person against whom the committal application is made (in this practice direction referred to as 'the respondent') but:

(1) the claim form together with copies of all written evidence in support must, unless the court otherwise directs, be served personally on the respondent,

(2) the claim form must set out in full the grounds on which the committal application is made and must identify, separately and numerically, each alleged act of contempt including, if known, the date of each alleged act,

(3) an amendment to the claim form can be made with the permission of the court but not otherwise,

(4) r. 8.4 does not apply, and

(5) the claim form must contain a prominent notice stating the possible consequences of the court making a committal order and of the respondent not attending the hearing. A form of notice, which may be used, is annexed to this practice direction.

2.6 If a committal application is commenced by the filing of an application notice, Part 23 shall, subject to the provisions of this practice direction, apply, but:

(1) the application notice together with copies of all written evidence in support must, unless the court otherwise directs, be served personally on the respondent,

(2) the application notice must set out in full the grounds on which the committal application is made and must identify, separately and numerically, each alleged act of contempt including, if known, the date of each of the alleged acts,

(3) an amendment to the application notice can be made with the permission of the court but not otherwise,

(4) the court may not dispose of the committal application without a hearing, and

(5) the application notice must contain a prominent notice stating the possible consequences of the court making a committal order and of the respondent not attending the hearing. A form of notice, which may be used, is annexed to this practice direction.

Written Evidence

para.3.1–3.4 **78.12**

3.1 Written evidence in support of or in opposition to a committal application must be given by affidavit.

3.2 Written evidence served in support of or in opposition to a committal application must, unless the court otherwise directs, be filed.

3.3 A respondent may give oral evidence at the hearing, whether or not he has filed or served any written evidence. If he does so, he may be cross-examined.

3.4 A respondent may, with the permission of the court, call a witness to give oral evidence at the hearing whether or not the witness has sworn an affidavit.

Case Management and Date of Hearing

para.4.1 **78.9**
para.4.2 **78.10**
paras.4.3–4.4 **78.13**
para.4.5 **78.13**
para.4.6(1)–(4) **78.13**

4.1 The applicant for the committal order must, when lodging the claim form or application notice with the court for issuing or filing, as the case may be, obtain from the court a date for the hearing of the committal application.

4.2 Unless the court otherwise directs, the hearing date of a committal application shall be not less than 14 days after service of the claim form or of the application notice, as the case may be, on the respondent. The hearing date must be specified in the claim form or application notice or in a notice of hearing or application attached to and served with the claim form or application notice.

4.3 The court may, however, at any time give case management directions, including directions for the service of written evidence by the respondent and written evidence in reply by the applicant, or may hold a directions hearing.

4.4 The court may on the hearing date:

(1) give case management directions with a view to a hearing of the committal application on a future date, or

(2) if the committal application is ready to be heard, proceed forthwith to hear it.

4.5 In dealing with any committal application, the court will have regard to the need for the respondent to have details of the alleged acts of contempt and the opportunity to respond to the committal application.

4.6 The court should also have regard to the need for the respondent to be:

(1) allowed a reasonable time for responding to the committal application including, if necessary, preparing a defence;

(2) made aware of the availability of assistance from the Community Legal Service and how to contact the Service;

(3) given the opportunity, if unrepresented, to obtain legal advice; and

(4) if unable to understand English, allowed to make arrangements, seeking the assistance of the court if necessary, for an interpreter to attend the hearing.

Striking Out

para.5 **78.14**

5 The court may, on application by the respondent or on its own initiative, strike out a committal application if it appears to the court:

(1) that the committal application and the evidence served in support of it disclose no reasonable ground for alleging that the respondent is guilty of a contempt of court,

(2) that the committal application is an abuse of the court's process or, if made in existing proceedings, is otherwise likely to obstruct the just disposal of those proceedings, or

(3) that there has been a failure to comply with a rule, practice direction or court order.

(Part 3 contains general powers for the management by the court.)

Miscellaneous

para.7 **78.12**
para.8 **78.14**
para.10 **78.14**

6 Rules 35.7 (court's power to direct that evidence is to be given by a single joint expert), 35.8 (instructions to single joint expert) and 35.9 (power of court to direct a party to provide information) do not apply to committal applications.

7 An order under r. 18.1 (order for a party to give additional information) may not be made against a respondent to a committal application.

8 A committal application may not be discontinued without the permission of the court.

9 A committal application should normally be heard in public (see r. 39.2), but if it is heard in private and the court finds the respondent guilty of contempt of court, the judge shall, when next sitting in public, state:

(1) the name of the respondent,

(2) in general terms the nature of the contempt or contempts found proved, and

(3) the penalty (if any) imposed.

10 The court may waive any procedural defect in the commencement or conduct of a committal application if satisfied that no injustice has been caused to the respondent by the defect.

11 Except where under an enactment a master or district judge has power to make a committal order,[1] a committal order can only be made:

(1) in High Court proceedings, by a High Court judge or a person authorised to act as such,[2]

(2) in county court proceedings by a circuit judge or a person authorised to act or capable by virtue of his office of acting as such.[3]

[1] E.g. County Courts Act 1984, ss. 14 and 118.

[2] See Supreme Court Act 1981, s. 9(1).

[3] See County Courts Act 1984, s. 5(3).

PART II

para.12 **78.15**	para.13(4)(e) **78.15**
para.13 **78.6, 78.15**	para.13(5)(a)–(c) **78.15**
para.13(1)–(3) **78.15**	para.13(6) **78.15**

12 Where the committal application relates to a contempt in the face of the court the following matters should be given particular attention. Normally, it will be appropriate to defer consideration of the behaviour to allow the respondent time to reflect on what has occurred. The time needed for the following procedures should allow such a period of reflection.

13 A Part 8 claim form and an application notice are not required for Part II, but other provisions of this practice direction should be applied, as necessary, or adapted to the circumstances. In addition the judge should:

(1) tell the respondent of the possible penalty he faces;

(2) inform the respondent in detail, and preferably in writing, of the actions and behaviour of the respondent which have given rise to the committal application;

(3) if he considers that an apology would remove the need for the committal application, tell the respondent;

(4) have regard to the need for the respondent to be:

(a) allowed a reasonable time for responding to the committal application, including, if necessary, preparing a defence;

(b) made aware of the availability of assistance from the Community Legal Service and how to contact the Service;

(c) given the opportunity, if unrepresented, to obtain legal advice;

(d) if unable to understand English, allowed to make arrangements, seeking the court's assistance if necessary, for an interpreter to attend the hearing; and

(e) brought back before the court for the committal application to be heard within a reasonable time;

(5) allow the respondent an opportunity to:

(a) apologise to the court;

(b) explain his actions and behaviour; and,

(c) if the contempt is proved, to address the court on the penalty to be imposed on him;

(6) if there is a risk of the appearance of bias, ask another judge to hear the committal application;

(7) where appropriate, nominate a suitable person to give the respondent the information.

(It is likely to be appropriate to nominate a person where the effective communication of information by the judge to the respondent was not possible when the incident occurred.)

14 Where the committal application is to be heard by another judge, a written statement by the judge before whom the actions and behaviour of the respondent which have given rise to the committal application took place may be submitted as evidence of those actions and behaviour.

ANNEX

annex **78.6**

Important Notice

The Court has power to send you to prison and to fine you if it finds that any of the allegations made against you are true and amount to a contempt of court.

You must attend court on the date shown on the front of this form. It is in your own interest to do so. You should bring with you any witnesses and documents which you think will help you put your side of the case.

If you consider the allegations are not true you must tell the court why. If it is established that they are true, you must tell the court of any good reason why they do not amount to a contempt of court, or, if they do, why you should not be punished.

If you need advice you should show this document at once to your solicitor or go to a Citizens' Advice Bureau.

PD RSC Ord. 54 Practice Direction — Application for Writ of Habeas Corpus

This practice direction supplements CPR Part 50, and Schedule 1 to the CPR

Terminology

1.1 In this practice direction:

(1) 'Order 54' means those provisions contained in Schedule 1, RSC Order 54 which were previously contained in the Rules of the Supreme Court (1965);

(2) a reference to a rule or Part prefixed with CPR is a reference to a rule or Part contained in the CPR rules; and

(3) a reference to a rule number alone is a reference to the rule so numbered in Order 54.

Scope

2.1 This practice direction supplements Order 54 (which sets out how to apply for a writ of habeas corpus) by providing further detail about the application.

2.2 This practice direction must be read together with Order 54.

2.3 It also lists at paragraph 7 other practice directions which governed procedure relating to Order 54 before 26 April 1999 and which will continue to do so.

Form to Be Used Where Court Directs Claim Form to Be Used

3.1 Where the court directs that an application be made by claim form, under:

(1) rule 2 (on hearing application under rule 1); or

(2) rule 4(2) (application in criminal proceedings ordered to be made to Divisional Court of the Queen's Bench Division),

the claimant must use Form 87 modified in accordance with the guidance set out in the Forms practice direction.

Form to Be Used for Notice of Adjourned Application Directed by Court

4.1 Where the court directs under rule 2(1)(c) that an application made under rule 1 is adjourned to allow for service of notice of the application, such notice must be given in modified Form 88.

Service

5.1 The party seeking the writ must serve:

(1) the claim form in accordance with rule 2(2); and

(2) the writ of habeas corpus ad subjiciendum and notice in Form 90, as modified, in accordance with rule 6.

(CPR rule 6.3 provides that the court will normally serve a document which it has issued or prepared.)

The Administrative Court

6.1 When the court directs that an application is to be made by claim form under:

(1) rule 2(1) (powers of court to whom application made under rule 1); or

(2) rule 4(2) (power of court where application made in criminal proceedings)

the application must be entered in the Administrative Court List in accordance with Practice Direction (Crown Office List) [1987] 1 WLR 232, [1987] 1 All ER 368.

Practice Directions etc., Which Apply to Order 54

7.1 On and after 26 April 1999, the practice directions, statements and practice notes set out in Table 1 continue to apply to proceedings under Order 54.

Table 1

Practice Direction etc.	Content
Practice Direction (Crown Office List: Criminal Proceedings) [1983] 1 WLR 925, [1983] 2 All ER 1020.	Urgent matters outside London — consultation of Crown Office and continuation in London
Practice Note (Crown Office List: Estimated Length of Hearing) [1987] 1 All ER 1184.	Need for accuracy in time estimates
Practice Direction (Crown Office List) [1987] 1 WLR 232, [1987] 1 All ER 368.	Parts of the List
Practice Direction (Crown Office List: Preparation for Hearings) [1994] 1 WLR 1551, [1994] 4 All ER 671.	Preparation for hearings; documentation; time limits; skeleton arguments; amendment of grounds.
Practice Direction (Crown Office List: Consent Orders) [1997] 1 WLR 825, [1997] 2 All ER 799.	Consent orders
Practice Statement (Supreme Court: Judgments) [1998] 1 WLR 825, [1998] 2 All ER 667.	Judgments

PD RSC Ord. 95 Practice Direction — Bills of Sale

This practice direction supplements RSC Order 95 (Schedule 1 to the CPR)

Entry of Satisfaction

1. Notwithstanding the provisions of RSC Order 95, rule 2(1), (1A) and (2), if a consent to the satisfaction signed by the person entitled to the benefit of the bill of sale can be obtained, the application under RSC Order 95, rule 2(1) can be made by affidavit or witness statement instead of by claim form.
2. If paragraph 1 applies and the application is made by affidavit or witness statement:
   (1) CPR Part 23 will apply to the application;
   (2) the affidavit or witness statement will constitute the application notice;
   (3) the affidavit or witness statement need not be served on any other person; and
   (4) the application will normally be dealt with without a hearing.
3. Where the consent of the person entitled to the benefit of the bill of sale cannot be obtained, the application under RSC Order 95, rule 2(1) must be made by claim form in accordance with CPR Part 8 and RSC Order 95, rule 2(3) will apply.

PD RSC Ord. 115 Practice Direction — Restraint Orders and Appointment of Receivers in Connection with Criminal Proceedings and Investigations

This practice direction supplements RSC Order 115 (Schedule 1 to the CPR)

Scope and Interpretation

1.1 This practice direction applies to applications to the High Court for a restraint order or the appointment of a receiver under:
(1) part VI of the Criminal Justice Act 1988 ('the 1988 Act');
(2) part I of the Drug Trafficking Act 1994 ('the 1994 Act'); or
(3) sch. 4 to the Terrorism Act 2000 ('the 2000 Act').
(Part VI of the 1988 Act and Part I of the 1994 Act are repealed by the Proceeds of Crime Act 2002 from a day to be appointed, but will continue to apply to pending and transitional cases. Following their repeal, applications for a restraint order or the appointment of a receiver which would previously have been made under those Acts will instead be made to the Crown Court under part 2 of the 2002 Act.)

1.2 In this practice direction:
(1) 'the prosecutor' means the person applying for a restraint order or the appointment of a receiver; and
(2) 'the defendant' means the person against whom criminal proceedings have been brought or a criminal investigation is taking place, and against whom a confiscation order or forfeiture order has been or might be made.

I RESTRAINT ORDERS

Form of Restraint Order

2. An example of a restraint order is annexed to this practice direction. This example may be modified as appropriate in any particular case.

Amount under Restraint

3.1 A restraint order may, where appropriate, apply to:
(1) all of the defendant's realisable property;
(2) the defendant's realisable property up to a specified value; or
(3) one or more particular specified assets.

3.2 Where:
(1) a confiscation order or forfeiture order has already been made against the defendant in a particular amount; or
(2) the prosecutor is able to make a reasonably accurate estimate of the amount of any confiscation order or forfeiture order that might be made against him,
and, in either case, it is clear that the defendant's realisable property is greater in value than the amount or estimated amount of that order, the court will normally limit the application of the restraint order in accordance with para. 3.1(2) or (3).

3.3 In such cases the prosecutor's draft order should normally either include an appropriate financial limit or specify the particular assets to which the order should apply.

Living Expenses and Legal Fees

4. A restraint order will normally, unless it is clear that a person restrained has sufficient assets which are not subject to the order, include an exception to the order permitting that person to spend assets:
(1) in the case of an individual, for reasonable living expenses; and

(2) in the case of either an individual or a company, to pay reasonable legal fees so that they may take advice in relation to the order and if so advised apply for its variation or discharge.

Restraint Orders against Third Parties

5.1 Where a restraint order applies to property held in the name of a person other than the defendant:

(1) the order must be addressed to that person in addition to the defendant; and

(2) in applying for the order, the prosecutor must consider the guidance given in *Re G (Restraint Order)* [2001] EWHC Admin 606.

5.2 Examples of additional persons to whom an order must, where appropriate, be addressed include:

(1) a person who has a joint bank account with the defendant;

(2) in proceedings under the 1988 Act or the 1994 Act, a person to whom the defendant is alleged to have made a gift which may be treated as realisable property of the defendant under the provisions of the relevant Act; or

(3) a company, where the prosecutor alleges that assets apparently belonging to the company are in reality those of the defendant.

5.3 However, an order should not normally be addressed:

(1) to a bank with whom a defendant has an account; or

(2) to the business name of a defendant who carries on an unincorporated business (such business not being a separate legal entity from the defendant).

Restraint Orders against Businesses

6. If an application for a restraint order is made against a company, partnership or individual apparently carrying on a legitimate business:

(1) the court will take into account the interests of the employees, creditors and customers of the business and, in the case of a company, any shareholders other than the defendant, before making an order which would or might prevent the business from being continued; and

(2) any restraint order made against that person will normally contain an exception enabling it to deal with its assets in the ordinary course of business.

Duration of Order Made on Application without Notice (Rules 4(2) and 27(2))

7.1 Rules 4(2) and 27(2) of RSC, ord. 115 in CPR, sch. 1, provide that, unless the court otherwise directs, a restraint order made without notice shall have effect until a day which shall be fixed for a further hearing where all parties may attend ('the return date').

7.2 Where a return date is fixed, it will normally be no more than 14 days after the date of the order.

7.3 Where no return date is fixed, the court will always include in the order a provision giving the defendant or anyone affected by the order permission to apply to vary or discharge the order (see para. 14 of the sample form of order).

II APPOINTMENT OF RECEIVER

8.1 Part 69 and PD 69 apply to the appointment of a receiver under the 1988, 1994 or 2000 Act, subject to the provisions of RSC, ord. 115, rr. 8 and 23(e) in CPR, sch. 1, where applicable.

8.2 In particular, r. 69.7, and PD 69, para. 9, apply in relation to the remuneration of the receiver.

8.3 Where no confiscation or forfeiture order has been made:

(1) an application for the appointment of a receiver should not be made without notice, unless the application is urgent or there is some other good reason for not giving notice to the defendant; and

(2) if the application is made without notice, the prosecutor's written evidence should explain the reasons for doing so.

8.4 Where the court appoints a receiver on an application without notice in the circumstances set out in para. 8.3, the order will normally limit the receiver's powers to manage, deal with or sell property (other than with the defendant's consent) to the extent that is shown to be urgently necessary. If the receiver seeks further powers, he should apply on notice for further directions.

[APPENDIX

The appendix, which consists of an example of a restraint order prohibiting disposal of assets, is on the CD-ROM version of *Blackstone's Civil Practice*. Please click on the title of the appendix to open it.]

CPR Schedule 2

sch.2 **1.5**. [For commentary on a specific CCR order, please refer to the cross-references after the title of the CCR rule.]

CCR ORDER 1 — CITATION, APPLICATION AND INTERPRETATION

Where by virtue of these rules or section 76 of the Act or otherwise any provision of the RSC is applied in relation to proceedings in a county court, that provision shall have effect with the necessary modifications and in particular—

(b) any reference in that provision to a Master, district judge of the Principal Registry of the Family Division, the Admiralty registrar, or a district judge or taxing officer shall be construed as a reference to the district judge of the county court; and

(d) any reference in that provision to an office of the Supreme Court having the conduct of the business of a division or court or a district registry shall be construed as a reference to the county court office.

CCR ORDER 5 — CAUSES OF ACTION AND PARTIES

Rule 3 Proceedings Related to Land

r.9 **14.46** r.9(2)–(3) **14.45**
r.9(1) **14.44**

(1) Subject to the provisions of any enactment, any two or more persons claiming to be entitled, or alleged to be liable, as partners in respect of a cause of action and carrying on business within England or Wales may sue or be sued in the name of the firm of which they were partners when the cause of action arose.

(2) Where partners sue or are sued in the name of the firm, the partners shall, on demand made in writing by any other party, forthwith deliver to the party making the demand and file a statement of the names and places of residence of all the persons who were partners in the firm when the cause of action arose.

(3) If the partners fail to comply with such a demand, the court, on application by any other party, may order the partners to furnish him with such a statement and to verify it on oath and may direct that in default—

   (a) if the partners are claimants, the proceedings be stayed on such terms as the court thinks fit; or

   (b) if the partners are defendants, they be debarred from defending the claim.

(4) When the names and places of residence of the partners have been stated in compliance with a demand or order under this rule, the proceedings shall continue in the name of the firm.

Rule 10 Defendant Carrying on Business in Another Name

r.10 **14.46**

(1) A person carrying on business in England or Wales in a name other than his own name may, whether or not he is within the jurisdiction, be sued—

   (a) in his own name, followed by the words 'trading as A.B.', or

   (b) in his business name, followed by the words '(a trading name)'.

(2) Where a person is sued in his business name in accordance with paragraph (1)(b), the provisions of these rules relating to claims against firms shall, subject to the provisions of any enactment, apply as if he were a partner and the name in which he carried on business were the name of his firm.

CCR ORDER 16 — TRANSFER OF PROCEEDINGS

Rule 7 Interpleader Proceedings under Execution

(1) This rule applies to interpleader proceedings under an execution which are ordered to be transferred from the High Court.

(1A) In this rule references to the sheriff shall be interpreted as including references to an individual authorised to act as an enforcement officer under the Courts Act 2003.

(2) Notice of the hearings or pre-trial review of the proceedings shall be given by the court officer to the sheriff as well as to every other party to the proceedings.

(3) The interpleader claimant shall, within 8 days of the receipt by him of the notice referred to in paragraph (2), file in triplicate particulars of any goods alleged to be his property and the grounds of his interpleader claim and the court officer shall send a copy to the execution creditor and to the sheriff, but the judge may hear the proceedings or, as the case may be, the district judge may proceed with the pre-trial review, if he thinks fit, notwithstanding that the particulars have not been filed.

(4) Subject to any directions in the order of the High Court, damages may be claimed against the execution creditor in the same manner as in interpleader proceedings commenced in a county court.

(5) On any day fixed for the pre-trial review of the proceedings or for the hearing of any application by the sheriff or other party for directions the court may order the sheriff—

(a) to postpone the sale of the goods seized;

(b) to remain in possession of such goods until the hearing of the proceedings; or

(c) to hand over possession of such goods to the district judge,

and, where a direction is given under sub-paragraph (c), the district judge shall be allowed reasonable charges for keeping possession of the goods, not exceeding those which might be allowed to the sheriff, and, if the district judge is directed to sell the goods, such charges for the sale as would be allowed under an execution issued by the county court.

(6) No order made in the proceedings shall prejudice or affect the rights of the sheriff to any proper charges and the judge may make such order with respect to them as may be just.

(7) The charges referred to in paragraphs (5) and (6) shall ultimately be borne in such manner as the judge shall direct.

(8) The order made at the hearing of the proceedings shall direct how any money in the hands of the sheriff is to be disposed of.

CCR ORDER 22 — JUDGMENTS AND ORDERS

Rule 8 Certificate of Judgment

r.8 **61.40, 76.2**

(1) Any person who wishes to have a certificate of any judgment or order given or made in a claim shall make a request in writing to the court stating—

(a) if he is a party to the claim whether the certificate—

(i) is required for the purpose of taking proceedings on the judgment or order in another court;

(ii) is required for the purpose of enforcing the judgment or order in the High Court; or

(iii) is for the purpose of evidence only;

(b) if he is not a party to the claim, the purpose for which the certificate is required, the capacity in which he asks for it and any other facts showing that the certificate may properly be granted.

(1A) Where the certificate is required for the purpose of enforcing the judgment or order in the High Court, the applicant shall also either—

(a) state that—

(i) it is intended to enforce the judgment or order by execution against goods; or

(ii) the judgment or order to be enforced is an order for possession of land made in a possession claim against trespassers; or

(b) confirm that an application has been made for an order under section 42 of the Act (transfer to High Court by order of a county court) and attach a copy of the application to the request for a certificate.

(2) Where the request is made by a person who is not a party to the claim, the request shall be referred to the district judge, who may, if he thinks fit, refer it to the judge.

(3) Without prejudice to paragraph (2), for the purposes of section 12(2) of the Act a certificate under this rule may be signed by the court manager or any other officer of the court acting on his behalf.

Rule 10 Variation of Payment

r.10–r.11 **61.40**

(1) Where a judgment or order has been given or made for the payment of money, the person entitled to the benefit of the judgment or order or, as the case may be, the person liable to make the payment (in this rule referred to as 'the judgment creditor' and 'the debtor' respectively) may apply in accordance with the provisions of this rule for a variation in the date or rate of payment.

(2) The judgment creditor may apply in writing, without notice being served on any other party, for an order that the money, if payable in one sum, be paid at a later date than that by which it is due or by instalments or, if the money is already payable by instalments, that it be paid by the same or smaller instalments, and the court officer may make an order accordingly unless no payment has been made under the judgment or order for 6 years before the date of the application in which case he shall refer the application to the district judge.

(3) The judgment creditor may apply to the district judge on notice for an order that the money, if payable in one sum, be paid at an earlier date than that by which it is due or, if the money is payable by instalments, that it be paid in one sum or by larger instalments, and any such application shall be made in writing stating the proposed terms and the grounds on which it is made.

(4) Where an application is made under paragraph (3)—
(a) the proceedings shall be automatically transferred to the debtor's home court if the judgment or order was not given or made in that court; and
(b) the court officer shall fix a day for the hearing of the application before the district judge and give to the judgment creditor and the debtor not less than 8 days' notice of the day so fixed,

and at the hearing the district judge may make such order as seems just.

(5) The debtor may apply for an order that the money, if payable in one sum, be paid at a later date than that by which it is due or by instalments or, if the money is already payable by instalments, that it be paid by smaller instalments, and any such application shall be in the appropriate form stating the proposed terms, the grounds on which it is made and including a signed statement of the debtor's means.

(6) Where an application is made under paragraph (5), the court officer shall—
(a) send the judgment creditor a copy of the debtor's application (and statement of means); and
(b) require the judgment creditor to notify the court in writing, within 14 days of service of notification upon him, giving his reasons for any objection he may have to the granting of the application.

(7) If the judgment creditor does not notify the court of any objection within the time stated, the court officer shall make an order in the terms applied for.

(8) Upon receipt of a notice from the judgment creditor under paragraph (6), the court officer may determine the date and rate of payment and make an order accordingly.

(9) Any party affected by an order made under paragraph (8) may, within 14 days of service of the order on him and giving his reasons, apply on notice for the order to be reconsidered and, where such an application is made—
(a) the proceedings shall be automatically transferred to the debtor's home court if the judgment or order was not given or made in that court; and
(b) the court officer shall fix a day for the hearing of the application before the district judge and give to the judgment creditor and the debtor not less than 8 days' notice of the day so fixed.

(10) On hearing an application under paragraph (9), the district judge may confirm the order or set it aside and make such new order as he thinks fit and the order so made shall be entered in the records of the court.

(11) Any order made under any of the foregoing paragraphs may be varied from time to time by a subsequent order made under any of those paragraphs.

Rule 11 Set-off of Cross-judgments

r.11 **61.40**

(1) An application under section 72 of the Act for permission to set off any sums, including costs, payable under several judgments or orders each of which was obtained in a county court shall be made in accordance with this rule.
(2) Where the judgments or orders have been obtained in the same county court, the application may be made to that court on the day when the last judgment or order is obtained, if both parties are present, and in any other case shall be made on notice.
(3) Where the judgments or orders have been obtained in different county courts, the application may be made to either of them on notice, and notice shall be given to the other court.
(4) The district judge of the court to which the application is made and the district judge of any other court to which notice is given under paragraph (3) shall forthwith stay execution on any judgment or order in his court to which the application relates and any money paid into court under the judgment or order shall be retained until the application has been disposed of.
(5) The application may be heard and determined by the court and any order giving permission shall direct how any money paid into court is to be dealt with.
(6) Where the judgments or orders have been obtained in different courts, the court in which an order giving permission is made shall send a copy of the order to the other court, which shall deal with any money paid into that court in accordance with the order.
(7) The court officer or, as the case may be, each of the court officers affected shall enter satisfaction in the records of his court for any sums ordered to be set off, and execution or other process for the enforcement of any judgment or order not wholly satisfied shall issue only for the balance remaining payable.
(8) Where an order is made by the High Court giving permission to set off sums payable under several judgments and orders obtained respectively in the High Court and a county court, the court officer of the county court shall, on receipt of a copy of the order, proceed in accordance with paragraph (7).

Rule 13 Order of Appellate Court

r.13 **61.40**

Where the Court of Appeal or High Court has heard and determined an appeal from a county court, the party entitled to the benefit of the order of the Court of Appeal or High Court shall deposit the order or an office copy thereof in the office of the county court.

CCR ORDER 24 — SUMMARY PROCEEDINGS FOR THE RECOVERY OF LAND

Part I Land

Rule 6 Warrant of Possession

r.6 **35.12**

(1) Subject to paragraphs (2) and (3), a warrant of possession to enforce an order for possession in a possession claim against trespassers under Part 55 may be issued at any time after the making of the order and subject to the provisions of Order 26, rule 17, a warrant of restitution may be issued in aid of the warrant of possession.
(2) No warrant of possession shall be issued after the expiry of 3 months from the date of the Order without the permission of the court, and an application for such permission may be made without notice being served on any other party unless the court otherwise directs.
(3) Nothing in this rule shall authorise the issue of a warrant of possession before the date on which possession is ordered to be given.

CCR ORDER 25 — ENFORCEMENT OF JUDGMENTS AND ORDERS: GENERAL

ord.25 **76.1, 76.38**

Rule 1 Judgment Creditor and Debtor

In this Order and Orders 26 to 29 'judgment creditor' means the person who has obtained or is entitled to enforce a judgment or order and 'debtor' means the person against whom it was given or made.

Rule 6 Description of Parties

Where the name or address of the judgment creditor or the debtor as given in the request for the issue of a warrant of execution or delivery, judgment summons or warrant of committal differs from his name or address in the judgment or order sought to be enforced and the judgment creditor satisfies the court officer that the name or address as given in the request is applicable to the person concerned, the judgment creditor or the debtor, as the case may be, shall be described in the warrant or judgment summons as 'C.D. of [name and address as given in the request] suing [or sued] as A.D. of [name and address in the judgment or order]'.

Rule 7 Recording and Giving Information as to Warrants and Orders

(1) Subject to paragraph (1A), every district judge by whom a warrant or order is issued or received for execution shall from time to time state in the records of his court what has been done in the execution of the warrant or order.

(1A) Where a warrant of execution issued by a court ('the home court') is sent to another court for execution ('the foreign court'), paragraph (1) shall not apply to the district judge of the home court, but when such a warrant is returned to the home court under paragraph (7), the court officer of the home court shall state in the records of his court what has been done in the execution of the warrant or order.

(2) If the warrant or order has not been executed within one month from the date of its issue or receipt by him, the court officer of the court responsible for its execution shall, at the end of that month and every subsequent month during which the warrant remains outstanding, send notice of the reason for non-execution to the judgment creditor and, if the warrant or order was received from another court, to that court.

(3) The district judge responsible for executing a warrant or order shall give such information respecting it as may reasonably be required by the judgment creditor and, if the warrant or order was received by him from another court, by the district judge of that court.

(4) Where money is received in pursuance of a warrant of execution or committal sent by one court to another court, the foreign court shall, subject to paragraph (5) and to section 346 of Insolvency Act 1986 and section 326 of the Companies Act 1948 send the money to the judgment creditor in the manner prescribed by the Court Funds Rules 1987 and, where the money is received in pursuance of a warrant of committal, make a return to the home court.

(5) Where interpleader proceedings are pending, the court shall not proceed in accordance with paragraph (4) until the interpleader proceedings are determined and the district judge shall then make a return showing how the money is to be disposed of and, if any money is payable to the judgment creditor, the court shall proceed in accordance with paragraph (4).

(6) Where a warrant of committal has been received from another court, the foreign court shall, on the execution of the warrant, send notice thereof to the home court.

(7) Mere a warrant of execution has been received from another court, either—
  (a) on the execution of the warrant; or
  (b) if the warrant is not executed—
    (i) on the making of a final return to the warrant; or
    (ii) on suspension of the warrant under rule 8 (suspension of judgment or execution) or Order 26, rule 10 (withdrawal and suspension of warrant at creditor's request),

  the foreign court shall return the warrant to the home court.

Rule 8 Suspension of Judgment or Execution

r.8 **76.3**

(1) The power of the court to suspend or stay a judgment or order or to stay execution of any warrant may be exercised by the district judge or, in the case of the power to stay execution of a warrant of execution and in accordance with the provisions of this rule, by the court officer.

(2) An application by the debtor to stay execution of a warrant of execution shall be in the appropriate form stating the proposed terms, the grounds on which it is made and including a signed statement of the debtor's means.

(3) Where the debtor makes an application under paragraph (2), the court shall—

(a) send the judgment creditor a copy of the debtor's application (and statement of means); and

(b) require the creditor to notify the court in writing, within 14 days of service of notification upon him, giving his reasons for any objection he may have to the granting of the application.

(4) If the judgment creditor does not notify the court of any objection within the time stated, the court officer may make an order suspending the warrant on terms of payment.

(5) Upon receipt of a notice by the judgment creditor under paragraph (3)(b), the court officer may, if the judgment creditor objects only to the terms offered, determine the date and rate of payment and make an order suspending the warrant on terms of payment.

(6) Any party affected by an order made under paragraph (5) may, within 14 days of service of the order on him and giving his reasons, apply on notice for the order to be reconsidered and the court shall fix a day for the hearing of the application before the district judge and give to the judgment creditor and the debtor not less than 8 days' notice of the day so fixed.

(7) On hearing an application under paragraph (6), the district judge may confirm the order or set it aside and make such new order as he thinks fit and the order so made shall be entered in the records of the court.

(8) Where the judgment creditor states in his notice under paragraph (3)(b) that he wishes the bailiff to proceed to execute the warrant, the court shall fix a day for a hearing before the district judge of the debtor's application and give to the judgment creditor and to the debtor not less than 2 days' notice of the day so fixed.

(9) Subject to any directions given by the district judge, where a warrant of execution has been suspended, it may be re-issued on the judgment creditor's filing a request showing that any condition subject to which the warrant was suspended has not been complied with.

(10) Where an order is made by the district judge suspending a warrant of execution, the debtor may be ordered to pay the costs of the warrant and any fees or expenses incurred before its suspension and the order may authorise the sale of a sufficient portion of any goods seized to cover such costs, fees and expenses and the expenses of sale.

Rule 9 Enforcement of Judgment or Order against Firm

r.9(1)–(4) **76.36**

(1) Subject to paragraph (2), a judgment or order against a firm may be enforced against—

(a) any property of the firm;

(b) any person who admitted in the proceedings that he was a partner or was adjudged to be a partner;

(c) any person who was served as a partner with the claim form if—

(i) judgment was entered under CPR Part 12, in default of defence or under CPR Part 14 on admission; or

(iii) the person so served did not appear at the trial or hearing of the proceedings.

(2) A judgment or order may not be enforced under paragraph (1) against a member of the firm who was out of England and Wales when the claim form was issued unless he—

(a) was served within England and Wales with the claim form as a partner; or

(b) was, with the permission of the court under CPR rule 6.20 served out of England and Wales with the claim form as a partner,

and, except as provided by paragraph (1)(a) and by the foregoing provisions of this paragraph, a judgment or order obtained against a firm shall not render liable, release or otherwise affect a member of the firm who was out of England and Wales when the claim form was issued.

(3) A judgment creditor who claims to be entitled to enforce a judgment or order against any other person as a partner may apply to the court for permission to do so by filing an application notice in accordance with CPR Part 23.

(4) An application notice under paragraph (3) shall be served on the alleged partner, not less than three days before the hearing of the application, in the manner set out in CPR rule 6.2 and on the hearing of the application, if the alleged partner does not dispute his liability, the court may, subject to paragraph (2), give permission to enforce the judgment or order against him and, if he disputes liability, the court may order that the question of his liability be tried and determined in such a manner as the court thinks fit.

(5) The foregoing provisions of this rule shall not apply where it is desired to enforce in a county court a judgment or order of the High Court, or a judgment, order, decree or award of any court or arbitrator which is or has become enforceable as if it were a judgment or order of the High Court, and in any such case the provisions of the RSC relating to the enforcement of a judgment or order against a firm shall apply.

Rule 10 Enforcing Judgment between a Firm and Its Members

(1) Execution to enforce a judgment or order given or made in—
(a) proceedings by or against a firm, in the name of the firm against or by a member of the firm; or
(b) proceedings by a firm in the name of the firm against a firm in the name of the firm where those firms have one or more members in common,
shall not issue without the permission of the court.
(2) On an application for permission the court may give such directions, including directions as to the taking of accounts and the making of inquiries, as may be just.

Rule 13 Transfer to High Court for Enforcement

r.13 **76.2**

(1) Where the judgment creditor makes a request for a certificate of judgment under Order 22, rule 8(1) for the purpose of enforcing the judgment or order in the High Court—
(a) by execution against goods; or
(b) where the judgment or order to be enforced is an order for possession of land made in a possession claim against trespassers,
the grant of a certificate by the court shall take effect as an order to transfer the proceedings to the High Court and the transfer shall have effect on the grant of that certificate.
(2) On the transfer of proceedings in accordance with paragraph (1), the court shall give notice to the debtor or the person against whom the possession order was made that the proceedings have been transferred and shall make an entry of that fact in the records of his court.
(3) In a case where a request for a certificate of judgment is made under Order 22, rule 8(1) for the purpose of enforcing a judgment or order in the High Court and—
(a) an application for a variation in the date or rate of payment of money due under a judgment or order;
(b) an application under either CPR rule 39.3(3) or CPR rule 13.4;
(c) a request for an administration order; or
(d) an application for a stay of execution under section 88 of the Act,
is pending, the request for the certificate shall not be dealt with until those proceedings are determined.

CCR ORDER 26 — WARRANTS OF EXECUTION, DELIVERY AND POSSESSION

ord.26 **76.1, 76.38**

Rule 1 Application for Warrant of Execution

(1) A judgment creditor desiring a warrant of execution to be issued shall file a request in that behalf certifying—
(a) the amount remaining due under the judgment or order; and
(b) where the order made is for payment of a sum of money by instalments—
(i) that the whole or part of any instalment due remains unpaid; and
(ii) the amount for which the warrant is to be issued.
(1A) The court officer shall discharge the functions—
(a) under section 85(2) of the Act of issuing a warrant of execution;
(b) under section 85(3) of the Act of entering in the record mentioned in that subsection and on the warrant the precise time of the making of the application to issue the warrant, and
(c) under section 103(1) of the Act of sending the warrant of execution to another county court.

(2) Where the court has made an order for payment of a sum of money by instalments and default has been made in payment of such an instalment, a warrant of execution may be issued for the whole of the said sum of money and costs then remaining unpaid or, subject to paragraph (3), for such part as the judgment creditor may request, not being in the latter case less than £50 or the amount of one monthly instalment or, as the case may be, 4 weekly instalments, whichever is the greater.

(3) In any case to which paragraph (2) applies no warrant shall be issued unless at the time when it is issued—

(a) the whole or part of an instalment which has already become due remains unpaid; and

(b) any warrant previously issued for part of the said sum of money and costs has expired or has been satisfied or abandoned.

(4) Where a warrant is issued for the whole or part of the said sum of money and costs, the court officer shall, unless the district judge responsible for execution of the warrant directs otherwise, send a warning notice to the person against whom the warrant is issued and, where such a notice is sent, the warrant shall not be levied until 7 days thereafter.

(5) Where judgment is given or an order made for payment otherwise than by instalments of a sum of money and costs to be assessed in accordance with CPR Part 47 (detailed assessment procedure) and default is made in payment of the sum of money before the costs have been assessed, a warrant of execution may issue for recovery of the sum of money and a separate warrant may issue subsequently for the recovery of the costs if default. is made in payment of them.

Rule 2 Execution of High Court Judgment

(1) Where it is desired to enforce by warrant of execution a judgment or order of the High Court, or a judgment, order, decree or award which is or has become enforceable as if it were a judgment of the High Court, the request referred to in rule 1(1) may be filed in any court in the district of which execution is to be levied.

(2) Subject to Order 25, rule 9(5), any restriction imposed by these rules on the issue of execution shall apply as if the judgment, order, decree or award were a judgment or order of the county court, but permission to issue execution shall not be required if permission has already been given by the High Court.

(3) Notice of the issue of the warrant shall be sent by the county court to the High Court.

Rule 3 Execution against Farmer

If after the issue of a warrant of execution the district judge for the district in which the warrant is to be executed has reason to believe that the debtor is a farmer, the execution creditor shall, if so required by the district judge, furnish him with an official certificate, dated not more than three days beforehand, of the result of a search at the Land Registry as to the existence of any charge registered against the debtor under the Agricultural Credits Act 1928.

Rule 4 Concurrent Warrants

Two or more warrants of execution may be issued concurrently for execution in different districts, but—

(a) no more shall be levied under all the warrants together than is authorised to be levied under one of them; and

(b) the costs of more than one such warrant shall not be allowed against the debtor except by order of the court.

Rule 5 Permission to Issue Certain Warrants

r.5 **76.7**

(1) A warrant of execution shall not issue without the permission of the court where—

(a) six years or more have elapsed since the date of the judgment or order;

(b) any change has taken place, whether by death or otherwise in the parties entitled to enforce the judgment or order or liable to have it enforced against them;

(c) the judgment or order is against the assets of a deceased person coming into the hands of his executors or administrators after the date of the judgment or order and it is sought to issue execution against such assets; or

(d) any goods to be seized under a warrant of execution are in the hands of a receiver appointed by a court.

(2) An application for permission shall be supported by a witness statement or affidavit establishing the applicant's right to relief and may be made without notice being served on any other party in the first instance but the court may direct the application notice to be served on such persons as it thinks fit.

(3) Where, by reason of one and the same event, a person seeks permission under paragraph (1)(b) to enforce more judgments or orders than one, he may make one application only, specifying in a schedule all the judgments or orders in respect of which it is made, and if the application notice is directed to be served on any person, it need set out only such part of the application as affects him.

(4) Paragraph (1) is without prejudice to any enactment, rule or direction by virtue of which a person is required to obtain the permission of the court for the issue of a warrant or to proceed to execution or otherwise to the enforcement of a judgment or order.

Rule 6 Duration and Renewal of Warrant

(1) A warrant of execution shall, for the purpose of execution, be valid in the first instance for 12 months beginning with the date of its issue, but if not wholly executed, it may be renewed from time to time, by order of the court, for a period of 12 months at any one time, beginning with the day next following that on which it would otherwise expire, if an application for renewal is made before that day or such later day (if any) as the court may allow.

(2) A note of any such renewal shall be indorsed on the warrant and it shall be entitled to priority according to the time of its original issue or, where appropriate, its receipt by the district judge responsible for its execution.

Rule 7 Notice on Levy

Any bailiff upon levying execution shall deliver to the debtor or leave at the place where execution is levied a notice of the warrant.

Rule 8 Bankruptcy or Winding Up of Debtor

(1) Where the district judge responsible for the execution of a warrant is required by any provision of the Insolvency Act 1986 or any other enactment relating to insolvency to retain the proceeds of sale of goods sold under the warrant or money paid in order to avoid a sale, the court shall, as soon as practicable after the sale or the receipt of the money, send notice to the execution creditor and, if the warrant issued out of another court, to that court.

(2) Where the district judge responsible for the execution of a warrant—

(a) receives notice that a bankruptcy order has been made against the debtor or, if the debtor is a company, that a provisional liquidator has been appointed or that an order has been made or a resolution passed for the winding up of the company; and

(b) withdraws from possession of goods seized or pays over to the official receiver or trustee in bankruptcy or, if the debtor is a company, to the liquidator the proceeds of sale of goods sold under the warrant or money paid in order to avoid a sale or seized or received in part satisfaction of the warrant,

the court shall send notice to the execution creditor and, if the warrant issued out of another court, to that court.

(3) Where the court officer of a court to which a warrant issued out of another court has been sent for execution receives any such notice as is referred to in paragraph (2)(a) after he has sent to the home court any money seized or received in part satisfaction of the warrant, he shall forward the notice to that court.

Rule 10 Withdrawal and Suspension of Warrant at Creditor's Request

(1) Where an execution creditor requests the district judge responsible for executing a warrant to withdraw from possession, he shall, subject to the following paragraphs of this rule, be treated as having abandoned the execution, and the court shall mark the warrant as withdrawn by request of the execution creditor.

(2) Where the request is made in consequence of a claim having been made under Order 33, rule 1, to goods seized under the warrant, the execution shall be treated as being abandoned in respect only of the goods claimed.

(3) If the district judge responsible for executing a warrant is requested by the execution creditor to suspend it in pursuance of an arrangement between him and the debtor, the court shall mark the warrant as suspended by request of the execution creditor and the execution creditor may subsequently apply to the district judge holding the warrant for it to be re-issued and, if he does so, the application shall be deemed for the purpose of section 85(3) of the Act to be an application to issue the warrant.

(4) Nothing in this rule shall prejudice any right of the execution creditor to apply for the issue of a fresh warrant or shall authorise the re-issue of a warrant which has been withdrawn or has expired or has been superseded by the issue of a fresh warrant.

Rule 11 Suspension of Part Warrant

Where a warrant issued for part of a sum of money and costs payable under a judgment or order is suspended on payment of instalments, the judgment or order shall, unless the court otherwise directs, be treated as suspended on those terms as respects the whole of the sum of money and costs then remaining unpaid.

Rule 12 Inventory and Notice Where Goods Removed

(1) Where goods seized in execution are removed, the court shall forthwith deliver or send to the debtor a sufficient inventory of the goods removed and shall, not less than 4 days before the time fixed for the sale, give him notice of the time and place at which the goods will be sold.

(2) The inventory and notice shall be given to the debtor by delivering them to him personally or by sending them to him by post at his place of residence or, if his place of residence is not known, by leaving them for him, or sending them to him by post, at the place from which the goods were removed.

Rule 13 Account of Sale

Where goods are sold under an execution, the court shall furnish the debtor with a detailed account in writing of the sale and of the application of the proceeds.

Rule 14 Notification to Foreign Court of Payment Made

Where, after a warrant has been sent to a foreign court for execution but before a final return has been made to the warrant, the home court is notified of a payment made in respect of the sum for which the warrant is issued, the home court shall send notice of the payment to the foreign court.

Rule 15 Order for Private Sale

(1) Subject to paragraph (6), an order of the court under section 97 of the Act that a sale under an execution may be made otherwise than by public auction may be made on the application of the execution creditor or the debtor or the district judge responsible for the execution of the warrant.

(2) Where he is not the applicant for an order under this rule, the district judge responsible for the execution of the warrant shall, on the demand of the applicant, furnish him with a list containing the name and address of every execution creditor under any other warrant or writ of execution against the goods of the debtor of which the district judge has notice, and where the district judge is the applicant, he shall prepare such a list.

(3) Not less than 4 days before the day fixed for the hearing of the application, the applicant shall give notice of the application to each of the other persons by whom the application might have been made and to every person named in the list referred to in paragraph (2).

(4) The applicant shall produce the list to the court on the hearing of the application.

(5) Every person to whom notice of the application was given may attend and be heard on the hearing of the application.

(6) Where the district judge responsible for the execution of the warrant is the district judge by whom it was issued and he has no notice of any other warrant or writ of execution against the goods of the debtor, an order under this rule may be made by the court of its own motion with

the consent of the execution creditor and the debtor or after giving them an opportunity of being heard.

Rule 16 Warrant of Delivery

(1) Except where an Act or rule provides otherwise, a judgment or order for the delivery of any goods shall be enforceable by warrant of delivery in accordance with this rule.
(2) If the judgment or order does not give the person against whom it was given or made the alternative of paying the value of the goods, it may be enforced by a warrant of specific delivery, that is to say, a warrant to recover the goods without alternative provision for recovery of their value.
(3) If the judgment or order is for the delivery of the goods or payment of their value, it may be enforced by a warrant of delivery to recover the goods or their value.
(4) Where a warrant of delivery is issued, the judgment creditor shall be entitled, by the same or a separate warrant, to execution against the debtor's goods for any money payable under the judgment or order which is to be enforced by the warrant of delivery.
(4A) Where a judgment or order is given or made for the delivery of goods or payment of their value and a warrant is issued to recover the goods or their value, money paid into court under the warrant shall be appropriated first to any sum of money and costs awarded.
(5) The foregoing provisions of this Order, so far as applicable, shall have effect, with the necessary modifications, in relation to warrants of delivery as they have effect in relation to warrants of execution.

Rule 17 Warrant of Possession

r.17(4) **76.32**

(1) A judgment or order for the recovery of land shall be enforceable by warrant of possession.
(2) Without prejudice to paragraph (3A), the person desiring a warrant of possession to be issued shall file a request in that behalf certifying that the land has not been vacated in accordance with the judgment or order for the recovery of the said land.
(3) Where a warrant of possession is issued, the judgment creditor shall be entitled, by the same or a separate warrant, to execution against the debtor's goods for any money payable under the judgment or order which is to be enforced by the warrant of possession.
(3A) In a case to which paragraph (3) applies or where an order for possession has been suspended on terms as to payment of a sum of money by instalments, the judgment creditor shall in his request certify—
  (a) the amount of money remaining due under the judgment or order; and
  (b) that the whole or part of any instalment due remains unpaid.
(4) A warrant of restitution may be issued, with the permission of the court, in aid of any warrant of possession.
(5) An application for permission under paragraph (4) may be made without notice being served on any other party and shall be, supported by evidence of wrongful re-entry into possession following the execution of the warrant of possession and of such further facts as would, in the High Court, enable the judgment creditor to have a writ of restitution issued.
(6) Rules 5 and 6 shall apply, with the necessary modifications, in relation to a warrant of possession and any further warrant in aid of such a warrant as they apply in relation to a warrant of execution.

Rule 18 Saving for Enforcement by Committal

Nothing in rule 16 or 17 shall prejudice any power to enforce a judgment or order for the delivery of goods or the recovery of land by an order of committal.

CCR ORDER 27 — ATTACHMENT OF EARNINGS

ord.27 **76.1, 76.38**

Part I General

Rule 1 Interpretation

(1) In this Order—

'the Act of 1971' means the Attachment of Earnings Act 1971 and, unless the context otherwise requires, expressions used in that Act have the same meanings as in that Act.

Rule 2 Index of Orders

(1) The court officer of every court shall keep a nominal index of the debtors residing within the district of his court in respect of whom there are in force attachment of earnings orders which have been made by that court or of which the court officer has received notice from another court.

(2) Where a debtor in respect of whom a court has made an attachment of earnings order resides within the district of another court, the court officer of the first-mentioned court shall send a copy of the order to the court officer of the other court for entry in his index.

(3) The court officer shall, on the request of any person having a judgment or order against a person believed to be residing within the district of the court, cause a search to be made in the index of the court and issue a certificate of the result of the search.

Rule 3 Appropriate Court

(1) Subject to paragraphs (2) and (3), an application for an attachment of earnings order may be made to the court for the district in which the debtor resides.

(2) If the debtor does not reside within England or Wales, or the creditor does not know where he resides, the application may be made to the court in which, or for the district in which, the judgment or order sought to be enforced was obtained.

(3) Where the creditor applies for attachment of earnings orders in respect of two or more debtors jointly liable under a judgment or order, the application may be made to the court for the district in which any of the debtors resides, so however that if the judgment or order was given or made by any such court, the application shall be made to that court.

Rule 4 Mode of Applying

(1) A judgment creditor who desires to apply for an attachment of earnings order shall file his application certifying the amount of money remaining due under the judgment or order and that the whole or part of any instalment due remains unpaid and, where it is sought to enforce an order of a magistrates' court—

(a) a certified copy of the order; and

(b) a witness statement or affidavit verifying the amount due under the order or, if payments under the order are required to be made to the designated officer for the magistrates' court, a certificate by that designated officer to the same effect.

(2) On the filing of the documents mentioned in paragraph (1) the court officer shall, where the order to be enforced is a maintenance order, fix a day for the hearing of the application.

Rule 5 Service and Reply

(1) Notice of the application together with a form of reply in the appropriate form, shall be served on the debtor in the manner set out in CPR rule 6.2.

(2) The debtor shall, within 8 days after service on him of the documents mentioned in paragraph (1), file a reply in the form provided, and the instruction to that effect in the notice to the debtor shall constitute a requirement imposed by virtue of section 14(4) of the Act of 1971:

Provided that no proceedings shall be taken for an offence alleged to have been committed under section 23(2)(c) or (f) of the Act of 1971 in relation to the requirement unless the said documents have been served on the debtor personally or the court is satisfied that they came to his knowledge in sufficient time for him to comply with the requirement.

(2A) Nothing in paragraph (2) shall require a defendant to file a reply if, within the period of time mentioned in that paragraph, he pays to the judgment creditor the money remaining due under the judgment or order and, where such payment is made, the judgment creditor shall so inform the court officer.

(3) On receipt of a reply the court officer shall send a copy to the applicant.

Rule 6 Notice to Employer

Without prejudice to the powers conferred by section 14(1) of the Act of 1971, the court officer may, at any stage of the proceedings, send to any person appearing to have the debtor in his employment a notice requesting him to give to the court, within such period as may be specified in the notice, a statement of the debtor's earnings and anticipated earnings with such particulars as may be so specified.

Rule 7 Attachment of Earnings Order

r.7(1) **76.19**

(1) On receipt of the debtor's reply, the court officer may, if he has sufficient information to do so, make an attachment of earnings order and a copy of the order shall be sent to the parties and to the debtor's employer.
(2) Where an order is made under paragraph (1), the judgment creditor or the debtor may, within 14 days of service of the order on him and giving his reasons, apply on notice for the order to be re-considered and the court officer shall fix a day for the hearing of the application and give to the judgment creditor and the debtor not less than 2 days' notice of the day so fixed.
(3) On hearing an application under paragraph (2), the district judge may confirm the order or set it aside and make such new order as he thinks fit and the order so made shall be entered in the records of the court.
(4) Where an order is not made under paragraph (1), the court officer shall refer the application to the district judge who shall, if he considers that he has sufficient information to do so without the attendance of the parties, determine the application.
(5) Where the district judge does not determine the application under paragraph (4), he shall direct that a day be fixed for the hearing of the application whereupon the court officer shall fix such a day and give to the judgment creditor and the debtor not less than 8 days' notice of the day so fixed.
(6) Where an order is made under paragraph (4), the judgment creditor or the debtor may, within 14 days of service of the order on him and giving his reasons, apply on notice for the order to be re-considered; and the court officer shall fix a day for the hearing of the application and give to the judgment creditor and the debtor not less than 2 days' notice of the day so fixed.
(7) On hearing an application under paragraph (6), the district judge may confirm the order or set it aside and make such new order as he thinks fit and the order so made shall be entered in the records of the court.
(8) If the creditor does not appear at the hearing of the application under paragraph (5) but—
    (a) the court has received a witness statement or affidavit of evidence from him; or
    (b) the creditor requests the court in writing to proceed in his absence,
    the court may proceed to hear the application and to make an order thereon.
(9) An attachment of earnings order may be made to secure the payment of a judgment debt if the debt is—
    (a) of not less than £50; or
    (b) for the amount remaining payable under a judgment for a sum of not less than £50.

Rule 7A Failure by Debtor

(1) If the debtor has failed to comply with rule 5(2) or to make payment to the judgment creditor, the court officer may issue an order under section 14(1) of the Act of 1971 which shall—
    (a) be indorsed with or incorporate a notice warning the debtor of the consequences of disobedience to the order;
    (b) be served on the debtor personally; and
    (c) direct that any payments made thereafter shall be paid into the court and not direct to the judgment creditor.
(2) Without prejudice to rule 16, if the person served with an order made pursuant to paragraph (1) fails to obey it or to file a statement of his means or to make payment, the court officer shall issue a notice calling on that person to show good reason why he should not be imprisoned and any such notice shall be served on the debtor personally not less than 5 days before the hearing.

(3) Order 29, rule 1 shall apply, with the necessary modifications and with the substitution of references to the district judge for references to the judge, where a notice is issued under paragraph (2) or (4) of that rule.
(4) In this rule 'statement of means' means a statement given under section 14(1) of the Act of 1971.

Rule 7B Suspended Committal Order

(1) If the debtor fails to attend at an adjourned hearing of an application for an attachment of earnings order and a committal order is made, the judge or district judge may direct that the committal order shall be suspended so long as the debtor attends at the time and place specified in the committal order and paragraphs (2), (4) and (5) of Order 28, rule 7 shall apply, with the necessary modifications, where such a direction is given as they apply where a direction is given under paragraph (1) of that rule.
(2) Where a committal order is suspended under paragraph (1) and the debtor fails to attend at the time and place specified under paragraph (1), a certificate to that effect given by the court officer shall be sufficient authority for the issue of a warrant of committal.

Rule 8 Failure by Debtor — Maintenance Orders

(1) An order made under section 23(1) of the Act of 1971 for the attendance of the debtor at an adjourned hearing of an application for an attachment of earnings order to secure payments under a maintenance order shall—
  (a) be served on the debtor personally not less than 5 days before the day fixed for the adjourned hearing; and
  (b) direct that any payments made thereafter shall be paid into the court and not direct to the judgment creditor.
(2) An application by a debtor for the revocation of an order committing him to prison and, if he is already in custody, for his discharge under subsection (7) of the said section 23 shall be made to the judge or district judge in writing without notice to any other party showing the reasons for the debtor's failure to attend the court or his refusal to be sworn or to give evidence, as the case may be, and containing an undertaking by the debtor to attend the court or to be sworn or to give evidence when next ordered or required to do so.
(3) The application shall, if the debtor has already been lodged in prison, be attested by the governor of the prison (or any other officer of the prison not below the rank of principal officer) and in any other case be made on witness statement or affidavit.
(4) Before dealing with the application the judge or district judge may, if he thinks fit, cause notice to be given to the judgment creditor that the application has been made and of a day and hour when he may attend and be heard.

Rule 9 Costs

(1) Where costs are allowed to the judgment creditor on an application for an attachment of earnings order, there may be allowed—
  (a) a charge of a solicitor for attending the hearing and, if the court so directs, for serving the application;
  (b) if the court certifies that the case is fit for counsel, a fee to counsel; and
  (c) the court fee on the issue of the application.
(2) For the purpose of paragraph (1)(a) a solicitor who has prepared on behalf of the judgment creditor a witness statement or affidavit or request under rule 7(8) shall be treated as having attended the hearing.
(3) The costs may be fixed and allowed without detailed assessment under CPR Part 47.

Rule 10 Contents and Service of Order

(1) An attachment of earnings order shall contain such of the following particulars relating to the debtor as are known to the court, namely—
  (a) his full name and address;
  (b) his place of work; and
  (c) the nature of his work and his works number, if any, and those particulars shall be the prescribed particulars for the purposes of section 6(3) of the Act of 1971.

(2) An attachment of earnings order and any order varying or discharging such an order shall be served on the debtor and on the person to whom the order is directed, and CPR Part 6 and CPR rules 40.4 and 40.5 shall apply with the further modification that where the order is directed to a corporation which has requested the court that any communication relating to the debtor or to the class of persons to whom he belongs shall be directed to the corporation at a particular address, service may, if the district judge thinks fit, be effected on the corporation at that address.

(3) Where an attachment of earnings order is made to enforce a judgment or order of the High Court or a magistrates' court, a copy of the attachment of earnings order and of any order discharging it shall be sent by the court officer of the county court to the court officer of the High Court, or, as the case may be, the designated officer for the magistrates' court.

Rule 11 Application to Determine Whether Particular Payments Are Earnings

An application to the court under section 16 of the Act of 1971 to determine whether payments to the debtor of a particular class or description are earnings for the purpose of an attachment of earnings order may be made to the district judge in writing and the court officer shall thereupon fix a date and time for the hearing of the application by the court and give notice thereof to the persons mentioned in the said section 16(2)(a), (b) and (c).

Rule 12 Notice of Cesser

Where an attachment of earnings order ceases to have effect under section 8(4) of the Act of 1971, the court officer of the court in which the matter is proceeding shall give notice of the cesser to the person to whom the order was directed.

Rule 13 Variation and Discharge by Court of Own Motion

(1) Subject to paragraph (9), the powers conferred by section 9(1) of the Act of 1971 may be exercised by the court of its own motion in the circumstances mentioned in the following paragraphs.

(2) Where it appears to the court that a person served with an attachment of earnings order directed to him has not the debtor in his employment, the court may discharge the order.

(3) Where an attachment of earnings order which has lapsed under section 9(4) of the Act of 1971 is again directed to a person who appears to the court to have the debtor in his employment, the court may make such consequential variations in the order as it thinks fit.

(4) Where, after making an attachment of earnings order, the court makes or is notified of the making of another such order in respect of the same debtor which is not to secure the payment of a judgment debt or payments under an administration order, the court may discharge or vary the first-mentioned order having regard to the priority accorded to the other order by paragraph 8 of Schedule 3 to the Act of 1971.

(5) Where, after making an attachment of earnings order, the court makes an order under section 4(1)(b) of the Act of 1971 or makes an administration order, the court may discharge the attachment of earnings order or, if it exercises the power conferred by section 5(3) of the said Act, may vary the order in such manner as it thinks fit.

(6) On making a consolidated attachment of earnings order the court may discharge any earlier attachment of earnings order made to secure the payment of a judgment debt by the same debtor.

(7) Where it appears to the court that a bankruptcy order has been made against a person in respect of whom an attachment of earnings order is in force to secure the payment of a judgment debt, the court may discharge the attachment of earnings order.

(8) Where an attachment of earnings order has been made to secure the payment of a judgment debt and the court grants permission to issue execution for the recovery of the debt, the court may discharge the order.

(9) Before varying or discharging an attachment of earnings order of its own motion under any of the foregoing paragraphs of this rule, the court shall, unless it thinks it unnecessary in the circumstances to do so, give the debtor and the person on whose application the order was made an opportunity of being heard on the question whether the order should be varied or discharged, and for that purpose the court officer may give them notice of a date, time and place at which the question will be considered.

Rule 14 Transfer of Attachment Order

(1) Where the court by which the question of making a consolidated attachment order falls to be considered is not the court by which any attachment of earnings order has been made to secure the payment of a judgment debt by the debtor, the district judge of the last-mentioned court shall, at the request of the district judge of the first-mentioned court, transfer to that court the matter in which the attachment of earnings order was made.

(2) Without prejudice to paragraph (1), if in the opinion of the judge or district judge of any court by which an attachment of earnings order has been made, the matter could more conveniently proceed in some other court, whether by reason of the debtor having become resident in the district of that court or otherwise, he may order the matter to be transferred to that court.

(3) The court to which proceedings arising out of an attachment of earnings are transferred under this rule shall have the same jurisdiction in relation to the order as if it has been made by that court.

Rule 15 Exercise of Power to Obtain Statement of Earnings etc.

(1) An order under section 14(1) of the Act of 1971 shall be indorsed with or incorporate a notice warning the person to whom it is directed of the consequences of disobedience to the order and shall be served on him personally.

(2) Order 34, rule 2, shall apply, with the necessary modifications, in relation to any penalty for failure to comply with an order under the said section 14(1) or, subject to the proviso to rule 5(2), any penalty for failure to comply with a requirement mentioned in that rule, as it applies in relation to a fine under section 55 of the County Courts Act 1984.

Rule 16 Offences

(1) Where it is alleged that a person has committed any offence mentioned in section 23(2)(a), (b), (d), (e) or (f) of the Act of 1971 in relation to proceedings in, or to an attachment of earnings order made by, a county court, the district judge shall, unless it is decided to proceed against the alleged offender summarily, issue a summons calling upon him to show cause why he should not be punished for the alleged offence.
The summons shall be served on the alleged offender personally not less than 14 days before the return day.

(2) Order 34, rules 3 and 4, shall apply, with the necessary modifications, to proceedings for an offence under section 23(2) of the Act of 1971 as they apply to proceedings for offences under the County Courts Act 1984.

Rule 17 Maintenance Orders

(1) The foregoing rules of this Order shall apply in relation to maintenance payments as they apply in relation to a judgment debt, subject to the following paragraphs.

(2) An application for an attachment of earnings order to secure payments under a maintenance order made by a county court shall be made to that county court.

(3) Any application under section 32 of the Matrimonial Causes Act 1973 for permission to enforce the payment of arrears which became due more than 12 months before the application for an attachment of earnings order shall be made in that application.

(3A) Notice of the application together with a form of reply in the appropriate form, shall be served on the debtor in the manner set out in CPR rule 6.2.

(3B) Service of the notice shall be effected not less than 21 days before the hearing, but service may be effected at any time before the hearing on the applicant satisfying the court by witness statement or affidavit that the respondent is about to remove from his address for service.

(3C) Rule 5(2A) shall not apply.

(4) An application by the debtor for an attachment of earnings order to secure payments under a maintenance order may be made on the making of the maintenance order or an order varying the maintenance order, and rules 4 and 5 shall not apply.

(5) Rule 7 shall have effect as if for paragraphs (1) to (8) there were substituted the following paragraph—

'(1) An application for an attachment of earnings order may be heard and determined by the district judge, who shall hear the application in private.'

(6) Rule 9 shall apply as if for the reference to the amount payable under the relevant adjudication there were substituted a reference to the arrears due under the related maintenance order.

(7) Where an attachment of earnings order made by the High Court designates the court officer of a county court as the collecting officer, that officer shall, on receipt of a certified copy of the order from the court officer of the High Court, send to the person to whom the order is directed a notice as to the mode of payment.

(8) Where an attachment of earnings order made by a county court to secure payments under a maintenance order ceases to have effect and—

(a) the related maintenance order was made by that court; or

(b) the related maintenance order was an order of the High Court and—

(i) the court officer of the county court has received notice of the cessation from the court officer of the High Court; or

(ii) a committal order has been made in the county court for the enforcement of the related maintenance order,

the court officer of the county court shall give notice of the cessation to the person to whom the attachment of earnings order was directed.

(9) Where an attachment of earnings order has been made by a county court to secure payments under a maintenance order, notice under section 10(2) of the Act of 1971 to the debtor and to the person to whom the district judge is required to pay sums received under the order shall be in the form provided for that purpose, and if the debtor wishes to request the court to discharge the attachment of earnings order or to vary it otherwise than by making the appropriate variation, he shall apply to the court, within 14 days after the date of the notice, for the remedy desired.

(10) Rule 13 shall have effect as if for paragraphs (4) to (7) there were substituted the following paragraph—

'(4) Where it appears to the court by which an attachment of earnings order has been made that the related maintenance order has ceased to have effect, whether by virtue of the terms of the maintenance order or under section 28 of the Matrimonial Causes Act 1973 or otherwise, the court may discharge or vary the attachment of earnings order.'

Part II Consolidated Attachment of Earnings Orders

Rule 18 Cases in Which Consolidated Order May be Made

Subject to the provisions of rules 19 to 21, the court may make a consolidated attachment order where—

(a) two or more attachment of earnings orders are in force to secure the payment of judgment debts by the same debtor; or

(b) on an application for an attachment of earnings order to secure the payment of a judgment debt, or for a consolidated attachment order to secure the payment of two or more judgment debts, it appears to the court that an attachment of earnings order is already in force to secure the payment of a judgment debt by the same debtor.

Rule 19 Application for Consolidated Order

(1) An application for a consolidated attachment order may be made—

(a) by the debtor in respect of whom the order is sought; or

(b) by any person who has obtained or is entitled to apply for an attachment of earnings order to secure the payment of a judgment debt by that debtor.

(2) An application under paragraph (1) may be made in the proceedings in which any attachment of earnings order (other than a priority order) is in force and rules 3, 4 and 5 of this Order shall not apply.

(3) Where the judgment which it is sought to enforce was not given by the court which made the attachment of earnings order, the judgment shall be automatically transferred to the court which made the attachment of earnings order.

(3A) An application under paragraph (1)(b) shall certify the amount of money remaining due under the judgment or order and that the whole or part of any instalment due remains unpaid.

(3B) Where an application for a consolidated attachment of earnings order is made, the court officer shall—

(a) notify any party who may be affected by the application of its terms; and

(b) require him to notify the court in writing, within 14 days of service of notification upon him, giving his reasons for any objection he may have to the granting of the application.

(3C) If notice of any objection is not given within the time stated, the court officer shall make a consolidated attachment of earnings order.

(3D) If any party objects to the making of a consolidated attachment of earnings order, the court officer shall refer the application to the district judge who may grant the application after considering the objection made and the reasons given.

(3E) In the foregoing paragraphs of this rule, a party affected by the application means—

(a) where the application is made by the debtor, the creditor in the proceedings in which the application is made and any other creditor who has obtained an attachment of earnings order which is in force to secure the payment of a judgment debt by the debtor;

(b) where the application is made by the judgment creditor, the debtor and every person who, to the knowledge of the applicant, has obtained an attachment of earnings order which is in force to secure the payment of a judgment debt by the debtor.

(4) A person to whom two or more attachment of earnings orders are directed to secure the payment of judgment debts by the same debtor may request the court in writing to make a consolidated attachment order to secure the payment of those debts, and on receipt of such a request paragraphs (3B) to (3E) shall apply, with the necessary modifications, as if the request were an application by the judgment creditor.

Rule 20 Making of Consolidated Order by Court of Its Own Motion

Where an application is made for an attachment of earnings order to secure the payment of a judgment debt by a debtor in respect of whom an attachment of earnings order is already in force to secure the payment of another judgment debt and no application is made for a consolidated attachment order, the court officer may make such an order of his own motion after giving all persons concerned an opportunity of submitting written objections.

Rule 21 Extension of Consolidated Order

(1) Where a consolidated attachment order is in force to secure the payment of two or more judgment debts, any creditor to whom another judgment debt is owed by the same judgment debtor may apply to the court by which the order was made for it to be extended so as to secure the payment of that debt as well as the first-mentioned debts and, if the application is granted, the court may either vary the order accordingly or may discharge it and make a new consolidated attachment order to secure payment of all the aforesaid judgment debts.

(2) An application under this rule shall be treated for the purposes of rules 19 and 20 as an application for a consolidated attachment order.

Rule 22 Payments under Consolidated Order

Instead of complying with section 13 of the Act of 1971, a court officer who receives payments made to him in compliance with a consolidated attachment order shall, after deducting such court fees, if any, in respect of proceedings for or arising out of the order as are deductible from those payments, deal with the sums paid as he would if they had been paid by the debtor to satisfy the relevant adjudications in proportion to the amounts payable thereunder, and for that purpose dividends may from time to time be declared and distributed among the creditors entitled thereto.

CCR ORDER 28 — JUDGMENT SUMMONSES

ord.28 **76.1**, **76.38**

Rule 1 Application for Judgment Summons

(1) An application for the issue of a judgment summons may be made to the court for the district in which the debtor resides or carries on business or, if the summons is to issue against two or more persons jointly liable under the judgment or order sought to be enforced, in the court for the district in which any of the debtors resides or carries on business.

(2) The judgment creditor shall make his application by filing a request in that behalf certifying the amount of money remaining due under the judgment or order, the amount in respect of which the judgment summons is to issue and that the whole or part of any instalment due remains unpaid.

(3) The judgment creditor must file with the request all written evidence on which he intends to rely.

Rule 2 Mode of Service

(1) Subject to paragraph (2), a judgment summons shall be served personally on every debtor against whom it is issued.

(2) Where the judgment creditor or his solicitor gives a certificate for postal service in respect of a debtor residing or carrying on business within the district of the court, the judgment summons shall, unless the district judge otherwise directs, be served on that debtor by an officer of the court sending it to him by first-class post at the address stated in the request for the judgment summons and, unless the contrary is shown, the date of service shall be deemed to be the seventh day after the date on which the judgment summons was sent to the debtor.

(3) Where a judgment summons has been served on a debtor in accordance with paragraph (2), no order of commitment shall be made against him unless—
   (a) he appears at the hearing; or
   (b) it is made under section 110(2) of the Act.

(4) The written evidence on which the judgment creditor intends to rely must be served with the judgment summons.

Rule 3 Time for Service

(1) The judgment summons and written evidence must be served not less than 14 days before the day fixed for the hearing.

(2) A notice of non-service shall be sent pursuant to CPR rule 6.11 in respect of a judgment summons which has been sent by post under rule 2(2) and has been returned to the court office undelivered.

(3) CPR rules 7.5 and 7.6 shall apply, with the necessary modifications, to a judgment summons as they apply to a claim form.

Rule 4 Enforcement of Debtor's Attendance

(1) Order 27, rules 711 and 8, shall apply, with the necessary modifications, to an order made under section 110(1) of the Act for the attendance of the debtor at an adjourned hearing of a judgment summons as they apply to an order made under section 23(1) of the Attachment of Earnings Act 1971 for the attendance of the debtor at an adjourned hearing of an application for an attachment of earnings order.

(1A) An order made under section 110(1) of the Act must be served personally on the judgment debtor.

(1B) Copies of—
   (a) the judgment summons; and
   (b) the written evidence,

must be served with the order.

(2) At the time of service of the order there shall be paid or tendered to the debtor a sum reasonably sufficient to cover his expenses in travelling to and from the court, unless such a sum was paid to him at the time of service of the judgment summons.

Rule 5 Evidence

(1) No person may be committed on an application for a judgment summons unless—
   (a) the order is made under section 110(2) of the Act; or
   (b) the judgment creditor proves that the debtor—
      (i) has or has had since the date of the judgment or order the means to pay the sum in respect of which he has made default; and
      (ii) has refused or neglected or refuses or neglects to pay that sum.

(2) The debtor may not be compelled to give evidence.

Rule 7 Suspension of Committal Order

(1) If on the hearing of a judgment summons a committal order is made, the judge may direct execution of the order to be suspended to enable the debtor to pay the amount due.

(2) A note of any direction given under paragraph (1) shall be entered in the records of the court and notice of the suspended committal order shall be sent to the debtor.

(3) Where a judgment summons is issued in respect of one or more but not all of the instalments payable under a judgment or order for payment by instalments and a committal order is made and suspended under paragraph (1), the judgment or order shall, unless the judge otherwise orders, be suspended for so long as the, execution of the committal order is suspended.

(4) Where execution of a committal order is suspended under paragraph (1) and the debtor subsequently desires to apply for a further suspension, the debtor shall attend at or write to the court office and apply for the suspension he desires, stating the reasons for his inability to comply with the terms of the original suspension, and the court shall fix a day for the hearing of the application by the judge and give at least 3 days' notice thereof to the judgment creditor and the debtor.

(5) The district judge may suspend execution of the committal order pending the hearing of an application under paragraph (4).

Rule 8 New Order on Judgment Summons

(1) Where on the hearing of a judgment summons, the judge makes a new order for payment of the amount of the judgment debt remaining unpaid, there shall be included in the amount payable under the order for the purpose of any enforcement proceedings, otherwise than by judgment summons, any amount in respect of which a committal order has already been made and the debtor imprisoned.

(2) No judgment summons under the new order shall include any amount in respect of which the debtor was imprisoned before the new order was made, and any amount subsequently paid shall be appropriated in the first instance to the amount due under the new order.

Rule 9 Notification of Order on Judgment of High Court

(1) Notice of the result of the hearing of a judgment summons on a judgment or order of the High Court shall be sent by the county court to the High Court.

(2) If a committal order or a new order for payment is made on the hearing, the office copy of the judgment or order filed in the county court shall be deemed to be a judgment or order of the court in which the judgment summons is heard.

Rule 10 Costs on Judgment Summons

(1) No costs shall be allowed to the judgment creditor on the hearing of a judgment summons unless—
   (a) a committal order is made; or
   (b) the sum in respect of which the judgment summons was issued is paid before the hearing.

(2) Where costs are allowed to the judgment creditor,
   (a) there may be allowed—
      (i) a charge of the judgment creditor's solicitor for attending the hearing and, if the judge so directs, for serving the judgment summons;
      (ii) a fee to counsel if the court certifies that the case is fit for counsel;

(iii) any travelling expenses paid to the debtor, and
(iv) the court fee on the issue of the judgment summons;
(b) the costs may be fixed and allowed without detailed assessment under CPR Part 47;

Rule 11 Issue of Warrant of Committal

(1) A judgment creditor desiring a warrant to be issued pursuant to a committal order shall file a request in that behalf.
(2) Where two or more debtors are to be committed in respect of the same judgment or order, a separate warrant of committal shall be issued for each of them.
(3) Where a warrant of committal is sent to a foreign court for execution, that court shall indorse on it a notice as to the effect of section 122(3) of the Act addressed to the governor of the prison of that court.

Rule 12 Notification to Foreign Court of Part Payment before Debtor Lodged in Prison

Where, after a warrant of committal has been sent to a foreign court for execution but before the debtor is lodged in prison, the home court is notified that an amount which is less than the sum on payment of which the debtor is to be discharged has been paid, the home court shall send notice of the payment to the foreign court.

Rule 13 Payment after Debtor Lodged in Prison

(1) Where, after the debtor has been lodged in prison under a warrant of committal, payment is made of the sum on payment of which the debtor is to be discharged, then—
(a) if the payment is made to the court responsible for the execution of the warrant, the court officer shall make and sign a certificate of payment and send it by post or otherwise to the gaoler;
(b) if the payment is made to the court which issued the warrant of committal after the warrant has been sent to a foreign court for execution, the home court shall send notice of the payment to the foreign court, and the court officer at the foreign court shall make and sign a certificate of payment and send it by post or otherwise to the gaoler;
(c) if the payment is made to the gaoler, he shall sign a certificate of payment and send the amount to the court which made the committal order.
(2) Where, after the debtor has been lodged in prison under a warrant of committal, payment is made of an amount less than the sum on payment of which the debtor is to be discharged, then subject to paragraph (3), paragraph (1)(a) and (b) shall apply with the substitution of references to a notice of payment for the references to a certificate of payment and paragraph (1)(c) shall apply with the omission of the requirement to make and sign a certificate of payment.
(3) Where, after the making of a payment to which paragraph (2) relates, the balance of the sum on payment of which the debtor is to be discharged is paid, paragraph (1) shall apply without the modifications mentioned in paragraph (2).

Rule 14 Discharge of Debtor Otherwise than on Payment

(1) Where the judgment creditor lodges with the district judge a request that a debtor lodged in prison under a warrant of committal may be discharged from custody, the district judge shall make an order for the discharge of the debtor in respect of the warrant of committal and the court shall send the gaoler a certificate of discharge.
(2) Where a debtor who has been lodged in prison under a warrant of committal desires to apply for his discharge under section 121 of the Act, the application shall be made to the judge in writing and without notice showing the reasons why the debtor alleges that he is unable to pay the sum in respect of which he has been committed and ought to be discharged and stating any offer which he desires to make as to the terms on which his discharge is to be ordered, and Order 27, rule 8(3) and (4), shall apply, with the necessary modifications, as it applies to an application by a debtor for his discharge from custody under section 23(7) of the Attachment of Earnings Act 1971.

(3) If in a case to which paragraph (2) relates the debtor is ordered to be discharged from custody on terms which include liability to re-arrest if the terms are not complied with, the judge may, on the application of the judgment creditor if the terms are not complied with, order the debtor to be re-arrested and imprisoned for such part of the term of imprisonment as remained unserved at the time of discharge.

(4) Where an order is made under paragraph (3), a duplicate warrant of committal shall be issued, indorsed with a certificate signed by the court officer as to the order of the judge.

CCR ORDER 29 — COMMITTAL FOR BREACH OF ORDER OR UNDERTAKING

ord.29 **76.1, 76.38, 78.18**

Rule 1 Enforcement of Judgment to Do or Abstain from Doing Any Act

r.1(1) **78.3**
r.1(2)–(3) **78.4**
r.1(4A) **78.8, 78.10**
r.1(5) **78.15**
r.1(6) **78.4**
r.1(7) **78.4, 78.10**
r.1(8) **78.15**

(1) Where a person required by a judgment or order to do an act refuses or neglects to do it within the time fixed by the judgment or order or any subsequent order, or where a person disobeys a judgment or order requiring him to abstain from doing an act, then, subject to the Debtors Acts 1869 and 1878 and to the provisions of these rules, the judgment or order may be enforced, by order of the judge, by a committal order against that person or, if that person is a body corporate, against any director or other officer of the body.

(2) Subject to paragraphs (6) and (7), a judgment or order shall not be enforced under paragraph (1) unless—
(a) a copy of the judgment or order has been served personally on the person required to do or abstain from doing the act in question and also, where that person is a body corporate, on the director or other officer of the body against whom a committal order is sought; and
(b) in the case of a judgment or order requiring a person to do an act, the copy has been so served before the expiration of the time within which he was required to do the act and was accompanied by a copy of any order, made between the date of the judgment or order and the date of service, fixing that time.

(3) Where a judgment or order enforceable by committal order under paragraph (1) has been given or made, the court officer shall, if the judgment or order is in the nature of an injunction, at the time when the judgment or order is drawn up, and in any other case on the request of the judgment creditor, issue a copy of the judgment or order, indorsed with or incorporating a notice as to the consequences of disobedience, for service in accordance with paragraph (2).

(4) If the person served with the judgment or order fails to obey it, the judgment creditor may issue a claim form or, as the case may be, an application notice seeking the committal for contempt of court of that person and subject to paragraph (7), the claim form or application notice shall be served on him personally.

(4A) The claim form or application notice (as the case may be) shall—
(a) identify the provisions of the injunction or undertaking which it is alleged have been disobeyed or broken;
(b) list the ways in which it is alleged that the injunction has been disobeyed or the undertaking has been broken;
(c) be supported by an affidavit stating the grounds on which the application is made, and unless service is dispensed with under paragraph (7), a copy of the affidavit shall be served with the claim form or application notice.

(5) If a committal order is made, the order shall be for the issue of a warrant of committal and, unless the judge otherwise orders—
(a) a copy of the order shall be served on the person to be committed either before or at the time of the execution of the warrant; or
(b) where the warrant has been signed by the judge, the order for issue of the warrant may be served on the person to be committed at any time within 36 hours after the execution of the warrant.

(5A) A warrant of committal shall not, without further order of the court, be enforced more than 2 years after the date on which the warrant is issued.

(6) A judgment or order requiring a person to abstain from doing an act may be enforced under paragraph (1) notwithstanding that service of a copy of the judgment or order has not been effected in accordance with paragraph (2) if the judge is satisfied that, pending such service, the person against whom it is sought to enforce the judgment or order has had notice thereof either—
  (a) by being present when the judgment or order was given or made; or
  (b) by being notified of the terms of the judgment or order whether by telephone, telegram or otherwise.

(7) Without prejudice to its powers under Part 6 of the CPR, the court may dispense with service of a copy of a judgment or order under paragraph (2) or a claim form or application notice under paragraph (4) if the court thinks it just to do so.

(8) Where service of the claim form or application notice has been dispensed with under paragraph (7) and a committal order is made in the absence of the respondent, the judge may on his own initiative fix a date and time when the person to be committed is to be brought before him or before the court.

Rule 1A Undertaking Given by Party

r.1A **78.19**

Rule 1 (except paragraph (6)) shall apply to undertakings as it applies to orders with the necessary modifications and as if—
  (a) for paragraph (2) of that rule there were substituted the following—
    '(2) A copy of the document recording the undertaking shall be delivered by the court officer to the party giving the undertaking—
      (a) by handing a copy of the document to him before he leaves the court building; or
      (b) where his place of residence is known, by posting a copy to him at his place of residence; or
      (c) through his solicitor,
    and, where delivery cannot be effected in this way, the court officer shall deliver a copy of the document to the party for whose benefit the undertaking is given and that party shall cause it to be served personally as soon as is practicable'.
  (b) in paragraph (7), the words from 'a copy of' to 'paragraph (2) or' were omitted.

Rule 2 Solicitor's Undertaking

r.2(1)–(3) **78.19**

(1) An undertaking given by a solicitor in relation to any proceeding in a county court may be enforced, by order of the judge of that court, by committal order against the solicitor.

(2) Where it appears to the judge that a solicitor has failed to carry out any such undertaking, he may of his own initiative direct the court officer to issue a notice calling on the solicitor to show cause why he should not be committed to prison.

(3) Where any party to the proceedings desires to have the undertaking enforced by committal order, the court officer shall, on the application of the party supported by an affidavit setting out the facts on which the application is based, issue such a notice as is referred to in paragraph (2).

Rule 3 Discharge of Person in Custody

r.3(1)–(3) **78.17**

(1) Where a person in custody under a warrant or order, other than a warrant of committal to which Order 27, rule 8, or Order 28, rule 4 or 14, relates, desires to apply to the court for his discharge, he shall make his application in writing attested by the governor of the prison (or any other officer of the prison not below the rank of principal officer) showing that he has purged or is desirous of purging his contempt and shall, not less than one day before the application is made, serve notice of it on the party, if any, at whose instance the warrant or order was issued.

(2) If the committal order—

(a) does not direct that any application for discharge shall be made to a judge; or
(b) was made by the district judge under section 118 of the Act,
any application for discharge may be made to the district judge.

(3) Nothing in paragraph (1) shall apply to an application made by the Official Solicitor in his official capacity for the discharge of a person in custody.

CCR ORDER 33 — INTERPLEADER PROCEEDINGS

ord.33 **12.1, 14.15**

Part I Under Execution

Rule 1 Notice of Claim

r.1(1) **14.19** r.1(2)(a)–(b) **14.19**

(A1) In this Part of this Order 'the interpleader claimant' means any person making a claim to or in respect of goods seized in execution or the proceeds or value thereof and 'the interpleader claim' means that claim.

(1) The interpleader claimant shall deliver to the bailiff holding the warrant of execution, or file in the office of the court for the district in which the goods were seized, notice of his claim stating—
(a) the grounds of the interpleader claim or, in the case of a claim for rent, the particulars required by section 102(2) of the Act; and
(b) the interpleader claimant's full name and address.

(2) On receipt of an interpleader claim made under this rule, the court shall—
(a) send notice thereof to the execution creditor; and
(b) except where the interpleader claim is to the proceeds or value of the goods, send to the interpleader claimant a notice requiring him to make a deposit or give security in accordance with section 100 of the Act.

Rule 2 Reply to Interpleader Claim

r.2 **14.19**

(1) Within 4 days after receiving notice of an interpleader claim under rule 1(2) the execution creditor shall give notice to the court informing him whether he admits or disputes the interpleader claim or requests the district judge to withdraw from possession of the goods or money claimed.

(2) If, within the period aforesaid, the execution creditor gives notice to the court admitting the interpleader claim or requesting the district judge to withdraw from possession of the goods or money claimed, the execution creditor shall not be liable to the district judge for any fees or expenses incurred after receipt of the notice.

Rule 3 Order Protecting District Judge

Where the execution creditor gives the court such a notice as is mentioned in rule 2(2), the district judge shall withdraw from possession of the goods or money claimed and may apply to the judge, on notice to the interpleader claimant, for an order restraining the bringing of a claim against the district judge for or in respect of his having taken possession of the goods or money and on the hearing of the application the judge may make such order as may be just.

Rule 4 Issue of Interpleader Proceedings

(1) Where the execution creditor gives notice under rule 2(1) disputing an interpleader claim made under rule 1 or fails, within the period mentioned in rule 2(1), to give the notice required by that rule, the district judge shall, unless the interpleader claim is withdrawn, issue an interpleader notice to the execution creditor and the interpleader claimant.

(2) On the issue of an interpleader notice under paragraph (1) the court officer shall enter the proceedings in the records of the court, fix a day for the hearing by the judge and prepare sufficient copies of the notice for service under this rule.

(3) Subject to paragraph (4) the notice shall be served on the execution creditor and the interpleader claimant in the manner set out in CPR rule 6.2.
(4) Service shall be effected not less than 14 days before the return day.

Rule 5 Claim for Damages

Where in interpleader proceedings under an execution the interpleader claimant claims from the execution creditor or the district judge, or the execution creditor claims from the district judge, damages arising or capable of arising out of the execution—
(a) the party claiming damages shall, within 8 days after service of the notice on him under rule 4(3), give notice of this claim to the court and to any other party against whom the claim is made, stating the amount and the grounds of the claim; and
(b) the party from whom damages are claimed may pay money into court in satisfaction of the claim as if the interpleader proceedings were a claim brought in accordance with CPR Part 7 by the person making the claim.

Part II Otherwise Than under Execution

Rule 6 Application for Relief

r.6(2)–(3) **14.20**

(1) Where a person (in this Part of this Order called 'the applicant') is under a liability in respect of a debt or any money or goods and he is, or expects to be, sued for or in respect of the debt, money or goods by two or more persons making adverse claims thereto ('the interpleader claimants'), he may apply to the court, in accordance with these rules, for relief by way of interpleader.
(2) The application shall be made to the court in which the claim is pending against the applicant or, if no claim is pending against him, to the court in which he might be sued.
(3) The application shall be made by filing a witness statement or affidavit showing that—
  (a) the applicant claims no interest in the subject-matter in dispute other than for charges or costs;
  (b) the applicant does not collude with any of the interpleader claimants; and
  (c) the applicant is willing to pay or transfer the subject-matter into court or to dispose of it as the court may direct,
together with as many copies of the witness statement or affidavit as there are interpleader claimants.

Rule 7 Relief in Pending Claim

r.7 **14.20**

Where the applicant is a defendant in a pending claim—
(a) the witness statement or affidavit and copies required by rule 6(3) shall be filed within 14 days after service on him of the claim form;
(b) the return day of the application shall be a day fixed for the pre-trial review of the claim including the interpleader proceedings and, if a day has already been fixed for the pre-trial review or hearing of the claim, the court shall, if necessary, postpone it;
(c) the interpleader claimant, the applicant and the claimant in the claim shall be given notice of the application, which shall be prepared by the court together with sufficient copies for service;
(d) the notice to the interpleader claimant shall be served on him, together with a copy of the witness statement or affidavit filed under rule 6(3) and of the claim form and particulars of claim in the claim, not less than 21 days before the return day in the same manner as an interpleader notice in accordance with rule 4(3);
(e) the notices to the applicant and the claimant shall be sent to them by the court and the notice to the claimant shall be accompanied by a copy of the said witness statement or affidavit.

Rule 8 Relief Otherwise Than in Pending Claim

r.8 **14.20**

Where the applicant is not a defendant in a pending claim—
(a) the court shall enter the proceedings in the records of the court;
(b) the court shall fix a day for the pre-trial review or, if the court so directs, a day for the hearing of the proceedings and shall prepare and issue an interpleader notice, together with sufficient copies for service;

(c) the notice together with a copy of the witness statement or affidavit filed under rule 6(3), shall be served on each of the claimants not less than 21 days before the return day in the same manner as an interpleader notice to be served under rule 4(3); and
(d) the court shall deliver or send a notice of issue to the applicant.

Rule 9 Payment into Court etc.

Before or after the court officer proceeds under rule 7 or 8 the district judge may direct the applicant to bring the subject-matter of the proceedings into court, or to dispose of it in such manner as the district judge thinks fit, to abide the order of the court.

Rule 10 Reply by Interpleader Claimant

r.10 **14.20**

(1) An interpleader claimant shall, within 14 days after service on him of the notice under rule 7(c) or the interpleader notice under rule 8(c), file—
  (a) a notice that he makes no interpleader claim; or
  (b) particulars stating the grounds of his interpleader claim to the subject matter,
  together in either case with sufficient copies for service under paragraph (2).
(2) The court shall send to each of the other parties a copy of any notice or particulars filed under paragraph (1).
(3) The court may, if it thinks fit, hear the proceedings although no notice or particulars have been filed.

Rule 11 Order Barring Interpleader Claim etc.

r.11(1)–(3) **14.21**

(1) Where an interpleader claimant does not appear on any day fixed for a pre-trial review or the hearing of interpleader proceedings, or fails or refuses to comply with an order made in the proceedings, the court may make an order barring his interpleader claim.
(2) If, where the applicant is a defendant in a pending claim, the claimant does not appear on any day fixed for a pre-trial review or the hearing of the interpleader proceedings, the claim including the interpleader proceedings may be struck out.
(3) In any other case where a day is fixed for the hearing of interpleader proceedings, the court shall hear and determine the proceedings and give judgment finally determining the rights and claims of the parties.
(4) Where the court makes an order barring the interpleader claim of an interpleader claimant, the order shall declare the interpleader claimant, and all persons claiming under him, forever barred from prosecuting his interpleader claim against the applicant and all persons claiming under him, but unless the interpleader claimant has filed a notice under rule 10 that he makes no interpleader claim, such an order shall not affect the rights of the interpleader claimants as between themselves.

CCR ORDER 34 — PENAL AND DISCIPLINARY PROVISIONS

ord.34 **12.1**

Rule 1 Issue and Service of Summons for Offence under Section 14, 92 or 124 of the Act

Where—
(a) it is alleged that any person has committed an offence under section 14, 92 or 118 of the Act by assaulting an officer of the court while in the execution of his duty, or by rescuing or attempting to rescue any goods seized in execution, or by wilfully insulting a judge, juror, witness or any officer of the court, and the alleged offender has not been taken into custody and brought before the judge; or
(b) a complaint is made against an officer of the court under section 124 of the Act for having lost the opportunity of levying execution,

the court officer shall issue a summons, which shall be served on the alleged offender personally not less than 8 days before the return day appointed in the summons.

Rule 1A Committal under Section 14, 92 or 118 of the Act

Rule 1(5) of Order 29 shall apply, with the necessary modifications, where an order is made under section 14, 92 or 118 of the Act committing a person to prison.

Rule 2 Notice to Show Cause before or after Fine under Section 55 of the Act

r.2 **55.7**

Before or after imposing a fine on any person under section 55 of the Act for disobeying a witness summons or refusing to be sworn or give evidence, the judge may direct the court officer to give to that person notice that if he has any cause to show why a fine should not be or should not have been imposed on him, he may show cause in person or by witness statement or affidavit or otherwise on a day named in the notice, and the judge after considering the cause shown may make such order as he thinks fit.

Rule 3 Non-payment of Fine

r.3(1) **55.7**

(1) If a fine is not paid in accordance with the order imposing it, the court officer shall forthwith report the matter to the judge.
(2) Where by an order imposing a fine, the amount of the fine is directed to be paid by instalments and default is made in the payment of any instalment, the same proceedings may be taken as if default had been made in payment of the whole of the fine.
(3) If the judge makes an order for payment of a fine to be enforced by warrant of execution, the order shall be treated as an application made to the district judge for the issue of the warrant at the time when the order was received by him.

Rule 4 Repayment of Fine

r.4 **55.7**

If, after a fine has been paid, the person on whom it was imposed shows cause sufficient to satisfy the judge that, if it had been shown at an earlier date, he would not have imposed a fine or would have imposed a smaller fine or would not have ordered payment to be enforced, the judge may order the fine or any part thereof to be repaid.

CCR ORDER 39 — ADMINISTRATION ORDERS

ord.39 **76.1**

Rule 1 Exercise of Powers by District Judge

Any powers conferred on the court by Part VI of the Act, section 4 of the Attachment of Earnings Act 1971 or this Order may be exercised by the district judge or, in the circumstances mentioned in this Order, by the court officer.

Rule 2 Request and List of Creditors

(1) A debtor who desires to obtain an administration order under Part VI of the Act shall file a request in that behalf in the court for the district in which he resides or carries on business.
(2) Where on his examination under CPR Part 71, or otherwise, a debtor furnishes to the court on oath a list of his creditors and the amounts which he owes to them respectively and sufficient particulars of his resources and needs, the court may proceed as if the debtor had filed a request under paragraph (1).
(3) Where a debtor is ordered to furnish a list under section 4(1)(b) of the said Act of 1971, then, unless otherwise directed, the list shall be filed within 14 days after the making of the order.

Rule 3 Verification on Oath

The statements in the request mentioned in rule 2(1) and the list mentioned in rule 2(3) shall be verified by the debtor on oath.

Rule 5 Orders Made by the Court Officer

(1) The question whether an administration order should be made, and the terms of such an order, may be decided by the court officer in accordance with the provisions of this rule.

(2) On the filing of a request or list under rule 2, the court officer may, if he considers that the debtor's means are sufficient to discharge in full and within a reasonable period the total amount of the debts included in the list, determine the amount and frequency of the payments to be made under such an order ('the proposed rate') and—

(a) notify the debtor of the proposed rate requiring him to give written reasons for any objection he may have to the proposed rate within 14 days of service of notification upon him;

(b) send to each creditor mentioned in the list provided by the debtor a copy of the debtor's request or of the list together with the proposed rate;

(c) require any such creditor to give written reasons for any objection he may have to the making of an administration order within 14 days of service of the documents mentioned in sub-paragraph (b) upon him.

Objections under sub-paragraph (c) may be to the making of an order, to the proposed rate or to the inclusion of a particular debt in the order.

(3) Where no objection under paragraph (2)(a) or (c) is received within the time stated, the court officer may make an administration order providing for payment in full of the total amount of the debts included in the list.

(4) Where the debtor or a creditor notifies the court of any objection within the time stated, the court officer shall fix a day for a hearing at which the district judge will decide whether an administration order should be made and the court officer shall give not less than 14 days' notice of the day so fixed to the debtor and to each creditor mentioned in the list provided by the debtor.

(5) Where the court officer is unable to fix a rate under paragraph (2) (whether because he considers that the debtor's means are insufficient or otherwise), he shall refer the request to the district judge.

(6) Where the district judge considers that he is able to do so without the attendance of the parties, he may fix the proposed rate providing for payment of the debts included in the list in full or to such extent and within such a period as appears practicable in the circumstances of the case.

(7) Where the proposed rate is fixed under paragraph (6), paragraphs (2) to (4) shall apply with the necessary modifications as if the rate had been fixed by the court officer.

(8) Where the district judge does not fix the proposed rate under paragraph (6), he shall direct the court officer to fix a day for a hearing at which the district judge will decide whether an administration order should be made and the court officer shall give not less than 14 days' notice of the day so fixed to the debtor and to each creditor mentioned in the list provided by the debtor.

(9) Where an administration order is made under paragraph (3), the court officer may exercise the power of the court under section 5 of the Attachment of Earnings Act 1971 to make an attachment of earnings order to secure the payments required by the administration order.

Rule 6 Notice of Objection by Creditor

(1) Any creditor to whom notice has been given under rule 5(8) and who objects to any debt included in the list furnished by the debtor shall, not less than 7 days before the day of hearing, give notice of his objection, stating the grounds thereof, to the court officer, to the debtor and to the creditor to whose debt he objects.

(2) Except with the permission of the court, no creditor may object to a debt unless he has given notice of his objection under paragraph (1).

Rule 7 Procedure on Day of Hearing

On the day of the hearing—

(a) any creditor, whether or not he is mentioned in the list furnished by the debtor, may attend and prove his debt or, subject to rule 6, object to any debt included in that list;

(b) every debt included in that list shall be taken to be proved unless it is objected to by a creditor or disallowed by the court or required by the court to be supported by evidence;

(c) any creditor whose debt is required by the court to be supported by evidence shall prove his debt;
(d) the court may adjourn proof of any debt and, if it does so, may either adjourn consideration of the question whether an administration order should be made or proceed to determine the question, in which case, if an administration order is made, the debt, when proved, shall be added to the debts scheduled to the order;
(e) any creditor whose debt is admitted or proved, and, with the permission of the court, any creditor the proof of whose debt has been adjourned, shall be entitled to be heard and to adduce evidence on the question whether an administration order should be made and, if so, in what terms.

Rule 8 Direction for Order to Be Subject to Review

(1) The court may, on making an administration order or at any subsequent time, direct that the order shall be subject to review at such time or at such intervals as the court may specify.
(2) Where the court has directed that an administration order shall be subject to review, the court officer shall give to the debtor and to every creditor who appeared when the order was made not less than 7 days' notice of any day appointed for such a review.
(3) Nothing in this rule shall require the court officer to fix a day for a review under rule 13A.

Rule 9 Service of Order

Where an administration order is made, the court officer shall send a copy to—
(a) the debtor;
(b) every creditor whose name was included in the list furnished by the debtor;
(c) any other creditor who has proved his debt; and
(d) every other court in which, to the knowledge of the district judge, judgment has been obtained against the debtor or proceedings are pending in respect of any debt scheduled to the order.

Rule 10 Subsequent Objection by Creditor

(1) After an administration order has been made, a creditor who has not received notice under rule 5 and who wishes to object to a debt scheduled to the order, or to the manner in which payment is directed to be made by instalments, shall give notice to the court officer of his objection and of the grounds thereof.
(2) On receipt of such notice the court shall consider the objection and may—
  (a) allow it;
  (b) dismiss it; or
  (c) adjourn it for hearing on notice being given to such persons and on such terms as to security for costs or otherwise as the court thinks fit.
(3) Without prejudice to the generality of paragraph (2), the court may dismiss an objection if it is not satisfied that the creditor gave notice of it within a reasonable time of his becoming aware of the administration order.

Rule 11 Subsequent Proof by Creditor

(1) Any creditor whose debt is not scheduled to an administration order, and any person who after the date of the order became a creditor of the debtor, shall, if he wishes to prove his debt, send particulars of his claim to the court officer, who shall give notice of it to the debtor and to every creditor whose debt is so scheduled.
(2) If neither the debtor nor any creditor gives notice to the court officer, within 7 days after receipt of notice under paragraph (1), that he objects to the claim, then, unless it is required by the court to be supported by evidence, the claim shall be taken to be proved.
(3) If the debtor or a creditor gives notice of objection within the said period of 7 days or the court requires the claim to be supported by evidence, the court officer shall fix a day for consideration of the claim and give notice of it to the debtor, the creditor by whom the claim was made and the creditor, if any, making the objection, and on the hearing the court may either disallow the claim or allow it in whole or in part.
(4) If a claim is taken to be proved under paragraph (2) or allowed under paragraph (3), the debt shall be added to the schedule to the order and a copy of the order shall then be sent to the creditor by whom the claim was made.

Rule 12 Permission to Present Bankruptcy Petition

An application by a creditor under section 112(4) of the Act for permission to present or join in a bankruptcy petition shall be made on notice to the debtor in accordance with CPR Part 23, but the court may, if it thinks fit, order that notice be given to any other creditor whose debt is scheduled to the administration order.

Rule 13 Conduct of Order

(1) The court manager or such other officer of the court as the court making an administration order shall from time to time appoint shall have the conduct of the order and shall take all proper steps to enforce the order (including exercising the power of the court under section 5 of the Attachment of Earnings Act 1971 to make an attachment of earnings order to secure payments required by the administration order) or to bring to the attention of the court any matter which may make it desirable to review the order.

(2) Without prejudice to section 115 of the Act, any creditor whose debt is scheduled to the order may, with the permission of the court, take proceedings to enforce the order.

(3) The debtor or, with the permission of the court, any such creditor may apply to the court to review the order.

(4) When on a matter being brought to its attention under paragraph (1) the court so directs or the debtor or a creditor applies for the review of an administration order, rule 8(2) shall apply as if the order were subject to review under that rule.

(5) Nothing in this rule shall require the court officer to fix a day for a review under rule 13A.

Rule 13A Review by Court Officer in Default of Payment

(1) Where it appears that the debtor is failing to make payments in accordance with the order, the court officer shall (either of his own initiative or on the application of a creditor whose debt is scheduled to the administration order) send a notice to the debtor—
  (a) informing him of the amounts which are outstanding; and
  (b) requiring him (within 14 days of service of the notice upon him) to—
    (i) make the payments as required by the order; or
    (ii) explain his reasons for failing to make the payments; and
    (iii) make a proposal for payment of the amounts outstanding; or
    (iv) make a request to vary the order.

(2) If the debtor does not comply with paragraph (1)(b) within the time stated, the court officer shall revoke the administration order.

(3) The court officer shall refer a notice given by a debtor under paragraph (1)(b)(ii), (iii) or (iv) to the district judge who may—
  (a) without requiring the attendance of the parties—
    (i) revoke the administration order or vary it so as to provide for payment of the debts included in the order in full or to such extent and within such a period as appears practicable in the circumstances of the case; or
    (ii) suspend the operation of the administration order for such time and on such terms as he thinks fit; or
  (b) require the court officer to fix a day for the review of the administration order and to give to the debtor and to every creditor whose debt is scheduled to the administration order not less than 8 days' notice of the day so fixed.

(4) Any party affected by an order made under paragraph (2) or (3)(a) may, within 14 days of service of the order on him and giving his reasons, apply on notice for the district judge to consider the matter afresh and the court officer shall fix a day for the hearing of the application before the district judge and give to the debtor and to every creditor whose debt is scheduled to the administration order not less than 8 days' notice of the day so fixed.

(5) On hearing an application under paragraph (4), the district judge may confirm the order or set it aside and make such new order as he thinks fit and the order so made shall be entered in the records of the court.

Rule 14 Review of Order

(1) On the review of an administration order the court may—
  (a) if satisfied that the debtor is unable from any cause to pay any instalment due under the order, suspend the operation of the order for such time and on such terms as it thinks fit;
  (b) if satisfied that there has been a material change in any relevant circumstances since the order was made, vary any provision of the order made by virtue of section 112(6) of the Act;
  (c) if satisfied that the debtor has failed without reasonable cause to comply with any provision of the order or that it is otherwise just and expedient to do so, revoke the order, either forthwith or on failure to comply with any condition specified by the court; or
  (d) make an attachment of earnings order to secure the payments required by the administration order or vary or discharge any such attachment of earnings order already made.

(2) The court officer shall send a copy of any order varying or revoking an administration order to the debtor, to every creditor whose debt is scheduled to the administration order and, if the administration order is revoked, to any other court to which a copy of the administration order was sent pursuant to rule 9.

Rule 16 Discharge of Attachment of Earnings Order

On the revocation of an administration order any attachment of earnings order made to secure the payments required by the administration order shall be discharged.

Rule 17 Declaration of Dividends

(1) The officer having the conduct of an administration order shall from time to time declare dividends and distribute them among the creditors entitled to them.
(2) When a dividend is declared, notice shall be sent by the officer to each of the creditors.

Rule 18 Creditors to Rank Equally

All creditors scheduled under section 113(d) of the Act before an administration order is superseded under section 117(2) of the Act shall rank equally in proportion to the amount of their debts subject to the priority given by the said paragraph (d) to those scheduled as having been creditors before the date of the order, but no payment made to any creditor by way of dividend or otherwise shall be disturbed by reason of any subsequent proof by any creditor under the said paragraph (d).

Rule 19 Change of Debtor's Address

(1) A debtor who changes his residence shall forthwith inform the court of his new address.
(2) Mere the debtor becomes resident in the district of another court, the court in which the administration order is being conducted may transfer the proceedings to that other court.

CCR ORDER 44 — THE AGRICULTURAL HOLDINGS ACT 1986

Rule 1 Order to Arbitrator to State Case

(1) An application under paragraph 26 of Schedule 11 to the Agricultural Holdings Act 1986 for an order directing an arbitrator to state, in the form of a special case for the opinion of the court, a question of law arising in the course of the arbitration shall include a concise statement of the question of law.
(2) The arbitrator shall not be made a respondent to the application, but if the judge grants the application, a copy of the order shall be served on the arbitrator.

Rule 2 Special Case Stated by Arbitrator

(1) Where, pursuant to the said paragraph 26, an arbitrator states, in the form of a special case for the opinion of the court, any question of law arising in the course of the arbitration, the case shall contain a statement of such facts and reference to such documents as may be necessary to enable the judge to decide the question of law.
(2) The case shall be signed by the arbitrator and shall be lodged in the court office by the arbitrator or any party to the arbitration, together with a copy for the use of the judge.
(3) The court officer shall fix a day for the hearing of the special case and give notice thereof to the parties.

(4) On the hearing the judge shall be at liberty to draw any inferences of fact from the case and the documents referred to therein.
(5) The judge may remit the case to the arbitrator for restatement or further statement.
(6) A copy of the order made by the judge on the hearing shall be served on the parties to the arbitration and on the arbitrator.

Rule 3 Removal of Arbitrator or Setting Aside Award

(1) An application under paragraph 27 of Schedule 11 to the said Act of 1986 for the removal of an arbitrator on the ground of his misconduct or for an order setting aside an award on the ground that the arbitrator has misconducted himself or that an arbitration or award has been improperly procured or that there is an error of law on the face of the award shall be made within 21 days after the date of the award.
(2) The arbitrator and all parties to the arbitration, other than the applicant, shall be made respondents.

Rule 4 Enforcement of Order Imposing Penalty

(1) When taking any proceedings for the enforcement in a county court of an order under section 27 of the Agricultural Holdings Act 1986, the party in whose favour the order was made shall file—
  (a) a certified copy of the order; and
  (b) a certificate specifying the amount due under the order and stating whether any previous proceedings have been taken for its enforcement and, if so, the nature of the proceedings and their result.
(2) Where it is desired to enforce the order by warrant of execution, the proceedings may be taken in any court in the district of which execution is to be levied.

CCR ORDER 45 — THE REPRESENTATION OF THE PEOPLE ACT 1983

Rule 1 Application for Detailed Assessment of Returning Officer's Account

(1) An application by the Secretary of State under section 30 of the Representation of the People Act 1983 for the detailed assessment of a returning officer's account shall be made by claim form and on issuing the claim form the court will fix a day for the hearing which shall be a day for proceeding with the detailed assessment if the application is granted.
(2) Where on the application the returning officer desires to apply to the court to examine any claim made against him in respect of matters charged in the account, the application shall be made in writing and filed, together with a copy thereof, within 7 days after service on the returning officer of the copy of the application for detailed assessment.
(3) On the filing of an application under paragraph (2) the court officer shall fix a day for the hearing and give notice thereof to the returning officer, and a copy of the application and of the notice shall be served on the claimant in the manner set out in CPR rule 6.2.
(4) The examination and detailed assessment may, if the court thinks fit, take place on the same day, but the examination shall be determined before the detailed assessment is concluded.
(5) The application for detailed assessment and any application under paragraph (2) may be heard and determined by the district judge and a copy of the order made on the application shall be served on the Secretary of State and the returning officer and, in the case of an application under paragraph (2), on the claimant.

Rule 2 Appeal from Decision of Registration Officer

(1) Where notice of appeal from a decision of a registration officer is given pursuant to regulations made under section 53 of the said Act of 1983 the registration officer shall, within 7 days after receipt of the notice by him, forward the notice by post to the court in which the appeal is required to be brought, together with the statement mentioned in those regulations.
(2) The appeal shall be brought in the court for the district in which the qualifying premises are situated.
In this paragraph 'qualifying premises' means the premises in respect of which—
  (a) the person whose right to be registered in the register of electors is in question on the appeal is entered on the electors' list or is registered or claims to be entitled to be registered; or

(b) the person whose right to vote by proxy or by post is in question on the appeal is or will be registered in the register of electors; or

(c) the elector whose proxy's right to vote by post is in question on the appeal is or will be registered in the register of electors,

as the case may be.

(3) The respondents to the appeal shall be the registration officer and the party (if any) in whose favour the decision of the registration officer was given.

(4) On the hearing of the appeal—

(a) the statement forwarded to the court by the registration officer and any document containing information furnished to the court by the registration officer pursuant to the regulations mentioned in paragraph (1) shall be admissible as evidence of the facts stated therein; and

(b) the judge shall have power to draw all inferences of fact which might have been drawn by the registration officer and to give any decision and make any order which ought to have been given or made by the registration officer.

(5) A respondent to an appeal other than the registration officer shall not be liable for or entitled to costs, unless he appears before the court in support of the decision of the registration officer.

Rule 3 Selected Appeals

(1) Where two or more appeals to which rule 2 relates involve the same point of law, the judge may direct that one appeal shall be heard in the first instance as a test case and thereupon the court shall send a notice of the direction to the parties to the selected appeal and the parties to the other appeals.

(2) If within 7 days after service of such notice on him any party to an appeal other than the selected appeal gives notice to the court that he desires the appeal to which he is a party to be heard—

(a) the appeal shall be heard after the selected appeal is disposed of;

(b) the court shall give the parties to the appeal notice of the day on which it will be heard;

(c) the party giving notice under this paragraph shall not be entitled to receive any costs occasioned by the separate hearing of the appeal to which he is a party, unless the judge otherwise orders.

(3) If no notice is given under paragraph (2) within the time limited—

(a) the decision on the selected appeal shall bind the parties to each other appeal without prejudice to their right to appeal to the Court of Appeal;

(b) an order similar to the order in the selected appeal shall be made in each other appeal without further hearing;

(c) the party to each other appeal who is in the same interest as the unsuccessful party to the selected appeal shall be liable for the costs of the selected appeal in the same manner and to the same extent as the unsuccessful party to that appeal and an order directing him to pay such costs may be made and enforced accordingly.

CCR ORDER 46 — THE LEGITIMACY ACT 1976

Rule 1 Manner of Application

(1) An application to a county court under section 45(2) of the Matrimonial Causes Act 1973 for a declaration of legitimation by virtue of the Legitimacy Act 1976 shall be made by claim form stating—

(a) the grounds on which the applicant relies;

(b) the date and place of birth of the applicant and the maiden name of his mother and, if it be the case, that the applicant is known by a name other than that which appears in the certificate of his birth; and

(c) particulars of every person whose interest may be affected by the proceedings and his relationship, if any, to the applicant, including any person other than the applicant's father to whom his mother was married at the date of his birth.

(2) The application may be filed in the court for the district in which the applicant resides or the marriage leading to the legitimation was celebrated, or if neither the residence of the applicant nor the place of the marriage is in England or Wales, then in the Westminster County Court.

(3) The applicant shall file with the claim form—
  (a) a witness statement or affidavit by him (or, if he is a child, by his litigation friend) verifying the application; and
  (b) any birth, death or marriage certificate intended to be relied on at the hearing.

Rule 2 Preliminary Consideration and Service

(1) On the filing of the documents mentioned in rule 1, the court officer shall fix a day for a case management hearing and give notice thereof to the Attorney-General.
(2) It shall not be necessary to serve the application on the Attorney-General otherwise than by delivering a copy of it to him in accordance with section 45(6) of the Matrimonial Causes Act 1973.
(3) At the case management hearing the court shall give directions as to the persons, if any, other than the Attorney-General, who are to be made respondents to the application.
(4) Where in the opinion of the court it is impracticable to serve a respondent other than the Attorney-General in accordance with the rules relating to service or it is otherwise necessary or expedient to dispense with service of the claim form on any such respondent, the court may make an order dispensing with service on him.

Rule 3 Answer

(1) The Attorney-General may file an answer to the application within 14 days after directions have been given at the case management hearing.
(2) Any other respondent who wishes to oppose the application or to dispute any of the facts alleged in it shall, within 14 days after service of the application on him, file an answer to the application.
(3) A respondent who files an answer shall file with it as many copies as there are other parties to the proceedings and the court shall send one of the copies to each of those parties.

CCR ORDER 47 — DOMESTIC AND MATRIMONIAL PROCEEDINGS

Rule 5 Family Law Reform Act 1969

(1) In this rule—
  'bodily samples' and 'scientific tests' have the meanings assigned to them by section 25 of the Family Law Reform Act 1969; and
  'direction' means a direction for the use of scientific tests under section 20(1) of that Act.
(2) Except with the permission of the court, an application in any proceedings for a direction shall be made on notice to every party to the proceedings (other than the applicant) and to any other person from whom the direction involves the taking of bodily samples.
(3) Where an application is made for a direction involving the taking of bodily samples from a person who is not a party to the proceedings in which the application is made, the application notice shall be served on him personally and the court may at any time direct him to be made a party to the proceedings.
(4) Where an application is made for a direction in respect of a person (in this paragraph referred to as a person under disability) who is either—
  (a) under 16; or
  (b) suffering from mental disorder within the meaning of the Mental Health Act 1983 and incapable of understanding the nature and purpose of scientific tests,

  the notice of application shall state the name and address of the person having the care and control of the person under disability and shall be served on him instead of on the person under disability.
(5) Where the court gives a direction in any proceedings, the court officer shall send a copy to every party to the proceedings and to every other person from whom the direction involves the taking of bodily samples, and, unless otherwise ordered, the proceedings shall stand adjourned until the court receives a report pursuant to the direction.
(6) On receipt by the court of a report made pursuant to a direction, the court officer shall send a copy to every party to the proceedings and to every other person from whom the direction involved the taking of bodily samples.

CCR ORDER 49 — MISCELLANEOUS STATUTES

ord.49 **1.5**

Rule 7 Injunctions to Prevent Environmental Harm: Town and Country Planning Act 1990 etc.

(1) An injunction under—

(a) section 187B or 214A of the Town and Country Planning Act 1990;

(b) section 44A of the Planning (Listed Buildings and Conservation Areas) Act 1990; or

(c) section 26AA of the Planning (Hazardous Substances) Act 1990,

may be granted against a person whose identity is unknown to the applicant; and in the following provisions of this rule such an injunction against such a person is referred to as 'an injunction under paragraph (1)', and the person against whom it is sought is referred to as 'the respondent'.

(2) An applicant for an injunction under paragraph (1) shall describe the respondent by reference to—

(a) a photograph;

(b) a thing belonging to or in the possession of the respondent; or

(c) any other evidence,

with sufficient particularity to enable service to be effected, and the form of the claim form used shall be modified accordingly.

(3) An applicant for an injunction under paragraph (1) shall file evidence by witness statement or affidavit—

(a) verifying that he was unable to ascertain, within the time reasonably available to him, the respondent's identity;

(b) setting out the action taken to ascertain the respondent's identity; and

(c) verifying the means by which the respondent has been described in the claim form and that the description is the best that the applicant is able to provide.

(4) Paragraph (2) is without prejudice to the power of the court to make an order in accordance with CPR Part 6 for service by an alternative method or dispensing with service.

Rule 12 Mental Health Act 1983

(1) In this rule—

a section referred to by number means the section so numbered in the Mental Health Act 1983 and 'Part II' means Part II of that Act;

'place of residence' means, in relation to a patient who is receiving treatment as an in-patient in a hospital or other institution, that hospital or institution;

'hospital authority' means the managers of a hospital as defined in section 145(1).

(2) An application to a county court under Part II shall be made by a claim form filed in the court for the district in which the patients' place of residence is situated or, in the case of an application made under section 30 for the discharge or variation of an order made under section 29, in that court or in the court which made the order.

(3) Where an application is made under section 29 for an order that the functions of the nearest relative of the patient shall be exercisable by some other person—

(a) the nearest relative shall be made a respondent to the application unless the application is made on the grounds set out in subsection (3)(a) of the said section or the court otherwise orders; and

(b) the court may order that any other person shall be made a respondent.

(4) On the hearing of the application the court may accept as evidence of the facts stated therein any report made by a medical practitioner and any report made in the course of his official duties by—

(a) a probation officer; or

(b) an officer of a local authority or of a voluntary organisation exercising statutory functions on behalf of a local authority; or

(c) an officer of a hospital authority,

provided that the respondent shall be told the substance of any part of the report bearing on his fitness or conduct which the judge considers to be material for the fair determination of the application.

(5) Unless otherwise ordered, an application under Part II shall be heard and determined by the court sitting in private.

(6) For the purpose of determining the application the judge may interview the patient either in the presence of or separately from the parties and either at the court or elsewhere, or may direct the district judge to interview the patient and report to the judge in writing.

Rule 17 Sex Discrimination Act 1975, Race Relations Act 1976, Disability Discrimination Act 1995 and Disability Rights Commission Act 1999

(1) In this rule—

(a) 'the Act of 1975', 'the Act of 1976', 'the Act of 1995' and 'the Act of 1999' mean respectively the Sex Discrimination Act 1975, the Race Relations Act 1976, the Disability Discrimination Act 1995 and the Disability Rights Commission Act 1999;

(aa) 'the Religion or Belief Regulations' means the Employment Equality (Religion or Belief) Regulations 2003 and 'the Sexual Orientation Regulations' means the Employment Equality (Sexual Orientation) Regulations 2003;

(b) in relation to proceedings under any of those Acts or Regulations, expressions which are used in the Act or Regulations concerned have the same meanings in this rule as they have in that Act or those Regulations;

(c) in relation to proceedings under the Act of 1976 'court' means a designated county court and 'district' means the district assigned to such a court for the purposes of that Act.

(2) A claimant who brings a claim under section 66 of the Act of 1975, section 57 of the Act of 1976 or section 25 of the Act of 1995 shall forthwith give notice to the Commission of the commencement of the proceedings and file a copy of the notice.

(3) CPR Rule 35.15 shall have effect in relation to an assessor who is to be appointed in proceedings under section 66(1) of the Act of 1975.

(4) Proceedings under section 66, 71 or 72 of the Act of 1975, section 57, 62 or 63 of the Act of 1976, regulation 31 of the Religion or Belief Regulations or regulation 31 of the Sexual Orientation Regulations, section 17B or 25 of the Act of 1995 or section 6 of the Act of 1999 may be commenced—

(a) in the court for the district in which the defendant resides or carries on business; or

(b) in the court for the district in which the act or any of the acts in respect of which the proceedings are brought took place.

(5) An appeal under section 68 of the Act of 1975, section 59 of the Act of 1976 or paragraph 10 of Schedule 3 to the Act of 1999 against a requirement of a non-discrimination notice shall be brought in the court for the district in which the acts to which the requirement relates were done.

(6) Where the claimant in any claim alleging discrimination has questioned the defendant under section 74 of the Act of 1975, section 65 of the Act of 1976, section 56 of the Act of 1995, regulation 33 of the Religion or Belief Regulations or regulation 33 of the Sexual Orientation Regulations, —

(a) either party may make an application to the court in accordance with CPR Part 23 to determine whether the question or any reply is admissible under that section; and

(b) CPR Rule 3.4 shall apply to the question and any answer as it applies to any statement of case.

(7) Where in any claim the Commission claim a charge for expenses incurred by them in providing the claimant with assistance under section 75 of the Act of 1975, section 66 of the Act of 1976 or section 7 of the Act of 1999—

(a) the Commission shall, within 14 days after the determination of the claim, give notice of the claim to the court and the claimant and thereafter no money paid into court for the benefit of the claimant, so far as it relates to any costs or expenses, shall be paid out except in pursuance of an order of the court; and

(b) the court may order the expenses incurred by the Commission to be assessed whether by the summary or detailed procedure as if they were costs payable by the claimant to his own solicitor for work done in connection with the proceedings.

(8) Where an application is made for the removal or modification of any term of a contract to which section 77(2) of the Act of 1975, section 72(2) of the Act of 1976, section 26 of or Schedule 3A to the Act of 1995, paragraph 1(1) or (2) of Schedule 4 to the Religion or Belief Regulations or paragraph 1(1) or (2) of Schedule 4 to the Sexual Orientation Regulations applies, all persons affected shall be made respondents to the application, unless in any particular case the court otherwise directs, and the proceedings may be commenced—
(a) in the court for the district in which the respondent or any of the respondents resides or carries on business; or
(b) in the court for the district in which the contract was made.

Rule 18A Telecommunications Act 1984

CPR Rule 35.15 applies to proceedings under paragraph 5 of Schedule 2 to the Telecommunications Act 1984.

Rule 19 Trade Union and Labour Relations Consolidation Act 1992

(1) Where a complainant desires to have an order of the Certification Officer under section 82 of the Trade Union and Labour Relations Consolidation Act 1992 recorded in the county court, he shall produce the order and a copy thereof to the court for the district in which he resides or the head or main office of the trade union is situate.
(2) The order shall be recorded by filing it, and the copy shall be sealed and dated and returned to the complainant.
(3) The sealed copy shall be treated as if it were the notice of issue in a claim begun by the complainant.
(4) The costs, if any, allowed for recording the order shall be recoverable as if they were payable under the order.
(5) The order shall not be enforced until proof is given to the satisfaction of the court that the order has not been obeyed and, if the order is for payment of money, of the amount remaining unpaid.

Notes on Text of the CPR

The text of the CPR printed above incorporates the amendments in the following list. The date after an amendment is the date on which it came into force. The notes at the end set out transitional provisions. The list does not include amendments of contents lists and cross-references.

The titles of the statutory instruments referred to are:

SI 1999/1008: Civil Procedure (Amendment) Rules 1999
SI 2000/221: Civil Procedure (Amendment) Rules 2000
SI 2000/940: Civil Procedure (Amendment No. 2) Rules 2000
SI 2000/1317: Civil Procedure (Amendment No. 3) Rules 2000
SI 2000/2092: Civil Procedure (Amendment No. 4) Rules 2000
SI 2001/256: Civil Procedure (Amendment) Rules 2001
SI 2001/1388: Civil Procedure (Amendment No. 2) Rules 2001
SI 2001/1769: Civil Procedure (Amendment No. 3) Rules 2001
SI 2001/2792: Civil Procedure (Amendment No. 4) Rules 2001
SI 2001/4015: Civil Procedure (Amendment No. 5) Rules 2001
SI 2001/4016: Civil Procedure (Amendment No. 6) Rules 2001
SI 2002/2058: Civil Procedure (Amendment) Rules 2002
SI 2002/3219: Civil Procedure (Amendment No. 2) Rules 2002
SI 2003/364: Civil Procedure (Amendment) Rules 2003
SI 2003/1242: Civil Procedure (Amendment No. 2) Rules 2003
SI 2003/1329: Civil Procedure (Amendment No. 3) Rules 2003
SI 2003/2113: Civil Procedure (Amendment No. 4) Rules 2003
SI 2003/3361: Civil Procedure (Amendment No. 5) Rules 2003
SI 2004/1306: Civil Procedure (Amendment) Rules 2004
SI 2004/2072: Civil Procedure (Amendment No. 2) Rules 2004
SI 2004/3129: Civil Procedure (Amendment No. 3) Rules 2004
SI 2004/3419: Civil Procedure (Amendment No. 4) Rules 2004
SI 2005/352: Civil Procedure (Amendment) Rules 2005
SI 2005/656: Civil Procedure (Amendment No. 2) Rules 2005
SI 2005/2292: Civil Procedure (Amendment No. 3) Rules 2005
SI 2005/2292: Civil Procedure (Amendment No. 4) Rules 2005

r. 1.2 amended by SI 2005/656, r. 3 (14 March 2005);
r. 2.1 amended by: (a) SI 1999/1008, r. 3 (26 April 1999); (b) SI 2003/1242, r. 3 (2 June 2003); (c) SI 2005/3515, r. 3 (6 April 2006);
r. 2.3(1) amended by: (a) SI 2000/2092, r. 3 (2 October 2000); (b) SI 2004/2072, r. 3 (1 October 2004);
r. 2.3(2) amended by SI 2001/4015, r. 3 (25 March 2002);
r. 3.1(2) amended by SI 2005/2292, r. 3 (1 October 2005);
r. 3.1(6A) inserted by SI 1999/1008, r. 4 (26 April 1999);
r. 3.3 amended by: (a) SI 2004/2072, r. 4 (1 October 2004); (b) SI 2005/2292, r. 4 (1 October 2005);
r. 3.4 amended by SI 2004/2072, r. 5 (1 October 2004);
r. 3.5 amended by SI 2000/221, r. 3 (2 May 2000);
r. 3.7(1) substituted by SI 2000/2092, r. 4 (2 October 2000); amended by SI 2002/2058, r. 3 (2 December 2002);
r. 3.7(2) substituted by SI 2000/2092, r. 4 (2 October 2000);
r. 3.7(4) and (6) amended by SI 2005/2292, r. 5 (1 October 2005);
r. 3.7(7) substituted and r. 3.7(8) inserted by SI 2003/1242, r. 4 (2 June 2003);
r. 3.7A inserted by SI 2005/2292, r. 6 (1 October 2005);
r. 3.7B inserted by SI 2005/2292, r. 7 (1 October 2005);
r. 5.2 amended by SI 2001/2792, r. 3 (25 March 2002);

r. 5.4 substituted by SI 2004/2072, r. 7 (1 October 2004); amended by SI 2005/2292, r. 8 (1 October 2005);
r. 5.4A inserted by SI 2004/1306, r. 3 (1 Junc 2004);
r. 5.5 inserted by SI 2002/2058, r. 4 (2 December 2002);
r. 6.2 amended by SI 2005/3515, r. 4(a) (6 April 2006);
r. 6.4 amended by SI 2005/2292, r. 10 (1 October 2005);
r. 6.5 amended by: (a) SI 2000/221, r. 4(3) (2 May 2000); (b) SI 2005/2292, r. 11 (6 April 2006 (amendment of para. (2)) and 1 October 2005 (insertion of para. (8)); (c) SI 2005/3515, r. 4(b) (6 April 2006);
r. 6.7 amended by: (a) SI 2000/221, r. 4(4) (2 May 2000); (b) SI 2005/3515, r. 4(c) (6 April 2006);
r. 6.10 amended by SI 2004/1306, r. 4 (30 June 2004);
r. 6.11 substituted by SI 2005/2292, r. 13 (1 October 2005);
r. 6.11A inserted by SI 2005/2292, r. 13 (1 October 2005);
r. 6.15 amended by SI 2000/940, r. 4 (2 May 2000);
rr. 6.17 to 6.31 inserted by SI 2000/221, r. 4(5) (2 May 2000);
r. 6.18 amended by: (a) SI 2001/1388, r. 3 (31 May 2001); (b) SI 2001/4015, r. 4 (1 March 2002); (c) SI 2002/2058, r. 5(b) (2 December 2002);
r. 6.19 amended by: (a) SI 2001/4015, rr. 5 and 6 (1 March 2002); (b) SI 2002/2058, r. 5(c) (2 December 2002);
r. 6.20(3) amended by SI 2004/2072, r. 8 (1 October 2004);
r. 6.20(3A) inserted by SI 2000/1317, r. 3 (3 July 2000);
r. 6.20(16) amended by SI 2005/2292, r. 15 (1 October 2005);
r. 6.20(17A) inserted by SI 2001/4015, r. 7 (25 March 2002);
r. 6.20(18) amended by SI 2001/1388, r. 4 (31 May 2001);
r. 6.21(2A) inserted by SI 2000/940, r. 5 (2 May 2000);
r. 6.22 amended by SI 2001/4015, r. 9 (1 March 2002);
r. 6.23 amended by SI 2001/4015, r. 10 (1 March 2002);
r. 6.24 amended by: (a) SI 2001/256, r. 4 (26 March 2001); (b) SI 2001/1388, r. 5 (31 May 2001);
r. 6.25 amended by SI 2001/1388, r. 6 (31 May 2001);
r. 6.26 amended by SI 2001/1388, r. 7 (31 May 2001);
r. 6.26A inserted by SI 2001/1388, r. 8 (31 May 2001);
rr. 6.32 to 6.35 inserted by SI 2002/2058, r. 5(d) and sch. 1 (2 December 2002);
r. 7.11 inserted by SI 2000/2092, r. 6 (2 October 2000);
r. 7.12 inserted by SI 2003/3361, r. 3 (1 February 2004);
r. 8.2A inserted by SI 2000/221, r. 5 (2 May 2000); amended by SI 2001/256, r. 5 (26 March 2001);
r. 8.3(4) revoked by SI 2001/4015, r. 11 (25 March 2002);
r. 10.3 amended by: (a) SI 2000/940, r. 6 (2 May 2000); (b) SI 2005/2292, r. 17 (1 October 2005);
r. 11 amended by: (a) SI 2001/4015, r. 12 (25 March 2002); (b) SI 2005/2292, r. 18 (1 October 2005);
r. 12.3 amended by SI 2000/221, r. 6 (2 May 2000);
r. 12.4(2) amended by SI 2005/2292, r. 19(a) (6 April 2006);
r. 12.4(4) inserted by SI 2005/2292, r. 19(b) (1 October 2005);
r. 12.10 amended by: (a) SI 2000/940, r. 7 (2 May 2000); (b) SI 2001/4015, r. 13 (1 March 2002); (c) SI 2005/2292, r. 20 (1 October 2005);
r. 12.11 amended by: (a) SI 2000/940, r. 8 (2 May 2000); (b) SI 2001/4015, r. 14 (1 March 2002); (c) SI 2005/2292, r. 21 (1 October 2005);
r. 13.4(1A) inserted by SI 1999/1008, r. 5 (26 April 1999), and revoked by SI 2000/2092, r. 7 (2 October 2000);
r. 13.5 revoked by SI 2004/1306, r. 21 (30 June 2004);
r. 14.2 amended by SI 2000/940, r. 9 (2 May 2000);
r. 15.4 amended by SI 2000/940, r. 10 (2 May 2000);
r. 16.2(1) amended by SI 2005/3515, r. 5 (6 April 2006);
r. 16.2(1A) inserted by SI 2005/2292, r. 22 (1 October 2005);
r. 16.3(4) substituted by SI 1999/1008, r. 6 (26 April 1999);
r. 17.1 amended by SI 2000/221, r. 7 (2 May 2000);
r. 17.4 amended by SI 2001/256, r. 7 (26 March 2001);
Part 19 substituted by SI 2000/221, r. 9 and sch. 2 (2 May 2000);

r. 19.4(4A) inserted by SI 2005/2292, r. 23 (1 October 2005);
r. 19.4A inserted by SI 2000/2092, r. 8 (2 October 2000);
r. 19.5 amended by SI 2001/256, r. 8 (26 March 2001);
r. 19.5A inserted by SI 2001/256, r. 9 (26 March 2001);
r. 19.7A inserted by SI 2002/2058, r. 6(a) (2 December 2002);
r. 19.7B inserted by SI 2005/2292, r. 24 (1 October 2005);
r. 19.8A inserted by SI 2001/256, r. 10 (26 March 2001); substituted by SI 2002/2058, r. 6(b) (2 December 2002);
Part 20 substituted by SI 2005/3515, r. 6 and sch. (6 April 2006);
r. 21.1 amended by SI 2003/3361, r. 4 (1 April 2004);
r. 21.10 amended by SI 2004/3419, r. 3 (1 April 2005);
r. 21.11A inserted by SI 2005/2292, r. 25 (1 October 2005);
r. 22.1 amended by: (a) SI 2001/1769, r. 3 (31 May 2001); (b) SI 2001/1769, r. 4 (15 October 2001); (c) SI 2001/4015, r. 16 (25 March 2002); (d) SI 2004/3419, r. 4 (1 April 2005);
r. 23.10(1) substituted by SI 2000/221, r. 11 (2 May 2000);
r. 23.12 inserted by SI 2004/2072, r. 9 (1 October 2004); amended by SI 2005/2292, r. 26 (1 October 2005);
r. 24.2 amended by SI 2000/1317, r. 9 (3 July 2000);
r. 24.3(2) amended by: (a) SI 1999/1008, r. 7 (26 April 1999); (b) SI 2000/2092, r. 9 (2 October 2000);
r. 24.4(1A) inserted by SI 2005/2292, r. 27 (1 October 2005);
r. 24.4(4) inserted by SI 2000/221, r. 12 (2 May 2000);
Part 25 title amended by SI 2000/221, r. 13(1) (2 May 2000);
r. 25.1 amended by: (a) SI 2002/2058, r. 7 (2 December 2002); (b) SI 2005/3515, r. 7(a) (6 April 2006);
r. 25.2(3) substituted by SI 2005/3515, r. 7(b) (6 April 2006);
r. 25.7 amended by SI 2004/3419, r. 5 (1 April 2005);
r. 25.10 amended by SI 2001/4015 (25 March 2002);
r. 25.11 inserted by SI 1999/1008, r. 8 (26 April 1999);
r. 25.12 inserted by SI 2000/221, r. 13(2) (2 May 2000);
r. 25.13 inserted by SI 2000/221, r. 13(2) (2 May 2000); amended by: (a) SI 2001/4015, r. 18 (1 March 2002); (b) SI 2002/3219, r. 3 (1 April 2003);
rr. 25.14 and 25.15 inserted by SI 2000/221, r. 13(2) (2 May 2000);
r. 26.3(6A) inserted by SI 2001/4015, r. 19 (25 March 2002);
r. 26.4(20) amended by SI 2005/2292, r. 28 (1 October 2005);
r. 26.7(3) amended by SI 2000/221, r. 14 (2 May 2000);
r. 26.11 inserted by SI 2000/2092, r. 10 (2 October 2000);
r. 27.2(1) amended by: (a) SI 2000/221, r. 15 (2 May 2000); (b) SI 2005/2292, r. 29(a) (1 October 2005);
r. 27.2(3) inserted by SI 2005/2292, r. 29(b) (1 October 2005);
r. 27.9(1) substituted by SI 2005/2292, r. 30 (1 October 2005);
rr. 27.12 and 27.13 revoked by SI 2000/2092, r. 11 (2 October 2000) (see note 1);
r. 27.14(2) amended by: (a) SI 1999/1008, r. 9 (26 April 1999); (b) SI 2000/2092, r. 12 (2 October 2000);
r. 27.14(2A) inserted by SI 2005/2292, r. 31(a) (1 October 2005);
r. 27.14(3) amended by SI 2005/2292, r. 31(b) (1 October 2005);
r. 27.14(5) substituted by SI 2005/2292, r. 31(c) (1 October 2005);
r. 27.14(6) inserted by SI 2005/2292, r. 31(c) (1 October 2005);
r. 28.4 amended by SI 2002/2058, r. 8 (2 December 2002);
r. 28.5 substituted by SI 2002/2058, r. 9 (2 December 2002); amended by SI 2005/2292, r. 32 (1 October 2005);
r. 28.6 amended by SI 2002/2058, r. 8 (2 December 2002);
r. 29.2 amended by SI 2002/2058, r. 8 (2 December 2002);
r. 29.5 amended by SI 2002/2058, r. 8 (2 December 2002);
r. 29.6 substituted by SI 2002/2058, r. 10 (2 December 2002); amended by SI 2005/2292, r. 33 (1 October 2005);
r. 29.7 amended by SI 2002/2058, r. 11 (2 December 2002);

r. 29.8 amended by SI 2002/2058, r. 8 (2 December 2002);
r. 30.1 amended by SI 2003/2113, r. 5 (6 October 2003);
r. 30.3(2) amended by: (a) SI 2000/2092, r. 13 (2 October 2000); (b) SI 2005/2292, r. 34 (1 October 2005);
r. 30.5 amended by SI 2005/3515, r. 8 (6 April 2006);
r. 30.8 revoked by SI 2000/2092, r. 14 (2 October 2000); new r. 30.8 inserted by SI 2003/3361, r. 5 (1 May 2004); substituted by SI 2004/1306, r. 5 (1 June 2004); amended by SI 2005/2292, r. 35 (1 October 2005);
r. 31.14 amended by SI 2001/4015, r. 20 (25 March 2002);
r. 31.23 inserted by SI 2000/221, r. 16 (2 May 2000);
r. 32.6 amended by SI 2000/221, r. 17 (2 May 2000);
r. 32.13 amended by SI 2001/256, r. 12 (26 March 2001);
r. 32.20 inserted by SI 2005/2292, r. 36 (1 October 2005);
r. 33.3 amended by SI 1999/1008, r. 10 (26 April 1999);
r. 33.9 inserted by SI 2000/2092, r. 15 (2 October 2000);
Part 34 title amended by SI 2002/2058, r. 12(a) (2 December 2002);
r. 34.1 substituted by SI 2002/2058, r. 12(c) (2 December 2002);
r. 34.13 amended by: (a) SI 1999/1008, r. 11(a) (26 April 1999); (b) SI 2003/2113, r. 7 (1 January 2004);
r. 34.13A inserted by SI 2003/3361, r. 6 (1 February 2004);
r. 34.14 amended by SI 1999/1008, r. 11(b) (26 April 1999);
rr. 34.16 to 34.21 inserted by SI 2002/2058, r. 12(d) and sch. 2 (2 December 2002);
r. 34.16 amended by: (a) SI 2003/2113, r. 8 (1 January 2004); (b) SI 2004/1306, r. 6 (1 June 2004);
r. 34.22 inserted by SI 2003/2113, r. 9 and sch. 1, part II (1 January 2004);
r. 34.23 inserted by SI 2003/2113, r. 9 and sch. 1, part II (1 January 2004); amended by: (a) SI 2003/3361, r. 7 (1 February 2004); (b) SI 2004/1306, r. 7 (1 June 2004);
r. 34.24 inserted by SI 2003/2113, r. 9 and sch. 1, part II (1 January 2004);
r. 35.12 amended by SI 2001/4015, r. 21 (25 March 2002);
r. 35.14 amended by SI 2001/4015, r. 22 (25 March 2002);
r. 36.2A inserted by SI 2004/3129, r. 4 (in force by SI 2005/547) (1 April 2005);
r. 36.3 amended by SI 2004/3129, r. 3 (in force by SI 2005/547) (1 April 2005);
r. 36.4 amended by: (a) SI 1999/1008, r. 12 (26 April 1999); (b) SI 2004/3129, r. 5 (in force by SI 2005/547) (1 April 2005);
r. 36.6(3) amended by: (a) SI 1999/1008, r. 13 (26 April 1999); (b) SI 2002/3219, r. 4(a) (1 April 2003);
r. 36.6(4) revoked by SI 2002/3219, r. 4(b) (1 April 2003);
r. 36.6(5) amended by SI 2000/2092, r. 16 (2 October 2000);
r. 36.10 amended by SI 2004/3129, r. 6 (in force by SI 2005/547) (1 April 2005);
r. 36.17(3) amended by SI 1999/1008, r. 14 (26 April 1999);
r. 36.20(1) amended by: (a) SI 1999/1008, r. 15 (26 April 1999); (b) SI 2004/3129, r. 7 (in force by SI 2005/547) (1 April 2005);
r. 36.21(1) amended by SI 2004/3129, r. 8 (in force by SI 2005/547) (1 April 2005);
r. 36.21(6) substituted by SI 2000/2092, r. 17 (2 October 2000);
r. 36.23 amended by SI 2004/3129, r. 9 (in force by SI 2005/547) (1 April 2005);
r. 37.1 amended by SI 2002/3219, r. 5 (1 April 2003);
r. 37.5 inserted by SI 2001/4015, r. 23 (25 March 2002);
r. 38.8 amended by SI 2000/1317, r. 10 (3 July 2000);
r. 39.3(4) amended by SI 2000/2092, r. 18 (2 October 2000);
r. 39.8 inserted by SI 2001/1388, r. 12 (31 May 2001);
Part 40, title amended by SI 2000/221, r. 18(1) (2 May 2000);
r. 40.1 substituted by SI 2000/221, r. 18(3) (2 May 2000); amended by SI 2004/3419, r. 6 (1 April 2005);
r. 40.2 amended by: (a) SI 2001/2792, r. 4 (25 March 2002); (b) SI 2005/3515, r. 9 (6 April 2006);
r. 40.3 amended by SI 2005/2292, r. 37 (1 October 2005);
rr. 40.15 to 40.19 inserted by SI 2000/221, r. 18(4) (2 May 2000);

r. 40.20 inserted by SI 2001/256, r. 13 (26 March 2001);
Part 41 title amended by SI 2004/3129, r. 10 (in force by SI 2005/547) (1 April 2005);
r. 41.3 amended by SI 2004/3419, r. 7 (1 April 2005);
rr. 41.4 to 41.10 inserted by SI 2004/3129, r. 11 and sch. 1 (in force by SI 2005/547) (1 April 2005);
r. 42.2(1) amended by SI 1999/1008, r. 16 (26 April 1999);
r. 42.2(5) inserted by SI 2004/1306, r. 8 (1 June 2004);
r. 42.2(6) substituted and (7) inserted by SI 2000/1317, r. 11 (3 July 2000);
r. 43.2 amended by: (a) SI 2000/1317, r. 12 (3 July 2000); (b) SI 2001/256, r. 14 (26 March 2001); (c) SI 2003/1242, r. 5(b) (2 June 2003) (see note 10); (d) SI 2003/1329, r. 3 (9 June 2003); (e) SI 2003/2113, r. 10 (6 October 2003);
rr. 44.3A and 44.3B inserted by SI 2000/1317, r. 14 (3 July 2000);
r. 44.4(5) revoked by SI 2000/1317, r. 15 (3 July 2000);
r. 44.8 amended by SI 2000/1317, r. 16 (3 July 2000);
r. 44.9(2) substituted by SI 1999/1008, r. 17 (26 April 1999);
r. 44.12A inserted by SI 2000/1317, r. 17 (3 July 2000); amended by: (a) SI 2002/2058, r. 14 (2 December 2002); (b) SI 2003/2113, r. 11 (6 October 2003); (c) SI 2004/3419, r. 8 (1 April 2005);
r. 44.13 amended by SI 2001/4015, r. 24 (25 March 2002);
r. 44.14 amended by: (a) SI 2000/1317, r. 18 (3 July 2000); SI 2005/2292, r. 38 (1 October 2005);
r. 44.15 inserted by SI 2000/1317, r. 19 (3 July 2000) (see note 2); amended by SI 2002/2058, r. 15 (2 December 2002);
r. 44.16 inserted by SI 2000/1317, r. 19 (3 July 2000) (see note 2); amended by SI 2002/2058, r. 16 (2 December 2002); substituted by SI 2005/3515, r. 10 (6 April 2006);
r. 44.17 inserted by SI 2000/1317, r. 19 (3 July 2000) (see note 2);
rr. 45.1 and 45.2 substituted by SI 2004/3419, r. 9 and sch. 1 (1 April 2005);
r. 45.2A inserted by SI 2004/3419, r. 9 and sch. 1 (1 April 2005);
rr. 45.3 and 45.4 substituted by SI 2004/3419, r. 9 and sch. 1 (1 April 2005);
r. 45.4A inserted by SI 2004/3419, r. 9 and sch. 1 (1 April 2005);
r. 45.5 substituted by SI 2004/3419, r. 9 and sch. 1 (1 April 2005);
r. 45.6 inserted by SI 2001/4015, r. 26 (25 March 2002) (see note 8); substituted by SI 2004/3419, r. 9 and sch. 1 (1 April 2005);
Part 45, Section II, heading amended by SI 2004/3419, r. 10 (1 April 2005);
r. 45.7 inserted by SI 2003/2113, r. 12(d) and sch. 2, part II (6 October 2003) (see note 11); amended by SI 2004/3419, r. 11 (1 April 2005);
rr. 45.8 and 45.9 inserted by SI 2003/2113, r.12(d) and sch. 2, part II (6 October 2003) (see note 11);
r. 45.10 inserted by SI 2003/2113, r. 12(d) and sch. 2, part II (6 October 2003) (see note 11); amended by: (a) SI 2003/3361, r. 8 (1 February 2004); (b) SI 2004/2072, r. 11 (1 October 2004);
r. 45.11 inserted by SI 2003/2113, r. 12(d) and sch. 2, part II (6 October 2003) (see note 11); amended by SI 2003/3361, r. 9 (1 March 2004);
rr. 45.12 and 45.13 inserted by SI 2003/2113, r. 12(d) and sch. 2, part II (6 October 2003) (see note 11);
r. 45.14 inserted by SI 2003/2113, r. 12(d) and sch.2, part II (6 October 2003) (see note 11); amended by SI 2004/3419, r. 12 (1 April 2005);
rr. 45.15 to 45.17 inserted by SI 2004/1306, r. 9 and sch. 1 (1 June 2004);
r. 45.18 inserted by SI 2004/1306, r. 9 and sch. 1 (1 June 2004); amended by SI 2004/3419, r. 13 (1 April 2005);
r. 45.19 inserted by SI 2004/1306, r. 9 and sch. 1 (1 June 2004);
r. 45.20 inserted by SI 2004/2072, r. 12 and sch. (1 October 2004); amended by SI 2005/2292, r. 39 (1 October 2005);
rr. 45.21 and 45.22 inserted by SI 2004/2072, r. 12 and sch. (1 October 2004);
rr. 45.23 to 45.26 inserted by SI 2005/2292, r. 40 and sch. 1 (1 October 2005);
r. 46.3(2A) inserted by SI 2000/1317, r. 21 (3 July 2000);
r. 47.8 amended by SI 2000/1317, r. 23 (3 July 2000);
r. 47.10(2) substituted by SI 2000/1317, r. 24 (3 July 2000);
r. 47.11(3) inserted by SI 1999/1008, r. 18 (26 April 1999);
r. 47.14 amended by SI 2002/2058, r. 17 (2 December 2002);

r. 47.16 amended by SI 1999/1008, r. 20 (26 April 1999);
Part 47, Section VI, heading substituted by SI 2000/1317, r. 26 (3 July 2000);
r. 47.17 amended by: (a) SI 1999/1008, r. 19 (26 April 1999); (b) SI 2000/1317, r. 27 (3 July 2000); (c) SI 2000/2092, r. 19 (2 October 2000);
r. 47.17A inserted by SI 2000/1317, r. 28 (3 July 2000);
Part 47, Section VIII, substituted by SI 2000/940, r. 11 (2 May 2000);
r. 47.20 amended by SI 2000/1317, r. 30 (3 July 2000);
r. 47.22 amended by SI 2000/1317, r. 31 (3 July 2000);
r. 48.2 amended by SI 2000/1317, r. 33 (3 July 2000);
r. 48.4 amended by: (a) SI 1999/1008, r. 23 (26 April 1999); (b) SI 2001/4015, r. 27 (25 March 2002);
r. 48.5 amended by: (a) SI 2004/3419, r. 14 (1 April 2005); (b) SI 2005/2292, r. 41 (1 October 2005);
r. 48.6 amended by SI 2002/2058, r. 19 (2 December 2002) (see note 9);
r. 48.6A inserted by SI 2000/1317, r. 34 (3 July 2000);
r. 48.7(3) revoked by SI 2000/1317, r. 35 (3 July 2000);
r. 48.7(4) amended by SI 2002/2058, r. 20 (2 December 2002);
r. 48.8(1) amended by SI 2000/1317, r. 36 (3 July 2000); substituted by SI 2001/256, r. 16.1(a) (26 March 2001);
r. 48.8(1A) inserted by SI 1999/1008, r. 24(a) (26 April 1999);
r. 48.8(2) amended by SI 1999/1008, r. 24(b) (26 April 1999);
r. 48.8(3) and (4) inserted by SI 2001/256, r. 16(1)(b) (26 March 2001);
r. 48.9 amended by SI 2000/1317, r. 37 (3 July 2000); revoked by SI 2001/256, r. 16(2) (26 March 2001);
r. 48.10(1) amended by SI 1999/1008, r. 25 (26 April 1999);
Part 49 amended by: (a) SI 2001/1388, r. 13 (15 October 2001); (b) SI 2001/4015, r. 28 (25 March 2002); (c) SI 2002/3219, r. 6 (1 April 2003);
Part 51 amended by SI 2001/2792, r. 5 (15 October 2001);
Part 52 inserted by SI 2000/221, r. 19 (2 May 2000) (see note 3);
r. 52.1(2) substituted by SI 2000/2092, r. 21 (2 October 2000) (see note 1);
r. 52.3 amended by SI 2005/3515, r. 11(b) (6 April 2006);
r. 52.4 amended by SI 2005/3515, r. 11(c) (6 April 2006);
r. 52.10 amended by SI 2004/2072, r. 13 (1 October 2004);
r. 52.12 amended by SI 2003/3361, r. 10 (1 April 2004);
r. 52.16 amended by SI 2003/3361, r. 11 (1 February 2004);
r. 52.17 inserted by SI 2003/2113, r. 14 (6 October 2003);
Part 53 inserted by SI 2000/221, r. 20 (28 February 2000);
Part 54 inserted by SI 2000/2092, r. 22 (2 October 2000) (see note 4);
r. 54.1 amended by: (a) SI 2003/364, r. 5(a) and (b) (1 April 2003 by SI 2003/754); (b) SI 2003/3361, r. 12 (1 May 2004);
r. 54.2 amended by SI 2003/364, r. 5(c) (1 April 2003 by SI 2003/754);
r. 54.3 amended by: (a) SI 2003/364, r. 5(c) (1 April 2003 by SI 2003/754); (b) SI 2003/3361, r. 13 (1 May 2004);
r. 54.4 amended by SI 2003/364, r. 5(d) (1 April 2003 by SI 2003/754);
r. 54.16 amended by: (a) SI 2002/2058, r. 21 (2 December 2002); (b) SI 2003/364, r. 5(d) (1 April 2003 by SI 2003/754);
r. 54.20 amended by SI 2003/364, r. 5(e) (1 April 2003 by SI 2003/754);
rr. 54.21 to 54.27 inserted by SI 2003/364, r. 5(f) and sch. (1 April 2003 by SI 2003/754);
r. 54.22 amended by SI 2003/1329, r. 4 (9 June 2003);
r. 54.24 amended by SI 2005/352, r. 4 (4 April 2005);
r. 54.25 amended by SI 2005/352, r. 5 (4 April 2005);
r. 54.26 amended by SI 2005/352, r. 6 (4 April 2005);
r. 54.28 inserted by SI 2005/352, r. 7 and sch. (4 April 2005) (see note 14); amended by SI 2005/3515, r. 12(a) (6 April 2006);
rr. 54.28A and 54.28B inserted by SI 2005/3515, r. 12(b) (6 April 2006);
r. 54.29 inserted by SI 2005/352, r. 7 and sch. (4 April 2005) (see note 14); amended by SI 2005/3515, r. 12(c) (6 April 2006);

rr. 54.30 and 54.31 inserted by SI 2005/352, r. 7 and sch. (4 April 2005) (see note 14);
r. 54.32 inserted by SI 2005/352, r. 7 and sch. (4 April 2005) (see note 14); amended by SI 2005/3515, r. 12(d) (6 April 2006);
r. 54.33 inserted by SI 2005/352, r. 7 and sch. (4 April 2005) (see note 14);
r. 54.34 inserted by SI 2005/352, r. 7 and sch. (4 April 2005) (see note 14); amended by SI 2005/3515, r. 12(e) (6 April 2006);
r. 54.35 inserted by SI 2005/352, r. 7 and sch. (4 April 2005) (see note 14);
Part 55 inserted by SI 2001/256, r. 17 (15 October 2001) (see note 5);
r. 55.1 amended by: (a) SI 2004/1306, r. 10 (30 June 2004); (b) SI 2005/2292, r. 42 (1 October 2005);
r. 55.2 amended by SI 2002/2058, r. 22(b) (2 December 2002);
r. 55.9 amended by SI 2004/1306, r. 12 (30 June 2004);
r. 55.10A inserted by SI 2005/2292, r. 44 (1 October 2005);
r. 55.11 amended by SI 2004/1306, r. 13 (30 June 2004);
r. 55.12 amended by SI 2004/1306, r. 14 (30 June 2004);
r. 55.13 amended by SI 2005/3515, r. 13 (6 April 2006);
rr. 55.20 to 55.28 inserted by SI 2002/2058, r. 22(c) and sch. 3 (2 December 2002);
Part 56 inserted by SI 2001/256, r. 18 (15 October 2001) (see note 5);
r. 56.2 amended by SI 2004/1306, r. 15 (1 June 2004) (see note 12);
r. 56.3 substituted by SI 2004/1306, r. 16 (30 June 2004) (see note 12);
r. 56.4 amended by SI 2002/3219, r. 7 (1 April 2003);
Part 57 inserted by SI 2001/1388, r. 14 (15 October 2001) (see note 6); title amended by SI 2002/2058, r. 23(a) (2 December 2002);
r. 57.1 amended by SI 2002/2058, r. 23(c) (2 December 2002);
r. 57.2 amended by SI 2003/2113, r. 15 (6 October 2003);
r. 57.9 amended by SI 2003/3361, r. 14 (1 April 2004);
rr. 57.14 to 57.16 inserted by SI 2002/2058, r. 23(d) and sch. 4 (2 December 2002);
r. 57.16 amended by SI 2004/1306, r. 17 (30 June 2004);
Part 58 inserted by SI 2001/4015, r. 29 (25 March 2002);
r. 58.4 amended by SI 2005/3515, r. 14 (6 April 2006);
Part 59 inserted by SI 2001/4015, r. 29 (25 March 2002);
r. 59.3 amended by SI 2005/3515, r. 15 (6 April 2006);
Part 60 inserted by SI 2001/4015, r. 29 (25 March 2002);
r. 60.7 inserted by SI 2005/2292, r. 45 (1 October 2005);
Part 61 inserted by SI 2001/4015, r. 29 (25 March 2002);
r. 61.2 amended by SI 2005/3515, r. 16 (6 April 2006);
Part 62 inserted by SI 2001/4015, r. 29 (25 March 2002);
r. 62.3 amended by SI 2005/3515, r. 17 (6 April 2006);
r. 62.20 amended by SI 2002/2058, r. 24 (2 December 2002);
r. 62.21 amended by SI 2002/2058, r. 25 (2 December 2002);
Part 63 inserted by SI 2002/3219, r. 8 and sch. (1 April 2003);
r. 63.1 amended by: (a) SI 2005/2292, r. 46 (1 October 2005); (b) SI 2005/3515, r. 18(a) (6 April 2006);
r. 63.4A inserted by SI 2005/2292, r. 47 (1 October 2005);
r. 63.7 amended by SI 2003/3361, r. 15 (1 April 2004);
r. 63.9 title amended by SI 2003/3361, r. 16 (1 April 2004);
r. 63.13 amended by SI 2004/3419, r. 15 (1 April 2005);
r. 63.16 substituted by SI 2003/3361, r. 17 (1 April 2004);
Part 64 inserted by SI 2002/2058, r. 26(a) and sch. 5 (2 December 2002);
Part 65 inserted by SI 2004/1306, r. 18 and sch. 2 (1 June 2004) (see note 13);
r. 65.3 amended by SI 2004/2072, r. 14 (1 September 2004);
Part 65, Section III, heading amended by SI 2005/2292, r. 48(a) (1 October 2005);
r. 65.11 amended by SI 2005/2292, r. 48(b) and (c) (1 October 2005);
r. 65.12 amended by SI 2005/2292, r. 48(d) (1 October 2005);
r. 65.13 amended by SI 2005/2292, r. 48(e) (1 October 2005);
r. 65.14 amended by SI 2005/2292, r. 48(f) (1 October 2005);
r. 65.17 amended by SI 2005/2292, r. 48(g) (1 October 2005);

r. 65.18 amended by SI 2005/2292, r. 48(h) (1 October 2005);
r. 65.19 amended by SI 2005/2292, r. 48(i) (1 October 2005);
Part 66 inserted by SI 2005/2292, r. 49 and sch. 2 (1 October 2005);
Part 67 inserted by SI 2004/3419, r. 16 and sch. 2 (1 April 2005);
Part 68 inserted by SI 2002/2058, r. 26(b) and sch. 6 (2 December 2002);
Part 69 inserted by SI 2002/2058, r. 26(c) and sch. 7 (2 December 2002);
r. 69.10 amended by SI 2004/1306, r. 19 (30 June 2004);
Part 70 inserted by SI 2001/2792, r. 6 (25 March 2002) (see note 7);
r. 70.5 amended by (a) SI 2001/4015, r. 30 (25 March 2002); (b) SI 2002/2058, r. 28 (2 December 2002); (c) SI 2003/2113, r. 16 (6 October 2003);
Part 71 inserted by SI 2001/2792, r. 6 (25 March 2002) (see note 7);
r. 71.8 amended by SI 2001/4015, r. 31 (25 March 2002);
Part 72 inserted by SI 2001/2792, r. 6 (25 March 2002) (see note 7);
rr. 72.1 and 72.6 amended by SI 2001/4015, rr. 32 and 33 (25 March 2002);
Part 73 inserted by SI 2001/2792, r. 6 (25 March 2002) (see note 7);
Part 74 inserted by SI 2002/2058, r. 29(a) and sch. 8 (2 December 2002);
r. 74.1 amended by SI 2005/2292, r. 50 (21 October 2005);
r. 74.19 amended by SI 2003/3361, r. 18 (1 April 2004);
rr. 74.27 to 74.33 inserted by SI 2005/2292, r. 52 and sch. 3 (21 October 2005);
Part 75 inserted by SI 2002/2058, r. 29(b) and sch. 9 (1 October 2002);
r. 75.3 amended by SI 2005/3515, r. 19 (6 April 2006);
Part 76 inserted by SI 2005/656, r. 4 and sch. (14 March 2005);
sch. 1, RSC, ord. 10, revoked by SI 2001/256, sch. 3 (15 October 2001);
sch. 1, RSC, ord. 11, revoked by SI 2000/221, sch. 8 (2 May 2000);
sch. 1, RSC, ord. 15, rr. 6A and 7, revoked by SI 2000/221, sch. 8 (2 May 2000);
sch. 1, RSC, ord. 15, r. 9, amended by SI 2000/940, r. 12 (2 May 2000); revoked by SI 2002/2058, r. 36 and sch. 10 (2 December 2002);
sch. 1, RSC, ord. 15, rr. 11, 12, 12A and 13, revoked by SI 2000/221, sch. 8 (2 May 2000);
sch. 1, RSC, ord. 15, r. 13A, revoked by SI 2001/256, r. 19 (26 March 2001);
sch. 1, RSC, ord. 15, r. 14, amended by SI 2001/2792, r. 7 (15 October 2001); revoked by SI 2002/2058, r. 36 and sch. 10 (2 December 2002);
sch. 1, RSC, ord. 15, r. 15, revoked by SI 2000/221, sch. 8 (2 May 2000);
sch. 1, RSC, ord. 15, r. 16, revoked by SI 2001/256, r. 19 (26 March 2001);
sch. 1, RSC, ord. 15, r. 17, revoked by SI 2000/221, sch. 8 (2 May 2000);
sch. 1, RSC, ord. 17, r. 1, amended by SI 2003/3361, r. 19 (1 April 2004);
sch. 1, RSC, ord. 17, r. 8, amended by SI 1999/1008, r. 27 (26 April 1999);
sch. 1, RSC, ord. 23, revoked by SI 2000/221, sch. 8 (2 May 2000);
sch. 1, RSC, ord. 30, amended by SI 1999/1008, r. 28 (26 April 1999); revoked by SI 2002/2058, r. 36 and sch. 10 (2 December 2002);
sch. 1, RSC, ord. 31, revoked by SI 2000/221, sch. 8 (2 May 2000);
sch. 1, RSC, ord. 44, rr. 1 to 11, revoked by SI 2002/2058, r. 36 and sch. 10 (2 December 2002);
sch. 1, RSC, ord. 44, r. 12, revoked by SI 2000/221, sch. 8 (2 May 2000);
sch. 1, RSC, ord. 45, r. 1A, inserted by SI 2003/3361, r. 20 (1 April 2004);
sch. 1, RSC, ord. 45, r. 1(1), (2) and (3), revoked by SI 2001/2792, sch. 5 (25 March 2002);
sch. 1, RSC, ord. 45, r. 2, amended by SI 2003/3361, r. 21 (1 April 2004);
sch. 1, RSC, ord. 45, r. 3, amended by SI 2001/256, r. 20 (15 October 2001);
sch. 1, RSC, ord. 45, r. 8, amended by SI 2003/3361, r. 22 (1 May 2004);
sch. 1, RSC, ord. 45, rr. 9, 10, 13 and 14, revoked by SI 2001/2792, sch. 5 (25 March 2002);
sch. 1, RSC, ord. 46, r. 8, amended by SI 2003/3361, r. 23 (1 April 2004);
sch. 1, RSC, ord. 46, r. 9, amended by SI 2003/3361, r. 24 (1 April 2004);
sch. 1, RSC, ord. 47, r. 2, revoked by SI 2003/3361, r. 25 (1 April 2004);
sch. 1, RSC, ord. 47, r. 4, amended by SI 2003/3361, r. 26 (1 April 2004);
sch. 1, RSC, ord. 47, r. 5, amended by SI 2003/3361, r. 27 (1 April 2004);
sch. 1, RSC, ord. 47, r. 6, amended by SI 2003/3361, r. 28 (1 April 2004);
sch. 1, RSC, ord. 48, amended by SI 1999/1008, r. 31 (26 April 1999); revoked by SI 2001/2792, sch. 5 (25 March 2002);

sch. 1, RSC, ord. 49, revoked by SI 2001/2792, sch. 5 (25 March 2002);
sch. 1, RSC, ord. 50, revoked by SI 2001/2792, sch. 5 (25 March 2002);
sch. 1, RSC, ord. 51, amended by SI 2001/2792, r. 7 (15 October 2001); revoked by SI 2002/2058, r. 36 and sch. 10 (2 December 2002);
sch. 1, RSC, ord. 52, r. 1, amended by SI 2002/2058, r. 30 (2 December 2002);
sch. 1, RSC, ord. 52, r. 6, amended by SI 1999/1008, r. 32 (26 April 1999);
sch. 1, RSC, ord. 52, r. 7A, inserted by SI 2003/3361, r. 29 (1 April 2004);
sch. 1, RSC, ord. 53, revoked by SI 2000/2092, r. 23 (2 October 2000) (see note 4);
sch. 1, RSC. ord. 54, r. 9, amended by SI 1999/1008, r. 62 (26 April 1999);
sch. 1, RSC, ord. 55, revoked by SI 2000/221, sch. 8 (2 May 2000);
sch. 1, RSC, ord. 56, revoked by SI 2000/221, sch. 8 (2 May 2000);
sch. 1, RSC, ord. 57, revoked by SI 2000/2092, r. 24 (2 October 2000);
sch. 1, RSC, ord. 58, revoked by SI 2000/221, sch. 8 (2 May 2000);
sch. 1, RSC, ord. 59, revoked by SI 2000/221, sch. 8 (2 May 2000);
sch. 1, RSC, ord. 60, revoked by SI 2000/221, sch. 8 (2 May 2000);
sch. 1, RSC, ord. 61, revoked by SI 2000/221, sch. 8 (2 May 2000);
sch. 1, RSC, ord. 62, revoked by SI 2004/3419, r. 17 (1 April 2005);
sch. 1, RSC, ord. 64, r. 4(b), revoked by SI 2000/2092, r. 25 (2 October 2000);
sch. 1, RSC, ord. 64, r. 4(c) and (d), revoked by SI 2000/221, sch. 8 (2 May 2000);
sch. 1, RSC, ord. 69, revoked by SI 2002/2058, r. 36 and sch. 10 (2 December 2002);
sch. 1, RSC, ord. 70, revoked by SI 2002/2058, r. 36 and sch. 10 (2 December 2002);
sch. 1, RSC, ord. 71, amended by: (a) SI 1999/1008, r. 62 (26 April 1999); (b) SI 2000/221, r. 22 (2 May 2000); (c) SI 2001/4015, r. 35 (1 March 2002); revoked by SI 2002/2058, r. 36 and sch. 10 (2 December 2002);
sch. 1, RSC, ord. 74, r. 1, revoked by SI 2001/4015, r. 37 (25 March 2002);
sch. 1, RSC, ord. 74, r. 2, revoked by SI 2000/221, sch. 8 (2 May 2000);
sch. 1, RSC, ord. 77, revoked by SI 2005/2292, r. 55(a) (1 October 2005);
sch. 1, RSC, ord. 79, r. 8, amended by SI 1999/1008, r. 62 (26 April 1999);
sch. 1, RSC, ord. 79, r. 9, amended by: (a) SI 1999/1008, rr. 40, 41 and 62 (26 April 1999); (b) SI 2001/256, r. 22 (1 April 2001); (c) SI 2003/3361, r. 30 (1 May 2004); (d) Courts Act 2003 (Consequential Provisions) (No. 2) Order 2005 (SI 2005/617), sch., para. 175 (1 April 2005);
sch. 1, RSC, ord. 81, r. 4, amended by SI 1999/1008, r. 42 (26 April 1999);
sch. 1, RSC, ord. 81, r. 5(3), amended by SI 2000/221, r. 23 (2 May 2000);
sch. 1, RSC, ord. 81, r. 7, amended by SI 2001/2792, r. 10 (25 March 2002);
sch. 1, RSC, ord. 81, r. 10, amended by SI 1999/1008, r. 43 (26 April 1999);
sch. 1, RSC, ord. 82, revoked by SI 2000/221, r. 40 (28 February 2000);
sch. 1, RSC, ord. 85, revoked by SI 2002/2058, r. 36 and sch. 10 (2 December 2002);
sch. 1, RSC, ord. 87, revoked by SI 2002/2058, r. 36 and sch. 10 (2 December 2002);
sch. 1, RSC, ord. 88, rr. 1 to 5, revoked by SI 2001/256, sch. 3 (15 October 2001);
sch. 1, RSC, ord. 88, r. 5A, revoked by SI 2001/2792, r. 3 (25 March 2002);
sch. 1, RSC, ord. 88, r. 7, revoked by SI 2001/256, sch. 3 (15 October 2001);
sch. 1, RSC, ord. 91, r. 1, revoked by SI 2003/2113, r. 19(a) (6 October 2003);
sch. 1, RSC, ord. 91, rr. 2, 3, 4, 5, 5A and 6, revoked by SI 2000/221, sch. 8 (2 May 2000);
sch. 1, RSC, ord. 92, rr. 1 and 2, revoked by SI 2002/2058, r. 36 and sch. 10 (2 December 2002);
sch. 1, RSC, ord. 92, r. 3A, revoked by SI 2001/4015, r. 37 (14 January 2002);
sch. 1, RSC, ord. 92, rr. 4 and 5, revoked by SI 2002/2058, r. 36 and sch. 10 (2 December 2002);
sch. 1, RSC, ord. 93, r. 1, amended by SI 1999/1008, r. 62 (26 April 1999);
sch. 1, RSC, ord. 93, r. 6, revoked by SI 2002/2058, r. 36 and sch. 10 (2 December 2002);
sch. 1, RSC, ord. 93, rr. 10(2) and (3), 11 and 12 revoked by SI 2000/221, sch. 8 (2 May 2000);
sch. 1, RSC, ord. 93, r. 15, revoked by SI 2001/256, sch. 3 (15 October 2001);
sch. 1, RSC, ord. 93, r. 16(2) and (3), revoked by SI 2000/221, sch. 8 (2 May 2000);
sch. 1, RSC, ord. 93, r. 20, revoked by SI 2001/1388, r. 15 (15 October 2001);
sch. 1, RSC, ord. 93, r. 21, revoked by SI 2002/2058, r. 36 and sch. 10 (2 December 2002);
sch. 1, RSC, ord. 93, r. 22, amended by: (a) SI 2001/4015, r. 38(a) (14 January 2002); (b) SI 2003/3361, r. 31 (1 May 2004);

sch. 1, RSC, ord. 93, r. 23, revoked by SI 2001/4015, r. 38(b) (14 January 2002);
sch. 1, RSC, ord. 94, r. 5(5), amended by SI 1999/1008, r. 47 (26 April 1999);
sch. 1, RSC, ord. 94, rr. 6 and 7, revoked by SI 2000/221, sch. 8 (2 May 2000);
sch. 1, RSC, ord. 94, r. 8 substituted by SI 2000/221, r. 25 (2 May 2000);
sch. 1, RSC, ord. 94, rr. 10, 10A and 11, revoked by SI 2000/221, sch. 8 (2 May 2000);
sch. 1, RSC, ord. 94, r. 12, amended by: (a) SI 1999/1008, r. 63; (b) SI 2000/221, r. 25 (2 May 2000);
sch. 1, RSC, ord. 94, r. 13, amended by SI 2000/221, r. 25 (2 May 2000);
sch. 1, RSC, ord. 94, r. 16, inserted by SI 1999/1008, r. 48 (26 April 1999); revoked by SI 2004/1306, r. 21 (30 June 2004);
sch. 1, RSC, ord. 95, r. 2, amended by SI 1999/1008, r. 49 (26 April 1999);
sch. 1, RSC, ord. 96, r. 7, amended by SI 1999/1008, r. 50 (26 April 1999);
sch. 1, RSC, ord. 97, amended by SI 1999/1008, r. 51 (26 April 1999); revoked by SI 2001/256, sch. 3 (15 October 2001);
sch. 1, RSC, ord. 98, revoked by SI 2004/1306, r. 21 (30 June 2004);
sch. 1, RSC, ord. 99, rr. A1 to 3, revoked by SI 2002/2058, r. 36 and sch. 10 (2 December 2002);
sch. 1, RSC, ord. 99, r. 4, amended by SI 2000/221, r. 26 (2 May 2000); revoked by SI 2002/2058, r. 36 and sch. 10 (2 December 2002);
sch. 1, RSC, ord. 99, rr. 5 to 7, revoked by SI 2002/2058, r. 36 and sch. 10 (2 December 2002);
sch. 1, RSC, ord. 99, r. 8, revoked by SI 1999/1008, r. 53 (26 April 1999);
sch. 1, RSC, ord. 99, rr. 9 and 10, revoked by SI 2002/2058, r. 36 and sch. 10 (2 December 2002);
sch. 1, RSC, ord. 101, revoked by SI 2000/221, sch. 8 (2 May 2000);
sch. 1, RSC, ord. 106, revoked by SI 2004/3419, r. 17 (1 April 2005);
sch. 1, RSC, ord. 108, amended by SI 2000/221, r. 28 (2 May 2000); revoked by SI 2002/2058, r. 36 and sch. 10 (2 December 2002);
sch. 1, RSC, ord. 109, r. 1, amended by SI 1999/1008, r. 55 (26 April 1999);
sch. 1, RSC, ord. 109, rr. 2 and 3, amended by SI 2000/221, r. 29 (2 May 2000);
sch. 1, RSC, ord. 109, r. 4, amended by: (a) SI 2001/256, r. 23 (1 April 2001); (b) Courts Act 2003 (Consequential Provisions) (No. 2) Order 2005 (SI 2005/617), sch., para. 175 (1 April 2005);
sch. 1, RSC, ord. 110, r. 1, amended by SI 1999/1008, r. 56 (26 April 1999);
sch. 1, RSC, ord. 111, revoked by SI 2000/221, sch. 8 (2 May 2000);
sch. 1, RSC, ord. 112, amended by: (a) SI 1999/1008, r. 57 (26 April 1999); (b) SI 2001/256, r. 24 (1 April 2001);
sch. 1, RSC, ord. 113, rr. 1 to 6, amended by SI 1999/1008, r. 58 (26 April 1999); revoked by SI 2001/256, sch. 3 (15 October 2001);
sch. 1, RSC, ord. 113, r. 7, amended by SI 2001/256, r. 25 (15 October 2001);
sch. 1, RSC, ord. 114, amended by: (a) SI 1999/1008, r. 59 (26 April 1999); (b) SI 2000/221, r. 30 (2 May 2000); revoked by SI 2002/2058, r. 36 and sch. 10 (2 December 2002);
sch. 1, RSC, ord. 115, r. 2, amended by SI 1999/1008, r. 62 (26 April 1999);
sch. 1, RSC, ord. 115, r. 4, amended by SI 2001/2792, r. 11 (25 March 2002);
sch. 1, RSC, ord. 115, rr. 5 and 6, amended by SI 1999/1008, r. 60 (26 April 1999);
sch. 1, RSC, ord. 115, r. 8, amended by SI 2002/2058, r. 3 (2 December 2002);
sch. 1, RSC, ord. 115, r. 12, amended by SI 1999/1008, r. 60 (26 April 1999);
sch. 1, RSC, ord. 115, r. 17, amended by SI 2000/221, r. 31 (2 May 2000);
sch. 1, RSC, ord. 115, sect. III, heading amended by SI 2001/1388, r. 16(a) (31 May 2001);
sch. 1, RSC, ord. 115, r. 24, amended by: (a) SI 2001/1388, r. 16(b) (31 May 2001); (b) SI 2001/4016, r. 2(a) (in force by SI 2001/4019) (20 December 2001);
sch. 1, RSC, ord. 115, r. 25, amended by SI 1999/1008, r. 62 (26 April 1999);
sch. 1, RSC, ord. 115, r. 26, amended by: (a) SI 2001/1388, r. 16(c) and (d) (31 May 2001); (b) SI 2001/4016, r. 2(b) (in force by SI 2001/4019) (20 December 2001);
sch. 1, RSC, ord. 115, r. 27, amended by: (a) SI 2001/1388, r. 16(e) (31 May 2001); (b) SI 2001/4016, r. 2(c) (in force by SI 2001/4019) (20 December 2001);
sch. 1, RSC, ord. 115, r. 29, amended by: SI 2001/1388, r. 16(f) (31 May 2001);
sch. 1, RSC, ord. 115, r. 32, amended by: SI 2001/1388, r. 16(g) (31 May 2001);
sch. 1, RSC, ord. 115, r. 33, amended by SI 2000/221, r. 31 (2 May 2000);

sch. 1, RSC, ord. 115, r. 35, amended by SI 2001/1388, r. 16(h) (31 May 2001);
sch. 1, RSC, ord. 115, rr. 37 and 38, inserted by SI 2003/2113, r. 17 (6 October 2003);
sch. 1, RSC, ord. 116, inserted by SI 1999/1008, r. 61 (26 April 1999); amended by SI 2001/256, r. 26 (1 April 2001); amended by Courts Act 2003 (Consequential Provisions) (No. 2) Order 2005 (SI 2005/617), sch., para. 175 (1 April 2005);
sch. 2, CCR, ord. 3, revoked by SI 2000/221, sch. 8 (2 May 2000);
sch. 2, CCR, ord. 4, r. 3, revoked by SI 2003/2113, r. 19(b) (6 October 2003);
sch. 2, CCR, ord. 5, rr. 5 to 8, revoked by SI 2000/221, sch. 8 (2 May 2000);
sch. 2, CCR, ord. 5, rr. 12 to 14, revoked by SI 2002/2058, r. 36 and sch. 10 (2 December 2002);
sch. 2, CCR, ord. 6, rr. 3, 5 and 5A, revoked by SI 2001/256, sch. 3 (15 October 2001);
sch. 2, CCR, ord. 6, r. 6, revoked by SI 2003/1242, r. 3 (2 June 2003);
sch. 2, CCR, ord. 7, revoked by SI 2001/256, sch. 3 (15 October 2001);
sch. 2, CCR, ord. 13, revoked by SI 2000/221, sch. 8 (2 May 2000);
sch. 2, CCR, ord. 16, r. 7, amended by SI 2003/3361, r. 32 (1 April 2004);
sch. 2, CCR, ord. 19, revoked by SI 2002/2058, r. 36 and sch. 10 (2 December 2002);
sch. 2, CCR, ord. 22, r. 8, amended by; (a) SI 2001/2792, r. 13 (15 October 2001); (b) SI 2001/2792, r. 13 (25 March 2002);
sch. 2, CCR, ord. 24, rr. 1 to 5, amended by SI 1999/1008, r. 66 (26 April 1999); revoked by SI 2001/256, sch. 3 (15 October 2001); revoked by SI 2002/2058, r. 36 and sch. 10 (2 December 2002);
sch. 2, CCR, ord. 24, r. 6, amended by SI 2001/256, r. 27(a) (15 October 2001);
sch. 2, CCR, ord. 24, r. 7, revoked by SI 2001/256, sch. 3 (15 October 2001);
sch. 2, CCR, ord. 24, rr. 8 to 15, amended by SI 2001/256, r. 27(b) to (d) (15 October 2001); revoked by SI 2002/2058, r. 36 and sch. 10 (2 December 2002)
sch. 2, CCR, ord. 25, r. 2, revoked by SI 2001/2792, sch. 5 (25 March 2002);
sch. 2, CCR, ord. 25, r. 3, amended by SI 2000/221, r. 32 (2 May 2000); revoked by SI 2001/2792, sch. 5 (25 March 2002);
sch. 2, CCR, ord. 25, rr. 4, 5 and 5A, revoked by SI 2001/2792, sch. 5 (25 March 2002);
sch. 2, CCR, ord. 25, r. 8, amended by SI 2001/2792, r. 14 (25 March 2002);
sch. 2, CCR, ord. 25, r. 9, amended by: (a) SI 2000/221, r. 32 (2 May 2000); (b) SI 2001/2792, r. 14 (25 March 2002);
sch. 2, CCR, ord. 25, rr. 11 and 12, revoked by SI 2001/2792, sch. 5 (25 March 2002);
sch. 2, ord. 25, r. 13, amended by: (a) SI 2001/2792, r. 15 (15 October 2001); (b) SI 2001/2792, r. 15 (25 March 2002);
sch. 2, CCR, ord. 27, r. 4, amended by: (a) SI 2001/256, r. 28(a) (1 April 2001); (b) Courts Act 2003 (Consequential Provisions) (No. 2) Order 2005 (SI 2005/617), sch., para. 176 (1 April 2005);
sch. 2, CCR, ord. 27, r. 5, amended by: (a) SI 2000/221, r. 33 (2 May 2000); (b) SI 2001/2792, r. 16 (25 March 2002);
sch. 2, CCR, ord. 27, r. 10, amended by: (a) SI 2001/256, r. 28(b) (1 April 2001); (b) Courts Act 2003 (Consequential Provisions) (No. 2) Order 2005 (SI 2005/617), sch., para. 176 (1 April 2005);
sch. 2, CCR, ord. 27, r. 17, amended by: (a) SI 1999/1008, r. 67 (26 April 1999); (b) SI 2000/221, r. 33 (2 May 2000); (c) SI 2001/2792, r. 17 (25 March 2002);
sch. 2, CCR, ord. 28, rr. 1 to 4, amended by SI 2001/4015, r. 39(a) to (d) (25 March 2002);
sch. 2, CCR, ord. 28, r. 5, substituted by SI 2001/4015, r. 39(e) (25 March 2002);
sch. 2, CCR, ord. 28, r. 9, amended by SI 2001/2792, r. 17 (25 March 2002);
sch. 2, CCR, ord. 28, r. 10(3), revoked by SI 2001/4015, r. 39(f) (25 March 2002);
sch. 2, CCR, ord. 28, r. 13, amended by SI 1999/1008, r. 68 (26 April 1999);
sch. 2, CCR, ord. 29, r. 1, amended by SI 2003/3361, r. 33 (1 April 2004);
sch. 2, CCR, ord. 30, amended by SI 2000/221, r. 34 (2 May 2000); revoked by SI 2001/2792, sch. 5 (25 March 2002);
sch. 1, CCR, ord. 31, revoked by SI 2001/2792, sch. 5 (25 March 2002);
sch. 2, CCR, ord. 33, r. 4, amended by: (a) SI 2000/221, r. 35 (2 May 2000); (b) SI 2001/2792, r. 18 (25 March 2002);
sch. 2, CCR, ord. 34, r. 1, amended by SI 2001/4015, r. 40 (14 January 2002);

sch. 2, CCR, ord. 35, amended by SI 2001/4015, r. 41 (1 March 2002); revoked by SI 2002/2058, r. 36 and sch. 10 (2 December 2002);
sch. 2, CCR, ord. 37, r. 1, revoked by SI 2002/2058, r. 36 and sch. 10 (2 December 2002);
sch. 2, CCR, ord. 37, r. 6, revoked by SI 2000/221, sch. 8 (2 May 2000);
sch. 2, CCR, ord. 37, r. 8(1) and (2), revoked by SI 2002/2058, r. 36 and sch. 10 (2 December 2002);
sch. 2, CCR, ord. 37, r. 8(3), revoked by SI 2001/2792, sch. 5 (25 March 2002);
sch. 2, CCR, ord. 38, revoked by SI 2004/3419, r. 17 (1 April 2005);
sch. 2, CCR, ord. 39, r. 2, amended by SI 2001/2792, r. 19 (25 March 2002);
sch. 2, RSC, ord. 42, revoked by SI 2005/2292, r. 55(b) (1 October 2005);
sch. 2, CCR, ord. 43, revoked by SI 2001/256, sch. 3 (15 October 2001);
sch. 2, CCR, ord. 44. r. 18, revoked and r. 20 amended by SI 1999/1008, r. 70 (26 April 1999);
sch. 2, CCR, ord. 45, r. 1, amended by: (a) SI 2000/221, r. 37 (2 May 2000); (b) SI 2001/2792, r. 21 (25 March 2002);
sch. 2, CCR, ord. 47, r. 5, amended by SI 2001/256, r. 30 (1 April 2001);
sch. 2, CCR, ord. 48B, amended by: (a) SI 1999/1008, r. 71 (26 April 1999); (b) SI 2001/1388, r. 17 (1 June 2001); (c) SI 2001/2792, r. 22 (25 March 2002);
sch. 2, CCR, ord. 48D, inserted by SI 1999/1008, r. 72 (26 April 1999); revoked by SI 2003/2113, r. 19(c) (6 October 2003);
sch. 2, CCR, ord. 49, r. 1, amended by SI 1999/1008, r. 73 (26 April 1999); revoked by SI 2001/256, sch. 3 (15 October 2001);
sch. 2, CCR, ord. 49, rr. 1A, 2 and 4, revoked by SI 2001/256, sch. 3 (15 October 2001);
sch. 2, CPR, ord. 49, rr. 4A and 5, revoked by SI 2003/2113, r. 19(d) (6 October 2003);
sch. 2, CCR, ord. 49, r. 6, revoked by SI 2000/2092, r. 27 (2 October 2000);
sch. 2, CCR, ord. 49, r. 6A, amended by: (a) SI 1999/1008, r. 73 (26 April 1999); (b) SI 2000/221, r. 38 (2 May 2000); (c) SI 2000/2092, r. 28 (2 October 2000); revoked by SI 2001/256, sch. 3 (15 October 2001);
sch. 2, CCR, ord. 49, r. 6B, amended by: (a) SI 1999/1008, r. 73 (26 April 1999); (b) SI 2001/2792, r. 23 (in force by SI 2001/2792, r. 1(b), and SI 2001/3164) (15 October 2001); revoked by SI 2004/1306, r. 21 (30 June 2004);
sch. 2, CCR, ord. 49, rr. 8 and 9, revoked by SI 2001/256, sch. 3 (15 October 2001);
sch. 2, CCR, ord. 49, rr. 10 and 11, revoked by SI 2000/221, sch. 8 (2 May 2000);
sch. 2, CCR, ord. 49, r. 12, amended by SI 2005/352, r. 8 (4 April 2005);
sch. 2, CCR, ord. 49, r. 13, amended by SI 1999/1008, r. 73 (26 April 1999); revoked by SI 2001/256, sch. 3 (15 October 2001);
sch. 2, CCR, ord. 49, r. 15, revoked by SI 2005/2292, r. 55(c) (1 October 2005);
sch. 2, CCR, ord. 49, r. 16, revoked by SI 2001/256, sch. 3 (15 October 2001);
sch. 2, CCR, ord. 49, r. 17, amended by: (a) SI 2000/1317, r. 38 (3 July 2000); (b) SI 2003/3361, r. 34 (1 February 2004); (c) SI 2004/2072, r. 15 (1 October 2004);
sch. 2, CCR, ord. 49, r. 18, revoked by SI 1999/1008, r. 73 (26 April 1999);
sch. 2, CCR, ord. 49; r. 18B, revoked by SI 2003/2113, r. 19(d) (6 October 2003);
sch. 2, CCR, ord. 49, r. 20, revoked by SI 2002/2058, r. 36 and sch. 10 (2 December 2002);

Note 1. The following transitional provision is made by SI 2000/2092, r. 29:

Where a person has, before 2nd October 2000, filed a notice of appeal in a claim allocated to the small claims track—
(a) Part 52 shall not apply to the appeal to which that notice relates; and
(b) rules 27.12 and 27.13 shall apply to that appeal as if they had not been revoked.

Note 2. The following transitional provision is made by SI 2000/1317, r. 39:

(1) This rule applies where a person has—
 (a) entered into a funding arrangement, and
 (b) started proceedings in respect of a claim the subject of that funding arrangement,
 before the date on which these Rules come into force [i.e., 3 July 2000].
(2) Any requirement imposed—
 (a) by any provision of the Civil Procedure Rules 1998 amended by these Rules, or

(b) by a practice direction

in respect of that funding arrangement may be complied with within 28 days of the coming into force of these Rules, and that compliance shall be treated as compliance with the relevant rule or practice direction.

(3) For the purpose of this rule, 'funding arrangement' means an arrangement where a person has—
   (a) entered into a conditional fee agreement which provides for a success fee within the meaning of section 58(2) of the Courts and Legal Services Act 1990;
   (b) taken out an insurance policy to which section 29 of the Access to Justice Act 1999 (recovery of insurance premiums by way of costs) applies; or
   (c) made an agreement with a membership organisation prescribed for the purpose of section 30 of the Access to Justice Act 1999 (recovery where body undertakes to meet cost liabilities) to meet his legal costs.

Note 3. The following transitional provision is made by SI 2000/221, r. 39, as substituted by SI 2000/940, r. 2:

Where a person has filed a notice of appeal or applied for permission to appeal before 2 May 2000—

(a) rule 19 of these Rules shall not apply to the appeal to which that notice or application relates; and

(b) the rules of court relating to appeals in force immediately before 2 May 2000 shall apply to that appeal as if they had not been revoked.

Note 4. The following transitional provision is made by SI 2000/2092, r. 30:

Where a person has, before 2nd October 2000, filed an application for permission to make an application for judicial review in accordance with RSC Order 53—

(a) Part 54 shall not apply to that application for permission or the application for judicial review to which it relates; and

(b) RSC Order 53 shall apply to those applications as if it had not been revoked.

Note 5. The following transitional provision is made by SI 2001/256, r. 31:

Where a claim form—

(a) relates to proceedings to which Part 55 or Part 56 would apply if it was issued on or after the date of entry into force of rules 17 and 18 of these Rules [i.e., 15 October 2001], but

(b) is issued before that date,

those rules shall not apply, and the rules of court in force immediately before that date shall apply as if they had not been amended or revoked.

Note 6. The following transitional provision is made by SI 2001/1388, r. 19:

Where a claim form—

(a) relates to proceedings to which Part 57 would apply if it was issued on or after 15th October 2001, but

(b) is issued before that date,

that Part shall not apply to the proceedings, and the rules of court in force immediately before that date shall apply as if they had not been amended or revoked.

Note 7. The following transitional provision is made by SI 2001/2792, r. 24:

(1) Parts 70 to 73 shall not apply to any enforcement proceedings specified in paragraph (2) which are issued before 25th March 2002, and the rules of court in force immediately before that date shall apply to those proceedings as if they had not been amended or revoked.

(2) The enforcement proceedings to which this rule applies are—
   (a) an application for an order for oral examination;
   (b) an application for a garnishee order;
   (c) an application by a judgment creditor for an order for the payment to him of money standing in court to the credit of a judgment debtor;
   (d) an application for a charging order;
   (e) a claim for the enforcement of a charging order by sale of the property charged; and

(f) an application for a stop order.

Note 8. The following transitional provision is made by SI 2001/4015, r. 43:

(1) Where proceedings for the possession of land are issued before 25th March 2002, rule 42(b) shall not apply, and CCR Order 38 shall apply as if it had not been amended.
(2) Where on or after 25th March 2002 fixed costs are to be awarded in enforcement proceedings which, pursuant to rule 24 of the Civil Procedure (Amendment No. 4) Rules 2001, continue to be governed by rules in Schedule 1 or Schedule 2 to the Civil Procedure Rules 1998 rather than rules in Parts 70 to 73, the rules governing enforcement costs in force immediately before 25th March 2002 shall continue to apply as if they had not been revoked.

Note 9. The following transitional provision is made by SI 2002/2058, r. 34:

Where before 2nd December 2002 proceedings have begun under rule 47.6(1) for the detailed assessment of the costs of a litigant in person, rule 48.6 shall continue to apply to those proceedings as if it had not been amended.

Note 10. The following transitional provision is made by SI 2003/1242, r. 6:

Rule 5(b) of these Rules has effect only where the conditional fee agreement which is in issue was entered into on or after 2nd June 2003.

Note 11. The following transitional provision is made by SI 2003/2113, r. 18:

Section II of Part 45 shall not apply to any costs-only proceedings arising out of a dispute, where the road traffic accident which gave rise to the dispute occurred before 6th October 2003.

Note 12. The following transitional provision is made by SI 2004/1306, r. 20(1):

(1) In the circumstances where article 29(1) or (4) of the Regulatory Reform (Business Tenancies) (England and Wales) Order 2003 applies—
    (a) the amendments to Part 56 made by rules 15 and 16 of these Rules shall not apply; and
    (b) Part 56 shall continue to apply on and after 1st June 2004 as if those amendments had not been made.

Note 13. The following transitional provision is made by SI 2004/1306, r. 20(2):

(2) Where an application for an injunction under Chapter III of Part V of the Housing Act 1996 has been issued before 30th June 2004—
    (a) Section I of Part 65 shall not apply in relation to that application; and
    (b) CCR Order 49, rule 6B shall continue to apply on and after 30th June 2004 as if it had not been revoked.

Note 14. The following transitional provision is made by SI 2005/352, r. 9:

(1) This rule applies where, by virtue of transitional provisions contained in an order made under section 48(3)(a) of the 2004 Act—
    (a) an application to the Immigration Appeal Tribunal for permission to appeal against an adjudicator's decision on an appeal, which was pending immediately before 4th April 2005, continues on and after 4th April 2005 as an application under section 103A of the 2002 Act; or
    (b) an application is made under section 103A of the 2002 Act on or after 4th April 2005 for an order requiring the Asylum and Immigration Tribunal to reconsider an adjudicator's decision on an appeal.
(2) [Section] III of Part 54 shall apply to the application, subject to the modifications set out in paragraphs (3) and (4).
(3) In rules 54.28(2)(c), 54.29(2) to (4) and 54.33(3) and (5)(a), references to the Tribunal shall be construed as references to the adjudicator who decided the appeal.
(4) In rules 54.28(2)(g) and 54.33(4)(b) and (5), the references to the Tribunal's decision on the appeal shall be construed as references to the adjudicator's decision.

Practice Direction — Insolvency Proceedings

PART ONE

1. General

1.1 In this practice direction:

(1) 'the Act' means the Insolvency Act 1986 and includes the Act as applied to limited liability partnerships by the Limited Liability Partnerships Regulations 2001 (SI 2001/1090);

(2) 'the Insolvency Rules' means the rules for the time being in force and made under s. 411 and s. 412 of the Act in relation to insolvency proceedings;*

(3) 'CPR' means the Civil Procedure Rules and 'CPR' followed by a Part or rule by number means the Part or rule with that number in those Rules;

(4) 'RSC' followed by an Order by number means the Order with that number set out in sch. 1 to the CPR;

(5) 'insolvency proceedings' means any proceedings under the Act, the Insolvency Rules, the Administration of Insolvent Estates of Deceased Persons Order 1986 (SI 1986/1999), the Insolvent Partnerships Order 1986 (SI 1986/2124), the Insolvent Partnerships Order 1994 (SI 1994/2421) or the Limited Liability Partnerships Regulations 2001.

(6) References to a 'company' shall include a limited liability partnership and references to a 'contributory' shall include a member of a limited liability partnership.

1.2 This practice direction shall come into effect on 26 April 1999 and shall replace all previous practice notes and practice directions relating to insolvency proceedings.

1.3 Except where the Insolvency Rules otherwise provide, service of documents in insolvency proceedings in the High Court will be the responsibility of the parties and will not be undertaken by the court.

1.4 Where r. 2.4 of the CPR provides for the court to perform any act, that act may be performed by a registrar in bankruptcy for the purpose of insolvency proceedings in the High Court.

1.5 A writ of execution to enforce any order made in insolvency proceedings in the High Court may be issued on the authority of a registrar.

1.6 (1) This paragraph applies where an insolvency practitioner ('the outgoing office holder') holds office as a liquidator, administrator, trustee or supervisor in more than one case and dies, retires from practice as an insolvency practitioner or is otherwise unable or unwilling to continue in office.

(2) A single application may be made to a judge of the Chancery Division of the High Court by way of ordinary application in form 7.2 for the appointment of a substitute office holder or office holders in all cases in which the outgoing office holder holds office, and for the transfer of each such case to the High Court for the purpose only of making such an order.

(3) The application may be made by any of the following:

(i) the outgoing office holder (if he is able and willing to do so);

(ii) any person who holds office jointly with the outgoing office holder;

(iii) any person who is proposed to be appointed as a substitute for the outgoing office holder; or

(iv) any creditor in the cases where the substitution is proposed to be made.

(4) The outgoing office holder (if he is not the applicant) and every person who holds office jointly with the office holder must be made a respondent to the application, but it is not necessary to join any other person as a respondent or to serve the application upon any other person unless the judge or registrar in the High Court so directs.

(5) The application should contain schedules setting out the nature of the office held, the identity of the court currently having jurisdiction over each case and its name and number.

(6) The application must be supported by evidence setting out the circumstances which have given rise to the need to make a substitution and exhibiting the written consent to act of each person who is proposed to be appointed in place of the outgoing office holder.

[* These are the Insolvency Rules 1986 (SI 1986/1925), abbreviated as IR 1986.]

(7) The judge will in the first instance consider the application on paper and make such order as he thinks fit. In particular he may do any of the following:
   (i) make an order directing the transfer to the High Court of those cases not already within its jurisdiction for the purpose only of the substantive application;
   (ii) if he considers that the papers are in order and that the matter is straightforward, make an order on the substantive application;
   (iii) give any directions which he considers to be necessary including (if appropriate) directions for the joinder of any additional respondents or requiring the service of the application on any person or requiring additional evidence to be provided;
   (iv) if he does not himself make an order on the substantive application when the matter is first before him, give directions for the further consideration of the substantive application by himself or another judge of the Chancery Division or adjourn the substantive application to the registrar for him to make such order upon it as is appropriate.

(8) An order of the kind referred to in [sub-paragraph (7)(i)*] shall follow the draft order in form PDIP 3 set out in the schedule hereto and an order granting the substantive application shall follow the draft order in form PDIP 4 set out in the schedule hereto (subject in each case to such modifications as may be necessary or appropriate).

(9) It is the duty of the applicant to ensure that a sealed copy of every order transferring any case to the High Court and of every order which is made on a substantive application is lodged with the court having jurisdiction over each case affected by such order for filing on the court file relating to that case.

(10) It will not be necessary for the file relating to any case which is transferred to the High Court in accordance with this paragraph to be sent to the High Court unless a judge or registrar so directs.

PART TWO COMPANIES

2. Advertisement of Winding-up Petition

2.1 Rule 4.11(2)(b) of IR 1986 is mandatory, and designed to ensure that the class remedy of winding up by the court is made available to all creditors, and is not used as a means of putting pressure on the company to pay the petitioner's debt. Failure to comply with the rule, without good reason accepted by the court, may lead to the summary dismissal of the petition on the return date (IR 1986, r. 4.11(5)). If the court, in its discretion, grants an adjournment, this will be on condition that the petition is advertised in due time for the adjourned hearing. No further adjournment for the purpose of advertisement will normally be granted.

2.2 Copies of every advertisement published in connection with a winding-up petition must be lodged with the court as soon as possible after publication and in any event not later than the day specified in IR 1986, r. 4.14. This direction applies even if the advertisement is defective in any way (e.g. is published at a date not in accordance with the Insolvency Rules, or omits or misprints some important words) or if the petitioner decides not to pursue the petition (e.g. on receiving payment).

3. Certificate of Compliance — Time for Filing

3.1 In the High Court in order to assist practitioners and the court the time laid down by IR 1986, r. 4.14, for filing a certificate of compliance and a copy of the advertisement, is hereby extended to not later than 4.30 p.m. on the Friday preceding the day on which the petition is to be heard. Applications to file the certificate and the copy advertisement after 4.30 p.m. on the Friday will only be allowed if some good reason is shown for the delay.

4. Errors in Petitions

4.1 Applications for leave to amend errors in petitions which are discovered subsequent to a winding-up order being made should be made to the court manager in the High Court and to the district judge in the county court.

[* The text issued by the Department for Constitutional Affairs mistakenly refers to sub-paragraph (6)(i).]

4.2 Where the error is an error in the name of the company, the court manager in the High Court and the district judge in the county court may make any necessary amendments to ensure that the winding-up order is drawn with the correct name of the company inserted. If there is any doubt, e.g. where there might be another company in existence which could be confused with the company to be wound up, the court manager will refer the application to the registrar and the district judge may refer it to the judge.

4.3 Where an error is an error in the registered office of the company and any director or member of the company claims that the company was unaware of the petition by reason of it having been served at the wrong registered office, it will be open to them to apply to rescind the winding-up order in the usual way.

4.4 Where it is discovered that the company had been struck off the register of companies prior to the winding-up order being made, the matter must be restored to the list before the order is entered to enable an order for the restoration of the name to be made as well as the order to wind up.

5. Distribution of Business

5.1 The following applications shall be made direct to the judge and, unless otherwise ordered, shall be heard in public:
(1) applications to commit any person to prison for contempt;
(2) applications for urgent interim relief (e.g. applications pursuant to s. 127 of the Act prior to any winding-up order being made);
(3) applications to restrain the presentation or advertisement of a petition to wind up; or
(4) applications for the appointment of a provisional liquidator;
(5) petitions for administration orders or an interim order upon such a petition;
(6) applications after an administration order has been made pursuant to s. 14(3) of the Act (for directions) or s. 18(3) of the Act (to vary or discharge the order);
(7) petitions to discharge administration orders and to wind up;
(8) applications pursuant to s. 5(3) of the Act (to stay a winding up or discharge an administration order or for directions) where a voluntary arrangement has been approved;
(9) appeal s from a decision made by a county court or by a registrar of the High Court.

5.2 Subject to para. 5.4 below all other applications shall be made to the registrar or the district judge in the first instance who may give any necessary directions and may, in the exercise of his discretion, either hear and determine it himself or refer it to the judge.

5.3 The following matters will also be heard in public:
(1) petitions to wind up;
(2) public examinations;
(3) all matters and applications heard by the judge, except those referred by the registrar or the district judge to be heard in private or so directed by the judge to be heard.

5.4 In accordance with directions given by the Lord Chancellor the registrar has authorised certain applications in the High Court to be dealt with by the court manager of the Companies Court, pursuant to IR 1986, r. 13.2(2). The applications are:
(1) to extend or abridge time prescribed by the Insolvency Rules in connection with winding up (IR 1986, rr. 4.3 and 12.9);
(2) for substituted service of winding-up petitions (IR 1986, r. 4.8(6));
(3) to withdraw petitions (IR 1986, r. 4.15);
(4) for the substitution of a petitioner (IR 1986, r. 4.19);
(5) by the official receiver for limited disclosure of a statement of affairs (IR 1986, r. 4.35);
(6) by the official receiver for relief from duties imposed upon him by the rules (IR 1986, r. 4.47);
(7) by the official receiver for permission to give notice of a meeting by advertisement only (IR 1986, r. 4.59);
(8) to transfer proceedings from the High Court to a county court (IR 1986, r. 7.11);
(9) For permission to amend any originating application.
(NB In district registries all such applications must be made to the district judge.)

6. Drawing Up of Orders

6.1 The court will draw up all orders except orders on the application of the official receiver or for which the Treasury Solicitor is responsible under the existing practice.

7. Rescission of a Winding-up Order

7.1 Any application for the rescission of a winding-up order shall be made within seven days after the date on which the order was made (IR 1986, r. 7.47(4)). Notice of any such application must be given to the official receiver.

7.2 Applications will only be entertained if made (a) by a creditor, or (b) by a contributory, or (c) by the company jointly with a creditor or with a contributory. The application must be supported by written evidence of assets and liabilities.

7.3 In the case of an unsuccessful application the costs of the petitioning creditor, the supporting creditors and of the official receiver will normally be ordered to be paid by the creditor or the contributory making or joining in the application. The reason for this is that if the costs of an unsuccessful application are made payable by the company, they fall unfairly on the general body of creditors.

7.4 Cases in which the making of the winding-up order has not been opposed may, if the application is made promptly, be dealt with on a statement by the applicant's legal representative of the circumstances; but apart from such cases, the court will normally require any application to be supported by written evidence.

7.5 There is no need to issue a form of application (form 7.2) as the petition is restored before the court.

8. Restraint of Presentation of a Winding-up Petition

8.1 An application to restrain presentation of a winding-up petition must be made to the judge by the issue of an originating application (form 7.1).

PART THREE PERSONAL INSOLVENCY — BANKRUPTCY

9. Distribution of Business

9.1 The following applications shall be made direct to the judge and unless otherwise ordered shall be heard in public:

(1) applications for the committal of any person to prison for contempt;
(2) application for injunctions or for the modification or discharge of injunctions;
(3) applications for interlocutory relief or directions after the matter has been referred to the judge.

9.2 All other applications shall be made to the registrar or the district judge in the first instance. He shall give any necessary directions and may, if the application is within his jurisdiction to determine, in his discretion either hear and determine it himself or refer it to the judge.

9.3 The following matters shall be heard in public:

(1) the public examination of debtors;
(2) opposed applications for discharge or for the suspension or lifting of the suspension of discharge;
(3) opposed applications for permission to be a director;
(4) in any case where the petition was presented or the receiving order or order for adjudication was made before the appointed day, those matters and applications specified in r. 8 of the Bankruptcy Rules 1952;
(5) all matters and applications heard by the judge, except matters and applications referred by the registrar or the district judge to be heard by the judge in private or directed by the judge to be so heard.

9.4 All petitions presented will be listed under the name of the debtor.

9.5 In accordance with directions given by the Lord Chancellor the registrar has authorised certain applications in the High Court to be dealt with by the court manager of the Bankruptcy Court pursuant to IR 1986, r. 13.2(2). The applications are:

(1) by petitioning creditors: to extend time for hearing petitions (s. 376 of the Act);
(2) by the official receiver:
(a) to transfer proceedings from the High Court to a county court (IR 1986, r. 7.13);
(b) to amend the full title of the proceedings (IR 1986, rr. 6.35 and 6.47).
(NB In district registries all such applications must be made to the district judge.)

10. Service Abroad of Statutory Demand

10.1 A statutory demand is not a document issued by the court. Leave to serve out of the jurisdiction is not, therefore, required.

10.2 Rule 6.3(2) of IR 1986 (requirements as to service) applies to service of the statutory demand whether outside or within the jurisdiction.

10.3 A creditor wishing to serve a statutory demand outside the jurisdiction in a foreign country with which a civil procedure convention has been made (including the Hague Convention) may and, if the assistance of a British consul is desired, must adopt the procedure prescribed by CPR, r. 6.25. In the case of any doubt whether the country is a 'convention country', enquiries should be made of the Queen's Bench Masters' Secretary Department, Room E216, Royal Courts of Justice.

10.4 In all other cases, service of the demand must be effected by private arrangement in accordance with IR 1986, r. 6.3(2), and local foreign law.

10.5 When a statutory demand is to be served out of the jurisdiction, the time limits of 21 days and 18 days respectively referred to in the demand must be amended. For this purpose reference should be made to the table set out in PD 6B.

10.6 A creditor should amend the statutory demand as follows:
(1) for any reference to 18 days there must be substituted the appropriate number of days set out in the table plus four days, and
(2) for any reference to 21 days must be substituted the appropriate number of days in the table plus seven days.
Attention is drawn to the fact that in all forms of the statutory demand the figure 18 and the figure 21 occur in more than one place.

11. Substituted Service

Statutory Demands

11.1 The creditor is under an obligation to do all that is reasonable to bring the statutory demand to the debtor's attention and, if practicable, to cause personal service to be effected. Where it is not possible to effect prompt personal service, service may be effected by other means such as first class post or by insertion through a letter box.

11.2 Advertisement can only be used as a means of substituted service where:
(1) the demand is based on a judgment or order of any court;
(2) the debtor has absconded or is keeping out of the way with a view to avoiding service; and
(3) there is no real prospect of the sum due being recovered by execution or other process.
As there is no statutory form of advertisement, the court will accept an advertisement in the following form:

STATUTORY DEMAND

(Debt for liquidated sum payable immediately following a judgment or order of the court)

To (Block letters)

of

TAKE NOTICE that a statutory demand has been issued by:

Name of Creditor:

Address:

The creditor demands payment of £ the amount now due on a judgment or order of the (High Court of Justice Division) (.................. County Court) dated the day of 200 .

The statutory demand is an important document and it is deemed to have been served on you on the date of the first appearance of this advertisement. You must deal with this demand within 21 days of the service upon you or you could be made bankrupt and your property and goods taken away from you. If you are in any doubt as to your position, you should seek advice immediately from a solicitor or your nearest Citizens' Advice Bureau. The statutory demand can be obtained or is available for inspection and collection from:

Name:

Address:

(Solicitor for) the Creditor

Tel. No. Reference:

You have only 21 days from the date of the first appearance of this advertisement before the creditor may present a bankruptcy petition. You have only 18 days from that date within which to apply to the court to set aside the demand.

11.3 In all cases where substituted service is effected, the creditor must have taken all those steps which would justify the court making an order for substituted service of a petition. The steps to be taken to obtain an order for substituted service of a petition are set out below. Failure to comply with these requirements may result in the court declining to file the petition (IR 1986, r. 6.11(9)).

Petitions

11.4 In most cases, evidence of the following steps will suffice to justify an order for substituted service:

(1) One personal call at the residence and place of business of the debtor where both are known or at either of such places as is known. Where it is known that the debtor has more than one residential or business address, personal calls should be made at all the addresses.

(2) Should the creditor fail to effect service, a first class prepaid letter should be written to the debtor referring to the call(s), the purpose of the same and the failure to meet with the debtor, adding that a further call will be made for the same purpose on the day of 20 at hours at (place). At least two business days' notice should be given of the appointment and copies of the letter sent to all known addresses of the debtor. The appointment letter should also state that:

(a) in the event of the time and place not being convenient, the debtor is to name some other time and place reasonably convenient for the purpose;

(b) (Statutory Demands) if the debtor fails to keep the appointment the creditor proposes to serve the debtor by [advertisement] [post] [insertion through a letter box] or as the case may be, and that, in the event of a bankruptcy petition being presented, the court will be asked to treat such service as service of the demand on the debtor;

(c) (Petitions) if the debtor fails to keep the appointment, application will be made to the court for an order for substituted service either by advertisement, or in such other manner as the court may think fit.

(3) In attending any appointment made by letter, inquiry should be made as to whether the debtor has received all letters left for him. If the debtor is away, inquiry should also be made as to whether or not letters are being forwarded to an address within the jurisdiction (England and Wales) or elsewhere.

(4) If the debtor is represented by a solicitor, an attempt should be made to arrange an appointment for personal service through such solicitor. The Insolvency Rules enable a Solicitor to accept service of a statutory demand on behalf of his client but there is no similar provision in respect of service of a bankruptcy petition.

(5) The written evidence filed pursuant to IR 1986, r. 6.11, should deal with all the above matters including all relevant facts as to the debtor's whereabouts and whether the appointment letter(s) have been returned.

11.5 Where the court makes an order for service by first class ordinary post, the order will normally provide that service be deemed to be effected on the seventh day after posting. The same method of calculating service may be applied to calculating the date of service of a statutory demand.

12. Setting Aside a Statutory Demand

12.1 The application (form 6.4) and written evidence in support (form 6.5) exhibiting a copy of the statutory demand must be filed in court within 18 days of service of the statutory demand on the debtor. Where service is effected by advertisement in a newspaper the period of 18 days is calculated from the date of the first appearance of the advertisement. Three copies of each document must be lodged with the application to enable the court to serve notice of the hearing date on the applicant, the creditor and the person named in part B of the statutory demand.

12.2 Where, to avoid expense, copies of the documents are not lodged with the application in the High Court, any order of the registrar fixing a venue is conditional upon copies of the documents being lodged on the next business day after the registrar's order otherwise the application will be deemed to have been dismissed.

12.3 Where the statutory demand is based on a judgment or order, the court will not at this stage go behind the judgment or order and inquire into the validity of the debt nor, as a general rule, will it adjourn the application to await the result of an application to set aside the judgment or order.

12.4 Where the debtor (a) claims to have a counterclaim, set-off or cross-demand (whether or not he could have raised it in the action in which the judgment or order was obtained) which equals or exceeds the amount of the debt or debts specified in the statutory demand or (b) disputes the debt (not being a debt subject to a judgment or order) the court will normally set aside the statutory demand if, in its opinion, on the evidence there is a genuine triable issue.

12.5 A debtor who wishes to apply to set aside a statutory demand after the expiration of 18 days from the date of service of the statutory demand must apply for an extension of time within which to apply. If the applicant wishes to apply for an injunction to restrain presentation of a petition the application must be made to the judge. Paragraphs 1 and 2 of form 6.5 (affidavit in support of application to set aside statutory demand) should be used in support of the application for an extension of time with the following additional paragraphs:

'3. That to the best of my knowledge and belief the creditor(s) named in the demand has/have not presented a petition against me.

4. That the reasons for my failure to apply to set aside the demand within 18 days after service are as follows: . . .'

If application is made to restrain presentation of a bankruptcy petition the following additional paragraph should be added:

'5. Unless restrained by injunction the creditor(s) may present a bankruptcy petition against me.'

13. Proof of Service of a Statutory Demand

13.1 Rule 6.11(3) of IR 1986 provides that, if the statutory demand has been served personally, the written evidence must be provided by the person who effected that service. Rule 6.11(4) of IR 1986 provides that, if service of the demand (however effected) has been acknowledged in writing, the evidence of service must be provided by the creditor or by a person acting on his behalf. Rule 6.11(5) of IR 1986 provides that, if neither paras (3) or (4) apply, the written evidence must be provided by a person having direct knowledge of the means adopted for serving the demand.

13.2 Form 6.11 (evidence of personal service of the statutory demand): this form should only be used where the demand has been served personally and acknowledged in writing (see IR 1986, r. 6.11(4)). If the demand has not been acknowledged in writing, the written evidence should be provided by the process server and paras 2 and 3 (part of form 6.11) should be omitted (see IR 1986, r. 6.11(3)).

13.3 Form 6.12 (evidence of substituted service of the statutory demand): this form can be used whether or not service of the demand has been acknowledged in writing. Paragraphs 4 and 5 (part) provide for the alternatives. Practitioners are reminded, however, that the appropriate person to provide the written evidence may not be the same in both cases. If the demand has been acknowledged in writing, the appropriate person is the creditor or a person acting on his behalf. If the demand has not been acknowledged, that person must be someone having direct knowledge of the means adopted for serving the demand.

Practitioners may find it more convenient to allow process servers to carry out the necessary investigation whilst reserving to themselves the service of the demand. In these circumstances para. 1 should be deleted and the following paragraph substituted:

'1. Attempts have been made to serve the demand, full details of which are set out in the accompanying affidavit of . . .'.

13.4 'Written evidence' means an affidavit or a witness statement.

14. Extension of Hearing Date of Petition

14.1 Late applications for extension of hearing dates under IR 1986, r. 6.28, and failure to attend on the listed hearing of a petition, will be dealt with as follows:

(1) If an application is submitted less than two clear working days before the hearing date (for example, later than Monday for Thursday, or Wednesday for Monday) the costs of the application will not be allowed under IR 1986, r. 6.28(3).

(2) If the petition has not been served and no extension has been granted by the time fixed for the hearing of the petition, and if no one attends for the hearing, the petition will be relisted for hearing about 21 days later. The court will notify the petitioning creditor's solicitors (or the petitioning creditor in person), and any known supporting or opposing creditors or their solicitors, of the new date and times. Written evidence should then be filed on behalf of the petitioning creditor explaining fully the reasons for the failure to apply for an extension or to appear at the hearing, and (if appropriate) giving reasons why the petition should not be dismissed.

(3) On the relisted hearing the court may dismiss the petition if not satisfied it should be adjourned or a further extension granted.

14.2 All applications for extension should include a statement of the date fixed for the hearing of the petition.

14.3 The petitioning creditor should attend (by solicitors or in person) on or before the hearing date to ascertain whether the application has reached the file and been dealt with. It should not be assumed that an extension will be granted.

15. Bankruptcy Petition

To help in the completion of the form of a creditor's bankruptcy petition, attention is drawn to the following points:

15.1 The petition does not require dating, signing or witnessing.

15.2 In the title it is only necessary to recite the debtor's name e.g. Re John William Smith or Re J W Smith (Male). Any alias or trading name will appear in the body of the petition. This also applies to all other statutory forms other than those which require the 'full title'.

15.3 Where the petition is based on a statutory demand, only the debt claimed in the demand may be included in the petition.

15.4 In completing para. 2 of the petition, attention is drawn to IR 1986, r. 6.8(1)(a) to (c), particularly where the 'aggregate sum' is made up of a number of debts.

15.5 Date of service of the statutory demand (para. 4 of the petition):

(1) In the case of personal service, the date of service as set out in the affidavit of service should be recited and whether service is effected *before/after* 1700 hours on Monday to Friday or at any time on a Saturday or a Sunday: see CPR, r. 6.7(2) and (3).

(2) In the case of substituted service (otherwise than by advertisement), the date alleged in the affidavit of service should be recited: see para. 11 above.

(3) In the strictly limited case of service by advertisement under IR 1986, r. 6.3, the date to be alleged is the date of the advertisement's appearance or, as the case may be, its first appearance: see IR 1986, rr. 6.3(3) and 6.11(8).

15.6 There is no need to include in the petition details of the person authorised to present it.

15.7 Certificates at the end of the petition:

(1) The period of search for prior petitions has been reduced to 18 months.

(2) Where a statutory demand is based wholly or in part on a county court judgment, the following certificate is to be added:

'I/We certify that on the day of 20 I/We attended on the County Court and was/were informed by an officer of the Court that no money had been paid into Court in the action or matter v Claim No. pursuant to the statutory demand.'

This certificate will not be required when the demand also requires payment of a separate debt, not based on a county court judgment, the amount of which exceeds the bankruptcy level (at present £750).

15.8 Deposit on petition: the deposit will be taken by the court and forwarded to the official receiver. In the High Court, the petition fee and deposit should be handed to the Supreme Court Accounts Office, Fee Stamping Room, who will record the receipt and will impress two entries on the original petition, one in respect of the court fee and the other in respect of the deposit. In the county court, the petition fee and deposit should be handed to the duly authorised officer of the court's staff who will record its receipt.

In all cases cheque(s) for the whole amount should be made payable to 'HM Paymaster General'.

15.9 On the hearing of a petition for a bankruptcy order, in order to satisfy the court that the debt on which the petition is founded has not been paid or secured or compounded the court will normally accept as sufficient a certificate signed by the person representing the petitioning creditor in the following form:

'I certify that I have/my firm has made enquiries of the petitioning creditor(s) within the last business day prior to the hearing/adjourned hearing and to the best of my knowledge and belief the debt on which the petition is founded is still due and owing and has not been paid or secured or compounded save as to. . . . .

Signed . . . . Dated . . . .'

For convenience in the High Court this certificate will be incorporated in the attendance slip, which will be filed after the hearing. A fresh certificate will be required on each adjourned hearing.

15.10 On the occasion of the adjourned hearing of a petition for a bankruptcy order, in order to satisfy the court that the petitioner has complied with IR 1986, r. 6.29, the petitioner will be required to file written evidence of the manner in which notice of the making of the order of adjournment and of the venue for the adjourned hearing has been sent to:

(i) the debtor, and

(ii) any creditor who has given notice under IR 1986, r. 6.23, but was not present at the hearing when the order for adjournment was made.

16. Orders without Attendance

16.1 In suitable cases the court will normally be prepared to make orders under Part VIII of the Act (individual voluntary arrangements), without the attendance of either party, provided there is no bankruptcy order in existence and (so far as is known) no pending petition. The orders are:

(1) A 14-day interim order with the application adjourned 14 days for consideration of the nominee's report, where the papers are in order, and the nominee's signed consent to act includes a waiver of notice of the application or a consent by the nominee to the making of an interim order without attendance.

(2) A standard order on consideration of the nominee's report, extending the interim order to a date seven weeks after the date of the proposed meeting, directing the meeting to be summoned and adjourning to a date about three weeks after the meeting. Such an order may be made without attendance if the nominee's report has been delivered to the court and complies with s. 256(1) of the Act and IR 1986, r. 5.10(2) and (3), and proposes a date for the meeting not less than 14 days from that on which the nominee's report is filed in court under IR 1986, r. 5.10, nor more than 28 days from that on which that report is considered by the court under IR 1986, r. 5.12.

(3) A 'concertina' order, combining orders as under (1) and (2) above. Such an order may be made without attendance if the initial application for an interim order is accompanied by a report of the nominee and the conditions set out in (1) and (2) above are satisfied.

(4) A final order on consideration of the chairman's report. Such an order may be made without attendance if the chairman's report has been filed and complies with IR 1986,

r. 5.22(1). The order will record the effect of the chairman's report and may discharge the interim order.

16.2 Provided that the conditions as under para. 16.1(2) and (4) above are satisfied and that the appropriate report has been lodged with the court in due time the parties need not attend or be represented on the adjourned hearing for consideration of the nominee's report or of the chairman's report (as the case may be) unless they are notified by the court that attendance is required. Sealed copies of the order made (in all four cases as above) will be posted by the court to the applicant or his solicitor and to the nominee.

16.3 In suitable cases the court may also make consent orders without attendance by the parties. The written consent of the parties will be required. Examples of such orders are as follows:

(1) On applications to set aside a statutory demand, orders:

(a) dismissing the application, with or without an order for costs as may be agreed (permission will be given to present a petition on or after the seventh day after the date of the order, unless a different date is agreed);

(b) setting aside the demand, with or without an order for costs as may be agreed; or

(c) giving permission to withdraw the application with or without an order for costs as may be agreed.

(2) On petitions: where there is a list of supporting or opposing creditors in form 6.21, or a statement signed by or on behalf of the petitioning creditor that no notices have been received from supporting or opposing creditors, orders:

(a) dismissing the petition, with or without an order for costs as may be agreed; or

(b) if the petition has not been served, giving permission to withdraw the petition (with no order for costs).

(3) On other applications, orders:

(a) for sale of property, possession of property, disposal of proceeds of sale;

(b) giving interim directions;

(c) dismissing the application, with or without an order for costs as may be agreed;

(d) giving permission to withdraw the application, with or without an order for costs as may be agreed.

If (as may often be the case with orders under sub-paras (3)(a) or (b) above) an adjournment is required, whether generally with liberty to restore or to a fixed date, the order by consent may include an order for the adjournment. If adjournment to a date is requested, a time estimate should be given and the court will fix the first available date and time on or after the date requested.

16.4 The above lists should not be regarded as exhaustive, nor should it be assumed that an order will be made without attendance as requested.

16.5 The procedure outlined above is designed to save time and costs but is not intended to discourage attendance.

16.6 Applications for consent orders without attendance should be lodged at least two clear working days (and preferably longer) before any fixed hearing date.

16.7 Whenever a document is lodged or a letter sent, the correct case number, code (if any) and year (for example 123/SD/99 or 234/99) should be quoted. A note should also be given of the date and time of the next hearing (if any).

16.8 Attention is drawn to [PD 43–48, para. 13.4*].

16A. Bankruptcy Restrictions Orders

Making the application

16A.1 An application for a bankruptcy restrictions order is made as an ordinary application in the bankruptcy.

16A.2 The application must be made within one year beginning with the date of the bankruptcy order unless the court gives permission for the application to be made after that period. The one year period does not run while the bankrupt's discharge has been suspended under the Insolvency Act 1986, s. 279(3).

[* The text issued by the Department for Constitutional Affairs refers to an earlier version of the practice direction.]

16A.3 An application for a bankruptcy restrictions order may be made by the Secretary of State or the Official Receiver ('the Applicant'). The application must be supported by a report which must include:

(a) a statement of the conduct by reference to which it is alleged that it is appropriate for a bankruptcy restrictions order to be made; and

(b) the evidence relied on in support of the application (IR 1986, r. 6.241).

16A.4 The report is treated as if it were an affidavit (IR 1986, r. 7.9(2)) and is prima facie evidence of any matter contained in it (IR 1986, r. 7.9(3)).

16A.5 The application may be supported by evidence from other witnesses which may be given by affidavit or (by reason of IR 1986, r. 7.57(5)) by witness statement verified by a statement of truth.

16A.6 The court will fix a first hearing which must be not less than eight weeks from the date when the hearing is fixed (IR 1986, r. 6.241(4)).

16A.7 Notice of the application and the venue fixed by the court must be served by the applicant on the bankrupt not more than 14 days after the application is made. Service of notice must be accompanied by a copy of the application together with the evidence in support and a form of acknowledgment of service.

16A.8 The bankrupt must file in court an acknowledgment of service not more than 14 days after service of the application on him, indicating whether or not he contests the application. If he fails to do so he may attend the hearing of the application but may not take part in the hearing unless the court gives permission.

Opposing the application

16A.9 If the bankrupt wishes to oppose the application, he must within 28 days of service on him of the application and the evidence in support (or such longer period as the court may allow) file in court and (within three days thereof) serve on the applicant any evidence which he wishes the court to take into consideration. Such evidence should normally be in the form of an affidavit or a witness statement verified by a statement of truth.

16A.10 The applicant must file any evidence in reply within 14 days of receiving the evidence of the bankrupt (or such longer period as the court may allow) and must serve it on the bankrupt as soon as reasonably practicable.

Hearings

16A.11 Any hearing of an application for a bankruptcy restrictions order must be in public (IR 1986, r. 6.241(5)). The hearing will generally be before the registrar or district judge in the first instance who may:

(1) adjourn the application and give directions;

(2) make a bankruptcy restrictions order; or

(3) adjourn the application to the judge.

Making a bankruptcy restrictions order

16A.12 When the court is considering whether to make a bankruptcy restrictions order, it must not take into account any conduct of the bankrupt prior to 1 April 2004 (Enterprise Act (Commencement No. 4 and Transitional Provisions and Savings) Order 2003, SI 2003/2093, art. 7).

16A.13 The court may make a bankruptcy restrictions order in the absence of the bankrupt and whether or not he has filed evidence (IR 1986, r. 6.244).

16A.14 When a bankruptcy restrictions order is made the court must send two sealed copies of the order to the applicant (IR 1986, r. 6.244(2)), and as soon as reasonably practicable after receipt, the applicant must send one sealed copy to the bankrupt (r. 6.244(3)).

16A.15 A bankruptcy restrictions order comes into force when it is made and must specify the date on which it will cease to have effect, which must be between two and 15 years from the date on which it is made.

Interim bankruptcy restriction orders

16A.16 An application for an interim bankruptcy restrictions order may be made any time between the institution of an application for a bankruptcy restrictions order and the determination of that application (Insolvency Act 1986, sch. 4A, para. 5). The application is made as an ordinary application in the bankruptcy.

16A.17 The application must be supported by a report as evidence in support of the application (IR 1986, r. 6.246(1)) which must include evidence of the bankrupt's conduct which is alleged to constitute the grounds for making an interim bankruptcy restrictions order and evidence of matters relating to the public interest in making the order.

16A.18 Notice of the application must be given to the bankrupt at least two business days before the date fixed for the hearing unless the court directs otherwise (IR 1986, r. 6.245).

16A.19 Any hearing of the application must be in public (IR 1986, r. 6.245).

16A.20 The court may make an interim bankruptcy restrictions order in the absence of the bankrupt and whether or not he has filed evidence (IR 1986, r. 6.247).

16A.21 The bankrupt may apply to the court to set aside an interim bankruptcy restrictions order. The application is made by ordinary application in the bankruptcy and must be supported by an affidavit or witness statement verified by a statement of truth stating the grounds on which the application is made (IR 1986, r. 6.248(2)).

16A.22 The bankrupt must send the Secretary of State, not less than seven days before the hearing, notice of his application, notice of the venue, a copy of his application and a copy of the supporting affidavit. The Secretary of State may attend the hearing and call the attention of the court to any matters which seem to him to be relevant, and may himself give evidence or call witnesses.

16A.23 Where the court sets aside an interim bankruptcy restrictions order, two sealed copies of the order must be sent by the court, as soon as reasonably practicable, to the Secretary of State.

16A.24 As soon as reasonably practicable after receipt of sealed copies of the order, the Secretary of State must send a sealed copy to the bankrupt.

Bankruptcy restrictions undertakings

16A.25 Where a bankrupt has given a bankruptcy restrictions undertaking, the Secretary of State must file a copy in court and send a copy to the bankrupt as soon as reasonably practicable (IR 1986, r. 6.250).

16A.26 The bankrupt may apply to annul a bankruptcy restrictions undertaking. The application is made as an ordinary application in the bankruptcy and must be supported by an affidavit or witness statement verified by a statement of truth stating the grounds on which it is made.

16A.27 The bankrupt must give notice of his application and the venue together with a copy of his affidavit in support to the Secretary of State at least 28 days before the date fixed for the hearing.

16A.28 The Secretary of State may attend the hearing and call the attention of the court to any matters which seem to him to be relevant and may himself give evidence or call witnesses.

16A.29 The court must send a sealed copy of any order annulling or varying the bankruptcy restrictions undertaking to the Secretary of State and the bankrupt.

PART FOUR

17. Appeals in Insolvency Proceedings

17.1 This Part shall come into effect on 2 May 2000 and shall replace and revoke para. 17 of, and be read in conjunction with PD Insolvency Proceedings which came into effect on 26 April 1999 as amended.

17.2 (1) An appeal from a decision of a county court (whether made by a district judge or a circuit judge) or of a registrar of the High Court in insolvency proceedings ('a first appeal') lies to a judge of the High Court pursuant to s. 375(2) of the Act and IR 1986, rr. 7.47(2) and 7.48(2) (as amended by s. 55 of the Access to Justice Act 1999).

(2) The procedure and practice for a first appeal are governed by IR 1986, r. 7.49, which imports the procedure and practice of the Court of Appeal. The procedure and practice of the Court of Appeal are governed by CPR, Part 52, and PD 52, which are subject to the provisions of the Act, the Insolvency Rules and this practice direction: see CPR, r. 52.1(4).

(3) A first appeal (as defined above) does not include an appeal from a decision of a judge of the High Court.

17.3 (1) Section 55 of the Access to Justice Act 1999 has amended s. 375(2) of the Act and IR 1986, rr. 7.47(2) and 7.48(2), so that an appeal from a decision of a judge of the High Court made on a first appeal lies, with the permission of the Court of Appeal, to the Court of Appeal.

(2) An appeal from a judge of the High Court in insolvency proceedings which is not a decision on a first appeal lies, with the permission of the judge or of the Court of Appeal, to the Court of Appeal (see CPR, r. 52.3).

(3) The procedure and practice for appeals from a decision of a judge of the High Court in insolvency proceedings (whether made on a first appeal or not) are also governed by IR 1986, r. 7.49, which imports the procedure and practice of the Court of Appeal as stated at para. 17.2(2) above.

17.4 Part 52 of the CPR and its practice direction [PD 52] and forms apply to appeals from a decision of a judge of the High Court in insolvency proceedings.

17.5 An appeal from a decision of a judge of the High Court in insolvency proceedings requires permission as set out in para. 17.3(1) and (2) above.

17.6 A first appeal does not require the permission of any court.

17.7 Except as provided in this Part, CPR, Part 52, and its practice direction [PD 52] and forms do not apply to first appeals, but paras 17.8 to 17.23 inclusive of this Part apply only to first appeals.

17.8 Interpretation:

(a) the expressions 'appeal court', 'lower court', 'appellant', 'respondent' and 'appeal notice' have the meanings given in CPR, r. 52.1(3);

(b) 'registrar of appeals' means in relation to an appeal filed at the Royal Courts of Justice in London a bankruptcy registrar, and in relation to an appeal filed in a district registry in accordance with para. 17.10(2) and (3) below a district judge of the relevant district registry.

(c) 'appeal date' means the date fixed by the appeal court for the hearing of the appeal or the date fixed by the appeal court upon which the period within which the appeal will be heard commences.

17.9 An appellant's notice and a respondent's notice shall be in form PDIP 1 and PDIP 2 set out in the schedule hereto.

17.10 (1) An appeal from a decision of a Registrar in Bankruptcy shall, or from any decision made in any county court may, be filed at the Royal Courts of Justice in London.

(2) An appeal from a decision made in the county court exercising jurisdiction over an area within the Birmingham, Bristol, Cardiff, Leeds, Liverpool, Manchester, Newcastle upon Tyne or Preston Chancery district registries may be filed in the Chancery district registry of the High Court appropriate to the area in which the decision was made.

17.11 (1) Where a party seeks an extension of time in which to file an appeal notice it must be requested in the appeal notice and the appeal notice should state the reason for the delay and the steps taken prior to the application being made; the court will fix a date for the hearing of the application and notify the parties of the date and place of hearing;

(2) The appellant must file the appellant's notice at the appeal court within:

(a) such period as may be directed by the lower court; or

(b) where the court makes no such direction, 14 days after the date of the decision of the lower court which the appellant wishes to appeal.

(3) Unless the appeal court orders otherwise, an appeal notice must be served by the appellant on each respondent:

(a) as soon as practicable; and

(b) in any event not later than seven days, after it is filed.

17.12 (1) A respondent may file and serve a respondent's notice.

(2) A respondent who wishes to ask the appeal court to uphold the order of the lower court for reasons different from or additional to those given by the lower court must file a respondent's notice.

(3) A respondents notice must be filed within:

(a) such period as may be directed by the lower court; or
(b) where the court makes no such direction, 14 days after the date on which the respondent is served with the appellant's notice.

(4) Unless the appeal court orders otherwise a respondent's notice must be served by the respondent on the appellant and any other respondent:
(a) as soon as practicable; and
(b) in any event not later than seven days, after it is filed.

17.13 (1) An application to vary the time limit for filing an appeal notice must be made to the appeal court.
(2) The parties may not agree to extend any date or time limit set by:
(a) this practice direction; or
(b) an order of the appeal court or the lower court.

17.14 Unless the appeal court or the lower court orders otherwise an appeal shall not operate as a stay of any order or decision of the lower court.

17.15 An appeal notice may not be amended without the permission of the appeal court.

17.16 A judge of the appeal court may strike out the whole or part of an appeal notice where there is compelling reason for doing so.

17.17 (1) In relation to an appeal the appeal court has all the powers of the lower court.
(2) The appeal court has power to:
(a) affirm, set aside or vary any order or judgment made or given by the lower court;
(b) refer any claim or issue for determination by the lower court;
(c) order a new trial or hearing;
(d) make a costs order.
(3) The appeal court may exercise its powers in relation to the whole or part of an order of the lower court.

17.18 (1) Every appeal shall be limited to a review of the decision of the lower court.
(2) Unless it orders otherwise, the appeal court will not receive:
(a) oral evidence; or
(b) evidence which was not before the lower court.
(3) The appeal court will allow an appeal where the decision of the lower court was:
(a) wrong; or
(b) unjust because of a serious procedural or other irregularity in the proceedings in the lower court.
(4) The appeal court may draw any inference of fact which it considers justified on the evidence.
(5) At the hearing of the appeal a party may not rely on a matter not contained in his appeal notice unless the appeal court gives permission.

17.19 The following applications shall be made to a judge of the appeal court:
(1) for injunctions pending a substantive hearing of the appeal;
(2) for expedition or vacation of the hearing date of an appeal;
(3) for an order striking out the whole or part of an appeal notice pursuant to para. 17.16 above;
(4) for a final order on paper pursuant to para. 17.22(8) below.

17.20 (1) All other interim applications shall be made to the registrar of appeals in the first instance who may in his discretion either hear and determine it himself or refer it to the judge.
(2) An appeal from a decision of a registrar of appeals lies to a judge of the appeal court and does not require the permission of either the registrar of appeals or the judge.

17.21 The procedure for interim applications is by way of ordinary application (see IR 1986, r. 12.7 and sch. 4, form 7.2).

17.22 The following practice applies to all first appeals to a judge of the High Court whether filed at the Royal Courts of Justice in London, or filed at one of the other venues referred to in para. 17.10 above:
(1) on filing an appellant's notice in accordance with para. 17.11(2) above, the appellant must file:

Civil Procedure Rules & Practice Directions

(a) two copies of the appeal notice for the use of the court, one of which must be stamped with the appropriate fee, and a number of additional copies equal to the number of persons who are to be served with it pursuant to para. 17.22(4) below;
(b) a copy of the order under appeal; and
(c) an estimate of time for the hearing.

(2) The above documents may be lodged personally or by post and shall be lodged at the address of the appropriate venue listed below:
(a) if the appeal is to be heard at the Royal Courts of Justice in London the documents must be lodged at Room 110, Thomas More Building, The Royal Courts of Justice, Strand, London WC2A 2LL;
(b) if the appeal is to be heard in Birmingham, the documents must be lodged at the District Registry of the Chancery Division of the High Court, 33 Bull Street, Birmingham B4 6DS;
(c) if the appeal is to be heard in Bristol the documents must be lodged at the District Registry of the Chancery Division of the High Court, Third Floor, Greyfriars, Lewins Mead, Bristol BS1 2NR;
(d) if the appeal is to be heard in Cardiff the documents must be lodged at the District Registry of the Chancery Division of the High Court, First Floor, 2 Park Street, Cardiff CF10 1ET;
(e) if the appeal is to be heard in Leeds the documents must be lodged at the District Registry of the Chancery Division of the High Court, The Court House, 1 Oxford Row, Leeds LS1 3BG;
(f) if the appeal is to be heard in Liverpool the documents must be lodged at the District Registry of the Chancery Division of the High Court, Liverpool Combined Court Centre, Derby Square, Liverpool L2 1XA;
(g) if the appeal is to be heard in Manchester the documents must be lodged at the District Registry of the Chancery Division of the High Court, Courts of Justice, Crown Square, Manchester M60 9DJ;
(h) if the appeal is to be heard at Newcastle upon Tyne the documents must be lodged at the District Registry of the Chancery Division of the High Court, The Law Courts, Quayside, Newcastle upon Tyne NE1 3LA;
(i) if the appeal is to be heard in Preston the documents must be lodged at the District Registry of the Chancery Division of the High Court, The Combined Court Centre, Ringway, Preston PR1 2LL.

(3) If the documents are correct and in order the court at which the documents are filed will fix the appeal date and will also fix the place of hearing. That court will send letters to all the parties to the appeal informing them of the appeal date and of the place of hearing and indicating the time estimate given by the appellant. The parties will be invited to notify the court of any alternative or revised time estimates. In the absence of any such notification the estimate of the appellant will be taken as agreed. The court will also send to the appellant a document setting out the courts requirement concerning the form and content of the bundle of documents for the use of the judge. Not later than seven days before the appeal date the bundle of documents must be filed by the appellant at the address of the relevant venue as set out in para. 17.22(2) above and a copy of it must be served by the appellant on each respondent. The bundle should include an approved transcript of the judgment of the lower court or, where there is no officially recorded judgment, the document(s) referred to in PD 52, para. 5.12.

(4) The appeal notice must be served on all parties to the proceedings in the lower court who are directly affected by the appeal. This may include the official receiver, liquidator or trustee in bankruptcy.

(5) the appeal notice must be served by the appellant or by the legal representative of the appellant and may be effected by:
(a) any of the methods referred to in CPR, r. 6.2; or
(b) with permission of the court, an alternative method pursuant to CPR, r. 6.8.

(6) Service of an appeal notice shall be proved by a certificate of service in accordance with CPR, r. 6.10 (form N215) which must be filed at the relevant venue referred to at para. 17.22(2) above immediately after service.

(7) Skeleton arguments, accompanied by a written chronology of events relevant to the appeal, should be filed at the address of the appropriate venue as set out in para. 17.22(2) above, at least two clear days before the date fixed for the hearing. Failure to lodge may result in an adverse costs order being made by the judge on the hearing of the appeal.

(8) Where an appeal has been settled or where an appellant does not wish to continue with the appeal, the appeal may be disposed of on paper without a hearing. It may be dismissed by consent but the appeal court will not make an order allowing an appeal unless it is satisfied that the decision of the lower court was wrong. Any consent order signed by each party or letters of consent from each party must be lodged not later than 24 hours before the date fixed for the hearing of the appeal at the address of the appropriate venue as set out in para. 17.22(2) above and will be dealt with by the judge of the appeal court. Attention is drawn to [PD 43–48, para. 13.4*] regarding costs where an order is made by consent without attendance.

17.23 Only the following paragraphs of PD 52, with any necessary modifications, shall apply to first appeals: 5.12 and 5.14 to 5.20 inclusive.

17.24 (1) Where, under the procedure relating to appeals in, insolvency proceedings prior to the coming into effect of this part of this practice direction, an appeal has been set down in the High Court or permission to appeal to the Court of Appeal has been granted before 2 May 2000, the procedure and practice set out in this part of this practice direction shall apply to such an appeal after that date.

(2) Where, under the procedure relating to appeals in insolvency proceedings prior to the coming into effect of this part of this practice direction, any person has failed before 2 May 2000 either:

(a) in the case of a first appeal, to set down in the High Court an appeal which relates to an order made (county court) or sealed (High Court) after 27 March 2000 and before 2 May 2000, or

(b) in the case of an appeal from a decision of a judge of the High Court, to obtain any requisite permission to appeal to the Court of Appeal which relates to an order sealed in the same period,

the time for filing an appeal notice is extended to 16 May 2000 and application for any such permission should be made in the appeal notice.

17.25 This paragraph applies where a judge of the High Court has made a bankruptcy order or a winding-up order or dismissed an appeal against such an order and an application is made for a stay of proceedings pending appeal.

(1) The judge will not normally grant a stay of all proceedings but will confine himself to a stay of advertisement of the proceedings.

(2) Where the judge has granted permission to appeal any stay of advertisement will normally be until the hearing of the appeal but on terms that the stay will determine without further order if an appellant's notice is not filed within the period prescribed by the rules.

(3) Where the judge has refused permission to appeal any stay of advertisement will normally be for a period not exceeding 28 days. Application for any further stay of advertisement should be made to the Court of Appeal.

THE SCHEDULE

[The schedule consists of forms which are on the CD-ROM version of *Blackstone's Civil Practice*. Click on the number of a form to open it.

PDIP1 appellant's notice — insolvency proceedings
PDIP2 respondent's notice — insolvency proceedings
PDIP3 draft order — multiple transfer of proceedings
PDIP4 draft order — multiple appointments of office holder]

[* The text issued by the Department for Constitutional Affairs refers to an earlier version of the practice direction.]

Practice Direction — Directors Disqualification Proceedings

PART ONE

1. Application and Interpretation

1.1 In this practice direction:

(1) 'the Act' means the Company Directors Disqualification Act 1986;

(2) 'the Disqualification Rules' means the rules for the time being in force made under s. 411 of the Insolvency Act 1986 in relation to disqualification proceedings;[1]

(3) 'the Insolvency Rules' means the rules for the time being in force made under ss. 411 and 412 of the Insolvency Act 1986 in relation to insolvency proceedings;

(4) 'CPR' means the Civil Procedure Rules 1998 and 'CPR' followed by 'Part' or 'rule' and a number means the Part or rule with that number in those Rules;

(5) 'disqualification proceedings' has the meaning set out in para. 1.3 below;

(6) 'a disqualification application' is an application under the Act for the making of a disqualification order;

(7) 'registrar' means any judge of the High Court or the county court who is a registrar within the meaning of the Insolvency Rules;

(8) 'Companies Court registrar' means any judge of the High Court sitting in the Royal Courts of Justice in London who is a registrar within the meaning of the Insolvency Rules;

(9) except where the context otherwise requires references to:

(a) 'company' or 'companies' shall include references to 'partnership' or 'partnerships' and to 'limited liability partnership' and 'limited liability partnerships';

(b) 'director' shall include references to an 'officer' of a partnership and to a 'member' of a limited liability partnership;

(c) 'shadow director' shall include references to a 'shadow member' of a limited liability partnership

and, in appropriate cases, the forms annexed to this practice direction shall be varied accordingly;

(10) 'disqualification order' has the meaning set out in s. 1 of the Act and 'disqualification undertaking' has the meaning set out in s. 1A or s. 9B of the Act (as the context requires);

(11) a 'section 8A application' is an application under s. 8A of the Act to reduce the period for which a disqualification undertaking is in force or to provide for it to cease to be in force;

(12) 'specified regulator' has the meaning set out in s. 9E(2) of the Act.

1.2 This practice direction shall come into effect on 26 April 1999 and shall replace all previous practice directions relating to disqualification proceedings.

1.3 This practice direction applies to the following proceedings ('disqualification proceedings'):

(1) disqualification applications made:

(a) under s. 2(2)(a) of the Act (after the person's conviction of an indictable offence in connection with the affairs of a company);

(b) under s. 3 of the Act (on the ground of persistent breaches of provisions of companies legislation);

(c) under s. 4 of the Act (on the ground of fraud etc.);

(d) by the Secretary of State or the official receiver under s. 7(1) of the Act (on the ground that the person is or has been a director of a company which has at any time become

---

[1] The current rules are the Insolvent Companies (Disqualification of Unfit Directors) Proceedings Rules 1987 (SI 1987/2023). For convenience relevant references to the Insolvent Companies (Disqualification of Unfit Directors) Proceedings Rules 1987, which apply to disqualification applications under ss. 7, 8 and 9A of the Act (see r. 1(3)) are set out in footnotes to this practice direction. This practice direction applies certain provisions contained in the Insolvent Companies (Disqualification of Unfit Directors) Proceedings Rules 1987 to disqualification proceedings other than applications under ss. 7, 8 and 9A of the Act.

insolvent and his conduct makes him unfit to be concerned in the management of a company);

(e) by the Secretary of State under s. 8 of the Act (on it appearing to the Secretary of State from investigative material that it is expedient in the public interest that a disqualification order should be made); or

(f) by the Office of Fair Trading or a specified regulator under s. 9A of the Act (on the ground of breach of competition law by an undertaking and unfitness to be concerned in the management of a company);

(2) any application made under s. 7(2) or 7(4) of the Act;

(3) any application for permission to act made under s. 17 of the Act for the purposes of any of ss. 1(1)(a), 1A(1)(a) or 9B(4), or made under s. 12(2) of the Act;

(4) any application for a court order made under CPR Part 23 in the course of any of the proceedings set out in sub-paras (1) to (3) above;

(5) any application under the Act to the extent provided for by subordinate legislation;[2]

(6) any section 8A application.

2. Multi-track

2.1 All disqualification proceedings are allocated to the multi-track. The CPR relating to allocation questionnaires and track allocation shall not apply.

3. Rights of Audience

3.1 Official receivers and deputy official receivers have right of audience in any proceedings to which this practice direction applies, including cases where a disqualification application is made by the Secretary of State or by the official receiver at his direction, and whether made in the High Court or a county court.[3]

PART TWO DISQUALIFICATION APPLICATIONS

4. Commencement

4.1 Sections 2(2)(a), 3(4), 4(2), 6(3) and 8(3) of the Act identify the civil courts which have jurisdiction to deal with disqualification applications.

4.1A A disqualification application must be commenced by a claim form issued:

(1) in the case of a disqualification application under s. 9A of the Act, in the High Court out of the office of the Companies Court registrar at the Royal Courts of Justice;

(2) in any other case:

(a) in the High Court out of the office of the Companies Court registrar or a Chancery district registry; and

(b) in the county court, out of a county court office.

4.2 Disqualification applications shall be made by the issue of a claim form in the form annexed hereto and the use of the procedure set out in CPR, Part 8,[4] as modified by this practice direction and (where the application is made under ss. 7, 8 or 9A of the Act) the Disqualification Rules. Rule 8.1(3) of the CPR (power of the court to order the application to continue as if the claimant had not used the Part 8 procedure) shall not apply.

4.3 When the claim form is issued, the claimant will be given a date for the first hearing of the disqualification application. This date is to be not less than eight weeks from the date of issue of the claim form.[5] The first hearing will be before a registrar.

[2] Current subordinate legislation includes the Insolvent Partnerships Order 1994 (SI 1994/2421) and the Limited Liability Partnerships Regulations 2001 (SI 2001/1090).

[3] Rule 10 of the Insolvent Companies (Disqualification of Unfit Directors) Proceedings Rules 1987.

[4] Rule 2(2) of the Insolvent Companies (Disqualification of Unfit Directors) Proceedings Rules 1987 as amended.

[5] Rule 7(1) of the Insolvent Companies (Disqualification of Unfit Directors) Proceedings Rules 1987.

5. Headings

5.1 Every claim form by which an application under the Act is begun and all affidavits, notices and other documents in the proceedings must be entitled in the matter of the company or companies in question and in the matter of the Act. In the case of any disqualification application under ss. 7 or 9A of the Act it is not necessary to mention in the heading any company other than that referred to in s. 6(1)(a) or 9A(2) of the Act (as the case may be).

6. The Claim Form

6.1 Rule 8.2 of the CPR does not apply. The claim form must state:

(1) that CPR, Part 8 (as modified by this practice direction), applies, and (if the application is made under ss. 7, 8 or 9A of the Act) that the application is made in accordance with the Disqualification Rules;[6]

(2) that the claimant seeks a disqualification order, and the section of the Act pursuant to which the disqualification application is made;

(3) the period for which, in accordance with the Act, the court has power to impose a disqualification period.
The periods are as follows:
(a) where the application is under s. 2 of the Act, for a period of up to 15 years;
(b) where the application is under s. 3 of the Act, for a period of up to five years;
(c) where the application is under s. 4 of the Act, for a period of up to 15 years;
(d) where the application is under s. 7 of the Act, for a period of not less than two, and up to 15, years;[7]
(e) where the application is under ss. 8 or 9A of the Act, for a period of up to 15 years.[8]

(4) in cases where the application is made under ss. 7 or 8 of the Act, that on the first hearing of the application, the court may hear and determine it summarily, without further or other notice to the defendant, and that, if the application is so determined, the court may impose a period of disqualification of up to five years but that if at the hearing of the application the court, on the evidence then before it, is minded to impose, in the case of any defendant, disqualification for any period longer than five years, it will not make a disqualification order on that occasion but will adjourn the application to be heard (with further evidence, if any) at a later date that will be notified to the defendant;[9]

(5) that any evidence which the defendant wishes the court to take into consideration must be filed in court in accordance with the time limits set out in paragraph 9 below (which time limits shall be set out in the notes to the claim form).[10]

7. Service of the Claim Form

7.1 Service of claim forms in disqualification proceedings will be the responsibility of the parties and will not be undertaken by the court.

7.2 The claim form shall be served by the claimant on the defendant. It may be served by sending it by first class post to his last known address; and the date of service shall, unless the contrary is shown, be deemed to be the seventh day following that on which the claim form was posted.[11] Rule 6.7(1) of the CPR shall be modified accordingly. Otherwise Sections I and II of Part 6 apply.[12]

7.3 Where any claim form or order of the court or other document is required under any disqualification proceedings to be served on any person who is not in England and Wales, the court may order service on him to be effected within such time and in such manner as it thinks fit, may require such proof of service as it thinks fit,[13] and may give such directions as to acknowledgment of service as it thinks fit. Section III of CPR, Part 6, shall not apply.

---

[6] Rule 4(a) of the Insolvent Companies (Disqualification of Unfit Directors) Proceedings Rules 1987.
[7] Rule 4(b)(i) of the Insolvent Companies (Disqualification of Unfit Directors) Proceedings Rules 1987.
[8] Rule 4(b)(ii) of the Insolvent Companies (Disqualification of Unfit Directors) Proceedings Rules 1987.
[9] Rule 4(c) and (d) of the Insolvent Companies (Disqualification of Unfit Directors) Proceedings Rules 1987.
[10] Rule 4(e) of the Insolvent Companies (Disqualification of Unfit Directors) Proceedings Rules 1987.
[11] Rule 5(1) of the Insolvent Companies (Disqualification of Unfit Directors) Proceedings Rules 1987.
[12] Attention is drawn to CPR, r. 6.14(2), regarding a certificate of service of the claim form.
[13] Rule 5(2) of the Insolvent Companies (Disqualification of Unfit Directors) Proceedings Rules 1987.

7.4 The claim form served on the defendant shall be accompanied by an acknowledgment of service.

8. Acknowledgment of Service

8.1 The form of acknowledgment of service is annexed to this practice direction. CPR rules 8.3(2) and 8.3(3)(a) do not apply to disqualification applications.

8.2 In cases brought under ss. 7, 8 or 9A of the Act, the form of acknowledgment of service shall state that the defendant should indicate:[14]

(1) whether he contests the application on the grounds that, in the case of any particular company:

(a) he was not a director or shadow director of that company at a time when conduct of his, or of other persons, in relation to that company is in question; or

(b) his conduct as director or shadow director of that company was not as alleged in support of the application for a disqualification order;

(c) in the case of an application made under s. 7 of the Act, the company has at no time become insolvent within the meaning of s. 6; or

(d) in the case of an application under s. 9A of the Act, the undertaking which is a company did not commit a breach of competition law within the meaning of that section.

(2) whether, in the case of any conduct of his, he disputes the allegation that such conduct makes him unfit to be concerned in the management of a company; and

(3) whether he, while not resisting the application for a disqualification order, intends to adduce mitigating factors with a view to reducing the period of disqualification.

8.3 The defendant shall:

(1) (subject to any directions to the contrary given under para. 7.3 above) file an acknowledgment of service in the prescribed form not more than 14 days after service of the claim form; and

(2) serve the acknowledgment of service on the claimant and any other party.

8.4 Where the defendant has failed to file an acknowledgment of service and the time period for doing so has expired, the defendant may attend the hearing of the application but may not take part in the hearing unless the court gives permission.

9. Evidence

9.1 Evidence in disqualification applications shall be by affidavit, except where the official receiver is a party, in which case his evidence may be in the form of a written report (with or without affidavits by other persons) which shall be treated as if it had been verified by affidavit by him and shall be prima facie evidence of any matter contained in it.[15]

9.2 In the affidavits or (as the case may be) the official receiver's report in support of the application, there shall be included:

(1) a statement of the matters by reference to which it is alleged that a disqualification order should be made against the defendant;[16] and

(2) a statement of the steps taken to comply with any requirements imposed by ss. 16(1) and 9C(4) of the Act.

9.3 When the claim form is issued:

(1) the affidavit or report in support of the disqualification application must be filed in court;

(2) exhibits must be lodged with the court where they shall be retained until the conclusion of the proceedings; and

[14] Rule 5(4) of the Insolvent Companies (Disqualification of Unfit Directors) Proceedings Rules 1987. Note that the requirements of para. 8.2(1)(c) and (d) of this practice direction are additional to the provisions in the said r. 5(4). [In the text issued by the Department for Constitutional Affairs the last sentence of this footnote is erroneously located in the next footnote and erroneously refers to para. 8.1(2) instead of r. 8.2(1).]

[15] Rule 3(2) of the Insolvent Companies (Disqualification of Unfit Directors) Proceedings Rules 1987. Section 441 of the Companies Act 1985 makes provision for the admissibility in legal proceedings of a certified copy of a report of inspectors appointed under part XIV of the Companies Act 1985.

[16] Rule 3(3) of the Insolvent Companies (Disqualification of Unfit Directors) Proceedings Rules 1987.

(3) copies of the affidavit/report and exhibits shall be served with the claim form on the defendant.[17]

9.4 The defendant shall, within 28 days from the date of service of the claim form:[18]

(1) file in court any affidavit evidence in opposition to the disqualification application that he or she wishes the court to take into consideration; and

(2) lodge the exhibits with the court where they shall be retained until the conclusion of the proceedings; and

(3) at the same time, serve upon the claimant a copy of the affidavits and exhibits.

9.5 In cases where there is more than one defendant, each defendant is required to serve his evidence on the other defendants unless the court otherwise orders.

9.6 The claimant shall, within 14 days from receiving the copy of the defendant's evidence:[19]

(1) file in court any further affidavit or report in reply he wishes the court to take into consideration; and

(2) lodge the exhibits with the court where they shall be retained until the conclusion of the proceedings; and

(3) at the same time serve a copy of the affidavits/reports and exhibits upon the defendant.

9.7 Prior to the first hearing of the disqualification application, the time for serving evidence may be extended by written agreement between the parties. After the first hearing, the extension of time for serving evidence is governed by CPR rules 2.11 and 29.5.

9.8 So far as is possible all evidence should be filed before the first hearing of the disqualification application.

10. The First Hearing of the Disqualification Application

10.1 The date fixed for the hearing of the disqualification application shall be not less than eight weeks from the date of issue of the claim form.[20]

10.2 The hearing shall in the first instance be before the registrar.[21]

10.3 The registrar shall either determine the case on the date fixed or give directions and adjourn it.[22]

10.4 All interim directions should in so far as possible be sought at the first hearing of the disqualification application so that the disqualification application can be determined at the earliest possible date. The parties should take all such steps as they respectively can to avoid successive directions hearings.

10.5 In the case of a disqualification application made under ss. 7, 8 or 9A of the Act, the registrar shall adjourn the case for further consideration if:

(1) he forms the provisional opinion that a disqualification order ought to be made, and that a period of disqualification longer than five years is appropriate,[23]

or

(2) he is of opinion that questions of law or fact arise which are not suitable for summary determination.[24]

10.6 If the registrar adjourns the application for further consideration he shall:

(1) direct whether the application is to be heard by a registrar or by a judge.[25] This direction may at any time be varied by the court either on application or of its own initiative. If the court varies the direction in the absence of any of the parties, notice will be given to the parties;

(2) consider whether or not to adjourn the application to a judge so that the judge can give further directions;

---

17 Rule 3(1) of the Insolvent Companies (Disqualification of Unfit Directors) Proceedings Rules 1987.

18 Rule 6(1) of the Insolvent Companies (Disqualification of Unfit Directors) Proceedings Rules 1987.

19 Rule 6(2) of the Insolvent Companies (Disqualification of Unfit Directors) Proceedings Rules 1987.

20 Rule 7(1) of the Insolvent Companies (Disqualification of Unfit Directors) Proceedings Rules 1987.

21 Rule 7(2) of the Insolvent Companies (Disqualification of Unfit Directors) Proceedings Rules 1987.

22 Rule 7(3) of the Insolvent Companies (Disqualification of Unfit Directors) Proceedings Rules 1987.

23 Rule 7(4)(a) of the Insolvent Companies (Disqualification of Unfit Directors) Proceedings Rules 1987.

24 Rule 7(4)(b) of the Insolvent Companies (Disqualification of Unfit Directors) Proceedings Rules 1987.

25 Rule 7(5)(a) of the Insolvent Companies (Disqualification of Unfit Directors) Proceedings Rules 1987.

(3) consider whether or not to make any direction with regard to fixing the trial date or a trial window;
(4) state the reasons for the adjournment.[26]

11. Case Management

11.1 On the first or any subsequent hearing of the disqualification application, the registrar may also give directions as to the following matters:
(1) the filing in court and the service of further evidence (if any) by the parties;[27]
(2) the timetable for the steps to be taken between the giving of directions and the hearing of the application;
(3) such other matters as the registrar thinks necessary or expedient with a view to an expeditious disposal of the application or the management of it generally;[28]
(4) the time and place of the adjourned hearing;[29] and
(5) the manner in which and the time within which notice of the adjournment and the reasons for it are to be given to the parties.[30]

11.2 Where a case is adjourned other than to a judge, it may be heard by the registrar who originally dealt with the case or by another registrar.[31]

11.3 If the Companies Court registrar adjourns the application to a judge, all directions having been complied with and the evidence being complete, the application will be referred to the Listing Office and any practice direction relating to listing shall apply accordingly.

11.4 In all disqualification applications, the court may direct a pre-trial review ('PTR'), a case management conference or pre-trial checklists (listing questionnaires) (in the form annexed to this practice direction) and will fix a trial date or trial period in accordance with the provisions of CPR, Part 29 (the multi-track), as modified by any relevant practice direction made thereunder.

11.5 At the hearing of the PTR, the registrar may give any further directions as appropriate and, where the application is to be heard in the Royal Courts of Justice in London, unless the trial date has already been fixed, may direct the parties (by counsel's clerks if applicable) to attend the registrar at a specified time and place in order solely to fix a trial date. The court will give notice of the date fixed for the trial to the parties.

11.6 In all cases, the parties must inform the court immediately of any material change to the information provided in a pre-trial checklist.

12. The Trial

12.1 Trial bundles containing copies of:
(1) the claim form;
(2) the acknowledgment of service;
(3) all evidence filed by or on behalf of each of the parties to the proceedings, together with the exhibits thereto;
(4) all relevant correspondence; and
(5) such other documents as the parties consider necessary;
shall be lodged with the court.

12.2 Skeleton arguments should be prepared by all the parties in all but the simplest cases whether the case is to be heard by a registrar or a judge. They should comply with all relevant guidelines.

12.3 The advocate for the claimant should also in all but the simplest cases provide: (a) a chronology; (b) a dramatis personae; (c) in respect of each defendant, a list of references to the relevant evidence.

[26] Rule 7(5)(b) of the Insolvent Companies (Disqualification of Unfit Directors) Proceedings Rules 1987.
[27] Rule 7(5)(c)(ii) of the Insolvent Companies (Disqualification of Unfit Directors) Proceedings Rules 1987.
[28] Rule 7(5)(c)(iii) of the Insolvent Companies (Disqualification of Unfit Directors) Proceedings Rules 1987.
[29] Rule 7(5)(c)(iv) of the Insolvent Companies (Disqualification of Unfit Directors) Proceedings Rules 1987.
[30] Rule 7(5)(c)(i) of the Insolvent Companies (Disqualification of Unfit Directors) Proceedings Rules 1987.
[31] Rule 7(6) of the Insolvent Companies (Disqualification of Unfit Directors) Proceedings Rules 1987.

12.4 The documents mentioned in paras 12.1–12.3 above must be delivered to the court in accordance with any order of the court and/or any relevant practice direction.[32]

(1) If the case is to be heard by a judge sitting in the Royal Courts of Justice, London, but the name of the judge is not known, or the judge is a deputy judge, these documents must be delivered to the Clerk of the Lists. If the name of the judge (other than a deputy judge) is known, these documents must be delivered to the judge's clerk.

(2) If the case is to be heard by a Companies Court registrar, these documents must be delivered to Room 409, Thomas More Building, Royal Courts of Justice. Copies must be provided to the other party so far as possible when they are delivered to the court.

(3) If the case is to be heard in the Chancery district registries in Birmingham, Bristol, Cardiff, Leeds, Liverpool, Manchester or Newcastle, the addresses for delivery are set out in annex 1.

(4) If the case is to be heard in a county court, the documents should be delivered to the relevant county court office.

12.5 Copies of documents delivered to the court must, so far as possible, be provided to each of the other parties to the claim.

12.6 The provisions in paras 12.1 to 12.5 above are subject to any order of the court making different provision.

13. Summary Procedure

13.1 If the parties decide to invite the court to deal with the application under the procedure adopted in *Re Carecraft Construction Co. Ltd* [1994] 1 WLR 172, they should inform the court immediately and obtain a date for the hearing of the application.

13.2 Whenever the *Carecraft* procedure is adopted, the claimant must:

(1) except where the court otherwise directs, submit a written statement containing in respect of each defendant any material facts which (for the purposes of the application) are either agreed or not opposed (by either party); and

(2) specify in writing the period of disqualification which the parties accept that the agreed or unopposed facts justify or the band of years (e.g. 4 to 6 years) or bracket (i.e. 2 to 5 years; 6 to 10 years; 11 to 15 years) into which they will submit the case falls.

13.3 Paragraph 12.4 above applies to the documents mentioned in para. 13.2 above unless the court otherwise directs.

13.4 Unless the court otherwise orders, a hearing under the *Carecraft* procedure will be held in private.

13.5 If the court is minded to make a disqualification order having heard the parties' representations, it will usually give judgment and make the disqualification order in public. Unless the court otherwise orders, the written statement referred to in para. 13.2 shall be annexed to the disqualification order.

13.6 If the court refuses to make the disqualification order under the *Carecraft* procedure, the court shall give further directions for the hearing of the application.

14. Making and Setting Aside of Disqualification Order

14.1 The court may make a disqualification order against the defendant, whether or not the latter appears, and whether or not he has completed and returned the acknowledgment of service of the claim form, or filed evidence.[33]

14.2 Any disqualification order made in the absence of the defendant may be set aside or varied by the court on such terms as it thinks just.[34]

[32] Attention is drawn to the provisions of the Chancery Guide. Chapter 7 of that Guide dated September 2000 provides guidance on the preparation of trial bundles and skeleton arguments. Unless the court otherwise orders, para. 7.16 of the Chancery Guide requires that trial bundles be delivered to the court seven days before trial and para. 7.21 requires that skeleton arguments be delivered to the court not less than two clear days before trial.

[33] Rule 8(1) of the Insolvent Companies (Disqualification of Unfit Directors) Proceedings Rules 1987.

[34] Rule 8(2) of the Insolvent Companies (Disqualification of Unfit Directors) Proceedings Rules 1987.

15. Service of Disqualification Orders

15.1 Service of disqualification orders will be the responsibility of the claimant.

16. Commencement of Disqualification Order

16.1 Unless the court otherwise orders, the period of disqualification imposed by a disqualification order shall begin at the end of the period of 21 days beginning with the date of the order.[35]

PART THREE APPLICATIONS UNDER SECTIONS 7(2) AND 7(4) OF THE ACT

17. Applications for Permission to Make a Disqualification Application after the End of the Period of 2 Years Specified in Section 7(2) of the Act

17.1 Such applications shall be made by form N208 under CPR, Part 8, save where it is sought to join a director or former director to existing proceedings, in which case such application shall be made by application notice under CPR, Part 23, and PD 23 shall apply save as modified below.

18. Applications for Extra Information Made under Section 7(4) of the Act

18.1 Such applications may be made:
(1) by form N208 under CPR, Part 8;
(2) by application notice in existing disqualification proceedings; or
(3) by application under the Insolvency Rules 1986 in the relevant insolvency, if the insolvency practitioner against whom the application is made remains the office-holder.

19. Provisions Applicable to Applications under Sections 7(2) and 7(4) of the Act

19.1 *Headings:* Every claim form and notice by which such an application is begun and all affidavits, notices and other documents in relation thereto must be entitled in the matter of the company or companies in question and in the matter of the Act.

19.2 *Service:*
(1) Service of claim forms and application notices seeking orders under s. 7(2) or 7(4) of the Act will be the responsibility of the applicant and will not be undertaken by the court.
(2) Where any claim form, application notice or order of the court or other document is required in any application under s. 7(2) or (4) of the Act to be served on any person who is not in England and Wales, the court may order service on him to be effected within such time and in such manner as it thinks fit, may require such proof of service as it thinks fit, and may make such directions as to acknowledgment of service as it thinks fit. Section III of CPR, Part 6, does not apply.

PART FOUR APPLICATIONS FOR PERMISSION TO ACT

20. Commencing an Application for Permission to Act

20.1 This practice direction governs applications for permission made under:
(1) s. 17 of the Act for the purposes of any of ss. 1(1)(a), 1A(1)(a) or 9B(4); and
(2) s. 12(2) of the Act.

20.2 Sections 12 and 17 of the Act identify the courts which have jurisdiction to deal with applications for permission to act. Subject to these sections, such applications may be made:
(1) by form N208 under CPR, Part 8; or
(2) by application notice in an existing disqualification application.

20.3 In the case of a person subject to disqualification under s. 12A or 12B of the Act (by reason of being disqualified in Northern Ireland), permission to act notwithstanding disqualification can only be granted by the High Court of Northern Ireland.

[35] Section 1(2) of the Act (as amended).

21. Headings

21.1 Every claim form or application notice by which an application for permission to act is begun, and all affidavits, notices and other documents in the application must be entitled in the matter of the company or companies in question and in the matter of the Act.

21.2 Every application notice by which an application for permission to act is made and all affidavits, notices and other documents in the application shall be entitled in the same manner as the heading of the claim form in the existing disqualification application.

22. Evidence

22.1 Evidence in support of an application for permission to act shall be by affidavit.

23. Service[36]

23.1 Where a disqualification application has been made under s. 9A of the Act or a disqualification undertaking has been accepted under s. 9B of the Act, the claim form or application notice (as appropriate), together with the evidence in support thereof, must be served on the Office of Fair Trading or specified regulator which made the relevant disqualification application or accepted the disqualification undertaking (as the case may be).

23.2 In all other cases, the claim form or application notice (as appropriate), together with the evidence in support thereof, must be served on the Secretary of State.

PART FIVE APPLICATIONS

24. Form of Application

24.1 CPR, Part 23, and PD 23 (general rules about applications for court orders) shall apply in relation to applications governed by this practice direction (see para. 1.3(4) above) save as modified below.

25. Headings

25.1 Every notice and all affidavits in relation thereto must be entitled in the same manner as the claim form in the proceedings in which the application is made.

26. Service

26.1 Service of application notices in disqualification proceedings will be the responsibility of the parties and will not be undertaken by the court.

26.2 Where any application notice or order of the court or other document is required in any application to be served on any person who is not in England and Wales, the court may order service on him to be effected within such time and in such manner as it thinks fit, and may also require such proof of service as it thinks fit. Section III of CPR, Part 6, does not apply.

PART SIX DISQUALIFICATION PROCEEDINGS OTHER THAN IN THE ROYAL COURTS OF JUSTICE

27.1 Where a disqualification application or a section 8A application is made by a claim form issued other than in the Royal Courts of Justice this practice direction shall apply with the following modifications:

(1) Upon the issue of the claim form the court shall endorse it with the date and time for the first hearing before a district judge. The powers exercisable by a registrar under this practice direction shall be exercised by a district judge.

(2) If the district judge (either at the first hearing or at any adjourned hearing before him) directs that the disqualification claim or section 8A application is to be heard by a High

[36] Addresses for service on government departments are set out in the List of Authorised Government Departments issued by the Cabinet Office under the Crown Proceedings Act 1947, s. 17, which [follows the text of the Crown Proceedings Act 1947 in appendix 7.]

Court judge or by an authorised circuit judge he will direct that the case be entered forthwith in the list for hearing by that judge and the court will allocate (i) a date for the hearing of the trial by that judge and (ii) unless the district judge directs otherwise a date for the hearing of a PTR by the trial judge.

PART SEVEN DISQUALIFICATION UNDERTAKINGS

28. Costs

28.1 The general rule is that the court will order the defendant to pay:

(1) the costs of the Secretary of State (and, in the case of a disqualification application made under s. 7(1)(b) of the Act, the costs of the official receiver) if:

(a) a disqualification application under s. 7 or 8 of the Act has been commenced; and

(b) that application is discontinued because the Secretary of State has accepted a disqualification undertaking under s. 1A of the Act;

(2) the costs of the Office of Fair Trading or a specified regulator if:

(a) a disqualification application under s. 9A of the Act has been commenced; and

(b) that application is discontinued because the Office of Fair Trading or specified regulator (as the case may be) has accepted a disqualification undertaking under s. 9B of the Act.

28.2 The general rule will not apply where the court considers that the circumstances are such that it should make another order.

APPLICATIONS UNDER SECTION 8A OF THE ACT TO REDUCE THE PERIOD FOR WHICH A DISQUALIFICATION UNDERTAKING IS IN FORCE OR TO PROVIDE FOR IT TO CEASE TO BE IN FORCE

29. Headings

29.1 Every claim form by which a section 8A application is begun and all affidavits, notices and other documents in the proceedings must be entitled in the matter of a disqualification undertaking and its date and in the matter of the Act.

30. Commencement: The Claim Form

30.1 Section 8A(3) of the Act identifies the courts which have jurisdiction to deal with section 8A applications.

30.1A A section 8A application must be commenced by a claim form issued:

(1) in the case of a disqualification undertaking given under s. 9B of the Act, in the High Court out of the office of the Companies Court registrar at the Royal Courts of Justice;

(2) in any other case,

(a) in the High Court out of the office of the Companies Court registrar or a Chancery district registry; and

(b) in the county court, out of a county court office.

30.2 A section 8A application shall be made by the issue of a Part 8 claim form in the form annexed hereto and the use of the procedure set out in CPR, Part 8, as modified by this practice direction. Rule 8.1(3) of the CPR (power of the court to order the application to continue as if the claimant had not used the Part 8 procedure) shall not apply.

30.3 When the claim form is issued, the claimant will be given a date for the first hearing of the section 8A application. This date is to be not less than eight weeks from the date of issue of the claim form. The first hearing will be before [a] registrar.

30.4 Rule 8.2 of the CPR does not apply. The claim form must state:

(1) that CPR, Part 8 (as modified by this practice direction), applies;

(2) the form of order the claimant seeks.

30.5 In the case of a disqualification undertaking given under s. 9B of the Act, the defendant to the s. 8A application shall be the Office of Fair Trading or specified regulator which accepted the undertaking. In all other cases, the Secretary of State shall be made the defendant to the section 8A application.

30.6 Service of claim forms in section 8A applications will be the responsibility of the claimant and will not be undertaken by the court. The claim form may be served by sending it by first-class post and the date of service shall, unless the contrary is shown, be deemed to be the seventh day following that on which the claim form was posted. Rule 6.7(1) of the CPR shall be modified accordingly. Otherwise Sections I and II of CPR, Part 6, apply.[37]

30.7 Where any order of the court or other document is required to be served on any person who is not in England and Wales, the court may order service on him to be effected within such time and in such manner as it thinks fit and may require such proof of service as it thinks fit. Part 6 of the CPR shall not apply.

30.8 The claim form served on the defendant shall be accompanied by an acknowledgment of service in the form annexed hereto.

31. Acknowledgment of Service

31.1 The defendant shall:

(1) file an acknowledgment of service in the relevant practice form not more than 14 days after service of the claim form; and

(2) serve a copy of the acknowledgment of service on the claimant and any other party.

31.2 Where the defendant has failed to file an acknowledgment of service and the time period for doing so has expired, the defendant may nevertheless attend the hearing of the application and take part in the hearing as provided for by s. 8A(2) or (2A) of the Act. However, this is without prejudice to the court's case management powers and its powers to make costs orders.

32. Evidence

32.1 Evidence in section 8A applications shall be by affidavit. The undertaking (or a copy) shall be exhibited to the affidavit.

32.2 When the claim form is issued:

(1) the affidavit in support of the section 8A application must be filed in court;

(2) exhibits must be lodged with the court where they shall be retained until the conclusion of the proceedings; and

(3) copies of the affidavit and exhibits shall be served with the claim form on the defendant.

32.3 The defendant shall, within 28 days from the date of service of the claim form:

(1) file in court any affidavit evidence that he wishes the court to take into consideration on the application; and

(2) lodge the exhibits with the court where they shall be retained until the conclusion of the proceedings; and

(3) at the same time, serve upon the claimant a copy of the affidavits and exhibits.

32.4 The claimant shall, within 14 days from receiving the copy of the defendant's evidence:

(1) file in court any further affidavit evidence in reply he wishes the court to take into consideration; and

(2) lodge the exhibits with the court where they shall be retained until the conclusion of the proceedings; and

(3) at the same time serve a copy of the affidavits and exhibits upon the defendant.

32.5 Prior to the first hearing of the section 8A application, the time for serving evidence may be extended by written agreement between the parties. After the first hearing, the extension of time for serving evidence is governed by CPR, rr. 2.11 and 29.5.

32.6 So far as is possible all evidence should be filed before the first hearing of the section 8A application.

33. Hearings and Case Management

33.1 The date fixed for the first hearing of the section 8A application shall be not less than eight weeks from the date of issue of the claim form.

33.2 The hearing shall in the first instance be before the registrar.

[37] Attention is drawn to CPR, r. 6.14(2), regarding a certificate of service of the claim form.

33.3 The registrar shall either determine the case on the date fixed or give directions and adjourn it.

33.4 All interim directions should in so far as possible be sought at the first hearing of the section 8A application so that the section 8A application can be determined at the earliest possible date. The parties should take all such steps as they respectively can to avoid successive directions hearings.

33.5 If the registrar adjourns the application for further consideration he shall:

(1) direct whether the application is to be heard by a registrar or by a judge. This direction may at any time be varied by the court either on application or of its own initiative. If the court varies the direction in the absence of any of the parties, notice will be given to the parties;

(2) consider whether or not to adjourn the application to a judge so that the judge can give further directions;

(3) consider whether or not to make any direction with regard to fixing the trial date or a trial window.

33.6 On the first or any subsequent hearing of the section 8A application, the registrar may also give directions as to the following matters:

(1) the filing in court and the service of further evidence (if any) by the parties;

(2) the timetable for the steps to be taken between the giving of directions and the hearing of the section 8A application;

(3) such other matters as the registrar thinks necessary or expedient with a view to an expeditious disposal of the section 8A application or the management of it generally;

(4) the time and place of the adjourned hearing.

33.7 Where a case is adjourned other than to a judge, it may be heard by the registrar who originally dealt with the case or by another registrar.

33.8 If the Companies Court registrar adjourns the application to a judge, all directions having been complied with and the evidence being complete, the application will be referred to the Listing Office and any practice direction relating to listing shall apply accordingly.

33.9 In all section 8A applications, the court may direct a pre-trial review ('PTR'), a case management conference or pre-trial checklists (listing questionnaires) (in the form annexed to this practice direction) and will fix a trial date or trial period in accordance with the provisions of CPR, Part 29, as modified by any relevant practice direction made thereunder.

33.10 At the hearing of the PTR, the registrar may give any further directions as appropriate and, where the application is to be heard in the Royal Courts of Justice in London, unless the trial date has already been fixed, may direct the parties (by counsel's clerks, if applicable) to attend the registrar at a specified time and place in order solely to fix a trial date. The court will give notice of the date fixed for the trial to the parties.

33.11 In all cases, the parties must inform the court immediately of any material change to the information provided in a pre-trial checklist.

34. The Trial

34.1 Trial bundles containing copies of:

(1) the claim form;

(2) the acknowledgment of service;

(3) all evidence filed by or on behalf of each of the parties to the proceedings, together with the exhibits thereto;

(4) all relevant correspondence; and

(5) such other documents as the parties consider necessary;

shall be lodged with the court.

34.2 Skeleton arguments should be prepared by all the parties in all but the simplest cases whether the case is to be heard by a registrar or a judge. They should comply with all relevant guidelines.

34.3 The advocate for the claimant should also in all but the simplest cases provide: (a) chronology; (b) a dramatis personae.

34.4 The documents mentioned in paras 34.1 to 34.3 above must be delivered to the court in accordance with any order of the court and/or [any] relevant practice direction.[38]

(1) If the case is to be heard by a judge sitting in the Royal Courts of Justice, London, but the name of the judge is not known, or the judge is a deputy judge, these documents must be delivered to the Clerk of the Lists. If the name of the judge (other than a deputy judge) is known, these documents must be delivered to the judge's clerk.

(2) If the case is to be heard by a Companies Court registrar, these documents must be delivered to Room 409, Thomas More Building, Royal Courts of Justice. Copies must be provided to the other party so far as possible when they are delivered to the court.

(3) If the case is to be heard in the Chancery district registries in Birmingham, Bristol, Cardiff, Leeds, Liverpool, Manchester, Newcastle, or Preston, the addresses for delivery are set out in Annex 1.

(4) If the case is to be heard in a county court, the documents should be delivered to the relevant county court office.

34.5 Copies of documents delivered to the court must, so far as possible, be provided to each of the other parties to the claim.

34.6 The provisions in paras 34.1 to 34.5 above are subject to any order of the court making different provision.

35. Appeals

35.1 Rules 7.47 and 7.49 of the Insolvency Rules, as supplemented by Part Four of PD Insolvency Proceedings, apply to an appeal from, or review of, a decision made by the court in the course of:

(1) disqualification proceedings under any of ss. 6 to 8A or 9A of the Act;

(2) an application made under s. 17 of the Act for the purposes of any of ss. 1(1)(a), 1A(1)(a) or 9B(4), for permission to act notwithstanding a disqualification order made, or a disqualification undertaking accepted, under any of ss. 6 to 10.

Any such decision, and any appeal from it, constitutes 'insolvency proceedings' for the purposes of PD Insolvency Proceedings.

35.2 An appeal from a decision made by the court in the course of disqualification proceedings under any of ss. 2(2)(a), 3 or 4 of the Act or on an application for permission to act notwithstanding a disqualification order made under any of those sections is governed by CPR, Part 52, and PD 52.[39]

ANNEX 1

Birmingham: The Chancery Listing Officer, The District Registry of the Chancery Division of the High Court, 33 Bull Street, Birmingham B4 6DS.

Bristol: The Chancery Listing Officer, The District Registry of the Chancery Division of the High Court, 3rd Floor, Greyfriars, Lewins Mead, Bristol BS1 2NR.

Cardiff: The Chancery Listing Officer, The District Registry of the Chancery Division of the High Court, 1st Floor, 2 Park Street, Cardiff CF10 1EE.

Leeds: The Chancery Listing Officer, The District Registry of the Chancery Division of the High Court, Leeds Combined Court Centre, The Court House, 1 Oxford Row, Leeds LS1 3BG.

Liverpool and Manchester: The Chancery Listing Officer, The District Registry of the Chancery Division of the High Court, Manchester Courts of Justice, Crown Square, Manchester M60 9DJ.

---

[38] Attention is drawn to the provisions of the Chancery Guide. Chapter 7 of that Guide dated September 2000 provides guidance on the preparation of trial bundles and skeleton arguments. Unless the court otherwise orders, para. 7.16 of the Chancery Guide requires that trial bundles be delivered to the court seven days before trial and para. 7.21 requires that skeleton arguments be delivered to the court not less than two clear days before trial. Addresses for service on government departments are set out in the List of Authorised Government Departments issued by the Cabinet Office under the Crown Proceedings Act 1947, s. 17, which is [after the text of the Crown Proceedings Act 1947 in **appendix** 7].

[39] CPR, r. 2.1(2), and s. 21(2) of the Act. See also the Insolvent Companies (Disqualification of Unfit Directors) Proceedings Rules 1987, r. 2(4), and *Re Tasbian Ltd (No. 2)* [1991] BCLC 59; *Re Probe Data Systems Ltd (No. 3)* [1992] BCLC 405; and *Secretary of State for Trade and Industry v Paulin* [2005] EWHC 888 (Ch), *The Times*, 26 May 2005.

Newcastle: The Chancery Listing Officer, The District Registry of the Chancery Division of the High Court, The Law Courts, Quayside, Newcastle upon Tyne NE1 3LA.

Preston: The Chancery Listing Officer, The District Registry of the Chancery Division of the High Court, The Combined Court Centre, Ringway, Preston PR1 2LL.

[FORMS

The forms annexed to this practice direction are on the CD-ROM version of *Blackstone's Civil Practice.* Click on the title of a form to open it.

N500	Claim form: directors disqualification application
N500A	Notes for claimant on completing claim form N500: directors disqualification application
N500B	Notes for defendant: directors disqualification application
N501	Claim form: directors disqualification: section 8A application
N501A	Notes for claimant on completing claim form N501: directors disqualification: section 8A application
N501B	Notes for defendant: directors disqualification: section 8A application
N502	Acknowledgment of service: directors disqualification application
N503	Acknowledgment of service: directors disqualification: section 8A application
N504	Pre-trial checklist: directors disqualification

Practice Direction Relating to the Use of the Welsh Language in Cases in the Civil Courts in Wales

The purpose of this practice direction is to reflect the principle of the Welsh Language Act 1993 that in the administration of justice in Wales, the English and Welsh languages should be treated on the basis of equality.

1. General

1.1 This practice direction applies to civil proceedings in courts in Wales.

1.2 The existing practice of conducting a hearing entirely in the Welsh language on an ad hoc basis and without notice will continue to apply when all parties and witnesses directly involved at the time consent to the proceedings being so conducted.

1.3 In every case in which it is possible that the Welsh language may be used by any party or witness (or in any document which may be placed before the court), the parties or their legal representatives must inform the court of that fact so that appropriate arrangements can be made for the management and listing of the case.

1.4 If costs are incurred as a result of a party failing to comply with this direction, a costs order may be made against him or his legal representative.

1.5 Where a case is tried with a jury, the law does not permit the selection of jurors in a manner which enables the court to discover whether a juror does or does not speak Welsh or to secure a jury whose members are bilingual to try a case in which the Welsh language may be used.

2. The Allocation Questionnaire

2.1 In any proceedings in which a party is required to complete an allocation questionnaire, he must include details relating to the possible use of Welsh i.e. details of any person wishing to give oral evidence in Welsh and of any documents in Welsh (e.g. documents to be disclosed under Part 31 or witness statements) which that party expects to use.

2.2 A party must include the details mentioned in para. 2.1 in the allocation questionnaire even if he has already informed the court of the possible use of Welsh in accordance with the provisions of section 1 above.

3. Case Management

3.1 At any interlocutory hearing, the court will take the opportunity to consider whether it should give case management directions. To assist the court, a party or his legal representative should draw the court's attention to the possibility of Welsh being used in the proceedings, even where he has already done so in compliance with other provisions of this direction.

3.2 In any case where a party is required to complete a pre-trial checklist (listing questionnaire) and has already intimated the intention to use Welsh, he should confirm the intended use of Welsh in the pre-trial checklist and provide any details which have not been set out in the allocation questionnaire.

4. Listing by the Court

4.1 The diary manager, in consultation with the designated civil judge, will ensure that a case in which the Welsh language is to be used is listed:

(a) wherever practicable before a Welsh speaking judge; and

(b) where translation facilities are needed, at a court with simultaneous translation facilities.

5. Interpreters

5.1 Whenever an interpreter is needed to translate evidence from English to Welsh or from Welsh to English, the court manager in whose court the case is to be heard will take steps to secure the attendance of an interpreter whose name is included in the list of approved court interpreters.

6. Witnesses and Jurors

6.1 When each witness is called, the court officer administering the oath or affirmation will inform the witness that he or she may be sworn or may affirm in Welsh or English as he or she wishes.

6.2 Where a case is tried with a jury, the court officer swearing in the jury will inform the jurors in open court that each juror may take the oath or may affirm in Welsh or English as he or she wishes.

7. Role of the Liaison Judge

7.1 If any question or difficulty arises concerning the implementation of this practice direction, contact should in the first place be made with the Liaison Judge for the Welsh language.

Practice Direction — Devolution Issues

This Practice Direction is divided into 4 parts:

Part I Introduction
Part II Directions applicable to all proceedings
Part III Directions applicable to specific proceedings
Part IV Appeals

PART I INTRODUCTION

Definitions

1. In this Practice Direction:
   'the Assembly' means the National Assembly for Wales or Cynulliad Cenedlaethol Cymru
   'the GWA' means the Government of Wales Act 1998
   'the NIA' means the Northern Ireland Act 1998
   'the SA' means the Scotland Act 1998
   'the Acts' mean the GWA, the NIA and the SA
   'the Judicial Committee' means the Judicial Committee of the Privy Council
   'the CPR' means the Civil Procedure Rules 1998
   'the FPR' means the Family Proceedings Rules 1991
   'the FPC' means the Family Proceedings Courts (Children Act 1989) Rules 1991
   'devolution issue' has the same meaning as in paragraph 1, schedule 8 to the GWA; paragraph 1, schedule 10 to the NIA; and paragraph 1, schedule 6 of the SA
   'devolution issue notice' means a notice that a devolution issue has arisen in proceedings.

Scope

2.1 This Practice Direction supplements the provisions dealing with devolution issues in the Acts. It deals specifically with the position if a devolution issue arises under the GWA. If a devolution issue arises under the NIA or the SA the procedure laid down in this Practice Direction should be adapted as required.

The Devolution Legislation

3.1 Schedule 8 to the GWA contains provisions dealing with devolution issues arising out of the GWA; schedule 10 to the NIA contains provisions dealing with devolution issues arising out of the NIA; and schedule 6 to the SA contains provisions dealing with devolution issues arising out of the SA.

3.2 Broadly a devolution issue will involve a question whether a devolved body has acted or proposes to act within its powers (which includes not acting incompatibly with Convention rights[1] and Community law[2]) or has failed to comply with a duty imposed on it. Reference should be made to the Acts where 'devolution issue' is defined.

3.3 (1) If a devolution issue under the GWA arises in proceedings, the court must order notice of it to be given to the Attorney General and the Assembly if they are not already a party. They have a right to take part as a party in the proceedings so far as they relate to a devolution issue, if they are not already a party (paragraph 5, schedule 8 to the GWA.) If they do take

[1] The rights and fundamental freedoms set out in: (a) Articles 2 to 12 and 14 of the European Convention on Human Rights ('ECHR'), (b) Articles 1 to 3 of the First Protocol (agreed at Paris on 20th March 1952), and (c) Articles 1 and 2 of the Sixth Protocol (agreed at Strasbourg on 11th May 1994), as read with Articles 16 and 18 of the ECHR (Section 1 Human Rights Act 1998; s. 107(1) and (5) GWA; sections 6(2); 24(1) and 98(1) NIA; sections 29(2); 57(2) and 126(1) SA).

[2] All the rights, powers, liabilities, obligations and restrictions from time to time created or arising by or under the Community Treaties; and all the remedies and procedures from time to time provided for by or under the Community Treaties (sections 106(7) and 155(1), GWA; sections 6(2); 24(1) and 98(1), NIA; sections 29(2); 57(2) and 126(9) SA).

part, they may require the court to refer the devolution issue to the Judicial Committee (paragraph 30, schedule 8 to the GWA).[3]

(2) There are similar provisions in the NIA and the SA although the persons to be notified are different (paragraphs 13,14, and 33, schedule 10 to the NIA; paragraphs 16,17 and 33, schedule 6 to the SA).

3.4 Under all the Acts the court may refer a devolution issue to another court as follows:

(1) A magistrates' court may refer a devolution issue arising in civil or summary proceedings to the High Court (paragraphs 6 and 9, schedule 8 to the GWA; paragraphs 15 and 18, schedule 10 to the NIA; and paragraphs 18 and 21, schedule 6 to the SA).

(2) The Crown Court may refer a devolution issue arising in summary proceedings to the High Court and a devolution issue arising in proceedings on indictment to the Court of Appeal (paragraph 9, schedule 8 to the GWA; paragraph 18, schedule 10 to the NIA; paragraph 21, schedule 6 to the SA).

(3) A county court, the High Court (unless the devolution issue has been referred to the High Court),[4] and the Crown Court[5] may refer a devolution issue arising in civil proceedings to the Court of Appeal (paragraph 7, schedule 8 to the GWA; paragraph 16, schedule 10 to the NIA; paragraph 19, schedule 6 to the SA).

(4) A tribunal from which there is no appeal must, and any other tribunal may, refer a devolution issue to the Court of Appeal (paragraph 8, schedule 8 to the GWA; paragraph 17, schedule 10 to the NIA; paragraph 20, schedule 6 to the SA).

(5) The Court of Appeal may refer a devolution issue to the Judicial Committee, unless the devolution issue was referred to it by another court (paragraph 10, schedule 8 to the GWA; paragraph 19, schedule 10 to the NIA; paragraph 22, schedule 6 to the SA).

(6) An appeal against the determination of a devolution issue by the High Court or the Court of Appeal on a reference lies to the Judicial Committee with the leave of the court concerned, or, failing such leave, with special leave of the Judicial Committee (paragraph 11, schedule 8 to the GWA; paragraph 20, schedule 10 to the NIA; paragraph 23, schedule 6 to the SA).

3.5 A court may take into account additional expense which the court considers that a party has incurred as a result of the participation of the Attorney General or the Assembly in deciding any question as to costs (paragraph 35, schedule 8 to the GWA).

PART II DIRECTIONS APPLICABLE TO ALL PROCEEDINGS

Scope

4. Paragraphs 5 to 13 apply to proceedings in England and Wales in the magistrates' courts, the county courts, the Crown Court, the High Court and the Court of Appeal (Civil and Criminal Division). Paragraph 10 also applies to the form and procedure for a reference to the Court of Appeal by a tribunal.

Raising the Question as to Whether a Devolution Issue Arises

5.1 Where a party to any form of proceedings wishes to raise an issue which may be a devolution issue whether as a claim (or part of a claim) to enforce or establish a legal right or to seek a remedy or as a defence (or part of a defence), the provisions of this Practice Direction apply in addition to the rules of procedure applicable to the proceedings in which the issue arises.

[3] If the Attorney General or the Assembly had become a party to the original proceedings but did not exercise their right to require the devolution issue to be referred to the Judicial Committee and the court decided the case, they would have the same rights of appeal as parties. These would not allow them to appeal a decision made in proceedings on indictment, although the Attorney General has a power under section 36 of the Criminal Justice Act 1972 to refer a point of law to the Court of Appeal where the defendant has been acquitted in a trial on indictment.

Paragraph 31, schedule 8 to the GWA, allows the Attorney General and Assembly to refer to the Judicial Committee any devolution issue which is not the subject of proceedings. This power could possibly be used if a court reached a decision where they had not been parties and so had no rights of appeal but such a reference could not affect the decision of the court.

[4] If an appeal by way of case stated in criminal proceedings goes to the Divisional Court there appears to be no power for the Divisional Court to refer a devolution issue to the Court of Appeal.

[5] E.g. in appeals from a magistrates' court in a licensing matter.

5.2 A court may, of its own volition, require the question of whether a devolution issue arises to be considered, if the materials put before the court indicate such an issue may arise, even if the parties have not used the term 'devolution issue'.

Determination by a Court of Whether a Devolution Issue Arises

6.1 The court may give such directions as it considers appropriate to obtain clarification or additional information to establish whether a devolution issue arises.

6.2 In determining whether a devolution issue arises the court, notwithstanding the contention of a party to the proceedings, may decide that a devolution issue shall *not* be taken to arise if the contention appears to the court to be frivolous or vexatious (paragraph 2 of schedule 8 to the GWA).

6.3 If the court determines that a devolution issue arises it must state what that devolution issue is clearly and concisely.

Notice of Devolution Issue to the Attorney General and the Assembly

7.1 If a court determines that a devolution issue arises in the proceedings, it must order a devolution issue notice substantially in the form numbered 'DI 1' in Annex 1 to be given to the Attorney General and the Assembly unless they are already a party to the proceedings (paragraph 5(1), schedule 8 to the GWA).

7.2 A court receiving a reference does not have to serve a devolution issue notice unless it determines that a devolution issue that was not identified by the court making the reference has arisen. In that case the court receiving the reference must serve a devolution issue notice which must:
(1) state what devolution issue has been referred to it;
(2) state what further devolution issue has arisen; and
(3) identify the referring court.

7.3 If the devolution issue has arisen in criminal proceedings, the devolution issue notice must state:
(1) whether the proceedings have been adjourned;
(2) whether the defendant is remanded in custody; and
(3) if the defendant has been remanded in custody and his trial has not commenced, when the custody time limit expires.[6]

7.4 If the devolution issue arises in an appeal, the devolution issue notice must:
(1) state that the devolution issue arises in an appeal;
(2) identify the court whose decision is being appealed; and
(3) state whether the devolution issue is raised for the first time on appeal; or, if it is not, state that the devolution issue was raised in the court whose decision is being appealed, what decision was reached by that court, and the date of the previous notice to the Attorney General and the Assembly.

7.5 The devolution issue notice will specify a date which will be 14 days, or such longer period as the court may direct (see below), after the date of the devolution issue notice as the date by which the Attorney General or the Assembly must notify the court that he or it wishes to take part as a party to the proceedings, so far as they relate to a devolution issue.

7.6 The court may, in exceptional circumstances, specify a date longer than 14 days after the date of the devolution issue notice as the date by which the Attorney General and the Assembly must notify the court that he or it wishes to take part as a party to the proceedings. The court may do this before the notice is given, or before or after the expiry of the period given in the notice.

7.7 (1) On the date of the devolution issue notice,
(a) the devolution issue notice for the Attorney General must be faxed to him by the court;[7] and
(b) the devolution issue notice for the Assembly must be faxed by the court to the Counsel General for the Assembly.

[6] Custody time limits are imposed by the Prosecution of Offences (Custody Time Limits) Regulations 1987 as amended.

[7] See Annex 2 for information about fax numbers and addresses.

(2) On the same day as a fax is sent a copy of the devolution issue notice must be sent by the court by first class post to the Attorney General and the Counsel General for the Assembly.

7.8 The court may, on such terms as it considers appropriate, order such additional documents to be served (e.g. in civil proceedings, the claim form) or additional information to be supplied with the devolution issue notice.

7.9 (1) When a court orders a devolution issue notice to be given the court may make such further orders as it thinks fit in relation to any adjournment, stay, continuance of the proceedings, or interim measures, during the period within which the Attorney General and the Assembly have to notify the court if they intend to take part as a party to the proceedings.

(2) Before ordering an adjournment in criminal proceedings, the court will consider all material circumstances, including whether it would involve delay that might extend beyond the custody time limits if the defendant is remanded in custody and his trial has not commenced.

7.10 If neither the Attorney General nor the Assembly notify the court within the specified time that he or it wishes to take part as a party to the proceedings:

(1) the proceedings should immediately continue on expiry of the period within which they had to notify the court; and

(2) the court has no duty to inform them of the outcome of the proceedings apart from the duty to notify them if the court decides to refer the devolution issue to another court (see paragraph 10.3(5)).[8]

Adding the Attorney General or the Assembly to the Proceedings and Their Right to Require Referral of a Devolution Issue to the Judicial Committee

8.1 If the Attorney General or the Assembly wishes to take part as a party to the proceedings so far as they relate to a devolution issue, he or it must send to the court and the other parties (and to each other if only one of them has become a party) a notice substantially in the form numbered 'DI 2' shown in Annex 1 within the time specified in the devolution issue notice.

8.2 On receipt of this form the court may give such consequential directions as it considers necessary.

8.3 If the Attorney General or the Assembly is a party to the proceedings, and either of them wishes to require the court to refer the devolution issue to the Judicial Committee, he or it must as soon as practicable send to the court and the other parties (and to each other if only one of them has become a party) a notice substantially in the form numbered 'DI 3' shown in Annex 1.

Determination by the Court of Whether or Not to Make a Reference of a Devolution Issue If the Attorney General or the Assembly Do Not Require a Reference

9.1 If the court is not required to refer the devolution issue to the Judicial Committee, the court will decide whether it should refer the devolution issue to the relevant court as specified in paragraph 3.4.

9.2 Before deciding whether to make a reference the court may hold a directions hearing or give written directions as to the making of submissions on the question of whether to make a reference.

9.3 The court may make a decision on the basis of written submissions if its procedures permit this and it wishes to do so, or the court may have a hearing before making a decision.

9.4 In exercising its discretion as to whether to make a reference, the court will have regard to all relevant circumstances and in particular to:

(1) the importance of the devolution issue to the public in general;

(2) the importance of the devolution issue to the original parties to the proceedings;

(3) whether a decision on the reference of the devolution issue will be decisive of the matters in dispute between the parties;

(4) whether all the relevant findings of fact have been made (a devolution issue will not, unless there are exceptional circumstances, be suitable for a reference if it has to be referred on the basis of assumed facts);

[8] If there is an appeal, the appeal court will serve a devolution issue notice on the Attorney General and the Assembly (see paragraph 7.4).

Civil Procedure Rules & Practice Directions

(5) the delay that a reference would entail particularly in cases involving children and criminal cases (including whether the reference is likely to involve delay that would extend beyond the expiry of the custody time limits if the defendant is remanded in custody and his trial has not commenced); and

(6) additional costs that a reference might involve.[9]

9.5 The court should state its reasons for making or declining to make a reference.

9.6 If the court decides not to refer the case, it will give directions for the future conduct of the action, which will include directions as to the participation of the Attorney General and the Assembly if they are parties.

Form and Procedure for References

10.1 If the court or tribunal is required by the Attorney General or the Assembly (in relation to any proceedings before the court to which he or it is a party) to refer the devolution issue to the Judicial Committee:

(1) the court or tribunal will make the reference as soon as practicable after receiving the notice from the Attorney General or the Assembly substantially in the form numbered 'DI 3' shown in Annex 1, and follow the procedure for references in the Judicial Committee (Devolution Issues) Rules Order 1999; and

(2) the court or tribunal may order the parties, or any of them, to draft the reference.

10.2 If the Court of Appeal decides to refer the devolution issue to the Judicial Committee:

(1) It will follow the procedure in the Judicial Committee (Devolution Issues) Rules Order 1999; and

(2) the court may order the parties, or any of them, to draft the reference.

10.3 If any other court or tribunal decides, or if a tribunal is required, to refer the devolution issue to another court:

(1) the reference must be substantially in the form numbered 'DI 4' shown in Annex 1 and must set out the following:

(a) the question referred;

(b) the addresses of the parties, except in the case of family proceedings, for which see paragraphs 15.2–4

(c) a concise statement of the background of the matter including:

(i) the facts of the case, including any relevant findings of fact by the referring court or lower courts; and

(ii) the main issues in the case and the contentions of the parties with regard to them;

(d) the relevant law, including the relevant provisions of the GWA;

(e) the reasons why an answer to the question is considered necessary for the purpose of disposing of the proceedings;

(2) all judgments already given in the proceedings will be annexed to the reference;

(3) the court may order the parties, or any of them, to draft the reference;

(4) the court or tribunal will transmit the reference to:

(a) the Civil Appeals Office Registry if the reference is to the Court of Appeal from a county court, the High Court or the Crown Court in civil proceedings, or from a tribunal;

(b) the Registrar of Criminal Appeals if the reference is to the Court of Appeal from the Crown Court in proceedings on indictment; and

(c) the Administrative Court Office if the reference is to the High Court from a magistrates' court in civil or summary proceedings or from the Crown Court in summary proceedings.[10]

---

[9] In criminal cases section 16 of the Prosecution of Offences Act 1985 does not enable a court receiving a reference to make a defendant's costs order. If the defendant is subsequently acquitted by the court who made the reference that court can make a defendant's costs order. However it would not cover the costs of the reference as 'proceedings' is defined in section 21 as including proceedings in any court below but makes no mention of proceedings on a reference.

[10] See Annex 2 for the relevant addresses. It shows The Law Courts, Cathays Park, Cardiff CF10 3PG and the Royal Courts of Justice, Strand, London WC2A 2LL as alternative addresses for transmitting documents to the Administrative Court Office. If the order is transmitted to Cardiff, the additional copy will be forwarded by the Cardiff Office to the Administrative Court Office in London.

If the reference is transmitted to Cardiff an additional copy of the reference must be filed so that it can be retained by the Cardiff Office. The original reference will be forwarded to the Administrative Court Office in London.

(5) at the same time as the reference is transmitted to the court receiving the reference a copy of the reference will be sent by first class post to:
   (a) the parties;
   (b) the Attorney General if he is not already a party; and
   (c) the Assembly if it is not already a party;

(6) each person on whom a copy of the reference is served must within 21 days notify the court to which the reference is transmitted and the other persons on whom the reference is served whether they wish to be heard on the reference;

(7) the court receiving the reference (either the Court of Appeal or the High Court) will give directions for the conduct of the reference, including the lodging of cases or skeleton arguments; and transmit a copy of the determination on the reference to the referring court; and

(8) if there has been an appeal to the Judicial Committee against a decision of the High Court or the Court of Appeal on a reference, and a copy of the Judicial Committee's decision on that appeal has been sent to the High Court or Court of Appeal (as the case may be), that court will send a copy to the court which referred the devolution issue to it.

10.4 When a court receives notification of the decision on a reference, it will determine how to proceed with the remainder of the case.

Power of the Court to Deal with Pending Proceedings if a Reference Is Made (Whether by the Attorney General, the Assembly or the Court)

11. If a reference is made the court will adjourn or stay the proceedings in which the devolution issue arose, unless it otherwise orders; and will make such further orders as it thinks fit in relation to any adjournment or stay.

The Welsh Language

12.1 If any party wishes to put forward a contention in relation to a devolution issue that involves comparison of the Welsh and English texts of any Assembly subordinate legislation, that party must give notice to the court as soon as possible.

12.2 Upon receipt of the notification, the court will consider the appropriate means of determining the issue, including, if necessary, the appointment of a Welsh speaking judicial assessor to assist the court.

12.3 Parties to any proceedings in which the Welsh language may be used must also comply with the Practice Direction of 16th October 1998 (relating to proceedings in the Crown Court) and the Practice Direction of 26th April 1999 (relating to civil proceedings). These Practice Directions apply, as appropriate, to proceedings involving a devolution issue in which the Welsh language may be used.

Crown Proceedings Act 1947 (Section 19)

13. Where the court has determined that a devolution issue arises, the Attorney General will give any necessary consent to:

(1) the proceedings being transferred to The Law Courts, Cathays Park, Cardiff CF10 3PG, or to such other district registry as shall (exceptionally) be directed by the court; and

(2) to the trial taking place at Cardiff or at such other trial location as shall (exceptionally) be directed by the court.

PART III DIRECTIONS APPLICABLE TO SPECIFIC PROCEEDINGS

Judicial Review Proceedings in Wales

14.1 PD 54 (judicial review) contains provisions about when judicial review proceedings may be brought in the Administrative Court in Wales.

Family Proceedings in the Magistrates' Courts, the County Courts and the High Court

15.1 In any proceedings in which any question with respect to the upbringing of a child arises, the court shall have regard to the general principle that any delay in determining the question is likely to prejudice the welfare of the child.[12]

15.2 If the FPR apply, the court will comply with rule 10.21.[13]

15.3 If Part IV of the FPR applies, the court will comply with rule 4.23.[14]

15.4 If the FPC apply, the court will comply with Rules 23 and 33A.[15]

15.5 If the proceedings are listed in column (1) of Appendix 3 to the FPR or Schedule 2 to the FPC, a copy of any notice to be given to the parties must also be given to the persons set out in column (iv) of Appendix 3 or Schedule 2 as the case may be.

15.6 A party wishing to raise a devolution issue must, wherever possible, raise it (giving full particulars of the provisions relied on) in the application or answer or at the first directions hearing where appropriate.

15.7 If a party has not raised a devolution issue as above, the party must seek the permission of the court to raise it at a later stage.

15.8 Where a court has referred the devolution issue to another court and has received notification of the decision on the reference, the matter should so far as is practicable be placed before the same judge or magistrates who dealt with the case before the reference.

Civil Proceedings in the County Courts and the High Court

16.1 A party wishing to raise a devolution issue must specify in the claim form, or if he is a defendant, in the defence (or written evidence filed with the acknowledgment of service in a Part 8 claim) that the claim raises a devolution issue and the relevant provisions of the GWA.

16.2 The particulars of claim or defence if the devolution issue is raised by the defendant (or written evidence filed with the acknowledgment of service in a Part 8 claim) must contain the facts and circumstances and points of law on the basis of which it is alleged that a devolution issue arises in sufficient detail to enable the court to determine whether a devolution issue arises in the proceedings.

16.3 Whether or not the allocation rules apply, if a question is raised during the proceedings that might be a devolution issue, then a directions hearing must take place and the matter must be referred to a circuit judge (in county court actions) or a High Court judge (in High Court actions) for determination as to whether a devolution issue arises and for further directions.

---

[12] Section 1(2), Children Act 1989. [Footnote 11 has been deleted but subsequent footnotes have not been renumbered in the text issued by the Department for Constitutional Affairs.]

[13] Rule 10.21 states: (1) Subject to rule 2.3 [of the FPR] nothing in these rules shall be construed as requiring any party to reveal the address of their private residence (or that of any child) save by order of the court. (2) Where a party declines to reveal an address in reliance upon paragraph (1) above, he shall give notice of that address to the court in Form C8 and that address shall not be revealed to any person save by order of the court.

[14] Rule 4.23 states: (1) Notwithstanding any rule of court to the contrary, no document, other than a record of an order, held by the court and relating to proceedings to which [Part IV] applies shall be disclosed, other than to— (a) a party, (b) the legal representative of a party, (c) the guardian ad litem, (d) the Legal Aid Board, or (e) a welfare officer, without the leave of the judge or the district judge. (2) Nothing in this rule shall prevent the notification by the court or the proper officer of a direction under section 37(1) to the authority concerned. (3) Nothing in this rule shall prevent the disclosure of a document prepared by a guardian ad litem for the purpose of— (a) enabling a person to perform functions required by regulations made under section 41(7); (b) assisting a guardian ad litem or a reporting officer (within the meaning of section 65(1)(b) of the Adoption Act 1976) who is appointed under any enactment to perform his functions.

[15] Rule 23 states: (1) No document, other than a record of an order, held by the court and relating to relevant proceedings shall be disclosed, other than to— (a) a party, (b) the legal representative of a party, (c) the guardian ad litem, (d) the Legal Aid Board, or (e) a welfare officer, without leave of the justices' clerk or the court. (2) Nothing in this rule shall prevent the notification by the court or the justices' clerk of a direction under section 37(1) to the authority concerned. (3) Nothing in this rule shall prevent the disclosure of a document prepared by a guardian ad litem for the purpose of— (a) enabling a person to perform functions required by regulations made under section 41(7); (b) assisting a guardian ad litem or a reporting officer (within the meaning of section 65(1)(b) of the Adoption Act 1976) who is appointed under any enactment to perform his functions.

Rule 33A states: (1) Nothing in these Rules shall be construed as requiring any party to reveal the address of their private residence (or that of any child) except by order of the court. (2) Where a party declines to reveal an address in reliance upon paragraph (1) he shall give notice of that address to the court in Form C8 and that address shall not be revealed to any person except by order of the court.

16.4 If a party fails to specify in the appropriate document that a devolution issue arises but that party subsequently wishes to raise a devolution issue, that party must seek the permission of the court.

16.5 Where any party has specified that a devolution issue arises, no default judgment can be obtained.

Criminal Proceedings in the Crown Court

17. If the defendant wishes to raise a devolution issue he should do so at the Plea and Directions Hearing.

Criminal and Civil Proceedings in the Magistrates' Courts

18.1 (1) Where a defendant, who has been charged or has had an information laid against him in respect of a criminal offence and has entered a plea of 'Not Guilty', wishes to raise a devolution issue he should, wherever possible, give full particulars of the provisions relied on by notice in writing.

(2) Where a party to a complaint, or applicant for a licence wishes to raise a devolution issue he should, wherever possible, give full particulars of the provisions relied on by notice in writing.

(3) Such notice should be given to the prosecution (and other party if any) and the court as soon as practicable after the 'Not Guilty' plea is entered or the complaint or application is made as the case may be.

18.2 Where proceedings are to be committed or transferred to the Crown Court by the magistrates, the question as to whether a devolution issue arises shall be a matter for the Crown Court.

PART IV APPEALS

Appeals to the Court of Appeal (Civil and Criminal Division)

19.1 This paragraph applies if a devolution issue is raised in any appeal to either the Civil or the Criminal Division of the Court of Appeal.

19.2 The devolution issue may already have been raised in the court whose decision is being appealed. The devolution issue may, however, be raised for the first time on appeal.

19.3 Where an application for permission to appeal is made, or an appeal is brought where permission is not needed, the appellant must specify in the application notice (or the notice of appeal or notice of motion as the case may be):

(1) that the appeal raises a devolution issue and the relevant provisions of the GWA;

(2) the facts and circumstances and points of law on the basis of which it is alleged that a devolution issue arises in sufficient detail to enable the court to determine whether a devolution issue arises; and

(3) whether the devolution issue was considered in the court below, and, if so, provide details of the decision.

19.4 An appellant may not seek to raise a devolution issue without the permission of the court after he has filed an application notice; or a notice of appeal or notice of motion (if no application notice).

19.5 Where permission to appeal is sought and a party to the appeal wishes to raise a devolution issue which was not raised in the lower court, the court will determine if a devolution issue arises before deciding whether to grant leave to appeal.

Appeals to the Crown Court

20. A notice of appeal from a decision of the magistrates' courts to the Crown Court must specify whether the devolution issue was considered in the court below and if so, provide details of the decision. If it was not so considered, the notice should specify:

(1) that the appeal raises a devolution issue and the relevant provisions of the GWA; and

(2) the facts and circumstances and points of law on the basis of which it is alleged that a devolution issue arises in sufficient detail to enable the court to determine whether a devolution issue arises.

ANNEX 1

DI 1 Devolution Issues

Notice of Devolution Issue to Attorney General and The National Assembly For Wales

[NAME OF CASE]

Take notice that the above mentioned case has raised a devolution issue as defined by Schedule 8 to the Government of Wales Act 1998. Details of the devolution issue are given in the attached schedule.

This notice meets the notification requirements under paragraph 5(1) of Schedule 8 to the Government of Wales Act 1998. You may take part as a party to these proceedings, so far as they relate to a devolution issue (paragraph 5(2) of Schedule 8). If you want to do this you must notify the court by completing the attached form, and returning it to the court at [address] by [date].

DATED

To: The Attorney General
The National Assembly for Wales
Other parties (where appropriate)

DI 2 Devolution Issues

Notice of Intention of Attorney General or The National Assembly For Wales to Become Party to Proceedings, So Far As They Relate To a Devolution Issue, Under Paragraph 5(2) Schedule 8 to The Government of Wales Act 1998

In the [name of court]

[case name]

Take notice that the [Attorney General] [the National Assembly for Wales] intends to take part as a party to proceedings so far as they relate to a devolution issue as permitted by paragraph 5(2) of Schedule 8 to the Government of Wales Act 1998 in relation to the devolution issue raised by [ ], of which notice was received by the [Attorney General] [Assembly] on [ ].

[The [ ] also gives notice that it [requires the matter to be referred to] [is still considering whether to require the matter to be referred to] the Judicial Committee of the Privy Council under paragraph 30 of Schedule 8 to the Government of Wales Act 1998.]

[DATE]

On behalf of the [Attorney General]
[National Assembly for Wales]

To: The clerk of the court at [ ]
The parties to the case
[Attorney General] [National Assembly for Wales]

DI 3 Devolution Issues

Notice by Attorney General or National Assembly For Wales That They Require Devolution Issue to be Referred to The Judicial Committee of the Privy Council

In the [court]

[case name]

The [Attorney General] [National Assembly for Wales] gives notice that the devolution issue, which has been raised in the above case and to which [he] [it] is a party, must be referred to the Judicial Committee of the Privy Council under paragraph 30 of Schedule 8 to the Government of Wales Act 1998.

[DATE]

On behalf of the [Attorney General]
[National] Assembly for Wales]

To: The clerk of the court at [ ]
The parties to the case
[Attorney General] [National Assembly for Wales]

DI 4 Devolution Issues

Reference by The Court or Tribunal of Devolution Issue to [High Court] [Court of Appeal] [Judicial Committee of The Privy Council]

In the [court]

[case name]

It is ordered that the devolution issue(s) set out in the schedule be referred to the [High Court] [Court of Appeal] [Judicial Committee of the Privy Council] for determination in accordance with paragraph [ ] of Schedule 8 to the Government of Wales Act 1998.

It is further ordered that the proceedings be stayed until the [High Court] [Court of Appeal] [Judicial Committee of the Privy Council] determine the devolution issue[s] or until further order.

DATED

Judge/clerk to the magistrates' court
Chairman of the Tribunal
[Address]

Skeleton Reference to Be Attached to Form DI 4

In the [court]

[case name]

(a) [The question referred.]
(b) [The addresses of the parties]
(c) [A concise statement of the background to the matters including—
  (i) The facts of the case including any relevant findings of fact by the referring court or lower courts; and
  (ii) The main issues in the case and the contentions of the parties with regard to them;]
(d) [the relevant law including the relevant provisions of the Government of Wales Act 1998]
(e) [the reasons why an answer to the question is considered necessary for the purpose of disposing of the proceedings.]

[All judgments already given in the proceedings are annexed to this reference.]

ANNEX 2 ADDRESSES

1. Notices to the National Assembly for Wales (Cynulliad Cenedlaethol Cymru) must be sent to the Counsel General to the National Assembly for Wales, Crown Buildings, Cathays Park, Cardiff CF99 1NA. Fax number: (01222) 826798.
2. Notices to the Attorney General must be sent to the Attorney General's Chambers, 9 Buckingham Gate, London SW1E 6JP. Fax number (0171) 271 2433.
3 References to the Crown Office under paragraph 9.3(1)c of the Practice Direction may be sent to the Crown Office, Royal Courts of Justice, Strand, London WC2A 2LL; or the Law Courts, Cathays Park, Cardiff CF10 3PG (2 copies).

Explanatory Note

4. The addresses and fax numbers above are the best information available. However it is possible that these (particularly the fax numbers and address for Notices to the Assembly) may change. It would therefore be advisable to confirm the numbers before sending information.

Practice Direction — Application for a Warrant under the Competition Act 1998

Interpretation

1. In this practice direction:
   (1) 'the Act' means the Competition Act 1998;
   (2) 'the Commission' means the European Commission;
   (3) 'Commission official' means a person authorised by the Commission for any of the purposes set out in s. 62(10), 62A(12) or 63(10) of the Act;
   (4) 'the OFT' means the Office of Fair Trading;
   (5) 'officer' means an officer of the OFT;
   (6) 'named officer' means the person identified in a warrant as the principal officer in charge of executing that warrant, and includes a named authorised officer under s. 63 of the Act; and
   (7) 'warrant' means a warrant under s. 28, 62 or 63 of the Act.

Application for a Warrant

2.1 An application by the OFT for a warrant must be made to a High Court judge using the Part 8 procedure as modified by this practice direction.

2.2 The application should be made to a judge of the Chancery Division at the Royal Courts of Justice (if available).

2.3 The application is made without notice and the claim form may be issued without naming a defendant. Rules 8.1(3), 8.3, 8.4, 8.5(2)–(6), 8.6(1), 8.7 and 8.8 do not apply.

Confidentiality of Court Documents

3.1 The court will not effect service of any claim form, warrant, or other document filed or issued in an application to which this practice direction applies, except in accordance with an order of the judge hearing the application.

3.2 Rule 5.4 does not apply, and paras 3.3 and 3.4 have effect in its place.

3.3 When a claim form is issued the court file will be marked 'Not for disclosure' and, unless a High Court judge grants permission, the court records relating to the application (including the claim form and documents filed in support and any warrant or order that is issued) will not be made available by the court for any person to inspect or copy, either before or after the hearing of the application.

3.4 An application for permission under para. 3.3 must be made on notice to the OFT in accordance with Part 23.
(Rule 23.7(1) requires a copy of the application notice to be served as soon as practicable after it is filed, and in any event at least three days before the court is to deal with the application.)

Contents of Claim Form, Affidavit and Documents in Support

4.1 The claim form must state:
   (1) the section of the Act under which the OFT is applying for a warrant;
   (2) the address or other identification of the premises to be subject to the warrant; and
   (3) the anticipated date or dates for the execution of the warrant.

4.2 The application must be supported by affidavit evidence, which must be filed with the claim form.

4.3 The evidence must set out all the matters on which the OFT relies in support of the application, including all material facts of which the court should be made aware. In particular it must state:
   (1) the subject matter (i.e. the nature of the suspected infringement of the chapter I or II prohibitions in the Act, or of arts 81 or 82 of the Treaty establishing the European Community) and purpose of the investigation to which the application relates;
   (2) the identity of the undertaking or undertakings suspected to have committed the infringement;
   (3) the grounds for applying for the issue of the warrant and the facts relied upon in support;

(4) details of the premises to be subject to the warrant and of the possible occupier or occupiers of those premises;
(5) the connection between the premises and the undertaking or undertakings suspected to have committed the infringement;
(6) the name and position of the officer who it is intended will be the named officer;
(7) if it is intended that the warrant may pursuant to a relevant provision of the Act authorise any person (other than an officer or a Commission official) to accompany the named officer in executing the warrant, the name and job title of each such person and the reason why it is intended that he may accompany the named officer.

4.4 There must be exhibited to an affidavit in support of the application:
(1) the written authorisation of the OFT containing the names of:
(a) the officer who it is intended will be the named officer; and
(b) the other persons who it is intended may accompany him in executing the warrant; and
(2) in the case of an application under s. 62, 62A or 63 of the Act, if it is intended that Commission officials will accompany the named officer in executing the warrant, the written authorisations of the Commission containing the names of the Commission officials.

4.5 There must also be filed with the claim form:
(1) drafts of:
(a) the warrant; and
(b) an explanatory note to be produced and served with it; and
(2) the written undertaking by the named officer required by para. 6.2 of this practice direction.
(Examples of forms of warrant under ss. 28 and 62 of the Act, and explanatory notes to be produced and served with them, are annexed to this practice direction. These forms and notes should be used with appropriate modifications in applications for warrants under other sections of the Act.)

4.6 If possible the draft warrant and explanatory note should also be supplied to the court on disk in a form compatible with the word processing software used by the court.

Listing

5. The application will be listed by the court on any published list of cases as 'An application by D'.

Hearing of the Application

6.1 An application for a warrant will be heard and determined in private, unless the judge hearing it directs otherwise.

6.2 The court will not issue a warrant unless there has been filed a written undertaking, signed by the named officer, to comply with para. 8.1 of this practice direction.

The Warrant

7.1 The warrant must:
(1) contain the information required by s. 29(1), s. 64(1) or 65I(1) of the Act;
(2) state the address or other identification of the premises to be subject to the warrant;
(3) state the names of:
(a) the named officer; and
(b) any other officers, Commission officials or other persons who may accompany him in executing the warrant;
(4) set out the action which the warrant authorises the persons executing it to take under the relevant section of the Act;
(5) give the date on which the warrant is issued;
(6) include a statement that the warrant continues in force until the end of the period of one month beginning with the day on which it issued; and
(7) state that the named officer has given the undertaking required by para. 6.2.

7.2 Rule 40.2 applies to a warrant.
(Rule 40.2 requires every judgment or order to state the name and judicial title of the person making it, to bear the date on which it is given or made, and to be sealed by the court.)

7.3 Upon the issue of a warrant the court will provide to the OFT:
(1) the sealed warrant and sealed explanatory note; and
(2) a copy of the sealed warrant and sealed explanatory note for service on the occupier or person in charge of the premises subject to the warrant.

Execution of Warrant

8.1 A named officer attending premises to execute a warrant must, if the premises are occupied:
(1) produce the warrant and an explanatory note on arrival at the premises; and
(2) as soon as possible thereafter personally serve a copy of the warrant and the explanatory note on the occupier or person appearing to him to be in charge of the premises.

8.2 The named officer must also comply with any order which the court may make for service of any other documents relating to the application.

8.3 Unless the court otherwise orders:
(1) the initial production of a warrant and entry to premises under the authority of the warrant must take place between 9.30 a.m. and 5.30 p.m. Monday to Friday; but
(2) once persons named in the warrant have entered premises under the authority of a warrant, they may, whilst the warrant remains in force:
(a) remain on the premises; or
(b) re-enter the premises to continue executing the warrant,
outside those times.

8.4 If the officers executing a warrant propose to remove any items from the premises they must, unless it is impracticable:
(1) make a list of all the items to be removed;
(2) supply a copy of the list to the occupier or person appearing to be in charge of the premises; and
(3) give that person a reasonable opportunity to check the list before removing any of the items.

Application to Vary or Discharge Warrant

9.1 The occupier or person in charge of premises in relation to which a warrant has been issued may apply to vary or discharge the warrant.

9.2 An application under para. 9.1 to stop a warrant from being executed must be made immediately upon the warrant being served.

9.3 A person applying to vary or discharge a warrant must first inform the named officer that he is making the application.

9.4 The application should be made to the judge who issued the warrant, or, if he is not available, to another High Court judge.

Application under the Criminal Justice and Police Act 2001, Section 59

10.1 Attention is drawn to the Criminal Justice and Police Act 2001, s. 59, which makes provision about applications relating to property seized in the exercise of the powers conferred by (among other provisions) s. 28(2) of the Act.

10.2 An application under s. 59:
(1) must be made by application notice in accordance with Part 23; and
(2) should be made to a judge of the Chancery Division at the Royal Courts of Justice (if available).

[ANNEX

The annex, which consists of examples of the forms of warrant and explanatory notes, is on the CD-ROM version of *Blackstone's Civil Practice*. Click on the title of the annex to open it.]

Practice Direction — Civil Recovery Proceedings

Scope and Interpretation

1.1 Section I of this practice direction contains general provisions about proceedings in the High Court under parts 5 and 8 of the Proceeds of Crime Act 2002 and part 5 of the Proceeds of Crime Act 2002 (External Requests and Orders) Order 2005 (SI 2005/3181).

1.2 Section II contains provisions about:

(1) applications to the High Court under part 5 of the Act and part 5 of the Order in Council for:

(a) a recovery order;

(b) a property freezing order; and

(c) an interim receiving order; and

(2) the register of external orders.

1.3 Section III contains provisions about applications to the High Court under part 8 of the Act for any of the following types of order or warrant in connection with a civil recovery investigation:

(a) a production order;

(b) a search and seizure warrant;

(c) a disclosure order;

(d) a customer information order; and

(e) an account monitoring order.

1.4 Section IV of this practice direction contains further provisions about applications for each of the specific types of order and warrant listed in para. 1.3 above.

1.5 In this practice direction:

(1) 'the Act' means the Proceeds of Crime Act 2002;

(2) 'the Director' means the Director of the Assets Recovery Agency, or any person authorised by him to act on his behalf in accordance with s. 1(6) of the Act;

(3) 'the Order in Council' means the Proceeds of Crime Act 2002 (External Requests and Orders) Order 2005 (SI 2005/3181);

(4) 'civil recovery proceedings' means proceedings under part 5 of the Act or part 5 of the Order in Council (as appropriate);

(5) 'the Regulations' means the Proceeds of Crime Act 2002 (Legal Expenses in Civil Recovery Proceedings) Regulations 2005 (SI 2005/3382); and

(6) other expressions used have the same meaning as in the Act or the Order in Council (as appropriate).

I GENERAL PROVISIONS

Venue

2.1 A claim or application to the High Court under part 5 or part 8 of the 2002 Act or part 5 of the Order in Council must be issued in the Administrative Court.

2.2 The Administrative Court will thereupon consider whether to transfer the claim or application to another Division or Court of the High Court.

Use of Pseudonyms by Agency Staff

3.1 If a member of staff of the Assets Recovery Agency gives written or oral evidence in any proceedings using a pseudonym in accordance with s. 449 of the Act:

(1) the court must be informed that the witness is using a pseudonym; and

(2) a certificate under s. 449(3) of the Act must be filed or produced.

II CIVIL RECOVERY PROCEEDING UNDER PART 5 OF THE ACT OR PART 5 OF THE ORDER IN COUNCIL

Claim for a Recovery Order

4.1 A claim by the Director for a recovery order must be made using the Part 8 procedure.

4.2 In a claim for a rrecovery order based on an external order, the claim must include an application to register the external order.

4.3 The claim form must:

(1) identify the property in relation to which a recovery order is sought;

(2) state, in relation to each item or description of property:

(a) whether the property is alleged to be recoverable property or associated property; and

(b) either:

(i) who is alleged to hold the property; or

(ii) where the Director is unable to identify who holds the property, the steps that have been taken to try to establish their identity;

(3) set out the matters relied upon in support of the claim;

(4) give details of the person nominated by the Director to act as trustee for civil recovery in accordance with s. 267 of the Act or art. 178 of the Order in Council; and

(5) in a claim which includes an application to register an external order, be accompanied by a copy of the external order.

4.4 The evidence in support of the claim must include the signed, written consent of the person nominated by the Director to act as trustee for civil recovery if appointed by the court.

4.5 In a claim which includes an application to register an external order, where:

(1) the sum specified in the external order is expressed in a currency other than sterling; and

(2) there are not funds held in the United Kingdom in the currency in which the sum specified is expressed sufficient to satisfy the external order,

the claim form, or particulars of claim if served subsequently, must state the sterling equivalent of the sum specified.

(Article 145(2) of the Order in Council provides that the sterling equivalent is to be calculated in accordance with the exchange rate prevailing at the end of the day on which the external order is made.)

Application for Property Freezing Order or Interim Receiving Order

5.1 An application for a property freezing order or an interim receiving order must be made:

(1) to a High Court judge; and

(2) in accordance with Part 23.

5.2 Rule 23.10(2) and Section I of Part 25 do not apply to applications for property freezing orders and interim receiving orders.

5.3 The application may be made without notice in the circumstances set out in:

(1) s. 245A(3) of the Act and art. 147(3) of the Order in Council (in the case of an application for a property freezing order); and

(2) s. 246(3) of the Act and art. 151(3) of the Order in Council (in the case of an application for an interim receiving order).

5.4 An application for a property freezing order must be supported by written evidence which must:

(1) set out the grounds on which the order is sought; and

(2) give details of each item or description of property in respect of which the order is sought, including:

(a) an estimate of the value of the property; and

(b) the additional information referred to in para. 5.5(2).

5.5 Part 69 (court's power to appoint a receiver) and PD 69 apply to an application for an interim receiving order with the following modifications:

(1) PD 69, para. 2.1, does not apply;

(2) the Director's written evidence must, in addition to the matters required by PD 69, para. 4.1, also state in relation to each item or description of property in respect of which the order is sought:

(a) whether the property is alleged to be:

(i) recoverable property; or

(ii) associated property,

and the facts relied upon in support of that allegation; and

(b) in the case of any associated property:

(i) who is believed to hold the property; or

(ii) if the Director is unable to establish who holds the property, the steps that have been taken to establish their identity; and

(3) the Director's written evidence must always identify a nominee and include the information in PD 69, para. 4.2.

5.6 A draft of the order which is sought must be filed with the application notice. This should if possible also be supplied to the court in an electronic form compatible with the word processing software used by the court.

Property Freezing Order or Interim Receiving Order Made before Commencement of Claim for Recovery Order

5A A property freezing order or interim receiving order which is made before a claim for a recovery order has been commenced shall:

(1) specify a period within which the Director must either start the claim or apply for the continuation of the order while he carries out his investigations; and

(2) provide that the order shall be set aside if the Director does not start the claim or apply for its continuation before the end of that period.

Exclusions When Making Property Freezing Order or Interim Receiving Order

5B.1 When the court makes a property freezing order or interim receiving order on an application without notice, it will normally make an initial exclusion from the order for the purpose of enabling the respondent to meet his reasonable legal costs so that he may:

(1) take advice in relation to the order;

(2) prepare a statement of assets in accordance with para. 7A.3; and

(3) if so advised, apply for the order to be varied or set aside.

The total amount specified in the initial exclusion will not normally exceed £3,000.

5B.2 When it makes a property freezing order or interim receiving order before a claim for a recovery order has been commenced, the court may also make an exclusion to enable the respondent to meet his resonable legal costs so that (for example) when the claim is commenced:

(1) he may file an acknowledgment of service and any written evidence on which he intends to rely; or

(2) he may apply for a further exclusion for the purpose of enabling him to meet his reasonable costs of the proceedings.

5B.3 Paragraph 7A contains general provisions about exclusions made for the purpose of enabling a person to meet his reasonable legal costs.

Interim Receiving Order: Application for Directions

6.1 An application for directions as to the exercise of the interim receiver's functions may, under s. 251 of the Act or art. 156 of the Order in Council, be made at any time by:

(1) the interim receiver;

(2) every party to the proceedings; and

(3) any person affected by any action taken by the interim receiver, or who may be affected by any action proposed to be taken by him.

6.2 The application must always be made by application notice, which must be served on:

(1) the interim receiver (unless he is the applicant);

(2) every party to the proceedings; and

(3) any other person who may be interested in the application.

Application to Vary or Set Aside Property Freezing Order or Interim Receiving Order

7.1 An application to vary or set aside a property freezing order or an interim receiving order (including an application for, or relating to, an exclusion from the order) may be made at any time by:

(1) the Director; or

(2) any person affected by the order.

7.2 Unless the court otherwise directs or exceptional circumstances apply, a copy of the application notice must be served on:

(1) every party to the proceedings;
(2) in the case of an application to vary or set aside an interim receiving order, the interim receiver; and
(3) any other person who may be affected by the court's decision.

7.3 The evidence in support of an application for an exclusion from a property freezing order or interim receiving order for the purpose of enabling a person to meet his reasonable legal costs must:
(1) contain full details of the stage or stages in civil recovery proceedings in respect of which the costs in question have been or will be incurred;
(2) include an estimate of the costs which the person has incurred and will incur in relation to each stage to which the application relates, substantially in the form illustrated in Precedent H in the Schedule of Costs Precedents annexed to PD 43–48;
(3) include a statement of assets containing the information set out in para. 7A.3 (unless the person has previously filed such a statement in the same civil recovery proceedings and there has been no material change in the facts set out in that statement);
(4) where the court has previously made an exclusion in respect of any stage to which the application relates, explain why the person's costs will exceed the amount specified in the exclusion for that stage; and
(5) state whether the terms of the exclusion have been agreed with the Director.

Exclusions for the Purpose of Meeting Legal Costs: General Provisions

7A.1 Subject to para. 7A.2, when the court makes an order or gives directions in civil recovery proceedings it will at the same time consider whether it is appropriate to make or vary an exclusion for the purpose of enabling any person affected by the order or directions to meet his reasonable legal costs.

7A.2 The court will not make an exclusion for the purpose of enabling a person to meet his reasonable legal costs, other than an exclusion to meet the costs of taking any of the steps referred to in para. 5B.1, unless that person has made and filed a statement of assets.

7A.3 A statement of assets is a witness statement which sets out all the property which the maker of the statement owns, holds or controls, or in which he has an interest, giving the value, location and details of all such property. Information given in a statement of assets under this practice direction will be used only for the purpose of the civil recovery proceedings.

7A.4 The court:
(1) will not make an exclusion for the purpose of enabling a person to meet his reasonable legal costs (including an initial exclusion under para. 5B.1); and
(2) may set aside any exclusion which it has made for that purpose or reduce any amount specified in such an exclusion,

if it is satisfied that the person has property to which the property freezing order or interim receiving order does not apply from which he may meet those costs.

7A.5 The court will normally refer to a costs judge any question relating to the amount which an exclusion should allow for reasonable legal costs in respect of proceedings or a stage in proceedings.

7A.6 Attention is drawn to s. 245C of the Act and art. 149 of the Order in Council (in relation to exclusions from property freezing orders) and to s. 252 of the Act and art. 157 of the Order in Council (in relation to exclusions from interim receiving orders). An exclusion for the purpose of enabling a person to meet his reasonable legal costs must be made subject to the 'required conditions' specified in part 2 of the Regulations.

7A.7 An exclusion made for the purpose of enabling a person to meet his reasonable legal costs will specify:
(1) the stage or stages in civil recovery proceedings to which it relates;
(2) the maximum amount which may be released in respect of legal costs for each specified stage; and
(3) the total amount which may be released in respect of legal costs pursuant to the exclusion.

7A.8 A person who becomes aware that his legal costs:
(1) in relation to any stage in civil recovery proceedings have exceeded or will exceed the maximum amount specified in the exclusion for that stage; or

(2) in relation to all the stages to which the exclusion relates have exceeded or will exceed the total amount that may be released pursuant to the exclusion,

should apply for a further exclusion or a variation of the existing exclusion as soon as reasonably practicable.

Assessment of Costs Where Recovery Order Is Made

7B.1 Where the court:

(1) makes a recovery order in respect of property which was the subject of a property freezing order or interim receiving order; and

(2) had made an exclusion from the property freezing order or interim receiving order for the purpose of enabling a person to meet his reasonable legal costs,

the recovery order will make provision under s. 266(8A) of the Act or art. 177(10) of the Order in Council (as appropriate) for the payment of those costs.

7B.2 Where the court makes a recovery order which provides for the payment of a person's reasonable legal costs in respect of civil recovery proceedings, it will at the same time order the detailed assessment of those costs. Parts 4 and 5 of the Regulations, Part 47 of the CPR and Section 49A of PD 43–48 apply to a detailed assessment pursuant to such order.

Registers

7C There will be kept in the Central Office of the Supreme Court at the Royal Courts of Justice, under the direction of the Senior Master, a register of external orders which the High Court has ordered to be registered.

III APPLICATIONS UNDER PART 8 OF THE ACT

How to Apply for an Order or Warrant

8.1 An application by the Director for an order or warrant under part 8 of the Act in connection with a civil recovery investigation must be made:

(1) to a High Court judge;

(2) by filing an application notice.

8.2 The application may be made without notice.

Confidentiality of Court Documents

9.1 CPR, r. 5.4, does not apply to an application under part 8 of the Act, and paras 9.2 and 9.3 below have effect in its place.

9.2 When an application is issued, the court file will be marked 'Not for disclosure' and, unless a High Court judge grants permission, the court records relating to the application (including the application notice, documents filed in support, and any order or warrant that is made) will not be made available by the court for any person to inspect or copy, either before or after the hearing of the application.

9.3 An application for permission under para. 9.2 must be made on notice to the Director in accordance with Part 23.

(Rule 23.7(1) requires a copy of the application notice to be served as soon as practicable after it is filed, and in any event at least three days before the court is to deal with the application.)

Application Notice and Evidence

10.1 The application must be supported by written evidence, which must be filed with the application notice.

10.2 The evidence must set out all the matters on which the Director relies in support of the application, including any matters required to be stated by the relevant sections of the Act, and all material facts of which the court should be made aware.

10.3 There must also be filed with the application notice a draft of the order sought. This should if possible also be supplied to the court on disk in a form compatible with the word processing software used by the court.

Hearing of the Application

11.1 The application will be heard and determined in private, unless the judge hearing it directs otherwise.

Variation or Discharge of Order or Warrant

12.1 An application to vary or discharge an order or warrant may be made by:
(1) the Director; or
(2) any person affected by the order or warrant.

12.2 An application under para. 12.1 to stop an order or warrant from being executed must be made immediately upon it being served.

12.3 A person applying to vary or discharge a warrant must first inform the Director that he is making the application.

12.4 The application should be made to the judge who made the order or issued the warrant or, if he is not available, to another High Court judge.

IV FURTHER PROVISIONS ABOUT SPECIFIC APPLICATIONS UNDER PART 8 OF THE ACT

Production Order

13.1 The application notice must name as a respondent the person believed to be in possession or control of the material in relation to which a production order is sought.

13.2 The application notice must specify:
(1) whether the application is for an order under para. (a) or (b) of s. 345(4) of the Act;
(2) the material, or description of material, in relation to which the order is sought; and
(3) the person who is believed to be in possession or control of the material.

13.3 An application under s. 347 of the Act for an order to grant entry may be made either:
(1) together with an application for a production order; or
(2) by separate application, after a production order has been made.

13.4 An application notice for an order to grant entry must:
(1) specify the premises in relation to which the order is sought; and
(2) be supported by written evidence explaining why the order is needed.

13.5 A production order, or an order to grant entry, must contain a statement of the right of any person affected by the order to apply to vary or discharge the order.

Search and Seizure Warrant

14.1 The application notice should name as respondent the occupier of the premises to be subject to the warrant, if known.

14.2 The evidence in support of the application must state:
(1) the matters relied on by the Director to show that one of the requirements in s. 352(6) of the Act for the issue of a warrant is satisfied;
(2) details of the premises to be subject to the warrant, and of the possible occupier or occupiers of those premises;
(3) the name and position of the member of the staff of the Agency who it is intended will execute the warrant.

14.3 There must be filed with the application notice drafts of:
(1) the warrant; and
(2) a written undertaking by the person who is to execute the warrant to comply with para. 13.8 of this practice direction.

14.4 A search and seizure warrant must:
(1) specify the statutory power under which it is issued and, unless the court orders otherwise, give an indication of the nature of the investigation in respect of which it is issued;
(2) state the address or other identification of the premises to be subject to the warrant;
(3) state the name of the member of staff of the Agency who is authorised to execute the warrant;

(4) set out the action which the warrant authorises the person executing it to take under the relevant sections of the Act;
(5) give the date on which the warrant is issued;
(6) include a statement that the warrant continues in force until the end of the period of one month beginning with the day on which it is issued;
(7) contain a statement of the right of any person affected by the order to apply to discharge or vary the order.

14.5 An example of a search and seizure warrant is annexed to this practice direction. This example may be modified as appropriate in any particular case.

14.6 CPR, r. 40.2, applies to a search and seizure warrant.
(Rule 40.2 requires every judgment or order to state the name and judicial title of the person making it, to bear the date on which it is given or made, and to be sealed by the court.)

14.7 Upon the issue of a warrant the court will provide to the Director:
(1) the sealed warrant; and
(2) a copy of it for service on the occupier or person in charge of the premises subject to the warrant.

14.8 A person attending premises to execute a warrant must, if the premises are occupied produce the warrant on arrival at the premises, and as soon as possible thereafter personally serve a copy of the warrant and an explanatory notice on the occupier or the person appearing to him to be in charge of the premises.

14.9 The person executing the warrant must also comply with any order which the court may make for service of any other documents relating to the application.

Disclosure Order

15.1 The application notice should normally name as respondents the persons on whom the Director intends to serve notices under the disclosure order sought.

15.2 A disclosure order must:
(1) give an indication of the nature of the investigation for the purposes of which the order is made;
(2) set out the action which the order authorises the Director to take in accordance with s. 357(4) of the Act;
(3) contain a statement of:
(a) the offences relating to disclosure orders under s. 359 of the Act; and
(b) the right of any person affected by the order to apply to discharge or vary the order.

15.3 Where, pursuant to a disclosure order, the Director gives to any person a notice under s. 357(4) of the Act, he must also at the same time serve on that person a copy of the disclosure order.

Customer Information Order

16.1 The application notice should normally (unless it is impracticable to do so because they are too numerous) name as respondents the financial institution or institutions to which it is proposed that an order should apply.

16.2 A customer information order must:
(1) specify the financial institution, or description of financial institutions, to which it applies;
(2) state the name of the person in relation to whom customer information is to be given, and any other details to identify that person;
(3) contain a statement of:
(a) the offences relating to disclosure orders under s. 366 of the Act; and
(b) the right of any person affected by the order to apply to discharge or vary the order.

16.3 Where, pursuant to a customer information order, the Director gives to a financial institution a notice to provide customer information, he must also at the same time serve a copy of the order on that institution.

Account Monitoring Order

17.1 The application notice must name as a respondent the financial institution against which an account monitoring order is sought.

17.2 The application notice must:

(1) state the matters required by s. 370(2) and (3) of the Act; and
(2) give details of:
(a) the person whose account or accounts the application relates to;
(b) each account or description of accounts in relation to which the order is sought, including if known the number of each account and the branch at which it is held;
(c) the information sought about the account or accounts;
(d) the period for which the order is sought;
(e) the manner in which, and the frequency with which, it is proposed that the financial institution should provide account information during that period.

17.3 An account monitoring order must contain a statement of the right of any person affected by the order to apply to vary or discharge the order.

[ANNEX

The annex, which contains an example of a search and seizure warrant, is on the CD-ROM version of *Blackstone's Civil Practice*. Click on the title of the annex to open it.]

Practice Direction — Competition Law — Claims Relating to the Application of Articles 81 and 82 of the EC Treaty and Chapters I and II of the Competition Act 1998

Scope and Interpretation

1.1 This practice direction applies to any claim relating to the application of:
(a) art. 81 or art. 82 of the Treaty establishing the European Community; or
(b) chapter I or chapter II of part I of the Competition Act 1998.

1.2 In this practice direction:
(a) 'the Act' means the Competition Act 1998;
(b) 'the Commission' means the European Commission;
(c) 'the Competition Regulation' means Council Regulation (EC) No. 1/2003 of 16 December 2002 on the implementation of the rules on competition laid down in arts 81 and 82 of the Treaty;
(d) 'national competition authority' means:
(i) the Office of Fair Trading; and
(ii) any other person or body designated pursuant to art. 35 of the Competition Regulation as a national competition authority of the United Kingdom;
(e) 'the Treaty' means the Treaty establishing the European Community.

Venue

2.1 A claim to which this practice direction applies:
(a) must be commenced in the High Court at the Royal Courts of Justice; and
(b) will be assigned to the Chancery Division, unless it comes within the scope of r. 58.1(2), in which case it will be assigned to the Commercial Court of the Queen's Bench Division.

2.2 Any party whose statement of case raises an issue relating to the application of art. 81 or 82 of the Treaty, or chapter I or II of part I of the Act, must:
(a) state that fact in his statement of case; and
(b) apply for the proceedings to be transferred to the Chancery Division at the Royal Courts of Justice, if they have not been commenced there, or in the Commercial or Admiralty Courts; or
(c) apply for the transfer of the proceedings to the Commercial Court, in accordance with rr. 58.4(2) and 30.5(3). If such application is refused, the proceedings must be transferred to the Chancery Division of the High Court at the Royal Courts of Justice.

2.3 Rule 30.8 provides that where proceedings are taking place in the Queen's Bench Division (other than proceedings in the Commercial or Admiralty Courts), a district registry of the High Court or a county court, the court must transfer the proceedings to the Chancery Division at the Royal Courts of Justice if the statement of case raises an issue relating to the application of art. 81 or 82, or chapter I or II. However, if any such proceedings which have been commenced in the Queen's Bench Division or a Mercantile Court fall within the scope of r. 58.1(2), any party to those proceedings may apply for the transfer of the proceedings to the Commercial Court, in accordance with rr. 58.4(2) and 30.5(3). If the application is refused, the proceedings must be transferred to the Chancery Division of the High Court at the Royal Courts of Justice.

2.4 Where proceedings are commenced in or transferred to the Chancery Division at the Royal Courts of Justice in accordance with this paragraph, that court may transfer the proceedings or any part of the proceedings to another court if:
(a) the issue relating to the application of art. 81 or 82, or chapter I or II, has been resolved; or
(b) the judge considers that the proceedings or part of the proceedings to be transferred does not involve any issue relating to the application of art. 81 or 82, or chapter I or II.

(Rule 30.3 sets out the matters to which the court must have regard when considering whether to make a transfer order.)

Notice of Proceedings

3. Any party whose statement of case raises or deals with an issue relating to the application of art. 81 or 82, or chapter I or II, must serve a copy of the statement of case on the Office of Fair Trading at the same time as it is served on the other parties to the claim (addressed to the Director of Competition Policy Coordination, Office of Fair Trading, Fleetbank House, 2–6 Salisbury Square, London EC4Y 8JX).

Case Management

4.1 Attention is drawn to the provisions of art. 15.3 of the Competition Regulation (cooperation with national courts), which entitles competition authorities and the Commission to submit written observations to national courts on issues relating to the application of art. 81 or 82 and, with the permission of the court in question, to submit oral observations to the court.

4.1A A national competition authority may also make written observations to the court, or apply for permission to make oral observations, on issues relating to the application of chapter I or II.

4.2 If a national competition authority or the Commission intends to make written observations to the court, it must give notice of its intention to do so by letter to Chancery Chambers at the Royal Courts of Justice (including the claim number and addressed to the Court Manager, Room TM 6.06, Royal Courts of Justice, Strand, London WC2A 2LL) at the earliest reasonable opportunity.

4.3 An application by a national competition authority or the Commission for permission to make oral representations at the hearing of a claim must be made by letter to Chancery Chambers (including the claim number and addressed to the Court Manager, Room TM 6.06, Royal Courts of Justice, Strand, London WC2A 2LL) at the earliest reasonable opportunity, identifying the claim and indicating why the applicant wishes to make oral representations.

4.4 If a national competition authority or the Commission files a notice under para. 4.2 or an application under para. 4.3, it must at the same time serve a copy of the notice or application on every party to the claim.

4.5 Any request by a national competition authority or the Commission for the court to send it any documents relating to a claim should be made at the same time as filing a notice under para. 4.2 or an application under para. 4.3.

4.6 Where the court receives a notice under para. 4.2 it may give case management directions to the national competition authority or the Commission, including directions about the date by which any written observations are to be filed.

4.7 The court will serve on every party to the claim a copy of any directions given or order made:
(a) on an application under para. 4.3; or
(b) under para. 4.6.

4.8 In any claim to which this practice direction applies, the court shall direct a pre-trial review to take place shortly before the trial, if possible before the judge who will be conducting the trial.

Avoidance of Conflict with Commission Decisions

5.1 In relation to claims which raise an issue relating to the application of art. 81 or 82 of the Treaty, attention is drawn to the provisions of art. 16 of the Competition Regulation (uniform application of Community competition law).

5.2 Every party to such a claim, and any national competition authority which has been served with a copy of a party's statement of case, is under a duty to notify the court at any stage of the proceedings if they are aware that:
(a) the Commission has adopted, or is contemplating adopting, a decision in relation to proceedings which it has initiated; and
(b) the decision referred to in (a) above has or would have legal effects in relation to the particular agreement, decision or practice in issue before the court.

5.3 Where the court is aware that the Commission is contemplating adopting a decision as mentioned in para. 5.2(a), it shall consider whether to stay the claim pending the Commission's decision.

Judgments

6. Where any judgment is given which decides on the application of art. 81 or art. 82 of the Treaty, the judge shall direct that a copy of the transcript of the judgment shall be sent to the Commission.

   Judgments may be sent to the Commission electronically to comp-amicus@cec.eu.int or by post to the European Commission: DG Competition, B-1049, Brussels.

Queen's Bench Masters' Practice Direction (11) — Claims, Judgments and Enforcement of Judgments in Foreign Currency

[*This practice direction is still in force, to the extent that it has not been superseded by the CPR and practice directions (see 61.16). The passages in square brackets have been reworded editorially to reflect changes in terminology and procedure made by the CPR.*]

1 Subject to any order or direction which the court may make or give in any particular case, the following practice shall be followed in relation to the making of claims and the enforcement of judgments expressed in a foreign currency.

2 [*Deals with the statement of value to be endorsed on the claim form. Superseded by PD 16, para. 9.1.*]

Pleading Claims in Foreign Currency

3 Where the [claimant] seeks to obtain a judgment expressed in a foreign currency, he should expressly state in his [claim form], whether [it includes particulars] of [claim] or not, that he makes his claim for payment in a specified foreign currency and unless the facts themselves clearly show this, he should plead the facts relied on to support such a claim in his [particulars] of claim. (See *Federal Commerce and Navigation Co. Ltd v Tradax Export SA* [1977] QB 324.)

Default Judgment for Debts or [Claims for Specified Amounts] in Foreign Currency

4 [*Wording of the judgment is now to be found in PD 40B, para. 10.*]

[Summary] Judgment

5 [*Wording of the judgment is now to be found in PD 40B, para. 10.*] The amount of the fixed costs will be calculated on the sterling equivalent of the foreign currency claimed as [stated in the claim form], unless the court orders otherwise.

6 [*Revoked 26 June 1991.*]

Payment of Foreign Currency into Court in Satisfaction

7 [*Superseded by PD 36, paras 9.1 to 9.4.*]

Orders for Conditional Payment of Foreign Currency into Court

8 Where the court makes a conditional order for payment of money into court, e.g., when [making a conditional order] on an application for summary judgment under [Part 24], or when setting aside a default judgment or granting an adjournment of [a case management hearing] or the trial or hearing of [a claim] or making any other order conditional upon payment of money into court, the court may order that such monies be paid into court in a foreign currency, and the court may further order that such money should be placed in a foreign currency account and if practicable should be placed in such an account which is an interest-bearing account.

Entry of Judgment in Foreign Currency

9 [*Wording of the judgment is now to be found in PD 40B, para. 10.*]

Interest on Judgment Debt in Foreign Currency

10 A judgment entered in foreign currency will carry the statutory rate of interest on the amount of the judgment in foreign currency and such interest will be added to the amount of the judgment itself for the purposes of enforcement of the judgment.

Enforcement of Judgment Debt in Foreign Currency by Writ of Fi. Fa.

11 (a) Where the [judgment creditor] desires to proceed to enforce a judgment expressed in foreign currency by the issue of a writ of fieri facias, the praecipe for the issue of the writ must first

be endorsed and signed by or on behalf of the solicitor for the [judgment creditor] or by the [judgment creditor] if he is acting in person with the following certificate:

Sterling equivalent of judgment

I / We certify that the rate current in London for the purpose of (*state the unit of foreign currency in which the judgment is expressed*) at the close of business on the day of 200 (*being the date nearest to or most nearly preceding the date of the issue of the writ of fi. fa.*) was to the £ sterling and at this rate the sum of (*state the amount of the judgment debt in foreign currency*) amounts to £ .

Dated the day of 200 .

Signed

(Solicitor for the [judgment debtor]).

(b) The amount so certified will then be entered in the writ of fi. fa. by adapting [form No. 53, writ of fieri facias] to meet the circumstances of the case but substituting the following recital:

Whereas in the above-named [claim] it was the day of 200 adjudged (or ordered) that the defendant CD do pay the [claimant] AB (*state the sum of the foreign currency for which judgment was entered*) or the sterling equivalent at the time of payment, and whereas the sterling equivalent at the date of issue of this writ is £ as appears by the certificate endorsed and signed by or on behalf of the [judgment creditor] on the praecipe for the issue of this writ.

Enforcement of Judgment Debt in Foreign Currency by [Third Party Debt] Proceedings

12 (a) Where the [judgment creditor] desires to proceed to enforce a judgment in foreign currency by [third party debt] proceedings, the [written evidence] made in support of an application for an order under [CPR, r. 72.2] must contain words to the following effect:

The rate current in London for the purpose of (*state the amount of the judgment in foreign currency*) at the close of business on the day of 200 (*being the date nearest to or most nearly preceding the [signing of the written evidence]*) was to the £ sterling, and at this rate the sum of (*state the amount of the judgment debt in foreign currency*) amounts to £ sterling. I have ascertained the above information (*state the source of the information*) and [believe] the same to be true.

The master will then make an [interim order] for the sterling equivalent of the judgment debt as so verified.

(b) Where the [judgment creditor] desires to attach a debt due or accruing due to the defendant within the jurisdiction in the unit of foreign currency in which the judgment debt is itself expressed, the [written evidence] made in support of an application for an order under [r. 72.2] must state all the relevant facts relied on and in such event the master may make the order to attach such debt due or accruing due in that foreign currency.

[Third Party Debt] Proceedings Where the Judgment Debt Is in Sterling and the Debt to Be [Attached Is] in Foreign Currency

13 For the procedure to be followed see *Choice Investments Ltd v Jeromnimon* [1981] QB 149.

Enforcement of Judgment Debt in Foreign Currency by Other Modes of Enforcement

14 Where the [judgment creditor] desires to proceed to enforce a judgment expressed in a foreign currency by other means of enforcement, e.g. by obtaining an order imposing a charge on land or interest in land under [CPR, r. 73.2], or by obtaining an order imposing a charge on securities under [CPR, r. 73.6], or some other similar order or by obtaining an order for the appointment of a receiver by way of equitable execution, under [CPR, r. 69.2], the [written evidence] made in respect of any such application shall contain words similar to those set out in para. 12(a) above. The master will then make an order for the sterling equivalent of the judgment expressed in foreign currency as so verified by such [written evidence].

15 These directions are issued with the concurrence of the Chief Chancery Master acting on the authority of the Vice-Chancellor so far as they apply to the practice in the Chancery Division, and of the Senior District Judge of the Family Division so far as they apply to the practice in that Division.

16 [*Superseded by the Insolvency Rules 1986 (SI 1986/1925), r. 4.91.*]

Appendix 3 Pre-action Protocols

Each protocol begins with a list of its contents

Practice Direction — Protocols

GENERAL

1.1 This practice direction applies to the pre-action protocols which have been approved by the Head of Civil Justice.

1.2 The pre-action protocols which have been approved are set out in para. 5.1. Other pre-action protocols may subsequently be added.

1.3 Pre-action protocols outline the steps parties should take to seek information from and to provide information to each other about a prospective legal claim.

1.4 The objectives of pre-action protocols are:

(1) to encourage the exchange of early and full information about the prospective legal claim,

(2) to enable parties to avoid litigation by agreeing a settlement of the claim before the commencement of proceedings,

(3) to support the efficient management of proceedings where litigation cannot be avoided.

COMPLIANCE WITH PROTOCOLS

2.1 The Civil Procedure Rules enable the court to take into account compliance or non-compliance with an applicable protocol when giving directions for the management of proceedings (see rr. 3.1(4) and (5) and 3.9(e)) and when making orders for costs (see r. 44.3(5)(a)).

2.2 The court will expect all parties to have complied in substance with the terms of an approved protocol.

2.3 If, in the opinion of the court, non-compliance has led to the commencement of proceedings which might otherwise not have needed to be commenced, or has led to costs being incurred in the proceedings that might otherwise not have been incurred, the orders the court may make include:

(1) an order that the party at fault pay the costs of the proceedings, or part of those costs, of the other party or parties;

(2) an order that the party at fault pay those costs on an indemnity basis;

(3) if the party at fault is a claimant in whose favour an order for the payment of damages or some specified sum is subsequently made, an order depriving that party of interest on such sum and in respect of such period as may be specified, and/or awarding interest at a lower rate than that at which interest would otherwise have been awarded;

(4) if the party at fault is a defendant and an order for the payment of damages or some specified sum is subsequently made in favour of the claimant, an order awarding interest on such sum and in respect of such period as may be specified at a higher rate, not exceeding 10 per cent above base rate (cf. r. 36.21(2)), than the rate at which interest would otherwise have been awarded.

2.4 The court will exercise its powers under paras 2.1 and 2.3 with the object of placing the innocent party in no worse a position than he would have been in if the protocol had been complied with.

3.1 A claimant may be found to have failed to comply with a protocol by, for example:

(a) not having provided sufficient information to the defendant, or

(b) not having followed the procedure required by the protocol to be followed (e.g. not having followed the medical expert instruction procedure set out in the Personal Injury Protocol).

3.2 A defendant may be found to have failed to comply with a protocol by, for example:

(a) not making a preliminary response to the letter of claim within the time fixed for that purpose by the relevant protocol (21 days under the Personal Injury Protocol, 14 days under the Clinical Negligence Protocol),

(b) not making a full response within the time fixed for that purpose by the relevant protocol (three months of the letter of claim under the Clinical Negligence Protocol, three months from the date of acknowledgment of the letter of claim under the Personal Injury Protocol),

(c) not disclosing documents required to be disclosed by the relevant protocol.

3.3 The court is likely to treat this practice direction as indicating the normal, reasonable way of dealing with disputes. If proceedings are issued and parties have not complied with this practice direction or a specific protocol, it will be for the court to decide whether sanctions should be applied.

3.4 The court is not likely to be concerned with minor infringements of the practice direction or protocols. The court is likely to look at the effect of non-compliance on the other party when deciding whether to impose sanctions.

3.5 This practice direction does not alter the statutory time limits for starting court proceedings. A claimant is required to start proceedings within those time limits and to adhere to subsequent time limits required by the rules or ordered by the court. If proceedings are for any reason started before the parties have followed the procedures in this practice direction, the parties are encouraged to agree to apply to the court for a stay of the proceedings while they follow the practice direction.

PRE-ACTION BEHAVIOUR IN OTHER CASES

4.1 In cases not covered by any approved protocol, the court will expect the parties, in accordance with the overriding objective and the matters referred to in r. 1.1(2)(a), (b) and (c), to act reasonably in exchanging information and documents relevant to the claim and generally in trying to avoid the necessity for the start of proceedings.

4.2 Parties to a potential dispute should follow a reasonable procedure, suitable to their particular circumstances, which is intended to avoid litigation. The procedure should not be regarded as a prelude to inevitable litigation. It should normally include:

(a) the claimant writing to give details of the claim;
(b) the defendant acknowledging the claim letter promptly;
(c) the defendant giving within a reasonable time a detailed written response; and
(d) the parties conducting genuine and reasonable negotiations with a view to settling the claim economically and without court proceedings.

4.3 The claimant's letter should:

(a) give sufficient concise details to enable the recipient to understand and investigate the claim without extensive further information;
(b) enclose copies of the essential documents which the claimant relies on;
(c) ask for a prompt acknowledgment of the letter, followed by a full written response within a reasonable stated period;

(For many claims, a normal reasonable period for a full response may be one month.)

(d) state whether court proceedings will be issued if the full response is not received within the stated period;
(e) identify and ask for copies of any essential documents, not in his possession, which the claimant wishes to see;
(f) state (if this is so) that the claimant wishes to enter into mediation or another alternative method of dispute resolution; and
(g) draw attention to the court's powers to impose sanctions for failure to comply with this practice direction and, if the recipient is likely to be unrepresented, enclose a copy of this practice direction.

4.4 The defendant should acknowledge the claimant's letter in writing within 21 days of receiving it. The acknowledgment should state when the defendant will give a full written response. If the time for this is longer than the period stated by the claimant, the defendant should give reasons why a longer period is needed.

4.5 The defendant's full written response should as appropriate:

(a) accept the claim in whole or in part and make proposals for settlement; or
(b) state that the claim is not accepted.

If the claim is accepted in part only, the response should make clear which part is accepted and which part is not accepted.

4.6 If the defendant does not accept the claim or part of it, the response should:

(a) give detailed reasons why the claim is not accepted, identifying which of the claimant's contentions are accepted and which are in dispute;
(b) enclose copies of the essential documents which the defendant relies on;
(c) enclose copies of documents asked for by the claimant, or explain why they are not enclosed;

(d) identify and ask for copies of any further essential documents, not in his possession, which the defendant wishes to see; and
(The claimant should provide these within a reasonably short time or explain in writing why he is not doing so.)
(e) state whether the defendant is prepared to enter into mediation or another alternative method of dispute resolution.

4.7 The parties should consider whether some form of alternative dispute resolution procedure would be more suitable than litigation, and if so, endeavour to agree which form to adopt. Both the claimant and defendant may be required by the court to provide evidence that alternative means of resolving their dispute were considered. The courts take the view that litigation should be a last resort, and that claims should not be issued prematurely when a settlement is still actively being explored. Parties are warned that if the protocol is not followed (including this paragraph) then the court must have regard to such conduct when determining costs.

It is not practicable in this protocol to address in detail how the parties might decide which method to adopt to resolve their particular dispute. However, summarised below are some of the options for resolving disputes without litigation:

- Discussion and negotiation.
- Early neutral evaluation by an independent third party (for example, a lawyer experienced in that field or an individual experienced in the subject matter of the claim).
- Mediation — a form of facilitated negotiation assisted by an independent neutral party.

The Legal Services Commission has published a booklet on *Alternatives to Court* (CLS Direct Information Leaflet 23) (www.clsdirect.org.uk/legalhelp/leaflet23.jsp), which lists a number of organisations that provide alternative dispute resolution services.

It is expressly recognised that no party can or should be forced to mediate or enter into any form of ADR.

4.8 Documents disclosed by either party in accordance with this practice direction may not be used for any purpose other than resolving the dispute, unless the other party agrees.

4.9 The resolution of some claims, but by no means all, may need help from an expert. If an expert is needed, the parties should wherever possible and to save expense engage an agreed expert.

4.10 Parties should be aware that, if the matter proceeds to litigation, the court may not allow the use of an expert's report, and that the cost of it is not always recoverable.

INFORMATION ABOUT FUNDING ARRANGEMENTS

4A.1 Where a person enters into a funding arrangement within the meaning of r. 43.2(1)(k) he should inform other potential parties to the claim that he has done so.

4A.2 Paragraph 4A.1 applies to all proceedings whether proceedings to which a pre-action protocol applies or otherwise.
(Rule 44.3B(1)(c) provides that a party may not recover any additional liability for any period in the proceedings during which he failed to provide information about a funding arrangement in accordance with a rule, practice direction or court order)

COMMENCEMENT

5.1 The following table sets out the protocols currently in force, the date they came into force and their date of publication:

Protocol	Coming into force	Publication
Personal Injury	26 April 1999	January 1999
Clinical Negligence	26 April 1999	January 1999
Construction and Engineering Disputes	2 October 2000	September 2000
Defamation	2 October 2000	September 2000
Professional Negligence	16 July 2001	May 2001
Judicial Review	4 March 2002	3 December 2001
Disease and Illness	8 December 2003	September 2003
Housing Disrepair	8 December 2003	September 2003

5.2 The court will take compliance or non-compliance with a relevant protocol into account where the claim was started after the coming into force of that protocol but will not do so where the claim was started before that date.

5.3 Parties in a claim started after a relevant protocol came into force, who have, by work done before that date, achieved the objectives sought to be achieved by certain requirements of that protocol, need not take any further steps to comply with those requirements. They will not be considered to have not complied with the protocol for the purposes of paras 2 and 3.

5.4 Parties in a claim started after a relevant protocol came into force, who have not been able to comply with any particular requirements of that protocol because the period of time between the publication date and the date of coming into force was too short, will not be considered to have not complied with the protocol for the purposes of paras 2 and 3.

Pre-action Protocol for Personal Injury Claims

1 INTRODUCTION

1.1 Lord Woolf in his final Access to Justice Report of July 1996 recommended the development of pre-action protocols:

> To build on and increase the benefits of early but well informed settlement which genuinely satisfy both parties to dispute.

1.2 The aims of pre-action protocols are:
- more pre-action contact between the parties
- better and earlier exchange of information
- better pre-action investigation by both sides
- to put the parties in a position where they may be able to settle cases fairly and early without litigation
- to enable proceedings to run to the court's timetable and efficiently, if litigation does become necessary
- to promote the provision of medical or rehabilitation treatment (not just in high-value cases) to address the needs of the claimant.

1.3 The concept of protocols is relevant to a range of initiatives for good litigation and pre-litigation practice, especially:
- predictability in the time needed for steps pre-proceedings
- standardisation of relevant information, including documents to be disclosed.

1.4 The courts will be able to treat the standards set in protocols as the normal reasonable approach to pre-action conduct. If proceedings are issued, it will be for the court to decide whether non-compliance with a protocol should merit adverse consequences. Guidance on the court's likely approach will be given from time to time in practice directions.

1.5 If the court has to consider the question of compliance after proceedings have begun, it will not be concerned with minor infringements, e.g. failure by a short period to provide relevant information. One minor breach will not exempt the 'innocent' party from following the protocol. The court will look at the effect of non-compliance on the other party when deciding whether to impose sanctions.

2 NOTES OF GUIDANCE

2.1 The protocol has been kept deliberately simple to promote ease of use and general acceptability. The notes of guidance which follow relate particularly to issues which arose during the piloting of the protocol.

Scope of the Protocol

2.2 This protocol is intended to apply to all claims which include a claim for personal injury (except those claims covered by the Pre-action Protocol for the Resolution of Clinical Disputes and the Pre-action Protocol for Disease and Illness Claims) and to the entirety of those claims: not only to the personal injury element of a claim which also includes, for instance, property damage.

2.3 This protocol is primarily designed for those road traffic, tripping and slipping and accident at work cases which include an element of personal injury with a value of less than £15,000 which are likely to be allocated to the fast track. This is because time will be of the essence, after proceedings are issued, especially for the defendant, if a case is to be ready for trial within 30 weeks of allocation. Also, proportionality of work and costs to the value of what is in dispute is particularly important in lower-value claims. For some claims within the value 'scope' of the fast track some flexibility in the timescale of the protocol may be necessary; see also para. 3.8.

2.4 However, the 'cards on the table' approach advocated by the protocol is equally appropriate to some higher-value claims. The spirit, if not the letter of the protocol, should still be followed for multi-track type claims. In accordance with the sense of the civil justice reforms, the court will expect to see the spirit of reasonable pre-action behaviour applied in all cases, regardless of the existence of a specific protocol. In particular with regard to personal injury cases worth more than £15,000, with a view to avoiding the necessity of proceedings parties are expected to comply with the protocol as far as possible, e.g. in respect of letters before action, exchanging information and documents and agreeing experts.

2.5 The timetable and the arrangements for disclosing documents and obtaining expert evidence may need to be varied to suit the circumstances of the case. Where one or both parties consider the detail of the protocol is not appropriate to the case, and proceedings are subsequently issued, the court will expect an explanation as to why the protocol has not been followed, or has been varied.

Early Notification

2.6 The claimant's legal representative may wish to notify the defendant and/or his insurer as soon as they know a claim is likely to be made, but before they are able to send a detailed letter of claim, particularly for instance, when the defendant has no or limited knowledge of the incident giving rise to the claim or where the claimant is incurring significant expenditure as a result of the accident which he hopes the defendant might pay for, in whole or in part. If the claimant's representative chooses to do this, it will not start the timetable for responding.

The Letter of Claim

2.7 The specimen letter of claim at Annex A will usually be sent to the individual defendant. In practice, he/she may have no personal financial interest in the financial outcome of the claim/dispute because he/she is insured. Court-imposed sanctions for non-compliance with the protocol may be ineffective against an insured. This is why the protocol emphasises the importance of passing the letter of claim to the insurer and the possibility that the insurance cover might be affected. If an insurer receives the letter of claim only after some delay by the insured, it would not be unreasonable for the insurer to ask the claimant for additional time to respond.

2.8 In road traffic cases, the letter of claim should always contain the name and address of the hospital where the claimant was treated and, where available, the claimant's hospital reference number.

2.9 The priority at letter-of-claim stage is for the claimant to provide sufficient information for the defendant to assess liability. Sufficient information should also be provided to enable the defendant to estimate the likely size of the claim.

2.10 Once the claimant has sent the letter of claim no further investigation on liability should normally be carried out until a response is received from the defendant indicating whether liability is disputed.

Reasons for Early Issue

2.11 The protocol recommends that a defendant be given three months to investigate and respond to a claim before proceedings are issued. This may not always be possible, particularly where a claimant only consults a solicitor close to the end of any relevant limitation period. In these circumstances, the claimant's solicitor should give as much notice of the intention to issue proceedings as is practicable and the parties should consider whether the court might be invited to extend time for service of the claimant's supporting documents and for service of any defence, or alternatively, to stay the proceedings while the recommended steps in the protocol are followed.

Status of Letters of Claim and Response

2.12 Letters of claim and response are not intended to have the same status as a statement of case in proceedings. Matters may come to light as a result of investigation after the letter of claim has been sent, or after the defendant has responded, particularly if disclosure of documents takes place outside the recommended three-month period. These circumstances could mean that the 'pleaded' case of one or both parties is presented slightly differently than in the letter of claim and response. It would not be consistent with the spirit of the protocol for a party to 'take a point' on this in the proceedings, provided that there was no obvious intention by the party who changed their position to mislead the other party.

Disclosure of Documents

2.13 The aim of the early disclosure of documents by the defendant is not to encourage 'fishing expeditions' by the claimant, but to promote an early exchange of relevant information to help in clarifying or resolving issues in dispute. The claimant's solicitor can assist by identifying in the letter of claim or in a subsequent letter the particular categories of documents which they consider are relevant.

Experts

2.14 The protocol encourages joint selection of, and access to, experts. The report produced is not a joint report for the purposes of CPR, Part 35. Most frequently this will apply to the medical expert, but on occasions also to liability experts, e.g. engineers. The protocol promotes the practice of the claimant obtaining a medical report, disclosing it to the defendant who then asks questions and/or agrees it and does not obtain his own report. The protocol provides for nomination of the expert by the claimant in personal injury claims because of the early stage of the proceedings and the particular nature of such claims. If proceedings have to be issued, a medical report must be attached to these proceedings. However, if necessary after proceedings have commenced and with the permission of the court, the parties may obtain further expert reports. It would be for the court to decide whether the costs of more than one expert's report should be recoverable.

2.15 Some solicitors choose to obtain medical reports through medical agencies, rather than directly from a specific doctor or hospital. The defendant's prior consent to the action should be sought and, if the defendant so requests, the agency should be asked to provide in advance the names of the doctor(s) whom they are considering instructing.

Alternative Dispute Resolution

2.16 The parties should consider whether some form of alternative dispute resolution procedure would be more suitable than litigation, and if so, endeavour to agree which form to adopt. Both the claimant and defendant may be required by the court ro provide evidence that alternative means of resolving their dispute were considered. The courts take the view that litigation should be a last resort, and that claims should not be issued prematurely when a settlement is still actively being explored. Parties are warned that if the protocol is not followed (including this paragraph) then the court must have regard to such conduct when determining costs.

2.17 It is not practicable in this protocol to address in detail how the parties might decide which method to adopt to resolve their particular dispute. However, summarised below are some of the options for resolving disputes without litigation:

- Discussion and negotiation.
- Early neutral evaluation by an independent third party (for example, a lawyer experienced in the field of personal injury or an individual experienced in the subject matter of the claim).
- Mediation — a form of facilitated negotiation assisted by an independent neutral party.

2.18 The Legal Services Commission has published a booklet on *Alternatives to Court* (CLS Direct Information Leaflet 23) (www.clsdirect.org.uk/legalhelp/leaflet23.jsp), which lists a number of organisations that provide alternative dispute resolution services.

2.19 *It is expressly recognised that no party can or should be forced to mediate or enter into any form of ADR.*

Stocktake

2.20 Where a claim is not resolved when the protocol has been followed, the parties might wish to carry out a 'stocktake' of the issues in dispute, and the evidence that the court is likely to need to decide those issues, before proceedings are started. Where the defendant is insured and the pre-action steps have been conducted by the insurer, the insurer would normally be expected to nominate solicitors to act in the proceedings and the claimant's solicitor is recommended to invite the insurer to nominate solicitors to act in the proceedings and do so 7–14 days before the intended issue date.

3 THE PROTOCOL

Letter of Claim

3.1 The claimant shall send to the proposed defendant two copies of a letter of claim, immediately sufficient information is available to substantiate a realistic claim and before issues of quantum are addressed in detail. One copy of the letter is for the defendants, the second for passing on to his insurers.

3.2 The letter shall contain a **clear summary of the facts** on which the claim is based together with an indication of the **nature of any injuries** suffered and of **any financial loss incurred.** In cases of road traffic accidents, the letter should provide the name and address of the hospital where treatment has been obtained and the claimant's hospital reference number. Where the case is funded by a conditional fee agreement (or collective conditional fee agreement), notification should be given of the existence of the agreement and where appropriate, that there is a success fee and/or insurance premium, although not the level of the success fee or premium.

3.3 Solicitors are recommended to use a **standard format** for such a letter — an example is at Annex A: this can be amended to suit the particular case.

3.4 The letter should ask for **details of the insurer** and that a copy should be sent by the proposed defendant to the insurer where appropriate. If the insurer is known, a copy shall be sent directly to the insurer. Details of the claimant's National Insurance number and date of birth should be supplied to the defendant's insurer once the defendant has responded to the letter of claim and confirmed the identity of the insurer. This information should not be supplied in the letter of claim.

3.5 **Sufficient information** should be given in order to enable the defendant's insurer/solicitor to commence investigations and at least put a broad valuation on the 'risk'.

3.6 The **defendant should reply within 21 calendar days** of the date of posting of the letter identifying the insurer (if any) and, if necessary, identifying specifically any significant omissions from the letter of claim. If there has been no reply by the defendant or insurer within 21 days, the claimant will be entitled to issue proceedings.

3.7 The **defendant**('s insurers) will have a **maximum of three months** from the date of acknowledgment of the claim **to investigate**. No later than the end of that period the defendant (insurer) shall reply, stating whether liability is denied and, if so, giving reasons for their denial of liability including any alternative version of events relied upon.

3.8 Where the accident occurred outside England and Wales and/or where the defendant is outside the jurisdiction, the time periods of 21 days and three months should normally be extended up to 42 days and six months.

3.9 Where **liability is admitted**, the presumption is that the defendant will be bound by this admission for all claims with a total value of up to £15,000. Where the claimant's investigation indicates that the value of the claim has increased to more than £15,000 since the letter of claim, the claimant should notify the defendant as soon as possible.

Documents

3.10 If the **defendant denies liability**, he should enclose with the letter of reply, **documents** in his possession which are **material to the issues** between the parties, and which would be likely to be ordered to be disclosed by the court, either on an application for pre-action disclosure, or on disclosure during proceedings.

3.11 Attached at Annex B are **specimen**, but non-exhaustive, **lists** of documents likely to be material in different types of claim. Where the claimant's investigation of the case is well advanced, the letter of claim could indicate which classes of documents are considered relevant for early disclosure. Alternatively these could be identified at a later stage.

3.12 Where the defendant admits primary liability, but alleges contributory negligence by the claimant, the defendant should give reasons supporting those allegations and disclose those documents from Annex B which are relevant to the issues in dispute. The claimant should respond to the allegations of contributory negligence before proceedings are issued.

3.13 No charge will be made for providing copy documents under the protocol.

Special Damages

3.14 The claimant will send to the defendant as soon as practicable a schedule of special damages with supporting documents, particularly where the defendant has admitted liability.

Experts

3.15 Before any party instructs an expert he should give the other party a list of the **name**(s) of **one or more experts** in the relevant speciality whom he considers are suitable to instruct.

3.16 Where a medical expert is to be instructed the claimant's solicitor will organise access to relevant medical records — see specimen letter of instruction at Annex C.

3.17 **Within 14 days** the other party may indicate **an objection** to one or more of the named experts. The first party should then instruct a mutually acceptable expert (which is not the same as a joint expert). It must be emphasised that if the claimant nominates an expert in the original letter of claim, the defendant has 14 days to object to one or more of the named experts after expiration of the period of 21 days within which he has to reply to the letter of claim, as set out in para. 3.6.

3.18 If the second party objects to all the listed experts, the parties may then instruct **experts of their own choice**. It would be for the court to decide subsequently, if proceedings are issued, whether either party had acted unreasonably.

3.19 If the **second party does not object to an expert nominated**, he shall not be entitled to rely on his own expert evidence within that particular speciality unless:
(a) the first party agrees,
(b) the court so directs, or
(c) the first party's expert report has been amended and the first party is not prepared to disclose the original report.

3.20 **Either party may send to an agreed expert written questions** on the report, relevant to the issues, via the first party's solicitors. The expert should send answers to the questions separately and directly to each party.

3.21 The cost of a report from an agreed expert will usually be paid by the instructing first party: the costs of the expert replying to questions will usually be borne by the party which asks the questions.

4 REHABILITATION

4.1 The claimant or the defendant or both shall consider as early as possible whether the claimant has reasonable needs that could be met by rehabilitation treatment or other measures.

4.2 The parties shall consider, in such cases, how those needs might be addressed. The Rehabilitation Code (which is attached at Annex D) may be helpful in considering how to identify the claimant's needs and how to address the cost of providing for those needs.

4.3 The time limit set out in para. 3.7 of this protocol shall not be shortened, except by consent to allow these issues to be addressed.

4.4 The provision of any report obtained for the purposes of assessment of provision of a party's rehabilitation needs shall not be used in any litigation arising out of the accident, the subject of the claim, save by consent and shall in any event be exempt from the provisions of paras 3.15 to 3.21 inclusive of this protocol.

5 RESOLUTION OF ISSUES

5.1 Where the defendant admits liability in whole or in part, before proceedings are issued, any medical reports obtained under this protocol on which a party relies should be disclosed to the other party. The claimant should delay issuing proceedings for 21 days from disclosure of the report (unless such delay would cause his claim to become time-barred), to enable the parties to consider whether the claim is capable of settlement.

5.2 Part 36 of the CPR permits claimants and defendants to make offers to settle pre-proceedings. Parties should always consider before issuing if it is appropriate to make Part 36 offers. If such an offer is made, the party making the offer must always supply sufficient evidence and/or information to enable the offer to be properly considered.

5.3 Where the defendant has admitted liability, the claimant should send to the defendant schedules of special damages and loss at least 21 days before proceedings are issued (unless that would cause the claimant's claim to become time-barred).

ANNEX A LETTER OF CLAIM

To

Defendant

Dear Sirs

Re: **Claimant's full name**
Claimant's full address
Claimant's Clock or Works Number
Claimant's Employer (*name and address*)

We are instructed by the above named to claim damages in connection with *an accident at work/a road traffic accident/a tripping accident* on day of (*year*) at (*place of accident which must be sufficiently detailed to establish location*)

Please confirm the identity of your insurers. Please note that the insurers will need to see this letter as soon as possible and it may affect your insurance cover and/or the conduct of any subsequent legal proceedings if you do not send this letter to them.

The circumstances of the accident are:
(*brief outline*)

The reason why we are alleging fault is:
(*simple explanation e.g. defective machine, broken ground*)

A description of our client's injuries is as follows:
(*brief outline*)

(In cases of road traffic accidents)

Our client (*state hospital reference number*) received treatment for the injuries at (*name and address of hospital*).

Our client is still suffering from the effects of his/her injury. We invite you to participate with us in addressing his/her immediate needs by use of rehabilitation.

He is employed as (*occupation*) and has had the following time off work (*dates of absence*). His approximate weekly income is (*insert if known*).

If you are our client's employers, please provide us with the usual earnings details which will enable us to calculate his financial loss.

We are obtaining a police report and will let you have a copy of the same upon your undertaking to meet half the fee.

We have also sent a letter of claim to (*name and address*) and a copy of that letter is attached. We understand their insurers are (*name, address and claims number if known*).

At this stage of our enquiries we would expect the documents contained in parts (*insert appropriate parts of standard disclosure list*) to be relevant to this action.

Please note that we have entered into a conditional fee agreement with our client dated in relation to this claim which provides for a success fee within the meaning of section 58(2) of the Courts and Legal Services Act 1990. Our client has taken out an insurance policy with [name of insurance company] of [address of insurance company] to which section 29 of the Access to Justice Act 1999 applies. The policy number is and the policy is dated . [Where the funding arrangement is an insurance policy, the party must state the name and address of the insurer, the policy number and the date of the policy, and must identify the claim or claims to which it relates (including Part 20 claims if any).]

A copy of this letter is attached for you to send to your insurers. Finally we expect an acknowledgment of this letter within 21 days by yourselves or your insurers.

Yours faithfully

ANNEX B PRE-ACTION PERSONAL INJURY PROTOCOL STANDARD DISCLOSURE LISTS

FAST TRACK DISCLOSURE

Road Traffic Accident Cases

Section A

In all cases where liability is at issue—

(i) Documents identifying nature, extent and location of damage to defendant's vehicle where there is any dispute about point of impact.

(ii) MOT certificate where relevant.

(iii) Maintenance records where vehicle defect is alleged or it is alleged by defendant that there was an unforeseen defect which caused or contributed to the accident.

Section B

Accident involving commercial vehicle as potential defendant—

(i) Tachograph charts or entry from individual control book.

(ii) Maintenance and repair records required for operators' licence where vehicle defect is alleged or it is alleged by defendant that there was an unforeseen defect which caused or contributed to the accident.

Section C

Cases against local authorities where highway design defect is alleged—

(i) Documents produced to comply with the Road Traffic Act 1988, s. 39, in respect of the duty designed to promote road safety to include studies into road accidents in the relevant area and documents relating to measures recommended to prevent accidents in the relevant area.

Highway tripping claims

Documents from highway authority for a period of 12 months prior to the accident—

(i) Records of inspection for the relevant stretch of highway.

(ii) Maintenance records including records of independent contractors working in relevant area.

(iii) Records of the minutes of highway authority meetings where maintenance or repair policy has been discussed or decided.

(iv) Records of complaints about the state of highways.

(v) Records of other accidents which have occurred on the relevant stretch of highway.

Workplace claims

(i) Accident book entry.

(ii) First aider report.

(iii) Surgery record.

(iv) Foreman/supervisor accident report.

(v) Safety representatives accident report.

(vi) RIDDOR report to HSE.

(vii) Other communications between defendants and HSE.

(viii) Minutes of Health and Safety Committee meeting(s) where accident/matter considered.

(ix) Report to DSS.

(x) Documents listed above relative to any previous accident/matter identified by the claimant and relied upon as proof of negligence.

(xi) Earnings information where defendant is employer.

Documents produced to comply with requirements of the Management of Health and Safety at Work Regulations 1999 (SI 1999/3242):*

(i) Pre-accident risk assessment required by reg. 3.

(ii) Post-accident reassessment required by reg. 3.

(iii) Accident investigation report prepared in implementing the requirements of regs 5, 7 and 11.

[* The protocol refers to an earlier version of these regulations and has been updated editorially.]

(iv) Health surveillance records in appropriate cases required by reg. 6.
(v) Information provided to employees under reg. 10.
(vi) Documents relating to the employee's health and safety training required by reg. 13.

Workplace Claims — Disclosure Where Specific Regulations Apply

Section A — Workplace (Health, Safety and Welfare) Regulations 1992 (SI 1992/3004)

(i) Repair and maintenance records required by reg. 5.
(ii) Housekeeping records to comply with the requirements of reg. 9.
(iii) Hazard warning signs or notices to comply with reg. 17 (traffic routes).

Section B — Provision and Use of Work Equipment Regulations 1998 (SI 1998/2306)

(i) Manufacturers' specifications and instructions in respect of relevant work equipment establishing its suitability to comply with reg. 4.*
(ii) Maintenance log/maintenance records required to comply with reg. 5.*
(iii) Documents providing information and instructions to employees to comply with reg. 8.
(iv) Documents provided to the employee in respect of training for use to comply with reg. 9.
(v) Any notice, sign or document relied upon as a defence to alleged breaches of regs 14 to 18 dealing with controls and control systems.
(vi) Instruction/training documents issued to comply with the requirements of reg. 22 in so far as it deals with maintenance operations where the machinery is not shut down.
(vii) Copies of markings required to comply with reg. 23.
(viii) Copies of warnings required to comply with reg. 24.

Section C — Personal Protective Equipment at Work Regulations 1992 (SI 1992/2966)

(i) Documents relating to the assessment of the personal protective equipment to comply with reg. 6.
(ii) Documents relating to the maintenance and replacement of personal protective equipment to comply with reg. 7.
(iii) Record of maintenance procedures for personal protective equipment to comply with reg. 7.
(iv) Records of tests and examinations of personal protective equipment to comply with reg. 7.
(v) Documents providing information, instruction and training in relation to the personal protective equipment to comply with reg. 9.
(vi) Instructions for use of personal protective equipment to include the manufacturers' instructions to comply with reg. 10.

Section D — Manual Handling Operations Regulations 1992 (SI 1992/2793)

(i) Manual handling risk assessment carried out to comply with the requirements of reg. 4(1)(b)(i).
(ii) Reassessment carried out post-accident to comply with requirements of reg. 4(1)(b)(i).
(iii) Documents showing the information provided to the employee to give general indications related to the load and precise indications on the weight of the load and the heaviest side of the load if the centre of gravity was not positioned centrally to comply with reg. 4(1)(b)(iii).
(iv) Documents relating to training in respect of manual handling operations and training records.

Section E — Health and Safety (Display Screen Equipment) Regulations 1992 (SI 1992/2792)

(i) Analysis of work stations to assess and reduce risks carried out to comply with the requirements of reg. 2.
(ii) Reassessment of analysis of work stations to assess and reduce risks following development of symptoms by the claimant.

[* Reference corrected editorially.]

(iii) Documents detailing the provision of training including training records to comply with the requirements of reg. 6.
(iv) Documents providing information to employees to comply with the requirements of reg. 7.

Section F — Control of Substances Hazardous to Health Regulations 2002 (SI 2002/2677)*

(i) Risk assessment carried out to comply with the requirements of reg. 6.
(ii) Reviewed risk assessment carried out to comply with the requirements of reg. 6.
(iii) Copy labels from containers used for storage handling and disposal of carcinogens to comply with the requirements of reg. 7(5)(e).
(iv) Warning signs identifying designation of areas and installations which may be contaminated by carcinogens to comply with the requirements of reg. 7(5)(d).
(v) Documents relating to the assessment of the personal protective equipment to comply with reg. 7(3A).
(vi) Documents relating to the maintenance and replacement of personal protective equipment to comply with reg. 7(9).
(vii) Record of maintenance procedures for personal protective equipment to comply with reg. 7(9).
(viii) Records of tests and examinations of personal protective equipment to comply with reg. 7(9).
(ix) Documents providing information, instruction and training in relation to the personal protective equipment to comply with reg. 7(9).
(x) Instructions for use of personal protective equipment to include the manufacturers' instructions to comply with reg. 7(9).
(xi) Air monitoring records for substances assigned a maximum exposure limit or occupational exposure standard to comply with the requirements of reg. 7.
(xii) Maintenance examination and test of control measures records to comply with reg. 9.
(xiii) Monitoring records to comply with the requirements of reg. 10.
(xiv) Health surveillance records to comply with the requirements of reg. 11.
(xv) Documents detailing information, instruction and training including training records for employees to comply with the requirements of reg. 12.
(xvi) Labels and health and safety data sheets supplied to the employers to comply with the Chemicals (Hazard Information and Packaging for Supply) Regulations 1994 (SI 1994/3247).

Section G — Construction (Design and Management) Regulations 1994 (SI 1994/3140) as amended by the Construction (Design and Management) (Amendment) Regulations 2000 (SI 2000/2380)

(i) Notification of a project form (HSE F10) to comply with the requirements of reg. 7.
(ii) Health and safety plan to comply with requirements of reg. 15.
(iii) Health and safety file to comply with the requirements of regs 12 and 14.
(iv) Information and training records provided to comply with the requirements of reg. 17.
(v) Records of advice from and views of persons at work to comply with the requirements of reg. 18.

Section H — Pressure Systems and Transportable Gas Containers Regulations 1989 (SI 1989/2169)†

(i) Information and specimen markings provided to comply with the requirements of reg. 5.
(ii) Written statements specifying the safe operating limits of a system to comply with the requirements of reg. 7.
(iii) Copy of the written scheme of examination required to comply with the requirements of reg. 8.
(iv) Examination records required to comply with the requirements of reg. 9.

[* The protocol refers to an earlier version of these regulations and has been updated editorially.]
[† These regulations were revoked by the Pressure Systems Safety Regulations 2000 (SI 2000/128), reg. 18(2).]

(v) Instructions provided for the use of operator to comply with reg. 11.
(vi) Records kept to comply with the requirements of reg. 13.
(vii) Records kept to comply with the requirements of reg. 22.

Section I — Lifting Operations and Lifting Equipment Regulations 1998 (SI 1998/2307)

(i) Record kept to comply with the requirements of reg. 10.*

Section J — Noise at Work Regulations 1989 (SI 1989/1790)

(i) Any risk assessment records required to comply with the requirements of regs 4 and 5.
(ii) Manufacturers' literature in respect of all ear protection made available to claimant to comply with the requirements of reg. 8.
(iii) All documents provided to the employee for the provision of information to comply with reg. 11.

Section K — Construction (Head Protection) Regulations 1989 (SI 1989/2209)

(i) Pre-accident assessment of head protection required to comply with reg. 3(4).
(ii) Post-accident reassessment required to comply with reg. 3(5).

Section L — Construction (General Provisions) Regulations 1961 (SI 1961/1580)

(i) Report prepared following inspections and examinations of excavations etc. to comply with the requirements of reg. 9.
(ii) Report prepared following inspections and examinations of work in cofferdams and caissons to comply with the requirements of regs 17 and 18.

Section M — Pressure Systems and Transportable Gas Containers Regulations 1989 (SI 1989/2169)†

(i) Information and specimen markings provided to comply with the requirements of reg. 5.
(ii) Written statements specifying the safe operating limits of a system to comply with the requirements of reg. 7.
(iii) Copy of the written scheme of examination required to comply with the requirements of reg. 8.
(iv) Examination records required to comply with the requirements of reg. 9.
(v) Instructions provided for the use of operator to comply with reg. 11.

ANNEX C LETTER OF INSTRUCTION TO MEDICAL EXPERT

Dear Sir,
Re: (*Name and Address*)
D.O.B. —
Telephone No. —
Date of Accident —

We are acting for the above named in connection with injuries received in an accident which occurred on the above date. The main injuries appear to have been (*main injuries*).

We should be obliged if you would examine our Client and let us have a full and detailed report dealing with any relevant pre-accident medical history, the injuries sustained, treatment received and present condition, dealing in particular with the capacity for work and giving a prognosis.

It is central to our assessment of the extent of our Client's injuries to establish the extent and duration of any continuing disability. Accordingly, in the prognosis section we would ask you to specifically comment on any areas of continuing complaint or disability or impact on daily living. If there is such continuing disability you should comment upon the level of suffering

or inconvenience caused and, if you are able, give your view as to when or if the complaint or disability is likely to resolve.

[* Reference corrected editorially.]

[† These regulations were revoked by the Pressure Systems Safety Regulations 2000 (SI 2000/128), reg. 18(2). Section M of annex B repeats section H, omitting items (vi) and (vii).]

Please send our Client an appointment direct for this purpose. Should you be able to offer a cancellation appointment please contact our Client direct. We confirm we will be responsible for your reasonable fees.

We are obtaining the notes and records from our Client's GP and Hospitals attended and will forward them to you when they are to hand/or please request the GP and Hospital records direct and advise that any invoice for the provision of these records should be forwarded to us.

In order to comply with Court Rules we would be grateful if you would insert above your signature a statement that the contents are true to the best of your knowledge and belief.

In order to avoid further correspondence we can confirm that on the evidence we have there is no reason to suspect we may be pursuing a claim against the hospital or its staff.

We look forward to receiving your report within   weeks. If you will not be able to prepare your report within this period please telephone us upon receipt of these instructions.

When acknowledging these instructions it would assist if you could give an estimate as to the likely time scale for the provision of your report and also an indication as to your fee.

Yours faithfully

ANNEX D THE REHABILITATION CODE

Code of Best Practice on Rehabilitation, Early Intervention and Medical Treatment in Personal Injury Claims

The main aim of this Code, first introduced in 1999, is to promote the use of rehabilitation and early intervention in the claims process so that the injured person makes the best and quickest possible medical, social and psychological recovery. This objective applies whatever the severity of the injury sustained by the claimant. The Code provides a framework supported by all the main associations for insurers and personal injury lawyers in the UK, but is neither compulsory nor the only way to approach rehabilitation. The objectives of the Rehabilitation Code will be met whenever the parties cooperate to assess and then provide for the claimant's rehabilitation needs.

1. Introduction

1.1 It is recognised that, in many claims for damages for personal injuries, the claimant's current medical situation, and/or the long-term prognosis, may be improved by appropriate medical treatment, including surgery, being given at the earliest practicable opportunity, rather than waiting until the claim has been settled. Similarly, claims may involve a need for non-medical treatment, such as physiotherapy, counselling, occupational therapy, speech therapy and so forth ('rehabilitation'): again, there is a benefit in these services being provided as early as practicable.

1.2 It is also recognised that (predominantly in cases of serious injury) the claimant's quality of life can be immediately improved by undertaking some basic home adaptations and/or by the provision of aids and equipment and/or appropriate medical treatment as soon as these are needed ('early intervention'), rather than when the claim is finally settled.

1.3 It is further recognised that, where these medical or other issues have been dealt with, there may be employment issues that can be addressed for the benefit of the claimant, to enable the claimant to keep his/her existing job, to obtain alternative suitable employment with the same employer or to retrain for new employment. Again, if these needs are addressed at the proper time, the claimant's quality of life and long-term prospects may be greatly improved.

1.4 Solicitors acting for claimants understand that, taking all these matters into account, they can achieve more for the claimant — by making rehabilitation available — than just the payment of compensation. The insurance industry realises that great benefit may be had in considering making funds available for these purposes.

1.5 The aim of this Rehabilitation Code is therefore to ensure that the claimant's solicitor and the insurer (and the insurer's solicitor or handling agent) both actively consider the use of rehabilitation services and the benefits of an early assessment of the claimant's needs.

The further aim is that both should treat the possibility of improving the claimant's quality of life and their present and long-term physical and mental well-being as issues equally as important as the payment of just, full and proper compensation.

1.6 The report mentioned in section 6 of the Code focuses on the early assessment of the claimant's needs in terms of treatment and/or rehabilitation. The assessment report is not intended to determine the claimant's long-term needs for care or medical treatment, other than by way of general indication and comment.

2. The Claimant's Solicitor's Duty

2.1 It shall be the duty of every claimant's solicitor to consider, from the earliest practicable stage, and in consultation with the claimant and/or the claimant's family, whether it is likely or possible that early intervention, rehabilitation or medical treatment would improve their present and/or long-term physical or mental well-being. This duty is ongoing throughout the life of the case but is of most importance in the early stages.

2.2 It shall be the duty of a claimant's solicitor to consider, with the claimant and/or the claimant's family, whether there is an immediate need for aids, adaptations or other matters that would seek to alleviate problems caused by disability, and then to communicate with the insurer as soon as practicable about any rehabilitation needs, with a view to putting this Code into effect.

2.3 It shall not be the responsibility of the solicitor to decide on the need for treatment or rehabilitation or to arrange such matters without appropriate medical consultation. Such medical consultation should involve the claimant and/or the claimant's family, the claimant's primary care physician and, where appropriate, any other medical practitioner currently treating the claimant.

2.4 Nothing in this Code shall in any way affect the obligations placed on a claimant's solicitor by the Pre-action Protocol for Personal Injury Claims ('the Protocol'). However, it must be appreciated that very early communication with the insurer will enable the matters dealt with here to be addressed more effectively.

2.5 It must be recognised that the insurer will need to receive from the claimant's solicitor sufficient information for the insurer to make a proper decision about the need for intervention, rehabilitation or treatment. To this extent, the claimant's solicitor must comply with the requirements of the Protocol to provide the insurer with full and adequate details of the injuries sustained by the claimant, the nature and extent of any, or any likely, continuing disability and any suggestions that may already have been made concerning rehabilitation and/or early intervention. There is no requirement under the Protocol, or this Code, for the claimant's solicitor to have obtained a full medical report. It is recognised that many cases will be identified for consideration under this Code before medical evidence has actually been commissioned.

3. The Insurer

3.1 It shall be the duty of the insurer to consider, from the earliest practicable stage in any appropriate case, whether it is likely that the claimant will benefit in the immediate, medium or longer term from further medical treatment, rehabilitation or early intervention. This duty is ongoing throughout the life of the case but is of most importance in the early stages.

3.2 If the insurer considers that a particular claim might be suitable for intervention, rehabilitation or treatment, the insurer will communicate this to the claimant's solicitor as soon as practicable.

3.3 On receipt of such communication, the claimant's solicitor will immediately discuss these issues with the claimant and/or the claimant's family pursuant to his duty as set out above and, where appropriate, will seek advice from the claimant's treating physicians/surgeons.

3.4 Nothing in this or any other Code of Practice shall in any way modify the obligations of the insurer under the Protocol to investigate claims rapidly and in any event within three months (except where time is extended by the claimant's solicitor) from the date of the formal claim letter. It is recognised that, although the rehabilitation assessment can be done even where liability investigations are outstanding, it is essential that such investigations proceed with the appropriate speed.

4. Assessment

4.1 Unless the need for intervention, rehabilitation or treatment has already been identified by medical reports obtained and disclosed by either side, the need for and extent of such intervention, rehabilitation or treatment will be considered by means of an independent assessment.

4.2 'Independent assessment' in this context means that the assessment will be carried out by either:

(a) one or more of the treating physicians/surgeons, or

(b) by an agency suitably qualified and/or experienced in such matters, which is financially and managerially independent of the claimant's solicitor's firm and the insurers dealing with the claim.

4.3 It is essential that the process of assessment and recommendation be carried out by those who have an appropriate qualification (to include physiotherapists, occupational therapists, psychologists, psychotherapists and so forth). It would be inappropriate for assessments to be done by someone who does not have a medical or other appropriate qualification. Those doing the assessments should not only have an appropriate qualification but should have experience in treating the type of disability from which the individual claimant suffers.

5. The Assessment Process

5.1 Where possible, the agency to be instructed to provide the assessment should be agreed between the claimant's solicitor and the insurer. The instruction letter will be sent by the claimant's solicitor to the medical agency and a copy of the instruction letter will be sent to the insurer.

5.2 The medical agency will be asked to interview the claimant at home (or in hospital, if the claimant is still in hospital, with a subsequent visit to the claimant's home) and will be asked to produce a report, which covers the following headings:

(1) the injuries sustained by the claimant;

(2) the claimant's present medical condition (medical conditions that do not arise from the accident should also be noted where relevant to the overall picture of the claimant's needs);

(3) the claimant's domestic circumstances (including mobility, accommodation and employment), where relevant;

(4) the injuries/disability in respect of which early intervention or early rehabilitation is suggested;

(5) the type of intervention or treatment envisaged;

(6) the likely cost;

(7) the likely short/medium-term benefit to the claimant.

5.3 The report will not deal with diagnostic criteria, causation issues or long-term care requirements.

6. The Assessment Report

6.1 The reporting agency will, on completion of the report, send copies to both the instructing solicitor and the insurer simultaneously. Both parties will have the right to raise queries on the report, disclosing such correspondence to the other party.

6.2 It is recognised that for this independent assessment report to be of benefit to the parties, it should be prepared and used wholly outside the litigation process. Neither side can therefore rely on its contents in any subsequent litigation. With that strict proviso, to be confirmed in writing by the individual solicitor and insurer if required, the report shall be disclosed to both parties.

6.3 The report, any correspondence relating to it and any notes created by the assessing agency will be covered by legal privilege and will not under any circumstances be disclosed in any legal proceedings. Any notes or documents created in connection with the assessment process will not be disclosed in any litigation, and any person involved in the preparation of the report or involved in the assessment process shall not be a compellable witness at court.

6.4 The provision in para. 6.3 above as to treating the report, etc. as outside the litigation process is limited to the assessment report and any notes relating to it. Once the parties have agreed, following an assessment report, that a particular regime of rehabilitation or treatment should be put in place, the case management of that regime falls outside this Code and para. 6.3 does not therefore apply. Any notes and reports created during the subsequent case management will be governed by the usual principles relating to disclosure of documents and medical records relating to the claimant.

6.5 The insurer will pay for the report within 28 days of receipt.

6.6 The need for any further or subsequent assessment shall be agreed between the claimant's solicitor and the insurer. The provisions of this Code shall apply to such assessments.

7. Recommendations

7.1 When the assessment report is disclosed to the insurer, the insurer will be under a duty to consider the recommendations made and the extent to which funds will be made available to implement all or some of the recommendations. The insurer will not be required to pay for intervention or treatment that is unreasonable in nature, content or cost. The claimant will be under no obligation to undergo intervention, medical investigation or treatment that is unreasonable in all the circumstances of the case.

7.2 Any funds made available shall be treated as an interim payment on account of damages. However, if the funds are provided to enable specific intervention, rehabilitation or treatment to occur, the insurers warrant that they will not, in any legal proceedings connected with the claim, dispute the reasonableness of that treatment nor the agreed cost, provided of course that the claimant has had the recommended treatment.

Pre-action Protocol for the Resolution of Clinical Disputes

EXECUTIVE SUMMARY

1. The Clinical Disputes Forum is a multi-disciplinary body which was formed in 1997, as a result of Lord Woolf's 'Access to Justice' inquiry. One of the aims of the Forum is to find less adversarial and more cost-effective ways of resolving disputes about healthcare and medical treatment. The names and addresses of the Chairman and Secretary of the Forum can be found at Annex E.
2. This protocol is the Forum's first major initiative. It has been drawn up carefully, including extensive consultations with most of the key stakeholders in the medico-legal system.
3. The protocol—
   - encourages a climate of openness when something has 'gone wrong' with a patient's treatment or the patient is dissatisfied with that treatment and/or the outcome. This reflects the new and developing requirements for clinical governance within healthcare;
   - provides **general guidance** on how this more open culture might be achieved when disputes arise;
   - recommends a **timed sequence** of steps for patients and healthcare providers, and their advisers, to follow when a dispute arises. This should facilitate and speed up exchanging relevant information and increase the prospects that disputes can be resolved without resort to legal action.
4. This protocol has been prepared by a working party of the Clinical Disputes Forum. It has the support of the Lord Chancellor's Department, the Department of Health and NHS Executive, the Law Society, the Legal Aid Board and many other key organisations.

1 WHY THIS PROTOCOL?

Mistrust in Healthcare Disputes

1.1 The number of complaints and claims against hospitals, GPs, dentists and private healthcare providers is growing as patients become more prepared to question the treatment they are given, to seek explanations of what happened, and to seek appropriate redress. Patients may require further treatment, an apology, assurances about future action, or compensation. These trends are unlikely to change. The Patients' Charter encourages patients to have high expectations, and a revised NHS Complaints Procedure was implemented in 1996. The civil justice reforms and new Rules of Court should make litigation quicker, more user friendly and less expensive.

1.2 It is clearly in the interests of patients, healthcare professionals and providers that patients' concerns, complaints and claims arising from their treatment are resolved as quickly, efficiently and professionally as possible. A climate of mistrust and lack of openness can seriously damage the patient/clinician relationship, unnecessarily prolong disputes (especially litigation), and reduce the resources available for treating patients. It may also cause additional work for, and lower the morale of, healthcare professionals.

1.3 At present there is often mistrust by both sides. This can mean that patients fail to raise their concerns with the healthcare provider as early as possible. Sometimes patients may pursue a complaint or claim which has little merit, due to a lack of sufficient information and understanding. It can also mean that patients become reluctant, once advice has been taken on a potential claim, to disclose sufficient information to enable the provider to investigate that claim efficiently and, where appropriate, resolve it.

1.4 On the side of the healthcare provider this mistrust can be shown in a reluctance to be honest with patients, a failure to provide prompt clear explanations, especially of adverse outcomes (whether or not there may have been negligence) and a tendency to 'close ranks' once a claim is made.

What Needs to Change

1.5 If that mistrust is to be removed, and a more cooperative culture is to develop—
- healthcare professionals and providers need to adopt a constructive approach to complaints and claims. They should accept that concerned patients are entitled to an explanation and an apology, if warranted, and to appropriate redress in the event of negligence. An overly defensive approach is not in the long-term interest of their main goal: patient care;
- patients should recognise that unintended and/or unfortunate consequences of medical treatment can only be rectified if they are brought to the attention of the healthcare provider as soon as possible.

1.6 A protocol which sets out 'ground rules' for the handling of disputes at their early stages should, if it is to be subscribed to, and followed—
- encourage greater openness between the parties;
- encourage parties to find the most appropriate way of resolving the particular dispute;
- reduce delay and costs;
- reduce the need for litigation.

Why This Protocol Now?

1.7 Lord Woolf in his Access to Justice Report in July 1996, concluded that major causes of costs and delay in medical negligence litigation occur at the pre-action stage. He recommended that patients and their advisers, and healthcare providers, should work more closely together to try to resolve disputes cooperatively, rather than proceed to litigation. He specifically recommended a pre-action protocol for medical negligence cases.

1.8 A fuller summary of Lord Woolf 's recommendations is at Annex D.

Where the Protocol Fits In

1.9 Protocols serve the needs of litigation and pre-litigation practice, especially—
- predictability in the time needed for steps pre-proceedings;
- standardisation of relevant information, including records and documents to be disclosed.

1.10 Building upon Lord Woolf's recommendations, the Lord Chancellor's Department is now promoting the adoption of protocols in specific areas, including medical negligence.

1.11 It is recognised that contexts differ significantly. For example: patients tend to have an ongoing relationship with a GP, more so than with a hospital; clinical staff in the National Health Service are often employees, while those in the private sector may be contractors; providing records quickly may be relatively easy for GPs and dentists, but can be a complicated procedure in a large multi-department hospital. The protocol which follows is intended to be sufficiently broadly based, and flexible, to apply to all aspects of the health service: primary and secondary; public and private sectors.

Enforcement of the Protocol and Sanctions

1.12 The civil justice reforms will be implemented in April 1999. One new set of Court Rules and procedures is replacing the existing rules for both the High Court and county courts. This and the personal injury protocol are being published with the Rules, practice directions and key court forms. The courts will be able to treat the standards set in protocols as the normal reasonable approach to pre-action conduct.

1.13 If proceedings are issued it will be for the court to decide whether non-compliance with a protocol should merit sanctions. Guidance on the court's likely approach will be given from time to time in practice directions.

1.14 If the court has to consider the question of compliance after proceedings have begun it will not be concerned with minor infringements, e.g. failure by a short period to provide relevant information. One minor breach will not entitle the 'innocent' party to abandon following the protocol. The court will look at the effect of non-compliance on the other party when deciding whether to impose sanctions.

2 THE AIMS OF THE PROTOCOL

2.1 The *general* aims of the protocol are—
- to maintain/restore the patient/healthcare provider relationship;
- to resolve as many disputes as possible without litigation.

2.2 The *specific* objectives are—

Openness

- to encourage early communication of the perceived problem between patients and healthcare providers;
- to encourage patients to voice any concerns or dissatisfaction with their treatment as soon as practicable;
- to encourage healthcare providers to develop systems of early reporting and investigation for serious adverse treatment outcomes and to provide full and prompt explanations to dissatisfied patients;
- to ensure that sufficient information is disclosed by both parties to enable each to understand the other's perspective and case, and to encourage early resolution.

Timeliness

- to provide an early opportunity for healthcare providers to identify cases where an investigation is required and to carry out that investigation promptly;
- to encourage primary and private healthcare providers to involve their defence organisations or insurers at an early stage;
- to ensure that all relevant medical records are provided to patients or their appointed representatives on request, to a realistic timetable by any healthcare provider;
- to ensure that relevant records which are not in healthcare providers' possession are made available to them by patients and their advisers at an appropriate stage;
- where a resolution is not achievable to lay the ground to enable litigation to proceed on a reasonable timetable, at a reasonable and proportionate cost and to limit the matters in contention;
- to discourage the prolonged pursuit of unmeritorious claims and the prolonged defence of meritorious claims.

Awareness of Options

- to ensure that patients and healthcare providers are made aware of the available options to pursue and resolve disputes and what each might involve.

2.3 This protocol does not attempt to be prescriptive about a number of related clinical governance issues which will have a bearing on healthcare providers' ability to meet the standards within the protocol. Good clinical governance requires the following to be considered—

(a) **Clinical risk management:** the protocol does not provide any detailed guidance to healthcare providers on clinical risk management or the adoption of risk management systems and procedures. This must be a matter for the NHS Executive, the National Health Service Litigation Authority, individual trusts and providers, including GPs, dentists and the private sector. However, effective co-ordinated, focused clinical risk management strategies and procedures can help in managing risk and in the early identification and investigation of adverse outcomes.

(b) **Adverse outcome reporting:** the protocol does not provide any detailed guidance on which adverse outcomes should trigger an investigation. However, healthcare providers should have in place procedures for such investigations, including recording of statements of key witnesses. These procedures should also cover when and how to inform patients that an adverse outcome has occurred.

(c) **The professional's duty to report:** the protocol does not recommend changes to the codes of conduct of professionals in healthcare, or attempt to impose a specific duty on those professionals to report known adverse outcomes or untoward incidents. Lord Woolf in his final report suggested that the professional bodies might consider this. The General Medical Council is preparing guidance to doctors about their duty to report adverse incidents and to cooperate with inquiries.

3 THE PROTOCOL

3.1 This protocol is not a comprehensive code governing all the steps in clinical disputes. Rather it attempts to set out **a code of good practice** which parties should follow when litigation might be a possibility.

3.2 The **commitments** section of the protocol summarises the guiding principles which healthcare providers and patients and their advisers are invited to endorse when dealing with patient dissatisfaction with treatment and its outcome, and with potential complaints and claims.

3.3 The **steps** section sets out in a more prescriptive form, a recommended sequence of actions to be followed if litigation is a prospect.

Good Practice Commitments

3.4 **Healthcare providers** should—

(i) ensure that **key staff**, including claims and litigation managers, are appropriately trained and have some knowledge of healthcare law, and of complaints procedures and civil litigation practice and procedure;

(ii) develop an approach to **clinical governance** that ensures that clinical practice is delivered to commonly accepted standards and that this is routinely monitored through a system of clinical audit and clinical risk management (particularly adverse outcome investigation);

(iii) set up **adverse outcome reporting systems** in all specialties to record and investigate unexpected serious adverse outcomes as soon as possible. Such systems can enable evidence to be gathered quickly, which makes it easier to provide an accurate explanation of what happened and to defend or settle any subsequent claims;

(iv) use the results of **adverse incidents and complaints positively** as a guide to how to improve services to patients in the future;

(v) ensure **that patients receive clear and comprehensible information** in an accessible form about how to raise their concerns or complaints;

(vi) establish **efficient and effective systems of recording and storing patient records,** notes, diagnostic reports and X-rays, and to retain these in accordance with Department of Health guidance (currently for a minimum of eight years in the case of adults, and all obstetric and paediatric notes for children until they reach the age of 25);

(vii) **advise patients** of a serious adverse outcome and provide on request to the patient or the patient's representative an oral or written explanation of what happened, information on further steps open to the patient, including where appropriate an offer of future treatment to rectify the problem, an apology, changes in procedure which will benefit patients and/or compensation.

3.5 **Patients and their advisers** should—

(i) **report any concerns and dissatisfaction** to the healthcare provider as soon as is reasonable to enable that provider to offer clinical advice where possible, to advise the patient if anything has gone wrong and take appropriate action;

(ii) consider the **full range of options** available following an adverse outcome with which a patient is dissatisfied, including a request for an explanation, a meeting, a complaint, and other appropriate dispute resolution methods (including mediation) and negotiation, not only litigation;

(iii) **inform the healthcare provider when the patient is satisfied** that the matter has been concluded: legal advisers should notify the provider when they are no longer acting for the patient, particularly if proceedings have not started.

Protocol Steps

3.6 The steps of this protocol which follow have been kept deliberately simple. An illustration of the likely sequence of events in a number of healthcare situations is at Annex A.

Obtaining the Health Records

3.7 Any request for records by the **patient** or their adviser should—

- **provide sufficient information** to alert the healthcare provider where an adverse outcome has been serious or had serious consequences;
- be as **specific as possible** about the records which are required.

3.8 Requests for copies of the patient's clinical records should be made using the Law Society and Department of Health approved **standard forms** (enclosed at Annex B), adapted as necessary.

3.9 The copy records should be provided **within 40 days** of the request and for a cost not exceeding the charges permissible under the Access to Health Records Act 1990 (currently a maximum of £10 plus photocopying and postage).

3.10 In the rare circumstances that the healthcare provider is in difficulty in complying with the request within 40 days, the **problem should be explained** quickly and details given of what is being done to resolve it.

3.11 It will not be practicable for healthcare providers to investigate in detail each case when records are requested. But healthcare providers should **adopt a policy on which cases will be investigated** (see paragraph 3.5 on clinical governance and adverse outcome reporting).

3.12 If the healthcare provider fails to provide the health records within 40 days, the patient or their adviser can then apply to the court for an **order for pre-action disclosure**. The new Civil Procedure Rules should make pre-action applications to the court easier. The court will also have the power to impose costs sanctions for unreasonable delay in providing records.

3.13 If either the patient or the healthcare provider considers **additional health records are required from a third party**, in the first instance these should be requested by or through the patient. Third party healthcare providers are expected to cooperate. The Civil Procedure Rules will enable patients and healthcare providers to apply to the court for pre-action disclosure by third parties.

Letter of Claim

3.14 Annex C1 to this protocol provides **a template for the recommended contents of a letter of claim:** the level of detail will need to be varied to suit the particular circumstances.

3.15 If, following the receipt and analysis of the records, and the receipt of any further advice (including from experts if necessary — see Section 4), the patient/adviser decides that there are grounds for a claim, they should then send, as soon as practicable, to the healthcare provider/potential defendant, a **letter of claim.**

3.16 This letter should contain a **clear summary of the facts** on which the claim is based, including the alleged adverse outcome, and the **main allegations of negligence.** It should also describe the **patient's injuries**, and present condition and prognosis. The **financial loss** incurred by the plaintiff should be outlined with an indication of the heads of damage to be claimed and the scale of the loss, unless this is impracticable.

3.17 In more complex cases a **chronology** of the relevant events should be provided, particularly if the patient has been treated by a number of different healthcare providers.

3.18 The letter of claim **should refer to any relevant documents**, including health records, and if possible enclose copies of any of those which will not already be in the potential defendant's possession, e.g. any relevant general practitioner records if the plaintiff 's claim is against a hospital.

3.19 **Sufficient information** must be given to enable the healthcare provider defendant to **commence investigations** and to put an initial valuation on the claim.

3.20 Letters of claim are **not** intended to have the same formal status as a **pleading**, nor should any sanctions necessarily apply if the letter of claim and any subsequent statement of claim in the proceedings differ.

3.21 **Proceedings should not be issued until after three months from the letter of claim**, unless there is a limitation problem and/or the patient's position needs to be protected by early issue.

3.22 The patient or their adviser may want to make an **offer to settle** the claim at this early stage by putting forward an amount of compensation which would be satisfactory (possibly including any costs incurred to date). If an offer to settle is made, generally this should be supported by a medical report which deals with the injuries, condition and prognosis, and by a schedule of loss and supporting documentation. The level of detail necessary will depend on the value of the claim. Medical reports may not be necessary where there is no significant continuing injury, and a detailed schedule may not be necessary in a low value case. The Civil Procedure Rules are expected to set out the legal and procedural requirements for making offers to settle.

The Response

3.23 Attached at Annex C2 is a template for the suggested contents of the **letter of response.**

3.24 The healthcare provider should **acknowledge** the letter of claim **within 14 days of receipt** and should identify who will be dealing with the matter.

3.25 The healthcare provider should, **within three months** of the letter of claim, provide a **reasoned answer**—

- if the **claim is admitted** the healthcare provider should say so in clear terms;
- if only **part of the claim is admitted** the healthcare provider should make clear which issues of breach of duty and/or causation are admitted and which are denied and why;
- if it is intended that any **admissions will be binding;**
- if the claim is denied, this should include specific comments on the allegations of negligence, and if a synopsis or chronology of relevant events has been provided and is disputed, the healthcare provider's version of those events;
- where additional documents are relied upon, e.g. an internal protocol, copies should be provided.

3.26 If the patient has made an offer to settle, the healthcare provider should **respond to that offer** in the response letter, preferably with reasons. The provider may make its own offer to settle at this stage, either as a counter-offer to the patient's, or of its own accord, but should accompany any offer by any supporting medical evidence, and/or by any other evidence in relation to the value of the claim which is in the healthcare provider's possession.

3.27 If the parties reach agreement on liability, but time is needed to resolve the value of the claim, they should aim to agree a reasonable period.

4 EXPERTS

4.1 In clinical negligence disputes **expert opinions** may be needed—

- on breach of duty and causation;
- on the patient's condition and prognosis;
- to assist in valuing aspects of the claim.

4.2 The civil justice reforms and the new **Civil Procedure Rules** will encourage economy in the use of experts and a **less adversarial expert culture.** It is recognised that in clinical negligence disputes, the parties and their advisers will require flexibility in their approach to expert evidence. Decisions on whether experts might be instructed jointly, and on whether reports might be disclosed sequentially or by exchange, should rest with the parties and their advisers. Sharing expert evidence may be appropriate on issues relating to the value of the claim. However, this protocol does not attempt to be prescriptive on issues in relation to expert evidence.

4.3 Obtaining expert evidence will often be an expensive step and may take time, especially in specialised areas of medicine where there are limited numbers of suitable experts. Patients and healthcare providers, and their advisers, will therefore need to consider carefully how best to obtain any necessary expert help quickly and cost-effectively. Assistance with locating a suitable expert is available from a number of sources.

5 ALTERNATIVE DISPUTE RESOLUTION

5.1 The parties should consider whether some form of alternative dispute resolution procedure would be more suitable than litigation, and if so, endeavour to agree which form to adopt. Both the claimant and defendant may be required by the court to provide evidence that alternative means of resolving their dispute were considered. The courts take the view that litigation should be a last resort, and that claims should not be issued prematurely when a settlement is still actively being explored. Parties are warned that if the protocol is not followed (including this paragraph) then the court must have regard to such conduct when determining costs.

5.2 It is not practicable in this protocol to address in detail how the parties might decide which method to adopt to resolve their particular dispute. However, summarised below are some of the options for resolving disputes without litigation:

- Discussion and negotiation. Parties should bear in mind that carefully planned face-to-face meetings may be particularly helpful in exploring further treatment for the patient, in reaching understandings about what happened, and on both parties' positions, in narrowing the issues in dispute and, if the timing is right, in helping to settle the whole matter especially if the patient wants an apology, explanation, or assurances about how other patients will be affected.
- Early neutral evaluation by an independent third party (for example, a lawyer experienced in the field of clinical negligence or an individual experienced in the subject matter of the claim).
- Mediation — a form of facilitated negotiation assisted by an independent neutral party. The Clinical Disputes Forum has published a *Guide to Mediation* which will assist — available on the Clinical Disputes Forum website at www.clinicaldisputesforum.org.uk.
- The **NHS Complaints Procedure** is designed to provide patients with an explanation of what happened and an apology if appropriate. It is not designed to provide compensation for cases of negligence. However, patients might choose to use the procedure if their only, or main, goal is to obtain an explanation, or to obtain more information to help them decide what other action might be appropriate.

5.3 The Legal Services Commission has published a booklet on *Alternatives to Court* (CLS Direct Information Leaflet 23) (www.clsdirect.org.uk/legalhelp/leaflet23.jsp), which lists a number of organisations that provide alternative dispute resolution services.

5.4 *It is expressly recognised that no party can or should be forced to mediate or enter into any form of ADR.*

ANNEX A ILLUSTRATIVE FLOWCHART

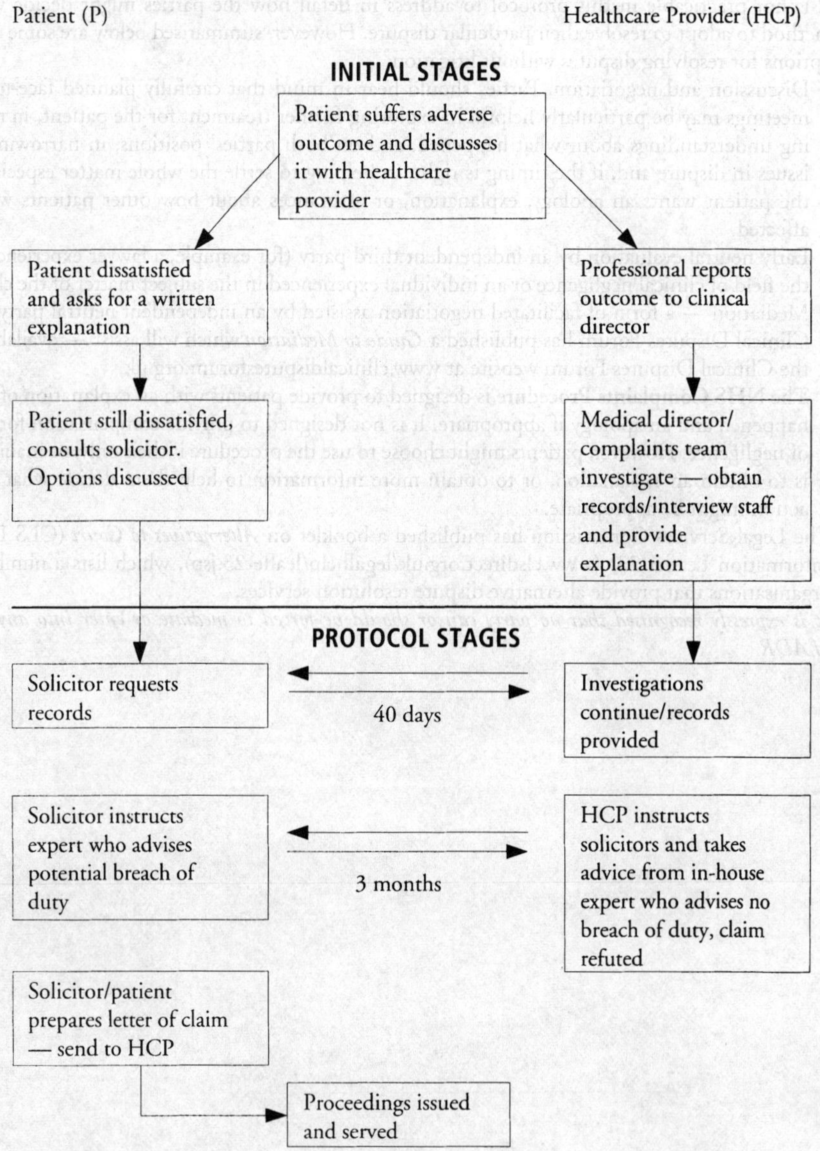

ANNEX B MEDICAL NEGLIGENCE AND PERSONAL INJURY CLAIMS

A PROTOCOL FOR OBTAINING HOSPITAL MEDICAL RECORDS

Application on Behalf of a Patient for Hospital Medical Records for Use When Court Proceedings Are Contemplated

Purpose of the Forms

This application form and response forms have been prepared by a working party of the Law Society's Civil Litigation Committee and approved by the Department of Health for use in NHS and Trust hospitals.

The purpose of the forms is to standardise and streamline the disclosure of medical records to a patient's solicitors, who are investigating pursuing a personal injury claim against a third party, or a medical negligence claim against the hospital to which the application is addressed and/or other hospitals or general practitioners.

Use of the Forms

Use of the forms is entirely voluntary and does not prejudice any party's right under the Access to Health Records Act 1990, the Data Protection Act 1984, or ss. 33 and 34 of the Supreme Court Act 1981. However, it is Department of Health policy that patients be permitted to see what has been written about them, and that healthcare providers should make arrangements to allow patients to see all their records, not only those covered by the Access to Health Records Act 1990. The aim of the forms is to save time and costs for all concerned for the benefit of the patient and the hospital and in the interests of justice. Use of the forms should make it unnecessary in most cases for there to be exchanges of letters or other enquiries. If there is any unusual matter not covered by the form, the patient's solicitor may write a separate letter at the outset.

Charges for Records

The Access to Health Records Act 1990 prescribes a maximum fee of £10. Photocopying and postage costs can be charged in addition. No other charges may be made.

The NHS Executive guidance makes it clear to healthcare providers that 'it is a perfectly proper use' of the 1990 Act to request records in that framework for the purpose of potential or actual litigation, whether against a third party or against the hospital or trust.

The 1990 Act does not permit differential rates of charges to be levied if the application is made by the patient, or by a solicitor on his or her behalf, or whether the response to the application is made by the healthcare provider directly (the medical records manager or a claims manager) or by a solicitor.

The NHS Executive guidance recommends that the same practice should be followed with regard to charges when the records are provided under a voluntary agreement as under the 1990 Act, except that in those circumstances the £10 access fee will not be appropriate.

The NHS Executive also advises—

- that the cost of photocopying may include 'the cost of staff time in making copies' and the costs of running the copier (but not costs of locating and sifting records);
- that the common practice of setting a standard rate for an application or charging an administration fee is not acceptable because there will be cases when this fails to comply with the 1990 Act.

Records: What Might Be Included

X-rays and test results form part of the patient's records. Additional charges for copying X-rays are permissible. If there are large numbers of X-rays, the records officer should check with the patient/solicitor before arranging copying.

Reports on an 'adverse incident' and reports on the patient made for risk management and audit purposes may form part of the records and be disclosable: the exception will be any specific record or report made solely or mainly in connection with an actual or potential claim.

Records: Quality Standards

When copying records healthcare providers should ensure—

1. All documents are legible, and complete, if necessary by photocopying at less than 100% size.
2. Documents larger than A4 in the original, e.g. ITU charts, should be reproduced in A3, or reduced to A4 where this retains readability.
3. Documents are only copied on one side of paper, unless the original is two sided.
4. Documents should not be unnecessarily shuffled or bound and holes should not be made in the copied papers.

Enquiries/Further Information

Any enquiries about the forms should be made initially to the solicitors making the request. Comments on the use and content of the forms should be made to the Secretary, Civil Litigation Committee, The Law Society, 113 Chancery Lane, London WC2A 1PL, telephone (020) 7320 5739, or to the NHS Management Executive, Quarry House, Quarry Hill, Leeds LS2 7UE.

The Law Society

May 1998

Application on Behalf of a Patient for Hospital Medical Records for Use When Court Proceedings Are Contemplated

This should be completed as fully as possible

Insert Hospital Name and Address	TO: Medical Records Officer Hospital

1(a)	Full name of patient (including previous surnames)	
(b)	Address now	
(c)	Address at start of treatment	
(d)	Date of birth (and death, if applicable)	
(e)	Hospital ref. number, if available	
(f)	N.I. number, if available	
2	This application is made because the patient is considering	
	(a) a claim against your hospital as detailed in para. 7 overleaf	YES/NO
	(b) pursuing an action against someone else	YES/NO
3	Department(s) where treatment was received	
4	Name(s) of consultant(s) at your hospital in charge of the treatment	
5	Whether treatment at your hospital was private or NHS, wholly or in part	
6	A description of the treatment received, with approximate dates	
7	If the answer to Q 2(a) is 'Yes' details of (a) the likely nature of the claim	
	(b) grounds for the claim	
	(c) approximate dates of the events involved	
8	If the answer to Q2(b) is 'Yes' insert (a) the names of the proposed defendants	
	(b) whether legal proceedings yet begun	YES/NO
	(c) if appropriate, details of the claim and action number	
9	We confirm we will pay reasonable copying charges	

10	We request prior details of	YES/NO
	(a) photocopying and administration charges for medical records	
	(b) number of and cost of copying X-ray and scan films	YES/NO
11	Any other relevant information, particular requirements, or any particular documents *not* required (e.g. copies of computerised records)	
	Signature of Solicitor	
	Name	
	Address	
	Ref.	
	Telephone Number	
	Fax number	

Please print name beneath each signature.
Signature by child over 12 but under
18 years also requires signature by parent

Signature of patient

Signature of parent or next friend if appropriate

Signature of personal representative where patient has died

First Response to Application for Hospital Records

NAME OF PATIENT Our ref. Your ref.		
1	Date of receipt of patient's application	
2	We intend that copy medical records will be dispatched within 6 weeks of that date	YES/NO
3	We require prepayment of photocopying charges	YES/NO
4	If estimate of photocopying charges requested or prepayment required the amount will be	£ / notified to you
5	The cost of X-ray and scan films will be	£ / notified to you
6	If there is any problem, we shall write to you within those 6 weeks	YES/NO
7	Any other information	
	Please address further correspondence to	
	Signed	
	Direct telephone number	
	Direct fax number	
	Dated	

Second Response Enclosing Patient's Hospital Medical Records

Address Our Ref.
Your Ref.

1	NAME OF PATIENT: We confirm that the enclosed copy medical records are all those within the control of the hospital, relevant to the application which you have made to the best of our knowledge and belief, subject to paras 2–5 below	YES/NO
2	Details of any other documents which have not yet been located	
3	Date by when it is expected that these will be supplied	
4	Details of any records which we are not producing	
5	The reasons for not doing so	
6	An invoice for copying and administration charges is attached	YES/NO
	Signed	
	Date	

ANNEX C TEMPLATES FOR LETTERS OF CLAIM AND RESPONSE

C1 Letter of Claim

Essential Contents

1. **Client's name, address, date of birth, etc.**
2. **Dates of allegedly negligent treatment**
3. **Events giving rise to the claim:**
   - an outline of what happened, including details of other relevant treatments to the client by other healthcare providers.
4. **Allegation of negligence and causal link with injuries:**
   - an outline of the allegations or a more detailed list in a complex case;
   - an outline of the causal link between allegations and the injuries complained of.
5. **The Client's injuries, condition and future prognosis**
6. **Request for clinical records (if not previously provided)**
   - use the Law Society form if appropriate or adapt;
   - specify the records required;
   - if other records are held by other providers, and may be relevant, say so;
   - state what investigations have been carried out to date, e.g. information from client and witnesses, any complaint and the outcome, if any clinical records have been seen or experts advice obtained.
7. **The likely value of the claim**
   - an outline of the main heads of damage, or, in straightforward cases, the details of loss.

Optional information

What investigations have been carried out
An offer to settle without supporting evidence
Suggestions for obtaining expert evidence
Suggestions for meetings, negotiations, discussion or mediation
Possible enclosures
Chronology
Clinical records request form and client's authorisation
Expert report(s)
Schedules of loss and supporting evidence

C2 Letter of Response

Essential Contents

1. Provide **requested records** and invoice for copying:
   - explain if records are incomplete or extensive records are held and ask for further instructions;
   - request additional records from third parties.
2. **Comments on events and/or chronology:**
   - if events are disputed or the healthcare provider has further information or documents on which they wish to rely, these should be provided, e.g. internal protocol;
   - details of any further information needed from the patient or a third party should be provided.
3. **If breach of duty and causation are accepted:**
   - suggestions might be made for resolving the claim and/or requests for further information;
   - a response should be made to any offer to settle.
4. **If breach of duty and/or causation are denied:**
   - a bare denial will not be sufficient. If the healthcare provider has other explanations for what happened, these should be given at least in outline;
   - suggestions might be made for the next steps, e.g. further investigations, obtaining expert evidence, meetings/negotiations or mediation, or an invitation to issue proceedings.

Optional Matters

An offer to settle if the patient has not made one, or a counter offer to the patient's with supporting evidence

Possible enclosures:

Clinical records
Annotated chronology
Expert reports

ANNEX D LORD WOOLF'S RECOMMENDATIONS

1. Lord Woolf in his Access to Justice Report in July 1996, following a detailed review of the problems of medical negligence claims, identified that one of the major sources of **costs and delay** is **at the pre-litigation** stage because—
   (a) Inadequate incident reporting and record keeping in hospitals, and mobility of staff, make it difficult to establish facts, often several years after the event.
   (b) Claimants must incur the cost of an expert in order to establish whether they have a viable claim.
   (c) There is often a long delay before a claim is made.
   (d) Defendants do not have sufficient resources to carry out a full investigation of every incident, and do not consider it worthwhile to start an investigation as soon as they receive a request for records, because many cases do not proceed beyond that stage.
   (e) Patients often give the defendant little or no notice of a firm intention to pursue a claim. Consequently, many incidents are not investigated by the defendants until after proceedings have started.
   (f) Doctors and other clinical staff are traditionally reluctant to admit negligence or apologise to, or negotiate with, claimants for fear of damage to their professional reputations or career prospects.
2. Lord Woolf acknowledged that under the present arrangements **healthcare providers**, faced with possible medical negligence claims, have a number of **practical problems** to contend with—
   (a) Difficulties of finding patients' records and tracing former staff, which can be exacerbated by late notification and by the health care provider's own failure to identify adverse incidents.
   (b) The healthcare provider may have only treated the patient for a limited time or for a specific complaint: the patient's previous history may be relevant but the records may be in the possession of one of several other healthcare providers.
   (c) The large number of potential claims which do not proceed beyond the stage of a request for medical records, or an explanation; and that it is difficult for healthcare providers to investigate fully every case whenever a patient asks to see the records.

ANNEX E HOW TO CONTACT THE FORUM

The Clinical Disputes Forum

Chairman
Dr Alastair Scotland
Medical Director and Chief Officer
National Clinical Assessment Authority
9th Floor, Market Towers
London
SW8 5NQ Telephone: (020) 7273 0850

Secretary
Sarah Leigh
c/o Margaret Dangoor
3 Clydesdale Gardens
Richmond
Surrey
TW10 5EG Telephone: (020) 8408 1012

Pre-action Protocol for Construction and Engineering Disputes

1 INTRODUCTION

1.1 This pre-action protocol applies to all construction and engineering disputes (including professional negligence claims against architects, engineers and quantity surveyors).

Exceptions

1.2 A claimant shall not be required to comply with this protocol before commencing proceedings to the extent that the proposed proceedings (i) are for the enforcement of the decision of an adjudicator to whom a dispute has been referred pursuant to s. 108 of the Housing Grants, Construction and Regeneration Act 1996 ('the 1996 Act'), (ii) include a claim for interim injunctive relief, (iii) will be the subject of a claim for summary judgment pursuant to Part 24 of the Civil Procedure Rules, or (iv) relate to the same or substantially the same issues as have been the subject of recent adjudication under the 1996 Act, or some other formal alternative dispute resolution procedure.

Objectives

1.3 The objectives of this protocol are as set out in PD Protocols, namely:

(i) to encourage the exchange of early and full information about the prospective legal claim;

(ii) to enable parties to avoid litigation by agreeing a settlement of the claim before commencement of proceedings; and

(iii) to support the efficient management of proceedings where litigation cannot be avoided.

Compliance

1.4 If proceedings are commenced, the court will be able to treat the standards set in this protocol as the normal reasonable approach to pre-action conduct. If the court has to consider the question of compliance after proceedings have begun, it will be concerned with substantial compliance and not minor departures, e.g. failure by a short period to provide relevant information. Minor departures will not exempt the 'innocent' party from following the protocol. The court will look at the effect of non-compliance on the other party when deciding whether to impose sanctions. For sanctions generally, see PD Protocols, para. 2 'Compliance with Protocols'.

2 OVERVIEW OF PROTOCOL

General Aim

2 The general aim of this protocol is to ensure that before court proceedings commence:

(i) the claimant and the defendant have provided sufficient information for each party to know the nature of the other's case;

(ii) each party has had an opportunity to consider the other's case, and to accept or reject all or any part of the case made against him at the earliest possible stage;

(iii) there is more pre-action contact between the parties;

(iv) better and earlier exchange of information occurs;

(v) there is better pre-action investigation by the parties;

(vi) the parties have met formally on at least one occasion with a view to

Pre-action Protocols

- defining and agreeing the issues between them; and
- exploring possible ways by which the claim may be resolved;

(vii) the parties are in a position where they may be able to settle cases early and fairly without recourse to litigation; and

(viii) proceedings will be conducted efficiently if litigation does become necessary.

3 THE LETTER OF CLAIM

3.1 Prior to commencing proceedings, the claimant or his solicitor shall send to each proposed defendant (if appropriate to his registered address) a copy of a letter of claim which shall contain the following information:

(i) the claimant's full name and address;

(ii) the full name and address of each proposed defendant;

(iii) a clear summary of the facts on which each claim is based;

(iv) the basis on which each claim is made, identifying the principal contractual terms and statutory provisions relied on;

(v) the nature of the relief claimed: if damages are claimed, a breakdown showing how the damages have been quantified; if a sum is claimed pursuant to a contract, how it has been calculated; if an extension of time is claimed, the period claimed;

(vi) where a claim has been made previously and rejected by a defendant, and the claimant is able to identify the reason(s) for such rejection, the claimant's grounds of belief as to why the claim was wrongly rejected;

(vii) the names of any experts already instructed by the claimant on whose evidence he intends to rely, identifying the issues to which that evidence will be directed.

4 DEFENDANT'S RESPONSE

The Defendant's Acknowledgment

4.1 Within 14 calendar days of receipt of the letter of claim, the defendant should acknowledge its receipt in writing and may give the name and address of his insurer (if any). If there has been no acknowledgment by or on behalf of the defendant within 14 days, the claimant will be entitled to commence proceedings without further compliance with this protocol.

Objections to the Court's Jurisdiction or the Named Defendant

4.2.1 If the defendant intends to take any objection to all or any part of the claimant's claim on the grounds that (i) the court lacks jurisdiction, (ii) the matter should be referred to arbitration, or (iii) the defendant named in the letter of claim is the wrong defendant, that objection should be raised by the defendant within 28 days after receipt of the letter of claim. The letter of objection shall specify the parts of the claim to which the objection relates, setting out the grounds relied on, and, where appropriate, shall identify the correct defendant (if known). Any failure to take such objection shall not prejudice the defendant's rights to do so in any subsequent proceedings, but the court may take such failure into account when considering the question of costs.

4.2.2 Where such notice of objection is given, the defendant is not required to send a letter of response in accordance with para. 4.3.1 in relation to the claim or those parts of it to which the objection relates (as the case may be).

4.2.3 If at any stage before the claimant commences proceedings, the defendant withdraws his objection, then para. 4.3 and the remaining part of this protocol will apply to the claim or those parts of it to which the objection related as if the letter of claim had been received on the date on which notice of withdrawal of the objection had been given.

The Defendant's Response

4.3.1 Within 28 days from the date of receipt of the letter of claim, or such other period as the parties may reasonably agree (up to a maximum of four months), the defendant shall send a letter of response to the claimant which shall contain the following information:

(i) the facts set out in the letter of claim which are agreed or not agreed, and if not agreed, the basis of the disagreement;

(ii) which claims are accepted and which are rejected, and if rejected, the basis of the rejection;
(iii) if a claim is accepted in whole or in part, whether the damages, sums or extensions of time claimed are accepted or rejected, and if rejected, the basis of the rejection;
(iv) if contributory negligence is alleged against the claimant, a summary of the facts relied on;
(v) whether the defendant intends to make a counterclaim, and if so, giving the information which is required to be given in a letter of claim by para. 3(iii) to (vi) above;
(vi) the names of any experts already instructed on whose evidence it is intended to rely, identifying the issues to which that evidence will be directed.

4.3.2 If no response is received by the claimant within the period of 28 days (or such other period as has been agreed between the parties), the claimant shall be entitled to commence proceedings without further compliance with this protocol.

Claimant's Response to Counterclaim

4.4 The claimant shall provide a response to any counterclaim within the equivalent period allowed to the defendant to respond to the letter of claim under para. 4.3.1 above.

5 PRE-ACTION MEETING

5.1 As soon as possible after receipt by the claimant of the defendant's letter of response, or (if the claimant intends to respond to the counterclaim) after receipt by the defendant of the claimant's letter of response to the counterclaim, the parties should normally meet.

5.2 The aim of the meeting is for the parties to agree what are the main issues in the case, to identify the root cause of disagreement in respect of each issue, and to consider (i) whether, and if so how, the issues might be resolved without recourse to litigation, and (ii) if litigation is unavoidable, what steps should be taken to ensure that it is conducted in accordance with the overriding objective as defined in r. 1.1 of the Civil Practice Rules.

5.3 In some circumstances, it may be necessary to convene more than one meeting. It is not intended by this protocol to prescribe in detail the manner in which the meetings should be conducted. But the court will normally expect that those attending will include:
(i) where the party is an individual, that individual, and where the party is a corporate body, a representative of that body who has authority to settle or recommend settlement of the dispute;
(ii) a legal representative of each party (if one has been instructed);
(iii) where the involvement of insurers has been disclosed, a representative of the insurer (who may be its legal representative); and
(iv) where a claim is made or defended on behalf of some other party (such as, for example, a claim made by a main contractor pursuant to a contractual obligation to pass on sub-contractor claims), the party on whose behalf the claim is made or defended and/or his legal representatives.

5.4 In respect of each agreed issue or the dispute as a whole, the parties should consider whether some form of alternative dispute resolution procedure would be more suitable than litigation, and if so, endeavour to agree which form to adopt.

5.5 If the parties are unable to agree on a means of resolving the dispute other than by litigation they should use their best endeavours to agree:
(i) whether, if there is any area where expert evidence is likely to be required, a joint expert may be appointed, and if so, who that should be; and (so far as is practicable)
(ii) the extent of disclosure of documents with a view to saving costs; and
(iii) the conduct of the litigation with the aim of minimising cost and delay.

5.6 Any party who attended any pre-action meeting shall be at liberty to disclose to the court:
(i) that the meeting took place, when and who attended;
(ii) the identity of any party who refused to attend, and the grounds for such refusal;
(iii) if the meeting did not take place, why not; and
(iv) any agreements concluded between the parties.

5.7 Except as provided in para. 5.6, everything said at a pre-action meeting shall be treated as 'without prejudice'.

6 LIMITATION OF ACTION

6.1 If by reason of complying with any part of this protocol a claimant's claim may be time-barred under any provision of the Limitation Act 1980, or any other legislation which imposes a time limit for bringing an action, the claimant may commence proceedings without complying with this protocol. In such circumstances, a claimant who commences proceedings without complying with all, or any part, of this protocol must apply to the court on notice for directions as to the timetable and form of procedure to be adopted, at the same time as he requests the court to issue proceedings. The court will consider whether to order a stay of the whole or part of the proceedings pending compliance with this protocol.

Pre-action Protocol for Defamation

1 INTRODUCTION

1.1 Lord Irvine of Lairg, in his foreword to the Pre-action Protocol for Personal Injury Claims identified the value of creating pre-action protocols as a key part of the civil justice reforms. He hoped that pre-action protocols would set effective and enforceable standards for the efficient conduct of pre-action litigation.

1.2 Lord Irvine went on to state that:

> The protocol aims to improve pre-action communication between the parties by establishing a timetable for the exchange of information relevant to the dispute and by setting standards for the content of correspondence. Compliance with the protocol will enable parties to make an informed judgement on the merits of their cases earlier than tends to happen today, because they will have earlier access to the information they need. This will provide every opportunity for improved communications between the parties designed to lead to an increase in the number of pre-action settlements.

1.3 It is against this background that a Pre-action Protocol for Claims in Defamation is submitted. This protocol is intended to encourage exchange of information between parties at an early, stage and to provide a clear framework within which parties to a claim in defamation, acting in good faith, can explore the early and appropriate resolution of that claim.

1.4 There are important features which distinguish defamation claims from other areas of civil litigation, and these must be borne in mind when both applying, and reviewing the application of, the pre-action protocol. In particular, time is always 'of the essence' in defamation claims; the limitation period is (uniquely) only one year, and almost invariably, a claimant will be seeking an immediate correction and/or apology as part of the process of restoring his/her reputation.

1.5 This pre-action protocol embraces the spirit of the reforms to the civil justice system envisaged by Lord Woolf, and now enacted in the Civil Procedure Rules. It aims to incorporate the concept of the overriding objective, as provided by the Rules at Part 1, before the commencement of any court proceedings, namely: dealing with a case justly includes, so far as is practicable:

- ensuring that the parties are on an equal footing;
- saving expense;

dealing with the case in ways which are proportionate:

- to the amount of money involved;
- to the importance of the case;
- to the complexity of the issues; and
- to the financial position of each party;
- ensuring that it is dealt with expeditiously and fairly; and
- allotting to it an appropriate share of the court's resources, while taking into account the need to allot resources to other cases.

2 AIMS OF THE PROTOCOL

- This protocol aims to set out a code of good practice which parties should follow when litigation is being considered.
- It encourages early communication of a claim.
- It aims to encourage both parties to disclose sufficient information to enable each to understand the other's case and to promote the prospect of early resolution.
- It sets a timetable for the exchange of information relevant to the dispute.
- It sets standards for the content of correspondence.
- It identifies options which either party might adopt to encourage settlement of the claim.

- Should a claim proceed to litigation, the extent to which the protocol has been followed both in practice and in spirit by the parties will assist the court in dealing with liability for costs and making other orders.
- Letters of claim and responses sent pursuant to this protocol are not intended to have the same status as a statement of case in proceedings.
- It aims to keep the costs of resolving disputes subject to this protocol proportionate.

3 PRE-ACTION PROTOCOL

Letter of Claim

3.1 The claimant should notify the defendant of his/her claim in writing at the earliest reasonable opportunity.

3.2 The letter of claim should include the following information:
- name of claimant;
- sufficient details to identify the publication or broadcast which contained the words complained of;
- the words complained of and, if known, the date of publication; where possible, a copy or transcript of the words complained of should be enclosed;
- factual inaccuracies or unsupportable comment within the words complained of; the claimant should give a sufficient explanation to enable the defendant to appreciate why the words are inaccurate or unsupportable;
- the nature of the remedies sought by the claimant.
- Where relevant, the letter of claim should also include:
- any facts or matters which make the claimant identifiable from the words complained of;
- details of any special facts relevant to the interpretation of the words complained of and/or any particular damage caused by the words complained of.

3.3 It is desirable for the claimant to identify in the letter of claim the meaning(s) he/she attributes to the words complained of.

Defendant's Response to Letter of Claim

3.4 The defendant should provide a full response to the letter of claim as soon as reasonably possible. If the defendant believes that he/she will be unable to respond within 14 days (or such shorter time limit as specified in the letter of claim), then he/she should specify the date by which he/she intends to respond.

3.5 The response should include the following:
- whether or to what extent the claimant's claim is accepted, whether more information is required or whether it is rejected;
- if the claim is accepted in whole or in part, the defendant should indicate which remedies it is willing to offer;
- if more information is required, then the defendant should specify precisely what information is needed to enable the claim to be dealt with and why;
- if the claim is rejected, then the defendant should explain the reasons why it is rejected, including a sufficient indication of any facts on which the defendant is likely to rely in support of any substantive defence;
- It is desirable for the defendant to include in the response to the letter of claim the meaning(s) he/she attributes to the words complained of.

Proportionality of Costs

3.6 In formulating both the letter of claim and response and in taking any subsequent steps, the parties should act reasonably to keep costs proportionate to the nature and gravity of the case and the stage the complaint has reached.

Alternative Dispute Resolution

3.7 The parties should consider whether some form of alternative dispute resolution procedure would be more suitable than litigation, and if so, endeavour to agree which form to adopt. Both the claimant and defendant may be required by the court to provide evidence that alternative means of resolving their dispute were considered. The courts take the view that litigation should be a last resort, and that claims should not be issued prematurely when a settlement is still actively being explored. Parties are warned that if the protocol is not followed (including this paragraph) then the court must have regard to such conduct when determining costs.

3.8 It is not practicable in this protocol to address in detail how the parties might decide which method to adopt to resolve their particular dispute. However, summarised below are some of the options for resolving disputes without litigation:

- Discussion and negotiation.
- Early neutral evaluation by an independent third party (for example, a lawyer experienced in the field of defamation or an individual experienced in the subject matter of the claim).
- Mediation — a form of facilitated negotiation assisted by an independent neutral party.
- The Reference to the Press Complaints Commission (an independent body which deals with complaints from members of the public about the editorial content of newspapers and magazines).

3.9 The Legal Services Commission has published a booklet on *Alternatives to Court* (CLS Direct Information Leaflet 23) (www.clsdirect.org.uk/legalhelp/leaflet23.jsp), which lists a number of organisations that provide alternative dispute resolution services.

3.10 *It is expressly recognised that no party can or should be forced to mediate or enter into any form of ADR.*

Professional Negligence Pre-action Protocol

This protocol merges the two protocols previously produced by the Solicitors Indemnity Fund (SIF) and Claims against Professionals (CAP).

A INTRODUCTION

A1 This protocol is designed to apply when a claimant wishes to claim against a professional (other than construction professionals and healthcare providers) as a result of that professional's alleged negligence or equivalent breach of contract or breach of fiduciary duty. Although these claims will be the usual situation in which the protocol will be used, there may be other claims for which the protocol could be appropriate. For a more detailed explanation of the scope of the protocol see Guidance Note C2.

A2 The aim of this protocol is to establish a framework in which there is an early exchange of information so that the claim can be fully investigated and, if possible, resolved without the need for litigation. This includes:

(a) ensuring that the parties are on an equal footing;
(b) saving expense;
(c) dealing with the dispute in ways which are proportionate:
  (i) to the amount of money involved;
  (ii) to the importance of the case;
  (iii) to the complexity of the issues;
  (iv) to the financial position of each party;
(d) ensuring that it is dealt with expeditiously and fairly.

A3 This protocol is not intended to replace other forms of pre-action dispute resolution (such as internal complaints procedures, the Surveyors and Valuers Arbitration Scheme, etc.). Where such procedures are available, parties are encouraged to consider whether they should be used. If, however, these other procedures are used and fail to resolve the dispute, the protocol should be used before litigation is started, adapting it where appropriate. See also Guidance Note C3.

A4 The courts will be able to treat the standards set in this protocol as the normal reasonable approach. If litigation is started, it will be for the court to decide whether sanctions should be imposed as a result of substantial non-compliance with a protocol. Guidance on the courts' likely approach is given in PD Protocols. The court is likely to disregard minor departures from this protocol and so should the parties as between themselves.

A5 Both in operating the timetable and in requesting and providing information during the protocol period, the parties are expected to act reasonably, in line with the court's expectations of them. See also Guidance Note C1.2.

B THE PROTOCOL

B1 Preliminary Notice

(See also Guidance Note C3.1)

B1.1 As soon as the claimant decides there is a reasonable chance that he will bring a claim against a professional, the claimant is encouraged to notify the professional in writing.

B1.2 This letter should contain the following information:

(a) the identity of the claimant and any other parties;
(b) a brief outline of the claimant's grievance against the professional;
(c) if possible, a general indication of the financial value of the potential claim.

B1.3 This letter should be addressed to the professional and should ask the professional to inform his professional indemnity insurers, if any, immediately.

B1.4 The professional should acknowledge receipt of the claimant's letter within 21 days of receiving it. Other than this acknowledgment, the protocol places no obligation upon either party to take any further action.

B2 Letter of Claim

B2.1 As soon as the claimant decides there are grounds for a claim against the professional, the claimant should write a detailed letter of claim to the professional.

B2.2 The letter of claim will normally be an open letter (as opposed to being 'without prejudice') and should include the following:

(a) The identity of any other parties involved in the dispute or a related dispute.

(b) A clear chronological summary (including key dates) of the facts on which the claim is based. Key documents should be identified, copied and enclosed.

(c) The allegations against the professional. What has he done wrong? What has he failed to do?

(d) An explanation of how the alleged error has caused the loss claimed.

(e) An estimate of the financial loss suffered by the claimant and how it is calculated. Supporting documents should be identified, copied and enclosed. If details of the financial loss cannot be supplied, the claimant should explain why and should state when he will be in a position to provide the details. This information should be sent to the professional as soon as reasonably possible.
If the claimant is seeking some form of non-financial redress, this should be made clear.

(f) Confirmation whether or not an expert has been appointed. If so, providing the identity and discipline of the expert, together with the date upon which the expert was appointed.

(g) A request that a copy of the letter of claim be forwarded immediately to the professional's insurers, if any.

B2.3 The letter of claim is not intended to have the same formal status as a statement of case. If, however, the letter of claim differs materially from the statement of case in subsequent proceedings, the court may decide, in its discretion, to impose sanctions.

B2.4 If the claimant has sent other letters of claim (or equivalent) to any other party in relation to this dispute or related dispute, those letters should be copied to the professional. (If the claimant is claiming against someone else to whom this protocol does not apply, please see Guidance Note C4.)

B3 The Letter of Acknowledgment

B3.1 The professional should acknowledge receipt of the letter of claim within 21 days of receiving it.

B4 Investigations

B4.1 The professional will have three months from the date of the letter of acknowledgment to investigate.

B4.2 If the professional is in difficulty in complying with the three-month time period, the problem should be explained to the claimant as soon as possible. The professional should explain what is being done to resolve the problem and when the professional expects to complete the investigations. The claimant should agree to any reasonable request for an extension of the three-month period.

B4.3 The parties should supply promptly, at this stage and throughout, whatever relevant information or documentation is reasonably requested. (Please see Guidance Note C5). (If the professional intends to claim against someone who is not currently a party to the dispute, please see Guidance Note C4.)

B5 Letter of Response and Letter of Settlement

B5.1 As soon as the professional has completed his investigations, the professional should send to the claimant:

(a) a letter of response; or

(b) a letter of settlement; or
(c) both.

The letters of response and settlement can be contained within a single letter.

The letter of response

B5.2 The letter of response will normally be an open letter (as opposed to being 'without prejudice') and should be a reasoned answer to the claimant's allegations:

(a) If the claim is admitted the professional should say so in clear terms.
(b) If only part of the claim is admitted the professional should make clear which parts of the claim are admitted and which are denied.
(c) If the claim is denied in whole or in part, the letter of response should include specific comments on the allegations against the professional and, if the claimant's version of events is disputed, the professional should provide his version of events.
(d) If the professional is unable to admit or deny the claim, the professional should identify any further information which is required.
(e) If the professional disputes the estimate of the claimant's financial loss, the letter of response should set out the professional's estimate. If an estimate cannot be provided, the professional should explain why and should state when he will be in a position to provide an estimate. This information should be sent to the claimant as soon as reasonably possible.
(f) Where additional documents are relied upon, copies should be provided.

B5.3 The letter of response is not intended to have the same formal status as a defence. If, however, the letter of response differs materially from the defence in subsequent proceedings, the court may decide, in its discretion, to impose sanctions.

The letter of settlement

B5.4 The letter of settlement will normally be a without prejudice letter and should be sent if the professional intends to make proposals for settlement. It should:

(a) Set out the professional's views to date on the claim identifying those issues which the professional believes are likely to remain in dispute and those which are not. (The letter of settlement does not need to include this information if the professional has sent a letter of response.)
(b) Make a settlement proposal or identify any further information which is required before the professional can formulate its proposals.
(c) Where additional documents are relied upon, copies should be provided.

Effect of letter of response and/or letter of settlement

B5.5 If the letter of response denies the claim in its entirety and there is no letter of settlement, it is open to the claimant to commence proceedings.

B5.6 In any other circumstance, the professional and the claimant should commence negotiations with the aim of concluding those negotiations within six months of the date of the letter of acknowledgment (*not* from the date of the letter of response).

B5.7 If the claim cannot be resolved within this period:

(a) The parties should agree within 14 days of the end of the period whether the period should be extended and, if so, by how long.
(b) The parties should seek to identify those issues which are still in dispute and those which can be agreed.
(c) If an extension of time is not agreed it will then be open to the claimant to commence proceedings.

B6 Alternative Dispute Resolution

B6.1 The parties should consider whether some form of alternative dispute resolution procedure would be more suitable than litigation, and if so, endeavour to agree which form to adopt. Both the claimant and defendant may be required by the court to provide evidence that alternative means of resolving their dispute were considered. The courts take the view that litigation should be a last resort, and that claims should not be issued prematurely when a settlement is still actively being explored. Parties are warned that if the protocol is not followed (including this paragraph) then the court must have regard to such conduct when determining costs.

B6.2 It is not practicable in this protocol to address in detail how the parties might decide which method to adopt to resolve their particular dispute. However, summarised below are some of the options for resolving disputes without litigation:

- Discussion and negotiation.
- Early neutral evaluation by an independent third party (for example, a lawyer experienced in the field of professional negligence or an individual experienced in the subject matter of the claim).
- Mediation — a form of facilitated negotiation assisted by an independent neutral party.

B6.3 The Legal Services Commission has published a booklet on *Alternatives to Court* (CLS Direct Information Leaflet 23) (www.clsdirect.org.uk/legalhelp/leaflet23.jsp), which lists a number of organisations that provide alternative dispute resolution services.

B6.4 *It is expressly recognised that no party can or should be forced to mediate or enter into any form of ADR.*

B7 Experts

(The following provisions apply where the claim raises an issue of professional expertise whose resolution requires expert evidence.)

B7.1 If the claimant has obtained expert evidence prior to sending the letter of claim, the professional will have equal right to obtain expert evidence prior to sending the letter of response/letter of settlement.

B7.2 If the claimant has not obtained expert evidence prior to sending the letter of claim, the parties are encouraged to appoint a joint expert. If they agree to do so, they should seek to agree the identity of the expert and the terms of the expert's appointment.

B7.3 If agreement about a joint expert cannot be reached, all parties are free to appoint their own experts.

(For further details on experts see Guidance Note C6.)

B8 Proceedings

B8.1 Unless it is necessary (for example, to obtain protection against the expiry of a relevant limitation period) the claimant should not start court proceedings until:

(a) the letter of response denies the claim in its entirety and there is no letter of settlement (see para. B5.5 above); or

(b) the end of the negotiation period (see paras B5.6 and B5.7 above).

(For further discussion of statutory time limits for the commencement of litigation, please see Guidance Note C7.)

B8.2 Where possible 14 days' written notice should be given to the professional before proceedings are started, indicating the court within which the claimant is intending to commence litigation.

B8.3 Proceedings should be served on the professional, unless the professional's solicitor has notified the claimant in writing that he is authorised to accept service on behalf of the professional.

C GUIDANCE NOTES

C1 Introduction

C1.1 The protocol has been kept simple to promote ease of use and general acceptability. The guidance notes which follow relate particularly to issues on which further guidance may be required.

C2.2 The Woolf reforms envisages that parties will act reasonably in the pre-action period. Accordingly, in the event that the protocol and the guidelines do not specifically address a problem, the parties should comply with the spirit of the protocol by acting reasonably.

C2 Scope of Protocol

C2.1 The protocol is specifically designated for claims of negligence against professionals. This will include claims in which the allegation against a professional is that they have breached a contractual term to take reasonable skill and care. The protocol is also appropriate for claims of breach of fiduciary duty against professionals.

C2.2 The protocol is not intended to apply to claims:

(a) against architects, engineers and quantity surveyors — parties should use the Construction and Engineering Disputes (CED) protocol;
(b) against healthcare providers — parties should use the Pre-action Protocol for the Resolution of Clinical Disputes;
(c) concerning defamation — parties should use the Pre-action Protocol for Defamation.

C2.3 'Professional' is deliberately left undefined in the protocol. If it becomes an issue as to whether a defendant is or is not a professional, parties are reminded of the overriding need to act reasonably (see paras A4 and C1.2 above). Rather than argue about the definition of 'professional', therefore, the parties are invited to use this protocol, adapting it where appropriate.

C2.4 The protocol may not be suitable for disputes with professionals concerning intellectual property claims, etc. Until specific protocols are created for those claims, however, parties are invited to use this protocol, adapting it where necessary.

C2.5 Allegations of professional negligence are sometimes made in response to an attempt by the professional to recover outstanding fees. Where possible these allegations should be raised before litigation has commenced, in which case the parties should comply with the protocol before either party commences litigation. If litigation has already commenced it will be a matter for the court whether sanctions should be imposed against either party. In any event, the parties are encouraged to consider applying to the court for a stay to allow the protocol to be followed.

C3 Interaction with Other Pre-action Methods of Dispute Resolution

C3.1 There are a growing number of methods by which disputes can be resolved without the need for litigation, e.g., internal complaints procedures, the Surveyors and Valuers Arbitration Scheme, and so on. The preliminary notice procedure of the protocol (see para. B1) is designed to enable both parties to take stock at an early stage and to decide before work starts on preparing a letter of claim whether the grievance should be referred to one of these other dispute resolution procedures. (For the avoidance of doubt, however, there is no obligation on either party under the protocol to take any action at this stage other than giving the acknowledgment provided for in para. B1.4.)

C3.2 Accordingly, parties are free to use (and are encouraged to use) any of the available pre-action procedures in an attempt to resolve their dispute. If appropriate, the parties can agree to suspend the protocol timetable whilst the other method of dispute resolution is used.

C3.3 If these methods fail to resolve the dispute, however, the protocol should be used before litigation is commenced. Because there has already been an attempt to resolve the dispute, it may be appropriate to adjust the protocol's requirements. In particular, unless the parties agree otherwise, there is unlikely to be any benefit in duplicating a stage which has in effect already been undertaken. However, if the protocol adds anything to the earlier method of dispute resolution, it should be used, adapting it where appropriate. Once again, the parties are expected to act reasonably.

C4 Multi-party Disputes

C4.1 Paragraph B2.2(a) of the protocol requires a claimant to identify any other parties involved in the dispute or a related dispute. This is intended to ensure that all relevant parties are identified as soon as possible.

C4.2 If the dispute involves more than two parties, there are a number of potential problems. It is possible that different protocols will apply to different defendants. It is possible that defendants will claim against each other. It is possible that other parties will be drawn into the dispute. It is possible that the protocol timetable against one party will not be synchronised with the protocol timetable against a different party. How will these problems be resolved?

C4.3 As stated in para. C1.2 above, the parties are expected to act reasonably. What is 'reasonable' will, of course, depend upon the specific facts of each case. Accordingly, it would be inappropriate for the protocol to set down generalised rules. Whenever a problem arises, the parties are encouraged to discuss how it can be overcome. In doing so, parties are reminded of the protocol's aims which include the aim to resolve the dispute without the need for litigation (para. A2 above).

C5 Investigations

C5.1 Paragraph B4.3 is intended to encourage the early exchange of relevant information, so that issues in the dispute can be clarified or resolved. It should not be used as a 'fishing expedition' by either party. No party is obliged under para. B4.3 to disclose any document which a court could not order them to disclose in the pre-action period.

C5.2 This protocol does not alter the parties' duties to disclose documents under any professional regulation or under general law.

C6 Experts

C6.1 Expert evidence is not always needed, although the use and role of experts in professional negligence claims is often crucial. However, the way in which expert evidence is used in, say, an insurance brokers' negligence case, is not necessarily the same as in, say, an accountants' case. Similarly, the approach to be adopted in a £10,000 case does not necessarily compare with the approach in a £10 million case. The protocol therefore is designed to be flexible and does not dictate a standard approach. On the contrary it envisages that the parties will bear the responsibility for agreeing how best to use experts.

C6.2 If a joint expert is used, therefore, the parties are left to decide issues such as: the payment of the expert, whether joint or separate instructions are used, how and to whom the expert is to report, how questions may be addressed to the expert and how the expert should respond, whether an agreed statement of facts is required, and so on.

C6.3 If separate experts are used, the parties are left to decide issues such as: whether the experts' reports should be exchanged, whether there should be an experts' meeting, and so on.

C6.4 Even if a joint expert is appointed, it is possible that parties will still want to instruct their own experts. The protocol does not prohibit this.

C7 Proceedings

C7.1 This protocol does not alter the statutory time limits for starting court proceedings. A claimant is required to start proceedings within those time limits.

C7.2 If proceedings are for any reason started before the parties have followed the procedures in this protocol, the parties are encouraged to agree to apply to the court for a stay whilst the protocol is followed.

Pre-action Protocol for Judicial Review

INTRODUCTION

This protocol applies to proceedings within England and Wales only. It does not affect the time limit specified by CPR, r. 54.5(1), which requires that any claim form in an application for judicial review must be filed promptly and in any event not later than three months after the grounds to make the claim first arose.[1]

1. Judicial review allows people with a sufficient interest in a decision or action by a public body to ask a judge to review the lawfulness of:
   - an enactment; or
   - a decision, action or failure to act in relation to the exercise of a public function.[2]
2. Judicial review may be used where there is no right of appeal or where all avenues of appeal have been exhausted.

Alternative Dispute Resolution

3.1 The parties should consider whether some form of alternative dispute resolution procedure would be more suitable than litigation, and if so, endeavour to agree which form to adopt. Both the claimant and defendant may be required by the court to provide evidence that alternative means of resolving their dispute were considered. The courts take the view that litigation should be a last resort, and that claims should not be issued prematurely when a settlement is still actively being explored. Parties are warned that if the protocol is not followed (including this paragraph) then the court must have regard to such conduct when determining costs. However, parties should also note that a claim for judicial review must be filed promptly and in any event not later than three months after the grounds to make the claim first arose.

3.2 It is not practicable in this protocol to address in detail how the parties might decide which method to adopt to resolve their particular dispute. However, summarised below are some of the options for resolving disputes without litigation:

- Discussion and negotiation.
- Ombudsmen — the Parliamentary and Health Service and the Local Government Ombudsmen have discretion to deal with complaints relating to maladministration. The British and Irish Ombudsman Association provide information about Ombudsman schemes and other complaint handling bodies and this is available from their website at www.bioa.org.uk. Parties may wish to note that the ombudsmen are not able to look into a complaint once court action has been commenced.
- Early neutral evaluation by an independent third party (for example, a lawyer experienced in the field of administrative law or an individual experienced in the subject matter of the claim).
- Mediation — a form of facilitated negotiation assisted by an independent neutral party.

3.3 The Legal Services Commission has published a booklet on *Alternatives to Court* (CLS Direct Information Leaflet 23) (www.clsdirect.org.uk/legalhelp/leaflet23.jsp), which lists a number of organisations that provide alternative dispute resolution services.

3.4 *It is expressly recognised that no party can or should be forced to mediate or enter into any form of ADR.*

[1] While the court does have the discretion under r. 3.1(2)(a) to allow a late claim, this is only used in exceptional circumstances. Compliance with the protocol alone is unlikely to be sufficient to persuade the court to allow a late claim.

[2] Rule 54.1(2).

4. Judicial review may not be appropriate in every instance.

Claimants are strongly advised to seek appropriate legal advice when considering such proceedings and, in particular, before adopting this protocol or making a claim. Although the Legal Services Commission will not normally grant Full Representation before a letter before claim has been sent and the proposed defendant given a reasonable time to respond, initial funding may be available, for eligible claimants, to cover the work necessary to write this. (See Annex C for more information.)

5. This protocol sets out a code of good practice and contains the steps which parties should generally follow before making a claim for judicial review.
6. This protocol does not impose a greater obligation on a public body to disclose documents or give reasons for its decision than that already provided for in statute or common law. However, where the court considers that a public body should have provided *relevant* documents and/or information, particularly where this failure is a breach of a statutory or common law requirement, it may impose sanctions.

This protocol *will not be appropriate* where the defendant does not have the legal power to change the decision being challenged, for example decisions issued by tribunals such as the Immigration Appeal Authorities.

This protocol *will not be appropriate* in urgent cases, for example, when directions have been set, or are in force, for the claimant's removal from the UK, or where there is an urgent need for an interim order to compel a public body to act where it has unlawfully refused to do so (for example, the failure of a local housing authority to secure interim accommodation for a homeless claimant) a claim should be made immediately. A letter before claim will not stop the implementation of a disputed decision in all instances.

7. All claimants will need to satisfy themselves whether they should follow the protocol, depending upon the circumstances of his or her case. Where the use of the protocol is appropriate, the court will normally expect all parties to have complied with it and will take into account compliance or non-compliance when giving directions for case management of proceedings or when making orders for costs.[3] However, even in emergency cases, it is good practice to fax to the defendant the draft claim form which the claimant intends to issue. A claimant is also normally required to notify a defendant when an interim mandatory order is being sought.

THE LETTER BEFORE CLAIM

8. Before making a claim, the claimant should send a letter to the defendant. The purpose of this letter is to identify the issues in dispute and establish whether litigation can be avoided.
9. Claimants should normally use the suggested standard format for the letter outlined at Annex A.
10. The letter should contain the date and details of the decision, act or omission being challenged and a clear summary of the facts on which the claim is based. It should also contain the details of any relevant information that the claimant is seeking and an explanation of why this is considered relevant.
11. The letter should normally contain the details of any interested parties[4] known to the claimant. They should be sent a copy of the letter before claim for information. Claimants are strongly advised to seek appropriate legal advice when considering such proceedings and, in particular, before sending the letter before claim to other interested parties or making a claim.
12. A claim should not normally be made until the proposed reply date given in the letter before claim has passed, unless the circumstances of the case require more immediate action to be taken.

THE LETTER OF RESPONSE

13. Defendants should normally respond within 14 days using the standard format at Annex B. Failure to do so will be taken into account by the court and sanctions may be imposed unless there are good reasons.[5]

[3] PD 43–48.

[4] See CPR, r. 54.1(2)(f).

[5] See PD Protocols, paras 2 and 3.

14. Where it is not possible to reply within the proposed time limit the defendant should send an interim reply and propose a reasonable extension. Where an extension is sought, reasons should be given and, where required, additional information requested. This will not affect the time limit for making a claim for judicial review[6] nor will it bind the claimant where he or she considers this to be unreasonable. However, where the court considers that a subsequent claim is made prematurely it may impose sanctions.
15. If the claim is being conceded in full, the reply should say so in clear and unambiguous terms.
16. If the claim is being conceded in part or not being conceded at all, the reply should say so in clear and unambiguous terms, and:
    (a) where appropriate, contain a new decision, clearly identifying what aspects of the claim are being conceded and what are not, or, give a clear timescale within which the new decision will be issued;
    (b) provide a fuller explanation for the decision, if considered appropriate to do so;
    (c) address any points of dispute, or explain why they cannot be addressed;
    (d) enclose any relevant documentation requested by the claimant, or explain why the documents are not being enclosed; and
    (e) where appropriate, confirm whether or not they will oppose any application for an interim remedy.
17. The response should be sent to all interested parties[7] identified by the claimant and contain details of any other parties who the defendant considers also have an interest.

ANNEX A LETTER BEFORE CLAIM

Section 1 Information Required in a Letter before Claim

Proposed Claim for Judicial Review

1. To (Insert the name and address of the proposed defendant — see details in section 2)
2. The claimant (Insert the title, first and last name and the address of the claimant)
3. Reference details (When dealing with large organisations it is important to understand that the information relating to any particular individual's previous dealings with it may not be immediately available, therefore it is important to set out the relevant reference numbers for the matter in dispute and/or the identity of those within the public body who have been handling the particular matter in dispute — see details in section 3)
4. The details of the matter being challenged (Set out clearly the matter being challenged, particularly if there has been more than one decision)
5. The issue (Set out the date and details of the decision, or act or omission being challenged, a brief summary of the facts and why it is contended to be wrong)
6. The details of the action that the defendant is expected to take (Set out the details of the remedy sought, including whether a review or any interim remedy is being requested)
7. The details of the legal advisers, if any, dealing with this claim (Set out the name, address and reference details of any legal advisers dealing with the claim)
8. The details of any interested parties (Set out the details of any interested parties and confirm that they have been sent a copy of this letter)
9. The details of any information sought (Set out the details of any information that is sought. This may include a request for a fuller explanation of the reasons for the decision that is being challenged)
10. The details of any documents that are considered relevant and necessary (Set out the details of any documentation or policy in respect of which the disclosure is sought and explain why these are relevant. If you rely on a statutory duty to disclose, this should be specified)
11. The address for reply and service of court documents (Insert the address for the reply)
12. Proposed reply date (The precise time will depend upon the circumstances of the individual case. However, although a shorter or longer time may be appropriate in a particular case, 14 days is a reasonable time to allow in most circumstances)

[6] See CPR, r. 54.5(1).
[7] See CPR, r. 54.1(2)(f).

Section 2 Address for Sending the Letter before Claim

Public bodies have requested that, for certain types of cases, in order to ensure a prompt response, letters before claim should be sent to specific addresses.

Where the claim concerns a decision in an immigration, asylum or nationality case:

Judicial Review Unit
Immigration and Nationality Directorate
St Anne's House
20–26 Wellesley Road
Croydon
CR9 2RL

Where the claim concerns a decision by the Legal Services Commission:

The address on the decision letter/notification; and
Policy and Legal Department
Legal Services Commission
85 Gray's Inn Road
London WC1X 8TX

Where the claim concerns a decision by a local authority:

The address on the decision letter/notification; and
Their legal department[8]

Where the claim concerns a decision by a department or body for whom Treasury Solicitor acts *and the Treasury Solicitor has already been involved in the case* a copy should also be sent, quoting the Treasury Solicitor's reference, to:

Treasury Solicitor
Queen Anne's Chambers
28 Broadway
London SW1H 9JS

In all other circumstances, the letter should be sent to the address on the letter notifying the decision.

Section 3 Specific Reference Details Required

Public bodies have requested that the following information should be provided in order to ensure prompt response.

Where the claim concerns an immigration, asylum or nationality case, dependent upon the nature of the case:

The Home Office reference number
The port reference number
The Immigration Appellate Authority reference number
The National Asylum Support Service reference number

Or, if these are unavailable:

The full name, nationality and date of birth of the claimant.

Where the claim concerns a decision by the Legal Services Commission:

The certificate reference number.

ANNEX B RESPONSE TO A LETTER BEFORE CLAIM

Information Required in a Response to a Letter before Claim

Proposed Claim for Judicial Review

1. The claimant (Insert the title, first and last names and the address to which any reply should be sent)
2. From (Insert the name and address of the defendant)

[8] The relevant address should be available from a range of sources such as the *Phone Book, Business and Services Directory, Thomson Local,* CAB, etc.

3. Reference details (Set out the relevant reference numbers for the matter in dispute and the identity of those within the public body who have been handling the issue)
4. The details of the matter being challenged (Set out details of the matter being challenged, providing a fuller explanation of the decision, where this is considered appropriate)
5. Response to the proposed claim (Set out whether the issue in question is conceded in part, or in full, or will be contested. Where it is not proposed to disclose any information that has been requested, explain the reason for this. Where an interim reply is being sent and there is a realistic prospect of settlement, details should be included)
6. Details of any other interested parties (Identify any other parties who you consider have an interest who have not already been sent a letter by the claimant)
7. Address for further correspondence and service of court documents (Set out the address for any future correspondence on this matter)

ANNEX C NOTES ON PUBLIC FUNDING FOR LEGAL COSTS IN JUDICIAL REVIEW

Public funding for legal costs in judicial review is available from legal professionals and advice agencies which have contracts with the Legal Services Commission as part of the Community Legal Service. Funding may be provided for:

- Legal Help to provide initial advice and assistance with any legal problem; or
- Legal Representation to allow you to be represented in court if you are taking or defending court proceedings. This is available in two forms:
  - — Investigative Help is limited to funding to investigate the strength of the proposed claim. It includes the issue and conduct of proceedings only so far as is necessary to obtain disclosure of relevant information or to protect the client's position in relation to any urgent hearing or time limit for the issue of proceedings. This includes the work necessary to write a letter before claim to the body potentially under challenge, setting out the grounds of challenge, and giving that body a reasonable opportunity, typically 14 days, in which to respond.
  - — Full Representation is provided to represent you in legal proceedings and includes litigation services, advocacy services, and all such help as is usually given by a person providing representation in proceedings, including steps preliminary or incidental to proceedings, and/or arriving at or giving affect to a compromise to avoid or bring to an end any proceedings. Except in emergency cases, a proper letter before claim must be sent and the other side must be given an opportunity to respond before Full Representation is granted.

Further information on the type(s) of help available and the criteria for receiving that help may be found in the *Legal Service Manual*, vol. 3, *The Funding Code*. This may be found on the Legal Services Commission website at:

http://www.legalservices.co.uk/

A list of contracted firms and advice agencies may be found on the Community Legal Service website at: http://www.justask.org.uk/

Pre-action Protocol for Disease and Illness Claims

1 INTRODUCTION

1.1 Lord Woolf in his *Final Report* of July 1996 recommended the development of protocols: 'to build on and increase the benefits of early but well-informed settlements which genuinely satisfy both parties to a dispute'.

1.2 The aims of these protocols are:
- more contact between the parties;
- better and earlier exchange of information;
- better investigation by both sides;
- to put the parties in a position where they may be able to settle cases fairly and early without litigation;
- to enable proceedings to run to the court's timetable and efficiently, if litigation does become necessary.

1.3 The concept of protocols is relevant to a range of initiatives for good claims practice, especially:
- predictability in the time needed for steps to be taken;
- standardisation of relevant information, including documents to be disclosed.

1.4 The courts will be able to treat the standards set in protocols as the normal reasonable approach. If proceedings are issued, it will be for the court to decide whether non-compliance with a protocol should merit adverse consequences. Guidance on the court's likely approach will be given from time to time in practice directions.

1.5 If the court has to consider the question of compliance after proceedings have begun, it will not be concerned with minor infringements, e.g., failure by a short period to provide relevant information. One minor breach will not exempt the 'innocent' party from following the protocol. The court will look at the effect of non-compliance on the other party when deciding whether to impose sanctions.

2 NOTES OF GUIDANCE

Scope of the Protocol

2.1 This protocol is intended to apply to all personal injury claims where the injury is not as the result of an accident but takes the form of an illness or disease.

2.2 This protocol covers disease claims which are likely to be complex and frequently not suitable for fast track procedures even though they may fall within fast track limits. Disease for the purpose of this protocol primarily covers any illness physical or psychological, any disorder, ailment, affliction, complaint, malady, or derangement other than a physical or psychological injury solely caused by an accident or other similar single event.

2.3 This protocol is not limited to diseases occurring in the workplace but will embrace diseases occurring in other situations for example through occupation of premises or the use of products. It is not intended to cover those cases, which are dealt with as a 'group' or 'class' action.

2.4 The 'cards on the table' approach advocated by the personal injury protocol is equally appropriate to disease claims. The spirit of that protocol, and of the clinical negligence protocol is followed here, in accordance with the sense of the civil justice reforms.

2.5 The timetable and the arrangements for disclosing documents and obtaining expert evidence may need to be varied to suit the circumstances of the case. If a party considers the detail of the protocol to be inappropriate they should communicate their reasons to all of the parties at that stage. If proceedings are subsequently issued, the court will expect an explanation as to why the protocol has not been followed, or has been varied. In a terminal disease claim with short life expectancy, for instance for a claimant who has a disease such as mesothelioma, the timescale of the protocol is likely to be too long. In such a claim, the claimant may not be able to follow the protocol and the defendant would be expected to treat the claim with urgency.

2A ALTERNATIVE DISPUTE RESOLUTION

2A.1 The parties should consider whether some form of alternative dispute resolution procedure would be more suitable than litigation, and if so, endeavour to agree which form to adopt. Both the claimant and defendant may be required by the court to provide evidence that alternative means of resolving their dispute were considered. The courts take the view that litigation should be a last resort, and that claims should not be issued prematurely when a settlement is still actively being explored. Parties are warned that if the protocol is not followed (including this paragraph) then the court must have regard to such conduct when determining costs.

2A.2 It is not practicable in this protocol to address in detail how the parties might decide which method to adopt to resolve their particular dispute. However, summarised below are some of the options for resolving disputes without litigation:

- Discussion and negotiation.
- Early neutral evaluation by an independent third party (for example, a lawyer experienced in the field of disease or illness, or an individual experienced in the subject matter of the claim).
- Mediation — a form of facilitated negotiation assisted by an independent neutral party.

2A.3 The Legal Services Commission has published a booklet on *Alternatives to Court* (CLS Direct Information Leaflet 23) (www.clsdirect.org.uk/legalhelp/leaflet23.jsp), which lists a number of organisations that provide alternative dispute resolution services.

2A.4 *It is expressly recognised that no party can or should be forced to mediate or enter into any form of ADR.*

3 THE AIMS OF THE PROTOCOL

3.1 The *general* aims of the protocol are:

- to resolve as many disputes as possible without litigation;
- where a claim cannot be resolved to identify the relevant issues which remain in dispute.

3.2 The *specific* objectives are:

Openness

- to encourage early communication of the perceived problem between the parties or their insurers;
- to encourage employees to voice any concerns or worries about possible work-related illness as soon as practicable;
- to encourage employers to develop systems of early reporting and investigation of suspected occupational health problems and to provide full and prompt explanations to concerned employees or former employees;
- to apply such principles to perceived problems outside the employer/employee relationship, for example occupiers of premises or land and producers of products;
- to ensure that sufficient information is disclosed by both parties to enable each to understand the other's perspective and case, and to encourage early resolution;

Timeliness

- to provide an early opportunity for employers (past or present) or their insurers to identify cases where an investigation is required and to carry out that investigation promptly;
- to encourage employers (past or present) or other defendants to involve and identify their insurers at an early stage;
- to ensure that all relevant records including health and personnel records are provided to employees

(past or present) or their appointed representatives promptly on request, by any employer (past or present) or their insurers. This should be complied with to a realistic timetable;
- to ensure that relevant records which are in the claimant's possession are made available to the employers or their insurers by claimants or their advisers at an appropriate stage;
- to proceed on a reasonable timetable where a resolution is not achievable to lay the ground to enable litigation to proceed at a reasonable and proportionate cost, and to limit the matters in contention;
- to communicate promptly where any of the requested information is not available or does not exist;
- to discourage the prolonged pursuit of unmeritorious claims and the prolonged defence of meritorious claims;
- to encourage all parties, at the earliest possible stage, to disclose voluntarily any additional documents which will assist in resolving any issue.

4 THE PROTOCOL

This protocol is not a comprehensive code governing all the steps in disease claims. Rather it attempts to set out *a code of good practice* which parties should follow.

Obtaining Occupational Records Including Health Records

4.1 In appropriate cases, a *potential claimant* may request occupational records including health records and personnel records before sending a letter of claim.

4.2 Any request for records by the *potential claimant* or his adviser should *provide sufficient information* to alert the *potential defendant* or his insurer where a possible disease claim is being investigated. Annex A1 provides a suggested form for this purpose for use in cases arising from employment. Similar forms can be prepared and used in other situations.

4.3 The copy records should be provided *within a maximum of 40 days* of the request at no cost. Although these will primarily be occupational records, it will be good practice for a *potential defendant* to disclose product data documents identified by a *potential claimant* at this stage which may resolve a causation issue.

4.4 In the rare circumstances that the *potential defendant* or his insurer is in difficulty in providing information quickly details should be given of what is being done to resolve it with a reasonable time estimate for doing so.

4.5 If the *potential defendant* or his insurer fails to provide the records including health records within 40 days and fails to comply with para. 4.4 above, the *potential claimant* or his adviser may then apply to the court for an *order for pre-action disclosure.* The CPR make pre-action applications to the court easier. The court also has the power to impose costs sanctions for unreasonable delay in providing records.

5 COMMUNICATION

5.1 If either the *potential claimant* or his adviser considers *additional records are required from a third party,* such as records from previous employers or general practitioner records, in the first instance these should be requested by the *potential claimant* or their advisers. Third party record holders would be expected to cooperate. The CPR enable parties to apply to the court for pre-action disclosure by third parties.

5.2 As soon as the records have been received and analysed, the *potential claimant* or his adviser should consider whether a claim should be made. General practitioner records will normally be obtained before a decision is reached.

5.3 If a decision is made not to proceed further at this stage against a party identified as a *potential defendant,* the *potential claimant* or his adviser should notify that *potential defendant* as soon as practicable.

6 LETTER OF CLAIM

6.1 Where a decision is made to make a claim, the claimant shall send to the proposed defendant two copies of a letter of claim, as soon as sufficient information is available to substantiate a realistic claim and before issues of quantum are addressed in detail. One copy is for the defendants, the second for passing on to his insurers.

6.2 This letter shall contain a *clear summary of the facts* on which the claim is based, including details of the illness alleged, and the *main allegations of fault.* It shall also give details of present condition and prognosis. The *financial loss* incurred by the claimant should be outlined. Where the case is funded by a conditional fee agreement, notification should be given of the existence of the agreement and where appropriate, that there is a success fee and insurance premium, although not the level of the success fee or premium.

6.3 Solicitors are recommended to use *a standard format* for such a letter — an example is at annex B: this can be amended to suit the particular case, for example, if the client has rehabilitation needs these can also be detailed in the letter.

6.4 A *chronology* of the relevant events (e.g. dates or periods of exposure) should be provided. In the case of alleged occupational disease an appropriate employment history should also be provided, particularly if the claimant has been employed by a number of different employers and the illness in question has a long latency period.

6.5 The letter of claim should identify any *relevant documents,* including health records not already in the defendant's possession e.g. any relevant general practitioner records. These will need to be disclosed in confidence to the nominated insurance manager or solicitor representing the defendant following receipt of their letter of acknowledgment. Where the action is brought under the Law Reform (Miscellaneous Provisions) Act 1934 or the Fatal Accidents Act 1976 then *relevant documents* will normally include copies of the death certificate, the post mortem report, the inquest depositions and if obtained by that date the grant of probate or letters of administration.

6.6 The letter of claim should indicate whether a claim is also being made against any *other potential defendant* and identify any known insurer involved.

6.7 Sufficient information should be given to enable the defendant's insurer/solicitor to commence *investigations* and at least to put a broad valuation on the 'risk'.

6.8 It is not a requirement for the claimant to provide *medical evidence* with the letter of claim, but the claimant may choose to do so in very many cases.

6.9 *Letters of claim and response* are not intended to have the same *status* as a statement of case in proceedings. Matters may come to light as a result of investigation after the letter of claim has been sent, or after the defendant has responded, particularly if disclosure of documents takes place outside the recommended three-month period. These circumstances could mean that the 'pleaded' case of one or both parties is presented slightly differently than in the letter of claim or response. It would not be consistent with the spirit of the protocol for a party to 'take a point' on this in the proceedings, provided that there was no obvious intention by the party who changed their position to mislead the other party.

6.10 *Proceedings should not be issued until after three months from the date of acknowledgment* (see para. 7), unless there is a limitation problem and/or the claimant's position needs to be protected by early issue (see para. 2.5).

7 THE RESPONSE

7.1 The defendant should *send an acknowledgment within 21 calendar days* of the date of posting of the letter of claim, identifying the liability insurer (if any) who will be dealing with the matter and, if necessary, identifying specifically any significant omissions from the letter of claim. If there has been no acknowledgment by the defendant or insurer within 21 days, the claimant will be entitled to issue proceedings.

7.2 The identity of all relevant insurers, if more than one, should be notified to the claimant by the insurer identified in the acknowledgment letter, within one calendar month of the date of that acknowledgment.

7.3 The defendant or his representative should, *within three months of the date of the acknowledgment letter,* provide a *reasoned answer*:

- if the *claim is admitted,* they should say so in clear terms;
- if only *part of the claim is admitted* they should make clear which issues of fault and/or causation and/or limitation are admitted and which remain in issue and why;

- if the *claim is not admitted in full*, they should explain why and should, for example, include comments on the employment status of the claimant (including job description(s) and details of the department(s) where the claimant worked), the allegations of fault, causation and of limitation, and if a synopsis or chronology of relevant events has been provided and is disputed, their version of those events;
- if the *claim is not admitted in full*, the defendant should enclose with his letter of reply *documents* in his possession which are *material to the issues* between the parties and which would be likely to be ordered to be disclosed by the court, either on an application for pre-action disclosure, or on disclosure during proceedings. Reference can be made to the documents annexed to the personal injury protocol.
- where more than one defendant receives a letter of claim, the timetable will be activated for each defendant by the date on the letter of claim addressed to them. If any defendant wishes to extend the timetable because the number of defendants will cause complications, they should seek agreement to a different timetable as soon as possible.

7.4 If the parties reach agreement on liability and/or causation, but time is needed to resolve other issues including the value of the claim, they should aim to agree a reasonable period.

7.5 Where it is not practicable for the defendant to complete his investigations within three months, the defendant should indicate the difficulties and outline the further time needed. Any request for an extension of time should be made, with reasons, as soon as the defendant becomes aware that an extension is needed and normally before the three-month period has expired. Such an extension of time should be agreed in circumstances where reasonable justification has been shown. Lapse of many years since the circumstances giving rise to the claim does not, by itself, constitute reasonable justification for further time.

7.6 Where the relevant negligence occurred outside England and Wales and/or where the defendant is outside the jurisdiction, the time periods of 21 days and three months should normally be extended up to 42 days and six months.

8 SPECIAL DAMAGES

8.1 The claimant will send to the defendant as soon as practicable a schedule of special damages with supporting documents, particularly where the defendant has admitted liability.

9 EXPERTS

9.1 In disease claims expert opinions will usually be needed:

- on knowledge, fault and causation;
- on condition and prognosis;
- to assist in valuing aspects of the claim.

9.2 The civil justice reforms and the CPR encourage economy in the use of experts and a less adversarial expert culture. It is recognised that in disease claims, the parties and their advisers will require flexibility in their approach to expert evidence. Decisions on whether experts might be instructed jointly, and on whether reports might be disclosed sequentially or by exchange, should rest with the parties and their advisers. Sharing expert evidence may be appropriate on various issues including those relating to the value of the claim. However, this protocol does not attempt to be prescriptive on issues in relation to expert evidence.

9.3 Obtaining expert evidence will often be an expensive step and may take time, especially in specialised areas where there are limited numbers of suitable experts. Claimants, defendants and their advisers, will therefore need to consider carefully how best to obtain any necessary expert help quickly and cost-effectively.

9.4 The protocol recognises that a flexible approach must be adopted in the obtaining of medical reports in claims of this type. There will be very many occasions where the claimant will need to obtain a medical report before writing the letter of claim. In such cases the defendant will be entitled to obtain their own medical report. In some other instances it may be more appropriate to send the letter of claim before the medical report is obtained. Defendants will usually need to see a medical report before they can reach a view on causation.

9.5 Where the parties agree the nomination of a single expert is appropriate, before any party instructs an expert he should give the other party a list of the *name(s) of one or more experts* in the relevant speciality whom he considers are suitable to instruct. The parties are encouraged to agree the instruction of a single expert to deal with discrete areas such as cost of care.

9.6 *Within 14 days* the other party may indicate an objection to one or more of the named experts. The first party should then instruct a mutually acceptable expert. If the Claimant nominates an expert in the original letter of claim, the 14 days is in addition to the 21 days in para. 7.1.

9.7 If the second party objects to all the listed experts, the parties may then instruct *experts of their own choice.* It would be for the court to decide subsequently, if proceedings are issued, whether either party had acted unreasonably.

9.8 If the *second party does not object to an expert nominated,* he shall not be entitled to rely on his own expert evidence within that particular speciality unless:

(a) the first party agrees,
(b) the court so directs, or
(c) the first party's expert report has been amended and the first party is not prepared to disclose the original report.

9.9 *Either party may send to an agreed expert written questions* on the report, relevant to the issues, via the first party's solicitors. The expert should send answers to the questions separately and directly to each party.

9.10 The cost of a report from an agreed expert will usually be paid by the instructing first party: the costs of the expert replying to questions will usually be borne by the party which asks the questions.

9.11 Where the defendant admits liability in whole or in part, before proceedings are issued, any medical report obtained under this protocol which *the claimant* relies upon, should be disclosed to the other party.

9.12 Where the defendant admits liability in whole or in part before proceedings are issued, any medical report obtained under this protocol which *the defendant* relies upon, should be disclosed to the claimant.

10 RESOLUTION OF ISSUES

10.1 Part 36 of the CPR enables claimants and defendants to make formal offers to settle before proceedings are started. Parties should consider making such an offer, since to do so often leads to settlement. If such an offer is made, the party making the offer must always supply sufficient evidence and/or information to enable the offer to be properly considered.

10.2 Where a claim is not resolved when the protocol has been followed, the parties might wish to carry out a 'stocktake' of the issues in dispute, and the evidence that the court is likely to need to decide those issues, before proceedings are started.

10.3 Prior to proceedings it will be usual for all parties to disclose those expert reports relating to liability and causation upon which they propose to rely.

10.4 The claimant should delay issuing proceedings for 21 days from disclosure of reports to enable the parties to consider whether the claim is capable of settlement.

10.5 Where the defendant is insured and the pre-action steps have been conducted by the insurer, the insurer would normally be expected to nominate solicitors to act in the proceedings and the claimant's solicitor is recommended to invite the insurer to nominate solicitors to act in the proceedings and to do so seven to 14 days before the intended issue date.

11 LIMITATION

11.1 If by reason of complying with any part of this protocol a claimant's claim may be time-barred under any provision of the Limitation Act 1980, or any other legislation which imposes a time limit for bringing an action, the claimant may commence proceedings without complying with this protocol. In such circumstances, a claimant who commences proceedings without complying with all, or any part, of this protocol may apply to the court on notice for directions as to the timetable and form of procedure to be adopted, at the same time as he requests the court to issue proceedings. The court will consider whether to order a stay of the whole or part of the proceedings pending compliance with this protocol.

ANNEX A LETTER REQUESTING OCCUPATIONAL RECORDS INCLUDING HEALTH RECORDS

Dear Sirs,

We are acting on behalf of the above-named who has developed the following *(disease)*. We are investigating whether this disease may have been caused:

- during the course of his employment with [you] [*(name of employer if different)*;
- whilst at your premises at *(address)*;
- as a result of your product *(name)*.

We are writing this in accordance with the Pre-action Protocol for Disease and Illness Claims.

We seek the following records:

(details, e.g., personnel, occupational health)

Please note your insurers may require you to advise them of this request.

We enclose a request form and expect to receive the records within 40 days.

If you are not able to comply with this request within this time, please advise us of the reason.

Yours faithfully

ANNEX A1 APPLICATION ON BEHALF OF A POTENTIAL CLAIMANT FOR USE WHERE A DISEASE CLAIM IS BEING INVESTIGATED

This should be completed as fully as possible.

Company

Name

Address

1 (a) Full name of claimant (including previous surnames)
1 (b) Address now
1 (c) Address at date of termination of employment, if different
1 (d) Date of birth (and death, if applicable)
1 (e) National Insurance number, if available
2 Department(s) where claimant worked
3 This application is made because the claimant is considering:
 (a) a claim against you as detailed in point 4 YES/NO
 (b) pursuing an action against someone else YES/NO
4 If the answer to point 3(a) is 'Yes' details of:
 (a) the likely nature of the claim, e.g., dermatitis
 (b) grounds for the claim, e.g., exposure to chemical
 (c) approximate dates of the events involved
5 If the answer to point 3(b) is 'Yes' insert:
 (a) the names of the proposed defendants
 (b) have legal proceedings been started? YES/NO
 (c) if appropriate, details of the claim and action number
6 Any other relevant information or documents requested

Signature of solicitor

Name

Address

Ref.

Telephone number

Fax number

I authorise you to disclose all of your records relating to me/the claimant to my solicitor and to your legal and insurance representatives.

Signature of claimant

Signature of personal representative where claimant has died

ANNEX B TEMPLATE FOR LETTER OF CLAIM

To Defendant

Dear Sirs

Re: *(Claimant's full name)*

(Claimant's full address)

National Insurance number:

Date of birth:

Clock or works number:

Employer: *(name and address)*

We are instructed by the above named to claim damages in connection with a claim for:

(specify occupational disease)

We are writing this letter in accordance with the Pre-action Protocol for Disease and Illness Claims.

Please confirm the identity of your insurers. Please note that your insurers will need to see this letter as soon as possible and it may affect your insurance cover if you do not send this to them.

The Claimant was employed by you *(if the claim arises out of public or occupiers' liability give appropriate details)* as *(job description)* from *(date)* to *(date)*. During the relevant period of his employment he worked:

(description of precisely where the claimant worked and what he did to include a description of any machines used and details of any exposure to noise or substances)

The circumstances leading to the development of this condition are as follows:

(give chronology of events)

The reason why we are alleging fault is:

(details should be given of contemporary and comparable employees who have suffered from similar problems if known; any protective equipment provided; complaints; the supervisors concerned, if known)

Our client's employment history is attached.

[We have also made a claim against:

(insert details)

Their insurers' details are:

(insert if known)]

We have the following documents in support of our client's claim and will disclose these in confidence to your nominated insurance manager or solicitor when we receive their acknowledgment letter:

(e.g., occupational health notes; GP notes)

[We have obtained a medical report from *(name)* and will disclose this when we receive your acknowledgment of this letter.

(This is optional at this stage.)]

From the information we presently have:

(i) the Claimant first became aware of symptoms on *(insert approximate date)*;

(ii) the Claimant first received medical advice about those symptoms on *(insert date) (give details of advice given if appropriate)*.

(iii) the Claimant first believed that those symptoms might be due to exposure leading to this claim on *(insert approximate date)*.

A description of our client's condition is as follows:

(this should be sufficiently detailed to allow the defendant to put a broad value on the claim)

He has the following time off work:

(insert dates)

He is presently employed as a *(job description)* and his average net weekly income is £____.

If you are our client's employers, please provide us with the usual earnings details, which will enable us to calculate his financial loss.

[Please note that we have entered into a conditional fee agreement with our client dated ____ in relation to this claim which provides for a success fee within the meaning of section 58(2) of the Courts and Legal Services Act 1990. Our client has taken out an insurance policy dated with *(name of insurance company)* to which section 29 of the Access to Justice Act 1999 applies in respect of this claim.]

A copy of this letter is attached for you to send to your insurers. Finally we expect an acknowledgment of this letter within 21 days by yourselves or your insurers.

Yours faithfully

Pre-action Protocol for Housing Disrepair Cases

1 INTRODUCTION

Following a review of the problems of civil housing disrepair claims, Lord Woolf recommended in his *Final Report* in July 1996 that there should be a pre-action protocol.

The protocol, which covers claims in England and Wales, is intended to encourage the exchange of information between parties at an early stage and to provide a clear framework within which parties in a housing disrepair claim can attempt to achieve an early and appropriate resolution of the issues. An attempt has been made to draft the protocol in plain English and to keep the contents straightforward in order to make the protocol accessible and easy to use by all, including those representing themselves.

The protocol embraces the spirit of the Woolf reforms to the civil justice system. As Lord Woolf noted, landlords and tenants have a common interest in maintaining housing stock in good condition. It is generally common ground that in principle court action should be treated as a last resort, and it is hoped that the protocol will lead to the avoidance of unnecessary litigation. Before using the protocol tenants should therefore ensure that the landlord is aware of the disrepair. Tenants should also consider whether other options for having repairs carried out and/or obtaining compensation are more appropriate. Examples of other options are set out in para. 4.1(a).

Should a claim proceed to litigation, the court will expect all parties to have complied with the protocol as far as possible. The court has the power to order parties who have unreasonably failed to comply with the protocol to pay costs or be subject to other sanctions.

2 AIMS OF THE PROTOCOL

PD Protocols provides that the objectives of pre-action protocols are:

(1) to encourage the exchange of early and full information about the prospective legal claim,
(2) to enable parties to avoid litigation by agreeing a settlement of the claim before the commencement of proceedings,
(3) to support the efficient management of proceedings where litigation cannot be avoided. The specific aims of this protocol are:
  - To avoid unnecessary litigation.
  - To promote the speedy and appropriate carrying out of any repairs which are the landlord's responsibility.
  - To ensure that tenants receive any compensation to which they are entitled as speedily as possible.
  - To promote good pre-litigation practice, including the early exchange of information and to give guidance about the instruction of experts.
  - To keep the costs of resolving disputes down.

3 PROTOCOL

When using this protocol, please refer to the guidance notes in para. 4.

3.1 Definitions

For the purposes of this protocol:

(a) A disrepair claim is a civil claim arising from the condition of residential premises and may include a related personal injury claim. (See para. 4.4 (c), (d) and (e) of the guidance notes.) It does not include disrepair claims which originate as counterclaims or set-offs in other proceedings.

(b) The types of claim which this protocol is intended to cover include those brought under the Landlord and Tenant Act 1985, s. 11, the Defective Premises Act 1972, s. 4, common law nuisance and negligence, and those brought under the express terms of a tenancy agreement or lease. It does not cover claims brought under the Environmental Protection Act 1990, s. 82 (which are heard in the magistrates' court).

(c) This protocol covers claims by any person with a disrepair claim as referred to in paragraphs (a) and (b) above, including tenants, lessees and members of the tenant's family. The use of the term 'tenant' in this protocol is intended to cover all such people. (See also paragraph 4.4(e).)

3.2 Early Notification Letter

(a) Notice of the claim should be given to the landlord as soon as possible. In order to avoid delay in notifying the landlord it may be appropriate to send a letter notifying the landlord of the claim (early notification letter) before sending a letter setting out the full details of the claim (letter of claim). An early notification letter is intended to be a helpful tool, but it will not be necessary in every case. It might be appropriate where, for example, a repair is urgent or there is likely to be some delay before enough details are available to make a claim. The early notification letter to the landlord should give the following information:
   - (i) tenant's name, the address of the property, tenant's address if different, tenant's telephone number and when access is available;
   - (ii) details of the defects, including any defects outstanding, in the form of a schedule, if appropriate. Attached at annex G is a specimen schedule which can be used to inform the landlord of the disrepair;
   - (iii) details of any notification previously given to the landlord of the need for repair or information as to why the tenant believes that the landlord has knowledge of the need for repair;
   - (iv) proposed expert (see para. 3.6);
   - (v) proposed letter of instruction to expert (see annex C);
   - (vi) tenant's disclosure of such relevant documents as are readily available.

(b) The early notification letter should also request the following disclosure from the landlord: All relevant records or documents including:
   - (i) copy of tenancy agreement including tenancy conditions;
   - (ii) documents or computerised records relating to notice given, disrepair reported, inspection reports or repair works to the property.

(c) The early notification letter should include the authorisation for release of the information (except in a case where the tenant is acting in person).

(d) Specimen early notification letters are attached at annex A. They may be suitably adapted as appropriate.

3.3 Letter of Claim

(a) The tenant should send to the landlord a letter of claim at the earliest reasonable opportunity. The letter of claim should contain the following details *(if they have not already been provided in an early notification letter)*:
   - (i) tenant's name, the address of the property, tenant's address if different, the tenant's telephone number and when access is available;
   - (ii) details of the defects, including any defects outstanding, in the form of a schedule, if appropriate. Attached at annex G is a specimen schedule which can be used to inform the landlord of the disrepair;
   - (iii) history of the defects, including attempts to rectify them;
   - (iv) details of any notification previously given to the landlord of the need for repair or information as to why the tenant believes that the landlord has knowledge of the need for repair;
   - (v) the effect of the defects on the tenant (see para. 4.4(c), (d) and (e) regarding personal injury claims);

(vi) details of any special damages (see form attached at annex E and definition of 'special damages' at para. 4.10);
(vii) proposed expert (see para. 3.6);
(viii) proposed letter of instruction to the expert (see annex C);
(ix) tenant's disclosure of relevant documents.

(b) If not already requested in an early notification letter, the letter of claim should also request the following disclosure from the landlord:
All relevant records or documents including:
(i) copy of tenancy agreement including tenancy conditions;
(ii) tenancy file;
(iii) documents relating to notice given, disrepair reported, inspection reports or requirements to the property;
(iv) computerised records.

(c) If not requested in an early notification letter, the letter of claim should also include the authorisation for release of the information (except in a case where the tenant is acting in person).

(d) Specimen letters of claim are attached at annex B. It will be seen that there are different versions depending on whether or not an early notification letter has been sent. The letters may be suitably adapted as appropriate.

3.4 Limitation Period

The procedures in this protocol do not extend statutory limitation periods. If a limitation period is about to expire, the tenant may need to issue proceedings immediately unless the landlord confirms that they will not rely on limitation as a defence in subsequent proceedings. (See para. 4.8 for guidance about the limitation period, and para. 4.10 for a definition of 'limitation period'.) Alternatively the tenant can ask the landlord to agree to extend the limitation period.

3.5 Landlord's Response

3.5.1 Response to first letter

The landlord should normally reply within 20 working days of the date of receipt of the first letter from the tenant, i.e., the early notification letter or the letter of claim if no early notification letter is sent. (See para. 4.10 for a definition of 'working days'.) The landlord's response to the first letter, whether an early notification letter or a letter of claim, should include the following:

Disclosure

(a) All relevant records or documents including:
(i) copy of tenancy agreement including tenancy conditions;
(ii) documents or computerised records relating to notice given, disrepair reported, inspection reports or requirements to the property.

Expert

(b) A response to the tenant's proposals for instructing an expert including:
(i) whether or not the proposed single joint expert is agreed;
(ii) whether the letter of instruction is agreed;
(iii) if the single joint expert is agreed but with separate instructions, a copy of the letter of instruction;
(iv) if the appointment of a single joint expert is not agreed, whether the landlord agrees to a joint inspection.

3.5.2 Response to letter of claim

(a) The landlord's response to the tenant's letter of claim should include:
(i) whether liability is admitted and if so, in respect of which defects. If liability is disputed in respect of some or all of the defects, the reasons for this;
(ii) any point which the landlord wishes to make regarding lack of notice of the repair or regarding any difficulty in gaining access;
(iii) a full schedule of intended works including anticipated start and completion dates and a timetable for the works;
(iv) any offer of compensation;

(v) any offer in respect of costs;
(vi) the information set out at para. 3.5.1(a) and (b), if it has not already been provided.

(b) On receipt of the letter of claim (whether or not an early notification letter was sent), the landlord may provide a response to the issues set out at paragraph (a) above either:
(i) within 20 working days of the date of receipt of the letter of claim (see para. 4.10 for a definition of 'working days'); or
(ii) within 20 working days of the date of receipt of the report of the single joint expert (see para. 3.6(h)) or date of receipt of the experts' agreed schedule following a joint inspection (see para. 3.6(g)).

3.5.3 If landlord does not respond

(a) If no response is received from the landlord to the early notification letter within 20 working days, the tenant should send a letter of claim giving as many of the details outlined at para. 3.3 as possible, on the basis of the information the tenant has to hand.

(b) Failure to respond within the time limits set out in paras 3.5.1 and 3.5.2, or at all, to the early notification letter or the letter of claim will be a breach of the protocol. (See para. 4.7(a) and (b) regarding time limits and the power of the court if the protocol is breached.)

3.6 Experts

General

See para. 4.6 for guidance regarding the use of experts.

(a) Tenants should remember that in some cases it might not be necessary to instruct an expert to provide evidence of disrepair, for example, if the only issue relates to the level of any damages claimed. It may be advisable to take photographs of any defects before and after works, and consideration should be given to the use of video footage, particularly if an expert has not been instructed.

(b) The expert should be instructed to report on all items of disrepair which the landlord ought reasonably to know about, or which the expert ought reasonably to report on. The expert should be asked to provide a schedule of works, an estimate of the costs of repair, and to list any urgent works.

(c) Information is given at para. 4.6(a) about obtaining lists of independent experts who can be instructed in disrepair cases.

Single joint expert

(d) If the landlord does not raise an objection to the proposed expert or letter of instruction within 20 working days of the date of receipt of the early notification letter or letter of claim, the expert should be instructed as a single joint expert, using the tenant's proposed letter of instruction. Attached at annex C are specimen letters of instruction to an expert. Alternatively, if the parties cannot agree joint instructions, the landlord and tenant should send their own separate instructions to the single joint expert. If sending separate instructions, the landlord should send the tenant a copy of the landlord's letter of instruction with their response to the first letter. (The tenant has already forwarded the proposed letter of instruction to the landlord.)

Joint inspection

(e) If it is not possible to reach agreement to instruct a single joint expert, even with separate instructions, the parties should attempt to arrange a joint inspection, i.e., an inspection by different experts instructed by each party to take place at the same time. If the landlord wishes to send their own expert to a joint inspection, they should inform both the tenant's expert and the tenant's solicitor. If the landlord instructs their own expert to inspect then the tenant can also instruct their own expert. It will be for the court to decide subsequently, if proceedings are issued, whether or not either party has acted reasonably.

Time limits

(f) Whether a single joint expert or a joint inspection is used, the property should be inspected within 20 working days of the date that the landlord responds to the tenant's first letter.

(g) If there is a joint inspection, the experts should produce an agreed schedule of works detailing:
(i) the defects and required works which are agreed and a timetable for the agreed works;
(ii) the areas of disagreement and the reasons for disagreement.

The agreed schedule should be sent to both the landlord and the tenant within 10 working days of the joint inspection.

(h) If there is a single joint expert, a copy of the report should be sent to both the landlord and the tenant within 10 working days of the inspection. Either party can ask relevant questions of the expert.

(i) At annex D are flowcharts showing the time limits in the protocol.

Urgent cases

(j) The protocol does not prevent a tenant from instructing an expert at an earlier stage if this is considered necessary for reasons of urgency, and the landlord should give access in such cases. Appropriate cases may include:
   (i) where the tenant reasonably considers that there is a significant risk to health and safety;
   (ii) where the tenant is seeking an interim injunction;
   (iii) where it is necessary to preserve evidence.

Access

(k) Tenants must give reasonable access to the landlord for inspection and repair in line with the tenancy agreement. The landlord should give reasonable notice of the need for access, except in the case of an emergency. The landlord must give access to common parts as appropriate, e.g., for the inspection of a shared heating system.

Costs

(l) Terms of appointment should be agreed at the outset and should include:
   (i) the basis of the expert's charges (either daily or hourly rates and an estimate of the time likely to be required, or a fee for the services);
   (ii) any travelling expenses and other relevant expenses;
   (iii) rates for attendance at court should this become necessary, and provisions for payment on late notice of cancellation of a court hearing;
   (iv) time for delivery of report;
   (v) time for making payment;
   (vi) whether fees are to be paid by a third party; and
   (vii) arrangements for dealing with questions for experts and discussions between experts and for providing for the cost involved.

(m) If a single joint expert is instructed, each party will pay one half of the cost of the report. If a joint inspection is carried out, each party will pay the full cost of the report from their own expert. (See para. 3.7.)

(n) The expert should send separately and directly to both parties answers to any questions asked.

3.7 Costs

(a) If the tenant's claim is settled without litigation on terms which justify bringing it, the landlord will pay the tenant's reasonable costs or out-of-pocket expenses. (See para. 4.10 for a definition of 'costs' and 'out-of-pocket expenses'.)

(b) Attached at annex F is a statement of costs form which can be used to inform the landlord of the costs of the claim.

4 GUIDANCE NOTES

4.1 Alternative Dispute Resolution

(a) The parties should consider whether some form of alternative dispute resolution procedure (see para. 4.10 for a definition of alternative dispute resolution) would be more suitable than litigation, and if so, endeavour to agree which form to adopt. Both the claimant and defendant may be required by the court to provide evidence that alternative means of resolving their dispute were considered. The courts take the view that litigation should be a last resort, and that claims should not be issued prematurely when a settlement is still actively being explored. Parties are warned that if the protocol is not followed (including this paragraph) then the court must have regard to such conduct when determining costs.

(b) It is not practicable in this protocol to address in detail how the parties might decide which method to adopt to resolve their particular dispute. However, summarised below are some of the options for resolving disputes without litigation:

- Discussion and negotiation.
- Early neutral evaluation by an independent third party (for example, a lawyer experienced in the field of housing disrepair or an individual experienced in the subject matter of the claim).
- Mediation — a form of facilitated negotiation assisted by an independent neutral party.
- Other options in respect of the following specific categories:
  (i) For council tenants:
    - Local authority repairs, complaints and/or arbitration procedures.
    - The Right to Repair Scheme. The scheme is only suitable for small, urgent repairs of less than £250 in value.
      Information and leaflets about the scheme in England can be obtained from the Office of the Deputy Prime Minister, Eland House, Bressenden Place, London SW1E 5DU. Tel: (020) 7944 3672.
      Information about the scheme in Wales can be obtained from the National Assembly for Wales, Cathays Park, Cardiff, CF10 3NQ. Tel: (029) 2082 5111.
    - Commission for Local Administration in England. Tel: 0845 602 1983.
    - The Local Government Ombudsman for Wales. Tel: (01656) 661325.

  (ii) For tenants of social landlords who are not council tenants, and for tenants of qualifying private landlords:
    - In England, the Independent Housing Ombudsman, 3rd Floor, Norman House, 105–109 Strand, London WC2R 0AA. Tel: (020) 7836 3630.
    - In Wales, the National Assembly for Wales, Cathays Park, Cardiff CF10 3NQ. Tel: (029) 2082 5111.
    - Local authority environmental health officers.

  (iii) For private tenants:
    - Local authority environmental health officers.

(c) The Legal Services Commission has published a booklet on *Alternatives to Court* (CLS Direct Information Leaflet 23) (www.clsdirect.org.uk/legalhelp/leaflet23.jsp), which lists a number of organisations that provide alternative dispute resolution services.

(d) *It is expressly recognised that no party can or should be forced to mediate or enter into any form of ADR.*

(e) Information about repair rights generally is available free of charge from the following web pages: www.shelter.org.uk/housingadvice/index.asp and www.legalservices.gov.uk/leaflets/cls/index.htm.

(f) The former Department for Transport, Local Government and the Regions issued *Good Practice Guidance on Housing Disrepair Legal Obligations* in January 2002. Copies of the Guidance (ISBN 185112 523X) can be obtained from ODPM Publications Sales Centre, Cambertown House, Goldthorpe Industrial Estate, Rotherham S63 9BL. A summary, Housing Research Summary No. 154, is available free from the Housing Support Unit, ODPM, Zone 2/C6, Eland House, Bressenden Place, London SW1E 5DU (Fax: (020) 7944 4527). The ODPM housing website www.housing.odpm.gov.uk is a general source of information for landlords and tenants.

4.2 Scope of the Protocol*

(a) This protocol is intended to apply to all civil law claims which include a claim for disrepair, but not to counterclaims or set-offs in disrepair claims which originate as other proceedings. (See para. 4.10 for an explanation of 'counterclaim' and 'set-off'.) In cases which involve a counterclaim or set-off, the landlord and tenant will still be expected to act reasonably in exchanging information and trying to settle the case at an early stage.

(b) In practice, most disrepair cases will have a value of more than £1,000 but less than £15,000 and so are likely to be allocated to the fast track if they come to court. (See para. 4.10 for an explanation of 'the fast track'.) The protocol is aimed at this type of case. The need to keep costs down is especially important in claims of lower value. The approach of the protocol is however, equally appropriate to all claims and the protocol should also be followed in small claims track and multi-track claims. (See para. 4.10 for an explanation of 'small claims track' and 'multi-track'.) The court will expect to see reasonable pre-action behaviour applied in all cases.

[* The text issued by the Department for Constitutional Affairs mistakenly omits paras 4.2 to 4.10.]

4.3 Early Notification Letter

(a) The early notification letter is not intended to replace the direct reporting of defects to the landlord at an early stage, using any procedure the landlord may have established. The protocol is for use in those cases where, despite the landlord's knowledge of the disrepair, the matter remains unresolved.

(b) It is recognised that disrepair cases can range from straightforward to highly complex, and that it is not always possible to obtain detailed information at an early stage. In order to avoid unnecessary delay and to ensure that notice of the claim is given to the landlord at the earliest possible opportunity, the protocol suggests the use of two letters in some cases; an early notification letter and a later letter of claim. (See para. 3.2(a) and annexes A and B.)

(c) A copy of the protocol need only be sent to the landlord if the tenant has reason to believe that the landlord will not have access to the protocol, e.g., because the landlord is an individual or small organisation. If in doubt, a copy should be sent.

4.4 Letters of Claim and Landlord's Response

(a) Letters of claim and a landlord's response are not intended to have the same status as a statement of case in court proceedings. Matters may come to light after the letter of claim has been sent, or after the landlord has responded, which could mean that the case of one or both parties is presented slightly differently than in the letters of claim or in the landlord's response. It would be inconsistent with the spirit of the protocol to seek to capitalise on this in the proceedings, provided that there was no intention to mislead. In particular, advantage should not be taken regarding discrepancies relating to the general details of notice given in the early notification letter.

(b) See para. 4.3(c) regarding the sending of a copy of the protocol by the tenant to the landlord.

Cases with a personal injury element

(c) Housing disrepair claims may contain a personal injury element. This should be set out in the letter of claim, as should a clear indication of the identities of all persons who plan to make a personal injury claim.

(d) There is also a Pre-action Protocol for Personal Injury Claims. This protocol should be followed for that part of the disrepair claim which forms a personal injury claim, unless it is insufficient to warrant separate procedures and would therefore be dealt with only as part of the disrepair claim and evidenced by a general practitioner's letter. The Pre-action Protocol for Personal Injury Claims should be followed for any claim which requires expert evidence other than a general practitioner's letter. If the disrepair claim is urgent, it would be reasonable to pursue separate disrepair and personal injury claims, which could then be case-managed or consolidated at a later date.

(e) Paragraph 3.3(a)(v) refers to the effect of the defects on 'the tenant'. This should be taken to include all persons who have a personal injury claim. The details of any such claim and of all likely claimants should be set out in the letter of claim.

4.5 Disclosure of Documents

(a) When giving disclosure, the landlord should copy all relevant documents. In housing disrepair claims, this includes any and all documents relating in particular to the disrepair and to notice given by the tenant to the landlord of the disrepair. Notice is often given by personal attendance at the landlord's office, and copies of any notes of meetings and oral discussions should also be copied, along with other relevant documents. Documents regarding rent arrears or tenants' disputes will not normally be relevant.

(b) The aim of the early disclosure of documents by the landlord is not to encourage 'fishing expeditions' by the tenant, but to promote an early exchange of relevant information to help in clarifying or resolving issues in dispute. The tenant should assist by identifying the particular categories of documents which they consider relevant.

(c) The 20 working days time limit specified in para. 3.5 runs from the date of receipt of either letter. Receipt of the letter is deemed to have taken place two days after the date of the letter. If necessary, a written request for extra time should be made by the landlord to the tenant. Should a case come to court, the court will decide whether the parties have acted reasonably, and whether any sanctions, including costs orders, are appropriate. The principles regarding time limits are referred to again at para. 4.7.

(d) Nothing in the protocol restricts the right of the tenant to look personally at their file or to request a copy of the whole file. Neither is the landlord prevented from sending to the tenant a copy of the whole file, should the landlord wish.

4.6 Experts

(a) Information about independent experts can be obtained from:
   (i) The Chartered Institute of Environmental Health, Chadwick Court, 15 Hatfields, London SE1 8DJ. Tel: (020) 7928 6006. Ask for a copy of the Consultants and Trainers Directory.
   (ii) The Law Society, 113 Chancery Lane, London WC2A 1PL, Tel: (020) 7831 0344. Refer to the Society's Expert Witness Directory.
   (iii) The Royal Institution of Chartered Surveyors, 12 Great George Street, Parliament Square, London SW1P 3AD, Tel: 0845 304 4111. Ask for a copy of the relevant regional directory.

(b) The protocol encourages the use of a single joint expert. In order to make it less likely that a second expert will be necessary, the protocol provides for the landlord to forward their own instructions directly to the single joint expert if they cannot agree joint instructions. Both parties can ask relevant questions of the expert. If the parties cannot agree on a single joint expert, either with joint or separate instructions, the protocol suggests a joint inspection by each party's expert.

(c) The specimen letters at annexes A and B ask for reasons to be given as to why the landlord objects to the expert proposed by the tenant. Should a case come to court, it will be for the court to decide whether the parties have acted reasonably and whether the costs of more than one expert should be recoverable.

(d) Parties should bear in mind that it may not always be necessary to obtain expert evidence of disrepair, and in view of this, the protocol encourages the use of photos before and after works, and if appropriate, video evidence.

(e) Parties are reminded that the CPR provide that expert evidence should be restricted to that which is necessary and that the court's permission is required to use an expert's report. The court may limit the amount of experts' fees and expenses recoverable from another party.

(f) When instructing an expert, regard should be had to any approved Code of Guidance for Experts and whether a copy of the protocol should be sent to the expert.

4.7 Time Limits

(a) The timescales given in the protocol are longstops and every attempt should be made to comply with the protocol as soon as possible. If parties are able to comply earlier than the timescales provided, they should do so.

(b) Time limits in the protocol may be changed by agreement. However, it should always be borne in mind that the court will expect an explanation as to why the protocol has not been followed or has been varied and breaches of the protocol may lead to costs or other orders being made by the court.

4.8 Limitation Period

(a) In cases where the limitation period will shortly expire, the tenant should ask in the first letter for an extension of the limitation period. The extension requested should be only so long as is necessary to avoid the cost of starting court proceedings.

(b) It will be for the court to decide whether refusal to grant the request is reasonable and whether any sanctions, including costs orders, are appropriate.

4.9 Contact Point

Where a landlord is not an individual, a person should be designated to act as a point of contact for the tenant as soon as possible after the landlord receives the first letter from the tenant and (if one is involved) their solicitor. The appointee's name and contact details should be sent to the tenant and their solicitor as soon as possible after the appointment is made.

4.10 Glossary

alternative dispute resolution. Mediation, or other dispute resolution method, which seeks to settle disputes without the need for court proceedings.

counterclaim. A claim that either party makes in response to an initial claim by the other.

costs. Legal fees or, in a small track claim, out-of-pocket expenses incurred as a result of a claim. (See **out-of-pocket expenses** below.)

damages. Money obtained as the result of a claim to compensate for inconvenience and/or distress suffered because of the condition of the property. (See also **special damages** below.)

defect/disrepair. A fault or problem with a property, for which the landlord is responsible.

disclosure. The making available by one party to the other of documentation relevant to the claim.

fast track/multi-track/small claims track. Cases which proceed to court will be allocated to separate tracks depending on their value. The separate tracks have different rules and procedures. Housing cases worth between £1,000 and £15,000 where there is a claim for works to be done will usually be allocated to the **fast track**. Housing cases where the costs of the repairs and/or the damages do not exceed £1,000 will usually be dealt with on the **small claims track**. Cases over £15,000 will usually be allocated to the **multi-track**.

joint inspection. An inspection of a property carried out at the same time by one expert instructed by the tenant and by one expert instructed by the landlord.

limitation period. The time limit after which a legal action cannot be started. In most housing cases it is six years. In personal injury cases it is three years.

litigation. A court case or court proceedings. The taking of legal action by someone.

notice. Notification of a disrepair, either directly by the tenant in writing or orally to the landlord or his employee, or indirectly, by inspection of the property by the landlord or his employee.

out-of-pocket expenses. Expenses incurred in a small track claim as a result of the claim, such as loss of earnings and experts' fees.

protocol. A code or procedure — in this case for dealing with housing disrepair.

set-off. Where one party agrees with the other's claim or part of it, but sets up one which counterbalances it.

single joint expert. An expert who is instructed by both the tenant and the landlord, either with joint or separate instructions.

special damages. Compensation for loss of or damage to specific items, e.g., clothes, carpets, curtains, wallpaper, bedding or extra electricity costs.

tenant. Someone who rents land (including property) owned by another. (See also the definition at para. 3.1(c).)

third party. Someone other than the landlord or tenant.

working days. All days other than Saturdays, Sundays and bank holidays.

5 ANNEXES

Specimen Letters

It will be noted that the attached specimen letters are in pairs for use by solicitors and by tenants acting in person respectively.

It is emphasised that they may be suitably adapted as appropriate.

The letters, with the paragraph of the protocol to which each one relates, are as follows:

Annex A early notification letter (see para. 3.2).

Annex B letter of claim (see para. 3.3).

Note: There are two versions of this:

(a) for use where an early notification letter has been sent;

(b) for other cases.

Annex C letter of instruction to expert (see para. 3.6).

Annex D early notification letter flowchart.

Annex E special damages form.

Annex F statement of costs.

Annex G schedule.

ANNEX A EARLY NOTIFICATION LETTER

(i) Letter from Solicitor

To Landlord

Dear Sirs,

Re: *(tenant's name and address of property)*

We are instructed by your above-named tenant. *(Include a sentence stating how the case is being funded.)* We are using the Housing Disrepair Protocol. [We enclose a copy of the protocol for your information.*]

REPAIRS

Your tenant complains of the following defects at the property *(set out nature of defects).*

[We enclose a schedule, which sets out the disrepair in each room.*]

You received notice of the defects as follows: *(list details of notice relied on).*

Please arrange to inspect the property as soon as possible. Access will be available on the following dates and times: *(list dates and times as appropriate)*

Please let us know what repairs you propose to carry out and the anticipated date for completion of the works.

DISCLOSURE

Please also provide within 20 working days of receipt of this letter, the following:

All relevant records or documents including:

(i) copy of tenancy agreement including tenancy conditions;

(ii) documents or computerised records relating to notice given, disrepair, reported, inspection reports or repair works to the property.

We enclose a signed authority from our clients for you to release this information to ourselves.

We also enclose copies of the following relevant documents from our client: *(list documents enclosed)*

EXPERT

If agreement is not reached about the carrying out of repairs within 20 working days of this letter, we propose to jointly instruct a single joint expert *(insert expert's name and address)* to carry out an inspection of the property and provide a report. We enclose a copy of their CV, plus a draft letter of instruction. Please let us know if you agree to his/her appointment. If you object, please let us know your reasons within 20 working days.

If you do not object to the expert being instructed as a single joint expert, but wish to provide your own instructions, you should send those directly to *(insert expert's name)* within 20 working days of this letter. Please send to ourselves a copy of your letter of instruction. If you do not agree to a single joint expert, we will instruct *(insert expert's name)* to inspect the property in any event. In those circumstances, if you wish to instruct your expert to attend at the same time, please let ourselves and *(insert expert's name)* know within 20 working days of this letter.

CLAIM

Our client's disrepair claim requires further investigation. We will write to you as soon as possible with further details of the history of the defects and of notice relied on, along with details of our client's claim for general and special damages.

Yours faithfully,

* Delete as appropriate

(ii) Letter from Tenant

To Landlord

Dear

Re: *(your name and address of property)*

I write regarding disrepair at the above address. I am using the Housing Disrepair Protocol. [I enclose a copy of the protocol for your information.*]

REPAIRS

The following defects exist at the property *(set out nature of defects).*

[I enclose a schedule which sets out the disrepair in each room.*]

Please arrange to inspect the property as soon as possible. Access will be available on the following dates and times: *(list dates and time as appropriate)*

You received notice of the defects as follows: *(list details of notice relied on).*

Please let me know what repairs you propose to carry out and the anticipated date for completion of the works.

DISCLOSURE

Please also provide within 20 working days of receipt of this letter, the following:

All relevant records or documents including:

(i) copy of tenancy agreement including tenancy conditions;

(ii) documents or computerised records relating to notice given, disrepair reported, inspection reports or repair works to the property.

I also enclose copies of the following relevant documents: *(list documents enclosed)*

EXPERT

If agreement is not reached about the carrying out of repairs within 20 working days, I propose that we jointly instruct a single joint expert *(insert expert's name and address)* to carry out an inspection of the property and provide a report. I enclose a copy of their CV, plus a draft letter of instruction. Please let me know if you agree to his/her appointment. If you object, please let me know your reasons within 20 working days.

If you do not object to the expert being appointed as a single joint expert but wish to provide your own instructions, you should send those directly to *(insert expert's name)* within 20 working days. Please send a copy of your letter of instruction to me. If you do not agree to a single joint expert I will instruct *(insert expert's name)* to inspect the property in any event. In those circumstances if you wish your expert to attend at the same time, please let me and *(insert expert's name)* know within 20 working days.

CLAIM

I will write to you as soon as possible with further details of the history of the defects and of notice relied on, along with details of my claim for general and special damages.

Yours sincerely

ANNEX B LETTER OF CLAIM

(a) For Use Where an Early Notification Letter Has Been Sent (As Set Out in Annex A)

(i) Letter from Solicitor

To Landlord

Dear Sirs,

Re: *(tenant's name and address of property)*

We write further to our letter of *(insert date)* regarding our client's housing disrepair claim. We have now taken full instructions from our client.

* Delete as appropriate

REPAIRS

The history of the disrepair is as follows: *(set out history of defects).*

[I enclose a schedule which sets out the disrepair in each room.*]

You received notice of the defects as follows: *(list details of notice relied on).*

The defects at the property are causing *(set out the effects of the disrepair on the client and their family, including any personal injury element; specify if there will be any additional claimant).*

Please forward to us within 20 working days of receipt of this letter a full schedule of works together with the anticipated date for completion of the works proposed.

CLAIM

We take the view that you are in breach of your repairing obligations. Please provide us with your proposals for compensation. *(Alternatively, set out suggestions for general damages, e.g., £x for x years).* [Our client also requires compensation for special damages, and we attach a schedule of the special damages claimed.*]

Yours faithfully,

(ii) Letter from Tenant

To Landlord

Dear

Re: *(your name and address of property)*

I write further to my letter of *(insert date)* regarding my housing disrepair claim. I am now able to provide you with further details.

REPAIRS

The history of the disrepair is as follows: *(set out history of defects).*

You received notice of the defects as follows: *(list details of notice relied on).*

The defects at the property are causing *(set out the effects of the disrepair on you and your family, including any personal injury element; specify if there will be any additional claimant).*

Please forward to me within 20 working days of receipt of this letter a full schedule of works together with the anticipated date for completion of the works proposed.

CLAIM

I take the view that you are in breach of your repairing obligations. Please provide me with your proposals for compensation. *(Alternatively, set out suggestions for general damages, e.g., £x for x years).* [I also require compensation for special damages, and I attach a schedule of the special damages claimed.*]

Yours sincerely,

(b) For Use Where an Early Notification Letter Has Not Been Sent

(i) Letter from Solicitor

To Landlord

Dear Sirs,

Re: *(tenant's name and address of property)*

We are instructed by your above-named tenant. *(Insert a sentence stating how the case is being funded.)* We are using the Housing Disrepair Protocol. [We enclose a copy of the protocol for your information.*]

* Delete as appropriate

REPAIRS

Your tenant complains of the following defects at the property: *(set out nature and history of defects).*

[We enclose a schedule which sets out the disrepair in each room.*]

You received notice of the defects as follows: *(list details of notice relied on).*

The defects at the property are causing *(set out the effects of the disrepair on the client and their family, including any personal injury element, specifying if there are any additional claimants).*

Please provide within 20 working days of receipt of this letter a full schedule of the works you propose to carry out to remedy the above defects and the anticipated date for completion of the works.

DISCLOSURE

Please also provide within 20 working days of this letter the following:

All relevant records or documents including:
(i) copy of tenancy agreement including tenancy conditions;
(ii) tenancy file;
(iii) documents relating to notice given, disrepair reported, inspection reports or repair works to the property;
(iv) computerised records.

We enclose a signed authority from our clients for you to release this information to ourselves.

We also enclose copies of the following relevant documents: *(list documents enclosed)*

EXPERT

If agreement is not reached about the carrying out of repairs within 20 working days of receipt of this letter, we propose to jointly instruct a single joint expert *(insert expert's name and address)* to carry out an inspection of the property and provide a report. We enclose a copy of their CV, plus a draft letter of instruction. Please let me know if you agree to his/her appointment. If you object, please let me know your reasons within 20 working days.

If you do not object to the expert being instructed a single joint expert, but wish to provide your own instructions, you should send those directly to *(insert expert's name)* within 20 working days. Please send a copy of your letter of instruction to ourselves. If you do not agree to a single joint expert, we will instruct *(insert expert's name)* to inspect the property in any event. In those circumstances, if you wish to instruct your expert to attend at the same time please let ourselves and *(insert expert's name)* know within 20 working days.

CLAIM

We take the view that you are in breach of your repairing obligations. Please provide us with your proposals for compensation. *(Alternatively, set out suggestions for general damages, e.g., £x for x years.)* [Our client also requires compensation for the special damages, and we attach a schedule of the special damages claimed.*]

Yours faithfully,

(ii) Letter from Tenant

To Landlord

Dear

Re: *(your name and address of property)*

I write regarding the disrepair at the above address. I am using the Housing Disrepair Protocol. [I enclose a copy of the protocol for your information.*]

REPAIRS

The property has the following defects: *(set out nature and history of defects).*

[I enclose a schedule which sets out the disrepair in each room.*]

You received notice of the defects as follows: *(list details of notice relied on).*

* Delete as appropriate

The defects at the property are causing *(set out the effects of the disrepair on you and your family, including any personal injury element, specifying if there are any additional claimants).*

Please provide within 20 working days of receipt of this letter a full schedule of the works you propose to carry out to remedy the above defects and the anticipated date for completion of the works.

DISCLOSURE

Please also provide within 20 working days of receipt of this letter the following:

All relevant records or documents including:

(i) copy of tenancy agreement including tenancy conditions;
(ii) tenancy file;
(iii) documents relating to notice given, disrepair reported, inspection reports or repair works to the property;
(iv) computerised records.

I also enclose copies of the following relevant documents: *(list documents enclosed).*

EXPERT

If agreement is not reached about the carrying out of repairs within 20 working days of receipt of this letter, I propose that we jointly instruct a single joint expert *(insert expert's name and address)* to carry out an inspection of the property and provide a report. I enclose a copy of their CV, plus a draft letter of instruction. Please let me know if you agree to his/her appointment. If you object, please let me know your reasons within 20 working days.

If you do not object to the expert being instructed as a single joint expert, but wish to provide your own instructions, you should send those directly to *(insert expert's name)* within 20 working days. Please also send a copy of the letter of instruction to me. If you do not agree to a single joint expert, I will instruct *(insert expert's name)* to inspect the property in any event. In those circumstances, if you wish to instruct your expert to attend at the same time please let me and *(insert expert's name)* know within 20 working days.

CLAIM

I take the view that you are in breach of your repairing obligations. Please provide me with your proposals for compensation. *(Alternatively, set out suggestions for general damages, e.g. £x for x years.)* [I also require compensation for special damages, and I attach a schedule of the special damages claimed.*]

Yours sincerely

ANNEX C LETTER OF INSTRUCTION TO EXPERT

(i) Letter from Solicitor

Dear

Re: *(tenant's name and address of property)*

We act for the above-named in connection with a housing disrepair claim at the above property. We are using the Housing Disrepair Protocol. [We enclose a copy of the Protocol for your information.*]

Please carry out an inspection of the above property by *(date †)* and provide a report covering the following points:

(a) whether you agree that the defects are as claimed;
(b) whether any of the defects is structural;
(c) the cause of the defect(s);
(d) the age, character and prospective life of the property.

Access will be available on the following dates and times: *(list dates and times as appropriate)*

[You are instructed as a single joint expert.] [The landlord is *(landlord's name and details).*] [The landlord will be providing you with their own instructions direct.] [The landlord will contact you to confirm that their expert will attend at the same time as you to carry out a joint inspection.]*

* Delete as appropriate

† The date to be inserted should be 20 working days from the date of the letter, in accordance with para. 3.6(f) of the protocol.

Please provide the report within 10 working days of the inspection. Please contact us immediately if there are any works which require an interim injunction.

If the case proceeds to court, the report may be used in evidence. In order to comply with court rules we would be grateful if you would insert above your signature a statement that the contents are true to the best of your knowledge and belief. We refer you to Part 35 of the Civil Procedure Rules which specifies experts' responsibilities, the contents of any report, and the statements experts must sign.

(Insert details as to cost and payment.)

Yours sincerely

(ii) Letter from Tenant

Dear

Re: *(your name and address of property)*

I am currently in dispute with my landlord about disrepair at the above property. I am using the Housing Disrepair Protocol. [I enclose a copy of the protocol for your information.*]

Please carry out an inspection of the above property by *(date †)* and provide a report covering the following points:

(a) whether you agree that the defects are as claimed;
(b) whether any of the defects is structural;
(c) the cause of the defect(s);
(d) the age, character and prospective life of the property.

Access will be available on the following dates and times: *(list dates and times as appropriate).*

[You are instructed as a single joint expert.] [The landlord is *(landlord's name and details)*.] [The landlord will be providing you with their own instructions direct.] [The landlord will contact you to confirm that their expert will attend at the same time as you to carry out a joint inspection.]*

Please provide the report within 10 working days of the inspection. Please contact me immediately if there are any works which require an interim injunction.

If the case proceeds to court, the report may be used in evidence. In order to comply with court rules I would be grateful if you would insert above your signature a statement that the contents are true to the best of your knowledge and belief. I refer you to Part 35 of the Civil Procedure Rules which specifies experts' responsibilities, the contents of any report, and the statements experts must sign.

(Insert details as to cost and payment.)

Yours sincerely

* Delete as appropriate

ANNEX D EARLY NOTIFICATION LETTER FLOWCHART

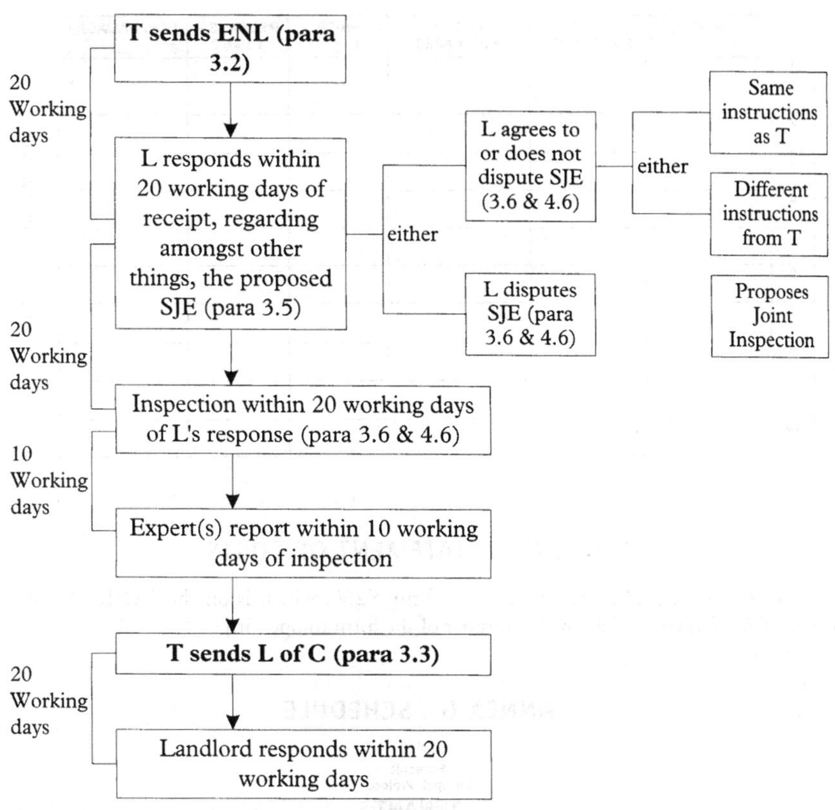

ANNEX E SPECIAL DAMAGES FORM

	ITEM	DATE PURCHASED	WHERE PURCHASED	PRICE	RECEIPTS – YES/NO	HOW DAMAGED
1						
2						
3						
4						
5						
6						
7						
8						
9						
10						

SPECIAL DAMAGES FORM

[ANNEX F STATEMENT OF COSTS

Annex F is not reproduced here, because it is form N260, which is on the CD-ROM version of *Blackstone's Civil Practice.* Click on the number of the form to open it.]

ANNEX G SCHEDULE

Schedule
Disrepair Protocol
TENANT

	Item Number	Room (tick where appropriate	Disrepair (identify briefly)	Notice given (How was the landlord made aware of the problem)	Inconvenience suffered (How has the disrepair affected you)
Exterior of premises, roof and access Comment:					
Entrance, hall and storage Comment:					
Living room (s) Comment:					
Kitchen Comment:					
Bathroom Comment:					
Bedroom 1 Comment:					
Bedroom 2 Comment:					
Bedroom 3 Comment:					
Other Comment					

Appendix 4 Court Guides

Each guide begins with a list of its contents.

The following items are on the CD-ROM version of *Blackstone's Civil Practice*. Click on the title of an item to open it:

A Guide to Emailing the Civil and Family Courts

1 INTRODUCTION

A new rule and practice direction (PD 5B) which came into force on 6 October 2003 permit parties in a case to communicate and file certain documents at specified county courts and the Commercial Court by email.

Filing by email is limited to the courts listed here which have received the appropriate technology to operate email. As more courts are able to receive email they will be added to this schedule.

THE COURTS

Please be advised that the county courts and the Commercial Court deal with different types of work. Please ensure that you are contacting the correct court before continuing. You can communicate with the following courts by email:

Barnsley County Court, Basildon County Court, Birkenhead County Court, Birmingham Civil Justice Centre, Blackburn County Court, Blackpool County Court, Bolton County Court, Bournemouth County Court, Bow County Court, Bradford County Court, Brighton County Court, Burnley County Court, Canterbury County Court, Cardiff County Court, Carlisle County Court, Chancery Division of the High Court, Chester County Court, the Commercial Court, Coventry County Court, Croydon County Court, Derby Combined Court Centre, Doncaster County Court, Dudley County Court, Edmonton County Court, Grimsby County Court, Haywards Heath County Court, Huddersfield County Court, Kingston-upon-Hull County Court, Lambeth County Court, Leeds County Court, Leicester County Court, Lewes Combined Court Centre, Lincoln County Court, Liverpool County Court, Manchester County Court, Milton Keynes County Court, Newcastle County Court, Northampton County Court, Norwich County Court, Nuneaton County Court, Oldham County Court, Oxford County Court, Preston County Court, Reading County Court, Romford County Court, Salford County Court, Sheffield County Court, Stockport County Court, Sunderland County Court, Taunton County Court, Walsall County Court, Watford County Court, Wolverhampton Combined Court Centre, York County Court.

COURT USER EMAIL GUIDANCE

1. What You Can File by Email

If you are filing a document by email that contains a statement of truth you are reminded that you should retain the document containing the original signature. The version of the document which is filed by email must satisfy one of the following requirements:

(a) the name of the person who has signed the statement of truth is typed underneath the statement; or

(b) the person who has signed the statement of truth has applied a facsimile of his signature to the statement in the document by mechanical means; or

(c) the document that is filed is a scanned version of the document containing the signed original statement of truth.

Below is a list of the work that will be accepted by the court if filed by email in accordance with PD 5B. *Please consider this list carefully before continuing with your email correspondence with the court.*

- Pre-trial checklist (listing questionnaire), provided that no fee is payable by the party filing the checklist (N170).
- Allocation questionnaire, provided that no fee is payable by the party filing the questionnaire (N150).
- Particulars of claim (after filing of claim form).
- Notice by solicitor of acting (N434).
- List of documents (N265).
- Certificate of service (N215).
- Notice of change of address.
- Request for judgment in default under r. 12.4(1), or for judgment upon admission under r. 14.4(3), 14.5(6), 14.6(4) or 14.7(5) (N225).
- Acknowledgment of service (N9).
- Claimant's response to notice of admission under r. 14.5(3) or r. 14.7(3) (N225A).
- Admission, other than one under r. 14.4 (N9C).
- Claimant's response to notice under r. 15.10, where defence is that money claimed has been paid (N236).
- Defence, provided that no counterclaim is made (N9B) .
- Notice of discontinuance, provided that the claimant does not require permission to discontinue, and is not required to attach to the notice the consent of another party (N279).
- Reply to defence.
- Notice of change of solicitor (N434).
- Reissue/amend process, no hearing (provided that no fee is payable) (N446).
- Reissue/amend process, hearing (provided that no fee is payable) (N446).
- Admission of liability (unspecified amount) (N226).
- Notice of admission — return of goods (N228).
- Amended defence.
- Part admission not accepted (N225A).
- Intention to proceed with states paid defence.
- Statement of witness (provided the document is no more than 10 pages and the total size of the email does not exceed 2 Mb as set out in PD 5B, para. 3.5).
- Claimant/Defendant list of documents (provided documents comply with PD 5B, para. 3.5) (N265).
- Experts' reports.
- Skeleton arguments/case summaries.
- Draft judgments and editorial suggestions for them.
- Request for judgment by default (provided that no fee is payable) (N227).
- Notice of acceptance and request for payment (N243A).
- Application to claimant to vary judgment (N294).
- Request for certificate of judgment (N293A).
- Any other document which the court has specifically directed to be filed by email.

You may also correspond with the court by email, making general enquiries about the progress of a case, or providing information to the court, for example:

- Information for the bailiff.
- Confirmation of appointments.
- Listing information such as dates to avoid.
- Chasing up replies.

2. What You Cannot File by Email

- A party must not use email to take any step in a claim which requires a fee to be paid. If a party sends a document by email for which a fee is payable upon filing, the document will be treated as not having been filed.
- Anything in family proceedings. PD 5B does not apply to family proceedings but general correspondence may be addressed to the court by email provided that it does not contain sensitive information.
- Anything in insolvency or adoption proceedings.

3. Form and Content of Emails

When you email the court the subject line of your email must contain (in the following order):
- The claim number.
- The title of the claim (abbreviated if necessary).[1]
- The subject matter (e.g., defence).
- If relating to a hearing the date and time of hearing.

Your message should also contain the name, telephone number and email address of the sender. If you email us we will normally send any reply to you by email.

Correspondence and documents may be sent as either text or attachments. Where there is a practice form, it must be sent in that form by attachment.

Attachments must be in one of the following formats and the complete email (including any attachment(s)) must not exceed 2 Mb:

Document file types
- Rich text format files (.rtf).
- Plain/formatted text files (.txt).
- Hypertext documents files (.htm).
- Microsoft Word viewer/reader files (.doc) minimum Word 97 format.
- Adobe Acrobat files (.pdf) minimum viewer version 4.

Spreadsheet file types
- Hypertext document files (.htm).
- Delimited files (.csv).

Presentation file types
- Hypertext document files (.htm).

General and compressed file types
- Zipped (compressed) files (.zip, .gz, .tgz, .tar).

Graphics file types
- Joint Photographic Experts Group (ISO 10918) files (.jpg).

Vector graphics file types
- Scalable vector graphics files (.svg).

4. Where to Send Your Email

Document filing
Participating courts will have a single email address for filing of documents at court, e.g.: efiling@leicester.countycourt.gsi.gov.uk

Correspondence
There are four or five standard email addresses to choose from when sending correspondence by email to the court (depending whether the court has family jurisdiction).

[1] If your email is in relation to a family matter please refer to the initials only.

The name of the appropriate court must be added to each email address followed by a dot, e.g.: enquiries@leicester.countycourt.gsi.gov.uk

Court email addresses
e-filing@[name of court].countycourt.gsi.gov.uk
family@[name of court].countycourt.gsi.gov.uk
bailiffs@[name of court].countycourt.gsi.gov.uk
hearings@[name of court].countycourt.gsi.gov.uk
enquiries@[name of court].countycourt.gsi.gov.uk

NOTE: The family@ email address should only be used at courts with family jurisdiction. Please check the jurisdiction of the court before continuing.

To decide which address to send your email to there are some examples listed below to help.

e-filing@[name of court].countycourt.gsi.gov.uk

- Experts' reports.
- List of documents.
- Skeleton arguments/case summaries.

family@[name of court].countycourt.gsi.gov.uk

- Progress in family cases.

bailiffs@[name of court].countycourt.gsi.gov.uk

- Progress on a warrant.
- Confirmation of appointment.
- Correspondence for a bailiff.

hearings@[name of court].countycourt.gsi.gov.uk

- Queries about dates of hearings.
- Dates to avoid.

enquiries@[name of court].countycourt.gsi.gov.uk

- Chase-up letters.
- Court opening hours.

5. What the Court Will Do with Your Email

The court will check your email and either respond to your enquiry or, where further action is required, will confirm in due course:

(a) that your document has been accepted, and
(b) the date of filing.

The date of filing will normally be the date of receipt unless the time of receipt is recorded as after 16.00 in which case the date of filing will be the next day the court office is open.

If your email does not comply with the requirements of PD 5B you will be sent a reply stating that it has been rejected and the reasons why.

The court will, where possible, reply to you electronically, although for the present, orders of the court will generally be dispatched by post as they are not currently produced in electronic form.

6. Points to Remember

- This guide does not replace PD 5B.
- When you file documents by email you must still comply with any rule or practice direction requiring the document to be served on any other person.
- There is nothing in PD 5B that requires any person to accept service of a document by email.
- Where a time limit applies it is the parties' responsibility to ensure that the document is filed in time.
- *Warning.* Internet email is not a secure medium. Any message or reply to your message could be intercepted and read by someone else. Please bear that in mind when deciding whether to send an email.
- If you require any assistance or have an enquiry regarding the email service please contact the appropriate court direct.

FORMS FOR FILING BY EMAIL

Below is a list of forms that will be accepted by the court if filed by email in accordance with PD 5B. There are other types of work that are accepted by email. For a list of work accepted and more information see Court User Email Guidance, above.

N9 Response pack.
N9B Defence and counterclaim (specified amount).
N9C Admission (unspecified amount, non-money and return of goods claims).
N150 Allocation questionnaire.
N170 Listing questionnaire (pre-trial checklist).
N215 Certificate of service
N225 Request for judgment and reply to admission (specified amount).
N225A Notice of part admission (specified amount).
N226 Notice of admission (unspecified amount).
N227 Request for judgment by default (amount to be decided by the court).
N228 Notice of admission — return of goods (hire-purchase or conditional sale).
N236 Notice of defence that amount claimed has been paid.
N243A Notice of acceptance and request for payment (Part 36).
N265 List of documents: standard disclosure.
N279 Notice of discontinuance.
N293A Combined certificate of judgment and request for writ of fieri facias or writ of possession.
N294 Claimant's application for a variation order (without hearing).
N434 Notice of change of solicitor.
N446 Request for reissue of enforcement or an order to obtain information from judgment debtor (not warrant).

PROTOCOL FOR EMAIL COMMUNICATIONS WITH THE CHANCERY DIVISION OF THE HIGH COURT AT THE ROYAL COURTS OF JUSTICE

Introduction

1 This protocol (the 'Email Protocol') sets out how parties may communicate by email on certain matters with the Chancery Division of the High Court of Justice at the Royal Courts of Justice. It applies with effect from 18 April 2005

Types of Documents Which May Be Sent by Email

2 PD 5B applies to the Chancery Division of the High Court of Justice at the Royal Courts of Justice in respect of the categories of documents referred to below.
3 For the purpose of PD 5B, para. 2.1(1), the 'specified court' is the Chancery Division of the High Court of Justice at the Royal Courts of Justice.
4 For the purpose of PD 5B, para. 2.1(2), the 'specified documents' are:
(a) Skeleton arguments, chronologies, reading lists, lists of issues, lists of authorities (but not the authorities themselves) and lists of the persons involved in the facts of the case ('dramatis personae') sent in advance of a hearing. The relevant email addresses for these documents are:

For a hearing before a	Use this address
Judge	rcjchancery.judgeslisting@hmcourts-service.gsi.gov.uk
Master	rcjchancery.mastersappointments@hmcourts-service.gsi.gov.uk
Bankruptcy registrar	rcjbankruptcy.registrarshearings@hmcourts-service.gsi.gov.uk
Registrar of the Companies Court	rcjcompanies.orders@hmcourts-service.gsi.gov.uk

(b) The agreed terms of an order which is ready to be sealed following the conclusion of a hearing. The relevant email addresses for these documents are:

For a hearing before a	Use this address
Judge	rcjchancery.ordersandaccounts@hmcourts-service.gsi.gov.uk
Master	rcjchancery.ordersandaccounts@hmcourts-service.gsi.gov.uk
Bankruptcy registrar	rcjbankruptcy.registrarshearings@hmcourts-service.gsi.gov.uk
Registrar of the Companies Court	rcjcompanies.orders@hmcourts-service.gsi.gov.uk

5 The above provisions take precedence over the provisions of the Chancery Guide in at least two respects:

(a) Notwithstanding paras 7.26, 7.41 and 7.43 of the Chancery Guide (2002 edition),* the email addresses specified above should be used for sending the relevant documents by email even if the name of the judge, master or registrar is known (unless the judge, master or registrar orders otherwise).

(b) Paragraph 7.44 of the Chancery Guide (2002 edition)† states that, where a skeleton argument is required, photocopies of any authorities to be relied upon should be attached to the skeleton argument. However, when lodging skeleton arguments by email in accordance with this Email Protocol, no authorities may be lodged with the skeleton argument (unless the judge, master or registrar orders otherwise). The authorities must be lodged on paper in the traditional way, even if the skeleton argument itself is lodged by email.

6 No other documents, aside from those specifically referred to in para. 4 above, can be accepted by email at present (except by specific arrangement with the judge, master or registrar concerned for an individual case). In particular, email cannot be used to file statements of case, application notices, affidavits, witness statements, experts' reports, allocation questionnaires, listing questionnaires, pre-trial checklists or statements of costs. If a party sends by email any type of document aside from one specifically referred to in para. 4 above, the document will be treated as not having been lodged.

7 This Email Protocol is not intended to limit the discretion of the judge, master or registrar to use information technology to a greater or lesser extent in an appropriate case, as envisaged in ch. 14 of the Chancery Guide (2002 edition).‡

8 Where a party sends a document by email he should still comply with any rule or practice direction requiring the document to be served on any other person.

9 For the avoidance of doubt, the Chancery Division of the High Court of Justice at the Royal Courts of Justice does not currently accept documents filed electronically via the online forms service referred to in PD 5B, Section II.

10 Nothing in this Email Protocol:

(a) Requires any person to accept service of a document by email.

(b) Affects any arrangements for communicating with any district registry or county court, whether or not on Chancery business.

11 Email is not a secure communications medium. Parties must not use email to send documents which are confidential or sensitive. This must be borne in mind particularly in cases to be heard in secret.

Form of the Email and Attachments

12 If the name of the judge, master or registrar concerned is known, the body of the email should state this name clearly.

13 PD 5B, para. 4.1, is varied so as to read that the email message 'should be in plain text or HTML rather than rich text format', but the remainder of that paragraph continues to apply.

14 For the purpose of PD 5B, para. 4.5, the following formats for attachments are supported:

(a) Microsoft Word format (Word 97 or Word 2000) (.doc files).

(b) Adobe Acrobat format (also known as Portable Document Format) (.pdf files).

(c) Rich text format (.rtf files).

(d) Plain text (.txt files).

15. For the purpose of PD 5B, para. 4.7, the total size of the email (including all of its attachments) must not exceed 8 MB.

[* Paragraphs 7.26, 7.43, 7.47 of the 2005 edition.

† Paragraph 7.48 of the 2005 edition.

‡ Chapter 14 of the 2005 edition.]

Receipt of Emails by the Court

An acknowledgment of the receipt of an email will be sent. This is not an acknowledgment that the email has been received by its ultimate intended recipient, merely an acknowledgment that the email has been received by one of the central mailboxes listed in para. 4 above.

COMMERCIAL AND ADMIRALTY COURTS: EMAIL COMMUNICATIONS WITH THE COURT: GUIDANCE

Introduction

1. This guidance sets out how parties may communicate by email with the Commercial and Admiralty Courts on certain matters with effect from 17 March 2003.

Initial Period of Application

2. This guidance will apply for an initial period of six months. Towards the end of that period, the guidance will be reviewed in the light of the experience gained. It may then be revised as necessary.*

Documents for Which Email May Be Used

3. Email may only be used:
   (a) to communicate with the Case Management Unit, including the lodging of progress monitoring information sheets;
   (b) to communicate with the Registry in relation to the approval by the judge of draft order following a hearing before that judge, queries on orders made, requests to transfer a case into or out of the Commercial Court and general correspondence, including questions on practice;
   (Note: Orders submitted for sealing must be submitted on paper.)
   (c) to communicate with the Listing Office in matters relating to listing (including the lodging of pre-trial checklists) and to lodge skeleton arguments with the Listing Office;
   (d) to communicate with the Admiralty Marshal (except for out-of-hours business).
   (Note: The court cannot accept any other documents by email at present. In particular email cannot be used to lodge pleadings, affidavits, witness statements, case memoranda and lists of issues.)

Restrictions

4. A party should not use email to take any step in a claim which requires a fee to be paid for that step. If a party sends by email a document for which a fee is payable upon filing, the document will be treated as not having been filed.
5. Where a party sends or lodges a document by email he should still comply with any rule or practice direction requiring the document to be served on any other person.
6. Nothing in this guidance requires any person to accept service of a document by email.

Sending Emails to the Court: Addresses

7. For listing matters, the email addresses are:
   (a) For all matters relating to listing (except Friday applications), for the lodging of pre-trial check lists and for all skeleton arguments:
   ComCt.Listing@courtservice.gsi.gov.uk
   (b) For matters relating to Friday applications (except skeleton arguments)
   ComCt.Friday@courtservice.gsi.gov.uk

[* The following note was published on the Court Service website on 8 October 2003:

The pilot scheme for email communications was introduced on 17 March 2003 for an initial period of six months. The take-up by users has been very encouraging and continues to grow. The guidance for users of the scheme, drawn up by the Admiralty and Commercial judiciary, provided for a review of the scheme after the initial six-month period.

Having now reviewed the scheme the judiciary have decided to extend the pilot, in its present form, for an indefinite period to allow time for further assessment and for analysis of the feedback generated by the recent customer survey. The impact of a general rule and practice direction dealing with email communications to courts, soon to be introduced to the CPR, will also need to be considered.]

8. For matters relating to case management and the Case Management Unit (including the lodging of progress monitoring sheets), the address is: ComCt.CMU@courtservice.gsi.gov.uk
9. For all correspondence for the Registry the address is: ComCt.Registry@courtservice.gsi.gov.uk
10. For all matters for the Admiralty Marshal or the business of the Admiralty Marshal, the address is: Admiralty.bus@courtservice.gsi.gov.uk

The Subject Line

11. The subject line of the email should contain only the following information which should be in the following order:
    (a) First, the proper title of the claim (abbreviated as necessary) with the claimant named first and the defendant named second; unless the action is an Admiralty action, the name of the ship should not be used:
    (b) Second, the claim number.

Form and Content of the Email

12. Correspondence and documents may be sent either as text or attachments, except that documents required to be in a practice form should be sent in that form as attachments using one of the formats specified in para. 17.
13. Parties must not use email to send any document which exceeds 40 pages in the aggregate of normal typescript in length or 2 MB whichever is the smaller. Documents may not be subdivided to comply with this requirement.
14. Where a party files a document by email, he should not send a hard copy in addition, unless there are good reasons for so doing or the Court requires.
15. Parties are advised to bear in mind when sending correspondence or documents of a confidential or sensitive nature that the security of emails cannot be guaranteed.
16. Where a time limit applies, it remains the responsibility of the party to ensure that the document is filed in time. Parties are advised to allow for delays or downtime on their server or the servers used by the Court.

Attachments

17. Attachments should be in one of the following formats:
    (a) Microsoft Word viewer/reader (.doc) in Word 97 or later format;
    (b) rich text format as (.rtf) files;
    (c) plain/formatted text as (.txt) files;
    (d) hypertext documents as (.htm) files;
    (e) Adobe Acrobat as (.pdf) files minimum viewer version 4.

Receipt of Email by the Court

18. A document is not filed until the email is received by the court at the addressee's computer terminal, whatever time it is shown to have been sent.
19. The time of receipt of an email at the addressee's computer terminal will be recorded.
20. If an email is received after 4 p.m. it will be treated as having been received on the next day the court office is open.
21. No automatic acknowledgment of the receipt of an email will be sent; the subject matter of the email will be considered in the ordinary way. If a response to the subject matter of the email is not received within a reasonable period, the sender should assume that the court has not received it and should send the email again, or file the document by another means.
22. Parties should not telephone to enquire as to the receipt of an email. They should observe the procedure set out in para. 21.

Replies to Emails Sent to the Court

23. The court will normally send any reply by email to documents or correspondence sent by email.
    (a) All replies will be sent to the email address from which the email has been sent. If the sender

wishes the reply to be copied to other parties or to another email address used by the sender of the message, such email addresses must be specified in the copy line.

(b) The court will not send copies to clients or others not on the record; the copy line must therefore not contain the addresses of such persons.

(c) The email should also contain in the body of the email the name and telephone number of the sender.

(Note: It is important that each firm or set of chambers considers putting in place a system to deal with the absence of the individual who has sent the email and to whom the court will ordinarily reply. Two possible solutions are:

(a) A central mailbox within each firm, either from which the email is sent to the court (and which will therefore receive the reply) or to which it is copied by the individual sender who sends it direct to the court (and who will receive a copy of the reply);

(b) a second individual email address within the firm to which the reply will be copied so that any reply can be monitored.

It must be for each firm and set of chambers to devise its own system.)

Communication with the Clerk to a Commercial Judge

24. No documents or correspondence should be sent by email to the clerk to a commercial judge dealing with a case, unless:

(a) an arrangement is made with the clerk in each specific instance in which email is to be used;

(b) if such an arrangement is made, the email must be copied to the appropriate Listing Office address, the Case Management Unit address, the Registry address, or the Admiralty Marshal address, as the case may be.

(Note: Draft orders for the approval of the judge must be submitted through the Registry.)

Admiralty and Commercial Courts Guide

INTRODUCTION

This edition of the Admiralty and Commercial Courts Guide is published to coincide with the introduction of Parts 58, 61 and 62 of the Civil Procedure Rules dealing with commercial and Admiralty proceedings and proceedings relating to arbitrations respectively. Most of the provisions which have hitherto been contained in the practice directions made under Part 49 and the 5th edition of the Commercial Court Guide are now to be found in these new rules and their associated practice directions, although the Guide still contains a number of additional provisions which are necessary to ensure the efficient conduct of business in the Admiralty and Commercial Courts.

For some time now the administration of the Admiralty and Commercial Courts has been undertaken by a single Registry and Listing Office and the two Courts have shared many common procedures. It seemed only natural, therefore, that this edition of the Guide should reflect that fact, both in its title and in the inclusion of a separate section dealing with admiralty proceedings.

This edition of the Guide draws heavily on its predecessor, but the introduction of the new rules has necessitated a substantial revision of the text. Moreover, the need to describe in detail various respects in which the procedure applicable to commercial proceedings diverges from that generally applicable under the Civil Procedure Rules, has diminished in importance as practitioners have become familiar both with the operation of the Rules themselves and with the procedures applicable in the Commercial and Admiralty Courts. We have therefore taken the opportunity to remove much of the explanatory material which we consider no longer serves a useful purpose in an attempt to produce a concise manual which meets the day-to-day needs of those who use the Courts. We have also taken the opportunity to review the Courts' procedures as a whole. This has resulted in the removal of some provisions which seemed to be otiose or to have outlived their usefulness and the introduction of others which we consider will enable the Courts to function more efficiently.

The fact that some provisions to be found in the 5th edition do not reappear in this edition should not necessarily be taken as an indication that they are no longer regarded as reflecting approved practice. In the interests of brevity we have not thought it necessary to reproduce all those provisions which were essentially matters of common sense or good practice, preferring in many cases to rely on the good sense and judgment of those who use the Courts. The Guide is not intended to be a blueprint to which all litigation must unthinkingly conform: as in the past, it seeks to provide a modern and flexible framework within which litigation can be conducted efficiently and in the interests of justice. We would emphasise that there has been no change in the Courts' approach to the business which comes before them or in their expectation that those who use the Courts will display the highest professional standards.

This Guide has been produced in order to set out in a convenient manner the practice which applies in the Admiralty and Commercial Courts. It should be read in conjunction with the Civil Procedure Rules and practice directions. For ease of reference we have included wherever possible references to the relevant rules and practice directions to which the reader should refer as necessary.

The Hon. Mr Justice David Steel — The Hon. Mr Justice Moore-Bick
Admiralty Judge — Judge in Charge of the Commercial List
February 2002

A PRELIMINARY

A1 The Procedural Framework

A1.1 Proceedings in the Commercial Court are governed by the Civil Procedure Rules ('CPR') and practice directions. CPR, Part 58, and PD 58 deal specifically with the Commercial Court. CPR, Part 61, deals with the Admiralty Court and Part 62 deals with arbitration applications.

A1.2 The Admiralty and Commercial Courts Guide is published with the approval of the Lord Chief Justice and the Head of Civil Justice in consultation with the judges of the Admiralty and Commercial Courts and with the advice and support of the Admiralty Court and Commercial Court Committees. It is intended to provide guidance about the conduct of proceedings in the Admiralty and Commercial Courts and, within the framework of the Civil Procedure Rules and practice directions, to establish the practice to be followed in those courts.

A1.3 In matters for which specific provision is not made by the Guide, the parties, their solicitors and counsel will be expected to act reasonably and in accordance with the spirit of the Guide.

A1.4 The requirements of the Guide are designed to ensure effective management of proceedings in the Admiralty and Commercial Courts. If parties fail to comply with these requirements the court may impose sanctions including orders for costs and (where appropriate) wasted costs orders.

A1.5 Pre-trial matters in the Admiralty and Commercial Courts are dealt with by the judges of those courts (PD 58, para. 1.2).

A1.6 The Court expects a high level of cooperation and realism from the legal representatives of the parties. This applies to dealings (including correspondence) between legal representatives as well as to dealings with the Court.

A1.7 In order to avoid excessive repetition, the Guide has been written by reference to proceedings in the Commercial Court. Practitioners should treat the guidance as applicable to proceedings in the Admiralty Court unless the content of CPR, Part 61, or section N of this Guide ('Admiralty') specifically requires otherwise.

A2 The Admiralty and Commercial Registry; The Commercial Court Listing Office

A2.1 The administrative office for the Admiralty Court and the Commercial Court is the Admiralty and Commercial Registry ('the Registry') which is located at Room E200 in the Royal Courts of Justice, Strand, London WC2A 2LL. The Commercial Court Listing Office ('the Listing Office') is located at Room E201 in the Royal Courts of Justice, Strand, London WC2A 2LL.

A2.2 It is important that there is close liaison between legal representatives of the parties and both the Registry and the Listing Office.

A3 The Commercial Court Committee

A3.1 The success of the Court's ability to meet the special problems and continually changing needs of the commercial community depends in part upon a steady flow of information and constructive suggestions between the Court, litigants and professional advisers.

A3.2 The Commercial Court Committee has assisted in this process for many years. It is expected to play an important part in helping to ensure that the procedures of the Court enable the achievement of the 'overriding objective'. All concerned with the Court are encouraged to make the fullest use of this important channel of communication. Correspondence raising matters for the consideration of the Committee should be addressed to the Clerk to the Commercial Court, Royal Courts of Justice, Strand, London WC2A 2LL.

A4 Specialist Associations

A4.1 There are a number of associations of legal representatives which liaise closely with the Commercial Court. These will also play an important part in helping to ensure that the Court remains responsive to the 'overriding objective'.

A4.2 The associations include the Commercial Bar Association ('COMBAR'), the London Common Law and Commercial Bar Association ('LCLCBA'), the City of London Law Society, the London Solicitors Litigation Association and the Admiralty Solicitors Group.

B COMMENCEMENT, TRANSFER AND REMOVAL

B1 Commercial Cases

CPR, r. 58.1(2), describes a 'commercial claim' as follows:

any claim arising out of the transaction of trade and commerce and includes any claim relating to—

(a) a business document or contract;
(b) the export or import of goods;
(c) the carriage of goods by land, sea, air or pipeline;
(d) the exploitation of oil and gas reserves or other natural resources;
(e) insurance and re-insurance;
(f) banking and financial services;
(g) the operation of markets and exchanges;
(h) the purchase and sale of commodities;
(i) the construction of ships;
(j) business agency; and
(k) arbitration.

B2 Starting a Case in the Commercial Court

B2.1 Except for arbitration applications which are governed by the provisions of CPR, Part 62, and section O of the Guide, the case will be begun by a claim form under CPR, Part 7 or Part 8.

B2.2 Save where otherwise specified, references in this Guide to a claim form are to a Part 7 claim form.

B2.3 The Commercial Court may give a fixed date for trial (see section D16), but it does not give a fixed date for a hearing when it issues a claim. CPR, rr. 7.9 and 7.10, and PD 7B and PD 7C do not apply to the Commercial Court.

B3 Part 7 Claims

The form

B3.1 A claimant starting proceedings in the Commercial Court must use form N1(CC) for Part 7 claims (PD 58, para. 2.4).

Marketing

B3.2 In accordance with PD 58, para. 2.3, the claim form should be marked in the top right-hand corner with the words 'Queen's Bench Division, Commercial Court', and on the issue of the claim form out of the Registry the case will be entered in the Commercial List. Marking the claim form in this way complies sufficiently with PD 7, para. 3.6(3).

Statement of value

B3.3 CPR, r. 16.3, which provides for a statement of value to be included in the claim form, does not apply in the Commercial Court (r. 58.5(2)).

Particulars of claim and the claim form

B3.4 Although particulars of claim may be served with the claim form, this is not a requirement in the Commercial Court. However, if the particulars of claim are not contained in or served with the claim form, the claim form must contain a statement that if an acknowledgment of service is filed indicating an intention to defend the claim, particulars of claim will follow (r. 58.5(1)(a)).

B3.5 If particulars of claim do not accompany the claim form they must be served within 28 days after the defendant has filed an acknowledgment of service indicating an intention to defend the claim (r. 58.5(1)(c)).

B3.6 The three forms specified in r. 7.8(1) must be served with the claim form. One of these is a form for acknowledging service (r. 58.5(1)(b)).

Statement of truth

B3.7 (a) A claim form must be verified by a statement of truth (r. 22.1). Unless the court otherwise orders, any amendment to a claim form must also be verified (r. 22.1(2)).
(b) The required form of statement of truth is set out at PD 7, para. 7.2.
(c) A claim form will remain effective even where not verified by a statement of truth, unless it is struck out (PD 22, para. 4.1).
(d) In certain cases the statement of truth may be signed by a person other than the party on whose behalf it is served or its legal representative (section C1.8 and 1.9).

Trial without service of particulars of claim or a defence

B3.8 The attention of the parties and their legal representatives is drawn to r. 58.11 which allows the court to order (before or after the issue of a claim form) that the case shall proceed without the filing or service of particulars of claim or defence or of any other statement of case.

Interest

B3.9 The claim form (and not only the particulars of claim) must comply with the requirements of r. 16.4(1)(b) and (2) concerning interest (r. 58.5(3)).

B3.10 References to particulars of claim in r. 12.6(1)(a) (referring to claims for interest where there is a default judgment) and r. 14.14(1)(a) (referring to claims for interest where there is a judgment on admissions) may be treated as references to the claim form (rr. 58.8(2) and 58.9(3)).

Issue of a claim form when the Registry is closed

B3.11 A request for the issue of a Part 7 claim form may be made by fax at certain times when the Registry is closed to the public (PD 58, para. 2.2). The procedure is set out in appendix 3. Any further details may be obtained from the Registry. The fax number is (020) 7947 6667.

B4 Part 8 Claims

Form

B4.1 A claimant who wishes to commence a claim under CPR, Part 8, must use form N208(CC) (PD 58, para. 2.4).

B4.2 Attention is drawn to the requirement in r. 8.2(a) that where a claimant uses the Part 8 procedure his claim form must state that Part 8 applies. Similarly, PD 7, para. 3.3, requires that the claim form state (if it be the case) that the claimant wishes his claim to proceed under Part 8 or that the claim is required to proceed under Part 8.

Marking and statement of truth

B4.3 Sections B3.2 (marking) and B3.7 (statement of truth) also apply to a claim form issued under Part 8.

Issue of a claim form when the Registry is closed

B4.4 A request for the issue of a Part 8 claim form may be made by fax at certain times when the Registry is closed to the public (PD 58, para. 2.2). The procedure is set out in appendix 3.

Time for filing evidence in opposition to a Part 8 claim

B4.5 A defendant to a Part 8 claim who wishes to rely on written evidence must file and serve it within 28 days after filing an acknowledgment of service (r. 58.12).

B5 Part 20 Claims

Form

Adapted versions of the Part 20 claim form (N211(CC)) and acknowledgment of service (N213(CC)) and of the related notes to Part 20 claimant and Part 20 defendant (N211C(CC)) have been approved for use in the Commercial Court.

B6 Service of the Claim Form

Service by the parties

B6.1 Claim forms issued in the Commercial List are to be served by the parties, not by the Registry (PD 58, para. 9).

Methods of service

B6.2 Methods of service are set out in CPR, Part 6, and PD 6.

B6.3 PD 6, paras 2.1 and 3.1, concern service by document exchange and by fax. Service of the claim form on the legal representative of the defendant by document exchange or fax will not be effective unless that legal representative has authority to accept service. It is desirable to obtain confirmation from the legal representative in writing that he has instructions to accept service of a claim form on behalf of the defendant.

Applications for extension of time

B6.4 Applications for an extension of time in which to serve a claim form are governed by CPR, r. 7.6. Rule 7.6(3)(a), which refers to service of the claim form by the court, does not apply in the Commercial Court.

B6.5 The evidence required on an application for an extension of time is set out in PD 7, para. 8.2.

Certificate of service

B6.6 When the claimant has served the claim form he must file a certificate of service (CPR, r. 6.14(2)). Satisfaction of this requirement is relevant, in particular, to the claimant's ability to obtain judgment in default (see Part 12) and to the right of a non-party to search for, inspect and take a copy of the claim form under r. 5.4(2)(a).

B7 Service of the Claim Form Out of the Jurisdiction

B7.1 Applications for permission to serve a claim form out of the jurisdiction are governed by rr. 6.19 to 6.31. A guide to the appropriate practice is set out in appendix 15.

B7.2 Service of process in some foreign countries may take a long time to complete; it is therefore important that solicitors take prompt steps to effect service.

B8 Acknowledgment of Service

Part 7 claims

B8.1 (a) A defendant must file an acknowledgment of service in every case (CPR, r. 58.6(1)). [Form N9(CC) is the form of acknowledgment of service for Part 7 claims which has been approved for use in the Commercial Court.]

(b) The period for filing an acknowledgment of service is calculated from the service of the claim form, whether or not particulars of claim are contained in or accompany the claim form or are to follow service of the claim form. Rule 9.1(2), which provides that in certain circumstances the defendant need not respond to the claim until particulars of claim have been served on him, does not apply (r. 58.6(1)).

Part 8 claims

B8.2 (a) A defendant must file an acknowledgment of service in every case (r. 58.6(1)). [Form N210(CC) is the form of acknowledgment of service for Part 8 claims which has been approved for use in the Commercial Court.]

(b) The time for filing an acknowledgment of service is calculated from the service of the claim form.

Acknowledgment of service in a claim against a firm

B8.3 (a) PD 10, para. 4.4, allows an acknowledgment of service to be signed on behalf of a partnership by any of the partners or a person having the control or management of the partnership business, whether he be a partner or not.

(b) However, attention is drawn to sch. 1 to the CPR which includes, with modifications, provisions previously contained in RSC, ord. 81, concerning acknowledgment of service by a person served as a partner who denies his liability as such. (See also the note at the end of CPR, Part 10.)

Time for filing acknowledgment of service

B8.4 (a) Except in the circumstances described in section B8.4(b) and B8.4(c), or when otherwise ordered by the court, the period for filing an acknowledgment of service is 14 days after service of the claim form.

(b) If the claim form has been served out of the jurisdiction without the permission of the court under r. 6.19, the time for filing an acknowledgment of service is governed by r. 6.22, save that in all cases time runs from the service of the claim form (r. 58.6(3)).

(c) If the claim form has been served out of the jurisdiction with the permission of the court under r. 6.20 the time for filing an acknowledgment of service is governed by r. 6.21(4)(a), PD 6B and the table in PD 6B, save that in all cases time runs from the service of the claim form (CPR, r. 58.6(3)).

B9 Disputing the Court's Jurisdiction

Part 7 claims

B9.1 (a) If the defendant intends to dispute the court's jurisdiction or contend that the court should not exercise its jurisdiction he must:

(i) file an acknowledgment of service (CPR, r. 11(2)); and

(ii) issue an application notice seeking the appropriate relief.

(b) An application to dispute the court's jurisdiction must be made within 28 days of filing an acknowledgment of service (r. 58.7(2)).

(c) If the defendant wishes to rely on written evidence in support of that application, he must file and serve that evidence when he issues the application.

(d) If the defendant makes an application under r. 11(1), the claimant is not bound to serve particulars of claim until that application has been disposed of (r. 58.7(3)).

Part 8 claims

B9.2 (a) The provisions of section B9.1(a)–(c) also apply in the case of Part 8 claims.

(b) If the defendant makes an application under r. 11(1), he is not bound to serve any written evidence on which he wishes to rely in opposition to the substantive claim until that application has been disposed of (r. 11(9)).

Effect of an application challenging the jurisdiction

B9.3 An acknowledgment of service of a Part 7 or Part 8 claim form which is followed by an application challenging the jurisdiction under Part 11 does not constitute a submission by the defendant to the jurisdiction (r. 11(3) and (7)).

B9.4 If an application under Part 11 is unsuccessful, and the court then considers giving directions for filing and serving statements of case (in the case of a Part 7 claim) or evidence (in the case of a Part 8 claim), a defendant does not submit to the jurisdiction merely by asking for time to serve and file his statement of case or evidence, as the case may be.

B10 Default Judgment

Default judgment is governed by CPR, Part 12, and PD 12. However, because in the Commercial Court the period for filing the acknowledgment of service is calculated from service of the claim form, the reference to 'particulars of claim' in PD 12, para. 4.1(1), should be read as referring to the claim form (PD 58, para. 6(1)).

B11 Admissions

(a) Admissions are governed by CPR, Part 14, and PD 14, except that the references to 'particulars of claim' in PD 14, paras 2.1, 3.1 and 3.2, should be read as referring to the claim form (PD 58, para. 6(2)).

(b) [Forms N9A(CC) and N9C(CC) have been approved for use in the Commercial Court.]

B12 Transfer of Cases into and out of the Commercial List

B12.1 The procedure for transfer and removal is set out in PD 58, para. 4. All such applications must be made to the Commercial Court (CPR, r. 30.5(3)).

B12.2 Although an order to transfer a case to the Commercial List may be made at any stage, any application for such an order should normally be made at an early stage in the proceedings.

B12.3 Transfer to the Commercial List may be ordered for limited purposes only, but a transferred case will normally remain in the Commercial List until its conclusion.

B12.4 An order transferring a case out of the Commercial List may be made at any stage, but will not usually be made after a pre-trial timetable has been fixed at the case management conference (see section D8).

B12.5 Some commercial cases may more suitably, or as suitably, be dealt with in one of the Mercantile Courts. Parties should consider whether it would be more appropriate to begin proceedings in one of those courts and the commercial judge may on his own initiative order the case to be transferred there.

C PARTICULARS OF CLAIM, DEFENCE AND REPLY

C1 Form, Content, Serving and Filing

C1.1 (a) Particulars of claim, the defence and any reply must be set out in separate consecutively numbered paragraphs and be as brief and concise as possible.

(b) If it is necessary for the proper understanding of the statement of case to include substantial parts of a lengthy document the passages in question should be set out in a schedule rather than in the body of the case.

(c) The document must be signed by the individual person or persons who drafted it, not, in the case of a solicitor, in the name of the firm alone.

C1.2 (a) Particulars of claim, the defence and also any reply must comply with the provisions of CPR, rr. 16.4 and 16.5, save that paras (6) and (8) of r. 16.5 do not apply.

(b) The requirements of PD 16, paras 8.4 to 9.1 (which relate to claims based upon oral agreements, agreements by conduct and consumer credit agreements and to reliance upon evidence of certain matters under the Civil Evidence Act 1968) should be treated as applying to the defence and reply as well as to the particulars of claim.

(c) (i) Full and specific details must be given of any allegation of fraud, dishonesty, malice or illegality; and

(ii) where an inference of fraud or dishonesty is alleged, the facts on the basis of which the inference is alleged must be fully set out.

(d) Any legislative provision upon which an allegation is based must be clearly identified and the basis of its application explained.

(e) Any provision of the Human Rights Act 1998 (including the Convention) on which a party relies in support of its case must be clearly identified and the basis of its application explained.

(f) Any principle of foreign law or foreign legislative provision upon which a party's case is based must be clearly identified and the basis of its application explained.

C1.3 (a) PD 16, para. 7.3, relating to a claim based upon a written agreement should be treated as also applying to the defence, unless the claim and the defence are based on the same agreement.

(b) In most cases attaching documents to or serving documents with a statement of case does not promote the efficient conduct of the proceedings and should be avoided.

(c) If documents are to be served at the same time as a statement of case they should normally be served separately from rather than attached to the statement of case.

(d) Only those documents which are obviously of critical importance and necessary for a proper understanding of the statement of case should be attached to or served with it. The statement of case must itself refer to the fact that documents are attached to or served with it.

(e) An expert's report should not be attached to the statement of case and should not be filed with the statement of case at the Registry. A party must obtain permission from the court in order to adduce expert evidence at trial and therefore any party which serves an expert's report without obtaining such permission does so at his own risk as to costs.

(f) Notwithstanding PD 16, para. 7.3(1), a true copy of the complete written agreement may be made available at any hearing unless the court orders otherwise.

Summaries

C1.4 If a statement of case exceeds 25 pages (excluding schedules), a summary, not exceeding four pages, must also be filed and served. The summary should cross-refer to the paragraph numbering of the full statement of case. The summary is to be included in the case management bundle (section D7.2(ii)).

Length

C1.5 Parties serving statements of case should bear in mind that the court will take into account the length of the document served when considering any application by another party for further time within which to respond.

Statement of truth

C1.6 Particulars of claim, a defence and any reply must be verified by a statement of truth (CPR, r. 22.1). So too must any amendment, unless the court otherwise orders (r. 22.1(2); see also section C5.4.)

C1.7 The required form of statement of truth is as follows:

(i) for particulars of claim, as set out in PD 7, para. 7.2 or PD 16, para. 3.4;

(ii) for a defence, as set out in PD 15, para. 2.2 or PD 16, para. 12.2;

(iii) for a reply the statement of truth should follow the form for the particulars of claim, but substituting the word 'reply' for the words 'particulars of claim' (see PD 22, para. 2.1).

C1.8 A party may apply to the court for permission that a statement of truth be signed by a person other than one of those required by CPR, r. 22.1(6).

C1.9 If insurers are conducting proceedings on behalf of many claimants or defendants a statement of truth may be signed by a senior person responsible for the case at a lead insurer, but:

(i) the person signing must specify the capacity in which he signs;

(ii) the statement of truth must be a statement that the lead insurer believes that the facts stated in the document are true; and

(iii) the court may order that a statement of truth also be signed by one or more of the parties.

See PD 22, para. 3.6.

C1.10 A statement of case remains effective (although it may not be relied on as evidence) even where it is not verified by a statement of truth, unless it is struck out (PD 22, paras 4.1 to 4.3).

Service

C1.11 All statements of case are served by the parties, not by the court (PD 58, para. 9).

Filing

C1.12 The statements of case filed with the court form part of the permanent record of the court.

C2 Serving and Filing Particulars of Claim

C2.1 Subject to any contrary order of the court and unless particulars of claim are contained in or accompany the claim form:

(i) the period for serving particulars of claim is 28 days after filing an acknowledgment of service (CPR, r. 58.5(1)(c));

(ii) the parties may agree extensions of the period for serving the particulars of claim. However, any such agreement must be evidenced in writing and notified to the court, addressed to the Case Management Unit (PD 58, para. 7.1);

(iii) any notification of an agreed extension exceeding six weeks, or which when taken together with preceding extensions exceeds six weeks in total, must be accompanied by a brief statement of the reasons for the extension.

C2.2 The court may make an order overriding any agreement by the parties varying a time limit (PD 58, para. 7.2).

C2.3 The claimant must serve the particulars of claim on all other parties. A copy of the claim form will be filed at the Registry on issue. If the claimant serves particulars of claim separately from the claim form he must file a copy within seven days of service together with a certificate of service (CPR, r. 7.4(3)).

C3 Serving and Filing a Defence

C3.1 The defendant must serve the defence on all other parties and must at the same time file a copy with the court.

C3.2 (a) If the defendant files an acknowledgment of service which indicates an intention to defend the period for serving and filing a defence is 28 days after service of the particulars of claim, subject to the provisions of CPR, r. 15.4(2). (See also appendix 15 for cases where the claim form has been served out of the jurisdiction.)

(b) The defendant and the claimant may agree that the period for serving and filing a defence shall be extended by up to 28 days (r. 15.5(1)).

(c) An application to the court is required for any further extension. If the parties are able to agree that a further extension should be granted, a draft consent order should be provided together with a brief explanation of the reasons for the extension.

C3.3 The general power to agree variations to time limits contained in r. 2.11 and PD 58, para. 7.1) enables parties to agree extensions of the period for serving and filing a defence that exceed 28 days. The length of extension must in all cases be specified. Any such agreement must be evidenced in writing and comply with the requirements of section C2.1.

C3.4 (a) Where an extension is agreed the defendant must, in accordance with CPR, r. 15.5(2) , notify the court in writing; the notification should be addressed to the Case Management Unit.

(b) Any notification of an agreed extension exceeding six weeks, or which when taken together with preceding extensions exceeds six weeks in total, must be accompanied by a brief statement (agreed by the claimant and the defendant) of the reasons for the extension. The reasons will be brought to the attention of the judge in charge of the Commercial List.

C3.5 The claimant must notify the Case Management Unit by letter when all defendants who intend to serve a defence have done so. This information is material to the fixing of the case management conference (see section D3.1).

C4 Serving and Filing a Reply

C4.1 Subject to section C4.3, the period for serving and filing a reply is 21 days after service of the defence (CPR, r. 58.10(1)).

C4.2 (a) A reply must be filed at the same time as it is served (r. 15.8(b)); r. 15.8(a) does not apply in proceedings in the Commercial List.

(b) The reply should be served before case management information sheets are provided to the court (see section D8.5). In the normal case, this will allow the parties to consider any reply before completing the case management information sheet, and allow time for the preparation of the case memorandum and the list of issues each of which is required for the case management conference (see sections D4 to D7).

C4.3 In some cases, more than 21 days may be needed for the preparation, service and filing of a reply. In such cases an application should be made on paper for an extension of time and for a postponement of the case management conference. The procedure to be followed when making an application on paper is set out in section F4.

C4.4 Any reply must be served by the claimant on all other parties (r. 58.10(1)).

C5 Amendment

C5.1 (a) Amendments to a statement of case must show the original text, unless the court orders otherwise (PD 58, para. 8).

(b) Amendments may be shown by using footnotes or marginal notes, provided they identify precisely where and when an amendment has been made.

(c) Unless the court so orders, there is no need to show amendments by colour coding.

(d) If there have been extensive amendments it may be desirable to prepare a fresh copy of the statement of case. However, a copy of the statement of case showing where and when amendments have been made must also be made available.

C5.2 All amendments to any statement of case must be verified by a statement of truth unless the court orders otherwise (CPR, r. 22.1(2)).

C5.3 Questions of amendment, and consequential amendment, should wherever possible be dealt with by consent. A party should consent to a proposed amendment unless he has substantial grounds for objecting to it.

C5.4 Late amendments should be avoided and may be disallowed.

D CASE MANAGEMENT IN THE COMMERCIAL COURT

D1 Generally

D1.1 All proceedings in the Commercial List will be subject to management by the court.

D1.2 All proceedings in the Commercial List are automatically allocated to the multi-track and consequently CPR, Part 26, and the rules relating to allocation do not apply (CPR, r. 58.13(1)).

D1.3 Except for r. 29.3(2) (legal representatives to attend case management conferences and pre-trial reviews) and r. 29.5 (variation of case management timetable), Part 29 does not apply to proceedings in the Commercial List (r. 58.13(2)).

D2 Key Features of Case Management in the Commercial Court

Case management is governed by CPR, r. 58.13, and PD 58, para. 10. In a normal commercial case commenced by a Part 7 claim form, case management will include the following 10 key features:

(1) statements of case will be exchanged within fixed or monitored time periods;

(2) a case memorandum, a list of issues and a case management bundle will be produced at an early point in the case;

(3) the case memorandum, list of issues and case management bundle will be amended and updated or revised on a running basis throughout the life of the case and will be used by the court at every stage of the case;

(4) a mandatory case management conference will be held shortly after statements of case have been served, if not before (and preceded by the parties lodging case management information sheets identifying their views on the requirements of the case);

(5) at the case management conference the court will (as necessary) discuss the issues in the case and the requirements of the case with the advocates retained in the case. The court will set a pre-trial timetable and give any other directions as may be appropriate;

(6) before the progress monitoring date the parties will report to the court, using a progress monitoring information sheet, the extent of their compliance with the pre-trial timetable;

(7) on or shortly after the progress monitoring date a judge will (without a hearing) consider progress and give such further directions as he thinks appropriate;

(8) if at the progress monitoring date all parties have indicated that they will be ready for trial, all parties will complete a pre-trial checklist;

(9) in many cases there will be a pre-trial review; in such cases the parties will be required to prepare a trial timetable for consideration by the court;

(10) throughout the case there will be regular reviews of the estimated length of trial.

D3 Fixing a Case Management Conference

D3.1 A mandatory case management conference will normally take place on the first available date six weeks after all defendants who intend to serve a defence have done so. This will normally allow time for the preparation and service of any reply (see section C4).

D3.2 (a) If proceedings have been started by service of a Part 7 claim form, the claimant must take steps to fix the date for the case management conference with the Listing Office in cooperation with the other parties within 14 days of the date when all defendants who intend to file and serve a defence have done so (PD 58, para. 10.2(a)). The parties should bear in mind the need to allow time for the preparation and service of any reply.

(b) If proceedings have been begun by service of a Part 8 claim form, the claimant must take steps to fix a date for the case management conference with the Listing Office in cooperation with the other parties within 14 days of the date when all defendants who wish to serve evidence have done so (PD 58, para. 10.2(b)).

D3.3 (a) In accordance with section C3 the Registry will expect a defence to be served and filed by the latest of:

(i) 28 days after service of particulars of claim (as certified by the certificate of service); or

(ii) any extended date for serving and filing a defence as notified to the court in writing following agreement between the parties; or

(iii) any extended date for serving and filing a defence as ordered by the court on an application.

(b) If within 28 days after the latest of these dates has passed for each defendant, the parties have not taken steps to fix the date for the case management conference, the Case Management Unit will inform the judge in charge of the List, and at his direction will take steps to fix a date for the case management conference without further reference to the parties.

D3.4 If the proceedings have been transferred to the Commercial List, the claimant must apply for a case management conference within 14 days of the date of the order transferring them, unless the judge held, or gave directions for, a case management conference when he made the order transferring the proceedings (PD 58, para. 10.3).

D3.5 If the claimant fails to make an application as required by the rules, any other party may apply for a case management conference (PD 58, para. 10.5).

D3.6 (a) In some cases it may be appropriate for a case management conference to take place at an earlier date.

(b) Any party may apply to the court in writing at an earlier time for a case management conference (PD 58, para. 10.4). A request by any party for an early case management conference should be made in writing to the judge in charge of the List, on notice to all other parties, at the earliest possible opportunity.

D3.7 If before the date on which the case management conference would be held in accordance with section D3 there is a hearing in the case at which the parties are represented, the business of the case management conference will normally be transacted at that hearing and there will be no separate case management conference.

D3.8 The court may fix a case management conference at any time on its own initiative. If it does so, the court will normally give at least seven days' notice to the parties (PD 58, para. 10.6).

D3.9 A case management conference may not be postponed or adjourned without an order of the court.

D4 Two-judge Team System

D4.1 (a) Cases which are exceptional in size or complexity or in having a propensity to give rise to numerous pre-trial applications may be allocated to a management team of two designated judges.

(b) An application for the appointment of a two-judge management team should be made in writing to the judge in charge of the List at the time of fixing the case management conference.

(c) If an order is made for allocation to a two-judge team, one of the designated judges will preside at the case management conference.

D4.2 Except for an application for an interim payment, all applications in the case, and the trial itself will be heard by one or other of the designated judges.

D5 Case Memorandum

D5.1 In order that the judge conducting the case management conference may be informed of the general nature of the case and the issues which are expected to arise, after service of the defence and any reply the solicitors and counsel for each party shall draft an agreed case memorandum.

D5.2 The case memorandum should contain:

(i) a short and uncontroversial description of what the case is about; and

(ii) a very short and uncontroversial summary of the material procedural history of the case.

D5.3 Unless otherwise ordered, the solicitors for the claimant are to be responsible for producing and filing the case memorandum.

D5.4 The case memorandum should not refer to any application for an interim payment, to any order for an interim payment, to any voluntary interim payment, or to any payment or offer under CPR, Part 36 or Part 37.

D5.5 (a) It should be clearly understood that the only purpose of the case memorandum is to help the judge understand broadly what the case is about. The case memorandum does not play any part in the trial. It is unnecessary, therefore, for parties to be unduly concerned about the precise terms in which it is drafted, provided it contains a reasonably fair and balanced description of the case.

(b) Accordingly, in all but the most exceptional cases it should be possible for the parties to draft an agreed case memorandum. However, if it proves impossible to do so, the claimant must draft the case memorandum and send a copy to the defendant. The defendant may provide its comments to the court (with a copy to the claimant) separately.

(c) The failure of the parties to agree a case memorandum is a matter which the court may wish to take into account when dealing with the costs of the case management conference.

D6 List of Issues

D6.1 After service of the defence (and any reply), the solicitors and counsel for each party shall produce an agreed list of the important issues in the case. The list should include both issues of fact and issues of law. A separate section of the document should list what is common ground between the parties (or any of them, specifying which).

D6.2 Unless otherwise ordered, the solicitors and counsel for the claimant are to have responsibility for the production and revision of the list of issues.

D7 Case Management Bundle

Preparation

D7.1 Before the case management conference (see sections D3 and D8), a case management bundle should be prepared by the solicitors for the claimant (PD 58, para. 10.8).

Contents

D7.2 The case management bundle should only contain the documents listed below (where the documents have been created by the relevant time):

(i) the claim form;

(ii) all statements of case (excluding schedules), except that, if a summary has been prepared, the bundle should contain the summary, not the full statement of case;

(iii) the case memorandum (see section D5);

(iv) the list of issues (see section D6);

(v) the case management information sheets and the pre-trial timetable if one has already been established (see sections D8.5 and D8.9);

(vi) the principal orders in the case; and

(vii) any agreement in writing made by the parties to disclose documents without making a list or any agreement in writing that disclosure (or inspection or both) shall take place in stages.

See generally PD 58, para. 10.8.

D7.3 The case management bundle must not include a copy of any order for an interim payment.

Lodging the case management bundle

D7.4 The case management bundle should be lodged with the Listing Office at least seven days before the (first) case management conference (or earlier hearing at which the parties are represented and at which the business of the case management conference may be transacted: see section D3.7).

Preparation and upkeep

D7.5 The claimant (or other party responsible for the preparation and upkeep of the case management bundle), in consultation with the other parties, must revise and update the case management bundle as the case proceeds (PD 58, para. 10.9). The claimant should attend at the Case Management Unit for this purpose at the following stages:

(i) within 10 days of the case management conference, in order to add the pre-trial timetable (or any other order made at the case management conference) and an updated case memorandum;

Court Guides

(ii) within 10 days of an order being made on an application, if in the light of the order or the application it is necessary to add a copy of the order made (as a principal order in the case) or an updated case memorandum;

(iii) within 14 days of the service of any amended statement of case (or summary), in order to substitute a copy of the amended statement of case (or summary) for that which it replaces and to incorporate an updated case memorandum and (if appropriate) a revised list of issues;

(iv) within 10 days of any other revision to the case memorandum or list of issues, in order to incorporate the revised document.

D8 Case Management Conference

Application to postpone the case management conference

D8.1 (a) An application to postpone the case management conference must be made within 21 days after all defendants who intend to serve a defence have done so.

(b) The application will be dealt with on paper unless the court considers it appropriate to direct an oral hearing.

Attendance at the case management conference

D8.2 Clients need not attend a case management conference unless the court otherwise orders. A representative who has conduct of the case must attend from each firm of solicitors instructed in the case. At least one of the advocates retained in the case on behalf of each party should also attend.

D8.3 The case management conference is a very significant stage in the case. It is not simply a substitute for the summons for directions under the former Rules of the Supreme Court and although parties are encouraged to agree proposals for directions for the consideration of the court, directions will not normally be made by consent without the need for attendance.

Applications

D8.4 (a) If by the time of the case management conference a party wishes to apply for an order in respect of a matter not covered by questions (1) to (16) in the case management information sheet, he should make that application at the case management conference.

(b) In some cases notice of such an application may be given in the case management information sheet itself: see section D8.5(c).

(c) In all other cases the applicant should ensure that an application notice and any supporting evidence is filed and served in time to enable the application to be heard at the case management conference.

Materials: case management information sheet and case management bundle

D8.5 (a) All parties attending a case management conference must complete a case management information sheet (PD 58, para. 10.7). A standard form of case management information sheet is set out in appendix 6. The information sheet is intended to include reference to all applications which the parties would wish to make at a case management conference.

(b) A completed case management information sheet must be provided by each party to the court (and copied to all other parties) at least seven days before the case management conference.

(c) Applications not covered by the standard questions raised in the case management information sheet should be entered under question (17). No other application notice is necessary if written evidence will not be involved and the seven-day notice given by entering the application on the information sheet will in all the circumstances be sufficient to enable all other parties to deal with the application.

D8.6 The case management bundle must be provided to the court at least seven days before the case management conference (PD 58, para. 10.8). Only where it is essential for the court on the case management conference to see the full version of a statement of case that has been summarised in accordance with section C1.4 above should a copy of that statement of case be lodged for the case management conference.

The hearing

D8.7 The court's power to give directions at the case management conference is to be found in CPR, rr. 3.1 and 58.13(4). At the case management conference the judge will:

(i) discuss the issues in the case, and the requirements of the case, with the advocates retained in the case;
(ii) fix the entire pre-trial timetable, or, if that is not practicable, fix as much of the pre-trial timetable as possible; and
(iii) in appropriate cases make an ADR order.

D8.8 (a) Rules 3.1(2) and 58.13(4) enable the court at the case management conference to stay the proceedings while the parties try to settle the case by alternative means. The case management information sheet requires the parties to indicate whether a stay for such purposes is sought.
(b) In an appropriate case an ADR order may be made without a stay of proceedings. The parties should consider carefully whether it may be possible to provide for ADR in the pre-trial timetable without affecting the date of trial.
(c) Where a stay has been granted for a fixed period for the purposes of ADR the court has power to extend it. If an extension of the stay is desired by all parties, a judge will normally be prepared to deal with an application for such an extension if it is made before the expiry of the stay by letter from the legal representatives of one of the parties. The letter should confirm that all parties consent to the application.
(d) An extension will not normally be granted for more than four weeks unless clear reasons are given to justify a longer period, but more than one extension may be granted.

The pre-trial timetable

D8.9 The pre-trial timetable will normally include:
(i) a progress monitoring date (see section D12 below); and
(ii) a direction that the parties attend upon the Clerk to the Commercial Court to obtain a fixed date for trial.

Variations to the pre-trial timetable

D8.10 The parties may agree minor variations to the time periods set out in the pre-trial timetable without the case needing to be brought back to the court provided that the variation:
(i) will not jeopardise the date fixed for trial;
(ii) does not relate to the progress monitoring date; and
(iii) does not provide for the completion after the progress monitoring date of any step which was previously scheduled to have been completed by that date.

D8.11 If in any case it becomes apparent that variations to the pre-trial timetable are required which do not fall within section D8.10 above, the parties should apply to have the case management conference reconvened immediately. The parties should not wait until the progress monitoring date.

D9 Case Management Conference: Part 8 Claims

In a case commenced by the issue of a Part 8 claim form, a case management conference will normally take place on the first available date six weeks after service and filing of the defendant's evidence. At that case management conference the court will make such pre-trial directions as are necessary, adapting (where useful in the context of the particular claim) those of the case management procedures used for a claim commenced by the issue of a Part 7 claim form.

D10 Case Management Conference: Part 20 Claims

D10.1 Wherever possible, any party who intends to make a Part 20 claim should do so before the hearing of the case management conference dealing with the main claim.

D10.2 Where permission to make a Part 20 claim is required it should be sought at the case management conference in the main claim.

D10.3 If the Part 20 claim is a counterclaim by a defendant against a claimant alone, the court will give directions in the Part 20 claim at the case management conference in the main claim.

D10.4 If the Part 20 claim is not a counterclaim by a defendant against a claimant alone, the case management conference in the main claim will be reconvened on the first available date six weeks after service of the defence to the Part 20 claim.

D10.5 All parties to the proceedings (i.e. the parties to the main claim and the parties to the Part 20 claim) must attend the reconvened case management conference. There will not be a separate case management conference for the Part 20 claim alone.

Court Guides

D10.6 In any case involving a Part 20 claim the court will give case management directions at the same case management conferences as it gives directions for the main claim (PD 58, para. 12). The court will therefore normally only give case management directions at hearings attended by all parties to the proceedings.

D11 Management Throughout the Case

The court will continue to take an active role in the management of the case throughout its progress to trial. Parties should be ready at all times to provide the court with such information and assistance as it may require for that purpose.

D12 Progress Monitoring

Fixing the progress monitoring date

D12.1 The progress monitoring date will be fixed at the case management conference and will normally be after the date in the pre-trial timetable for exchange of witness statements and expert reports.

Progress monitoring information sheet

D12.2 At least three days (i.e. three clear days) before the progress monitoring date the parties must each send to the Case Management Unit (with a copy to all other parties) a progress monitoring information sheet to inform the court:

(i) whether they have complied with the pre-trial timetable, and if they have not, the respects in which they have not; and

(ii) whether they will be ready for a trial commencing on the fixed date specified in the pre-trial timetable, and if they will not be ready, why they will not be ready.

D12.3 A standard form of progress monitoring information sheet is set out in appendix 12.

D13 Reconvening the Case Management Conference

D13.1 If in the view of the court the information given in the progress monitoring sheets justifies this course, the court may direct that the case management conference be reconvened.

D13.2 At a reconvened hearing of the case management conference the court may make such orders and give such directions as it considers appropriate.

D14 Pre-trial Checklist

Not later than three weeks before the date fixed for trial each party must send to the Listing Office (with a copy to all other parties) a completed checklist confirming final details for trial (a 'pre-trial checklist') in the form set out in appendix 13.

D15 Further Information

D15.1 (a) If a party declines to provide further information requested under CPR, Part 18, the solicitors or counsel for the parties concerned must communicate directly with each other in an attempt to reach agreement before any application is made to the court.

(b) No application for an order that a party provide further information will normally be listed for hearing without prior written confirmation from the applicant that the requirements of section D15.1(a) have been complied with.

D15.2 Because it falls within the definition of a statement of case (see CPR, r. 2.3(1)) a response providing further information under CPR, Part 18, must be verified by a statement of truth.

D16 Fixed Trial Dates

D16.1 Most cases will be given fixed trial dates immediately after the pre-trial timetable has been set at the case management conference.

D16.2 A fixed date for trial is given on the understanding that if previous fixtures have been substantially underestimated or other urgent matters need to be heard, the trial may be delayed. Where such delay might cause particular inconvenience to witnesses or others involved in the trial, the Clerk to the Commercial Court should be informed well in advance of the fixed date.

D17 Estimates of Length of Trial

D17.1 At the case management conference an estimate will be made of the minimum and maximum lengths of the trial. The estimate will appear in the pre-trial timetable and will be the basis on which a date for trial will be fixed.

D17.2 If a party subsequently instructs new advocate(s) to appear on its behalf at the trial, the Listing Office should be notified of that fact within 14 days. Advocates newly instructed should review the estimate of the minimum and maximum lengths of the trial, and submit to the Listing Office a signed note revising or confirming the estimate as appropriate.

D17.3 A confirmed estimate of the minimum and maximum lengths of the trial, signed by the advocates who are to appear at the trial, should be attached to the pre-trial checklist.

D17.4 It is the duty of all advocates who are to appear at the trial to seek agreement, if possible, on the estimated minimum and maximum lengths of trial.

D17.5 The provisional estimate and (after it is given) the confirmed estimate must be kept under review by the advocates who are to appear at the trial. If at any stage an estimate needs to be revised, a signed revised estimate (whether agreed or not) must be submitted by the advocates to the Clerk to the Commercial Court.

D17.6 Accurate estimation of trial length is of great importance to the efficient functioning of the court. The court will be guided by, but will not necessarily accept, the estimates given by the parties

D18 Pre-trial Review and Trial Timetable

D18.1 The court will order a pre-trial review in any case in which it considers it appropriate to do so.

D18.2 A pre-trial review will normally take place between eight and four weeks before the date fixed for trial.

D18.3 Whenever possible the pre-trial review will be conducted by the trial judge. It should be attended by the advocates who are to appear at the trial (PD 58, para. 11.2).

D18.4 Before the pre-trial review the parties must attempt to agree a timetable for the trial providing for oral submissions, witnesses of fact and expert evidence (PD 58, para. 11.3). The claimant must file a copy of the draft timetable at least two days before the date fixed for the pre-trial review; any differences of view should be clearly identified (PD 58, para. 11.4). At the pre-trial review the judge may set a timetable for the trial and give such other directions for the conduct of the trial as he considers appropriate.

D19 Orders

D19.1 (a) Except for orders made by the court on its own initiative under CPR, r. 3.3, and unless the court otherwise orders, every judgment or order will be drawn up by the parties and r. 40.3 is modified accordingly (r. 58.15(1)).

(b) Consent orders are to be drawn up in accordance with the procedure described in section F9.

(c) All other orders are to be drawn up in draft by the parties and dated in the draft with the date of the judge's decision. The claimant is to have responsibility for drafting the order, unless it was made on the application of another party in which case that other party is to have the responsibility.

(d) Two copies of the draft, signed by the parties themselves, or by their solicitors or counsel, must be lodged with the Registry *within five days* of the decision of the court reflected in the draft.

D19.2 If the court orders that an act be done by a certain date without specifying a time for compliance, the latest time for compliance is 4.30 p.m. on the day in question.

D19.3 Orders that are required to be served must be served by the parties, unless the court otherwise directs.

E DISCLOSURE

E1 Generally

The court will seek to ensure that disclosure is no wider than appropriate. Anything wider than standard disclosure (see section E3) will need to be justified.

E2 Procedure

E2.1 At the case management conference the court will normally wish to consider one or more of the following:
(i) ordering standard disclosure (CPR, r. 31.5(1));
(ii) dispensing with or limiting standard disclosure (r. 31.5(2));
(iii) ordering sample disclosure;
(iv) ordering disclosure in stages;
(v) ordering disclosure otherwise than by service of a list of documents, for example, by service of copy documents; and
(vi) ordering specific disclosure (r. 31.12).

E2.2 The obligations imposed by an order for disclosure continue until the proceedings come to an end. If, after a list of documents has been prepared and served, the existence (present or past) of further documents to which the order applies comes to the attention of the disclosing party, that party must prepare and serve a supplemental list.

E3 Standard Disclosure

E3.1 Standard disclosure is defined by r. 31.6. Where standard disclosure is ordered a party is required to disclose only:
(i) the documents on which he relies; and
(ii) documents which:
— adversely affect his own case;
— adversely affect another party's case; or
— support another party's case; and
(iii) documents which he is required to disclose by any relevant practice direction.

E3.2 A party who contends that to search for a category or class of document under r. 31.6(b) would be unreasonable must indicate this in his case management information sheet (see appendix 6).

E3.3 In order to comply with r. 31.10(3) (which requires the list to identify the documents in a convenient order and manner and as concisely as possible) it will normally be necessary to list the documents in date order, to number them consecutively and to give each a concise description. However, where there is a large number of documents all falling within a particular category the disclosing party may (unless otherwise ordered) list those documents as a category rather than individually.

E3.4 Each party to the proceedings must serve a separate list of documents. This applies even if two or more parties are represented by the same firm of solicitors.

E3.5 If the physical structure of a file may be of evidential value (e.g. a placing or chartering file) solicitors should make one complete copy of the file in the form in which they received it before any documents are removed for the purpose of giving disclosure or inspection.

E3.6 Unless the court directs otherwise, the disclosure statement must comply with the requirements of rr. 31.7(3) and 31.10(6). In particular, it should:
(i) expressly state that the disclosing party believes the extent of the search to have been reasonable in all the circumstances; and
(ii) draw attention to any particular limitations on the extent of the search adopted for reasons of proportionality and give the reasons why they were adopted.

E3.7 The disclosure statement for standard disclosure should begin with the following words:

[I/we], [name(s)] state that [I/we] have carried out a reasonable and proportionate search to locate all the documents which [I am/ *here name the party* is] required to disclose under [the order made by the Court or the agreement in writing made between the parties] on the [ ] day of [ ] 20[ ].

E3.8 The disclosure statement for standard disclosure should end with the following certificate:

[I/we] certify that [I/we] understand the duty of disclosure and to the best of [my/our] knowledge [I have/ *here name the party* has] carried out that duty. [I/we] certify that the list above is a complete list of all documents which are or have been in [my/*here name the party's]* control and which [I am/ *here name the party* is] obliged under [the said order or the said agreement in writing] to disclose.

E3.9 [**Form N265(CC)** is an adapted version of form N265 (list of documents: standard disclosure) which has been approved for use in the Commercial Court.] The court may at any stage order that a disclosure statement be verified by affidavit.

E3.10 (a) For the purposes of PD 31, para. 4.3, the court will normally regard as an appropriate person any person who is in a position responsibly and authoritatively to search for the documents required to be disclosed by that party and to make the statements contained in the disclosure statement concerning the documents which must be disclosed by that party

(b) A legal representative may in certain cases be an appropriate person.

(c) An explanation why the person is considered an appropriate person must still be given in the disclosure statement.

(d) A person holding an office or position in the disclosing party but who is not in a position responsibly and authoritatively to make the statements contained in the disclosure statement will not be regarded as an appropriate person to make the disclosure statement of the party.

(e) The court may of its own initiative or on application require that a disclosure statement also be signed by another appropriate person.

E4 Specific Disclosure

E4.1 Specific disclosure is defined by CPR, r. 31.12(2).

E4.2 An order for specific disclosure under r. 31.12 may in an appropriate case direct a party to carry out a thorough search for any documents which it is reasonable to suppose may adversely affect his own case or support the case of the party applying for disclosure or which may lead to a train of enquiry which has either of these consequences and to disclose any documents located as a result of that search (PD 31, para. 5.5).

E4.3 The court may at any stage order that specific disclosure be verified by affidavit or witness statement.

E4.4 Applications for ship's papers are provided for in r. 58.14.

F APPLICATIONS

F1 Generally

F1.1 (a) Applications are governed by CPR, Part 23, and PD 23 as modified by Part 58 and PD 58. As a result:

(i) PD 23, paras 1 and 2.3 to 2.6 do not apply;

(ii) PD 23, paras 2.8 and 2.10, apply only if the proposed (additional) application will not increase the time estimate already given for the hearing for which a date has been fixed; and

(iii) PD 23, para. 3, is subject in all cases to the judge's agreeing that the application may proceed without an application notice being served.

(b) [Form N244(CC) is an adapted version of form N244 (application notice) which has been approved for use in the Commercial Court.]

F1.2 An application for a consent order must include a draft of the proposed order signed on behalf of all parties to whom it relates (PD 58, para. 14.1).

F1.3 The requirement in PD 23, para. 12.1, that a draft order be supplied on disk does not apply in the Commercial Court since orders are generally drawn up by the parties (PD 58, para. 14.2).

Service

F1.4 Application notices are served by the parties, not by the court (PD 58, para. 9).

Court Guides

Evidence

F1.5 (a) Particular attention is drawn to PD 23, para. 9.1, which points out that even where no specific requirement for evidence is set out in the rules or practice directions the court will in practice often need to be satisfied by evidence of the facts that are relied on in support of, or in opposition to, the application.

(b) Where convenient the written evidence relied on in support of an application may be included in the application notice, which may be lengthened for this purpose.

Time for service of evidence

F1.6 The time allowed for the service of evidence in relation to applications is governed by PD 58, para. 13.

Hearings

F1.7 (a) Applications (other than arbitration applications) will be heard in public in accordance with CPR, r. 39.2, save where otherwise ordered.

(b) With certain exceptions, arbitration applications will normally be heard in private: r. 62.10(3). See section O.

(c) An application without notice for a freezing injunction or a search order will normally be heard in private.

F1.8 Parties should pay particular attention to PD 23, para. 2.9, which warns of the need to anticipate the court's wish to review the conduct of the case and give further management directions. The parties should be ready to give the court their assistance and should be able to answer any questions that the court may ask for this purpose.

F1.9 PD 23, paras 6.1 to 6.5 and 7, deal with the hearing of applications by telephone (other than an urgent application out of court hours) and the hearing of applications using video-conferencing facilities. These methods may be considered when an application needs to be made before a particular commercial judge who is currently on circuit. In most other cases applications are more conveniently dealt with in person.

F2 Applications Without Notice

F2.1 All applications should be made on notice, even if that notice has to be short, unless:

(i) any rule or practice direction provides that the application may be made without notice; or

(ii) there are good reasons for making the application without notice, for example, because notice would or might defeat the object of the application.

F2.2 Where an application without notice does not involve the giving of undertakings to the court, it will normally be made and dealt with on paper, as, for example, applications for permission to serve a claim form out of the jurisdiction, and applications for an extension of time in which to serve a claim form.

F2.3 Any application for an interim injunction or similar remedy will require an oral hearing.

F2.4 (a) A party wishing to make an application without notice which requires an oral hearing before a judge should contact the Clerk to the Commercial Court at the earliest opportunity.

(b) If a party wishes to make an application without notice at a time when no commercial judge is available he should apply to the Queen's Bench judge in chambers (see section P1.1).

F2.5 On all applications without notice it is the duty of the applicant and those representing him to make full and frank disclosure of all matters relevant to the application.

F2.6 The papers lodged for the application should include two copies of a draft of the order sought. Save in exceptional circumstances where time does not permit, all the evidence relied upon in support of the application and any other relevant documents must be lodged in advance with the Clerk to the Commercial Court. If the application is urgent, the Clerk to the Commercial Court should be informed of the fact and of the reasons for the urgency.

F3 Expedited Applications

F3.1 The court will expedite the hearing of an application on notice in cases of sufficient urgency and importance.

F3.2 Where a party wishes to make an expedited application a request should be made to the Clerk to the Commercial Court on notice to all other parties.

F4 Paper Applications

F4.1 (a) Although contested applications are usually best determined at an oral hearing, some applications may be suitable for determination on paper.

(b) Attention is drawn to the provisions of CPR, r. 23.8, and PD 23, para. 11. If the applicant considers that the application is suitable for determination on paper, he should ensure before lodging the papers with the court:

(i) that the application notice together with any supporting evidence has been served on the respondent;

(ii) that the respondent has been allowed the appropriate period of time in which to serve evidence in opposition;

(iii) that any evidence in reply has been served on the respondent; and

(iv) that there is included in the papers:

(A) the written consent of the respondent to the disposal of the application without a hearing; or

(B) a statement by the applicant of the grounds on which he seeks to have the application disposed of without a hearing, together with confirmation that a copy has been served on the respondent.

(c) Only in exceptional cases will the court dispose of an application without a hearing in the absence of the respondent's consent.

F4.2 (a) Certain applications relating to the management of proceedings may conveniently be made in correspondence without issuing an application notice.

(b) It must be clearly understood that such applications are not applications without notice and the applicant must therefore ensure that a copy of the letter making the application is sent to all other parties to the proceedings.

(c) Accordingly, the following procedure should be followed when making an application of this kind:

(i) the applicant should first ascertain whether the application is opposed by the other parties;

(ii) if it is, the applicant should apply to the court by letter stating the nature of the order which it seeks and the grounds on which the application is made;

(iii) a copy the letter should be sent (by fax, where possible) to all other parties at the same time as it is sent to the court;

(iv) any other party wishing to make representations should do so by letter within two days (i.e. two clear days) of the date of the applicant's letter of application. The representations should be sent (by fax, where possible) to the applicant and all other parties at the same time as they are sent to the court;

(v) the court will advise its decision by letter to the applicant. The applicant must forthwith copy the court's letter to all other parties, by fax where possible.

F5 Ordinary Applications

F5.1 Applications likely to require an oral hearing lasting half a day or less are regarded as 'ordinary' applications.

F5.2 Ordinary applications will generally be heard on Fridays, but may be heard on other days. Where possible, the Listing Office will have regard to the availability of advocates when fixing hearing dates.

F5.3 Many ordinary applications, especially those in the non-counsel list on Fridays, are very short indeed (e.g. applications to extend time). As in the past, it is likely that many, if not most, of such applications can be heard without evidence and on short (i.e. a few days') notice. The parties should however have in mind what is said in section F1.5(a) above.

F5.4 (a) The timetable for ordinary applications is set out in PD 58, para. 13.1, and is as follows:

(i) evidence in support must be filed and served with the application;

(ii) evidence in answer must be filed and served within 14 days thereafter;

(iii) evidence in reply (if any) must be filed and served within seven days thereafter.

(b) This timetable may be abridged or extended by agreement between the parties provided that any date fixed for the hearing of the application is not affected (PD 58, para. 13.4). In appropriate cases, this timetable may be abridged by the court.

Court Guides

F5.5 An application bundle (see section F11) must be lodged with the Listing Office by 1 p.m. one clear day before the date fixed for the hearing. The case management bundle will also be required on the hearing; this file will be passed by the Listing Office to the judge. Only where it is essential for the court on the hearing of the ordinary application to see the full version of a statement of case that has been summarised in accordance with section C1.4 above should a copy of that statement of case be lodged for the ordinary application.

F5.6 Save in very short and simple cases, skeleton arguments must be provided by all parties. These must be lodged with the Listing Office and served on the advocates for all other parties to the application by 1 p.m. on the day before the date fixed for the hearing (i.e. the immediately preceding day). Guidelines on the preparation of skeleton arguments are set out in part 1 of appendix 9.

F5.7 Thus, for an application estimated for a half day or less and due to be heard on a Friday:
(i) the application bundle must be lodged by 1 p.m. on Wednesday; and
(ii) skeleton arguments must be lodged by 1 p.m. on Thursday.

F5.8 The applicant should, as a matter of course, provide all other parties to the application with a copy of the application bundle at the cost of the receiving party. Further copies should be supplied on request, again at the cost of the receiving party.

F5.9 Problems with the lodging of bundles or skeleton arguments should be notified to the Clerk to the Commercial Court as far in advance as possible. *If the application bundle or skeleton argument is not lodged by the time specified, the application may be stood out of the list without further warning.*

F6 Heavy Applications

F6.1 Applications likely to require an oral hearing lasting more than half a day are regarded as 'heavy' applications.

F6.2 Heavy applications normally involve a greater volume of evidence and other documents and more extensive issues. They accordingly require a longer lead time for preparation and exchange of evidence. Where possible the Listing Office will have regard to the availability of advocates when fixing hearing dates.

F6.3 The timetable for heavy applications is set out in PD 58, para. 13.2, and is as follows:
(i) evidence in support must be filed and served with the application;
(ii) evidence in answer must be filed and served within 28 days thereafter;
(iii) evidence in reply (if any) must be filed and served as soon as possible, and in any event within 14 days of service of the evidence in answer.

F6.4 (a) An application bundle (see section F11) must be lodged with the Listing Office by 4 p.m. two days (i.e. two clear days) before the date fixed for the hearing. The case management bundle will also be required on the hearing; this file will be passed by the Listing Office to the judge.
(b) Only where it is essential for the court on the hearing of the application to see the full version of a statement of case that has been summarised in accordance with section C1.4 above should a copy of that statement of case be lodged for the application.

F6.5 Skeleton arguments must be lodged with the Listing Office and served on the advocates for all other parties to the application as follows:
(i) applicant's skeleton argument (with chronology unless one is unnecessary, and with a dramatis personae if one is warranted), by 4 p.m. two days (i.e. two clear days) before the hearing;
(ii) respondent's skeleton argument, by 4 p.m. one day (i.e. one clear day) before the hearing.
Guidelines on the preparation of skeleton arguments are set out in part 1 of appendix 9.

F6.6 Thus, for an application estimated for more than half a day and due to be heard on a Thursday:
(i) the application bundle and the applicant's skeleton argument must be lodged by 4 p.m. on Monday;
(ii) the respondent's skeleton argument must be lodged by 4 p.m. on Tuesday.

F6.7 The applicant must, as a matter of course, provide all other parties to the application with a copy of the application bundle at the cost of the receiving party. Further copies must be supplied on request, again at the cost of the receiving party.

F6.8 Problems with the lodging of bundles or skeleton arguments should be notified to the Clerk to the Commercial Court as far in advance as possible. *If the application bundle or skeleton argument is not lodged by the time specified, the application may be stood out of the list without further warning.*

F7 Evidence

F7.1 Although evidence may be given by affidavit, it should generally be given by witness statement, except where PD 32 requires evidence to be given on affidavit (as, for example, in the case of an application for a freezing injunction or a search order (PD 32, para. 1.4)). In other cases the court may order that evidence be given by affidavit (PD 32, paras 1.4(1) and 1.6).

F7.2 Witness statements and affidavits must comply with the requirements of PD 32, save that photocopy documents should be used unless the court orders otherwise.

F7.3 (a) Witness statements must be verified by a statement of truth signed by the maker of the statement (CPR, r. 22.1).

(b) At hearings other than trial an applicant may rely on the application notice itself, and a party may rely on his statement of case, if the application notice or statement of case (as the case may be) is verified by a statement of truth (r. 32.6(2)).

(c) A statement of truth in an application notice may also be signed as indicated in sections C1.8 and C1.9 above.

F7.4 Proceedings for contempt of court may be brought against a person who makes, or causes to be made, a false statement in a witness statement (or any other document verified by a statement of truth) without an honest belief in its truth (r. 32.14(1)).

F8 Reading Time

(a) It is essential for the efficient conduct of the court's business that the parties inform the court of the reading required in order to enable the judge to dispose of the application within the time allowed for the hearing and of the time likely to be required for that purpose. Accordingly:

(i) each party must lodge with the Listing Office by 1 p.m. on the day before the date fixed for the hearing of an application (i.e. the immediately preceding day) a reading list with an estimate of the time required to complete the reading;

(ii) each party's reading list should identify the material *on both sides* which the court needs to read; and

(iii) if any advocate considers that the time required for reading is likely to exceed 2½ hours, the Listing Office must be warned of that fact *not later than 4.00 p.m. one clear day before the hearing of the application.*

(b) *Failure to comply with these requirements may result in the adjournment of the hearing.*

F9 Applications Disposed of by Consent

F9. 1 (a) Consent orders may be submitted to the court in draft for approval and initialling without the need for attendance.

(b) Two copies of the draft, one of which (or a counterpart) must be signed on behalf of all parties to whom it relates, should be lodged at the Registry. The copies should be undated. The order will be dated with the date on which the judge initials it, but that does not prevent the parties acting on their agreement immediately if they wish.

(c) The parties should act promptly in lodging the copies at the Registry. If it is important that the orders are made by a particular date, that fact (and the reasons for it) should be notified in writing to the Registry.

F9.2 For the avoidance of doubt, this procedure is not normally available in relation to a case management conference or a pre-trial review. Whether or not the parties are agreed as between themselves on the directions that the court should be asked to consider giving at a case management conference or a pre-trial review, attendance will normally be required. See section D8.3.

F9.3 Where an order provides a time by which something is to be done the order should wherever possible state the particular date by which the thing is to be done rather than specify a period of time from a particular date or event (r. 2.9).

F10 Hearing Dates, Times Estimates and Time Limits

F10.1 Dates for the hearing of applications to be attended by advocates are normally fixed after discussion with the counsel's clerks or with the solicitor concerned.

F10.2 The efficient working of the court depends on accurate estimates of the time needed for the oral hearing of an application. Overestimating can be as wasteful as underestimating.

F10.3 Subject to section F10.4, the Clerk to the Commercial Court will not accept or act on time estimates for the oral hearing of applications where those estimates exceed the following maxima:

Application to set aside service:	4 hours
Application for summary judgment:	4 hours
Application to set aside or vary interim remedy:	4 hours
Application to set aside or vary default judgment:	2 hours
Application to amend statement of case:	1 hour
Application for specific disclosure:	1 hour
Application for security for costs:	1 hour

F10.4 A longer listing time will only be granted upon application in writing specifying the additional time required and giving reasons why it is required. A copy of the written application should be sent to the advocates for all other parties in the case at the same time as it is sent to the Listing Office.

F10.5 (a) Not later than five days before the date fixed for the hearing the applicant must provide the Listing Office with his current estimate of the time required to dispose of the application.

(b) If at any time either party considers that there is a material risk that the hearing of the application will exceed the time currently allowed it must inform the Listing Office immediately.

F10.6 (a) All time estimates should be given on the assumption that the judge will have read in advance the skeleton arguments and the documents identified in the reading list. In this connection attention is drawn to section F8.

(b) A time estimate for an ordinary application should allow time for judgment and consequential matters; a time estimate for a heavy application should not.

F10.7 Save in the situation referred to at section F10.8, a separate estimate must be given for each application, including any application issued after, but to be heard at the same time as, another application.

F10.8 A separate estimate need not be given for any application issued after, but to be heard at the same time as, another application where the advocate in the case certifies in writing that:

(i) the determination of the application first issued will necessarily determine the application issued subsequently; or

(ii) the matters raised in the application issued subsequently are not contested.

F10.9 If it is found at the hearing that the time required for the hearing has been significantly underestimated, the judge hearing the application may adjourn the matter and may make any special costs orders (including orders for the immediate payment of costs and wasted costs orders) as may be appropriate.

F10.10 Failure to comply with the requirements for lodging bundles for the application will normally result in the application not being heard on the date fixed at the expense of the party in default (see further sections F5.9 and F6.8 above). An order for immediate payment of costs may be made.

F11 Application Bundles

(a) Bundles for use on applications may be compiled in any convenient manner but must contain the following documents (preferably in separate sections in the following order):

(i) a copy of the application notice;

(ii) a draft of the order which the applicant seeks;

(iii) a copy of the statements of case;

(iv) copies of any previous orders which are relevant to the application;

(v) copies of the witness statements and affidavits filed in support of, or in opposition to, the application, together with any exhibits.

(b) Copies of the statements of case and of previous orders in the action should be provided in a separate section of the bundle. They should not be exhibited to witness statements.

(c) Witness statements and affidavits previously filed in the same proceedings should be included in the bundle at a convenient location. They should not be exhibited to witness statements.

F12 Chronologies, Indices and Dramatis Personae

F12.1 For most applications it is of assistance for the applicant to provide a chronology. Dramatis personae are often useful as well.

F12.2 Guidelines on the preparation of chronologies and indices are set out in part 2 of appendix 9.

F13 Authorities

F13.1 On some applications there will be key authorities that it would be useful for the judge to read before the oral hearing of the application. Copies of these authorities should be provided with the skeleton arguments.

F13.2 It is also desirable for bundles of the authorities on which the parties wish to rely to be provided to the judge hearing the application as soon as possible after skeleton arguments have been exchanged.

F13.3 Unreported cases should only be cited where the advocate is ready to give an assurance that the transcript contains a statement of some principle of law, relevant to an issue on the application, of which the substance, as distinct from some mere choice of phraseology, is not to be found in any judgment that has appeared in one of the recognised series of law reports.

F14 Costs

F14.1 Costs are dealt with generally at section J13.

F14.2 Reference should be also be made to the rules governing the summary assessment of costs for shorter hearings contained in CPR, Parts 43 and 44.

F14.3 In carrying out a summary assessment of costs, the court may have regard amongst other matters to:

(i) advice from a commercial costs judge or from the Chief Costs Judge on costs of specialist solicitors and counsel;

(ii) any survey published by the London Solicitors Litigation Association showing the average hourly expense rate for solicitors in London;

(iii) any information provided to the court at its request by one or more of the specialist associations (referred to at section A4.2) on average charges by specialist solicitors and counsel.

F15 Interim Injunctions

Generally

F15.1 (a) Applications for interim injunctions are governed by CPR, Part 25.

(b) Applications must be made on notice in accordance with the procedure set out in CPR, Part 23, unless there are good reasons for proceeding without notice.

F15.2 A party who wishes to make an application for an interim injunction must give the Clerk to the Commercial Court as much notice as possible.

F15.3 (a) Except when the application is so urgent that there has not been any opportunity to do so, the applicant must issue his claim form and obtain the evidence on which he wishes to rely in support of the application before making the application.

(b) On applications of any weight, and unless the urgency means that this is not possible, the applicant should provide the court at the earliest opportunity with a skeleton argument.

(c) An affidavit, and not a witness statement, is required on an application for a freezing injunction or a search order (PD 25, para. 3.1).

Fortification of undertakings

F15.4 (a) Where the applicant for an interim remedy is not able to show sufficient assets within the jurisdiction of the court to provide substance to the undertakings given, particularly the

Court Guides

undertaking in damages, he may be required to reinforce his undertakings by providing security.

(b) Security will be ordered in such form as the judge decides is appropriate but may, for example, take the form of a payment into court, a bond issued by an insurance company or a first demand guarantee or standby credit issued by a first-class bank.

(c) In an appropriate case the judge may order a payment to be made to the applicant's solicitors to be held by them as officers of the court pending further order. Sometimes the undertaking of a parent company may be acceptable.

Form of order

F15.5 Standard forms of wording for freezing injunctions and search orders are set out in appendix 5. The forms have been adapted for use in the Commercial Court and should be followed unless the judge hearing a particular application considers there is good reason for adopting a different form.

F15.6 A phrase indicating that an interim remedy is to remain in force until judgment or further order means that it remains in force until the delivery of a final judgment. If an interim remedy continuing after judgment is required, say until judgment has been satisfied, an application to that effect must be made (see further section K1).

F15.7 It is good practice to draft an order for an interim remedy so that it includes a proviso which permits acts which would otherwise be a breach of the order to be done with the written consent of the claimant's solicitors. This enables the parties to agree in effect to variations (or the discharge) of the order without the necessity of coming back to the court.

Freezing injunctions

F15.8 (a) Freezing injunctions made on an application without notice will provide for a return date, unless the judge otherwise orders (PD 25, para. 5.1(3)). In the usual course, the return date given will be a Friday (unless a date for a case management conference has already been fixed, in which event the return date given will in the usual course be that date).

(b) If, after service or notification of the injunction, one or more of the parties considers that more than 15 minutes will be required to deal with the matter on the return date the Listing Office should be informed forthwith and in any event no later than 4 p.m. on the Wednesday before the Friday fixed as the return date.

(c) If the parties agree, the return date may be postponed to a later date on which all parties will be ready to deal with any substantive issues. In this event, an agreed form of order continuing the injunction to the postponed return date should be submitted for consideration by a judge and if the order is made in the terms submitted there will be no need for the parties to attend on the day originally fixed as the return date.

(d) In such a case the defendant and any other interested party will continue to have liberty to apply to vary or set aside the order.

F15.9 A provision for the defendant to give notice of any application to discharge or vary the order is usually included as a matter of convenience but it is not proper to attempt to fetter the right of the defendant to apply without notice or on short notice if need be.

F15.10 As regards freezing injunctions in respect of assets outside the jurisdiction, the standard wording in relation to effects on third parties should normally incorporate wording to enable overseas branches of banks or similar institutions which have offices within the jurisdiction to comply with what they reasonably believe to be their obligations under the laws of the country where the assets are located or under the proper law of the relevant banking or other contract relating to such assets.

F15.11 Any bank or third party served with, notified of or affected by a freezing injunction may apply to the court without notice to any party for directions, or notify the court in writing without notice to any party, in the event that the order affects or may affect the position of the bank or third party under legislation, regulations or procedures aimed to prevent money laundering.

Search orders

F15.12 Attention is drawn to the detailed requirements in respect of search orders set out in PD 25, paras 7.1 to 8.3. The applicant for the search order will normally be required to undertake not to inform any third party of the search order or of the case until after a specified date.

Applications to discharge or vary freezing injunctions and search orders

F15.13 Applications to discharge or vary freezing injunctions and search orders are treated as matters of urgency for listing purposes. Those representing applicants for discharge or variation should ascertain before a date is fixed for the hearing whether, having regard to the evidence which they wish to adduce, the claimant would wish to adduce further evidence in opposition. If so, all reasonable steps must be taken by all parties to agree upon the earliest practicable date at which they can be ready for the hearing, so as to avoid the last-minute need to vacate a fixed date. In cases of difficulty the matter should be referred to a judge who may be able to suggest temporary solutions pending the hearing.

F15.14 If a freezing injunction or search order is discharged on an application to discharge or vary, or on the return date, the judge will consider whether it is appropriate that he should assess damages at once and direct immediate payment by the applicant.

Applications under section 25 of the Civil Jurisdiction and Judgments Act 1982

F15.15 A Part 8 claim form (rather than an application notice: cf. CPR, r. 25.4(2)) must be used for an application under the Civil Jurisdiction and Judgments Act 1982, s. 25 (interim relief in England and Wales and Northern Ireland in the absence of substantive proceedings). The modified Part 8 procedure used in the Commercial Court is referred to at section B4 above.

F16 Security for Costs

F16.1 Applications for security for costs are governed by CPR, rr. 25.12 to 25.14.

F16.2 The applicable practice is set out in appendix 16.

G ALTERNATIVE DISPUTE RESOLUTION (ADR)

G1 Generally

G1.1 While emphasising its primary role as a forum for deciding commercial cases, the Commercial Court encourages parties to consider the use of ADR (such as, but not confined to, mediation and conciliation) as an alternative means of resolving disputes or particular issues.

G1.2 Whilst the Commercial Court remains an entirely appropriate forum for resolving most of the disputes which are entered in the Commercial List, the view of the Commercial Court is that the settlement of disputes by means of ADR:

(i) significantly helps parties to save costs;
(ii) saves parties the delay of litigation in reaching finality in their disputes;
(iii) enables parties to achieve settlement of their disputes while preserving their existing commercial relationships and market reputation;
(iv) provides parties with a wider range of solutions than those offered by litigation; and
(v) is likely to make a substantial contribution to the more efficient use of judicial resources.

G1.3 The commercial judges will in appropriate cases invite the parties to consider whether their dispute, or particular issues in it, could be resolved through ADR.

G1.4 Legal representatives in all cases should consider with their clients and the other parties concerned the possibility of attempting to resolve the dispute or particular issues by ADR and should ensure that their clients are fully informed as to the most cost-effective means of resolving their dispute.

G1.5 Parties who consider that ADR might be an appropriate means of resolving the dispute or particular issues in the dispute may apply for directions at any stage, including before service of the defence and before the case management conference.

G1.6 At the case management conference if it should appear to the judge that the case before him or any of the issues arising in it are particularly appropriate for an attempt at settlement by means of ADR but that the parties have not previously attempted settlement by such means, he may invite the parties to use ADR.

G1.7 The judge may, if he considers it appropriate, adjourn the case for a specified period of time to encourage and enable the parties to use ADR. He may for this purpose extend the time for compliance by the parties or any of them with any requirement under the rules, the Guide or any order of the court.

G1.8 The judge may further consider in an appropriate case making an ADR Order in the terms set out in appendix 7.

G1.9 (a) The Clerk to the Commercial Court keeps some published information on individuals and bodies that offer ADR and arbitration services. If the parties are unable to agree upon a neutral individual or panel of individuals to act as a mediator, they may by consent refer to the judge for assistance in reaching such agreement.

(b) The court will not recommend any individual or body to act as a mediator or arbitrator.

G1.10 At the case management conference or at any other hearing in the course of which the judge makes an order providing for ADR he may make such order as to the costs that the parties may incur by reason of their using or attempting to use ADR as may in all the circumstances seem appropriate.

G2 Early Neutral Evaluation

G2.1 In appropriate cases and with the agreement of all parties the court will provide a without-prejudice, non-binding, early neutral evaluation (ENE) of a dispute or of particular issues.

G2.2 The approval of the judge in charge of the List must be obtained before any ENE is undertaken.

G2.3 If, after discussion with the advocates representing the parties, it appears to a judge that an ENE is likely to assist in the resolution of the dispute or of particular issues, he will, with the agreement of the parties, refer the matter to the judge in charge of the List.

G2.4 (a) The judge in charge of the List will nominate a judge to conduct the ENE.

(b) The judge who is to conduct the ENE will give such directions for its preparation and conduct as he considers appropriate.

G2.5 The judge who conducts the ENE will take no further part in the case, either for the purpose of the hearing of applications or as the judge at trial, unless the parties agree otherwise.

H EVIDENCE FOR TRIAL

H1 Witnesses of Fact

Preparation and form of witness statements

H1.1 Witness statements must comply with the requirements of PD 32. The following points are also emphasised:

(i) the function of a witness statement is to set out in writing the evidence-in-chief of the witness; as far as possible, therefore, the statement should be in the witness's own words;

(ii) it should be as concise as the circumstances of the case allow without omitting any significant matters;

(iii) it should not contain lengthy quotations from documents;

(iv) it should not engage in argument;

(v) it must indicate which of the statements made in it are made from the witness's own knowledge and which are made on information or belief, giving the source for any statement made on information or belief;

(vi) it must contain a statement by the witness that he believes the matters stated in it are true; proceedings for contempt of court may be brought against a person if he makes, or causes to be made, a false statement in a witness statement without an honest belief in its truth (CPR, r. 32.14(1)).

H1.2 It is improper to put pressure of any kind on a witness to give anything other than his own account of the matters with which his statement deals. It is also improper to serve a witness statement which is known to be false or which it is known the maker does not in all respects actually believe to be true.

Fluency of witnesses

H1.3 If a witness is not sufficiently fluent in English to give his evidence in English, the witness statement should be in the witness's own language and a translation provided.

H1.4 If a witness is not fluent in English but can make himself understood in broken English and can understand written English, the statement need not be in his own words provided that these matters are indicated in the statement itself It must however be written so as to express as accurately as possible the substance of his evidence.

Witness statement as evidence-in-chief

H1.5 (a) Where a witness is called to give oral evidence, his witness statement is to stand as his evidence-in-chief unless the court orders otherwise (r. 32.5(2)).

(b) In an appropriate case the trial judge may direct that the whole or any part of a witness's evidence-in-chief is to be given orally. Any application for such an order should be made at the beginning of the trial.

Additional evidence from a witness

H1.6 (a) A witness giving oral evidence at trial may with the permission of the court amplify his witness statement and give evidence in relation to new matters which have arisen since the witness statement was served (r. 32.5(3)). Permission will be given only if the court considers that there is good reason not to confine the evidence of the witness to the contents of his witness statement (r. 32.5(4)).

(b) A supplemental witness statement should normally be served where the witness proposes materially to add to, alter, correct or retract from what is in his original statement. Permission will be required for the service of a supplemental statement.

Notice of decision not to call a witness

H1.7 (a) A party who has decided not to call to give oral evidence at trial a witness whose statement has been served must give prompt notice of this decision to all other parties. He must at the same time state whether he proposes to put the statement in as hearsay evidence.

(b) If the party who has served the statement does not put it in as hearsay evidence, any other party may do so (r. 32.5(5)).

Witness summonses

H1.8 (a) Rules 34.2 to 34.8 deal with witness summonses, including a summons for a witness to attend court or to produce documents in advance of the date fixed for trial.

(b) Witness summonses are served by the parties, not the court.

H2 Expert Witnesses

Application for permission to call an expert witness

H2.1 Any application for permission to call an expert witness or serve an expert's report should normally be made at the case management conference.

H2.2 Parties should bear in mind that expert evidence can lead to unnecessary expense and they should be prepared to consider the use of single joint experts in appropriate cases. In many cases the use of single joint experts is not appropriate and each party will generally be given permission to call one expert in each field requiring expert evidence. These are referred to in the Guide as 'separate experts'.

H2.3 When the use of a single joint expert is contemplated, the court will expect the parties to cooperate in developing, and agreeing to the greatest possible extent, terms of reference for that expert. In most cases the terms of reference will (in particular) identify in detail what the expert is asked to do, identify any documentary materials he is asked to consider and specify any assumptions he is asked to make.

Provisions of general application in relation to expert evidence

H2.4 The provisions set out in appendix 11 to the Guide apply to all aspects of expert evidence (including expert reports, meetings of experts and expert evidence given orally) unless the court orders otherwise. Parties should ensure that they are drawn to the attention of any experts they instruct at the earliest opportunity.

Form and content of experts' reports

H2.5 Experts' reports must comply with the requirements of PD 35, paras 1 and 2.

H2.6 (a) In stating the substance of all material instructions on the basis of which his report is written as required by CPR, r. 35.10(3), and PD 35, para. 1.2(8), an expert witness should state the facts or assumptions upon which his opinion is based.

(b) The expert must make it clear which, if any, of the facts stated are within his own direct knowledge.

(c) If a stated assumption is, in the opinion of the expert witness, unreasonable or unlikely he should state that clearly.

Court Guides

H2.7 It is useful if a report contains a glossary of significant technical terms.

Statement of truth

H2.8 (a) The report must be signed by the expert and must contain a statement of truth in accordance with CPR, Part 35.

(b) Proceedings for contempt of court may be brought against a person if he makes, or causes to be made, without an honest belief in its truth, a false statement in an expert's report verified in the manner set out in this section.

Request by an expert to the court for directions

H2.9 An expert may file with the court a written request for directions to assist him in carrying out his function as expert, but

(i) at least seven days before he does so (or such shorter period as the court may direct) he should provide a copy of his proposed request to the party instructing him; and

(ii) at least four days before he does so (or such shorter period as the court may direct) he should provide a copy of his proposed request to all other parties.

Exchange of reports

H2.10 In appropriate cases the court will direct that the reports of expert witnesses be exchanged sequentially rather than simultaneously. This is an issue that the court will normally wish to consider at the case management conference.

Meetings of expert witnesses

H2.11 The court will normally direct a meeting or meetings of expert witnesses before trial. Sometimes it may be useful for there to be further meetings during the trial itself

H2.12 The purposes of a meeting of experts are to give the experts the opportunity:

(i) to discuss the expert issues;

(ii) to decide, with the benefit of that discussion, on which expert issues they share or can come to share the same expert opinion and on which expert issues there remains a difference of expert opinion between them (and what that difference is).

H2.13 Subject to section H2.16 below, the content of the discussion between the experts at or in connection with a meeting is without prejudice and shall not be referred to at the trial unless the parties so agree (r. 35.12(4)).

H2.14 Subject to any directions of the court, the procedure to be adopted at a meeting of experts is a matter for the experts themselves, not the parties or their legal representatives.

H2.15 Neither the parties nor their legal representatives should seek to restrict the freedom of experts to identify and acknowledge the expert issues on which they agree at, or following further consideration after, meetings of experts.

H2.16 Unless the court orders otherwise, at or following any meeting the experts should prepare a joint memorandum for the court recording:

(i) the fact that they have met and discussed the expert issues;

(ii) the issues on which they agree;

(iii) the issues on which they disagree; and

(iv) a brief summary of the reasons for their disagreement.

H2.17 If experts reach agreement on an issue that agreement shall not bind the parties unless they expressly agree to be bound by it.

Written questions to experts

H2.18 (a) Under r. 35.6 a party may, without the permission of the court, put written questions to an expert instructed by another party (or to a single joint expert) about his report. Unless the court gives permission or the other party agrees, such questions must be for the purpose only of clarifying the report.

(b) The court will pay close attention to the use of this procedure (especially where separate experts are instructed) to ensure that it remains an instrument for the helpful exchange of information. The court will not allow it to interfere with the procedure for an exchange of professional opinion at a meeting of experts, or to inhibit that exchange of professional opinion. In cases where (for example) questions that are oppressive in number or content are put, or questions are put for any purpose other than clarification of the report, the court will not hesitate to disallow the questions and to make an appropriate order for costs against the party putting them.

Documents referred to in experts' reports

H2.19 Unless they have already been provided on inspection of documents at the stage of disclosure, copies of any photographs, plans, analyses, measurements, survey reports or other similar documents relied on by an expert witness as well as copies of any unpublished sources must be provided to all parties at the same time as his report.

H2.20 (a) Rule 31.14(e) provides that (subject to r. 35.10(4)) a party may inspect a document mentioned in an expert's report. In a commercial case an expert's report will frequently, and helpfully, list all or many of the relevant previous papers (published or unpublished) or books written by the expert or to which the expert has contributed. Requiring inspection of this material may often be unrealistic, and the collating and copying burden could be huge.

(b) Accordingly, a party wishing to inspect a document in an expert report should (failing agreement) make an application to the court. The court will not permit inspection unless it is satisfied that it is necessary for the just disposal of the case and that the document is not reasonably available to the party making the application from an alternative source.

Trial

H2.21 At trial the evidence of expert witnesses is usually taken as a block, after the evidence of witnesses of fact has been given.

H3 Evidence by Video Link

H3.1 In an appropriate case permission may be given for the evidence of a witness to be given by video link. If permission is given the court will give directions for the conduct of this part of the trial.

H3.2 The party seeking permission to call evidence by video link should prepare and serve on all parties and lodge with the court a memorandum dealing with the matters out-lined in the videoconferencing guidance contained in annex 3 to PD 32 (see appendix 14) and setting out precisely what arrangements are proposed. Where the proposal involves transmission from a location with no existing video-link facility, experience shows that questions of feasibility, timing and cost will require particularly close investigation.

H3.3 An application for permission to call evidence by video link should be made, if possible, at the case management conference or, at the latest, at any pre-trial review. However, an application may be made at an even later stage if necessary.

H3.4 In considering whether to give permission for evidence to be given in this way the court will be concerned in particular to balance any potential savings of costs against the inability to observe the witness at first hand when giving evidence.

H4 Taking Evidence Abroad

H4.1 In an appropriate case permission may be given for the evidence of a witness to be taken abroad. CPR, Part 34, contains provisions for the taking of evidence by deposition, and the issue of letters of request.

H4.2 In a very exceptional case, and subject in particular to all necessary approvals being obtained and diplomatic requirements being satisfied, the court may be willing to conduct part of the proceedings abroad. However, if there is any reasonable opportunity for the witness to give evidence by video link, the court is unlikely to take that course.

J TRIAL

J1 Expedited Trial

J1.1 The Commercial Court is able to provide an expedited trial in cases of sufficient urgency and importance.

J1.2 A party seeking an expedited trial should apply to the judge in charge of the Commercial List on notice to all parties at the earliest possible opportunity. The application should normally be made after issue and service of the claim form but before service of particulars of claim.

Court Guides

J2 Split Trials

It will sometimes be advantageous to try liability first. Assessment of damages can be referred to a judge of the Technology and Construction Court or to a master, or the parties may choose to ask an arbitrator to decide them. The same approach can be applied to other factual questions.

J3 Documents for Trial

J3.1 Bundles of documents for the trial must be prepared in accordance with appendix 10.

J3.2 The number, content and organisation of the trial bundles must be approved by the advocates with the conduct of the trial.

J3.3 Consideration must always be given to what documents are and are not relevant and necessary. Where the court is of the opinion that costs have been wasted by the copying of unnecessary documents it will have no hesitation in making a special order for costs against the person responsible.

J3.4 The number, content and organisation of the trial bundles should be agreed in accordance with the following procedure:

(i) the claimant must submit proposals to all other parties at least six weeks before the date fixed for trial; and

(ii) the other parties must submit details of additions they require and any suggestions for revision of the claimant's proposals to the claimant at least four weeks before the date fixed for trial.

This information must be supplied in a form that will be most convenient for the recipient to understand and respond to. The form to be used should be discussed between the parties before the details are supplied.

J3.5 (a) It is the claimant's responsibility to prepare and lodge the agreed trial bundles.

(b) If another party wishes to put before the court a bundle that the claimant regards as unnecessary he must prepare and lodge it himself

J3.6 (a) Preparation of the trial bundles must be completed not later than two weeks before the date fixed for trial unless the court orders otherwise.

(b) Any party preparing a trial bundle should, as a matter of course, provide all other parties who are to take part in the trial with a copy, at the cost of the receiving party. Further copies should be supplied on request, again at the cost of the receiving party.

J3.7 Unless the court orders otherwise, a full set of the trial bundles must be lodged with the Listing Office at least seven days before the date fixed for trial.

J3.8 Failure to comply with the requirements for lodging bundles for the trial may result in the trial not commencing on the date fixed, at the expense of the party in default. An order for immediate payment of costs may be made.

J3.9 If oral evidence is to be given at trial, the claimant must provide a clean unmarked set of all relevant trial bundles for use in the witness box. The claimant is responsible for ensuring that these bundles are kept up to date throughout the trial.

J4 Information Technology at Trial

J4.1 The use of information technology at trial is encouraged where it is likely substantially to save time and cost or to increase accuracy.

J4.2 If any party considers that it might be advantageous to make use of information technology in preparation for, or at, trial, the matter should be raised at the case management conference. This is particularly important if it is considered that document handling systems would assist disclosure and inspection of documents or the use of documents at trial.

J4.3 Where information technology is to be used for the purposes of presenting the case at trial the same system must be used by all parties and must be made available to the court.

J5 Reading Lists, Authorities and Trial Timetable

J5.1 Unless the court orders otherwise, a single reading list approved by all advocates must be lodged with the Listing Office not later than 1 p.m. two days (i.e. two clear days) before the date fixed for trial together with an estimate of the time required for reading.

J5.2 (a) If any party objects to the judge reading any document in advance of the trial, the

objection and its grounds should be clearly stated in a letter accompanying the trial bundles and in the skeleton argument of that party.
(b) Parties should consider in particular whether they have any objection to the judge's reading the witness statements before the trial.
(c) In the absence of objection, the judge will be free to read the witness statements and documents in advance.

J5.3 (a) A composite bundle of the authorities referred to in the skeleton arguments should be lodged with the Listing Office as soon as possible after skeleton arguments have been exchanged.
(b) Unless otherwise agreed, the preparation of the bundle of authorities is the responsibility of the claimant, who should provide copies to all other parties. Advocates should liaise in relation to the production of bundles of authorities to ensure that the same authority does not appear in more than one bundle.

J5.4 Unreported cases should normally only be cited where the advocate is ready to give an assurance that the transcript contains a statement of some relevant principle of law of which the substance, as distinct from some mere choice of phraseology, is not to be found in any judgment that has appeared in one of the general or specialised series of law reports.

J5.5 (a) When lodging the reading list the claimant should also lodge a trial timetable.
(b) A trial timetable may have been fixed by the judge at the pre-trial review (section D18.4 above). If it has not, a trial timetable should be prepared by the advocate(s) for the claimant after consultation with the advocate(s) for all other parties.
(c) If there are differences of view between the advocate(s) for the claimant and the advocate(s) for other parties, these should be shown.
(d) The trial timetable will provide for oral submissions, witness evidence and expert evidence over the course of the trial. On the first day of the trial the judge may fix the trial timetable, subject to any further order.

Court Guides

J6 Skeleton Arguments etc. at Trial

J6.1 Written skeleton arguments should be prepared by each party. Guidelines on the preparation of skeleton arguments are set out in part 1 of appendix 9.

J6.2 Unless otherwise ordered, the skeleton arguments should be served on all other parties and lodged with the court as follows:
(i) by the claimant, not later than 1 p.m. two days (i.e. two clear days) before the start of the trial;
(ii) by each of the defendants, not later than 1 p.m. one day (i.e. one clear day) before the start of the trial.

J6.3 In heavier cases it will often be appropriate for skeleton arguments to be served and lodged at earlier times than indicated at section J6.2. The timetable should be discussed between the advocates and may be the subject of a direction in the pre-trial timetable or at any pre-trial review.

J6.4 The claimant should provide a chronology with his skeleton argument. Indices (i.e. documents that collate key references on particular points, or a substantive list of the contents of a particular bundle or bundles) and dramatis personae should also be provided where these are likely to be useful. Guidelines on the preparation of chronologies and indices are set out in part 2 of appendix 9.

J7 Trial Sitting Days and Hearing Trials in Public

J7.1 Trial sitting days will not normally include Fridays.

J7.2 Where it is necessary in order to accommodate hearing evidence from certain witnesses or types of witness, the court may agree to sit outside normal hours.

J7.3 The general rule is that a hearing is to be in public (CPR, r. 39.2(1)).

J8 Oral Opening Statements at Trial

J8.1 Oral opening statements should as far as possible be uncontroversial and in any event no longer than the circumstances require. Even in a very heavy case, oral opening statements may be very short.

J8.2 At the conclusion of the opening statement for the claimant the advocates for each of the other parties will usually each be invited to make a short opening statement.

J9 Applications in the Course of Trial

J9.1 It will not normally be necessary for an application notice to be issued for an application which is to be made during the course of the trial, but all other parties should be given adequate notice of the intention to apply.

J9.2 Unless the judge directs otherwise the parties should prepare skeleton arguments for the hearing of the application

J10 Oral Closing Submissions at Trial

J10.1 All parties will be expected to make oral closing submissions, whether or not closing submissions have been made in writing. It is a matter for the advocate to consider how in all the circumstances these oral submissions should be presented.

J10.2 Unless the trial judge directs otherwise, the claimant will make his oral closing submissions first, followed by the defendant(s) in the order in which they appear on the claim form with the claimant having a right of reply.

J11 Written Closing Submissions at Trial

J11.1 (a) In a more substantial trial, the court will normally also require closing submissions in writing before oral closing submissions.

(b) In such a case the court will normally allow an appropriate period of time after the conclusion of the evidence to allow the preparation of these submissions.

(c) Even in a less substantial trial the court will normally require a skeleton argument on matters of law.

J12 Judgment

J12.1 (a) When judgment is reserved the judge may deliver judgment orally or by handing down a written judgment.

(b) If the judge intends to hand down a written judgment a copy of the draft text marked:

'Unapproved Judgment. No permission is granted to copy or use in Court'

and bearing the rubric:

'Confidential to Counsel and Solicitors, but the substance may be communicated to clients not more than one hour before the giving of judgment'.

will normally be supplied to the advocates one clear day before the judgment is to be delivered.

(c) Advocates should inform the judge's clerk not later than noon on the day before judgment is to be handed down of any typographical or other errors of a similar nature which the judge might wish to correct.

(d) The requirement to treat the text as confidential must be strictly observed. Failure to do so amounts to a contempt of court.

J12.2 (a) Judgment is not delivered until it is formally pronounced in open court.

(b) Copies of the approved judgment will be made available to the parties, to law reporters and to any other person wanting a copy.

(c) The judge may direct that the written judgment stand as the definitive record and that no transcript need be made. Any editorial corrections made at the time of handing down will be incorporated in an approved official text as soon as possible, and the approved official text, so marked, will be available from the Mechanical Recording Department.

J13 Costs

J13.1 The rules governing the award and assessment of costs are contained in CPR, Parts 43 to 48.

J13.2 The summary assessment procedure provided for in Parts 43 and 44 also applies to trials lasting one day or less.

K AFTER TRIAL

K1 Continuation, Variation and Discharge of Interim Remedies and Undertakings

(a) Applications to continue, vary or discharge interim remedies or undertakings should be made to a commercial judge, even after trial.

(b) If a party wishes to continue a freezing injunction after trial or judgment, care should be taken to ensure that the application is made before the existing freezing injunction has expired.

K2 Accounts and Enquiries

The court may order that accounts and inquiries be referred to a judge of the Technology and Construction Court or to a master. Alternatively, the parties may choose to refer the matter to arbitration.

K3 Enforcement

K3.1 Unless the court orders otherwise, all proceedings for the enforcement of any judgment or order for the payment of money given or made in the Commercial Court will be referred automatically to a master of the Queen's Bench Division or a district judge (PD 58, para. 1.2(2)).

K3.2 Applications in connection with the enforcement of a judgment or order for the payment of money should accordingly be directed to the Registry which will allocate them to the Admiralty Registrar or to one of the Queen's Bench masters as appropriate.

K4 Assessment of Damages or Interest After a Default Judgment

Unless the court orders otherwise, the assessment of damages or interest following the entry of a default judgment for damages or interest to be assessed will be carried out by the Admiralty Registrar or one of the Queen's Bench masters to whom the case is allocated by the Registry.

L MULTI-PARTY DISPUTES

L1 Early Consideration

L1.1 Cases which involve, or are expected to involve, a large number of claimants or defendants require close case management from the earliest point. The same is true where there are, or are likely to be, a large number of separate cases involving the same or similar issues. Both classes of case are referred to as 'multi-party' disputes.

L1.2 (a) The judge in charge of the List should be informed as soon as it becomes apparent that a multi-party dispute exists or is likely to exist and an early application for directions should be made.

(b) In an appropriate case an application for directions may be made before issue of a claim form. In some cases it may be appropriate for an application to be made without notice in the first instance.

L2 Available Procedures

L2.1 In some cases it may be appropriate for the court to make a Group Litigation Order under CPR, Part 19. In other cases it may be more convenient for the court to exercise its general powers of management. These include powers:

(i) to dispense with statements of case;
(ii) to direct parties to serve outline statements of case;
(iii) to direct that cases be consolidated or managed and tried together;
(iv) to direct that certain cases or issues be determined before others and to stay other proceedings in the meantime;
(v) to advance or put back the usual time for pre-trial steps to be taken (for example the disclosure of documents by one or more parties or a payment into court).

L2.2 Attention is drawn to the provisions of Section III of Part 19, rr. 19.10 to 19.15 and PD 19B. Practitioners should note that the provisions of Section III of Part 19 give the court additional

Court Guides

powers to manage disputes involving multiple claimants or defendants. They should also note that a Group Litigation Order may not be made without the consent of the Lord Chief Justice (PD 19B, para. 3.3(1)).

L2.3 An application for a Group Litigation Order should be made in the first instance to the judge in charge of the List (PD 19B, para. 3.5).

M LITIGANTS IN PERSON

M1 The Litigant In Person

Litigants in person appear less often in the Commercial Court than in some other courts. Their position requires special consideration.

M2 Represented Parties

M2.1 Where a litigant in person is involved in a case the court will expect solicitors and counsel for other parties to do what they reasonably can to ensure that he has a fair opportunity to prepare and put his case.

M2.2 The duty of an advocate to ensure that the court is informed of all relevant decisions and legislative provisions of which he is aware (whether favourable to his case or not) and to bring any procedural irregularity to the attention of the court during the hearing is of particular importance in a case where a litigant in person is involved.

M2.3 Further, the court will expect solicitors and counsel appearing for other parties to ensure that the case memorandum, the list of issues and all necessary bundles are prepared and provided to the court in accordance with the Guide, even where the litigant in person is unwilling or unable to participate.

M2.4 If the claimant is a litigant in person the judge at the case management conference will normally direct which of the parties is to have responsibility for the preparation and upkeep of the case management bundle.

M2.5 At the case management conference the court may give directions relating to the costs of providing application bundles and trial bundles to the litigant in person.

M3 Companies Without Representation

Although CPR, r. 39.6, allows a company or other corporation with the permission of the court to be represented at trial by an employee, the complexity of most cases in the Commercial Court makes that unsuitable. Accordingly, permission is likely to be given only in unusual circumstances.

N ADMIRALTY

N1 General

N1.1 Proceedings in the Admiralty Court are dealt with in CPR, Part 61, and PD 61.

N1.2 The Admiralty and Commercial Courts Guide has been prepared in consultation with the Admiralty judge. It has been adopted to provide guidance about the conduct of proceedings in the Admiralty Court. The Guide must be followed in the Admiralty Court unless the content of Part 61, PD 61 or the terms of this section N require otherwise.

N1.3 One significant area of difference between practice in the Commercial Court and practice in the Admiralty Court is that many interlocutory applications are heard by the Admiralty Registrar who has all the powers of the Admiralty judge save as provided otherwise (CPR, r. 61.1(4)).

N2 The Admiralty Court Committee

The Admiralty Court Committee provides a specific forum for contact and consultation between the Admiralty Court and its users. Any correspondence should be addressed to the Deputy Admiralty Marshal, Royal Courts of Justice, Strand, London WC2A 2LL.

N3 Commencement of Proceedings, Service of Statements of Case and Associated Matters

Sections B and C of this guide apply to all Admiralty claims except:

(i) a claim *in rem*;
(ii) a collision claim; and
(iii) a limitation claim.

N4 Commencement and Early Stages of a Claim *In Rem*

N4.1 The early stages of an *in rem* claim differ from those of other claims. The procedure is governed generally by r. 61.3 and PD 61, paras 3.1 to 3.11.

N4.2 In addition, the following sections of the Guide apply to claims *in rem*: B3.3, B3.7 to B3.11, B6.4 to B6.6, C1.1 to C1.9, C1.11 and C2.1(ii) to C5.4.

N4.3 Subject to PD 61, para. 3.7, section C1.10 of the Guide also applies to claims *in rem*.

N4.4 After an acknowledgment of service has been filed a claim *in rem* follows the procedure applicable to a claim proceeding in the Commercial List, save that the claimant is allowed 75 days in which to serve his particulars of claim (PD 61, para. 3.10).

N5 The Early Stages of a Collision Claim

N5.1 Where a collision claim is commenced *in rem*, the general procedure applicable to claims *in rem* applies subject to CPR, r. 61.4, and PD 61, paras 4.1 to 4.5.

N5.2 Where a collision claim is not commenced *in rem* the general procedure applicable to claims proceeding in the Commercial List applies subject to CPR, r. 61.4, and PD 61, paras 4.1 to 4.5.

N5.3 Service of a claim form out of the jurisdiction in a collision claim (other than a claim *in rem*) is permitted in the circumstances identified in CPR, r. 61.4(7), only and the procedure set out in appendix 15 of the Guide should be adapted accordingly.

N5.4 One particular feature of a collision action is that the parties must prepare and file a collision statement of case. Prior to the coming into force of Part 61, a collision statement of case was known as a preliminary act and the law relating to preliminary acts continues to apply to collision statements of case (PD 61, para. 4.5).

N5.5 The provisions of appendix 4 apply to part 2 of a collision statement of case (but not to part 1).

N5.6 Every party is required, so far as it is able, to provide full and complete answers to the questions contained in part 1 of the collision statement of case. The answers should descend to a reasonable level of particularity.

N5.7 The answers to the questions contained in part 1 are treated as admissions made by the party answering the questions and leave to amend such answers will be granted only in exceptional circumstances.

N6 The Early Stages of a Limitation Claim

N6.1 The procedure governing the early stages of a limitation claim differs significantly from the procedure relating to other claims and is contained in CPR, r. 61.11, and PD 61, para. 10.1.

N6.2 Service of a limitation claim form out of the jurisdiction is permitted in the circumstances identified in CPR, r. 61.11(5) only and the procedure set out in appendix 15 of the Guide should be adapted accordingly.

N7 Issue of Documents When the Registry is Closed

N7.1 When the Registry is closed (and only when it is closed) an Admiralty claim form may be issued on the following designated fax machine: (020) 7947 6667 and only on that machine.

N7.2 The procedure to be followed is set out in appendix 3 of the Guide.

N7.3 The issue of an Admiralty claim form in accordance with the procedure set out in appendix 3 shall have the same effect for all purposes as a claim form issued in accordance with the relevant provisions of CPR, Part 61, and PD 61.

Court Guides

N7.4 When the Registry is closed (and only when it is closed) a notice requesting a caution against release may be filed on the following designated fax machine: (020) 7947 6056 and only on that machine. This machine is manned 24 hours a day by court security staff (telephone (020) 7947 6260).

N7.5 The notice requesting the caution should be transmitted with a note in the following form for ease of identification by security staff:

'CAUTION AGAINST RELEASE

Please find notice requesting caution against release of the . . . (*name ship/identify cargo*) . . . for filing in the Admiralty and Commercial Registry.'

N7.6 The notice must be in Admiralty form ADM11 and signed by a solicitor acting on behalf of the applicant.

N7.7 Subject to the provisions of sections N7.9 and N7.10 below, the filing of the notice takes place when the fax is recorded as having been received.

N7.8 When the Registry is next open to the public, the filing solicitor or his agent shall attend and deliver to the Registry the document which was transmitted by fax together with the transmission report. Upon satisfying himself that the document delivered fully accords with the document received by the Registry, the court officer shall stamp the document delivered with the time and date on which the notice was received, enter the same in the caution register and retain the same with the faxed copy.

N7.9 Unless otherwise ordered by the court, the stamped notice shall be conclusive proof that the notice was filed at the time and on the date stated.

N7.10 If the filing solicitor does not comply with the foregoing procedure, or if the notice is not stamped, the notice shall be deemed never to have been filed.

N8 Case Management

N8.1 The case management provisions of the Guide apply to Admiralty claims save that:

(i) In Admiralty claims the case management provisions of the Guide are supplemented by PD 61, paras 2.1 to 2.3 which make provision for the early classification and streaming of cases;

(ii) In a collision case the claimant should apply for a case management conference within seven days after the last collision statement of case is filed;

(iii) In a limitation claim where the right to limit is not admitted and the claimant seeks a general limitation decree, the claimant must, within seven days after the date of the filing of the defence of the defendant last served or the expiry of the time for doing so, apply to the Admiralty Registrar for a case management conference (PD 61, para. 10.7);

(iv) In a collision claim or a limitation claim a mandatory case management conference will normally take place on the first available date five weeks after the date when the claimant is required to take steps to fix a date for the case management conference;

(v) In a limitation claim, case management directions are initially given by the Registrar (PD 61, para. 10.8);

(vi) In the Admiralty Court, the case management information sheet should be in the form in appendix 6 of this Guide but should also include the following questions:

1. Do any of the issues contained in the list of issues involve questions of navigation or other particular matters of an essentially Admiralty nature which require the trial to be before the Admiralty judge?
2. Is the case suitable to be tried before a deputy judge nominated by the Admiralty judge?
3. Do you consider that the court should sit with nautical or other assessors? If you intend to ask that the court sit with one or more assessors who is not a Trinity master, please state the reasons for such an application.

N8.2 The two-judge team system referred to in section D. 4 of the Guide does not apply to Admiralty claims.

N9 Evidence

N9.1 In collision claims, section H1.5 and appendix 8 are subject to the proviso that experience has shown that it is usually desirable for the main elements of a witness's evidence-in-chief to be adduced orally.

Authenticity

N9.2 Where:

(i) the authenticity of any document or entry in any document is challenged;

(ii) it will be suggested at trial that a document or entry in a document was not made at the time or by the person stated; or

(iii) a document or entry in a document will be i n any other way challenged in a manner which may require a witness to be produced at trial to support the document or entry in a document;

such challenge:

(i) must be raised in good time in advance of the trial to enable any such witness to be produced; and

(ii) must be contained in the skeleton argument.

Skeleton arguments in collision claims

N9.3 In collision claims the skeleton argument of each party must be accompanied by a plot or plots of that party's case or alternative cases as to the navigation of vessels during and leading to the collision. All plots must contain a sufficient indication of the assumptions used in the preparation of the plot.

N10 Split Trials, Accounts, Enquiries and Enforcement

N10.1 In collision claims it is usual for liability to be tried first and for the assessment of damages and interest to be referred to the Admiralty Registrar.

N10.2 Where the Admiralty Court refers an account, enquiry or enforcement, it will usually refer the matter to the Admiralty Registrar.

N11 Release of Vessels Out of Hours

N11.1 This section makes provision for release from arrest when the Registry is closed.

N11.2 An application for release under CPR, r. 61.8(4)(c) or (d), may, when the Registry is closed, be made in, and only in, the following manner:

(i) The solicitor for the arrestor or the other party applying must telephone the security staff at the Royal Courts of Justice ((020) 7947 6260) and ask to be contacted by the Admiralty Marshal, who will then respond as soon as practicably possible.

(ii) Upon being contacted by the Admiralty Marshal the solicitor must give oral instructions for the release and an oral undertaking to pay the fees and expenses of the Admiralty Marshal as required in form ADM12.

(iii) The arrestor or other party applying must then send a written request and undertaking on form ADM12 by fax to a number given by the Admiralty Marshal.

(iv) The solicitor must provide written consent to the release from all persons who have entered cautions against release (and from the arrestor if the arrestor is not the party applying) by sending such consents by fax to the number supplied by the Admiralty Marshal.

(v) Upon the Admiralty Marshal being satisfied that no cautions against release are in force, or that all persons who have entered cautions against release, and if necessary the arrestor, have given their written consent to the release, the Admiralty Marshal shall effect the release as soon as practicable.

N11.3 Practitioners should note that the Admiralty Marshal is not formally on call and therefore at times may not be available to assist. Similarly the practicalities of releasing a ship in some localities may involve the services of others who may not be available outside court hours.

N11.4 This service is offered to practitioners for use during reasonable hours and on the basis that if the Admiralty Marshal is available and can be contacted he will use his best endeavours to effect instructions to release but without guarantee as to their success.

N12 Use of Postal Facilities in the Registry

N12.1 Applications together with the requisite documents may be posted to:
The Admiralty and Commercial Registry, Room E200,
Royal Courts of Justice,
Strand, London WC2A 2LL.

N12.2 In addition to the classes of business for which the use of postal facilities is permitted by the CPR or the Commercial Court Guide, the filing of the following classes of documents is also permitted in Admiralty matters:

(i) requests for cautions;

(ii) collision statements of case.

N12.3 (a) Documents sent by post for filing must be accompanied by two copies of a list of the documents sent and an envelope properly addressed to the sender.

(b) On receipt of the documents in the Registry, the court officer will, if the circumstances are such that had the documents been presented personally they would have been filed, cause them to be filed and will, by post, notify the sender that this has been done. If the documents would not have been accepted if presented personally the court officer will not file them but will retain them in the Registry for collection by the sender and will, by post, so inform the sender.

(c) When documents received through the post are filed by the court officer they will be sealed and entered as filed on the date on which they were received in the Registry.

N13 Insurance of Arrested Property

N13.1 The Marshal will not insure any arrested property for the benefit of parties at any time during the period of arrest (whether before or after the lodging of an application for sale, if any).

N13.2 The Marshal will use his best endeavours (but without any legal liability for failure to do so) to advise all parties known to him as being on the record in actions *in rem* against the arrested property, including those who have filed cautions against release of that property, before any such property moves or is moved beyond the area covered by the usual port risks policy.

N13.3 In these circumstances, practitioners' attention is drawn to the necessity of considering the questions of insuring against port risks for the amount of their clients' interest in any property arrested in an Admiralty action and the inclusion in any policy of a 'held covered' clause in case the ship moves or is moved outside the area covered by the usual port risks policy. The usual port risks policy provides, among other things, for a ship to be moved or towed from one berth to another up to a distance of five miles within the port where she is lying.

N14 Assessors

N14.1 In collision claims and other cases involving issues of navigation and seamanship, the Admiralty Court usually sits with assessors. The parties are not permitted to call expert evidence on such matters without the leave of the court (CPR, r. 61.13).

N14.2 Provision is made in r. 35.15 for assessors' remuneration. The usual practice is for the court to seek an undertaking from the claimant to pay the remuneration on demand after the case has concluded.

O ARBITRATION

O1 Arbitration Claims

(a) Applications to the court under the Arbitration Acts 1950 to 1996 and other applications relating to arbitrations are known as 'arbitration claims'.

(b) The procedure applicable to arbitration claims is to be found in CPR, Part 62, and PD 62. Separate provision is made:

(i) by Section I of CPR, Part 62, for claims relating to arbitrations to which the Arbitration Act 1996 applies;

(ii) by Section II for claims relating to arbitrations to which the Arbitration Acts 1950 to 1979 ('the old law') apply; and

(iii) by Section III for enforcement proceedings.

(c) For a full definition of the expression 'arbitration claim' see r. 62.2(1) (claims under the 1996 Act) and r. 62.11(2) (claims under the old law).

(d) Part 58 applies to arbitration claims in the Commercial Court in so far as no specific provision is made by Part 62 (r. 62.1(3)).

Claims Under the Arbitration Act 1996

O2 Starting an Arbitration Claim

O2.1 Subject to section O2.3 an arbitration claim must be started by the issue of an arbitration claim form in accordance with the Part 8 procedure (r. 62.3(1)).

O2.2 The claim form must be substantially in the form set out in appendix A to PD 62 (PD 62, para. 2.2).

O2.3 An application to stay proceedings under the Arbitration Act 1996, s. 9, must be made by application notice in the proceedings (CPR, r. 62.3(2)).

O3 The Arbitration Claim Form

O3.1 The arbitration claim form must contain, among other things, a concise statement of the remedy claimed and, if an award is challenged, the grounds for that challenge (r. 62.4(1)).

O3.2 Reference in the arbitration claim form to a witness statement or affidavit filed in support of the claim is not sufficient to comply with the requirements of r. 62.4(1).

O4 Service of the Arbitration Claim Form

O4.1 An arbitration claim form issued in the Admiralty and Commercial Registry must be served by the claimant.

O4.2 (a) The rules governing service of the claim form are set out in CPR, Part 6.
(b) Unless the court orders otherwise an arbitration claim form must be served on the defendant within one month from the date of issue (r. 62.4(2)).

O4.3 (a) An arbitration claim form may be served out of the jurisdiction with the permission of the court (r. 62.5(1)).
(b) Rules 6.24 to 6.29 apply to the service of an arbitration claim form out of the jurisdiction (r. 62.5(3)).

O4.4 The court may exercise its powers under r. 6.8 to permit service of an arbitration claim form on a party at the address of the solicitor or other representative acting for him in the arbitration (PD 62, para. 3.1).

O4.5 The claimant must file a certificate of service within seven days of serving the arbitration claim form (PD 62, para. 3.2).

O5 Acknowledgment of Service

O5.1 (a) A defendant must file an acknowledgment of service of the arbitration claim form in every case (CPR, r. 58.6(1)).
(b) [Form N210(CC) is an adapted version of form N210 (acknowledgment of service of a Part 8 claim form) which has been approved for use in the Commercial Court.]

O5.2 The time for filing an acknowledgment of service is calculated from the service of the arbitration claim form.

O6 Standard Directions

O6.1 The directions set out in PD 62, para. 6.2 to 6.7 apply unless the court orders otherwise.

O6.2 The claimant should apply for a hearing date as soon as possible after issuing an arbitration claim form or (in the case of an appeal) obtaining permission to appeal.

O6.3 A defendant who wishes to rely on evidence in opposition to the claim must file and serve his evidence within 21 days after the date by which he was required to acknowledge service (PD 62, para. 6.2).

O6.4 A claimant who wishes to rely on evidence in response to evidence served by the defendant must file and serve his evidence within seven days after the service of the defendant's evidence (PD 62, para. 6.3).

O6.5 An application for directions in a pending arbitration claim should be made by application notice under CPR, Part 23.

Court Guides

O7 Interim Remedies

An application for an interim remedy under the Arbitration Act 1996, s. 44, must be made in an arbitration claim form (PD 62, para. 8.1).

O8 Challenging the Award

Challenge by way of appeal

O8.1 A party wishing to appeal against the award of an arbitrator or umpire must set out in the arbitration claim form:
(i) the question of law on which the appeal is based; and
(ii) a succinct statement of the grounds of appeal, identifying the relevant part(s) of the award and reasons.

O8.2 If the appeal is brought with the agreement of the other parties to the proceedings, a copy of their agreement in writing must be filed with the arbitration claim form.

O8.3 A party seeking permission to appeal must:
(i) state in his arbitration claim form the grounds on which he contends that permission to appeal should be given (PD 62, para. 12.1); and
(ii) file and serve with the arbitration claim form any written evidence on which he wishes to rely for the purposes of satisfying the court of the matters referred to in s. 69(3) of the 1996 Act (PD 62, para. 12.2).

O8.4 (a) If the defendant wishes to oppose the claimant's application for permission to appeal he must file a witness statement setting out:
(i) the grounds on which he opposes the grant of permission; and
(ii) any evidence on which he relies in relation to the matters mentioned in s. 69(3) of the 1996 Act (PD 62, paras 12.3(1) and (2)).
(b) If the defendant wishes to contend that that the award should be upheld for reasons other than those expressed in the award, he must set out those reasons in his witness statement (PD 62, para. 12.3(3)).

O8.5 The court will normally determine applications for permission to appeal without an oral hearing. If the court considers that an oral hearing is required, it will give further directions as appropriate.

Challenging an award for serious irregularity

O8.6 (a) An arbitration claim challenging an award on the ground of serious irregularity under s. 68 of the 1996 Act is appropriate only in cases where there are grounds for thinking:
(i) that an irregularity has occurred which
(ii) has caused or will cause *substantial* injustice to the party making the challenge.
(b) An application challenging an award on the ground of serious irregularity should therefore not be regarded as an alternative to, or a means of supporting, an application for permission to appeal.

O8.7 The challenge to the award must be supported by evidence of the circumstances on which the claimant relies as giving rise to the irregularity complained of and the nature of the injustice which has been or will be caused to him.

O8.8 If the nature of the challenge itself or the evidence filed in support of it leads the court to consider that the claim has no real prospect of success, the court may exercise its powers under CPR, r. 3.3(4), to dismiss the application summarily. In such cases the applicant will have the right to apply to the court to set aside the order and to seek directions for the hearing of the application.

Multiple claims

O8.9 If the arbitration claim form includes both a challenge to an award by way of appeal and a challenge on the ground of serious irregularity, the applications should be set out in separate sections of the arbitration claim form and the grounds on which they are made separately identified.

O8.10 In such cases the papers will be placed before a judge to consider how the applications may most appropriately be disposed of. It is usually more appropriate to dispose of the application to set aside or remit the award before considering the application for permission to appeal.

O9 Time Limits

O9.1 An application to challenge an award under ss. 67 or 68 of the 1996 Act or to appeal under s. 69 of the Act must be brought within 28 days of the date of the award: see s. 70(3).

O9.2 The court has power to vary the period of 28 days fixed by s. 70(3) of the 1996 Act (CPR, r. 62.9(1)). However, it is important that any challenge to an award be pursued without delay and the court will require cogent reasons for extending time.

O9.3 An application to extend time made *before* the expiry of the period of 28 days must be made in a Part 23 application notice, but the application notice need not be served on any other party (r. 62.9(2) and PD 62, para. 11.1(1)).

O9.4 An application to extend time made *after* the expiry of the period of 28 days must be made in the arbitration claim form in which the applicant is seeking substantive relief (r. 62.9(3)(a)).

O9.5 An application to vary the period of 28 days will normally be determined without a hearing and prior to the consideration of the substantive application (PD 62, para. 10.2).

Claims Under the Arbitration Acts 1950–1979

O10 Starting an Arbitration Claim

O10.1 Subject to section O10.2 an arbitration claim must be started by the issue of an arbitration claim form in accordance with the Part 8 procedure (CPR, r. 62.13(1)).

O10.2 The claim form must be substantially in the form set out in appendix A to PD 62, para. 2.2.

O10.3 An application to stay proceedings on the grounds of an arbitration agreement must be made by application notice in the proceedings (CPR, r. 62.13(2)).

O11 The Arbitration Claim Form

O11.1 An arbitration claim form must state the grounds of the claim or appeal (CPR, r. 62.15(5)(a)).

O11.2 Reference in the arbitration claim form to the witness statement or affidavit filed in support of the claim is not sufficient to comply with the requirements of r. 62.15(5)(a).

O12 Service of the Arbitration Claim Form

O12.1 An arbitration claim form issued in the Admiralty and Commercial Registry must be served by the claimant.

O12.2 The rules governing service of the claim form are set out in CPR, Part 6.

O12.3 (a) An arbitration claim form may be served out of the jurisdiction with the permission of the court (r. 62.16(1)).

(b) Rules 6.24 to 6.29 apply to the service of an arbitration claim form out of the jurisdiction (r. 62.16(4)).

O12.4 Although not expressly covered by PD 62, the court may in an appropriate case exercise its powers under CPR, r. 6.8, to permit service of an arbitration claim form on a party at the address of the solicitor or other representative acting for him in the arbitration.

O12.5 The claimant must file a certificate of service within seven days of serving the claim form.

O13 Acknowledgment of Service

O13.1 (a) A defendant must file an acknowledgment of service in every case (r. 58.6(1)).

(b) [Form N210(CC) is an adapted version of practice form N210 (acknowledgment of service of a Part 8 claim form) which has been approved for use in the Commercial Court.]

O13.2 The time for filing an acknowledgment of service is calculated from the service of the arbitration claim form.

O14 Standard Directions

O14.1 Where the claim or appeal is based on written evidence, a copy of that evidence must be served with the arbitration claim form (CPR, r. 62.15(5)(b)).

Court Guides

O14.2 Where the claim or appeal is made with the consent of the arbitrator or umpire or other parties, a copy of every written consent must be served with the arbitration claim form (r. 62.15(5)(c)).

O14.3 An application for directions in a pending arbitration claim should be made by application notice under CPR, Part 23.

O15 Interim Remedies

O15.1 An application for an interim remedy under s. 12(6) of the 1950 Act must be made in accordance with CPR, Part 25.

O15.2 The application must be made by arbitration claim form.

O15.3 A claim under s. 12(4) of the 1950 Act for an order for the issue of a witness summons to compel the attendance of a witness before an arbitrator or umpire where the attendance of the witness is required within the district of a district registry may be started in that registry (CPR, r. 62.14).

O16 Challenging the Award

Challenge by way of appeal

O16.1 A party wishing to appeal against the award of an arbitrator or umpire must file and serve with the arbitration claim form a statement of the grounds for the appeal, specifying the relevant part(s) of the award and reasons (CPR, r. 62.15(6)).

O16.2 A party seeking permission to appeal must also file and serve with the arbitration claim form any written evidence in support of the contention that the question of law concerns a term of the contract or an event which is not 'one off' (r. 62.15(6)).

O16.3 Any written evidence in reply must be filed and served not less than two days before the hearing of the application for permission to appeal (r. 62.15(7)).

O16.4 A party who wishes to contend that the award should be upheld for reasons other than those set out in the award and reasons must file and serve on the claimant a notice specifying the grounds of his contention not less than two days before the hearing of the application for permission to appeal (r. 62.15(8)).

O16.5 Applications for permission to appeal will be heard orally, but will not normally be listed for longer than half an hour. Skeleton arguments should be lodged.

Claims to set aside or remit the award

O16.6 A claim to set aside or remit an award on the grounds of misconduct should not be regarded as an alternative to, or a means of supporting, an application for permission to appeal.

O16.7 The directions set out in PD 62, paras 6.2 to 6.7, should be followed unless the court orders otherwise.

Multiple claims

O16.8 If the arbitration claim form includes both an appeal and an application to set aside or remit the award, the applications should be set out in separate sections of the arbitration claim form and the grounds on which they are made separately identified.

O16.9 The court may direct that one application be heard before the other or may direct that they be heard together, as may be appropriate. It is usually more appropriate to dispose of the application to set aside or remit the award before considering the application for permission to appeal.

O17 Time Limits

(a) Time limits governing claims under the 1950 and 1979 Acts are set out in CPR, r. 62.15.

(b) Different time limits apply to different claims. *It is important to consult r. 62.15 to ensure that applications are made within the time prescribed.*

(c) The court has power under r. 3.1(2) to vary the time limits prescribed by r. 62.15, but will require cogent reasons for doing so.

Provisions Applicable to All Arbitrations

O18 Enforcement of Awards

O18.1 All applications for permission to enforce awards are governed by Section III of CPR, Part 62 (r. 62.17).

O18.2 An application for permission to enforce an award in the same manner as a judgment may be made without notice, but the court may direct that the arbitration claim form be served, in which case the application will continue as an arbitration claim in accordance with the procedure set out in Section I of Part 62 (r. 62.18(1) to (3)).

O18.3 An application for permission to enforce an award in the same manner as a judgment must be supported by written evidence in accordance with r. 62.18(6).

O18.4 (a) Two copies of the draft order must accompany the application.
(b) If the claimant wishes to enter judgment, the form of the judgment must correspond to the terms of the award.
(c) The defendant has the right to apply to the court to set aside an order made without notice giving permission to enforce the award and the order itself must state in terms:
(i) that the defendant may apply to set it aside within 14 days after service of the order or, if the order is to be served out of the jurisdiction, within such other period as the court may set; and
(ii) that it may not be enforced until after the end of that period or any application by the defendant to set it aside has been finally disposed of (r. 62.18(9) and (10)).

Matters of General Application

O19 Transfer of Arbitration Claims

O19.1 An arbitration claim which raises no significant point of arbitration law or practice will normally be transferred:
(i) if a rent-review arbitration, to the Chancery Division;
(ii) if a construction or engineering arbitration, to the Technology and Construction Court;
(iii) if an employment arbitration, to the Central London County Court Mercantile List.

O19.2 Salvage arbitrations will normally be transferred to the Admiralty Court.

O20 Appointment of a Commercial Judge as Sole Arbitrator or Umpire

O20.1 Section 93 of the Arbitration Act 1996 provides for the appointment of a commercial judge as sole arbitrator or umpire. The Act limits the circumstances in which a judge may accept such an appointment.

O20.2 Enquiries should be directed to the judge in charge of the Commercial List or the Clerk to the Commercial Court.

P MISCELLANEOUS

P1 Out-of-hours Emergency Arrangements

P1.1 (a) When the Listing Office is closed, solicitors or counsel's clerks should in an emergency contact the Clerk to the Queen's Bench judge in chambers by telephone through the security desk at the Royal Courts of Justice (PD 58, para. 2.2).
(b) The telephone number of the security desk is included in the list of addresses and contact details at the end of the Guide.

P1.2 When the Listing Office is closed an urgent hearing will initially be dealt with by the Queen's Bench judge in chambers who may dispose of the application himself or make orders allowing the matter to come before a commercial judge at the first available opportunity.

P2 Index of Unreported Decisions

P2.1 An index has been prepared on a subject-matter basis of unreported Commercial Court and Admiralty Court judgments from 1995 onwards. The index is updated regularly.

P2.2 The index is provided as a service to litigants and to the legal profession, and to assist the Commercial Court and the Admiralty Court to maintain reasonable consistency of approach in those areas of law and procedure most frequently before them.

P2.3 The index is available on disk to counsel and solicitors from the Listing Office, free of charge, in exchange for new unused 1.44 MB disks. Except in special circumstances no more than one disk will be issued to each set of chambers or firm of solicitors. Copies of the disk should not be made except for copies that are to be made available to members of the set of chambers or firm of solicitors to which it has been issued.

P2.4 The judgments referred to in the index are kept in the Registry. They may be consulted there.

P2.5 Copies of the judgments referred to in the index may be obtained from the Registry (or where there is difficulty, from the clerk to the judge) unless the judgment is in the form of a transcript, in which case copies should be obtained from the shorthand writers or other transcript agency.

[APPENDIX 1 CPR, PART 58, PD 58, CPR, PART 61, AND PD 61
APPENDIX 2 CPR, PART 62, AND PD 62

Appendices 1 and 2 are not printed here. They consist of CPR, Parts 58, 61 and 62, PD 58, PD 61 and PD 62, which are all printed in **appendix** 2 of *Blackstone's Civil Practice*.]

APPENDIX 3 PROCEDURE FOR ISSUE OF CLAIM FORM WHEN REGISTRY CLOSED

(See generally sections B3.11 and B4.4 of the Guide.)

Procedure

The procedure is as follows:

1. The claim form must be signed by a solicitor acting on behalf of the claimant, and must not require the permission of the court for its issue (unless such permission has already been given).
2. The solicitor causing the claim form to be issued ('the issuing solicitor') must
   (i) endorse on the claim form the endorsement shown below and sign that endorsement;
   (ii) send a copy of the claim form so endorsed to the Registry by fax for issue under this section; and
   (iii) when he has received a transmission report stating that the transmission of the claim form to the Registry was completed in full and the time and the date of the transmission, complete and sign the certificate shown below.
3. When the Registry is next open to the public after the issue of a claim form in accordance with this procedure the issuing solicitor or his agent shall attend and deliver to the Registry the document which was transmitted by fax (including the endorsement and the certificate), or if that document has been served, a true and certified copy of it, together with as many copies as the Registry shall require and the transmission report.
4. When the proper officer at the Registry has checked and is satisfied that the document delivered under para. 3 fully accords with the document received under para. 2, and that all proper fees for issue have been paid, he shall allocate a number to the case, and seal, mark as 'original' and date the claim form with the date on which it was issued (being, as indicated below, the date when the fax is recorded at the Registry as having been received).
5. As soon as practicable thereafter the issuing solicitor shall inform any person served with the unsealed claim form of the case number, and (on request) shall serve any such person with a copy of the claim form sealed and dated under para. 4 above (at such address in England and Wales as the person may request) and the person may, without paying a fee, inspect and take copies of the documents lodged at the Registry under paras 2 and 3 above.

Effect of issue following request by fax

The issue of a claim form in accordance with this procedure takes place when the fax is recorded at the Registry as having been received, and the claim form bearing the endorsement shall have the same effect for all purposes as a claim form issued under CPR, Part 7 or 8, as the case may be. Unless otherwise ordered the sealed version of the claim form retained by the Registry shall be conclusive proof that the claim form was issued at the time and on the date stated. If the procedure set out in this appendix is not complied with, the court may declare (on its own initiative or on application) that the claim form shall be treated as not having been issued.

Endorsement

A claim form issued pursuant to a request by fax must be endorsed as follows:

1. This claim form is issued under section B3.11/B4.4 of the Commercial Court Guide and may be served notwithstanding that it does not bear the seal of the Court.
2. A true copy of this claim form and endorsement has been transmitted to the Admiralty and Commercial Registry, Royal Courts of Justice, Strand, London WC2A 2LL, at the time and date certified below by the undersigned solicitor.
3. It is the duty of the undersigned solicitor or his agent to attend at the Registry when it is next open to the public for the claim form to be sealed.
4. Any person upon whom this unsealed claim form is served will be notified by the undersigned solicitor of the number of the case and may require the undersigned solicitor to serve a copy of the sealed claim form at an address in England and Wales and may inspect without charge the documents which have been lodged at the Registry by the undersigned solicitor.
5. I, the undersigned solicitor, undertake to the Court, to the defendants named in this claim form, and to any other person upon whom this claim form may be served:
   (i) that the statement in paragraph 2 above is correct;
   (ii) that the time and date given in the certificate at the foot of this endorsement are correct;
   (iii) that this claim form is a claim form which may be issued under section B3.11 (or B4.4, as the case may be) of the Commercial Court Guide;
   (iv) that I will comply in all respects with the requirements of section B3.11/B4.4 of the Commercial Court Guide;
   (v) that I will indemnify any person served with the claim form before it is sealed against any loss suffered as a result of the claim form being or becoming invalid in accordance with section B3.11/B4.4 of the Commercial Court Guide.

(*Signed*)
Solicitor for the claimant

[Note: the endorsement may be signed in the name of the firm of solicitors rather than an individual solicitor, or by solicitors' agents in their capacity as agents acting on behalf of their professional clients.]

Certificate

A solicitor who causes a claim form to be issued pursuant to a request sent by fax must sign a certificate in the following form:

> I, the undersigned solicitor, certify that I have received a transmission report confirming that the transmission of a copy of this claim form to the Registry by fax was fully completed and that the time and date of transmission to the Registry were [*enter the time and date shown on the transmission report*].
> Dated
> (*Signed*)
> Solicitor for the claimant.

[Note: the certificate may be signed in the name of the firm of solicitors rather than an individual solicitor, or by solicitors' agents in their capacity as agents acting on behalf of their professional clients.]

Court Guides

APPENDIX 4 STATEMENTS OF CASE

The following principles apply to all statements of case and should, as far as possible, also be observed when drafting a Part 8 claim form, which will not contain, or be followed by, particulars of claim:

1. The document must be as brief and concise as possible.
2. The document must be set out in separate consecutively numbered paragraphs and sub-paragraphs.
3. So far as possible each paragraph or sub-paragraph should contain no more than one allegation.

4. The document must deal with the case on a point-by-point basis to allow a point-by-point response.
5. Where particulars are given of any allegation or reasons given for a denial, the allegation or denial should be stated first and the particulars or reasons for it listed one by one in separate numbered sub-paragraphs.
6. A party wishing to advance a positive case should set that case out in the document; a simple denial is not sufficient.
7. Any matter which, if not stated, might take another party by surprise should be stated.
8. Where they will assist:
   (i) headings should be used; and
   (ii) abbreviations and definitions should be established and used, and a glossary annexed.
9. Contentious headings, abbreviations and definitions should not be used. Every effort should be made to ensure that headings, abbreviations and definitions are in a form that will enable them to be adopted without issue by the other parties.
10. Particulars of primary allegations should be stated as particulars and not as primary allegations.
11. If it is necessary to rely upon a substantial amount of detailed factual information or lengthy particulars in support of an allegation, these should be set out in schedules or appendices.
12. Particular care should be taken to set out only those factual allegations which are necessary to support the case. Evidence should not be included.
13. A response to particulars set out in a schedule should be set out in a corresponding schedule.
14. If it is necessary for the proper understanding of the statement of case to include substantial parts of a lengthy document the passages in question should be set out in a schedule rather than in the body of the case.
15. Contentious paraphrasing should be avoided.
16. The document must be signed by the individual person or persons who drafted it, not, in the case of a solicitor, in the name of the firm alone.

APPENDIX 5 SEARCH ORDER AND FREEZING INJUNCTION

[The forms of search order and freezing injunction appended to the Admiralty and Commercial Courts Guide are the same as those appended to PD 25, except that they are headed 'Queen's Bench Division, Commercial Court' and the section 'Communications with the court', is:

Communications with the court

All communications to the court about this order should be sent to Room E201, Royal Courts of Justice, Strand, London WC2A 2LL quoting the case number. The telephone number is (020) 7947 6826.

The offices are open between 10 a.m. and 4.30 p.m. Monday to Friday.]

APPENDIX 6 CASE MANAGEMENT INFORMATION SHEET

Party lodging information sheet:
Name of solicitors:
Name(s) of advocates for trial:
[Note: This sheet should normally be completed with the involvement of the advocate(s) instructed for trial. If the claimant is a litigant in person this fact should be noted at the foot of the sheet and proposals made as to which party is to have responsibility for the preparation and upkeep of the case management bundle.]

(1) By what date can you give standard disclosure?
(2) In relation to standard disclosure, do you contend in relation to any category or class of document under rule 31.6(b) that to search for that category or class would be unreasonable? If so, what is the category or class and on what grounds do you so contend?
(3) Is specific disclosure required on any issue? If so, please specify.
(4) By what dates can you (a) give specific disclosure or (b) comply with a special disclosure order?
(5) May the time periods for inspection at rule 31.15 require adjustment, and if so by how much?
(6) Are amendments to or is information about any statement of case required? If yes, please give brief details of what is required.

(7) Can you make any additional admissions? If yes, please give brief details of the additional admissions.

(8) Are any of the issues in the case suitable for trial as preliminary issues?

(9) (a) On the evidence of how many witnesses of fact do you intend to rely at trial (subject to the directions of the Court)? Please give their names, or explain why this is not being done.
(b) By what date can you serve signed witness statements?
(c) How many of these witnesses of fact do you intend to call to give oral evidence at trial (subject to the directions of the Court)? Please give their names, or explain why this is not being done.
(d) Will interpreters be required for any witness?
(e) Do you wish any witness to give oral evidence by video link? Please give his or her name, or explain why this is not being done. Please state the country and city from which the witness will be asked to give evidence by video link.

(10) (a) On what issues may expert evidence be required?
(b) Is this a case in which the use of a single joint expert might be suitable (see rule 35.7)?
(c) On the evidence of how many expert witnesses do you intend to rely at trial (subject to the directions of the Court)? Please give their names, or explain why this is not being done. Please identify each expert's field of expertise.
(d) By what date can you serve signed expert reports?
(e) When will the experts be available for a meeting or meetings of experts?
(f) How many of these expert witnesses do you intend to call to give oral evidence at trial (subject to the directions of the Court)? Please give their names, or explain why this is not being done.
(g) Will interpreters be required for any expert witness?
(h) Do you wish any expert witness to give oral evidence by video link? Please give his or her name, or explain why this is not being done. Please state the country and city from which the witness will be asked to give evidence by video link.

(11) What are the advocates' present provisional estimates of the minimum and maximum lengths of the trial?

(12) What is the earliest date by which you believe you can be ready for trial?

(13) Is this a case in which a pre-trial review is likely to be useful?

(14) Is there any way in which the Court can assist the parties to resolve their dispute or particular issues in it without the need for a trial or a full trial?

(15) (a) Might some form of Alternative Dispute Resolution procedure assist to resolve or narrow the dispute or particular issues in it?
(b) Has the question at (a) been considered between the client and legal representatives (including the advocate(s) retained)?
(c) Has the question at (a) been explored with the other parties in the case?
(d) Do you request that the case is adjourned while the parties try to settle the case by Alternative Dispute Resolution or other means?
(e) Would an ADR order in the form of appendix 7 to the Admiralty and Commercial Courts Guide be appropriate?
(f) Are any other special directions needed to allow for Alternative Dispute Resolution?

(16) What other applications will you wish to make at the Case Management Conference?

(17) Does provision need to be made in the pre-trial timetable for any application or procedural step not otherwise dealt with above? If yes, please specify the application or procedural step.

(18) Are there, or are there likely in due course to be, any related proceedings (e.g. a Part 20 claim)? Please give brief details.

[Signature of solicitors]

Note: This information sheet must be lodged with the Clerk to the Commercial Court at least 7 days before the Case Management Conference (with a copy to all other parties): see section D8.5 of the Admiralty and Commercial Courts Guide.

APPENDIX 7 DRAFT ADR ORDER

1. On or before [*] the parties shall exchange lists of 3 neutral individuals who are available to conduct ADR procedures in this case prior to [*]. Each party may [in addition] [in the

alternative] provide a list identifying the constitution of one or more panels of neutral individuals who are available to conduct ADR procedures in this case prior to [*].

2. On or before [*] the parties shall in good faith endeavour to agree a neutral individual or panel from the lists so exchanged and provided.
3. Failing such agreement by [*] the Case Management Conference will be restored to enable the Court to facilitate agreement on a neutral individual or panel.
4. The parties shall take such serious steps as they may be advised to resolve their disputes by ADR procedures before the neutral individual or panel so chosen by no later than [*].
5. If the case is not finally settled, the parties shall inform the Court by letter prior to [disclosure of documents/exchange of witness statements/exchange of experts' reports] what steps towards ADR have been taken and (without prejudice to matters of privilege) why such steps have failed. If the parties have failed to initiate ADR procedures the Case Management Conference is to be restored for further consideration of the case.
6. [Costs].

Note: The term 'ADR procedures' is deliberately used in the draft ADR order. This is in order to emphasise that (save where otherwise provided) the parties are free to use the ADR procedure that they regard as most suitable, be it mediation, early neutral evaluation, non-binding arbitration etc.

APPENDIX 8 STANDARD PRE-TRIAL TIMETABLE

1. [Standard disclosure is to be made by [*], with inspection [*] days after notice.]
2. Signed statements of witnesses of fact, and hearsay notices where required by rule 33.2, are to be exchanged not later than [*].
3. Unless otherwise ordered, witness statements are to stand as the evidence-in-chief of the witness at trial.
4. Signed reports of experts
   (i) are to be confined to one expert for each party from each of the following fields of expertise: [*];
   (ii) are to be confined to the following issues: [*];
   (iii) are to be exchanged [sequentially/simultaneously];
   (iv) are to be exchanged not later than [date or dates for each report in each field of expertise].
5. Meeting of experts
   (i) The meeting of experts is to be by [*];
   (ii) The joint memorandum of the experts is to be completed by [*];
   (iii) Any short supplemental expert reports are to be exchanged [sequentially/simultaneously] by not later than [date or dates for each supplemental report].
6. [If the experts' reports cannot be agreed, the parties are to be at liberty to call expert witnesses at the trial, limited to those experts whose reports have been exchanged pursuant to 4. above.]
   [Or: The parties are to be at liberty to apply to call as expert witnesses at the trial those experts whose reports they have exchanged pursuant to 4. above, such application to be made not earlier than [*] and not later than [*]]
7. Preparation of trial bundles to be completed in accordance with appendix 10 to the Admiralty and Commercial Courts Guide by not later than [*].
8. The provisional estimated length of the trial is [*].
9. Within [*] days the parties are to attend on the Clerk to the Commercial Court to fix the date for trial which shall be not before [*].
10. The progress monitoring date is [*]. Each party is to lodge a completed progress monitoring information sheet with the Clerk to the Commercial Court at least 3 days before the progress monitoring date (with a copy to all other parties).
11. Each party is to lodge a completed pre-trial checklist not later than 3 weeks before the date fixed for trial.
12. [There is to be a pre-trial review not earlier than [*] and not later than [*]].
13. Save as varied by this order or further order, the practice and procedures set out in the Admiralty and Commercial Courts Guide are to be followed.
14. Costs in the case.
15. Liberty to restore the Case Management Conference.

APPENDIX 9 SKELETON ARGUMENTS, CHRONOLOGIES AND INDICES

Part 1 Skeleton arguments

1. A skeleton argument is intended to identify both for the parties and the court those points which are, and are not, in issue and the nature of the argument in relation to those points that are in issue. It is not a substitute for oral argument.
2. Skeleton arguments must therefore:
   (a) identify concisely:
      (i) the nature of the case generally and the background facts in so far as they are relevant to the matter before the court;
      (ii) the propositions of law relied on with references to the relevant authorities;
      (iii) the submissions of fact to be made with references to the evidence;
   (b) be in numbered paragraphs and state the name of the advocate(s) who prepared them; and
   (c) should avoid arguing the case at length.

Part 2 Chronologies and indices

3. As far as possible chronologies and indices should not be prepared in a tendentious form. The ideal is that the court and the parties should have a single point of reference that all find useful and are happy to work with.
4. Where there is disagreement about a particular event or description, it is useful if that fact is indicated in neutral terms and the competing versions shortly stated.
5. If time and circumstances allow its preparation, a chronology or index to which all parties have contributed and agreed can be invaluable.
6. Chronologies and indices once prepared can be easily updated and are of continuing usefulness throughout the life of the case.

APPENDIX 10 PREPARATION OF BUNDLES

1. The preparation of bundles requires a high level of cooperation between legal representatives for all parties. It is the duty of all legal representatives to cooperate to this high level.
2. Bundles should be prepared as follows:
   (i) No more than one copy of any one document should be included, unless there is good reason for doing otherwise.
   (ii) Contemporaneous documents, and correspondence, should be included in chronological order.
   (iii) Where a contract or similar document is central to the case it may be included in a separate place provided that a page is inserted in the chronological run of documents to indicate:
      (A) the place the contract or similar document would have appeared had it appeared chronologically; and
      (B) where it may be found instead.
   (iv) Documents in manuscript, or not fully legible, should be transcribed; the transcription should be marked and placed adjacent to the document transcribed.
   (v) Documents in a foreign language should be translated; the translation should be marked and placed adjacent to the document transcribed; the translation should be agreed, or, if it cannot be agreed, each party's proposed translation should be included.
   (vi) If a document has to be read across rather than down the page, it should be so placed in the bundle as to ensure that the top of the text is nearest the spine.
   (vii) No bundle should contain more than 300 pages.
   (viii) Bundles should not be overfilled, and should allow sufficient room for later insertions. Subject to this, the size of file used should not be a size that is larger than necessary for the present and anticipated contents.
   (ix) Bundles should be paginated, in the bottom right-hand corner and in a form that can clearly be distinguished from any existing pagination on the document.
   (x) Bundles should be indexed, save that a chronological bundle of contemporaneous documents need not be indexed if an index is unlikely to be useful.

Court Guides

(xi) Bundles should be numbered and named on the outside and on the inside front cover, the label to include the short title of the case, and a description of the bundle (including its number, where relevant).

3. Documents within bundles should be marked as follows:
   (i) When copy documents from exhibits have been included in the bundle(s), then unless clearly unnecessary, the copy of the affidavit or witness statement to which the documents were exhibited should be marked in the right-hand margin (in manuscript if need be) to show where the document referred to may be found in the bundle(s).
   (ii) Unless clearly unnecessary, where copy documents in a bundle are taken from the disclosure of more than one party the documents should be marked in the top right-hand corner (in manuscript if need be) to show from which party's disclosure the copy document has been taken.
   (iii) Where there is a reference in a statement of case or witness statement to a document which is contained in the trial bundles a note should be made in the margin (if necessary in manuscript) identifying the place where that document is to be found. Unless otherwise agreed this is the responsibility of the party tendering the statement of case or witness statement.
4. For the trial a handy-sized core bundle should normally be provided containing the really important documents in the case. The documents in this bundle should be paginated, but each page should also bear its bundle and page number reference in the main bundles. It is particularly important to allow sufficient room for later insertions (see para. 2(viii) above).
5. Large documents, such as plans, should be placed in an easily accessible file.
6. (a) When agreeing bundles for trial, the parties should also establish through their legal representatives, and record in correspondence, whether the agreement of bundles:
   (i) extends no further than agreement of the composition and preparation of the bundles; or
   (ii) includes agreement that the documents in the bundles are authentic (see further CPR, r. 32.19); or
   (iii) includes agreement that the documents may be treated as evidence of the facts stated in them.

   (b) The court will normally expect parties to agree that the documents or at any rate the great majority of them may be treated as evidence of the facts stated in them. A party not willing so to agree should, when the trial bundles are lodged, write a letter to the court (with a copy to all other parties) stating that it is not willing so to agree, and explaining why that is so.

APPENDIX 11 EXPERT EVIDENCE — REQUIREMENTS OF GENERAL APPLICATION

1. It is the duty of an expert to help the court on the matters within his expertise (CPR, r. 35.3(1)). This duty is paramount and overrides any obligation to the person from whom the expert has received instructions or by whom he is paid (r. 35.3(2)).
2. Expert evidence presented to the court should be, and should be seen to be, the independent product of the expert uninfluenced by the pressures of litigation.
3. An expert witness should provide independent assistance to the court by way of objective unbiased opinion in relation to matters within his expertise. An expert witness should never assume the role of an advocate.
4. An expert witness should not omit to consider material facts which could detract from his concluded opinion.
5. An expert witness should make it clear when a particular question or issue falls outside his expertise.
6. If an expert's opinion is not properly researched because he considers that insufficient data are available, this must be stated in his report with an indication that the opinion is no more than a provisional one.
7. In a case where an expert witness who has prepared a report is unable to confirm that the report contains the truth, the whole truth and nothing but the truth without some qualification, that qualification must be stated in the report.

8. If, after exchange of reports, an expert witness changes his view on a material matter having read another expert's report or for any other reason, such change of view should be communicated in writing (through the party's legal representatives) to the other side without delay, and when appropriate to the court.

APPENDIX 12 PROGRESS MONITORING INFORMATION SHEET

[Short Title of Case and Folio Number]

Fixed trial date/provisional range of dates for trial specified in the pre-trial timetable: Party lodging information sheet:

Name of solicitors:

Name(s) of advocates for trial:

[Note: this information sheet should normally be completed with the involvement of the advocate(s) instructed for trial]

(1) Have you complied with the pre-trial timetable in all respects?

(2) If you have not complied, in what respects have you not complied?

(3) Will you be ready for a trial commencing on the fixed date (or, where applicable, within the provisional range of dates) specified in the pre-trial timetable?

(4) If you will not be ready, why will you not be ready?

[*Signature of solicitors*]

Note: This information sheet must be lodged with the Case Management Unit at least 3 days before the progress monitoring date (with a copy to all other parties): see section D12.2 of the Guide.

APPENDIX 13 PRE-TRIAL CHECKLIST

[Short Title of Case and Folio Number]

a. Trial date:
b. Party lodging checklist:
c. Name of solicitors:
d. Name(s) of advocates for trial:

[Note: this checklist should normally be completed with the involvement of the advocate(s) instructed for trial]

1. Have you completed preparation of trial bundles in accordance with appendix 10 to the Admiralty and Commercial Courts Guide?
2. If not, when will the preparation of the trial bundles be completed?
3. Which witnesses of fact do you intend to call?
4. Which expert witness(es) do you intend to call (if directions for expert evidence have been given)?
5. Will an interpreter be required for any witness and if so, have any necessary directions already been given?
6. Have directions been given for any witness to give evidence by video link? If so, have all necessary arrangements been made?
7. What are the advocates' confirmed estimates of the minimum and maximum lengths of the trial? (A confirmed estimate of length signed by the advocates should be attached.)
8. What is your estimate of costs already incurred and to be incurred at trial for the purposes of section 46 of PD 43–48? (If the trial is not expected to last more than *one day* the estimate should be substantially in the form of a statement of costs as illustrated in Form H of the Schedule of Costs Precedents annexed to PD 43–48.)

[Signature of solicitors]

APPENDIX 14 VIDEOCONFERENCING GUIDANCE

[Appendix 14 is not reproduced here because it consists of annex 3 to PD 32, which is in **appendix 2** of *Blackstone's Civil Practice*.]

APPENDIX 15 SERVICE OUT OF THE JURISDICTION: RELATED PRACTICE

Service out of the jurisdiction without permission

1. Before issuing a claim form or seeking permission to serve out of the jurisdiction, it is necessary to consider whether the jurisdiction of the English courts is affected by the Civil Jurisdiction and Judgments Act 1982. Where each claim in the claim form is a claim which the court has by virtue of the Civil Jurisdiction and Judgments Act 1982 power to hear and determine, service of the claim form out of the jurisdiction may be effected without permission provided that the requirements of CPR, r. 6.19, are satisfied and the claim form is endorsed before issue with a statement that the court has power under the Act to hear and determine the claim against the defendant, and that no proceedings involving the same claim are pending between the parties in Scotland, Northern Ireland or another convention country. Care must be taken to see that the endorsement is not made unless the statement is accurate.

Application for permission: affidavit or witness statement

2. (a) On applications for permission under r. 6.20 the written evidence must, amongst other things:
   - (i) identify the paragraph or paragraphs of r. 6.20 relied on as giving the court jurisdiction to order service out, together with a summary of the facts relied on as bringing the case within each such paragraph;
   - (ii) state the belief of the deponent that there is a good claim and state in what place or country the defendant is or probably may be found;
   - (iii) summarise the considerations relied upon as showing that the case is a proper one in which to subject a party outside the jurisdiction to proceedings within it;
   - (iv) draw attention to any features which might reasonably be thought to weigh against the making of the order sought;
   - (v) state the deponent's grounds of belief and sources of information;
   - (vi) exhibit copies of the documents referred to and any other significant documents.

   (b) Where convenient the written evidence should be included in the form of application notice, rather than in a separate witness statement. The form of application notice may be extended for this purpose.

Application for permission: copies of draft order

3. The documents submitted with the application must include two copies of a draft of the order sought which must state the time allowed for acknowledgment of service in accordance with any applicable practice direction and paras 6 and 7 below.

Application for permission: copy or draft of claim form

4. A copy or draft of the claim form which the applicant intends to issue and serve must be provided for the judge to initial. If the endorsement to the claim form includes causes of action or claims not covered by the grounds on which permission to serve out of the jurisdiction can properly be granted, permission will be refused unless the draft is amended to restrict it to proper claims. Where the application is for the issue of a concurrent claim form, the documents submitted must also include a copy of the original claim form.

Arbitration matters

5. Service out of the jurisdiction in arbitration matters is governed by CPR, Part 62. As to the 1968 Convention on Jurisdiction in the context of arbitration, see art. 1(4).

Practice under rules 6.19 *and* 6.20

6. (a) Although a Part 7 claim form may contain or be accompanied by particulars of claim, there is no need for it to do so and in many cases particulars of claim will be served after the claim form (r. 58.5).

   (b) A defendant should acknowledge service in every case (r. 58.6(1)).

   (c) The period for filing acknowledgment of service will be calculated from the service of the claim form, whether or not particulars of claim are to follow (r. 58.6).

   (d) The period for serving, and filing, particulars of claim (where they were not contained in the claim form and did not accompany the claim form) will be calculated from acknowledgment of service (r. 58.5(1)(c)).

(e) The period for serving and filing the defence will be calculated from service of the particulars of claim (r. 58.10(2)).

7. Time for serving and filing a defence is calculated as follows:
   (i) where particulars of claim were included in or accompanied the claim form the period for serving and filing a defence is 21 or 31 days as prescribed by r. 6.23, or the number of days shown in the table in PD 6B, in either case plus an additional 14 days;
   (ii) where particulars of claim were not included in and did not accompany the claim form, the period for serving and filing a defence is 28 days from the service of the particulars of claim.

APPENDIX 16 SECURITY FOR COSTS: RELATED PRACTICE

First applications

1. First applications for security for costs should not be made later than at the case management conference and in any event any application should not be left until close to the trial date. Delay to the prejudice of the other party or the administration of justice will probably cause the application to fail, as will any use of the application to harass the other party. Where it is intended to make an application for security at the case management conference the procedure, and timetable for evidence, for an ordinary application must be followed (see section F5 of the Guide).

Successive applications

2. Successive applications for security can be granted where the circumstances warrant. If a claimant wishes to seek to preclude any further application it is incumbent on him to make that clear.

Evidence

3. An affidavit or witness statement in support of an application for security for costs should deal not only with the residence of the claimant (or other respondent to the application) and the location of his assets but also with the practical difficulties (if any) of enforcing an order for costs against him.

Investigation of the merits of the case

4. Investigation of the merits of the case on an application for security is strongly discouraged. Only in those cases where it can be shown without detailed investigation of evidence or law that the claim is certain or almost certain to succeed or fail will the merits be taken into consideration.

Undertaking by the applicant

5. In appropriate cases an order for security for costs may only be made on terms that the applicant gives an undertaking to comply with any order that the court may make if the court later finds that the order for security for costs has caused loss to the claimant and that the claimant should be compensated for such loss. Such undertakings are intended to compensate claimants in cases where no order for costs is ultimately made in favour of the applicant.

Stay of proceedings

6. It is not usually convenient or appropriate to order an automatic stay of the proceedings pending the provision of the security. It leads to delay and may disrupt the preparation of the case for trial, or other hearing. Experience has shown that it is usually better to give the claimant (or other relevant party) a reasonable time within which to provide the security and the other party liberty to apply to the court in the event of default. This enables the court to put the claimant to his election and then, if appropriate, to dismiss the case.

Amount of security

7. Where the dispute on an application for security for costs relates to the correct evaluation of the amount of costs likely to be allowed to a successful defendant on an assessment of costs, parties should consider whether it would be advantageous for the judge hearing the application to sit with a costs judge as an informal assessor. The judge himself may take such an initiative.

ADDRESSES AND CONTACT DETAILS

THE ADMIRALTY MARSHAL
Room E203
Royal Courts of Justice
Strand
London WC2A 2LL
Tel: (020) 7947 6111
Fax: (020) 7947 7671

THE ADMIRALTY AND COMMERCIAL REGISTRY
Room E200
Royal Courts of Justice
Strand
London WC2A 2LL
Tel: (020) 7947 6112
Fax: (020) 7947 6245
DX 44450 STRAND

THE ADMIRALTY AND COMMERCIAL COURT LISTING OFFICE
Room E201
Royal Courts of Justice
Strand
London WC2A 2LL
Tel: (020) 7947 6826
Fax: (020) 7947 7670
DX 44450 STRAND

THE ADMIRALTY AND COMMERCIAL CASE MANAGEMENT UNIT
Room E206
Royal Courts of Justice
Strand
London WC2A 2LL
Tel: (020) 7947 6256
Fax: (020) 7947 7672

THE SECRETARY TO THE COMMERCIAL COURT COMMITTEE
Mrs Angela Hodgson
Room E201
Royal Courts of Justice
Strand
London WC2A 2LL
Tel: (020) 7947 6826
Fax: (020) 7947 7670
DX 44450 STRAND

OUT-OF-HOURS EMERGENCY NUMBER
(Security Office at Royal Courts of Justice)
(020) 7947 6000

Fax number for the procedure under sections B3.11 and B4.4 of the Guide for the issue of claim forms when the Registry is closed: (020) 7947 6667.

Chancery Guide

October 2005 updated 16 January 2006

Abbreviations used in this Guide

Civil Procedure Rules	CPR
HM Courts Service	HMCS
Practice Direction supplementing a Civil Procedure Rule	PD
Rules of the Supreme Court 1965	RSC
Pre-trial review	PTR

As from October 2005, the effective head of the Chancery Division is the Chancellor of the High Court, formerly the Vice-Chancellor.

PREFACE

This is the fifth edition of the Chancery Guide. It is published 10 years after the publication of the first. The changes made in the conduct of civil proceedings generally and in the Chancery Division in particular in the intervening period have been profound. The substitution of the old Rules of the Supreme Court with the Civil Procedure Rules is now virtually complete and amendments to the first editions of the Civil Procedure Rules are coming through.

As I wrote in the Preface to the fourth edition, the Chancery Guide is no substitute for the Civil Procedure Rules and associated practice directions. It seeks to give practical guidance on the conduct of cases in the Chancery Division within the framework of those rules and practice directions.

This edition has been produced under the supervision of Sir Lawrence Collins. I am very grateful to him for undertaking the task. The amount of work involved is considerable. It is additional to the normal workload of a judge of the Chancery Division and, in his case, to the editorial responsibility for *Dicey and Morris on the Conflict of Laws.* He has been assisted with regard to various topics by many others to whom I send my thanks too. It is always dangerous to mention them by name lest

Court Guides

someone is inadvertently omitted; nevertheless I would like to pay particular tribute to: Chief Master Winegarten; Master Bragge; Registrar Derrett; Mrs V. C. Bell; Mr A. D. Parkinson; Miss R. Warner; Mr J. Smethurst; Mr S. Adamyk.

The pattern of the last 10 years has been for a new edition to appear every two to three years. The proposals for changes to civil litigation now under consideration suggest that this pattern, at least, will continue in the future. In the meantime I hope and believe that this edition will be of considerable use to all those who, in whatever capacity, have occasion to participate in litigation in the Chancery Division.

Andrew Morritt
Chancellor of the High Court
October 2005

Chapter 1 Introductory

The overriding objective

1.1 The aim of the Civil Procedure Rules and the practice directions which supplement them is to remove excessive delay and expense, and to improve access to justice through quicker, cheaper and more proportionate justice. As an integral part of the reforms, cases are more closely monitored through to trial by the judiciary.

1.2 To achieve these aims, all procedural decisions under the CPR are guided by the overriding objective stated in r. 1.1. The court must deal with cases justly; dealing justly with a case includes, so far as practicable, ensuring that the parties are on an equal footing, saving expense, dealing with the case in ways which are proportionate to the sum at stake, to the importance of the case, to its complexity and to each party's financial position, ensuring expedition and fairness and allotting to each case an appropriate share of the court's resources.

About the Chancery Division

1.3 The Chancery Division is one of the three parts, or Divisions, of the High Court of Justice, the other two being the Queen's Bench Division and the Family Division. The effective head of the Chancery Division is the Chancellor of the High Court ('the Chancellor'). There are currently 17 High Court judges attached to the Division. In addition, in the Royal Courts of Justice in London, there are six judges who are referred to as masters (one of whom is the Chief Master), and six judges who are referred to as bankruptcy registrars (one of whom is the Chief Registrar). In the district registries (see ch. 12) the work done by masters in London is performed by district judges. References in this Guide to a master include, in the case of proceedings in a district registry, references to a district judge. Deputies sit on a regular basis for both judges and masters. Any reference to a judge or master in the Guide includes a reference to a person sitting as a deputy.

1.4 In general, trials of claims are heard by the judges, as are interim applications involving injunctions (including applications for freezing and search orders), while the majority of other work, including most procedural work and most post-trial work (e.g. accounts and inquiries) is conducted by the masters. Masters may, however, direct that a matter be listed before a judge although they have jurisdiction, for example in the case of lengthy inquiries as to damages (see paras 3.2 and 9.20 below).

1.5 The Chancery Division undertakes civil work of many kinds, including specialist work such as companies, patents and contentious probate. The range of cases heard in the Chancery Division is wide and varied. The major part of the caseload today involves business disputes of one kind or another. Often these are complex and involve substantial sums of money.

1.6 In many types of case (e.g. claims for professional negligence against solicitors, accountants, valuers or other professionals) the claimant has a choice whether to bring the claim in the Chancery Division or elsewhere in the High Court. But there are other types of case which, in the High Court, must be brought in the Chancery Division including claims (other than claims in the Commercial Court) relating to the application of arts 81 and 82 of the EC Treaty and the equivalent provisions in the Competition Act 1998. The specialist work of the Chancery Division is dealt with in Section B of this Guide. There are also certain claims which must be started in the Chancery Division either in the High Court or in a district registry where there is a Chancery district registry or in the Central London Trial Centre (Chancery List).

About this Guide

1.7 The aim of this Guide is to provide additional practical information not already contained in the CPR or the practice directions supplementing them. Litigants and their advisers are expected to be familiar with the CPR. It is not the function of this Guide to summarise the CPR, nor should it be regarded as a substitute for them.

1.8 This Guide is published as part of a series of Guides to various civil courts. Where information is more readily available in another Guide, this Guide may simply refer to it. A separate book* contains practice forms for use in the Chancery Division and in the Queen's Bench Division. Some of the forms most commonly used in the Chancery Division are found in the appendices to this Guide. Forms may also be downloaded from the HMCS website and [are on the CD-ROM version of *Blackstone's Civil Practice*].

1.9 Section A of this Guide is concerned with general civil work. Section B deals with specialist work. Some subjects are covered in more detail in the appendices, and appendix 1 sets out some contact details which may be useful.

1.10 Material which used to be contained in the Chancery Division Practice Directions and which remains relevant has been incorporated into either Section A or Section B of this Guide, as appropriate.

1.11 A reference in this Guide to a Part is to that Part of the CPR, and to a rule is to the relevant rule in the CPR, unless otherwise stated.

1.12 This Guide states the position as at September 2005. During the currency of the Guide, and even in some cases before publication, there are likely to be changes in matters covered in the text, including room numbers and other contact details; these should be checked as necessary. The Guide will be kept under review in the light of practical experience and of changes to the rules and practice directions. Any comments on the text of the Guide are welcome and should be addressed to the Clerk to the Chancellor.

1.13 The text of the Guide is also to be found, together with other court guides and other useful information concerning the administration of justice in the Chancery Division and elsewhere, on the HMCS website. Amendments will appear on the Guide on the website as appropriate: www.hmcourts-service.gov.uk.

SECTION A GENERAL CIVIL WORK

Chapter 2 Starting Proceedings, Service, Allocation and Statements of Case

Key rules: CPR, Parts 6, 7, 8, 9, 10, 15, 16, 18, 20 and 26 and CPR, sch. 1

How to start a claim

2.1 Claims are issued out of the High Court of Justice, Chancery Division, either in the Royal Courts of Justice (Chancery Chambers) or in a district registry. There is no production centre for Chancery claims.

2.2 The claim form must be issued either as a Part 7 claim under CPR, Part 7, or as a Part 8 claim under the alternative procedure for claims in Part 8.

2.3 When issuing proceedings, the general rule is that the title of the claim should contain only the names of the parties to the proceedings. To this there are four exceptions: (a) proceedings relating to the administration of an estate, which should be entitled 'In the estate of AB deceased' (some cases relating to the estates of deceased Lloyd's names require additional wording: see para. 26.53 below); (b) contentious probate proceedings, which should be entitled 'In the estate of AB deceased (probate)'; (c) proceedings under the Inheritance (Provision for Family and Dependants) Act 1975, which should be entitled 'In the Matter of the Inheritance (Provision for Family and Dependants) Act 1975'; and (d) proceedings relating to pension schemes, which may be entitled 'In the Matter of the [ ] Pension Scheme'. In addition, proceedings in the Companies Court are entitled in the matter of the relevant company or other person and of the relevant legislation: see para. 20.5.

Service

2.4 Part 6 of the CPR applies to the service of documents, including claim forms. Unless the claimant notifies the court that he or she wishes to serve the claim form, it will be served by

* [*Practice Forms for Use in Proceedings in the High Court* (London: Royal Courts of Justice, 2000).]

Court Guides

the court. Many solicitors, however, will prefer to serve the claim form themselves and will notify the court that they wish to do so.

Allocation

2.5 The vast majority of claims issued, and all those retained, in the Chancery Division will be either expressly allocated to the multi-track or in the case of Part 8 claims, deemed allocated to that track. Chapter 13 deals with transfer to county courts.

Statements of case

2.6 In addition to the matters which PD 16 requires to be set out specifically in the particulars of claim, a party must set out in any statement of case:
(1) full particulars of any allegation of fraud, dishonesty, malice or illegality;
(2) where any inference of fraud or dishonesty is alleged, the facts on the basis of which the inference is alleged.

2.7 A party should not set out allegations of fraud or dishonesty unless there is material admissible in evidence to support the contentions made. Setting out such matters without such material being available may result in the particular allegations being struck out and may result in wasted costs orders being made against the legal advisers responsible.

2.8 Points of law may be set out in any statement of case, and any point to be taken under the Human Rights Act 1998 must be so set out.

2.9 In the preparation of statements of case, the guidelines in appendix 2 should be followed.

2.10 The guidelines apply to: the claim form (unless no particulars are given in it); particulars of claim; defence; Part 20 claim; reply to a defence; and a response to a request for further information under CPR, Part 18.

2.11 Parties should not attach copies of documents or any expert's report to their statement of case if they are bulky.

2.12 Notwithstanding r. 15.8, claimants should if possible serve any reply before they file their allocation questionnaire. This will enable other parties to consider the reply before they file their allocation questionnaire.

Part 8 claims

2.13 This procedure is appropriate in particular where there is no substantial dispute of fact, such as where the case raises only questions of the construction of a document or a statute. Additionally, however, a large number of particular claims are also brought under Part 8 pursuant to PD 8B. Of particular relevance will be applications to enforce charging orders by sale, contested applications with respect to funds in court, contentious probate claims and proceedings relating to solicitors. Subject to jurisdiction, applications to enforce charging orders are now issued in the court in which the charging order was made. Proceedings to enforce charging orders made in any Division of the High Court and the Court of Appeal are issued in the Chancery Division.

2.14 Provision is also made in CPR, Part 8, for a claim form to be issued without naming a defendant with the permission of the court. No separate application for permission is required where personal representatives seek permission to distribute the estate of a deceased Lloyd's name nor for applications under the Administration of Justice Act 1985, s. 48 (see further ch. 26 — Trusts). Where permission is needed, it is to be sought by application notice under CPR, Part 23.

2.15 Part 8 claims will generally be disposed of on written evidence. The features of the Part 8 procedure are:
(1) no particulars of claim;
(2) no defence;
(3) no allocation questionnaire;
(4) no judgment in default;
(5) normally no oral evidence.

2.16 Defendants who wish to contest a Part 8 claim or to take part in the proceedings should complete and file the acknowledgment of service in form N210 which accompanies the claim form. Alternatively the information required to be contained in the acknowledgment of service can be provided by letter. A party who does not wish to contest a claim should indicate that fact on the form acknowledging service or by letter.

2.17 Claimants must file the written evidence, namely evidence by witness statement, on which they intend to rely with the claim form. Defendants are required to file and serve their evidence when they file their acknowledgment of service, namely within 14 days after service of the claim form (r. 8.5(3)). By PD 8, para. 5.6, a defendant's time for filing evidence may be extended by agreement for not more than 14 days from the filing of the acknowledgment of service. Any such agreement must be filed with the court by the defendant at the same time as he or she files an acknowledgment of service. The claimant has 14 days for filing evidence in reply but this period may be extended by agreement for not more than 28 days from service of the defendant's evidence. Again, any such agreement must be filed with the court. Any longer extension either for the defendant or the claimant requires an application to the court. It is recognised that in substantial matters the provisions in CPR, Part 8, may be burdensome upon defendants and in such matters the court will readily grant an extension. If the parties are in agreement that such an extension should be granted the application should be made in writing by letter. The parties should at all times act cooperatively.

2.18 Defendants who acknowledge service but do not intend to file evidence should notify the court in writing when they file their acknowledgment of service that they do not intend to file evidence. This enables the court to know what each defendant's intention is when it considers the file.

2.19 The general rule (exceptions include, for example, some claims under the Variation of Trusts Act 1958 or where a party has made a Part 24 application) is that the court file will be considered by the court after the time for acknowledgment of service has expired, or, if the time for serving the defendant's evidence has been extended, after the expiry of that period.

2.20 In some cases if the papers are in order the court will not require any oral hearing, but will be able to deal with the matter on paper by making a final order. In other cases the court will direct that the Part 8 claim is listed either for a disposal hearing or for a case management conference.

Chapter 3 The Court's Case Management Powers

Key rules: CPR, r. 1.4, and Parts 3, 18, 26, 29, 31, 39

3.1 A key feature of the CPR is that cases are closely monitored by the court. Case management by the court includes: identifying disputed issues at an early stage; fixing timetables; dealing with as many aspects of the case as possible on the same occasion; controlling costs; disposing of cases summarily where they disclose no case or defence; dealing with the case without the parties having to attend court; and giving directions to ensure that the trial of a case proceeds quickly and efficiently. The court will expect the parties to cooperate with each other. Where appropriate the court will encourage the parties to use alternative dispute resolution (on which see ch. 17) or otherwise help them settle the case. In particular, the court will readily grant a short stay at allocation or at any other stage to accommodate mediation or any other form of settlement negotiations. The court will not, however, normally, grant an open-ended stay for such purposes and if, for any reason, a lengthy stay is granted it will be on terms that the parties report to the court on a regular basis in respect of their negotiations.

3.2 In the Chancery Division case management is normally carried out by the masters, but a judge may be nominated by the Chancellor to hear the case and to deal with the case management where it is appropriate due to the size or complexity of the case or for other reasons. A request by any or all parties for such a nomination should be addressed to the Chancellor.

Directions

3.3 It is expected that parties and their advisers will endeavour to agree proposals for management of the case at the allocation stage in accordance with CPR, r. 29.4, and PD 29, paras 4.6 to 4.8. In particular, the parties should act cooperatively and seek to agree directions and a list of the issues to be tried. The court will approve the parties' proposals, if they are suitable, and give directions accordingly without a hearing. If it does not approve the agreed directions it may give modified directions or its own directions or, more usually, direct a case management conference. If the parties cannot agree directions then each party should put forward its own proposals for the future management of the case for consideration by the court. Draft orders commonly made by the masters on allocation and at case management conferences are set out at appendix 3, and parties drafting proposed directions for submission to a master on allocation or at a case management conference should have regard to and make use, as appropriate, of those draft orders.

3.4 If parties do not, at the allocation stage, agree or attempt to agree directions and if, in consequence, the court is unable to give directions without ordering a case management conference, the parties should not expect to recover any costs in respect of such a case management conference.

3.5 In many claims the court will give directions without holding a case management conference.

3.6 Any party who considers that a case management conference should be held before any directions are given should so state in his or her allocation questionnaire (or, in the case of a Part 8 claim, inform the court in writing) and give reasons why he or she considers that a case management conference is required. The court when sending out allocation questionnaires will also send out a questionnaire inviting the parties to give their time estimate for any case management conference and to specify any dates or times inconvenient for the holding of a case management conference.

3.7 Wherever possible, the advocate(s) instructed or expected to be instructed to appear at the trial should attend any hearing at which case management directions are likely to be given. To this end the court when ordering a case management conference, otherwise than upon allocation, will normally send out questionnaires to the parties in respect of their availability. Parties must not, however, expect that a case management conference will be held in abeyance for a substantial length of time in order to accommodate the advocates' convenience.

3.8 Case management conferences are intended to deal with the general management of the case. They are not an opportunity to make controversial interim applications without appropriate notice to the opposing party. Accordingly, as provided by PD 29, para. 5.8(1), where a party wishes to obtain an order not routinely made at a case management conference (such as an order for specific disclosure or summary disposal) such application should be made by separate Part 23 application to be heard at the case management conference and the case management conference should be listed for a sufficient period of time to allow the application to be heard. Where parties fail to comply with this paragraph it is highly unlikely that the court will entertain, other than by consent, an application which is not of a routine nature. It is the obligation of the parties to ensure that a realistic time estimate for hearings is given to the court.

3.9 Even where routine orders are sought (i.e. orders falling within the topics set out in PD 29, para. 5.3) care should be taken to ensure that the opposing party is given notice of the orders intended to be sought.

Applications for information and disclosure

3.10 Before a party applies to the court for an order that another party provides him or her with any further information or specific disclosure of documents he or she must communicate directly with the other party in an attempt to reach agreement or narrow the issues before the matter is raised with the court. If not satisfied that the parties have taken steps to reach agreement or narrow the issues, the court will normally require such steps to be taken before hearing the application.

Preliminary issues

3.11 Costs can sometimes be saved by identifying decisive issues, or potentially decisive issues, and ordering that they are tried first. The decision of one issue, although not itself decisive in law of the whole case, may enable the parties to settle the remainder of the dispute. In such cases a preliminary issue may be appropriate.

3.12 At the allocation stage, at any case management conference and again at any PTR, consideration will be given to the possibility of the trial of preliminary issues the resolution of which is likely to shorten proceedings. The court may suggest the trial of a preliminary issue, but it will rarely make an order without the concurrence of at least one of the parties.

Group litigation orders

3.13 Under CPR, r. 19.11, where there are likely to be a number of claims giving rise to common or related issues of fact, the court may make a group litigation order ('GLO') for their case management. Such orders may be appropriate in Chancery proceedings and there are a number in existence. A list of GLOs is published on the HMCS website. An application for a GLO is made under Part 23. The procedure is set out in PD 19B, which provides that the application should be made to the Chief Master, except for claims in a specialist list (such as the business of the Patents Court), when the application should be made to the senior judge of that list.

3.14 Claimants wishing to join in group litigation should issue proceedings in the normal way and should then apply (by letter) to be entered on the group register set up by a GLO. The details required for entry will be specified in the GLO. In the Chancery Division the register is usually kept by the management court and is maintained either by the court or by the lead solicitors, as specified in the GLO. Where the register is kept in the Chancery Division at the Royal Courts of Justice, it is kept by Mrs V. C. Bell, Chancery Lawyer (Room TM5.06, tel. (020) 7947 6080). Any initial enquiries regarding GLOs may be addressed to her.

Trial timetable

3.15 The judge at trial, or sometimes at the PTR, may determine the timetable for the trial. The advocates for the parties should be ready to assist the court in this respect if so required. The time estimate given for the trial should have been based on an approximate forecast of the trial timetable, and must be reviewed by each party at the stage of the PTR and as preparation for trial proceeds thereafter. If that review requires a change in the estimate the other parties' advocates and the court must be informed.

3.16 When a trial timetable is set by the court, it will ordinarily fix the time for the oral submissions and factual and expert evidence, and it may do so in greater or lesser detail. Trial timetables are always subject to any further order by the trial judge.

Pre-trial review

3.17 In cases estimated to take more than 10 days and in other cases where the circumstances warrant it, the court may direct that a PTR be held (see CPR, r. 29.7).

3.18 Such a PTR will normally be heard by a judge. The date and time should be fixed with the Chancery Judges' Listing Officer. If the trial judge has already been nominated, the application will if possible be heard by that judge. The advocates' clerks must attend the Chancery Judges' Listing Office in sufficient time so that the PTR can be fixed between four and eight weeks before the trial date.

3.19 A PTR should be attended by advocates who are to represent the parties at the trial.

3.20 Not less than seven days before the date fixed for the PTR the claimant, or another party if so directed by the court, must circulate a list of matters to be considered at the PTR, including proposals as to how the case should be tried, to the other parties, who must respond with their comments at least two days before the PTR.

3.21 The claimant, or another party if so directed by the court, should deliver a bundle containing the lists of matters to be considered and proposals served by the parties on each other and the trial timetable, together with the results of the discussions between the parties as to those matters, and any other documents the court is likely to need in order to deal with the PTR, to the Chancery Judges' Listing Office by 10 a.m. on the day before the day fixed for the hearing of the PTR.

3.22 At the PTR the court will review the state of preparation of the case, and deal with outstanding procedural matters, not limited to those apparent from the lists of matters lodged by the parties. The court may give directions as to how the case is to be tried, including directions as to the order in which witnesses are to be called (for example, all witnesses of fact before all expert witnesses) or as to the time to be allowed for particular stages in the trial.

Chapter 4 Disclosure of Documents and Expert Evidence

Key rules: CPR, Parts 18, 29, 31 and 35; PD 31 and PD 35

4.1 As part of its management of a case, the court will give directions about the disclosure of documents and any expert evidence. Attention is drawn to paras 3.8 to 3.10 above. An application for specific disclosure should be made by a specific Part 23 application and is not to be regarded as a matter routinely dealt with at a case management conference.

Disclosure of documents

4.2 Under the CPR, the normal order for disclosure is an order for standard disclosure, which requires disclosure of:

(1) *a party's own documents* — that is, the documents on which a party relies;

(2) *adverse documents* — that is, documents which adversely affect his or her own or another party's case or support another party's case; and

(3) *required documents* — that is, documents which a practice direction requires him or her to disclose.

4.3 The court may make an order for specific disclosure going beyond the limits of standard disclosure if it is satisfied that standard disclosure is inadequate.

4.4 The court will not make such an order readily. One of the clear principles underlying the CPR is that the burden and cost of disclosure should be reduced. The court will, therefore, seek to ensure that any specific disclosure ordered is proportionate in the sense that the cost of such disclosure does not outweigh the benefits to be obtained from such disclosure. The court will, accordingly, seek to tailor the order for disclosure to the requirements of the particular case. The financial position of the parties, the importance of the case and the complexity of the issues will be taken into account when considering whether more than standard disclosure should be ordered.

4.5 If specific disclosure is sought, the parties should give careful thought to the ways in which such disclosure can be limited, for example, by requiring disclosure in stages or by requiring disclosure simply of sufficient documents to show a specified matter and so on. They should also consider whether the need for disclosure could be avoided by requiring a party to provide information under Part 18.

Expert evidence

General

4.6 Part 35 contains particular provisions designed to limit the amount of expert evidence to be placed before the court and to reinforce the obligation of impartiality which is imposed upon an expert witness.

4.7 Fundamentally, Part 35 states that expert evidence must be restricted to what is reasonably required to resolve the proceedings and makes provision for the court to direct that expert evidence is given by a single joint expert. The parties should consider from the outset of the proceedings whether appointment of a single joint expert is appropriate.

Duties of an expert

4.8 It is the duty of an expert to help the court on the matters within his or her expertise; this duty overrides any obligation to the person from whom the expert has received instructions or by whom he or she is paid (r. 35.3). Attention is drawn to PD 35.

4.9 In fulfilment of this duty, an expert must for instance make it clear if a particular question or issue falls outside his or her expertise or he or she considers that insufficient data are available on which to express an opinion. Any material change of view by an expert should be communicated in writing (through legal representatives) to the other parties without delay, and when appropriate to the court.

Single joint expert

4.10 The introduction to PD 35 states that, where possible, matters requiring expert evidence should be dealt with by a single expert.

4.11 In very many cases it is possible for the question of expert evidence to be dealt with by a single expert. Single experts are, for example, often appropriate to deal with questions of quantum in cases where the primary issues are as to liability. Likewise, where expert evidence is required in order to acquaint the court with matters of expert fact, as opposed to opinion, a single expert will usually be appropriate. There remains, however, a substantial body of cases where liability will turn upon expert opinion evidence or where quantum is a primary issue and where it will be appropriate for the parties to instruct their own experts. For example, in cases where the issue for determination is as to whether a party acted in accordance with proper professional standards, it will often be of value to the court to hear the opinions of more than one expert as to the proper standard in order that the court becomes acquainted with the range of views existing upon the question and in order that the evidence can be tested in cross-examination.

4.12 It is not necessarily a sufficient objection to the making by the court of an order for a single joint expert that the parties have already appointed their own experts. An order for a single joint expert does not prevent a party from having his or her own expert to advise him or her, but he or she may well be unable to recover the cost of employing his or her own expert from the other party. The duty of an expert who is called to give evidence is to help the court.

4.13 When the use of a single joint expert is contemplated the court will expect the parties to cooperate in developing and agreeing to the greatest possible extent, terms of reference for the expert. In most cases the terms of reference will (in particular) detail what the expert is asked to do, identify any documentary material he or she is asked to consider and specify any assumptions he or she is asked to make.

More than one expert — exchange of reports

4.14 In an appropriate case the court will direct that experts' reports are delivered sequentially. Sequential reports may, for example, be appropriate if the service of the first expert's report would help to define and limit the issues on which such evidence may be relevant.

Discussion between experts

4.15 The court will normally direct discussion between experts before trial. Sometimes it may be useful for there to be further discussions during the trial itself. The purpose of these discussions is to give the experts the opportunity:

(1) to discuss the expert issues; and

(2) to identify the expert issues on which they share the same opinion and those on which there remains a difference of opinion between them (and what that difference is).

4.16 Unless the court otherwise directs, the procedure to be adopted at these discussions is a matter for the experts. It may be sufficient if the discussion takes place by telephone.

4.17 Parties must not seek to restrict their expert's participation in any discussion directed by the court, but they are not bound by any agreement on any issue reached by their expert unless they expressly so agree.

Written questions to experts

4.18 It is emphasised that this procedure is only for the purpose (generally) of seeking clarification of an expert's report where the other party is unable to understand it. Written questions going beyond this can only be put with the agreement of the parties or with the permission of the court. The procedure of putting written questions to experts is not intended to interfere with the procedure for an exchange of professional opinion in discussions between experts or to inhibit that exchange of professional opinion. If questions that are oppressive in number or content are put or questions are put without permission for any purpose other than clarification of an expert's report, the court will not hesitate to disallow the questions and to make an appropriate order for costs against the party putting them.

Request by an expert to the court for directions

4.19 An expert may file with the court a written request for directions to assist him or her in carrying out his or her function as expert (CPR, r. 35.14). Copies of any such request must be provided to the parties in accordance with r. 35.14(2) save where the court orders otherwise. The expert should guard against accidentally informing the court about, or about matters connected with, communications or potential communications between the parties that are without prejudice or privileged. The expert may properly be privy to the content of these communications because he or she has been asked to assist the party instructing him or her to evaluate them.

Assessors

4.20 Under r. 35.15 the court may appoint an assessor to assist it in relation to any matter in which the assessor has skill and experience. The report of the assessor is made available to the parties. The remuneration of the assessor is determined by the court and forms part of the costs of the proceedings.

Chapter 5 Applications

Key rules: CPR, Parts 23 and 25, PD 23 and PD 25

5.1 This chapter deals with applications to a judge, including applications for interim remedies, and applications to a master. As regards the practical arrangements for making, listing and adjourning applications, the chapter is primarily concerned with hearings at the Royal Courts of Justice. Hearings before Chancery judges outside London are dealt with in ch. 12.

5.2 Only applications which need to be heard by a judge (e.g. most applications for an injunction) should be made to a judge. Any procedural application (e.g. for directions) should be made to a master unless there is some special reason for making it to a judge. Otherwise the application may be dismissed with costs. If an application is to be made to a judge, the application notice should state that it is a judge's application.

5.3 CPR, Part 23, contains rules as to how an application may be made. In some circumstances it may be dealt with without a hearing, or by a telephone hearing.

Applications without notice

5.4 Generally it is wrong to make an application without giving prior notice to the respondent. There are, however, two classes of exceptions.

(1) First, there are cases where the giving of notice might frustrate the order (e.g. a search order) or where there is such urgency that there has not been time to give notice. Even in an urgent case, however, the applicant should notify the respondent informally of the application if possible, unless secrecy is essential.

(2) Secondly, there are in the Chancery Division some procedural applications normally made without notice relating to such matters as service out of the jurisdiction, service, extension of the validity of claim forms, permission to issue writs of possession etc. All of these are properly made without notice but will be subjected by the rules to an express provision in any order made that the absent party will be entitled to apply to set aside or vary the order provided that application is so made within a given number of days of service of the order.

(3) Thirdly, there are cases in which the defendant can only be identified by description and not by name (*Bloomsbury Publishing Group Ltd v News Group Newspapers Ltd* [2003] EWHC 1205 (Ch), [2003] 1 WLR 1633).

An application made without giving notice which does not fall within the classes of cases where absence of notice is justified, may be dismissed or adjourned until proper notice has been given.

Applications without a hearing

5.5 Part 23 makes provision for applications to be dealt with without a hearing. This is a useful provision in cases where the parties consent to the terms of the order sought or agree that a hearing is not necessary (often putting in written representations by letter or otherwise). It is also a useful provision in cases where, although the parties have not agreed to dispense with a hearing and the order is not consented to, the order sought by the application is, essentially, non-contentious. In such circumstances, the order made will, in any event, be treated as being made on the court's own initiative and will set out the right of any party affected by the application who has not been heard to apply to vary or set aside the order.

5.6 These provisions should not be used to deal with contentious matters without notice to the opposing party and without a hearing. Usually, this will result in delay since the court will simply order a hearing. It may also give rise to adverse costs orders. It will normally be wrong to seek an order which imposes sanctions in the event of non-compliance without notice and without a hearing. An application seeking such an order may well be dismissed.

Applications to a judge

5.7 If an application is made to a judge in existing proceedings, e.g. for an injunction, it should be made by application notice. This is called an interim application. Normally three clear days' notice to the other party is required but in an emergency or for other good reason the application can be made without giving notice, or the full three days' notice, to the other side. Permission to serve on short notice may be obtained on application without notice to the interim applications judge. Such permission will not be given by the master. Except in an emergency a party notifies the court of his or her wish to bring an application by delivering the requisite documents to the Chancery Judges' Listing Office (Room WG4) and paying the appropriate fee. He or she should at the same time deliver a completed 'Judge's Application Information Form' in the form set out in part 1 of appendix 4. An application will only be listed if (1) two copies of the claim form and (2) two copies of the application notice (one stamped with the appropriate fee) are lodged in the Chancery Judges' Listing Office before 12 noon on the working day before the date for which notice of the application has been given.

5.8 The current practice is that one judge combines the functions of interim applications judge and companies judge. His or her name will be found in the daily cause list and also in the Chancery Division term list.

5.9 The interim applications judge is available to hear applications each day in term and an application notice can be served for any day in term except the last. If the volume of applications requires it, any other judge who is available to assist with interim applications will hear such applications as the interim applications judge may direct. Special arrangements are made for hearing applications out of hours and in vacation, for which see paras 5.28 to 5.34 below.

5.10 At the beginning of each day's hearing the interim applications judge calls on each of the applications to be made that day in turn. This enables him or her to establish the identity of the parties, their state of readiness, their estimates of the duration of the hearing, and where relevant the degree of urgency of the case. On completion of this process, the judge decides the order in which he or she will hear applications and gives any other directions that may be necessary. Sometimes cases are released to other judges at this point. If cases are likely to take two hours or more (including pre-reading and oral delivery of judgment), the judge may order that they are given a subsequent fixed date for hearing (they are then called 'interim applications by order') and hears any application for a court order to last until the application is heard fully. Where on or before the day preceding the hearing it becomes likely that the time required for the application (including pre-reading and oral delivery of judgment) will exceed two hours, the Chancery Judges' Listing Officer (or, in appropriate cases, the clerk to the applications judge) must be notified immediately.

5.11 In such a case the solicitors or the clerks to counsel concerned should apply to the Chancery Judges' Listing Officer for a date for the hearing. Before so doing there must be lodged with the Chancery Judges' Listing Office a certificate signed by the advocate stating the estimated length of the hearing. Applications by order may be entered in the interim hearings list and, if not fixed by arrangement with the Chancery Judges' Listing Officer, will be liable to be listed for hearing in accordance with the timetable fixed by the judge.

5.12 Parties and their representatives should arrive at least 10 minutes before the court sits. This will assist the usher to take a note of the names of those proposing to address the court and of their estimate of the hearing time. This information is given to the judge before he or she sits. Parties should also allow time before the court sits to agree any form of order with any other party if this has not already been done. If the form of the order is not agreed before the court sits, the parties may have to wait until there is a convenient break in the list before they can ask the court to make any agreed order. If an application, not being an interim application by order, is adjourned the associate in attendance will notify the Chancery Judges' Listing Office of the day to which it has been adjourned so that it may be relisted for the new date.

Agreed adjournment of interim applications

5.13 If all parties to an interim application agree, it can be adjourned for not more than 14 days by counsel or solicitors attending the Chancery Judges' Listing Officer in Room WG4 at any time before 4 p.m. on the day before the hearing of the application and producing consents signed by solicitors or counsel for all parties agreeing to the adjournment. A litigant in person must attend before the Chancery Judges' Listing Officer as well as signing a consent. This procedure may not be used for more than three successive adjournments and no adjournment may be made by this procedure to the last two days of any sitting.

Interim applications by order by agreement

5.14 This procedure should also be used where the parties agree that the hearing of the application will take two hours or more and that, in consequence, the application should be adjourned to be heard as an interim application by order. In that event, the consents set out above should also contain an agreed timetable for the filing of evidence or confirmation that no further evidence is to be filed. Any application arising from the failure of a party to abide by the timetable and any application to extend the timetable must be made to the judge. Interim applications by order will, initially at least, enter the interim hearings warned list on the first Monday after close of evidence.

5.15 Undertakings given to the court may be continued unchanged over any adjournment. If, however, on an adjournment an undertaking is to be varied or a new undertaking given then that must be dealt with by the court.

The duty of disclosure

5.16 On all applications made in the absence of the respondent the applicant and his or her legal representatives owe a duty to the court to disclose fully all matters relevant to the application, including matters, whether of fact or law, which are, or may be, adverse to it. If there is a failure to comply with this duty and an order is made, the court may subsequently set aside the order on that ground alone. The disclosure, if made orally, must be confirmed by witness statement or affidavit. The representatives for the applicant must specifically direct the court to passages in the evidence which disclose matters adverse to the application.

5.17 A party wishing to apply urgently to a judge for remedies without notice to the respondent must notify the clerk to the interim applications judge by telephone (the number will be set out in the daily cause list). Where such an urgent application is made, two copies of the order sought and an electronic copy on disk (in Word for Windows) and a completed judge's application information form in the form in part 1 of appendix 4 should, where possible, be included with the papers handed to the judge's clerk. Where an application is very urgent and the interim applications judge is unable to hear it promptly, it may be heard by any judge who is available, though the request for this must be made to the clerk to the interim applications judge, or, in default, to the Chancery Judges' Listing Officer. Every effort should be made to issue the claim form before the application is made. If this is not practicable, the party making the application must give an undertaking to the court to issue the claim form forthwith even if the court makes no order, unless the court orders otherwise. A party making an urgent application must ensure that all necessary fees are paid.

Freezing injunctions and search orders

5.18 The grant of freezing injunctions (both domestic and worldwide) and search orders is a staple feature of the work of the interim applications judge. Applications for such orders are invariably made without notice in the first instance; and in a proper case the court will sit in private in order to hear them. Where such an application is to be listed, two copies of the order sought, together with the application notice, should be lodged with the Chancery Judges' Listing Officer. If the application is to be made in private, it will be listed as 'Application without notice' without naming the parties. The judge will consider, in each case, whether publicity might defeat the object of the hearing and, if so, may hear the application in private.

5.19 Freezing injunctions and search orders are never granted as a matter of course. A strong case must be made out, and applications need to be prepared with great care. The application should always be accompanied by a draft of the order which the court is to be invited to make.

Period for which an injunction or an order appointing a receiver is granted if the application was without notice

5.20 When an application for an injunction is heard without notice, and the judge decides that an injunction should be granted, it will normally be granted for a limited period only — usually not more than seven days. The same applies to an interim order appointing a receiver. The applicant will be required to give the respondent notice of his or her intention to apply to the court at the expiration of that period for the order to be continued. In the meantime the respondent will be entitled to apply, though generally only after giving notice to the applicant, for the order to be varied or discharged.

Opposed applications without notice

5.21 These are applications of which proper notice has not been given to the respondents but which are made in the presence of both parties in advance of a full hearing of the application. The judge may impose time limits on the parties if, having regard to the pressure of business or for any other reason, he or she considers it appropriate to do so. On these applications, the judge may, in an appropriate case, make an order which will have effect until trial or further order as if proper notice had been given.

Implied cross-undertakings in damages where undertakings are given to the court

5.22 Often the party against whom an injunction is sought gives to the court an undertaking which avoids the need for the court to grant the injunction. In these cases, there is an implied undertaking in damages by the party applying for the injunction in favour of the other. The position is less clear where the party applying for the injunction also gives an undertaking to the court. The parties should consider and, if necessary, raise with the judge whether the party in whose favour the undertaking is given must give a cross-undertaking in damages in those circumstances.

Orders on applications

5.23 The judge may direct the parties to agree, sign and deliver to the court a statement of the terms of the order made by the court (commonly still referred to as a minute of order), particularly where complex undertakings are given.

Consents by parties not attending hearing

5.24 It is commonly the case that on an interim application the respondent does not appear either in person or by solicitors or counsel but the applicant seeks a consent order based upon a letter of consent from the respondent or his or her solicitors or a draft statement of agreed terms signed by the respondent's solicitors. This causes no difficulty where the agreed relief falls wholly within the relief claimed in the application notice.

5.25 If, however, the agreed relief goes outside that which is claimed in the application notice or even in the claim form or when undertakings are offered then difficulties can arise. A procedure has been established for this purpose to be applied to all applications in the Chancery Division.

5.26 Subject always to the discretion of the court, no order will be made in such cases unless a consent signed by or on behalf of the respondent to an application is put before the court in accordance with the following provisions:

(1) Where there are solicitors on the record for the respondent the court will normally accept as sufficient a written consent signed by those solicitors on their headed notepaper.

(2) Where there are solicitors for the respondent who are not on the record, the court will normally accept as sufficient a written consent signed by those solicitors on their headed notepaper only if in the consent (or some other document) the solicitors certify that they have fully explained to the respondent the effect of the order and that the respondent appeared to have understood the explanation.

(3) Where there is a written consent signed by a respondent acting in person the court will not normally accept it as sufficient unless the court is satisfied that the respondent understands the effect of the order either by reason of the circumstances (for example, the respondent is himself a solicitor or barrister) or by means of other material (for example, the respondent's consent is given in reply to a letter explaining in simple terms the effect of the order).

(4) Where the respondent offers any undertaking to the court (a) the document containing the undertaking must be signed by the respondent personally, (b) solicitors must certify on their headed notepaper that the signature is that of the respondent and (c) if the case falls within (2) or (3) above, solicitors must certify that they have explained to the respondent the consequences of giving the undertaking and that the respondent appeared to understand the explanation.

Bundles and skeleton arguments

5.27 See ch. 7 below.

Out-of-hours emergency arrangements

5.28 An application should not be made out of hours unless it is essential. An explanation will be required as to why it was not made or could not be made during normal court hours. Applications made during legal vacations must also constitute vacation business.

5.29 There is always a duty Chancery judge available to hear urgent out-of-hours applications. The following is a summary of the procedure:

(1) All requests for the duty Chancery judge to hear urgent matters are to be made through the judge's clerk. There may be occasions when the duty Chancery judge is not immediately available. The clerk will be able to inform the applicant of the judge's likely availability.

(2) Initial contact should be through the Security Office at the Royal Courts of Justice (tel: (020) 7947 6260), who should be requested to contact the duty Chancery judge's clerk. The applicant must give a telephone number for the return call.

(3) When the clerk contacts the applicant, he or she will need to know:

(a) the name of the party on whose behalf the application is to be made;

(b) the name of the person who is to make the application and his or her status (counsel or solicitor);

(c) the nature of the application;

(d) the degree of urgency;

(e) the contact telephone numbers.

Court Guides

(4) The duty judge will indicate to his or her clerk whether he or she is prepared to deal with the matter by telephone or whether it will be necessary for the matter to be dealt with by a hearing, in court or elsewhere. The clerk will inform the applicant and make the necessary arrangements.

(5) Applications for interim remedies will (normally) be heard by telephone only where the applicant is represented by counsel or solicitors (PD 25, para. 4.5). If, however, an applicant not so represented indicates reasons why, exceptionally, the application should be heard by telephone, the judge may require that the applicant be attended by a responsible person who can confirm the identity of the applicant and the accuracy of what is said: see PD 23, paras 6.3 and 8. If satisfied that it is really necessary, the judge may grant an injunction on such an application, but it is likely to be granted for as short a time as possible pending a hearing on notice to the respondent.

5.30 Which judge will, in appropriate cases, hear an out-of-hours application varies according to when the application is made.

(1) *Weekdays.* Out-of-hours duty, during term time, is the responsibility of the applications judge. He or she is normally available from 4.15 p.m. until 10.15 a.m. Monday to Thursday.

(2) *Weekends.* A duty Chancery judge is nominated by rota for weekends, commencing 4.15 p.m. Friday until 10.15 a.m. Monday.

(3) *Vacation.* The vacation judge also undertakes out-of-hours applications.

5.31 *Sealing orders out of hours.* In normal circumstances it is not possible to issue a sealed order out of hours. The judge may direct the applicant to lodge a draft of the order made at Chancery Chambers Registry by 10 a.m. on the following working day.

5.32 *County court matters.* Similar arrangements exist for making urgent applications out of hours in county court matters in certain parts of England and Wales. Contact with the circuit judge on duty for the London county courts can be made through the Security Office of the Royal Courts of Justice.

Vacation arrangements

5.33 There is a Chancery judge available to hear applications in vacation. Applications must generally constitute vacation business in that, in particular, they require to be immediately or promptly heard. Special arrangements exist, however, in the Companies Court for certain schemes of arrangement and reductions of capital to be heard in the Long Vacation (see PD 49B, para. 8).

5.34 In the long vacation, the vacation judge sits each day to hear vacation business. In other vacations there are no regular sittings. Mondays and Thursdays are made available for urgent interim applications on notice. The judge is available on the remaining days for urgent business.

Applications to a master

5.35 Applications to a master should be made by application notice. Application notices are issued by the masters' appointments section in Room TM7.09. If the master has already directed a case management conference the parties should ensure that all applications in the proceedings are properly issued and listed to be heard at the case management conference. If the available listed time is likely to be insufficient to give directions and hear any application the parties should cooperate and invite the court to arrange a longer appointment. It is the duty of the parties to seek to agree directions if possible and to provide a draft of the order for consideration by the master.

5.36 Applications to a master estimated to last in excess of two hours will require serious cooperation between the parties and will require the master's directions before they are listed. The master will normally give his permission to list such an application on condition that there is compliance with directions given by the master.

5.37 Those directions are likely to require:

(1) that the applicant agrees the time estimate (see below) with his opponent;

(2) that, if the time allowed subsequently becomes insufficient, the court is informed and a new and longer appointment given;

(3) that the parties agree an appropriate timetable for filing evidence such that the hearing will be effective on the date listed;

(4) that positive confirmation is to be given to the master five working days before the hearing date that the hearing remains effective; and
(5) that, in the event of settlement, the master be informed of that fact.

5.38 The agreed time estimate must take into account not only the hearing time of the application but the time for the master to give any judgment at the conclusion of the hearing. It should also take into account any further time that may be required for the master to assess costs, and for any application for permission to appeal.

5.39 Failure to comply with the master's directions given in respect of the listing of an appointment in excess of two hours may result, depending upon the circumstances, in the application not being heard or in adverse costs orders being made.

5.40 On any matter of substance, the master is likely to require a bundle and skeleton arguments to be provided before the hearing as detailed in paras 7.40 to 7.50 below. Where directions are given in respect of an application to which para. 5.36 applies, the provision of a bundle and skeleton arguments should form part of the agreed timetable.

5.41 The masters may also allow applications to be made to them informally. The masters are normally listed to hear oral applications without notice between 2.15 p.m. and 2.45 p.m. (see para. 6.32 below). Such applications should not be used in place of a Part 23 application and care must be taken to notify in appropriate cases parties likely to be affected by any order made on the application. Letters should not be used in place of a Part 23 application, and parties should be particularly careful to keep any correspondence with the masters to a minimum and to ensure that opposing parties receive copies of any correspondence. Failure in this regard will mean that the master will refuse to deal with the correspondence. Correspondence should state that it has been copied to the other parties (or should state why it has not been copied). Unless the matter is one of urgency correspondence and any other documents should be sent by post. If, in a case of real urgency, a letter is sent by fax, it should not be followed by a hard copy, unless it contains an original document which needs to be filed. Further guidance is set out in the Chief Master's practice note reproduced at appendix 5.

5.42 There is no distinction between term time and vacation so far as business before the Chancery masters is concerned. They will deal with all types of business throughout the year. When a master is on holiday, his or her list will normally be taken by a deputy master.

Applications for payment out of court

5.43 Applications for payment out of money held in court under PD 37, para. 4.2 (for example, where money has been paid into court following compulsory purchase or repossession of property), must be made by Part 23 application notice (form N244). The required documents should be sent to Room TM5.04. The following must be included:
(1) the reasons why the payment should be made (in part C of the application notice);
(2) any relevant documents such as birth, marriage or death certificate, title deeds etc. (exhibited to the application notice);
(3) a statement whether or not anyone else has any claim to the money (in the statement of truth);
(4) bank details, i.e. the name and address of the relevant bank/building society branch, its sort code, and the account title and number;
(5) the court fee of £50.

5.44 If there is a dispute as to entitlement to money in court, the master may order the matter to proceed by Part 8 claim (see para. 2.13 above). In all other cases the master will consider the file without a hearing and make an order for payment.

Chapter 6 Listing Arrangements

Key rules: CPR, Parts 29 and 39

6.1 This chapter deals with listing arrangements for hearings before judges and masters in the Royal Courts of Justice.

Hearings before judges

Responsibility for listing

6.2 Subject to the direction of the Chancellor the clerk of the lists (Room WG3, Royal Courts of

Court Guides

Justice) has overall responsibility for listing. Day-by-day management of Chancery listing is dealt with by the Chancery Judges' Listing Officer (Room WG4). All applications relating to listing should, in the first instance, be made to the Chancery Judges' Listing Officer, who will refer matters, as necessary, to the clerk of the lists. Any party dissatisfied with any decision of the clerk of the lists may, on one clear day's notice to all other parties, apply to the judge in charge of the list. Any such application should be made within seven days of the decision of the clerk of the lists and be arranged through the Chancery Judges' Listing Officer.

6.3 There are three main lists in the Chancery Division: the trial list, the general list and the interim hearings list. In addition there is a separate patents list which is also controlled on a day-to-day basis by the Chancery Judges' Listing Officer in Room WG4 (see ch. 23).

The trial list

6.4 This comprises a list of all trials to be heard with witnesses.

The interim hearings list

6.5 This list comprises interim applications and appeals from masters.

The general list

6.6 This list comprises other matters including revenue, bankruptcy and pension appeals, Part 8 proceedings, applications for judgment and all company matters.

6.7 The procedure for listing Chancery cases to be heard in the Royal Courts of Justice and listed in the trial list is that at an early stage in the claim the court will give directions with a view to fixing the period during which the case will be heard. In a Part 7 claim that period (the trial window) will be determined by the court either when the case is allocated or subsequently at any case management conference or other directions hearing. In a Part 8 claim covered by this procedure, that is to say a Part 8 claim to be heard with witnesses, similar directions will be given when the Part 8 claim is listed for preliminary directions or for a case management conference. It is only in a small minority of Part 8 claims that the claim is tried by a judge in the trial list and the trial window procedure applies. The bulk of Part 8 claims are heard on written evidence either by the master or by the judge. Additionally, many Part 8 claims, even where oral evidence is to be called, will be heard by the master pursuant to the jurisdiction set out in PD 2B, para. 4.1.

6.8 In determining the trial window the court will have regard to the listing constraints created by the existing court list and will determine a trial window which provides the parties with enough time to complete their preparations for trial. A trial window, once fixed, will not readily be altered. A list of current trial windows is published on the HMCS website. When determining the trial window the court will direct that one party, normally the claimant, makes an appointment to attend on the Chancery Judges' Listing Officer (Room WG4) to fix a trial date within the trial window, by such date as may be specified in the order and gives notice of that appointment to all other parties. It is to be understood that an order to attend on the Chancery Judges' Listing Officer imposes a strict obligation of compliance, without which the trial window that has been given will be lost.

6.9 At the listing appointment, the Chancery Judges' Listing Officer will take account, in so far as it is practical to do so, of any difficulties the parties may have as to the availability of counsel, experts and witnesses. The Chancery Judges' Listing Officer will, nevertheless, try to ensure the speedy disposal of the trial by arranging a firm trial date as soon as possible within the trial window. If a case summary has been prepared (see PD 29, paras 5.6 and 5.7) the claimant must produce a copy at the listing appointment together with a copy of the particulars of claim and any orders relevant to the fixing of the trial date. If, exceptionally, at the listing appointment, it appears to the Chancery Judges' Listing Officer that a trial date cannot be provided by the court within the trial window, he may fix the trial date outside the trial window at the first available date.

6.10 A party wishing to appeal a date allocated by the Chancery Judges' Listing Officer must, within seven days of the allocation, make an application to the judge nominated to hear such applications. The application notice should be filed in the Chancery Judges' Listing Office and served, giving one clear day's notice to the other parties.

6.11 A trial date once fixed will, like a trial window, only rarely be altered or vacated. An application to adjourn a trial date will normally be made to the judge nominated to hear such applications (see further para. 7.38). Such an application will, however, be entertained by the master if, for example, on the hearing of an interim application or case management conference it becomes clear that the trial date cannot stand without injustice to one or both parties.

Warned list — general and interim hearings lists

6.12 On each Friday of term and on such other days as may be appropriate, the Chancery Judges' Listing Officer will publish a warned list, showing the matters that are liable to be heard in the following week. Any matters for which no date has been arranged will be liable to appear in the list for hearing with no warning save that given by the next day's list of cases, posted each afternoon outside Room WG4. Where a case is listed in the warned list, the parties may agree to offer the case for a specified date, in accordance with the statement of Chancery Judges' Listing Office practice on offering cases issued by the clerk of the lists.

Estimate of duration

6.13 If after a case is listed the estimated length of the hearing is varied, or if the case is settled, withdrawn or discontinued, the solicitors for the parties must forthwith inform the Chancery Judges' Listing Officer in writing. Failure so to do may result in an adverse costs order being made. If the case is settled but the parties wish the master to make a consent order, the solicitor must notify the Chancery Judges' Listing Officer in writing, whereupon he or she will take the case out of the list and notify the master. The master may then make the consent order.

6.14 Seven days before the date for the hearing, the claimant's solicitors must inform the Chancery Judges' Listing Officer whether there is any variation in the estimate of duration, and, in particular, whether the case is likely to be disposed of in some summary way. If the claimant is a litigant in person, this must be done by the solicitor for the first-named defendant who has instructed a solicitor. If a summary disposal is likely, the solicitor must keep the Chancery Judges' Listing Officer informed of any developments as soon as they occur.

Applications after listing

6.15 Where a case has been listed for hearing and because of the timing of the hearing an application is urgent, any application in the case may be made to the interim applications judge if the application cannot be heard by a master without the hearing being delayed. Parties should not however list an application before the interim applications judge without first consulting the masters' clerks (Room TM7.09) as to the availability of the assigned master or, in an appropriate case, applying to the master himself. Provision can be made for urgent applications to be dealt with by the Chief Master or a deputy (see further para. 6.29).

Appeals

6.16 All appeals for hearing by High Court judges in the Division are issued by the Clerk of the Lists, High Court Appeals Office (Room WG8). Enquiries relating to such appeals are to be made in the first instance to that office, except as provided by para. 6.18 below.

Daily list of cases

6.17 This list, known as the Daily Cause List, is available on the Courts Service website: www.hmcourts-service.gov.uk.

Listing of particular business

Appeals from masters

6.18 (1) Appeals from masters, where permission has been given, will appear in the appeals warned list. Such appeals (stamped with the appropriate fee) must be filed with the Clerk of the Lists' Office in Room WG7. When an appeal is filed an appeal number will be allocated and any future order will bear both the original claim number and the appeal number. On being satisfied that the case has been placed in the warned list, solicitors should forthwith inform the Chancery Judges' Listing Officer whether they intend to instruct counsel and, if so, the name or names of counsel.

(2) Any order made on appeal from a master will be placed on the court file. However, practitioners should cooperate by ensuring that a copy of any relevant order is available to the master at any subsequent hearing.

Applications for permission to appeal from masters

6.19 Applications for permission to appeal from a decision of a master (stamped with the appropriate fee) must be lodged in the Clerk of the Lists' Office in Room WG7. If permission to appeal is granted the appeal will appear in the interim hearings list and the procedure set out above will apply.

Bankruptcy appeals

6.20 Notice of appeal from the decision of a registrar or of a county court should be lodged in the Clerk of the Lists' Office, Room WG7. The appeal will be entered in the appeals warned list, usually with a fixed date. The date of the hearing will be fixed by the Chancery Judges' Listing Officer in the usual way.

Bankruptcy applications

6.21 All originating applications to the judge should be lodged with the deputy court manager in bankruptcy. Urgent applications without notice for (i) the committal of any person to prison for contempt or (ii) injunctions or the modification or discharge of injunctions will be passed directly to the clerk to the interim applications judge for hearing by that judge. All applications on notice for (i) and (ii) above, and applications referred to the judge by the registrar, will be listed by the Chancery Judges' Listing Officer. Applications estimated not to exceed two hours will be heard by the interim applications judge. The Chancery Judges' Listing Officer is to give at least three clear days' notice of the hearing to the applicant and to any respondent who attended before the registrar. Applications over two hours will be placed in the general list and listed accordingly.

Companies Court

6.22 Matters for hearing before the companies judge, such as [applications] for an administration order, petitions for approval by the court of schemes of arrangement and applications for the appointment of provisional liquidators, may be issued for hearing on any day of the week in term time (other than the last day of each term) and will be dealt with by the interim applications judge as companies judge. Applications or petitions which are estimated to exceed two hours are liable to be stood over to a date to be fixed by the Chancery Judges' Listing Officer. Urgent applications will also be dealt with by the interim applications judge. Applications and petitions referred to the judge by the registrar will be placed in the general list and listed accordingly.

Applications referred to the judge

6.23 Applications referred by the master to the judge will be added to the interim hearings list. The power to refer applications made to the master and in respect of which the master has jurisdiction is now very sparingly exercised. The proper use of judicial resources dictates that where the master has jurisdiction in respect of an interlocutory matter he should ordinarily exercise that jurisdiction.

Judge's applications

6.24 Reference should be made to ch. 5.

Revenue appeals

6.25 Appeals will be entered in the appeals warned list, usually with fixed dates, and will be heard by such judges as are available. The dates for hearing are settled in the usual way on application to the Chancery Judges' Listing Officer. Where it would assist counsel and solicitor with their other commitments, the Chancery Judges' Listing Officer, if requested, will endeavour to fix two or more revenue appeals so that they will come on consecutively.

Short applications

6.26 An application for judgment in default made to a judge (because the master has no jurisdiction) should be made to the interim applications judge.

Summary judgment

6.27 Where an application for summary judgment includes an application for an injunction, it usually has to be made to a judge because in most cases the master cannot grant an injunction save in terms agreed by the parties. In such cases the application should be made returnable before the judge instead of the master and will be listed in the general list. The return date to be inserted in the application notice should be a Monday at least 14 clear days after the application notice has been served. The application notice should be issued in the Chancery Judges' Listing Office (Room WG4) when there must be lodged two copies of the application notice and the witness statements or affidavits in support together with their exhibits. On the return date the application will normally be adjourned to a date to be fixed if the hearing is likely to take longer than 30 minutes. The adjourned date will be fixed in the usual way through the Chancery Judges' Listing Officer, and a certificate signed by an advocate as to the estimated length of the hearing must be lodged with the Chancery Judges' Listing Officer.

If the applicant informs the Chancery Judges' Listing Officer at the time of issue of an application notice for summary judgment returnable before a judge that directions have been agreed, or are not necessary, the application will be listed for a substantive hearing without being listed for directions.

If, subsequent to issue, the parties agree directions the Chancery Judges' Listing Officer will, on application, relist the application for a substantive hearing and any directions hearing will be vacated. Time estimates should be agreed.

Variation of trusts: application to a judge

6.28 Applications under the Variation of Trusts Act 1958 for a hearing before the judge may be listed for hearing in the general list without any direction by a master on the lodgment in Room WG4 of a certificate signed by advocates for all the parties, stating (i) that the evidence is complete and has been filed; (ii) that the application is ready for hearing; and (iii) the estimated length of the hearing.

Hearings before masters

Assignment of cases before masters

6.29 The general rule is that cases are assigned to the masters in accordance with the last digit of the claim number. At present cases are allocated as follows:

0 and 1 Master Bragge
2 and 3 Master Teverson
4 and 5 Master Bowles
6 and 7 Master Price
8 and 9 Master Moncaster

In view of administrative responsibilities, the Chief Master does not have assigned cases. He will take individual cases or classes of case in his own discretion and arrangements will be made accordingly through the court manager. Where an application is required to be heard at short notice or is urgent but the assigned master's list cannot accommodate an early date for the length of hearing necessary, arrangements can often be made for it to be listed before the Chief Master. Application should first be made to the assigned master, who will determine whether the case is one which it is appropriate to release to the Chief Master. In that event arrangements are made by the court manager (Room TM6.06).

Applications by the Official Solicitor under CPR, r. 21.12, to be appointed a guardian of a minor's estate are normally dealt with by the Chief Master. All applications for a Group Litigation Order in the Chancery Division have to be made to the Chief Master: see para. 3.13.

6.30 An important exception to the general rule is that all registered trade mark claims are assigned to Master Bragge. Practitioners must, therefore, ensure, both at the date of issue of proceedings and when any application is to be made, that the court staff are aware that the claim is a registered trade mark claim and that, irrespective of the claim number, the claim and any application in the claim is assigned to and should be listed before Master Bragge. Each month in term time a day or more is usually set aside in Master Bragge's list specifically for trade mark applications and practitioners should, if possible, seek to have applications listed on that day. If the provisions of this paragraph are ignored and an application in a registered trade mark claim is listed other than before Master Bragge, it is likely that the master before whom it is listed will refuse to hear it. If Master Bragge is away it is to be expected that the claim will be heard by the deputy sitting for him.

6.31 In addition, from time to time, the Chief Master assigns particular classes of case to particular masters. This will normally relate to managed litigation where the particular parties will be aware that their cases have been specifically assigned.

Oral applications without notice to the masters

6.32 Masters are normally available to hear oral applications without notice at Applications without Notice Time between 2.15 p.m. and 2.45 p.m. on working days. Notice should be given to the Master's Appointments Section in Room TM7.09, or by telephone or fax, by 4.30 p.m. on the previous working day (except in cases of real emergency when notice may be given at any time) so that the file will be before the master. If this procedure is not followed the master may well refuse to deal with the application. The master will expect notice of such an application to have been given in an appropriate case to the other party. Applications without Notice Time must not be used as a substitute for cases where the issue and service of an application notice is appropriate. (See para. 5.41 above.)

6.33 If the assigned master is not available on any particular day, the applicant will be informed and (except in cases of emergency) asked to come when the assigned master is next available. Applications will only be heard by another master in cases of emergency or when the assigned master is on vacation.

6.34 See also paras 5.35 to 5.42 (applications to masters).

Chapter 7 Preparation for Hearings

Key rules: CPR, Parts 29 and 39

7.1 This chapter contains guidance on the preparation of cases for hearings before judges and masters. Guidelines about the conduct of trials are given in ch. 8 of this Guide. When an affidavit or witness statement (or other document) is filed in Chancery Chambers in preparation for a hearing or for any other purpose, it should be accompanied by a written evidence lodgment form as set out in part 2 of appendix 4, unless it accompanies an application notice. The preparation of witness statements is covered in ch. 8.

Hearings before judges

7.2 To ensure court time is used efficiently there must be adequate preparation of cases prior to the hearing. This covers, among other things, the preparation and exchange of skeleton arguments, compiling bundles of documents and dealing out of court with queries which need not concern the court. The parties should also use their best endeavours to agree before any hearing what are the issues or the main issues.

Estimates

7.3 Realistic estimates of the length of time a hearing is expected to take must be given.

7.4 In estimating the length of a hearing, sufficient time must be allowed for reading any documents required to be read, the length of the speeches, the time required to examine witnesses (if any), and, if appropriate, an immediate judgment, together with the summary assessment of costs, in cases where that may arise, and any application for permission to appeal.

7.5 Except as mentioned below, a written estimate signed by the advocates for all the parties is required in the case of any hearing before a judge. This should be delivered to the Chancery Judges' Listing Officer:

(1) in the case of a trial, on the application to fix the trial date; and

(2) in any other case, as soon as possible after the application notice or case papers have been lodged with the Chancery Judges' Listing Office.

7.6 If the estimate given in the application notice for an application to the interim applications judge (other than applications by order) or for an application listed before the companies judge requires to be revised, the revised estimate should be given to the court orally when the application is called on.

Changes in estimate

7.7 The parties must inform the court immediately of any material change in a time estimate. They should keep each other informed of any such change. In any event a further time estimate signed by the advocates to the parties must be lodged when bundles are lodged (see para. 7.17 below).

Inaccurate estimates

7.8 Where estimates prove inaccurate, a hearing may have to be adjourned to a later date and the party responsible for the adjournment is likely to be ordered to pay the costs thrown away.

Bundles

7.9 Bundles of documents for use in court will generally be required for all hearings if more than 25 pages are involved (and may be appropriate even if fewer pages are involved). The efficient preparation of bundles of documents is very important. Where bundles have been properly prepared, the case will be easier to understand and present, and time and costs are likely to be saved. Where documents are copied unnecessarily or bundled incompetently the cost may be disallowed.

7.10 Where the provisions of this Guide as to the preparation or delivery of bundles are not followed, the bundle may be rejected by the court or be made the subject of a special costs order.

7.11 The claimant or applicant (as the case may be) should begin his or her preparation of the bundles in sufficient time to enable:

(1) the bundles to be agreed with the other parties (so far as possible);
(2) references to the bundles to be used in skeleton arguments; and
(3) the bundles to be delivered to the court at the required time.

7.12 The representatives for all parties involved must cooperate in agreeing bundles for use in court. The court and the advocates should all have exactly the same bundles.

7.13 When agreeing bundles for trial, the parties should establish through their legal representatives, and record in correspondence, whether the agreement of bundles:

(1) extends no further than agreement of the composition and preparation of the bundles; or
(2) includes agreement that the documents in the bundles are authentic (see CPR, r. 32.19); or
(3) includes agreement that the documents may be treated as evidence of the facts stated in them.

The court will normally expect parties to agree that the documents, or at any rate the great majority of them, may be treated as evidence of the facts stated in them. A party not willing to agree should, when the trial bundles are lodged, write a letter to the court (with a copy to all other parties) stating that it is not willing to agree, and explaining why.

7.14 Documents disclosed are in general deemed to be admitted to be authentic under r. 32.19.

7.15 Detailed guidelines on the preparation of bundles are set out in appendix 6 in addition to those in PD 39, para. 3. These should always be followed unless there is good reason not to do so. Particular attention is drawn to the need to consider the preparation of a core bundle.

7.16 The general rule is that the claimant/applicant must ensure that one copy of a properly prepared bundle is delivered at the Chancery Judges' Listing Office not less than two clear days (and not more than seven days) before a trial or application by order. However, the court may direct the delivery of bundles earlier than this. Where oral evidence is to be given a second copy of the bundle must be available in court for the use of the witnesses. In the case of bundles to be used on judge's applications (other than applications by order) the bundles must be delivered to the clerk to the interim applications judge by 10 a.m. on the morning preceding the day of the hearing unless the court directs otherwise. A bundle delivered to the court should always be in final form and parties should not make a request to alter the bundle after it has been delivered to the court save for good reason.

7.17 When lodging the agreed bundles there should also be lodged a further agreed time estimate, together with an agreed reading list and an agreed time estimate in respect of that reading list. The time estimates and reading list must be signed by the advocates for the parties. Failing agreement as to the time estimates or reading list then separate reading lists and time estimates must be submitted signed by the appropriate advocate. See appendix 7 as to reading lists.

7.18 If the case is one which does not require the preparation of a bundle, the advocate should check before the hearing starts that all the documents to which he or she wishes to refer and which ought to have been filed have been filed, and, if possible, indicate to the associate which they are.

7.19 Bundles provided for the use of the court should be removed promptly after the conclusion of the hearing unless the court directs otherwise.

Skeleton arguments

7.20 The general rule is that for the purpose of all hearings before a judge skeleton arguments should be prepared. The exceptions to this general rule are where the application does not warrant one, for example because it is likely to be short, or where the application is so urgent that preparation of a skeleton argument is impracticable or where an application is ineffective and the order is agreed by all parties (see also paras 26.26 and 26.33).

Time for delivery of skeleton arguments

7.21 *In the more substantial matters (e.g. trials and applications by order)* — not less than two clear days before the date or first date on which the application or trial is due to come on for hearing.

Court Guides

7.22 *On judge's applications without notice* — with the papers which the judge is asked to read on the application.

7.23 *On all other applications to a judge, including interim applications* — as soon as possible and not later than 10 a.m. on the day preceding the hearing.

7.24 Where a case is liable to be placed in the warned list, consideration should be given to the preparation of skeleton arguments as soon as the case is placed in the warned list, so that the skeleton arguments are ready to be delivered to the court on time. Preparation of skeleton arguments should not be left until notice is given that the case is to be heard. Notice may be given that the case is to be heard the next day.

Place to which skeleton arguments should be delivered

7.25 If the name of the judge is not known, or the judge is a deputy judge, skeleton arguments should be delivered to the Chancery Judges' Listing Office (Room WG4).

7.26 If the name of the judge (other than a deputy judge) is known, skeleton arguments should be delivered to the judge's clerk.

Content of skeleton arguments

7.27 Appendix 7 contains guidelines which should be followed on the content of skeleton arguments and chronologies, as well as indices and reading lists.

7.28 In most cases before a judge, a list of the persons involved in the facts of the case, a chronology and a list of issues will also be required. The chronology and list of issues should be agreed where possible. The claimant/applicant is responsible for preparing the list of persons involved and the chronology, and he or she should deliver these and his or her list of issues (if required) to the court with his or her skeleton argument.

7.29 Unless the court gives any other direction, the parties shall, as between themselves, arrange for the delivery, exchange, or sequential service of skeleton arguments and any list of persons involved, list of issues or chronology. Where there are no such arrangements, all such documents should, where possible, be given to the other parties (if any) in sufficient time before the hearing to enable them properly to consider them.

Failure to lodge bundles or skeleton arguments on time

7.30 Failure to lodge skeleton arguments and bundles in accordance with this Guide may result in:
(1) the matter not being heard on the date in question;
(2) the costs of preparation being disallowed; and
(3) an adverse costs order being made.

7.31 In the Royal Courts of Justice, a log will be maintained of all late skeletons and bundles. The log will regularly be inspected by the Chancellor who will consider such further action as appropriate in relation to any recurrent failure by any chambers, barrister, or solicitors firm to comply with the requirements of the CPR and the Guide.

Authorities

7.32 Unless photocopies of authorities are provided, lists of authorities should be supplied to the usher by 9 a.m. on the first day of the hearing. Delivery of skeleton arguments does not relieve a party of his or her duty to deliver his or her list of authorities to the usher by the time stated.

7.33 Advocates should exchange lists of authorities by 4 p.m. on the day before the hearing. Any failure in this regard which has the effect of increasing the length of a hearing or of giving rise to delay in the hearing of an application may give rise to an adverse costs order.

7.34 Excessive citation of authority should be avoided and practitioners must have full regard to the matters contained in Practice Direction (Citation of Authorities) [2001] 1 WLR 1001. In particular, the citation of authority should be restricted to the expression of legal principle rather than the application of such principle to particular facts. Practitioners must also, when citing authority, seek to ensure that their citations comply with Practice Direction (Judgments: Neutral Citations) [2002] 1 WLR 346.

Oral argument

7.35 The court may indicate the issues on which it wishes to be addressed and those on which it wishes to be addressed only briefly.

Documents and authorities

7.36 Only the key part of any document or authority should be read aloud in court.

7.37 At any hearing, handing in written material designed to reduce or remove the need for the court to take a manuscript note will assist the court and save time.

Adjournments

7.38 As a timetable for the case will have been fixed at an early stage, applications for adjournment of a trial should only be necessary where there has been a change of circumstances not known when the timetable was fixed.

When to apply:

(1) A party who seeks to have a hearing before a judge adjourned must inform the Chancery Judges' Listing Officer of his or her application as soon as possible.

(2) Applications for an adjournment immediately before a hearing begins should be avoided as they take up valuable time which could be used for dealing with effective business and, if successful, they may result in a loss of court time altogether.

How to apply:

(3) If the application is agreed, the parties should, in writing, apply to the Chancery Judges' Listing Officer. The officer will consult the judge nominated for such matters. The judge may grant the application on conditions and give directions as to a new hearing date. But the judge may direct that the application be listed for a hearing and that all parties attend.

(4) If the adjournment is opposed the party asking for it should apply to the judge nominated for such matters or to the judge to whom the matter has been allocated. A hearing should be arranged, at the first opportunity, through the Chancery Judges' Listing Office.

(5) A short summary of the reasons for the adjournment should be delivered to the Chancery Judges' Listing Office, where possible by 12 noon on the day before the application is made. A witness statement or affidavit is not generally required.

(6) The party requesting an adjournment will, in general, be expected to show that he or she has conducted his or her own case diligently. Parties should take all reasonable steps to ensure that their cases are adequately prepared in sufficient time to enable a hearing before the court to proceed. Likewise, they should take reasonable steps to prepare and serve any document (including any written evidence) required to be served on any other party in sufficient time to enable the other party similarly to be adequately prepared.

(7) If a failure to take reasonable steps necessitates an adjournment, the court may disallow costs as between solicitor and client, or order the person responsible to pay the costs under CPR, r. 48.7, or dismiss the application, or make any other order (including an order for the payment of costs on an indemnity basis).

(8) A trial date may, on occasion, also be vacated by the master in the circumstances envisaged in para. 6.11.

Hearings before masters and registrars

7.39 As in the case of hearings before judges, there must be adequate preparation of cases prior to a hearing before the masters and registrars. Parties must ensure when issuing applications to be heard by the masters and registrars that time estimates are realistic and make proper allowance for the time taken to read any documents required to be read, give judgment and deal with the summary assessment of costs and any application for permission to appeal. The parties must inform the court and all other parties immediately of any material change in a time estimate. Where estimates prove inaccurate, the hearing may have to be adjourned to a later date and the party responsible for the adjournment is likely to be ordered to pay the costs thrown away.

7.40 In the case of a hearing before a master or registrar which is listed for one hour or more and in any other hearing before a master or registrar such as a case management conference, where a bundle would assist, a bundle should be provided.

7.41 Bundles must be provided for a trial or equivalent hearing (such as an account or inquiry or a Part 8 claim with oral evidence) which is listed before a master or a registrar. Such bundles must comply with appendix 6 and contain or be accompanied by a reading list and an estimate of reading time as set out in para. 7.17 above.

7.42 Bundles provided for the use of the master and registrars should be removed promptly after the conclusion of the hearing unless the master or registrar directs otherwise.

Delivery of bundles for hearings before masters

7.43 (1) Bundles should be delivered to Masters' Appointments, Room TM7.09, not less than two (and not more than seven) clear working days before the hearing. They should be clearly marked 'For hearing on [*date*] before Master '. They must not be taken to the Registry (Room TM5.04) or the Chancery Judges' Listing Office, and no document required for any hearing must be taken to the RCJ post room. Documents delivered to the wrong place are unlikely to reach the master in time for the hearing, resulting in probable postponement and the party responsible for the adjournment is likely to be ordered to pay the costs thrown away.

(2) Detailed guidance on where to deliver documents in Chancery Chambers is at appendix 8.

(3) Where no bundle is provided for the use of the master, but a party intends to rely on the exhibits to a witness statement or affidavit, that party must ensure that those documents are filed with the court in sufficient time to be available to be read by the master in advance of the hearing. Documents filed less than 10 days before a hearing must be taken to Masters' Appointments, Room TM7.09, for filing and marked 'For hearing on [*date*] before Master '. (Documents filed before that time should be filed in the Registry, Room TM5.04, in the normal way.) Exhibits should not be placed in lever arch files but should be fastened securely, for example by treasury tags.

Delivery of bundles for hearings before bankruptcy registrars

7.44 Bundles should be delivered to Room TM1.10 not less than two (and not more than seven) clear working days before the hearing. They should be clearly marked 'For hearing on [*date*] before Registrar '.

Delivery of bundles for hearings before Companies Court registrars

7.45 Bundles should be delivered to Room TM4.04 not less than two (and not more than seven) clear working days before the hearing. They should be clearly marked 'For hearing on [*date*] before Registrar '.

Late delivery of bundles for hearings before masters and registrars

7.46 Parties delivering bundles should note that a log will be kept recording the time of their delivery to Rooms TM1.10, TM4.04 and TM7.09. Any failure to comply with these requirements which results in the postponement of a hearing may render that party liable to pay the costs occasioned by the adjournment.

Note: Bundles for hearings before a Chancery judge must be delivered to the Chancery Judges' Listing Office (Room WG4).

Skeleton arguments

7.47 Skeleton arguments should normally be prepared in respect of any application before the master or registrar of one or more hours' duration and certainly for any trial or similar hearing. They are to be delivered to the same place and at the same time as bundles. The contents of the skeleton argument should be in accordance with appendix 7.

7.48 Where a skeleton argument is required, photocopies of any authorities to be relied upon should be attached to the skeleton argument.

7.49 If pursuant to the email protocol for communications with the Chancery Division (para. 14.8 below), a skeleton argument is sent electronically, then the provisions of the protocol as well as the time limits set out above must be followed. In particular, any authorities relied on should be delivered in hard form and, where it would assist, be accompanied by a copy of the skeleton argument in hard form.

7.50 Failure to deliver skeleton arguments or bundles in accordance with this Guide is likely to result in the matter not being heard on the date fixed, the costs of preparation being disallowed and an adverse costs order being made.

Compromise or settlement of hearings

7.51 When hearings before masters are compromised or settled, Masters' Appointments (Room TM7.09) should be informed in writing immediately and in any event no later than 4 p.m. on the day preceding the hearing. In the case of substantial hearings involving pre-reading Masters'

Appointments should be informed immediately if it appears likely that a hearing will be ineffective, with a request that the master is immediately notified. Written notification must be given to Room TM1.10 for bankruptcy hearings and Room TM4.04 for companies hearings. Failure to notify and consequent waste of court time may result in an adverse costs order being made.

Chapter 8 Conduct of a Trial

Key rules: CPR, Parts 32 and 39

8.1 An important aim of all concerned must be to ensure that at trial court time is used as efficiently as possible. Thorough preparation of the case prior to trial is the key to this.

8.2 Chapter 7 of this Guide applies to preparation for a trial as well as for other hearings in court. This chapter contains matters which principally affect trials.

Time limits

8.3 The court may, either at the outset of the trial or at any time thereafter, fix time limits for oral submissions, speeches and the examination and cross-examination of witnesses. (See paras 3.15–16.)

Oral submissions

8.4 In general, and subject to any direction to the contrary by the trial judge, there should be a short opening statement on behalf of the claimant, at the conclusion of which the judge will invite short opening statements on behalf of the other parties.

8.5 Unless notified otherwise, advocates should assume that the judge will have read their skeleton arguments and the principal documents referred to in the reading list lodged in advance of the hearing (see para. 7.17). The judge will state at an early stage how much he or she has read and what arrangements are to be made about reading any documents not already read, for which an adjournment of the trial after opening speeches may be appropriate. If the judge needs to read any documents additional to those mentioned in the reading list lodged in advance of the hearing, a list should be provided during the opening.

8.6 It is normally convenient for any outstanding procedural matters to be dealt with in the course of, or immediately after, the opening speech.

8.7 After the evidence is concluded, and subject to any direction to the contrary by the trial judge, oral closing submissions will be made on behalf of the claimant first, followed by the defendant(s) in the order in which they appear on the claim form, followed by a reply on behalf of the claimant. In a lengthy and complex case each party should provide written summaries of their closing submissions.

8.8 The court may require the written summaries to set out the principal findings of fact for which a party contends.

Witness statements

8.9 In the preparation of witness statements for use at trial, the guidelines in appendix 9 should be followed.

8.10 Unless the court orders otherwise, a witness statement will stand as the witness's evidence-in-chief if he or she is called and confirms that he or she believes the facts stated in the statement are true (CPR, r. 32.5).

8.11 A witness may be allowed to supplement his or her witness statement orally at the trial before submitting to cross-examination, for example to deal with events occurring, or matters discovered, after his or her statement was served, or in response to matters dealt with by another party's witness, but a party seeking to examine in chief a witness who has provided a witness statement must satisfy the judge that there is good reason not to confine the evidence to the contents of his or her witness statement (see r. 32.5(3) and (4)). Where practicable a supplementary witness statement should be prepared and served on the other parties to deal with matters not dealt with in the original witness statement. Permission is required to adduce a supplementary witness statement at trial if any other party objects to it. This need not be sought prior to service; it can be sought at a case management conference if convenient or, if need be, at trial.

8.12 Witnesses are expected to have re-read their witness statements shortly before they are called to give evidence.

8.13 Where a party decides not to call a witness whose witness statement has been served to give oral

Court Guides

evidence at trial, prompt notice of this decision should be given to all other parties. The party should make plain when he or she gives this notice whether he or she proposes to put, or seek to put, the witness statement in as hearsay evidence. If he or she does not put the witness statement in as hearsay evidence, r. 32.5(5) allows any other party to put it in as hearsay evidence.

8.14 Facilities may be available to assist parties or witnesses with special needs, whether as regards access to the court, or audibility in court, or otherwise. The Chancery Judges' Listing Office should be notified of any such needs prior to the hearing. The customer service officer (tel: (020) 7947 7731) can also assist with parking, access etc.

Cross-examination

8.15 The party cross-examining is not necessarily obliged to put his or her case to each witness even if they deal in chief with the same point. It may be sufficient if he or she puts it to one of the other side's witnesses. If that witness makes any admission or expresses any opinion or otherwise adds a qualification to his or her evidence, the party cross-examining can rely on it in argument but he or she cannot assume that other witnesses would have made the same admission or qualification and expressed the same opinion: see *Re Yarn Spinners' Agreement* [1959] 1 All ER 299 at p. 309 per Devlin J.

Expert evidence

8.16 The trial judge may disallow expert evidence which either is not relevant for any reason, or which he or she regards as excessive and disproportionate in all the circumstances, even though permission for the evidence has been given.

8.17 The evidence of experts (or of the experts on a particular topic) is commonly taken together at the same time and after the factual evidence has been given. If this is to be done it should be agreed by the parties before the trial and should be raised with the judge at the PTR, if there is one, or otherwise at the start of the trial. Expert evidence should as far as possible be given by reference to the reports exchanged.

8.18 The evidence of experts must be impartial, complying with r. 35.3. If it is not it may be disregarded.

Physical exhibits

8.19 Some cases involve a number of physical exhibits. The parties should endeavour to agree the exhibits in advance and their system of labelling. Where it would be desirable, a scheme of display should be agreed (e.g. on a board with labels readable from a distance). Where witness statements refer to these, a note in the margin (which can be handwritten) of the exhibit number should be added.

Chapter 9 Judgments, Orders and Proceedings after Judgment

Key rules: CPR, Part 40; PD 40, PD 40B and PD 40D

Judgments

9.1 Where judgment is reserved, the judge will normally deliver his or her judgment by handing down the written text without reading it out in open court. Where this course is adopted, the advocates will be supplied with the full text of the judgment in advance of delivery. In such cases, the advocates should familiarise themselves with the text of the judgment and be ready to deal with any points which may arise when judgment is delivered.

9.2 The text may be shown, in confidence, to the parties, but only for the purpose of obtaining instructions and on the strict understanding that the judgment, or its effect, is not to be disclosed to any other person, or used in the public domain, and that no action is taken (other than internally) in response to the judgment. Advocates should notify the judge's clerk of any obvious errors or omissions.

9.3 The judgment does not take effect until formally delivered in court, when, if requested and so far as practicable, it will be made available to the law reporters and the press. The judge will normally direct that the written judgment may be used for all purposes as the text of the judgment, and that no transcript of the judgment need be made. Where such a direction is made, copies of the judgment may be obtained from the Mechanical Recording Department.

Orders

9.4 It may often be possible for the court to prepare and seal an order more quickly if a draft of the order is handed in. Speed may be particularly important where the order involves the grant of an interim injunction or the appointment of a receiver without notice. In all but the most simple cases a draft order should be prepared and brought to the hearing.

9.5 The court may in any case direct the parties to agree and sign a statement of the terms of the order made by the court (still commonly called a minute of order). Where the proceedings are in the Royal Courts of Justice, the statement should, when agreed and signed, be delivered to Chancery Chambers Registry and Issue Section (Room TM5.04) unless otherwise requested. The statement must, under PD 40B, be filed no later than seven days from the date of the order, unless the court directs otherwise. In the case of any dispute or difficulty as to the contents of the order, the parties should mention the matter to the judge or master who heard the application.

9.6 Where a draft or an agreed statement of the terms of an order exists in electronic form, it is often helpful if the draft or agreed statement is provided to the court by email or on disk as well as in hard copy, particularly if the order needs to be drawn quickly. Any disk supplied for this purpose must be new and newly formatted before writing the material on it so as to minimise the risk of transferring a computer virus. The current word processing system used by the Chancery associates is Word for Windows 2000. Enquiries regarding the provision of disks should be made of the associate responsible for drawing the order in question.

Drafting and service of orders

9.7 Where a judge or master directs that a statement of the terms of an order be agreed and signed, the agreed statement should be lodged in Room TM5.04 as set out in para. 9.5 above. Agreed statements will normally be adopted as the order of the court.

9.8 Orders will be drawn up by the court, unless the judge or master directs that no order be drawn. Unless a contrary order is made, or the party concerned has asked to serve the order, a sealed order will be sent to each party.

9.9 Where a particular order is required to be served personally, the party concerned (see above) will be responsible for service.

9.10 If the order is to be drawn up by a party, three engrossments of the order proposed should be lodged at or posted to:

Chancery Chambers Registry
Room TM5.04 Thomas More Building
Royal Courts of Justice
Strand
London WC2A 2LL

Forms of order

9.11 Recitals will be kept to a minimum and the body of the order will be confined to setting out the decision of the court and the directions required to give effect to it. If upon receipt of an order any party is of the view that it is not drawn up in such a way as to give effect to the decision of the court, prompt notice must be given to the Chancery Chambers Registry in Room TM5.04 and to all other parties setting out the reasons for dissatisfaction. If the differences cannot be resolved, the objecting party may apply on notice for the order to be amended and should do so promptly.

Copies of orders

9.12 Copies of orders may be obtained from Room TM5.04 upon payment of the appropriate fee.

Consent orders

9.13 All consent orders filed in Chancery Chambers and in respect of which a fee has been paid are referred to the master for approval before the order is sealed.

Consent orders under the Inheritance (Provision for Family and Dependants) Act 1975

9.14 Every final order embodying terms of compromise made in proceedings in the Chancery Division under the 1975 Act must under PD 57, para. 18.2, contain a direction that a memorandum of the order shall be endorsed on or permanently annexed to the grant and a copy of the order shall be sent to the Principal Registry of the Family Division with the relevant grant of probate or letters of administration for endorsement notwithstanding that any particular order may not, strictly speaking, be an order under the 1975 Act.

Consents by parties not attending the hearing

9.15 This is covered in paras 5.24 to 5.26 above.

Tomlin orders

9.16 Where proceedings are to be stayed on agreed terms to be scheduled to the order, the draft order should be drawn so as to read, with any appropriate provision in respect of costs, as follows:

> And the parties having agreed to the terms set out in the attached schedule
> IT IS BY CONSENT ORDERED
>
> That all further proceedings in this claim be stayed except for the purpose of carrying such terms into effect
>
> AND for that purpose the parties have permission to apply.

This form of order is called a 'Tomlin order '.

Proceedings after judgment

9.17 Proceedings under judgments and orders in the Chancery Division are now regulated by PD 40, PD 40B and PD 40D.

Directions

9.18 Where a judgment or order directs further proceedings or steps, such as accounts or inquiries, it will often give directions as to how the accounts and inquiries are to be conducted, for example:

for accounts:

(1) who is to lodge the account and within what period;
(2) within what period objection is to be made;
(3) arrangements for inspection of vouchers or other relevant documents;

for inquiries:

(4) whether the inquiry is to proceed on written evidence or with statements of case;
(5) directions for service of such evidence or statements; and
(6) directions as to disclosure.

9.19 If directions are not given in the judgment or order an application should be made to the appropriate master as soon as possible asking for such directions. The application notice should specify the directions sought. Before making the application, applicants should write to the other parties setting out the directions they seek and inviting their response within 14 days. The application to the court should not be made until after the expiry of that period unless there is some special urgency. The application must state that the other parties have been consulted and have attached to it copies of the applicant's letter to the other parties and of any response from them. The master will then consider what directions are appropriate. In complex cases he or she may direct a case management conference.

9.20 If any inquiry is estimated to last more than two days and involves very large sums of money or strongly contested issues of fact or difficult points of law, the master may direct that it be heard by a judge. The parties are under an obligation to consider whether in any particular case the inquiry is more suitable to be heard by a judge and should assist the master in this. Accounts, however long they are estimated to take, will normally be heard by the master. The master is likely to want to give detailed directions in connection with the account and the form of it.

Chapter 10 Appeals

Key rules: CPR, Part 52; PD 52; PD Insolvency Proceedings, para. 17

General

10.1 This chapter is concerned with the following appeals affecting the Chancery Division:

(1) appeals within the ordinary work of the Division, from masters to High Court judges;
(2) insolvency appeals from High Court registrars and from county courts to High Court judges;
(3) appeals to High Court judges in the Chancery Division from orders in claims proceeding in a county court;
(4) statutory appeals from tribunals and others to the Chancery Division.

Proceedings under the Companies Acts are specialist proceedings for the purposes of CPR, r. 49(2), and therefore as regards the destination of appeals. In those cases appeals from final decisions by a registrar of the Companies Court go direct to the Court of Appeal. Such appeals are not covered in this chapter.

10.2 This chapter does not deal with appeals from High Court judges of the Division, except as regards permission to appeal, and as to giving notice to the court of an appeal in a contempt case. It does not deal with appeals in the course of the detailed assessment of costs.

10.3 The detailed procedure for appeals is set out in Part 52 and in PD 52, and in PD Insolvency Proceedings, to which reference should be made. This chapter only refers to some of the salient points.

Permission to appeal

10.4 Permission to appeal is required in all cases except: (a) appeals against committal orders, (b) certain insolvency appeals and (c) certain statutory appeals. Permission to appeal will only be given where the court considers that the appeal would have a real prospect of success or there is some other compelling reason why the appeal should be heard (CPR, r. 52.3(6)).

10.5 An application for permission may be made to the lower court, but only if it is made at the hearing at which the decision to be appealed was made (CPR, r. 52.3(2)(a)). Permission may be granted, or refused, or granted in part (whether as to a part of the order, a ground of appeal or an issue) and refused as to the rest. It may be granted conditionally.

10.6 If the lower court refuses permission, or if permission is not applied for to the lower court at the original hearing, an application for permission may be made to the appeal court, by appeal notice.

10.7 An application to the appeal court for permission may be dealt with without a hearing, but if refused without a hearing the applicant may request that it be reconsidered at a hearing. Notice of the hearing is often given to the respondent; the respondent may submit written representations or attend the hearing but will not necessarily be awarded any costs of so doing even if permission to appeal is refused.

10.8 Guidance for litigants in relation to appeals to the High Court is available by way of a practice statement which may be obtained from the High Court Appeals Office at the Royal Courts of Justice (Room WG4).

10.9 If a party who wishes to appeal cannot lodge all the documents which are required at the time when the appellant's notice is issued, the Appeals Office is able to allow some further time by way of an extension, but beyond this any further extension has to be allowed by a judge, who will consider the case on paper. If there is a delay in obtaining a transcript of the judgment to be appealed, the appellant should endeavour to obtain a note of the judgment, which the lawyers representing any party at the hearing below ought to be able to provide, at least as an interim measure before a transcript is obtained.

10.10 If the documents required for consideration of an application for permission to appeal have not been lodged, despite any extension which has been allowed, the case may be listed for oral hearing in the dismissal list, for the appellant to show cause why the case should not be dismissed. The respondent will not normally be notified of such a hearing.

Time for appealing

10.11 The time limit for an appeal notice to be filed at the appeal court is 14 days after the decision of the lower court to be appealed, unless the lower court fixes some other period, which may be longer or shorter. The lower court can only fix a different period if it does so at the time it makes the order to be appealed from. Otherwise only the appeal court can alter the time limits.

Stay

10.12 Unless the lower court or the appeal court orders otherwise, an appeal does not operate as a stay of any order or decision of the lower court. A stay of execution may be applied for in the appellant's notice. If it is, it may be dealt with on paper. If the stay is required as a matter of great urgency, or before the appellant's notice can be filed, an application should be made to the applications judge.

Appeals from masters in cases proceeding in the Chancery Division

10.13 If permitted, an appeal from a decision of a master in a case proceeding in the Chancery Division usually lies to a High Court judge of the Division. An appeal from a final decision of a master in a claim allocated to the multi-track lies direct to the Court of Appeal.

10.14 Every such appeal is limited to a review of the decision of the lower court, unless the court considers that, in the circumstances of the individual appeal, it would be in the interests of justice to hold a rehearing. This principle applies to all appeals dealt with in this chapter except where some other provision is made, as mentioned below. Unless the court does decide, exceptionally, to hold a rehearing, the appeal will be allowed if the decision of the lower court was wrong or if it was unjust because of a serious procedural or other irregularity in the proceedings in the lower court.

Insolvency appeals

10.15 An appeal lies from a county court (circuit or district judge) or a High Court registrar in bankruptcy or company insolvency matters to a High Court judge of the Chancery Division, for which permission is not required.

10.16 Appeals in proceedings under the Company Directors Disqualification Act 1986 are treated as being in insolvency proceedings.

10.17 The time limit for such an appeal is the same as for ordinary Chancery appeals. An appeal is limited to a review of the decision of the lower court.

Appeals from orders made in county court claims

10.18 An appeal against a decision of a circuit judge in a claim proceeding in a county court lies to the High Court, unless, either, the decision is a final decision in a claim allocated to the multi-track or in specialist proceedings to which r. 49(2) applies, or the decision is itself on an appeal; in either of these cases the appeal lies direct to the Court of Appeal. This does not apply, however, where the allocation to the multi-track is deemed, rather than the result of a specific order, so that in cases begun by a Part 8 claim form, even though they are deemed to be so allocated, appeals lie to the High Court. The general rules as to the requirement for permission described above apply to these appeals.

Statutory appeals

10.19 The Chancery Division hears a variety of appeals and cases stated under statute from decisions of tribunals and other persons. Some of these are listed or referred to in PD 52, but this is not exhaustive. Particular cases include appeals under the Taxes Management Act 1970 and the Inheritance Tax Act 1984, appeals from the Value Added Tax and Duties Tribunal, from the Pensions Ombudsman and the Occupational Pensions Regulatory Authority, from the Comptroller-General of Patents, Designs and Trade Marks, from the Chief Land Registrar, from the Commons Commissioners, and from the Charity Commissioners under the Charities Act 1993.

10.20 Tax and VAT appeals are dealt with in ch. 25 below, and appeals in patent, design and trade mark matters in ch. 23. For other appeals reference should be made to the relevant statute and to PD 52.

Appeals to the Court of Appeal: permission to appeal

10.21 An appeal lies from a judgment of a High Court judge of the Division to the Court of Appeal (unless an enactment makes it final and unappealable), but permission is required in all cases except where the order is for committal. Permission may be granted by the High Court judge, if applied to at the hearing at which the decision to be appealed was made, unless the order of the High Court judge was itself on an appeal, in which case permission may only be granted by the Court of Appeal.

Appeals in cases of contempt of court

10.22 Appellant's notices which by PD 52, para. 21.4, are required to be served on 'the court from whose order or decision the appeal is brought' may be served, in the case of appeals from the Chancery Division, on the Chief Master of the Chancery Division; service may be effected by leaving a copy of the notice of appeal with the clerk of the lists in Room WG4, Royal Courts of Justice, Strand, London WC2A 2LL.

Dismissal by consent

10.23 The practice is as set out in PD 52, para. 12, for all appeals except first appeals in insolvency matters. A document signed by solicitors for all parties must be lodged with the High Court Appeals Office (Room WG7), Royal Courts of Justice, Strand, London WC2A 2LL, requesting dismissal of the appeal. The appeal can be dismissed without any hearing by an order made in the name of the Chancellor. Any orders with directions as to costs will be drawn by the Chancery associates. In the case of a first appeal in an insolvency matter, reference should be made to PD Insolvency Proceedings, para. 17.22(8).

Chapter 11 Costs

Key rules: CPR, Parts 43 to 48 and PD 43–48

11.1 This chapter does not set out to do more than refer to some salient points on costs relevant to proceedings in the Chancery Division. In particular it does not deal with the processes of detailed assessment or appeals in relation to such assessments.

11.2 A number of provisions in respect of costs in the CPR and in PD 43–48 are likely to be relevant to Chancery proceedings:

(1) *Informing the client of costs orders:* Solicitors have a duty to tell their clients, within seven days, if an order for costs is made against them and they were not present at the hearing. Solicitors must also tell anyone else who has instructed them to act on the case or who is liable to pay their fees. They must inform these persons how the order came to be made (CPR, r. 44.2; PD 43–48, para. 7.1).

(2) *Providing the court with estimates of costs:* The court can order a party to file an estimate of costs and to serve it on the other parties (PD 43–48, para. 6.3). This is to assist the court in deciding what case management orders to make and also to inform other parties as to their potential liability for costs. In addition parties must file estimates of costs when they file their allocation questionnaire or any listing questionnaire (PD 43–48, para. 6.4).

(3) *Summary assessment of costs:* An outline of these provisions is given below. Their effect is that in the majority of contested hearings lasting no more than a day the court will decide, at the end of the hearing, not only who is to pay the costs but also how much those costs should be, and will order them to be paid, usually within 14 days. As a result the paying party will have to pay the costs at a much earlier stage than before.

(4) *Interim orders for costs:* Where the court decides immediately who is to pay particular costs, but does not assess the costs summarily, for example, after a trial lasting more than a day, so that the final amount of costs payable has to be fixed by a detailed assessment, the court may order the paying party to pay a sum or sums on account of the ultimate liability for costs.

(5) *Interest on costs:* The court has power to award interest on costs from a date before the date of the order, so compensating the receiving party for the delay between incurring the costs and receiving a payment in respect of them from the paying party.

Summary assessment

11.3 The court will generally make a summary assessment of costs whenever the hearing lasts for less than one day. The judge or master who heard the application or other hearing (which will include a trial, or the hearing of a Part 8 claim, lasting less than a day) carries out the summary assessment. The court may decide not to assess costs summarily either because it orders the costs to be 'costs in the case' or because it considers the case to be otherwise inappropriate for summary assessment, typically because substantial issues arise as to the amount of the costs claimed. Costs payable to a party funded by the Legal Services Commission cannot be assessed summarily.

11.4 In order that the court can assess costs summarily at the end of the hearing each party who intends to claim costs must, no later than 24 hours before the time fixed for the hearing, serve on the other party, and file with the court, his or her statement of costs. PD 43–48, para. 13.5, contains requirements about the information to be included in this statement, and the form of the statement. Failure by a party to file and serve his or her statement of costs as required by PD 43–48, para. 13.5, will be taken into account by the court in deciding what order to make about costs and could result in a very much reduced assessment, in no order being made as to costs, or in the party being penalised in respect of the costs of any further hearing or detailed assessment hearing which may be required as a result of the party's failure.

11.5 Where the receiving party (the party to whom the costs are to be paid) is funded by the Legal Services Commission the court cannot assess costs summarily. It is not, however, prevented from assessing costs summarily by the fact that the paying party (the party by whom the costs are to be paid) is so funded. A summary assessment of costs payable by a person funded by the Legal Services Commission is not by itself a determination of the amount of those costs which the funded party is to pay (as to which see the Access to Justice Act 1999, s. 11, and the Community Legal Service (Costs) Regulations 2000, reg. 10). Ordinarily, where costs are summarily assessed and ordered to be paid by a funded person the order will provide that the determination of any amount which the person who is or was in receipt of services funded by the Legal Services Commission is to pay shall be dealt with in accordance with reg. 10 of the Regulations.

11.6 The amount of costs to be paid by one person to another can be determined on the standard basis or the indemnity basis. The basis to be used is determined when the court decides that a person should pay the costs of another. The usual basis is the standard basis and this is the basis that will apply if the order does not specify the basis of assessment. Costs that are unreasonably incurred or are unreasonable in amount are not allowed on either basis.

11.7 On the standard basis the court only allows costs which are proportionate to the matters in issue. If it has any doubt as to whether the costs were reasonably incurred or reasonable and proportionate in amount, it resolves the doubt in favour of the paying party. The concept of proportionality will always require the court to consider whether the costs which have been incurred were warranted having regard to the issues involved. A successful party who incurs costs which are disproportionate to the issues involved and upon which he or she has succeeded will only recover an amount of costs which the court considers to have been proportionate to those issues.

11.8 On the indemnity basis the court resolves any doubt it may have as to whether the costs were reasonably incurred or were reasonable in amount in favour of the receiving party.

11.9 The court must take into account all the circumstances, including the parties' conduct and the other matters mentioned in CPR, r. 44.5. Indemnity costs are not confined to cases of improper or reprehensible conduct. They will not, however, usually be awarded unless there has been conduct by the paying party which the court regards as unreasonable or unless the case falls within r. 48.4 (see para. 11.13 below).

11.10 A party must normally pay costs which are awarded against him or her and summarily assessed within 14 days of the assessment. But the court can extend that time (rr. 44.8, 3.1(2)(a)). The court may therefore direct payment by instalments, or defer the liability to pay costs until the end of the proceedings so that the costs can then be set against any costs or judgment to which the paying party then becomes entitled.

11.11 If the parties have agreed the amount of costs, they do not need to file a statement of the costs, and summary assessment is unnecessary. If the parties to an application are able to agree an order by consent without the parties attending they should also agree a figure for costs to be inserted in the order or agree that there should be no order as to costs. If the costs position cannot be agreed then the parties will have to attend on the appointment but unless good reason can be shown for the failure of the parties to deal with costs as set out above no costs will be allowed for that attendance. The court finds it most unsatisfactory if parties agree the terms of a consent order but not the provision for costs. Depending on the facts and circumstances, the court may not be able to decide on the question of costs without hearing the application fully, but it is not likely to be consistent with the overriding objective to allow the necessary amount of court time to the dispute on costs in such a case. The court may then have to decide the costs issue on a broad-brush approach, making an order against one party or the other only if it is clear, without spending too much time on it, that such an order would be appropriate, and otherwise making no order as to the costs.

Conditional fee agreements

11.12 The court should be informed, on any application for the payment of costs, if any party has entered into a conditional fee agreement. The court can then consider whether, in the light of that agreement, to stay the payment of any costs which have been summarily assessed until the end of the action, or to decline to order the payment of costs on account under r. 44.3(8).

Other provisions

11.13 Parts 45 to 48, and PD 43–48, contain provisions regarding:

(1) special cases in which costs are payable;

(2) wasted costs;

(3) fixed costs (these are payable for instance if judgment for a sum of money is given in default); and
(4) detailed assessment.

In the context of Chancery litigation attention is drawn to r. 48.2 (costs orders in favour of or against non-parties); r. 48.3 (amount of costs where costs are payable pursuant to a contract) (see further PD 43–48, para. 50, and see also ch. 21 — mortgage claims); and r. 48.4 and PD 43–48, para. 50A (limitations on court's power to award costs in favour of trustee or personal representative). Reference may also be made to ch. 26 as regards costs orders in trust litigation.

Chapter 12 District Registries

General

12.1 Many Chancery cases are heard outside London. There are eight Chancery district registries: Birmingham, Bristol, Cardiff, Leeds, Liverpool, Manchester, Newcastle upon Tyne, and Preston. High Court or circuit Chancery judges sit regularly at all of these centres.

12.2 Outside London, county courts have exclusive jurisdiction in bankruptcy, and proceedings in bankruptcy must therefore be brought in the relevant county court which has bankruptcy jurisdiction rather than in the district registries.

Judges

12.3 Two Chancery judges supervise the arrangements for the hearing of Chancery cases out of London. Mr Justice Hart is the Chancery supervising judge for the Western, Wales and Chester, and Midland circuits. Mr Justice Patten, as Vice-Chancellor of the County Palatine of Lancaster, is concerned with Chancery hearings on the Northern and North Eastern circuits. Both these judges regularly take substantial Chancery matters for hearing outside London. Mr Justice Hart sits regularly in Birmingham, Bristol and Cardiff, but if appropriate will sit elsewhere on the relevant circuit, for example in Chester. Mr Justice Patten sits regularly in Manchester, Liverpool, Leeds and Newcastle, and may sit in Preston or in other court centres on either circuit (e.g. Carlisle or Sheffield) if business so requires.

12.4 There are also specialist circuit judges who have the authority to exercise the powers of a judge of the Chancery Division (under the Supreme Court Act 1981, s. 9, therefore known as section 9 judges) and who normally sit out of London. They exercise a general Chancery jurisdiction, subject to exceptions. Those exceptions are proceedings directly concerning revenue, and proceedings before the Patents Court constituted as part of the Chancery Division under the Patents Act 1977, s. 96.

12.5 Currently the circuit judges who sit regularly in Chancery out of London are:

Judge Weeks QC (Bristol)
Judge Norris QC (Birmingham)
Judge Wyn Williams QC (Cardiff)
Judge Howarth (Manchester, Liverpool and Preston)
Judge Behrens (Leeds and Newcastle)
Judge Kaye QC (Leeds and Newcastle)
Judge Hodge QC (Manchester, Liverpool and Preston)
Judge Gilliland QC (who normally sits in Salford hearing technology and construction cases) and Judges Kershaw QC and Hegarty QC (who are the local mercantile judges based in Manchester and Liverpool) and Judge Raynor QC also assist in the disposal of Chancery business on the Northern Circuit. So also, on the North-Eastern Circuit, does Judge Langan QC who is the mercantile judge for Leeds and Newcastle. The Chancery, Mercantile and TCC judges assist each other in Birmingham, Bristol and Cardiff as well.

12.6 In addition certain other circuit judges and some Queen's counsel are authorised to take Chancery cases on the same basis.

Trials

12.7 If a Chancery case is proceeding in any district registry other than a Chancery district registry, the case should normally be transferred to the appropriate Chancery district registry upon the first occasion the case comes before the court.

12.8 The venue of a Chancery trial out of London will normally be one of the centres mentioned above. However, in many circumstances (e.g. because of the number or age of local witnesses, the need for a site visit, or travel problems) arrangements can be made for a Chancery judge to sit elsewhere.

12.9 In cases of great difficulty or importance the trial may be by a High Court judge. Arrangements can also be made in exceptional circumstances for a High Court judge to deal with any of the matters excepted from the jurisdiction of an authorised circuit judge. Such a judge may be one of the Chancery judges other than Hart or Patten JJ.

12.10 Where it is desired that a case be heard by a specialist Chancery judge outside one of the normal Chancery centres, or be taken by a High Court judge, inquiries should normally be made in the first instance to the listing officer for the nearest Chancery district registry on the relevant circuit. If the need arises, inquiries can also be made to the clerk to Mr Justice Hart or the clerk to Mr Justice Patten, as the case may be. If no relevant clerk is available, inquiries should be made to the Chancery Listing Officer at the Royal Courts of Justice in London. The clerks' contact numbers are in appendix 1.

Applications

12.11 Subject to the following paragraphs any application should normally be made to a district judge (unless it relates to a matter which a district judge does not have power to hear).

12.12 A district judge may of his or her own initiative (for instance because of the complexity of the matter or the need for specialist attention) direct that an application be referred to a High Court or an authorised circuit judge.

12.13 If all or any of the parties consider that the matter should be dealt with by a judge (High Court or circuit), the parties or any of them may arrange that the matter be listed on one of the ordinary application days (see para. 12.14 below). The district judges, who will consult where necessary with one of the Chancery judges (High Court or circuit), are usually available by post or telephone to give guidance on procedural matters, for example the court before which the matter should come or whether the matter may be dealt with in writing.

Application days before a judge

12.14 Application days are listed regularly before a judge, when applications and short appeals, including all interim matters are heard. Normally all matters will be called into court at the commencement of the day in order to work out a running order. Matters will be heard without the court going into private session unless good reason is shown. Rights of audience are unaffected. Application days in Newcastle are subject to the Newcastle telephone application pilot scheme (see PD 23B), and many applications there are dealt with by telephone hearings.

12.15 Application days are: Monday in Birmingham, Thursday in Bristol and Friday in Cardiff. In Manchester and Liverpool application days are on Friday of each week alternating between Manchester and Liverpool. In Leeds and Newcastle Chancery and Mercantile application days are combined. In Leeds applications are heard most Fridays. In Newcastle there is at least one application day each month, on a Friday. An application which needs to be heard urgently may be made, by telephone or in person, on a day other than the regular applications day: the listing officer for the relevant centre should be approached as soon as possible when the need for an urgent hearing arises.

Applications out of hours and telephone applications

12.16 These are governed by the general rules, save that in the case of applications out of hours, the party applying should contact the relevant court office. The main relevant contact numbers are set out in appendix 1. In case of difficulty, contact the Royal Courts of Justice, on the number given in appendix 1.

Agreed interim orders

12.17 Normally a hearing will not be necessary. The procedure is as in the general rules.

12.18 A judge is unlikely to agree to more than two consent adjournments of an interim application. Applications to vacate a trial date will require substantial justification and a hearing, normally before the trial judge.

Local listing arrangements

12.19 Listing arrangements may vary at different centres, depending on availability of judges and courtrooms. The current details are described below.

Birmingham: shared listing

The shared list

12.20 The shared list is primarily for use by the three specialised lists of the Birmingham district registry — those operated by the Chancery, Mercantile and Technology and Construction Courts.

The shared list is in addition to the normal lists of those courts and allows better use to be made of judicial time. Given the settlement rate of trials in the three divisions, two additional cases, the fourth and fifth fixtures, will be listed at any one time, in addition to the three cases listed before the three specialist courts. Those two additional cases will be taken by any of the section 9 judges who become available. Cases are only entered into the shared list if there is a very strong expectation that they will be heard on the day fixed.

In order, therefore, for a case to enter the shared list it must be suitable for hearing before any of the section 9 specialist judges.

Suitability for listing a case in the shared list may be suggested by the district judge at directions stage, or by the parties when applying for the case to be listed. It is likely that fourth and fifth fixtures will be allocated an earlier trial date than a case which has to be heard by the appropriate specialist judge.

The final decision to list a case in the shared list will lie with Judge Norris QC for Chancery cases, Judge Alton for mercantile cases, and Judge Kirkham for technology and construction cases.

Bristol: reserve listing

12.21 In order to make available earlier hearing dates than would otherwise be possible, a reserve list is operated for Chancery cases listed to be heard in the Bristol district registry. Cases in the reserve list are given a fixed date, usually as a second fixture. A second fixture will only be given when there is a very strong expectation of the case being heard on that date. Other judges are called upon in the event of both first and second fixtures being effective.

Cardiff: reserve listing

12.22 Judge Wyn Williams QC sits both as a Chancery judge and a judge of the Technology and Construction Court. His list contains both categories of case. All cases are allocated a fixed starting date but some are first and some reserve fixtures. Other judges are called upon in the event of both first and reserve fixtures being effective. All the judges who sit at the Cardiff Civil Justice Centre (Judges Price QC, Masterman, Chambers QC and Hickinbottom) are authorised to sit as Chancery judges. Any discussions concerning listing should be with the Chancery listing clerk in Cardiff.

Manchester, Liverpool and Preston

The shared list

12.23 When sitting at the same court centre Judge Howarth and Judge Hodge QC will assist each other in the disposal of their respective daily lists. If necessary and if they are available at the relevant court centre, Judge Kershaw QC and Judge Hegarty QC (who are the local mercantile judges) and other circuit judges will assist in the disposal of business. Listing for all Chancery matters in Manchester, Liverpool and Preston is dealt with from Manchester.

Second fixtures

Given the very high settlement rate, most cases will be given a second fixture date as well as a first fixture date. Parties to second fixtures are notified in advance of the hearing date if the case will not be reached on that date. The amount of notice depends on the circumstances of the case. In some cases it may not be until the previous working day but it is usually farther ahead, and longer may be guaranteed in the case of particular difficulties.

Leeds and Newcastle

12.24 When sitting at the same time in Leeds or Newcastle any of Judge Behrens, Judge Langan QC and Judge Kaye QC will assist each other in the disposal of their respective daily lists. The Chancery and Mercantile Court lists are run on a shared basis in both Leeds and Newcastle. Second fixtures are used in the same way as on the Northern Circuit, and on the same basis.

Chapter 13 County Courts

Key rules: CPR, Part 30; PD 7, para. 2

Unified procedure

13.1 A key feature of the civil justice reforms is the introduction of a unified procedure for the High Court and for county courts. The procedure to be followed in both courts is therefore the same.

Chancery cases brought in the county court

13.2 Any county court has jurisdiction to hear a Chancery case, subject to two principal exceptions: (1) a probate claim in a county court must be brought in a county court where there is a Chancery district registry (CPR, r. 57.2(3)); (2) an intellectual property claim must be brought in any such county court or in the Patents County Court (r. 63.13; PD 63, para. 18).

13.3 If a case of a Chancery nature is brought in any county court, the claim form should be marked 'Chancery business' in the top left-hand corner (PD 7, para. 2.5).

13.4 If a Chancery case is brought in a county court which does not coincide with a Chancery district registry, consideration ought to be given at an early stage to whether it needs to have specialist case management or a specialist trial judge, because of the nature of the issues. If it needs either, then it may be necessary to transfer the case to a county court at a Chancery district registry. If there are good reasons against such a transfer, for example because of the distance involved and the convenience of parties or witnesses, then it may be possible, with enough notice, to arrange that the trial is heard by a recorder with Chancery experience or even by a Chancery circuit judge. Guidance has been given to district judges by the Chancery supervising judges as to the circumstances and types of case in respect of which either a transfer or a special arrangement for trial by a judge or recorder with specialist experience may be appropriate.

Transfer to a county court

13.5 Any case which does not require to be heard by a High Court judge, and falls within the jurisdiction of the county courts, may be transferred to a county court. Where a case has been so transferred, the papers must be marked 'Chancery Business' so as to ensure, so far as possible, suitable listing.

13.6 The jurisdiction of county courts is set out in the High Court and County Courts Jurisdiction Order 1991 as amended, and in enactments amended by that Order.

13.7 The jurisdiction of the High Court to transfer cases to a county court is contained in the County Courts Act 1984, s. 40, as substituted by the Courts and Legal Services Act 1990, s. 2(1). Under that section, the court has jurisdiction in certain circumstances to strike out actions which ought to have been begun in a county court.

13.8 A claim with an estimated value of less than £50,000 will generally be transferred to a county court, if the county court has jurisdiction, unless it is either within a specialist list or is within the criteria in CPR, r. 30.3(2).

13.9 If the case is one of a specifically Chancery nature a transfer from the High Court will ordinarily be to the Central London County Court (Chancery list) ('the CLCC') where cases are heard by specialist Chancery circuit judges or recorders and a continuous Chancery list is maintained, unless the parties prefer a transfer to a local county court.

13.10 Even where the estimated value of the claim is more than £50,000 transfer to the CLCC may still be ordered if the criteria in r. 30.3(2) point in that direction, in particular having regard to the criteria in r. 30.3(2)(d), namely the complexity of the facts, legal issues, remedies or procedures involved.

13.11 If a claim is transferred to a county court at the allocation stage no other directions will usually be given and all case management will be left to the county court.

13.12 The Chancery list at the CLCC is managed by the Business Chancery and Patents Section at 26 Park Crescent, London W1N 4HT. The telephone number of the section manager is set out in appendix 1. A guide to the Chancery list may be obtained from the section manager.

13.13 As an alternative to starting the case in the Chancery Division and transferring to the CLCC a case (if appropriate to be started there) may be started at the CLCC and a request made there for it to be transferred to the Chancery list. The request will receive judicial consideration and a transfer will be made if appropriate.

13.14 It should be noted that only in very limited circumstances may freezing orders or search orders be granted in the county court. If necessary, an application may be made in the High Court in aid of the county court proceedings if such an order is to be sought in a case where it cannot be granted in the county court.

13.15 Practitioners should continue to take care that Chancery cases requiring Chancery expertise are dealt with in a county court with a Chancery district registry.

Patents County Court

13.16 See ch. 23 below.

Chapter 14 Use of Information Technology

Key rules: CPR, r. 1.4; CPR, Part 6; PD 6; PD 32, annex 3

General

14.1 The CPR contain certain provisions about the use of information technology in the conduct of cases. Apart from these provisions, no standard practice has evolved or been prescribed for the use of information technology in civil cases, but it is possible to identify certain areas in which electronic techniques may be used which should encourage the efficient and economical conduct of litigation.

14.2 It must be remembered, however, that it is unlikely that the number of litigants in person will diminish, and the number may well increase, in the future and that not all solicitors have available sophisticated IT facilities. Use of IT is acceptable only if no party to the case will be unfairly prejudiced and its use will save time or money.

14.3 A number of specific applications of information technology have been well developed in recent years. The use of fax, the provision of skeleton arguments on disk, and daily transcripts on disk (with or without appropriate software) have become commonplace. Short applications may be economically heard by a conference telephone call, provided that the parties ensure that the judge or master has the relevant documents and a draft order. Taking evidence by video link has become more common, and the available technology has improved considerably. There is still little experience of the intensive use of information technology in the ordinary course of the trial by, for example, providing documents as images to be displayed.

14.4 In any case in which it is proposed to use information technology in the preparation, management and presentation of a case in a manner which is not provided for by the CPR, it may be necessary for directions to be given by the judge who is to hear the case. It is unlikely to be satisfactory for parties and their solicitors to agree to a particular application of information technology (for example, using imaging techniques to deal either with disclosure or with the preparation of documents for use in court, in effect by way of electronic bundles) without the agreement of the judge. Accordingly it is likely, particularly in heavy cases, that it will be desirable for a judge to be nominated to conduct the case. Where a nomination is desired, application should be made to the Chancellor in writing by letter addressed to his clerk for a judge to be nominated.

14.5 In every case in which it is proposed to use information technology, the first step will be for the solicitors for all parties to determine whether it is possible to establish a common protocol for the electronic exchange and management of information. It is recommended that the protocol provided by the Technology and Construction Solicitors Association ('TeCSA') be used. The TeCSA protocol has enjoyed success and is available from TeCSA's website at www.tecsa.org.uk/protocol/protocol.htm. The CPR's underlying policy of cooperation and collaboration is particularly important in this context. In a large case the parties must facilitate the task of the judge by providing any additional help and IT know-how, including for example, demonstrations, which he or she requires in order to control the case properly.

14.6 The Judges of the Chancery Division and their clerks are equipped with IBM-compatible computers running Windows (usually NT 4.0 but in some cases another version) and MS Office 97 or 2000. To avoid compatibility problems it is preferable that text files to be provided for use by a judge or clerk be provided in Rich Text Format (RTF).

Provision of information on disk: skeleton arguments etc.

14.7 Skeleton arguments, chronologies, witness statements, experts' reports and other documents (if available in electronic form) should be provided on disk (or by email) if the judge requests it.

Enquiry should be made of the judge's clerk for this purpose. Where the complexity of the case justifies it, attention must be given to providing the judge with versions of the documents containing links to enable cross-references to be followed up in a convenient manner. Disks provided to judges must be checked for virus contamination and be clean.

Email communications with the Chancery Division

14.8 A protocol for email communications with the Chancery Division sets out how parties may communicate by email on certain matters, and [is in the section of **appendix** 4 headed **A Guide to Emailing the Civil and Family Courts**]. The protocol applies PD 5B on electronic communication and filing of documents in respect of specified documents: skeleton arguments, chronologies, reading lists, lists of issues, lists of authorities (but not the authorities themselves) and lists of dramatis personae sent in advance of a hearing. The protocol sets out the relevant email addresses, which are also to be found in appendix 1. The clerk to the judge concerned should be contacted to find out whether the judge will accept other documents by email and whether documents should be sent by email direct to the judge's clerk's email address.

Transcripts

14.9 The various shorthand writers provide a number of different transcript services. These range from an immediately displayed transcript which follows the evidence as it is given (usually with about 10 seconds' delay) to provision of transcripts of a day's proceedings one or two days in arrears. The use of transcripts is always of assistance if they can be justified on the ground of cost and in long cases they are a considerable advantage. If an instantaneous service is proposed, inquiries should be made of the judge's clerk, and sufficient time for the installation of the equipment necessary and for any familiarisation on the part of the judge with the system should be found. If special transcript-handling software is to be used by the parties, consideration should be given to making the software available to the judge.

14.10 If the shorthand writers make disks available (and nearly all do) the judge should be provided with disks as they appear if he or she requires them.

Fax communications

14.11 The use of fax in the service of documents is now authorised by CPR, r. 6.2(1), and PD 6.

14.12 Each of the judges sitting in the Chancery Division may be reached by fax if the occasion warrants it. The respective judges' clerks' telephone and fax numbers are set out in appendix 1. Where the name of the judge is not known, short documents may be sent to the Chancery Judges' Listing Office, whose fax number is also given in appendix 1. Written evidence should not be sent by fax to this number. All fax messages should have a cover sheet setting out the name of the case, the case number and the judge's name, if known.

Telephone hearings

14.13 Applications may be heard by telephone, if the court so orders, but normally only if all parties entitled to be given notice agree, and none of them intends to be present in person. Special provisions apply where the applicant or another party is in person: see PD 23, para. 6.3. Guidance on other aspects of telephone hearings, and in particular how to set them up, is contained in PD 23, para. 6.5. When putting that guidance into practice once an order has been made for a hearing to take place by a telephone conference call, the following points may be useful:

(1) A telephone hearing may be set up by calling the BT Legal Call Centre on 0800 028 4194. The caller's name and EB account number will have to be given. Other telecommunications providers may also be able to offer the same facility.

(2) The names and telephone numbers of the participants in the hearing including the judge must be provided.

(3) The coordinator should be told the date, time and likely approximate duration of the hearing.

(4) The name and address of the court and the court case reference should be given, for delivery of the tape of the hearing.

(5) Then tell the court that the hearing has been arranged.

It is necessary to ensure that all participants in the hearing have all documents that it may be necessary for any of them to refer to by the time the hearing begins.

Videoconferencing

14.14 The court may allow evidence to be taken using videoconferencing facilities (CPR, r. 32.3). Experience has shown that normally taking evidence by this means is comparatively straightforward, but its suitability may depend on the particular witness, and the case, and on such matters as the volume and nature of documents which need to be referred to in the course of the evidence.

14.15 A video link may also be used for an application, or otherwise in the course of any hearing.

14.16 Annex 3 to PD 32 provides further detail on the manner in which videoconferencing facilities are to be used in civil proceedings.

14.17 Videoconferencing facilities are available at the RCJ in Court 38. It is convenient that these facilities should be used if at all possible in relation to proceedings which are under way in the RCJ. Attention is drawn to the following matters:

(a) Permission to use videoconferencing during a hearing should be obtained as early as possible in the proceedings. If all parties are agreed that the use of videoconferencing is appropriate, then a hearing may not be necessary to obtain such permission.

(b) Before an order fixing the appointment for the use of the facilities at the RCJ is obtained their availability must be ascertained from the video managers (Roger Little/Norman Muller, tel. (020) 7947 7609, fax (020) 7947 6357). When the order is made the video managers must be informed immediately so as to ensure that all necessary arrangements can be made well in advance of the hearing.

(c) If it is necessary for other facilities to be used, whether because the RCJ facilities are unavailable or for any other reason, consideration should be given to using the facilities available at the Bar Council or the Law Society. The party seeking to use the facilities will be responsible for making all the necessary arrangements.

(d) If the use of facilities other than those at the RCJ, the Bar Council or the Law Society is proposed, approval must first be obtained to the use of the particular facilities even if the parties are agreed.

Chapter 15 Miscellaneous Matters

Key rules: CPR, Part 39; PD 39

Litigants in person

15.1 The provisions of this Guide in general apply to litigants in person. Thus, for example, litigants in person should, unless they have good reason for not doing so:

(1) prepare a written summary of their argument in the same circumstances as those in which a represented party is required to produce a skeleton argument;

(2) prepare a bundle of documents in the same way that a represented party is required to produce a bundle of documents; and

(3) be prepared to put forward their argument within a limited time if they are directed to do so by the court.

15.2 This means that litigants in person should identify in advance of the hearing those points which they consider to be their strongest points, and that they should put those points at the forefront of their oral and written submissions to the court.

15.3 It is not the function of court officials to give legal advice. However, subject to that, they will do their best to assist any litigant. Litigants in person who need further assistance should contact the Community Legal Service (CLS) through their Information Points. The CLS is developing local networks of people giving legal assistance such as law centres, local solicitors or the Citizens' Advice Bureaux. CLS Information Points are being set up in libraries and other public places. Litigants can telephone the CLS to find their nearest CLS Information Point on 0845 608 1122 or can log on to the CLS website at www.justask.org.uk for the CLS directory and for legal information.

15.4 The RCJ Advice Bureau off the Main Hall at the Royal Courts of Justice is open from Monday to Friday from 10 a.m. to 1 p.m. and from 2 p.m. to 5 p.m. The bureau is run by lawyers in conjunction with the Citizens' Advice Bureau and is independent of the court. The Bureau operates on a 'first come first served' basis, or telephone advice is available on 0845 120 3715 (or (020) 7947 6880) from Monday to Friday between 11 a.m. and 12 noon and between 3 and 4 p.m. The Bureau also operates a Bankruptcy Court Advice Desk on

Monday and Wednesday mornings (10 a.m. to 1 p.m.) in the Consultation Room, 1st Floor, Thomas More Building.

15.5 Where a litigant in person is the applicant, the court may ask one of the represented parties to open the matter briefly and impartially, and to summarise the issues.

15.6 It is the duty of an advocate to ensure that the court is informed of all relevant decisions and enactments of which the advocate is aware (whether favourable or not to his or her case) and to draw the court's attention to any material irregularity.

15.7 Representatives for other parties must treat litigants in person with consideration. They should where possible be given photocopies of any authorities which are to be cited before the case starts in addition to the skeleton argument. They should be asked to give their names to the usher if they have not already done so. Representatives for other parties should explain the court's order after the hearing if the litigant in person does not appear to understand it.

15.8 If a litigant in person wishes to give oral evidence he or she will generally be required to do so from the witness box in the same manner as any other witness of fact.

15.9 A litigant in person must give an address for service in England or Wales. If he or she is a claimant, the address will be in the claim form or other document by which the proceedings are brought. If he or she is a defendant, it will be in the acknowledgment of service form which he or she must send to the court on being served with the proceedings. It is essential that any change of address should be notified in writing to Chancery Chambers and to all other parties to the case.

15.10 Notice of hearing dates will be given by post to litigants at the address shown in the court file. A litigant in person will generally be given a fixed date for trial on application. A litigant in person who wishes to apply for a fixed date should ask the Chancery Judges' Listing Office for a copy of its Guidance Notes for Litigants in Person.

Assistance to litigants in person

15.11 A litigant who is acting in person may be assisted at a hearing by another person, often referred to as a McKenzie friend (see *McKenzie v McKenzie* [1971] P 33). The litigant must be present at the hearing. If the hearing is in private, it is a matter of discretion for the court whether such an assistant is allowed to attend the hearing. That may depend, among other things, on the nature of the proceedings.

15.12 The McKenzie friend is allowed to help by taking notes, quietly prompting the litigant and offering advice and suggestions to the litigant. The court can, and sometimes does, permit the McKenzie friend to address the court on behalf of the litigant, by making an order to that effect under the Courts and Legal Services Act 1990, s. 27(2)(c) (by reference to ss. 17 and 18 of that Act), but this is an exceptional course. Some factors which may be relevant to whether this should be permitted have been discussed in reported judgments, including *Izzo v Ross* [2002] BIPR 310 and *Paragon Finance plc v Noueiri* [2001] EWCA Civ 1402, [2001] 1 WLR 2357.

15.13 The Personal Support Unit (Room M104) offers personal support for litigants in person, witnesses and others. The PSU will sometimes be able to accompany litigants into court to provide emotional support and give other guidance, but it does not give legal advice.

Representation on behalf of companies

15.14 Rule 39.6 of the CPR allows a company or other corporation to be represented at trial by an employee if the employee has been authorised by the company or corporation to appear on its behalf and the court gives permission. PD 39, para. 5, describes what is needed to obtain permission from the court for this purpose and mentions some of the considerations relevant to the grant or refusal of permission.

Robed and unrobed hearings

15.15 Advocates (and judges) wear robes at hearings by High Court judges of trials (including preliminary issues) and statutory appeals or cases stated. Robes are not worn for other hearings, including appeals from masters, bankruptcy registrars and county courts. The daily cause list states, in relation to each judge's list, whether the matter is to be heard robed or unrobed. Robes are not worn at hearings before masters. Robes are worn at the following hearings before bankruptcy and Companies Court registrars: public examinations of bankrupts and of directors or other officers of companies; applications for discharge from bankruptcy or for suspension of such discharge; all proceedings under the Company Directors

Disqualification Act 1986; petitions to wind up companies; final hearings of petitions for the reduction of capital of companies.

Solicitors' rights of audience

15.16 At hearings in chambers before 26 April 1999 solicitors had general rights of audience. The fact that a matter which would then have been heard in chambers is now heard in public under CPR, Part 39, does not affect rights of audience, so in such matters as would have been heard in chambers previously, the general right of audience for solicitors continues to apply. Such cases included appeals from masters, applications for summary judgment, and those concerned with pleadings, security for costs and the like, pre-trial reviews, and applications concerned with the administration of a deceased person's estate, a trust or a charity. They did not include applications in what is now the interim applications list or the Companies Court, nor appeals from county courts or insolvency appeals. Solicitors do, however, have general rights of audience in personal insolvency matters; this is not affected by whether the hearing is in public or private.

15.17 If a solicitor who does not have the appropriate special right of audience wishes to be heard in a case which is not one which, before 26 April 1999, would have been heard in chambers nor a personal insolvency case, an application may be made for the grant of a special right of audience before the particular court and for the particular proceedings under the Courts and Legal Services Act 1990, s. 27(2)(c).

Recording at hearings

15.18 In the Royal Courts of Justice it is normal to record all oral evidence and any judgment delivered during a hearing before a judge. If any party wishes a recording to be made of any other part of the proceedings, this should be mentioned in advance or at the time of the hearing.

15.19 At hearings before masters, it is not normally practicable to record anything other than any oral evidence and the judgment, but these will be recorded. No party or member of the public may use recording equipment without the court's permission.

Chapter 16 Suggestions for Improvement and Court Users' Committees

16.1 Suggestions for improvements in this Guide or in the practice or procedure of the Chancery Division are welcome. If they do not fall within the remit of the committees mentioned at paras 16.3 to 16.7 below, they should be sent to the clerk to the Chancellor.

Chancery Division Court Users' Committee

16.2 The Chancery Division Court Users' Committee's function is to review, as may from time to time be required, the practice and procedure of all courts forming part of the Chancery Division, to ensure that they continue to provide a just, economical and expeditious system for the resolution of disputes. The Chancellor is the chairman. Its membership includes judges, a master, barristers, solicitors and other representatives of court staff and users. Meetings are held three times a year, and more often if necessary. Suggestions for points to be considered by the committee should be sent to the clerk to the Chancellor.

Insolvency Court Users' Committee

16.3 Proposals for change in insolvency matters fall within the remit of the Insolvency Court Users' Committee unless they relate to the Insolvency Rules 1986. The members of the Insolvency Court Users' Committee include members of the Bar, the Law Society, the Insolvency Service and the Society of Practitioners of Insolvency. Meetings are held three times a year, and more often if necessary. Suggestions for points to be considered by the committee should be sent to the clerk to the Chancellor.

Insolvency Rules Committee

16.4 The Insolvency Rules Committee must be consulted before any changes to the Insolvency Rules 1986 are made. The Chairman of the Insolvency Rules Committee is Mr Justice David Richards. Proposals for changes in the Rules should be sent to The Insolvency Service, Room 502, PO Box 203, 21 Bloomsbury Street, London WC1B 3QW, with a copy to the clerk to Mr Justice David Richards.

Intellectual Property Court Users' Committee

16.5 This considers the problems and concerns of intellectual property litigation generally. Membership of the committee includes the principal patent judges, a representative of each of the Patent Bar Association, the Intellectual Property Lawyers Association, the Chartered Institute of Patent Agents, the Institute of Trade Mark Agents and the Trade Marks Designs and Patents Federation. It will also include one or more other Chancery judges. The chairman is Mr Justice Pumfrey. Anyone having views concerning the improvement of intellectual property litigation is invited to make his or her views known to the committee, preferably through the relevant professional representative on the committee.

Pension Litigation Court Users' Committee

16.6 This consists of a judge and a master, two barristers and two solicitors. Its chairman is Mr Justice Etherton. Any suggestions for consideration by the committee should be sent to the clerk to Mr Justice Etherton.

Court users' committees outside London

16.7 There are several court users' committees relating to Chancery work on circuit. They are as follows:

(1) The Northern Circuit and the North-Eastern Circuit Court Users' Committees: the Northern Circuit Chancery Court Users' Committee, which meets in Manchester; the Leeds Chancery and Mercantile Court Users' Committee; and the Newcastle Joint Chancery Mercantile and TCC Court Users' Committee. Each of these meets two or three times a year, and has a membership including judges, court staff, barristers and solicitors. The Vice-Chancellor of the County Palatine of Lancaster chairs these three committees, and the Vice-Chancellor's clerk acts as secretary to each committee. All communications should be to the clerk.

(2) The Western Circuit, Wales and Chester and Midland Circuits Court User Committees: the circuit committees normally meet three or four times per year. They have a membership including judges, court staff, barristers and solicitors.

(a) *Western Circuit:* Judge Weeks chairs the committee in Bristol (or Mr Justice Hart when there), Mrs Liz Bodman acts as secretary. All communications should be addressed to her at Chancery Listing Section, Bristol Crown Court, Small Street, Bristol.

(b) *Wales and Chester Circuit:* Judge Williams chairs the committee in Cardiff (or Mr Justice Hart when there), the diary manager, Annette Parsons acts as secretary. All communications should be addressed to her at Cardiff Civil Justice Centre, 2 Park Street, Cardiff.

(c) *Midland Circuit:* Judge Norris chairs the committee in Birmingham (or Mr Justice Hart when there), the Chancery listing officer, Amanda Lee acts as secretary. All communications should be addressed to her at Chancery Listing Section, Birmingham Civil Justice Centre, 33 Bull Street, Birmingham.

Chapter 17 Alternative Dispute Resolution

Key rules: CPR, rr. 3.1 and 26.4

17.1 While emphasising the primary role of the court as a forum for deciding cases, the court encourages parties to consider the use of ADR (such as, but not confined to, mediation and conciliation) as a possible means of resolving disputes or particular issues.

17.2 The settlement of disputes by means of ADR can:

(1) significantly help litigants to save costs;

(2) save litigants the delay of litigation in reaching finality in their disputes;

(3) enable litigants to achieve settlement of their disputes while preserving their existing commercial relationships and market reputation;

(4) provide litigants with a wider range of solutions than those offered by litigation; and

(5) make a substantial contribution to the more efficient use of judicial resources.

17.3 The court will in an appropriate case invite the parties to consider whether their dispute, or particular issues in it, could be resolved through ADR. In particular, it is to be expected that the judge or master at any case management conference will inquire what steps can usefully be taken to resolve the dispute by settlement discussion, alternative dispute resolution or other means. The parties should be in a position to tell the court what steps have been taken or are proposed to be taken. The court may also adjourn the case for a specified period of time to encourage and enable the parties to use ADR and for this purpose extend the time for compliance by the parties or any of them with any requirement under the CPR or this Guide or any order of the court. The court may make such order as to the costs that the parties may incur by reason of the adjournment or their using or attempting to use ADR as may in all the circumstances seem appropriate.

17.4 Legal representatives in all cases should consider with their clients and the other parties concerned the possibility of attempting to resolve the dispute or particular issues by ADR and they should ensure that their clients are fully informed as to the most cost-effective means of resolving their dispute.

17.5 Parties who consider that ADR might be an appropriate means of resolving their dispute, or particular issues in the dispute, may apply for directions at any stage.

17.6 The clerk to the Commercial Court keeps some published information as to individuals and bodies that offer ADR services. (The list also includes individuals and bodies that offer arbitration services.) If the parties are unable to agree upon a neutral individual, or panel of individuals, for ADR, they may refer to the judge for assistance, though the court will not recommend any particular body or individual to act as mediator or arbitrator.

SECTION B SPECIALIST WORK

Chapter 18 Introduction to the Specialist Work of the Chancery Division

18.1 As explained in ch. 1 of this Guide, some proceedings in the High Court must be brought in the Chancery Division. These matters include:

(1) claims for the sale, exchange or partition of land, or the raising of charges on land;
(2) mortgage claims;
(3) claims relating to the execution of trusts;
(4) claims relating to the administration of the estates of deceased persons;
(5) bankruptcy matters;
(6) claims for the dissolution of partnerships or the taking of partnership or other accounts;
(7) claims for the rectification, setting aside or cancellation of deeds or other instruments in writing;
(8) contentious probate business;
(9) claims relating to patents, trade marks, registered designs, copyright or design right;
(10) claims for the appointment of a guardian of a minor's estate;
(11) jurisdiction under the Companies Act 1985 and the Insolvency Act 1986 relating to companies;
(12) some revenue matters;
(13) claims relating to charities;
(14) some proceedings under the Solicitors Act 1974;
(15) proceedings under the Landlord and Tenant Act 1927, part I, the Landlord and Tenant Act 1954, part II, the Landlord and Tenant Act 1987 and the Leasehold Reform Act 1967;
(16) proceedings (other than those in the Commercial Court) relating to the application of arts 81 and 82 of the EC Treaty and the equivalent provisions of the Competition Act 1998; and
(17) proceedings under other miscellaneous statutory jurisdictions.

18.2 There is concurrent jurisdiction with the Family Division under the Inheritance (Provision for Family and Dependants) Act 1975.

18.3 Certain appeals lie to the Chancery Division under statute. These are dealt with in para. 10.19. Intellectual property appeals and revenue appeals are also covered in ch. 23 and 25 respectively.

18.4 The Chancery judges are the nominated judges of the Court of Protection but this Guide does not deal with the Court of Protection.

Chapter 19 The Bankruptcy Court

Key rules: PD Insolvency Proceedings; Insolvency Rules 1986 (SI 1986/1925)

19.1 The Bankruptcy Court is part of the Chancery Division and disposes of proceedings relating to insolvent individuals arising under parts VIII to XI of the Insolvency Act 1986 and related legislation. These include applications for interim orders to support an individual voluntary arrangement, applications to set aside a statutory demand, bankruptcy petitions and various applications concerned with the realisation and distribution of the assets of individuals who have been adjudged bankrupt, as well as proceedings concerning the administration in bankruptcy of the insolvent estate of a deceased person. The procedure in the Bankruptcy Court is governed by the Insolvency Rules 1986 and PD Insolvency Proceedings. Appeals in bankruptcy matters are covered in ch. 10.

19.2 Proceedings in the Bankruptcy Court are issued in the Bankruptcy Issue and Search Room and are dealt with by the registrars in bankruptcy, not the masters. Proceedings under parts VIII to XI of the Insolvency Act 1986 should be entitled 'IN BANKRUPTCY'.

19.3 Certain matters, such as applications for injunctions or for committal for contempt, are heard by a judge. A judge is available to hear such matters each day in term time and applications may be listed for any such day. The judge will normally also be hearing the interim applications list for the day, but one or more other judges may be available to assist if necessary.

19.4 The registrar may refer or adjourn proceedings to the judge, having regard to such matters as the complexity of the proceedings, whether the proceedings raise new or controversial points of law, the likely date and length of the hearing, public interest in the proceedings, and the availability of relevant specialist expertise. When proceedings have been referred or adjourned to the judge, interim applications and applications for directions or case management will be listed before a judge, except where liberty to apply to the registrar has been given.

19.5 There are prescribed forms for use in connection with all types of statutory demand and of petitions for bankruptcy orders. Every other type of application is either an originating application in form 7.1 (meaning an application to the court which is not an application in pending proceedings before the court) or an ordinary application in form 7.2 (meaning any other application to the court).

Statutory demands

19.6 All applications to set aside a statutory demand are referred initially to a registrar. The application may be dismissed by the court without a hearing if it fails to disclose sufficient grounds (see PD Insolvency Proceedings, para. 12.4, and Insolvency Rules 1986, r. 6.5(4)). If it is not dismissed summarily, it will be allocated a hearing date when the registrar may either dispose of it summarily or give directions for its disposal at a later date. Such directions will commonly include an order for the filing and service of written evidence and a listing certificate of compliance (see para. 19.13 below).

Bankruptcy petitions

19.7 The court will not normally allow more than one bankruptcy petition to be presented against an individual at any one time.

19.8 In cases where the statutory demand relied on has not been personally served on the debtor or where execution of the debt has been returned unsatisfied in whole or in part, the permission of the registrar is required before a petition may be presented to the court. For service of statutory demands PD Insolvency Proceedings, paras 10, 11 and 13.

19.9 On presentation to the court a bankruptcy petition is given a distinctive number. The details of the name and address of the petitioner, of his solicitors and of the debtor are entered on a computerised record which may be searched by attendance at the Issue and Search Room. It will also be endorsed with a hearing date which may be extended on application without notice if the petitioner has been unable to serve the petition on the debtor before the hearing date (see PD Insolvency Proceedings, para. 14).

19.10 A debtor who intends to oppose the making of a bankruptcy order should file and serve a written notice in the prescribed form stating his grounds for opposing the petition not less than seven days before the hearing date. The court may give such further directions as to the filing of evidence and of certificates of compliance (see para. 19.13 below) as it considers appropriate to the disposal of the petition.

Other applications

19.11 Many different types of application may be made to the court for the purpose of the administration of the estate and affairs of a bankrupt individual or insolvent person who is subject to an individual voluntary arrangement (IVA). These may involve such matters as the examination of the bankrupt or of persons having knowledge of his affairs, the realisation of assets in his estate and the determination of disputes regarding the validity of a creditor's claim to dividend or entitlement to vote at a creditors' meeting. Such applications will be given a hearing date when the registrar will give such directions as are appropriate to the type of case, which may include directions for the filing and service of written evidence, for the cross-examination of witnesses and for the filing of certificates of compliance (see para. 19.13 below).

Orders without attendance

19.12 In suitable cases the court will normally be prepared to make orders under part VIII of the Insolvency Act 1986 (interim orders for IVAs) and consent orders without attendance by the parties. Details of these types of order are set out in PD Insolvency Proceedings, para. 16.

Listing certificates

19.13 In order to prevent waste of the court's time each party to insolvency proceedings may be required by the court to file a listing certificate in which he will be required to certify whether the directions previously given by the court have been complied with, whether and by whom he will be represented at the final hearing, his estimate of the time required for such hearing and his and his representative's dates to avoid. On the filing of the certificates in any particular case the court will fix a date for the final hearing of the case and notify the parties.

Preparation for hearings before the registrars

19.14 Paragraphs 7.39 to 7.50 apply to hearings before the bankruptcy registrars. Skeleton arguments and bundles should be delivered to the Bankruptcy Registry.

General information

19.15 Inspection of the court's record and court file in any insolvency proceedings is governed by the Insolvency Rules 1986, rr. 7.28 and 7.31.

19.16 The following publications regarding practice and procedure in the Bankruptcy Court are available free from the Bankruptcy Issue and Search Room and from Room TM1.10 Thomas More Building, Royal Courts of Justice:

(1) *Current Practice Direction and Practice Notes.*
(2) *A Concise Guide to Procedure in the Bankruptcy Court.*
(3) *'I Want to Set Aside My Statutory Demand — What Do I Do?'*
(4) *'I Have a Petition against Me — What Do I Do?'*
(5) *'I Want to Appeal an Order Made by a District Judge or an Order Made by a Bankruptcy Registrar of the High Court — What Can I Do?'*
(6) *'I Wish to Apply for my Certificate of Discharge from Bankruptcy — What Do I Do?'*
(7) *Dealing with Debt — How to Make Someone Bankrupt.*
(8) *Dealing with Debt — How to Petition for Your Own Bankruptcy.*

Chapter 20 The Companies Court

Key rules: PD 49B; PD Insolvency Proceedings; Insolvency Rules 1986 (SI 1986/1925); Insolvent Companies (Disqualification of Unfit Directors) Proceedings Rules 1987 (SI 1987/2023); PD Directors Disqualification Proceedings

20.1 The Companies Court is a part of the Chancery Division. Applications in the High Court under the Companies Act 1985, the Insurance Companies Act 1982, the Financial Services and Markets Act 2002, the Insolvency Act 1986 in relation to companies registered in England and Wales, and the Company Directors Disqualification Act 1986, must be commenced in the Companies Court. Proceedings concerning insolvent partnerships, under the Insolvent Partnerships Order 1994 (SI 1994/2421), are also brought in the Companies Court (unlike proceedings against partners separately, which, if the partner is an individual, are brought in bankruptcy). Many other kinds of application are brought in the Companies Court. Appeals in Companies Court matters are dealt with in ch. 10.

20.2 Applications, other than in insolvency, are governed by the CPR and PD 49B.

20.3 Applications in insolvency relating to companies (and to insolvent partnerships) are governed by the Insolvency Rules 1986 and PD Insolvency Proceedings.

20.4 Proceedings under the Company Directors Disqualification Act 1986 are governed by the Insolvent Companies (Disqualification of Unfit Directors) Proceedings Rules 1987 and PD Directors Disqualification Proceedings.

20.5 Proceedings in the Companies Court under a particular statute should be entitled accordingly, thus:

In the matter of [*name and registration number of the company*] And in the matter of the Companies Act 1985 [*and of any other statute as appropriate*]

In the matter of [*name of the relevant company*] And in the matter of the Company Directors Disqualification Act 1986

In the matter of [*name of the debtor*] And in the matter of the Insolvency Act 1986 [*and of any appropriate order, such as the Insolvent Partnerships Order 1994*]

20.6 The Companies Court has a separate administrative procedure. Proceedings are issued in the Companies Court General Office, and they are dealt with by the registrars.

20.7 Petitions for winding up, petitions for confirmation by the court of reduction of capital, and interim applications for directions in proceedings by shareholders are among the principal matters heard by the registrars. A registrar may direct that any case be heard by a judge even if it is a kind of application which would normally be heard by a registrar.

20.8 Certain matters such as applications for an administration order under part II of the Insolvency Act 1986, petitions for approval by the court of schemes of arrangement and applications for the appointment of provisional liquidators are heard by a judge. A judge is available to hear companies matters each day in term time, and applications to be heard by that judge may be listed for any such day. The judge will normally also be hearing the interim applications list for the day, but one or more other judges may be available to assist if necessary. The registrar may refer or adjourn proceedings to the judge in accordance with the criteria set out in para. 19.4 above.

Preparation for hearings before the registrars

20.9 Paragraphs 7.39 to 7.50 apply to hearings before the registrars of the Companies Court. Skeleton arguments and bundles should be delivered to the Companies Court Issue Section.

Aadministration orders

20.10 The statutory regime for administrations commencing on or after 15 September 2003, with certain exceptions, is found in the Insolvency Act 1986, sch. B1, which should be read with the new part 2 of the Insolvency Rules 1986. Administrations commenced before 15 September 2003 and administrations of certain bodies (building societies, insolvent partnerships, limited liability partnerships, certain insurers, and public utility companies listed in the Enterprise Act 2002, s. 249(1)(a) to (d)) continue to be governed by part II of the Insolvency Act 1986 (as enacted before the introduction of sch. B1) and the former part 2 of the Insolvency Rules 1986. Administration creates a statutory moratorium and allows the affairs, business and property of the company to be managed by an administrator.

20.11 Administrators may be appointed by the court or out of court. By the Insolvency Act 1986, sch. B1, para. 3(1), the administrator must perform his duties with the objective of:

(1) rescuing the company as a going concern, or

(2) achieving a better result for the company's creditors as a whole than would be likely if the company were wound up (without first being in administration), or

(3) realising property in order to make a distribution to one or more secured or preferential creditors.

Court order

20.12 An application to the court must be commenced by the prescribed form of application (form 2.1B under the new regime) and must be supported by an affidavit. The Act and Rules specify the information which must be included in the affidavit. The application may be made by the company, its directors, one or more creditors, the [designated officer*] for a magistrates' court

[* Text updated editorially.]

(in relation to a fine) or any combination of the above. The application will be listed before a judge.

20.13 To make the order the court must be satisfied that the company is or is likely to become unable to pay its debts and that the administration order is likely to achieve the purpose of the administration.

Out of court

20.14 Under the new regime, the holder of a qualifying floating charge, the company or its directors, may appoint an administrator without going through the court process. The appointment becomes effective when a notice of appointment in the prescribed form accompanied by the administrator's consent to act and a statement by him that in his opinion the purpose of the administration is likely to be achieved has been filed with the court. Rule 2.19 of the Insolvency Rules 1986 makes special provision for filing notice of appointment by fax out of business hours (form 2.7B). The fax number for filing notice in the Royal Courts of Justice is (020) 7947 6607.

Schemes of arrangement

20.15 A scheme under the Companies Act 1985, s. 425, can be proposed whether or not a company is in liquidation. It is necessary to obtain the sanction of the court to a scheme which has been approved by the requisite majority of members or creditors of each class at separately convened meetings directed by the court. If the company is insolvent the objective of the scheme may be more simply and economically achieved by a company voluntary arrangement under part I of the Insolvency Act 1986. However, a scheme under the Companies Act 1985, s. 425, has the advantage that the court may approve the distribution of assets otherwise than in accordance with creditors' strict legal rights.

20.16 The application for an order to convene meetings of members or creditors under s. 425(1) is made by a CPR, Part 8, claim form. The application will usually be heard by a registrar, unless it is thought that issues of difficulty may arise, in which case it can be heard by a judge. The relevant practice is set out in Practice Statement (Companies: Schemes of Arrangement) [2002] 1 WLR 1345.

20.17 The application to sanction a scheme of arrangement, once approved by members or creditors by the statutory majority, is made by petition. The hearing of the petition at which the sanction of the court is sought will be before a judge. If the petition also seeks confirmation of a reduction of capital, there will first be an application to the registrar for directions. In other cases the petition will go straight to a judge.

Winding-up petitions

20.18 Proceedings to wind up a company are commenced by presenting a petition to the court. The presentation of a winding-up petition can cause substantial damage to a company. A winding-up petition should not be presented when it is known that there is a real dispute about the debt. Practitioners should make reasonable enquiries from their client as to the existence of any such dispute. The court may order a petitioner to pay the company's costs of a petition based on a disputed debt on the indemnity basis.

20.19 When a winding-up petition is presented to either the Companies Court, a Chancery district registry or a county court having jurisdiction, particulars including the name of the company and the petitioner's solicitors are entered in a computerised register. This is called the Central Registry of Winding-up Petitions. It may be searched by personal attendance at the Companies Court General Office, or by telephone on (020) 7947 7328.

20.20 The requirement to advertise the petition (Insolvency Rules 1986, r. 4.11(2)(b)) is mandatory, and designed to ensure that the class remedy of winding up by the court is made available to all creditors, and is not used simply as a means of putting pressure on the company to pay the petitioner's debt. Failure to comply with the rule, without good reason accepted by the court, may lead to the summary dismissal of the petition on the return date (Insolvency Rules 1986, r. 4.11(5)). If the court, in its discretion, grants an adjournment, this will be on condition that the petition is advertised in due time for the adjourned hearing. No further adjournment for the purpose of advertisement will normally be granted.

20.21 If an order is made restraining advertisement while an application is made to the court to stop the proceedings, the case is listed in the daily cause list by number only so that the name of the company is not given.

Proceedings for relief from unfairly prejudicial conduct under the Companies Act 1985, section 459

20.22 Cases under the Companies Act 1985, s. 459, are liable to involve extensive factual enquiry and many of the measures summarised in Section A of this Guide which are designed to avoid unnecessary cost and delay are particularly relevant to them. Procedure is governed by the Companies (Unfair Prejudice Applications) Proceedings Rules 1986 (SI 1986/2000).

20.23 Where applications are brought in the Companies Court and in a related case in the Chancery Division at the same time, special arrangements can be made on request to the Chancery Judges' Listing Officer for the applications to be heard by the same judge.

Applications for leave to act as director of a company with a prohibited name

20.24 The Insolvency Act 1986, s. 216, restricts the use of a company name by any person who was a director or shadow director of the company in the 12-month period ending with the day upon which it went into insolvent liquidation — except with the leave of the court (s. 216(3)).

20.25 The application for leave is governed by the Insolvency Rules 1986, rr. 4.226 to 4.230. These rules provide for certain exceptions to the prohibition. The application for leave is by originating application supported by written evidence.

20.26 By r. 4.227 the court may call upon the liquidator for a report of the circumstances in which the company became insolvent and the extent of the applicant's apparent responsibility. However, if the liquidator consents to the application it is helpful if his views are put before the court at the outset. The registrar who then hears the application may be prepared to grant it at the first hearing.

20.27 Notice should be given to the Secretary of State and/or the official receiver.

General

20.28 Inspection of the court's records and the court file in any insolvency proceedings is governed by Insolvency Rules 1986, rr. 7.28 and 7.31.

20.29 The following leaflets are available from the Companies Court General Office:

(1) *Current Practice Directions and Practice Notes.*
(2) *'I Want to Wind up a Company: What Do I Do?'*
(3) *Treasury Solicitors' — A Guide to Company Restoration*
(4) *'I Want to Apply to Extend Time for Registration of a Charge or to Rectify a Misstatement or Omission (in the Registered Particulars of a Charge or of a Memorandum of Satisfaction): What Do I Do?'*
(5) *Dealing with Debt: How to Wind up Your Own Company*

Chapter 21 Mortgage Claims

Key rules: CPR, Parts 55 and 73; PD 55; PD 73

21.1 Under CPR, Part 55, mortgage possession claims commenced since 15 October 2001, whether in respect of residential or commercial property, are generally heard in the county courts. The only exceptions to this are (a) a relatively small number of cases where either the county court has no jurisdiction or where the claimant can certify, verified by a statement of truth, the reasons for bringing the claim in the High Court and (b) any remaining transitional cases, i.e. mortgage possession claims commenced before 15 October 2001, and proceedings to enforce charging orders commenced prior to 25 March 2002, as to which directions should be sought from the assigned master.

21.2 PD 55 emphasises that High Court claims are to be regarded as exceptional and that while the value of the property and the size of the claim may well be relevant circumstances they will not, taken alone, normally justify the issue of proceedings in the High Court. High Court proceedings may, however, be justified where there are complicated disputes of fact or where a claim gives rise to points of law of general importance. Where a mortgage possession claim is issued in the High Court it is assigned to the Chancery Division. The provisions of CPR, Part 55, will apply to it.

21.3 The most common instance where, notwithstanding Part 55, the Chancery Division will retain jurisdiction in a mortgage possession case is where proceedings are brought seeking an order for sale under an equitable charge, ordinarily that created by a charging order, but where part of the relief claimed ancillary to the order for sale is an order for possession. Although r. 73.10 now provides that proceedings to enforce charging orders by sale should be made in the court in which the charging order was made, that provision is expressly subject to that court having jurisdiction. The jurisdiction of a county court to enforce a charge is confined to those cases where the amount secured by the charge falls within the relevant county court limit (currently £30,000) and it follows that in many cases where judgments have been obtained in county courts and charging orders made enforcement will nonetheless require proceedings in the High Court.

21.4 Such proceedings, as well as proceedings to enforce charging orders made in other Divisions of the High Court, are assigned to the Chancery Division. The evidence required in support of such proceedings is that set out in PD 73, para. 4.3.

21.5 There remain in the Chancery Division a number of mortgage possession proceedings issued prior to CPR, Part 55, coming into force (on 15 October 2001). Of those proceedings, some may never have been adjudicated upon and many will have given rise to suspended possession orders, in respect of which applications to issue execution may arise in reducing numbers.

21.6 Practitioners should also have regard to the fact that 'old' proceedings which have not been adjudicated upon and which were issued prior to 26 April 1999 will fall within the 'automatic stay' provisions of PD 51, para. 19, so that a claimant wishing to proceed with such a claim will have to apply to lift the stay. Such an application may be made at the same time as the application for possession but the court will require sufficient evidence to allow it to determine properly whether it is appropriate to lift the stay. The application to lift the automatic stay should form one of the heads of relief in the application notice seeking possession. If the evidence in support exhibits a mortgage account sufficient to show what has happened on the account since the last time the claim was before the court (*ex hypothesi* from before 26 April 1999) no additional evidence will be likely to be necessary in support of the stay application.

21.7 The Chancery Division retains its jurisdiction in respect of redemption and foreclosure of mortgages and kindred matters.

21.8 CPR, r. 48.3, and PD 43–48, para. 50 (amount of costs where costs are payable under a contract), are of particular relevance to mortgage claims.

21.9 In summary, where under a mortgage a mortgagee has a contractual right to his or her costs, the court's discretion in respect of costs under the Supreme Court Act 1981, s. 51, should be exercised so as to reflect that contractual right. The power of the court to disallow a mortgagee's costs sought to be added to the security stems not from s. 51 but from the power of the courts of equity to fix the terms upon which redemption will be allowed. A decision by the court to refuse costs to a mortgagee litigant may be a decision in the exercise of the court's discretion under s. 51, or pursuant to its power to fix the terms upon which redemption will be allowed, or a decision as to the extent of the mortgagee's contractual right, in a given case, to add costs to his or her security, or any combination of these three things. A mortgagee is not to be deprived of a contractual or equitable right to add costs to his or her security without reference to the mortgagee's contractual or equitable rights to such costs and without a proper adjudication as to whether or not the mortgagee should be deprived of his or her costs.

Chapter 22 Partnership Claims and Receivers

Key rules: CPR, Part 69; PD 24 and PD 40; RSC, ord. 81 in CPR, sch. 1

Partnership claims

22.1 In claims for or arising out of the dissolution of a partnership often the only matters in dispute between the partners are matters of accounting. In such cases there will be no trial. The court will, if appropriate, make a summary order under PD 24, para. 6, for the taking of an account. This will be taken before the master.

22.2 Only if there is a dispute as to the existence of a partnership (whether it is claimed that there never was a partnership or that the partnership is still continuing and has not been dissolved) or if there is a material dispute as to the terms of the partnership (e.g. as to the profit-sharing ratios) will there be a trial, at which the judge will decide those issues. In such cases there will be a two-stage procedure with the judge deciding these issues at the trial and ordering the winding up of the partnership which will involve the taking of the partnership accounts by the Master (see PD 40).

22.3 In some cases and in order to reduce costs, it may be appropriate for the parties to invite the master to determine factual issues as a preliminary to the account, e.g. issues as to terms of the partnership or assets comprised in it. At any case management conference it will be particularly

Court Guides

important to identify issues to be determined before an effective account or inquiry can be made. The court will not simply order accounts and inquiries without identifying the issues.

22.4 The expense of taking an account in court is usually wholly disproportionate to the amount at stake. Parties are strongly encouraged to refer disputes on accounts to a jointly instructed accountant for determination or mediation.

22.5 The functions of a receiver in a partnership action are limited. It is not his or her duty to wind up the partnership, like the liquidator of a company. His or her primary function is to get in the debts and preserve the assets pending winding up by the court and he or she has no power of sale without the permission of the court.

Receivers

22.6 The procedure for the appointment of receivers by the court is comprehensively governed by Part 69 and PD 69. A new Guide for Receivers in the Chancery Division is available. Copies of the Guide can be obtained from an associate or from the Court Manager, Chancery Chambers. The Guide is also reproduced at appendix 10. Particular attention should be paid to remuneration and the fact that it must be authorised on the basis specified in an order of the court.

Chapter 23 The Patents Court and Trade Marks etc.

Key rules: CPR, Part 63; PD 63

23.1 The matters assigned to the Patents Court are essentially all those concerned with patents or registered designs. CPR, Part 63, and PD 63 deal with its particular procedures. Appeals in patent, design and trade mark cases are governed by CPR, Part 52 (see r. 63.17); reference should be made to ch. 10 for the general procedure as regards such appeals.

23.2 The principal patents judges are Mr Justice Pumfrey and Mr Justice Kitchin. The other assigned patents judges currently nominated are:

Mr Justice Patten
Mr Justice Lewison
Mr Justice Mann

Several senior practitioners have also been appointed to sit as deputy High Court judges to hear Patents Court matters.

23.3 Mr Justice Pumfrey is the judge in charge of the patents list.

23.4 In cases of great urgency, when a nominated judge or deputy judge is not available an application can be made to any other judge of the High Court, preferably a judge of the Chancery Division.

23.5 The procedure of the Patents Court is broadly that of the Chancery Division as a whole, but there are important differences.

23.6 The Patents Court has its own court guide which is [printed in this appendix]. That Guide must be consulted for detailed guidance as to the procedure in the Patents Court.

23.7 The Court's diary can be accessed on its website (www.hmcourts-service.gov.uk). The Patents Court will endeavour, if the parties so desire and the case is urgent, to sit in September.

Patents County Court

23.8 Special provisions relate to the transfer of cases between the Patents Court and the Patents County Court. The Patents Court has no power to order the transfer to it of cases commenced in the Patents County Court which fall within the latter court's special jurisdiction (i.e. matters relating to patents and designs). On the other hand it does have the power to transfer cases commenced in the High Court to the Patents County Court.

Registered trade marks and other intellectual property rights

23.9 CPR, rr. 63.13 to 63.15, and PD 63, paras 18 to 27, apply to claims relating to matters arising out of the Trade Marks Act 1994 and other intellectual property rights (such as copyright, passing off, design rights, etc.) as set out in PD 63, para. 18. Claims under the Trade Marks Act 1994 must be brought in the Chancery Division. Among the Chancery masters trade mark cases are assigned to Master Bragge.

23.10 Appeals from decisions of the Registrar of Trade Marks are brought to the Chancery Division as a whole, not the Patents Court. Permission to appeal is not required.

Chapter 24 Probate and Inheritance Claims

Key rules: CPR, Part 57, and PD 57

Probate

24.1 In general, contentious probate proceedings follow the same pattern as an ordinary claim but there are important differences and CPR, Part 57, and PD 57 should be carefully studied. Particular regard should be had to the following:

(1) The claim form must be issued out of Chancery Chambers or out of the Chancery district registries, or if the claim is suitable to be heard in the county court, a county court where there is also a Chancery district registry, or the Central London County Court.

(2) A defendant must file an acknowledgment of service. An additional 14 days is provided for doing so.

(3) Save where the court orders otherwise, the parties must at the outset of proceedings lodge all testamentary documents in their possession and control with the court. At the same time parties must file written evidence describing any testamentary document of the deceased of which they have knowledge, stating, if any such document is not in the party's possession or control, the name and address, if known, of the person in whose possession or under whose control the document is. In the case of a claimant, these materials must be lodged at the time when the claim form is issued. In the case of a defendant, these materials must be lodged when service is acknowledged. If these requirements are not complied with it is likely that the claim will not be issued and, correspondingly, that the acknowledgment of service will not be permitted to be lodged.

(4) The court will generally ensure that all persons with any potential interest in the proceedings are joined as parties or served with notice under CPR, r. 19.8A.

(5) A default judgment cannot be obtained in a probate claim. Where, however, no defendant acknowledges service or files a defence, the claimant may apply for an order that the claim proceed to trial and seek a direction that the claim be tried on written evidence.

(6) If an order pronouncing for a will in solemn form is sought under Part 24, the evidence in support must include written evidence proving due execution of the will. In such a case, if a defendant has given notice under r. 57.7(5) that he raises no positive case but requires that the will be proved in solemn form and that, to that end, he wishes to cross-examine the attesting witnesses, then the claimant's application for summary judgment is subject to the right of such a defendant to require the attesting witnesses to attend for cross-examination.

(7) A defendant who wishes to do more than test the validity of the will by cross-examining the attesting witnesses must set up by counterclaim his positive case in order to enable the court to make an appropriate finding or declaration as to which is the valid will, or whether a person died intestate or as the case may be.

(8) The proceedings may not be discontinued without permission. Even if they are compromised, it will usually be necessary to have an order stating to whom the grant is to be made, either under r. 57.11 (leading to a grant in common form), or after a trial on written evidence under PD 57, para. 6.1(1) (leading to a grant in solemn form) or under the Administration of Justice Act 1985, s. 49, and PD 57, para. 6.1(3) (again leading to a grant in solemn form). Practitioners should refer to PF 38 CH and adapt as appropriate.

24.2 When the court orders trial of a contentious probate claim on written evidence, or where the court is asked to pronounce in solemn form under CPR, Part 24, it is normally necessary for an attesting witness to sign a witness statement or swear an affidavit of due execution of any will or codicil sought to be admitted to probate. The will or codicil is at that stage in the court's possession and cannot be handed out of court for use as an exhibit to the witness statement or affidavit, so that the attesting witness has to attend at the Royal Courts of Justice.

24.3 Where an attesting witness is unable to attend the Royal Courts of Justice in order to sign his or her witness statement or swear his or her affidavit in the presence of an officer of the court, the solicitor concerned may request from Room TM7.09, a photographic copy of the will or codicil in question. This will be certified as authentic by the court and may be exhibited to the witness statement or affidavit of due execution in lieu of the original. The witness statement or affidavit must in that case state that the exhibited document is an authenticated copy of the document signed in the witness's presence.

24.4 When a probate claim is listed for trial outside London, the solicitor for the party responsible for preparing the court bundle must write to Room TM7.09 and request that the testamentary documents be forwarded to the appropriate district registry.

Inheritance (Provision for Family and Dependants) Act 1975

24.5 Claims under the Inheritance (Provision for Family and Dependants) Act 1975 in the Chancery Division are issued by way of a Part 8 claim. Ordinarily they will be heard by the master unless an order is made transferring the claim to a county court for trial. They are governed by CPR, Part 57, and PD 57.

24.6 The written evidence filed by the claimant with the claim form must exhibit an official copy of the grant of probate or letters of administration together with every testamentary document in respect of which probate or letters of administration was granted.

24.7 A defendant must file and serve acknowledgment of service not later than 21 days after service of the Part 8 claim form. Any written evidence (subject to any extension agreed or directed) must likewise be served and filed no later than 21 days after service.

24.8 The personal representatives of the deceased are necessary defendants to a claim under the 1975 Act and the written evidence filed by a defendant who is a personal representative must comply with PD 57, para. 15.

24.9 On the hearing of a claim under the 1975 Act, the personal representatives must produce the original grant of representation to the deceased's estate. If the court makes an order under the Act, the original grant together with a sealed copy of the order must, under PD 57, para. 18.2, be sent to the Principal Registry of the Family Division, First Avenue House, 42-49 High Holborn, London WC1V 6NP for a memorandum of the order to be endorsed on or permanently annexed to the grant.

24.10 Where claims under the 1975 Act are compromised the consent order filed must comply with para. 9.14 of this Guide.

Chapter 25 Revenue Proceedings

Key rules: CPR, Part 52, PD 52, paras 23.2(11) to (16), 23.3 to 23.5, 23.8

25.1 Several kinds of revenue proceedings are heard in the Chancery Division. Usually the parties are HM Revenue and Customs on one side and a taxpayer on the other. The main examples are described below. Almost all of them are appeals against decisions made by lower level tribunals at first instance. The appeals are governed by CPR, Part 52. Reference should be made to chapter 10 for the general procedure relating to such appeals.

Appeals from decisions of the general commissioners relating to income tax, corporation tax or capital gains tax

25.2 The general commissioners are a first-instance appeal tribunal for cases concerning these three taxes. Appeals from their decisions, whether by the Revenue or by a taxpayer, are conducted on the basis of a case stated, drawn up by the general commissioners, which sets out the facts, the arguments, and the general commissioners' decision. The case stated is usually backed up by whatever documents were before the commissioners. These appeals are limited to questions of law. The judge never hears evidence, and the appeal will almost certainly fail if the appellant's real complaint is that the general commissioners got the facts wrong. The judge does have power to remit a case to the general commissioners for them to hear further evidence and find further facts, but this is only rarely done.

25.3 The rules provide that, when the party who is appealing from the general commissioners receives the case stated in its final form from the general commissioners' clerk, the party has to transmit it to the High Court within 30 days. The court has no power to extend this time limit, which must be strictly observed if the court is to be able to hear the appeal: (*New World Medical Ltd v Cormack* [2002] EWHC 1245 (Ch), [2002] STC 1245).

Appeals from decisions of the special commissioners relating to income tax, corporation tax, capital gains tax or inheritance tax

25.4 The special commissioners are the other first-instance appeal tribunal for tax purposes, and hear cases relating to all four taxes mentioned above, known as the direct taxes. Appeals from their decisions, whether by the Revenue or by a taxpayer, are conducted, not on the basis of a case stated, but on the basis of the special commissioners' decision and the papers which they had before them. Those papers may include a transcript of the evidence or the special commissioners' notes of the evidence, but, as with appeals from general commissioners, appeals to the Chancery Division are limited to questions of law. The judge never hears evidence. Again as with the general commissioners, the judge has power to remit a case to the special commissioners for them to hear further evidence and find further facts, but this is only rarely done. There are time limits for filing an appellant's notice for an appeal from a decision of the special commissioners. In most cases the limit is 56 days from the date of the commissioners' decision, but in some cases it is shorter. For details reference should be made to PD 52, para. 23.5.

25.5 Exceptionally, appeals from the special commissioners in relation to the direct taxes may go directly to the Court of Appeal, so leapfrogging the Chancery Division.

25.6 Some inheritance tax appeals are exceptions to the normal procedure and do not start before the special commissioners, so that the Chancery Division is the court of first instance. These are limited to cases where the issues to be decided are wholly or mainly issues of law and there is no substantial dispute about the facts. Detailed procedural rules about appeals of this nature are to be found in PD 52, para. 23.3.

Stamp duty appeals

25.7 These are heard in the Chancery Division, and are conducted on the basis of a case stated drawn up by HM Revenue and Customs. Usually there is no oral evidence, but it has occasionally been heard.

25.8 Appeals relating to stamp duty reserve tax are also heard in the Chancery Division. Rules relating such appeals have been made, but no such appeal has yet arisen.

Appeals from the Value Added Tax and Duties Tribunal

25.9 Most of these appeals relate to VAT, but occasionally appeals on other duties, such as excise duty, arise. An appeal may be brought either by HM Revenue and Customs or by the taxpayer. As with appeals from the special commissioners relating to the direct taxes, exceptionally leapfrog appeals may lie direct to the Court of Appeal, but normally the appeal will be to the Chancery Division.

25.10 As with appeals from the special commissioners, VAT appeals are based on the tribunal's decision and the documents in the case. The judge never hears evidence. The documents usually include a transcript of the evidence before the tribunal or the tribunal's notes of the evidence. Nevertheless, like appeals from the special commissioners concerning the direct taxes, an appeal lies only on a point of law. Usually the time limit for filing the appellant's notice is 56 days from the decision of the tribunal.

Chapter 26 Trusts

Key rules: CPR, Parts 8, 19 and PD 64

Introduction

26.1 This chapter contains material about a number of aspects of proceedings concerning trusts, the estates of deceased persons (other than probate claims) and charities.

26.2 The topics covered in this chapter are (a) applications by trustees for directions and related matters; (b) the Variation of Trusts Act 1958; (c) the Administration of Justice Act 1985, s. 48; (d) vesting orders as regards property in Scotland; (e) trustees under a disability; (f) lodgment of funds; (g) the estates of deceased Lloyd's names; and (h) judicial trustees.

Trustees' applications for directions

26.3 Applications to the court by trustees for directions in relation to the administration of a trust or charity, or by personal representatives in relation to a deceased person's estate, are to be brought by Part 8 claim form, and are governed by CPR, Part 64, PD 64 and PD 64B; CPR, r. 8.2A, is also relevant.

26.4 If confidentiality of the directions sought is important (for example, where the directions relate to actual or proposed litigation with a third party who could find out what directions the claimants are seeking through access to the claim form under r. 5.4) the statement of the remedy sought, for the purposes of r. 8.2(b), may be expressed in general terms. The trustees must, in that case, state specifically in the evidence what it is that they seek to be allowed to do.

Court Guides

26.5 The proceedings will normally be listed and heard in private (r. 39.2(3)(f) and PD 39, para. 1.5). Accordingly the order made, and the other documents among the court records (apart from a claim form which has been served), will not be open to inspection by third parties without the court's permission (CPR, r. 5.4(2)). If the matter is disposed of without a hearing, the order made will be expressed to have been made in private.

26.6 Part 64 deals with the joining of beneficiaries as defendants. Often, especially in the case of a private trust, it will be clear that some, and which, beneficiaries need to be joined as defendants. Sometimes, if there are only two views as to the appropriate course, and one is advocated by one beneficiary who will be joined, it may not be necessary for other beneficiaries to be joined since the trustees may be able to present the other arguments. Equally, in the case of a pension trust, it may not be necessary for a member of every possible different class of beneficiaries to be joined.

26.7 In some cases, it may be that the court will or might be able to assess whether or not to give the directions sought, or what directions to give, without hearing from any party other than the trustees. If the trustees consider that their case is in that category they may apply to the court under r. 8.2A for permission to issue the claim form without naming any defendants. They must apply to the court before the claim form is issued, and include a copy of the claim form that they propose to issue. Practitioners should note that this procedure may enable directions to be obtained about matters concerning the administration of a trust or estate in circumstances which would fall outside the relatively narrow confines of the Administration of Justice Act 1985, s. 48, where the expense and delay associated with an application naming defendants may not be in the interests of beneficiaries.

26.8 In other cases the trustees may know that beneficiaries need to be joined as defendants, or to be given notice, but may be in doubt as to which. Examples could include a case concerning a pension scheme with many beneficiaries and a number of different categories of interest, especially if they may be differently affected by the action for which directions are sought, or a private trust with a large class of discretionary beneficiaries. In those cases the trustees may apply for permission to issue the claim form without naming any defendants under r. 8.2A. The application may be combined with an application for directions as to which persons to join as parties or to give notice to under r. 19.8A.

26.9 In the case of a charitable trust the Attorney-General is always the appropriate defendant, and almost always the only one.

26.10 Applications for directions whether or not to take or defend or pursue litigation (see *Re Beddoe* [1893] 1 Ch 547) must be made by Part 8 claim, independently of the main litigation, to a master not involved with the main case. They should be supported by evidence including the advice of an appropriately qualified lawyer as to the prospects of success and other matters relevant to be taken into account, including a cost estimate for the proceedings and any known facts concerning the means of the opposite party to the proceedings, and a draft of any proposed statement of case. There are cases in which it is likely to be so clear that the trustees ought to proceed as they wish that the costs of making the application, even on a simplified procedure without a hearing and perhaps without defendants, are not justified in comparison with the size of the fund or the matters at issue.

26.11 References to an appropriately qualified lawyer mean one whose qualifications and experience are appropriate to the circumstances of the case. The qualifications should be stated. If the advice is given on formal instructions, the instructions should always be put in evidence as well, so that the court can see the basis on which the advice was given. If it is not, the advice must state fully the basis on which it is given. If a hearing is necessary the lawyer whose opinion is relied on should if possible be the advocate at the hearing.

26.12 All applications for directions should be supported by evidence showing the value of the trust assets, the significance of the proposed litigation or other course of action for the trust, and why the court's directions are needed. In the case of a pension trust the evidence should include the latest actuarial valuation, and should describe the membership profile and, if a deficit on winding up is likely, the priority provisions and their likely effect.

26.13 On an application for directions about actual or possible litigation, the evidence should also state (i) whether any relevant pre-action protocol has been followed, and (ii) whether the trustees have proposed or undertaken, or intend to propose, ADR, and (in each case) if not why not.

26.14 If a beneficiary of the trust is a party to the litigation about which directions are sought, with an interest opposed to that of the trustees, that beneficiary should be a defendant to the trustees' application, but any material which would be privileged as regards that beneficiary in the litigation should be put in evidence as exhibits to the trustees' witness statement, and should not be served on the beneficiary. However, if the claimant's representatives consider that no harm would be done by the disclosure of all or some part of the material then that material should be served on that defendant. That defendant may also be excluded from part of the hearing, including that which is devoted to discussion of the material withheld: see *Re Moritz* [1960] Ch 251; *Re Eaton* [1964] 1 WLR 1269.

Case management directions

26.15 The claim will be referred to the master once a defendant has acknowledged service, or otherwise on expiry of the period for acknowledgment of service (or, if no defendant is named, as soon as the claimant's evidence has been filed) to consider directions for the management of the case. Such directions may be given without a hearing in some cases; these might include directions as to parties or as to notice of proceedings, as mentioned in para. 26.8 above.

26.16 Case management directions will be given where the court grants an application to issue the claim form without naming a defendant under r. 8.2A.

Proceeding without a hearing

26.17 The court will always consider whether it is possible to deal with the application on paper without a hearing. The trustees must always consider whether a hearing is needed for any reason. If they consider that it is they should say so and explain why in their evidence. If a defendant considers that a hearing is needed, this should be stated, and the reasons explained, in his evidence, if any, or otherwise in a letter to the court.

26.18 If the court would be minded to refuse to give the directions asked for on a consideration of the papers alone, the parties will be notified and given the opportunity, within a stated time, to ask for a hearing.

26.19 In charity cases, the master may deal with the case without a hearing on the basis of a letter from or on behalf of the Attorney-General setting out his attitude to the application.

26.20 Cases in which the directions can be given without a hearing include those where personal representatives apply to be allowed to distribute the estate of a deceased Lloyd's name, following the decision in *Re Yorke* [1997] 4 All ER 907 (see paras 26.50 to 26.55 below), as well as applications under the Administration of Justice Act 1985, s. 48 (see paras 26.37 to 26.42 below).

Evidence

26.21 The trustees' evidence should be given by witness statement. In order to ensure that, if directions are given, the trustees are properly protected by the order, they must ensure full disclosure of relevant matters, even if the case is to proceed with the participation of beneficiaries as defendants.

Consultation with beneficiaries

26.22 The evidence must explain what, if any, consultation there has been with beneficiaries, and with what result. In preparation for an application for directions in respect of litigation, the following guidance is to be followed.

(1) If the trust is a private trust where the beneficiaries principally concerned are not numerous and are all or mainly adult, identified and traceable, the trustees will be expected to have canvassed with all the adult beneficiaries the proposed or possible courses of action before applying for directions.

(2) If it is a private trust with a larger number of beneficiaries, including those not yet born or identified, or children, it is likely that there will nevertheless be some adult beneficiaries principally concerned, with whom the trustees must consult.

(3) In relation to a charitable trust the trustees must have consulted the Attorney-General, through the Treasury Solicitor, as well as the Charity Commissioners, whose consent to the application will have been needed under the Charities Act 1993, s. 33.

(4) In relation to a pension trust, unless the members are very few in number, no particular steps by way of consultation with beneficiaries (including, where relevant, employers) or

their representatives are required in preparation for the application, though the trustees' evidence should describe any consultation that has in fact taken place. If no consultation has taken place, the court could in some cases direct that meetings of one or more classes of beneficiaries be held to consider the subject matter of the application, possibly as a preliminary to deciding whether a member of a particular class ought to be joined as a defendant, though in a case concerning actual or proposed litigation, steps would need to be considered to protect privileged material from too wide disclosure.

26.23 If the court gives directions allowing the claimant to take, defend or pursue litigation it may do so up to a particular stage in the litigation, requiring the trustees, before they carry on beyond that point, to renew their application to the court. What stage that should be will depend on the likely management of the litigation under the CPR. If the application is to be renewed after disclosure of documents, and disclosed documents need to be shown to the court, it may be necessary to obtain permission to do this from the court in which the other litigation is proceeding. However, the implied undertaking limiting the use of documents disclosed by another party to the litigation does not preclude their use on an application by trustee parties for directions, since that is use for the purposes of the litigation (*White v Biddulph* (1998) LTL 22/5/98).

26.24 In such a case the court may sometimes direct that the case be dealt with at that stage without a hearing if the beneficiaries obtain and lodge an opinion of an appropriately qualified lawyer supporting the continuation of the directions. Any such opinion will be considered by the court and, if thought fit, the trustees will be given a direction allowing them to continue pursuing the proceedings without a hearing.

26.25 In a case of urgency, such as where a limitation period or period for service of proceedings is about to expire, the court may give directions on a summary consideration of the evidence to cover the steps which need to be taken urgently, but limiting those directions so that the application needs to be renewed for fuller consideration at an early stage.

26.26 On any application for directions where a child is a defendant, the court will expect to have put before it the instructions to and advice of an appropriately qualified lawyer as to the benefits and disadvantages of the proposed, and any other relevant, course of action from the point of view of the child beneficiary. Where the matters to be drawn to the attention of the court are fully covered in the instructions and written opinion, it should not be necessary for a separate skeleton argument to be lodged, but the court needs to be informed that this is the case. The opinion should be given by the lawyer who is to be the advocate at the hearing.

Hearing

26.27 The master may give the directions sought though, if the directions relate to actual or proposed litigation, only if it is a plain case, and therefore usually without a hearing: see PD 2B, paras 4.1 and 5.1(e), and see also paras 26.17 to 26.20 above. Otherwise the case will be referred to the judge.

Representation orders

26.28 It is not the normal practice of the court to make representation orders under CPR, r. 19.7, on an application for directions, and sometimes it would not be possible, for lack of separate representatives among the parties of all relevant classes of beneficiaries, but such orders can be useful in an appropriate case and they are sometimes made.

Costs

26.29 Normally the trustees' costs of a proper application will be allowed out of the trust fund, on an indemnity basis, as will the assessed (or agreed) costs of beneficiaries joined as defendants, subject to their conduct of the proceedings having been proper and reasonable.

Prospective costs orders

26.30 In proceedings brought by one or more beneficiaries against trustees, the court has power to direct that the beneficiaries be indemnified out of the trust fund in any event for any costs incurred by them and any costs which they may be ordered to pay to any other party, known as a prospective costs order: see *McDonald v Horn* [1995] 1 All ER 961. Such an order may provide for payments out of the trust fund from time to time on account of the indemnity so that the beneficiaries' costs may be paid on an interim basis. Applications for prospective costs orders should be made on notice to the trustees. The court will require to be satisfied that there are matters which need to be investigated. How far the court will wish to go into that question, and in what way it should be done, will depend on the circumstances of the particular case. The order may be expressed to cover costs incurred only up to a particular stage in the proceedings, so that the application has to be renewed, if necessary, in the light of what has occurred in the proceedings in the meantime. See PD 64, para. 6, to which is annexed a model form of order.

Charity trustees' applications for permission to bring proceedings

26.31 In the case of a charitable trust, if the Charity Commissioners refuse their consent to the trustees applying to the court for directions, under Charities Act 1993, s. 33(2), and also refuse to give the trustees the directions under their own powers, under ss. 26 or 29, the trustees may appeal to the court under s. 33(5). On such an application, which may be dealt with on paper, the judge may call for a statement from the Charity Commissioners of their reasons for refusing permission, if not already apparent from the papers. The court may require the trustees to attend before deciding whether to grant permission for the proceedings. It is possible to require notice of the hearing to be given to the Attorney-General, but this would not normally be appropriate.

Variation of Trusts Act 1958

26.32 An application under the Variation of Trusts Act 1958 should be made by a Part 8 claim form. As to listing of such applications see para. 6.27. The master will not consider the file without an application.

26.33 Where any children or unborn beneficiaries will be affected by an arrangement under the Variation of Trusts Act 1958, evidence must normally be before the court which shows that their litigation friends or the trustees support the arrangements as being in the interests of the children or unborn beneficiaries, and exhibits a written opinion to this effect. In complicated cases a written opinion is usually essential to the understanding of the litigation friends and the trustees, and to the consideration by the court of the merits and fiscal consequences of the arrangement. If the written opinion was given on formal instructions, those instructions must be exhibited. Otherwise the opinion must state fully the basis on which it was given. The opinion must be given by the advocate who will appear on the hearing of the application. A skeleton argument may not be needed where a written opinion has been put in evidence and no matters not appearing from the instructions or the opinion are to be relied on: see para. 26.26 above.

26.34 Where the interests of two or more children, or two or more of the children and unborn beneficiaries, are similar, a single written opinion will suffice; and no written opinion is required in respect of those who fall within the proviso to s. 1(1) of the Act (discretionary interests under protective trusts). Further, in proper cases the requirement of a written opinion may at any stage be dispensed with by the master or the judge.

Stamp duty

26.35 An undertaking by solicitors with regard to stamping is not required to be included in an order under the Variation of Trusts Act 1958 whether made by a judge or master.

26.36 The Commissioners of Inland Revenue consider that the stamp duty position of duplicate orders is as follows:

(1) Orders confined to the lifting of protective trusts. These orders are not liable for duty at all and should not be presented to a stamp office.

(2) Orders effecting voluntary dispositions *inter vivos*. These orders may be certified under the Stamp Duty (Exempt Instruments) Regulations 1987 (SI 1987/516), as within category L in the schedule to those regulations, in which case they should not be presented to a stamp office. Without such a certificate they attract [£5 duty under the head 'transfer otherwise than on sale'*].

(3) Orders outside those described at paragraphs (1) and (2) above that contain declarations of the trust, i.e. that effect no disposition of trust property. These orders attract [£5 duty under the head 'declaration of use or trust'*]. They may be presented for stamping at any stamp office in the usual way, or sent for adjudication if preferred.

[* Updated editorially. Liability to stamp duty reserve tax or stamp duty land tax should also be considered.]

Applications under the Administration of Justice Act 1985, s. 48

26.37 Applications under the Administration of Justice Act 1985, s. 48, should be made by Part 8 claim form without naming a defendant, under CPR, r. 8.2A. No separate application for permission under r. 8.2A need be made. The claim should be supported by a witness statement or affidavit to which are exhibited: (a) copies of all relevant documents; (b) instructions to a person with a 10-year High Court qualification within the meaning of the Courts and Legal Services Act 1990 ('the qualified person'); (c) the qualified person's opinion; and (d) draft terms of the desired order.

26.38 The witness statement or affidavit (or exhibits thereto) should state: (a) the names of all persons who are, or may be, affected by the order sought; (b) all surrounding circumstances admissible and relevant in construing the document; (c) the date of qualification of the qualified person and his or her experience in the construction of trust documents; (d) the approximate value of the fund or property in question; and (e) whether it is known to the applicant that a dispute exists and, if so, details of such dispute.

26.39 When the file is placed before the master he will consider whether the evidence is complete and if it is send the file to the judge.

26.40 The judge will consider the papers and, if necessary, direct service of notices under CPR, r. 19.8A, or request such further information as he or she may desire. If the judge is satisfied that the order sought is appropriate, the order will be made and sent to the claimant.

26.41 If following service of notices under r. 19.8A any acknowledgment of service is received, the claimant must apply to the master (on notice to the parties who have so acknowledged service) for directions. If the claimant desires to pursue the application to the court, in the ordinary case the master will direct that the case proceeds as a Part 8 claim.

26.42 If on the hearing of the claim the judge is of the opinion that any party who entered an acknowledgment of service has no reasonably tenable argument contrary to the qualified person's opinion, in the exercise of his or her discretion he or she may order such party to pay any costs thrown away, or part thereof.

Vesting orders — property in Scotland

26.43 In applications for vesting orders under the Trustee Act 1925 any investments or property situate in Scotland should be set out in a separate schedule to the claim form, and the claim form should ask that the trustees may have permission to apply for a vesting order in Scotland in respect thereto.

26.44 The form of the order to be made in such cases will (with any necessary variation) be as follows:

> It is ordered that the as Trustees have permission to take all steps that may be necessary to obtain a vesting order in Scotland relating to [the securities] specified in the schedule herein.

Disability of trustee

26.45 There must be medical evidence showing incapacity to act as a trustee at the date of issue of the claim form and that the incapacity is continuing at the date of signing the witness statement or swearing the affidavit. The witness statement or affidavit should also show incapacity to execute transfers, where a vesting order of stocks and shares is asked for.

26.46 The trustee under disability should be made a defendant to the claim but need not be served unless he or she is sole trustee or has a beneficial interest.

Lodgment of funds

26.47 Lodgment into the High Court of amounts of cash or securities of less than £500 under the Trustee Act 1925, s. 63, and the Court Funds Rules 1987, r. 14(1), will not be accepted by the Accountant-General unless the Chief Master so signifies in writing.

26.48 The Accountant-General will refer the applicant to the Chief Master who will consider whether there is a more economical method of preserving the fund than lodging it in the High Court or, failing that, may suggest that the money be lodged in a county court (which has power to accept sums of up to £30,000 lodged under the Trustee Act 1925, s. 63).

26.49 If the Chief Master decides that a particular lodgment should be made in the High Court, he will so signify on the back of the request (in respect of applications under r. 14(1)(ii)(a)) or the office copy schedule to the affidavit (in respect of applications under r. 14(1)(ii)(b)).

Estates of deceased Lloyd's names

26.50 The procedure concerning the estates of deceased Lloyd's names is governed by Practice Note (Deceased Lloyd's Names: Applications to Distribute Estates) [2001] 3 All ER 765.

26.51 Personal representatives who wish to apply to the court for permission to distribute the estate of a deceased Lloyd's name following *Re Yorke* [1997] 4 All ER 907, or trustees who wish to administer any will trusts arising in such an estate, may, until further notice and if appropriate in the particular estate, adopt the following procedure.

26.52 The procedure will be appropriate where:

(1) the only, or only substantial, reason for delaying distribution of the estate is the possibility of personal liability to Lloyd's creditors; and

(2) all liabilities of the estate in respect of syndicates of which the name was a member have for the years 1992 and earlier (if any) been reinsured (whether directly or indirectly) into the Equitas group; and

(3) all liabilities of the estate in respect of syndicates of which the name was a member have for the years 1993 and later (if any) arise in respect of syndicates which have closed by reinsurance in the usual way or are protected by the terms of an Estate Protection Plan issued by Centrewrite Ltd or are protected by the terms of EXEAT insurance cover provided by Centrewrite Ltd.

26.53 In these circumstances personal representatives may apply by a Part 8 claim form headed 'In the Matter of the Estate of [ ] deceased (a Lloyd's estate) and In the Matter of the Practice Direction dated May 25, 2001' for permission to distribute the estate (and, if applicable, to administer the will trusts) on the footing that no or no further provision need be made for Lloyd's creditors. Ordinarily, the claim form need not name any other party. It may be issued in this form without a separate application for permission under CPR, r. 8.2A.

26.54 The claim should be supported by a witness statement or an affidavit substantially in the form set out in appendix 11 adapted as necessary to the particular circumstances and accompanied by a draft of the desired order substantially in the form also set out in appendix 11. If the amount of costs has been agreed with the residuary beneficiaries (or, if the costs are not to be taken from residue, with the beneficiaries affected) their signed consent to those costs should also be submitted. If the claimants are inviting the court to make a summary assessment they should submit a statement of costs in the form specified in PD 43–48. If in his discretion the master (or outside London the district judge) thinks fit, he will summarily assess the costs but with permission for the paying party to apply within 14 days of service of the order on him to vary or discharge the summary assessment. Subject to the foregoing, the order will provide for a detailed assessment unless subsequently agreed.

26.55 The application will be considered in the first instance by the master who, if satisfied that the order should be made, may make the order without requiring the attendance of the applicants, and the court will send it to them. If not so satisfied, the master may give directions for the further disposal of the application.

Judicial trustees

26.56 Judicial trustees are appointed by the court under the Judicial Trustees Act 1896, in accordance with the Judicial Trustee Rules 1983. An application for the appointment of a judicial trustee should be made by Part 8 claim (or, if in an existing claim, by an application notice in that claim) which must be served (subject to any directions by the court) on every existing trustee who is not an applicant and on such of the beneficiaries as the applicant thinks fit. Once appointed, a judicial trustee may obtain non-contentious directions from the assigned master informally by letter, without the need for a Part 23 application (unless the court directs otherwise). Applications for directions can be sought from the court as to the trust or its administration by the Judicial Trustee Rules 1983, r. 8.

26.57 Where it is proposed to appoint the Official Solicitor as judicial trustee, inquiries must first be made to his office for confirmation that he is prepared to act if appointed. The Official Solicitor will not be required to give security.

26.58 A judicial trustee is entitled under r. 11 of the 1983 rules to such remuneration as is reasonable in respect of work reasonably performed. Applications for payment by the trustee must be by letter to the court, submitted with the accounts. A practice note issued by the Chief Chancery Master, with the authority of the Vice-Chancellor, on 1 July 2003 sets out the best practice to be followed in determining the amount of remuneration. The practice note mirrors the position regarding receivers' remuneration under CPR, r. 69.7, and is reproduced at appendix 12.

APPENDIX 1 ADDRESSES AND OTHER CONTACT DETAILS

1 Clerks to the Chancery Judges

Clerk to:	Telephone	Fax
The Chancellor	(020) 7947 6412	(020) 7947 6572
Mr Justice Lindsay	(020) 7947 6253	(020) 7947 7185
Mr Justice Evans-Lombe	(020) 7947 6657	(020) 7947 6719
Mr Justice Blackburne	(020) 7947 6589	(020) 7947 7379
Mr Justice Lightman	(020) 7947 6671	(020) 7947 6291
Mr Justice Rimer	(020) 7947 6418	(020) 7947 6649
Mr Justice Park	(020) 7947 6741	(020) 7947 6196
Mr Justice Pumfrey	(020) 7947 7482	(020) 7947 6593
Mr Justice Hart	(020) 7947 6419	(020) 7947 6062
Mr Justice Lawrence Collins	(020) 7947 7467	(020) 7947 7298
Mr Justice Patten	(020) 7947 7617	(020) 7947 6650
Mr Justice Etherton	(020) 7947 6116	(020) 7947 6165
Mr Justice Peter Smith	(020) 7947 6183	(020) 7947 6133
Mr Justice Lewison	(020) 7947 6039	(020) 7947 6894
Mr Justice David Richards	(020) 7947 7419	(020) 7947 6743
Mr Justice Mann	(020) 7947 7964	(020) 7947 6739
Mr Justice Warren	(020) 7947 7260	(020) 7947 7740
Mr Justice Kitchin	(020) 7947 6518	(020) 7947 6439

2 Email Communications

The email protocol sets out how parties may communicate by email on certain matters with the Chancery Division, and [is in **appendix 4** under the heading **A Guide to Emailing the Civil and Family Courts**].

The relevant email addresses are:

(a) For skeleton arguments, chronologies, reading lists, list of issues, lists of authorities (but not the authorities themselves) and lists of the persons involved in the facts of the case sent in advance of a hearing:

Judge:
rcjchancery.judgeslisting@hmcourts-service.gsi.gov.uk

[*Note:* The clerk to the judge concerned should be contacted to find out whether other documents will be accepted by email, and whether documents should be sent direct to the judge's clerk's email address.]

Chancery master:
rcjchancery.mastersappointments@hmcourts-service.gsi.gov.uk

Bankruptcy Registrar:
rcjbankruptcy.registrarshearings@hmcourts-service.gsi.gov.uk

Companies Court registrar:
rcjcompanies.orders@hmcourts-service.gsi.gov.uk

(b) For the agreed terms of an order which is ready to be sealed following the conclusion of a hearing:

Judge:
rcjchancery.ordersandaccounts@hmcourts-service.gsi.gov.uk

Chancery master:
rcjchancery.ordersandaccounts@hmcourts-service.gsi.gov.uk

Bankruptcy registrar:
rcjbankruptcy.registrarshearings@hmcourts-service.gsi.gov.uk

Companies Court registrar:
rcjcompanies.orders@hmcourts-service.gsi.gov.uk

3 At the Royal Courts of Justice, Thomas More Building

1st floor

TM1.10 Bankruptcy registrars' clerks, applications without notice, registrars' hearings and orders: telephone (020) 7947 6444.
Bankruptcy registrars' chambers: telephone (020) 7947 6444; (020) 7947 7387.
Bankruptcy Court fax number: (020) 7947 6378.

2nd floor

TM2.04 Deputy Court Manager: telephone (020) 7947 6812.

TM2.07 Court Manager, Companies, Bankruptcy Courts: telephone (020) 7947 6870.

TM2.09 Companies Court General Office: issue of all winding-up petitions and all other Companies Court applications; filing of documents: telephone (020) 7947 6294.
Central Index: telephone (020) 7947 7328.

TM2.11 Bankruptcy Issue and Search Room: issue of all petitions presented by creditors and debtors and applications to set aside statutory demands and applications for interim orders:
search room: telephone (020) 7947 6448.
setting down appeals from registrars and district and circuit judges: telephone (020) 7947 6863.
Companies Court fax number: (020) 7947 6958.

3rd floor

TM3.08 Bankruptcy and Companies Registry. Filing affidavits, witness statements and documents and requesting bankruptcy and company files for applications without notice to be made in chambers; requests for office copies, lodging applications for certificates of discharge in bankruptcy: telephone (020) 7947 6441.

4th floor

TM4.04 Companies schemes and reductions of capital: telephone (020) 7947 6727.

TM4.05 Companies Orders Section: Winding-up Court: telephone (020) 7947 6780.
Registrars' orders and disqualification of directors: telephone (020) 7947 6822.

5th floor

TM5.04 Chancery Chambers Registry and Issue Section: issue and amendment of all Chancery process, filing affidavits and witness statements (save those lodged within two days of a hearing before a master which are to be filed in Room TM7.09); filing acknowledgments of service, searches of cause book; applications for office copy documents, including orders; transfers in and out: telephone (020) 7947 6148; (020) 7947 6167.

TM5.05 Deputy Court Manager, Chancery Chambers. Certification of documents for use abroad: telephone (020) 7947 6754.

TM5.06 Lawyer, Chancery Chambers: telephone (020) 7947 6080.

TM5.07 Orders and Accounts Section. Associates: preparation of all Chancery orders and Companies and Bankruptcy Court orders; small payments; bills of costs for assessment; settlement of payment and lodgment schedules; accounts of receivers, judicial trustees, guardians and administrators; applications relating to security set by the court; matters arising out of accounts and inquiries ordered by the court: telephone (020) 7947 6855.
Chancery orders and accounts fax number: (020) 7947 7049.

6th floor

TM6.04 Chancery masters' library.

TM6.05 Master Price.

TM6.06 Court Manager, Chancery Chambers: telephone (020) 7947 6075.

TM6.07 Master Bowles.

TM6.08 Secretary to masters: telephone (020) 7947 6777.

TM6.09 Master Bragge.

7th floor

TM7.05 Master Teverson.

TM7.06 Master Moncaster.

TM7.08 Chief Master Winegarten.

TM7.09 Masters' appointments. Issue of masters' applications, including applications without notice to masters; filing affidavits and witness statements in proceedings before masters (only if filed within two working days of hearing before the master); applications to serve out of jurisdiction; filing stop notices; filing testamentary documents in contested probate cases; filing grants lodged under CPR, Part 57; filing affidavits relating to funds paid into court under the Trustee Act 1925, Compulsory Purchase Act 1965 and the Lands Clauses Consolidation Act 1845.
Manager: telephone (020) 7947 6095.
Clerks to Chancery Masters: telephone (020) 7947 6702; (020) 7947 7391.
Masters' appointments fax number: (020) 7947 7422.

4 At the Royal Courts of Justice but outside Thomas More Building

RCJ Switchboard: telephone (020) 7947 6000.
RCJ Security Office: telephone (020) 7947 6260.
Fees Office, Room E01: telephone (020) 7947 6527.
Clerk of the Lists, Room WG3: telephone (020) 7947 6318.
Chancery Judges' Listing Office, Room WG4: telephone (020) 7947 6778; (020) 7947 6690.
High Court Appeals Office, Room WG7: telephone (020) 7947 7518.
Chancery Judges' Listing Office fax number:* (020) 7947 7345.
Officer in charge of mechanical recording, Room WB.14: telephone (020) 7947 6154.
Head Usher: telephone (020) 7947 6356, fax (020) 7947 6668.
Customer Service Officer: telephone (020) 7947 7731.
Videoconferencing managers: telephone (020) 7947 6581, fax (020) 7947 6613.
RCJ Advice Bureau: telephone 0845 120 3715 or (020) 7947 6880, fax (020) 7947 7167.
Personal Support Unit, Room M104: telephone (020) 7947 7701, (020) 7947 7703, fax (020) 7947 7702.

5 London, outside the Royal Courts of Justice

Central London County Court
Civil Trial Centre, Chancery List, 26-29 Park Crescent, London W1N 4HT
DX 97325 Regents Park 2
Business Chancery and Patents section: telephone (020) 7917 7821, (020) 7917 7887.
Fax (020) 7917 7935, (020) 7917 7940.

6 Outside London

The following are the court addresses, telephone and fax numbers for the courts at which there are regular Chancery sittings outside London:
Birmingham: The Priory Courts, 33 Bull Street, Birmingham B4 6DS.
Telephone: (0121) 681 3033. Fax: (0121) 681 3121.
Bristol: The Law Courts, Small Street, Bristol BS1 1DA.
Telephone: (0117) 976 3098. Fax: (0117) 976 3074.
Cardiff: The Civil Justice Centre, 2 Park Street, Cardiff CF1 1ET.
Telephone: (01222) 376402. Fax: (01222) 376470.
Leeds: The Court House, 1 Oxford Row, Leeds LS1 3BG.
Telephone: (0113) 283 0040. Fax: (0113) 244 8507.
Liverpool: Queen Elizabeth II Law Courts, Derby Square, Liverpool L2 1XA.
Telephone: (0151) 473 7373. Fax: (0151) 227 2806.
Manchester: The Courts of Justice, Crown Square, Manchester M3 3FL.
Telephone: (0161) 954 1800. Fax: (0161) 832 5179.

[* See para. 14.12.]

Newcastle: The Law Courts, Quayside, Newcastle upon Tyne NE1 3LB.
Telephone: (0191) 201 2000. Fax: (0191) 201 2001.
Preston: The Law Courts, Openshaw Place, Ringway, Preston PR1 2LL.
Telephone: (01772) 832300. Fax: (01772) 832476.

In some centres resources do not permit the listing telephone numbers to be attended personally at all times. In cases of urgency, solicitors, counsel and counsel's clerks may come into the Chancery Court and leave messages with the member of staff sitting in court.

Urgent court business officer pager numbers for out-of-hours applications:
Birmingham (Midland Circuit):
West Side: 07699 618079
East Side: 07699 618078
Bristol: 07699 618088
Cardiff: 07699 618086
Manchester and Liverpool: 07699 618080
Preston: 07699 618081
Newcastle: 01399 618083
Leeds and Bradford: 01399 618082
In case of difficulty out of hours, contact the Royal Courts of Justice on (020) 7947 6260.

APPENDIX 2 GUIDELINES ON STATEMENTS OF CASE

1. The document must be as brief and concise as possible.
2. The document must be set out in separate consecutively numbered paragraphs and sub-paragraphs.
3. So far as possible each paragraph or sub-paragraph should contain no more than one allegation.
4. The document should deal with the case on a point-by-point basis, to allow a point-by-point response.
5. Where the CPR require a party to give particulars of an allegation or reasons for a denial (see r. 16.5(2)), the allegation or denial should be stated first and then the particulars or reasons listed one by one in separate numbered sub-paragraphs.
6. A party wishing to advance a positive case must identify that case in the document; a simple denial is not sufficient.
7. Any matter which if not stated might take another party by surprise should be stated.
8. Where they will assist, headings, abbreviations and definitions should be used and a glossary annexed.
9. Contentious headings, abbreviations, paraphrasing and definitions should not be used; every effort should be made to ensure that headings, abbreviations and definitions are in a form that will enable them to be adopted without issue by the other parties.
10. Particulars of primary allegations should be stated as particulars and not as primary allegations.
11. Schedules or appendices should be used if this would be helpful, for example, where lengthy particulars are necessary.
12. The names of any witness to be called may be given, and necessary documents (including an expert's report) can be attached or served contemporaneously if not bulky (PD 16; Guide para. 2.11). Otherwise evidence should not be included.
13. A response to particulars stated in a schedule should be stated in a corresponding schedule.
14. A party should not set out lengthy extracts from a document in his or her statement of case. If an extract has to be included, it should be placed in a schedule.
15. The document must be signed by the individual person or persons who drafted it not, in the case of a solicitor, in the name of the firm only. It must be accompanied by a statement of truth.

APPENDIX 3 CASE MANAGEMENT DIRECTIONS

[Appendix 3 is on the CD-ROM version of *Blackstone's Civil Practice*. Click on the title of the appendix to open it.]

APPENDIX 4 JUDGE'S APPLICATION INFORMATION FORM AND WRITTEN EVIDENCE LODGMENT FORM

[Appendix 4 is on the CD-ROM version of *Blackstone's Civil Practice.* Click on the title of the appendix to open it.]

APPENDIX 5 CORRESPONDENCE WITH CHANCERY MASTERS — PRACTICE NOTE

1. One of the consequences of the new rules and practice directions has been a significant increase in letters to the court from parties and their solicitors. This imposes a heavy extra burden on the staff and masters. It also means that court files have to be moved more often, which itself gives rise to problems. It would therefore be greatly appreciated if parties and solicitors involved in litigation before the Chancery masters had regard to the following points.
2. When corresponding, please consider carefully (a) whether your letter is really necessary and (b) if it is who the correct addressee should be. Only address letters to the master if the letter needs to be seen by him. If not address the letter to his clerk.
3. Letters and other documents should only be sent by fax if there is a real urgency, and should not be followed up with a hard copy. (If, exceptionally, a fax has contained a document the original of which needs to go on the court file, then the hard copy enclosing the original should be marked clearly 'confirmation of fax'.)
4. As a general rule all correspondence, whether letter or fax, must be copied to the other parties. Correspondence should therefore state that it has been copied to the other parties (or else it should state that it has not and explain why).
5. Correspondence should not be used in place of a Part 23 application (which requires payment of a fee, a draft order and a statement of truth).

J. Winegarten
Chief Chancery Master
July 2001

APPENDIX 6 GUIDELINES ON BUNDLES

Bundles of documents must comply with PD 39, para. 3. These guidelines are additional to those requirements, and they should be followed wherever possible.

1. The preparation of bundles requires cooperation between the legal representatives for all parties, and in many cases a high level of cooperation. It is the duty of all legal representatives to cooperate to the necessary level. Where a party is acting in person it is also that party's duty to cooperate as necessary with the other parties' legal representatives.
2. Bundles should be prepared in accordance with the following guidance.

Avoidance of duplication

3. No more than one copy of any one document should be included, unless there is good reason for doing otherwise. One such reason may be the use of a separate core bundle.
4. If the same document is included in the chronological bundles and is also an exhibit to an affidavit or witness statement, it should be included in the chronological bundle and where it would otherwise appear as an exhibit to an affidavit a sheet should instead be inserted. This sheet should state the page and bundle number in the chronological bundles where the documents can be found.
5. Where the court considers that costs have been wasted by copying unnecessary documents, a special costs order may be made against the relevant person. In no circumstances should rival bundles be presented to the court.

Chronological order and organisation

6. In general documents should be inserted in date order commencing with the earliest document.
7. If a contract or other transactional document is central to the case it may be included in a separate place provided that a page is inserted in the chronological run of documents to indicate where it would have appeared chronologically and where it is to be found instead. Alternatively transactional documents may be placed in a separate bundle as a category.

Pagination

8. This is covered by PD 39, para. 3, but it is permissible, instead of numbering the whole bundle, to number documents separately within tabs. An exception to consecutive page numbering arises in the case of the core bundle. For this it may be preferable to retain the original numbering with each bundle represented by a separate divider.
9. Page numbers should be inserted in bold figures, at the bottom of the page and in a form that can clearly be distinguished from any other pagination on the document.

Format and presentation

10. Where possible, the documents should be in A4 format. Where a document has to be read across rather than down the page, it should so be placed in the bundle as to ensure that the top of the text starts nearest the spine.
11. Where any marking or writing in colour on a document is important, for example, on a conveyancing plan, the document must be copied in colour or marked up correctly in colour.
12. Documents in manuscript, or not easily legible, should be transcribed; the transcription should be marked and placed adjacent to the document transcribed.
13. Documents in a foreign language should be translated; the translation should be marked and placed adjacent to the document translated; the translation should be agreed or, if it cannot be agreed, each party's proposed translation should be included.
14. The size of any bundle should be tailored to its contents. There is no point having a large lever-arch file with just a few pages inside. On the other hand bundles should not be overloaded as they tend to break. *No bundle should contain more than 300 pages.*
15. Binders and files must be strong enough to withstand heavy use.
16. Large documents, such as plans, should be placed in an easily accessible file. If they will need to be opened up often, it may be sensible for the file to be larger than A4 size.

Indices and labels

17. Indices should, if possible, be on a single sheet. It is not necessary to waste space with the full heading of the action. Documents should be identified briefly but properly, e.g. 'AGS3 — Defendant's Accounts'.
18. Outer labels should use large lettering, e.g. 'A. Pleadings'. The full title of the action and solicitors' names and addresses should be omitted. A label should be used on the front as well as on the spine.
19. A label should also be stuck on to the front inside cover of a file at the top left, in such a way that it can be seen even when the file is open.

Staples etc.

20. All staples, heavy metal clips etc. should be removed.

Statements of case

21. Statements of case should be assembled in 'chapter' form, i.e. claim form followed by particulars of claim, followed by further information, irrespective of date.
22. Redundant documents, e.g. particulars of claim overtaken by amendments, requests for further information recited in the answers given, should generally be excluded. Backsheets to statements of case should also be omitted.

Witness statements, affidavits and expert reports

23. Where there are witness statements, affidavits and/or expert reports from two or more parties, each party's witness statements etc. should, in large cases, be contained in separate bundles.
24. The copies of the witness statements, affidavits and expert reports in the bundles should have written on them, next to the reference to any document, the reference to that document in the bundles. This can be done in manuscript.
25. Documents referred to in, or exhibited to, witness statements, affidavits and expert reports should be put in a separate bundle and not placed behind the statement concerned, so that the reader can see both the text of the statement and the document referred to at the same time.
26. Backsheets to affidavits and witness statements should be omitted.

New documents

27. Before a new document is introduced into bundles which have already been delivered to the

court — indeed before it is copied — steps should be taken to ensure that it carries an appropriate bundle/page number, so that it can be added to the court documents. It should not be stapled, and it should be prepared with punch holes for immediate inclusion in the binders in use.

28. If it is expected that a large number of miscellaneous new documents will from time to time be introduced, there should be a special tabbed empty loose-leaf file for that purpose. An index should be produced for this file, updated as necessary.

Inter-solicitor correspondence

29. It is seldom that all inter-solicitor correspondence is required. Only those letters which are likely to be referred to should be copied. They should normally be placed in a separate bundle.

Core bundle

30. Where the volume of documents needed to be included in the bundles, and the nature of the case, makes it sensible, a separate core bundle should be prepared for the trial, containing those documents likely to be referred to most frequently.

Basis of agreement of bundles

31. See para. 7.13.

Photocopy authorities

32. If authorities, extracts from textbooks etc. are photocopied for convenience for use in court, the photocopies should be placed in a separate bundle with an index and dividers. Reduced-size copies (i.e. two pages of original to each A4 sheet) should not be used. Where only a short passage from a long case is needed, the headnote and key pages only should be copied and the usher should be asked to have the full volume in court. Whenever possible the parties' advocates should liaise about these bundles in order to avoid duplication of copies.

APPENDIX 7 GUIDELINES ON SKELETON ARGUMENTS, CHRONOLOGIES, INDICES AND READING LISTS

Skeleton arguments

1. A skeleton argument is intended to identify both for the parties and the court those points which are, and those that are not, in issue, and the nature of the argument in relation to those points which are in issue. It is not a substitute for oral argument.
2. Every skeleton argument should therefore:
   (1) identify concisely:
      (a) the nature of the case generally, and the background facts in so far as they are relevant to the matter before the court;
      (b) the propositions of law relied on with references to the relevant authorities;
      (c) the submissions of fact to be made with reference to the evidence;
   (2) be as brief as the nature of the issues allows — it should not normally exceed 20 pages of double-spaced A4 paper and in many cases it should be much shorter than this;
   (3) be in numbered paragraphs and state the name (and contact details) of the advocate(s) who prepared it;
   (4) avoid arguing the case at length;
   (5) avoid formality and make use of abbreviations, e.g. C for Claimant, A/345 for bundle A page 345, 1.1.95 for 1 January 1995 etc.
3. Paragraph 1 also applies to written summaries of opening speeches and final speeches. Even though in a large case these may necessarily be longer, they should still be as brief as the case allows.

Reading lists

4. The documents which the judge should if possible read before the hearing may be identified in a skeleton argument, but must in any event be listed in a separate reading list, if possible agreed between the advocates, which must be lodged with the agreed bundles, together with an estimate, if possible agreed, of the time required for the reading.

Chronologies and indices

5. Chronologies and indices should be non-contentious and agreed with the other parties if

possible. If there is a material dispute about any event stated in the chronology, that should be stated in neutral terms and the competing versions shortly stated.

6. If time and circumstances allow its preparation, a chronology or index to which all parties have contributed and agreed can be invaluable.
7. Chronologies and indices once prepared can be easily updated and may be of continuing usefulness throughout the case.

APPENDIX 8 DELIVERY OF DOCUMENTS IN CHANCERY CHAMBERS

Delivery of Documents for Masters' Hearings

1 (a) Deliver bundles and skeletons (if required) to Masters' Appointments, Room TM7.09, two clear working days (not more than seven) before the hearing.
(b) Mark clearly 'for hearing on (*date*) before Master '.
(c) Insert a reading list and estimate of reading time if appropriate.
(d) Bundles may be presented in ring binders or lever arch files, or as appropriate.
(e) Documents for masters' hearings should not be taken direct to the master's room unless in any particular case the master has directed otherwise.
(f) Documents required for masters' hearings should never be taken to:
(i) the Registry (Room TM5.04);
(ii) the Chancery Judges' Listing Office (Room WG 4); or
(iii) the RCJ Post Room — if they are they may well not reach the master in time.

Note:
Documents required for hearings before a Chancery judge must not be delivered to Chancery Chambers. They must be delivered to the Chancery Judges' Listing Office (Room WG 4).

Filing of Documents

2 (a) Take or send documents required to be filed (i.e. placed on the court file, either under the CPR or under an order of the court (e.g. statements of case, defences, allocation questionnaires, some witness statements) to the Chancery Registry, Room TM5.04 for filing.
(b) But documents (e.g. witness statements, exhibits) required to be filed which are needed for a masters' hearing within 10 working days must be delivered for filing to Masters' Appointments, Room 7.09 not the Registry.
(c) If bulky, use treasury tags, not files or ring binders.

APPENDIX 9 GUIDELINES ON WITNESS STATEMENTS

1. The function of a witness statement is to set out in writing the evidence-in-chief of the maker of the statement. Accordingly witness statements should, so far as possible, be expressed in the witness's own words. This guideline applies unless the perception or recollection of the witness of the events in question is not in issue.
2. Witness statements should be as concise as the circumstances of the case allow. They should be written in consecutively numbered paragraphs. They should present the evidence in an orderly and readily comprehensible manner. They must be signed by the witness, and contain a statement that he or she believes that the facts stated in his or her witness statement are true. They must indicate which of the statements made are made from the witness's own knowledge and which are made on information and belief, giving the source of the information or basis for the belief.
3. Inadmissible material should not be included. Irrelevant material should likewise not be included.
4. Any party on whom a witness statement is served who objects to the relevance or admissibility of material contained in a witness statement should notify the other party of his or her objection within 28 days after service of the witness statement in question and the parties concerned should attempt to resolve the matter as soon as possible. If it is not possible to resolve the matter, the party who objects should make an appropriate application, normally at the PTR, if there is one, or otherwise at trial.
5. It is incumbent on solicitors and counsel not to allow the costs of preparation of witness statements to be unnecessarily increased by over-elaboration of the statements. Any unnecessary elaboration may be the subject of a special order as to costs.
6. Witness statements must contain the truth, the whole truth and nothing but the truth on the

issues covered. Great care must be taken in the preparation of witness statements. No pressure of any kind should be placed on a witness to give other than a true and complete account of his or her evidence. It is improper to serve a witness statement which is known to be false or which the maker does not in all respects actually believe to be true. In addition, a professional adviser may be under an obligation to check where practicable the truth of facts stated in a witness statement if he or she is put on enquiry as to their truth. If a party discovers that a witness statement which he or she has served is incorrect he or she must inform the other parties immediately.

7. A witness statement should simply cover those issues, but only those issues, on which the party serving the statement wishes that witness to give evidence-in-chief. Thus it is not, for example, the function of a witness statement to provide a commentary on the documents in the trial bundle, nor to set out quotations from such documents, nor to engage in matters of argument. Witness statements should not deal with other matters merely because they may arise in the course of the trial.
8. Witness statements very often refer to documents. If there could be any doubt as to what document is being referred to, or if the document has not previously been made available on disclosure, it may be helpful for the document to be exhibited to the witness statement. If, to assist reference to the documents, the documents referred to are exhibited to the witness statement, they should nevertheless not be included in trial bundles in that form: see appendix 6, para. 4. If (as is normally preferable) the documents referred to in the witness statement are not exhibited, care should be taken in identifying them, for example, by reference to the lists of documents exchanged on disclosure. In preparation for trial, it will be necessary to insert cross-references to the trial bundles so as to identify the documents: see appendix 6, para. 24.
9. If a witness is not sufficiently fluent in English to give his evidence in English, the witness statement should be in the witness's own language and a translation provided. If a witness is not fluent in English but can make himself understood in broken English and can understand written English, the statement need not be in his own words provided that these matters are indicated in the statement itself. It must, however, be written so as to express as accurately as possible the substance of his evidence.

APPENDIX 10 A GUIDE FOR RECEIVERS IN THE CHANCERY DIVISION

[Appendix 10 is on the CD-ROM version of *Blackstone's Civil Practice.* Click on the title of the appendix to open it.]

APPENDIX 11 LLOYD'S NAMES' ESTATE APPLICATIONS: FORMS

[Appendix 11 is on the CD-ROM version of *Blackstone's Civil Practice.* Click on the title of the appendix to open it.]

APPENDIX 12 PRACTICE NOTE: REMUNERATION OF JUDICIAL TRUSTEES

[Appendix 12 is on the CD-ROM version of *Blackstone's Civil Practice.* Click on the title of the appendix to open it.]

Patents Court Guide

Issued 12 November 2003 and subsequently updated. By authority of the Chancellor of the High Court.

1 Introduction

The general guidance applicable to matters in the Chancery Division, as set out in the Chancery Guide, also applies to patent actions unless specifically mentioned below. 'PD 63' refers to the Practice Direction — Patents and Other Intellectual Property Claims which supplements CPR, Part 63. This Guide applies as appropriate to both the Patents Court and the Patents County Court.

2 General

Actions proceeding in the Patents Court are allocated to the multi-track (CPR, r. 63.7(1)). Attention is drawn to r. 63.7 and PD 63, paras 4.1 to 4.12.

3 The Patents Judges

The patents judges and their clerks are as set out below.
Pumfrey J (Clerk: Richard Trout — telephone (020) 7947 7482, fax (020) 7947 6593, email: richard.trout@courtservice.gsi.gov.uk)
Patten J (Clerk: Anne Bateman — telephone (020) 7947 7617, fax (020) 7947 6650, email: anne.bateman@courtservice.gsi.gov.uk)
Lewison J (Clerk: temporary clerk — telephone (020) 7947 6039, fax (020) 7947 6894)
Mann J (Clerk: Amanda Dennis — telephone (020) 7947 7964, fax (020) 7947 6739, email: amanda.dennis@courtservice.gsi.gov.uk)
Kitchin J (Clerk: Ranjit Singh — telephone (020) 7947 6518, fax (020) 7947 6439, email ranjit.singh@hmcourts-service.gsi.gov.uk)

4 Patents County Court

Claim forms for the Patents County Court and general enquiries relating to procedure, fees and forms may be addressed to:
The Specialist Section
Central London Civil Justice Section
26 Park Crescent
London W1N 4HT

Telephone: (020) 7073 4251
Fax: (020) 7073 4253

Enquiries relating to listing and existing patents cases may be addressed to:
Clerk to His Honour Judge Fysh QC
Field House
15–25 Breams Buildings
London EC4A 1DX
Telephone: (020) 7073 4251
Fax: (020) 7073 4253

5 Arrangements for Listing

The Chancery Listing Officer is responsible for the listing of all patents work.

The Chancery Listing Officer and his staff are located in Room WG04 in the Royal Courts of Justice. The office is open to the public from 10.00 a.m. to 4.30 p.m. each day. The telephone numbers are (020) 7947 6778 and (020) 7947 6690 and the fax number is (020) 7947 7345.

Appointments to fix trials and interlocutory applications are dealt with on Mondays and Thursdays between 11.00 a.m. and 12.00 noon. The applicant should first obtain an appointment from the Chancery Listing Officer and notify all interested parties of the date and time fixed.

Short applications (before the normal court day starts at 10.30 a.m.) can be issued and the hearing date arranged at any time by attendance at the Chancery Listing Office.

These are listed for hearing before the normal court day starts at 10.30, for instance at 9.30 or 10 a.m. Attention is drawn to PD 63, para. 6. Accurate time estimates are essential and a guillotine may be imposed on oral submissions if estimates show signs of being exceeded.

6 September Sittings

The Patents Court will endeavour, if the parties so desire and the case is urgent, to sit in September.

7 Appeals from the Comptroller General of Patents, Trade Marks and Designs

Patents

By virtue of statute these lie only to the High Court and not the Patents County Court. They are now governed by CPR, Part 52 (see r. 63.17). Permission to appeal is not required. Note that the Comptroller must be served with a notice of appeal (r. 63.17(3)). The appellant has the conduct of the appeal and he or his representative should within two weeks of lodging the appeal, contact the Chancery Listing Officer with a view to arranging a hearing date. The appellant shall ensure that the appeal is set down as soon as is reasonably practicable after service of the notice of appeal. Parties are reminded that the provisions about the service of skeleton arguments apply to appeals from the Comptroller.

Trade Marks

These are assigned to the Chancery Division as a whole, not the Patents Court (r. 63.17(2)). Permission to appeal is not required.

Appeals on paper only

The court will hear appeals on the papers only if that is what the parties desire. If the appellant is willing for the appeal to be heard on paper only, he should contact the respondent and the Patent Office at the earliest opportunity to discover whether such a way of proceeding is agreed. If it is, the Chancery Listing Office should be informed as soon as possible. The parties (and the Chancery Listing Officer if he/she desires) should liaise amongst themselves for early preparation of written submissions and bundles and provide the court with all necessary materials.

Appeals concerning registered designs

These go to the Registered Designs Appeal Tribunal. This consists of one of the patents judges sitting as a tribunal. The CPR and practice directions do not apply to such appeals. Where such an appeal is desired, contact should be made direct to the Chancery Listing Officer.

8 Applications without Notice

A party wishing to apply without notice to the respondent(s) should contact the Chancery Listing Office. In cases of emergency in vacation or out of normal court hours the application should be made to the duty Chancery judge. In the Patents County Court, contact should be made with the Court Office.

9 Documents

(a) Bundling is of considerable importance and should be approached intelligently. The general guidance given in appendix [6] to the Chancery Guide should be followed. Solicitors or patent agents who fail to do so may be required to explain why and may be penalised personally in costs.

(b) Copies of documents referred to in a statement of case (e.g., an advertisement referred to in a claim of infringement form or documents cited in grounds of invalidity) should be served with the statement of case. Where any such document requires translation, a translation should be served at the same time.

(c) If it is known which judge will be taking the case, papers for the case should be lodged directly with that judge's clerk. Faxed documents of significance (and particularly skeleton arguments) should be followed up by clean direct prints. By agreement documents may also be sent by email to the clerk of the judge concerned.

(d) It is the responsibility of both parties to ensure that all relevant documents are lodged with the clerk of the judge who will be taking the case by noon two days before the date fixed for hearing unless some longer or shorter period has been ordered by the judge or is prescribed by this Guide.

(e) The judges request that all important documents also be supplied to them on disk in a format convenient for the judge's use (normally Microsoft Word 7 for Windows). These will include skeleton arguments, the witness statements and expert reports.

10 Streamlined Procedure

(a) Nature of a streamlined procedure

A streamlined procedure is one in which, save and to the extent that it is otherwise ordered:

- all factual and expert evidence is in writing;
- there is no requirement to give disclosure of documents;
- there are no experiments;
- cross-examination is only permitted on any topic or topics where it is necessary and is confined to those topics;
- the total duration of the trial fixed is and will normally be not more than one day;
- the date for trial will be fixed when the order for a streamlined trial is made and will normally be about six months thereafter.

A streamlined procedure also includes minor variants of the above (e.g., disclosure confined to a limited issue).

(b) Criteria for a streamlined procedure

The court will order a streamlined procedure by agreement or, in the absence of agreement, where application of the overriding objective indicates that it is appropriate. Particular emphasis will be placed on proportionality, the financial position of each of the parties, degree of complexity and the importance of the case.

(c) When to apply for streamlined procedure

Any party may apply at any time after commencement of the action for a streamlined procedure. Any such application should be made at the earliest time reasonably possible, which will generally be at the case management conference required by PD 63 within 14 days after service of the defence.

(d) How to apply for a streamlined procedure

A party wishing for a streamlined procedure should, in the first instance, invite the other party(ies) to agree, setting out the proposed procedural steps in a draft order. If there is agreement, the court will normally make the order on a written application signed on behalf of each party. The parties should liaise with each other and the Chancery Listing Officer or the Patents County Court concerning a date for trial so that this can be fixed.

If there is no agreement, the party wishing for a streamlined procedure must make an application for it, setting forth the proposed procedural directions in his application notice and requesting that the application be determined on paper. He should support the application by a witness statement addressing the criteria in CPR, r. 1.1(2). The opposing party must, unless he obtains an extension of time (by consent or from the court) make and serve on the opposite party a witness statement in response within 10 days of service upon him of the application notice.

The court will determine the matter provisionally on paper alone and make a provisional judgment and order accordingly. Unless either side seeks an oral hearing the provisional order will come into effect seven days after its service on the parties.

If a party is desirous of an oral hearing, it must, within seven days of service upon it of the provisional order, seek an oral hearing in the immediate future by contacting the clerk to the judge in charge of the patents list. Such an oral hearing will be fixed as soon as is practicable, either by way of a telephone hearing or a short application.

(e) Duty to inform clients

The parties' legal advisers must draw their clients' attention to the availability of a streamlined procedure in the Patents Court and the Patents County Court.

11 Timetable for Trial, Reading Guide, Time Estimates, Common General Knowledge

Attention is drawn to PD 63, para. 7. Further the parties should endeavour to produce a composite document setting forth the matters alleged to form part of the common general knowledge and, where they disagree, what that disagreement is.

12 Narrowing of Issues

As early as possible the patentee should identify which of the claims of its patent are contended to have independent validity and which of those claims are said to be infringed and should communicate a list of those claims to the other party.

This position should be kept under constant review. If there is any alteration in the number of claims said to have independent validity the patentee must forthwith notify the other parties.

13 Admissions

With a view to early elimination of non-issues, practitioners are reminded of the necessity of making admissions in accordance with CPR, r. 32.18, at an early stage. It should be done as early as possible, for instance, in a defence or reply. Thus in a defence a party may admit the acts complained of or that his article/process has certain of the features of a claim. In a reply a patentee may be able to admit prior publication of cited documents.

Parties should also consider making a request to identify points not in dispute. Technically a request seeking admissions in respect of particular integers of a claim may involve a mixed question of fact and law and so not be within the rules about admissions. By asking whether or not the defendant disputes that his article/process has certain features of the claim the real dispute can be narrowed. Thus the ambit of disclosure and of witness and expert statements will be narrowed.

14 Skeleton Arguments, Pre-trial and after the Evidence

In addition to the reading guide parties should lodge skeleton arguments in time for the judge to read them before trial. That should normally be at least two days before commencement of the trial, but in substantial cases a longer period (to be discussed with the clerk to the judge concerned) may be needed. It is desirable that each party should summarise what it contends to be the common general knowledge of the man skilled in the art.

Following the evidence in a substantial trial a short adjournment may be granted to enable the parties to summarise their arguments in writing before oral argument.

In trials where a transcript of evidence is being made and supplied to the judge, the transcript should be accompanied by a version on disk.

15 Jurisdiction of Masters

Masters have only a limited jurisdiction in patent matters (see PD 63, para. 8). Generally it is more convenient for consent orders (on paper or in court) to be made by a judge even where a master has jurisdiction to do so.

Where a master makes a consent order disposing of an action which has been fixed, it is the duty of all the parties' representatives to inform both the clerk in charge of the patents list and the Listing Office that the case has settled.

16 Agreed Orders

The court is normally willing to make consent orders without the need for the attendance of any parties. A draft of the agreed order and the written consent of all the parties' respective solicitors or counsel should be supplied to the clerk in charge of the patents list. Where a draft has been substantially amended by hand, it is helpful for a disk of the unamended version to be supplied in accordance with para. 9.6 of the Chancery Guide. Unless the judge considers a hearing is needed he will make the order in the agreed terms by initialling it. It will be drawn up accordingly and sent to the parties.

17 Telephone Applications

For short (20 minutes or less) matters, the patents judges are willing, unless a matter of general public importance is involved, to hear applications by telephone conference in accordance with PD 23.

It is possible for the application to be recorded, and if recording by the Patents Court rather than by British Telecom (or other service provider) is requested arrangements should be made with the clerk in charge of the patents list. The recording will not be transcribed. The tape will be kept for a period of six months. Arrangements for transcription, if needed, must be made by the parties.

This procedure should be used where it will save costs.

18 Patents Judges Able and Willing to Sit out of London

If the parties so desire, for the purpose of saving time or costs, the Patents Court will sit out of London. Before any approach is made to the clerk in charge of the patents list, the parties should discuss between themselves the desirability of such course. If there is a dispute as to venue the court will resolve the matter on an application. Where there is no dispute, the clerk should be contacted as soon as possible so that arrangements can be put in place well before the date of the proposed hearing. The Patents County Court may also be able to sit out of London.

19 Intellectual Property Court Users' Committee

This considers the problems and concerns of intellectual property litigation generally. Membership of the committee includes the principal patents judges, the Patents County Court judge, a representative of each of the Patent Bar Association, the Intellectual Property Lawyers Association, the Chartered Institute of Patent Agents, the Institute of Trade Mark Agents and the Trade Marks Designs and Patents Federation. It will also include one or more other Chancery judges. Anyone having views concerning the improvement of intellectual property litigation is invited to make his or her views known to the committee, preferably through the relevant professional representative on the committee. The Patents County Court also has a Users' Committee.

20 Orders Following Judgment

Where a judgment is made available in draft before being given in open court the parties should, in advance of that occasion, exchange drafts of the desired consequential order. It is highly undesirable that one party should spring a proposal on the other for the first time when judgment is given. Where the parties are agreed as to the consequential order and have supplied a copy of the same signed by all parties or their representatives, attendance at the handing down of the judgment is not necessary.

21 Applications for Interim Remedies: Trial Dates

When an application for an interim remedy is made the claimant should, where practicable, make prior investigations as to the estimated length of trial and possible trial dates.

22 Specimen Minute of Order for Directions

The standard form of order for directions annexed to this practice direction has the approval of the patents judges. It is intended only as a guide and may need adaptation for particular circumstances.

Standard Form of Order for Directions

(* indicates a provision which may be necessary when a rule has not been compiled with, for example, standard disclosure in accordance with PD 63.)

[RECITALS AS NECESSARY]

Transfer

1 [This Action and Counterclaim be transferred to the Patents County Court.] (*If this order is made, no other order will generally be necessary, though it will generally be desirable for procedural orders to be made at this time to save the costs of a further conference in the county court.*)

Proof of Documents

2 Legible copies of the specification of the patent in suit [and any patent specifications or other documents cited in the particulars of objections] may be used at the trial without further proof thereof or of their contents.

Amendments to Pleadings

3 The claimants have leave to amend their claim form as shown in red on the copy [annexed to the application notice/as signed by the solicitors for the parties/annexed hereto] and [to reserve the same on or before [*date*]/ that re-service be dispensed with] and that the defendants have leave to serve a consequentially amended defence within [*number*] days [thereafter/hereafter] and that the claimants have leave to serve a consequentially amended reply (if so advised) within [*number*] days thereafter.

4 (a) The defendants have leave to amend their defence [and Part 20 claim and grounds of invalidity] as shown in red on the copy [annexed to the application notice/as signed by the solicitors for the parties/annexed hereto] and [to re-serve the same within [*number*] days/on or before [*date*]] [that re-service be dispensed with] and that the claimants have leave to serve a consequentially amended reply (if so advised) within [*number*] days thereafter.

(b) The claimants do on or before [*date*] elect whether they will discontinue this claim and withdraw their defence to Part 20 claim and consent to an order for the revocation of patent No. [*number*] (' the patent in suit') AND IF the claimants shall so elect and give notice thereof in the time aforesaid IT IS ORDERED THAT the patent in suit be revoked [and that it be referred to the costs judge to assess the costs of the defendants and this action and grounds of invalidity up to and including [*date*] being the date of service of the [amended] grounds of invalidity and Part 20 claim to the date of this order [except so far as the same have been increased by the failure of the defendants originally to deliver the defence and grounds of invalidity in its amended form], and to assess the costs of the claimants in this action and Part 20 claim from [*date*] [in so far as they have been increased by the failure of the defendants aforesaid] AND IT IS ORDERED that the said costs judge is to set off the costs of the defendants and of the claimants when so assessed as aforesaid and to certify to which of them the balance after such set-off is due.]/[*Order for payment of sums determined by the court on a summary assessment*].

Further Information and Clarification

5 (a) The [claimants/defendants] do on or before [*date*] serve on the [defendants/claimants] the further information or clarification of the [*specify statement of case*] as requested by the [claimants/defendants] by their request served on the [defendants/claimants] on [*date*] [and/or]

(b) The [claimants/defendants] do on or before [*date*] serve on the [defendants/claimants] a response to their request for further information or clarification of the [*identify statement of case*] served on the [defendants/claimants] on [*date*].

*Admissions**

6 The [claimants/defendants] do on or before [*date*] state in writing whether or not they admit the facts specified in the [defendants'/ claimants'] notice to admit facts dated [*date*].

Security

7 The claimants do provide security for the defendants' costs in the sum of £[*state sum*] by [*specify manner in which security to be given*] and that in the meantime all further proceedings be stayed.

*Lists of Documents**

8 (a) The claimants and the defendants respectively do on or before [*state date*] make and serve on the other of them a list in accordance with form N264 of the documents in their control which they are required to disclose in accordance with the obligation of standard disclosure in accordance with CPR, Part 31, as modified by PD 63, para. 5.

(b) In respect of those issues identified in schedule [*number*] hereto disclosure shall be limited to those [documents/categories of documents] listed in schedule [*number*].

*Inspection**

9 If any party wishes to inspect or have copies of such documents as are in another party's control it shall give notice in writing that it wishes to do so and such inspection shall be allowed at all reasonable times upon reasonable notice and any copies shall be provided within [*number*] working days of the request upon the undertaking of the party requesting the copies to pay the reasonable copying charges.

*Experiments**

10 (a) Where a party desires to establish any fact by experimental proof, including an experiment conducted for the purposes of litigation or otherwise not being an experiment conducted in the normal course of research, that party shall on or before [*date*] serve on all the other parties a notice stating the facts which it desires to establish and giving full particulars of the experiments proposed to establish them.

(b) A party upon whom a notice is served under the preceding sub-paragraph shall within [*number*] days serve on the party serving the notice a notice stating in respect of each fact whether or not that party admits it.

(c) Where any fact which a party wishes to establish by experimental proof is not admitted that party shall apply to the court for further directions in respect of such experiments.

[Or where para. 9 of PD 63 has been complied with.]

11 (a) The claimants/defendants are to afford to the other parties an opportunity, if so requested, of inspecting a repetition of the experiments identified in paragraphs [*specify them*] of the notice[s] of experiments served on [*date*]. Any such inspection must be requested within [*number*] days of the date of this order and shall take place within [*number*] days of the date of the request.

(b) If any party shall wish to establish any fact in reply to experimental proof that party shall on or before [*date*] serve on all the other parties a notice stating the facts which it desires to establish and giving full particulars of the experiments proposed to establish them.

(c) A party upon whom a notice is served under the preceding sub-paragraph shall within [*number*] days serve on the party serving the notice a notice stating in respect of each fact whether or not that party admits it.

(d) Where any fact which a party wishes to establish by experimental proof in reply is not admitted the party may apply to the court for further directions in respect of such experiments.

Notice of Models, etc.

12 (a) If any party wishes to rely at the trial of this action upon any model, apparatus, drawing, photograph, cinematograph or video film whether or not the same is contained in a witness statement, affidavit or expert's report that party shall on or before [*date*] give notice thereof to all the other parties; shall afford the other parties an opportunity within [*number*] days of the service of such notice of inspecting the same and shall, if so requested, furnish the other party with copies of any such drawing or photograph and a sufficient drawing photograph or other illustration of any model or apparatus.

(b) If any party wishes to rely upon any such materials in reply to any matter of which notice was given under sub-paragraph (a) of this paragraph, that party shall within [*number*] days after the last inspection to be made in pursuance of the said sub-paragraph (a) give to the other parties a like notice, and if so requested within [*number*] days of delivery of such notice shall afford like opportunities of inspection which shall take place within [*number*] days of such request; and shall in like manner furnish copies of any drawing or photograph and illustration of any such model or apparatus.

(c) No further or other model apparatus drawing photograph cinematograph or video film shall be relied upon in evidence by either party save with consent or by leave of the court.

Written Evidence

13 (a) Each party may call up to [*number*] expert witnesses in this action and Part 20 claim provided that the said party:

(i) supplies the name of such expert to the other parties and to the court on or before [*date*]; and

(ii) no later than [*date*]/[[*number*] days before the date set for the hearing of this action and Part 20 claim] serve upon the other parties a report of each such expert comprising the evidence which that expert intends to give at trial.

(b) Each party shall on or before [*date*] serve on the other parties [signed] written statements of the oral evidence which the party intends to lead on any issues of fact to be decided at the trial, such statements to stand as the evidence-in-chief of the witness unless the court otherwise directs.

(c) The parties shall [*here insert the particular directions sought, e.g., within 21 days after service of the other party's expert reports and written statements state in writing the facts and matters in those reports and statements which are admitted*].

Admissibility of Evidence

14 A party who objects to any statements of any witness being read by the judge prior to hearing of the trial, shall serve upon each other party a notice in writing to that effect setting out the grounds of the objection.

Non-compliance

15 Where either party fails to comply with the directions relating to experiments and written evidence it shall not be entitled to adduce evidence to which such directions relate without the leave of the court.

Trial Bundles

16 Each party shall no later than [*number*] days before the date fixed for the trial of this action and counterclaim serve upon the parties a list of all the documents to be included in the trial bundles. The claimants shall no later than [*number*] days before the date fixed for trial serve upon the defendants [*number*] sets of bundles for use at trial.

Trial

17 The trial of these proceedings shall be before an assigned judge alone in [London], estimated length [*number*] days and a pre-reading estimate for the judge of [*number*] days.

Liberty to Apply

18 The parties are to be at liberty on two days' notice to apply for further directions and generally.

Costs

19 The costs of this application are to be costs in the action and Part 20 claim.

Queen's Bench Guide
May 2000

1 INTRODUCTION

1.1 The Guide

1.1.1 This Guide has been prepared by the Senior Master, acting under the authority of the Lord Chief Justice, and provides a general explanation of the work and practice of the Queen's Bench Division with particular regard to proceedings started in the Central Office, and is designed to make it easier for parties to use and proceed in the Queen's Bench Division.

1.1.2 The Guide must be read with the Civil Procedure Rules ('the CPR') and the supporting practice directions. Litigants and their advisers are responsible for acquainting themselves with the CPR; it is not the task of this Guide to summarise the CPR, nor should anyone regard it as a substitute for the CPR. It is intended to bring the Guide up to date at regular intervals as necessary.

1.1.3 The Guide does not have the force of law, but parties using the Queen's Bench Division will be expected to act in accordance with this Guide. Further guidance as to the practice of the Queen's Bench Division may be obtained from the practice master (see paragraph 6.1 below).

1.1.4 It is assumed throughout the Guide that the litigant intends to proceed in the Royal Courts of Justice. For all essential purposes, though, the Guide is equally applicable to the work of the district registries, which deal with the work of the Queen's Bench Division outside London, but it should be borne in mind that there are some differences.

1.1.5 The telephone numbers and room numbers quoted in the Guide are correct at the time of going to press. However, the room numbers quoted for the Clerk of the Lists and the Listing Office are effective as from 2 October 2000.

1.2 The Civil Procedure Rules

1.2.1 The overriding objective set out in Part 1 of the CPR is central to the new culture which enables the court to deal with cases justly. To further this aim the work is allocated to one of three tracks — the small claims track, the fast track and the multi-track — so as to dispose of the work in the most appropriate and effective way combined with active case management by the court.

1.2.2 The CPR are divided into Parts. A particular Part is referred to in the Guide as Part 7, etc., as the case may be. Any particular rule within a Part is referred to as r. 6.4(2), and so on.

1.3 The Practice Directions

1.3.1 Each Part — or almost each Part — has an accompanying practice direction or directions, and other practice directions deal with matters such as the pre-action protocols and the former Rules of the Supreme Court and the County Court Rules which are scheduled to Part 50.

1.3.2 The practice directions are made pursuant to statute, and have the same authority as do the CPR themselves.[1] However, in case of any conflict between a rule and a practice direction, the rule will prevail.[2] […]

[1] Civil Procedure Act 1997, ss. 1 and 5, and sch. 1, paras 3 and 6.
[2] There is one exception: Part 8.

1.4 The Forms

1.4.1 PD 4 lists the practice forms that are required by or referred to in the CPR, and also those referred to in such of the Rules of the Supreme Court and the County Court Rules as are still in force (see Part 50 of the CPR; sch. 1 and 2).

1.4.2 Those listed in Table 1 with a number prefixed by the letter N are new forms, a number of these forms have been published with the CPR. Those listed in Table 2 are forms still in use in the High Court but altered so as to conform to the CPR. They may be used as precedents and are set out in a separate Appendix to this Guide and include:

(1) Forms that were previously prescribed forms; these are listed under the same numbers that previously identified them.
(2) Former practice forms common to both the Chancery and Queen's Bench Divisions; these forms have been given numbers starting with the letters PF.
(3) Former practice forms used mainly in the Queen's Bench Division; these forms have been given numbers ending with the letters QB.
(4) Former practice forms used mainly in the Chancery Division; these forms have been given numbers ending with the letters CH.

1.4.3 The forms may be modified as circumstances in individual cases require,[3] but it is essential that a modified form contains at least as full information or guidance as would have been given if the original form had been used.

1.4.4 Where the Royal Arms appears on any listed form it must appear on any modification of that form. The same format for the Royal Arms as is used on the listed forms need not be used. All that is necessary is that there is a complete Royal Arms.

1.5 The Queen's Bench Division

1.5.1 The Queen's Bench Division is one of the three Divisions of the High Court, together with the Chancery Division and Family Division. The Lord Chief Justice is President of the Queen's Bench Division, and certain High Court judges and masters are assigned to it. A Lord Justice of Appeal (currently Lord Justice Kennedy) has been appointed by the Lord Chief Justice to be the Vice-President of the Division; a High Court judge is appointed as judge in charge of the Jury List (currently Mr Justice Moreland); another is appointed as judge in charge of the Trial List (currently Mr Justice Buckley).

1.5.2 Outside London, the work of the Queen's Bench Division is administered in provincial offices known as district registries. In London, the work is administered in the Central Office at the Royal Courts of Justice. The work in the Central Office of the Queen's Bench Division is the responsibility of the Senior Master, acting under the authority of the Lord Chief Justice.

1.5.3 The work of the Queen's Bench Division is (with certain exceptions) governed by the CPR. The Divisional Court, the Admiralty Court, the Commercial Court and the Technology and Construction Court are all part of the Queen's Bench Division. However, each does specialised work requiring a distinct procedure that to some extent modifies the CPR. For that reason each publishes its own guide or practice direction, to which reference should be made by parties wishing to proceed in the specialist courts.

1.5.4 The work of the Queen's Bench Division consists mainly of claims for:

(1) damages in respect of:
  (a) personal injury,
  (b) negligence,
  (c) breach of contract, and
  (d) libel and slander (defamation),
(2) non-payment of a debt, and
(3) possession of land or property.

Proceedings retained to be dealt with in the Central Office of the Queen's Bench Division will almost invariably be multi-track claims.

1.5.5 In many types of claim — for example, claims in respect of negligence by solicitors, accountants, etc. or claims for possession of land — the claimant has a choice whether to

[3] See r. 4.3.

bring the claim in the Queen's Bench Division or in the Chancery Division. However, there are certain claims that may be brought only in the Queen's Bench Division, namely:

(1) sheriffs interpleader proceedings,
(2) enrolment of deeds,
(3) registration of foreign judgments under the Civil Jurisdiction and Judgments Act 1982,
(4) applications for bail in criminal proceedings,
(5) applications under the Administration of Justice Act 1920 and the Foreign Judgments (Reciprocal Enforcement) Act 1933,
(6) registration and satisfaction of bills of sale,
(7) election petitions,
(8) obtaining evidence for foreign courts.

1.6 The Central Office

1.6.1 The information in this and the following paragraph is to be found in the PD 2, para. 2; it is reproduced here for the convenience of litigants. The Central Office is open for business from 10 a.m. to 4.30 p.m. (except during August when it is open from 10 a.m. to 2.30 p.m.) on every day of the year except:

(1) Saturdays and Sundays,
(2) Good Friday and the day after Easter Monday,
(3) Christmas Day and, if that day is a Friday or Saturday, then 28 December,
(4) Bank Holidays in England and Wales (under the Banking and Financial Dealings Act 1971), and
(5) such other days as the Lord Chancellor, with the concurrence of the Lord Chief Justice, the Master of the Rolls, the President of the Family Division and the Vice-Chancellor, may direct.

1.6.2 One of the masters of the Queen's Bench Division is present at the Central Office on every day on which the office is open for the purpose of superintending the business administered there and giving any directions that may be required on questions of practice and procedure. He is normally referred to as the 'Practice Master'. (See paragraph 6.1 below for information about the Practice Master and masters in general.)

1.6.3 The Central Office consists of the Action Department, the Masters' Secretary's Department, the Queen's Bench Associates' Department, the Clerk of the Lists, the Registry of the Technology and Construction Court and the Admiralty and Commercial Registry.

1.6.4 The Action Department deals with the issue of claims, responses to claims, admissions, undefended and summary judgments, enforcement, drawing up certain orders, public searches, provision of copies of court documents, enrolment of deeds, submission of references to the Court of Justice of the European Communities and registration of foreign judgments.

1.6.5 The Masters' Secretary's Department covers three discrete areas of work;

(1) the Masters' Support Unit which provides support (a) to the Masters, including assisting with case management, and (b) to the Senior Master,
(2) foreign process, and
(3) investment of children's funds.

1.6.6 The Queen's Bench associates sit in court with the judges during trials and certain interim hearings. The Chief Associate manages the Queen's Bench associates and also provides support to the Senior Master as the Queen's Remembrancer and as the prescribed officer for election petitions. The associates draw up the orders made in court at trial and those interim orders that the parties do not wish to draw up themselves.

1.6.7 The Clerk of the Lists lists all trials and matters before the judges (see paragraph 8 below).

1.6.8 The Technology and Construction Court deals with claims which involve issues or questions which are technically complex or for which a trial by a judge of that court is for any other reason desirable (see [CPR, Part 60 and PD 60]).

1.6.9 The Admiralty and Commercial Court deals mainly with shipping collision claims and claims concerning charters and insurance, and commercial arbitrations. See the [Admiralty and Commercial Court Guide and CPR, Parts 58, 59 and 61, PD 58, PD 59 and PD 61.]

1.7 The Judiciary

1.7.1 The judiciary in the Queen's Bench Division consist of the High Court judges (The Honourable Mr/Mrs Justice ...... and addressed in court as my Lord/my Lady) and in the Royal Courts of Justice the masters (Master ....); in the district registries the work of the masters is conducted by district judges.

1.7.2 Trial normally takes place before a High Court judge (or deputy High Court judge[4]) who may also hear pre-trial reviews and other interim applications. Wherever possible the judge before whom a trial has been fixed will hear any pre-trial review. A High Court judge will hear applications to commit for contempt of court, applications for injunctions[5] and most appeals from masters' orders. (See PD 2B, and see paragraphs 7.11 and 7.12 below for more information on hearings and applications.)

1.7.3 The masters deal with interim and some pre-action applications, and manage the claims so that they proceed without delay. The masters' rooms are situated in the East Block of the Royal Courts of Justice. Hearings take place in these rooms or (short hearings only) in the Bear Garden.

1.7.4 Cases are assigned on issue by a court officer in the Action Department to masters on a random basis, and that master is then known as the assigned master in relation to that case. (See paragraphs 6.2 and 6.3 below for more information about assignment and the masters' lists.)

1.7.5 General enquiries about the business dealt with by the masters should initially be made in writing to the Masters' Support Unit in Room E14.

2 GENERAL

2.1 Essential Matters

2.1.1 Before bringing any proceedings, the intending claimant should think carefully about the implications of so doing. (See paragraph 3 below about steps to be taken before issuing a claim form.)

2.1.2 A litigant who is acting in person faces a heavier burden in terms of time and effort than does a litigant who is legally represented, but all litigation calls for a high level of commitment from the parties. No intending claimant should underestimate this.

2.1.3 The overriding objective of the CPR is to deal with cases justly, which means dealing with the claim in a way which is proportionate (amongst other things) to the amount of money involved.[6] However, in all proceedings there are winners and losers; the loser is generally ordered to pay the costs of the winner and the costs of litigation can still be large. The risk of large costs is particularly acute in cases involving expert witnesses, barristers and solicitors. Also, the costs of an interim hearing are almost always summarily assessed and made payable by the unsuccessful party usually within 14 days after the order for costs is made.[7] There may be a number of interim hearings before the trial itself is reached, so the costs must be paid as the claim progresses. (See also paragraph 2.5 below.)

2.1.4 The intending claimant should also keep in mind that every claim must be proved, unless of course the defendant admits the allegations. There is little point in incurring the risks and expense of litigating if the claim cannot be proved. An intending claimant should therefore be taking steps to obtain statements from his prospective witnesses before starting the claim; if he delays until later, it may turn out that he is in fact unable to obtain the evidence that he needs to prove his claim. A defendant faces a similar task.

2.1.5 Any party may, if he is to succeed, need an opinion from one or more expert witnesses, such as medical practitioners, engineers, accountants, or as the case may be. However he must remember that no expert evidence may be given at trial without the permission of the court. If the claim is for compensation for personal injuries, the claimant must produce a medical report with his particulars of claim.

[4] A deputy High Court judge may be a circuit judge or a Queen's counsel. A retired High Court judge may also sit as a High Court judge.

[5] See Part 25 and PD 25 for more information about injunctions and who may hear them, and interim remedies in general.

[6] See r. 1.1.

[7] See r. 44.8.

2.1.6 The services of such experts are in great demand, especially as in some fields of expertise there are few of them. It may take many months to obtain an opinion, and the cost may be high. (See paragraph 7.9 below for information about experts' evidence.) The claimant must remember also not to allow the time limit for starting his claim to pass (see paragraph 2.3 below for information about time limits).

2.1.7 Any intending claimant should also have in mind that he will usually be required to give standard disclosure of the documents on which he relies. Although r. 31.3(2) makes provision for a party not to be required to disclose documents if disclosure would be disproportionate to the value of the claim, in complex cases it may still be necessary to disclose relatively large quantities of documents, and this invariably involves much time, effort and expense. (See paragraph 7.8 below for information about disclosure.)

2.1.8 In many cases the parties will need legal assistance, whether by way of advice, drafting, representation at hearings or otherwise. It is not the function of court staff to give legal advice, however, subject to that, they will do their best to assist any litigant. Litigants in person who need assistance or funding should contact the Community Legal Service through their information points. The CLS are developing local networks of people giving legal assistance such as law centres, local solicitors or the Citizens Advice Bureaux. CLS Information Points are being set up in libraries and other public places. Litigants can telephone the CLS to find their nearest CLS Information Point on 0845 608 1122 or can log on to the CLS website at www.justask.org.uk for the CLS directory and for legal information.

2.1.9 The RCJ Advice Bureau off the Main Hall at the Royal Courts of Justice is open Monday to Friday from 10.00 a.m. to 1.00 p.m. and from 2.00 p.m. to 5.00 p.m. The Bureau is run by lawyers in conjunction with the Citizens Advice Bureau and is independent of the court. The Bureau operates on a 'first come first served' basis, or telephone advice is available on (020) 7947 7604 Monday to Friday from 11.00 a.m. to 12.00 p.m. and from 3.00 p.m. to 4.00 p.m.

2.2 Inspection and Copies of Documents

2.2.1 Intending claimants must not expect to be able to keep the details of a claim away from public scrutiny. In addition to the right of a party to obtain copies of documents in the proceedings to which he is a party from the court record (on payment of the prescribed fee), a claim form when it has been served, and the particulars of claim where they are included in or served with the claim form, may be inspected by anyone simply on payment of the fee. Any judgment or order made in public may also be inspected on payment of the fee. Additionally, other documents may be inspected with the permission of the court.[8]

2.2.2 Witness statements[9] used at trial are open to inspection unless the court directs otherwise.[10] Considerations of publicity are often particularly important in deciding whether to commence proceedings in respect of an alleged libel or slander; such a claim may by its attendant publicity do more damage than was ever inflicted by the original publication. In such proceedings the claimant may decide to serve his particulars of claim separately from the claim form.[11]

2.3 Time Limits

2.3.1 There are strict time limits that apply to every claim. First, there are time limits fixed by the Limitation Act 1980 within which proceedings must be brought. There are circumstances in which the court may extend those time limits, but this should be regarded as exceptional. In all other cases, once the relevant time limit has expired, it is rarely possible to start a claim.

2.3.2 Secondly, in order to try and bring the proceedings to an early trial date, a timetable will be set with which all parties must comply. Unless the CPR or a practice direction provide otherwise, or the court orders otherwise, the timetable may be varied by the written agreement of the parties.[12] However, there are certain 'milestone' events in the timetable in which the time limits may not be varied by the parties. Examples of these are:

[8] See r. 5.4 and PD 5.

[9] See paragraph 7.10 below about evidence.

[10] See r. 32.13.

[11] See Part 53 and PD 53 for matters to be included in the claim form in a defamation claim where the particulars of claim are served separately.

[12] See r. 2.11.

(1) return of the allocation questionnaire
(2) date for the case management conference
(3) return of the listing questionnaire
(4) date fixed for trial.

Where parties have extended a time limit by agreement, the party for whom the time has been extended must advise the Masters' Support Unit in writing of the event in the proceedings for which the time has been extended and the new date by which it must be done. For example, if an extension is agreed for the filing of the defence, it is for the defendant to inform the Masters' Support Unit.

2.3.3 The court has power to penalise any party who fails to comply with a time limit. If the court considers that a prior warning should be given before a penalty is imposed, it will make an 'unless' order; in other words, the court will order that, unless that party performs his obligation by the time specified, he will be penalised in the manner set out in the order. This may involve the party in default having his claim or statement of case struck out and judgment given against him.

2.4 Legal Representation

2.4.1 A party may act in person or be represented by a lawyer. A party who is acting in person may be assisted at any hearing by another person (often referred to as a McKenzie friend) subject to the discretion of the court. The McKenzie friend is allowed to help by taking notes, quietly prompting the litigant and offering advice and suggestions. The litigant, however, must conduct his own case; the McKenzie friend may not represent him and may only in very exceptional circumstances be allowed to address the court on behalf of the litigant under s. 27(2)(c) of the Courts and Legal Services Act 1990.

2.4.2 A written statement should be provided to the court at any hearing concerning the representation of the parties in accordance with PD 39, para. 5.1.

2.4.3 At a trial, a company or corporation may be represented by an employee if the company or corporation authorise him to do so and the court gives permission. Where this is to be the case, the permission of the judge who is to hear the case may be sought informally; PD 39, para. 5 describes what is needed to obtain permission from the court for this purpose and mentions some of the considerations relevant to the grant or refusal of permission. A further statement concerning representation should be provided in accordance with PD 39, para. 5.2.

2.4.4 The practice of allowing experienced outdoor clerks to appear before the masters will continue.

2.5 Costs

2.5.1 Costs are dealt with in Parts 43 to 48.[13] There are important new provisions in the costs rules, particularly with respect to:
(1) informing the client of costs orders,
(2) providing the court with estimates of costs,
(3) summary assessment of costs,
(4) interim orders for costs, and
(5) interest on costs.

2.5.2 Solicitors now have a duty under r. 44.2 to notify their client within seven days if an order for costs is made against him in his absence. Solicitors must also notify any other person who has instructed them to act in the proceedings or who is liable to pay their fees (such as an insurer, trade union or the Legal Services Commission (LSC)). They must also inform these persons how the order came to be made (PD 43–48, paras 7.1 and 7.2).

2.5.3 The court may at any stage order any party to file an estimate of base costs (substantially in the form of precedent H in the Schedule of Costs Precedents annexed to PD 43–48) and serve copies on all the other parties (para. 6.3). This will both assist the court in deciding what case management directions to make and inform the other parties as to their potential liability for payment of costs.

[13] Rule 43.2 and sections 1 and 2 of PD 43–48 contain the definitions and applications used throughout Parts 43 to 48 and PD 43–48.

Court Guides

2.5.4 If a party seeks an order for his costs, in order to assist the court in making a summary assessment, he must prepare a written statement of the costs he intends to claim in accordance with PD 43–48, para. 13.5, following as closely as possible form N260. In addition, when an allocation questionnaire or a listing questionnaire is filed, the party filing it must file and serve an estimate of costs on all the other parties.

2.5.5 If the parties have agreed the amount of costs, they do not need to file a statement of the costs, and summary assessment is unnecessary. Or, where the parties agree a consent order without any party attending on the application, the parties should insert either an agreed figure for costs or that there should be no order for costs in the order (PD 43–48, para. 13.4).

2.5.6 Unless the court decides not to order an assessment of costs where, for example, it orders costs to be 'costs in the case',[14] it may either make a summary assessment of costs or order a detailed assessment to take place.[15]

The court will generally make a summary assessment of costs at any hearing which lasts for less than one day:

(1) 'summary assessment' is where the court, when making an order for costs, assesses those costs and orders payment of a sum of money in respect of them,[16] and

(2) 'detailed assessment' is the procedure by which the amount of costs is decided by a costs officer at a later date in accordance with Part 47.

The provision of summary assessment means that the paying party is likely to be paying the costs at an earlier stage than he would have done under the previous rules (and see paragraph 2.5.15 below).

2.5.7 The court will not make a summary assessment of the costs of a receiving party (the party to whom the costs are to be paid) where he is:

(1) a child or patient within the meaning of Part 21 unless the solicitor acting for the child or patient has waived the right to further costs,[17] or

(2) an assisted person or a person in receipt of funded services under the Access to Justice Act 1999, ss. 4 to 11.

The costs payable by a party who is an assisted person or a person in receipt of funded services may be summarily assessed as the assessment is not by itself a determination of the assisted person's liability to pay those costs.[18]

2.5.8 Rule 44.3A prevents the court from assessing an additional liability in respect of a funding agreement before the conclusion of the proceedings. At an interim hearing therefore, the court will assess only the base costs. (See PD 43–48, para. 14.9 for assessing an additional liability and Section 19 for information about funding arrangements.)

2.5.9 Interim orders for costs: where the court decides immediately who is to pay particular costs, but does not assess the costs summarily, for example, after a trial lasting more than a day, so that the final amount of costs payable has to be fixed by a detailed assessment, the court may order the paying party to pay a sum or sums on account of the ultimate liability for costs.[19]

2.5.10 Interest on costs: the court has power to award interest on costs from a date before the date of the order, so compensating the receiving party for the delay between incurring the costs and receiving payment in respect of them.

2.5.11 Parties should note that where the court makes an order which does not mention costs, no party is entitled to costs in relation to that order.[20]

2.5.12 Rule 44.3 describes the court's discretion as to costs and the circumstances to be taken into account when exercising its discretion. Rules 44.4 and 44.5 set out the basis of assessment and the factors to be taken into account in deciding the amount of costs. (See also PD 43–48 Sections 8 and 11.)

[14] See the table in PD 43–48, para. 8.5, for some of the most common costs orders the court may make.

[15] See r. 44.7 and PD 43–48, section 12.

[16] See PD 43–48, sections 12 and 13.

[17] See PD 43–48, paras 13.11 and 51.1.

[18] See PD 43–48, para. 13.10.

[19] See r. 44.3(8).

[20] See r. 44.13(1).

2.5.13 The amount of costs to be paid by one party to another can be assessed on the standard basis or on the indemnity basis. The basis to be used is decided when the court decides that a party should pay the costs of another. Costs that are unreasonably incurred or are unreasonable in amount are not allowed on either basis.

2.5.14 The standard basis is the usual basis for assessment, where only costs which are proportionate to the matters in issue are allowed, and any doubt as to whether the costs were reasonably incurred or reasonable and proportionate in amount is resolved in favour of the paying party. On the indemnity basis, any such doubts are resolved in favour of the receiving party.

2.5.15 A party must normally pay summarily assessed costs awarded against him within 14 days of the assessment, but the court can extend that time, direct payment by instalments, or defer the liability to pay the costs until the end of the proceedings so that they can then be set off against any costs or judgment to which the paying party becomes entitled.

2.5.16 Fixed costs relating to default judgments, certain judgments on admissions and summary judgments etc. are set out in Part 45 (see also PD 43–48, Section 25). Part 46 relates to fast track costs.

2.5.17 Part 47 and PD 43–48, Sections 28 to 49, contain the procedure for detailed assessment together with the default provisions. Precedents A, B, C and D set out in the Schedule of Costs Precedents annexed to PD 43–48 are model forms of bills of costs for detailed assessment. Section 43 deals with costs payable out of the Community Legal Service fund, Section 44 deals with costs payable out of a fund other than the CLS fund and Section 49 deals with costs payable by the LSC. Part 48 and PD 43–48, Sections 50 to 56 deal with special cases, in particular:
(1) costs payable by or to a child or patient,
(2) litigants in person, and
(3) wasted costs orders — personal liability of the legal representative.

2.5.18 Costs only proceedings are dealt with in r. 44.12A and PD 43–48, Section 17. They may be brought in the High Court only where the dispute was of such a value or type that had proceedings been brought they would have been commenced in the High Court. Proceedings are brought under Part 8 by the issue of a claim form in the Supreme Court Costs Office at Clifford's Inn, Fetter Lane, London EC4A 1DQ. (See also paragraphs 4.1.16 and 6.8.13 below.)

2.6 Court Fees

2.6.1 The fees payable in the High Court are set out in sch. 1 to the [Civil Proceedings Fees Order 2004].

2.6.2 In the Royal Courts of Justice fees are paid in the Fees Room E01 and are usually stamped on the document to which they relate.

2.7 Information Technology

2.7.1 To support the work of the Central Office in operating the provisions of the CPR, and to facilitate effective case management, a computerised system will be introduced to provide a record of proceedings and a search facility, and to produce court forms and orders. The full system is not yet available, but an interim system has been in use since 26 April 1999.

2.7.2 A number of specific applications of information technology have been well developed in recent years; the use of fax, the provision of skeleton arguments on disk and daily transcripts on disk have become more commonplace. Short applications may be dealt with more economically by a conference telephone call, and taking evidence by video link has become more common and the available technology has improved considerably. The CPR contain certain provisions about the use of information technology, for example, Part 6 and PD 6 deal with service of documents by fax or other electronic means, PD 23 refers to telephone hearings and videoconferencing, r. 32.3 allows the use of evidence given by video link and the PD 5 refers to the filing of documents at court by fax.

2.7.3 Parties may agree to use information technology in the preparation, management and presentation of a case, however, the agreement of the judge or master should be sought before providing the court with material in electronic form. Where permission has been given, the material for use at a hearing or in support of an application can be provided on a floppy disk.

The parties should check with the court which word-processing format should be used. This will normally be Word 6 for Windows or WordPerfect for DOS 5.1.

2.7.4 A protocol has been prepared as a guide to all persons who are involved in the use of videoconferencing equipment in civil proceedings in the High Court. It covers its use in courtrooms where the equipment may be installed, and also the situation where the court assembles in a commercial studio or conference room containing videoconferencing equipment. Copies of the Videoconferencing Protocol may be obtained from the Bar Council at a charge of £2.50 to cover expenses. A room has now been made available as an audio-video-conferencing courtroom for applications to masters, as a pilot measure. More information may be obtained from the Senior Master through the Masters' Secretary's Department.*

3 STEPS BEFORE ISSUE OF A CLAIM FORM

3.1 Settlement

3.1.1 So far as reasonably possible, a claimant should try to resolve his claim without litigation. The court is increasingly taking the view that litigation should be a last resort and parties may wish to consider the use of alternative dispute resolution ('ADR'). (See paragraph 6.6 below.)

3.1.2 There are codes of practice for preliminary negotiations in certain types of claim. These codes of practice are called 'protocols' and are set out in a schedule to PD Protocols. At present there are protocols covering only the areas of personal injury and clinical negligence. Even if there is no protocol that applies to the claim, the parties will nonetheless be expected to comply with the spirit of the overriding objective.[21]

3.1.3 An offer to settle a claim may be made by either party[22] whether before or after a claim is brought. The court will take account of any offer to settle made before proceedings are started when making any order as to costs after proceedings have started.[23]

3.2 Disclosure Before Proceedings Are Started

3.2.1 An intending claimant may need documents to which he does not yet have access. Rule 31.16 sets out the provisions for making an application for disclosure of documents before proceedings have started.

3.2.2 Essentially, the court must be satisfied that the applicant and respondent to the application are likely to be parties when proceedings are brought, that the required documents are those that the respondent would be required to disclose under r. 31.6 when proceedings are brought and that their early disclosure might dispose of or assist the disposal of anticipated proceedings or save costs.

3.3 Defamation Proceedings

3.3.1 Application may be made to the court before a claim is brought for the court's assistance in accepting an offer of amends under the Defamation Act 1996, s. 3. The application is made by Part 8 claim form. For more information see paragraphs 4.1. 15 and 12.7 below.

4 STARTING PROCEEDINGS IN THE CENTRAL OFFICE

4.1 Issuing the Claim Form

4.1.1 All claims must be started by issuing a claim form. The great majority of claims involve a dispute of fact, and the claim form should be issued in accordance with Part 7 of the CPR. The Part 8 procedure may be followed in the types of claim described in paragraphs 4.1.14 to 4.1.16 below.

4.1.2 The requirements for issuing a claim form are set out in Part 7 and PD 7, the main points of which are summarised in the following paragraphs.

4.1.3 PD 7, at paras 2, 3 and 4, provides information as to:

[* See now PD 32, annex 3]

[21] See PD Protocols, para. 4.

[22] See [paragraphs 5.1 to 5.3] of the Pre-action Protocol for Personal Injury Claims and paragraphs 3.22 and 3.26 of the Pre-action Protocol for the Resolution of Clinical Disputes.

[23] See r. 36.10 and r. 44.3(4)(c) .

(1) where a claim should be started,
(2) certain matters that must be included in the claim form, and
(3) how the heading of the claim should be set out on the claim form.

In defamation cases see Part 53 and PD 53 for matters that should be included in the claim form and particulars of claim. See also paragraph 12.7 below.

4.1.4 Proceedings are started when the court issues a claim form, and a claim form is issued on the date entered on the claim form by the court.[24] However, where a claim form is received in the court office on an earlier date than the date of issue, then, for the purposes of the Limitation Act 1980, the claim is brought on the earlier date (see PD 7, paras 5.1 to 5.4).

4.1.5 To start proceedings in the Central Office, a claimant must use form N1 or form N208 for a Part 8 claim (or a form suitably modified as permitted by Part 4), and should take or send the claim form to Room E17, Action Department, Central Office, Royal Courts of Justice, Strand, London WC2A 2LL. If the court is to serve the claim form, the claimant must provide sufficient copies for each defendant. A claimant who wishes to retain for his file a copy of the claim form as issued should provide a further copy of the claim form which the court will seal and return it to him marked 'claimant's copy'. This copy will bear any amendments which have been made to the court's copy and the copies for service. Copies of practice forms relevant to the work of the Action Department (including the claim form and response pack) are available from that office. Alternatively, claimants may produce their own forms, which may be modified as the circumstances require, provided that all essential information, especially any information or guidance that the form gives to the recipient, is included. (See Part 4.)

4.1.6 On issuing the claim form, the court will give or send the claimant a notice of issue endorsed with the date of issue of the claim form. If the claimant requires the court to serve the claim form, the date of posting and deemed date of service will also be endorsed on the notice of issue. Claimants, especially solicitors who have been accustomed to using the Action Department, are encouraged to continue to serve their own documents but must inform the court when service has been effected (see paragraph 4.2.4 in relation to service by the claimant and the certificate of service). For certain types of claims, the notice of issue contains the request for judgment. (See paragraph 5 below for information about default judgments.)

4.1.7 A claim form must be served within four months after the date of issue (r. 7.5) unless it is to be served out of the jurisdiction, when the period is six months; and r. 7.6 and PD 7, para. [8] set out how an extension of time for service of the claim form may be sought. (See paragraph 4.2 below about service.)

4.1.8 The particulars of claim may be:
(1) included in the claim form,
(2) in a separate document served with the claim form, or
(3) in a separate document served within 14 days of service of the claim form provided that the particulars of claim are served within the latest time for serving the claim form.[25]

4.1.9 A claim form that does not include particulars of claim must nonetheless contain a concise statement of the nature of the claim.[26] Any claim form that:
(1) does not comply with the requirements of r. 16.2, or
(2) is garbled or abusive,

will be referred to a master and is likely to be struck out by the court.[27]

4.1.10 Where the particulars of claim are neither included in nor served with the claim form;
(1) the claim form must contain a statement that particulars of claim will follow, and
(2) the particulars of claim must be served by the claimant.[28]

However, where a claim form is to be served out of the jurisdiction,[29] the particulars of claim must accompany the claim form. (See paragraph 4.2.13 below.)

[24] See r. 7.2.
[25] See r. 7.4.
[26] See r. 16.2(1), and [PD 53, para.2] in respect of defamation claims.
[27] See r. 3.2.
[28] See r. 7.4(1)(b).
[29] See r. 2.3 for the definition of 'jurisdiction'.

Court Guides

4.1.11 Certain forms must accompany the particulars of claim when they are served on the defendant. These forms are listed in r. 7.8 and are included in a response pack, which is available from the Action Department.

4.1.12 A party who has entered into a funding arrangement and who wishes to claim an additional liability must give the court and any other party information about that claim if he is to recover the additional liability. Where the funding arrangement has been entered into before proceedings are commenced, the claimant should file a notice of funding in form N251 when the claim form is issued.[30]

4.1.13 Part 22 requires the particulars of claim, and where they are not included in the claim form itself, the claim form to be verified by a statement of truth; see PD 7, para. [7], and PD 22.

4.1.14 Part 16 and PD 16 deal with statements of case, and in particular the contents of the claim form and the particulars of claim. Part 16 does not apply to claims in respect of which the Part 8 alternative procedure for claims is being used. See paragraph 5.6 below for more about statements of case.

4.1.15 A claimant may use the Part 8 procedure where:
(1) he seeks the court's decision on a question that is unlikely to involve a substantial dispute of fact, or
(2) a rule or practice direction requires or permits the use of the Part 8 procedure,[31]
however, the court may at any stage order the claim to continue as if the claimant had not used the Part 8 procedure.[32]

4.1.16 Certain matters that must be included on the claim form when the Part 8 procedure is being used are set out in r. 8.2. The types of claim for which the Part 8 procedure may be used include:[33]
(1) a claim by or against a child or patient that has been settled before the commencement of proceedings, the sole purpose of the claim being to obtain the approval of the court to the settlement,
(2) provided there is unlikely to be a substantial dispute of fact, a claim for a summary order for possession against named or unnamed defendants occupying land or premises without the licence or consent of the person claiming possession (RSC, ord. 113 in CPR, sch. 1),
(3) a claim for provisional damages that has been settled before the commencement of proceedings, the sole purpose of the claim being to obtain a judgment by consent,
(4) a claim under the Defamation Act 1996, s. 3 (made other than in existing proceedings), and
(5) a claim under r. 44.12A where the parties have agreed all issues before the commencement of proceedings except the amount of costs and an order for costs is required.

4.1.17 In addition to the provisions of r. 8.1, attention is drawn also to PD 8B which deals with proceedings brought under 'the schedule rules'.[34]
See paragraph 6.7 below for more information regarding the Part 8 procedure.

4.2 Service

4.2.1 Service of documents is dealt with in Part 6; Section I (rr. 6.1 to 6.11) contains provisions relating to service generally and Section II (rr. 6.12 to 6.16) contains special provisions relating to service of the claim form. Section III (rr. 6.17 to 6.31) deals with service out of the jurisdiction. Some of the more important provisions are described below.

Within the jurisdiction

4.2.2 The methods by which a document may be served are to be found in r. 6.2. The court will serve a document that it has issued or prepared unless:
(1) the party on whose behalf it is to be served notifies the court that he wishes to serve it himself,

[30] See r. 44.15 and PD 43–48, Section19.
[31] See r. 8.1.
[32] See r. 8.1(3).
[33] See PD 8, para. 1.4.
[34] See PD 8B, para. 1.1.

(2) the court orders otherwise, or
(3) a rule or practice direction provides otherwise.[35]
It is anticipated that practitioners familiar with Central Office procedures will wish to continue to serve their own documents.

4.2.3 Where a party has entered into a funding agreement the notice of funding (form N251) must be served on all the other parties. If a claimant files his notice of funding when his claim form is issued, the court will serve it on the other parties provided sufficient copies are provided. Otherwise the claimant must serve the notice of funding with the claim form.[36] A defendant should file his notice of funding with his first document, i.e. his defence or acknowledgment of service etc. Sufficient copies of the notice should be provided for the court to serve.

4.2.4 In all other circumstances a party must serve a notice of funding within seven days of entering into the funding agreement.[37]

4.2.5 Where the court has tried to serve a document but has been unable to serve it, the court will send a notice of non-service to the party on whose behalf it was to be served stating the method attempted.[38] On receipt of this notice, the party should take steps to serve the document himself, as the court is under no further duty to effect service. The method of service used by the court will normally be first-class post.

4.2.6 Where a claimant has served a claim form, he must file a certificate of service that complies with the provisions of r. 6.10. The certificate of service must be filed within seven days of service of the claim form, and the claimant may not obtain judgment in default if it has not been filed.[39]

4.2.7 Information as to how personal service is to be effected and as to service by electronic means is to be found in PD 6. Rule 6.6 deals with service on a child or patient.

4.2.8 A party must give an address for service within the jurisdiction. Rule 6.5 contains information as to the address for service.

4.2.9 A party may make an application for permission to serve a document by an alternative method[40] to those set out in r. 6.2. The application may be made without notice, and PD 6, para. 9.1 sets out the evidence that will be required in support of the application. (Paragraph 7.12 below contains information in relation to applications.)

Out of the jurisdiction

4.2.10 The provisions for service out of the jurisdiction are contained in rr. 6.17 to 6.31. Rule 6.19 sets out the provisions whereby a claim form may be served out of the jurisdiction without the permission of the court, and r. 6.20 sets out the circumstances where the court's permission is required. Parties should also see PD 6B.

4.2.11 A claimant may issue a claim form against defendants, one or some of whom appear to be out of the jurisdiction, without first having obtained permission for service out of the jurisdiction, provided that where the claim form is not one which may be served without the permission of the court under r. 6.19, the claim form is endorsed by the court that it is 'not for service out of jurisdiction'.

4.2.12 Where a claim form is to be served in accordance with r. 6.19 it must contain a statement of the grounds on which the claimant is entitled to serve it out of the jurisdiction. The statement should be as follows:
(1) 'I, (*name*) state that the High Court of England and Wales has power under the Civil Jurisdiction and Judgments Act 1982 to hear this claim and that no proceedings are pending between the parties in Scotland, Northern Ireland or another Convention territory of any contracting State as defined by section 1(3) of the Act.', or
(2) where the proceedings are those to which art. 16 of sch. 1,3C or 4 to the Act refers,
'I, (*name*) state that the High Court of England and Wales has power under the Civil Jurisdiction and Judgments Act 1982, the claim having as its object rights *in rem* in

[35] See r. 6.3.
[36] See r. 44.15 and PD 43–48, Section19.
[37] See PD 43–48, para. 19.2.
[38] See r. 6.11.
[39] See r. 6.14(2)(b).
[40] See r. 6.8.

Court Guides

immovable property or tenancies in immovable property (or otherwise in accordance with the provisions of article 16 of schedule 1, 3C or 4 to that Act) to which article 16 of schedule 1, 3C or 4 to that Act applies, to hear the claim and that no proceedings are pending between the parties in Scotland, Northern Ireland or another Convention territory of any contracting State as defined by section 1(3) of the Act.', or

(3) where the defendant is party to an agreement conferring jurisdiction to which art. 17 of sch. 1, 3C or 4 to that Act applies,

'I, (*name*) state that the High Court of England and Wales has power under the Civil Jurisdiction and Judgments Act 1982, the defendant being a party to an agreement conferring jurisdiction to which article 17 of schedule 1, 3C or 4 to that Act applies, to hear the claim and that no proceedings are pending between the parties in Scotland, Northern Ireland or another Convention territory of any contracting State as defined by section 1(3) of the Act.'.

4.2.13 The above statement should be signed and have set out the full name of the signatory. If a claim form as specified in paragraph 4.2.10 above does not bear the above statement, the claim form will be endorsed 'not for service out of the jurisdiction'.

4.2.14 An application for an order for permission to issue a claim form for service out of the jurisdiction or to serve the claim form out of the jurisdiction should be made in accordance with Part 23 (form PF 6(A) may be used). The application must be supported by written evidence, and may be made without notice. The written evidence should state the requirements set out in r. 6.21(1) and (2).

4.2.15 An order giving permission for service out of the jurisdiction will be drawn up by the court (in form PF 6(B)), unless a party wishes to do so, and will:

(1) specify the country in which, or place at which, service is to be effected, and

(2) specify the number of days within which the defendant may either

(a) file an acknowledgment of service,

(b) file or serve an admission, or

(c) file a defence

to the claim, and where an acknowledgment of service is filed, specify a further 14 days within which the defendant may file a defence.

4.2.16 Where service is to be effected in a country which requires a translation of the documents to be served,[41] it is the claimant's responsibility to provide the translation of all the documents for each defendant. In every case, it is the claimant's duty to ensure that the response pack clearly states the appropriate period for responding to the claim form, and form N9, form N1C and other relevant forms must be modified accordingly. Every translation must be accompanied by a statement by the person making it:

(1) that it is a correct translation, and

(2) including the person's name, address and qualifications for making the translation.[42]

4.2.17 The periods for acknowledging service of a claim form served out of the jurisdiction are set out in r. 6.22 and in the Table contained in PD 6C, and the periods for serving a defence to a claim form served out of the jurisdiction are set out in r. 6.23 and in the Table in the practice direction. Rule 6.24 describes the methods of service.

4.2.18 Where the claim form is to be served through;

(1) the judicial authorities of the country where the claim form is to be served,

(2) a British consular authority in that country,

(3) the authority designated under the Hague Convention in respect of that country, or

(4) the government of that country, or

(5) where the court permits service on a State, the Foreign and Commonwealth Office,

the claimant should provide the Senior Master with the following documents by forwarding them to the Foreign Process Section, Room E02:

(a) a request for service by the chosen method (in form PF 7),

(b) a sealed copy and a duplicate copy of the claim form,

(c) the response pack as referred to in paragraph 4.2.14,

[41] See r. 6.28.

[42] Rule 6.28(3).

(d) a translation in duplicate, and the statement referred to in paragraph 4.2.13, and
(e) any other relevant documents.

4.2.19 Where service has been requested in accordance with paragraph 4.2.16, the particulars of claim, if not included in the claim form, must accompany the claim form (in duplicate). Where the claimant is effecting service of the claim form direct (and not as in paragraph 4.2.16) and the claim form states that particulars of claim are to follow, the permission of the court is not required to serve the particulars of claim out of the jurisdiction.

4.2.20 Where an official certificate of service[43] is received in a foreign language, it is the responsibility of the claimant to obtain a translation of the certificate. Where a defendant served out of the jurisdiction fails to attend a hearing, the official certificate of service is evidence of service. Otherwise the claimant may take no further steps against the defendant until written evidence showing that the claim form has been duly served is filed.[44]

4.2.21 Further advice on service out of the jurisdiction may be obtained from the Foreign Process Section, Room E02.

5 RESPONSE TO A PART 7 CLAIM

5.1 General

5.1.1 Responding to particulars of claim is dealt with in Part 9. A defendant may respond to the service of particulars of claim by:[45]
(1) filing or serving an admission in accordance with Part 14,
(2) filing a defence in accordance with Part 15,
(3) doing both if part only of the claim is admitted, or
(4) filing an acknowledgment of service in accordance with Part 10.

5.1.2 Where a defendant receives a claim form that states that particulars of claim are to follow, he need not respond to the claim until the particulars of claim have been served on him.[46]

5.1.3 If a defendant fails to:
(1) file an acknowledgment of service within the time specified in r. 10.3, and
(2) file a defence within the time specified in r. 15.4, or
(3) file or serve an admission in accordance with Part 14,
the claimant may obtain default judgment if Part 12 allows it.[47] (See paragraph 5.5 below for information about default judgments.)

5.2 Acknowledgment of Service

5.2.1 Acknowledgments of service are dealt with in Part 10. A defendant may file an acknowledgment of service if:
(1) he is unable to file a defence within the period specified in r. 15.4, or
(2) he wishes to dispute the Court's jurisdiction.[48]
Filing an acknowledgment of service extends the time for filing the defence by 14 days.

5.2.2 A defendant who wishes to acknowledge service of a claim form should do so by using form N9. Rule 10.5 states that the acknowledgment of service must:
(1) be signed by the defendant or his legal representative, and
(2) include the defendant's address for service. PD 10 contains information relating to the acknowledgment of service and how it may be signed.

5.3 Admissions

5.3.1 The manner in which a defendant may make an admission of a claim or part of a claim is set out in rr. 14.1 and 14.2, and rr. 14.3 to 14.7 set out how judgment may be obtained on a written admission.

43 See rr. 6.26(5) and 6.27(4).
44 Rule 6.31.
45 See r. 9.2.
46 See r. 9.1(2).
47 See r. 10.2.
48 See r. 10.1(3).

5.3.2 Included in the response pack that will accompany the particulars of claim when they are served on the defendant is an admission form (form N9A for a specified amount and form N9C for an unspecified amount). If the defendant makes an admission and requests time to pay, he should complete as fully as possible the statement of means contained in the admission form, or otherwise give in writing the same details of his means as could have been given in the admission form.

5.3.3 Where the defendant has:
(1) made an admission in respect of a specified sum and requested time to pay, or
(2) made an admission in respect of an unspecified sum, offered a sum in satisfaction (which is accepted) and requested time to pay,
and the claimant has not accepted the request for time to pay, on receipt of the claimant's notice the court will enter judgment for the amount admitted or offered (less any payments made) to be paid at the time and rate of payment determined by the court.[49]

5.3.4 Where the defendant has:
(1) made an admission for an unspecified amount, or
(2) made an admission for an unspecified amount and offered in satisfaction a sum that the claimant has not accepted,
on receipt of the claimant's request for judgment the court will enter judgment for an amount to be decided by the court and costs.[50]

5.3.5 The matters that the court will take into account when determining the time and rate of payment are set out in PD 14, para. 5.1.

5.3.6 The court may determine the time and rate of payment with or without a hearing, but, where a hearing is to take place, the proceedings must, where the provisions of r. 14.12(2) apply, be transferred to the defendant's home court. Where the claim form was issued in the Royal Courts of Justice the defendant's home court will be the district registry for the district in which the defendant's address given in the admission form is situated. If there is no such district registry the proceedings will remain in the Royal Courts of Justice.[51]

5.3.7 The procedure for an application for redetermination of a decision determining the time and rate of payment is to be found in r. 14.13 and PD 14, paras 5.3 to 5.6.

5.3.8 Where judgment has been entered for an amount to be decided by the court and costs, the court will give any directions that it considers appropriate, which may include allocating the case to a track.[52] (See paragraph 6.5 below about allocation.)

5.3.9 Judgment will not be entered on an admission where:
(1) the defendant is a child or patient, or
(2) the claimant is a child or patient and the admission is made in respect of:
(a) a specified amount of money, or
(b) a sum offered in satisfaction of a claim for an unspecified amount of money.
See Part 21 and PD 21, and in particular r. 21.10 which provides that, where a claim is made by or on behalf of a child or patient or against a child or patient, no settlement, compromise or payment shall be valid, so far as it relates to that person's claim, without the approval of the court.

5.4 Defence

5.4.1 A defendant who wishes to defend all or part of a claim must file a defence, and if he fails to do so, the claimant may obtain default judgment if Part 12 allows it.[53] The time for filing a defence is set out in r. 15.4.

5.4.2 A form for defending the claim[54] is included in the response pack. The form for defending the claim also contains provision for making a counterclaim.[55] Part 22 requires a defence to be verified by a statement of truth (see PD 15, para. 2; and see also Part 22 and PD 22).

49 See r. 14.10(4).
50 See rr. 14.6(7) and 14.7(10).
51 Derived from r. 2.3.
52 See r. 14.8.
53 See rr. 15.2 and 15.3.
54 Forms N9B and N9D.
55 See Part 20.

5.4.3 The parties may, by agreement, extend the period specified in r. 15.4 for filing a defence by up to 28 days.[56] If the parties do so, the defendant must notify the court in writing of the date by which the defence must be filed.

5.5 Default Judgment

5.5.1 A party may obtain default judgment under Part 12 except in the circumstances set out in r. 12.2 and PD 12, paras 1.2 and 1.3 which list the circumstances where default judgment may not be obtained.

5.5.2 To obtain default judgment under the circumstances set out in rr. 12.4(1) and 12.9(1), a party may do so by filing a request.[57] A request is dealt with by a court officer and provided he is satisfied that the provisions of PD 12, para. 4.1, have been complied with, he will enter the default judgment.

5.5.3 Default judgment in respect of claims specified in rr. 12.4(2)(a), 12.9 and 12.10 must be obtained by making an application to a master. The following are some of the types of claim which require an application for default judgment:

(1) against children and patients,
(2) for costs (other than fixed costs) only,
(3) by one spouse against the other on a claim in tort,
(4) for delivery up of goods where the defendant is not allowed the alternative of paying their value,
(5) against the Crown, and
(6) against persons or organisations who enjoy immunity from civil jurisdiction under the provisions of the International Organisations Acts 1968 and 1981.

PD 12, para. 4, provides information about the evidence required in support of an application for default judgment.

5.5.4 Where default judgment has been obtained for an amount to be decided by the court, the matter will be referred to a master for directions to be given concerning the management of the case and any date to be fixed for a hearing.

5.6 Statements of Case

5.6.1 Statements of case comprise the particulars of claim and defence in the main proceedings and also in any Part 20 proceedings, and are dealt with in Part 16. (Part 16 does not apply to claims proceeding under Part 8.)

5.6.2 The particulars of claim, whether contained in the claim form or served separately, should set out the claimant's claim clearly and fully. The same principle applies to the defence.

5.6.3 Part 16 sets out certain matters which must be included in a statement of case. Paragraphs [4 to 8] of PD 16 contain matters which should be included in the particulars of claim in specific types of claim, and para. [9] lists matters which must be set out in the particulars of claim if relied on. In addition to the matters listed in para. [9], full particulars of any allegation of dishonesty or malice and, where any inference of fraud or dishonesty is alleged, the basis on which the inference is alleged should also be included. Points of law may be set out in any statement of case. For information in respect of statements of case in defamation claims see PD 53.

5.6.4 In addition to the information contained in Part 16 and PD 16, the following guidelines on preparing a statement of case should be followed;

(1) a statement of case must be as brief and concise as possible,
(2) a statement of case should be set out in separate consecutively numbered paragraphs and sub-paragraphs,
(3) so far as possible each paragraph or sub-paragraph should contain no more than one allegation,
(4) the facts and other matters alleged should be set out as far as reasonably possible in chronological order,

[56] See r. 15.5.

[57] Forms N205A, N255, N225B or N227.

(5) the statement of case should deal with the claim on a point-by-point basis, to allow a point-by-point response,
(6) where a party is required to give reasons,[58] the allegation should be stated first and then the reasons listed one by one in separate numbered sub-paragraphs,
(7) a party wishing to advance a positive claim must identify that claim in the statement of case,
(8) any matter which if not stated might take another party by surprise should be stated,
(9) where they will assist, headings, abbreviations and definitions should be used and a glossary annexed; contentious headings, abbreviations, paraphrasing and definitions should not be used and every effort should be made to ensure that they are in a form acceptable to the other parties,
(10) particulars of primary allegations should be stated as particulars and not as primary allegations,
(11) schedules or appendices should be used if this would be helpful, for example, where lengthy particulars are necessary, and any response should also be stated in a schedule or appendix,
(12) any lengthy extracts from documents should be placed in a schedule.

5.6.5 A statement of case should be verified by a statement of truth.[59] If a party fails to verify his statement of case, it will remain effective unless struck out, but that party may not rely on the statement of case as evidence of any of the matters contained in it.[60] Any party may apply to the court for an order to strike out a statement of case which has not been verified.[61]

6 PRELIMINARY CASE MANAGEMENT

6.1 The Practice Master

6.1.1 On every working day, the practice master is available from 10.30 a.m. to 1.00 p.m. and from 2.00 p.m. to 4.30 p.m. to answer questions about the practice of the Queen's Bench Division. Usually, one master takes the morning practice, and another master takes the afternoon practice. This will be shown on the case-lists for the day and on the notice boards in the masters' corridors. Also, a board is placed on the door of the master who is sitting as practice master.

6.1.2 The practice master cannot give advice, whether about a given case or about the law generally. He is there simply to answer general questions about the CPR and practice governing the work of the Queen's Bench Division, and can deal with any consent order, notwithstanding that the claim in which it is to be made has been assigned to another master. The practice master may grant stays of execution and deal with urgent applications which do not require notice to be given to the respondent. It is unnecessary to make an appointment to see the practice master, litigants are generally seen in order of arrival.

6.2 Assignment to Masters

6.2.1 A claim issued in the Central Office will normally be assigned at the issue stage to a particular master as the procedural judge responsible for managing the claim. The Action Department will endorse the name of the assigned master on the claim form. However, assignment may be triggered at an earlier stage, for example, by one of the following events:
(1) an application for pre-action disclosure under r. 31.16,
(2) an application for an interim remedy before the commencement of a claim or where there is no relevant claim (Part 25).

It occasionally happens that a claim is assigned to a master who may have an 'interest' in the claim. In such cases the Senior Master will re-assign the claim to another master.

6.2.2 Where either an application notice or Part 8 claim form is issued which requires a hearing date to be given immediately, the Masters' Support Unit will give a hearing date and assign it to

[58] See r. 16.5(2).
[59] See r. 22.1.
[60] See r. 22.2(1).
[61] See r. 22.2(2) and (3).

the master who has the next available date for the hearing. The Masters' Support Unit will endorse the name of that master on the application notice or Part 8 claim form at the time of entering it in the list for hearing.

6.2.3 The Senior Master may assign a particular master to a class/group of claims or may re-assign work generally. At present clinical negligence claims are assigned to Master Murray and Master Ungley. In the event of an assigned master being on leave or for any other reason temporarily absent from the Royal Courts of Justice then the Masters' Support Unit may endorse on the appropriate document the name of another master.

6.2.4 A court file will normally be opened when a defence is filed, provided that the claim is not one that will automatically be transferred (see paragraph 6.4 below). The court file will be endorsed with the name of the assigned master. Any application notice in an assigned claim for hearing before a master should have the name of the assigned master entered on it by the solicitors making the application.

6.3 Listing Before Masters

6.3.1 The masters' lists consist of;

(1) the ordinary list — short applications in Rooms E102 and E110 ('the Bear Garden lists'),
(2) the floating list,
(3) private room appointments,[62] and
(4) the sheriffs first return applications.

6.3.2 Parties attending on all applications before the masters are requested to complete the court record sheet (form PF 48) which will be used to record details of the claim, representation and the nature of the application, and will be used by the master for his notes. Copies of this form may be found in the writing desks in the masters' corridors and the Bear Garden.

6.3.3 Masters will sit each day at 10.30 a.m. in the Bear Garden to hear applications in the Bear Garden lists. Applications of up to 20 minutes duration are listed at 10.30 a.m., 11.00 a.m., 11.30 a.m. and 12 noon. Solicitors and counsel may attend any application in these lists although the costs of being represented by counsel may be disallowed if not fully justified. If an application is estimated to take longer than 20 minutes the applicant must request a private room appointment. To do so the applicant must complete the PRA form giving details of the parties' availability as fully as possible. Failure to do so may result in the request form being returned for further information thereby delaying the hearing date.

6.3.4 Hearing dates for the Bear Garden lists are given by the Masters' Support Unit. Hearing dates for private room appointments are given by the assigned master personally. The parties or their legal representatives must inform the Masters' Support Unit of any settlements as soon as possible. All time estimates must be updated as necessary.

6.3.5 Applications in the Bear Garden list may, by agreement or where the application notice has not been served, be transferred (in the case of a 10 minute application) to the next available 12 noon list or (in either case) for a private room appointment on a date to be specified by the master. In all other cases an application for a postponement of the hearing date must be made to the master to whom the claim has been assigned. An application may be relisted in the Bear Garden list without permission of a master if for any reason the application has not been heard or has not been fully disposed of.

6.3.6 When an application in the Bear Garden list is adjourned by a master he will specify the date to which it is adjourned. An application for the adjournment of a private room appointment must be made to the master who gave the appointment unless the application is by agreement of all parties and the master approves. The master will usually require details of parties' availability. Any adjournment will normally now be to a new hearing date.

6.3.7 Where an application for which a master has given a private room appointment has been settled, it is the duty of the parties or their legal representatives, particularly those who obtained that appointment, to notify the master immediately.

6.3.8 If the master hearing an application considers that the result might affect the date fixed for a trial, he may refer the application to the judge in charge of the list. This possibility should be

[62] A private room appointment is given where the hearing will be more than 20 minutes and takes place in the master's private room rather than a Bear Garden room. The appointment must be made by the master personally.

Court Guides

considered when making an application and a request should be included in the application notice asking the master to refer the application to the judge.

6.3.9 If the master considers that an application should more properly be heard by a judge, he may either during the hearing or before it takes place refer the application to the interim applications judge. Among the circumstances that may make this appropriate are:

(1) that the time required for the hearing is longer than a master could ordinarily make available,

(2) that, whatever the master's decision on the application, an appeal to the judge is considered inevitable,

(3) that the application raises issues of unusual difficulty or importance, etc., or

(4) that the outcome is likely to affect the trial date or window.

However, it is emphasised that no single factor or combination of factors is necessarily decisive, and the master has a complete discretion.

6.3.10 The sheriffs first return applications are interpleader applications (under RSC ord. 17 in CPR, sch. 1) and are listed at monthly intervals.

6.3.11 The floating list is run by the Masters' Support Unit. Applications in this list will usually have a time estimate of not more than 30 minutes and are released by the assigned master, if he considers them suitable, when the request for a private room appointment is made. Dates and times of hearings are allocated by staff in Room E14. The parties should assemble at Room E14 well before the appointed time in order to facilitate the allocation of the application to a master or deputy who is free.

6.4 Automatic Transfer

6.4.1 Part 26 requires certain claims to be transferred automatically.[63] Where;

(1) the claim is for a specified amount of money,

(2) the claim has not been issued in a specialist list,[64]

(3) the defendant, or one of the defendants is an individual,

(4) the claim has not been issued in the individual defendant's home court, and

(5) the claim has not already been transferred to another individual defendant's home court,

the claim will, on receipt of the defence, be transferred to the individual defendant's home court.

6.4.2 Where the claim form was issued in the Royal Courts of Justice the defendant's home court will be the district registry for the district in which the defendant's address for service as shown on the defence is situated. If there is no such district registry the proceedings will remain in the Royal Courts of Justice.[65] If the claim is against more than one individual defendant, the claim will be transferred to the home court of the defendant who first files his defence. (See paragraph 6.9 below about transfer following an order.)

6.5 Allocation

6.5.1 When a defence to a claim is received in the Central Office from all the defendants, or from one or more of the defendants and the time for filing a defence has expired, the Action Department Registry will send an allocation questionnaire to those defendants who have filed a defence,[66] unless it has been dispensed with.

6.5.2 The allocation questionnaire to be used in accordance with Part 26 is form N150. The allocation questionnaire will state the time within which it must be filed, which will normally be at least 14 days after the day on which it is deemed served. Where proceedings are automatically transferred to a defendant's home court, notwithstanding that the issuing court will send out the allocation questionnaire before transfer, the allocation questionnaire should nevertheless be returned to the receiving court.

6.5.3 Each party should state in his allocation questionnaire if there is any reason why the claim should be managed and tried at a court other than the Royal Courts of Justice or the trial

[63] See rr. 26.1 and 26.2.
[64] See Part 49.
[65] See r. 2.3(1)(b).
[66] See Part 26 and PD 26.

centre for a particular district registry. PD 29, para. 2.6 sets out certain types of claim which are suitable for trial in the Royal Courts of Justice. Form PF 49 will be sent out to parties with the allocation questionnaire requesting the parties to state convenient dates for a case management conference, if one should be ordered, or for other hearings. Parties are encouraged to agree directions for the management of the claim.

6.5.4 Where a party fails to file his allocation questionnaire within the specified time the court officer will refer the proceedings to the master for his directions. The master's directions may include 'the standard unless order', that is that unless the defaulting party files his allocation questionnaire within three days, his statement of case will be struck out.[67]

6.5.5 Where one but not all of the parties has filed an allocation questionnaire the master may allocate the claim to the multi-track where he considers that he has sufficient information to do so. Alternatively, the master may order that an allocation hearing take place and that all or any particular parties must attend. The court officer will then send out a notice of allocation hearing (form N153) giving reasons for the hearing and any other directions.

6.5.6 Parties requesting a stay to settle the proceedings should do so in their allocation questionnaire or otherwise in writing. The court encourages parties to consider the use of ADR (see paragraph 6.6 below). The master will normally direct the proceedings to be stayed for one month, but parties may by agreement seek an extension of the stay. PD 26, para. 3, sets out the procedure for seeking an extension.

6.5.7 Parties are reminded that an estimate of costs must be filed and served when the allocation questionnaire is filed (PD 43–48, para. 6.4).

6.5.8 On receipt of the allocation questionnaires or on an allocation hearing the master will allocate the claim to the multi-track or transfer the claim to the appropriate county court.[68] Rule 26.6 sets out the scope of each track. Claims proceeding in the Royal Courts of Justice must be allocated to the multi-track.

6.6 Alternative Dispute Resolution ('ADR')

6.6.1 Parties are encouraged to use ADR (such as, but not confined to, mediation and conciliation) to try to resolve their disputes or particular issues. Legal representatives should consider with their clients and the other parties the possibility of attempting to resolve the dispute or particular issues by ADR and they should ensure that their clients are fully informed as to the most cost-effective means of resolving their dispute.

6.6.2 The settlement of disputes by ADR can;

(1) significantly reduce parties' costs,
(2) save parties the delay of litigation in resolving their disputes,
(3) assist parties to preserve their existing commercial relationships while resolving their disputes, and
(4) provide a wider range of remedies than those available through litigation.

The master will in an appropriate case invite the parties to consider whether their dispute; or particular issues in it, could be resolved by ADR. The master may also either adjourn proceedings for a specified period of time or extend the time for compliance with an order, a rule or practice direction to encourage and enable the parties to use ADR. Parties may apply for directions seeking a stay for ADR at any time.

6.6.3 Information concerning ADR may be obtained from the Admiralty and Commercial Court Registry.

6.7 Part 8 — Alternative Procedure For Claims

6.7.1 Paragraphs 4.1.14 to 4.1.16 above deal with issuing a Part 8 claim form. The alternative procedure set out in Part 8 ('the Part 8 procedure') may not be used if a practice direction disapplies it in respect of a particular type of claim. A practice direction may require or permit the Part 8 procedure and may disapply or modify any of the rules contained in Part 8. PD 8B deals with commencement of proceedings under the Rules of the Supreme Court and the County Court Rules the provisions of which remain in force in sch. 1 and 2 to the CPR

[67] See PD 26, para. 2.5.

[68] County Courts Act 1984, ss. 40 to 42 and Part 30.

Court Guides

('the schedule rules'). The schedule rules and the practice directions supporting them may require certain proceedings to be commenced by the issue of a Part 8 claim form with appropriate modifications to the Part 8 procedure.

6.7.2 The main features of the Part 8 procedure are:
(1) Part 16 (statements of case) does not apply,
(2) Part 15 (defence and reply) does not apply,
(3) judgment in default may not be obtained (r. 12.2),
(4) rr. 14.4 to 14.7 (judgment by request on an admission) do not apply,
(5) a Part 8 claim shall be treated as being allocated to the multi-track.[69]

6.7.3 A master may give directions for managing the claim as soon as the Part 8 claim form is issued. In certain circumstances this may include fixing a hearing date. Where a hearing date is fixed, notice of the hearing date must be served with the claim form.[70] Where the master does not fix a hearing date when the claim form is issued he will give directions for the disposal of the claim as soon as practicable after the receipt of the acknowledgment of service or, as the case may be, the expiry of the period for acknowledging service.

6.7.4 Where a Part 8 claim form has been issued for the purpose of giving effect to a consent order for an award of damages to a child or patient or an award of provisional damages as in paragraph 4.1.15(1) and (2) above, a draft of the order sought should be attached to the claim form. For more information see paragraphs 6.8.1 to 6.8.8 and 9.3.8 to 9.3.10 below about children and patients, and paragraphs 6.8.12, 9.3.11 and 9.3.12 below about provisional damages.

6.7.5 A defendant who wishes to respond to a Part 8 claim form should acknowledge service of it and may do so either by using form N210 or otherwise in writing giving the following information:
(1) whether he contests the claim, and
(2) where he is seeking a different remedy from that set out in the claim form, what that remedy is.

If a defendant does not acknowledge service of the claim form within the specified time, he may attend the hearing of the claim but may not take part in the hearing unless the court gives permission.[71]

6.7.6 Rules 8.5 and 8.6 and PD 8, para. 5, (alternative procedure) deal with evidence to be relied on in Part 8 proceedings; the claimant's evidence must be filed and served with the claim form, and the defendant's evidence (if any) must be filed with his acknowledgment of service. If the defendant files written evidence he must at the same time serve it on the other parties. It is helpful to the court if, where the defendant does not intend to rely on written evidence, he notifies the court in writing to that effect.

6.7.7 Where a defendant contends that the Part 8 procedure should not be used, he should state the reasons for his contention on his acknowledgment of service. On receipt of the acknowledgment of service, the master will give appropriate directions for the future management of the claim.

6.8 Specific Matters Which May Be Dealt With Under the Part 8 Procedure

Settlements on behalf of children and patients

6.8.1 Part 21 and PD 21 set out the requirements for litigation by or against children and patients. References in Part 21, PD 21 and in this guide to:
(1) 'child' means a person under 18, and
(2) 'patient' means a person who by reason of mental disorder within the meaning of the Mental Health Act 1983 is incapable of managing and administering his own affairs.[72]

No settlement or compromise of a claim by or against a child or patient will be binding unless and until it has been approved by the court. In addition, a party may not obtain a default judgment against a child or patient without the permission of the court, and may not enter judgment on an admission against a child or patient.

[69] Rule 8.9.
[70] See PD 8, para.4.
[71] See r. 8.4.
[72] See r. 21.1(2).

6.8.2 A patient must have a litigation friend to conduct proceedings on his behalf, and so must a child unless the court makes an order permitting the child to act on his own behalf. A litigation friend is someone who can fairly and competently conduct proceedings on behalf of the child or patient. He must have no interest in the proceedings adverse to that of the child or patient, and all steps he takes in the proceedings must be taken for the benefit of the child or patient. Rules 21.5 to 21.8 and PD 21, paras 2 and 3, set out how a person may become a litigation friend.

6.8.3 Applications for the approval of settlements or compromises of claims by or against a child or patient proceeding in the Central Office are heard by a master. If the purpose of starting the claim is for the approval of a settlement, a Part 8 claim form should be issued in accordance with form PF 170(A) which must contain a request for approval of the settlement (or compromise) and, in addition to the details of the claim, must set out the terms of the settlement (or compromise) or must have attached to it a draft consent order. The draft consent order should be in form N292. See PD 21, para. 6, for further information which the master will require.

6.8.4 Where parties reach a settlement (or compromise) in proceedings started by the issue of a Part 7 claim form (where the trial has not started) an application may be made to the master in accordance with Part 23 for the approval of the settlement. The application notice should be in form PF 170(B) and should have attached to it a draft consent order in form N292. The application notice should be filed in Room E16. (See paragraph 7.12 below for information about applications.) However, where the trial hearing has been listed, the application notice should be filed in Room WG5. If the trial has started, oral application may be made to the trial judge. Applications for approval of a settlement on behalf of a child or patient will normally be heard in public unless the judge or master orders otherwise.[73] If a settlement is approved in private, the terms of settlement can be announced in public.

6.8.5 PD 21, para. 8, gives information about control of money recovered by or on behalf of a child or patient. Paragraph 10 deals with investment of money on behalf of a child and para. 11 deals with investment on behalf of a patient. Enquiries concerning investment for a child are dealt with in Room E13.

6.8.6 In respect of investment on behalf of a child, the litigation friend or his legal representative should provide the master with form PF 172 (request for investment) for completion by the master. The child's birth certificate should also be provided. The PF 172 will then be forwarded to the Court Funds Office for their investment managers to make the appropriate investment. The Court of Protection is responsible for the administration of patients' funds (unless they are small). PD 21, para. 11, gives full information about procedure for investment by the Court of Protection. These procedures may also be used for investment of money on behalf of a child or patient following an award of damages at trial.

6.8.7 Damages may also be paid to a child or patient by way of a structured settlement. A structured settlement on behalf of a child or patient must be approved by a judge or master. A structured settlement on behalf of a patient must also be approved by the Court of Protection. (For more information about structured settlements see PD 40C.)

6.8.8 Control of a child's fund, provided he is not also a patient, passes to him when he reaches the age of 18 (see PD 21, para. 12.2).

Summary order for possession

6.8.9 Where there is unlikely to be a substantial dispute of fact, a claim for a summary order for possession against named or unnamed defendants occupying land or premises without the licence or consent of the person claiming possession under RSC, ord. 113 in CPR, sch. 1, may be started by the issue of a Part 8 claim form.

6.8.10 When the claim form has been issued in the Action Department it will be passed to the Masters' Support Unit who will assign a master to the claim and fix a hearing date. Parties should check that they have sufficient time for service.

6.8.11 At the hearing the master may make the order sought or such other order as appropriate including directions for the management of the claim.

[73] See r. 39.2.

Settlement of a provisional damages claim

6.8.12 A claim for provisional damages may proceed under Part 8 where the claim form is issued solely for the purpose of obtaining a consent judgment.[74]

The claimant must state in his claim form in addition to the matters set out in PD 16, para. 4.4, that the parties have reached agreement and request a consent judgment. A draft order in accordance with PD 41, para. 4.2, should be attached to the claim form. The claimant or his legal representative must lodge the case file documents (set out in the draft order) in Room E14 for the case file to be compiled and preserved by the court. For more information about provisional damages claims and orders see Part 41 and PD 41, and paragraph 9.3 below.

Costs-only proceedings

6.8.13 Proceedings may be brought under Part 8 where the parties to a dispute have reached a written agreement before proceedings have been started but have been unable to agree an amount of costs. The costs-only proceedings may be started by the issue of a claim form in the Supreme Court Costs Office at Clifford's Inn, Fetter Lane, London EC4A 1DQ. PD 43–48 at Section 17 sets out in detail the provisions for issue and proceeding with the claim.

6.9 Transfer

6.9.1 Part 30 and PD 30 deal with transfer of proceedings, within the High Court, and between county courts. The jurisdiction of the High Court to transfer proceedings to the county courts is contained in the County Courts Act 1984, s. 40, as substituted by the Courts and Legal Services Act 1990, s. 2(1). Under that section the court has jurisdiction in certain circumstances to strike out claims which should have been started in a county court.

6.9.2 Rule 30.2 sets out the provisions for the transfer of proceedings between:

(1) county courts,
(2) the Royal Courts of Justice and a district registry of the High Court, and
(3) between district registries.

Rule 30.3 sets out the criteria to which the court will have regard when making an order for transfer. The High Court may order proceedings in any Division of the High Court to be transferred to another Division or to or from a specialist list. An application for the transfer of proceedings to or from a specialist list must be made to a judge dealing with claims in that list.[75] (See paragraph 6.4 above about automatic transfer.)

6.9.3 A claim with an estimated value of less than £50,000 will generally be transferred to a county court, if the county court has jurisdiction, unless it is to proceed in the High Court under an enactment or in a specialist list.

6.9.4 An order for transfer takes effect from the date it is made.[76] When an order for transfer is made the court officer will immediately send notice of the transfer to the receiving court. The notice will contain the title of the proceedings and the claim number. At the same time, the court officer will also notify all parties of the transfer.

6.9.5 PD 30, para. 5, sets out the procedure for appealing an order for transfer. Where an order for transfer is made in the absence of a party, that party may apply to the court which made the order to have it set aside.[77] The transferring court will normally retain the court file until the time for appealing the order or applying to set it aside has expired, whereupon the court officer will send the court file to the court manager of the receiving court. If at the time an order for transfer is made a court file has not been compiled, the court officer will send to the receiving court those documents which have been filed at that time.

6.9.6 Where money has been paid into court before an order for transfer is made, the court may direct transfer of the money to the control of the receiving court.

---

[74] See PD 8, para. 1.4(2).

[75] See r. 30.5.

[76] See PD 30, para.3.

[77] See PD 30, para.6.

6.10 Part 20 Proceedings

6.10.1 Part 20 deals with (a) counterclaims and (b) other additional claims, being claims for contribution or indemnity and what were formerly called 'third party' claims. A Part 20 claim is treated as a claim for the purpose of the CPR with certain exceptions, for which see r. 20.3.

6.10.2 A defendant may make a counterclaim by completing the defence and counterclaim form provided in the response pack. If the counterclaim is not filed with the defence, the permission of the court is required.[78] Where a counterclaim brings in a new party, the defendant (Part 20 claimant) must apply to the court for an order in form PF 21A adding the new party as defendant.[79]

6.10.3 A defendant claiming contribution or indemnity from another defendant may do so by filing a notice, in form PF 22, containing a statement of the nature and grounds of his claim and serving the notice on the other defendant.[80]

6.10.4 Any other additional claim may be brought by the issue of a Part 20 claim form, N211. If the Part 20 claim form is issued at a time other than when the defence is filed, the permission of the court is required. Rule 20.8 deals with service of a Part 20 claim form and r. 20.12 sets out the forms which must accompany the Part 20 claim form.

6.11 Summary Judgment

6.11.1 The court may give summary judgment under Part 24 against a claimant or defendant:

(1) if it considers that (a) the claimant has no real prospect of succeeding on the claim or issue, or (b) the defendant has no real prospect of successfully defending the claim, and

(2) there is no other reason why the claim or issue should be disposed of at a trial.

6.11.2 The court may give summary judgment against a claimant in any type of proceedings, and against a defendant in any type of proceedings except (a) proceedings for possession of residential premises against a mortgagor, or a tenant or person holding over after the end of his tenancy where occupancy is protected within the meaning of the Rent Act 1977 or the Housing Act 1988, (b) proceedings for an Admiralty claim *in rem*, and (c) contentious probate proceedings.[81] For information about summary disposal of defamation claims see Part 53, PD 53 and paragraph 12.7 below.

6.11.3 An application for summary judgment should be made in accordance with Part 23 and the application notice should contain the information set out in PD 24, para. 2 (parties may use forms PF 11 and PF 12 as precedents). The application notice should be filed and served on the respondent giving at least 14 days' notice of the date fixed for the hearing and the issues to be decided at the hearing. Unless the application notice contains all the evidence on which the applicant relies, the application notice should identify that evidence. In claims which include a claim for:

(1) specific performance of an agreement,

(2) rescission of such an agreement, or

(3) forfeiture or return of a deposit made under such an agreement, the application notice and any evidence in support must be served on the defendant not less than four days before the hearing.[82]

6.11.4 The application will normally be listed before a master unless, for example, an injunction is also sought. In that case the application notice should state that the application is intended to be made to a judge.

6.11.5 Where an order made on an application for summary judgment does not dispose of the claim or issue, the court will give case management directions in respect of the claim or issue.

[78] Rule 20.4.

[79] Rule 20.5.

[80] Rule 20.6.

[81] See r. 24.3 but see also RSC, ord. 77, r. 7(1) in CPR, sch. 1.

[82] See PD 24, para. 7.

6.12 Offers to Settle and Payments Into and Out Of Court

6.12.1 A party may offer to settle a claim at any time. Part 36 deals with offers to settle and payments into court. An offer to settle made in accordance with Part 36 will have the costs and other consequences specified in that Part and may be made at any time after proceedings have started. PD 36, para. 1, defines an offer made in accordance with Part 36. See also PD 36, para. 5, which contains general provisions concerning Part 36 offers and Part 36 payments.

6.12.2 A Part 36 offer may be made by any party, but to comply with Part 36 a defendant who makes an offer to settle for a specified sum must do so by way of a Part 36 payment into court. PD 36, para. 4.1(2), sets out the requirements for making a Part 36 payment in respect of a claim proceeding in the Royal Courts of Justice. If a defendant has made a pre-action offer to settle and proceedings are then started, in order for the court to take account of his offer he must make a Part 36 payment of not less than the amount offered within 14 days of service of the claim form. See also PD 36, para. 10, which deals with compensation recovery in respect of Part 36 payments.

6.12.3 The times for accepting a Part 36 offer or Part 36 payment are set out in rr. 36.11 and 36.12; the general rule is that a Part 36 offer or Part 36 payment made more than 21 days before the start of the trial may be accepted without the permission of the court, within 21 days after it was made. Otherwise, the permission of the court must be obtained. A Part 36 offer is made when received by the offeree. A Part 36 payment is made when the Part 36 payment notice (form N242A) is served on the claimant.

6.12.4 A party may accept a Part 36 offer or Part 36 payment by serving on the offeror a notice of acceptance (form N243 may be used to accept a Part 36 payment) within the times set out in rr. 36.11 and 36.12. When a Part 36 offer or Part 36 payment is accepted within those times, the general rule is that the claimant will be entitled to his costs up to the date of service of the notice of acceptance.

6.12.5 To obtain money out of court on acceptance of a Part 36 payment, the claimant should file a request for payment (form N243) in the Action Department of the Central Office, and file a completed Court Funds Office form 201 in the Court Funds Office. See PD 36, para. 8, for more information about obtaining payment out of court.

6.12.6 The court's permission is required for acceptance of a Part 36 offer or Part 36 payment:
(1) which is not made or accepted within the times set out in rr. 36.11 and 36.12,
(2) where acceptance is by or on behalf of a child or patient,[83] or
(3) where a defence of tender has been put forward, or
(4) otherwise as mentioned in r. 36.17.

6.12.7 Where a Part 36 offer or Part 36 payment is not accepted and a trial of the claim takes place, r. 36.20 sets out the costs consequences where a claimant fails to do better than the Part 36 offer or Part 36 payment, and r. 36.21 sets out the costs and other consequences where a claimant does better than he proposed in his Part 36 offer.

7 CASE MANAGEMENT AND INTERIM REMEDIES

7.1 Case Management — General

7.1.1 The CPR require the court to provide a high degree of case management. Case management includes: identifying disputed issues at an early stage; fixing timetables; dealing with as many aspects of the claim as possible on the same occasion; controlling costs; disposing of proceedings summarily where appropriate; dealing with the applications without a hearing where appropriate; and giving directions to ensure that the trial of a claim proceeds quickly and efficiently. The court will expect the parties to cooperate with each other, and where appropriate, will encourage the parties to use ADR or otherwise help them settle the case.

7.1.2 Parties and their legal representatives will be expected to do all that they can to agree proposals for the management of the claim in accordance with r. 29.4 and PD 29, paras 4.6 to 4.8. There is provision in the allocation questionnaire for proposing certain directions to be made, otherwise parties may use form PF 50 for making the application (attaching to it the draft

[83] See r. 21.10.

form of order in form PF 52) and file it for the master's approval. If the master approves the proposals he will give directions accordingly.

7.1.3 Parties should consider whether a case summary would assist the master in dealing with the issues before him. PD 29, para. 5.7, sets out the provisions for preparation of a case summary.

7.2 The Case Management Conference

7.2.1 Parties who are unable to agree proposals for the management of the case, should notify the court of the matters which they are unable to agree.

7.2.2 Where:

(1) the parties' proposed directions are not approved, or
(2) parties are unable to agree proposed directions, or
(3) the master wishes to make further directions,

the master will generally either consult the parties or direct that a case management conference be held.

7.2.3 In relatively straightforward claims, the court will give directions without holding a case management conference.

7.2.4 Any party who considers that a case management conference should be held before any directions are given should so state in his allocation questionnaire (or in a Part 8 claim should notify the master in writing), giving his reasons and supplying a realistic time estimate for the case management conference, with a list of any dates or times convenient to all parties, or most of them, in form PF 49.

7.2.5 Where a case management conference has been fixed, parties should ensure that any other applications are listed or made at that hearing. A party applying for directions at the case management conference should use form PF 50 for making their application and attach to it the draft order for directions (form PF 52).

7.2.6 The advocates instructed or expected to be instructed to appear at the trial should attend any hearing at which case management directions are likely to be given. In any event, the legal representatives who attend the case management conference must be familiar with the case and have sufficient authority to deal with any issues which may arise. Where necessary, the court may order the attendance of a party.[84]

7.3 Preliminary Issues

7.3.1 Costs can sometimes be saved by identifying decisive issues, or potentially decisive issues, and by the court ordering that they be tried first. The decision of one issue, although not necessarily itself decisive of the claim as a whole, may enable the parties to settle the remainder of the dispute. In such a case, the trial of a preliminary issue may be appropriate.

7.3.2 At the allocation stage, at any case management conference and again at any pre-trial review, the court will consider whether the trial of a preliminary issue may be helpful. Where such an order is made, the parties and the court should consider whether the costs of the issue should be in the issue or in the claim as a whole.

7.3.3 Where there is an application for summary judgment, and issues of law or construction may be determined in the respondent's favour, it will usually be in the interests of the parties for such issues to be determined conclusively, rather than that the application should simply be dismissed.

7.4 Trial Timetable

7.4.1 To assist the court to set a trial timetable,[85] a draft timetable should be prepared by the claimant's advocate(s) after consulting the other parties' advocates. If there are differing views, those differences should be clearly indicated in the timetable. The draft timetable should be filed with the trial bundle.

7.4.2 The trial timetable will normally include times for giving evidence (whether of fact or opinion) and for oral submissions during the trial.

[84] See r. 3.1(c).

[85] See rr. 29.8 and 39.4.

Court Guides

7.4.3 The trial timetable may be fixed at the case management conference, at any pre-trial review or at the beginning of the trial itself.

7.5 Listing Questionnaire

7.5.1 The court may send out a listing questionnaire (N170) to all parties for completion, specifying the date by which it must be returned. The master will then fix the trial date or period ('the trial window'). It is likely however, that the master will already have sufficient information to enable him to fix a trial window, and will dispense with the need for a listing questionnaire subject to any requirement of the Clerk of the Lists for one to be filed. Instead, the master will direct the parties within a specified time to attend before the Clerk of the Lists to fix a trial date within that window.

7.5.2 PD 43–48, para. 6.4, requires an estimate of costs to be filed and served with the listing questionnaire. If the filing of a listing questionnaire has been dispensed with, the estimate of costs should be filed on attendance before the Clerk of the Lists.

7.6 Pre-trial Review

7.6.1 Where the trial of a claim is estimated to last more than 10 days, or where the circumstances require it, the master may direct that a pre-trial review ('PTR') should be held.[86] The PTR may be heard by a Master, but more usually is heard by a Judge.

7.6.2 Application should normally be made to the Clerk of the Lists for the PTR to be heard by the trial judge (if known), and the applicant should do all that he can to ensure that it is heard between eight and four weeks before the trial date, and in any event long enough before the trial date to allow a realistic time in which to complete any outstanding matters.

7.6.3 The PTR should be attended by the advocates who are to represent the parties at the trial.

7.6.4 At least seven days before the date fixed for the PTR, the applicant must serve the other parties with a list of matters to be considered at the PTR, and those other parties must serve their responses at least two days before the PTR. Account must be taken of the answers in any listing questionnaires filed. Realistic proposals must be put forward and if possible agreed as to the time likely to be required for each stage of the trial and as to the order in which witnesses are to be called.

7.6.5 The applicant should lodge a properly indexed bundle containing the listing questionnaires (if directed to be filed) and the lists of matters and the proposals, together with the results of discussions between the parties, and any other relevant material, in the Listing Office, Room WG5, by no later than 10.00 a.m. on the day before the day fixed for the hearing of the PTR. If the PTR is to take place before a master and he asks for the bundle in advance, it should be lodged in the Masters' Support Unit, Room E14. Otherwise it should be lodged at the hearing.

7.6.6 At the PTR, the court will review the parties' state of preparation, deal with any outstanding matters, and give any directions or further directions that may be necessary.

7.7 Requests for Further Information

7.7.1 A party seeking further information or clarification under Part 18 should serve a written request on the party from whom the information is sought before making an application to the court. PD 18, para. 1, deals with how the request should be made, and para. 2 deals with the response. A response should be verified by a statement of truth.[87] Parties may use form PF 56 for a combined request and reply, if they so wish.

7.7.2 If a party who has been asked to provide further information or clarification objects or is unable to do so, he must notify the party making the request in writing.[88]

7.7.3 Where it is necessary to apply for an order for further information or clarification the party making the application should set out in or have attached to his application notice:

(1) the text of the order sought specifying the matters on which further information or clarification is sought, and

[86] See r. 29.7.

[87] See Part 22.

[88] See PD 18, para.4.

(2) whether a request has been made and, if so, the result of that request.[89]

Applicants may use form PF 57 for their application notice.

7.8 Disclosure

7.8.1 Under Part 31, there is no longer any general duty to disclose documents. Instead, a party is prevented from relying on any document that he has not disclosed, and is required to give inspection of any document to which he refers in his statement of case or in any witness statement, etc.[90] The intention is that disclosure should be proportionate to the value of the claim.

7.8.2 If an order for disclosure is made, unless the contrary is stated, the court will order standard disclosure, namely disclosure of only:

(1) the documents on which a party relies,

(2) the documents that adversely affect his own or another party's case,

(3) the documents that support another party's case, and

(4) the documents required to be disclosed by a relevant practice direction.

Parties should give standard disclosure by completing **form N265** but may also list documents by category.[91]

7.8.3 The court may either limit or dispense with disclosure (and the parties may agree to do likewise). The court may also order disclosure of specified documents or specified classes of documents. In deciding whether to make any such order for specific disclosure, the court will want to be satisfied that the disclosure is necessary, that the cost of disclosure will not outweigh the benefits of disclosure and that a party's ability to continue the litigation would not be impaired by any such order.

7.8.4 The court will therefore seek to ensure that any specific disclosure ordered is appropriate to the particular case, taking into account the financial position of the parties, the importance of the case and the complexity of the issues.

7.8.5 If specific disclosure is sought, a separate application for specific disclosure should be made in accordance with Part 23; it is not a matter that would be routinely dealt with at the CMC. The parties should give careful thought to ways of limiting the burdens of such disclosure, whether by giving disclosure in stages, by dispensing with the need to produce copies of the same document, by requiring disclosure of documents sufficient merely for a limited purpose, or otherwise. They should also consider whether the need for disclosure could be reduced or eliminated by a request for further information.

7.8.6 A party who has the right to inspect a document[92] should give written notice of his wish to inspect to the party disclosing the document. That party must permit inspection not more than seven days after receipt of the notice.

7.9 Experts and Assessors

7.9.1 The parties in a claim must bear in mind that under Part 35 no party may call an expert or put in evidence an expert's report without the court's express permission, and the court is under a duty to restrict such evidence to what is reasonably required.

7.9.2 The duty of an expert called to give evidence is to assist the court. This duty overrides any obligation to the party instructing him or by whom he is being paid (see PD 35). In fulfilment of this duty, an expert must for instance make it clear if a particular question or issue falls outside his expertise or if he considers that insufficient information is available on which to express an opinion.

7.9.3 Before the master gives permission, he must be told the field of expertise of the expert on whose evidence a party wishes to rely and where practicable the identity of the expert. Even then, he may, before giving permission, impose a limit on the extent to which the cost of such evidence may be recovered from the other parties in the claim.[93]

[89] See PD 18, para. 5.

[90] Rules 31.14 and 31.21.

[91] See PD 31, para. 3.2.

[92] See rr. 31.3 and 31.15.

[93] Rule 35.4.

Court Guides

7.9.4 Parties should always consider whether a single expert could be appointed in a particular claim or to deal with a particular issue. Before giving permission for the parties to call separate experts, the master will always consider whether a single joint expert ought to be used, whether in relation to the issues as a whole or to a particular issue.[94]

7.9.5 In very many cases it is possible for the question of expert evidence to be dealt with by a single expert. Single experts are, for example, often appropriate to deal with questions of quantum in cases where primary issues are as to liability. Likewise, where expert evidence is required in order to acquaint the court with matters of expert fact, as opposed to opinion, a single expert will usually be appropriate. There remain, however, a body of cases where liability will turn upon expert opinion evidence and where it will be appropriate for the parties to instruct their own experts. For example, in cases where the issue for determination is as to whether a party acted in accordance with proper professional standards, it will often be of value to the court to hear the opinions of more than one expert as to the proper standard in order that the court becomes acquainted with a range of views existing upon the question and in order that the evidence can be tested in cross-examination.

7.9.6 It will not be a sufficient ground for objecting to an order for a single joint expert that the parties have already chosen their own experts. An order for a single joint expert does not prevent a party from having his own expert to advise him, though that is likely to be at his own cost, regardless of the outcome.

7.9.7 When the use of a single joint expert is being considered, the master will expect the parties to cooperate in agreeing terms of reference for the expert. In most cases, such terms of reference will include a statement of what the expert is asked to do, will identify any documents that he will be asked to consider and will specify any assumptions that he is asked to make.

7.9.8 The court will generally also order that experts in the same field confer on a without-prejudice basis, and then report in writing to the parties and the court on the extent of any agreement, giving reasons at least in summary for any continuing disagreement. A direction to 'confer' gives the experts the choice of discussing the matter by telephone or in any other convenient way, as an alternative to attending an actual meeting. Any material change of view of an expert should be communicated in writing to the other parties through their legal representatives, and when appropriate, to the court.

7.9.9 Written questions may be put to an expert within 28 days after service of his report, but are for purposes of clarification of the expert's report when the other party does not understand it. Questions going beyond this can only be put with the agreement of the parties or the master's permission. The procedure of putting written questions to experts is not intended to interfere with the procedure for an exchange of professional opinion in discussions between experts or to inhibit that exchange of professional opinion. If questions that are oppressive in number or content are put without permission for any purpose other than clarification of the expert's report, the court is likely to disallow the questions and make an appropriate order for costs against the party putting them. (See PD 35, para. 5.3, with respect to payment of an expert's fees for answering questions under r. 35.6.)

7.9.10 An expert may file with the court a written request for directions to assist him in carrying out his function as an expert.[95] The expert should guard against accidentally informing the court about, or about matters connected with, communications or potential communications between the parties that are without prejudice or privileged. The expert may properly be asked to be privy to the content of these communications because he has been asked to assist the party instructing him to evaluate them.

7.9.11 Under r. 35.15 the court may appoint an assessor to assist it in relation to any matter in which the assessor has skill and experience. The report of the assessor is made available to the parties. The remuneration of the assessor is decided by the court and forms part of the costs of the proceedings.

7.10 Evidence

7.10.1 Evidence is dealt with in the CPR in Parts 32, 33 and 34.

[94] Rule 35.7.

[95] See r. 35.14.

7.10.2 The most common form of written evidence is a witness statement. PD 32 at para. 17, 18 and 19 contains information about the heading, body (what it must contain) and format of a witness statement. The witness must sign a statement of truth to verify the witness statement; the wording of the statement of truth is set out in PD 32, para. 20.2.

7.10.3 A witness statement may be used as evidence in support of an interim application and, where it has been served on any other party to a claim, it may be relied on as a statement of the oral evidence of the witness at the trial. Part 33 contains provisions relating to the use of hearsay evidence in a witness statement.

7.10.4 In addition to the information and provisions for making a witness statement mentioned in paragraph 7.10.2, the following matters should be borne in mind:

(1) a witness statement must contain the truth, the whole truth and nothing but the truth on the issues it covers,
(2) those issues should consist only of the issues on which the party serving the witness statement wishes that witness to give evidence-in-chief and should not include commentary on the trial bundle or other matters which may arise during the trial,
(3) a witness statement should be as concise as the circumstances allow, inadmissible or irrelevant material should not be included,
(4) the cost of preparation of an over-elaborate witness statement may not be allowed,
(5) r. 32.14 states that proceedings for contempt of court may be brought against a person if he makes, or causes to be made, a false statement in a document verified by a statement of truth without an honest belief in its truth,
(6) if a party discovers that a witness statement which they have served is incorrect they must inform the other parties immediately.

7.10.5 Evidence may also be given by affidavit[96] but unless an affidavit is specifically required either in compliance with a court order, a rule or practice direction, or an enactment, the party putting forward the affidavit may not recover from another party the cost of making an affidavit unless the court so orders.[97]

7.10.6 PD 32 at paras 3 to 6 contains information about the heading, body, jurat (the sworn statement which authenticates the affidavit) and the format of an affidavit. The court will normally give directions as to whether a witness statement or, where appropriate, an affidavit is to be filed.[98]

7.10.7 A statement of case which has been verified by a statement of truth and an application notice containing facts which have been verified by a statement of truth may also stand as evidence other than at the trial.

7.10.8 Evidence by deposition is dealt with in Part 34. A party may apply to a master for an order for a person to be examined before a hearing takes place (r. 34.8). Evidence obtained on an examination under that rule is referred to as a deposition. The master may order the person to be examined before either a judge, an examiner of the court or such other person as the court appoints. PD 34 at para. 4 sets out in detail how the examination should take place.

7.10.9 Provisions relating to applications for evidence by deposition to be taken either:

(1) in this country for use in a foreign court,[99] or
(2) abroad for use in proceedings within the jurisdiction[100]

are set out in detail in PD 34 at paras 5 and 6.

7.10.10 The procedure for issuing a witness summons is also dealt with in Part 34 and PD 34. A witness summons may require a witness to;

(1) attend court,
(2) produce documents to the court, or
(3) both,

on either a date fixed for the hearing or another date as the court may direct[101] (but see also r. 31.17 which may be used when there are areas of contention).

[96] See r. 32.15(2).
[97] See r. 32.15(1) and (2).
[98] See r. 32.4(3)(b).
[99] See RSC, ord. 70 in CPR, sch. 1.
[100] See r. 34.13.
[101] See r. 34.2(4).

7.10.11 The court may also issue a witness summons in aid of a court or tribunal which does not have the power to issue a witness summons in relation to the proceedings before it (and see PD 34 at paras 1, 2 and 3).

7.10.12 To issue a witness summons, two copies should be filed in the Action Department, Room E14 for sealing; one copy will be retained on the court file.

7.11 Hearings

Hearings generally

7.11.1 All hearings are in principle open to the public, even though in practice most of the hearings until the trial itself will be attended only by the parties and their representatives. However, in an appropriate case the court may decide to hold a hearing in private. Rule 39.2 lists the circumstances where it may be appropriate to hold a hearing in private. In addition, PD 39, para. 1.5, sets out certain types of hearings which may be listed in private.

7.11.2 The court also has the power under the Contempt of Court Act 1981, s. 11, to make an order forbidding publication of any details that might identify one or more of the parties. Such orders are granted only in exceptional cases.

7.11.3 References in the CPR and practice directions to hearings being in public or private do not restrict any existing rights of audience or confer any new rights of audience in respect of applications or proceedings which under the rules previously in force would have been heard in court or chambers respectively.[102] Advocates (and judges) do not wear robes at interim hearings before High Court judges, including appeals from masters, district judges and the county courts. Robes are worn for trials and certain other proceedings such as preliminary issues, committals etc. It is not intended that the new routes of appeal should restrict the advocate's right of audience, in that, a solicitor who appeared in a county court matter which is the subject of an appeal to a High Court judge would normally be allowed to appear at the appeal hearing.

7.11.4 Parties are reminded that they are expected to act with courtesy and respect for the other parties present and for the proceedings of the court. Punctuality is particularly important; being late for hearings is unfair to the other parties and other court users, as well as being discourteous to them and to the court.

Preparation for hearings

7.11.5 To ensure court time is used efficiently there must be adequate preparation prior to the hearing. This includes the preparation and exchange of skeleton arguments, the compilation of bundles of documents and giving realistic time estimates. Where estimates prove inaccurate, a hearing may have to be adjourned to a later date, and the party responsible for the adjournment is likely to be ordered to pay the costs thrown away.

7.11.6 The parties should use their best endeavours to agree beforehand the issues, or main issues between them, and must cooperate with the court and each other to enable the court to deal with claims justly; parties may expect to be penalised for failing to do so.

7.11.7 A bundle of documents must be compiled for the court's use at the trial, and also for hearings before the interim applications judge or a master where the documents to be referred to total 25 pages or more. The party lodging a trial bundle should supply identical bundles to all parties and for the use of witnesses. The efficient preparation of bundles is very important. Where bundles have been properly prepared, the claim will be easier to understand and present, and time and costs are likely to be saved. Where documents are copied unnecessarily or bundled incompetently, the costs may be disallowed. PD 39, para. 3, sets out in full the requirements for compiling bundles of documents for hearings or trial.

7.11.8 The trial bundle must be filed not more than seven and not less than three days before the start of the trial. Bundles for a master's hearing should be brought to the hearing unless the master directs otherwise. The contents of the trial bundle should be agreed where possible, and it should be made clear whether in addition, they are agreeing that the documents in the bundle are authentic even if not previously disclosed and are evidence of the facts stated in them even if a notice under the Civil Evidence Act 1995 has not been served.

[102] See PD 39, para. 1.14.

7.11.9 Lists of authorities for use at trial or at substantial hearings before a judge should be provided to the usher by 9.00 a.m. on the first day of the hearing. For other applications before a judge, or applications before a master, copies of the authorities should be included in the bundle.

7.11.10 For trial and most hearings before a judge, and substantial hearings before a master, a chronology, a list of the persons involved and a list of the issues should be prepared and filed with the skeleton argument. A chronology should be non-contentious and agreed with the other parties if possible. If there is a material dispute about any event stated in the chronology, that should be stated.

7.11.11 Skeleton arguments should be prepared and filed:

(1) for trials, not less than two days before the trial in the Listing Office, and

(2) for substantial applications or appeals, not later than one day before the hearing in the Listing Office and, where the master has requested papers in advance of the hearing, in the Masters' Support Unit Room E16.

7.11.12 A skeleton argument should:

(1) concisely summarise the party's submissions in relation to each of the issues,

(2) cite the main authorities relied on, which may be attached,

(3) contain a reading list and an estimate of the time it will take the judge to read,

(4) be as brief as the issues allow and not normally be longer than 20 pages of double-spaced A4 paper,

(5) be divided into numbered paragraphs and paged consecutively,

(6) avoid formality and use understandable abbreviations, and

(7) identify any core documents which it would be helpful to read beforehand.

7.11.13 Where a party decides not to call a witness whose witness statement has been served, to give oral evidence at trial, prompt notice of this decision should be given to all other parties. The party should also indicate whether he proposes to put, or seek to put, the witness statement in as hearsay evidence. If he does not, any other party may do so.[103]

Recording of proceedings

7.11.14 At any hearing, including the trial, any oral evidence, the judgment or decision (including reasons) and any summing up to a jury will be recorded. At hearings before masters, it is not normally practicable to record anything other than oral evidence and any judgment, but these will be recorded. A party to the proceedings may obtain a transcript of the proceedings on payment of the appropriate charge, from the Mechanical Recording Department, Room WG5. A person who is not a party to the proceedings may not obtain a transcript of a hearing which took place in private without the permission of the court.

7.11.15 No person or party may use unofficial recording equipment at a hearing without the permission of the court; to do so constitutes a contempt of court.[104]

7.12 Applications

7.12.1 Applications for court orders are governed by Part 23 and PD 23. Rule 23.6 and PD 23, para. 2, set out the matters an application notice must include. PD 23 states that form N244 may be used, however, parties may prefer to use form PF 244 which is available for use in the Royal Courts of Justice only. To make an application the applicant must file an application notice unless a rule or practice direction permits otherwise or the court dispenses with the requirement for an application notice.[105] Except in cases of extreme urgency, or where giving notice might frustrate the order (as with a search order), an application notice must be served on every party unless a rule or practice direction or a court order dispenses with service[106] (see paragraph 7.12.3 below).

7.12.2 Applications for remedies which a master has jurisdiction to grant should ordinarily be made to a master. PD 28 contains information about the types of applications which may be dealt with by masters and judges. An application notice for hearing by:

[103] Rule 32.5(5).

[104] Contempt of Court Act 1981, s. 9.

[105] See r. 23.3.

[106] See r. 23.4.

(1) a judge should be issued in the Listing Office, Room WG5, and
(2) a master should be issued in the Masters' Support Unit, Room E16,

and wherever possible should be accompanied by a draft in double spacing of the order sought.

7.12.3 The following are examples of applications which may be heard by a master where service of the application notice is not required:

(1) service by an alternative method (r. 6.8),
(2) service of a claim form out of the jurisdiction (section III of Part 6),
(3) default judgment under r. 12.11(4) or (5),
(4) substituting a party under r. 19.1(4),
(5) permission to issue a witness summons under r. 34.3(2),
(6) deposition for use in a foreign court (RSC, ord. 70 in CPR, sch. 1),
(7) charging order to show cause (RSC, ord. 50, r. 1(2) in CPR, sch. 1),
(8) garnishee order to show cause (RSC, ord. 49, r. 2(1) in CPR, sch. 1).

7.12.4 PD 23, para. 3, states in addition that an application may be made without serving an application notice:

(1) where there is exceptional urgency,
(2) where the overriding objective is best furthered by doing so,
(3) by consent of all parties, and
(4) where a date for a hearing has been fixed and a party wishes to make an application at that hearing but does not have sufficient time to serve an application notice.[107]

With the court's permission an application may also be made without serving an application notice where secrecy is essential.

7.12.5 Where an application is heard in the absence of one or more of the parties, it is the duty of the party attending to disclose fully all matters relevant to the application, even those matters adverse to the applicant. Failure to do so may result in the order being set aside. Any party who does not attend a hearing may apply to have the order set aside.[108]

7.12.6 Where notice of an application is to be given, the application notice should be served as soon as practicable after issue and, if there is to be a hearing, at least three clear days before the hearing date.[109] Where there is insufficient time to serve an application notice, informal notice of the application should be given unless the circumstances of the application require secrecy.

7.12.7 The court may deal with an application without a hearing if:

(1) the parties agree the terms of the order sought,
(2) the parties agree that the application should be dealt with without a hearing, or
(3) the court does not consider that a hearing would be appropriate.[110]

7.12.8 The court may deal with an application or part of an application by telephone where it is convenient to do so or in matters of extreme urgency. See PD 23, para. 6, and PD 25, para. 4.5.

7.12.9 Applications of extreme urgency may be made out of hours and will be dealt with by the duty judge. An explanation will be required as to why it was not made or could not be made during normal court hours.

7.12.10 Initial contact should be made through the Security Office on (020) 7947 6260 who will require the applicants phone number. The clerk to the duty judge will then contact the applicant and will require the following information:

(1) the name of the party on whose behalf the application is to be made,
(2) the name and status of the person making the application,
(3) the nature of the application,
(4) the degree of urgency, and
(5) the contact telephone number(s).

[107] See PD 23, para. 2.10.
[108] See r. 23.11.
[109] See r. 23.7(1)(b).
[110] See r. 23.8.

7.12.11 The duty judge will indicate to his clerk if he thinks it appropriate for the application to be dealt with by telephone or in court. The clerk will inform the applicant and make the necessary arrangements. Where the duty judge decides to deal with the application by telephone, and the facility is available, it is likely that the judge will require a draft order to be faxed to him. An application for an injunction will be dealt with by telephone only where the applicant is represented by counsel or solicitors.

7.12.12 It is not normally possible to seal an order out of hours. The judge is likely to order the applicant to file the application notice and evidence in support on the same or next working day, together with two copies of the order for sealing.

7.13 Interim Remedies

7.13.1 Interim remedies which the court may grant are listed in r. 25.1. An order for an interim remedy may be made at any time including before proceedings are started and after judgment has been given.[111] Some of the most commonly sought remedies are injunctions, most of which are heard by the Interim Applications Judge.

7.13.2 An application notice for an injunction should be filed in the Listing Office, Room WG5, and may be made without giving notice to the other parties in the first instance. This is most likely to be appropriate in applications for search orders and freezing injunctions which may also be heard in private if the judge thinks it appropriate to do so. Where the injunction is granted without the other party being present it will normally be for a limited period, seldom more than seven days. PD 25 at para. 4 deals fully with making urgent applications and those without notice, and para. 6,7 and 8 deal specifically with search orders and freezing injunctions, examples of which are annexed to the practice direction.

7.13.3 Applications for interim payments are heard by a master. The application notice should be filed in the Masters' Support Unit, Room E14. The requirements for obtaining an order for an interim payment are fully dealt with in PD 25.

8 LISTING BEFORE JUDGES

8.1 Responsibility For Listing

8.1.1 The Clerk of the Lists (Room WG3, Royal Courts of Justice) is in general responsible for listing. All applications relating to listing should in the first instance be made to him. Any party dissatisfied with any decision of the Clerk of the Lists may, on one day's notice to all other parties, apply to the judge in charge of the list.

8.1.2 The application should be made within seven days of the decision of the Clerk of the Lists and should be arranged through the Queen's Bench Listing Office, Room WG5.

8.2 The Lists

8.2.1 There are three lists, namely:
(1) the jury list
(2) the trial list, and
(3) the interim hearings list.
The lists are described below.

8.3 The Jury List

8.3.1 Claims for damages for libel and slander (defamation), fraud, malicious prosecution and false imprisonment will be tried by a judge and jury unless the court orders trial by a judge alone.

8.3.2 Where a claim is being tried by a judge and jury it is vitally important that the jury should not suffer hardship and inconvenience by having been misled by an incorrect time estimate. It is therefore essential that time estimates given to the court are accurate and realistic.

8.3.3 Dates for the trial of substantial claims will be fixed by the Listing Office after consideration of the parties' views. In such cases the Listing Office may, in addition, impose an alternative reserve date several weeks or months in advance of the trial date, in an endeavour to dispose of claims more quickly and to fill gaps in the list created by frequent settlements. When a

[111] See r. 25.2(1).

Court Guides

reserve date is so allocated a 'cut-off' date will be stated by the Clerk of the Lists again, after consideration of any views expressed by the parties and having regard to the complexity of the claim and the commitments of counsel and expert witnesses. On the cut-off date a decision will be made by the Clerk of the Lists to break or confirm the reserved date for trial.

8.3.4 If a party considers that he will suffer significant prejudice as the result of the decision of the Clerk of the Lists relating to either a reserved date or the cut-off date he may apply to the judge in charge of the jury list for reversal or variation of the decision, as set out in paragraph 8.1.1 above.

8.3.5 Jury applications will enter the interim warned list not less than two weeks from the date the application notice is filed. Parties may 'offer' a date for hearing the application within the week for which they are warned. Subject to court availability, the application will be listed on the offered date. Any application not reached on the offered date will return to the current warned list and will be taken from that list as and when required.

8.3.6 Applications in defamation claims in respect of 'meaning' (for an explanation of 'meaning' see PD 53, para. 4.1) may be listed in private on a specific day allocated for such matters.

8.3.7 Jury applications of length and/or complexity may be fixed by the same manner as set out in paragraph 8.3.6 above. (See the section below on The Trial List for general information about fixing trials.)

8.3.8 Applications for directions and other applications within the master's jurisdiction should firstly be made to a master unless:

(1) a direction has been given for the arranging of a trial date, or

(2) a date has been fixed or a window given for the trial.

Interim applications made after (1) or (2) above should be made to the judge. The master will use his discretion to refer a matter to the judge if he thinks it right to do so.

8.3.9 If a party believes that the master is very likely to refer the application to the judge, for example, where there is a substantial application to strike out, the matter should first be referred to the master or practice master on notice to the other parties without waiting for a private room appointment. The master will then decide whether the application should be referred to the judge.

8.4 The Trial List

8.4.1 This list consists of trials (other than jury trials), preliminary questions or issues ordered to be tried and proceedings to commit for contempt of court.

8.4.2 The Royal Courts of Justice presents unique problems in terms of fixing trial dates. The number of judges and masters involved and their geographical location has caused, for the time being at least, a different approach to the fixing of trials in the Chancery and Queen's Bench Divisions.

8.4.3 The requirement of judges to go on circuit, sit in the Criminal Division of the Court of Appeal, deal with cases in the Crown Office and other lists make it difficult to fix dates for trials before particular judges. Accordingly the following will only apply to the Listing Offices in the Royal Courts of Justice.

8.4.4 At as early an interim stage as practicable, the court will give directions with a view to fixing the trial date, week, or other short period within which the trial is to begin (the trial window).

8.4.5 For that purpose the court may:

(1) direct that the trial do not begin earlier than a specified date calculated to provide enough time for the parties to complete any necessary preparations for trial, and/or

(2) direct that the trial date be within a specified period, and/or

(3) specify the trial date or window.

8.4.6 If directions under 8.4.5(1) or (2) are given the court will direct the parties to attend upon the Clerk of the Lists in Room WG5 in order to fix the trial date or trial window.

8.4.7 The claimant must, unless some other party agrees to do so, take out an appointment with the Clerk of the Lists within seven days of obtaining the direction in paragraph 8.4. 6 above. If an appointment is not taken out within the seven days, the Listing Office will appoint a date for a listing hearing and give notice of the date to all parties.

8.4.8 At the listing hearing the Clerk of the Lists will take account, in so far as it is practical to do so, of any difficulties the parties may have as to availability of counsel, experts and witnesses.

The Clerk of the Lists will, nevertheless, try to ensure the speedy disposal of the trial by arranging a firm trial date as soon as possible within the trial period or, as the case may be, after the 'not before' date directed by the court under paragraph 8.4.5 above. If exceptionally it appears to the Clerk of the Lists at the listing hearing that a trial date cannot be provided within a trial window, he may fix the trial date outside the trial period at the first available date. (If a case summary has been prepared (see PD 29, paras 5.6 and 5.7) the claimant must produce a copy at the listing hearing together with a copy of particulars of claim and any orders relevant to the fixing of the trial date.)

8.4.9 The Listing Office will notify the Masters' Support Unit of any trial date or trial window given. In accordance with r. 29.2(3) notice will also be given to all the parties.

8.4.10 A party who wishes to appeal a date or window allocated by the listing officer must, within seven days of the notification, make an application to the judge nominated by each Division to hear such applications. The application notice should be filed in the Listing Office and served, giving one day's notice, on the other parties.

8.5 The Interim Hearings List

8.5.1 This list consists of interim applications, appeals and applications for judgment.

8.5.2 On each Thursday of term and on such other days as may be appropriate, the Clerk of the Lists will publish a warned list showing the matters in the interim hearings list that are liable to be heard in the following week. Any matters for which no date has been arranged will be liable to appear in the list for hearing with no warning save that given by the cause list for the following day, posted each afternoon outside Room WG5.

8.5.3 Fixtures will only be given in exceptional circumstances. The parties may by agreement 'offer' preferred dates for their matter to be heard, to be taken from the list on designated days, within the week following entry into the warned list in accordance with Listing Office practice. Matters lasting less than a day are usually offered for two preferred consecutive days and matters lasting more than a day are usually offered for three preferred consecutive days.

8.6 General

8.6.1 In addition to the matters listed to be heard by individual judges, the daily cause list for each day may list 'unassigned cases'. These are matters from the two lists to be heard that day but not assigned to a particular judge. If on any day a matter assigned to a particular judge proves to be ineffective, he will hear an unassigned case. It is hoped that the great majority of unassigned cases will be heard on the day that they are listed but this cannot be absolutely guaranteed. Parties engaged in matters listed as unassigned should attend outside the court where the matter is listed. The Clerk of the Lists will notify them as soon as possible which judge is to hear the matter. It is not the practice to list cases as unassigned unless the parties consent and there are no witnesses.

8.6.2 Appeals from masters' decisions will appear in the interim hearings list. The appeal notice (stamped with the appropriate fee) must be filed in Room WG7. On filing the appeal notice the solicitors should inform the Clerk of the Lists whether they intend to instruct counsel and, if so, the names of counsel.

8.7 Listing Before the Interim Applications Judge

8.7.1 All interim applications on notice to the interim applications judge will initially be entered in a List for hearing. They will be listed for hearing in Room E101 or some other nominated venue on any day of the week. Any matter which cannot be disposed of with within one hour will not be taken on the date given for the listed hearing.

8.7.2 If the parties agree that a matter cannot be disposed of within one hour, the applicant/appellant:

(1) may, on filing the application notice/notice of appeal, seek to have the matter placed directly into the interim hearings warned list, or

(2) must as soon as practicable and in any event not later than 24 hours before the hearing date transfer the matter into the interim hearings list.

Court Guides

If the parties do not so agree, or agree less than 24 hours before the hearing date, the parties must attend on that date.

8.7.3 Matters in the interim hearings list will be listed by the Clerk of the Lists in Room WG3, and the parties will be notified by the Listing Office (Room WG5) of the date on which the matter will enter the warned list. Matters in the warned list may be listed for hearing at any time on or after that date.

8.7.4 In order to ensure that a complete set of papers in proper order is available for the judge to read before the hearing, the parties must in advance of the hearing lodge in room WG4 a bundle, properly paginated in date order, and indexed, containing copies of the following documents;

(1) the application notice or notice of appeal,
(2) any statements of case,
(3) copies of all written evidence (together with copy exhibits) on which any party intends to rely, and
(4) any relevant order made in the proceedings.

8.7.5 The bundle should be agreed if possible. In all but simple cases a skeleton argument and, where that would be helpful, a chronology should also be lodged. (See paragraph 8.9.1 and 8.9.2 below in respect of skeleton arguments.)

8.7.6 Where a date for the hearing has been arranged the bundle must be lodged not later than three clear days before the fixed date. For application or appeals where there is no fixed date for hearing, the bundle must be lodged not later than 48 hours after the parties have been notified that the matter is to appear in the warned list. (For information concerning trial bundles see PD 39.)

8.7.7 Except with the permission of the judge no document may be used in evidence or relied on unless a copy of it has been included in the bundle referred to in paragraph 8.7. 6 above. If any party seeks to rely on written evidence which has not been included in the bundle, that party should lodge the original (with copy exhibits) in Room WG5 in advance of the hearing, or otherwise with the court associate before the hearing commences.

8.7.8 In appeals from circuit and district judges the provisions of paragraphs 8.7.4, 8.7.5, 8.7.6 and 8.7.7 should be complied with. In addition, the notes (if any) of reasons given by the circuit judge or district judge, prepared by the judge, counsel or solicitors should be lodged.

8.7.9 Subject to the discretion of the judge, any application or appeal normally made to the interim applications judge may be made in the month of September. In the month of August, except with the permission of a judge, only appeals in respect of orders:

(1) to set aside a claim form, or service of a claim form,
(2) to set aside judgment,
(3) for stay of execution,
(4) for any order by consent,
(4) for permission to enter judgment,
(5) for approval of settlements or for interim payment,
(6) for relief from forfeiture,
(7) for a charging order,
(8) for a garnishee order,
(9) for appointment or discharge of a receiver,
(10) for relief by way of sheriffs interpleader,
(11) for transfer to a county court or for trial by master, or
(12) for time where time is running in the month of August, may be heard, and only applications of real urgency will be dealt with, for example, urgent applications in respect of injunctions, or for possession (under RSC, ord. 113 in CPR, sch. 1).

8.7.10 It is desirable, where this is practical, that application notices or appeal notices are submitted to the practice master or a judge prior to the hearing of the application or appeal so that they can be marked 'fit for August' or 'fit for vacation'. If they are so marked, then normally the judge will be prepared to hear the application or appeal in August, if marked 'fit for August' or in September if marked 'fit for vacation'. The application to a judge to have the papers so marked should normally be made in writing, the application shortly setting out the nature of the application or appeal and the reasons why it should be dealt with in August or in September, as the case maybe.

8.8 The Lists Generally

8.8.1 Where a fixed date has been given it is the duty of the parties to keep the Clerk of the Lists fully informed as to the current position of the matter with regard to negotiations for settlement, whether all aspects of the claim are being proceeded with, an estimate of the length of the hearing, and so on.

8.8.2 Applications for adjournments will not be granted except for the most cogent reasons. If an application is made because solicitors were unaware of the state of the list they may be ordered personally to pay the costs of the application.

8.8.3 A party who seeks to have a hearing before a judge adjourned must inform the Clerk of the Lists of his application as soon as possible. Applications for an adjournment immediately before a hearing begins should be avoided as they take up valuable time which could be used for dealing with effective matters and, if successful, may result in court time being wasted.

8.8.4 If the application is made by agreement, the parties should, in writing, apply to the Clerk of the Lists who will consult the judge nominated to deal with such matters. The judge may grant the application on conditions which may include giving directions for a new hearing date.

8.8.5 If the application is opposed the applicant should apply to either the nominated judge or the judge to whom the matter has been allocated. A hearing should then be arranged through the Clerk of the Lists. A short summary of the reasons for the adjournment should be lodged with the Listing Office where possible by 10.30 a.m. on the day before the application is to be made. Formal written evidence is not normally required.

8.8.6 The applicant will be expected to show that he has conducted his own case diligently. Any party should take all reasonable steps:

(1) to ensure his case is adequately prepared in sufficient time to enable the hearing to proceed, and

(2) to prepare and serve any document (including any evidence) required to be served on any other party in sufficient time to enable that party also to be prepared.

8.8.7 If a party or his solicitor's failure to take reasonable steps necessitates an adjournment, the court may dismiss the application or make any other order including an order penalising the defaulting party in costs.

8.9 Listing Office — General Matters

8.9.1 To facilitate the efficient listing of proceedings, parties are reminded that skeleton arguments concisely summarising each party's submissions must be prepared and filed with the Listing Office;

(1) for trials, not less than three days before the trial, and

(2) for substantial applications or appeals, not later than one day before the hearing.

8.9.2 If it is anticipated that a skeleton argument will be filed late, a letter of explanation should accompany it which will be shown to the judge before whom the trial or hearing is to take place.

8.9.3 For parties' information, the following targets for the disposal of matters in the lists have been agreed as set out below:

Interim hearings warned list	within 4 weeks
From date of fixing;	
Trials under 5 days	within 4 months
Trials over 5 but under 10 days	within 6 months
Trials over 10 but under 20 days	within 9 months
Trials over 20 days	within 12 months.

9 TRIAL, JUDGMENTS AND ORDERS

9.1 General

9.1.1 The trial of a claim in the Royal Courts of Justice normally takes place before a High Court judge or a deputy sitting as a High Court judge. A master may assess the damages or sum due to a party under a judgment and, subject to any practice direction, may try a claim which is:
(1) treated as being allocated to the multi-track because it is proceeding under Part 8, or
(2) with the consent of the parties, allocated to the multi-track under Part 26.[112]

9.1.2 Claims for defamation, malicious prosecution or false imprisonment will be tried by a judge sitting with a jury unless the court orders otherwise.

9.2 The Trial

9.2.1 See paragraphs 2.4.2 and 2.4.3 above about representation at the trial, and paragraphs 7.11.14 and 7.11.15 above about recording of proceedings.

9.2.2 Rule 39.3 sets out the consequences of a party's failure to attend the trial and see also PD 39, para. 2.

9.2.3 The judge may fix a timetable for evidence and submissions if it has not already been fixed. The claimant's advocate will normally begin the trial with a short opening speech, and the judge may then allow the other party to make a short speech. Each party should provide written summaries of their opening speeches if the points are not covered in their skeleton arguments

9.2.4 It is normally convenient for any outstanding procedural matters or applications to be dealt with in the course of, or immediately after, the opening speech. In a jury trial such matters would normally be dealt with before the jury is sworn in.

9.2.5 Unless the court orders otherwise, a witness statement will stand as the evidence-in-chief of the witness, provided he is called to give oral evidence. With the court's permission, a witness may amplify his witness statement or give evidence in relation to new matters which have arisen since the witness statement was served on the other parties.[113]

9.2.6 The court associate will be responsible for any exhibits produced as evidence during the trial. After the trial, the exhibits are the responsibility of the party who produced them. Where a number of physical exhibits are involved, it is desirable, if possible, for the parties to agree a system of labelling and the manner of display, beforehand. The associate will normally draw the judgment or order made at the trial.

9.2.7 At a jury trial, it is the parties' responsibility to provide sufficient bundles of documents for the use of the jury.

9.2.8 Facilities are available to assist parties or witnesses with special needs. The Listing Office should be notified of any needs or requirements prior to the trial.

9.3 Judgments and Orders

9.3.1 Part 40 deals with judgments and orders. Rule 40.2 contains the standard requirements of a judgment or order and r. 40.3 contains provisions about drawing them up, see also PD 40B, para. 1 for more information.

9.3.2 Provisions concerning consent orders are contained in r. 40.6 which sets out in para. (3) the types of consent judgments and orders that may be sealed and entered by a court officer, provided:
(1) that none of the parties is a litigant in person, and
(2) the approval of the court is not required by a rule, a practice direction or an enactment.
Other types of consent order require an application to be made to a master or judge for approval. It is common for a respondent to a consent order not to attend the hearing but to provide a written consent. The consent may either be written on the document or contained in a letter, and must be signed by the respondent, or where there are solicitors on record as

[112] See PD 2B, para. 4.
[113] Rule 32.5.

acting for him, by his solicitors. Paragraph 3 of PD 40B contains further information about consent orders.

9.3.3 Rule 40.11 sets out the time for complying with a judgment or order, which is 14 days unless the judgment or order specifies otherwise (for example, by instalments), or a rule specifies a different time, or the judgment or proceedings have been stayed.

9.3.4 PD 40B contains further information about the effect of non-compliance with a judgment or order (and sets out the penal notice), adjustment of the final judgment sum in respect of interim payments and compensation recovery, and refers to various precedents for types of judgments and orders. See also:
(1) PD 40, and
(2) PD 40C which sets out the procedure to be followed both on settlement and after trial. Precedents for structured settlement orders, Parts 1 and 2, are annexed to PD 40C.

9.3.5 Where judgment is reserved, the judge may deliver his judgment by handing down the written text without reading it out in open court. Where this is the case, the advocates will be supplied with the full text of the judgment in advance of delivery. The advocates should then familiarise themselves with the contents and be ready to deal with any points which may arise when the judgment is delivered. Any direction or requirement as to confidentiality must be complied with.

9.3.6 The judgment does not take effect until formally delivered in court. If the judgment is to be handed down in writing copies will then be made available to the parties and, if requested and so far as practicable, to the law reporters and the press.

9.3.7 The judge will usually direct that the written judgment may be used for all purposes as the text of the judgment, and that no transcript need be made. Where such a direction is made, a copy will be provided to the Mechanical Recording Department from where further copies may be obtained (and see paragraph 7.11.14 above).

Judgment or order for payment of money on behalf of a child or patient

9.3.8 The usual order made at trial will make provision for any immediate payment to the litigation friend or his legal representative and for the balance of the award to be placed to a special investment account pending application to a master or district judge (in the case of a child) or the Court of Protection (in the case of a patient) for investment directions. The order will specify the time within which the application should be made.

9.3.9 The litigation friend or his legal representative should then write to or make an appointment with:
(1) in the case of a child, the master or district judge in accordance with paragraph 6.8.6 above and PD 21, or
(2) in the case of a patient, the Court of Protection in accordance with PD 21, para. 11.

9.3.10 Where after trial the judge has found in favour of a child or patient, instead of judgment being given, the proposed award of damages may be paid by way of a structured settlement. The structure must be approved by the judge, and in the case of a patient must also be approved by the Court of Protection. (See also PD 40C.)

Provisional damages

9.3.11 Rule 41.1 defines an award of provisional damages. Where there is a chance that a claimant may in the future develop a particular disease or deterioration as a result of the event giving rise to the claim, he can seek an award of damages for personal injury on the assumption that he will not develop the disease or deterioration, with provision for him to make a further application within the time specified in the order, if he does so develop the disease or deterioration.

9.3.12 PD 41 gives further information about provisional damages awards and, in particular, about the preservation of the case file for the time specified in the order for making a further application, and the documents to be included in the case file. A precedent for a provisional damages judgment is annexed to PD 41.

Court Guides

10 APPEALS

10.1 General

10.1.1 Appeals are governed by Part 52 and PD 52. The contents of Part 52 are divided into two sections: general rules about appeals and special provisions applying to the Court of Appeal. The practice direction is divided into three sections: general provisions about appeals, general provisions about statutory appeals and appeals by way of case stated, and provisions about specific appeals. The following paragraphs apply to orders made after 2 May 2000 and are intended only to draw parties' attention to the basic provisions for making an appeal in or from the Queen's Bench Division. For further information about these procedures and about other specific types of appeal, parties should refer to PD 52 and the Civil Appeals Guide.

10.1.2 In the Queen's Bench Division an appeal from a master will lie to a High Court judge unless it is a final decision in a claim allocated to the multi-track or in specialist proceedings referred to in Part 49 in which case the appeal will lie to the Court of Appeal. An appeal from a High Court judge will lie to the Court of Appeal.

10.1.3 Unless the lower court or the appeal court orders otherwise, an appeal does not operate as a stay of any order or decision of the lower court.

10.2 Permission to Appeal

10.2.1 Permission is required to appeal from a decision of a judge in a county court or the High Court, except where the appeal is in respect of:

(1) a committal order,
(2) a refusal to grant habeas corpus,
(3) certain insolvency appeals, and
(4) certain statutory appeals.

For the purposes of Part 52 and PD 52, the term 'judge' includes a master or district judge.
(For more information see r. 52.3.)

10.2.2 Permission should be sought at the hearing at which the decision to be appealed against is made. If it is not, or if it is sought and refused, permission should be sought from the court appealed to ('the appeal court'). Where permission is sought from the appeal court it must be requested in the appellant's notice. Permission may be granted, or refused, or granted in part (whether as to a part of the order, a ground of appeal or an issue) and refused as to the rest. Paragraphs 4.1 to 4.12 of PD 52 deal with permission to appeal including the matters to be stated in the notice and the documents to be filed with it.

10.2.3 An application to the appeal court for permission may be dealt with without a hearing, but if refused without a hearing the applicant may request that it be reconsidered at a hearing; the court need not require that notice of the hearing be given to the respondent.

10.3 Notices

10.3.1 Rule 52.4 and PD 52, para. 5, deal with the appellant's notice. The appellant must file his notice at the appeal court either within a period specified by the court appealed from ('the lower court') or, if no such period is specified, within 14 days of the date of the decision appealed from. The notice must be served on each respondent as soon as practicable and in any event not later than seven days after it is filed.

10.3.2 A respondent must file a notice where:

(1) he also wishes to appeal the lower court's decision,
(2) he wishes to uphold the decision of the lower court for different or additional reasons to those given by the lower court, or
(3) he is seeking permission to appeal from the appeal court.

10.3.3 The respondent's notice must be filed either within a period specified by the lower court or, if no such period is specified, within 14 days of:

(1) the date the respondent is served with the appellant's notice where:
    (a) permission to appeal was given by the lower court, or

(b) permission to appeal is not required,
(2) the date the respondent is served with notification that the appeal court has given the appellant permission to appeal, or
(3) the date the respondent is served with notification that the application for permission to appeal and the appeal itself are to be heard together.
(Paragraph 7 of PD 52 deals with the respondent's notice of appeal.)

10.3.4 The notices to be used are as follows:
(1) the appellant's notice is form N161, and
(2) the respondent's notice is form N162.
There is a leaflet available from the Listing Office, Room WG5 entitled 'I want to appeal', which provides information about appealing other than to the Court of Appeal.

10.4 Appeals in Cases of Contempt of Court

10.4.1 Appellant's notices which by PD 52, para. 21.4, are required to be served on 'the court from whose order or decision the appeal is brought' may be served, in the case of appeals from the Queen's Bench Division, on the Senior Master of the Queen's Bench Division; service may be effected by leaving a copy of the notice of appeal with the Clerk of the Lists in Room WG5, Royal Courts of Justice, Strand, London WC2A 2LL.

11 ENFORCEMENT

11.1 General

11.1.1 Enforcement in the High Court is still governed by RSC, ord. 17, 45 to 52 and 71 in CPR, sch. 1.*

11.1.2 RSC, ord. 45 in CPR, sch. 1, deals with enforcement generally. A judgment or order for payment of money (other than into court) may be enforced by a writ of fieri facias, garnishee proceedings, a charging order or the appointment of a receiver.[114] A judgment or order to do or abstain from doing an act may be enforced by a writ of sequestration (with the permission of the court) or an order of committal.[115] A judgment or order for possession of land may be enforced by a writ of possession,[116] and a judgment or order for delivery of goods without the alternative of paying their value by a writ of specific delivery.[117] In each case, where RSC, ord. 45, r. 5, applies enforcement may also be by a writ of sequestration or an order of committal.

11.2 Writs of Execution

11.2.1 RSC, ord. 46, in CPR, sch. 1, deals with writs of execution generally. Rules 2 and 3 set out the circumstances when permission to issue a writ is necessary.[118] Rule 4 contains provisions for making an application for permission. Rule 5 deals with applications for permission to issue a writ of sequestration. RSC, ord. 47, in CPR, sch. 1, contains provisions concerning writs of fieri facias. Forms of writs of execution may be used as follows:
(1) writs of fieri facias in form Nos. 53 to 63,
(2) writs of delivery in form Nos. 64 and 65,
(3) writs of possession in form Nos. 66 and 66A,
(4) writ of sequestration in form No. 67,
(5) writ of restitution in form No. 68,
(6) writ of assistance in form No. 69.

11.2.2 With certain exceptions, writs of execution issued in the Royal Courts of Justice are executed by the sheriff of the county in which the debtor has assets, or his officer. RSC, ord. 46, r. 6, sets out the provisions for issue of writs of execution. In the Queen's Bench Division writs of

[* Orders 48 to 51 and 71 have been replaced by CPR, Parts 69 and 71 to 74, and supplementing practice directions.]

114 RSC, ord. 45, r. 1 in CPR, sch. 1.

115 RSC, ord. 45, r. 5.

116 RSC, ord. 45, r. 3.

117 RSC, ord. 45, r. 4.

118 See also RSC, ord. 45, r. 3.

Court Guides

execution are issued in the Central Office in Room E17. Before the writ can be sealed for issue, a signed praecipe for its issue must be filed[119] in one of forms PF 86 to 90, as appropriate, stamped with the appropriate fee. A copy of the judgment or order requiring enforcement should also be provided.

11.2.3 On an application for permission to issue a writ of possession under RSC, ord. 45, r. 3(2), if the property consists of a house of which various parts are sublet to, or in the occupation of, different persons, the evidence in support should show the nature and length of the notice which has been given to the various occupiers. Where the defendant or any other persons are in actual possession of the premises of which possession is sought, the evidence must contain the following information:

(1) whether the premises or any part of it is residential,
(2) if so,
    (a) what is the rateable value of the residential premises, and
    (b) whether it is let furnished or unfurnished and, if furnished, the amount of furniture it contains, and
(3) any other matters that will assist the master in deciding whether any occupier is protected by the Rent Acts.

11.2.4 Where a party wishes to enforce a judgment or order expressed in a foreign currency by the issue of a writ of fieri facias, the praecipe must be endorsed with the following certificate:

I/We certify that the rate current in London for the purchase of (*state the unit of foreign currency in which the judgment is expressed*) at the close of business on (*state the nearest preceding date to the date of issue of the writ of fieri facias*) was (   ) to the £ sterling and at this rate the sum of (*state amount of the judgment debt in the foreign currency*) amounts to £   .

The schedule to the writ of fieri facias should be amended;

(1) showing the amount of the judgment or order in the foreign currency at paragraph 1.
(2) inserting a new paragraph 2 as follows:
    2. Amount of the sterling equivalent as appears from the certificate endorsed on the praecipe for issue of the writ £   .
(3) renumbering the remaining paragraphs accordingly.

11.2.5 County court judgments or orders to which art. 8(1) of the High Court and County Courts Jurisdiction Order 1991 applies may be enforced in the High Court, and since 26 April 1999, any county court judgment for over £600 may be transferred to the High Court sheriff for enforcement (except where it is a judgment arising from a regulated agreement under the Consumer Credit Act 1974).

11.2.6 The party seeking enforcement should obtain from the appropriate county court a certificate of judgment of the county court in compliance with CCR, ord. 22, r. 8(1A) in sch. 2, setting out details of the judgment or order to be enforced, sealed with the seal of that court and dated and signed by an officer of that court and stating on its face that it is granted for the purpose of enforcing the judgment or order by execution against goods in the High Court. Form N293A is a 'Combined Certificate of Judgment and Request for Writ of Fieri Facias' and should be used.

11.2.7 A correctly completed form N293A together with a copy should be filed in Room E17 where the court officer will:

(1) allocate a reference number,
(2) date seal the certificate and copy, returning the original to the party and retaining the copy, and
(3) enter the proceedings in a register kept for that purpose. The certificate shall be treated for enforcement purposes as a High Court judgment and interest at the appropriate rate shall run from the date of the certificate.

11.2.8 The title of all subsequent documents shall be set out as follows:

[119] RSC, ord. 46, r. 6(3).

IN THE HIGH COURT OF JUSTICE
QUEEN'S BENCH DIVISION
High Court Claim No.
County Court Claim No.
(Sent from the [ ] County Court by Certificate dated (*date*))
Claimant
Defendant

When the writ of fieri facias is issued, the certificate of judgment retained by the party shall be date sealed by the court officer on the bottom left-hand corner and endorsed with the designation of the sheriff to whom the writ is directed.

11.2.9 The Sheriff's Lodgment Centre at 2 Serjeant's Inn, Fleet Street, London EC4Y 1NX provides a service for arranging transfer up of county court judgments, and will complete the required forms and take all the above steps on behalf of the judgment creditor. (A helpline is provided on (020) 7353 3640.)

11.2.10 It is important to remember in these cases that although any application for a stay of execution may be made to a master in the High Court by application notice filed in accordance with Part 23, all other applications for enforcement or other relief must be made to the issuing county court. This practice is followed in the district registries with such variations as circumstances require.

11.2.11 When a writ of execution has been issued in the Royal Courts of Justice it may then be delivered to the Sheriff's Lodgment Centre. Value added tax is payable in addition to the sheriff's fee on the services for which the fee is payable, and must be paid at the time of delivery. If the goods, chattels and property to be seized in execution are not within Greater London, the sheriff will direct the writ to the sheriff of the appropriate county. Goods which may not be seized in execution of a writ are set out in the Supreme Court Act 1981, s. 138(3A), as follows:

(1) such tools, books, vehicles and other items of equipment as are necessary to that person for use personally by him in his employment, business or vocation,
(2) such clothing, bedding, furniture, household equipment and provisions as are necessary for satisfying the basic domestic needs of that person and his family,
(3) any money, banknotes, bills of exchange, promissory notes, bonds, specialties or securities for money belonging to that person.

11.2.12 When first executing a writ of fieri facias the sheriff will deliver to the debtor or leave at each place where execution is levied a notice of seizure in form No. 55.[120] This is commonly known as 'walking possession' and the notice explains to the debtor the situation with regard to the goods seized and what he then has to do.

11.2.13 After execution of a writ of execution, the sheriff will endorse on the writ a statement of the manner in which he has executed it and will send a copy of the statement to the party issuing the writ.

11.3 Interpleader Proceedings (RSC, Ord. 17)

11.3.1 Where a person is under liability in respect of a debt or property and has been, or expects to be claimed against by two or more persons claiming the same debt or property, if the person under liability does not dispute the debt or claim the property, he may apply to the court for relief by way of interpleader, i.e. for the entitlement of the persons claiming the same debt or property to be established in separate proceedings between them.

11.3.2 Where the sheriff has seized goods in execution and a person other than the person against whom the writ of execution was issued wishes to claim the goods seized, he must give notice of his claim to the sheriff, including in his notice a statement of his address which will be his address for service. The sheriff will then give notice of that claim to the claimant on whose behalf the goods were seized, in form PF 23. The notice requires the claimant to state whether he admits or disputes the claim. The claimant must do so within seven days of receipt of the sheriff's notice and may use form PF 24 to do so.

[120] RSC, ord. 45, r. 2.

11.3.3 Where the claimant admits the claim, the sheriff will withdraw from possession of the goods and may apply under RSC, ord. 17, r. 2(4) for an order to restrain a claim being brought against him for having taken possession of the goods. Where the claimant disputes the claim, the sheriff may apply for interpleader relief. An application for interpleader relief if made in existing proceedings is made by an application in accordance with Part 23, otherwise it is made by the issue of a Part 8 claim form.

11.3.4 The master may deal with the claims summarily, or may direct an issue to be tried between the parties in dispute (see RSC, ord. 17, r. 5 in CPR, sch. 1) or make such other order as is appropriate.

11.4 Examination of Judgment Debtor (RSC, Ord. 48)*

11.4.1 Where a person ('the judgment creditor') has obtained a judgment or order for payment of a sum of money against a person ('the judgment debtor'), the judgment creditor may apply for an order requiring the judgment debtor to attend to be orally examined concerning his assets and means.[121] If the judgment debtor is a company or corporation, the court will order an officer of the company or corporation to attend for examination. In the case of a judgment or order which is not for payment of a sum of money, the court may make an order for the attendance of the party liable for his examination on such questions as may be specified in the order.

11.4.2 An application for an order under RSC, ord. 48, r. 1, should be made in accordance with Part 23 without notice to any other party. The application must be supported by evidence giving details of the judgment or order, including the amount still owing, and showing that the judgment creditor is entitled to enforce the judgment or order. Where the judgment debtor is a company or corporation the evidence must give details of the officer to be examined. Form PF 98 may be used as a precedent for the evidence in support. Where a judgment creditor has obtained judgments in several different proceedings against the same judgment debtor, only one application need be made, setting out in the body of the application details of all the judgments on which examination is sought.

11.4.3 The examination will take place before a master, registrar, district judge or nominated officer, as may be ordered, and will normally be at the court where the least expense will be incurred, usually the county court for the area where the judgment debtor lives. If a different court is requested the reason why should be given.

11.4.4 The application notice/evidence should be filed in the Masters' Support Unit Room E16 for consideration by a master who will, if satisfied, make the order sought. Where the examination is to take place in a county court, the judgment creditor should lodge a copy of the order with the county court and obtain an appointment for the examination. If the examination is to take place in the Royal Courts of Justice, the order should be taken to Room E17 where the appointment will be endorsed on the order. In the Central Office the nominated officer is nominated at the discretion of the Senior Master and their names may be obtained from Room E17.

11.4.5 The order (endorsed with the penal notice as set out in PD 40B, para. 9.1.) together with details of the appointment must be served personally on the judgment debtor or on the officer of the judgment debtor company or corporation to be examined. A judgment debtor should be offered his conduct money, i.e. expenses of travelling to and from the examination and of attending to give evidence.

11.4.6 The officer conducting the examination will take down, or arrange to have taken down in writing the judgment debtor's statement. The officer will read the statement to the judgment debtor and will ask him to sign it. If he refuses to do so the officer will sign the statement. If the judgment debtor refuses to answer any question or if any other difficulties arise, the matter will be referred to the Senior Master or the practice master who will give such direction as he thinks fit.

[* See now CPR, Part 71, and PD 71.]

121 RSC, ord. 48, r. 1 in CPR, sch. 1.

11.5 Garnishee Proceedings (RSC, Ord. 49)*

11.5.1 Where a judgment creditor has obtained a judgment or order for payment of a sum of money of at least £50 against a judgment debtor, and another person ('the garnishee') is indebted to the judgment debtor, the judgment creditor may apply to the master for an order that the garnishee pays to the judgment creditor the amount of the debt due to the judgment debtor, or sufficient of it to satisfy the judgment debt.

11.5.2 The application should be made in accordance with Part 23 but the application notice need not be served on the judgment debtor. The application will normally be dealt with without a hearing and must be supported by evidence as set out in RSC, ord. 49, r. 2 in CPR, sch. 1. Parties may use form PF 100 for their evidence in support. If the master is satisfied that such an order is appropriate, he will make an order in form No. 72 specifying the debt attached and appointing a time for the garnishee to attend and show cause why the order should not be made absolute.

11.5.3 The garnishee order to show cause must be served personally on the garnishee, and served on the judgment debtor, in accordance with RSC, ord. 49 r. 3. Where the garnishee fails to attend the hearing or attends but does not dispute the debt, the master may make a garnishee order absolute against the garnishee under RSC, ord. 49, r. 1. The order absolute may be enforced in the same manner as any other order for the payment of money.[122] Where the garnishee disputes the debt, the master may dispose of the matter as set out in RSC, ord. 49, r. 5.

11.5.4 Where the judgment creditor seeks to enforce a judgment expressed in a foreign currency by garnishee proceedings, the evidence in support of the application must contain words to the following effect:

> The rate current in London for the purchase of (*state the unit of foreign currency in which the judgment is expressed*) at the close of business on (*state the nearest preceding date to the date of verifying the evidence*) was (   ) to the £ sterling, and at this rate the sum of (*state the amount of the judgment debt in the foreign currency*) amounts to £   . I have obtained this information from (*state source*) and believe it to be true.

11.6 Charging Orders (RSC, Ord. 50)†

11.6.1 A judgment creditor may apply for a charging order on the property or assets of the judgment debtor, which will have the effect of providing him with security over the property of the judgment debtor. The High Court has jurisdiction to impose a charging order in the following cases:

(1) where the property is a fund lodged in the High Court,
(2) where the order to be enforced is a maintenance order[123] of the High Court, and
(3) where the judgment or order is made in the High Court and exceeds £5,000.[124]

The property and assets of the judgment debtor on which a charge may be imposed by a charging order are specified by the Charging Orders Act 1979, s. 2.

11.6.2 A charging order to show cause imposing a charge on land will be drawn in respect of the judgment debtor's interest in the land and not the land itself, unless the court orders otherwise. If a charging order to show cause is made on stocks or shares in more than one company, a separate order must be drawn in respect of each company. If the judgment debt is expressed in a foreign currency, the evidence in support of any application for a charging order should contain a similar provision to that set out in paragraph 11.5. 4 above.

11.6.3 The application for a charging order is made to a master and should be made in accordance with Part 23 but the application is made without being served on the judgment debtor. The application will normally be dealt with without a hearing and must be supported by evidence as set out in RSC, ord. 50, r. 3. Parties may use form PF 101 for their evidence in support. If the master is satisfied that such an order is appropriate, he will make an order in form

[* See now CPR, Part 72, and PD 72.]

122 RSC, ord. 49, r. 4(2).

[† See now CPR, Part 73, and PD 73.]

123 See Attachment of Earnings Act 1971, s. 2(a).

124 In the case of sub-paras (2) and (3) the county court also has jurisdiction.

No. 75 appointing a time for the judgment debtor to attend and show cause why the order should not be made absolute.

11.6.4 The order to show cause and the evidence in support should be served in accordance with RSC, ord. 50, r. 2, or otherwise as directed by the master. After further consideration at the hearing the master will either make the order absolute (with or without modifications) as in form No. 76, or discharge it. Where the order is discharged, the order of discharge must be served in accordance with RSC, ord. 50 r. 7.

11.6.5 See RSC, ord. 50, r. 4 for provisions concerning imposing a charge on an interest held by a trustee. RSC, ord. 50, r. 5 deals with the effects of a charging order in relation to securities out of court, and RSC, ord. 50, r. 6 with funds in court. Proceedings for the enforcement of a charging order by sale of the property charged must be begun by a Part 8[125] claim form issued out of Chancery Chambers or a Chancery district registry (RSC, ord. 50, r. 9A).

11.7 Receivers; Equitable Execution (RSC Ord. 51)*

11.7.1 Equitable execution is a process which enables a judgment creditor to obtain payment of the judgment debt where the interest of the judgment debtor in property cannot be reached by ordinary execution.

11.7.2 An application for appointment of a receiver by way of equitable execution may be made to a master, who also has jurisdiction to grant an injunction if, and only so far as, the injunction is ancillary or incidental to the order. The procedure follows that set out in RSC, ord. 30, rr. 1 to 6 in CPR, sch. 1, and the application should be made in accordance with Part 23 and PD 23 as described in the following paragraphs.

11.7.3 If the judgment creditor seeks an injunction (as in 11.7.2 above) he should file his application notice based on form No. 82 but setting out in addition the injunction sought, together with a witness statement or affidavit in support stating:

(1) the date and particulars of the judgment, and that it remains wholly unsatisfied, or to what extent it remains unsatisfied,
(2) the particulars and result of any execution which has been issued, and the nature of the sheriffs return (if any),
(3) that the judgment debtor has no property which can be taken by the ordinary process of execution, (*if he has, give reasons showing that legal execution would be futile*),
(4) particulars of the property in respect of which it is proposed to appoint a receiver,
(5) the name and address of the receiver proposed to be appointed, and that in the deponent's judgment he is a fit and proper person to be appointed receiver, and
(6) that the judgment debtor is in financial difficulties (that the immediate appointment of a receiver without the delay of giving security is of great importance] and that the deponent believes that the judgment debtor may assign or dispose of his estate or interest in (*give details of property*) unless restrained from doing so by the order and injunction of the court.

11.7.4 The judgment creditor need not give notice of this application which will normally be dealt with without a hearing. If the master is satisfied with the evidence he will make an order in form No. 83 for a hearing to take place in respect of the application for the appointment of the receiver and granting an injunction meanwhile.

11.7.5 If the judgment creditor does not seek an injunction, the application notice should be filed and served together with the evidence in support (as in paragraph 11.7.3 above but without paragraph (6)).

11.7.6 At the hearing of the application to appoint the receiver, the master will, if he thinks fit, make an order in form No. 84. A copy of the order appointing the receiver shall be served by the judgment creditor on the receiver and all other parties to the proceedings.[126]

11.7.7 Where a receiver has been ordered to give security under RSC, ord. 30, r. 2, the judgment creditor should obtain an appointment before the master who made the order appointing the receiver, to settle the form and amount of the security. Unless otherwise ordered, the security

[125] See PD 8B, Table 1.
[* See now CPR, Part 69, and PD 69.]
[126] RSC, ord. 30, r. 4.

will be in the form of a guarantee. The judgment creditor should have prepared a draft form of guarantee for the master to approve at the appointment. Form PF 30CH may be used as a precedent for the guarantee.

11.7.8 RSC, ord. 30, r. 3 deals with the remuneration of the receiver which may either be assessed by the master or referred to a costs judge. Rule 5 contains the provisions for submitting the receiver's accounts.

11.8 Committals, etc. (RSC, Ord. 52)

11.8.1 The court has power to punish contempt of court by an order of committal to prison or by other means. These may be by ordering the payment of a fine, by the issue of a writ of sequestration, or by making a hospital or guardianship order under certain provisions of the Mental Health Act 1983. Committal applications under RSC, ord. 52, r. 4, are always dealt with by a High Court judge. The following provisions apply to applications made under RSC, ord. 52, r. 4.

11.8.2 The application should be made in existing proceedings by filing an application notice. If not in existing proceedings, a Part 8 Claim Form should be issued[127] (see PD RSC, ord. 52, paras 2.1 and 2.2). Evidence in support of a committal application must be by affidavit[128] and, together with the Part 8 claim form or application notice, must be served personally on the person sought to be committed. A date for the hearing must be obtained from the Listing Office, Room WG5 and endorsed on or served with the claim form or application notice.

11.8.3 Paragraphs 2.5, 2.6 and 3.1 to 3.4 of PD RSC, ord. 52 deal with the content of the evidence, and serving and filing, and para. 4 deals with the hearing date and management of the proceedings.

11.8.4 Committal proceedings will normally be heard in public, but see RSC, ord. 52, r. 6, which sets out certain types of cases which may be heard in private, and see PD RSC, ord. 52, para. 9.

11.8.5 Where the court makes a finding of contempt, details of the contempt and of the order or undertaking breached (where appropriate) must be set out in the order. The term of any period of committal must be stated in the order and must not exceed two years.[129] A fine must be expressed as payable to Her Majesty the Queen and the order must state the amount of the fine and the date and time within which it must be paid. A contemnor and his solicitors will be notified separately as to how the fine should be paid. A precedent of the order is in form No. 85 and will normally be drawn by the court.

11.8.6 When an order for committal to prison is made, the court will issue a warrant to the tipstaff authorising him to convey the contemnor to the appropriate prison. A copy of the order should be served on the prison governor. RSC, ord. 52, r. 8, deals with the discharge of a person committed.

11.9 Execution against Property of Foreign or Commonwealth States

11.9.1 In cases where judgment has been obtained against a foreign or Commonwealth State and it is sought to execute the judgment by a writ of fieri facias, a charging order or a garnishee order, the following provisions apply:

(1) Before the writ of fieri facias is issued, the master must be informed in writing and his direction sought. In cases where an application is to be made for a charging order to show cause or a garnishee order to show cause, the evidence in support of the application must include a statement that the execution sought is against a foreign or Commonwealth State.

(2) The master, having been so informed will, as soon as practicable, inform the Foreign and Commonwealth Office ('FCO') of the application and will not permit the issue of a writ of fieri facias, nor grant an order to show cause until the FCO has been so informed. The Privileges and Immunities Section of the Protocol Department of the FCO may be contacted by telephone on (020) 7210 4053 or by fax on (020) 7270 4126.

[127] See PD 8B, Table 1.

[128] RSC, ord. 52, r. 4(2).

[129] Contempt of Court Act 1981, s. 14.

(3) Having regard to all the circumstances of the case, the master may postpone the decision whether to issue the writ or grant the order to show cause for so long as he considers reasonable for the purpose of enabling the FCO to furnish further information relevant to his decision, but not for longer than three days from the time of his contacting the FCO. In the event that no further information is received from the FCO within 24 hours of its being informed, then the writ of fieri facias may be issued or the order to show cause may be sealed without further delay.

11.10 Recovery of Enforcement Costs

11.10.1 The Courts and Legal Services Act 1990, s. 15(3), enables a person taking steps to enforce a money judgment in the High Court to recover the costs of any previous attempt to enforce that judgment. Section 15(4) excludes costs that the court considers to have been unreasonably incurred.

11.10.2 The application for an enforcement costs order is made to a master and should be made in accordance with Part 23 but the application notice need not be served on the judgment debtor. The application will normally be dealt with without a hearing and must be supported by evidence substantially as set out in form PF 205. The deponent should exhibit sufficient vouchers, receipts or other documents as are reasonably necessary to verify the amount of the costs of previous attempts to enforce the judgment.

11.10.3 If the master is satisfied that such an order is appropriate, he will make an order for payment of the amount of such costs as he considers may be recoverable under s. 15(3). If the amount of such costs is less than that claimed by the judgment creditor, the master may either disallow the balance or give directions for a detailed assessment or other determination of the balance. If after assessment or other determination it appears that the judgment creditor is entitled to further costs beyond those originally allowed, he may issue a further writ of fieri facias or take other lawful steps to enforce those costs. Interest on the costs runs either from the date the master made the enforcement costs order or from the date of the costs certificate.

11.11 Enforcement of Magistrates' Courts' Orders

11.11.1 The Magistrates' Courts Act 1980, s. 87, provides that payment of a sum ordered to be paid on a conviction of a magistrates' court may be enforced by the High Court or a county court (otherwise than by the issue of a writ of fieri facias or other process against goods or by imprisonment or attachment of earnings) as if the sum were due to the clerk of the magistrates' court under a judgment of the High Court or county court, as the case may be.

11.11.2 In the Central Office, the application is made to a master and should be made in accordance with Part 23. Where enforcement is sought by a garnishee or charging order to show cause, the application will normally be dealt with without a hearing. Otherwise the application notice and evidence in support should be served on the defendant.

11.11.3 The application must be supported by a witness statement or affidavit in a form appropriate to the type of execution sought and must have exhibited to it the authority of the magistrates' court to take the proceedings which will recite the conviction, the amount outstanding and the nature of the proceedings authorised to be taken (Magistrates' Courts Forms Rules 1981, form 63).

11.11.4 The application notice and evidence in support together with an additional copy of the exhibit should be filed in Room E15 where it will be assigned a reference number from the register kept for that purpose. The matter will then be dealt with by the master according to the type of enforcement sought.

11.11.5 This practice will also be followed in the district registries with such variations as circumstances may render necessary.

11.12 Reciprocal Enforcement of Judgments and Enforcement of European Community Judgments and Recommendations etc. Under the Merchant Shipping (Liner Conferences) Act 1982 (RSC, Ord. 71)*

Reciprocal enforcement; the Administration of Justice Act 1920 and the Foreign Judgments (Reciprocal Enforcement) Act 1933

11.12.1 Rule 2 of RSC, ord. 71 in CPR, sch. 1, sets out how an application under s. 9 of the Act of 1920 or under s. 2 of the Act of 1933 for registration of a foreign judgment in the High Court may be made. The application should be made without notice being served on any other party, but the master may direct that a Part 8 claim form should be issued and served.

11.12.2 Rule 3 of RSC, ord. 71, sets out what the evidence in support of the application should contain or have exhibited to it. The title of the witness statement or affidavit should:

(1) expressly state whether it is made 'In the matter of the Administration of Justice Act 1920' or 'In the matter of the Foreign Judgments (Reciprocal Enforcement) Act 1933', and

(2) identify the judgment by reference to the court in which it was obtained and the date it was given.

The foreign judgment will be registered in the foreign currency in which it is expressed and must not be converted into sterling in the evidence in support. When it comes to enforcing the foreign judgment, the amount should then be converted in accordance with the instructions set out above in paragraph 11 in respect of the type of enforcement sought.

11.12.3 The order giving permission to register the judgment must be drawn up by, or on behalf of the judgment creditor (form PF 154 may be used as a precedent) and will be entered in the register of judgments kept in the Central Office for that purpose.[130] The order will usually contain a direction that the costs of and caused by the application and the registration be assessed and added to the judgment as registered. Notice of registration of the judgment must state the matters set out in RSC, ord. 71, r. 7(3), including the right of the judgment debtor to apply, and the time within [which] he may do so, to have the registration set aside. The notice must be served on the judgment debtor in accordance with ord. 71, r. 7(1).

11.12.4 An application to set aside the registration of a judgment under RSC, ord. 71, r. 9 must be made in accordance with Part 23 and be supported by a witness statement or affidavit.

11.12.5 An application for a certified copy of a judgment entered in the High Court must be made without notice by witness statement or affidavit in accordance with RSC, ord. 71, r. 13. The certified copy will be endorsed with a certificate signed by the master in accordance with ord. 71, r. 13(4). Where the application was made under s. 10 of the Act of 1933, an additional certificate will be issued and signed by the master as in form PF 155. Judgment creditors who intend to seek enforcement abroad should ensure that their judgment is endorsed as follows:

This judgment carries interest from (*date*) at the rate of 8% per annum in accordance with the provisions of the Judgments Act 1838.

Enforcement of European Community judgments

11.12.6 Rules 15 to 24 of RSC, ord. 71 in CPR, sch. 1, contain provisions concerning applications for enforcement of Community judgments and Euratom inspection orders under the European Communities (Enforcement of Community Judgments) Order 1972 and for their enforcement. The application for registration may be made without notice being served on any other party and must be supported by a witness statement or affidavit containing or having exhibited to it the matters referred to in ord. 71, r. 18. Form PF 156 may be used as a precedent.

11.12.7 The order for registration (form PF 157) will be entered in the register of the Community judgments and Euratom inspection orders kept in the Central Office for that purpose. The court will serve notice of the registration in form PF 158 in accordance with ord. 71, r. 20.

[* See now CPR, Part 74, and PD 74.]

[130] RSC, ord. 71, rr. 5 and 6.

Court Guides

11.12.8 An application to vary or cancel a registration under the provisions of ord. 71, r. 22, shall be made by application notice in accordance with Part 23, supported by a witness statement or an affidavit.

Reciprocal enforcement; the Civil Jurisdiction and Judgments Act 1982

Applications under s. 4 of the Act of 1982

11.12.9 The provisions concerning applications for registration of judgments of another contracting State under s. 4 of the Act of 1982 are set out in RSC, ord. 71, rr. 25 to 35 in CPR, sch. 1. The application is made without notice being served on any other party and must be supported by evidence as set out in ord. 71, r. 28. Form PF 159 may be used as a precedent.

11.12.10 The order for registration (form PF 160) will be entered in the register of judgments ordered to be registered under s. 4 of the Act of 1982 kept in the Central Office for that purpose. The notice of registration in form PF 161 should be served in accordance with RSC, ord. 71, r. 32 in CPR, sch. 1.

11.12.11 An appeal against registration must be made to a judge under the provisions of ord. 71, r. 33(2), by application notice in accordance with Part 23, and should be served in accordance with ord. 71, r. 33(2)(a) and (b).

Applications under s. 12 of the Act of 1982

11.12.12 Rule 36 of RSC, ord. 71 in CPR, sch. 1, deals with applications for enforcement of High Court judgments in other contracting States under s. 12 of the Act of 1982. The application for a certified copy of the judgment entered in the High Court must be made without notice being served on any other party and must be supported by evidence as set out in RSC, ord. 71, r. 36(2) in CPR, sch. 1. Form PF 163 may be used as a precedent.

11.12.13 The court will issue a certified copy of the judgment together with a certificate in form PF 110 signed by the master, and having annexed to it a copy of the claim form by which the proceedings were begun.

Applications under s. 18 of the Act of 1982; judgment containing money provisions

11.12.14 Rule 37 of RSC, ord. 71 in CPR, sch. 1, deals with applications for registration in the High Court of a certificate in respect of any money provisions contained in a judgment given in another part of the United Kingdom. The certificate may be obtained by filing a draft certificate in form No. 111 together with a witness statement or affidavit in accordance with ord. 71, r. 37(3). Form PF 164 may be used as a precedent.

11.12.15 The certificate must be filed for registration in Room E13 in the Central Office within six months from the date of its issue. Under para. 9 of sch. 6 to the Act of 1982 an application may be made to stay the enforcement of the certificate. The application may be made without notice being served on any other party supported by a witness statement or affidavit stating that the applicant is entitled and intends to apply to the judgment court to set aside or stay the judgment.

Applications under s. 18 of the Act of 1982; judgment containing non-money provisions

11.12.16 Rule 38 of RSC, ord. 71 in CPR, sch. 1, deals with applications for registration in the High Court of a judgment which contains non-money provisions, given in another part of the United Kingdom. The application should be made broadly in accordance with paragraphs 11.12.11 and 11.12.12 above, without notice being served on any other party, but the master may direct that a Part 8 claim form should be issued and served.

11.12.17 The application should be accompanied by a draft certificate in form No. 112 and must be supported by a witness statement or affidavit in accordance with ord. 71, r. 37(3) (with the necessary modifications). Form PF 165 may be used as a precedent. An application to set aside registration of a judgment under sch. 7 to the Act of 1982 may be made in accordance with ord. 71, r. 9(1) and (2).

11.12.18 The certificates will be entered in the register of certificates in respect of judgments ordered to be registered under sch. 6 or 7 to the Act of 1982 kept in the Central Office for that purpose.

Enforcement of recommendations etc. under the Merchant Shipping (Liner Conferences) Act 1982

11.12.19 Applications under s. 9 of the Act of 1982 for registration of a recommendation, determination or award, are dealt with by a commercial judge and shall be made by the issue of a Part 8 claim form.[131] The application should be supported by evidence in accordance with RSC, ord. 71, r. 42 in CPR, sch. 1.

11.12.20 The order giving permission to register the recommendation, determination or award must be drawn up by or on behalf of the party making the application, and entered in the register of the recommendations, determinations and awards ordered to be registered under s. 9 of the Act of 1982, directed by the Senior Master to be kept in the Admiralty and Commercial Registry.

12 MISCELLANEOUS

12.1 Service of Foreign Process (RSC, Ord. 69)*

12.1.1 RSC, ord. 69 in CPR, sch. 1 applies to the service on a person in England or Wales of any process in connection with civil or commercial proceedings in a foreign court or tribunal. A request for service is made to the Senior Master from either Her Majesty's Principal Secretary of State for Foreign and Commonwealth Affairs, or where the foreign court or tribunal is in a convention country,[132] from a consular or other authority of that country.

12.1.2 Where the foreign court or tribunal certifies that the person to be served understands the language of the process, it is not necessary to provide a translation. Order 69, r. 3 deals with the manner of service; the process may be served through the machinery of the county court and the usual practice is for the Senior Master to provide a certificate for the bailiff or county court officer to use. The Senior Master may make an order for service by an alternative method based on the bailiffs certificate.

12.1.3 When service has been effected, the Senior Master will send a certificate, together with a copy of the process served, to the authority who requested service, stating how service was effected, or why service could not be effected. There is a discretion to charge for the costs of service or attempted service, but recovery is usually sought only where the country requesting service does not provide a reciprocal free service.

12.2 Rectification of Register of Deeds of Arrangement (RSC, Ord. 94, r. 4)

12.2.1 Deeds of arrangement must be registered.[133] The registration office is at the Department of Trade [and Industry].

12.2.2 An application for an order as set out in RSC, ord. 94, r. 4(1)(a) or (b), must be made to a master of the Queen's Bench Division. Notice need not be served on any other party and the application must be supported by a witness statement or affidavit as described in ord. 94, r. 4(2).

12.3 Exercise of Jurisdiction under the Representation of the People Acts (RSC, Ord. 94, r. 5)

12.3.1 Rule 5 of RSC, ord. 94 in CPR, sch. 1, describes the jurisdiction of the High Court under the above Acts. The practice is governed by the Election Petition Rules 1960 (as amended).

12.3.2 Under Part III of the Representation of the People Act 1983, the result of a parliamentary or local government election may be questioned on the grounds of some irregularity either before or during the election. The provisions of Part III have also been applied to European Parliamentary elections.

12.3.3 The challenge is made by the issue of an election petition:

(a) in respect of a Parliamentary election by one or more electors or

(b) in respect of a local government election by four or more electors,

or by an unsuccessful or alleged candidate. The member/councillor whose election is complained of is a respondent to the petition as is the returning officer if his conduct is complained of. The petition is issued in the Election Petitions Office, Room E218, normally within 21 days of the election, although this may be extended in certain circumstances.

[131] RSC, ord. 71, r. 41, and PD 8B, Table 1.

[* See now CPR, rr. 6.32 to 6.35.]

[132] For definition of 'convention country' see ord. 69, r. 1.

[133] Deeds of Arrangement Act 1914, as amended by the Administration of Justice Act 1925, s. 22.

12.3.4 The petition is tried by two High Court judges of the Queen's Bench Division in respect of parliamentary elections or by a commissioner in respect of local government elections. The commissioner must be a lawyer of not less than 10 years' standing who neither resides nor practises in the area concerned. The trial usually takes place in the constituency/local government area although preliminary matters are dealt with at the Royal Courts of Justice.

12.3.5 The election court may confirm the result of the election, or substitute another candidate as the member/councillor, or may order the election to be rerun.

12.3.6 Applications for remedies under various sections of the Representation of the People Act 1983 are also issued in the Election Petitions Office, and are usually heard by an election rota judge.

12.3.7 Outside the court offices' opening times, but while the building is still open to the public, election petitions and applications may be left in the letter box fixed to the door of Room E218. When the building is closed, election petitions and applications may be left with Security at the Main Entrance, up until midnight.

12.4 Bills of Sale Acts 1878 and 1882 and the Industrial and Provident Societies Act 1967 (RSC, Ord. 95)

12.4.1 Every bill of sale and absolute bill of sale to which the Act of 1878 applies must be registered under s. 8 of that Act, within seven clear days of its making, and, under s. 11 of the Act of 1878, the registration of a bill of sale must be renewed at least once every five years. The register for the purpose of the Bills of Sale Acts contains the particulars of registered bills of sale and an alphabetical index of the names of the grantors, and is kept in the Action Department in Room E10.

12.4.2 An application to register a bill of sale which is made within the prescribed time should be made by filing in Room E17 the original bill of sale and any document annexed to it together with a witness statement or affidavit in form PF 179 or PF 180. An application to re-register a bill of sale which is made within the prescribed time should be made by filing in Room E17 a witness statement or affidavit in form PF 181.

12.4.3 An application to rectify:

(1) an omission to register, by extending the time for registration, or

(2) an omission or misstatement of the name, residence or occupation of a person in the register, by correcting the registration,

must be made by witness statement or affidavit to a master of the Queen's Bench Division. In addition to the matters set out in forms PF 179 or PF 180, the evidence in support must also set out the particulars of the omission and state the grounds on which the application is made.

12.4.4 Where the residence of the grantor of the bill of sale or the person against whom the process is issued is outside the London bankruptcy district, or where the bill of sale describes the goods as being in a place outside that district, the Central Office will send copies of the bill of sale to the appropriate county court district judge.[134]

12.4.5 The master, on being satisfied that the omission or misstatement of name, residence or occupation of a person in the register was accidental or due to inadvertence, may order the omission or misstatement to be rectified by the insertion in the register of the correct name, residence or occupation of the person.

12.4.6 Where the master is satisfied that the omission to register a bill of sale or a witness statement or affidavit of renewal within the prescribed time was accidental or due to inadvertence, he may extend the time for registration on such terms as he thinks fit. In order to protect any creditors who have accrued rights of property in the assets in respect of which the bill of sale was granted between the date of the bill and its actual registration, any order to extend the time for registration will normally be made 'without prejudice' to those creditors. The order will be drawn up in form PF 182.

12.4.7 An application for an order that a memorandum of satisfaction be written on a registered copy of a bill of sale, made without the consent of the person entitled to the benefit of the bill of sale, must be made by the issue of a Part 8 claim form. Where the consent of the person

[134] Bills of Sale Act 1882, s. 11, and the Bills of Sale (Local Registration) Rules 1960.

entitled to the benefit of the bill of sale has been obtained, the application may be made by a witness statement or affidavit[135] containing that consent and verifying the signature on it. Form PF 183 contains precedents for the evidence and forms of consent. Where the application is made with consent, the evidence need not be served on any other person. If the master is satisfied on the evidence, he will endorse his approval on the witness statement or affidavit (an order is not normally drawn up) and send it to Room E17 for satisfaction to be entered. If a copy of the bill of sale has been sent to a county court district judge, a notice of satisfaction will be sent to that district judge.

12.4.8 Where the consent has not been obtained, the claim form must be served on the person entitled to the benefit of the bill of sale and must be supported by evidence that the debt (if any) for which the bill of sale was made has been satisfied or discharged.

12.4.9 An application to restrain removal on sale of goods seized in accordance with RSC, ord. 95, r. 3, and under the proviso to s. 7 of the Bills of Sale Act (1878) Amendment Act 1882 must be made by the issue of a Part 8 claim form for hearing before the interim applications judge.

12.4.10 Under the Industrial and Provident Societies Act 1967 an application to record an instrument creating a fixed or floating charge on the assets of a registered society or to rectify any omission or misstatement in it must be made within 14 days beginning with the date of its execution.

12.4.11 Under RSC, ord. 95, r. 5 in CPR, sch. 1, and in accordance with s. 1(5) of the Act of 1967 the court may order:

(1) that the period for making an application for recording a charge be extended, or

(2) an omission or misstatement in such an application be rectified.

The procedure for obtaining an order as in (1) or (2) above is similar to that under s. 14 of the Bills of Sale Act 1878 and must be made by witness statement or affidavit to a master of the Queen's Bench Division as in paragraph 12.4. 3 above and must exhibit a copy of the instrument duly authenticated in the prescribed manner together with any other particulars relating to the charge.

12.4.12 Rule 3 of RSC, ord. 95 in CPR, sch. 1, refers to the assignment of book debts; the register of assignments of book debts is kept in Room E10 in the Central Office. An application for registration under the Insolvency Act 1986, s. 344, should be made in accordance with RSC, ord. 95, r. 6(2). Parties may use form PF 186 for their evidence in support. It is helpful if the original assignment is also produced.

12.5 Enrolment of Deeds and Other Documents

12.5.1 Any deed or document which by virtue of any enactment is required or authorised to be enrolled in the Supreme Court may be enrolled in the Central Office. See PD 5, para. 6, which fully sets out the procedure for enrolment and contains in an appendix the Enrolment of Deeds (Change of Name) Regulations 1994.

12.6 Bail (RSC, Ord. 79, r. 9)

12.6.1 Under the provisions of the Criminal Justice Act 1967, s. 22(1) and (2) (as amended by the Bail Act 1976, sch. 2) the High Court may grant bail in criminal proceedings to a defendant in custody who has been refused bail, or vary the arrangements for bail of an inferior court.

12.6.2 The application must be made to the interim applications judge by the issue of a Part 8 claim form in form No. 97 or 97A, and supported by a witness statement or affidavit in accordance with RSC, ord. 79, r. 9(1) to (3) in CPR, sch. 1. The claim form should be issued in the Listing Office, Room WG5, and will be given a bail number from the register kept there for recording bail applications.

12.6.3 If a defendant wishing to apply for bail is unable to instruct a solicitor to act for him through lack of means, he may write to the interim applications judge to that effect and requesting

[135] See PD RSC, ord. 95.

that the Official Solicitor act for him. The letter should be addressed to the Listing Office, Room WG5, marked for the attention of the interim applications judge. Where the judge assigns the Official Solicitor to act for the defendant, he may dispense with the issue of a claim form and a witness statement or affidavit in support.

12.6.4 Where the Judge grants bail, the order will be drawn up in form No. 98 which provides for the conditions to be complied with both before release, including the provision of sureties, and after release. An order varying the arrangements for bail will be drawn up in form No. 98A. Copies of those orders must be sent to the appropriate officer of the Crown Court or of the court which committed the defendant.

12.7 Defamation

12.7.1 Defamation claims are governed by Part 53 and PD 53. Paragraph 2 of PD 53 sets out the information which should be included in a statement of case.

Offer to make amends

12.7.2 Under the Defamation Act 1996, s. 2, a person who has published a statement alleged to be defamatory of another may offer to make amends ('a s. 2 offer'). The s. 2 offer must:

(1) be in writing,
(2) be expressed to be an offer to make amends under s. 2 of the Act, and
(3) state whether it is a qualified offer, and if so, set out the defamatory meaning in relation to which it is made.

A s. 2 offer is an offer:

(1) to make a suitable correction of the statement complained of and sufficient apology,
(2) to publish the correction and apology in a manner that is reasonable and practicable in the circumstances, and
(3) to pay to the aggrieved party compensation (if any) and costs as may be agreed or determined to be payable.

12.7.3 Where a s. 2 offer is accepted by an aggrieved person he may not bring or continue defamation proceedings against the person making the offer, but he may apply to the court under s. 3 of the Act for an order that the other party fulfil his offer by taking the agreed steps. If the parties are unable to agree the amount of compensation or costs, the aggrieved party may apply to the court for the amount to be decided.

12.7.4 In the event that the parties are unable to agree on the steps to be taken, the person making the offer may take such steps as he thinks appropriate, including making an application for the court's approval of the terms of a statement to be read in court containing a correction and apology. He may also give an undertaking to the court as to the manner of their publication.

12.7.5 In existing proceedings the above applications may be made in accordance with Part 23, otherwise a Part 8 claim form should be issued. The application or claim must be supported by written evidence as set out in PD 53, para. 3.3, and should be made to a master. If the application or claim involves the court's approval for a statement to be read in court, it should be made to the Senior Master. The claim form or application notice should be issued or filed in the Masters' Support Unit, Room E17.

Ruling on meaning

12.7.6 An application for an order determining whether or not a statement complained of is capable of:

(1) having any meaning or meanings attributed to it in a statement of case,
(2) being defamatory of the claimant, or
(3) bearing any other meaning defamatory of the claimant,

should be made in accordance with Part 23 and may be made at any time after service of the particulars of claim. Paragraphs 4.3 and 4.4 of PD 53 state the information which must be included in the application notice and evidence in support.

12.7.7 The application notice should be filed in the Listing Office, Room WG5, for hearing by the judge in charge of the jury list, or another designated judge.

Summary disposal

12.7.8 Section 8 of the Act gives the court power to dispose summarily of the claimant's claim. The court may:

(1) dismiss the claim if it appears that it has no realistic prospect of success and there is no reason why it should be tried, or

(2) give judgment for the claimant and grant him summary relief.

12.7.9 Summary relief includes the following:

(1) a declaration that the statement was false and defamatory of the claimant,

(2) an order that the defendant publish or cause to be published a suitable correction and apology,

(3) damages not exceeding £10,000,

(4) an order restraining the defendant from publishing or further publishing the matter complained of.

12.7.10 Applications for summary disposal are dealt with in r. 53.2 and PD 53, paras 5.1 to 5.3. Substantial claims and those involving the police authorities or the media or those seeking an order restraining publication will be dealt with by the judge in charge of the jury list or another designated judge, and the application notice should be filed in the Listing Office, Room WG5. Applications for summary disposal in other defamation claims may be made at first instance to a master.

12.7.11 An application notice for summary disposal must state:

(1) that it is an application for summary disposal made in accordance with s. 8 of the Act,

(2) the matters set out in PD 24, para. 2(3), and

(3) whether or not the defendant has made an offer to make amends under s. 2 of the Act, and whether or not it has been withdrawn.

The application may be made at any time after service of the particulars of claim and the provisions of r. 24.4(1)(a) and (b) do not apply.

12.7.12 Where the court has made an order for summary relief as in 12.7.9(2) above (specifying the date by which the parties should agree the content, time, manner, form and place of publication of the correction and apology) and the parties are unable to comply within the specified time, the claimant must prepare a summary of the court's judgment and serve it on the other parties within three days following the date specified in the order for the content to be agreed by the parties.[136]

12.7.13 If the parties are unable to agree the summary, they must within three days of its receipt, apply to the court by:

(1) filing an application notice, and

(2) filing and serving on all the other parties a copy of the summary showing the revisions they wish to make to it.

The court (normally the judge who delivered the judgment) will then settle the summary.

Statements read in court

12.7.14 PD 53, para. 6, only applies where a party wishes to accept a Part 36 offer, Part 36 payment or other offer of settlement.

12.7.15 An application for permission to make the statement before a judge in court may be made before or after acceptance of the Part 36 offer, Part 36 payment or other offer to settle, and should be made in accordance with Part 23 to the Senior Master, or if he is not available, to the practice master. The application notice, together with a copy of the statement, should be filed in the Masters' Support Unit, Room E17.

12.7.16 Where permission has been given, the parties may take a copy of the order to the Listing Office, Room WG5 for the matter will be listed before the judge in charge of the jury list for mention. Otherwise, the Action Department will send the court file to the Listing Office for the matter to be listed.

[136] PD 53, para. 5.3.

12.8 References to the Court of Justice of the European Communities*

12.8.1 A party wishing to apply for an order[137] under RSC, ord. 114 in CPR, sch. 1, may do so by application before or at the trial or hearing. An application made before the trial or hearing should be made in accordance with Part 23.

12.8.2 Before making an order for reference, the court will pay close attention to the terms of the appropriate article, to RSC, ord. 114, to form PF 109 and to the 'Guidance of the Court of Justice of the European Communities on References by National Courts for Preliminary Rulings' which may be found in the Practice Direction (ECJ References: Procedure) [1999] 1 WLR 260.

12.8.3 It is the responsibility of the court, rather than the parties, to settle the terms of the reference. This should identify as clearly, succinctly and simply as the nature of the case permits the question to which the British court seeks an answer and it is very desirable that language should be used which lends itself readily to translation.

12.8.4 The referring court should, in a single document scheduled to the order (in form PF 109):

(1) identify the parties and summarise the nature and history of the proceedings,
(2) summarise the salient facts, indicating whether these are proved or admitted or assumed,
(3) make reference to the rules of national law (substantive and procedural) relevant to the dispute,
(4) summarise the contentions of the parties as far as relevant,
(5) explain why a ruling of the European Court is sought, identifying the EC provisions whose effect is in issue, and
(6) formulate, without avoidable complexity, the question(s) to which an answer is requested.

12.8.5 Where the document is in the form of a judgment, passages which are not relevant to the reference should be omitted from the text scheduled to the order. Incorporation of appendices, annexes or enclosures as part of the document should be avoided, unless the relevant passages lend themselves readily to translation and are clearly identified.

12.8.6 When the order of reference has been approved by the judge and sealed by the court, the order, together with any other necessary documents should be promptly passed to Room E13 for the attention of the Senior Master of the Queen's Bench Division, for transmission to Luxembourg without avoidable delay.

12.9 Group Litigation Orders 'GLOs'

12.9.1 Section III of Part 19 and PD 19B deal with claims where multiple parties are claimants.

12.9.2 When considering applying for a GLO, the applicant should contact the Law Society at 113 Chancery Lane, London WC2A 1PL, who may be able to assist in putting the applicant in contact with other parties who may also be interested in applying for a GLO in the same matter.

12.9.3 The consent of either the Lord Chief Justice or the Vice-Chancellor to the GLO is required. In the Queen's Bench Division the application should be made to the Senior Master in accordance with Part 23. If the Senior Master is minded to make the GLO he will forward a copy of the application notice and any written evidence to the Lord Chief Justice. The application notice should include the information set out in PD 19B, para. 3.2.

12.9.4 A group register will be set up and maintained in the court of all the parties to the group of claims to be managed under the GLO. In order to publicise the GLO when it has been made, a copy should be supplied to the Law Society and to the Senior Master. A record of each GLO made will be maintained in the Central Office.

12.9.5 PD 19B sets out how the group litigation will be managed. In particular, a managing judge will be appointed. The case management directions are likely to direct:

[* See now CPR, Part 68, and PD 68.]

137 An 'order' means an order referring a question to the European Court for a preliminary ruling under art. 234 (formerly art. 177) of the Treaty establishing the European Community, art. 150 of the Treaty establishing the European Atomic Energy Community or art. 41 of the Treaty establishing the European Coal and Steel Community, or for a ruling on the interpretation of any of the Brussels Conventions (within the meaning of the Civil Jurisdiction and Judgments Act 1982, s. 1(1)) or any of the instruments referred to in the Contracts (Applicable Law) Act 1990, s. 1.

(1) that a 'group particulars of claim' containing the various claims of the claimants on the group register are served,
(2) that one claim proceed as a 'test' claim, and
(3) a cut-off date after which no additions may be made to the group register.

ANNEX 1 FEES TO BE TAKEN

[Annex 1 is omitted. It consists of sch. 1 to the Supreme Court Fees Order 1999, which has been replaced by the Civil Proceedings Fees Order 2004, which is reproduced in **appendix 6**.]

ANNEX 2 MASTERS' ABBREVIATIONS

The following is a list of the abbreviations commonly used by masters on endorsements of orders, though there may be some variation as between individual masters.

A.D.R	alternative dispute resolution
Aff.	affidavit
A.M-T	allocate to multi-track
A.N.	appointment notice
App.	application
A.Q.	allocation questionnaire
A.S.	assessed summarily
B.N.L.T.	by no later than
C.C.	county court
C.I.A.	costs in the application
C.I.A.E.	costs in any event
C.I.C.	costs in the case
Cl.	claimant
Col.	certificate for counsel
C.M.C.	case management conference
C.O.A.	charging order absolute
C.O.C.B.	costs of and caused by
C.O.S.C.	charging order to show cause
C.R.	costs reserved
C.T.R.	costs of today reserved
D./Def	defendant/defence
D.A.I/N.A.	detailed assessment if not agreed
Disc.	disclosure
Dism.	dismissed
Disp. C/S.	dispense with requirement of certificate of service
F.C.	fixed costs
F.I.	further information
F.O.	further order
F.O.D.	first open date
G.O.A.	garnishee order absolute
G.O.S.C.	garnishee order to show cause
I.A.E.	in any event
I.B.	indemnity basis
Insp.	inspection
J.	judgment (as in Part 24 applications)
L.A.	legal aid
L.A.A.	legal aid assessment
L.Q.	listing questionnaire
O.	order
On C.Serv.	on producing certificate of service
O.	Exam. oral examination
P/C	particulars of claim
P.D.	practice direction

Court Guides

Pm.	permission
Pm. A.	permission to apply
Pm. R.	permission to restore
Pm. R.F.D.	permission to restore for further directions
Pt.	part
P.R.A.	private room appointment
R.	rule
S.A.	set aside; special allowance
S.O.J.	service out of the jurisdiction
S/C	statement of case
S.B.	standard basis
S/T	statement of truth
Tfr.	transfer
W.N.	without notice
W.C.O.	wasted costs order
W.S.	witness statement

Appendix 5 Forms

FORMS IN THE CD-ROM VERSION

What is in Appendix 5

This appendix provides a list of all the forms in the CD-ROM version of *Blackstone's Civil Practice.* The list is in order of form number. In the CD-ROM version, clicking on the form number in this list will open the form.

There are subheadings in the list where forms concerned with particular types of proceedings are grouped together (see the Contents at the beginning of the appendix).

At the end of this appendix, in the book, there is a printed copy of form PF 52, the standard form of multi-track case management directions.

Printing Forms from the CD-ROM Version

A form can be printed from the CD-ROM version and filled in. All the forms are provided as Adobe Acrobat documents. Some are also provided as Microsoft Word documents. Most of the Adobe Acrobat forms can be filled in on-screen (see **Filling in Adobe Acrobat Forms On-screen** below). Adobe Acrobat forms which can be filled in on-screen have comments attached to assist in filling them in. When printing a form which has comments, the Print dialog box will include a check box labelled Comments. If there is a tick in this check box, the comments will be printed on the form. If you do not want the comments to be printed, please ensure that there is no tick in this check box.

Filling in Adobe Acrobat Forms On-screen

In the following list the Adobe Acrobat forms which have '(FILL IN ON-SCREEN)' after the title of the form may be completed on-screen from the CD-ROM version of *Blackstone's Civil Practice.* To fill in a form on-screen, make sure you are using the hand tool. If the form can be filled in on-screen, the hand tool will change to the I-beam cursor when it is over an area of the form which can be filled in (a 'field'). Click on the field to be filled in and type in the text which you want to appear there (or paste in text from the Windows clipboard). Strike the tab key on your keyboard to confirm the entered text and move to the next field. Alternatively, strike the Enter key to confirm the entered text without moving to another field. You may return to any field to amend it. Use the tab key alone to move forwards through fields; use the tab key with the shift key to move backwards. When you have completed a form it may be printed (see **Printing Forms from the CD-ROM Version** above). If you print without also closing the form, you can proofread your print and make any required amendments on-screen. You can also copy any particular item from a completed form on to the Windows clipboard and paste it into a Word or text document for subsequent use: this may be a convenient way of dealing with, for example, an address which has to be put into a number of different forms. It is not possible to save a completed form using Acrobat Reader alone: if you wish to save completed forms you must use the full Adobe Acrobat product or Adobe Acrobat Approval.

LIST OF FORMS IN THE CD-ROM VERSION

Administration

2.1B	Administration application *2.1B Microsoft Word version*
2.2B	Statement of proposed administrator *2.2B Microsoft Word version*
2.3B	Affidavit of service of administration application *2.3B Microsoft Word version*

Winding up

4.1	Statutory demand under the Insolvency Act 1986, s. 123(1)(a) or 222(1)(a) *4.1 Microsoft Word version*
4.2	Winding-up petition *4.2 Microsoft Word version*
4.4	Affidavit of service of winding-up petition at registered office *4.4 Microsoft Word version*
4.5	Affidavit of service of winding-up petition other than at registered office or on an oversea company *4.5 Microsoft Word version*

Bankruptcy

6.1	Statutory demand under the Insolvency Act 1986, s. 268(1)(a). Debt for liquidated sum payable immediately *6.1 Microsoft Word version*
6.2	Statutory demand under the Insolvency Act 1986, s. 269(1)(a). Debt for liquidated sum payable immediately following a judgment or order of the court
6.3	Statutory demand under the Insolvency Act 1986, s. 268(2). Debt payable at future date *6.3 Microsoft Word version*
6.4	Application to set aside a statutory demand *6.4 Microsoft Word version*
6.5	Affidavit in support of application to set aside statutory demand *6.5 Microsoft Word version*
6.7	Creditor's bankruptcy petition on failure to comply with a statutory demand for a liquidated sum payable immediately *6.7 Microsoft Word version*
6.11	Affidavit of personal service of statutory demand *6.11 Microsoft Word version*
6.13	Affidavit of truth of statements in bankruptcy petition
6.17	Affidavit of personal service of bankruptcy petition *6.17 Microsoft Word version*
6.27	Debtor's bankruptcy petition *6.27 Microsoft Word version*
6.28	Statement of affairs (debtor's petition) *6.28 Microsoft Word version*
6.28 debtors guidance	Statement of affairs (debtor's petition) (guidance notes) *6.28 debtorsguidance Microsoft Word version*
7.2	Ordinary application *7.2 Microsoft Word version*

Admiralty

ADM1	Claim form (Admiralty claim *in rem*) (FILL IN ON-SCREEN)
ADM1A	Claim form (Admiralty claim) (FILL IN ON-SCREEN)
ADM1C	Notes for defendant
ADM2	Acknowledgment of service (Admiralty claim) (FILL IN ON-SCREEN)
ADM3	Collision statement of case (FILL IN ON-SCREEN)
ADM4	Application and undertaking for arrest and custody (FILL IN ON-SCREEN)
ADM5	Declaration in support of application for warrant of arrest (FILL IN ON-SCREEN)
ADM6	Notice to consular officer of intention to apply for warrant of arrest (FILL IN ON-SCREEN)
ADM7	Request for caution against arrest (FILL IN ON-SCREEN)
ADM9	Warrant of arrest (FILL IN ON-SCREEN)
ADM10	Standard directions to the Admiralty Marshal (FILL IN ON-SCREEN)
ADM11	Request for caution against release (FILL IN ON-SCREEN)
ADM12	Request and undertaking for release (FILL IN ON-SCREEN)
ADM12A	Request for withdrawal of caution against release (FILL IN ON-SCREEN)
ADM13	Application for judgment in default of filing an acknowledgment of service and/or defence or collision statement of case (FILL IN ON-SCREEN)
ADM14	Order for sale of a ship (FILL IN ON-SCREEN)
ADM15	Claim form (Admiralty limitation claim) (FILL IN ON-SCREEN)
ADM15B	Notes for defendant (Admiralty limitation claim)
ADM16	Notice of admission of right of claimant to limit liability (FILL IN ON-SCREEN)
ADM16A	Defence to Admiralty limitation claim (FILL IN ON-SCREEN)
ADM16B	Acknowledgment of service (Admiralty limitation claim) (FILL IN ON-SCREEN)
ADM17	Application for restricted limitation decree (FILL IN ON-SCREEN)
ADM17A	Application for general limitation decree (FILL IN ON-SCREEN)
ADM18	Restricted limitation decree (FILL IN ON-SCREEN)
ADM19	General limitation decree (FILL IN ON-SCREEN)
ADM20	Defendant's claim in a limitation claim (FILL IN ON-SCREEN)
ADM21	Declaration as to inability of a defendant to file and serve statement of case under a decree of limitation (FILL IN ON-SCREEN)

General forms EX

EX80A	Legal aid / Legal Services Commission assessment certificate (FILL IN ON-SCREEN)
EX107	Tape transcription (FILL IN ON-SCREEN)
EX107 Info	Authorised members of the Tape Transcription Panel
EX140	Record of examination (individual)
EX141	Record of examination (officer of company or corporation)
EX160	Application for a fee exemption or remission (FILL IN ON-SCREEN)
EX550	Affidavit (order to attend for questioning and suspended committal order) (FILL IN ON-SCREEN)

Court Funds Office

Form 100	Request for lodgment (FILL IN ON-SCREEN)
Form 108	Cash lodgment into the Supreme Court
Form 200	Payment schedule
Form 212	Request for investment decision

See also N243A/Form201

General Forms N

N1	Claim form (CPR, Part 7) (FILL IN ON-SCREEN)
N1(CC)	Claim form (CPR, Part 7) (Commercial Court) (FILL IN ON-SCREEN)
N1A	Notes for claimant
N1C	Notes for defendant on replying to the claim form
N1C(CC)	Notes for defendant on replying to the Part 7 claim form (Commercial Court)
N1(FD)	Notes for defendant on replying to the claim form (Consumer Credit Act claim)
N2	Claim form (probate claim) (FILL IN ON-SCREEN)
N2A	Probate claim — notes for claimant on completing a claim form
N2B	Probate claim — notes for the defendant
N3	Acknowledgment of service (probate claim) (FILL IN ON-SCREEN)
N5	Claim form for possession of property (FILL IN ON-SCREEN)
N5A	Claim form for relief against forfeiture (FILL IN ON-SCREEN)
N5B	Claim form for possession of property (accelerated procedure) (assured shorthold tenancy) (FILL IN ON-SCREEN)
N5C	Notes for the claimant (accelerated procedure)
N6	Claim form for demotion of tenancy (PD 65, para. 5.2) (FILL IN ON-SCREEN)
N7	Notes for defendant — mortgaged residential premises
N7A	Notes for defendant — rented residential premises claim
N7B	Notes for defendant – forfeiture of the lease (residential premises)
N7D	Notes for defendant – demotion/suspension claim
N8	Claim form (arbitration) (FILL IN ON-SCREEN)
N8A	Arbitration claim — notes for the claimant
N8B	Arbitration claim — notes for the defendant
N9	Response pack (FILL IN ON-SCREEN)
N9(CC)	Acknowledgment of service (Commercial Court) (FILL IN ON-SCREEN)
N9A	Admission (specified amount) (FILL IN ON-SCREEN)
N9B	Defence and counterclaim (specified amount) (FILL IN ON-SCREEN)
N9C	Admission (unspecified amount, non-money and return of goods claims) (FILL IN ON-SCREEN)
N9D	Defence and counterclaim (unspecified amount, non-money and return of goods claims) (FILL IN ON-SCREEN)
N10	Notice that acknowledgment of service has been filed
N11	Defence form (FILL IN ON-SCREEN)
N11B	Defence form (accelerated possession procedure) (assured shorthold tenancy) (FILL IN ON-SCREEN)
N11D	Defence form (demotion of tenancy) (PD 65, para. 5.2) (FILL IN ON-SCREEN)

N11M	Defence form (mortgaged residential premises) (FILL IN ON-SCREEN)
N11R	Defence form (rented residential premises) (FILL IN ON-SCREEN)
N15	Acknowledgment of service (arbitration claim) (FILL IN ON-SCREEN)
N16A	General form of application for injunction (FILL IN ON-SCREEN)
N19	Limited civil restraint order
N19A	Extended civil restraint order
N19B	General civil restraint order
N20	Witness summons (FILL IN ON-SCREEN)
N21	Order for examination of deponent (before the hearing)
N24	General form of judgment or order (FILL IN ON-SCREEN)
N56	Form for replying to an attachment of earnings application (statement of means) (FILL IN ON-SCREEN)
N77	Notice as to consequences of disobedience to court order (FILL IN ON-SCREEN)
N92	Request for administration order (FILL IN ON-SCREEN)
N93	List of creditors (FILL IN ON-SCREEN)
N117	General form of undertaking (FILL IN ON-SCREEN)
N119	Particulars of claim for possession (rented residential premises) (FILL IN ON-SCREEN)
N119A	Notes of guidance on completing particulars of claim (rented residential premises)
N120	Particulars of claim (mortgaged rented residential premises) (FILL IN ON-SCREEN)
N121	Particulars of claim (trespassers) (FILL IN ON-SCREEN)
N122	Particulars of claim for demotion of tenancy (PD 65, para. 5.2) (FILL IN ON-SCREEN)
N130	Application for an interim possession order (FILL IN ON-SCREEN)
N131	Notice of application for interim possession order (FILL IN ON-SCREEN)
N133	Witness statement of the defendant to oppose the making of an interim possession order (FILL IN ON-SCREEN)
N134	Interim possession order
N136	Order for possession
N149	Allocation questionnaire (small claims track) (FILL IN ON-SCREEN)
N150	Allocation questionnaire (FILL IN ON-SCREEN)
N152	Notice that a defence/counterclaim has been filed
N153	Notice of allocation or listing hearing
N154	Notice of allocation to the fast track
N155	Notice of allocation to the multi-track
N156	Request for further information (allocation)
N157	Notice of allocation to the small claims track
N158	Notice of allocation to the small claims track (preliminary hearing)
N159	Notice of allocation to the small claims track (no hearing)
N160	Notice of allocation to the small claims track (with parties' consent)
N161	Appellant's notice (FILL IN ON-SCREEN)
N161A	Guidance notes on completing the appellant's notice
N161B	Important notes for respondent
N162	Respondent's notice (FILL IN ON-SCREEN)
N162A	Guidance notes for completing the respondent's notice

N163	Skeleton argument (FILL IN ON-SCREEN)
N164	Appellant's notice (small claims track only)
N170	Listing questionnaire (pre-trial checklist) (FILL IN ON-SCREEN)
N173	Notice to pay fee
N200	Petition
N205D	Notice of issue (probate claim) (FILL IN ON-SCREEN)
N206A	Notice of issue (accelerated possession procedure) (assured shorthold tenancy)
N206B	Notice of issue (possession claim)
N208	Claim form (CPR, Part 8)
N208(CC)	Claim form (CPR, Part 8) (Commercial Court) (FILL IN ON-SCREEN)
N208A	Notes for claimant (CPR, Part 8)
N208C	Notes for defendant (CPR, Part 8)
N208C(CC)	Notes for defendant on replying to the Part 8 claim form (Commercial Court)
N209	Notice of issue (Part 8 claim)
N210	Acknowledgment of service (Part 8 claim) (FILL IN ON-SCREEN)
N210A	Acknowledgment of service (Part 8 costs-only claim) (FILL IN ON-SCREEN)
N210(CC)	Acknowledgment of service (Part 8 claim) (Commercial Court) (FILL IN ON-SCREEN)
N211	Claim form (additional claims — CPR, Part 20) (FILL IN ON-SCREEN)
N211(CC)	Claim form (additional claims — CPR, Part 20) (Commercial Court)
N211A	Notes for claimant Part 20
N211C	Notes for defendant on replying to the Part 20 claim form
N211C(CC)	Notes for Part 20 defendant on replying to the Part 20 claim form (Commercial Court)
N212	Notice of issue (Part 20 claim)
N213	Acknowledgment of service (Part 20 claim) (FILL IN ON-SCREEN)
N213(CC)	Acknowledgment of service (Part 20 claim) (Commercial Court)
N215	Certificate of service (FILL IN ON-SCREEN)
N218	Notice of service on partner (FILL IN ON-SCREEN)
N219	Application for European enforcement order certificate (judgment by agreement/admission/settlement)
N219A	Application for European enforcement order certificate (judgment in default of a defence or objection)
N225	Request for judgment and reply to admission (specified amount) (FILL IN ON-SCREEN)
N225A	Notice of part admission (specified amount)
N226	Notice of admission (unspecified amount)
N227	Request for judgment by default (amount to be decided by the court) (FILL IN ON-SCREEN)
N228	Notice of admission — return of goods (hire-purchase or conditional sale)
N235	Certificate of suitability of litigation friend (FILL IN ON-SCREEN)
N236	Notice of defence that amount claimed has been paid
N242	Notice of payment into court (under order — Part 37) (FILL IN ON-SCREEN)
N242A	Notice of payment into court (in settlement) (FILL IN ON-SCREEN)

N243A/Form201	Notice of acceptance and request for payment (Part 36) (FILL IN ON-SCREEN)
N244	Application notice (FILL IN ON-SCREEN)
N245	Application for suspension of a warrant and/or variation of an instalment order (FILL IN ON-SCREEN)
N251	Notice of funding of case or claim (FILL IN ON-SCREEN)
N252	Notice of commencement of assessment of bill of costs (FILL IN ON-SCREEN)
N253	Notice of amount allowed on provisional assessment
N254	Request for default costs certificate (FILL IN ON-SCREEN)
N255	Default costs certificate (county court)
N255HC	Default costs certificate (High Court)
N256	Final costs certificate (county court)
N256HC	Final costs certificate (High Court)
N257	Interim costs certificate
N258	Request for detailed assessment hearing (general form) (FILL IN ON-SCREEN)
N258A	Request for detailed assessment (Legal aid/Legal Services Commission only) (FILL IN ON-SCREEN)
N258B	Request for detailed assessment (costs payable out of a fund other than the Community Legal Service Fund) (FILL IN ON-SCREEN)
N258C	Request for detailed assessment hearing pursuant to an order under part III of the Solicitors Act 1974 (FILL IN ON-SCREEN)
N259	Notice of appeal (FILL IN ON-SCREEN)
N260	Statement of costs (summary assessment) (FILL IN ON-SCREEN)
N265	List of documents: standard disclosure (FILL IN ON-SCREEN)
N265(CC)	List of documents: standard disclosure (Commercial Court) (FILL IN ON-SCREEN)
N266	Notice to admit facts (FILL IN ON-SCREEN)
N268	Notice to prove documents at trial (FILL IN ON-SCREEN)
N270	Notes for guidance (application for administration order)
N279	Notice of discontinuance (FILL IN ON-SCREEN)
N285	General form of affidavit (FILL IN ON-SCREEN)
N292	Order on settlement on behalf of child or patient
N293A	Combined certificate of judgment and request for writ of fieri facias or writ of possession (FILL IN ON-SCREEN)
N294	Claimant's application for a variation order (without hearing) (FILL IN ON-SCREEN)
N316	Application for order that debtor attend court for questioning (FILL IN ON-SCREEN)
N316A	Application for order that officer of debtor company attend court for questioning (FILL IN ON-SCREEN)
N322A	Application to enforce an award (FILL IN ON-SCREEN)
N323	Request for warrant of execution (FILL IN ON-SCREEN)
N324	Request for warrant of delivery of goods (FILL IN ON-SCREEN)
N325	Request for warrant of possession of land (FILL IN ON-SCREEN)
N336	Request for and result of search in the attachment of earnings index (FILL IN ON-SCREEN)
N337	Request for attachment of earnings order (FILL IN ON-SCREEN)
N342	Request for judgment summons

N349	Application for third party debt order (FILL IN ON-SCREEN)
N379	Application for charging order on land or property
N380	Application for charging order on securities
N434	Notice of change of solicitor (FILL IN ON-SCREEN)
N440	Notice of application for time order by debtor or hirer (FILL IN ON-SCREEN)
N441	Notification of request for certificate of satisfaction or cancellation (FILL IN ON-SCREEN)
N445	Request for reissue of warrant (FILL IN ON-SCREEN)
N446	Request for reissue of enforcement or oral examination (not warrant) (FILL IN ON-SCREEN)
N461	Judicial review claim form (FILL IN ON-SCREEN)
N461Notes	Guidance notes on completing the judicial review claim form
N462	Judicial review — acknowledgment of service (FILL IN ON-SCREEN)
N463	Judicial review — application for urgent consideration (FILL IN ON-SCREEN)
N500	Claim form: directors disqualification application
N500A	Notes for claimant on completing claim form N500: directors disqualification application
N500B	Notes for defendant: directors disqualification application
N501	Claim form: directors disqualification: section 8A application
N501A	Notes for claimant on completing claim form N501: directors disqualification: section 8A application
N501B	Notes for defendant: directors disqualification: section 8A application
N502	Acknowledgment of service: directors disqualification application
N503	Acknowledgment of service: directors disqualification: section 8A application
N504	Pre-trial checklist: directors disqualification

Practice Forms No.

No. 32	Order for examination within jurisdiction of witness before trial (r. 34.8)
No. 33	Application for issue of letter of request to judicial authority out of jurisdiction (r. 34.13)
No. 34	Order for issue of letter of request to judicial authority out of jurisdiction (r. 34.13)
No. 35	Letter of request for examination of witness out of jurisdiction (r. 34.13)
No. 37	Order for appointment of special examiner to take evidence of witness out of jurisdiction (r. 34.13(4); PD 34, para. 5)
No. 41	Default judgment in claim relating to detention of goods (r. 12.4(1)(c))
No. 42	Default judgment in claim for possession of land (r. 12.4(2)(a))
No. 42A	Order for possession (RSC, ord. 113 in CPR, sch. 1)
No. 44	Part 24 judgment for claimant
No. 44A	Part 24 judgment for defendant
No. 45	Judgment after trial before judge without jury (PD 40B, para. 14)
No. 46	Judgment after trial before judge with jury (PD 40B, para. 14)
No. 47	Judgment after trial before a judge of the Technology and Construction Court, or a master or district judge (PD 40B, para. 14)
No. 48	Order after trial of issue directed to be tried under r. 3.1(2)(i)
No. 49	Judgment against personal representatives (PD 40B, para. 14.3)
No. 52	Notice of claim (r. 19.8A(4)(a))

No. 52A	Notice of judgment or order to an interested party
No. 53	Writ of fieri facias (RSC, ord. 45, r. 12 in CPR, sch. 1)
No. 54	Writ of fieri facias on order for costs (RSC, ord. 45, r. 12 in CPR, sch. 1)
No. 55	Notice of seizure (RSC, ord. 45, r. 2 in CPR, sch. 1)
No. 56	Writ of fieri facias after levy of part (RSC, ord. 45, r. 12 in CPR, sch. 1)
No. 57	Writ of fieri facias against personal representatives (RSC, ord. 45, r. 12 in CPR, sch. 1)
No. 58	Writ of fieri facias de bonis ecclesiasticis (RSC, ord. 45, r. 12 in CPR, sch. 1)
No. 59	Writ of sequestrari de bonis ecclesiasticis (RSC, ord. 45, r. 12 in CPR, sch. 1)
No. 62	Writ of fieri facias to enforce Northern Irish or Scottish judgment (RSC, ord. 45, r. 12 in CPR, sch. 1)
No. 63	Writ of fieri facias to enforce foreign registered judgment (RSC, ord. 45, r. 12 in CPR, sch. 1)
No. 64	Writ of delivery: delivery of goods, damages and costs (RSC, ord. 45, r. 4 in CPR, sch. 1)
No. 65	Writ of delivery: delivery of goods or value, damages and costs (RSC, ord. 45, r. 12(2) in CPR, sch. 1)
No. 66	Writ of possession (RSC, ord. 45, r. 12(3) in CPR, sch. 1)
No. 66A	Writ of possession (RSC, ord. 113, r. 7 in CPR, sch. 1)
No. 67	Writ of sequestration (RSC, ord. 45, r. 12(4) in CPR, sch. 1; RSC, ord. 46, r. 5 in CPR, sch. 1)
No. 68	Writ of restitution (RSC, ord. 46, rr. 1 and 3 in CPR, sch. 1)
No. 69	Writ of assistance (RSC, ord. 46, rr. 1 and 3 in CPR, sch. 1)
No. 71	Notice of renewal of writ of execution (RSC, ord. 46, r. 8 in CPR, sch. 1)
No. 82	Application for appointment of a receiver
No. 83	Order directing application for appointment of receiver and granting injunction meanwhile
No. 84	Order appointing receiver by way of equitable execution (Supreme Court Act 1981, s. 37)
No. 85	Order of committal or other penalty upon finding of contempt of court (RSC, ord. 52 in CPR, sch. 1)
No. 93	Order under the Evidence (Proceedings in Other Jurisdictions) Act 1975
No. 94	Order for production of documents in marine insurance claim (r. 58.14)
No. 95	Certificate of order against the Crown (RSC, ord. 77, r. 15 in CPR, sch. 1; Crown Proceedings Act 1947, s. 25)
No. 96	Certificate of order for costs against the Crown (RSC, ord. 77, r. 15 in CPR, sch. 1; Crown Proceedings Act 1947, s. 25)
No. 97	Claim form to grant bail (criminal proceedings) (RSC, ord. 79, r. 9(1) in CPR, sch. 1)
No. 97A	Claim form to vary arrangements for bail (criminal proceedings) (RSC, ord. 79, r. 9(1) in CPR, sch. 1)
No. 98	Order to release prisoner on bail (RSC, ord. 79, r. 9(6), (6A) and (6B) in CPR, sch. 1)
No. 98A	Order varying arrangements for bail (RSC, ord. 79, r. 9(10) in CPR, sch. 1)
No. 99	Order of Court of Appeal to admit prisoner to bail
No. 100	Notice of bail (RSC, ord. 79, r. 9(7) in CPR, sch. 1)
No. 104	Attachment of earnings order (Attachment of Earnings Act 1971)

No. 105	Notice under the Attachment of Earnings Act 1971, s. 10(2)
No. 109	Order for reference to the European Court
No. 110	Certificate under [the Administration of Justice Act 1920, s. 10] [the Foreign Judgments (Reciprocal Enforcement) Act 1933] [the Civil Jurisdiction and Judgments Act 1982, s. 12] (FILL IN ON-SCREEN)
No. 111	Certificate of money provisions contained in a judgment for registration in another part of the United Kingdom (Civil Jurisdiction and Judgments Act 1982, sch. 6) (FILL IN ON-SCREEN)
No. 112	Certificate of non-money provisions in a judgment for registration in another part of the United Kingdom (Civil Jurisdiction and Judgments Act 1982, sch. 7) (FILL IN ON-SCREEN)

PD Insolvency Proceedings

PDIP1	Appellant's notice — insolvency proceedings (FILL IN ON-SCREEN)
PDIP2	Respondent's notice — insolvency proceedings (FILL IN ON-SCREEN)
PDIP3	Draft order — multiple transfer of proceedings
PDIP4	Draft order — multiple appointments of office holder

Practice Forms PF

PF 1	Application for time (r. 3.1(2)(a))
PF 2	Order for time (r. 3.1(2)(a))
PF 3	Application for an extension of time for serving a claim form (r. 7.6)
PF 4	Order for an extension of time for serving a claim form (r. 7.6)
PF 6A	Application for permission to serve claim form out of jurisdiction (r. 6.21)
PF 6B	Order for service out of the jurisdiction (r. 6.21(4))
PF 7 QB	Request for service of document abroad (rr. 6.26(2)(a) and 6.27(2)(a))
PF 8	Standard 'unless' order (r. 26.5(5); PD 26, para. 2. 5; N150A)
PF 9	Application for default judgment for possession of land (r. 12.4(2))
PF 10 CH	Judgment in beneficiaries' administration action
PF 11	Application for Part 24 judgment (whole claim) (r. 24.2)
PF 12	Application for Part 24 judgment (one or some of several claims) (r. 24.2)
PF 12 CH	Advertisement for creditors (PD 40, para. 10)
PF 13	Order under Part 24 (No. 1)
PF 13 CH	Advertisement for claimants other than creditors
PF 14	Order under Part 24 (No. 2)
PF 14 CH	[Witness statement] [Affidavit] verifying list of creditors' claims
PF 15	Judgment under Part 24 for amount found due upon detailed assessment of solicitor's bill of costs
PF 15 CH	List of claims by persons claiming to be creditors following advertisement (Exhibit A referred to in [witness statement] [affidavit] in PF 14 CH)
PF 16	Notice of court's intention to make an order of its own initiative (r. 3.3(2) and (3))
PF 16 CH	List of claims by persons claiming to be creditors other than those sent in following advertisement (Exhibit B referred to in [witness statement] [affidavit] in PF 14 CH)
PF 17	Order made on court's own initiative without a hearing (r. 3.3(4) and (5))
PF 17 CH	List of sums of money which may be due in respect of which no claim has been received (Exhibit C referred to in [witness statement] [affidavit] in PF 14 CH)
PF 18 CH	Notice to creditor to prove claim

PF 19 CH	Notice to creditor or other claimant to produce documents or particulars in support of claim
PF 20	Application for Part 20 directions PF 21 Order for Part 20 directions
PF 20 CH	Notice to creditor of allowance of claim
PF 21A	Order to add person as defendant to counterclaim (r. 20.5)
PF 21 CH	Notice to creditor of disallowance of claim in whole or in part
PF 22	Notice claiming contribution or indemnity against another defendant (r. 20.6)
PF 22 CH	Order for administration: beneficiaries' action reconstituted as creditors' claim (Van Oppen order)
PF 23	Group litigation order
PF 23 CH	[Witness statement] [Affidavit] verifying list of claims other than creditors' claims
PF 23 QB	Notice by sheriff of claim to goods taken in execution (RSC, ord. 17, r. 2(2) in CPR, sch. 1)
PF 24 CH	List of claims not being creditors' claims sent following advertisement (Exhibit D referred to in [witness statement] [affidavit] in PF 23 CH)
PF 24 QB	Notice by execution creditor of admission or dispute of title of interpleader claimant
PF 25 CH	List of claims not being creditors' claims other than those sent in following advertisement (Exhibit E referred to in [witness statement] [affidavit] in PF 23 CH)
PF 25 QB	Interpleader application (RSC, ord. 17, r. 3 in CPR, sch. 1)
PF 26 CH	Notice to claimant other than a creditor to prove claim
PF 26 QB	Interpleader application by an enforcement officer
PF 27 CH	[Witness statement] [Affidavit] verifying accounts and answering usual enquiries in administration claim (rr. 32.8 and 32.16)
PF 27 QB	Evidence in support of interpleader application (RSC, ord. 17, r. 3(4) in CPR, sch. 1)
PF 28 CH	Executors' [or administrators'] account (account A in PF 27 CH)
PF 28 QB	Interpleader order (1) — claim barred where an enforcement officer interpleads
PF 29 CH	Master's order stating the results of proceedings before him on the usual accounts and inquiries in an administration claim
PF 29 QB	Interpleader order (1a) — enforcement officer to withdraw
PF 30 CH	Security of receiver or administrator pending determination of a probate claim (PD 44)
PF 30 QB	Interpleader order (2) — interpleader claimant substituted as defendant (RSC, ord. 17 in CPR, sch. 1)
PF 31 CH	Consent to act as trustee (r. 33.8)
PF 31 QB	Interpleader order (3) — trial of issue
PF 32 QB	Interpleader order (4) — conditional order for an enforcement officer to withdraw and trial of issue
PF 32 CH	[Witness statement] [Affidavit] in support of application for appointment of new litigation friend of child claimant
PF 33 CH	Order for distribution of a Lloyd's estate
PF 34 CH	Order in inquiry as to title in proceedings to enforce charging order where the defendant's title is not disclosed
PF 34 QB	Interpleader order (6) — summary disposal
PF 36 CH	Order appointing administrator pending determination
PF 37 CH	Witness statement or affidavit of testamentary scripts

PF 38 CH	Order in probate claim involving compromise
PF 39 CH	Order for an injunction (intended action)
PF 40 CH	Order for interim injunction
PF 43	Application for security for costs (r. 25.12; also Companies Act 1985, s. 726)
PF 44	Order for security for costs (r. 25.12; also Companies Act 1985, s. 726)
PF 48	Court record form
PF 49	Request to parties to state convenient dates for hearing of 1st CMC— form to be returned with allocation questionnaire
PF 50	Application for directions (Part 29)
PF 52	Order for case management directions in the multi-track CPR, Part 29) (FILL IN ON-SCREEN) also printed on page 2547
PF 53	Order for separate trial of an issue (r. 3.1(2)(i))
PF 56	Request for further information (PD 18, para. 1.6(2))
PF 57	Application for clarification or further information (Part 18 and PD 18, para. 5)
PF 58	Order for clarification or further information (r. 18.1)
PF 63	Interim order for receiver in pending claim
PF 67	Evidence in support of application to make order of House of Lords an order of the High Court (PD 40B, para. 13.2)
PF 68	Order making an order of the House of Lords an order of the High Court (PD 40B, para. 13.3)
PF 72	List of exhibits handed in at trial (PD 39, para. 7)
PF 74	Order for trial of whole claim or of an issue by master or district judge (PD 2B, para. 4. 1)
PF 78 QB	Solicitor's undertaking as to expenses (r. 34.13(6)(b) and PD 34, para. 5.3.(5))
PF 83	Judgment (non-attendance of party) (r. 39.3)
PF 84A	Order on application arising from a failure to comply with an order or condition (r. 3.1(3))
PF 84B	Judgment on application arising from a failure to comply with an order (r. 3.5(1) and (4))
PF 85A	Request for judgment (r. 3.5(2))
PF 85B	Judgment on request arising from a failure to comply with an order (r. 3.5(2))
PF 86	Praecipe for writ of fieri facias (RSC, ord. 45, r. 12(1) in CPR, sch. 1; RSC, ord. 46, r. 6 in CPR, sch. 1)
PF 87	Praecipe for writ of sequestration (RSC, ord. 45, r. 12(4) in CPR, sch. 1; RSC, ord. 46, r. 6 in CPR, sch. 1)
PF 88	Praecipe for writ of possession (RSC, ord. 45, r. 12(3) in CPR, sch. 1; RSC, ord. 46, r. 6 in CPR, sch. 1; RSC, ord. 113, r. 7 in CPR, sch. 1)
PF 89	Praecipe for writ of possession and fieri facias combined (RSC, ord. 45, r. 12 in CPR, sch. 1; RSC, ord. 46, r. 6 in CPR, sch. 1)
PF 90	Praecipe for writ of delivery (RSC, ord. 45, r. 12(2) in CPR, sch. 1; RSC, ord. 46, r. 6 in CPR, sch. 1)
PF 91	Evidence in support of application to enforce judgment for possession (RSC, ord. 45, r. 3 in CPR, sch. 1)
PF 97 QB	Order for sale by an enforcement officer by private contract
PF 102	Bench warrant (RSC, ord. 52 in CPR, sch. 1)
PF 103	Warrant of committal (general) (RSC, ord. 52 in CPR, sch. 1)

PF 104	Warrant of committal (contempt in face of court) (RSC, ord. 52 in CPR, sch. 1)
PF 105	Bench warrant (failure of witness to attend) (RSC, ord. 52 in CPR, sch. 1)
PF 106	Warrant of committal (of prisoner) (RSC, ord. 52 in CPR, sch. 1)
PF 113	Evidence on application for service by an alternative method (r. 6.8; PD 6, para. 9. 1)
PF 130	Form of advertisement (r. 6.8)
PF 141	Witness statement/affidavit of personal service of judgment or order (RSC, ord. 45, r. 7 in CPR, sch. 1)
PF 147	Application for order declaring that solicitor has ceased to act through death etc. (r. 42.4; PD 42, para. 4)
PF 148	Order declaring solicitor has ceased to act (r. 42.4)
PF 149	Application by solicitor for declaration that he has ceased to act (r. 42.3; PD 42, para. 3)
PF 150	Order declaring solicitor has ceased to act (r. 42.3; PD 42, para. 3.3)
PF 152 QB	Evidence in support of application for examination of witness under the Evidence (Proceedings in Other Jurisdictions) Act 1975
PF 153 QB	Certificate under the Evidence (Proceedings in Other Jurisdictions) Act 1975
PF 154 QB	Order for registration of a foreign judgment under the Administration of Justice Act 1920 or the Foreign Judgments (Reciprocal Enforcement) Act 1933
PF 155	Certificates under the Foreign Judgments (Reciprocal Enforcement) Act 1933, s. 10
PF 156 QB	Evidence in support of application for registration of a Community judgment
PF 157 QB	Order for registration of a Community judgment
PF 158 QB	Notice of registration of a Community judgment
PF 159 QB	Evidence in support of application for registration of a judgment of another Contracting State or Regulation State
PF 160 QB	Order for registration of a judgment of another Contracting State or Regulation State under the Civil Jurisdiction and Judgments Act 1982, s. 4
PF 161 QB	Notice of registration of a judgment of another Contracting State or Regulation State
PF 163 QB	Evidence in support of application for certified copy of a judgment for enforcement in another Contracting State or Regulation State
PF 164	Evidence in support of application for certificate as to money provisions contained in a judgment of the High Court for registration elsewhere in the United Kingdom
PF 165	Evidence in support of application for registration in the High Court of a judgment of a court in another part of the United Kingdom containing non-money provisions
PF 166 QB	Certificate as to finality etc. of arbitration award for enforcement abroad (Arbitration Act 1996, s. 58)
PF 167 QB	Order to stay proceedings under the Arbitration Act 1996, s. 9 (r. 62.8)
PF 168	Order to transfer claim from the High Court to county court (County Courts Act 1984, s. 40; High Court and County Courts Jurisdiction Order 1991; CPR, r. 30. 3)
PF 170A	Application for child or patient's settlement in personal injury or Fatal Accidents Act claims before proceedings begun (r. 21.10(2); PD 21, paras 6 and 7)

PF 170B	Application for child or patient's settlement in personal injury or Fatal Accidents Act claims in existing proceedings (r. 21.10(2); PD 21, paras 6 and 7)
PF 172 QB	Request for directions in respect of funds in court or to be brought into court (r. 21.11 and PD 21, para. 8)
PF 177	Order for written statement as to partners in firm (RSC, ord. 81, r. 2 in CPR, sch. 1)
PF 179 QB	Evidence on registration of a Bill of Sale (Bills of Sale Act 1878; RSC, ord. 95 in CPR, sch. 1)
PF 180 QB	Evidence on registration of an absolute bill of sale, settlement and deed of gift (RSC, ord. 95 in CPR, sch. 1)
PF 181 QB	Evidence on re-registration of a bill of sale (Bills of Sale Act 1878, s. 11; RSC, ord. 95 in CPR, sch. 1)
PF 182 QB	Order for extension of time to register or re-register a bill of sale (Bills of Sale Act 1878, s. 14; RSC, ord. 95, r. 1 in CPR, sch. 1)
PF 183 QB	Evidence for permission to enter a memorandum of satisfaction on a bill of sale (Bills of Sale Act 1878, s. 15; RSC, ord. 95, r. 2 in CPR, sch. 1; PD RSC Ord. 95, para. 1)
PF 184 QB	Claim form for entry of satisfaction on a registered bill of sale (Bills of Sale Act 1878, s. 15; RSC, ord. 95, r. 2 in CPR, sch. 1; PD RSC Ord. 95, para. 3)
PF 185 QB	Order for entry of satisfaction on a registered bill of sale (Bills of Sale Act 1878, s. 14; RSC, ord. 95, r. 2 in CPR, sch. 1)
PF 186 QB	Evidence on registration of assignment of book debts (Insolvency Act 1986, s. 344; RSC, ord. 95, r. 6(2) in CPR, sch. 1)
PF 187	Application for solicitor's charging order (Solicitors Act 1974, s. 73; RSC, ord. 106, r. 2 in CPR, sch. 1)
PF 188	Charging order; solicitor's costs (Solicitors Act 1974, s. 73; RSC, ord. 106, r. 2 in CPR, sch. 1)
PF 197	Application for order for transfer from the Royal Courts of Justice to a district registry or vice versa or from one district registry to another (r. 30.2(4))
PF 198	Order for transfer from the Royal Courts of Justice to a district registry or vice versa or from one district registry to another (r. 30.2(4))
PF 205	Evidence in support of application for permission to execute for earlier costs of enforcement under the Courts and Legal Services Act 1990, s. 15(3) and (4)
PF 244 (ACO)	Application notice (Part 23) statutory review of decision of Immigration Appeal Tribunal (Nationality, Immigration and Asylum Act 2002, s. 101)
PF 244 RCJ	Application notice

Costs Precedents (Schedule to PD 43–48)

PRECEDENT A:	Model form of bill of costs (receiving party's solicitor and counsel on CFA terms)
PRECEDENT B:	Model form of bill of costs (detailed assessment of additional liability only)
PRECEDENT C:	Model form of bill of costs (payable by defendant and the LSC)
PRECEDENT D:	Model form of bill of costs (alternative form, single column for amounts claimed, separate parts for costs payable by the LSC only)
PRECEDENT E:	Legal aid/LSC schedule of costs
PRECEDENT F:	Certificates for inclusion in bill of costs
PRECEDENT G:	Points of dispute

PRECEDENT H: Estimate of costs served on other parties
PRECEDENT J: Solicitors Act 1974: Part 8 claim form under part III of the Act
PRECEDENT K: Solicitors Act 1974: order for delivery of bill
PRECEDENT L: Solicitors Act 1974: order for detailed assessment (client)
PRECEDENT M: Solicitors Act 1974: order for detailed assessment (solicitors)
PRECEDENT P: Solicitors Act 1974: breakdown of costs

Technology and Construction Court

TCC/CM1 Case management information sheet (FILL IN ON-SCREEN)
TCC/PTR1 Pre-trial review questionnaire (FILL IN ON-SCREEN)

FORM PF 52
Order for case management directions in the multi-track
(CPR, Part 29)

IN THE HIGH COURT OF JUSTICE
[CHANCERY] [QUEEN'S BENCH] DIVISION
[DISTRICT REGISTRY]
[IN THE COUNTY COURT]

Claim No.

Before (*Master or District Judge*) [sitting in Private]

Claimant

Defendant

An Application was made by [application notice/letter] dated (*date*) or by [Counsel] [solicitor] for (*party*) and was attended by ( )

The Master [District Judge] read the written evidence filed

[**The parties** having agreed the directions set out in paragraph(s) ( ) below which are made by consent],

IT IS ORDERED that:

1. ALLOCATION
   the case be allocated to the multi-track.
2. TRANSFER
   (1) the claim be transferred to:
      (a) the ( ) Division of the High Court,
      (b) the ( ) District Registry [Mercantile List], or
      (c) the ( ) County Court [Chancery List][Business List],
   (2) the issue(s) (*define issue(s)*) be transferred to (*insert one of (a) to (c) above*) for detemination.
   (3) the (*party*) apply by (*date*) to a Judge of the Technology and Construction Court [or other Specialist List] for an order to transfer the claim to that court.
   (4) the claim (*give title and claim number*) commenced in the (*name*) County Court be transferred from that court to the [Chancery][Queen's Bench] Division of the High Court.
3. ALTERNATIVE DISPUTE RESOLUTION
   the claim be stayed until (*date*) while the parties try to settle it by mediation or other means. [The parties shall notify the Court in writing at the end of that period whether settlement has or has not been reached, and shall submit a draft consent order of any settlement]. The claim will be listed on (*date*) for the court to make further directions unless:
   (a) the claim has been settled and the claimant advises the court of the settlement in writing and files a draft consent order, or
   (b) the parties apply not later than 3 days before the hearing for further directions without a hearing, or
   (c) the parties apply for an extension of the stay and the extension is granted, upon which the hearing will be relisted on the date to which the extension is granted.
4. PROBATE CASES ONLY
   the [Claimant] [Defendant] file his witness statement or affidavit of testamentary scripts and lodge any testamentary script at Room TM7.09 Thomas More Building, Royal Courts of Justice, Strand WC2A 2LL [District Registry/ County Court, at (*address*)] by (*date*).

5. CASE SUMMARY
the (*party*) by (*date*) prepare and serve a Case Summary [not exceeding ( ) words] on all other parties, to be agreed by (*date*) and filed by (*date*) and if it is not agreed the parties by that date file their own Case Summaries.

6. CASE MANAGEMENT CONFERENCE etc.
[(a) there be a [further] Case Management Conference/Listing Hearing before the Master/ District Judge in [Court/Room No.] [[Thomas More Building] Royal Courts of Justice] [Court (trial centre)] on (*date*) at (*time*) of hours/ minutes duration.] *or*
[(b) there be a Case Management Conference/Listing Hearing of hours/ minutes duration. In order for the Court to fix a date the parties are to complete the accompanying questionnaire and file it by (*date*).] *or*
[(c) the (*party*) apply for an appointment for a [further] Case Management Conference/Listing Hearing by (*date*).]
At the Case Management Conference, except for urgent matters in the meantime, the Court will hear any further applications for Directions or Orders and any party must file an Application Notice for any such Directions or Orders and serve it and supporting evidence (if any) by (*date*).

7. AMENDMENTS TO STATEMENTS OF CASE
(1) the (*party*) has permission to amend his statement of case in accordance with the attached draft initialled by the [Master] [District Judge].
(2) the amended statement of case be verified by a statement of truth.
(3) the amended statement of case be filed by (*date*).
(4) the amended statement of case be served by (*date*) *or* service of the amended statement of case be dispensed with.
(5) any consequential amendments to other statements of case be filed and served by (*date*).
(6) the costs of and caused by the amendment to the statement of case be (*party*) in any event *or* are assessed in the sum of £ and are to be paid by (*party*).

8. ADDITION OF PARTIES
(1) the (*party*) has permission:
   (a) to [add] [substitute] [remove] (*name of party*) as a (*party*), and
   (b) to amend his statement of case in accordance with the attached draft initialled by the [Master] [District Judge].
(2) the amended statement of case be verified by a statement of truth.
(3) the amended statement of case be:
   (a) filed by (*date*) and
   (b) served on (*new party, existing parties or removed party, as appropriate*) by (*date*).
(4) a copy of this order be served on (*new party, existing parties or removed party, as appropriate*) by (*date*).
(5) any consequential amendments to other statements of case be filed and served by (*date*).
(6) the costs of and caused by the amendment to the statement of case be (*party*) in any event *or* are assessed in the sum of £ and are to be paid by (*party*).

9. CONSOLIDATION this claim be consolidated with claim number (*give number and title of claim*), the lead claim to be claim number (*give number*). [The title to the consolidated case shall be as set out in the Schedule to this order.]

10. TRIAL OF ISSUE
the issue of (*define issue*) be tried as follows:
(1) with the consent of the parties, before a Master:
   (a) on (*date*) in Room ( ) at the Royal Courts of Justice,
   (b) with an estimated length of hearing ( ) hours,
   (c) with the filing of listing questionnaires dispensed with, *or*
(2) before a Judge:

Forms

(a) with the trial of the issue to take place within (*period*) after (*date*) ('the trial window')
(b) with the (*party*) to apply to the Clerk of the Lists at Room [W14] [W15] by (*date*) for a trial date within the trial window
(c) with the issue:
(i) to be entered in the [Jury List] [Trial List] [General List] category 'A' 'B' or 'C', with a time estimate of (*specify number of days/weeks*), and
(ii) to take place in London (*or identify venue*)
[(d) the filing of listing questionnaires be dispensed with [unless directed by the Clerk of the Lists] *or* each party file his completed listing questionnaire by (*date*)], *or*

(3) before a [District Judge, with the consent of the parties] [Circuit Judge] [High Court Judge] [listing category [A] [B] [C]], at a hearing details of which [accompany this order] [will be sent shortly] with an estimated length of hearing ( ) hours.

11. FURTHER INFORMATION
(1) the (*party*) provide by (*date*) the [further information] [clarification] sought in the Request dated (*date*) attached and initialled by the [Master] [District Judge].
(2) any request for [further information] [clarification] be served by (*date*).

12. DISCLOSURE OF DOCUMENTS
(1) no disclosure is required.
(2) each party give by (*date*) standard disclosure to every other party by list [by categories].
(3) the (*party/parties*) give specific disclosure of documents [limited to the issues of (*define issues*)] described in the Schedule to this order [initialled by the Master/District Judge] by list [by categories] by (*date*).
(4) the (*party*) give by (*date*) standard disclosure by list [by categories] to (*party*) of documents limited to the issue(s) of (*define issues*) by list.

13. INSPECTION OF DOCUMENTS
Any requests for inspection or copies of disclosed documents shall be made within days after service of the list.

14. PRESERVATION OF PROPERTY
the (*party*) preserve (*give details of relevant property*) until trial of the claim or further order *or other remedy under rule 25.1(1).*

15. WITNESS STATEMENTS
(1) each party serve on every other party the witness statement of the oral evidence which the party serving the statement intends to rely on in relation to [any issues of fact] [the following issues of fact (*define issues*)] to be decided at the trial, those statements and any Notices of intention to rely on hearsay evidence to be:
(a) exchanged by (*date*) *or*
(b) served by (*party*) by (*date*) and by (*party*) by (*date*).
(2) the (*party*) has permission to serve a witness summary relating to the evidence of (*name*) of (*address*) on every other party by (*date*).

16. NO EXPERT EVIDENCE
(1) no expert evidence being necessary, [no party has permission to call or rely on expert evidence] [permission to call or rely on expert evidence is refused].

17. SINGLE EXPERT
(1) evidence be given by the report of a single expert in the field of (*define field*), instructed jointly by the parties, on the issue of (*define issue*) [and his fees shall be limited to £].
(2) the claimant advise the court in writing by (*date*) whether or not the single expert has been instructed.
(3) if the parties are unable to agree [by that date] who that expert is to be and about the payment of his fees any party may apply for further directions.
(4) unless the parties agree in writing or the court orders otherwise, the fees and expenses of the single expert shall be paid to him [by the parties equally] (*or as ordered*).

(5) each party give his instructions to the single expert by (*date*).
(6) the report of the single expert be filed by (*date*).
(7) the evidence of the expert be given at the trial by written report/oral evidence of the expert.

18. SEPARATE EXPERTS

[(1) each party has permission to adduce [oral] expert evidence in the field of [limited to expert(s) [per party] [on each side]].
(2) the experts' reports shall be exchanged by (*date*).
(3) the experts shall hold a discussion for the purpose of:
(a) identifying the issues, if any, between them; and
(b) where possible, reaching agreement on those issues.
(4) the experts shall by [*specify date after discussion*] prepare and file a statement for the Court showing:
(a) those issues on which they did agree; and
(b) those issues on which they disagree and a summary of their reasons for disagreeing.
(5) no party shall be entitled to recover by way of costs from any other party more than £ for the fees or expenses of an expert.]
or
[(1) the parties (*party*) have permission to rely on expert evidence as follows:

Party	Identity of Expert	Field of Expertise	Issue to be addressed
Claimant			
Defendant			
(other parties)			

(2) the number of expert witnesses in each field be limited to [one] for the (*party/parties*) and to [one] for the (*party/parties*).
[(3) the amount of the fees and expenses of the experts in the field[s] of (*define field(s)*) that the (*party/parties*) may recover from the (*party/parties*) be limited to £].
(4) the experts in the field(s) of (*define field(s)*) prepare reports which are to be served as follows:
(a) by simultaneous exchange by (*date*)
(b) by (*party/parties*) by (*date*) and by (*party/parties*) by (*date*).
(5) the reports be agreed if possible by (*date*).
(6) (a) if the reports are not agreed by that date, then the experts in the same field(s) shall, by (*date*), seek to identify, by 'without prejudice' discussion, the issues between them and, where possible, to reach agreement on all/any issue(s),
(b) the experts shall by (*date*) prepare and file a statement showing those issues on which they are agreed, those issues on which they disagree and a summary of their reasons for disagreeing.
(7) the expert evidence relied on by the (*party/parties*) in the field of (*define field(s)*) be given at the trial by written report(s)/ written summary of agreement/oral evidence of the expert(s).
(8) no party shall be entitled to recover by way of costs from any other party more than £ for the fees or expenses of an expert.]

19. TRIAL AND PRE-TRIAL CHECKLISTS

(1) (a) the trial of the claim/issue(s) take place [within (*period*) after (*date*)] [between (*date*) and (*date*)] ('the trial window').
(b) the (*party*) make an appointment to attend on the Clerk of the Lists/Listing Officer at Room [W14] [W15] in order to fix a trial date within the trial window, such appointment to be [within 14 days after] [on] [not later than] (*date*) and give notice of the appointment to all other parties.

Forms

(c) the claim

(i) be entered in the [Jury List] [Trial List] [General List] category 'A' 'B' or 'C', with a time estimate of (*specify number of days/weeks*), and

(ii) take place in London (*or identify venue*), *or*

(2) (a) Trial Date: the trial take place [on (*date*)] [on a date to be fixed], a Notice of Hearing [accompanies this order] [will be sent shortly], at [Court] [a venue to be notified],

or

(b) Trial Window: the trial take place during the period beginning on (*date*) and ending on (*date*) at a venue to be notified,

(c) the present estimate of the time to be allowed for the trial is (*specify number of days/weeks*).

(3) Pre-trial Checklists:

[(a) the filing of pre-trial checklists be dispensed with [unless directed by the Clerk of the Lists/Listing Officer]], *or*

[(b) each party file his completed pre-trial checklist by [4.30pm] [4.00pm] on (*date*)],

(4) the parties inform the Court forthwith of any change in the trial time estimate.

20. PRE-TRIAL REVIEW

[[The trial being estimated to last more than 10 days], There be a Pre-Trial Review on a date to be arranged by the Clerk of the Lists/Listing Officer in Room [W14] [W15]] [there be a Pre-Trial Review on (*date*) at (*time*)] before the Judge at the [Royal Courts of Justice] [Court (trial centre)] at which, except for urgent matters in the meantime, the Court will hear any further applications for Directions or Orders.

21. DEFINITION AND REDUCTION OF ISSUES

by (*date*) the parties list and discuss the issues in the claim [including the experts' reports and statements] and attempt to define and narrow the issues [including those issues the subject of discussion by the experts].

22. TRIAL BUNDLE

The parties agree and file a trial bundle and exchange and file skeleton arguments and chronologies not more than 7 and not less than 3 days before the start of the trial.

23. TRIAL TIMETABLE (*only for use at final CMC or PTR*)

(1) the parties agree a timetable for the trial, subject to the approval of the trial Judge, and file it with the trial bundle,

(2) subject to the approval of the trial Judge, the timetable for the trial will be:

(a) opening speeches to last no more than minutes,

(b) the statements served stand as the evidence-in-chief of the Claimants' witnesses of fact who are to give evidence on the [first] morning/afternoon/day of the trial,

(c) the statements served stand as the evidence-in-chief of the Defendants' witnesses of fact who are to give evidence on the [second] morning/afternoon/day of the trial,

(d) the reports of the experts served stand as their evidence-in-chief and the experts in the field(s) of (*specify*) give oral evidence on the [third] morning/afternoon/day of the trial,

(e) closing submissions be made on the [fourth] morning/afternoon/day of the trial.

24. SETTLEMENT

If the claim or part of the claim is settled the parties must immediately inform the Court, whether or not it is then possible to file a draft Consent Order to give effect to the settlement.

25. OTHER DIRECTIONS

(*The parties may here set out drafts of other Directions or Orders sought*).

26. COSTS

the costs of this application be:

(a) in the case, or

(b) summarily assessed at £ and paid by , or

(c) the (*party/parties*) in any event to be the subject of a detailed assessment,

(d) the (*party*) pay the (*party*) the sum of £ on account of such costs on or before (*date*).

DATED

Appendix 6 Court Fees Orders

Civil Proceedings Fees Order 2004

(SI 2004/3121)

The Lord Chancellor, in exercise of the powers conferred upon him by sections 92 and 108(6) of the Courts Act 2003, sections 414 and 415 of the Insolvency Act 1986, and section 128 of the Finance Act 1990, with the consent of the Treasury under section 92(1) of the Courts Act 2003 and after consultation with the Lord Chief Justice, the Master of the Rolls, the President of the Family Division, the Vice-Chancellor, the Head of Civil Justice and the Deputy Head of Civil Justice and the Civil Justice Council under section 92(5) and (6) of the Courts Act 2003 and with the sanction of the Treasury under sections 414(1) and 415(1) of the Insolvency Act 1986, hereby makes the following Order:

1 Citation, commencement and interpretation

(1) This Order may be cited as the Civil Proceedings Fees Order 2004 and shall come into force on the 4th January 2005.
(2) In this Order —
  (a) a fee referred to by number means the fee so numbered in Schedule 1 to this Order;
  (b) 'CCBC' means County Court Bulk Centre;
  (c) 'CPC' means Claim Production Centre;
  (d) 'the CPR' means the Civil Procedure Rules 1998;
  (e) expressions also used in the CPR have the same meaning as in those Rules;
  (f) 'family proceedings' means family proceedings in the High Court or in a county court as appropriate;
  (g) 'LSC' means the Legal Services Commission established under section 1 of the Access to Justice Act 1999;
  (h) 'Funding Code' means the code approved under section 9 of the Access to Justice Act 1999;
  (i) 'GLO' means a Group Litigation Order.

2 Fees to be taken

The fees set out in column 2 of Schedule 1 to this Order shall be taken in the Supreme Court and in county courts respectively in respect of the items described in column 1 in accordance with and subject to the directions specified in column 1.

3

The provisions of this Order shall not apply to —
(a) non-contentious probate business;
(b) proceedings in the Court of Protection, except in so far as fees 1, 2, 3, 6, 9 and 10 in Schedule 1 (High Court only) are applicable;
(c) the enrolment of documents;
(d) criminal proceedings (except proceedings on the Crown side of the Queen's Bench Division to which the fees contained in Schedule 1 are applicable);
(e) proceedings by sheriffs, under-sheriffs, deputy-sheriffs or other officers of the sheriff; and
(f) family proceedings.

4 Exemptions, reductions, remissions and refunds

(1) No fee shall be payable under this Order by a party who, at the time when a fee would otherwise become payable —
  (a) is in receipt of any qualifying benefit, and
  (b) is not in receipt of, as appropriate, either —
    (i) representation under Part IV of the Legal Aid Act 1988 for the purposes of the proceedings; or

(ii) funding provided by the LSC for the purposes of the proceedings and for which a certificate has been issued under the Funding Code certifying a decision to fund services for that party.

(2) The following are qualifying benefits for the purposes of paragraph (1)(a) above —
   (a) income support under the Social Security Contributions and Benefits Act 1992;
   (b) working tax credit, provided that —
      (i) child tax credit is being paid to the party, or otherwise following a claim for child tax credit made jointly by the members of a couple (as defined in section 3(5A) of the Tax Credits Act 2002) which includes the party; or
      (ii) there is a disability element or severe disability element (or both) to the tax credit received by the party;

   and that the gross annual income taken into account for the calculation of the working tax credit is £15,460 or less;
   (c) income-based jobseeker's allowance under the Jobseekers Act 1995; and
   (d) guarantee credit under the State Pension Credit Act 2002.

(3) In the county courts paragraph (1) shall not apply to fee 7.8 (fee payable on a consolidated attachment of earnings order or an administration order).

5

Where it appears to the Lord Chancellor that the payment of any fee prescribed by this Order would, owing to the exceptional circumstances of the particular case, involve undue financial hardship, he may reduce or remit the fee in that case.

6

(1) Subject to paragraph (2), where a fee has been paid at a time —
   (a) when, under article 4, it was not payable, the fee shall be refunded;
   (b) where the Lord Chancellor, if he had been aware of all the circumstances, would have reduced the fee under article 5, the amount by which the fee would have been reduced shall be refunded; and
   (c) where the Lord Chancellor, if he had been aware of all the circumstances, would have remitted the fee under article 5, the fee shall be refunded.

(2) No refund shall be made under paragraph (1) unless the party who paid the fee applies within 6 months of paying the fee.

(3) The Lord Chancellor may extend the period of 6 months referred to in paragraph (2) if he considers that there is good reason for an application being made after the end of the period of 6 months.

7

Where by any convention entered into by Her Majesty with any foreign power it is provided that no fee shall be required to be paid in respect of any proceedings, the fees specified in this Order shall not be taken in respect of those proceedings.

8 Revocations

The Orders specified in Schedule 2, in so far as they were made under sections 414 and 415 of the Insolvency Act 1986 and section 128 of the Finance Act 1990, shall be revoked.

SCHEDULE 1 FEES TO BE TAKEN

[Schedule introduced by article 2]

Column 1 *Number and description of fee*	*Column 2* *Amount of fee*
1 Commencement of proceedings (High Court and county court)	
1.1 On the commencement of originating proceedings in the High Court (including originating proceedings issued after permission to issue is granted) to recover a sum of money where the sum claimed:	
(a) does not exceed £50,000	£400
(b) exceeds £50,000 but does not exceed £100,000	£700
(c) exceeds £100,000 but does not exceed £150,000	£900
(d) exceeds £150,000 but does not exceed £200,000	£1,100
(e) exceeds £200,000 but does not exceed £250,000	£1,300
(f) exceeds £250,000 but does not exceed £300,000	£1,500
(g) exceeds £300,000 or is not limited	£1,700
1.2 On the commencement of originating proceedings in the county court (including originating proceedings issued after permission to issue is granted) to recover a sum of money, except in CPC cases brought by Centre users:	
(a) does not exceed £300	£30
(b) exceeds £300 but does not exceed £500	£50
(c) exceeds £500 but does not exceed £1,000	£80
(d) exceeds £1,000 but does not exceed £5,000	£120
(e) exceeds £5,000 but does not exceed £15,000	£250
(f) exceeds £15,000 but does not exceed £50,000	£400
(g) exceeds £50,000 but does not exceed £100,000	£700
(h) exceeds £100,000 but does not exceed £150,000	£900
(i) exceeds £150,000 but does not exceed £200,000	£1,100
(j) exceeds £200,000 but does not exceed £250,000	£1,300
(k) exceeds £250,000 but does not exceed £300,000	£1,500
(l) exceeds £300,000 or is not limited	£1,700
1.3 On the commencement of originating proceedings in the county court to recover a sum of money in Claim Production Centre cases brought by Centre users, where the sum claimed:	
(a) does not exceed £300	£20
(b) exceeds £300 but does not exceed £500	£40
(c) exceeds £500 but does not exceed £1,000	£70
(d) exceeds £1,000 but does not exceed £5,000	£110
(e) exceeds £5,000 but does not exceed £15,000	£240
(f) exceeds £15,000 but does not exceed £50,000	£390
(g) exceeds £50,000 but does not exceed £100,000	£690
Fee 1.3 Claims above £99,999.99 cannot be issued through the Claim Production Centre. Parties should issue the claim in the relevant court.	
Fees 1.1, 1.2 and 1.3 Where the claimant is making a claim for interest on a specified sum of money, the sum claimed for the purposes of calculating fees 1.1, 1.2 and 1.3 shall be taken to include the interest in addition to that specified sum.	
1.4 On the commencement of originating proceedings for any other remedy or relief (including originating proceedings issued after permission to issue is granted):	
— in the High Court	£400
— in the county court	£150

Column 1 *Number and description of fee*	*Column 2* *Amount of fee*

Fees 1.1, 1.2 and 1.4 Recovery of land or goods
Where a claim for money is additional or alternative to a claim for recovery of land or goods, only fee 1.4 shall be payable.

Fees 1.1, 1.2 and 1.4 Claims other than recovery of land or goods
Where a claim for money is additional to a non money claim (other than a claim for recovery of land or goods), then fee 1.1 or fee 1.2 as appropriate shall be payable in addition to fee 1.4. Where a claim for money is alternative to a non money claim (other than a claim for recovery of land or goods), only fee 1.1 shall be payable in the High Court, and, in the county court, fee 1.2 or fee 1.4 shall be payable, whichever is the greater.

Fees 1.1 or 1.2 as appropriate and 1.4 — Generally
Where more than one non money claim is made in the same proceedings, fee 1.4 shall be payable once only, in addition to any fee which may be payable under fee 1.1 or fee 1.2 as appropriate.
Fees 1.1 or fee 1.2 as appropriate and fee 1.4 shall not be payable where fee 1.7(b), fee 1.8(a) (in the High Court only), fee 9.1 (in the High Court only) or fee 3 apply.

Fees 1.1 or 1.2 as appropriate and 1.4 — Amendment of claim or counterclaim
Where the claim or counterclaim is amended, and the fee paid before amendment is less than that which would have been payable if the document, as amended, had been so drawn in the first instance, the party amending the document shall pay the difference.

1.5 On the filing of proceedings against a party or parties not named in the originating proceedings:	
— in the High Court	£50
— in the county court	£35

Fee 1.5
Fee 1.5 shall be payable by a defendant who adds or substitutes a party or parties to the proceedings or by a claimant who adds or substitutes a defendant or defendants.

1.6 On the filing of a counterclaim	The same fee as if the relief or remedy sought were the subject of separate proceedings

Fee 1.6
No fee is payable on a counterclaim which a defendant is required to make under the CPR because he contends that he has any claim or is entitled to any remedy relating to a grant of probate of a will, or letters of administration of an estate, of a deceased person.

1.7(a) On an application for leave to issue originating proceedings:	
— in the High Court	£50
— in the county court	£35
1.7(b) On an application for an order under Part III of the Solicitors Act 1974 for the assessment of costs payable to a solicitor by his client or on the commencement of costs-only proceedings	
— in the High Court	£50
— in the county court	£35
1.8(a) On the commencement of the judicial review procedure (High Court only)	£50

Where the court has made an order giving permission to proceed with a claim for judicial review, there shall be payable by the claimant within 7 days of service on the claimant of that order:

1.8(b) if the judicial review procedure has been commenced	£180

Court Fees Orders

Column 1 *Number and description of fee*	*Column 2* *Amount of fee*
1.8(c) if the claim for judicial review was commenced otherwise than by using the judicial review procedure	£50

2 General Fees (High Court and county court)

2.1 On the claimant filing an allocation questionnaire; or

- where the court dispenses with the need for an allocation questionnaire, within 14 days of the date of despatch of the notice of allocation to track; or
- where the CPR or a Practice Direction provide for automatic allocation or provide that the rules on allocation shall not apply, within 28 days of the filing of the defence (or the filing of the last defence if there is more than one defendant), or within 28 days of the expiry of the time permitted for filing all defences if sooner:

— in the High Court	£200
— in the county court	£100

Fee 2.1

Fee 2.1 shall be payable by the claimant except where the action is proceeding on the counterclaim alone, when it shall be payable by the defendant—

- on the defendant filing an allocation questionnaire; or
- where the court dispenses with the need for an allocation questionnaire, within 14 days of the date of despatch of the notice of allocation to track; or
- where the CPR or a Practice Direction provide for automatic allocation or provide that the rules on allocation shall not apply, within 28 days of the filing of the defence to the counterclaim (or the filing of the last defence to the counterclaim if there is more than one party entitled to file a defence to a counterclaim), or within 28 days of the expiry of the time permitted for filing all defences to the counterclaim if sooner.

2.2 On the claimant filing a listing questionnaire; or where the court fixes the trial date or trial week without the need for a listing questionnaire, within 14 days of the date of despatch of the notice (or the date when oral notice is given if no written notice is given) of the trial week or the trial date if no trial week is fixed

— in the High Court	£600
— in the county court if the case is on the multi-track	£500
— in the county court in any other case	£275

Fee 2.2

Fee 2.2 shall be payable by the claimant except where the action is proceeding on the counterclaim alone, when it shall be payable by the defendant—

— on the defendant filing a listing questionnaire; or

— where the court fixes the trial date or trial week without the need for a listing questionnaire, within 14 days of the date of despatch of the notice (or the date when oral notice is given if no written notice is given) of the trial week or the trial date if no trial week is fixed.

Where the court receives notice in writing—

— before the trial date has been fixed or,

— where a trial date has been fixed, at least 14 days before the trial date,

from the party who paid fee 2.2 that the case is settled or discontinued, fee 2.2 shall be refunded.

Fees 2.1 and 2.2 in the High Court and the county court

Fees 2.1 and 2.2 shall be payable as appropriate where the court allocates a case to track for a trial of the assessment of damages.

Fees 2.1 and 2.2 shall not be payable in relation to claims managed under a GLO after that GLO is made.

Fees 2.1 and 2.2 shall be payable once only in the same proceedings.

Fee 2.1 shall not be payable where the procedure in Part 8 of the CPR is used.

Fees 2.1 and 2.2 in the county court

Fee 2.1 shall not be payable in proceedings where the only claim is a claim to recover a sum of money and the sum claimed does not exceed £1,500.

Fee 2.2 shall not be payable in respect of a small claims hearing.

Column 1 *Number and description of fee*	*Column 2* *Amount of fee*
2.3 In the High Court on filing: — an appellant's notice, or — a respondent's notice where the respondent is appealing or wishes to ask the appeal court to uphold the order of the lower court for reasons different from or additional to those given by the lower court.	£200
2.4 In the county court on filing— — an appellant's notice, or — a respondent's notice where the respondent is appealing or wishes to ask the appeal court to uphold the order of the lower court for reasons different from or additional to those given by the lower court:	
(a) in a claim allocated to the small claims track	£100
(b) in all other claims	£120
Fees 2.3 and 2.4 Fees 2.3 and 2.4 do not apply on appeals against a decision made in detailed assessment proceedings.	
2.5 On an application on notice where no other fee is specified	
— in the High Court	£100
— in the county court	£65
2.6 On an application by consent or without notice for a judgment or order where no other fee is specified	
— in the High Court	£50
— in the county court	£35
For the purpose of fee 2.6 a request for a judgment or order on admission or in default shall not constitute an application and no fee shall be payable. Fee 2.6 shall not be payable in relation to an application by consent for an adjournment of a hearing where the application is received by the court at least 14 days before the date set for that hearing.	
Fees 2.5 and 2.6 Fees 2.5 and 2.6 shall not be payable when an application is made in an appeal notice or is filed at the same time as an appeal notice.	
2.7 On an application for a summons or order for a witness to attend court to be examined on oath or an order for evidence to be taken by deposition, other than an application for which fee 6.2 or 7.3 is payable	
— in the High Court	£50
— in the county court	£35
2.8 On an application to vary a judgment or suspend enforcement (where more than one remedy is sought in the same application only one fee shall be payable)	
— in the High Court	£50
— in the county court	£35
2.9 Register of judgments etc kept under section 98 of the Courts Act 2003 On a request for the issue of a certificate of satisfaction	£15
3 Companies Act 1985 and Insolvency Act 1986 (High Court and county court)	
3.1 On entering a bankruptcy petition:	
(a) if presented by a debtor or the personal representative of a deceased debtor	£150
(b) if presented by a creditor or other person	£190
3.2 On entering a petition for an administration order	£150
3.3 On entering any other petition One fee only is payable where more than one petition is presented in relation to a partnership.	£190

Column 1 *Number and description of fee*	*Column 2* *Amount of fee*
3.4(a) On a request for a certificate of discharge from bankruptcy	£60
3.4(b) and after the first certificate for each copy	£1
3.5 On an application under the Companies Act 1985 or the Insolvency Act 1986 other than one brought by petition and where no other fee is specified.	£130
Fee 3.5 Fee 3.5 is not payable where the application is made in existing proceedings.	
3.6 On an application for the conversion of a voluntary arrangement into a winding up or bankruptcy under Article 37 of Council Regulation (EC) No 1346/2000.	£130
3.7 On an application, for the purposes of Council Regulation (EC) No 1346/2000, for an order confirming creditors' voluntary winding up (where the company has passed a resolution for voluntary winding up, and no declaration under section 89 of the Insolvency Act 1986 has been made).	£30
3.8 On filing — a notice of intention to appoint an administrator under paragraph 14 of Schedule B1 to the Insolvency Act 1986 or in accordance with paragraph 27 of that Schedule; or — a notice of appointment of an administrator in accordance with paragraphs 18 or 29 of that Schedule.	£30
Fee 3.8 Where a person pays fee 3.8 on filing a notice of intention to appoint an administrator, no fee shall be payable on that same person filing a notice of appointment of that administrator.	
3.9 On submitting a nominee's report under section 2(2) of the Insolvency Act 1986	£30
3.10 On filing documents in accordance with paragraph 7(1) of Schedule A1 to the Insolvency Act 1986	£30
3.11 On an application by consent or without notice within existing proceedings where no other fee is specified	£30
3.12 On an application with notice within existing proceedings where no other fee is specified	£60
Requests and applications with no fee No fee is payable on a request or on an application to the Court by the Official Receiver when applying only in the capacity of Official Receiver to the case (and not as trustee or liquidator), or on an application to set aside a statutory demand.	
4 Copy Documents (High Court, Court of Appeal and county court)	
4.1 On a request for a copy of any document (other than where fee 4.2 applies):	
(a) for the first page (except the first page of a subsequent copy of the same document supplied at the same time)	£1
(b) per page in any other case	20p
Fee 4.1 Fee 4.1 shall be payable for a faxed copy or for examining a plain copy and marking it as an examined copy. Fee 4.1 shall be payable whether or not the copy is issued as an office copy.	
4.2 On a request for a copy of a document required in connection with proceedings and supplied by the party making the request at the time of copying, for each page.	20p
4.3 On a request for a copy of a document on a computer disk or in other electronic form, for each such copy.	£3

Column 1 *Number and description of fee*	*Column 2* *Amount of fee*
5 **Determination of costs** (Supreme Court and county court)	
5.1 **On the filing of a request for detailed assessment** where the party filing the request is legally aided or is funded by the LSC and no other party is ordered to pay the costs of the proceedings	
— in the Supreme Court	£120
— in the county court	£105
5.2 **On the filing of a request for a detailed assessment hearing in any case where fee 5.1 does not apply; or on the filing of a request for a hearing date for the assessment of costs payable to a solicitor by his client pursuant to an order under Part III of the Solicitors Act 1974**	
— in the Supreme Court	£600
— in the county court	£300
Where there is a combined party and party and legal aid, or a combined party and party and LSC, or a combined party and party, legal aid and LSC determination of costs, fee 5.2 shall be attributed proportionately to the party and party, legal aid, or LSC (as the case may be) portions of the bill on the basis of the amount allowed.	
5.3 **On a request for the issue of a default costs certificate**	
— in the Supreme Court	£50
— in the county court	£45
5.4 **On an appeal against a decision made in detailed assessment proceedings**	
— in the Supreme Court	£200
— in the county court	£105
5.5 **On applying for the court's approval of a certificate of costs payable from the Community Legal Service Fund**	
— in the Supreme Court	£50
— in the county court	£35
Fee 5.5 Fee 5.5 is payable at the time of applying for the court's approval and is recoverable only against the Community Legal Service Fund.	
5.6 **On a request or application to set aside a default costs certificate**	
— in the Supreme Court	£100
— in the county court	£65
6 **Enforcement in the High Court**	
6.1 **On sealing a writ of execution/possession/delivery** Where the recovery of a sum of money is sought in addition to a writ of possession and delivery, no further fee is payable.	£50
6.2 **On an application for an order requiring a judgment debtor or other person to attend court to provide information in connection with enforcement of a judgment or order**	£50
6.3(a) **On an application for a third party debt order or the appointment of a receiver by way of equitable execution**	£100
6.3(b) **On an application for a charging order**	£100
Fee 6.3(a) and (b) Fee 6.3(a) shall be payable in respect of each third party against whom the order is sought. Fee 6.3(b) shall be payable in respect of each application issued.	
6.4 **On an application for a judgment summons**	£100

Column 1 *Number and description of fee*	*Column 2* *Amount of fee*
6.5 On a request or application to register a judgment or order, or for permission to enforce an arbitration award, or for a certificate or a certified copy of a judgment or order for use abroad	£50
7 Enforcement in the county court	
7.1 On an application for or in relation to enforcement of a judgment or order of a county court or through a county court:	
In cases other than CCBC cases brought by Centre users, by the issue of a warrant of execution against goods except a warrant to enforce payment of a fine:	
(a) Where the amount for which the warrant issues does not exceed £125	£35
(b) Where the amount for which the warrant issues exceeds £125	£55
In CCBC cases brought by Centre users, by the issue of a warrant of execution against goods except a warrant to enforce payment of a fine:	
(c) Where the amount for which the warrant issues does not exceed £125	£25
(d) Where the amount for which the warrant issues exceeds £125	£45
7.2 On a request for a further attempt at execution of a warrant at a new address following a notice of the reason for non-execution (except a further attempt following suspension and CCBC cases brought by Centre users)	£25
7.3 On an application for an order requiring a judgment debtor or other person to attend court to provide information in connection with enforcement of a judgment or order	£45
7.4(a) On an application for a third party debt order or the appointment of a receiver by way of equitable execution	£55
7.4(b) On an application for a charging order	£55
Fee 7.4(a) and (b) Fee 7.4(a) shall be payable in respect of each third party against whom the order is sought. Fee 7.4(b) shall be payable in respect of each application issued.	
7.5 On an application for a judgment summons	£95
7.6 On the issue of a warrant of possession or a warrant of delivery Where the recovery of a sum of money is sought in addition, no further fee is payable.	£95
7.7 On an application for an attachment of earnings order (other than a consolidated attachment of earnings order) to secure payment of a judgment debt	£65
Fee 7.7 Fee 7.7 is payable for each defendant against whom an order is sought. Fee 7.7 is not payable where the attachment of earnings order is made on the hearing of a judgment summons.	
7.8 On a consolidated attachment of earnings order or on an administration order	For every £1 or part of a £1 of the money paid into court in respect of debts due to creditors 10p
Fee 7.8 Fee 7.8 shall be calculated on any money paid into court under any order at the rate in force at the time when the order was made (or, where the order has been amended, at the time of the last amendment before the date of payment).	
7.9 On the application for the recovery of a tribunal award	£35

Column 1 *Number and description of fee*	*Column 2* *Amount of fee*
7.10 On a request for an order to recover a sum that is: — a specified debt within the meaning of the Enforcement of Road Traffic Debts Order 1993 as amended from time to time; or — pursuant to an enactment, treated as a specified debt for the purposes of that Order No fee is payable on: — an application for an extension of time to serve a statutory declaration in connection with any such order; or — a request to issue a warrant of execution to enforce any such order	£5
8 Sale (county court only)	
8.1 For removing or taking steps to remove goods to a place of deposit	The reasonable expenses incurred
Fee 8.1 is to include the reasonable expenses of feeding and caring for any animals.	
8.2 For advertising a sale by public auction pursuant to section 97 of the County Courts Act 1984	The reasonable expenses incurred
8.3 For the appraisement of goods	5p in the £1 or part of a £1 of the appraised value
8.4 For the sale of goods (including advertisements, catalogues, sale and commission and delivery of goods)	15p in the £1 or part of a £1 on the amount realised by the sale or such other sum as the district judge may consider to be justified in the circumstances
8.5 Where no sale takes place by reason of an execution being withdrawn, satisfied or stopped	(a) 10p in the £1 or part of a £1 on the value of the goods seized, the value to be the appraised value where the goods have been appraised or such other sum as the district judge may consider to be justified in the circumstances; and in addition (b) any sum payable under fee 8.1, 8.2 or 8.3

Court Fees Orders

Column 1 *Number and description of fee*	*Column 2* *Amount of fee*
FEES PAYABLE IN HIGH COURT ONLY	
9 Miscellaneous proceedings or matters (High Court only)	
Bills of Sale	
9.1 On filing any document under the Bills of Sale Acts 1878 and the Bills of Sale Act (1878) Amendment Act 1882 or on an application under section 15 of the Bills of Sale Act 1878 for an order that a memorandum of satisfaction be written on a registered copy of the bill	£10
Searches	
9.2 For an official certificate of the result of a search for each name, in any register or index held by the court; or in the Court Funds Office, for an official certificate of the result of a search of unclaimed balances for a specified period of up to 50 years	£5
9.3 On a search in person of the bankruptcy and companies records, including inspection, for each 15 minutes or part of 15 minutes	£5
Judge sitting as arbitrator	
9.4 On the appointment of—	
(a) a judge of the Commercial Court as an arbitrator or umpire under section 93 of the Arbitration Act 1996; or	£1,800
(b) a judge of the Technology and Construction Court as an arbitrator or umpire under section 93 of the Arbitration Act 1996	£1,400
9.5 For every day or part of a day (after the first day) of the hearing before—	
(a) a judge of the Commercial Court; or	£1,800
(b) a judge of the Technology and Construction Court, so appointed as arbitrator or umpire	£1,400
Where fee 9.4 has been paid on the appointment of a judge of the Commercial Court or a judge of the Technology and Construction Court as an arbitrator or umpire but the arbitration does not proceed to a hearing or an award, the fee shall be refunded.	
10 Fees payable in Admiralty matters (High Court only) **In the Admiralty Registrar and Marshal's Office—**	
10.1 On the issue of a warrant for the arrest of a ship or goods	£100
10.2 On the sale of a ship or goods— Subject to a minimum fee of £200,	
(a) for every £100 or fraction of £100 of the price up to £100,000	£1
(b) for every £100 or fraction of £100 of the price exceeding £100,000	50p
Where there is sufficient proceeds of sale in court, fee 10.2 shall be taken by transfer from the proceeds of sale in court.	
10.3 On entering a reference for hearing by the Registrar	£50
FEES PAYABLE IN HIGH COURT AND COURT OF APPEAL ONLY	
11 Affidavits	
11.1 On taking an affidavit or an affirmation or attestation upon honour in lieu of an affidavit or a declaration except for the purpose of receipt of dividends from the Accountant General and for a declaration by a shorthand writer appointed in insolvency proceedings — for each person making any of the above	£5
11.2 For each exhibit referred to in an affidavit, affirmation, attestation or declaration for which fee 11.1 is payable	£2

Column 1 *Number and description of fee*	*Column 2* *Amount of fee*
FEES PAYABLE IN COURT OF APPEAL ONLY	
12 Fees payable in appeals to the Court of Appeal	
12.1(a) **Where in an appeal notice** permission to appeal or an extension of time for appealing is applied for (or both are applied for) — — on filing an appellant's notice, or — where the respondent is appealing, on filing a respondent's notice	£200
12.1(b) **Where permission to appeal** is not required or has been granted by the lower court— — on filing an appellant's notice, or — on filing a respondent's notice where the respondent is appealing	£400
12.1(c) **On the appellant filing an appeal questionnaire** (unless the appellant has paid fee 12.1(b)), or on the respondent filing an appeal questionnaire (unless the respondent has paid fee 12.1(b))	£400
12.2 **On filing a respondent's notice** where the respondent wishes to ask the appeal court to uphold the order of the lower court for reasons different from or additional to those given by the lower court	£200
12.3 **On filing an application notice**	£200
Fee 12.3 Fee 12.3 shall not be payable for an application made in an appeal notice.	

SCHEDULE 2 ORDERS REVOKED

[Schedule introduced by article 8]

Title	*Reference*
The Supreme Court Fees Order 1999	S.I. 1999/687
The Supreme Court Fees (Amendment) Order 1999	S.I. 1999/2569
The Supreme Court Fees (Amendment) Order 2000	S.I. 2000/641
The Supreme Court Fees (Amendment) Order 2003	S.I. 2003/646
The Supreme Court Fees (Amendment) Order 2004	S.I. 2004/2100
The Supreme Court Fees (Amendment No. 2) Order 2000	S.I. 2000/937
The Supreme Court Fees (Amendment No. 2) Order 2003	S.I. 2003/717
The County Court Fees Order 1999	S.I. 1999/689
The County Court Fees (Amendment) Order 1999	S.I. 1999/2548
The County Court Fees (Amendment) Order 2000	S.I. 2000/639
The County Court Fees (Amendment) Order 2003	S.I. 2003/648
The County Court Fees (Amendment) Order 2004	S.I. 2004/2098
The County Court Fees (Amendment No. 2) Order 2000	S.I. 2000/939
The County Court Fees (Amendment No. 2) Order 2003	S.I. 2003/718
The County Court Fees (Amendment No. 4) Order 2000	S.I. 2000/2310

NOTES ON TEXT

The text printed above incorporates the following amendments:
art. 4 amended by: (a) Civil Proceedings Fees (Amendment) Order 2005 (SI 2005/473), art. 2; (b) Civil Proceedings Fees (Amendment) Order 2005 (SI 2005/3445), art 2; (c) Civil Proceedings Fees (Amendment) Order 2006 (SI 2006/719), art. 2;
sch. 1 substituted by Civil Proceedings Fees (Amendment) Order 2005 (SI 2005/3445), art. 3 and sch.; amended by Civil Proceedings Fees (Amendment) Order 2006 (SI 2006/719), art. 3; in fee 12.1(c) a closing parenthesis has been added editorially after 'fee 12.1(b)' the first time it occurs.

Non-Contentious Probate Fees (Indian Ocean Tsunami) Order 2005

(SI 2005/266)

The Lord Chancellor, in exercise of the powers conferred upon him by sections 92 and 108(6) of the Courts Act 2003 and section 128 of the Finance Act 1990, with the consent of the Treasury under section 92(1) of the Courts Act 2003 and after consultation with the Lord Chief Justice, the Master of the Rolls, the President of the Family Division, the Vice-Chancellor, the Head of Civil Justice and the Deputy Head of Civil Justice and the Civil Justice Council under section 92(5) and (6) of the Courts Act 2003, hereby makes the following Order:

1 Citation, commencement and interpretation

(1) This Order may be cited as the Non-Contentious Probate Fees (Indian Ocean Tsunami) Order 2005 and shall come into force on the 4th March 2005.

(2) In this Order 'the 2004 Order' means the Non-Contentious Probate Fees Order 2004.

2 Remission of fees

Notwithstanding the provisions of Article 4 of the 2004 Order, where it appears to the Lord Chancellor that an application for a grant is in respect of a death occurring as a result of the earthquake and tsunami in the Indian Ocean on 26th December 2004, he shall remit any fee prescribed by that Order in that case.

3 Transitional provision

Where—

(a) a fee has been paid under the 2004 Order after 26th December 2004 but before 4th March 2005 and

(b) if this Order had been in force when the fee was paid, the Lord Chancellor would have remitted the fee,

the fee shall be refunded.

Non-Contentious Probate Fees (London Terrorist Bombings) Order 2005

(SI 2005/3359)

The Lord Chancellor makes the following Order in exercise of the powers conferred upon him by sections 92 and 108(6) of the Courts Act 2003 and section 128 of the Finance Act 1990. In accordance with section 92 of the Courts Act 2003, he has consulted the Lord Chief Justice, the Master of the Rolls, the President of the Queen's Bench Division, the President of the Family Division, the Chancellor of the High Court, the Head of Civil Justice, the Deputy Head of Civil Justice, and the Civil Justice Council.

1 Citation, Commencement and Interpretation

(1) This order may be cited as the Non-Contentious Probate Fees (London Terrorist Bombings) Order 2005 and shall come into force on 29th December 2005.

(2) In this Order 'the 2004 Order' means the Non-Contentious Probate Fees Order 2004.

2 Remission of fees

Notwithstanding the provisions of Article 4 of the 2004 Order, where it appears to the Lord Chancellor that an application for a grant is in respect of—

(a) a death occurring as a result of another person's detonation of a bomb in London on 7th July 2005, or

(b) a death occurring as a result of action taken in a police operation following another person's attempted detonation of a bomb in London on 21st July 2005,

he shall remit any fee prescribed by the 2004 Order.

3 Transitional provision

Where—

(a) a fee has been paid under the 2004 Order after 7th July 2005 but before 29th December 2005 and

(b) if this Order had been in force when the fee was paid, the Lord Chancellor would have remitted the fee,

the fee shall be refunded.

Non-Contentious Probate Fees Order 2004

(SI 2004/3120)

The Lord Chancellor, in exercise of the powers conferred upon him by sections 92 and 108(6) of the Courts Act 2003, and section 128 of the Finance Act 1990 with the consent of the Treasury under section 92(1) of the Courts Act 2003 and after consultation with the Lord Chief Justice, the Master of the Rolls, the President of the Family Division, the Vice-Chancellor, the Head of Civil Justice and the Deputy Head of Civil Justice and the Civil Justice Council under section 92(5) and (6) of the Courts Act 2003, hereby makes the following Order:

1 Citation, commencement and interpretation

(1) This Order may be cited as the Non-Contentious Probate Fees Order 2004 and shall come into force on the 4th January 2005.

(2) In this Order—

- (a) a fee referred to by number means the fee so numbered in Schedule 1 to this Order;
- (b) 'assessed value' means the value of the net real and personal estate (excluding settled land if any) passing under the grant as shown —
  - (i) in the Inland Revenue affidavit (for a death occurring before 13th March 1975), or
  - (ii) in the Inland Revenue account (for a death occurring on or after 13th March 1975), or
  - (iii) in the case in which, in accordance with arrangements made between the President of the Family Division and the Commissioners of the Inland Revenue, or regulations made under section 256(1)(a) of the Inheritance Tax Act 1984 and from time to time in force, no such affidavit or account is required to be delivered, in the oath which is sworn to lead to the grant,

  and in the case of an application to reseal means the value, as shown, passing under the grant upon its being resealed;
- (c) 'authorised place of deposit' means any place in which, by virtue of a direction given under section 124 of the Supreme Court Act 1981 original wills and other documents under the control of the High Court (either in the principal registry or in any district registry) are deposited and preserved;
- (d) 'grant' means a grant of probate or letters of administration;
- (e) 'district registry' includes the probate registry of Wales, any district probate registry and any sub-registry attached to it;
- (f) 'the principal registry' means the Principal Registry of the Family Division and any sub-registry attached to it.

2 Fees to be taken

The fees set out in column 2 of Schedule 1 to this Order shall be taken in the principal registry and in each district registry in respect of the items described in column 1 in accordance with and subject to any directions specified in column 1.

3 Exclusion of certain death gratuities

In determining the value of any personal estate for the purposes of this Order there shall be excluded the value of a death gratuity payable under section 17(2) of the Judicial Pensions Act 1981 or section 4(3) of the Judicial Pensions and Retirement Act 1993, or payable to the personal representatives of a deceased civil servant by virtue of a scheme made under section 1 of the Superannuation Act 1972.

4 Exemptions, reductions, remissions and refunds

Where it appears to the Lord Chancellor that the payment of any fee prescribed by this Order would, owing to the exceptional circumstances of the particular case, involve undue financial hardship, he may reduce or remit the fee in that case.

5

(1) Subject to paragraph (2) where a fee has been paid at a time —
(a) where the Lord Chancellor, if he had been aware of all the circumstances, would have reduced the fee under article 4, the amount by which the fee would have been reduced shall be refunded; and
(b) where the Lord Chancellor, if he had been aware of all the circumstances, would have remitted the fee under article 4, the fee shall be refunded.
(2) No refund shall be made under paragraph (1) unless the party who paid the fee applies within 6 months of paying the fee.
(3) The Lord Chancellor may extend the period of 6 months referred to in paragraph (2) if he considers that there is good reason for an application being made after the end of the period of 6 months.

6

(1) Where by any convention entered into by Her Majesty with any foreign power it is provided that no fee shall be required to be paid in respect of any proceedings, the fees specified in this Order shall not be taken in respect of those proceedings.
(2) Where any application for a grant is withdrawn before the issue of a grant, a registrar may reduce or remit a fee.
(3) Fee 7 shall not be taken where a search is made for research or similar purposes by permission of the President of the Family Division for a document over 100 years old filed in the principal registry or a district registry or another authorised place of deposit.

7 Special exemption — Armed Forces

Where a fee has been paid or fees have been paid for the application of a grant (other than fee 3.2) and at the time of payment of that fee or those fees —
(a) the application for the grant was in respect of an estate exempt from Inheritance Tax by virtue of section 154 of the Inheritance Tax Act 1984 (exemption for members of the armed forces etc); and
(b) was in respect of a death occurring before 20th March 2003;
the Lord Chancellor shall upon receiving a written application refund the difference between any fee or fees paid and fee 3.2.

8 Revocation

The Order specified in Schedule 2 in so far as it was made under section 128 of the Finance Act 1990 shall be revoked.

SCHEDULE 1 FEES TO BE TAKEN

[Schedule introduced by article 2]

Column 1 *Number and description of fee*	*Column 2* *Amount of fee*
1. Application for a grant On an application for a grant (or for resealing a grant) other than on an application to which fee 3 applies, where the assessed value of the estate exceeds £5,000	£40
2. Personal application fee Where the application under fee 1 is made by a personal applicant (not being an application to which fee 3 applies) fee 2 is payable in addition to fee 1, where the assessed value of the estate exceeds £5,000	£50
3. Special applications 3.1 For a duplicate or second or subsequent grant (including one following a revoked grant) in respect of the same deceased person, other than a grant preceded only by a grant limited to settled land, to trust property, or to part of the estate	£15

Column 1 *Number and description of fee*	*Column 2* *Amount of fee*
3.2 On an application for a grant relating to a death occurring on or after 20th March 2003 and in respect of an estate exempt from inheritance tax by virtue of section 154 of the Inheritance Tax Act 1984 (exemption for members of the armed forces etc)	£8
4. Caveats For the entry or the extension of a caveat	£15
5. Search On an application for a standing search to be carried out in an estate, for each period of six months including the issue of a copy grant and will, if any (irrespective of the number of pages)	£5
6. Deposit of wills On depositing a will for safe custody in the principal registry or a district registry	£15
7. Inspection On inspection of any will or other document retained by the registry (in the presence of an officer of the registry)	£15
8. Copy documents On a request for a copy of any document whether or not provided as a certified copy:	
(a) for the first copy	£5
(b) for every subsequent copy of the same document if supplied at the same time	£1
(c) where copies of any document are made available on a computer disk or in other electronic form, for each such copy	£3
(d) where a search of the index is required, in addition to fee 8(a), (b) or (c) as appropriate, for each period of 4 years searched after the first 4 years	£3
9. Oaths Except on a personal application for a grant, for administering an oath,	
9.1 for each deponent to each affidavit	£5
9.2 for marking each exhibit	£2
10. Determination of costs For determining costs	The same fees as are payable from time to time for determining costs under the Civil Proceedings Fees Order 2004, (the relevant fees are set out in fee 5 in Schedule 1 to that Order)
11. Settling documents For perusing and settling citations, advertisements, oaths, affidavits, or other documents, for each document settled	£10

SCHEDULE 2 ORDER REVOKED

[Schedule introduced by article 8]

Title	*Reference*
The Non-Contentious Probate Fees (Amendment) Order 2000	S.I. 2000/642

Appendix 7 Selected Legislation

The following items are on the CD-ROM version of *Blackstone's Civil Practice*. Click on the title of an item to open it:

Access to Justice Act 1999

(1999 CHAPTER 22)

An Act to establish the Legal Services Commission, the Community Legal Service and the Criminal Defence Service; to amend the law of legal aid in Scotland; to make further provision about legal services; to make provision about appeals, courts, judges and court proceedings; to amend the law about magistrates and magistrates' courts; and to make provision about immunity from action and costs and indemnities for certain officials exercising judicial functions. [27th July 1999]

PART I LEGAL SERVICES COMMISSION

Commission

1. Legal Services Commission

(1) There shall be a body known as the Legal Services Commission (in this Part referred to as 'the Commission').

(2) The Commission shall have the functions relating to—
- (a) the Community Legal Service, and
- (b) the Criminal Defence Service,

which are conferred or imposed on it by the provisions of this Act or any other enactment.

(3) The Commission shall consist of—
- (a) not fewer than seven members, and
- (b) not more than twelve members;

but the Secretary of State may by order substitute for either or both of the numbers for the time being specified in paragraphs (a) and (b) such other number or numbers as he thinks appropriate.

(4) The members of the Commission shall be appointed by the Secretary of State; and the Secretary of State shall appoint one of the members to chair the Commission.

(5) In appointing persons to be members of the Commission the Secretary of State shall have regard to the desirability of securing that the Commission includes members who (between them) have experience in or knowledge of—
- (a) the provision of services which the Commission can fund as part of the Community Legal Service or Criminal Defence Service,
- (b) the work of the courts,
- (c) consumer affairs,
- (d) social conditions, and
- (e) management.

(6) Schedule 1 (which makes further provision about the Commission) has effect.

2. Power to Replace Commission With Two Bodies

(1) The Secretary of State may by order establish in place of the Commission two bodies—
- (a) one to have functions relating to the Community Legal Service, and
- (b) the other to have functions relating to the Criminal Defence Service.

(2) The order may make any consequential, incidental, supplementary or transitional provisions, and any savings, which appear to the Secretary of State to be appropriate.

(3) The order shall include amendments of—
- (a) any provisions of, or amended by, this Part which refer to the Commission, and
- (b) any other enactments which so refer,

to replace references to the Commission with references to either or both of the bodies established by the order.

3. Powers of Commission

(1) Subject to the provisions of this Part, the Commission may do anything which it considers—
- (a) is necessary or appropriate for, or for facilitating, the discharge of its functions, or
- (b) is incidental or conducive to the discharge of its functions.

(2) In particular, the Commission shall have power—
   (a) to enter into any contract,
   (b) to make grants (with or without conditions),
   (c) to make loans,
   (d) to invest money,
   (e) to promote or assist in the promotion of publicity relating to its functions,
   (f) to undertake any inquiry or investigation which it may consider appropriate in relation to the discharge of any of its functions, and
   (g) to give the Secretary of State any advice which it may consider appropriate in relation to matters concerning any of its functions.

(3) Subsections (1) and (2) do not confer on the Commission power to borrow money.

(4) The Commission may make such arrangements as it considers appropriate for the discharge of its functions, including the delegation of any of its functions.

(5) The Secretary of State may by order require the Commission—
   (a) to delegate any function specified in the order or to delegate any function so specified to a person (or person of a description) so specified,
   (b) not to delegate any function so specified or not to delegate any function so specified to a person (or person of a description) so specified, or
   (c) to make arrangements such as are specified in the order in relation to the delegation of any function so specified.

Community Legal Service

4. Community Legal Service

(1) The Commission shall establish, maintain and develop a service known as the Community Legal Service for the purpose of promoting the availability to individuals of services of the descriptions specified in subsection (2) and, in particular, for securing (within the resources made available, and priorities set, in accordance with this Part) that individuals have access to services that effectively meet their needs.

(2) The descriptions of services referred to in subsection (1) are—
   (a) the provision of general information about the law and legal system and the availability of legal services,
   (b) the provision of help by the giving of advice as to how the law applies in particular circumstances,
   (c) the provision of help in preventing, or settling or otherwise resolving, disputes about legal rights and duties,
   (d) the provision of help in enforcing decisions by which such disputes are resolved, and
   (e) the provision of help in relation to legal proceedings not relating to disputes.

(3) Services which the Commission is required to fund as part of the Criminal Defence Service do not fall within subsection (2).

(4) Every person who exercises any function relating to the Community Legal Service shall have regard to the desirability of exercising it, so far as is reasonably practicable, so as to—
   (a) promote improvements in the range and quality of services provided as part of the Community Legal Service and in the ways in which they are made accessible to those who need them,
   (b) secure that the services provided in relation to any matter are appropriate having regard to its nature and importance, and
   (c) achieve the swift and fair resolution of disputes without unnecessary or unduly protracted proceedings in court.

(5) The Commission shall fund services of the descriptions specified in subsection (2) as part of the Community Legal Service in accordance with the following sections.

(6) The Commission shall also inform itself about the need for, and the provision of, services of the descriptions specified in subsection (2) and about the quality of the services provided and, in co-operation with such authorities and other bodies and persons as it considers appropriate—
   (a) plan what can be done towards meeting that need by the performance by the Commission of its functions, and

(b) facilitate the planning by other authorities, bodies and persons of what can be done by them to meet that need by the use of any resources available to them;

and the Commission shall notify the Secretary of State of what it has done under this subsection.

(7) The Commission may set and monitor standards in relation to services of the descriptions specified in subsection (2).

(8) In particular, the Commission may accredit, or authorise others to accredit, persons or bodies providing services of the descriptions specified in subsection (2); and any system of accreditation shall include provision for the monitoring of the services provided by accredited persons and bodies and for the withdrawal of accreditation from any providing services of unsatisfactory quality.

(9) The Commission may charge—

(a) for accreditation,

(b) for monitoring the services provided by accredited persons and bodies, and

(c) for authorising accreditation by others;

and persons or bodies authorised to accredit may charge for accreditation, and for such monitoring, in accordance with the terms of their authorisation.

(10) The Secretary of State may by order require the Commission to discharge the functions in subsections (6) to (9) in accordance with the order.

5. Funding of Services

(1) The Commission shall establish and maintain a fund known as the Community Legal Service Fund from which it shall fund services as part of the Community Legal Service.

(2) The Secretary of State—

(a) shall pay to the Commission the sums which he determines are appropriate for the funding of services by the Commission as part of the Community Legal Service, and

(b) may determine the manner in which and times at which the sums are to be paid to the Commission and may impose conditions on the payment of the sums.

(3) In making any determination under subsection (2) the Secretary of State shall take into account (in addition to such other factors as he considers relevant) the need for services of the descriptions specified in subsection (2) of section 4 as notified to him by the Commission under subsection (6) of that section.

(4) The Secretary of State shall lay before each House of Parliament a copy of every determination under subsection (2)(a).

(5) The Commission shall pay into the Community Legal Service Fund—

(a) sums received from the Secretary of State under subsection (2), and

(b) sums received by the Commission by virtue of regulations under section 10 or 11.

(6) The Secretary of State may by direction impose requirements on the Commission as to the descriptions of services to be funded from any specified amount paid into the Community Legal Service Fund.

(7) In funding services as part of the Community Legal Service the Commission shall aim to obtain the best possible value for money.

6. Services Which May Be Funded

(1) The Commission shall set priorities in its funding of services as part of the Community Legal Service and the priorities shall be set—

(a) in accordance with any directions given by the Secretary of State, and

(b) after taking into account the need for services of the descriptions specified in section 4(2).

(2) Subject to that (and to subsection (6)), the services which the Commission may fund as part of the Community Legal Service are those which the Commission considers appropriate.

(3) The Commission may fund services as part of the Community Legal Service by—

(a) entering into contracts with persons or bodies for the provision of services by them,

(b) making payments to persons or bodies in respect of the provision of services by them,

(c) making grants or loans to persons or bodies to enable them to provide, or facilitate the provision of, services,

(d) establishing and maintaining bodies to provide, or facilitate the provision of, services,

(e) making grants or loans to individuals to enable them to obtain services,
(f) itself providing services, or
(g) doing anything else which it considers appropriate for funding services.

(4) The Secretary of State may by order require the Commission to discharge the function in subsection (3) in accordance with the order.

(5) The Commission may fund as part of the Community Legal Service different descriptions of services or services provided by different means—
(a) in relation to different areas or communities in England and Wales, and
(b) in relation to different descriptions of cases.

(6) The Commission may not fund as part of the Community Legal Service any of the services specified in Schedule 2.

(7) Regulations may amend that Schedule by adding new services or omitting or varying any services.

(8) The Secretary of State—
(a) may by direction require the Commission to fund the provision of any of the services specified in Schedule 2 in circumstances specified in the direction, and
(b) may authorise the Commission to fund the provision of any of those services in specified circumstances or, if the Commission request him to do so, in an individual case.

(9) The Secretary of State shall either—
(a) publish, or
(b) require the Commission to publish,
any authorisation under subsection (8)(b) unless it relates to an individual case (in which case he or the Commission may publish it if appropriate).

7. Individuals for Whom Services May Be Funded

(1) The Commission may only fund services for an individual as part of the Community Legal Service if his financial resources are such that, under regulations, he is an individual for whom they may be so funded.

(2) Regulations may provide that, in prescribed circumstances and subject to any prescribed conditions, services of a prescribed description may be so funded for individuals without reference to their financial resources.

(3) Regulations under this section may include provision requiring the furnishing of information.

8. Code about Provision of Funded Services

(1) The Commission shall prepare a code setting out the criteria according to which it is to decide whether to fund (or continue to fund) services as part of the Community Legal Service for an individual for whom they may be so funded and, if so, what services are to be funded for him.

(2) In settling the criteria to be set out in the code the Commission shall consider the extent to which they ought to reflect the following factors—
(a) the likely cost of funding the services and the benefit which may be obtained by their being provided,
(b) the availability of sums in the Community Legal Service Fund for funding the services and (having regard to present and likely future demands on that Fund) the appropriateness of applying them to fund the services,
(c) the importance of the matters in relation to which the services would be provided for the individual,
(d) the availability to the individual of services not funded by the Commission and the likelihood of his being able to avail himself of them,
(e) if the services are sought by the individual in relation to a dispute, the prospects of his success in the dispute,
(f) the conduct of the individual in connection with services funded as part of the Community Legal Service (or an application for funding) or in, or in connection with, any proceedings,
(g) the public interest, and
(h) such other factors as the Secretary of State may by order require the Commission to consider.

(3) The criteria set out in the code shall reflect the principle that in many family disputes mediation will be more appropriate than court proceedings.
(4) The code shall seek to secure that, where more than one description of service is available, the service funded is that which (in all the circumstances) is the most appropriate having regard to the criteria set out in the code.
(5) The code shall also specify procedures for the making of decisions about the funding of services by the Commission as part of the Community Legal Service, including—
(a) provision about the form and content of applications for funding,
(b) provision imposing conditions which must be satisfied by an individual applying for funding,
(c) provision requiring applicants to be informed of the reasons for any decision to refuse an application,
(d) provision for the giving of information to individuals whose applications are refused about alternative ways of obtaining or funding services, and
(e) provision establishing procedures for appeals against decisions about funding and for the giving of information about those procedures.
(6) The code may make different provision for different purposes.
(7) The Commission may from time to time prepare a revised version of the code.
(8) Before preparing the code the Commission shall undertake such consultation as appears to it to be appropriate; and before revising the code the Commission shall undertake such consultation as appears to it to be appropriate unless it considers that it is desirable for the revised version to come into force without delay.
(9) The Secretary of State may by order require the Commission to discharge its functions relating to the code in accordance with the order.

9. Procedure Relating to Funding Code

(1) After preparing the code or a revised version of the code the Commission shall send a copy to the Secretary of State.
(2) If he approves it he shall lay it before each House of Parliament.
(3) The Commission shall publish—
(a) the code as first approved by the Secretary of State, and
(b) where he approves a revised version, either the revisions or the revised code as appropriate.
(4) The code as first approved by the Secretary of State shall not come into force until it has been approved by a resolution of each House of Parliament.
(5) A revised version of the code which does not contain changes in the criteria set out in the code shall not come into force until it has been laid before each House of Parliament.
(6) Subject as follows, a revised version of the code which does contain such changes shall not come into force until it has been approved by a resolution of each House of Parliament.
(7) Where the Secretary of State considers that it is desirable for a revised version of the code containing such changes to come into force without delay, he may (when laying the revised version before Parliament) also lay before each House a statement of his reasons for so considering.
(8) In that event the revised version of the code—
(a) shall not come into force until it has been laid before each House of Parliament, and
(b) shall cease to have effect at the end of the period of 120 days beginning with the day on which it comes into force unless a resolution approving it has been made by each House (but without that affecting anything previously done in accordance with it).

10. Terms of Provision of Funded Services

(1) An individual for whom services are funded by the Commission as part of the Community Legal Service shall not be required to make any payment in respect of the services except where regulations otherwise provide.
(2) Regulations may provide that, in prescribed circumstances, an individual for whom services are so funded shall—
(a) pay a fee of such amount as is fixed by or determined under the regulations,

(b) if his financial resources are, or relevant conduct is, such as to make him liable to do so under the regulations, pay the cost of the services or make a contribution in respect of the cost of the services of such amount as is so fixed or determined, or

(c) if the services relate to a dispute and he has agreed to make a payment (which may exceed the cost of the services) only in specified circumstances, make in those circumstances a payment of the amount agreed, or determined in the manner agreed, by him;

and in paragraph (b) 'relevant conduct' means conduct in connection with the services (or any application for their funding) or in, or in connection with, any proceedings in relation to which they are provided.

(3) The regulations may include provision for any amount payable in accordance with the regulations to be payable by periodical payments or one or more capital sums, or both.

(4) The regulations may also include provision for the payment by an individual of interest (on such terms as may be prescribed) in respect of—

(a) any loan made to him by the Commission as part of the Community Legal Service,

(b) any payment in respect of the cost of services required by the regulations to be made by him later than the time when the services are provided, or

(c) so much of any payment required by the regulations to be made by him which remains unpaid after the time when it is required to be paid.

(5) The regulations shall include provision for the repayment to an individual of any payment made by him in excess of his liability under the regulations.

(6) The regulations may—

(a) include provision requiring the furnishing of information, and

(b) make provision for the determination of the cost of services for the purposes of the regulations.

(7) Except so far as regulations otherwise provide, where services have been funded by the Commission for an individual as part of the Community Legal Service—

(a) sums expended by the Commission in funding the services (except to the extent that they are recovered under section 11), and

(b) other sums payable by the individual by virtue of regulations under this section,

shall constitute a first charge on any property recovered or preserved by him (whether for himself or any other person) in any proceedings or in any compromise or settlement of any dispute in connection with which the services were provided.

(8) Regulations may make provision about the charge, including—

(a) provision as to whether it is in favour of the Commission or the body or person by whom the services were provided, and

(b) provision about its enforcement.

11. Costs in Funded Cases

(1) Except in prescribed circumstances, costs ordered against an individual in relation to any proceedings or part of proceedings funded for him shall not exceed the amount (if any) which is a reasonable one for him to pay having regard to all the circumstances including—

(a) the financial resources of all the parties to the proceedings, and

(b) their conduct in connection with the dispute to which the proceedings relate;

and for this purpose proceedings, or a part of proceedings, are funded for an individual if services relating to the proceedings or part are funded for him by the Commission as part of the Community Legal Service.

(2) In assessing for the purposes of subsection (1) the financial resources of an individual for whom services are funded by the Commission as part of the Community Legal Service, his clothes and household furniture and the tools and implements of his trade shall not be taken into account, except so far as may be prescribed.

(3) Subject to subsections (1) and (2), regulations may make provision about costs in relation to proceedings in which services are funded by the Commission for any of the parties as part of the Community Legal Service.

(4) The regulations may, in particular, make provision—

(a) specifying the principles to be applied in determining the amount of any costs which may be awarded against a party for whom services are funded by the Commission as part of the Community Legal Service,

(b) limiting the circumstances in which, or extent to which, an order for costs may be enforced against such a party,

(c) as to the cases in which, and extent to which, such a party may be required to give security for costs and the manner in which it is to be given,

(d) requiring the payment by the Commission of the whole or part of any costs incurred by a party for whom services are not funded by the Commission as part of the Community Legal Service,

(e) specifying the principles to be applied in determining the amount of any costs which may be awarded to a party for whom services are so funded,

(f) requiring the payment to the Commission, or the person or body by which the services were provided, of the whole or part of any sum awarded by way of costs to such a party, and

(g) as to the court, tribunal or other person or body by whom the amount of any costs is to be determined and the extent to which any determination of that amount is to be final.

Supplementary

19. Foreign Law

(1) The Commission may not fund as part of the Community Legal Service or Criminal Defence Service services relating to any law other than that of England and Wales, unless any such law is relevant for determining any issue relating to the law of England and Wales.

(2) But the Secretary of State may, if it appears to him necessary to do so for the purpose of fulfilling any obligation imposed on the United Kingdom by any international agreement, by order specify that there may be funded as part of the Community Legal Service or Criminal Defence Service (or both) services relating to the application of such other law as may be specified in the order.

20. Restriction of Disclosure of Information

(1) Subject to the following provisions of this section, information which is furnished—

(a) to the Commission or any court, tribunal or other person or body on whom functions are imposed or conferred by or under this Part, and

(b) in connection with the case of an individual seeking or receiving services funded by the Commission as part of the Community Legal Service or Criminal Defence Service,

shall not be disclosed except as permitted by subsection (2).

(2) Such information may be disclosed—

(a) for the purpose of enabling or assisting the Commission to discharge any functions imposed or conferred on it by or under this Part,

(b) for the purpose of enabling or assisting the Secretary of State to discharge any functions imposed or conferred on him by or under this Part,

(c) for the purpose of enabling or assisting any court, tribunal or other person or body to discharge any functions imposed or conferred on it by or under this Part,

(d) except where regulations otherwise provide, for the purpose of the investigation or prosecution of any offence (or suspected offence) under the law of England and Wales or any other jurisdiction,

(e) in connection with any proceedings relating to the Community Legal Service or Criminal Defence Service, or

(f) for the purpose of facilitating the proper performance by any tribunal of disciplinary functions.

(3) Subsection (1) does not limit the disclosure of—

(a) information in the form of a summary or collection of information so framed as not to enable information relating to any individual to be ascertained from it, or

(b) information about the amount of any grant, loan or other payment made to any person or body by the Commission.

(4) Subsection (1) does not prevent the disclosure of information for any purpose with the consent of the individual in connection with whose case it was furnished and, where he did not furnish it himself, with that of the person or body who did.

(5) A person who discloses any information in contravention of this section shall be guilty of an offence and liable on summary conviction to a fine not exceeding level 4 on the standard scale.

(6) Proceedings for an offence under this section shall not be brought without the consent of the Director of Public Prosecutions.

(7) Nothing in this section applies to information furnished to a person providing services funded as part of the Community Legal Service or the Criminal Defence Service by or on behalf of an individual seeking or receiving such services.

21. Misrepresentation etc.

(1) Any person who—
 (a) intentionally fails to comply with any requirement imposed by virtue of this Part as to the information to be furnished by him, or
 (b) in furnishing any information required by virtue of this Part makes any statement or representation which he knows or believes to be false,

shall be guilty of an offence.

(2) A person guilty of an offence under subsection (1) is liable on summary conviction to—
 (a) a fine not exceeding level 4 on the standard scale, or
 (b) imprisonment for a term not exceeding three months, or to both.

(3) Proceedings in respect of an offence under subsection (1) may (despite anything in the Magistrates' Courts Act 1980) be brought at any time within the period of six months beginning with the date on which evidence sufficient in the opinion of the prosecutor to justify a prosecution comes to his knowledge.

(4) But subsection (3) does not authorise the commencement of proceedings for an offence at a time more than two years after the date on which the offence was committed.

(5) A county court shall have jurisdiction to hear and determine any action brought by the Commission to recover loss sustained by reason of—
 (a) the failure of any person to comply with any requirement imposed by virtue of this Part as to the information to be furnished by him, or
 (b) a false statement or false representation made by any person in furnishing any information required by virtue of this Part.

22. Position of Service Providers and Other Parties etc.

(1) Except as expressly provided by regulations, the fact that services provided for an individual are or could be funded by the Commission as part of the Community Legal Service or Criminal Defence Service shall not affect—
 (a) the relationship between that individual and the person by whom they are provided or any privilege arising out of that relationship, or
 (b) any right which that individual may have to be indemnified in respect of expenses incurred by him by any other person.

(2) A person who provides services funded by the Commission as part of the Community Legal Service or Criminal Defence Service shall not take any payment in respect of the services apart from—
 (a) that made by way of that funding, and
 (b) any authorised by the Commission to be taken.

(3) The withdrawal of a right to representation previously granted to an individual shall not affect the right of any person who has provided to him services funded by the Commission as part of the Criminal Defence Service to remuneration for work done before the date of the withdrawal.

(4) Except as expressly provided by regulations, any rights conferred by or by virtue of this Part on an individual for whom services are funded by the Commission as part of the Community Legal Service or Criminal Defence Service in relation to any proceedings shall not affect—
 (a) the rights or liabilities of other parties to the proceedings, or
 (b) the principles on which the discretion of any court or tribunal is normally exercised.

(5) Regulations may make provision about the procedure of any court or tribunal in relation to services funded by the Commission as part of the Community Legal Service or Criminal Defence Service.

(6) Regulations made under subsection (5) may in particular authorise the exercise of the functions of any court or tribunal by any member or officer of that or any other court or tribunal.

23. Guidance

(1) The Secretary of State may give guidance to the Commission as to the manner in which he considers it should discharge its functions.

(2) The Commission shall take into account any such guidance when considering the manner in which it is to discharge its functions.

(3) Guidance may not be given under this section in relation to individual cases.

(4) The Secretary of State shall either—

(a) publish, or

(b) require the Commission to publish, any guidance given under this section.

25. Orders, Regulations and Directions

(1) Any power of the Secretary of State under this Part to make an order or regulations is exercisable by statutory instrument.

(2) Before making any remuneration order relating to the payment of remuneration to barristers or solicitors the Secretary of State shall consult the General Council of the Bar and the Law Society.

(3) When making any remuneration order the Secretary of State shall have regard to—

(a) the need to secure the provision of services of the description to which the order relates by a sufficient number of competent persons and bodies,

(b) the cost to public funds, and

(c) the need to secure value for money.

(4) In subsections (2) and (3) 'remuneration order' means an order under section 6(4), 13(3) or 14(3) which relates to the payment by the Commission of remuneration—

(a) for the provision of services by persons or bodies in individual cases, or

(b) by reference to the provision of services by persons or bodies in specified numbers of cases.

(5) No directions may be given by the Secretary of State to the Commission under this Part in relation to individual cases.

(6) Any directions given by the Secretary of State to the Commission under this Part may be varied or revoked.

(7) The Secretary of State shall either—

(a) publish, or

(b) require the Commission to publish, any directions given by him under this Part.

(8) Orders, regulations and directions of the Secretary of State under this Part may make different provision for different purposes (including different areas).

(9) No order shall be made under section 2 or 8 or paragraph 5(3) of Schedule 3, and no regulations shall be made under section 6(7), 11(1) or (4)(b) or (d) or 15(2)(a) or (5) or paragraph 4 of Schedule 3, unless a draft of the order or regulations has been laid before, and approved by a resolution of, each House of Parliament.

(10) A statutory instrument containing any other order or regulations under this Part shall be subject to annulment in pursuance of a resolution of either House of Parliament.

26. Interpretation

In this Part—

'the Commission' means the Legal Services Commission,

'the Community Legal Service Fund' has the meaning given by section 5(1),

'criminal proceedings' has the meaning given in section 12(2),

'prescribed' means prescribed by regulations and 'prescribe' shall be construed accordingly,

'regulations' means regulations made by the Secretary of State, and 'representation' means representation for the purposes of proceedings and includes the assistance which is usually given by a representative in the steps preliminary or incidental to any proceedings and, subject to any time limits which may be prescribed, advice and assistance as to any appeal.

PART II OTHER FUNDING OF LEGAL SERVICES

Conditional Fee and Litigation Funding Agreements

27. Conditional Fee Agreements

[(1) *Substitutes s. 58 of, and inserts s. 58A into, the Courts and Legal Services Act 1990.*]

(2) In section 120(4) of the Courts and Legal Services Act 1990 (orders and regulations subject to affirmative procedure), for '58,' substitute '58(4),'.

28. Litigation Funding Agreements

In the Courts and Legal Services Act 1990, after section 58A (inserted by section 27 above) insert—

'58B Litigation Funding Agreements

(1) A litigation funding agreement which satisfies all of the conditions applicable to it by virtue of this section shall not be unenforceable by reason only of its being a litigation funding agreement.

(2) For the purposes of this section a litigation funding agreement is an agreement under which
- (a) a person ("the funder") agrees to fund (in whole or in part) the provision of advocacy or litigation services (by someone other than the funder) to another person ("the litigant"); and
- (b) the litigant agrees to pay a sum to the funder in specified circumstances.

(3) The following conditions are applicable to a litigation funding agreement—
- (a) the funder must be a person, or person of a description, prescribed by the Secretary of State;
- (b) the agreement must be in writing;
- (c) the agreement must not relate to proceedings which by virtue of section 58A(1) and (2) cannot be the subject of an enforceable conditional fee agreement or to proceedings of any such description as may be prescribed by the Secretary of State;
- (d) the agreement must comply with such requirements (if any) as may be so prescribed;
- (e) the sum to be paid by the litigant must consist of any costs payable to him in respect of the proceedings to which the agreement relates together with an amount calculated by reference to the funder's anticipated expenditure in funding the provision of the services; and
- (f) that amount must not exceed such percentage of that anticipated expenditure as may be prescribed by the Secretary of State in relation to proceedings of the description to which the agreement relates.

(4) Regulations under subsection (3)(a) may require a person to be approved by the Secretary of State or by a prescribed person.

(5) The requirements which the Secretary of State may prescribe under subsection (3)(d)—
- (a) include requirements for the funder to have provided prescribed information to the litigant before the agreement is made; and
- (b) may be different for different descriptions of litigation funding agreements.

(6) In this section (and in the definitions of "advocacy services" and "litigation services" as they apply for its purposes) "proceedings" includes any sort of proceedings for resolving disputes (and not just proceedings in a court), whether commenced or contemplated.

(7) Before making regulations under this section, the Secretary of State shall consult—
- (a) the designated judges;
- (b) the General Council of the Bar;
- (c) the Law Society; and
- (d) such other bodies as he considers appropriate.

(8) A costs order made in any proceedings may, subject in the case of court proceedings to rules of court, include provision requiring the payment of any amount payable under a litigation funding agreement.

(9) Rules of court may make provision with respect to the assessment of any costs which include fees payable under a litigation funding agreement.'

Costs

29. Recovery of Insurance Premiums by Way of Costs

Where in any proceedings a costs order is made in favour of any party who has taken out an insurance policy against the risk of incurring a liability in those proceedings, the costs payable to him may, subject in the case of court proceedings to rules of court, include costs in respect of the premium of the policy.

30. Recovery Where Body Undertakes to Meet Costs Liabilities

(1) This section applies where a body of a prescribed description undertakes to meet (in accordance with arrangements satisfying prescribed conditions) liabilities which members of the body or other persons who are parties to proceedings may incur to pay the costs of other parties to the proceedings.

(2) If in any of the proceedings a costs order is made in favour of any of the members or other persons, the costs payable to him may, subject to subsection (3) and (in the case of court proceedings) to rules of court, include an additional amount in respect of any provision made by or on behalf of the body in connection with the proceedings against the risk of having to meet such liabilities.

(3) But the additional amount shall not exceed a sum determined in a prescribed manner; and there may, in particular, be prescribed as a manner of determination one which takes into account the likely cost to the member or other person of the premium of an insurance policy against the risk of incurring a liability to pay the costs of other parties to the proceedings.

(4) In this section 'prescribed' means prescribed by regulations made by the Secretary of State by statutory instrument; and a statutory instrument containing such regulations shall be subject to annulment in pursuance of a resolution of either House of Parliament.

(5) Regulations under subsection (1) may, in particular, prescribe as a description of body one which is for the time being approved by the Secretary of State or by a prescribed person.

31. Rules as to Costs

In section 51 of the Supreme Court Act 1981 (costs), in subsection (2) (rules regulating matters relating to costs), insert at the end 'or for securing that the amount awarded to a party in respect of the costs to be paid by him to such representatives is not limited to what would have been payable by him to them if he had not been awarded costs.'

PART IV APPEALS, COURTS, JUDGES AND COURT PROCEEDINGS

Appeals

54. Permission to Appeal

(1) Rules of court may provide that any right of appeal to—
 (a) a county court,
 (b) the High Court, or
 (c) the Court of Appeal, may be exercised only with permission.

(2) This section does not apply to a right of appeal in a criminal cause or matter.

(3) For the purposes of subsection (1) rules of court may make provision as to—
 (a) the classes of case in which a right of appeal may be exercised only with permission,
 (b) the court or courts which may give permission for the purposes of this section,
 (c) any considerations to be taken into account in deciding whether permission should be given, and
 (d) any requirements to be satisfied before permission may be given, and may make different provision for different circumstances.

(4) No appeal may be made against a decision of a court under this section to give or refuse permission (but this subsection does not affect any right under rules of court to make a further application for permission to the same or another court).

(5) For the purposes of this section a right to make an application to have a case stated for the opinion of the High Court constitutes a right of appeal.

(6) For the purposes of this section a right of appeal to the Court of Appeal includes—
   (a) the right to make an application for a new trial, and
   (b) the right to make an application to set aside a verdict, finding or judgment in any cause or matter in the High Court which has been tried, or in which any issue has been tried, by a jury.

55. Second Appeals

(1) Where an appeal is made to a county court or the High Court in relation to any matter, and on hearing the appeal the court makes a decision in relation to that matter, no appeal may be made to the Court of Appeal from that decision unless the Court of Appeal considers that—
   (a) the appeal would raise an important point of principle or practice, or
   (b) there is some other compelling reason for the Court of Appeal to hear it.
(2) This section does not apply in relation to an appeal in a criminal cause or matter.

56. Power to Prescribe Alternative Destination of Appeals

(1) The Lord Chancellor may by order provide that appeals which would otherwise lie to—
   (a) a county court,
   (b) the High Court, or
   (c) the Court of Appeal,

   shall lie instead to another of those courts, as specified in the order.
(2) This section does not apply to an appeal in a criminal cause or matter.
(3) An order under subsection (1)—
   (a) may make different provision for different classes of proceedings or appeals, and
   (b) may contain consequential amendments or repeals of enactments.
(4) Before making an order under subsection (1) the Lord Chancellor shall consult—
   (a) the Lord Chief Justice,
   (b) the Master of the Rolls,
   (c) the President of the Queen's Bench Division,
   (d) the President of the Family Division, and
   (e) the Chancellor of the High Court.
(5) An order under subsection (1) shall be made by statutory instrument.
(6) No such order may be made unless a draft of it has been laid before and approved by resolution of each House of Parliament.
(7) For the purposes of this section an application to have a case stated for the opinion of the High Court constitutes an appeal.
(8) The Lord Chief Justice may nominate a judicial office holder (as defined in section 109(4) of the Constitutional Reform Act 2005) to exercise his functions under this section.

57. Assignment of Appeals to Court of Appeal

(1) Where in any proceedings in a county court or the High Court a person appeals, or seeks permission to appeal, to a court other than the Court of Appeal or the House of Lords—
   (a) the Master of the Rolls, or
   (b) the court from which or to which the appeal is made, or from which permission to appeal is sought,

   may direct that the appeal shall be heard instead by the Court of Appeal.
(2) The power conferred by subsection (l)(b) shall be subject to rules of court.

69. Vice-president of Queen's Bench Division

(1) The Lord Chief Justice may, after consulting the Lord Chancellor, appoint one of the ordinary judges of the Court of Appeal as vice-president of the Queen's Bench Division; and any person so appointed shall hold that office in accordance with the terms of his appointment.
(1A) The Lord Chief Justice may nominate a judicial office holder (as defined in section 109(4) of the Constitutional Reform Act 2005) to exercise his functions under subsection (1).

72. Reporting of Proceedings Relating to Children

In section 97 of the Children Act 1989 (privacy for children involved in certain proceedings)—

(a) in subsection (2) (which prohibits the publication of material intended or likely to identify a child as being involved in proceedings before a magistrates' court in which powers under that Act may be exercised), after 'before' insert 'the High Court, a county court or', and
(b) in subsection (8) (which makes provision about the application of certain provisions of the Magistrates' Courts Act 1980 in relation to proceedings to which section 97 applies), after 'any proceedings' insert '(before a magistrates' court)'.

PART VII SUPPLEMENTARY

105. Transitional Provisions and Savings

Schedule 14 (transitional provisions and savings) has effect.

107. Crown Application

This Act binds the Crown.

108. Commencement

(1) Subject to subsections (2) and (3), the preceding provisions of this Act shall come into force on such day as the Lord Chancellor or Secretary of State may by order made by statutory instrument appoint; and different days may be appointed for different purposes and, in the case of section 67(2), for different areas.
(2) Section 45 shall come into force on the day on which this Act is passed.
(3) The following provisions shall come into force at the end of the period of two months beginning with the day on which this Act is passed—
(a) in Part II, sections 32 to 34,
(b) Part IV, apart from section 66 and Schedule 9 and sections 67(2) and 71,
(c) in Part V, sections 74 to 76, 81, 82, 84, 86 and 87 and Schedule 10,
(d) in Part VI, section 104,
(e) Schedule 14,
(f) in Schedule 15, Part III and Part V(1) and (5), apart from the provisions specified in subsection (4), and
(g) section 107.
(4) The provisions excepted from subsection (3)(f) are the repeal of section 67(8) of the Magistrates' Courts Act 1980 (and that in Schedule 11 to the Children Act 1989) contained in Part V(1) of Schedule 15.

[*For commencement dates see the note at the end of the Act.*]

109. Extent

(1) Sections 32 to 34 and 73(2) extend to Scotland.
(2) Sections 98(2) and (3) and 104(2) extend to Northern Ireland.
(3) Sections 68, 101, 102 and 103 extend to England and Wales, Scotland and Northern Ireland.
(4) The other provisions of this Act which make amendments or repeals or revocations in other enactments also have the same extent as the enactments which they amend or repeal or revoke.
(5) Subject to subsection (4), the provisions of this Part (including paragraph 1, but not the rest, of Schedule 14) extend to England and Wales, Scotland and Northern Ireland.
(6) Subject to the preceding provisions, this Act extends to England and Wales.
(7) For the purposes of the Scotland Act 1998 this Act, so far as it extends to Scotland, shall be taken to be a pre-commencement enactment within the meaning of that Act.

110. Short title

This Act may be cited as the Access to Justice Act 1999.

Section 6

SCHEDULE 2 COMMUNITY LEGAL SERVICE: EXCLUDED SERVICES

The services which may not be funded as part of the Community Legal Service are as follows.

1. Services consisting of the provision of help (beyond the provision of general information about the law and the legal system and the availability of legal services) in relation to—
   (a) allegations of personal injury or death, other than allegations relating to clinical negligence,
   (aa) allegations of negligently caused damage to property,
   (b) conveyancing,
   (c) boundary disputes,
   (d) the making of wills,
   (e) matters of trust law,
   (f) defamation or malicious falsehood,
   (g) matters of company or partnership law,
   (h) other matters arising out of the carrying on of a business, or
   (i) attending an interview conducted on behalf of the Secretary of State with a view to his reaching a decision on a claim for asylum (as defined by section 167(1) of the Immigration and Asylum Act 1999).
2. Advocacy in any proceedings except—
   (1) proceedings in—
      (a) the House of Lords in its judicial capacity,
      (b) the Judicial Committee of the Privy Council in the exercise of its jurisdiction under the Government of Wales Act 1998, the Scotland Act 1998 or the Northern Ireland Act 1998,
      (c) the Court of Appeal,
      (d) the High Court,
      (e) any county court,
      (f) the Employment Appeal Tribunal,
      (g) any Mental Health Review Tribunal,
      (h) the Asylum and Immigration Tribunal,
      (ha) the Special Immigration Appeals Commission,
      (i) the Proscribed Organisations Appeal Commission,
   (2) proceedings in the Crown Court—
      (a) for the variation or discharge of an order under section 5 of the Protection from Harassment Act 1997,
      (b) which relate to an order under section 10 of the Crime and Disorder Act 1998,
      (d) which relate to an order under paragraph 6 of Schedule 1 to the Anti-terrorism, Crime and Security Act 2001, or
      (e) under the Proceeds of Crime Act 2002 to the extent specified in paragraph 3,
   (3) proceedings in a magistrates' court—
      (a) under section 43 or 47 of the National Assistance Act 1948, section 22 of the Maintenance Orders Act 1950, section 4 of the Maintenance Orders Act 1958 or section 106 of the Social Security Administration Act 1992,
      (b) under Part I of the Maintenance Orders (Reciprocal Enforcement) Act 1972 relating to a maintenance order made by a court of a country outside the United Kingdom,
      (c) in relation to an application for leave of the court to remove a child from a person's custody under section 36 of the Adoption and Children Act 2002 or in which the making of a placement order or adoption order (within the meaning of the Adoption and Children Act 2002) or an order under section 41 or 84 of that Act is opposed by any party to the proceedings,
      (d) for or in relation to an order under Part I of the Domestic Proceedings and Magistrates' Courts Act 1978 or Schedule 6 to the Civil Partnership Act 2004,
      (e) under the Children Act 1989,
      (f) under section 30 of the Human Fertilisation and Embryology Act 1990,
      (g) under section 20 of the Child Support Act 1991,
      (h) under Part IV of the Family Law Act 1996,
      (i) for the variation or discharge of an order under section 5 of the Protection from Harassment Act 1997,
      (j) under section 8 or 11 of the Crime and Disorder Act 1998,

(k) for an order or direction under paragraph 3, 5, 6, 9 or 10 of Schedule 1 to the Anti-terrorism, Crime and Security Act 2001,

(l) for an order or direction under section 295, 297, 298, 301 or 302 of the Proceeds of Crime Act 2002, and

(4) proceedings before any person to whom a case is referred (in whole or in part) in any proceedings within paragraphs (1) to (3).

3. (1) These are the proceedings under the Proceeds of Crime Act 2002—

(za) an application under section 42 for a restraint order;

(a) an application under section 42(3) to vary or discharge a restraint order or an order under section 41(7);

(b) proceedings which relate to a direction under section 54(3) or 56(3) as to the distribution of funds in the hands of a receiver;

(c) an application under section 62 relating to action taken or proposed to be taken by a receiver;

(d) an application under section 63 to vary or discharge an order under any of sections 48 to 53 for the appointment of or conferring powers on a receiver;

(e) an application under section 72 or 73 for the payment of compensation;

(f) proceedings which relate to an order under section 298 for the forfeiture of cash;

(g) an application under section 351(3), 362(3), 369(3) or 375(2) to vary or discharge certain orders made under Part 8.

(2) But sub-paragraph (1) does not authorise the funding of the provision of services to a defendant (within the meaning of Part 1 of that Act) in relation to—

(a) proceedings mentioned in paragraph (b);

(b) an application under section 73 for the payment of compensation if the confiscation order was varied under section 29.

Section 105

SCHEDULE 14 TRANSITIONAL PROVISIONS AND SAVINGS

PART I GENERAL

1.—(1) The Lord Chancellor may by order made by statutory instrument make such transitional provisions and savings he considers appropriate in connection with the coming into force of any provision of this Act.

(2) Nothing in the following provisions of this Schedule limits sub-paragraph (1).

(3) Nothing in this Schedule limits the operation of sections 16 and 17 of the Interpretation Act 1978 (effect of repeals).

PART II LEGAL SERVICES COMMISSION

Replacement of Legal Aid Board by Legal Services Commission

2.—(1) When section 1 of this Act comes into force—

(a) the functions of the Legal Aid Board, and

(b) the property, rights and liabilities of the Board,

shall by virtue of this paragraph be transferred to the Legal Services Commission.

(2) Sub-paragraph (1)(b) has effect in relation to any property, rights or liabilities to which it applies in spite of any provision (of whatever nature) which would otherwise prevent or restrict their transfer.

3.—(1) Anything which, immediately before section 1 of this Act comes into force, is in the process of being done by or in relation to the Legal Aid Board may, if it relates to anything transferred by paragraph 2(1), be continued by or in relation to the Legal Services Commission.

(2) Anything done (or having effect as if done) by or in relation to the Legal Aid Board before the time when section 1 of this Act comes into force for the purpose of, or in connection with, anything transferred by paragraph 2(1) shall, so far as is required for continuing its effect after that time, have effect as if done by or in relation to the Legal Services Commission.

(3) Any reference to the Legal Aid Board in any document, including any enactment, constituting or relating to anything transferred by paragraph 2(1) shall, so far as is required for giving effect to that paragraph, be construed as a reference to the Legal Services Commission.

Further Provision for Legal Aid Board and Legal Services Commission

8.—(1) The Lord Chancellor may by order made by statutory instrument make any consequential, incidental, supplementary or transitional provisions, and any savings, which appear to him to be appropriate in consequence of or otherwise in connection with—

(a) the transfers effected by paragraph 2(1), or

(b) the abolition of the Legal Aid Board.

(2) An order under sub-paragraph (1) may include provisions in the form of amendments or repeals of this Part of this Schedule or any other enactment.

PART III LEGAL SERVICES

Conditional Fee Agreements

10. Any order made under section 58(4) or (5) of the Courts and Legal Services Act 1990 and in force immediately before the time when section 27 of this Act comes into force shall have effect after that time (until revoked) as if made under section 58(4) as substituted by that section.

11. Any regulations made under section 58(1)(c) of the Courts and Legal Services Act 1990 and in force immediately before the time when section 27 of this Act comes into force shall have effect after that time (until revoked) as if made under section 58(3)(c) as substituted by that section.

PART IV REPORTING OF PROCEEDINGS ABOUT CHILDREN

18. Section 97(2) of the Children Act 1989 (as amended by section 72 of this Act) shall not apply in relation to proceedings before a county court or the High Court which have begun before the coming into force of that section.

COMMENCEMENT

The commencement dates of the provisions printed above are:
ss. 1–11, 19–23, 25, 26 and 27 (see note 1): 1 April 2000, by SI 2000/774, art. 2;
s. 28: to be brought into force by order of the Lord Chancellor under s. 108(1);
ss. 29 (see note 1) and 30 (see note 1): 1 April 2000, by SI 2000/774, art. 2;
s. 31: to be brought into force by order of the Lord Chancellor under s. 108(1);
ss. 54–7, 69(1), 70 and 72: 27 September 1999, by s. 108(3);
s. 105: 27 September 1999, by SI 1999/2657;
s. 107: 27 September 1999, by s. 108(3);
ss. 108–10: 27 July 1999;
sch. 2: 1 April 2000, by SI 2000/774, art. 2;
sch. 14: 27 September 1999, by s. 108(3).

Note 1. SI 2000/900 makes the following transitional provisions:

1. This Order may be cited as the Access to Justice Act 1999 (Transitional Provisions) Order 2000 and shall come into force on 1st April 2000.

(2) In this Order a reference to a section by number alone means the section so numbered in the Access to Justice Act 1999.

2.—(1) Section 58A(6) and (7) of the Courts and Legal Services Act 1990 shall not apply, as regards a party to proceedings, to:

(a) any proceedings in relation to which that party entered into a conditional fee agreement before 1st April 2000; or

(b) any proceedings arising out of the same cause of action as any proceedings to which sub-paragraph (a) refers.

(2) The coming into force of section 27 (Conditional fee agreements) shall not affect the validity of any conditional fee agreement entered into before 1st April 2000, and any such agreement shall continue to have effect after that date as if section 27 had not come into force.

(3) In paragraphs 1(a) and (2) 'conditional fee agreement' has the same meaning as in section 58 of the Courts and Legal Services Act 1990 as that section stands immediately before the coming into force of section 27 of the Access to Justice Act 1999.

3. Section 29 (Recovery of insurance premiums by way of costs) shall not apply, as regards a party to proceedings, to:
   (a) any proceedings in relation to which that party took out an insurance policy of the sort referred to in section 29 before 1st April 2000; or
   (b) any proceedings arising out of the same cause of action as any proceedings to which sub-paragraph (a) refers.

4. Section 30 (Recovery where body undertakes to meet costs liabilities) shall not apply, as regards a party to proceedings, to:
   (a) any proceedings in relation to which that party gave an undertaking before 1st April 2000 which, if it had been given after that date, would have been an undertaking to which section 30(1) applied; or
   (b) any proceedings arising out of the same cause of action as any proceedings to which sub-paragraph (a) refers.

NOTES ON TEXT

Only selected provisions of the Act are printed above, incorporating the following amendments:

ss. 1 to 6, 8, 9, 19, 20, 23, 25 and 26 amended by Secretary of State for Constitutional Affairs Order 2003 (SI 2003/1887), sch. 2, para. 11(1)(a);

s. 28 (inserted s. 58B of Courts and Legal Services Act 1990) amended by Secretary of State for Constitutional Affairs Order 2003 (SI 2003/1887), sch. 2, para. 11(1)(b);

s. 30 amended by Secretary of State for Constitutional Affairs Order 2003 (SI 2003/1887), sch. 2, para. 11(1)(c);

s. 56 amended by Constitutional Reform Act 2005, sch. 4, para. 280 (in force by SI 2005/2505 and by SI 2006/2014);

s. 69 amended by Constitutional Reform Act 2005, sch. 4, para. 282 (in force by SI 2006/1014);

s. 108 amended by Secretary of State for Constitutional Affairs Order 2003 (SI 2003/1887), sch. 2, para. 11(2);

sch. 2, para. 1, amended by: (a) Community Legal Service (Scope) Regulations 2004 (SI 2004/1055); (b) Community Legal Service (Scope) Regulations 2005 (SI 2005/2008), reg. 2;

sch. 2, para. 2, amended by: (a) Community Legal Service (Scope) Regulations 2000 (SI 2000/822); (b) Terrorism Act 2000, sch. 15, para. 19, and sch. 16, part I (in force by SI 2001/421); (c) Child Support, Pensions and Social Security Act 2000, sch. 9, part IX (in force by SI 2001/774); (d) Anti-terrorism, Crime and Security Act 2001, s. 2(1) to (3) and sch. 8, part 1 (in force by SI 2001/4019); (e) Proceeds of Crime Act 2002, sch. 11, para. 36(1)–(3), and sch. 12 (in force by SI 2002/3015); (f) Nationality, Immigration and Asylum Act 2002, s. 116 (in force by SI 2003/754); (g) Asylum and Immigration (Treatment of Claimants, etc.) Act 2004, sch. 2, para. 14 (in force by SI 2005/565); (h) Adoption and Children Act 2002, sch. 3, para. 102 (in force by SI 2005/2213); (i) Civil Partnership Act 2004, sch. 27, para. 156 (in force by SI 2005/3175);

sch. 2, para. 3, inserted by Proceeds of Crime Act 2002, sch. 11, para. 36(1) and (4) (in force by SI 2002/3015); amended by Community Legal Service (Scope) Regulations 2005 (SI 2005/2008), reg. 3.

Access to Justice Act 1999 (Destination of Appeals) Order 2000

(SI 2000/1071)

The Lord Chancellor, in exercise of the powers conferred on him by section 56(1) and (3) of the Access to Justice Act 1999, having consulted as required by section 56(4), makes the following Order of which a draft has, in accordance with section 56(6), been laid before and approved by resolution of each House of Parliament:

1. Citation, Commencement and Interpretation

(1) This Order maybe cited as the Access to Justice Act 1999 (Destination of Appeals) Order 2000 and shall come into force on 2nd May 2000.

(2) In this Order—

- (a) 'decision' includes any judgment, order or direction of the High Court or a county court;
- (b) 'family proceedings' means proceedings which are business of any description which in the High Court is for the time being assigned to the Family Division and to no other Division by or under section 61 of (and Schedule 1 to) the Supreme Court Act 1981; and
- (c) 'final decision' means a decision of a court that would finally determine (subject to any possible appeal or detailed assessment of costs) the entire proceedings whichever way the court decided the issues before it.

(3) A decision of a court shall be treated as a final decision where it—

- (a) is made at the conclusion of part of a hearing or trial which has been split into parts: and
- (b) would, if made at the conclusion of that hearing or trial, be a final decision under paragraph (2)(c).

(4) Articles 2 to 6—

- (a) do not apply to an appeal in family proceedings: and
- (b) are subject to—
  - (i) any enactment that provides a different route of appeal (other than section 16(1) of the Supreme Court Act 1981 or section 77(1) of the County Courts Act 1984); and
  - (ii) any requirement to obtain permission to appeal.

2. Appeals from the High Court

Subject to articles 4 and 5, an appeal shall lie to a judge of the High Court where the decision to be appealed is made by—

- (a) a person holding an office referred to in Part II of Schedule 2 to the Supreme Court Act 1981;
- (b) a district judge of the High Court; or
- (c) a person appointed to act as a deputy for any person holding such an office as is referred to in sub-paragraphs (a) and (b) or to act as a temporary additional officer in any such office.

3. Appeals from a County Court

(1) Subject to articles 4 and 5 and to paragraph (2), an appeal shall lie from a decision of a county court to the High Court.

(2) Subject to articles 4 and 5, where the decision to be appealed is made by a district judge or deputy district judge of a county court, an appeal shall lie to a judge of a county court.

4. Appeals in a Claim Allocated to the Multi-track or in Specialist Proceedings

An appeal shall lie to the Court of Appeal where the decision to be appealed is a final decision—

- (a) in a claim made under Part 7 of the Civil Procedure Rules 1998 and allocated to the multi-track under those Rules; or
- (b) made in proceedings under the Companies Act 1985 or the Companies Act 1989 or to which Sections I, II or III of Part 57 or any of Parts 58 to 63 of the Civil Procedure Rules 1998 apply.

5. Appeals Where Decision Was Itself Made on Appeal

Where—

(a) an appeal is made to a county court or the High Court (other than from the decision of an officer of the court authorised to assess costs by the Lord Chancellor); and

(b) on hearing the appeal the court makes a decision,

an appeal shall lie from that decision to the Court of Appeal and not to any other court.

6. Transitional Provisions

Where a person has filed a notice of appeal or applied for permission to appeal before 2nd May 2000—

(a) this Order shall not apply to the appeal to which that notice or application relates; and

(b) that appeal shall lie to the court to which it would have lain before 2nd May 2000.

NOTES ON TEXT

The text printed above incorporates the following amendments:

art. 4 amended by: (a) Civil Procedure (Modification of Enactments) Order 2002 (SI 2002/439), art. 12; (b) Civil Procedure (Modification of Enactments) Order 2003 (SI 2003/490), art. 2

The following provisions are omitted: arts 7 and 8 (consequential amendments).

Access to Justice (Membership Organisation) Regulations 2005

(SI 2005/2306)

The Secretary of State, in exercise of the powers conferred upon the Lord Chancellor by sections 30(1) and (3) to (5) of the Access to Justice Act 1999 and now vested in him makes the following Regulations:

1. Citation, Commencement and Interpretation

(1) These Regulations may be cited as the Access to Justice (Membership Organisation) Regulations 2005 and shall come into force on 1st November 2005.

(2) In these Regulations a reference to a section by number alone is a reference to the section so numbered in the Access to Justice Act 1999.

2. Revocation and Transitional

(1) Subject to paragraph (2), the Access to Justice (Membership Organisation) Regulations 2000 (the '2000 Regulations') are revoked.

(2) The 2000 Regulations shall continue to have effect for the purposes of arrangements entered into before 1st November 2005 as if these Regulations had not come into force.

3. Bodies of a Prescribed Description

The bodies which are prescribed for the purpose of section 30 (recovery where body undertakes to meet costs liabilities) are those bodies which are for the time being approved by the Secretary of State for that purpose.

4. Requirements for Arrangements to Meet Costs Liabilities

(1) Section 30(1) applies to arrangements which satisfy the following conditions.

(2) The arrangements must be in writing.

(3) The arrangements must contain a statement specifying the circumstances in which the member may be liable to pay costs of the proceedings.

5. Recovery of Additional Amount for Insurance Costs

(1) Where an additional amount is included in costs by virtue of section 30(2) (costs payable to a member of a body or other person party to the proceedings to include an additional amount in respect of provision made by the body against the risk of having to meet the member's or other person's liabilities to pay other parties' costs), that additional amount must not exceed the following sum.

(2) That sum is the likely cost to the member of the body or, as the case may be, the other person who is a party to the proceedings in which the costs order is made of the premium of an insurance policy against the risk of incurring a liability to pay the costs of other parties to the proceedings.

Access to Justice (Membership Organisations) Regulations 2000

(SI 2000/693)

The Lord Chancellor, in exercise of the powers conferred on him by section 30(1) and (3) to (5) of the Access to Justice Act 1999 and all other powers enabling him hereby makes the following Regulations:

1. Citation, Commencement and Interpretation

(1) These Regulations may be cited as the Access to Justice (Membership Organisations) Regulations 2000.
(2) These Regulations come into force on 1st April 2000.

2. Bodies of a Prescribed Description

The bodies which are prescribed for the purpose of section 30 of the Access to Justice Act 1999 (recovery where body undertakes to meet costs liabilities) are those bodies which are for the time being approved by the Lord Chancellor for that purpose.

3. Requirements for Arrangements to Meet Costs Liabilities

(1) Section 30(1) of the Access to Justice Act 1999 applies to arrangements which satisfy the following conditions.
(2) The arrangements must be in writing.
(3) The arrangements must contain a statement specifying—
(a) the circumstances in which the member or other party may be liable to pay costs of the proceedings,
(b) whether such a liability arises—
(i) if those circumstances only partly occur,
(ii) irrespective of whether those circumstances occur, and
(iii) on the termination of the arrangements for any reason,
(c) the basis on which the amount of the liability is calculated, and
(d) the procedure for seeking assessment of costs.
(4) A copy of the part of the arrangements containing the statement must be given to the member or other party to the proceedings whose liabilities the body is undertaking to meet as soon as possible after the undertaking is given.

4. Recovery of Additional Amount for Insurance Costs

(1) Where an additional amount is included in costs by virtue of section 30(2) of the Access to Justice Act 1999 (costs payable to a member of a body or other person party to the proceedings to include an additional amount in respect of provision made by the body against the risk of having to meet the member's or other person's liabilities to pay other parties' costs), that additional amount must not exceed the following sum.
(2) That sum is the likely cost to the member of the body or, as the case may be, the other person who is a party to the proceedings in which the costs order is made of the premium of an insurance policy against the risk of incurring a liability to pay the costs of other parties to the proceedings.

REVOCATION

As from 1 November 2005, these regulations are revoked by the Access to Justice (Membership Organisation) Regulations 2005 (SI 2005/2306), reg. 2(1). These regulations continue to have effect for the purposes of arrangements entered into before 1 November 2005 as if the 2005 regulations had not come into force (SI 2005/2306, reg. 2(2)).

Administration of Justice Act 1960

(1960 CHAPTER 65)

An Act to make further provision for appeals to the House of Lords in criminal cases; to amend the law relating to contempt of court, habeas corpus and certiorari; and for purposes connected with the matters aforesaid. [27th October 1960]

Contempt of Court, Habeas Corpus and Certiorari

12. Publication of Information Relating to Proceedings in Private

(1) The publication of information relating to proceedings before any court sitting in private shall not of itself be contempt of court except in the following cases, that is to say—
  (a) where the proceedings—
    (i) relate to the exercise of the inherent jurisdiction of the High Court with respect to minors;
    (ii) are brought under the Children Act 1989; or
    (iii) otherwise relate wholly or mainly to the maintenance or upbringing of a minor;
  (b) where the proceedings are brought under Part VIII of the Mental Health Act 1959, or under any provision of that Act authorising an application or reference to be made to a Mental Health Review Tribunal or to a county court;
  (c) where the court sits in private for reasons of national security during that part of the proceedings about which the information in question is published;
  (d) where the information relates to a secret process, discovery or invention which is in issue in the proceedings;
  (e) where the court (having power to do so) expressly prohibits the publication of all information relating to the proceedings or of information of the description which is published.

(2) Without prejudice to the foregoing subsection, the publication of the text or a summary of the whole or part of an order made by a court sitting in private shall not of itself be contempt of court except where the court (having power to do so) expressly prohibits the publication.

(3) In this section references to a court include references to a judge and to a tribunal and to any person exercising the functions of a court, a judge or a tribunal; and references to a court sitting in private include references to a court sitting in camera or in chambers.

(4) Nothing in this section shall be construed as implying that any publication is punishable as contempt of court which would not be so punishable apart from this section.

13. Appeal in Cases of Contempt of Court

(1) Subject to the provisions of this section, an appeal shall lie under this section from any order or decision of a court in the exercise of jurisdiction to punish for contempt of court (including criminal contempt); and in relation to any such order or decision the provisions of this section shall have effect in substitution for any other enactment relating to appeals in civil or criminal proceedings.

(2) An appeal under this section shall lie in any case at the instance of the defendant and, in the case of an application for committal or attachment, at the instance of the applicant; and the appeal shall lie—
  (a) from an order or decision of any inferior court not referred to in the next following paragraph, to the High Court;
  (b) from an order or decision of a county court or any other inferior court from which appeals generally lie to the Court of Appeal, and from an order or decision (other than a decision on an appeal under this section) of a single judge of the High Court, or of any court having the powers of the High Court or of a judge of that court, to the Court of Appeal;
  (bb) from an order or decision of the Crown Court to the Court of Appeal;
  (c) from a decision of a single judge of the High Court on an appeal under this section, from an order or decision of a Divisional Court or the Court of Appeal (including a decision of

Selected Legislation

either of those courts on an appeal under this section), and from an order or decision of the Court of Criminal Appeal or the Courts-Martial Appeal Court, to the House of Lords.

(3) The court to which an appeal is brought under this section may reverse or vary the order or decision of the court below, and make such other order as may be just; and without prejudice to the inherent powers of any court referred to in subsection (2) of this section, provision may be made by rules of court for authorising the release on bail of an appellant under this section.

(4) Subsections (2) to (4) of section one and section two of this Act shall apply to an appeal to the House of Lords under this section as they apply to an appeal to that House under the said section one, except that so much of the said subsection (2) as restricts the grant of leave to appeal shall apply only where the decision of the court below is a decision on appeal to that court under this section.

(5) In this section 'court' includes any tribunal or person having power to punish for contempt; and references in this section to an order or decision of a court in the exercise of jurisdiction to punish for contempt of court include references—

(a) to an order or decision of the High Court, the Crown Court or a county court under any enactment enabling that court to deal with an offence as if it were contempt of court;

(b) to an order or decision of a county court, or of any court having the powers of a county court, under section 14,92 or 118 of the County Courts Act 1984;

(c) to an order or decision of a magistrates' court under subsection (3) of section 63 of the Magistrates' Courts Act 1980,

but do not include references to orders under section five of the Debtors Act 1869, or under any provision of the Magistrates' Courts Act 1980, or the County Courts Act 1984 except those referred to in paragraphs (b) and (c) of this subsection and except sections 38 and 142 of the last mentioned Act so far as those sections confer jurisdiction in respect of contempt of court.

(6) This section does not apply to a conviction or sentence in respect of which an appeal lies under Part I of the Criminal Appeal Act 1968, or to a decision of the criminal division of the Court of Appeal under that Part of that Act.

14. Procedure on Application For Habeas Corpus

(2) Notwithstanding anything in any enactment or rule of law, where a criminal or civil application for habeas corpus has been made by or in respect of any person, no such application shall again be made by or in respect of that person on the same grounds, whether to the same court or judge or to any other court or judge, unless fresh evidence is adduced in support of the application; and no such application shall in any case be made to the Lord Chancellor.

(3) In every case where the person by or in respect of whom an application for habeas corpus is made is restrained as a person liable, or treated by virtue of any enactment as liable, to be detained in pursuance of an order or direction under Part V of the Mental Health Act 1959 (otherwise than by virtue of paragraph (e) or paragraph

(f) of subsection (2) of section seventy-three of that Act), the application shall be deemed for the purposes of this section and of any appeal in the proceedings to constitute a criminal cause or matter.

15. Appeal in Habeas Corpus Proceedings

(1) Subject to the provisions of this section, an appeal shall lie, in any proceedings upon application for habeas corpus, whether civil or criminal, against an order for the release of the person restrained as well as against the refusal of such an order.

(3) In relation to a decision of the High Court on a criminal application for habeas corpus, section one of this Act shall have effect as if so much of subsection (2) as restricts the grant of leave to appeal were omitted.

(4) Except as provided by section five of this Act in the case of an appeal against an order of the High Court on a criminal application, an appeal brought by virtue of this section shall not affect the right of the person restrained to be discharged in pursuance of the order under appeal and (unless an order under subsection (1) of that section is in force at the determination of the appeal) to remain at large regardless of the decision on appeal.

Supplementary

17. Interpretation

(1) In this Act any reference to the defendant shall be construed—
  (a) in relation to proceedings for an offence, and in relation to an application for an order of mandamus, prohibition or certiorari in connection with such proceedings, as a reference to the person who was or would have been the defendant in those proceedings;
  (b) in relation to any proceedings or order for or in respect of contempt of court, as a reference to the person against whom the proceedings were brought or the order was made;
  (c) in relation to a criminal application for habeas corpus, as a reference to the person by or in respect of whom that application was made,

and any reference to the prosecutor shall be construed accordingly.

(2) In this Act 'application for habeas corpus' means an application for a writ of habeas corpus ad subjiciendum and references to a criminal application or civil application shall be construed according as the application does or does not constitute a criminal cause or matter.

(3) In this Act any reference to the court below shall, in relation to any function of a Divisional Court, be construed as a reference to the Divisional Court or to a judge according as the function is by virtue of rules of court exercisable by the Divisional Court or a judge.

(4) An appeal under section one of this Act shall be treated for the purposes of this Act as pending until any application for leave to appeal is disposed of and, if leave to appeal is granted, until the appeal is disposed of; and for the purposes of this Act an application for leave to appeal shall be treated as disposed of at the expiration of the time within which it may be made, if it is not made within that time.

(6) Any reference in this Act to any other enactment is a reference thereto as amended by or under any other enactment, including this Act.

[*In s. 17(1)(a), by the Supreme Court Act 1981, s. 29(5), the reference to an order of mandamus is to be read as a reference to a mandatory order, the reference to an order of prohibition is to be read as a reference to a prohibiting order and the reference to an order of certiorari is to be read as a reference to a quashing order.*]

20. Short Title and Extent

(1) This Act may be cited as the Administration of Justice Act 1960.

(2) Except so far as it relates to appeals from the Courts-Martial Appeal Court and to proceedings preliminary or incidental to such appeals, this Act shall not extend to Scotland.

NOTES ON TEXT

Only ss. 12 to 15, 17 and 20 are printed here. The text incorporates the following amendments:

s. 12 amended by Children Act 1989, sch. 13, para. 14 (in force by SI 1991/828, art. 3(2));

s. 13 amended by: (a) Criminal Appeal Act 1968, sch. 5, part I (in force by s. 55(2) of that Act and SI 1967/1234, sch. 3); (b) Courts Act 1971, sch. 8, para. 40 and sch. 11, part II (in force by SI 1971/1151); (c) Magistrates' Courts Act 1980, sch. 7, para. 36 (in force by SI 1981/457); (d) Supreme Court Act 1981, sch. 7; (e) County Courts Act 1984, sch. 2, para. 25; (f) Access to Justice Act 1999, s. 64 and sch. 15, part III (in force by s. 108(3) of that Act);

ss. 14(1) and 15(2) repealed by Access to Justice Act 1999, s. 65(1) and sch. 15, part III (in force by s. 108(3) of that Act);

s. 15(3) amended by Access to Justice Act 1999, s. 65(2) (in force by s. 108(3) of that Act);

s. 17(5) repealed by Criminal Appeal Act 1966, sch. 3 (in force by SI 1966/1018).

Administration of Justice Act 1969

(1969 CHAPTER 58)

An Act . . . to make further provision for appeals from the High Court (whether in England and Wales or in Northern Ireland) to the House of Lords; . . . and for purposes connected with the matters aforesaid. [22nd October 1969]

PART II APPEAL FROM HIGH COURT TO HOUSE OF LORDS

12. Grant of Certificate by Trial Judge

(1) Where on the application of any of the parties to any proceedings to which this section applies the judge is satisfied—

(a) that the relevant conditions are fulfilled in relation to his decision in those proceedings, and

(b) that a sufficient case for an appeal to the House of Lords under this Part of this Act has been made out to justify an application for leave to bring such an appeal, and

(c) that all the parties to the proceedings consent to the grant of a certificate under this section,

the judge, subject to the following provisions of this Part of this Act, may grant a certificate to that effect.

(2) This section applies to any civil proceedings in the High Court which are either—

(a) proceedings before a single judge of the High Court,

(c) proceedings before a Divisional Court.

(3) Subject to any Order in Council made under the following provisions of this section, for the purposes of this section the relevant conditions, in relation to a decision of the judge in any proceedings, are that a point of law of general public importance is involved in that decision and that that point of law either—

(a) relates wholly or mainly to the construction of an enactment or of a statutory instrument, and has been fully argued in the proceedings and fully considered in the judgment of the judge in the proceedings, or

(b) is one in respect of which the judge is bound by a decision of the Court of Appeal or of the House of Lords in previous proceedings, and was fully considered in the judgments given by the Court of Appeal or the House of Lords (as the case may be) in those previous proceedings.

(4) Any application for a certificate under this section shall be made to the judge immediately after he gives judgment in the proceedings:

Provided that the judge may in any particular case entertain any such application made at any later time before the end of the period of fourteen days beginning with the date on which that judgment is given or such other period as may be prescribed by rules of court.

(5) No appeal shall lie against the grant or refusal of a certificate under this section.

(6) Her Majesty may by Order in Council amend subsection (3) of this section by altering, deleting, or substituting one or more new paragraphs for, either or both of paragraphs (a) and (b) of that subsection, or by adding one or more further paragraphs.

(7) Any Order in Council made under this section shall be subject to annulment in pursuance of a resolution of either House of Parliament.

(8) In this Part of this Act 'civil proceedings' means any proceedings other than proceedings in a criminal cause or matter, and 'the judge', in relation to any proceedings to which this section applies, means the judge or commissioner referred to in paragraph (a) or paragraph (b) of subsection (2) of this section, or the Divisional Court referred to in paragraph (c) of that subsection, as the case may be.

13. Leave to Appeal to House of Lords

(1) Where in any proceedings the judge grants a certificate under section 12 of this Act, then, at any time within one month from the date on which that certificate is granted or such extended time as in any particular case the House of Lords may allow, any of the parties to the proceedings may make an application to the House of Lords under this section.

(2) Subject to the following provisions of this section, if on such an application it appears to the House of Lords to be expedient to do so, the House may grant leave for an appeal to be brought directly to the House; and where leave is granted under this section—
   (a) no appeal from the decision of the judge to which the certificate relates shall lie to the Court of Appeal, but
   (b) an appeal shall lie from that decision to the House of Lords.
(3) Applications under this section shall be determined without a hearing.
(4) Any order of the House of Lords which provides for applications under this section to be determined by a committee of the House—
   (a) shall direct that the committee shall consist of or include not less than three of the persons designated as Lords of Appeal in accordance with section 5 of the Appellate Jurisdiction Act 1876, and
   (b) may direct that the decision of the committee on any such application shall be taken on behalf of the House.
(5) Without prejudice to subsection (2) of this section, no appeal shall lie to the Court of Appeal from a decision of the judge in respect of which a certificate is granted under section 12 of this Act until—
   (a) the time within which an application can be made under this section has expired, and
   (b) where such an application is made, that application has been determined in accordance with the preceding provisions of this section.

14. Appeal Where Leave Granted

In relation to any appeal which lies to the House of Lords by virtue of subsection (2) of section 13 of this Act—
(a) section 4 of the Appellate Jurisdiction Act 1876 (which provides for the bringing of appeals to the House of Lords by way of petition),
(b) section 5 of that Act (which regulates the composition of the House for the hearing and determination of appeals), and
(c) except in so far as those orders otherwise provide, any orders of the House of Lords made with respect to the matters specified in section 11 of that Act (which relates to the procedure on appeals),
shall have effect as they have effect in relation to appeals under that Act.

15. Cases Excluded From s. 12

(1) No certificate shall be granted under section 12 of this Act in respect of a decision of the judge in any proceedings where by virtue of any enactment, apart from the provisions of this Part of this Act, no appeal would lie from that decision to the Court of Appeal, with or without the leave of the judge or of the Court of Appeal.
(2) No certificate shall be granted under section 12 of this Act in respect of a decision of the judge where—
   (b) by virtue of any enactment, apart from the provisions of this Part of this Act, no appeal would (with or without the leave of the Court of Appeal or of the House of Lords) lie from any decision of the Court of Appeal on an appeal from the decision of the judge.
(3) Where by virtue of any enactment, apart from the provisions of this Part of this Act, no appeal would lie to the Court of Appeal from the decision of the judge except with the leave of the judge or of the Court of Appeal, no certificate shall be granted under section 12 of this Act in respect of that decision unless it appears to the judge that apart from the provisions of this Part of this Act it would be a proper case for granting such leave.
(4) No certificate shall be granted under section 12 of this Act where the decision of the judge, or any order made by him in pursuance of that decision, is made in the exercise of jurisdiction to punish for contempt of court.

PART IV MISCELLANEOUS AND SUPPLEMENTARY PROVISIONS

36. Short Title, Extent and Commencement

(1) This Act may be cited as the Administration of Justice Act 1969.

(2) This Act (except section 24, subsections (1) and (2) of section 27, sections 30, 31, 34, 35 and this section and Schedules 1 and 2) shall not extend to Scotland.
(3) This Act (except Part II and sections 20, 21, 24, 27, 30, 31, 33 to 35 and this section and Schedules 1 and 2) shall not extend to Northern Ireland.
(4) Section 24 of this Act shall extend to the Isle of Man.
[*Sections 12 to 15 were brought into force by SI 1970/672, s. 36 by SI 1969/1607.*]

NOTES ON TEXT

Only ss. 12 to 15 and 36 are printed here. The text incorporates the following amendments:
s. 12(2)(a) amended by Supreme Court 1981, sch. 7;
s. 12(2)(b) repealed by Courts Act 1971, sch. 11, part IV (in force by SI 1971/1151);
s. 15(2)(a) repealed by Administration of Justice Act 1977, sch. 5, part IV;
s. 36(5) and (6) repealed by Statute Law (Repeals) Act 2004, sch. 1, part 1, group 4.

Attachment of Earnings Act 1971

(1971 CHAPTER 53)

Cases in which attachment is available

1. Courts with Power to Attach Earnings

(1) The High Court may make an attachment of earnings order to secure payments under a High Court maintenance order.

(2) A county court may make an attachment of earnings order to secure—
  (a) payments under a High Court or a county court maintenance order;
  (b) the payment of a judgment debt, other than a debt of less than £5 or such other sum as may be prescribed by county court rules; or
  (c) payments under an administration order.

(3) A magistrates' court may make an attachment of earnings order to secure—
  (a) payments under a magistrates' court maintenance order;
  (b) the payment of any sum adjudged to be paid by a conviction or treated (by any enactment relating to the collection and enforcement of fines, costs, compensation or forfeited recognisances) as so adjudged to be paid; or
  (c) the payment of any sum required to be paid by [an] order under section 17(2) of the Access to Justice Act 1999.

(4) The following provisions of this Act apply, except where otherwise stated, to attachment of earnings orders made, or to be made, by any court.

(5) Any power conferred by this Act to make an attachment of earnings order includes a power to make such an order to secure the discharge of liabilities arising before the coming into force of this Act.

2. Principal Definitions

In this Act—

(a) 'maintenance order' means any order specified in Schedule 1 to this Act and includes such an order which has been discharged if any arrears are recoverable thereunder;

(b) 'High Court maintenance order', 'county court maintenance order' and 'magistrates' court maintenance order' mean respectively a maintenance order enforceable by the High Court, a county court and a magistrates' court;

(c) 'judgment debt' means a sum payable under—
  (i) a judgment or order enforceable by a court in England and Wales (not being a magistrates' court);
  (ii) an order of a magistrates' court for the payment of money recoverable summarily as a civil debt; or
  (iii) an order of any court which is enforceable as if it were for the payment of money so recoverable,

  but does not include any sum payable under a maintenance order or an administration order;

(d) 'the relevant adjudication', in relation to any payment secured or to be secured by an attachment of earnings order, means the conviction, judgment, order or other adjudication from which there arises the liability to make the payment; and

(e) 'the debtor', in relation to an attachment of earnings order, or to proceedings in which a court has power to make an attachment of earnings order, or to proceedings arising out of such an order, means the person by whom payment is required by the relevant adjudication to be made.

3. Application for Order and Conditions of Court's Power to Make It

(1) The following persons may apply for an attachment of earnings order:—
  (a) the person to whom payment under the relevant adjudication is required to be made (whether directly or through an officer of any court);

(b) where the relevant adjudication is an administration order, any one of the creditors scheduled to the order;

(c) without prejudice to paragraph (a) above, where the application is to a magistrates' court for an order to secure maintenance payments, and there is in force an order under section 59 of the Magistrates' Courts Act 1980, or section 19(2) of the Maintenance Orders Act 1950, that those payments be made to the designated officer for a magistrates' court, that officer;

(d) in the following cases the debtor—

(i) where the application is to a magistrates' court; or

(ii) where the application is to the High Court or a county court for an order to secure maintenance payments.

(3) Subject to subsection (3A) below for an attachment of earnings order to be made on the application of any person other than the debtor it must appear to the court that the debtor has failed to make one or more payments required by the relevant adjudication.

(3A) Subsection (3) above shall not apply where the relevant adjudication is a maintenance order.

(3B) Where—

(a) a magistrates' court imposes a fine on a person in respect of an offence, and

(b) that person consents to an order being made under this subsection,

the court may at the time it imposes the fine, and without the need for an application, make an attachment of earnings order to secure the payment of the fine.

(3C) Where—

(a) a magistrates' court makes in the case of a person convicted of an offence an order under section 130 of the Powers of Criminal Courts (Sentencing) Act 2000 (a compensation order) requiring him to pay compensation or to make other payments, and

(b) that person consents to an order being made under this subsection,

the court may at the time it makes the compensation order, and without the need for an application, make an attachment of earnings order to secure the payment of the compensation or other payments.

(4) Where proceedings are brought—

(a) in the High Court or a county court for the enforcement of a maintenance order by committal under section 5 of the Debtors Act 1869; or

(b) in a magistrates' court for the enforcement of a maintenance order under section 76 of the Magistrates' Courts Act 1980 (distress or committal),

then the court may make an attachment of earnings order to secure payments under the maintenance order, instead of dealing with the case under section 5 of the said Act of 1869 or, as the case may be, section 76 of the said Act of 1980.

Administration Orders in the County Court

4. Extension of Power to Make Administration Order

(1) Where, on an application to a county court for an attachment of earnings order to secure the payment of a judgment debt, it appears to the court that the debtor also has other debts, the court—

(a) shall consider whether the case may be one in which all the debtor's liabilities should be dealt with together and that for that purpose an administration order should be made; and

(b) if of opinion that it may be such a case, shall have power (whether or not it makes the attachment of earnings order applied for), with a view to making an administration order, to order the debtor to furnish to the court a list of all his creditors and the amounts which he owes to them respectively.

(2) If, on receipt of the list referred to in subsection (1)(b) above, it appears to the court that the debtor's whole indebtedness amounts to not more than the amount which for the time being is the county court limit for the purposes of section 112 of the County Courts Act 1984 (limit of total indebtedness governing county court's power to make administration order on application of debtor), the court may make such an order in respect of the debtor's estate.

(2A) Subsection (2) above is subject to section 112(3) and (4) of the County Courts Act 1984 (which require that, before an administration order is made, notice is to be given to all the creditors and thereafter restricts the right of any creditor to institute bankruptcy proceedings).

(4) Nothing in this section is to be taken as prejudicing any right of a debtor to apply, under section 112 of the County Courts Act 1984, for an administration order.

Consequences of Attachment Order

6. Effect and Contents of Order

(1) An attachment of earnings order shall be an order directed to a person who appears to the court to have the debtor in his employment and shall operate as an instruction to that person—
  (a) to make periodical deductions from the debtor's earnings in accordance with Part I of Schedule 3 to this Act; and
  (b) at such times as the order may require, or as the court may allow, to pay the amounts deducted to the collecting officer of the court, as specified in the order.

(2) For the purposes of this Act, the relationship of employer and employee shall be treated as subsisting between two persons if one of them as a principal and not as a servant or agent, pays to the other any sums defined as earnings by section 24 of this Act.

(3) An attachment of earnings order shall contain prescribed particulars enabling the debtor to be identified by the employer.

(4) Except where it is made to secure maintenance payments, the order shall specify the whole amount payable under the relevant adjudication (or so much of that amount as remains unpaid), including any relevant costs.

(5) The order shall specify—
  (a) the normal deduction rate, that is to say, the rate (expressed as a sum of money per week, month or other period) at which the court thinks it reasonable for the debtor's earnings to be applied to meeting his liability under the relevant adjudication; and
  (b) the protected earnings rate, that is to say the rate (so expressed) below which, having regard to the debtor's resources and needs, the court thinks it reasonable that the earnings actually paid to him should not be reduced.

(6) In the case of an order made to secure payments under a maintenance order (not being an order for the payment of a lump sum), the normal deduction rate—
  (a) shall be determined after taking account of any right or liability of the debtor to deduct income tax when making the payments; and
  (b) shall not exceed the rate which appears to the court necessary for the purpose of—
    (i) securing payment of the sums falling due from time to time under the maintenance order, and
    (ii) securing payment within a reasonable period of any sums already due and unpaid under the maintenance order.

(7) For the purposes of an attachment of earnings order, the collecting officer of the court shall be (subject to later variation of the order under section 9 of this Act)—
  (a) in the case of an order made by the High Court, either—
    (i) the proper officer of the High Court, or
    (ii) the appropriate officer of such county court as the order may specify;
  (b) in the case of an order made by a county court, the appropriate officer of that court; and
  (c) in the case of an order made by a magistrates' court, the designated officer for that court or for another magistrates' court specified in the order.

(8) In subsection (7) above 'appropriate officer' means an officer designated by the Lord Chancellor.

7. Compliance with Order by Employer

(1) Where an attachment of earnings order has been made, the employer shall, if he has been served with the order, comply with it; but he shall be under no liability for non-compliance before seven days have elapsed since the service.

(2) Where a person is served with an attachment of earnings order directed to him and he has not the debtor in his employment, or the debtor subsequently ceases to be in his employment, he shall (in either case), within ten days from the date of service or, as the case may be, the cesser, give notice of that fact to the court.

8. Interrelation with Alternative Remedies Open to Creditor

(1) Where an attachment of earnings order has been made to secure maintenance payments, no order or warrant of commitment shall be issued in consequence of any proceedings for the enforcement of the related maintenance order begun before the making of the attachment of earnings order.

(2) Where a county court has made an attachment of earnings order to secure the payment of a judgment debt—

(a) no order or warrant of commitment shall be issued in consequence of any proceedings for the enforcement of the debt begun before the making of the attachment of earnings order; and

(b) so long as the order is in force, no execution for the recovery of the debt shall issue against any property of the debtor without the leave of the county court.

(3) An attachment of earnings order made to secure maintenance payments shall cease to have effect upon the making of an order of commitment or the issue of a warrant of commitment for the enforcement of the related maintenance order, or upon the exercise for that purpose of the power conferred on a magistrates' court by section 77(2) of the Magistrates' Courts Act 1980 to postpone the issue of such a warrant.

(4) An attachment of earnings order made to secure the payment of a judgment debt shall cease to have effect on the making of an order of commitment or the issue of a warrant of commitment for the enforcement of the debt.

(5) An attachment of earnings order made to secure any payment specified in section 1(3)(b) or (c) of this Act shall cease to have effect on the issue of a warrant committing the debtor to prison for default in making that payment.

Subsequent Proceedings

9. Variation, Lapse and Discharge of Orders

(1) The court may make an order discharging or varying an attachment of earnings order.

(2) Where an order is varied, the employer shall, if he has been served with notice of the variation, comply with the order as varied; but he shall be under no liability for non-compliance before seven days have elapsed since the service.

(3) Rules of court may make provision—

(a) as to the circumstances in which an attachment of earnings order may be varied or discharged by the court of its own motion;

(b) in the case of an attachment of earnings order made by a magistrates' court, for enabling a single justice, on an application made by the debtor on the ground of a material change in his resources and needs since the order was made or last varied, to vary the order for a period of not more than four weeks by an increase of the protected earnings rate.

(4) Where an attachment of earnings order has been made and the person to whom it is directed ceases to have the debtor in his employment, the order shall lapse (except as respects deduction from earnings paid after the cesser and payment to the collecting officer of amounts deducted at any time) and be of no effect unless and until the court again directs it to a person (whether the same as before or another) who appears to the court to have the debtor in his employment.

(5) The lapse of an order under subsection (4) above shall not prevent its being treated as remaining in force for other purposes.

Administrative Provisions

14. Power of Court to Obtain Statements of Earnings etc.

(1) Where in any proceedings a court has power to make an attachment of earnings order, it may—

(a) order the debtor to give to the court, within a specified period, a statement signed by him of—

(i) the name and address of any person by whom earnings are paid to him:

(ii) specified particulars as to his earnings and anticipated earnings, as to his resources and needs; and

(iii) specified particulars for the purpose of enabling the debtor to be identified by any employer of his;

(b) order any person appearing to the court to have the debtor in his employment to give to the court, within a specified period, a statement signed by him or on his behalf of specified particulars of the debtor's earnings and anticipated earnings.

(2) Where an attachment of earnings order has been made, the court may at any time thereafter while the order is in force—

(a) make such an order as is described in subsection (1)(a) or (b) above; and

(b) order the debtor to attend before it on a day and at a time specified in the order to give the information described in subsection (1)(a) above.

(3) In the case of an application to a magistrates' court for an attachment of earnings order, or for the variation or discharge of such an order, the power to make an order under subsection (1) or (2) above shall be exercisable also, before the hearing of the application, by a single justice.

(4) Without prejudice to subsections (1) to (3) above, rules of court may provide that where notice of an application for an attachment of earnings order is served on the debtor, it shall include a requirement that he shall give to the court, within such period and in such manner as may be prescribed, a statement in writing of the matters specified in subsection (1)(a) above and of any other prescribed matters which are, or may be, relevant under section 6 of this Act to the determination of the normal deduction rate and the protected earnings rate to be specified in any order made on the application.

(5) In any proceedings in which a court has power to make an attachment of earnings order, and in any proceedings for the making, variation or discharge of such an order, a document purporting to be a statement given to the court in compliance with an order under subsection (1)(a) or (b) above, or with any such requirement of a notice of application for an attachment of earnings order as is mentioned in subsection (4) above, shall, in the absence of proof to the contrary, be deemed to be a statement so given and shall be evidence of the facts stated therein.

16. Power of Court to Determine Whether Particular Payments are Earnings

(1) Where an attachment of earnings order is in force, the court shall, on the application of a person specified in subsection (2) below, determine whether payments to the debtor of a particular class or description specified by the application are earnings for the purposes of the order; and the employer shall be entitled to give effect to any determination for the time being in force under this section.

(2) The persons referred to in subsection (1) above are—

(a) the employer;

(b) the debtor;

(c) the person to whom payment under the relevant adjudication is required to be made (whether directly or through an officer of any court); and

(d) without prejudice to paragraph (c) above, where the application is in respect of an attachment of earnings order made to secure payments under a magistrates' court maintenance order, the collecting officer.

(3) Where an application under this section is made by the employer, he shall not incur any liability for non-compliance with the order as respects any payments of the class or description specified by the application which are made by him to the debtor while the application, or any appeal in consequence thereof, is pending; but this subsection shall not, unless the court otherwise orders, apply as respects such payments if the employer subsequently withdraws the application or, as the case may be, abandons the appeal.

17. Consolidated Attachment Orders

(1) The powers of a county court under sections 1 and 3 of this Act shall include power to make an attachment of earnings order to secure the payment of any number of judgment debts; and the powers of a magistrates' court under those sections shall include power to make an attachment of earnings order to secure the discharge of any number of such liabilities as are specified in section 1(3).

(2) An attachment of earnings order made by virtue of this section shall be known as a consolidated attachment order.

(3) The power to make a consolidated attachment order shall be exercised subject to and in accordance with rules of court; and rules made for the purposes of this section may provide—

(a) for the transfer from one court to another—
(i) of an attachment of earnings order, or any proceedings for or arising out of such an order; and
(ii) of functions relating to the enforcement of any liability capable of being secured by attachment of earnings;
(b) for enabling a court to which any order, proceedings or functions have been transferred under the rules to vary or discharge an attachment of earnings order made by another court and to replace it (if the court thinks fit) with a consolidated attachment order;
(c) for the cases in which any power exercisable under this section or the rules may be exercised by a court of its own motion or on the application of a prescribed person;
(d) for requiring the officer of a court who receives payments made to him in compliance with an attachment of earnings order, instead of complying with section 13 of this Act, to deal with them as directed by the court or the rules; and
(e) for modifying or excluding provisions of this Act or Part III of the Magistrates' Courts Act 1980, but only so far as may be necessary or expedient for securing conformity with the operation of rules made by virtue of paragraphs (a) to (d) of this subsection.

Miscellaneous Provisions

23. Enforcement Provisions

(1) If, after being served with notice of an application to a county court for an attachment of earnings order or for the variation of such an order or with an order made under section 14(2)(b) above, the debtor fails to attend on the day and at the time specified for any hearing of the application or specified in the order, the court may adjourn the hearing and order him to attend at a specified time on another day; and if the debtor—
(a) fails to attend at that time on that day; or
(b) attends, but refuses to be sworn or give evidence,
he may be ordered by the judge to be imprisoned for not more than fourteen days.

(1A) In any case where the judge has power to make an order of imprisonment under subsection (1) for failure to attend, he may, in lieu of or in addition to making that order, order the debtor to be arrested and brought before the court either forthwith or at such time as the judge may direct.

(2) Subject to this section, a person commits an offence if—
(a) being required by section 7(1) or 9(2) of this Act to comply with an attachment of earnings order, he fails to do so; or
(b) being required by section 7(2) of this Act to give a notice for the purposes of that subsection, he fails to give it, or fails to give it within the time required by that subsection; or
(c) he fails to comply with an order under section 14(1) of this Act or with any such requirement of a notice of application for an attachment of earnings order as is mentioned in section 14(4), or fails (in either case) to comply within the time required by the order or notice; or
(d) he fails to comply with section 15 of this Act; or
(e) he gives a notice for the purposes of section 7(2) of this Act, or a notification for the purposes of section 15, which he knows to be false in a material particular, or recklessly gives such a notice or notification which is false in a material particular; or
(f) in purported compliance with section 7(2) or 15 of this Act, or with an order under section 14(1), or with any such requirement of a notice of application for an attachment of earnings order as is mentioned in section 14(4), he makes any statement which he knows to be false in a material particular, or recklessly makes any statement which is false in a material particular.

(3) Where a person commits an offence under subsection (2) above in relation to proceedings in, or to an attachment of earnings order made by the High Court or a county court, he shall be liable on summary conviction to a fine of not more than level 2 on the standard scale or he may be ordered by a judge of the High Court or the county court judge (as the case may be) to pay a fine of not more than £250 or, in the case of an offence specified in subsection (4) below, to be imprisoned for not more than fourteen days; and where a person commits an offence under

subsection (2) otherwise than as mentioned above in this subsection, he shall be liable on summary conviction to a fine of not more than level 2 on the standard scale.

(4) The offences referred to above in the case of which a judge may impose imprisonment are—
  (a) an offence under subsection (2)(c) or (d), if committed by the debtor; and
  (b) an offence under subsection (2)(e) or (f), whether committed by the debtor or any other person.

(5) It shall be a defence—
  (a) for a person charged with an offence under subsection (2)(a) above to prove that he took all reasonable steps to comply with the attachment of earnings order in question;
  (b) for a person charged with an offence under subsection (2)(b) to prove that he did not know, and could not reasonably be expected to know, that the debtor was not in his employment, or (as the case may be) had ceased to be so, and that he gave the required notice as soon as reasonably practicable after the fact came to his knowledge.

(6) Where a person is convicted or dealt with for an offence under subsection (2)(a), the court may order him to pay, to whoever is the collecting officer of the court for the purposes of the attachment of earnings order in question, any sums deducted by that person from the debtor's earnings and not already paid to the collecting officer.

(7) Where under this section a person is ordered by a judge of the High Court or a county court to be imprisoned, the judge may at any time revoke the order and, if the person is already in custody, order his discharge.

(8) Any fine imposed by a judge of the High Court under subsection (3) above and any sums ordered by the High Court to be paid under subsection (6) above shall be recoverable in the same way as a fine imposed by that court in the exercise of its jurisdiction to punish for contempt of court; section 129 of the County Courts Act 1984 (enforcement of fines) shall apply to payment of a fine imposed by a county court judge under subsection (3) and of any sums ordered by a county court judge to be paid under subsection (6); and any sum ordered by a magistrates' court to be paid under subsection (6) shall be recoverable as a sum adjudged to be paid on a conviction by that court.

(9) For the purposes of section 13 of the Administration of Justice Act 1960 (appeal in cases of contempt of court), subsection (3) above shall be treated as an enactment enabling the High Court or a county court to deal with an offence under subsection (2) above as if it were contempt of court.

(10) In this section references to proceedings in a court are to proceedings in which that court has power to make an attachment of earnings order or has made such an order.

(11) A district judge, assistant district judge or deputy district judge shall have the same powers under this section as a judge of a county court.

24. Meaning of 'Earnings'

(1) For the purposes of this Act, but subject to the following subsection, 'earnings' are any sums payable to a person—
  (a) by way of wages or salary (including any fees, bonus, commission, overtime pay or other emoluments payable in addition to wages or salary or payable under a contract of service);
  (b) by way of pension (including an annuity in respect of past services, whether or not rendered to the person paying the annuity, and including periodical payments by way of compensation for the loss, abolition or relinquishment, or diminution in the emoluments, of any office or employment);
  (c) by way of statutory sick pay.

(2) The following shall not be treated as earnings:—
  (a) sums payable by any public department of the Government of Northern Ireland or of a territory outside the United Kingdom;
  (b) pay or allowances payable to the debtor as a member of Her Majesty's forces other than pay or allowances payable by his employer to him as a special member of a reserve force (within the meaning of the Reserve Forces Act 1996);
  (c) pension, allowances or benefit payable under any enactment relating to social security;
  (d) pension or allowances payable in respect of disablement or disability;

(e) except in relation to a maintenance order, wages payable to a person as a seaman, other than wages payable to him as a seaman of a fishing boat;
(f) guaranteed minimum pension within the meaning of the Pension Schemes Act 1993.

25. General Interpretation

(1) In this Act, except where the context otherwise requires—
'administration order' means an order made under, and so referred to in, Part VI of the County Courts Act 1984;
'the court', in relation to an attachment of earnings order, means the court which made the order, subject to rules of court as to the venue for, and the transfer of, proceedings in county courts and magistrates' courts;
'debtor' and 'relevant adjudication' have the meanings given by section 2 of this Act;
'the employer', in relation to an attachment of earnings order, means the person who is required by the order to make deductions from earnings paid by him to the debtor;
'judgment debt' has the meaning given by section 2 of this Act;
'maintenance order' has the meaning given by section 2 of this Act;
'maintenance payments' means payments required under a maintenance order;
'prescribed' means prescribed by rules of court.

(2) Any reference in this Act to sums payable under a judgment or order, or to the payment of such sums, includes a reference to costs and the payment of them; and the references in sections 6(4) and 12(2) to relevant costs are to any costs of the proceedings in which the attachment of earnings order in question was made, being costs which the debtor is liable to pay.

(3) References in sections 6(5)(b), 9(3)(b) and 14(1)(a) of this Act to the debtor's needs include references to the needs of any person for whom he must, or reasonably may, provide.

(5) Any power to make rules which is conferred by this Act is without prejudice to any other power to make rules of court.

(6) This Act, so far as it relates to magistrates' courts, and Part III of the Magistrates' Courts Act 1980 shall be construed as if this Act were contained in that Part.

(7) References in this Act to any enactment include references to that enactment as amended by or under any other enactment, including this Act.

Charging Orders Act 1979

(1979 CHAPTER 53)

An Act to make provision for imposing charges to secure payment of money due, or to become due, under judgments or orders of court; to provide for restraining and prohibiting dealings with, and the making of payments in respect of, certain securities; and for connected purposes. [6th December 1979]

Charging Orders

1. Charging Orders

(1) Where, under a judgment or order of the High Court or a county court, a person (the 'debtor') is required to pay a sum of money to another person (the 'creditor') then, for the purpose of enforcing that judgment or order, the appropriate court may make an order in accordance with the provisions of this Act imposing on any such property of the debtor as may be specified in the order a charge for securing the payment of any money due or to become due under the judgment or order.

(2) The appropriate court is—

(a) in a case where the property to be charged is a fund in court, the court in which that fund is lodged;

(b) in a case where paragraph (a) above does not apply and the order to be enforced is a maintenance order of the High Court, the High Court or a county court;

(c) in a case where neither paragraph (a) nor paragraph (b) above applies and the judgment or order to be enforced is a judgment or order of the High Court for a sum exceeding the county court limit, the High Court or a county court; and

(d) in any other case, a county court.

In this section 'county court limit' means the county court limit for the time being specified in an Order in Council under section 145 of the County Courts Act 1984, as the county court limit for the purposes of this section and 'maintenance order' has the same meaning as in section 2(a) of the Attachment of Earnings Act 1971.

(3) An order under subsection (1) above is referred to in this Act as a 'charging order'.

(4) Where a person applies to the High Court for a charging order to enforce more than one judgment or order, that court shall be the appropriate court in relation to the application if it would be the appropriate court, apart from this subsection, on an application relating to one or more of the judgments or orders concerned.

(5) In deciding whether to make a charging order the court shall consider all the circumstances of the case and, in particular, any evidence before it as to—

(a) the personal circumstances of the debtor, and

(b) whether any other creditor of the debtor would be likely to be unduly prejudiced by the making of the order.

[*The county court limit for the purposes of this section was specified as £5,000 by the County Courts Jurisdiction Order 1981 (SI 1981/1123), which has effect as if made under the County Courts Act 1984, s. 145, by virtue of the Interpretation Act 1978, s. 17(2)(b).*]

2. Property Which May be Charged

(1) Subject to subsection (3) below, a charge may be imposed by a charging order only on—

(a) any interest held by the debtor beneficially—

(i) in any asset of a kind mentioned in subsection (2) below, or

(ii) under any trust; or

(b) any interest held by a person as trustee of a trust (' the trust'), if the interest is in such an asset or is an interest under another trust and—

(i) the judgment or order in respect of which a charge is to be imposed was made against that person as trustee of the trust, or

(ii) the whole beneficial interest under the trust is held by the debtor unencumbered and for his own benefit, or

(iii) in a case where there are two or more debtors all of whom are liable to the creditor for the same debt, they together hold the whole beneficial interest under the trust unencumbered and for their own benefit.

(2) The assets referred to in subsection (1) above are—

(a) land,

(b) securities of any of the following kinds—

(i) government stock,

(ii) stock of any body (other than a building society) incorporated within England and Wales.

(iii) stock of any body incorporated outside England and Wales or of any state or territory outside the United Kingdom, being stock registered in a register kept at any place within England and Wales,

(iv) units of any unit trust in respect of which a register of the unit holders is kept at any place within England and Wales, or

(c) funds in court.

(3) In any case where a charge is imposed by a charging order on any interest in an asset of a kind mentioned in paragraph (b) or (c) of subsection (2) above, the court making the order may provide for the charge to extend to any interest or dividend payable in respect of the asset.

3. Provisions Supplementing Sections 1 and 2

(1) A charging order may be made either absolutely or subject to conditions as to notifying the debtor or as to the time when the charge is to become enforceable, or as to other matters.

(2) The Land Charges Act 1972 and the Land Registration Act 1925 shall apply in relation to charging orders as they apply in relation to other orders or writs issued or made for the purpose of enforcing judgments.

(3) In section 49 of the Land Registration Act 1925 (protection of certain interests by notice) there is inserted at the end of subsection (1) the following paragraph—

'(g) charging orders (within the meaning of the Charging Orders Act 1979) which in the case of unregistered land may be protected by registration under the Land Charges Act 1972 and which, notwithstanding section 59 of this Act, it may be deemed expedient to protect by notice instead of by caution.'.

(4) Subject to the provisions of this Act, a charge imposed by a charging order shall have the like effect and shall be enforceable in the same courts and in the same manner as an equitable charge created by the debtor by writing under his hand.

(5) The court by which a charging order was made may at any time, on the application of the debtor or of any person interested in any property to which the order relates, make an order discharging or varying the charging order.

(6) Where a charging order has been protected by an entry registered under the Land Charges Act 1972 or the Land Registration Act 1925, an order under subsection (5) above discharging the charging order may direct that the entry be cancelled.

(7) The Lord Chancellor may by order made by statutory instrument amend section 2(2) of this Act by adding to, or removing from, the kinds of asset for the time being referred to there, any asset of a kind which in his opinion ought to be so added or removed.

(8) Any order under subsection (7) above shall be subject to annulment in pursuance of a resolution of either House of Parliament.

Stop Orders and Notices

5. Stop Orders and Notices

(1) In this section—

'stop order' means an order of the court prohibiting the taking, in respect of any of the securities specified in the order, of any of the steps mentioned in subsection (5) below;

'stop notice' means a notice requiring any person or body on whom it is duly served to refrain from taking, in respect of any of the securities specified in the notice, any of those steps without first notifying the person by whom, or on whose behalf, the notice was served; and 'prescribed securities' means securities (including funds in court) of a kind prescribed by rules of court made under this section.

(2) The power to make rules of court under section 1 of, and Schedule 1 to, the Civil Procedure Act 1997 shall include power by any such rules to make provision—

(a) for the High Court to make a stop order on the application of any person claiming to be entitled to an interest in prescribed securities; and

(b) for the service of a stop notice by any person claiming to be entitled to an interest in prescribed securities.

(4) Rules of court made by virtue of subsection (2) above shall prescribe the person or body on whom a copy of any stop order or a stop notice is to be served.

(5) The steps mentioned in subsection (1) above are—

(a) the registration of any transfer of the securities;

(b) in the case of funds in court, the transfer, sale, delivery out, payment or other dealing with the funds, or of the income thereon;

(c) the making of any payment by way of dividend, interest or otherwise in respect of the securities; and

(d) in the case of units of a unit trust, any acquisition of or other dealing with the units by any person or body exercising functions under the trust.

(6) Any rules of court made by virtue of this section may include such incidental, supplemental and consequential provisions as the authority making them consider necessary or expedient, and may make different provision in relation to different cases or classes of case.

Supplemental

6. Interpretation

(1) In this Act—

'building society' has the same meaning as in the Building Societies Act 1986;

'charging order' means an order made under section 1(1) of this Act

'debtor' and 'creditor' have the meanings given by section 1(1) of this Act;

'dividend' includes any distribution in respect of any unit of a unit trust;

'government stock' means any stock issued by Her Majesty's government in the United Kingdom or any funds of, or annuity granted by, that government;

'stock' includes shares, debentures and any securities of the body concerned, whether or not constituting a charge on the assets of that body;

'unit trust' means any trust established for the purpose, or having the effect, of providing, for persons having funds available for investment, facilities for the participation by them, as beneficiaries under the trust, in any profits or income arising from the acquisition, holding, management or disposal of any property whatsoever.

(2) For the purposes of section 1 of this Act references to a judgment or order of the High Court or a county court shall be taken to include references to a judgment, order, decree or award (however called) of any court or arbitrator (including any foreign court or arbitrator) which is or has become enforceable (whether wholly or to a limited extent) as if it were a judgment or order of the High Court or a county court.

(3) References in section 2 of this Act to any securities include references to any such securities standing in the name of the Accountant General.

7. Consequential Amendment, Repeals and Transitional Provisions

(3) Any order made or notice given under any enactment repealed by this Act or under any rules of court revoked by rules of court made under this Act (the 'new rules') shall, if still in force when the provisions of this Act or, as the case may be, the new rules come into force, continue to have effect as if made under this Act or, as the case may be, under the new rules.

(4) Any notice of such an order registered in the register maintained under the Land Registration Act 1925 which would have been registrable by virtue of the paragraph inserted in section 49(1) of that Act by section 3(3) of this Act, if section 3(3) had been in force when the notice was registered, shall have effect as it registered by virtue of that paragraph.

8. Short Title, Commencement and Extent

(1) This Act may be cited as the Charging Orders Act 1979.
(2) This Act comes into force on such day as the Lord Chancellor may appoint by order made by statutory instrument.
(3) This Act does not extend to Scotland or Northern Ireland.
[*The whole Act was brought into force by SI 1980/627.*]

NOTES ON TEXT

The text incorporates the following amendments:
s. 1(2) amended by: (a) County Courts Jurisdiction Order 1981 (SI 1981/1123), art. 2; (b) Administration of Justice Act 1982, s. 34(3) and sch. 3, paras 2, 3(b)(iv) and 6 (in force by s. 76(11) of that Act);
s. 4 repealed by Insolvency Act 1985, sch. 10 (in force by SI 1986/1924, art. 2);
s. 5 amended by: (a) Supreme Court Act 1981, sch. 5; (b) County Courts Act 1984, sch. 2, para. 72; (c) Civil Procedure (Modification of Enactments) Order 2002 (SI 2002/439), art. 5;
s. 6(1) amended by Building Societies Act 1986, sch. 18, para. 14 (in force by SI 1986/1560, sch. 2);
s. 7(1) repealed by County Courts Act 1984, sch. 4.
s. 7(2) repealed by Supreme Court Act 1981, sch. 7, and County Courts Act 1984, sch. 4.

Civil Jurisdiction and Judgments Act 1982

(1982 CHAPTER 27)

An Act to make further provision about the jurisdiction of courts and tribunals in the United Kingdom and certain other territories and about the recognition and enforcement of judgments given in the United Kingdom or elsewhere; to provide for the modification of certain provisions relating to legal aid; and for connected purposes. [13th July 1982]

PART I IMPLEMENTATION OF THE CONVENTIONS

Main Implementing Provisions

1. Interpretation of References to the Conventions and Contracting States

(1) In this Act—

'the 1968 Convention' means the Convention on jurisdiction and the enforcement of judgments in civil and commercial matters (including the Protocol annexed to that Convention), signed at Brussels on 27th September 1968;

'the 1971 Protocol' means the Protocol on the interpretation of the 1968 Convention by the European Court, signed at Luxembourg on 3rd June 1971;

'the Accession Convention' means the Convention on the accession to the 1968 Convention and the 1971 Protocol of Denmark, the Republic of Ireland and the United Kingdom, signed at Luxembourg on 9th October 1978;

'the 1982 Accession Convention' means the Convention on the accession of the Hellenic Republic to the 1968 Convention and the 1971 Protocol, with the adjustments made to them by the Accession Convention, signed at Luxembourg on 25th October 1982;

'the 1989 Accession Convention' means the Convention on the accession of the Kingdom of Spain and the Portuguese Republic to the 1968 Convention and the 1971 Protocol, with the adjustments made to them by the Accession Convention and the 1982 Accession Convention, signed at Donostia — San Sebastián on 26th May 1989;

'the 1996 Accession Convention' means the Convention on the accession of the Republic of Austria, the Republic of Finland and the Kingdom of Sweden to the 1968 Convention and the 1971 Protocol, with the adjustments made to them by the Accession Convention, the 1982 Accession Convention and the 1989 Accession Convention, signed at Brussels on 29th November 1996;

'the Brussels Conventions' means the 1968 Convention, the 1971 Protocol, the Accession Convention, the 1982 Accession Convention, the 1989 Accession Convention and the 1996 Accession Convention;

'the Lugano Convention' means the Convention on jurisdiction and the enforcement of judgments in civil and commercial matters (including the Protocols annexed to that Convention) opened for signature at Lugano on 16th September 1988 and signed by the United Kingdom on 18th September 1989;

'the Regulation' means Council Regulation (EC) No. 44/2001 of 22nd December 2000 on jurisdiction and the recognition and enforcement of judgments in civil and commercial matters.

(2) In this Act, unless the context otherwise requires—

(a) references to, or to any provision of, the 1968 Convention or the 1971 Protocol are references to that Convention, Protocol or provision as amended by the Accession Convention, the 1982 Accession Convention, the 1989 Accession Convention and the 1996 Accession Convention;

(aa) references to, or to any provision of, the Lugano Convention are references to that Convention as amended on the accession to it of Poland; and

(b) any reference in any provision to a numbered Article without more is a reference—

(i) to the Article so numbered of the 1968 Convention, in so far as the provision applies in relation to that Convention, and

Selected Legislation

(ii) to the Article so numbered of the Lugano Convention, in so far as the provision applies in relation to that Convention,

and any reference to a sub-division of a numbered Article shall be construed accordingly.

(3) In this Act—

'Contracting State', without more, in any provision means—

(a) in the application of the provision in relation to the Brussels Conventions, a Brussels Contracting State; and

(b) in the application of the provision in relation to the Lugano Convention, a Lugano Contracting State;

'Brussels Contracting State' means Denmark (which is not bound by the Regulation, but was one of the parties acceding to the 1968 Convention under the Accession Convention);

'Lugano Contracting State' means—

(a) one of the original parties to the Lugano Convention, that is to say Austria, Belgium, Denmark, Finland, France, the Federal Republic of Germany, the Hellenic Republic, Iceland, the Republic of Ireland, Italy, Luxembourg, the Netherlands, Norway, Portugal, Spain, Sweden, Switzerland and the United Kingdom; or

(b) a party who has subsequently acceded to that Convention, that is to say, Poland,

being a State in relation to which that Convention has taken effect in accordance with paragraph 3 or 4 of Article 61.

'Regulation State' in any provision, in the application of that provision in relation to the Regulation, has the same meaning as 'Member State' in the Regulation, that is all Member States except Denmark.

(4) Any question arising as to whether it is the Regulation, any of the Brussels Conventions, or the Lugano Convention which applies in the circumstances of a particular case shall be determined as follows—

(a) in accordance with Article 54B of the Lugano Convention (which determines the relationship between the Brussels Conventions and the Lugano Convention); and

(b) in accordance with Article 68 of the Regulation (which determines the relationship between the Brussels Conventions and the Regulation).

2. The Conventions to Have the Force of Law

(1) The Brussels Conventions shall have the force of law in the United Kingdom, and judicial notice shall be taken of them.

(2) For convenience of reference there are set out in Schedules 1, 2, 3, 3A, 3B and 3C respectively the English texts of—

(a) the 1968 Convention as amended by Titles II and III of the Accession Convention, by Titles II and III of the 1982 Accession Convention, by Titles II and III of, and Annex I(d) to, the 1989 Accession Convention and by Titles II and III of the 1996 Accession Convention;

(b) the 1971 Protocol as amended by Title IV of the Accession Convention, by Title IV of the 1982 Accession Convention, by Title IV of the 1989 Accession Convention and by Title IV of the 1996 Accession Convention ;

(c) Titles V and VI of the Accession Convention (transitional and final provisions) as amended by Title V of the 1989 Accession Convention;

(d) Titles V and VI of the 1982 Accession Convention (transitional and final provisions);

(e) Titles VI and VII of the 1989 Accession Convention (transitional and final provisions); and

(f) Titles V and VI of the 1996 Accession Convention (transitional and final provisions),

being texts prepared from the authentic English texts referred to in Articles 37 and 41 of the Accession Convention, in Article 17 of the 1982 Accession Convention, in Article 34 of the 1989 Accession Convention and in Article 18 of the 1996 Accession Convention.

3. Interpretation of the Conventions

(1) Any question as to the meaning or effect of any provision of the Brussels Conventions shall, if not referred to the European Court in accordance with the 1971 Protocol, be determined in accordance with the principles laid down by and any relevant decision of the European Court.

(2) Judicial notice shall be taken of any decision of, or expression of opinion by, the European Court on any such question.

(3) Without prejudice to the generality of subsection (1), the following reports (which are reproduced in the Official Journal of the Communities), namely—
(a) the reports by Mr P. Jenard on the 1968 Convention and the 1971 Protocol; and
(b) the report by Professor Peter Schlosser on the Accession Convention; and
(c) the report by Professor Demetrios I. Evrigenis and Professor K. D. Kerameus on the 1982 Accession Convention; and
(d) the report by Mr Martinho de Almeida Cruz, Mr Manuel Desantes Real and Mr P. Jenard on the 1989 Accession Convention,
may be considered in ascertaining the meaning or effect of any provision of the Conventions and shall be given such weight as is appropriate in the circumstances.

[*The reports referred to in s. 3(3) were published as follows: para. (a) [1979] OJ C591 and 66; para. (b) [1979] OJ C5971; para. (c) [1986] OJ C2981; para. (d) [1990] OJ C189 35.*]

3A. The Lugano Convention To Have The Force Of Law

(1) The Lugano Convention shall have the force of law in the United Kingdom, and judicial notice shall be taken of it.
(2) For convenience of reference there is set out in Schedule 3C the English text of the Lugano Convention as amended on the accession of Poland to that Convention.

3B. Interpretation Of The Lugano Convention

(1) In determining any question as to the meaning or effect of a provision of the Lugano Convention, a court in the United Kingdom shall, in accordance with Protocol No. 2 to that Convention, take account of any principles laid down in any relevant decision delivered by a court of any other Lugano Contracting State concerning provisions of the Convention.
(2) Without prejudice to any practice of the courts as to the matters which may be considered apart from this section, the report on the Lugano Convention by Mr P. Jenard and Mr G. Möller (which is reproduced in the Official Journal of the Communities of 28th July 1990) may be considered in ascertaining the meaning or effect of any provision of the Convention and shall be given such weight as is appropriate in the circumstances.

PART IV MISCELLANEOUS PROVISIONS

Provisions Relating to Jurisdiction

24. Interim Relief and Protective Measures in Cases of Doubtful Jurisdiction

(1) Any power of a court in England and Wales or Northern Ireland to grant interim relief pending trial or pending the determination of an appeal shall extend to a case where—
(a) the issue to be tried, or which is the subject of the appeal, relates to the jurisdiction of the court to entertain the proceedings; or
(b) the proceedings involve the reference of any matter to the European Court under the 1971 Protocol; or
(c) the proceedings involve a reference of any matter relating to the Regulation to the European Court under Article 68 of the Treaty establishing the European Community.
(2) Any power of a court in Scotland to grant protective measures pending the decision of any hearing shall apply to a case where—
(a) the subject of the proceedings includes a question as to the jurisdiction of the court to entertain them; or
(b) the proceedings involve the reference of a matter to the European Court under the 1971 Protocol; or
(c) the proceedings involve a reference of any matter relating to the Regulation to the European Court under Article 68 of the Treaty establishing the European Community.
(3) Subsections (1) and (2) shall not be construed as restricting any power to grant interim relief or protective measures which a court may have apart from this section.

25 Interim Relief in England and Wales and Northern Ireland in the Absence of Substantive Proceedings

(1) The High Court in England and Wales or Northern Ireland shall have power to grant interim relief where—

(a) proceedings have been or are to be commenced in a Brussels or Lugano Contracting State other than the United Kingdom or in a part of the United Kingdom other than that in which the High Court in question exercises jurisdiction; and

(b) they are or will be proceedings whose subject-matter is within the scope of the 1968 Convention as determined by Article 1 (whether or not that or any other Convention has effect in relation to the proceedings).

(2) On an application for any interim relief under subsection (1) the court may refuse to grant that relief if, in the opinion of the court, the fact that the court has no jurisdiction apart from this section in relation to the subject-matter of the proceedings in question makes it inexpedient for the court to grant it.

(3) Her Majesty may by Order in Council extend the power to grant interim relief conferred by subsection (1) so as to make it exercisable in relation to proceedings of any of the following descriptions, namely—

(a) proceedings commenced or to be commenced otherwise than in a Brussels or Lugano Contracting State;

(b) proceedings whose subject-matter is not within the scope of the 1968 Convention as determined by Article 1;

(c) arbitration proceedings.

(4) An Order in Council under subsection (3)—

(a) may confer power to grant only specified descriptions of interim relief;

(b) may make different provision for different classes of proceedings, for proceedings pending in different countries or courts outside the United Kingdom or in different parts of the United Kingdom, and for other different circumstances; and

(c) may impose conditions or restrictions on the exercise of any power conferred by the Order.

(5) An Order in Council under subsection (3) which confers power to grant interim relief in relation to arbitration proceedings may provide for the repeal of any provision of section 12(6) of the Arbitration Act 1950 or section 21(1) of the Arbitration Act (Northern Ireland) 1937 to the extent that it is superseded by the provisions of the Order.

(6) Any Order in Council under subsection (3) shall be subject to annulment in pursuance of a resolution of either House of Parliament.

(7) In this section 'interim relief', in relation to the High Court in England and Wales or Northern Ireland, means interim relief of any kind which that court has power to grant in proceedings relating to matters within its jurisdiction, other than—

(a) a warrant for the arrest of property; or

(b) provision for obtaining evidence.

PART V SUPPLEMENTARY AND GENERAL PROVISIONS

Domicile

41. Domicile of Individuals

(1) Subject to Article 52 (which contains provisions for determining whether a party is domiciled in a Contracting State), the following provisions of this section determine, for the purposes of the 1968 Convention or, as the case may be, the Lugano Convention and this Act, whether an individual is domiciled in the United Kingdom or in a particular part of, or place in, the United Kingdom or in a state other than a Contracting State.

(2) An individual is domiciled in the United Kingdom if and only if—

(a) he is resident in the United Kingdom; and

(b) the nature and circumstances of his residence indicate that he has a substantial connection with the United Kingdom.

(3) Subject to subsection (5), an individual is domiciled in a particular part of the United Kingdom if and only if—

(a) he is resident in that part; and
(b) the nature and circumstances of his residence indicate that he has a substantial connection with that part.

(4) An individual is domiciled in a particular place in the United Kingdom if and only if he—
(a) is domiciled in the part of the United Kingdom in which that place is situated; and
(b) is resident in that place.

(5) An individual who is domiciled in the United Kingdom but in whose case the requirements of subsection (3)(b) are not satisfied in relation to any particular part of the United Kingdom shall be treated as domiciled in the part of the United Kingdom in which he is resident.

(6) In the case of an individual who—
(a) is resident in the United Kingdom, or in a particular part of the United Kingdom; and
(b) has been so resident for the last three months or more,
the requirements of subsection (2)(b) or, as the case may be, subsection (3)(b) shall be presumed to be fulfilled unless the contrary is proved.

(7) An individual is domiciled in a state other than a Contracting State if and only if—
(a) he is resident in that state; and
(b) the nature and circumstances of his residence indicate that he has a substantial connection with that state.

42. Domicile and Seat of Corporation or Association

(1) For the purposes of this Act the seat of a corporation or association (as determined by this section) shall be treated as its domicile.

(2) The following provisions of this section determine where a corporation or association has its seat—
(a) for the purpose of Article 53 (which for the purposes of the 1968 Convention or, as the case may be, the Lugano Convention equates the domicile of such a body with its seat; and
(b) for the purposes of this Act other than the provisions mentioned in section 43(1)(b) and (c).

(3) A corporation or association has its seat in the United Kingdom if and only if—
(a) it was incorporated or formed under the law of a part of the United Kingdom and has its registered office or some other official address in the United Kingdom; or
(b) its central management and control is exercised in the United Kingdom.

(4) A corporation or association has its seat in a particular part of the United Kingdom if and only if it has its seat in the United Kingdom and—
(a) it has its registered office or some other official address in that part; or
(b) its central management and control is exercised in that part; or
(c) it has a place of business in that part.

(5) A corporation or association has its seat in a particular place in the United Kingdom if and only if it has its seat in the part of the United Kingdom in which that place is situated and—
(a) it has its registered office or some other official address in that place; or
(b) its central management and control is exercised in that place; or
(c) it has a place of business in that place.

(6) Subject to subsection (7), a corporation or association has its seat in a state other than the United Kingdom if and only if—
(a) it was incorporated or formed under the law of that state and has its registered office or some other official address there; or
(b) its central management and control is exercised in that state.

(7) A corporation or association shall not be regarded as having its seat in a Contracting State other than the United Kingdom if it is shown that the courts of that state would not regard it as having its seat there.

(8) In this section—
'business' includes any activity carried on by a corporation or association, and 'place of business' shall be construed accordingly;
'official address', in relation to a corporation or association, means an address which it is required by law to register, notify or maintain for the purpose of receiving notices or other communications.

General

50. Interpretation: General

In this Act, unless the context otherwise requires—

'the Accession Convention', 'the 1982 Accession Convention', 'the 1989 Accession Convention' and 'the 1996 Accession Convention' have the meaning given by section 1(1);

'Article' and references to sub-divisions of numbered Articles are to be construed in accordance with section 1(2)(b);

'association' means an unincorporated body of persons;

'Brussels Contracting State' has the meaning given by section 1(3);

'the Brussels Conventions' has the meaning given by section 1(1);

'Contracting State' has the meaning given by section 1(3);

'the 1968 Convention' has the meaning given by section 1(1), and references to that Convention and to provisions of it are to be construed in accordance with section 1(2)(a);

'corporation' means a body corporate, and includes a partnership subsisting under the law of Scotland;

'court', without more, includes a tribunal;

'court of law', in relation to the United Kingdom, means any of the following courts, namely—

(a) the House of Lords,
(b) in England and Wales or Northern Ireland, the Court of Appeal, the High Court, the Crown Court, a county court and a magistrates' court,
(c) in Scotland, the Court of Session and a sheriff Court;

'the Crown' is to be construed in accordance with section 51(2);

'enactment' includes an enactment comprised in Northern Ireland legislation;

'judgment', subject to sections 15(1) and 18(2) and to paragraph 1 of Schedules 6 and 7, means any judgment or order (by whatever name called) given or made by a court in any civil proceedings;

'Lugano Contracting State' has the meaning given by section 1(3);

'the Lugano Convention' has the meaning given by section 1(1);

'magistrates' court', in relation to Northern Ireland, means a court of summary jurisdiction;

'modifications' includes additions, omissions and alterations;

'overseas country' means any country or territory outside the United Kingdom;

'part of the United Kingdom' means England and Wales, Scotland or Northern Ireland;

'the 1971 Protocol' has the meaning given by section 1(1), and references to that Protocol and to provisions of it are to be construed in accordance with section 1(2)(a);

'the Regulation' has the meaning given by section 1(1);

'Regulation State' has the meaning given by section 1(3);

'rules of court', in relation to any court, means rules, orders or regulations made by the authority having power to make rules, orders or regulations regulating the procedure of that court, and includes—

(a) in Scotland, Acts of Sederunt;
(b) in Northern Ireland, Judgment Enforcement Rules;

'statutory provision' means any provision contained in an Act, or in any Northern Ireland legislation, or in—

(a) subordinate legislation (as defined in section 21(1) of the Interpretation Act 1978); or
(b) any instrument of a legislative character made under any Northern Ireland legislation;

'tribunal'—

(a) means a tribunal of any description other than a court of law;
(b) in relation to an overseas country, includes, as regards matters relating to maintenance within the meaning of the 1968 Convention, any authority having power to give, enforce, vary or revoke a maintenance order.

51. Application to Crown

(1) This Act binds the Crown.

(2) In this section and elsewhere in this Act references to the Crown do not include references to Her

Majesty in Her private capacity or to Her Majesty in right of Her Duchy of Lancaster or to the Duke of Cornwall.

55. Short Title

This Act may be cited as the Civil Jurisdiction and Judgments Act 1982.

SCHEDULE 1 TEXT OF 1968 CONVENTION, AS AMENDED

[Schedule 1 is on the CD-ROM version of *Blackstone's Civil Practice.* Please click on the title of the schedule to open it.]

NOTES ON TEXT

Only selected provisions of the Act are printed above, incorporating the following amendments:

s. 1(1) amended by (a) SI 1989/1346, art. 3; (b) SI 1990/2591, arts 3 and 4; (c) Civil Jurisdiction and Judgments Act 1991, s. 2(1) to (3); (d) SI 2000/1824, art. 3; (e) SI 2001/3929, sch. 2, para. 1(a);
s. 1(2) amended by (a) SI 1990/2591, art. 5; (b) Civil Jurisdiction and Judgments Act 1991, s. 2(1) and (4); (c) SI 2000/1824, arts 4 and 9;
s. 1(3) amended by (a) SI 1990/2591, art. 6; (b) Civil Jurisdiction and Judgments Act 1991, s. 2(1), (5) and (6); (c) SI 2000/1824, arts 5 and 10; (d) SI 2001/3929, sch. 2, para. 1(b);
s. 1(4) inserted by SI 2001/3929, sch. 2, para. 1(c);
s. 2(1) amended by Civil Jurisdiction and Judgments Act 1991, sch. 2, para. 1;
s. 2(2) substituted by SI 1990/2591, art. 7; amended by SI 2000/1824, art. 6;
s. 3 amended by: (a) SI 1989/1346, art. 8; (b) SI 1990/2591, art. 8; (c) Civil Jurisdiction and Judgments Act 1991, sch. 2, para. 1;
s. 3A inserted by Civil Jurisdiction and Judgments Act 1991, s. 1(1); amended by SI 2000/1824, art. 11;
s. 3B inserted by Civil Jurisdiction and Judgments Act 1991, s. 1(1);
s. 24 amended by SI 2001/3929, sch. 2, para. 9;
s. 25 amended by Civil Jurisdiction and Judgments Act 1991, sch. 2, para. 12;
s. 41 amended by Civil Jurisdiction and Judgments Act 1991, sch. 2, para. 16;
s. 42 amended by Civil Jurisdiction and Judgments Act 1991, sch. 2, para. 17;
s. 50 amended by: (a) SI 1990/2591, art. 9; (b) Civil Jurisdiction and Judgments Act 1991, sch. 2, para. 25; (c) SI 2000/1824, art. 7; (d) SI 2001/3929, sch. 2, para. 18;
sch. 1 substituted by SI 2000/1824, art. 8(1) and sch. 1.

The titles of the statutory instruments referred to above are: Civil Jurisdiction and Judgments Act 1982 (Amendment) Order 1989 (SI 1989/1346); Civil Jurisdiction and Judgments Act 1982 (Amendment) Order 1990 (SI 1990/2591) (which came into force on 1 December 1991); Civil Jurisdiction and Judgments Act 1982 (Amendment) Order 2000 (SI 2000/1824) (part of which came into force on 1 August 2000 and the remainder on 1 January 2001); Civil Jurisdiction and Judgments Order 2001 (SI 2001/3929).

The Civil Jurisdiction and Judgments Act 1991 was brought into force by SI 1992/745.

Civil Liability (Contribution) Act 1978

(1978 CHAPTER 47)

1. Entitlement to Contribution

(1) Subject to the following provisions of this section, any person liable in respect of any damage suffered by another person may recover contribution from any other person liable in respect of the same damage (whether jointly with him or otherwise).

(2) A person shall be entitled to recover contribution by virtue of subsection (1) above notwithstanding that he has ceased to be liable in respect of the damage in question since the time when the damage occurred, provided that he was so liable immediately before he made or was ordered or agreed to make the payment in respect of which the contribution is sought.

(3) A person shall be liable to make contribution by virtue of subsection (1) above notwithstanding that he has ceased to be liable in respect of the damage in question since the time when the damage occurred, unless he ceased to be liable by virtue of the expiry of a period of limitation or prescription which extinguished the right on which the claim against him in respect of the damage was based.

(4) A person who has made or agreed to make any payment in bona fide settlement or compromise of any claim made against him in respect of any damage (including a payment into court which has been accepted) shall be entitled to recover contribution in accordance with this section without regard to whether or not he himself is or ever was liable in respect of the damage, provided, however, that he would have been liable assuming that the factual basis of the claim against him could be established.

(5) A judgment given in any action brought in any part of the United Kingdom by or on behalf of the person who suffered the damage in question against any person from whom contribution is sought under this section shall be conclusive in the proceedings for contribution as to any issue determined by that judgment in favour of the person from whom the contribution is sought.

(6) References in this section to a person's liability in respect of any damage are references to any such liability which has been or could be established in an action brought against him in England and Wales by or on behalf of the person who suffered the damage; but it is immaterial whether any issue arising in any such action was or would be determined (in accordance with the rules of private international law) by reference to the law of a country outside England and Wales.

2. Assessment of Contribution

(1) Subject to subsection (3) below, in any proceedings for contribution under section 1 above the amount of the contribution recoverable from any person shall be such as may be found by the court to be just and equitable having regard to the extent of that person's responsibility for the damage in question.

(2) Subject to subsection (3) below, the court shall have power in any such proceedings to exempt any person from liability to make contribution or to direct that the contribution to be recovered from any person shall amount to a complete indemnity.

(3) Where the amount of the damages which have or might have been awarded in respect of the damage in question in any action brought in England and Wales by or on behalf of the person who suffered it against the person from whom the contribution is sought was or would have been subject to—

(a) any limit imposed by or under any enactment or by any agreement made before the damage occurred;

(b) any reduction by virtue of section 1 of the Law Reform (Contributory Negligence) Act 1945 or section 5 of the Fatal Accidents Act 1976; or

(c) any corresponding limit or reduction under the law of a country outside England and Wales;

the person from whom the contribution is sought shall not by virtue of any contribution awarded under section 1 above be required to pay in respect of the damage a greater amount than the amount of those damages as so limited or reduced.

3. Proceedings Against Persons Jointly Liable For the Same Debt or Damage

Judgment recovered against any person liable in respect of any debt or damage shall not be a bar to an action, or to the continuance of an action, against any person who is (apart from any such bar) jointly liable with him in respect of the same debt or damage.

4. Successive Actions Against Persons Liable (Jointly or Otherwise) For the Same Damage

If more than one action is bought in respect of any damage by or on behalf of the person by whom it was suffered against persons liable in respect of the damage (whether jointly or otherwise) the plaintiff shall not be entitled to costs in any of those actions, other than that in which judgment is first given, unless the court is of the opinion that there was reasonable ground for bringing the action.

5. Application to the Crown

Without prejudice to section 4(1) of the Crown Proceedings Act 1947 (indemnity and contribution), this Act shall bind the Crown, but nothing in this Act shall be construed as in any way affecting Her Majesty in Her private capacity (including in right of Her Duchy of Lancaster) or the Duchy of Cornwall.

6. Interpretation

(1) A person is liable in respect of any damage for the purposes of this Act if the person who suffered it (or anyone representing his estate or dependants) is entitled to recover compensation from him in respect of that damage (whatever the legal basis of his liability, whether tort, breach of contract, breach of trust or otherwise).

(2) References in this Act to an action brought by or on behalf of the person who suffered any damage include references to an action brought for the benefit of his estate or dependants.

(3) In this Act 'dependants' has the same meaning as in the Fatal Accidents Act 1976.

(4) In this Act, except in section 1(5) above, 'action' means an action brought in England and Wales.

7. Savings

(3) The right to recover contribution in accordance with section 1 above supersedes any right, other than an express contractual right, to recover contribution (as distinct from indemnity) otherwise than under this Act in corresponding circumstances; but nothing in this Act shall affect—

(a) any express or implied contractual or other right to indemnity; or

(b) any express contractual provision regulating or excluding contribution;

which would be enforceable apart from this Act (or render enforceable any agreement for indemnity or contribution which would not be enforceable apart from this Act).

Civil Procedure Act 1997

(1997 CHAPTER 12)

An Act to amend the law about civil procedure in England and Wales; and for connected purposes. [27th February 1997]

Rules and Directions

1. Civil Procedure Rules

(1) There are to be rules of court (to be called 'Civil Procedure Rules') governing the practice and procedure to be followed in—
 (a) the civil division of the Court of Appeal,
 (b) the High Court, and
 (c) county courts.

(2) Schedule 1 (which makes further provision about the extent of the power to make Civil Procedure Rules) is to have effect.

(3) The power to make Civil Procedure Rules is to be exercised with a view to securing that the civil justice system is accessible, fair and efficient.

[*When the Courts Act 2003, s. 82, is brought into force, the following will be substituted for the Civil Procedure Act 1997, s. 1(3):*

(3) Any power to make Civil Procedure Rules is to be exercised with a view to securing that—
 (a) the system of civil justice is accessible, fair and efficient, and
 (b) the rules are both simple and simply expressed.]

2. Rule Committee

(1) Civil Procedure Rules are to be made by a committee known as the Civil Procedure Rule Committee, which is to consist of the following persons—
 (a) the Head of Civil Justice;
 (b) the Deputy Head of Civil Justice (if there is one);
 (c) the persons currently appointed in accordance with subsections (1A) and (1B).

(1A) The Lord Chief Justice must appoint the persons falling within paragraphs (a) to (d) of subsection (2).

(1B) The Lord Chancellor must appoint the persons falling within paragraphs (e) to (g) of subsection (2).

(2) The persons to be appointed in accordance with subsections (1A) and (1B) are—
 (a) either two or three judges of the Supreme Court,
 (b) one Circuit judge,
 (c) one district judge,
 (d) one person who is a Master referred to in Part II of Schedule 2 to the Supreme Court Act 1981,
 (e) three persons who have a Supreme Court qualification (within the meaning of section 71 of the Courts and Legal Services Act 1990), including at least one with particular experience of practice in county courts,
 (f) three persons who have been granted by an authorised body, under Part II of that Act, the right to conduct litigation in relation to all proceedings in the Supreme Court, including at least one with particular experience of practice in county courts,
 (g) two persons with experience in and knowledge of the lay advice sector or consumer affairs.

(3) Before appointing a person in accordance with subsection (1A), the Lord Chief Justice must consult the Lord Chancellor.

(4) Before appointing a person in accordance with subsection (1B), the Lord Chancellor must consult the Lord Chief Justice and, if the person falls within paragraph (e) or (f) of subsection (2), must also consult any body which—
 (a) has members who are eligible for appointment under that paragraph, and

(b) is an authorised body for the purposes of section 27 or 28 of the Courts and Legal Services Act 1990.

(5) The Lord Chancellor may reimburse the members of the Civil Procedure Rule Committee their travelling and out-of-pocket expenses.

(6) The Civil Procedure Rule Committee must, before making or amending Civil Procedure Rules—

(a) consult such persons as they consider appropriate, and

(b) meet (unless it is inexpedient to do so).

(7) The Civil Procedure Rule Committee must, when making Civil Procedure Rules, try to make rules which are both simple and simply expressed.

(8) Rules made by the Civil Procedure Rule Committee must be signed by at least eight members of the Committee and be submitted to the Lord Chancellor, who may allow or disallow them.

(9) The Lord Chief Justice may nominate a judicial office holder (as defined in section 109(4) of the Constitutional Reform Act 2005) to exercise his functions under this section.

[*The following subsection (which has the same number as the preceding subsection) is in force until the Courts Act 2003, s. 85(1), comes into force.*]

(9) If the Lord Chancellor disallows rules under subsection (8), he must give the Civil Procedure Rules Committee written reasons for doing so.

[*When the Courts Act 2003, s. 85(1), is brought into force, subsections (6) to (8) of the Civil Procedure Act 1997, s. 2, will be repealed.*]

2A. Power to Change Certain Requirements Relating to Committee

(1) The Lord Chancellor may by order—

(a) amend section 2(2), (3) or (4), and

(b) make consequential amendments in any other provision of section 2.

(2) The Lord Chancellor may make an order under this section only with the concurrence of the Lord Chief Justice.

(2A) Before making an order under this section the Lord Chancellor must consult the following persons—

(a) the Head of Civil Justice;

(b) the Deputy Head of Civil Justice (if there is one).

(2B) The Lord Chief Justice may nominate a judicial office holder (as defined in section 109(4) of the Constitutional Reform Act 2005) to exercise his functions under this section.

(3) The power to make an order under this section is exercisable by statutory instrument.

(4) A statutory instrument containing such an order is subject to annulment in pursuance of a resolution of either House of Parliament.

3. Section 2: Supplementary

(1) Rules made and allowed under section 2 are to—

(a) come into force on such day as the Lord Chancellor may direct, and

(b) be contained in a statutory instrument to which the Statutory Instruments Act 1946 is to apply as if it contained rules made by a Minister of the Crown.

(2) A statutory instrument containing Civil Procedure Rules shall be subject to annulment in pursuance of a resolution of either House of Parliament.

[*When the Courts Act 2003, s. 85(2), is brought into force, the following will be substituted for the Civil Procedure Act 1997, s. 3:*

3. Process for Making Civil Procedure Rules

(1) The Civil Procedure Rule Committee must, before making Civil Procedure Rules—

(a) consult such persons as they consider appropriate, and

(b) meet (unless it is inexpedient to do so).

(2) Rules made by the Civil Procedure Rule Committee must be—

(a) signed by a majority of the members of the Committee, and

(b) submitted to the Lord Chancellor.

(3) The Lord Chancellor may allow or disallow rules so made.

(4) If the Lord Chancellor disallows Rules, he must give the Committee written reasons for doing so.

(5) Rules so made and allowed by the Lord Chancellor—
(a) come into force on such day as the Lord Chancellor directs, and
(b) are to be contained in a statutory instrument to which the Statutory Instruments Act 1946 applies as if the instrument contained rules made by a Minister of the Crown.
(6) A statutory instrument containing Civil Procedure Rules is subject to annulment in pursuance of a resolution of either House of Parliament.]

3A. Rules to Be Made If Required by Lord Chancellor

(1) This section applies if the Lord Chancellor gives the Civil Procedure Rules [*sic*] Committee written notice that he thinks it is expedient for Civil Procedure Rules to include provision that would achieve a purpose specified in the notice.
(2) The Committee must make such Rules as it considers necessary to achieve the specified purpose.
(3) Those rules must be—
(a) made within a reasonable period after the Lord Chancellor gives notice to the Committee;
(b) made in accordance with section 3.

4. Power to Make Consequential Amendments

(1) The Lord Chancellor may, after consulting the Lord Chief Justice, by order amend, repeal or revoke any enactment to the extent he considers necessary or desirable in consequence of—
(a) section 1 or 2, or
(b) Civil Procedure Rules.
(2) The Lord Chancellor may, after consulting the Lord Chief Justice, by order amend, repeal or revoke any enactment passed or made before the commencement of this section to the extent he considers necessary or desirable in order to facilitate the making of Civil Procedure Rules.
(3) Any power to make an order under this section is exercisable by statutory instrument.
(4) A statutory instrument containing an order under subsection (1) shall be subject to annulment in pursuance of a resolution of either House of Parliament.
(5) No order may be made under subsection (2) unless a draft of it has been laid before and approved by resolution of each House of Parliament.
(6) The Lord Chief Justice may nominate a judicial office holder (as defined in section 109(4) of the Constitutional Reform Act 2005) to exercise his functions under subsection (1) or (2).

5. Practice Directions

(1) Practice directions may be given in accordance with Part 1 of Schedule 2 to the Constitutional Reform Act 2005.
(2) Practice directions given otherwise than under subsection (1) may not be given without the approval of—
(a) the Lord Chancellor, and
(b) the Lord Chief Justice.
(3) Practice directions (whether given under subsection (1) or otherwise) may provide for any matter which, by virtue of paragraph 3 of Schedule 1, may be provided for by Civil Procedure Rules.
(4) The power to give practice directions under subsection (1) includes power—
(a) to vary or revoke directions given by any person;
(b) to give directions containing different provision for different cases (including different areas);
(b) to give directions containing provision for a specific court, for specific proceedings or for a specific jurisdiction.
(5) Subsection (2)(a) does not apply to directions to the extent that they consist of guidance about any of the following—
(a) the application or interpretation of the law;
(b) the making of judicial decisions.
(6) Subsection (2)(a) does not apply to directions to the extent that they consist of criteria for determining which judges may be allocated to hear particular categories of case; but the directions may, to that extent, be given only—
(a) after consulting the Lord Chancellor, and
(b) with the approval of the Lord Chief Justice.

Civil Justice Council

6. Civil Justice Council

(1) The Lord Chancellor is to establish and maintain an advisory body, to be known as the Civil Justice Council.

(2) The Council must include—

(a) members of the judiciary,

(b) members of the legal professions,

(c) civil servants concerned with the administration of the courts,

(d) persons with experience in and knowledge of consumer affairs,

(e) persons with experience in and knowledge of the lay advice sector, and

(f) persons able to represent the interests of particular kinds of litigants (for example, businesses or employees).

(2A) The Lord Chancellor must decide the following questions, after consulting the Lord Chief Justice—

(a) how many members of the Council are to be drawn from each of the groups mentioned in subsection (2);

(b) how many other members the Council is to have.

(2B) It is for—

(a) the Lord Chief Justice to appoint members of the judiciary to the Council, after consulting the Lord Chancellor;

(b) the Lord Chancellor to appoint other persons to the Council.

(3) The functions of the Council are to include—

(a) keeping the civil justice system under review,

(b) considering how to make the civil justice system more accessible, fair and efficient,

(c) advising the Lord Chancellor and the judiciary on the development of the civil justice system,

(d) referring proposals for changes in the civil justice system to the Lord Chancellor and the Civil Procedure Rule Committee, and

(e) making proposals for research.

(4) The Lord Chancellor may reimburse the members of the Council their travelling and out-of-pocket expenses.

(5) The Lord Chief Justice may nominate a judicial office holder (as defined in section 109(4) of the Constitutional Reform Act 2005) to exercise his functions under this section.

Court Orders

7. Power of Courts to Make Orders for Preserving Evidence, etc.

(1) The court may make an order under this section for the purpose of securing, in the case of any existing or proposed proceedings in the court—

(a) the preservation of evidence which is or may be relevant, or

(b) the preservation of property which is or may be the subject-matter of the proceedings or as to which any question arises or may arise in the proceedings.

(2) A person who is, or appears to the court likely to be, a party to proceedings in the court may make an application for such an order.

(3) Such an order may direct any person to permit any person described in the order, or secure that any person so described is permitted—

(a) to enter premises in England and Wales, and

(b) while on the premises, to take in accordance with the terms of the order any of the following steps.

(4) Those steps are—

(a) to carry out a search for or inspection of anything described in the order, and

(b) to make or obtain a copy, photograph, sample or other record of anything so described.

(5) The order may also direct the person concerned—

(a) to provide any person described in the order, or secure that any person so described is provided, with any information or article described in the order, and

(b) to allow any person described in the order, or secure that any person so described is allowed, to retain for safe keeping anything described in the order.

(6) An order under this section is to have effect subject to such conditions as are specified in the order.

(7) This section does not affect any right of a person to refuse to do anything on the ground that to do so might tend to expose him or his spouse to proceedings for an offence or for the recovery of a penalty.

(8) In this section—

'court' means the High Court, and

'premises' includes any vehicle;

and an order under this section may describe anything generally, whether by reference to a class or otherwise.

8. Disclosure etc. of Documents before Action Begun

(1) The Lord Chancellor may by order amend the provisions of section 33(2) of the Supreme Court Act 1981, or section 52(2) of the County Courts Act 1984 (power of court to order disclosure etc. of documents where claim may be made in respect of personal injury or death), so as to extend the provisions—

(a) to circumstances where other claims may be made, or

(b) generally.

(2) The power to make an order under this section is exercisable by statutory instrument which shall be subject to annulment in pursuance of a resolution of either House of Parliament.

General

9. Interpretation

(1) A court the practice and procedure of which is governed by Civil Procedure Rules is referred to in this Act as being 'within the scope' of the rules; and references to a court outside the scope of the rules are to be read accordingly.

(2) In this Act—

'enactment' includes an enactment contained in subordinate legislation (within the meaning of the Interpretation Act 1978), and

'practice directions' means directions as to the practice and procedure of any court within the scope of Civil Procedure Rules.

11. Short Title, Commencement and Extent

(1) This Act may be cited as the Civil Procedure Act 1997.

(2) Sections 1 to 10 are to come into force on such day as the Lord Chancellor may by order made by statutory instrument appoint, and different days may be appointed for different purposes.

(3) This Act extends to England and Wales only.

[*Section 11 came into force on royal assent (27 February 1997). All other provisions of the Act printed here were brought into force on 27 April 1997 by the Civil Procedure Act 1997 (Commencement No. 1) Order 1997 (SI 1997/841).*]

Section 1

SCHEDULES

SCHEDULE 1 CIVIL PROCEDURE RULES

Matters Dealt with by the Former Rules

1. Among the matters which Civil Procedure Rules may be made about are any matters which were governed by the former Rules of the Supreme Court or the former county court rules (that is, the Rules of the Supreme Court (Revision) 1965 and the County Court Rules 1981).

Exercise of Jurisdiction

2. Civil Procedure Rules may provide for the exercise of the jurisdiction of any court within the scope of the rules by officers or other staff of the court.

Removal of Proceedings

3. (1) Civil Procedure Rules may provide for the removal of proceedings at any stage—
   (a) within the High Court (for example, between different divisions or different district registries), or
   (b) between county courts.
 (2) In sub-paragraph (1)—
   (a) 'provide for the removal of proceedings' means—
     (i) provide for transfer of proceedings, or
     (ii) provide for any jurisdiction in any proceedings to be exercised (whether concurrently or not) elsewhere within the High Court or, as the case may be, by another county court without the proceedings being transferred, and
   (b) 'proceedings' includes any part of proceedings.

Evidence

4. Civil Procedure Rules may modify the rules of evidence as they apply to proceedings in any court within the scope of the rules.

Application of Other Rules

5.—(1) Civil Procedure Rules may apply any rules of court which relate to a court which is outside the scope of Civil Procedure Rules.
 (2) Any rules of court, not made by the Civil Procedure Rule Committee, which apply to proceedings of a particular kind in a court within the scope of Civil Procedure Rules may be applied by Civil Procedure Rules to other proceedings in such a court.
 (3) In this paragraph 'rules of court' includes any provision governing the practice and procedure of a court which is made by or under an enactment.
 (4) Where Civil Procedure Rules may be made by applying other rules, the other rules may be applied—
   (a) to any extent,
   (b) with or without modification, and
   (c) as amended from time to time.

Practice Directions

6. Civil Procedure Rules may, instead of providing for any matter, refer to provision made or to be made about that matter by directions.

Different Provision for Different Cases etc.

7. The power to make Civil Procedure Rules includes power to make different provision for different cases or different areas, including different provision—
   (a) for a specific court or specific division of a court, or
   (b) for specific proceedings, or a specific jurisdiction, specified in the rules.

Selected Legislation

NOTES ON TEXT

The text printed above incorporates the following amendments:
s. 1 as prospectively amended by Courts Act 2003, s. 82, amended by Constitutional Reform Act 2005, sch. 4, para. 262, and sch. 18, part 2 (in force by SI 2006/1014);
s. 2 amended by: (a) Courts Act 2003, s. 83 (in force by SI 2003/3345); (b) Constitutional Reform Act 2005, sch. 4, paras 263 and 385 (in force by SI 2006/1014);
s. 2A inserted by Courts Act 2003, s. 84 (in force by SI 2003/3345); Constitutional Reform Act 2005, sch. 4, para. 264 (in force by SI 2006/1014);
s. 3 as prospectively amended by Courts Act 2003, s. 85(2), amended by Constitutional Reform Act 2005, sch. 4, para. 265, and sch. 18, part 2 (in force by SI 2006/1014);
s. 3A inserted by Constitutional Reform Act 2005, sch. 4, para. 266 (in force by SI 2006/1014);
s. 4 amended by Constitutional Reform Act 2005, sch. 4, para. 267 (in force by SI 2006/1014);

s. 5 substituted by Constitutional Reform Act 2005, sch. 2, para. 6 (in force by SI 2006/1014);
s. 6 amended by Constitutional Reform Act 2005, sch. 4, para. 268 (in force by SI 2006/1014);

The following provisions have been omitted: s. 10 and sch. 2 (minor and consequential amendments).

Collective Conditional Fee Agreements Regulations 2000

(SI 2000/2988)

The Lord Chancellor, in exercise of the powers conferred upon him by sections 58(3)(c), 58A(3) and 119 of the Courts and Legal Services Act 1990 hereby makes the following Regulations:

1. Citation, Commencement and Interpretation

(1) These regulations may be cited as the Collective Conditional Fee Agreements Regulations 2000, and shall come into force on 30th November 2000.

(2) In these Regulations, except where the context requires otherwise—

'client' means a person who will receive advocacy or litigation services to which the agreement relates;

'collective conditional fee agreement' has the meaning given in regulation 3;

'conditional fee agreement' has the same meaning as in section 58 of the Courts and Legal Services Act 1990;

'funder' means the party to a collective conditional fee agreement who, under that agreement, is liable to pay the legal representative's fees;

'legal representative' means the person providing the advocacy or litigation services to which the agreement relates.

2. Transitional Provisions

These Regulations shall apply to agreements entered into on or after 30th November 2000, and agreements entered into before that date shall be treated as if these Regulations had not come into force.

3. Definition of 'Collective Conditional Fee Agreement'

(1) Subject to paragraph (2) of this regulation, a collective conditional fee agreement is an agreement which—

(a) disregarding section 58(3)(c) of the Courts and Legal Services Act 1990, would be a conditional fee agreement; and

(b) does not refer to specific proceedings, but provides for fees to be payable on a common basis in relation to a class of proceedings, or, if it refers to more than one class of proceedings, on a common basis in relation to each class.

(2) An agreement may be a collective conditional fee agreement whether or not—

(a) the finder is a client; or

(b) any clients are named in the agreement.

4. Requirements for Contents of Collective Conditional Fee Agreements: General

(1) A collective conditional fee agreement must specify the circumstances in which the legal representative's fees and expenses, or part of them, are payable.

(1A) The circumstances referred to in paragraph (1) may include the fact that the legal representative's fees and expenses are payable only to the extent that sums are recovered in respect of the proceedings, whether by way of costs or otherwise.

(2) A collective conditional fee agreement must provide that, when accepting instructions in relation to any specific proceedings the legal representative must—

(a) inform the client as to the circumstances in which the client or his estate may be liable to pay the costs of the legal representative; and

(b) if the client requires any further explanation, advice or other information about the matter referred to in sub-paragraph (a), provide such further explanation, advice or other information about it as the client may reasonably require.

(3) Paragraph (2) does not apply in the case of an agreement between a legal representative and an additional legal representative.

(4) A collective conditional fee agreement must provide that, after accepting instructions in relation to

Selected Legislation

any specific proceedings, the legal representative must confirm his acceptance of instructions in writing to the client.

5. Requirements for Contents of Collective Conditional Fee Agreements Providing for Success Fees

(1) Where a collective conditional fee agreement provides for a success fee the agreement must provide that, when accepting instructions in relation to any specific proceedings the legal representative must prepare and retain a written statement containing—

(a) his assessment of the probability of the circumstances arising in which the percentage increase will become payable in relation to those proceedings ('the risk assessment');

(b) his assessment of the amount of the percentage increase in relation to those proceedings, having regard to the risk assessment; and

(c) the reasons, by reference to the risk assessment, for setting the percentage increase at that level.

(2) If the agreement relates to court proceedings it must provide that where the success fee becomes payable as a result of those proceedings, then—

(a) if—

(i) any fees subject to the increase are assessed, and

(ii) the legal representative or the client is required by the court to disclose to the court or any other person the reasons for setting the percentage increase at the level assessed by the legal representative,

he may do so,

(b) if—

(i) any such fees are assessed by the court, and

(ii) any amount in respect of the percentage increase is disallowed on the assessment on the ground that the level at which the increase was set was unreasonable in view of facts which were or should have been known to the legal representative at the time it was set

that amount ceases to be payable under the agreement, unless the court is satisfied that it should continue to be so payable, and

(c) if—

(i) sub-paragraph (b) does not apply, and

(ii) the legal representative agrees with any person liable as a result of the proceedings to pay fees subject to the percentage increase that a lower amount than the amount payable in accordance with the conditional fee agreement is to be paid instead,

the amount payable under the collective conditional fee agreement in respect of those fees shall be reduced accordingly, unless the court is satisfied that the full amount should continue to be payable under it.

(3) In this regulation 'percentage increase' means the percentage by which the amount of the fees which would have been payable if the agreement were not a conditional fee agreement is to be increased under the agreement.

(4) Sub-paragraphs (b) and (c) of paragraph (2) do not apply to a collective conditional fee agreement under which, except in the circumstances set out in paragraphs (6) and (7), the client is liable to pay his legal representative's fees and expenses only to the extent that sums are recovered in respect of the proceedings, whether by way of costs or otherwise.

(5) In determining for the purposes of paragraph (4) the circumstances in which a client is liable to pay his legal representative's fees and expenses, no account is to be taken of any obligation to pay costs in respect of the premium of a policy taken out to insure against the risk of incurring a liability in the relevant proceedings.

(6) A collective conditional fee agreement to which paragraph (4) applies may specify that the client will be liable to pay his legal representative's fees and expenses whether or not sums are recovered in respect of the relevant proceedings, if the client—

(a) fails to cooperate with the legal representative;

(b) fails to attend any medical or expert examination or court hearing which the legal representative reasonably requests him to attend;

(c) fails to give necessary instructions to the legal representative;

(d) withdraws instructions from the legal representative;

(e) *is an individual who is adjudged bankrupt or enters into an arrangement or a composition with his creditors, or against whom an administration order is made; or*

(f) *is a company for which a receiver, administrative receiver or liquidator is appointed.*

(7) *A collective conditional fee agreement to which paragraph (4) applies may specify that, in the event of the client dying in the course of the relevant proceedings, his estate will be liable for the legal representative's fees and expenses, whether or not sums are recovered in respect of those proceedings.*

6. Form and Amendment of Collective Conditional Fee Agreement

(1) *Subject to paragraph (2), a collective conditional fee agreement must be signed by the funder, and by the legal representative.*

(2) *Paragraph (1) does not apply in the case of an agreement between a legal representative and an additional legal representative.*

(3) *Where a collective conditional fee agreement is amended, regulations 4 and 5 apply to the amended agreement as if it were a fresh agreement made at the time of the amendment.*

NOTES ON TEXT

The text printed above incorporates the following amendments:

reg. 4 amended by (a): Conditional Fee Agreements (Miscellaneous Amendments) Regulations 2003 (SI 2003/1240), reg. 3(2); (b) Conditional Fee Agreements (Miscellaneous Amendments) (No. 2) Regulations 2003 (SI 2003/3344), reg. 3(1) and (2);

reg. 5 amended by (a): Conditional Fee Agreements (Miscellaneous Amendments) Regulations 2003 (SI 2003/1240), reg. 3(3); (b) Conditional Fee Agreements (Miscellaneous Amendments) (No. 2) Regulations 2003 (SI 2003/3344), reg. 3(1) and (3).

The following provision has been omitted: reg. 7 (amendment of Conditional Fee Agreements Regulations 2000).

REVOCATION

As from 1 November 2005, these regulations are revoked by the Conditional Fee Agreements (Revocation) Regulations 2005 (SI 2005/2305), reg. 2. These regulations continue to have effect for the purposes of a collective conditional fee agreement entered into before 1 November 2005 (SI 2005/2305, reg. 3).

Community Legal Service (Cost Protection) Regulations 2000

(SI 2000/824)

The Lord Chancellor, in exercise of the powers conferred on him by sections 11(1), (3) and (4)(b) and (d) of the Access to Justice Act 1999, and all other powers enabling him in that behalf, makes the following Regulations, a draft of which has been laid before and approved by resolution of each House of Parliament:

1. Citation and Commencement

These Regulations may be cited as the Community Legal Service (Cost Protection) Regulations 2000 and shall come into force on 1st April 2000.

2. Interpretation

(1) In these Regulations:

'the Act' means the Access to Justice Act 1999;

'certificate' means a certificate issued under the Funding Code certifying a decision to fund services for the client and 'emergency certificate' means a certificate certifying a decision to fund Legal Representation for the client in a case of emergency;

'client' means an individual who receives funded services;

'Commission' means the Legal Services Commission established under section 1 of the Act;

'costs judge' has the same meaning as in the Civil Procedure Rules 1998;

'costs order' means an order that a party pay all or part of the costs of proceedings;

'cost protection' means the limit on costs awarded against a client set out in section 11(1) of the Act;

'court' includes any tribunal having the power to award costs in favour of, or against, a party;

'family proceedings' means—

(a) all proceedings under any one or more of the following—
   (i) the Matrimonial Causes Act 1973;
   (ii) the Domestic Proceedings and Magistrates' Courts Act 1978;
   (iii) Part III of the Matrimonial and Family Proceedings Act 1984;
   (iv) the Child Abduction and Custody Act 1985;
   (v) Parts I and II of and Schedule 1 to the Children Act 1989;
   (vi) section 53 of and Schedule 7 to the Family Law Act 1996; and

(b) proceedings which arise out of family relationships under either or both of the following—
   (i) the Inheritance (Provision for Family and Dependants) Act 1975;
   (ii) the Trusts of Land and Appointment of Trustees Act 1996;

'family relationships' has the same meaning as in the Funding Code which came into force on 1st April 2000 and the Funding Code Guidance published on 1st April 2000 by the Commission for the purpose of making decisions under the Funding Code;

'full costs' means, where a section 11(1) costs order is made against a client, the amount of costs which that client would, but for section 11(1) of the Act, have been ordered to pay;

'funded proceedings' means proceedings (including prospective proceedings) in relation to which the client receives funded services or, as the case may be, that part of proceedings during which the client receives funded services;

'funded services' means services which are provided directly for a client and funded for that client by the Commission as part of the Community Legal Service under sections 4 to 11 of the Act;

'Funding Code' means the code approved under section 9 of the Act;

'non-funded party' means a party to proceedings who has not received funded services in relation to those proceedings under a certificate, other than a certificate which has been revoked;

'partner' means a person with whom the person concerned lives as a couple, and includes a person with whom the person concerned is not currently living but from whom he is not living separate and apart;

'proceedings' include proceedings in any tribunal which is a court, as defined in this paragraph;
'receiving party' means a party in favour of whom a costs order is made;
'section 11(1) costs order' means a costs order against a client where cost protection applies;
'solicitor' means a solicitor or another person who is an authorised litigator within the meaning of section 119(1) of the Courts and Legal Services Act 1990.

(2) References to the levels of service listed in paragraph (3) shall be construed as references to the receipt or provision of those levels of service granted in accordance with the Funding Code.

(3) The levels of service referred to in paragraph (2) are:
(a) Legal Help;
(b) Help at Court;
(c) Legal Representation;
(d) General Family Help and Help with Mediation.

3. Cost Protection

(1) Cost protection shall not apply in relation to such parts of proceedings, or prospective proceedings, as are funded for the client by way of:
(a) Help at Court;
(b) [*revoked*]
(c) subject to paragraph (2), Legal Help;
(d) General Family Help and Help with Mediation in family proceedings;
(e) Legal Representation in family proceedings.

(2) Subject to paragraph (4), where the client receives Legal Help, but later receives Legal Representation or General Family Help or Help with Mediation in respect of the same dispute, other than Legal Representation in family proceedings or General Family Help or Help with Mediation in family proceedings, cost protection shall apply, both in respect of:
(a) the costs incurred by the receiving party before the commencement of proceedings which, as regards the client, are funded proceedings by virtue of the client's receipt of Legal Help, and
(b) the costs incurred by the receiving party in the course of proceedings which, as regards the client, are funded proceedings by virtue of the client's receipt of Legal Representation, General Family Help or Help with Mediation.

(3) Subject to paragraph (4), cost protection shall apply only to costs incurred by the receiving party in relation to proceedings which, as regards the client, are funded proceedings, and:
(a) where work is done before the issue of a certificate, cost protection shall (subject to paragraphs (2) and (5)) apply only to costs incurred after the issue of the certificate;
(b) where funding is withdrawn by discharging the client's certificate, cost protection shall apply only to costs incurred before the date when funded services under the certificate ceased to be provided.

(4) Where funding is withdrawn by revoking the client's certificate, cost protection shall not apply, either in respect of work done before or after the revocation.

(5) Cost protection shall apply to work done immediately before the grant of an emergency certificate, other than an emergency certificate granted in relation to family proceedings, if:
(a) no application for such a certificate could be made because the Commission's office was closed; and
(b) the client's solicitor applies for an emergency certificate at the first available opportunity, and the certificate is granted.

4. Enforcement of Costs Order against Client

Where, in a case where costs protection applies, for the purpose of enforcing a costs order against a client (alone or together with any other judgment or order), a charging order under section 1 of the Charging Orders Act 1979 is made in respect of the client's interest in the main or only dwelling in which he resides:

(a) that charging order shall operate to secure the amount payable under the costs order (including, without limitation, any interest) only to the extent of the amount (if any) by which the proceeds of sale of the client's interest in the dwelling (having deducted any mortgage debts) exceed £100,000; and

(b) an order for the sale of the dwelling shall not be made in favour of the person in whose favour the charging order is made.

5. Costs Order against Commission

(1) The following paragraphs of this regulation apply where:
 (a) funded services are provided to a client in relation to proceedings;
 (b) those proceedings are finally decided in favour of a non-funded party; and
 (c) cost protection applies.

(2) The court may, subject to the following paragraphs of this regulation, make an order for the payment by the Commission to the non-funded party of the whole or any part of the costs incurred by him in the proceedings (other than any costs that the client is required to pay under a section 11(1) costs order).

(3) An order under paragraph (2) may only be made if all the conditions set out in sub-paragraphs (a), (b), (c) and (d) are satisfied:
 (a) a section 11(1) costs order is made against the client in the proceedings, and the amount (if any) which the client is required to pay under that costs order is less than the amount of the full costs;
 (b) unless there is a good reason for the delay, the non-funded party makes a request under regulation 10(2) of the Community Legal Service (Costs) Regulations 2000 within three months of the making of the section 11(1) costs order;
 (c) as regards costs incurred in a court of first instance, the proceedings were instituted by the client, the non-funded party is an individual, and the court is satisfied that the non-funded party will suffer financial hardship unless the order is made; and
 (d) in any case, the court is satisfied that it is just and equitable in the circumstances that provision for the costs should be made out of public funds.

(3A) An order under paragraph (2) may be made—
 (a) in relation to proceedings in the House of Lords, by the Clerk to the Parliaments;
 (b) in relation to proceedings in the Court of Appeal, High Court or a county court, by a costs judge or a district judge;
 (c) in relation to proceedings in a magistrates' court, by a single justice or by the justices' clerk;
 (d) in relation to proceedings in the Employment Appeal Tribunal, by the Registrar of that tribunal.

(4) Where the client receives funded services in connection with part only of the proceedings, the reference in paragraph (2) to the costs incurred by the non-funded party in the relevant proceedings shall be construed as a reference to so much of those costs as is attributable to the part of the proceedings which are funded proceedings.

(5) Where a court decides any proceedings in favour of the non-funded party and an appeal lies (with or without permission) against that decision, any order made under this regulation shall not take effect:
 (a) where permission to appeal is required, unless the time limit for applications for permission to appeal expires without permission being granted;
 (b) where permission to appeal is granted or is not required, unless the time limit for appeal expires without an appeal being brought.

(6) Subject to paragraph (7), in determining whether the conditions in paragraph (3)(c) and (d) are satisfied, the court shall have regard to the resources of the non-funded party and of his partner.

(7) The court shall not have regard to the resources of the partner of the non-funded party if the partner has a contrary interest in the funded proceedings.

(8) Where the non-funded party is acting in a representative, fiduciary or official capacity and is entitled to be indemnified in respect of his costs from any property, estate or fund, the court shall, for the purposes of paragraph (3), have regard to the value of the property, estate or fund and the resources of the persons, if any, including that party where appropriate, who are beneficially interested in that property, estate or fund.

7. Effect Of These Regulations

(1) No order to pay costs in favour of a non-funded party shall be made against the Commission in respect of funded proceedings except in accordance with these Regulations, and any costs to be paid under such an order shall be paid out of the Community Legal Service Fund.

(2) Nothing in these Regulations shall be construed, in relation to proceedings where one or more parties are receiving, or have received, funded services, as:

(a) requiring a court to make a costs order where it would not otherwise have made a costs order; or

(b) affecting the court's power to make a wasted costs order against a legal representative.

NOTES ON TEXT

The text printed above incorporates the following amendments:

reg. 2 amended by: (a) Community Legal Service (Cost Protection) (Amendment) Regulations 2001 (SI 2001/823), reg. 2; (b) Community Legal Service (Cost Protection) (Amendment) Regulations 2005 (SI 2005/2006), reg. 2;

reg. 3 amended by Community Legal Service (Cost Protection) (Amendment) Regulations 2005 (SI 2005/2006), reg. 3;

reg. 4 amended by Community Legal Service (Cost Protection) (Amendment) Regulations 2005 (SI 2005/2006), reg. 4;

reg. 5 amended by: (a) Community Legal Service (Cost Protection) (Amendment) Regulations 2001 (SI 2001/823), reg. 3; (b) Community Legal Service (Cost Protection) (Amendment No. 2) Regulations 2001 (SI 2001/3812), reg. 4;

reg. 6 revoked by Community Legal Service (Cost Protection) (Amendment) Regulations 2005 (SI 2005/2006), reg. 5.

Community Legal Service (Costs) Regulations 2000

(SI 2000/441)

The Lord Chancellor, in exercise of the powers conferred on him by sections 10, 11(2), (3) and (4)(a), (c) and (e) to (g) and section 22(1), (5) and (6) of the Access to Justice Act 1999, and all other powers enabling him in that behalf, makes the following Regulations:

PART I GENERAL

1. Citation and Commencement

These Regulations may be cited as the Community Legal Service (Costs) Regulations 2000 and shall come into force on 1st April 2000.

2. Interpretation

In these Regulations:

'the Act' means the Access to Justice Act 1999;

'certificate' means a certificate issued under the Funding Code certifying a decision to fund services for the client;

'child' means a person under 18;

'client' means an individual who receives funded services;

'Commission' means the Legal Services Commission established under section 1 of the Act;

'costs judge' has the same meaning as in the CPR;

'costs order' means an order that a party pay all or part of the costs of proceedings;

'costs order against the Commission' means an order, made under regulation 5 of the Community Legal Service (Cost Protection) Regulations 2000 (but not one under regulation 6 of those Regulations), that the Commission pay all or part of the costs of a part to proceedings who has not received funded services in relation to those proceedings under a certificate, other than a certificate which has been revoked;

'cost protection' means the limit on costs awarded against a client set out in section 11(1) of the Act;

'court' includes any tribunal having the power to award costs in favour of, or against, a party;

'CPR' means the Civil Procedure Rules 1998, and a reference to a Part or rule, prefixed by 'CPR', means the Part or rule so numbered in the CPR;

'Financial Regulations' means the Community Legal Service (Financial) Regulations 2000;

'full costs' means, where a section 11(1) costs order is made against a client, the amount of costs which that client would, but for section 11(1) of the Act, have been ordered to pay;

'funded services' means services which are provided directly for a client and funded for that client by the Commission as part of the Community Legal Service under sections 4 to 11 of the Act;

'Funding Code' means the code approved under section 9 of the Act;

'litigation friend' has the meaning given by CPR Part 21;

'partner', in relation to a party to proceedings, means a person with whom that party lives as a couple, and includes a person with whom the party is not currently living but from whom he is not living separate and apart;

'patient' means a person who by reason of mental disorder within the meaning of the Mental Health Act 1983 is incapable of managing and administering his own affairs;

'proceedings' include proceedings in any tribunal which is a court, as defined, in this paragraph;

'receiving party' means a party in favour of whom a costs order is made;

'Regional Director' means any Regional Director appointed by the Commission in accordance with the Funding Code and any other person authorised to act on his behalf, except a supplier;

'rules of court', in relation to a tribunal, means rules or regulations made by the authority having power to make rules or regulations regulating the practice and procedure of that tribunal and, in relation to any court, includes practice directions;

'section 11(1) costs order' means a costs order against a client where cost protection applies;

'solicitor' means solicitor or other person who is an authorised litigator within the meaning of section 119(1) of the Courts and Legal Services Act 1990;

'statement of resources' means:

(a) a statement, verified by a statement of truth, made by a party to proceedings setting out:
   (i) his income and capital and financial commitments during the previous year and, if applicable, those of his partner;
   (ii) his estimated future financial resources and expectations and, if applicable, those of his partner; and
   (iii) a declaration stating whether he, and if applicable his partner, has deliberately foregone or deprived himself of any resources or expectations, together (if applicable and as far as is practical) with details of those resources or expectations and the manner in which they have been foregone or deprived;
   (iv) particulars of any application for funding made by him in connection with the proceedings; and
   (v) any other facts relevant to the determination of his resources; or
(b) a statement, verified by a statement of truth, made by a client receiving funded services, setting out the information provided by the client under regulation 6 of the Financial Regulations, and stating that there has been no significant change in the client's financial circumstances since the date on which the information was provided or, as the case may be, details of any such change;

'statement of truth' has the same meaning as in CPR Part 22;

'supplier' means any person or body providing funded services to the client, including any authorised advocate (within the meaning of section 119(1) of the Courts and Legal Services Act 1990) engaged by the client's solicitor to act in proceedings.

3. Effect of These Regulations

Nothing in these Regulations shall be construed, in relation to proceedings where one or more parties are receiving, or have received, funded services, as:

(a) requiring a court to make a costs order where it would not otherwise have made a costs order; or
(b) affecting the court's power to make a wasted costs order against a legal representative.

4. Termination of Retainer Where Funding is Withdrawn

(1) The following paragraphs of this regulation apply where funding is withdrawn by revoking or discharging the client's certificate.

(2) Subject to paragraphs (3) and (4), on the revocation or discharge of the client's certificate, the retainer of any supplier acting under that certificate shall terminate immediately.

(3) Termination of retainers under paragraph (2) shall not take effect unless and until any procedures under the Funding Code for review of the decision to withdraw the client's funding are concluded, and confirm the decision to withdraw finding.

(4) The solicitor's retainer shall not terminate until he has complied with any procedures under the Funding Code that require him to send or serve notices.

PART II COSTS ORDERS AGAINST CLIENT AND AGAINST COMMISSION

5. Application of Regulations 6 to 13

Regulations 6 to 13 apply only where cost protection applies.

6. Security for Costs

Where in any proceedings a client is required to give security for costs, the amount of that security shall not exceed the amount (if any) which is a reasonable one having regard to all the circumstances, including the client's financial resources and his conduct in relation to the dispute to which the proceedings relate.

7. Assessment of Resources

(1) The first £100,000 of the value of the client's interest in the main or only dwelling in which he

Selected Legislation

resides shall not be taken into account in having regard to the client's resources for the purposes of section 11(1) of the Act.

(2) Where, but only to the extent that, the court considers that the circumstances are exceptional, having regard in particular to the quantity or value of the items concerned, the court may take into account the value of the client's clothes and household furniture, or the tools and implements of his trade, in having regard to the client's resources for the purposes of section 11(1) of the Act.

(3) Subject to paragraph (4), in having regard to the resources of a party for the purposes of section 11(1) of the Act, the resources of his partner shall be treated as his resources.

(4) The resources of a party's partner shall not be treated as that party's resources if the partner has a contrary interest in the dispute in respect of which the funded services are provided.

(5) Where a party is acting in a representative, fiduciary or official capacity, the court shall not take the personal resources of the party into account for the purposes of section 11(1) of the Act, but shall have regard to the value of any property or estate, or the amount of any fund out of which he is entitled to be indemnified, and may also have regard to the resources of the persons, if any, including that party where appropriate, who are beneficially interested in that property, estate or fund.

(6) For the purposes of section 11(1) of the Act, where a party is acting as a litigation friend to a client who is a child or a patient, the court shall not take the personal resources of the litigation friend into account in assessing the resources of the client.

8. Statements of Resources

(1) Any person who is a party to proceedings in which another party is a client may make a statement of resources, and file it with the court.

(2) A person making and filing a statement of resources under paragraph (1) shall serve a copy of it on the client.

(3) Where a copy of a statement of resources has been served under paragraph (2) not less than seven days before the date fixed for a hearing at which the amount to be paid under a section 11(1) costs order falls, or may fall, to be decided, the client shall also make a statement of resources, and shall produce it at that hearing.

9. Procedures for Ordering Costs against Client and Commission

(1) Where the court is considering whether to make a section 11(1) costs order, it shall consider whether, but for cost protection, it would have made a costs order against the client and, if so, whether it would, on making the costs order, have specified the amount to be paid under that order.

(2) If the court considers that it would have made a costs order against the client, but that it would not have specified the amount to be paid under it, the court shall, when making the section 11(1) costs order:
   (a) specify the amount (if any) that the client is to pay under that order if, but only if:
      (i) it considers that it has sufficient information before it to decide what amount is, in that case, a reasonable amount for the client to pay, in accordance with section 11(1) of the Act; and
      (ii) it is satisfied that, if it were to determine the full costs at that time, they would exceed the amount referred to in sub-paragraph (i);
   (b) otherwise, it shall not specify the amount the client is to pay under the costs order.

(3) If the court considers that it would have made a costs order against the client, and that it would have specified the amount to be paid under it, the court shall, when making the section 11(1) costs order:
   (a) specify the amount (if any) that the client is to pay under that order if, but only if, it considers that it has sufficient information before it to decide what amount is, in that case, a reasonable amount for the client to pay, in accordance with section 11(1) of the Act;
   (b) otherwise, it shall not specify the amount the client is to pay under the costs order.

(4) Any order made under paragraph (3) shall state the amount of the full costs.

(5) The amount (if any) to be paid by the client under an order made under paragraph (2)(b) or paragraph (3)(b), and any application for a costs order against the Commission, shall be

determined in accordance with regulation 10, and at any such determination following an order made under paragraph (2)(b), the amount of the full costs shall also be assessed.

(6) Where the court makes a section 11(1) costs order that does not specify the amount which the client is to pay under it, it may also make findings of fact, as to the parties' conduct in the proceedings or otherwise, relevant to the determination of that amount, and those findings shall be taken into consideration in that determination.

10.

(1) The following paragraphs of this regulation apply where the amount to be paid under a section 11(1) costs order, or an application for a costs order against the Commission, is to be determined under this regulation, by virtue of regulation 9(5).

(2) The receiving party may, within three months after a section 11(1) costs order is made, request a hearing to determine the costs payable to him.

(3) A request under paragraph (2) shall be accompanied by:
- (a) if the section 11(1) costs order does not state the full costs, the receiving party's bill of costs, which shall comply with any requirements of relevant rules of court relating to the form and content of a bill of costs where the court is assessing a party's costs;
- (b) unless the conditions set out in paragraph (3A) are satisfied, a statement of resources; and
- (c) if the receiving party is seeking, or, subject to the determination of the amount to be paid under the section 11(1) costs order, may seek, a costs order against the Commission, written notice to that effect.

(3A) The conditions referred to in paragraph (3)(b) above are that—
- (a) the court is determining an application for a costs order against the Commission;
- (b) the costs were not incurred in a court of first instance.

(4) The receiving party shall file the documents referred to in paragraph (3) with the court and at the same time serve copies of them:
- (a) on the client, if a determination of costs payable under section 11(1) of the Act is sought; and
- (b) on the Regional Director, if notice has been given under paragraph (3)(c).

(5) Where documents are served on the client under paragraph (4)(a), the client shall make a statement of resources.

(6) The client shall file the statement of resources made under paragraph (5) with the court, and serve copies of it on the receiving party and, if notice has been given under paragraph (3)(c), on the Regional Director, not more than 21 days after the client receives a copy of the receiving party's statement of resources.

(7) The client may, at the same time as filing and serving a statement of resources under paragraph (6), file, and serve on the same persons, a statement setting out any points of dispute in relation to the bill of costs referred to in paragraph (3)(a).

(8) If the client, without good reason, fails to file a statement of resources in accordance with paragraph (6), the court shall determine the amount which the client shall be required to pay under the section 11(1) costs order (and, if relevant, the full costs), having regard to the statement made by the receiving party, and the court need not hold an oral hearing for such determination.

(9) If the client files a statement of resources in accordance with paragraph (6), or the period for filing such notice expires, or if the costs payable by the client have already been determined, the court shall set a date for the hearing and, at least 14 days before that date, serve notice of it on:
- (a) the receiving party;
- (b) the client (unless the costs payable by the client have already been determined); and
- (c) if a costs order against the Commission is or may be sought, the Regional Director.

(10) The court's functions under this regulation may be exercised:
- (a) in relation to proceedings in the House of Lords, by the Clerk to the Parliaments;
- (b) in relation to proceedings in the Court of Appeal, High Court or a county court, a costs judge or a district judge;
- (c) in relation to proceedings in a magistrates' court, by a single justice or by the justices' clerk;
- (d) in relation to proceedings in the Employment Appeal Tribunal, by the Registrar of that Tribunal.

(11) The amount of costs to be determined under this regulation may include the costs incurred in relation to a request made under this regulation.

10A.

(1) Subject to paragraph (2), where the court makes a section 11(1) costs order but does not specify the amount which the client is to pay under it, the court may order the client to pay an amount on account of the costs which are the subject of the order.

(2) The court may order a client to make a payment on account of costs under this regulation only if it has sufficient information before it to decide the minimum amount which the client is likely to be ordered to pay on a determination under regulation 10.

(3) The amount of the payment on account of costs shall not exceed the minimum amount which the court decides that the client is likely to be ordered to pay on such a determination.

(4) Where the court orders a client to make a payment on account of costs—

(a) it shall order the client to make the payment into court; and

(b) the payment shall remain in court unless and until the court—

(i) makes a determination under regulation 10 of the amount which the client should pay to the receiving party under the section 11(1) costs order, and orders the payment on account or part of it to be paid to the receiving party in satisfaction or part satisfaction of the client's liability under that order; or

(ii) makes an order under paragraph (5)(b) or (5)(c) of this regulation that the payment on account or part of it be repaid to the client.

(5) Where a client has made a payment on account of costs pursuant to an order under paragraph (1) of this regulation—

(a) the receiving party shall request a hearing under regulation 10 to determine the amount of costs payable to him;

(b) if the receiving party fails to request such a hearing within the time permitted by regulation 10(2), the payment on account shall be repaid to the client;

(c) if upon the hearing under regulation 10 the amount of costs which it is determined that the client should pay is less than the amount of the payment on account, the difference shall be repaid to the client.

11. Appeals, etc.

(1) Subject to the following paragraphs of this regulation, and to regulation 12, any determination made under regulation 9 or regulation 10 shall be final.

(2) Any party with a financial interest in an assessment of the full costs may appeal against that assessment, if and to the extent that that party would, but for these Regulations, be entitled to appeal against an assessment of costs by the court in which the relevant proceedings are taking place.

(3) Where, under regulation 9(2)(a), the court has specified the amount which a client is required to pay under a section 11(1) costs order, the client may apply to the court for a determination of the full costs and if, on that determination, the amount of the full costs is less than the amount which the court previously specified under regulation 9(2)(a), the client shall instead be required to pay the amount of the full costs.

(4) The receiving party or the Commission may appeal, on a point of law, against the making of a costs order against the Commission (including the amount of costs which the Commission is required to pay under the order), or against the court's refusal to make such an order.

12. Variation and Late Determination of Amount of Costs

(1) The following paragraphs of this regulation apply where the court makes a section 11(1) costs order.

(2) Where the amount (if any) which the client is required to pay under the section 11(1) costs order, together with the amount which the Commission is required to pay under any costs order against the Commission, is less than the full costs, the receiving party may, on the ground set out in paragraph (4)(a), apply to the court for an order varying the amount which the client is required to pay under the section 11(1) costs order.

(3) Where the court has not specified the amount to be paid under the section 11(1) costs order, and

the receiving party has not, within the time limit in regulation 10(2), applied to have that amount determined in accordance with regulation 10, the receiving party may, on any of the grounds set out in paragraph (4), apply for a determination of the amount that the client is required to pay.

(4) The grounds referred to in paragraphs (2) and (3) are the grounds that:
  (a) there has been a significant change in the client's circumstances since the date of the order;
  (b) material additional information as to the client's financial resources is available, and that information could not with reasonable diligence have been obtained by the receiving party in time to make an application in accordance with regulation 10; or
  (c) there were other good reasons justifying the receiving party's failure to make an application within the time limit in regulation 10(2).

(5) Any application under paragraph (2) or (3) shall be made by the receiving party within six years from the date on which the section 11(1) costs order is first made.

(6) On any application under paragraph (2), the order may be varied as the court thinks fit, but the amount of costs ordered (excluding any costs ordered to be paid under paragraph (9)) shall not exceed the amount of the full costs as stated in any previous order of the court.

(7) When the amount which the client is required to pay under the section 11(1) costs order has been determined under regulation 9(2)(a), and the receiving party applies under paragraph (2) for an order varying that amount:
  (a) the receiving party shall file with the application under paragraph (2) his bill of costs, which shall comply with any requirements of relevant rules of court relating to the form and content of a bill of costs where the court is assessing a party's costs; and
  (b) the court shall, when determining the application, assess the full costs.

(8) Where the receiving party has received funded services in relation to the proceedings, the Commission may make an application under paragraph (2) or paragraph (3), and:
  (a) when making the application the Commission shall file with the court a statement of the receiving party's costs or, if those costs have not been assessed, the receiving party's bill of costs; and
  (b) paragraphs (4) to (6) shall apply to that application as if 'the Commission' were substituted for 'the receiving party' in those paragraphs.

(9) The amount of costs to be determined under this regulation may include the costs incurred in relation to an application made under this regulation.

13. Rights to Appear

(1) The Regional Director may appear at:
  (a) any hearing in relation to which notice has been given under regulation 10(3)(c);
  (b) the hearing of any appeal under regulation 11(4); or
  (c) the hearing of any application under regulation 12(8).

(2) The Regional Director may, instead of appearing under paragraph (1), give evidence in the form of a written statement to the court, verified by a statement of truth.

(3) The Regional Director shall file with the court any statement under paragraph (2), and serve a copy on the receiving party, not less than seven days before the hearing to which it relates.

PART III PROPERTY AND COSTS RECOVERED FOR A FUNDED CLIENT

14. Application of This Part

(1) In this Part:

'the awarded sum' means the amount of costs to be paid in accordance with a client's costs order or a client's costs agreement;

'client's costs order' and 'client's costs agreement' mean, respectively, an order and an agreement that another party to proceedings or prospective proceedings pay all or part of the costs of a client;

'Fund' means the Community Legal Service Fund established under section 5 of the Act;

'the funded sum' means the amount of remuneration payable by the Commission to a supplier for the relevant work under a contract or any other arrangements that determine that supplier's remuneration, including those that apply by virtue of article 4 of the Community

Legal Service (Funding) Order 2000; and, where funding is provided by the Commission under a contract which does not differentiate between the remuneration for the client's case and remuneration for other cases, means such part of the remuneration payable under the contract as may be specified in writing by the Commission as being the funded sum;

'relevant work' means the funded services provided in relation to the dispute or proceedings to which the client's costs order or client's costs agreement relates;

'remuneration' includes fees and disbursements and value added tax on fees and disbursements;

'statutory charge' means the charge created by section 10(7) of the Act.

15. Amount of Costs under Client's Costs Order or Client's Costs Agreement

(1) Subject to the following paragraphs of this regulation, the amount of the costs to be paid under a client's costs order or client's costs agreement shall, subject to regulation 16, be determined on the same basis as it would be if the costs were to be paid to a person who had not received funded services.

(2) Subject to paragraph (3), the amount of the awarded sum shall not be limited to the amount of the funded sum by any rule of law which limits the costs recoverable by a party to proceedings to the amount he is liable to pay to his legal representatives.

(3) Paragraph (2) applies only to the extent that the Commission has authorised the supplier under section 22(2)(b) of the Act to take payment for the relevant work other than that funded by the Commission.

16. Costs of Serving Notices and Other Documents

The amount of costs to be paid under a client's costs order or client's costs agreement may include costs incurred in filing with the court, or serving on any other party to proceedings, notices or any other documents in accordance with these Regulations, the Financial Regulations or the Funding Code.

17. Application of Regulations 18 to 24

(1) Regulations 18 to 24 apply only where funded services have been provided under a certificate.

(2) If the client is no longer being represented by a solicitor, all money to which regulation 18(1) applies shall be paid (or repaid) to the Commission, and all references in regulations 18(1) and 19 to the client's solicitor shall be construed as references to the Commission.

18. Money Recovered to Be Paid to Solicitor

(1) Subject to the following paragraphs of this regulation, and to regulation 17(2), all money payable to or recovered by a client in connection with a dispute by way of damages, costs or otherwise, whether or not proceedings were begun, and whether under an order of the court or an agreement or otherwise, shall be paid to the client's solicitor, and only the client's solicitor shall be capable of giving a good discharge for that money.

(2) Paragraph (1) shall not apply to:
- (a) any periodical payment of maintenance; or
- (b) any money recovered or preserved by a client in any proceedings which:
  - (i) has been paid into, or remains in, court, and is invested for the client's benefit; and
  - (ii) under regulation 50 of the Financial Regulations, is not subject to the statutory charge.

(3) Where the client's solicitor has reason to believe that an attempt may be made to circumvent the provisions of paragraph (1), he shall inform the Commission immediately.

19. Notice to Third Parties

(1) Where money is payable under regulation 18, and that money is payable by a trustee in bankruptcy, a trustee or assignee of a deed of arrangement, a liquidator of a company in liquidation, a trustee of a pension fund or any other third party ('the third party') the client's solicitor shall send to the third party notice that funded services have been funded for the client by the Commission.

(2) Notice under paragraph (1) shall operate as a request by the client that money payable under regulation 18 be paid to his solicitor, and shall be a sufficient authority for that purpose.

20. Solicitor to Pay Money Recovered to Commission

(1) The client's solicitor shall forthwith:
  (a) inform the Regional Director of any money or other property recovered or preserved, and send him a copy of the order or agreement by virtue of which the property was recovered or preserved;
  (b) subject to the following paragraphs of this regulation, pay to the Commission all money or other property received by him under regulation 18.

(2) Paragraph (1)(b) shall not apply to any money or other property to which the statutory charge does not apply, by virtue of the Financial Regulations.

(3) Where he considers it essential to protect the client's interests or welfare, the Regional Director shall pay, or direct the client's solicitor to pay, to the client any money received by way of any interim payment made in accordance with an order made under CPR rule 25.6, or in accordance with an agreement having the same effect as such an order.

(4) The Regional Director may direct the client's solicitor to:
  (a) pay to the Commission under paragraph (1)(b) only such sums as, in the Regional Director's opinion, should be retained by the Commission in order to safeguard its interests; and
  (b) pay any other money to the client.

(5) Where the solicitor pays money to the Commission in accordance with this regulation, he shall identify what sums relate respectively to:
  (a) costs;
  (b) damages;
  (c) interest on costs; and
  (d) interest on damages.

21. Postponement of Statutory Charge

(1) In this regulation:
'conveyancer' means a solicitor or any other person who lawfully provides conveyancing services;
'family proceedings' means proceedings which arise out of family relationships, including proceedings in which the welfare of children is determined. Family proceedings also include all proceedings under any one or more of the following:
  (a) the Matrimonial Causes Act 1973;
  (b) the Inheritance (Provision for Family and Dependants) Act 1975;
  (c) the Adoption Act 1976;
  (d) the Domestic Proceedings and Magistrates' Courts Act 1978;
  (e) Part III of the Matrimonial and Family Proceedings Act 1984;
  (f) Parts I, II and IV of the Children Act 1989;
  (g) Part IV of the Family Law Act 1996;
  (ga) the Adoption and Children Act 2002;
  (h) the inherent jurisdiction of the High Court in relation to children; and
  (i) the Civil Partnership Act 2004;
'purchase money' means money recovered or preserved by the client in family proceedings which, by virtue of an order of the court or an agreement, is to be used to purchase a home to be used by the client or the client's dependants, and 'the purchased property' means the property purchased or to be purchased with that money.

(2) The following paragraphs of this regulation apply, and (subject to paragraph (6)) regulation 20(1)(b) does not apply, where the Commission decides to postpone enforcement of the statutory charge under regulation 52 of the Financial Regulations.

(3) The solicitor may release the purchase money to the seller or the seller's representative on completion of the purchase of the purchased property; and shall as soon as practicable provide the Commission with sufficient information to enable it to protect its interest in accordance with regulation 52(1)(c) of the Financial Regulations.

(4) The client's solicitor may release the purchase money to a conveyancer acting for the client in the purchase of the purchased property, if he is satisfied that adequate steps have been, or will be, taken to protect the interests of the Commission.

(5) The steps referred to in paragraph (4) shall include, but are not limited to, the securing of an undertaking from the conveyancer referred to in that paragraph to:

Selected Legislation

(a) provide the information referred to in paragraph (3); and
(b) repay the purchase money under paragraph (6).

(6) Where the purchase of the purchased property has not been completed within 12 months after the date of the Commission's decision referred to in paragraph (2), or such longer period as the Commission considers reasonable, regulation 20(1)(b) shall apply and the purchase money shall accordingly be repaid to the Commission.

22. Retention and Payment Out of Money by the Commission

(1) The Commission shall deal with the money paid to it under this Part in accordance with this regulation.

(2) The Commission shall retain:
(a) an amount equal to the costs incurred in taking steps under regulation 23;
(b) an amount equal to that part of the funded sum already paid to the supplier in respect of the relevant work; and
(c) where costs are paid to the Commission together with interest, an amount equal to that interest, less the amount of any interest payable to the supplier under paragraph (3)(b)(ii).

(3) The Commission shall pay to the supplier:
(a) any outstanding amount of the funded sum payable to him in respect of the relevant work;
(b) where costs are ordered or agreed to be paid to the client, and those costs are received by the Commission, and those costs (less any amount retained under paragraph (2)(a) or payable under paragraph (5)) exceed the funded sum:
(i) an amount equal to the amount of the excess; and
(ii) where those costs are paid to the Commission together with interest, an amount equal to the interest attributable to the excess referred to in sub-paragraph (i).

(4) Paragraph (5) applies where a solicitor has acted on behalf of the client in proceedings before that client receives funded services in respect of the same proceedings, or has a lien on any documents necessary to proceedings to which a client is a party, and has handed them over subject to the lien, but applies only so far as is consistent with the express terms of any contract between the Commission and the solicitor.

(5) Where the solicitor referred to in paragraph (4) gives the Commission written notice that this paragraph applies, the Commission shall pay to that solicitor the costs to which that solicitor would have been entitled if those costs had been assessed on an indemnity basis.

(6) Where the amount of costs payable under paragraph (5) have not been assessed by the court, they may instead be assessed by the Commission.

(7) Where the amount received by the Commission, less any amount retained under paragraph (2)(a), is insufficient to meet the funded sum and any sum payable under paragraph (5), the Commission shall apportion the amount received proportionately between the two.

(8) The Commission shall pay all the money paid to it under this Part, which is not paid or retained under paragraphs (2) to (5), to the client.

23. Enforcement of Orders etc. in Favour of Client

(1) Where, in relation to any dispute to which a client is a party, whether or not proceedings are begun:
(a) an order or agreement is made providing for the recovery or preservation of property by the client (whether for himself or any other person); or
(b) there is a client's costs order or client's costs agreement

the Commission may take any steps, including proceedings in its own name, as may be necessary to enforce or give effect to that order or agreement.

(2) A client may, with the consent of the Regional Director, take proceedings to give effect to an order or agreement under which he is entitled to recover or preserve money or other property.

(3) Subject to paragraph (4), the client's solicitor may take proceedings for the recovery of costs where a client's costs order or a client's costs agreement has been made.

(4) Where the client's costs order or client's costs agreement relates wholly or partly to costs incurred in carrying out work which is remunerated, or to be remunerated, in the funded sum, but those costs have not been reimbursed by payment from any other party in favour of the client, the solicitor shall require the consent of the Regional Director before taking proceedings to which paragraph (3) refers.

(5) Where the Commission takes proceedings, it may authorise any person to make a statement, file a proof or take any other step in the proceedings in its name.
(6) The costs incurred by the Commission in taking any step to enforce an order or agreement where paragraph (1) applies shall be a first charge on any property or sum so recovered.

24. Interest on Damages

(1) Where the Commission receives damages paid in favour of a client it shall, subject to the following paragraphs, pay to the client a sum representing gross interest earned while the damages are being held by the Commission.
(2) Without prejudice to its other powers to invest money, the Commission shall maintain and may deposit damages to which this regulation refers in one general account at a deposit-taker.
(3) The rate of interest payable to the client under this regulation shall be 0.5% per annum less than the rate payable on damages deposited in the general account.
(4) The Commission shall not be required to pay interest where the damages received do not exceed £500 or where the period during which they are held by the Commission is less than 28 days.
(5) Interest shall be payable for the period beginning on the third business day after the date on which damages are received by the Commission to and including the date on which the Commission determines the amount to be paid under regulation 22(8).
(6) In this regulation:
'business day' means a day other than a Saturday, a Sunday, Christmas Day, Good Friday or a bank holiday under the Banking and Financial Dealings Act 1971;
'deposit taker' means the Bank of England, or the branch, situated in England or Wales, of either—
(a) a person with permission under Part 4 of the Financial Services and Markets Act 2000 to accept deposits, or
(b) an EEA firm of the kind mentioned in paragraph 5(b) of Schedule 3 to that Act, which has permission under paragraph 15 of that Schedule (as a result of qualifying for authorisation under paragraph 12(1) of that Schedule) to accept deposits;
'general account' means an interest bearing account opened in the name of the Commission, the title of which does not identify any client.
(7) The definition of 'deposit taker' in paragraph (6) must be read with—
(a) section 22 of the Financial Services and Markets Act 2000;
(b) any relevant order under that section; and
(c) Schedule 2 to that Act.

NOTES ON TEXT

The text printed above incorporates the following amendments:
reg. 2 amended by Community Legal Service (Costs) (Amendment) Regulations 2003 (SI 2003/649), reg. 3; the definition of 'Funding Code' has been moved to its correct alphabetical position editorially;
reg. 7 amended by Community Legal Service (Costs) (Amendment) Regulations 2003 (SI 2003/649), reg. 4;
reg. 9 amended by Community Legal Service (Costs) (Amendment) Regulations 2001 (SI 2001/822), regs 2 and 3;
reg. 10 amended by Community Legal Service (Costs) (Amendment) Regulations 2003 (SI 2003/649), reg. 5;
reg. 10A inserted by Community Legal Service (Costs) (Amendment) Regulations 2001 (SI 2001/822), reg. 4;
reg. 21(1) amended by: (a) Civil Partnership Act 2004 (Amendments to Subordinate Legislation) Order 2005 (SI 2005/2114), sch. 7, para. 1; (b) Adoption and Children Act 2002 (Consequential Amendments) Order 2005 (SI 2005/3504), art. 3;
reg. 24 amended by Financial Services and Markets Act 2000 (Consequential Amendments and Repeals) Order 2001 (SI 2001/3649), art. 588.

Conditional Fee Agreements Order 2000

(SI 2000/823)

The Lord Chancellor, in exercise of the powers conferred on him by section 58(4)(a) and (c) of the Courts and Legal Services Act 1990, and all other powers enabling him in that behalf, having consulted in accordance with section 58A(5) of that Act, makes the following Order, a draft of which has been laid before and approved by resolution of each House of Parliament:

1. Citation, Commencement and Interpretation

(1) This Order may be cited as the Conditional Fee Agreements Order 2000 and shall come into force on 1st April 2000.

(2) In this Order 'the Act' means the Courts and Legal Services Act 1990.

2. Revocation of 1998 Order

The Conditional Fee Agreements Order 1998 is revoked.

3. Agreements Providing For Success Fees

All proceedings which, under section 58 of the Act, can be the subject of an enforceable conditional fee agreement, except proceedings under section 82 of the Environmental Protection Act 1990, are proceedings specified for the purposes of section 58(4)(a) of the Act.

4. Amount of Success Fees

In relation to all proceedings specified in article 3, the percentage specified for the purposes of section 58(4)(c) of the Act shall be 100%.

Conditional Fee Agreements Regulations 2000

(SI 2000/692)

The Lord Chancellor, in exercise of the powers conferred on him by sections 58(3)(c), 58A(3) and 119 of the Courts and Legal Services Act 1990 and all other powers enabling him hereby makes the following Regulations:

1. Citation, Commencement and Interpretation

(1) These Regulations may be cited as the Conditional Fee Agreements Regulations 2000.

(2) These Regulations come into force on 1st April 2000.

(3) In these Regulations—

'client' includes, except where the context otherwise requires, a person who—

(a) has instructed the legal representative to provide the advocacy or litigation services to which the conditional fee agreement relates, or

(b) is liable to pay the legal representative's fees in respect of those services; and 'legal representative' means the person providing the advocacy or litigation services to which the conditional fee agreement relates.

2. Requirements for Contents of Conditional Fee Agreements: General

(1) A conditional fee agreement must specify—

(a) the particular proceedings or parts of them to which it relates (including whether it relates to any appeal, counterclaim or proceedings to enforce a judgment or order),

(b) the circumstances in which the legal representative's fees and expenses, or part of them, are payable,

(c) what payment, if any, is due—

(i) if those circumstances only partly occur,

(ii) irrespective of whether those circumstances occur, and

(iii) on the termination of the agreement for any reason, and

(d) the amounts which are payable in all the circumstances and cases specified or the method to be used to calculate them and, in particular, whether the amounts are limited by reference to the damages which may be recovered on behalf of the client.

(2) A conditional fee agreement to which regulation 4 applies must contain a statement that the requirements of that regulation which apply in the case of that agreement have been complied with.

3. Requirements for Contents of Conditional Fee Agreements Providing For Success Fees

(1) A conditional fee agreement which provides for a success fee—

(a) must briefly specify the reasons for setting the percentage increase at the level stated in the agreement, and

(b) must specify how much of the percentage increase, if any, relates to the cost to the legal representative of the postponement of the payment of his fees and expenses.

(2) If the agreement relates to court proceedings, it must provide that where the percentage increase becomes payable as a result of those proceedings, then—

(a) if—

(i) any fees subject to the increase are assessed, and

(ii) the legal representative or the client is required by the court to disclose to the court or any other person the reasons for setting the percentage increase at the level stated in the agreement,

he may do so,

(b) if—

(i) any such fees are assessed, and

(ii) any amount in respect of the percentage increase is disallowed on the assessment on the ground that the level at which the increase was set was unreasonable in view of facts which were or should have been known to the legal representative at the time it was set,

Selected Legislation

that amount ceases to be payable under the agreement, unless the court is satisfied that it should continue to be so payable, and

(c) if—

(i) sub-paragraph (b) does not apply, and

(ii) the legal representative agrees with any person liable as a result of the proceedings to pay fees subject to the percentage increase that a lower amount than the amount payable in accordance with the conditional fee agreement is to be paid instead,

the amount payable under the conditional fee agreement in respect of those fees shall be reduced accordingly, unless the court is satisfied that the full amount should continue to be payable under it.

(3) In this regulation 'percentage increase' means the percentage by which the amount of the fees which would be payable if the agreement were not a conditional fee agreement is to be increased under the agreement.

3A. Requirements Where the Client's Liability Is Limited to Sums Recovered

(1) This regulation applies to a conditional fee agreement under which, except in the circumstances set out in paragraphs (5) and (5A), the client is liable to pay his legal representative's fees and expenses only to the extent that sums are recovered in respect of the relevant proceedings, whether by way of costs or otherwise.

(2) In determining for the purposes of paragraph (1) the circumstances in which a client is liable to pay his legal representative's fees and expenses, no account is to be taken of any obligation to pay costs in respect of the premium of a policy taken out to insure against the risk of incurring a liability in the relevant proceedings.

(3) Regulations 2, 3 and 4 do not apply to a conditional fee agreement to which this regulation applies.

(4) A conditional fee agreement to which this regulation applies must—

(a) specify—

(i) the particular proceedings or parts of them to which it relates (including whether it relates to any appeal, counterclaim or proceedings to enforce a judgment or order); and

(ii) the circumstances in which the legal representative's fees and expenses, or part of them, are payable; and

(b) if it provides for a success fee—

(i) briefly specify the reasons for setting the percentage increase at the level stated in the agreement; and

(ii) provide that if, in court proceedings, the percentage increase becomes payable as a result of those proceedings and the legal representative or the client is ordered to disclose to the court or any other person the reasons for setting the percentage increase at the level stated in the agreement, he may do so.

(5) A conditional fee agreement to which this regulation applies may specify that the client will be liable to pay the legal representative's fees and expenses whether or not sums are recovered in respect of the relevant proceedings, if the client—

(a) fails to cooperate with the legal representative;

(b) fails to attend any medical or expert examination or court hearing which the legal representative reasonably requests him to attend;

(c) fails to give necessary instructions to the legal representative;

(d) withdraws instructions from the legal representative;

(e) is an individual who is adjudged bankrupt or enters into an arrangement or a composition with his creditors, or against whom an administration order is made; or

(f) is a company for which a receiver, administrative receiver or liquidator is appointed.

(5A) A conditional fee agreement to which this regulation applies may specify that, in the event of the client dying in the course of the relevant proceedings, his estate will be liable for the legal representative's fees and expenses, whether or not sums are recovered in respect of those proceedings.

(6) Before a conditional fee agreement to which this regulation applies is made, the legal representative must inform the client as to the circumstances in which the client or his estate may be liable to pay the legal representative's fees and expenses, and provide such further explanation, advice or other information as to those circumstances as the client may reasonably require.

4. Information to Be Given before Conditional Fee Agreements Made

(1) Before a conditional fee agreement is made the legal representative must—
- *(a) inform the client about the following matters, and*
- *(b) if the client requires any further explanation, advice or other information about any of those matters, provide such further explanation, advice or other information about them as the client may reasonably require.*

(2) Those matters are—
- *(a) the circumstances in which the client may be liable to pay the costs of the legal representative in accordance with the agreement,*
- *(b) the circumstances in which the client may seek assessment of the fees and expenses of the legal representative and the procedure for doing so,*
- *(c) whether the legal representative considers that the client's risk of incurring liability for costs in respect of the proceedings to which agreement relates is insured against under an existing contract of insurance,*
- *(d) whether other methods of financing those costs are available, and, if so, how they apply to the client and the proceedings in question,*
- *(e) whether the legal representative considers that any particular method or methods of financing any or all of those costs is appropriate and, if he considers that a contract of insurance is appropriate or recommends a particular such contract—*
  - *(i) his reasons for doing so, and*
  - *(ii) whether he has an interest in doing so.*

(3) Before a conditional fee agreement is made the legal representative must explain its effect to the client.

(4) In the case of an agreement where—
- *(a) the legal representative is a body to which section 30 of the Access to Justice Act 1999 (recovery where body undertakes to meet costs liabilities) applies, and*
- *(b) there are no circumstances in which the client may be liable to pay any costs in respect of the proceedings,*

paragraph (1) does not apply.

(5) Information required to be given under paragraph (1) about the matters in paragraph (2)(a) to (d) must be given orally (whether or not it is also given in writing), but information required to be so given about the matters in paragraph (2)(e) and the explanation required by paragraph (3) must be given both orally and in writing.

(6) This regulation does not apply in the case of an agreement between a legal representative and an additional legal representative.

5. Form of Agreement

(1) A conditional fee agreement must be signed by the client and the legal representative.

(2) This regulation does not apply in the case of an agreement between a legal representative and an additional legal representative.

6. Amendment of Agreement

Where an agreement is amended to cover further proceedings or parts of them—
- *(a) regulations 2,3, 3A and 5 apply to the amended agreement as if it were a fresh agreement made at the time of the amendment, and*
- *(b) the obligations under regulation 4 apply in relation to the amendments in so far as they affect the matters mentioned in that regulation.*

7. Revocation of 1995 Regulations

The Conditional Fee Agreements Regulations 1995 are revoked.

8. Exclusion of Collective Conditional Fee Agreements

These Regulations shall not apply to collective conditional fee agreements within the meaning of regulation 3 of the Collective Conditional Fee Agreements Regulations 2000.

NOTES ON TEXT

The text printed above incorporates the following amendment:

reg. 3A inserted by Conditional Fee Agreements (Miscellaneous Amendments) Regulations 2003 (SI 2003/1240), reg. 2(2); amended by Conditional Fee Agreements (Miscellaneous Amendments) (No. 2) Regulations 2003 (SI 2003/3344), reg. 2;

reg. 6 amended by Conditional Fee Agreements (Miscellaneous Amendments) Regulations 2003 (SI 2003/1240), reg. 2(3);

reg. 8 inserted by Collective Conditional Fee Agreements Regulations 2000 (SI 2000/2988), reg. 7.

REVOCATION

As from 1 November 2005, these regulations are revoked by the Conditional Fee Agreements (Revocation) Regulations 2005 (SI 2005/2305), reg. 2. These regulations continue to have effect for the purposes of a conditional fee agreement entered into before 1 November 2005 (SI 2005/2305, reg. 3(1)).

County Court Remedies Regulations 1991

(SI 1991/1222)

The Lord Chancellor, in exercise of the powers conferred on him by section 38 of the County Courts Act 1984, hereby makes the following Regulations a draft of which has, in accordance with section 38(7) of that Act, been laid before and approved by resolution of each House of Parliament:

1. These Regulations may be cited as the County Court Remedies Regulations 1991 and shall come into force on 1st July 1991.

2. In these Regulations, 'prescribed relief' means relief of any of the following kinds—
   (a) an order requiring a party to admit any other party to premises for the purpose of inspecting or removing documents or articles which may provide evidence in any proceedings, whether or not the proceedings have been commenced;
   (b) an interlocutory injunction—
      (i) restraining a party from removing from the jurisdiction of the High Court assets located within that jurisdiction; or
      (ii) restraining a party from dealing with assets whether located within the jurisdiction of the High Court or not.

3.—(1) Subject to the following provisions of this regulation, a county court shall not grant prescribed relief or vary or revoke an order made by the High Court granting such relief.

(2) Paragraph (1) shall not apply to—
   (a) any county court held by a judge of the Court of Appeal or judge of the High Court sitting as a judge for any county court district;
   (b) a patents county court held by a person nominated under section 291 of the Copyright, Designs and Patents Act 1988 to sit as a judge of that court.

(3) A county court may grant relief of a kind referred to in regulation 2(b)—
   (a) when exercising jurisdiction in family proceedings within the meaning of Part V of the Matrimonial and Family Proceedings Act 1984;
   (b) for the purpose of making an order for the preservation, custody or detention of property which forms or may form the subject matter of proceedings;
   (c) in aid of execution of a judgment or order made in proceedings in a county court to preserve assets until execution can be levied upon them; or
   (d) where the proceedings are to be or are included in the Central London County Court Mercantile List and the application is made to a Circuit judge nominated by the Senior Presiding Judge.

(3A) In paragraph (3)(d)—
   'the Central London County Court Mercantile List' means the Mercantile Court established at the Central London County Court pursuant to Part 59 of the Civil Procedure Rules 1998;
   'the Senior Presiding Judge' means the judge appointed as such under section 72(2) of the Courts and Legal Services Act 1990.

(4) Paragraph (1) shall not—
   (a) affect or modify powers expressly conferred on a county court by or under any enactment other than section 38 of the County Courts Act 1984; or
   (b) prevent a county court from varying an order granting prescribed relief where all the parties are agreed on the terms of the variation.

4. An application to the High Court for relief of a kind referred to in regulation 2(a) in county court proceedings shall be deemed to include an application for transfer of the proceedings to the High Court.

5.—(1) After an application for prescribed relief has been disposed of by the High Court, the proceedings shall, unless the High Court orders otherwise, be transferred to a county court if—
   (a) they were transferred to the High Court; or
   (b) apart from these Regulations. they should have been commenced in a county court.

(2) Where an order is made on an ex parte application, the application shall not be treated as disposed of for the purposes of paragraph (1) until any application to set aside or vary the order has been heard, or until the expiry of 28 days (or such other period as the Court may specify) during which no such application has been made.

NOTES ON TEXT

The text printed above incorporates the following amendments:

reg. 3(3) amended by: (a) County Court Remedies (Amendment) Regulations 1995 (SI 1995/206), reg. 2(a); (b) Civil Procedure (Modification of Enactments) Order 2002 (SI 2002/439), art. 10(a);

reg. 3(3A) inserted by County Court Remedies (Amendment) Regulations 1995 (SI 1995/206), reg. 2(b); amended by Civil Procedure (Modification of Enactments) Order 2002 (SI 2002/439), art. 10(b).

County Courts Act 1984

(1984 CHAPTER 28)

An Act to consolidate certain enactments relating to county courts. [26th June 1984]

PART I CONSTITUTION AND ADMINISTRATION

County Courts and Districts

1. County Courts to Be Held for Districts

(1) For the purposes of this Act, England and Wales shall be divided into districts, and a court shall be held under this Act for each district at one or more places in it; and each court shall have such jurisdiction and powers as are conferred by this Act and any other enactment for the time being in force.

(2) Every court so held shall be called a county court and shall be a court of record and shall have a seal.

(3) Nothing in this section affects the operation of section 42 of the Courts Act 1971 (City of London).

2. County Court Districts etc.

(1) The Lord Chancellor may, after consulting the Lord Chief Justice, by order specify places at which county courts are to be held and the name by which the court held at any place so specified is to be known.

(2) Any order under this section shall be made by statutory instrument, which shall be laid before Parliament after being made.

(3) The districts for which county courts are to be held shall be determined in accordance with directions given, after consulting the Lord Chief Justice, by or on behalf of the Lord Chancellor.

(4) Subject to any alterations made by virtue of this section, county courts shall continue to be held for the districts and at the places and by the names appointed at the commencement of this Act.

(5) The Lord Chief Justice may nominate a judicial office holder (as defined in section 109(4) of the Constitutional Reform Act 2005) to exercise his functions under subsection (1) or (3).

Places and Times of Sittings of Courts

3. Places and Times of Sittings

(1) In any district the places at which the court sits, and the days and times when the court sits at any place, shall be determined in accordance with directions given, after consulting the Lord Chief Justice, by or on behalf of the Lord Chancellor.

(2) A judge may from time to time adjourn any court held by him, and a registrar may from time to time adjourn—

(a) any court held by him, or

(b) in the absence of the judge, any court to be held by the judge.

(4) References in this Act to sittings of the court shall include references to sittings by any registrar in pursuance of any provision contained in, or made under, this Act.

(5) The Lord Chief Justice may nominate a judicial office holder (as defined in section 109(4) of the Constitutional Reform Act 2005) to exercise his functions under subsection (1).

[*By the Courts and Legal Services Act 1990, s. 74(1) and (3), any reference to the office of registrar is to be construed as a reference to the office of district judge.*]

4. Use of Public Buildings for Courts

(1) Where, in any place in which a county court is held, there is a building, being a town hall, court-house or other public building belonging to any local or other public authority, that building shall, with all necessary rooms, furniture and fittings in it, be used for the purpose of holding the

court, without any charge for rent or other payment, except the reasonable and necessary charges for lighting, heating and cleaning the building when used for that purpose.

(2) Where any such building is used for the purpose of holding any court, the sittings of the court shall be so arranged as not to interfere with the business of the local or other public authority usually transacted in the building or with any purpose for which the building may be used by virtue of any local Act.

(3) This section shall not apply to any place in which a building was erected before 1st January 1889 for the purpose of holding and carrying on the business of a county court.

Judges

5. Judges of County Courts

(1) Every Circuit judge shall, by virtue of his office, be capable of sitting as a judge for any county court district in England and Wales, and the Lord Chief Justice shall, after consulting the Lord Chancellor, assign one or more Circuit judges to each district and may from time to time vary the assignment of Circuit judges among the districts.

(2) Subject to any directions given by the Lord Chief Justice after consulting the Lord Chancellor, in any case where more than one Circuit judge is assigned to a district under subsection (1), any function conferred by or under this Act on the judge for a district may be exercised by any of the Circuit judges for the time being assigned to that district.

(3) The following, that is—
every judge of the Court of Appeal,
every judge of the High Court,
every Recorder,
shall, by virtue of his office, be capable of sitting as a judge for any county court district in England and Wales and, if he consents to do so, shall sit as such a judge at such times and on such occasions as the Lord Chief Justice considers desirable after consulting the Lord Chancellor.

(4) Notwithstanding that he is not for the time being assigned to a particular district, a Circuit judge—
(a) shall sit as a judge of that district at such times and on such occasions as the Lord Chief Justice may, after consulting the Lord Chancellor, direct; and
(b) may sit as a judge of that district in any case where it appears to him that the judge of that district is not, or none of the judges of that district is, available to deal with the case.

(5) The Lord Chief Justice may nominate a judicial office holder (as defined in section 109(4) of the Constitutional Reform Act 2005) to exercise his functions under this section.

Registrars, Assistant Registrars and Deputy Registrars

6. District Judges

(1) Her Majesty may, on the recommendation of the Lord Chancellor, appoint district judges.

(2) The Lord Chief Justice, after consulting the Lord Chancellor—
(a) must assign each district judge to one or more districts;
(b) may change an assignment so as to assign the district judge to a different district or districts.

(3) A reference in any enactment or other instrument to the district judge for a district or of a county court is a reference to any district judge assigned to the district concerned.

(4) Every district judge is, by virtue of his office, capable of acting in any district whether or not assigned to it, but may do so only in accordance with arrangements made by or on behalf of the Lord Chief Justice.

(5) A district judge is to be paid such salary as may be determined by the Lord Chancellor with the concurrence of the Treasury.

(6) A salary payable under this section may be increased but not reduced by a determination or further determination under this section.

8. Deputy Registrars

(1) If it appears to the Lord Chancellor that it is expedient as a temporary measure to make an appointment under this subsection in order to facilitate the disposal of business in county courts, he may appoint a person to be deputy district judge for any county court district during

such period or on such occasions as the Lord Chancellor thinks fit; and a deputy district judge, while acting under his appointment, shall have the same powers and be subject to the same liabilities as if he were the district judge.

(1A) Any appointment of a person as a deputy district judge—
(a) if he has previously held office as a district judge, shall not be such as to extend beyond the day on which he attains the age of 75 years; and
(b) in any other case, shall not be such as to extend beyond the day on which he attains the age of 70 years, but subject to section 26(4) to (6) of the Judicial Pensions and Retirement Act 1993 (power to authorise continuance in office up to the age of 75).

(3) The Lord Chancellor may pay to any person appointed under this section as deputy district judge such remuneration and allowances as he may, with the approval of the Treasury, determine.

9. Qualifications

No person shall be appointed a district judge or deputy district judge unless he has a 7 year general qualification, within the meaning of section 71 of the Courts and Legal Services Act 1990.

11. Tenure of Office

(1) This subsection applies to the office of district judge.
(2) Subject to the following provisions of this section and to subsections (4) to (6) of section 26 of the Judicial Pensions and Retirement Act 1993 (Lord Chancellor's power to authorise continuance in office up to the age of 75), a person who holds an office to which subsection (1) applies shall vacate his office on the day on which he attains the age of 70 years.
(4) A person appointed to an office to which subsection (1) applies shall hold that office during good behaviour.
(5) The power to remove such a person from his office on account of misbehaviour shall be exercisable by the Lord Chancellor, but only with the concurrence of the Lord Chief Justice.
(6) The Lord Chancellor may, with the concurrence of the Lord Chief Justice, also remove such a person from his office on account of inability to perform the duties of his office.

12. Records of Proceedings to Be Kept by Registrars

(1) The district judge for every district shall keep or cause to be kept such records of and in relation to proceedings in the court for that district as the Lord Chancellor may by regulations made by statutory instrument prescribe.
(2) Any entry in a book or other document required by the said regulations to be kept for the purposes of this section, or a copy of any such entry or document purporting to be signed and certified as a true copy by the district judge, shall at all times without further proof be admitted in any court or place whatsoever as evidence of the entry and of the proceeding referred to by it and of the regularity of that proceeding.
(3) The Lord Chancellor must consult the Lord Chief Justice before making regulations under this section.
(4) The Lord Chief Justice may nominate a judicial office holder (as defined in section 109(4) of the Constitutional Reform Act 2005) to exercise his functions under this section.

Miscellaneous Provisions as to Officers

13. Officers of Court Not to Act as Solicitors in That Court

(1) Subject to the provisions of this section, no officer of a court shall, either by himself or his partner, be directly or indirectly engaged as legal representative or agent for any party in any proceedings in that court.
(2) Every person who contravenes this section shall for each offence be liable on summary conviction to a fine of an amount not exceeding level 3 on the standard scale.
(3) Subsection (1) does not apply to a person acting as registrar by virtue of section 6(5).
(4) Subsection (1) does not apply to a deputy registrar; but a deputy registrar shall not act as such in relation to any proceedings in which he is, either by himself or his partner, directly or indirectly engaged as legal representative or agent for any party.

[*By the Courts and Legal Services Act 1990, s. 74(1) and (3), any reference to the office of deputy registrar is to be construed as a reference to the office of deputy district judge.*]

14. Penalty for Assaulting Officers

(1) If any person assaults an officer of a court while in the execution of his duty, he shall be liable—
- (a) on summary conviction, to imprisonment for a term not exceeding 3 months or to a fine of an amount not exceeding level 5 on the standard scale, or both; or
- (b) on an order made by the judge in that behalf, to be committed for a specified period not exceeding 3 months to prison or to such a fine as aforesaid, or to be so committed and to such a fine,

and a bailiff of the court may take the offender into custody, with or without warrant, and bring him before the judge.

(2) The judge may at any time revoke an order committing a person to prison under this section and, if he is already in custody, order his discharge.

(3) A district judge, assistant district judge or deputy district judge shall have the same powers under this section as a judge.

PART II JURISDICTION AND TRANSFER OF PROCEEDINGS

Actions of Contract and Tort

15. General Jurisdiction in Actions of Contract and Tort

(1) Subject to subsection (2), a county court shall have jurisdiction to hear and determine any action founded on contract or tort.

(2) A county court shall not, except as in this Act provided, have jurisdiction to hear and determine—
- [(a) repealed]
- (b) any action in which the title to any toll, fair, market or franchise is in question; or
- (c) any action for libel or slander.

16. Money Recoverable by Statute

A county court shall have jurisdiction to hear and determine an action for the recovery of a sum recoverable by virtue of any enactment for the time being in force, if—
- (a) it is not provided by that or any other enactment that such sums shall only be recoverable in the High Court or shall only be recoverable summarily.
- [(b) repealed]

17. Abandonment of Part of Claim to Give Court Jurisdiction

(1) Where a plaintiff has a cause of action for more than the county court limit in which, if it were not for more than the county court limit, a county court would have jurisdiction, the plaintiff may abandon the excess, and thereupon a county court shall have jurisdiction to hear and determine the action, but the plaintiff shall not recover in the action an amount exceeding the county court limit.

(2) Where the court has jurisdiction to hear and determine an action by virtue of this section, the judgment of the court in the action shall be in full discharge of all demands in respect of the cause of action, and entry of the judgment shall be made accordingly.

18. Jurisdiction by Agreement in Certain Actions

If the parties to any action, other than an action which, if commenced in the High Court, would have been assigned to the Chancery Division or to the Family Division or have involved the exercise of the High Court's Admiralty jurisdiction, agree, by a memorandum signed by them or by their respective legal representatives, that a county court specified in the memorandum shall have jurisdiction in the action, that court shall have jurisdiction to hear and determine the action accordingly.

Recovery of Land and Cases Where Title in Question

21. Actions for Recovery of Land and Actions Where Title Is in Question

(1) A county court shall have jurisdiction to hear and determine any action for the recovery of land.

(2) A county court shall have jurisdiction to hear and determine any action in which the title to any hereditament comes in question.

(3) Where a mortgage of land consists of or includes a dwelling-house and no part of the land is situated in Greater London then, subject to subsection (4), if a county court has jurisdiction by virtue of this section to hear and determine an action in which the mortgagee under that mortgage claims possession of the mortgaged property, no court other than a county court shall have jurisdiction to hear and determine that action.

(4) Subsection (3) shall not apply to an action for foreclosure or sale in which a claim for possession of the mortgaged property is also made.

(7) In this section—

'dwelling-house' includes any building or part of a building which is used as a dwelling;

'mortgage' includes a charge and 'mortgagor' and 'mortgagee' shall be construed accordingly;

'mortgagor' and 'mortgagee' includes any person deriving title under the original mortgagor or mortgagee.

(8) The fact that part of the premises comprised in a dwelling-house is used as a shop or office or for business, trade or professional purposes shall not prevent the dwelling-house from being a dwelling-house for the purposes of this section.

(9) This section does not apply to a mortgage securing an agreement which is a regulated agreement within the meaning of the Consumer Credit Act 1974.

Equity Proceedings

23. Equity Jurisdiction

A county court shall have all the jurisdiction of the High Court to hear and determine—

(a) proceedings for the administration of the estate of a deceased person, where the estate does not exceed in amount or value the county court limit;

(b) proceedings—

(i) for the execution of any trust, or

(ii) for a declaration that a trust subsists, or

(iii) under section 1 of the Variation of Trusts Act 1958,

where the estate or fund subject, or alleged to be subject, to the trust does not exceed in amount or value the county court limit;

(c) proceedings for foreclosure or redemption of any mortgage or for enforcing any charge or lien, where the amount owing in respect of the mortgage, charge or lien does not exceed the county court limit;

(d) proceedings for the specific performance, or for the rectification, delivery up or cancellation, of any agreement for the sale, purchase or lease of any property, where, in the case of a sale or purchase, the purchase money, or in the case of a lease, the value of the property, does not exceed the county court limit;

(e) proceedings relating to the maintenance or advancement of a minor, where the property of the minor does not exceed in amount or value the county court limit;

(f) proceedings for the dissolution or winding-up of any partnership (whether or not the existence of the partnerships is in dispute), where the whole assets of the partnership do not exceed in amount or value the county court limit;

(g) proceedings for relief against fraud or mistake, where the damage sustained or the estate or fund in respect of which relief is sought does not exceed in amount or value the county court limit.

[*The county court limit for the purposes of the predecessor to this section in the County Courts Act 1959 was specified as £30,000 by the County Courts Jurisdiction Order 1981 (SI 1981/1123), which is to be construed as referring to this section by virtue of the Interpretation Act 1978, s. 17(2)(a), and has effect as if made under the County Courts Act 1984, s. 145, by virtue of the Interpretation Act 1978, s. 17(2)(b).*]

24. Jurisdiction by Agreement in Certain Equity Proceedings

(1) If, as respects any proceedings to which this section applies, the parties agree, by a memorandum signed by them or by their respective legal representatives or agents, that a county court specified

in the memorandum shall have jurisdiction in the proceedings, that court shall, notwithstanding anything in any enactment, have jurisdiction to hear and determine the proceedings accordingly.

(2) Subject to subsection (3), this section applies to any proceedings in which a county court would have jurisdiction by virtue of—
(a) section 113(3) of the Settled Land Act 1925,
(b) section 63A of the Trustee Act 1925,
(c) sections 3(7), 49(4), 66(4), 89(7), 90(3), 91(8), 92(2), 136(3), 181(2), 188(2) of, and paragraph 3A of Part III and paragraph 1(3A) and (4A) of Part IV of Schedule 1 to, the Law of Property Act 1925,
(d) sections 17(2), 38(4), 41(1A), and 43(4) of the Administration of Estates Act 1925,
(e) section 6(1) of the Leasehold Property (Repairs) Act 1938,
(f) sections 1(6A) and 5(11) of the Land Charges Act 1972, and
(g) section 23 of this Act,
but for the limits of the jurisdiction of the court provided in those enactments.

(3) This section does not apply to proceedings under section 1 of the Variation of Trusts Act 1958.

Family Provision Proceedings

25. Jurisdiction under Inheritance (Provision For Family and Dependants) Act 1975

A county court shall have jurisdiction to hear and determine any application for an order under section 2 of the Inheritance (Provision for Family and Dependants) Act 1975 (including any application for permission to apply for such an order and any application made, in the proceedings on an application for such an order, for an order under any other provision of that Act).

Probate Proceedings

32. Contentious Probate Jurisdiction

(1) Where—
(a) an application for the grant or revocation of probate or administration has been made through the principal registry of the Family Division or a district probate registry under section 105 of the Supreme Court Act 1981; and
(b) it is shown to the satisfaction of a county court that the value at the date of the death of the deceased of his net estate does not exceed the county court limit,
the county court shall have the jurisdiction of the High Court in respect of any contentious matter arising in connection with the grant or revocation.

(2) In subsection (1) 'net estate', in relation to a deceased person, means the estate of that person exclusive of any property he was possessed of or entitled to as a trustee and not beneficially, and after making allowances for funeral expenses and for debts and liabilities.

[*The county court limit for the purposes of the predecessor to this section in the County Courts Act 1959 was specified as £30,000 by the County Courts Jurisdiction Order 1981 (SI 1981/1123), which is to be construed as referring to this section by virtue of the Interpretation Act 1978, s. 17(2)(a), and has effect as if made under the County Courts Act 1984, s. 145, by virtue of the Interpretation Act 1978, s. 17(2)(b).*]

33. Effect of Order of Judge in Probate Proceedings

Where an order is made by a county court for the grant or revocation of probate or administration, in pursuance of any jurisdiction conferred upon the court by section 32—
(a) the registrar of the county court shall transmit to the principal registry of the Family Division or a district probate registry, as he thinks convenient, a certificate under the seal of the court certifying that the order has been made; and
(b) on the application of a party in favour of whom the order has been made, probate or administration in compliance with the order shall be issued from the registry to which the certificate was sent or, as the case may require, the probate or letters of administration previously granted shall be recalled or varied by, as the case may be, a registrar of the principal registry of the Family Division or the district probate registrar according to the effect of the order.

[*By the Courts and Legal Services Act 1990, s. 74(1) to (3), any reference to the office of registrar is to be construed as a reference to the office of district judge and any reference to the office of registrar of the principal registry of the Family Division is to be construed as a reference to the office of district judge of the principal registry of the Family Division.*]

Miscellaneous Provisions as to Jurisdiction

35. Division of Causes of Action

It shall not be lawful for any plaintiff to divide any cause of action for the purpose of bringing two or more actions in one or more of the county courts.

36. No Action on Judgment of High Court

No action shall be brought in a county court on any judgment of the High Court.

Exercise of Jurisdiction and Ancillary Jurisdiction

37. Persons Who May Exercise Jurisdiction of Court

(1) Any jurisdiction and powers conferred by this or any other Act—
(a) on a county court; or
(b) on the judge of a county court,
may be exercised by any judge of the court.
(2) Subsection (1) applies to jurisdiction and powers conferred on all county courts or judges of county courts or on any particular county court or the judge of any particular county court.

38. Remedies Available in County Courts

(1) Subject to what follows, in any proceedings in a county court the court may make any order which could be made by the High Court if the proceedings were in the High Court.
(2) Any order made by a county court may be—
(a) absolute or conditional;
(b) final or interlocutory.
(3) A county court shall not have power—
(a) to order mandamus, certiorari or prohibition; or
(b) to make any order of a prescribed kind.
(4) Regulations under subsection (3)—
(a) may provide for any of their provisions not to apply in such circumstances or descriptions of case as may be specified in the regulations;
(b) may provide for the transfer of the proceedings to the High Court for the purpose of enabling an order of a kind prescribed under subsection (3) to be made; [and]
(d) may make provision amending or repealing any provision made by or under any enactment, so far as may be necessary or expedient in consequence of the regulations.
(4A) If regulations are made under subsection (3), rules may be made in accordance with Part 1 of Schedule 1 to the Constitutional Reform Act 2005 about procedure relevant to the matters prescribed in the regulations.
(5) In this section 'prescribed' means prescribed by regulations made under this section by the Lord Chancellor after consulting the Lord Chief Justice.
(6) The power to make regulations under this section shall be exercised by statutory instrument.
(7) No such statutory instrument shall be made unless a draft of the instrument has been approved by both Houses of Parliament.

[*In s. 38(3)(a), by the Supreme Court Act 1981, s. 29(5), the reference to mandamus is to be read as a reference to a mandatory order, the reference to certiorari is to be read as a reference to a quashing order and the reference to prohibition is to be read as a reference to a prohibiting order.*]

Transfer of Proceedings

40. Transfer of Proceedings to County Court

(1) Where the High Court is satisfied that any proceedings before it are required by any provision of a kind mentioned in subsection (8) to be in a county court it shall—
(a) order the transfer of the proceedings to a county court; or

Selected Legislation

(b) if the court is satisfied that the person bringing the proceedings knew, or ought to have known, of that requirement, order that they be struck out.

(2) Subject to any such provision, the High Court may order the transfer of any proceedings before it to a county court.

(3) An order under this section may he made either on the motion of the High Court itself or on the application of any party to the proceedings.

(4) Proceedings transferred under this section shall be transferred to such county court as the High Court considers appropriate, having taken into account the convenience of the parties and that of any other persons likely to he affected and the state of business in the courts concerned.

(5) The transfer of any proceedings under this section shall not affect any right of appeal from the order directing the transfer.

(6) Where proceedings for the enforcement of any judgment or order of the High Court are transferred under this section—

(a) the judgment or order may be enforced as if it were a judgment or order of a county court; and

(b) subject to subsection (7), it shall be treated as a judgment or order of that court for all purposes.

(7) Where proceedings for the enforcement of any judgment or order of the High Court are transferred under this section—

(a) the powers of any court to set aside, correct, vary or quash a judgment or order of the High Court, and the enactments relating to appeals from such a judgment or order, shall continue to apply; and

(b) the powers of any court to set aside, correct, vary or quash a judgment or order of a county court, and the enactments relating to appeals from such a judgment or order, shall not apply.

(8) The provisions referred to in subsection (1) are any made—

(a) under section 1 of the Courts and Legal Services Act 1990; or

(b) by or under any other enactment.

(9) This section does not apply to family proceedings within the meaning of Part V of the Matrimonial and Family Proceedings Act 1984.

41. Transfer to High Court by Order of High Court

(1) If at any stage in proceedings commenced in a county court or transferred to a county court under section 40 the High Court thinks it desirable that the proceedings, or any part of them, should be heard and determined in the High Court, it may order the transfer to the High Court of the proceedings or, as the case may be, of that part of them.

(2) The power conferred by subsection (1) is without prejudice to section 29 of the Supreme Court Act 1981 (power of High Court to issue prerogative orders) but shall be exercised in relating to family proceedings (within the meaning of Part V of the Matrimonial and Family Proceedings Act 1984) in accordance with any directions given under section 37 of that Act (directions as to distribution and transfer of family business and proceedings).

(3) The power conferred by subsection (1) shall be exercised subject to any provision made—

(a) under section 1 of the Courts and Legal Services Act 1990; or

(b) by or under any other enactment.

42. Transfer to High Court by Order of a County Court

(1) Where a county court is satisfied that any proceedings before it are required by any provision of a kind mentioned in subsection (7) to be in the High Court, it shall—

(a) order the transfer of the proceedings to the High Court; or

(b) if the court is satisfied that the person bringing the proceedings knew, or ought to have known, of that requirement, order that they be struck out.

(2) Subject to any such provision, a county court may order the transfer of any proceedings before it to the High Court.

(3) An order under this section may be made either on the motion of the court itself or on the application of any party to the proceedings.

(4) The transfer of any proceedings under this section shall not affect any right of appeal from the order directing the transfer.

(5) Where proceedings for the enforcement of any judgment or order of a county court are transferred under this section—
   (a) the judgment or order may be enforced as if it were, a judgment or order of the High Court; and
   (b) subject to subsection (6), it shall be treated as a judgment or order of that court for all purposes.

(6) Where proceedings for the enforcement of any judgment or order of a county court are transferred under this section—
   (a) the powers of any court to set aside, correct, vary or quash a judgment or order of a county court, and the enactments relating to appeals from such a judgment or order, shall continue to apply; and
   (b) the powers of any court to set aside, correct, vary or quash a judgment or order of the High Court, and the enactments relating to appeals from such a judgment or order, shall not apply.

(7) The provisions referred to in subsection (1) are any made—
   (a) under section 1 of the Courts and Legal Services Act 1990; or
   (b) by or under any other enactment.

(8) This section does not apply to family proceedings within the meaning of Part V of the Matrimonial and Family Proceedings Act 1984.

45. Costs in Transferred Cases

(1) Where an action, counterclaim or matter is ordered to be transferred—
   (a) from the High Court to a county court; or
   (b) from a county court to the High Court; or
   (c) from one county court to another county court,

the costs of the whole proceedings both before and after the transfer shall, subject to any order of the court which ordered the transfer, be in the discretion of the court to which the proceedings are transferred; and that court shall have power to make orders with respect to the costs, and the costs of the whole proceedings shall be taxed in that court.

PART III PROCEDURE

Parties

46. Proceedings by the Crown

(1) Subject to the provisions of any enactment limiting the jurisdiction of a county court, whether by reference to the subject matter of the proceedings to be brought or the amount sought to be recovered in the proceedings or otherwise, proceedings by the Crown may be instituted in a county court.

(2) Subject to section 40(5), all rules of law and enactments regulating the removal or transfer of proceedings from a county court to the High Court and the transfer of proceedings in the High Court to a county court shall apply respectively to the removal or transfer of proceedings by the Crown in a county court and to the transfer of proceedings by the Crown in the High Court.

(3) Nothing in this section shall apply to proceedings affecting Her Majesty in Her private capacity.

48. Persons Jointly Liable

(1) Where a plaintiff has a demand recoverable under this Act against two or more persons jointly liable, it shall be sufficient to serve any of those persons with process, and judgment may be obtained and execution issued against any person so served, notwithstanding that others jointly liable may not have been served or sued or may not be within the jurisdiction of the court.

(2) Where judgment is so obtained against any person by virtue of subsection (1) and is satisfied by that person, he shall be entitled to recover in the court contribution from any other person jointly liable with him.

49. Bankruptcy of Plaintiff

(1) The bankruptcy of the plaintiff in any action in a county court which the trustee might maintain

Selected Legislation

for the benefit of the creditors shall not cause the action to abate if, within such reasonable time as the court orders, the trustee elects to continue the action and to give security for the costs of the action.

(2) The hearing of the action may be adjourned until such an election is made.

(3) Where the trustee does not elect to continue the action and to give such security as is mentioned in subsection (1) within the time limited by the order, the defendant may avail himself of the bankruptcy as a defence to the action.

Interim Payments in Pending Proceedings

50. Orders for Interim Payment

(1) Provision may be made by rules of court for enabling the court, in such circumstances as may be prescribed, to make an order requiring a party to the proceedings to make an interim payment of such amount as may be specified in the order, with provision for the payment to be made to such other party to the proceedings as may be so specified or, if the order so provides, by paying it into court.

(2) Any rules of court which make provision in accordance with subsection (1) may include provision for enabling a party to any proceedings who, in pursuance of such an order, has made an interim payment to recover the whole or part of the amount of the payment in such circumstances, and from such other party to the proceedings, as may be determined in accordance with the rules.

(3) Any rules made by virtue of this section may include such incidental, supplementary and consequential provisions as the Civil Procedure Rule Committee may consider necessary or expedient.

(4) Nothing in this section shall be construed as affecting the exercise of any power relating to costs, including any power to make rules of court relating to costs.

(5) In this section 'interim payment', in relation to a party to any proceedings, means a payment on account of any damages, debt or other sum (excluding any costs) which that party may be held liable to pay to or for the benefit of another party to the proceedings if a final judgment or order of the court in the proceedings is given or made in favour of that other party; and any reference to a party to any proceedings includes a reference to any person who for the purposes of the proceedings acts as next friend or guardian of a party to the proceedings.

Provisional Damages for Personal Injuries

51. Orders for Provisional Damages for Personal Injuries

(1) This section applies to an action for damages for personal injuries in which there is proved or admitted to be a chance that at some definite or indefinite time in the future the injured person will, as a result of the act or omission which gave rise to the cause of action, develop some serious disease or suffer some serious deterioration in his physical or mental condition.

(2) Subject to subsection (4), as regards any action for damages to which this section applies in which a judgment is given in the county court, provision may be made by rules of court for enabling the court, in such circumstances as may be prescribed, to award the injured person—

(a) damages assessed on the assumption that the injured person will not develop the disease or suffer the deterioration in his condition; and

(b) further damages at a future date if he develops the disease or suffers the deterioration.

(3) Any rules made by virtue of this section may include such incidental, supplementary and consequential provisions as the Civil Procedure Rule Committee may consider necessary or expedient.

(4) Nothing in this section shall be construed—

(a) as affecting the exercise of any power relating to costs, including any power to make rules of court relating to costs; or

(b) as prejudicing any duty of the court under any enactment or rule of law to reduce or limit the total damages which would have been recoverable apart from any such duty.

(5) In this section 'personal injuries' includes any disease and any impairment of a person's physical or mental condition.

Discovery and Related Procedures

52. Powers of Court Exercisable before Commencement of Action

(1) On the application of any person in accordance with rules of court, a county court shall, in such circumstances as may be prescribed, have power to make an order providing for any one or more of the following matters, that is to say—
 (a) the inspection, photographing, preservation, custody and detention of property which appears to the court to be property which may become the subject-matter of subsequent proceedings in the court, or as to which any question may arise in any such proceedings; and
 (b) the taking of samples of any such property as is mentioned in paragraph (a), and the carrying out of any experiment on or with any such property.

(2) On the application, in accordance with rules of court, of a person who appears to a county court to be likely to be a party to subsequent proceedings in that court the county court shall, in such circumstances as may be prescribed, have power to order a person who appears to the court to be likely to be a party to the proceedings and to be likely to have or to have had in his possession, custody or power any documents which are relevant to an issue arising or likely to arise out of that claim—
 (a) to disclose whether those documents are in his possession, custody or power; and
 (b) to produce such of those documents as are in his possession, custody or power to the applicant or, on such conditions as may be specified in the order,—
  (i) to the applicant's legal advisers: or
  (ii) to the applicant's legal advisers and any medical or other professional adviser of the applicant; or
  (iii) if the applicant has no legal adviser, to any medical or other professional adviser of the applicant.

(3) This section is subject to any provision made under section 38.

53. Power of Court to Order Disclosure of Documents, Inspection of Property etc. in Proceedings for Personal Injuries or Death

(2) On the application, in accordance with rules of court, of a party to any proceedings, a county court shall, in such circumstances as may be prescribed, have power to order a person who is not a party to the proceedings and who appears to the court to be likely to have in his possession, custody or power any documents which are relevant to an issue arising out of the said claim—
 (a) to disclose whether those documents are in his possession, custody or power; and
 (b) to produce such of those documents as are in his possession, custody or power to the applicant or, on such conditions as may be specified in the order,—
  (i) to the applicant's legal advisers; or
  (ii) to the applicant's legal advisers and any medical or other professional adviser of the applicant; or
  (iii) if the applicant has no legal adviser, to any medical or other professional adviser of the applicant.

(3) On the application, in accordance with rules of court, of a party to any proceedings, a county court shall, in such circumstances as may be prescribed, have power to make an order providing for any one or more of the following matters, that is to say—
 (a) the inspection, photographing, preservation, custody and detention of property which is not the property of, or in the possession of, any party to the proceedings but which is the subject-matter of the proceedings or as to which any question arises in the proceedings;
 (b) the taking of samples of any such property as is mentioned in paragraph (a) and the carrying out of any experiment on or with any such property.

(4) The preceding provisions of this section are without prejudice to the exercise by a county court of any power to make orders which is exercisable apart from those provisions.

(5) This section is subject to any provision made under section 38.

54. Provisions Supplementary to Sections 52 and 53

(1) A county court shall not make an order under section 52 or 53 if it considers that compliance with the order, if made, would be likely to be injurious to the public interest.

(2) Rules of court may make provision as to the circumstances in which an order under section 52 or 53 can be made; and any rules making such provision may include such incidental, supplementary and consequential provisions as the Civil Procedure Rule Committee may consider necessary or expedient.

(3) Without prejudice to the generality of subsection (2), rules of court shall be made for the purpose of ensuring that the costs of and incidental to proceedings for an order under section 52(2) or 53 incurred by the person against whom the order is sought shall be awarded to that person unless the court otherwise directs.

(4) Sections 52(2) and 53 and this section bind the Crown; and section 52(1) binds the Crown so far as it relates to property as to which, it appears to the court that it may become the subject-matter of subsequent proceedings involving a claim in respect of personal injuries to a person or in respect of a person's death.

In this subsection references to the Crown do not include references to Her Majesty in Her private capacity or to Her Majesty in right of Her Duchy of Lancaster or to the Duke of Cornwall.

(5) In sections 52 and 53 and this section—

'property' includes any land, chattel or other corporeal property of any description:

'personal injuries' includes any disease and any impairment of a person's physical or mental condition.

(6) This section is subject to any provision made under section 38.

Witnesses and Evidence

55. Penalty for Neglecting or Refusing to Give Evidence

(1) Subject to subsections (2) and (3), any person who—

(a) having been summoned in pursuance of rules of court as a witness in a county court refuses or neglects, without sufficient cause, to appear or to produce any documents required by the summons to be produced; or

(b) having been so summoned or being present in court and being required to give evidence, refuses to be sworn or give evidence,

shall forfeit such fine as the judge may direct.

(2) A judge shall not have power under subsection (1) to direct that a person shall forfeit a fine of an amount exceeding £1,000.

(3) No person summoned in pursuance of rules of court as a witness in a county court shall forfeit a fine under this section unless there has been paid or tendered to him at the time of the service of the summons such sum in respect of his expenses (including, in such cases as may be prescribed, compensation for loss of time) as may be prescribed for the purposes of this section.

(4) The judge may at his discretion direct that the whole or any part of any such fine, after deducting the costs, shall be applicable towards indemnifying the party injured by the refusal or neglect.

(4A) A district judge, assistant district judge or deputy district judge shall have the same powers under this section as a judge.

(5) This section does not apply to a debtor summoned to attend by a judgment summons.

56. Examination of Witnesses Abroad

The High Court shall have the same power to issue a commission, request or order to examine witnesses abroad for the purpose of proceedings in a county court as it has for the purpose of an action or matter in the High Court.

57. Evidence of Prisoners

(1) Subject to subsection (2), in any proceedings pending before a county court, the judge may, if he thinks fit, upon application on affidavit by any party, issue an order under his hand for bringing up before the court any person (in this section referred to as a 'prisoner') confined in any place under any sentence or under committal for trial or otherwise, to be examined as a witness in the proceedings.

(2) No such order shall be made with respect to a person confined under process in any civil action or matter.

(3) Subject to subsection (4), the prisoner mentioned in any such order shall be brought before the court under the same custody, and shall be dealt with in the same manner in all respects, as a prisoner required by a writ of habeas corpus to be brought before the High Court and examined there as a witness.

(4) The person having the custody of the prisoner shall not be bound to obey the order unless there is tendered to him a reasonable sum for the conveyance and maintenance of a proper officer or officers and of the prisoner in going to, remaining at, and returning from, the court.

58. Persons Who May Take Affidavits for Use in County Courts

(1) An affidavit to be used in a county court may be sworn before—
 (a) the judge or registrar of any court; or
 (b) any justice of the peace; or
 (c) an officer of any court appointed by the judge of that court for the purpose,
 as well as before a commissioner for oaths or any other person authorised to take affidavits under the Commissioners for Oaths Acts 1889 and 1891.

(2) An affidavit sworn before a judge or registrar or before any such officer may be sworn without the payment of any fee.

[*See the note to s. 3.*]

Right of Audience

60. Right of Audience

(2) Where an action is brought in a county court by a local authority for either or both of the following—
 (a) the recovery of possession of a house belonging to the authority;
 (b) the recovery of any rent, mesne profits, damages or other sum claimed by the authority in respect of the occupation by any person of such a house,
 then, in so far as the proceedings in the action are heard by the registrar, any officer of the authority authorised by the authority in that behalf may address the registrar.

(3) In this section—
 'local authority' means a county council, a district council, the Broads Authority, any National Park Authority, a London borough council, a police authority established under section 3 of the Police Act 1996, the Metropolitan Police Authority, the Service Authority for the National Criminal Intelligence Service, the Service Authority for the National Crime Squad, a joint authority established by Part IV of the Local Government Act 1985 or the Common Council of the City of London; and
 'house' includes a part of a house, a flat or any other dwelling and also includes any yard, garden, outhouse or appurtenance occupied with a house or part of a house or with a flat or other dwelling.
 and any reference to the occupation of a house by a person includes a reference to anything done by that person, or caused or permitted by him to be done, in relation to the house as occupier of the house, whether under a tenancy or licence or otherwise.

[*See the note to s. 3. Section 60(3) is, by the Waste Regulation and Disposal (Authorities) Order 1985 (SI 1985/1884), sch. 3, para. 4, to have effect as if the reference to a joint authority established by Part IV of the Local Government Act 1985 included a reference to an authority established by that Order.*]

61. Right of Audience by Direction of Lord Chancellor

(1) The Lord Chancellor may, with the concurrence of the Lord Chief Justice, at any time direct that such categories of persons in relevant legal employment as may be specified in the direction may address the court in any proceedings in a county court, or in proceedings in a county court of such description as may be so specified.

(2) In subsection (1), 'relevant legal employment' means employment which consists of or includes giving assistance in the conduct of litigation to a legal representative whether in private practice or not.

(3) A direction under this section may be given subject to such conditions and restrictions as appear to the Lord Chancellor to be necessary or expedient, and may be expressed to have effect as

respects every county court or as respects a specified county court or as respects one or more specified places where a county court sits.

(4) The power to give directions conferred by this section includes a power to vary or rescind any direction given under this section.

(5) The Lord Chief Justice may nominate a judicial office holder (as defined in section 109(4) of the Constitutional Reform Act 2005) to exercise his functions under this section.

Mode of Trial

62. General Power of Judge to Determine Questions of Law and Fact

Subject to the provisions of this Act and of rules of court, the judge of a county court shall be the sole judge in all proceedings brought in the court, and shall determine all questions of fact as well as of law.

63. Assessors

(1) In any proceedings the judge may, if he thinks fit, summon to his assistance, in such manner as may be prescribed, one or more persons of skill and experience in the matter to which the proceedings relate who may be willing to sit with the judge and act as assessors.

(3) Subject to subsection (4), the remuneration of assessors for sitting under this section shall be determined by the judge and shall be costs in the proceedings unless otherwise ordered by the judge.

(4) Where one or more assessors are summoned for the purposes of assisting the judge in reviewing the taxation by the district judge of the costs of any proceedings the remuneration of any such assessor—

(a) shall be at such rate as may be determined by the Lord Chancellor with the approval of the Treasury; and

(b) shall be payable out of moneys provided by Parliament.

(5) Where any person is proposed to be summoned as an assessor, objection to him, either personally or in respect of his qualification, may be taken by any party in the prescribed manner.

64. Reference to Arbitration

(1) Rules of court—

(a) may prescribe cases in which proceedings are (without any order of the court) to be referred to arbitration, and

(b) may prescribe the manner in which and the terms on which cases are to be so referred, and

(c) may, where cases are so referred, require other matters within the jurisdiction of the court in dispute between the parties also to be referred to arbitration.

(2) Rules of court—

(a) may prescribe cases in which proceedings may be referred to arbitration by order of the court, and

(b) may authorise the court also to order other matters in dispute between the parties and within the jurisdiction of the court to be so referred.

(2A) Rules of court may prescribe the procedures and rules of evidence to be followed on any reference under subsection (1) or (2).

(2B) Rules made under subsection (2A) may, in particular, make provision with respect to the manner of taking and questioning evidence.

(3) On a reference under subsection (1) or (2) the award of the arbitrator, arbitrators or umpire shall be entered as the judgment in the proceedings and shall be as binding and effectual to all intents, subject to subsection (4), as if it had been given by the judge.

(4) The judge may, if he thinks fit, on application made to him within such time as may be prescribed, set aside the award, or may, with the consent of the parties, revoke the reference or order another reference to be made in the manner specified in this section.

(5) In this section 'award' includes an interim award.

65. Power of Judge to Refer to Registrar or Referee

(1) Subject to rules of court, the judge may refer to the registrar or a referee for inquiry and report—

(a) any proceedings which require any prolonged examination of documents or any scientific or local investigation which cannot, in the opinion of the judge, conveniently be made before him;
(b) any proceedings where the question in dispute consists wholly or in part of matters of account;
(c) with the consent of the parties, any other proceedings;
(d) subject to any right to have particular cases tried with a jury, any question arising in any proceedings.

(2) In such cases as may be prescribed by, and subject to, rules of court the registrar may refer to a referee for inquiry and report any question arising in any proceedings.

(3) Where any proceedings or question are referred under subsection (1) or (2), the judge or, as the case may be, the registrar may direct how the reference shall be conducted, and may remit any report for further inquiry and report, and on consideration of any report or further report may give such judgment or make such order in the proceedings as may be just.

(4) The judge may, after deciding or reserving any question of liability, refer to the registrar any mere matter of account which is in dispute between the parties and, after deciding the question of liability, may give judgment on the registrar's report.

[*See the note to s. 3.*]

Juries

66. Trial by Jury

(1) In the following proceedings in a county court the trial shall be without a jury—
(a) Admiralty proceedings;
(b) proceedings arising—
(i) under Part I, II or III of the Rent (Agriculture) Act 1976, or
(ii) under any provision of the Rent Act 1977 other than a provision contained in Part V, sections 103 to 106 or Part IX, or
(iii) under Part I of the Protection from Eviction Act 1977, or
(c) any appeal to the county court under the Housing Act 1985.

(2) In all other proceedings in a county court the trial shall be without a jury unless the court otherwise orders on an application made in that behalf by any party to the proceedings in such manner and within such time before the trial as may be prescribed.

(3) Where, on any such application, the court is satisfied that there is in issue—
(a) a charge of fraud against the party making the application; or
(b) a claim in respect of libel, slander, malicious prosecution or false imprisonment; or
(c) any question or issue of a kind prescribed for the purposes of this paragraph,
the action shall be tried with a jury, unless the court is of opinion that the trial requires any prolonged examination of documents or accounts or any scientific or local investigation which cannot conveniently be made with a jury.

(4) There shall be payable, in respect of the trial with a jury of proceedings in a county court, such fees as may be prescribed by an order under section 92 of the Courts Act 2003 (fees).

67. Impanelling and Swearing of Jury

At any county court where proceedings are to be tried with a jury, eight jurymen shall be impanelled and sworn as occasion requires to give their verdicts in the proceedings brought before them, and being once sworn need not be re-sworn in each trial.

68. Duty of Judge to Determine Foreign Law in Jury Trials

Where, for the purpose of disposing of any proceedings which are being tried in a county court by the judge with a jury, it is necessary to ascertain the law of any other country which is applicable to the facts of the case, any question as to the effect of the evidence given with respect to that law shall, instead of being submitted to the jury, be decided by the judge alone.

Interest on Debts and Damages

69. Power to Award Interest on Debts and Damages

(1) Subject to rules of court, in proceedings (whenever instituted) before a county court for the recovery of a debt or damages there may be included in any sum for which judgment is given simple interest, at such rate as the court thinks fit or as may be prescribed, on all or any part of the debt or damages in respect of which judgment is given, or payment is made before judgment, for all or any part of the period between the date when the cause of action arose and—
   (a) in the case of any sum paid before judgment, the date of the payment; and
   (b) in the case of the sum for which judgment is given, the date of the judgment.

(2) In relation to a judgment given for damages for personal injuries or death which exceed £200 subsection (1) shall have effect—
   (a) with the substitution of 'shall be included' for 'may be included'; and
   (b) with the addition of 'unless the court is satisfied that there are special reasons to the contrary' after 'given', where first occurring.

(3) Subject to rules of court, where—
   (a) there are proceedings (whenever instituted) before a county court for the recovery of a debt; and
   (b) the defendant pays the whole debt to the plaintiff (otherwise than in pursuance of a judgment in the proceedings),

   the defendant shall be liable to pay the plaintiff simple interest, at such rate as the court thinks fit or as may be prescribed, on all or any part of the debt for all or any part of the period between the date when the cause of action arose and the date of the payment.

(4) Interest in respect of a debt shall not be awarded under this section for a period during which, for whatever reason, interest on the debt already runs.

(5) Interest under this section may be calculated at different rates in respect of different periods.

(6) In this section 'plaintiff' means the person seeking the debt or damages and 'defendant' means the person from whom the plaintiff seeks the debt or damages and 'personal injuries' includes any disease and any impairment of a person's physical or mental condition.

(7) Nothing in this section affects the damages recoverable for the dishonour of a bill of exchange.

(8) In determining whether the amount of any debt or damages exceeds that prescribed by or under any enactment, no account shall be taken of any interest payable by virtue of this section except where express provision to the contrary is made by or under that or any other enactment.

Judgments and Orders

70. Finality of Judgments and Orders

Every judgment and order of a county court shall, except as provided by this or any other Act or as may be prescribed, be final and conclusive between the parties.

71. Satisfaction of Judgments and Orders for Payment of Money

(1) Where a judgment is given or an order is made by a county court under which a sum of money of any amount is payable, whether by way of satisfaction of the claim or counterclaim in the proceedings or by way of costs or otherwise, the court may, as it thinks fit, order the money to be paid either—
   (a) in one sum, whether forthwith or within such period as the court may fix; or
   (b) by such instalments payable at such times as the court may fix.

(2) If at any time it appears to the satisfaction of the court that any party to any proceedings is unable from any cause to pay any sum recovered against him (whether by way of satisfaction of the claim or counterclaim in the proceedings or by way of costs or otherwise) or any instalment of such a sum, the court may, in its discretion, suspend or stay any judgment or order given or made in the proceedings for such time and on such terms as the court thinks fit, and so from time to time until it appears that the cause of inability has ceased.

72. Set-off in Cases of Cross Judgments in County Courts and High Court

(1) Where one person has obtained a judgment or order in a county court against another person, and that other person has obtained a judgment or order against the first-mentioned person in the same or in another county court or in the High Court, either such person may, in accordance with rules of court, give notice in writing to the court or the several courts as the case may be, and may apply to the court or any of the said courts in accordance with rules of court for leave to set off any sums, including costs, payable under the several judgments or orders.

(2) Upon any such application, the set-off may be allowed in accordance with the practice for the time being in force in the High Court as to the allowance of set-off and in particular in relation to any solicitor's lien for costs.

(3) Where the cross judgments or orders have not been obtained in the same court, a copy of the order made on any such application shall be sent by the proper officer of the court to which the application is made to the proper officer of the other court.

74. Interest on Judgment Debts etc.

(1) The Lord Chancellor may by order made with the concurrence of the Treasury provide that any sums to which this subsection applies shall carry interest at such rate and between such times as may be prescribed by the order.

(2) The sums to which subsection (1) applies are—

- (a) sums payable under judgments or orders given or made in a county court, including sums payable by instalments; and
- (b) sums which by virtue of any enactment are, if the county court so orders, recoverable as if payable under an order of that court, and in respect of which the county court has so ordered.

(3) The payment of interest due under subsection (1) shall be enforceable as a sum payable under the judgment or order.

(4) The power conferred by subsection (1) includes power—

- (a) to specify the descriptions of judgment or order in respect of which interest shall be payable;
- (b) to provide that interest shall be payable only on sums exceeding a specified amount;
- (c) to make provision for the manner in which and the periods by reference to which the interest is to be calculated and paid;
- (d) to provide that any enactment shall or shall not apply in relation to interest payable under subsection (1) or shall apply to it with such modifications as may be specified in the order; and
- (e) to make such incidental or supplementary provisions as the Lord Chancellor considers appropriate.

(5) Without prejudice to the generality of subsection (4), an order under subsection (1) may provide that the rate of interest shall be the rate specified in section 17 of the Judgments Act 1838 as that enactment has effect from time to time.

(5A) The power conferred by subsection (1) includes power to make provision enabling a county court to order that the rate of interest applicable to a sum expressed in a currency other than sterling shall be such rate as the court thinks fit (instead of the rate otherwise applicable).

(6) The power to make an order under subsection (1) shall be exercisable by statutory instrument subject to annulment in pursuance of a resolution of either House of Parliament.

General Rules of Procedure

76. Application of Practice of High Court

In any case not expressly provided for by or in pursuance of this Act, the general principles of practice in the High Court may be adopted and applied to proceedings in a county court.

PART IV APPEALS ETC.

Appeals

77. Appeals: General Provisions

(1) Subject to the provisions of this section and the following provisions of this Part of this Act and to any order made by the Lord Chancellor under section 56(1) of the Access to Justice Act 1999, if any party to any proceedings in a county court is dissatisfied with the determination of the judge or jury, he may appeal from it to the Court of Appeal in such manner and subject to such conditions as may be provided by Civil Procedure Rules.

(1A) Without prejudice to the generality of the power to make county court rules under section 75, such rules may make provision for any appeal from the exercise by a district judge, assistant district judge or deputy district judge of any power given to him by virtue of any enactment to be to a judge of a county court.

(5) Subject to the provisions of this section and the following provisions of this Part of this Act, where an appeal is brought under subsection (1) in any action, an appeal may be brought under that subsection in respect of any claim or counterclaim in the action notwithstanding that there could have been no such appeal if that claim had been the subject of a separate action.

(6) In proceedings in which either the plaintiff or the defendant is claiming possession of any premises this section shall not confer any right of appeal on any question of fact if by virtue of—
- (a) section 13(4) of the Landlord and Tenant Act 1954; or
- (b) Cases III to IX in Schedule 4 to the Rent (Agriculture) Act 1976; or
- (c) section 98 of the Rent Act 1977, as it applies to Cases 1 to 6 and 8 and 9 in Schedule 15 to that Act, or that section as extended or applied by any other enactment; or
- (d) section 99 of the Rent Act 1977, as it applies to Cases 1 to 6 and 9 in Schedule 15 to that Act; or
- (e) section 84(2)(a) of the Housing Act 1985; or
- (ee) section 7 of the Housing Act 1988, as it applies to the grounds in Part II of Schedule 2 to that Act; or
- (f) any other enactment,

the court can only grant possession on being satisfied that it is reasonable to do so.

(7) This section shall not—
- (a) confer any right of appeal from any judgment or order where a right of appeal is conferred by some other enactment; or
- (b) take away any right of appeal from any judgment or order where a right of appeal is so conferred,

and shall have effect subject to any enactment other than this Act.

(8) In this section 'enactment' means an enactment whenever passed.

79. Agreement Not to Appeal

(1) No appeal shall lie from any judgment, direction, decision or order of a judge of county courts if, before the judgment, direction, decision or order is given or made, the parties agree, in writing signed by themselves or their legal representatives or agents, that it shall be final.

80. Judge's Note on Appeal

(1) At the hearing of any proceedings in a county court in which there is a right of appeal or from which an appeal may be brought with leave, the judge shall, at the request of any party, make a note—
- (a) of any question of law raised at the hearing; and
- (b) of the facts in evidence in relation to any such question; and
- (c) of his decision on any such question and of his determination of the proceedings.

(2) Where such a note has been taken, the judge shall (whether notice of appeal has been served or not), on the application of any party to the proceedings, and on payment by that party of such fee as may be prescribed by an order under section 92 of the Courts Act 2003 (fees), furnish him with a copy of the note, and shall sign the copy, and the copy so signed shall be used at the hearing of the appeal.

81. Powers of Court of Appeal on Appeal from County Court

(1) On the hearing of an appeal, the Court of Appeal — may draw any inference of fact and either—
   (a) order a new trial on such terms as the court thinks just; or
   (b) order judgment to be entered for any party; or
   (c) make a final or other order on such terms as the court thinks proper to ensure the determination on the merits of the real question in controversy between the parties.

(2) Subject to Civil Procedure Rules, on any appeal from a county court the Court of Appeal may reverse or vary, in favour of a party seeking to support the judgment or order of the county court in whole or in part, any determinations made in the county court on questions of fact, notwithstanding that the appeal is an appeal on a point of law only, or any such determinations on points of law, notwithstanding that the appeal is an appeal on a question of fact only.

(3) Subsection (2) shall not enable the Court of Appeal to reverse or vary any determination, unless the party dissatisfied with the determination would have been entitled to appeal in respect of it if aggrieved by the judgment or order.

82. Decision of Court of Appeal on Probate Appeals to Be Final

No appeal shall lie from the decision of the Court of Appeal on any appeal from a county court in any probate proceedings.

Certiorari and Prohibition

83. Stay of Proceedings in Case of Certiorari or Prohibition

(1) The grant by the High Court of leave to make an application for an order of certiorari or prohibition to a county court shall, if the High Court so directs, operate as a stay of the proceedings in question until the determination of the application, or until the High Court otherwise orders.

(2) Where any proceedings are so stayed, the judge of the county court shall from time to time adjourn the hearing of the proceedings to such day as he thinks fit.

[*In s. 83(1), by the Supreme Court Act 1981, s. 29(5), the reference to an order of certiorari is to be read as a reference to a quashing order and the reference to an order of prohibition is to be read as a reference to a prohibiting order.*]

84. Prohibition

(1) Where an application is made to the High Court for an order of prohibition addressed to any county court, the matter shall be finally disposed of by order.

(2) Upon any such application, the judge of the county court shall not be served with notice of it, and shall not, except by the order of a judge of the High Court—
   (a) be required to appear or be heard; or
   (b) be liable to any order for the payment of the costs of the application;

   but the application shall be proceeded with and heard in the same manner in all respects as an appeal duly brought from a decision of the judge, and notice of the application shall be given to or served upon the same parties as in the case of an order made or refused by a judge in a matter within his jurisdiction.

PART V ENFORCEMENT OF JUDGMENTS AND ORDERS

Execution against Goods

85. Execution of Judgments or Orders for Payment of Money

(1) Subject to article 8 of the High Court and County Courts Jurisdiction Order 1991, any sum of money payable under a judgment or order of a county court may be recovered, in case of default or failure of payment, forthwith or at the time or times and in the manner thereby directed, by execution against the goods of the party against whom the judgment or order was obtained.

(2) The registrar, on the application of the party prosecuting any such judgment or order, shall issue

a warrant of execution in the nature of a writ of fieri facias whereby the registrar shall be empowered to levy or cause to be levied by distress and sale of the goods, wherever they may be found within the district of the court, the money payable under the judgment or order and the costs of the execution.

(3) The precise time of the making of the application to the registrar to issue such a warrant shall be entered by him in the record prescribed for the purpose under section 12 and on the warrant.

(4) It shall be the duty of every constable within his jurisdiction to assist in the execution of every such warrant.

[*See the note to s. 3.*]

86. Execution of Orders for Payment by Instalments

(1) Where the court has made an order for payment of any sum of money by instalments, execution on the order shall not be issued until after default in payment of some instalment according to the order.

(2) Rules of court may prescribe the cases in which execution is to issue if there is any such default and limit the amounts for which and the times at which execution may issue.

(3) Except so far as may be otherwise provided by rules of court made for those purposes, execution or successive executions may issue if there is any such default for the whole of the said sum of money and costs then remaining unpaid or for such part as the court may order either at the time of the original order or at any subsequent time; but except so far as nay be otherwise provided by such rules, no execution shall issue unless at the time when it issues the whole or some part of an instalment which has already become due remains unpaid.

87. Execution to Be Superseded on Payment

(1) In or upon every warrant of execution issued from a county court against the goods of any person, the registrar shall cause to be inserted or indorsed the total amount to be levied, inclusive of the fee for issuing the warrant but exclusive of the fees for its execution.

(2) If the person against whom the execution is issued, before the actual sale of the goods, pays or causes to be paid or tendered to the registrar of the court from which the warrant is issued, or to the bailiff holding the warrant, the amount inserted in, or indorsed upon, the warrant under subsection (1), or such part as the person entitled agrees to accept in full satisfaction, together with the amount stated by the officer of the court to whom the payment or tender is made to be the amount of the fees for the execution of the warrant, the execution shall be superseded, and the goods shall be discharged and set at liberty.

[*See the note to s. 3.*]

88. Power to Stay Execution

If at any time it appears to the satisfaction of the court that any party to any proceedings is unable from any cause to pay any sum recovered against him (whether by way of satisfaction of the claim or counterclaim in the proceedings or by way of costs or otherwise), or any instalment of such a sum, the court may, in its discretion, stay any execution issued in the proceedings for such time and on such terms as the court thinks fit, and so from time to time until it appears that the cause of inability has ceased.

Seizure and Custody of Goods etc.

89. Goods Which May Be Seized

(1) Every bailiff or officer executing any warrant of execution issued from a county court against the goods of any person may by virtue of it seize—
   (a) any of that person's goods except—
      (i) such tools, books, vehicles and other items of equipment as are necessary to that person for use personally by him in his employment, business or vocation;
      (ii) such clothing, bedding, furniture, household equipment and provisions as are necessary for satisfying the basic domestic needs of that person and his family;
   (b) any money, banknotes, bills of exchange, promissory notes, bonds, specialities or securities for money belonging to that person.

(2) Any reference to the goods of an execution debtor in this Part of this Act includes a reference to anything else of his that may lawfully be seized in execution.

90. Custody of Goods Seized

Goods seized in execution under process of a county court shall, until sale,—

(a) be deposited by the bailiff in some fit place; or

(b) remain in the custody of a fit person approved by the registrar to be put in possession by the bailiff; or

(c) be safeguarded in such other manner as the registrar directs.

91. Disposal of Bills of Exchange, etc., Seized

The registrar shall hold any bills of exchange, promissory notes, bonds, specialties or other securities for money seized in execution under process of a county court as security for the amount directed to be levied by the execution, or for so much of that amount as has not been otherwise levied or raised, for the benefit of the plaintiff, and the plaintiff may sue in the name of the defendant, or in the name of any person in whose, name the defendant might have sued, for the recovery of the sum secured or made payable thereby, when the time of payment arrives.

[*See the note to s. 3.*]

92. Penalty for Rescuing Goods Seized

(1) If any person rescues or attempts to rescue any goods seized in execution under process of a county court, he shall be liable—

  (a) on summary conviction, to imprisonment for a term not exceeding one month or to a fine of an amount not exceeding level 4 on the standard scale, or both; or

  (b) on an order made by the judge in that behalf, to be committed for a specified period not exceeding one month to prison or to a fine of an amount not exceeding level 4 on the standard scale or to be so committed and to such a fine,

  and a bailiff of the court may take the offender into custody, with or without warrant, and bring him before the judge.

(2) The judge may at any time revoke an order committing a person to prison under this section and, if he is already in custody, order his discharge.

Sale of Goods Seized

93. Period to Elapse before Sale

No goods seized in execution under process of a county court shall be sold for the purpose of satisfying the warrant of execution until the expiration of a period of at least 5 days next following the day on which the goods have been so seized unless—

(a) the goods are of a perishable nature; or

(b) the person whose goods have been seized so requests in writing.

94. Goods Not to Be Sold Except by Brokers or Appraisers

No goods seized in execution under process of a county court shall be sold for the purpose of satisfying the warrant of execution except by one of the brokers or appraisers appointed under this Part of this Act.

95. Appointment of Brokers, Appraisers etc.

(1) The registrar may from time to time as he thinks fit appoint such number of persons for keeping possession, and such number of brokers and appraisers for the purpose of selling or valuing any goods seized in execution under process of the court, as appears to him to be necessary.

(2) The registrar may direct security to be taken from any broker, appraiser or other person so appointed for such sum and in such manner as he thinks fit for the faithful performance of his duties without injury or oppression.

(3) The judge or registrar may dismiss any broker, appraiser or other person so appointed,

(4) There shall be payable to brokers and appraisers so appointed in respect of their duties, out of the

Selected Legislation

produce of goods distrained or sold, such fees as may be prescribed by an order under section 92 of the Courts Act 2003 (fees).

[*See the note to s. 3.*]

96. Power to Appoint Bailiffs to Act as Brokers and Appraisers

(1) The judge may appoint in writing any bailiff of the court to act as a broker or appraiser for the purpose of selling or valuing any goods seized in execution under process of the court.

(2) A bailiff so appointed may, without other licence in that behalf, perform all the duties which brokers or appraisers appointed under section 95 may perform under this Act.

97. Sales under Executions to be Public Unless Otherwise Ordered

(1) Where any goods are to be sold under execution for a sum exceeding £20 (including legal incidental expenses), the sale shall, unless the court from which the warrant of execution issued otherwise orders, be made by public auction and not by bill of sale or private contract, and shall be publicly advertised by the registrar on, and during 3 days next preceding, the day of sale.

(2) Where any goods are seized in execution and the registrar has notice of another execution or other executions, the court shall not consider an application for leave to sell privately until the prescribed notice has been given to the other execution creditor or creditors, who may appear before the court and be heard upon the application.

[*See the note to s. 3.*]

98. Protection of Registrar Selling Goods under Execution without Notice of Claim by Third Party

(1) Where any goods in the possession of an execution debtor at the time of seizure by a registrar or other officer charged with the enforcement of a warrant or other process of execution issued from a county court are sold by that registrar or other officer without any claims having been made to them—

(a) the purchaser of the goods so sold shall acquire a good title to those goods; and

(b) no person shall be entitled to recover against the district judge or other officer, or anyone lawfully acting under his authority—

(i) for any sale of the goods, or

(ii) for paying over the proceeds prior to the receipt of a claim to the goods,

unless it is proved that the person from whom recovery is sought had notice, or might by making reasonable inquiry have ascertained, that the goods were not the property of the execution debtor.

(2) Nothing in this section shall affect the right of any claimant, who may prove that at the time of sale he had a title to any goods so seized and sold, to any remedy to which he may be entitled against any person other than the registrar or other officer.

(3) The provisions of this section shall have effect subject to those of sections 183,184 and 346 of the Insolvency Act 1986.

[*See the note to s. 3.*]

Claims in Respect of Goods Seized

99. Effect of Warrants of Execution

(1) Subject—

(a) to subsection (2); and

(b) to section 103(2),

a warrant of execution against goods issued from a county court shall bind the property in the goods of the execution debtor as from the time at which application for the warrant was made to the registrar of the county court.

(2) Such a warrant shall not prejudice the title to any goods of the execution debtor acquired by a person in good faith and for valuable consideration unless he had at the time when he acquired his title—

(a) notice that an application for the issue of a warrant of execution against the goods of the execution debtor had been made to the registrar of a county court and that the warrant issued on the application either—
   (i) remained unexecuted in the hands of the registrar of the court from which it was issued; or
   (ii) had been sent for execution to, and received by, the registrar of another county court, and remained unexecuted in the hands of the registrar of that court; or

(b) notice that a writ of fieri facias or other writ of execution by virtue of which the goods of the execution debtor might be seized or attached had been delivered to an enforcement officer or other officer charged with the execution of the writ and remained unexecuted in the hands of that person.

(3) It shall be the duty of the registrar (without fee) on application for a warrant of execution being made to him to endorse on its back the hour, day, month and year when he received the application.

(4) For the purposes of this section—
   (za) 'enforcement officer' means an individual who is authorised to act as an enforcement officer under the Courts Act 2003;
   (a) 'property' means the general property in goods, and not merely a special property; and
   (c) a thing shall be treated as done in good faith if it is in fact done honestly whether it is done negligently or not.

[*See the note to s. 3.*]

100. Sales of Goods to Which Claim is Made

(1) Where a claim is made to or in respect of any goods seized in execution under process of a county court, the claimant may—
   (a) deposit with the bailiff either—
      (i) the amount of the value of the goods claimed; or
      (ii) the sum which the bailiff is allowed to charge as costs for keeping possession of the goods until the decision of the judge can be obtained on the claim or
   (b) give the bailiff in the prescribed manner security for the value of the goods claimed.

(2) For the purpose of this section, the amount of the value of the goods claimed shall, in case of dispute, be fixed by appraisement, and where that amount is deposited it shall be paid by the bailiff into court to abide the decision of the judge upon the claim.

(3) Subject to subsection (4), in default of the claimant's complying with this section, the bailiff shall sell the goods as if no such claim had been made, and shall pay into court the proceeds of the sale to abide the decision of the judge.

(4) The goods shall not be sold if the registrar decides that, in all the circumstances, the decision of the judge on the claim made to or in respect of them ought to be awaited.

[*See the note to s. 3.*]

101. Interpleader by Registrar

(1) If a claim is made to or in respect of any goods seized in execution under process of a county court, or in respect of the proceeds or value of any such goods, the registrar may, as well before as after any action brought against him, issue a summons calling before the court the party at whose instance the process issued and the party making the claim.

(2) Upon the issue of the summons, any action brought in any county court or other court in respect of the claim or of any damage arising out of the execution of the warrant shall be stayed.

(3) On the hearing of the summons, the judge shall adjudicate upon the claim, and shall also adjudicate between the parties or either of them and the registrar upon any claim to damages arising or capable of arising out of the execution of the warrant by the registrar, and shall make such order in respect of any such claim and the costs of the proceedings as he thinks fit.

[*See the note to s. 3.*]

102. Claims for Rent Where Goods Seized in Execution

(1) Section 1 of the Landlord and Tenant Act 1709 shall not apply to goods seized in execution

under process of a county court, but the following provisions of this section shall apply in substitution.

(2) The landlord of any tenement in which any goods are seized may claim the rent of the tenement in arrear at the date of the seizure, at any time within the 5 days next following that date, or before the removal of the goods, by delivering to the bailiff or officer making the levy a claim in writing, signed by himself or his agent, stating—
 (a) the amount of rent claimed to be in arrear; and
 (b) the period in respect of which the rent is due.

(3) Where such a claim is made, the bailiff or officer making the levy shall in addition distrain for the rent so claimed and the cost of the distress, and shall not, within 5 days next after the distress, sell any part of the goods seized, unless—
 (a) the goods are of a perishable nature; or
 (b) the person whose goods have been seized so requests in writing.

(4) The bailiff shall afterwards sell under the execution and distress such of the goods as will satisfy—
 (a) first, the costs of and incidental to the sale;
 (b) next, the claim of the landlord not exceeding—
  (i) in a case where the tenement is let by the week, 4 weeks' rent;
  (ii) in a case where the tenement is let for any other term less than a year, the rent of two terms of payment;
  (iii) in any other case, one year's rent; and
 (c) lastly, the amount for which the warrant of execution issued.

(5) If any replevin is made of the goods seized, the bailiff shall nevertheless sell such portion of them as will satisfy the costs of and incidental to the sale under the execution and the amount for which the warrant of execution issued.

(6) In any event the surplus of the sale, if any, and the residue of the goods shall be returned to the execution debtor.

(7) The fees of the registrar and broker for keeping possession, appraisement and sale under any such distress shall be the same as would have been payable if the distress had been an execution of the court, and no other fees shall be demanded or taken in respect thereof.

(8) Nothing in this section affects section 346 of the Insolvency Act 1986.

[*See the note to s. 3.*]

Execution Out of Jurisdiction of Court

103. Execution Out of Jurisdiction of Court

(1) Where a warrant of execution has been issued from a county court (hereafter in this section referred to as a 'home court') against the goods of any person and the goods are out of the jurisdiction of that court, the registrar of that court may send the warrant of execution to the registrar of any other county court within the jurisdiction of which the goods are or are believed to be, with a warrant endorsed on it or annexed to it requiring execution of the original warrant.

(2) The original warrant shall bind the property in goods of the execution debtor which are within the jurisdiction of the court to which it is sent as from the time when it is received by the registrar of that court.

(3) It shall be the duty of the registrar of the court to which the warrant is sent (without fee) on receipt of the warrant to endorse on its back the hour, day, month and year when he received it.

(4) On the receipt of the warrant, the registrar of the other county court shall act in all respects as if the original warrant of execution had been issued by the court of which he is registrar and shall within the prescribed time—
 (a) report to the registrar of the home court what he has done in the execution of the warrant; and
 (b) pay over all moneys received in pursuance of the warrant.

(5) Where a warrant of execution is sent by the registrar of a home court to the registrar of another court for execution under this section, that other court shall have the same power as the home

court of staying the execution under section 88 as respects any goods within the jurisdiction of that other court.

(6) Rules of court may make provision for the suspension of an judgment or order, on terms, in connection with any warrant issued with respect to any instalment payable under the judgment or order.

[*See the note to s. 3.*]

104. Information as to Writs and Warrants of Execution

(1) Where a writ against the goods of any person issued from the High Court is delivered to an enforcement officer who is under a duty to execute the writ or to a sheriff, then on demand from the district judge of a county court that person shall—

(a) in the case of an enforcement officer, by writing signed by that officer or a person acting under his authority, and

(b) in the case of a sheriff, by writing signed by any clerk in the office of the under-sheriff,

inform the district judge of the precise time the writ was delivered to him.

(2) A bailiff of a county court shall on demand show his warrant to any enforcement officer, any person acting under the authority of an enforcement officer and any sheriff's officer.

(3) Any writing purporting to be signed as mentioned in subsection (1) and the endorsement on any warrant issued from a county court shall respectively be sufficient justification to any district judge, or enforcement officer or sheriff, acting on it.

(4) In this section 'enforcement officer' means an individual who is authorised to act as an enforcement officer under the Courts Act 2003.

Receivers and Attachment of Debts

107. Receivers

(1) The power of the county court to appoint a receiver by way of equitable execution shall operate in relation to all legal estates and interests in land.

(2) The said power may be exercised in relation to an estate or interest in land whether or not a charge has been imposed on that land under section 1 of the Charging Orders Act 1979 for the purpose of enforcing the judgment, decree, order or award in question, and the said power shall be in addition to and not in derogation of any power of any court to appoint a receiver in proceedings for enforcing such a charge.

(3) Where an order under section 1 of the Charging Orders Act 1979 imposing a charge for the purpose of enforcing a judgment, decree, order or award has been registered under section 6 of the Land Charges Act 1972, subsection (4) of that section (which provides that, amongst other things, an order appointing a receiver and any proceedings pursuant to the order or in obedience to it, shall be void against a purchaser unless the order is for the time being registered under that section) shall not apply to an order appointing a receiver made either in proceedings for enforcing the charge or by way of equitable execution of the judgment, decree, order or award or, as the case may be, of so much of it as requires payment of moneys secured by the charge.

108. Attachment of Debts

(1) Subject to any order for the time being in force under subsection (4), this section applies to any deposit account, and any withdrawable share account, with a deposit-taker.

(2) In determining whether, for the purposes of the jurisdiction of the county court to attach debts for the purpose of satisfying judgments or orders for the payment of money, a sum standing to the credit of a person in an account to which this section applies is a sum due or accruing to that person and, as such, attachable in accordance with rules of court, any condition mentioned in subsection (3) which applies to the account shall be disregarded.

(3) Those conditions are—

(a) any condition that notice is required before any money or share is withdrawn;

(b) any condition that a personal application must be made before any money or share is withdrawn;

(c) any condition that a deposit book or share-account book must be produced before any money or share is withdrawn; or

Selected Legislation

(d) any other prescribed condition.

(4) The Lord Chancellor may by order make such provision as he thinks fit, by way of amendment of this section or otherwise, for all or any of the following purposes, namely—

(a) including in, or excluding from, the accounts to which this section applies accounts of any description specified in the order;

(b) excluding from the accounts to which this section applies all accounts with any particular deposit-taker so specified or with any deposit-taker of a description so specified.

(5) An order under subsection (4) shall be made by statutory instrument subject to annulment in pursuance of a resolution of either House of Parliament.

109. Administrative and Clerical Expenses of Garnishees

(1) Where an interim third party debt order made in the exercise of the jurisdiction mentioned in subsection (2) of the preceding section is served on any deposit-taker, it may, subject to the provisions of this section, deduct from the relevant debt or debts an amount not exceeding the prescribed sum towards its administrative and clerical expenses in complying with the order; and the right to make a deduction under this subsection shall be exercisable as from the time the interim third party debt order is served on it.

(1A) In subsection (1) 'the relevant debt or debts', in relation to an interim third party debt order served on a deposit-taker, means the amount, as at the time the order is served on it, of the debt or debts of which the whole or a part is expressed to be attached by the order.

(1B) A deduction may be made under subsection (1) in a case where the amount referred to in subsection (1A) is insufficient to cover both the amount of the deduction and the amount of the judgment debt and costs in respect of which the attachment was made, notwithstanding that the benefit of the attachment to the creditor is reduced as a result of the deduction.

(2) An amount may not in pursuance of subsection (1) be deducted or, as the case may be, retained in a case where by virtue of section 346 of the Insolvency Act 1986 or section 325 of the Companies Act 1948 or otherwise, the creditor is not entitled to retain the benefit of the attachment.

(3) In this section 'prescribed' means prescribed by an order made by the Lord Chancellor.

(4) An order under this section—

(a) may make different provision for different cases;

(b) without prejudice to the generality of paragraph (a) may prescribe sums differing according to the amount due under the judgment or order to be satisfied.

(c) may provide for this section not to apply to deposit-takers of any prescribed description.

(5) Any such order shall be made by statutory instrument subject to annulment in pursuance of a resolution of either House of Parliament.

[*By virtue of the Interpretation Act 1978, s. 17(2)(b), the reference to the Companies Act 1948, s. 325, is to be construed as a reference to the Insolvency Act 1986, s. 183.*]

Miscellaneous Provisions as to Enforcement of Judgments and Orders

110. Penalty for Non-attendance on Judgment Summons

(1) If a debtor summoned to attend a county court by a judgment summons fails to attend on the day and at the time fixed for any hearing of the summons, the judge may adjourn or further adjourn the summons to a specified time on a specified day and order the debtor to attend at that time on that day.

(2) If—

(a) a debtor, having been ordered under subsection (1) to attend at a specified time on a specified day, fails to do so;

the judge may make an order committing him to prison for a period not exceeding 14 days in respect of the failure or refusal.

(3) In any case where the judge has power to make an order of committal under subsection (2) for failure to attend, he may in lieu of or in addition to making that order, order the debtor to be arrested and brought before the court either forthwith or at such time as the judge may direct.

(4) A debtor shall not be committed to prison under subsection (2) for having failed to attend as required by an order under subsection (1) unless there was paid to him at the time of the service of the judgment summons, or paid or tendered to him at the time of the service of the order, such sum in respect of his expenses as may be prescribed for the purposes of this section.

(5) The judge may at any time revoke an order committing a person to prison under this section and, if he is already in custody, order his discharge.

111. Provisions as to Warrants of Possession

(1) For the purpose of executing a warrant to give possession of any premises, it shall not be necessary to remove any goods from those premises.

(2) The duration of any warrant of possession issued by a county court to enforce a judgment or order for the recovery of land or for the delivery of possession of land shall be such as may be fixed by or in accordance with rules of court.

PART VI ADMINISTRATION ORDERS

112. Power to Make Administration Order

(1) Where a debtor—
 (a) is unable to pay forthwith the amount of a judgment obtained against him; and
 (b) alleges that his whole indebtedness amounts to a sum not exceeding the county court limit, inclusive of the debt for which the judgment was obtained;

a county court may make an order providing for the administration of his estate.

(2) In this Part of this Act—
'administration order' means an order under this section; and
'the appropriate court', in relation to an administration order, means the court which has the power to make the order.

(3) Before an administration order is made, the appropriate court shall, in accordance with rules of court, send to every person whose name the debtor has notified to the appropriate court as being a creditor of his, a notice that that person's name has been so notified.

(4) So long as an administration order is in force, a creditor whose name is included in the schedule to the order shall not, without the leave of the appropriate court, be entitled to present, or join in, a bankruptcy petition against the debtor unless—
 (a) his name was so notified; and
 (b) the debt by virtue of which he presents, or joins in, the petition, exceeds £400; and
 (c) the notice given under subsection (3) was received by the creditor within 28 days immediately preceding the day on which the petition is presented.

(5) An administration order shall not be invalid by reason only that the total amount of the debts is found at any time to exceed the county court limit, but in that case the court may, if it thinks fit, set aside the order.

(6) An administration order may provide for the payment of the debts of the debtor by instalments or otherwise, and either in full or to such extent as appears practicable to the court under the circumstances of the case, and subject to any conditions as to his future earnings or income which the court may think just.

(7) The Secretary of State may by regulations increase or reduce the sum for the time being specified in subsection (4)(b); but no such increase in the sum so specified shall affect any case in which the bankruptcy petition was presented before the coming into force of the increase.

(8) The power to make regulations under subsection (7) shall be exercisable by statutory instrument; and no such regulations shall be made unless a draft of them has been approved by resolution of each House of Parliament.

113. Notice of Order and Proof of Debts

Where an administration order has been made—
(a) notice of the order—
 (ii) shall be posted in the office of the county court for the district in which the debtor resides, and

(iii) shall be sent to every person whose name the debtor has notified to the appropriate court as being a creditor of his or who has proved;

(b) any creditor of the debtor, on proof of his debt before the registrar, shall be entitled to be scheduled as a creditor of the debtor for the amount of his proof;

(c) any creditor may object in the prescribed manner to any debt scheduled, or to the manner in which payment is directed to be made by instalments;

(d) any person who, after the date of the order, becomes a creditor of the debtor shall, on proof of his debt before the registrar, be scheduled as a creditor of the debtor for the amount of his proof, but shall not be entitled to any dividend under the order until the creditors who are scheduled as having been creditors before the date of the order have been paid to the extent provided by the order.

114. Effect of Administration Order

(1) Subject to sections 115 and 116, when an administration order is made, no creditor shall have any remedy against the person or property of the debtor in respect of any debt—

(a) of which the debtor notified the appropriate court before the administration order was made; or

(b) which has been scheduled to the order,

except with the leave of the appropriate court, and on such terms as that court may impose.

(2) Subject to subsection (3), any county court in which proceedings are pending against the debtor in respect of any debt so notified or scheduled shall, on receiving notice of the administration order, stay the proceedings, but may allow costs already incurred by the creditor, and such costs may, on application, be added to the debt.

(3) The requirement to stay proceedings shall not operate as a requirement that a county court in which proceedings in bankruptcy against the debtor are pending shall stay those proceedings.

115. Execution by Registrar

(1) Where it appears to the registrar of the appropriate court at any time while an administration order is in force that property of the debtor exceeds in value £10, he shall, at the request of any creditor, and without fee, issue execution against the debtor's goods.

(2) Section 89 applies on an execution under this section as it applies on an execution under Part V.

[*See the note to s. 3.*]

116. Right of Landlord to Distrain Notwithstanding Order

A landlord or other person to whom any rent is due from a debtor in respect of whom an administration order is made, may at any time, either before or after the date of the order, distrain upon the goods or effects of the debtor for the rent due to him from the debtor, with this limitation, that if the distress for rent is levied after the date of the order, it shall be available only for six months' rent accrued due prior to the date of the order and shall not be available for rent payable in respect of any period subsequent to the date when the distress was levied, but the landlord or other person to whom the rent may be due from the debtor may prove under the order for the surplus due for which the distress may not have been available.

117. Appropriation of Money Paid under Order and Discharge of Order

(1) Money paid into court under an administration order shall be appropriated—

(a) first in satisfaction of the costs of administration (which shall not exceed 10 pence in the pound on the total amount of the debts); and

(b) then in liquidation of debts in accordance with the order.

(2) Where the amount received is sufficient to pay—

(a) each creditor scheduled to the order to the extent provided by the order;

(b) the costs of the plaintiff in the action in respect of which the order was made; and

(c) the costs of the administration,

the order shall be superseded, and the debtor shall be discharged from his debts to the scheduled creditors.

PART VII COMMITTALS

118. Power to Commit for Contempt

(1) If any person—
  (a) wilfully insults the judge of a county court, or any juror or witness, or any officer of the court during his sitting or attendance in court, or in going to or returning from the court; or
  (b) wilfully interrupts the proceedings of a county court or otherwise misbehaves in court;

any officer of the court, with or without the assistance of any other person, may, by order of the judge, take the offender into custody and detain him until the rising of the court, and the judge may, if he thinks fit,—
    (i) make an order committing the offender for a specified period not exceeding one month to prison; or
    (ii) impose upon the offender, for every offence, a fine of an amount not exceeding £2,500 or may both make such an order and impose such a fine.

(2) The judge may at any time revoke an order committing a person to prison under this section and, if he is already in custody, order his discharge.

(3) A district judge, assistant district judge or deputy district judge shall have the same powers under this section in relation to proceedings before him as a judge.

119. Issue and Execution of Orders of Committal

(1) Whenever any order or warrant for the committal of any person to prison is made or issued by a county court (whether in pursuance of this or any other Act or of rules of court), the order or warrant shall be directed to the registrar of the court, who shall thereby be empowered to take the body of the person against whom the order is made or warrant issued.

(2) It shall be the duty of every constable within his jurisdiction to assist in the execution of every such order or warrant.

(3) The governor of the prison mentioned in any such order or warrant shall be bound to receive and keep the person mentioned in it until he is lawfully discharged.

120. Prisons to Which Committals May Be Made

Any person committed to prison by the judge of any county court, in pursuance of this or any other Act or of rules of court, shall be committed to such prison as may from time to time be directed in the case of that court by order of the Secretary of State.

121. Power of Judge to Order Discharge

(1) If at any time it appears to the satisfaction of a judge of a county court that any debtor arrested or confined in prison by order of the court is unable from any cause to pay any sum recovered against him (whether by way of satisfaction of a clam or counterclaim or by way of costs or otherwise), or any instalment thereof, and ought to be discharged, the judge may order his discharge upon such terms (including liability to re-arrest if the terms are not complied with) as the judge thinks fit.

[*This is designated subsection (1) in the Queen's Printer's copy, but there is no other subsection.*]

122. Execution of Committal Orders Out of Jurisdiction of Court

(1) Where any order or warrant for the committal of an person to prison has been made or issued (whether in pursuance of this or any other Act or of county court rules) by a county court (hereafter in this section referred to as a 'home court' and that person is out of the jurisdiction of that court, the registrar may send the order or warrant to the registrar of any other county court within the jurisdiction of which that person is or is believed to be, with a warrant endorsed on it or annexed to it requiring execution of the original order or warrant.

(2) On receipt of the warrant, the registrar of the other county court shall act in all respects as if the original order or warrant had been issued by the court of which he is registrar and shall within the prescribed time—
  (a) report to the registrar of the home court what he has done in the execution of the order or warrant; and
  (b) pay over all moneys received in pursuance of the order or warrant.

(3) Where a person is apprehended under the order or warrant, he shall be forthwith conveyed, in custody of the officer apprehending him, to the prison of the court within the jurisdiction of which he was apprehended and kept there, unless sooner discharged by law, until the expiration of the period mentioned in the order or warrant.
(4) It shall be the duty of every constable within his jurisdiction to assist in the execution of every such order or warrant.
(5) Where an order of committal—
 (a) under the Debtors Act 1869; or
 (b) under section 110.
 is sent by the registrar of a home court to the registrar of another court for execution under this section, the judge of that other court shall have the same powers to order the debtor's discharge as the judge of the home court would have under section 110 or 121.

[*See the note to s. 3.*]

PART VIII RESPONSIBILITY AND PROTECTION OF OFFICERS

123. Registrar to Have Same Responsibilities as Sheriff

Every registrar shall be responsible for the acts and defaults of himself and of the bailiffs appointed to assist him in like manner as the sheriff of any county in England or Wales is responsible for the acts and defaults of himself and his officers.

[*See the note to s. 3.*]

124. Liability of Bailiff for Neglect to Levy Execution

(1) Where a bailiff of a county court, being employed to levy any execution against goods, loses the opportunity of levying the execution by reason of neglect, connivance or omission, any party aggrieved thereby may complain to the judge of that court.
(2) On any such complaint the judge, if the neglect, connivance or omission is proved to his satisfaction, shall order the bailiff to pay such damages as it appears that the complainant has sustained by reason of it, not exceeding in any case the sum for which the execution issued.

125. Irregularity in Executing Warrants

(1) No officer of a county court in executing any warrant of a court, and no person at whose instance any such warrant is executed, shall be deemed a trespasser by reason of any irregularity or informality—
 (a) in any proceeding on the validity of which the warrant depends; or
 (b) in the form of the warrant or in the mode of executing it
 but any person aggrieved may bring an action for any special damage sustained by him by reason of the irregularity or informality against the person guilty of it.
(2) No costs shall be recovered in such an action unless the damages awarded exceed £2.

126. Actions against Bailiffs Acting under Warrants

(1) No action shall be commenced against any bailiff for anything done in obedience to a warrant issued by the registrar, unless—
 (a) a demand for inspection of the warrant and for a copy of it is made or left at the office of the bailiff by the party intending to bring the action, or his legal representative or agent; and
 (b) the bailiff refuses or neglects to comply with the demand within six days after it is made.
(2) The demand must be in writing and signed by the person making it.
(3) If an action is commenced against a bailiff in a case where such a demand has been made and not complied with, judgment shall be given for the bailiff if the warrant is produced or proved at the trial, notwithstanding any defect of jurisdiction or other irregularity in the warrant; but the registrar who issued the warrant may be joined as a defendant in the action, and if the registrar is so joined and judgment is given against him, the costs to be recovered by the plaintiff against the registrar shall include such costs as the plaintiff is liable to pay to the bailiff.
(4) In this section (except in paragraph (a) of subsection (1)) 'bailiff' includes any person acting by the order and in aid of a bailiff.

[*See the note to s. 3.*]

127. Warrants Evidence of Authority

In any action commenced against a person for anything done in pursuance of this Act, the production of the warrant of the county court shall be deemed sufficient proof of the authority of the court previous to the issue of the warrant.

PART IX MISCELLANEOUS AND GENERAL

Financial Provisions

129. Enforcement of Fines

Payment of any fine imposed by any court under this Act may be enforced upon the order of the judge in like manner—

(a) as payment of a debt adjudged by the court to be paid may be enforced under this Act; or
(b) as payment of a sum adjudged to be paid by a conviction of a magistrates' court may be enforced under the Magistrates' Courts Act 1980 (disregarding section 81(1) of that Act).

130. Payment and Application of Fees, Fines, etc.

(1) Subject to subsection (2), all fees, forfeitures and fines payable under this Act and any penalty payable to an officer of a county court under any other Act shall be paid to officers designated by the Lord Chancellor and dealt with by them in such manner as the Lord Chancellor, after consultation with the Treasury, may direct.
(2) Subsection (1) does not apply to fines imposed on summary conviction or to so much of a fine as is applicable under section 55(4) to indemnify a party injured.
(3) The Lord Chancellor, with the concurrence of the Treasury, shall from time to time make such rules as he thinks fit for securing the balances and other sums of money in the hands of any officers of a county court, and for the due accounting for and application of those balances and sums.

131. Appointment of Auditors and Other Officers

The Lord Chancellor may, subject to the consent of the Treasury as to numbers and salaries, appoint as officers in his department such auditors and other officers as he may consider necessary for the purpose of controlling the accounts of county courts.

132. Payment of Salaries and Expenses

There shall be paid out of money provided by Parliament—

(a) all salaries, remuneration and other sums payable under Part I of this Act or under section 131;
(b) the expenses of supplying the courts and offices with law and office books and stationery and postage stamps;
(c) expenses incurred in conveying to prison persons committed by the courts; and
(d) all other expenses arising out of any jurisdiction for the time being conferred on the courts or any officer of the courts.

Summonses and Other Documents

133. Proof of Service of Summonses etc.

(1) Where any summons or other process issued from a county court is served by an officer of a court, the service may be proved by a certificate in a prescribed form showing the fact and mode of the service.
(2) Any officer of a court wilfully and corruptly giving a false certificate under subsection (1) in respect of the service of a summons or other process shall be guilty of an offence and, on conviction thereof, shall be removed from office and shall be liable—
   (a) on conviction on indictment, to imprisonment for any term not exceeding 2 years; or
   (b) on summary conviction, to imprisonment for any term not exceeding 6 months or to a fine not exceeding the statutory maximum or to both such imprisonment and fine.

135. Penalty for Falsely Pretending to Act under Authority of Court

Any person who—

(a) delivers or causes to be delivered to any other person any paper falsely purporting to be a copy of any summons or other process of a county court, knowing it to be false; or

(b) acts or professes to act under any false colour or pretence of the process or authority of a county court;

shall be guilty of an offence and shall for each offence be liable on conviction on indictment to imprisonment for a term not exceeding 7 years.

136. Penalty for Falsely Representing Document to Have Been Issued from County Court

(1) It shall not be lawful to deliver or cause to be delivered to any person any document which was not issued under the authority of a county court but which, by reason of its form or contents or both, has the appearance of having been issued under such authority.

(2) If any person contravenes this section, he shall for each offence be liable on summary conviction to a fine of an amount not exceeding level 3 on the standard scale.

(3) Nothing in this section shall be taken to prejudice section 135.

137. Lessee to Give Notice of Summons for Recovery of Land

(1) Every lessee to whom there is delivered any summons issued from a county court for the recovery of land demised to or held by him, or to whose knowledge any such summons comes, shall forthwith give notice of the summons to his lessor or his bailiff or receiver.

(2) If a lessee fails to give notice as required by subsection (1), he shall be liable to forfeit to the person of whom he holds the land an amount equal to the value of 3 years' improved or rack rent of the land to be recovered by action in any county court or other court having jurisdiction in respect of claims for such an amount.

Forfeiture for Non-payment of Rent

138. Provisions as to Forfeiture for Non-payment of Rent

(1) This section has effect where a lessor is proceeding by action in a county court (being an action in which the county court has jurisdiction) to enforce against a lessee a right of re-entry or forfeiture in respect of any land for non-payment of rent.

(2) If the lessee pays into court or to the lessor not less than 5 clear days before the return day all the rent in arrear and the costs of the action, the action shall cease, and the lessee shall hold the land according to the lease without any new lease.

(3) If—

(a) the action does not cease under subsection (2); and

(b) the court at the trial is satisfied that the lessor is entitled to enforce the right of re-entry or forfeiture,

the court shall order possession of the land to be given to the lessor at the expiration of such period, not being less than 4 weeks from the date of the order, as the court thinks fit, unless within that period the lessee pays into court or to the lessor all the rent in arrear and the costs of the action.

(4) The court may extend the period specified under subsection (3) at any time before possession of the land is recovered in pursuance of the order under that subsection.

(5) If—

(a) within the period specified in the order; or

(b) within that period as extended under subsection (4), the lessee pays into court—

(i) all the rent in arrear; and

(ii) the costs of the action,

he shall hold the land according to the lease without any new lease.

(6) Subsection (2) shall not apply where the lessor is proceeding in the same action to enforce a right of re-entry or forfeiture on any other ground as well as for non-payment of rent, or to enforce any other claim as well as the right of re-entry or forfeiture and the claim for arrears of rent.

(7) If the lessee does not—

(a) within the period specified in the order; or
(b) within that period as extended under subsection (4), pay into court or to the lessor—
(i) all the rent in arrear; and
(ii) the costs of the action,
the order shall be enforceable in the prescribed manner and so long as the order remains unreversed the lessee shall, subject to subsections (8) and (9A), be barred from all relief.

(8) The extension under subsection (4) of a period fixed by a court shall not be treated as relief from which the lessee is barred by subsection (7) if he fails to pay into court or to the lessor all the rent in arrear and the costs of the action within that period.

(9) Where the court extends a period under subsection (4) at a time when—
(a) that period has expired; and
(b) a warrant has been issued for the possession of the land, the court shall suspend the warrant for the extended period; and, if, before the expiration of the extended period, the lessee pays into court or to the lessor all the rent in arrear and all the costs of the action, the court shall cancel the warrant.

(9A) Where the lessor recovers possession of the land at any time after the making of the order under subsection (3) (whether as a result of the enforcement of the order or otherwise) the lessee may, at any time within six months from the date on which the lessor recovers possession, apply to the court for relief; and on any such application the court may, if it thinks fit, grant to the lessee such relief, subject to such terms and conditions, as it thinks fit.

(9B) Where the lessee is granted relief on an application under subsection (9A) he shall hold the land according to the lease without any new lease.

(9C) An application under subsection (9A) may be made by a person with an interest under a lease of the land derived (whether immediately or otherwise) from the lessee's interest therein in like manner as if he were the lessee; and on any such application the court may make an order which (subject to such terms and conditions as the court thinks fit) vests the land in such a person, as lessee of the lessor, for the remainder of the term of the lease under which he has any such interest as aforesaid, or for any lesser term.

In this subsection any reference to the land includes a reference to a part of the land.

(10) Nothing in this section or section 139 shall be taken to affect—
(a) the power of the court to make any order which it would otherwise have power to make as respects a right of re-entry or forfeiture on any ground other than non-payment of rent; or
(b) section 146(4) of the Law of Property Act 1925 (relief against forfeiture).

139. Service of Summons and Re-entry

(1) In a case where section 138 has effect, if—
(a) one-half-year's rent is in arrear at the time of the commencement of the action; and
(b) the lessor has a right to re-enter for non-payment of that rent; and
(c) no sufficient distress is to be found on the premises countervailing the arrears then due,
the service of the summons in the action in the prescribed manner shall stand in lieu of a demand and re-entry.

(2) Where a lessor has enforced against a lessee, by re-entry without action, a right of re-entry or forfeiture as respects any land for non-payment of rent, the lessee may, at any time within six months from the date on which the lessor re-entered apply to the county court for relief, and on any such application the court may, if it thinks fit, grant to the lessee such relief as the High Court could have granted.

(3) Subsections (9B) and (9C) of section 138 shall have effect in relation to an application under subsection (2) of this section as they have effect in relation to an application under subsection (9A) of that section.

140. Interpretation of Sections 138 and 139

For the purposes of sections 138 and 139—
'lease' includes—
(a) an original or derivative under-lease;
(b) an agreement for a lease where the lessee has become entitled to have his lease granted; and
(c) a grant at a fee farm rent, or under a grant securing a rent by condition;

'lessee' includes—

(a) an original or derivative under-lessee;
(b) the persons deriving title under a lessee;
(c) a grantee under a grant at a fee farm rent, or under a grant securing a rent by condition; and
(d) the persons deriving title under such a grantee;

'lessor' includes—

(a) an original or derivative under-lessor;
(b) the persons deriving title under a lessor;
(c) a person making a grant at a fee farm rent, or a grant securing a rent by condition; and
(d) the persons deriving title under such a grantor;

'under-lease' includes an agreement for an under-lease where the under-lessee has become entitled to have his under-lease granted; and

'under-lessee' includes any person deriving title under an under-lessee.

Solicitors

142. Power to Enforce Undertakings of Solicitors

A county court shall have the same power to enforce an undertaking given by a solicitor in relation to any proceedings in that court as the High Court has to enforce an undertaking so given in relation to any proceedings in the High Court.

143. Prohibition on Persons Other Than Solicitors Receiving Remuneration for Business Done in County Courts

(1) No person other than—

(a) a legal representative; or
(b) a person exercising a right of audience or a right to conduct litigation by virtue of an order made under section 11 of the Courts and Legal Services Act 1990 (representation in county courts).

shall be entitled to have or recover any fee or reward for acting on behalf of a party in proceedings in a county court.

Replevin

144. Replevin

Schedule 1 to this Act shall have effect.

Power to Raise Monetary Limits

145. Power to Raise Monetary Limits

(1) If it appears to Her Majesty in Council—

(a) that the county court limit for the purposes of any enactment referring to that limit, or
(b) that the higher limit or the lower limit referred to in section 20 of this Act, should be increased, Her Majesty may by Order in Council direct that the limit in question shall be such amount as may be specified in the Order.

(2) An Order under subsection (1) may contain such incidental or transitional provisions as Her Majesty considers appropriate.

(2A) It is for the Lord Chancellor to recommend to Her Majesty the making of an Order under subsection (1).

(3) No recommendation shall be made to Her Majesty in Council to make an Order under this section unless a draft of the Order has been laid before Parliament and approved by resolution of each House of Parliament.

General

146. Lords Commissioners to Represent Lord Chancellor When Great Seal in Commission

When the Great Seal is in commission, the Lords Commissioners shall represent the Lord Chancellor for the purposes of this Act; but the powers vested in him by this Act in relation to the appointment of officers may be exercised by the senior Lord Commissioner for the time being.

147. Interpretation

(1) In this Act, unless the context otherwise requires—

'action' means any proceedings in a county court which may be commenced as prescribed by plaint;

'Admiralty county court' means a county court appointed to have Admiralty jurisdiction by order under this Act;

'Admiralty proceedings' means proceedings in which the claim would not be within the jurisdiction of a county court but for sections 26 and 27;

'bailiff' includes a registrar;

'the county court limit' means—

(a) in relation to any enactment contained in this Act for which a limit is for the time being specified by an Order under section 145, that limit,

(c) in relation to any enactment contained in this Act and not within paragraph (a), the county court limit for the time being specified by any other Order in Council or order defining the limit of county court jurisdiction for the purposes of that enactment;

'court' and 'county court' mean a court held for a district under this Act;

'deposit-taking institution'* means any person who may, in the course of his business, lawfully accept deposits in the United Kingdom;

'district' and 'county court district' mean a district for which a court is to be held under section 2;

'hearing' includes trial, and 'hear' and 'heard' shall be construed accordingly;

'hereditament' includes both a corporeal and an incorporeal hereditament;

'judge', in relation to a county court, means a judge assigned to the district of that court under subsection (1) of section 5 and any person sitting as a judge for that district under subsection (3) or (4) of that section;

'judgment summons' means a summons issued on the application of a person entitled to enforce a judgment or order under section 5 of the Debtors Act 1869 requiring a person, or where two or more persons are liable under the judgment or order, requiring any one or more of them, to attend court;

'landlord', in relation to any land, means the person entitled to the immediate reversion or, if the property therein is held in joint tenancy, any of the persons entitled to the immediate reversion;

'legal representative' means an authorised advocate or authorised litigator, as defined by section 119(1) of the Courts and Legal Services Act 1990.

'matter' means every proceeding in a county court which may be commenced as prescribed otherwise than by plaint;

'officer', in relation to a court, means any registrar, deputy registrar or assistant registrar of that court, and any clerk, bailiff, usher or messenger in the service of that court;

'part-time registrar' and 'part-time assistant registrar' have the meaning assigned to them by section 10(3);

'party' includes every person served with notice of, or attending, any proceeding, whether named as a party to that proceeding or not;

'prescribed' means prescribed by rules of court;

'probate proceedings' means proceedings brought in a county court by virtue of section 32 or transferred to that court under section 40;

'proceedings' includes both actions and matters;

'registrar' and 'registrar of a county court' mean a registrar appointed for a district under this Act, or in a case where two or more registrars are appointed jointly, either or any of those registrars;

'return day' means the day appointed in any summons or proceeding for the appearance of the defendant or any other day fixed for the hearing of any proceedings;

'ship' includes any description of vessel used in navigation;

'solicitor' means solicitor of the Supreme Court.

(1A) The definition of 'deposit-taking institution'* in subsection (1) must be read with—
- (a) section 22 of the Financial Services and Markets Act 2000;
- (b) any relevant order under that section; and
- (c) Schedule 2 to that Act.

[*By the Courts and Legal Services Act 1990, s. 74(1) and (3), any reference to the office of registrar is to be construed as a reference to the office of district judge; any reference to the office of assistant registrar is to be construed as a reference to the office of assistant district judge; and any reference to the office of deputy registrar is to be construed as a reference to the office of deputy district judge.*]

148. Amendments of Other Acts, Transitory Provisions, Transitional Provisions, Savings and Repeals

(1) The enactments specified in Schedule 2 shall have effect subject to the amendments there specified.

(2) This Act shall have effect subject to the transitory provisions and transitional provisions and savings contained in Schedule 3.

(3) The enactments specified in Schedule 4 are hereby repealed to the extent specified in the third column of that Schedule.

149. Extent

(1) Section 148(1) and Schedule 2 extend to Scotland so far as they amend enactments extending to Scotland.

(2) Section 148(1) and Schedule 2 extend to Northern Ireland so far as they amend enactments extending to Northern Ireland.

(3) Subject to subsections (1) and (2), this Act extends to England and Wales only.

150. Commencement

This Act shall come into force on 1st August 1984.

151. Short Title

This Act may be cited as the County Courts Act 1984.

Section 144

SCHEDULE 1 REPLEVIN

1.—(1) The sheriff shall have no power or responsibility with respect to replevin bonds or replevins.

(2) The registrar for the district in which any goods subject to replevin are taken shall have power, subject to the provisions of this Schedule, to approve of replevin bonds and to grant replevins and to issue all necessary process in relation to them, and any such process shall be executed by a bailiff of the court.

(3) The registrar shall, at the instance of the party whose goods have been seized, cause the goods to be replevied to that party on his giving such security as is provided in this Schedule.

[*See the note to s. 3.*]

2.—(1) It shall be a condition of any security given under paragraph 1 that the replevisor will—
- (a) commence an action of replevin against the seizor in the High Court within one week from the date when the security is given; or
- (b) commence such an action in a county court within one month from that date.

(2) In either case—
- (a) the replevisor shall give security, to be approved by the registrar having power in the matter, for such an amount as the registrar thinks sufficient to cover both the probable costs of the action and either—
  - (i) the alleged rent or damage in respect of which the distress has been made; or
  - (ii) in a case where the goods replevied have been seized otherwise than under colour of distress, the value of the goods; and

[* 'deposit-taking institution' should be 'deposit-taker'.]

(b) it shall be a further condition of the security that the replevisor will—
   (i) prosecute the action with effect and without delay; and
   (ii) make a return of the goods, if a return of them is ordered in the action.

[*See the note to s. 3.*]

Section 148(2)

SCHEDULE 3 TRANSITORY AND TRANSITIONAL PROVISIONS AND SAVINGS

Administration Orders

4.—(1) Any reference in Part VI of this Act to an administration order includes a reference to an administration order made under an enactment repealed by this Act.

County Court

5. References in any enactment or document to a county court constituted under the County Courts Act 1888 or the County Courts Act 1934 or the County Courts Act 1959 shall be construed as references to a county court constituted under this Act and anything done or proceedings taken in respect of any action or matter whatsoever before the commencement of this Act in a county court under any of the enactments mentioned above shall be deemed to have been done or taken in a county court constituted under this Act.

Former Enactments

6. Any document referring to any former enactment relating to county courts shall be construed as referring to the corresponding enactment in this Act. In this paragraph 'former enactment relating to county courts' means any enactment repealed by the County Courts Act 1959, by the County Courts Act 1934 or by the County Courts Act 1888.

High Bailiffs

7. References to a high bailiff in any enactment, Order in Council, order, rule, regulation or any document whatsoever shall be construed as a reference to a registrar.

[*See the note to s. 3.*]

Periods of Time

8. Where a period of time specified in an enactment repealed by this Act is current at the coming into force of this Act, this Act shall have effect as if the corresponding provision of it had been in force when that period began to run.

Offences

9. Nothing in this Act renders a person liable to punishment by way of fine or imprisonment for an offence committed before the coming into force of this Act which differs from the punishment to which he would have been liable if this Act had not been passed.

General

11. Without prejudice to any express amendment made by this Act, a reference in an enactment or other document, whether express or implied, to an enactment repealed by this Act shall, unless the context otherwise requires, be construed as, or as including, a reference to this Act or to the corresponding provisions of this Act.

12. Nothing in this Schedule shall be taken as prejudicing the operation of the provisions of the Interpretation Act 1978 as respects the effect of repeals.

NOTES ON TEXT

The text printed above incorporates the following amendments:

s. 1(1) amended by Civil Procedure Act 1997, sch. 2, para. 2(1) and (4) (in force by SI 1997/841);

s. 2 amended by Constitutional Reform Act 2005, sch. 4, para. 161 (in force by SI 2006/1014);

s. 3 amended by Constitutional Reform Act 2005, sch. 4, para. 162 (in force by SI 2006/1014);
s. 3(3) repealed by Civil Procedure Act 1997, sch. 2, para. 2(1) and (5) (in force by SI 1997/841);
s. 5 amended by Constitutional Reform Act 2005, sch. 4, para. 163 (in force by SI 2006/1014);
s. 6 substituted by Constitutional Reform Act 2005, sch. 3, para. 1(1) (in force by SI 2006/1014);
s. 7 repealed by Judicial Pensions and Retirement Act 1993, sch. 8, para. 17, and sch. 9 (in force by SI 1995/631);
s. 8 amended by: (a) Courts and Legal Services Act 1990, sch. 18, para. 42 (in force by SI 1990/2484); (b) Judicial Pensions and Retirement Act 1993, sch. 6, para. 17(1), and sch. 9 (in force by SI 1995/631);
s. 9 amended by: (a) Courts and Legal Services Act 1990, sch. 10, para. 57, and sch. 18, para. 42 (in force by SI 1990/2484); (b) Judicial Pensions and Retirement Act 1993, sch. 8, para. 17, and sch. 9 (in force by SI 1995/631);
s. 10 repealed by Courts and Legal Services Act 1990, sch. 20 (in force by SI 1990/2484);
s. 11 amended by: (a) Judicial Pensions and Retirement Act 1993, sch. 6, para. 17(2) to (4), and sch. 9 (in force by SI 1995/631); (b) Constitutional Reform Act 2005, sch. 4, para. 164 (in force by SI 2006/1014);
s. 12 amended by: (a) Courts and Legal Services Act 1990, sch. 18, para. 42 (in force by SI 1990/2484); (b) Constitutional Reform Act 2005, sch. 4, para. 165 (in force by SI 2006/1014);
s. 13(1) and (4) amended by Courts and Legal Services Act 1990, sch. 18, para. 49(2) (in force by SI 1991/608);
s. 14(1)(b) amended by Statute Law (Repeals) Act 1986, sch. 1, part I, group 1;
s. 14(3) inserted by Courts and Legal Services Act 1990, s. 74(4) (in force by SI 1991/1364);
ss. 15 and 16 amended by High Court and County Courts Jurisdiction Order 1991 (SI 1991/724), sch., part I;
s. 18 amended by Courts and Legal Services Act 1990, sch. 18, para. 49(3) (in force by SI 1991/608);
ss. 19 and 20 repealed by Courts and Legal Services Act 1990, sch. 20 (in force by SI 1991/1364);
s. 21 amended by High Court and County Courts Jurisdiction Order 1991 (SI 1991/724), sch., part I;
s. 22 repealed by Courts and Legal Services Act 1990, sch. 20 (in force by SI 1991/1364);
s. 24(1) amended by Courts and Legal Services Act 1990, sch. 18, para. 49(3) (in force by SI 1991/608);
s. 24(2) amended by: (a) High Court and County Courts Jurisdiction Order 1991 (SI 1991/724), sch., part I; (b) Statute Law (Repeals) Act 2004, sch. 1, part 1, group 4;
s. 25 amended by High Court and County Courts Jurisdiction Order 1991 (SI 1991/724), sch., part I;
s. 32 substituted by Administration of Justice Act 1985, s. 51(1) (in force by SI 1986/1503, art. 2);
s. 33 amended by Administration of Justice Act 1985, sch. 7, para. 7 (in force by SI 1986/1503, art. 2);
s. 34 repealed by Courts and Legal Services Act 1990, sch. 20 (in force by SI 1991/1364);
s. 38 substituted by Courts and Legal Services Act 1990, s. 3 (in force by SI 1991/1364); amended by Constitutional Reform Act 2005, sch. 1, para. 17, sch. 4, para. 167, and sch. 18, part 1 (in force by SI 2006/1014); s. 39 repealed by Courts and Legal Services Act 1990, s. 3 (in force by SI 1991/1364);
s. 40 substituted by Courts and Legal Services Act 1990, s. 2(1) (in force by SI 1991/1364);
s. 41(2) amended by Matrimonial and Family Proceedings Act 1984, sch. 1, para. 30 (in force by SI 1986/635, art. 2(b));
s. 41(3) inserted by Courts and Legal Services Act 1990, s. 2(2) (in force by SI 1991/1364);
s. 42 substituted by Courts and Legal Services Act 1990, s. 2(3) (in force by SI 1991/1364);
ss. 43 and 44 repealed by Courts and Legal Services Act 1990, sch. 20 (in force by SI 1991/1364);
s. 45(1) amended and s. 45(2) repealed by Courts and Legal Services Act 1990, sch. 20 (in force by SI 1992/1221);
s. 47 repealed by Civil Procedure (Modification of Enactments) Order 1998 (SI 1998/2940), art. 6(a);
s. 50(1) and (2) amended by Civil Procedure Act 1997, sch. 2, para. 2(1) and (2) (in force by SI 1997/841, arts 3 and 4);

s. 50(3) amended by Civil Procedure Act 1997, sch. 2, para. 2(1) and (3) (in force by SI 1999/1009);
s. 50(4) amended by Civil Procedure Act 1997, sch. 2, para. 2(1) and (2) (in force by SI 1997/841, arts 3 and 4);
s. 51(2) amended by Civil Procedure Act 1997, sch. 2, para. 2(1) and (2) (in force by SI 1997/841, arts 3 and 4);
s. 51(3) amended by Civil Procedure Act 1997, sch. 2, para. 2(1) and (3) (in force by SI 1999/1009);
s. 51(4) amended by Civil Procedure Act 1997, sch. 2, para. 2(1) and (2) (in force by SI 1997/841, arts 3 and 4);
s. 52(1) amended by Civil Procedure Act 1997, sch. 2, para. 2(1) and (2) (in force by SI 1997/841, arts 3 and 4);
s. 52(2) amended by: (a) Civil Procedure Act 1997, sch. 2, para. 2(1) and (2) (in force by SI 1997/841, arts 3 and 4); (b) Civil Procedure (Modification of Enactments) Order 1998 (SI 1998/2940), art. 6(b);
s. 52(3) inserted by Courts and Legal Services Act 1990, sch. 18, para. 43 (in force by SI 1991/1364);
s. 53(1) repealed by Civil Procedure (Modification of Enactments) Order 1998 (SI 1998/2940), art. 6(c);
s. 53(2) and (3) amended by: (a) Civil Procedure Act 1997, sch. 2, para. 2(1) and (2) (in force by SI 1997/841, arts 3 and 4); (b) Civil Procedure (Modification of Enactments) Order 1998 (SI 1998/2940), art. 6(c);
s. 53(5) inserted by Courts and Legal Services Act 1990, sch. 18, para. 44 (in force by SI 1991/1364);
s. 54(2) amended by: (a) Civil Procedure Act 1997, sch. 2, para. 2(1) and (2) (in force by SI 1997/841, arts 3 and 4); (b) Civil Procedure Act 1997, sch. 2, para. 2(1) and (3) (in force by SI 1999/1009);
s. 54(3) amended by Civil Procedure Act 1997, sch. 2, para. 2(1) and (2) (in force by SI 1997/841, arts 3 and 4);
s. 54(6) inserted by Courts and Legal Services Act 1990, sch. 18, para. 45 (in force by SI 1991/1364);
s. 55(1) amended by Civil Procedure Act 1997, sch. 2, para. 2(1) and (2) (in force by SI 1997/841, arts 3 and 4);
s. 55(2) amended by Criminal Justice Act 1991, sch. 4, part I (in force by SI 1992/333, sch. 2);
s. 55(3) amended by Civil Procedure Act 1997, sch. 2, para. 2(1) and (2) (in force by SI 1997/841, arts 3 and 4);
s. 55(4A) inserted by Courts and Legal Services Act 1990, s. 74(5) (in force by SI 1991/1364);
s. 58(1) amended by Administration of Justice Act 1985, sch. 7, para. 8 and sch. 8, part II (in force by s. 69(4) of Act);
s. 60(1) repealed and s. 60(2) amended by Courts and Legal Services Act 1990, sch. 20 (in force by SI 1990/2484);
s. 60(3) amended by (a) Local Government Act 1985, sch. 14, para. 63, and sch. 17 (in force by ss. 1 and 102 of Act); (b) Norfolk and Suffolk Broads Act 1988, sch. 6, para. 24 (in force by SI 1988/955, art. 3); (c) Education Reform Act 1988, sch. 13; (d) Police and Magistrates' Courts Act 1994, sch. 4, para. 57 (in force by SI 1994/3262, art. 4(1) and sch.); (e) Environment Act 1995, sch. 10, para. 23 (in force by SI 1995/2950, art. 2(1)); (f) Police Act 1996, sch. 7, para. 1; (g) Police Act 1997, sch. 9, para. 45 (in force by SI 1998/354, art. 2); (h) Greater London Authority Act 1999, sch. 27, para. 49 (in force by SI 2000/1648);
s. 61 amended by: (a) Courts and Legal Services Act 1990, sch. 18, para. 49(2) (in force by SI 1991/608); (b) Constitutional Reform Act 2005, sch. 4, para. 168 (in force by SI 2006/1014);
s. 62 amended by Civil Procedure Act 1997, sch. 2, para. 2(1) and (2) (in force by SI 1997/841, arts 3 and 4);
s. 63 amended by Civil Procedure (Modification of Enactments) Order 1998 (SI 1998/2940), art. 6(d);
s. 64(1), (2) and (2A) amended by Civil Procedure Act 1997, sch. 2, para. 2(1) and (2) (in force by SI 1997/841, arts 3 and 4);
s. 64(2A) and (2B) inserted by Courts and Legal Services Act 1990, s. 6 (in force by s. 124(2) of Act);
s. 65(1) and (2) amended by Civil Procedure Act 1997, sch. 2, para. 2(1) and (2) (in force by SI 1997/841, arts 3 and 4);
s. 66(1)(b) amended by Housing Act 1988, sch. 17, para. 35(1) (in force by SI 1988/2152, art. 3);

s. 66(1)(c) amended by Housing (Consequential Provisions) Act 1985, sch. 2, para. 57(1) and (2);
s. 66(4) amended by Courts Act 2003, sch. 8, para. 271 (in force by SI 2005/910);
s. 69(1) and (3) amended by Civil Procedure Act 1997, sch. 2, para. 2(1) and (2) (in force by SI 1997/841, arts 3 and 4);
s. 69(8) substituted by Courts and Legal Services Act 1990, sch. 18, para. 46 (in force by SI 1991/1364);
ss. 73 and 73A repealed by Courts Act 2003, sch. 10 (in force by SI 2005/3518);
s. 74(5A) inserted by Private International Law (Miscellaneous Provisions) Act 1995, s. 2 (in force by SI 1996/2515);
s. 74A inserted by Civil Procedure Act 1997, s. 5(2) (in force by SI 1997/841); repealed by Constitutional Reform Act 2005, sch. 4, para. 169, and sch. 18, part 2 (in force by SI 2005/2505 and SI 2006/1014);
s. 75 repealed by Civil Procedure Act 1997, sch. 2, para. 2(1) and (6) (in force by SI 1999/1009);
s. 77(1) amended by: (a) Civil Procedure Act 1997, sch. 2, para. 2(1) and (7) (in force by SI 1999/1009); (b) Access to Justice Act 1999 (Destination of Appeals) Order 2000 (SI 2000/1071), art. 8;
s. 77(1A) inserted by Courts and Legal Services Act 1990, sch. 17, para. 15 (in force by SI 1990/2484);
s. 77(2) to (4) repealed by Access to Justice Act 1999, sch. 15, part III (in force by s. 108(3) of Act);
s. 77(6)(e) amended by Housing (Consequential Provisions) Act 1985, sch. 2, para. 57(1) and (3);
s. 77(6)(ee) inserted by Housing Act 1988, sch. 17, para. 35(2) (in force by SI 1988/2152, art. 3);
s. 79(1) amended by Courts and Legal Services Act 1990, sch. 18, para. 49(3) (in force by SI 1991/608);
s. 79(2) repealed by Statute Law (Repeals) Act 1986, sch. 1, part I, group 1;
s. 80(2) amended by Courts Act 2003, sch. 8, para. 271 (in force by SI 2005/910);
s. 81(2) amended by Civil Procedure Act 1997, sch. 2, para. 2(1) and (8) (in force by SI 1999/1009);
s. 85(1) amended by High Court and County Courts Jurisdiction Order 1991 (SI 1991/724), art. 8(2);
s. 86(2) and (3) amended by Civil Procedure Act 1997, sch. 2, para. 2(1) and (2) (in force by SI 1997/841, arts 3 and 4);
s. 89(1)(a) substituted by Courts and Legal Services Act 1990, s. 15(2) (in force by SI 1991/1364);
s. 89(3) repealed by Courts and Legal Services Act 1990, sch. 20 (in force by SI 1991/1364);
s. 92(1)(b) amended by Statute Law (Repeals) Act 1986, sch. 1, part I, group 1;
s. 95(4) amended by Courts Act 2003, sch. 8, para. 271 (in force by SI 2005/910);
s. 98(1) amended by Courts Act 2003, sch. 8, para. 273 (in force by SI 2005/910);
s. 98(3) substituted by Insolvency Act 1986, sch. 14 (in force by SI 1986/1924, art. 3, and Insolvency Act 1986, s. 443);
s. 99 amended by Courts Act 2003, sch. 8, para. 274, and sch. 10 (in force by SI 2004/401);
s. 102(8) substituted by Insolvency Act 1986, sch. 14 (in force by SI 1986/1924, art. 3, and Insolvency Act 1986, s. 443);
s. 103(6) inserted by Courts and Legal Services Act 1990, sch. 17, para. 16 (in force by s. 124(2) of Act); amended by Civil Procedure Act 1997, sch. 2, para. 2(1) and (2) (in force by SI 1997/841, arts 3 and 4);
s. 104 substituted by Courts Act 2003, sch. 8, para. 275 (in force by SI 2004/401);
ss. 105 and 106 repealed by Courts and Legal Services Act 1990, sch. 20 (in force by SI 1991/1364);
s. 108 amended by: (a) Civil Procedure Act 1997, sch. 2, para. 2(1) and (2) (in force by SI 1997/841, arts 3 and 4); (b) Financial Services and Markets Act 2000 (Consequential Amendments and Repeals) Order 2001 (SI 2001/3649), art. 294;
s. 109(1) substituted and s. 109(1A) and (1B) inserted by Administration of Justice Act 1985, s. 52(1) and (2) (in force by s. 69(4) of Act); s. 109(1) and (1A) amended by: (a) Financial Services and Markets Act 2000 (Consequential Amendments and Repeals) Order 2001 (SI 2001/3649), art. 295(1), (2) and (3); (b) Civil Procedure (Modification of Enactments) Order 2002 (SI 2002/439), art. 7;
s. 109(2) amended by: (a) Administration of Justice Act 1985, s. 52(1) and (3) (in force by s. 69(4) of

Act); and (b) Insolvency Act 1985, sch. 8, para. 38, and Insolvency Act 1986, sch. 14 (in force by SI 1986/1924, art. 3, and Insolvency Act 1986, s. 443);

s. 109(4) amended by: (a) Administration of Justice Act 1985, s. 52(1) and (4) and sch. 8, part II (in force by s. 69(4) of Act); (b) Financial Services and Markets Act 2000 (Consequential Amendments and Repeals) Order 2001 (SI 2001/3649), art. 295(1) and (4);

s. 110(2)(b) repealed by Civil Procedure (Modification of Enactments) Order 2002 (SI 2002/439), art. 8;

s. 111(2) amended by Civil Procedure Act 1997, sch. 2, para. 2(1) and (2) (in force by SI 1997/841, arts 3 and 4);

s. 112(3) amended by Civil Procedure Act 1997, sch. 2, para. 2(1) and (2) (in force by SI 1997/841, arts 3 and 4);

s. 113(a)(i) repealed by Administration of Justice Act 1985, sch. 8, part II (in force by s. 69(4) of Act);

s. 118(1) amended by: (a) Statute Law (Repeals) Act 1986, sch. 1, part I, group 1; (b) Criminal Justice Act 1991, sch. 4, part I (in force by SI 1992/333, sch. 2);

s. 118(3) inserted by Courts and Legal Services Act 1990, s. 75(6) (in force by SI 1991/1364);

s. 119(1) amended by Civil Procedure Act 1997, sch. 2, para. 2(1) and (2) (in force by SI 1997/841, arts 3 and 4);

s. 120 amended by Civil Procedure Act 1997, sch. 2, para. 2(1) and (2) (in force by SI 1997/841, arts 3 and 4);

s. 126(1) amended by Courts and Legal Services Act 1990, sch. 18, para. 49(2) (in force by SI 1991/608);

s. 128 repealed by Courts Act 2003, sch. 8, para. 276, and sch. 10 (in force by SI 2004/3123);

s. 133(1) amended by Civil Procedure (Modification of Enactments) Order 1998 (SI 1998/2940), art. 6(e);

s. 134 repealed by Civil Procedure (Modification of Enactments) Order 1998 (SI 1998/2940), art. 6(f);

s. 138 amended by: (a) Administration of Justice Act 1985, s. 55(1) to (4) and sch. 8, part III (in force by SI 1986/1503, art. 2); (b) Courts and Legal Services Act 1990, sch. 17, para. 17 (in force by SI 1991/1364);

s. 139(2) amended by High Court and County Courts Jurisdiction Order 1991 (SI 1991/724), sch., part I;

s. 139(3) inserted by Administration of Justice Act 1985, s. 51(5) (in force by SI 1986/1503, art. 2);

s. 141 repealed by Statute Law (Repeals) Act 1986, sch. 1, part I, group 1;

s. 143(1) substituted by Courts and Legal Services Act 1990, sch. 18, para. 48 (in force by SI 1991/608);

s. 143(2) repealed by Courts and Legal Services Act 1990, sch. 20 (in force by SI 1991/608);

s. 145 amended by Constitutional Reform Act 2005, sch. 4, para. 170 (in force by SI 2006/1014);

s. 147(1) amended by (a) Matrimonial and Family Proceedings Act 1984, sch. 3 (in force by SI 1986/635, art. 2(c)); (b) Banking Act 1987, sch. 6, para. 15 (in force by SI 1988/644); (c) Courts and Legal Services Act 1990, sch. 18, para. 49(1) (in force by SI 1991/608); (d) Statute Law (Repeals) Act 1993, sch. 1, part XIV, group 2; (e) Civil Procedure Act 1997, sch. 2, para. 2(1) and (2) (in force by SI 1997/841, arts 3 and 4); (f) Civil Procedure Act 1997, sch. 2, para. 2(1) and (9) (in force by SI 1999/1009); (g) Financial Services and Markets Act 2000 (Consequential Amendments and Repeals) Order 2001 (SI 2001/3649), art. 296; (h) Civil Procedure (Modification of Enactments) Order 2002 (SI 2002/439), art. 9;

s. 147(2) and (3) repealed by Local Government Finance (Repeals, Savings and Consequential Amendments) Order 1990 (SI 1990/776), sch. 1;

sch. 1, paras 2(3) and 3, repealed by Courts and Legal Services Act 1990, sch. 17, para. 18, and sch. 20 (in force by SI 1991/1364);

sch. 3, paras 1 to 3, 4(2) and 10, repealed by Statute Law (Repeals) Act 1989, sch. 1, part I.

Sections 26 to 31, 59 and 78 (admiralty proceedings), sch. 2 (amendments of other enactments) and sch. 4 (repeals) have been omitted.

Courts and Legal Services Act 1990

(1990 CHAPTER 41)

An Act to make provision with respect to the procedure in, and allocation of business between, the High Court and other courts; to make provision with respect to legal services; . . . and for connected purposes. [1st November 1990]

PART I PROCEDURE ETC. IN CIVIL COURTS

Allocation and Transfer of Business

1. Allocation of Business between High Court and County Courts

(1) The Lord Chancellor may by order make provision—
 (a) conferring jurisdiction on the High Court in relation to proceedings in which county courts have jurisdiction;
 (b) conferring jurisdiction on county courts in relation to proceedings in which the High Court has jurisdiction;
 (c) allocating proceedings to the High Court or to county courts;
 (d) specifying proceedings which may be commenced only in the High Court;
 (e) specifying proceedings which may be commenced only in a county court;
 (f) specifying proceedings which may be taken only in the High Court;
 (g) specifying proceedings which may be taken only in a county court.

(1A) An order under subsection (1)(a) or (b) may be made only with the concurrence of the Lord Chief Justice.

(2) Without prejudice to the generality of section 120(2), any such order may differentiate between categories of proceedings by reference to such criteria as the Lord Chancellor sees fit to specify in the order.

(3) The criteria so specified may, in particular, relate to—
 (a) the value of an action (as defined by the order);
 (b) the nature of the proceedings;
 (c) the parties to the proceedings;
 (d) the degree of complexity likely to be involved in any aspect of the proceedings; and
 (e) the importance of any question likely to be raised by, or in the course of, the proceedings.

(4) An order under subsection (1)(b), (e) or (g) may specify one or more particular county courts in relation to the proceedings so specified.

(5) Any jurisdiction exercisable by a county court, under any provision made by virtue of subsection (4), shall be exercisable throughout England and Wales.

(6) Rules of court may provide for a matter—
 (a) which is pending in one county court; and
 (b) over which that court has jurisdiction under any provision made by virtue of subsection (4),

to be heard and determined wholly or partly in another county court which also has jurisdiction in that matter under any such provision.

(7) Any such order may—
 (a) amend or repeal any provision falling within subsection (8) and relating to—
  (i) the jurisdiction, practice or procedure of the Supreme Court; or
  (ii) the jurisdiction, practice or procedure of any county court,

 so far as the Lord Chancellor considers it to be necessary, or expedient, in consequence of any provision made by the order; or
 (b) make such incidental or transitional provision as the Lord Chancellor considers necessary, or expedient, in consequence of any provision made by the, order.

(8) A provision falls within this subsection if it is made by any enactment other than this Act or made under any enactment.

(9) Before making any such order the Lord Chancellor shall consult the Lord Chief Justice, the Master of the Rolls, the President of the Queen's Bench Division, the President of the Family Division, the Chancellor of the High Court and the Senior Presiding Judge (appointed under section 72).

(10) No such order shall be made so as to confer jurisdiction on any county court to hear any application for judicial review.

(11) For the purposes of this section the commencement of proceedings may include the making of any application in anticipation of any proceedings or in the course of any proceedings.

(12) The Lord Chancellor shall, within one year of the coming into force of the first order made under this section, and annually thereafter, prepare and lay before both Houses of Parliament a report as to the business of the Supreme Court and county courts.

(13) The Lord Chancellor may nominate a judicial office holder (as defined in section 109(4) of the Constitutional Reform Act 2005) to exercise his functions under this section.

Evidence

5. Witness Statements

(1) Rules of court may make provision—

(a) requiring, in specified circumstances, any party to civil proceedings to serve on the other parties a written statement of the oral evidence which he intends to adduce on any issue of fact to be decided at the trial;

(b) enabling the court to direct any party to civil proceedings to serve such a statement on the other party; and

(c) prohibiting a party who fails to comply with such a requirement or direction from adducing oral evidence on the issue of fact to which it relates.

(2) Where a party to proceedings has refused to comply with such a requirement or direction, the fact that his refusal was on the ground that the required statement would have been a document which was privileged from disclosure shall not affect any prohibition imposed by virtue of subsection (1)(c).

(3) This section is not to be read as prejudicing in any way any other power to make rules of court.

Appeals

8. Powers of Court of Appeal to Award Damages

(1) In this section 'case' means any case where the Court of Appeal has power to order a new trial on the ground that damages awarded by a jury are excessive or inadequate.

(2) Rules of court may provide for the Court of Appeal, in such classes of case as may be specified in the rules, to have power, in place of ordering a new trial, to substitute for the sum awarded by the jury such sum as appears to the court to be proper.

(3) This section is not to be read as prejudicing in any way any other power to make rules of court.

Miscellaneous

12. Penalty for Failure to Warn That Hearing Will Not Be Attended

(1) This section applies where an appointment has been fixed for any hearing in the High Court or in any county court, but a party to the proceedings—

(a) has failed to appear; or

(b) has failed to give the court due notice of his desire to cancel the hearing or of his inability to appear at it.

(2) The court may summon the party concerned, or the person conducting the proceedings on his behalf, to explain his failure.

(3) Where a court—

(a) has summoned a person under subsection (2); and

(b) is not satisfied that he took reasonable steps to give due notice to the court of his desire to cancel the hearing or (as the case may be) of his inability to appear at it, the court may declare that person to be in contravention of this section.

(4) On declaring a person to be in contravention of this section a court may impose on him a penalty equivalent to a fine not exceeding level 3 on the standard scale.
(5) Before deciding whether or not to impose any such penalty, the court shall consider the extent to which (if any) the person concerned will, or is likely to—
 (a) suffer any financial loss (by way of a reduction of costs or otherwise); or
 (b) be subject to any disciplinary action,
 as a result of his failure.
(6) Sections 129 and 130 of the County Courts Act 1984 (enforcement, payment and application of fines) shall apply with respect to any penalty imposed by a county court under this section as they apply with respect to any fine imposed by any county court under that Act.
(7) In subsection (1) 'due notice' means—
 (a) such notice as is required by rules of court; or
 (b) where there is no such requirement applicable to the circumstances of the case, such notice as the court considers reasonable.

[*Section 12 has not yet been brought into force.*]

PART II LEGAL SERVICES

Miscellaneous

58. Conditional Fee Agreements

(1) A conditional fee agreement which satisfies all of the conditions applicable to it by virtue of this section shall not be unenforceable by reason only of its being a conditional fee agreement; but (subject to subsection (5)) any other conditional fee agreement shall be unenforceable.
(2) For the purposes of this section and section 58A—
 (a) a conditional fee agreement is an agreement with a person providing advocacy or litigation services which provides for his fees and expenses, or any part of them, to be payable only in specified circumstances; and
 (b) a conditional fee agreement provides for a success fee if it provides for the amount of any fees to which it applies to be increased, in specified circumstances, above the amount which would be payable if it were not payable only in specified circumstances.
(3) The following conditions are applicable to every conditional fee agreement—
 (a) it must be in writing;
 (b) it must not relate to proceedings which cannot be the subject of an enforceable conditional fee agreement; and
 (c) it must comply with such requirements (if any) as may be prescribed by the Secretary of State.
(4) The following further conditions are applicable to a conditional fee agreement which provides for a success fee—
 (a) it must relate to proceedings of a description specified by order made by the Secretary of State;
 (b) it must state the percentage by which the amount of the fees which would be payable if it were not a conditional fee agreement is to be increased; and
 (c) that percentage must not exceed the percentage specified in relation to the description of proceedings to which the agreement relates by order made by the Secretary of State.
(5) If a conditional fee agreement is an agreement to which section 57 of the Solicitors Act 1974 (non-contentious business agreements between solicitor and client) applies, subsection (1) shall not make it unenforceable.

58A. Conditional Fee Agreements: Supplementary

(1) The proceedings which cannot be the subject of an enforceable conditional fee agreement are—
 (a) criminal proceedings; and
 (b) family proceedings, apart from proceedings under section 82 of the Environmental Protection Act 1990.
(2) In subsection (1) 'family proceedings' means proceedings under any one or more of the following—
 (a) the Matrimonial Causes Act 1973;

(b) the Adoption and Children Act 2002;
(c) the Domestic Proceedings and Magistrates' Courts Act 1978;
(d) Part III of the Matrimonial and Family Proceedings Act 1984;
(e) Parts I, II and IV of the Children Act 1989;
(f) Part IV of the Family Law Act 1996; and
(g) the inherent jurisdiction of the High Court in relation to children.

(3) The requirements which the Secretary of State may prescribe under section 58(3)(c)—
(a) include requirements for the person providing advocacy or litigation services to have provided prescribed information before the agreement is made; and
(b) may be different for different descriptions of conditional fee agreements (and, in particular, may be different for those which provide for a success fee and those which do not).

(4) In section 58 and this section (and in the definitions of 'advocacy services' and 'litigation services' as they apply for their purposes) 'proceedings' includes any sort of proceedings for resolving disputes (and not just proceedings in a court), whether commenced or contemplated.

(5) Before making an order under section 58(4), the Lord Chancellor shall consult—
(a) the designated judges;
(b) the General Council of the Bar;
(c) the Law Society; and
(d) such other bodies as he considers appropriate.

(6) A costs order made in any proceedings may, subject in the case of court proceedings to rules of court, include provision requiring the payment of any fees payable under a conditional fee agreement which provides for a success fee.

(7) Rules of court may make provision with respect to the assessment of any costs which include fees payable under a conditional fee agreement (including one which provides for a success fee).

61. Right of Barrister to Enter into Contract for the Provision of His Services

(1) Any rule of law which prevents a barrister from entering into a contract for the provision of his services as a barrister is hereby abolished.

(2) Nothing in subsection (1) prevents the General Council of the Bar from making rules (however described) which prohibit barristers from entering into contracts or restrict their right to do so.

62. Immunity of Advocates from Actions in Negligence and for Breach of Contract

(1) A person—
(a) who is not a barrister; but
(b) who lawfully provides any legal services in relation to any proceedings,
shall have the same immunity from liability for negligence in respect of his acts or omissions as he would have if he were a barrister lawfully providing those services.

(2) No act or omission on the part of any barrister or other person which is accorded immunity from liability for negligence shall give rise to an action for breach of any contract relating to the provision by him of the legal services in question.

63. Legal Professional Privilege

(1) This section applies to any communication made to or by a person who is not a barrister or solicitor at any time when that person is—
(a) providing advocacy or litigation services as an authorised advocate or authorised litigator;
(b) providing conveyancing services as an authorised practitioner; or
(c) providing probate services as a probate practitioner.

(2) Any such communication shall in any legal proceedings be privileged from disclosure in like manner as if the person in question had at all material times been acting as his client's solicitor.

(3) In subsection (1), 'probate practitioner' means a person to whom section 23(1) of the Solicitors Act 1974 (unqualified person not to prepare probate papers etc.) does not apply.

[*The provisions of s. 63 in italics have not yet been brought into force.*]

Selected Legislation

PART VI MISCELLANEOUS AND SUPPLEMENTAL

Miscellaneous

113. Administration of Oaths and Taking of Affidavits

(1) In this section—
'authorised person' means—
(a) any authorised advocate or authorised litigator, other than one who is a solicitor (in relation to whom provision similar to that made by this section is made by section 81 of the Solicitors Act 1974); or
(b) any person who is a member of a professional or other body prescribed by the Secretary of State for the purposes of this section; and
'general notary' means any public notary other than—
(a) an ecclesiastical notary; or
(b) one who is a member of the Incorporated Company of Scriveners (in relation to whom provision similar to that made by this section is made by section 65 of the Administration of Justice Act 1985).

(2) Section 1(1) of the Commissioners for Oaths Act 1889 (appointment of commissioners by Lord Chancellor) shall cease to have effect.

(3) Subject to the provisions of this section, every authorised person shall have the powers conferred on a commissioner for oaths by the Commissioners for Oaths Acts 1889 and 1891 and section 24 of the Stamp Duties Management Act 1891; and any reference to such a commissioner in an enactment or instrument (including an enactment passed or instrument made after the commencement of this Act) shall include a reference to an authorised person unless the context otherwise requires.

(4) Subject to the provisions of this section, every general notary shall have the powers conferred on a commissioner for oaths by the Commissioners for Oaths Acts 1889 and 1891; and any reference to such a commissioner in an enactment or instrument (including an enactment passed or instrument made after the commencement of this Act) shall include a reference to a general notary unless the context otherwise requires.

(5) No person shall exercise the powers conferred by this section in any proceedings in which he is interested.

(6) A person exercising such powers and before whom any oath or affidavit is taken or made shall state in the jurat or attestation at which place and on what date the oath or affidavit is taken or made.

(7) A document containing such a statement and purporting to be sealed or signed by an authorised person or general notary shall be admitted in evidence without proof of the seal or signature, and without proof that he is an authorised person or general notary.

(8) The Secretary of State may, with the concurrence of the Lord Chief Justice and the Master of the Rolls, by order prescribe the fees to be charged by authorised persons exercising the powers of commissioners for oaths by virtue of this section in respect of the administration of an oath or the taking of an affidavit.

(9) in this section 'affidavit' has the same meaning as in the Commissioners for Oaths Act 1889.

(10) Every—
(a) solicitor who holds a practising certificate which is in force;
(b) authorised person;
(c) general notary; and
(d) member of the Incorporated Company of Scriveners ('the Company') who has been admitted to practise as a public notary within the jurisdiction of the Company,
shall have the right to use the title 'Commissioner for Oaths'.

Supplemental

119. Interpretation

(1) In this Act—
'administration', in relation to letters of administration, has the same meaning as in section 128 of the Supreme Court Act 1981;

'advocacy services' means any services which it would be reasonable to expect a person who is exercising, or contemplating exercising, a right of audience in relation to any proceedings, or contemplated proceedings, to provide;

'authorised advocate' means any person (including a barrister or solicitor) who has a right of audience granted by an authorised body in accordance with the provisions of this Act;

'authorised body' and 'appropriate authorised body'—

(a) in relation to any right of audience or proposed right of audience, have the meanings given in section 27; and

(b) in relation to any right to conduct litigation or proposed right to conduct litigation, have the meanings given in section 28;

'authorised litigator' means any person (including a solicitor) who has a right to conduct litigation granted by an authorised body in accordance with the provisions of this Act;

'authorised practitioner' has the same meaning as in section 37;

'conveyancing services' means the preparation of transfers, conveyances, contracts and other documents in connection with, and other services ancillary to the disposition or acquisition of estates or interests in land;

'court' includes—

(a) any tribunal which the Council on Tribunals is under a duty to keep under review;

(b) any court-martial; and

(c) a statutory inquiry within the meaning of section 19(1) of the Tribunals and Inquiries Act 1971;

'designated judge' means the Lord Chief Justice, the Master of the Rolls, the President of the Queen's Bench Division, the President of the Family Division or the Chancellor of the High Court;

'the Director' means the Director General of Fair Trading;

'duly certificated notary public' has the same meaning as it has in the Solicitors Act 1974 by virtue of section 87(1) of that Act:

'the general principle' has the meaning given in section 17(4);

'licensed conveyancer' has the same meaning as it has in the Administration of Justice Act 1985 by virtue of section 11 of that Act:

'litigation services' means any services which it would be reasonable to expect a person who is exercising, or contemplating exercising, a right to conduct litigation in relation to any proceedings, or contemplated proceedings, to provide;

'member', in relation to any professional or other body (other than any body established by this Act), includes any person who is not a member of that body but who may be subject to disciplinary sanctions for failure to comply with any of that body's rules;

'multi-national partnership' has the meaning given by section 89(9);

'probate services' means the drawing or preparation of any papers on which to found or oppose a grant of probate or a grant of letters of administration and the administration of the estate of a deceased person;

'prescribed' means prescribed by regulations under this Act;

'proceedings' means proceedings in any court;

'qualification regulations' and 'rules of conduct'—

(a) in relation to any right of audience or proposed right of audience, have the meanings given in section 27; and

(b) in relation to any right to conduct litigation or proposed right to conduct litigation, have the meanings given in section 28;

'qualified person' has the meaning given in section 36(6);

'registered foreign lawyer' has the meaning given by section 89(9);

'right of audience' means the right to appear before and address a court including the right to call and examine witnesses;

'right to conduct litigation' means the right—

(a) to issue proceedings before any court; and

(b) to perform any ancillary functions in relation to proceedings (such as entering appearances to actions);

'solicitor' means solicitor of the Supreme Court; and

'the statutory objective' has the meaning given in section 17(2).

(2) For the purposes of the definition of 'conveyancing services' in subsection (1)—
'disposition'—
(i) does not include a testamentary disposition or any disposition in the case of such a lease as is referred to in section 54(2) of the Law of Property Act 1925 (short leases); but
(ii) subject to that, includes in the case of leases both their grant and their assignment; and
'acquisition' has a corresponding meaning.

(3) In this Act any reference (including those in sections 27(9) and 28(5)) to rules of conduct includes a reference to rules of practice.

124. Commencement

(1) The following provisions come into force on the passing of this Act—
(a) sections 1, 5, 119 to 123, this section and section 125(1); and
(b) paragraphs 2 and 3 of Schedule 17.

(2) The following provisions come into force at the end of the period of two months beginning on the day on which this Act is passed—
(a) sections 6, 8, 11, 16, 64, 65, 72, 73, 85, 87 and 88, 90 to 92, 94 to 97, 98 and 108 to 110;
(b) paragraphs 1, 11, 12, 16 and 20 of Schedule 17;
(c) paragraphs 7, 8, 14 to 16, 55 and 57 of Schedule 18; and
(d) paragraph 1 of Schedule 19.

(3) The other provisions of this Act shall come into force on such date as may be appointed by order made by the Lord Chancellor or by the Secretary of State or by both, acting jointly.

(4) Different dates may be appointed for different provisions of this Act and for different purposes.

[*Section 58 was brought into force by SI 1993/2132, ss. 61 and 62 by SI 1990/2484, ss. 63(1)(a) and (2) and 113 by SI 1991/608.*]

125. Short Title, Minor and Consequential Amendments, Transitional and Repeals

(1) This Act may be cited as the Courts and Legal Services Act 1990.

NOTES ON TEXT

Only selected provisions of the Act are printed above, incorporating the following amendments:

s. 1 amended by Constitutional Reform Act 2005, sch. 4, para. 212 (in force by SI 2005/2505 and SI 2006/1014);

s. 58 substituted and s. 58A inserted by Access to Justice Act 1999, s. 27(1) (in force by SI 2000/774, art. 2); for a transitional provision see the notes on commencement at the end of the Access to Justice Act 1999 in this appendix; ss. 58 and 58A amended by Secretary of State for Constitutional Affairs Order 2003 (SI 2003/1887), sch. 2, para. 8(1); s. 58A amended by Adoption and Children Act 2002, sch. 3, para. 80 (in force by SI 2005/2213);

s. 113 amended by Secretary of State for Constitutional Affairs Order 2003 (SI 2003/1887), sch. 2, para. 8(1);

s. 119 amended by: (a) Access to Justice Act 1999, sch. 6, para. 10 (in force by SI 1999/2657, art. 2(a)); (b) Constitutional Reform Act 2005, sch. 4, para. 216 (in force by SI 2005/2505).

Crown Proceedings Act 1947

(10 & 11 GEO. 6 CHAPTER 44)

An Act to amend the law relating to the civil liabilities and rights of the Crown and to civil proceedings by and against the Crown, to amend the law relating to the civil liabilities of persons other than the Crown in certain cases involving the affairs or property of the Crown, and for purposes connected with the matters aforesaid. [31st July 1947]

PART I SUBSTANTIVE LAW

1. Right to Sue the Crown

Where any person has a claim against the Crown after the commencement of this Act, and, if this Act had not been passed, the claim might have been enforced, subject to the grant of His Majesty's fiat, by petition of right, or might have been enforced by a proceeding provided by any statutory provision repealed by this Act, then, subject to the provisions of this Act, the claim may be enforced as of right, and without the fiat of His Majesty, by proceedings taken against the Crown for that purpose in accordance with the provisions of this Act.

2. Liability of the Crown in Tort

(1) Subject to the provisions of this Act, the Crown shall be subject to all those liabilities in tort to which, if it were a private person of full age and capacity, it would be subject:—

(a) in respect of torts committed by its servants or agents;

(b) in respect of any breach of those duties which a person owes to his servants or agents at common law by reason of being their employer; and

(c) in respect of any breach of the duties attaching at common law to the ownership, occupation, possession or control of property:

Provided that no proceedings shall lie against the Crown by virtue of paragraph (a) of this subsection in respect of any act or omission of a servant or agent of the Crown unless the act or omission would apart from the provisions of this Act have given rise to a cause of action in tort against that servant or agent or his estate.

(2) Where the Crown is bound by a statutory duty which is binding also upon persons other than the Crown and its officers then, subject to the provisions of this Act, the Crown shall, in respect of a failure to comply with that duty, be subject to all those liabilities in tort (if any) to which it would be so subject if it were a private person of full age and capacity.

(3) Where any functions are conferred or imposed upon an officer of the Crown as such either by any rule of the common law or by statute, and that officer commits a tort while performing or purporting to perform those functions, the liabilities of the Crown in respect of the tort shall be such as they would have been if those functions had been conferred or imposed solely by virtue of instructions lawfully given by the Crown.

(4) Any enactment which negatives or limits the amount of the liability of any Government department, part of the Scottish administration or officer of the Crown in respect of any tort committed by that department, part or officer shall, in the case of proceedings against the Crown under this section in respect of a tort committed by that department, part or officer, apply in relation to the Crown as it would have applied in relation to that department, part or officer if the proceedings against the Crown had been proceedings against that department, part or officer.

(5) No proceedings shall lie against the Crown by virtue of this section in respect of anything done or omitted to be done by any person while discharging or purporting to discharge any responsibilities of a judicial nature vested in him, or any responsibilities which he has in connection with the execution of a judicial process.

(6) No proceedings shall lie against the Crown by virtue of this section in respect of any act, neglect or default of any officer of the Crown, unless that officer has been directly or indirectly appointed by the Crown and was at the material time paid in respect of his duties as an officer of the Crown wholly out of the Consolidated Fund of the United Kingdom, moneys provided by Parliament, the Scottish Consolidated Fund or any other Fund certified by the Treasury for the

purposes of this subsection or was at the material time holding an office in respect of which the Treasury certify that the holder thereof would normally be so paid.

3. Infringement of Intellectual Property Rights

(1) Civil proceedings lie against the Crown for an infringement committed by a servant or agent of the Crown, with the authority of the Crown, of—
  (a) a patent,
  (b) a registered trade mark,
  (c) the right in a registered design,
  (d) design right, or
  (e) copyright;

but save as provided by this subsection no proceedings lie against the Crown by virtue of this Act in respect of an infringement of any of those rights.

(2) Nothing in this section, or any other provision of this Act, shall be construed as affecting—
  (a) the rights of a government department or any part of the Scottish Administration under section 55 of the Patents Act 1977, Schedule 1 to the Registered Designs Act 1949 or section 240 of the Copyright, Designs and Patents Act 1988 (Crown use of patents and designs), or
  (b) the rights of the Secretary of State under section 22 of the Patents Act 1977 or section 5 of the Registered Designs Act 1949 (security of information prejudicial to defence or public safety).

4. Application of Law as to Indemnity, Contribution, Joint and Several Tortfeasors, and Contributory Negligence

(1) Where the Crown is subject to any liability by virtue of this Part of this Act, the law relating to indemnity and contribution shall be enforceable by or against the Crown in respect of the liability to which it is so subject as if the Crown were a private person of full age and capacity.

(3) Without prejudice to the general effect of section one of this Act, the Law Reform (Contributory Negligence) Act, 1945 (which amends the law relating to contributory negligence) shall bind the Crown.

PART II JURISDICTION AND PROCEDURE

The High Court

13. Civil Proceedings in the High Court

Subject to the provisions of this Act, all such civil proceedings by or against the Crown as are mentioned in the First Schedule to this Act are hereby abolished, and all civil proceedings by or against the Crown in the High Court shall be instituted and proceeded with in accordance with rules of court and not otherwise.

In this section the expression 'rules of court' means, in relation to any claim against the Crown in the High Court which falls within the jurisdiction of that court as a prize court, rules of court made under section three of the Prize Courts Act 1894.

14. Summary Applications to High Court in Certain Revenue Matters

(1) Subject to and in accordance with rules of court, the Crown may apply in a summary manner to the High Court:—
  (a) for the furnishing of information required to be furnished by any person under the enactments relating to [inheritance tax];
  (b) for the delivery of accounts and payment of [inheritance tax] under the [Inheritance Tax Act 1984];
  (c) for the delivery of an account under section two of the Stamp Duties Management Act 1891, or under that section as amended or applied by any subsequent enactment;
  (d) for the payment of sums improperly withheld or retained within the meaning of the said section two.

(2) Subject to and in accordance with rules of court, the Crown may apply in a summary manner to the High Court:—
(a) for the payment of duty under the enactments relating to excise duties;
(b) for the delivery of any accounts required to be delivered, or the furnishing of any information required to be furnished, by the enactments relating to excise duties or by any regulations relating to such duties;
(c) for the payment of tax under the enactments relating to value added tax;
(d) for the delivery of any accounts, the production of any books, or the furnishing of any information, required to be delivered, produced or furnished under the enactments relating to value added tax.

County Courts

15. Civil Proceedings In the County Court

(1) Subject to the provisions of this Act, and to any enactment limiting the jurisdiction of a county court (whether by reference to the subject matter of the proceedings to be brought or the amount sought to be recovered in the proceedings or otherwise) any civil proceedings against the Crown may be instituted in a county court.
(2) Any proceedings by or against the Crown in a county court shall be instituted and proceeded with in accordance with rules of court and not otherwise.

General

16. Interpleader

The Crown may obtain relief by way of interpleader proceedings, and may be made a party to such proceedings, in the same manner in which a subject may obtain relief by way of such proceedings or be made a party thereto, and may be made a party to such proceedings notwithstanding that the application for relief is made by a sheriff or other like officer; and all rules of court relating to interpleader proceedings shall, subject to the provisions of this Act, have effect accordingly.

17. Parties to Proceedings

(1) [The Minister for the Civil Service] shall publish a list specifying the several Government departments which are authorised departments for the purposes of this Act, and the name and address for service of the person who is, or is acting for the purposes of this Act as, the solicitor for each such department, and may from time to time amend or vary the said list.

Any document purporting to be a copy of a list published under this section and purporting to be printed under the superintendence or the authority of His Majesty's Stationery Office shall in any legal proceedings be received as evidence for the purpose of establishing what departments are authorised departments for the purposes of this Act, and what person is, or is acting for the purposes of this Act as, the solicitor for, any such department.
(2) Civil proceedings by the Crown may be instituted either by an authorised Government department in its own name, whether that department was or was not at the commencement of this Act authorised to sue, or by the Attorney General.
(3) Civil proceedings against the Crown shall be instituted against the appropriate authorised Government department, or, if none of the authorised Government departments is appropriate or the person instituting the proceedings has any reasonable doubt whether any and if so which of those departments is appropriate, against the Attorney General.
(4) Where any civil proceedings against the Crown are instituted against the Attorney General, an application may at any stage of the proceedings be made to the court by or on behalf of the Attorney General to have such of the authorised Government departments as may be specified in the application substituted for him as defendant to the proceedings; and where any such proceedings are brought against an authorised Government department, an application may at any stage of the proceedings be made to the court on behalf of that department to have the Attorney General or such of the authorised Government departments as may be specified in the application substituted for the applicant as the defendant to the proceedings.

Upon any such application the court may if it thinks fit make an order granting the application on such terms as the court thinks just; and on such an order being made the proceedings shall continue as if they had been commenced against the department specified in that behalf in the order, or, as the case may require, against the Attorney General.

(5) No proceedings instituted in accordance with this Part of this Act by or against the Attorney General or an authorised Government department shall abate or be affected by any change in the person holding the office of Attorney General or in the person or body of persons constituting the department.

18. Service of Documents

All documents required to be served on the Crown for the purpose of or in connection with any civil proceedings by or against the Crown shall, if those proceedings are by or against an authorised Government department, be served on the solicitor, if any, for that department, or the person, if any, acting for the purposes of this Act as solicitor for that department, or if there is no such solicitor and no person so acting, or if the proceedings are brought by or against the Attorney General, on the Solicitor for the affairs of His Majesty's Treasury.

20. Removal and Transfer of Proceedings

(2) All rules of law and enactments relating to the removal or transfer of proceedings from a county court to the High Court, or the transfer of proceedings from the High Court to a county court, shall apply in relation to proceedings against the Crown.

21. Nature of Relief

(1) In any civil proceedings by or against the Crown the court shall, subject to the provisions of this Act, have power to make all such orders as it has power to make in proceedings between subjects, and otherwise to give such appropriate relief as the case may require: Provided that:—

(a) where in any proceedings against the Crown any such relief is sought as might in proceedings between subjects be granted by way of injunction or specific performance, the court shall not grant an injunction or make an order for specific performance, but may in lieu thereof make an order declaratory of the rights of the parties; and

(b) in any proceedings against the Crown for the recovery of land or other property the court shall not make an order for the recovery of the land or the delivery of the property, but may in lieu thereof make an order declaring that the plaintiff is entitled as against the Crown to the land or property or to the possession thereof.

(2) The court shall not in any civil proceedings grant any injunction or make any order against an officer of the Crown if the effect of granting the injunction or making the order would be to give any relief against the Crown which could not have been obtained in proceedings against the Crown.

22. Appeals and Stay of Execution

Subject to the provisions of this Act, all enactments and rules of court relating to appeals and stay of execution shall, with any necessary modifications, apply to civil proceedings by or against the Crown as they apply to proceedings between subjects.

23. Scope of Part II

(1) Subject to the provisions of this section, any reference in this Part of this Act to civil proceedings by the Crown shall be construed as a reference to the following proceedings only:—

(a) proceedings for the enforcement or vindication of any right or the obtaining of any relief which, if this Act had not been passed, might have been enforced or vindicated or obtained by any such proceedings as are mentioned in paragraph 1 of the First Schedule to this Act;

(b) proceedings for the enforcement or vindication of any right or the obtaining of any relief which, if this Act had not been passed, might have been enforced or vindicated or obtained by an action at the suit of any Government department or any officer of the Crown as such;

(c) all such proceedings as the Crown is entitled to bring by virtue of this Act;

and the expression 'civil proceedings by or against the Crown' shall be construed accordingly.

(2) Subject to the provisions of this section, any reference in this Part of this Act to civil proceedings against the Crown shall be construed as a reference to the following proceedings only:—

(a) proceedings for the enforcement or vindication of any right or the obtaining of any relief which, if this Act had not been passed, might have been enforced or vindicated or obtained by any such proceedings as are mentioned in paragraph 2 of the First Schedule to this Act;

(b) proceedings for the enforcement or vindication of any right or the obtaining of any relief which, if this Act had not been passed, might have been enforced or vindicated or obtained by an action against the Attorney General, any Government department, or any officer of the Crown as such; and

(c) all such proceedings as any person is entitled to bring against the Crown by virtue of this Act;

and the expression 'civil proceedings by or against the Crown' shall be construed accordingly.

(3) Notwithstanding anything in the preceding provisions of this section, the provisions of this Part of this Act shall not have effect with respect to any of the following proceedings, that is to say:—

(a) proceedings brought by the Attorney General on the relation of some other person;

(b) proceedings by or against the Public Trustee;

(c) proceedings by or against the Charity Commissioners;

(f) proceedings by or against the Registrar of the Land Registry or any officers of that registry.

(4) Subject to the provisions of any Order in Council made under the provisions hereinafter contained, this part of this Act shall not affect proceedings initiated in any court other than the High Court or a county court.

PART III JUDGMENTS AND EXECUTION

24. Interest on Debts Damages and Costs

(1) Section seventeen of the Judgments Act 1838 (which provides that a judgment debt shall carry interest) and section 44A of the Administration of Justice Act 1970 (which enables the court to order an appropriate rate for a judgment debt expressed in a currency other than sterling) shall apply to judgment debts due from or to the Crown.

(2) Where any costs are awarded to or against the Crown in the High Court, interest shall be payable upon those costs unless the court otherwise orders, and any interest so payable shall be at the same rate as that at which interest is payable upon judgment debts due from or to the Crown.

(3) Section 35A of the Supreme Court Act 1981 and section 69 of the County Courts Act 1984 (which respectively empower the High Court and county courts to award interest on debts and damages) and section 3 of the Law Reform (Miscellaneous Provisions) Act 1934 (which empowers other courts of record to do so) shall apply to judgments given in proceedings by and against the Crown.

25. Satisfaction of Orders against the Crown

(1) Where in any civil proceedings by or against the Crown, or in any proceedings on the Crown side of the King's Bench Division, or in connection with any arbitration to which the Crown is a party, any order (including an order for costs) is made by any court in favour of any person against the Crown or against a Government department or against an officer of the Crown as such, the proper officer of the court shall, on an application in that behalf made by or on behalf of that person at any time after the expiration of twenty-one days from the date of the order or, in case the order provides for the payment of costs and the costs require to be taxed, at any time after the costs have been taxed, whichever is the later, issue to that person a certificate in the prescribed form containing particulars of the order:

Provided that, if the court so directs, a separate certificate shall be issued with respect to the costs (if any) ordered to be paid to the applicant.

(2) A copy of any certificate issued under this section may be served by the person in whose favour the order is made upon the person for the time being named in the record as the solicitor, or as the person acting as solicitor, for the Crown or for the Government department or officer concerned.

(3) If the order provides for the payment of any money by way of damages or otherwise, or of any costs, the certificate shall state the amount so payable, and the appropriate Government department shall, subject as hereinafter provided, pay to the person entitled or to his solicitor the amount appearing by the certificate to be due to him together with the interest, if any, lawfully due thereon:

Provided that the court by which any such order as aforesaid is made or any court to which an appeal against the order lies may direct that, pending an appeal or otherwise, payment of the whole of any amount so payable, or any part thereof, shall be suspended, and if the certificate has not been issued may order any such directions to be inserted therein.

(4) Save as aforesaid no execution or attachment or process in the nature thereof shall be issued out of any court for enforcing payment by the Crown of any such money or costs as aforesaid and no person shall be individually liable under any order for the payment by the Crown, or any Government department, or any officer of the Crown as such, of any such money or costs.

26. Execution by the Crown

(1) Subject to the provisions of this Act, any order made in favour of the Crown against any person in any civil proceedings to which the Crown is a party may be enforced in the same manner as an order made in an action between subjects, and not otherwise.

(2) Sections four and five of the Debtors Act, 1869 (which provide respectively for the abolition of imprisonment for debt, and for saving the power of committal in case of small debts), shall apply to sums of money payable and debts due to the Crown:

Provided that for the purpose of the application of the said section four to any sum of money payable or debt due to the Crown, the section shall have effect as if there were included among the exceptions therein mentioned default in payment of any sum payable in respect of death duties.

[*The reference to death duties in s. 26(2) has effect as if it included a reference to capital transfer tax and inheritance tax (Capital Transfer Tax Act 1984, sch. 6, para. 1; Finance Act 1986, s. 100).*]

(3) Nothing in this section shall affect any procedure which immediately before the commencement of this Act was available for enforcing an order made in favour of the Crown in proceedings brought by the Crown for the recovery of any fine or penalty, or the forfeiture or condemnation of any goods, or the forfeiture of any ship or any share in a ship.

27. Attachment of Moneys Payable by the Crown

(1) Where any money is payable by the Crown to some person who, under any order of any court, is liable to pay any money to any other person, and that other person would, if the money so payable by the Crown were money payable by a subject, be entitled under rules of court to obtain an order for the attachment thereof as a debt due or accruing due, or an order for the appointment of a sequestrator or receiver to receive the money on his behalf, the High Court may, subject to the provisions of this Act and in accordance with rules of court, make an order restraining the first-mentioned person from receiving that money and directing payment thereof to that other person, or to the sequestrator or receiver:

Provided that no such order shall be made in respect of:—

(a) any wages or salary payable to any officer of the Crown as such;

(b) any money which is subject to the provisions of any enactment prohibiting or restricting assignment or charging or taking in execution.

(2) The provisions of the preceding subsection shall, so far as they relate to forms of relief falling within the jurisdiction of a county court, have effect in relation to county courts as they have effect in relation to the High Court.

PART IV MISCELLANEOUS AND SUPPLEMENTAL

Miscellaneous

28. Discovery

(1) Subject to and in accordance with rules of court:—

(a) in any civil proceedings in the High Court or a county court to which the Crown is a party, the Crown may be required by the court to make discovery of documents and produce documents for inspection; and

(b) in any such proceedings as aforesaid, the Crown may be required by the court to answer interrogatories:

Provided that this section shall be without prejudice to any rule of law which authorises or requires the withholding of any document or the refusal to answer any question on the ground that the disclosure of the document or the answering of the question would be injurious to the public interest.

Any order of the court made under the powers conferred by paragraph (b) of this subsection shall direct by what officer of the Crown the interrogatories are to be answered.

(2) Without prejudice to the proviso to the preceding subsection, any rules made for the purposes of this section shall be such as to secure that the existence of a document will not be disclosed if, in the opinion of a Minister of the Crown, it would be injurious to the public interest to disclose the existence thereof.

29. Exclusion of Proceedings In Rem Against the Crown

(1) Nothing in this Act shall authorise proceedings in rem in respect of any claim against the Crown, or the arrest, detention or sale of any of His Majesty's ships or aircraft, or of any cargo or other property belonging to the Crown, or give to any person any lien on any such ship, aircraft, cargo or other property.

(2) Where proceedings in rem have been instituted in the High Court or in a county court against any such ship, aircraft, cargo or other property, the court may, if satisfied, either on an application by the plaintiff for an order under this subsection or an application by the Crown to set aside the proceedings, that the proceedings were so instituted by the plaintiff in the reasonable belief that the ship, aircraft, cargo or other property did not belong to the Crown, order that the proceedings shall be treated as if they were in personam duly instituted against the Crown in accordance with the provisions of this Act, or duly instituted against any other person whom the court regards as the proper person to be sued in the circumstances, and that the proceedings shall continue accordingly.

Any such order may be made upon such terms, if any, as the court thinks just; and where the court makes any such order it may make such consequential orders as the court thinks expedient.

38. Interpretation

(1) Any reference in this Act to the provisions of this Act shall, unless the context otherwise requires, include a reference to rules of court made for the purposes of this Act.

(2) In this Act, except in so far as the context otherwise requires or it is otherwise expressly provided, the following expressions have the meanings hereby respectively assigned to them, that is to say:—

'Agent', when used in relation to the Crown, includes an independent contractor employed by the Crown;

'Civil proceedings' includes proceedings in the High Court or the county court for the recovery of fines or penalties, but does not include proceedings on the Crown side of the King's Bench Division;

'His Majesty's aircraft' does not include aircraft belonging to His Majesty otherwise than in right of His Government in the United Kingdom or the Scottish Administration;

'His Majesty's ships' means ships of which the beneficial interest is vested in His Majesty or which are registered as Government ships for the purposes of the Merchant Shipping Act 1995, or which are for the time being demised or subdemised to or in the exclusive possession of the Crown, except that the said expression does not include any ship in which His Majesty is interested otherwise than in right of His Government in the United Kingdom or the Scottish Administration unless that ship is for the time being demised or subdemised to His Majesty in right of His said Government or Administration or in the exclusive possession of His Majesty in that right;

'Officer', in relation to the Crown, includes any servant of His Majesty, and accordingly (but without prejudice to the generality of the foregoing provision) includes a Minister of the Crown and a member of the Scottish Executive;

'Order' includes a judgment, decree, rule, award or declaration;

'Prescribed' means prescribed by rules of court;

'Proceedings against the Crown' includes a claim by way of set-off or counterclaim raised in proceedings by the Crown:

'Ship' has the same meaning as in the Merchant Shipping Act 1995:

'Statutory duty' means any duty imposed by or under any Act of Parliament.

(3) Any reference in this Act to His Majesty in His private capacity shall be construed as including a reference to His Majesty in right of His Duchy of Lancaster and to the Duke of Cornwall.

(4) Any reference in Parts III or IV of this Act to civil proceedings by or against the Crown, or to civil proceedings to which the Crown is a party, shall be construed as including a reference to civil proceedings to which the Attorney General, or any Government department, or any officer of the Crown as such is a party:

Provided that the Crown shall not for the purposes of Parts III and IV of this Act be deemed to be a party to any proceedings by reason only that they are brought by the Attorney General upon the relation of some other person.

(6) References in this Act to any enactment shall be construed as references to that enactment as amended by or under any other enactment, including this Act.

40. Savings

(1) Nothing in this Act shall apply to proceedings by or against, or authorise proceedings in tort to be brought against, His Majesty in His private capacity.

(2) Except as therein otherwise expressly provided, nothing in this Act shall:—

(a) affect the law relating to prize salvage, or apply to proceedings in causes or matters within the jurisdiction of the High Court as a prize court or to any criminal proceedings; or

(b) authorise proceedings to be taken against the Crown under or in accordance with this Act in respect of any alleged liability of the Crown arising otherwise than in respect of His Majesty's Government in the United Kingdom or the Scottish Administration, or affect proceedings against the Crown in respect of any such alleged liability as aforesaid; or

(c) affect any proceedings by the Crown otherwise than in right of His Majesty's Government in the United Kingdom or the Scottish Administration; or

(d) subject the Crown to any greater liabilities in respect of the acts or omissions of any independent contractor employed by the Crown than those to which the Crown would be subject in respect of such acts or omissions if it were a private person; or

(f) affect any rules of evidence or any presumption relating to the extent to which the Crown is bound by any Act of Parliament; or

(g) affect any right of the Crown to demand a trial at bar or to control or otherwise intervene in proceedings affecting its rights, property or profits; or

(h) affect any liability imposed on the public trustee or on the Consolidated Fund of the United Kingdom by the Public Trustee Act 1906;

and, without prejudice to the general effect of the foregoing provisions, Part III of this Act shall not apply to the Crown except in right of His Majesty's Government in the United Kingdom or the Scottish Administration.

(3) A certificate of a Secretary of State—

(a) to the effect that any alleged liability of the Crown arises otherwise than in respect of His Majesty's Government in the United Kingdom;

(b) to the effect that any proceedings by the Crown are proceedings otherwise than in right of His Majesty's Government in the United Kingdom;

shall, for the purposes of this Act, be conclusive as to the matter so certified.

(3A) A certificate of the Scottish Ministers to the effect that—

(a) any alleged liability of the Crown arises otherwise than in respect of the Scottish Administration,

(b) any proceedings by the Crown are proceedings otherwise than in right of the Scottish Administration,

shall, for the purposes of this Act, be conclusive as to that matter.

(4) Where any property vests in the Crown by virtue of any rule of law which operates independently of the acts or the intentions of the Crown, the Crown shall not by virtue of this Act be subject to any liabilities in tort by reason only of the property being so vested; but the provisions of this subsection shall be without prejudice to the liabilities of the Crown under this Act in respect of any period after the Crown or any person acting for the Crown has in fact taken possession or control of any such property, or entered into occupation thereof.

(5) This Act shall not operate to limit the discretion of the court to grant relief by way of mandamus in cases in which such relief might have been granted before the commencement of this Act, notwithstanding that by reason of the provisions of this Act some other and further remedy is available.

[In s. 40(5), by the Supreme Court Act 1981, s. 29(5), the reference to mandamus is to be read as a reference to a mandatory order.]

PART VI EXTENT, COMMENCEMENT, SHORT TITLE, ETC.

54. Short Title and Commencement

(1) This Act may be cited as the Crown Proceedings Act 1947.

Section 23 FIRST SCHEDULE PROCEEDINGS ABOLISHED BY THIS ACT

1.—(1) Latin informations and English informations.

(2) Writs of capias ad respondendum, writs of subpoena ad respondendum, and writs of appraisement.

(3) Writs of scire facias.

(4) Proceedings for the determination of any issue upon a writ of extent or of diem clausit extremum.

(5) Writs of summons under Part V of the Crown Suits Act, 1865.

2.—(1) Proceedings against His Majesty by way of petition of right, including proceedings by way of petition of right intituled in the Admiralty Division under section fifty-two of the Naval Prize Act, 1864.

(2) Proceedings against His Majesty by way of monstrans de droit.

NOTES ON TEXT

The text incorporates the following amendments:

s. 2 amended by: (a) Statute Law (Repeals) Act 1981, sch. 1, part I; (b) Scotland Act 1998 (Consequential Modifications) (No. 1) Order 1999 (SI 1999/1042), sch. 2, para. 4(1) and (2); (c) Scotland Act 1998 (Consequential Modifications) (No. 2) Order 1999 (SI 1999/1820), sch. 2, para. 21;

s. 3 substituted by Copyright, Designs and Patents Act 1988, sch. 7, para. 4 (in force by SI 1989/816); amended by: (a) Trade Marks Act 1994, sch. 5 (in force by SI 1994/2550); (b) Scotland Act 1998 (Consequential Modifications) (No. 1) Order 1999 (SI 1999/1042), sch. 2, para. 4(1) and (3);

s. 4(2) repealed by Civil Liability (Contribution) Act 1978, sch. 2;

ss. 5 to 8 repealed by Merchant Shipping Act 1995, sch. 12;

s. 9 repealed by Post Office Act 1969, sch. 11, part II (in force by SI 1969/1066);

s. 10 repealed by Crown Proceedings (Armed Forces) Act 1987, s. 1;

s. 14(1) amended by: (a) Finance Act 1975, sch. 12, para. 8; (b) Capital Transfer Tax Act 1984, sch. 8, para. 2; the words in square brackets give effect to Finance Act 1986, s. 100;

s. 14(2) amended by Finance Act 1972, s. 55(1) (in force by s. 55(7));

s. 15(2) amended by Civil Procedure (Modification of Crown Proceedings Act 1947) Order 2005 (SI 2005/2712), sch. 1, para. 1;

s. 16 amended by Civil Procedure (Modification of Crown Proceedings Act 1947) Order 2005 (SI 2005/2712), sch. 1, para. 2;

in s. 17(1) the words in square brackets give effect to the Minister for the Civil Service Order 1968 (SI 1968/1656), art. 3(2) as read with arts 1(3), 2(2) and sch.;

s. 19 repealed by Civil Procedure (Modification of Crown Proceedings Act 1947) Order 2005 (SI 2005/2712), sch. 1, para. 3;

s. 20(1) repealed by Civil Procedure (Modification of Crown Proceedings Act 1947) Order 2005 (SI 2005/2712), sch. 1, para. 4(a);

s. 20(2) amended by: (a) Supreme Court Act 1981, sch. 7; (b) Civil Procedure (Modification of Crown Proceedings Act 1947) Order 2005 (SI 2005/2712), sch. 1, para. 4(b);

s. 22 amended by Civil Procedure (Modification of Crown Proceedings Act 1947) Order 2005 (SI 2005/2712), sch. 1, para. 5;

s. 23(3)(d) repealed by Charities Act 1960, sch. 7, part I;
s. 23(3)(e) repealed by Education Act 1973, sch. 2, part III (in force by s. 1(5) of that Act and SI 1973/1661);
s. 24(1) amended by Private International Law (Miscellaneous Provisions) Act 1995, s. 4(1) (in force by SI 1996/2515);
s. 24(3) amended by: (a) Administration of Justice Act 1982, sch. 1, part III (in force by SI 1983/236); (b) County Courts Act 1984, sch. 2, para. 21;
ss. 24(4) and 25(5) repealed, and s. 26(1) amended, by Statute Law (Repeals) Act 1993, sch. 1, part I, group 1;
s. 26(2) amended by Finance Act 1972, sch. 28, part II (in force by SI 1982/87);
s. 27(1) amended by Supreme Court Act 1981, sch. 7;
s. 27(2) amended by Civil Procedure (Modification of Crown Proceedings Act 1947) Order 2005 (SI 2005/2712), sch. 1, para. 6;
s. 28(1) amended by Civil Procedure (Modification of Crown Proceedings Act 1947) Order 2005 (SI 2005/2712), sch. 1, para. 7;
s. 30 repealed by Merchant Shipping Act 1995, sch. 12;
s. 34 repealed by Administration of Justice Act 1977, sch. 5, part V;
s. 36 repealed by Statute Law (Repeals) Act 1993, sch. 1, part I, group 1;
s. 38(1) amended by Civil Procedure (Modification of Crown Proceedings Act 1947) Order 2005 (SI 2005/2712), sch. 1, para. 9(a);
s. 38(2) amended by: (a) Merchant Shipping Act 1995, sch. 13, para. 21; (b) Scotland Act 1998, sch. 8, para. 7(1) and (2) (in force by SI 1998/3178); (c) s. 15(2) Civil Procedure (Modification of Crown Proceedings Act 1947) Order 2005 (SI 2005/2712), sch. 1, para. 9(b);
s. 38(5) repealed by Armed Forces Act 1981, sch. 5, part I;
s. 39(1) repealed by Statute Law Revision Act 1950, sch. 1;
s. 39(2) repealed by Secretary of State for the Environment Order 1970 (SI 1970/1681), art. 5(3) and sch. 4;
s. 40(2)(e) repealed by Highways (Miscellaneous Provisions) Act 1961, s. 1(6) (in force by s. 1(8));
s. 40(2) amended and s. 40(3A) inserted by Scotland Act 1998, sch. 8, para. 7(1) and (3) (in force by SI 1998/3178);
s. 54(2) and sch. 2 repealed by Statute Law Revision Act 1950, sch. 1;
Sections 11, 12, 31–3, 35, 37, 41–53 are omitted.

LIST OF AUTHORISED GOVERNMENT DEPARTMENTS

List of authorised government departments and the names and addresses for service of the person who is, or is acting for the purposes of the Act as, solicitor for such departments, published by the Minister for the Civil Service in pursuance of section 17 of the Crown Proceedings Act 1947.

Authorised Government departments	Solicitors and addresses for service
Departments whose solicitor is the Treasury Solicitor	
Advisory, Conciliation and Arbitration Service	The Treasury Solicitor
Assets Recovery Agency	Queen Anne's Chambers
Board of Trade	28 Broadway
Cabinet Office	Westminster
Central Office of Information	London SW1H 9JS
Crown Prosecution Service	
Department for Constitutional Affairs[1]	
Department for Culture, Media and Sport	
Department for Education and Skills	
Department for International Development	
Department for Transport	
Department of Trade and Industry	
Export Credits Guarantee Department	
Foreign and Commonwealth Office	
Government Actuary's Department	

[1] The reference to the Department for Constitutional Affairs includes a reference to the Lord Chancellor's Department.

Authorised Government departments	Solicitors and addresses for service
Health and Safety Executive Her Majesty's Chief Inspector of Schools in England Her Majesty's Chief Inspector of Schools in Wales Her Majesty's Treasury Home Office The International Rail Regulator Ministry of Defence National Savings and Investments Northern Ireland Office Office of the Deputy Prime Minister Office of Rail Regulation Ordnance Survey Privy Council Office Public Record Office Public Works Loan Board Royal Mint Serious Fraud Office Wales Office (Office of the Secretary of State for Wales)[2]	
Other departments	
Commissioners of Customs and Excise	The Solicitor for the Customs and Excise New King's Beam House 22 Upper Ground London SE1 9PJ
Commissioners of Inland Revenue	The Solicitor of Inland Revenue Somerset House The Strand London WC2R 1LB
Crown Estate Commissioners	Head of Legal The Crown Estate 16 Carlton House Terrace London SW1Y 5AH
Department for Environment, Food and Rural Affairs[2] Forestry Commissioners	The Solicitor to the Department for Environment, Food and Rural Affairs Nobel House 17 Smith Square London SW1P 3JR
Department of Health Department for Work and Pensions Food Standards Agency Office for National Statistics	The Solicitor to the Department for Work and Pensions and the Department of Health New Court 48 Carey Street London WC2A 2LS
Director General of Water Services	Head of Legal Services The Office of Water Services Centre City Tower 7 Hill Street Birmingham B5 4UA

[2] The solicitor and address for service for the purposes of or in connection with civil proceedings brought by or against the Crown which relate to those matters for which the Secretary of State is responsible in Wales and for which the Secretary of State for Environment, Food and Rural Affairs is responsible is the Solicitor to the Department for Environment, Food and Rural Affairs, Nobel House, 17 Smith Square, London SW1P 3JR. The Treasury Solicitor is the solicitor acting for the Wales Office (Office of the Secretary of State for Wales) in all other civil proceedings affecting that Office.

Authorised Government departments	Solicitors and addresses for service
Gas and Electricity Markets Authority	General Counsel Office of Gas and Electricity Markets 9 Millbank London SW1P 3GE
Her Majesty's Revenue and Customs	The Solicitor to Her Majesty's Revenue and Customs Somerset House The Strand London WC2R 1LB
National Assembly for Wales	The Director of Legal Services to the Welsh Assembly Government Cathays Park Cardiff CF10 3NQ
Office of Fair Trading	The Solicitor to the Office of Fair Trading Fleetbank House 2-6 Salisbury Square London EC4Y 8JX
Postal Services Commission	The Chief Legal Adviser Postal Services Commission Hercules House 6 Hercules Road London SE1 7DB

Data Protection Act 1998

(1998 CHAPTER 29)

An Act to make new provision for the regulation of the processing of information relating to individuals, including the obtaining, holding, use or disclosure of such information.

[16th July 1998]

PART I PRELIMINARY

1. Basic Interpretative Provisions

(1) In this Act, unless the context otherwise requires—

'data' means information which—

(a) is being processed by means of equipment operating automatically in response to instructions given for that purpose,

(b) is recorded with the intention that it should be processed by means of such equipment,

(c) is recorded as part of a relevant filing system or with the intention that it should form part of a relevant filing system,

(d) does not fall within paragraph (a), (b) or (c) but forms part of an accessible record as defined by section 68, or

(e) is recorded information held by a public authority and does not fall within any of paragraphs (a) to (d);

'data controller' means, subject to subsection (4), a person who (either alone or jointly or in common with other persons) determines the purposes for which and the manner in which any personal data are, or are to be, processed;

'data processor', in relation to personal data, means any person (other than an employee of the data controller) who processes the data on behalf of the data controller;

'data subject' means an individual who is the subject of personal data;

'personal data' means data which relate to a living individual who can be identified—

(a) from those data, or

(b) from those data and other information which is in the possession of, or is likely to come into the possession of, the data controller,

and includes any expression of opinion about the individual and any indication of the intentions of the data controller or any other person in respect of the individual;

'processing', in relation to information or data, means obtaining, recording or holding the information or data or carrying out any operation or set of operations on the information or data, including—

(a) organisation, adaptation or alteration of the information or data,

(b) retrieval, consultation or use of the information or data,

(c) disclosure of the information or data by transmission, dissemination or otherwise making available, or

(d) alignment, combination, blocking, erasure or destruction of the information or data;

'public authority' means a public authority as defined by the Freedom of Information Act 2000 or a Scottish public authority as defined by the Freedom of Information (Scotland) Act 2002;

'relevant filing system' means any set of information relating to individuals to the extent that, although the information is not processed by means of equipment operating automatically in response to instructions given for that purpose, the set is structured, either by reference to individuals or by reference to criteria relating to individuals, in such a way that specific information relating to a particular individual is readily accessible.

(2) In this Act, unless the context otherwise requires—

(a) 'obtaining' or 'recording', in relation to personal data, includes obtaining or recording the information to be contained in the data, and

(b) 'using' or 'disclosing', in relation to personal data, includes using or disclosing the information contained in the data.

(3) In determining for the purposes of this Act whether any information is recorded with the intention—
   (a) that it should be processed by means of equipment operating automatically in response to instructions given for that purpose, or
   (b) that it should form part of a relevant filing system,
   it is immaterial that it is intended to be so processed or to form part of such a system only after being transferred to a country or territory outside the European Economic Area.
(4) Where personal data are processed only for purposes for which they are required by or under any enactment to be processed, the person on whom the obligation to process the data is imposed by or under that enactment is for the purposes of this Act the data controller.
(5) In paragraph (e) of the definition of 'data' in subsection (1), the reference to information 'held' by a public authority shall be construed in accordance with section 3(2) of the Freedom of Information Act 2000 or section 3(2), (4) and (5) of the Freedom of Information (Scotland) Act 2002.
(6) Where—
   (a) section 7 of the Freedom of Information Act 2000 prevents Parts I to V of that Act; or
   (b) section 7(1) of the Freedom of Information (Scotland) Act 2002 prevents that Act,
   from applying to certain information held by a public authority, that information is not to be treated for the purposes of paragraph (e) of the definition of 'data' in subsection (1) as held by a public authority.

PART II RIGHTS OF DATA SUBJECTS AND OTHERS

7. Right of Access to Personal Data

(1) Subject to the following provisions of this section and to sections 8 and 9, an individual is entitled—
   (a) to be informed by any data controller whether personal data of which that individual is the data subject are being processed by or on behalf of that data controller,
   (b) if that is the case, to be given by the data controller a description of—
      (i) the personal data of which that individual is the data subject,
      (ii) the purposes for which they are being or are to be processed, and
      (iii) the recipients or classes of recipients to whom they are or may be disclosed,
   (c) to have communicated to him in an intelligible form—
      (i) the information constituting any personal data of which that individual is the data subject, and
      (ii) any information available to the data controller as to the source of those data, and
   (d) where the processing by automatic means of personal data of which that individual is the data subject for the purpose of evaluating matters relating to him such as, for example, his performance at work, his creditworthiness, his reliability or his conduct, has constituted or is likely to constitute the sole basis for any decision significantly affecting him, to be informed by the data controller of the logic involved in that decision-taking.
(2) A data controller is not obliged to supply any information under subsection (1) unless he has received—
   (a) a request in writing, and
   (b) except in prescribed cases, such fee (not exceeding the prescribed maximum) as he may require.
(3) Where a data controller—
   (a) reasonably requires further information in order to satisfy himself as to the identity of the person making a request under this section and to locate the information which that person seeks, and
   (b) has informed him of that requirement,
   the data controller is not obliged to comply with the request unless he is supplied with that further information.
(4) Where a data controller cannot comply with the request without disclosing information relating to another individual who can be identified from that information, he is not obliged to comply with the request unless—

(a) the other individual has consented to the disclosure of the information to the person making the request, or
(b) it is reasonable in all the circumstances to comply with the request without the consent of the other individual.

(5) In subsection (4) the reference to information relating to another individual includes a reference to information identifying that individual as the source of the information sought by the request; and that subsection is not to be construed as excusing a data controller from communicating so much of the information sought by the request as can be communicated without disclosing the identity of the other individual concerned, whether by the omission of names or other identifying particulars or otherwise.

(6) In determining for the purposes of subsection (4)(b) whether it is reasonable in all the circumstances to comply with the request without the consent of the other individual concerned, regard shall be had, in particular, to—
(a) any duty of confidentiality owed to the other individual,
(b) any steps taken by the data controller with a view to seeking the consent of the other individual,
(c) whether the other individual is capable of giving consent, and
(d) any express refusal of consent by the other individual.

(7) An individual making a request under this section may, in such cases as may be prescribed, specify that his request is limited to personal data of any prescribed description.

(8) Subject to subsection (4), a data controller shall comply with a request under this section promptly and in any event before the end of the prescribed period beginning with the relevant day.

(9) If a court is satisfied on the application of any person who has made a request under the foregoing provisions of this section that the data controller in question has failed to comply with the request in contravention of those provisions, the court may order him to comply with the request.

(10) In this section—
'prescribed' means prescribed by the Secretary of State by regulations;
'the prescribed maximum' means such amount as may be prescribed;
'the prescribed period' means forty days or such other period as may be prescribed;
'the relevant day', in relation to a request under this section, means the day on which the data controller receives the request or, if later, the first day on which the data controller has both the required fee and the information referred to in subsection (3).

(11) Different amounts or periods may be prescribed under this section in relation to different cases.

15. Jurisdiction and Procedure

(1) The jurisdiction conferred by sections 7 to 14 is exercisable by the High Court or a county court or, in Scotland, by the Court of Session or the sheriff.

(2) For the purpose of determining any question whether an applicant under subsection (9) of section 7 is entitled to the information which he seeks (including any question whether any relevant data are exempt from that section by virtue of Part IV) a court may require the information constituting any data processed by or on behalf of the data controller and any information as to the logic involved in any decision-taking as mentioned in section 7(1)(d) to be made available for its own inspection but shall not, pending the determination of that question in the applicant's favour, require the information sought by the applicant to be disclosed to him or his representatives whether by discovery (or, in Scotland, recovery) or otherwise.

PART VI MISCELLANEOUS AND GENERAL

Unlawful Obtaining etc. of Personal Data

55. Unlawful Obtaining etc. of Personal Data

(1) A person must not knowingly or recklessly, without the consent of the data controller—
(a) obtain or disclose personal data or the information contained in personal data, or
(b) procure the disclosure to another person of the information contained in personal data.

(2) Subsection (1) does not apply to a person who shows—
(a) that the obtaining, disclosing or procuring—
(i) was necessary for the purpose of preventing or detecting crime, or
(ii) was required or authorised by or under any enactment, by any rule of law or by the order of a court,
(b) that he acted in the reasonable belief that he had in law the right to obtain or disclose the data or information or, as the case may be, to procure the disclosure of the information to the other person,
(c) that he acted in the reasonable belief that he would have had the consent of the data controller if the data controller had known of the obtaining, disclosing or procuring and the circumstances of it, or
(d) that in the particular circumstances the obtaining, disclosing or procuring was justified as being in the public interest.
(3) A person who contravenes subsection (1) is guilty of an offence.
(4) A person who sells personal data is guilty of an offence if he has obtained the data in contravention of subsection (1).
(5) A person who offers to sell personal data is guilty of an offence if—
(a) he has obtained the data in contravention of subsection (1), or
(b) he subsequently obtains the data in contravention of that subsection.
(6) For the purposes of subsection (5), an advertisement indicating that personal data are or may be for sale is an offer to sell the data.
(7) Section 1(2) does not apply for the purposes of this section; and for the purposes of subsections (4) to (6), 'personal data' includes information extracted from personal data.
(8) References in this section to personal data do not include references to personal data which by virtue of section 28 are exempt from this section.

General

70. Supplementary Definitions

(1) In this Act, unless the context otherwise requires—
. . .
'enactment' includes an enactment passed after this Act and any enactment comprised in, or in any instrument made under, an Act of the Scottish Parliament; . . .
'recipient', in relation to any personal data, means any person to whom the data are disclosed, including any person (such as an employee or agent of the data controller, a data processor or an employee or agent of a data processor) to whom they are disclosed in the course of processing the data for the data controller, but does not include any person to whom disclosure is or may be made as a result of, or with a view to, a particular inquiry by or on behalf of that person made in the exercise of any power conferred by law; . . .

75. Short Title, Commencement and Extent

(1) This Act may be cited as the Data Protection Act 1998.
(2) The following provisions of this Act—
(a) sections 1 to 3, . . .
(d) sections 67 to 71,
(e) this section, . . . and
(i) so much of any other provision of this Act as confers any power to make subordinate legislation,
shall come into force on the day on which this Act is passed.
(3) The remaining provisions of this Act shall come into force on such day as the Secretary of State may by order appoint; and different days may be appointed for different purposes. . . .
(5) Subject to subsection (6), this Act extends to Northern Ireland.
(6) Any amendment, repeal or revocation made by Schedule 15 or 16 has the same extent as that of the enactment or instrument to which it relates.

[*Provisions of the Act printed above, which did not come into force on royal assent, were brought into force on 1 March 2000 by SI 2000/183.*]

NOTES ON TEXT

Only selected provisions of the Act are printed above, incorporating the following amendments:

s. 1 amended by: (a) Freedom of Information Act 2000, s. 68(1), (2) and (3) (in force by SI 2004/3122); (b) Freedom of Information (Scotland) Act 2002 (Consequential Modifications) Order 2004 (SI 2004/3089), art. 2;

s. 7 amended by: (a) Freedom of Information Act 2000, sch. 6, para. 1 (in force by SI 2001/1637); (b) Transfer of Functions (Miscellaneous) Order 2001 (SI 2001/3500), sch. 2, para. 6(1)(b); (c) Secretary of State for Constitutional Affairs Order 2003 (SI 2003/1887), sch. 2, para. 9(1)(a);

s. 70 amended by Scotland Act 1998 (Consequential Modifications) (No. 2) Order 1999 (SI 1999/1820), sch. 2, para. 133.

European Communities (Rights against Insurers) Regulations 2002

(SI 2002/3061)

The Lord Chancellor, being a Minister designated for the purpose of section 2(2) of the European Communities Act 1972 in relation to a direct right of action against the insurer of the person responsible by any person claiming compensation in respect of loss or injury caused by a motor vehicle or trailer, in exercise of the powers conferred by that section, makes the following Regulations:

1. Citation and Commencement

These Regulations may be cited as the European Communities (Rights against Insurers) Regulations 2002 and shall come into force on 19th January 2003.

2. Interpretation

(1) In these Regulations—
'the 1981 Order' means the Road Traffic (Northern Ireland) 1981;
'the 1988 Act' means the Road Traffic Act 1988;
'accident' means an accident on a road or other public place in the United Kingdom caused by, or arising out of, the use of any insured vehicle;
'entitled party' means any person who is—
(a) a resident of a Member State; or
(b) a resident of any other State which is a Contracting Party to the Agreement on the European Economic Area signed at Oporto on 2nd May 1992 and the Protocol adjusting the Agreement signed at Brussels on 17th March 1993;
'insured person' means a person insured under a policy of insurance satisfying the conditions set out in paragraph (3) of this regulation;
'vehicle' means any motor vehicle intended for travel on land and propelled by mechanical power, but not running on rails, and any trailer whether or not coupled, which is normally based (within the meaning of paragraph (2) of this Regulation) in the United Kingdom.

(2) The territory in which a vehicle is normally based is—
(a) the territory of the State of which the vehicle bears a registration plate; or
(b) in cases where no registration is required for the type of vehicle, but the vehicle bears an insurance plate or a distinguishing sign analogous to a registration plate, the territory of the State in which the insurance plate or the sign is issued; or
(c) in cases where neither registration plate nor insurance plate nor distinguishing sign is required for the type of vehicle, the territory of the State in which the keeper of the vehicle is permanently resident.

(3) For the purposes of these Regulations, a vehicle is insured if there is in force in relation to the use of that vehicle on a road or other public place in the United Kingdom by the insured person a policy of insurance (including a covering note) which fulfils the requirements of section 145 of the 1988 Act or article 92 of the 1981 Order.

3. Right of Action

(1) Paragraph (2) of this regulation applies where an entitled party has a cause of action against an insured person in tort or (as the case may be) delict, and that cause of action arises out of an accident.

(2) Where this paragraph applies, the entitled party may, without prejudice to his right to issue proceedings against the insured person, issue proceedings against the insurer which issued the policy of insurance relating to the insured vehicle, and that insurer shall be directly liable to the entitled party to the extent that he is liable to the insured person.

Fatal Accidents Act 1976

(1976 CHAPTER 30)

1. Right of Action for Wrongful Act Causing Death

(1) If death is caused by any wrongful act, neglect or default which is such as would (if death had not ensued) have entitled the person injured to maintain an action and recover damages in respect thereof, the person who would have been liable if death had not ensued shall be liable to an action for damages, notwithstanding the death of the person injured.

(2) Subject to section 1A(2) below, every such action shall be for the benefit of the dependants of the person ('the deceased') whose death has been so caused.

(3) In this Act 'dependant' means—

(a) the wife or husband or former wife or husband of the deceased;

(b) any person who—

(i) was living with the deceased in the same household immediately before the date of the death; and

(ii) had been living with the deceased in the same household for at least two years before that date; and

(iii) was living during the whole of that period as the husband or wife of the deceased;

(c) any parent or other ascendant of the deceased;

(d) any person who was treated by the deceased as his parent;

(e) any child or other descendant of the deceased;

(f) any person (not being a child of the deceased) who, in the case of any marriage to which the deceased was at any time a party, was treated by the deceased as a child of the family in relation to that marriage;

(g) any person who is, or is the issue of, a brother, sister, uncle or aunt of the deceased.

(4) The reference to the former wife or husband of the deceased in subsection (3)(a) above includes a reference to a person whose marriage to the deceased has been annulled or declared void as well as a person whose marriage to the deceased has been dissolved.

(5) In deducing any relationship for the purposes of subsection (3) above—

(a) any relationship by affinity shall be treated as a relationship of consanguinity, any relationship of the half blood as a relationship of the whole blood, and the stepchild of any person as his child, and

(b) an illegitimate person shall be treated as the legitimate child of his mother and reputed father.

(6) Any reference in this Act to injury includes any disease and any impairment of a person's physical or mental condition.

1A. Bereavement

(1) An action under this Act may consist of or include a claim for damages for bereavement.

(2) A claim for damages for bereavement shall only be for the benefit—

(a) of the wife or husband of the deceased; and

(b) where the deceased was a minor who was never married—

(i) of his parents, if he was legitimate; and

(ii) of his mother, if he was illegitimate.

(3) Subject to subsection (5) below, the sum to be awarded as damages under this section shall be £7,500.

(4) Where there is a claim for damages under this section for the benefit of both the parents of the deceased, the sum awarded shall be divided equally between them (subject to any deduction falling to be made in respect of costs not recovered from the defendant).

(5) The Lord Chancellor may by order made by statutory instrument, subject to annulment in pursuance of a resolution of either House of Parliament, amend this section by varying the sum for the time being specified in subsection (3) above.

2. Persons Entitled to Bring the Action

(1) The action shall be brought by and in the name of the executor or administrator of the deceased.

(2) If—

(a) there is no executor or administrator of the deceased, or

(b) no action is brought within six months after the death by and in the name of an executor or administrator of the deceased,

the action may be brought by and in the name of all or any of the persons for whose benefit an executor or administrator could have brought it.

(3) Not more than one action shall lie for and in respect of the same subject matter of complaint.

(4) The plaintiff in the action shall be required to deliver to the defendant or his solicitor full particulars of the persons for whom and on whose behalf the action is brought and of the nature of the claim in respect of which damages are sought to be recovered.

3. Assessment of Damages

(1) In the action such damages, other than damages for bereavement, may be awarded as are proportioned to the injury resulting from the death to the dependants respectively.

(2) After deducting the costs not recovered from the defendant any amount recovered otherwise than as damages for bereavement shall be divided among the dependants in such shares as may be directed.

(3) In an action under this Act where there fall to be assessed damages payable to a widow in respect of the death of her husband there shall not be taken into account the re-marriage of the widow or her prospects of re-marriage.

(4) In an action under this Act where there fall to be assessed damages payable to a person who is a dependant by virtue of section 1(3)(b) above in respect of the death of the person with whom the dependant was living as husband or wife there shall be taken into account (together with any other matter that appears to the court to be relevant to the action) the fact that the dependant had no enforceable right to financial support by the deceased as a result of their living together.

(5) If the dependants have incurred funeral expenses in respect of the deceased, damages may be awarded in respect of those expenses.

(6) Money paid into court in satisfaction of a cause of action under this Act may be in one sum without specifying any person's share.

4. Assessment of Damages; Disregard of Benefits

In assessing damages in respect of a person's death in an action under this Act, benefits which have accrued or will or may accrue to any person from his estate or otherwise as a result of his death shall be disregarded.

5. Contributory Negligence

Where any person dies as the result partly of his own fault and partly of the fault of any other person or persons, and accordingly if an action were brought for the benefit of the estate under the Law Reform (Miscellaneous Provisions) Act 1934 the damages recoverable would be reduced under section 1(1) of the Law Reform (Contributory Negligence) Act 1945, any damages recoverable in an action under this Act shall be reduced to a proportionate extent.

High Court and County Courts Jurisdiction Order 1991

(SI 1991/724)

The Lord Chancellor, in exercise of the powers conferred upon him by sections 1 and 120 of the Courts and Legal Services Act 1990, having consulted as required by section 1(9) of that Act, hereby makes the following Order a draft of which has, in accordance with section 120(4) of that Act, been laid before and approved by resolution of each House of Parliament—

1. Title and Commencement

This Order may be cited as the High Court and County Courts Jurisdiction Order 1991 and shall come into force on 1st July 1991.

2. Jurisdiction

(1) A county court shall have jurisdiction under—
  (a) sections 146 and 147 of the Law of Property Act 1925,
  (b) [*Revoked*]
  (c) section 26 of the Arbitration Act 1950,
  (d) section 63(2) of the Landlord and Tenant Act 1954,
  (e) section 28(3) of the Mines and Quarries (Tips) Act 1969,
  (f) section 66 of the Taxes Management Act 1970,
  (g) section 41 of the Administration of Justice Act 1970,
  (h) section 139(5)(b) of the Consumer Credit Act 1974,
  (i) section 13 of the Torts (Interference with Goods) Act 1977,
  (j) section 87 of the Magistrates' Courts Act 1980,
  (k) sections 19 and 20 of the Local Government Finance Act 1982,
  (l) sections 15, 16, 21, 25 and 139 of the County Courts Act 1984,
  (m) section 39(4) of, and paragraph 3(1) of Schedule 3 to, the Legal Aid Act 1988,
  (n) sections 99, 102(5), 114, 195, 204, 230, 231 and 235(5) of the Copyright, Designs and Patents Act 1988,
  (o) section 40 of the Housing Act 1988, and
  (p) sections 13 and 14 of the Trusts of Land and Appointment of Trustees Act 1996,

whatever the amount involved in the proceedings and whatever the value of any fund or asset connected with the proceedings.

(2) A county court shall have jurisdiction under—
  (a) section 10 of the Local Land Charges Act 1975, and
  (b) section 10(4) of the Rentcharges Act 1977,

where the sum concerned or amount claimed does not exceed £5,000.

(3) A county court shall have jurisdiction under the following provisions of the Law of Property Act 1925 where the capital value of the land or interest in land which is to be dealt with does not exceed £30,000;
  (a) sections 3, 49, 66, 181, and 188;
  (b) proviso (iii) to paragraph 3 of Part III of Schedule 1;
  (c) proviso (v) to paragraph 1(3) of Part IV of Schedule 1.
  (d) provisos (iii) and (iv) to paragraph 1(4) of Part IV of Schedule 1.

(4) A county court shall have jurisdiction under sections 89, 90, 91 and 92 of the Law of Property Act 1925 where the amount owing in respect of the mortgage or charge at the commencement of the proceedings does not exceed £30,000.

(5) A county court shall have jurisdiction under the proviso to section 136(1) of the Law of Property Act 1925 where the amount or value of the debt or thing in action does not exceed £30,000.

(6) A county court shall have jurisdiction under section 1(6) of the Land Charges Act 1972—
  (a) in the case of a land charge of Class C(i), C(ii) or D(i), if the amount does not exceed £30,000;

Selected Legislation

(b) in the case of a land charge of Class C(iii), if it is for a specified capital sum of money not exceeding £30,000 or, where it is not for a specified capital sum, if the capital value of the land affected does not exceed £30,000;

(c) in the case of a land charge of Class A, Class B, Class C(iv), Class D(ii), Class D(iii) or Class E, if the capital value of the land affected does not exceed £30,000;

(d) in the case of a land charge of Class F, if the land affected by it is the subject of an order made by the court under section 1 of the Matrimonial Homes Act 1983 or an application for an order under that section relating to that land has been made to the court;

(e) in a case where an application under section 23 of the Deeds of Arrangement Act 1914 could be entertained by the court.

(7) A county court shall have jurisdiction under sections 69, 70 and 71 of the Solicitors Act 1974 where a bill of costs relates wholly or partly to contentious business done in a county court and the amount of the bill does not exceed £5,000.

(7A) A patents county court and the county courts listed in paragraph (7B) shall have jurisdiction under the following provisions of the Trade Marks Act 1994—

(a) sections 15, 16, 19, 23(5), 25(4)(b), 30, 31, 46, 47, 64, 73 and 74;

(b) paragraph 12 of Schedule 1; and

(c) paragraph 14 of Schedule 2,

to include jurisdiction to hear and determine any claims or matters ancillary to, or arising from proceedings brought under such provisions.

(7B) For the purposes of paragraph (7A), the county courts at—

(a) Birmingham;

(b) Bristol;

(c) Cardiff;

(d) Leeds;

(e) Liverpool;

(f) Manchester; and

(e) Newcastle upon Tyne,

shall have jurisdiction.

3. Injunctions

The High Court shall have jurisdiction to hear an application for an injunction made in the court of or in anticipation of proceedings in a county court where a county court may not, by virtue of regulations under section 38(3)(b) of the County Courts Act 1984 or otherwise, grant such an injunction.

4. Allocation — Commencement of Proceedings

Subject to articles 4A, 5, 6 and 6A, proceedings in which both the county courts and the High Court have jurisdiction may be commenced either in a county court or in the High Court.

4A.

Except for proceedings to which article 5 applies, a claim for money in which county courts have jurisdiction may only be commenced in the High Court if the financial value of the claim is more than £15,000.

5.

(1) Proceedings which include a claim for damages in respect of personal injuries may only be commenced in the High Court if the financial value of the claim is £50,000 or more.

(2) In this article 'personal injuries' means personal injuries to the claimant or any other person, and includes disease, impairment of physical or mental condition, and death.

(3) This article does not apply to proceedings which include a claim for damages in respect of an alleged breach of duty of care committed in the course of the provision of clinical or medical services (including dental or nursing services).

6.

Applications and appeals under section 19 of the Local Government Finance Act 1982 and appeals under section 20 of that Act shall be commenced in the High Court.

6A.

Applications under section 1 of the Access to Neighbouring Land Act 1992 shall be commenced in a county court.

8. Enforcement

(1) Subject to paragraph (1A) a judgment or order of a county court for the payment of a sum of money which it is sought to enforce wholly or partially by execution against goods—
- (a) shall be enforced only in the High Court where the sum which it is sought to enforce is £5,000 or more;
- (b) shall be enforced only in a county court where the sum which it is sought to enforce is less than £600;
- (c) in any other case may be enforced in either the High Court or a county court.

(1A) A judgment or order of a county court for the payment of a sum of money in proceedings arising out of an agreement regulated by the Consumer Credit Act 1974 shall be enforced only in a county court.

(2) Section 85(1) of the County Courts Act 1984 is amended by the insertion, at the beginning of the subsection, of the words 'Subject to article 8 of the High Court and County Courts Jurisdiction Order 1991,'.

8A. Enforcement of Traffic Penalties

(1) Proceedings for the recovery of—
- (a) increased penalty charges provided for in charge certificates issued under—
  - (i) paragraph 6 of Schedule 6 to the 1991 Act; and
  - (ii) paragraph 8 of Schedule 1 to the London Local Authorities Act 1996;
- (b) amounts payable by a person other than a local authority under an adjudication of a parking adjudicator pursuant to section 73 of the 1991 Act; and
- (c) fixed penalties payable under fixed penalty notices issued under regulation 5 of the Road Traffic (Vehicle Emissions) (Fixed Penalty) Regulations 1997,

shall be taken in Northampton County Court.

(2) In this article, 'the 1991 Act' means the Road Traffic Act 1991 and expressions which are used in the 1991 Act have the same meaning in this article as they have in that Act.

(3) In this article, 'a local authority' means: —
- (a) in England, a London authority, a county or district council or the Council of the Isles of Scilly; and
- (b) in Wales, a county or county borough council.

8B. Enforcement of Possession Orders Against Trespassers

(1) A judgment or order of a county court for possession of land made in a possession claim against trespassers may be enforced in the High Court or a county court.

(2) In this article 'a possession claim against trespassers' has the same meaning as in Part 55 of the Civil Procedure Rules 1998.

9. Financial Value of Claim

For the purposes of Articles 4A and 5, the financial value of the claim shall be calculated in accordance with rule 16.3(6) of the Civil Procedure Rules 1998.

11. Crown Proceedings — Transitional Provisions

For a period of two years from the date upon which this Order comes into force no order shall be made transferring proceedings in the High Court to which the Crown is a party to a county court, except—
- (a) when the proceedings are set down to be tried or heard; or
- (b) with the consent of the Crown.

12. Savings

This Order shall not apply to:

(a) family proceedings within the meaning of Part V of the Matrimonial and Family Proceedings Act 1984.

NOTES ON TEXT

The text printed above incorporates the following amendments:

art. 2 amended by: (a) High Court and County Courts Jurisdiction (Amendment) Order 1996 (SI 1996/3141), art. 2; (b) High Court and County Courts Jurisdiction (Amendment) Order 2005 (SI 2005/587), art. 3;

art. 4 amended by: (a) Access to Neighbouring Land Act 1992, s. 7 (in force by SI 1992/3349); (b) High Court and County Courts Jurisdiction (Amendment) Order 1999 (SI 1999/1014), art. 4;

art. 4A inserted by High Court and County Courts Jurisdiction (Amendment) Order 1999 (SI 1999/1014), art. 5;

art. 5 amended by High Court and County Courts Jurisdiction (Amendment) Order 1999 (SI 1999/1014), arts 3 and 6;

art. 6 amended by High Court and County Courts Jurisdiction (Amendment) Order 1993 (SI 1993/1407), art. 3;

art. 6A inserted by Access to Neighbouring Land Act 1992, s. 7 (in force by SI 1992/3349);

art. 7 revoked by High Court and County Courts Jurisdiction (Amendment) Order 1999 (SI 1999/1014), art. 7;

art. 8 amended by: (a) High Court and County Courts Jurisdiction (Amendment) Order 1993 (SI 1993/1407), art. 4; (b) High Court and County Courts Jurisdiction (Amendment) Order 1995 (SI 1995/205), art. 5; (c) High Court and County Courts Jurisdiction (Amendment) Order 1996 (SI 1996/3141), art. 3; (d) High Court and County Courts Jurisdiction (Amendment) Order 1999 (SI 1999/1014), art. 8;

art. 8A inserted by High Court and County Courts Jurisdiction (Amendment) Order 1993 (SI 1993/1407), art. 5, and amended by: (a) High Court and County Courts Jurisdiction (Amendment) Order 1996 (SI 1996/3141), art. 4; (b) High Court and County Courts Jurisdiction (Amendment) Order 2001 (SI 2001/1387);

art. 8B inserted by High Court and County Courts Jurisdiction (Amendment No. 2) Order 2001 (SI 2001/2685);

art. 9 substituted by High Court and County Courts Jurisdiction (Amendment) Order 1999 (SI 1999/1014), art. 9;

art. 10 revoked by High Court and County Courts Jurisdiction (Amendment) Order 1999 (SI 1999/1014), art. 10;

art. 12(b) revoked by High Court and County Courts Jurisdiction (Amendment) Order 1999 (SI 1999/1014), art. 11;

Article 2(8) and the schedule (amendments of other legislation) have been omitted.

Highways Act 1980

(1980 CHAPTER 66)

40. Adoption of Private Streets

The foregoing provisions of this Part of this Act are without prejudice to the power or, as the case may be, the duty of the council of a county, metropolitan district or London borough, or the Common Council, to adopt private streets as highways maintainable at the public expense under Part XI of this Act.

41. Duty to Maintain Highways Maintainable at Public Expense

(1) The authority who are for the time being the highway authority for a highway maintainable at the public expense are under a duty, subject to subsections (2) and (4) below, to maintain the highway.

(2) An order made by the Minister under section 10 above directing that a highway proposed to be constructed by him shall become a trunk road may, as regards—
- (a) a highway to which this subsection applies which becomes a trunk road by virtue of the order, or
- (b) a part of a highway to which this subsection applies, being a part which crosses the route of the highway to be so constructed,

contain such a direction as is specified in subsection (4) below.

(3) Subsection (2) above applies to—
- (a) any highway maintainable at the public expense by a local highway authority, and
- (b) any highway other than a highway falling within paragraph (a) above or a highway maintainable under a special enactment or by reason of tenure, enclosure or prescription.

(4) The direction referred to in subsection (2) above is—
- (a) in a case where the highway or part of a highway falls within subsection (3)(a) above, a direction that, notwithstanding subsection (1) above, it shall be maintained by the highway authority for that highway until such date, not being later than the date on which the new route is opened for the purposes of through traffic, as may be specified in a notice given by the Minister to that authority; and
- (b) in a case where the highway or part of a highway falls within subsection (3)(b) above, a direction that, notwithstanding subsection (1) above, the Minister is to be under no duty to maintain it until such date as aforesaid.

(5) Where an order under section 10 above contains a direction made in pursuance of subsections (2) to (4) above, then, until the date specified in the notice given by the Minister pursuant to the direction, in accordance with subsection (4) above, the powers of a highway authority under sections 97, 98, 270 and 301 below as respects the highway to which the direction relates are exercisable by the highway authority to whom the notice is required to be given, as well as by the Minister.

Human Rights Act 1998

(1998 CHAPTER 42)

An Act to give further effect to rights and freedoms guaranteed under the European Convention on Human Rights; to make provision with respect to holders of certain judicial offices who become judges of the European Court of Human Rights; and for connected purposes.

[9th November 1998]

Introduction

1. The Convention Rights

(1) In this Act 'the Convention rights' means the rights and fundamental freedoms set out in—
(a) Articles 2 to 12 and 14 of the Convention,
(b) Articles 1 to 3 of the First Protocol, and
(c) Article 1 of the Thirteenth Protocol,
as read with Articles 16 to 18 of the Convention.

(2) Those Articles are to have effect for the purposes of this Act subject to any designated derogation or reservation (as to which see sections 14 and 15).

(3) The Articles are set out in Schedule 1.

(4) The Secretary of State may by order make such amendments to this Act as he considers appropriate to reflect the effect, in relation to the United Kingdom, of a protocol.

(5) In subsection (4) 'protocol' means a protocol to the Convention—
(a) which the United Kingdom has ratified; or
(b) which the United Kingdom has signed with a view to ratification.

(6) No amendment may be made by an order under subsection (4) so as to come into force before the protocol concerned is in force in relation to the United Kingdom.

2. Interpretation of Convention Rights

(1) A court or tribunal determining a question which has arisen in connection with a Convention right must take into account any—
(a) judgment, decision, declaration or advisory opinion of the European Court of Human Rights,
(b) opinion of the Commission given in a report adopted under Article 31 of the Convention,
(c) decision of the Commission in connection with Article 26 or 27(2) of the Convention, or
(d) decision of the Committee of Ministers taken under Article 46 of the Convention,
whenever made or given, so far as, in the opinion of the court or tribunal, it is relevant to the proceedings in which that question has arisen.

(2) Evidence of any judgment, decision, declaration or opinion of which account may have to be taken under this section is to be given in proceedings before any court or tribunal in such manner as may be provided by rules.

(3) In this section 'rules' means rules of court or, in the case of proceedings before a tribunal, rules made for the purposes of this section—
(a) by the Secretary of State, in relation to any proceedings outside Scotland;
(b) by the Secretary of State, in relation to proceedings in Scotland; or
(c) by a Northern Ireland department, in relation to proceedings before a tribunal in Northern Ireland—
(i) which deals with transferred matters; and
(ii) for which no rules made under paragraph (a) are in force.

Legislation

3. Interpretation of Legislation

(1) So far as it is possible to do so, primary legislation and subordinate legislation must be read and given effect in a way which is compatible with the Convention rights.

(2) This section—
 (a) applies to primary legislation and subordinate legislation whenever enacted;
 (b) does not affect the validity, continuing operation or enforcement of any incompatible primary legislation; and
 (c) does not affect the validity, continuing operation or enforcement of any incompatible subordinate legislation if (disregarding any possibility of revocation) primary legislation prevents removal of the incompatibility.

4. Declaration of Incompatibility

(1) Subsection (2) applies in any proceedings in which a court determines whether a provision of primary legislation is compatible with a Convention right.
(2) If the court is satisfied that the provision is incompatible with a Convention right, it may make a declaration of that incompatibility.
(3) Subsection (4) applies in any proceedings in which a court determines whether a provision of subordinate legislation, made in the exercise of a power conferred by primary legislation, is compatible with a Convention right.
(4) If the court is satisfied—
 (a) that the provision is incompatible with a Convention right, and
 (b) that (disregarding any possibility of revocation) the primary legislation concerned prevents removal of the incompatibility,
 it may make a declaration of that incompatibility.
(5) In this section 'court' means—
 (a) the House of Lords;
 (b) the Judicial Committee of the Privy Council;
 (c) the Courts-Martial Appeal Court;
 (d) in Scotland, the High Court of Justiciary sitting otherwise than as a trial court or the Court of Session;
 (e) in England and Wales or Northern Ireland, the High Court or the Court of Appeal.
(6) A declaration under this section ('a declaration of incompatibility')—
 (a) does not affect the validity, continuing operation or enforcement of the provision in respect of which it is given; and
 (b) is not binding on the parties to the proceedings in which it is made.

5. Right of Crown to Intervene

(1) Where a court is considering whether to make a declaration of incompatibility, the Crown is entitled to notice in accordance with rules of court.
(2) In any case to which subsection (1) applies—
 (a) a Minister of the Crown (or a person nominated by him),
 (b) a member of the Scottish Executive,
 (c) a Northern Ireland Minister,
 (d) a Northern Ireland department,
 is entitled, on giving notice in accordance with rules of court, to be joined as a party to the proceedings.
(3) Notice under subsection (2) may be given at any time during the proceedings.
(4) A person who has been made a party to criminal proceedings (other than in Scotland) as the result of a notice under subsection (2) may, with leave, appeal to the House of Lords against any declaration of incompatibility made in the proceedings.
(5) In subsection (4)—
 'criminal proceedings' includes all proceedings before the Courts-Martial Appeal Court; and
 'leave' means leave granted by the court making the declaration of incompatibility or by the House of Lords.

Public Authorities

6. Acts of Public Authorities

(1) It is unlawful for a public authority to act in a way which is incompatible with a Convention right.

(2) Subsection (1) does not apply to an act if—

(a) as the result of one or more provisions of primary legislation, the authority could not have acted differently; or

(b) in the case of one or more provisions of, or made under, primary legislation which cannot be read or given effect in a way which is compatible with the Convention rights, the authority was acting so as to give effect to or enforce those provisions.

(3) In this section 'public authority' includes—

(a) a court or tribunal, and

(b) any person certain of whose functions are functions of a public nature,

but does not include either House of Parliament or a person exercising functions in connection with proceedings in Parliament.

(4) In subsection (3) 'Parliament' does not include the House of Lords in its judicial capacity.

(5) In relation to a particular act, a person is not a public authority by virtue only of subsection (3)(b) if the nature of the act is private.

(6) 'An act' includes a failure to act but does not include a failure to—

(a) introduce in, or lay before, Parliament a proposal for legislation; or

(b) make any primary legislation or remedial order.

7. Proceedings

(1) A person who claims that a public authority has acted (or proposes to act) in a way which is made unlawful by section 6(1) may—

(a) bring proceedings against the authority under this Act in the appropriate court or tribunal, or

(b) rely on the Convention right or rights concerned in any legal proceedings,

but only if he is (or would be) a victim of the unlawful act.

(2) In subsection (1)(a) 'appropriate court or tribunal' means such court or tribunal as may be determined in accordance with rules; and proceedings against an authority include a counter-claim or similar proceeding.

(3) If the proceedings are brought on an application for judicial review, the applicant is to be taken to have a sufficient interest in relation to the unlawful act only if he is, or would be, a victim of that act.

(4) If the proceedings are made by way of a petition for judicial review in Scotland, the applicant shall be taken to have title and interest to sue in relation to the unlawful act only if he is, or would be, a victim of that act.

(5) Proceedings under subsection (1)(a) must be brought before the end of—

(a) the period of one year beginning with the date on which the act complained of took place; or

(b) such longer period as the court or tribunal considers equitable having regard to all the circumstances,

but that is subject to any rule imposing a stricter time limit in relation to the procedure in question.

(6) In subsection (1)(b) 'legal proceedings' includes—

(a) proceedings brought by or at the instigation of a public authority; and

(b) an appeal against the decision of a court or tribunal.

(7) For the purposes of this section, a person is a victim of an unlawful act only if he would be a victim for the purposes of Article 34 of the Convention if proceedings were brought in the European Court of Human Rights in respect of that act.

(8) Nothing in this Act creates a criminal offence.

(9) In this section 'rules' means—

(a) in relation to proceedings before a court or tribunal outside Scotland, rules made by the Secretary of State for the purposes of this section or rules of court,

(b) in relation to proceedings before a court or tribunal in Scotland, rules made by the Secretary of State for those purposes,
(c) in relation to proceedings before a tribunal in Northern Ireland—
(i) which deals with transferred matters; and
(ii) for which no rules made under paragraph (a) are in force,
rules made by a Northern Ireland department for those purposes,
and includes provision made by order under section 1 of the Courts and Legal Services Act 1990.

(10) In making rules, regard must be had to section 9.

(11) The Minister who has power to make rules in relation to a particular tribunal may, to the extent he considers it necessary to ensure that the tribunal can provide an appropriate remedy in relation to an act (or proposed act) of a public authority which is (or would be) unlawful as a result of section 6(1), by order add to—
(a) the relief or remedies which the tribunal may grant; or
(b) the grounds on which it may grant any of them.

(12) An order made under subsection (11) may contain such incidental, supplemental, consequential or transitional provision as the Minister making it considers appropriate.

(13) 'The Minister' includes the Northern Ireland department concerned.

8. Judicial Remedies

(1) In relation to any act (or proposed act) of a public authority which the court finds is (or would be) unlawful, it may grant such relief or remedy, or make such order, within its powers as it considers just and appropriate.

(2) But damages may be awarded only by a court which has power to award damages, or to order the payment of compensation, in civil proceedings.

(3) No award of damages is to be made unless, taking account of all the circumstances of the case, including—
(a) any other relief or remedy granted, or order made, in relation to the act in question (by that or any other court), and
(b) the consequences of any decision (of that or any other court) in respect of that act,
the court is satisfied that the award is necessary to afford just satisfaction to the person in whose favour it is made.

(4) In determining—
(a) whether to award damages, or
(b) the amount of an award,
the court must take into account the principles applied by the European Court of Human Rights in relation to the award of compensation under Article 41 of the Convention.

(5) A public authority against which damages are awarded is to be treated—
(a) in Scotland, for the purposes of section 3 of the Law Reform (Miscellaneous Provisions) (Scotland) Act 1940 as if the award were made in an action of damages in which the authority has been found liable in respect of loss or damage to the person to whom the award is made;
(b) for the purposes of the Civil Liability (Contribution) Act 1978 as liable in respect of damage suffered by the person to whom the award is made.

(6) In this section—
'court' includes a tribunal;
'damages' means damages for an unlawful act of a public authority; and
'unlawful' means unlawful under section 6(1).

9. Judicial Acts

(1) Proceedings under section 7(1)(a) in respect of a judicial act may be brought only—
(a) by exercising a right of appeal;
(b) on an application (in Scotland a petition) for judicial review; or
(c) in such other forum as may be prescribed by rules.

(2) That does not affect any rule of law which prevents a court from being the subject of judicial review.

(3) In proceedings under this Act in respect of a judicial act done in good faith, damages may not be awarded otherwise than to compensate a person to the extent required by Article 5(5) of the Convention.
(4) An award of damages permitted by subsection (3) is to be made against the Crown; but no award may be made unless the appropriate person, if not a party to the proceedings, is joined.
(5) In this section—
'appropriate person' means the Minister responsible for the court concerned, or a person or government department nominated by him;
'court' includes a tribunal;
'judge' includes a member of a tribunal, a justice of the peace and a clerk or other officer entitled to exercise the jurisdiction of a court;
'judicial act' means a judicial act of a court and includes an act done on the instructions, or on behalf, of a judge; and
'rules' has the same meaning as in section 7(9).

Remedial Action

10. Power to Take Remedial Action

(1) This section applies if—
(a) a provision of legislation has been declared under section 4 to be incompatible with a Convention right and, if an appeal lies—
(i) all persons who may appeal have stated in writing that they do not intend to do so;
(ii) the time for bringing an appeal has expired and no appeal has been brought within that time; or
(iii) an appeal brought within that time has been determined or abandoned; or
(b) it appears to a Minister of the Crown or Her Majesty in Council that, having regard to a finding of the European Court of Human Rights made after the coming into force of this section in proceedings against the United Kingdom, a provision of legislation is incompatible with an obligation of the United Kingdom arising from the Convention.
(2) If a Minister of the Crown considers that there are compelling reasons for proceeding under this section, he may by order make such amendments to the legislation as he considers necessary to remove the incompatibility.
(3) If, in the case of subordinate legislation, a Minister of the Crown considers—
(a) that it is necessary to amend the primary legislation under which the subordinate legislation in question was made, in order to enable the incompatibility to be removed, and
(b) that there are compelling reasons for proceeding under this section,
he may by order make such amendments to the primary legislation as he considers necessary.
(4) This section also applies where the provision in question is in subordinate legislation and has been quashed, or declared invalid, by reason of incompatibility with a Convention right and the Minister proposes to proceed under paragraph 2(b) of Schedule 2.
(5) If the legislation is an Order in Council, the power conferred by subsection (2) or (3) is exercisable by Her Majesty in Council.
(6) In this section 'legislation' does not include a Measure of the Church Assembly or of the General Synod of the Church of England.
(7) Schedule 2 makes further provision about remedial orders.

Other Rights and Proceedings

11. Safeguard for Existing Human Rights

A person's reliance on a Convention right does not restrict—
(a) any other right or freedom conferred on him by or under any law having effect in any part of the United Kingdom; or
(b) his right to make any claim or bring any proceedings which he could make or bring apart from sections 7 to 9.

12. Freedom of Expression

(1) This section applies if a court is considering whether to grant any relief which, if granted, might affect the exercise of the Convention right to freedom of expression.

(2) If the person against whom the application for relief is made ('the respondent') is neither present nor represented, no such relief is to be granted unless the court is satisfied—
  (a) that the applicant has taken all practicable steps to notify the respondent; or
  (b) that there are compelling reasons why the respondent should not be notified.

(3) No such relief is to be granted so as to restrain publication before trial unless the court is satisfied that the applicant is likely to establish that publication should not be allowed.

(4) The court must have particular regard to the importance of the Convention right to freedom of expression and, where the proceedings relate to material which the respondent claims, or which appears to the court, to be journalistic, literary or artistic material (or to conduct connected with such material), to—
  (a) the extent to which—
    (i) the material has, or is about to, become available to the public; or
    (ii) it is, or would be, in the public interest for the material to be published;
  (b) any relevant privacy code.

(5) In this section—
'court' includes a tribunal; and
'relief' includes any remedy or order (other than in criminal proceedings).

13. Freedom of Thought, Conscience and Religion

(1) If a court's determination of any question arising under this Act might affect the exercise by a religious organisation (itself or its members collectively) of the Convention right to freedom of thought, conscience and religion, it must have particular regard to the importance of that right.

(2) In this section 'court' includes a tribunal.

Derogations and Reservations

14. Derogations

(1) In this Act 'designated derogation' means any derogation by the United Kingdom from an Article of the Convention, or of any protocol to the Convention, which is designated for the purposes of this Act in an order made by the Secretary of State.

(3) If a designated derogation is amended or replaced it ceases to be a designated derogation.

(4) But subsection (3) does not prevent the Secretary of State from exercising his power under subsection (1) to make a fresh designation order in respect of the Article concerned.

(5) The Secretary of State must by order make such amendments to Schedule 3 as he considers appropriate to reflect—
  (a) any designation order; or
  (b) the effect of subsection (3).

(6) A designation order may be made in anticipation of the making by the United Kingdom of a proposed derogation.

15. Reservations

(1) In this Act 'designated reservation' means—
  (a) the United Kingdom's reservation to Article 2 of the First Protocol to the Convention; and
  (b) any other reservation by the United Kingdom to an Article of the Convention, or of any protocol to the Convention, which is designated for the purposes of this Act in an order made by the Secretary of State.

(2) The text of the reservation referred to in subsection (1)(a) is set out in Part II of Schedule 3.

(3) If a designated reservation is withdrawn wholly or in part it ceases to be a designated reservation.

(4) But subsection (3) does not prevent the Secretary of State from exercising his power under subsection (1)(b) to make a fresh designation order in respect of the Article concerned.

(5) The Secretary of State must by order make such amendments to this Act as he considers appropriate to reflect—

(a) any designation order; or
(b) the effect of subsection (3).

16. Period for Which Designated Derogations Have Effect

(1) If it has not already been withdrawn by the United Kingdom, a designated derogation ceases to have effect for the purposes of this Act at the end of the period of five years beginning with the date on which the order designating it was made.

(2) At any time before the period—
(a) fixed by subsection (1), or
(b) extended by an order under this subsection,
comes to an end, the Secretary of State may by order extend it by a further period of five years.

(3) An order under section 14(1) ceases to have effect at the end of the period for consideration, unless a resolution has been passed by each House approving the order.

(4) Subsection (3) does not affect—
(a) anything done in reliance on the order; or
(b) the power to make a fresh order under section 14(1).

(5) In subsection (3) 'period for consideration' means the period of forty days beginning with the day on which the order was made.

(6) In calculating the period for consideration, no account is to be taken of any time during which—
(a) Parliament is dissolved or prorogued; or
(b) both Houses are adjourned for more than four days.

(7) If a designated derogation is withdrawn by the United Kingdom, the Secretary of State must by order make such amendments to this Act as he considers are required to reflect that withdrawal.

17. Periodic Review of Designated Reservations

(1) The appropriate Minister must review the designated reservation referred to in section 15(1)(a)—
(a) before the end of the period of five years beginning with the date on which section 1(2) came into force; and
(b) if that designation is still in force, before the end of the period of five years beginning with the date on which the last report relating to it was laid under subsection (3).

(2) The appropriate Minister must review each of the other designated reservations (if any)—
(a) before the end of the period of five years beginning with the date on which the order designating the reservation first came into force; and
(b) if the designation is still in force, before the end of the period of five years beginning with the date on which the last report relating to it was laid under subsection (3).

(3) The Minister conducting a review under this section must prepare a report on the result of the review and lay a copy of it before each House of Parliament.

Parliamentary Procedure

19. Statements of Compatibility

(1) A Minister of the Crown in charge of a Bill in either House of Parliament must, before Second Reading of the Bill—
(a) make a statement to the effect that in his view the provisions of the Bill are compatible with the Convention rights ('a statement of compatibility'); or
(b) make a statement to the effect that although he is unable to make a statement of compatibility the government nevertheless wishes the House to proceed with the Bill.

(2) The statement must be in writing and be published in such manner as the Minister making it considers appropriate.

Supplemental

20. Orders etc. Under This Act

(1) Any power of a Minister of the Crown to make an order under this Act is exercisable by statutory instrument.

(2) The power of the Secretary of State to make rules (other than rules of court) under section 2(3) or 7(9) is exercisable by statutory instrument.
(3) Any statutory instrument made under section 14, 15 or 16(7) must be laid before Parliament.
(4) No order may be made by the Secretary of State under section 1(4), 7(11) or 16(2) unless a draft of the order has been laid before, and approved by, each House of Parliament.
(5) Any statutory instrument made under section 18(7) or Schedule 4, or to which subsection (2) applies, shall be subject to annulment in pursuance of a resolution of either House of Parliament.
(6) The power of a Northern Ireland department to make—
(a) rules under section 2(3)(c) or 7(9)(c), or
(b) an order under section 7(11),
is exercisable by statutory rule for the purposes of the Statutory Rules (Northern Ireland) Order 1979.
(7) Any rules made under section 2(3)(c) or 7(9)(c) shall be subject to negative resolution; and section 41(6) of the Interpretation Act (Northern Ireland) 1954 (meaning of 'subject to negative resolution') shall apply as if the power to make the rules were conferred by an Act of the Northern Ireland Assembly.
(8) No order may be made by a Northern Ireland department under section 7(11) unless a draft of the order has been laid before, and approved by, the Northern Ireland Assembly.

21. Interpretation etc.

(1) In this Act—
'amend' includes repeal and apply (with or without modifications);
'the appropriate Minister' means the Minister of the Crown having charge of the appropriate authorised government department (within the meaning of the Crown Proceedings Act 1947);
'the Commission' means the European Commission of Human Rights;
'the Convention' means the Convention for the Protection of Human Rights and Fundamental Freedoms, agreed by the Council of Europe at Rome on 4th November 1950 as it has effect for the time being in relation to the United Kingdom;
'declaration of incompatibility' means a declaration under section 4;
'Minister of the Crown' has the same meaning as in the Ministers of the Crown Act 1975;
'Northern Ireland Minister' includes the First Minister and the deputy First Minister in Northern Ireland;
'primary legislation' means any—
(a) public general Act;
(b) local and personal Act;
(c) private Act;
(d) Measure of the Church Assembly;
(e) Measure of the General Synod of the Church of England;
(f) Order in Council—
(i) made in exercise of Her Majesty's Royal Prerogative;
(ii) made under section 38(1)(a) of the Northern Ireland Constitution Act 1973 or the corresponding provision of the Northern Ireland Act 1998; or
(iii) amending an Act of a kind mentioned in paragraph (a), (b) or (c);
and includes an order or other instrument made under primary legislation (otherwise than by the National Assembly for Wales, a member of the Scottish Executive, a Northern Ireland Minister or a Northern Ireland department) to the extent to which it operates to bring one or more provisions of that legislation into force or amends any primary legislation;
'the First Protocol' means the protocol to the Convention agreed at Paris on 20th March 1952;
'the Eleventh Protocol' means the protocol to the Convention (restructuring the control machinery established by the Convention) agreed at Strasbourg on 11th May 1994;
'the Thirteenth Protocol' means the protocol to the Convention (concerning the abolition of the death penalty in all circumstances) agreed at Vilnius on 3rd May 2002;

'remedial order' means an order under section 10;
'subordinate legislation' means any—
(a) Order in Council other than one—
(i) made in exercise of Her Majesty's Royal Prerogative;
(ii) made under section 38(1)(a) of the Northern Ireland Constitution Act 1973 or the corresponding provision of the Northern Ireland Act 1998; or
(iii) amending an Act of a kind mentioned in the definition of primary legislation;
(b) Act of the Scottish Parliament;
(c) Act of the Parliament of Northern Ireland;
(d) Measure of the Assembly established under section 1 of the Northern Ireland Assembly Act 1973;
(e) Act of the Northern Ireland Assembly;
(f) order, rules, regulations, scheme, warrant, byelaw or other instrument made under primary legislation (except to the extent to which it operates to bring one or more provisions of that legislation into force or amends any primary legislation);
(g) order, rules, regulations, scheme, warrant, byelaw or other instrument made under legislation mentioned in paragraph (b), (c), (d) or (e) or made under an Order in Council applying only to Northern Ireland;
(h) order, rules, regulations, scheme, warrant, byelaw or other instrument made by a member of the Scottish Executive, a Northern Ireland Minister or a Northern Ireland department in exercise of prerogative or other executive functions of Her Majesty which are exercisable by such a person on behalf of Her Majesty;

'transferred matters' has the same meaning as in the Northern Ireland Act 1998; and
'tribunal' means any tribunal in which legal proceedings may be brought.

(2) The references in paragraphs (b) and (c) of section 2(1) to Articles are to Articles of the Convention as they had effect immediately before the coming into force of the Eleventh Protocol.
(3) The reference in paragraph (d) of section 2(1) to Article 46 includes a reference to Articles 32 and 54 of the Convention as they had effect immediately before the coming into force of the Eleventh Protocol.
(4) The references in section 2(1) to a report or decision of the Commission or a decision of the Committee of Ministers include references to a report or decision made as provided by paragraphs 3,4 and 6 of Article 5 of the Eleventh Protocol (transitional provisions).
(5) Any liability under the Army Act 1955, the Air Force Act 1955 or the Naval Discipline Act 1957 to suffer death for an offence is replaced by a liability to imprisonment for life or any less punishment authorised by those Acts; and those Acts shall accordingly have effect with the necessary modifications.

22. Short Title, Commencement, Application and Extent

(1) This Act may be cited as the Human Rights Act 1998.
(2) Sections 18, 20 and 21(5) and this section come into force on the passing of this Act.
(3) The other provisions of this Act come into force on such day as the Secretary of State may by order appoint; and different days may be appointed for different purposes.
(4) Paragraph (b) of subsection (1) of section 7 applies to proceedings brought by or at the instigation of a public authority whenever the act in question took place; but otherwise that subsection does not apply to an act taking place before the coming into force of that section.
(5) This Act binds the Crown.
(6) This Act extends to Northern Ireland.
(7) Section 21(5), so far as it relates to any provision contained in the Army Act 1955, the Air Force Act 1955 or the Naval Discipline Act 1957, extends to any place to which that provision extends.

[*Section 19 was brought into force on 24 November 1998 by the Human Rights Act 1998 (Commencement) Order 1998 (SI 1998/2882). All remaining provisions were brought into force on 2 October 2000 by the Human Rights Act 1998 (Commencement No. 2) Order 2000 (SI 2000/1851).*]

Section 1(3)

SCHEDULE 1 THE ARTICLES

PART I THE CONVENTION

Rights and Freedoms

Article 2 Right to life

1. Everyone's right to life shall be protected by law. No one shall be deprived of his life intentionally save in the execution of a sentence of a court following his conviction of a crime for which this penalty is provided by law.
2. Deprivation of life shall not be regarded as inflicted in contravention of this Article when it results from the use of force which is no more than absolutely necessary:
   (a) in defence of any person from unlawful violence;
   (b) in order to effect a lawful arrest or to prevent the escape of a person lawfully detained;
   (c) in action lawfully taken for the purpose of quelling a riot or insurrection.

Article 3 Prohibition of torture

No one shall be subjected to torture or to inhuman or degrading treatment or punishment.

Article 4 Prohibition of slavery and forced labour

1. No one shall be held in slavery or servitude.
2. No one shall be required to perform forced or compulsory labour.
3. For the purpose of this Article the term 'forced or compulsory labour' shall not include:
   (a) any work required to be done in the ordinary course of detention imposed according to the provisions of Article 5 of this Convention or during conditional release from such detention;
   (b) any service of a military character or, in case of conscientious objectors in countries where they are recognised, service exacted instead of compulsory military service;
   (c) any service exacted in case of an emergency or calamity threatening the life or well-being of the community;
   (d) any work or service which forms part of normal civic obligations.

Article 5 Right to liberty and security

1. Everyone has the right to liberty and security of person. No one shall be deprived of his liberty save in the following cases and in accordance with a procedure prescribed by law:
   (a) the lawful detention of a person after conviction by a competent court;
   (b) the lawful arrest or detention of a person for non-compliance with the lawful order of a court or in order to secure the fulfilment of any obligation prescribed by law;
   (c) the lawful arrest or detention of a person effected for the purpose of bringing him before the competent legal authority on reasonable suspicion of having committed an offence or when it is reasonably considered necessary to prevent his committing an offence or fleeing after having done so;
   (d) the detention of a minor by lawful order for the purpose of educational supervision or his lawful detention for the purpose of bringing him before the competent legal authority;
   (e) the lawful detention of persons for the prevention of the spreading of infectious diseases, of persons of unsound mind, alcoholics or drug addicts or vagrants;
   (f) the lawful arrest or detention of a person to prevent his effecting an unauthorised entry into the country or of a person against whom action is being taken with a view to deportation or extradition.
2. Everyone who is arrested shall be informed promptly, in a language which he understands, of the reasons for his arrest and of any charge against him.
3. Everyone arrested or detained in accordance with the provisions of paragraph 1(c) of this Article shall be brought promptly before a judge or other officer authorised by law to exercise judicial power and shall be entitled to trial within a reasonable time or to release pending trial. Release may be conditioned by guarantees to appear for trial.
4. Everyone who is deprived of his liberty by arrest or detention shall be entitled to take proceed-

ings by which the lawfulness of his detention shall be decided speedily by a court and his release ordered if the detention is not lawful.

5. Everyone who has been the victim of arrest or detention in contravention of the provisions of this Article shall have an enforceable right to compensation.

Article 6 Right to a fair trial

1. In the determination of his civil rights and obligations or of any criminal charge against him, everyone is entitled to a fair and public hearing within a reasonable time by an independent and impartial tribunal established by law. Judgment shall be pronounced publicly but the press and public may be excluded from all or part of the trial in the interest of morals, public order or national security in a democratic society, where the interests of juveniles or the protection of the private life of the parties so require, or to the extent strictly necessary in the opinion of the court in special circumstances where publicity would prejudice the interests of justice.
2. Everyone charged with a criminal offence shall be presumed innocent until proved guilty according to law.
3. Everyone charged with a criminal offence has the following minimum rights:
   (a) to be informed promptly, in a language which he understands and in detail, of the nature and cause of the accusation against him;
   (b) to have adequate time and facilities for the preparation of his defence;
   (c) to defend himself in person or through legal assistance of his own choosing or, if he has not sufficient means to pay for legal assistance, to be given it free when the interests of justice so require;
   (d) to examine or have examined witnesses against him and to obtain the attendance and examination of witnesses on his behalf under the same conditions as witnesses against him;
   (e) to have the free assistance of an interpreter if he cannot understand or speak the language used in court.

Article 7 No punishment without law

1. No one shall be held guilty of any criminal offence on account of any act or omission which did not constitute a criminal offence under national or international law at the time when it was committed. Nor shall a heavier penalty be imposed than the one that was applicable at the time the criminal offence was committed.
2. This Article shall not prejudice the trial and punishment of any person for any act or omission which, at the time when it was committed, was criminal according to the general principles of law recognised by civilised nations.

Article 8 Right to respect for private and family life

1. Everyone has the right to respect for his private and family life, his home and his correspondence.
2. There shall be no interference by a public authority with the exercise of this right except such as is in accordance with the law and is necessary in a democratic society in the interests of national security, public safety or the economic well being of the country, for the prevention of disorder or crime, for the protection of health or morals, or for the protection of the rights and freedoms of others.

Article 9 Freedom of thought, conscience and religion

1. Everyone has the right to freedom of thought, conscience and religion; this right includes freedom to change his religion or belief and freedom, either alone or in community with others and in public or private, to manifest his religion or belief, in worship, teaching, practice and observance.
2. Freedom to manifest one's religion or beliefs shall be subject only to such limitations as are prescribed by law and are necessary in a democratic society in the interests of public safety, for the protection of public order, health or morals, or for the protection of the rights and freedoms of others.

Article 10 Freedom of expression

1. Everyone has the right to freedom of expression. This right shall include freedom to hold opinions and to receive and impart information and ideas without interference by public authority and regardless of frontiers. This Article shall not prevent States from requiring the licensing of broadcasting, television or cinema enterprises.
2. The exercise of these freedoms, since it carries with it duties and responsibilities, may be subject to such formalities, conditions, restrictions or penalties as are prescribed by law and are necessary in a democratic society, in the interests of national security, territorial integrity or public safety, for the prevention of disorder or crime, for the protection of health or morals, for the protection of the reputation or rights of others, for preventing the disclosure of information received in confidence, or for maintaining the authority and impartiality of the judiciary.

Article 11 Freedom of assembly and association

1. Everyone has the right to freedom of peaceful assembly and to freedom of association with others, including the right to form and to join trade unions for the protection of his interests.
2. No restrictions shall be placed on the exercise of these rights other than such as are prescribed by law and are necessary in a democratic society in the interests of national security or public safety, for the prevention of disorder or crime, for the protection of health or morals or for the protection of the rights and freedoms of others. This Article shall not prevent the imposition of lawful restrictions on the exercise of these rights by members of the armed forces, of the police or of the administration of the State.

Article 12 Right to marry

Men and women of marriageable age have the right to marry and to found a family, according to the national laws governing the exercise of this right.

Article 14 Prohibition of discrimination

The enjoyment of the rights and freedoms set forth in this Convention shall be secured without discrimination on any ground such as sex, race, colour, language, religion, political or other opinion, national or social origin, association with a national minority, property, birth or other status.

Article 16 Restrictions on political activity of aliens

Nothing in Articles 10, 11 and 14 shall be regarded as preventing the High Contracting Parties from imposing restrictions on the political activity of aliens.

Article 17 Prohibition of abuse of rights

Nothing in this Convention may be interpreted as implying for any State, group or person any right to engage in any activity or perform any act aimed at the destruction of any of the rights and freedoms set forth herein or at their limitation to a greater extent than is provided for in the Convention.

Article 18 Limitation on use of restrictions on rights

The restrictions permitted under this Convention to the said rights and freedoms shall not be applied for any purpose other than those for which they have been prescribed.

PART II THE FIRST PROTOCOL

Article 1 Protection of property

Every natural or legal person is entitled to the peaceful enjoyment of his possessions. No one shall be deprived of his possessions except in the public interest and subject to the conditions provided for by law and by the general principles of international law.

The preceding provisions shall not, however, in any way impair the right of a State to enforce such laws as it deems necessary to control the use of property in accordance with the general interest or to secure the payment of taxes or other contributions or penalties.

Article 2 Right to education

No person shall be denied the right to education. In the exercise of any functions which it assumes in relation to education and to teaching, the State shall respect the right of parents to ensure such education and teaching in conformity with their own religious and philosophical convictions.

Article 3 Right to free elections

The High Contracting Parties undertake to hold free elections at reasonable intervals by secret ballot, under conditions which will ensure the free expression of the opinion of the people in the choice of the legislature.

PART III ARTICLE 1 OF THE THIRTEENTH PROTOCOL

Abolition of the death penalty

The death penalty shall be abolished. No one shall be condemned to such penalty or executed.

SCHEDULE 2 REMEDIAL ORDERS

Orders

1.—(1) A remedial order may—

(a) contain such incidental, supplemental, consequential or transitional provision as the person making it considers appropriate;

(b) be made so as to have effect from a date earlier than that on which it is made;

(c) make provision for the delegation of specific functions;

(d) make different provision for different cases.

(2) The power conferred by sub-paragraph (1)(a) includes—

(a) power to amend primary legislation (including primary legislation other than that which contains the incompatible provision); and

(b) power to amend or revoke subordinate legislation (including subordinate legislation other than that which contains the incompatible provision).

(3) A remedial order may be made so as to have the same extent as the legislation which it affects.

(4) No person is to be guilty of an offence solely as a result of the retrospective effect of a remedial order.

Procedure

2. No remedial order may be made unless—

(a) a draft of the order has been approved by a resolution of each House of Parliament made after the end of the period of 60 days beginning with the day on which the draft was laid; or

(b) it is declared in the order that it appears to the person making it that, because of the urgency of the matter, it is necessary to make the order without a draft being so approved.

Orders Laid in Draft

3.—(1) No draft may be laid under paragraph 2(a) unless—

(a) the person proposing to make the order has laid before Parliament a document which contains a draft of the proposed order and the required information; and

(b) the period of 60 days, beginning with the day on which the document required by this sub-paragraph was laid, has ended.

(2) If representations have been made during that period, the draft laid under paragraph 2(a) must be accompanied by a statement containing—

(a) a summary of the representations; and

(b) if, as a result of the representations, the proposed order has been changed, details of the changes.

Urgent Cases

4.—(1) If a remedial order ('the original order') is made without being approved in draft, the person making it must lay it before Parliament, accompanied by the required information, after it is made.

(2) If representations have been made during the period of 60 days beginning with the day on which the original order was made, the person making it must (after the end of that period) lay before Parliament a statement containing—

(a) a summary of the representations; and

(b) if, as a result of the representations, he considers it appropriate to make changes to the original order, details of the changes.

(3) If sub-paragraph (2)(b) applies, the person making the statement must—

(a) make a further remedial order replacing the original order; and

(b) lay the replacement order before Parliament.

(4) If, at the end of the period of 120 days beginning with the day on which the original order was made, a resolution has not been passed by each House approving the original or replacement order, the order ceases to have effect (but without that affecting anything previously done under either order or the power to make a fresh remedial order).

Definitions

5. In this Schedule—

'representations' means representations about a remedial order (or proposed remedial order) made to the person making (or proposing to make) it and includes any relevant Parliamentary report or resolution; and

'required information' means

(a) an explanation of the incompatibility which the order (or proposed order) seeks to remove, including particulars of the relevant declaration, finding or order; and

(b) a statement of the reasons for proceeding under section 10 and for making an order in those terms.

Calculating Periods

6. In calculating any period for the purposes of this Schedule, no account is to be taken of any time during which—

(a) Parliament is dissolved or prorogued; or

(b) both Houses are adjourned for more than four days.

7.—(1) This paragraph applies in relation to—

(a) any remedial order made, and any draft of such an order proposed to be made,—

(i) by the Scottish Ministers; or

(ii) within devolved competence (within the meaning of the Scotland Act 1998) by Her Majesty in Council; and

(b) any document or statement to be laid in connection with such an order (or proposed order).

(2) This Schedule has effect in relation to any such order (or proposed order), document or statement subject to the following modifications.

(3) Any reference to Parliament, each House of Parliament or both Houses of Parliament shall be construed as a reference to the Scottish Parliament.

(4) Paragraph 6 does not apply and instead, in calculating any period for the purposes of this Schedule, no account is to be taken of any time during which the Scottish Parliament is dissolved or is in recess for more than four days.

SCHEDULE 3 DEROGATION AND RESERVATION

PART II RESERVATION

At the time of signing the present (First) Protocol, I declare that, in view of certain provisions of the Education Acts in the United Kingdom, the principle affirmed in the second sentence of Article 2 is accepted by the United Kingdom only so far as it is compatible with the provision of efficient instruction and training, and the avoidance of unreasonable public expenditure.

Dated 20 March 1952. Made by the United Kingdom Permanent Representative to the Council of Europe.

NOTES ON TEXT

The text printed above incorporates the following amendments:

s. 1 amended by: (a) Transfer of Functions (Miscellaneous) Order 2001 (SI 2001/3500), sch. 2, para. 7; (b) Secretary of State for Constitutional Affairs Order 2003 (SI 2003/1887), sch. 2, para. 10(1); (c) Human Rights Act 1998 (Amendment) Order 2004 (SI 2004/1574), art. 2(1);

s. 2 amended by Secretary of State for Constitutional Affairs Order 2003 (SI 2003/1887), sch. 2, para. 10(2);

s. 7 amended by Secretary of State for Constitutional Affairs Order 2003 (SI 2003/1887), sch. 2, para. 10(2);

s. 14 amended by: (a) Human Rights Act (Amendment) Order 2001 (SI 2001/1216), art. 2; (b) Transfer of Functions (Miscellaneous) Order 2001 (SI 2001/3500), sch. 2, para. 7; (c) Secretary of State for Constitutional Affairs Order 2003 (SI 2003/1887), sch. 2, para. 10(1);

s. 15 amended by Transfer of Functions (Miscellaneous) Order 2001 (SI 2001/3500), sch. 2, para. 7; (c) Secretary of State for Constitutional Affairs Order 2003 (SI 2003/1887), sch. 2, para. 10(1);

s. 16 amended by: (a) Human Rights Act (Amendment) Order 2001 (SI 2001/1216), art. 3; (b) Transfer of Functions (Miscellaneous) Order 2001 (SI 2001/3500), sch. 2, para. 7; (c) Secretary of State for Constitutional Affairs Order 2003 (SI 2003/1887), sch. 2, para. 10(1);

s. 20 amended by Secretary of State for Constitutional Affairs Order 2003 (SI 2003/1887), sch. 2, para. 10(2);

s. 21 amended by Human Rights Act 1998 (Amendment) Order 2004 (SI 2004/1574), art. 2(2);

sch. 2, para. 7, inserted by Scotland Act 1998 (Consequential Modifications) Order 2000 (SI 2000/2040), sch., para. 21;

sch. 3, part I, repealed by Human Rights Act (Amendment) Order 2001 (SI 2001/1216), art. 4; new part I inserted by Human Rights Act 1998 (Amendment No. 2) Order 2001 (SI 2001/4032); repealed by Human Rights Act 1998 (Amendment) Order 2005 (SI 2005/1071);

sch. 3, part III, substituted by Human Rights Act 1998 (Amendment) Order 2004 (SI 2004/1574), art. 2(3).

The following provisions are omitted:

s. 18 (appointment of judges to the European Court of Human Rights); sch. 4 (judicial pensions).

Interpretation Act 1978

(1978 CHAPTER 30)

An Act to consolidate the Interpretation Act 1889 and certain other enactments relating to the construction and operation of Acts of Parliament and other instruments, with amendments to give effect to recommendations of the Law Commission and the Scottish Law Commission.

[20th July 1978]

Interpretation and Construction

7. References to Service by Post

Where an Act authorises or requires any document to be served by post (whether the expression 'serve' or the expression 'give' or 'send' or any other expression is used) then, unless the contrary intention appears, the service is deemed to be effected by properly addressing, pre-paying and posting a letter containing the document and, unless the contrary is proved, to have been effected at the time at which the letter would be delivered in the ordinary course of post.

Supplementary

21. Interpretation etc.

(1) In this Act 'Act' includes a local and personal or private Act; and 'subordinate legislation' means Orders in Council, orders, rules, regulations, schemes, warrants, byelaws and other instruments made or to be made under any Act.

(2) This Act binds the Crown.

22. Application to Acts and Measures

(1) This Act applies to itself, to any Act passed after the commencement of this Act and, to the extent specified in Part I of Schedule 2, to Acts passed before the commencement of this Act. . . .

23. Application to other instruments

(1) The provisions of this Act, except sections 1 to 3 and 4(b), apply, so far as applicable and unless the contrary intention appears, to subordinate legislation made after the commencement of this Act and, to the extent specified in Part II of Schedule 2, to subordinate legislation made before the commencement of this Act, as they apply to Acts. . . .

26. Commencement

This Act shall come into force on 1st January 1979.

27. Short Title

This Act may be cited as the Interpretation Act 1978.

SCHEDULE 2 APPLICATION OF ACT TO EXISTING ENACTMENTS

PART 1 ACTS

3. The following apply to Acts passed after the year 1889:—
. . . Section 7. . . .

Judgments Act 1838

(1 & 2 VICT. CHAPTER 110)

An Act for extending the remedies of creditors against the property of debtors.

[16 August 1838]

17. Judgment Debts to Carry Interest

(1) Every judgment debt shall carry interest at the rate of 8 per cent per annum from such time as shall be prescribed by rules of court, until the same shall be satisfied, and such interest may be levied under a writ of execution on such judgment.

(2) Rules of court may provide for the court to disallow all or part of any interest otherwise payable under subsection (1).

18. Decrees and Orders of Courts of Equity, etc. to Have Effect of Judgments

All decrees and orders of courts of equity, and all rules of courts of common law, whereby any sum of money, or any costs, charges, or expenses, shall be payable to any person, shall have the effect of judgments in the superior courts of common law, and the persons to whom any such moneys, or costs, charges, or expenses, shall be payable, shall be deemed judgment creditors within the meaning of this Act; and all powers hereby given to the judges of the superior courts of common law with respect to matters depending in the same courts shall and may be exercised by courts of equity with respect to matters therein depending; and all remedies hereby given to judgment creditors are in like manner given to persons to whom any moneys, or costs, charges, or expenses, are by such orders or rules respectively directed to be paid.

NOTES ON TEXT

Only ss. 17 and 18 are printed above. Spelling and capitalisation have been modernised. The text incorporates the following amendments:

short title given by Short Titles Act 1896;

long title amended by Statute Law Revision (No. 2) Act 1888, sch.;

s. 17 amended by: (a) Civil Procedure Acts Repeal Act 1879, sch.; (b) Statute Law Revision (No. 2) Act 1888, sch.; (c) Judgment Debts (Rate of Interest) Order 1993 (SI 1993/564); Civil Procedure (Modification of Enactments) Order 1998 (SI 1998/2940), art. 3;

s. 18 amended by: (a) Bankruptcy Repeal and Insolvent Court Act 1869, sch.; (b) Statute Law Revision (No. 2) Act 1888, sch.; (c) Mental Health Act 1959, sch. 8, part I (in force by SI 1960/1698).

Law Reform (Contributory Negligence) Act 1945

(8 & 9 GEO. 6 CHAPTER 28)

1. Apportionment of Liability in Case of Contributory Negligence

(1) Where any person suffers damage as the result partly of his own fault and partly of the fault of any other person or persons, a claim in respect of that damage shall not be defeated by reason of the fault of the person suffering the damage, but the damages recoverable in respect thereof shall be reduced to such extent as the court thinks just and equitable having regard to the claimant's share in the responsibility of the damage: Provided that—

(a) this subsection shall not operate to defeat any defence arising under a contract;

(b) where any contract or enactment providing for the limitation of liability is applicable to the claim, the amount of damages recoverable by the claimant by virtue of this subsection shall not exceed the maximum limit so applicable.

(2) Where damages are recoverable by any person by virtue of the foregoing subsection subject to such reduction as is therein mentioned, the court shall find and record the total damages which would have been recoverable if the claimant had not been at fault.

(5) Where, in any case to which subsection (1) of this section applies, one of the persons at fault avoids liability to any other such person or his personal representative by pleading the Limitation Act 1939, or any other enactment limiting the time within which proceedings may be taken, he shall not be entitled to recover any damages from that other person or representative by virtue of the said subsection.

(6) Where any case to which subsection (1) of this section applies is tried with a jury, the jury shall determine the total damages which would have been recoverable if the claimant had not been at fault and the extent to which those damages are to be reduced.

4. Interpretation

The following expressions have the meanings hereby respectively assigned to them, that is to say—

'court' means, in relation to any claim, the court or arbitrator by or before whom the claim falls to be determined;

'damage' includes loss of life and personal injury;

'fault' means negligence, breach of statutory duty or other act or omission which gives rise to liability in tort or would, apart from this Act, give rise to the defence of contributory negligence.

Law Reform (Frustrated Contracts) Act 1943

(6 & 7 GEO. 6 CHAPTER 40)

1. Adjustment of Rights and Liabilities of Parties to Frustrated Contracts

(1) Where a contract governed by English law has become impossible of performance or been otherwise frustrated, and the parties thereto have for that reason been discharged from the further performance of the contract, the following provisions of this section shall, subject to the provisions of section two of this Act, have effect in relation thereto.

(2) All sums paid or payable to any party in pursuance of the contract before the time when the parties were so discharged (in this Act referred to as 'the time of discharge') shall, in the case of sums so paid, be recoverable from him as money received by him for the use of the party by whom the sums were paid, and, in the case of sums so payable, cease to be so payable:
Provided that, if the party to whom the sums were so paid or payable incurred expenses before the time of discharge in, or for the purpose of, the performance of the contract, the court may, if it considers it just to do so having regard to all the circumstances of the case, allow him to retain or, as the case may be, recover the whole or any part of the sums so paid or payable, not being an amount in excess of the expenses so incurred.

(3) Where any party to the contract has, by reason of anything done by any other party thereto in, or for the purpose of, the performance of the contract, obtained a valuable benefit (other than a payment of money to which the last foregoing subsection applies) before the time of discharge there shall be recoverable from him by the said other party such sum (if any), not exceeding the value of the said benefit to the party obtaining it, as the court considers just, having regard to all the circumstances of the case and, in particular,—
   (a) the amount of any expenses incurred before the time of discharge by the benefited party in, or for the purpose of, the performance of the contract, including any sums paid or payable by him to any other party in pursuance of the contract and retained or recoverable by that party under the last foregoing subsection, and
   (b) the effect, in relation to the said benefit, of the circumstances giving rise to the frustration of the contract.

(4) In estimating, for the purposes of the foregoing provisions of this section, the amount of any expenses incurred by any party to the contract, the court may, without prejudice to the generality of the said provisions, include any sum as appears to be reasonable in respect of overhead expenses and in respect of any work or services performed personally by the said party.

(5) In considering whether any sum ought to be recovered or retained under the foregoing provisions of this section by any party to the contract, the court shall not take into account any sums which have, by reason of the circumstances giving rise to the frustration of the contract, become payable to that party under any contract of insurance unless there was an obligation to insure imposed by an express term of the frustrated contract or by or under any enactment.

(6) Where any person has assumed obligations under the contract in consideration of the conferring of a benefit by any other party to the contract upon any other person, whether a party to the contract or not, the court may, if in all the circumstances of the case it considers it just to do so, treat for the purposes of subsection (3) of this section any benefit so conferred as a benefit obtained by the person who has assumed the obligations as aforesaid.

2. Provision as to Application of This Act

(1) This Act shall apply to contracts, whether made before or after the commencement of this Act, as respects which the time of discharge is on or after the first day of July, nineteen hundred and forty-three, but not to contracts as respects which the time of discharge is before the said date.

(2) This Act shall apply to contracts to which the Crown is a party in like manner as to contracts between subjects.

(3) Where any contract to which this Act applies contains any provision which, upon the true construction of the contract, is intended to have effect in the event of circumstances arising which operate, or would but for the said provision operate, to frustrate the contract, or is

intended to have effect whether such circumstances arise or not, the court shall give effect to the said provision and shall only give effect to the foregoing section of this Act to such extent, if any, as appears to the court to be consistent with the said provision.

(4) Where it appears to the court that a part of any contract to which this Act applies can be properly severed from the remainder of the contract, being a part wholly performed before the time of discharge, or so performed except for the payment in respect of that part of the contract of sums which are or can be ascertained under the contract, the court shall treat that part of the contract as if it were a separate contract and had not been frustrated and shall treat the foregoing section of this Act as only applicable to the remainder of that contract.

(5) This Act shall not apply—
- (a) to any charterparty, except a time charterparty or a charterparty by way of demise, or to any contract (other than a charterparty) for the carriage of goods by sea; or
- (b) to any contract of insurance, save as is provided by subsection (5) of the foregoing section; or
- (c) to any contract to which section 7 of the Sale of Goods Act 1979 (which avoids contracts for the sale of specific goods which perish before the risk has passed to the buyer) applies, or to any other contract for the sale, or for the sale and delivery, of specific goods, where the contract is frustrated by reason of the fact that the goods have perished.

3. Short Title and Interpretation

(1) This Act may be cited as the Law Reform (Frustrated Contracts) Act 1943.

(2) In this Act the expression 'court' means, in relation to any matter, the court or arbitrator by or before whom the matter falls to be determined.

Law Reform (Miscellaneous Provisions) Act 1934

(24 & 25 GEO. 5 CHAPTER 41)

1. Effect of Death on Certain Causes of Action

(1) Subject to the provisions of this section, on the death of any person after the commencement of this Act all causes of action subsisting against or vested in him shall survive against, or, as the case may be, for the benefit of, his estate. Provided that this subsection shall not apply to causes of action for defamation.

(1A) The right of a person to claim under section 1A of the Fatal Accidents Act 1976 (bereavement) shall not survive for the benefit of his estate on his death.

(2) Where a cause of action survives as aforesaid for the benefit of the estate of a deceased person, the damages recoverable for the benefit of the estate of that person:—

(a) shall not include—

(i) any exemplary damages;

(ii) any damages for loss of income in respect of any period after that person's death;

(c) where the death of that person has been caused by the act or omission which gives rise to the cause of action, shall be calculated without reference to any loss or gain to his estate consequent on his death, except that a sum in respect of funeral expenses may be included.

(4) Where damage has been suffered by reason of any act or omission in respect of which a cause of action would have subsisted against any person if that person had not died before or at the same time as the damage was suffered, there shall be deemed, for the purposes of this Act, to have been subsisting against him before his death such cause of action in respect of that act or omission as would have subsisted if he had died after the damage was suffered.

(5) The rights conferred by this Act for the benefit of the estates of deceased persons shall be in addition to and not in derogation of any rights conferred on the dependants of deceased persons by the Fatal Accidents Acts 1846 to 1908* and so much of this Act as relates to causes of action against the estates of deceased persons shall apply in relation to causes of action under the said Act as it applies in relation to other causes of action not expressly excepted from the operation of subsection (1) of this section.

(6) In the event of the insolvency of an estate against which proceedings are maintainable by virtue of this section, any liability in respect of the cause of action in respect of which the proceedings are maintainable shall be deemed to be a debt provable in the administration of the estate, notwithstanding that it is a demand in the nature of unliquidated damages arising otherwise than by a contract, promise or breach of trust.

* [Includes a reference to the Fatal Accidents Act 1976.]

Law Reform (Personal Injuries) Act 1948

(11 & 12 GEO. 6 CHAPTER 41)

1. Common Employment

(1) It shall not be a defence to an employer who is sued in respect of personal injuries caused by the negligence of a person employed by him, that that person was at the time the injuries were caused in common employment with the person injured.

(3) Any provision contained in a contract of service or apprenticeship, or in an agreement collateral thereto, (including a contract or agreement entered into before the commencement of this Act) shall be void in so far as it would have the effect of excluding or limiting any liability of the employer in respect of personal injuries caused to the person employed or apprenticed by the negligence of persons in common employment with him.

2. Measure of Damages

(4) In an action for damages for personal injuries (including any such action arising out of a contract), there shall be disregarded, in determining the reasonableness of any expenses, the possibility of avoiding those expenses or part of them by taking advantage of facilities available under the National Health Service Act 1977, or the National Health Service (Scotland) Act 1978, or of any corresponding facilities in Northern Ireland.

3. Definition of 'Personal Injury'

In this Act the expression 'personal injury' includes any disease and any impairment of a person's physical or mental condition, and the expression 'injured' shall be construed accordingly.

Limitation Act 1980

(1980 CHAPTER 58)

An Act to consolidate the Limitation Acts 1939 to 1980. [13th November 1980]

PART I ORDINARY TIME LIMITS FOR DIFFERENT CLASSES OF ACTION

Time Limits Under Part I Subject to Extension or Exclusion Under Part II

1. Time Limits Under Part I Subject to Extension or Exclusion Under Part II

(1) This Part of this Act gives the ordinary time limits for bringing actions of the various classes mentioned in the following provisions of this Part.

(2) The ordinary time limits given in this Part of this Act are subject to extension or exclusion in accordance with the provisions of Part II of this Act.

Actions Founded on Tort

2. Time Limit For Actions Founded on Tort

An action founded on tort shall not be brought after the expiration of six years from the date on which the cause of action accrued.

3. Time Limit in Case of Successive Conversions and Extinction of Title of Owner of Converted Goods

(1) Where any cause of action in respect of the conversion of a chattel has accrued to any person and, before he recovers possession of the chattel, a further conversion takes place, no action shall be brought in respect of the further conversion after the expiration of six years from the accrual of the cause of action in respect of the original conversion.

(2) Where any such cause of action has accrued to any person and the period prescribed for bringing that action has expired and he has not during that period recovered possession of the chattel, the title of that person to the chattel shall be extinguished.

4. Special Time Limit in Case of Theft

(1) The right of any person from whom a chattel is stolen to bring an action in respect of the theft shall not be subject to the time limits under sections 2 and 3(1) of this Act, but if his title to the chattel is extinguished under section 3(2) of this Act he may not bring an action in respect of a theft preceding the loss of his title, unless the theft in question preceded the conversion from which time began to run for the purposes of section 3(2).

(2) Subsection (1) above shall apply to any conversion related to the theft of a chattel as it applies to the theft of a chattel; and, except as provided below, every conversion following the theft of a chattel before the person from whom it is stolen recovers possession of it shall be regarded for the purposes of this section as related to the theft.

If anyone purchases the stolen chattel in good faith neither the purchase nor any conversion following it shall be regarded as related to the theft.

(3) Any cause of action accruing in respect of the theft or any conversion related to the theft of a chattel to any person from whom the chattel is stolen shall be disregarded for the purpose of applying section 3(1) or (2) of this Act to his case.

(4) Where in any action brought in respect of the conversion of a chattel it is proved that the chattel was stolen from the plaintiff or anyone through whom he claims it shall be presumed that any conversion following the theft is related to the theft unless the contrary is shown.

(5) In this section 'theft' includes—

(a) any conduct outside England and Wales which would be theft if committed in England and Wales; and

(b) obtaining any chattel (in England and Wales or elsewhere) in the circumstances described in section 15(1) of the Theft Act 1968 (obtaining by deception) or by blackmail within the meaning of section 21 of that Act;

and references in this section to a chattel being 'stolen' shall be construed accordingly.

4A. Time Limit for Actions for Defamation or Malicious Falsehood

The time limit under section 2 of this Act shall not apply to an action for—

(a) libel or slander, or

(b) slander of title, slander of goods or other malicious falsehood,

but no such action shall be brought after the expiration of one year from the date on which the cause of action accrued.

Actions Founded on Simple Contract

5. Time Limit for Actions Founded on Simple Contract

An action founded on simple contract shall not be brought after the expiration of six years from the date on which the cause of action accrued.

6. Special Time Limit for Actions in Respect of Certain Loans

(1) Subject to subsection (3) below, section 5 of this Act shall not bar the right of action on a contract of loan to which this section applies.

(2) This section applies to any contract of loan which—

(a) does not provide for repayment of the debt on or before a fixed or determinable date; and

(b) does not effectively (whether or not it purports to do so) make the obligation to repay the debt conditional on a demand for repayment made by or on behalf of the creditor or on any other matter;

except where in connection with taking the loan the debtor enters into any collateral obligation to pay the amount of the debt or any part of it (as, for example, by delivering a promissory note as security for the debt) on terms which would exclude the application of this section to the contract of loan if they applied directly to repayment of the debt.

(3) Where a demand in writing for repayment of the debt under a contract of loan to which this section applies is made by or on behalf of the creditor (or, where there are joint creditors, by or on behalf of any one of them) section 5 of this Act shall thereupon apply as if the cause of action to recover the debt had accrued on the date on which the demand was made.

(4) In this section 'promissory note' has the same meaning as in the Bills of Exchange Act 1882.

7. Time Limit for Actions to Enforce Certain Awards

An action to enforce an award, where the submission is not by an instrument under seal, shall not be brought after the expiration of six years from the date on which the cause of action accrued.

General Rule for Actions on a Specialty

8. Time Limit for Actions on a Specialty

(1) An action upon a specialty shall not be brought after the expiration of twelve years from the date on which the cause of action accrued.

(2) Subsection (1) above shall not affect any action for which a shorter period of limitation is prescribed by any other provision of this Act.

Actions for Sums Recoverable by Statute

9. Time Limit for Actions for Sums Recoverable by Statute

(1) An action to recover any sum recoverable by virtue of any enactment shall not be brought after the expiration of six years from the date on which the cause of action accrued.

(2) Subsection (1) above shall not affect any action to which section 10 of this Act applies.

10. Special Time Limit for Claiming Contribution

(1) Where under section 1 of the Civil Liability (Contribution) Act 1978 any person becomes entitled to a right to recover contribution in respect of any damage from any other person, no action to recover contribution by virtue of that right shall be brought after the expiration of two years from the date on which that right accrued.

(2) For the purposes of this section the date on which a right to recover contribution in respect of any damage accrues to any person (referred to below in this section as 'the relevant date') shall be ascertained as provided in subsections (3) and (4) below.

(3) If the person in question is held liable in respect of that damage—
(a) by a judgment given in any civil proceedings; or
(b) by an award made on any arbitration;
the relevant date shall be the date on which the judgment is given, or the date of the award (as the case may be).

For the purposes of this subsection no account shall be taken of any judgment or award given or made on appeal in so far as it varies the amount of damages awarded against the person in question.

(4) If, in any case not within subsection (3) above, the person in question makes or agrees to make any payment to one or more persons in compensation for that damage (whether he admits any liability in respect of the damage or not), the relevant date shall be the earliest date on which the amount to be paid by him is agreed between him (or his representative) and the person (or each of the persons, as the case may be) to whom the payment is to be made.

(5) An action to recover contribution shall be one to which sections 28, 32 and 35 of this Act apply, but otherwise Parts II and III of this Act (except sections 34, 37 and 38) shall not apply for the purposes of this section.

Actions in Respect of Wrongs Causing Personal Injuries or Death

11. Special Time Limit for Actions in Respect of Personal Injuries

(1) This section applies to any action for damages for negligence, nuisance or breach of duty (whether the duty exists by virtue of a contract or of provision made by or under a statute or independently of any contract or any such provision) where the damages claimed by the plaintiff for the negligence, nuisance or breach of duty consist of or include damages in respect of personal injuries to the plaintiff or any other person.

(1A) This section does not apply to any action brought for damages under section 3 of the Protection from Harassment Act 1997.

(2) None of the time limits given in the preceding provisions of this Act shall apply to an action to which this section applies.

(3) An action to which this section applies shall not be brought after the expiration of the period applicable in accordance with subsection (4) or (5) below.

(4) Except where subsection

(5) below applies, the period applicable is three years from—
(a) the date on which the cause of action accrued; or
(b) the date of knowledge (if later) of the person injured.

(5) If the person injured dies before the expiration of the period mentioned in subsection (4) above, the period applicable as respects the cause of action surviving for the benefit of his estate by virtue of section 1 of the Law Reform (Miscellaneous Provisions) Act 1934 shall be three years from—
(a) the date of death; or
(b) the date of the personal representative's knowledge, whichever is the later.

(6) For the purposes of this section 'personal representative' includes any person who is or has been a personal representative of the deceased, including an executor who has not proved the will (whether or not he has renounced probate) but not anyone appointed only as a special personal representative in relation to settled land; and regard shall be had to any knowledge acquired by any such person while a personal representative or previously.

(7) If there is more than one personal representative, and their dates of knowledge are different, subsection (5)(b) above shall be read as referring to the earliest of those dates.

11A. Actions in Respect of Defective Products

(1) This section shall apply to an action for damages by virtue of any provision of Part I of the Consumer Protection Act 1987.
(2) None of the time limits given in the preceding provisions of this Act shall apply to an action to which this section applies.
(3) An action to which this section applies shall not be brought after the expiration of the period of ten years from the relevant time. within the meaning of section 4 of the said Act of 1987; and this subsection shall operate to extinguish a right of action and shall do so whether or not that right of action had accrued, or time under the following provisions of this Act had begun to run, at the end of the said period of ten years.
(4) Subject to subsection (5) below, an action to which this section applies in which the damages claimed by the plaintiff consist of or include damages in respect of personal injuries to the plaintiff or any other person or loss of or damage to any property. shall not be brought after the expiration of the period of three years from whichever is the later of—
   (a) the date on which the cause of action accrued: and
   (b) the date of knowledge of the injured person or, in the case of loss of or damage to property, the date of knowledge of the plaintiff or (if earlier) of any person in whom his cause of action was previously vested.
(5) If in a case where the damages claimed by the plaintiff consist of or include damages in respect of personal injuries to the plaintiff or any other person the injured person died before the expiration of the period mentioned in subsection (4) above, that subsection shall have effect as respects the cause of action surviving for the benefit of his estate by virtue of section I of the Law Reform (Miscellaneous Provisions) Act 1934 as if for the reference to that period there were substituted a reference to the period of three years from whichever is the later of—
   (a) the date of death; and
   (b) the date of the personal representative's knowledge.
(6) For the purposes of this section 'personal representative' includes any person who is or has been a personal representative of the deceased, including an executor who has not proved the will (whether or not he has renounced probate) but not anyone appointed only as a special personal representative in relation to settled land; and regard shall be had to any knowledge acquired by any such person while a personal representative or previously.
(7) If there is more than one personal representative and their dates of knowledge are different, subsection (5)(b) above shall be read as referring to the earliest of those dates.
(8) Expressions used in this section or section 14 of this Act and in Part I of the Consumer Protection Act 1987 have the same meanings in this section or that section as in that Part; and section 1(1) of that Act (Part I to be construed as enacted for the purpose of complying with the product liability Directive) shall apply for the purpose of construing this section and the following provisions of this Act so far as they relate to an action by virtue of any provision of that Part as it applies for the purpose of construing that Part.

12. Special Time Limit for Actions Under Fatal Accidents Legislation

(1) An action under the Fatal Accidents Act 1976 shall not be brought if the death occurred when the person injured could no longer maintain an action and recover damages in respect of the injury (whether because of a time limit in this Act or in any other Act, or for any other reason).
   Where any such action by the injured person would have been barred by the time limit in section 11 or 11A of this Act, no account shall be taken of the possibility of that time limit being overridden under section 33 of this Act.
(2) None of the time limits given in the preceding provisions of this Act shall apply to an action under the Fatal Accidents Act 1976, but no such action shall be brought after the expiration of three years from—
   (a) the date of death; or
   (b) the date of knowledge of the person for whose benefit the action is brought;
   whichever is the later.
(3) An action under the Fatal Accidents Act 1976 shall be one to which sections 28, 33 and 35 of this Act apply, and the application to any such action of the time limit under subsection (2) above

shall be subject to section 39; but otherwise Parts II and III of this Act shall not apply to any such action.

13. Operation of Time Limit Under Section 12 in Relation to Different Dependants

(1) Where there is more than one person for whose benefit an action under the Fatal Accidents Act 1976 is brought, section 12(2)(b) of this Act shall be applied separately to each of them.

(2) Subject to subsection (3) below, if by virtue of subsection (1) above the action would be outside the time limit given by section 12(2) as regards one or more, but not all, of the persons for whose benefit it is brought, the court shall direct that any person as regards whom the action would be outside that limit shall be excluded from those for whom the action is brought.

(3) The court shall not give such a direction if it is shown that if the action were brought exclusively for the benefit of the person in question it would not be defeated by a defence of limitation (whether in consequence of section 28 of this Act or an agreement between the parties not to raise the defence, or otherwise).

14. Definition of Date of Knowledge for Purposes of Section 11 and 12

(1) Subject to subsection (1A) below, in sections 11 and 12 of this Act references to a person's date of knowledge are references to the date on which he first had knowledge of the following facts—

(a) that the injury in question was significant; and

(b) that the injury was attributable in whole or in part to the act or omission which is alleged to constitute negligence, nuisance or breach of duty; and

(c) the identity of the defendant; and

(d) if it is alleged that the act or omission was that of a person other than the defendant, the identity of that person and the additional facts supporting the bringing of an action against the defendant;

and knowledge that any acts or omissions did or did not, as a matter of law, involve negligence, nuisance or breach of duty is irrelevant.

(1A) In section 11A of this Act and in section 12 of this Act so far as that section applies to an action by virtue of section 6(1)(a) of the Consumer Protection Act 1987 (death caused by defective product) references to a person's date of knowledge are references to the date on which he first had knowledge of the following facts—

(a) such facts about the damage caused by the defect as would lead a reasonable person who had suffered such damage to consider it sufficiently serious to justify his instituting proceedings for damages against a defendant who did not dispute liability and was able to satisfy a judgment; and

(b) that the damage was wholly or partly attributable to the facts and circumstances alleged to constitute the defect; and

(c) the identity of the defendant;

but, in determining the date on which a person first had such knowledge there shall be disregarded both the extent (if any) of that person's knowledge on any date of whether particular facts or circumstances would or would not, as a matter of law, constitute a defect and, in a case relating to loss of or damage to property, any knowledge which that person had on a date on which he had no right of action by virtue of Part I of that Act in respect of the loss or damage.

(2) For the purposes of this section an injury is significant if the person whose date of knowledge is in question would reasonably have considered it sufficiently serious to justify his instituting proceedings for damages against a defendant who did not dispute liability and was able to satisfy a judgment.

(3) For the purposes of this section a person's knowledge includes knowledge which be might reasonably have been expected to acquire—

(a) from facts observable or ascertainable by him; or

(b) from facts ascertainable by him with the help of medical or other appropriate expert advice which it is reasonable for him to seek;

but a person shall not be fixed under this subsection with knowledge of a fact ascertainable only with the help of expert advice so long as he has taken all reasonable steps to obtain (and, where appropriate, to act on) that advice.

Actions in Respect of Latent Damage Not Involving Personal Injuries

14A. Special Time Limit for Negligence Actions Where Facts Relevant to Cause of Action are Not Known at Date of Accrual

(1) This section applies to any action for damages for negligence, other than one to which section 11 of this Act applies, where the starting date for reckoning the period of limitation under subsection (4)(b) below falls after the date on which the cause of action accrued.

(2) Section 2 of this Act shall not apply to an action to which this section applies.

(3) An action to which this section applies shall not be brought after the expiration of the period applicable in accordance with subsection (4) below.

(4) That period is either—
- (a) six years from the date on which the cause of action accrued; or
- (b) three years from the starting date as defined by subsection (5) below, if that period expires later than the period mentioned in paragraph (a) above.

(5) For the purposes of this section, the starting date for reckoning the period of limitation under subsection (4)(b) above is the earliest date on which the plaintiff or any person in whom the cause of action was vested before him first had both the knowledge required for bringing an action for damages in respect of the relevant damage and a right to bring such an action.

(6) In subsection (5) above 'the knowledge required for bringing an action for damages in respect of the relevant damage' means knowledge both—
- (a) of the material facts about the damage in respect of which damages are claimed; and
- (b) of the other facts relevant to the current action mentioned in subsection (8) below.

(7) For the purposes of subsection (6)(a) above, the material facts about the damage are such facts about the damage as would lead a reasonable person who had suffered such damage to consider it sufficiently serious to justify his instituting proceedings for damages against a defendant who did not dispute liability and was able to satisfy a judgment.

(8) The other facts referred to in subsection (6)(b) above are—
- (a) that the damage was attributable in whole or in part to the act or omission which is alleged to constitute negligence: and
- (b) the identity of the defendant; and
- (c) if it is alleged that the act or omission was that of a person other than the defendant, the identity of that person and the additional facts supporting the bringing of an action against the defendant.

(9) Knowledge that any acts or omissions did or did not, as a matter of law, involve negligence is irrelevant for the purposes of subsection (5) above.

(10) For the purposes of this section a person's knowledge includes knowledge which he might reasonably have been expected to acquire—
- (a) from facts observable or ascertainable by him; or
- (b) from facts ascertainable by him with the help of appropriate expert advice which it is reasonable for him to seek;

but a person shall not be taken by virtue of this subsection to have knowledge of a fact ascertainable only with the help of expert advice so long as he has taken all reasonable steps to obtain (and, where appropriate, to act on) that advice.

14B. Overriding Time Limit for Negligence Actions Not Involving Personal Injuries

(1) An action for damages for negligence, other than one to which section 11 of this Act applies, shall not be brought after the expiration of fifteen years from the date (or, if more than one, from the last of the dates) on which there occurred any act or omission—
- (a) which is alleged to constitute negligence; and
- (b) to which the damage in respect of which damages are claimed is alleged to be attributable (in whole or in part).

(2) This section bars the right of action in a case to which subsection (1) above applies notwithstanding that—
- (a) the cause of action has not yet accrued; or
- (b) where section 14A of this Act applies to the action, the date which is for the purposes of that

section the starting date for reckoning the period mentioned in subsection (4)(b) of that section has not yet occurred;

before the end of the period of limitation prescribed by this section.

Actions to Recover Land and Rent

15. Time Limit for Actions to Recover Land

(1) No action shall be brought by any person to recover any land after the expiration of twelve years from the date on which the right of action accrued to him or, if it first accrued to some person through whom he claims, to that person.

(2) Subject to the following provisions of this section, where—

(a) the estate or interest claimed was an estate or interest in reversion or remainder or any other future estate or interest and the right of action to recover the land accrued on the date on which the estate or interest fell into possession by the determination of the preceding estate or interest; and

(b) the person entitled to the preceding estate or interest (not being a term of years absolute) was not in possession of the land on that date;

no action shall be brought by the person entitled to the succeeding estate or interest after the expiration of twelve years from the date on which the right of action accrued to the person entitled to the preceding estate or interest or six years from the date on which the right of action accrued to the person entitled to the succeeding estate or interest, whichever period last expires.

(3) Subsection (2) above shall not apply to any estate or interest which falls into possession on the determination of an entailed interest and which might have been barred by the person entitled to the entailed interest.

(4) No person shall bring an action to recover any estate or interest in land under an assurance taking effect after the right of action to recover the land had accrued to the person by whom the assurance was made or some person through whom he claimed or some person entitled to a preceding estate or interest, unless the action is brought within the period during which the person by whom the assurance was made could have brought such an action.

(5) Where any person is entitled to any estate or interest in land in possession and, while so entitled, is also entitled to any future estate or interest in that land, and his right to recover the estate or interest in possession is barred under this Act, no action shall be brought by that person, or by any person claiming through him, in respect of the future estate or interest, unless in the meantime possession of the land has been recovered by a person entitled to an intermediate estate or interest.

(6) Part I of Schedule 1 to this Act contains provisions for determining the date of accrual of rights of action to recover land in the cases there mentioned.

(7) Part II of that Schedule contains provisions modifying the provisions of this Section in their application to actions brought by, or by a person claiming through, the Crown or any spiritual or eleemosynary corporation sole.

16. Time Limit for Redemption Actions

When a mortgagee of land has been in possession of any of the mortgaged land for a period of twelve years, no action to redeem the land of which the mortgagee has been so in possession shall be brought after the end of that period by the mortgagor or any person claiming through him.

17. Extinction of Title to Land After Expiration of Time Limit

Subject to—

(a) section 18 of this Act; and

(b) section 75 of the Land Registration Act 1925

at the expiration of the period prescribed by this Act for any person to bring an action to recover land (including a redemption action) the title of that person to the land shall be extinguished.

18. Settled Land and Land Held on Trust

(1) Subject to section 21(1) and (2) of this Act, the provisions of this Act shall apply to equitable interests in land as they apply to legal estates.

Accordingly a right of action to recover the land shall, for the purposes of this Act but not otherwise, be treated as accruing to a person entitled in possession to such an equitable interest in the like manner and circumstances, and on the same date, as it would accrue if his interest were a legal estate in the land (and any relevant provision of Part I of Schedule 1 to this Act shall apply in any such case accordingly).

(2) Where the period prescribed by this Act has expired for the bringing of an action to recover land by a tenant for life or a statutory owner of settled land—

(a) his legal estate shall not be extinguished if and so long as the right of action to recover the land of any person entitled to a beneficial interest in the land either has not accrued or has not been barred by this Act; and

(b) the legal estate shall accordingly remain vested in the tenant for life or statutory owner and shall devolve in accordance with the Settled Land Act 1925;

but if and when every such right of action has been barred by this Act, his legal estate shall be extinguished.

(3) Where any land is held upon trust and the period prescribed by this Act has expired for the bringing of an action to recover the land by the trustees, the estate of the trustees shall not be extinguished if and so long as the right of action to recover the land of any person entitled to a beneficial interest in the land either has not accrued or has not been barred by this Act; but if and when every such right of action has been so barred the estate of the trustees shall be extinguished.

(4) Where—

(a) any settled land is vested in a statutory owner; or

(b) any land is held upon trust;

an action to recover the land may be brought by the statutory owner or trustees on behalf of any person entitled to a beneficial interest in possession in the land whose right of action has not been barred by this Act, notwithstanding that the right of action of the statutory owner or trustees would apart from this provision have been barred by this Act.

19. Time Limit for Actions to Recover Rent

No action shall be brought, or distress made, to recover arrears of rent, or damages in respect of arrears of rent, after the expiration of six years from the date on which the arrears became due.

Actions to Recover Money Secured by a Mortgage or Charge or to Recover Proceeds of the Sale of Land

20. Time Limit for Actions to Recover Money Secured by a Mortgage or Charge or to Recover Proceeds of the Sale of Land

(1) No action shall be brought to recover—

(a) any principal sum of money secured by a mortgage or other charge on property (whether real or personal); or

(b) proceeds of the sale of land;

after the expiration of twelve years from the date on which the right to receive the money accrued.

(2) No foreclosure action in respect of mortgaged personal property shall be brought after the expiration of twelve years from the date on which the right to foreclose accrued.

But if the mortgagee was in possession of the mortgaged property after that date, the right to foreclose on the property which was in his possession shall not be treated as having accrued for the purposes of this subsection until the date on which his possession discontinued.

(3) The right to receive any principal sum of money secured by a mortgage or other charge and the right to foreclose on the property subject to the mortgage or charge shall not be treated as accruing so long as that property comprises any future interest or any life insurance policy which has not matured or been determined.

(4) Nothing in this section shall apply to a foreclosure action in respect of mortgaged land, but the provisions of this Act relating to actions to recover land shall apply to such an action.

(5) Subject to subsections (6) and (7) below, no action to recover arrears of interest payable in respect of any sum of money secured by a mortgage or other charge or payable in respect of proceeds of the sale of land, or to recover damages in respect of such arrears shall be brought after the expiration of six years from the date on which the interest became due.

(6) Where—
   (a) a prior mortgagee or other encumbrancer has been in possession of the property charged; and
   (b) an action is brought within one year of the discontinuance of that possession by the subsequent encumbrancer;

the subsequent encumbrancer may recover by that action all the arrears of interest which fell due during the period of possession by the prior encumbrancer or damages in respect of those arrears, notwithstanding that the period exceeded six years.

(7) Where—
   (a) the property subject to the mortgage or charge comprises any future interest or life insurance policy; and
   (b) it is a term of the mortgage or charge that arrears of interest shall be treated as part of the principal sum of money secured by the mortgage or charge;

interest shall not be treated as becoming due before the right to recover the principal sum of money has accrued or is treated as having accrued.

Actions in Respect of Trust Property or the Personal Estate of Deceased Persons

21. Time Limit for Actions in Respect of Trust Property

(1) No period of limitation prescribed by this Act shall apply to an action by a beneficiary under a trust, being an action—
   (a) in respect of any fraud or fraudulent breach of trust to which the trustee was a party or privy; or
   (b) to recover from the trustee trust property or the proceeds of trust property in the possession of the trustee, or previously received by the trustee and converted to his use.

(2) Where a trustee who is also a beneficiary under the trust receives or retains trust property or its proceeds as his share on a distribution of trust property under the trust, his liability in any action brought by virtue of subsection (1)(b) above to recover that property or its proceeds after the expiration of the period of limitation prescribed by this Act for bringing an action to recover trust property shall be limited to the excess over his proper share.

This subsection only applies if the trustee acted honestly and reasonably in making the distribution.

(3) Subject to the preceding provisions of this section, an action by a beneficiary to recover trust property or in respect of any breach of trust, not being an action for which a period of limitation is prescribed by any other provision of this Act, shall not be brought after the expiration of six years from the date on which the right of action accrued.

For the purposes of this subsection, the right of action shall not be treated as having accrued to any beneficiary entitled to a future interest in the trust property until the interest fell into possession.

(4) No beneficiary as against whom there would be a good defence under this Act shall derive any greater or other benefit from a judgment or order obtained by any other beneficiary than he could have obtained if he had brought the action and this Act had been pleaded in defence.

22. Time Limit for Actions Claiming Personal Estate of a Deceased Person

Subject to section 21(1) and (2) of this Act—

(a) no action in respect of any claim to the personal estate of a deceased person or to any share or interest in any such estate (whether under a will or on intestacy) shall be brought after the expiration of twelve years from the date on which the right to receive the share or interest accrued; and

(b) no action to recover arrears of interest in respect of any legacy, or damages in respect of such arrears, shall be brought after the expiration of six years from the date on which the interest became due.

Actions for an Account

23. Time Limit in Respect of Actions for an Account

An action for an account shall not be brought after the expiration of any time limit under this Act which is applicable to the claim which is the basis of the duty to account.

Miscellaneous and Supplemental

24. Time Limit for Actions to Enforce Judgments

(1) An action shall not be brought upon any judgment after the expiration of six years from the date on which the judgment became enforceable.

(2) No arrears of interest in respect of any judgment debt shall be recovered after the expiration of six years from the date on which the interest became due.

25. Time Limit for Actions to Enforce Advowsons and Extinction of Title to Advowsons

(1) No person shall bring an action to enforce a right to present to or bestow any ecclesiastical benefice as patron of that benefice after the expiration of whichever of the following periods last expires, that is to say—

(a) a period during which three clerks in succession have held the benefice adversely to the right of presentation or gift of the person in question (or of some person through whom he claims); or

(b) a period of sixty years during which the benefice has been held adversely to that right;

and in no case after the expiration of a period of one hundred years during which the benefice has been held adversely to that right or to the right of some person entitled to a preceding estate or interest or an undivided share or alternate right of presentation or gift held or derived under the same title.

This subsection shall apply to the Crown or a bishop claiming a right to present to or bestow any ecclesiastical benefice as patron, but shall not affect the right of the Crown or a bishop to present or collate to any ecclesiastical benefice by reason of a lapse.

(2) Where any benefice becomes void after being held adversely to the right of presentation or gift of the patron of the benefice and a clerk is presented or collated to the benefice by Her Majesty or the ordinary—

(a) the possession of that clerk shall be treated as adverse; but

(b) where the benefice is avoided in consequence of the incumbent being made a bishop, the incumbency of the new clerk shall, for the purpose of subsection (1)(a) above, be treated as a continuation of the prior incumbency.

(3) Subject to section 75 of the Land Registration Act 1925, at the expiration of the period prescribed by this Act for any person to bring an action to enforce an advowson the title of that person to the advowson shall be extinguished.

26. Administration to Date Back to Death

For the purposes of the provisions of this Act relating to actions for the recovery of land and advowsons an administrator of the estate of a deceased person shall be treated as claiming as if there had been no interval of time between the death of the deceased person and the grant of the letters of administration.

27. Cure of Defective Disentailing Assurance

(1) This section applies where—

(a) a person entitled in remainder to an entailed interest in any land makes an assurance of his interest which fails to bar the issue in tail or the estates and interests taking effect on the determination of the entailed interest, or fails to bar those estates and interests only; and

(b) any person takes possession of the land by virtue of the assurance.

(2) If the person taking possession of the land by virtue of the assurance, or any other person whatsoever (other than a person entitled to possession by virtue of the settlement) is in possession of the land for a period of twelve years from the commencement of the time when the assurance could have operated as an effective bar, the assurance shall thereupon operate, and be

treated as having always operated, to bar the issue in tail and the estates and interests taking effect on the determination of the entailed interest.

(3) The reference in subsection (2) above to the time when the assurance could have operated as an effective bar is a reference to the time at which the assurance, if it had then been executed by the person entitled to the entailed interest, would have operated, without the consent of any other person, to bar the issue in tail and the estates and interests taking effect on the determination of the entailed interest.

PART II EXTENSION OR EXCLUSION OF ORDINARY TIME LIMITS

Disability

28. Extension of Limitation Period in Case of Disability

(1) Subject to the following provisions of this section, if on the date when any right of action accrued for which a period of limitation is prescribed by this Act, the person to whom it accrued was under a disability, the action may be brought at any time before the expiration of six years from the date when he ceased to be under a disability or died (whichever first occurred) notwithstanding that the period of limitation has expired.

(2) This section shall not affect any case where the right of action first accrued to some person (not under a disability) through whom the person under a disability claims.

(3) When a right of action which has accrued to a person under a disability accrues, on the death of that person while still under a disability, to another person under a disability, no further extension of time shall be allowed by reason of the disability of the second person.

(4) No action to recover land or money charged on land shall be brought by virtue of this section by any person after the expiration of thirty years from the date on which the right of action accrued to that person or some person through whom he claims.

(4A) If the action is one to which section 4A of this Act applies, subsection (1) above shall have effect—

- (a) in the case of an action for libel or slander, as if for the words from 'at any time' to 'occurred) ' there were substituted the words 'by him at any time before the expiration of one year from the date on which he ceased to be under a disability'; and
- (b) in the case of an action for slander of title, slander of goods or other malicious falsehood, as if for the words 'six years' there were substituted the words 'one year'.

(5) If the action is one to which section 10 of this Act applies, subsection (1) above shall have effect as if for the words 'six years' there were substituted the words 'two years'.

(6) If the action is one to which section 11 or 12(2) of this Act applies, subsection (1) above shall have effect as if for the words 'six years' there were substituted the words 'three years'.

(7) If the action is one to which section 11A of this Act applies or one by virtue of section 6(1)(a) of the Consumer Protection Act 1987 (death caused by defective product), subsection (1) above—

- (a) shall not apply to the time limit prescribed by subsection (3) of the said section 11A or to that time limit as applied by virtue of section 12(1) of this Act; and
- (b) in relation to any other time limit prescribed by this Act shall have effect as if for the words 'six years' there were substituted the words 'three years'.

28A. Extension for Cases Where the Limitation Period is the Period Under Section 14A(4)(b)

(1) Subject to subsection (2) below, if in the case of any action for which a period of limitation is prescribed by section 14A of this Act—

- (a) the period applicable in accordance with subsection (4) of that section is the period mentioned in paragraph (b) of that subsection;
- (b) on the date which is for the purposes of that section the starting date for reckoning that period the person by reference to whose knowledge that date fell to be determined under subsection (5) of that section was under a disability; and
- (c) Section 28 of this Act does not apply to

the action; the action may be brought at any time before the expiration of three years from the date when he ceased to be under a disability or died (whichever first occurred) notwithstanding that the period mentioned above has expired.

(2) An action may not be brought by virtue of subsection (1) above after the end of the period of limitation prescribed by section 14B of this Act.

Acknowledgment and Part Payment

29. Fresh Accrual of Action on Acknowledgment or Part Payment

(1) Subsections (2) and (3) below apply where any right of action (including a foreclosure action) to recover land or an advowson or any right of a mortgagee of personal property to bring a foreclosure action in respect of the property has accrued.

(2) If the person in possession of the land, benefice or personal property in question acknowledges the title of the person to whom the right of action has accrued—

(a) the right shall be treated as having accrued on and not before the date of the acknowledgment; and

(b) in the case of a right of action to recover land which has accrued to a person entitled to an estate or interest taking effect on the determination of an entailed interest against whom time is running under section 27 of this Act, section 27 shall there upon cease to apply to the land.

(3) In the case of a foreclosure or other action by a mortgagee, if the person in possession of the land, benefice or personal property in question or the person liable for the mortgage debt makes any payment in respect of the debt (whether of principal or interest) the right shall be treated as having accrued on and not before the date of the payment.

(4) Where a mortgagee is by virtue of the mortgage in possession of any mortgaged land and either—

(a) receives any sum in respect of the principal or interest of the mortgage debt; or

(b) acknowledges the title of the mortgagor, or his equity of redemption;

an action to redeem the land in his possession may be brought at any time before the expiration of twelve years from the date of the payment or acknowledgment.

(5) Subject to subsection (6) below, where any right of action has accrued to recover—

(a) any debt or other liquidated pecuniary claim; or

(b) any claim to the personal estate of a deceased person or to any share or interest in any such estate;

and the person liable or accountable for the claim acknowledges the claim or makes any payment in respect of it the right shall be treated as having accrued on and not before the date of the acknowledgment or payment.

(6) A payment of a part of the rent or interest due at any time shall not extend the period for claiming the remainder then due, but any payment of interest shall be treated as a payment in respect of the principal debt.

(7) Subject to subsection (6) above, a current period of limitation may be repeatedly extended under this section by further acknowledgments or payments, but a right of action, once barred by this Act, shall not be revived by any subsequent acknowledgment or payment.

30. Formal Provisions as to Acknowledgments and Part Payments

(1) To be effective for the purposes of section 29 of this Act, an acknowledgment must be in writing and signed by the person making it.

(2) For the purposes of section 29, any acknowledgment or payment—

(a) may be made by the agent of the person by whom it is required to be made under that section; and

(b) shall be made to the person, or to an agent of the person, whose title or claim is being acknowledged or, as the case may be, in respect of whose claim the payment is being made.

31. Effect of Acknowledgment or Part Payment on Persons Other Than the Maker or Recipient

(1) An acknowledgment of the title to any land, benefice, or mortgaged personalty by any person in possession of it shall bind all other persons in possession during the ensuing period of limitation.

(2) A payment in respect of a mortgage debt by the mortgagor or any other person liable for the debt, or by any person in possession of the mortgaged property, shall, so far as any right of the mortgagee to foreclose or otherwise to recover the property is concerned, bind all other persons in possession of the mortgaged property during the ensuing period of limitation.

(3) Where two or more mortgagees are by virtue of the mortgage in possession of the mortgaged land, an acknowledgment of the mortgagor's title or of his equity of redemption by one of the mortgagees shall only bind him and his successors and shall not bind any other mortgagee or his successors.

(4) Where in a case within subsection (3) above the mortgagee by whom the acknowledgment is given is entitled to a part of the mortgaged land and not to any ascertained part of the mortgage debt the mortgagor shall be entitled to redeem that part of the land on payment, with interest, of the part of the mortgage debt which bears the same proportion to the whole of the debt as the value of the part of the land bears to the whole of the mortgaged land.

(5) Where there are two or more mortgagors, and the title or equity of redemption of one of the mortgagors is acknowledged as mentioned above in this section, the acknowledgment shall be treated as having been made to all the mortgagors.

(6) An acknowledgment of any debt or other liquidated pecuniary claim shall bind the acknowledger and his successors but not any other person.

(7) A payment made in respect of any debt or other liquidated pecuniary claim shall bind all persons liable in respect of the debt or claim.

(8) An acknowledgment by one of several personal representatives of any claim to the personal estate of a deceased person or to any share or interest in any such estate, or a payment by one of several personal representatives in respect of any such claim, shall bind the estate of the deceased person.

(9) In this section 'successor', in relation to any mortgagee or person liable in respect of any debt or claim, means his personal representatives and any other person on whom the rights under the mortgage or, as the case may be, the liability in respect of the debt or claim devolve (whether on death or bankruptcy or the disposition of property or the determination of a limited estate or interest in settled property or otherwise).

Fraud, Concealment and Mistake

32. Postponement of Limitation Period in Case of Fraud, Concealment or Mistake

(1) Subject to subsections (3) and (4A) below, where in the case of any action for which a period of limitation is prescribed by this Act, either—
  (a) the action is based upon the fraud of the defendant; or
  (b) any fact relevant to the plaintiff's right of action has been deliberately concealed from him by the defendant; or
  (c) the action is for relief from the consequences of a mistake;

the period of limitation shall not begin to run until the plaintiff has discovered the fraud, concealment or mistake (as the case may be) or could with reasonable diligence have discovered it.

References in this subsection to the defendant include references to the defendant's agent and to any person through whom the defendant claims and his agent.

(2) For the purposes of subsection (1) above, deliberate commission of a breach of duty in circumstances in which it is unlikely to be discovered for some time amounts to deliberate concealment of the facts involved in that breach of duty.

(3) Nothing in this section shall enable any action—
  (a) to recover, or recover the value of, any property; or
  (b) to enforce any charge against, or set aside any transaction affecting, any property;

to be brought against the purchaser of the property or any person claiming through him in any case where the property has been purchased for valuable consideration by an innocent third party since the fraud or concealment or (as the case may be) the transaction in which the mistake was made took place.

(4) A purchaser is an innocent third party for the purposes of this section—
  (a) in the case of fraud or concealment of any fact relevant to the plaintiff's right of action, if he was not a party to the fraud or (as the case may be) to the concealment of that fact and

did not at the time of the purchase know or have reason to believe that the fraud or concealment had taken place; and

(b) in the case of mistake, if he did not at the time of the purchase know or have reason to believe that the mistake had been made.

(4A) Subsection (1) above shall not apply in relation to the time limit prescribed by section 11A(3) of this Act or in relation to that time limit as applied by virtue of section 12(1) of this Act).

(5) Sections 14A and 14B of this Act shall not apply to any action to which subsection (1)(b) above applies (and accordingly the period of limitation referred to in that subsection, in any case to which either of those sections would otherwise apply, is the period applicable under section 2 of this Act).

Discretionary Exclusion of Time Limit for Actions for Defamation or Malicious Falsehood

32A. Discretionary Exclusion of Time Limit for Actions for Defamation or Malicious Falsehood

(1) If it appears to the court that it would be equitable to allow an action to proceed having regard to the degree to which—

(a) the operation of section 4A of this Act prejudices the plaintiff or any person whom he represents, and

(b) any decision of the court under this subsection would prejudice the defendant or any person whom he represents,

the court may direct that that section shall not apply to the action or shall not apply to any specified cause of action to which the action relates.

(2) In acting under this section the court shall have regard to all the circumstances of the case and in particular to—

(a) the length of, and the reasons for, the delay on the part of the plaintiff;

(b) where the reason or one of the reasons for the delay was that all or any of the facts relevant to the cause of action did not become known to the plaintiff until after the end of the period mentioned in section 4A—

(i) the date on which any such facts did become known to him, and

(ii) the extent to which he acted promptly and reasonably once he knew whether or not the facts in question might be capable of giving rise to an action; and

(c) the extent to which, having regard to the delay, relevant evidence is likely—

(i) to be unavailable, or

(ii) to be less cogent than if the action had been brought within the period mentioned in section 4A.

(3) In the case of an action for slander of title, slander of goods or other malicious falsehood brought by a personal representative—

(a) the references in subsection (2) above to the plaintiff shall be construed as including the deceased person to whom the cause of action accrued and any previous personal representative of that person; and

(b) nothing in section 28(3) of this Act shall be construed as affecting the court's discretion under this section.

(4) In this section 'the court' means the court in which the action has been brought.

Discretionary Exclusion of Time Limit for Actions in Respect of Personal Injuries or Death

33. Discretionary Exclusion of Time Limit for Actions in Respect of Personal Injuries or Death

(1) If it appears to the court that it would be equitable to allow an action to proceed having regard to the degree to which—

(a) the provisions of section 11 or 11A or 12 of this Act prejudice the plaintiff or any person whom he represents; and

(b) any decision of the court under this subsection would prejudice the defendant or any person whom he represents;

the court may direct that those provisions shall not apply to the action, or shall not apply to any specified cause of action to which the action relates.

(1A) The court shall not under this section disapply—
(a) subsection (3) of section 11A; or
(b) where the damages claimed by the plaintiff are confined to damages for loss of or damage to any property, any other provision in its application to an action by virtue of Part I of the Consumer Protection Act 1987.

(2) The court shall not under this section disapply section 12(1) except where the reason why the person injured could no longer maintain an action was because of the time limit in section 11 or subsection (4) of section 11A.

If, for example, the person injured could at his death no longer maintain an action under the Fatal Accidents Act 1976 because of the time limit in Article 29 in Schedule 1 to the Carriage by Air Act 1961, the court has no power to direct that section 12(1) shall not apply.

(3) In acting under this section the court shall have regard to all the circumstances of the case and in particular to—
(a) the length of, and the reasons for, the delay on the part of the plaintiff;
(b) the extent to which, having regard to the delay, the evidence adduced or likely to be adduced by the plaintiff or the defendant is or is likely to be less cogent than if the action had been brought within the time allowed by section 11, by section 11A or (as the case may be) by section 12;
(c) the conduct of the defendant after the cause of action arose, including the extent (if any) to which he responded to requests reasonably made by the plaintiff for information or inspection for the purpose of ascertaining facts which were or might be relevant to the plaintiff's cause of action against the defendant;
(d) the duration of any disability of the plaintiff arising after the date of the accrual of the cause of action;
(e) the extent to which the plaintiff acted promptly and reasonably once he knew whether or not the act or omission of the defendant, to which the injury was attributable, might be capable at that time of giving rise to an action for damages;
(f) the steps, if any, taken by the plaintiff to obtain medical, legal or other expert advice and the nature of any such advice he may have received.

(4) In a case where the person injured died when, because of section 11 or subsection (4) of section 11A, he could no longer maintain an action and recover damages in respect of the injury, the court shall have regard in particular to the length of, and the reasons for, the delay on the part of the deceased.

(5) In a case under subsection (4) above, or any other case where the time limit, or one of the time limits, depends on the date of knowledge of a person other than the plaintiff, subsection (3) above shall have effect with appropriate modifications, and shall have effect in particular as if references to the plaintiff included references to any person whose date of knowledge is or was relevant in determining a time limit.

(6) A direction by the court disapplying the provisions of section 12(1) shall operate to disapply the provisions to the same effect in section 1(1) of the Fatal Accidents Act 1976.

(7) In this section 'the court' means the court in which the action has been brought.

(8) References in this section to section 11 or 11A include references to that section as extended by any of the preceding provisions of this Part of this Act or by any provision of Part III of this Act.

PART III MISCELLANEOUS AND GENERAL

35. New Claims in Pending Actions: Rules of Court

(1) For the purposes of this Act, any new claim made in the course of any action shall be deemed to be a separate action and to have been commenced—
(a) in the case of a new claim made in or by way of third party proceedings, on the date on which those proceedings were commenced; and
(b) in the case of any other new claim, on the same date as the original action.

(2) In this section a new claim means any claim by way of set-off or counterclaim, and any claim involving either—
(a) the addition or substitution of a new cause of action; or
(b) the addition or substitution of a new party;

and 'third party proceedings' means any proceedings brought in the course of any action by any party to the action against a person not previously a party to the action, other than proceedings brought by joining any such person as defendant to any claim already made in the original action by the party bringing the proceedings.

(3) Except as provided by section 33 of this Act or by rules of court, neither the High Court nor any county court shall allow a new claim within subsection (1)(b) above, other than an original set-off or counterclaim, to be made in the course of any action after the expiry of any time limit under this Act which would affect a new action to enforce that claim.

For the purposes of this subsection, a claim is an original set-off or an original counterclaim if it is a claim made by way of set-off or (as the case may be) by way of counterclaim by a party who has not previously made any claim in the action.

(4) Rules of court may provide for allowing a new claim to which subsection (3) above applies to be made as there mentioned, but only if the conditions specified in subsection (5) below are satisfied, and subject to any further restrictions the rules may impose.

(5) The conditions referred to in subsection (4) above are the following—

(a) in the case of a claim involving a new cause of action, if the new cause of action arises out of the same facts or substantially the same facts as are already in issue on any claim previously made in the original action; and

(b) in the case of a claim involving a new party, if the addition or substitution of the new party is necessary for the determination of the original action.

(6) The addition or substitution of a new party shall not be regarded for the purposes of subsection (5)(b) above as necessary for the determination of the original action unless either—

(a) the new party is substituted for a party whose name was given in any claim made in the original action in mistake for the new party's name; or

(b) any claim already made in the original action cannot be maintained by or against an existing party unless the new party is joined or substituted as plaintiff or defendant in that action.

(7) Subject to subsection (4) above, rules of court may provide for allowing a party to any action to claim relief in a new capacity in respect of a new cause of action notwithstanding that he had no title to make that claim at the date of the commencement of the action.

This subsection shall not be taken as prejudicing the power of rules of court to provide for allowing a party to claim relief in a new capacity without adding or substituting a new cause of action.

(8) Subsections (3) to (7) above shall apply in relation to a new claim made in the course of third party proceedings as if those proceedings were the original action, and subject to such other modifications as may be prescribed by rules of court in any case or class of case.

36. Equitable Jurisdiction and Remedies

(1) The following time limits under this Act, that is to say—

(a) the time limit under section 2 for actions founded on tort;

(aa) the time limit under section 4A for actions for libel or slander, or for slander of title, slander of goods or other malicious falsehood;

(b) the time limit under section 5 for actions founded on simple contract;

(c) the time limit under section 7 for actions to enforce awards where the submission is not by an instrument under seal;

(d) the time limit under section 8 for actions on a specialty;

(e) the time limit under section 9 for actions to recover a sum recoverable by virtue of any enactment; and

(f) the time limit under section 24 for actions to enforce a judgment;

shall not apply to any claim for specific performance of a contract or for an injunction or for other equitable relief, except in so far as any such time limit may be applied by the court by analogy in like manner as the corresponding time limit under any enactment repealed by the Limitation Act 1939 was applied before 1st July 1940.

(2) Nothing in this Act shall affect any equitable jurisdiction to refuse relief on the ground of acquiescence or otherwise.

37. Application to the Crown and the Duke of Cornwall

(1) Except as otherwise expressly provided in this Act, and without prejudice to section 39, this Act shall apply to proceedings by or against the Crown in like manner as it applies to proceedings between subjects.

(2) Notwithstanding subsection (1) above, this Act shall not apply to—
- (a) any proceedings by the Crown for the recovery of any tax or duty or interest on any tax or duty;
- (b) any forfeiture proceedings under the customs and excise Acts (within the meaning of the Customs and Excise Management Act 1979); or
- (c) any proceedings in respect of the forfeiture of a ship.

In this subsection 'duty' includes any debt due to Her Majesty under section 16 of the Tithe Act 1936, and 'ship' includes every description of vessel used in navigation not propelled by oars.

(3) For the purposes of this section, proceedings by or against the Crown include—
- (a) proceedings by or against Her Majesty in right of the Duchy of Lancaster;
- (b) proceedings by or against any Government department or any officer of the Crown as such or any person acting on behalf of the Crown; and
- (c) proceedings by or against the Duke of Cornwall.

(4) For the purpose of the provisions of this Act relating to actions for the recovery of land and advowsons, references to the Crown shall include references to Her Majesty in right of the Duchy of Lancaster; and those provisions shall apply to lands and advowsons forming part of the possessions of the Duchy of Cornwall as if for the references to the Crown there were substituted references to the Duke of Cornwall as defined in the Duchy of Cornwall Management Act 1863.

(5) For the purposes of this Act a proceeding by petition of right (in any case where any such proceeding lies, by virtue of any saving in section 40 of the Crown Proceedings Act 1947, notwithstanding the general abolition by that Act of proceedings by way of petition of right) shall be treated as being commenced on the date on which the petition is presented.

(6) Nothing in this Act shall affect the prerogative right of Her Majesty (whether in right of the Crown or of the Duchy of Lancaster) or of the Duke of Cornwall to any gold or silver mine.

38. Interpretation

(1) In this Act, unless the context otherwise requires—

'action' includes any proceeding in a court of law, including an ecclesiastical court

'land' includes corporeal hereditaments, tithes and rent charges and any legal or equitable estate or interest therein but except as provided above in this definition does not include any incorporeal hereditament;

'personal estate' and 'personal property' do not include chattels real;

'personal injuries' includes any disease and any impairment of a person's physical or mental condition, and 'injury' and cognate expressions shall be construed accordingly;

'rent' includes a rentcharge and a rent service;

'rentcharge' means any annuity or periodical sum of money charged upon or payable out of land, except a rent service or interest on a mortgage on land;

'settled land', 'statutory owner' and 'tenant for life' have the same meanings respectively as in the Settled Land Act 1925;

'trust' and 'trustee' have the same meanings respectively as in the Trustee Act 1925.

(2) For the purposes of this Act a person shall be treated as under a disability while he is an infant, or of unsound mind.

(3) For the purposes of subsection (2) above a person is of unsound mind if he is a person who, by reason of mental disorder within the meaning of the Mental Health Act 1983 is incapable of managing and administering his property and affairs.

(4) Without prejudice to the generality of subsection (3) above, a person shall be conclusively presumed for the purposes of subsection (2) above to be of unsound mind—
- (a) while he is liable to be detained or subject to guardianship under the Mental Health Act 1983 (otherwise than by virtue of section 35 or 89); and
- (b) while he is receiving treatment as an inpatient in any hospital within the meaning of the Mental Health Act 1983 or mental nursing home within the meaning of the Nursing Homes Act 1975 without being liable to be detained under the said Act of 1983 (otherwise than by virtue of section 35 or 89), being treatment which follows without any interval a

period during which he was liable to be detained or subject to guardianship under the Mental Health Act 1959, or the said Act of 1983 (otherwise than by virtue of section 35 or 89) or by virtue of any enactment repealed or excluded by the Mental Health Act 1959.

(5) Subject to subsection (6) below, a person shall be treated as claiming through another person if he became entitled by, through, under, or by the act of that other person to the right claimed, and any person whose estate or interest might have been barred by a person entitled to an entailed interest in possession shall be treated as claiming through the person so entitled.

(6) A person becoming entitled to any estate or interest by virtue of a special power of appointment shall not be treated as claiming through the appointor.

(7) References in this Act to a right of action to recover land shall include references to a right to enter into possession of the land or, in the case of rentcharges and tithes, to distrain for arrears of rent or tithe, and references to the bringing of such an action shall include references to the making of such an entry or distress.

(8) References in this Act to the possession of land shall, in the case of tithes and rentcharges, be construed as references to the receipt of the tithe or rent, and references to the date of dispossession or discontinuance of possession of land shall, in the case of rent charges, be construed as references to the date of the last receipt of rent.

(9) References in Part II of this Act to a right of action shall include references to—

(a) a cause of action;

(b) a right to receive money secured by a mortgage or charge on any property;

(c) a right to recover proceeds of the sale of land; and

(d) a right to receive a share or interest in the personal estate of a deceased person.

(10) References in Part II to the date of the accrual of a right of action shall be construed—

(a) in the case of an action upon a judgment, as references to the date on which the judgment became enforceable; and

(b) in the case of an action to recover arrears of rent or interest, or damages in respect of arrears of rent or interest, as references to the date on which the rent or interest became due.

39. Saving for Other Limitation Enactments

This Act shall not apply to any action or arbitration for which a period of limitation is prescribed by or under any other enactment (whether passed before or after the passing of this Act) or to any action or arbitration to which the Crown is a party and for which, if it were between subjects, a period of limitation would be prescribed by or under any such other enactment.

40. Transitional Provisions, Amendments and Repeals

(1) Schedule 2 to this Act, which contains transitional provisions, shall have effect.

(2) The enactments specified in Schedule 3 to this Act shall have effect subject to the amendments specified in that Schedule, being amendments consequential on the provisions of this Act; but the amendment of any enactment by that Schedule shall not be taken as prejudicing the operation of section 17(2) of the Interpretation Act 1978 (effect of repeals).

(3) The enactments specified in Schedule 4 to this Act are hereby repealed to the extent specified in column 3 of that Schedule.

41. Short Title, Commencement and Extent

(1) This Act may be cited as the Limitation Act 1980.

(2) This Act, except section 35, shall come into force on 1st May 1981.

(3) Section 35 of this Act shall come into force on 1st May 1981 to the extent (if any) that the section substituted for section 28 of the Limitation Act 1939 by section 8 of the Limitation Amendment Act 1980 is in force immediately before that date; but otherwise section 35 shall come into force on such day as the Lord Chancellor may by order made by statutory instrument appoint, and different days may be appointed for different purposes of that section (including its application in relation to different courts or proceedings).

(4) The repeal by this Act of section 14(1) of the Limitation Act 1963 and the corresponding saving in paragraph 2 of Schedule 2 to this Act shall extend to Northern Ireland, but otherwise this Act does not extend to Scotland or to Northern Ireland.

[*Section 35 was brought into force on 1 May 1981 by SI 1981/588.*]

Section 15(6)(7)

SCHEDULE 1 PROVISIONS WITH RESPECT TO ACTIONS TO RECOVER LAND

PART I ACCRUAL OF RIGHTS OF ACTION TO RECOVER LAND

Accrual of Right of Action in Case of Present Interests in Land

1. Where the person bringing an action to recover land, or some person through whom he claims, has been in possession of the land, and has while entitled to the land been dispossessed or discontinued his possession, the right of action shall be treated as having accrued on the date of the dispossession or discontinuance.

2. Where any person brings an action to recover any land of a deceased person (whether under a will or on intestacy) and the deceased person—
(a) was on the date of his death in possession of the land or, in the case of a rentcharge created by will or taking effect upon his death, in possession of the land charged; and
(b) was the last person entitled to the land to be in possession of it;
the right of action shall be treated as having accrued on the date of his death.

3. Where any person brings an action to recover land, being an estate or interest in possession assured otherwise than by will to him, or to some person through whom he claims, and—
(a) the person making the assurance was on the date when the assurance took effect in possession of the land or, in the case of a rentcharge created by the assurance, in possession of the land charged; and
(b) no person has been in possession of the land by virtue of the assurance;
the right of action shall be treated as having accrued on the date when the assurance took effect.

Accrual of Right of Action in Case of Future Interests

4. The right of action to recover any land shall, in a case where—
(a) the estate or interest claimed was an estate or interest in reversion or remainder or any other future estate or interest; and
(b) no person has taken possession of the land by virtue of the estate or interest claimed;
be treated as having accrued on the date on which the estate or interest fell into possession by the determination of the preceding estate or interest.

5.—(1) Subject to sub-paragraph (2) below, a tenancy from year to year or other period, without a lease in writing, shall for the purposes of this Act be treated as being determined at the expiration of the first year or other period; and accordingly the right of action of the person entitled to the land subject to the tenancy shall be treated as having accrued at the date on which in accordance with this sub-paragraph the tenancy is determined.

(2) Where any rent has subsequently been received in respect of the tenancy, the right of action shall be treated as having accrued on the date of the last receipt of rent.

6.—(1) Where—
(a) any person is in possession of land by virtue of a lease in writing by which a rent of not less than ten pounds a year is reserved; and
(b) the rent is received by some person wrongfully claiming to be entitled to the land in reversion immediately expectant on the determination of the lease; and
(c) no rent is subsequently received by the person rightfully so entitled;
the right of action to recover the land of the person rightfully so entitled shall be treated as having accrued on the date when the rent was first received by the person wrongfully claiming to be so entitled and not on the date of the determination of the lease.

(2) Sub-paragraph (1) above shall not apply to any lease granted by the Crown.

Accrual of Right of Action in Case of Forfeiture or Breach of Condition

7.—(1) Subject to sub-paragraph (2) below, a right of action to recover land by virtue of a forfeiture or breach of condition shall be treated as having accrued on the date on which the forfeiture was incurred or the condition broken.

(2) If any such right has accrued to a person entitled to an estate or interest in reversion or remainder and the land was not recovered by virtue of that right, the right of action to

recover the land shall not be treated as having accrued to that person until his estate or interest fell into possession, as if no such forfeiture or breach of condition had occurred.

Right of Action Not to Accrue or Continue Unless There is Adverse Possession

8.—(1) No right of action to recover land shall be treated as accruing unless the land is in the possession of some person in whose favour the period of limitation can run (referred to below in this paragraph as 'adverse possession'); and where under the preceding provisions of this Schedule any such right of action is treated as accruing on a certain date and no person is in adverse possession on that date, the right of action shall not be treated as accruing unless and until adverse possession is taken of the land.

(2) Where a right of action to recover land has accrued and after its accrual, before the right is barred, the land ceases to be in adverse possession, the right of action shall no longer be treated as having accrued and no fresh right of action shall be treated as accruing unless and until the land is again taken into adverse possession.

(3) For the purposes of this paragraph—

(a) possession of any land subject to a rentcharge by a person (other than the person entitled to the rentcharge) who does not pay the rent shall be treated as adverse possession of the rentcharge; and

(b) receipt of rent under a lease by a person wrongfully claiming to be entitled to the land in reversion immediately expectant on the determination of the lease shall be treated as adverse possession of the land.

(4) For the purpose of determining whether a person occupying any land is in adverse possession of the land it shall not be assumed by implication of law that his occupation is by permission of the person entitled to the land merely by virtue of the fact that his occupation is not inconsistent with the latter's present or future enjoyment of the land.

This provision shall not be taken as prejudicing a finding to the effect that a person's occupation of any land is by implied permission of the person entitled to the land in any case where such a finding is justified on the actual facts of the case.

Possession of Beneficiary Not Adverse to Others Interested in Settled Land or Land Held on Trust for Sale

9. Where any settled land or any land subject to a trust of land is in the possession of a person entitled to a beneficial interest in the land (not being a person solely or absolutely entitled to the land), no right of action to recover the land shall be treated for the purposes of this Act as accruing during that possession to any person in whom the land is vested as tenant for life, statutory owner or trustee, or to any other person entitled to a beneficial interest in the land.

PART II MODIFICATIONS OF SECTION 15 WHERE CROWN OR CERTAIN CORPORATIONS SOLE ARE INVOLVED

10. Subject to paragraph 11 below, section 15(1) of this Act shall apply to the bringing of an action to recover any land by the Crown or by any spiritual or eleemosynary corporation sole with the substitution for the reference to twelve years of a reference to thirty years.

11.—(1) An action to recover foreshore may be brought by the Crown at any time before the expiration of sixty years from the date mentioned in section 15(1) of this Act.

(2) Where any right of action to recover land which has ceased to be foreshore but remains in the ownership of the Crown accrued when the land was foreshore, the action may be brought at any time before the expiration of—

(a) sixty years from the date of accrual of the right of action; or

(b) thirty years from the date when the land ceased to be fore-shore;

whichever period first expires.

(3) In this paragraph 'foreshore' means the shore and bed of the sea and of any tidal water, below the line of the medium high tide between the spring tides and the neap tides.

12. Notwithstanding section 15(1) of this Act, where in the case of any action brought by a person other than the Crown or a spiritual or eleemosynary corporation sole the right of action first

accrued to the Crown or any such corporation sole through whom the person in question claims, the action may be brought at any time before the expiration of—

(a) the period during which the action could have been brought by the Crown or the corporation sole; or

(b) twelve years from the date on which the right of action accrued to some person other than the Crown or the corporation sole;

whichever period first expires.

13. Section 15(2) of this Act shall apply in any case where the Crown or a spiritual or eleemosynary corporation sole is entitled to the succeeding estate or interest with the substitution—

(a) for the reference to twelve years of a reference to thirty years; and

(b) for the reference to six years of a reference to twelve years.

SCHEDULE 2 TRANSITIONAL PROVISIONS

1. Nothing in this Act shall affect the operation of section 4 of the Limitation Act 1963, as it had effect immediately before 1 January 1979 (being the date on which the Civil Liability (Contribution) Act 1978 came in to force), in relation to any case where the damage in question occurred before that date.

2. The amendment made by section 14(1) of the Limitation Act 1963 in section 5 of the Limitation (Enemies and War Prisoners) Act 1945 (which provides that section 5 shall have effect as if for the words 'in force in Northern Ireland at the date of the passing of this Act' there were substituted the words 'for the time being in force in Northern Ireland') shall continue to have effect notwithstanding the repeal by this Act of section 14(1).

3. It is hereby declared that a decision taken at any time by a court to grant, or not to grant, leave under Part I of the Limitation Act 1963 (which, so far as it related to leave, was repealed by the Limitation Act 1975) does not affect the determination of any question in proceedings under any provision of this Act which corresponds to a provision of the Limitation Act 1975, but in such proceedings account may be taken of evidence admitted in proceedings under Part I of the Limitation Act 1963.

4.—(1) In section 33(6) of this Act the reference to section 1(1) of the Fatal Accidents Act 1976 shall be construed as including a reference to section 1 of the Fatal Accidents Act 1846.

(2) Any other reference in that section, or in section 12 or 13 of this Act, to the Fatal Accidents Act 1976 shall be construed as including a reference to the Fatal Accidents Act 1846.

5. Notwithstanding anything in section 29(7) of this Act or in the repeals made by this Act, the Limitation Act 1939 shall continue to have effect in relation to any acknowledgment or payment made before the coming into force of section 6 of the Limitation Amendment Act 1980 (which amended section 23 of the Limitation Act 1939 and made certain repeals in sections 23 and 25 of that Act so as to prevent the revival by acknowledgment or part payment of a right of action barred by that Act) as it had effect immediately before section 6 came into force.

6. Section 28 of the Limitation Act 1939 (provisions as to set-off or counterclaim) shall continue to apply (as originally enacted) to any claim by way of set-off or counterclaim made in an action to which section 35 of this Act does not apply, but as if the reference in section 28 to that Act were a reference to this Act; and, in relation to any such action, references in this Act to section 35 of this Act shall be construed as references to section 28 as it applies by virtue of this paragraph.

7. Section 37(2)(c) of this Act shall be treated for the purposes of the Hovercraft Act 1968 as if it were contained in an Act passed before that Act.

8. In relation to a lease granted before the coming into force of section 3(2) of the Limitation Amendment Act 1980 (which substituted 'ten pounds a year' for 'twenty shillings' in section 9(3) of the Limitation Act 1939), paragraph 6(1)(a) of Schedule 1 to this Act shall have effect as if for the words 'ten pounds a year' there were substituted the words 'twenty shillings'.

9.—(1) Nothing in any provision of this Act shall—

(a) enable any action to be brought which was barred by this Act or (as the case may be) by the Limitation Act 1939 before the relevant date; or

(b) affect any action or arbitration commenced before that date or the title to any property which is the subject of any such action or arbitration.

(2) In sub-paragraph (1) above 'the relevant date' means—

(a) in relation to section 35 of this Act, the date on which that section comes into force in relation to actions of the description in question or, if section 8 of the Limitation Amendment Act 1980 (which substituted the provisions reproduced in section 35 for section 28 of the Limitation Act 1939) is in force immediately before 1st May 1981 in relation to actions of that description, the date on which section 8 came into force in relation to actions of that description; and

(b) in relation to any other provision of this Act, 1st August 1980 (being the date of coming into force of the remaining provisions of the Limitation Amendment Act 1980, apart from section 8).

NOTES ON TEXT

The text printed above incorporates the following amendments:

s. 4A inserted by Administration of Justice Act 1985, s. 57(1) and (2) (see note 1), and substituted by Defamation Act 1996, s. 5(1) and (2) (see note 2);

s. 11(1A) inserted by Protection from Harassment Act 1997, s. 6 (in force by SI 1997/1498);

s. 11A inserted by Consumer Protection Act 1987, sch. 1, para. 1 (see note 3);

s. 12(1) amended by Consumer Protection Act 1987, sch. 1, para. 2 (see note 3);

s. 14(1) amended and (1A) inserted by Consumer Protection Act 1987, sch. 1, para. 3 (see note 3);

ss. 14A and 14B inserted by Latent Damage Act 1986, s. 1 (see note 4);

s. 18 amended by Trusts of Land and Appointment of Trustees Act 1996, sch. 4 (in force by SI 1996/2974);

s. 28(4A) inserted by Administration of Justice Act 1985, s. 57(1) and (3), 1 and substituted by Defamation Act 1996, s. 5(1) and (3) (see note 2);

s. 28(7) inserted by Consumer Protection Act 1987, sch. 1, para. 4 (see note 3);

s. 28A inserted by Latent Damage Act 1986, s. 2(1) (see note 4);

s. 32(1) amended and (4A) inserted by Consumer Protection Act 1987, sch. 1, para. 5 (see note 3);

s. 32(5) inserted by Latent Damage Act 1986, s. 2(2) (see note 4);

s. 32A inserted by Administration of Justice Act 1985, s. 57(1) and (4) (see note 1), and substituted by Defamation Act 1996, s. 5(1) and (4) (see note 2);

s. 33 amended by Consumer Protection Act 1987, sch. 1, para. 6 (see note 3);

s. 34 repealed by Arbitration Act 1996, sch. 4 (in force by SI 1996/3146, art. 3);

s. 35(9) repealed by Supreme Court Act 1981, sch. 7;

s. 36(1)(aa) inserted by Administration of Justice Act 1985, s. 57(1) and (5) (see note 1), and substituted by Defamation Act 1996, s. 5(1) and (5) (see note 2);

s. 38(1) amended by Trusts of Land and Appointment of Trustees Act 1996, sch. 4 (in force by SI 1996/2974);

s. 38(3) and (4) amended by: (a) Mental Health (Amendment) Act 1982, sch. 3, para. 58; (b) Mental Health Act 1983, sch. 4, para. 55;

sch. 1, para. 9, amended by Trusts of Land and Appointment of Trustees Act 1996, sch. 3, para. 18, and sch. 4 (in force by SI 1996/2974).

Schedules 3 (consequential amendments) and 4 (repeals) are omitted.

Note 1. The amendments made by the Administration of Justice Act 1985, s. 57 do not apply in relation to an action if the cause of action accrued before 30 December 1985 (by the 1985 Act, s. 69(4) and sch. 9, para. 14).

Note 2. The amendments made by the Defamation Act 1996 apply only to causes of action arising after 4 September 1996 (by ss. 5(6) and 19(2) of the 1996 Act).

Note 3. In force by SI 1987/1680, art. 4.

Note 4. The amendments made by the Latent Damage Act 1986, ss. 1 and 2, are subject to s. 4 of the Act, which provides:

(1) Nothing in section 1 or 2 of this Act shall—

(a) enable any action to be brought which was barred by [the Limitation Act 1980] or (as the case may be) by the Limitation Act 1939 before this Act comes into force; or

(b) affect any action commenced before this Act comes into force.

(2) Subject to subsection (1) above, sections 1 and 2 of this Act shall have effect in relation to causes of action accruing before, as well as in relation to causes of action accruing after, this Act comes into force.

The 1986 Act came into force on 18 September 1986 (by s. 5(3) of the Act).

Misrepresentation Act 1967

(1967 CHAPTER 7)

1. Removal of Certain Bars to Rescission for Innocent Misrepresentation

Where a person has entered into a contract after a misrepresentation has been made to him, and—
(a) the misrepresentation has become a term of the contract, or
(b) the contract has been performed;
or both, then, if otherwise he would be entitled to rescind the contract without alleging fraud, he shall be so entitled, subject to the provisions of this Act, notwithstanding the matters mentioned in paragraphs (a) and (b) of this section.

2. Damages for Misrepresentation

(1) Where a person has entered into a contract after a misrepresentation has been made to him by another party thereto and as a result thereof he has suffered loss, then, if the person making the misrepresentation would be liable to damages in respect thereof had the misrepresentation been made fraudulently, that person shall be so liable notwithstanding that the misrepresentation was not made fraudulently, unless he proves that he had reasonable ground to believe and did believe up to the time the contract was made that the facts represented were true.

(2) Where a person has entered into a contract after a misrepresentation has been made to him otherwise than fraudulently, and he would be entitled, by reason of the misrepresentation, to rescind the contract, then, if it is claimed, in any proceedings arising out of the contract, that the contract ought to be or has been rescinded, the court or arbitrator may declare the contract subsisting and award damages in lieu of rescission, if of opinion that it would be equitable to do so having regard to the nature of the misrepresentation and the loss that would be caused by it if the contract were upheld, as well as to the loss that rescission would cause to the other party.

(3) Damages may be awarded against a person under subsection (2) of this section whether or not he is liable to damages under subsection (1) thereof, but where he is so liable any award under the said subsection (2) shall be taken into account in assessing his liability under the said subsection (1).

3. Avoidance of Provision Excluding Liability for Misrepresentation

If a contract contains a term which would exclude or restrict—
(a) any liability to which a party to a contract may be subject by reason of any misrepresentation made by him before the contract was made; or
(b) any remedy available to another party to the contract by reason of such a misrepresentation,
that term shall be of no effect except in so far as it satisfies the requirement of reasonableness as stated in section II (1) of the Unfair Contract Terms Act 1977; and it is for those claiming that the term satisfies that requirement to show that it does.

5. Saving for Past Transactions

Nothing in this Act shall apply in relation to any misrepresentation or contract of sale which is made before the commencement of this Act.
[*The Act came into force on 22 April 1967.*]

Occupiers' Liability Act 1957

(5 & 6 ELIZ. 2 CHAPTER 31)

1. Preliminary

(1) The rules enacted by the two next following sections shall have effect, in place of the rules of the common law, to regulate the duty which an occupier of premises owes to his visitors in respect of dangers due to the state of the premises or to things done or omitted to be done on them.

(2) The rules so enacted shall regulate the nature of the duty imposed by law in consequence of a person's occupation or control of premises and of any invitation or permission he gives (or is to be treated as giving) to another to enter or use the premises, but they shall not alter the rules of the common law as to the persons on whom a duty is so imposed or to whom it is owed; and accordingly for the purpose of the rules so enacted the persons who are to be treated as an occupier and as his visitors are the same (subject to subsection (4) of this section) as the persons who would at common law be treated as an occupier and as his invitees or licensees.

(3) The rules so enacted in relation to an occupier of premises and his visitors shall also apply, in like manner and to the like extent as the principles applicable at common law to an occupier of premises and his invitees or licensees would apply, to regulate—

(a) the obligations of a person occupying or having control over any fixed or moveable structure, including any vessel, vehicle or aircraft; and

(b) the obligations of a person occupying or having control over any premises or structure in respect of damage to property, including the property of persons who are not themselves his visitors.

(4) A person entering any premises in exercise of rights conferred by virtue of an access agreement or order under the National Parks and Access to the Countryside Act 1949, is not, for the purposes of this Act, a visitor of the occupier of those premises.

2. Extent of Occupier's Ordinary Duty

(1) An occupier of premises owes the same duty, the 'common duty of care', to all his visitors, except in so far as he is free to and does extend, restrict, modify or exclude his duty to any visitor or visitors by agreement or otherwise.

(2) The common duty of care is a duty to take such care as in all the circumstances of the case is reasonable to see that the visitor will be reasonably safe in using the premises for the purposes for which he is invited or permitted by the occupier to be there.

(3) The circumstances relevant for the present purposes include the degree of care, and of want of care, which would ordinarily be looked for in such a visitor, so that (for example) in proper cases—

(a) an occupier must be prepared for children to be less careful than adults; and

(b) an occupier may expect that a person, in the exercise of his calling, will appreciate and guard against any special risks ordinarily incident to it, so far as the occupier leaves him free to do so.

(4) In determining whether the occupier of premises has discharged the common duty of care to a visitor, regard is to be had to all the circumstances, so that (for example)—

(a) where damage is caused to a visitor by a danger of which he had been warned by the occupier, the warning is not to be treated without more as absolving the occupier from liability, unless in all the circumstances it was enough to enable the visitor to be reasonably safe; and

(b) where damage is caused to a visitor by a danger due to the faulty execution of any work of construction, maintenance or repair by an independent contractor employed by the occupier, the occupier is not to be treated without more as answerable for the danger if in all the circumstances he had acted reasonably in entrusting the work to an independent contractor and had taken such steps (if any) as he reasonably ought in order to satisfy himself that the contractor was competent and that the work had been properly done.

(5) The common duty of care does not impose on an occupier any obligation to a visitor in respect of risks willingly accepted as his by the visitor (the question whether a risk was so accepted to be decided on the same principles as in other cases in which one person owes a duty of care to another).

(6) For the purposes of this section, persons who enter premises for any purpose in the exercise of a right conferred by law are to be treated as permitted by the occupier to be there for that purpose, whether they in fact have his permission or not.

3. Effect of Contract on Occupier's Liability to Third Party

(1) Where an occupier of premises is bound by contract to permit persons who are strangers to the contract to enter or use the premises, the duty of care which he owes to them as his visitors cannot be restricted or excluded by that contract, but (subject to any provision of the contract to the contrary) shall include the duty to perform his obligations under the contract, whether undertaken for their protection or not, in so far as those obligations go beyond the obligations otherwise involved in that duty.

(2) A contract shall not by virtue of this section have the effect, unless it expressly so provides, of making an occupier who has taken all reasonable care answerable to strangers to the contract for dangers due to the faulty execution of any work of construction, maintenance or repair or other like operation by persons other than himself, his servants and persons acting under his direction and control.

(3) In this section, 'stranger to the contract' means a person not for the time being entitled to the benefit of the contract as a party to it or as the successor by assignment or otherwise of a party to it, and accordingly includes a party to the contract who has ceased to be so entitled.

(4) Where by the terms or conditions governing any tenancy (including a statutory tenancy which does not in law amount to a tenancy) either the landlord or the tenant is bound, though not by contract, to permit persons to enter or use premises of which he is the occupier, this section shall apply as if the tenancy were a contract between the landlord and the tenant.

(5) This section, in so far as it prevents the common duty of care from being restricted or excluded, applies to contracts entered into and tenancies created before the commencement of this Act, as well as to those entered into or created after its commencement; but, in so far as it enlarges the duty owed by an occupier beyond the common duty of care, it shall have effect only in relation to obligations which are undertaken after the commencement or which are renewed by agreement (whether express or implied) after that commencement.

5. Implied Term in Contracts

(1) Where persons enter or use, or bring or send goods to, any premises in exercise of a right conferred by contract with a person occupying or having control of the premises, the duty he owes them in respect of dangers due to the state of the premises or to things done or omitted to be done on them, in so far as the duty depends on a term to be implied in the contract by reason of its conferring that right, shall be the common duty of care.

(2) The foregoing subsection shall apply to fixed and moveable structures as it applies to premises.

(3) This section does not affect the obligations imposed on a person by or by virtue of any contract for the hire of, or for the carriage for reward of persons or goods in, any vehicle, vessel, aircraft or other means of transport, or by or by virtue of any contract of bailment.

(4) This section does not apply to contracts entered into before the commencement of this Act.

6. Application to Crown

This Act shall bind the Crown, but as regards the Crown's liability in tort shall not bind the Crown further than the Crown is made liable in tort by the Crown Proceedings Act 1947, and that Act and in particular section two of it shall apply in relation to duties under sections two to four of this Act as statutory duties.

Occupiers' Liability Act 1984

(1984 CHAPTER 3)

1. Duty of Occupier to Persons Other Than His Visitors

(1) The rules enacted by this section shall have effect, in place of the rules of the common law, to determine—

(a) whether any duty is owed by a person as occupier of premises to persons other than his visitors in respect of any risk of their suffering injury on the premises by reason of any danger due to the state of the premises or to things done or omitted to be done on them; and

(b) if so, what that duty is.

(2) For the purposes of this section, the persons who are to be treated respectively as an occupier of any premises (which, for those purposes, include any fixed or movable structure) and as his visitors are—

(a) any person who owes in relation to the premises the duty referred to in section 2 of the Occupiers' Liability Act 1957 (the common duty of care), and

(b) those who are his visitors for the purposes of that duty.

(3) An occupier of premises owes a duty to another (not being his visitor) in respect of any such risk as is referred to in subsection (1) above if—

(a) he is aware of the danger or has reasonable grounds to believe that it exists;

(b) he knows or has reasonable grounds to believe that the other is in the vicinity of the danger concerned or that he may come into the vicinity of the danger (in either case, whether the other has lawful authority for being in that vicinity or not); and

(c) the risk is one against which, in all the circumstances of the case, he may reasonably be expected to offer the other some protection.

(4) Where, by virtue of this section, an occupier of premises owes a duty to another in respect of such a risk, the duty is to take such care as is reasonable in all the circumstances of the case to see that he does not suffer injury on the premises by reason of the danger concerned.

(5) Any duty owed by virtue of this section in respect of a risk may, in an appropriate case, be discharged by taking such steps as are reasonable in all the circumstances of the case to give warning of the danger concerned or to discourage persons from incurring the risk.

(6) No duty is owed by virtue of this section to any person in respect of risks willingly accepted as his by that person (the question whether a risk was so accepted to be decided on the same principles as in other cases in which one person owes a duty of care to another).

(7) No duty is owed by virtue of this section to persons using the highway, and this section does not affect any duty owed to such persons.

(8) Where a person owes a duty by virtue of this section, he does not, by reason of any breach of the duty, incur any liability in respect of any loss of or damage to property.

(9) In this section—

'highway' means any part of a highway other than a ferry or waterway;

'injury' means anything resulting in death or personal injury, including any disease and any impairment of physical or mental condition; and

'movable structure' includes any vessel, vehicle or aircraft.

3. Application to Crown

Section 1 of this Act shall bind the Crown, but as regards the Crown's liability in tort shall not bind the Crown further than the Crown is made liable in tort by the Crown Proceedings Act 1947.

Protection from Harassment Act 1997

(1997 CHAPTER 40)

1. Prohibition of Harassment

(1) A person must not pursue a course of conduct—
 (a) which amounts to harassment of another, and
 (b) which he knows or ought to know amounts to harassment of the other.

(2) For the purposes of this section, the person whose course of conduct is in question ought to know that it amounts to harassment of another if a reasonable person in possession of the same information would think the course of conduct amounted to harassment of the other.

(3) Subsection (1) does not apply to a course of conduct if the person who pursued it shows—
 (a) that it was pursued for the purpose of preventing or detecting crime,
 (b) that it was pursued under any enactment or rule of law or to comply with any condition or requirement imposed by any person under any enactment, or
 (c) that in the particular circumstances the pursuit of the course of conduct was reasonable.

2. Offence of Harassment

(1) A person who pursues a course of conduct in breach of section 1 is guilty of an offence.

(2) A person guilty of an offence under this section is liable on summary conviction to imprisonment for a term not exceeding six months, or a fine not exceeding level 5 on the standard scale, or both.

3. Civil Remedy

(1) An actual or apprehended breach of section 1 may be the subject of a claim in civil proceedings by the person who is or maybe the victim of the course of conduct in question.

(2) On such a claim, damages may be awarded for (among other things) any anxiety caused by the harassment and any financial loss resulting from the harassment.

(3) Where—
 (a) in such proceedings the High Court or a county court grants an injunction for the purpose of restraining the defendant from pursuing any conduct which amounts to harassment, and
 (b) the plaintiff considers that the defendant has done anything which he is prohibited from doing by the injunction,

the plaintiff may apply for the issue of a warrant for the arrest of the defendant.

(4) An application under subsection (3) may be made—
 (a) where the injunction was granted by the High Court, to a judge of that court, and
 (b) where the injunction was granted by a county court, to a judge or district judge of that or any other county court.

(5) The judge or district judge to whom an application under subsection (3) is made may only issue a warrant if—
 (a) the application is substantiated on oath, and
 (b) the judge or district judge has reasonable grounds for believing that the defendant has done anything which he is prohibited from doing by the injunction.

(6) Where—
 (a) the High Court or a county court grants an injunction for the purpose mentioned in subsection (3)(a), and
 (b) without reasonable excuse the defendant does anything which he is prohibited from doing by the injunction,

he is guilty of an offence.

(7) Where a person is convicted of an offence under subsection (6) in respect of any conduct, that conduct is not punishable as a contempt of court.

(8) A person cannot be convicted of an offence under subsection (6) in respect of any conduct which has been punished as a contempt of court.

(9) A person guilty of an offence under subsection (6) is liable—
(a) on conviction on indictment, to imprisonment for a term not exceeding five years, or a fine, or both, or
(b) on summary conviction, to imprisonment for a term not exceeding six months, or a fine not exceeding the statutory maximum, or both.

4. Putting People in Fear of Violence

(1) A person whose course of conduct causes another to fear, on at least two occasions, that violence will be used against him is guilty of an offence if he knows or ought to know that his course of conduct will cause the other so to fear on each of those occasions.
(2) For the purposes of this section, the person whose course of conduct is in question ought to know that it will cause another to fear that violence will be used against him on any occasion if a reasonable person in possession of the same information would think the course of conduct would cause the other so to fear on that occasion.
(3) It is a defence for a person charged with an offence under this section to show that—
(a) his course of conduct was pursued for the purpose of preventing or detecting crime,
(b) his course of conduct was pursued under any enactment or rule of law or to comply with any condition or requirement imposed by any person under any enactment, or
(c) the pursuit of his course of conduct was reasonable for the protection of himself or another or for the protection of his or another's property.
(4) A person guilty of an offence under this section is liable—
(a) on conviction on indictment, to imprisonment for a term not exceeding five years, or a fine, or both, or
(b) on summary conviction, to imprisonment for a term not exceeding six months, or a fine not exceeding the statutory maximum, or both.
(5) If on the trial on indictment of a person charged with an offence under this section the jury find him not guilty of the offence charged, they may find him guilty of an offence under section 2.
(6) The Crown Court has the same powers and duties in relation to a person who is by virtue of subsection (5) convicted before it of an offence under section 2 as a magistrates' court would have on convicting him of the offence.

5. Restraining Orders

(1) A court sentencing or otherwise dealing with a person ('the defendant') convicted of an offence under section 2 or 4 may (as well as sentencing him or dealing with him in any other way) make an order under this section.
(2) The order may, for the purpose of protecting the victim of the offence, or any other person mentioned in the order, from further conduct which—
(a) amounts to harassment, or
(b) will cause a fear of violence,
prohibit the defendant from doing anything described in the order.
(3) The order may have effect for a specified period or until further order.
(4) The prosecutor, the defendant or any other person mentioned in the order may apply to the court which made the order for it to be varied or discharged by a further order.
(5) If without reasonable excuse the defendant does anything which he is prohibited from doing by an order under this section, he is guilty of an offence.
(6) A person guilty of an offence under this section is liable—
(a) on conviction on indictment, to imprisonment for a term not exceeding five years, or a fine, or both, or
(b) on summary conviction, to imprisonment for a term not exceeding six months, or a fine not exceeding the statutory maximum, or both.

7. Interpretation of This Group of Sections

(1) This section applies for the interpretation of sections 1 to 5.
(2) References to harassing a person include alarming the person or causing the person distress.
(3) A 'course of conduct' must involve conduct on at least two occasions.
(4) 'Conduct' includes speech.

12. National Security, etc.

(1) If the Secretary of State certifies that in his opinion anything done by a specified person on a specified occasion related to—
  (a) national security,
  (b) the economic well-being of the United Kingdom, or
  (c) the prevention or detection of serious crime,

and was done on behalf of the Crown, the certificate is conclusive evidence that this Act does not apply to any conduct of that person on that occasion.

(2) In subsection (1), 'specified' means specified in the certificate in question.

(3) A document purporting to be a certificate under subsection (1) is to be received in evidence and, unless the contrary is proved, be treated as being such a certificate.

Regulation (EC) No. 44/2001

of 22 December 2000 on jurisdiction and the recognition and enforcement of judgments in civil and commercial matters (OJ L 012, 16.01.2001, pp. 0001–0023)

THE COUNCIL OF THE EUROPEAN UNION,

Having regard to the Treaty establishing the European Community, and in particular Article 61(c) and Article 67(1) thereof,

Having regard to the proposal from the Commission,[1]

Having regard to the opinion of the European Parliament,[2]

Having regard to the opinion of the Economic and Social Committee,[3]

Whereas:

(1) The Community has set itself the objective of maintaining and developing an area of freedom, security and justice, in which the free movement of persons is ensured. In order to establish progressively such an area, the Community should adopt, amongst other things, the measures relating to judicial cooperation in civil matters which are necessary for the sound operation of the internal market.

(2) Certain differences between national rules governing jurisdiction and recognition of judgments hamper the sound operation of the internal market. Provisions to unify the rules of conflict of jurisdiction in civil and commercial matters and to simplify the formalities with a view to rapid and simple recognition and enforcement of judgments from Member States bound by this Regulation are essential.

(3) This area is within the field of judicial cooperation in civil matters within the meaning of Article 65 of the Treaty.

(4) In accordance with the principles of subsidiarity and proportionality as set out in Article 5 of the Treaty, the objectives of this Regulation cannot be sufficiently achieved by the Member States and can therefore be better achieved by the Community. This Regulation confines itself to the minimum required in order to achieve those objectives and does not go beyond what is necessary for that purpose.

(5) On 27 September 1968 the Member States, acting under Article 293, fourth indent, of the Treaty, concluded the Brussels Convention on Jurisdiction and the Enforcement of Judgments in Civil and Commercial Matters, as amended by Conventions on the Accession of the New Member States to that Convention (hereinafter referred to as the 'Brussels Convention').[4] On 16 September 1988 Member States and EFTA States concluded the Lugano Convention on Jurisdiction and the Enforcement of Judgments in Civil and Commercial Matters, which is a parallel Convention to the 1968 Brussels Convention. Work has been undertaken for the revision of those Conventions, and the Council has approved the content of the revised texts. Continuity in the results achieved in that revision should be ensured.

(6) In order to attain the objective of free movement of judgments in civil and commercial matters, it is necessary and appropriate that the rules governing jurisdiction and the recognition and enforcement of judgments be governed by a Community legal instrument which is binding and directly applicable.

(7) The scope of this Regulation must cover all the main civil and commercial matters apart from certain well-defined matters.

(8) There must be a link between proceedings to which this Regulation applies and the territory of the Member States bound by this Regulation. Accordingly common rules on jurisdiction should, in principle, apply when the defendant is domiciled in one of those Member States.

(9) A defendant not domiciled in a Member State is in general subject to national rules of jurisdic-

[1] OJ C 376, 28.12.1999, p. 1.

[2] OJ C 146, 17.5.2001, p. 101.

[3] OJ C 117, 26.4.2000, p. 6.

[4] OJ L 299, 31.12.1972, p. 32. OJ L 304, 30.10.1978, p. 1. OJ L 388, 31.12.1982, p. 1. OJ L 285, 3.10.1989, p. 1. OJ C 15, 15.1.1997, p. 1. For a consolidated text, see OJ C 27, 26.1.1998, p. 1.

tion applicable in the territory of the Member State of the court seised, and a defendant domiciled in a Member State not bound by this Regulation must remain subject to the Brussels Convention.

(10) For the purposes of the free movement of judgments, judgments given in a Member State bound by this Regulation should be recognised and enforced in another Member State bound by this Regulation, even if the judgment debtor is domiciled in a third State.

(11) The rules of jurisdiction must be highly predictable and founded on the principle that jurisdiction is generally based on the defendant's domicile and jurisdiction must always be available on this ground save in a few well-defined situations in which the subject-matter of the litigation or the autonomy of the parties warrants a different linking factor. The domicile of a legal person must be defined autonomously so as to make the common rules more transparent and avoid conflicts of jurisdiction.

(12) In addition to the defendant's domicile, there should be alternative grounds of jurisdiction based on a close link between the court and the action or in order to facilitate the sound administration of justice.

(13) In relation to insurance, consumer contracts and employment, the weaker party should be protected by rules of jurisdiction more favourable to his interests than the general rules provide for.

(14) The autonomy of the parties to a contract, other than an insurance, consumer or employment contract, where only limited autonomy to determine the courts having jurisdiction is allowed, must be respected subject to the exclusive grounds of jurisdiction laid down in this Regulation.

(15) In the interests of the harmonious administration of justice it is necessary to minimise the possibility of concurrent proceedings and to ensure that irreconcilable judgments will not be given in two Member States. There must be a clear and effective mechanism for resolving cases of *lis pendens* and related actions and for obviating problems flowing from national differences as to the determination of the time when a case is regarded as pending. For the purposes of this Regulation that time should be defined autonomously.

(16) Mutual trust in the administration of justice in the Community justifies judgments given in a Member State being recognised automatically without the need for any procedure except in cases of dispute.

(17) By virtue of the same principle of mutual trust, the procedure for making enforceable in one Member State a judgment given in another must be efficient and rapid. To that end, the declaration that a judgment is enforceable should be issued virtually automatically after purely formal checks of the documents supplied, without there being any possibility for the court to raise of its own motion any of the grounds for non-enforcement provided for by this Regulation.

(18) However, respect for the rights of the defence means that the defendant should be able to appeal in an adversarial procedure, against the declaration of enforceability, if he considers one of the grounds for non-enforcement to be present. Redress procedures should also be available to the claimant where his application for a declaration of enforceability has been rejected.

(19) Continuity between the Brussels Convention and this Regulation should be ensured, and transitional provisions should be laid down to that end. The same need for continuity applies as regards the interpretation of the Brussels Convention by the Court of Justice of the European Communities and the 1971 Protocol[5] should remain applicable also to cases already pending when this Regulation enters into force.

(20) The United Kingdom and Ireland, in accordance with Article 3 of the Protocol on the position of the United Kingdom and Ireland annexed to the Treaty on European Union and to the Treaty establishing the European Community, have given notice of their wish to take part in the adoption and application of this Regulation.

(21) Denmark, in accordance with Articles 1 and 2 of the Protocol on the position of Denmark annexed to the Treaty on European Union and to the Treaty establishing the European Community, is not participating in the adoption of this Regulation, and is therefore not bound by it nor subject to its application.

[5] OJ L 204, 2.8.1975, p. 28. OJ L 304, 30.10.1978, p. 1. OJ L 388, 31.12.1982, p. 1. OJ L 285, 3.10.1989, p. 1. OJ C 15, 15.1.1997, p. 1. For a consolidated text see OJ C 27, 26.1.1998, p. 28.

(22) Since the Brussels Convention remains in force in relations between Denmark and the Member States that are bound by this Regulation, both the Convention and the 1971 Protocol continue to apply between Denmark and the Member States bound by this Regulation.

(23) The Brussels Convention also continues to apply to the territories of the Member States which fall within the territorial scope of that Convention and which are excluded from this Regulation pursuant to Article 299 of the Treaty.

(24) Likewise for the sake of consistency, this Regulation should not affect rules governing jurisdiction and the recognition of judgments contained in specific Community instruments.

(25) Respect for international commitments entered into by the Member States means that this Regulation should not affect conventions relating to specific matters to which the Member States are parties.

(26) The necessary flexibility should be provided for in the basic rules of this Regulation in order to take account of the specific procedural rules of certain Member States. Certain provisions of the Protocol annexed to the Brussels Convention should accordingly be incorporated in this Regulation.

(27) In order to allow a harmonious transition in certain areas which were the subject of special provisions in the Protocol annexed to the Brussels Convention, this Regulation lays down, for a transitional period, provisions taking into consideration the specific situation in certain Member States.

(28) No later than five years after entry into force of this Regulation the Commission will present a report on its application and, if need be, submit proposals for adaptations.

(29) The Commission will have to adjust Annexes I to IV on the rules of national jurisdiction, the courts or competent authorities and redress procedures available on the basis of the amendments forwarded by the Member State concerned; amendments made to Annexes V and VI should be adopted in accordance with Council Decision 1999/468/EC of 28 June 1999 laying down the procedures for the exercise of implementing powers conferred on the Commission,[6]

HAS ADOPTED THIS REGULATION:

CHAPTER I SCOPE

Article 1

1. This Regulation shall apply in civil and commercial matters whatever the nature of the court or tribunal. It shall not extend, in particular, to revenue, customs or administrative matters.
2. The Regulation shall not apply to:
   (a) the status or legal capacity of natural persons, rights in property arising out of a matrimonial relationship, wills and succession;
   (b) bankruptcy, proceedings relating to the winding-up of insolvent companies or other legal persons, judicial arrangements, compositions and analogous proceedings;
   (c) social security;
   (d) arbitration.
3. In this Regulation, the term 'Member State' shall mean Member States with the exception of Denmark.

CHAPTER II JURISDICTION

Section 1 General Provisions

Article 2

1. Subject to this Regulation, persons domiciled in a Member State shall, whatever their nationality, be sued in the courts of that Member State.
2. Persons who are not nationals of the Member State in which they are domiciled shall be governed by the rules of jurisdiction applicable to nationals of that State.

[6] OJ L 184, 17.7.1999, p. 23.

Article 3

1. Persons domiciled in a Member State may be sued in the courts of another Member State only by virtue of the rules set out in Sections 2 to 7 of this Chapter.
2. In particular the rules of national jurisdiction set out in Annex I shall not be applicable as against them.

Article 4

1. If the defendant is not domiciled in a Member State, the jurisdiction of the courts of each Member State shall, subject to Articles 22 and 23, be determined by the law of that Member State.
2. As against such a defendant, any person domiciled in a Member State may, whatever his nationality, avail himself in that State of the rules of jurisdiction there in force, and in particular those specified in Annex I, in the same way as the nationals of that State.

Section 2 Special Jurisdiction

Article 5

A person domiciled in a Member State may, in another Member State, be sued:

1. (a) in matters relating to a contract, in the courts for the place of performance of the obligation in question;
   (b) for the purpose of this provision and unless otherwise agreed, the place of performance of the obligation in question shall be:
   — in the case of the sale of goods, the place in a Member State where, under the contract, the goods were delivered or should have been delivered,
   — in the case of the provision of services, the place in a Member State where, under the contract, the services were provided or should have been provided,
   (c) if sub-paragraph (b) does not apply then sub-paragraph (a) applies;
2. in matters relating to maintenance, in the courts for the place where the maintenance creditor is domiciled or habitually resident or, if the matter is ancillary to proceedings concerning the status of a person, in the court which, according to its own law, has jurisdiction to entertain those proceedings, unless that jurisdiction is based solely on the nationality of one of the parties;
3. in matters relating to tort, delict or quasi-delict, in the courts for the place where the harmful event occurred or may occur;
4. as regards a civil claim for damages or restitution which is based on an act giving rise to criminal proceedings, in the court seised of those proceedings, to the extent that that court has jurisdiction under its own law to entertain civil proceedings;
5. as regards a dispute arising out of the operations of a branch, agency or other establishment, in the courts for the place in which the branch, agency or other establishment is situated;
6. as settlor, trustee or beneficiary of a trust created by the operation of a statute, or by a written instrument, or created orally and evidenced in writing, in the courts of the Member State in which the trust is domiciled;
7. as regards a dispute concerning the payment of remuneration claimed in respect of the salvage of a cargo or freight, in the court under the authority of which the cargo or freight in question:
   (a) has been arrested to secure such payment, or
   (b) could have been so arrested, but bail or other security has been given;
   provided that this provision shall apply only if it is claimed that the defendant has an interest in the cargo or freight or had such an interest at the time of salvage.

Article 6

A person domiciled in a Member State may also be sued:

1. where he is one of a number of defendants, in the courts for the place where any one of them is domiciled, provided the claims are so closely connected that it is expedient to hear and determine them together to avoid the risk of irreconcilable judgments resulting from separate proceedings;
2. as a third party in an action on a warranty or guarantee or in any other third party proceedings, in the court seised of the original proceedings, unless these were instituted solely with the object of removing him from the jurisdiction of the court which would be competent in his case;

3. on a counterclaim arising from the same contract or facts on which the original claim was based, in the court in which the original claim is pending;
4. in matters relating to a contract, if the action may be combined with an action against the same defendant in matters relating to rights *in rem* in immovable property, in the court of the Member State in which the property is situated.

Article 7

Where by virtue of this Regulation a court of a Member State has jurisdiction in actions relating to liability from the use or operation of a ship, that court, or any other court substituted for this purpose by the internal law of that Member State, shall also have jurisdiction over claims for limitation of such liability.

Section 3 Jurisdiction in Matters Relating to Insurance

Article 8

In matters relating to insurance, jurisdiction shall be determined by this Section, without prejudice to Article 4 and point 5 of Article 5.

Article 9

1. An insurer domiciled in a Member State may be sued:
   (a) in the courts of the Member State where he is domiciled, or
   (b) in another Member State, in the case of actions brought by the policyholder, the insured or a beneficiary, in the courts for the place where the plaintiff is domiciled,
   (c) if he is a co-insurer, in the courts of a Member State in which proceedings are brought against the leading insurer.
2. An insurer who is not domiciled in a Member State but has a branch, agency or other establishment in one of the Member States shall, in disputes arising out of the operations of the branch, agency or establishment, be deemed to be domiciled in that Member State.

Article 10

In respect of liability insurance or insurance of immovable property, the insurer may in addition be sued in the courts for the place where the harmful event occurred. The same applies if movable and immovable property are covered by the same insurance policy and both are adversely affected by the same contingency.

Article 11

1. In respect of liability insurance, the insurer may also, if the law of the court permits it, be joined in proceedings which the injured party has brought against the insured.
2. Articles 8, 9 and 10 shall apply to actions brought by the injured party directly against the insurer, where such direct actions are permitted.
3. If the law governing such direct actions provides that the policyholder or the insured may be joined as a party to the action, the same court shall have jurisdiction over them.

Article 12

1. Without prejudice to Article 11(3), an insurer may bring proceedings only in the courts of the Member State in which the defendant is domiciled, irrespective of whether he is the policyholder, the insured or a beneficiary.
2. The provisions of this Section shall not affect the right to bring a counterclaim in the court in which, in accordance with this Section, the original claim is pending.

Article 13

The provisions of this Section may be departed from only by an agreement:
1. which is entered into after the dispute has arisen, or
2. which allows the policyholder, the insured or a beneficiary to bring proceedings in courts other than those indicated in this Section, or

3. which is concluded between a policyholder and an insurer, both of whom are at the time of conclusion of the contract domiciled or habitually resident in the same Member State, and which has the effect of conferring jurisdiction on the courts of that State even if the harmful event were to occur abroad, provided that such an agreement is not contrary to the law of that State, or
4. which is concluded with a policyholder who is not domiciled in a Member State, except in so far as the insurance is compulsory or relates to immovable property in a Member State, or
5. which relates to a contract of insurance in so far as it covers one or more of the risks set out in Article 14.

Article 14

The following are the risks referred to in Article 13(5):

1. any loss of or damage to:
   (a) seagoing ships, installations situated offshore or on the high seas, or aircraft, arising from perils which relate to their use for commercial purposes;
   (b) goods in transit other than passengers' baggage where the transit consists of or includes carriage by such ships or aircraft;
2. any liability, other than for bodily injury to passengers or loss of or damage to their baggage:
   (a) arising out of the use or operation of ships, installations or aircraft as referred to in point 1(a) in so far as, in respect of the latter, the law of the Member State in which such aircraft are registered does not prohibit agreements on jurisdiction regarding insurance of such risks;
   (b) for loss or damage caused by goods in transit as described in point 1(b);
3. any financial loss connected with the use or operation of ships, installations or aircraft as referred to in point 1(a), in particular loss of freight or charter-hire;
4. any risk or interest connected with any of those referred to in points 1 to 3;
5. notwithstanding points 1 to 4, all 'large risks' as defined in Council Directive 73/239/EEC,[7] as amended by Council Directives 88/357/EEC[8] and 90/618/EEC,[9] as they may be amended.

Section 4 Jurisdiction Over Consumer Contracts

Article 15

1. In matters relating to a contract concluded by a person, the consumer, for a purpose which can be regarded as being outside his trade or profession, jurisdiction shall be determined by this Section, without prejudice to Article 4 and point 5 of Article 5, if:
   (a) it is a contract for the sale of goods on instalment credit terms; or
   (b) it is a contract for a loan repayable by instalments, or for any other form of credit, made to finance the sale of goods; or
   (c) in all other cases, the contract has been concluded with a person who pursues commercial or professional activities in the Member State of the consumer's domicile or, by any means, directs such activities to that Member State or to several States including that Member State, and the contract falls within the scope of such activities.
2. Where a consumer enters into a contract with a party who is not domiciled in the Member State but has a branch, agency or other establishment in one of the Member States, that party shall, in disputes arising out of the operations of the branch, agency or establishment, be deemed to be domiciled in that State.
3. This Section shall not apply to a contract of transport other than a contract which, for an inclusive price, provides for a combination of travel and accommodation.

[7] OJ L 228, 16.8.1973, p. 3. Directive as last amended by Directive 2000/26/EC of the European Parliament and of the Council (OJ L 181, 20.7.2000, p. 65). OJ L 330, 29.11.1990, p. 44.

[8] OJ L 172, 4.7.1988, p. 1. Directive as last amended by Directive 2000/26/EC.

[9] OJ L 160, 30.6.2000, p. 37.

Article 16

1. A consumer may bring proceedings against the other party to a contract either in the courts of the Member State in which that party is domiciled or in the courts for the place where the consumer is domiciled.
2. Proceedings may be brought against a consumer by the other party to the contract only in the courts of the Member State in which the consumer is domiciled.
3. This Article shall not affect the right to bring a counterclaim in the court in which, in accordance with this Section, the original claim is pending.

Article 17

The provisions of this Section may be departed from only by an agreement:

1. which is entered into after the dispute has arisen; or
2. which allows the consumer to bring proceedings in courts other than those indicated in this Section; or
3. which is entered into by the consumer and the other party to the contract, both of whom are at the time of conclusion of the contract domiciled or habitually resident in the same Member State, and which confers jurisdiction on the courts of that Member State, provided that such an agreement is not contrary to the law of that Member State.

Section 5 Jurisdiction Over Individual Contracts of Employment Article 18

1. In matters relating to individual contracts of employment, jurisdiction shall be determined by this Section, without prejudice to Article 4 and point 5 of Article 5.
2. Where an employee enters into an individual contract of employment with an employer who is not domiciled in a Member State but has a branch, agency or other establishment in one of the Member States, the employer shall, in disputes arising out of the operations of the branch, agency or establishment, be deemed to be domiciled in that Member State.

Article 19

An employer domiciled in a Member State may be sued:

1. in the courts of the Member State where he is domiciled; or
2. in another Member State:
   (a) in the courts for the place where the employee habitually carries out his work or in the courts for the last place where he did so, or
   (b) if the employee does not or did not habitually carry out his work in any one country, in the courts for the place where the business which engaged the employee is or was situated.

Article 20

1. An employer may bring proceedings only in the courts of the Member State in which the employee is domiciled.
2. The provisions of this Section shall not affect the right to bring a counterclaim in the court in which, in accordance with this Section, the original claim is pending.

Article 21

The provisions of this Section may be departed from only by an agreement on jurisdiction:

1. which is entered into after the dispute has arisen; or
2. which allows the employee to bring proceedings in courts other than those indicated in this Section.

Section 6 Exclusive Jurisdiction

Article 22

The following courts shall have exclusive jurisdiction, regardless of domicile:

1. in proceedings which have as their object rights *in rem* in immovable property or tenancies of immovable property, the courts of the Member State in which the property is situated.

However, in proceedings which have as their object tenancies of immovable property concluded for temporary private use for a maximum period of six consecutive months, the courts of the Member State in which the defendant is domiciled shall also have jurisdiction, provided that the tenant is a natural person and that the landlord and the tenant are domiciled in the same Member State;

2. in proceedings which have as their object the validity of the constitution, the nullity or the dissolution of companies or other legal persons or associations of natural or legal persons, or of the validity of the decisions of their organs, the courts of the Member State in which the company, legal person or association has its seat. In order to determine that seat, the court shall apply its rules of private international law;
3. in proceedings which have as their object the validity of entries in public registers, the courts of the Member State in which the register is kept;
4. in proceedings concerned with the registration or validity of patents, trade marks, designs, or other similar rights required to be deposited or registered, the courts of the Member State in which the deposit or registration has been applied for, has taken place or is under the terms of a Community instrument or an international convention deemed to have taken place.

   Without prejudice to the jurisdiction of the European Patent Office under the Convention on the Grant of European Patents, signed at Munich on 5 October 1973, the courts of each Member State shall have exclusive jurisdiction, regardless of domicile, in proceedings concerned with the registration or validity of any European patent granted for that State;
5. in proceedings concerned with the enforcement of judgments, the courts of the Member State in which the judgment has been or is to be enforced.

Section 7 Prorogation of Jurisdiction

Article 23

1. If the parties, one or more of whom is domiciled in a Member State, have agreed that a court or the courts of a Member State are to have jurisdiction to settle any disputes which have arisen or which may arise in connection with a particular legal relationship, that court or those courts shall have jurisdiction. Such jurisdiction shall be exclusive unless the parties have agreed otherwise. Such an agreement conferring jurisdiction shall be either:
   (a) in writing or evidenced in writing; or
   (b) in a form which accords with practices which the parties have established between themselves; or
   (c) in international trade or commerce, in a form which accords with a usage of which the parties are or ought to have been aware and which in such trade or commerce is widely known to, and regularly observed by, parties to contracts of the type involved in the particular trade or commerce concerned.
2. Any communication by electronic means which provides a durable record of the agreement shall be equivalent to 'writing'.
3. Where such an agreement is concluded by parties, none of whom is domiciled in a Member State, the courts of other Member States shall have no jurisdiction over their disputes unless the court or courts chosen have declined jurisdiction.
4. The court or courts of a Member State on which a trust instrument has conferred jurisdiction shall have exclusive jurisdiction in any proceedings brought against a settlor, trustee or beneficiary, if relations between these persons or their rights or obligations under the trust are involved.
5. Agreements or provisions of a trust instrument conferring jurisdiction shall have no legal force if they are contrary to Articles 13, 17 or 21, or if the courts whose jurisdiction they purport to exclude have exclusive jurisdiction by virtue of Article 22.

Article 24

Apart from jurisdiction derived from other provisions of this Regulation, a court of a Member State before which a defendant enters an appearance shall have jurisdiction. This rule shall not apply where appearance was entered to contest the jurisdiction, or where another court has exclusive jurisdiction by virtue of Article 22.

Section 8 Examination as to Jurisdiction and Admissibility

Article 25

Where a court of a Member State is seised of a claim which is principally concerned with a matter over which the courts of another Member State have exclusive jurisdiction by virtue of Article 22, it shall declare of its own motion that it has no jurisdiction.

Article 26

1. Where a defendant domiciled in one Member State is sued in a court of another Member State and does not enter an appearance, the court shall declare of its own motion that it has no jurisdiction unless its jurisdiction is derived from the provisions of this Regulation.
2. The court shall stay the proceedings so long as it is not shown that the defendant has been able to receive the document instituting the proceedings or an equivalent document in sufficient time to enable him to arrange for his defence, or that all necessary steps have been taken to this end.
3. Article 19 of Council Regulation (EC) No. 1348/2000 of 29 May 2000 on the service in the Member States of judicial and extrajudicial documents in civil or commercial matters[10] shall apply instead of the provisions of paragraph 2 if the document instituting the proceedings or an equivalent document had to be transmitted from one Member State to another pursuant to this Regulation.
4. Where the provisions of Regulation (EC) No. 1348/2000 are not applicable, Article 15 of the Hague Convention of 15 November 1965 on the Service Abroad of Judicial and Extrajudicial Documents in Civil or Commercial Matters shall apply if the document instituting the proceedings or an equivalent document had to be transmitted pursuant to that Convention.

Section 9 Lis Pendens — Related Actions

Article 27

1. Where proceedings involving the same cause of action and between the same parties are brought in the courts of different Member States, any court other than the court first seised shall of its own motion stay its proceedings until such time as the jurisdiction of the court first seised is established.
2. Where the jurisdiction of the court first seised is established, any court other than the court first seised shall decline jurisdiction in favour of that court.

Article 28

1. Where related actions are pending in the courts of different Member States, any court other than the court first seised may stay its proceedings.
2. Where these actions are pending at first instance, any court other than the court first seised may also, on the application of one of the parties, decline jurisdiction if the court first seised has jurisdiction over the actions in question and its law permits the consolidation thereof.
3. For the purposes of this Article, actions are deemed to be related where they are so closely connected that it is expedient to hear and determine them together to avoid the risk of irreconcilable judgments resulting from separate proceedings.

Article 29

Where actions come within the exclusive jurisdiction of several courts, any court other than the court first seised shall decline jurisdiction in favour of that court.

Article 30

For the purposes of this Section, a court shall be deemed to be seised:

1. at the time when the document instituting the proceedings or an equivalent document is lodged with the court, provided that the plaintiff has not subsequently failed to take the steps he was required to take to have service effected on the defendant, or

[10] OJ L 160, 30.6.2000, p. 37.

2. if the document has to be served before being lodged with the court, at the time when it is received by the authority responsible for service, provided that the plaintiff has not subsequently failed to take the steps he was required to take to have the document lodged with the court.

Section 10 Provisional, Including Protective, Measures

Article 31

Application may be made to the courts of a Member State for such provisional, including protective, measures as may be available under the law of that State, even if, under this Regulation, the courts of another Member State have jurisdiction as to the substance of the matter.

CHAPTER III RECOGNITION AND ENFORCEMENT

Article 32

For the purposes of this Regulation, 'judgment' means any judgment given by a court or tribunal of a Member State, whatever the judgment may be called, including a decree, order, decision or writ of execution, as well as the determination of costs or expenses by an officer of the court.

Section 1 Recognition

Article 33

1. A judgment given in a Member State shall be recognised in the other Member States without any special procedure being required.
2. Any interested party who raises the recognition of a judgment as the principal issue in a dispute may, in accordance with the procedures provided for in Sections 2 and 3 of this Chapter, apply for a decision that the judgment be recognised.
3. If the outcome of proceedings in a court of a Member State depends on the determination of an incidental question of recognition that court shall have jurisdiction over that question.

Article 34

A judgment shall not be recognised:

1. if such recognition is manifestly contrary to public policy in the Member State in which recognition is sought;
2. where it was given in default of appearance, if the defendant was not served with the document which instituted the proceedings or with an equivalent document in sufficient time and in such a way as to enable him to arrange for his defence, unless the defendant failed to commence proceedings to challenge the judgment when it was possible for him to do so;
3. if it is irreconcilable with a judgment given in a dispute between the same parties in the Member State in which recognition is sought;
4. if it is irreconcilable with an earlier judgment given in another Member State or in a third State involving the same cause of action and between the same parties, provided that the earlier judgment fulfils the conditions necessary for its recognition in the Member State addressed.

Article 35

1. Moreover, a judgment shall not be recognised if it conflicts with Sections 3,4 or 6 of Chapter II, or in a case provided for in Article 72.
2. In its examination of the grounds of jurisdiction referred to in the foregoing paragraph, the court or authority applied to shall be bound by the findings of fact on which the court of the Member State of origin based its jurisdiction.
3. Subject to the paragraph 1, the jurisdiction of the court of the Member State of origin may not be reviewed. The test of public policy referred to in point 1 of Article 34 may not be applied to the rules relating to jurisdiction.

Article 36

Under no circumstances may a foreign judgment be reviewed as to its substance.

Article 37

1. A court of a Member State in which recognition is sought of a judgment given in another Member State may stay the proceedings if an ordinary appeal against the judgment has been lodged.
2. A court of a Member State in which recognition is sought of a judgment given in Ireland or the United Kingdom may stay the proceedings if enforcement is suspended in the State of origin, by reason of an appeal.

Section 2 Enforcement

Article 38

1. A judgment given in a Member State and enforceable in that State shall be enforced in another Member State when, on the application of any interested party, it has been declared enforceable there.
2. However, in the United Kingdom, such a judgment shall be enforced in England and Wales, in Scotland, or in Northern Ireland when, on the application of any interested party, it has been registered for enforcement in that part of the United Kingdom.

Article 39

1. The application shall be submitted to the court or competent authority indicated in the list in Annex II.
2. The local jurisdiction shall be determined by reference to the place of domicile of the party against whom enforcement is sought, or to the place of enforcement.

Article 40

1. The procedure for making the application shall be governed by the law of the Member State in which enforcement is sought.
2. The applicant must give an address for service of process within the area of jurisdiction of the court applied to. However, if the law of the Member State in which enforcement is sought does not provide for the furnishing of such an address, the applicant shall appoint a representative *ad litem.*
3. The documents referred to in Article 53 shall be attached to the application.

Article 41

The judgment shall be declared enforceable immediately on completion of the formalities in Article 53 without any review under Articles 34 and 35. The party against whom enforcement is sought shall not at this stage of the proceedings be entitled to make any submissions on the application.

Article 42

1. The decision on the application for a declaration of enforceability shall forthwith be brought to the notice of the applicant in accordance with the procedure laid down by the law of the Member State in which enforcement is sought.
2. The declaration of enforceability shall be served on the party against whom enforcement is sought, accompanied by the judgment, if not already served on that party.

Article 43

1. The decision on the application for a declaration of enforceability may be appealed against by either party.
2. The appeal is to be lodged with the court indicated in the list in Annex III.
3. The appeal shall be dealt with in accordance with the rules governing procedure in contradictory matters.
4. If the party against whom enforcement is sought fails to appear before the appellate court in proceedings concerning an appeal brought by the applicant, Article 26(2) to (4) shall apply even where the party against whom enforcement is sought is not domiciled in any of the Member States.

5. An appeal against the declaration of enforceability is to be lodged within one month of service thereof. If the party against whom enforcement is sought is domiciled in a Member State other than that in which the declaration of enforceability was given, the time for appealing shall be two months and shall run from the date of service, either on him in person or at his residence. No extension of time may be granted on account of distance.

Article 44

The judgment given on the appeal may be contested only by the appeal referred to in Annex IV.

Article 45

1. The court with which an appeal is lodged under Article 43 or Article 44 shall refuse or revoke a declaration of enforceability only on one of the grounds specified in Articles 34 and 35. It shall give its decision without delay.
2. Under no circumstances may the foreign judgment be reviewed as to its substance.

Article 46

1. The court with which an appeal is lodged under Article 43 or Article 44 may, on the application of the party against whom enforcement is sought, stay the proceedings if an ordinary appeal has been lodged against the judgment in the Member State of origin or if the time for such an appeal has not yet expired; in the latter case, the court may specify the time within which such an appeal is to be lodged.
2. Where the judgment was given in Ireland or the United Kingdom, any form of appeal available in the Member State of origin shall be treated as an ordinary appeal for the purposes of paragraph 1.
3. The court may also make enforcement conditional on the provision of such security as it shall determine.

Article 47

1. When a judgment must be recognised in accordance with this Regulation, nothing shall prevent the applicant from availing himself of provisional, including protective, measures in accordance with the law of the Member State requested without a declaration of enforceability under Article 41 being required.
2. The declaration of enforceability shall carry with it the power to proceed to any protective measures.
3. During the time specified for an appeal pursuant to Article 43(5) against the declaration of enforceability and until any such appeal has been determined, no measures of enforcement may be taken other than protective measures against the property of the party against whom enforcement is sought.

Article 48

1. Where a foreign judgment has been given in respect of several matters and the declaration of enforceability cannot be given for all of them, the court or competent authority shall give it for one or more of them.
2. An applicant may request a declaration of enforceability limited to parts of a judgment.

Article 49

A foreign judgment which orders a periodic payment by way of a penalty shall be enforceable in the Member State in which enforcement is sought only if the amount of the payment has been finally determined by the courts of the Member State of origin.

Article 50

An applicant who, in the Member State of origin has benefited from complete or partial legal aid or exemption from costs or expenses, shall be entitled, in the procedure provided for in this Section, to benefit from the most favourable legal aid or the most extensive exemption from costs or expenses provided for by the law of the Member State addressed.

Article 51

No security, bond or deposit, however described, shall be required of a party who in one Member State applies for enforcement of a judgment given in another Member State on the ground that he is a foreign national or that he is not domiciled or resident in the State in which enforcement is sought.

Article 52

In proceedings for the issue of a declaration of enforceability, no charge, duty or fee calculated by reference to the value of the matter at issue may be levied in the Member State in which enforcement is sought.

Section 3 Common Provisions

Article 53

1. A party seeking recognition or applying for a declaration of enforceability shall produce a copy of the judgment which satisfies the conditions necessary to establish its authenticity.
2. A party applying for a declaration of enforceability shall also produce the certificate referred to in Article 54, without prejudice to Article 55.

Article 54

The court or competent authority of a Member State where a judgment was given shall issue, at the request of any interested party, a certificate using the standard form in Annex *V* to this Regulation.

Article 55

1. If the certificate referred to in Article 54 is not produced, the court or competent authority may specify a time for its production or accept an equivalent document or, if it considers that it has sufficient information before it, dispense with its production.
2. If the court or competent authority so requires, a translation of the documents shall be produced. The translation shall be certified by a person qualified to do so in one of the Member States.

Article 56

No legalisation or other similar formality shall be required in respect of the documents referred to in Article 53 or Article 55(2), or in respect of a document appointing a representative *ad litem.*

CHAPTER IV AUTHENTIC INSTRUMENTS AND COURT SETTLEMENTS

Article 57

1. A document which has been formally drawn up or registered as an authentic instrument and is enforceable in one Member State shall, in another Member State, be declared enforceable there, on application made in accordance with the procedures provided for in Articles 38, et seq. The court with which an appeal is lodged under Article 43 or Article 44 shall refuse or revoke a declaration of enforceability only if enforcement of the instrument is manifestly contrary to public policy in the Member State addressed.
2. Arrangements relating to maintenance obligations concluded with administrative authorities or authenticated by them shall also be regarded as authentic instruments within the meaning of paragraph 1.
3. The instrument produced must satisfy the conditions necessary to establish its authenticity in the Member State of origin.
4. Section 3 of Chapter III shall apply as appropriate. The competent authority of a Member State where an authentic instrument was drawn up or registered shall issue, at the request of any interested party, a certificate using the standard form in Annex VI to this Regulation.

Article 58

A settlement which has been approved by a court in the course of proceedings and is enforceable in the Member State in which it was concluded shall be enforceable in the State addressed under the same conditions as authentic instruments. The court or competent authority of a Member State where a court settlement was approved shall issue, at the request of any interested party, a certificate using the standard form in Annex V to this Regulation.

CHAPTER V GENERAL PROVISIONS

Article 59

1. In order to determine whether a party is domiciled in the Member State whose courts are seised of a matter, the court shall apply its internal law.
2. If a party is not domiciled in the Member State whose courts are seised of the matter, then, in order to determine whether the party is domiciled in another Member State, the court shall apply the law of that Member State.

Article 60

1. For the purposes of this Regulation, a company or other legal person or association of natural or legal persons is domiciled at the place where it has its:
   (a) statutory seat, or
   (b) central administration, or
   (c) principal place of business.
2. For the purposes of the United Kingdom and Ireland 'statutory seat' means the registered office or, where there is no such office anywhere, the place of incorporation or, where there is no such place anywhere, the place under the law of which the formation took place.
3. In order to determine whether a trust is domiciled in the Member State whose courts are seised of the matter, the court shall apply its rules of private international law.

Article 61

Without prejudice to any more favourable provisions of national laws, persons domiciled in a Member State who are being prosecuted in the criminal courts of another Member State of which they are not nationals for an offence which was not intentionally committed may be defended by persons qualified to do so, even if they do not appear in person. However, the court seised of the matter may order appearance in person; in the case of failure to appear, a judgment given in the civil action without the person concerned having had the opportunity to arrange for his defence need not be recognised or enforced in the other Member States.

Article 62

In Sweden, in summary proceedings concerning orders to pay (betalningsföreläggande) and assistance (handräckning), the expression 'court' includes the 'Swedish enforcement service' (kronofogdemyndighet).

Article 63

1. A person domiciled in the territory of the Grand Duchy of Luxembourg and sued in the court of another Member State pursuant to Article 5(1) may refuse to submit to the jurisdiction of that court if the final place of delivery of the goods or provision of the services is in Luxembourg.
2. Where, under paragraph 1, the final place of delivery of the goods or provision of the services is in Luxembourg, any agreement conferring jurisdiction must, in order to be valid, be accepted in writing or evidenced in writing within the meaning of Article 23(1)(a).
3. The provisions of this Article shall not apply to contracts for the provision of financial services.
4. The provisions of this Article shall apply for a period of six years from entry into force of this Regulation.

Article 64

1. In proceedings involving a dispute between the master and a member of the crew of a seagoing ship registered in Greece or in Portugal, concerning remuneration of other conditions of service, a court in a Member State shall establish whether the diplomatic or consular officer responsible for the ship has been notified of the dispute. It may act as soon as that officer has been notified.

2. The provisions of this Article shall apply for a period of six years from entry into force of this Regulation.

Article 65

1. The jurisdiction specified in Article 6(2), and Article 11 in actions on a warranty [or*] guarantee or in any other third party proceedings may not be resorted to [in†] Germany, Austria and Hungary. Any person domiciled in another Member State may be sued in the courts:
   (a) of Germany, pursuant to Articles 68 and 72 to 74 of the Code of Civil Procedure (Zivilprozessordnung) concerning third-party notices,
   (b) of Austria, pursuant to Article 21 of the Code of Civil Procedure (Zivilprozessordnung) concerning third-party notices;
   (c) of Hungary, pursuant to Articles 58 to 60 of the Code of Civil Procedure (Polgári perrendtartás) concerning third-party notices;
2. Judgments given in other Member States by virtue of Article 6(2), or Article 11 shall be recognised and enforced in Germany, Austria and Hungary in accordance with Chapter III. Any effects which judgments given in these States may have on third parties by application of the provisions in paragraph 1 shall also be recognised in the other Member States.

CHAPTER VI TRANSITIONAL PROVISIONS

Article 66

1. This Regulation shall apply only to legal proceedings instituted and to documents formally drawn up or registered as authentic instruments after the entry into force thereof.
2. However, if the proceedings in the Member State of origin were instituted before the entry into force of this Regulation, judgments given after that date shall be recognised and enforced in accordance with Chapter III,
   (a) if the proceedings in the Member State of origin were instituted after the entry into force of the Brussels or the Lugano Convention both in the Member State or origin and in the Member State addressed;
   (b) in all other cases, if jurisdiction was founded upon rules which accorded with those provided for either in Chapter II or in a convention concluded between the Member State of origin and the Member State addressed which was in force when the proceedings were instituted.

CHAPTER VII RELATIONS WITH OTHER INSTRUMENTS

Article 67

This Regulation shall not prejudice the application of provisions governing jurisdiction and the recognition and enforcement of judgments in specific matters which are contained in Community instruments or in national legislation harmonised pursuant to such instruments.

Article 68

1. This Regulation shall, as between the Member States, supersede the Brussels Convention, except as regards the territories of the Member States which fall within the territorial scope of that Convention and which are excluded from this Regulation pursuant to Article 299 of the Treaty.
2. In so far as this Regulation replaces the provisions of the Brussels Convention between Member States, any reference to the Convention shall be understood as a reference to this Regulation.

Article 69

Subject to Article 66(2) and Article 70, this Regulation shall, as between Member States, supersede the following conventions and treaty concluded between two or more of them:

[* In the Official Journal this word is 'of'.]

[† This word is omitted in the Official Journal.]

- the Agreement between the Federative People's Republic of Yugoslavia and the Republic of Austria on the Mutual Recognition and Enforcement of Arbitral Awards and Arbitral Settlements in Commercial Matters, signed at Belgrade on 18 March 1960,
- the Agreement between the Federative People's Republic of Yugoslavia and the Republic of Austria on the Mutual Recognition and Enforcement of Decisions in Alimony Matters, signed at Vienna on 10 October 1961,
- the Agreement between the Republic of Cyprus and the Republic of Greece on Legal Cooperation in Matters of Civil, Family, Commercial and Criminal Law, signed at Nicosia on 5 March 1984,
- the Agreement between the Republic of Cyprus and the Socialist Federal Republic of Yugoslavia on Legal Assistance in Civil and Criminal Matters, signed at Nicosia on 19 September 1984, now in force between Cyprus and Slovenia,
- the Agreement between the Republic of Latvia, the Republic of Estonia and the Republic of Lithuania on Legal Assistance and Legal Relationships, signed at Tallinn on 11 November 1992,
- the Agreement between the Republic of Poland and the Republic of Lithuania on Legal Assistance and Legal Relations in Civil, Family, Labour and Criminal Matters, signed in Warsaw on 26 January 1993,
- the Agreement between the Republic of Latvia and the Republic of Poland on Legal Assistance and Legal Relationships in Civil, Family, Labour and Criminal Matters, signed at Riga on 23 February 1994,
- the Agreement between the Republic of Cyprus and the Republic of Poland on Legal Cooperation in Civil and Criminal Matters, signed at Nicosia on 14 November 1996,
- the Agreement between Estonia and Poland on Granting Legal Assistance and Legal Relations on Civil, Labour and Criminal Matters, signed at Tallinn on 27 November 1998.
- the Convention between Belgium and France on Jurisdiction and the Validity and Enforcement of Judgments, Arbitration Awards and Authentic Instruments, signed at Paris on 8 July 1899,
- the Convention between Belgium and the Netherlands on Jurisdiction, Bankruptcy, and the Validity and Enforcement of Judgments, Arbitration Awards and Authentic Instruments, signed at Brussels on 28 March 1925,
- the Convention between the Czechoslovak Republic and Portugal on the Recognition and Enforcement of Court Decisions, signed at Lisbon on 23 November 1927, still in force between the Czech Republic and Portugal,
- the Convention between France and Italy on the Enforcement of Judgments in Civil and Commercial Matters, signed at Rome on 3 June 1930,
- the Convention between the United Kingdom and the French Republic providing for the reciprocal enforcement of judgments in civil and commercial matters, with Protocol, signed at Paris on 18 January 1934,
- the Convention between the United Kingdom and the Kingdom of Belgium providing for the reciprocal enforcement of judgments in civil and commercial matters, with Protocol, signed at Brussels on 2 May 1934,
- the Convention between Germany and Italy on the Recognition and Enforcement of Judgments in Civil and Commercial Matters, signed at Rome on 9 March 1936,
- the Convention between the Federative People's Republic of Yugoslavia and the Republic of Austria on Mutual Judicial Cooperation, signed at Vienna on 16 December 1954,
- the Convention between Belgium and Austria on the Reciprocal Recognition and Enforcement of Judgments and Authentic Instruments relating to Maintenance Obligations, signed at Vienna on 25 October 1957,
- the Convention between Germany and Belgium on the Mutual Recognition and Enforcement of Judgments, Arbitration Awards and Authentic Instruments in Civil and Commercial Matters, signed at Bonn on 30 June 1958,
- the Convention between the Netherlands and Italy on the Recognition and Enforcement of Judgments in Civil and Commercial Matters, signed at Rome on 17 April 1959,
- the Convention between the Polish People's Republic and the Hungarian People's Republic on the Legal Assistance in Civil, Family and Criminal Matters, signed at Budapest on 6 March 1959,
- the Convention between Germany and Austria on the Reciprocal Recognition and Enforcement of Judgments, Settlements and Authentic Instruments in Civil and Commercial Matters, signed at Vienna on 6 June 1959,

- the Convention between Belgium and Austria on the Reciprocal Recognition and Enforcement of Judgments, Arbitral Awards and Authentic Instruments in Civil and Commercial Matters, signed at Vienna on 16 June 1959,
- the Convention between the Federative People's Republic of Yugoslavia and the Kingdom of Greece on the Mutual Recognition and Enforcement of Judgments, signed at Athens on 18 June 1959,
- the Convention between the Polish People's Republic and the Federative People's Republic of Yugoslavia on the Legal Assistance in Civil and Criminal Matters, signed at Warsaw on 6 February 1960, now in force between Poland and Slovenia,
- the Convention between the United Kingdom and the Federal Republic of Germany for the reciprocal recognition and enforcement of judgments in civil and commercial matters, signed at Bonn on 14 July 1960,
- the Convention between the United Kingdom and Austria providing for the reciprocal recognition and enforcement of judgments in civil and commercial matters, signed at Vienna on 14 July 1961, with amending Protocol signed at London on 6 March 1970,
- the Convention between Greece and Germany for the Reciprocal Recognition and Enforcement of Judgments, Settlements and Authentic Instruments in Civil and Commercial Matters, signed in Athens on 4 November 1961,
- the Convention between Belgium and Italy on the Recognition and Enforcement of Judgments and other Enforceable Instruments in Civil and Commercial Matters, signed at Rome on 6 April 1962,
- the Convention between the Netherlands and Germany on the Mutual Recognition and Enforcement of Judgments and Other Enforceable Instruments in Civil and Commercial Matters, signed at The Hague on 30 August 1962,
- the Convention between the Netherlands and Austria on the Reciprocal Recognition and Enforcement of Judgments and Authentic Instruments in Civil and Commercial Matters, signed at The Hague on 6 February 1963,
- the Convention between Poland and Austria on Mutual Relations in Civil Matters and on Documents, signed at Vienna on 11 December 1963,
- the Convention between the United Kingdom and the Republic of Italy for the reciprocal recognition and enforcement of judgments in civil and commercial matters, signed at Rome on 7 February 1964, with amending Protocol signed at Rome on 14 July 1970,
- the Convention between France and Austria on the Recognition and Enforcement of Judgments and Authentic Instruments in Civil and Commercial Matters, signed at Vienna on 15 July 1966,
- the Convention between Poland and France on Applicable Law, Jurisdiction and the Enforcement of Judgments in the Field of Personal and Family Law, concluded in Warsaw on 5 April 1967,
- the Convention between the United Kingdom and the Kingdom of the Netherlands providing for the reciprocal recognition and enforcement of judgments in civil matters, signed at The Hague on 17 November 1967,
- the Convention between Spain and France on the Recognition and Enforcement of Judgment Arbitration Awards in Civil and Commercial Matters, signed at Paris on 28 May 1969,
- the Convention between the Governments of Yugoslavia and France on the Recognition and Enforcement of Judgments in Civil and Commercial Matters, signed at Paris on 18 May 1971,
- the Convention between Luxembourg and Austria on the Recognition and Enforcement of Judgments and Authentic Instruments in Civil and Commercial Matters, signed at Luxembourg on 29 July 1971,
- the Convention between Italy and Austria on the Recognition and Enforcement of Judgments in Civil and Commercial Matters, of Judicial Settlements and of Authentic Instruments, signed at Rome on 16 November 1971,
- the Convention between Spain and Italy regarding Legal Aid and the Recognition and Enforcement of Judgments in Civil and Commercial Matters, signed at Madrid on 22 May 1973,
- the Convention between the Federative Socialist Republic of Yugoslavia and the Kingdom of Belgium on the Recognition and Enforcement of Court Decisions in Alimony Matters, signed at Belgrade on 12 December 1973,
- the Convention between Finland, Iceland, Norway, Sweden and Denmark on the Recognition and Enforcement of Judgments in Civil Matters, signed at Copenhagen on 11 October 1977,

- the Convention between Hungary and Greece on Legal Assistance in Civil and Criminal Matters, signed at Budapest on 8 October 1979,
- the Convention between Poland and Greece on Legal Assistance in Civil and Criminal Matters, signed at Athens on 24 October 1979,
- the Convention between Hungary and France on Legal Assistance in Civil and Family Law, on the Recognition and Enforcement of Decisions and on Legal Assistance in Criminal Matters and on Extradition, signed at Budapest on 31 July 1980,
- the Convention between the Republic of Cyprus and the Hungarian People's Republic on Legal Assistance in Civil and Criminal Matters, signed at Nicosia on 30 November 1981,
- the Convention between Austria and Sweden on the Recognition and Enforcement of Judgments in Civil Matters, signed at Stockholm on 16 September 1982,
- the Convention between Spain and the Federal Republic of Germany on the Recognition and Enforcement of Judgments, Settlements and Enforceable Authentic Instruments in Civil and Commercial Matters, signed at Bonn on 14 November 1983,
- the Convention between Austria and Spain on the Recognition and Enforcement of Judgments, Settlements and Enforceable Authentic Instruments in Civil and Commercial Matters, signed at Vienna on 17 February 1984,
- the Convention between Finland and Austria on the Recognition and Enforcement of Judgments in Civil Matters, signed at Vienna on 17 November 1986,
- the Convention between Poland and Italy on Judicial Assistance and the Recognition and Enforcement of Judgments in Civil Matters, signed at Warsaw on 28 April 1989,
- the Treaty between Belgium, the Netherlands and Luxembourg in Jurisdiction, Bankruptcy, and the Validity and Enforcement of Judgments, Arbitration Awards and Authentic Instruments, signed at Brussels on 24 November 1961, in so far as it is in force.
- the Treaty between the Czechoslovak Socialist Republic and the Socialist Federative Republic of Yugoslavia on Settlement of Legal Relations in Civil, Family and Criminal Matters, signed at Belgrade on 20 January 1964, still in force between the Czech Republic, Slovakia and Slovenia,
- the Treaty between the Czechoslovak Socialist Republic and the Hellenic Republic on Legal Aid in Civil and Criminal Matters, signed at Athens on 22 October 1980, still in force between the Czech Republic, Slovakia and Greece,
- the Treaty between the Czechoslovak Socialistic Republic and the Republic of Cyprus on Legal Aid in Civil and Criminal Matters, signed at Nicosia on 23 April 1982, still in force between the Czech Republic, Slovakia and Cyprus,
- the Treaty between the Government of the Czechoslovak Socialist Republic and the Government of the Republic of France on Legal Aid and the Recognition and Enforcement of Judgments in Civil, Family and Commercial Matters, signed at Paris on 10 May 1984, still in force between the Czech Republic, Slovakia and France,
- the Treaty between the Czechoslovak Socialist Republic and the Italian Republic on Legal Aid in Civil and Criminal Matters, signed at Prague on 6 December 1985, still in force between the Czech Republic, Slovakia and Italy,
- the Treaty between the Czechoslovak Socialist Republic and the Kingdom of Spain on Legal Aid, Recognition and Enforcement of Court Decisions in Civil Matters, signed at Madrid on 4 May 1987, still in force between the Czech Republic, Slovakia and Spain,
- the Treaty between the Czechoslovak Socialist Republic and the Polish People's Republic on Legal Aid and Settlement of Legal Relations in Civil, Family, Labour and Criminal Matters, signed at Warsaw on 21 December 1987, still in force between the Czech Republic, Slovakia and Poland,
- the Treaty between the Czechoslovak Socialist Republic and the Hungarian People's Republic on Legal Aid and Settlement of Legal Relations in Civil, Family and Criminal Matters, signed at Bratislava on 28 March 1989, still in force between the Czech Republic, Slovakia and Hungary, and
- the Treaty between the Czech Republic and the Slovak Republic on Legal Aid provided by Judicial Bodies and on Settlements of Certain Legal Relations in Civil and Criminal Matters, signed at Prague on 29 October 1992.

Article 70

1. The Treaty and the Conventions referred to in Article 69 shall continue to have effect in relation to matters to which this Regulation does not apply.
2. They shall continue to have effect in respect of judgments given and documents formally drawn up or registered as authentic instruments before the entry into force of this Regulation.

Article 71

1. This Regulation shall not affect any conventions to which the Member States are parties and which in relation to particular matters, govern jurisdiction or the recognition or enforcement of judgments.
2. With a view to its uniform interpretation, paragraph 1 shall be applied in the following manner:
   (a) this Regulation shall not prevent a court of a Member State, which is a party to a convention on a particular matter, from assuming jurisdiction in accordance with that convention, even where the defendant is domiciled in another Member State which is not a party to that convention. The court hearing the action shall, in any event, apply Article 26 of this Regulation;
   (b) judgments given in a Member State by a court in the exercise of jurisdiction provided for in a convention on a particular matter shall be recognised and enforced in the other Member States in accordance with this Regulation.

   Where a convention on a particular matter to which both the Member State of origin and the Member State addressed are parties lays down conditions for the recognition or enforcement of judgments, those conditions shall apply. In any event, the provisions of this Regulation which concern the procedure for recognition and enforcement of judgments may be applied.

Article 72

This Regulation shall not affect agreements by which Member States undertook, prior to the entry into force of this Regulation pursuant to Article 59 of the Brussels Convention, not to recognise judgments given, in particular in other Contracting States to that Convention, against defendants domiciled or habitually resident in a third country where, in cases provided for in Article 4 of that Convention, the judgment could only be founded on a ground of jurisdiction specified in the second paragraph of Article 3 of that Convention.

CHAPTER VIII FINAL PROVISIONS

Article 73

No later than five years after the entry into force of this Regulation, the Commission shall present to the European Parliament, the Council and the Economic and Social Committee a report on the application of this Regulation. The report shall be accompanied, if need be, by proposals for adaptations to this Regulation.

Article 74

1. The Member States shall notify the Commission of the texts amending the lists set out in Annexes I to IV. The Commission shall adapt the Annexes concerned accordingly.
2. The updating or technical adjustment of the forms, specimens of which appear in Annexes V and VI, shall be adopted in accordance with the advisory procedure referred to in Article 75(2).

Article 75

1. The Commission shall be assisted by a committee.
2. Where reference is made to this paragraph, Articles 3 and 7 of Decision 1999/468/EC shall apply.
3. The Committee shall adopt its rules of procedure.

Article 76

This Regulation shall enter into force on 1 March 2002.

This Regulation is binding in its entirety and directly applicable in the Member States in accordance with the Treaty establishing the European Community.
Done at Brussels, 22 December 2000.
For the Council
The President
C. Pierret

ANNEX I
RULES OF JURISDICTION REFERRED TO IN ARTICLE 3(2) AND ARTICLE 4(2)

The rules of jurisdiction referred to in Article 3(2) and Article 4(2) are the following:

- in Belgium: Article 15 of the Civil Code (Code civil/Burgerlijk Wetboek) and Article 638 of the Judicial Code (Code judiciaire/Gerechtelijk Wetboek);
- in the Czech Republic: Article 86 of Act No. 99/1963 Coll., the Code of Civil Procedure (občanský soudní řád), as amended,
- in Germany: Article 23 of the Code of Civil Procedure (Zivilprozessordnung),
- in Estonia: Article 139, paragraph 2 of the Code of Civil Procedure (tsiviilkohtumenetluse seadustik),
- in Greece, Article 40 of the Code of Civil Procedure (*Κώδικας Πολιτικής Δικονομίας*);
- in France: Articles 14 and 15 of the Civil Code (Code civil),
- in Ireland: the rules which enable jurisdiction to be founded on the document instituting the proceedings having been served on the defendant during his temporary presence in Ireland,
- in Italy: Articles 3 and 4 of Act 218 of 31 May 1995,
- in Cyprus: section 21(2) of the Courts of Justice Law No. 14 of 1960, as amended,
- in Latvia: section 27 and paragraphs 3, 5, 6 and 9 of section 28 of the Civil Procedure Law (Civilprocesa likums),
- in Lithuania: Article 31 of the Code of Civil Procedure (Civilinio proceso kodeksas),
- in Luxembourg: Articles 14 and 15 of the Civil Code (Code civil),
- in Hungary: Article 57 of Law Decree No. 13 of 1979 on International Private Law (a nemzetközi magánjogról szóló 1979. évi 13. törvényerejű rendelet),
- in Malta: Articles 742, 743 and 744 of the Code of Organisation and Civil Procedure—Cap. 12 (Kodiċi ta' Organizzazzjoni u Proċedura Ċivili — Kap. 12) and Article 549 of the Commercial Code — Cap. 13 (Kodiċi tal-kummerċ — Kap. 13),
- in Austria: Article 99 of the Court Jurisdiction Act (Jurisdiktionsnorm),
- in Poland: Articles 1103 and 1110 of the Code of Civil Procedure (Kodeks postępowania cywilnego),
- in Portugal: Articles 65 and 65A of the Code of Civil Procedure (Código de Processo Civil) and Article 11 of the Code of Labour Procedure (Código de Processo de Trabalho),
- in Slovenia: Article 48(2) of the Private International Law and Procedure Act (Zakon o mednarodnem zasebnem pravu in postopku) in relation to Article 47(2) of Civil Procedure Act (Zakon o pravdnem postopku) and Article 58(1) of the Private International Law and Procedure Act (Zakon o mednarodnem zasebnem pravu in postopku) in relation to Article 57(1) and 47(2) of Civil Procedure Act (Zakon o pravdnem postopku),
- in Slovakia: Articles 37 to 37e of Act No. 97/1963 on Private International Law and the Rules of Procedure relating thereto,
- in Finland: the second, third and fourth sentences of the first paragraph of Section 1 of Chapter 10 of the Code of Judicial Procedure (oikeudenkäymiskaari/rättegångsbalken),
- in Sweden: the first sentence of the first paragraph of Section 3 of Chapter 10 of the Code of Judicial Procedure (rättegångsbalken),
- in the United Kingdom: rules which enable jurisdiction to be founded on:
  (a) the document instituting the proceedings having been served on the defendant during his temporary presence in the United Kingdom; or
  (b) the presence within the United Kingdom of property belonging to the defendant; or
  (c) the seizure by the plaintiff of property situated in the United Kingdom.

ANNEX II

The courts or competent authorities to which the application referred to in Article 39 may be submitted are the following:

- in Belgium, the 'tribunal de première instance' or 'rechtbank van eerste aanleg' or 'erstinstanzliches Gericht',
- in the Czech Republic, the 'okresní soud' or 'soudní exekutor',
- in Germany:
  (a) the presiding Judge of a chamber of the 'Landgericht';
  (b) a notary ('. . .'*) in a procedure of declaration of enforcement of an authentic instrument.
- in Estonia, the 'maakohus' or the 'linnakohus',
- in Greece, the '*Μονμελές Πρωτοδικείο*',
- in Spain, the 'Juzgado de Primera Instancia',
- in France:
  (a) the 'greffier en chef du tribunal de grande instance',
  (b) the 'président de la chambre départementale des notaires' in the case of application for a declaration of enforceability of a notarial authentic instrument,
- in Ireland, the High Court,
- in Italy, the 'Corte d'appello',
- in Cyprus, the '*Επαρχιακό Δικαστήριο*' or in the case of a maintenance judgment the '*Οικογεωειακό Δικαστήριο*
- in Latvia, the 'rajona (pilsētas) tiesa',
- in Lithuania, the 'Lietuvos apeliacinis teismas',
- in Luxembourg, the presiding judge of the 'tribunal d'arrondissement',
- in Hungary, the 'megyei bíróság székhelyén működő helyi bíróság', and in Budapest the 'Budai Központi Kerületi Bíróság',
- in Malta, the 'Prim' Awla tal-Qorti Ċivili' or 'Qorti tal-Maġistrati ta' Għawdex fil-ġurisdizzjoni superjuri tagħha', or, in the case of a maintenance judgment, the 'Reġistratur tal-Qorti' on transmission by the 'Ministru responsabbli għall-Ġustizzja',
- in the Netherlands, the 'voorzieningenrechter van de rechtbank';
- in Austria, the 'Bezirksgericht',
- in Poland, the 'Sąd Okręgowy',
- in Portugal, the 'Tribunal de Comarca',
- in Slovenia, the 'okrozno sodišče',
- in Slovakia, the 'okresný súd',
- in Finland, the 'käräjäoikeus/tingsrätt',
- in Sweden, the 'Svea hovrätt',
- in the United Kingdom:
  (a) in England and Wales, the High Court of Justice, or in the case of a maintenance judgment, the Magistrate's Court on transmission by the Secretary of State;
  (b) in Scotland, the Court of Session, or in the case of a maintenance judgment, the Sheriff Court on transmission by the Secretary of State;
  (c) in Northern Ireland, the High Court of Justice, or in the case of a maintenance judgment, the Magistrate's Court on transmission by the Secretary of State;
  (d) in Gibraltar, the Supreme Court of Gibraltar, or in the case of a maintenance judgment, the Magistrates' Court on transmission by the Attorney General of Gibraltar.

ANNEX III

The courts with which appeals referred to in Article 43(2) may be lodged are the following:

- in Belgium,
  (a) as regards appeal by the defendant: the 'tribunal de première instance' or 'rechtbank van eerste aanleg' or 'erstinstanzliches Gericht',
  (b) as regards appeal by the applicant: the 'Cour d'appel' or 'hof van beroep',

[* It is likely that this should be 'Notar'.]

– in the Czech Republic, the 'okresní soud',
– in the Federal Republic of Germany, the 'Oberlandesgericht',
– in Estonia, the 'ringkonnakohus',
– in Greece, the '*Εφετείο*',
– in Spain, the 'Audiencia Provincial',
– in France:
  (a) the 'cour d'appel' on decisions allowing the application,
  (b) the presiding judge of the 'tribunal de grande instance', on decisions rejecting the application,
– in Ireland, the High Court,
– in Italy, the 'corte d'appello',
– in Cyprus, the '*Επαρχιακό Δικαστήριο*' or in the case of a maintenance judgment the '*Οικογενειακό Δικαστήριο*',
– in Latvia, the 'Apgabaltiesa',
– in Lithuania, the 'Lietuvos apeliacinis teismas',
– in Luxembourg, the 'Cour supérieure de Justice' sitting as a court of civil appeal,
– in Hungary, the 'megyei bíróság'; in Budapest, the 'Fővárosi Bíróság',
– in Malta, the 'Qorti ta' l-Appell' in accordance with the procedure laid down for appeals in the Kodiċi ta' Organizzazzjoni u Proċedura Ċivili — Kap. 12 or in the case of a maintenance judgment by 'ċitazzjoni' before the 'Prim' Awla tal-Qorti [Ċivili*] jew il-Qorti tal-Maġistrati ta' Għawdex fil-ġurisdizzjoni superjuri tagħha'',
– in the Netherlands:
  (a) for the defendant: the 'arrondissementsrechtbank',
  (b) for the applicant: the 'gerechtshof',
– in Austria, the 'Bezirksgericht',
– in Poland, the 'Sąd Apelacyjny',
– in Portugal, the 'Tribunalde Relação',
– in Slovenia, the 'okrožno sodišče',
– in Slovakia, the 'okresný súd',
– in Finland, the 'hovioikeus/hovrätt',
– in Sweden, the 'Svea hovrätt',
– in the United Kingdom:
  (a) in England and Wales, the High Court of Justice, or in the case of a maintenance judgment, the Magistrate's Court;
  (b) in Scotland, the Court of Session, or in the case of a maintenance judgment, the Sheriff Court;
  (c) in Northern Ireland, the High Court of Justice, or in the case of a maintenance judgment, the Magistrate's Court;
  (d) in Gibraltar, the Supreme Court of Gibraltar, or in the case of a maintenance judgment, the Magistrates' Court.

ANNEX IV

The appeals which may be lodged pursuant to Article 44 are the following:
– in Belgium, Greece, Spain, France, Italy, Luxembourg and the Netherlands, an appeal in cassation,
– in the Czech Republic, a 'dovolání' and a 'žaloba pro zmatečnost',
– in Germany, a 'Rechtsbeschwerde',
– in Estonia, a 'kassatsioonkaebus',
– in Ireland, an appeal on a point of law to the Supreme Court,
– in Cyprus, an appeal to the Supreme Court,
– in Latvia, an appeal to the 'Augstākā tiesa',
– in Lithuania, an appeal to the 'Lietuvos Aukščiausiasis Teismas',
– in Hungary, 'felülvizsgálati kérelem',
– in Malta, no further appeal lies to any other court; in the case of a maintenance judgment the 'Qorti ta' l-Appell' in accordance with the procedure laid down for appeal in the 'kodiċi ta' Organizzazzjoni u Procedura Ċivili — Kap. 12',
– in Austria, a 'Revisionsrekurs',

[* In the Official Journal this word is 'ivili'.]

– in Poland, by an appeal in cassation to the 'Sąd Najwyższy',
– in Portugal, an appeal on a point of law,
– in Slovenia, an appeal to the 'Vrhovno sodišče Republike Slovenije',
– in Slovakia ['odvolanie'†],
– in Finland, an appeal to the 'korkein oikeus/högsta domstolen',
– in Sweden, an appeal to the 'Högsta domstolen',
– in the United Kingdom, a single further appeal on a point of law.

ANNEX V
CERTIFICATE REFERRED TO IN ARTICLES 54 AND 58 OF THE REGULATION ON JUDGMENTS AND COURT SETTLEMENTS

(English, inglés, anglais, inglese, . . .)

1. Member State of origin
2. Court or competent authority issuing the certificate
   2.1 Name
   2.2 Address
   2.3 Tel./fax/e-mail
3. Court which delivered the judgment/approved the court settlement*
   3.1 Type of court
   3.2 Place of court
4. Judgment/court settlement*
   4.1 Date
   4.2 Reference number
   4.3 The parties to the judgment/court settlement*
      4.3.1 Name(s) of plaintiff(s)
      4.3.2 Name(s) of defendant(s)
      4.3.3 Name(s) of other party(ies), if any
   4.4 Date of service of the document instituting the proceedings where judgment was given in default of appearance
   4.5 Text of the judgment/court settlement* as annexed to this certificate
5. Names of parties to whom legal aid has been granted

The judgment/court settlement* is enforceable in the Member State of origin (Articles 38 and 58 of the Regulation) against:

Name:

Done at . . ., date . . .

Signature and/or stamp . . .

* Delete as appropriate.

ANNEX VI
CERTIFICATE REFERRED TO IN ARTICLE 57(4) OF THE REGULATION ON AUTHENTIC INSTRUMENTS

(English, inglés, anglais, inglese . . .)

1. Member State of origin
2. Competent authority issuing the certificate
   2.1 Name
   2.2 Address
   2.3 Tel./fax/e-mail
3. Authority which has given authenticity to the instrument
   3.1 Authority involved in the drawing up of the authentic instrument (if applicable)
      3.1.1 Name and designation of authority
      3.1.2 Place of authority

[† In the Official Journal this word is 'dovolanie'.]

3.2 Authority which has registered the authentic instrument (if applicable)
  3.2.1 Type of authority
  3.2.2 Place of authority
4. Authentic instrument
  4.1 Description of the instrument
  4.2 Date
    4.2.1 on which the instrument was drawn up
    4.2.2 if different: on which the instrument was registered
  4.3 Reference number
  4.4 Parties to the instrument
    4.4.1 Name of the creditor
    4.4.2 Name of the debtor
5. Text of the enforceable obligation as annexed to this certificate

The authentic instrument is enforceable against the debtor in the Member State of origin (Article 57(1) of the Regulation)

Done at . . ., date . . .

Signature and/or stamp . . .

NOTES ON TEXT

The text printed above incorporates the corrigendum published in [2001] OJ L 307 28 and the following amendments:

art. 65 amended by Act of Accession, annex II, point 18.A.3(a);

art. 69 amended by Act of Accession, annex II, point 18.A.3(b);

annex I amended by: (a) Regulation (EC) No. 1496/2002, art. 1; (b) Act of Accession, annex II, point 18.A.3(c); (c) Regulation (EC) No. 2245/2004, art. 1(1);

annex II amended by: (a) Regulation (EC) No. 1496/2002, arts 2 and 3; (b) Act of Accession, annex II, point 18.A.3(d); (c) Regulation (EC) No. 2245/2004, art. 1(2);

annex III amended by: (a) Act of Accession, annex II, point 18.A.3(e); (b) Regulation (EC) No. 2245/2004, art. 1(3);

annex IV amended by: (a) Act of Accession, annex II, point 18.A.3(f); (b) Regulation (EC) No. 2245/2004, art. 1(4);

The Act of Accession referred to above is the Act concerning the conditions of accession of the Czech Republic, the Republic of Estonia, the Republic of Cyprus, the Republic of Latvia, the Republic of Lithuania, the Republic of Hungary, the Republic of Malta, the Republic of Poland, the Republic of Slovenia and the Slovak Republic and the adjustments to the Treaties on which the European Union is founded [2003] OJ L 236 33.

Sale of Goods Act 1979

(1979 CHAPTER 54)

PART I CONTRACTS TO WHICH ACT APPLIES

1. Contracts to Which Act Applies

(1) This Act applies to contracts of sale of goods made on or after (but not to those made before) 1 January 1894.
(2) In relation to contracts made on certain dates, this Act applies subject to the modification of certain of its sections as mentioned in Schedule 1 below.
(3) Any such modification is indicated in the section concerned by a reference to Schedule 1 below.
(4) Accordingly, where a section does not contain such a reference, this Act applies in relation to the contract concerned without such modification of the section.

PART II FORMATION OF THE CONTRACT

Contract of Sale

2. Contract of Sale

(1) A contract of sale of goods is a contract by which the seller transfers or agrees to transfer the property in goods to the buyer for a money consideration, called the price.
(2) There may a contract of sale between one part owner and another.
(3) A contract of sale may be absolute or conditional.
(4) Where under a contract of sale the property in the goods is transferred from the seller to the buyer the contact is called a sale.
(5) Where under a contract of sale the transfer of the property in the goods is to take place at a future time or subject to some condition later to be fulfilled the contract is called an agreement to sell.
(6) An agreement to sell becomes a sale when the time elapses or the conditions are fulfilled subject to which the property in the goods is to be transferred.

3. Capacity to Buy and Sell

(1) Capacity to buy and sell is regulated by the general law concerning capacity to contract and to transfer and acquire property.
(2) Where necessaries are sold and delivered to a minor or to a person who by reason of mental incapacity or drunkenness is incompetent to contract, he must pay a reasonable price for them.
(3) In subsection (2) above 'necessaries' means goods suitable to the condition in life of the minor or other person concerned and to his actual requirements at the time of the sale and delivery.

[The words 'to a minor or' in s. 3(2) and 'minor or other' in s. 3(3) were repealed, for Scotland only, by the Age of Legal Capacity (Scotland) Act 1991, s. 10 and sch. 2.]

Formalities of Contract

4. How Contract of Sale is Made

(1) Subject to this and any other Act, a contract of sale may be made in writing (either with or without seal), or by word of mouth, or partly in writing and partly by word of mouth, or may be implied from the conduct of the parties.
(2) Nothing in this section affects the law relating to corporations.

Subject Matter of Contract

5. Existing or Future Goods

(1) The goods which form the subject of a contract of sale may be either existing goods, owned or possessed by the seller, or goods to be manufactured or acquired by him after the making of the contract of sale, in this Act called future goods.

(2) There may be a contract for the sale of goods the acquisition of which by the seller depends on a contingency which may or may not happen.
(3) Where by a contract of sale the seller purports to effect a present sale of future goods, the contract operates as an agreement to sell the goods.

6. Goods Which Have Perished

Where there is a contract for the sale of specific goods, and the goods without the knowledge of the seller have perished at the time when a contract is made, the contract is void.

7. Goods Perishing before Sale but after Agreement to Sell

Where there is an agreement to sell specific goods and subsequently the goods, without any fault on the part of the seller or buyer, perish before the risk passes to the buyer, the agreement is avoided.

The Price

8. Ascertainment of Price

(1) The price in a contract of sale may be fixed by the contract, or may be left to be fixed in a manner agreed by the contract, or may be determined by the course of dealing between the parties.
(2) Where the price is not determined as mentioned in subsection (1) above the buyer must pay a reasonable price.
(3) What is a reasonable price is a question of fact dependent on the circumstances of each particular case.

9. Agreement to Sell at Valuation

(1) Where there is an agreement to sell goods on the terms that the price is to be fixed by the valuation of a third party, and he cannot or does not make the valuation, the agreement is avoided; but if the goods or any part of them have been delivered to and appropriated by the buyer he must pay a reasonable price for them.
(2) Where the third party is prevented from making the valuation by the fault of the seller or buyer, the party not at fault may maintain an action for damages against the party at fault.

[Implied Terms etc.]

10. Stipulations about Time

(1) Unless a different intention appears from the terms of the contract, stipulations as to time of payment are not of the essence of a contract of sale.
(2) Whether any other stipulation as to time is or is not of the essence of the contract depends on the terms of the contract.
(3) In a contract of sale 'month' prima facie means calendar month.

11. When Condition to Be Treated as Warranty

(1) This section does not apply to Scotland.
(2) Where a contract of sale is subject to a condition to be fulfilled by the seller, the buyer may waive the condition, or may elect to treat the breach of the condition as a breach of warranty and not as a ground for treating the contract as repudiated.
(3) Whether a stipulation in a contract of sale is a condition, the breach of which may give rise to a right to treat the contract as repudiated, or a warranty, the breach of which may give rise to a claim for damages but not to a right to reject the goods and treat the contract as repudiated, depends in each case on the construction of the contract; and a stipulation may be a condition, though called a warranty in the contract.
(4) Subject to section 35A below where a contract of sale is not severable and the buyer has accepted the goods or part of them, the breach of a condition to be fulfilled by the seller can only be treated as a breach of warranty, and not as a ground for rejecting the goods and treating the contract as repudiated, unless there is an express or implied term of the contract to that effect.
(6) Nothing in this section affects a condition or warranty whose fulfilment is excused by law by reason of impossibility or otherwise.

(7) Paragraph 2 of Schedule 1 below applies in relation to a contract made before 22 April 1967 or (in the application of this Act to Northern Ireland) 28 July 1967.

12. Implied Terms about Title, etc.

(1) In a contract of sale, other than one to which subsection (3) below applies, there is an implied term on the part of the seller that in the case of a sale he has a right to sell the goods, and in the case of an agreement to sell he will have such a right at the time when the property is to pass.

(2) In a contract of sale, other than one to which subsection (3) below applies, there is also an implied term that—

(a) the goods are free, and will remain free until the time when the property is to pass, from any charge or encumbrance not disclosed or known to the buyer before the contract is made, and

(b) the buyer will enjoy quiet possession of the goods except so far as it may be disturbed by the owner or other person entitled to the benefit of any charge or encumbrance so disclosed or known.

(3) This subsection applies to a contract of sale in the case of which there appears from the contract or is to be inferred from its circumstances an intention that the seller should transfer only such title as he or a third person may have.

(4) In a contract to which subsection (3) above applies there is an implied term that all charges or encumbrances known to the seller and not known to the buyer have been disclosed to the buyer before the contract is made.

(5) In a contract to which subsection (3) above applies there is also an implied term that none of the following will disturb the buyer's quiet possession of the goods, namely—

(a) the seller;

(b) in a case where the parties to the contract intend that the seller should transfer only such title as a third person may have, that person;

(c) anyone claiming through or under the seller or that third person otherwise than under a charge or encumbrance disclosed or known to the buyer before the contract is made.

(5A) As regards England and Wales and Northern Ireland, the term implied by subsection (1) above is a condition and the terms implied by subsections (2), (4) and (5) above are warranties.

(6) Paragraph 3 of Schedule 1 below applies in relation to a contract made before 18 May 1973.

13. Sale by Description

(1) Where there is a contract for the sale of goods by description, there is an implied term that the goods will correspond with the description.

(1A) As regards England and Wales and Northern Ireland, the term implied by subsection (1) above is a condition.

(2) If the sale is by sample as well as by description it is not sufficient that the bulk of the goods corresponds with the sample if the goods do not also correspond with the description.

(3) A sale of goods is not prevented from being a sale by description by reason only that, being exposed for sale or hire, they are selected by the buyer.

(4) Paragraph 4 of Schedule 1 below applies in relation to a contract made before 18 May 1973.

14. Implied Terms about Quality or Fitness

(1) Except as provided by this section and section 15 below and subject to any other enactment, there is no implied term about the quality or fitness for any particular purpose of goods supplied under a contract of sale.

(2) Where the seller sells goods in the course of a business, there is an implied term that the goods supplied under the contract are of satisfactory quality.

(2A) For the purposes of this Act, goods are of satisfactory quality if they meet the standard that a reasonable person would regard as satisfactory, taking account of any description of the goods, the price (if relevant) and all the other relevant circumstances.

(2B) For the purposes of this Act, the quality of goods includes their state and condition and the following (among others) are in appropriate cases aspects of the quality of goods—

(a) fitness for all the purposes for which goods of the kind in question are commonly supplied,

(b) appearance and finish,

(c) freedom from minor defects,
(d) safety, and
(e) durability.

(2C) The term implied by subsection (2) above does not extend to any matter making the quality of goods unsatisfactory—
(a) which is specifically drawn to the buyer's attention before the contract is made,
(b) where the buyer examines the goods before the contract is made, which that examination ought to reveal, or
(c) in the case of a contract for sale by sample, which would have been apparent on a reasonable examination of the sample.

(2D) If the buyer deals as consumer or, in Scotland, if a contract of sale is a consumer contract, the relevant circumstances mentioned in subsection (2A) above include any public statements on the specific characteristics of the goods made about them by the seller, the producer or his representative, particularly in advertising or on labelling.

(2E) A public statement is not by virtue of subsection (2D) above a relevant circumstance for the purposes of subsection (2A) above in the case of a contract of sale, if the seller shows that—
(a) at the time the contract was made, he was not, and could not reasonably have been, aware of the statement,
(b) before the contract was made, the statement had been withdrawn in public or, to the extent that it contained anything which was incorrect or misleading, it had been corrected in public, or
(c) the decision to buy the goods could not have been influenced by the statement.

(2F) Subsections (2D) and (2E) above do not prevent any public statement from being a relevant circumstance for the purposes of subsection (2A) above (whether or not the buyer deals as consumer or, in Scotland, whether or not the contract of sale is a consumer contract) if the statement would have been such a circumstance apart from those subsections.

(3) Where the seller sells goods in the course of a business and the buyer, expressly or by implication, makes known—
(a) to the seller, or
(b) where the purchase price of part of it is payable by instalments and the goods were previously sold by a credit-broker to the seller, to that credit-broker, any particular purpose for which the goods are being bought,

there is an implied term that the goods supplied under the contract are reasonably fit for that purpose, whether or not that is a purpose for which such goods are commonly supplied, except where the circumstances show that the buyer does not rely, or that it is unreasonable for him to rely, on the skill or judgment of the seller or credit-broker.

(4) An implied term about quality or fitness for a particular purpose may be annexed to a contract of sale by usage.

(5) The preceding provisions of this section apply to a sale by a person who in the course of a business is acting as agent for another as they apply to a sale by a principal in the course of a business, except where that other is not selling in the course of a business and either the buyer knows that fact or reasonable steps are taken to bring it to the notice of the buyer before the contract is made.

(6) As regards England and Wales and Northern Ireland, the terms implied by subsections (2) and (3) above are conditions.

(7) Paragraph 5 of Schedule 1 below applies in relation to a contract made on or after 18 May 1973 and before the appointed day, and paragraph 6 in relation to one made before 18 May 1973.

(8) In subsection (7) above and paragraph 5 of Schedule 1 below references to the appointed day are to the day appointed for the purposes of those provisions by an order of the Secretary of State made by statutory instrument.

Sale by Sample

15. Sale by Sample

(1) A contract of sale is a contract for sale by sample where there is an express or implied term to that effect in the contract.

(2) In the case of a contract for sale by sample there is an implied term—
   (a) that the bulk will correspond with the sample in quality;
   (c) that the goods will be free from any defect, making their quality unsatisfactory, which would not be apparent on reasonable examination of the sample.
(3) As regards England and Wales and Northern Ireland, the term implied by subsection (2) above is a condition.
(4) Paragraph 7 of Schedule 1 below applies in relation to a contract made before 18 May 1973.

Miscellaneous

15A. Modification of Remedies for Breach of Condition in Non-consumer Cases

(1) Where in the case of a contract of sale—
   (a) the buyer would, apart from this subsection, have the right to reject goods by reason of a breach on the part of the seller of a term implied by section 13, 14 or 15 above, but
   (b) the breach is so slight that it would be unreasonable for him to reject them,
   then, if the buyer does not deal as consumer, the breach is not to be treated as a breach of condition but may be treated as a breach of warranty.
(2) This section applies unless a contrary intention appears in, or is to be implied from, the contract.
(3) It is for the seller to show that a breach fell within subsection (1)(b) above.
(4) This section does not apply to Scotland.

PART III EFFECTS OF THE CONTRACT

Transfer of Property as Between Seller and Buyer

16. Goods Must Be Ascertained

Subject to section 20A below where there is a contract for the sale of unascertained goods no property in the goods is transferred to the buyer unless and until the goods are ascertained.

17. Property Passes When Intended to Pass

(1) Where there is a contract for the sale of specific or ascertained goods the property in them is transferred to the buyer at such time as the parties to the contract intend it to be transferred.
(2) For the purpose of ascertaining the intention of the parties regard shall be had to the terms of the contract, the conduct of the parties and the circumstances of the case.

18. Rules for Ascertaining Intention

Unless a different intention appears, the following are rules for ascertaining the intention of the parties as to the time at which the property in the goods is to pass to the buyer.

Rule 1.—Where there is an unconditional contract for the sale of specific goods in a deliverable state the property in the goods passes to the buyer when the contract is made, and it is immaterial whether the time of payment or the time of delivery, or both, be postponed.

Rule 2.—Where there is a contract for the sale of specific goods and the seller is bound to do something to the goods for the purpose of putting them into a deliverable state, the property does not pass until the thing is done and the buyer has notice that it has been done.

Rule 3.—Where there is a contract for the sale of specific goods in a deliverable state but the seller is bound to weigh, measure, test, or do some other act or thing with reference to the goods for the purpose of ascertaining the price, the property does not pass until the act or thing is done and the buyer has notice that it has been done.

Rule 4.—When goods are delivered to the buyer on approval or on sale or return or other similar terms the property in the goods passes to the buyer:—
(a) when he signifies his approval or acceptance to the seller or does any other act adopting the transaction;
(b) if he does not signify his approval or acceptance to the seller but retains the goods without giving notice of rejection, then, if a time has been fixed for the return of the goods, on the expiration of that time, and, if no time has been fixed, on the expiration of a reasonable time.

Rule 5.—(1) Where there is a contract for the sale of unascertained or future goods by description, and goods of that description and in a deliverable state are unconditionally appropriated to the contract, either by the seller with the assent of the buyer or by the buyer with the assent of the seller, the property in the goods then passes to the buyer; and the assent may be express or implied, and may be given either before of after the appropriation is made.

(2) Where, in pursuance of the contract, the seller delivers the goods to the buyer or to a carrier or other bailee or custodier (whether named by the buyer or not) for the purpose of transmission to the buyer, and does not reserve the right of disposal, he is to be taken to have unconditionally appropriated the goods to the contract.

(3) Where there is a contract for the sale of a specified quantity of unascertained goods in a deliverable state forming part of a bulk which is identified either in the contract or by subsequent agreement between the parties and the bulk is reduced to (or to less than) that quantity, then, if the buyer under that contract is the only buyer to whom goods are then due out of the bulk—

(a) the remaining goods are to be taken as appropriated to that contract at the time when the bulk is so reduced; and

(b) the property in those goods then passes to that buyer.

(4) Paragraph (3) above applies also (with the necessary modifications) where a bulk is reduced to (or to less than) the aggregate of the quantities due to a single buyer under separate contracts relating to that bulk and he is the only buyer to whom goods are then due out of that bulk.

19. Reservation of Right of Disposal

(1) Where there is a contract for the sale of specific goods or where goods are subsequently appropriated to the contract, the seller may, by the terms of the contract or appropriation, reserve the right of disposal of the goods until certain conditions are fulfilled; and in such a case, notwithstanding the delivery of the goods to the buyer, or to a carrier or other bailee or custodier for the purpose of transmission to the buyer, the property in the goods does not pass to the buyer until the conditions imposed by the seller are fulfilled.

(2) Where goods are shipped, and by the bill of lading the goods are deliverable to the order of the seller or his agent, the seller is prima facie to be taken to reserve the right of disposal.

(3) Where the seller of goods draws on the buyer for the price, and transmits the bill of exchange and bill of lading to the buyer together to secure acceptance or payment of the bill of exchange, the buyer is bound to return the bill of lading if he does not honour the bill of exchange, and if he wrongfully retains the bill of lading the property in the goods does not pass to him.

20. Passing of Risk

(1) Unless otherwise agreed, the goods remain at the seller's risk until the property in them is transferred to the buyer, but when the property in them is transferred to the buyer the goods are at the buyer's risk whether delivery has been made or not.

(2) But where delivery has been delayed through the fault of either buyer or seller the goods are at the risk of the party at fault as regards any loss which might not have occurred but for such fault.

(3) Nothing in this section affects the duties or liabilities of either seller or buyer as a bailee or custodier of the goods of the other party.

(4) In a case where the buyer deals as consumer or, in Scotland, where there is a consumer contract in which the buyer is a consumer, subsections (1) to (3) above must be ignored and the goods remain at the seller's risk until they are delivered to the consumer.

20A. Undivided Shares in Goods Forming Part of a Bulk

(1) This section applies to a contract for the sale of a specified quantity of unascertained goods if the following conditions are met—

(a) the goods or some of them form part of a bulk which is identified either in the contract or by subsequent agreement between the parties; and

(b) the buyer has paid the price for some or all of the goods which are the subject of the contract and which form part of the bulk.

(2) Where this section applies, then (unless the parties agree otherwise), as soon as the conditions specified in paragraphs (a) and (b) of subsection (1) above are met or at such later time as the parties may agree—
  (a) property in an undivided share in the bulk is transferred to the buyer, and
  (b) the buyer becomes an owner in common of the bulk.
(3) Subject to subsection (4) below, for the purposes of this section, the undivided share of a buyer in a bulk at any time shall be such share as the quantity of goods paid for and due to the buyer out of the bulk bears to the quantity of goods in the bulk at that time.
(4) Where the aggregate of the undivided shares of buyers in a bulk determined under subsection (3) above would at any time exceed the whole of the bulk at that time, the undivided share in the bulk of each buyer shall be reduced proportionately so that the aggregate of the undivided shares is equal to the whole bulk.
(5) Where a buyer has paid the price for only some of the goods due to him out of a bulk, any delivery to the buyer out of the bulk shall, for the purposes of this section, be ascribed in the first place to the goods in respect of which payment has been made.
(6) For the purposes of this section payment of part of the price for any goods shall be treated as payment for a corresponding part of the goods.

20B. PDeemed Consent by Co-owner to Dealings in Bulk Goods

(1) A person who has become an owner in common of a bulk by virtue of section 20A above shall be deemed to have consented to—
  (a) any delivery of goods out of the bulk to any other owner in common of the bulk, being goods which are due to him under his contract;
  (b) any dealing with or removal, delivery or disposal of goods in the bulk by any other person who is an owner in common of the bulk in so far as the goods fall within that co-owner's undivided share in the bulk at the time of the dealing, removal, delivery or disposal.
(2) No cause of action shall accrue to anyone against a person by reason of that person having acted in accordance with paragraph (a) or (b) of subsection (1) above in reliance on any consent deemed to have been given under that subsection.
(3) Nothing in this section or section 20A above shall—
  (a) impose an obligation on a buyer of goods out of a bulk to compensate any other buyer of goods out of that bulk for any shortfall in the goods received by that other buyer;
  (b) affect any contractual arrangement between buyers of goods out of a bulk for adjustments between themselves; or
  (c) affect the rights of any buyer under his contract.

Transfer of Title

21. Sale by Person Not the Owner

(1) Subject to this Act, where goods are sold by a person who is not their owner, and who does not sell them under the authority or with the consent of the owner, the buyer acquires no better title to the goods than the seller had, unless the owner of the goods is by his conduct precluded from denying the seller's authority to sell.
(2) Nothing in this Act affects—
  (a) the provisions of the Factors Acts or any enactment enabling the apparent owner of goods to dispose of them as if he were their true owner;
  (b) the validity of any contract of sale under any special common law or statutory power of sale or under the order of a court of competent jurisdiction.

22. Market Overt

(2) This section does not apply to Scotland.
(3) Paragraph 8 of Schedule 1 below applies in relation to a contract under which goods were sold before 1 January 1968 or (in the application of this Act to Northern Ireland) 29 August 1967.

23. Sale under Voidable Title

When the seller of goods has a voidable title to them, but his title has not been avoided at the time of

Selected Legislation

the sale, the buyer acquires a good title to the goods, provided he buys them in good faith and without notice of the seller's defect of title.

24. Seller in Possession after Sale

Where a person having sold goods continues or is in possession of the goods, or of the documents of title to the goods, the delivery or transfer by that person, or by a mercantile agent acting for him, of the goods or documents of title under any sale, pledge, or other disposition thereof, to any person receiving the same in good faith and without notice of the previous sale, has the same effect as if the person making the delivery or transfer were expressly authorised by the owner of the goods to make the same.

25. Buyer in Possession after Sale

(1) Where a person having bought or agreed to buy goods obtains, with the consent of the seller, possession of the goods or the documents of title to the goods, the delivery or transfer by that person, or by a mercantile agent acting for him, of the goods or documents of title, under any sale, pledge, or other disposition thereof, to any person receiving the same in good faith and without notice of any lien or other right of the original seller in respect of the goods, has the same effect as if the person making the delivery or transfer were a mercantile agent in possession of the goods or documents of title with the consent of the owner.

(2) For the purposes of subsection (1) above—
  (a) the buyer under a conditional sale agreement is to be taken not to be a person who has bought or agreed to buy goods, and
  (b) 'conditional sale agreement' means an agreement for the sale of goods which is a consumer credit agreement within the meaning of the Consumer Credit Act 1974 under which the purchase price or part of it is payable by instalments, and the property in the goods is to remain in the seller (notwithstanding that the buyer is to be in possession of the goods) until such conditions as to the payment of instalments or otherwise as may be specified in the agreement are fulfilled.

(3) Paragraph 9 of Schedule 1 below applies in relation to a contract under which a person buys or agrees to buy goods and which is made before the appointed day.

(4) In subsection (3) above and paragraph 9 of Schedule 1 below references to the appointed day are to the day appointed for the purposes of those provisions by an order of the Secretary of State made by statutory instrument.

26. Supplementary to Sections 24 and 25

In sections 24 and 25 above 'mercantile agent' means a mercantile agent having in the customary course of his business as such agent authority either—
(a) to sell goods, or
(b) to consign goods for the purpose of sale, or
(c) to buy goods, or
(d) to raise money on the security of goods.

PART IV PERFORMANCE OF THE CONTRACT

27. Duties of Seller and Buyer

It is the duty of the seller to deliver the goods, and of the buyer to accept and pay for them, in accordance with the terms of the contract of sale.

28. Payment and Delivery are Concurrent Conditions

Unless otherwise agreed, delivery of the goods and payment of the price are concurrent conditions, that is to say, the seller must be ready and willing to give possession of the goods to the buyer in exchange for the price and the buyer must be ready and willing to pay the price in exchange for possession of the goods.

29. Rules about Delivery

(1) Whether it is for the buyer to take possession of the goods or for the seller to send them to the

buyer is a question depending in each case on the contract, express or implied, between the parties.

(2) Apart from any such contract, express or implied, the place of delivery is the seller's place of business if he has one, and if not, his residence; except that, if the contract is for the sale of specific goods, which to the knowledge of the parties when the contract is made are in some other place, then that place is the place of delivery.

(3) Where under the contract of sale the seller is bound to send the goods to the buyer, but no time for sending them is fixed, the seller is bound to send them within a reasonable time.

(4) Where the goods at the time of sale are in the possession of a third person, there is no delivery by seller to buyer unless and until the third person acknowledges to the buyer that he holds the goods on his behalf; but nothing in this section affects the operation of the issue or transfer of any document of title to goods.

(5) Demand or tender of delivery may be treated as ineffectual unless made at a reasonable hour; and what is a reasonable hour is a question of fact.

(6) Unless otherwise agreed, the expenses of and incidental to putting the goods into a deliverable state must be borne by the seller.

30. Delivery of Wrong Quantity

(1) Where the seller delivers to the buyer a quantity of goods less than he contracted to sell, the buyer may reject them, but if the buyer accepts the goods so delivered he must pay for them at the contract rate.

(2) Where the seller delivers to the buyer a quantity of goods larger than he contracted to sell, the buyer may accept the goods included in the contract and reject the rest, or he may reject the whole.

(2A) A buyer who does not deal as consumer may not—

(a) where the seller delivers a quantity of goods less than he contracted to sell, reject the goods under subsection (1) above, or

(b) where the seller delivers a quantity of goods larger than he contracted to sell, reject the whole under subsection (2) above,

if the shortfall or, as the case may be, excess is so slight that it would be unreasonable for him to do so.

(2B) It is for the seller to show that a shortfall or excess fell within subsection (2A) above.

(2C) Subsections (2A) and (2B) above do not apply to Scotland.

(2D) Where the seller delivers a quantity of goods—

(a) less than he contracted to sell, the buyer shall not be entitled to reject the goods under subsection (1) above,

(b) larger than he contracted to sell, the buyer shall not be entitled to reject the whole under subsection (2) above,

unless the shortfall or excess is material.

(2E) Subsection (2D) above applies to Scotland only.

(3) Where the seller delivers to the buyer a quantity of goods larger than he contracted to sell and the buyer accepts the whole of the goods so delivered he must pay for them at the contract rate.

(5) This section is subject to any usage of trade, special agreement, or course of dealing between the parties.

31. Instalment Deliveries

(1) Unless otherwise agreed, the buyer of goods is not bound to accept delivery of them by instalments.

(2) Where there is a contract for the sale of goods to be delivered by stated instalments, which are to be separately paid for, and the seller makes defective deliveries in respect of one or more instalments, or the buyer neglects or refuses to take delivery of or pay for one or more instalments, it is a question in each case depending on the terms of the contract and the circumstances of the case whether the breach of contract is a repudiation of the whole contract or whether it is a severable breach giving rise to a claim for compensation but not to a right to treat the whole contract as repudiated.

32. Delivery to Carrier

(1) Where, in pursuance of a contract of sale, the seller is authorised or required to send the goods to the buyer, delivery of the goods to a carrier (whether named by the buyer or not) for the purpose of transmission to the buyer is prima facie deemed to be delivery of the goods to the buyer.

(2) Unless otherwise authorised by the buyer, the seller must make such contact with the carrier on behalf of the buyer as may be reasonable having regard to the nature of the goods and the other circumstances of the case; and if the seller omits to do so, and the goods are lost or damaged in course of transit, the buyer may decline to treat the delivery to the carrier as a delivery to himself or may hold the seller responsible in damages.

(3) Unless otherwise agreed, where goods are sent by the seller to the buyer by a route involving sea transit, under circumstances in which it is usual to insure, the seller must give such notice to the buyer as may enable him to insure them during their sea transit, and if the seller fails to do so, the goods are at his risk during such sea transit.

(4) In a case where the buyer deals as consumer or, in Scotland, where there is a consumer contract in which the buyer is a consumer, subsections (1) to (3) above must be ignored, but if in pursuance of a contract of sale the seller is authorised or required to send the goods to the buyer, delivery of the goods to the carrier is not delivery of the goods to the buyer.

33. Risk Where Goods Are Delivered at Distant Place

Where the seller of goods agrees to deliver them at his own risk at a place other than that where they are when sold, the buyer must nevertheless (unless otherwise agreed) take any risk of deterioration in the goods necessarily incident to the course of transit.

34. Buyer's Right of Examining the Goods

Unless otherwise agreed, when the seller tenders delivery of goods to the buyer, he is bound on request to afford the buyer a reasonable opportunity of examining the goods for the purpose of ascertaining whether they are in conformity with the contract and, in the case of a contract for sale by sample, of comparing the bulk with the sample.

35. Acceptance

(1) The buyer is deemed to have accepted the goods subject to subsection (2) below—
  (a) when he intimates to the seller that he has accepted them, or
  (b) when the goods have been delivered to him and he does any act in relation to them which is inconsistent with the ownership of the seller.

(2) Where goods are delivered to the buyer, and he has not previously examined them, he is not deemed to have accepted them under subsection (1) above until he has had a reasonable opportunity of examining them for the purpose—
  (a) of ascertaining whether they are in conformity with the contract, and
  (b) in the case of a contract for sale by sample, of comparing the bulk with the sample.

(3) Where the buyer deals as consumer or (in Scotland) the contract of sale is a consumer contract, the buyer cannot lose his right to rely on subsection (2) above by agreement, waiver or otherwise.

(4) The buyer is also deemed to have accepted the goods when after the lapse of a reasonable time he retains the goods without intimating to the seller that he has rejected them.

(5) The questions that are material in determining for the purposes of subsection (4) above whether a reasonable time has elapsed include whether the buyer has had a reasonable opportunity of examining the goods for the purpose mentioned in subsection (2) above.

(6) The buyer is not by virtue of this section deemed to have accepted the goods merely because—
  (a) he asks for, or agrees to, their repair by or under an arrangement with the seller, or
  (b) the goods are delivered to another under a sub-sale or other disposition.

(7) Where the contract is for the sale of goods making one or more commercial units, a buyer accepting any goods included in a unit is deemed to have accepted all the goods making the unit; and in this subsection 'commercial unit' means a unit division of which would materially impair the value of the goods or the character of the unit.

(8) Paragraph 10 of Schedule 1 below applies in relation to a contract made before 22 April 1967 or (in the application of this Act to Northern Ireland) 28 July 1967.

35A. Right of Partial Rejection

(1) If the buyer—
  (a) has the right to reject the goods by reason of a breach on the part of the seller that affects some or all of them, but
  (b) accepts some of the goods, including, where there are any goods unaffected by the breach, all such goods,

he does not by accepting them lose his right to reject the rest.

(2) In the case of a buyer having the right to reject an instalment of goods, subsection (1) above applies as if references to the goods were references to the goods comprised in the instalment.

(3) For the purposes of subsection (1) above, goods are affected by a breach if by reason of the breach they are not in conformity with the contract.

(4) This section applies unless a contrary intention appears in, or is to be implied from, the contract.

36. Buyer Not Bound to Return Rejected Goods

Unless otherwise agreed, where goods are delivered to the buyer, and he refuses to accept them, having the right to do so, he is not bound to return them to the seller, but it is sufficient if he intimates to the seller that he refuses to accept them.

37. Buyer's Liability for Not Taking Delivery of Goods

(1) When the seller is ready and willing to deliver the goods, and requests the buyer to take delivery, and the buyer does not within a reasonable time after such request take delivery of the goods, he is liable to the seller for any loss occasioned by his neglect or refusal to take delivery, and also for a reasonable charge for the care and custody of the goods.

(2) Nothing in this section affects the rights of the seller where the neglect or refusal of the buyer to take delivery amounts to a repudiation of the contract.

PART V RIGHTS OF UNPAID SELLER AGAINST THE GOODS

Preliminary

38. Unpaid Seller Defined

(1) The seller of goods is an unpaid seller within the meaning of this Act—
  (a) when the whole of the price has not been paid or tendered;
  (b) when a bill of exchange or other negotiable instrument has been received as conditional payment, and the condition on which it was received has not been fulfilled by reason of the dishonour of the instrument or otherwise.

(2) In this Part of this Act 'seller' includes any person who is in the position of a seller, as, for instance, an agent of the seller to whom the bill of lading has been indorsed, or a consignor or agent who has himself paid (or is directly responsible for) the price.

39. Unpaid Seller's Rights

(1) Subject to this and any other Act, notwithstanding that the property in the goods may have passed to the buyer, the unpaid seller of goods, as such, has by implication of law—
  (a) a lien on the goods or right to retain them for the price while he is in possession of them;
  (b) in the case of the insolvency of the buyer, a right of stopping the goods in transit after he has parted with the possession of them;
  (c) a right of re-sale as limited by this Act.

(2) Where the property in goods has not passed to the buyer, the unpaid seller has (in addition to his other remedies) a right of withholding delivery similar to and coextensive with his rights of lien or retention and stoppage in transit where the property has passed to the buyer.

PART 5A ADDITIONAL RIGHTS OF BUYER IN CONSUMER CASES

48A. Introductory

(1) This section applies if—

(a) the buyer deals as consumer or, in Scotland, there is a consumer contract in which the buyer is a consumer, and

(b) the goods do not conform to the contract of sale at the time of delivery.

(2) If this section applies, the buyer has the right—

(a) under and in accordance with section 48B below, to require the seller to repair or replace the goods, or

(b) under and in accordance with section 48C below—

(i) to require the seller to reduce the purchase price of the goods to the buyer by an appropriate amount, or

(ii) to rescind the contract with regard to the goods in question.

(3) For the purposes of subsection (1)(b) above goods which do not conform to the contract of sale at any time within the period of six months starting with the date on which the goods were delivered to the buyer must be taken not to have so conformed at that date.

(4) Subsection (3) above does not apply if—

(a) it is established that the goods did so conform at that date;

(b) its application is incompatible with the nature of the goods or the nature of the lack of conformity.

48B. Repair or Replacement of the Goods

(1) If section 48A above applies, the buyer may require the seller—

(a) to repair the goods, or

(b) to replace the goods.

(2) If the buyer requires the seller to repair or replace the goods, the seller must—

(a) repair or, as the case may be, replace the goods within a reasonable time but without causing significant inconvenience to the buyer;

(b) bear any necessary costs incurred in doing so (including in particular the cost of any labour, materials or postage).

(3) The buyer must not require the seller to repair or, as the case may be, replace the goods if that remedy is—

(a) impossible, or

(b) disproportionate in comparison to the other of those remedies, or

(c) disproportionate in comparison to an appropriate reduction in the purchase price under paragraph (a), or rescission under paragraph (b), of section 48C(1) below.

(4) One remedy is disproportionate in comparison to the other if the one imposes costs on the seller which, in comparison to those imposed on him by the other, are unreasonable, taking into account—

(a) the value which the goods would have if they conformed to the contract of sale,

(b) the significance of the lack of conformity, and

(c) whether the other remedy could be effected without significant inconvenience to the buyer.

(5) Any question as to what is a reasonable time or significant inconvenience is to be determined by reference to—

(a) the nature of the goods, and

(b) the purpose for which the goods were acquired.

48C. Reduction of Purchase Price or Rescission of Contract

(1) If section 48A above applies, the buyer may—

(a) require the seller to reduce the purchase price of the goods in question to the buyer by an appropriate amount, or

(b) rescind the contract with regard to those goods,

if the condition in subsection (2) below is satisfied.

(2) The condition is that—

(a) by virtue of section 48B(3) above the buyer may require neither repair nor replacement of the goods; or

(b) the buyer has required the seller to repair or replace the goods, but the seller is in breach of the requirement of section 48B(2)(a) above to do so within a reasonable time and without significant inconvenience to the buyer.

(3) For the purposes of this Part, if the buyer rescinds the contract, any reimbursement to the buyer may be reduced to take account of the use he has had of the goods since they were delivered to him.

48D. Relation to Other Remedies etc.

(1) If the buyer requires the seller to repair or replace the goods the buyer must not act under subsection (2) until he has given the seller a reasonable time in which to repair or replace (as the case may be) the goods.
(2) The buyer acts under this subsection if—
  (a) in England and Wales or Northern Ireland he rejects the goods and terminates the contract for breach of condition;
  (b) in Scotland he rejects any goods delivered under the contract and treats it as repudiated;
  (c) he requires the goods to be replaced or repaired (as the case may be).

48E. Powers of the Court

(1) In any proceedings in which a remedy is sought by virtue of this Part the court, in addition to any other power it has, may act under this section.
(2) On the application of the buyer the court may make an order requiring specific performance or, in Scotland, specific implement by the seller of any obligation imposed on him by virtue of section 48B above.
(3) Subsection (4) applies if—
  (a) the buyer requires the seller to give effect to a remedy under section 48B or 48C above or has claims to rescind under section 48C, but
  (b) the court decides that another remedy under section 48B or 48C is appropriate.
(4) The court may proceed—
  (a) as if the buyer had required the seller to give effect to the other remedy, or if the other remedy is rescission under section 48C
  (b) as if the buyer had claimed to rescind the contract under that section.
(5) If the buyer has claimed to rescind the contract the court may order that any reimbursement to the buyer is reduced to take account of the use he has had of the goods since they were delivered to him.
(6) The court may make an order under this section unconditionally or on such terms and conditions as to damages, payment of the price and otherwise as it thinks just.

48F. Conformity with the Contract

For the purposes of this Part, goods do not conform to a contract of sale if there is, in relation to the goods, a breach of an express term of the contract or a term implied by section 13, 14 or 15 above.

PART VI ACTIONS FOR BREACH OF THE CONTRACT

Seller's Remedies

49. Action for Price

(1) Where, under a contract of sale, the property in the goods has passed to the buyer and he wrongfully neglects or refuses to pay for the goods according to the terms of the contract, the seller may maintain an action against him for the price of the goods.
(2) Where, under a contract of sale, the price is payable on a day certain irrespective of delivery and the buyer wrongfully neglects or refuses to pay such price, the seller may maintain an action for the price, although the property in goods has not passed and the goods have not been appropriated to the contract.
(3) Nothing in this section prejudices the right of the seller in Scotland to recover interest on the price from the date of tender of the goods, or from the date on which the price was payable, as the case may be.

50. Damages for Non-acceptance

(1) Where the buyer wrongfully neglects or refuses to accept and pay for the goods, the seller may maintain an action against him for damages for non-acceptance.

(2) The measure of damages is the estimated loss directly and naturally resulting in the ordinary course of events, from the buyer's breach of contract.

(3) Where there is an available market for the goods in question the measure of damages is prima facie to be ascertained by the difference between the contract price and the market or current price at the time or times when the goods ought to have been accepted or (if no time was fixed for acceptance) at the time of the refusal to accept.

Buyer's Remedies

51. Damages for Non-delivery

(1) Where the seller wrongfully neglects or refuses to deliver the goods to the buyer, the buyer may maintain an action against the seller for damages for non-delivery.

(2) The measure of damages is the estimated loss directly and naturally resulting, in the ordinary course of events, from the seller's breach of contract.

(3) Where there is an available market for the goods in question the measure of damages is prima facie to be ascertained by the difference between the contract price and the market or current price of the goods at the time or times when they ought to have been delivered or (if no time was fixed) at the time of the refusal to deliver.

52. Specific Performance

(1) If any action for breach of contract to deliver specific or ascertained goods the court may, if it thinks fit, on the plaintiff's application, by its judgment or decree direct that the contract shall be performed specifically, without giving the defendant the option of retaining the goods on payment of damages.

(2) The plaintiff's application may be made at any time before judgment or decree.

(3) The judgment or decree may be unconditional, or on such terms and conditions as to damages, payment of the price and otherwise as seem just to the court.

(4) The provisions of this section shall be deemed to be supplementary to, and not in derogation of, the right of specific implement in Scotland.

53. Remedy for Breach of Warranty

(1) Where there is a breach of warranty by the seller, or where the buyer elects (or is compelled) to treat any breach of a condition on the part of the seller as a breach of warranty, the buyer is not by reason only of such breach of warranty entitled to reject the goods; but he may—

(a) set up against the seller the breach of warranty in diminution or extinction of the price, or

(b) maintain an action against the seller for damages for the breach of warranty.

(2) The measure of damages for breach of warranty is the estimated loss directly and naturally resulting, in the ordinary course of events, from the breach of warranty.

(3) In the case of breach of warranty of quality such loss is prima facie the difference between the value of the goods at the time of delivery to the buyer and the value they would have had if they had fulfilled the warranty.

(4) The fact that the buyer has set up the breach of warranty in diminution or extinction of the price does not prevent him from maintaining an action for the same breach of warranty if he has suffered further damage.

(5) This section does not apply to Scotland.

Interest, etc.

54. Interest, etc.

Nothing in this Act affects the right of the buyer or the seller to recover interest or special damages in any case where by law interest or special damages may be recoverable, or to recover money paid where the consideration for the payment of it has failed.

PART VII SUPPLEMENTARY

55. Exclusion of Implied Terms

(1) Where a right duty or liability would arise under a contract of sale of goods by implication of law, it may (subject to the Unfair Contract Terms Act 1977) be negatived or varied by express agreement, or by the course of dealing between the parties, or by such usage as binds both parties to the contract.
(2) An express term does not negative a term implied by this Act unless inconsistent with it.
(3) Paragraph 11 of Schedule 1 below applies in relation to a contract made on or after 18 May 1973 and before 1 February 1978, and paragraph 12 in relation to one made before 18 May 1973.

56. Conflict of Laws

Paragraph 13 of Schedule 1 below applies in relation to a contract made on or after 18 May 1973 and before 1 February 1978, so as to make provision about conflict of laws in relation to such a contract.

57. Auction Sales

(1) Where goods are put up for sale by auction in lots, each lot is prima facie deemed to be the subject of a separate contract of sale.
(2) A sale by auction is complete when the auctioneer announces its completion by the fall of the hammer, or in other customary manner; and until the announcement is made any bidder may retract his bid.
(3) A sale by auction may be notified to be subject to a reserve or upset price, and a right to bid may also be reserved expressly by or on behalf of the seller.
(4) Where a sale by auction is not notified to be subject to a right to bid by or on behalf of the seller, it is not lawful for the seller to bid himself or to employ any person to bid at the sale, or for the auctioneer knowingly to take any bid from the seller or any such person.
(5) A sale contravening subsection (4) above may be treated as fraudulent by the buyer.
(6) Where, in respect of a sale by auction, a right to bid is expressly reserved (but not otherwise) the seller or any one person on his behalf may bid at the auction.

59. Reasonable Time a Question of Fact

Where a reference is made in this Act to a reasonable time the question what is a reasonable time is a question of fact.

60. Rights etc. Enforceable by Action

Where a right, duty or liability is declared by this Act, it may (unless otherwise provided by this Act) be enforced by action.

61. Interpretation

(1) In this Act, unless the context or subject matter otherwise requires,—
'action' includes counterclaim and set-off, and in Scotland condescendence and claim and compensation;
'bulk' means a mass or collection of goods of the same kind which—
(a) is contained in a defined space or area; and
(b) is such that any goods in the bulk are interchangeable with any other goods therein of the same number or quantity;
'business' includes a profession and the activities of any government department (including a Northern Ireland department) or local or public authority;
'buyer' means a person who buys or agrees to buy goods;
'consumer contract' has the same meaning as in section 25(1) of the Unfair Contract Terms Act 1977; and for the purposes of this Act the onus of proving that a contract is not to be regarded as a consumer contract shall lie on the seller
'contract of sale' includes an agreement to sell as well as a sale,

'credit-broker' means a person acting in the course of a business of credit brokerage carried on by him, that is a business of effecting introductions of individuals desiring to obtain credit—

(a) to persons carrying on any business so far as it relates to the provision of credit, or
(b) to other persons engaged in credit brokerage;

'defendant' includes in Scotland defender, respondent, and claimant in a multiple-poinding;

'delivery' means voluntary transfer of possession from one person to another; except that in relation to sections 20A and 20B above it includes such appropriation of goods to the contract as results in property in the goods being transferred to the buyer;

'document of title to goods' has the same meaning as it has in the Factors Acts;

'Factors Acts' means the Factors Act 1889, the Factors (Scotland) Act 1890, and any enactment amending or substituted for the same;

'fault' means wrongful act or default;

'future goods' means goods to be manufactured or acquired by the seller after the making of the contract of sale;

'goods' includes all personal chattels other than things in action and money, and in Scotland all corporeal moveables except money; and in particular 'goods' includes emblements, industrial growing crops, and things attached to or forming part of the land which are agreed to be severed before sale or under the contract of sale; and includes an undivided share in goods;

'plaintiff' includes pursuer, complainer, claimant in a multiplepoinding and defendant or defender counter-claiming;

'producer' means the manufacturer of goods, the importer of goods into the European Economic Area or any person purporting to be a producer by placing his name, trade mark or other distinctive sign on the goods;

'property' means the general property in goods, and not merely a special property;

'repair' means, in cases where there is a lack of conformity in goods for the purposes of section 48F of this Act, to bring the goods into conformity with the contract;

'sale' includes a bargain and sale as well as a sale and delivery;

'seller' means a person who sells or agrees to sell goods;

'specific goods' means goods identified and agreed on at the time a contract of sale is made; and includes an undivided share, specified as a fraction or percentage, of goods identified and agreed on as aforesaid;

'warranty' (as regards England and Wales and Northern Ireland) means an agreement with reference to goods which are the subject of a contract of sale, but collateral to the main purpose of such contract, the breach of which gives rise to a claim for damages, but not to a right to reject the goods and treat the contract as repudiated.

(3) A thing is deemed to be done in good faith within the meaning of this Act when it is in fact done honestly, whether it is done negligently or not.

(4) A person is deemed to be insolvent within the meaning of this Act if he has either ceased to pay his debts in the ordinary course of business or he cannot pay his debts as they become due.

(5) Goods are in a deliverable state within the meaning of this Act when they are in such a state that the buyer would under the contract be bound to take delivery of them.

(5A) References in this Act to dealing as consumer are to be construed in accordance with Part I of the Unfair Contract Terms Act 1977; and, for the purposes of this Act, it is for a seller claiming that the buyer does not deal as consumer to show that he does not.

(6) As regards the definition of 'business' in subsection (1) above, paragraph 14 of Schedule 1 below applies in relation to a contract made on or after 18 May 1973 and before 1 February 1978, and paragraph 15 in relation to one made before 18 May 1973.

Solicitors Act 1974

(1974 CHAPTER 47)

An Act to consolidate the Solicitors Acts 1957 to 1974 and certain other enactments relating to solicitors. [31st July 1974]

PART I RIGHT TO PRACTISE AS SOLICITOR

Rights and Privileges of Solicitors

19. Rights of Practising and Rights of Audience

(1) Subject to subsection (2), every person qualified in accordance with section 1 may practise as a solicitor—

- (a) in the Supreme Court;
- (b) in any county court;
- (c) in all courts and before all persons having jurisdiction in ecclesiastical matters; and
- (d) in all matters relating to applications to obtain notarial faculties,

and shall be entitled to all the rights and privileges, and may exercise and perform all the powers and duties, formerly appertaining to the office or profession of a proctor in the provincial, diocesan or other jurisdictions in England and Wales.

(2) Nothing in subsection (1) shall affect the provisions of section 94 of the Supreme Court Act 1981, section 13 or 60 of the County Courts Act 1984 or any other enactment in force at the commencement of this Act which restricts the right of any solicitor to practise as such in any court.

(3) Nothing in subsection (1) or (2) shall prejudice or affect any right of practising or being heard in, before or by any court, tribunal or other body which immediately before the commencement of this Act was enjoyed by virtue of any enactment, rule, order or regulation or by custom or otherwise by persons qualified to act as solicitors.

Unqualified Persons Acting as Solicitors

20. Unqualified Person Not to Act as Solicitor

(1) No unqualified person shall—

- (a) act as a solicitor, or as such issue any writ or process, or commence, prosecute or defend any action, suit or other proceeding, in his own name or in the name of any other person, in any court of civil or criminal jurisdiction; or
- (b) act as a solicitor in any cause or matter, civil or criminal, to be heard or determined before any justice or justices or any commissioners of Her Majesty's revenue.

(2) Any person who contravenes the provisions of subsection (1)—

- (a) shall be guilty of an offence and liable on conviction on indictment to imprisonment for not more than two years or to a fine or to both; and
- (b) shall be guilty of contempt of the court in which the action, suit, cause, matter or proceeding in relation to which he so acts is brought or taken and may be punished accordingly.

21. Unqualified Person Not to Pretend to Be a Solicitor

Any unqualified person who wilfully pretends to be, or takes or uses any name, title, addition or description implying that he is, qualified or recognised by law as qualified to act as a solicitor shall be guilty of an offence and liable on summary conviction to a fine not exceeding the fourth level on the standard scale.

PART II PROFESSIONAL PRACTICE, CONDUCT AND DISCIPLINE OF SOLICITORS AND CLERKS

Disciplinary Proceedings before Supreme Court

50. Jurisdiction of Supreme Court over Solicitors

(1) Any person duly admitted as a solicitor shall be an officer of the Supreme Court.

(2) Subject to the provisions of this Act, the High Court, the Crown Court and the Court of Appeal respectively, or any division or judge of those courts, may exercise the same jurisdiction in respect of solicitors as any one of the superior courts of law or equity from which the Supreme Court was constituted might have exercised immediately before the passing of the Supreme Court of Judicature Act 1873 in respect of any solicitor, attorney or proctor admitted to practise there.

(3) An appeal shall lie to the Court of Appeal from any order made against a solicitor by the High Court or the Crown Court in the exercise of its jurisdiction in respect of solicitors under subsection (2).

PART III REMUNERATION OF SOLICITORS

Non-contentious Business

56. Orders as to Remuneration for Non-contentious Business

(1) For the purposes of this section there shall be a committee consisting of the following persons—
- (a) the Secretary of State;
- (b) the Lord Chief Justice;
- (c) the Master of the Rolls;
- (d) the President of the Society;
- (e) a solicitor, being the president of a local law society, nominated by the Secretary of State to serve on the committee during his tenure of office as president; and
- (f) for the purpose only of prescribing and regulating the remuneration of solicitors in respect of business done under the Land Registration Act 1925, the Chief Land Registrar appointed under that Act.

(2) The committee, or any three members of the committee (the Secretary of State being one), may make general orders prescribing and regulating in such manner as they think fit the remuneration of solicitors in respect of non-contentious business.

(3) The Secretary of State, before any order under this section is made, shall cause a draft of the order to be sent to the Council; and the committee shall consider any observations of the Council submitted to them in writing within one month of the sending of the draft, and may then make the order, either in the form of the draft or with such alterations or additions as they may think fit.

(4) An order under this section may prescribe the mode of remuneration of solicitors in respect of non-contentious business by providing that they shall be remunerated—
- (a) according to a scale of rates of commission or a scale of percentages, varying or not in different classes of business; or
- (b) by a gross sum; or
- (c) by a fixed sum for each document prepared or perused, without regard to length; or
- (d) in any other mode; or
- (e) partly in one mode and partly in another.

(5) An order under this section may regulate the amount of such remuneration with reference to all or any of the following, among other, considerations, that is to say—
- (a) the position of the party for whom the solicitor is concerned in the business, that is, whether he is vendor or purchaser, lessor or lessee, mortgagor or mortgagee, or the like;
- (b) the place where, and the circumstances in which, the business or any part of it is transacted;
- (c) the amount of the capital money or rent to which the business relates;
- (d) the skill, labour and responsibility on the part of the solicitor which the business involves;
- (e) the number and importance of the documents prepared or perused, without regard to length.

(6) An order under this section may authorise and regulate—
(a) the taking by a solicitor from his client of security for payment of any remuneration, to be ascertained by taxation or otherwise, which may become due to him under any such order; and
(b) the allowance of interest.
(7) So long as an order made under this section is in operation the taxation of bills of costs of solicitors in respect of non-contentious business shall, subject to the provisions of section 57, be regulated by that order.
(8) Any order made under this section may be varied or revoked by a subsequent order so made.
(9) The power to make orders under this section shall be exercisable by statutory instrument which shall be subject to annulment in pursuance of a resolution of either House of Parliament; and the Statutory Instruments Act 1946 shall apply to a statutory instrument containing such an order in like manner as if the order had been made by a Minister of the Crown.

57. Non-contentious Business Agreements

(1) Whether or not any order is in force under section 56, a solicitor and his client may, before or after or in the course of the transaction of any non-contentious business by the solicitor, make an agreement as to his remuneration in respect of that business.
(2) The agreement may provide for the remuneration of the solicitor by a gross sum or by reference to an hourly rate, or by a commission or percentage, or by a salary, or otherwise, and it may be made on the terms that the amount of the remuneration stipulated for shall or shall not include all or any disbursements made by the solicitor in respect of searches, plans, travelling, stamps, fees or other matters.
(3) The agreement shall be in writing and signed by the person to be bound by it or his agent in that behalf.
(4) Subject to subsections (5) and (7), the agreement may be sued and recovered on or set aside in the like manner and on the like grounds as an agreement not relating to the remuneration of a solicitor.
(5) If on any taxation of costs the agreement is relied on by the solicitor and objected to by the client as unfair or unreasonable, the taxing officer may enquire into the facts and certify them to the court, and if from that certificate it appears just to the court that the agreement should be set aside, or the amount payable under it reduced, the court may so order and may give such consequential directions as it thinks fit.
(6) Subsection (7) applies where the agreement provides for the remuneration of the solicitor to be by reference to an hourly rate.
(7) If, on the taxation of any costs, the agreement is relied on by the solicitor and the client objects to the amount of the costs (but is not alleging that the agreement is unfair or unreasonable), the taxing officer may enquire into—
(a) the number of hours worked by the solicitor; and
(b) whether the number of hours worked by him was excessive.

58. Remuneration of a Solicitor who is a Mortgagee

(1) Where a mortgage is made to a solicitor, either alone or jointly with any other person, he or the firm of which he is a member shall be entitled to recover from the mortgagor in respect of all business transacted and acts done by him or them in negotiating the loan, deducing and investigating the title to the property, and preparing and completing the mortgage, such usual costs as he or they would have been entitled to receive if the mortgage had been made to a person who was not a solicitor and that person had retained and employed him or them to transact that business and do those acts.
(2) Where a mortgage has been made to, or has become vested by transfer or transmission in, a solicitor, either alone or jointly with any other person, and any business is transacted or acts are done by that solicitor or by the firm of which lie is a member in relation to that mortgage or the security thereby created or the property thereby charged, he or they shall be entitled to recover from the person on whose behalf the business was transacted or the acts were done, and to charge against the security, such usual costs as he or they would have been entitled to receive if the mortgage had been made to and had remained vested in a person who was not a

solicitor and that person had retained and employed him or them to transact that business and do those acts.

(3) In this section 'mortgage' includes any charge on any property for securing money or money's worth.

Contentious Business

59. Contentious Business Agreements

(1) Subject to subsection (2), a solicitor may make an agreement in writing with his client as to his remuneration in respect of any contentious business done, or to be done, by him (in this Act referred to as a 'contentious business agreement') providing that he shall be remunerated by a gross sum or by reference to an hourly rate, or by a salary, or otherwise, and whether at a higher or lower rate than that at which he would otherwise have been entitled to be remunerated.

(2) Nothing in this section or in sections 60 to 63 shall give validity to—

(a) any purchase by a solicitor of the interest, or any part of the interest, of his client in any action, suit or other contentious proceeding; or

(b) any agreement by which a solicitor retained or employed to prosecute any action, suit or other contentious proceeding, stipulates for payment only in the event of success in that action, suit or proceeding; or

(c) any disposition, contract, settlement, conveyance, delivery, dealing or transfer which under the law relating to bankruptcy is invalid against a trustee or creditor in any bankruptcy or composition.

60. Effect of Contentious Business Agreements

(1) Subject to the provisions of this section and to sections 61 to 63, the costs of a solicitor in any case where a contentious business agreement has been made shall not be subject to taxation or (except in the case of an agreement which provides for the solicitor to be remunerated by reference to an hourly rate) to the provisions of section 69.

(2) Subject to subsection (3), a contentious business agreement shall not affect the amount of, or any rights or remedies for the recovery of, any costs payable by the client to, or to the client by, any person other than the solicitor, and that person may, unless he has otherwise agreed, require any such costs to be taxed according to the rules for their taxation for the time being in force.

(3) A client shall not be entitled to recover from any other person under an order for the payment of any costs to which a contentious business agreement relates more than the amount payable by him to his solicitor in respect of those costs under the agreement.

(4) A contentious business agreement shall be deemed to exclude any claim by the solicitor in respect of the business to which it relates other than—

(a) a claim for the agreed costs; or

(b) a claim for such costs as are expressly excepted from the agreement.

(5) A provision in a contentious business agreement that the solicitor shall not be liable for negligence, or that he shall be relieved from any responsibility to which he would otherwise be subject as a solicitor, shall be void.

61. Enforcement of Contentious Business Agreements

(1) No action shall be brought on any contentious business agreement, but on the application of any person who—

(a) is a party to the agreement or the representative of such a party; or

(b) is or is alleged to be liable to pay, or is or claims to be entitled to be paid, the costs due or alleged to be due in respect of the business to which the agreement relates,

the court may enforce or set aside the agreement and determine every question as to its validity or effect.

(2) On any application under subsection (1), the court—

(a) if it is of the opinion that the agreement is in all respects fair and reasonable, may enforce it;

(b) if it is of the opinion that the agreement is in any respect unfair or unreasonable, may set it aside and order the costs covered by it to be taxed as if it had never been made;

(c) in any case, may make such order as to the costs of the application as it thinks fit.

(3) If the business covered by a contentious business agreement (not being an agreement to which section 62 applies) is business done, or to be done, in any action, a client who is a party to the agreement may make application to a taxing officer of the court for the agreement to be examined.

(4) A taxing officer before whom an agreement is laid under subsection (3) shall examine it and may either allow it, or, if he is of the opinion that the agreement is unfair or unreasonable, require the opinion of the court to be taken on it, and the court may allow the agreement or reduce the amount payable under it, or set it aside and order the costs covered by it to be taxed as if it had never been made.

(4A) Subsection (4B) applies where a contentious business agreement provides for the remuneration of the solicitor to be by reference to an hourly rate.

(4B) If on the taxation of any costs the agreement is relied on by the solicitor and the client objects to the amount of the costs (but is not alleging that the agreement is unfair or unreasonable), the taxing officer may enquire into—

(a) the number of hours worked by the solicitor; and

(b) whether the number of hours worked by him was excessive.

(5) Where the amount agreed under any contentious business agreement is paid by or on behalf of the client or by any person entitled to do so, the person making the payment may at any time within twelve months from the date of payment, or within such further time as appears to the court to be reasonable, apply to the court, and, if it appears to the court that the special circumstances of the case require it to be re-opened, the court may, on such terms as may be just, re-open it and order the costs covered by the agreement to be taxed and the whole or any part of the amount received by the solicitor to be repaid by him.

(6) In this section and in sections 62 and 63 'the court' means—

(a) in relation to an agreement under which any business has been done in any court having jurisdiction to enforce and set aside agreements, any such court in which any of that business has been done;

(b) in relation to an agreement under which no business has been done in any such court, and under which more than £50 is payable, the High Court;

(c) in relation to an agreement under which no business has been done in any such court and under which not more than £50 is payable, any county court which would, but for the provisions of subsection (1) prohibiting the bringing of an action on the agreement, have had jurisdiction in any action on it;

and for the avoidance of doubt it is hereby declared that in paragraph (a) 'court having jurisdiction to enforce and set aside agreements' includes a county court.

62. Contentious Business Agreements by Certain Representatives

(1) Where the client who makes a contentious business agreement makes it as a representative of a person whose property will be chargeable with the whole or part of the amount payable under the agreement, the agreement shall be laid before a taxing officer of the court before payment.

(2) A taxing officer before whom an agreement is laid under subsection (1) shall examine it and may either allow it, or, if he is of the opinion that it is unfair or unreasonable, require the opinion of the court to be taken on it, and the court may allow the agreement or reduce the amount payable under it, or set it aside and order the costs covered by it to be taxed as if it had never been made.

(3) A client who makes a contentious business agreement as mentioned in subsection (1) and pays the whole or any part of the amount payable under the agreement without it being allowed by the officer or by the court shall be liable at any time to account to the person whose property is charged with the whole or any part of the amount so paid for the sum so charged, and the solicitor who accepts the payment may be ordered by the court to refund the amount received by him.

(4) A client makes a contentious business agreement as the representative of another person if he makes it—

(a) as his guardian,

(b) as a trustee for him under a deed or will,

(c) as his receiver appointed under Part VII of the Mental Health Act 1983, or

(d) as a person other than a receiver authorised under that Part of that Act to act on his behalf.

63. Effect on Contentious Business Agreement of Death, Incapability or Change of Solicitor

(1) If, after some business has been done under a contentious business agreement but before the solicitor has wholly performed it—
(a) the solicitor dies, or becomes incapable of acting; or
(b) the client changes his solicitor (as, notwithstanding the agreement, he shall be entitled to do),
any party to, or the representative of any party to, the agreement may apply to the court, and the court shall have the same jurisdiction as to enforcing the agreement so far as it has been performed, or setting it aside, as the court would have had if the solicitor had not died or become incapable of acting, or the client had not changed his solicitor.

(2) The court, notwithstanding that it is of the opinion that the agreement is in all respects fair and reasonable, may order the amount due in respect of business under the agreement to be ascertained by taxation, and in that case—
(a) the taxing officer, in ascertaining that amount, shall have regard so far as may be to the terms of the agreement; and
(b) payment of the amount found by him to be due may be enforced in the same manner as if the agreement had been completely performed.

(3) If in such a case as is mentioned in subsection (1)(b) an order is made for the taxation of the amount due to the solicitor in respect of the business done under the agreement, the court shall direct the taxing officer to have regard to the circumstances under which the change of solicitor has taken place, and the taxing officer, unless he is of the opinion that there has been no default, negligence, improper delay or other conduct on the part of the solicitor affording the client reasonable ground for changing his solicitor, shall not allow to the solicitor the full amount of the remuneration agreed to be paid to him.

64. Form of Bill of Costs for Contentious Business

(1) Where the remuneration of a solicitor in respect of contentious business done by him is not the subject of a contentious business agreement, then, subject to subsections (2) to (4), the solicitor's bill of costs may at the option of the solicitor be either a bill containing detailed items or a gross sum bill.

(2) The party chargeable with a gross sum bill may at any time—
(a) before he is served with a writ or other originating process for the recovery of costs included in the bill, and
(b) before the expiration of three months from the date on which the bill was delivered to him,
require the solicitor to deliver, in lieu of that bill, a bill containing detailed items; and on such a requirement being made the gross sum bill shall be of no effect.

(3) Where an action is commenced on a gross sum bill, the court shall, if so requested by the party chargeable with the bill before the expiration of one month from the service on that party of the writ or other originating process, order that the bill be taxed.

(4) If a gross sum bill is taxed, whether under this section or otherwise, nothing in this section shall prejudice any rules of court with respect to taxation, and the solicitor shall furnish the taxing officer with such details of any of the costs covered by the bill as the taxing officer may require.

65. Security for Costs and Termination of Retainer

(1) A solicitor may take security from his client for his costs, to be ascertained by taxation or otherwise, in respect of any contentious business to be done by him.

(2) If a solicitor who has been retained by a client to conduct contentious business requests the client to make a payment of a sum of money, being a reasonable sum on account of the costs incurred or to be incurred in the conduct of that business and the client refuses or fails within a reasonable time to make that payment, the refusal or failure shall be deemed to be a good cause whereby the solicitor may, upon giving reasonable notice to the client, withdraw from the retainer.

66. Taxations With Respect to Contentious Business

Subject to the provisions of any rules of court, on every taxation of costs in respect of any contentious business, the taxing officer may—

(a) allow interest at such rate and from such time as he thinks just on money disbursed by the solicitor for the client, and on money of the client in the hands of, and improperly retained by, the solicitor; and

(b) in determining the remuneration of the solicitor, have regard to the skill, labour and responsibility involved in the business done by him.

Remuneration— General

67. Inclusion of Disbursements in Bill of Costs

A solicitor's bill of costs may include costs payable in discharge of a liability properly incurred by him on behalf of the party to be charged with the bill (including counsel's fees) notwithstanding that those costs have not been paid before the delivery of the bill to that party; but those costs—

(a) shall be described in the bill as not then paid; and

(b) if the bill is taxed, shall not be allowed by the taxing officer unless they are paid before the taxation is completed.

68. Power of Court to Order Solicitor to Deliver Bill, etc.

(1) The jurisdiction of the High Court to make orders for the delivery by a solicitor of a bill of costs, and for the delivery up of, or otherwise in relation to, any documents in his possession, custody or power, is hereby declared to extend to cases in which no business has been done by him in the High Court.

(2) A county court shall have the same jurisdiction as the High Court to make orders making such provision as is mentioned in subsection (1) in cases where the bill of costs or the documents relate wholly or partly to contentious business done by the solicitor in that county court.

(3) In this section and in sections 69 to 71 'solicitor' includes the executors, administrators and assignees of a solicitor.

69. Action to Recover Solicitor's Costs

(1) Subject to the provisions of this Act, no action shall be brought to recover any costs due to a solicitor before the expiration of one month from the date on which a bill of those costs is delivered in accordance with the requirements mentioned in subsection (2); but if there is probable cause for believing that the party chargeable with the costs—

  (a) is about to quit England and Wales, to become bankrupt or to compound with his creditors, or

  (b) is about to do any other act which would tend to prevent or delay the solicitor obtaining payment,

  the High Court may, notwithstanding that one month has not expired from the delivery of the bill, order that the solicitor be at liberty to commence an action to recover his costs and may order that those costs be taxed.

(2) The requirements referred to in subsection (1) are that the bill—

  (a) must be signed by the solicitor, or if the costs are due to a firm, by one of the partners of that firm, either in his own name or in the name of the firm, or be enclosed in, or accompanied by, a letter which is so signed and refers to the bill; and

  (b) must be delivered to the party to be charged with the bill, either personally or by being sent to him by post to, or left for him at, his place of business, dwellinghouse, or last known place of abode;

  and, where a bill is proved to have been delivered in compliance with those requirements, it shall not be necessary in the first instance for the solicitor to prove the contents of the bill and it shall be presumed, until the contrary is shown, to be a bill bona fide complying with this Act.

(3) Where a bill of costs relates wholly or partly to contentious business done in a county court and the amount of the bill does not exceed £5,000, the powers and duties of the High Court under this section and sections 70 and 71 in relation to that bill may be exercised and performed by any county court in which any part of the business was done.

70. Taxation on Application of Party Chargeable or Solicitor

(1) Where before the expiration of one month from the delivery of a solicitor's bill an application is made by the party chargeable with the bill, the High Court shall, without requiring any sum to be paid into court, order that the bill be taxed and that no action be commenced on the bill until the taxation is completed.

(2) Where no such application is made before the expiration of the period mentioned in subsection (1), then, on an application being made by the solicitor or, subject to subsections (3) and (4), by the party chargeable with the bill, the court may on such terms, if any, as it thinks fit (not being terms as to the costs of the taxation), order—
(a) that the bill be taxed; and
(b) that no action be commenced on the bill, and that any action already commenced be stayed, until the taxation is completed.

(3) Where an application under subsection (2) is made by the party chargeable with the bill—
(a) after the expiration of 12 months from the delivery of the bill, or
(b) after a judgment has been obtained for the recovery of the costs covered by the bill, or
(c) after the bill has been paid, but before the expiration of 12 months from the payment of the bill,
no order shall be made except in special circumstances and, if an order is made, it may contain such terms as regards the costs of the taxation as the court may think fit.

(4) The power to order taxation conferred by subsection (2) shall not be exercisable on an application made by the party chargeable with the bill after the expiration of 12 months from the payment of the bill.

(5) An order for the taxation of a bill made on an application under this section by the party chargeable with the bill shall, if he so requests, be an order for the taxation of the profit costs covered by the bill.

(6) Subject to subsection (5), the court may under this section order the taxation of all the costs, or of the profit costs, or of the costs other than profit costs and, where part of the costs is not to be taxed, may allow an action to be commenced or to be continued for that part of the costs.

(7) Every order for the taxation of a bill shall require the taxing officer to tax not only the bill but also the costs of the taxation and to certify what is due to or by the solicitor in respect of the bill and in respect of the costs of the taxation.

(8) If after due notice of any taxation either party to it fails to attend, the officer may proceed with the taxation ex parte.

(9) Unless—
(a) the order for taxation was made on the application of the solicitor and the party chargeable does not attend the taxation, or
(b) the order for taxation or an order under subsection (10) otherwise provides,
the costs of a taxation shall be paid according to the event of the taxation, that is to say, if one-fifth of the amount of the bill is taxed off, the solicitor shall pay the costs, but otherwise the party chargeable shall pay the costs.

(10) The taxing officer may certify to the court any special circumstances relating to a bill or to the taxation of a bill, and the court may make such order as respects the costs of the taxation as it may think fit.

(11) Subsection (9) shall have effect in any case where the application for an order for taxation was made before the passing of the Solicitors (Amendment) Act 1974 and—
(a) the bill is a bill for contentious business, or
(b) more than half of the amount of the bill before taxation consists of costs for which a scale charge is provided by an order for the time being in operation under section 56,
as if for the reference to one-fifth of the amount of the bill there were substituted a reference to one-sixth of that amount.

(12) In this section 'profit costs' means costs other than counsel's fees or costs paid or payable in the discharge of a liability incurred by the solicitor on behalf of the party chargeable, and the reference in subsection (9) to the fraction of the amount of the bill taxed off shall be taken, where the taxation concerns only part of the costs covered by the bill, as a reference to that fraction of the amount of those costs which is being taxed.

71. Taxation on Application of Third Parties

(1) Where a person other than the party chargeable with the bill for the purposes of section 70 has paid, or is or was liable to pay, a bill either to the solicitor or to the party chargeable with the bill, that person, or his executors, administrators or assignees may apply to the High Court for an order for the taxation of the bill as if he were the party chargeable with it, and the court may make the same order (if any) as it might have made if the application had been made by the party chargeable with the bill.

(2) Where the court has no power to make an order by virtue of subsection (1) except in special circumstances it may, in considering whether there are special circumstances sufficient to justify the making of an order, take into account circumstances which affect the applicant but do not affect the party chargeable with the bill.

(3) Where a trustee, executor or administrator has become liable to pay a bill of a solicitor, then, on the application of any person interested in any property out of which the trustee, executor or administrator has paid, or is entitled to pay, the bill, the court may order—
   (a) that the bill be taxed on such terms, if any, as it thinks fit; and
   (b) that such payments, in respect of the amount found to be due to or by the solicitor and in respect of the costs of the taxation, be made to or by the applicant, to or by the solicitor, or to or by the executor, administrator or trustee, as it thinks fit.

(4) In considering any application under subsection (3) the court shall have regard—
   (a) to the provisions of section 70 as to applications by the party chargeable for the taxation of a solicitor's bill so far as they are capable of being applied to an application made under that subsection;
   (b) to the extent and nature of the interest of the applicant.

(5) If an applicant under subsection (3) pays any money to the solicitor, he shall have the same right to be paid that money by the trustee, executor or administrator chargeable with the bill as the solicitor had.

(6) Except in special circumstances, no order shall be made on an application under this section for the taxation of a bill which has already been taxed.

(7) If the court on an application under this section orders a bill to be taxed, it may order the solicitor to deliver to the applicant a copy of the bill on payment of the costs of that copy.

72. Supplementary Provisions as to Taxations

(1) Every application for an order for the taxation of a solicitor's bill or for the delivery of a solicitor's bill and for the delivery up by a solicitor of any documents in his possession, custody or power shall be made in the matter of that solicitor.

(2) Where a taxing officer is in the course of taxing a bill of costs, he may request the taxing officer of any other court to assist him in taxing any part of the bill, and the taxing officer so requested shall tax that part of the bill and shall return the bill with his opinion on it to the taxing officer making the request.

(3) Where a request is made as mentioned in subsection (2), the taxing officer who is requested to tax part of a bill shall have such powers, and may take such fees, in respect of that part of the bill, as he would have or be entitled to take if he were taxing that part of the bill in pursuance of an order of the court of which he is an officer; and the taxing officer who made the request shall not take any fee in respect of that part of the bill.

(4) The certificate of the taxing officer by whom any bill has been taxed shall, unless it is set aside or altered by the court, be final as to the amount of the costs covered by it, and the court may make such order in relation to the certificate as it thinks fit, including, in a case where the retainer is not disputed, an order that judgment be entered for the sum certified to be due with costs.

73. Charging Orders

(1) Subject to subsection (2), any court in which a solicitor has been employed to prosecute or defend any suit, matter or proceedings may at any time—
   (a) declare the solicitor entitled to a charge on any property recovered or preserved through his instrumentality for his taxed costs in relation to that suit, matter or proceeding; and
   (b) make such orders for the taxation of those costs and for raising money to pay or for paying them out of the property recovered or preserved as the court thinks fit;

and all conveyances and acts done to defeat, or operating to defeat, that charge shall, except in the case of a conveyance to a bona fide purchaser for value without notice, be void as against the solicitor.

(2) No order shall be made under subsection (1) if the right to recover the costs is barred by any statute of limitations.

74. Special Provisions as to Contentious Business Done in County Courts

(1) The remuneration of a solicitor in respect of contentious business done by him in a county court shall be regulated in accordance with sections 59 to 73, and for that purpose those sections shall have effect subject to the following provisions of this section.

(2) The registrar of a county court shall be the taxing officer of that court but any taxation of costs by him may be reviewed by a judge assigned to the county court district, or by a judge acting as a judge so assigned, on the application of any party to the taxation.

(3) The amount which may be allowed on the taxation of any costs or bill of costs in respect of any item relating to proceedings in a county court shall not, except in so far as rules of court may otherwise provide, exceed the amount which could have been allowed in respect of that item as between party and party in those proceedings, having regard to the nature of the proceedings and the amount of the claim and of any counterclaim.

[*By the Courts and Legal Services Act 1990. s. 74(1) and (3), any reference to the office of registrar is to be construed as a reference to the office of district judge.*]

PART IV MISCELLANEOUS AND GENERAL

Supplementary

87. Interpretation

(1) In this Act, except where the context otherwise requires,—

. . .

'the Charter' means the Royal Charter dated 26th February 1845, whereby the Society was incorporated, together with the Royal Charters supplemental to it dated respectively 26th November 1872,4th June 1903,2nd June 1909 and 10th March 1954; 'client' includes—

(a) in relation to contentious business, any person who as a principal or on behalf of another person retains or employs, or is about to retain or employ, a solicitor, and any person who is or may be liable to pay a solicitor's costs;

(b) in relation to non-contentious business, any person who, as a principal or on behalf of another, or as a trustee or executor, or in any other capacity, has power, express or implied, to retain or employ, and retains or employs or is about to retain or employ, a solicitor, and any person for the time being liable to pay to a solicitor for his services any costs;

. . .

'contentious business' means business done, whether as solicitor or advocate, in or for the purposes of proceedings begun before a court or before an arbitrator appointed under the Arbitration Act 1950, not being business which falls within the definition of non-contentious or common form probate business contained in section 128 of the Supreme Court Act 1981;

'contentious business agreement' means an agreement made in pursuance of section 59;

. . .

'costs' includes fees, charges, disbursements, expenses and remuneration;

'the Council' means the Council of the Society elected in accordance with the provisions of the Charter and this Act;

. . .

'employee' includes an articled clerk;

'local law society' means a society which is for the time being recognised by the Council as representative of solicitors in some particular part of England and Wales;

'non-contentious business' means any business done as a solicitor which is not contentious business as defined by this subsection;

'practising certificate' has the meaning assigned to it by section 1;

. . .

'the Society' means the Law Society, that is to say, the Society incorporated and regulated by the Charter;

. . .

'solicitor' means solicitor of the Supreme Court;

. . .

'trust' includes an implied or constructive trust and a trust where the trustee has a beneficial interest in the trust property, and also includes the duties incident to the office of a personal representative, and 'trustee' shall be construed accordingly;

'unqualified person' means a person who is not qualified under section 1 to act as a solicitor.

. . .

(3) In this Act, except where otherwise indicated—
   (a) a reference to a numbered Part, section or Schedule is a reference to the Part or section of, or the Schedule to, this Act so numbered;
   (b) a reference in a section to a numbered subsection is a reference to the subsection of that section so numbered;
   (c) a reference in a section, subsection or Schedule to a numbered paragraph is a reference to the paragraph of that section, subsection or Schedule so numbered; and
   (d) a reference in a paragraph to a numbered sub-paragraph is a reference to the sub-paragraph of that paragraph so numbered.

(4) Except where the context otherwise requires, references in this Act to any enactment shall be construed as references to that enactment as amended or applied by or under any other enactment, including this Act.

90. Short Title, Commencement and Extent

(1) This Act may be cited as the Solicitors Act 1974.

(2) This Act shall come into force on such day as the Lord Chancellor may by order made by statutory instrument appoint, not being earlier than the first day on which all the provisions of the Solicitors (Amendment) Act 1974 are in force.

(3) If any order made under section 19(7) of the Solicitors (Amendment) Act 1974 makes any savings from the effect of any provision of that Act which it brings into force, the order under subsection (2) may make corresponding savings from the effect of the corresponding provision of this Act.

(4) The provisions of this Act extend to England and Wales only, with the exception of—
   (a) section 4(4) and the repeal of section 5(3) of the Solicitors Act 1957, which extend to Scotland;
   (b) section 29 and the repeal of section 1 of the Solicitors (Amendment) Act 1974, which extend to Northern Ireland;
   (c) sections 5(3) and 86, and the repeals of section 5(2) of the Solicitors Act 1957 and paragraphs 1 and 5 of Schedule 2 to the Solicitors (Amendment) Act 1974, all of which extend both to Scotland and to Northern Ireland.

[*The Act was brought into force on 1 May 1975 by SI 1975/534.*]

NOTES ON TEXT

Only ss. 19 to 21,50,56 to 74 and 90 and relevant provisions of s. 87 are printed here. The text incorporates the following amendments:

s. 19 amended by: (a) Supreme Court Act 1981, sch. 5; (b) County Courts Act 1984, sch. 2, para. 49;

s. 20(2) amended by Courts and Legal Services Act, sch. 20 (in force by SI 1990/2484);

s. 21 amended by Administration of Justice Act 1985, s. 8 and sch. 1, para. 6 (in force by SI 1986/364);

s. 50(1) amended by Supreme Court Act 1981, sch. 7;

s. 50(3) inserted by Supreme Court Act 1981, s. 147;

s. 56 amended by Secretary of State for Constitutional Affairs Order 2003 (SI 2003/1887), sch. 2, para. 3;

ss. 57, 59, 60 and 61 amended by Courts and Legal Services Act 1990, s. 98 (in force by s. 124(2) of that Act);

s. 62(4) amended by Mental Health Act 1983, sch. 4, para. 38;
s. 69(3) amended by: (a) Administration of Justice Act 1982, sch. 3, paras 2 and 3(b)(iii) (in force by s. 76(11) of that Act); (b) High Court and County Courts Jurisdiction Order 1991 (SI 1991/724), sch., part I;
s. 69(4) inserted by Administration of Justice Act 1982, sch. 3, para. 4 (in force by s. 76(11) of that Act), repealed by High Court and County Courts Jurisdiction Order 1991 (SI 1991/724), sch., part I;
s. 87(1) definition of 'contentious business' amended by Administration of Justice Act 1985, sch. 1, para. 12 (in force by SI 1986/364);
s. 90(4) amended by House of Commons Disqualification Act 1975, sch. 3.

Supply of Goods and Services Act 1982

(1982 CHAPTER 29)

PART II SUPPLY OF SERVICES

12. The Contracts Concerned

(1) In this Act a 'contract for the supply of a service' means, subject to subsection (2) below a contract under which a person ('the supplier') agrees to carry out a service.

(2) For the purposes of this Act, a contract of service or apprenticeship is not a contract for the supply of a service.

(3) Subject to subsection (2) above, a contract is a contract for the supply of a service for the purposes of this Act whether or not goods are also—

(a) transferred or to be transferred, or

(b) bailed or to be bailed by way of hire,

under the contract, and whatever is the nature of the consideration for which the service is to be carried out.

(4) The Secretary of State may by order provide that one or more of sections 13 to 15 below shall not apply to services of a description specified in the order, and such an order may make different provision for different circumstances.

(5) The power to make an order under subsection (4) above shall be exercisable by statutory instrument subject to annulment in pursuance of a resolution of either House of Parliament.

13. Implied Term About Care and Skill

In a contract for the supply of a service where the supplier is acting in the course of a business, there is an implied term that the supplier will carry out the service with reasonable care and skill.

14. Implied Term About Time of Performance

(1) Where, under a contract for the supply of a service by a supplier acting in the course of a business, the time for the service to be carried out is not fixed by the contract, left to be fixed in a manner agreed by the contract or determined by the course of dealing between the parties, there is an implied term that the supplier will carry out the service within a reasonable time.

(2) What is a reasonable time is a question of fact.

15. Implied Term About Consideration

(1) Where, under a contract for the supply of a service, the consideration for the service is not determined by the contract, left to be determined in a manner agreed by the contract or determined by the course of dealing between the parties, there is an implied term that the party contracting with the supplier will pay a reasonable charge.

(2) What is a reasonable charge is a question of fact.

16. Exclusion of Implied Terms, etc.

(1) Where a right, duty or liability would arise under contract for the supply of a service by virtue of this Part of this Act, it may (subject to subsection (2) below and the 1977 Act) be negatived or varied by express agreement, or by the course of dealing between the parties, or by such usage as binds both parties to the contract.

(2) An express term does not negative a term implied by this Part of this Act unless inconsistent with it.

(3) Nothing in this Part of this Act prejudices—

(a) any rule of law which imposes on the supplier a duty stricter than that imposed by section 13 or 14 above; or

(b) subject to paragraph (a) above, any rule of law whereby any term not inconsistent with this Part of this Act is to be implied in a contract for the supply of a service.

(4) This Part of this Act has effect to any other enactment which defines or restricts the rights, duties or liabilities arising in connection with a service of any description.

PART III SUPPLEMENTARY

18. Interpretation: General

(1) In the preceding provisions of this Act and this section—

'bailee', in relation to a contract for the hire of goods means (depending on the context) a person to whom the goods are bailed under a contract, or a person to whom they are to be so bailed, or a person to whom the rights under the contract of either of those persons have passed;

'bailor', in relation to a contract for the hire of goods, means (depending on the context) a person who bails the goods under the contract, or a person who agrees to do so, or a person to whom the duties under the contract of either of those persons have passed;

'business' includes a profession and the activities of any government department or local or public authority;

'credit-broker' means a person acting in the course of a business of credit brokerage carried on by him;

'credit brokerage' means the effecting of introductions—

(a) of individuals desiring to obtain credit to persons carrying on any business so far as it relates to the provision of credit; or

(b) of individuals desiring to obtain goods on hire to persons carrying on a business which comprises or relates to the bailment or as regards Scotland the hire of goods under a contract for the hire of goods; or

(c) of individuals desiring to obtain credit, or to obtain goods on hire, to other credit-brokers;

'enactment' means any legislation (including subordinate legislation) of the United Kingdom or Northern Ireland;

'goods' includes all personal chattels, other than things in action and money, and as regards Scotland all corporeal moveables; and in particular 'goods' includes emblements, industrial growing crops, and things attached to or forming part of the land which are agreed to be severed before the transfer bailment or hire concerned or under the contract concerned;

'hire-purchase agreement' has the same meaning as in the 1974 Act;

'property', in relation to goods, means the general property in them and not merely a special property;

'transferee', in relation to a contract for the transfer of goods, means (depending on the context) a person to whom the property in the goods is transferred under the contract, or a person to whom the property is to be so transferred, or a person to whom the rights under the contract of either of those persons have passed;

'transferor', in relation to a contract for the transfer of goods, means (depending on the context) a person who transfers the property in the goods under the contract, or a person who agrees to do so, or a person to whom the duties under the contract of either of those persons have passed.

(2) In subsection (1) above, in the definitions of bailee, bailor, transferee and transferor, a reference to rights or duties passing is to their passing by assignment, assignation operation of law or otherwise.

(3) For the purposes of this Act, the quality of goods includes their state and condition and the following (among others) are in appropriate cases aspects of the quality of goods—

(a) fitness for all the purposes for which goods of the kind in question are commonly supplied,
(b) appearance and finish,
(c) freedom from minor defects,
(d) safety, and
(e) durability.

(4) References in this Act to dealing as consumer are to be construed in accordance with Part I of the Unfair Contract Terms Act 1977; and, for the purposes of this Act, it is for the transferor or bailor claiming that the transferee or bailee does not deal as consumer to show that he does not.

19. Interpretation: References to Acts

In this Act—

'the 1973 Act' means the Supply of Goods (Implied Terms) Act 1973;
'the 1974 Act' means the Consumer Credit Act 1974;
'the 1977 Act' means the Unfair Contract Terms Act 1977; and
'the 1979 Act' means the Sale of Goods Act 1979.

Supreme Court Act 1981

(1981 CHAPTER 54)

An Act to consolidate with amendments the Supreme Court of Judicature (Consolidation) Act 1925 and other enactments relating to the Supreme Court in England and Wales and the administration of justice therein; . . . and for connected purposes. [28 July 1981]

PART I CONSTITUTION OF SUPREME COURT

The Supreme Court

1. The Supreme Court

(1) The Supreme Court of England and Wales shall consist of the Court of Appeal, the High Court of Justice and the Crown Court, each having such jurisdiction as is conferred on it by or under this or any other Act.

(2) [*Repealed*]

The Court of Appeal

2. The Court of Appeal

(1) The Court of Appeal shall consist of ex-officio judges and not more than 37 ordinary judges.

(2) The following shall be ex-officio judges of the Court of Appeal—
- (a) [*repealed*]
- (b) any person who was Lord Chancellor before 12 June 2003;
- (c) any Lord of Appeal in Ordinary who at the date of his appointment was, or was qualified for appointment as, an ordinary judge of the Court of Appeal or held an office within paragraphs (d) to (g);
- (d) the Lord Chief Justice;
- (e) the Master of the Rolls;
- (f) the President of the Queen's Bench Division;
- (g) the President of the Family Division;
- (h) the Chancellor of the High Court;

but a person within paragraph (b) or (c) shall not be required to sit and act as a judge of the Court of Appeal unless at the request of the Lord Chief Justice he consents to do so.

(2A) The Lord Chief Justice may nominate a judicial office holder (as defined in section 109(4) of the Constitutional Reform Act 2005) to exercise his function under subsection (2) of making requests to persons within paragraphs (b) and (c) of that subsection.

(3) An ordinary judge of the Court of Appeal (including the vice-president, if any, of either division) shall be styled 'Lord Justice of Appeal' or 'Lady Justice of Appeal'.

(4) Her Majesty may by Order in Council from time to time amend subsection (1) so as to increase or further increase the maximum number of ordinary judges of the Court of Appeal.

(4A) It is for the Lord Chancellor to recommend to Her Majesty the making of an Order under subsection (4).

(5) No recommendation shall be made to Her Majesty in Council to make an order under subsection (4) unless a draft of the Order has been laid before Parliament and approved by resolution of each House of Parliament.

(6) The Court of Appeal shall be taken to be duly constituted notwithstanding any vacancy in the office of Lord Chief Justice, Master of the Rolls, President of the Queen's Bench Division, President of the Family Division or Chancellor of the High Court.

3. Divisions of Court of Appeal

(1) There shall be two divisions of the Court of Appeal, namely the criminal division and the civil division.

(2) The Lord Chief Justice shall be president of the criminal division of the Court of Appeal, and the Master of the Rolls shall be president of the civil division of that court.
(3) The Lord Chief Justice may, after consulting the Lord Chancellor appoint one of the ordinary judges of the Court of Appeal as vice-president of both divisions of that court, or one of those judges as vice-president of the criminal division and another of them as vice-president of the civil division.
(4) When sitting in a court of either division of the Court of Appeal in which no ex-officio judge of the Court of Appeal is sitting, the vice-president (if any) of that division shall preside.
(5) Any number of courts of either division of the Court of Appeal may sit at the same time.
(6) The Lord Chief Justice may nominate a judicial office holder (as defined in section 109(4) of the Constitutional Reform Act 2005) to exercise his functions under subsection (3).

The High Court

4. The High Court

(1) The High Court shall consist of—
(a) [*repealed*]
(b) the Lord Chief Justice;
(ba) the President of the Queen's Bench Division;
(c) the President of the Family Division;
(d) the Chancellor of the High Court;
(dd) the Senior Presiding Judge;
(ddd) the vice-president of the Queen's Bench Division;
(e) not more than 108 puisne judges of that court.
(2) The puisne judges of the High Court shall be styled 'Justices of the High Court'.
(3) All the judges of the High Court shall, except where this Act expressly provides otherwise, have in all respects equal power, authority and jurisdiction.
(4) Her Majesty may by Order in Council from time to time amend subsection (1) so as to increase or further increase the maximum number of puisne judges of the High Court.
(4A) It is for the Lord Chancellor to recommend to Her Majesty the making of an Order under subsection (4).
(5) No recommendation shall be made to Her Majesty in Council to make an Order under subsection (4) unless a draft of the Order has been laid before Parliament and approved by resolution of each House of Parliament.
(6) The High Court shall be taken to be duly constituted notwithstanding any vacancy in the office of Lord Chief Justice, President of the Queen's Bench Division, President of the Family Division, Chancellor of the High Court or Senior Presiding Judge and whether or not an appointment has been made to the office of vice-president of the Queen's Bench Division.

5. Divisions of High Court

(1) There shall be three divisions of the High Court namely—
(a) the Chancery Division, consisting of the Chancellor of the High Court, who shall be president thereof, and such of the puisne judges as are for the time being attached thereto in accordance with this section;
(b) the Queen's Bench Division, consisting of the Lord Chief Justice, the President of the Queen's Bench Division, the vice-president of the Queen's Bench Division and such of the puisne judges as are for the time being so attached thereto; and
(c) the Family Division, consisting of the President of the Family Division and such of the puisne judges as are for the time being so attached thereto.
(2) The puisne judges of the High Court shall be attached to the various Divisions by direction given by the Lord Chief Justice after consulting the Lord Chancellor; and any such judge may with his consent be transferred from one Division to another by direction given by the Lord Chief Justice after consulting the Lord Chancellor, but shall be so transferred only with the concurrence of the senior judge of the Division from which it is proposed to transfer him.
(3) Any judge attached to any Division may act as an additional judge of any other Division at the request of the Lord Chief Justice made with the concurrence of both of the following—
(a) the senior judge of the Division to which the judge is attached;

(b) the senior judge of the Division of which the judge is to act as an additional judge.

(4) Nothing in this section shall be taken to prevent a judge of any Division (whether nominated under section 6(2) or not) from sitting, whenever required, in a divisional court of another Division or for any judge of another Division.

(5) Without prejudice to the provisions of this Act relating to the distribution of business in the High Court, all jurisdiction vested in the High Court under this Act shall belong to all the Divisions alike.

(6) The Lord Chief Justice may nominate a judicial office holder (as defined in section 109(4) of the Constitutional Reform Act 2005) to exercise his functions under subsection (2).

6. The Patents, Admiralty and Commercial Courts

(1) There shall be—

(a) as part of the Chancery Division, a Patents Court; and

(b) as parts of the Queen's Bench Division, an Admiralty Court and a Commercial Court.

(2) The judges of the Patents Court, of the Admiralty Court and of the Commercial Court shall be such of the puisne judges of the High Court as the Lord Chief Justice may, after consulting the Lord Chancellor, from time to time nominate to be judges of the Patents Court, Admiralty Judges and Commercial Judges respectively.

(3) The Lord Chief Justice may nominate a judicial office holder (as defined in section 109(4) of the Constitutional Reform Act 2005) to exercise his functions under subsection (2).

7. Power to Alter Divisions or Transfer Certain Courts to Different Divisions

(1) Her Majesty may from time to time, on a recommendation of the Lord Chancellor and the judges mentioned in subsection (2), by Order in Council direct that—

(a) any increase or reduction in the number of Divisions of the High Court; or

(b) the transfer of any of the courts mentioned in section 6(1) to a different Division,

be carried into effect in pursuance of the recommendation.

(2) Those judges are the Lord Chief Justice, the Master of the Rolls, the President of the Queen's Bench Division, the President of the Family Division and the Chancellor of the High Court.

(3) An Order in Council under this section may include such incidental, supplementary or consequential provisions as appear to Her Majesty necessary or expedient, including amendments of provisions referring to particular Divisions contained in this Act or any other statutory provision.

(4) Any Order in Council under this section shall be subject to annulment in pursuance of a resolution of either House of Parliament.

Other Provisions

9. Assistance for Transaction of Judicial Business of Supreme Court

(1) A person within any entry in column 1 of the following Table may, subject to the proviso at the end of that Table, at any time, at the request of the appropriate authority, act—

(a) as a judge of a relevant court specified in the request; or

(b) if the request relates to a particular division of a relevant court so specified, as a judge of that court in that division.

Table

1 Judge or ex-judge	2 Where competent to act on request
1. A judge of the Court of Appeal.	The High Court and the Crown Court.
2. A person who has been a judge of the Court of Appeal.	The Court of Appeal, the High Court and the Crown Court.
3. A puisne judge of the High Court.	The Court of Appeal.
4. A person who has been a puisne judge of the High Court.	The Court of Appeal, the High Court and the Crown Court.
5. A Circuit judge.	The High Court and the Court of Appeal.
6. A Recorder.	The High Court.

The entry in column 2 specifying the Court of Appeal in relation to a Circuit judge only authorises such a judge to act as a judge of a court in the criminal division of the Court of Appeal.

(1A) A person shall not act as a judge by virtue of subsection (1) after the day on which he attains the age of 75.

(2) In subsection (1)—

'the appropriate authority' means—

(a) the Lord Chief Justice or a judicial office holder (as defined in section 109(4) of the Constitutional Reform Act 2005) nominated by him to exercise his functions under this section, or

(b) at any time when the Lord Chief Justice or the nominated judicial office holder is unable to make such a request himself, or there is a vacancy in the office of Lord Chief Justice, the Master of the Rolls;

'relevant court', in the case of a person within any entry in column 1 of the Table, means a court specified in relation to that entry in column 2 of the Table.

(2A) The power of the appropriate authority to make a request under subsection (1) is subject to subsections (2B) to (2D).

(2B) In the case of a request to a person within entry 1, 3, 5 or 6 in column 1 of the Table, the appropriate authority may make the request only after consulting the Lord Chancellor.

(2C) In any other case the appropriate authority may make a request only with the concurrence of the Lord Chancellor.

(2D) In the case of a request to a Circuit judge or Recorder to act as a judge of the High Court, the appropriate authority may make the request only with the concurrence of the Judicial Appointments Commission.

(3) In the case of—

(a) a request under subsection (1) to a Lord Justice of Appeal to act in the High Court; or

(b) any request under that subsection to a puisne judge of the High Court or a Circuit judge,

it shall be the duty of the person to whom the request is made to comply with it.

(4) Without prejudice to section 24 of the Courts Act 1971 (temporary appointment of deputy Circuit judges and assistant Recorders), if it appears to the Lord Chief Justice, after consulting the Lord Chancellor, that it is expedient as a temporary measure to make an appointment under this subsection in order to facilitate the disposal of business in the High Court or the Crown Court, he may appoint a person qualified for appointment as a puisne judge of the High Court to be a deputy judge of the High Court during such period or on such occasions as the Lord Chief Justice may, after consulting the Lord Chancellor, think fit; and during the period or on the occasions for which a person is appointed as a deputy judge under this subsection, he may act as a puisne judge of the High Court.

(4A) No appointment of a person as a deputy judge of the High Court shall be such as to extend beyond the day on which he attains the age of 70, but this subsection is subject to section 26(4) to (6) of the Judicial Pensions and Retirement Act 1993 (Lord Chancellor's power to authorise continuance in office up to the age of 75).

(5) Every person while acting under this section shall, subject to subsections (6) and (6A), be treated for all purposes as, and accordingly may perform any of the functions of, a judge of the court in which he is acting.

(6) A person shall not by virtue of subsection (5)—

(a) be treated as a judge of the court in which he is acting for the purposes of section 98(2) or of any statutory provision relating to—

(i) the appointment, retirement, removal or disqualification of judges of that court;

(ii) the tenure of office and oaths to be taken by such judges; or

(iii) the remuneration, allowances or pensions of such judges; or

(b) subject to section 27 of the Judicial Pensions and Retirement Act 1993, be treated as having been a judge of a court in which he has acted only under this Section.

(6A) A Circuit judge or Recorder shall not by virtue of subsection (5) exercise any of the powers conferred on a single judge by sections 31, 31B, 31C and 44 of the Criminal Appeal Act 1968 (powers of single judge in connection with appeals to the Court of Appeal and appeals from the Court of Appeal to the House of Lords).

(8) Such remuneration and allowances as the Lord Chancellor may, with the concurrence of the Minister for the Civil Service, determine may be paid out of money provided by Parliament—
  (a) to any person who has been—
    (i) a Lord of Appeal in Ordinary; or
    (ii) a judge of the Court of Appeal; or
    (iii) a judge of the High Court,
  and is by virtue of subsection (1) acting as mentioned in that subsection;
  (b) to any deputy judge of the High Court appointed under subsection (4).

(9) The Lord Chief Justice may nominate a judicial office holder (as defined in section 109(4) of the Constitutional Reform Act 2005) to exercise his functions under subsection (4).

10. Appointment of Judges of Supreme Court

(1) Whenever the office of Lord Chief Justice, Master of the Rolls, President of the Queen's Bench Division, President of the Family Division or Chancellor of the High Court is vacant, Her Majesty may, on the recommendation of the Lord Chancellor, by letters patent appoint a qualified person to that office.

(2) Subject to the limits on numbers for the time being imposed by sections 2(1) and 4(1), Her Majesty may, on the recommendation of the Lord Chancellor, from time to time by letters patent appoint qualified persons as Lords Justices of Appeal or as puisne judges of the High Court.

(3) No person shall be qualified for appointment—
  (a) as Lord Chief Justice, Master of the Rolls, President of the Queen's Bench Division, President of the Family Division or Chancellor of the High Court, unless he is qualified for appointment as a Lord Justice of Appeal or is a judge of the Court of Appeal;
  (b) as a Lord Justice of Appeal, unless—
    (i) he has a 10 year High Court qualification within the meaning of section 71 of the Courts and Legal Services Act 1990; or
    (ii) he is a judge of the High Court; or
  (c) as a puisne judge of the High Court, unless—
    (i) he has a 10 year High Court qualification, within the meaning of section 71 of the Courts and Legal Services Act 1990; or
    (ii) he is a Circuit judge who has held that office for at least 2 years.

(4) A person appointed—
  (a) to any of the offices mentioned in subsection (1),
  (b) as a Lord Justice of Appeal, or
  (c) as a puisne judge of the High Court,
shall take the required oaths as soon as may be after accepting office.

(5) In the case of a person appointed to the office of Lord Chief Justice, the required oaths are to be taken in the presence of all of the following—
  (a) the Master of the Rolls;
  (b) the President of the Queen's Bench Division;
  (c) the President of the Family Division;
  (d) the Chancellor of the High Court.

(6) Where subsection (5) applies but there is a vacancy in one or more (but not all) of the offices mentioned in that subsection, the required oaths are to be taken in the presence of the holders of such of the offices as are not vacant.

(7) In the case of a person appointed other than to the office of Lord Chief Justice, the required oaths are to be taken in the presence of—
  (a) the Lord Chief Justice, or
  (b) a judicial office holder (as defined in section 109(4) of the Constitutional Reform Act 2005) nominated by him for this purpose.

(8) In this section 'required oaths' means—
  (a) the oath of allegiance, and
  (b) the judicial oath,
as set out in the Promissory Oaths Act 1868.

11. Tenure of Office of Judges of Supreme Court

(1) This section applies to the office of any judge of the Supreme Court.

(2) A person appointed to an office to which this section applies shall vacate it on the day on which he attains the age of seventy years unless by virtue of this section he has ceased to hold it before then.

(3) A person appointed to an office to which this section applies shall hold that office during good behaviour, subject to a power of removal by Her Majesty on an address presented to Her by both Houses of Parliament.

(3A) It is for the Lord Chancellor to recommend to Her Majesty the exercise of the power of removal under subsection (3).

(4) A person holding an office within section 2(2)(d) to (g) shall vacate that office on becoming Lord Chancellor or a Lord of Appeal in Ordinary.

(5) A Lord Justice of Appeal shall vacate that office on becoming an ex-officio judge of the Court of Appeal.

(6) A puisne judge of the High Court shall vacate that office on becoming a judge of the Court of Appeal.

(7) A person who holds an office to which this section applies may at any time resign it by giving the Lord Chancellor notice in writing to that effect.

(8) The Lord Chancellor, if satisfied by means of a medical certificate that a person holding an office to which this section applies—

(a) is disabled by permanent infirmity from the performance of the duties of his office; and

(b) is for the time being incapacitated from resigning his office,

may, subject to subsection (9), by instrument under his hand declare that person's office to have been vacated; and the instrument shall have the like effect for all purposes as if that person had on the date of the instrument resigned his office.

(9) A declaration under subsection (8) with respect to a person shall be of no effect unless it is made—

(a) in the case of any of the Lord Chief Justice, the Master of the Rolls, the President of the Queen's Bench Division, the President of the Family Division and the Chancellor of the High Court, with the concurrence of two others of them;

(b) in the case of a Lord Justice of Appeal, with the concurrence of the Master of the Rolls;

(c) in the case of a puisne judge of any Division of the High Court, with the concurrence of the senior judge of that Division.

12. Salaries etc. of Judges of Supreme Court

(1) Subject to subsections (2) and (3), there shall be paid to judges of the Supreme Court such salaries as may be determined by the Lord Chancellor with the concurrence of the Minister for the Civil Service.

(2) Until otherwise determined under this section, there shall be paid to the judges mentioned in subsection (1) the same salaries as at the commencement of this Act.

(3) Any salary payable under this section may be increased, but not reduced, by a determination or further determination under this section.

(5) Salaries payable under this section shall be charged on and paid out of the Consolidated Fund.

(6) There shall be paid out of money provided by Parliament to any judge of the Court of Appeal or of the High Court, in addition to his salary, such allowances as may be determined by the Lord Chancellor with the concurrence of the Minister for the Civil Service.

(7) Pensions shall be payable to or in respect of the judges mentioned in subsection (1) in accordance with section 2 of the Judicial Pensions Act 1981 or, in the case of a judge who is a person to whom Part I of the Judicial Pensions and Retirement Act 1993 applies, in accordance with that Act.

13. Precedence of Judges of Supreme Court

(1) When sitting in the Court of Appeal—

(a) the Lord Chief Justice and the Master of the Rolls shall rank in that order; and

(b) Lords of Appeal in Ordinary and persons who have been Lord Chancellor shall rank next after the Master of the Rolls and, among themselves, according to the priority of the dates on which they respectively became Lords of Appeal in Ordinary or Lord Chancellor, as the case may be.

(2) Subject to subsection (1)(b), the President of the Queen's Bench Division shall rank next after the Master of the Rolls.

(2A) The President of the Family Division shall rank next after the President of the Queen's Bench Division.

(3) The Chancellor of the High Court shall rank next after the President of the Family Division.

(4) The vice-president or vice-presidents of the divisions of the Court of Appeal shall rank next after the Chancellor of the High Court; and if there are two vice-presidents of those divisions, they shall rank, among themselves, according to the priority of the dates on which they respectively became vice-presidents.

(5) The Lords Justices of Appeal (other than the vice-president or vice-presidents of the divisions of the Court of Appeal) shall rank after the ex-officio judges of the Court of Appeal and, among themselves, according to the priority of the dates on which they respectively became judges of that court.

(6) The puisne judges of the High Court shall rank next after the judges of the Court of Appeal and, among themselves, according to the priority of the dates on which they respectively became judges of the High Court.

14. Power of Judge of Supreme or Crown Court to Act in Cases Relating to Rates and Taxes

(1) A judge of the Supreme Court or of the Crown Court shall not be incapable of acting as such in any proceedings by reason of being, as one of a class of ratepayers, taxpayers or persons of any other description, liable in common with others to pay, or contribute to, or benefit from, any rate or tax which may be increased, reduced or in any way affected by those proceedings.

(2) In this section 'rate or tax' means any rate, tax, duty or liability, whether public, general or local, and includes—

(a) any fund formed from the proceeds of any such rate, tax, duty or liability; and

(b) any fund applicable for purposes the same as, or similar to, those for which the proceeds of any such rate, tax, duty or liability are or might be applied.

PART II JURISDICTION

THE COURT OF APPEAL

15. General Jurisdiction of Court of Appeal

(1) The Court of Appeal shall be a superior court of record.

(2) Subject to the provisions of this Act, there shall be exercisable by the Court of Appeal—

(a) all such jurisdiction (whether civil or criminal) as is conferred on it by this or any other Act; and

(b) all such other jurisdiction (whether civil or criminal) as was exercisable by it immediately before the commencement of this Act.

(3) For all purposes of or incidental to—

(a) the hearing and determination of any appeal to the civil division of the Court of Appeal; and

(b) the amendment, execution and enforcement of any judgment or order made on such an appeal,

the Court of Appeal shall have all the authority and jurisdiction of the court or tribunal from which the appeal was brought.

(4) It is hereby declared that any provision in this or any other Act which authorises or requires the taking of any steps for the execution or enforcement of a judgment or order of the High Court applies in relation to a judgment or order of the civil division of the Court of Appeal as it applies in relation to a judgment or order of the High Court.

16. Appeals from High Court

(1) Subject as otherwise provided by this or any other Act (and in particular to the provision in section 13(2)(a) of the Administration of Justice Act 1969 excluding appeals to the Court of

Appeal in cases where leave to appeal from the High Court directly to the House of Lords is granted under Part II of that Act), or as provided by any order made by the Lord Chancellor under section 56(1) of the Access to Justice Act 1999, the Court of Appeal shall have jurisdiction to hear and determine appeals from any judgment or order of the High Court.

(2) An appeal from a judgment or order of the High Court when acting as a prize court shall not be to the Court of Appeal, but shall be to Her Majesty in Council in accordance with the Prize Acts 1864 to 1944.

17. Applications for New Trial

(1) Where any cause or matter, or any issue in any cause or matter, has been tried in the High Court, any application for a new trial thereof, or to set aside a verdict, finding or judgment therein, shall be heard and determined by the Court of Appeal except where rules of court made in pursuance of subsection (2) provide otherwise.

(2) As regards cases where the trial was by a judge alone and no error of the court at the trial is alleged, or any prescribed class of such cases, rules of court may provide that any such application as is mentioned in subsection (1) shall be heard and determined by the High Court.

(3) Nothing in this section shall alter the practice in bankruptcy.

18. Restrictions on Appeals to Court of Appeal

(1) No appeal shall lie to the Court of Appeal—

(a) except as provided by the Administration of Justice Act 1960, from any judgment of the High Court in any criminal cause or matter;

(b) from any order of the High Court or any other court or tribunal allowing an extension of time for appealing from a judgment or order;

(c) from any order, judgment or decision of the High Court or any other court or tribunal which, by virtue of any provision (however expressed) of this or any other Act, is final;

(d) from a decree absolute of divorce or nullity of marriage, by a party who, having had time and opportunity to appeal from the decree nisi on which that decree was founded, has not appealed from the decree nisi;

(g) except as provided by Part I of the Arbitration Act 1996, from any decision of the High Court under that Part;

THE HIGH COURT

General Jurisdiction

19. General Jurisdiction of High Court

(1) The High Court shall be a superior court of record.

(2) Subject to the provisions of this Act, there shall be exercisable by the High Court—

(a) all such jurisdiction (whether civil or criminal) as is conferred on it by this or any other Act; and

(b) all such other jurisdiction (whether civil or criminal) as was exercisable by it immediately before the commencement of this Act (including jurisdiction conferred on a judge of the High Court by any statutory provision).

(3) Any jurisdiction of the High Court shall be exercised only by a single judge of that court, except in so far as it is—

(a) by or by virtue of rules of court or any other statutory provision required to be exercised by a divisional court; or

(b) by rules of court made exercisable by a master, registrar or other officer of the court, or by any other person.

(4) The specific mention elsewhere in this Act of any jurisdiction covered by subsection (2) shall not derogate from the generality of that subsection.

Admiralty Jurisdiction

20. Admiralty Jurisdiction of High Court

(1) The Admiralty jurisdiction of the High Court shall be as follows, that is to say—
- (a) jurisdiction to hear and determine any of the questions and claims mentioned in subsection (2);
- (b) jurisdiction in relation to any of the proceedings mentioned in subsection (3);
- (c) any other Admiralty jurisdiction which it had immediately before the commencement of this Act; and
- (d) any jurisdiction connected with ships or aircraft which is vested in the High Court apart from this section and is for the time being by rules of court made or coming into force after the commencement of this Act assigned to the Queen's Bench Division and directed by the rules to be exercised by the Admiralty Court.

(2) The questions and claims referred to in subsection (1)(a) are—
- (a) any claim to the possession or ownership of a ship or to the ownership of any share therein;
- (b) any question arising between the co-owners of a ship as to possession, employment or earnings of that ship;
- (c) any claim in respect of a mortgage of or charge on a ship or any share therein;
- (d) any claim for damage received by a ship;
- (e) any claim for damage done by a ship;
- (f) any claim for loss of life or personal injury sustained in consequence of any defect in a ship or in her apparel or equipment, or in consequence of the wrongful act, neglect or default of—
  - (i) the owners, charterers or persons in possession or control of a ship; or
  - (ii) the master or crew of a ship, or any other person for whose wrongful acts, neglects or defaults the owners, charterers or persons in possession or control of a ship are responsible,

  being an act, neglect or default in the navigation or management of the ship, in the loading, carriage or discharge of goods on, in or from the ship, or in the embarkation, carriage or disembarkation of persons on, in or from the ship;
- (g) any claim for loss of or damage to goods carried in a ship;
- (h) any claim arising out of any agreement relating to the carriage of goods in a ship or to the use or hire of a ship;
- (j) any claim—
  - (i) under the Salvage Convention 1989;
  - (ii) under any contract for or in relation to salvage services; or
  - (iii) in the nature of salvage not falling within (i) or (ii) above;

  or any corresponding claim in connection with an aircraft;
- (k) any claim in the nature of towage in respect of a ship or an aircraft;
- (l) any claim in the nature of pilotage in respect of a ship or an aircraft;
- (m) any claim in respect of goods or materials supplied to a ship for her operation or maintenance;
- (n) any claim in respect of the construction, repair or equipment of a ship or in respect of dock charges or dues;
- (o) any claim by a master or member of the crew of a ship for wages (including any sum allotted out of wages or adjudged by a superintendent to be due by way of wages);
- (p) any claim by a master, shipper, charterer or agent in respect of disbursements made on account of a ship;
- (q) any claim arising out of an act which is or is claimed to be a general average act;
- (r) any claim arising out of bottomry;
- (s) any claim for the forfeiture or condemnation of a ship or of goods which are being or have been carried, or have been attempted to be carried, in a ship, or for the restoration of a ship or any such goods after seizure, or for droits of Admiralty.

(3) The proceedings referred to in subsection (1)(b) are—
- (a) any application to the High Court under the Merchant Shipping Act 1995;
- (b) any action to enforce a claim for damage, loss of life or personal injury arising out of—

(i) a collision between ships; or
(ii) the carrying out of or omission to carry out a manoeuvre in the case of one or more of two or more ships; or
(iii) non-compliance, on the part of one or more of two or more ships, with the collision regulations;

(c) any action by shipowners or other persons under the Merchant Shipping Act 1995 for the limitation of the amount of their liability in connection with a ship or other property.

(4) The jurisdiction of the High Court under subsection (2)(b) includes power to settle any account outstanding and unsettled between the parties in relation to the ship, and to direct that the ship, or any share thereof, shall be sold, and to make such other order as the court thinks fit.

(5) Subsection (2)(e) extends to—
(a) any claim in respect of a liability incurred under Chapter III of Part VI of the Merchant Shipping Act 1995; and
(b) any claim in respect of a liability falling on the International Oil Pollution Compensation Fund, or on the International Oil Pollution Compensation Fund 1992, under Chapter IV of Part VI of the Merchant Shipping Act 1995.

(6) In subsection (2)(j)—
(a) the 'Salvage Convention 1989' means the International Convention on Salvage, 1989 as it has effect under section 224 of the Merchant Shipping Act 1995;
(b) the reference to salvage services includes services rendered in saving life from a ship and the reference to any claim under any contract for or in relation to salvage services includes any claim arising out of such a contract whether or not arising during the provision of the services;
(c) the reference to a corresponding claim in connection with an aircraft is a reference to any claim corresponding to any claim mentioned in sub-paragraph (i) or (ii) of paragraph (j) which is available under section 87 of the Civil Aviation Act 1982.

(7) The preceding provisions of this section apply—
(a) in relation to all ships or aircraft, whether British or not and whether registered or not and wherever the residence or domicile of their owners may be;
(b) in relation to all claims, wherever arising (including, in the case of cargo or wreck salvage, claims in respect of cargo or wreck found on land); and
(c) so far as they relate to mortgages and charges, to all mortgages or charges, whether registered or not and whether legal or equitable, including mortgages and charges created under foreign law;

Provided that nothing in this subsection shall be construed as extending the cases in which money or property is recoverable under any of the provisions of the Merchant Shipping Act 1995.

21. Mode of Exercise of Admiralty Jurisdiction

(1) Subject to section 22, an action in personam may be brought in the High Court in all cases within the Admiralty jurisdiction of that court.

(2) In the case of any such claim as is mentioned in section 20(2)(a), (c) or (s) or any such question as is mentioned in section 20(2)(b), an action in rem may be brought in the High Court against the ship or property in connection with which the claim or question arises.

(3) In any case in which there is a maritime lien or other charge on any ship, aircraft or other property for the amount claimed, an action in rem may be brought in the High Court against that ship, aircraft or property.

(4) In the case of any such claim as is mentioned in section 20(2)(e) to (r), where—
(a) the claim arises in connection with a ship; and
(b) the person who would be liable on the claim in an action in personam ('the relevant person') was, when the cause of action arose, the owner or charterer of, or in possession or in control of, the ship,

an action in rem may (whether or not the claim gives rise to a maritime lien on that ship) be brought in the High Court against—
(i) that ship, if at the time when the action is brought the relevant person is either the beneficial owner of that ship as respects all the shares in it or the charterer of it under a charter by demise; or

(ii) any other ship of which, at the time when the action is brought, the relevant person is the beneficial owner as respects all the shares in it.

(5) In the case of a claim in the nature of towage or pilotage in respect of an aircraft, an action in rem may be brought in the High Court against that aircraft if, at the time when the action is brought, it is beneficially owned by the person who would be liable on the claim in an action in personam.

(6) Where, in the exercise of its Admiralty jurisdiction, the High Court orders any ship, aircraft or other property to be sold, the court shall have jurisdiction to hear and determine any question arising as to the title to the proceeds of sale.

(7) In determining for the purposes of subsections (4) and (5) whether a person would be liable on a claim in an action in personam it shall be assumed that he has his habitual residence or a place of business within England or Wales.

(8) Where, as regards any such claim as is mentioned in section 20(2)(e) to (r), a ship has been served with a writ or arrested in an action in rem brought to enforce that claim, no other ship may be served with a writ or arrested in that or any other action in rem brought to enforce that claim; but this subsection does not prevent the issue, in respect of any one such claim, of a writ naming more than one ship or of two or more writs each naming a different ship.

22. Restrictions on Entertainment of Actions In Personam in Collision and Other Similar Cases

(1) This section applies to any claim for damage, loss of life or personal injury arising out of—

(a) a collision between ships; or

(b) the carrying out of, or omission to carry out, a manoeuvre in the case of one or more of two or more ships; or

(c) non-compliance, on the part of one or more of two or more ships, with the collision regulations.

(2) The High Court shall not entertain any action in personam to enforce a claim to which this section applies unless—

(a) the defendant has his habitual residence or a place of business within England or Wales; or

(b) the cause of action arose within inland waters of England or Wales or within the limits of a port of England or Wales; or

(c) an action arising out of the same incident or series of incidents is proceeding in the court or has been heard and determined in the court.

In this subsection—

'inland waters' includes any part of the sea adjacent to the coast of the United Kingdom certified by the Secretary of State to be waters falling by international law to be treated as within the territorial sovereignty of Her Majesty apart from the operation of that law in relation to territorial waters;

'port' means any port, harbour, river, estuary, haven, dock, canal or other place so long as a person or body of persons is empowered by or under an Act to make charges in respect of ships entering it or using the facilities therein, and 'limits of a port' means the limits thereof as fixed by or under the Act in question or, as the case may be, by the relevant charter or custom;

'charges' means any charges with the exception of light dues, local light dues and any other charges in respect of lighthouses, buoys or beacons and of charges in respect of pilotage.

(3) The High Court shall not entertain any action in personam to enforce a claim to which this section applies until any proceedings previously brought by the plaintiff in any court outside England and Wales against the same defendant in respect of the same incident or series of incidents have been discontinued or otherwise come to an end.

(4) Subsections (2) and 3 shall apply to counterclaims (except counterclaims in proceedings arising out of the same incident or series of incidents) as they apply to actions, the references to the plaintiff and the defendant being for this purpose read as references to the plaintiff on the counterclaim and the defendant to the counterclaim respectively.

(5) Subsections (2) and 3) shall not apply to any action or counterclaim if the defendant thereto submits or has agreed to submit to the jurisdiction of the court.

(6) Subject to the provisions of subsection (3), the High Court shall have jurisdiction to entertain an action in personam to enforce a claim to which this section applies whenever any of the

conditions specified in subsection (2)(a) to (c) is satisfied, and the rules of court relating to the service of process outside the jurisdiction shall make such provision as may appear to the rule-making authority to be appropriate having regard to the provisions of this subsection.

(7) Nothing in this section shall prevent an action which is brought in accordance with the provisions of this section in the High Court being transferred, in accordance with the enactments in that behalf, to some other court.

(8) For the avoidance of doubt it is hereby declared that this section applies in relation to the jurisdiction of the High Court not being Admiralty jurisdiction, as well as in relation to its Admiralty jurisdiction.

23. High Court Not to Have Jurisdiction in Cases Within Rhine Convention

The High Court shall not have jurisdiction to determine any claim or question certified by the Secretary of State to be a claim or question which, under the Rhine Navigation Convention, falls to be determined in accordance with the provisions of that Convention; and any proceedings to enforce such a claim which are commenced in the High Court shall be set aside.

24. Supplementary Provisions as to Admiralty Jurisdiction

(1) In sections 20 to 23 and this section, unless the context otherwise requires—

'collision regulations' means safety regulations under section 85 of the Merchant Shipping Act 1995;

'goods' includes baggage;

'master' has the same meaning as in the Merchant Shipping Act 1995, and accordingly includes every person (except a pilot) having command or charge of a ship;

'the Rhine Navigation Convention' means the Convention of the 7th October 1868 as revised by any subsequent Convention;

'ship' includes any description of vessel used in navigation and (except in the definition of 'port' in section 22(2) and in subsection (2)(c) of this section) includes, subject to section 2(3) of the Hovercraft Act 1968, a hovercraft;

'towage' and 'pilotage', in relation to an aircraft, mean towage and pilotage while the aircraft is water-borne.

(2) Nothing in sections 20 to 23 shall—

(a) be construed as limiting the jurisdiction of the High Court to refuse to entertain an action for wages by the master or a member of the crew of a ship, not being a British ship;

(b) affect the provisions of section 226 of the Merchant Shipping Act 1995 (power of a receiver of wreck to detain a ship in respect of a salvage claim); or

(c) authorise proceedings in rem in respect of any claim against the Crown, or the arrest, detention or sale of any of Her Majesty's ships or Her Majesty's aircraft, or, subject to section 2(3) of the Hovercraft Act 1968, Her Majesty's hovercraft, or of any cargo or other property belonging to the Crown.

(3) In this section—

'Her Majesty's ships' and 'Her Majesty's aircraft' have the meanings given by section 38(2) of the Crown Proceedings Act 1947;

'Her Majesty's hovercraft' means hovercraft belonging to the Crown in right of Her Majesty's Government in the United Kingdom or Her Majesty's Government in Northern Ireland.

Other Particular Fields of Jurisdiction

25. Probate Jurisdiction of High Court

(1) Subject to the provisions of Part V, the High Court shall, in accordance with section 19(2), have the following probate jurisdiction, that is to say all such jurisdiction in relation to probates and letters of administration as it had immediately before the commencement of this Act, and in particular all such contentious and non-contentious jurisdiction as it then had in relation to—

(a) testamentary causes or matters;

(b) the grant, amendment or revocation of probates and letters of administration; and
(c) the real and personal estate of deceased persons.

(2) Subject to the provisions of Part V, the High Court shall, in the exercise of its probate jurisdiction, perform all such duties with respect to the estates of deceased persons as fell to be performed by it immediately before the commencement of this Act.

26. Matrimonial Jurisdiction of High Court

The High Court shall, in accordance with section 19(2), have all such jurisdiction in relation to matrimonial causes and matters as was immediately before the commencement of the Matrimonial Causes Act 1857 vested in or exercisable by any ecclesiastical court or person in England or Wales in respect of—

(a) divorce a mensa et thoro (renamed judicial separation by that Act);
(b) nullity of marriage; and
(c) any matrimonial cause or matter except marriage licences.

27. Prize Jurisdiction of High Court

The High Court shall, in accordance with section 19(2), have as a prize court—

(a) all such jurisdiction as is conferred on it by the Prize Acts 1864 to 1944 (in which references to the High Court of Admiralty are by virtue of paragraph 1 of Schedule 4 to this Act to be construed as references to the High Court); and
(b) all such other jurisdiction on the high seas and elsewhere as it had as a prize court immediately before the commencement of this Act.

28. Appeals from Crown Court and Inferior Courts

(1) Subject to subsection (2), any order, judgment or other decision of the Crown Court may be questioned by any party to the proceedings, on the ground that it is wrong in law or is in excess of jurisdiction, by applying to the Crown Court to have a case stated by that court for the opinion of the High Court.

(2) Subsection (1) shall not apply to—
   (a) a judgment or other decision of the Crown Court relating to trial on indictment; or
   (b) any decision of that court under the Betting, Gaming and Lotteries Act 1963, the Licensing Act 1964 or the Gaming Act 1968 which, by any provision of any of those Acts, is to be final.

(3) Subject to the provisions of this Act and to rules of court, the High Court shall, in accordance with section 19(2), have jurisdiction to hear and determine—
   (a) any application, or any appeal (whether by way of case stated or otherwise), which it has power to hear and determine under or by virtue of this or any other Act; and
   (b) all such other appeals as it had jurisdiction to hear and determine immediately before the commencement of this Act.

(4) In subsection (2)(a) the reference to a decision of the Crown Court relating to trial on indictment does not include a decision relating to an order under section 17 of the Access to Justice Act 1999.

[*In s. 28(2)(b), for the words 'or the Gaming Act 1968' there shall be substituted the words ', the Gaming Act 1968 or the Local Government (Miscellaneous Provisions) Act 1982', by para. 27(6) of sch. 3 to the 1982 Act, which applies in any area to which the local authority has resolved, under s. 2 of the 1982 Act, that sch. 3 shall apply.*]

28A. Proceedings on Case Stated by Magistrates' Court or Crown Court

(1) This section applies where a case is stated for the opinion of the High Court—
   (a) by a magistrates' court under section 111 of the Magistrates' Courts Act 1980; or
   (b) by the Crown Court under section 28(1) of this Act.

(2) The High Court may, if it thinks fit, cause the case to be sent back for amendment and, where it does so, the case shall be amended accordingly.

(3) The High Court shall hear and determine the question arising on the case (or the case as amended) and shall—
   (a) reverse, affirm or amend the determination in respect of which the case has been stated; or

(b) remit the matter to the magistrates' court, or the Crown Court, with the opinion of the High Court,

and may make such other order in relation to the matter (including as to costs) as it thinks fit.

(4) Except as provided by the Administration of Justice Act 1960 (right of appeal to House of Lords in criminal cases), a decision of the High Court under this section is final.

29. Mandatory, Prohibiting and Quashing Orders

(1) The orders of mandamus, prohibition and certiorari shall be known instead as mandatory, prohibiting and quashing orders respectively.

(1A) The High Court shall have jurisdiction to make mandatory, prohibiting and quashing orders in those classes of case in which, immediately before 1st May 2004, it had jurisdiction to make orders of mandamus, prohibition and certiorari respectively.

(2) Every such order shall be final, subject to any right of appeal therefrom.

(3) In relation to the jurisdiction of the Crown Court, other than its jurisdiction in matters relating to trial on indictment, the High Court shall have all such jurisdiction to make mandatory, prohibiting or quashing orders as the High Court possesses in relation to the jurisdiction of an inferior court.

(3A) The High Court shall have no jurisdiction to make mandatory, prohibiting or quashing orders in relation to the jurisdiction of a court-martial in matters relating to—

(a) trial by court-martial for an offence, or

(b) appeals from a Standing Civilian Court;

and in this subsection 'court-martial' means a court-martial under the Army Act 1955, the Air Force Act 1955 or the Naval Discipline Act 1957.

(4) The power of the High Court under any enactment to require justices of the peace or a judge or officer of a county court to do any act relating to the duties of their respective offices, or to require a magistrates' court to state a case for the opinion of the High Court, in any case where the High Court formerly had by virtue of any enactment jurisdiction to make a rule absolute, or an order, for any of those purposes, shall be exercisable by mandatory order.

(5) In any statutory provision—

(a) references to mandamus or to a writ or order of mandamus shall be read as references to a mandatory order;

(b) references to prohibition or to a writ or order of prohibition shall be read as references to a prohibiting order;

(c) references to certiorari or to a writ or order of certiorari shall be read as references to a quashing order; and

(d) references to the issue or award of a writ of mandamus, prohibition or certiorari shall be read as references to the making of the corresponding mandatory, prohibiting or quashing order.

(6) In subsection (3) the reference to the Crown Court's jurisdiction in matters relating to trial on indictment does not include its jurisdiction relating to orders under section 17 of the Access to Justice Act 1999.

30. Injunctions to Restrain Persons From Acting in Offices in Which They Are Not Entitled to Act

(1) Where a person not entitled to do so acts in an office to which this section applies, the High Court may—

(a) grant an injunction restraining him from so acting; and

(b) if the case so requires, declare the office to be vacant.

(2) This section applies to any substantive office of a public nature and permanent character which is held under the Crown or which has been created by any statutory provision or royal charter.

31. Application for Judicial Review

(1) An application to the High Court for one or more of the following forms of relief, namely—

(a) a mandatory, prohibiting or quashing order;

(b) a declaration or injunction under subsection (2); or

(c) an injunction under section 30 restraining a person not entitled to do so from acting in an office to which that section applies,

shall be made in accordance with rules of court by a procedure to be known as an application for judicial review.

(2) A declaration may be made or an injunction granted under this subsection in any case where an application for judicial review, seeking that relief, has been made and the High Court considers that, having regard to—

(a) the nature of the matters in respect of which relief may be granted by mandatory, prohibiting or quashing orders;

(b) the nature of the persons and bodies against whom relief may be granted by such orders; and

(c) all the circumstances of the case,

it would be just and convenient for the declaration to be made or the injunction to be granted, as the case may be.

(3) No application for judicial review shall be made unless the leave of the High Court has been obtained in accordance with rules of court; and the court shall not grant leave to make such an application unless it considers that the applicant has a sufficient interest in the matter to which the application relates.

(4) On an application for judicial review the High Court may award to the applicant damages, restitution or the recovery of a sum due if—

(a) the application includes a claim for such an award arising from any matter to which the application relates; and

(b) the court is satisfied that such an award would have been made if the claim had been made in an action begun by the applicant at the time of making the application.

(5) If, on an application for judicial review seeking a quashing order, the High Court quashes the decision to which the application relates, the High Court may remit the matter to the court, tribunal or authority concerned, with a direction to reconsider it and reach a decision in accordance with the findings of the High Court.

(6) Where the High Court considers that there has been undue delay in making an application for judicial review, the court may refuse to grant—

(a) leave for the making of the application; or

(b) any relief sought on the application,

if it considers that the granting of the relief sought would be likely to cause substantial hardship to, or substantially prejudice the rights of, any person or would be detrimental to good administration.

(7) Subsection (6) is without prejudice to any enactment or rule of court which has the effect of limiting the time within which an application for judicial review may be made.

Powers

32. Orders for Interim Payment

(1) As regards proceedings pending in the High Court, provision may be made by rules of court for enabling the court, in such circumstances as may be prescribed, to make an order requiring a party to the proceedings to make an interim payment of such amount as may be specified in the order, with provision for the payment to be made to such other party to the proceedings as may be so specified or, if the order so provides, by paying it into court.

(2) Any rules of court which make provision in accordance with subsection (1) may include provision for enabling a party to any proceedings who, in pursuance of such an order, has made an interim payment to recover the whole or part of the amount of the payment in such circumstances, and from such other party to the proceedings, as may be determined in accordance with the rules.

(3) Any rules made by virtue of this section may include such incidental, supplementary and consequential provisions as the rule-making authority may consider necessary or expedient.

(4) Nothing in this section shall be construed as affecting the exercise of any power relating to costs, including any power to make rules of court relating to costs.

(5) In this section 'interim payment', in relation to a party to any proceedings, means a payment on account of any damages, debt or other sum (excluding any costs) which that party may be held

liable to pay to or for the benefit of another party to the proceedings if a final judgment or order of the court in the proceedings is given or made in favour of that other party.

32A. Orders for Provisional Damages for Personal Injuries

(1) This section applies to an action for damages for personal injuries in which there is proved or admitted to be a chance that at some definite or indefinite time in the future the injured person will, as a result of the act or omission which gave rise to the cause of action, develop some serious disease or suffer some serious deterioration in his physical or mental condition.

(2) Subject to subsection (4) below, as regards any action for damages to which this section applies in which a judgment is given in the High Court, provision may be made by rules of court for enabling the court, in such circumstances as may be prescribed, to award the injured person—

(a) damages assessed on the assumption that the injured person will not develop the disease or suffer the deterioration in his condition; and

(b) further damages at a future date if he develops the disease or suffers the deterioration.

(3) Any rules made by virtue of this section may include such incidental, supplementary and consequential provisions as the rule-making authority may consider necessary or expedient.

(4) Nothing in this section shall be construed—

(a) as affecting the exercise of any power relating to costs, including any power to make rules of court relating to costs; or

(b) as prejudicing any duty of the court under any enactment or rule of law to reduce or limit the total damages which would have been recoverable apart from any such duty.

33. Powers of High Court Exercisable before Commencement of Action

(1) On the application of any person in accordance with rules of court, the High Court shall, in such circumstances as may be specified in the rules, have power to make an order providing for any one or more of the following matters, that is to say—

(a) the inspection, photographing, preservation, custody and detention of property which appears to the court to be property which may become the subject-matter of subsequent proceedings in the High Court, or as to which any question may arise in any such proceedings; and

(b) the taking of samples at any such property as is mentioned in paragraph (a), and the carrying out of any experiment on or with any such property.

(2) On the application, in accordance with rules of court, of a person who appears to the High Court to be likely to be a party to subsequent proceedings in that court the High Court shall, in such circumstances as may be specified in the rules, have power to order a person who appears to the court to be likely to be a party to the proceedings and to be likely to have or to have had in his possession, custody or power any documents which are relevant to an issue arising or likely to arise out of that claim—

(a) to disclose whether those documents are in his possession, custody or power; and

(b) to produce such of those documents as are in his possession, custody or power to the applicant or, on such conditions as may be specified in the order—

(i) to the applicant's legal advisers; or

(ii) to the applicant's legal advisers and any medical or other professional adviser of the applicant; or

(iii) if the applicant has no legal adviser, to any medical or other professional adviser of the applicant.

34. Power of High Court to Order Disclosure of Documents, Inspection of Property etc. in Proceedings for Personal Injuries or Death

(2) On the application, in accordance with rules of court, of a party to any proceedings, the High Court shall, in such circumstances as may be specified in the rules, have power to order a person who is not a party to the proceedings and who appears to the court to be likely to have in his possession, custody or power any documents which are relevant to an issue arising out of the said claim—

(a) to disclose whether those documents are in his possession, custody or power; and

(b) to produce such of those documents as are in his possession, custody or power to the applicant or, on such conditions as may be specified in the order—
(i) to the applicant's legal advisers; or
(ii) to the applicant's legal advisers and any medical or other professional adviser of the applicant; or
(iii) if the applicant has no legal adviser, to any medical or other professional adviser of the applicant.

(3) On the application, in accordance with the rules of court, of a party to any proceedings, the High Court shall, in such circumstances as may be specified in the rules, have power to make an order providing for any one or more of the following matters, that is to say—
(a) the inspection, photographing, preservation, custody and detention of property which is not the property of, or in the possession of, any party to the proceedings but which is the subject-matter of the proceedings or as to which any question arises in the proceedings;
(b) the taking of samples of any such property as is mentioned in paragraph (a) and the carrying out of any experiment on or with any such property.

(4) The preceding provisions of this section are without prejudice to the exercise by the High Court of any power to make orders which is exercisable apart from those provisions.

35. Provisions Supplementary to ss. 33 and 34

(1) The High Court shall not make an order under section 33 or 34 if it considers that compliance with the order, if made, would be likely to be injurious to the public interest.

(2) Rules of court may make provision as to the circumstances in which an order under section 33 or 34 can be made; and any rules making such provision may include such incidental, supplementary and consequential provisions as the rule-making authority may consider necessary or expedient.

(3) Without prejudice to the generality of subsection (2), rules of court shall be made for the purpose of ensuring that the costs of and incidental to proceedings for an order under section 33(2) or 34 incurred by the person against whom the order is sought shall be awarded to that person unless the court otherwise directs.

(4) Sections 33(2) and 34 and this section bind the Crown; and section 33(1) binds the Crown so far as it relates to property as to which it appears to the court that it may become the subject-matter of subsequent proceedings involving a claim in respect of personal injuries to a person or in respect of a person's death.

In this subsection references to the Crown do not include references to Her Majesty in Her private capacity or to Her Majesty in right of Her Duchy of Lancaster or to the Duke of Cornwall.

(5) In sections 32A, 33 and 34 and this section—
'property' includes any land, chattel or other corporeal property of any description;
'personal injuries' includes any disease and any impairment of a person's physical or mental condition.

35A. Power of High Court to Award Interest on Debts and Damages

(1) Subject to rules of court, in proceedings (whenever instituted) before the High Court for the recovery of a debt or damages there may be included in any sum for which judgment is given simple interest, at such rate as the court thinks fit or as rules of court may provide, on all or any part of the debt or damages in respect of which judgment is given, or payment is made before judgment, for all or any part of the period between the date when the cause of action arose and—
(a) in the case of any sum paid before judgment, the date of the payment; and
(b) in the case of the sum for which judgment is given, the date of the judgment.

(2) In relation to a judgment given for damages for personal injuries or death which exceed £200 subsection (1) shall have effect—
(a) with the substitution of 'shall be included' for 'may be included'; and
(b) with the addition of 'unless the court is satisfied that there are special reasons to the contrary' after 'given', where first occurring.

(3) Subject to rules of court, where—
 (a) there are proceedings (whenever instituted) before the High Court for the recovery of a debt; and
 (b) the defendant pays the whole debt to the plaintiff (otherwise than in pursuance of a judgment in the proceedings),

the defendant shall be liable to pay the plaintiff simple interest at such rate as the court thinks fit or as rules of court may provide on all or any part of the debt for all or any part of the period between the date when the cause of action arose and the date of the payment.

(4) Interest in respect of a debt shall not be awarded under this section for a period during which, for whatever reason, interest on the debt already runs.

(5) Without prejudice to the generality of section 84, rules of court may provide for a rate of interest by reference to the rate specified in section 17 of the Judgments Act 1838 as that section has effect from time to time or by reference to a rate for which any other enactment provides.

(6) Interest under this section may be calculated at different rates in respect of different periods.

(7) In this section 'plaintiff' means the person seeking the debt or damages and 'defendant' means the person from whom the plaintiff seeks the debt or damages and 'personal injuries' includes any disease and any impairment of a person's physical or mental condition.

(8) Nothing in this section affects the damages recoverable for the dishonour of a bill of exchange.

36. Subpoena Issued by High Court to Run Throughout United Kingdom

(1) If in any cause or matter in the High Court it appears to the court that it is proper to compel the personal attendance at any trial of a witness who may not be within the jurisdiction of the court, it shall be lawful for the court, if in the discretion of the court it seems fit so to do, to order that a writ of subpoena ad testificandum or writ of subpoena duces tecum shall issue in special form commanding the witness to attend the trial wherever he shall be within the United Kingdom; and the service of any such writ in any part of the United Kingdom shall be as valid and effectual for all purposes as if it had been served within the jurisdiction of the High Court.

(2) Every such writ shall have at its foot a statement to the effect that it is issued by the special order of the High Court, and no such writ shall issue without such a special order.

(3) If any person served with a writ issued under this section does not appear as required by the writ, the High Court, on proof to the satisfaction of the court of the service of the writ and of the default, may transmit a certificate of the default under the seal of the court or under the hand of a judge of the court—
 (a) if the service was in Scotland, to the Court of Session at Edinburgh; or
 (b) if the service was in Northern Ireland, to the High Court of Justice in Northern Ireland at Belfast;

and the court to which the certificate is sent shall thereupon proceed against and punish the person in default in like manner as if that person had neglected or refused to appear in obedience to process issued out of that court.

(4) No court shall in any case proceed against or punish any person for having made such default as aforesaid unless it is shown to the court that a reasonable and sufficient sum of money to defray—
 (a) the expenses of coming and attending to give evidence and of returning from giving evidence; and
 (b) any other reasonable expenses which he has asked to be defrayed in connection with his evidence,

was tendered to him at the time when the writ was served upon him.

(5) Nothing in this section shall affect—
 (a) the power of the High Court to issue a commission for the examination of witnesses out of the jurisdiction of the court in any case in which, notwithstanding this section, the court thinks fit to issue such a commission; or
 (b) the admissibility at any trial of any evidence which, if this section had not been enacted, would have been admissible on the ground of a witness being outside the jurisdiction of the court.

(6) In this section references to attendance at a trial include references to attendance before an

examiner or commissioner appointed by the High Court in any cause or matter in that court, including an examiner or commissioner appointed to take evidence outside the jurisdiction of the court.

37. Powers of High Court With Respect to Injunctions and Receivers

(1) The High Court may by order (whether interlocutory or final) grant an injunction or appoint a receiver in all cases in which it appears to the court to be just and convenient to do so.

(2) Any such order may be made either unconditionally or on such terms and conditions as the court thinks just.

(3) The power of the High Court under subsection (1) to grant an interlocutory injunction restraining a party to any proceedings from removing from the jurisdiction of the High Court, or otherwise dealing with, assets located within that jurisdiction shall be exercisable in cases where that party is, as well as in cases where he is not, domiciled, resident or present within that jurisdiction.

(4) The power of the High Court to appoint a receiver by way of equitable execution shall operate in relation to all legal estates and interests in land; and that power—

(a) may be exercised in relation to an estate or interest in land whether or not a charge has been imposed on that land under section 1 of the Charging Orders Act 1979 for the purpose of enforcing the judgment, order or award in question; and

(b) shall be in addition to, and not in derogation of, any power of any court to appoint a receiver in proceedings for enforcing such a charge.

(5) Where an order under the said section 1 imposing a charge for the purpose of enforcing a judgment, order or award has been, or has effect as if, registered under section 6 of the Land Charges Act 1972, subsection (4) of the said section 6 (effect of non-registration of writs and orders registrable under that section) shall not apply to an order appointing a receiver made either—

(a) in proceedings for enforcing the charge; or

(b) by way of equitable execution of the judgment, order or award or, as the case may be, of so much of it as requires payment of moneys secured by the charge.

38. Relief Against Forfeiture for Non-payment of Rent

(1) In any action in the High Court for the forfeiture of a lease for non-payment of rent, the court shall have power to grant relief against forfeiture in a summary manner, and may do so subject to the same terms and conditions as to the payment of rent, costs or otherwise as could have been imposed by it in such an action immediately before the commencement of this Act.

(2) Where the lessee or a person deriving title under him is granted relief under this section, he shall hold the demised premises in accordance with the terms of the lease without the necessity for a new lease.

39. Execution of Instrument by Person Nominated by High Court

(1) Where the High Court has given or made a judgment or order directing a person to execute any conveyance, contract or other document, or to indorse any negotiable instrument, then, if that person—

(a) neglects or refuses to comply with the judgment or order; or

(b) cannot after reasonable inquiry be found,

the High Court may, on such terms and conditions, if any, as may be just, order that the conveyance, contract or other document shall be executed, or that the negotiable instrument shall be indorsed, by such person as the court may nominate for that purpose.

(2) A conveyance, contract, document or instrument executed or indorsed in pursuance of an order under this section shall operate, and be for all purposes available, as if it had been executed or indorsed by the person originally directed to execute or indorse it.

40. Attachment of Debts

(1) Subject to any order for the time being in force under subsection (4), this section applies to any deposit account, and any withdrawable share account, with a deposit-taker.

(2) In determining whether, for the purposes of the jurisdiction of the High Court to attach debts

for the purpose of satisfying judgments or orders for the payment of money, a sum standing to the credit of a person in an account to which this section applies is a sum due or accruing to that person and, as such, attachable in accordance with rules of court, any condition mentioned in subsection (3) which applies to the account shall be disregarded.

(3) Those conditions are—
  (a) any condition that notice is required before any money or share is withdrawn;
  (b) any condition that a personal application must be made before any money or share is withdrawn;
  (c) any condition that a deposit book or share-account book must be produced before any money or share is withdrawn; or
  (d) any other prescribed condition.

(4) The Lord Chancellor may by order make such provision as he thinks fit, by way of amendment of this section or otherwise, for all or any of the following purposes, namely—
  (a) including in, or excluding from, the accounts to which this section applies accounts of any description specified in the order;
  (b) excluding from the accounts to which this section applies all accounts with any particular deposit-taker so specified or with any deposit-taker of a description so specified.

(5) Any order under subsection (4) shall be made by statutory instrument subject to annulment in pursuance of a resolution of either House of Parliament.

(6) 'Deposit-taker' means a person who may, in the course of his business, lawfully accept deposits in the United Kingdom.

(7) Subsection (6) must be read with—
  (a) section 22 of the Financial Services and Markets Act 2000;
  (b) any relevant order under that section; and
  (c) Schedule 2 to that Act.

40A. Administrative and Clerical Expenses of Garnishees

(1) Where an interim third party debt order made in the exercise of the jurisdiction mentioned in subsection (2) of the preceding section is served on any deposit-taker, it may, subject to the provisions of this section, deduct from the relevant debt or debts an amount not exceeding the prescribed sum towards its administrative and clerical expenses in complying with the order; and the right to make a deduction under this subsection shall be exercisable as from the time the interim third party debt order is served on it.

(1A) In subsection (1) 'the relevant debt or debts', in relation to an interim third party debt order served on a deposit-taker, means the amount, as at the time the order is served on it, of the debt or debts of which the whole or part is expressed to be attached by the order.

(1B) A deduction may be made under subsection (1) in a case where the amount referred to in subsection (1A) is insufficient to cover both the amount of the deduction and the amount of the judgment debt and costs in respect of which the attachment was made, notwithstanding that the benefit of the attachment to the creditor is reduced as a result of the deduction.

(2) An amount may not in pursuance of subsection (1) be deducted or, as the case may be, retained in a case where, by virtue of section 346 of the Insolvency Act 1986 or section 183 of the Insolvency Act 1986 or otherwise, the creditor is not entitled to retain the benefit of the attachment.

(3) In this section—
'deposit-taker' has the meaning given by section 40(6); and
'prescribed' means prescribed by an order made by the Lord Chancellor.

(4) An order under this section—
  (a) may make different provision for different cases;
  (b) without prejudice to the generality of paragraph (a) of this subsection, may prescribe sums differing according to the amount due under the judgment or order to be satisfied;
  (c) may provide for this section not to apply to deposit-takers of any prescribed description.

(5) Any such order shall be made by statutory instrument subject to annulment in pursuance of a resolution of either House of Parliament.

42. Restriction of Vexatious Legal Proceedings

(1) If, on an application made by the Attorney General under this section, the High Court is satisfied that any person has habitually and persistently and without any reasonable ground—
   (a) instituted vexatious civil proceedings, whether in the High Court or any inferior court, and whether against the same person or against different persons; or
   (b) made vexatious applications in any civil proceedings, whether in the High Court or any inferior court, and whether instituted by him or another; or
   (c) instituted vexations prosecutions (whether against the same person or different persons),

the court may, after hearing that person or giving him an opportunity of being heard, make a civil proceedings order, a criminal proceedings order or an all proceedings order.

(1A) In this section—

'civil proceedings order' means an order that—
   (a) no civil proceedings shall without the leave of the High Court be instituted in any court by the person against whom the order is made;
   (b) any civil proceedings instituted by him in any court before the making of the order shall not be continued by him without the leave of the High Court; and
   (c) no application (other than one for leave under this section) shall be made by him, in any civil proceedings instituted in any court by any person, without the leave of the High Court;

'criminal proceedings order' means an order that—
   (a) no information shall be laid before a justice of the peace by the person against whom the order is made without the leave of the High Court; and
   (b) no application for leave to prefer a bill of indictment shall be made by him without the leave of the High Court; and

'all proceedings order' means an order which has the combined effect of the two other orders.

(2) An order under subsection (1) may provide that it is to cease to have effect at the end of a specified period, but shall otherwise remain in force indefinitely.

(3) Leave for the institution or continuance of, or for the making of an application in, any civil proceedings by a person who is the subject of an order for the time being in force under subsection (1) shall not be given unless the High Court is satisfied that the proceedings or application are not an abuse of the process of the court in question and that there are reasonable grounds for the proceedings or application.

(3A) Leave for the laying of an information or for an application for leave to prefer a bill of indictment by a person who is the subject of an order for the time being in force under subsection (1) shall not be given unless the High Court is satisfied that the institution of the prosecution is not an abuse of the criminal process and that there are reasonable grounds for the institution of the prosecution by the applicant.

(4) No appeal shall lie from a decision of the High Court refusing leave required by virtue of this section.

(5) A copy of any order made under subsection (1) shall be published in the London Gazette.

43A. Specific Powers of Arbitrator Exercisable by High Court

In any cause or matter proceeding in the High Court in connection with any contract incorporating an arbitration agreement which confers specific powers upon the arbitrator, the High Court may, if all parties to the agreement agree, exercise any such powers.

GENERAL PROVISIONS

Law and Equity

49. Concurrent Administration of Law and Equity

(1) Subject to the provisions of this or any other Act, every court exercising jurisdiction in England or Wales in any civil cause or matter shall continue to administer law and equity on the basis that, wherever there is any conflict or variance between the rules of equity and the rules of the common law with reference to the same matter, the rules of equity shall prevail.

(2) Every such court shall give the same effect as hitherto—
(a) to all equitable estates, titles, rights, reliefs, defences and counterclaims, and to all equitable duties and liabilities; and
(b) subject thereto, to all legal claims and demands and all estates, titles, rights, duties, obligations and liabilities existing by the common law or by any custom or created by any statute,

and, subject to the provisions of this or any other Act, shall so exercise its jurisdiction in every cause or matter before it as to secure that, as far as possible, all matters in dispute between the parties are completely and finally determined, and all multiplicity of legal proceedings with respect to any of those matters is avoided.

(3) Nothing in this Act shall affect the power of the Court of Appeal or the High Court to stay any proceedings before it, where it thinks fit to do so, either of its own motion or on the application of any person, whether or not a party to the proceedings.

50. Power to Award Damages As Well As, or in Substitution For, Injunction or Specific Performance

Where the Court of Appeal or the High Court has jurisdiction to entertain an application for an injunction or specific performance, it may award damages in addition to, or in substitution for, an injunction or specific performance.

Costs

51. Costs in Civil Division of Court of Appeal, High Court and County Courts

(1) Subject to the provisions of this or any other enactment and to rules of court, the costs of and incidental to all proceedings in—
(a) the civil division of the Court of Appeal;
(b) the High Court; and
(c) any county court,

shall be in the discretion of the court.

(2) Without prejudice to any general power to make rules of court, such rules may make provision for regulating matters relating to the costs of those proceedings including, in particular, prescribing scales of costs to be paid to legal or other representatives or for securing that the amount awarded to a party in respect of the costs to be paid by him to such representatives is not limited to what would have been payable by him to them if he had not been awarded costs.

(3) The court shall have full power to determine by whom and to what extent the costs are to be paid.

(4) In subsections (1) and (2) 'proceedings' includes the administration of estates and trusts.

(5) Nothing in subsection (1) shall alter the practice in any criminal cause, or in bankruptcy.

(6) In any proceedings mentioned in subsection (1), the court may disallow, or (as the case may be) order the legal or other representative concerned to meet, the whole of any wasted costs or such part of them as may be determined in accordance with rules of court.

(7) In subsection (6), 'wasted costs' means any costs incurred by a party—
(a) as a result of any improper, unreasonable or negligent act or omission on the part of any legal or other representative or any employee of such a representative; or
(b) which, in the light of any such act or omission occurring after they were incurred, the court considers it is unreasonable to expect that party to pay.

(8) Where—
(a) a person has commenced proceedings in the High Court; but
(b) those proceedings should, in the opinion of the court, have been commenced in a county court in accordance with any provision made under section 1 of the Courts and Legal Services Act 1990 or by or under any other enactment,

the person responsible for determining the amount which is to be awarded to that person by way of costs shall have regard to those circumstances.

(9) Where, in complying with subsection (8), the responsible person reduces the amount which would otherwise be awarded to the person in question—

Selected Legislation

(a) the amount of that reduction shall not exceed 25 per cent; and
(b) on any taxation of the costs payable by that person to his legal representative, regard shall be had to the amount of the reduction.

(10) The Lord Chancellor may by order amend subsection (9)(a) by substituting, for the percentage for the time being mentioned there, a different percentage.

(11) Any such order shall be made by statutory instrument and may make such transitional or incidental provision as the Lord Chancellor considers expedient.

(12) No such statutory instrument shall be made unless a draft of the instrument has been approved by both Houses of Parliament.

(13) In this section 'legal or other representative', in relation to a party to proceedings, means any person exercising a right of audience or right to conduct litigation on his behalf.

PART III PRACTICE AND PROCEDURE
THE COURT OF APPEAL

Distribution of Business

53. Distribution of Business between Civil and Criminal Divisions

(1) Rules of court may provide for the distribution of business in the Court of Appeal between the civil and criminal divisions, but subject to any such rules business shall be distributed in accordance with the following provisions of this section.

(2) The criminal division of the Court of Appeal shall exercise—
(a) all jurisdiction of the Court of Appeal under Parts I and II of the Criminal Appeal Act 1968;
(b) the jurisdiction of the Court of Appeal under section 13 of the Administration of Justice Act 1960 (appeals in cases of contempt of court) in relation to appeals from orders and decisions of the Crown Court;
(c) all other jurisdiction expressly conferred on that division by this or any other Act; and
(d) the jurisdiction to order the issue of writs of venire de novo.

(3) The civil division of the Court of Appeal shall exercise the whole of the jurisdiction of that court not exercisable by the criminal division.

(4) Where any class of proceedings in the Court of Appeal is by any statutory provision assigned to the criminal division of that court, rules of court may provide for any enactment relating to—
(a) appeals to the Court of Appeal under Part I of the Criminal Appeal Act 1968; or
(b) any matter connected with or arising out of such appeals,

to apply in relation to proceedings of that class or, as the case may be, to any corresponding matter connected with or arising out of such proceedings, as it applies in relation to such appeals or, as the case may be, to the relevant matter within paragraph (b), with or without prescribed modifications in either case.

Composition of Court

54. Court of Civil Division

(1) This section relates to the civil division of the Court of Appeal; and in this section 'court', except where the context otherwise requires, means a court of that division.

(2) Subject as follows, a court shall be duly constituted for the purpose of exercising any of its jurisdiction if it consists of one or more judges.

(3) The Master of the Rolls may, with the concurrence of the Lord Chancellor, give (or vary or revoke) directions about the minimum number of judges of which a court must consist if it is to be duly constituted for the purpose of any description of proceedings.

(4) The Master of the Rolls, or any Lord Justice of Appeal designated by him, may (subject to any directions under subsection (3)) determine the number of judges of which a court is to consist for the purpose of any particular proceedings.

(4A) The Master of the Rolls may give directions as to what is to happen in any particular case where one or more members of a court which has partly heard proceedings are unable to continue.

(5) Where—
(a) an appeal has been heard by a court consisting of an even number of judges; and
(b) the members of the court are equally divided,
the case shall, on the application of any party to the appeal, be reargued before and determined by an uneven number of judges not less than three, before any appeal to the House of Lords.
(8) Subsections (1) and (2) of section 70 (assessors in the High Court) shall apply in relation to causes and matters before the civil division of the Court of Appeal as they apply in relation to causes and matters before the High Court.
(9) Subsections (3) and (4) of section 70 (scientific advisers to assist the Patents Court in proceedings under the Patents Act 1949 and the Patents Act 1977) shall apply in relation to the civil division of the Court of Appeal and proceedings on appeal from any decision of the Patents Court in proceedings under those Acts as they apply in relation to the Patents Court and proceedings under those Acts.

56. Judges Not to Sit on Appeal from Their Own Judgments, etc.

(1) No judge shall sit as a member of the civil division of the Court of Appeal on the hearing of, or shall determine any application in proceedings incidental or preliminary to, an appeal from a judgment or order made in any case by himself or by any court of which he was a member.
(2) No judge shall sit as a member of the criminal division of the Court of Appeal on the hearing of, or shall determine any application in proceedings incidental or preliminary to, an appeal against—
(a) a conviction before himself or a court of which he was a member; or
(b) a sentence passed by himself or such a court.

Sittings and Vacations

57. Sittings and Vacations

(1) Sittings of the Court of Appeal may be held, and any other business of the Court of Appeal may be conducted, at any place in England or Wales.
(2) Subject to rules of court—
(a) the places at which the Court of Appeal sits outside the Royal Courts of Justice; and
(b) the days and times at which the Court of Appeal sits at any place outside the Royal Courts of Justice,
shall be determined in accordance with directions given by the Lord Chancellor after consulting the Lord Chief Justice.
(3) Rules of court may make provision for regulating the vacations to be observed by the Court of Appeal and in the offices of that court.
(4) Rules of court—
(a) may provide for securing such sittings of the civil division of the Court of Appeal during vacation as the Master of the Rolls may with the concurrence of the Lord Chancellor determine;
(b) without prejudice to paragraph (a), shall provide for the transaction during vacation by judges of the Court of Appeal of all such business in the civil division of that court as may require to be immediately or promptly transacted; and
(c) shall provide for securing sittings of the criminal division of that court during vacation if necessary.
(5) The Lord Chief Justice may nominate a judicial office holder (as defined in section 109(4) of the Constitutional Reform Act 2005) to exercise his functions under this section.

Other Provisions

58. Calling Into Question of Incidental Decisions in Civil Division

(1) Rules of court may provide that decisions of the Court of Appeal which—
(a) are taken by a single judge or any officer or member of staff of that court in proceedings incidental to any cause or matter pending before the civil division of that court; and

(b) do not involve the determination of an appeal or of an application for permission to appeal, may be called into question in such manner as may be prescribed.

(2) No appeal shall lie to the House of Lords from a decision which may be called into question pursuant to rules under subsection (1).

60. Rules of Court, and Decisions of Court of Appeal, as to Whether Judgment or Order is Final or Interlocutory

(1) Rules of court may provide for orders or judgments of any prescribed description to be treated for any prescribed purpose connected with appeals to the Court of Appeal as final or as interlocutory.

(2) No appeal shall lie from a decision of the Court of Appeal as to whether a judgment or order is, for any purpose connected with an appeal to that court, final or interlocutory.

THE HIGH COURT

Distribution of Business

61. Distribution of Business among Divisions

(1) Subject to any provision made by or under this or any other Act (and in particular to any rules of court made in pursuance of subsection (2) and any order under subsection (3)), business in the High Court of any description mentioned in Schedule 1, as for the time being in force, shall be distributed among the Divisions in accordance with that Schedule.

(2) Rules of court may provide for the distribution of business in the High Court among the Divisions; but any rules made in pursuance of this subsection shall have effect subject to any orders for the time being in force under subsection (3).

(3) Subject to subsection (5), the Lord Chief Justice may, with the concurrence of the Lord Chancellor, by order—

(a) direct that any business in the High Court which is not for the time being assigned by or under this or any other Act to any Division be assigned to such Division as may be specified in the order;

(b) if at any time it appears to the Lord Chief Justice and the Lord Chancellor desirable to do so with a view to the more convenient administration of justice, direct that any business for the time being assigned by or under this or any other Act to any Division be assigned to such other Division as may be specified in the order; and

(c) amend Schedule 1 so far as may be necessary in consequence of provision made by order under paragraph (a) or (b).

(4) The powers conferred by subsection (2) and subsection (3) include power to assign business of any description to two or more Divisions concurrently.

(5) No order under subsection (3(b) relating to any business shall be made without the concurrence of the senior judge of—

(a) the Division or each of the Divisions to which the business is for the time being assigned; and

(b) the Division or each of the Divisions to which the business is to be assigned by the order.

(6) Subject to rules of court, the fact that a cause or matter commenced in the High Court falls within a class of business assigned by or under this Act to a particular Division does not make it obligatory for it to be allocated or transferred to that Division.

(7) Without prejudice to subsections (1) to (5) and section 63, rules of court may provide for the distribution of the business (other than business required to be heard by a divisional court) in any Division of the High Court among the judges of that Division.

(8) Any order under subsection (3) shall be made by statutory instrument, which shall be laid before Parliament after being made.

(9) The Lord Chief Justice may nominate a judicial office holder (as defined in section 109(4) of the Constitutional Reform Act 2005) to exercise his functions under subsection (3).

62. Business of Patents, Admiralty and Commercial Courts

(1) The Patents Court shall take such proceedings relating to patents as are within the jurisdiction conferred on it by the Patents Act 1977, and such other proceedings relating to patents or other matters as may be prescribed.

(2) The Admiralty Court shall take Admiralty business, that is to say causes and matters assigned to the Queen's Bench Division and involving the exercise of the High Court's Admiralty jurisdiction or its jurisdiction as a prize court.

(3) The Commercial Court shall take such causes and matters as may in accordance with rules of court be entered in the commercial list.

63. Business Assigned to Specially Nominated Judges

(1) Any business assigned, in accordance with this or any other Act or rules of court, to one or more specially nominated judges of the High Court may—
   (a) during vacation; or
   (b) during the illness or absence of that judge or any of those judges; or
   (c) for any other reasonable cause,

   be dealt with by any judge of the High Court named for that purpose by the Lord Chief Justice after consulting the Lord Chancellor.

(2) If at any time it appears to the Lord Chief Justice, after consulting the Lord Chancellor, to be desirable to do so with a view to the more convenient administration of justice, he may by order direct that business of any description which is for the time being assigned, in accordance with this or any other Act or rules of court, to one or more specially nominated judges of the High Court shall cease to be so assigned and may be dealt with by any one or more judges of the High Court.

(3) An order under subsection (2) shall not be made in respect of any business without the concurrence of the senior judge of the Division to which the business is for the time being assigned.

(4) The Lord Chief Justice may nominate a judicial office holder (as defined in section 109(4) of the Constitutional Reform Act 2005) to exercise his functions under subsection (1) or (2).

64. Choice of Division by Plaintiff

(1) Without prejudice to the power of transfer under section 65, the person by whom any cause or matter is commenced in the High Court shall in the prescribed manner allocate it to whichever Division he thinks fit.

(2) Where a cause or matter is commenced in the High Court, all subsequent interlocutory or other steps or proceedings in the High Court in that cause or matter shall be taken in the Division to which the cause or matter is for the time being allocated (whether under subsection (1) or in consequence of its transfer under section 65).

65. Power of Transfer

(1) Any cause or matter may at any time and at any stage thereof, and either with or without application from any of the parties, be transferred, by such authority and in such manner as rules of Court may direct, from one Division or judge of the High Court to another Division or judge thereof.

(2) The transfer of a cause or matter under subsection (1) to a different Division or judge of the High Court shall not affect the validity of any steps or proceedings taken or order made in that cause or matter before the transfer.

Divisional Courts

66. Divisional Courts of High Court

(1) Divisional courts may be held for the transaction of any business in the High Court which is, by or by virtue of rules of court or any other statutory provision, required to be heard by a divisional court.

(2) Any number of divisional courts may sit at the same time.

(3) A divisional court shall be constituted of not less than two judges.

(4) Every judge of the High Court shall be qualified to sit in any divisional court.

(5) The judge who is, according to the order of precedence under this Act, the senior of the judges constituting a divisional court shall be the president of the court.

Mode of Conducting Business

67. Proceedings in Court and in Chambers

Business in the High Court shall be heard and disposed of in court except in so far as it may, under this or any other Act, under rules of court or in accordance with the practice of the court, be dealt with in chambers.

68. Exercise of High Court Jurisdiction Otherwise Than by Judges of That Court

(1) Provision may be made by rules of court as to the cases in which jurisdiction of the High Court may be exercised by—
   (a) such Circuit judges, deputy Circuit judges or Recorders as the Lord Chief Justice may, after consulting the Lord Chancellor, from time to time nominate to deal with official referees' business; or
   (b) special referees.

(2) Without prejudice to the generality of subsection (1), rules of court may in particular—
   (b) authorise any question arising in any cause or matter to be referred to a special referee for inquiry and report.

(3) Rules of court shall not authorise the exercise of powers of attachment and committal by a special referee or any officer or other staff of the court.

(4) Subject to subsection (5), the decision of—
   (a) any such person as is mentioned in subsection (1); or
   (b) any officer or other staff of the court,

   may be called in question in such manner as may be prescribed by rules of court, whether by appeal to the Court of Appeal, or by an appeal or application to a divisional court or a judge in court or a judge in chambers, or by an adjournment to a judge in court or a judge in chambers.

(5) Rules of court may provide either generally or to a limited extent for decisions of persons nominated under subsection (1)(a) being called in question only by appeal on a question of law.

(6) The cases in which jurisdiction of the High Court may be exercised by persons nominated under subsection (1)(a) shall be known as 'official referees' business'; and, subject to rules of court, the distribution of official referees' business among persons so nominated shall be determined in accordance with directions given by the Lord Chief Justice after consulting the Lord Chancellor.

(7) Any reference to an official referee in any enactment, whenever passed, or in rules of court or in rules of court or any other instrument or document, whenever made, shall, unless the context otherwise requires, be construed as, or (where the context requires) as including, a reference to a person nominated under subsection (1)(a).

(8) The Lord Chief Justice may nominate a judicial office holder (as defined in section 109(4) of the Constitutional Reform Act 2005) to exercise his functions under subsections (1)(a) and (6).

69. Trial by Jury

(1) Where, on the application of any party to an action to be tried in the Queen's Bench Division, the court is satisfied that there is in issue—
   (a) a charge of fraud against that party; or
   (b) a claim in respect of libel, slander, malicious prosecution or false imprisonment; or
   (c) any question or issue of a kind prescribed for the purposes of this paragraph,

   the action shall be tried with a jury, unless the court is of opinion that the trial requires any prolonged examination of documents or accounts or any scientific or local investigation which cannot conveniently be made with a jury.

(2) An application under subsection (1) must be made not later than such time before the trial as may be prescribed.

(3) An action to be tried in the Queen's Bench Division which does not by virtue of subsection (1) fall to be tried with a jury shall be tried without a jury unless the court in its discretion orders it to be tried with a jury.

(4) Nothing in subsections (1) to (3) shall affect the power of the court to order, in accordance with rules of court, that different questions of fact arising in any action be tried by different modes of trial; and where any such order is made, subsection (1) shall have effect only as respects questions relating to any such charge, claim, question or issue as is mentioned in that subsection.

(5) Where for the purpose of disposing of any action or other matter which is being tried in the High Court by a judge with a jury it is necessary to ascertain the law of any other country which is applicable to the facts of the case, any question as to the effect of the evidence given with respect to that law shall, instead of being submitted to the jury, be decided by the judge alone.

70. Assessors and Scientific Advisers

(1) In any cause or matter before the High Court the court may, if it thinks it expedient to do so, call in the aid of one or more assessors specially qualified, and hear and dispose of the cause or matter wholly or partially with their assistance.

(2) The remuneration, if any, to be paid to an assessor for his services under subsection (1) in connection with any proceedings shall be determined by the court, and shall form part of the costs of the proceedings.

(3) Rules of court shall make provision for the appointment of scientific advisers to assist the Patents Court in proceedings under the Patents Act 1949 and the Patents Act 1977 and for regulating the functions of such advisers.

(4) The remuneration of any such adviser shall be determined by the Lord Chancellor with the concurrence of the Minister for the Civil Service and shall be defrayed out of money provided by Parliament.

Sittings and Vacations

71. Sittings and Vacations

(1) Sittings of the High Court may be held, and any other business of the High Court may be conducted, at any place in England or Wales.

(2) Subject to rules of court—
  (a) the places at which the High Court sits outside the Royal Courts of Justice; and
  (b) the days and times when the High Court sits at any place outside the Royal Courts of Justice,

shall be determined in accordance with directions given by the Lord Chancellor after consulting the Lord Chief Justice.

(3) Rules of court may make provision for regulating the vacations to be observed by the High Court and in the offices of that court.

(4) Rules of court—
  (a) may provide for securing such sittings of any Division of the High Court during vacation as the senior judge of that Division may with the concurrence of the Lord Chancellor determine; and
  (b) without prejudice to paragraph (a), shall provide for the transaction during vacation by judges of the High Court of all such business in the High Court as may require to be immediately or promptly transacted.

(5) Different provision may be made in pursuance of subsection (3) for different parts of the country.

(6) The Lord Chief Justice may nominate a judicial office holder (as defined in section 109(4) of the Constitutional Reform Act 2005) to exercise his functions under this section.

Other Provisions

72. Withdrawal of Privilege Against Incrimination of Self or Spouse in Certain Proceedings

(1) In any proceedings to which this subsection applies a person shall not be excused, by reason that

Selected Legislation

to do so would tend to expose that person, or his or her spouse, to proceedings for a related offence or for the recovery of a related penalty—

(a) from answering any question put to that person in the first-mentioned proceedings; or

(b) from complying with any order made in those proceedings.

(2) Subsection (1) applies to the following civil proceedings in the High Court, namely—

(a) proceedings for infringement of rights pertaining to any intellectual property or for passing off;

(b) proceedings brought to obtain disclosure of information relating to any infringement of such rights or to any passing off; and

(c) proceedings brought to prevent any apprehended infringement of such rights or any apprehended passing off.

(3) Subject to subsection (4), no statement or admission made by a person—

(a) in answering a question put to him in any proceedings to which subsection (1) applies; or

(b) in complying with any order made in any such proceedings,

shall, in proceedings for any related offence or for the recovery of any related penalty, be admissible in evidence against that person or (unless they married after the making of the statement or admission) against the spouse of that person.

(4) Nothing in subsection (3) shall render any statement or admission made by a person as there mentioned inadmissible in evidence against that person in proceedings for perjury or contempt of court.

(5) In this section—

'intellectual property' means any patent, trade mark, copyright, design right, registered design, technical or commercial information or other intellectual property;

'related offence', in relation to any proceedings to which subsection (1) applies, means—

(a) in the case of proceedings within subsection (2)(a) or (b)—

(i) any offence committed by or in the course of the infringement or passing off to which those proceedings relate; or

(ii) any offence not within sub-paragraph (i) committed in connection with that infringement or passing off, being an offence involving fraud or dishonesty;

(b) in the case of proceedings within subsection (2)(c), any offence revealed by the facts on which the plaintiff relies in those proceedings;

'related penalty', in relation to any proceedings to which subsection (1) applies means—

(a) in the case of proceedings within subsection (2)(a) or (b), any penalty incurred in respect of anything done or omitted in connection with the infringement or passing off to which those proceedings relate;

(b) in the case of proceedings within subsection (2)(c), any penalty incurred in respect of any act or omission revealed by the facts on which the plaintiff relies in those proceedings.

(6) Any reference in this section to civil proceedings in the High Court of any description includes a reference to proceedings on appeal arising out of civil proceedings in the High Court of that description.

PART IV OFFICERS AND OFFICES

Appointment of Certain Officers of Supreme Court

88. Qualification for Office

A person shall not be qualified for appointment to any office in the Supreme Court listed in column 1 of any Part of Schedule 2 unless he is a person of any description specified in relation to that office in column 2 of that Part.

89. Masters and Registrars [version applying to appointments to offices listed in sch. 2, part II]

(1) The power to make appointments to the offices in the Supreme Court listed in column 1 of [Part II] of Schedule 2 shall be exercisable by Her Majesty.

(1A) The maximum number of appointments under subsection (1) is such as may be determined from time to time by the Lord Chancellor with the concurrence of the Treasury.

(2) The person appointed to the office of Queen's coroner and attorney and master of the Crown Office and Registrar of criminal appeals shall, by virtue of his appointment, be a master of the Queen's Bench Division.

(3) Her Majesty shall, on the recommendation of the Lord Chancellor, appoint a person to each office listed in the first column of the table in subsection (3C) ('a senior office').

(3A) A person may be appointed to a senior office only if—
- (a) he holds the office in the corresponding entry in the second column of that table ('the qualifying office'), or
- (b) he does not hold the qualifying office but could be appointed to it in compliance with section 88.

(3B) Where a person who is to be appointed to a senior office meets the condition in subsection (3A)(b) he shall, when appointed to the senior office, also be appointed to the qualifying office.

(3C) This is the table referred to in subsections (3) and (3A)—

Senior office	*Qualifying office*
Senior Master of the Queen's Bench Division	Master of the Queen's Bench Division
Chief Chancery Master	Master of the Chancery Division
Chief Taxing Master	Taxing master of the Senior Courts
Chief Bankruptcy Registrar	Registrar in bankruptcy of the High Court
Senior District Judge of the Family Division	Registrar of the Principal Registry of the Family Division

(4) The person appointed Senior Master under subsection (3)(a) shall hold and perform the duties of the offices of the Queen's Remembrancer and registrar of judgments.

(7A) A person appointed under subsection (1) is to be paid such salary, and a person appointed to a senior office is to be paid such additional salary, as may be determined by the Lord Chancellor with the concurrence of the Treasury.

(7B) A salary payable under or by virtue of this section—
- (a) may in any case be increased, but
- (b) may not, in the case of a salary payable in respect of an office listed in column 1 of Part 2 of Schedule 2 or of a senior office, be reduced,

by a determination or further determination under this section.

(8) Salaries payable under or by virtue of this section shall be paid out of money provided by Parliament.

[*In s. 89(1) the words in square brackets have been substituted editorially for 'Parts II and III' to clarify the temporary effect of amendments which are only partially in force.*]

89. Masters and Registrars [version applying to appointments to offices listed in sch. 2, part III]

(1) The power to make appointments to the offices in the Supreme Court listed in column 1 of [Part III] of Schedule 2 shall be exercisable by the Lord Chancellor, with the concurrence of the Minister for the Civil Service as to numbers and salaries.

(2) The person appointed to the office of Queen's coroner and attorney and master of the Crown Office and Registrar of criminal appeals shall, by virtue of his appointment, be a master of the Queen's Bench Division.

(3A) A person may be appointed to a senior office only if—
- (a) he holds the office in the corresponding entry in the second column of that table ('the qualifying office'), or
- (b) he does not hold the qualifying office but could be appointed to it in compliance with section 88.

(3B) Where a person who is to be appointed to a senior office meets the condition in subsection (3A)(b) he shall, when appointed to the senior office, also be appointed to the qualifying office.

(3C) This is the table referred to in subsections (3) and (3A)—

Selected Legislation

Senior office	*Qualifying office*
Senior Master of the Queen's Bench Division	Master of the Queen's Bench Division
Chief Chancery Master	Master of the Chancery Division
Chief Taxing Master	Taxing master of the Senior Courts
Chief Bankruptcy Registrar	Registrar in bankruptcy of the High Court
Senior District Judge of the Family Division	Registrar of the Principal Registry of the Family Division

(4) The person appointed Senior Master under subsection (3)(a) shall hold and perform the duties of the offices of the Queen's Remembrancer and registrar of judgments.

(8) Salaries payable under or by virtue of this section shall be paid out of money provided by Parliament.

[*In s. 89(1) the words in square brackets have been substituted editorially for 'Parts II and III' to clarify the temporary effect of amendments which are only partially in force.*]

90. Official Solicitor

(1) There shall continue to be an Official Solicitor to the Supreme Court, who shall be appointed by the Lord Chancellor.

(2) There shall be paid to the Official Solicitor out of money provided by Parliament such salary as the Lord Chancellor may, with the concurrence of the Minister for the Civil Service, determine.

(3) The Official Solicitor shall have such powers and perform such duties as may for the time being be conferred or imposed on the holder of that office—

(a) by or under this or any other Act; or

(b) by or in accordance with any direction given (before or after the commencement of this Act) by the Lord Chancellor.

(3A) The holder for the time being of the office of Official Solicitor shall have the right to conduct litigation in relation to any proceedings.

(3B) When acting as Official Solicitor a person who would otherwise have the right to conduct litigation by virtue of section 28(2)(a) of the Courts and Legal Services Act 1990 shall be treated as having acquired that right solely by virtue of subsection (3A).

(4) If—

(a) the Official Solicitor is not available because of his absence or for some other reason; or

(b) his office is vacant,

then, during such unavailability or vacancy, any powers or duties of the Official Solicitor shall be exercisable or fall to be performed by any person for the time being appointed by the Lord Chancellor as deputy to the Official Solicitor (and any property vested in the Official Solicitor may accordingly be dealt with by any such person in all respects as if it were vested in him instead).

91. Deputies and Temporary Appointments

(1) If it appears to the Lord Chief Justice, after consulting the Lord Chancellor, that it is expedient to do so in order to facilitate the disposal of business in the Supreme Court, he may appoint a person—

(a) to act as a deputy for any person holding an office listed in column 1 of Part II of Schedule 2; or

(b) to act as a temporary additional officer in any such office,

during such period or on such occasions as the Lord Chief Justice may, after consulting the Lord Chancellor, think fit.

(1A) If it appears to the Lord Chancellor that it is expedient to do so in order to facilitate the disposal of business in the Senior Courts, he may appoint a person—

(a) to act as a deputy for any person holding an office listed in column 1 of Part 3 of Schedule 2; or

(b) to act as a temporary additional officer in any such office,

during such period or on such occasions as the Lord Chancellor may think fit.

(2) Subject to subsection (3), a person shall not be qualified for appointment under this section if the office in which he would act by virtue of the appointment is one to which he is not qualified for permanent appointment.

(3) A person may be appointed under this section if he would, but for his age, be qualified for permanent appointment to the office in question and he has previously held a permanent appointment to that office or—

(a) where the office in question is listed in column 1 of Part II of Schedule 2, to any other office so listed; or

(b) where the office in question is listed in column 1 of Part III of that Schedule, to any other office listed in column 1 of either Part II or Part III; or

(c) (whatever the office in question) to the office of county court registrar,

but no appointment by virtue of this subsection shall be such as to extend beyond the day on which the person in question attains the age of seventy-five years.

(4) Every person, while acting under this section, shall have all the jurisdiction of a person permanently appointed to the office in which he is acting.

(6) The Lord Chancellor may, out of money provided by Parliament, pay to any person appointed under this section such remuneration and allowances as he may, with the concurrence of the Minister for the Civil Service, determine.

(7) The Lord Chief Justice may nominate a judicial office holder (as defined in section 109(4) of the Constitutional Reform Act 2005) to exercise his functions under subsection (1).

Other Provisions Relating to Officers of Supreme Court

92. Tenure of Office

(1) Subject to the following provisions of this section and to subsections (4) to (6) of section 26 of the Judicial Pensions and Retirement Act 1993 (Lord Chancellor's power to authorise continuance in office up to the age of 75), a person who holds an office to which this subsection applies shall vacate it on the day on which he attains the age of seventy years.

(2) Subsection (1) applies to the offices listed in column 1 of Part II of Schedule 2.

(2A) Subject to the following provisions of this section, a person who holds an office to which this subsection applies shall vacate it at the end of the completed year of service in the course of which he attains the age of sixty-two years.

(2B) Subsection (2A) applies to the offices listed in column 1 of Part I of Schedule 2.

(3A) Where the Lord Chancellor considers it desirable in the public interest to retain in office a person who holds an office to which subsection (2A) applies after the time when he would otherwise retire in accordance with that subsection, the Lord Chancellor may from time to time authorise the continuance in office of that person until such date, not being later than the date on which he attains the age of sixty-five years, as he thinks fit.

(4) A person appointed to an office listed in column 1 of Part I or II of Schedule 2 shall hold that office during good behaviour.

(5) The power to remove such a person from his office on account of misbehaviour shall be exercisable by the Lord Chancellor with the concurrence of the Lord Chief Justice.

(6) The Lord Chancellor may also, with the concurrence of the Lord Chief Justice, remove such a person from his office on account of inability to perform the duties of his office.

(7) A person appointed to an office listed in column 1 of Part III of Schedule 2 shall hold that office during Her Majesty's pleasure.

(8) It is for the Lord Chancellor to recommend to Her Majesty the exercise of any power under subsection (7).

93. Status of Officers for Purposes of Salary and Pension

(1) Subject to subsection (2), any person who holds qualifying judicial office, within the meaning of the Judicial Pensions and Retirement Act 1993.

(2) Subsection (1), so far as it relates to pension, shall not apply to a person holding an office within paragraph 1 of Schedule 1 to the Judicial Pensions Act 1981 (pensions of certain judicial officers).

Selected Legislation

95. Property Held by Officers

Any property held in his official capacity by a person holding an office listed in column 1 of Part II of Schedule 2 or by the Official Solicitor shall, on his dying or ceasing to hold office, vest in the person appointed to succeed him without any conveyance, assignment or transfer.

Central Office and Accountant General

96. Central Office

(1) The Central Office of the Supreme Court shall perform such business as the Lord Chief Justice may, with the concurrence of the Lord Chancellor, direct.
(2) Subject to any direction under subsection (1), the Central Office shall perform such business as it performed immediately before the commencement of this Act.
(3) The Lord Chief Justice may nominate a judicial office holder (as defined in section 109(4) of the Constitutional Reform Act 2005) to exercise his functions under this section.

97. Accountant General

(1) There shall continue to be an Accountant General of, and an accounting department for, the Supreme Court.
(2) The Lord Chancellor shall appoint such person as he thinks fit to the office in the Supreme Court of Accountant General of the Supreme Court and the person so appointed shall hold and vacate office in accordance with the terms of his appointment.
(3) The Accountant General shall be paid such salary or fees as the Lord Chancellor determines with the consent of the Treasury.
(4) If one person holds office both as the Accountant General and as the Public Trustee then, if he ceases to be the Public Trustee, he shall also cease to be the Accountant General unless the Lord Chancellor otherwise directs.
(5) If a vacancy occurs in the office of Accountant General or the person appointed to hold the office is for any reason unable to act for any period such person as the Lord Chancellor appoints as deputy in that office shall, during the vacancy or that period, perform the functions of that office (and any property vested in the Accountant General may accordingly be dealt with by the deputy in all respects as if it were vested in him instead).

Judges' Clerks and Secretaries

98. Judges' Clerks and Secretaries

(1) A clerk and a secretary shall be attached to each of the following judges of the Supreme Court, namely the Lord Chief Justice, the Master of the Rolls, the President of the Queen's Bench Division, the President of the Family Division and the Chancellor of the High Court.
(2) A clerk shall be attached to each of the following judges of the Supreme Court, namely the Lords Justices of Appeal and the puisne judges of the High Court.
(3) Any clerk or secretary attached as mentioned in subsection (1) or (2)—
  (a) shall be appointed by the Lord Chancellor; and
  (b) if not already employed in the civil service of the State shall be deemed for all purposes to be so employed.
(4) If at any time it appears to any of the judges mentioned in subsection (1) desirable that there should be attached to him a legal secretary (that is to say a secretary with legal qualifications) in addition to the secretary provided for by that subsection, he may, with the concurrence of the Lord Chancellor, appoint a person who has a general qualification (within the meaning of section 71 of the Courts and Legal Services Act 1990) as his legal secretary.
(5) An appointment under subsection (4) may be on either a full-time or a part-time basis; and a person appointed by a judge as his legal secretary shall, except as regards remuneration, hold and vacate that office in accordance with such terms as the judge may, with the concurrence of the Lord Chancellor, determine when making the appointment.
(6) A person appointed under subsection (4)—
  (a) shall not be treated as employed in the civil service of the State by reason only of that appointment; and

(b) if the Lord Chancellor so determines in his case, shall be paid out of money provided by Parliament such remuneration as the Lord Chancellor may, with the concurrence of the Minister for the Civil Service, determine.

District Registries and District Registrars

99. District Registries

(1) The Lord Chancellor may, after consulting the Lord Chief Justice, by order direct that there shall be district registries of the High Court at such places and for such districts as are specified in the order.
(2) Any order under this section shall be made by statutory instrument, which shall be laid before Parliament after being made.
(3) The Lord Chief Justice may nominate a judicial office holder (as defined in section 109(4) of the Constitutional Reform Act 2005) to exercise his functions under this section.

100. District Registrars

(1) Subject to subsection (2), for each district registry the Lord Chancellor shall appoint a person who is a district judge for a county court district, appointed under section 6 of the County Courts Act 1984, as a district judge of the High Court.
(2) The Lord Chancellor may, if he thinks fit, appoint two or more persons who are district judges for county court districts to execute jointly the office of district judge in any district registry.
(3) Where joint district judges are appointed under subsection (2), the Lord Chancellor may—
   (a) give directions with respect to the division between them of the duties of the office of district registrar; and
   (b) as he thinks fit, on the death, resignation or removal of one of them, either appoint in place of that person another person to be joint district judge, or give directions that the continuing district judge shall act as sole district judge or (as the case may be) that the continuing district judge shall execute jointly the office of district judge.
(4) Subsections (4) to (6) of section 92 shall apply in relation to a person appointed as a district judge as they apply in relation to a person appointed to an office to which subsection (1) of that section applies, except that he shall vacate his office as district judge at such time as, for any cause whatever, he vacates his office as district judge for a county court district.

101. Power of One District Registrar to Act for Another

(1) A district judge of any registry shall be capable of acting in any other district registry for a district judge of that registry; and, where a district judge is so acting, the district judge of the other registry may divide the duties of his office as he thinks fit between himself and the district judge acting for him.

102. Deputy District Registrars

(1) If it appears to the Lord Chancellor that it is expedient to do so in order to facilitate the disposal of business in the High Court, he may appoint a person to be a deputy district judge in any district registry during such period or on such occasions as the Lord Chancellor thinks fit.
(2) Subject to subsection (3), a person shall not be qualified for appointment as a deputy district judge unless he is, or is qualified for appointment as, a district judge for a county court district.
(3) A person may be appointed as a deputy district judge if he would, but for his age, be qualified for appointment as a district judge for a county court district and he has previously held the office of district judge for a county court district; but no appointment by virtue of this subsection shall be such as to extend beyond the day on which the person in question attains the age of seventy-five years.
(4) A deputy district judge, while acting under this section, shall have the same jurisdiction as the district judge.
(5) Subsection (6) of section 91 applies in relation to a deputy district judge appointed under this section as it applies in relation to a person appointed under that section.

103. Assistant District Registrars

(1) The Lord Chancellor may appoint assistant district judges of the High Court in aid of district judges.
(2) A person shall not be qualified for appointment as an assistant district judge unless he is a district judge for a county court district or an assistant district judge for a county court district.
(3) An assistant district judge of any district registry shall be capable of discharging any of the functions of the district judge, and in so doing shall have the same jurisdiction as the district judge.
(4) A district judge of any registry where there is an assistant district judge may divide the duties of his office as he thinks fit between himself and the assistant district judge.
(5) Subsections (4) to (6) of section 92 shall apply in relation to a person appointed as an assistant district judge as they apply in relation to a person appointed to an office to which subsection (1) of that section applies, except that he shall vacate his office as assistant district judge at such time as, for any cause whatever, he vacates his office as district judge for a county court district or, as the case may be, assistant district judge for a county court district (unless in the latter case he is thereupon appointed a district judge for a county court district).

PART VI MISCELLANEOUS AND SUPPLEMENTARY

Miscellaneous Provisions

129. Lords Commissioners to Represent Lord Chancellor When Great Seal in Commission

When the Great Seal is in commission, the Lords Commissioners shall represent the Lord Chancellor for the purposes of this Act; but the powers vested in him by this Act in relation to—
(a) the appointment of officers, and
(b) any act for which the concurrence or presence of the Lord Chancellor is required by this Act,
may be exercised by the senior Lord Commissioner for the time being.

131. Conveyancing Counsel of Supreme Court

(1) The conveyancing counsel of the Supreme Court shall be persons who have a 10 year High Court qualification, within the meaning of section 71 of the Courts and Legal Services Act 1990 who have practised as such for not less than ten years.
(2) The conveyancing counsel of the court shall be not more than six, nor less than three, in number, and shall be appointed by the Lord Chancellor with the concurrence of the Lord Chief Justice.
(3) The Lord Chief Justice may nominate a judicial office holder (as defined in section 109(4) of the Constitutional Reform Act 2005) to exercise his functions under this section.

132. Proof of Documents Bearing Seal or Stamp of Supreme Court or Any Office Thereof

Every document purporting to be sealed or stamped with the seal or stamp of the Supreme Court or of any office of the Supreme Court shall be received in evidence in all parts of the United Kingdom without further proof.

133. Enrolment and Engrossment of Instruments

(1) The Master of the Rolls may make regulations for authorising and regulating the enrolment or filing of instruments in the Supreme Court, and for prescribing the form in which certificates of enrolment or filing are to be issued.
(2) Regulations under subsection (1) shall not affect the operation of any enactment requiring or authorising the enrolment of any instrument in the Supreme Court or prescribing the manner in which any instrument is to be enrolled there.
(3) Any instrument which is required or authorised by or under this or any other Act to be enrolled or engrossed in the Supreme Court shall be deemed to have been duly enrolled or engrossed if it is written on material authorised or required by regulations under subsection (1) and has been filed or otherwise preserved in accordance with regulations under that subsection.

(4) The Lord Chancellor may, with the concurrence of the Master of the Rolls and of the Treasury, make regulations prescribing the fees to be paid on the enrolment or filing of any instrument in the Supreme Court, including any additional fees payable on the enrolment or filing of any instrument out of time.

(5) Any regulations under this section shall be made by statutory instrument, which shall be laid before Parliament after being made; and the Statutory Instruments Act 1946 shall apply to a statutory instrument containing regulations under subsection (1) in like manner as if the regulations had been made by a Minister of the Crown.

134. Powers of Attorney Deposited before October 1971

(1) This section applies to any instrument creating, or verifying the execution of, a power of attorney which was deposited in the Central Office of the Supreme Court before 1st October 1971.

(2) A separate file of such instruments shall continue to be kept and, subject to payment of any fee prescribed by an order under section 92 of the Courts Act 2003 (fees)—
   (a) any person may search that file, and may inspect any such instrument; and
   (b) an office copy of any such instrument shall be issued to any person on request.

(3) A document purporting to be an office copy of any such instrument shall, in any part of the United Kingdom, without further proof be sufficient evidence of the contents of the instrument and of its having been deposited as mentioned in subsection (1).

135. Bonds Given under Order of Court

(1) A bond to be given by any person under or for the purposes of any order of the High Court or the civil division of the Court of Appeal shall be given in such form and to such officer of the court as may be prescribed and, if the court so requires, with one or more sureties.

(2) An officer of the court to whom a bond is given in accordance with subsection (1) shall as such have power to enforce it or to assign it, pursuant to an order of the court under subsection (4), to some other person.

(3) Where by rules of court made for the purposes of this section another officer is at any time substituted for the officer previously prescribed as the officer to whom bonds of any class are to be given, the rules may provide that bonds of that class given before the rules come into operation shall have effect as if references in the bonds to the officer previously prescribed were references to the substituted officer.

(4) Where it appears to the court that the condition of a bond given in accordance with subsection (1) has been broken, the court may, on an application in that behalf, order the bond to be assigned to such person as may be specified in the order.

(5) A person to whom a bond is ordered to be assigned under subsection (4) shall be entitled by virtue of the order to sue on the bond in his own name as if it had been originally given to him, and to recover on it as trustee for all persons interested the full amount recoverable in respect of the breach of condition.

136. Production of Documents Filed in, or in Custody of, Supreme Court

(1) Rules may be made in accordance with Part 1 of Schedule 1 to the Constitutional Reform Act 2005 for providing that, in any case where a document filed in, or in the custody of, any office of the Supreme Court is required to be produced to any court or tribunal (including an umpire or arbitrator) sitting elsewhere than at the Royal Courts of Justice—
   (a) it shall not be necessary for any officer, whether served with a subpoena in that behalf or not, to attend for the purpose of producing the document; but
   (b) the document may be produced to the court or tribunal by sending it to the court or tribunal, in the manner prescribed in the rules, together with a certificate, in the form so prescribed, to the effect that the document has been filed in, or is in the custody of, the office;

   and any such certificate shall be prima facie evidence of the facts stated in it.

(2) Rules under this section may contain—
   (a) provisions for securing the safe custody and return to the proper office of the Supreme Court of any document sent to a court or tribunal in pursuance of the rules; and

(b) such incidental and supplementary provisions as appear to the person making the rules to be necessary or expedient.

137. Money Paid into Court under Enactment Subsequently Repealed

Where in pursuance of any enactment, whenever passed, any money has (before or after the commencement of this Act) been paid—

(a) into the Bank of England in the name of the Accountant General of the Supreme Court; or

(b) into the Supreme Court, then, if that enactment has been or is subsequently repealed—

(i) the Accountant General may continue to deal with the money; and

(ii) any powers of the High Court with respect to the money shall continue to be exercisable,

in all respects as if that enactment had not been repealed.

139. Attachment of National Savings Bank Deposits

(1) In section 27 of the Crown Proceedings Act 1947 (attachment of moneys payable by the Crown)—

(a) in subsection (1), paragraph (c) of the proviso (which precludes the making of orders under that subsection by the High Court or a county court in respect of money payable on account of a deposit in the National Savings Bank) shall cease to have effect; and

(b) after subsection (2) there shall be added—

'(3) In their application to England and Wales the preceding provisions of this section shall have effect subject to any order for the time being in force under section 139(2) of the Supreme Court Act 1981.'.

(2) The Lord Chancellor may by order direct that section 27(1) and (2) of the Crown Proceedings Act 1947 (attachment of moneys payable by the Crown) shall not apply in relation to any money payable by the Crown to any person on account of—

(a) any deposit in the National Savings Bank; or

(b) a deposit in that Bank of any description specified in the order.

(3) Any order under subsection (2) shall be made by statutory instrument subject to annulment in pursuance of a resolution of either House of Parliament.

(4) Without prejudice to section 153(4), this section extends to England and Wales only.

140. Enforcement of Fines and Forfeited Recognisances

(1) Payment of a fine imposed, or sum due under a recognisance forfeited, by the High Court or the civil division of the Court of Appeal may be enforced upon the order of the court—

(a) in like manner as a judgment of the High Court for the payment of money; or

(b) in like manner as a fine imposed by the Crown Court.

(2) Where payment of a fine or other sum falls to be enforced as mentioned in paragraph (a) of subsection (1) upon an order of the High Court or the civil division of the Court of Appeal under that subsection—

(a) the court shall, if the fine or other sum is not paid in full forthwith or within such time as the court may allow, certify to Her Majesty's Remembrancer the sum payable; and

(b) Her Majesty's Remembrancer shall thereupon proceed to enforce payment of that sum as if it were due to him as a judgment debt.

(3) Where payment of a fine or other sum falls to be enforced as mentioned in paragraph (b) of subsection (1) upon an order of the High Court or the civil division of the Court of Appeal under that subsection, the provisions of sections 139 and 140 of the Powers of Criminal Courts (Sentencing) Act 2000 shall apply to that fine or other sum as they apply to a fine imposed by the Crown Court.

(4) Where payment of a fine or other sum has become enforceable by Her Majesty's Remembrancer by virtue of this section or section 16 of the Contempt of Court Act 1981, any payment received by him in respect of that fine or other sum shall be dealt with by him in such manner as the Lord Chancellor may direct.

(5) In this section, and in sections 31 and 32 of the Powers of Criminal Courts Act 1973 as extended by this section, 'fine' includes a penalty imposed in civil proceedings.

151. Interpretation of This Act, and Rules of Construction for Other Acts and Documents

(1) In this Act, unless the context otherwise requires

'action' means any civil proceedings commenced by writ or in any other manner prescribed by rules of court;

'appeal', in the context of appeals to the civil division of the Court of Appeal, includes—

(a) an application for a new trial, and

(b) an application to set aside a verdict, finding or judgment in any cause or matter in the High Court which has been tried, or in which any issue has been tried, by a jury;

'arbitration agreement' has the same meaning as it has in Part I of the Arbitration Act 1996;

'cause' means any action or any criminal proceedings;

'Division', where it appears with a capital letter, means a division of the High Court;

'judgment' includes a decree;

'jurisdiction' includes powers;

'matter' means any proceedings in court not in a cause;

'party', in relation to any proceedings, includes any person who pursuant to or by virtue of rules of court or any other statutory provision has been served with notice of, or has intervened in, those proceedings;

'prescribed' means—

(a) except in relation to fees, prescribed by rules of court;

'senior judge', where the reference is to the senior judge of a Division, means the president of that Division;

'solicitor' means a solicitor of the Supreme Court;

'statutory provision' means any enactment, whenever passed, or any provision contained in subordinate legislation (as defined in section 21(1) of the Interpretation Act 1978), whenever made;

'this or any other Act' includes an Act passed after this Act.

(2) Section 128 contains definitions of expressions used in Part V and in the other provisions of this Act relating to probate causes and matters.

(3) Any reference in this Act to rules of court under section 84 includes a reference to rules of court in relation to the Supreme Court under any provision of this or any other Act which confers on the Civil Procedure Rule Committee or the Crown Court Rule Committee power to make rules of court.

(4) Except where the context otherwise requires, in this or any other Act—

'Criminal Appeal Rules' means rules of court made by the Crown Court Rule Committee in relation to the criminal division of the Court of Appeal;

'Crown Court Rules' means rules of court made by the Crown Court Rule Committee in relation to the Crown Court;

'divisional court' (with or without capital letters) means a divisional court constituted under section 66;

'judge of the Supreme Court' means—

(a) a judge of the Court of Appeal other than an ex-officio judge within paragraph (b) or (c) of section 2(2), or

(b) a judge of the High Court,

and accordingly does not include, as such, a judge of the Crown Court;

'official referees' business' has the meaning given by section 68(6).

(5) The provisions of Schedule 4 (construction of references to superseded courts and officers) shall have effect.

153. Citation, Commencement and Extent

(1) This Act may be cited as the Supreme Court Act 1981.

(2) This Act, except the provisions mentioned in subsection (3), shall come into force on 1st January 1982; and references to the commencement of this Act shall be construed as references to the beginning of that day.

(3) Sections 72, 143 . . . and this section shall come into force on the passing of this Act.

(4) In this Act—

. . .

(c) the following provisions extend to Scotland and Northern Ireland, namely—
section 36;
sections 132 and 134(3) . . .;
but, save as aforesaid, the provisions of this Act, other than those mentioned in subsection (5), extend to England and Wales only.

(5) The provisions of this Act whose extent is not restricted by subsection (4) are—
section 27; . . .
section 151(1); . . .
this section . . .

Section 61(1)(3)

SCHEDULE 1 DISTRIBUTION OF BUSINESS IN HIGH COURT

Chancery Division

1. To the Chancery Division are assigned all causes and matters relating to—
   (a) the sale, exchange or partition of land, or the raising of charges on land;
   (b) the redemption or foreclosure of mortgages;
   (c) the execution of trusts;
   (d) the administration of the estates of deceased persons;
   (e) bankruptcy;
   (f) the dissolution of partnerships or the taking of partnership or other accounts;
   (g) the rectification, setting aside or cancellation of deeds or other instruments in writing;
   (h) probate business, other than non-contentious or common form business;
   (i) patents, trade marks, registered designs, copyright or design right;
   (j) the appointment of a guardian of a minor's estate,

   and all causes and matters involving the exercise of the High Court's jurisdiction under the enactments relating to companies.

Queen's Bench Division

2. To the Queen's Bench Division are assigned—
   (a) applications for writs of habeas corpus, except applications made by a parent or guardian of a minor for such a writ concerning the custody of the minor;
   (b) applications for judicial review;
   (ba) all control order proceedings (within the meaning of the Prevention of Terrorism Act 2005);
   (c) all causes and matters involving the exercise of the High Court's Admiralty jurisdiction or its jurisdiction as a prize court; and
   (d) all causes and matters entered in the commercial list.

Family Division

3. To the Family Division are assigned—
   (a) all matrimonial causes and matters (whether at first instance or on appeal);
   (b) all causes and matters (whether at first instance or on appeal) relating to—
      (i) legitimacy;
      (ii) the exercise of the inherent jurisdiction of the High Court with respect to minors, the maintenance of minors and any proceedings under the Children Act 1989. except proceedings solely for the appointment of a guardian of a minor's estate;
      (iii) adoption;
      (iv) non-contentious or common form probate business;
   (c) applications for consent to the marriage of a minor or for a declaration under section 27B(5) of the Marriage Act 1949;
   (d) proceedings on appeal under section 13 of the Administration of Justice Act 1960 from an order or decision made under section 63(3) of the Magistrates' Courts Act 1980 to enforce an order of a magistrates' court made in matrimonial proceedings or proceedings

under Part IV of the Family Law Act 1996 or with respect to the guardianship of a minor.

(e) applications under Part III of the Family Law Act 1986;

(f) all proceedings under:—
   (i) the Part IV of the Family Law Act 1996;
   (ii) the Child Abduction and Custody Act 1985;
   (iii) the Family Law Act 1986;
   (iv) section 30 of the Human Fertilisation and Embryology Act 1990;
   (v) Council Regulation (EC) No 2201/2003 of 27th November 2003 concerning jurisdiction and the recognition and enforcement of judgments in matrimonial matters and matters of parental responsibility, so far as that Regulation relates to jurisdiction, recognition and enforcement in parental responsibility matters;

(g) all proceedings for the purpose of enforcing an order made in any proceedings of a type described in this paragraph;

(h) all proceedings under the Child Support Act 1991;

(i) all proceedings under sections 6 and 8 of the Gender Recognition Act 2004.

Sections 88 to 95

SCHEDULE 2 LIST OF OFFICES IN SUPREME COURT FOR PURPOSES OF PART IV

Part I

1. **Office**	2. **Persons qualified**
2. Official Solicitor.	2. A person who has a 10 year general qualification.

Part II

3. Master, Queen's Bench Division.	3. A person who has a 7 year general qualification.
4. Queen's Coroner and Attorney and Master of the Crown Office and Registrar of Criminal Appeals.	4. A person who has a 10 year general qualification.
5. Admiralty Registrar.	5. A person who has a 7 year general qualification.
6. Master, Chancery Division.	6. A person who has a 7 year general qualification.
7. Registrar in Bankruptcy of the High Court.	7. A person who has a 7 year general qualification.
8. Taxing Master of the Supreme Court.	8. A person who has a 7 year general qualification.
9. District judge of the principal registry of the Family Division.	9.—(1) A person who has a 7 year general qualification. (2) A district probate registrar who either— (a) is of at least 5 years' standing; or (b) has, during so much of the 10 years immediately preceding his appointment as he has not been a district probate registrar, served as a civil servant in the principal registry or a district probate registry. (3) A civil servant who has served at least 10 years in the principal registry or a district probate registry.
11. Master of the Court of Protection.	11. A person who has a 7 year general qualification.

Part III

12. District probate registrar.	12.—(1) A person who has a 5 year general qualification. (2) A civil servant who has served at least 5 years in the principal registry of the Family Division or a district probate registry.

NOTES ON TEXT

The text printed above incorporates the following amendments:

s. 1 amended by Constitutional Reform Act 2005, s. 7(5), and sch. 18, part 2 (in force by SI 2006/1014);

s. 2 amended by: (a) Maximum Number of Judges Order 2002 (SI 2002/2837), art. 2; (b) Courts Act 2003, s. 63 (in force by SI 2003/3345); (c) Constitutional Reform Act 2005, sch. 4, para. 115, and sch. 18, part 2 (in force by SI 2005/2505 and SI 2006/1014);

s. 3 amended by Constitutional Reform Act 2005, sch. 4, para. 116 (in force by SI 2005/2505 and SI 2006/1014);

s. 4 amended by: (a) Courts and Legal Services Act 1990, s. 72(6) (in force by s. 124(2) of that Act); (b) Access to Justice Act 1999, s. 69(2) (in force by s. 108(3) of that Act); (c) Maximum Number of Judges Order 2003 (SI 2003/778); (d) Constitutional Reform Act 2005, sch. 4, para. 117, and sch. 18, part 2 (in force by SI 2005/2505 and SI 2006/1014);

s. 5 amended by: (a) Courts and Legal Services Act 1990, sch. 17, para. 12 (in force by SI 1991/608); (b) Access to Justice Act 1999, s. 69(3) (in force by s. 108(3) of that Act); (c) Constitutional Reform Act 2005, sch. 4, para. 118 (in force by SI 2005/2505 and SI 2006/1014);

s. 6 amended by Constitutional Reform Act 2005, sch. 4, para. 119 (in force by SI 2006/1014);

s. 7 amended by Constitutional Reform Act 2005, sch. 4, para. 120, and sch. 18, part 2 (in force by SI 2005/2505 and SI 2006/1014);

s. 9(1) amended by: (a) Administration of Justice Act 1982, s. 58 (in force by s. 76(11) of that Act); (b) Criminal Justice and Public Order Act 1994, s. 52(1) and (2) (in force by SI 1994/3258);

s. 9(1A) inserted by Judicial Pensions and Retirement Act 1993, sch. 6, para. 5 (in force by SI 1995/631);

s. 9(2) amended by: (a) Criminal Justice and Public Order Act 1994, s. 52(1) and (3) (in force by SI 1994/3258); (b) Constitutional Reform Act 2005, sch. 4, para. 121(1) and (2) (in force by SI 2006/1014);

s. 9(2A) to (2D) inserted by Constitutional Reform Act 2005, sch. 4, para. 121(1) and (3) (in force by SI 2006/1014);

s. 9(4) amended by Constitutional Reform Act 2005, sch. 4, para. 121(1) and (4) (in force by SI 2006/1014);

s. 9(4A) inserted by Judicial Pensions and Retirement Act 1993, sch. 6, para. 5 (in force by SI 1995/631);

s. 9(5) amended by Criminal Justice and Public Order Act 1994, s. 52(1) and (4) (in force by SI 1994/3258);

s. 9(6) amended by Judicial Pensions and Retirement Act 1993, sch. 6, para. 5 (in force by SI 1995/631);

s. 9(6A) inserted by Criminal Justice and Public Order Act 1994, s. 52(1) and (5) (in force by SI 1994/3258); amended by Courts Act 2003, sch. 8, para. 260 (in force by SI 2005/910);

s. 9(7) repealed by Judicial Pensions and Retirement Act 1993, sch. 9 (in force by SI 1995/631);

s. 9(8) inserted by Constitutional Reform Act 2005, sch. 4, para. 121(1) and (5) (in force by SI 2006/1014);

s. 10 amended by: (a) Courts and Legal Services Act 1990, s. 71(1) (in force by SI 1990/2484); (b) Constitutional Reform Act 2005, sch. 4, para. 122 (in force by SI 2005/2505 and SI 2006/1014);

s. 11 amended by: (a) Judicial Pensions and Retirement Act 1993, sch. 6, para. 4 (in force by SI 1995/631); (b) Constitutional Reform Act 2005, sch. 4, para. 123, and sch. 18, part 2 (in force by SI 2005/2505 and SI 2006/1014);
s. 12(1) amended by Constitutional Reform Act 2005, sch. 4, para. 124, and sch. 18, part 2 (in force by SI 2006/1014);
s. 12(4) repealed by Courts and Legal Services Act 1990, s. 84 and sch. 20 (in force by SI 1990/2484);
s. 12(7) amended by Judicial Pensions and Retirement Act 1993, sch. 8, para. 15(1) (in force by SI 1995/631);
s. 13 amended by Constitutional Reform Act 2005, sch. 4, para. 125 (in force by SI 2005/2505);
s. 16(1) amended by Access to Justice Act 1999 (Destination of Appeals) Order 2000 (SI 2000/1071), art. 7;
s. 18(1)(e), (f)and (h) and (2) repealed and (1A) and (1B) inserted by Courts and Legal Services Act 1990, s. 7(1), (2) and (3) and sch. 20 (in force by SI 1993/2132); s. 18(1A) and (1B) repealed by Access to Justice Act 1999, sch. 15, part III (in force by s. 108(3) of that Act);
s. 18(1)(g) substituted by Arbitration Act 1996, sch. 3, para. 37(1) and (2) (in force by SI 1996/3146, art. 3);
s. 20 amended by: (a) Merchant Shipping (Salvage and Pollution) Act 1994, sch. 2, para. 6 (in force by SI 1994/2971); (b) Merchant Shipping Act 1995, sch. 13, para. 59(1) and (2); (c) Merchant Shipping and Maritime Security Act 1997, sch. 6, para. 2 (in force by SI 1997/1539); (i) was not used when lettering the paragraphs in s. 20(2) when it was originally enacted;
s. 24 amended by Merchant Shipping Act 1995, sch. 13, para. 59(1) and (3);
s. 26(b) amended by Family Law Act 1986, sch. 1, para. 25 and sch. 2 (in force by SI 1988/375);
s. 28(4) inserted by Access to Justice Act 1999, sch. 4, paras 21 and 22 (in force by SI 2001/916);
s. 28A inserted by Statute Law (Repeals) Act 1993, sch. 2, para. 9; substituted by Access to Justice Act 1999, s. 61 (in force by s. 108(3) of that Act);
s. 29 amended by: (a) Access to Justice Act 1999, sch. 4, paras 21 and 23 (in force by SI 2001/916); (b) Armed Forces Act 2001, s. 23 (in force by SI 2002/345); (c) Civil Procedure (Modification of Supreme Court Act 1981) Order 2004 (SI 2004/1033), arts 2 and 3;
s. 31 amended by Civil Procedure (Modification of Supreme Court Act 1981) Order 2004 (SI 2004/1033), arts 2 and 4;
s. 32A inserted by Administration of Justice Act 1982, s. 6(1) (in force by SI 1983/236);
s. 33(2) amended by Civil Procedure (Modification of Enactments) Order 1998 (SI 1998/2940), art. 5(a);
s. 34 amended by Civil Procedure (Modification of Enactments) Order 1998 (SI 1998/2940), art. 5(b);
s. 35(5) amended by Administration of Justice Act 1982, s. 6(2) (in force by SI 1983/236);
s. 35A inserted by Administration of Justice Act 1982, s. 15(1) and sch. 1 (in force by SI 1983/236, art. 2);
s. 36(4) amended by Courts and Legal Services Act 1990, sch. 17, para. 13 (in force by SI 1991/608);
s. 40 amended by Financial Services and Markets Act 2000 (Consequential Amendments and Repeals) Order 2001 (SI 2001/3649), art. 290;
s. 40A inserted by Administration of Justice Act 1982, s. 55(1) and sch. 4, part I (in force by s. 76(11) of that Act); s. 40A(1) substituted and (1A) and (1B) inserted by Administration of Justice Act 1985, s. 52(1) and (2) (in force by s. 69(4) of that Act); s. 40A(1) and (1A) amended by: (a) Financial Services and Markets Act 2000 (Consequential Amendments and Repeals) Order 2001 (SI 2001/3649), art. 291(1), (2) and (3); (b) Civil Procedure (Modification of Enactments) Order 2002 (SI 2002/439), art. 6; s. 40A(2) amended by (a) Administration of Justice Act 1985, s. 52(1) and (3) (in force by s. 69(4) of that Act); (b) Companies Consolidation (Consequential Provisions) Act 1985, sch. 2; (c) Insolvency Act 1985, sch. 8, para. 35 (in force by SI 1986/1924, art. 2); (d) Insolvency Act 1986, sch. 14 (in force by s. 443 of that Act and SI 1986/1924, art. 3); s. 40A(3) amended by Financial Services and Markets Act 2000 (Consequential Amendments and Repeals) Order 2001 (SI 2001/3649), art. 291(1) and (4); s. 40A(4) amended by: (a) Administration of Justice Act 1985, s. 52(1) and (4) and sch. 8, part II (in force by s. 69(4) of that Act); (b)

Financial Services and Markets Act 2000 (Consequential Amendments and Repeals) Order 2001 (SI 2001/3649), art. 291(1) and (5);

s. 42 amended by Prosecution of Offences Act 1985, s. 24 (in force by SI 1985/1849);

s. 43A inserted by Courts and Legal Services Act 1990, s. 100 (in force by SI 1991/608);

s. 47 repealed by Powers of Criminal Courts (Sentencing) Act 2000, sch. 12, part I;

s. 51 substituted by Courts and Legal Services Act 1990, s. 4(1) (in force by SI 1991/1883); amended by Access to Justice Act 1999, s. 31 (in force by SI 2003/1241);

s. 54(2) to (4) substituted and (4A) inserted by Access to Justice Act 1999, s. 59 (in force by s. 108(3) of that Act);

s. 56A inserted by Criminal Justice and Public Order Act 1994, s. 52(1), (6) and (8) (in force by SI 1994/3258); repealed by Courts Act 2003, s. 67 and sch. 10 (in force by SI 2003/3345);

s. 57 amended by Constitutional Reform Act 2005, sch. 4, para. 128 (in force by SI 2006/1014);

s. 58 substituted by Access to Justice Act 1999, s. 60 (in force by s. 108(3) of that Act);

s. 61 amended by Constitutional Reform Act 2005, sch. 4, para. 129 (in force by SI 2006/1014);

s. 63 amended by Constitutional Reform Act 2005, sch. 4, para. 130 (in force by SI 2006/1014);

s. 68 amended by: (a) Administration of Justice Act 1982, s. 59 (in force by s. 76(11) of that Act); (b) Civil Procedure Act 1997, sch. 2, para. 1(1) and (3) (in force by SI 1999/1009); (c) Constitutional Reform Act 2005, sch. 4, para. 131 (in force by SI 2006/1014);

s. 71 amended by Constitutional Reform Act 2005, sch. 4, para. 132 (in force by SI 2006/1014);

s. 72(5) amended by Copyright, Designs and Patents Act 1988, sch. 7, para. 28(1) and (2) (in force by SI 1989/816);

s. 83 repealed by Access to Justice Act 1999, sch. 15, part II (in force by SI 2000/1920, art. 2(c));

s. 85 repealed by Civil Procedure Act 1997, sch. 2, para. 1(1) and (5) (in force by SI 1999/1009);

s. 89 amended by: (a) Courts and Legal Services Act 1990, sch. 18, para. 37 (in force by SI 1990/2484); (b) Constitutional Reform Act 2005, sch. 3, para. 3 (partially in force by SI 2006/1014);

s. 89(5), (6) and (7) repealed by Statute Law (Repeals) Act 1989, sch. 1, part I, group 5;

s. 90(3A) and (3B) inserted by Courts and Legal Services Act 1990, sch. 18, para. 39 (in force by SI 1990/2484);

s. 91 amended by: (a) Judicial Pensions and Retirement Act 1993, sch. 6, para. 15 (in force by SI 1995/631); (b) Constitutional Reform Act 2005, sch. 4, para. 139, and sch. 18, part 2 (in force by SI 2006/1014);

s. 91(5) repealed by Judicial Pensions and Retirement Act 1993, sch. 9 (in force by SI 1995/631);

s. 92 amended by: (a) Courts and Legal Services Act 1990, s. 77 (in force by SI 1990/2484); (b) Judicial Pensions and Retirement Act 1993, sch. 6, para. 14 and sch. 9 (in force by SI 1995/631); the 1993 Act repealed s. 92(2C); (c) Courts Act 2003, s. 89(1) and sch. 10 (in force by SI 2005/910); (d) Constitutional Reform Act 2005, sch. 4, para. 140 (in force by SI 2006/1014);

s. 93(1) amended by Judicial Pensions and Retirement Act 1993, sch. 8, para. 15(2) (in force by SI 1995/631);

s. 94 repealed by Courts and Legal Services Act 1990, sch. 20 (in force by SI 1990/2484);

s. 96 amended by Constitutional Reform Act 2005, sch. 4, para. 141 (in force by SI 2006/1014);

s. 97 amended by Public Trustee and Administration of Funds Act 1986, sch. 1, para. 3 (in force by SI 1986/2261);

s. 98(1) amended by Constitutional Reform Act 2005, sch. 4, para. 142 (in force by SI 2005/2505);

s. 98(4) amended by Courts and Legal Services Act 1990, sch. 10, para. 47 (in force by SI 1990/2484);

s. 99 amended by Constitutional Reform Act 2005, sch. 4, para. 143 (in force by SI 2006/1014);

ss. 100 to 103 amended by Courts and Legal Services Act 1990, sch. 18, para. 40 and sch. 20 (in force by SI 1990/2484);

s. 102(3) amended by Judicial Pensions and Retirement Act 1993, sch. 6, para. 16 (in force by SI 1995/631);

s. 102(5) substituted by Judicial Pensions and Retirement Act 1993, sch. 8, para. 15(3) (in force by SI 1995/631);

s. 130 repealed by Courts Act 2003, sch. 8, para. 263, and sch. 10 (in force by SI 2004/3123);

s. 131 amended by: (a) Courts and Legal Services Act 1990, sch. 10, para. 48 (in force by SI 1990/2484); (b) Constitutional Reform Act 2005, sch. 4, para. 145 (in force by SI 2006/1014);
s. 134 amended by Courts Act 2003, sch. 8, para. 262 (in force by SI 2005/910);
s. 136 amended by Constitutional Reform Act 2005, sch. 1, para. 13, and sch. 18, part 1 (in force by SI 2006/1014);
s. 138 repealed by Courts Act 2003, sch. 8, para. 264, and sch. 10 (in force by SI 2004/401);
ss. 138A and 138B inserted by Statute Law (Repeals) Act 1989, sch. 2, para. 4; repealed by Courts Act 2003, sch. 8, para. 264, and sch. 10 (in force by SI 2004/401);
s. 140(3) amended by Powers of Criminal Courts (Sentencing) Act 2000, sch. 9, para. 88;
s. 141 repealed by Statute Law (Repeals) Act 2004, sch. 1, part 1, group 4;
s. 143 repealed by Administration of Justice Act 1982, sch. 9 (in force by s. 76(11) of that Act);
s. 144 repealed by Mental Health Act 1983, sch. 6;
s. 148 repealed by Arbitration Act 1996, sch. 4 (in force by SI 1996/3146, art. 3);
s. 149 repealed by County Courts Act 1984, sch. 4;
s. 151(1) amended by: (a) Courts and Legal Services Act 1990, sch. 18, para. 41 (in force by SI 1991/608); (b) Arbitration Act 1996, sch. 3, para. 37(1) and (3) (in force by SI 1996/3146, art. 3); (c) Courts Act 2003, sch. 8, para. 265, and sch. 10 (in force by SI 2005/910); (d) Constitutional Reform Act 2005, para. 146 (in force by SI 2006/1014);
s. 151(3) amended by Civil Procedure Act 1997, sch. 2, para. 1(1) and (7)(a) (in force by SI 1999/1009);
s. 151(4) amended by: (a) Civil Procedure Act 1997, sch. 2, para. 1(1) and (7)(b) (in force by SI 1999/1009); (b) Courts Act 2003 (Consequential Amendments) Order 2004 (SI 2004/2035), sch., para. 18;
sch. 1, para. 1, amended by Copyright, Designs and Patents Act 1988, sch. 7, para. 28(1) and (3) (in force by SI 1989/816);
sch. 1, para. 2, amended by Prevention of Terrorism Act 2005, sch., para. 10;
sch. 1, para. 3, amended by: (a) Marriage (Prohibited Degrees of Relationship) Act 1986, s. 5 (in force by SI 1986/1343); (b) Family Law Act 1986, sch. 1, para. 26 (in force by SI 1988/375); (c) Family Law Reform Act 1987, sch. 4 (in force by SI 1989/382); (d) Children Act 1989, sch. 13, para. 45(3) (in force by SI 1991/828); (e) High Court (Distribution of Business) Order 1991 (SI 1991/1210), sch.; (f) High Court (Distribution of Business) Order 1993 (SI 1993/622), art. 3; (g) Family Law Act 1996, sch. 8, para. 51 (in force by SI 1991/1892, art. 3(1)); (h) High Court (Distribution of Business) Order 2004 (SI 2004/3418), art. 3; (i) European Communities (Jurisdiction and Judgments in Matrimonial and Parental Responsibility Matters) Regulations 2005 (SI 2005/265), reg. 5;
sch. 2 substituted by Courts and Legal Services Act 1990, sch. 10, para. 49 (in force by SI 1990/2484); amended by: (a) Supreme Court (Offices) Act 1997, s. 1; (b) Access to Justice Act 1999, sch. 15, part III (in force by s. 108(3) of that Act);
sch. 3 repealed by County Courts Act 1984, sch. 4.

The following provisions are omitted:
s. 8 (Crown Court); s. 41 (wards of court); ss. 43 and 43ZA (variation of sentence); s. 44 (extraordinary functions of judges); ss. 45, 46 and 48 (Crown Court); s. 52 (costs in Crown Court); ss. 55, 56B and 59 (criminal division of Court of Appeal); ss. 73 to 82 (Crown Court); ss. 84, 86 and 87 (rules of court for Crown Court and criminal division of Court of Appeal); ss. 104 to 128 (probate); s. 142 (judges to try election petitions); ss. 145, 146 and 147 (amendments of other Acts); s. 150 (extension of Admiralty jurisdiction); s. 152 (amendments of other Acts, transitional provisions, savings and repeals); words in s. 153 relating to omitted provisions; sch. 4 (construction of references to superseded courts and officers); sch. 5 (consequential amendments); sch. 6 (transitional provisions and savings); sch. 7 (repeals).

Third Parties (Rights against Insurers) Act 1930

(20 & 21 GEO. 5 CHAPTER 25)

1. Rights of Third Parties against Insurers on Bankruptcy, etc., of the Insured

(1) Where under any contract of insurance a person (hereinafter referred to as the insured) is insured against liabilities to third parties which he may incur, then

(a) in the event of the insured becoming bankrupt or making a composition or arrangement with his creditors; or

(b) in the case of the insured being a company, in the event of a winding-up order or an administration order being made, or a resolution for a voluntary winding-up being passed, with respect to the company, or of a receiver or manager of the company's business or undertaking being duly appointed, or of possession being taken, by or on behalf of the holders of any debentures secured by a floating charge, of any property comprised in or subject to that charge or of a voluntary arrangement proposed for the purposes of Part I of the Insolvency Act 1986 being approved under that Part; if,

either before or after that event, any such liability as aforesaid is incurred by the insured, his rights against the insurer under the contract in respect of the liability shall, notwithstanding anything in any Act or rule of law to the contrary, be transferred to and vest in the third party to whom the liability was so incurred.

(2) Where the estate of any person falls to be administered in accordance with an order under section 421 of the Insolvency Act 1986 then, if any debt provable in bankruptcy (in Scotland, any claim accepted in the sequestration) is owing by the deceased in respect of a liability against which he was insured under a contract of insurance as being a liability to a third party, the deceased debtor's rights against the insurer under the contract in respect of that liability shall, notwithstanding anything in any such order, be transferred to and vest in the person to whom the debt is owing.

(3) In so far as any contract of insurance made after the commencement of this Act in respect of any liability of the insured to third parties purports, whether directly or indirectly, to avoid the contract or to alter the rights of the parties thereunder upon the happening to the insured of the events specified in paragraph (a) or paragraph (b) of subsection (1) of this section or upon the estate of any person falling to be administered in accordance with an order under section 421 of the Insolvency Act 1986, the contract shall be of no effect.

(4) Upon a transfer under subsection (1) or subsection (2) of this section, the insurer shall, subject to the provisions of section three of this Act, be under the same liability to the third party as he would have been under to the insured, but—

(a) if the liability of the insurer to the insured exceeds the liability of the insured to the third party, nothing in this Act shall affect the rights of the third party against the insured in respect of the excess; and

(b) if the liability of the insurer to the insured is less than the liability of the insured to the third party, nothing in this Act shall affect the rights of the third party against the insured in respect of the balance.

(5) For the purposes of this Act, the expression 'liabilities to third parties', in relation to a person insured under any contract of insurance, shall not include any liability of that person in the capacity of insurer under some other contract of insurance.

(6) This Act shall not apply—

(a) where a company is wound up voluntarily merely for the purposes of reconstruction or of amalgamation with another company; or

(b) to any case to which subsections (1) and (2) of section seven of the Workmen's Compensation Act 1925 applies.

2. Duty to Give Necessary Information to Third Parties

(1) In the event of any person becoming bankrupt or making a composition or arrangement with his creditors, or in the event of the estate of any person falling to be administered in accordance

with an order under section 421 of the Insolvency Act 1986, or in the event of a winding-up order or an administration order being made, or a resolution for a voluntary winding-up being passed, with respect to any company or of a receiver or manager of the company's business or undertaking being duly appointed, or of possession being taken, by or on behalf of the holders of any debentures secured by a floating charge, of any property comprised in or subject to the charge it shall be the duty of the bankrupt, debtor, personal representative of the deceased debtor or company, and, as the case may be, of the trustee in bankruptcy, trustee, liquidator, administrator, receiver, or manager, or person in possession of the property to give at the request of any person claiming that the bankrupt, debtor, deceased debtor, or company is under a liability to him such information as may be reasonably required by him for the purpose of ascertaining whether any rights have been transferred to and vested in him by this Act and for the purpose of enforcing such rights, if any, and any contract of insurance, in so far as it purports, whether directly or indirectly, to avoid the contract or to alter the rights of the parties thereunder upon the giving of any such information in the events aforesaid or otherwise to prohibit or prevent the giving thereof in the said events shall be of no effect.

(1A) The reference in subsection (1) of this section to a trustee includes a reference to the supervisor of a voluntary arrangement proposed for the purposes of, and approved under, Part I or Part VIII of the Insolvency Act 1986.

(2) If the information given to any person in pursuance of subsection (1) of this section discloses reasonable ground for supposing that there have or may have been transferred to him under this Act rights against any particular insurer, that insurer shall be subject to the same duty as is imposed by the said subsection on the persons therein mentioned.

(3) The duty to give information imposed by this section shall include a duty to allow all contracts of insurance, receipts for premiums, and other relevant documents in the possession or power of the person on whom the duty is so imposed to be inspected and copies thereof to be taken.

3. Settlement between Insurers and Insured Persons

Where the insured has become bankrupt or where in the case of the insured being a company, a winding-up order or an administration order has been made or a resolution for a voluntary winding-up has been passed, with respect to the company, no agreement made between the insurer and the insured after liability has been incurred to a third party and after the commencement of the bankruptcy or winding-up or the day of the administration order, as the case may be, nor any waiver, assignment, or other disposition made by, or payment made to the insured after the commencement or day aforesaid shall be effective to defeat or affect the rights transferred to the third party under this Act, but those rights shall be the same as if no such agreement, waiver, assignment, disposition or payment had been made.

Torts (Interference with Goods) Act 1977

(1977 CHAPTER 32)

1. Definition of 'Wrongful Interference with Goods'

In this Act 'wrongful interference', or 'wrongful interference with goods', means—

(a) conversion of goods (also called trover),

(b) trespass to goods,

(c) negligence so far as it results in damage to goods or to an interest in goods,

(d) subject to section 2, any other tort so far as it results in damage to goods or to an interest in goods

and references in this Act (however worded) to proceedings for wrongful interference or to a claim or right to claim for wrongful interference shall include references to proceedings by virtue of Part I of the Consumer Protection Act 1987 (product liability) in respect of any damage to goods and to the interest in goods or, as the case may be, to a claim or right to claim by virtue of that Part in respect of any such damage.

2. Abolition of Detinue

(1) Detinue is abolished.

(2) An action lies in conversion for loss or destruction of goods which a bailee has allowed to happen in breach of his duty to his bailor (that is to say it lies in a case which is not otherwise conversion, but would have been detinue before detinue was abolished).

3. Forms of Judgment where Goods are Detained

(1) In proceedings for wrongful interference against a person who is in possession or in control of the goods relief may be given in accordance with this section, so far as appropriate.

(2) The relief is—

(a) an order for delivery of goods, and for payment of any consequential damages, or

(b) an order for delivery of the goods, but giving the defendant the alternative of paying damages by reference to the value of the goods, together in either alternative with payment of any consequential damages, or

(c) damages.

(3) Subject to rules of court—

(a) relief shall be given under only one of paragraphs (a), (b) and (c) of subsection (2),

(b) relief under paragraph (a) of subsection (2) is at the discretion of the court, and the claimant may choose between the others.

(4) If it is shown to the satisfaction of the court that an order under subsection (2)(a) had not been complied with, the court may—

(a) revoke the order, or the relevant part of it, and

(b) make an order for payment of damages by reference to the value of the goods.

(5) Where an order is made under subsection (2)(b) the defendant may satisfy the order by returning the goods at any time before execution of judgment, but without prejudice to liability to pay any consequential damages.

(6) An order for delivery of the goods under subsection (2)(a) or (b) may impose such conditions as may be determined by the court, or pursuant to rules of court, and in particular, where damages by reference to the value of the goods would not be the whole of the value of the goods, may require an allowance to be made by the claimant to reflect the difference.

For example, a bailor's action against the bailee may be one in which the measure of damages is not the full value of the goods, and then the court may order delivery of the goods, but require the bailor to pay the bailee a sum reflecting the difference.

(7) Where under subsection (1) or subsection (2) of section 6 an allowance is to be made in respect of an improvement of the goods, and an order is made under subsection (2)(a) or (b), the court may assess the allowance to be made in respect of the improvement, and by the

order require, as a condition for delivery of the goods, that allowance to be made by the claimant.

(8) This section is without prejudice—
   (a) to the remedies afforded by section 133 of the Consumer Credit Act, or
   (b) to the remedies afforded by sections 35, 42 and 44 of the Hire-Purchase Act 1965, or to those sections of the Hire-Purchase Act (Northern Ireland) 1966 (so long as those sections respectively remain in force), or
   (c) to any jurisdiction to afford ancillary or incidental relief.

4. Interlocutory Relief where Goods are Detained

(1) In this section 'proceedings' means proceedings for wrongful interference.

(2) On the application of any person in accordance with rules of court, the High Court shall, in such circumstances as may be specified in the rules, have power to make an order providing for the delivery up of any goods which are or may become subject matter of subsequent proceedings in the court, or as to which any question may arise in proceedings.

(3) Delivery shall be, as the order may provide, to the claimant or to a person appointed by the court for the purpose, and shall be on such terms and conditions as may be specified in the order.

5. Extinction of Title on Satisfaction of Claim for Damages

(1) Where damages for wrongful interference are, or would fall to be, assessed on the footing that the claimant is being compensated—
   (a) for the whole of his interest in the goods, or
   (b) for the whole of his interest in the goods subject to a reduction for contributory negligence,

payment of the assessed damages (under all heads), or as the case may be settlement of a claim for damages for the wrong (under all heads), extinguishes the claimant's title to that interest.

(2) In subsection (1) the reference to the settlement of the claim includes—
   (a) where the claim is made in court proceedings, and the defendant has paid a sum into court to meet the whole claim, the taking of that sum by the claimant, and
   (b) where the claim is made in court proceedings, and the proceedings are settled or compromised, the payment of what is due in accordance with the settlement or compromise, and
   (c) where the claim is made out of court and is settled or compromised, the payment of what is due in accordance with the settlement or compromise.

(3) It is hereby declared that subsection (1) does not apply where damages are assessed on the footing that the claimant is being compensated for the whole of his interest in the goods, but the damages paid are limited to some lesser amount by virtue of any enactment or rule of law.

(4) Where under section 7(3) the claimant accounts over to another person (the 'third party') so as to compensate (under all heads) the third party for the whole of his interest in the goods, the third party's title to that interest is extinguished.

(5) This section has effect subject to any agreement varying the respective rights of the parties to the agreement, and where the claim is made in court proceedings has effect subject to any court.

6. Allowance for Improvement of the Goods

(1) If in proceedings for wrongful interference against a person (the 'improver') who has improved the goods, it is shown that the improver acted in the mistaken but honest belief that he had a good title to them, an allowance shall be made for the extent to which, at the time as at which the goods fall to be valued in assessing damages, the value of the goods is attributable to the improvement.

(2) If, in proceedings for wrongful interference against a person ('the purchaser') who has purported to purchase the goods—
   (a) from the improver, or
   (b) where after such a purported sale the goods passed by a further purported sale on one or more occasions, on any such occasion,

it is shown that the purchaser acted in good faith, an allowance shall be made on the principle set out in subsection (1).

For example, where a person in good faith buys a stolen car from the improver and is sued in conversion by the true owner the damages may be reduced to reflect the improvement, but if the person who bought the stolen car from the improver sues the improver for failure of consideration, and the improver acted in good faith, subsection (3) below will ordinarily make a comparable reduction in the damages he recovers from the improver.

(3) If in a case within subsection (2) the person purporting to sell the goods acted in good faith, then in proceedings by the purchaser for recovery of the purchase price because of failure of consideration, or in any other proceedings founded on that failure of consideration, an allowance shall, where appropriate, be made on the principle set out in subsection (1).

(4) This section applies, with the necessary modifications, to a purported bailment or other disposition of goods as it applies to a purported sale of goods.

7. Double Liability

(1) In this section 'double liability' means the double liability of the wrongdoer which can arise—

(a) where one of two or more rights of action for wrongful interference is founded on a possessory title, or

(b) where the measure of damages in an action for wrongful interference founded on a proprietary title is or includes the entire value of the goods, although the interest is one of two or more interests in the goods.

(2) In proceedings to which any two or more claimants are parties, the relief shall be such as to avoid double liability of the wrongdoer as between those claimants.

(3) On satisfaction, in whole or in part, of any claim for an amount exceeding that recoverable if subsection (2) applied, the claimant is liable to account over to the other person having a right to claim to such extent as will avoid double liability.

(4) Where, as the result of enforcement of a double liability, any claimant is unjustly enriched to an extent, he shall be liable to reimburse the wrongdoer to that extent.

For example, if a converter of goods pays damages first to a finder of the goods, and then to the true owner, the finder is unjustly enriched unless he accounts over to the true owner under subsection (3); and then the true owner is unjustly enriched and becomes liable to reimburse the converter of the goods.

8. Competing Rights to the Goods

(1) The defendant in an action for wrongful interference shall be entitled to show, in accordance with rules of court, that a third party has a better right than the plaintiff as respects all or any part of the interest claimed by the plaintiff, or in right of which he sues, and any rule of law (sometimes called jus tertii) to the contrary is abolished.

(2) Rules of court relating to proceedings for wrongful interference may—

(a) require the plaintiff to give particulars of his title,

(b) require the plaintiff to identify any person who, to his knowledge, has or claims any interest in the goods,

(c) authorise the defendant to apply for directions as to whether any person should be joined with a view to establishing whether he has a better right than the plaintiff, or has a claim of a result of which the defendant might be doubly liable,

(d) where a party fails to appear on an application within paragraph (c), or to comply with any direction given by the court on such an application, authorise the court to deprive him of any right of action against the defendant for the wrong either unconditionally, or subject to such terms or conditions as may be specified.

(3) Subsection (2) is without prejudice to any power of making rules of court.

9. Concurrent Actions

(1) This section applies where goods are the subject of two or more claims for wrongful interference (whether or not the claims are founded on the same wrongful act, and whether or not any of the claims relates also to other goods).

(2) Where the goods are the subject of two or more claims under section 6 this section shall apply as if any claim under section 6(3) were a claim for wrongful interference.

(3) If proceedings have been brought in a county court on one of those claims, county court rules may waive, or allow a court to waive, any limit (financial or territorial) on the jurisdiction of county courts in the County Courts Act 1984 or the County Courts Act (Northern

Ireland) Order 1980 so as to allow another of those claims to be brought in the same county court.

(4) If proceedings are brought on one of the claims in the High Court, and proceedings on any other are brought in a county court, whether prior to the High Court proceedings or not, the High Court may, on the application of the defendant, after notice has been given to the claimant in the county court proceedings—
   (a) order that the county court proceedings be transferred to the High Court, and
   (b) order security for costs or impose such other terms as the court thinks fit.

10. Co-owners

(1) Co-ownership is no defence to an action founded on conversion or trespass to goods where the defendant without the authority of the other co-owner—
   (a) destroys the goods, or disposes of the goods in a way giving a good title to the entire property in the goods, or otherwise does anything equivalent to the destruction of the other's interest in the goods, or
   (b) purports to dispose of the goods in a way which would give a good title to the entire property in the goods if he was acting with the authority of all co-owners of the goods.

(2) Subsection (1) shall not affect the law concerning execution or enforcement of judgments, or concerning any form of distress.

(3) Subsection (1)(a) is by the way of restatement of existing law so far as it relates to conversion.

Unfair Contract Terms Act 1977

(1977 CHAPTER 50)

PART I

1. Scope of Part I

(1) For the purposes of this Part of this Act, 'negligence' means the breach—
  (a) of any obligation, arising from the express or implied terms of a contract, to take reasonable care or exercise reasonable skill in the performance of the contract;
  (b) of any common law duty to take reasonable care or exercise reasonable skill (but not any stricter duty);
  (c) of the common duty of care imposed by the Occupiers' Liability Act 1957 or the Occupier's Liability Act (Northern Ireland) 1957.
(2) This Part of the Act is subject to Part III; and in relation to contracts, the operation of sections 2 to 4 and 7 is subject to the exceptions made by Schedule I.
(3) In the case of both contract and tort, sections 2 to 7 apply (except where the contrary is stated in section 6(4)) only to business liability, that is liability to breach of obligations or duties arising—
  (a) from things done or to be done by a person in the course of a business (whether his own business or another's); or
  (b) from the occupation of premises used for business purposes of the occupier; and references to liability are to be read accordingly but liability of an occupier of premises for breach of an obligation or duty towards a person obtaining access to the premises for recreational or educational purposes, being liability for loss or damage suffered by reason of the dangerous state of the premises, is not a business liability of the occupier unless granting that person such access for the purposes concerned falls within the business purposes of the occupier.
(4) In relation to any breach of duty or obligation, it is immaterial for any purpose of this Part of this Act whether the breach was inadvertent or intentional, or whether liability for it arises directly or vicariously.

2. Negligence Liability

(1) A person cannot by reference to any contract term or to a notice given to persons generally or to particular persons exclude or restrict his liability for death or personal injury resulting from negligence.
(2) In the case of other loss or damage, a person cannot so exclude or restrict his liability for negligence except in so far as the term or notice satisfies the requirement of reasonableness.
(3) Where a contract term or notice purports to exclude or restrict liability for negligence a person's agreement to or awareness of it is not of itself to be taken as indicating his voluntary acceptance of any risk.

3. Liability Arising in Contract

(1) This section applies as between contracting parties where one of them deals as consumer or on the other's written standard terms of business.
(2) As against that party, the other cannot by reference to any contract term—
  (a) when himself in breach of contract, exclude or restrict any liability of his in respect of the breach; or
  (b) claim to be entitled—
    (i) to render a contractual performance substantially different from that which was reasonably expected of him, or
    (ii) in respect of the whole of any part of his contractual obligation, to render no performance at all,

except in so far as (in any of the cases mentioned above in this subsection) the contract term satisfies the requirement of reasonableness.

6. Sale and Hire-purchase

(1) Liability for breach of the obligations arising from—
  (a) section 12 of the Sale of Goods Act 1979 (seller's implied undertakings as to title, etc.);
  (b) section 8 of the Supply of Goods (Implied Terms) Act 1973 (the corresponding thing in relation to hire-purchase),

cannot be excluded or restricted by reference to any contract term.

(2) As against a person dealing as consumer, liability for breach of the obligations arising from—
  (a) section 13,14 or 15 of the 1979 Act (seller's implied undertakings as to conformity of goods with description or sample, or as to their quality of fitness for a particular purpose);
  (b) section 9,10 or 11 of the 1973 Act (the corresponding things in relation to hire-purchase),

cannot be excluded or restricted by reference to any contract term.

(3) As against a person dealing otherwise than as consumer, the liability specified in subsection (2) above can be excluded or restricted by reference to a contract term, but only in so far as the term satisfies the requirement of reasonableness.

(4) The liabilities referred to in this section are not only the business liabilities defined by section 1(3), but include those arising under any contract of sale of goods or hire-purchase agreement.

11. The 'Reasonableness' Test

(1) In relation to a contract term, the requirement of reasonableness for the purposes of this Part of this Act, section 3 of the Misrepresentation Act 1967 and section 3 of the Misrepresentation Act (Northern Ireland) 1967 is that the term shall have been a fair and reasonable one to be included having regard to the circumstances which were, or ought reasonably to have been, known to or in the contemplation of the parties when the contract was made.

(2) In determining for the purposes of section 6 or 7 above whether a contract term satisfies the requirement of reasonableness, regard shall be had in particular to the matters specified in Schedule 2 to this Act; but this subsection does not prevent the court or arbitrator from holding, in accordance with any rule of law, that a term which purports to exclude or restrict any relevant liability is not a term of the contract.

(3) In relation to a notice (not being a notice having contractual effect), the requirement of reasonableness under this Act is that it should be fair and reasonable to allow reliance on it, having regard to all the circumstances obtaining when the liability arose or (but for the notice) would have arisen.

(4) Where by reference to a contract term or notice a person seeks to restrict liability to a specified sum of money, and the question arises (under this or any other Act) whether the term or notice satisfies the requirement of reasonableness, regard shall be had in particular (but without prejudice to subsection (2) above in the case of contract terms) to—
  (a) the resources which he could expect to be available to him for the purpose of meeting the liability should it arise; and
  (b) how far it was open to him to cover himself by insurance.

(5) It is for those claiming that a contract term or notice satisfies the requirement of reasonableness to show that it does.

12. 'Dealing as Consumer'

(1) A party to contract 'deals as consumer' in relation to another party if—
  (a) he neither makes the contract in the course of a business nor holds himself out as doing so; and
  (b) the other party does make the contract in the course of a business; and
  (c) in the case of a contract governed by the law of sale of goods or hire-purchase, or by section 7 of this Act, the goods passing under or in pursuance of the contract are of a type ordinarily supplied for private use or consumption.

(1A) But if the first party mentioned in subsection (1) is an individual paragraph (c) of that subsection must be ignored.

(2) But the buyer is not in any circumstances to be regarded as dealing as consumer—
  (a) if he is an individual and the goods are second hand goods sold at public auction at which individuals have the opportunity of attending the sale in person;
  (b) if he is not an individual and the goods are sold by auction or by competitive tender.

(3) Subject to this, it is for those claiming that a party does not deal as consumer to show that he does not.

13. Varieties of Exemption Clause

(1) To the extent that this Part of this Act prevents the exclusion or restriction of any liability it also prevents—
 (a) making the liability or its enforcement subject to restrictive or onerous conditions;
 (b) excluding or restricting any right or remedy in respect of the liability, or subjecting a person to any prejudice in consequence of his pursuing any such right or remedy;
 (c) excluding or restricting rules of evidence or procedure;
 and (to that extent) sections 2 and 5 to 7 also prevent excluding or restricting liability by reference to terms and notices which exclude or restrict the relevant obligation or duty.

(2) But an agreement in writing to submit present or future differences to arbitration is not to be treated under this Part of this Act as excluding or restricting any liability.

14. Interpretation of Part I

In this Part of the Act—

'business' includes a profession and the activities of any government department or local or public authority;

'goods' has the same meaning as in the Sale of Goods Act 1979;

'hire-purchase agreement' has the same meaning as in the Consumer Credit Act 1974;

'negligence' has the meaning given by section 1(1);

'notice' includes an announcement, whether or not in writing, and any other communication or pretended communication; and

'personal injury' includes any disease and any impairment of physical or mental condition.

Section 1(2)

SCHEDULE 1 SCOPE OF SECTIONS 2 TO 4 AND 7

1. Sections 2 to 4 of this Act do not extend to—
 (a) any contract of insurance (including a contract to pay an annuity on human life);
 (b) any contract so far as it relates to the creation or transfer of an interest in land, or to the termination of such an interest, whether by extinction, merger, surrender, forfeiture or otherwise;
 (c) any contract so far as it relates to the creation or transfer of a right or interest in any patent, trade mark, copyright, registered design, technical or commercial information or other intellectual property, or relates to the termination of any such right or interest;
 (d) any contract so far as it relates—
  (i) to the formation or dissolution of a company (which means any body corporate or unincorporated association and includes a partnership), or
  (ii) to its constitution or the rights or obligations of its corporators or members;
 (e) any contract so far as it relates to the creation or transfer of securities or of any right or interest in securities.

2. Section 2(1) extends to—
 (a) any contract of marine salvage or towage;
 (b) any charterparty of a ship or hovercraft; and
 (c) any contract for the carriage of goods by ship or hovercraft;
 but subject to this sections 2 to 4 and 7 do not extend to any such contract except in favour of a person dealing as a consumer.

3. Where goods are carried by ship or hovercraft in pursuance of a contract which either—
 (a) specifies that as the means of carriage over part of the journey to be covered, or
 (b) makes no provision as to the means of carriage and does not exclude that means, then sections 2(2), 3 and 4 do not, except in favour of a person dealing as consumer, extend to the contract as it operates for and in relation to the carriage of the goods by that means.

4. Section 2(1) and (2) do not extend to a contract of employment, except in favour of the employee.

5. Section 2(1) does not affect the validity of any discharge and indemnity given by a person, on or in connection with an award to him of compensation for pneumoconiosis attributable to

employment in the coal industry, in respect of any further claim arising from his contracting the disease.

Sections 11(2) and 24(2)

SCHEDULE 2
'GUIDELINES' FOR APPLICATION OF REASONABLENESS TEST

The matters to which regard is to be had in particular for the purposes of sections 6(3), 7(3) and (4), 20 and 21 are any of the following which appear to be relevant—

(a) the strength of the bargaining positions of the parties relative to each other, taking into account (among other things) alternative means by which the customer's requirements could have been met;

(b) whether the customer received an inducement to agree to the term, or in accepting it had an opportunity of entering into a similar contract with other persons, but without having to accept a similar term;

(c) whether the customer knew or ought reasonably to have known of the existence and extent of the term (having regard, among other things, to any custom of the trade and any previous course of dealing between the parties);

(d) where the term excludes or restricts any relevant liability if some condition is not complied with, whether it was reasonable at the time of the contract to expect that compliance with that condition would be practicable;

(e) whether the goods were manufactured, processed or adapted to the special order of the customer.

Index

This is a subject index to the contents of **chapters 1** to **98** and **appendix 1 and** 2 of *Blackstone's Civil Practice*. Each heading in chapters 1 to 98 is numbered. The first heading in **chapter 2** is **2.1**, the second is **2.2**, and so on. This index refers to headings by their numbers.

appendix 1 consists of 38 procedural checklists.
appendix 2 consists of the Civil Procedure Rules (CPR) and supplementing practice directions (PDs).
The Civil Procedure Rules are divided into numbered Parts. The Parts are divided into rules.
In this index, **CPR** followed by a number is a reference to a rule in the Civil Procedure Rules in **appendix 2**.
For example, **CPR** 55.7 is a reference to rule 55.7 in **appendix 2**.

A Part of the Civil Procedure Rules may have one or more supplementing practice directions. A practice direction is given the same number as the Part which it supplements. For example, the first practice direction supplementing Part 8 is **PD 8**, the second is **PD 8B**, and so on. Those numbers are used in this index to identify practice directions supplementing Parts of the Civil Procedure Rules. The other practice directions in **appendix** 2 are identified as follows:

PD Civil Recovery Proceedings	Practice Direction — Civil Recovery Proceedings
PD Competition Act 1998	Practice Direction — Application for a Warrant under the Competition Act 1998
PD Devolution Issues	Practice Direction — Devolution Issues
PD Directors Disqualification Proceedings	Practice Direction — Directors Disqualification Proceedings
PD Insolvency Proceedings	Practice Direction — Insolvency Proceedings
PD Welsh Language	Practice Direction Relating to the Use of the Welsh Language in the Civil Courts in Wales
QB Masters' PD(11)	Practice Direction — Queen's Bench Masters